YEARBOOK OF INTERNATIONAL ORGANIZATIONS 2023 - 2024

Copyright 2023 Union of International Associations

Publication history

1905 – 1907
Institut International de la Paix, Monaco
- *Annuaire de la Vie internationale*: 1905–1906–1907 (1ère série).

1908 – 1911
Union of International Associations / Central Office of International Associations
- *Annuaire de la Vie internationale* (with the collaboration of the Institut International de Bibliographie and the Institut International de la Paix) 1908–1909 (2ème série)
- *Annuaire de la Vie internationale* (with the support of the Carnegie Endowment for International Peace) 1910–1911 (2ème série)

1921 – 1939
Continuation by the League of Nations (Geneva) of the initiative of the Union of International Associations
- *Répertoire des Organisations internationales*: 1925, 1936 (French ed.)
- *Handbook of International Organizations*: 1926, 1929, 1938 (English ed.)
- *Répertoire des Organisations internationales / Handbook of International Organizations*: 1921, 1923 (bi-lingual ed.)

1948 (1st ed.) – 1950 (3rd ed.)
Editions de l'Annuaire des Organisations Internationales S.A. (Geneva)
- *Annuaire des Organisations Internationales / Yearbook of International Organizations*. 1948 (1st ed.), 1949 (2nd ed.), 1950 (3rd ed.) (with the collaboration of the Union of International Associations)

1951 (4th ed.) – 1980 (18th ed.)
Union of International Associations (Brussels) based on an agreement with the United Nations resulting from a resolution of the Economic and Social Council
- *Yearbook of International Organizations*, 1951/52 (4th ed.), 1954/55 (5th ed.)
- *Annuaire des Organisations Internationales*, 1956/57 (6th ed.)
- *Yearbook of International Organizations*, 1958/59 (7th ed.)
- *Annuaire des Organisations Internationales*, 1960/61 (8th ed.)
- *Yearbook of International Organizations*, 1962/63 (9th ed.), 1964/65 (10th ed.), 1966/67 (11th ed.), 1968/69 (12th ed.), 1970/71 (13th ed.), 1972/73 (14th ed.)
- *Yearbook of International Organizations / Annuaire des Organisations Internationales*, 1974 (15th ed.)
- *Yearbook of International Organizations*, 1976/77 (16th ed.), 1978/79 (17th ed.)
- *Annuaire des Organisations Internationales*, 1980 (16/18th ed.)

1981 (19th ed.)
Edited by the Union of International Associations (Brussels). Published jointly with the International Chamber of Commerce (Paris)
- *Yearbook of International Organizations*, 1981 (19th ed.)

1983 (20th ed.) – 2010 (47th ed.)
Edited by the Union of International Associations (Brussels). Published, with four supplementary volumes, by K.G. Saur Verlag (Munich)
- *Yearbook of International Organizations*
  - Volume 1: Organization descriptions, from 1983 (20th ed.) to 1998 (35th ed.) and in 2 parts (1A and 1B) since 1999 (36th ed.)
  - Volume 2: Geographic Volume: International Organization Participation; Country directory of secretariats and membership, since 1983 (1st ed.)
  - Volume 3: Subject volume: Global Action Networks; Classified directory by subject and region, since 1983 (1st ed.)
  - Volume 4: Bibliographic volume: International Organization Bibliography and Resources, since 1996 (1st ed.)
  - Volume 5: Statistics, Visualizations and Patterns, since 2001 (1st ed.)
  - Volume 6: Who's Who in International Organizations, since 2007 (1st ed.)
  - CD-ROM version: Yearbook / Annuaire Plus, 1995 (1st ed.) – 2008 (15th ed.)

2011 (48th ed.) – 2017 (54th ed.)
Edited by the Union of International Associations (Brussels). Published by Brill / Martinus Nijhoff Publishers (Leiden/Boston)
- *Yearbook of International Organizations: Guide to Global Civil Society Networks*
  - Volume 1: Organization Descriptions and Cross-references, in 2 parts (1A and 1B)
  - Volume 2: Geographical Index: country directory of secretariats and memberships
  - Volume 3: Global Action Networks: subject directory and index
  - Volume 4: International Organization Bibliography and Resources
  - Volume 5: Statistics, Visualizations and Patterns
  - Volume 6: Who's Who in International Organizations

2018 (55th ed.) –
Edited by the Union of International Associations (Brussels). Published by Brill / Martinus Nijhoff Publishers (Leiden/Boston)
- *Yearbook of International Organizations: Guide to Global Civil Society Networks*
  - Volume 1: Organization Descriptions and Cross-references, in 2 parts (1A and 1B)
  - Volume 2: Geographical Index: country directory of secretariats and memberships
  - Volume 3: Global Action Networks: subject directory and index
  - Volume 4: International Organization Bibliography and Resources
  - Volume 5: Statistics, Visualizations and Patterns
  - Volume 6: Global Civil Society and the United Nations Sustainable Development Goals

The *Yearbook of International Organizations* is also available online. See https://uia.org/

The editors

Union of International Associations (UIA)
Rue Washington 40, B-1050 Brussels, Belgium
Tel: (32 2) 640 18 08
E-mail: uia@uia.org
Website: https://uia.org/

EDITED BY THE UNION OF INTERNATIONAL ASSOCIATIONS

YEARBOOK OF INTERNATIONAL ORGANIZATIONS 2023 - 2024

GUIDE TO GLOBAL CIVIL SOCIETY NETWORKS
EDITION 60

VOLUME 1A (*A* TO *INS*)
ORGANIZATION DESCRIPTIONS AND CROSS-REFERENCES

BRILL

The following people contributed to this edition:
- Carine Faveere
- Carol Williams
- Chloé Houyoux
- Christelle Behets
- Clara Fernández López
- Frédéric Magin
- João Andrade
- Joel Fischer
- Judy Wickens
- Kimberly Trathen
- Leslie Selvais
- Liesbeth Van Hulle *(Editor-in-Chief)*
- Nordine Bittich
- Rachele Dahle
- Ryan Brubaker
- Jacques de Mévius
- Sylvie Hosselet
- Yolande Vlaminck

Special thanks to:
- Alessandro Cortese
- Brigitte Motte
- Cyril Ritchie
- Danièle Vranken
- Dianne Dillon-Ridgley
- Dragana Avramov
- Esperanza Duran
- Jacqueline Staniforth
- Jacques de Mévius
- Judy Wickens
- Marc Bontemps
- Marilyn Mehlmann
- Marisha Wojciechowska-Shibuya
- Rolf Reinhardt
- Seya Immonen
- Sheila Bordier
- Simone Van Beek
- Tim Casswell
- Yves Moreau

The Editors dedicate this edition to

Régine Toussaint, editor from 1981 to 2021

and

Nancy Carfrae, editor from 1984 to 2021

Thank you, ladies!

Information researched and edited by
Union of International Associations
Rue Washington 40
B-1050 Brussels, Belgium

Koninklijke Brill NV, Leiden, The Netherlands.
Koninklijke Brill NV incorporates the imprints Brill, Brill Nijhoff, Brill Hotei, Brill Schöningh, Brill Fink, Brill mentis, Vandenhoeck & Ruprecht, Böhlau, V&R unipress and Wageningen Academic.

Typeset by
bsix information exchange GmbH
Sophienstraße 40
D-38118 Braunschweig, Germany

Printed on acid free paper.

Copyright 2023 by Union of International Associations. All rights reserved. No part of this publication may be reproduced, translated, stored in a retrieval system, or transmitted in any form or by any means, electronic, mechanical, photocopying, recording or otherwise, without written permission from the Secretary General, Union of International Associations.

Library of Congress Card Number: 49-22132
ISSN: 2211-3010
ISBN: Yearbook Volume 1 (A and B): 978-90-04-54680-6
        Yearbook Volumes 1-6 Set: 978-90-04-54794-0
UIA Publication Number: 501

The publisher and editor do not assume and hereby disclaim any liability to any party for any loss or damage caused by errors or omissions in the *Yearbook of International Organizations*, whether such errors or omissions result from negligence, accident or any other cause.

Contents	Table des matières
This Volume	**Ce volume**

Organization descriptions / Descriptions des organisations

Appearing in alphabetical order of title, with index of abbreviations, other language titles, previous and alternative titles and abbreviations, subsidiary titles and abbreviations all inserted in the same alphabetical sequence.	Classées par ordre alphabétique du nom en anglais, ou du sigle, si celui-ci est plus connu, dans une séquence unique qui contient également: les sigles, les noms dans d'autres langues que l'anglais, les noms et abréviations alternatifs et du passé, les noms et abréviations secondaires.

Part 1A / Partie 1A

Notes to the user / Notes pour l'utilisateur

Organization descriptions: *A to INS* / Description des organisations: *A à INS*

Part 1B / Partie 1B

Organization descriptions: *INT to Z* / Description des organisations: *INT à Z*

Appendices / Annexes (en anglais)
1. Contents of organization descriptions
4. Editorial problems and policies

Other Volumes / **Autres volumes**

Volume 2: Geographical Index: country directory of secretariats and memberships

Volume 3: Global Action Networks: subject directory and index

Volume 4: International Organization Bibliography and Resources

Volume 5: Statistics, Visualizations and Patterns

Volume 6: Global Civil Society and the United Nations Sustainable Development Goals

Further information can be found at https://uia.org / Informations complémentaires sur le web https://uia.org

The YEARBOOK series

All these publications are also available online. For further information please see https://uia.org/

VOLUME 1 (Parts 1A and 1B): ORGANIZATION DESCRIPTIONS AND CROSS-REFERENCES
Descriptions of intergovernmental and non-governmental organizations, covering every field of human activity. Listed in alphabetic order of title.
Contents of descriptions: Descriptions, varying in length from several lines to several pages, include: organization names in all relevant languages; principal and secondary addresses; main activities and programmes; personnel and finances; technical and regional commissions; history, goals, structure; inter-organizational links; languages used; membership by country.
Cross-references: Integrated into the alphabetic sequence of descriptions are cross-references to related organizations. Access is possible via organization names in English, French and other working languages and via all initials or abbreviations in various languages.

VOLUME 2: GEOGRAPHICAL INDEX: COUNTRY DIRECTORY OF SECRETARIATS AND MEMBERSHIPS
– Organizations classified by country of secretariat(s)
– Organizations classified by countries of location of membership
– Statistics by country and city
Can be used to locate international organizations by country of secretariat or membership. Each organization is listed with its complete address under the country or countries in which it has established a main secretariat.

VOLUME 3: GLOBAL ACTION NETWORKS: SUBJECT DIRECTORY AND INDEX
– Organizations classified by subject concerns
– Organizations classified by regional concerns
– Organizations classified by type
– Statistics by subject
– Index (with introductory comments):
    – subject keywords in all available languages
    – keywords from organization names in English and French
Groups organizations into general and detailed subject categories. Can be used as an index to descriptions in Volume 1. Each organization is listed with its complete address.

VOLUME 4: INTERNATIONAL ORGANIZATION BIBLIOGRAPHY AND RESOURCES
– Bibliography of studies on international non-profit organizations
– Organization publications
– Indexes
Includes major and periodical publications of international organizations, together with bibliographic information on research on NGOs.

VOLUME 5: STATISTICS, VISUALIZATIONS AND PATTERNS
- Detailed statistical tables of information in Volumes 1, 2, 3, 4 and 6.
- Historical statistical summaries and analyses
- Visual representations of statistical data and networks
- Statistical data on the meetings of international organizations

VOLUME 6: GLOBAL CIVIL SOCIETY AND THE UNITED NATIONS SUSTAINABLE DEVELOPMENT GOALS
In 2015 the United Nations adopted a set of seventeen goals "to end poverty, protect the planet and ensure prosperity for all", with specific targets for each goal to be achieved by 2030. These are the Sustainable Development Goals [SDGs] of the United Nations, or "Transforming our World: the 2030 Agenda for Sustainable Development". The UN calls on governments, the private sector, individuals and civil society bodies to join together to achieve these goals.
This volume groups international organizations by the seventeen UN Sustainable Development Goals, indicating which organizations are – or could be - concerned with which SDGs. It can also be used as an index to descriptions in Volume 1. Each organization is listed with its complete address.

INTERNATIONAL CONGRESS CALENDAR
Lists future international meetings with details of place, date, subject and organizer, including complete address, and cross-referencing the Yearbook where possible. Geographical and chronological listings. Index by subject.

HISTORICAL INTERNATIONAL ORGANIZATION DOCUMENTS
– *Annuaire de la Vie Internationale*. Editions 1905, 1906, 1907, 1908-9, 1910-11, totalling 4,741 pages
– *Code des Voeux Internationaux* (Classification of resolutions of international organizations) Edition 1923, 940 pages

La série YEARBOOK

Tous ces publications sont également disponible en ligne. Pour plus d'informations, veuillez consulter https://uia.org/

VOLUME 1 (Parties 1A et 1B): DESCRIPTIONS DES ORGANISATIONS ET LEURS LIENS
Descriptions des organisations intergouvernementales et non-gouvernementales qui couvrent tous les domaines d'activités. Présentation par ordre alphabétique des titres.
Contenu des descriptions: titres de l'organisation; adresses principale et secondaires; activités et programmes; personnel et finances; commissions; historique, buts, structure; liens avec d'autres organisations; langues utilisées; membrariat par pays.
Références croisées: Des références croisées à des organisations apparentées sont intégrées dans la séquence alphabétique des descriptions. L'accès à ces organisations est possible via les titres et les abréviations en toutes langues de travail.

VOLUME 2: INDEX GEOGRAPHIQUE : REPERTOIRE DES SECRETARIATS ET MEMBRARIATS PAR PAYS
– Organisations classées selon le pays siège de leur secrétariat
– Organisations classées selon les pays de leurs membres
– Statistiques par pays et par ville
Peut-être utilisé pour localiser des organisations internationales par pays de secrétariat ou de membrariat. Chaque organisation est reprise avec son adresse complète.

VOLUME 3: RESEAUX D'ACTION GLOBALE : REPERTOIRE THEMATIQUE ET INDEX
– Organisations classées par sujet, par région, et par catégorie
– Statistiques par sujet
– Index des mots clés
Regroupe les organisations internationales en catégories de sujets. Ces catégories, générales ou spécifiques, peuvent être utilisées comme index aux notices du Volume 1. Chaque organisation est reprise avec son adresse complète.

VOLUME 4: BIBLIOGRAPHIE ET RESSOURCES DES ORGANISATIONS INTERNATIONALES
– Bibliographie des études sur les organisations internationales sans but lucratif
– Publications des organisations
– Indexes
Regroupe les publications principales et périodiques des organisations internationales, de même qu'une information bibliographique sur des études réalisées sur les ONG.

VOLUME 5: STATISTIQUES, VISUALIZATIONS ET REPRESENTATIONS
- Tableaux statistiques détaillés des informations incorporés dans les volumes 1, 2, 3, 4 et 6.
- Résumés statistiques historiques et analyses
- Présentation visuelle des données statistiques et des réseaux.
- Données statistiques sur les réunions des organisations.

VOLUME 6: LA SOCIÉTÉ CIVILE MONDIALE ET LES OBJECTIFS DES NATIONS UNIES POUR LE DÉVELOPPEMENT DURABLE
En 2015, les Nations Unies ont adopté un ensemble de dix-sept objectifs «pour mettre fin à la pauvreté, protéger la planète et assurer la prospérité pour tous», avec des cibles spécifiques pour chaque objectif à atteindre d'ici 2030. Ce sont les objectifs de développement durable (ODD) des Nations Unies, ou «Transformer notre monde: l'Agenda 2030 pour le développement durable. L'ONU appelle les gouvernements, le secteur privé, les individus et les organismes de la société civile à se regrouper pour atteindre ces objectifs.
Ce volume regroupe les organisations internationales selon les dix-sept objectifs de développement durable des Nations Unies, indiquant quelles organisations sont - ou pourraient être - concernées par les ODD. Il peut également être utilisé comme répertoire pour les descriptions du Volume 1. Chaque organisation y figure avec son adresse complète.

INTERNATIONAL CONGRESS CALENDAR
Recense les futures réunions internationales, mentionnant le lieu, la date, le sujet, l'organisateur, l'adresse complète et, dans la mesure du possible, le renvoi à l'Annuaire. Listes géographique et chronologique. Index thématique.

HISTORICAL INTERNATIONAL ORGANIZATION DOCUMENTS
– *Annuaire de la Vie Internationale*. Editions 1905, 1906, 1907, 1908-9, 1910-11, totalling 4,741 pages
– *Code des Voeux Internationaux* (Classification of resolutions of international organizations) Edition 1923, 940 pages

Notes to the user

To find the description of an organization in the Yearbook:

- **If you know the name or abbreviation of the organization:**
  Locate the organization in the alphabetic sequence in Volume 1. All names in all official languages and abbreviations are included in the alphabetic sequence. Note that the alphabetic sequence does not take account of prepositions or articles.
  You may find the name in the form of a cross-reference to the sequence number where the description is given. The sequence number follows the alphabetic order.

- **If you know keywords in the name of the organization:**
  Consult the index in Volume 3. It will refer you to the sequence number of the description in Volume 1.

- **If you know the field in which the organization is active (e.g. its aims or activities):**
  Consult the classified list of organizations by subject in Volume 3. It will refer you to the sequence number of the description in Volume 1.

- **If you know where the organization is located, or where it has members:**
  Consult the listing of organizations by country in Volume 2. This will refer you to the sequence number of the description in Volume 1.

- **If you know the name of another organization that has a formal relationship with the one you want:**
  The description of the other organization in Volume 1 will refer you to the sequence number of the description of the organization you want in Volume 1.

Note that, due to the limitations of printing and binding, this volume does not include full descriptions of all organizations. All descriptions can be found in the online version.

Notes pour l'utilisateur

Pour trouver la notice descriptive d'une organisation:

- **A partir du nom (ou de son abréviation):**
  Consultez d'abord la séquence alphabétique du Volume 1. Les noms et abréviations y sont repris dans toutes les langues officielles.
  Vous constaterez que la séquence alphabétique ne tient pas compte des prépositions et articles.
  Le nom que vous recherchez peut vous renvoyer à un numéro de séquence sous lequel est reprise la notice descriptive de l'organisation. La numérotation suit l'ordre alphabétique.

- **A partir d'un mot clé:**
  Consultez l'index dans le volume 3 qui renvoie au numéro de séquence de la notice descriptive dans le Volume 1.

- **A partir d'un sujet ou d'une matière spécifique:**
  Consultez la liste classifiée par sujet dans le volume 3. Cette liste renvoie au numéro de séquence de la notice descriptive du Volume 1.

- **A partir d'un pays:**
  Consultez la liste par pays de secrétariat et de membrariat dans le volume 2. Cette liste renvoie au numéro de séquence de la notice descriptive du Volume 1.

- **A partir d'une organisation en relations officielles avec celle que vous cherchez:**
  La description de la première dans le Volume 1 vous donnera le numéro de notice de la deuxième dans ce même Volume 1.

A noter qu'à la suite de limitations d'impression et de reliure ce volume ne comprendra pas toutes les descriptions détaillées de toutes les organisations. Toutes les descriptions sont reprises dans la version online.

Codes used

Number codes
Organization descriptions are numbered sequentially (e.g. •00023) following the alphabetical order. It is this number that is used in any cross-reference or index referring to the entry (e.g. •00023). Organizations are renumbered sequentially for each edition. The number is therefore not a permanent reference point from one edition to the next. The permanent number (e.g. B2345) by which organizations were ordered prior to the 29th edition now appears (for information only) at the end of the description. It continues to be used for computer-based editorial purposes.

Letter codes in upper case
Organizations are coded by type, indicated by a single upper case letter printed in bold at the end of the description. In brief, these type codes have the following significance:
- A = federations of international organizations
- B = universal membership organizations
- C = intercontinental membership organizations
- D = limited or regionally defined membership organizations
- E = organizations emanating from places, persons or other bodies
- F = organizations having a special form, including foundations, funds
- G = internationally-oriented national organizations
- H = inactive or dissolved international organizations
- J = recently reported or proposed international organizations
- K = subsidiary and internal bodies
- N = national organizations
- R = religious orders, fraternities and secular institutes
- S = autonomous conference series
- T = multilateral treaties and agreements
- U = currently inactive non-conventional bodies

For further information, see the Appendix: "Types of organization".

Letter codes in lower case
The type code may be preceded by a letter code printed in lower case. These codes have the following significance:
- b = bilateral
- c = conference series
- d = dissolved, dormant
- e = commercial enterprise
- f = foundation, fund
- j = research institute
- n = has become national
- p = proposed body
- s = information suspect
- v = individual membership only
- x = no recent information received
- y = international organization membership

Asterisks
- *Intergovernmental organizations:* An asterisk as the final code in the description indicates the organization is intergovernmental.
- *Translated organization names:* An asterisk following the name of an organization indicates a title that has been translated by the editors for the purposes of multilingual indexing.

Codes utilisés

Codes numériques
Les notices descriptives sont numérotées dans l'ordre séquentiel qui suit l'ordre alphabétique. Le numéro apparaît à la droite du titre de chaque notice (p.ex. •00023). Toute référence donnée renvoie exclusivement à ce numéro (p.ex. •00023). Cela a pour conséquence que chaque édition de l'Annuaire a sa numérotation propre. Le numéro n'est donc plus permanent, faisant un lien entre les différentes éditions. Le numéro permanent de référence (p.ex. B2345) qui était propre à chaque organisation jusqu'à la 29ème édition apparaît désormais (à titre d'information) à la fin de la description. Il continue à être utilisé pour des raisons de facilité d'ordre interne.

Codes alphabétiques: lettres majuscules
Les organisations sont codifiées par catégorie à l'aide d'une lettre majuscule en caractère gras, apparaissant à la fin de la notice descriptive. Voici leur signification:
- A = fédérations d'organisations internationales
- B = organisations à membrariat universel
- C = organisations à membrariat intercontinental
- D = organisations à membrariat limité ou régional
- E = organisations émanant de lieus, de personnes ou d'autres organes
- F = organisations ayant une forme particulière, y compris fondations, fonds
- G = organisations nationales à orientation internationale
- H = organisations internationales dissoutes et inactives
- J = organisations internationales récemment rapportées ou proposées
- K = organes subsidiaires et internes
- N = organisations nationales
- R = ordres religieux, fraternités et instituts séculaires
- S = séries de conférences autonomes
- T = traités et accords multilatéraux
- U = organes non-conventionnels momentanément inactifs

Voir aussi l'Annexe: "Types d'organisation".

Codes alphabétiques: lettres minuscules
Le code de la catégorie peut être précédé par une ou deux lettres minuscules. Voici leur signification:
- b = bilatérale
- c = série de conférences
- d = inactive, dissoute
- e = entreprise commerciale
- f = fondation
- j = institut de recherche
- n = devenue nationale
- p = organisation en projet
- s = information suspecte
- v = membres individuels seulement
- x = aucune information récente
- y = ayant comme membres des organisations internationales

Astérisques
- *Organisations intergouvernementales:* Un astérisque à la fin de la description indique la nature intergouvernementale de l'organisation.
- *Traduction du nom d'organisation:* Le titre d'une organisation suivi d'un astérisque indique que la traduction de ce titre a été faite par la rédaction pour l'indexation multilingue.

Abbreviations used

Function names
Title of organization officers may be abbreviated as follows:

Admin	Administrator
CEO	Chief Executive Officer
Dir	Director
Dir Gen	Director General
Exec Dir	Executive Director
Exec Sec	Executive Secretary
Gen Sec	General Secretary
Hon Sec	Honorary Secretary
Pres	President
Sec	Secretary
Sec-Treas	Secretary-Treasurer
SG	Secretary-General
Vice-Pres	Vice-President

Organization forms

NGO	non-governmental organization
IGO	intergovernmental organization

Names of countries
The names of countries given in each entry or in the index may not be the complete official names of those countries as abridged names are used to simplify consultation. In a few cases, such as in the description of an organization's history, it has been considered appropriate to leave the old form of a country's name.

Note
It is not the intention of the editors to take a position with regard to the political or diplomatic implications of geographical names or continental groupings used.

The geographical names used in this publication are chosen for the sake of brevity and common usage. Wherever possible, the country (or territory) name preferred by the organization concerned is used, providing this is possible within the limits of standardization required for mailing or statistical purposes. It is important to note that some organizations insist on the inclusion of territories on the same basis as countries, or on the inclusion of countries or territories that are not recognized by other organizations.

Political changes over the years may lead to some questions in an organization's description. Briefly: countries referred to in an organization's description retain their old form when referring to a date prior to the change. For example, towns referred to in events prior to 1991 still retain their country as German DR (Democratic Republic) or Germany FR (Federal Republic), while subsequent dates refer simply to Germany.

Abréviations utilisées

Fonctions et titres
Les fonction ou les titres des directeurs peuvent être abrégés de la façon suivante:

Admin	administrateur
CEO	Chef de l'exécutif
Dir	directeur
Dir Gen	directeur général
Exec Dir	directeur exécutif
Exec Sec	secrétaire exécutif
Gen Sec	secrétaire général
Hon Sec	secrétaire honoraire
Pres	président
Sec	secrétaire
Sec Treas	secrétaire-trésorier
SG	secrétaire général
Vice-Pres	vice-président

Formes d'organisation

NGO	Organisation non-gouvernementale
IGO	Organisation intergouvernementale

Noms de pays
Les noms des pays apparaissant dans chaque notice ou dans l'index ne correspondent pas toujours exactement à l'appellation officielle de ces pays. Des abréviations ont été utilisées pour faciliter la lecture. Dans quelques cas, par exemple dans la partie historique, il a été jugé préférable de conserver l'ancien nom du pays cité.

Note
Il n'entre pas dans les intentions des éditeurs de prendre position au regard des implications politiques ou diplomatiques résultant du choix et de l'utilisation des noms géographiques ou de groupements continentaux.

Le choix des noms géographiques – pays ou territoires – dans cet ouvrage est fait en fonction de leur brièveté et de l'usage commun. Dans la mesure du possible, c'est le nom tel qu'adopté par l'organisation qui est retenu, mais seulement dans les limites d'une normalisation nécessaire pour les services postaux ou les statistiques. Il est important de rappeler que certaines organisations insistent sur l'inclusion de territoires au même titre que les pays ou sur l'inclusion de pays et de territoires qui ne sont pas reconnus comme tels par d'autres organisations.

Les changements politiques au cours des années peuvent poser de questions pour la description des organisations. En résumé: les pays mentionnés dans la description d'une organisation ont gardé leur ancienne appellation dans le cas où l'on se réfère à une date antérieure au changement. Par exemple, la section "Events", qui concerne le passé, conserve la vérité historique de la division de l'Allemagne d'avant 1991. Dans les adresses, les pays sont mentionnés sous leur nouveau nom.

Warning

Coverage
The Yearbook attempts to cover all "international organizations", according to a broad range of criteria. It therefore includes many bodies that may be perceived as not being fully international, or as not being organizations as such, or as not being of sufficient significance to merit inclusion. Such bodies are nevertheless included, so as to enable users to make their own evaluation in the light of their own criteria. See the Appendix "Types of organization" for further information.

Sources
The descriptions of organizations in this Yearbook are based on information received from a variety of sources. Priority is normally given to information received from the organizations themselves, and every effort is made by the editors to check this information against other sources (periodicals, official documents, media, etc.). Organizations may over time change their purpose or characteristics. The editors therefore use information from a variety of sources to present the most appropriate static picture of what is essentially a dynamic situation. See the Appendix "Editorial problems" for further information.

Reliability of sources
Because an organization's view of itself has been given priority, and because secondary sources confirming this view are not always available or reliable, the editors cannot take responsibility for any resulting inaccuracies in the information presented. The editors apologize for any inconvenience this might cause the user. See the Appendix "Editorial problems" for further information.

Censorship
Users should be aware that the editors are subject to pressure from some international bodies to suppress certain categories of information. In most cases, the editors resist these pressures; in some cases, the entry is reworded to respect the concern of the body in question. No entries have been eliminated as a result of such pressure. See the Appendix "Editorial problems" for further information.

Evaluation
The final evaluation of the information presented here must be left to the users of this volume. See the Appendices "Contents of organization descriptions", "Types of organization" and "Editorial problems and policies" for further information.

Avertissement

Contenu
L'objectif du *Yearbook of International Organizations* est de couvrir tous les types d'organisations internationales, à partir d'un large éventail de critères. On peut donc y trouver des organismes qui, selon certaines définitions plus étroites, n'y auraient pas place – pas assez "internationaux" par exemple, ou pas une "vrai" organisation, ou d'importance trop réduite. Voir aussi Annexe: "Types of organization".

Sources
La description des organisations telle qu'elle est présentée dans ce Yearbook est basée sur un ensemble de sources différentes. Priorité est normalement donnée à l'information reçue des organisations elles-mêmes, et en même temps tous les efforts sont faits par la rédaction pour contrôler cette information à l'aide d'autres sources (périodiques, documents officiels, médias, etc). Il peut arriver, qu'au cours des années, des organisations modifient leurs objectifs ou changent leurs caractéristiques. Les rédacteurs du *Yearbook* recueillent des informations auprès de multiples sources afin de présenter de façon appropriée, mais inévitablement statique, la physionomie d'une situation essentiellement dynamique. Voir aussi Annexe: "Editorial problems".

Fiabilité des sources
Quoiqu'il en soit, l'évaluation finale de l'information présentée incombe à l'utilisateur qui l'établira à la lumière de ses critères personnels. La rédaction décline toute responsabilité pour les inexactitudes qui se glisseraient dans l'information présentée et s'excuse des inconvénients qui pourraient en découler pour l'utilisateur. Voir aussi Annexe: "Editorial problems".

Censure
Peut-être est-ce le lieu de rappeler ici que, en ce qui concerne certaines catégories d'information, la rédaction du Yearbook est l'objet de pressions de la part d'organisations qui en demandent la suppression. Dans la plupart des cas, la rédaction du Yearbook résiste à de telles pressions. Sinon, mention est faite de la préoccupation de l'organisation concernée. Aucune notice n'a été éliminée du fait d'une quelconque pression. Voir aussi Annexe: "Editorial problems".

Evaluation
L'évaluation finale de l'information présentée dans ce volume est laissée aux utilisateurs. Voir aussi les Annexes " Contenu des notices descriptives", "Types d'organisation" et " Politique rédactionnelle".

DISCLAIMER. The organizations described in this Yearbook are invited annually to update their profiles. By updating or approving a profile, the organization gives its fully informed permission to the Union of International Associations (UIA) to collect, save and use the data the organization thus submits, in order to execute UIA's core activities as set out in https://uia.org/core-activities. At any time an organization described in this Yearbook may ask UIA to remove, free of charge, its contact details by writing to uia@uia.org. UIA is responsible for processing the data it receives in accordance with the *General Data Protection Regulation* of the European Union. UIA will take all reasonable measures to ensure the protection of the data it holds. Those who submit data acknowledge and agree that the transmission of data is never without risk and therefore potential damage due to the unlawful use of information by third parties cannot be claimed from UIA. For more information, please see https://uia.org/privacypolicy

alphabetic sequence excludes articles and prepositions

AAEDC
00001

- **A2ii** Access to Insurance Initiative (#00051)
- **A2IP** Association internationale interactions de la psychanalyse (#11968)
- **A2M2** – Attack Avoidable Maternal Mortality/Morbidity (internationally oriented national body)
- **A2R** / see UN Climate Resilience Initiative (#20284)
- **A2R** UN Climate Resilience Initiative (#20284)
- **A3P** / see Association pour les Produits Propres et Parentéraux
- **A3P** – Association pour les Produits Propres et Parentéraux (internationally oriented national body)
- **A4A** – Airlines for America (internationally oriented national body)
- **A4AH** Action for Animal Health (#00088)
- **A4AI** Alliance for Affordable Internet (#00651)
- **A4E** Airlines for Europe (#00607)
- **A4HP** Alliance for Health Promotion (#00687)
- **A4ID** – Advocates for International Development (internationally oriented national body)
- **A4LE** – Association for Learning Environments (internationally oriented national body)
- **A4LE** – Learning Environments Australasia (internationally oriented national body)
- **AAAA** Alps-Adria Acoustics Association (#00746)
- **AAAA** / see Asian Athletics Association (#01348)
- **AAAA** Association for Applied Animal Andrology (#02371)
- **AAA** African Acarology Association (#00194)
- **AAA** – African Action on AIDS (internationally oriented national body)
- **AAA** – ASEAN Airlines Association (no recent information)
- **AAA** ASEAN International Airports Association (#01204)
- **AAA** / see Asian Anti-Counterfeit Association (#01308)
- **AAA** Asian Anti-Counterfeit Association (#01308)
- **AAA** Asian Apicultural Association (#01309)
- **AAA** Asian Athletics Association (#01348)
- **AAA** – Asociación Andina de Armadores (no recent information)
- **AAAC** Asian Association for Algorithms and Computation (#01314)
- **AAAC** Association of Asian Athletics Coaches (#02376)
- **AAAC** / see Confederation of African Athletics (#04504)
- **AAACU** Asian Association of Agricultural Colleges and Universities (#01312)
- **AAAE** African Association of Agricultural Economists (#00205)
- **AAAE** Asian Association for Agricultural Engineering (#01313)
- **AAAE** Association of Accountants and Auditors in Europe (#02344)
- **AAAE** – Association of Arts Administration Educators (internationally oriented national body)
- **AAAF** – Asian Allergy and Asthma Foundation (internationally oriented national body)
- **AAAH** Asia Pacific Action Alliance on Human Resources for Health (#01817)
- **AAAI** / see Association for the Advancement of Artificial Intelligence
- **AAAI** – Association for the Advancement of Artificial Intelligence (internationally oriented national body)
- **AAAI** – Association africaine des administrateurs africains des impôts (no recent information)
- **AAAID** Arab Authority for Agricultural Investment and Development (#00902)
- **AAALAC** / see AAALAC International
- **AAALAC** International (internationally oriented national body)
- **AAALC** All Africa Anglican-Lutheran Commission (#00638)
- **AAAM** – Advances Against Aspergillosis and Mucormycosis (meeting series)
- **AAAM** – Association for the Advancement of Automotive Medicine (internationally oriented national body)
- **AAAP** / see Asian-Australasian Association of Animal Production Societies (#01349)
- **AAAP** Asian-Australasian Association of Animal Production Societies (#01349)
- **AAAPM** Association africaine pour l'administration publique et le management (#00215)
- **AAAPS** / see Australian Association for Pacific Studies
- **AAAPT** Asian African Association for Plasma Training (#01302)
- **AAASA** – Association for the Advancement of Agricultural Sciences in Africa (no recent information)
- **A-AASA** / see Association for the Study of Australasia in Asia (#02937)
- **AAAS** – American Association for the Advancement of Science (internationally oriented national body)
- **AAASS** / see Association for Slavic, East European, and Eurasian Studies
- **AAAST** – African Association for the Advancement of Science and Technology (no recent information)
- **AAA Symposium** – European Symposium on Ambulatory Anesthesia and Analgesia (meeting series)
- **AAATE** Association for the Advancement of Assistive Technology in Europe (#02346)
- **AAATP** / see Asian Alliance of Appropriate Technology Practitioners (#01306)
- **AABA** / see African Boxing Confederation (#00228)
- **AAB** – Association of Applied Biologists (internationally oriented national body)
- **AABB** (internationally oriented national body)
- **AABB** – Advancing Transfusion and Cellular Therapies Worldwide / see AABB
- **AABC** / see Association for Biblical Higher Education
- **AABC** Afro-Asian Book Council (#00535)
- **AABE** Asian Association for Biology Education (#01315)
- **AABF** All Africa Baptist Fellowship (#00639)
- **AABFS** – Arab Academy of Banking and Financial Sciences (internationally oriented national body)
- **AABNF** African Association for Biological Nitrogen Fixation (#00206)
- **AABS** – Anglican Association of Biblical Scholars (internationally oriented national body)
- **AABS** Association of African Business Schools (#02351)
- **AABT** / see Association for Behavioural and Cognitive Therapies
- **AACA** / see Americas Apparel Producers Network
- **AACA** – Asia Archipelago Cruise Alliance (unconfirmed)
- **AAC** – African Accounting Council (no recent information)
- **AAC** – Arctic Athabaskan Council (internationally oriented national body)
- **AAC** – Asia Arthroscopy Congress (meeting series)
- **AACB** / see Australasian Association for Clinical Biochemistry and Laboratory Medicine
- **AACB** Association of African Central Banks (#02352)
- **AACB** – Australasian Association for Clinical Biochemistry and Laboratory Medicine (internationally oriented national body)
- **AACC** – Airport Associations Coordinating Council (inactive)
- **AACC** All Africa Conference of Churches (#00640)
- **AACC** / see Cereals and Grains Association (#03830)
- **AACC EUROPE SECTION** / see Cereals and Europe (#03829)
- **AACC International** / see Cereals and Grains Association (#03830)
- **AACCLA** – Association of American Chambers of Commerce in Latin America (internationally oriented national body)
- **AACE** / see AACE International (#00001)
- **AACE** – Africa Annual Congress Europe (meeting series)
- **AACE** Alliance africaine pour le commerce électronique (#00652)
- **AACE** – Association for the Advancement of Computing in Education (internationally oriented national body)
- **AACED** Association Africaine des Centres d'Enseignement à Distance (#02354)

- **AACE International** **00001**
  Exec Dir 726 East Park Avenue, Suite 180, Fairmont WV 26554, USA. T. +13042968444. Fax +13042915728. E-mail: info@aacei.org.
  URL: https://web.aacei.org/

History Founded as *American Association of Cost Engineers (AACE)*. Present name adopted 1992. Also referred to as *AACE International – Association for the Advancement of Cost Engineering*. Constitution and bylaws adopted 2 Jun 1956; amended 7 Mar 1998; 5 Apr 2002; 19 Apr 2008. Registration: Non-profit 501(c)(3), No/ID: EIN: 54-1364306, Start date: 2017, USA, West Virginia. **Aims** Advocate use of the principles of *Total Cost Management* (TCM), an integrated package for managing the cost, *planning*, and *control* activities that take a product or project from the concept stage through development into implementation. **Structure** Annual Meeting. Board of Directors, comprising Officers, 8 Directors-Regions and Executive Director. Officers: President; President-Elect; Vice President-Regions; Vice President-Finance; Vice President-Administration; Vice President-TEC (Technical, Education, Certification); immediate Past President. Education Board. Certification Board. Technical Board, comprising 3 divisions: Product Division (including 7 Project Teams); Technical Committee Division, (including 11 Technical Committees); Special Interest Groups (SIG) Division (including 14 SIGs). Standing Committees (3): Awards; Constitution and Bylaws; Nominating. Other Committees (3): Inter-Organizational Liaison; Marketing Advisory; Government Liaison. African Chapter: *Southern African Project Controls Institute (SAPCI)*. **Languages** English. **Staff** 15.00 FTE, paid. **Finance** Members' dues. **Activities** Organizes: Annual Meeting; International Cost Engineering Congress; periodically hosts World Cost Congress; seminars; training courses. *'Programmes'* (2): Scholarship; Certification. *'Project Teams'* (7): Recommended Practices and Standards; Professional Practice Guides; Terminology; Books and Publications; Internet and Electronic Media; External Liaison; Cost Engineers' Notebook. *'Technical Committees'* (12): Business and Program Planning; Contract Management; Cost Estimating; Decision and Risk Management; Economic and Financial Analysis; Enabling Technologies; Materials Management; Planning and Scheduling; Productivity; Program and Project Management; Project and Control; Value Engineering and Constructability. *'Special Interest Groups (SIGs)'* (11): Aerospace; Appraisals; Claims and Dispute Resolution; Construction; Environmental; Forest Products; Government and Public Works; International Projects; Manufacturing; Oil/Gas/Chemicals; Utilities/Energy. **Events** *Annual Meeting* Chicago, IL (USA) 2023, *Annual Meeting* San Antonio, TX (USA) 2022, *Annual Meeting* Boston, MA (USA) 2021, *Annual Meeting* Morgantown, WV (USA) 2020, *Annual Meeting* New Orleans, LA (USA) 2019. **Publications** *Cost Engineering* (12 a year) – technical journal; *AACE Transactions*. *Certification Study Guide*; *Professional Practice Guide*; *Recommmended Practices and Standards*. Guides; skills and knowledge of cost engineering. Information Services: Virtual library available to members.
Members Categories Member (Fellows, Emeritus Members, Life Members); Associate Member; Student Member. Cost managers and engineers, project managers, planners, schedulers, estimators, bidders, value engineers, students and others (over 7,500) mostly in North America but in a total of 92 countries and territories:
Afghanistan, Algeria, Angola, Argentina, Australia, Austria, Azerbaijan, Bahamas, Bahrain, Bangladesh, Barbados, Belgium, Bosnia-Herzegovina, Botswana, Brazil, Bulgaria, Burkina Faso, Canada, Cayman Is, Chile, China, Colombia, Cyprus, Czechia, Denmark, Dominican Rep, Ecuador, Egypt, Finland, France, Germany, Ghana, Greece, Grenada, Hong Kong, Hungary, India, Indonesia, Iran Islamic Rep, Ireland, Israel, Italy, Jamaica, Japan, Jordan, Kazakhstan, Kenya, Korea Rep, Kuwait, Lebanon, Libya, Madagascar, Malaysia, Mexico, Nepal, Netherlands, New Zealand, Nigeria, Norway, Oman, Pakistan, Papua New Guinea, Peru, Philippines, Poland, Portugal, Qatar, Romania, Russia, Saudi Arabia, Singapore, South Africa, Spain, Sri Lanka, St Lucia, Sudan, Sweden, Switzerland, Taiwan, Tanzania UR, Thailand, Trinidad-Tobago, Türkiye, Uganda, UK, Ukraine, United Arab Emirates, USA, Venezuela, Vietnam, Yemen, Zimbabwe.
NGO Relations *International Cost Engineering Council (ICEC, #12976)*; national organizations.

[2022/XF4965/v/F]

- **AACG** – Asian Association of Carbon Groups (unconfirmed)
- **AACG** – Australasian Association of Clinical Geneticists (internationally oriented national body)
- **AACGC** Asian Angle-Closure Glaucoma Club (#01307)
- **AACI** Afro-Arab Institute for Culture and Strategic Studies (#00534)
- **AACI** / see Airports Council International (#00611)
- **AAC Internationale** / see Africa Culture Internationale Human Rights
- **AACL** – Arab Association for Comparative Literature (inactive)
- **AACLS** ASEAN Association for Clinical Laboratory Sciences (#01139)
- **AACMA** – All Africa Church Music Association (inactive)
- **AACM** – Asian-Australasian Association for Composite Materials (unconfirmed)
- **AAC/MIS** / see International Cooperative and Mutual Insurance Federation / Regional Association for The Americas (#12949)
- **AACMP** Asian Association of Career Management Professionals (#01317)
- **AACO** Afro-Asian Council of Ophthalmology (#00536)
- **AACO** Arab Air Carriers Organization (#00896)
- **AACO** – Arab Anti-Corruption Organization (no recent information)
- **AA** – Congregatio Augustinianorum ab Assumptione (religious order)
- **AACP** / see Asian Association of Christian Philosophers (#01318)
- **AACP** Asian Association of Christian Philosophers (#01318)
- **AACP** – Association of African Church Planters (inactive)
- **AACPCS** – Australasian Association for Communist and Post-Communist Studies (internationally oriented national body)
- **AACS** Alliance Against Counterfeit Spirits (#00654)
- **AACS** Asia Association of Coaching Science (#01252)
- **AACSB** / see AACSB International – Association to Advance Collegiate Schools of Business
- **AACSB International** – Association to Advance Collegiate Schools of Business (internationally oriented national body)
- **AACSB** – The International Association for Management Education / see AACSB International – Association to Advance Collegiate Schools of Business
- **AAC** / see Starch Europe (#19966)
- **AACT** / see Association européenne des chasses traditionnelles (#02557)
- **AACTS** – Arab Association of Cardiothoracic Surgery (unconfirmed)
- **AACUHO** / see Asia-Pacific Student Accommodation Association (#02058)
- **AACVB** Asian Association of Convention and Visitor Bureaus (#01319)
- **AACW** Association for the Advancement of Consumerism in the World (#02347)
- **AADA** – Arab Academy of Dermatology and Aesthetics (unconfirmed)
- **AAD** – African Artists for Development (internationally oriented national body)
- **AAD** – Arab Association for Democracy (unconfirmed)
- **AAD** Association des anciens députés au Parlement européen (#08151)
- **AADE** – African Association for Distance Education (no recent information)
- **AADFI** Association of African Development Finance Institutions (#02353)
- **aaDH** – Australasian Association for Digital Humanities (internationally oriented national body)
- **AADI** Association africaine de droit international (#00208)
- **AADLC** Association of African Distance Learning Centres (#02354)
- **AADL** / see European Association for Local Democracy (#06110)
- **AADMER** – ASEAN Agreement on Disaster Management and Emergency Response (2005 treaty)
- **AADO** Asian Association for Dynamic Osteosynthesis (#01320)
- **AADV** – Asian Academy of Dermatology and Venereology (unconfirmed)
- **AAEA** – African Adult Education Association (inactive)
- **AAEA** Arab Atomic Energy Agency (#00901)
- **AAEA** Association of African Election Authorities (#02355)
- **AAEA** Association of Asian Election Authorities (#02379)
- **AAE** Actuarial Association of Europe (#00105)
- **AAE** – Archery Association of Europe (internationally oriented national body)
- **AAE** Asian-Pacific Association of Echocardiography (#01597)
- **AAE** Association Africaine de l'Eau (#00497)
- **AAE** Association of African Entrepreneurs (#02356)
- **AAE** – Association des astronautes européens (inactive)
- **AAE** Associazione Archivistica Ecclesiastica (#05279)
- **AAEDC** – Association africaine pour l'environnement et le développement communautaire (no recent information)

- ♦ AAEE – Australasian Association for Engineering Education (internationally oriented national body)
- ♦ **AAEEN** African Agricultural Economics Education Network (#00198)
- ♦ AAE / see European Food Safety Authority (#07287)
- ♦ AAEFA – Association africaine des educateurs et formateurs à l'assurance (inactive)
- ♦ AAEN – Associação de Ambientalistas a Favor da Energia Nuclear (internationally oriented national body)
- ♦ **AAERE** Asian Association of Environmental and Resource Economics (#01322)
- ♦ AAESC – Association pour l'avancement des études scandinaves au Canada (internationally oriented national body)
- ♦ AAESEE – Association of Agricultural Engineering of South Eastern Europe (inactive)
- ♦ **AAET** ASEAN Academy of Engineering and Technology (#01135)
- ♦ **AAEU** Arab Agricultural Engineers Union (#00895)
- ♦ **AAFA** African Accounting and Finance Association (#00195)
- ♦ **AAFA** Association africaine du fer et de l'acier (#00346)
- ♦ **AaFaNet** All Africa Farmers Network (#00641)
- ♦ **AAF** Animals Asia Foundation (#00842)
- ♦ **AAF** ASEAN Automotive Federation (#01142)
- ♦ **AAF** Asian Aerosol Federation (#01300)
- ♦ AAFD – Arabic Alliance for Freedom and Democracy (unconfirmed)
- ♦ **AAFI-AFICS Geneva** Association of Former International Civil Servants – Geneva (#02599)
- ♦ **AAFI New York** Association des anciens fonctionnaires internationaux – New York (#02600)
- ♦ **AAFITN** Asian-Australasian Federation of Interventional and Therapeutic Neuroradiology (#01350)
- ♦ **AAFPS** Asian Australasian Federation of Pain Societies (#01351)
- ♦ AAFPS – Australasian Academy of Facial Plastic Surgery (internationally oriented national body)
- ♦ AAFRA / see African Airlines Association (#00200)
- ♦ AAFRC / see Giving Institute: Leading Consultants to Non-Profits
- ♦ AAFS / see AFS Intercultural Programs (#00541)
- ♦ **AAFS** Asian Association for Foundation of Software (#01323)
- ♦ **AAFS** Asian Association for Frailty and Sarcopenia (#01324)
- ♦ AAFSRET – African Association of Farming Systems for Research, Extension and Training (inactive)
- ♦ AAF / see Starch Europe (#19966)
- ♦ AAFT – Asian Academy of Family Therapy (unconfirmed)
- ♦ AAFU – All African Farmers' Union (inactive)
- ♦ **AAFU Paris** Association des anciens fonctionnaires de l'UNESCO (#02601)
- ♦ AAF / see World Archery Asia (#21107)
- ♦ **AAG** Alliance Against Genocide (#00655)
- ♦ AAG – Association of American Geographers (internationally oriented national body)
- ♦ **AAG** Association of Applied Geochemists (#02372)
- ♦ AAGL / see Advancing Minimally Invasive Gynecology Worldwide (#00130)
- ♦ **AAGL** Advancing Minimally Invasive Gynecology Worldwide (#00130)
- ♦ AAGRA – Australasian Association of Genealogists and Record Agents (internationally oriented national body)
- ♦ **AAGS** Asia Association for Global Studies (#01253)
- ♦ AAGS – Association of African Geological Surveys (inactive)
- ♦ **AAGSC** Australasian Aviation Ground Safety Council (#03021)
- ♦ AAGT / see International Association for the Advancement of Gestalt Therapy
- ♦ AAGT-AIC / see International Association for the Advancement of Gestalt Therapy
- ♦ AAH – Aktion Afrika Hilfe (internationally oriented national body)
- ♦ AAHC International – Association of Academic Health Centers International (internationally oriented national body)
- ♦ **AAHM** Asian Academy for Heritage Management (#01294)
- ♦ AAHNA – European Equine Health and Nutrition Association (internationally oriented national body)
- ♦ AAHO – Afro-Asian Housing Organization (inactive)
- ♦ AAHPRID – African Association for Human and Peoples' Rights in Development (inactive)
- ♦ AAHRA – Asia and Australasia Hotel and Restaurant Association (inactive)
- ♦ AAHRED – Africa Alliance for Health Research and Economic Development (internationally oriented national body)
- ♦ **AAHRS** Asian Association of Hair Restoration Surgeons (#01325)
- ♦ **AAHSA** ASEAN Alliance of Health Supplement Associations (#01137)
- ♦ AAI / see Africa-America Institute
- ♦ **AAI** Académie des affaires internationales (#00040)
- ♦ AAI / see Academy of International Business (#00040)
- ♦ AAI – Access Aid International (internationally oriented national body)
- ♦ AAI / see Accountability International (#00059)
- ♦ AAI / see ActionAid (#00087)
- ♦ AAI – Africa-America Institute (internationally oriented national body)
- ♦ AAI – Afro-Asiatisches Institut Salzburg (internationally oriented national body)
- ♦ **AAI** AIESEC Alumni International (#00594)
- ♦ AAI – Airline Ambassadors International (internationally oriented national body)
- ♦ AAI – Anti-Atom-International (internationally oriented national body)
- ♦ **AAI** Association actuarielle internationale (#11586)
- ♦ **AAI** Atheist Alliance International (#03003)
- ♦ **AAIB** Association of African Insurance Brokers (#02358)
- ♦ AAIBBA / see Association of African Insurance Brokers (#02358)
- ♦ AAIBC / see Association of African Insurance Brokers (#02358)
- ♦ AAIBS / see IB Schools Australasia (#11039)
- ♦ AAIC – Association for the Advancement of Industrial Crops (internationally oriented national body)
- ♦ AAIC – Association of Asian Insurance Commissioners (no recent information)
- ♦ **AAICP** Asian Association of Indigenous and Cultural Psychology (#01326)
- ♦ AAICU – Association of American International Colleges and Universities (internationally oriented national body)
- ♦ AAID – African Agency For Integrated Development (internationally oriented national body)
- ♦ AAIE – Association for the Advancement of International Education (internationally oriented national body)
- ♦ AAIET – Association of African Insurance Educators and Trainers (inactive)
- ♦ **AAIG** Association Académique Internationale de Gouvernance (#02342)
- ♦ **AAII** Animal Assisted Intervention International (#00834)
- ♦ **AAIL** African Association of International Law (#00208)
- ♦ AAIN – African Agribusiness Incubators Network (internationally oriented national body)
- ♦ AAIO – Afro-Asian Islamic Organization (inactive)
- ♦ AAIR – Australasian Association for Institutional Research (internationally oriented national body)
- ♦ AAISA – Association of African Insurance Supervisory Authorities (no recent information)
- ♦ **AAIS** African Association of Insect Scientists (#00207)
- ♦ AAIS – Australasian Association for Information Systems (internationally oriented national body)
- ♦ AAITO – Association of African Industrial Technology Organizations (inactive)
- ♦ AAITS – Arab Association for Information and Technology Systems (no recent information)
- ♦ AAI – World Water Institute (internationally oriented national body)
- ♦ **AAJ** American Association of Jurists (#02110)
- ♦ **AAJ** Asociación Americana de Juristas (#02110)
- ♦ **AAJ** Associação Americana de Juristas (#02110)
- ♦ AAJWA – Asian Agricultural Journalists and Writers Association (inactive)
- ♦ AAKF – Asian Amateur Kabaddi Federation (inactive)
- ♦ AAKKL – Aasian ja Afrikan kielten ja kulttuurien laitos (internationally oriented national body)
- ♦ AAKNet – Africa Adaptation Knowledge Network (unconfirmed)
- ♦ AALA – Asociación de Abogados Latinoamericanos por la Defensa de los Derechos Humanos (no recent information)
- ♦ AALA – Asociación Andina de Lineas Aéreas (no recent information)
- ♦ AALAE – African Association for Literacy and Adult Education (inactive)
- ♦ **AAL Assocation** Ambient Assisted Living Association (#00770)
- ♦ Aalborg Centre / see Aalborg Centre for Problem Based Learning in Engineering Science and Sustainability
- ♦ Aalborg Centre for Problem Based Learning in Engineering Science and Sustainability (internationally oriented national body)
- ♦ AALCC / see Asian-African Legal Consultative Organization (#01303)
- ♦ **AALCO** Asian-African Legal Consultative Organization (#01303)
- ♦ AALE / see Association des Loteries d'Afrique (#02791)
- ♦ AALEP – Association of Accredited Public Policy Advocates to the European Union (unconfirmed)
- ♦ AALMA – Association africaine pour la liturgie, la musique et les arts (inactive)
- ♦ Aalmoezeniers van de Arbeid (religious order)
- ♦ AALS – Association of Arid Lands Studies (internationally oriented national body)
- ♦ AAMA – Asian America MultiTechnology Association (internationally oriented national body)
- ♦ AAM – African Association for Management (inactive)
- ♦ **AAM** Arab Academy of Music (#00890)
- ♦ **AAM** Asia Academy of Management (#01249)
- ♦ AAM – Association africaine pour le management (inactive)
- ♦ AA and MDSIF – Aplastic Anemia and MDS International Foundation (unconfirmed)
- ♦ AAMETI – ASEAN Association of Maritime Education and Training Institutions (no recent information)
- ♦ **AAMHA** Association africaine de microbiologie et d'hygiène alimentaire (#02350)
- ♦ **AAMISS** Asian Academy of Minimally Invasive Spinal Surgery (#01295)
- ♦ **AAMLS** Asia Association of Medical Laboratory Scientists (#01254)
- ♦ AAMLT / see ASEAN Association for Clinical Laboratory Sciences (#01139)
- ♦ AAMMH – African Alliance for Maternal Mental Health (unconfirmed)
- ♦ **AAMO** Asian Association of Management Organizations (#01329)
- ♦ AAMOCIOS / see Asian Association of Management Organizations (#01329)
- ♦ AAMPS – Association for African Medicinal Plants Standards (no recent information)
- ♦ AAM / see Starch Europe (#19966)
- ♦ **AAMT** Asia-Pacific Association for Machine Translation (#01845)
- ♦ AAMTI – Association of African Maritime Training Institutes (no recent information)
- ♦ AANA – Arthroscopy Association of North America (internationally oriented national body)
- ♦ **AAN** Asia Arsenic Network (#01251)
- ♦ **AAN** Asian Aquaculture Network (#01310)
- ♦ AAN – Australasian Association of Nematologists
- ♦ **AANM** African Association of Nuclear Medicine (#00210)
- ♦ **AANOA** ASEAN Academy of Neurotology Otology and Audiology (#01136)
- ♦ Aansteeklike Siektesvereniging van Suider Afrika / see Infectious Diseases Society of Southern Africa
- ♦ AANZUPJ / see Union for Progressive Judaism
- ♦ AAOAA – Afro-Asia-Oceania Association of Anatomists (no recent information)
- ♦ **AAO** Asian Academy of Osseointegration (#01297)
- ♦ AAOE – Association of African Optometric Educators (no recent information)
- ♦ **AAOEH** Asian Association of Occupational and Environmental Health (#01330)
- ♦ AAOH / see Asian Association of Occupational and Environmental Health (#01330)
- ♦ **AAOIFI** Accounting and Auditing Organization for Islamic Financial Institutions (#00062)
- ♦ AAOMFS / see Asian Association of Oral and Maxillofacial Surgeons (#01332)
- ♦ AAONMS / see Shriners International
- ♦ **AAOT** Asian Academy of Orofacial Pain and Temporomandibular Disorders (#01296)
- ♦ **AAOU** Asian Association of Open Universities (#01331)
- ♦ **AAPA** African Association for Precision Agriculture (#00213)
- ♦ AAPA – Afro-Asian Philosophy Association (inactive)
- ♦ AAPA – Afro-Asian Psychological Association (unconfirmed)
- ♦ **AAPA** All Africa Pool Association (#00643)
- ♦ **AAPA** American Association of Port Authorities (#00775)
- ♦ **AAPA** Asian Association for Public Administration (#01334)
- ♦ **AAPA** Association of Asia Pacific Airlines (#02385)
- ♦ **AAPA** Audiovisual Anti-Piracy Alliance (#03015)
- ♦ AAPAC – African Association of Pure and Applied Chemistry (inactive)
- ♦ AAPAF / see Association of Asian and Pacific Arts Festivals (#02380)
- ♦ **AAPAF** Association of Asian and Pacific Arts Festivals (#02380)
- ♦ **AAPAM** African Association for Public Administration and Management (#00215)
- ♦ **AAPAM** Association of Asia Pacific Advertising Media (#02384)
- ♦ **AAPAP** African Association of Psychiatrists and Allied Professions (#00214)
- ♦ AAP – Arab Academy of Pharmacy (no recent information)
- ♦ **AAP** Asian Academy of Prosthodontics (#01299)
- ♦ AAP – Australasian Association of Philosophy (internationally oriented national body)
- ♦ **AAPBS** Association of Asia-Pacific Business Schools (#02386)
- ♦ AAPC – All African Peoples' Conference (inactive)
- ♦ **AAPD** Asian Academy of Preventive Dentistry (#01298)
- ♦ AAPDMAC – Action d'appui pour la protection des droits des minorités en Afrique centrale (internationally oriented national body)
- ♦ AAPG – American Association of Petroleum Geologists (internationally oriented national body)
- ♦ AAPM / see Asian Pacific Federation of Human Resource Management (#01611)
- ♦ AAPN / see Americas Apparel Producers Network
- ♦ AAPN – Americas Apparel Producers Network (internationally oriented national body)
- ♦ AAPN – Asian Animal Protection Network (internationally oriented national body)
- ♦ AAPN – Associazione Ambientalisti per il Nucleare (internationally oriented national body)
- ♦ AAPO – All-African People's Organization (internationally oriented national body)
- ♦ **AAPOCAD** Association des agents pensionnés des organisations coordonnées et de leurs ayants droit (#02363)
- ♦ **AAPPAC** Association of Asia Pacific Performing Arts Centres (#02387)
- ♦ AAPP – Arab Association of Petroleum Professionals (unconfirmed)
- ♦ AAPP / see Asian Parliamentary Assembly (#01653)
- ♦ **AAPPS** Association of Asia Pacific Physical Societies (#02388)
- ♦ AAPRD – Association for the Advancement of Policy, Research and Development in the Third World (inactive)
- ♦ **AAPS** African Association of Physics Students (#00211)
- ♦ **AAPS** African Association of Physiological Sciences (#00212)
- ♦ AAPS – African Association of Political Science (unconfirmed)
- ♦ **AAPS** Asian Association of Pediatric Surgeons (#01333)
- ♦ **AAPS** Association of African Planning Schools (#02359)
- ♦ AAPS – Australian Association for Pacific Studies (internationally oriented national body)
- ♦ **AAPSO** Afro-Asian Peoples' Solidarity Organization (#00537)
- ♦ AAPW – Academic Associates Peace Works (internationally oriented national body)
- ♦ AAQG – Americas Aerospace Quality Group (internationally oriented national body)
- ♦ **AAQS** Africa Association of Quantity Surveyors (#00156)
- ♦ AAR / see Association for Aid and Relief – Japan
- ♦ **AARA** Asian Aerosol Research Assembly (#01301)
- ♦ **AAR** Artists Against Racism (#01123)
- ♦ **AAR** ASEAN Association of Radiology (#01140)
- ♦ AAR – Association for Aid and Relief – Japan (internationally oriented national body)

♦ AARC – Arab and African Research Centre (internationally oriented national body)
♦ **AARC** Rectors' Conference of the Universities of the Adriatic Universities (#18632)
♦ **AARDO** African-Asian Rural Development Organization (#00203)
♦ **AARG** Aerial Archaeology Research Group (#00144)
♦ AARI – Arctic and Antarctic Research Institute (internationally oriented national body)
♦ **AARINENA** Association of Agricultural Research Institutions in the Near East and North Africa (#02364)
♦ AARINENA Regional Date Palm Network / see Date Palm Global Network (#05013)
♦ **AArk** Amphibian Ark (#00803)
♦ **AARNET** ASEAN-AVRDC Regional Network on Vegetable Research and Development (#01143)
♦ AARO – Association of Americans Resident Overseas (internationally oriented national body)
♦ AARON Groep / see TRIAS
♦ AARP / see AARP International

♦ AARP Global Network 00002

Main Office 601 E St NW, Washington DC 20049, USA. T. +12024342450.
URL: http://www.aarpglobalnetwork.org/

History 2006, by *AARP International.* **Languages** English. **Activities** Organizes: annual workshop; monthly peer group meeting. **Events** *Seminar on affordability and safety of livable communities* Washington, DC (USA) 2010, *Annual workshop / Workshop* Washington, DC (USA) 2008, *Annual workshop / Workshop* Utrecht (Netherlands) 2007, *Annual workshop / Workshop* Anaheim, CA (USA) 2006. **Publications** *Around the Network Newsletter.*
Members National associations in 7 countries:
Canada, Chile, Denmark, India, Italy, Netherlands, USA.
[2010.08.11/XM8212/**E**]

♦ AARP International (internationally oriented national body)
♦ **AARR** Asian Association for Radiation Research (#01335)
♦ AARRO / see African-Asian Rural Development Organization (#00203)
♦ **AARS** Asian Association on Remote Sensing (#01336)
♦ **AARSE** African Association of Remote Sensing of the Environment (#00216)
♦ **AARU** Association of Arab Universities (#02374)
♦ **AASA** Airlines Association of Southern Africa (#00606)
♦ AASA – Association of Academies of Science for Asia (inactive)
♦ AASA / see Association for the Study of Australasia in Asia (#02937)
♦ **AAS** African Academy of Sciences (#00193)
♦ **AAS** Asian Allelopathy Society (#01305)
♦ AAS – Association arabe de sociologie (no recent information)
♦ AAS – Association for Asian Studies, Ann Arbor (internationally oriented national body)
♦ AASBi – Association of Asian Societies for Bioinformatics (unconfirmed)
♦ AASCA – Association of American Schools of Central America (see: #02367)
♦ **AASC** Association of African Sports Confederations (#02360)
♦ AASD – Andean Alliance for Sustainable Development (internationally oriented national body)
♦ **AASD** Asian Association for the Study of Diabetes (#01341)
♦ **AASD** Australasian Association of Schools of Dentistry (#03020)
♦ AASE – African Association of Science Editors (no recent information)
♦ AASF – African Asian Studies Association (internationally oriented national body)
♦ AASF – Afrikanisch-Asiatische Studienförderung (internationally oriented national body)
♦ **AASF** Asia Swimming Federation (#02099)
♦ AASG – American Anti-Slavery Group (internationally oriented national body)
♦ AASGON – Africa Asia Scholars Global Network (internationally oriented national body)
♦ **A-ASIA** Association for Asian Studies in Africa (#02383)
♦ Aasian ja Afrikan kielten ja kulttuurien laitos (internationally oriented national body)
♦ AASLD – American Association for the Study of Liver Diseases (internationally oriented national body)
♦ AASLE – Asian and Australasian Society of Labour Economics (unconfirmed)
♦ **AASM** Asian-African Society of Mycobacteriology (#01304)
♦ **AASM** Asian Association for Sport Management (#01340)
♦ **AASNS** Asian-Australasian Society of Neurological Surgeons (#01352)
♦ AASO – African Aeronautics & Space Organisation (internationally oriented national body)
♦ **AASP** Asian Association of Schools of Pharmacy (#01337)
♦ **AASP** Asian Association of Social Psychology (#01338)
♦ AASP – Association of African Studies Programs (internationally oriented national body)
♦ AASP – Association arabe de science politique (inactive)
♦ **AASPN** Asian-Australasian Society for Pediatric Neurosurgery (#01353)
♦ **AASPP** Asian Association of Societies for Plant Pathology (#01339)
♦ **AASR** African Association for the Study of Religions (#00217)
♦ AASSA / see American International Schools in the Americas
♦ **AASSA** Association of Academies and Societies of Sciences in Asia (#02341)
♦ **AASS** Association africaine de la science du sol (#00520)
♦ AASSC / see Australasian Association for Communist and Post-Communist Studies
♦ AASSC – Association for the Advancement of Scandinavian Studies in Canada (internationally oriented national body)
♦ **AASSE** Athletic Association of the Small States of Europe (#03006)
♦ **AASSFN** Asian-Australasian Society for Stereotactic and Functional Neurosurgery (#01354)
♦ Aassociation internationale médico-sportive / see International Federation of Sports Medicine (#13554)
♦ **AASSREC** Association of Asian Social Science Research Councils (#02382)
♦ **AASTMT** Arab Academy for Science, Technology and Maritime Transport (#00891)
♦ AASU / see All-Africa Students Union (#00644)
♦ **AASU** All-Africa Students Union (#00644)
♦ AASVET – Asian Academic Society for Vocational Education and Training (unconfirmed)
♦ AATAA – All African Travel Agents Association (inactive)
♦ AATA / see Animal Transportation Association (#00844)
♦ AATA – Association of African Tax Administrators (no recent information)
♦ **AATE** Association africaine de la télédétection et de l'environnement (#00216)
♦ **AATF** African Agricultural Technology Foundation (#00199)
♦ AATFS – Asian Association of Track and Field Statisticians (inactive)
♦ AATO – All Africa Teachers' Organization (no recent information)
♦ AATPO – Association of African Trade Promotion Organizations (no recent information)
♦ AATUF – All African Trade Union Federation (inactive)
♦ **AAU** Arab Association of Urology (#00900)
♦ **AAU** Association of African Universities (#02361)
♦ AAUS / see Asian Association of UTI and STI (#01343)
♦ **AAUS** Asian Association of UTI and STI (#01343)
♦ **AAV** Association of Avian Veterinarians (#02389)
♦ AAVDI – Australasian Association of Veterinary Diagnostic Imaging (internationally oriented national body)
♦ AAVIS / see International Society for Pelviperineology (#15348)
♦ AAVMF – Arab Association of Veterinary Medical Faculties (inactive)
♦ AAVP – African AIDS Vaccine Partnership (unconfirmed)
♦ **AAVS** Asian Association of Veterinary Schools (#01345)
♦ AAWA – Afro-Asian Writers' Association (inactive)
♦ **AAW** Alliance for Arab Women (#00657)
♦ AAWC / see Asian Associated Wrestling Committee (#01311)
♦ **AAWC** Asian Associated Wrestling Committee (#01311)
♦ AAWC / see Pan African Women's Organization (#18074)
♦ AAWG / see African Association of Women in Geosciences (#00219)
♦ **AAWG** African Association of Women in Geosciences (#00219)
♦ **AAWH** Asian Association for World Historians (#01347)
♦ **AAWORD** Association of African Women for Research and Development (#02362)
♦ **AAWS** Alcoholics Anonymous World Services (#00624)
♦ **AAWS** Asian Association of Women's Studies (#01346)
♦ AAXO – Association of African Exhibition Organisers (internationally oriented national body)
♦ **AAYC** Arab African Youth Council (#00894)
♦ ABA / see African Bar Association (#00220)
♦ **ABA** Arab Beverage Association (#00908)
♦ **ABA** ASEAN Bankers Association (#01144)
♦ **ABA** Asian Bankers Association (#01355)
♦ **ABA** Asian Biophysics Association (#01358)
♦ **ABA** Asian Buffalo Association (#01367)
♦ ABA – Association belge des africanistes (internationally oriented national body)
♦ ABA CEELI / see Central and Eastern European Law Initiative (#03693)
♦ Abacusking International Abacus Mental-Arithmetic Alliance (unconfirmed)
♦ **ABAECA** Association of Psychological and Educational Counsellors of Asia (#02878)
♦ **ABAI** Association for Behavior Analysis International (#02395)
♦ ABA International / see Association for Behavior Analysis International (#02395)
♦ AB – Alliance balkanique (inactive)

♦ ABANTU for Development 00003

Office HNo A30, Adjacent Belfort School, Spintex Road, Baatsoona, PO Box KD 4, Kanda, Accra, Ghana. T. +23321816113. Fax +23321816114. E-mail: abanturowa@yahoo.com.
Nigeria Country Office PO Box 2604, Kaduna, Nigeria. T. +23462233066. Fax +23462233066.
Regional Office for Eastern and Southern Africa Mbaaze Ave, PO Box 56241, 00200 City Square, Nairobi, Kenya. T. +2542570343. Fax +2542570668. E-mail: roesa@abantu.org.
URL: http://www.abantu-rowa.org/

History 1991, by African women. **Aims** Increase participation of African, especially women in the political and economic structures of African countries; eradicate the cultural, legal and political obstacles to women attaining *economic independence* and equality before the law; ensure the advancement of women's interests, benefits the entire community. **Structure** Board of Directors. **Languages** English. **Staff** 11.00 FTE, paid. **Finance** Funded by individuals and by the following bodies: *Christian Aid*; *Commonwealth Secretariat (#04362)*; *Department for International Development (DFID, inactive)*; *Ford Foundation (#09858)*; *Humanistisch Instituut voor Ontwikkelingssamenwerking (Hivos)*; National Lottery (UK) Charities Board; *Oxfam Novib*; *Oxfam GB*; *DANIDA*. **Activities** Advocacy/lobbing/activissm; guidance/assistance/consulting; training/education; knowledge management/information dissemination. **Events** *Policy forum on gender and poverty alleviation* Accra (Ghana) 1999, *Policy seminar on good governance and poverty alleviation in Nigeria* Brussels (Belgium) 1999, *Policy seminar on the gender dimension of international and regional peacekeeping in Africa* New York, NY (USA) 1999, *Gender equity, social and economic empowerment of women* Lusaka (Zambia) 1998, *Gender sensitive constitutional reform* Nairobi (Kenya) 1998. **Publications** *GAP Matters* (4 a year) – magazine. *ABANTU for Development's Training Brochure.* Annual Report. Books; pamphlets; training materials; papers; brochures; fact sheets. **Members** Not a membership organization. **Consultative Status** Consultative status granted from: *ECOSOC (#05331)* (Special). **IGO Relations** *African Centre for Gender (ACG).* Associated with Department of Global Communications of the United Nations. **NGO Relations** Member of: *EarthAction (EA, #05159)*; *PMNCH (#18410)*; *Think Global – Development Education Association (DEA).*
[2011.08.11/XE2924/**E**]

♦ ABAO – Association des banquiers de l'Afrique de l'Ouest (no recent information)
♦ ABAO – Association des botanistes de l'Afrique de l'ouest (no recent information)
♦ ABASU / see Confederación Sudamericana de Básquetbol (#04482)
♦ ABA-UNDP International Legal Resource Centre (internationally oriented national body)
♦ ABB – Association Belgique – Bolivie – Amérique latine (internationally oriented national body)
♦ ABBF / see Asian Bodybuilding and Physique Sports Federation (#01361)
♦ **ABBF** Asian Bodybuilding and Physique Sports Federation (#01361)
♦ ABB – International Conference on Applied Biochemistry and Biotechnology (meeting series)
♦ **ABBS** Association of BRICS Business Schools (#02398)
♦ **ABCA** Association des banques centrales africaines (#02352)
♦ **ABC** African Bird Club (#00224)
♦ **ABC** African Books Collective (#00226)
♦ **ABC** African Boxing Confederation (#00228)
♦ **ABC** Arab Banking Corporation (#00906)
♦ ABC – Asian Battery Conference (meeting series)
♦ ABC – Asian Billiards Confederation (inactive)
♦ **ABC** Association of the Balkan Chambers (#02392)
♦ ABC – Association for Business Communication (internationally oriented national body)
♦ ABC / see Badminton Asia (#03056)
♦ ABCDEF – Association des responsables des bibliothèques et centres de documentation universitaires et de recherche d'expression française (inactive)
♦ **ABCD** European Advisory Board on Cat Diseases (#05830)
♦ ABC / see FIBA-Asia (#09746)
♦ ABCG – Africa Biodiversity Collaborative Group (internationally oriented national body)

♦ ABC Global Alliance 00004

Contact c/o Fundação Champalimaud, Avenida de Brasilia s/n, 1400-038 Lisbon, Portugal. T. +41918200956. E-mail: info@abcglobalalliance.org.
URL: https://www.abcglobalalliance.org/

History 3 Nov 2016, Paris (France). Launched during World Cancer Congress, as an initiative of *European School of Oncology (ESO, #08434).* "ABC" derives from "advanced breast cancer". Registration: Start date: 19 Nov 2019, Portugal; EU Transparency Register, No/ID: 470824037205-61, Start date: 3 Feb 2020. **Aims** Develop, promote and support tangible improvements that will ultimately create awareness and actions that will improve and extend the lives of patients living with advanced breast cancer (ABC) worldwide. **Structure** General Assembly; Board of Directors. **Languages** English. **Staff** 1.00 FTE, paid. **Activities** Advocacy/lobbying/activism; events/meetings. **Events** *Advanced Breast Cancer International Consensus Conference (ABC6)* Lisbon (Portugal) 2023, *Advanced Breast Cancer International Consensus Conference (ABC6)* 2021, *Advanced Breast Cancer International Consensus Conference (ABC5)* Lisbon (Portugal) 2019, *Advanced Breast Cancer International Consensus Conference (ABC4)* Lisbon (Portugal) 2017, *Advanced Breast Cancer International Consensus Conference (ABC3)* Lisbon (Portugal) 2015. **Information Services** *ABC Global Charter* in Arabic, Chinese, Dutch, English, French, German, Greek, Hindi, Italian, Japanese, Malaysian Sign Language, Polish, Portuguese, Russian, Spanish, Swedish – The ABC Global Charter aims to drive change in the care of patients with ABC, tailoring actions to make them relevant and feasible for different geographies and capacities. **Members** Members (186) from 84 countries. Membership countries not specified. **NGO Relations** Member of (1): *Global Cancer Coalitions Network (GCCN, #10270).* Cooperates with (8): *Europa Donna – The European Breast Cancer Coalition (#05745)*; *European Cancer Patient Coalition (ECPC, #06433)*; *European Oncology Nursing Society (EONS, #08086)*; *European School of Oncology (ESO, #08434)*; *European Society of Breast Cancer Specialists (EUSOMA, #08534)*; *Reach to Recovery International (RRI, #18625)*; *Société internationale d'oncologie gériatrique (SIOG, #19493)*; *Union for International Cancer Control (UICC, #20415).* Many other national associations worldwide.
[2021/XM8704/**E**]

♦ ABC Group (inactive)
♦ **ABCPI** Association du Barreau près la Cour Pénale Internationale (#13109)
♦ ABCS – Associazione Bertoni Cooperazione Sviluppo Terzo Mondo (internationally oriented national body)
♦ ABCSR – Arab Bank Centre for Scientific Research (see: #00903)
♦ ABCT – Association for Behavioural and Cognitive Therapies (internationally oriented national body)

- ♦ **ABCW** Asian Brotherhood of Clerical Workers (#01366)
- ♦ **ABDA** Asian Breast Diseases Association (#01365)
- ♦ **ABDGN** African Black Diaspora Global Network (#00225)
- ♦ Abdul Hameed Shoman Foundation (see: #00903)

♦ Abdus Salam International Centre for Theoretical Physics (ICTP) .. 00005

Centre international Abdus Salam de physique théorique (CIPT)

Dir Strada Costiera 11, 34151 Trieste TS, Italy. T. +39402240111. Fax +3940224163. E-mail: pio@ictp.it – sci_info@ictp.it – director@ictp.it.
URL: http://www.ictp.it/

History 1964, Trieste (Italy). Founded by *International Atomic Energy Agency (IAEA, #12294)*, with the support of the Italian Government. Operated jointly by IAEA and *UNESCO (#20322)*, with major financial assistance from the Government of Italy, from 1970 to 1 Jan 1996, when administrative management transferred from IAEA to UNESCO. Present name adopted to honour the memory of the founder and inspirational leader. Former names and other names: *International Centre for Theoretical Physics* – former. **Aims** Foster growth of advanced studies and research in physical and *mathematical* sciences, especially in support of excellence in developing countries; develop high-level scientific programmes, minding the needs of developing countries; provide an international forum of scientific contact for scientists worldwide; conduct research at the highest international standards; maintain conducive environment of scientific inquiry for the entire ICTP community. **Structure** Scientific Council; Steering Committee. **Languages** English. **Staff** Small permanent staff including resident scientists plus visiting and guest scientists, staff associates and senior and junior research scientists (by invitation, one month to one year). Over 100 general service staff; part-time consultants. **Finance** Regular budget: contributions from Italian Government, IAEA and UNESCO. Programme funding from various scientific institutions and international organizations. Grants for fellowships. Annual budget: 27,000,000 USD. **Activities** Awards/prizes/competitions; events/meetings; research/documentation; training/education. **Events** *Adiabatic Quantum Computing Conference* Trieste (Italy) 2022, *Adiabatic Quantum Computing Conference* Trieste (Italy) 2020, *Joint Workshop on Physics and Technology of Innovative Nuclear Energy Systems* Trieste (Italy) 2018, *Workshop on Space Weather Effects on Global Navigation Satellite Systems Operations at Low Latitudes* Trieste (Italy) 2018, *Workshop on Research Reactors for Development of Materials and Fuels for Innovative Nuclear Energy Systems* Trieste (Italy) 2017. **Publications** *News from ICTP* – newsletter. Annual Report; brochures. **IGO Relations** United Nations organizations. **NGO Relations** Cooperates with (1): *Adiabatic Quantum Computing Conference (AQC).* [2022/XF2724/y/**E***]

- ♦ **ABE** Assemblée des bibliothèques de l'Eurasie (#16458)
- ♦ **ABE** Association bancaire pour l'Euro (#05647)
- ♦ **ABEGS** Arab Bureau of Education for the Gulf States (#00910)
- ♦ ABET (internationally oriented national body)
- ♦ **ABF** African Bridge Federation (#00230)
- ♦ **ABF** ASEAN Business Forum (#01147)
- ♦ **ABF** Asian Bird Fair Network (#01359)
- ♦ **ABF** Asian Bowling Federation (#01362)
- ♦ ABF – Asian Bukido Federation (unconfirmed)
- ♦ ABF / see Asia Pacific Baptist Federation (#01857)
- ♦ ABFA – Wellbeing Foundation Africa (internationally oriented national body)
- ♦ ABF / see Badminton Confederation of Africa (#03057)
- ♦ **ABFER** Asian Bureau of Finance and Economic Research (#01369)
- ♦ ABFM / see Global Interaction
- ♦ ABFMS / see American Baptist International Ministries
- ♦ **ABF Norden** Arbetarnas Bildningsförbund i Norden (#17377)
- ♦ ABG / see Advertising Business Group (#00136)
- ♦ **ABG** Advertising Business Group (#00136)
- ♦ **ABGTS** Asia Baptist Graduate Theological Seminary (#01255)
- ♦ ABHE – Association for Biblical Higher Education (internationally oriented national body)
- ♦ ABI – Action biblique internationale (internationally oriented national body)
- ♦ ABI – Arnold Bergstraesser Institut für Kulturwissenschaftliche Forschung (internationally oriented national body)
- ♦ **ABIC Foundation** Agricultural Biotechnology International Conference Foundation (#00568)
- ♦ Abidjan convention – Convention for Cooperation in the Protection and Development of the Marine and Coastal Environment of the West and Central African Region (1981 treaty)
- ♦ Abidjan Regional Maritime Academy / see Regional Academy of Maritime Science and Technology (#18744)
- ♦ Abilis Foundation (internationally oriented national body)
- ♦ **ABINIA** Asociación de Estados Iberoamericanos para el Desarrollo de las Bibliotecas Nacionales de Iberoamérica (#02638)
- ♦ ABINIA / see Association of Ibero-American States for the Development of National Libraries (#02638)
- ♦ **ABINIA** Association of Ibero-American States for the Development of National Libraries (#02638)
- ♦ ABioNET / see African Society for Bioinformatics and Computational Biology (#00459)
- ♦ ABIPALC – Asociación de Bibliotecas Públicas de América Latina y el Caribe (no recent information)
- ♦ ABI ROLI – American Bar Association Rule of Law Initiative (internationally oriented national body)
- ♦ **ABIS** Academy of Business in Society (#00032)
- ♦ Abkommen zur erhaltung der fledermäuse in Europa (1991 treaty)
- ♦ Abkommen zur Erhaltung der Kleinwale in der Nord- und Ostsee, des Nordostatlantiks und der Irischen See (1992 treaty)
- ♦ Abkommen über den austausch von kriegsbeschädigten zwischen den mitgliedsländern des Europarats zum zwecke der ärztlichen behandlung (1955 treaty)
- ♦ Abkommen über die zusammenarbeit auf dem gebiet der seefischerei (1962 treaty)
- ♦ ABLA – Association of Binational Centers in Latin America (inactive)
- ♦ **ABL** Alliance of Business Lawyers (#00660)
- ♦ **ABLCC** Arab-Belgian-Luxembourg Chamber of Commerce (#00907)
- ♦ ABLD – Academic Business Library Directors (internationally oriented national body)
- ♦ AbleChildAfrica / see Able Child Africa
- ♦ Able Child Africa (internationally oriented national body)
- ♦ ABLE International – Association for Better Living and Education (see: #03922)
- ♦ ABLFA – African Business Law Firms Association (unconfirmed)
- ♦ ABLH – Association for Better Land Husbandry (internationally oriented national body)
- ♦ **ABMA** Asian Building Maintenance Association (#01368)
- ♦ ABM – Academy of Breastfeeding Medicine (internationally oriented national body)
- ♦ **ABM** AgroBioMediterraneao (#00579)
- ♦ **ABMF** ASEAN+3 Bond Market Forum (#01133)
- ♦ ABMS / see Global Interaction
- ♦ ABMTRR – Australasian Bone Marrow Transplant Recipient Registry (internationally oriented national body)
- ♦ ABMU / see American Baptist International Ministries
- ♦ **ABNA** Association of the Balkan News Agencies (#02393)
- ♦ **ABN** African Biodiversity Network (#00222)
- ♦ **ABN** Arbetarrörelsens Barnorganisationer i Norden (#01084)
- ♦ **ABN** Association of Baltic Numismatists (#02394)
- ♦ **ABN** Autorité du bassin du Niger (#17134)
- ♦ ABNP – Association of Baltic National Parks (inactive)
- ♦ **ABO** Alliance of Blood Operators (#00659)
- ♦ Abogados Europeos Democraticos (#03049)
- ♦ Abogados Sin Fronteras (#03050)
- ♦ **Abolition 2000** Abolition 2000 – Global Network to Eliminate Nuclear Weapons (#00006)

♦ Abolition 2000 – Global Network to Eliminate Nuclear Weapons (Abolition 2000) 00006

Contact c/o Western States Legal Foundation, 655 13th St, Ste 201, Preservation Park, Oakland CA 94612, USA. T. +15108395877. E-mail: wslf@earthlink.net.
URL: http://www.abolition2000.org/

History Apr 1995, New York NY (USA), as 'The Abolition Caucus', during the *Conference to Review and Extend the Non-Proliferation Treaty*. Has also been referred to as *NGO Abolition Caucus*. Current title adopted, Nov 1995, The Hague (Netherlands). Absorbed activities of *Global Anti-Nuclear Alliance (GANA, inactive)* and *International Coalition for Nuclear Non-Proliferation and Disarmament (inactive)*. **Aims** Achieve a world free of nuclear weapons and redress the *environmental degradation* and human *suffering* arising from 50 years of nuclear weapons testing and production. **Structure** International Coordinating Committee of 9 members. Global Council. Regions (7): North America; Central and South America; Europe; Pacific; Asia; Africa; Middle East. Working Groups. **Activities** Working Groups (16): Abolition Days; Communications; CTBT; Depleted Uranium; European Security; Finance; Fissile Materials; Grassroots; NATO; Non-Aligned Movement (NAM); Nuclearization of Space; Nuclear Threats/Legal Issues; Nuclear Weapons Convention; Radiation Effects; Religious Organizations; Sustainable Energy. **Events** *International Meeting on Nuclear Security in Europe after the Collapse of the INF Treaty* Brussels (Belgium) 2019, *Annual General Meeting / Meeting* New York, NY (USA) 2015, *Annual General Meeting / Meeting* New York, NY (USA) 2014, *Annual General Meeting / Meeting* Edinburgh (UK) 2013, *Annual General Meeting / Meeting* Vienna (Austria) 2012. **Publications** *Abolition 2000 Grassroots Newsletter.*

Members Network of organizations endorsing the Abolition Statement (currently over 2,000). Signatories in 109 countries and territories:
Afghanistan, Albania, Algeria, Andorra, Argentina, Armenia, Australia, Austria, Bahrain, Bangladesh, Belarus, Belgium, Bhutan, Bosnia-Herzegovina, Botswana, Brazil, Bulgaria, Burundi, Cameroon, Canada, Central African Rep, China, Colombia, Congo Brazzaville, Congo DR, Costa Rica, Côte d'Ivoire, Croatia, Cuba, Cyprus, Czechia, Denmark, Egypt, El Salvador, Eritrea, Estonia, Eswatini, Ethiopia, Fiji, Finland, France, Germany, Ghana, Greece, Guatemala, Hungary, India, Indonesia, Iran Islamic Rep, Iraq, Ireland, Israel, Italy, Japan, Jordan, Kazakhstan, Kenya, Korea Rep, Kyrgyzstan, Madagascar, Malaysia, Marshall Is, Mauritius, Mexico, Micronesia FS, Moldova, Mongolia, Morocco, Mozambique, Namibia, Nepal, Netherlands, New Zealand, Nigeria, Norway, Pakistan, Palau, Palestine, Peru, Philippines, Poland, Portugal, Puerto Rico, Qatar, Romania, Russia, Serbia, Sierra Leone, Singapore, Slovakia, Slovenia, Somalia, South Africa, Spain, Sudan, Sweden, Switzerland, Taiwan, Thailand, Togo, Türkiye, Uganda, UK, Ukraine, Uruguay, USA, Vanuatu, Zambia, Zimbabwe.

Included in the above, 92 organizations listed in this Yearbook:
- *Abolition des armes nucléaires – Maison de Vigilance*;
- *Anti-Atom-International (AAI)*;
- *Arab Coordination Center for NGOs (ACCN, no recent information)*;
- *Arab Office for Youth and Environment (AOYE)*;
- *Arab Organization for Human Rights (AOHR, #01020)*;
- *Association of Women of the Mediterranean Region (AWMR, no recent information)*;
- *Basel Peace Office*;
- *Campaign for a More Democratic United Nations (CAMDUN, inactive)*;
- *Campaign for International Cooperation and Disarmament (CICD)*;
- *Canadian Peace Alliance (CPA)*;
- *Canadian Voice of Women for Peace (VOW)*;
- *Center for Science and International Security (CENSIS)*;
- *Centre for International Peacebuilding (no recent information)*;
- *Church Women United (CWU)*;
- *Citizens for a United Earth (CUE)*;
- *Deutscher Friedensrat (DFR)*;
- *Development Center International, Dhaka (DCI)*;
- *Economists for Peace and Security (EPS, #05322)*;
- *Forest Movement Europe (FME, #09864)*;
- *Foundation for Universal Responsibility of His Holiness The Dalai Lama*;
- *Friends of the Earth International (FoEI, #10002)*;
- *Fundación para la Aplicación y Enseñanza de las Ciencias (FUNDAEC)*;
- *Geneva International Peace Research Institute (GIPRI)*;
- *Global Justice Now*;
- *Global Resource Action Center for the Environment (GRACE)*;
- *Graduate Women International (GWI, #10688)*;
- *Grandmothers for Peace International*;
- *Greenpeace International (#10727)*;
- *Hague Appeal for Peace (HAP, #10848)*;
- *Hiroshima Peace Culture Foundation (HPCF)*;
- *Indian Institute for Peace, Disarmament and Environmental Protection (IIPDEP)*;
- *Institute for Cultural Conflict and Peace Research and Inter-Cultural Cooperation, Hannover (no recent information)*;
- *Institute for Resource and Security Studies (IRSS, no recent information)*;
- *International Alliance of Atomic Veterans (no recent information)*;
- *International Architects, Designers, Planners for Social Responsibility (ARC-PEACE, #11666)*;
- *International Association of Educators for World Peace (IAEWP)*;
- *International Association of Lawyers Against Nuclear Arms (IALANA, #11994)*;
- *International Association of Peace Messenger Cities (IAPMC, #12073)*;
- *International Network of Engineers and Scientists Against Proliferation (INESAP, see: #14260)*;
- *International Peace Bureau (IPB, #14535)*;
- *International Peace Research Association (IPRA, #14537)*;
- *International Physicians for the Prevention of Nuclear War (IPPNW, #14578)*;
- *International Secretariat Committee of Nuclear Free Zone Local Authorities (#14820)*;
- *Labour Action for Peace (LAP)*;
- *Latin American Circle for International Studies (LACIS)*;
- *Lawyers Alliance for World Security (LAWS)*;
- *Lutheran Peace Fellowship (LPF)*;
- *Mayors for Peace (#16605)*;
- *Medact*;
- *Missionary Sisters of Our Lady of Africa (White Sisters)*;
- *Nagasaki Foundation for the Promotion of Peace*;
- *Nagasaki Peace Institute*;
- *New Global Freedom Movement (no recent information)*;
- *Norwegian Peace Association (NPA)*;
- *Norwegian Peace Council*;
- *Nuclear-Free and Independent Pacific Movement (NFIP Movement, #17617)*;
- *Pacific Concerns Resource Centre (PCRC)*;
- *Pacific Islands Association of Non-Governmental Organizations (PIANGO, #17961)*;
- *Pan-African Reconciliation Council (PARC, #18063)*;
- *Parliamentarians for Global Action (PGA, #18208)*;
- *Pax Christi – International Catholic Peace Movement (#18266)*;
- *Pax World Service (PWS)*;
- *Peace Farm*;
- *Peace Pledge Union (PPU)*;
- *Physicians for Global Survival, Canada (PGS)*;
- *Quaker Peace and Social Witness (QPSW, see: #10004)*;
- *Ribbon International*;
- *Science for Peace (SFP)*;
- *Scientists for Global Responsibility (SGR)*;
- *SERVAS International (#19234)*;
- *Sisters of the Sacred Hearts of Jesus and Mary (SHJM)*;
- *Soka Gakkai International (SGI, #19672)*;
- *Swedish Peace Council (no recent information)*;
- *The Other Economic Summit (TOES, no recent information)*;
- *UNESCO (#20322)*;
- *Unitarian Universalist Association (UUA, #20494)*;
- *United Network of Young Peacebuilders (UNOY, #20653)*;
- *Veterans for Peace (VFP)*;
- *War and Peace Foundation*;
- *War Resisters' International (WRI, #20818)*;
- *War Resisters League (WRL)*;
- *Women for Peace, Switzerland*;
- *Women's Environmental Network (WEN)*;
- *Women's Environment and Development Organization (WEDO, #21016)*;

– *Women's International Democratic Federation (WIDF, #21022)*;
– *Women's International League for Peace and Freedom (WILPF, #21024)*;
– *Women Strike for Peace (WSP, no recent information)*;
– *World Court Project (WCP, inactive)*;
– *World Federalist Movement – Movement for a Just World Order through a Strengthened United Nations (WFM, #21404)*;
– *World Information Service on Energy (WISE, #21582)*;
– *World Peace Prayer Society*;
– *World Young Women's Christian Association (World YWCA, #21947)*.

NGO Relations Represented on the Organizing Committee of: Hague Appeal for Peace (HAP). Member of: *EarthAction (EA, #05159)*; *International Campaign to Abolish Nuclear Weapons (ICAN, #12426)*.
[2018/XF4131/y/**F**]

♦ Abolition des armes nucléaires – Maison de Vigilance (internationally oriented national body)
♦ D'abord ne pas nuire (#10875)
♦ **ABORNE** The African Borderlands Research Network (#00227)

♦ Abortion and Postabortion Care Consortium (APAC) 00007

Contact address not obtained. E-mail: contactus@ipas.org.

History Founded 1993, by *IPAS (#16010)*, AVSC (now *EngenderHealth*), *Johns Hopkins Program for International Education in Gynecology and Obstetrics (JHPIEGO)*, *Pathfinder International (#18261)* and *International Planned Parenthood Federation (IPPF, #14589)*. Former names and other names: *Postabortion Care Consortium (PAC Consortium)* – former; *Consorcio para la Atención Postaborto* – former. **Aims** Inform the reproductive health community about complications related to miscarriage and incomplete abortion; promote Postabortion Care (PAC) as an effective strategy for addressing this global problem. **Structure** Steering Committee. Task Forces (varying). **Languages** English. **Activities** Works through voluntary Task Forces (4): Essential Supplies; Misoprostol for PAC; Service Delivery; Youth-Friendly PAC. Promotes coordination and information sharing on the issue of postabortion care; advocates at the international level for policy changes and increased resources for PAC services and the prevention of unsafe abortion; informs the broader reproductive health community about health issues related to unsafe abortion and strategies to confront this through PAC, and to promote PAC as an effective strategy for addressing this global problem, especially in countries where abortion is highly restricted. **Events** *Meeting* Kuala Lumpur (Malaysia) 2013, *Meeting* Washington, DC (USA) 2012, *Meeting* Washington, DC (USA) 2006, *Meeting* San Francisco, CA (USA) 2003, *Meeting* Washington, DC (USA) 2003. **Publications** Available on website.

Members National and international organizations (over 100) worldwide, including 16 organizations listed in this Yearbook:
EngenderHealth; *FHI 360*; *International Planned Parenthood Federation (IPPF, #14589)*; *IntraHealth International*; *IPAS (#16010)*; *Johns Hopkins Program for International Education in Gynecology and Obstetrics (JHPIEGO)*; *Management Sciences for Health (MSH)*; *MSI Reproductive Choices*; *Pacific Institute for Women's Health (PIWH)*; *PAI (#18025)*; *PATH (#18260)*; *Pathfinder International (#18261)*; *Population Council (#18458)*; *Save the Children UK (SC UK)*; *United States Agency for International Development (USAID)*; *World Vision International (WVI, #21904)*.
[2017/XF4805/y/**F**]

♦ ABOS / see Directorate-General for Development Cooperation
♦ **ABPA** ASEAN Book Publishers Association (#01145)
♦ ABPCD – Association des banques populaires pour la coopération et le développement (internationally oriented national body)
♦ ABP' / see Helen Keller International (#10902)
♦ ABPMP International – Association of Business Process Management Professionals International (internationally oriented national body)
♦ ABPN / see AME World Ecology Foundation
♦ ABPTOE – Association of Bookseller and Publisher Training Organizations in Europe (inactive)
♦ ABPVD / see Association des banques populaires pour la coopération et le développement
♦ **ABRA** Association of Behavioural Researchers on Asians (#02396)
♦ **ABR** African Business Roundtable (#00232)
♦ **ABR** Arts-Based Research Global Consortium (#01126)
♦ **ABRE** Associação de Brasilianistas na Europa (#02324)
♦ ABR Global Consortium / see Arts-Based Research Global Consortium (#01126)
♦ Abri Fellowship / see L'Abri Fellowship International (#00008)

♦ L'Abri Fellowship International 00008

Swiss Contact c/o Swiss L'Abri, Chalet Bellevue, 1884 Huémoz VD, Switzerland. T. +41244952139. Fax +41244957647. E-mail: swiss@labri.org.
URL: http://www.labri.org/

History 1955, Switzerland, by Francis August Schaeffer (30 Jan 1912 – 15 May 1984). Also referred to as *Abri Fellowship*. **Aims** Function as a *Protestant* fundamentalist *religious* fellowship. **Finance** Donations. **Events** *Annual Conference* Rochester, MN (USA) 2013, *Annual Conference* Huémoz (Switzerland) 2012, *Annual Conference* Rochester, MN (USA) 2012, *Annual Conference* Rochester, MN (USA) 2009, *Annual Conference* Midrand (South Africa) 2008. **Publications** *International Newsletter* (2-3 a year).

Members Branches in 7 countries:
Canada, Korea Rep, Netherlands, Sweden, Switzerland, UK, USA.
[2012.07.24/XF5854/**F**]

♦ Abri international (internationally oriented national body)
♦ ABRN – Asian Borderlands Research Network (internationally oriented national body)
♦ ABRW – African Bureau for the Defence of the Rights of Writers (no recent information)
♦ ABSA – Advisory Board on Statistics in Africa (inactive)
♦ **ABSA** Africa Baseball and Softball Association (#00158)
♦ **ABS** Association for Baha'i Studies (#02391)
♦ **ABS** Association for Borderlands Studies (#02397)
♦ **ABSC** African Billiards and Snooker Confederation (#00221)
♦ ABSF / see African Billiards and Snooker Confederation (#00221)
♦ ABS – International Conference on Agricultural and Biological Sciences (meeting series)
♦ ABSTD – Association of Basic Science Teachers in Dentistry (internationally oriented national body)
♦ **ABTA** Asia Business Trade Association (#01256)
♦ Abteilung Internationale Beziehungen/Friedens- und Konfliktforschung (internationally oriented national body)
♦ Abteilung für Tropenhygiene und Öffentliches Gesundheitswesen, Heidelberg / see Heidelberg Institute of Global Health
♦ ABTSA / see Association for the Treatment of Sexual Abusers
♦ **ABU** African Boxing Union (#00229)
♦ **ABU** Alliance biblique universelle (#20498)
♦ **ABU** Asia-Pacific Broadcasting Union (#01863)
♦ Abu Dhabi Fund – Abu Dhabi Fund for Development (internationally oriented national body)
♦ Abu Dhabi Fund for Arab Economic Development / see Abu Dhabi Fund for Development
♦ Abu Dhabi Fund for Development (internationally oriented national body)
♦ Abu Dhabi Fund for Economic Development / see Abu Dhabi Fund for Development
♦ Abu Dhabi Global Environmental Data Initiative (internationally oriented national body)

♦ Abu Hafs al-Masri Brigade 00009

Address not obtained.

History 2001, after Abu Hafs al-Masri aka Muhammad Atef, a training commander of *Al-Qa'ida (#00748)*. An Islamic terrorist organization.
[2008/XM0474/s/**F**]

♦ Abuja MOU – Memorandum of Understanding on Port State Control in West and Central Africa (1999 treaty)
♦ Abuja treaty – Treaty Establishing the African Economic Community (1991 treaty)
♦ ABV – Australian Business Volunteers (internationally oriented national body)
♦ **ABV** Autorité du Bassin de la Volta (#20808)
♦ ABVMI – Suore Ancelle di Beata Vergine Maria Immacolata (religious order)
♦ ABWA – Asia Middle East Bottled Water Association (inactive)
♦ **ABWA** Association of Accountancy Bodies in West Africa (#02343)
♦ ABWAid / see Baptist World Aid Australia
♦ ABWARC / see Baptist World Aid Australia
♦ ABWCW / see Asian Brotherhood of Clerical Workers (#01366)
♦ ABWE – Association of Baptists for World Evangelism (internationally oriented national body)
♦ ABWI – Alliance of Business Women International (internationally oriented national body)
♦ **ABWU** Asian Baptist Women's Union (#01356)
♦ **AC21** Academic Consortium for the 21st Century (#00018)
♦ **ACAA** American Coal Ash Association (#00777)
♦ ACAA – Asian Christian Art Association (internationally oriented national body)
♦ **ACAA** Association des courtiers africains d'assurance (#02358)
♦ **ACA** Academic Cooperation Association (#00019)
♦ ACA – Adult Children of Alcoholics – World Service Organization (internationally oriented national body)
♦ **ACA** Africa Capacity Alliance (#00160)
♦ **ACA** African Cashew Alliance (#00234)
♦ **ACA** African Cricket Association (#00279)
♦ **ACA** Agence pour l'Assurance du Commerce en Afrique (#00485)
♦ **ACAAI** Agencia Centroamericana de Acreditación de Programas de Arquitectura y de Ingenieria (#00549)
♦ **ACA** Airline Catering Association (#00604)
♦ ACA – Amazon Conservation Association (internationally oriented national body)
♦ ACA – American Citizens Abroad (internationally oriented national body)
♦ **ACA** ASEAN Cosmetic Association (#01162)
♦ ACA – Asia Color Association (unconfirmed)
♦ **ACA** Asia Competition Association (#01260)
♦ ACA – Asian Christian Association (no recent information)
♦ **ACA** Asian Control Association (#01405)
♦ **ACA** Association cotonnière africaine (#00270)
♦ **ACA** The Australasian Corrosion Association (#03023)
♦ ACACC – Asociación Centroamericana de Ciencias Cosméticas (unconfirmed)
♦ ACACIA UK – Action for Children and Communities in Africa (internationally oriented national body)
♦ ACADB – Association of Culture and Art Development in Balkans (internationally oriented national body)
♦ Academia Africana de Línguas (#00192)
♦ Academia de Centroamérica, San José (internationally oriented national body)

♦ Academia de Ciencias de América Latina (ACAL) 00010

Académie de sciences de l'Amérique latine – Latin American Academy of Sciences

Contact Palacio de las Academias, Edificio Anexo, Piso 2 De Bolsa a San Francisco, Av Universidad, Apartado Postal 1010-A, Distrito Capital, Caracas DF, Venezuela. T. +582124841310. E-mail: info@acal-scientia.org.
URL: http://acal-scientia.org/

History 25 Sep 1982, Rome (Italy). Founded during a meeting sponsored by the *Pontifical Academy of Sciences (#18433)*. Set up in Caracas (Venezuela) in 1983 to honour the memory of Simon Bolivar. Statutes adopted 25-26 Sep 1982, Rome; modified 21-22 Oct 1983, Caracas; 21-24 Apr 1987; 6-7 Oct 1994. **Aims** Promote, contribute to the advancement of mathematical, physical, chemical, earth and life sciences, and to human, cultural and integration of Latin America and the Caribbean. **Structure** President; Council, consisting of President, Past President, 6 Councillors and Chancellor. The permanent office of the Academy is care of the Chancellor assisted by the Executive Director and the International Relations. **Finance** Annual resources from the 'Fundación Simón Bolivar para la ACAL'. Subsidies from 'Procter and Gamble'; *UNESCO (#20322)*. **Activities** Research/documentation; knowledge management/information dissemination; events/meetings; networking/liaising; awards/prizes/competitions; training/education. *Centre for Latin American Science Studies (no recent information)*. Instrumental in setting up *Information Network for Latin America and the Caribbean (REDALC, inactive)*. **Events** *Congress* Bogota (Colombia) 2001, *Congress* Cancún (Mexico) 2000, *Congress* Santiago (Chile) 1999, *Congress* Asunción (Paraguay) 1996, *Congress* Concepción (Chile) 1996. **Publications** *Boletin Ciencia on América Latina* (2 a year). *Directorio de Instituciones Cientificas de América Latina* (1990). **Information Services** *Database Inventory of Scientific Institution in Latin America*.

Members Academicians; Honorary members, Correspondent members. Members in 16 countries:
Argentina, Brazil, Chile, Colombia, Costa Rica, Cuba, Ecuador, France, Guatemala, Honduras, Italy, Mexico, Peru, Uruguay, USA, Venezuela.

Consultative Status Consultative status granted from: *OAS (#17629)*. **NGO Relations** Member of: *Consortium on Science, Technology and Innovation for the South (COSTIS, no recent information)*; *InterAcademy Partnership (IAP, #11376)*; *InterAmerican Network of Academies of Science (IANAS, #11441)*.
[2020/XF0462/v/**F**]

♦ Academia de Creatividad (unconfirmed)
♦ Academia Diplomatica Internacional (#00024)

♦ Academia Europaea 00011

Exec Sec Room 251 – 2nd Floor, Senate House, Malet St, London, WC1E 7HU, UK.
Admin address not obtained. T. +442078625784.
URL: http://www.ae-info.org/

History 1988. Former names and other names: *Academia Europaea – The Academy of Europe* – alias. Registration: Registered Charity, No/ID: 1133902, England and Wales. **Aims** Advance and propagate excellence in scholarship in the humanities, law, the economic, social and political sciences, mathematics, medicine and all branches of natural and technological sciences for public benefit and for advancement of education of the public of all ages in Europe. **Structure** Board of Trustees; Regional Knowledge Hubs (7); Data Centre in Graz (Austria); Secretariat in London (UK). **Languages** English. **Staff** Secretariat: 2. Hubs: 2 staff each. **Finance** Sources: members' dues. Other sources: governmental organizations; charities; public and private sector charitable foundations; national academies. **Activities** Awards/prizes/competitions; events/meetings; knowledge management/information dissemination; monitoring/evaluation; politics/policy/regulatory; publishing activities; research and development; research/documentation; training/education. **Events** *Annual Plenary Conference* Barcelona (Spain) 2021, *Annual Plenary Conference* Barcelona (Spain) 2019, *Annual Plenary Conference* Barcelona (Spain) 2018, *Annual Plenary Conference* Budapest (Hungary) 2017, *Conference on New Nationalisms* Wroclaw (Poland) 2017. **Publications** *European Review* (6 a year); *Academia Europaea Directory* (annual).

Members Individuals (about 4,500) in 54 countries and territories:
Australia, Austria, Belarus, Belgium, Brazil, Bulgaria, Canada, China, Croatia, Cyprus, Czechia, Denmark, Estonia, Finland, France, Georgia, Germany, Ghana, Gibraltar, Greece, Hong Kong, Hungary, Iceland, India, Ireland, Israel, Italy, Japan, Kenya, Latvia, Lithuania, Luxembourg, Monaco, Montenegro, Netherlands, New Zealand, Norway, Poland, Portugal, Romania, Russia, Saudi Arabia, Serbia, Singapore, Slovakia, Slovenia, South Africa, Spain, Sweden, Switzerland, Türkiye, UK, Ukraine, USA.

Consultative Status Consultative status granted from: *UNESCO (#20322)* (Consultative Status). **NGO Relations** Member of (1): *European Alliance for the Social Sciences and Humanities (EASSH, #05885)*. Cooperates with (5): *ALLEA – ALL European Academies (#00647)*; *European Academies' Science Advisory Council (EASAC, #05778)*; *European Council of Applied Sciences, Technologies and Engineering (Euro-CASE, #06804)*; *Federation of European Academies of Medicine (FEAM, #09490)*; *Young Academy of Europe (YAE, #21979)*.
[2021.05.20/XF1775/v/**F**]

♦ Academia Europaea – The Academy of Europe / see Academia Europaea (#00011)
♦ Academia Europa Nostra (internationally oriented national body)
♦ Academia Europea de Ciencias, Artes y Letras (#05781)
♦ Academia Europea de Dirección y Economia de la Empresa (#05801)
♦ Academia Europea per la Medicina per Ambiente Ecologico (#05790)
♦ Academia Europeana HIV/SIDA – Academia Europeana HIV/SIDA si de Boli Infectioase (internationally oriented national body)

Academia Europeana HIV
00011
alphabetic sequence excludes
For the complete listing, see Yearbook Online at

♦ Academia Europeana HIV/SIDA si de Boli Infectioase (internationally oriented national body)
♦ Academia Europeana Pentru Cercetare de Viata, Integrare si Societate Civila (#05799)

♦ Academia Iberoamericana de Criminalistica y Estudios Forenses (AICEF) 00012

Ibero-American Academy of Criminal and Forensic Studies

Pres c/o IUICP, Fac de Derecho, Col Max de Jesuitas, C/ Libreros 27, 28802 Alcala de Henares, Madrid, Spain. E-mail: iuicp@uah.es.
URL: http://www.aicef.net/

History 2004. **Structure** Board.
Members Full in 18 countries:
Argentina, Bolivia, Brazil, Chile, Colombia, Costa Rica, Ecuador, El Salvador, Guatemala, Honduras, Mexico, Nicaragua, Panama, Paraguay, Peru, Portugal, Spain, Uruguay.
NGO Relations Member of: *International Forensic Strategic Alliance (IFSA, #13626).* [2011/XJ3956/**D**]

♦ Academia Iberoamericana de Derecho del Trabajo y de la Seguridad Social (AIADTSS) 00013

Academia Iberoamericana do Direito do Trabalho e da Segurança Social

Contact address not obtained. T. +582512317013. E-mail: academiaiberoamericana.org@gmail.com.
URL: http://www.iberoamericana.com/

History 27 Sep 1972, Sao Paulo (Brazil). **Aims** Promote and stimulate the study and diffusion of matters related to *labour laws* and *social security*; organize and patronize scientific meetings of these matters. **Structure** Officers: President; 2 Vice-Presidents; Secretary-General; Vice Secretary-General. **Events** *Meeting* Lisbon (Portugal) 2006, *Meeting* Lisbon (Portugal) 2003, *Iberoamerican days* Lima (Peru) 1999, *Meeting* Panama 1998, *Meeting* Seville (Spain) 1992. **Publications** Books.
Members Individuals in 17 countries:
Argentina, Bolivia, Brazil, Chile, Colombia, Costa Rica, Cuba, Dominican Rep, Ecuador, Mexico, Panama, Paraguay, Peru, Portugal, Spain, Uruguay, Venezuela. [2013/XE4699/v/**E**]

♦ Academia Iberoamericana do Direito do Trabalho e da Segurança Social (#00013)
♦ Academia Iberoamericana de Neurologia Pediatrica (#11013)
♦ Academia Ibero-Latinoamericana de Disfunción Craneo-Mandibular y Dolor Facial (internationally oriented national body)
♦ Academia Ibero-Latinoamericana de Valoración del Daño Corporal (unconfirmed)
♦ Academia Interamericana de las Fuerzas Aéreas (internationally oriented national body)
♦ Academia pro Interlingua (inactive)
♦ Academia Internacional de Arquitectura (#11535)
♦ Academia Internacional de Astronautica (#11536)
♦ Academia Internacional de la Ceramica (#11540)
♦ Academia Internacional de Citologia (#11544)
♦ Academia Internacional de Medicina Aeronautica y Espacial (#11537)

♦ Academia Internacional de Odontologia Integral (AIOI) 00014

International Academy of Integrated Dentistry

Contact Rua Pelotas 763, Sao Paulo SP, 04012-002, Brazil. T. +551155721176.

History 1992. Founded on the initiative of Dr Mariano Flores Rubio. **Aims** Facilitate creation of multidisciplinary dentists in member countries. **Activities** Events/meetings. **Events** *World Congress* Rosario (Argentina) 2021, *World Congress* Rosario (Argentina) 2020, *World Congress* Sao Paulo (Brazil) 2017, *World congress* Asunción (Paraguay) 2008, *Congress* Lima (Peru) 2004.
Members in 30 countries:
Argentina, Bolivia, Brazil, Canada, Chile, Colombia, Cuba, Dominican Rep, Ecuador, Egypt, Germany, Guatemala, India, Italy, Japan, Korea Rep, Mexico, Morocco, Panama, Paraguay, Peru, Puerto Rico, Singapore, Spain, Thailand, Türkiye, UK, Uruguay, USA, Venezuela. [2020/XE4140/**E**]

♦ Academia Internacional de Patologia (#11567)
♦ Academia Internacional de la Paz / see International Peace Institute (#14536)
♦ Academia Internacional de Sexologia Médica (#11552)
♦ Academia Internationalis Historiae Medicinae (inactive)
♦ Academia de Iusprivatistas Europeos (#00036)

♦ Academia Latinitati Fovendae (ALF) 00015

Sec Via Angelo Tittoni 4, 00153 Rome RM, Italy. T. +3965880811. E-mail: ottaviode@katamail.com.
URL: http://www.academialatinitatifovendae.org/

History 1966, Rome (Italy), during an international congress. **Aims** Increase the knowledge and study of *Latin*. **Structure** General Assembly (annual, at study convention). **Activities** Study Commissions (2): *'Consilium de novis verbis latinis creandis vel recipiendis'* – dealing with new Latin words; *'De investigandis scriptoribus quod ad dicendi rationem spectat'* – research on the "dicenti ratio" of latin writers. Organizes: annual meeting at Rome (Italy) headquarters; annual study convention in Rome; international congress (about every 4 years) in various countries. **Events** *Congress / Quadrennial International Congress* Vienna (Austria) 2013, *Quadrennial International Congress* Regensburg (Germany) 2009, *World congress of Latin / Quadrennial International Congress* Jyväskylä (Finland) 1997, *Quadrennial International Congress* Louvain-la-Neuve (Belgium) / Antwerp (Belgium) 1993, *Quadrennial International Congress* East Berlin (German DR) 1989. **Publications** *Acta* – series; *Biliotheca Scriptorum Latinorum* – series; *Comentarii* – series; *Opuscula* – series; *Varia* – series.
Members Membership Full (50); Honorary; Benefactor. Members in 28 countries:
Austria, Belgium, Brazil, Bulgaria, Croatia, Finland, France, Germany, Greece, Holy See, Hungary, Italy, Lithuania, Malta, Mexico, Netherlands, Poland, Portugal, Romania, Russia, Senegal, Slovakia, Slovenia, Spain, Sweden, Switzerland, UK, USA. [2013/XF3543/v/**F**]

♦ Academia Latinoamericana de Médicos Intervencionistas en Dolor (ALMID) 00016

Contact José Aguirre Acha y calle 1 de Los Pinos, La Paz, Bolivia. T. +59122791956 – +59170199955. E-mail: info@clidla.com.
URL: https://almid.net/

History 2012. **Structure** Board. **Activities** Events/meetings; training/education. **Events** *Congress* La Paz (Bolivia) 2020. [2020/XM5558/**D**]

♦ Academia Multidisciplinaria Neurotraumatologica (#00042)
♦ Academia Mundial de Arte y Ciencia (#21065)
♦ Academia Mundial de la Juventud (#21948)
♦ Academia de Negocios Internacionales (#00040)
♦ Academia Norteamericana de la Lengua Española (internationally oriented national body)

♦ Academia Ophthalmologica Internationalis (AOI) 00017

International Academy of Ophthalmology

SG Dept of Opthalmology, Univ of California San Francisco, 54 Topside Way, Mill Valley CA 94941, USA. T. +14153079860.
URL: http://www.a-o-int.org/

History 1975, within the framework of *International Council of Ophthalmology (ICO, #13057).* Registered in accordance with Switzerland law, 2001. **Aims** Monitor and uphold ethical standards of ophthalmology; record, preserve and pass on to future generations their heritage of ophthalmic custom and tradition; encourage study of the history of ophthalmology; advance the art and science of ophthalmology. **Structure** Officers: President; 1st and 2nd Vice-Presidents; Secretary-General; Treasurer. **Languages** English, French, German, Spanish. **Staff** None. **Finance** Members' dues. Other sources: grants; donations. **Activities** Events/meetings; training/education; guidance/assistance/consulting; standards/guidelines. **Events** *Annual Meeting* Guadalajara (Mexico) 2016, *Annual Meeting* Ghent (Belgium) 2015, *Annual Meeting* Tokyo (Japan) 2014, *Annual Meeting* Hyderabad (India) 2013, *Annual Meeting* Abu Dhabi (United Arab Emirates) 2012. **Publications** Newsletter.
Members Ordinary: ophthalmologists (82) working in the field for at least 15 years and having published not less than 100 papers and at least one book. Emeritus members (31). Members in 36 countries:
Argentina, Australia, Austria, Belgium, Brazil, Bulgaria, Canada, Chile, China, Colombia, Finland, France, Germany, Greece, Hungary, India, Israel, Italy, Japan, Malaysia, Mexico, Netherlands, New Zealand, Panama, Peru, Poland, Portugal, Russia, Singapore, South Africa, Spain, Sweden, Switzerland, Türkiye, UK, USA. [2019.10.04/XD6697/v/**E**]

♦ Academia Scientiarum et Artium Europaea (#05814)
♦ Academia Svizra da Scienzas Moralas a Socialas (internationally oriented national body)
♦ Academia de los Trastornos de la Alimentación (#00034)
♦ Academic Associates Peace Works (internationally oriented national body)
♦ Academic Business Library Directors (internationally oriented national body)

♦ Academic Consortium for the 21st Century (AC21) 00018

Secretariat Nagoya Univ, Furcho, Chikusa-ku, Nagoya AICHI, 464-8601 Japan. T. +81527886122. Fax +81527892045. E-mail: office@ac21.org.
URL: http://www.ac21.org/

History 24 Jun 2002, Nagoya (Japan). Founded at the International Forum 2002. **Aims** Promote cooperation in education and research, bridging between different societies worldwide and delivering wisdom to all people to mutually understand and share values, knowledge and cultures necessary to improve quality of life and foster co-existence beyond national and regional boundaries in the 21st century. **Activities** Events/meetings. **Events** *International Forum* Nagoya (Japan) 2022, *International Forum* Bangkok (Thailand) 2020, *International Forum* Changchun (China) 2018, *International Forum* Chemnitz (Germany) 2016, *International Forum* Stellenbosch (South Africa) 2014. **Publications** *AC21 Newsletter*.
Members Universities in 10 countries:
Australia, China, France, Germany, Indonesia, Japan, New Zealand, South Africa, Thailand, USA. [2020/AA1512/**C**]

♦ Academic Consortium for Integrative Medicine & Health (internationally oriented national body)

♦ Academic Cooperation Association (ACA) 00019

Association pour la coopération académique

Dir Rue d'Egmont 15, 1000 Brussels, Belgium. T. +3225132241. Fax +3225131776. E-mail: secretariat@aca-secretariat.be – info@aca-secretariat.be.
URL: http://www.aca-secretariat.be/

History Jul 1993, by leading academic agencies of 10 European countries. Registered in accordance with Belgian law. **Aims** Promote internationalization in education and training; set the agenda in international cooperation; be a think-tank on all matters related to internationalization; promote quality enhancement in *higher education* cooperation; facilitate contact and cooperation among member organizations. **Structure** General Assembly (1-2 a year); Administrative Council; Director. Secretariat in Brussels (Belgium). **Languages** English, French. **Staff** 4.00 FTE, paid. Various temporary and part-time posts. **Finance** Members' dues. Other sources: contract-based activities; donations. **Activities** Training/education; research/documentation; events/meetings. **Events** *"Inclusive Excellence" – a Global Approach for European Higher Education?* Brussels (Belgium) 2022, *Strategic Summit* Brussels (Belgium) 2022, *What's New in Brussels?* Brussels (Belgium) 2022, *European Policy Seminar* Brussels (Belgium) 2021, *European Policy Seminar* Brussels (Belgium) 2020. **Publications** *ACA Newsletter* (periodic). *ACA Papers on International Cooperation in Education* – series. Books; handbooks; guides; brochures.
Members Full: academic organizations (21) in Europe in 16 countries:
Austria, Belgium, Estonia, Finland, France, Germany, Greece, Lithuania, Netherlands, Norway, Poland, Slovakia, Spain, Sweden, Switzerland, UK.
Included in the above, 5 organizations listed in this Yearbook:
British Council (Brussels office); *Centre for International Mobility (CIMO)*; *Netherlands Organization for International Cooperation in Higher Education (NUFFIC)*; *Norwegian Centre for International Cooperation in Higher Education (SIU)*; *Österreichische Austauschdienst (OeAD).*
Associate: academic organizations outside Europe in 2 countries:
Mexico, USA.
Included in the above, 1 organization listed in this Yearbook:
Institute of International Education (IIE). [2020/XD2803/y/**D**]

♦ Academic Council on the United Nations System (ACUNS) 00020

Conseil universitaire pour le système des Nations Unies – Consejo Académico para el Sistema de las Naciones Unidas

Administrative Coordinator address not obtained. E-mail: admin@acuns.org.
Pres address not obtained.
URL: http://www.acuns.org/

History 1987, Hanover, NH (USA). Founded by specialists in international affairs from Canada, Mexico and USA, to bridge the gap between the UN and scholars working on topics related to the UN and the field of international cooperation. **Aims** As a professional association of educational and research institutions, individual scholars, and practitioners active in the work and study of the United Nations, multilateral relations, global governance and international cooperation; promote teaching on these topics, as well as dialogue and mutual understanding across and between academics, practitioners, civil society and students. **Structure** Annual Meeting; Board of Directors; Secretariat located in a university or other institution for a 5-year period. Liaison Offices (5): New York NY (USA); Geneva (Switzerland); Delhi (India); Vienna (Austria); Tokyo (Japan). **Languages** English. **Staff** 3.50 FTE, paid; 6.00 FTE, voluntary. **Finance** Sources: grants; members' dues; sale of publications. Supported by: *Centre for International Governance Innovation (CIGI)*; *One Earth Future Foundation (OEF)*; *The Hague Institute for Global Justice (The Hague Institute)*; United Nations University; Wilfrid Laurier University. Annual budget: 400,000 USD. **Activities** Awards/prizes/competitions; events/meetings; training/education. **Events** *Annual Meeting* Rome (Italy) 2018, *International Peace Studies Conference* Vienna (Austria) 2018, *Annual Meeting* Seoul (Korea Rep) 2017, *Vienna UN Conference on the Implementation of the 2030 Agenda* Vienna (Austria) 2017, *Workshop on Youth Empowerment for Agenda 2030 Action through Social Entrepreneurship and Digital Social Currencies* Vienna (Austria) 2017. **Publications** *ACUNS Quarterly Newsletter* (4 a year); *Global Governance: A Review of Multilateralism and International Organizations* – journal, jointly with Lynne Rienner Publishers and Brigham Young University. *Mirror, Tool or Linchpin for Change ? The UN and Development* (2003) by Jacques Fomer; *Reforming the United Nations: Lessons from a History in Progress* (2003) by Edward Luck; *The United Nations and Disarmament* (2002) by Derek Boothby; *Informal Ad Hoc Groupings of States and the Workings of the United Nations* (2002) by Jochen Prantl and Jean Krasno; *The Role of the United Nations in Forming Global Norms* (2002) by Joe Sills; *Financing the United Nations* (2001) by Jeffrey Laurenti; *Global Governance and the Changing Face of International Law* (2001) by Charlotte Ku; *Letting the People Decide: The Evolution of United Nations Electoral Assistance* (2001) by Robin Ludwig; *The Founding of the United Nations: International Cooperation as an Evolutionary Process* (2001) by Jean Krasno; *Putting ACUNS Together* (1999) by Lyons; *The Quiet Revolutionary: A Biographical Sketch of James S Sutterlin* (1998) by Jean E Krasso; *ACUNS Membership Directory* (1998); *Toward Understanding Global Governance: The International Law and International Relations Toolbox* (1998) by Charlotte Ku and Thomas G Weiss; *Beyond UN Subcontracting: Task-Sharing with Regional Security Arrangements and Service-Providing NGOs* (1997) by Thomas G Weiss; *The Imperative of Idealism* (1997) by James S Sutterlin; *Human Development: The World After Copenhagen* (1996) by Richard Jolly; *The Ethics of Globalism* (1995) by Donald J Puchala; *Ten Years After Esquipula: Looking Toward the Future* by Oscar Arias Sanchez; *NGOs, the UN and Global Governance*; *John Holmes Memorial Lectures (2002-2005).* Pamphlets; occasional papers and reports.
Members Institutional and Individual members. Institutional members (44) in 20 countries:
Austria, Belgium, Brazil, Canada, China, Gambia, Germany, Greece, India, Italy, Japan, Netherlands, Norway, Pakistan, Serbia, Sweden, Switzerland, Trinidad-Tobago, UK, USA.
Included in the above, 30 organizations listed in this Yearbook:
- *Dag Hammarskjöld Foundation (DHF, #04995)*;
- *Deutsches Institut für Entwicklungspolitik (DIE)*;
- *Diplomatic Academy of Vienna (DA)*;
- *Ecologic Institut (#05303)*;
- *Elliott School of International Affairs*;
- *Environmental Ambassadors for Sustainable Development (Environmental Ambassadors)*;
- *Euclid University (EUCLID, #05575)*;
- *European Association of Development Research and Training Institutes (EADI, #06012)*;
- *Fletcher School of Law and Diplomacy* (Edwin Ginn Library);
- *Friedrich-Ebert-Stiftung (FES)*;
- *Geneva Centre for Security Policy (GCSP)*;
- *Institut de hautes études internationales et du développement (IHEID)*;
- *Institute for Human Rights, Turku*;

– *Institut für Entwicklung und Frieden, Duisburg (INEF);*
– *International Association for Humanitarian Medicine Chisholm-Gunn (IAHM, #11946);*
– *International Cooperation Research Association (ICRA);*
– *International Jurist Organization (IJO, #13979);*
– *Jan Masaryk Centre of International Studies (JMCIS);*
– *John Sloan Dickey Center for International Understanding;*
– *Kroc Institute for International Peace Studies;*
– *Leuven Centre for Global Governance Studies;*
– *New World Hope Organization (NWHO);*
– *Norwegian Institute of International Affairs (NUPI);*
– *Ralph Bunche Institute for International Studies;*
– *Raoul Wallenberg Institute of Human Rights and Humanitarian Law (RWI);*
– *Stanley Center for Peace and Security;*
– *Stiftung Entwicklung und Frieden (SEF);*
– *UNDP (#20292);*
– *United States Institute of Peace (USIP);*
– *World Federation of United Nations Associations (WFUNA, #21499).*

Individual members (600) in 68 countries and territories:
Afghanistan, Argentina, Australia, Austria, Bahrain, Bangladesh, Barbados, Belgium, Brazil, Brunei Darussalam, Cameroon, Canada, Chile, China, Côte d'Ivoire, Cyprus, Czechia, Denmark, Egypt, Ethiopia, Finland, France, Gambia, Germany, Ghana, Greece, Honduras, Hong Kong, Hungary, India, Ireland, Israel, Italy, Japan, Jordan, Kazakhstan, Korea Rep, Latvia, Lebanon, Malaysia, Mauritius, Mexico, Netherlands, New Zealand, Nicaragua, Nigeria, Norway, Pakistan, Peru, Philippines, Portugal, Russia, Serbia, Singapore, Slovakia, Slovenia, South Africa, Spain, Sweden, Switzerland, Taiwan, Thailand, Trinidad-Tobago, Türkiye, UK, United Arab Emirates, USA, Venezuela.

Consultative Status Consultative status granted from: *ECOSOC (#05331)* (General); *UNESCO (#20322)* (Associate Status); *UNEP (#20299)*. **NGO Relations** Member of: *NGO Committee on Sustainable Development, Vienna (#17119)*. [2021/XF2992/y/**E**]

♦ Academic Forum for Foreign Affairs – Austria / see United Nations Youth and Student Association of Austria – Academic Forum for Foreign Affairs

♦ Academic Network Public and Political Leadership (PUPOL) 00021

Contact address not obtained. E-mail: info@pupolnetwork.com.
URL: http://www.pupolnetwork.com/

History 2012, Netherlands. Initially a national network; since 2015 international. **Aims** Contribute to solutions, and help societies and their leaders address such challenges through scholarship specifically focusing on the role of leaders and leadership in the public and political domain. **Structure** Board of Directors; Board of Executives. **Activities** Knowledge management/information dissemination; research/documentation; events/meetings. **Events** *Conference* The Hague (Netherlands) 2020, *Conference* Wellington (New Zealand) 2019, *Conference* Stockholm (Sweden) 2018. **Publications** *PUPOL Newsletter*. [2019/XM8320/**F**]

♦ Academic Network for Sexual and Reproductive Health and Rights Policy (ANSER) 00022

Contact ICRH, C Heymanslaan 10, 9000 Ghent, Belgium. T. +3293323564. E-mail: anser@ugent.be.
URL: https://www.ugent.be/anser/en

Structure Secretariat; General Assembly; Management Committee; Ad Hoc working Groups. **Activities** Events/meetings; research/documentation; training/education. **Events** *Conference* Ghent (Belgium) 2019.
Members Partner institutions in 22 countries:
Albania, Armenia, Australia, Azerbaijan, Belgium, China, Ecuador, Ethiopia, Georgia, Germany, Kenya, Latvia, Moldova, Mozambique, Netherlands, Norway, Portugal, South Africa, Sweden, Uganda, UK, USA. [2022/AA0276/**F**]

♦ Academic Permanent Forum LAC-EU (#09874)
♦ Academics Without Borders (internationally oriented national body)

♦ Academic Scientific Research Organization (ASRO) 00023

Austria Office Schiesstattgasse 4/3, 8010 Graz, Austria. T. +436641116669. E-mail: info@asrongo.org.
Norway Office Nordbotnvegen 172, 9027 Ramfjordbotn, Norway.
URL: http://asrongo.org/

History 2011, as *Arabian Scientific Research Organization (ASRO)*. Current title adopted 2015. Registered in accordance with Norwegian law: 915 742 653. **Aims** Stimulate scientific thinking in developing countries; build a network between scientists helping them to find good infrastructure for their research projects. **Structure** Board; General Secretariat. Committees (5): Regional; Scientific; Ethics; Academic Promotion; Non-Scientific Member. **Languages** Arabic, English, French, German, Norwegian. **Finance** Donations from members. **Activities** Research/documentation. Active in: Africa, Middle East, Asia and Europe. **Events** *Geological Congress* El Jadida (Morocco) 2017. **Publications** *Arabian Journal of Earth Sciences*; *Arabian Journal of Science*; *Arabian Journal of Science Education*.
Members Full in 22 countries:
Afghanistan, Algeria, Austria, Chad, Czechia, Egypt, Germany, Iran Islamic Rep, Italy, Kuwait, Libya, Morocco, Norway, Portugal, Qatar, Saudi Arabia, Sudan, Thailand, Tunisia, UK, United Arab Emirates, USA.
NGO Relations *African Network for Geo-Education (ANGE, #00387)*; national organizations. [2015.10.25/XJ9994/**E**]

♦ Academic University Radiologists in Europe (inactive)
♦ Académie des affaires internationales (#00040)
♦ Académie africaine des langues (#00192)
♦ Académie africaine des sciences (#00193)
♦ Académie de l'Afrique de l'Est (inactive)
♦ Académie arabe pour la musique (#00890)
♦ Académie arabe des sciences, des technologies et des transports maritimes (#00891)
♦ Académie des arcades (inactive)

♦ Académie diplomatique internationale (ADI) 00024

International Diplomatic Academy – Academia Diplomatica Internacional
Contact address not obtained. T. +33142128250. Fax +33142128251.
URL: http://www.academiediplomatique.org/

History 1926, Paris (France), on signature of an Agreement by representatives of 91 Governments. **Aims** Promote diplomacy and contribute to understanding and analysis of dynamics in international affairs by convening conferences and conducting training programmes. **Structure** Board, consisting of 8-20 members. Officers: President; Secretary General. **Languages** English, French. **Finance** Annual contributions from Member-States. **Activities** Organizes training, research, conferences. Plenary Sessions (12 a year) in Paris (France). **Events** *Meeting* Paris (France) 2008, *Colloque international sur les vingt ans de diplomatie pontificale sous Jean-Paul II* Rome (Italy) 1998, *International university training on development* Paris (France) 1994, *Influence de la Révolution française dans le monde* Paris (France) 1989, *La naissance d'un état moderne* Paris (France) 1988. **Publications** *Les Cahiers de la diplomatie* (4 a year). *Dictionnaire diplomatique* (1933-).
Members Members (90) represented by their Ambassador in France. [2018/XF1793/**F***]

♦ Académie diplomatique de Vienne (internationally oriented national body)
♦ Académie diplomatique de Vienne/Ecole des hautes Etudes Internationale de Vienne / see Diplomatic Academy of Vienna
♦ Académie de Droit Européen (#00035)
♦ Académie de droit international de La Haye (internationally oriented national body)
♦ Académie d'environnement d'expression francophone, philosophique et scientifique (internationally oriented national body)
♦ Académie d'espéranto (#05543)

♦ Académie européenne 00025

Contact 147 avenue de Suffren, 75015 Paris, France. T. +33142407750. Fax +33142407750.
History 1 Jul 1995, Rome (Italy). Registration: France. **Structure** Board of Advisors; Board of Directors, comprising President and 3 members. [2009/XM3853/**F**]

♦ Académie européenne d'allergie / see European Academy of Allergy and Clinical Immunology (#05779)
♦ Académie européenne d'allergologie et d'immunologie clinique (#05779)
♦ Académie européenne d'anesthésiologie (inactive)
♦ Académie européenne Berlin (internationally oriented national body)
♦ Académie européenne de commerce international (#07585)
♦ Académie européenne de dermatologie et vénéréologie (#05788)
♦ Académie européenne de direction et économie de l'entreprise (#05801)
♦ Académie européenne de formation médicale continue (inactive)
♦ Académie européenne de médecine de l'environnement (#05790)

♦ Académie européenne de médecine de réadaptation 00026

European Academy of Rehabilitation Medicine
Pres address not obtained.
Gen Sec address not obtained.
URL: http://www.aemr.eu/

History Founded 28 Jun 1969, Geneva (Switzerland). **Aims** Encourage improvement of all areas of rehabilitation to benefit those in need; promote education and research across Europe; act as a reference point in science, education, research and knowledge transfer; engage in moral and ethical debate; facilitate exchange of PRM doctors between different countries. **Structure** General Assembly (2 a year); Council; Committees (4). **Languages** English, French. **Staff** Voluntary. **Finance** Members' dues. **Activities** Awards/prizes/competitions; events/meetings. **Events** *General Assembly* Helsinki (Finland) 2018, *Biennial Congress* Athens (Greece) 2000. **Publications** Books; monographies; papers.
Members Individuals (34) in 18 countries:
Belgium, Denmark, Finland, France, Germany, Greece, Hungary, Ireland, Italy, Lithuania, Netherlands, Norway, Portugal, Slovenia, Spain, Sweden, Switzerland, UK. [2019/XE4728/v/**E**]

♦ Académie européenne, Paris (internationally oriented national body)
♦ Académie européenne de pédodontie (#05810)
♦ Académie européenne de recherche en marketing (#07745)
♦ Académie Européenne des Sciences (#05813)
♦ Académie européenne des sciences et des arts (#05814)
♦ Académie européenne des sciences, des arts et des lettres (#05781)
♦ Académie Européenne des Sciences du Foncier (#05797)
♦ Académie Européenne des Sciences de Nutrition (#00045)
♦ Académie européenne pour la sécurité aérienne (inactive)
♦ Académie européenne de théorie du droit (#05798)
♦ Académie européenne des troubles cranio-faciaux (#05785)
♦ Académie des heritages culturels (unconfirmed)
♦ Académie interaméricaine de la police (inactive)
♦ Académie internationale (inactive)
♦ Académie internationale d'architecture (#11535)
♦ Académie internationale de l'art moderne (internationally oriented national body)
♦ Académie internationale des arts et des lettres, Paris (internationally oriented national body)
♦ Académie internationale d'astronautique (#11536)
♦ Académie Internationale de la Céramique (#11540)
♦ Académie internationale du chant (inactive)
♦ Académie internationale de comptabilité (inactive)
♦ Académie internationale de culture française (inactive)
♦ Académie internationale de cytologie (#11544)
♦ Académie internationale de cytologie gynécologique (inactive)

♦ Académie internationale de droit comparé (AIDC) 00027

International Academy of Comparative Law
SG 28 rue Saint-Guillaume, 75007 Paris, France. T. +33144398629. Fax +33144398628. E-mail: secretariat@aidc-iacl.org.
URL: https://aidc-iacl.org/

History 14 Sep 1924, The Hague (Netherlands). Current statutes: adopted by titular members 22 Jul 2006, Utrecht (Netherlands); modified 31 Jul 2010, Washington DC (USA), but changes not yet registered. Current by-laws adopted by Executive Committee, 16 Mar 2007, Paris (France). **Aims** Unite scholars in the comparative study of legal systems. **Structure** General Meeting; Executive Committee; National Committees; Secretariat in Paris (France). **Languages** English, French. **Staff** None. **Finance** Sources: grants; members' dues. Other sources: proportion of congress fees. **Activities** Events/meetings; research/documentation. **Events** *Quadrennial Congress* Asunción (Paraguay) 2022, *Intermediate Congress* Pretoria (South Africa) 2021, *Quadrennial Congress* Fukuoka (Japan) 2018, *Colloquium on Comparative Human Rights* Strasbourg (France) 2018, *Intermediate Congress* Montevideo (Uruguay) 2016. **Publications** *Annuaire de l'Académie – Directory of the Academy* in English, French. Congress reports.
Members Emeritus (68); Titular (149); Associate (710). Members in 75 countries and territories:
Algeria, Argentina, Australia, Austria, Belarus, Belgium, Bosnia-Herzegovina, Brazil, Bulgaria, Cameroon, Canada, Chile, China, Colombia, Congo Brazzaville, Costa Rica, Croatia, Cuba, Denmark, Dominican Rep, Egypt, Ethiopia, Finland, France, Gabon, Georgia, Germany, Ghana, Greece, Hungary, India, Indonesia, Iran Islamic Rep, Ireland, Israel, Italy, Japan, Kazakhstan, Korea Rep, Lebanon, Lithuania, Luxembourg, Mexico, Netherlands, New Zealand, Nicaragua, Norway, Pakistan, Paraguay, Peru, Poland, Portugal, Qatar, Romania, Russia, Senegal, Serbia, Singapore, Slovakia, South Africa, Spain, Sri Lanka, Sweden, Switzerland, Syrian AR, Taiwan, Thailand, Tunisia, Türkiye, UK, Ukraine, Uruguay, USA, Uzbekistan, Venezuela.
NGO Relations Member of (1): *World Society of Mixed Jurisdiction Jurists (WSMJJ, #21805)*. Close links with: Alumni Association of the International Faculty of Comparative Law, Strasbourg; *The Hague Academy of International Law*. [2022/XD5163/v/**C**]

♦ Académie internationale de droit linguistique (#11556)
♦ Académie internationale de droit et de santé mentale (#11554)
♦ Académie internationale de l'équipement des piscines, des sports et des loisirs (#13211)
♦ Académie internationale pour les études du tourisme (#11576)
♦ Académie internationale du Fiqh islamique (#13960)
♦ Académie internationale de la gastronomie (unconfirmed)

♦ Académie internationale de généalogie (AIG) 00028

International Academy of Genealogy (IAG)
Pres Via Baronio 14, 47899 Serravalle, San Marino. E-mail: info@geneacademie.org.
URL: http://www.geneacademie.org/

History 22 Sep 1998, Turin (Italy). Registration: France. **Aims** Coordinate and centralize studies and research in the field of genealogy. **Structure** General Assembly (annual); Bureau. **Finance** Members' dues. **Events** *International Colloquium of Genealogy* Madrid (Spain) 2023, *Colloquium* Messina (Italy) 2021, *Colloquium* Warsaw (Poland) 2019, *Colloquium* Montréal, QC (Canada) 2017, *Colloque* Madrid (Spain) 2015. **Publications** Bulletin.
Members Full; Associate. Individuals in 28 countries:
Argentina, Azerbaijan, Belgium, Bolivia, Brazil, Canada, Costa Rica, Denmark, Estonia, France, Georgia, Germany, Greece, Hungary, Italy, Mexico, Morocco, Netherlands, Poland, Portugal, Romania, Russia, San Marino, Spain, Switzerland, UK, Uruguay, USA. [2022/XJ3929/**E**]

♦ Académie internationale de gnathologie (internationally oriented national body)
♦ Académie internationale d'héraldique (#11549)
♦ Académie internationale d'histoire de la médecine (inactive)
♦ Académie internationale d'histoire de la pharmacie (no recent information)
♦ Académie internationale d'histoire des sciences (#11550)
♦ Académie internationale IMOS – Organisation interalliée 'Sphinx' (internationally oriented national body)
♦ Académie internationale d'informatisation (#13850)
♦ Académie internationale de lutte contre la corruption (#11654)
♦ Académie internationale de management (internationally oriented national body)
♦ Académie internationale de Manternach (inactive)

Académie internationale médecine
00028
alphabetic sequence excludes
For the complete listing, see Yearbook Online at

♦ Académie internationale de médecine aéronautique et spatiale (#11537)
♦ Académie internationale de médecine légale (#11555)
♦ Académie internationale de médecine légale et de médecine sociale / see International Academy of Legal Medicine (#11555)
♦ Académie internationale de médecine ostéopathique (inactive)
♦ Académie internationale de musique pour les jeunes musiciens des instruments à cordes (internationally oriented national body)
♦ Académie internationale olympique (#14406)
♦ Académie internationale de parodontologie (#11569)
♦ Académie internationale de pathologie (#11567)
♦ Académie internationale de philosophie des sciences (#11570)

♦ Académie internationale de la pipe (AIP) 00029

International Pipe Academy

Administrator Pipe House Chapel, Garth Road, Garth, Llangollen, LL20 7UY, UK. E-mail: admin@pipeacademy.org.
URL: http://www.pipeacademy.org/

History 1984, on the initiative of André-Paul Bastien. **Aims** Promote awareness of the *tobacco* pipe as a cultural, artistic and social phenomenon; highlight its place in history; collect, preserve and disseminate evidence relating to its history; encourage research on the subject. **Structure** Board. **Activities** Events/meetings. **Events** *Conference* Vilnius (Lithuania) 2021, *Conference* Germany 2020, *Conference* Budapest (Hungary) 2019, *Conference* Gouda (Netherlands) 2018, *Conference* Stoke-on-Trent (UK) 2017. **Publications** *AIP Journal* (annual); *AIP Newsletter* (occasional).
Members Individuals in 18 countries:
Australia, Belgium, Czechia, France, Germany, Hungary, Ireland, Japan, Lithuania, Netherlands, Poland, Portugal, Romania, Serbia, Singapore, Sweden, UK, USA. [2022/XG6590/**E**]

♦ Académie internationale de protection de l'environnement (internationally oriented national body)

♦ Académie internationale des sciences Ararat (AISA) 00030

Ararat International Academy of Sciences

SG BP 929, 75829 Paris CEDEX, France. T. +33627920467. E-mail: ararat-academy@reso.net.
Founding Pres address not obtained.
Registered Office 106 boulevard de Courcelles, BP 929, 75829 Paris CEDEX, France.
URL: http://www.ararat-academy.org/

History 1966, Paris (France). Registration: Start date: 2 May 1986, France. **Aims** Promote development of science, arts and letters; work for friendship among peoples; assist cultural activities of philanthropic and scientific organizations; contribute to a just and lasting world peace; create or contribute to creation of cultural and scientific centres, open universities, museums, libraries and publications. **Structure** General Assembly (every 3 years, at International Congress). Honorary Committee. International Committee, including President, one or more Vice-Presidents, Secretary-General with one or more assistants, Treasurer-General. **Languages** Armenian, English, French. **Activities** Events/meetings. **Events** *World Congress* France 2021, *World Congress* Paris (France) 2019, *World Congress* Geneva (Switzerland) 2017, *World Congress* Geneva (Switzerland) 2016, *Armenian World Congress* Jerusalem (Israel) 2014.
Members A mainly French national organization, but members in a total of 33 countries and territories:
Argentina, Armenia, Australia, Austria, Belgium, Bulgaria, Canada, Croatia, Egypt, France, Georgia, Germany, Greece, Iran Islamic Rep, Israel, Italy, Lebanon, Morocco, Netherlands, Portugal, Romania, Russia, Saudi Arabia, Spain, Sweden, Switzerland, Syrian AR, Taiwan, Thailand, UK, United Arab Emirates, USA, Uzbekistan.
IGO Relations *UNESCO (#20322).* Has or has had links with: *Council of Europe (CE, #04881).* **NGO Relations** Has or has had links with: *Association médicale arménienne mondiale*; *Calouste Gulbenkian Foundation*; *International Astronomical Union (IAU, #12287)*; *International Council for Science (ICSU, inactive)*; *International Solvay Institutes for Physics and Chemistry*; *International Society of Orthopaedic Surgery and Traumatology (#15335).* [2023/XE2013/**E**]

♦ Académie internationale des sciences du bois (#11581)
♦ Académie internationale des sciences moléculaires quantiques (#11558)

♦ Académie internationale des sciences religieuses (AISR) 00031

International Academy of Religious Sciences

Pres Rue Marie de Bourgogne 8, 1050 Brussels, Belgium. T. +3225121549. E-mail: academies@skynet.be.
URL: http://www.lesacademies.net/fr/a-i-s-r

History Founded 31 May 1966, Heverlee (Belgium). One of two academies constituting *International Institute for Theoretical Sciences.* **Structure** General Assembly. **Languages** English, French, German. **Staff** None. **Finance** Members' dues. Subsidized by Patrimoine de l'Institut International des Sciences Théoriques (PIIST). **Events** *Ecumenism from the 1960s to the 21st century – evaluation, changing trends and future perspectives* Louvain-la-Neuve (Belgium) 2016, *Colloquium* Klingenthal (France) 2014, *Colloquium* Athens (Greece) 2013, *Colloquium* Bologna (Italy) 2012, *Colloquium* Lille (France) 2011. **Publications** *Gospel, Morality and Civil Law, 2ème partie* (2014); *Conciliarité et Consensus* (2013); *Gospel, Morality and Civil Law* (2012); *L' ecclésiologie des églises orientales* (2011); *La Parole de Dieu* (2010); *Evolutionism and Religion* (2009); *L'ecclésiologie eucharistique* (2008); *Jesus Christ Today, Studies in Various Contexts* (2007); *L'homme, image de Dieu* (2005); *Béatitude eschatologique et bonheur humain* (2004); *Science and Ethics* (2003); *Comment faire de la théologie aujourd'hui? Continuité et renouveau* (2002); *Temps, temps marqué, temps neuf* (2000); *Le Péché* (1999); *Life, Interpretation and the Sense of Illness within the human Condition* (1998); *Le Christianisme vis-à-vis des Religions – A la rencontre du Bouddhisme* (1997); *Christianisme, Judaïsme et Islam* (1996); *Le christianisme vis-à-vis des religions* (1995); *La tolérance* (1994); *Perspectives actuelles sur l'oecuménisme* (1993); *Interprétation actuelle de l'homme: philosophie, science et religion* (1992); *Conception chrétienne du salut* (1991); *Fondements, spécificité et problématiques actuelles de l'éthique chrétienne* (1990); *Christian Unity: 550 years since the Council of Ferrara-Florence (1439-1989) – Disappointements, Tensions, Perspectives* (1989); *Temps et eschatologie* (1987, 1989); *Parole de Dieu et éthique* (1986); *Parole de Dieu et expérience mystique* (1985); *Salut universel et regard pluraliste* (1984); *Formes et problèmes actuels de la chrétienté* (1983); *The Incarnation* (1978); *Christian Theology in the Context of Scientific Revolution* (1977); *L'appartenance à l'Eglise* (1976); *La Trinité – Toward an Ecumenical Consensus on the Trinity* (1975); *Une contribution aux recherches de Foi et Constitution sur le ministère ordonné* (1974); *La portée de l'Eglise des Apôtres pour l'Eglise d'aujourd'hui* (1973); *Les sacrements d'initiation et les ministères sacrés* (1967); *L'Esprit Saint et l'Eglise* (1966); *Unité des Eglises dans leur union commune au Christ* (1965); *La Collégialité épiscopale* (1964).
Members Individuals (79) in 15 countries:
Belgium, Brazil, Canada, France, Germany, Greece, Italy, Netherlands, Romania, Russia, Spain, Switzerland, Syrian AR, UK, USA. [2015.06.25/XU5091/v/**D**]

♦ Académie internationale des sciences, San Marino (#00617)
♦ Académie internationale des sciences et techniques du sport (internationally oriented national body)
♦ Académie internationale du tourisme (inactive)
♦ Académie islamique du Fiqh / see International Islamic Fiqh Academy (#13960)
♦ Académie pour une langue internationale (inactive)
♦ Académie maritime régionale d'Accra / see Regional Maritime University, Accra (#18796)
♦ Académie mondiale des arts et des sciences (#21065)
♦ Académie mondiale pour la paix / see Academy of Peace
♦ Académie mondiale pour la paix / see International Peace Institute (#14536)
♦ Académie mondiale des technologies biomédicales (internationally oriented national body)
♦ Académie d'ophtalmologie pour l'Asie et le Pacifique (#01814)
♦ Académie de la paix (internationally oriented national body)
♦ Académie pour la paix mondiale / see Professors World Peace Academy (#18520)
♦ Académie de la paix et de la sécurité internationale / see Academy of Peace
♦ Académie pontificale mariale internationale (#18453)
♦ Académie pontificale des sciences (#18433)
♦ Académie pontificale des sciences sociales (#18434)
♦ Académie pontificale pour la vie (#18432)
♦ Académie des privatistes européens (#00036)
♦ Académie des professeurs pour la paix mondiale (#18520)
♦ Académie des recherches islamiques (#16049)
♦ Académie Régionale des Sciences et Techniques de la Mer d'Abidjan (#18744)
♦ Académie royale des sciences d'outre-mer (internationally oriented national body)
♦ Académie de sciences de l'Amérique latine (#00010)
♦ Académie des sciences coloniales / see Académie des sciences d'outre-mer
♦ Académie des sciences de criminologie (internationally oriented national body)
♦ Académie des sciences d'outre-mer (internationally oriented national body)
♦ Académie pour la science et la technique des piscines et des bains / see Internationale Akademie für Bäder-, Sport-, und Freizeitbauten (#13211)
♦ Académie scientifique internationale Coménius (#14795)
♦ Académie suisse des sciences humaines et sociales (internationally oriented national body)
♦ Academy of Arab Music / see Arab Academy of Music (#00890)
♦ Academy of Breastfeeding Medicine (internationally oriented national body)

♦ Academy of Business in Society (ABIS) 00032

CEO Av Molière 128, 1050 Brussels, Belgium. T. +3225393702. E-mail: info@abis-global.org.
URL: https://www.abis-global.org/

History 2001, as *European Academy of Business in Society (EABIS).* **Aims** Advance the role of business in society through research and education; contribute to the debate and the practice involved in equipping current and future business leaders with knowledge, skills and capabilities related to business in society. **Structure** General Assembly (annual); Supervisory Board; Management Board; Audit Committee; Academic and Business Network Boards. Coordination Office, headed by Director General. **Languages** English. **Staff** 7.00 FTE, paid. **Finance** Members' dues. Additional public funding. **Activities** Training/education; research and development; networking/liaising; knowledge management/information dissemination; guidance/assistance/consulting. **Events** *Annual Colloquium* Brussels (Belgium) 2022, *Knowlege Into Action Forum* Brussels (Belgium) 2022, *Annual Colloquium* Brussels (Belgium) 2021, *Knowlege Into Action Forum* Brussels (Belgium) 2021, *Annual Colloquium* Brussels (Belgium) 2020. **Members** International corporations and high-level academic institutions (over 100). Membership countries not specified. **NGO Relations** Member of (2): *CEEMAN – International Association for Management Development in Dynamic Societies (CEEMAN, #03625)* (Exchange member); *EFMD – The Management Development Network (#05387).* Represented on the Steering Committee of: *Principles for Responsible Management Education (PRME, #18500).* [2020/XM0472/**D**]

♦ Academy of Creativity (unconfirmed)
♦ Academy of Criminal Justice Sciences (internationally oriented national body)
♦ Academy of Cultural Heritages (unconfirmed)

♦ Academy of Dental Materials (ADM) 00033

Contact 4425 Cass St, Suite A, San Diego CA 92109, USA. T. +18582721018. Fax +18582727687. E-mail: admin@academydentalmaterials.org.
URL: http://www.academydentalmaterials.org/

History Set up 1940, as *Academy for Plastics Research in Dentistry.* Current title adopted, 1983. **Aims** Provide a forum for information exchange on all aspects of dental materials; enhance communication between industry, researchers and dentists; encourage dental materials research and its applications; promote dental materials through its activities. **Structure** Board of Directors. **Finance** Sources: members' dues. **Activities** Awards/prizes/competitions; events/meetings. **Events** *Annual Meeting* Dublin (Ireland) 2020, *Annual Meeting* Jackson Hole, WY (USA) 2019, *Annual Meeting* Porto de Galinhas (Brazil) 2018, *Annual Meeting* Nürburg (Germany) 2017, *Annual Meeting* Chicago, IL (USA) 2016. **Publications** *Academy of Dental Materials Newsletter*, *Dental Materials* – journal. **Members** Fellow; Active; Student; Emeritus; Honorary. Membership countries not specified. [2021/XJ6984/**C**]

♦ Academy of Dentistry International (internationally oriented national body)
♦ Academy of East Asian Studies (internationally oriented national body)

♦ Academy of Eating Disorders (AED) 00034

Academia de los Trastornos de la Alimentación

Exec Dir 11130 Sunrise Valley Dr, Ste 350, Reston VA 20191, USA. T. +17036269087. Fax +17034354390. E-mail: info@aedweb.org.
URL: http://www.aedweb.org/

History 1993, Tulsa, OK (USA). Registration: USA. **Aims** Promote excellence in research, treatment and prevention of eating disorders. **Structure** Council; Board; Regional Chapters (4). **Languages** English, Spanish. Many publications in 10 or more languages. **Staff** 6.00 FTE, paid. **Finance** Annual budget: 2,200,000 USD. **Activities** Advocacy/lobbying/activism; awards/prizes/competitions; awareness raising; capacity building; certification/accreditation; events/meetings; financial and/or material support; guidance/assistance/consulting; humanitarian/emergency aid; knowledge management/information dissemination; networking/liaising; politics/policy/regulatory; publishing activities; research and development; training/education. **Events** *International Conference on Eating Disorders (ICED)* New York, NY (USA) 2024, *International Conference on Eating Disorders (ICED)* Washington, DC (USA) 2023, *International Conference on Eating Disorders (ICED)* Monterrey (Mexico) 2022, *International Conference on Eating Disorders (ICED)* Reston, VA (USA) 2021, *International Conference on Eating Disorders (ICED)* Sydney, NSW (Australia) 2020. **Publications** *International Journal of Eating Disorders. Medical Care Standards Guide.* Newsletters; books; studies; databases.
Members Organizations in 40 countries and territories:
Argentina, Australia, Austria, Belgium, Bolivia, Brazil, Canada, Chile, China, Colombia, Czechia, Denmark, Egypt, Finland, France, Georgia, Germany, Hong Kong, Iceland, India, Ireland, Israel, Italy, Mexico, Netherlands, New Zealand, Nigeria, Norway, Peru, Philippines, Poland, Portugal, Saudi Arabia, Singapore, Spain, Sweden, Tanzania UR, United Arab Emirates, USA, Venezuela.
NGO Relations US Food and Drug Administration; US National Institute of Mental Health; Dubai Ministry of Health; Substance Abuse and Mental Health Agency;. [2020.05.06/XM0601/**E**]

♦ Academy of European Law 00035

Europäische Rechtsakademie (ERA) – Académie de Droit Européen

Main Office Metzer Allee 4, 54295 Trier, Germany. T. +49651937370. Fax +496519373790. E-mail: info@era.int.
URL: http://www.era.int/

History 1992, Trier (Germany). Founded by the Grand Duchy of Luxembourg, Rheinland-Pfalz, the city of Trier and the Promotion Association, on the initiative of *European Parliament (EP, #08146).* Former names and other names: *Accademia di Diritto Europeo* – former. Registration: Germany; EU Transparency Register, No/ID: 97138128231-58. **Aims** Enable individuals and authorities involved in the application and implementation of European Union law in *European Union* member states, and in other European states interested in close cooperation with the EU, to gain a wider knowledge of EU law and its application and to make possible a mutual and comprehensive exchange of experience. **Structure** Governing Board; Executive Board; Board of Trustees. **Finance** Sources: government support; international organizations; revenue from activities/projects. Income from: *European Commission (EC, #06633)*; State of Rhineland-Palatinate. Annual budget: 5,900,000 EUR. **Activities** Events/meetings; training/education. **Events** *Annual Conference on Artificial Intelligence Systems and Fundamental Rights* Brussels (Belgium) 2022, *Annual Conference on EU Financial Regulation and Supervision* Brussels (Belgium) 2022, *Annual Conference on EU Law in the Food Sector* Brussels (Belgium) 2022, *Annual Conference on European Media Law* Brussels (Belgium) 2022, *Conference on Data Protection in the European Institutions* Brussels (Belgium) 2022. **Publications** *ERA e-Newsletter* (4 a year); *ERA-Forum* (4 a year). Brochure; RSS feeds. Maintains a library. **Members** States (27) and regions (17, including all German Länder). Membership countries not specified. **IGO Relations** Cooperates with (5): *Court of Justice of the European Union (CJEU, #04938)*; *Eurojust (#05698)*; *European Commission (EC, #06633)*; *European Parliament (EP, #08146)*; *European Union Agency for Fundamental Rights (FRA, #08969).* **NGO Relations** Cooperates with (3): *Council of Bars and Law Societies of Europe (CCBE, #04871)*; *European Company Lawyers Association (ECLA, #06686)*; *European Criminal Bar Association (ECBA, #06859).* [2023.02.14/XE4754/**E**]

♦ Academy of European Law, Florence (see: #09034)

♦ Academy of European Private Lawyers 00036

Académie des privatistes européens – Academia de Iusprivatistas Europeos – Akademie Europäischer Privatrechtswissenschaftler – Accademia dei Giusprivatisti Europei

Co-Pres Secretariat, Piazza Velasca 6, 20122 Milan MI, Italy. T. +392861622. Fax +3928693129. E-mail: accadgiuspriveur@interfree.it.

Registered Office Dipto di Scienze Politiche e Sociali, Univ Pavia, Strada Nuova 65, 27100 Pavia PV, Italy. T. +3938233955 – +39382504435 – +39382504440. Fax +39382504435.

URL: http://www.accademiagiusprivatistieuropei.it/

History 9 Nov 1992, Pavia (Italy), originating from a meeting of European jurists, 21 Oct 1990, Pavia (Italy). Statutes adopted in 1995. Registered in accordance with Italian law: 483/2011. **Aims** Contribute, through scientific research, to the unification and future interpretation and enforcement of private law in Europe; promote the development of a *legal culture* leading to European unification. **Structure** Meeting of Members (twice a year). Senate of 30 members. Managing Council, including President, Co-President, Secretary and Administrator. Board of Auditors. Chancellor. **Languages** English, French, German, Italian, Spanish. **Staff** 1.00 FTE, paid. Other voluntary. **Finance** Contributions from: Italian Government; *European Commission (EC, #06633)*; public and private bodies. **Activities** Drafts "European contracts code" in conformity with *European Parliament (EP, #08146)* Resolution of 6 May 1989. Book I of this draft code on "contracts in general" completed 1999, discussed before European Parliament Oct and Nov 2000 and considered by *European Commission (EC, #06633)* 11 Jul 2001. Title I on "sale of goods and collateral contracts" of Book II completed 2006. Currently writing Book II on services contracts. Formulates proposals and expresses opinions to national and community authorities, to academic and business bodies. Organizes meetings and conferences. **Publications** *Annals of Private Law* (2011, 2013); *Book II – Specific contracts* (2008); *Book II, Title 1* (2007); *European Contracts Code – Book I – Code européen des contrats – Book I* (2001, 2003, 2004).

Members Active private lawyers of EU countries and Switzerland; Foreign private lawyers of other States; Ordinary jurists not exclusively specialized in Private Law; Honorary; Contributing. Members in 40 countries:

Argentina, Austria, Belgium, Brazil, Bulgaria, Chile, China, Croatia, Cyprus, Czechia, Denmark, Estonia, Finland, France, Germany, Greece, Hungary, Ireland, Italy, Japan, Latvia, Lithuania, Luxembourg, Malta, Netherlands, Peru, Poland, Portugal, Romania, Russia, Slovakia, Slovenia, Spain, Sweden, Switzerland, Türkiye, UK, Ukraine, Uruguay, USA.

[2013.04.16/XD5592/v/**D**]

♦ Academy of European Public Law 00037

Secretariat European Public Law Centre, 16 Achaiou St, Kolonaki, 106 75 Athens, Greece. T. +302107258801. Fax +302107258040. E-mail: academy@eplo.eu.

URL: http://www.eploacademy.eu/

History Sep 1994, Athens (Greece), by *European Public Law Organization (EPLO, #08299)*. **Aims** Promote European public law through education and training. **Structure** Honorary Board; Curatorium; Directorate. Included within *European Public Law Organization (EPLO, #08299)*. **Languages** English, French. **Activities** Training/education.

Members Universities (40) in 18 countries:

Austria, Belgium, Denmark, France, Germany, Iceland, Italy, Moldova, Netherlands, Portugal, Romania, Serbia, Slovakia, Spain, Sweden, Türkiye, UK, Ukraine.

NGO Relations *European Group of Public Law (EGPL, #07431)*. [2016/XK1725/**E**]

♦ Academy for Future Science (internationally oriented national body)

♦ Academy of Human Resource Development (AHRD) 00038

Contact 1000 Westgate Drive, Ste 252, St Paul MN 55114, USA. T. +16512907466. Fax +16512902266. E-mail: office@ahrd.org.

URL: http://www.ahrd.org/

Aims Encourage systematic study of human resource development (HRD) theories, processes and practices; disseminate information about HRD; encourage the application of HRD research findings; provide opportunities for social interaction among individuals with scholarly and professional interests in HRD from multiple disciplines and from across the globe. **Structure** Board of Directors of 12 members. Executive Committee, comprising President, President Elect and Immediate Past President. Chapters (2): Asian; European. **Activities** Standing Committees (11); Awards Committees (11). **Events** *Asia Conference* Kuala Lumpur (Malaysia) 2021, *Americas Conference* Atlanta, GA (USA) 2020, *Asia Conference* Kuala Lumpur (Malaysia) 2020, *Asia Conference* Hanoi (Vietnam) 2019, *Asia Conference* Bangkok (Thailand) 2018. **Publications** *Advances in Developing Human Resources* – journal; *Human Resource Development International* – journal; *Human Resource Development Quarterly* – journal; *Human Resource Development Review*. Conference proceedings.

[2021/XM1724/**E**]

♦ Academy of Improbable Research 00039

Contact 44-C Sacramento St, Cambridge MA 01238, USA. T. +16174914437. Fax +16176610927.

URL: http://www.improbable.com/

History 1994, Cambridge MA (USA), replacing *Society for Basic Irreproducible Research (inactive)* set up 1955, Jerusalem (Israel). **Aims** Publish scientific *satire* and *humour*. **Languages** English. **Finance** Members' dues. **Activities** Ig Nobel Prize Ceremony (annual). **Publications** *Mini-AIR* (12 a year) – on Internet; *Annals of Improbable Research (AIR)* (6 a year).

Members Individuals in 62 countries and territories:

Argentina, Australia, Austria, Belarus, Bolivia, Brazil, Canada, Chile, China, Colombia, Costa Rica, Czechia, Denmark, Egypt, Estonia, Fiji, Finland, France, Georgia, Germany, Greece, Hong Kong, Hungary, Iceland, India, Indonesia, Ireland, Israel, Italy, Japan, Kenya, Korea Rep, Kuwait, Latvia, Lebanon, Lithuania, Mexico, Netherlands, New Zealand, Norway, Pakistan, Panama, Papua New Guinea, Peru, Portugal, Puerto Rico, Romania, Russia, Saudi Arabia, Singapore, Slovakia, South Africa, Spain, Sweden, Switzerland, Taiwan, Thailand, Türkiye, UK, Uruguay, USA, Venezuela. [2018/XF3386/**F**]

♦ Academy of International Business (AIB) 00040

Académie des affaires internationales (AAI) – Academia de Negocios Internacionales (ANI)

Exec Dir 667 N Shaw Ln, Suite 413, Eppley Center, Michigan State Univ, East Lansing MI 48824-1121, USA. T. +15174321452. E-mail: aib@aib.msu.edu.

URL: https://www.aib.world/

History 1959, USA. Former names and other names: *Association for Education in International Business (AEIB)* – former (1959 to 1973); *Académie des affaires internationales (AAI)* – former (1959 to 1973); *Academia de Negocios Internacionales (ANI)* – former (1959 to 1973). Registration: State of Michigan – Domestic Nonprofit Corporation Registration, No/ID: 800941399, Start date: 7 Jul 2015, USA, Michigan; U.S. Internal Revenue Service – 501(c)(3) Nonprofit Determination, No/ID: 30-0876454, Start date: 7 Jul 2015, USA. **Aims** Create, nurture and empower a global community of scholars focused on creating, advancing and disseminating knowledge in international business research, education, policy and practice. **Structure** Executive Board; Chapters (13); Special Interest Groups (5); Fellows. **Languages** English. **Staff** 4.00 FTE, paid. **Finance** Sources: donations; meeting proceeds; members' dues; revenue from activities/projects; sale of publications; sponsorship. Annual budget: 950,000 USD (2020). **Activities** Capacity building; events/meetings; financial and/or material support; knowledge management/information dissemination; networking/liaising; research/documentation. **Events** *Annual Conference* Warsaw (Poland) 2023, *Annual Conference* Miami, FL (USA) 2022, *US-Northeast Chapter Conference* Fairfield, CT (USA) 2021, *Asia Pacific Chapter Conference* Nakhon Pathom (Thailand) 2021, *US-Southeast Chapter Conference* Panama City, FL (USA) 2021. **Publications** *AIB Insights* (4 a year) in English; *AIB Newsletter* (4 a year); *Journal of International Business Policy (JIBP)* (4 a year); *Journal of International Business Studies (JIBS)* (9 a year). *International Business Curricula: Internationalizing the Business School – Global Survey of Institutions of Higher Learning in the Year 2000* (2000). Conference proceedings.

Members Institutional; Individual. Academics, researchers, business executives, government officials and postgraduate students (3,483) in 93 countries and territories:

Afghanistan, Algeria, Argentina, Australia, Austria, Bangladesh, Barbados, Belgium, Bermuda, Bolivia, Bosnia-Herzegovina, Botswana, Brazil, Bulgaria, Canada, Chile, China, Colombia, Costa Rica, Croatia, Cyprus, Czechia, Denmark, Dominican Rep, Ecuador, Egypt, Estonia, Finland, France, Germany, Ghana, Greece, Hong Kong, Hungary, Iceland, India, Indonesia, Iran Islamic Rep, Ireland, Israel, Italy, Jamaica, Japan, Jordan, Kazakhstan, Kenya, Korea Rep, Kuwait, Kyrgyzstan, Latvia, Lebanon, Lithuania, Luxembourg, Macau, Malaysia, Malta, Mexico, Mozambique, Netherlands, New Zealand, Nicaragua, Nigeria, North Macedonia, Norway, Oman, Pakistan, Peru, Philippines, Poland, Portugal, Qatar, Romania, Russia, Rwanda, Saudi Arabia, Singapore, Slovakia, Slovenia, South Africa, Spain, St Vincent-Grenadines, Sweden, Switzerland, Taiwan, Tanzania UR, Thailand, Türkiye, Uganda, UK, Ukraine, United Arab Emirates, USA, Vietnam. [2022.05.03/XC4421/v/**F**]

♦ Academy for International Health Studies (internationally oriented national body)
♦ Academy for an International Language (inactive)
♦ Academy of the Lincei / see Pontifical Academy of Sciences (#18433)

♦ Academy of the Mediterranean 00041

Accademia del Mediterraneo

Contact c/o Fondazione Laboratorio Mediterraneo, Via A Depretis 130, 80133 Naples NA, Italy. T. +39815523033. Fax +39814203273.

URL: http://www.euromedi.org/accademiamed/

History 10 Oct 1998, Naples (Italy), by *Fondazione Mediterraneo*. Previously referred to in English as *Mediterranean Academy*. **Aims** Create a critical inventory of the culture of the Mediterranean; establish a complete ecology of Mediterranean culture. **Publications** Information Services: Databases. **Members** Institutions (561), of which 168 universities, 67 national and regional academies, 200 cultural and research institutes and 48 cities. Membership countries not specified. **NGO Relations** Instrumental in setting up: *Maison de la méditerranée, Naples (MdM, no recent information)*. [2015/XD8419/**D**]

♦ Academy for Multidisciplinary Neurotraumatology (World AMN) 00042

Akademie für multidisziplinäre Neurotraumatologie – Academia Multidisciplinaria Neurotraumatologica

Gen Sec c/o SSNN, Mircea Eliade 37, Cluj-Napoca, Romania. T. +40264431924. E-mail: dafinm@ssnn.ro – office@brain-amn.org.

Pres Div of Neurosurgery, Dept of Surgery, Prince of Wales Hops, Chinese Univ of Hong Kong, Shatin, Hong Kong. T. +85226322211. Fax +85226377974.

URL: http://www.brain-amn.org/

History 19 May 2003, Germany. Registered in accordance with German law. **Aims** Advance neurotraumatology in research, practical application and teaching. **Structure** Management Committee. **Events** *Annual International Congress* Eforie (Romania) 2016, *Annual International Congress / Congress* Cancún (Mexico) 2015, *Annual International Congress / Congress* Dubai (United Arab Emirates) 2014, *Annual International Congress / Congress* Istanbul (Turkey) 2013, *Annual International Congress / Congress* Taipei (Taiwan) 2012.

Members Founding members in 5 countries and territories:

Egypt, Germany, Hong Kong, Italy, Japan. [2020/XJ8176/**F**]

♦ Academy of Operative Dentistry – European Section (AODES) 00043

Sec Athens Univ School of Dentistry, 2 Thivon Str, Goudi, 115 27 Athens, Greece. T. +302107461146.

Hon Sec Restorative Dentistry, Univ Dental Hospital of Manchester, Higher Cambridge Street, Manchester, M15 6FH, UK.

URL: http://academyofoperativedentistry.com/

History 1997, within (US) Academy of Operative Dentistry (AOD). **Aims** Promote excellence in operative dentistry within Europe; share knowledge, information and experience; discuss new trends and evolutions; stimulate research. **Structure** Executive Council, comprising President, Past President, President-Elect, Secretary, Secretary-assistant, Treasurer, Editor and 3 members. **Finance** Supported by AOD. Other sources: donations; proceeds from scientific meetings. **Activities** Organizes: annual scientific meeting in Europe (in October); annual scientific meeting in Chicago Il (USA) (in February). Grants research award. **Events** *Meeting* Nijmegen (Netherlands) 2015, *Meeting* Edinburgh (UK) 2014, *Meeting* Paris (France) 2013, *Meeting* Seville (Spain) 2009, *Meeting* Athens (Greece) 2008. **Publications** *Eurocondensor* (3 a year) – newsletter. **NGO Relations** Full member of: *European Federation of Conservative Dentistry (EFCD, #07087)*.

[2016/XE4578/**E**]

♦ Academy of Peace (internationally oriented national body)
♦ Academy for Peace and International Security / see Academy of Peace
♦ Academy for Peace Research (internationally oriented national body)
♦ Academy for Peace Research, Santa Cruz (internationally oriented national body)
♦ Academy for Plastics Research in Dentistry / see Academy of Dental Materials (#00033)
♦ Academy for Regional Research and Planning (internationally oriented national body)
♦ Academy of World Economics, Washington DC (inactive)
♦ ACADIA – Association for Computer Aided Design in Architecture (internationally oriented national body)
♦ ACADI – Arab Centre for Agricultural Documentation (no recent information)
♦ ACAE – Asociación Centroamericana de Aeronautica y del Espacio (internationally oriented national body)
♦ **ACA-Europe** Association of the Councils of State and Supreme Administrative Jurisdictions of the European Union (#02458)
♦ ACAFADE – Asociación Centroamericana de Familiares de Detenidos Desaparecidos (no recent information)
♦ ACAFAM – Asociación Centroamericana de Facultades de Medicina (no recent information)
♦ ACAFI – Association canadienne des anciens fonctionnaires internationaux (internationally oriented national body)
♦ ACAG – Australasian Council of Auditors-General (internationally oriented national body)
♦ ACAHD – African Centre for Advocacy and Human Development (internationally oriented national body)
♦ **ACAL** Academia de Ciencias de América Latina (#00010)
♦ **ACALAN** African Academy of Languages (#00192)
♦ **ACALASP** Asociación de Agregados Culturales de Latinoamérica, España y Portugal (#02462)
♦ **ACALIN** Academia Africana de Línguas (#00192)
♦ ACAMAR – Asociación Centroamericana de Armadores (no recent information)
♦ ACAM – Atlantic Centre for Atomistic Modelling (internationally oriented national body)
♦ ACAM – Australasian College of Advancement in Medicine (internationally oriented national body)
♦ ACAM – Australasian College of Aesthetic Medicine (internationally oriented national body)
♦ **ACAME** Association africaine des centrales d'achats de médicaments essentiels (#02348)
♦ ACAMH – Association for Child and Adolescent Mental Health (internationally oriented national body)
♦ ACAMIS – Association of China and Mongolia International Schools (internationally oriented national body)
♦ ACAMS – Association of Certified Anti-Money Laundering Specialists (internationally oriented national body)
♦ **ACAO** Arab Civil Aviation Organization (#00920)
♦ Ação Mundo Solidario (internationally oriented national body)
♦ Ação Serviço Cidadão Europeu / see European Citizen Action Service (#06555)
♦ ACAP – Agreement on the Conservation of Albatrosses and Petrels (2001 treaty)
♦ ACAP – Arctic Contaminants Action Program (see: #01097)
♦ ACAP – Asociación Centroamericana de Psiquiatria (no recent information)
♦ ACAPES – Association culturelle d'aide à la promotion éducative et sociale (internationally oriented national body)
♦ ACAPHEI – ASEAN-China Alliance of Private Higher Education Institutions (unconfirmed)
♦ ACAPI – Asociación de Conductas Adictivas y Patologia Dual de Iberoamérica (unconfirmed)

♦ ACAPS 00044

Contact Av de France 23, 1202 Geneva, Switzerland. E-mail: info@acaps.org.

URL: http://www.acaps.org/

History Set up 2009, as a non-profit project of *HelpAge International (#10904)*, *Norwegian Refugee Council (NRC)* and *Save the Children International (#19058)*. Original title: *Assessment Capacities Project*. **Aims** Provide independent, ground-breaking *humanitarian* analysis to help humanitarian workers, influencers, fundraisers and donors make better decisions. **Languages** English. **Activities** Monitoring/evaluation; knowledge management/information dissemination. **Events** *International Congress* Paris (France) 2019. **Publications** Humanitarian analysis reports; infographics; maps; methodologies; technical tools. **IGO Relations** *International Organization for Migration (IOM, #14454)*. **NGO Relations** *CartONG (#03591)*; *IMPACT Initiatives*; *MapAction*; *Start Network (#19969)*. [2019.12.11/XM7205/**F**]

♦ **ACARE** Advisory Council for Aeronautics Research in Europe (#00140)

- ♦ **ACARE** African Centre for Aquatic Research and Education (#00238)
- ♦ ACARM – Association of Commonwealth Archivists and Records Managers (inactive)
- ♦ **ACARTSOD** African Centre for Applied Research and Training in Social Development (#00237)
- ♦ ACASA – Arts Council of the African Studies Association (internationally oriented national body)
- ♦ **ACAS** Asociación Centroamericana de Sociologia (#02115)
- ♦ ACAS – Association of Concerned Africa Scholars (internationally oriented national body)
- ♦ **AC** Asociación de Cervantistas (#02117)
- ♦ **ACATAP** Arab Centre for Arabization, Translation, Authorship and Publication (#00914)
- ♦ **ACAT International** Africa Cooperative Action Trust – International (#00165)
- ♦ ACAT Lilima / see Africa Cooperative Action Trust – International (#00165)
- ♦ ACAV – Associazione Centro Aiuti Volontari Cooperazione Sviluppo Terzo Mondo (internationally oriented national body)
- ♦ **ACA WG** Applications of Computer Algebra Working Group (#00878)
- ♦ ACB / see African Centre for Biodiversity
- ♦ ACB – African Central Bank (unconfirmed)
- ♦ ACB – African Centre for Biodiversity (internationally oriented national body)
- ♦ ACBAR – Agency Coordinating Body for Afghan Relief (internationally oriented national body)
- ♦ **ACB** ASEAN Centre for Biodiversity (#01149)
- ♦ ACB – Association of Savings Banks of CIS (no recent information)
- ♦ ACB / see Council of Arab Central Banks and Monetary Agencies' Governors (#04858)
- ♦ **ACBF** The African Capacity Building Foundation (#00233)
- ♦ **ACBF** ASEAN Central Bank Forum (#01148)
- ♦ **ACBLPE** Associação de Crioulos de Base Lexical Portuguesa e Espanhola (#02325)
- ♦ **ACBO** Association of Caribbean Beekeepers Organisations (#02401)
- ♦ ACBO – Australasian College of Behavioural Optometrists (internationally oriented national body)
- ♦ **ACBS** Arab Committee on Banking Supervision (#00925)
- ♦ **ACBS** Asian Confederation of Billiards Sports (#01396)
- ♦ **ACBS** Association for Contextual Behavioral Science (#02452)
- ♦ ACBSP – Accreditation Council for Business Schools and Programs (internationally oriented national body)
- ♦ **ACBTA** Asian Cognitive Behaviour Therapy Association (#01383)
- ♦ **ACCA** African Coalition for Corporate Accountability (#00252)
- ♦ **ACCA** Asia Cloud Computing Association (#01258)
- ♦ **ACCA** Asian Corrugated Case Association (#01407)
- ♦ ACCA – Asociación para la Conservación de la Cuenca Amazónica (internationally oriented national body)
- ♦ ACCA – Association of Chartered Certified Accountants (internationally oriented national body)
- ♦ Accademia di Diritto Europeo / see Academy of European Law (#00035)
- ♦ Accademia Europea di Bolzano (internationally oriented national body)
- ♦ Accademia Europea del Quartetto / see European Chamber Music Academy (#06515)
- ♦ Accademia Europea per la ricerca applicata ed il perfezionamento professionale – Bolzano / see European Academy of Bozen/Bolzano
- ♦ Accademia Europea di Scienza dell'Alimentazione / see Accademia Europea di Scienza della Nutrizione (#00045)

♦ Accademia Europea di Scienza della Nutrizione 00045

European Academy of Nutritional Sciences (EANS) – Académie Européenne des Sciences de Nutrition – Europäische Akademie der Ernährungswissenschaften

Sec Dipto di Scienze Cliniche e di Comunita, Univ of Milan, Fondawione IRCCS Ca Ganda – Ospedale Maggiore Policlinico, Via della Commenda 9, 20122 Milan MI, Italy. T. +39255032497 – +39250320202. Fax +39250320226.

Pres Dipto di Scienze della Sallute – Ospedale San Paolo, Via di Rudini 8, 20142 Milan MI, Italy. T. +39250323098. Fax +39250323097.

History 1961, as *Gruppo di Nutrizionisti Europea – Group of European Nutritionists (GEN) – Groupe européen de nutritionnistes – Studiengruppe Europäischer Ernährungswissenschaftler.* Subsequently also referred to as *Accademia Europea di Scienza dell'Alimentazione.* **Aims** Promote personal contacts and cooperation among European nutritionists and international organizations; promote the quality of nutritional science. **Structure** General Assembly; Praesidium; Council. **Languages** English. **Staff** Voluntary. **Finance** Members' dues. **Activities** Events/meetings; research/documentation. **Events** *Annual Symposium* Milan (Italy) 2014, *Annual Symposium* Milan (Italy) 2012, *Annual Symposium* Milan (Italy) 2010, *Annual Symposium* Milan (Italy) 2008, *Annual Symposium* Durban (South Africa) 2005. **Publications** *European Academy of Nutritional Sciences Newsletter.* Symposium reports; workshop reports.

Members Nutritional scientists and organisations. Members 26 countries:
Australia, Austria, Belgium, Bulgaria, Croatia, Czechia, Denmark, Finland, France, Germany, Greece, Iceland, Ireland, Italy, Mexico, Netherlands, Norway, Poland, Portugal, Russia, Spain, Sweden, Switzerland, Türkiye, UK, USA.

IGO Relations Collaborates with: *FAO (#09260); WHO (#20950).* **NGO Relations** Collaborates with: *International Union of Nutritional Sciences (IUNS, #15796).* [2015.01.08/XD1002/**D**]

- ♦ Accademia Europeista del Friuli-Venezia Giulia (internationally oriented national body)
- ♦ Accademia Europeistica del Friuli Venice Giulia / see Accademia Europeista del Friuli-Venezia Giulia
- ♦ Accademia dei Giusprivatisti Europei (#00036)
- ♦ Accademia Internazionale d'Arte Moderna (internationally oriented national body)
- ♦ Accademia Internazionale Melitense (internationally oriented national body)
- ♦ Accademia Internazionale delle Scienze, San Marino (#00617)
- ♦ Accademia del Mediterraneo (#00041)
- ♦ Accademia Svizzera di Science Morali e Sociali (internationally oriented national body)
- ♦ ACC – African Conservation Centre (internationally oriented national body)
- ♦ ACC / see African Cricket Association (#00279)
- ♦ ACCAINC / see African Aid Organization
- ♦ **ACC** Allied Coordination Committee (#00733)
- ♦ **ACC** Anglican Consultative Council (#00828)
- ♦ ACC – Arab Cooperation Council (inactive)
- ♦ ACCAS – Association of Colombian-Caribbean American Schools (see: #02367)
- ♦ **ACC** ASEAN Chess Confederation (#01153)
- ♦ **ACC** ASEAN-China Centre (#01154)
- ♦ **ACC** ASEAN Cocoa Club (#01155)
- ♦ **ACC** Asia Cohort Consortium (#01259)
- ♦ **ACC** Asian Cricket Council (#01412)
- ♦ **ACC** Asian Cycling Confederation (#01417)
- ♦ **ACC** Asociación para la Conservación del Caribe (#03481)
- ♦ ACC / see Association of Asian Constitutional Courts and Equivalent Institutions (#02378)
- ♦ **ACC** Association of Asian Constitutional Courts and Equivalent Institutions (#02378)
- ♦ **ACC** Association for Community Colleges (#02441)
- ♦ ACCC – Asian Conference on Coordination Chemistry (meeting series)
- ♦ **ACCCLATAM** Asociación de Centros de Convenciones del Caribe y Latinoamérica (#02116)
- ♦ ACCCP / see ASEAN Committee on Consumer Protection (#01157)
- ♦ **ACCCSA** Association of Caribbean, Central and South American Corrugators (#02402)
- ♦ **ACCD** Arab Council for Childhood and Development (#00929)
- ♦ **ACCE** African Council for Communication Education (#00273)
- ♦ **ACCEAO** Association des conseils chrétiens et eglises en afrique de l'ouest (#09724)
- ♦ ACCE / see Association of European Film Archives and Cinémathèques (#02511)
- ♦ ACCEDE – African Centre for Citizenship and Democracy (internationally oriented national body)
- ♦ ACCED-I – Association of Collegiate Conference and Events Directors – International (internationally oriented national body)
- ♦ ACCEE – Architects' Council of Central and Eastern Europe (no recent information)

♦ ACCELERATE 00046

Registered Address Veldkapelgaarde 30, bte 1-30-30, 1200 Sint-Lambrechts-Woluwe, Belgium. E-mail: contact@accelerate-platform.org.

URL: https://www.accelerate-platform.org/

History 2015. Founded by *SIOP Europe (SIOPE, #19288)*, *Innovative Therapies for Children with Cancer Consortium (ITCC, #11222)* and *Cancer Drug Development Forum (CDDF, #03413).* CDDF terminated its cooperation, Mar 2018. Registration: Banque-Carrefour des Entreprises, No/ID: 0733.539.041, Start date: 30 Aug 2019, Belgium; EU Transparency Register, No/ID: 553056941424-52, Start date: 15 Feb 2021. **Aims** Accelerate innovation in drug development for children and adolescents with cancer. **Structure** Steering Committee; Project Management Team. Working Groups. **Finance** Supported by: *Innovative Therapies for Children with Cancer Consortium (ITCC, #11222); SIOP Europe (SIOPE, #19288).* **Activities** Events/meetings. **Events** *ACCELERATE Paediatric Oncology Conference* 2022, *ACCELERATE Paediatric Oncology Conference* Brussels (Belgium) 2021, *ACCELERATE Paediatric Oncology Conference* Brussels (Belgium) 2020, *ACCELERATE Paediatric Oncology Conference* Brussels (Belgium) 2019, *ACCELERATE Paediatric Oncology Conference* Brussels (Belgium) 2018. [2021/AA1570/**F**]

- ♦ Accelerating International Mission Strategies (internationally oriented national body)
- ♦ Accelerator, HomeMaker, Incubator, MatchMaker, SenseMaker, Art ambassador / see Ahimsa Fund (#00586)
- ♦ ACCEO – Association of Chief Education Officers in the Caribbean (no recent information)
- ♦ Acceso (internationally oriented national body)
- ♦ ACCESS / see Keystone Accountability (#16186)
- ♦ **ACCESS** ACCESS Facility (#00048)
- ♦ **ACCESS** Africa Centre for Climate and Earth Systems Science (#00161)

♦ Access Agriculture 00047

Exec Dir Rue Washington 40, 1050 Brussels, Belgium. E-mail: info@accessagriculture.org.

URL: https://www.accessagriculture.org/

History 2012. Founded by 2 media companies: Agro-Insight and Countrywise Communication. Registration: Banque-Carrefour des Entreprises, No/ID: 0723.866.755, Start date: 1 Apr 2019, Belgium. **Aims** Improve agroecological principles and rural entrepreneurship. **Structure** Governing Board. **Activities** Capacity building; networking/liaising; training/education. **IGO Relations** Partner of (4): *Centre on Integrated Rural Development for Asia and the Pacific (CIRDAP, #03750); Inter-American Institute for Cooperation on Agriculture (IICA, #11434); International Center for Agricultural Research in the Dry Areas (ICARDA, #12466); International Crops Research Institute for the Semi-Arid Tropics (ICRISAT, #13116).*

NGO Relations Member of (1): *Federation of European and International Associations Established in Belgium (FAIB, #09508).*

Partner of (28):
- *ACT Alliance EU (#00082);*
- *African Forum for Agricultural Advisory Services (AFAAS, #00320);*
- *Biovision Africa Trust (BvAT);*
- *Catholic Relief Services (CRS, #03608);*
- *Eastern African Farmers Federation (EAFF, #05223);*
- *Eastern and Southern Africa small scale Farmers' Forum (ESAFF, #05256);*
- *Fairtrade Africa (FTA, #09239);*
- *Farm Concern International (FCI, #09272);*
- *Farm Radio International (#09274);*
- *Folkekirkens Nødhjaelp (FKN);*
- *Global Forum for Rural Advisory Services (GFRAS, #10378);*
- *Grameen Foundation (GF, #10694);*
- *IFOAM – Organics International (IFOAM, #11105);*
- *International Institute of Rural Reconstruction (IIRR, #13921);*
- *International Institute of Tropical Agriculture (IITA, #13933);*
- *Latin American and Caribbean Network of Small Fairtrade Producers (#16282);*
- *Mercy Corps International (MCI);*
- *More and Better (#16855);*
- *Network of Asia and Pacific Producers (NAPP, #16995);*
- *Pacific Organic & Ethical Trade Community (POETCom, #17986);*
- *Practical Action (#18475);*
- *PROLINNOVA (#18537);*
- *Red Latinoamericana de Servicios de Extensión Rural (RELASER, #18719);*
- *Regional Universities Forum for Capacity Building in Agriculture (RUFORUM, #18818);*
- *Research Institute of Organic Agriculture (#18857);*
- *Swiss Interchurch Aid (EPER);*
- *TRIAS;*
- *World Overview of Conservation Approaches and Technologies (WOCAT, see: #21192).* [2022.02.09/AA1254/**F**]

- ♦ Access Aid International (internationally oriented national body)
- ♦ Access Alliance (internationally oriented national body)

♦ ACCESS Facility (ACCESS) 00048

Managing Dir Vierambachtsstraat 137A-2, 3022 AL Rotterdam, Netherlands. T. +31641253065. E-mail: secretariat@accessfacility.org.

URL: http://www.accessfacility.org/

History Launched Dec 2012. Original working title: *CSR Conflict Management Center (CCMC).* Registered in accordance with Dutch law, as a foundation. **Aims** Promote collaborative processes and provide access to local and global expertise, facilitation and mediation services to help companies, communities and governments work better together to improve the relationships, identify joint opportunities and find common solutions to their differences. **Structure** Governing Board. **Staff** 5.00 FTE, paid. **Activities** Projects/programmes. [2017.10.11/XJ6264/**F**]

- ♦ **Access** Global Movement for Digital Freedom (#10478)

♦ ACCESS Health International 00049

Chairman/Pres 1016 Fifth Ave, Ste 11A/C, New York NY 10028, USA. E-mail: sofi@accessh.org – info@accessh.org.

URL: http://www.accessh.org/

History Registered in accordance with US law. **Aims** Conduct practical research to improve health systems and healthcare delivery; foster health innovation by equipping entrepreneurs with technical expertise, education and networking opportunities. **Structure** Board of Directors; Special Advisors. **Activities** Healthcare; advocacy/lobbying/activism; events/meetings; research/documentation. **Publications** Books; monographs; articles. [2019.02.13/XJ7460/**F**]

♦ The Access Initiative (TAI) 00050

Dir c/o WRI, 10 G St NE, Ste 800, Washington DC 20002, USA. T. +12027297767. E-mail: access@wri.org.

URL: http://www.accessinitiative.org/

History Founded 1999. **Aims** Improve decisions and policies that affect the environment and human lives by establishing common global practices for public access to *information,* participation and justice in *environmental decision-making.*

Members Founding members (4) in 4 countries:
Chile, Hungary, Thailand, USA.

Included in the above, 1 organization listed in this Yearbook:
World Resources Institute (WRI, #21753).

Associations in 23 countries:
Argentina, Bolivia, Brazil, Bulgaria, Chile, Congo DR, Ecuador, El Salvador, Estonia, Guatemala, Hungary, Ireland, Latvia, Mexico, Paraguay, Portugal, South Africa, Türkiye, Uganda, UK, Uruguay, Venezuela, Zimbabwe.

NGO Relations Member of: *Freedom of Information Advocates Network (FOIAnet, #09985).* Cooperates with: *Global Call for Climate Action (GCCA, inactive).* [2014.12.05/XF6360/**F**]

♦ **Access to Insurance Initiative (A2ii)** 00051
Secretariat c/o GIZ, Dag-Hammarskjöld-Weg 1-5, 65760 Eschborn, Germany. T. +496196796176. Fax +4961967980617 6.
URL: https://a2ii.org/
History Created by *Microinsurance Network (#16747)* and *International Association of Insurance Supervisors (IAIS, #11966)* and their Joint Working Group. **Aims** Strengthen the capacity and understanding of supervisors to facilitate the promotion of inclusive and *responsible* insurance, thereby reducing vulnerability. **Structure** Governing Council; Executive Committee; Secretariat. Hosted by: *Deutsche Gesellschaft für Internationale Zusammenarbeit (GIZ)*. **Finance** Core funding from German Federal Ministry for Economic Cooperation and Development (BMZ) and The Netherlands' Ministry of Foreign Affairs (DGIS). Additional contributions from: *International Association of Insurance Supervisors (IAIS, #11966); FSD Africa (#10010); Multilateral Investment Fund (MIF, #16887); FinMark Trust (FMT, #09775)*. **Activities** Advocacy/lobbying/activism; capacity building; knowledge management/information dissemination; standards/guidelines; training/education. **Events** *Consultative Forum* Johannesburg (South Africa) 2019, *Consultative Forum* Panama (Panama) 2019, *Consultative Forum* Accra (Ghana) 2018, *Consultative Forum* Buenos Aires (Argentina) 2018, *Consultative Forum* Colombo (Sri Lanka) 2018. **Publications** *A2ii Newsletter*.
Members Founding partners (6):
Consultative Group to Assist the Poor (CGAP, #04768); FinMark Trust (FMT, #09775); German Ministry for Economic Cooperation and Development (BMZ); *ILO (#11123); International Association of Insurance Supervisors (IAIS, #11966); United Nations Capital Development Fund (UNCDF, #20524).*
NGO Relations Member of (1): *Microinsurance Network (#16747).* [2023/XM7417/y/**E**]

♦ Accession Partnership (inactive)

♦ **Access Now** 00052
Address not obtained.
URL: http://www.accessnow.org/
History 2009. EU Transparency Register: 71149477682-53. **Aims** Defend and extend *digital rights* of users at risk around the world. **Structure** Board; International Advisory Board; Technical Advisory Board. **Events** *RightsCon Summit* Costa Rica 2023, *RightsCon Summit* 2022, *RightsCon Summit* Brussels (Belgium) 2017. **Consultative Status** Consultative status granted from: *ECOSOC (#05331)* (Special). **NGO Relations** Member of: *Global Net Neutrality Coalition (#10480); International Corporate Accountability Roundtable (ICAR, #12968)*. Affiliate of: *Internet Society (ISOC, #15952).* [2020/XJ8986/**C**]

♦ **Access Quality International (AQI)** 00053
CEO PO Box 18, Chiangmai Univ Post Office, Muang 50202, Chiang Mai, Thailand. T. +66818836388.
URL: http://www.accessquality.org/
History A technical assistance NGO derived from *Asian Harm Reduction Network (AHRN, #01501)*. **Aims** Improve quality of life of *marginalized*, vulnerable people and communities by increasing availability, accessibility and quality of a comprehensive package of services. [2014/XJ7759/**E**]

♦ **Access VetMed** 00054
Technical Dir Espace Meeûs, Square de Meeûs 38/40, 1000 Brussels, Belgium. T. +3224018795. E-mail: info@accessvetmed.eu.
Communications and PR address not obtained.
URL: https://accessvetmed.eu/
History 15 Apr 2002. Former names and other names: *European Group for Generic Veterinary Products (EGGVP)* – former. Registration: Banque-Carrefour des Entreprises, Belgium; EU Transparency Register, No/ID: 894642514444-82. **Aims** Increase ACCESS – availability, compliance, convenience, efficacy, safety, and savings – of veterinary medicines to veterinarians, and farm and companion animal owners in Europe. **Structure** General Assembly; Board of Directors. **Languages** English. **Staff** 1.00 FTE, paid. **Finance** Sources: members' dues. **Activities** Research/documentation; standards/guidelines. Active in Europe. **Publications** Position papers.
Members Full (24) in 14 countries:
Austria, Belgium, France, Germany, Hungary, Ireland, Italy, Netherlands, Poland, Portugal, Romania, Slovenia, Spain, UK.
IGO Relations Also links with national organizations. [2023.02.14/XJ8488/**D**]

♦ ACCFA – Asian Conference of Correctional Facilities and Planners (meeting series)
♦ **ACCF** Association des cours constitutionnelles Francophone (#02459)
♦ ACCF / see Caribbean Philanthropy Network (#03538)

♦ **ACC International** 00055
Contact Heart House, 2400 N St NW, Washington DC 20037, USA. E-mail: international@acc.org.
URL: http://www.acc.org/membership/sections-and-councils/international-center
History Set up as the international arm of *American College of Cardiology (ACC)*. Also referred to as *ACC International Center*. **Aims** Enhance *cardiovascular* health through the collaboration and exchange of knowledge and resources. **Structure** Assembly of International Governors.
Members Chapters in 30 countries:
Argentina, Australia, Brazil, Canada, Chile, China, Egypt, Germany, Greece, Hong Kong, Indonesia, Israel, Italy, Jamaica, Jordan, Korea Rep, Lebanon, Malaysia, Mexico, Pakistan, Philippines, Saudi Arabia, Singapore, Spain, Taiwan, Thailand, Türkiye, UK, United Arab Emirates, Venezuela. [2014/XJ8530/**E**]

♦ ACC International Center / see ACC International (#00055)
♦ ACC / see International Coconut Community (#12628)
♦ Acción Andina (internationally oriented national body)
♦ Acción Climática (unconfirmed)
♦ Acción para las Comarcas Mineras / see Association of Europe's Coalfield Regions (#02585)
♦ Acción contra el Hambre (#00086)
♦ Accion para el Desarrollo Sostenible (unconfirmed)
♦ Acción Frente a la Resistencia Bacteriana (#00089)
♦ Acción Global de los Pueblos contra el comercio 'libre' y la OCM (#18304)
♦ Acción Internacional en pro de los Recursos Genéticos / see GRAIN (#10691)

♦ **Acción Internacional por la Salud – Latinoamérica and Caribe (AIS-LAC)** 00056
Exec Dir Av General Garzón 938, Dpto C – Jesús Maria, Lima, Peru. T. +5117233310.
URL: http://www.aislac.org/
Aims Improve health conditions of people in Latin America and the Caribbean; promote access to essential medicines.
Members Institutional; Individual. Members in 16 countries:
Argentina, Bolivia, Brazil, Chile, Colombia, Dominican Rep, Ecuador, Guatemala, Honduras, Mexico, Nicaragua, Paraguay, Peru, Spain, Uruguay, USA.
NGO Relations Member of (1): *Health Action International (HAI, #10868)*. Supports (1): *Global Call for Action Against Poverty (GCAP, #10263).* [2021/XK1818/**E**]

♦ Acción Internacional Técnica / see ACCION International
♦ ACCION International (internationally oriented national body)
♦ Acción Mundial de Parlamentarios (#18208)
♦ Acción Mundo Solidario (internationally oriented national body)
♦ Acción Permanente por la Paz (internationally oriented national body)
♦ Acción para la Salud Internacional (#10868)
♦ Acción Sanitaria y Desarrollo Social (internationally oriented national body)
♦ Acción Sin Fronteras (internationally oriented national body)
♦ **ACCIP** Federation of African Chambers of Commerce, Industry, Agriculture and Professions (#09401)
♦ **ACCIS** Association of Consumer Credit Information Suppliers (#02451)
♦ ACCM – Africa Continent Care for Migration (internationally oriented national body)
♦ **ACCMAL** Asociación Centroamericana, del Caribe y Mexicana de Animales de Laboratorio (#02113)
♦ **ACCMS** Asian Consortium for Computational Materials Science (#01402)
♦ ACCO – Africa Centre for Citizens Orientation (internationally oriented national body)

♦ ACCOBAMS – Agreement on the Conservation of Cetaceans of the Black Sea, Mediterranean Sea and contiguous Atlantic Area (1996 treaty)
♦ ACCOP – Asian Conference of Criminal and Operations Psychology (meeting series)
♦ ACCOPRA – Central American Association of Orthotists, Prosthetics, Rehabilitation Professionals and Affiliates (inactive)
♦ Accord de 1971 sur les navires à passagers qui effectuent des transports spéciaux (1971 treaty)
♦ Accord de 2005 sur l'huile d'olive et les olives de table (2005 treaty)
♦ Accord additionnel à l'arrangement de Nyon (1937 treaty)
♦ Accord aéronautique en vue d'assurer l'application de l'article 128 du Traité de Trianon (1927 treaty)
♦ Accord aéronautique en vue d'assurer l'application de l'article 144 du Traité de Saint-Germain-en-Laye (1927 treaty)
♦ Accord aéronautique en vue d'assurer l'application de l'article 198 du Traité de Versailles (1926 treaty)
♦ Accord aéronautique en vue d'assurer l'application de l'article 89 du Traité de Neuilly (1927 treaty)
♦ ACCORD – African Centre for the Constructive Resolution of Disputes (internationally oriented national body)
♦ Accord sur l'application de la clause de la nation la plus favorisée (1934 treaty)
♦ Accord pour l'application de garanties (1970 treaty)
♦ Accord sur les arrangements administratifs pour le plan d'aménagement énergétique et d' irrigation du Perk Thnot – Cambodge (1968 treaty)
♦ Accord sur les arrangements provisoires relatifs aux nodules polymétalliques des grands fonds marins (1982 treaty)
♦ Accord de l' ASEAN sur la conservation de la nature et des ressources naturelles (1985 treaty)
♦ Accord d'assistance mutuelle exceptionnelle entre les pays nordiques en cas d'accidents impliquant des dommages dus aux rayonnements (1973 treaty)
♦ Accord sur les bateaux-feux gardés se trouvant hors de leur post normal (1930 treaty)
♦ Accord BDLN (1986 treaty)
♦ Accord de Bonn (#00564)
♦ Accord de Carthagène – Accord d'intégration sous-régionale andine (1969 treaty)
♦ Accord centraméricain relatif aux stimulants fiscaux du développement industriel, 1962 (1962 treaty)
♦ Accord centroaméricain sur la circulation routière (1958 treaty)
♦ Accord centroaméricain sur l'unification de la signalisation routière (1958 treaty)
♦ Accord commercial à long terme (1967 treaty)
♦ Accord complémentaire pour l'application de la Convention européenne de sécurité sociale (1972 treaty)
♦ Accord concernant l' accès réciproque des zones de pêche du Skagerrak et du Kattegat (1966 treaty)
♦ Accord concernant l'adoption de conditions uniformes applicables au controle technique périodique des véhicules a roues et la reconnaissance réciproque des controles (1997 treaty)
♦ Accord concernant l'adoption de Règlements techniques harmonisés de l'ONU applicables aux véhicules à roues et aux équipements et pièces susceptibles d'être montés ou utilisés sur les véhicules à roues et les conditions de reconnaissance réciproque des homologations délivrées conformément à ces Règlements (1958 treaty)
♦ Accord concernant l'aide au Kenya dans le domaine des coopératives (1967 treaty)
♦ Accord concernant l'application de l'accord du 11 février 1977, en matière de conception et de technologie des réacteurs refroidis par gaz (1977 treaty)
♦ Accord concernant la cession d'un réacteur d'enseignement et d'uranium enrichi destiné à ce réacteur (1970 treaty)
♦ Accord concernant les cimetières militaires britanniques (1917 treaty)
♦ Accord concernant les conditions de travail des bateliers rhénans (1954 treaty)
♦ Accord concernant la Convention internationale pour régler la police de la pêche dans la Mer du Nord (1955 treaty)
♦ Accord concernant la coopération régionale dans la lutte contre la pollution par les hydrocarbones et autres substances nuisibles en cas de situation critique dans le Pacifique du Sud-Est (1981 treaty)
♦ Accord concernant la coopération transfrontière pour prévenir et limiter, en cas d'accident, les conséquences dangereuses pour la santé, la propriété et l'environnement (1989 treaty)
♦ Accord concernant l'enregistrement de la population (1968 treaty)
♦ Accord concernant l'établissement de règlements techniques mondiaux applicables aux véhicules à roues, ainsi qu'aux équipements et pièces qui peuvent être et/ou utilisés sur les vehicules à roues (1998 treaty)
♦ Accord concernant une exécution commune de mesures visant visant à lutter contre le commerce illégal de faune et de flore sauvages (1994 treaty)
♦ Accord concernant la libération des échanges des produits de la pêche (1956 treaty)
♦ Accord concernant un marché commun nordique du travail pour les infirmiers et les infirmières (1968 treaty)
♦ Accord concernant un marché commun nordique du travail pour les pharmaciens (1969 treaty)
♦ Accord concernant les mesures à prendre pour la protection des peuplements de grosses crevettes (1952 treaty)
♦ Accord concernant l'octroi de garanties financières à certaines entreprises de transports aériens, 1951 (1951 treaty)
♦ Accord concernant l'octroi de garanties financières à certaines entreprises de transports aériens, 1955 (1955 treaty)
♦ Accord concernant l'octroi de garanties financières à certaines entreprises de transports aériens, 1959 (1959 treaty)
♦ Accord concernant la poursuite et le châtiment des grands criminels de guerre des puissances européennes de l'Axe (1945 treaty)
♦ Accord concernant la préparation d'un programme de gestion tripartite de l' environnement du lac Victoria (1994 treaty)
♦ Accord concernant les problèmes pratiques liés aux grands fonds miniers marins (1987 treaty)
♦ Accord Concernant la Protection de la Meuse (1994 treaty)
♦ Accord concernant la protection des phoques de la mer des Wadden (1990 treaty)
♦ Accord concernant des recherches en commun en science des réactions (1970 treaty)
♦ Accord concernant des recherches sur les effets de la radioactivité dans la mer (1961 treaty)
♦ Accord concernant la réglementation de la pêche de la plie et du flet dans la mer Baltique (1929 treaty)
♦ Accord concernant les règles relatives à la validation des périodes d'affiliation et autres conditions déterminant l'ouverture du droit à l'indemnité des personnes assurées contre le chômage (1976 treaty)
♦ Accord concernant les règles relatives à la validation des périodes de cotisation et des périodes d'emploi pour les personnes assurées contre le chômage qui passent d'un pays à l'autre (1959 treaty)
♦ Accord concernant la sécurité sociale des bateliers rhénans, 1950 (1950 treaty)
♦ Accord concernant la sécurité sociale des bateliers rhénans, 1961 (1961 treaty)
♦ Accord concernant la sécurité sociale des bateliers rhénans, 1979 (1979 treaty)
♦ Accord concernant le séjour des réfugiés au sens de la Convention relative au statut des réfugiés (1965 treaty)
♦ Accord concernant le statut juridique du personnel employé auprès des institutions nordiques (1974 treaty)
♦ Accord concernant les transferts d'une caisse-maladie à une autre et les prestations de maladie en cas de séjours temporaires (1956 treaty)
♦ Accord concernant les transferts de personnes affiliées à l'assurance-maladie ainsi que les prestations de maladies au cours de séjours temporaires (1967 treaty)
♦ Accord concernant le transit des personnes expulsées (1965 treaty)
♦ Accord concernant le transport international direct de marchandises par rail et par eau (1959 treaty)

- Accord de concertation communauté-COST relatif à une action concertée dans le domaine de l'analyse des micropolluants organiques dans l'eau (1980 treaty)
- Accord de concertation Communauté-COST relatif à une action concertée dans le domaine du comportement physico-chimique des polluants atmosphériques (1980 treaty)
- Accord de concertation Communauté-COST relatif à une action concertée dans le domaine de l'effet des traitements sur les propriétés physiques des denrées alimentaires (1980 treaty)
- Accord de concertation Communauté-COST relatif à une action concertée dans le domaine de la téléinformatique (1981 treaty)
- Accord de concertation communauté-COST relatif à une action concertée dans le domaine du traitement et de l'utilisation des boues d'épuration (1979 treaty)
- Accord conclu à la conférence monétaire et économique de Londres, en 1933 (1933 treaty)
- Accord sur la conservation des albatros et pétrels (2001 treaty)
- Accord sur la conservation des cétacés de la mer Noire, de la Méditerranée et de la zone atlantique adjacente (1996 treaty)
- Accord sur la conservation des petits cétacés de la mer Baltique, du nord-est de l'Atlantique et des mers d'Irlande et du Nord (1992 treaty)
- Accord de coopération (1962 treaty)
- Accord de coopération et d'assistance mutuelle entre les directions nationales et les douanes (1981 treaty)
- Accord de coopération pour assurer l'application du règlement relatif à la prévention de la pollution des eaux de la mer par les hydrocarbures (1967 treaty)
- Accord de coopération commerciale et économique pour le Pacifique-sud (1980 treaty)
- Accord de coopération commerciale et économique pour le Pacifique-sud, 1980 (1980 treaty)
- Accord de coopération concernant la quarantaine et la protection des plantes contre les parasites et les maladies (1959 treaty)
- Accord de coopération et de concertation entre les états d'Afrique centrale sur la conservation de la faune sauvage (1983 treaty)
- Accord de coopération culturelle (1971 treaty)
- Accord de coopération pour un développement durable du bassin du Mekong (1995 treaty)
- Accord de coopération économique (1952 treaty)
- Accord de coopération économique et technique (1970 treaty)
- Accord de coopération en matière de contrôle technique et de classification des navires (1961 treaty)
- Accord de coopération en matière monétaire, économique et financière (1960 treaty)
- Accord de coopération en matière vétérinaire (1959 treaty)
- Accord de coopération pour la pêche en mer (1962 treaty)
- Accord de coopération pour la protection des côtes et des eaux de l'Atlantique du Nord-Est contre la pollution (1990 treaty)
- Accord de coopération relatif à l'assistance entre les pays nordiques (1981 treaty)
- Accord de coopération relatif à un plan de développement rural intégré en Amérique latine (1966 treaty)
- Accord de coopération en vue de la mise au point et de l'exploitation du procédé de la centrifugation gazeuse pour la production d'uranium enrichi (1970 treaty)
- Accord sur la coordination de la répartition des canaux pour le service maritime mobile dans la bande de 2065 à 2107 khz (1980 treaty)
- Accord de Cotonou (2000 treaty)
- Accord de défense (1960 treaty)
- Accord sur l'échange des mutilés de guerre entre les pays membres du Conseil de l'Europe aux fins de traitement médical (1955 treaty)
- Accord entre les états de l'Afrique centrale pour la création d'un fonds spécial pour la conservation de la faune sauvage (1983 treaty)
- Accord entre les Etats membres du Conseil de l'Europe sur l'attribution aux mutilés de guerre militaires et civils d'un carnet international de bons de réparation d'appareils de prothèse et d'orthopédie (1962 treaty)
- Accord entre les Etats parties au Traité de l'Atlantique Nord, 1955 (1955 treaty)
- Accord entre les états parties au Traité de l'Atlantique Nord sur la coopération dans le domaine des renseignements atomiques, 1964 (1964 treaty)
- Accord étendant la compétence territoriale de la Commission du Pacifique Sud (1951 treaty)
- **Accord EUR-OPA risques majeurs** Accord partiel ouvert en matière de prévention, de protection et d'organisation des secours contre les risques naturels et technologiques majeurs (#17762)
- Accord européen sur la circulation des jeunes sous couvert du passeport collectif entre les pays membres du Conseil de l'Europe (1961 treaty)
- Accord européen complétant la Convention sur la circulation routière (1971 treaty)
- Accord européen complétant la Convention sur la signalisation routière (1971 treaty)
- Accord européen concernant l'entraide médicale dans le domaine des traitements spéciaux et des ressources thermo-climatiques (1962 treaty)
- Accord européen concernant l'octroi des soins médicaux aux personnes en séjour temporaire (1980 treaty)
- Accord européen concernant les personnes participant aux procédures devant la Commission et Cour européenne des droits de l'homme (1969 treaty)
- Accord européen concernant les personnes participant aux procédures devant la Cour européenne des droits de l'homme (1996 treaty)
- Accord Européen Concernant la Sécurité Sociale des Bateliers de la Navigation Intérieure (1993 treaty)
- Accord européen sur l'échange de réactifs pour la détermination des groupes tissulaires (1974 treaty)
- Accord européen sur les grandes lignes internationales de chemin de fer (1985 treaty)
- Accord européen sur les grandes lignes de transport international combiné et les installations connexes (1991 treaty)
- Accord européen sur les grandes routes de trafic international (1975 treaty)
- Accord européen sur les grandes voies navigables d'importance internationale (1996 treaty)
- Accord européen sur l'instruction et la formation des infirmières (1967 treaty)
- Accord européen sur la limitation de l'emploi de certains détergents dans les produits de lavage et de nettoyage (1968 treaty)
- Accord européen sur le maintien du paiement des bourses aux étudiants poursuivant leurs études à l'étranger (1969 treaty)
- Accord européen sur le placement au pair (1969 treaty)
- Accord européen portant application de l'article 23 de la convention sur la circulation routière de 1949 (1950 treaty)
- Accord européen sur le régime de la circulation des personnes entre les pays membres du Conseil de l'Europe (1957 treaty)
- Accord européen relatif à l'échange des réactifs pour la détermination des groupes sanguins (1962 treaty)
- Accord européen relatif à l'échange de substances thérapeutiques d'origine humaine (1958 treaty)
- Accord européen relatif aux marques routières (1957 treaty)
- Accord européen relatif à la suppression des visas pour les réfugiés (1959 treaty)
- Accord européen relatif au transport international des marchandises dangereuses par route (1957 treaty)
- Accord européen relatif au transport international des marchandises dangereuses par voies de navigation intérieures (2000 treaty)
- Accord européen relatif au travail des équipages des véhicules effectuant des transports internationaux par route, 1970 (1970 treaty)
- Accord européen pour la répression des émissions de radiodiffusion effectués par des stations hors des territoires nationaux (1965 treaty)
- Accord européen sur le transfert de la responsabilité à l'égard des réfugiés (1980 treaty)
- Accord européen sur la transmission des demandes d'assistance judiciaire (1977 treaty)
- Accord sur la facilitation de échanges (2014 treaty)
- Accord de financement collectif des stations océaniques de l'Atlantique Nord (1974 treaty)
- Accord général sur le commerce des services (1994 treaty)
- Accord général sur les privilèges et immunités du Conseil de l'Europe (1949 treaty)
- Accord général sur les tarifs douaniers et le commerce (inactive)
- Accord général sur les tarifs douaniers et le commerce, 1947 (1947 treaty)
- Accord général sur les tarifs douaniers et le commerce, 1994 (1994 treaty)
- Accord entre les gouvernements représentés à la Conférence des télécommunications des Bermudes (1945 treaty)
- Accordia – Accordia Global Health Foundation (internationally oriented national body)
- Accordia Global Health Foundation (internationally oriented national body)
- Accord pour l'importation d'objets de caractère éducatif, scientifique ou culturel (1950 treaty)
- Accord pour l'importation temporaire en franchise de douane, à titre de prêt gratuit et à des fins diagnostiques ou thérapeutiques, de matériel médico-chirurgical et de laboratoire destiné aux établissements sanitaires (1960 treaty)
- Accord d'intégration sous-régionale andine (1969 treaty)
- Accord interaméricain du café (1940 treaty)
- Accord interaméricain des radiocommunications, 1949 (1949 treaty)
- Accord interaméricain relatif au service d'amateurs (1987 treaty)
- Accord inter-arabe sur le commerce et le transit (1953 treaty)
- Accord intérimaire sur l'aviation civile internationale (1944 treaty)
- Accord intérimaire européen concernant les régimes de sécurité sociale relatifs à la vieillesse, à l'invalidité et aux survivants (1953 treaty)
- Accord intérimaire européen concernant la sécurité sociale à l'exclusion des régimes relatifs à la vieillesse, à l'invalidité et aux survivants (1953 treaty)
- Accord international de 2015 sur l'huile d'olive et les olives de tables (2015 treaty)
- Accord international sur le blé (1986 treaty)
- Accord international sur le blé, 1971 (treaty)
- Accord international sur le blé, 1971 (1971 treaty)
- Accord international sur le blé, 1986 (1986 treaty)
- Accord international sur les bois tropicaux, 1983 (1983 treaty)
- Accord international sur les bois tropicaux, 1994 (1994 treaty)
- Accord international sur les bois tropicaux, 2006 (2006 treaty)
- Accord international sur le cacao, 1972 (1972 treaty)
- Accord international sur le cacao, 1975 (1975 treaty)
- Accord international sur le cacao, 1980 (1980 treaty)
- Accord international sur le cacao, 1986 (1986 treaty)
- Accord international sur le cacao, 1993 (1993 treaty)
- Accord international sur le cacao, 2001 (2001 treaty)
- Accord international sur le cacao, 2010 (2010 treaty)
- Accord international sur le café, 1962 (1962 treaty)
- Accord international sur le café, 1968 (1968 treaty)
- Accord international sur le café, 1976 (1976 treaty)
- Accord international sur le café, 1982 (1982 treaty)
- Accord international sur le café, 1994 (1994 treaty)
- Accord international sur le café, 2001 (2000 treaty)
- Accord international sur le caoutchouc naturel (1979 treaty)
- Accord international sur le caoutchouc naturel, 1987 (1987 treaty)
- Accord international sur l'étain, 1954 (1954 treaty)
- Accord international sur l'étain, 1975 (1975 treaty)
- Accord international sur l'étain, 1981 (1981 treaty)
- Accord international sur l'huile d'olive, 1956 (1956 treaty)
- Accord international sur l'huile d'olive, 1963 (1963 treaty)
- Accord international sur l'huile d'olive, 1979 (1979 treaty)
- Accord international sur l'huile d'olive et les olives de tables, 1986 (1986 treaty)
- Accord international sur le jute et les articles en jute (1982 treaty)
- Accord International sur la Meuse (2002 treaty)
- Accord international sur la procédure applicable à l'établissement des tarifs des services aériens réguliers (1967 treaty)
- Accord international pour la réglementation de la chasse à la baleine (1937 treaty)
- Accord international relatif à la stabilisation des prix du caoutchouc naturel (1976 treaty)
- Accord international sur le sucre, 1953 (1953 treaty)
- Accord international sur le sucre, 1958 (1958 treaty)
- Accord international sur le sucre, 1968 (1968 treaty)
- Accord international sur le sucre, 1973 (1973 treaty)
- Accord international sur le sucre, 1977 (1977 treaty)
- Accord international sur le sucre, 1984 (1984 treaty)
- Accord international sur le sucre, 1987 (1987 treaty)
- Accord international sur le sucre, 1992 (1992 treaty)
- Accord interne relatif au financement et à la gestion des aides de la communauté (1979 treaty)
- Accord interne relatif aux mesures à prendre et aux procédures à suivre pour l'application de la deuxième convention ACP-CEE de Lomé (1979 treaty)
- Accord de libre échange asiatique (1992 treaty)
- Accord de libre-échange centre-européen (1992 treaty)
- Accord de Lisbonne – Accord de coopération pour la protection des côtes et des eaux de l'Atlantique du Nord-Est contre la pollution (1990 treaty)
- Accord pour le maïs, le sorgho, le blé ordinaire, le riz et la volaille (1962 treaty)
- Accord de Manille (1963 treaty)
- Accord pour la mise en oeuvre d'une action concertée européenne dans le domaine de la métallurgie sur le thème – Matériaux pour turbines à gaz (1971 treaty)
- Accord pour la mise en oeuvre d'une action concertée européenne dans le domaine de la métallurgie sur le thème – Matériaux pour les usines de dessalement de l'eau de mer (1971 treaty)
- Accord pour la mise en oeuvre d'une action européenne dans le domaine des nuisances sur le thème 'analyse des micropolluants organiques dans l'eau' (1971 treaty)
- Accord pour la mise en oeuvre d'une action européenne dans le domaine des nuisances sur le thème 'recherches sur le comportement physico-chimique de l'anhydride sulfureux dans l'atmosphère' (1971 treaty)
- Accord pour la mise en oeuvre d'une action européenne dans le domaine des nuisances sur le thème 'traitement des boues d'épuration' (1971 treaty)
- Accord pour la mise en oeuvre d'une action européenne dans le domaine des télécommunications sur le thème: antennes avec premiers lobes secondaires réduits et rapport G/T maximal (1971 treaty)
- Accord pour la mise en oeuvre d'une action européenne dans le domaine des télécommunications sur le thème 'réseau d'antennes à commande de phase' (1972 treaty)
- Accord pour la mise en oeuvre de l'article III 1 et 4 du Traité sur la non-prolifération des armes nucléaires (1973 treaty)
- Accord modifiant la convention nordique du 19 novembre 1934 relative à l'héritage et à la liquidation des successions (1975 treaty)
- Accord modifiant la Convention nordique du 7 novembre 1933 relative aux faillites (1977 treaty)
- Accord monétaire centroaméricain (1974 treaty)
- Accord multifibre – Arrangement concernant le commerce international des textiles (1973 treaty)
- Accord multilatéral sur les droits commerciaux pour les transports aériens non réguliers en Europe (1956 treaty)
- Accord multilatéral relatif aux certificats de navigabilité des aéronefs importés (1960 treaty)
- Accord multilatéral relatif à la perception des redevances de route (1970 treaty)

articles and prepositions
http://www.brill.com/yioo

Accord réorganisation administrative
00057

♦ Accord Network (internationally oriented national body)
♦ Accord Nord-Américain de coopération dans le domaine de l'environnement (1993 treaty)
♦ Accordo complementare di applicazione della Convenzione europea di sicurezza sociale (1972 treaty)
♦ Accordo europeo di assistenza medica in materia di trattamenti speciali e di risorse termo-climatiche (1962 treaty)
♦ Accordo europeo sulla circolazione dei giovani con passaporto collettivo fra i paesi membri del Consiglio d'Europa (1961 treaty)
♦ Accordo europeo sulla circolazione delle persone fra i paesi membri del Consiglio d'Europa (1957 treaty)
♦ Accordo europeo concernente le persone partecipanti alle procedure davanti alla Commissione e alla Corte europee dei diritti dell'uomo (1969 treaty)
♦ Accordo europeo concernente lo scambio dei reagenti per la determinazione dei gruppi sanguigni (1962 treaty)
♦ Accordo europeo sull'istruzione e formazione delle infermiere (1967 treaty)
♦ Accordo europeo sulla limitazione dell'impiego di taluni detersivi nei prodotti di lavatura e pulitura (1968 treaty)
♦ Accordo europeo sulle persone "alla pari" (1969 treaty)
♦ Accordo europeo sulle persone partecipanti alla procedura davanti la Corte europea dei diritti dell'uomo (1996 treaty)
♦ Accordo europeo per la protezione delle emissioni televisive (1960 treaty)
♦ Accordo europeo relativo alla soppressione dei visti per i rifugiati (1959 treaty)
♦ Accordo europeo per la repressione di radiodiffuzioni effettuate da stazioni fuori dei territori nazionali (1965 treaty)
♦ Accordo europeo sullo scambio di programmi attraverso film televisivi (1958 treaty)
♦ Accordo europeo sullo scambio di reattivi per la determinazione dei gruppi tissulari (1974 treaty)
♦ Accordo europeo sul mantenimento delle borse di studio versate a studenti che proseguono i loro studi all'estero (1969 treaty)
♦ Accordo europeo sul trasferimento di responsabilità relativa ai rifugiati (1980 treaty)
♦ Accordo europeo sulla trasmissione delle domande di assistenza giudiziaria (1977 treaty)
♦ Accordo generale su i privilegi e le immunità del Consiglio d'Europa (1949 treaty)
♦ Accordo per l'importazione temporanea in franchigia doganale, come prestito gratuito e a scopi diagnostici o terapeutici, di materiale medico-chirurgico e di laboratorio, destinato agli istituti sanitari (1960 treaty)
♦ Accord sur les oiseaux d'eau migrateurs d'Afrique-Eurasie (1995 treaty)
♦ Accordo tra i paesi membri del Consiglio d'Europa sull'attribuzione ai mutilati di guerra, militari e civili, di un blocchetto internazionale di buoni per le riparazioni di protesi ed apparecchi ortopedici (1962 treaty)
♦ Accordo provvisorio europeo concernente la sicurezza sociale con esclusione dei regimi relativi la vecchiaia, l'invalidità ed i superstiti (1953 treaty)
♦ Accordo provvisorio europeo su i regimi di sicurezza sociale relativi all'anzianità, l'invalidità ed i superstiti (1953 treaty)
♦ Accordo RAMOGE (#00057)
♦ Accordo relativo all'applicazione della Convenzione europea sull'arbitrato commerciale internazionale (1962 treaty)
♦ Accordo sullo scambio dei mutilati di guerra tra i paesi membri del Consiglio d'Europa per trattamento medico (1955 treaty)
♦ Accordo sul traffico illecito via mare, che applica l'articolo 17 della Convenzione delle Nazioni unite contro il traffico illecito di stupefacenti e di sostanze psicotrope (1995 treaty)
♦ Accordo sul trasferimento delle persone decedute (1973 treaty)
♦ Accord OTAN sur la communication, à des fins de défense, d'informations techniques (1970 treaty)
♦ Accord de Paris (2015 treaty)
♦ Accord de participation aux recherches et d'échange technique dans les programmes de recherche effectuée dans CABRI et dans le réacteur pulsé à coeur annulaire relatifs à la sûreté des réacteurs à neutrons rapides (1978 treaty)
♦ Accord partiel dans le domaine social et de la santé publique (inactive)
♦ Accord partiel élargi sur les Itinéraires culturels (#05486)
♦ Accord partiel élargi sur le sport (#05487)
♦ Accord partiel ouvert en matière de prévention, de protection et d'organisation des secours contre les risques naturels et technologiques majeurs (#17762)
♦ Accord sur la pêche au thon dans le Pacifique Est (1983 treaty)
♦ Accord sur un plan d'action pour la gestion écologiquement rationnelle du bassin hydrographique commun du Zambèze (1987 treaty)
♦ Accord politique (1922 treaty)
♦ Accord portant réglementation commune sur la faune et la flore (1977 treaty)
♦ Accord sur la préservation du caractère confidentiel des données relatives aux sites faisant l'objet d'une demande dans les grands fonds marins (1984 treaty)
♦ Accord sur la préservation du caractère confidentiel des données relatives aux sites des fonds marins (1986 treaty)
♦ Accord prévoyant la réadmission des étrangers qui sont entrés illégalement sur le territoire d'un de ces pays (1952 treaty)
♦ Accord sur la prise en charge de personnes à la frontière (1965 treaty)
♦ Accord sur les privilèges et immunités de la Cour pénale internationale (2002 treaty)
♦ Accord sur la propriété artistique et littéraire (1911 treaty)
♦ Accord sur la protection du saumon dans la Mer Baltique (1962 treaty)
♦ Accord sur la protection des végétaux dans la région de l'Asie et du Pacifique (1956 treaty)
♦ Accord provisoire pour la réglementation de la pêche dans les eaux baignant les côtes septentrionales du territoire de l'Union des Républiques soviétiques socialistes (1930 treaty)
♦ Accord quadripartite (1972 treaty)

♦ Accord RAMOGE 00057

Accordo RAMOGE

Exec Sec 36 Avenue de l'Annonciade, 98000 Monte Carlo, Monaco. T. +37798984229. Fax +37798984007. E-mail: contact@ramoge.org.

URL: http://www.ramoge.org/

History Established on signature of *Agreement Concerning the Protection of the Waters of the Mediterranean Shores (RAMOGE agreement, 1976)* between the governments of France, Italy and Monaco. Original title: *RAMOGE Commission – Commission RAMOGE.* **Aims** Protect the *marine environment* along the *coasts* of Provence, Monaco and Liguria. **Structure** Commission. **Languages** French, Italian. **Finance** Contributions from the governments of France, Italy and Monaco. **IGO Relations** *Regional Activity Centre for Specially Protected Areas (RAC/SPA, #18746).* [2018/XE4395/E*]

♦ Accord sur le rapport entre l'obligation de service militaire et la nationalité en Norvège, au Danemark et en Suède (1956 treaty)
♦ Accord sur des recherches météorologiques à l'échelle mondiale (1979 treaty)
♦ Accord régional sur l'accès à l'information, la participation publique et l'accès à la justice à propos des questions environnementales en Amérique latine et dans les Caraïbes (2018 treaty)
♦ Accord régional de l'Amérique du Sud sur les radiocommunications, 1935 (1935 treaty)
♦ Accord régional de l'Amérique du Sud sur les radiocommunications, 1937 (1937 treaty)
♦ Accord régional de l'Amérique du Sud sur les radiocommunications, 1940 (1940 treaty)
♦ Accord régional concernant les mouvements transfrontières des déchets dangereux (1992 treaty)
♦ Accord régional de coopération sur le développement, la recherche et la formation dans le domaine de la science et de la technologie nucléaires (1972 treaty)
♦ Accord régional relatif à l'importation temporaire des véhicules routiers (1956 treaty)
♦ Accord régissant les activités des Etats sur la Lune et les autres corps célestes (1979 treaty)
♦ Accord sur la réglementation de la chasse à la baleine dans le Pacifique nord (1970 treaty)
♦ Accord relatif à une action concertée dans le domaine de l'enregistrement des anomalies congénitales (1979 treaty)
♦ Accord relatif à l'aide volontaire à fournir pour l'exécution du projet de préservation et de mise en valeur de l'ensemble monumental de Mohenjodaro (1980 treaty)
♦ Accord relatif à l'aide volontaire à fournir pour l'exécution du projet de sauvegarde de Borobudur (1973 treaty)
♦ Accord relatif à l'aide volontaire à fournir pour l' exécution du projet de sauvegarde des temples d'Abou Simbel (1963 treaty)
♦ Accord relatif à l' aide volontaire à fournir pour l' exécution du projet de sauvegarde des temples de Philae (1970 treaty)
♦ Accord relatif à l'allocation des fréquences sur le continent Nord-américain (1929 treaty)
♦ Accord relatif à l'application de la partie XI de la Convention des nations unies sur le droit de la mer du 10 décembre 1982 (1994 treaty)
♦ Accord relatif à l'application provisoire des projets de conventions douanières internationales sur le tourisme, sur les véhicules routiers commerciaux et sur le transports international des marchandises pour la route (1949 treaty)
♦ Accord relatif au balisage uniforme des eaux navigables (1962 treaty)
♦ Accord relatif aux bases navales et aériennes cédées à bail aux Etats-Unis d'Amérique (1941 treaty)
♦ Accord relatif à certaines questions touchant le régime applicable à la navigation du Rhin (1939 treaty)
♦ Accord relatif aux cimetières de guerre britanniques en Irak (1935 treaty)
♦ Accord relatif aux cimetières et sépultures de guerre britanniques en Egypte (1937 treaty)
♦ Accord relatif au commerce des aéronefs civils (1979 treaty)
♦ Accord relatif aux conditions générales d'exécution des transports internationaux de voyageurs par autocar (1970 treaty)
♦ Accord relatif à la conservation des chauves-souris en Europe (1991 treaty)
♦ Accord relatif à une coopération en matière de transports aériens (1951 treaty)
♦ Accord relatif à la coopération pour le sauvetage des vies humaines et à l'assistance aux navires et aéronefs en détresse dans la Mer Noire (1956 treaty)
♦ Accord relatif à la coopération transfrontière entre les pays nordiques au niveau des collectivités locales (1977 treaty)
♦ Accord relatif à la coordination, à la répartition et à l'utilisation de la radiodiffusion en modulation de fréquence dans la bande 88-108 MHz (1980 treaty)
♦ Accord relatif au développement économique (1952 treaty)
♦ Accord relatif aux documents d'identité du personnel des aéronefs, 1940 (1940 treaty)
♦ Accord relatif aux documents d'identité du personnel des aéronefs, Bruxelles (1938 treaty)
♦ Accord relatif aux documents d'identité pour le personnel des aéronefs, Paris (1938 treaty)
♦ Accord relatif au droit de libre survol des aéronefs au-dessus des territoires antarctiques britanniques et français (1938 treaty)
♦ Accord relatif aux échanges commerciaux et la libre circulation des capitaux (1953 treaty)
♦ Accord relatif à l'enseignement supérieur (1960 treaty)
♦ Accord relatif à l'entraînement de pilotes d'hélicoptères (1977 treaty)
♦ Accord relatif à l'établissement d'une réserve de diamants d'industrie sur le continent Nord-américain (1943 treaty)
♦ Accord relatif à l'extension de certaines dispositions de sécurité sociale (1977 treaty)
♦ Accord relatif à la gestion de projets nordiques communs d'aide aux pays en développement (1968 treaty)
♦ Accord relatif à l'harmonisation des droits à pension prévus par les régimes de pensions de l'Etat (1973 treaty)
♦ Accord relatif à l'harmonisation des mesures fiscales destinées à stimuler l'industrie (1973 treaty)
♦ Accord Relatif à L'importation de la Viande Bovine en Provenance du Groupe des Etats D'Afrique, Caraïbes et Pacifique (1979 treaty)
♦ Accord relatif à un marché commun scandinave du travail pour les dentistes (1966 treaty)
♦ Accord relatif à un marché commun scandinave du travail pour les médecins (1965 treaty)
♦ Accord relatif à un marché commun du travail (1954 treaty)
♦ Accord relatif aux marchés publics (1979 treaty)
♦ Accord relatif aux mesures propres à faciliter le contrôle sanitaire du trafic (1955 treaty)
♦ Accord relatif aux mesures du ressort l'état du port visant à prévenir, contrecarrer et éliminer la pêche illicite, non déclarée et non réglementée (2009 treaty)
♦ Accord relatif à la mise en oeuvre de certaines dispositions concernant la nationalité (1969 treaty)
♦ Accord relatif aux obstacles techniques au commerce (1979 treaty)
♦ Accord relatif à la pêche dans la Mer Noire (1959 treaty)
♦ Accord relatif aux prestations de maladie et aux prestations de grossesse et de maternité (1975 treaty)
♦ Accord relatif aux procédures en matière de licences d'importation (1979 treaty)
♦ Accord relatif aux produits céréaliers (1967 treaty)
♦ Accord relatif aux produits relevant de la Communauté européenne du charbon et de l'acier (treaty)
♦ Accord relatif à un programme international de l'énergie (1974 treaty)
♦ Accord relatif à la protection des eaux du littoral méditerranéen (1976 treaty)
♦ Accord relatif à la reconnaissance des brevets de pilote et de navigateur d'aviation comme tenant lieu de passeports nationaux (1937 treaty)
♦ Accord relatif à la reconnaissance mutuelle des documents d'identité pour le personnel des aéronefs (1938 treaty)
♦ Accord relatif au régime des droits d'invention dans le domaine de l'énergie atomique (1956 treaty)
♦ Accord relatif à la régulation du régime du lac Inari au moyen de la centrale hydro-électrique et du barrage de Kaitakoski (1959 treaty)
♦ Accord relatif à la responsabilité décennale et à l'assurance de certains architectes et entrepreneurs (1979 treaty)
♦ Accord relatif à la sécurité sociale (1977 treaty)
♦ Accord relatif aux services télégraphiques du Commonwealth, 1948 (1948 treaty)
♦ Accord relatif aux services télégraphiques du Commonwealth, 1963 (1963 treaty)
♦ Accord relatif aux signaux maritimes (1930 treaty)
♦ Accord relatif à la stabilisation du commerce des raisins secs – sultanes (1964 treaty)
♦ Accord relatif à la stabilisation des marchés des raisins secs (1963 treaty)
♦ Accord relatif à une station météo-flottante commune dans l'Atlantique Nord (1949 treaty)
♦ Accord relatif au statut juridique et aux privilèges des organisations internationales spécialisées de coopération (1966 treaty)
♦ Accord relatif à la suppression de la formalité du visa, 1971 (1971 treaty)
♦ Accord relatif à la suppression de la formalité du visa, 1974 (1974 treaty)
♦ Accord relatif à la suppression de l'habitude de fumer l'opium, 1931 (1931 treaty)
♦ Accord relatif à la suppression du visa, avril 1970 (1970 treaty)
♦ Accord relatif à la suppression du visa, octobre 1970 (1970 treaty)
♦ Accord relatif à la suppression du visa, septembre 1970 (1970 treaty)
♦ Accord relatif au trafic illicite par mer, mettant en oeuvre l'article 17 de la Convention des nations unies contre le trafic illicite de stupéfiants et de substances psychotropes (1995 treaty)
♦ Accord relatif au transit des services aériens internationaux (1944 treaty)
♦ Accord relatif au transport aérien international (1944 treaty)
♦ Accord relatif au transport de personnes et de marchandises par la route, 1958 (1958 treaty)
♦ Accord relatif au transport de personnes et de marchandises par la route, 1971 (1971 treaty)
♦ Accord relatif aux transports internationaux de denrées périssables et aux engins spéciaux à utiliser pour ces transports (1970 treaty)
♦ Accord relatif aux tribunaux chinois dans le 'Settlement' international de Shanghaï (1930 treaty)
♦ Accord pour la réorganisation administrative et technique du réseau de la Compagnie des chemins de fer du Sud (1923 treaty)

- ♦ Accord pour la sauvegarde mutuelle du secret des inventions intéressant la défense et ayant fait l'objet de demandes de brevet (1960 treaty)
- ♦ Accord sur le sauvetage des astronautes, le retour des astronautes et la restitution des objets lancés ans l'espace extra-atmosphérique (1968 treaty)
- ♦ Accord de Schengen (1985 treaty)
- ♦ Accord de Senningen (1996 treaty)
- ♦ Accord se rapportant à la coopération concernant les mesures prises contre la pollution des eaux de mer pas les hydrocarbures (1971 treaty)
- ♦ Accords aux fins des dispositions de la Convention des Nations Unies sur le droit de la mer du 10 décembre 1982 relatives à la conservation et la gestion des stocks de poissons dont les déplacements s' effectuent tant à l' intérieur qu' au-delà des zones économiques exclusives – stocks chevauchants – et des stocks de poissons grands migrateurs (1995 treaty)
- ♦ Accords généraux d'emprunts révisés (1962 treaty)
- ♦ Accord spécial centroaméricain sur l'uniformisation des droits à l'importation sur les textiles de rayonne et d'autres fibres artificielles ou synthétiques (1965 treaty)
- ♦ Accords relatifs à la réglementation de l'importation de la viande de boeuf dans le Royaume-Uni (1939 treaty)
- ♦ Accord sur les stations météorologiques flottantes de l'Atlantique du Nord (1949 treaty)
- ♦ Accord sud-américain relatif aux stupéfiants et aux substances psychotropes (1973 treaty)
- ♦ Accord au sujet des passeports et des visas (1922 treaty)
- ♦ Accord sur la surveillance de la stratosphère (1976 treaty)
- ♦ Accord touristique (1938 treaty)
- ♦ Accord sur le transfert des corps des personnes décédées (1973 treaty)
- ♦ Accord sur le transport routier (1955 treaty)
- ♦ Accord sur les Transports Routiers entre le Benelux et les Etats Baltes (1992 treaty)
- ♦ Accord de l'union douanière entre l'Afrique du Sud, le Botswana, le Lesotho et le Swaziland (1910 treaty)
- ♦ Accord visant la circulation internationale du matériel visuel et auditif de caractère éducatif, scientifique et culturel (1948 treaty)
- ♦ Accord visant à favoriser le respect par les navires de pêche en haute mer des mesures internationales de conservation et de gestion (1993 treaty)
- ♦ Accord volontaire entre armateurs de navires-citernes relatif à la responsabilité due à la pollution des hydrocarbures (inactive)
- ♦ **ACCOSCA** African Confederation of Cooperative Savings and Credit Associations (#00261)

♦ AccountAbility 00058

Communications Dir 477 Madison Avenue, Level 3, New York NY 10022, USA. T. +16465075900. E-mail: info@accountability.org.
CEO address not obtained.
URL: http://www.accountability.org/

History Founded at which time the primary areas of focus were research and standards. Launched the AA-1000 Series of Standards in 1995 and began providing Advisory Services to corporates in 2005. Former names and other names: *Institute of Social and Ethical Accountability* – former. **Aims** Provide research, standards and advisory services in the area of sustainability and corporate responsibility. **Structure** Advisory Board; Standards Board; Management Team. **Languages** Arabic, English, French, German, Spanish. **Staff** 10-20. **Activities** Events/meetings; guidance/assistance/consulting; research/documentation; standards/guidelines; training/education. **Events** *Responsible competitiveness conference / Conference* Copenhagen (Denmark) 2003. [2021.08.31/XE4623/**E**]

- ♦ Accountability Counsel (internationally oriented national body)

♦ Accountability International 00059

Exec Dir 54 Shortmarket Street, Greenmarket Square, Cape Town, 8000, South Africa. T. +27214242057. E-mail: info@accountability.international – communications@accountability.international.
Contact address not obtained.
URL: https://accountability.international/

History 2005. Former names and other names: *AIDS Accountability International (AAI)* – former. **Aims** Follow up on commitments to the *AIDS epidemic* that were made by governments. **Structure** Board of Trustees. Offices in: Cape Town (South Africa); Johannesburg (South Africa); Stockholm (Sweden); New York NY (USA). **Staff** 9.00 FTE, paid. **NGO Relations** Member of (2): *Girls not Brides (#10154)*; *ILGA World (International Lesbian, Gay, Bisexual, Trans and Intersex Association, #11120)*. Cooperates with (1): *ICASO (#11040)*. [2020/XJ9213/**F**]

- ♦ The Accountability Project / see Ending Clergy Abuse (#05460)

♦ Accountable Now 00060

Exec Dir Agricolastr 26, 10555 Berlin, Germany. T. +49302062469712 – +49302062469713. Fax +49302062469719. E-mail: info@accountablenow.org.
URL: http://accountablenow.org/

History Set up 2008, as *International NGO Charter of Accountability*, under which title it is still legally registered in the UK as a charity. **Aims** Support civil society organizations (CSOs) to be transparent, responsive to stakeholders and focused on delivering impact. **Structure** Board of Trustees. **Languages** English. **Staff** 4.00 FTE, paid. **Finance** Members' dues. **Activities** Advocacy/lobbying/activism; events/meetings; training/education.
Members CSO's (26); national entities. Included in the above, 21 organizations listed in this Yearbook:
ActionAid (#00087); *Adventist Development and Relief Agency International (ADRA, #00131)*; *Amnesty International (AI, #00801)*; *ARTICLE 19 (#01121)*; *CARE International (CI, #03429)*; *Christian Blind Mission (CBM)*; *CIVICUS: World Alliance for Citizen Participation (#03962)*; *EDUCO*; *European Environmental Bureau (EEB, #06996)*; *Greenpeace International (#10727)*; *Mediterranean Information Office for Environment, Culture and Sustainable Development (MIO-ECSDE, #16657)*; *Oxfam International (#17922)*; *Plan International (#18386)*; *Restless Development*; *Sightsavers International (#19270)*; *SOS-Kinderdorf International (#19693)*; *Terre des Hommes International Federation (TDHIF, #20133)*; *Transparency International (TI, #20223)*; *World Vision International (WVI, #21904)*; *World Young Women's Christian Association (World YWCA, #21947)*.
Affiliate members include 3 organizations listed in this Yearbook:
ChildFund Alliance (#03868); *ChildFund International (#03869)*; *TECHO (#20121)*. [2019.06.03/XM6761/y/**F**]

♦ Accountancy Europe 00061

CEO Avenue d'Auderghem 22-28 box 8, 1040 Brussels, Belgium. T. +3228933360. E-mail: info@accountancyeurope.eu.
URL: http://www.accountancyeurope.eu/

History 1986. Founded on merger of *European Union of Public Accountants (UEC, inactive)* and *Groupe d'études des experts comptables de la CEE (inactive)*, as *Fédération des experts-comptables européens (FEE) – European Federation of Accountants*. Current title adopted Dec 2016. Registration: Banque-Carrefour des Entreprises, No/ID: 0430.069.789, Start date: 30 Dec 1986, Belgium; EU Transparency Register, No/ID: 4713568401-18, Start date: 16 Sep 2008. **Aims** Translate the daily experience of professional accountants from across Europe to inform the European *policy* debate; ensure the high quality of work of professional accountants and their ethical behaviour. **Structure** Members' Assembly (3 per year); Board; Secretariat, headed by Chief Executive. **Languages** English, French. **Staff** 25.00 FTE, paid. **Finance** Members' dues. **Activities** Research/documentation. Active in: Corporate Reporting; Auditing; Small and Medium-sized Enterprises/Small and Medium-sized Practices; Ethics; Company Law and Corporate Governance; Sustainability; Tax Policy; Public Sector; Anti-Money Laundering; Qualification and Market Access. **Events** *ESG and Corporate Governance* Brussels (Belgium) 2022, *EU Anti-Money Laundering Reforms – Building a Resilient Framework* Brussels (Belgium) 2022, *Sustainable Tax System – Towards a Green Future* Brussels (Belgium) 2022, *The impact of bribery and corruption on SMEs* Brussels (Belgium) 2022, *Tax Day* Brussels (Belgium) 2020. **Publications** *Newsletter* (12 a year). Annual Report; fact sheets; comment letters; consultation responses; studies; surveys; discussions papers; position papers; events and conference summaries. Series of updates on specific areas: technology; tax; capital markets union; small- and medium-sized enterprises.
Members Professional organizations (50), representing about 1 million professional accountants, auditors and advisors, in 37 countries:
Austria, Belgium, Bosnia-Herzegovina, Bulgaria, Croatia, Cyprus, Czechia, Denmark, Estonia, Finland, France, Germany, Greece, Hungary, Iceland, Ireland, Israel, Italy, Latvia, Lithuania, Luxembourg, Malta, Monaco, Montenegro, Netherlands, Norway, Poland, Portugal, Romania, Serbia, Slovakia, Slovenia, Spain, Sweden, Switzerland, Türkiye, UK.
NGO Relations In liaison with technical committees of: *International Organization for Standardization (ISO, #14473)*. Member of: *European Financial Reporting Advisory Group (EFRAG, #07254)*; *European Organization of Regional External Public Audit Finance Institutions (EURORAI, #08113)*; *European Parliamentary Financial Services Forum (EPFSF, #08148)*; *European Services Forum (ESF, #08469)*. Institutional member of: *Centre for European Policy Studies (CEPS, #03741)*. [2020/XD0711/**D**]

♦ Accounting and Auditing Organization for Islamic Financial Institutions (AAOIFI) 00062

Sec Gen Al Nakheel Tower, 10th Floor – Office 1001, Building 1074, Road 3622 Seef Area 436, Manama, Bahrain. T. +97317244496. Fax +97317250194.
URL: http://www.aaoifi.com/

History Founded 26 Feb 1990, Algiers (Algeria). Registered 27 Mar 1991, in the State of Bahrain. Statutes amended Nov 2000. **Aims** Develop accounting, auditing and banking practices; prepare, promulgate and interpret accounting and auditing standards for Islamic financial institutions in order to harmonize accounting practices and auditing procedures; review and amend accounting and auditing standards; prepare, issue, review and adjust the statements and guidelines on banking, investment and insurance practices; work towards the implementation of these standards and statements. **Structure** General Assembly; Board of Trustees; Executive Committee; General Secretariat; Accounting and Auditing Standards Board; Shari'a Board. **Languages** Arabic, English. **Staff** 9.00 FTE, paid. **Activities** Training/education; research/documentation. **Events** *Conference on adapting to a rapidly changing regulatory and financial environment* Manama (Bahrain) 2003, *Sharia conference* Manama (Bahrain) 2003, *Conference on enhancing governance and transparency in Islamic financial institutions* Manama (Bahrain) 2001. **Publications** *Accounting, Auditing and Governance Standards for Islamic Financial Institutions* (2002); *Shari'a Standards Volume* (2002); *Statement on the Purpose and Calculation of the Capital Adequacy Ratio for Islamic Banks* (1999).
Members Financial services institutions (93) Founding; Associate; Observers. Founding members (5) in 3 countries:
Kuwait, Saudi Arabia, Switzerland.
Included in the above, 1 organization listen in this Yearbook:
Islamic Development Bank (IsDB, #16044).
Associate members (75) in 22 countries and territories:
Algeria, Bahrain, Bangladesh, Brunei Darussalam, Cayman Is, Egypt, Indonesia, Jordan, Kuwait, Malaysia, Pakistan, Palestine, Qatar, Russia, Saudi Arabia, South Africa, Sri Lanka, Sudan, Tunisia, Türkiye, United Arab Emirates, Yemen.
Included in the above, 1 organization listed in this Yearbook:
International Islamic Bank of Investment and Development (no recent information).
Affiliated Member (1):
Islamic Corporation for the Insurance of Investment and Export Credit (ICIEC, #16041).
Observing members (12) in 7 countries and territories:
Bahrain, Cyprus, Kuwait, Malaysia, Pakistan, Palestine, Saudi Arabia.
Included in the above, 1 organization listed in this Yearbook:
Gulf International Bank (GIB, #10832).
NGO Relations Instrumental in setting up: *International Shari'ah Council of the AAOIFI (#14844)*. [2019.07.30/XD7375/y/**D**]

- ♦ Accounting History International Conference (meeting series)
- ♦ **ACCP** Alliance for Cervical Cancer Prevention (#00663)
- ♦ **ACCP** ASEAN Committee on Consumer Protection (#01157)
- ♦ **ACCP** Asian Conference on Clinical Pharmacy (#01399)
- ♦ ACCP – Assembly of Caribbean Community Parliamentarians (no recent information)
- ♦ **ACCP** Association of Caribbean Commissioners of Police (#02403)
- ♦ ACCPR – Africa Chamber of Content Producers (unconfirmed)
- ♦ ACCPUF / see Association des cours constitutionnelles Francophone (#02459)
- ♦ ACCR / see European Network of Cultural Centres in Historic Monuments
- ♦ Accra Assembly (inactive)
- ♦ ACCR – Association des Centres culturels de rencontre – Réseau européen (internationally oriented national body)
- ♦ ACCREC – African Climate Change Research Centre (internationally oriented national body)
- ♦ Accreditation Board for Engineering and Technology / see ABET
- ♦ Accreditation Committee for Veterinary Nurse Education (unconfirmed)
- ♦ Accreditation Council for Business Schools and Programs (internationally oriented national body)

♦ Accreditation Council for Oncology in Europe (ACOE) 00063

Contact c/o European Cancer Organisation, Rue de la Science 41, 1040 Brussels, Belgium. T. +327750200. E-mail: acoe@europeancancer.org.
URL: https://acoe.europeancancer.org/

History 1989. **Aims** Promote accreditation of European continuing *medical education* activities in oncology. **Structure** Council, including Chairman. **Languages** English. **Staff** 0.50 FTE, paid. **Finance** Accreditation fees charged to event organizers. **Activities** Certification/accreditation; events/meetings.
Members One nominated member from each of 4 international organizations listed in this Yearbook:
European School of Oncology (ESO, #08434); *European SocieTy for Radiotherapy and Oncology (ESTRO, #08721)*; *European Society of Surgical Oncology (ESSO, #08753)*; *SIOP Europe (SIOPE, #19288)*.
NGO Relations Located at: *European Cancer Organisation (ECO, #06432)*. [2022/XJ3565/y/**E**]

♦ Accredited European Schools Network (AESN) 00064

Address not obtained.

History Launched 2011 as an informa network. Previously known as *Associated European Schools Network (AES)*. **Structure** Rotating Presidency. **Events** *Annual Plenary Meeting* Helsinki (Finland) 2018, *Annual Plenary Meeting* Strasbourg (France) 2014.
Members Accredited schools in 12 countries:
Belgium, Denmark, Estonia, Finland, France, Germany, Greece, Ireland, Italy, Luxembourg, Netherlands, UK.
IGO Relations *Board of Governors of the European Schools (#03295)*. [2018/XM7827/**F**]

- ♦ Accrediting Association of Bible Colleges / see Association for Biblical Higher Education
- ♦ Accrediting Association of Bible Institutes and Bible Colleges / see Association for Biblical Higher Education
- ♦ Accrediting Council for Theological Education in Africa / see Association for Christian Theological Education in Africa (#02431)
- ♦ ACCR – European Network of Cultural Centres in Historic Monuments (internationally oriented national body)
- ♦ ACCRI – Associazione di Cooperazione Cristiana Internazionale (internationally oriented national body)
- ♦ **ACCS** Association of Caribbean Copyright Societies (#02404)
- ♦ ACCS – Australasian College of Cosmetic Surgery (internationally oriented national body)
- ♦ **ACCU** Asia/Pacific Cultural Centre for UNESCO (#01879)
- ♦ **ACCU** Association of Asian Confederation of Credit Unions (#02377)
- ♦ ACCUGAZ – Association des fabricants européens de chauffe-eau à accumulation au gaz (inactive)
- ♦ ACC / see United Nations System Chief Executives Board for Coordination (#20636)
- ♦ ACDA – Action concertée pour le développement de l'Afrique (inactive)
- ♦ ACD – African and Caribbean Diversity (internationally oriented national body)
- ♦ ACDAR / see Arab Company for Livestock Development (#00927)
- ♦ **ACD** Asia Cooperation Dialogue (#01261)
- ♦ **ACDE** African Council for Distance Education (#00274)
- ♦ ACDE / see Renew Europe (#18840)

♦ ACDESS – African Centre for Development and Strategic Studies (internationally oriented national body)
♦ ACDF – African Citizens Development Foundation (internationally oriented national body)
♦ **ACDHRS** African Centre for Democracy and Human Rights Studies (#00239)
♦ **ACDIMA** Arab Company for Drug Industries and Medical Appliances (#00926)
♦ ACDI/VOCA (internationally oriented national body)
♦ ACEAA – Asociación Boliviana para la Investigación y Conservación de Ecosistemas Andino-Amazónicos (internationally oriented national body)
♦ **ACEA** Arab Campaign for Education for All (#00911)
♦ ACEA – Association canadienne des études africaines (internationally oriented national body)
♦ **ACEAB** Association of Commonwealth Examination and Accreditation Bodies (#02438)
♦ **ACEAC** Association des conférences épiscopales de l'Afrique centrale (#02448)
♦ ACE / see ACE Producers (#00067)
♦ **ACEA** European Automobile Manufacturers' Association (#06300)

♦ Ace Africa 00065

Treas c/o Lockton Companies LLP, The St Botolph Bldg, 138 Houndsditch, London, EC3A 7AG, UK. T. +442079332994. E-mail: info@ace-africa.org.
Kenya PO Box 1185, Bungoma, 50200, Kenya. T. +254722831834. E-mail: resources@ace-africa.org.
Tanzania PO Box 16416, Arusha, Tanzania UR. T. +255732971760. E-mail: infotz@ace-africa.org.
URL: http://www.ace-africa.org/

History Founded Sep 2003, Kenya, by Joanna Waddington (UK) and Augustine Wasonga and Anthony Okoti (Kenyans). ACE stands for *Action in the Community Environment.* Registered in Kenya (OP218/051/2003/0477/3060), Tanzania (63324), UK (1111283) and USA. **Aims** Empower *children* and their communities to improve and sustain their own health, wellbeing and development. **NGO Relations** Member of: *UK Consortium on AIDS and International Development.* [2014.10.29/XJ6052/**F**]

♦ **ACE** Alliance for Beverage Cartons and the Environment (#00658)
♦ ACE / see Allied Command Operations (#00731)
♦ ACE – Amitiés chrétiennes européennes (inactive)
♦ **ACE** Architects Council of Europe (#01086)
♦ **ACE** ASEAN Centre for Energy (#01150)
♦ **ACE** ASEAN Confederation of Employers (#01158)
♦ ACE – Asociación de Ciudadanos de Europa (inactive)
♦ **ACE** Association caraïbe pour l'environnement (#03481)
♦ ACE – Association of Caribbean Economists (no recent information)
♦ ACE – Association of Catering Excellence (unconfirmed)
♦ ACE / see Association of Chemistry and the Environment (#02426)
♦ **ACE** Association of Chemistry and the Environment (#02426)
♦ **ACE** Association des Cinémathèques Européennes (#02511)
♦ **ACE** Association for Competition Economics (#02443)
♦ ACE – Association des conseillers européens (inactive)
♦ ACE – Association for the Cooperation of Employers (no recent information)
♦ ACE / see Association for Cultural Economics International (#02463)
♦ **ACE** Association des cytogénéticiens européens (#06880)
♦ **ACECA** Association des coopératives d'épargne et de crédit d'Afrique (#00261)
♦ **ACECC** Asian Civil Engineering Coordinating Council (#01378)
♦ ACECCT/CAMEROUN / see Association of the Episcopal Conferences of the Central African Region (#02491)
♦ ACECCTC / see Association of the Episcopal Conferences of the Central African Region (#02491)
♦ ACECOMS – Asian Centre for Engineering Computations and Software (internationally oriented national body)
♦ ACED – Asian Council on Ergonomics and Design (unconfirmed)
♦ ACEDI – Association canadienne d'études du développement international (internationally oriented national body)
♦ **ACEE** Auditeurs consultants experts européens (#03016)
♦ ACEEDAC – Association pour la coopération des Eglises, l'environnement et le développement de l'Afrique centrale (no recent information)
♦ ACEEEO / see Association of European Election Officials (#02508)
♦ **ACEEEO** Association of European Election Officials (#02508)

♦ ACE Electoral Knowledge Network 00066

Coordination Unit address not obtained. E-mail: ace.facilitator@gmail.com.
URL: http://aceproject.org/

History 1998, as *Administration and Cost of Elections (ACE) Project* by *International Institute for Democracy and Electoral Assistance (International IDEA, #13872), International Foundation for Electoral Systems (IFES, #13669)* and UN Department of Economic and Social Affairs (UNDESA). Current title adopted 2006. **Aims** Promote credible and transparent electoral processes with emphasis on sustainability, professionalism and trust in the electoral process. **Structure** Steering Board; Coordination Unit. **Languages** Arabic, English, French, Spanish.
Members Partners (9):
Elections Canada; *Electoral Institute for Sustainable Democracy in Africa (EISA, #05415); International Foundation for Electoral Systems (IFES, #13669); International Institute for Democracy and Electoral Assistance (International IDEA, #13872)*; National Electoral Institute of Mexico; *The Carter Center, UNDP (#20292)*; UN Electoral Assistance Division. [2018.09.05/XJ7521/y/**E**]

♦ ACEER – Amazon Center for Environmental Education and Research (internationally oriented national body)
♦ **ACEG** African Centre for Economic Growth (#00240)
♦ ACEI / see Childhood Education International
♦ **ACEI** Alliance for a Competitive European Industry (#00670)
♦ **ACEI** Association for Cultural Economics International (#02463)
♦ ACELA – Asociación de Combustibles Eficientes de Latinoamérica (unconfirmed)
♦ ACELAC – Association canadienne des études latinoaméricaines et caraïbes (internationally oriented national body)
♦ ACELC – Asociación Canadiense de Estudios Latinoamericanos y del Caribe (internationally oriented national body)
♦ ACELE – Association centre-européenne de libre-échange (no recent information)
♦ **ACEM** Association des constructeurs européens de motocycles (#02450)
♦ ACEM – Australasian College for Emergency Medicine (internationally oriented national body)
♦ **ACEN** Asian-Pacific Chemical Education Network (#01604)
♦ **ACENDIO** Association for Common European Nursing Diagnoses, Interventions and Outcomes (#02437)
♦ **ACEO** Association of Caribbean Electoral Organizations (#02405)
♦ ACEPESA – Asociación Centroamericana para la Economia, la Salud y el Ambiente (internationally oriented national body)

♦ ACE Producers 00067

Contact WG Plein 508, 1054 SJ Amsterdam, Netherlands. T. +31202410777. E-mail: info@ace-producers.com.
URL: http://www.ace-producers.com/

History Founded 1993, Paris (France). Previous title: *Ateliers du cinéma européen (ACE).* Registered in accordance with French law. **Aims** As a network of experienced producers from Europe and beyond, encourage and enable international co-productions. **Structure** Board. **Languages** English. **Staff** 4.00 FTE, paid. **Finance** Supported by: *MEDIA Programme (MEDIA, inactive)* of European Union; Netherlands Film Fund; national institutions; private sponsors. **Activities** Training/education; events/meetings; networking/liaising. Producers with proven experience in their own countries may join the network after completing the ACE programme of advanced training. Senior members also participate as consultants.
Members Full (about 200) in 42 countries:
Argentina, Australia, Austria, Belgium, Bosnia-Herzegovina, Bulgaria, Canada, Chile, China, Colombia, Croatia, Czechia, Denmark, Estonia, Finland, France, Germany, Greece, Hungary, Iceland, Ireland, Israel, Italy, Japan, Lebanon, Luxembourg, Morocco, Netherlands, New Zealand, Norway, Palestine, Poland, Romania, Russia, Serbia, Slovakia, Slovenia, Spain, Sweden, Switzerland, Türkiye, UK. [2017.10.26/XF3581/v/**F**]

♦ ACE Project / see ACE Electoral Knowledge Network (#00066)
♦ **ACERAC** Association des conférences épiscopales de la région de l'Afrique centrale (#02491)
♦ **ACER** Agency for the Cooperation of Energy Regulators (#00552)
♦ ACE Rapid Reaction Corps / see Allied Rapid Reaction Corps (#00736)
♦ ACERI – African Child Education Right Initiative (internationally oriented national body)
♦ ACER-Russie (internationally oriented national body)
♦ **ACERWC** African Committee of Experts on the Rights and Welfare of the Child (#00257)
♦ **A.C.E.S.** African Confederation of Equestrian Sport (#00262)
♦ ACES – Annual Conference of Experimental Sociology (meeting series)
♦ **ACES** Applied Computational Electromagnetics Society (#00879)
♦ **ACES** Asian Chemical Editorial Society (#01375)
♦ ACES – Association for Comparative Economic Studies (internationally oriented national body)
♦ ACES – European Association of Air Conditioning Stockholders (inactive)
♦ **ACES Europe** European Capitals and Cities of Sport Federation (#06440)
♦ **ACESS** Asian Council of Exercise and Sports Science (#01409)
♦ ACET / see ACET International
♦ **ACETA** Associaçio Cristo para Educaçio Teológica em Africa (#02431)
♦ **ACET** African Center for Economic Transformation (#00235)
♦ ACET International (internationally oriented national body)
♦ ACEV – Anne Cocuk Egitim Vakfi (internationally oriented national body)
♦ ACEX – International Conference on Advanced Computational Engineering and Experimenting (meeting series)
♦ ACF / see Center for Humanitarian Outreach and Intercultural Exchange
♦ ACfA – African Crowdfunding Association (unconfirmed)
♦ **ACFA** Asian Clean Fuels Association (#01379)
♦ **ACFA** Asian Committee for Future Accelerators (#01390)
♦ **ACF** African Competition Forum (#00260)
♦ ACF – African Conservation Foundation (internationally oriented national body)
♦ **ACF** Arab Chess Federation (#00919)
♦ Acfas (internationally oriented national body)
♦ **ACF** ASEAN Coffee Federation (#01156)
♦ ACF – ASEAN Colorectal Forum (meeting series)
♦ **ACF** ASEAN Constructors Federation (#01160)
♦ ACF / see ASEAN Federation of Cardiology (#01172)
♦ Acfas – Faire avances les savoirs / see Acfas
♦ **ACF** Asian Chess Federation (#01376)
♦ ACF – Asian Competition Forum (unconfirmed)
♦ **ACF** Asian Concrete Federation (#01395)
♦ **ACF** Asian Couture Federation (#01410)
♦ ACF – Association de la cause freudienne (internationally oriented national body)
♦ **ACFD** African Centre for Fertilizer Development (#00241)
♦ **ACFEA** Asian Consumer and Family Economics Association (#01404)
♦ **ACFE** Association of Certified Fraud Examiners (#02421)
♦ **ACFF** Alliance for a Cavity-Free Future (#00661)
♦ ACFH – African Climate Finance Hub (internationally oriented national body)
♦ ACFID – Australian Council for International Development (internationally oriented national body)
♦ ACFIF – Asian Chemical Fiber Industries Federation (no recent information)
♦ ACF International / see Action Against Hunger (#00086)
♦ **ACF International** Association of Career Firms International (#02400)
♦ ACFM – Amitiés catholiques françaises dans le mondes (internationally oriented national body)
♦ ACFOA / see Australian Council for International Development
♦ **AC Forum** Associations and Conference Forum (#02909)
♦ ACFSE – Alliance for Consumer Fire Safety in Europe (internationally oriented national body)
♦ ACFTI – Association of Cyber Forensics and Threat Investigators (unconfirmed)
♦ **ACGA** Asian Corporate Governance Association (#01406)
♦ **ACG** Asia Pacific Central Securities Depository Group (#01866)
♦ ACGC – Alberta Council for Global Cooperation (internationally oriented national body)
♦ **ACGF** Arctic Coast Guard Forum (#01096)
♦ **ACGG** Asian Community of Glycoscience and Glycotechnology (#01392)
♦ ACGRC – Analytical Centre on Globalization and Regional Cooperation (internationally oriented national body)
♦ **ACGSSR** Arab Council for Graduate Studies and Scientific Research (#00930)
♦ ACHA / see African Christian Health Associations Platform (#00247)
♦ **ACHAC** Association des centres pour handicapés de l'Afrique centrale (#02419)
♦ **ACHAN** Asian Community Health Action Network (#01393)
♦ **ACHAP** African Christian Health Associations Platform (#00247)
♦ **ACH** Association of Caribbean Historians (#02407)
♦ **ACH** Association for Computers and the Humanities (#02446)
♦ **ACHEA** Association of Caribbean Higher Education Administrators (#02406)
♦ ACHE Internacional (unconfirmed)
♦ ACHE International (unconfirmed)
♦ ACHEMA – International Meeting on Chemical Engineering and Biotechnology (meeting series)
♦ ACHEST – African Centre for Global Health and Social Transformation (internationally oriented national body)
♦ ACHHRP – African Commission of Health and Human Rights Promoters (internationally oriented national body)

♦ ACHIEVE 00068

Address not obtained.
URL: https://achievehepatitiselimination.eu/

History 7 Jun 2017. Former names and other names: *Associations Collaborating on Hepatitis to Immunise and Eliminate the Viruses in Europe (ACHIEVE)* – full title. **Aims** Elimiate viral hepatitis in Europe by 2030.
Members Organizations (7):
Barcelona Institute for Global Health (ISGlobal); Correlation – European Harm Reduction Network (C-EHRN, #04848); European AIDS Treatment Group (EATG, #05850); European Liver Patients 'Association (ELPA, #07706); Hepatitis B and C Public Policy Association (#10910); Viral Hepatitis Prevention Board (VHPB, #20782); World Hepatitis Alliance (WHA, #21564). [2022/AA2337/y/**D**]

♦ ACHOC – Association Caritative et Humanitaire des Ordres de Chevalerie (unconfirmed)
♦ **ACHPR** African Commission on Human and Peoples' Rights (#00255)
♦ **ACHR** Arab Commission for Human Rights (#00924)
♦ ACHR – Asian Centre for Human Rights (internationally oriented national body)
♦ **ACHR** Asian Coalition for Housing Rights (#01381)
♦ ACHRO – Asian Coalition of Human Rights Organizations (inactive)
♦ ACHS – African Church of the Holy Spirit (internationally oriented national body)
♦ **ACHS** Association of Critical Heritage Studies (#02461)
♦ AChSHM – Australasian Chapter of Sexual Health Medicine (internationally oriented national body)
♦ ACHSTS – African Council for the Training and Promotion of Health Sciences Teachers and Specialists (inactive)
♦ ACIA – African Community Involvement Association (inactive)

ACI Africa
00069

alphabetic sequence excludes
For the complete listing, see Yearbook Online at

♦ **ACI Africa** **00069**

SG Académie International Mohammed VI, de l'Aviation Civile, Nouasseur, Casablanca, Morocco. T. +212660156916. Fax +212520300880. E-mail: aci-africa@aci-africa.aero.
URL: https://www.aci-africa.aero/

History Former names and other names: *ACI Africa – the Voice of African airports* – alias. **Aims** Represent and advance the collective interests of African airports, while promoting professional excellence in airport operations and management, to achieve a safe, secure and sustainable development of the air transport industry in Africa. **Structure** Board of Directors; Secretariat. **Activities** Awards/prizes/competitions; certification/accreditation; events/meetings; guidance/assistance/consulting; training/education. **Events** *Regional Conference* Kigali (Rwanda) 2023, *Regional Conference* Marrakech (Morocco) 2022, *Regional Conference* Mombasa (Kenya) 2022. **Members** Regular (over 70) in 53 African countries. Membership countries not specified. [2023/AA3181/**E**]

♦ ACI – African Concern International (internationally oriented national body)
♦ ACI – African Cultural Institute (inactive)
♦ ACI Africa – the Voice of African airports / see ACI Africa (#00069)
♦ **ACI** Agence de contrôles internationale (#15678)
♦ **ACI** Airports Council International (#00611)
♦ ACI / see Airports Council International – European Region (#00612)
♦ ACI – Akrofi-Christaller Institute of Theology, Mission and Culture (internationally oriented national body)
♦ **ACI** Alianza Cooperativa Internacional (#12944)
♦ **ACI** Alliance coopérative internationale (#12944)
♦ ACI – American Concrete Institute (internationally oriented national body)
♦ ACIAR – Australian Centre for International Agricultural Research (internationally oriented national body)
♦ **ACI** Asociación Cartografica Internacional (#12446)
♦ **ACI** Association Cartographique Internationale (#12446)
♦ ACICA – Australian Centre for International Commercial Arbitration (internationally oriented national body)
♦ **ACICAFOC** Asociación Coordinadora Indigena y Campesina de Agroforesteria Comunitaria (#02120)
♦ **ACIC** ASEAN Chemical Industries Council (#01152)
♦ ACIC – Atlantic Council for International Cooperation (internationally oriented national body)
♦ **ACICC** Arab Coalition for the International Criminal Court (#00922)
♦ **ACICI** Agence de coopération et d'information pour le commerce international (#00553)

♦ **Acid Deposition Monitoring Network in East Asia (EANET)** **00070**

Secretariat c/o UNEP RRC AP, Outreach Building, AIT PO Box 4, Klongluang, Pathum Thani, 12120, Thailand. T. +6625162124. Fax +6625162125.
ADORC / Network Centre 1182 Sowa, Nishi-ku, Niigata, 950-2144 Japan. T. +81252630550. Fax +81252630566.
URL: http://www.eanet.cc/

History Jan 2001, following expert meetings held in Japan (1993-1997) and a preparatory phase (1998-2000). **Aims** Create a common understanding of the state of the acid deposition problems in East Asia; provide useful inputs for decision making at local, national and regional levels aimed at preventing or reducing adverse impacts on the environment caused by acid deposition; contribute to cooperation on the issues related to acid deposition among the participating countries. **Activities** *Acid Deposition and Oxidant Research Center (ADORC)* in Niigata (Japan). Workshops; training programmes; research fellowships; technical missions; Intergovernmental Meeting. **Events** *Intergovernmental Meeting* Manila (Philippines) 2022, *Seminar on Learning Opportunity of IIASA Study on Urban and Rural Relations in Atmospheric Environment* Pathum Thani (Thailand) 2022, *Intergovernmental Meeting* Bangkok (Thailand) 2016, *Session* Bangkok (Thailand) 2016, *Seminar on the Periodic Report on State of Acid Deposition in East Asia* Busan (Korea Rep) 2016. **Publications** *Periodic Report on the State of Acid Deposition in East Asia*. Newsletter.
Members in 13 countries:
Cambodia, China, Indonesia, Japan, Korea Rep, Laos, Malaysia, Mongolia, Myanmar, Philippines, Russia, Thailand, Vietnam. [2014/XM8151/**D***]

♦ ACIEMP – Association catholique internationale d'études médico-psychologiques (inactive)
♦ **ACI EUROPE** Airports Council International – European Region (#00612)
♦ ACIEW – Arab Centre for Information and Early Warning (no recent information)
♦ ACIF – Asociación Católica Interamericana de Filosofia (inactive)
♦ ACIFI – Association des courtiers et intervenants frontaliers internationaux (internationally oriented national body)
♦ ACI – Financial Markets Association / see Financial Markets Association (#09767)
♦ ACI / see Financial Markets Association (#09767)
♦ ACI FMA / see Financial Markets Association (#09767)
♦ **ACIHL** Arab Centre for International Humanitarian Law and Human Right Education (#00915)
♦ ACI Human Rights – Africa Culture Internationale Human Rights (internationally oriented national body)
♦ **ACIIA** Asian Confederation of Institutes of Internal Auditors (#01397)
♦ **ACIIA** Association of Certified International Investment Analysts (#02422)
♦ ACI International / see Financial Markets Association (#09767)
♦ ACI International / see American Concrete Institute
♦ ACIJLP – Arab Centre for the Independence of the Judiciary and the Legal Profession (internationally oriented national body)
♦ ACIL – Amsterdam Center for International Law (internationally oriented national body)
♦ ACILS / see Solidarity Center
♦ ACIMA – Alexandria Centre for International Maritime Arbitration (internationally oriented national body)
♦ ACIM – Agence pour la coopération internationale et le développement local en Méditerranée (inactive)
♦ ACIMO – Association de coureurs internationaux en multicoques océaniques (inactive)
♦ ACIN – African Child in Need (internationally oriented national body)
♦ ACIOPJF / see Association Catholique Internationale de Services pour la Jeunesse Féminine (#02417)
♦ **ACIPAC** Asian Centre of International Parasite Control (#01373)
♦ ACIP – American College of International Physicians (internationally oriented national body)
♦ **ACISCA** Association of Christian Institutes for Social Concern in Asia (#02428)
♦ **ACISE** Association catholique internationale des sciences de l'éducation (#12448)
♦ ACISE / see International Catholic Association of Institutes of Educational Sciences (#12448)
♦ ACISF / see International Critical Incident Stress Foundation
♦ **ACIS** International Association for Computer and Information Science (#11801)
♦ **ACISJF/In Via** Association Catholique Internationale de Services pour la Jeunesse Féminine (#02417)
♦ ACISP – Australasian Conference on Information Security and Privacy (meeting series)
♦ AcIT – Académie internationale du tourisme (inactive)
♦ ACJA – African Criminology and Justice Association (internationally oriented national body)
♦ **ACJ** Alianza Mundial de Asociaciones Cristianas de Jóvenes (#21090)
♦ ACJ – Ancillae Sacri Cordis Jesu (religious order)
♦ **ACJ** Andean Commission of Jurists (#00816)
♦ ACJ – Arab Court of Justice (unconfirmed)
♦ **ACJP** Ambedkar Center for Justice and Peace (#00769)
♦ ACJPS – African Centre for Justice and Peace Studies (internationally oriented national body)
♦ ACJS – Academy of Criminal Justice Sciences (internationally oriented national body)
♦ ACK – American Committee for KEEP (internationally oriented national body)
♦ **ACKF** African Continental Korfball Federation (#00268)
♦ ACLAE – Arab Centre for Labour Administration and Employment (internationally oriented national body)
♦ **ACLALS** Association for Commonwealth Literature and Language Studies (#02439)
♦ **ACLARS** African Consortium for Law and Religion Studies (#00266)
♦ **ACL** Asian Composers League (#01394)
♦ ACL – Association for Computational Learning (unconfirmed)
♦ **ACL** Association for Computational Linguistics (#02445)
♦ **ACLCA** Association of Christian Lay Centres in Africa (#02429)
♦ ACLD – Agency for Christian Literature Development (inactive)
♦ ACLED – Armed Conflict Location & Event Data Project (internationally oriented national body)
♦ **ACLEU** Association of Charity Lotteries in Europe (#02425)
♦ ACLing – ACLing Conference on Arabic Computational Linguistics (meeting series)
♦ ACLing Conference on Arabic Computational Linguistics (meeting series)
♦ ACLN – Asia Cruise Leaders Network (unconfirmed)

♦ **ACL Study Group** **00071**

Contact Ms Cheri Baumann, 21474 Seabury Ave, Fairview Park OH 44126-2759, USA.
URL: http://aclstudygroup.net/

History By a group of orthopaedic surgeons. **Aims** Exchange information on anterior cruciate ligament (ACL) injuries. **Events** *Biennial Meeting* Cape Town (South Africa) 2014, *Biennial Meeting* Jackson Hole, WY (USA) 2012, *Biennial Meeting* Phuket (Thailand) 2010, *Biennial Meeting* Engelberg (Switzerland) 2008, *Biennial Meeting* Sardinia (Italy) 2004. [2018.06.30/XM3296/**E**]

♦ **ACMA** Arab Centre for Mediation and Arbitration (#00917)
♦ ACMA – Association des chercheurs du maïs en Afrique (no recent information)
♦ **ACMAD** African Centre of Meteorological Applications for Development (#00242)
♦ **ACM** Asian Consortium for the Conservation and Sustainable Use of Microbial Resources (#01403)
♦ **ACM** Association of Caribbean Media Workers (#02408)
♦ **ACM** Association for Computing Machinery (#02447)
♦ ACMC – Arts Cultural Management Conference (meeting series)
♦ ACMCU – Prince Alwaleed Bin Talal Center for Muslim-Christian Understanding (internationally oriented national body)
♦ **ACME** Association of Cotton Merchants in Europe (#02457)
♦ ACMI – Association of Christians Ministering Among Internationals (internationally oriented national body)
♦ ACML – Arab Centre for Medical Literature (no recent information)
♦ ACML – Asian Conference on Machine Learning (meeting series)
♦ ACMP / see ACMP – The Chamber Music Network (#00072)
♦ **ACMP** ACMP – The Chamber Music Network (#00072)
♦ **ACMP** Association of Change Management Professionals (#02424)

♦ **ACMP – The Chamber Music Network (ACMP)** **00072**

Association des amateurs de musique de chambre

Dir 1133 Broadway, Room 810, New York NY 10010-8046, USA. T. +12126457424. Fax +12127412678. E-mail: admin@acmp.net.
URL: http://www.acmp.net/

History Founded 1947, as *Amateur Chamber Music Players (ACMP)*. Incorporated, 1969, in New York State (USA). **Aims** Stimulate and expand the playing of chamber music for pleasure among musicians of all backgrounds, ages and skill levels. **Structure** Board of Directors. **Languages** English. **Staff** 1.50 FTE, paid. **Finance** Members' dues. Other sources: contributions; endowment. **Activities** Networking/liaising; knowledge management/information dissemination; financial and/or material support; publishing activities; training/education. **Publications** *ACMP Newsletter* (3 a year). Directory; Workshop Guide.
Members Individuals (mostly in USA) in 32 countries:
Argentina, Australia, Austria, Belgium, Brazil, Canada, China, Czechia, Denmark, France, Germany, Greece, Hungary, India, Ireland, Israel, Italy, Japan, Mexico, Netherlands, New Zealand, Norway, Panama, Portugal, Romania, Russia, Singapore, Spain, Sweden, Switzerland, UK, USA. [2019.02.13/XF3045/v/**F**]

♦ ACMRO – Australian Catholic Migrant and Refugee Office (internationally oriented national body)
♦ ACMS – African Centre for Migration and Society (internationally oriented national body)
♦ ACNA – African Child Neurology Association (unconfirmed)
♦ ACNA – Agencia Centroamericana de Navegación Aérea (see: #04837)
♦ ACNA – Association professionelle du caoutchouc naturel en Afrique (no recent information)
♦ ACN – Active Citizenship Network (internationally oriented national body)
♦ ACN / see Andean Community (#00817)
♦ **ACN** Anti-Corruption Network for Eastern Europe and Central Asia (#00853)
♦ **ACN** Asian Communication Network (#01391)
♦ **ACNOA** Association des comités nationaux olympiques d'Afrique (#02820)
♦ **ACNO** Association des comités nationaux olympiques (#02819)
♦ ACNOE / see European Olympic Committees (#08083)
♦ ACNS / see US Committee for Refugees and Immigrants
♦ **ACNS** Asian Congress of Neurological Surgeons (#01401)
♦ ACNS – Australasian Cognitive Neuroscience Society (internationally oriented national body)
♦ **ACNUDH** Oficina del Alto Comisionado para los Derechos Humanos (#17697)
♦ **ACNUR** Oficina del Alto Comisionado de las Naciones Unidas para los Refugiados (#20327)
♦ ACOA – African Council of Organic Associations (no recent information)
♦ ACO – Action Chrétienne en Orient (unconfirmed)
♦ ACO – African Curriculum Organization (no recent information)
♦ **ACO** Allied Command Operations (#00731)
♦ ACO / see Arab Towns Organization (#01059)
♦ ACODA – Association internationale pour la coopération et le développement en Afrique australe (no recent information)
♦ ACODE – Australasian Council on Open, Distance and E-Learning (internationally oriented national body)
♦ **ACODEPA** Asociación de Confederaciones Deportivas Panamericanas (#02119)
♦ ACODESU – Asociación de Confederaciones Deportivas Sudamericanas (no recent information)
♦ **ACODEV** Fédération francophone et germanophone des associations de coopération au développement (#09587)
♦ **ACOE** Accreditation Council for Oncology in Europe (#00063)
♦ **ACOLID** Arab Company for Livestock Development (#00927)
♦ ACOMPT – Asian Confederation of Orthopaedic Manipulative Physical Therapy (unconfirmed)
♦ **ACOPS** Advisory Committee on Protection of the Sea (#00139)
♦ ACOR – American Center of Oriental Research, Amman (internationally oriented national body)
♦ ACORBAT – Asociación para la Cooperación en la Investigación del Banano en el Caribe y la América Tropical (no recent information)

♦ **ACORD – Agency for Cooperation and Research in Development** ... **00073**

Agence de coopération et de recherche pour le développement

Exec Dir PO Box 61216 – 00200, Nairobi, Kenya. T. +254202721172 – +254202721185 – +254202721186. Fax +254202721166. E-mail: kristin.seljeflot@acordinternational.org – info@acordinternational.org.
Kenya street address ACK Garden Annex, 4th Floor, 1st Ngong Avenue, Nairobi, Kenya.
UK street address Grayston Ctr, 28 Charles Square, London, N1 6HT, UK. T. +442073244698 – +442073244708.
URL: http://www.acordinternational.org/

History Founded 1974, as *Euro Action – ACORD (EAA)*, by merger of *International Agency for Cooperation in Development (IACOD, inactive)*, set up 1972, and *Euro-Action Sahel*, also referred to in French as *Association internationale pour la coopération et le développement au Sahel (AICDS)*. Current title adopted 1987. Organizational change process transformed ACORD from a consortium of Northern NGOs to a Pan-African organization, when Head office was relocated from London (UK) to Nairobi (Kenya), 2003. Headquarters agreement with government of Kenya. UK registered Charity: 283302. **Aims** Work towards a society in which all citizens are equally able to achieve their rights and fulfil their responsibilities; work in

common cause with poor people and those who have been denied their rights to obtain social justice and development and be part of locally rooted citizen movements. **Structure** Assembly (annual); Board; Country Offices (15); Secretariat. **Languages** English, French, Portuguese. **Staff** 335.00 FTE, paid. **Finance** Sources: private; multilateral institutions; bilateral institutions; members. Annual budget: pounds7,833,000. **Activities** Research/documentation; capacity building; advocacy/lobbying/activism; events/meetings. Active in Africa, at local, national and regional levels. **Events** *Forum Asia* Singapore (Singapore) 2015, *African Women's Land Rights Conference* Nairobi (Kenya) 2011, *Pan African Conference* Kampala (Uganda) 2009, *Pan African Conference* Nairobi (Kenya) 2008. **Publications** *ACORD Newsletter* (irregular). *ACORD's Transformation: Overcoming Uncertainty* (2012) by Prof Alan Fowler. Research report series; development practice series. Books; reports; policy recommendations; handbooks; case studies; occasional papers; toolkits; films.
Members Presence across Africa, including in 12 African countries:
Burundi, Central African Rep, Chad, Ethiopia, Guinea, Kenya, Mali, Mauritania, Rwanda, South Sudan, Tanzania UR, Uganda.
International and internationally-oriented organizations (4):
Comité Catholique contre la Faim et pour le Développement-Terre Solidaire (CCFD-Terre Solidaire); Inter Pares; Mani Tese (MT); Rikolto.
Individuals, mainly in Africa. Membership countries not specified.
Consultative Status Consultative status granted from: *ECOSOC (#05331)* (Special); *UNEP (#20299)*. **IGO Relations** Cooperates with: *FAO (#09260)*; *UNDP (#20292)*; *UNHCR (#20327)*; *UNICEF (#20332)*; *United Nations Population Fund (UNFPA, #20612)*; *United Nations Democracy Fund (UNDEF, #20551)*; *UN Women (#20724)*; *World Food Programme (WFP, #21510)*. Associated with Department of Global Communications of the United Nations. **NGO Relations** Member of: *UK Consortium on AIDS and International Development*.
[2017.12.21/XD0119/y/**D**]

- ♦ **ACORD** Asian Centre for Organisation Research and Development (#01374)
- ♦ **ACORD** Association for Cooperative Operations Research and Development (#02456)
- ♦ Acôrdo de cooperação para a protecção das costas e aguas de Atlântico Nordeste contra a poluição (1990 treaty)
- ♦ Acôrdo interamericano de radiocomunicações, 1937 (1937 treaty)
- ♦ Acôrdo interamericano de radiocomunicações, 1940 (1940 treaty)
- ♦ Acôrdo Latino-americano sobre controle de navios pelo estado reitor (1992 treaty)
- ♦ Acôrdo de Lisboa – Acôrdo de cooperação para a protecção das costas e aguas de Atlântico Nordeste contra a poluição (1990 treaty)
- ♦ Acôrdo Sul-Americano regional de radiocomunicações, 1935 (1935 treaty)
- ♦ Acôrdo Sul-Americano regional de radiocomunicações, 1937 (1937 treaty)
- ♦ Acôrdo Sul-Americano regional de radiocomunicações, 1940 (1940 treaty)
- ♦ ACORN / see Communication Policy Research Latin America (#04382)
- ♦ ACOS – Asian Clinical Oncology Society (inactive)
- ♦ **ACOSHED** African Council for Sustainable Health Development (#00277)
- ♦ ACOTA / see African Contingency Operations Training and Assistance
- ♦ ACOTA – African Contingency Operations Training and Assistance (internationally oriented national body)
- ♦ ACOTA Program / see African Contingency Operations Training and Assistance
- ♦ Acoustical Society of Scandinavia / see Nordic Acoustic Association (#17165)
- ♦ ACOVENE – Accreditation Committee for Veterinary Nurse Education (unconfirmed)
- ♦ **ACPA** Asia Canine Protection Alliance (#01257)
- ♦ ACP / see Africa Platform (#00513)
- ♦ **ACP** Africa Platform (#00513)
- ♦ ACP – Alliance Genève ACP pour les Droits de l'Homme (internationally oriented national body)
- ♦ **ACP** Asian Co-Benefits Partnership (#01382)
- ♦ ACP – Association des chasseurs professionnels d'Afrique francophone (inactive)
- ♦ ACP / see Association of Clinical Research Professionals (#02434)
- ♦ **ACP** Association for Constraint Programming (#02449)
- ♦ ACP – Australasian College of Phlebology (internationally oriented national body)

♦ ACP Business Forum 00074

Address not obtained.
History 1998, by business representatives from Africa, the Caribbean and the Pacific (ACP). **Aims** Promote cooperation among ACP private sectors; articulate their interests at the global ACP-EU level. **Structure** Board, comprising 6 members.
[2014/XF4880/**F**]

- ♦ **ACPC** African Climate Policy Centre (#00251)
- ♦ ACPC – Asian Council for People's Culture (no recent information)
- ♦ **ACP Chambers** Association of ACP National Chambers of Commerce, Industry and Other Economic Operators (#02345)

♦ ACP Civil Society Forum (ACP CSF) 00075

Legal Advisor Kleine Wouwer 50/10, 1860 Meise, Belgium. T. +3222700750.
Chairman c/o Barbados Assn of NGOs (BANGO), No 10 Garrison, St Michael, ST MICHAEL, Barbados. T. +12468227707.
Facebook: https://www.facebook.com/acpcsf.org/
History Founded Oct 1997, Entebbe (Uganda). Also referred to as *ACP CSF Network*. Recognized by *European Commission (EC, #06633)* and *Organisation of African, Caribbean and Pacific States (OACPS, #17796)* as the legitimate body for participation of Civil Society in ACP-EU processes. EU Transparency Register: 36703913506-85. Registration: EU Transparency Register, No/ID: 36703913506-85. **Aims** Provide a platform for civil society actors in the African, Caribbean and Pacific countries to formulate common positions on issues of concern relevant to ACP-EU cooperation; articulate the views and concerns of marginalized social groups in ACP countries; facilitate dialogue between ACP civil society organizations and official institutions of the ACP Group and the EU; support and strengthen the participation of ACP civil society organizations in the ACP-EU development cooperation framework; regularly access, update and share information on developments at all levels of ACP-EU cooperation. **Structure** Bureau, comprising 12 Forum members: 2 from each ACP region – West Africa, East Africa, Central Africa, Southern Africa, Caribbean, Pacific. Officers: Chairman; Policy Advisor; Legal Advisor. Chairman's Assistant. **Languages** English, French, Portuguese, Spanish. **Staff** 16.00 FTE, voluntary. **Finance** ACP-EU. **Activities** Events/meetings. **Events** *Forum* Brussels (Belgium) 2009, *Forum* Brussels (Belgium) 2006, *Forum* Brussels (Belgium) 2001.
Members Full in 80 countries and territories:
Angola, Antigua-Barbuda, Bahamas, Barbados, Belize, Benin, Botswana, Burkina Faso, Burundi, Cameroon, Cape Verde, Central African Rep, Chad, Comoros, Congo Brazzaville, Congo DR, Cook Is, Côte d'Ivoire, Cuba, Djibouti, Dominica, Dominican Rep, Equatorial Guinea, Eritrea, Eswatini, Ethiopia, Fiji, Gabon, Gambia, Ghana, Grenada, Guinea, Guinea-Bissau, Guyana, Haiti, Jamaica, Kenya, Kiribati, Lesotho, Liberia, Madagascar, Malawi, Mali, Marshall Is, Mauritania, Mauritius, Micronesia FS, Mozambique, Namibia, Nauru, Niger, Nigeria, Niue, Palau, Papua New Guinea, Rwanda, Samoa, Sao Tomé-Principe, Senegal, Seychelles, Sierra Leone, Solomon Is, Somalia, South Africa, South Sudan, St Kitts-Nevis, St Lucia, St Vincent-Grenadines, Sudan, Suriname, Tanzania UR, Timor-Leste, Togo, Tonga, Trinidad-Tobago, Tuvalu, Uganda, Vanuatu, Zambia, Zimbabwe.
IGO Relations Recognized by: *European Commission (EC, #06633)* – DG Trade Civil Society Dialogue. Observer to EC CAP Advisory Group meetings on International Aspects of Agriculture.
[2019/XJ2722/**F**]

- ♦ ACP Countries / see Organisation of African, Caribbean and Pacific States (#17796)
- ♦ **ACP CSF** ACP Civil Society Forum (#00075)
- ♦ ACP CSF Network / see ACP Civil Society Forum (#00075)
- ♦ ACPD – Amman Center for Peace and Development (internationally oriented national body)
- ♦ ACPD – Asian Center for Population and Community Development (internationally oriented national body)
- ♦ acpDH / see Alliance Genève ACP pour les Droits de l'Homme
- ♦ ACPDT – Africa Community Publishing and Development Trust (internationally oriented national body)
- ♦ ACP-EC Council of Ministers / see ACP-EU Council of Ministers (#00076)
- ♦ ACP-EC Customs Cooperation Committee (inactive)
- ♦ ACP-EC Joint Assembly / see ACP-EU Joint Parliamentary Assembly (#00077)
- ♦ ACP-EC Joint Council / see ACP-EU Joint Parliamentary Assembly (#00077)
- ♦ ACP-EEC Article 193 Committee (inactive)
- ♦ ACP-EEC Convention (1975 treaty)
- ♦ ACPEL / see Advance Care Planning International (#00126)
- ♦ ACPEL Society / see Advance Care Planning International (#00126)
- ♦ ACPES – ASEAN Council of Physical Education and Sport (unconfirmed)
- ♦ ACPET – African Centre for Peace Education and Training (internationally oriented national body)

♦ ACP-EU Council of Ministers 00076

Conseil des Ministres ACP-UE
Dir General Secretariat, Rue de la Loi 175, 1048 Brussels, Belgium. T. +3222817712.
SG ACP Av Georges Henri 451, 1200 Brussels, Belgium. T. +3227430600. Fax +3227355573.
URL: http://www.acp.int/
History 1977, Brussels (Belgium), under *ACP-EEC Convention (Lomé convention, 1975)*; formalized following conclusion of *Second ACP-EEC Convention (Lomé II, 1979)*, Oct 1979; currently under *Fourth ACP-EEC Convention (Lomé IV, 1989)*, signed 15 Dec 1989, entered into force Mar 1990, for a period of 10 years, revised 4 Nov 1995, Mauritius. *ACP-EU Partnership Agreement (Cotonou agreement, 2000)*, signed 23 Jun 2000, Cotonou (Benin), and entered into force, Apr 2003, for a period of 20 years. Revised 25 Jun 2005, Luxembourg; 22 Jun 2010, Ouagadougou. Original title: *ACP-EC Council of Ministers – Conseil des Ministres ACP-CE*. **Aims** Establish broad lines of work to be undertaken under ACP-EU Partnership Agreement. **Structure** Council, meeting annually, brings together ministers from signatory states of the Cotonou Agreement, ie most member states of *Organisation of African, Caribbean and Pacific States (OACPS, #17796)* and all Member States of the *European Union (EU, #08967)*. It comprises members of *Council of the European Union (#04895)* and *European Commission (EC, #06633)*, and a member of government of each ACP state. President (6-month term) is alternately a member of the Council of the European Union and a member of government of an ACP state. It is assisted by *'ACP-EU Committee of Ambassadors'*. Secretaries (2), one appointed by ACP Group and one by the EU, run both the ACP-EU Council and the ACP-EU Committee of Ambassadors, as well as committees and sub-committees. ACP-EU Committee of Ambassadors is supervisory authority of *Centre technique de coopération agricole et rurale (CTA, inactive)*. **Languages** English, French, Portuguese, Spanish. **Activities** Politics/policy/regulatory. **Events** *Annual Session* Lomé (Togo) 2018, *Annual Session* Brussels (Belgium) 2017, *Annual Session* Dakar (Senegal) 2016, *Annual Session* Brussels (Belgium) 2015, *Annual Session* Nairobi (Kenya) 2014.
Members Parties that ratified the ACP-EU Partnership Agreement: governments of the 75 ACP countries and 28 EU member countries, 104 countries in all:
Angola, Antigua-Barbuda, Austria, Bahamas, Barbados, Belgium, Belize, Benin, Botswana, Bulgaria, Burkina Faso, Burundi, Cameroon, Cape Verde, Central African Rep, Chad, Comoros, Congo Brazzaville, Congo DR, Cook Is, Côte d'Ivoire, Croatia, Cyprus, Czechia, Denmark, Djibouti, Dominica, Dominican Rep, Eritrea, Estonia, Eswatini, Ethiopia, Fiji, Finland, France, Gabon, Gambia, Germany, Ghana, Greece, Grenada, Guinea, Guinea-Bissau, Guyana, Haiti, Hungary, Ireland, Italy, Jamaica, Kenya, Kiribati, Latvia, Lesotho, Liberia, Lithuania, Luxembourg, Madagascar, Malawi, Mali, Malta, Marshall Is, Mauritania, Mauritius, Micronesia FS, Mozambique, Namibia, Nauru, Netherlands, Niger, Nigeria, Niue, Palau, Papua New Guinea, Poland, Portugal, Romania, Rwanda, Samoa, Sao Tomé-Principe, Senegal, Seychelles, Sierra Leone, Slovakia, Slovenia, Solomon Is, Somalia, South Africa, Spain, St Kitts-Nevis, St Lucia, St Vincent-Grenadines, Suriname, Sweden, Tanzania UR, Timor-Leste, Togo, Tonga, Trinidad-Tobago, Tuvalu, Uganda, UK, Vanuatu, Zambia, Zimbabwe.
Observers, who signed but have not ratified the Agreement, in 3 countries:
Equatorial Guinea, South Sudan, Sudan.
[2019.06.14/XE4168/**E***]

- ♦ ACP-EU Joint Assembly / see ACP-EU Joint Parliamentary Assembly (#00077)

♦ ACP-EU Joint Parliamentary Assembly 00077

Assemblée parlementaire paritaire ACP-UE
Co-Secretariat ACP Rue de l'Aqueduc 118, 1050 Brussels, Belgium. T. +3227430600 ext 689. Fax +3227355573. E-mail: info@acp.int.
Co-Secretariat EU Rue Wiertz, 1047 Brussels, Belgium. T. +3222840723. Fax +3222842484. E-mail: acp@europarl.europa.eu.
URL: http://www.europarl.europa.eu/intcoop/acp/
History 8 Dec 1984, Lomé (Togo). Established on signature of *Third ACP-EEC Convention (Lomé III, 1984)*, as *ACP-EC Joint Assembly – Assemblée paritaire ACP-CE*, taking over the tasks of *ACP-EEC Consultative Assembly – Assemblée consultative ACP-CE*, set up 31 Oct 1979, on signature of *Second ACP-EEC Convention (Lomé II, 1979)* by representatives of the *European Community (inactive)* and the then 58 African, Caribbean and Pacific States – *Organisation of African, Caribbean and Pacific States (OACPS, #17796)* – and of *ACP-EEC Joint Committee – Comité paritaire ACP-CEE*, which comprised directly elected members of *European Parliament (EP, #08146)*. Current treaty: *Fourth ACP-EEC Convention (Lomé IV, 1989)*, signed 15 Dec 1989, amended 4 Nov 1995. *ACP-EU Partnership Agreement (Cotonou agreement, 2000)*, signed 23 Jun 2000, Cotonou (Benin), and replacing the Lomé conventions. **Aims** Provide a forum for regular and structured dialogue between designated members of the European Parliament and representatives from each ACP state in order to strengthen multilateral cooperation in terms of trade and development policy; provide information and policy input in ACP/EC decision-making. **Structure** Plenary Session (twice a year), alternately in an ACP country and in an EU country; Bureau meets several times a year. Standing Committees (3): Political Affairs; Economic Development, Finance and Trade; Social Affairs and the Environment. **Languages** Bulgarian, Croatian, Czech, Danish, Dutch, English, Estonian, Finnish, French, German, Greek, Hungarian, Italian, Latvian, Lithuanian, Maltese, Polish, Portuguese, Romanian, Slovakian, Slovene, Spanish, Swedish. **Staff** provided by Secretariat of the European Parliament and ACP Secretariat. **Finance** Partially financed from: *European Development Fund (EDF, #06914)*. Funding from: ACP Secretariat Budget and EU Parliament Budget; National Parliaments of ACP Member States who cover travel costs for Members to attend Sessions. **Activities** Events/meetings. The Joint Assembly may adopt resolutions on matters concerning or covered by the Cotonou Convention and may submit conclusions and resolutions to the Council of Ministers, in particular after examining the Council's annual report. It has the power to authorize joint missions of inquiry where the need arises. **Events** *Session* Strasbourg (France) 2022, *Regional Meeting* Maseru (Lesotho) 2020, *Session* Bucharest (Romania) 2019, *Session* Kigali (Rwanda) 2019, *Regional Meeting* Paramaribo (Suriname) 2019.
Members EU countries (27):
Austria, Belgium, Bulgaria, Croatia, Cyprus, Czechia, Denmark, Estonia, Finland, France, Germany, Greece, Hungary, Ireland, Italy, Latvia, Lithuania, Luxembourg, Malta, Netherlands, Poland, Portugal, Romania, Slovakia, Slovenia, Spain, Sweden.
ACP countries (78):
Angola, Antigua-Barbuda, Bahamas, Barbados, Belize, Benin, Botswana, Burkina Faso, Burundi, Cameroon, Cape Verde, Central African Rep, Chad, Comoros, Congo Brazzaville, Congo DR, Cook Is, Côte d'Ivoire, Djibouti, Dominica, Dominican Rep, Equatorial Guinea, Eritrea, Eswatini, Ethiopia, Fiji, Gabon, Gambia, Ghana, Grenada, Guinea, Guinea-Bissau, Guyana, Haiti, Jamaica, Kenya, Kiribati, Lesotho, Liberia, Madagascar, Malawi, Mali, Marshall Is, Mauritania, Mauritius, Micronesia FS, Mozambique, Namibia, Nauru, Niger, Nigeria, Niue, Palau, Papua New Guinea, Rwanda, Samoa, Sao Tomé-Principe, Senegal, Seychelles, Sierra Leone, Solomon Is, Somalia, South Africa, St Kitts-Nevis, St Lucia, St Vincent-Grenadines, Sudan, Suriname, Tanzania UR, Timor-Leste, Togo, Tonga, Trinidad-Tobago, Tuvalu, Uganda, Vanuatu, Zambia, Zimbabwe.
IGO Relations Participates in the activities of: *UNCTAD (#20285)*. Links with parliamentarians of: *Southern African Customs Union (SACU, #19842)*. **NGO Relations** Observer status with (1): *Inter-Parliamentary Union (IPU, #15961)*.
[2022.10.16/XE9068/**F***]

- ♦ ACP-EU Partnership Agreement (2000 treaty)
- ♦ **ACPF** African Child Policy Forum (#00246)
- ♦ **ACPF** Asia Crime Prevention Foundation (#01263)
- ♦ **ACPF** Asociación del Congreso Panamericano de Ferrocarriles (#18124)
- ♦ **ACP-i** Advance Care Planning International (#00126)
- ♦ **ACPM** Asian College of Psychosomatic Medicine (#01386)
- ♦ ACPO – Asian Committee for People's Organization (inactive)
- ♦ ACPP / see Association for Child and Adolescent Mental Health
- ♦ ACPP – Asamblea de Cooperación por la Paz (internationally oriented national body)
- ♦ ACPP – Asian Center for the Progress of Peoples (internationally oriented national body)
- ♦ ACPR – Asian Council of Peace Research (inactive)
- ♦ ACPRC – African Center for Prevention and Resolution of Conflicts (internationally oriented national body)
- ♦ ACPS – Australasian College of Podiatric Surgeons (internationally oriented national body)
- ♦ ACPSEM – Australasian College of Physical Scientists and Engineers in Medicine (internationally oriented national body)
- ♦ ACPSM / see Australasian College of Physical Scientists and Engineers in Medicine

♦ ACPSS – Al Ahram Centre for Political and Strategic Studies (internationally oriented national body)
♦ ACP States / see Organisation of African, Caribbean and Pacific States (#17796)

♦ ACP Sugar Group 00078

Hon Sec ACP Group, Ave Georges Henri 451, 1200 Brussels, Belgium. T. +3227430600. Fax +3227355573.
URL: https://acpsugar.org/

History on signature of the *Sugar Protocol* to *Fourth ACP-EEC Convention (Lomé IV, 1989)*, a trade agreement of indefinite duration between the *European Communities (EC, inactive)* – currently *European Union (EU, #08967)* – and 19 of the *Organisation of African, Caribbean and Pacific States (OACPS, #17796)*. Members are also signatory to the *Agreement on Special Preferential Sugar (SPS)*. ACP sugar has been an integral part of the *Sugar Régime* of the European Communities since 1975. From 23 Jun 2000, the Sugar Protocol is annexed to Annex V of *ACP-EU Partnership Agreement (Cotonou agreement, 2000)*. **Aims** Under the Sugar Protocol, while the *European Community* undertakes for an indefinite period to purchase and import, at guaranteed prices, specific quantities of raw or white cane sugar which originate in ACP states, the signatory ACP states undertake to deliver it. Under the Special Preferential Sugar agreement, if there is a deficit of raw sugar to meet the needs of EU sugar refiners, the European Community undertakes to open a special tariff quota for the import of raw cane sugar for refining originating in ACP states, on the basis of the needs determined by the European Commission. **Activities** Member suppliers to the EU market enjoy many of the same rights and obligations as those in the European beet sugar industry.
Members African, Caribbean and Pacific states signatory to the ACP/EU Sugar Protocol (19, not specified). Sugar industries in 10 countries:
Belize, Congo Brazzaville, Côte d'Ivoire, Eswatini, Guyana, Malawi, Mauritius, Tanzania UR, Zambia, Zimbabwe.
IGO Relations *European Commission (EC, #06633)*; *FAO (#09260)*; *International Sugar Organization (ISO, #15623)*; *World Trade Organization (WTO, #21864)*. **NGO Relations** *Comité européen des fabricants de sucre (CEFS, #04159)*. Sugar refiners in France, Finland, Portugal and UK. [2021/XE4544/**E***]

♦ **ACPT** Asian Confederation of Physical Therapy (#01398)
♦ ACPTC / see International Textile and Apparel Association
♦ Acqua Solidarità / see Programme Solidarité eau (#18529)
♦ ACR / see Caritas Australia
♦ **ACRAA** Association of Credit Rating Agencies in Asia (#02460)
♦ ACRA – Associazione di Cooperazione Rurale in Africa e America Latina (internationally oriented national body)
♦ ACRA – Australasian Container Reconditioners Association (internationally oriented national body)
♦ **ACRAN** African Communication Regulation Authorities Network (#00259)
♦ ACR / see Association of Cities and Regions for Sustainable Resource Management (#02433)
♦ ACR+ / see Association of Cities and Regions for Sustainable Resource Management (#02433)
♦ **ACR+** Association of Cities and Regions for Sustainable Resource Management (#02433)
♦ ACR – Association for Conflict Resolution (internationally oriented national body)
♦ ACRC – African Community Resource Center (internationally oriented national body)
♦ ACRE / see European Conservatives and Reformists Party (#06747)
♦ **ACRE** International Atmospheric Circulation Reconstructions over the Earth Initiative (#12293)
♦ ACRI / see African Contingency Operations Training and Assistance
♦ ACRI – International Conference on Cellular Automata for Research and Industry (meeting series)
♦ ACR / see International Confederation of Container Reconditioners (#12854)

♦ ACRISS EEIG 00079

Secretariat address not obtained. T. +447807386366. E-mail: secretariat@acriss.org – info@acriss.org.
URL: http://www.acriss.org/

History Set up 1989. Reconstituted 1992, as a grouping of the type *European Economic Interest Grouping (EEIG, #06960)* as *Association of Car Rental Industry Systems Standards (ACRISS EEIG)*. Constitution adopted 5 Feb 1992; revised 12 Jul 2012; Nov 2015. Currently known only under acronym. **Aims** Develop, implement and maintain standards for European Car Rental and Vehicle with Driver Service Industries for use in all distribution systems enabling customers to book with confidence. **Structure** Annual General Meeting; Secretariat. **Languages** English. **Staff** 1.00 FTE, paid. **Finance** Members' dues. Subscription fees. **Activities** Events/meetings. **Publications** Reference guides. **Members** Full; Associate. Membership countries not specified. **IGO Relations** UK Government Competitions and Market Authority. **NGO Relations** National associations. [2018.09.06/XJ9824/**D**]

♦ **ACRLI** Arab Center for the Development of the Rule of Law and Integrity (#00912)
♦ **ACRL-RfP** African Council of Religious Leaders – Religions for Peace (#00276)
♦ **ACRN** African Coffee Research Network (#00253)
♦ ACRON / see Alliance for Peacebuilding
♦ Acronym Institute for Disarmament Diplomacy (internationally oriented national body)
♦ ACRoRS / see Geoinformatics Center

♦ ACROSS 00080

Exec Dir PO Box 132, Buluk, off Ministries Rd, Juba, South Sudan. E-mail: acrossinfo@across-ssd.org.
International Liaison Office PO Box 21033, Ngong Road, Nairobi, 00505, Kenya. T. +254722923283.
URL: https://across-ssd.org/

History 1972. Founded by four mission societies: Africa Inland Mission *AIM* (AIM), Sudan United Mission *Pioneers UK*, Sudan Interior Mission *SIM International* (SIM), and Mission Aviation Fellowship *Mission Aviation Fellowship (MAF, #16829)* (MAF). Originally formed to allow these organisations a platform on which they could serve what was then Sudan. Former names and other names: *Africa Committee for Rehabilitation of Southern Sudan (ACROSS)* – full title; *Association of Christian Resource Organizations Serving Sudan (ACROSS)* – former; *Association of Christian Resource Organisation Service Sudan (ACROSS)* – current – now national. Registration: Charity Commission, No/ID: 1069973, England and Wales; Relief and Rehabilitation Commission, No/ID: 552, South Sudan; National Board of Non-Governmental Organisations, Uganda, No/ID: 683, Uganda; Kenya Non-Governmental Organizations Board, No/ID: OP>218/051/9381/152, Start date: 25 Jun 1993, Kenya; Department of Treasury, Internal Revenue Service, Tax Exempt and Government Entities, No/ID: 85-0783389, USA. **Aims** Transform communities in South Sudan and beyond through a holistic Christ-centred approach. **Structure** Board of Directors (meets annually). **Languages** English. **Finance** Programmes financed through international agencies. Annual budget: 7,000,000 USD. **Activities** Awareness raising; capacity building; healthcare; humanitarian/emergency aid; monitoring/evaluation; networking/liaising; projects/programmes; publishing activities; religious activities; training/education. Active in: Kenya, South Sudan, Uganda. **Publications** Annual Report.
Members Agencies and groups in 15 countries and territories:
Australia, Canada, Denmark, Finland, Germany, Hong Kong, Ireland, Kenya, Netherlands, New Zealand, South Sudan, Sweden, Switzerland, UK, USA.
IGO Relations Partner of (1): *UNHCR (#20327)*. **NGO Relations** Member of (3): *Association of Evangelicals in Africa (AEA, #02587)*; *CHS Alliance (#03911)*; *Micah Global (#16741)*. Partner of (5): *ICCO – Interchurch Organization for Development Cooperation*; *PMU Interlife*; *Red een Kind*; *TEAR Australia*; *Tearfund, UK*. [2022.05.18/XE6451/**E**]

♦ ACROSS / see ACROSS (#00080)
♦ ACRP / see Asian Conference of Religions for Peace (#01400)
♦ **ACRP** Asian Conference of Religions for Peace (#01400)
♦ **ACRP** Association of Clinical Research Professionals (#02434)
♦ ACRP – European Association for Construction Repair, reinforcement and protection (unconfirmed)
♦ **ACRPS** Arab Center for Research and Policy Studies (#00913)
♦ ACRS – Asian Cartilage Repair Society (unconfirmed)
♦ ACRS / see World Skate Africa (#21787)
♦ **ACRU** Association of the Carpathian Region Universities (#02414)
♦ Acrylonitrile Producers' Association (see: #04687)

♦ **ACSA** African Correctional Services Association (#00269)
♦ ACSA – Agencia Centroamericana de Seguridad Aeronautica (see: #04837)
♦ **ACSA** Anglican Church of Southern Africa (#00826)
♦ **ACSA** Asian Crop Science Association (#01414)
♦ **ACSAD** Arab Centre for the Studies of Arid Zones and Dry Lands (#00918)
♦ ACS – APRACA Consultancy Services (see: #02019)
♦ **ACS** Arab Computer Society (#00928)
♦ **ACS** Asia Cornea Society (#01262)
♦ ACS / see Asian Criminological Society (#01413)
♦ **ACS** Asian Criminological Society (#01413)
♦ **ACS** Association of Caribbean States (#02411)
♦ ACS – Association of Caribbean Studies (no recent information)
♦ **ACS** Association for Cultural Studies (#02464)
♦ ACS – Associazione Controllo Strutture (no recent information)
♦ ACS – Australasian Cytometry Society (internationally oriented national body)
♦ ACSB / see AACSB International – Association to Advance Collegiate Schools of Business
♦ **ACSC** Asian Carombole Sports Confederation (#01371)
♦ **ACSDA** Americas' Central Securities Depositories Association (#00792)
♦ AC/SDRC Yaoundé / see ECA Sub-Regional Office for Central Africa (#05274)
♦ ACSEA – African Coalition for Sustainable Energy and Access (unconfirmed)
♦ ACSEC – Association des conjoints du service extérieur de la commission européenne (internationally oriented national body)
♦ ACSEL – Asian Conference on Safety and Education in Laboratory (meeting series)
♦ ACSEP – Asia Centre for Social Entrepreneurship and Philanthropy (internationally oriented national body)
♦ ACSFT – Arab Council for Supporting Fair Trial (unconfirmed)
♦ **ACSI** Association of Christian Schools International (#02430)
♦ **ACSIC** Asian Credit Supplementation Institution Confederation (#01411)
♦ ACSIG – Asian Centre for Soil Improvement and Geosynthetics (internationally oriented national body)
♦ **ACSIS** Africa Civil Society for the Information Society (#00163)
♦ ACSM – Association canadienne pour la santé mondiale (internationally oriented national body)
♦ ACSN / see Anti-Corruption Student Network in South East Europe (#00854)
♦ **ACSN SEE** Anti-Corruption Student Network in South East Europe (#00854)
♦ **ACSO** African Civil Service Observatory (#00249)
♦ ACSPFT – Asian Committee for Standardization of Physical Fitness Tests (inactive)
♦ **ACSR** Asian College of Schizophrenia Research (#01387)
♦ **ACSRM** Asociación de Cientistas Sociales de la Religión del MERCOSUR (#02118)
♦ **ACSRT** African Center for the Study and Research on Terrorism (#00236)
♦ ACSS – Africa Center for Strategic Studies (internationally oriented national body)
♦ **ACSS** African Crop Science Society (#00280)
♦ **ACSS** Arab Council for the Social Sciences (#00932)
♦ ACSUR – Asociación para la Cooperación con el Sur – Las Segovias (internationally oriented national body)
♦ **ACSWE** Association of Caribbean Social Work Educators (#02410)
♦ Act4Africa (internationally oriented national body)
♦ **ACTA** Alliance pour le contrôle du tabac en Afrique (#00484)
♦ ACTA – Anti-Conterfeiting Trade Agreement (2011 treaty)
♦ **ACTA** Asia Cruise Terminal Association (#01264)
♦ Act for Africa International (internationally oriented national body)
♦ **ACT** African Conservation Tillage Network (#00265)
♦ ACT – African Conservation Trust (internationally oriented national body)
♦ ACT Alianza (#00081)

♦ ACT Alliance 00081

Alliance ACT – ACT Alianza
Head of Communications PO Box 2100, Route de Ferney 150, 1211 Geneva 2, Switzerland. T. +41227916434. E-mail: actcom@actalliance.org.
URL: http://www.actalliance.org/

History 1 Jan 2010. Founded upon merger of *Action by Churches Together (ACT International, inactive)* and *ACT Development (inactive)*. **Aims** Create positive and sustainable change in the lives of poor and marginalized people regardless of their religion, politics, gender, sexual orientation, race or nationality in keeping with the highest international codes and standards. **Structure** Assembly (every 4 years); Governing Board; Executive Committee; Secretariat, headed by General Secretary and Director/CEO, based in Geneva (Switzerland). Since Jan 2015, includes: *ACT Alliance EU (#00082)*. **Languages** English, French, Spanish. **Staff** 35.00 FTE, paid. **Finance** Sources: members' dues. Budget (2021): Secretariat: US$ 6.8 million; emergency response funding: US$ 11.85 million. **Activities** Advocacy/lobbying/activism; capacity building; humanitarian/emergency aid. **Publications** Annual Report; reports; specialist publications.
Members Organizations (145) in over 125 countries not specified but including the following 26 international organizations listed in this Yearbook:
- *Act for Peace*;
- *All Africa Conference of Churches (AACC, #00640)*;
- *Anglican Overseas Aid*;
- *Brot für die Welt*;
- *Canadian Lutheran World Relief (CLWR)*;
- *Centro Evangélico de Estudios Pastorales en Centro América (CEDEPCA)*;
- *Christian Aid*;
- *Church World Service (CWS)*;
- *Community World Service Asia (#04407)*;
- *Diakonie Katastrophenhilfe*;
- *Evangelical Lutheran Church in America (ELCA)*;
- *Evangelical Lutheran Church of Southern Africa (ELCSA)*;
- *Fellowship of Christian Councils and Churches in the Great Lakes and Horn of Africa (FECCLAHA, #09723)*;
- *Finn Church Aid (FCA)*;
- *Finnish Evangelical Lutheran Mission (FELM)*;
- *ICCO – Interchurch Organization for Development Cooperation* (Cordaid/ICCO);
- *Icelandic Church Aid*;
- *Latin American Council of Churches (LACC, #16309)*;
- *Norwegian Church Aid*;
- *Presbyterian World Service and Development (PWS and D)*;
- *Primate's World Relief and Development Fund (PWRDF)*;
- *Solidarité protestante*;
- *The Lutheran World Federation (LWF, #16532)*;
- *World Association for Christian Communication (WACC, #21126)*;
- *World Renew*;
- *World Student Christian Federation (WSCF, #21833)*.

Consultative Status Consultative status granted from: *ECOSOC (#05331)* (Special); *UNEP (#20299)*. **NGO Relations** Member of (6): *CHS Alliance (#03911)*; *Confédération européenne des ong d'urgence et de développement (CONCORD, #04547)*; *International Council of Voluntary Agencies (ICVA, #13092)*; *International Partnership on Religion and Sustainable Development (PaRD, #14524)*; *Joint Learning Initiative on Faith and Local Communities (JLI, #16139)*; *Steering Committee for Humanitarian Response (SCHR, #19978)*. Related to: *The Lutheran World Federation (LWF, #16532)*; *World Council of Churches (WCC, #21320)*. Represented on the Board of: *The Sphere Project (#19918)*. [2023.02.23/XJ1227/y/**E**]

♦ ACT Alliance Advocacy to the European Union / see ACT Alliance EU (#00082)

♦ ACT Alliance EU 00082

Dir Bd Charlemagne 28, 1000 Brussels, Belgium. T. +3222345660. E-mail: admin@actalliance.eu.
URL: http://actalliance.eu/

History Mar 1990. Founded at first inaugural meeting. Apr 2000, incorporated *Gender Orientation on Development (GOOD, inactive)*. Current name adopted when became part of: *ACT Alliance (#00081)*. Former names and other names: *Association of Protestant Development Organizations in Europe* – former; *Association of World Council of Churches Related Development Organizations in Europe (APRODEV)* – former; *ACT Alliance Advocacy to the European Union* – full title. Registration: EU Transparency Register, No/ID: 5189768701-12. **Aims** Represent member organizations, dealing mainly with development-related issues, to European institutions; influence decisions of the European Union on development and humanitarian aid policy and NGO activity; coordinate the work of members in their relations with Europe and reflect aspirations of partner NGOs in the South; share more effectively information, experience and skills among member organizations within and outside EU. **Structure** General Assembly (annual); Board; Policy and Advocacy Group; Working Groups. **Languages** English. **Staff** 5.60 FTE, paid. **Finance** Sources: members' dues. Annual budget: 642,000 EUR (2022). **Activities** Advocacy/lobbying/activism; capacity building; politics/policy/regulatory. **Events** *Annual Meeting* 2021, *Annual Meeting* 2020, *Annual Meeting* Brussels (Belgium) 2019, *Annual Meeting* Finland 2018, *Annual Meeting* Belgium 2017. **Publications** Occasional papers.
Members Full in 12 countries:
Austria, Czechia, Denmark, Finland, Germany, Iceland, Ireland, Netherlands, Norway, Sweden, Switzerland, UK.
Included in the above, 12 organizations:
Act Church of Sweden; Bread for the World – Protestant Development Service, Berlin; *Christian Aid*; Diaconia ECCB; *Diakonia*; Diakonie Austria; *Finn Church Aid (FCA)*; *Folkekirkens Nødhjaelp (FKN)*; Global Ministries of the United Churches in the Netherlands (KerkinActie); *Icelandic Church Aid*; *Norwegian Church Aid*; Swiss Interchurch Aid (EPER).
Observers (3):
ACT Alliance (#00081); *The Lutheran World Federation (LWF, #16532)* ('Lutheran World Service' Department); *World Council of Churches (WCC, #21320)*.
Consultative Status Consultative status granted from: *UNCTAD (#20285)* (General Category). **NGO Relations** Member of (5): *Climate Action Network Europe (CAN Europe, #04001)*; *Confédération européenne des ong d'urgence et de développement (CONCORD, #04547)*; *Human Rights and Democracy Network (HRDN, #10980)*; *SDG Watch Europe (#19162)*; *TP Organics – European Technology Platform (TP Organics, #20180)*.
[2022.02.03/XD2348/y/**E**]

♦ **ACT** Allied Command Transformation (#00732)
♦ **ACT** – Amazon Conservation Team (internationally oriented national body)
♦ Acta Odontologica Scandinavica Foundation / see Acta Odontologica Scandinavica Society (#00083)

♦ **Acta Odontologica Scandinavica Society** **00083**
Föreningen Acta Odontologica Scandinavica
Contact Dept of Dentistry/Periodontology, Aarhus Univ, Bldg 1610 – 284, Vennelyst Boulevard 9, 8000 Aarhus C, Denmark.
History 1939, as *Acta Odontologica Scandinavica Foundation* – – *Stiftelsen för Acta Odontologica Scandinavica*. Registered in accordance with Swedish law. **Aims** Make *dental research* in the *Nordic* countries known to an international forum. **Structure** Foundation Board; Editor. **Finance** Subscriptions: US$ 330. **Activities** Publishes the journal; awards prizes and scholarships to researchers in odontology. **Publications** *Acta Odontologica Scandinavica* (6 a year).
Members Faculties and societies of dentistry (18) in 5 countries:
Denmark, Finland, Iceland, Norway, Sweden.
[2010/XF1168/f/**F**]

♦ **ACT** ASEAN Council of Teachers (#01165)

♦ **ACTAsia** **00084**
Exec Dir PO Box 1264, High Wycombe, HP10 8WL, UK. T. +443000010104. E-mail: info@actasia.org.
USA 328 Town View Dr, Wappingers Falls NY 12590, USA. T. +19147641075.
URL: http://www.actasia.org/
History 2006. UK Registered Charity: 1127625; Registered in accordance with Dutch law, Dec 2007: 30232790; Also registered in accordance with US law. Previously known as *ACTAsia for Animals*. **Aims** Initiate education programmes aimed at children, consumers and professionals for gradual and sustainable social change. **Structure** Board of Directors; Advisory Board. **Languages** English, Mandarin Chinese. **Staff** 14.50 FTE, paid; 50.00 FTE, voluntary. **Finance** Grants; individual donors. Annual budget: about US$ 109,000. **Activities** Training/education; awareness raising; events/meetings. **Publications** Annual Report; country status reports; teacher manuals. **Members** Not a membership organization. **NGO Relations** Member of (1): *Species Survival Network (SSN, #19916)*. Affiliate of: *World Animal Net (WAN, inactive)*.
[2019.02.12/XJ9551/**F**]

♦ ACTAsia for Animals / see ACTAsia (#00084)
♦ **ACT** – Asian Community Trust (internationally oriented national body)
♦ **ACT** – Asian Confederation of Teachers (no recent information)
♦ **ACT** Association of Commercial Television in Europe (#02436)
♦ **ACT** – Association of Corporate Treasurers (internationally oriented national body)
♦ **ACTC** – Asian Consultancy on Tobacco Control (internationally oriented national body)
♦ ACTFA / see Association for Christian Theological Education in Africa (#02431)
♦ **ACTEA** Association for Christian Theological Education in Africa (#02431)
♦ **ACTE** – Association Civic Tech Europe (unconfirmed)
♦ **ACTE** Association des collectivités textiles européennes (#02435)
♦ ACTEC / see ACTEC – Association for Cultural, Technical and Educational Cooperation
♦ **ACTEC** – Association for Cultural, Technical and Educational Cooperation (internationally oriented national body)
♦ Acte de Clôture des Négociations sur les Effectifs des Forces Armées Conventionnelles en Europe (1992 treaty)
♦ ACTED – Agence d'aide à la coopération technique et au développement (internationally oriented national body)
♦ Acte final et accord portant révision de l'Accord relatif aux télécommunications (1949 treaty)
♦ Acte final de la Conférence intergouvernementale relative à l'adoption d'un titre de voyage pour réfugiés (1946 treaty)
♦ Acte final de la Conférence internationale pour la sauvegarde la vie humaine en mer (1948 treaty)
♦ Acte final de la Conférence des Nations Unies sur l'arbitrage commercial international (1958 treaty)
♦ Acte final de la Conférence des Nations Unies sur le commerce de transit des pays sans littoral (1965 treaty)
♦ Acte final de la Conférence des Nations Unies sur la déclaration de décès de personnes disparues, 1950 (1950 treaty)
♦ Acte final de la Conférence des Nations Unies sur le droit de la mer (1958 treaty)
♦ Acte final de la Conférence des Nations Unies sur les formalités douanières concernant l'importation temporaire des véhicules de tourisme et le tourisme (1954 treaty)
♦ Acte final de la Conférence des Nations Unies sur les obligations alimentaires (1956 treaty)
♦ Acte général de Berlin sur le trafic des esclaves en Afrique, 1885 (1885 treaty)
♦ Acte général de conciliation, d'arbitrage et de règlement judiciaire (1929 treaty)
♦ Acte de Genève à l'arrangement de Nice concernant la classification internationale des produits et des services aux fins de l'enregistrement des marques (1977 treaty)
♦ Acte international concernant la coopération intellectuelle (1938 treaty)
♦ Acte de navigation de l'Elbe (1922 treaty)
♦ Acte relatif à la navigation et à la coopération économique entre les états du bassin du Niger 1963 treaty)
♦ **ACTESA** Alliance for Commodity Trade in Eastern and Southern Africa (#00668)
♦ Acte unique européen (1986 treaty)
♦ **ACTI** Association of Caribbean Tertiary Institutions (#02412)
♦ Actie Dienst voor de Europese Burger (#06555)
♦ Het Actiefonds (internationally oriented national body)
♦ **ACTIF** African Cotton and Textile Industries Federation (#00271)

♦ Acting for Life (internationally oriented national body)
♦ Acting for Life International / see Acting for Life
♦ Acting for Women in Distressing Circumstances (internationally oriented national body)

♦ **ACTION** **00085**
Main Office c/o RESULTS Educational Fund, 1101 15th St NW, Ste 1200, Washington DC 20005, USA. T. +12027834800. Fax +12027832818. E-mail: info@action.org.
URL: http://www.action.org/
History 2004, as an international partnership. Original full title: *Advocacy to Control Tuberculosis Internationally (ACTION Project) – Promotion de la lutte contre la tuberculose au plan international – Promoción del Control de la Tuberculosis Internacionalmente*. Full title: *ACTION – Global Health Advocacy Partnership*. **Aims** Influence policy and mobilize resources to fight *diseases* of *poverty* and improve equitable access to *health* services. **Structure** Secretariat. **Languages** English, French, Hindi, Swahili. **Staff** 1.00 FTE, paid. **Finance** Funded by: *Bill and Melinda Gates Foundation (BMGF)*.
Members Partners in 9 countries:
Australia, Canada, India, Japan, Kenya, South Africa, UK, USA, Zambia.
Included in the above, 2 organizations listed in this Yearbook:
Global Health Advocates (#10400); *RESULTS*.
NGO Relations Member of: *PMNCH (#18410)*; *TB Europe Coalition (TBEC, #20104)*. Partner of: *1,000 Days*.
[2019/XM3961/**F**]

♦ Action10 (internationally oriented national body)
♦ Action4SD – Action for Sustainable Development (unconfirmed)

♦ **Action Against Hunger** **00086**
Action contre la faim – Acción contra el Hambre – Azione contro la Fame – Aktion gegen den Hunger
SG 14/16 bvd de Douaumont, CS 80060, 75854 Paris CEDEX 17, France. T. +33170847070. Fax +33170847071.
URL: http://www.actioncontrelafaim.org/
History 1979, France. Former names and other names: *Action internationale contre la faim (AICF)* – former; *ACF International* – alias. Registration: France. **Aims** Carry out *emergency relief* operations in situations of war, crisis and famine to bring aid to populations in extreme difficulty, such as displaced persons or refugees who no longer have access to food; define and carry out small-scale development and rehabilitation programmes in primary health care, nutrition, water supply, agriculture, education and training, in order to enable them in the longer term to regain autonomy; develop *disaster* preparedness programmes in order to anticipate and forecast *humanitarian* crises. **Structure** Head Offices in Paris (France), Madrid (Spain), London (UK), New York NY (USA) and Montréal (Canada). **Languages** English, French, Spanish. **Staff** 247.00 FTE, paid. **Finance** Donations from individuals, international institutions, foundations and companies. **Activities** Humanitarian/emergency aid; financial and/or material support; advocacy/lobbying/activism; events/meetings. **Events** *The urban bomb, how to feed towns and shanty towns in wartime* 2004, *Hunger as a weapon* 1997, *International colloquium* Paris (France) 1987. **Publications** *Geopolitics of Hunger*, *Interventions* – external newspaper. *Urban Misery, Hidden Hunger* (2006); *Visions of the World of the Faces of Hunger* (2004); *World Murmurs* (1998). Annual Report.
Members Organizations in 5 countries:
Canada, France, Spain, UK, USA.
Individuals in 50 countries and territories:
Afghanistan, Armenia, Bangladesh, Bolivia, Burkina Faso, Cambodia, Cameroon, Central African Rep, Chad, Colombia, Congo DR, Côte d'Ivoire, Djibouti, Egypt, Ethiopia, Georgia, Guatemala, Guinea, Haiti, India, Indonesia, Jordan, Kenya, Kurdish area, Lebanon, Liberia, Madagascar, Mali, Mauritania, Mongolia, Myanmar, Nepal, Nicaragua, Niger, Nigeria, Pakistan, Palestine, Paraguay, Peru, Philippines, Senegal, Sierra Leone, Somalia, South Sudan, Syrian AR, Türkiye, Uganda, Ukraine, Yemen, Zimbabwe.
Consultative Status Consultative status granted from: *ECOSOC (#05331)* (Special); *WHO (#20950)* (Official). **IGO Relations** Signatory to an agreement with: *World Food Programme (WFP, #21510)*. Participates as observer in the activities of: *Codex Alimentarius Commission (CAC, #04081)*. Partner of: *UNHCR (#20327)*. Operational links with: *UNDP (#20292)*; *UNICEF (#20332)*; *United Nations Office for the Coordination of Humanitarian Affairs (OCHA, #20593)*.
NGO Relations Member of:
– *Active Learning Network for Accountability and Performance in Humanitarian Action (ALNAP, #00101)*;
– *American Council for Voluntary International Action (InterAction)*;
– *The Butterfly Effect (BE, #03389)*;
– *CHS Alliance (#03911)*;
– *Coalition Eau*;
– *Coordination SUD*;
– *Emergency Telecommunications Cluster (ETC, #05438)*;
– *End Water Poverty (EWP, #05464)*;
– *Global WASH Cluster (GWC, #10651)*;
– *Inter-agency Network for Education in Emergencies (INEE, #11387)*;
– *International Campaign to Ban Landmines – Cluster Munition Coalition (ICBL-CMC, #12427)*;
– *NGO Working Group on the Security Council (#17128)*;
– *PMNCH (#18410)*;
– *Start Network (#19969)*.
Member of Board of: *Voluntary Organisations in Cooperation in Emergencies (VOICE, #20809)*. Operational collaboration with: *Coalition for the International Criminal Court (CICC, #04062)*; *Global Call for Action Against Poverty (GCAP, #10263)*; *International Federation of Red Cross and Red Crescent Societies (#13526)*; *Oxfam GB* – (Oxfam for Food Security and Nutrition); national organizations.
[2020/XD9042/**F**]

♦ **ActionAid** **00087**
Ecoliers du monde – Ayuda en Acción – Azione Aiuto
Head Office PostNet Ste 248, Private Bag X31, Saxonwold, Johannesburg, 2132, South Africa. T. +27117314500. Fax +27118808082. E-mail: mail.jhb@actionaid.org.
URL: http://www.actionaid.org/
History 1972, as *Action in Distress*. Present name adopted 1980. Also referred to in French as *Aide et action*. UK Registered Charity: 274467. Also referred to as *ActionAid International (AAI)*. **Aims** Overcome the *injustice* and *inequity* that cause *poverty*; contribute to and influence development cooperation policies, in particular on poverty eradication and education. **Structure** Regions: Africa; Asia; Europe – *ActionAid Alliance*; Latin America and the Caribbean; North America. Head Office/Registered Office in London (UK); Offices in Washington DC (USA) and Brussels (Belgium). **Staff** Asia – 444; Africa – 1,158; North America – 3; Latin America and the Caribbean – 36; Europe – 504 (ActionAid Alliance). **Activities** Advocacy/lobbying/activism.
Publications *ActionAid Annual Review*. Annual Report.
Members Comprises sister organizations in 6 countries:
France, Greece, Ireland, Italy, Spain, UK.
Works in 40 countries:
Bangladesh, Belgium, Bolivia, Brazil, Burundi, Canada, China, Dominican Rep, Ecuador, El Salvador, Ethiopia, France, Gambia, Ghana, Greece, Guatemala, Haiti, India, Ireland, Italy, Kenya, Liberia, Malawi, Mozambique, Nepal, Nicaragua, Nigeria, Pakistan, Peru, Rwanda, Sierra Leone, Somalia, Spain, Tanzania UR, Uganda, UK, USA, Vietnam, Zambia, Zimbabwe.
Consultative Status Consultative status granted from: *ECOSOC (#05331)* (Special); *UNCTAD (#20285)* (General Category); *World Intellectual Property Organization (WIPO, #21593)* (Permanent Observer Status); *UNESCO (#20322)* (Consultative Status). **IGO Relations** Accredited by (3): *Green Climate Fund (GCF, #10714)*; *UNEP (#20299)*; *United Nations Office at Vienna (UNOV, #20604)*. Lobbies: *European Commission (EC, #06633)*; *International Bank for Reconstruction and Development (IBRD, #12317)* (World Bank); US Government. Links with most UN Specialized Agencies, including: *International Fund for Agricultural Development (IFAD, #13692)*; *UNHCR (#20327)*. Associated with Department of Global Communications of the United Nations.
NGO Relations Support from: *Charities Aid Foundation of America (CAF America)*. Supports: *African Highland Initiative Eco-regional Programme (AHI, inactive)*; *Amref Health Africa (#00806)*; *Circle for International Reflect Action and Communication (CIRAC)*; *Cooperation Committee for Cambodia (CCC)*; *Global Call for Action Against Poverty (GCAP, #10263)*; *NGO Forum on Cambodia (#17124)*. Cooperates with: *Alliance Against Hunger and Malnutrition (AAHM, no recent information)*; *International Council for Adult Education (ICAE, #12983)*; *International Food Policy Research Institute (IFPRI, #13622)*; *Ockenden International*; *Panos Network (#18183)*;

Also cooperation with: *International Network of Resource Centers on Urban Agriculture and Food Security (RUAF Foundation, #14319)*. Provides secretariat for: *Bretton Woods Project*. Partner of: *Global Call for Climate Action (GCCA, inactive)*; *WorldFish (#21507)*. On the Board of: *European Network on Debt and Development (EURODAD, #07891)*. On Steering Committee of: *Campaña Latinoamericana por el Derecho a la Educación (CLADE, #03407)*. Houses and on Steering Committee of: *Right to Education Initiative (RTE, #18942)*.
Member of:
- *Accountable Now (#00060)*;
- *African Health Policy Network (AHPN)*;
- *African Smallholder Farmers Group (ASFG, inactive)*;
- *Association for Women's Rights in Development (AWID, #02980)*;
- *British Overseas Aid Group (BOAG)*;
- *British Overseas NGO's for Development (BOND)*;
- *CHS Alliance (#03911)* (various national sections);
- *CIVICUS: World Alliance for Citizen Participation (#03962)*;
- *Commonwealth HIV and AIDS Action Group (Para55, no recent information)*;
- *Communicating with Disaster Affected Communities Network (CDAC Network, #04379)*;
- *Confédération européenne des ong d'urgence et de développement (CONCORD, #04547)*;
- *Conference of Non-Governmental Organizations in Consultative Relationship with the United Nations (CONGO, #04635)*;
- *Copenhagen Initiative for Central America and Mexico (CIFCA, inactive)*;
- *Council for Education in the Commonwealth (CEC)*;
- *EarthAction (EA, #05159)*;
- *Environment Liaison Centre International (ELCI, no recent information)*;
- *Ethical Trading Initiative (ETI)*;
- *Financial Transparency Coalition (FTC, #09772)*;
- *Global Campaign for Education (GCE, #10264)*;
- *Global Gender and Climate Alliance (GGCA, no recent information)*;
- *End Corporal Punishment (#05457)*;
- *Inter-agency Network for Education in Emergencies (INEE, #11387)*;
- *International AIDS Women's Caucus (IAWC, #11603)*;
- *International Council of Voluntary Agencies (ICVA, #13092)*;
- *International Network for Economic, Social and Cultural Rights (ESCR-Net, #14255)*;
- *Jubilee Research (#16158)*;
- *Just Net Coalition (JNC, #16173)*;
- *National Council for Voluntary Organizations (NCVO)*;
- *NetHope (#16979)*;
- *Start Network (#19969)*;
- *Think Global – Development Education Association (DEA)*.

Member of the Coordinating Committee of: *More and Better (#16855)*. Ethiopian Office member of: *Consortium of Christian Relief and Development Association (CCRDA)*. UK Office member of: *Disasters Emergency Committee (DEC)*. European Office member of: *Fédération des employeurs ONG (FEONG)*. Links with other BOAG members:
- *Catholic Agency for Overseas Development (CAFOD)*;
- *Christian Aid*;
- *Oxfam GB*;
- *Save the Children UK (SC UK)*;
- *Voluntary Organisations in Cooperation in Emergencies (VOICE, #20809)*. [2020/XF5056/f/**F**]

♦ ActionAid France – Peuples Solidaires (internationally oriented national body)
♦ ActionAid International / see ActionAid (#00087)
♦ Action andine (internationally oriented national body)

♦ Action for Animal Health (A4AH) 00088

Senior Coordinator Brooke, 2nd Floor – Hallmark Bldg, 52-56 Leadenhall Street, London, EC3A 2BJ, UK.
URL: https://actionforanimalhealth.org/

Aims Advocacy for more investment in strong and resilient animal health systems that protect people, animals and the planet. **Activities** Advocacy/lobbying/activism; guidance/assistance/consulting; research/documentation.
Members Partners (12):
Centre for Supporting Evidence Based Interventions in Livestock (SEBI-Livestock); *Compassion in World Farming (CIWF, #04414)*; *Dogs Trust Worldwide*; *GALVmed (#10066)*; *Global Alliance for Rabies Control (GARC)*; *Interafrican Bureau for Animal Resources (AU-IBAR, #11382)*; *International Livestock Research Institute (ILRI, #14062)*; *Send a Cow*; *Soi Dog Foundation (#19670)*; *The Brooke (#03338)*; *Vétérinaires Sans Frontières International (VSF International, #20760)*; *World Veterinary Association (WVA, #21901)*.
[2022.02.09/AA2386/y/**C**]

♦ Action on Antibiotic Resistance (ReAct) 00089

Acción Frente a la Resistencia Bacteriana

Exec Dir Uppsala Univ, Box 256, SE-751 05 Uppsala, Sweden. T. +46184716607. E-mail: react@reactgroup.org.
Latin America Office Fac Ciencias Médicas, Univ de Cuenca, Cuenca, Ecuador.
Southeast Asia 97 Jalan SS22A/1, Damansara Jaya, 47400 Petaling Jaya, Selangor, Malaysia.
URL: http://www.reactgroup.org/

History 2005, Uppsala (Sweden). Pre-meeting held May 2004, Uppsala (Sweden). **Aims** Combat antibiotic resistance as a global threat to health. **Structure** Global Leadership Group. Nodes (5): Africa; Asia Pacific; Europe; Latin America; North America. **Finance** Supported by: *Swedish International Development Cooperation Agency (Sida)*. **Activities** Advocacy/lobbying/activism. **NGO Relations** National organizations are involved.
[2023/XM1532/**F**]

♦ Action d'appui pour la protection des droits des minorités en Afrique centrale (internationally oriented national body)
♦ Action on Armed Violence (internationally oriented national body)
♦ Action A B C en faveur de l'éducation et de la santé dans le Tiers-monde (internationally oriented national body)
♦ Action biblique internationale (internationally oriented national body)
♦ Action Without Borders (internationally oriented national body)
♦ Action de carême (internationally oriented national body)
♦ Action de carême des catholiques en Suisse / see Catholic Lenten Fund
♦ Action Children Aid (internationally oriented national body)
♦ Action for Children and Communities in Africa (internationally oriented national body)
♦ Action for Children in Conflict / see Action for Children and Communities in Africa
♦ Action Chrétienne des Etudiants Russes / see ACER-Russie
♦ Action Chrétienne en Orient (unconfirmed)
♦ Action commerciale pour l'Afrique (#03375)
♦ Action Committee for the Integration of Latin America (inactive)
♦ Action Committee Service for Peace (internationally oriented national body)
♦ Action Committee for a United States of Europe (inactive)
♦ Action communautaire en Europe (inactive)
♦ Action concertée pour le développement de l'Afrique (inactive)
♦ ACTION for Conflict Transformation (internationally oriented national body)
♦ Action contre la faim (#00086)
♦ Action for Development (internationally oriented national body)
♦ Action pour le développement / see Action pour le développement – SOS Faim
♦ Action pour le développement sanitaire en Europe du sud-est (#19807)
♦ Action pour le développement – SOS Faim (internationally oriented national body)
♦ Action on Disability and Development / see ADD International
♦ Action in Distress / see ActionAid (#00087)
♦ Action for Dolphins (internationally oriented national body)
♦ Action économique arabe commune (no recent information)
♦ Action européenne des handicapés (#05825)
♦ Action d'évangélisation mondiale (#20850)
♦ Action at External Frontiers (inactive)
♦ Action pour une fédération mondiale (inactive)
♦ Action Five – Action Five Percent for Development Aid (internationally oriented national body)
♦ Action Five Percent for Development Aid (internationally oriented national body)

♦ Action for Global Health (AfGH) 00090

Coordinator c/o STOPAIDS, The Grayston Centre, 28 Charles Square, Old Street, London, N1 6HT, UK.
URL: https://actionforglobalhealth.org.uk/

History Founded by 14 NGOs and charities. Registration: Charity Commission, No/ID: 1113204, England and Wales; Companies House, No/ID: 2589198, Start date: 6 Mar 1991, England. **Aims** Promote the realization of the universal right to health and access to quality healthcare for everyone without being forced into financial hardship. **Structure** Coordination Team. **Languages** English, French, German, Italian, Spanish. **Staff** 17.00 FTE, paid. **Finance** Supported by: *Bill and Melinda Gates Foundation (BMGF)*; *The Rockefeller Foundation (#18966)*.
Members Organizations in 6 countries:
Belgium, France, Germany, Italy, Spain, UK.
Included in the above, 5 organizations listed in this Yearbook:
Frontline AIDS (#10007); *Plan International (#18386)*.
NGO Relations Member of (1): *Gavi – The Vaccine Alliance (Gavi, #10077)* (CSO Constituency).
[2021/XM1531/y/**E**]

♦ ACTION – Global Health Advocacy Partnership / see ACTION (#00085)

♦ Action Group on Erosion, Technology and Concentration (ETC Group) 00091

Contact 2464 rue de l'Eglise, Val-David QC J0T 2N0, Canada. E-mail: etc@etcgroup.org.
URL: http://www.etcgroup.org/

History Founded 1983, as *International Genetic Resources Programme*. Name changed subsequently to: *Rural Advancement Fund International*, 1986; *Rural Advancement Foundation International (RAFI)*. Current name adopted Sep 2001. **Aims** Investigate ecological erosion (including erosion of cultures and human rights); develop new technologies (agricultural and other technologies working with genomics and matter); monitor global governance issues including corporate concentration and trade in technologies. **Structure** Board of Directors. **Languages** English, French, Spanish. **Staff** 9.00 FTE, paid. **Events** *Emerging technologies strategy discussion on nanotechnology, synthetic biology, genomics, geo-engineering* New York, NY (USA) 2009. **Publications** *ETC Group Communique* (about 6 a year). Books; annual report; occasional papers; videos. **Consultative Status** Consultative status granted from: *ECOSOC (#05331)* (Ros A); *FAO (#09260)* (Special Status); *UNCTAD (#20285)* (Special Category); *UNEP (#20299)*. **IGO Relations** Observer to: *Convention on Biological Diversity (Biodiversity convention, 1992)*; *United Nations Framework Convention on Climate Change – Secretariat (UNFCCC, #20564)*. International affiliations: *Commission on Genetic Resources for Food and Agriculture (CGRFA, #04215)*. **NGO Relations** ETC Group's Southern NGO Partnership listed in this Yearbook: *Southeast Asia Regional Initiatives for Community Empowerment (SEARICE, #19795)*. International Affiliations: *Friends of the Earth International (FoEI, #10002)*; *GRAIN (#10691)*; *Third World Network (TWN, #20151)*; *World Council of Churches (WCC, #21320)*. Endorses: *Ban Terminator Campaign (#03172)*; United Nations Moratorium on Geoengineering. Member of: *World Forum on Science and Democracy (WFSD, #21522)*. Links with numerous NGOs, not specified. [2018.06.18/XF0027/**F**]

♦ Action internationale contre la faim / see Action Against Hunger (#00086)
♦ Action internationale pour la paix et le développement dans la région des Grands Lacs, Switzerland (internationally oriented national body)
♦ Action internationale pour les ressources génétiques / see GRAIN (#10691)
♦ Action International Ministries (internationally oriented national body)
♦ Action médical missionnaire / see MEMISA
♦ Action for Mining Communities / see Association of Europe's Coalfield Regions (#02585)
♦ Action Mission and Leprosy Assistance Schiefbahn (internationally oriented national body)
♦ Action monde en solidarité (internationally oriented national body)
♦ Action mondiale contre la pauvreté (#10263)
♦ Action mondiale des parlementaires (#18208)
♦ Action mondiale des peuples / see Peoples' Global Action Against Free Trade and the WTO (#18304)
♦ Action mondiale des peuples contre le 'libre' échange et l'OMC (#18304)
♦ Action our le Développement Durable (unconfirmed)
♦ Action Partners / see Pioneers UK
♦ Action Partners-Pioneers / see Pioneers UK
♦ Action for Peace through Prayer and Aid (internationally oriented national body)
♦ Action for Peoples in Conflict / see Action for Children and Communities in Africa
♦ Action Plan for the Caribbean Environment Programme / see Caribbean Action Plan (#03432)
♦ Action Plan for Protection, Development and Management of the Marine Environment of the North-West Pacific Region / see Action Plan for Protection, Development and Management of the Marine Environment of the Northwest Pacific Region (#00092)

♦ Action Plan for Protection, Development and Management of the Marine Environment of the Northwest Pacific Region (NOWPAP) 00092

Dep Coordinator – Busan Office NOWPAP RCU, 216 Gijanghaean-ro, Gijang-eup, Gijang-gun, Busan 619 705, Korea Rep. T. +82517203001. Fax +82517203009.
Coordinator – Toyama Office 5-5 Ushijimashin-machi, Toyama City TOYAMA, 930 0856 Japan. T. +81764441611. Fax +81764442780.
URL: http://www.nowpap.org/

History 31 Oct 1991, USSR. Set up 31 Oct 1991, Vladivostok (USSR), at 1st consultative meeting of experts and national focal points. Adopted 14 Sep 1994, Seoul (Korea Rep), at intergovernmental meeting. Part of *Regional Seas Programme (#18814)* of *UNEP (#20299)*. Also referred to as *Northwest Pacific Action Plan* and *Action Plan for Protection, Development and Management of the Marine Environment of the North-West Pacific Region*. **Aims** Promote wise use, development and management of the marine and coastal environment so as to obtain the utmost long-term benefits for the human populations of the region, while securing the region's sustainability for future generations. **Structure** Intergovernmental Meeting (IGM); Regional Coordinating Units (2); Regional Activity Centres (4). **Languages** English. **Staff** RCU: 7; RACs: 15. **Finance** Members' dues to the Trust Fund. Budget (annual): about US$ 600,000. **Activities** Knowledge management/information dissemination; monitoring/evaluation. **Events** *Marine Litter Workshop* Busan (Korea Rep) 2019, *Marine Litter Management Workshop* Busan (Korea Rep) 2018, *Intergovernmental Meeting* Moscow (Russia) 2018, *International Maritime Disaster Response Conference* Busan (Korea Rep) 2017, *Intergovernmental Meeting* Toyama City (Japan) 2017. **Publications** Reports.
Members Participating States (4):
China, Japan, Korea Rep, Russia.
IGO Relations Participating in development and implementation of the Plan: *International Maritime Organization (IMO, #14102)*; *North Pacific Marine Science Organization (PICES, #17602)*; *UNESCO (#20322)*. **NGO Relations** Participating in the development and implementation of the Plan: international and local organizations involved in marine environment protection. [2015.09.22/XF5204/**F***]

♦ Action Plan for the Protection and Development of the Marine Environment and Coastal Areas of the East Asian Region (EAS) 00093

Coordination c/o UNEP/ROAP, UN Bldg 2nd Floor, Block B, Rajadamnern-Nok Avenue, Bangkok, 10200, Thailand. T. +6622881860 – +6622881889.
URL: http://www.cobsea.org/

History 1981. Also referred to as *East Asian Seas Action Plan*. One of a number of such plans implemented under the authority of the Executive Director of *UNEP (#20299)* within *Regional Seas Programme (#18814)*. Technical coordination originally through *UNEP Water Branch (inactive)*, currently through Regional Coordinating Unit (EAS/RCU) in Bangkok (Thailand). **Aims** Promote protection and *sustainable development* of coastal

and marine areas of participating countries. **Structure** Regional Coordinating Unit (EAS/RCU) – also acts as secretariat for meetings of *Coordinating Body on the Seas of East Asia (COBSEA, #04814)* and functions as UN lead agency in the region for marine environmental matters. Decisions on the Plan are made by UNEP Governing Council and by intergovernmental meetings of COBSEA. **Languages** English. **Staff** 5.00 FTE, paid. **Finance** Main source: East Asian Seas Trust Fund. Other sources: UNEP Environment Fund; bilateral and multilateral donors. **Activities** EAS/RCU organizes: annual meetings of COBSEA; regional meetings; twice-yearly meetings of experts on the Plan; ad hoc workshops, seminars and meetings. Projects approved at annual meetings of COBSEA are implemented by national institutions of participating countries. **Events** *Meeting* Thailand 1992. **Publications** *EAS/RCU Technical Reports* – series.
Members Participating states (10):
Australia, Cambodia, China, Indonesia, Korea Rep, Malaysia, Philippines, Singapore, Thailand, Vietnam.
IGO Relations Participating in development and implementation of the Plan: *ASEAN (#01141); ASEAN Council on Petroleum (ASCOPE, #01164); Asian Development Bank (ADB, #01422); FAO (#09260); Commission de l'Océan Indien (COI, #04236); International Atomic Energy Agency (IAEA, #12294); International Maritime Organization (IMO, #14102); UNDP (#20292); UNESCO (#20322); United Nations Economic and Social Commission for Asia and the Pacific (ESCAP, #20557); WHO (#20950); World Meteorological Organization (WMO, #21649).* Works with: *Global Programme of Action for the Protection of the Marine Environment from Land-Based Activities (GPA, see: #20299).* **NGO Relations** Participating in development and implementation of the Plan: *Advisory Committee on Protection of the Sea (ACOPS, #00139); International Union for Conservation of Nature and Natural Resources (IUCN, #15766).* RCU supports publication of newsletter of: *Association of Southeast Asian Marine Scientists (ASEAMS, no recent information).* [2017/XF2002/**F***]

♦ Action Plan for the Protection and Management of the South Asia Seas Region (SASP) 00094

Dir Gen 69/4 Maya Avenue, Colombo, 06, Sri Lanka. T. +94112589376. Fax +94112589369. E-mail: secretariat@sacep.org – info@sacep.org.
Administrative Officer address not obtained. T. +94112504708. Fax +94112589369.
URL: http://www.sacep.org/
History Mar 1995, when Plan was adopted. Technical coordination and secretariat provided through *South Asia Cooperative Environment Programme (SACEP, #19714)* with assistance from *UNEP (#20299)* through *Regional Seas Programme (#18814).* Implemented under the authority of UNEP Executive Director. Also referred to as *South Asian Seas Action Plan* and *SAS Action Plan.* **Aims** Protect and manage marine environment and related coastal ecosystems in the region by establishing and enhancing consultations and technical cooperation among States of the region; emphasize the economic and social importance of marine and coastal resources; establish a regional cooperative network of activities concerning concrete subjects/projects of mutual interest to the whole region. **Activities** Mandate is to focus specifically on: Integrated Coastal Zone Management (ICZM); Development and Implementation of National and Regional Oil and Chemical Spill Contingency Planning; Human Resources Development through Strengthening Regional Centres of Excellence; Protection of the Marine Environment from Land-Based Activities. Assists in development of ICRAN activities in South Asia. Organizes: workshops; training courses.
Members Participating states (5):
Bangladesh, India, Maldives, Pakistan, Sri Lanka.
IGO Relations Participating in development and implementation of the Plan: *Global Programme of Action for the Protection of the Marine Environment from Land-Based Activities (GPA, see: #20299); International Coral Reef Action Network (ICRAN, #12964); International Maritime Organization (IMO, #14102); UN Environment Programme World Conservation Monitoring Centre (UNEP-WCMC, #20295).* **NGO Relations** Participating in development and implementation of the Plan: Coral Reef Degradation in the Indian Ocean (CORDIO); *International Union for Conservation of Nature and Natural Resources (IUCN, #15766).* [2017/XF1833/**F***]

♦ Action Plan for the Protection of the Marine Environment and Coastal Areas in the South East Pacific (SE/PCF) 00095

Plan de Acción para la Protección del Medio Marino y Areas Costeras del Pacifico Sudeste
Coordinator Av Francisco de Orellana y Miguel H Allcivar, Las Camaras, Torre B Local 1, 090512 Guayaquil, Ecuador. T. +59343714390.
URL: http://www.cpps-int.org/
History Nov 1981, Lima (Peru). Also referred to as *South East Pacific Action Plan.* A joint project of *Comisión Permanente del Pacifico Sur (CPPS, #04141)* and *UNEP (#20299)*, within the framework of *Regional Seas Programme (#18814)*, carried out through CPPS. **Aims** Protect the marine environment and coastal areas of the South East Pacific. **Structure** CPPS acts as Executive Secretariat for programmes. National focal points. **Languages** English, Spanish. **Finance** UNEP; special contributions of CPPS member states and Panama. **Activities** Projects/programmes. Management of treaties and agreements: *Agreement on Regional Cooperation in Combating Pollution of the South-East Pacific by Hydrocarbons or other Harmful Substances in Cases of Emergency (1981)*, 12 Nov 1981, Lima (Peru); *Convention for the Protection of the Marine Environment and Coastal Area of the Southeast Pacific (Lima Convention, 1981)*, 12 Nov 1981, Lima; *Complementary Protocol to the Agreement on Regional Cooperation in Combating Pollution of the Southeast Pacific by Hydrocarbons and other Harmful Substances (1983)*, 22 Jul 1983, Quito (Ecuador); *Protocol for the Protection of the Southeast Pacific Against Pollution from Land-based Sources (1983)*, 22 Jul 1983, Quito; *Protocol for the Conservation and Management of Protected Marine and Coastal Areas of the Southeast Pacific (1989)*, 21 Sep 1989, Paipa (Colombia); *Protocol for the Protection of the South East Pacific Against Radioactive Contamination (1989)*, 21 Sep 1989, Paipa (Colombia). **Events** *Intergovernmental meeting* Lima (Peru) 1995, *General authority meeting* Santiago (Chile) 1993.
Members Participating States (5, " indicates CPPS member state):
Chile (*), Colombia (*), Ecuador (*), Panama, Peru (*).
IGO Relations International organizations participating in the development and implementation of the Plan: *FAO (#09260); Commission de l'Océan Indien (COI, #04236); International Atomic Energy Agency (IAEA, #12294); International Maritime Organization (IMO, #14102); OAS (#17629); UNDP (#20292); UNESCO (#20322); UNIDO (#20336); United Nations Economic Commission for Latin America and the Caribbean (ECLAC, #20556); WHO (#20950); World Meteorological Organization (WMO, #21649).* [2020.03.03/XF1831/**F***]

- ♦ Action Plan for the Protection of the Marine Environment and the Sustainable Development of the Coastal Areas of the Mediterranean / see Mediterranean Action Plan (#16638)
- ♦ Action Plan for the Protection of the Marine Environment and the Sustainable Development of the Mediterranean / see Mediterranean Action Plan (#16638)
- ♦ Action Plan for the Protection of the Mediterranean / see Mediterranean Action Plan (#16638)
- ♦ Action positive pour l'environnement et le développement en Afrique centrale (internationally oriented national body)
- ♦ Action for Post-Soviet Jewry (internationally oriented national body)
- ♦ Action on Poverty (internationally oriented national body)
- ♦ Action Programme for Economic Cooperation / see Research and Information System for Developing Countries, India
- ♦ ACTION Project / see ACTION (#00085)
- ♦ Action for Rational Drugs in Asia / see HAI – Asia-Pacific (#10852)
- ♦ Action Reconciliation Services for Peace (internationally oriented national body)
- ♦ Action pour les régions minières / see Association of Europe's Coalfield Regions (#02585)

♦ Action Research Network of the Americas (ARNA) 00096

Red de Investigación Acción de América – Rede de Pesquisa-Ação das Américas
Contact address not obtained.
URL: https://arnawebsite.org/
History 2012. Constitution introduced 2016; revised 2017. **Aims** Unite college and university students and faculty conducting practitioner inquiry into teaching and learning with fellow action researchers in public schools, private schools, community settings and workplaces throughout the Americas. **Structure** Executive Committee; Coordinating Group; Action Research Communities (ARCs). **Activities** Awards/prizes/competitions; events/meetings. **Events** *Annual Conference* Puerto Vallarta (Mexico) 2021, *Annual Conference* Montréal, QC (Canada) 2019. **Publications** Annual Report; conference proceedings. [2020.10.21/AA0403/**F**]

- ♦ Action Sans Frontières (internationally oriented national body)
- ♦ Action santé internationale (#10868)
- ♦ Action Santé Mondiale (#10400)

♦ Actions for Genuine Democratic Alternatives (AGENDA) 00097

Contact Corner of Benson and Lynch Streets, Monrovia, Liberia. T. +2316557728 – +2316542933.
URL: http://www.freeagenda.org/
Aims Promote citizens participation in governance, so as to promote good governance, transparency and accountability in the administration of public trust. **Structure** Board of Directors of 11 members, including Chair. **NGO Relations** Partners include: *African Democracy Forum (ADF, #00281); CIVICUS: World Alliance for Citizen Participation (#03962); Publish What You Pay Coalition (PWYP, #18573); West Africa Civil Society Forum (WACSOF, #20864).* [2011/XJ2225/**F**]

- ♦ Action pour la solidarité, l'équité, l'environnement et le développement (#00098)
- ♦ Action solidarité Tiers-monde (internationally oriented national body)
- ♦ Action in Solidarity with Asia and the Pacific (internationally oriented national body)
- ♦ Action for Solidarity, Equality, Environment and Development / see Action for Solidarity, Equality, Environment and Diversity (#00098)

♦ Action for Solidarity, Equality, Environment and Diversity (A SEED) . 00098

Action pour la solidarité, l'équité, l'environnement et le développement
A SEED Europe Plantage Doklaan 12A, 1018 CM Amsterdam, Netherlands. T. +31206682236. E-mail: info@aseed.net.
URL: http://www.aseed.net/
History Founded 1992, Germany, on creation of a global structure. Originally also referred to in English as *Action for Solidarity, Equality, Environment and Development.* **Aims** Coordinate youth efforts aiming to influence international policy-making on environment and development; promote mutual understanding and cooperation between youth activists in North and South; promote sustainable lifestyles and a just and sustainable international economy. **Structure** Council; Board. **Languages** Dutch, English. **Staff** 1.00 FTE, paid; 4.00 FTE, voluntary. **Finance** Support from individuals and organizations, including European Union departments. **Activities** Advocacy/lobbying/activism. **Events** *General Meeting* Brussels (Belgium) 1993, *International seminar on racism, North-South and environment* Brussels (Belgium) 1993, *Meeting* Copenhagen (Denmark) 1993, *Environment and development* Dhaka (Bangladesh) 1993. **Publications** Brochures; readers; films; toolkits; stickers. **Members** Not a membership organizations. **NGO Relations** Member of: *1% for the Planet; EarthAction (EA, #05159).* [2018.09.11/XF5289/**F**]

- ♦ Action in Solidarity with Indonesia and East Timor / see Action in Solidarity with Asia and the Pacific
- ♦ Action for Southern Africa (internationally oriented national body)
- ♦ Action for Soviet Jewry / see Action for Post-Soviet Jewry
- ♦ Actions de Solidarité Internationale (internationally oriented national body)
- ♦ Action for Sustainable Development (unconfirmed)
- ♦ Action for a United World (internationally oriented national body)
- ♦ Action d'urgence internationale (#13258)
- ♦ Action vivre ensemble (internationally oriented national body)
- ♦ Action for World Federation (inactive)
- ♦ Action for World Solidarity (internationally oriented national body)
- ♦ **ACTIP** Animal Cell Technology Industrial Platform (#00835)

♦ Activated Carbons Producers Association 00099

Manager c/o CEFIC, Rue Belliard 40, bte 15, 1040 Brussels, Belgium. T. +3224369460. E-mail: info@activatedcarbon.org.
History 1979. Founded as a sector group of *Conseil européen de l'industrie chimique (CEFIC, #04687).*
Members European producers of activated carbon (9) in 6 countries:
Belgium, France, Germany, Italy, Netherlands, UK. [2020.11.17/XE0887/**E**]

- ♦ Active 20-30 International (internationally oriented national body)
- ♦ Active Citizenship Network (internationally oriented national body)

♦ Active House Alliance 00100

Main Office Rue du Luxembourg 22-24, 1000 Brussels, Belgium.
Registered Office Rue Washington 40, 1050 Brussels, Belgium. E-mail: activehouse@activehouse.info.
URL: http://www.activehouse.info/
History Registration: Belgium. **Aims** Unite all parties finding it an advantage to support development of Active Houses; support knowledge sharing, specification and demonstration, and communication. **Structure** General Assembly (annual), in Brussels (Belgium); Board of Directors; Advisory Committee. **Languages** English. **Staff** 5.00 FTE, paid. **Finance** Members' dues. Sponsors. **Activities** Events/meetings. **Events** *Symposium* Rotterdam (Netherlands) 2022, *Active House Seminar* Brussels (Belgium) 2018, *General Assembly* Brussels (Belgium) 2011. **Publications** *Activehouse Newsletter.*
Members International partners (37) include: architect and engineering companies; consulting companies; research institutes; universities; construction companies; manufacturers. Partners in 14 countries:
Austria, Belgium, Denmark, Finland, France, Germany, Italy, Netherlands, Norway, Poland, Romania, Russia, Switzerland, USA.
Included in the above, 3 organizations listed in this Yearbook:
Buildings Performance Institute Europe (BPIE, #03354); European Solar Shading Organization (ES-SO, #08794); Union internationale des architectes (UIA, #20419). [2022/XJ2936/y/**D**]

- ♦ Active and Intelligent Packaging Industry Association (unconfirmed)

♦ Active Learning Network for Accountability and Performance in Humanitarian Action (ALNAP) 00101

Main Office c/o ODI, 203 Blackfriars Road, London, SE1 8NJ, UK. T. +442079220336. Fax +442079220399. E-mail: alnap@alnap.org.
URL: http://www.alnap.org/
History 1997. **Aims** Improve humanitarian performance through increased learning and accountability. **Structure** Steering Committee; Secretariat hosted by Overseas Development Institute in London (UK). **Languages** English, French, Spanish. **Staff** 11.00 FTE, paid. **Finance** Funded by member agencies. **Activities** Events/meetings; knowledge management/information dissemination; training/education. **Publications** *ALNAP Guides* – series; *Review of Humanitarian Action* – previously annual series, now discontinued. *Report on The State of the Humanitarian System* (2015); *Evaluating International Humanitarian Action: Reflections from practitioners.* Briefing papers; studies. **Information Services** *Evaluative Reports Database.*
Members Full (86); Associate (15): NGOs, UN agencies, members of the Red Cross/Crescent Movement, donors, academics, networks and consultants. Full in 22 countries:
Australia, Austria, Belgium, Canada, Denmark, Ethiopia, France, Germany, Hong Kong, India, Ireland, Italy, Kenya, Malaysia, Netherlands, New Zealand, Norway, Pakistan, Philippines, Senegal, Spain, Sweden, Switzerland, UK, USA.

- *Action Against Hunger (#00086);*
- *Africa Humanitarian Action (AHA);*
- *Agencia Española de Cooperación Internacional para el Desarrollo (AECID);*
- *Bureau international des Médecins sans frontières (MSF International, #03366);*
- *CARE International (CI, #03429);*
- *Catholic Agency for Overseas Development (CAFOD);*
- *Catholic Relief Services (CRS, #03608);*
- *Christian Aid;*
- *Community World Service Asia (#04407);*
- *DANIDA;*
- *Danish Refugee Council (DRC);*
- *DARA (#05009);*
- *Development and Humanitarian Learning in Action (Dahlia);*
- *European Commission (EC, #06633);*
- *Evidence Aid;*
- *FAO (#09260);*
- *Global Public Policy Institute (GPPi);*
- *GOAL;*

- *Groupe urgence, réhabilitation et développement (Groupe URD)*;
- *Human Appeal (#10961)*;
- *Humanitarian Aid Network for Distribution (Global Hand)*;
- *Institute of International Humanitarian Affairs (IIHA)*;
- *Instituto de Estudios sobre Conflictos y Acción Humanitaria (IECAH)*;
- *International Committee of the Red Cross (ICRC, #12799)*;
- *International Federation of Red Cross and Red Crescent Societies (#13526)*;
- *International Humanitarian Studies Association (IHSA, #13821)*;
- *International Institute for Environment and Development (IIED, #13877)*;
- *International Organization for Migration (IOM, #14454)*;
- *International Rescue Committee (IRC, #14717)*;
- *Irish Aid*;
- *Mercy Corps International (MCI)*;
- *Norwegian Agency for Development Cooperation (Norad)*;
- *Norwegian Refugee Council (NRC)*;
- *Overseas Development Institute (ODI)*;
- *Oxfam International (#17922)*;
- *Save the Children International (#19058)*;
- *Solidarités International*;
- *Swedish International Development Cooperation Agency (Sida)*;
- *Swiss Agency for Development and Cooperation (SDC)*;
- *Tearfund, UK*;
- *Transparency International (TI, #20223)*;
- *Trocaire – Catholic Agency for World Development*;
- *UNDP (#20292)*;
- *UNHCR (#20327)*;
- *UNICEF (#20332)*;
- *United Nations Office for the Coordination of Humanitarian Affairs (OCHA, #20593)*;
- *United Nations Population Fund (UNFPA, #20612)*;
- *United States Agency for International Development (USAID)*;
- *Voluntary Organisations in Cooperation in Emergencies (VOICE, #20809)*;
- *War Child International (#20817)*;
- *WHO (#20950)*;
- *World Food Programme (WFP, #21510)*;
- *World Vision International (WVI, #21904)*.

Associate (15), including organizations listed in this Yearbook:
CHS Alliance (#03911); *Communicating with Disaster Affected Communities Network (CDAC Network, #04379)*; *Disasters Emergency Committee (DEC)*; *International Council of Voluntary Agencies (ICVA, #13092)*; *Start Network (#19969)*; *Steering Committee for Humanitarian Response (SCHR, #19978)*; *The Sphere Project (#19918)*.
NGO Relations Member of: *DARA (#05009)*; *Global WASH Cluster (GWC, #10651)*; *International Organisation for Cooperation in Evaluation (IOCE, #14426)*. Affiliate member of: *International Council of Voluntary Agencies (ICVA, #13092)*. Cooperates with: *EvalPartners (#09208)*; *United Nations Evaluation Group (UNEG, #20560)*.
[2014.12.09/XF6345/y/**F**]

♦ Active Pharmaceutical Ingredients Committee (APIC) 00102

Contact c/o CEFIC, Rue Belliard 40, Box 15, 1040 Brussels, Belgium. T. +3226767202. Fax +3226767359.
Contact address not obtained.
URL: http://apic.cefic.org/
History Founded as a sector group of *Conseil européen de l'industrie chimique (CEFIC, #04687)*. Registration: EU Transparency Register, No/ID: 64879142323-90, Start date: 24 Sep 2009. **Structure** Plenary; Board; Executive Committee; Working Groups (3). **Activities** Events/meetings. **Events** *Conference* Berlin (Germany) 2021, *European Conference* Amsterdam (Netherlands) 2020, *European Conference* Prague (Czechia) 2019, *European Conference* Budapest (Hungary) 2018, *European Conference* Berlin (Germany) 2017.
Members Companies (62) and associations (3) in 18 countries:
Austria, Belgium, Czechia, Denmark, France, Germany, Hungary, Ireland, Italy, Latvia, Netherlands, Norway, Portugal, Slovenia, Spain, Sweden, Switzerland, UK.
NGO Relations Member of (1): *International Council on Harmonisation of Technical Requirements for Registration of Pharmaceuticals for Human Use (ICH, #13027)* (Observer). [2022/XE3482/**E**]

♦ Active Shipbuilding Experts' Federation (ASEF) 00103

Secretariat c/o CANSI, 5 Yuetan Beije, 100861 Beijing, China. T. +861059518756. E-mail: cansibj@163.com.
URL: http://www.asef2015.com/
History Inaugural assembly 26 Nov 2015. **Structure** Assembly; Council. **Activities** Events/meetings. **Events** *Forum* Osaka (Japan) 2019, *Forum* Dalian (China) 2018, *Accredited Persons Meeting* Busan (Korea Rep) 2017, *Assembly* Busan (Korea Rep) 2017, *Forum* Busan (Korea Rep) 2017.
Members Full in 10 countries:
China, India, Indonesia, Japan, Korea Rep, Malaysia, Sri Lanka, Thailand, Türkiye, Vietnam.
Consultative Status Consultative status granted from: *International Maritime Organization (IMO, #14102)*.
[2018/XM6509/**D**]

- ♦ Active – Sobriety, Friendship and Peace (inactive)
- ♦ ACTLAP Charity – African Computer and Technology Literacy Awareness Program Charity (internationally oriented national body)
- ♦ **ACTMalaria** Asian Collaborative Training Network for Malaria (#01384)
- ♦ ACTM / see Association for the Advancement of Consumerism in the World (#02347)
- ♦ **ACTM** Australasian College of Tropical Medicine (#03022)
- ♦ ACTnet / see African Conservation Tillage Network (#00265)
- ♦ **ACTO** Amazon Cooperation Treaty Organization (#00766)
- ♦ **ACTO** Asian Cellular Therapy Organization (#01372)
- ♦ Actors, Interpreting Artists Committee (no recent information)
- ♦ Act for Peace (internationally oriented national body)
- ♦ ACTR / see American Councils for International Education
- ♦ ACTR-ACCELS – American Councils for International Education (internationally oriented national body)
- ♦ Act Regarding Navigation and Economic Cooperation between the States of the Niger Basin (1963 treaty)

♦ ACTRiS 00104

Project Manager Finnish Meteorological Inst, PO Box 503, FI-00101 Helsinki, Finland. T. +358505728435.
URL: http://www.actris.eu/
History 2014. Designed; preparation phase started 2016. ACTRIS stands for *Aerosol, Clouds and Trace Gases Research Infrastructure*. **Aims** Provide a platform for researchers to combine their efforts more effectively; provide observational data of *aerosols*, *clouds* and trace *gases* openly to anyone who might want to use them. **Structure** Interim ACTRIS Council. **Activities** Research/documentation; events/meetings. **Events** *Meeting* 2020, *Meeting* 2020, *Meeting* Brussels (Belgium) 2020, *Meeting* Warsaw (Poland) 2019, *Meeting* Oslo (Norway) 2018. **Publications** *ACTRiS Newsletter*.
Members Research institutes and organizations in 20 countries:
Belgium, Bulgaria, Cyprus, Czechia, Denmark, Estonia, Finland, France, Germany, Greece, Ireland, Italy, Netherlands, Norway, Poland, Romania, Spain, Sweden, Switzerland, UK.
Associate members in 2 countries:
Austria, Portugal. [2021/XM8034/**F**]

- ♦ ACTSA – Action for Southern Africa (internationally oriented national body)
- ♦ ACTS – Africa Community Technical Service (internationally oriented national body)
- ♦ **ACTS** African Centre for Technology Studies (#00243)
- ♦ ACTS – Asia Center for Theological Studies and Mission (internationally oriented national body)
- ♦ **ACTS** Asian Crystallization Technology Society (#01415)
- ♦ **ACTSAU** Arab Council for the Training of Students of Arab Universities (#00933)
- ♦ ACTS International (internationally oriented national body)
- ♦ Acts of the International Telecommunication and Radio Conferences (1947 treaty)
- ♦ Acts for Peace / see World Without War Council
- ♦ ACTS University / see Asia Center for Theological Studies and Mission
- ♦ **ACTTCN** Autorité de coordination de transit et de transport du Corridor Nord (#17582)
- ♦ ACTT / see Northern Corridor Transit and Transport Coordination Authority (#17582)

♦ Actuarial Association of Europe (AAE) 00105

Association Actuarielle Européenne
Operations Manager Maison des Actuaires, Place du Samedi 1, 1000 Brussels, Belgium. T. +3222160121.
URL: http://actuary.eu/
History 1978. Former names and other names: *Groupe consultatif des associations d'actuaires des pays des Communautés européennes* – former; *European Actuarial Consultative Group* – former (2001 to 2014); *Groupe consultatif actuariel européen* – former (2001 to 2014). **Aims** Represent actuarial associations in Europe; provide advice and opinions to the various organizations of the European Union – Commission, Council of Ministers, European Parliament, EIOPA and their various committees – on actuarial issues in European legislation. **Structure** General Assembly (annual); Committees (5); Secretariat. **Languages** English, French. **Staff** 1.40 FTE, paid. **Finance** Sources: members' dues. **Activities** Advocacy/lobbying/activism; events/meetings; guidance/assistance/consulting. **Events** *Annual Meeting* Cologne (Germany) 2023, *European Congress of Actuaries* Madrid (Spain) 2022, *Annual Meeting* Rome (Italy) 2022, *European Congress of Actuaries* Madrid (Spain) 2021, *Annual Meeting* Oberkirch (Switzerland) 2021. **Publications** *The European Actuary*. Position papers; discussion papers; books.
Members National organizations. Full in 32 countries and territories:
Austria, Belgium, Bulgaria, Channel Is, Croatia, Cyprus, Czechia, Denmark, Estonia, Finland, France, Germany, Greece, Hungary, Iceland, Ireland, Italy, Latvia, Lithuania, Luxembourg, Netherlands, Norway, Poland, Portugal, Romania, Slovakia, Slovenia, Spain, Sweden, Switzerland, Türkiye, UK.
Observers in 3 countries:
Malta, Serbia, Ukraine. [2022.10.20/XE2540/**E**]

- ♦ ACTV – African Centre for Treatment and Rehabilitation of Torture Victims (internationally oriented national body)
- ♦ ACU – Academy of Cultural Heritages (unconfirmed)
- ♦ ACU / see Arab Chess Federation (#00919)
- ♦ **ACU** Asian Clearing Union (#01380)
- ♦ **ACU** Association of Commonwealth Universities, The (#02440)
- ♦ ACUC' / see IFCA International
- ♦ **ACUCA** Association of Christian Universities and Colleges in Asia (#02432)
- ♦ Acuerdo sobre buques de pasaje que prestan servicios especiales (1971 treaty)
- ♦ Acuerdo de Cartagena – Acuerdo de Integración Subregional Andina (1969 treaty)
- ♦ Acuerdo sobre compras del sector público (1979 treaty)
- ♦ Acuerdo sobre Facilitación del Comercio (2014 treaty)
- ♦ Acuerdo General sobre Aranceles Aduaneros y Comercio (inactive)
- ♦ Acuerdo para la implantación de objetos e caracter educativo, cientifico y cultural (1950 treaty)
- ♦ Acuerdo de Integración Subregional Andina (1969 treaty)
- ♦ Acuerdo interamericano de radiocomunicaciones, 1940 (1940 treaty)
- ♦ Acuerdo internacional del aceite de oliva y aceitunas, 1986 (1986 treaty)
- ♦ Acuerdo internacional del cacao, 1986 (1986 treaty)
- ♦ Acuerdo internacional del cacao, 1993 (1993 treaty)
- ♦ Acuerdo internacional del cacao, 2001 (2001 treaty)
- ♦ Acuerdo internacional del cacao, 2010 (2010 treaty)
- ♦ Acuerdo internacional sobre caucho natural (1987 treaty)
- ♦ Acuerdo internacional del estaño, 1981 (1981 treaty)
- ♦ Acuerdo internacional de yute y articulos de yute (1982 treaty)
- ♦ Acuerdo Latinoamericano sobre control de buques por el estado rector del puerto (1992 treaty)
- ♦ Acuerdo de Lima (unconfirmed)
- ♦ Acuerdo sobre medidas del estado rector del puerto destinadas a prevenir, desalentar y eliminar la pesca ilegal, no declarada y no reglamentada (2009 treaty)
- ♦ Acuerdo monetario centroamericano (1974 treaty)
- ♦ Acuerdo multifibras – Arreglo relativo al comercio internacional de textiles (1973 treaty)
- ♦ Acuerdo multilateral sobre la liberalización del transporte aereo internacional (2001 treaty)
- ♦ Acuerdo de Paris (2015 treaty)
- ♦ Acuerdo sobre privilegios e inmunidades de la Organización de los estados americanos (1949 treaty)
- ♦ Acuerdo sobre procedimientos para el tramite de licencias de importación (1979 treaty)
- ♦ Acuerdo sobre propiedad literaria y artistica (1911 treaty)
- ♦ Acuerdo por el que se establece una clasificación internacional de los elementos figurativos de las marcas (1973 treaty)
- ♦ Acuerdo Regional sobre el Acceso a la Información, la Participación Pública y el Acceso a la Justicia en Asuntos Ambientales en América Latina y el Caribe (2018 treaty)
- ♦ Acuerdo Regional de Cooperación para la Promoción de la Ciencia y Tecnologia Nucleares en América Latina y el Caribe (#18772)
- ♦ Acuerdo regional sobre movimiento transfronterizo de desechos peligrosos (1992 treaty)
- ♦ Acuerdo relativo al comercio de aeronaves civiles (1979 treaty)
- ♦ Acuerdo relativo a los obstaculos técnicos al comercio (1979 treaty)
- ♦ Acuerdo relativo al transito de los servicios aéreos internacionales (1944 treaty)
- ♦ Acuerdo rigiendo las actividades de los Estados sobre la Luna y demas cuerpos celestes (1979 treaty)
- ♦ Acuerdo sobre el salvamento de astronautas, el regreso de astronautas y la restitución de objetos lanzados en el espacio extra atmosférico (1968 treaty)
- ♦ Acuerdos generales de préstamos revisados (1962 treaty)
- ♦ Acuerdo sudamericano de radiocomunicaciones, 1935 (1935 treaty)
- ♦ Acuerdo sudamericano de radiocomunicaciones, 1937 (1937 treaty)
- ♦ Acuerdo sudamericano de radiocomunicaciones, 1940 (1940 treaty)
- ♦ Acuerdo de unión aduanera entre Sudafrica, Botswana, Lesotho y Swaziland (1910 treaty)
- ♦ Acuerdo voluntario de los armadores de buques tanque relativo a la responsabilidad originada por la contaminación por hidrocarburos (inactive)
- ♦ **ACUHIAM** Association of Catholic Universities and Higher Institutes of Africa and Madagascar (#02416)
- ♦ Acumen (internationally oriented national body)
- ♦ Acumen Fund / see Acumen
- ♦ **ACUNS** Academic Council on the United Nations System (#00020)
- ♦ ACUNS – Association of Canadian Universities for Northern Studies (internationally oriented national body)
- ♦ Acupuncture Without Borders (#00106)
- ♦ Acupuncture International Association (inactive)
- ♦ Acupuncture sans frontières / see Acupuncture sans frontières International (#00106)

♦ Acupuncture sans frontières International (ASF International) 00106

Acupuncture Without Borders (AWB) – Acupuntura para el Mundo – Agopuntura Senza Frontiere
Main Office 6 ave Dumas, 1206 Geneva, Switzerland. E-mail: contact@acupuncture-sfi.org.
URL: http://www.acupuncture-sfi.org/
History 23 Feb 1992, France. Chapters set up in Switzerland (1996), Belgium (2004), Pyrenees – France (2008), Canada (2008) and Spain (2008). International structure set up 20 Nov 2004, Geneva (Switzerland), and operational as of 9 Feb 2005. Former names and other names: *Acupuncture sans frontières (ASF)* – former. **Aims** Train acupuncture practitioners so that they can offer local people an efficient healing technique in addition to their existing healthcare practices, whether based on modern Western medicine or traditional medicine. **Structure** Committees (3): Ethics; Administrative; Pedagogic.
Members Chapters in 6 countries:
Belgium, Canada, China, France, Spain, Switzerland. [2021/XN4071/**F**]

♦ Acupuntura para el Mundo (#00106)
♦ **ACURIL** Association of Caribbean University, Research and Institutional Libraries (#02413)
♦ ACUS / see Atlantic Council

♦ Acute Leukemia Advocates Network (ALAN) 00107

Contact Leukemia Patient Advocates Foundation, POB 453, 3000 Bern 7, Switzerland. E-mail: info@acuteleuk.org.
URL: https://acuteleuk.org/

History 2017. **Aims** Change outcomes of patients with acute leukemias by strengthening patient advocacy in that area; build capacity to deliver tailored services to acute leukemia patients and carers on the national level, while joining forces between organizations on the policy and research level across countries. **Structure** Steering Committee. Hosted by *Leukemia Patient Advocates Foundation (LePAF)*. **Languages** English, French, German. **Activities** Advocacy/lobbying/activism; awareness raising; capacity building; networking/liaising; training/education. **Events** *Acute Leukemia Global Summit* 2021, *Drug Development* Bern (Switzerland) 2021, *Acute Leukemia Global Summit* Bern (Switzerland) 2020. **Publications** *Identifying differences in the quality of life of patients with acute leukemia: a global survey.* **Members** Organizations. Membership countries not specified. **NGO Relations** Member of (3): *European Cancer Organisation (ECO, #06432)*; *Project Harmony*; *Workgroup of European Cancer Patient Advocacy Networks (WECAN, #21054)*. [2022.05.04/AA0353/**F**]

♦ **ACUUS** Associated research Centres for the Urban Underground Space (#02420)
♦ **ACUUS** Association des Centres de recherche sur l'Utilisation Urbaine du Sous-sol (#02420)
♦ ACWAP – Australasian Council of Women and Policing (internationally oriented national body)
♦ ACWAY – A Common Word Among the Youth (unconfirmed)
♦ **ACWC** Asian Church Women's Conference (#01377)
♦ ACWECA – Association of Consecrated Women in Eastern and Central Africa (unconfirmed)
♦ **ACWL** Advisory Centre on WTO Law (#00138)
♦ **ACWO** ASEAN Confederation of Women's Organizations (#01159)
♦ ACWR – Centre for the World Religions, A (internationally oriented national body)
♦ ACWS – Asian Center for Women's Studies (internationally oriented national body)
♦ **ACWUA** Arab Countries Water Utilities Association (#00934)
♦ **ACWW** Associated Country Women of the World (#02338)
♦ ACYM / see América Cooperativa y Mutual (#00773)
♦ ADA / see ADA Microfinance
♦ ADAA – African Development Aid Association (internationally oriented national body)
♦ ADA – Africa Disability Alliance (unconfirmed)
♦ ADA – Americans for Democratic Action (internationally oriented national body)
♦ ADA – Arab Demographers' Association (no recent information)
♦ **ADA** Asia Development Alliance (#01266)
♦ ADA – Asia Diabolo Association (unconfirmed)
♦ ADA – Asian Dendrochronology Association (unconfirmed)
♦ **ADA** Asian Dermatological Association (#01421)
♦ ADA – Austrian Development Agency (internationally oriented national body)
♦ ADAC – African Development Assistance Consult (internationally oriented national body)

♦ Ada-Europe 00108

Pres Dept of Mathematics, Univ of Padua, Via Trieste 63, 35138 Padua PD, Italy. T. +39498271359. E-mail: president@ada-europe.org.
Vice-Pres c/o Offis Aubay Group, Rue Gatti de Gamond 145, 1180 Brussels, Belgium.
URL: http://www.ada-europe.org/

History Founded 1988. Registered in accordance with Belgian law. **Aims** Spread use and knowledge of Ada, the *computer language* named after Ada Lovelace, the first programmer; promote its introduction into academic and research establishments; represent European interests in Ada and Ada-related matters. **Structure** General Assembly; Board. **Languages** English, French. **Staff** Voluntary. **Finance** Members' dues. Donations. **Activities** Events/meetings. **Events** *International Conference on Reliable Software Technologies* Warsaw (Poland) 2019, *International Conference on Reliable Software Technologies* Lisbon (Portugal) 2018, *International Conference on Reliable Software Technologies* Vienna (Austria) 2017, *International Conference on Reliable Software Technologies* Pisa (Italy) 2016, *International Conference on Reliable Software Technologies* Madrid (Spain) 2015. **Publications** *Ada User Journal* (4 a year). *Rationale for Ada* (2012); *Reference Manual for Ada* (2012).
Members Ada national organizations and individuals (about 350) in 13 countries:
Austria, Belgium, Denmark, France, Germany, Italy, Norway, Poland, Portugal, Spain, Sweden, Switzerland, UK. [2017.10.25/XF1178/**F**]

♦ AdA / see International Association of Book and Paper Conservators (#11729)
♦ ADAIS – Association pour le développement agro-industriel du Sahel (internationally oriented national body)
♦ ADALC – Asociación de Directores de Academias Diplomaticas de América Latina y Estados del Caribe (no recent information)
♦ **ADALPI** Association Internationale pour le Développement de la Propriété Intellectuelle (#15056)
♦ ADAM – Association d'anthropologie méditerranéenne (internationally oriented national body)
♦ ADA Microfinance (internationally oriented national body)
♦ Adam Institute for Democracy and Peace (internationally oriented national body)

♦ Adaptation Fund (AF) 00109

Manager c/o Global Environment Facility, Mail stop N 7-700, 1818 H St NW, Washington DC 20433, USA. T. +12024587347.
URL: http://www.adaptation-fund.org/

History Established 29 Oct 2001, under *Kyoto Protocol to the United Nations Framework Convention on Climate Change (1997)* of *United Nations Framework Convention on Climate Change (UNFCCC, 1992)*. Adaptation Fund Board and other operational processes created, 3 Dec 2007. Legal capacity granted to Adaptation Fund Board by Federal Republic of Germany, 1 Feb 2011. **Aims** Finance concrete adaptation projects and programmes in *developing countries* that are parties to the Kyoto Protocol and are particularly vulnerable to the adverse effects of *climate change*. **Structure** Fund Board (AFB), comprising 16 members and 16 alternates; Adaptation Fund Board Secretariat. *International Bank for Reconstruction and Development (IBRD, #12317)* (World Bank) serves as trustee on an interim basis. Accreditation Panel. **Staff** 12.00 FTE, paid. **Finance** Financing mainly from sales of certified emission reductions. Other sources: contributions from governments, private sector and individuals. **Activities** Financial and/or material support; projects/programmes. **IGO Relations** Relevant treaty: *Kyoto Protocol to the United Nations Framework Convention on Climate Change (1997)*. Accredited by: *Green Climate Fund (GCF, #10714)*; *United Nations Framework Convention on Climate Change – Secretariat (UNFCCC, #20564)*. **NGO Relations** Member of: *International Aid Transparency Initiative (IATI, #11604)*. [2018/XJ7659/f/**F***]

♦ Adara Development 00110

CEO 300 Admiral Way, Ste 106, Edmonds WA 98020, USA. T. +14259675115. Fax +14259675439. E-mail: info@adaragroup.org.
Business Office Adara Advisors Pty Ltd, 1st Fl – 661 Darling Str, PO Box 887, Rozelle NSW 2039, Australia. T. +61293952800. Fax +61295555988.
URL: http://www.adaragroup.org/

History Set up 1998, Bermuda, as *The ISIS Foundation*. Current title adopted 2014. Collective known as *Adara Group*. Registered: as a charity in Bermuda, 1999; as a UK Charity, 2004 – 1098152 (under the name ADARA Development); in Nepal, 2006; in the US, 2011. Business office in Australia. **Aims** Improve health and education for women, children and communities in *need*. **Structure** Boards in Australia, Bermuda, UK, USA and Uganda. Advisors Board. Global Management Team. **Activities** Advocacy/lobbying/activism; healthcare; knowledge management/information dissemination. Active in: Nepal, Uganda. **NGO Relations** Member of: *Washington Global Health Alliance (WGHA)*. [2017/XM5945/f/**F**]

♦ Adara Group / see Adara Development (#00110)
♦ ADAR / see Association des Gestionnaires et Partenaires Africains de la Route (#02626)
♦ A and D – Architecture and Development (internationally oriented national body)
♦ ADASS – Astronomical Data Analysis Software & Systems (meeting series)
♦ **ADB** African Development Bank (#00283)
♦ **ADB** Asian Development Bank (#01422)
♦ **ADB Group** African Development Bank Group (#00284)
♦ **ADB Institute** Asian Development Bank Institute (#01423)
♦ ADBIS – European Conference on Advances in Databases and Information Systems (meeting series)
♦ ADC / see Development Bank of Latin America (#05055)
♦ ADCAM – Associação para o Desenvolvimento Coesivo da Amazônia (internationally oriented national body)
♦ ADC – American-Arab Anti-Discrimination Committee (internationally oriented national body)
♦ ADC – Applied Diamond Conference (meeting series)
♦ **ADC** Asian Dance Council (#01418)
♦ **ADC** Asian Draughts Confederation (#01432)
♦ ADC – Association of Diving Contractors International (internationally oriented national body)
♦ ADC Austria / see Hilfswerk International
♦ ADCC – Asia-Pacific Development and Communication Centre (internationally oriented national body)
♦ ADCCK – Association for the Development of Commonwealth Cultural Knowledge (inactive)
♦ **ADCE** Art Directors Club of Europe (#01115)
♦ ADCETE – Association for the Development and Coordination of European Touristic Exchanges (inactive)
♦ ADCLE – Asociación de Demócratas Cristianos Latinoamericanos Residentes en Europa (inactive)
♦ ADD / see ADD International
♦ **ADDE** Association des dépôts dentaires européens (#02466)
♦ ADDHMA – Association de défense des droits de l'homme et des libertés démocratiques dans le monde arabe (no recent information)

♦ Addiction and the Family International Network (AFINet) 00111

Sec address not obtained. E-mail: administrator@afinetwork.info.
URL: https://www.afinetwork.info/

History Feb 2014. Constitution adopted 1 Mar 2015. Registration: Charity Commission, No/ID: EW82750, Start date: 16 Nov 2017, England and Wales. **Aims** Promote, through research, practice and policy, the well-being of family members, friends and colleagues who are affected by, and/or concerned about another person's addiction. **Structure** Annual General Meeting; Trustees. **Activities** Events/meetings; politics/policy/regulatory; publishing activities; research/documentation; training/education. **Events** *Annual Conference* Helsinki (Finland) 2022, *Conference* 2021, *Conference* Rotterdam (Netherlands) 2020. **Publications** *AFINet Newsletter* (2 a year).
Members Over 450 members in 44 countries and territories:
Australia, Belgium, Brazil, Canada, Channel Is, China, Denmark, Egypt, England, Ethiopia, Finland, Germany, Greece, Guatemala, Hong Kong, India, Indonesia, Iran Islamic Rep, Ireland, Italy, Kenya, Luxembourg, Malaysia, Mexico, Morocco, Netherlands, New Zealand, Nigeria, Northern Ireland, Norway, Pakistan, Philippines, Scotland, Slovakia, South Africa, Spain, Sri Lanka, Sweden, Switzerland, Thailand, Türkiye, USA, Wales, Zimbabwe. [2022.06.14/AA1721/**F**]

♦ ADDIHAC – Agence de diffusion du droit international humanitaire en Afrique centrale (internationally oriented national body)
♦ ADD International (internationally oriented national body)
♦ Additional Act to the 1925 Agreement Concerning the International Deposit of Industrial Designs (1961 treaty)
♦ Additional Convention to the International Convention Signed at Rome on 23 Nov 1933 Concerning the Transport of Goods by Rail (1950 treaty)
♦ Additional Convention Relating to the Liability of the Railway for Death of and Personal Injury (1966 treaty)
♦ Additional Monetary Convention (1902 treaty)
♦ Additional Protocol to the Agreement on the Temporary Importation, Free of Duty, of Medical, Surgical and Laboratory Equipment for Use on Free Loan in Hospitals and other Medical Institutions for Purposes of Diagnosis or Treatment (1983 treaty)
♦ Additional Protocol to the American Convention on Human Rights in the Area of Economic, Social and Cultural Rights (1988 treaty)
♦ Additional Protocol to the Anti-doping Convention (2002 treaty)
♦ Additional Protocol to the Bilateral Agreements Relating to the Reciprocal Recognition of Driving Permits and Motorvehicle Registration Certificates (1956 treaty)
♦ Additional Protocol to the Convention of 31 January 1963 Supplementary to the Paris Convention of 29 July 1960 on Third Party Liability in the Field of Nuclear Energy (1964 treaty)
♦ Additional Protocol to the Convention Concerning Customs Facilities for Touring, Relating to the Importation of Tourist Publicity Documents and Material (1954 treaty)
♦ Additional Protocol to the Convention on the Contract for the International Carriage of Goods by Road (CMR) concerning the Electronic Consignment Note (2008 treaty)
♦ Additional Protocol to the Convention on Cybercrime, Concerning the Criminalisation of Acts of a Racist and Xenophobic Nature Committed through Computer Systems (2003 treaty)
♦ Additional Protocol to the Convention on Human Rights and Biomedicine, Concerning Biomedical Research (2005 treaty)
♦ Additional Protocol to the Convention on Human Rights and Biomedicine concerning Genetic Testing for Health Purposes (2008 treaty)
♦ Additional Protocol to the Convention on Human Rights and Biomedicine Concerning Transplantation of Organs and Tissues of Human Origin (2002 treaty)
♦ Additional Protocol to the Convention for the Protection of Human Rights and Dignity of the Human Being with Regard to the Application of Biology and Medicine, on the Prohibition of Cloning Human Beings (1998 treaty)
♦ Additional Protocol to the Convention for the Protection of Individuals with Regard to Automatic Processing of Personal Data, Regarding Supervisory Authorities and Transborder Data Flows (2001 treaty)
♦ Additional Protocol to the Convention on the Reduction of Cases of Multiple Nationality and Military Obligations in Cases of Multiple Nationality (1977 treaty)
♦ Additional Protocol to the Convention on the Régime of Navigable Waterways of International Concern (1921 treaty)
♦ Additional Protocol to the Convention on Third Party Liability in the Field of Nuclear Energy (1964 treaty)
♦ Additional Protocol to the Convention on the Transfer of Sentenced Persons (1997 treaty)
♦ Additional Protocol to the Council of Europe Convention on the Prevention of Terrorism (2015 treaty)
♦ Additional Protocol to the Criminal Law Convention on Corruption (2003 treaty)
♦ Additional Protocol to the EUROCONTROL International Convention Relating to Cooperation for the Safety of Air Navigation (1970 treaty)
♦ Additional Protocol to the European Agreement on the Exchanges of Blood-grouping Reagents (1983 treaty)
♦ Additional Protocol to the European Agreement on the Exchange of Therapeutic Substances of Human Origin (1983 treaty)
♦ Additional Protocol to the European Agreement on the Exchange of Tissue-typing Reagents (1976 treaty)
♦ Additional Protocol to the European Agreement on the Transmission of Applications for Legal Aid (2001 treaty)
♦ Additional Protocol to the European Charter of Local Self-Government on the right to participate in the affairs of a local authority (2009 treaty)
♦ Additional Protocol to the European Convention on Extradition (1975 treaty)
♦ Additional Protocol to the European Convention on Information on Foreign Law (1978 treaty)
♦ Additional Protocol to the European Convention on Mutual Assistance in Criminal Matters (1978 treaty)

- ♦ Additional Protocol to the European Convention for the Protection of Animals During International Transport (1979 treaty)
- ♦ Additional Protocol to the European Convention on State Immunity (1972 treaty)
- ♦ Additional Protocol to the European Outline Convention on Transfrontier Cooperation between Territorial Communities or Authorities (1995 treaty)
- ♦ Additional Protocol to the European Social Charter, 1988 (1988 treaty)
- ♦ Additional Protocol to the European Social Charter Providing for a System of Collective Complaints (1995 treaty)
- ♦ Additional Protocol to the General Convention of Inter-American Conciliation of 1929 (1933 treaty)
- ♦ Additional Protocol to the Inter-American Convention on Letters Rogatory (1979 treaty)
- ♦ Additional Protocol to the Inter-American Convention on the Taking of Evidence Abroad (1984 treaty)
- ♦ Additional Protocol to the Pan-American Sanitary Code, 1927 (1927 treaty)
- ♦ Additional Protocol to the Pan-American Sanitary Code, 1952 (1952 treaty)
- ♦ Additional Protocol to the Protocol to the European Agreement on the Protection of Television Broadcasts (1983 treaty)
- ♦ Additional Protocol to the Protocol to the European Agreement on the Protection of Television Broadcasts, 1974 (1974 treaty)
- ♦ Additional Protocol Relative to Non-intervention (1936 treaty)
- ♦ Additional Protocol to the Treaties on Private International Law (1940 treaty)
- ♦ Additional Protocol to the Treaties on Private International Law (1889 treaty)
- ♦ Additive Manufacturing Platform / see European Technology Platform in Additive Manufacturing (#08886)
- ♦ **ADEA** Association for the Development of Education in Africa (#02471)
- ♦ ADEA – Association des éducateurs à distance d'Afrique (no recent information)
- ♦ ADEALC / see Latin American and Caribbean Economics Association (#16274)
- ♦ **ADE** Association Européenne pour l'Etude de l'Alimentation et du Développement de l'Enfant (#02566)
- ♦ ADEC – Australasian Democratic Education Community (internationally oriented national body)
- ♦ ADECI – Association régionale pour le développement de la coopération industrielle internationale (internationally oriented national body)
- ♦ ADEC-NS – Agence pour le Développement Economique et Cultural Nord-Sud (internationally oriented national body)
- ♦ ADECRI – Agence pour le développement et la coordination des relations internationales (internationally oriented national body)
- ♦ **ADEE** Association for Dental Education in Europe (#02467)
- ♦ ADEFI – Asociación de Floristas Iberoamericanos (unconfirmed)
- ♦ **ADEG** Association déontologique européenne de graphologues (#02468)
- ♦ Adeia Azul Mundial (#21235)
- ♦ ADEKSO – International Power Engineering Association (inactive)
- ♦ ADELA – Atlantic Community Development Group for Latin America (inactive)
- ♦ **ADELF** Association des écrivains de langue française (#02481)
- ♦ **ADELF** Association des épidémiologistes de langue française (#02490)
- ♦ Ädelmetallbranchens Nordiska Samarbetskommitté (inactive)
- ♦ ADEO – African Development and Emergency Organization (internationally oriented national body)
- ♦ **ADEPA** Association ouest africaine pour le développement de la pêche artisanale (#20867)
- ♦ ADEPAC – Asociación del Desarrollo para America Central (no recent information)
- ♦ ADéPAT – Association pour le développement de la physique de l'atmosphère tropicale (no recent information)
- ♦ ADEPTA / see Association for the Development of International Exchanges in Agricultural and Agrifood Products and Techniques
- ♦ ADEPTA – Association pour le développement des échanges internationaux de produits et techniques agro-alimentaires (internationally oriented national body)
- ♦ **ADEPT** Africa-Europe Diaspora Development Platform (#00170)
- ♦ **ADERASA** Asociación de Entes Reguladores de Agua y Saneamiento de las Americas (#02124)
- ♦ Adeso / see African Development Solutions (#00287)
- ♦ **Adeso** African Development Solutions (#00287)
- ♦ ADESOL – Africa Development Solutions (internationally oriented national body)
- ♦ ADESPE – Association pour le développement de la science politique européenne (inactive)
- ♦ Adessium Foundation (internationally oriented national body)
- ♦ **ADEu** Assistance Dogs Europe (#02322)
- ♦ ADEVIA – Asociación de Editores para Deficientes Visuales de Ibero-América (inactive)
- ♦ ADFA – Australian Doctors for Africa (internationally oriented national body)
- ♦ ADFAED / see Abu Dhabi Fund for Development
- ♦ **ADF** African Democracy Forum (#00281)
- ♦ ADF – African Development Foundation (internationally oriented national body)
- ♦ **ADF** African Development Fund (#00285)
- ♦ ADF – America's Development Foundation (internationally oriented national body)
- ♦ **ADF** Arab Dental Federation (#00936)
- ♦ **ADF** ASEAN Development Fund (#01167)
- ♦ **ADF** ASEAN Disability Forum (#01168)
- ♦ **ADF** Asian Development Fund (#01425)
- ♦ **ADFIAP** Association of Development Financing Institutions in Asia and the Pacific (#02472)
- ♦ **ADFIMI** Association of National Development Finance Institutions in Member Countries of the Islamic Development Bank (#02817)

♦ ADF International 00112

Head Office Postfach 5, 1037 Vienna, Austria. T. +4319049555. E-mail: contact@adfinternational.org.
Contact 16 Old Queen Street, London, SW1H 9HP, UK.
URL: http://adfinternational.org/

History Name derives from USA organization *Alliance Defending Freedom.* Former names and other names: *Alliance Defending Freedom International* – alias. Registration: Companies House, No/ID: 09923116, Start date: 18 Dec 2015, England; Charity Commission, No/ID: 1173195, England and Wales; EU Transparency Register, No/ID: 69403354038-78, Start date: 20 Aug 2010. **Aims** Build alliances with lawyers and like-minded organizations, providing training, funding and advocacy. **Structure** Leadership Team; Advisory Council. Headquarters in Vienna (Austria). Offices in: Brussels (Belgium); Geneva (Switzerland); Strasbourg (France); London (UK); New York NY (USA); Washington DC (USA); India. **Activities** Advocacy/lobbying/activism; financial and/or material support; training/education. **Consultative Status** Consultative status granted from: *OAS (#17629).* **IGO Relations** Accredited by (1): *Organization for Security and Cooperation in Europe (OSCE, #17887).* Cooperates with (1): *European Court of Human Rights (#06855).* Participant in Fundamental Rights Platform of: *European Union Agency for Fundamental Rights (FRA, #08969).* **NGO Relations** Member of (1): *Forum of Catholic Inspired NGOs (#09905).* [2021.02.09/XM4208/**F**]

- ♦ **ADFIP** Association of Development Financing Institutions in the Pacific (#02473)
- ♦ ADG / see Democrat Union of Africa (#05036)

♦ ADHD-Europe 00113

Pres Rue Washington 40, 1050 Brussels, Belgium. E-mail: info@adhdeurope.eu – president@adhdeurope.eu.
URL: http://www.adhdeurope.eu/

History 2008. Registration: Banque-Carrefour des Entreprises, No/ID: 0810.982.059, Start date: 6 Apr 2009, Belgium. **Aims** Advance the rights of, and advocate on every level throughout Europe for people affected by *Attention Deficit Hyperactivity Disorder* (ADHD) and co-morbid conditions in order to help them reach their full potential. **Structure** Annual General Meeting; Board. **Languages** English. **Staff** Several voluntary. **Finance** Sources: members' dues; sale of publications. Annual budget: 4,000 EUR. **Activities** Advocacy/lobbying/activism; events/meetings. **Events** *Annual General Meeting* Brussels (Belgium) 2021, *Annual General Meeting* Helsinki (Finland) / Stockholm (Sweden) 2020, *Dyslexia, Dyscalculia Awareness Conference* Brussels (Belgium) 2016, *General Assembly* Brussels (Belgium) 2016, *International Conference* Athens (Greece) 2015. **Publications** *Treatment of ADHD in Europe* (2011) by Stephanie Clark; *Diagnosis and Treatment of ADHD in Europe* (2009) by Stephanie Clark.
Members Full in 22 countries and territories:
Belgium, Croatia, Cyprus, Denmark, Faeroe Is, Finland, France, Germany, Greece, Hungary, Iceland, Ireland, Italy, Luxembourg, Malta, Netherlands, Norway, Scotland, Slovenia, Spain, Sweden, UK.
IGO Relations Participant in Fundamental Rights Platform of *European Union Agency for Fundamental Rights (FRA, #08969).* **NGO Relations** Member of (6): *European Federation of Neurological Associations (EFNA, #07177); European Public Health Alliance (EPHA, #08297); Federation of European and International Associations Established in Belgium (FAIB, #09508); International Collaboration on ADHD and Substance Abuse (ICASA, #12635); Mental Health Europe (MHE, #16715); World Federation of ADHD (#21406).* [2021.06.08/XJ6180/**D**]

- ♦ **ADHILAC** Asociación de Historiadores Latinoamericanos y del Caribe (#02632)
- ♦ ADHILAC Internacional / see Association of Historians of Latin America and the Caribbean (#02632)
- ♦ **ADHO** Alliance of Digital Humanities Organizations (#00671)
- ♦ Ad Hoc Expert Group on the transition from institutional to community-based care / see European Expert Group on the transition from institutional to community-based care (#07014)
- ♦ Ad Hoc International Working Group on Contaminated Land / see International Committee on Contaminated Land (#12756)
- ♦ Ad Hoc Working Group on NGOs and Peacebuilding / see Canadian Peacebuilding Coordinating Committee
- ♦ **ADHS** Alcohol and Drugs History Society (#00623)
- ♦ Adiabatic Quantum Computing Conference (meeting series)
- ♦ **ADI** Académie diplomatique internationale (#00024)
- ♦ ADI – Academy of Dentistry International (internationally oriented national body)
- ♦ **ADI** African Development Institute (#00286)
- ♦ ADI – Aide au développement international (internationally oriented national body)
- ♦ **ADI** Alzheimer's Disease International (#00762)
- ♦ ADI – Animal Defenders International (internationally oriented national body)
- ♦ ADI – Asia Disability Institute (internationally oriented national body)
- ♦ ADI – Asian Dynamics Initiative (internationally oriented national body)
- ♦ **ADI** Assistance Dogs International (#02323)
- ♦ ADI – Australian Doctors International (internationally oriented national body)
- ♦ ADIC / see International Union for Intercultural and Interfaith Dialogue and Peace Education (#15783)
- ♦ **ADIC** International Union for Intercultural and Interfaith Dialogue and Peace Education (#15783)
- ♦ ADIE – Association pour le développement de l'information environnementale (inactive)
- ♦ ADIF – Asia Dyestuff Industry Federation (unconfirmed)
- ♦ ADIFLOR – Association pour la diffusion internationale francophone de livres, ouvrages et revues (internationally oriented national body)
- ♦ ADIN – Africa Development Interchange Network (internationally oriented national body)
- ♦ ADIPA – Association of Development Research and Training Institutes of Asia and the Pacific (inactive)
- ♦ ADIPS – Australasian Diabetes in Pregnancy Society (internationally oriented national body)
- ♦ ADIRH – Association internationale des diplômés de la restauration et de l'hôtellerie (no recent information)
- ♦ ADJC – Arme Dienstmägde Jesu Christi (religious order)

♦ Adjudicating Committee for the Nordic Council's Literature Prize .. 00114

Comité du Prix de littérature du Conseil nordique – Bedömningskommittén för Nordiska Rådets Litteraturpris – Pohjoismaiden Neuvoston Kirjallisuuspalkinnon Arvostelulautakunta

Secretariat Nordens hus, Sturlugötu 5, 101 Reykjavik, Iceland. T. +3545517030. Fax +3545526476.
URL: http://www.norden.org/en/nordic-council/nordic-council-prizes/

History 1961, when statutes and procedures were decided by the Nordic Governments in the framework of *Nordic Council (NC, #17256).* A cooperation body of *Nordic Council of Ministers (NCM, #17260)* within the framework of *Nordic Cultural Cooperation (1971).* **Aims** Increase interest in Nordic literature and establish a Nordic *book market.* **Structure** Committee of 10 members, 2 from each of the 5 Nordic countries; Auxiliary Committee Members are co-opted from autonomous regions. **Finance** Budget (annual): Danish Kr 1,000,000. **Activities** Awards/prizes/competitions.
Members Representatives of the 5 Nordic countries:
Denmark, Finland, Iceland, Norway, Sweden. [2014.12.05/XE8199/**E***]

- ♦ **ADLaF** Association des diatomistes de langue française (#02475)
- ♦ ADL – Anti-Defamation League of B'nai B'rith (internationally oriented national body)
- ♦ ADL Braun Holocaust Institute (internationally oriented national body)
- ♦ ADLF – Association des diététiciens de langue française (inactive)
- ♦ **ADLSN** African Digital Library Support Network (#00289)
- ♦ Ad Lucem – Association catholique de coopération internationale (inactive)
- ♦ **ADM** Academy of Dental Materials (#00033)
- ♦ ADMD – International Symposium on Advanced Display Materials and Devices (meeting series)
- ♦ ADME / see Association of Destination Management Executives International
- ♦ **ADMEE-Europe** Association pour le développement des méthodologies d'évaluation en éducation (#02474)
- ♦ ADMEI – Association of Destination Management Executives International (internationally oriented national body)
- ♦ Administración Conjunta de la Cultura y las Artes Turcas / see International Organization of Turkic Culture (#14482)
- ♦ Administration conjointe de la culture et des arts turcs / see International Organization of Turkic Culture (#14482)
- ♦ Administration and Cost of Elections / see ACE Electoral Knowledge Network (#00066)
- ♦ Administration des Nations Unies pour le secours et la reconstruction (inactive)
- ♦ Administration postale des Nations Unies (#20613)
- ♦ Administration des postes et télécommunications de l'Afrique de l'Est (inactive)
- ♦ Administration transitoire des Nations Unies au Timor oriental (inactive)

♦ Administration universitaire francophone et européenne en médecine et odontologie (AUFEMO) 00115

Association of French-Speaking and European University Administrations in Medicine and Odontology

Pres Fac de médecine, Chargé de mission auprès du Doyen, 4 rue Kirschleger, 67085 Strasbourg CEDEX, France. T. +33368853480 – +33390243496. Fax +33368853467 – +33368853468.
URL: http://udsmed.u-strasbg.fr/aufemo/

History Feb 1982, as *Association of Secretaries General of French-Speaking Faculties of Medicine and Odontology – Association des secrétaires généraux des facultés de médecine et d'odontologie francophones (ASGFMOF).* Current title adopted 1988. Registered in accordance with French law. **Aims** Bring together secretaries-general, heads of administrative services, administrative directors and those responsible for administration in faculties of medicine and dental surgery in France, French-speaking countries and countries of the European Community; understand and solve common administrative problems met with in day-to-day management; promote better understanding of medical and odontological training in French-speaking and European countries. **Structure** Bureau. **Languages** French. **Finance** Members' dues. **Activities** Events/meetings. **Events** *International housing summit* Rotterdam (Netherlands) 2011, *Meeting* London (UK) / Lille (France) 1995. **Publications** *La Chronique de l'AUFEMO* (8 a year); *Annuaire de l'Aufemo.*
Members Representatives of faculties (103) in 24 countries and territories:
Albania, Algeria, Belgium, Benin, Burundi, Canada, China, France, French Antilles, Germany, Laos, Lebanon, Luxembourg, Madagascar, Mali, Morocco, Netherlands, Portugal, Réunion, Senegal, Switzerland, Tunisia, UK, Vietnam.

Corresponding members – French and Belgian national bodies and 4 organizations listed in this Yearbook: *Association for Medical Education in Europe (AMEE, #02797); Conférence internationale des doyens des facultés de chirurgie dentaire d'expression totalement ou partiellement française (CIDCDF, #04615); Conférence internationale des doyens des facultés de médecine d'expression française (CIDMEF, #04616); European Association for International Education (EAIE, #06092).*
IGO Relations *TEMPUS IV (inactive).* [2016.06.23/XD2723/y/**D**]

♦ Administrative Centre of Social Security for Rhine Boatmen 00116

Centre administratif de la sécurité sociale pour les bateliers rhénans – Zentrale Verwaltungsstelle für die Soziale Sicherheit der Rheinschiffer

Sec CCNR, Palais du Rhin, 2 place de la République, 67082 Strasbourg CEDEX, France. T. +33388522010. Fax +33388321072. E-mail: ccnr@ccr-zkr.org.
URL: http://www.ccr-zkr.org/

History 27 Jul 1950, Paris (France). Established as *Centre administratif permanent pour la sécurité sociale des bateliers rhénans*, by virtue of Agreements signed at tripartite conference called by *ILO (#11123)*. Entered into force in 1953; amended 1961 and subsequently, the most recent amendment being 1979, entered into force 1 Dec 1987. For this application an "Administrative Arrangement" was also taken and is currently in force. Standing Board set up under Art 28 of 1950 Agreement. Art 71 of 1979 Agreement aims at issuing official statements on any question of interpretation or application of the Agreement and settling individual situations in close cooperation with national executive institutions. Agreement partly overlapped by Community law and especially regulation 883/2004 from *European Parliament (EP, #08146)* and *Council of Europe (CE, #04881)* of 29 apr 2004, on the coordination of social security systems. **Aims** Interpret the Agreement; facilitate its application by helping interested parties, notably Rhine boatmen and their families, with a view to the practical settlement of individual situations, and negotiating with competent bodies; act as a forum for discussion over the development of social security regulations for inland navigation boatmen. **Structure** Membership limited to the Contracting States; Permanent Secretariat, managed by Secretariat of *Central Commission for the Navigation of the Rhine (CCNR, #03687)*. **Languages** Dutch, French, German. **Staff** 1.00 FTE, paid. **Finance** Contributions from Member States. Annual budget: euro 45,000. **Activities** Advocacy/lobbying/activism. **Events** *Intergovernmental Conference* Bucharest (Romania) 1995, *Intergovernmental conference* Strasbourg (France) 1993, *Governmental conference / Intergovernmental Conference* Vienna (Austria) 1991.
Members Governments of 6 countries:
Belgium, France, Germany, Luxembourg, Netherlands, Switzerland.
Observer:
Liechtenstein.
IGO Relations *Central Commission for the Navigation of the Rhine (CCNR, #03687); European Commission (EC, #06633).* [2022/XD0007/**E***]

♦ Administrative Committee on Coordination / see United Nations System Chief Executives Board for Coordination (#20636)
♦ Administrative Council of the Eurasian Patent Organization / see Eurasian Patent Organization (#05613)

♦ Administrative Hierarchy of the Roman Catholic Church 00117

Address not obtained.
URL: http://www.vatican.va/

Structure *'Hierarchy of the Roman Catholic Church'*:
'Hierarchy of Order' is the orderly arrangement of ranks and orders of the clergy in one apostolic body to carry out the sacramental and pastoral ministry of the Church. Comprises: His Holiness, the Pope, Supreme Pastor of the Roman Catholic Church; and the Patriarchs, Archbishops, bishops, priests and deacons. *'Hierarchy of Jurisdiction'*, consisting of the Pope and bishops by divine law and other Church officials by ecclesiastical institution and mandate; has authority to govern and direct the faithful for spiritual ends. Cardinals, now always bishops, number about 150. They serve as the chief counsellors to the Pope. The Supreme Pastor is further assisted by the *Roman Curia – Curie romaine*, which consists of:
(a) Office of the Pope, including the Secretariat of State or the Papal Secretariat, within which is the Section for Relations with States, which replaced the Council for the Public Affairs of the Church. The Council of Cardinals and Bishops – *Consiglio di Cardinali e Vescovi*, previously part of the Council for the Public Affairs of the Church, is currently part of the Section for Relations with States.
(b) Office of the Sacred Congregations (9):
- *Congregation for the Doctrine of the Faith (#04669);*
- *Congregation for the Oriental Churches (CO, #04672)* – which includes *Riunione delle Opere per l'Aiuto alle Chiese Orientali (ROACO, see: #04672);*
- *Congregation for Bishops (#04664);*
- *Congregation for Divine Worship and the Discipline of the Sacraments (#04668);*
- *Congregation for the Causes of Saints (#04666);*
- *Congregation for the Clergy (#04667);*
- *Congregation for Institutes of Consecrated Life and Societies of Apostolic Life (CICSAL, #04671);*
- *Congregation for Catholic Education – for Seminaries and Educational Institutions (CEC, #04665);*
- *Congregation for the Evangelization of Peoples (CEP, #04670);*

(c) Pontifical Councils:
- *Pontifical Council for Culture (#18443)*, also referred to as *Consilium Pontificium de Cultura*, a fusion of a previous Pontifical Council of the same name, with *Pontificium Concilium pro Dialogo cum Non Credentibus (PCDNC, inactive)*, the latter previously *Secretariatus pro Non Credentibus;*
- *Pontifical Council for the Laity (inactive);*
- *Pontifical Council for Promoting Christian Unity (PCPCU, #18446)*, previously *Secretariat for Promoting Christian Unity;*
- *Pontifical Council for Legislative Texts (#18445);*
- *Pontifical Council for Interreligious Dialogue (PCID, #18444)*, previously *Secretariat for Non-Christian Religions;*
- *Pontifical Council for Pastoral Health Care (inactive);*
- *Pontifical Council 'Cor Unum' (inactive);*
- *Pontificium Consilium pro Familia (PCF, inactive);*
- *Pontifical Council for the Pastoral Care of Migrants and Itinerant People (inactive);*
- *Pontifical Council for Justice and Peace (inactive);*
- *Pontifical Council for Social Communications (#18447).*

(d) Tribunals (3).
- Apostolic Penitentiary;
- Supreme Tribunal of the Apostolic Signature;
- Tribunal of the Rota Romana.

(e) Pontifical Commissions (6):
- *Pontifical Commission for Latin America (#18440);*
- *Pontifical Commission for the Cultural Patrimony of the Church (#18438);*
- *Pontifical Commission "Ecclesia Dei" (#18439);*
- *Pontifical Commission for Sacred Archeology (#18441);*
- *Pontifical Biblical Commission (#18436);*
- *International Theological Commission (#15684).*

(f) Other organizations include -
- Academies (7):
  - *Pontifical Academy Cultorum Martyrum (#18430);*
  - *Illustrious Pontifical Academy of Fine Arts and Letters of the Virtuosi of the Pantheon (#11121);*
  - *Pontifical Academy of the Immaculate Conception (#18431);*
  - *Pontifical Academy of St Thomas Aquinas (#18435);*
  - *Pontifical Theological Academy (#18452);*
  - *Pontifical Academy of Sciences (#18433);*
  - *Pontifical Academy of Social Sciences (#18434);*
  - *Pontifical Academy for Life (#18432).*
- Secret archives of the Vatican;
- Vatican Apostolic Library;
- Central Statistical Office of the Church;
- Central Office for Work;
- Vatican Television Centre;
- Apostolic Chamber;
- Swiss Guard;
- *Institut pour les oeuvres de religion;*
- Office of Liturgical Celebrations of the Sovereign Pontiff;
- Prefecture of the Pontifical Household;
- Prefecture for Economic Affairs of the Holy See;
- *Centesimus Annus Pro Pontifice Foundation (CAPP, #03654);*
- *Peregrinatio ad Petri Sedem (PAPS, #18309);*
- *Radio Vaticana – Vatican News;*
- Secretariat General of *Synod of Bishops (#20083);*
- Fondo Assistenza Sanitaria, the social security system of Vatican City and Holy See employees.

The bishops, some bearing the title of Patriarch or Archbishop, are united with the Supreme Pastor in the government of the whole Church. When assigned to particular sees, they are individually responsible for the teaching, sanctification and governance of their particular jurisdictions of the Church. The Synod of Bishops, directly responsible to the Pope, acts as a system for communicating on questions of importance between the Pope and the bishops and among the bishops themselves.
The Papal territorial possessions are called the State of Vatican City, situated within the city of Rome (Italy) and occupying 108.7 acres. It is the smallest sovereign state in the world. Papal authority is recognized as supreme by virtue of a Concordat reached with the Italian State and ratified 7 Jun 1929. Included in Vatican City are the Vatican Palace, various museums, art galleries, libraries, apartments, offices, a post office and St Peter's Basilica.
The term *Holy See* stands for the central authority of the Church, which transcends, although includes, the sovereign State of Vatican City. Thus, the Holy See represents a world wide community and not only the citizens of Vatican City. Since the Holy See does not have the political, commercial, strategic interests of other countries, the focus of all its initiatives is always the "human person", its dignity, rights and duties. In keeping with this principle, the Holy See is mainly concerned with issues concerning human rights, justice, religious freedom, development and peace; it attempts to present, always respectfully but without fear, the principles of the Gospel.
Events *International Conference on the Religions and the Sustainable Development Goals (SDGs)* Vatican City (Vatican) 2019, *World Meeting of Families* Dublin (Ireland) 2018, *World Youth Day* Vatican 2018, *Conference on Governing a Common Good* Vatican City (Vatican) 2018, *World Youth Day* Vatican 2017. **IGO Relations** *United Nations (UN, #20515)*: The Holy See maintains a 'Permanent Observer Mission of the Holy See to the United Nations'. The status of 'observer state' ensures total neutrality as regards political issues. Although the Holy See does not cast a vote, it can and does make statements during the discussion of any item before the different Committees; and on special occasions it may address the General Assembly. *'Editor's Note'*: Although not disagreeing with the details as mentioned above, the Roman Catholic Church has strong reservations as to the inclusion of this entry in the Yearbook of International Organizations. We therefore point out that the Hierarchy as described refers only to the administration of the Church and not to the existence of the Church as such. [2010/XF8042/**F**]

♦ Administrative Tribunal of the International Bank of Reconstruction and Development, International Development Association and International Finance Corporation / see World Bank Administrative Tribunal (#21216)

♦ Administrative Tribunal of the International Labour Organization (ILO Tribunal) 00118

Tribunal administratif de l'Organisation internationale du travail (TAOIT)

Registrar ILO, Route des Morillons 4, 1211 Geneva 22, Switzerland. T. +41227997926 – +41227997928. Fax +41227998737. E-mail: trib@ilo.org.
URL: http://www.ilo.org/public/english/tribunal/

History 9 Oct 1946, Geneva (Switzerland), on adoption of Statute, as successor to *Administrative Tribunal of the League of Nations (inactive)*. Functions within *ILO (#11123)*. Statute amended: 1949; 1986; 1992; 1998; 2008; 2016. Rules of Court amended: 1953; 1957; 1972; 1984; 1991; 1993; 2011; 2014. **Aims** Hear *disputes* between approved organizations and their present or former *staff* members. **Structure** President, Vice-President. Tribunal comprising 7 judges, all of different nationalities, appointed by the International Labour Conference for renewable 3-year terms; 3 or, exceptionally, 5 or all 7 judges may sit in each case. Holds 2 sessions a year. **Languages** English, French. **Staff** 20.00 FTE, paid. **Finance** Through ILO regular budget. Annual cost paid by all organizations who recognized its jurisdiction; session costs paid by organizations concerned with the judgments of that session. **Events** *Session* Geneva (Switzerland) 2013. **Publications** *Judgments* – covering 40th (1978) and following sessions. Judgments delivered at earlier sessions were published in the ILO Official Bulletin. **Information Services** *Triblex* – database.
IGO Relations The jurisdiction of the Administrative Tribunal has been recognized by the following organizations:
- *Bioversity International (#03262);*
- *Bureau international des poids et mesures (BIPM, #03367);*
- *Centre technique de coopération agricole et rurale (CTA, inactive);*
- *EFTA (#05391);*
- *EFTA Court (#05390);*
- *EFTA Surveillance Authority (ESA, #05392);*
- *Energy Charter Conference;*
- *European and Mediterranean Plant Protection Organization (EPPO, #07773);*
- *European Molecular Biology Laboratory (EMBL, #07813);*
- *EUROCONTROL (#05667);*
- *European Organization for Astronomical Research in the Southern hemisphere (ESO, #08106);*
- *European Organization for Nuclear Research (CERN, #08108);*
- *European Patent Office (EPO, #08166)* of the European Patent Organization;
- *European Telecommunications Satellite Organization (EUTELSAT IGO, #08896);*
- *FAO (#09260)* (including *World Food Programme (WFP, #21510)*);
- *Global Fund to Fight AIDS, Tuberculosis and Malaria (Global Fund, #10383);*
- *ILO (#11123);*
- *International Atomic Energy Agency (IAEA, #12294);*
- *International Centre for Genetic Engineering and Biotechnology (ICGEB, #12494);*
- *International Centre for the Study of the Preservation and Restoration of Cultural Property (ICCROM, #12521);*
- *International Criminal Court (ICC, #13108);*
- *International Criminal Police Organization – INTERPOL (ICPO-INTERPOL, #13110);*
- *International Fund for Agricultural Development (IFAD, #13692);*
- *International Hydrographic Organization (IHO, #13825);*
- *International Institute for Democracy and Electoral Assistance (International IDEA, #13872);*
- *International Olive Council (IOC, #14405);*
- *International Organisation for the Development of Fisheries and Aquaculture in Europe (EUROFISH, #14427);*
- *International Organization of Legal Metrology (#14451);*
- *International Organization for Migration (IOM, #14454);*
- *International Organisation of Vine and Wine (OIV, #14435);*
- *International Telecommunication Union (ITU, #15673);*
- *International Training Centre of the ILO (ITC, #15717);*
- *ISSN International Centre (ISSNIC, #16069);*
- *ITER International Fusion Energy Organization (ITER Organization, #16072);*
- *OIE – World Organisation for Animal Health (#17703)* (International Office of Epizootics);
- *Organisation for the Prohibition of Chemical Weapons (OPCW, #17823);*
- *Pan American Health Organization (PAHO, #18108);*
- *Preparatory Commission for the Comprehensive Nuclear-Test-Ban Treaty Organization (CTBTO, #18482);*
- *South Centre (#19753);*
- *UNESCO (#20322);*
- *UNIDO (#20336);*
- *Union internationale pour la protection des obtentions végétales (UPOV, #20436);*
- *Universal Postal Union (UPU, #20682);*
- *WHO (#20950);*
- *World Customs Organization (WCO, #21350);*
- *World Intellectual Property Organization (WIPO, #21593);*
- *World Tourism Organization (UNWTO, #21861);*
- *World Trade Organization (WTO, #21864).*

NGO Relations Also competent in case of: *International Federation of Red Cross and Red Crescent Societies (#13526); Inter-Parliamentary Union (IPU, #15961).* [2018.09.11/XF4460/**F***]

♦ Administrative Tribunal of the League of Nations (inactive)

♦ Administrative Tribunal of the Organisation for Economic Co-operation and Development 00119

Tribunal administratif de l'Organisation de coopération et de développement économiques

Contact c/o OCDE, 2 rue André Pascal, 75775 Paris CEDEX 16, France. T. +33145248200. E-mail: administrative.tribunal@oecd.org.

URL: http://www.oecd.org/administrativetribunal/

History Dec 1991, as an internal organ of *OECD (#17693)*. Works in the framework of: regulations applying to staff, former officials, auxiliary staff and employees and to Council experts and consultants (Resolution of the Council adopted 12 Dec 1991); rules of procedure adopted by the Tribunal 20 Jan 1992. Replaces *Appeals Board of the Organisation for Economic Cooperation and Development (inactive)*. **Aims** As a genuine administrative tribunal, issue binding judgements on legal grounds in individual disputes arising from decisions by the Secretary-General of OECD which officials, former officials or duly qualified claimants consider as prejudicial to themselves. **Structure** Chairman, 2 judges of different nationalities and 3 deputies appointed by the Council and not on the staff of OECD (for 3 years); Registrar; Deputy Registrar. **Languages** English, French. [2018/XF5226/**F***]

- ♦ Administrative Tribunal of the Organization of American States (see: #17629)
- ♦ Administrative Tribunal of UNIDROIT (see: #13934)
- ♦ Administrative Tribunal of the United Nations (inactive)
- ♦ ADNA – Advocacy Network for Africa (internationally oriented national body)
- ♦ **ADN** Asia Democracy Network (#01265)
- ♦ **ADNDRC** Asian Domain Name Dispute Resolution Centre (#01429)
- ♦ ADN / see Fédération Internationale de la Diaspora Afar (#09626)
- ♦ **ADO** Asian Dance Organisers (#01419)
- ♦ Adoratrice del Sangue di Cristo (religious order)
- ♦ Adoratrices du Sang du Christ (religious order)
- ♦ Adorers of the Blood of Christ (religious order)
- ♦ Adorno Fathers – Clerics Regular Minor (religious order)
- ♦ ADP – African Development Programme (internationally oriented national body)
- ♦ ADPAI / see Asian Local Search and Media Association (#01531)
- ♦ ADPAN – Anti-Death Penalty Asia Network (unconfirmed)
- ♦ AD Partners – Avoided Deforestation Partners (internationally oriented national body)
- ♦ ADPC – African Diaspora Policy Centre (internationally oriented national body)
- ♦ **ADPC** Asian Disaster Preparedness Center (#01426)
- ♦ AD/PD – International Conference on Alzheimer's and Parkinson's Diseases (meeting series)
- ♦ ADPH – Association africaine pour le développement du palmier à huile (no recent information)
- ♦ **ADRA** Adventist Development and Relief Agency International (#00131)
- ♦ ADRAI / see Louvain Coopération
- ♦ ADRAO / see Africa Rice Center (#00518)
- ♦ **ADRC** Asian Disaster Reduction Center (#01427)
- ♦ ADR – European Agreement Concerning the International Carriage of Dangerous Goods by Road (1957 treaty)
- ♦ ADRF – Africa Asia Development Relief Foundation (internationally oriented national body)
- ♦ Adrian Dominican Sisters – Dominican Sisters of the Congregation of the Most Holy Rosary (religious order)
- ♦ Adriano Olivetti Foundation (internationally oriented national body)
- ♦ Adriatic Euroregion / see Adriatic Ionian Euroregion (#00120)

♦ Adriatic Ionian Euroregion (AIE) 00120

Secretariat Via Genova 11, 86100 Campobasso CB, Italy. T. +39874314342. Fax +39874437348. E-mail: secretariat@adriaticionianeuroregion.eu.

Registered Office Flanaticka 29, HR-52100 Pula, Croatia.

URL: http://www.adriaticionianeuroregion.eu/

History 30 Jun 2006, Pula (Croatia). Previously also referred to as *Adriatic Euroregion (AE)*. Current title adopted 15 Jan 2013, during 8th General Assembly. **Aims** Form an area of peace, stability and cooperation; protect *cultural heritage* and the environment; stimulate sustainable economic development, particularly in the area of *tourism*; work towards solutions in the fields of transport and infrastructure. **Structure** General Assembly; Executive Committee; Presidency; Thematic Commissions (7); Secretariat. **Languages** English. **Staff** 5.00 FTE, paid. **Finance** Members' dues. **Events** *General Assembly* Mostar (Bosnia-Herzegovina) 2019, *General Assembly* Termoli (Italy) 2018, *General Assembly* Dubrovnik (Croatia) 2017, *Extraordinary General Assembly* Pula (Croatia) 2016, *General Assembly* Brussels (Belgium) 2015. **Publications** Brochures.

Members Regional and local authorities (29) in 6 countries:

Albania, Bosnia-Herzegovina, Croatia, Greece, Italy, Montenegro.

IGO Relations *Congress of Local and Regional Authorities of the Council of Europe (#04677)*. [2019.02.13/XM2967/**D**]

♦ Adriatic and Ionian Initiative (AII) 00121

Permanent Secretariat Via della Cittadella snc, 60121 Ancona AN, Italy. T. +39712073715. Fax +39712076976. E-mail: aii-ps@aii-ps.org.

URL: http://www.aii-ps.org/

History Presented by the Italian Government, Oct 1999, Tampere (Finland). Established May 2000, Ancona (Italy), at Summit on Development and Security on the Adriatic and Ionian Seas, when 'Ancona Declaration' was signed by Heads of States of Governments of Italy, Albania, Bosnia-Herzegovina, Croatia, Greece and Slovenia, in the presence of the President of *European Commission (EC, #06633)*. **Aims** Strengthen regional *cooperation* so as to promote political and economic *stability*, thus creating a solid base for the process of European integration. **Structure** Council of Foreign Ministers (Adriatic-Ionian Council). Rotating Chairmanship. Permanent Secretariat.

Members Governments of 8 countries:

Albania, Bosnia-Herzegovina, Croatia, Greece, Italy, Montenegro, Serbia, Slovenia. [2021/XM4518/**F***]

♦ Adriatic Region Employers' Centre (AREC) 00122

Contact c/o IOE, Chemin de Joinville 26, PO Box 68, Cointrin, 1216 Geneva, Switzerland.

History under the auspices of *International Organisation of Employers (IOE, #14428)*, with initial support of *Swiss Agency for Development and Cooperation (SDC)*. Statutes adopted 27 Mar 2008. **Aims** Promote projects, cooperation and exchange of views and knowledge between partners in the region.

Members Full in 6 countries:

Albania, Bosnia-Herzegovina, Croatia, Montenegro, North Macedonia, Serbia.

IGO Relations *Regional Cooperation Council (RCC, #18773)*. [2011/XJ2473/**E**]

♦ Adriatic Society of Pathology (ASP) 00123

Contact c/o Ist Anatomia Patologica, Ospedale Maggiore, Via della Pietà 2/2, 34100 Trieste TS, Italy. T. +39407762236. E-mail: marina.delvecchio73@gmail.com.

Events *Meeting* Neum (Bosnia-Herzegovina) 2017, *Meeting* Grottammare (Italy) 2013, *Meeting* Duino (Italy) 2011, *Meeting* Dubrovnik (Croatia) 2008, *Meeting* Grottammare (Italy) 2007. [2019/XN5175/**D**]

♦ Adriatic Vascular Ultrasound Society (AVUS) 00124

Contact Ist Clinica Medica Generale, Universita di Firenze, Viale Morgagni 85, 50134 Florence FI, Italy. T. +39554277679. Fax +39554277608.

Vice-Pres Dept of Diagnostic Radiology, Univ Hosp Dubrava, Avenija G Suska 6, HR-10000 Zagreb, Croatia. T. +38512903669. Fax +38512903255. E-mail: rbobinac@kbd.hr.

History 2004, by Sergio Castellani, Boris Brkljacic and Sasa Rainer. **Events** *Adriatic Vascular Ultrasound and Imaging Symposium* 2018, *Meeting* Lovran (Croatia) 2016, *Meeting* Opatija (Croatia) 2014, *Annual meeting* Montecatini Terme (Italy) 2010, *Joint meeting* Opatija (Croatia) 2009. **NGO Relations** EUROSON School of *European Federation of Societies for Ultrasound in Medicine and Biology (EFSUMB, #07217)*. [2016/XJ1506/**D**]

- ♦ **ADRRN** Asian Disaster Reduction and Response Network (#01428)
- ♦ ADSA / see Australasian Association for Theatre, Drama and Performance Studies
- ♦ **ADSE** American Dental Society of Europe (#00779)
- ♦ ADSE / see Society for the Advancement of Socio-Economics (#19516)
- ♦ **ADSF** Asian Dance Sport Federation (#01420)
- ♦ ADSGM – Association of Deans of Southeast Asian Graduate Schools of Management (no recent information)
- ♦ ADTC – Asian Development Technology Centre (internationally oriented national body)
- ♦ ADTEL – Association for Development of Teaching, Education and Learning (internationally oriented national body)
- ♦ ADU – Americas Democrat Union (no recent information)
- ♦ Adult Children of Alcoholics – World Service Organization (internationally oriented national body)

♦ Adults Learning Mathematics: International Research Forum (ALM) 00125

Contact address not obtained. E-mail: info@alm-online.net.

URL: http://www.alm-online.net/

History Founded 1992. **Structure** Annual General Meeting; Trustees. **Finance** Members' dues. **Activities** Events/meetings. **Events** *Conference* London (UK) 2018. **Publications** *ALM International Journal*. Conference proceedings. **Members** Full (60) in about 15 countries. Membership countries not specified. [2020.03.17/XM7978/**F**]

♦ Advance Care Planning International (ACP-i) 00126

Internationale Gesellschaft für Behandlung im Voraus Planen und Betreuung am Lebensende

Registered Office c/o Würdezentrum, Geleitsstr 14, 60599 Frankfurt-Main, Germany. E-mail: office@acp-i.org.

URL: http://www.acp-i.org/

History Apr 2010, Melbourne, VIC (Australia). Founded at inaugural conference. Officially launched Jun 2011, London (UK). Former names and other names: *International Society of Advance Care Planning and End of Life Care (ACPEL)* – former (Apr 2010); *ACPEL Society* – alias. Registration: Germany. **Aims** Promote universal access to quality advance care planning; promote excellence in care for people near the end of life; promote the provision of physical, psycho-emotional and spiritual care in the context of advance care planning and end of life care. **Structure** Steering Committee, comprising President and 4 members. **Events** *International ACP-I Conference* Singapore (Singapore) 2023, *Annual Conference* Singapore (Singapore) 2022, *International ACP-I Digital Exchange Meeting* 2021, *International ACP-I Conference* Rotterdam (Netherlands) 2019, *Annual Conference* Banff, AB (Canada) 2017. [2022/XJ2320/**C**]

- ♦ Advanced Functional Materials and Devices (meeting series)
- ♦ Advanced Functional Polymers for Medicine (meeting series)

♦ Advanced Mathematical Methods for Finance (AMaMeF) 00127

Chair address not obtained.

URL: http://amamef.impan.pl/

History Originally a programme network of *European Science Foundation (ESF, #08441)*, 2005-2010. **Aims** Provide platforms of knowledge exchange at the frontiers of research; facilitate the interaction between young and experienced researchers; promote the growth of expert education in mathematical finance. **Structure** Acting Board. **Activities** Events/meetings. **Events** *General Conference* Paris (France) 2019, *General Conference* Amsterdam (Netherlands) 2017, *General Conference* Lausanne (Switzerland) 2015, *General Conference* Warsaw (Poland) 2013, *General Conference* Bled (Slovenia) 2010. [AA0895/**F**]

- ♦ Advanced Networked Cities and Regions Association (no recent information)
- ♦ Advanced School of Public Administration Central America / see Central American Institute of Public Administration (#03670)
- ♦ Advances Against Aspergillosis and Mucormycosis (meeting series)

♦ Advances in Modal Logic (AiML) 00128

Contact Dept of Philosophy – Univ of Helsinki, PO Box 24 (Unioninkatu 40 A), FI-00014 Helsinki, Finland.

URL: http://www.aiml.net/

History 1995. **Aims** Report on important new developments in pure and applied modal logic. **Structure** Steering Committee. **Activities** Events/meetings. **Events** *Advances in Modal Logic Conference* Helsinki (Finland) 2020. **Publications** *Advances in Modal Logic (AiML)*. [2020/AA1698/c/**F**]

♦ Advances in Neuroblastoma Research Association (ANRA) 00129

Sec Children's Hosp of Philadelphia, 3501 Civic Center Blvd, Philadelphia PA 19104-4302, USA.

URL: http://www.anrmeeting.org/

History Current bylaws adopted 10 Dec 2006 and amended 21 May 2008, 24 Jun 2008, 12 Jun 2009, Sept 2012 and Sept 2015. **Aims** Improve the diagnosis, treatment, and outcome of patients with neuroblastoma through biennial meetings to advance advancement and integration of laboratory and clinical research. **Structure** Steering Committee; Advisory Board Committee; Regional Committees (3): Europe including Russia; North and South Americas; Asia, Australia and Africa. **Languages** English. **Staff** No FTE. Voluntary. **Finance** Sources: donations; members' dues. Other sources: local support for biennial international meetings. No fixed annual budget. **Activities** Awards/prizes/competitions; events/meetings. **Events** *Conference* Amsterdam (Netherlands) 2022, *Conference* Amsterdam (Netherlands) 2021, *Conference* Amsterdam (Netherlands) 2020, *Building the bridges for neuroblastoma research* San Francisco, CA (USA) 2018, *Conference* Cairns, QLD (Australia) 2016. **Publications** Meeting abstracts. [2017.07.10/XJ6784/**C**]

- ♦ Advancing Girls' Education in Africa (internationally oriented national body)

♦ Advancing Minimally Invasive Gynecology Worldwide (AAGL) 00130

Main Office 6757 Katella Ave, Cypress CA 90630-5105, USA. T. +17145036200. Fax +17145036201. E-mail: generalmail@aagl.org.

URL: http://www.aagl.org/

History 1971, USA. Founded on the initiative of Dr Jordan M Phillips. Former names and other names: *American Association of Gynecologic Laparoscopists (AAGL)* – former (1971). **Aims** Develop and promote the safe, practical and skilled application of minimally invasive techniques in treating gynecologic conditions. **Structure** Board of Directors. **Events** *Global Congress on Minimally Invasive Gynecologic Surgery (MIGS)* Aurora, CO (USA) 2022, *Annual Meeting* Austin, TX (USA) 2021, *International Congress on Minimally Invasive Gynecological Surgery* Mumbai (India) 2021, *Annual Meeting* Cypress, CA (USA) 2020, *International Congress on Minimally Invasive Gynecological Surgery* Mumbai (India) 2020. **Publications** *News Scope* (4 a year); *The Journal of Minimaly Invasive Gynecology (JMIG)*. **Members** Full (about 7,500) in 110 countries and territories. Membership countries not specified. **NGO Relations** Affiliated with (6): *Asian Society for Gynecologic Robotic Surgery (ASGRS, #01721)*; *Asia Pacific Association for Gynecologic Endoscopy and Minimally Invasive Therapy (APAGE, #01842)*; *Australasian Gynaecological Endoscopy and Surgery (AGES)*; *Ibero-American Society of Gynecological Endoscopy and Images (#11030)*; *International Pelvic Pain Society (IPPS)*; *Southern African Society for Reproductive Medicine and Gynaecological Endoscopy (SASREG)*. [2021/XM0690/**C**]

- ♦ Advancing the Ministries of the Gospel International (internationally oriented national body)
- ♦ Advantage Africa (internationally oriented national body)

♦ Adventist Development and Relief Agency International (ADRA) . . . 00131

Agence Adventiste d'aide et de développement – Agencia Adventista de Desarrollo y Recursos Asistenciales – Adventistische Entwicklungs- Und Katastrophenhilfe

Main Office 12501 Old Columbia Pk, Silver Spring MD 20904, USA. T. +13016806380. Fax +13016806370.

URL: http://www.adra.org/

History 1956. EU Liaison Office is on EU Transparency Register: 84615015169-54. Former names and other names: *Seventh-day Adventist Welfare Service (SAWS)* – former (1956 to 1973); *Seventh-day Adventist World Service* – former (1973 to 1984). **Aims** Reflect the character of God through *humanitarian* and developmental activities; actively support communities in need; provide assistance in situations of crisis or chronic distress and work toward development of long-term solutions with those affected; work through equitable partnership

with those in need to achieve positive and sustainable change in communities; build networks that develop indigenous capacity, appropriate technology and skills at all levels; develop and maintain relationships with partners to provide effective channels for mutual growth and action; promote and expand equitable and participatory involvement of women in the development process; advocate for, and assist in, increased use of community capacity to care for and responsibly manage natural resources of their environment; facilitate the right and ability of all children to attain their full potential and assist in assuring the child's survival to achieve that potential. **Structure** Operates as a network of national entities, each autonomous and governed by its own board. Central office in Silver Spring MD (USA). Regional offices (9): Africa; Asia; Euro-Africa; Euro-Asia; Inter-America; North America; South America; South Pacific; Trans-Europe. **Staff** 4000.00 FTE, paid. **Finance** Donations from the public, Seventh-Day Adventist Church and other donor organizations. Programme budget (annual): over US$ 145 million. **Activities** Humanitarian/emergency aid. **Publications** *ADRA Works* (4 a year); *First Monday* (4 a year); *Heritage of Hope* (4 a year). Annual Report. Awareness/resource kits; gift catalog.
Members Offices; Supporting and Implementing members, in 122 countries:
Afghanistan, Albania, Angola, Argentina, Armenia, Australia, Austria, Azerbaijan, Bangladesh, Belarus, Belgium, Belize, Bolivia, Brazil, Bulgaria, Burkina Faso, Burundi, Cambodia, Cameroon, Canada, Cape Verde, Chad, Chile, China, Colombia, Congo DR, Costa Rica, Côte d'Ivoire, Croatia, Cuba, Czechia, Denmark, Dominican Rep, Ecuador, El Salvador, Equatorial Guinea, Ethiopia, Fiji, Finland, Georgia, Germany, Ghana, Guatemala, Guinea, Guinea-Bissau, Guyana, Haiti, Honduras, Hungary, India, Indonesia, Italy, Jamaica, Japan, Kazakhstan, Kenya, Korea Rep, Kyrgyzstan, Laos, Liberia, Luxembourg, Madagascar, Malawi, Mali, Mauritania, Mauritius, Mexico, Moldova, Mongolia, Morocco, Mozambique, Myanmar, Namibia, Nepal, Netherlands, New Zealand, Nicaragua, Niger, Nigeria, Norway, Pakistan, Panama, Papua New Guinea, Paraguay, Peru, Philippines, Portugal, Puerto Rico, Romania, Russia, Rwanda, Sao Tomé-Principe, Senegal, Serbia, Sierra Leone, Slovakia, Solomon Is, Somalia, South Africa, Spain, Sri Lanka, Sudan, Suriname, Sweden, Switzerland, Tajikistan, Tanzania UR, Thailand, Togo, Trinidad-Tobago, Tunisia, Türkiye, Uganda, UK, Ukraine, USA, Uzbekistan, Venezuela, Vietnam, Yemen, Zambia, Zimbabwe.
Consultative Status Consultative status granted from: *ECOSOC (#05331)* (General).
IGO Relations Donors, partners and friends include:
- *Asian Development Bank (ADB, #01422)*;
- *Australian Aid (inactive)*;
- *Canadian International Development Agency (CIDA, inactive)*;
- *DANIDA*;
- *Department for International Development (DFID, inactive)*;
- *Department for International Development Cooperation*;
- *European Commission (EC, #06633)*;
- *FAO (#09260)*;
- *Inter-American Institute for Cooperation on Agriculture (IICA, #11434)*;
- *International Bank for Reconstruction and Development (IBRD, #12317)* (World Bank);
- *International Organization for Migration (IOM, #14454)*;
- Ireland Aid Programme of *Irish Aid*;
- *New Zealand Ministry of Foreign Affairs and Trade – New Zealand Aid Programme*;
- *Norwegian Agency for Development Cooperation (Norad)*;
- *Swedish International Development Cooperation Agency (Sida)*;
- *Swiss Agency for Development and Cooperation (SDC)*;
- *UNDP (#20292)*;
- *UNESCO (#20322)*;
- *UNHCR (#20327)*;
- *UNICEF (#20332)*;
- *United Nations Office for the Coordination of Humanitarian Affairs (OCHA, #20593)*;
- *United Nations Office for Project Services (UNOPS, #20602)*;
- *United Nations Population Fund (UNFPA, #20612)*;
- *United Nations Volunteers (UNV, #20650)*;
- *United States Agency for International Development (USAID)*;
- *WHO (#20950)*;
- *World Food Programme (WFP, #21510)*.

NGO Relations Member of:
- *Accord Network*;
- *Accountable Now (#00060)*;
- *Alliance for Food Aid*;
- *American Council for Voluntary International Action (InterAction)*;
- *Christian Connections for International Health (CCIH)*;
- *Confédération européenne des ong d'urgence et de développement (CONCORD, #04547)*;
- *CORE Group*;
- *Danish Refugee Council (DRC)*;
- *Framework Convention Alliance (FCA, #09981)*;
- *Global Health Council (GHC, #10402)*;
- *GLOBAL RESPONSIBILITY – Austrian Platform for Development and Humanitarian Aid*;
- *Global WASH Cluster (GWC, #10651)*;
- *InsideNGO (inactive)*;
- *Inter-agency Network for Education in Emergencies (INEE, #11387)*;
- *Joint Learning Initiative on Faith and Local Communities (JLI, #16139)*;
- Canada branch member of: *Ontario Council for International Cooperation (OCIC)*;
- *Voluntary Organisations in Cooperation in Emergencies (VOICE, #20809)*.

Donors, partners and friends include:
- *American International Health Alliance (AIHA)*;
- *Americares Foundation*;
- *Blumont International*;
- *Bread for the World, USA (BFW)*;
- *Brother's Brother Foundation*;
- *CARE International (CI, #03429)*;
- *Catholic Relief Services (CRS, #03608)*;
- *Church of Jesus Christ of the Latter-day Saints (#03915)*;
- *Concern Worldwide*;
- *Counterpart International (FSP)*;
- *Comitato Europeo per la Formazione e l'Agricoltura (CEFA)*;
- *Feed the Children*;
- *General Conference of Seventh-Day Adventists (SDA, #10109)*;
- *Good360*;
- *Heart to Heart International (HHI)*;
- *Help International, USA*;
- *Hope International Development Agency*;
- *ICCO – Interchurch Organization for Development Cooperation*;
- *IMA World Health (IMA)*;
- *International Aid*;
- *International Federation of Red Cross and Red Crescent Societies (#13526)*;
- *International Fertilizer Development Center (IFDC, #13590)*;
- *International Medical Corps (IMC)*;
- *International Rescue Committee (IRC, #14717)*;
- *Management Sciences for Health (MSH)*;
- *Mercy Corps International (MCI)*;
- *PCI Global*;
- *Peace Corps*;
- *Plan International (#18386)*;
- *Project Harmony*;
- *Rotary International (RI, #18975)*;
- *Salesian Missionaries of Mary Immaculate (SMMI)*;
- *Salvation Army (#19041)*;
- *Samaritan's Purse (#19047)*;
- *Save the Children Federation (SCF)*;
- *Voluntary Service Overseas (VSO)*;
- *Welthungerhilfe*;
- *Winrock International*;
- *World Learning*;
- *World Vision International (WVI, #21904)*. [2020/XF1011/F]

♦ Adventist Frontier Missions (internationally oriented national body)

♦ Adventist Health Food Association (AHFA) 00132

Chairman Argentina Food Factory, Ave San Martin 4625, B1604CDH Florida, Buenos Aires, Argentina. E-mail: gerencia.general@granix.com.ar.
Sec Korean Sahmyook Food, 54-13 Seongjin-ro, Jiksan-eup, Seobuk-gu – Cheonan-si, Chungnam 330 811, Korea Rep.

History Founded 1967, as *International Health Food Association (IHFA)*, as a department of *General Conference of Seventh-Day Adventists (SDA, #10109)*. Subsequent title: *International Health Food Ministry (IHFM)*. Current title adopted when it became an independent organization, 2010. **Aims** Serve member institutions with know-how, technical support and product development. **Structure** Executive Committee. **Languages** English. **Staff** 2.00 FTE, voluntary. **Finance** Members' dues. **Events** *Convention* Argentina 2016, *Convention* Germany 2013, *Convention* Costa Rica 2011, *Convention* Sydney, NSW (Australia) 2008, *Convention* Buenos Aires (Argentina) 2006.
Members Full in 14 countries:
Argentina, Brazil, Colombia, Costa Rica, Dominican Rep, Germany, Guatemala, Haiti, Japan, Korea Rep, New Zealand, Panama, Spain, Trinidad-Tobago. [2017.03.14/XU4907/D]

♦ Adventist International Institute of Advanced Studies (internationally oriented national body)
♦ Adventistische Entwicklungs- Und Katastrophenhilfe (#00131)
♦ Adventist World Radio (see: #10109)

♦ Adventure Therapy International Committee (ATIC) 00133

Co-Chair address not obtained.
Co-Chair address not obtained.
Co-Chair address not obtained.
Co-Chair address not obtained. E-mail: adventuretherapy@icloud.com.
URL: https://internationaladventuretherapy.org/

History Predecessor founded Jul 1997 following first conference. Founded under current title, Feb 2006, Rotorua (New Zealand). **Aims** Promote and support professional practice, research and the development of adventure therapy worldwide. **Structure** Executive Committee. **Activities** Events/meetings. **Events** *Triennial Conference* Kristiansand (Norway) 2021, *Triennial Conference* Sydney, NSW (Australia) 2018. [2020/XM8007/E]

♦ Adventure Tourism Research Association (internationally oriented national body)

♦ Adventure Travel Conservation Fund (ATCF) 00134

Contact 14751 N Kelsey St, Suite 105, PMB 604, Monroe WA 98272, USA. T. +14258352493. E-mail: info@atconservationfund.org.
URL: http://adventuretravelconservationfund.org/

History 2016. Founded by *Adventure Travel Trade Association (ATTA, #00135)* and other leaders from the adventure travel industry. **Aims** Directly fund local projects engaged in the conservation of unique natural and cultural resources of adventure travel destinations. **Structure** Board ofDirectors. **Activities** Awards/prizes/competitions; financial and/or material support. **Members** Worldwide membership. Membership countries not specified. **NGO Relations** Partner of (1): *1% for the Planet*. [2020/AA0479/f/F]

♦ Adventure Travel Trade Association (ATTA) 00135

Contact 14751 N Kelsey St, Suite 105 PMB 604, Monroe WA 98272, USA. E-mail: info@adventuretravel.biz.
URL: https://www.adventuretravel.biz/

History 1990. **Aims** Empower the global travel community to protect natural and cultural capital while creating economic value that benefits both trade members and destinations. **Structure** Advisory Board; Global Development Team. **Activities** Advocacy/lobbying/activism; events/meetings; research/documentation; training/education. **Events** *Adventure Travel World Summit* Hokkaido (Japan) 2023, *Adventure Travel World Summit* Lugano (Switzerland) 2022, *Adventure Travel World Summit* Sapporo (Japan) 2021, *Adventure Travel World Summit* Adelaide, SA (Australia) 2020, *Adventure Travel World Summit* Gothenburg (Sweden) 2019.
Members Tour Operators; Accomodations; Tourism Boards; Industry Partners; Associations; Travel Advisors; Gear Suppliers; Media. Members in 84 countries and territories:
Albania, Argentina, Australia, Austria, Belgium, Bhutan, Bolivia, Bosnia-Herzegovina, Brazil, Bulgaria, Canada, Chile, China, Colombia, Costa Rica, Croatia, Cuba, Denmark, Dominica, Dominican Rep, Ecuador, Egypt, Estonia, Ethiopia, Finland, France, Georgia, Germany, Greece, Greenland, Guatemala, Guyana, Iceland, India, Ireland, Israel, Italy, Japan, Jordan, Kazakhstan, Kenya, Kyrgyzstan, Lebanon, Luxembourg, Madagascar, Malaysia, Mexico, Mongolia, Montenegro, Morocco, Namibia, Nepal, Netherlands, New Zealand, Nicaragua, Norway, Oman, Palestine, Panama, Papua New Guinea, Peru, Philippines, Portugal, Romania, Rwanda, Saudi Arabia, Slovenia, South Africa, Spain, Sri Lanka, St Lucia, Sweden, Switzerland, Tajikistan, Tanzania UR, Thailand, Trinidad-Tobago, Türkiye, Uganda, UK, United Arab Emirates, USA, Uzbekistan, Venezuela.
European Travel Commission (ETC, #08943); *FHI 360*; *World Indigenous Tourism Alliance (WINTA, #21581)*.
NGO Relations Partner of (4): *Adventure Travel Conservation Fund (ATCF, #00134)*; *End Child Prostitution, Child Pornography and Trafficking of Children for Sexual Purposes (ECPAT, #05456)*; *Global Sustainable Tourism Council (GSTC, #10619)*; *World Wide Fund for Nature (WWF, #21922)*. [2021/AA0478/et/C]

♦ Advertisers without Borders (unconfirmed)
♦ Advertisers Business Group / see Advertising Business Group (#00136)

♦ Advertising Business Group (ABG) 00136

Chairman c/o IAA-UAE, PO Box 71104, Dubai, United Arab Emirates. E-mail: charlotte@abg-me.com.
URL: http://www.abg-me.com/

History 20 Nov 1991, as *GCC Advertising Association (GCC AA)*, by *Gulf Cooperation Council (GCC, #10826)*. 1st Constituent Committee held in Jan 1992. 2005, name changed to *Advertisers Business Group (ABG)*. Previously referred to as *GCC Advertisers Association*. Registered in accordance with the laws of the State of Bahrain. **Aims** Further cooperation among the persons engaged in advertising business in GCC states; promote and enhance interest in advertising business, seeking to raise performance levels and establishing ethical and practical criteria among the parties involved in this business; create better awareness of the role of advertising in serving the *economy* and the community; contribute to the development of field studies and surveys associated with the advertising *market*; pay attention to training and instruction programmes for encouraging GCC nationals to be actively involved in advertising; cooperate with local, regional and international professional associations led by IAA. **Structure** Board of Directors, consisting of 2 representatives per GCC member country. **Finance** Members' dues. **Activities** Organizes conferences. **Events** *Advista Arabia conference* Manama (Bahrain) 1999, *Advista Arabia meeting* Abu Dhabi (United Arab Emirates) 1997. **Publications** *AdGulf Newsletter*.
Members Membership Full; Associate; Corporate; Honorary. Individuals and companies or firms in 7 countries:
Bahrain, Egypt, Kuwait, Oman, Qatar, Saudi Arabia, UK.
NGO Relations Member of: *International Council for Advertising Self-Regulation (ICAS, #12984)*. [2020/XE2005/E]

♦ Advertising Information Group (AIG) 00137

Contact c/o Advertising Assn, Artillery House, 11-19 Artillery Row, London, SW1P 1RT, UK. T. +442073401100.
URL: http://www.aigeurope.org/

History Oct 1996. **Activities** Events/meetings. **Publications** *AIG E-news* (bi-weekly).
Members Organizations in 3 countries:
Austria, Germany, UK.
NGO Relations Industry member of: *European Advertising Standards Alliance (EASA, #05829)*. Exchange partners include: *egta – association of television and radio sales houses (#05397)*; *European Magazine Media Association (EMMA, #07723)*; *European Publishers Council (EPC, #08304)*; *Federation of European Data & Marketing (FEDMA, #09499)*; *World Out of Home Organization (WOO, #21702)*. [2018.06.21/XF6075/F]

♦ Advice on Individual Rights in Europe Centre (internationally oriented national body)
♦ Advisory Board on Statistics in Africa (inactive)

♦ Advisory Centre on WTO Law (ACWL) 00138

Centre consultatif sur la législation de l'OMC – Centro de Asesoria Legal en Asuntos de la OMC
Exec Dir Av Giuseppe-Motta 31-33, CP 132, 1211 Geneva 20, Switzerland. T. +41229192121. Fax +41229192122. E-mail: info@acwl.ch.
Senior Office Admin address not obtained.
URL: http://www.acwl.ch/

History Jul 2001. Established following an agreement signed 13 Nov 1999, Seattle WA (USA), which entered into force, 15 July 2001. Became operational 17 July 2001. **Aims** Provide *legal training*, support and advice on World Trade Organization law and dispute settlement procedures to *developing countries* and least developed countries (LDCs). **Structure** General Assembly (twice a year); Management Board. **Languages** English, French, Spanish. **Staff** 15.00 FTE, paid. *Administrative Tribunal of the International Labour Organization (ILO Tribunal, #00118)* is competent to settle disputes. **Finance** Members' one-time contributions to Endowment Fund, based on share in world trade and GNP per capita. Several developed country members contribute specific amounts to annual budget. LDCs are not required to pay contributions. **Activities** Guidance/assistance/consulting; training/education.
Members Open to WTO Member countries or countries in the process of accession. Governments of 49 countries and territories:
Australia, Bolivia, Canada, Colombia, Costa Rica, Côte d'Ivoire, Cuba, Denmark, Dominican Rep, Ecuador, Egypt, El Salvador, Finland, Guatemala, Honduras, Hong Kong, India, Indonesia, Ireland, Italy, Jordan, Kazakhstan, Kenya, Mauritius, Morocco, Netherlands, Nicaragua, Norway, Oman, Pakistan, Panama, Paraguay, Peru, Philippines, Seychelles, South Africa, Sri Lanka, Sweden, Switzerland, Taiwan, Thailand, Tunisia, Türkiye, UK, Ukraine, United Arab Emirates, Uruguay, Venezuela, Vietnam.
Associate member:
Germany.
IGO Relations Cooperates with: *World Trade Organization (WTO, #21864).* [2022.12.02/XM0704/**E***]

- ♦ Advisory Committee on Oil Pollution of the Sea / see Advisory Committee on Protection of the Sea (#00139)
- ♦ Advisory Committee on Overseas Cooperative Development / see US Overseas Cooperative Development Council
- ♦ Advisory Committee on Pollution of the Sea / see Advisory Committee on Protection of the Sea (#00139)

♦ Advisory Committee on Protection of the Sea (ACOPS) 00139

Comité consultatif sur la protection des mers

Trustee One Bartholomew Close, London, EC1A 7BL, UK. E-mail: admin@acops.org.uk.
Chair address not obtained.
URL: http://www.acops.org.uk/

History 1952. Former names and other names: *Advisory Committee on Oil Pollution of the Sea* – former (1952 to 1981); *Advisory Committee on Pollution of the Sea* – former (1981 to 5 Dec 1990); *Comité consultatif sur la pollution des mers* – former (1981 to 5 Dec 1990). Registration: Charity Commission, No/ID: 290776, Start date: 3 Jan 1985, England and Wales. **Aims** Promote and implement strategies for sustainable development of the *coastal* and *marine environment*, through scientific, legal and policy research, advisory and public awareness activities. **Structure** Board of Trustees; Advisor; Volunteers **Languages** English, French. **Staff** 0.50 FTE, paid. **Finance** Recent and ongoing support to intergovernmental bodies rely primarily on global network of expert volunteers and early carrier ocean professionals (ECOPS) as well as consultation fees and donations. In the past, programmes have been carried out with the political and financial support of the following governments and international, intergovernmental, public and private organizations: Governments of Australia, Belgium, Canada, Denmark, Finland, France, Germany, Iceland, Netherlands, Norway, Portugal, Russia, Sweden, Saudi Arabia, UK, USA; *European Commission (EC, #06633)*; *Intergovernmental Oceanographic Commission (IOC, #11496)*; *UNDP (#20292)* – global and regional offices; *UNEP (#20299)*; *International Bank for Reconstruction and Development (IBRD, #12317)* (World Bank); EXPO '98; local authorities worldwide. URL: https://www.acops.org.uk/donate/ **Activities** Awareness raising; events/meetings; guidance/assistance/consulting; research and development. **Events** *International conference on the promotion of ocean security in the Mediterranean sea* Tripoli (Libyan AJ) 2005, *African preparatory meeting to the world summit on sustainable development* Abuja (Nigeria) 2002, *Global conference* Cape Town (South Africa) 1998, *Global conference* Philippines 1998, *Towards enhanced ocean security into the third millennium conference* Stockholm (Sweden) 1998. **Publications** *ACOPS Newsletter* – Studies. Studies; surveys; papers; reports; recommendations; proceedings.
Members Representatives of various organizations (including 24 UK organizations and observers from 1 UK body) in 34 countries and territories:
Australia, Belgium, Bulgaria, Colombia, Costa Rica, Denmark, Egypt, Finland, France, Germany, Hong Kong, Iceland, Italy, Japan, Jordan, Kiribati, Malaysia, Mexico, Netherlands, New Zealand, Norway, Philippines, Portugal, Russia, Samoa, Saudi Arabia, Senegal, Seychelles, South Africa, Sweden, Thailand, UK, Ukraine, Yemen.
Representatives of 5 international organizations:
Council of European Municipalities and Regions (CEMR, #04891); *European Environmental Bureau (EEB, #06996)*; *International Association of Independent Tanker Owners (INTERTANKO, #11959)*; *International Association of Ports and Harbors (IAPH, #12096)*; *International Institute for Environment and Development (IIED, #13877)*.
Consultative Status Consultative status granted from: *International Maritime Organization (IMO, #14102)*; *UNEP (#20299)*. **IGO Relations** Accredited by (1): *International Whaling Commission (IWC, #15879)*. Observer status with (2): *Arctic Monitoring and Assessment Programme (AMAP, #01100)*; *OSPAR Commission for the Protection of the Marine Environment of the North-East Atlantic (OSPAR Commission, #17905)*. **NGO Relations** Member of (1): *EarthAction (EA, #05159)*. Cooperates with (1): *Asian Network on Climate Science and Technology (ANCST, #01548)*. [2023.02.13/XE0530/y/**E**]

- ♦ Advisory Committee on Television (inactive)

♦ Advisory Council for Aeronautics Research in Europe (ACARE) 00140

Address not obtained.
URL: https://www.acare4europe.org/

History Jun 2001, Paris (France). **Aims** Provide a network for strategic research in aeronautics and air transport so that aviation satisfies the needs of society and secures global leadership for Europe in this important sector. **Structure** Forum; General Assembly; Strategy and Integration Board; Implementation Review Group. [2017/AA1574/**D**]

- ♦ ADVOA – African Dermatovenereology Officers Association (unconfirmed)

♦ ADVOC 00141

Contact 1 New Fetter Lane, London, EC4A 1AN, UK. T. +442075442406.
URL: http://www.advoc.com/

History 1989. Trade Mark Registered 1990. Former names and other names: *International Network of Independent Law Firms* – alias. Registration: Start date: 1991, UK. **Aims** Share international expertise in jurisdictions worldwide. **Structure** Annual General Meeting; Global Committees (4); Secretariat. **Languages** English. **Staff** 1.00 FTE, paid. **Finance** Sources: members' dues. **Activities** Events/meetings. **Events** *Europe Annual General Meeting* Aarhus (Denmark) 2021, *International Business Law Conference* Bangkok (Thailand) 2020, *Europe Annual General Meeting* Bristol (UK) 2020, *Europe Annual General Meeting* Lyon (France) 2018, *Europe Annual General Meeting* Copenhagen (Denmark) 2017.
Members Firms (93) in 72 countries and territories:
Argentina, Australia, Austria, Bangladesh, Belgium, Bolivia, Brazil, Bulgaria, Cambodia, Chile, China, Colombia, Costa Rica, Croatia, Cyprus, Czechia, Dominican Rep, Ecuador, England, Estonia, Fiji, Finland, France, Germany, Gibraltar, Greece, Guatemala, Hungary, India, Indonesia, Ireland, Israel, Italy, Japan, Korea Rep, Latvia, Liechtenstein, Lithuania, Luxembourg, Malaysia, Malta, Mexico, Myanmar, Netherlands, New Zealand, Nigeria, North Macedonia, Norway, Pakistan, Panama, Paraguay, Peru, Philippines, Poland, Portugal, Romania, Russia, Scotland, Serbia, Singapore, Slovakia, South Africa, Spain, Sri Lanka, Sweden, Switzerland, Thailand, Türkiye, United Arab Emirates, Uruguay, USA, Vietnam. [2021.09.06/XM6277/**F**]

- ♦ Advocacy to Control Tuberculosis Internationally / see ACTION (#00085)
- ♦ Advocacy Network for Africa (internationally oriented national body)
- ♦ Advocacy for the Prevention of Alcohol related Harm in Europe / see European Alcohol Policy Alliance (#05856)
- ♦ Advocaten Zonder Grenzen (#03050)
- ♦ Advocates for Human Rights (internationally oriented national body)
- ♦ Advocates International (internationally oriented national body)
- ♦ Advocates for International Development (internationally oriented national body)
- ♦ Advocates for Youth, Washington DC (internationally oriented national body)
- ♦ Advogados para África / see LEX Africa (#16449)
- ♦ ADVT – Association Defending Victims of Terrorism (internationally oriented national body)
- ♦ ADVTNGO / see Association Defending Victims of Terrorism
- ♦ ADW – Aktion Dritte Welt (internationally oriented national body)
- ♦ **ADWN** Asian Domestic Workers Network (#01430)
- ♦ ADWOC – Arab Drilling and Workover Company (see: #17854)
- ♦ ADWU – Asian Domestic Workers' Union (unconfirmed)
- ♦ ADWU – Asian Domestic Workers' Union (no recent information)
- ♦ ADYFE – African Diaspora Youth Forum in Europe (unconfirmed)
- ♦ **ADYNE** African Diaspora Youth Network in Europe (#00288)
- ♦ **AEAA** Association for Educational Assessment in Africa (#02482)
- ♦ **AEAA** Association Européenne des Agents Artistiques (#02554)
- ♦ AEA / see AEA – International Lawyers Network (#00142)
- ♦ **AEA** AEA – International Lawyers Network (#00142)
- ♦ **AEA** Asia Evangelical Alliance (#01275)
- ♦ AEA – Asociación de Empresarios de la Amazonia (inactive)
- ♦ AEA – Association of Enterprise Architects (unconfirmed)
- ♦ AEA – Association for Environmental Archaeology (internationally oriented national body)
- ♦ AEA – Association of European Airlines (inactive)
- ♦ AEA – Association for European Astronauts (inactive)
- ♦ **AEA** Association européenne d'archéologie (#05940)
- ♦ **AEA** Association européenne des avocats (#07661)
- ♦ **AEA** Association of Evangelicals in Africa (#02587)
- ♦ AEA – Australasian Epidemiological Association (internationally oriented national body)
- ♦ AEAC – Action économique arabe commune (no recent information)
- ♦ AEAC – Association for Euro-Atlantic Cooperation (no recent information)
- ♦ AE / see Adriatic Ionian Euroregion (#00120)
- ♦ **AEAEH** Association for East Asian Environmental History (#02476)
- ♦ **AEA** European Association of Hearing Aid Professionals (#06066)
- ♦ **AEA Europe** Association for Educational Assessment – Europe (#02483)
- ♦ AEAI / see Federation of European Risk Management Associations (#09539)

♦ AEA – International Lawyers Network (AEA) 00142

Contact Avda Maisonnave 30, ALICANTE, 03003 Alicante, Castellón, Spain. T. +34965986540. Fax +34965133092. E-mail: europea1@aeuropea.com.
URL: http://www.aeuropea.com/

History 1 Jan 2002, Alicante (Spain). Originally covering the countries of the European Union. Former names and other names: *Asociación Europea de Abogados (AEA)* – former; *Association européenne des avocats* – former; *European Association of Attorneys* – former; *Europäisches Anwaltsverein* – former; *Associazione Europea di Avvocati* – former. **Aims** Offer services on a global scale. **Structure** Board of Directors. **Languages** English, French, German, Italian, Spanish. **Finance** Sources: members' dues. **Activities** Events/meetings. **Events** *Congress*. Vienna (Austria) 2023, *Congress* Barcelona (Spain) 2022, *Congress* Barcelona (Spain) 2020, *Congress* Nice (France) 2019, *Working together – joining forces internationally* Palermo (Italy) 2018.
Members in 199 countries and territories:
Afghanistan, Albania, Algeria, Andorra, Angola, Antigua-Barbuda, Argentina, Armenia, Australia, Austria, Azerbaijan, Bahamas, Bahrain, Bangladesh, Barbados, Belarus, Belgium, Belize, Benin, Bermuda, Bhutan, Bolivia, Bosnia-Herzegovina, Botswana, Brazil, Brunei Darussalam, Burkina Faso, Burundi, Cambodia, Cameroon, Canada, Cape Verde, Cayman Is, Chad, Chile, China, Colombia, Comoros, Congo Brazzaville, Congo DR, Costa Rica, Côte d'Ivoire, Croatia, Cuba, Cyprus, Czechia, Denmark, Djibouti, Dominica, Dominican Rep, Ecuador, Egypt, El Salvador, Equatorial Guinea, Eritrea, Estonia, Eswatini, Ethiopia, Fiji, Finland, France, Gabon, Gambia, Georgia, Germany, Ghana, Greece, Grenada, Guatemala, Guinea, Guyana, Haiti, Honduras, Hungary, Iceland, India, Indonesia, Iran Islamic Rep, Iraq, Ireland, Israel, Italy, Jamaica, Japan, Jordan, Kazakhstan, Kenya, Kiribati, Korea DPR, Korea Rep, Kosovo, Kuwait, Kyrgyzstan, Laos, Latvia, Lebanon, Lesotho, Liberia, Libya, Liechtenstein, Lithuania, Luxembourg, Madagascar, Malawi, Malaysia, Maldives, Mali, Malta, Marshall Is, Mauritania, Mauritius, Mexico, Micronesia FS, Moldova, Monaco, Mongolia, Montenegro, Morocco, Mozambique, Myanmar, Namibia, Nauru, Nepal, Netherlands, New Caledonia, New Zealand, Nicaragua, Niger, Nigeria, Norfolk Is, North Macedonia, Norway, Oman, Pakistan, Palau, Palestine, Panama, Papua New Guinea, Paraguay, Peru, Philippines, Poland, Portugal, Qatar, Romania, Russia, Rwanda, Samoa, San Marino, Sao Tomé-Principe, Saudi Arabia, Senegal, Serbia, Seychelles, Sierra Leone, Singapore, Slovakia, Slovenia, Solomon Is, Somalia, South Africa, South Sudan, Spain, Sri Lanka, St Kitts-Nevis, St Lucia, St Maarten, St Vincent-Grenadines, Sudan, Suriname, Sweden, Switzerland, Syrian AR, Taiwan, Tajikistan, Tanzania UR, Timor-Leste, Togo, Tonga, Trinidad-Tobago, Tunisia, Türkiye, Turkmenistan, Turks-Caicos, Tuvalu, Uganda, UK, Ukraine, United Arab Emirates, Uruguay, USA, Uzbekistan, Vanuatu, Venezuela, Vietnam, Virgin Is USA, Yemen, Zambia, Zimbabwe. [2022.11.05/XJ0714/**C**]

- ♦ AEA / see International Mastic Asphalt Association (#14119)
- ♦ **AEAJ** Association of European Administrative Judges (#02497)
- ♦ AEALC / see Latin American and Caribbean Economics Association (#16274)
- ♦ **AEALC** Asociación de Economistas de América Latina y el Caribe (#02480)
- ♦ AEALCD – Association européenne des administrateurs locaux démocrates-chrétiens (no recent information)
- ♦ AEALDC – Asociación Europea de Administradores Locales Demócrata Cristianos (no recent information)
- ♦ **AE** Alumni Europae (#00760)
- ♦ **AE** Alzheimer Europe (#00761)
- ♦ AEAM / see Association of Evangelicals in Africa (#02587)
- ♦ AEAO – Association économique de l'Afrique de l'Ouest (inactive)
- ♦ AEAO / see International Association of Assay Offices (#11715)
- ♦ **AEARU** Association of East Asian Research Universities (#02477)
- ♦ AEAS – Academy of East Asian Studies (internationally oriented national body)
- ♦ AEASHS – Association européenne des assistants sociaux hospitaliers et de la santé (inactive)
- ♦ AE – Assoziation Europa für Sozialen und Kulturellen Fortschritt (inactive)
- ♦ **AEATG** Association Européenne pour l'Analyse Transculturelle de Groupe (#06258)
- ♦ **AE** Autisme-Europe (#03040)
- ♦ **AE** Autism-Europe (#03040)
- ♦ **AEBA** Association of Eye Banks of Asia (#02591)
- ♦ AEB – Art Education for the Blind (internationally oriented national body)
- ♦ **AEB** Asiatische Entwicklungsbank (#01422)
- ♦ **AEBF** Asian Exim Banks Forum (#01448)
- ♦ AEBIOM / see Bioenergy Europe (#03247)
- ♦ **AEBR** Association of European Border Regions (#02499)
- ♦ AEC / see African Energy Commission (#00298)
- ♦ AEC / see Caribbean Studies Association (#03559)
- ♦ AECA – American European Community Association (internationally oriented national body)
- ♦ **A and ECA** Anglican and Eastern Churches Association (#00829)
- ♦ **AECA** Asian Electroceramics Association (#01434)
- ♦ **AECA** Association Européenne des Cadres de l'Assurance (#02556)
- ♦ AECA – Association européenne des centres d'audiophonologie (inactive)
- ♦ **AECAC** Association Européenne de Commerce d'Armes Civiles (#05975)
- ♦ **AEC** African Economic Community (#00290)
- ♦ AEC – African Entrepreneur Collective (internationally oriented national body)
- ♦ **AECAL** Academia Europea de Ciencias, Artes y Letras (#05781)
- ♦ **AEC** Antilles Episcopal Conference (#00856)
- ♦ AEC – Asian Eye Care (internationally oriented national body)
- ♦ **AEC** Asociación de Estados del Caribe (#02411)
- ♦ **AEC** Asociación Europea de Coleopterologia (#02125)
- ♦ **AEC** Assemblée européenne des citoyens (#05922)
- ♦ **AEC** Association des Etats de la Caraïbe (#02411)
- ♦ AEC – Association of European Consumers (no recent information)
- ♦ AEC – Association européenne de céramique (inactive)
- ♦ **AEC** Association européenne des cheminots (#02558)

- ♦ **AEC** Association Européenne des Conservatoires, Académies de Musique et Musikhochschulen (#02560)
- ♦ AEC – Association européenne pour la coopération (inactive)
- ♦ AEC – Association européenne de cyclosport (internationally oriented national body)
- ♦ AEC – Association européenne des fabricants de feuilles, membranes et revêtements en matière plastique (inactive)
- ♦ **AEC** Association évangélique des Caraïbes (#09210)
- ♦ AEC – Associazione Europea per la Cooperazione (inactive)
- ♦ AECAWA – Association of Episcopal Conferences of Anglophone West Africa (inactive)
- ♦ AECB / see European Federation of Managers in the Banking Sector (#07161)
- ♦ AECC / see AECC University College
- ♦ **AECC** Association for Emissions Control by Catalyst (#02486)
- ♦ **AECCJ** Association européenne des centres communautaires juifs (#06097)
- ♦ AECCP – Association of European Comparative Clinical Pathology (inactive)
- ♦ AECC University College (internationally oriented national body)
- ♦ AECE – Association of Eastern Caribbean Exporters (no recent information)
- ♦ **AECEC** Association d'études canadiennes en Europe Centrale (#03704)
- ♦ **AECEF** Association of European Civil Engineering Faculties (#02503)
- ♦ **AECEM** Association européenne des centres d'éthique médicale (#05968)
- ♦ **AECEN** Asian Environmental Compliance and Enforcement Network (#01437)
- ♦ **AEC** European Association of Conservatories (#02560)
- ♦ **AECF** Africa Enterprise Challenge Fund (#00168)
- ♦ AECF – Association européenne des clubs de figurinistes (inactive)
- ♦ AECF / see European Federation of Christian Student Associations (#07076)
- ♦ AECI / see Agencia Española de Cooperación Internacional para el Desarrollo
- ♦ AECID – Agencia Española de Cooperación Internacional para el Desarrollo (internationally oriented national body)
- ♦ **AECJ** Association européenne des Cartes jeunes (#09137)
- ♦ **AECLJ** Association of European Competition Law Judges (#02505)
- ♦ AECMA – European Association of Aerospace Industries (inactive)
- ♦ AECM – Association of European Candle Makers (inactive)
- ♦ **AECM** Association européenne de Cautionnement (#06061)
- ♦ AECM – Association européenne des classes moyennes (inactive)
- ♦ AECM / see European Association of Guarantee Institutions (#06061)
- ♦ **AECNP** Association européenne des centres nationaux de productivité (#06130)
- ♦ **AECO** Association of Arctic Expedition Cruise Operators (#02375)
- ♦ AECOPSD – Association Européenne de membres de Corps et Organismes Publics de Sécurité et de Défense (internationally oriented national body)
- ♦ **AECOS** American-European Congress of Ophthalmic Surgery (#00780)
- ♦ AECOWA / see Regional Episcopal Conference of West Africa (#18783)
- ♦ AECR / see European Conservatives and Reformists Party (#06747)
- ♦ **AECSD** Association of Eurasian Central Securities Depositories (#02496)
- ♦ AECS / see European Association for Distance Learning (#06015)
- ♦ AECV – Association européenne de chirurgie viscérale (no recent information)
- ♦ **AECVP** Association for the European Cardiovascular Pathology (#02501)
- ♦ **AEDA** Association Européenne pour le Droit de l'Alimentation (#07286)
- ♦ **AED** Abogados Europeos Democraticos (#03049)
- ♦ **AED** Academy of Eating Disorders (#00034)
- ♦ AED – Associated European Divers (internationally oriented national body)
- ♦ **AED** Avocats européens démocrates (#03049)
- ♦ AEDBCS / see Association Européenne des Agents Artistiques (#02554)
- ♦ **AEDBF** Association européenne pour le droit bancaire et financier (#02564)
- ♦ **AEDE** Association européenne des enseignants (#02565)
- ♦ **AEDEM** Académie européenne de direction et économie de l'entreprise (#05801)
- ♦ AEDEM / see European Academy of Management and Business Economics (#05801)
- ♦ **AEDES** Association européenne pour le développement et la santé (#02562)
- ♦ AEDESC – Association pour l'étude du développement économique, social et culturel (inactive)
- ♦ **AEDET** Asociación Europea de Estaciones Termales (#08805)
- ♦ AEDEV – Association l'e-développement (internationally oriented national body)
- ♦ AEDG – Asociación Europea de Derecho y Gastronomia (internationally oriented national body)
- ♦ AEDH / see Agir ensemble pour les droits humains
- ♦ **AEDH** Association européenne des directeurs d'hôpitaux (#06073)
- ♦ AEDH – European Association for the Defence of Human Rights (no recent information)
- ♦ AEDIDH – Asociación Española para el Derecho Internacional de los Derechos Humanos (internationally oriented national body)
- ♦ AEDP / see European Association for People Management (#06146)
- ♦ AEDT – European Association of Fashion Retailers (inactive)
- ♦ **AEDTF** Association européenne pour le développement du transport ferroviaire (#06011)
- ♦ **AEEA** African Engineering Education Association (#00299)
- ♦ **AEEA** Association européenne pour l'enseignement de l'architecture (#05941)
- ♦ AEEADE / see Euro-American Association of Economic Development Studies
- ♦ AEEADE – Asociación de Estudios Euro-Americana de Desarrollo Económico (internationally oriented national body)
- ♦ **AEE** Association for Experiential Education (#02590)
- ♦ **AEEBC** Association of European Experts in Building and Construction (The) (#02510)
- ♦ **AEEBC** Association d'experts européens du bâtiment et de la construction (#02510)
- ♦ AEEC – Association of European Express Carriers (inactive)
- ♦ **AEEC** Association européenne d'études chinoises (#05973)
- ♦ **AEEC** Association européenne des officiers de l'Etat civil (#05760)
- ♦ **AEED** Association européenne des enseignants dentaires (#02467)
- ♦ **AEEE** Association of European Economics Education (#02507)
- ♦ **AEEEV** Association Européenne des Etablissements d'Enseignement Vétérinaire (#06031)
- ♦ **AEEF** Asia Europe Economic Forum (#01269)
- ♦ AEEF – Association européenne de l'ethnie française (inactive)
- ♦ AEEF – Association européenne des exploitations frigorifiques (inactive)
- ♦ **AEEMA** Association européenne pour l'éducation aux médias audiovisuels (#05946)
- ♦ **AEEP** Alliance européenne pour l'éthique en publicité (#05829)
- ♦ AEEP – Association of European Engineering Periodicals (inactive)
- ♦ **AEERPA** Association Européenne des Entreprises de Restauration du Patrimoine Architectural (#05942)
- ♦ AEESCA – Association for Engineering Education in South and Central Asia (no recent information)
- ♦ AEESEA / see Association for Engineering Education in Southeast Asia and the Pacific (#02487)
- ♦ **AEESEAP** Association for Engineering Education in Southeast Asia and the Pacific (#02487)
- ♦ **AEET** Association européenne pour l'éducation technologique (#08757)
- ♦ AEETC – Asia-Europe Environmental Technology Centre (inactive)
- ♦ **AEETD** Association européenne pour l'enseignement de la théorie du droit (#06250)
- ♦ AEFA – Association of European Federations of Agro-Engineers (inactive)
- ♦ **AEFA** CARTOON – Association européenne du film d'animation (#03592)
- ♦ AEF – Africa Energy Forum (meeting series)
- ♦ **AEF** African Elephant Fund (#00297)
- ♦ **AEF** African Engineers Forum (#00300)
- ♦ AEF – African Enterprise Fund (inactive)
- ♦ AEF – Afrique équatoriale française (inactive)
- ♦ **AEF** Agroecology Fund (#00583)
- ♦ AEF – Asian Electronics Forum (meeting series)
- ♦ **AEF** Asian Equestrian Federation (#01441)
- ♦ **AEFCA** Alliance of European Football Coaches' Associations (#00674)
- ♦ AEFC – Association of European Financial Centres (inactive)
- ♦ AEF – Centre d'action européenne fédéraliste (inactive)
- ♦ AEF / see European Festivals Association (#07242)
- ♦ **AEFJ** Association européenne de formation au journalisme (#07613)
- ♦ **AEFJN** Africa-Europe Faith and Justice Network (#00171)
- ♦ **AEFLib** Association Européenne des Facultés Libres (#02569)
- ♦ **AEFMUTA** Association européenne des fabricants de médicaments utilisés en thérapeutique anthroposophique (#02568)
- ♦ **AEFP** Association européenne pour le fleurissement et le paysage (#02570)
- ♦ **AEFP** Association européenne pour la formation professionnelle (#09075)
- ♦ AEFPR – Association européenne de formation paysanne et rurale (inactive)
- ♦ AEFR – Association Europe-Finances-Régulations (internationally oriented national body)
- ♦ AEFRV / see Diagnostics For Animals (#05062)
- ♦ **AEG** Asian EUS Group (#01446)
- ♦ AEG / see Association of Applied Geochemists (#02372)
- ♦ **AEG** Association of Esperantist Greens (#02494)
- ♦ AEGC – Australasian Exploration Geoscience Conference (meeting series)
- ♦ AEGDU / see European Association of Lawyers for Democracy and World Human Rights (#06105)
- ♦ **AEGEE-Europe** Association des états généraux des étudiants de l'Europe (#02495)
- ♦ **AEGIS** Africa-Europe Group for Interdisciplinary Studies (#00172)
- ♦ AEGIS Europe (unconfirmed)
- ♦ AEGIS Trust (internationally oriented national body)
- ♦ AEGPL / see Liquid Gas Europe (#16488)
- ♦ **AEGRAFLEX** Association européenne des graveurs et des flexographes (#02572)
- ♦ **AEGS** Association of European Geological Societies (#02513)
- ♦ **AEH** Action européenne des handicapés (#05825)
- ♦ **AEHD** Association européenne des historiens de la danse (#06004)
- ♦ **AeHIN** Asia eHealth Information Network (#01268)
- ♦ **AEHMS** Aquatic Ecosystem Health and Management Society (#00889)
- ♦ **AEHN** African Economic History Network (#00291)
- ♦ **AEHT** Association européenne des écoles d'hôtellerie et de tourisme (#06075)
- ♦ AEHWO – Association of European Home Warranty Organisations (see: #13816)
- ♦ AEI – Agency for European Integration and Economic Development (internationally oriented national body)
- ♦ **AEI** Aircraft Engineers International (#00602)
- ♦ AEI – American Enterprise Institute (internationally oriented national body)
- ♦ **AEIAR** Association européenne des institutions d'aménagement rural (#06198)
- ♦ **AEI** Asian Energy Institute (#01436)
- ♦ AEI – Association des études internationales (internationally oriented national body)
- ♦ AEI – Association of European Inventors (inactive)
- ♦ **AEI** Association européenne Inédits (#02574)
- ♦ AEI – Association européenne des investisseurs individuels (inactive)
- ♦ AEIB / see Academy of International Business (#00040)
- ♦ AEIBS / see European Association for Health Information and Libraries (#06064)
- ♦ **AEIC** ASEAN Earthquake Information Centre (#01169)
- ♦ AEICO – Arab Engineering Industries Company (inactive)
- ♦ **AEIDL** Association européenne pour l'information sur le développement local (#00143)

♦ AEIDL – European Association for Information on Local Development 00143

Association européenne pour l'information sur le développement local (AEIDL)

Dir Gen Chaussée Saint Pierre 260, 1040 Brussels, Belgium. T. +3227364960. Fax +3227360434.
URL: http://www.aeidl.eu/

History 1988, Brussels (Belgium). Latest statutes adopted by General Assembly, 21 Oct 1995. Registered in accordance with Belgian law. **Aims** Help build a *citizens* Europe; through its activities, encourage local development initiatives that take into account local, social, economic and environmental aspects and which engender a development process based on partnership and people's *rights.* **Structure** General Assembly (annual). Governing Board of at least 5 members. Officers: President; Treasurer; Secretary. **Languages** English, French, German, Italian, Portuguese, Romanian, Spanish. **Staff** 25.00 FTE, paid. Staff backed up by freelance professionals. **Activities** Networking/liaising; knowledge management/information dissemination; training/education; events/meetings; guidance/assistance/consulting; publishing activities. **Events** *Workshop on European Social Fund Actions to Promote Local Employment Initiatives* Brussels (Belgium) 2011, *Meeting* Brussels (Belgium) 2010, *European citizens panel meeting* Brussels (Belgium) 2007, *Meeting* Brussels (Belgium) 1998, *Meeting* Brussels (Belgium) 1992. **Publications** *Euclide* (weekly) – newsletter; *INFOREGIO News* (12 a year) – for EC DG on Regional Policy; *PANORAMA* (4 a year) – magazine; *LIFE Focus.* CD-ROMs. **Members** Associate; Adhering. Individuals in 8 countries:
Belgium, France, Germany, Hungary, Portugal, Spain, Sweden, UK. [2019/XE1673/v/**E**]

- ♦ AEIE – Association pour l'étude de l'intégration européenne (inactive)
- ♦ AEIF – Association européenne pour l'interopérabilité ferroviaire (inactive)
- ♦ AEIMS / see Association Européenne des Illustrateurs Médicaux et Scientifiques (#02573)
- ♦ **AEIMS** Association Européenne des Illustrateurs Médicaux et Scientifiques (#02573)
- ♦ AEIOU – Association européenne pour une interaction entre les organismes universitaires (inactive)
- ♦ AEIP / see Association Européenne des Institutions Paritaires de la Protection Sociale (#02575)
- ♦ **AEIP** Association Européenne des Institutions Paritaires de la Protection Sociale (#02575)
- ♦ **AEIRSP** Association Européenne des institutions de retraite du secteur public (#06180)
- ♦ AEIU – Asia Electronics and Info-Communications Union (no recent information)
- ♦ **AEJ** Association of European Journalists (#02516)
- ♦ AEJDH / see European Association of Lawyers for Democracy and World Human Rights (#06105)
- ♦ **AEJDT** Asociación Europea de Juegos y Deportes Tradicionales (#08931)
- ♦ **AEJE** Association Européenne des Jeunes Entrepreneurs (#02576)
- ♦ **AEJE** Association européenne des juristes d'entreprises (#06686)
- ♦ **AEJeST** Association européenne des jeux et sports traditionnels (#08931)
- ♦ AEJI – Association of European Jute Industries (inactive)
- ♦ **AEJM** Association of European Jewish Museums (#02515)
- ♦ AEJM – Association européenne des jeunes médiateurs (no recent information)
- ♦ **AEKMP** Association Europe des kinésithérapeutes pour la maladie de Parkinson (#02860)
- ♦ AEKPC – Association européenne des kinésithérapeutes photographes et cinéastes (inactive)
- ♦ AELAC – Asociación de Educadores de Latinoamérica y del Caribe (unconfirmed)
- ♦ **AELAC** Association of Economists of Latin America and the Caribbean (#02480)
- ♦ **AEL** Alliance for European Logistics (#00675)
- ♦ **AEL** Associazione Europea Maestri Liutai e Archettai (#06273)
- ♦ AELDH / see European Association of Lawyers for Democracy and World Human Rights (#06105)
- ♦ **AELE** Association européenne de libre-échange (#05391)
- ♦ AELE / see European State Lotteries and Toto Association (#08833)
- ♦ AELERT – Australasian Environmental Law Enforcement and Regulators Network (internationally oriented national body)
- ♦ AELIA – Association d'études linguistiques interculturelles africaines (inactive)
- ♦ AELPL – Association européenne des linguistes et des professeurs de langues (no recent information)
- ♦ AELSC / see European Landscape Contractors Association (#07642)
- ♦ AEMA – Asphalt Emulsion Manufacturers Association (internationally oriented national body)

AEM Action évangélisation
00143
alphabetic sequence excludes
For the complete listing, see Yearbook Online at

- ♦ **AEM** Action d'évangélisation mondiale (#20850)
- ♦ **AEM** Alianza Evangélica Mundial (#21393)
- ♦ **AEM** Alliance évangélique universelle (#21393)
- ♦ AEM AMS – Atlantic Euro Mediterranean Academy of Medical Science (internationally oriented national body)
- ♦ AEM – Arbeitsgemeinschaft Evangelikaler Missionen (internationally oriented national body)
- ♦ AEM – Asociación de Elevadores del Mercosur (unconfirmed)
- ♦ **AEM** Association des Echanges Méditerranéens pour l'eau, la forêt, l'énergie, et le développement durable des territoires (#02478)
- ♦ **AEM** Association européenne des élus de montagne (#06021)
- ♦ **AEMB** Association européenne des marchés aux bestiaux (#06109)
- ♦ AEMCP – Association of European Manufacturers of Carbonless Paper (no recent information)
- ♦ **AEMDA** Alliance européenne des associations de myopathes (#05876)
- ♦ **AEME** Association pour l'enseignement médical en Europe (#02797)
- ♦ **AEME Foundation** Austrian Economics Meeting Europe Foundation (#03037)
- ♦ **AEMH** Association européenne des médecins des hôpitaux (#02577)
- ♦ **AEMHSM** Association européenne des musées de l'histoire des sciences médicales (#06125)
- ♦ **AEMI** Association of European Migration Institutions (#02524)
- ♦ AEMIC – Asociación para el Estudio de los Exilios y Migraciones Ibéricos Contemporaneos (internationally oriented national body)
- ♦ AEMIE / see European Federation of Internal Medicine (#07147)
- ♦ AEMI / see European Federation of Internal Medicine (#07147)
- ♦ AEMRI / see Alliance of International Market Research Institutes (#00695)
- ♦ **AEMRN** Afro-European Medical and Research Network (#00538)
- ♦ AEMSM – Association of European Metal Sink Manufacturers (inactive)
- ♦ AEMThB – Association européenne de médecine thermale et bioclimatologie (inactive)
- ♦ AEMTM / see Aide médicale et développement
- ♦ AEN – Academia Europa Nostra (internationally oriented national body)
- ♦ **AEN** Africa Evidence Network (#00173)
- ♦ AEN – Afrika-Europa Netwerk (internationally oriented national body)
- ♦ **AEN** Agence de l'OCDE pour l'énergie nucléaire (#17615)
- ♦ AEN – Alliance Européenne Numismatique (internationally oriented national body)
- ♦ **AEN** Asian Ecotourism Network (#01433)
- ♦ **AEN** Audiences Europe Network (#03013)
- ♦ AEN – Australasian Ethics Network (internationally oriented national body)
- ♦ **AENEAS** Association for European NanoElectronics ActivitieS (#02525)
- ♦ **AENE** Association européenne de neuroendocrinologie (#08040)
- ♦ AENOC / see European Olympic Committees (#08083)
- ♦ AEOA – Association européenne des orchestres d'amateurs (inactive)
- ♦ **AEO** Association of European Ocularists (#02526)
- ♦ **AEOM** Association of European Open Air Museums (#02527)
- ♦ AEOPSP – Association européenne des officiers professionnels sapeurs-pompiers (no recent information)
- ♦ AEPA – Asia-Pacific Symposium on Engineering Plasticity and its Applications (meeting series)
- ♦ AEP – Association européenne des podologues (inactive)
- ♦ **AEP** Association européenne de psychiatrie (#08290)
- ♦ AEP – Association européenne de recherche sur les protéagineux (inactive)
- ♦ AEPC / see Association for European Paediatric and Congenital Cardiology (#02529)
- ♦ **AEPC** Association for European Paediatric and Congenital Cardiology (#02529)
- ♦ **AEPC** Association of European Police Colleges (#02531)
- ♦ **AE-PCOS** Androgen Excess and PCOS Society (#00821)
- ♦ AEPDP – Association européenne des producteurs de papier décoratif (no recent information)
- ♦ AEPDSPSF – Association Européenne de promotion des droits et de soutien des Personnes en Situation de Fragilité (unconfirmed)
- ♦ **AEPEA** Association européenne de psychopathologie de l'enfant et de l'adolescent (#02581)
- ♦ AEPE – Asociación para los Estudios de los Problemas de Europa (inactive)
- ♦ **AEPE** Asociación Europea de Profesores de Español (#02127)
- ♦ AEPE – Association pour l'étude des problèmes de l'Europe (inactive)
- ♦ **AEPE** Association Européenne pour l'enseignement de la pédiatrie (#02847)
- ♦ **AEPF** Asia-Europe People's Forum (#01274)
- ♦ AEPF – Association d'églises de professants des pays francophones (inactive)
- ♦ **AEPL** Asociación Europea de Pensamiento Libre (#06048)
- ♦ **AEPL** Association Européenne de la Pensée Libre (#06048)
- ♦ **AEPL** Associazione Europea del Pensiero Libero (#06048)
- ♦ **AEPM** Asociación Europea de Productores de Moluscos (#07818)
- ♦ **AEPM** Association of European Printing Museums (#02532)
- ♦ **AEPM** Association européenne de producteurs de mollusques (#07818)
- ♦ **AEPM** Associazione Europea di Produttori di Molluschi (#07818)
- ♦ AEPN – Association des écologistes pour le nucléaire (internationally oriented national body)
- ♦ AEPO / see Association of European Performers' Organisations (#02530)
- ♦ **AEPO-ARTIS** Association of European Performers' Organisations (#02530)
- ♦ AEPOC / see Audiovisual Anti-Piracy Alliance (#03015)
- ♦ AEPPC / see INSOL Europe (#11231)
- ♦ AEPS / see European network for health promotion and economic development (#07920)
- ♦ AEPS Indigenous Peoples' Secretariat / see Arctic Council Indigenous Peoples' Secretariat (#01098)
- ♦ AEPVD – Association européenne pour la vente à distance (no recent information)
- ♦ **AEPW** Alliance to End Plastic Waste (#00673)
- ♦ AEQ – Association européenne de fabricants de tuyaux métalliques flexibles et de compensateurs de dilatation de qualité (inactive)
- ♦ AEqualia (unconfirmed)
- ♦ AER – Agri-Energy Roundtable (internationally oriented national body)
- ♦ AERAM – Association européenne de réassurance et d'assurances mutuelles (inactive)
- ♦ AERAP – African-European Radio Astronomy Platform (unconfirmed)
- ♦ Aeras Global TB Vaccine Foundation (internationally oriented national body)
- ♦ **AER** Assembly of European Regions (#02316)
- ♦ **AER** Association of European Radios (#02535)
- ♦ AER – Association européenne de radiologie (inactive)
- ♦ **AER** Association européenne des radios (#02535)
- ♦ AER – Association européenne du rhum (no recent information)
- ♦ AER – Association for Eye Research (inactive)
- ♦ AER – Avenir pour l'Enfant des Rizières (internationally oriented national body)
- ♦ **AERC** African Economic Research Consortium (#00292)
- ♦ AERC / see Association of Executive Search and Leadership Consultants (#02588)
- ♦ AER / see Comprehensive System International Rorschach Association (#04421)
- ♦ AERDO / see Accord Network
- ♦ AERDQ – Association européenne des régies de quartier (internationally oriented national body)
- ♦ AEREA / see Association of European Research Establishments in Aeronautics (#02539)
- ♦ AERE – Association of Environmental and Resource Economists (internationally oriented national body)
- ♦ **AERG** Association of ERC Grantees (#02492)

♦ Aerial Archaeology Research Group (AARG) 00144

Hon Sec address not obtained.
Events Sec address not obtained.
URL: https://a-r-g.eu/

History 1983. Current constitution approved Sep 1990; revised Sep 2007, Sep 2009, Sep 2010 and Sep 2013. Registration: Scottish Charity Regulator, No/ID: SC023162, Start date: 26 Sep 1990, Scotland. **Aims** Advance the education of the public in archaeology. **Structure** Annual General Meeting; Committee. **Finance** Sources: members' dues. **Activities** Advocacy/lobbying/activism; events/meetings; financial and/or material support. **Events** *Meeting* 2022, *Annual Conference* Trondheim (Norway) 2020, *Annual Conference* Constantza (Romania) 2019, *Annual Conference* Venice (Italy) 2018, *Annual Conference* Pula (Croatia) 2017. **Publications** *AARGnews* (2 a year). [2021/AA1798/**F**]

- ♦ **AERM** Alliance of European Republican Movements (#00676)
- ♦ **AERN** African Educational Research Network (#00294)
- ♦ AEROARCTIC – International Study Society for the Exploration of Arctic Regions by Airship (inactive)
- ♦ AEROBAL / see International Organization of Aluminium Aerosol Container Manufacturers (#14437)
- ♦ **AEROBAL** International Organization of Aluminium Aerosol Container Manufacturers (#14437)
- ♦ AeroMed Australasia – Aeromedical Society of Australasia (internationally oriented national body)
- ♦ Aero Medical Association / see Aerospace Medical Association
- ♦ Aeromedical Society of Australasia (internationally oriented national body)
- ♦ Aerophilatelic Society of Southern Africa (internationally oriented national body)

♦ Les Aéroports Francophones 00145

Pres Aéroport La Rochelle-Ile de Ré, rue du Jura, 17000 La Rochelle, France.
SG c/o Aéroports de Paris-Orly, DCM, Zone Sud Bât 651, 103 aérogare Sud, CS 90055, 94396 Orly-Aérogare CEDEX, France.

History Founded 6 Nov 1991, to unite French-speaking members of *Airports Council International (ACI, #00611)*. Original title: *Aéroports de langue française associés à l'ACI (ALFA-ACI) – Association of French-Speaking Airports*. Previously also referred to as *Association francophone des aéroports*. Current title adopted Dec 2016. Full title: *Les Aéroports Francophones – Associés à l'ACI*. **Aims** Study subjects concerning *French-speaking airports* in order to establish common policies and promote *civil airports*; present these common policies on behalf of French-speaking civil airports to authorities and organizations in *aviation* and other related fields. **Structure** Global Board; Management Board; Management Committee; Committees (15). **Languages** French. **Staff** None. **Finance** Members' dues. Budget (annual): euro 100,000. **Activities** Events/meetings. **Events** *Congrès Annuel* Montpellier (France) 2017, *Congrès Annuel* Fort de France (Martinique) 2016, *Congrès Annuel* Geneva (Switzerland) 2015, *Congrès Annuel* Abidjan (Côte d'Ivoire) 2014, *Congrès Annuel* Paris (France) 2013.
Members Airports (150) in 20 countries and territories:
Algeria, Belgium, Cameroon, Canada, Comoros, Congo Brazzaville, Côte d'Ivoire, France, French Antilles, Gabon, Guyana, Madagascar, Moldova, Monaco, Morocco, New Caledonia, Switzerland, Tahiti Is, Togo, Tunisia. [2018/XE2743/**E**]

- ♦ Les Aéroports Francophones – Associés à l'ACI / see Les Aéroports Francophones (#00145)
- ♦ Aéroports de langue française associés à l'ACI / see Les Aéroports Francophones (#00145)
- ♦ Aerosol, Clouds and Trace Gases Research Infrastructure / see ACTRiS (#00104)

♦ Aerospace and Defence Industries Association of Europe (ASD) ... 00146

SG Rue Montoyer 10, 1000 Brussels, Belgium. T. +3227758110. Fax +3227758112. E-mail: info@asd-europe.org.
URL: http://asd-europe.org/

History 2004, by merger of *Association of European Space Industry (EUROSPACE, #02544)*, *European Association of Aerospace Industries (AECMA, inactive)* and *European Defence Industries Group (EDIG, inactive)*. Registered in accordance with Belgian law. EU Transparency Register: 72699997886-57. **Aims** Enhance the competitive development of the aeronautic, space, security and defence industry in Europe. **Structure** General Assembly; Board. Business Units (4): Civil Aviation; Space; Security; Defence. Commissions (6): ELT; R and T; Environment; Services; Supply Chair and SMEs; External Affairs. **Languages** English. **Staff** 23.00 FTE, paid. **Events** *IPS User Forum 2022* Vienna (Austria) 2022, *EU Aeronautics Conference* Brussels (Belgium) 2020, *EU Aeronautics Conference* Brussels (Belgium) 2018, *EU Aeronautics Conference* Brussels (Belgium) 2017, *Annual Conference* Brussels (Belgium) 2016. **Publications** *FOCUS Magazine*. Newsletter; yearly facts and figures; annual reviews.
Members European aerospace and defence companies (16) and national associations (27), in 20 countries:
Austria, Belgium, Bulgaria, Czechia, Denmark, Finland, France, Germany, Greece, Ireland, Italy, Netherlands, Norway, Poland, Portugal, Spain, Sweden, Switzerland, Türkiye, UK.
NGO Relations Affiliated associations: ASD-CERT; *ASD-STAN Standardization (ASD-STAN, #01132)*; *European Aerospace Quality Group (EAQG, #05838)*. Member of: *Council for Environmentally Friendly Aviation (CEFA, #04880)*; *European Organisation for Security (EOS, #08102)*; *Federation of European and International Associations Established in Belgium (FAIB, #09508)*; *Industry4Europe (#11181)*; *International Coordinating Council of Aerospace Industry Associations (ICCAIA, #12956)*. Cooperates closely with: *Comité européen de normalisation (CEN, #04162)*. [2020/XJ4116/t/**D**]

- ♦ Aerospace Medical Association (internationally oriented national body)
- ♦ AERPF – Association européenne pour la réduction de la pollution due aux fibres (inactive)
- ♦ **AERTE** Association européenne de représentants territoriaux de l'état (#06220)
- ♦ AERTEL – Association européenne rubans, tresses, tissus élastiques (inactive)
- ♦ **AESA** Africa Electric Sport Association (#00167)
- ♦ AESA – Alliance for Accelerating Excellence in Science in Africa (unconfirmed)
- ♦ AESA – Association pour l'enseignement social en Afrique (inactive)
- ♦ AES / see Accredited European Schools Network (#00064)
- ♦ AESAD – Association européenne de soins et aides à domicile (inactive)
- ♦ AES – African Econometric Society (inactive)
- ♦ **AESAL** Académie européenne des sciences, des arts et des lettres (#05781)
- ♦ **AES** Aquacultural Engineering Society (#00884)
- ♦ AES / see Arab Endodontic Society (#00939)
- ♦ **AES** Arab Endodontic Society (#00939)
- ♦ **AES** Asian Environmental Society (#01438)
- ♦ AES – ASKO Europa-Stiftung (internationally oriented national body)
- ♦ AES – Association of European Studies, Moscow (internationally oriented national body)
- ♦ AES – Association Européenne SIBIU2020 pour L'Éducation et la Culture (unconfirmed)
- ♦ AESAU – Association of Eastern and Southern African Universities (inactive)
- ♦ **AES** Audio Engineering Society (#03014)
- ♦ **AESC** Arab Economic and Social Council (#00937)
- ♦ **AESC** Asian Epilepsy Surgery Society (#01440)
- ♦ AESC – Association européenne de la sécurité sur les campus (inactive)
- ♦ AESC / see Association of Executive Search and Leadership Consultants (#02588)
- ♦ **AESC** Association of Executive Search and Leadership Consultants (#02588)
- ♦ AESCO – Aide à l'équipement scolaire et culturelle (internationally oriented national body)
- ♦ AESEA / see Benthological Society of Asia (#03208)
- ♦ AESEDA – Alliance for Earth Sciences, Engineering and Development in Africa (internationally oriented national body)
- ♦ AES / see European Aeroallergen Network (#05832)
- ♦ **AESF** Asian Electronic Sports Federation (#01435)
- ♦ **AESGP** Association européenne des spécialités pharmaceutiques grand public (#02543)
- ♦ **AESIEAP** Association of the Electricity Supply Industry of East Asia and the Western Pacific (#02485)
- ♦ AES / see International Atlantic Economic Society (#12291)
- ♦ AES – International Conference on Antennas and Electromagnetic Systems (meeting series)
- ♦ **AESIS** Network for Advancing and Evaluating the Societal Impact of Science (#16983)
- ♦ **AESM** Agence européenne pour la sécurité maritime (#07744)
- ♦ **AESMEAF** Association européenne de pratiques multidisciplinaires en santé mentale de l'enfant, l'adolescent et de la famille (#02580)
- ♦ **AESN** Accredited European Schools Network (#00064)
- ♦ AESOP / see Australian Business Volunteers
- ♦ **AESOP** Association of European Schools of Planning (#02542)

♦ AESOR / see Confédération Interalliée des Sous-Officiers de Réserve (#04556)
♦ **AESP** Association européenne pour les soins palliatifs (#06141)
♦ **AESPRE** Association des écoles de santé publique de la région européenne (#02904)
♦ **AESSD** Association Européenne pour les Soins de Soutien au Développement (#06009)
♦ AESSEA – Agricultural Economics Society of South East Asia (inactive)

♦ Aesthetic Multispecialty Society (AMS) 00147

Contact address not obtained. E-mail: secretariat@multispecialtysociety.com.
Facebook: https://www.facebook.com/WOSIAM.ORG/

Aims Disseminate high knowledge in medical aesthetic and anti-aging prevention/treatment; federate scientific associations with shared values. **Structure** Board. **Activities** Awards/prizes/competitions; events/meetings. **Events** *International Congress of Aesthetic Dermatology* Bangkok (Thailand) 2022, *International Congress of Aesthetic Dermatology* Bangkok (Thailand) 2020, *International Congress of Aesthetic Dermatology* Bangkok (Thailand) 2019, *International Congress of Aesthetic Dermatology* Bangkok (Thailand) 2018, *International Congress of Aesthetic Dermatology* Bangkok (Thailand) 2016. **Publications** *WOSIAM Newsletter.*
[2019/XM8073/**C**]

♦ AESTM – Association européenne des sciences et techniques de la mer (no recent information)
♦ **AETAL** Associação Evangélica de Educação Teológica na América Latina (#02326)
♦ **AETAP** Association of European Threat Assessment Professionals (#02547)
♦ **AET** Association for European Transport (#02548)
♦ **AET** Association européenne de terminologie (#06252)
♦ AET – Association européenne de thanatologie (inactive)
♦ AET – Association européenne de thermographie (inactive)
♦ **AET** Association européenne de thermologie (#06254)
♦ **AETC** Alliance européenne pour la télévision et la culture (#05888)
♦ **AETC** Association européenne de théologie catholique (#08540)
♦ **AETC** Association européenne du thermalisme et du climatisme (#08805)
♦ **AETC** Associazione Europea del Termalismo e Climatismo (#08805)
♦ **AETE** Association européenne de théologiens évangéliques (#09727)
♦ **AETE** Association européenne de transfert embryonnaire (#02582)
♦ AET / see European Thyroid Association (#08913)
♦ **AETF** All Europe Taekwon-Do Federation (#00649)
♦ **AETFAT** Association pour l'étude taxonomique de la flore d'Afrique tropicale (#02948)

♦ Aetherius Society (AS) 00148

European Headquarters 757 Fulham Rd, London, SW6 5UU, UK. T. +442077364187. Fax +442077311067. E-mail: info@aetherius.co.uk.
American Headquarters 6202 Afton Place, Hollywood CA 90028, USA. E-mail: info@aetherius.org.
URL: http://www.aetherius.org/

History 1955. Founded by Dr George King. **Aims** Spread the Teachings of the Master Aetherius, the Master *Jesus* and other Cosmic Masters, through classes on spiritual healing, *yoga* and cosmic teachings; prepare the way for the Coming of the Next Master; perform and support certain missions for mass healing and world peace and enlightenment; promote spiritual healing on an individual and global level. **Activities** Religious activities. **Publications** *The Aetherius Society e-Newsletter* (12 a year). Books; CD-ROMs; DVDs; ebooks; audio downloads.
Members Branches and Groups in 9 countries:
Australia, Canada, Ghana, New Zealand, Nigeria, Portugal, South Africa, UK, USA.
[2023.02.20/XF9673/**F**]

♦ AETR – Accord européen relatif au travail des équipages des véhicules effectuant des transports internationaux par route, 1970 (1970 treaty)
♦ AETR – European Agreement Concerning the Work of Crews of Vehicles Engaged in International Road Transport, 1962 (1962 treaty)
♦ AETR – European Agreement Concerning the Work of Crews of Vehicles Engaged in International Road Transport, 1970 (1970 treaty)
♦ AETSCA – Association pour l'éducation technique dans le Sud et le centre asiatiques (inactive)
♦ AETV – Association européenne de tisseurs de verre (no recent information)
♦ **AEUA** Association of Arab and European Universities (#02373)
♦ AEUSCO – European Association of Universities, Schools and Colleges of Optometry (inactive)
♦ **AEVV** Asociación Europea de Vias Verdes (#07412)
♦ **AEVV** Association Européenne des voies vertes (#07412)
♦ AEWA – African-Eurasian Migratory /Water Bird/ Agreement (1995 treaty)
♦ AEW – Aktion Eine Welt (internationally oriented national body)
♦ **AEXEA** Association des experts européens agréés (#02538)
♦ AF / see Forum for Former African Heads of State and Government (#09915)
♦ AFA / see United Nations Youth and Student Association of Austria – Academic Forum for Foreign Affairs
♦ AFAA / see ASEAN Automotive Federation (#01142)
♦ **AFAA** Asian Federation of Advertising Associations (#01452)
♦ AFAA – Association des facultés agronomiques d'Afrique (inactive)
♦ AFA – African Farmers Association (inactive)
♦ AFA – AID FOR AIDS International (internationally oriented national body)
♦ AFA – Akademisches Forum für Aussenpolitik – Hochschulliga für die Vereinten Nationen (internationally oriented national body)
♦ AfA – Alliances for Africa (internationally oriented national body)
♦ **AFA** Arab Fertilizer Association (#00958)
♦ AFA – Arab Forum for Alternatives (unconfirmed)
♦ AFA – Ark Foundation of Africa (internationally oriented national body)
♦ **AFAAS** African Forum for Agricultural Advisory Services (#00320)
♦ **AFA** ASEAN Federation of Accountants (#01171)
♦ **AfA** Asia for Animals Coalition (#01250)
♦ **AFA** Asian Farmers'Association for Sustainable Rural Development (#01450)
♦ **AFA** Asian Ferroelectric Association (#01477)
♦ AFA – Association of AfricaFreeAid (internationally oriented national body)
♦ AFABA / see FIBA Africa (#09744)
♦ **AFAC** Arab Fund for Arts and Culture (#00964)
♦ AFAC – Australasian Fire Authorities Council (internationally oriented national body)
♦ **AFACI** Asian Food and Agriculture Cooperation Initiative (#01485)
♦ **AFACT** Asia Pacific Council for Trade Facilitation and Electronic Business (#01877)
♦ **AF** Adaptation Fund (#00109)
♦ **AFAD** Asian Federation Against Involuntary Disappearances (#01453)
♦ **AFAEMME** Asociación de Federaciones y Asociaciones de Empresarias del Mediterraneo (#02840)
♦ AFAEMME / see Association of Organisations of Mediterranean Businesswomen (#02840)
♦ AFAEP / see Association of Photographers
♦ AFAF – Asian Federation of American Football (inactive)
♦ AFAHPER-SD – Africa Association for Health, Physical Education, Recreation, Sport and Dance (no recent information)
♦ AFAI – Alliance canadienne féministe pour l'action internationale (internationally oriented national body)
♦ AFAID – African Aid Organization (internationally oriented national body)
♦ AFA International (unconfirmed)
♦ **AFALA** African Assembly of Linguistic Anthropology (#00204)
♦ **AFAL** Association francophone d'amitié et de liaison (#02605)
♦ AFALMA – Africa Association for Liturgy, Music and Arts (inactive)
♦ **AFAN** African ALARA Network (#00201)
♦ **AFAO** Association des femmes de l'Afrique de l'Ouest (#20900)
♦ **AFAP** African Fertilizer and Agribusiness Partnership (#00314)
♦ **AFAPDP** Association francophone des autorités de protection des données personnelles (#02606)
♦ **AFARD** Association des femmes africaines pour la recherche et le développement (#02362)
♦ Afar Diaspora International Federation (#09626)
♦ Afar Diaspora Network / see Fédération Internationale de la Diaspora Afar (#09626)
♦ af – Asahi Glass Foundation (internationally oriented national body)
♦ AFAS – ASEAN Framework Agreement on Services (1995 treaty)
♦ **AFAS** Asian Fisheries Acoustics Society (#01481)
♦ Afasirådet i Norden (#17174)
♦ AFASLD – African Association for the Study of Liver Diseases (no recent information)
♦ AFASPA – Association française d'amitié et de solidarité avec les peuples d'Afrique (internationally oriented national body)
♦ AFASTOF – Afro-Asian Federation for Tobacco Producers and Manufacturers (inactive)
♦ AfATAP – African Association of Threat Assessment Professionals (internationally oriented national body)
♦ AFATTA – Association francophone pour l'avancement des technologies en transformation des aliments (no recent information)
♦ **AFAVAS** Asian Foundation for the Advancement of Veterinary and Animal Science (#01495)
♦ **AfBAA** African Business Aviation Association (#00231)
♦ **AFBA** African Bar Association (#00220)
♦ **AFBE** Asian Forum on Business Education (#01490)
♦ AFBF / see Asian Bodybuilding and Physique Sports Federation (#01361)
♦ AfBMT – African Blood and Marrow Transplantation Society (unconfirmed)
♦ **AfBSA** African Biological Safety Association (#00223)
♦ AfC / see Action for Children and Communities in Africa
♦ **AFCA** African Fine Coffees Association (#00316)
♦ AFCA – Asian Financial Cooperation Association (internationally oriented national body)
♦ **AFCAC** African Civil Aviation Commission (#00248)
♦ AFC / see African Forestry and Wildlife Commission (#00319)
♦ AFC – Ambassadors for Children (internationally oriented national body)
♦ **AFC** Arab Federation for the Consumer (#00942)
♦ **AFC** Arab Fisheries Company (#00959)
♦ **AFCAR** Alliance for the Freedom of Car Repair in the EU (#00682)
♦ AFC – Artists for Conservation (internationally oriented national body)
♦ **AFCAS** African Commission on Agricultural Statistics (#00254)
♦ **AFC** Asian Federation of Cheerleading (#01456)
♦ **AFC** Asian Football Confederation (#01487)
♦ **AFC** Association francophone de comptabilité (#02609)
♦ **AFCB** Arab Federation of Clinical Biology (#00941)
♦ **AFCC** African Federation of Clinical Chemistry (#00306)
♦ **AFCC** Agri-Food Chain Coalition (#00577)
♦ AFCEA International – Armed Forces Communications and Electronics Association International (internationally oriented national body)
♦ **AFCE** Association francophone de chirurgie endocrinienne (#02607)
♦ **AFC-ENG** Alliance for Childhood European Network Group (#00666)
♦ AFCENT / see Allied Joint Force Command Brunssum (#00734)
♦ AFC / see Fencing Confederation of Asia (#09735)
♦ AFCFP / see Arab Fertilizer Association (#00958)
♦ **AfCFTA** African Continental Free Trade Area (#00267)
♦ AFCG / see Australasian Cytometry Society
♦ AFCG / see Arab Fisheries Company (#00959)
♦ **AfCHPR** African Court on Human and Peoples' Rights (#00278)
♦ **AFCI** Ambassadors for Christ International (#00768)
♦ **AFCI** Association of Film Commissioners International (#02595)
♦ AFCLIST – African Forum for Children's Literacy in Science and Technology (internationally oriented national body)
♦ **AFCMA** Asian Federation of Catholic Medical Associations (#01455)
♦ AFCM-ASEAN-CCI / see ASEAN Federation of Cement Manufacturers (#01173)
♦ **AFCM** ASEAN Federation of Cement Manufacturers (#01173)
♦ AFC Merchant Bank / see ASEAN Finance Corporation (#01186)
♦ **AFCNDH** Association francophone des commissions nationales des droits de l'Homme (#02608)
♦ **AFCNet** Asian Film Commissions Network (#01478)
♦ **AFCO** African Council of Optometry (#00275)
♦ AFCO – Aluminium Foil Conference (inactive)
♦ AFCOD – African Centre for Community and Development (unconfirmed)
♦ **AFCONE** African Commission on Nuclear Energy (#00256)
♦ AFCP / see Asia Pacific Federation of Coloproctology (#01897)
♦ AFCPI – Arab Federation of Chemical and Petrochemical Industries (no recent information)
♦ **AFCTWS** African Confederation of Traditional Wrestling Sports (#00263)
♦ AFCUD – Asia Fund for Credit Union Development (see: #02377)
♦ AFCW / see Fédération panafricaine des employés (#09700)
♦ **AFDA** Asian Federation of Dietetic Associations (#01458)
♦ AFD – Action for Dolphins (internationally oriented national body)
♦ AFD – Agence française de développement (internationally oriented national body)
♦ AF – Damien Foundation – Voluntary Organization for Leprosy and TB Control (internationally oriented national body)
♦ AfDB / see African Development Bank (#00283)
♦ AFDEAA – Association des femmes et des jeunes de la diaspora africaine pour le développement socio-éducatif et agricole de l'afrique (internationally oriented national body)
♦ **AfDEA** African Dental Education Association (#00282)
♦ **AFDE** Association des facultés de droit en Europe (#07656)
♦ AFDEM – Association francophone pour le développement de l'éducation médicale (inactive)
♦ AfDF / see African Development Fund (#00285)
♦ AFDHA – Association francophone des droits de l'homme âgé (internationally oriented national body)
♦ AFDI – Agriculteurs français et développement international (internationally oriented national body)
♦ AFDI – Asia-Pacific Finance and Development Institute (internationally oriented national body)
♦ AFDIP – Association africaine des formateurs et directeurs de personnel (inactive)
♦ AFDP / see Asian Federation of Dietetic Associations (#01458)
♦ AFDWEA – Arab Federation for Democracy and Workers Education Associations (no recent information)
♦ AFEA – African Finance and Economics Association (internationally oriented national body)
♦ **AFEA** Alliance des Femmes Evangeliques en Afrique (#18043)
♦ AFEA – Association française d'études américaines (internationally oriented national body)
♦ **AFE** Arab Federation of Exchanges (#00944)
♦ **AFE** Association for Fire Ecology (#02597)
♦ **AFE** Atlas Florae Europaeae (#04268)
♦ **AFECA** Asian Federation of Exhibition and Convention Associations (#01459)
♦ AFEC – Asian Federation of Electronic Circuits (unconfirmed)
♦ **AFEC** Association francophone d'éducation comparée (#02610)
♦ AFECI – Association des fabricants européens de chauffe-bains et chauffe-eau instantanés et de chaudières murales au gaz (inactive)
♦ **AfECN** Africa Early Childhood Network (#00166)
♦ AFECOGAZ / see Association des fabricants européens d'appareils de contrôle et de régulation (#02592)

- ♦ **AFECOR** Association des fabricants européens d'appareils de contrôle et de régulation (#02592)
- ♦ AFECTI / see Association francophone des experts et des consultants de la coopération technique internationale
- ♦ AFÉCTI – Association francophone des experts et des consultants de la coopération technique internationale (internationally oriented national body)
- ♦ **AFED** Arab Forum for Environment and Development (#00960)
- ♦ AFED – Association Femmes et développement (internationally oriented national body)
- ♦ AFEDEF – Association des fabricants européens d'équipements ferroviaires (inactive)
- ♦ **AFEDI** Association Francophone Européenne des Diagnostics Interventions Résultats Infirmiers (#02612)
- ♦ AFEE – Association for Evolutionary Economics (internationally oriented national body)
- ♦ AFÉE – Association Française d'Études Européennes (internationally oriented national body)
- ♦ **AFEEB** Association francophone européenne d'études baha'ies (#02613)
- ♦ **AFEEC** ASEAN Federation of Electrical Engineering Contractors (#01174)
- ♦ AFEHC – Asociación para el Fomento de los Estudios Históricos en Centroamérica (internationally oriented national body)
- ♦ **AFEI** Arab Federation for Engineering Industries (#00943)
- ♦ **AFEIDAL** Asociación de Facultades, Escuelas e Institutos de Derecho de América Latina (#02129)
- ♦ **AFEIEAL** Asociación de Facultades, Escuelas e Institutos de Economia de América Latina (#02784)
- ♦ AFEJ / see Asia-Pacific Forum of Environmental Journalists (#01910)
- ♦ **AFELSH** Association des facultés ou établissements de lettres et sciences humaines des universités d'expression française (#02593)
- ♦ **AFEM** African Federation for Emergency Medicine (#00307)
- ♦ **AFEM** Association des femmes de l'Europe méridionale (#02594)
- ♦ AFEM – European Natural Disasters Training Centre, Ankara (internationally oriented national body)
- ♦ **AFEMS** Association des fabricants européens de munitions de sport (#02522)
- ♦ **AFENET** African Field Epidemiology Network (#00315)
- ♦ **AFEO** ASEAN Federation of Engineering Organizations (#01176)
- ♦ AFEPA – Association des fabricants européens de pièces automobiles (inactive)
- ♦ **AFERA** Association des fonds d'entretien routier africains (#00443)
- ♦ AFERA / see European Adhesive Tape Association (#05826)
- ♦ **AFERA** European Adhesive Tape Association (#05826)
- ♦ **AFERT** Association européenne des femmes pour la recherche théologique (#08789)
- ♦ **AFERUP** Association Francophone pour l'Etude et la Recherche sur les Urgences Psychiatriques (#02611)
- ♦ AFES – Arbeitsgruppe Friedensforschung und Europäische Sicherheitspolitik (internationally oriented national body)
- ♦ **AFES** ASEAN Federation of Endocrine Societies (#01175)
- ♦ **AFESD** Arab Fund for Economic and Social Development (#00965)
- ♦ AFESIP International – Agir pour les femmes en situation précaire (internationally oriented national body)
- ♦ AFES-PRESS – Peace Research and European Security Studies (internationally oriented national body)
- ♦ AFEW – AIDS Foundation East-West (internationally oriented national body)
- ♦ AFEW International / see AIDS Foundation East-West
- ♦ AFEX – African Freedom of Expression Exchange (unconfirmed)
- ♦ **AFFA** ASEAN Federation of Forwarders Associations (#01177)
- ♦ **AFF** African Forest Forum (#00318)
- ♦ AFFAH – African Foundation For Human Advancement (internationally oriented national body)
- ♦ AFF – Anne Frank Fonds (internationally oriented national body)
- ♦ **AFF** Arab Foundations Forum (#00963)
- ♦ **AFFAS** Asian Federation of Foot and Ankle Surgeons (#01460)
- ♦ **AFF** ASEAN Football Federation (#01187)
- ♦ **AFF** Asia Fashion Federation (#01276)
- ♦ AFFC – ASEAN Federation of Flying Clubs (inactive)
- ♦ AFFHO – Australasian Federation of Family History Organizations (internationally oriented national body)
- ♦ **AFFI** Arab Federation for Food Industries (#00946)

♦ Affiliation of Rotational Moulding Organisations (ARMO) 00149

Contact c/o ARMA, PO Box 826, Ipswich QLD 4305, Australia. T. +61738121450. E-mail: info@rotationalmoulding.com.
URL: http://www.armo-global.org/

Aims Provide an equal forum for organizations serving the global rotational moulding industry. **Events** *Conference* Gold Coast, QLD (Australia) 2016, *Conference* Nottingham (UK) 2015. **Publications** *ARMO News*.
Members National and regional organizations in 12 countries:
Australia, China, France, Germany, India, Italy, Mexico, Norway, Poland, South Africa, UK, USA.
Included in the above, 6 organizations listed in this Yearbook:
Association Francophone du Rotomoulage (AFR); Association of Rotational Moulders Australasia (ARMA); Association of Rotational Moulders of Southern Africa (ARMSA); Association of Rotational Moulding – Central Europe (ARM-CE); Nordic Association of Rotational Moulders (Nordic ARM, #17203); Society of Asian Rotomoulders (StAR). [2015/XJ9198/y/**C**]

- ♦ AFF / see International Cultic Studies Association (#13121)
- ♦ AFFMA / see ASEAN Furniture Industries Council (#01192)
- ♦ AF / see Fondation des Alliances Françaises (#09814)
- ♦ **AF** Fondation des Alliances Françaises (#09814)
- ♦ Affordable Medicines for Africa (internationally oriented national body)

♦ Affordable Medicines Europe 00150

SG Rue des Deux Eglises 26, 1000 Brussels, Belgium. T. +32491255611. E-mail: info@affordablemedicines.eu.
URL: https://affordablemedicines.eu/

History 23 Jun 1998, Brussels (Belgium). Registration: Transparency Register Number, No/ID: 095858939393; EU Transparency Register, No/ID: 509882515669-01, Start date: 20 Jan 2015; Banque Carrefour des Entreprises, No/ID: 0465125985, Start date: 11 Feb 1999, Belgium. **Aims** Safeguard free movement of *medicines*; counteract attempts to restrict freedom of choice for the consumer; review, evaluate and react to development that affect parallel trade with medicines; keep members informed and involved; represent their interests with appropriate organizations at national and European levels. **Structure** General Assembly (biennial); Board of Directors; Working Groups. **Languages** English. **Staff** 5.00 FTE, paid. **Finance** Sources: members' dues. **Activities** Guidance/assistance/consulting; monitoring/evaluation. **Events** *Meeting* Vienna (Austria) 2015.
Members National associations and individual companies (about 85 companies) in 23 countries:
Austria, Belgium, Bulgaria, Czechia, Denmark, Estonia, Finland, France, Germany, Greece, Hungary, Ireland, Italy, Lithuania, Malta, Netherlands, Norway, Poland, Portugal, Romania, Spain, Sweden, UK.
NGO Relations Member of (2): *Alliance for Safe Online Pharmacy – EU (ASOP EU, #00720); Federation of European and International Associations Established in Belgium (FAIB, #09508).* Founding member of: *European Medicines Verification Organisation (EMVO, #07768).* [2021/XD6938/**D**]

- ♦ AFFORD – African Foundation for Development (internationally oriented national body)
- ♦ AFFORTHECC – Association Francophone de Formation et Recherche en Thérapie Comportementale et Cognitive (unconfirmed)
- ♦ **AFFP** Arab Federation of Fish Producers (#00945)
- ♦ AFFPI-ASEAN-CCI / see ASEAN Federation of Glass Manufacturers (#01178)
- ♦ AFFS – Academy for Future Science (internationally oriented national body)
- ♦ AFG – Association Francophone des Glycogénoses (internationally oriented national body)
- ♦ AFGE – African Federation of Gastroenterology (no recent information)
- ♦ **AfGH** Action for Global Health (#00090)
- ♦ Afghanistan World Foundation (internationally oriented national body)
- ♦ AfGJ – Alliance for Global Justice (internationally oriented national body)
- ♦ **AFGM** ASEAN Federation of Glass Manufacturers (#01178)
- ♦ **AFGT** African Federation for the Gifted and Talented (#00308)
- ♦ **AFH** ASEAN Federation of Haematology (#01179)
- ♦ **AfHEA** African Health Economics and Policy Association (#00335)
- ♦ **AfHF** African Hockey Federation (#00338)
- ♦ AFHF – ASEAN Federation of Heart Foundations (no recent information)
- ♦ **AFHIC** Asociación de Filosofía e Historia de la Ciencia del Cono Sur (#02130)
- ♦ AFIA – African Federation of Inventors' Associations (inactive)
- ♦ **AFIA** Australasian Forum for International Arbitration (#03024)
- ♦ **AFI** African Futures Institute (#00327)
- ♦ **AFI** Alliance for Financial Inclusion (#00679)
- ♦ AFI – American Film Institute (internationally oriented national body)
- ♦ AFI – Ancient Forest International (internationally oriented national body)
- ♦ **AFI** Ariel Foundation International (#01106)
- ♦ AFI – Association des foyers internationaux (internationally oriented national body)
- ♦ **AFI** Association fraternelle internationale (#11465)
- ♦ **AFIC** Africa Freedom of Information Centre (#00175)
- ♦ **AFIC** ASEAN Furniture Industries Council (#01192)
- ♦ **AFIC** Asia Fire Protection Inspection Council (#01277)
- ♦ AFIC – Asian Finance and Investment Corporation (inactive)
- ♦ AFIC – Asian Food Information Council (no recent information)
- ♦ **AFICS New York** Asociación de ex Funcionarios Públicos Internacionales – New York (#02600)
- ♦ **AFICS New York** Association of Former International Civil Servants – New York (#02600)
- ♦ **AfICTA** Africa Information and Communication Technologies Alliance (#00181)
- ♦ AFICUD / see Credit Union Foundation Australia
- ♦ **AFIDA** Asociación Internacional de Ferias de América (#11886)
- ♦ AFID – Association francophone internationale du diabète (inactive)
- ♦ **AFIDE** Association of Former United Nations Industry and Development Experts (#02602)
- ♦ AFIDEP – African Institute for Development Policy Research and Dialogue (internationally oriented national body)
- ♦ AFIDES – Association francophone internationale des directeurs d'établissements scolaires (inactive)
- ♦ **AFIGAP** Association francophone internationale des groupes d'animation de la paraplégie (#02614)
- ♦ AFI-ICA / see Inter-Cultural Association (#11465)
- ♦ **AFIIP** African International Institute for Peace (#00345)
- ♦ **AFIL** African Foundation for International Law (#00325)

♦ AFILIATYS 00151

Administrative Delegate Rue de la Science 29 – SC29 00/26, 1049 Brussels, Belgium. T. +3222981003. Fax +3222981005. E-mail: afiliatys@ec.europa.eu.
URL: http://www.afiliatys.eu/

History 1965, as *Union of Provident Associations of Officials of the European Union – Union des groupements de prévoyance des fonctionnaires européens (UGPFE) – Zusammenschluss der Vorsorgevereinigungen der Europäischen Beamten*, as a cooperative society. Formerly also referred to in English as *Providential Union of Officials of the European Union (UPFE)*. Subsequently changed title to *Union of Providence of European Officials – Union de prévoyance des fonctionnaires européens (UPFE) – Zusammenschluss der Vorsorgeunion der Europäischen Beamten*. Current title adopted when registered in accordance with Belgian law, 21 Dec 2006. **Aims** Contribute to the global and sustainable well-being of members; develop social and cultural links between members and the host country. **Structure** General Meeting; Board of up to 10 members. **Languages** English, French. **Activities** Provides assistance, advice and information to officials and other employees of European Union in such fields as: insurance, including the conclusion of insurance contracts (group insurance, individual insurance); supply of domestic heating oil; maintenance of heating installations; etc. Organizes: Welcome days; Kids days; Opera. **Publications** *AFILIATYS News* (5 a year); *AFILIATYS Review* – online.
Members Individuals staff, both active and pensioners (over 17,500) of the European Union. Members from 27 countries:
Austria, Belgium, Bulgaria, Cyprus, Czechia, Denmark, Estonia, Finland, France, Germany, Greece, Hungary, Ireland, Italy, Latvia, Lithuania, Luxembourg, Malta, Netherlands, Poland, Portugal, Romania, Slovakia, Slovenia, Spain, Sweden, UK.
[2019/XE5911/v/**E**]

- ♦ **AFINet** Addiction and the Family International Network (#00111)
- ♦ AFIPOCO – Association fédérale internationale des promoteurs et organisateurs de courses océaniques (inactive)
- ♦ **AFIR** Asian Forum of Insurance Regulators (#01492)
- ♦ **AFIRSE** Association francophone internationale de recherche scientifique en éducation (#02615)
- ♦ AFISAL – Asociación de Facultades de Ingenieria de Sistemas de América Latine (inactive)
- ♦ AFIS – Association for Improvement of Safety (no recent information)
- ♦ **AFISM** Association Internationale pour la promotion de Formations Spécialisées en Médecine et en Sciences Biologiques (#02733)
- ♦ AFISTAS – Association francophone internationale des spécialistes du traitement des abuseurs sexuels (no recent information)
- ♦ AFITA / see Asia-Pacific Federation for Information Technology in Agriculture (#01900)
- ♦ AFJEM – Association femmes et jeunesse dans l'environnement maghrébin (no recent information)
- ♦ AFJN – Africa Faith and Justice Network (internationally oriented national body)
- ♦ AFJN/E / see Africa-Europe Faith and Justice Network (#00171)
- ♦ AFK – Arbeitsgemeinschaft für Friedens-und Konfliktforschung (internationally oriented national body)
- ♦ AFK / see WKF Asia (#20973)
- ♦ **AFLA** Africa Legal Aid (#00186)
- ♦ AFLA – American Foreign Law Association (internationally oriented national body)
- ♦ **AFLA** Asian Federation of Laryngectomees' Associations (#01463)
- ♦ AFLA – Asian Federation of Library Associations (inactive)
- ♦ **AFLA** Austronesian Formal Linguistics Association (#03038)
- ♦ AFL – Acting for Life (internationally oriented national body)
- ♦ **AFLAG** ASEAN Federation of Land Surveying and Geomatics (#01180)
- ♦ AFLAR / see African League of Associations for Rheumatology (#00360)
- ♦ **AFLAR** African League of Associations for Rheumatology (#00360)
- ♦ **AFLAS** Asian Federation of Laboratory Animal Science Associations (#01462)
- ♦ Aflatoun / see Aflatoun International (#00152)

♦ Aflatoun International 00152

Mailing Address PO Box 15991, 1001 NL Amsterdam, Netherlands. T. +31206262025. E-mail: info@aflatoun.org.
URL: http://www.aflatoun.org/

History 2005, Amsterdam (Netherlands). Founded following the work of Jeroo Billimoria. Former names and other names: *Child Savings International (Aflatoun)* – former. Registration: Netherlands. **Aims** Develop and promote *child savings* programmes and child *rights* to combat *poverty*. **Structure** General Board; Regional Representatives (6). **Staff** 29.00 FTE, paid. **Activities** Events/meetings; training/education. **Events** *Aflatoun Day Meeting* Amsterdam (Netherlands) 2021. **Publications** *Aflatoun Newsletter* (6 a year). Annual Report. **NGO Relations** Member of (2): *International Centre for Social Franchising (ICSF); International Childhood and Youth Research Network (ICYRnet, #12549).* Stakeholder in: *Child and Youth Finance International (CYFI, inactive).*
[2021.03.05/XM4564/**C**]

- ♦ AFLF – Africa Family Life Federation (inactive)
- ♦ **AfLIA** African Library and Information Associations and Institutions (#00363)
- ♦ **AFLI** Africa Leadership Institute (#00184)

- ♦ **AFLI** Arab Federation for Libraries and Information (#00947)
- ♦ AfLSA / see African Law Students' Association
- ♦ AFMA / see Independent Film and Television Alliance
- ♦ **AfMA** Africa Medical Association (#00188)
- ♦ **AFMA** African Masters Athletics (#00368)
- ♦ **AFMA** Agricultural and Food Marketing Association for Asia and the Pacific (#00569)
- ♦ **AFMA** ASEAN Federation of Mining Associations (#01181)
- ♦ **AFMA** Asian Federation of Middle East Studies Associations (#01466)
- ♦ AFM – Adventist Frontier Missions (internationally oriented national body)
- ♦ AFMANENA – Agricultural Food Marketing Association for the Near East and North Africa Region (no recent information)
- ♦ AFM – Anglican Frontier Missions (internationally oriented national body)
- ♦ AFM – Arab Federation for Metrology (unconfirmed)
- ♦ **AFM** Articulación Feminista Marcosur (#09730)
- ♦ **AFM** Association of Futures Markets (#02621)
- ♦ AFMAT – Association Francophone de MAnagement du Tourisme (internationally oriented national body)
- ♦ **AFMC** Asian Federation of Medicinal Chemistry (#01464)
- ♦ **AFMC** Asian Fluid Mechanics Committee (#01484)
- ♦ AFMD – Advanced Functional Materials and Devices (meeting series)
- ♦ AFME – African Forum for Mathematical Ecology (no recent information)
- ♦ **AFME** Arab Foundation for Marine Environment (#00962)
- ♦ **AFME** Association for Financial Markets in Europe (#02596)
- ♦ AFMESA – Association of Food Marketing Enterprises in Eastern and Southern Africa (inactive)
- ♦ AFM Europe – Amis du Fonds mondial Europe (internationally oriented national body)
- ♦ **AFMIN** Africa Microfinance Network (#00189)
- ♦ AFMPO / see Asia-Oceania Federation of Organizations for Medical Physics (#01797)
- ♦ AFMR / see Asian Federation on Intellectual Disabilities (#01461)
- ♦ AFMVM – Australasian Federation for Medical and Veterinary Mycology (internationally oriented national body)
- ♦ **AFNA** Americas Federation of Netball Associations (#00793)
- ♦ AFNA / see Netball Asia (#16977)
- ♦ AFN – Asia Forest Network (internationally oriented national body)
- ♦ AFN – Australasian Facilitators' Network (internationally oriented national body)
- ♦ **AFNDA** Arab Federation of NGOs for Drug Abuse Prevention (#00948)
- ♦ AFN / see Fairtrade Africa (#09239)
- ♦ **AFNLP** Asian Federation of Natural Language Processing (#01467)
- ♦ **AfNOG** African Network Operators Group (#00392)
- ♦ AFNORTH / see Allied Joint Force Command Brunssum (#00734)
- ♦ **AFOB** Asian Federation of Biotechnology (#01454)
- ♦ AFOB / see Helen Keller International (#10902)
- ♦ **AFOC** ASEAN Forum on Coal (#01189)
- ♦ **AFoCO** Asian Forest Cooperation Organization (#01489)
- ♦ AFOCS – African Oil Chemists' Society (no recent information)
- ♦ AFOD / see Arab Federation of Organizations Working with the Deaf (#00949)
- ♦ **AFOG** African Federation of Obstetrics and Gynaecology (#00309)
- ♦ **AFOM** Association francophone oecuménique de missiologie (#02616)
- ♦ **AFOMEDI** Asian Federation of Mediterranean Studies Institutes (#01465)
- ♦ **AFOMP** Asia-Oceania Federation of Organizations for Medical Physics (#01797)
- ♦ AFOPDA – African Oil Palm Development Association (no recent information)
- ♦ **AFoPS** Asian Forum for Polar Sciences (#01494)
- ♦ AFORD – Action for Development (internationally oriented national body)
- ♦ AFOS / see Arab Federation of Shipping (#00953)
- ♦ **AFOS** Asian Federation of Osteoporosis Societies (#01468)
- ♦ AFOS – Association for the Foundations of Science, Language and Cognition (no recent information)
- ♦ **AFOWD** Arab Federation of Organizations Working with the Deaf (#00949)
- ♦ **AFPA** Asian Federation of Psychiatric Associations (#01470)
- ♦ **AFPAN** African Physical Activity Network (#00416)
- ♦ **AFP** Arab Federation of Psychiatrists (#00952)
- ♦ AfP – Artists for Peace Association (inactive)
- ♦ **AFP** Asian Federation for Psychotherapy (#01471)
- ♦ AFP – Association for Financial Professionals (internationally oriented national body)
- ♦ AFP – Association of Fundraising Professionals (internationally oriented national body)
- ♦ **AFPB** Asian Foundation for the Prevention of Blindness (#01496)
- ♦ **AFPBF** African Paintball Federation (#00408)
- ♦ AFPCA – Association Francophone contre la Polychondrite Chronique Atrophiante (internationally oriented national body)
- ♦ AFPC – American Foreign Policy Council (internationally oriented national body)
- ♦ AFPE International / see Seniors of the European Public Service (#19229)
- ♦ AFPERA – Association féminine pluridisciplinaire d'études et de recherches en Afrique (inactive)
- ♦ AFPE / see Seniors of the European Public Service (#19229)
- ♦ AFPG – International Conference on the Advances in Fusion and Processing of Glass (meeting series)
- ♦ **AFPHA** African Federation of Public Health Associations (#00310)
- ♦ **AFPI** ASEAN Federation of Plastic Industries (#01182)
- ♦ AfPiC / see Action for Children and Communities in Africa
- ♦ **AFPIPR** Arab Federation for the Protection of Intellectual Property Rights (#00951)
- ♦ **AFPLP** Associação de Farmacêuticos dos Paises de Lingua Portuguesa (#02327)
- ♦ AFPM – Advanced Functional Polymers for Medicine (meeting series)
- ♦ **AFPMH** ASEAN Federation for Psychiatry and Mental Health (#01184)
- ♦ **AFPNA** African Paediatric Nephrology Association (#00407)
- ♦ **AFPPD** Asian Forum of Parliamentarians on Population and Development (#01493)
- ♦ **AFPPPI** Asian Federation for Paper, Printing and Packaging Industries (#00950)
- ♦ AFPRA / see Africa Peace Research and Education Association (#00511)
- ♦ **AFPRC** Association francophone pour la prévention-réadaptation cardiovasculaire (#02617)
- ♦ **AFPREA** Africa Peace Research and Education Association (#00511)
- ♦ AFPSA – African Federation of Private Schools Associations (internationally oriented national body)
- ♦ **AfPS** African Physical Society (#00417)
- ♦ **AFPS** Asian Federation for Pharmaceutical Sciences (#01469)
- ♦ **AFPSS** Asian Facial Plastic Surgery Society (#01449)
- ♦ AFPU – Asia Freerunning Parkour Union (unconfirmed)
- ♦ AFQUAD / see European Quadricycle League (#08309)
- ♦ AFR / see International Association of Forensic Radiographers
- ♦ **AFRAA** African Airlines Association (#00200)
- ♦ AFRA – African Regional Cooperative Agreement for Research, Development and Training Related to Nuclear Science and Technology (treaty)
- ♦ **AFRACA** African Rural and Agricultural Credit Association (#00446)
- ♦ **AFRAC** African Accreditation Cooperation (#00196)
- ♦ AFRAD – African Association of Dermatology (no recent information)
- ♦ **AFRALTI** African Advanced Level Telecommunications Institute (#00197)
- ♦ **AFRAN** African Association of Nephrology (#00209)
- ♦ **AFRAN** African Research on Ageing Network (#00440)
- ♦ AFRAND – African Foundation for Research and Development (no recent information)
- ♦ **AFRAPS** Association francophone pour la recherche en activités physiques et sportives (#02619)
- ♦ **AFRAS** African Arachnological Society (#00202)
- ♦ AFRASEC – Afro-Asian Organization for Economic Cooperation (inactive)
- ♦ AFR – Association Francophone du Rotomoulage (internationally oriented national body)
- ♦ AFRATC – African Air Tariff Conference (no recent information)
- ♦ **AfrEA** African Evaluation Association (#00304)
- ♦ **AFREC** African Energy Commission (#00298)
- ♦ **AFREhealth** African Forum for Research and Education in Health (#00322)

♦ AFREPREN/FWD 00153

Dir PO Box 30979, Nairobi, 00100, Kenya. T. +254203866032 – +254203866032 – +254202535266. Fax +254203861464. E-mail: afreprenfwd16@gmail.com.
URL: https://www.afrepren.org/

History 1987. Founded as a Programme on Energy, Environment and Sustainable Development. **Aims** Provide key stakeholders with feasible technical, financing and policy options, information and skills for the delivery of affordable and cleaner energy services for the poor in Africa.. **Structure** Management team, Secretariat. **Languages** English. **Staff** 17.50 FTE, paid. **Finance** Sources: grants. **Activities** Events/meetings; research/documentation; training/education. **Events** *Workshop on energy* Lusaka (Zambia) 1994, *Energy planning seminar* Nairobi (Kenya) 1993. **Publications** *AFREPREN Newsletter* (4 a year). Dossier series. Books; working papers; occasional papers.
Members Energy researchers and policy makers in 10 countries:
Botswana, Kenya, Lesotho, Malawi, Mauritius, South Africa, Tanzania UR, Uganda, Zambia, Zimbabwe.
NGO Relations Member of: *Climate Action Network (CAN, #03999)*; *EarthAction (EA, #05159)*.
[2020/XF5252/v/**F**]

- ♦ **AfRES** African Real Estate Society (#00428)
- ♦ AFREWATCH – African Resources Watch (internationally oriented national body)
- ♦ **Afreximbank** African Export-Import Bank (#00305)
- ♦ Afri – Action from Ireland (internationally oriented national body)
- ♦ **AfriAlliance** Africa-EU Innovation Alliance for Water and Climate (#00169)
- ♦ Africa 2000 (internationally oriented national body)
- ♦ Africa 2000 Charity Foundation / see Africa 2000
- ♦ Africa 2000 Network / see Africa 2000 Plus Network, Harare (#00154)

♦ Africa 2000 Plus Network, Harare 00154

Contact GEF Small Grants Project, 60 Selous Ave, Takura House, Union Avenue, PO Box 4775, Harare, HARARE, Zimbabwe. T. +2634700939. Fax +2634700946.

History 1989, Harare (Zimbabwe), as *Africa 2000 Network – Réseau Afrique 2000*, on the initiative of *UNDP (#20292)*. Also previously referred to as *NGO Africa 2000 Network*. **Aims** Provide institutional support to foster environmentally sensitive *poverty* reduction policies; improve livelihoods and resource management of *rural communities* in Africa. **NGO Relations** Partner of: *International Centre for Tropical Agriculture (#12527)*.
[2008/XF2494/**F**]

- ♦ Africa 21 – Association Africa 21 (internationally oriented national body)
- ♦ Africa 70 (internationally oriented national body)
- ♦ Africa Action (internationally oriented national body)
- ♦ Africa Adaptation Knowledge Network (unconfirmed)
- ♦ Africa Advocacy Foundation (internationally oriented national body)
- ♦ Africa Alliance for Health Research and Economic Development (internationally oriented national body)
- ♦ Africa Alliance of YMCAs / see Africa Alliance of Young Men's Christian Associations (#00155)

♦ Africa Alliance of Young Men's Christian Associations 00155

Alliance africaine des unions chrétiennes de jeunes gens

Contact State House Crescent, PO Box 60856, Nairobi, 00200, Kenya. T. +254202724804. E-mail: aaymcas@africaymca.org.
URL: https://africaymca.org/

History Mar 1977, within the framework of *World Alliance of Young Men's Christian Associations (YMCA, #21090)*. Also known as *Africa Alliance of YMCAs – Alliance africaine des UCJG*. **Aims** Promote and strengthen local initiatives aimed at fostering: social justice; international understanding; leadership development; rehabilitation programmes for refugees; institutional capacity building; establishing viable sustainable national movements; personal growth and development of individual members of national movements, especially youth; youth and gender development. **Structure** General Meeting (every 3 years). Executive Committee (meets annually), comprising 15 members, including office bearers: Chairman, 2 Vice-Chairmen and Honorary Treasurer. Sub-Committees (4): Finances and Personnel; Leadership and Development; Inter-Movement Cooperation; Youth and Gender. National Movements grouped into 3 zones, each headed by Facilitator: Eastern; Southern; Western. Secretariat, headed by Executive Secretary. **Finance** Members' dues. Budget (annual): US$ 500,000. **Activities** Strategic Plan 2001-2005 – Programme Areas: HIV/AIDS; Civic Education; Peace Building; Gender Mainstreaming and Sensitization; Drug Control; Mine Awareness Campaign. **Events** *General Assembly* Johannesburg (South Africa) 2019, *General Meeting* Nairobi (Kenya) 2006, *Ordinary general meeting / General Meeting* Johannesburg (South Africa) 2002, *Youth and gender workshop* Lomé (Togo) 1997, *Ordinary general meeting* Port Said (Egypt) 1995. **Publications** *Africa Alliance Youth Newsletter* (4 a year).
Members National Movements (26, representing over 500,000 individuals) in 24 countries:
Angola, Benin, Burundi, Cameroon, Egypt, Ethiopia, Gabon, Gambia, Ghana, Kenya, Liberia, Madagascar, Mauritius, Nigeria, Rwanda, Sao Tomé-Principe, Senegal, Sierra Leone, South Africa, Sudan, Tanzania UR, Togo, Zambia, Zimbabwe.
NGO Relations *CARE International (CI, #03429)*; *Forum of African Voluntary Development Organizations (FAVDO, inactive)*; *International Youth Foundation (IYF)*; *World Organization of the Scout Movement (WOSM, #21693)*; *World Young Women's Christian Association (World YWCA, #21947)*. [2019/XE7502/**E**]

- ♦ Africa-America Institute (internationally oriented national body)
- ♦ Africa Annual Congress Europe (meeting series)
- ♦ Africa Asia Development Relief Foundation (internationally oriented national body)
- ♦ Africa Asia Scholars Global Network (internationally oriented national body)
- ♦ Africa Association, Hamburg (internationally oriented national body)
- ♦ Africa Association for Health, Physical Education, Recreation, Sport and Dance (no recent information)
- ♦ Africa Association for Liturgy, Music and Arts (inactive)

♦ Africa Association of Quantity Surveyors (AAQS) 00156

Liaison Officer Thornhill Office Park, Unit G6 – Building 27, Bekker Road – Vorna Valley Ext 21, Midrand, 1681, South Africa. T. +27113154140. Fax +27113153785. E-mail: admin@aaqs.org.
URL: http://www.aaqs.org/

History 2 Jun 1999, Sun City (South Africa). **Aims** Unite national bodies of quantity surveyors on the African continent on a democratic basis; foster co-operative, intellectual, cultural, educational and scientific ties among such bodies. **Structure** General Assembly. Council, comprising Executive Committee (President, Immediate Past-President, Eastern Region Vice-President, Southern Region Vice-President, Western Region Vice-President, Secretary-General, Honorary Treasurer, Chairman of Educational and Training Committee, Chairman of Ethics and Conduct Committee and Chairman of Services and Model Documentation) and regional representatives. **Events** *Joint Conference / World Congress* Accra (Ghana) 2024, *Joint Conference* Accra (Ghana) 2020, *General Assembly* Pretoria (South Africa) 2014, *International conference* Durban (South Africa) 2007, *Meeting* Abuja (Nigeria) 2005.
Members Full; Associate; Honorary. Full in 13 countries:
Angola, Botswana, Eswatini, Ghana, Kenya, Mauritius, Mozambique, Namibia, Nigeria, South Africa, Tanzania UR, Uganda, Zimbabwe.
NGO Relations *International Cost Management Standard Coalition (ICMS Coalition, #12978)*; *International Cost Engineering Council (ICEC, #12976)*. [2014/XD7065/**D**]

♦ Africa Atrocities Watch 00157

CEO Plot 16 Kyambogo Way, Ministers' Village Ntinda, PO Box 7785, Kampala, Uganda. T. +256751259952. E-mail: info@atrocitieswatch.org.
URL: http://www.atrocitieswatch.org/

Aims Provide leadership in matters pertaining to prevention of mass atrocities in Africa. **Structure** Board; Advisory Board. **Languages** English, French. **Staff** 5.00 FTE, paid; 1.00 FTE, voluntary. **Finance** Funded by foundations and philanthropies. Annual budget: about US$ 700,000. **Activities** Advocacy/lobbying/activism; knowledge management/information dissemination; research/documentation. **Publications** Weekly updates; reports.
Members Full in 8 countries:
Burundi, Congo DR, Gambia, Kenya, South Sudan, Tanzania UR, Uganda, Zimbabwe.
IGO Relations *African Commission on Human and Peoples' Rights (ACHPR, #00255); African Union (AU, #00488); East African Community (EAC, #05181).* **NGO Relations** *Freedom House; Open Society Foundations (OSF, #17763); Pan-African Lawyers Union (PALU, #18054); United Nations (UN, #20515).*
[2017.06.01/XM5095/**D**]

♦ Africa Baseball and Softball Association (ABSA) 00158
Association de baseball et softball de l'Afrique – Associação de Beisebol e Softbol da Africa
Exec Dir Paiko Road, Chanchaga, PMB 150, Minna, Niger, Nigeria. T. +23466224555. Fax +23466224555. E-mail: absa.secretariat@gmail.com – absasecretariat@yahoo.com.
URL: http://www.baseballsoftballinafrica.com/
History Jun 1990, Lagos (Nigeria). **Aims** Promote, encourage and develop baseball, softball and little league baseball in the continent of Africa and its islands and assist where practicable in other parts of the world; develop harmonious relationships between members leading to strong development of the *sports* through mutual cooperation; mediate in disputes. **Structure** Congress (every 4 years). Executive Council (meets annually); Executive Committee (meets 2 times a year); Secretariat headed by Executive Director; Zones (7). **Languages** English, French, Portuguese. **Staff** 6.00 FTE, paid. **Finance** Members' dues. Other sources: donations, grants; foundations; profits. **Activities** Sporting activities. **Events** *Congress* Nairobi (Kenya) 2006, *Congress* 2004, *Meeting* Kampala (Uganda) 2001, *Congress* Minna (Nigeria) 2001, *Biennial congress / Congress* South Africa 1998. **Publications** *The Gong* (12 a year).
Members Baseball federations in 19 countries:
Burundi, Comoros, Côte d'Ivoire, Ghana, Kenya, Lesotho, Liberia, Mali, Morocco, Namibia, Nigeria, Sierra Leone, South Africa, Tanzania UR, Togo, Tunisia, Uganda, Zambia, Zimbabwe.
Softball federations in 20 countries:
Botswana, Burundi, Comoros, Gambia, Guinea, Guinea-Bissau, Kenya, Lesotho, Liberia, Mali, Namibia, Nigeria, Senegal, Sierra Leone, South Africa, Tanzania UR, Tunisia, Uganda, Zambia, Zimbabwe.
NGO Relations Continental confederation of: *World Baseball Softball Confederation (WBSC, #21222).* Member of: *Association of African Sports Confederations (AASC, #02360).* Recognized by: *Association of National Olympic Committees of Africa (ANOCA, #02820).* Affiliated with: *Little League Baseball.* [2018/XD2383/**D**]

♦ AfricaBio 00159
CEO Ste U9 – 1st Floor, Enterprise Bldg, Mark Shuttle Worth Street, The Innovation Hub, Pretoria, 0087, South Africa. T. +27128440126. Fax +27866199399.
URL: http://www.africabio.com/
History 1999. **Aims** Provide accurate information and raise awareness about *biotechnology* and *biosafety* in South Africa and Africa. **Structure** Board of Directors; Executive Committee. **Finance** Members' dues. **Activities** Knowledge management/information dissemination; events/meetings; training/education; research and development; advocacy/lobbying/activism; capacity building. **Events** *Convention* Durban (South Africa) 2018. **Publications** Brochures. **Members** Research and tertiary education institutions; biotechnology companies; seed companies; farmer organizations; grain traders; food manufacturers; food retailers; professionals; scientists; consumers; students. Membership countries not specified. **NGO Relations** Member of: *CropLife International (#04966).* Instrumental in setting up: *International Council of Biotechnology Associations (ICBA).*
[2016.07.26/XJ7509/**D**]

♦ Africa Biodiversity Collaborative Group (internationally oriented national body)

♦ Africa Capacity Alliance (ACA) 00160
Exec Dir Morningside Office Park, 4th Floor, Wing B, Ngong Road, PO Box 16035, Nairobi, 00100, Kenya. T. +254202635929.
URL: http://africacapacityalliance.org/
History 1997, as a project under the auspices of Universities of Nairobi (Kenya) and Manitoba (Canada). Original title: *Regional AIDS Training Network (RATN).* Since 2003, registered as an international NGO. **Aims** Build, develop and strengthen the capacity of individuals and organizations towards an effective *health* response. **Structure** Board of Directors; Secretariat. **Languages** English. **Finance** Initial funding from: *Canadian International Development Agency (CIDA, inactive); International Bank for Reconstruction and Development (IBRD, #12317)* (World Bank). **Activities** Events/meetings; capacity building; knowledge management/information dissemination. **Publications** *ACA E-Newsletter.*
Members Institutions (37) in 12 countries:
Botswana, Eswatini, Kenya, Lesotho, Malawi, Namibia, Rwanda, South Africa, Tanzania UR, Uganda, Zambia, Zimbabwe.
Included in the above, 6 organizations listed in this Yearbook:
Amref Health Africa (#00806); Centre for African Family Studies (CAFS, #03726); Eastern and Southern African Management Institute (ESAMI, #05254); Network of AIDS Researchers of Eastern and Southern Africa (NARESA, #16990); Southern Africa HIV/AIDS Information Dissemination Service (SAfAIDS, #19831); SRHR Africa Trust (SAT, #19934). [2018/XF6850/**y/F**]

♦ **Africa CDC** Africa Centres for Disease Control and Prevention (#00162)
♦ Africa Center for Strategic Studies (internationally oriented national body)
♦ Africa Centre for Citizens Orientation (internationally oriented national body)

♦ Africa Centre for Climate and Earth Systems Science (ACCESS) . . . 00161
Dir Dept of Oceanography, Univ of Cape Town, RW James Building, University Ave, Rondebosch, 7701, South Africa. T. +27216505442. Fax +27216503283. E-mail: gphlder@princeton.edu – info@africaclimatescience.org.
URL: http://www.africaclimatescience.org/
Aims Promote research and knowledge transfer on climate related phenomena. **Structure** Governance Board (meets at least annually). Research Director. Committees (2): Education; Operational. **Activities** Offers educational programmes including workshops and seminars; coordinates research projects including computer modelling of the atmosphere and ocean; makes available operational products related to environmental conditions; provides information concerning future global warming. **Events** *EGU Alexander von Humboldt international conference* Cape Town (South Africa) 2009. [2011/XJ0110/**F**]

♦ Africa Centre, Finland (internationally oriented national body)
♦ Africa Centre, London (internationally oriented national body)
♦ Africa Centre for Open Governance (internationally oriented national body)

♦ Africa Centres for Disease Control and Prevention (Africa CDC) . . . 00162
Dir African Union HQ, PO Box 3243, Roosevelt Str, W21K19 Addis Ababa, Ethiopia. T. +251115517700. Fax +251115517844. E-mail: africacdc@africa-union.org.
URL: http://www.africacdc.org/
History Proposed following decision Assembly/AU/Dec 499 (XXII), adopted Jan 2014, Addis Ababa (Ethiopia), at Ordinary Session of the Assembly of *African Union (AU, #00488);* establishment endorsed in decision Assembly/AU/Dec 554 (XXIV), adopted Jan 2015, Addis Ababa (Ethiopia). **Aims** Strengthen Africa's public health institutions' capacities, capabilities and partnerships to detect and respond quickly and effectively to disease threats and outbreaks based on science, policy, and data-driven interventions and programs. **Structure** Governing Board; Advisory and Technical Council; Regional Collaborating Centres; Secretariat, headed by Director. Coordination Office located at Headquarters of *African Union (AU, #00488).* **Activities** Research/documentation; knowledge management/information dissemination. **Events** *Africa Health Agenda International Conference (AHAIC)* Kigali (Rwanda) 2023, *International Conference on Public Health in Africa (CPHIA 2022)* Kigali (Rwanda) 2022, *ICREID : International Conference on (Re-)Emerging Infectious Diseases* Addis Ababa (Ethiopia) 2019, *Joint Meeting on Ebola Virus Disease Preparedness, Vaccines and Therapeutics* Addis Ababa (Ethiopia) 2019, *Technical Workshop on Mortality Surveillance in Africa* Addis Ababa (Ethiopia) 2019. **IGO Relations** *WHO (#20950).* [2022/XM7710/**E***]

♦ Africa Chamber of Content Producers (unconfirmed)
♦ Africa Civil Society Centre / see Africans Rising For Justice, Peace and Dignity (#00474)

♦ Africa Civil Society for the Information Society (ACSIS) 00163
Société Civile Africaine pour la Société de l'Information (SCASI)
Contact address not obtained. T. +221772677273.
Contact 2675 Avenue Cheikh Ahmadou Bamba, Ouagou Naiyes II, Dakar, Senegal.
URL: http://www.acsis-scasi.org/
History Launched Jun 2003. Registered in accordance with the law of Ethiopia. **Structure** General Assembly; Cabinet; Sub-regional Coordinations; National Coordinations; Executive Secretariat.
Members Full in 31 countries:
Benin, Burkina Faso, Cameroon, Canada, Central African Rep, Chad, Congo Brazzaville, Congo DR, Côte d'Ivoire, Djibouti, Egypt, France, Gabon, Gambia, Ghana, Guinea, Kenya, Liberia, Madagascar, Mali, Morocco, Niger, Nigeria, Senegal, Sudan, Switzerland, Togo, Tunisia, Uganda, USA, Zambia.
Consultative Status Consultative status granted from: *ECOSOC (#05331)* (Special). [2018/XM7268/**D**]

♦ Africa Civil Society Initiative / see Africans Rising For Justice, Peace and Dignity (#00474)
♦ Africa Civil Society Platform on Principled Partnership / see Africa Platform (#00513)
♦ Africa Clean Energy Group (internationally oriented national body)
♦ AFRICACLEAN – Réseau pour la Qualité de l'Environnement en Afrique Sub-Saharienne (internationally oriented national body)

♦ Africa Committee 00164
Afrika Komitee (AK)
Exec Officer Rüdengasse 2, 4001 Basel BS, Switzerland. T. +41616916293. E-mail: info@afrikakomitee.ch.
URL: http://www.afrikakomitee.ch/
History 1973. **Aims** Address North-South relations and the current political, economic, social and cultural developments in Africa; promote cultural exchange and the richness of African culture. **Languages** German. **Finance** Sources: donations. **Publications** *Afrika-Bulletin* (4 a year) in German.
Members Organizations in 2 countries:
Germany, Switzerland.
Individuals in 10 countries:
Austria, Eritrea, France, Germany, Italy, Liechtenstein, South Africa, Switzerland, USA, Zimbabwe. [2023.02.15/XN3688/**E**]

♦ Africa Committee for Rehabilitation of Southern Sudan / see ACROSS (#00080)
♦ Africa Community Publishing and Development Trust (internationally oriented national body)
♦ Africa Community Technical Service (internationally oriented national body)
♦ Africa Concern / see Concern Worldwide
♦ Africa Continent Care for Migration (internationally oriented national body)

♦ Africa Cooperative Action Trust – International (ACAT International) 00165
Contact PO Box 283, Mbabane, Eswatini. T. +26824042446. E-mail: secretary@acat.org.sz.
URL: http://www.acat.org.sz/
History Mar 1979, South Africa. ACAT Swaziland set up, 1982 and renamed *ACAT Lilima,* 1992. **Aims** Demonstrate in word and action the love of the Lord Jesus *Christ;* generate community self-development in the rural areas of Africa by training community representatives in basic skills necessary to stimulate others to help themselves in such areas as food production, soil husbandry, money management, health care and income generation. **Structure** ACAT work is divided into regions or countries, each with its own Trust Deed and Board of Trustees, and with counselling and monitoring of performance through the Founding Trust ACAT International. **Activities** Teaches rural people how to use their resources of land, labour, money and time more effectively. Forms savings clubs of 20 to 60 members and teaches the virtues of saving towards an objective whose achievement will improve the quality of life. Nutrition and Farming Programme. Package programmes in production of maize, beans, potatoes, vegetables and chicken. ACAT Training Centres provide residential courses. Reconstruction and Development Department trains selected community members in: saving towards community projects; identifying marketable commodities; developing water supplies; improving stock development; building community facilities and roads. *'Food for Work'* projects organized during crisis periods. **NGO Relations** Associate member of: *Association of Evangelicals in Africa (AEA, #02587).* [2008.09.15/XF1612/**F**]

♦ Africa Cooperative Savings and Credit Association / see African Confederation of Cooperative Savings and Credit Associations (#00261)
♦ Africa Council for Food and Nutrition Sciences (no recent information)
♦ Africa CSO Platform on Principled Partnership / see Africa Platform (#00513)
♦ Africa Culture Internationale Human Rights (internationally oriented national body)
♦ Africa Development Interchange Network (internationally oriented national body)
♦ Africa Development Solutions (internationally oriented national body)
♦ Africa Disability Alliance (unconfirmed)

♦ Africa Early Childhood Network (AfECN) 00166
Exec Dir Hemingways Block, Karen Office Park, Nairobi, 24780-00502, Kenya. T. +254203882433. E-mail: info@afecn.org.
URL: https://africaecnetwork.org/
History 2013. Founder members include African champions for children. Registration: Start date: 2015. **Aims** Serve as a platform to champion excellence and collaboration in protecting children's rights, influence policy and practice, strengthen partnerships, and share experiences and knowledge in ECD on the African continent. **Structure** Board of Directors; Technical Committee; Working Groups; Secretariat. **Languages** English, French, Portuguese. **Staff** 10.00 FTE, paid. **Activities** Advocacy/lobbying/activism; knowledge management/information dissemination; networking/liaising; training/education. **Events** *Biennial Conference* Dakar (Senegal) 2020. **NGO Relations** Member of: *Early Childhood Development Action Network (ECDAN, #05155).* [2021/XM8790/**F**]

♦ Africa Educational Trust (internationally oriented national body)

♦ Africa Electric Sport Association (AESA) 00167
Founder/CEO address not obtained. E-mail: info@a-esa.org.
URL: https://a-esa.org/
History Registration: No/ID: 2018/475515/08, South Africa. **Aims** Promote the development and adoption of Electronic Sports (Esports) in Africa. **Structure** Annual General Meeting; Governing Board. **NGO Relations** Member of (1): *World Esports Consortium (WESCO, #21391).* [2022/AA3044/**D**]

♦ Africa Energy Forum (meeting series)

♦ Africa Enterprise Challenge Fund (AECF) 00168
CEO PO Box 1996 Westlands, Nairobi, 00606, Kenya. E-mail: info@aecfafrica.org.
URL: http://www.aecfafrica.org/
History A special partnership initiative of *Alliance for a Green Revolution in Africa (AGRA, #00685).* Not registered as a legal entity. **Aims** Make funding available through *competitions.* **Structure** Committee. **Finance** Stakeholders: *International Fund for Agricultural Development (IFAD, #13692); Department for International Development (DFID, inactive)* / UKaid; *Swedish International Development Cooperation Agency (Sida);* Australian Aid; Kingdom of Netherlands; *DANIDA.* **Activities** Financial and/or material support. **NGO Relations** Supports: *Farming First.* [2017/XJ9338/**f/F**]

♦ Africa-EU Innovation Alliance for Water and Climate (AfriAlliance) . 00169
Dir c/o IHE Delft, PO Box 3015, 2601 DA Delft, Netherlands. T. +31152151802.
URL: http://www.afrialliance.org/
History Set up as project led by *IHE Delft Institute for Water Education (#11110),* running 2016-2021. **Aims** Better prepare Africa for future climate change challenges by having African and European stakeholders work together in the areas of water innovation, research, policy, and capacity development. **Finance** Funding from *European Union (EU, #08967)* Horizon 2020. **Activities** Research/documentation; knowledge management/information dissemination. **Events** *Final Conference* Victoria Falls (Zimbabwe) 2020, *Conference* Ekurhuleni (South Africa) 2017.

Members Partners (16):
African Water Association (AfWA, #00497); Akvo Foundation; Both ENDS (#03307); CSIR, South Africa; *Global Water Partnership (GWP, #10653); IHE Delft Institute for Water Education (#11110); Institut International d'Ingénierie de l'Eau et de l'Environnement (2iE, #11313); International Network of Basin Organizations (INBO, #14235); International Office for Water (IOW, #14399);* ITC – University of Twente (Netherlands); *Local Governments for Sustainability (ICLEI, #16507);* Water, Environment and Business for Development (WE and B), Spain; *WaterNet (#20832);* Water Research Commission, South Africa; *West African Science Service Center on Climate Change and Adapted Land Use (WASCAL, #20897).* [2017/XM6082/y/E]

♦ Africa-Europe Diaspora Development Platform (ADEPT) 00170

Exec Dir Rue Washington 40, 1050 Brussels, Belgium. T. +3227310103. E-mail: info@adept-platform.org.
URL: http://www.adept-platform.org/

History Originated as a project running 2014-2017, before it transformed into a permanent platform. Registration: No/ID: 0670.947.812, Start date: 10 Feb 2017, Belgium; EU Transparency Register, No/ID: 483111039195-46, Start date: 2 Sep 2020. **Aims** Improve and enhance the capacity and impact of the African diaspora organizations that are involved in development activities in Africa. **Structure** Board of Trustees; Advisory Council. **Finance** Support from *European Union (EU, #08967), Swiss Agency for Development and Cooperation (SDC)* and *International Centre for Migration Policy Development (ICMPD, #12503).* **Publications** *ADEPT Newsletter.* Briefing papers. **NGO Relations** Member of (1): *Federation of European and International Associations Established in Belgium (FAIB, #09508).* [2020/XM6515/F]

♦ Africa-Europe Faith and Justice Network (AEFJN) 00171

Réseau foi et justice Afrique-Europe

International Secretariat Rue Joseph II 174, 1000 Brussels, Belgium. T. +3222346810. Fax +3222311413. E-mail: aefjn@aefjn.org.
URL: http://www.aefjn.org/

History Founded 1988, under the name of *Africa Faith and Justice Network / Europe (AFJN/E) – Réseau foi et justice Europe – Afrique.* Secretariat opened, 1989, in Brussels (Belgium). EU Transparency Register: 03904371831-43. **Aims** Promote equity and economic justice in the relationships between Europe and Africa; influence in a positive way decisions taken by the *European Union* which affect people in Africa. **Structure** General Assembly (annual); Executive Board, in Rome (Italy); Secretariat, located in Brussels (Belgium). **Languages** English, French. **Staff** 4.00 FTE, paid. **Finance** Contributions from members. **Activities** Research/documentation; knowledge management/information dissemination; advocacy/lobbying/activism; networking/liaising; meeting activities. *Meeting of Representatives of the European Antennae.* **Events** *Meeting on the European antennae representatives* Brussels (Belgium) 1998, *General information for African antennae representatives* Yaoundé (Cameroon) 1997, *International seminar on lobbying* Brussels (Belgium) 1995, *Annual meeting* Washington, DC (USA) 1995. **Publications** *NEWS from AEFJN* (12 a year); *Forum for Action* (3 a year). *ADFJN Manual on Economic Justice, vols 1-2.* Working documents.

Members Representatives (over 8,000) of religious and missionary congregations of men and women who work in Africa and Europe, or who have a great concern for Africa. Members in 68 countries:
Algeria, Angola, Austria, Belgium, Benin, Burkina Faso, Burundi, Cameroon, Cape Verde, Central African Rep, Chad, Congo Brazzaville, Congo DR, Côte d'Ivoire, Czechia, Egypt, Equatorial Guinea, Eritrea, Eswatini, Ethiopia, France, Gabon, Gambia, Germany, Ghana, Guinea, Guinea-Bissau, Holy See, Hungary, Ireland, Italy, Kenya, Lesotho, Liberia, Luxembourg, Madagascar, Malawi, Mali, Malta, Mauritania, Mauritius, Morocco, Mozambique, Namibia, Netherlands, Niger, Nigeria, Poland, Portugal, Rwanda, Sao Tomé-Principe, Senegal, Seychelles, Sierra Leone, Slovakia, Slovenia, Somalia, South Africa, Spain, Sudan, Sweden, Tanzania UR, Togo, Tunisia, Uganda, UK, Zambia, Zimbabwe.

National branches in 18 countries:
Belgium, Cameroon, Congo DR, Côte d'Ivoire, France, Germany, Ireland, Italy, Kenya, Malawi, Mozambique, Netherlands, Poland, Portugal, Spain, Switzerland, Uganda, UK.

Organization (one) listed in this Yearbook:
Afrika-Europa Netwerk (AEN).

Institutes (49):
- *Bethlehem Mission Society (SMB);*
- *Brothers of Christian Instruction of St Gabriel (SG)* (Ireland);
- *Brothers of the Christian Schools (Christian Brothers);*
- *Carmelite Sisters of Charity, Vedruna (CCV);*
- *Comboni Missionary Sisters (CMS);*
- *Company of the Daughters of Charity of St Vincent de Paul (DC);*
- *Congregatio Fratrum Christianorum (CFC);*
- *Congregatio Fratrum Immaculatae Conceptionis Beatae Mariae Virginis (FIC);*
- *Congregation of the Holy Spirit (Spiritans);*
- *Congregation of the Immaculate Heart of Mary (Missionaries of Scheut);*
- *Congregation of the Missionaries of Mariannhill (CMM);*
- *Daughters of Mary and Joseph (DMJ);*
- Dominican Sisters of the Visitation (SDV);
- *Franciscan Missionaries of Mary (FMM);*
- *Institut de la Bienheureuse Vierge Marie (Dames Anglaises);*
- *Institute of Consolata Missionaries (Consolata Fathers);*
- *Little Brothers of Mary (Marist Brothers);*
- *Little Sisters of the Assumption (LSA);*
- *Medical Mission Sisters;*
- *Missionarie Serve dello Spirito Santo (SSpS);*
- *Missionarii Comboniani Cordis Jesu (MCCI);*
- *Missionarii Sacratissimi Cordis Jesu (MSC);*
- *Missionary Oblates of Mary Immaculate (OMI);*
- *Missionary Sisters of Our Lady of Africa (White Sisters);*
- *Missionary Sisters of Our Lady of the Apostles;*
- *Missionary Sons of the Immaculate Heart of Mary (Claretians);*
- *Religious of the Holy Union of the Sacred Hearts (SUSC);*
- *Religious of the Sacred Heart of Mary (RSHM);*
- *School Sisters of Notre Dame (SSND);*
- *Sisters Mercedarian Missionaries of Bérriz (MMB);*
- *Sisters of Charity of Jesus and Mary (SCJM);*
- *Sisters of Mercy, 1823;*
- *Sisters of Our Lady of Charity of the Good Shepherd;*
- *Sisters of St Louis Juilly-Monaghan;*
- *Sisters of St Paul of Chartres;*
- *Sisters of the Holy Family of Bordeaux;*
- *Società del Verbo Divino (Verbiti);*
- *Society of African Missions (SMA);*
- *Society of Mary (Marist Fathers);*
- *Society of Missionaries of Africa (White Fathers);*
- *Society of St Francis Xavier for the Foreign Missions (Xaverians);*
- *Society of the Holy Child Jesus (SHCJ);*
- *Society of the Sacred Heart of Jesus (St Madeleine-Sophie Barat);*
- *Soeurs de Notre-Dame de Namur (SNDN);*
- *Soeurs Missionnaires de la Consolata (MC);*
- *Soeurs Missionnaires de la Société de Marie (SMSM);*
- *St Joseph's Missionary Society of Mill Hill (MHM);*
- *St Patrick's Society for the Foreign Missions (Kiltegan Fathers);*
- *Ursulines of the Roman Union.*

NGO Relations Member of: *Coalition Eau; Forum of Catholic Inspired NGOs (#09905); International Action Network on Small Arms (IANSA, #11585); Stamp Out Poverty.* [2019/XF5036/y/F]

♦ Africa-Europe Group for Interdisciplinary Studies (AEGIS) 00172

Groupe d'études interdisciplinaires Afrique-Europe

Mailing Address PO Box 9555, 2300 RB Leiden, Netherlands. E-mail: asc@ascleiden.nl.
URL: http://www.aegis-eu.org/

History 1991. Former names and other names: *Africa-Europe Group for Interdisciplinary Studies in Social Sciences and Humanities* – former; *Groupe d'études interdisciplinaires Afrique-Europe en sciences humaines et sociales* – former. Registration: Netherlands. **Aims** Improve understanding about contemporary African societies, with primary emphasis on social sciences and humanities. **Structure** Plenary Meeting (annual). A network of African studies centres throughout Europe, managed by Board of 4 members and headed by President. **Languages** English, French. **Finance** Members' contributions. **Activities** Organizes: Biennial European Conference of African Study; Summer School for post-graduate students and junior faculty; thematic conferences on state-of-the-art research. **Events** *European Conference on African Studies (ECAS)* Prague (Czechia) 2025, *European Conference on African Studies (ECAS)* Cologne (Germany) 2023, *Thematic conference* Lisbon (Portugal) 2021, *European Conference on African Studies* Edinburgh (UK) 2019, *European Conference on African Studies* Basel (Switzerland) 2017. **Publications** *Yearbook on African Affairs. Monograph Series.*

Members Centres of African Studies (19):
African Studies Centre Leiden (ASCL); African Studies, University of Oxford (UK); *Centre d'études africaines, Paris (CEAf); Centre for African Studies, Barcelona (CEA); Centre for African Studies, Basel (CASB); Centre for African Studies, Lisbon; Centre for Africa Studies, Gothenburg (CAS); Centre of African Studies, Copenhagen; Centre of African Studies, Edinburgh (CAS); Centre of African Studies, London; Centro de Estudos Africanos da Universidade do Porto (CEAUP); Institute for African Studies, University of Bayreuth (IAS); Institute of African Affairs, Hamburg (IAA); Institut für Afrikanistik, Leipzig; Institut für Ethnologie und Afrika-Studien (IFEAS)* (Mainz); *Les Afriques dans le monde (LAM)* (Bordeaux); *Nordic Africa Institute (NAI, #17168)* (Uppsala); Programme of African Studies, University of Trondheim (Norway); *University Institute of Oriental Studies.* [2022/XD6557/y/E]

♦ Africa-Europe Group for Interdisciplinary Studies in Social Sciences and Humanities / see Africa-Europe Group for Interdisciplinary Studies (#00172)

♦ Africa Evidence Network (AEN) 00173

Coordinator address not obtained. E-mail: cfar@uj.ac.za.
URL: http://www.africaevidencenetwork.org/

History Set up following colloquium held Dec 2012, Dhaka (Bangladesh). **Finance** Supported by: *Department for International Development (DFID, inactive).* **Events** *Colloquium* Johannesburg (South Africa) 2016, *Colloquium* Johannesburg (South Africa) 2014. **Publications** *AEN Newsletter.*

Members Individuals in 26 countries:
Australia, Bangladesh, Benin, Cameroon, Canada, Côte d'Ivoire, Egypt, Ethiopia, Germany, Ghana, India, Italy, Kenya, Liberia, Malawi, Nepal, Nigeria, Somalia, South Africa, Sri Lanka, Switzerland, Tanzania UR, Uganda, UK, USA, Zimbabwe.

NGO Relations Member of: *Effective Institutions Platform (EIP, #05384).* [2015/XJ9644/F]

♦ Africa Faith and Justice Network (internationally oriented national body)
♦ Africa Faith and Justice Network / Europe / see Africa-Europe Faith and Justice Network (#00171)
♦ Africa Family Life Federation (inactive)
♦ Africa Fire Mission (internationally oriented national body)
♦ **Africa Forum** Forum for Former African Heads of State and Government (#09915)
♦ Africa Foundation (internationally oriented national body)

♦ Africa Foundation for Sustainable Development (AFSD) 00174

Contact 1st Floor West Wing, Corner Main Office Park, Cnr Main and Payne Roads, Bryanston, 2191, South Africa. T. +27833804991.
URL: http://www.af-sd.com/

History Jan 2010. Registered in Mozambique, South Africa and Zambia. **Aims** Contribute to socio-economic development of Southern Africa. **Structure** Board of Directors; national country directors. **Languages** English. **Finance** Grants; corporate and project funding. **Activities** Guidance/assistance/consulting; advocacy/lobbying/activism; financial and/or material support.

Members Full in 3 countries:
Mozambique, South Africa, Zambia.

IGO Relations *Global Environment Facility (GEF, #10346); UNDP (#20292); UNIDO (#20336).* **NGO Relations** Member of: *GEF CSO Network (GCN, #10087); Global Gender and Climate Alliance (GGCA, no recent information).* Affiliated with national organizations. [2017.03.09/XJ9417/f/F]

♦ Africa Freedom of Information Centre (AFIC) 00175

Centre Africain pour la Liberté d'Information

Head Office Plot 5 Katego Road, Kamokya (Near Save the Children), PO Box 356443, Kampala, Uganda. T. +256414533554. Fax +256414533554.
URL: http://www.africafoicentre.org/

History Sep 2006, Lagos (Nigeria). **Aims** Promote the right of access to information through comparative research, coordinating regional advocacy, facilitating information-sharing and capacity building. **Structure** Steering Committee, comprising Chairperson, Secretary, Treasurer, 4 members and 1 Observer.

Members Civil Society Organizations; Non-Governmental Organizations; Individuals; Institutions. Members in 16 countries:
Botswana, Congo DR, Ghana, Kenya, Liberia, Morocco, Mozambique, Namibia, Nigeria, Senegal, Sierra Leone, South Africa, South Sudan, Tanzania UR, Uganda, Zimbabwe.

Included in the above, 6 organizations listed in this Yearbook:
African Network of Constitutional Lawyers (ANCL, #00384); ARTICLE 19 (#01121) (East Africa / West Africa); *Centre for Media Freedom in the Middle East and North Africa (CMF MENA, no recent information); International Federation of Journalists (IFJ, #13462); Media Foundation for West Africa (MFWA, #16617); Media Institute of Southern Africa (MISA, #16619).*

Consultative Status Consultative status granted from: *African Commission on Human and Peoples' Rights (ACHPR, #00255)* (Observer). **IGO Relations** Global partner of: *Global Partnership for Social Accountability (GPSA, #10541).* **NGO Relations** Member of: *African Freedom of Expression Exchange (AFEX); Freedom of Information Advocates Network (FOIAnet, #09985).* [2013/XJ7664/y/F]

♦ Africa Free Media Foundation 00176

Exec Dir PO Box 70147, Nairobi, Kenya. T. +2546651118. Fax +2546650836.
Street Address 00400 Tom Mboya Street, Nairobi, Kenya.
URL: http://www.freemediafoundation.org/

History Aug 1993, Harare (Zimbabwe), as *Network for the Defence of Independent Media in Africa (NDIMA).* Also referred to as *Africa Free Media Trust.* **Aims** Promote, encourage and safeguard freedom of expression and human rights in Africa, in particular for the press, print, electronic media, publishers and for individuals working for the right to life and human dignity, personal liberty, fair trial and equality before the law; promote artistic talent; support establishment of rural press; educate and create awareness among Africans on public issues, politics and international relations; address new forms of censorship and strengthen emerging independent media in Africa. **Structure** General Meeting (annual). Management Board comprising individual journalists and representatives of media groups. Programme Director. Headquarters in Nairobi (Kenya). **Languages** English, French, Swahili. **Finance** Members' dues. Other sources: sales of publications; donations; support from international sponsors, including: *Ford Foundation (#09858); Friedrich-Ebert-Stiftung (FES).* **Activities** Works through contact with governments and authorities, appeals and public meetings. Raises funds to support human rights and freedom of expression. Organizes training programmes for journalists. *'RECASU'* programme designed to cater to journalists escaping from repressive regimes, especially in Ethiopia, Burundi and Somalia. *'NIDMA'* programme involved in promoting and encouraging circulation of censored material or literature. **Events** *Annual Convention* Kampala (Uganda) 1998. **Publications** *Letter from Mairobi* (weekly); *Ngao* (12 a year) – newsletter. Special reports.

Members Independent media houses (10) and newspapers publishing for community readership in 24 countries:
Austria, Burkina Faso, Burundi, Congo Brazzaville, Côte d'Ivoire, Ethiopia, Germany, Ghana, Guinea, Kenya, Madagascar, Malawi, Mexico, Mozambique, Namibia, Niger, Nigeria, Sierra Leone, South Africa, Tanzania UR, Uganda, USA, Zambia, Zimbabwe.

IGO Relations Working relations with: *UNESCO (#20322).* **NGO Relations** Cooperates with: *Amnesty International (AI, #00801); ARTICLE 19 (#01121); Committee to Protect Journalists (CPJ, #04280); Digital Freedom Network (DFN); International Federation of Journalists (IFJ, #13462); International PEN (#14552); Media Institute of Southern Africa (MISA, #16619); World Free Press Institute (WFPI).* [2010/XF3974/f/F]

♦ Africa Free Media Trust / see Africa Free Media Foundation (#00176)
♦ Africa Free Trade Zone / see African Continental Free Trade Area (#00267)

♦ Africa Fund for Fungal Biodiversity and Mycotic Infections (internationally oriented national body)
♦ Africa Future (internationally oriented national body)

♦ Africa Gender and Development Evaluators Network (AGDEN) 00177

Contact PO Box 49475, Nairobi, 00800, Kenya. T. +254203745646 – +254203741647. E-mail: info@agdenworld.org.
Street Address Sociology Dept, Univ of Nairobi, Nairobi, Kenya.
URL: http://www.agdenworld.org/

History 2002. Founded by *African Evaluation Association (AfrEA, #00304)* and *United Nations Development Fund for Women (UNIFEM, inactive)*. Serves as Special Interest Group of AfrEA. **Aims** Strengthen effectiveness and gender responsiveness of development programmes and projects to human rights. **Structure** Steering Committee/Board. **Activities** Capacity building; research/documentation; training/education.
Members Individuals in 24 countries:
Benin, Burkina Faso, Cameroon, Congo DR, Côte d'Ivoire, Egypt, Eritrea, Ethiopia, Ghana, Guatemala, Kenya, Mali, Mauritania, Namibia, Niger, Nigeria, Rwanda, Senegal, Sierra Leone, South Africa, Tanzania UR, Uganda, Zambia, Zimbabwe.
IGO Relations *UN Women (#20724)*. **NGO Relations** Partners include: *EvalPartners (#09208)*; *Ford Foundation (#09858)*. [2019/XJ9844/v/F]

♦ Africa Genetics Association (inactive)
♦ Africa Governance Alert (internationally oriented national body)

♦ Africa Governance Institute (AGI) 00178

Exec Dir Sotrac Mermoz Sipres 32, Dakar, Senegal. T. +221301029488. Fax +221338246706.
URL: http://www.iag-agi.org/

History Jun 2005, at the initiative of *UNDP (#20292)*. **Aims** Generate innovative thinking on the governance challenges facing Africa and the solutions that African regional organizations, states, civil society and the private sector should develop in response to these challenges. **Structure** Board. **Finance** Technical assistance from UNDP during establishment phase. **Events** *Global forum on reinventing government* Vienna (Austria) 2007. **IGO Relations** Partner of: *African Union (AU, #00488)*. [2015/XM3185/j/E]

♦ Africa Grantmakers' Affinity Group (internationally oriented national body)

♦ Africa Groundwater Network (AGW-NET) 00179

Contact Inst of Water and Sanitation, 7 Maasdorp Avenue, Alexandra Park Harare Box MP422, Mount Pleasant, Harare, HARARE, Zimbabwe. T. +2634794728.
URL: http://agw-net.org/

History Jul 2008, Pretoria (South Africa), at *Network for Capacity Building in Integrated Water Resources Management (CAP-Net, #17000)*. **Aims** Increase awareness of the potential and value of groundwater across the continent; contribute to capacity building in the groundwater sector in Africa. **Structure** Steering Committee of 8 members.
Members Individuals in 33 countries and territories:
Bangladesh, Botswana, Burkina Faso, Burundi, Cameroon, Canaries, Cape Verde, Chad, Congo DR, Denmark, Ethiopia, Germany, Ghana, Kenya, Malawi, Mozambique, Namibia, Netherlands, Niger, Nigeria, Rwanda, Senegal, South Africa, Sudan, Sweden, Switzerland, Tanzania UR, Togo, Uganda, UK, USA, Zambia, Zimbabwe.
NGO Relations Member of: *Network for Capacity Building in Integrated Water Resources Management (CAP-Net, #17000)*. [2011/XJ2378/E]

♦ Africa Groups of Sweden (internationally oriented national body)
♦ Africa Health Budget Network (unconfirmed)
♦ Africa Health Organisation (internationally oriented national body)

♦ Africa Health Research Institute (AHRI) 00180

Dir Private Bag X7, Congella, Durban, 4013, South Africa. T. +27312604991. E-mail: info@ahri.org.
Street Address Nelson R Mandela School of Medicine, 3rd Floor – K-RITH Tower Bldg, 719 Umbilo Roa, Durban, South Africa.
Somkhele Address PO Box 198, Mtubatuba, 3935, South Africa. T. +27312604991. E-mail: communcation@ahri.org.
URL: http://www.ahri.org/

History 1 Oct 2016, on merger of *Africa Centre for Health and Population Studies (inactive)* and KwaZulu-Natal Research Institute for TB-HIV (K-RITH). **Aims** Work towards elimination of *HIV* and *TB* disease. **Structure** Board of Directors; Scientific Advisory Board. **Activities** Research and development; training/education. [2018/XM6743/D]

♦ Africa Hepatitis Initiative (unconfirmed)
♦ Africa Humanitarian Action (internationally oriented national body)
♦ Africa ICT Alliance / see Africa Information and Communication Technologies Alliance (#00181)

♦ Africa Information and Communication Technologies Alliance (AfICTA) 00181

Head Office CP9 Jimson Olufuye Street, behind High Court of Justice, Airport Road, Lugbe, PO Box 8576, Wuse, Abuja 900211, Federal Capital Territory, Nigeria. T. +2348068674380. E-mail: info@aficta.africa.
URL: https://aficta.africa/

History 1 May 2012. Current constitution adopted 1 Apr 2012. Former names and other names: *Africa ICT Alliance* – alias. Registration: Corporate Affairs Commission, No/ID: RC:1162034, Nigeria, FCT (Abuja). **Aims** Encourage multi-stakeholder dialogue fostering accelerated and ICT enabled development in Africa and use of cutting-edge innovative technologies including mobile, computing and satellite technologies to achieve an information society in Africa. **Structure** General Meeting (annual); Board. **Languages** Arabic, English, French. **Staff** 3.00 FTE, paid. **Finance** Sources: members' dues. **Activities** Events/meetings; research and development. **Events** *Summit* Abuja (Nigeria) 2019, *Summit* Nairobi (Kenya) 2018, *Summit* Abuja (Nigeria) 2017, *Summit* Windhoek (Namibia) 2016, *Summit* Johannesburg (South Africa) 2015. **Publications** *AfICTA eNewsletter* (26 a year). News articles.
Members Full in 32 countries:
Benin, Botswana, Burundi, Cameroon, Chad, Congo DR, Côte d'Ivoire, Egypt, Ethiopia, Gabon, Gambia, Ghana, Kenya, Lesotho, Libya, Mali, Mauritius, Morocco, Namibia, Niger, Nigeria, Rwanda, Senegal, Somalia, South Africa, Sudan, Tanzania UR, Togo, Tunisia, Uganda, Zambia, Zimbabwe.
NGO Relations Member of (2): *Alliance for Affordable Internet (A4AI, #00651)*; *Internet Corporation for Assigned Names and Numbers (ICANN, #15949)*. [2021.06.11/XJ8576/D]

♦ Africa Inland Mission / see Africa Inland Mission International (#00182)

♦ Africa Inland Mission International (AIM International) 00182

Contact PO Box 3611, Peachtree City GA 30269-7611, USA. E-mail: admin.io@aimint.org.
URL: http://www.aimint.org/

History 1895, Philadelphia, PA (USA). Former names and other names: *Africa Inland Mission (AIM)* – former. **Aims** Serve the church of Jesus Christ in its responsibility to make disciples of the peoples of Africa. **Structure** A cooperation of separate legal entities in Australia, Brazil, Canada, Europe, Korea Rep, South Africa and USA. **Languages** English. **Staff** 900.00 FTE, paid. **Finance** Sources: donations. Supported through churches and individual donors. **Activities** Healthcare; humanitarian/emergency aid; religious activities; training/education. Active in: Australia, Brazil, Canada, Central African Rep, Chad, Congo DR, France, Hong Kong, Kenya, Korea Rep, Lesotho, Madagascar, Mayotte, Mozambique, Namibia, Netherlands, New Zealand, Rwanda, South Africa, South Sudan, Tanzania UR, Uganda, UK, USA. [2022.05.05/XF1913/F]

♦ Africa Innovation Foundation / see African Innovation Foundation
♦ Africa Institute / see Netherlands-African Business Council
♦ Africa Institute of South Africa (internationally oriented national body)
♦ Africa Institute of the USSR Academy of Sciences / see Institute for African Studies of the Russian Academy of Sciences
♦ Africa Ju-Jitsu Belt Wrestling Federation (unconfirmed)

♦ Africa Leadership Forum (ALF) 00183

Exec Dir c/o ALF Plaza, Bells Univ of Technology, 1 Bells Drive Km 9, Idiroko Rd, Ota, Ogun, Nigeria. T. +2347031953465. E-mail: info@africaleadership.org.
URL: http://www.africaleadership.org/

History 1988. **Aims** Expose African leaders to recognized and accomplished leaders from within and outside Africa so as to exchange views in an informal setting and and profit from their specific experience, particularly in an African environment; encourage diagnosis, understanding and informed search for solutions to local, regional and global problems, taking into account their interrelationships and mutual consequences, involving both current and future leaders; generate greater understanding and enhance knowledge and awareness of *development* and *social problems* within a global context among young, potential leaders from all sectors of society, with a view to fostering close and enduring relationships and promoting lifelong association and cooperation among them; support and encourage the diagnosis and informed search for appropriate and effective solutions to local and regional African problems from an African perspective, within the framework of global interdependence; sensitize incumbent leaders and policy-makers, the media and the public at large, worldwide, on national, regional and global problems of *development*, *strategy*, *environment* and *management* in a way to facilitate their effective contributions to solutions. **Structure** Council of Convenors. Executive Committee of 8 members. Secretariat, headed by Executive Director. Includes Africa Leadership Foundations. Departments (5): Programmes; Information Technology; Publication; Finance; Administration. **Languages** English, French. **Finance** Contributions from: Norwegian Government; *DANIDA*; *African Union (AU, #00488)*; *UNDP (#20292)*; the private sector in Nigeria. **Activities** Organizes: seminars, meetings and face-to-face encounters on emerging key issues, disseminating findings and proposals on priority issues; Farmhouse Dialogue (6 a year), at Forum Centre in Ota (Nigeria), to discuss issues of a more national interest but which may have wider relevance and ramifications for other African countries. Organized first meeting of *African Elders Council for Peace (AECP, inactive)*, 25 Mar 1992, Arusha (Tanzania), and subsequently instrumental in setting up *Conference on Security, Stability, Development and Cooperation in Africa (CSSDCA, inactive)*. **Events** *Africa Governance, Leadership and Management Convention* Mombasa (Kenya) 2011, *Africa Regional Conference on Water* Ota (Nigeria) 2011, *Africa women's forum* Abuja (Nigeria) 2003, *Conference on corruption, accountability, and transparency for sustainable development* Abuja (Nigeria) 2003, *African women's forum* Ota (Nigeria) 2002. **Publications** *AFRICA Forum: Journal of Leadership and Development*; *Akuko* – online newsletter. Books; monographs; reports. **Members** Not a membership organization. **IGO Relations** *Economic Community of West African States (ECOWAS, #05312)*. **NGO Relations** Member of: *The Reality Of Aid (ROA, #18626)*. [2018/XF1629/F]

♦ Africa Leadership Institute (AFLI) 00184

Contact Fourways, Johannesburg, 2191, South Africa. E-mail: info@alinstitute.org.
URL: https://alinstitute.org/

History 2003. **Aims** Promote effective leadership in African governance, development, peace and security activities. **Finance** Donors include national government programmes in Europe and the USA. **Activities** Research/documentation; training/education. **Members** Individuals. Membership countries not specified. [2022.02.01/XM4542/j/E]

♦ Africa Leather and Leather Products Institute (ALLPI) 00185

Exec Dir PO Box 2358, 1110 Addis Ababa, Ethiopia. T. +251114390330. E-mail: executive.director@allpi.int.
URL: http://allpi.int/

History Formation approved by *Preferential Trade Area for Eastern and Southern African States (PTA, inactive)*, 1988, and established by signing of of the Charter, 23 Nov 1990, Mbabane (Swaziland). Since 8 Dec 1994, an instituttion of *Common Market for Eastern and Southern Africa (COMESA, #04296)*, follwing its replacement of TA. Former names and other names: *PTA Leather Institute* – former; *PTA Leather and Leather Products Institute* – former; *COMESA Leather and Leather Products Institute (COMESA/LLPI)* – former (8 Dec 1994 to 1 Jan 2018). **Aims** Support development of the leather sector in the region. **Structure** COMESA Summit; Council of Ministers; Board of Directors; Executive; Director; Experts. **Languages** Arabic, English, French. **Staff** 32.00 FTE, paid. **Finance** Assessed contributions of member countries. Other sources: service charge fees; consultancy; grants; assistance. **Activities** Research/documentation; events/meetings; training/education; knowledge management/information dissemination; networking/liaising; publishing activities. **Events** *World Leather Congress* Addis Ababa (Ethiopia) 2021. **Publications** *ALLPI Quarterly Newsletter* (4 a year).
Members Governments of 10 countries:
Burundi, Eritrea, Ethiopia, Kenya, Malawi, Rwanda, Sudan, Uganda, Zambia, Zimbabwe.
IGO Relations Memorandum of Understanding with (1): *Euclid University (EUCLID, #05575)*. *African Development Bank (ADB, #00283)*; *African Export-Import Bank (Afreximbank, #00305)*; *Arab Bank for Economic Development in Africa (#00904)*; *FAO (#09260)*; *ILO (#11123)*; *UNIDO (#20336)*. [2022/XK0222/j/E*]

♦ Africa Legal Aid (AFLA) 00186

Exec Dir Alexanderveld 5, 2585 DB The Hague, Netherlands. E-mail: communications@africalegalaid.com.
URL: http://www.africalegalaid.com/

History 21 Oct 1995, Maastricht (Netherlands). Registration: KVK, No/ID: 41078925, Netherlands. **Aims** Promote human rights and accountability in Africa **Structure** Governing Council. **Languages** English. **Activities** Events/meetings; guidance/assistance/consulting; knowledge management/information dissemination. **Publications** *AFLA Quarterly* – journal. *AFLA Special Book Series. The International Criminal Court and Africa: One Decade On.* **Members** Not a membership organization. **Consultative Status** Consultative status granted from: *African Commission on Human and Peoples' Rights (ACHPR, #00255)* (Observer). **NGO Relations** Member of: *Coalition for an Effective African Court on Human and Peoples' Rights (African Court Coalition, #04055)*. [2022.05.17/XF6175/F]

♦ Africa Legal Network / see ALN (#00740)
♦ Africalia (internationally oriented national body)
♦ Africa Liaison Program Initiative (internationally oriented national body)

♦ Africa Liberal Network (ALN) 00187

Réseau liberal africain

Coordinator PO Box 1475, Cape Town, 8000, South Africa. T. +27214651431.
Street address 2nd Floor, Theba Hoskin House, 16 Mill Street, 590, Cape Town, 8001, South Africa.
URL: http://www.africaliberalnetwork.org/

History Current constitution adopted Feb 2007, Dakar (Senegal); amended Aug 2008, Dar es Salaam (Tanzania UR). **Aims** Promote liberal *democratic* principles across the African continent. **Structure** General Assembly. Executive Committee. **Languages** English, French. **Staff** 1.00 FTE, paid. **Finance** Currently financed by donor partners: Liberal Democrats UK; *Westminster Foundation for Democracy (WFD)*; *Friedrich Naumann Foundation for Freedom*. **Events** *General Assembly* Zanzibar (Tanzania UR) 2013, *General Assembly* Abidjan (Côte d'Ivoire) 2012, *General Assembly* Kinshasa (Congo DR) 2011.
Members Political Parties (47) in 27 countries:
Botswana, Burkina Faso, Burundi, Comoros, Congo DR, Côte d'Ivoire, Eswatini, Ethiopia, Ghana, Guinea, Kenya, Madagascar, Malawi, Mali, Mauritania, Morocco, Niger, Senegal, Seychelles, Sierra Leone, Somalia, South Africa, South Sudan, Sudan, Tanzania UR, Togo, Zambia.
Included in the above, 1 organization listed in this Yearbook:
African Liberal Youth (OALY, #00362).
IGO Relations No official links. [2019.02.25/XJ8606/F]

♦ **AFRICALICS** African Network for Economics of Learning, Innovation and Competence Building Systems (#00385)
♦ Africa Logistics Network (unconfirmed)

♦ Africa Medical Association (AfMA) 00188

Contact PO Box 31253, Braamfontein, 2107, South Africa. E-mail: delon@africama.net.
Street Address 24th Floor – bldg 209, Smit Street, Braamfontein, 2001, South Africa.
URL: http://www.africama.net/

History Inaugural Assembly Oct 2006, Pilanesberg (South Africa). **Aims** Act as the collective voice of physicians in Africa. **Structure** Council, comprising President, Vice-President, Secretary-General, Treasurer and member.

Members Full in 15 countries:
Angola, Botswana, Cameroon, Eswatini, Ethiopia, Ghana, Kenya, Lesotho, Mozambique, Namibia, Nigeria, Seychelles, South Africa, Zambia, Zimbabwe.
NGO Relations Acts as regional office for: *World Medical Association (WMA, #21646).* [2013/XJ6841/**D**]

♦ Africa Microfinance Network (AFMIN) 00189

Réseau africain de microfinance

Acting CEO AFMIN Headquarters, 1066 Bd du Canada, Cadjehoun, 07 BP 530, Cotonou, Benin. T. +22921307441. Fax +22921307496.
URL: http://www.afminetwork.org/

History Nov 2000, Cotonou (Benin). *Africa Microfinance Network Initiative* was set up Jul 1997, South Africa, to formalize setting up of AFMIN. **Aims** Be an innovative and sustainable regional network to promote inclusive finance in Africa by enhancing the capacity of Country Networks (CLNs). **Structure** General Assembly (annual, in conjunction with Annual Conference). Board of 7 Directors, including Chairperson, Vice Chairperson, Treasurer and Secretary. Technical Committee. Executive Secretariat, headed by Chief Executive Officer. **Languages** English, French. **Staff** 7.00 FTE, paid. **Finance** Members' dues. Primary funding from: *United States Agency for International Development (USAID)* through *Small Enterprise Education and Promotion Network (SEEP)*; *Humanistisch Instituut voor Ontwikkelingssamenwerking (Hivos)*; *Directorate-General for Development Cooperation (DGDC)*; *International Fund for Agricultural Development (IFAD, #13692).* Other sources: income from activities. Budget (annual): US$ 847,770. **Activities** Capacity building; advocacy; social and financial performance building; knowledge management and sharing; research; information dissemination. **Events** *Annual Conference / General Assembly* Addis Ababa (Ethiopia) 2013, *Annual Conference / General Assembly* Kampala (Uganda) 2011, *General Assembly* Accra (Ghana) 2010, *General Assembly* Bujumbura (Burundi) 2010, *Annual conference / General Assembly* Dakar (Senegal) 2009. **Publications** *AFMIN Newsletter* (4 a year); *The Africa Mircofinance Tribune* (2 a year); *Africa Microfinance Mag.*
Members National networks of microfinance institutions (over 800) in 23 countries:
Benin, Burundi, Cameroon, Cape Verde, Congo Brazzaville, Congo DR, Côte d'Ivoire, Ethiopia, Gambia, Ghana, Guinea, Kenya, Madagascar, Malawi, Mali, Niger, Rwanda, Senegal, South Africa, Tanzania UR, Togo, Uganda, Zimbabwe.
IGO Relations *African Development Bank (ADB, #00283)*; Microfinance Capacity Building Funds. **NGO Relations** Member of: *Microfinance Centre (MFC, #16745).* [2013.08.26/XF6651/**F**]

♦ Africa Microfinance Network Initiative / see Africa Microfinance Network (#00189)

♦ Africa and Middle East Depositories Association (AMEDA) 00190

Pres Villa 53, unit 3, second district, Area 6, 90th street, Fifth Settlement, Cairo, Egypt. E-mail: support@ameda.org.eg – riham.khedr@ameda.org.eg.
Vice-Pres address not obtained.
URL: http://www.ameda.org.eg/

History 27 Apr 2005. Registered in accordance with Egyptian law. **Aims** Offer solutions and provide advice at international level on technical, economical, financial, legal and regulatory matters to reduce risk and increase efficiency in custory, pre-settlement and settlement arrangements for *securities* and related *payments* across Africa and Middle East for the benefit of issuers, *investors* and market participants. **Structure** General Assembly. Board of Directors. **Finance** Members' dues. **Events** *Meeting* Sharm el Sheikh (Egypt) 2016, *Meeting* Tangiers (Morocco) 2016, *Meeting* Abu Dhabi (United Arab Emirates) 2015, *Meeting* Manama (Bahrain) 2014, *Meeting* Muscat (Oman) 2014.
Members Full; Associate. Members in 25 countries:
Algeria, Bahrain, Botswana, Côte d'Ivoire, Egypt, Ghana, Iraq, Jordan, Kenya, Kuwait, Lebanon, Libya, Mauritius, Morocco, Nigeria, Oman, Palestine, Qatar, Rwanda, Saudi Arabia, South Africa, Tunisia, Türkiye, United Arab Emirates, Zimbabwe.
NGO Relations Member of: *World Forum of CSDs (WFC, #21514).* [2022/XJ8696/**D**]

♦ Africa and Middle East Refugee Assistance / see AMERA International
♦ Africa-Middle East Working Group / see CropLife Africa Middle East (#04963)

♦ Africa Mining Network (AMN) 00191

Address not obtained.
URL: http://www.seamic.org/projects.php

History Mar 2002, during World Mining Ministers Forum, at the initiative of *United Nations Economic Commission for Africa (ECA, #20554).* **Aims** Enhance capacity building and policy networking for sustainable resource-based development. **IGO Relations** *New Partnership for Africa's Development (NEPAD, #17091).* **NGO Relations** *International Union for Conservation of Nature and Natural Resources (IUCN, #15766)* – Commission on Environmental, Economic and Social Policy (CEESP). [2007/XM3453/**F**]

♦ Africa Ministry Resources (internationally oriented national body)
♦ Africa on the Move (unconfirmed)
♦ Africa Muslims Agency / see Direct Aid International (#05091)

♦ African Academy of Languages (ACALAN) 00192

Académie africaine des langues – Academia Africana de Línguas (ACALIN)

Exec Sec PO Box E2097, Hamdallaye ACI 2000, porte 232 – Rue 394, Bamako, Mali. T. +22320290459. Fax +22320290457. E-mail: info@acalan.tv.
URL: https://www.acalan-au.org/

History Founded Dec 2000, by Decree 00-630/PRM by the then President of Mali, His Excellency Alpha Oumar Konaré, as *Mission for the African Academy of Languages (MACALAN).* Subsequently became a specialized institution of *African Union (AU, #00488)*, when adopted current name, and moved headquarters to Bamako (Mali). **Aims** Develop and promote African languages in general and vehicular cross-border languages in particular, in partnership with the former colonial languages; promote convivial functional multilingualism at all levels, especially in the education sector; ensure development of African languages as a factor of integration an development. **Structure** AU Conference of Ministers of Culture; Governing Board; Scientific and Technical Committee; Assembly of Academicians; Executive Secretariat; National Language Structures (Focal Points); Vehicular Cross-border Language Commissions. **Staff** 5.00 FTE, paid. **NGO Relations** Member of: *Union académique internationale (UAI, #20345).* Instrumental in setting up: *World Network for Linguistic Diversity (Maaya, #21671).* Cooperates with: *International Communications Volunteers (ICVolunteers, #12817).* [2021/XM2921/**D**]

♦ African Academy of Sciences (AAS) 00193

Académie africaine des sciences

Pres PO Box24916-00502, Nairobi, 00502, Kenya. E-mail: communication@aasciences.africa.
URL: http://www.aasciences.africa/

History 10 Dec 1985, Trieste (Italy), at a meeting held at the headquarters of the *TWAS (#20270)*, at *Abdus Salam International Centre for Theoretical Physics (ICTP, #00005)*, when constitution was ratified. The inauguration took place on 1-2 Jun 1986, at *International Centre of Insect Physiology and Ecology (ICIPE, #12499)*, where the Secretariat of AAS was located up to 1992 before moving to its own headquarters at Nairobi (Kenya). **Aims** Promote and foster the growth of scientific community in Africa, and stimulate and nurture the spirit of scientific discovery and technological innovation so as to serve socio-economic development and regional integration and global peace and security; stimulate, design and coordinate regional interdisciplinary and transdisciplinary scientific research, development and demonstration projects or activities of major regional interest or concern; plan, convene and coordinate science education programmes; help in developing and nurturing high-level scientific and technological manpower by identifying young talented scientists and technologists, recognizing their merit and promoting growth of their creativity; facilitate, coordinate and undertake publication of scientific progress; foster dissemination of scientific knowledge throughout the continent; facilitate contacts between scientists in Africa. **Structure** General Assembly (every 3 years). Governing Council, consisting of Officers and 5 sub-regional representatives. Executive Committee, comprising President, Secretary-General, Treasurer, Secretary for International Affairs, 2 Vice-Presidents and 2 regional representatives appointed by the Governing Council. Officers: President, 5 Vice-Presidents (representing Eastern, Western, Northern, Southern and Central Africa), Secretary-General, Treasurer, Secretary for International Affairs, Editor-in-Chief and 5 representatives. **Languages** English, French. **Staff** 17.00 FTE, paid. **Finance** Members' dues. Other sources: grants, subventions, contracts, donations and legacies; net income from publications; revenue from capital investment. Donors: Governments of Kenya, Morocco and Norway; international and governmental agencies, including the following listed in this Yearbook – *Canadian International Development Agency (CIDA, inactive)*, *Carnegie Corporation of New York*, ICIPE, *International Development Research Centre (IDRC, #13162)*, *International Foundation for the Survival and Development of Humanity (no recent information)*, *The Rockefeller Foundation (#18966)*, *Swedish International Development Cooperation Agency (Sida)*, TWAS, *UNDP (#20292)*, *UNESCO (#20322).* **Activities** Core programme in 4 principal areas: 1. /Mobilization and strengthening of the African scientific community/ – comprising: *Network of African Scientific Organizations (NASO, no recent information)* and *African Research Information Network (AFRINET, no recent information)*; Profiles and Databank of African Scientists and Scientific Institutions; Specific Assistance to Regional Scientific and Professional Associations. 2. /Publication and dissemination of scientific materials/ – undertaken by Academy Science Publishers (ASP), a joint venture between AAS and TWAS. 3. /Research, development and public policy/ – including: *Special Commission on Africa (SCA)*; Drought, Desertification and Food Deficit (DDFD). 4. /Capacity building in science and technology/ – including: Capacity Building in Forestry Research (CBFR); Capacity Building in Soil and Water Management (SWM); Management of Environment and Natural Resources; Sustainable Development under Freshwater Poverty; *Virtual Institute of Advanced Study in Africa (VIASA)*; National Forests Programmes (NFPs) Initiative for Africa. In addition: carries out Sensitization Missions; organizes meetings, symposia and workshops; collaborates in projects with other organizations with similar objectives. **Events** *SFSA : Science Forum South Africa* Pretoria (South Africa) 2018, *Conference on climate change and food security* Nairobi (Kenya) 2011, *World population conference of the world's scientific academies* Delhi (India) 1993, *Meeting* Abidjan (Côte d'Ivoire) 1992, *Conference on economic cooperation and regional integration in Africa* Algiers (Algeria) 1992. **Publications** *Whydah* (4 a year) – newsletter; *Discovery and Innovations* (4 a year) – journal, together with TWAS; *Directory of Scholarly Journals Published in Africa. Profiles of African Scientific Institutions* (1992); *30 Years of Independence in Africa: The Lost Decades ?*; *Philosophy, Humanity and Ecology*; *Supporting Capacity Building in Forestry Research in Africa*; *Soil and Water Management and Biotechnology in Africa: A Report of the Fact Finding Mission*; *Science for Development in Africa*; *Regional Integration in Africa: Unfinished Agenda*; *Profiles of African Scientists* (3rd ed); *Mobilization of African Scientific Talent for Development*; *Africa in the Context of World Science*; *Industrialization at Bay: African Experiences*; *Guide to Directories on Science and Technology in Africa*; *Environment Crisis in Africa: Scientific Response*; *Enhancement of Agricultural Research in Francophone Africa*; *Economic Cooperation and Regional Integration*; *Arms and Daggers in the Heart of Africa: Studies on Internal Conflicts*; *The Greening of Africa.* Annual Report. Brochures; proceedings; strategic plan.
Members Founding Fellows; Fellows (elected); Foreign Fellows; Honorary Fellows. Fellows (162) in 30 African countries:
Algeria, Benin, Burkina Faso, Burundi, Cameroon, Central African Rep, Chad, Congo Brazzaville, Congo DR, Côte d'Ivoire, Egypt, Eswatini, Ethiopia, Ghana, Kenya, Madagascar, Malawi, Mauritius, Morocco, Mozambique, Nigeria, Senegal, Sierra Leone, South Africa, Sudan, Tanzania UR, Togo, Tunisia, Uganda, Zimbabwe.
Foreign Fellows in 3 countries:
India, Italy, USA.
NGO Relations Member of: *Consortium on Science, Technology and Innovation for the South (COSTIS, no recent information)*; *Global Research Collaboration for Infectious Disease Preparedness (GLOPID-R, #10573)*; *ICSC – World Laboratory (#11088)*; *InterAcademy Partnership (IAP, #11376)*; *International Foundation for Science (IFS, #13677)*; *International Science Council (ISC, #14796)*; *International Technical Tropical Timber Association (ITTTA, #15668)*; *Next Einstein Forum (NEF, #17098)*; *ORCID (#17790).* Collaborates with: *African Technology Policy Studies Network (ATPS, #00481).* Instrumental in setting up: *Forestry Research Network for Sub-Saharan Africa (FORNESSA, #09866)*; *Network of African Science Academies (NASAC, #16987)*; *Research and Development Forum for Science-Led Development in Africa (RANDFORUM, no recent information).* [2022/XF2052/v/**F**]

♦ African Acarology Association (AAA) 00194

Chairman address not obtained. E-mail: edalbert@lantic.net.
URL: http://www.africanacarologyassociation.com/

History 27 Nov 1998, Pretoria (South Africa). **Aims** Promote and support the study of mites and ticks in Africa; increase cooperation amongst acarologists in Africa. **Structure** Committee, comprising Chairman, Secretary, 4 regional members (South; East; West; North) and an additional member. **Languages** English. **Staff** None. **Finance** No budget. **Activities** Organizes symposia. **Events** *Symposium* Livingstone (Zambia) 2011, *Symposium* Tunis (Tunisia) 2007, *Symposium* Cairo (Egypt) 2004, *Novel approaches to tick and mite management in the new millennium* Nairobi (Kenya) 2001.
Members Full in 10 countries:
Benin, Egypt, Kenya, Namibia, Nigeria, South Africa, Sudan, Tunisia, Zambia, Zimbabwe. [2009.06.01/XD8235/**D**]

♦ African Accounting Council (no recent information)

♦ African Accounting and Finance Association (AAFA) 00195

Secretariat Dept of Accounting, Univ of Jos, PMB 2084, Jos 930001, Plateau, Nigeria. T. +2348033492313. E-mail: info@aafassociation.com.
URL: http://www.aafassociation.com/

History Founded Dec 2010. **Aims** Provide a platform for academics and practitioners to debate the role of accounting, finance, auditing, corporate governance and related fields in Africa; bring together academic, graduate students and practitioners from Africa and the rest of the accounting and finance community worldwide to share information, experiences and challenges while networking with peers and establishing professional contacts. **Structure** Executive Board; headquarters in Accra (Ghana). **Languages** English, French. **Finance** Members' dues. Support from: Chartered Institute of Management Accountants (CIMA) and Emerald. **Activities** Events/meetings; research/documentation; training/education. **Events** *Conference* Cairo (Egypt) 2022, *Conference* 2021, *Conference* Cairo (Egypt) 2020, *Conference* Dar es Salaam (Tanzania UR) 2019, *Conference* Dakar (Senegal) 2018. **Publications** *AAFA Newsletter*; *Research in Accounting in Emerging Economies* – peer-reviewed. [2018.01.27/XJ8860/**D**]

♦ African Accreditation Cooperation (AFRAC) 00196

Contact c/o SANAS, Libertas Office Park, Cnr Libertas Avenue and Highway Street, Equesstria, Pretoria, 0184, South Africa.
URL: http://www.intra-afrac.com/

History Set up 2010, as one of 4 pillars of *Pan-African Quality Infrastructure (PAQI)*, established by *New Partnership for Africa's Development (NEPAD, #17091).* **Aims** Facilitate the use of accreditation as a tool to support trade and industrial development, improve competitiveness of African products and enhance protection of health and safety of the public and the environment. **Structure** General Assembly; Executive Committee; MRA Council; Committees; Subcommittees; Secretariat. **Languages** English. **Staff** 2.00 FTE, paid. **Finance** Secretariat financed by South African Department of Trade and Industry. **Activities** Certification/accreditation; networking/liaising. **Events** *General Assembly* Cairo (Egypt) 2017, *General Assembly* Abuja (Nigeria) 2016, *General Assembly* Tunis (Tunisia) 2015, *General Assembly* Addis Ababa (Ethiopia) 2014, *General Assembly* Nairobi (Kenya) 2013. **Publications** *AFRAC Newsletter.*
Members Arrangement; Full; Associate; Stakeholder. Arrangement Members in 5 countries:
Egypt, Ethiopia, Kenya, Mauritius, South Africa.
Regional Arrangement Member:
Southern African Development Community Accreditation Service (SADCAS, #19844).
Full in 2 countries:
Nigeria, Tunisia.
Regional Full Member:
Système Ouest-Africain d'Accréditation (SOAC).
Associate in 1 country:
Sudan.
Stakeholder Members in 4 countries:
Ethiopia, Kenya, Nigeria, Senegal.
Included in the above, 5 organizations listed in this Yearbook:
African Society for Laboratory Medicine (ASLM, #00463); *Economic Community of West African States (ECOWAS, #05312)*; *FHI 360*; *Southern African Development Community (SADC, #19843)* (Cooperation in Accreditation SADCA); *Union internationale des laboratoires indépendants (UILI, #20429).*

African Action AIDS
00196

alphabetic sequence excludes
For the complete listing, see Yearbook Online at

IGO Relations *African Organisation for Standardisation (ARSO, #00404); Southern African Development Community (SADC, #19843).* Observer member of: *Intra-Africa Metrology System (AFRIMETS, #15992).* **NGO Relations** Regional cooperation body of: *International Laboratory Accreditation Cooperation (ILAC, #13995).* Member of: *International Accreditation Forum (IAF, #11584).* Memorandum of Understanding with: *Asia Pacific Accreditation Cooperation (APAC, #01816).* [2018.10.11/XM5875/y/**E**]

♦ African Action on AIDS (internationally oriented national body)
♦ African Adult Education Association (inactive)

♦ African Advanced Level Telecommunications Institute (AFRALTI) .. 00197

Main Office PO Box 58902, 00200 City Square, Nairobi, Kenya. T. +254202655011 – +254204440633. Fax +254204444483. E-mail: director@afralti.org – info@afralti.org.
URL: http://www.afralti.org/

History 1987, Nairobi (Kenya). Founded as a project of *UNDP (#20292).* Taken over by 9 countries in the eastern and southern Africa region in 1992. **Aims** Supplement and complement efforts by countries in the Eastern nd Southern African region to develop capacity in telecommunications and related fields. **Structure** Governing Council, comprising representatives of member States. Director; Heads of Departments. **Languages** English. **Staff** 23.00 FTE, paid. **Finance** Main source: tuition fees (55% of total revenue). Others: membership contributions (17%); internally generated revenue. **Activities** Conducts ICT courses in the areas of: Access Networks; Network Planning; Digital Technology; Management Information Systems; Regulatory Management Studies. **Events** *Meeting* Mbabane (Swaziland) 2004, *Meeting* Kampala (Uganda) 2003, *Meeting* Maseru (Lesotho) 2002, *Meeting* Nairobi (Kenya) 2002, *Meeting* Malawi 2000.
Members Covers 8 countries:
Angola, Eswatini, Kenya, Malawi, Mozambique, Tanzania UR, Uganda, Zimbabwe. [2021/XE0210/j/**E**]

♦ African Aeronautics & Space Organisation (internationally oriented national body)
♦ African Agency For Integrated Development (internationally oriented national body)
♦ African Agency For Integrated Development Uganda / see African Agency For Integrated Development
♦ African Agribusiness Incubators Network (internationally oriented national body)

♦ African Agricultural Economics Education Network (AAEEN) 00198

Contact c/o AERC, Mebank Towers, 4th Fl, Milimani Road, PO Box 62882, Nairobi, 00200, Kenya. E-mail: cmaae@aercafrica.org.
URL: http://www.agriculturaleconomics.net/

History as Agricultural Economics Education Board (AEEB). Present name adopted 2005. **Activities** Main programme: 'Collaborative Master in Science Programme in Agricultural and Applied Economics in Eastern and Southern Africa (CMAAE)'.
Members University departments (16) in 12 countries:
Botswana, Eswatini, Ethiopia, Kenya, Malawi, Mozambique, Rwanda, South Africa, Tanzania UR, Uganda, Zambia, Zimbabwe.
NGO Relations Located at: *African Economic Research Consortium (AERC, #00292).* [2007/XM2777/**F**]

♦ African Agricultural Technology Foundation (AATF) 00199

Exec Dir PO Box 30709, Nairobi, 00100, Kenya. T. +254204223700. Fax +254204223701. E-mail: aatf@aatf-africa.org.
URL: http://www.aatf-africa.org/

History 2003, Nairobi (Kenya). **Aims** Access and deliver affordable agricultural technologies for sustainable use by smallholders, and in particular resource-poor *farmers*, in Sub-Saharan Africa through innovative partnerships and effective technology/product stewardship along the entire food value chain. **Structure** Board, including Chair, Vice Chair and Executive Director. **Languages** English, French. **Staff** 11 internationally recruited; 11 nationally recruited. **Finance** Financed by: *Department for International Development (DFID, inactive); The Rockefeller Foundation (#18966); United States Agency for International Development (USAID); Bill and Melinda Gates Foundation (BMGF);* Howard G Buffett Foundation. **Activities** Negotiates royalty-free proprietary technologies; convenes and manages partnerships to support agricultural technology development and deployment; stewards technologies along the entire food value chain; organizes open fora for Agricultural Biotechnology in Africa (OFAB). **Publications** *AATF Partnerships Newsletter.* Annual Report.
Members in 8 countries:
Burkina Faso, Ghana, Kenya, Mozambique, Nigeria, South Africa, Tanzania UR, Uganda.
IGO Relations Located at: *International Livestock Research Institute (ILRI, #14062).* Permanent observer status with: *World Intellectual Property Organization (WIPO, #21593).* **NGO Relations** Supports: *International Institute of Tropical Agriculture (IITA, #13933).* [2015/XM0425/f/**D**]

♦ African Aid Organization (internationally oriented national body)
♦ African AIDS Vaccine Partnership (unconfirmed)

♦ African Airlines Association (AFRAA) 00200

Association des compagnies aériennes africaines

SG AFRAA Building, Red Cross Road PO Box 20116, Nairobi, 00200, Kenya. T. +254202320144. Fax +254206001173. E-mail: afraa@afraa.org.
URL: http://www.afraa.org/

History Founded 4 Apr 1968, Accra (Ghana), as *Association of African Airlines (AAFRA),* with 15 founder members. Present name adopted May 1974. **Aims** Promote and develop safe, regular, economical and efficient air transport services to, from and within Africa. **Structure** General Assembly (annual); Executive Committee; Steering Committees (5); Secretariat. **Languages** English, French. **Staff** 15.00 FTE, paid. **Finance** Members' dues. Other sources: partnership subscriptions; training; conferences; advertising; office rentals. **Activities** Research and development; networking/liaising; events/meetings; training/education. **Events** *Annual General Assembly* Brazzaville (Congo Brazzaville) 2015, *Aviation Stakeholders Convention* Johannesburg (South Africa) 2015, *Annual General Assembly* Algiers (Algeria) 2014, *Annual General Assembly* Mombasa (Kenya) 2013, *Annual General Assembly* Johannesburg (South Africa) 2012. **Publications** *AFRAA Bulletin* (12 a year); *Africa Wings* (4 a year) – magazine. Annual Reports.
Members Airlines (37) representing 31 countries:
Algeria, Angola, Botswana, Burkina Faso, Cameroon, Cape Verde, Congo Brazzaville, Egypt, Equatorial Guinea, Ethiopia, Ghana, Kenya, Libya, Madagascar, Malawi, Mali, Mauritius, Morocco, Mozambique, Namibia, Nigeria, Rwanda, Seychelles, South Africa, Sudan, Tanzania UR, Togo, Tunisia, Uganda, Zambia, Zimbabwe.
IGO Relations A specialized agency of: *African Union (AU, #00488).* [2019/XD4373/**D**]

♦ African Air Sports Federation (unconfirmed)
♦ African Air Tariff Conference (no recent information)

♦ African ALARA Network (AFAN) 00201

Secretariat Radiation Protection Inst, PO Box LG 80 Legon, Accra, Ghana. E-mail: rpi@gaecgh.org.
URL: https://african-alara.net/

History 5 Dec 2017, Antananarivo (Madagascar). **Activities** Events/meetings; training/education.
Members Full in 23 countries:
Botswana, Burkina Faso, Cameroon, Central African Rep, Chad, Congo Brazzaville, Congo DR, Egypt, Gabon, Ghana, Liberia, Madagascar, Malawi, Mali, Morocco, Namibia, Niger, Nigeria, Senegal, South Africa, Sudan, Tanzania UR, Tunisia. [2020/AA1212/**F**]

♦ Africana Librarians Council (internationally oriented national body)
♦ African Alliance for e-Commerce (#00652)
♦ African Alliance for Maternal Mental Health (unconfirmed)
♦ African Amateur Athletic Confederation / see Confederation of African Athletics (#04504)
♦ African Amateur Boxing Association / see African Boxing Confederation (#00228)
♦ African-American Institute / see Africa-America Institute
♦ African-American Islamic Institute (internationally oriented national body)
♦ African-American Society for Humanitarian Aid and Development (internationally oriented national body)

♦ African Arachnological Society (AFRAS) 00202

Chairman Dept of Zoology, Univ of Venda, Private Bag X5050, Thohoyandou, 0950, South Africa. T. +27159628492. Fax +27159628000.
URL: http://afras.ufs.ac.za/

History 1986, Pretoria (South Africa), as *Research Group for the Study of African Arachnids.* Present name adopted Nov 1996. **Aims** Promote study of African *Arachnida* (non-Acari); achieve closer cooperation and understanding between local and overseas professional arachnologists; provide a web-based expert information system. **Structure** General Meeting; Committee. **Languages** English. **Staff** 2.00 FTE, voluntary. **Finance** Donations; proceeds from colloquia. **Activities** Events/meetings; knowledge management/ information dissemination; publishing activities. **Events** *African Colloquium of Arachnology* South Africa 2020, *African Colloquium of Arachnology* South Africa 2017, *African colloquium of arachnology* South Africa 2011, *African Colloquium of Arachnology* Louis Trichardt (South Africa) 2008, *African arachnological colloquium* Bloemfontein (South Africa) 2005. **Publications** *AFRAS Newsletter.* **Information Services** *African Arachnida Database (AFRAD).*
Members Full (122) in 25 countries:
Argentina, Australia, Belgium, Brazil, Denmark, Egypt, Ethiopia, France, Germany, Ghana, Hungary, Kenya, Malawi, Namibia, Netherlands, New Zealand, Nigeria, Pakistan, Poland, Russia, Slovenia, South Africa, UK, USA, Zimbabwe. [2017.08.08/XD8234/**D**]

♦ African Artists for Development (internationally oriented national body)

♦ African-Asian Rural Development Organization (AARDO) 00203

Contact 2 State Guest Houses Complex, Chanakyapuri, Delhi 110021, DELHI 110021, India. T. +911126877783. Fax +911126115937. E-mail: aardohq@aardo.org.
URL: http://www.aardo.org/

History 31 Mar 1962, Cairo (Egypt). Established on adoption of Constitution by 5 nations at 2nd Afro-Asian Rural Reconstruction Conference, following a proposal approved by 1st Afro-Asian Rural Reconstruction Conference, Jan 1961, Delhi (India). Former names and other names: *Afro-Asian Rural Reconstruction Organization (AARRO)* – former (1962); *Organisation afro-asiatique pour la reconstruction rurale (OASRR)* – former (1962); *Organización Afro-Asiatica para la Reconstrucción Rural* – former (1962). **Aims** Catalyze efforts of Afro-Asian countries to help them restructure their rural societies and reconstruct the economy of their rural people. **Structure** General Conference (every 3 years); Executive Committee; Liaison Committee; Technical Programme Committee; Regional Offices (6); Secretariat, headed by Secretary-General. **Languages** Arabic, English, French. **Staff** 30.00 FTE, paid. **Finance** Sources: members' dues. **Activities** Events/meetings; financial and/or material support; knowledge management/information dissemination; networking/liaising; training/education. **Events** *General Session of Conference* Accra (Ghana) 2021, *Asia-Pacific Agricultural Policy Forum* Seoul (Korea Rep) 2019, *General Session of Conference* Kuala Lumpur (Malaysia) 2018, *General Session of Conference* Pointe aux Piments (Mauritius) 2015, *General Session of Conference* Cairo (Egypt) 2012. **Publications** *AARDO e-Newsletter* (4 a year); *African-Asian Journal of Rural Development* (2 a year). Annual Report.
Members Full: open to governments of countries invited to 1st or 2nd AARRO conference, to countries in the Afro-Asian region and members of the UN or its specialized agencies and to organizations (governmental or non-governmental) in these countries, approved by the government concerned. Governments of 31 countries and territories:
Bangladesh, Burkina Faso, Egypt, Ethiopia, Gambia, Ghana, India, Iraq, Jordan, Kenya, Korea Rep, Lebanon, Liberia, Libya, Malawi, Malaysia, Mauritius, Morocco, Namibia, Nigeria, Oman, Pakistan, Palestine, Sierra Leone, Sri Lanka, Sudan, Syrian AR, Taiwan, Tunisia, Yemen, Zambia.
Associates: Corporation and Bank in 2 countries:
Korea Rep, Sudan.
IGO Relations Cooperates with (1): *UNCTAD (#20285).* Relationship agreement with: *FAO (#09260).* [2022.12.05/XC0030/**C***]

♦ African Asian Studies Association (internationally oriented national body)
♦ African Assembly for the Defense of Human Rights (internationally oriented national body)

♦ African Assembly of Linguistic Anthropology (AFALA) 00204

Address not obtained.
2021 Conference: https://afala2021.uonbi.ac.ke/

Aims Redefine the way African language and society is viewed. **Languages** English. **Staff** 4.00 FTE, paid; 10.00 FTE, voluntary. **Activities** Advocacy/lobbying/activism; awards/prizes/competitions; awareness raising; capacity building; events/meetings; financial and/or material support; guidance/assistance/consulting; knowledge management/information dissemination; networking/liaising; publishing activities; research/documentation; training/education. **Events** *AFALA Conference on African Linguistic Anthropology* Nairobi (Kenya) 2021. **Publications** *The Journal of African Linguistic Anthropology (AFALA Journal).* **NGO Relations** Constitutes *Global Network in Linguistic Anthropology,* together with *Global Council for Anthropological Linguistics (GLOCAL, #10310), Conference on Mediterranean and European Linguistic Anthropology (COMELA, #04628), South and Central American Assembly on Linguistic Anthropology (SCAALA, #19752), Conference on Oceanian Linguistic Anthropology (COOLA, #04636)* and *Middle Eastern Association of Linguistic Anthropology (MEALA, #16760).* [2020.05.02/XM8718/c/**F**]

♦ African Association for the Advancement of Science and Technology (no recent information)

♦ African Association of Agricultural Economists (AAAE) 00205

Association africaine des agroéconomistes

Secretariat c/o Univ of Nairobi, College of Agriculture and Veterinary Sciences, Upper Kabete Campus, PO Box 63515, Nairobi, 00619, Kenya. T. +254572511300. E-mail: info@aaae-africa.org.
URL: http://www.aaae-africa.org/

History 2003, Durban (South Africa). Founded during the 25th conference of *International Association of Agricultural Economists (IAAE, #11695),* as a branch of IAAE. Officially launched, Dec 2004, Nairobi (Kenya). Currently functions as an autonomous association, complementing IAAE. Registration: Start date: 2005, Kenya. **Aims** Enhance the skills, knowledge and professional contributions of economists who help society solve agricultural, development and food security challenges in achieving a thriving, sustainable and well-nourished Africa. **Structure** Executive Committee; Secretariat. **Languages** English, French. **Staff** 3.00 FTE, paid. **Finance** Members' dues. Donor funding. Annual budget: about US$ 150,000. **Events** *African Conference of Agricultural Economists* Durban (South Africa) 2023, *African Conference of Agricultural Economists* Abuja (Nigeria) 2019, *Conference* Addis Ababa (Ethiopia) 2016, *Conference / Triennial Conference* Hammamet (Tunisia) 2013, *Conference / Triennial Conference* Cape Town (South Africa) 2010. **Publications** *African Journal of Agricultural and Resource Economics (AFJARE)* in English, French. **Members** Individuals in 67 countries. Membership countries not specified. **IGO Relations** *African Development Bank (ADB, #00283); Australian Centre for International Agricultural Research (ACIAR); FAO (#09260); International Development Research Centre (IDRC, #13162); International Livestock Research Institute (ILRI, #14062); Norwegian Agency for Development Cooperation (Norad); Swedish International Development Cooperation Agency (Sida).* [2021/XM0132/**E**]

♦ African Association for Biological Nitrogen Fixation (AABNF) 00206

Association africaine pour la fixation de l'azote

Congress Coordinator Lab de Microbiologie des Sols, Fac des Sciences et Techniques, Univ de Bamako BPE, Bamako, Mali. T. +22320223244. Fax +22320238168.

History 1982. **Aims** Act as a non-governmental multidisciplinary group, gathering specialists in soil sciences, nutrition, agronomy, microbiology, political decision makers and others interested in the promotion of research, education and the use of biological nitrogen fixation systems. **Languages** English, French. **Events** *Conference* Bamako (Mali) 2010, *Conference* Tunisia 2008, *International congress on nitrogen fixation* Cape Town (South Africa) 2007, *Impact of biological nitrogen fixation on agricultural development in Africa* Dakar (Senegal) 2004, *Conference* Legon (Ghana) 2002. **Publications** Conference proceedings.
Members Full in 31 countries:
Algeria, Benin, Burkina Faso, Burundi, Cameroon, Chad, Congo Brazzaville, Congo DR, Egypt, Ethiopia, Ghana, Kenya, Lesotho, Madagascar, Malawi, Mali, Mauritania, Mauritius, Morocco, Mozambique, Nigeria, Rwanda, Senegal, Sierra Leone, South Africa, Sudan, Tanzania UR, Tunisia, Uganda, Zambia, Zimbabwe. [2010/XD0331/**D**]

♦ African Association for the Defense of Human Rights (internationally oriented national body)
♦ African Association of Dermatology (no recent information)
♦ African Association for Development (inactive)
♦ African Association for Distance Education (no recent information)
♦ African Association of Education for Development (no recent information)
♦ African Association for the Environment and Community Development (no recent information)
♦ African Association of Farming Systems for Research, Extension and Training (inactive)
♦ African Association of Generic Essential Drugs Purchasing Centres (#02348)
♦ African Association for Human and Peoples' Rights in Development (inactive)

♦ African Association of Insect Scientists (AAIS) 00207

Mailing Address PO BOx 30772-00100, Nairobi, 00100, Kenya. E-mail: aaissecretary@gmail.com.
URL: https://aaisafrica.org/

History Dec 1978. Founded at inaugural meeting. Registration: Kenya. **Aims** Promote development, advancement and dissemination of knowledge in all aspects of insect science, particularly, but not exclusively, in relation to insects on the African continent; act as coordinating body for grants for problem-solving research areas and for development of insect science. **Structure** General Meeting (every 2 years, at Conference); Steering Committee; Executive Committee; Regional Representatives for the 5 regions of Africa (Northern, Southern, Eastern, Central, Western); Representative of international institutes; Representative of universities. **Languages** English, French. **Staff** 12.00 FTE, voluntary.
Finance Members' dues. Other sources: donors and supporters, national governments and the following international and internationally oriented bodies that have supported AAIS over the years include:
– *African Academy of Sciences (AAS, #00193)*;
– *African Biosciences Network (ABN, no recent information)*;
– *African Development Foundation (ADF)*;
– *Commonwealth Foundation (CF, #04330)*;
– *Commonwealth Secretariat (#04362)*;
– *FAO (#09260)*;
– *International Bank for Reconstruction and Development (IBRD, #12317)*;
– *International Centre of Insect Physiology and Ecology (ICIPE, #12499)*;
– *International Development Research Centre (IDRC, #13162)*;
– *International Fund for Agricultural Development (IFAD, #13692)*;
– *International Institute of Tropical Agriculture (IITA, #13933)*;
– *The Rockefeller Foundation (#18966)*;
– *TWAS (#20270)*;
– *UNEP (#20299)*;
– *UNDP (#20292)*;
– *UNESCO (#20322)*;
– *United Nations Economic Commission for Africa (ECA, #20554)*;
– *United States Agency for International Development (USAID)*.
Activities Knowledge management/information dissemination; events/meetings; awards/prizes/competitions. **Events** *Meeting and Scientific Conference* Addis Ababa (Ethiopia) 2022, *Meeting and Scientific Conference* Addis Ababa (Ethiopia) 2021, *Meeting and Scientific Conference* Abidjan (Côte d'Ivoire) 2019, *Meeting and Scientific Conference* Wad Medani (Sudan) 2017, *Meeting and Scientific Conference* Cotonou (Benin) 2015. **Publications** *AAIS Newsletter*; *Bulletin of African Insect Science* in English, French; *Insect Science and its Application* – journal. Proceedings of meetings.
Members Institutions in 7 countries:
Burkina Faso, Côte d'Ivoire, Ghana, Kenya, Nigeria, South Africa, Tanzania UR.
Individuals (200) in 42 countries and territories:
Australia, Benin, Burkina Faso, Cameroon, Chad, Congo Brazzaville, Congo DR, Côte d'Ivoire, Ethiopia, France, Gambia, Germany, Ghana, Guinea, India, Kenya, Libya, Madagascar, Malawi, Mauritius, Morocco, Mozambique, Netherlands, Niger, Nigeria, Réunion, Rwanda, Senegal, Sierra Leone, South Africa, Spain, Sri Lanka, Sudan, Switzerland, Tanzania UR, Togo, Uganda, UK, USA, Yemen, Zambia, Zimbabwe.
NGO Relations Secretariat provided by ICIPE. [2022/XD1445/D]

♦ African Association of International Law (AAIL) 00208

Association africaine de droit international (AADI)
Sec-Treas c/o PALU, PO Box 6065, Arusha, Tanzania UR. E-mail: secretariat@lawyersofafrica.org.
SG address not obtained. E-mail: info@aail-aadi.org.
URL: http://www.aail-aadi.org/

History 1986. Reactivated 2012. **Aims** Foster development and dissemination of African perspectives and practices of international law; assist in the development of international law, recognizing the special needs of Africa; promote teaching of international law in Africa and encourage and coordinate research on international law. **Structure** Executive Committee. **Events** *Annual Conference* Libreville (Gabon) 2015. **Publications** *African Yearbook of International Law*. **Consultative Status** Consultative status granted from: *African Commission on Human and Peoples' Rights (ACHPR, #00255)* (Observer). [2016/XD1001/D]

♦ African Association of Journalists of the Rural Press (inactive)
♦ African Association for Lexicography (internationally oriented national body)
♦ African Association for Literacy and Adult Education (inactive)
♦ African Association for Management (inactive)
♦ African Association of Microbiology and Food Hygiene (#02350)

♦ African Association of Nephrology (AFRAN) 00209

Association africaine de néphrologie
Sec-Treas Cairo University, Misr Kidney Centre, 55 Abde El Monheim Riad Street, Cairo, Egypt. T. +2023455782 – +2023024925. Fax +2023610558.
Pres Cairo Univ, Misr Kidney Center, 55 Abde El Monheim Riad Street, Mohandessin, Cairo, Egypt. T. +20233455782 – +20233024925. Fax +20233610558.

History Dec 1987, Cairo (Egypt). Also referred to as *Association africaine pour les maladies rénales*. **Aims** Improve education and promote research in nephrology in Africa. **Structure** Board, consisting of President; President Elect; 6 Past Presidents; Secretary/Treasurer; Deputy Secretary; Board of Trustees, comprising of 9 members. **Languages** English, French. **Staff** Full-time, voluntary. **Finance** Members' dues. **Activities** Organizes conferences and a student exchange programme. Setting up a research programme in collaboration with ISN. **Events** *African Nephrology and Transplantation Summit* Cairo (Egypt) 2023, *Joint Congress* Abidjan (Côte d'Ivoire) 2021, *Joint Congress* Mombasa (Kenya) 2019, *Congress* Yaoundé (Cameroon) 2017, *Working towards healthy kidneys* Accra (Ghana) 2013. **Publications** *African Journal of Nephrology* (3 a year); *AFRAN Newsletter* (2 a year). Registry of African nephrologists.
Members Full in 28 countries:
Algeria, Benin, Burkina Faso, Cameroon, Congo Brazzaville, Congo DR, Côte d'Ivoire, Egypt, Ethiopia, Gabon, Ghana, Guinea, Kenya, Libya, Madagascar, Mali, Morocco, Niger, Nigeria, Rwanda, Senegal, South Africa, Sudan, Tanzania UR, Tunisia, Uganda, Zambia, Zimbabwe.
NGO Relations Member of: *International Society of Nephrology (ISN, #15294)*. [2013.09.17/XD3785/D]

♦ African Association of Nuclear Medicine (AANM) 00210

SG Nuclear Medicine – Tygerberg Hospital, Tygerberg, 7505, South Africa.

History 1998, on the initiative of Dr Heinz R Morke. Also referred to as *Pan African Association of Nuclear Medicine*. **Events** *African conference of nuclear medicine / Conference* Réunion 2001. **NGO Relations** Affiliated to: *World Federation of Nuclear Medicine and Biology (WFNMB, #21467)*. [2013/XD8237/D]

♦ African Association of Physics Students (AAPS) 00211

Contact c/o AfPS, PO Box 197, Legon, Accra, Ghana. T. +233302544102. E-mail: fkallotey@gmail.com.
URL: http://www.africanphysicsstudents.org/

History 2005. Since 2007 a subsidiary body of *African Physical Society (AfPS, #00417)*. **Aims** Encourage physics students in their scientific and professional work in an African and an international context; promote relations between physics students from all over the world. **Structure** Executive Committee, comprising Chair, Vice-Chair, Treasurer, Secretary and 4 members. **Events** *African Conference for Physics Students* Dakar (Senegal) 2010, *African Conference for Physics Students* Abuja (Nigeria) 2005. [2012.07.02/XJ1876/E]

♦ African Association of Physiological Sciences (AAPS) 00212

SG Physiology Dept, Fac of Medicine, Suez Canal Univ, Ismailia, 41522, Egypt.
Secretariat 82 Bulwer Road, Durban, 4001, South Africa. T. +27312011392. Fax +27312013950. E-mail: toni.ebeigbe@gmail.com.
URL: http://www.aapsnet.org/

History Inaugurated 8 Jul 1989, Kuopio (Finland). Officially launched, 1992, Nairobi (Kenya). **Aims** Develop the capacity of basic medical scientists in Africa; disseminate the latest development in physiological sciences; promote advancement of African physiological sciences. **Structure** General Assembly; Council; Executive. **Activities** Events/meetings. **Events** *International Congress* Lagos (Nigeria) 2016, *International Congress* Ismailia (Egypt) 2012, *International Congress* Nairobi (Kenya) 2008, *International Congress* Tangiers (Morocco) 2004, *International Congress* Pretoria (South Africa) 2001. **NGO Relations** Member of: *International Society for Pathophysiology (ISP, #15343)*. Regional member of: *International Union of Physiological Sciences (IUPS, #15800)*. [2017/XU4179/D]

♦ African Association of Political Science (unconfirmed)

♦ African Association for Precision Agriculture (AAPA) 00213

Contact c/o APNI, Lot 660, Hay Moulay Rachid, 43150 Ben Guerir, Morocco. E-mail: info@paafrica.org.
URL: https://paafrica.org/AAPA

History 2020. Founded by *African Plant Nutrition Institute (APNI, #00418)*. **Aims** Promote he advancement and dissemination of Precision Agriculture tailored to the needs and aspirations of the African people. **Structure** Board. **Events** *African Conference on Precision Agriculture* Nairobi (Kenya) 2022, *African Conference on Precision Agriculture* 2020. **Publications** *AAPA Newsletter*. **NGO Relations** Cooperates with (1): *International Society of Precision Agriculture (ISPA, #15379)*. [2022/AA2973/D]

♦ African Association of Psychiatrists and Allied Professions (AAPAP) 00214

Pres KPA, PO Box 65 KNH 00202, Nairobi, Kenya.

Events *Joint Conference* Addis Ababa (Ethiopia) 2016, *Annual Conference* Legon (Ghana) 2015, *Annual Conference* Lagos (Nigeria) 2012, *Meeting* Nairobi (Kenya) 2011, *Meeting* Khartoum (Sudan) 2010. **Publications** *African Journal of Psychiatry*. **NGO Relations** Affiliate member of: *World Psychiatric Association (WPA, #21741)*. [2016/XJ1739/D]

♦ African Association for Public Administration and Management (AAPAM) 00215

Association africaine pour l'administration publique et le management (AAAPM)
SG UN Avenue, Magnolia 132 Fuchsia Close, Gigiri 254, Nairobi, 00100, Kenya. T. +254202629650. E-mail: aapam@aapam.org.
Pres Government Secretary, Head of Civil Service and Cabinet – Lesotho, PO Box 527, Maseru 100, Lesotho. T. +26622316332. Fax +26622310102.
URL: http://www.aapam.org/

History 1962, Dar es Salaam (Tanzania UR). Present name adopted during 10th Inter-African Seminar on Public Administration, following recommendations of previous seminar, 3 Oct 1970, Gaberone. Former names and other names: *Inter-African Public Administration Seminar* – former; *Association africaine d'administration et de gestion publiques* – former. **Aims** Promote best practices, excellence and professionalism in public administration and management in Africa through research, publication, training seminars/workshops and conferences so as to provide fora for senior public service officials to exchange ideas and learning experiences. **Structure** General Assembly (every 3 years); Council; Executive Committee; Secretariat. National Chapters have their own constitutions and elect national chapter officials and Committees. Secretariat. **Languages** English, French. **Staff** 6.00 FTE, paid. **Finance** Sources: members' dues. Annual subventions from African governments; grants from foundations and donors interested in development and professionalization of the public service. **Activities** Training/education; events/meetings; guidance/assistance/consulting; awards/prizes/competitions. **Events** *Annual Roundtable Conference* Bellville (South Africa) 2022, *Annual Roundtable Conference* Dubai (United Arab Emirates) 2019, *Annual Roundtable Conference* Gaborone (Botswana) 2018, *Annual Round Table Conference* El Jadida (Morocco) 2017, *Annual Round Table Conference* Lusaka (Zambia) 2016. **Publications** *AAPAM Newsletter* (3 a year); *African Journal for Public Administration and Management (AJPAM)* (2 a year). Monographs; surveys; annual roundtable reports; research findings; occasional papers of topical interest.
Members Individual and Honorary (over 600 top administrators and managers); Corporate (50): institutions and schools of public administration and management in Africa. Members in 34 countries:
Benin, Botswana, Cameroon, Canada, Côte d'Ivoire, Egypt, Eswatini, Ethiopia, Gambia, Ghana, Kenya, Lesotho, Liberia, Libya, Madagascar, Malawi, Mauritius, Morocco, Mozambique, Namibia, Netherlands, Nigeria, Rwanda, Senegal, Seychelles, Sierra Leone, South Africa, Sudan, Tanzania UR, Uganda, UK, USA, Zambia, Zimbabwe.
Corporate members include the following 3 regional organizations:
Eastern and Southern African Management Institute (ESAMI, #05254); *Institute of Development Management (IDM, #11253)*; *West African Management Development Institutes Network (WAMDEVIN, #20886)*.
NGO Relations Memorandum of Understanding with (1): *Asian Association for Public Administration (AAPA, #01334)*. Member of: *International Institute of Administrative Sciences (IIAS, #13859)*; *International Management Development Network (INTERMAN, no recent information)*. [2021/XD5399/y/D]

♦ African Association of Pure and Applied Chemistry (inactive)
♦ African Association for Quaternary Research (inactive)

♦ African Association of Remote Sensing of the Environment (AARSE) 00216

Association africaine de la télédétection et de l'environnement (AATE)
SG Chouaib Doukkali Univ, BP 20, El Jadida, Morocco. T. +212663107371.
Pres Dept of Estate Management, Obafemi Awolowo Univ, Ile Ife, Osun, Nigeria. T. +2348037251141.
URL: http://www.africanremotesensing.org/

History Aug 1992, Boulder, CO (USA). **Aims** Increase awareness of African governments and their institutions, the private sector and society at large about the empowering and enhancing benefits of developing, applying and utilizing responsibly, the products and services of *earth observation systems* and *geo-information technology*. **Structure** Secretariat; Sub-Regional zones (5). **Languages** English, French. **Staff** 13.00 FTE, voluntary. **Finance** Members' dues. Other sources: contributions; donations; grants. **Activities** Knowledge management/information dissemination; events/meetings; guidance/assistance/consulting. **Events** *AARSE Conference* Kigali (Rwanda) 2022, *AARSE Conference* Kigali (Rwanda) 2021, *AARSE Conference* Kigali (Rwanda) 2020, *AARSE Conference* Alexandria (Egypt) 2018, *AARSE Conference* Kampala (Uganda) 2016. **Publications** *AARSE Newsletter*. *AARSE Directory of Members*.
Members Institutions (73) in 48 countries:
Algeria, Benin, Botswana, Burkina Faso, Burundi, Cameroon, Canada, Chad, Congo DR, Côte d'Ivoire, Egypt, Eritrea, Ethiopia, Finland, France, Gambia, Germany, Ghana, India, Italy, Japan, Jordan, Kenya, Lesotho, Libya, Madagascar, Malawi, Mali, Mauritania, Morocco, Mozambique, Netherlands, Niger, Nigeria, Senegal, Sierra Leone, South Africa, Sudan, Tanzania UR, Thailand, Togo, Tunisia, Uganda, UK, United Arab Emirates, USA, Zambia, Zimbabwe.
Included in the above, 1 regional organization listed in this Yearbook:
African Regional Institute for Geospatial Information Science and Technology (AFRIGIST, #00433).
Individuals (454) in 47 countries:
Algeria, Belgium, Benin, Botswana, Burkina Faso, Burundi, Cameroon, Canada, Chad, Comoros, Congo DR, Côte d'Ivoire, Egypt, Eritrea, Ethiopia, France, Gambia, Ghana, India, Italy, Japan, Jordan, Kenya, Libya, Madagascar, Malawi, Mali, Mauritania, Morocco, Mozambique, Namibia, Netherlands, Niger, Nigeria, Senegal, Sierra Leone, South Africa, Sudan, Tanzania UR, Thailand, Togo, Tunisia, Türkiye, Uganda, UK, USA, Zimbabwe.
NGO Relations Member of: *International Society for Photogrammetry and Remote Sensing (ISPRS, #15362)*. [2018/XD3536/y/D]

♦ African Association of Science Editors (no recent information)
♦ African Association of States Lotteries / see Association des Loteries d'Afrique (#02791)
♦ African Association for the Study of Liver Diseases (no recent information)

♦ **African Association for the Study of Religions (AASR) 00217**
SG Centre for the Study of Religion, Leiden Univ, PO Box 9515, 2300 RA Leiden, Netherlands. T. +31715276903.
Pres Rice Univ, 6100 Main St MS-156, Houston TX 77005, USA. T. +17133482759.
URL: http://www.a-asr.org/
History 1992, Harare (Zimbabwe), at a Regional Conference of the International Association for the History of Religions, to which it has been affiliated since 1995. **Aims** Promote study of religions in Africa through international collaboration in research, publishing and teaching; provide a forum for multilateral communications between scholars of African religions; facilitate exchange of resources and information. **Structure** Meets during IAHR congress (every 5 years); Executive Committee. **Languages** English. **Staff** None. **Finance** Members' dues. **Activities** Events/meetings; knowledge management/information dissemination; publishing activities; financial and/or material support; networking/liaising. **Events** *Conference* 2022, *Conference* 2021, *Conference* Dakar (Senegal) 2020, *Revisiting Religion, Politics, and the State in Africa and the African Diaspora* Lusaka (Zambia) 2018, *Conference* Accra (Ghana) 2016. **Publications** *Journal for the Study of the Religions of Africa and Its Diaspora* (2 a year) – e-journal; *AASR Bulletin* (annual). Occasional conference proceedings. Formally affiliated with 'Journal of African Religions' and 'Journal of Religion in Africa'.
Members Individuals (257) – scholars of religions posted in universities in Africa and scholars of the religions of Africa posted in universities outside Africa. Members in 21 countries:
Botswana, Cameroon, Canada, Congo Brazzaville, Denmark, Germany, Ghana, Italy, Kenya, Morocco, Mozambique, Namibia, Netherlands, Nigeria, South Africa, Sweden, Uganda, UK, USA, Zambia, Zimbabwe.
NGO Relations Affiliate of: *International Association for the History of Religions (IAHR, #11936).*
[2020.03.03/XD5511/**D**]

♦ African Association of Threat Assessment Professionals (internationally oriented national body)
♦ African Association of Training and Personnel Management (inactive)

♦ **African Association for a Unified System of Business Laws (UNIDA) 00218**
Deputy SG A Single Business Law for Africa, 7 av de Ségur, 75007 Paris, France. T. +33153599605. Fax +33153599605.
IGO Relations *Organisation pour l'Harmonisation en Afrique du Droit des Affaires (OHADA, #17806).*
[2015/XD5588/**D**]

♦ **African Association of Women in Geosciences (AAWG) 00219**
Pres Chouaib Doukkali Univ, Fac of Sciences, BO 20, Geology Dept, 24000 El Jadida, Morocco. T. +212668038116. Fax +212523342187. E-mail: contact@aawg.org.
SG address not obtained.
URL: http://aawg.org/
History 1995, Nairobi (Kenya). Former names and other names: *African Association of Women Geoscientists (AAWG)* – former (1995). **Aims** Promote the advancement of scientific and technological knowledge in the field of geosciences; disseminate information on scientific and technical research and discoveries and promote public understanding of the role of geosciences in Africa's development; establish and maintain relations between African scientists and the international scientific community; provide a forum for discussion and cooperation in geosciences and other related professions in Africa; assist African governments in the quest for capacity building in geosciences and its applications; cooperate with relevant African governments in the formulation of policies and programme designed to encourage the development and application of geosciences for Africa's development; highlight and seek solutions to problems faced specifically by women and grassroots communities in Africa in the area of geosciences; encourage and mobilize support for education, training and research in order to assist African women in their acquisition of specialized skills for leadership in geosciences; identify, promote and advise on the importance and preservation of geological sites in Africa in collaboration with other stakeholders. **Structure** General Meeting; Governing Council. Regions (4): Eastern; Southern; Northern; Central. **Finance** Members' dues. **Activities** Events/meetings; knowledge management/information dissemination; awareness raising; networking/liaising; capacity building; guidance/assistance/consulting. **Events** *Biennial Conference* Luanda (Angola) 2020, *Biennial Conference* El Jadida (Morocco) 2018, *International Conference on Geoparks in Africa and Middle East* El Jadida (Morocco) 2018, *Biennial Conference* Sibiu (Romania) 2016, *Biennial Conference* Windhoek (Namibia) 2014.
Members Individuals in 34 countries:
Algeria, Angola, Botswana, Cameroon, Chad, Congo Brazzaville, Côte d'Ivoire, Djibouti, Egypt, Eswatini, Ethiopia, Finland, Gabon, Ghana, Kazakhstan, Kenya, Madagascar, Morocco, Mozambique, Namibia, Niger, Nigeria, Romania, Senegal, South Africa, Sudan, Tanzania UR, Togo, Tunisia, Türkiye, Uganda, USA, Zambia, Zimbabwe.
Affiliate members: one organization listed in this Yearbook:
African Geoparks Network (AGN, #00328). [2022/XJ0572/y/**D**]

♦ African Association of Women Geoscientists / see African Association of Women in Geosciences (#00219)
♦ Africana Studies and Research Center / see Institute for African Development, Ithaca NY
♦ African Badminton Federation / see Badminton Confederation of Africa (#03057)

♦ **African Bar Association (AFBA) 00220**
Association du Barreau Africain
Headquarters 19 Adeola Hopewell Street, CIBN Bldg, 5th Floor, Victoria Island, Lagos, Nigeria. T. +2348064938136. E-mail: support@afribar.org.
URL: http://www.afribar.org/
History 1971, Nairobi (Kenya). Former names and other names: *ABA* – former. **Aims** Assist and encourage the maintenance of the rule of *law* and the independence of the *judiciary*; improve *legal* services to the public. **Events** *Conference* Niamey (Niger) 2021, *Conference* Niamey (Niger) 2020, *Annual Conference* Nairobi (Kenya) 2018, *Conference* Lusaka (Zambia) 1985, *Conference* Nairobi (Kenya) 1981. **Members** Membership countries not specified. **Consultative Status** Consultative status granted from: *African Commission on Human and Peoples' Rights (ACHPR, #00255)* (Observer). **NGO Relations** Together with: *African Institute of Human Rights (inactive), Arab Lawyers' Union (ALU, #01002)* and *Conférence des avocats francophones (inactive)*, instrumental in setting up, 1980, *Inter-African Union of Lawyers (IAUL, inactive).* [2021/XD7302/**D**]

♦ **African Billiards and Snooker Confederation (ABSC) 00221**
Pres Villa 148, Neighbourhood 6, District 13, Sheikh Zayed, Cairo, 12593, Egypt. E-mail: africabsf@gmail.com.
URL: http://www.africabsc.com/
History 1991. Former names and other names: *African Billiards and Snooker Federation (ABSF)* – former. **Aims** Promote Billiards and Snooker in Africa. **Structure** General Meeting (annual); Council; Executive Board; Committees: Tournament committee, Referee committee, Legal committee, Marketing committee. **Languages** Arabic, English. **Staff** 6.00 FTE, paid. **Finance** Sources: sponsorship. Annual budget: 30,000 USD (2020). **Activities** Sporting activities.
Members Snooker federations in 13 countries:
Algeria, Cameroon, Egypt, Libya, Mauritius, Morocco, Mozambique, Senegal, South Africa, Sudan, Tanzania UR, Tunisia, Uganda.
NGO Relations Regional federation of: *International Billiards and Snooker Federation (IBSF, #12340).*
[2023.02.14/XD6964/**D**]

♦ African Billiards and Snooker Federation / see African Billiards and Snooker Confederation (#00221)
♦ African Biodiversity Foundation / see Biodiversity Foundation for Africa

♦ **African Biodiversity Network (ABN) 00222**
Contact Section 9, Mortgage House No 60, Off OAU Rd, Thika, Kenya. T. +254202675043. Fax +254206722338. E-mail: abnsecretariat@africanbiodiversity.org.
URL: http://www.africanbiodiversity.org/
History 2002. **Aims** Consolidate and expand an active and informed network of concerned Africans and their friends engaged in biodiversity issues on the ground; increase local and national capacity in Africa to protect biodiversity and community rights, and promote sustainable *ecological* practices; catalyze African civil society and governments to take action that will protect and enhance biodiversity and local livelihoods. **Structure** Secretariat located in Kenya. One overall Coordinator; 4 Coordinators for each thematic area, based in different countries. **Finance** Sources: *African Women's Development Fund (AWDF, #00504); Artists Project Earth (APE); Christensen Fund (TCF); Comic Relief*; Dutch Biodiversity Fund; *European Commission (EC, #06633); Gaia Foundation; Global Greengrants Fund; Humanistisch Instituut voor Ontwikkelingssamenwerking (Hivos)*; Network for Social Change; Restore UK; *Siemenpuu Foundation; Sigrid Rausing Trust*; Swedbio; Swedish Society for Nature Conservation; The Funders Network (TFN); Tudor Trust. **Publications** *ABN Newsletter* (4 a year).
Members No official membership. Partners (over 300) in 11 countries:
Benin, Botswana, Ethiopia, Ghana, Kenya, Mozambique, Senegal, South Africa, Tanzania UR, Uganda, Zambia.
Consultative Status Consultative status granted from: *UNEP (#20299).* **NGO Relations** Member of: *Climate Justice Now ! (CJN!, inactive); Global Alliance for the Rights of Nature (GARN, #10225); ICCA Consortium (#11041); More and Better (#16855); Yes to Life, No to Mining (YLNM, #21976).* [2011/XJ0880/**F**]

♦ African Bioinformatics Network / see African Society for Bioinformatics and Computational Biology (#00459)

♦ **African Biological Safety Association (AfBSA) 00223**
CEO Fairlane House, off Mbagathi Road, PO Box 35749-00200, Nairobi, Kenya. T. +254205213998. E-mail: afbsa@afbsa.org – admin@afbsa.org.
URL: http://www.afbsa.org/
History 31 May 2007, Nairobi (Kenya). **Aims** Congregate practitioners of biological safety for the promotion of biosafety and *biosecurity*; facilitate sharing of biosafety and biosecurity information in the African region. **Structure** Council; Board of Directors; Executive Director. **Finance** Members' dues. **Activities** Events/meetings; knowledge management/information dissemination. **NGO Relations** Member of: *International Federation of Biosafety Associations (IFBA, #13373); Virtual Biosecurity Centre (VBC).*
[2017.07.10/XJ8865/**D**]

♦ African Biological Union (inactive)

♦ **African Bird Club (ABC) 00224**
Chair c/o BirdLife International, The David Attenborough Building, Pembroke Street, Cambridge, CB2 3QZ, UK. E-mail: info@africanbirdclub.org – chairman@africanbirdclub.org.
Sec address not obtained. E-mail: secretary@africanbirdclub.org.
URL: http://www.africanbirdclub.org/
History 1994, London (UK). Founded within the framework of *BirdLife International (#03266).* Registration: Charitable Incorporated Organization (CIO), No/ID: 1184309, Start date: 8 Jul 2019, England and Wales; Unincorporated charitable association, No/ID: 1053920, Start date: 20 Mar 1996, UK. **Aims** Conserving birds and their habitats across Africa and related islands, and furthering ornithology in this region. **Structure** Board of Charity Trustees; Voting Membership (other than the Trustees); Country Representatives; Conservation Committee; Bulletin Editorial Board. **Languages** English. **Staff** 0.50 FTE, paid; 13.00 FTE, voluntary. **Finance** Sources: donations; gifts, legacies; sponsorship; subscriptions. Annual budget: 175,000 GBP (2020). **Activities** Advocacy/lobbying/activism; awareness raising; capacity building; events/meetings; financial and/or material support; knowledge management/information dissemination; monitoring/evaluation; networking/liaising; projects/programmes; publishing activities; training/education. Continental Africa and related islands, and the UK. **Events** *Annual Meeting* Cambridge (UK) 2021, *Annual Meeting* London (UK) 2020. **Publications** *Bulletin of the African Bird Club* (2 a year). **Information Services** *Birds of Africa* – birding app. **Members** Over 1,200 individuals and organizations in most African countries, UK, mainland Europe and USA. Membership countries not specified. **NGO Relations** Cooperates with (2): *BirdLife International (#03266); World Land Trust (WLT).* Supports (1): *Pan African Ornithological Congress (PAOC).* [2022.05.12/XM7116/**F**]

♦ **African Black Diaspora Global Network (ABDGN) 00225**
Managing Dir 2 Carlton Street, Ste 500, Toronto ON M5B 1J3, Canada. T. +14165937655. E-mail: info@abdgn.org.
URL: http://abdgn.org/
History Emerged from activities organized for the African and Black Diaspora stream at International AIDS Conference, 2006, Toronto ON (Canada). **Aims** Advocate for health and human rights for the diverse cultural, faith, and linguistic communities of African and black diaspora *migrant* and *refugee* (ABDMR) populations existing around the world. **Structure** Council. **Activities** Advocacy/lobbying/activism. **NGO Relations** *Caribbean Vulnerable Communities Coalition (CVC, #03565).* [2018/XM6518/**F**]

♦ African Blood and Marrow Transplantation Society (unconfirmed)

♦ **African Books Collective (ABC) 00226**
CEO PO Box 721, Oxford, OX1 9EN, UK. T. +441865589756. Fax +441865412431.
URL: http://www.africanbookscollective.com/
History Founded Oct 1989, London (UK), at African Publishers' Working Group Meeting. Started operations in 1990. A UK-registered company, limited by guarantee. Remodelled and self-financed, 2007. **Aims** Meet the needs of libraries and other book buyers in marketing and distributing books outside domestic markets. **Structure** Council of Management. **Languages** Afrikaans, English, French, Igbo, Ndebele, Portuguese, Shona, Swahili. **Staff** 3.50 FTE, paid. **Finance** Self-sustaining through sales. **Activities** Knowledge management/information dissemination; publishing activities; events/meetings.
Members Publishers (154) in 23 countries:
Benin, Botswana, Cameroon, Eswatini, Ethiopia, Gambia, Ghana, Kenya, Lesotho, Liberia, Malawi, Mali, Mauritius, Morocco, Namibia, Nigeria, Senegal, Sierra Leone, South Africa, Tanzania UR, Uganda, Zambia, Zimbabwe.
Included in the above, 9 organizations listed in this Yearbook:
Africa Community Publishing and Development Trust (ACPDT); Africa Institute of South Africa (AISA); African Research and Resource Forum (ARRF, #00441); Council for the Development of Social Science Research in Africa (CODESRIA, #04879); Organization for Social Science Research in Eastern and Southern Africa (OSSREA, #17888); Southern African Research and Documentation Centre (SARDC, #19861); Third World Network-Africa (TWN Africa); Union for African Population Studies (UAPS, #20346); Women and Law in Southern Africa Research Trust (WLSA, #21006). [2019.12.12/XF1867/y/**F**]

♦ **The African Borderlands Research Network (ABORNE) 00227**
Coordinator Ctr of African Studies, Univ of Edinburgh, 4-12 Chrystal Macmillan Bldg, 15a George Square, Edinburgh, EH8 9LD, UK. T. +441316513134.
URL: http://www.aborne.org/
History Jun 2007, Edinburgh (UK). **Aims** Provide a lively platform for debate, sharing of knowledge and coordination of research activity, conferences and publications on all aspects of international borders and *trans-boundary* phenomena in Africa. **Structure** Executive Committee. **Languages** English, French, German. **Staff** 2.00 FTE, paid. **Finance** Funding from: *European Science Foundation (ESF, #08441)* through Research Networking Programme (RNP), since Apr 2009. **Activities** Events/meetings; training/education. **Events** *Annual Conference* St Petersburg (Russia) / Joensuu (Finland) 2014, *Annual Conference* Edinburgh (UK) 2012, *Annual Conference* Lisbon (Portugal) 2011, *Annual Conference* Basel (Switzerland) 2010, *Annual Conference* Johannesburg (South Africa) 2009. **Publications** *ABORNE Newsletter. ABORNE-Palgrave Book Series.* Articles.
Members Institutional; Individual. Institutional in 7 countries:
Belgium, France, Germany, Italy, Portugal, Senegal, UK.
Included in the above, 4 organizations listed in this Yearbook:
Centre for African Studies, Lisbon; Centre of African Studies, Edinburgh (CAS); Institute for African Studies, University of Bayreuth (IAS); Institute for Anthropological Research in Africa (IARA).
Individuals in 38 countries:
Australia, Austria, Belgium, Brazil, Burkina Faso, Cameroon, Czechia, Denmark, Ethiopia, Finland, France, Germany, Israel, Italy, Japan, Kenya, Latvia, Luxembourg, Mozambique, Netherlands, Niger, Nigeria, Norway, Poland, Portugal, Senegal, Somalia, South Africa, Sudan, Sweden, Switzerland, Tanzania UR, Togo, Uganda, UK, USA, Zambia, Zimbabwe.
IGO Relations Memorandum of Understanding with: *African Union (AU, #00488).* [2014.07.10/XJ5513/y/**F**]

♦ **African Boxing Confederation (ABC) 00228**
Confédération africain de boxe (CAB)
Interim Pres address not obtained. E-mail: africanboxingconfederation@gmail.com.
URL: http://www.aiba.org/confederations-2/

History Founded 1960, as *African Amateur Boxing Association (AABA) – Association africaine de boxe amateur*. Restructured, 4-6 Nov 1986, Yaoundé (Cameroon), on request of *Supreme Council for Sport in Africa (SCSA, inactive)* and under aegis of AIBA, to incorporate professional boxing activities of *African Boxing Union (ABU, #00229)*, which then ceased to exist. Incorporation approved and current name adopted at extraordinary meeting, 1987, Nairobi (Kenya). ABU split from ABC again, 1996 and was relaunched. A regional confederation of *International Boxing Association (IBA, #12385)*. **Aims** Cater to and run *amateur* and *professional* boxing in line with WBC rules; ensure that boxers are not exploited. **Structure** Congress (annual). Executive Council (meets twice a year), comprising 14 members: President; General Secretary-Treasurer; Presidents of 7 zones; President of Professional Commission 4 further members. **Languages** English, French. **Staff** Voluntary. **Activities** Events/meetings. **Events** *Congress* Ouagadougou (Burkina Faso) 2002. [2017/XE2440/E]

♦ African Boxing Union (ABU) 00229
Union Africaine de Boxe
Address not obtained.
URL: http://www.abuboxing.com/
History 1973, as an association of professional boxers. Ceased to exist, 1987, when activities taken over by *African Boxing Confederation (ABC, #00228)*, 1987. Split from ABC, 1996 and relaunched again. **Structure** General Assembly. **Events** *General Assembly* Lusaka (Zambia) 2011.
Members Federations in 49 countries:
Algeria, Angola, Benin, Burkina Faso, Burundi, Cameroon, Cape Verde, Central African Rep, Chad, Comoros, Congo Brazzaville, Congo DR, Côte d'Ivoire, Djibouti, Egypt, Equatorial Guinea, Eswatini, Ethiopia, Gabon, Gambia, Ghana, Guinea-Bissau, Kenya, Lesotho, Liberia, Libya, Madagascar, Malawi, Mali, Mauritania, Mauritius, Morocco, Mozambique, Niger, Nigeria, Rwanda, Sao Tomé-Principe, Senegal, Seychelles, Sierra Leone, Somalia, South Africa, Sudan, Tanzania UR, Togo, Tunisia, Uganda, Zambia, Zimbabwe.
NGO Relations Member of: *World Boxing Council (WBC, #21242)*. [2015/XJ9571/D]

♦ African Bridge Federation (ABF) 00230
Pres 28 – 26th of July Street, Ezbekia, Cairo, 11511, Egypt. T. +20225752331.
Sec address not obtained.
History 1996. Founded as a subzone of then Bridge Federation of Africa, Asia & the Middle East - currently *Bridge Federation of Asia & the Middle East (BFAME, #03328)*. A zone of *World Bridge Federation (WBF, #21246)*. **Activities** Events/meetings.
Members Full in 8 countries and territories:
Botswana, Egypt, Kenya, Morocco, Réunion, South Africa, Tunisia, Zambia. [2019/AA0986/D]
♦ African Bureau for the Defence of the Rights of Writers (no recent information)
♦ African Bureau of Educational Sciences (no recent information)

♦ African Business Aviation Association (AfBAA) 00231
Contact 2 Kings Court, Newcomen Way, Severalls Business Park, Colchester, CO4 9RA, UK. T. +441206844288. Fax +441206844299. E-mail: info@afbaa.org.
URL: https://afbaa.org/
History 2012. Originally founded to deal with business aviation in Africa, but widened its remit, 2018, to also include general aviation. **Aims** Board. **Events** *AGM Conference* Johannesburg (South Africa) 2019. **NGO Relations** Member of (1): *International Business Aviation Council (IBAC, #12418)*. [2020/AA1953/D]
♦ African Business Law Firms Association (unconfirmed)

♦ African Business Roundtable (ABR) 00232
Table Ronde des Hommes d'Affaires d'Afrique
Headquarters ECOWAS Annex, Niger House, Plo 56 Ralph Shodeinde Str, Central Business District, Abuja, Federal Capital Territory, Nigeria. T. +2348163650193 – +2348127230731. E-mail: abrabuja@yahoo.com.
History Mar 1990, Cairo (Egypt), by *African Development Bank (ADB, #00283)*. Registered in accordance with the law of Côte d'Ivoire, 1991. Transferred to Johannesburg (South Africa), end 1996. **Aims** Realize Africa's full promise and potential through promotion of free markets and democratic governance. **Structure** Annual General Meeting; Board of Directors. Chapters (7): Southern African; Eastern African; Central African; West Africa; Senegal River Basin; North African; International. Specializes committees and Task Forces. **Languages** English, French. **Finance** Members' fees and annual dues. Other sources: grants from: *Canadian International Development Agency (CIDA, inactive)*; *UNDP (#20292)*; *United States Agency for International Development (USAID)*; FAPA grant (Japanese Government). **Activities** Advocacy/lobbying/activism; events/meetings; financial and/or material support. **Events** *Investor conference* Brussels (Belgium) 2009, *African World Business Congress* Accra (Ghana) 2005, *Annual General Assembly* Johannesburg (South Africa) 1996, *Annual General Assembly* Yaoundé (Cameroon) 1995, *Annual General Assembly* Arusha (Tanzania UR) 1994. **Publications** *African Business Report* (4 a year). Annual report.
Members Charter members chief executives of major enterprises based in Africa; Corporate members large corporations, based either in Africa or abroad, who sponsor senior-level executives handling African operations; Associate members chief executive officers of corporations that conduct business in Africa but are based abroad; Patrons eminent chief executive officers of large corporations in Africa and abroad. Members in 28 countries:
Angola, Benin, Burundi, Cameroon, Congo DR, Côte d'Ivoire, Egypt, France, Gabon, Gambia, Ghana, Guinea, Kenya, Malawi, Mauritania, Morocco, Mozambique, Netherlands, Nigeria, Senegal, South Africa, Sudan, Switzerland, Tanzania UR, Uganda, UK, USA, Zambia.
Consultative Status Consultative status granted from: ECOSOC (#05331) (Special); UNCTAD (#20285) (General Category). **IGO Relations** *African Development Bank (ADB, #00283)*; *Company for Habitat and Housing in Africa (Shelter-Afrique, #04408)*; *International Bank for Reconstruction and Development (IBRD, #12317)*; *UNIDO (#20336)*. **NGO Relations** *Centrist Democrat International (CDI, #03792)*; *Corporate Council on Africa (CCA)*; *International Resource Centre, Johannesburg (IRC, no recent information)*. [2017/XF5168/F]

♦ The African Capacity Building Foundation (ACBF) 00233
Fondation pour le renforcement des capacités en Afrique
Exec Sec 2 Fairbairn Drive, Mount Plesant, PO Box 1562, Harare, HARARE, Zimbabwe. T. +2634304663 – +2634304662 – +2634332002. E-mail: root@acbf-pact.org.
URL: http://www.acbf-pact.org/
History Feb 1991, Dakar (Senegal). Location: Harare (Zimbabwe). Pilot phase: 1992-1996. A Specialized Agency of *African Union (AU, #00488)*. Former names and other names: *African Capacity Building Initiative* – former. **Aims** Build sustainable human and institutional capacity for growth, poverty reduction and good governance in Africa. **Structure** Board of Governors (meets annually); Executive Board; Management Team; Secretariat. **Languages** English, French. **Staff** 73.00 FTE, paid. **Finance** Sponsored by: AfDB; UNDP; World Bank; IMF; bilateral donors and African Governments. **Activities** Capacity building; knowledge management/information dissemination. **Events** *Pan African Capacity Development Forum* Harare (Zimbabwe) 2016, *Pan-African Forum on the Modernization of Public Service and State Institutions / Annual Session* Marrakech (Morocco) 2015, *Pan African Forum on African Diplomacy and Diplomacy in Africa* Rabat (Morocco) 2015, *Conference on Evaluation of Strategies and Actions of African Countries in Pursuing the Objectives of Economic Emergence* Tangiers (Morocco) 2015, *Pan African Forum on African Women and the Challenges of Peace and Development* Tangiers (Morocco) 2015. **Publications** *Africa Capacity Indicators Reports*. Annual Report; research and analyses; occasional papers; working papers; development memoirs; books.
Members Full in 45 countries:
Benin, Botswana, Burkina Faso, Burundi, Cameroon, Canada, Central African Rep, Chad, Congo Brazzaville, Congo DR, Côte d'Ivoire, Denmark, Djibouti, Eswatini, Finland, France, Gabon, Ghana, Greece, Guinea, India, Ireland, Kenya, Liberia, Madagascar, Malawi, Mali, Mauritania, Mauritius, Netherlands, Niger, Nigeria, Norway, Rwanda, Sao Tomé-Principe, Senegal, Sierra Leone, Sudan, Sweden, Tanzania UR, Uganda, UK, USA, Zambia, Zimbabwe.
International organizations (4):
African Development Bank (ADB, #00283); *International Bank for Reconstruction and Development (IBRD, #12317)* (World Bank); *International Monetary Fund (IMF, #14180)*; *UNDP (#20292)*.
IGO Relations Partner of: *African Development Institute (ADI, #00286)*. Adheres to: *Global Partnership for Effective Development Co-operation (GPEDC, #10532)*. **NGO Relations** Member of (1): *Effective Institutions Platform (EIP, #05384)*. African non-state actors. [2022/XF3152/fy/F]

♦ African Capacity Building Initiative / see The African Capacity Building Foundation (#00233)
♦ African and Caribbean Diversity (internationally oriented national body)

♦ African Cashew Alliance (ACA) 00234
Acting Managing Dir 31 Boundary Road, East Legon, PMB 35A Osu, Accra, Ghana. T. +233302904951. Fax +233302904952. E-mail: masiedu@africancashewalliance.com.
URL: http://www.africancashewalliance.com/
History 2005. **Aims** Promote the African cashew sector from production to consumption. **Structure** General Assembly; Executive Committee; Advisory Board; Secretariat. **Events** *Annual Cashew Conference* Senegal 2023, *Annual Cashew Conference* Abuja (Nigeria) 2022, *Annual Cashew Conference* Accra (Ghana) 2021, *Annual Cashew Conference* Accra (Ghana) 2020, *Annual Conference* Lagos (Nigeria) 2013. **Publications** *ACA Newsletter* (4 a year).
Members Full in 22 countries:
Benin, Brazil, Côte d'Ivoire, Gambia, Germany, Ghana, Guinea-Bissau, India, Italy, Kenya, Lithuania, Mozambique, Netherlands, Nigeria, Senegal, Singapore, South Africa, Tanzania UR, Togo, UK, USA, Vietnam.
NGO Relations Signatory to: *Global Cashew Council (#10273)*. [2022/XJ3434/E]

♦ African Center for Economic Transformation (ACET) 00235
Dir Communications/External Relations Cantonments, PMB CT 4, Accra, Ghana. T. +233302210240ext118. E-mail: info@acetforafrica.org.
Street Address 50 Liberation Road, Ridge Residential Area, Accra, Ghana.
URL: http://acetforafrica.org/
History 2008, Accra (Ghana). **Aims** Promote policy and institutional reforms for sustained economic growth and transformation in Africa. **Structure** Board of Directors; President; Chief Economist; Directors (4). **Languages** English, French. **Staff** 30.00 FTE, paid. **Finance** Support from: governments of Ghana, Netherlands, and Norway; *Australian Aid (inactive)*; *Bill and Melinda Gates Foundation (BMGF)*; *Department for International Development (DFID, inactive)*; *Ford Foundation (#09858)*; *The William and Flora Hewlett Foundation*; *International Bank for Reconstruction and Development (IBRD, #12317)* (World Bank); *Open Society Initiative*; *The Rockefeller Foundation (#18966)*. Paid consultancies. **Activities** Politics/policy/regulatory; advocacy/lobbying/activism; research/documentation; guidance/assistance/consulting. **Events** *Seminar on the World Development Report 2022* Tokyo (Japan) 2022. **Publications** *The African Transformation Report* (every 2 years).
Members Partners (country-based policy think tanks) in 15 countries:
Botswana, Burkina Faso, Cameroon, Ethiopia, Ghana, Kenya, Mauritius, Mozambique, Nigeria, Rwanda, Senegal, South Africa, Tanzania UR, Uganda, Zambia.
NGO Relations Together with *International Food Policy Research Institute (IFPRI, #13622)*, organizes: *Global Research Consortium on Economic Structural Transformation (GReCEST)*. Founding member of: *Global Research Consortium on Economic Structural Transformation (GReCEST)*. [2015.09.14/XJ7324/E]

♦ African Center for Global Trends (unconfirmed)
♦ African Center for Peace / see African Center for Prevention and Resolution of Conflicts
♦ African Center for Prevention and Resolution of Conflicts (internationally oriented national body)
♦ African Center for Science and International Security (internationally oriented national body)

♦ African Center for the Study and Research on Terrorism (ACSRT) .. 00236
Centre Africain d'Etudes et de Recherches sur le Terrorisme (CAERT)
Dir 05 Rue Hammag Idir, Mohammadia 141, 16000 Algiers, Algeria. T. +21321520083. Fax +21321520374. E-mail: admin@acsrt.org.
URL: http://www.caert.org.dz/
History Inaugurated 2004, Algiers (Algeria), as a structure of *African Union (AU, #00488)* Commission, in conformity with *Protocol to the OAU Convention on the Prevention and Combating of Terrorism (2004)*. **Aims** Function as a research centre of excellence in matters concerning the prevention and combating of terrorism in Africa. **Structure** Advisory Council; Director. **Activities** Research/documentation. **Publications** *African Journal for the Prevention and Combating of Terrorism*. [2020/XM8550/E*]

♦ African Central Bank (unconfirmed)
♦ African Centre for Advanced Studies in Management (#03724)
♦ African Centre for Advocacy and Human Development (internationally oriented national body)
♦ African Centre for Applied Forestry Research and Development (internationally oriented national body)

♦ African Centre for Applied Research and Training in Social Development (ACARTSOD) 00237
Centre africain de recherche appliquée et de formation en matière de développement social (CAFRADES) – Centro Africano de Investigaciones Aplicadas y de Formación en Materia de Desarrollo Social
Address not obtained.
History 1977, Tripoli (Libyan AJ), by *Conference of African Ministers of Social Affairs (inactive)*, under the auspices of *Organization of African Unity (OAU, inactive)* and *United Nations Economic Commission for Africa (ECA, #20554)*. **Aims** Promote and coordinate applied research and training in social development; assist African countries in formulating national development strategies. **Structure** Conference of African Ministers of Social Affairs. Governing Board, comprising: Executive Secretary of ECA as ex officio Chairman, a representative of General Secretariat of OAU, and 2 representatives of each of the 4 sub-regions of Africa, designated by Conference of Ministers. Technical Advisory Committee. Executive Director. Research Coordinator; Training Coordinator; Librarian; Computer Programmer; Finance and Administration; General Service. **Languages** Arabic, English, French. **Staff** 5.00 FTE, paid. **Finance** Contributions from member States. **Activities** Provides training of high-level personnel; undertakes research programmes, including promotion of rural development programmes; assists national universities and institutes in the field of training; develops indigenous teaching and research materials; initiates and maintains relations with similar institutes within and outside the region. Organizes seminars; provides documentation service. Projects include: comparative study of African social security systems; evaluation of social development in the light of the '*Lagos Plan of Action*'; survey of social development and training institutes in Africa. **Events** *Regional conference on socio-economic impact of drought in Africa* Addis Ababa (Ethiopia) 1994, *Regional conference on youth and unemployment in Africa* Conakry (Guinea) 1994, *Regional conference on African integration within the perspective of a United Europe* Dakar (Senegal) 1994, *Annual regional conference* Tripoli (Libyan AJ) 1991, *Annual regional conference* Tripoli (Libyan AJ) 1990. **Publications** *ACARTSOD Newsletter* (3 a year). *African Social Challenges* – monograph series. General, research and training series; proceedings and reports of conferences, workshops, seminars, courses.
Members Governments of 27 countries:
Algeria, Angola, Benin, Burkina Faso, Burundi, Cameroon, Central African Rep, Congo Brazzaville, Congo DR, Egypt, Equatorial Guinea, Ethiopia, (member institutions), Gambia, Ghana, Guinea, Kenya, Liberia, Libya, Mali, Morocco, Niger, Senegal, Sierra Leone, Sudan, Togo, Tunisia, Uganda.
IGO Relations Formal agreement with: *UNESCO (#20322)*. Formal contacts with: *ILO (#11123)*; *UNDP (#20292)*; *African Training and Research Centre in Administration for Development (CAFRAD, #00486)*; *Arab League Educational, Cultural and Scientific Organization (ALECSO, #01003)*; *Centre for the Coordination of Research and Documentation in Social Science for Sub-Saharan Africa (no recent information)*. **NGO Relations** Member of: *Organization for Social Science Research in Eastern and Southern Africa (OSSREA, #17888)*. [2010/XE6282/E*]

♦ African Centre for Aquatic Research and Education (ACARE) 00238
Exec Dir 2200 Commonwealth Blvd, Ste 100, Ann Arbor MI 48105, USA. T. +17347302038. E-mail: info@agl-acare.org.
URL: http://www.agl-acare.org/
History 31 Jul 2017, Ann Arbor, MI (USA). Initially proposed by *United Nations University – Institute for Water, Environment and Health (UNU-INWEH, see: #20642)* and the Government of Malawi, 2005. Became dormant 2006. Officially relaunched Jul 2017. **Aims** Create highly collaborative systems that strengthen science to positively affect policy and management for healthy African Great Lakes. **Structure** Board of Directors. **Languages** English. **Staff** 5.00 FTE, paid; 4.00 FTE, voluntary. **Finance** Sources: grants. **Activities** Events/meetings; research/documentation; training/education. Active in: Burundi, Congo DR, Ethiopia, Kenya,

Malawi, Mozambique, Rwanda, Tanzania UR, Uganda, Zambia. **Events** *African Great Lakes Stakeholder Network Annual Meeting* Ann Arbor, MI (USA) 2020, *African Great Lakes Stakeholder Network Workshop* Entebbe (Uganda) 2019. [2021.02.16/XJ2613/**D**]

- ♦ African Centre for Assistance and Protection of the Environment of the Sahel (internationally oriented national body)
- ♦ African Centre for Biodiversity (internationally oriented national body)
- ♦ African Centre for Biosafety / see African Centre for Biodiversity
- ♦ African Centre for Citizenship and Democracy (internationally oriented national body)
- ♦ African Centre for Community and Development (unconfirmed)
- ♦ African Centre for the Constructive Resolution of Disputes (internationally oriented national body)

♦ African Centre for Democracy and Human Rights Studies (ACDHRS) 00239

Centre africain pour la démocratie et les études des droits de l'homme (CADEDH)

Executive Zoe Tembo Bldg, Kerr Sereign, PO Box 2728, Serekunda, Gambia. T. +2204462341. E-mail: admin@acdhrs.org – csec@acdhrs.org.
URL: http://www.acdhrs.org/

History 7 Jun 1989. Founded by an Act of the Parliament of The Gambia. Currently an independent, regional, human rights NGO, new Statutes having been adopted in Aug 1995. **Aims** Promote, in cooperation with other African and international institutions, the observance of human and *peoples' rights* and *democratic principles* throughout Africa. **Structure** Governing Council, comprising Executive Committee (Chairman, Vice-Chairman and 2 members), Executive Director, 7 members and Advisory Committee of 7 members. **Finance** Sources: donations; international organizations; revenue from activities/projects. Supported by: IPAS-Africa Alliance; *Office of the United Nations High Commissioner for Human Rights (OHCHR, #17697)* (East Africa Regional Office); Solidarity for African Women's Rights Coalition (SOAWR) (EU-PANAF Project); United Nations Office for West Africa (UNOWAS). **Activities** Events/meetings; research/documentation; training/education. **Events** *Forum on the Participation of NGOs* Banjul (Gambia) 2022, *Forum on the participation of NGOs* Banjul (Gambia) 2020, *African Court on Human and Peoples' Rights* Serekunda (Gambia) 2020, *Forum on the participation of NGOs* Sharm el Sheikh (Egypt) 2019, *Forum on the Participation of NGOs* Banjul (Gambia) 2018. **Publications** *African Human Rights Newsletter – Bulletin africain des droits de l'homme* (4 a year) in English, French. Occasional Papers. Studies; articles. **Members** Not a membership organization. **Consultative Status** Consultative status granted from: *African Commission on Human and Peoples' Rights (ACHPR, #00255)* (Observer Status); *ECOSOC (#05331)* (Special). **NGO Relations** Member of (2): *International Network for Economic, Social and Cultural Rights (ESCR-Net, #14255)*; *Sudan Consortium (#20031)*. [2022.02.01/XE1093/**E**]

- ♦ African Centre for Development and Strategic Studies (internationally oriented national body)

♦ African Centre for Economic Growth (ACEG) 00240

Exec Dir Longonot Place Apartment 3, Harry Thuku Rd, PO Box 55237, Nairobi, 00200, Kenya. T. +254202091031 – +254202091032. Fax +254202217315.
URL: http://www.aceg.org/

History 1993, as regional office of *International Center for Economic Growth (ICEG, inactive)*. Became autonomous under present title in 1999. **Aims** Undertake research and carry out analyses of socio-economic issues that are of interest to African governments and society; increase public awareness of the policies that work to expand socio-economic opportunities and foster development in Africa; produce research results and consultancy reports that are critical in accelerating economic growth and combating poverty in Africa. **Structure** Board of Directors. Secretariat, headed by Executive Director. **Languages** English, French. **Staff** Mostly outsourced. **Activities** Projects and consultancy services carried out by research and experts of member institutes in 26 countries in Sub-Saharan Africa. Current topics: Regional Integration; Private Enterprise Development; Democracy; Governance; Trade; Poverty Equity. **Publications** *Improving Financial Sector Performance in Kenya: Proceedings of the First Financial Sector Reforms Forum* (2006); *Democratic Transition in Kenya: The Struggle from Liberal to Social Democracy* (2005); *Growth and Transformation of Small Firms in Africa: Insights from Kenya, Ghana and Zimbabwe* (2003); *Steering East Africa Towards a Customs Union: Suggestions from a Pilot Study* (2003); *Zambia-Malawi-Mozambique Growth Triangle: Private Sector – Public Sector Partnership for Sub-Regional Development* (2003); *The Link Between Corruption and Poverty: Lessons from Kenya Case Studies* (2000); *Micro and Small Enterprises in Kenya: Agenda for Improving the Policy Environment* (1999). Policy briefs; research and conference reports. **IGO Relations** Cooperation agreement with: *Department for International Development (DFID, inactive)*; *International Institute for Democracy and Electoral Assistance (International IDEA, #13872)*; *UNDP (#20292)*; *United States Agency for International Development (USAID)*. [2013/XJ3050/**E**]

- ♦ African Centre for Empowerment and Gender Advocacy (internationally oriented national body)

♦ African Centre for Fertilizer Development (ACFD) 00241

Centre africain pour le développement des engrais (CADE)

Managing Dir PO Box A469, Avondale, Harare, HARARE, Zimbabwe. T. +2634860421 – +2634860422. Fax +2634860423.
Street Address Alpes Road, Hatcliffe Estate, 51283 Tevoitdale, Avondale, Harare, HARARE, Zimbabwe.

History 1987, Harare (Zimbabwe), by *Organization of African Unity (OAU, inactive)* Convention, as part of the larger strategy implementing the 1980 'Lagos Plan of Action', an OAU resolution establishing ACFD having been adopted in 1981. Also referred to as *African Fertilizer Development Centre*. Currently (2000) under reorganization. **Aims** Develop simple, affordable, accessible strategies to improve and stabilize *agriculture* in Africa through proper and adequate use of fertilizers and local organic material; develop collaborative projects with national, regional and international organizations; liaise with governments and the private sector on fertilizer use and *soil* management; conduct, foster and support training in all aspects of resource development, agri- *marketing* and use of fertilizers and other nutrients; conduct research on *soil fertility* management, leading to improved and *sustainable* agricultural *production* and *environmental* protection; undertake research on marketing costs, pricing and other factors affecting fertilizer use, and other inputs, especially in the small-scale *farming* sector. **Structure** Board of Directors, consisting of representatives from the 5 regions of Africa (currently from Congo DR, Libyan AJ, Niger, Sudan and Zambia) and of the host government, *International Fund for Agricultural Development (IFAD, #13692)* as executing agency, *International Fertilizer Development Center (IFDC, #13590)* and *United Nations Economic Commission for Africa (ECA, #20554)*. Technical Divisions (2): Research and Development; Technology Transfer. Administrative Unit. **Staff** 3 professional; 6 support (full quota would be 32 and 29 respectively). **Finance** Sources: Government of Zimbabwe; OAU Secretariat; OAU member states; donors, including IFAD, *Canadian International Development Agency (CIDA, inactive)*, *European Union (EU, #08967)*, *FAO (#09260)*, *OPEC Fund for International Development (OFID, #17745)*, *UNDP (#20292)* and *W K Kellogg Foundation (WKKF)*; commercial returns from farm. Budget (annual): US$ 500,000. **Activities** Events/meetings; training/education. **Publications** *Achievements and Constraints of ACFD 1991-2000* – report; *Empowering African Farmers to Increase Crop Production while Maintaining Soil Fertility* – booklet. Annual Report.
Members As at May 2019, ratified by 8 governments:
Benin, Burkina Faso, Comoros, Ethiopia, Gabon, Libya, Madagascar, Zimbabwe. [2019/XE5919/**E***]

- ♦ African Centre for Global Health and Social Transformation (internationally oriented national body)
- ♦ African Centre for Human Rights Education (internationally oriented national body)
- ♦ African Centre for Justice and Peace Studies (internationally oriented national body)

♦ African Centre of Meteorological Applications for Development (ACMAD) 00242

Centre africain pour les applications de la météorologie au développement

Dir Gen Avenue des Ministères 85, PO Box 13184, Niamey, Niger. T. +22720734992. Fax +22720723627.
URL: http://www.acmad.net/

History Apr 1987, at Conference of Ministers of *United Nations Economic Commission for Africa (ECA, #20554)*. A joint project of ECA and *World Meteorological Organization (WMO, #21649)*. **Aims** Assist member states in the development of meteorology and its applications; contribute to socio-economic development of African countries through use of meteorological / *climatological* products and assistance systems for *sustainable development*. **Structure** Director General. **Languages** English, French. **Finance** Members' contributions. Sponsored by United Nations bodies and by: *African Development Bank (ADB, #00283)*; *European Commission (EC, #06633)*. **Activities** Knowledge management/information dissemination; research/documentation; training/education. **Events** *Partners conference* 1996, *Session* Niamey (Niger) 1996. **Publications** *Bulletin climatologique* (12 a year); *Bulletin de Prévision Climatique Saisonnière* (6 a year); *Bulleting de Veille Climatique* (6 a year); *ACMAD Bulletin* (every 10 days). *Climate Impacts for Africa* (1993).
Members All African countries which are member of OAU and ECA (53):
Algeria, Angola, Benin, Botswana, Burkina Faso, Burundi, Cameroon, Cape Verde, Central African Rep, Chad, Comoros, Congo Brazzaville, Congo DR, Côte d'Ivoire, Djibouti, Egypt, Equatorial Guinea, Eritrea, Eswatini, Ethiopia, Gabon, Gambia, Ghana, Guinea, Guinea-Bissau, Kenya, Lesotho, Liberia, Libya, Madagascar, Malawi, Mali, Mauritania, Mauritius, Morocco, Mozambique, Namibia, Niger, Nigeria, Rwanda, Sao Tomé-Principe, Senegal, Seychelles, Sierra Leone, Somalia, South Africa, Sudan, Tanzania UR, Togo, Tunisia, Uganda, Zambia, Zimbabwe.
International member (1):
United Nations Economic Commission for Africa.
IGO Relations Accredited by: *United Nations Framework Convention on Climate Change – Secretariat (UNFCCC, #20564)*. Participates in: *Group on Earth Observations (GEO, #10735)*. Partner of: *West African Science Service Center on Climate Change and Adapted Land Use (WASCAL, #20897)*. **NGO Relations** Instrumental in setting up: *Conference of Directors of the West African National Meteorological and Hydrological Services (AFRIMET, #04589)*. Founding member of: *International Network for Climate and Health for Africa (ClimHEALTH Africa, #14244)*. [2015/XE1341/**E***]

- ♦ African Centre for Migration and Society (internationally oriented national body)
- ♦ African Centre for Peace Education and Training (internationally oriented national body)
- ♦ African Centre for Pluridisciplinary Research on Ethnicity / see Africa Governance Alert
- ♦ African Centre for the Prevention and Resolution of Conflicts (internationally oriented national body)

♦ African Centre for Technology Studies (ACTS) 00243

Secretariat Gigiri Court, Off United Nations Crescent, PO Box 45917, Nairobi, 00100, Kenya. T. +254207126889 – +254207126890 – +254207126894. Fax +254202339093. E-mail: info@acts-net.org.
URL: http://acts-net.org/

History 1982, Kenya, as *Technoscan*. Current name adopted 1988. **Aims** Undertake policy research on the application of *science* and technology to *sustainable development* in Africa. **Structure** Governing Council, consisting of 10 members. **Languages** English, French. **Staff** 15.00 FTE, paid. **Finance** Sources: grants; sale of services. Budget (annual): US$ 500,000. **Activities** Research/documentation; training/education; monitoring/evaluation; knowledge management/information dissemination; events/meetings. **Events** *Low-Carbon Development in Africa Workshop* Nairobi (Kenya) 2015, *Global diversity forum* Curitiba (Brazil) 2006, *India and South Asia sub-regional session of the Global Biodiversity Forum* Delhi (India) 2005, *Latin America regional session of the Global Biodiversity Forum* Lima (Peru) 2005, *Asia regional session of the Global Biodiversity Forum* Manila (Philippines) 2004. **Publications** *ACTS Press Books*; *Ecopolicy and Biopolicy Papers*; *Research Reports*. Conference Papers.
Members Full in 7 countries:
Kenya, Malawi, Norway, Poland, Sweden, Thailand, Uganda.
Consultative Status Consultative status granted from: *UNEP (#20299)*. **IGO Relations** Accredited by: *United Nations Framework Convention on Climate Change – Secretariat (UNFCCC, #20564)*. **NGO Relations** Member of: *Climate Action Network (CAN, #03999)*; *Global Open Data for Agriculture and Nutrition (GODAN, #10514)*; *Natural Capital Coalition (NCC, #16952)*; *Next Einstein Forum (NEF, #17098)*. Hosts: *African Network for Economics of Learning, Innovation and Competence Building Systems (AFRICALICS, #00385)*. Partner of: *Green Growth Knowledge Platform (GGKP, #10719)*. Collaborates with: *African Technology Policy Studies Network (ATPS, #00481)*; *International Union for Conservation of Nature and Natural Resources (IUCN, #15766)*; *World Resources Institute (WRI, #21753)*. [2016/XE0965/**E**]

- ♦ African Centre for Treatment and Rehabilitation of Torture Victims (internationally oriented national body)
- ♦ African Charter of Human and Peoples' Rights (1981 treaty)

♦ African Chess Confederation 00244

Confédération africaine des échecs (CAC)

Contact address not obtained. T. +22890130628. E-mail: generalsecretary@africa-chess.org.
URL: https://www.facebook.com/AfricanChessConfederation/

History 1976, Tripoli (Libyan AJ). **Members** in 22 countries. Membership countries not specified. [2017/XD3839/**D**]

♦ African Chess Union 00245

Pres Botswana Chess Federation, PO Box 41090, Gaborone, Botswana.
Members National chess organizations (6):
Botswana, Namibia, Somalia, South Africa, Uganda, Zambia.
NGO Relations Affiliated to: *Fédération internationale des échecs (FIDE, #09627)*. [2013/XJ0290/**D**]

- ♦ African Child Care Association / see African Aid Organization
- ♦ African Child Education Right Initiative (internationally oriented national body)
- ♦ African Child in Need (internationally oriented national body)
- ♦ African Child Neurology Association (unconfirmed)

♦ African Child Policy Forum (ACPF) 00246

Exec Dir PO Box 1179, Addis Ababa, Ethiopia. T. +251116628192 – +251116628196 – +251116628197. Fax +251116628200. E-mail: info@africanchildforum.org.
URL: http://www.africanchildforum.org/

History 2003, Addis Ababa (Ethiopia). **Aims** Work towards a more child-friendly and accountable Africa. **Structure** International Board of Trustees; Administrative Council; Secretariat, based in Addis Ababa (Ethiopia). **Languages** English, French. **Staff** 30.00 FTE, paid. **Finance** Supported by: *American Jewish World Service (AJWS)*; *ICS*; *Oak Foundation*; *Plan International (#18386)*; *Save the Children International (#19058)*; *Tides*; *UNICEF (#20332)*. Annual budget: 2,300,000 USD. **Activities** Awards/prizes/competitions; events/meetings; knowledge management/information dissemination. **Publications** *The African Report on Child Wellbeing (ARCW)* (every 2 years); *The African Child Newsletter*. Downloadable PDFs. **Members** Not a membership organization. **Consultative Status** Consultative status granted from: *African Commission on Human and Peoples' Rights (ACHPR, #00255)* (Observer); *African Committee of Experts on the Rights and Welfare of the Child (ACERWC, #00257)* (Observer Status); *ECOSOC (#05331)* (Special). **IGO Relations** Observer status with: *African Committee of Experts on the Rights and Welfare of the Child (ACERWC, #00257)*. **NGO Relations** Cooperates with: *ICS*; *Save the Children International (#19058)*; *Plan International (#18386)*. Member of: *Child Rights Connect (#03884)*; *Global Partnership to End Violence Against Children (End Violence Against Children, #10533)*; *Regional Inter-Agency Task Team on Children and AIDS in Eastern and Southern Africa (RIATT-ESA, #18791)*; *Girls not Brides (#10154)*; *Global Coalition to End Child Poverty (#10292)*; *International Coalition for the Optional Protocol to the Convention on the Rights of the Child on a Communications Procedure (Ratify OP3CRC, #12617)*. [2020.05.06/XM2962/**F**]

- ♦ African Childrens Haven (internationally oriented national body)
- ♦ African Child Right / see African Child Education Right Initiative
- ♦ African Christian Health Association / see African Christian Health Associations Platform (#00247)

♦ African Christian Health Associations Platform (ACHAP) 00247

Secretariat c/o CHAK, PO Box 30690-00100, Nairobi, Kenya. T. +25424441920. E-mail: communications@africachap.org.
URL: http://www.africachap.org/

History Founded May 2007, as *African Christian Health Association (ACHA)*. Registered under Kenyan law, 4 May 2012. **Aims** Promote continued, effective and efficient engagement of church health services in Africa towards achieving equitable access to quality health care. **Structure** General Assembly (every 2 years); Board; Thematic Working Groups; Secretariat, located in Nairobi (Kenya). **Languages** English, French. **Staff** 3.00 FTE, paid. **Activities** Advocacy/lobbying/activism; networking/liaising; training/education. **Events** *Biennial Conference* Nairobi (Kenya) 2015, *Biennial Conference* Lusaka (Zambia) 2013.
Members National associations in 32 countries:
Angola, Benin, Botswana, Burkina Faso, Burundi, Cameroon, Central African Rep, Chad, Congo DR, Côte d'Ivoire, Eswatini, Ethiopia, Ghana, Guinea, Kenya, Lesotho, Liberia, Madagascar, Malawi, Mali, Namibia, Niger, Nigeria, Rwanda, Sierra Leone, South Africa, Sudan, Tanzania UR, Togo, Uganda, Zambia, Zimbabwe.
IGO Relations *Joint United Nations Programme on HIV/AIDS (UNAIDS, #16149); WHO (#20950).* **NGO Relations** *Christian Connections for International Health (CCIH); Global Health Workforce Alliance (GHWA, inactive); Global Water; IMA World Health (IMA); World Council of Churches (WCC, #21320).*
[2018.09.06/XJ1576/**D**]

♦ African Christian Hospitals Foundation / see IHCF African Christian Hospitals (#11109)
♦ African Church of the Holy Spirit (internationally oriented national body)
♦ African Citizens Development Foundation (internationally oriented national body)

♦ African Civil Aviation Commission (AFCAC) 00248
Commission africaine de l'aviation civile (CAFAC)
SG Leopold Sedar Senghor Intl Airport Road, BP 8898, Dakar, Senegal. T. +221338598800. Fax +221338207018. E-mail: secretariat@afcac.org.
URL: http://www.afcac.org/
History Constitutive Conference organized 1969, Addis Ababa (Ethiopia), convened by *International Civil Aviation Organization (ICAO, #12581)* and *Organization of African Unity (OAU, inactive)* – currently *African Union (AU, #00488)* Commission. Began functioning 1969. Since 11 May 1978, became the OAU Specialized Agency in the field of civil aviation. Constitution adopted 1969; revised 2001. New constitution of 2009 provisionally entered into force 11 May 2010, and will definitively enter into force upon ratification by 15 African States. Since 11 May 2007, entrusted with responsibility of being Executing Agency for the implementation of the Yamoussoukro Decision by Ministers of Air Transport and endorsed by Assembly of Heads of States and Governments, 29 Jun 2007. Previously also referred to as *Pan-African Civil Aviation Commission*. Statutes registered in *'UNTS 1/14690'*. Became autonomous from ICAO management, 1 Jan 2017. **Aims** Facilitate cooperation and coordination among African States towards development of integrated and sustainable air transport systems; foster implementation if ICAO SARPs and development of harmonized rules and regulations consistent with best international practices in civil aviation. **Structure** Plenary (every 3 years); Bureau; Secretariat headed by Secretary-General. **Languages** Arabic, English, French. **Staff** 17.00 FTE, paid. **Finance** Member States' contributions. **Activities** Research and development; knowledge management/information dissemination; training/education; standards/guidelines; networking/liaising. **Events** *Capacity Building Workshop on Liberalising Aviation in Africa* Addis Ababa (Ethiopia) 2019, *Plenary Session* Zambia 2018, *Airport Excellence (APEX) In Safety Symposium* Dakar (Senegal) 2013, *(Extraordinary) plenary session* Addis Ababa (Ethiopia) 2005, *Plenary Session* Johannesburg (South Africa) 2004. **Publications** Yearbook; reports; circulars; directories.
Members Membership open to all African States members of OAU. Governments of 51 countries:
Algeria, Angola, Benin, Botswana, Burkina Faso, Burundi, Cameroon, Cape Verde, Central African Rep, Chad, Comoros, Congo Brazzaville, Congo DR, Côte d'Ivoire, Egypt, Equatorial Guinea, Eritrea, Ethiopia, Gabon, Gambia, Ghana, Guinea, Guinea-Bissau, Kenya, Lesotho, Liberia, Libya, Madagascar, Malawi, Mali, Mauritania, Mauritius, Mozambique, Namibia, Niger, Nigeria, Rwanda, Sao Tomé-Principe, Senegal, Seychelles, Sierra Leone, Somalia, South Africa, South Sudan, Sudan, Tanzania UR, Togo, Tunisia, Uganda, Zambia, Zimbabwe.
IGO Relations Agreement with: *International Civil Aviation Organization (ICAO, #12581).* Relevant Treaty: *Treaty Establishing the African Economic Community (Abuja treaty, 1991).* **NGO Relations** Joint projects and close cooperation with: *African Airlines Association (AFRAA, #00200); Arab Air Carriers Organization (AACO, #00896).* Instrumental in setting up: *African Air Tariff Conference (AFRATC, no recent information).*
[2019.12.20/XD0017/**D***]

♦ African Civil Service Observatory (ACSO) 00249
Observatoire des fonctions publiques africaines (OFPA)
Exec Sec La Patte d'Oie, 04 BP 0595, Cotonou, Benin. T. +22921303368. E-mail: ofpaofpa@yahoo.fr.
URL: http://www.ofpa.net/
History 5 Nov 1991, on the basis of the *'Cotonou Initiative'*. Commenced activities 1993. **Aims** Participate in reflections on the evolution of the state's role in facing the challenge with respect to the rule of law and of economic and social development by: collecting information on the state of African civil services; appreciating the problems these civil services face in common and considering possible solutions; identifying programmes or regional projects for better cooperation among these civil services, especially training, harmonization of statutes and exchange among civil servants of different states, and taking part in such activities. Provide for better exchange of information. **Structure** Board of Directors, comprising 10 representatives of Civil Service Ministers of member states of the Activities Monitoring Committee and 5 representatives of backers (including ACCT, UNDP and the World Bank). Officers: Chairperson, Standing Secretary, Assistant Standing Secretary. Headquarters in Benin. **Languages** French. **Finance** Sources: taxes of member states; funds from backers; own resources. **Activities** *'Human resources'*: the social dialogue; adaptation of statutes; training and recruiting; workers and job management. *'Structures and organization'*: devolution; computerization; internal organization; internal communication. *'Public Service assignments'*: services offered; relationship with users; external communication; public policy evaluation. Priorities: monitoring the effects of remuneration policy; reform and harmonization of public service statutes; devolution of national and local administration; professional training; setting up a system for civil service performance evaluation. Organizes conferences, seminars and workshops. **Events** *Conférence des ministres de la fonction publique africaine* Cotonou (Benin) 1997, *Conference on administrative reforms in Africa* Rabat (Morocco) 1995. **Publications** *Innov'Action* – bulletin. Papers; reviews; meeting proceedings. Information Services: Bibliographic database; database on African expertise in the civil service; database on salaries.
Members States (26):
Angola, Benin, Burkina Faso, Burundi, Cameroon, Cape Verde, Central African Rep, Chad, Comoros, Congo Brazzaville, Côte d'Ivoire, Djibouti, Equatorial Guinea, Gabon, Gambia, Guinea, Guinea-Bissau, Madagascar, Mali, Mauritania, Mozambique, Niger, Rwanda, Sao Tomé-Principe, Senegal, Togo.
IGO Relations Formal relations with: *ILO (#11123); International Bank for Reconstruction and Development (IBRD, #12317); UNDP (#20292).* Partner of: *United Nations Public Administration Network (UNPAN, #20615).* **NGO Relations** Formal relations with: *European Centre for Development Policy Management (ECDPM, #06473).*
[2018.07.10/XF3594/**F***]

♦ African Civil Society Network on Water and Sanitation (ANEW) 00250
Réseau africain de la société civile sur l'eau et l'assainissement
Head Office Mango Court, 4th Floor, Suite A403 WoodAvenue, Nairobi, 00100, Kenya. T. +2547012009988. E-mail: info@anew.africa.
URL: https://anew.africa/
Aims Promote the effective engagement of diverse African civil society voices in the formulation and implementation of policies and strategies for water, sanitation and hygiene. **Structure** General Assembly. Board; Secretariat based in Nairobi (Kenya). Regional offices in: Botswana (Southern Africa); Chad (Central African); Kenya (Eastern Africa); Senegal (Western Africa); Egypt (Northern Africa). **Activities** Advocacy/lobbying/activism.
Members Full in 28 countries:
Benin, Burkina Faso, Burundi, Cameroon, Chad, Congo DR, Egypt, Ethiopia, Gambia, Ghana, Kenya, Liberia, Madagascar, Malawi, Mauritania, Mauritius, Mozambique, Niger, Nigeria, Rwanda, Senegal, Sierra Leone, South Sudan, Sudan, Tanzania UR, Togo, Uganda, Zambia.
IGO Relations Partners: *Department for International Development (DFID, inactive); European Commission (EC, #06633).* **NGO Relations** Member of (1): *The Butterfly Effect (BE, #03389).* Partner in: *Sanitation and Water for All (SWA, #19051).* Partners: *Arab Office for Youth and Environment (AOYE); WaterAid (#20822);* national associations. Supports: *Global Call for Action Against Poverty (GCAP, #10263).* [2021/XJ5180/**D**]

♦ African Climate Change Research Centre (internationally oriented national body)
♦ African Climate Finance Hub (internationally oriented national body)

♦ African Climate Policy Centre (ACPC) 00251
Contact c/o UNECA, Menelik II Rd, PO Box 3001, Addis Ababa, Ethiopia. T. +25115517200. Fax +25115510350. E-mail: acpc@uneca.org.
URL: http://www.uneca.org/acpc/
Aims Address the need for greatly improved climate information for Africa; strengthen the use of such information for decision making, by improving analytical capacity, knowledge management and dissemination activities. **Activities** Knowledge generation, sharing and networking; Advocacy and consensus building; Advisory services and technical cooperation. **Events** *African Climate Conference* Arusha (Tanzania UR) 2013. **NGO Relations** *Africa Adaptation Knowledge Network (AAKNet).* Member of: *LEDS Global Partnership (LEDS GP, #16435).* [2018/XJ7052/**E***]

♦ African Coalition for Corporate Accountability (ACCA) 00252
Project Coordinator c/o Ctr for Human Rights, Fac of Law – Univ of Pretoria, Pretoria, 0002, South Africa. T. +27124204531. E-mail: accacoordinator@gmail.com – coordinator@accahumanrights.org.
URL: http://www.accahumanrights.org/
History Nov 2013. Launched with the support of *Global Rights*. **Aims** Facilitate an alliance that crosses borders and creates a strong and united African network of civil society organization and communities; protect and promote *human rights* in relation to business activity; provide a platform to share information and knowledge. **Structure** General Assembly; Steering Committee; Secretariat, headed by Coordinator. **Languages** English, French. **Staff** 1.00 FTE, paid. **Finance** Donor-advised funding. **Activities** Knowledge management/information dissemination; advocacy/lobbying/activism; capacity building; research/documentation. **Events** *General Assembly* Pretoria (South Africa) 2017, *Meeting* Nairobi (Kenya) 2016, *General Assembly* Pretoria (South Africa) 2016, *Meeting* Addis Ababa (Ethiopia) 2014. **Publications** *ACCA Quarterly Newsletter*.
Members Organizations (116) in 31 countries:
Benin, Burkina Faso, Burundi, Cameroon, Chad, Congo Brazzaville, Congo DR, Côte d'Ivoire, Egypt, Equatorial Guinea, Ethiopia, Ghana, Guinea, Kenya, Liberia, Madagascar, Malawi, Mali, Mauritania, Mozambique, Niger, Nigeria, Rwanda, Senegal, Sierra Leone, South Africa, Tanzania UR, Togo, Uganda, Zambia, Zimbabwe.
Included in the above, 8 organizations listed in this Yearbook:
African Law Foundation (AFRILAW); Centre for Human Rights and Democracy in Africa (CHRDA); Global Network for Good Governance (GNGG, #10490); Global Rights Alert (GRA); Great Lakes Institute for Strategic Studies (GLiSS); Leadership Initiative for Transformation and Empowerment (LITE-Africa); Organisation of African Youth (OAYouth, #17799); Southern African Resource Watch (SARW). [2022/XJ8790/y/**D**]

♦ African Coalition for Sustainable Energy and Access (unconfirmed)

♦ African Coffee Research Network (ACRN) 00253
Réseau de recherche caféière en Afrique (RECA)
Chairman Coffee Research Centre, Kituza, PO Box 185, Mukono, Uganda. T. +25641320512 – +25641320341 – +25641320342. Fax +25641321070.
URL: http://www.naro.go.ug/
History 27 Mar 1993, London (UK), under the auspices of *Inter-African Coffee Organization (IACO, #11383)*, as an intergovernmental network. **Aims** Revitalize and improve research in view of enhancing productivity and quality of African coffee. **Structure** General Assembly (annual), consisting of delegates representing a Member State or an Associate Member Institution. Coordination Committee, consisting of Chairman, Vice-Chairman, IACO Secretary General, 7 correspondents from amongst Members and 3 delegates from Associate Members. Coordination Office, headed by Coordinator. **Languages** English. **Staff** 27.00 FTE, paid. **Finance** Members' dues. Other sources: grants; legacies. **Activities** Promotes: cooperation, concertation and exchange of information between members; common research objectives; creation, coordination and development of regional research teams; collaboration with international coffee research institutions, regional or international organizations and donors; training of scientists and extension officials; exchange of scientific information and plant materials; mobilization of funds to finance activities. Facilitates coffee production projects for poverty reduction in Africa; organizes workshops. **Events** *General assembly* Abidjan (Côte d'Ivoire) 2003, *Annual general assembly* Abidjan (Côte d'Ivoire) 2001, *Extraordinary general assembly / Annual General Assembly* Luanda (Angola) 2000, *Annual General Assembly* Abidjan (Côte d'Ivoire) 1999, *Workshop on tracheomycosis of coffee in Africa* Kampala (Uganda) 1997. **Publications** Proceedings.
Members Member countries (16):
Angola, Benin, Burundi, Cameroon, Congo DR, Côte d'Ivoire, Ethiopia, Guinea, Kenya, Madagascar, Malawi, Rwanda, Tanzania UR, Togo, Uganda, Zimbabwe. [2008/XF3349/**F**]

♦ African Commission on Agricultural Statistics (AFCAS) 00254
Commission des statistiques agricoles pour l'Afrique
Statistician FAO ROA, PO Box 1628, Accra, Ghana. T. +233217010930 – +23321675000ext3407. Fax +233217010943.
URL: http://www.fao.org/africa/afcas/en/
History 1961, within the framework of *FAO (#09260)*, by Article VI-1 of its Constitution, at 11th session of the Conference. First session held Oct 1962. Based at *FAO Regional Office for Africa (FAO/RAF, #09265).* **Aims** Review the state of *food* and agricultural statistics in the region; advise members on the development and standardization of such statistics; convene expert consultations on matters relating to the improvement and development of agricultural statistics. **Languages** English, French. **Activities** Considers: use of population census results as a frame for agricultural censuses and surveys; improved gender disaggregation of agricultural statistics; use of agro-ecological zones as appropriate strata for agricultural censuses and surveys; statistical aspects of structural readjustment programmes; statistics on area and need in a mixed-cropping environment; statistical sampling designs; use of remote sensing. Monitors fishery and forestry statistics. **Events** *Session* Rabat (Morocco) 2013, *Session* Addis Ababa (Ethiopia) 2011, *Session* Accra (Ghana) 2009, *Session* Algiers (Algeria) 2007, *Session* Maputo (Mozambique) 2005.
Members Open to all Member Nations and Associate Members of FAO whose territories are situated wholly or partly in the region or who are responsible for the international relations of any non-self-governing territories in the region. Current membership comprises governments of 44 countries:
Algeria, Angola, Benin, Botswana, Burkina Faso, Burundi, Cameroon, Cape Verde, Central African Rep, Chad, Congo Brazzaville, Congo DR, Côte d'Ivoire, Equatorial Guinea, Eswatini, Ethiopia, Gabon, Gambia, Ghana, Guinea, Guinea-Bissau, Kenya, Lesotho, Liberia, Madagascar, Malawi, Mali, Mauritania, Mauritius, Morocco, Mozambique, Namibia, Niger, Nigeria, Rwanda, Senegal, Seychelles, Sierra Leone, Tanzania UR, Togo, Tunisia, Uganda, Zambia, Zimbabwe.
Observers (2 countries):
UK, USA. [2014/XE9654/**E***]

♦ African Commission of Health and Human Rights Promoters (internationally oriented national body)

♦ African Commission on Human and Peoples' Rights (ACHPR) 00255
Commission africaine des droits de l'homme et des peuples (CADHP)
Chairperson No 31 Bijilo Annex Layout, Kombo North District – Western Region, PO Box 673, Banjul, Gambia. T. +2204410505 – +2204410506. Fax +2204410504. E-mail: au-banjul@africa-union.org.
URL: http://www.achpr.org/
History 26 Jun 1981, Banjul (Gambia). Established within the framework of *Organization of African Unity (OAU, inactive)*, under the *African Charter of Human and Peoples' Rights (Banjul Protocol, 1981)*, which entered into force 21 Oct 1986, on ratification by an absolute majority of OAU member states. The Commission was officially installed in Banjul, 12 Jun 1989, and is the main organ entrusted with the enforcement of the Charter. Statutes registered in *OAU doc Cab/LEG/67/Rev 5*. Currently a legal organ of *African Union (AU, #00488).* **Aims** Promote human and *peoples'* rights; ensure protection of these rights under conditions laid down by the Charter; interpret all provisions of the Charter; perform all tasks which may be entrusted to it by the Assembly of Heads of States and Governments. **Structure** Commission (meeting in Ordinary Session twice a year) comprises 11 members, elected by Assembly of Heads of State. **Languages** Arabic, English, French, Portuguese. **Activities** Conflict resolution; events/meetings; research/documentation. **Events** *Ordinary Session* Banjul (Gambia) 2022, *Ordinary Session* Banjul (Gambia) 2022, *Ordinary Session* Banjul (Gambia) 2022, *Ordinary Session* Banjul (Gambia) 2022, *Ordinary Session* Dakar (Senegal) 2021. **Publications** *Indicative questions to State Parties in respect of Article 5 of the African Charter* (2019) in

English, French. *General Comment No. 6 On The Protocol To The African Charter On Human And Peoples Right On The Rights Of Women In Africa (Maputo Protocol): The Right To Property During Separation, Divorce Or Annulment Of Marriage (Article 7(D))* (2020) by ACHPR in English, French; *Rules of Procedure of the African Commission on Human and Peoples' Rights of 2020 – Règlement intérieur de la Commission africaine des droits de l'homme et des peuples de 2020 – Regulamento Interno da Comissão Africana dos Direitos Humanos e dos Povos de 2020* (2020) in English, French, Portuguese; *Addressing Human Rights issues in conflict situations* (2019) in English, French; *Study on Transitional Justice and Human and Peoples' Rights in Africa – Etude sur la justice transitionnelle et les droits de l'homme et des peuples en Afrique* (2019) by ACHPR in English, French; *General Comment No.5 on the African Charter on Human and Peoples' Rights: The Right to Freedom of Movement and Residence (Article 12(1))* (2019) by ACHPR in English, French; *Pilot Study on migration and respect for Human Rights focus on the responses provided by Niger* (2019) by ACHPR in English, French; *Guidelines on the Right to Water in Africa – Lignes directrices sur le droit à l'eau en Afrique* (2019) by ACHPR in English, French; *State Reporting Guidelines and Principles on Articles 21 And 24 of the African Charter relating to Extractive Industries, Human Rights and the Environment* (2018) by ACHPR in English, French; *Protocol to the African Charter on Human and Peoples' Rights on the Rights of Older Persons in Africa* (2018) by ACHPR in English, French; *Principles on the Decriminalisation of Petty Offences in Africa* (2018) by ACHPR in English, French; *Guidelines on Freedom of Association and Assembly in Africa* (2017) by ACHPR in English, French; *The Guidelines on Combating Sexual Violence and its Consequences in Africa* (2017) by ACHPR in English, French; *Guidelines on Access to Information and Elections in Africa* (2017) by ACHPR in English, French; *General Comment No. 4: The Right to Redress for Victims of Torture and Other Cruel, Inhuman or Degrading Punishment or Treatment (Article 5)* (2017) by ACHPR in English, French; *Guidelines for the Policing of Assemblies by Law Enforcement Officials in Africa* (2017) by ACHPR in English, French; *Principles and Guidelines on Human and Peoples' Rights while Countering Terrorism in Africa* (2016) in English, French; *Guidelines on the Conditions of Arrest, Police Custody and Pre-Trial Detention in Africa* (2015) in English, French; *Resolution on Granting Affiliate Status to National Human Rights Institutions*; *African Charter on the Rights and Welfare of the Child*; *Study on the Question of the Death Penalty in Africa*; *Declaration of Principles on Freedom of Expression in Africa*; *State Party Reporting Guidelines for Economic, Social and Cultural Rights in the African Charter on Human and Peoples' Rights*; *Declaration of the Pretoria Seminar on Economic, Social and Cultural Rights in Africa (ECOSOC)*; *Rules of Procedure of the African Commission on Human and Peoples' Rights*; *Resolution on the Criteria for Granting and Enjoying Observer Status to Non-Governmental Organizations Working in the Field of Human Rights with the Commission*; *Resolution on Guidelines and Measures for the Prohibition and Prevention of Torture, Cruel, Inhuman or Degrading Treatment or Punishment in Africa (The Robben Island Guidelines)*; *Protocol to the African Charter on Human and Peoples' Rights on the Rights of Women in Africa*; *Recommendations and Resolutions of the African Commission on Human and Peoples Rights*; *General Comment N3 on The African Charter On Human And Peoples' Rights: The Right To Life (Article 4)*; *Protocol to the African Charter on Human and Peoples' Rights on the Establishment of an African Court on Human and Peoples' Rights*; *Principles and Guidelines on the Right to a Fair Trial and Legal Assistance in Africa*; *Principles and Guidelines on the Implementation of Economic, Social and Cultural Rights in the African Charter on Human and Peoples' Rights*; *African Charter on Human and Peoples' Rights*; *General Comments N2 on Article 14 (1) (a), (b), (c) and (f) and Article 14 (2) (a) and (c) of the Protocol to the African Charter on Human and Peoples' Rights on the Rights of Women in Africa*; *Model Law on Access to Information in Africa*; *Guidelines for State Reporting under the Protocol to the African Charter on Human and Peoples Rights on the Rights of Women in Africa*; *Guidelines On Policing Assemblies in Africa*; *Principles and Guidelines on Human and Peoples' Rights while Countering Terrorism in Africa*. Information sheets.

Members States party to the African Charter on Human and Peoples' Rights (54):
Algeria, Angola, Benin, Botswana, Burkina Faso, Burundi, Cameroon, Cape Verde, Central African Rep, Chad, Comoros, Congo Brazzaville, Congo DR, Côte d'Ivoire, Djibouti, Egypt, Equatorial Guinea, Eritrea, Eswatini, Ethiopia, Gabon, Gambia, Ghana, Guinea, Guinea-Bissau, Kenya, Lesotho, Liberia, Libya, Madagascar, Malawi, Mali, Mauritania, Mauritius, Mozambique, Namibia, Niger, Nigeria, Rwanda, Sahara West, Sao Tomé-Principe, Senegal, Seychelles, Sierra Leone, Somalia, South Africa, South Sudan, Sudan, Tanzania UR, Togo, Tunisia, Uganda, Zambia, Zimbabwe.

IGO Relations Observer status granted to: *Organisation internationale de la Francophonie (OIF, #17809)*, replacing *Agence intergouvernementale de La Francophonie (inactive)*; *Commonwealth Secretariat (#04362)*. Instrumental in setting up: *African Court on Human and Peoples' Rights (AfCHPR, #00278)*. Cooperates with: *United Nations Institute for Training and Research (UNITAR, #20576)*.

NGO Relations Observer status granted to 514 organizations, including:
- *Action internationale pour la paix et le développement dans la région des Grands Lacs, Switzerland (AIPD-GL)*;
- *Advocates for Human Rights*;
- *Africa Disability Alliance (ADA)*;
- *Africa Freedom of Information Centre (AFIC, #00175)*;
- *Africa Human Rights and Justice Protection Network (AHRJP, no recent information)*;
- *Africa Legal Aid (AFLA, #00186)*;
- *African Association of International Law (AAIL, #00208)*;
- *African Bar Association (AFBA, #00220)*;
- *African Centre for Democracy and Human Rights Studies (ACDHRS, #00239)*;
- *African Centre for Treatment and Rehabilitation of Torture Victims (ACTV)*;
- *African Child Policy Forum (ACPF, #00246)*;
- *African Commission of Health and Human Rights Promoters (ACHHRP)*;
- *African Institute for Democracy (no recent information)*;
- *African Jurists' Association (AJA, #00351)*;
- *African Network for Integrated Development (ANID, #00390)*;
- *African Network for Prevention and Protection Against Child Abuse and Neglect (ANPPCAN, #00393)*;
- *African Policing Civilian Oversight Forum (APCOF, #00419)*;
- *African Studies Association (ASA)*;
- *African Union of the Blind (AFUB, #00489)*;
- *Afro-Asian Peoples' Solidarity Organization (AAPSO, #00537)*;
- *Agence de diffusion du droit international humanitaire en Afrique centrale (ADDIHAC)*;
- *Agir ensemble pour les droits humains*;
- *AIDS and Rights Alliance for Southern Africa (ARASA)*;
- *All Africa Conference of Churches (AACC, #00640)*;
- *Alliances for Africa (AfA)*;
- *Amnesty International (AI, #00801)*;
- *Anti-Slavery International (#00860)*;
- *Arab Institute for Human Rights (AIHR, #00983)*;
- *Arab Lawyers' Union (ALU, #01002)*;
- *Arab Organization for Human Rights (AOHR, #01020)*;
- *Arab Programme for Human Rights Activists (APHRA)*;
- *ARTICLE 19 (#01121)*;
- *Association for the Prevention of Torture (APT, #02869)*;
- *Avocats Sans Frontières (ASF, #03050)*;
- *Cairo Institute for Human Rights Studies (CIHRS, #03397)*;
- *Centre africain pour la démocratie, les droits de l'homme et la protection des détenus (CADEPROD, no recent information)*;
- *Centre africain pour l'éducation aux droits humains (CAEDHU)*;
- *Centre Afrika Obota (CAO, #03728)*;
- *Center for Civil and Human Rights, Notre Dame IN (CCHR)*;
- *Centre for Human Rights, Pretoria*;
- *Centre d'Information et de Formation en matière de Droits Humains en Afrique (CIFDHA)*;
- *Center for Justice and International Law (CEJIL, #03647)*;
- *CIVICUS: World Alliance for Citizen Participation (#03962)*;
- *Commonwealth Human Rights Initiative (CHRI, #04340)*;
- *Council for the Development of Social Science Research in Africa (CODESRIA, #04879)*;
- *Dignity International (#05086)*;
- *Eastern Africa Centre for Constitutional Development (Kituo Cha Katiba, #05220)*;
- *Eastern Africa Journalists Association (EAJA)*;
- *Egyptian Organization for Human Rights (EOHR)*;
- *English International Association of Lund*;
- *Equality Now (#05518)*;
- *Equitas – International Centre for Human Rights Education*;
- *Federation of African Journalists (FAJ, #09404)*;
- *Feinstein International Center (FIC)*;
- *Femmes Africa solidarité (FAS, #09732)*;
- *FIAN International (#09743)*;
- *Forest Peoples Programme (FPP, #09865)*;
- *Foundation for Women's Health Research and Development (FORWARD)*;
- *Franciscans International (FI, #09982)*;
- *Fund for Peace (FFP)*;
- *Global Initiative for Economic, Social and Cultural Rights (GI-ESCR)*;
- *Global Network for Good Governance (GNGG, #10490)*;
- *HelpAge International (#10904)*;
- *Human Rights First*;
- *Human Rights Information and Documentation Systems, International (HURIDOCS, #10985)*;
- *Human Rights Internet (HRI, #10986)*;
- *Human Rights Watch (HRW, #10990)*, especially its Africa Division;
- *Humanists International (#10972)*;
- *Indigenous Peoples of Africa Coordinating Committee (IPACC, #11163)*;
- *Institut des droits de l'homme, Lyon (IDHL)*;
- *Institute for Human Rights and Development in Africa (IHRDA)*;
- *International Alert (#11615)*;
- *International Association for Democracy in Africa (#11836)*;
- *International Association of Young Lawyers (#12282)*;
- *International Baby Food Action Network (IBFAN, #12305)*;
- *International Catholic Child Bureau (#12450)*;
- *International Center for Not-for-Profit Law (ICNL, #12471)*;
- *International Commission of Jurists (ICJ, #12695)*;
- *International Committee of the Red Cross (ICRC, #12799)*;
- *International Federation of ACATs – Action by Christians for the Abolition of Torture (#13334)*;
- *International Federation for Human Rights (#13452)*;
- *Front Line Defenders (FLD, #10008)*;
- *International Human Rights Association of American Minorities (IHRAAM)*;
- *International Institute of Human Rights – Fondation René Cassin (IIHR, #13887)*;
- *International Organization for the Elimination of All Forms of Racial Discrimination (EAFORD, #14445)*;
- *International PEN (#14552)*;
- *International Rehabilitation Council for Torture Victims (IRCT, #14712)*;
- *International Service for Human Rights (ISHR, #14841)*;
- *International Society for Human Rights (ISHR, #15183)*;
- *International Trade Union Confederation – African Regional Organization (#15709)*;
- *International Training Centre on Human Rights and Peace Teaching, Geneva (CIFEDHOP, see: #21184)*;
- *International Work Group for Indigenous Affairs (IWGIA, #15907)*;
- *IPAS (#16010)* Africa Alliance;
- *Kataliko Action for Africa (KAF)*;
- *Ligue des droits de la personne humaine dans la région des Grands-Lacs (LDGL)*;
- *Marangopoulos Foundation for Human Rights (MFHR)*;
- *Media Foundation for West Africa (MFWA, #16617)*;
- *Media Institute of Southern Africa (MISA, #16619)*;
- *Minority Rights Group International (MRG, #16820)*;
- *Network of African National Human Rights Institutions (NANHRI, #16984)*;
- *Pan African Movement (PAM)*;
- *Panos Network (#18183)* – Eastern Africa;
- *Pax Romana, International Catholic Movement for Intellectual and Cultural Affairs (ICMICA, #18267)*;
- *Penal Reform International (PRI, #18290)*;
- *Regional Episcopal Conference of West Africa (RECOWA, #18783)*;
- *Rencontre africaine pour la défense des droits de l'homme (RADDHO)*;
- *Reporters sans frontières (RSF, #18846)*;
- *Reprieve*;
- *Réseau des Défenseurs des Droits Humains en Afrique Centrale (REDHAC, #18870)*;
- *Sightsavers International (#19270)*;
- *Southern Africa Litigation Centre (SALC, #19832)*;
- *Southern African Development Community Lawyers Association (#19845)*;
- *Southern African Research and Documentation Centre (SARDC, #19861)*;
- *Strategic Initiative for Women in the Horn of Africa (SIHA, #20006)*;
- *Study and Research Group on Democracy, Economic and Social Development in Africa (GERDDES-Africa, #20021)*;
- *Survival International (#20047)*;
- *Swedish Foundation for Human Rights (SFHR)*;
- *Third World Network-Africa (TWN Africa)*;
- *WaterAid (#20822)*;
- *West Africa Network for Peacebuilding (WANEP, #20878)*;
- *West African Bar Association (WABA, #20870)*;
- *West African Institute for Legal Aid (WAILA)*;
- *West African Human Rights Defenders' Network (WAHRDN, #20882)*;
- *Witness*;
- *Women in Law and Development in Africa-Afrique de l'Ouest (WiLDAF-AO, #21005)*;
- *Women and Law in Southern Africa Research Trust (WLSA, #21006)*;
- *World Coalition Against the Death Penalty (#21281)*;
- *World Federalist Movement – Movement for a Just World Order through a Strengthened United Nations (WFM, #21404)*;
- *World Organisation Against Torture (OMCT, #21685)*;
- *World University Service (WUS, #21892)*. [2022.05.24/XE0982/**E***]

♦ African Commission on Mathematics Education (inactive)

♦ African Commission on Nuclear Energy (AFCONE) 00256

Exec Dir Unit B2003, Corobay Corner, 169 Corobay Avenue, Waterkloof Glen, Pretoria, 0010, South Africa. T. +27870960175.
Secretariat Dept of Foreign Affairs, Private Bag X152, Pretoria, 001, South Africa.
URL: https://www.afcone.org/

History Nov 2010. Established following signing of *African Nuclear-weapon-free-zone Treaty (Pelindaba Treaty, 1996)* for which it acts as its secretariat. **Aims** Ooversee and coordinate nuclear activities and cooperation in Africa, so as to foster international peace and security, and engender sustainable development in Africa. **Structure** Bureau, comprising Chairperson, Vice Chairperson and Executive Secretary. Headquarters based in South Africa. **Events** *Ordinary Session of the Conference of States Parties* Addis Ababa (Ethiopia) 2022, *Session* Addis Ababa (Ethiopia) 2011.

Members Elected members for 3-year-membership (12):
Algeria, Burkina Faso, Cameroon, Ethiopia, Kenya, Libya, Mali, Mauritius, Senegal, South Africa, Togo, Tunisia.

IGO Relations Memorandum of Understanding with (1): *Agency for the Prohibition of Nuclear Weapons in Latin America and the Caribbean (#00554)*. Partner of (10): *African Energy Commission (AFREC, #00298)*; *African Regional Cooperative Agreement for Research, Development and Training Related to Nuclear Science and Technology (AFRA)*; *African Union (AU, #00488)*; *European Safeguards Research and Development Association (ESARDA, #08417)*; *European Union (EU, #08967)*; *Forum of Nuclear Regulatory Bodies in Africa (FNRBA, #09927)*; *International Atomic Energy Agency (IAEA, #12294)*; *New Partnership for Africa's Development (NEPAD, #17091)*; *United Nations Office for Disarmament Affairs (UNODA, #20594)*; *United Nations Regional Centre for Peace and Disarmament in Africa (UNREC, #20616)*. **NGO Relations** Partner of (3): *United Nations – Nuclear Young Generation (UN-NYG, #20592)*; *Vienna Center for Disarmament and Non-Proliferation (VCDNP)*; *Women in Nuclear (WIN, #21009)*. [2022/XD8052/**E***]

♦ African Commission for the Promotion of Health and Human Rights / see African Commission of Health and Human Rights Promoters

♦ African Committee for the Coordination of Information Media (inactive)

♦ African Committee of Experts on the Rights and Welfare of the Child (ACERWC) 00257

Sec c/o Commission of the African Union, African Union Headquarters, PO Box 3243, Roosvelt Street, Addis Ababa, Ethiopia. T. +2511513522 – +2511517700 ext 300. Fax +2511535716. E-mail: info@acerwc.africa – dsocial@africa-union.org.
URL: https://www.acerwc.africa/

History Jul 2001, Lusaka (Zambia), mandated by articles 32-46 of the *African Charter on the Rights and Welfare of the Child*, adopted by Heads of State and Government of *Organization of African Unity (OAU, inactive)* – currently *African Union (AU, #00488)*, 11 Jul 1990 and came into force 29 Nov 1999. **Aims** Promote and protect the rights enshrined in the Charter; monitor implementation and ensure protection of the rights enshrined in the Charter; interpret the provisions of the Charter at the request of a state party, an institution of the OAU/AU or any other person or institution recognized by OAU/AU. **Events** *Ordinary Session*

Addis Ababa (Ethiopia) 2019, *Ordinary Session* Addis Ababa (Ethiopia) 2018, *Ordinary Session* Bamako (Mali) 2018, *Ordinary Session* Khartoum (Sudan) 2017, *Ordinary Session* Maseru (Lesotho) 2017. **NGO Relations** Observer Status granted the following organizations listed in this Yearbook:
- *African Child Policy Forum (ACPF, #00246);*
- *African Movement of Working Children and Youth (AMWCY);*
- *African Union of the Blind (AFUB, #00489);*
- *Child Helpline International (CHI, #03870);*
- *Defence for Children International (DCI, #05025);*
- *East African Centre for Human Rights (EACHRights);*
- *Institute for Human Rights and Development in Africa (IHRDA);*
- *International Social Service (ISS, #14886);*
- *Penal Reform International (PRI, #18290);*
- *Plan International (#18386);*
- *Rädda Barnen – Save the Children Sweden;*
- *REPSSI (#18848);*
- *Retrak;*
- *SOS-Kinderdorf International (#19693) – Africa and Middle East;*
- *Under The Same Sun (UTSS);*
- *World Vision International (WVI, #21904).* [2021/XJ5076/**E***]

♦ African Committee of Metrology 00258
Comité Africain de Métrologie (CAFMET)
Pres 5 rue Alexandre Fleming, 49000 Angers, France. T. +33673623262. E-mail: contact@cafmet.com.
URL: http://www.cafmet.com/
History 31 Mar 2005. **Aims** Make public or private companies aware of the importance of metrology for the sustainable development of a country; offer training courses delivered by internationally recognized technical experts; have the competence of companies and laboratories recognized by the quality assurance of services and the results they provide. **Structure** Management Committee; Council Board; International Technical Committee; Member State Committee; Technical Groups. **Activities** Capacity building; events/meetings; guidance/assistance/consulting; research/documentation; training/education. **Events** *International Metrology Conference* Casablanca (Morocco) 2021, *International Metrology Conference* Casablanca (Morocco) 2020, *International Metrology Conference* Marrakech (Morocco) 2018, *Forum Africain de Métrologie* Angers (France) 2015, *International Metrology Conference* Pretoria (South Africa) 2014. **Publications** *International Journal of Metrology and Quality Engineering.* **Members** Mostly industrialists, but open to all organizations and individuals interested in metrology. Membership countries not specified. **IGO Relations** Observer status with (1): *Intra-Africa Metrology System (AFRIMETS, #15992).* [2021.05.26/XM1555/**E**]

♦ African Communication Regulation Authorities Network (ACRAN) .. 00259
Réseau des instances africaines de régulation de la communication (RIARC) – Instâncias Africanas de Regulação e da Comunicação
Address not obtained.
URL: http://www.acran.org/
History 5 Jun 1998, Libreville (Gabon). Registered in accordance with the law of Cameroon. **Structure** Conference of Presidents (every 2 years); President; Secretariat in Cotonou (Benin). **Events** *Conference* Niamey (Niger) 2013, *Conference* Arusha (Tanzania UR) 2011, *Conference* Marrakech (Morocco) 2009, *Conference* Ouagadougou (Burkina Faso) 2007, *Conference* Maputo (Mozambique) 2005.
Members Full in 33 countries:
Angola, Benin, Botswana, Burkina Faso, Burundi, Cameroon, Cape Verde, Central African Rep, Chad, Congo Brazzaville, Congo DR, Côte d'Ivoire, Eswatini, Gabon, Ghana, Guinea, Guinea-Bissau, Lesotho, Mali, Mauritania, Morocco, Mozambique, Namibia, Niger, Nigeria, Rwanda, Sao Tomé-Principe, Senegal, South Africa, Tanzania UR, Togo, Tunisia, Zimbabwe. [2015/XM2242/**F**]

♦ African Community Involvement Association (inactive)
♦ African Community Resource Center (internationally oriented national body)

♦ African Competition Forum (ACF) 00260
Forum Africain de la Concurrence (FAC)
Head Intl Relations Competition Commission South Africa, DTI Campus- Mulayo Block C, 77 Meintjies Str, Sunnyside, Pretoria, South Africa.
URL: http://www.africancompetitionforum.org/
History Launched Mar 2011, Nairobi (Kenya), as an informal network of African national and multinational competition authorities. **Aims** Promote adoption of competition principles in the implementation of national and regional economic policies of African countries. **Structure** Steering Committee. **Languages** English, French. **Activities** Capacity building; research/documentation; advocacy/lobbying/activism; events/meetings. **Events** *Biennial Conference* Marrakech (Morocco) 2018, *Biennial Conference* Port Louis (Mauritius) 2016. **Publications** Books.
Members Authorities and agencies (36). National competition agencies of 31 countries:
Algeria, Benin, Botswana, Burkina Faso, Burundi, Cameroon, Congo Brazzaville, Côte d'Ivoire, Egypt, Eswatini, Ethiopia, Gabon, Gambia, Guinea, Kenya, Malawi, Mali, Mauritius, Morocco, Mozambique, Namibia, Nigeria, Rwanda, Senegal, Seychelles, South Africa, Tanzania UR, Togo, Tunisia, Zambia, Zimbabwe.
Regional agencies (5):
Common Market for Eastern and Southern Africa (COMESA, #04296); East African Community (EAC, #05181); Economic Community of West African States (ECOWAS, #05312) (Competition Authority Forum); *Southern African Development Community (SADC, #19843); Union économique et monétaire Ouest africaine (UEMOA, #20377)* (Competition Commission).
IGO Relations *OECD (#17693)* Competition Committee; *UNCTAD (#20285)* Competition Branch. [2017.09.20/XM5905/**F***]

♦ African Computer and Technology Literacy Awareness Program Charity (internationally oriented national body)
♦ African Concern International (internationally oriented national body)
♦ African Confederation of Christian Workers in Equatorial Africa (inactive)
♦ African Confederation of Christian Workers in West Africa (inactive)

♦ African Confederation of Cooperative Savings and Credit Associations (ACCOSCA) 00261
Association des coopératives d'épargne et de crédit d'Afrique (ACECA) – Confederación Africana de Asociaciones Cooperativas de Ahorro y Crédito
CEO PO Box 43278, Nairobi, 00100, Kenya. T. +254202714648 – +254202714649. Fax +254202714646.
URL: http://www.accosca.org/
History Sep 1968, Nairobi (Kenya), as *All African Credit Union Association*, at a meeting attended by delegates from 13 African countries. Also referred to as *Africa Cooperative Savings and Credit Association.* Registered under the Societies Act of Kenya. Ceased to exist 2001. Revived 2007. **Aims** Empower savings and credit associations (SACCOs) in Africa through financial, social and technical assistance so as to improve the livelihood of people living in African in accordance with cooperative principles. **Structure** General Assembly (every 2 years, at Conference); Board of Directors; Board of Trustees. CEO/Executive Director. **Languages** English, French. **Staff** 7.00 FTE, paid. **Finance** Members' dues. Support from *United States Agency for International Development (USAID)* and other international development agencies. **Activities** Training/education; events/meetings; guidance/assistance/consulting. **Events** *Congress* Matsapha (Eswatini) 2022, *Congress* Kwale (Kenya) 2021, *Congress* Mombasa (Kenya) 2019, *Congress* Accra (Ghana) 2018, *Congress* Lilongwe (Malawi) 2017. **Publications** *ACCOSCA Newsletter.* Annual report; technical manuals.
Members National cooperative savings and credit associations representing 20,000 savings and credit cooperatives with a total of over 5 million members in 28 countries:
Benin, Botswana, Burkina Faso, Cameroon, Congo Brazzaville, Congo DR, Côte d'Ivoire, Eswatini, Ethiopia, Gambia, Ghana, Kenya, Lesotho, Liberia, Malawi, Mauritius, Namibia, Nigeria, Rwanda, Senegal, Seychelles, Sierra Leone, South Africa, Tanzania UR, Togo, Uganda, Zambia, Zimbabwe.
IGO Relations Cooperates with: *UNICEF (#20332).* **NGO Relations** Contact maintained with several international development agencies. Member of: *World Council of Credit Unions (WOCCU, #21324).* Partner of: *Development Innovations and Networks (#05057).* Member of: *International Co-operative Alliance (ICA, #12944).* [2015/XD0010/**D**]

♦ African Confederation of Equestrian Sport (A.C.E.S.) 00262
SG Rue El Estad El Bahary, Nasr City, Cairo, Egypt. T. +263784863770. E-mail: admin@acesafrica.org.
Pres address not obtained.
URL: https://acesafrica.org/
Structure Board.
Members Federations in 21 countries:
Algeria, Angola, Botswana, Congo DR, Côte d'Ivoire, Egypt, Eswatini, Ethiopia, Kenya, Libya, Madagascar, Malawi, Mauritius, Morocco, Namibia, Senegal, South Africa, Sudan, Tunisia, Zambia, Zimbabwe.
NGO Relations Continental federation of *Fédération Équestre Internationale (FEI, #09484).* [2022/AA3099/**D**]

♦ African Confederation of Futsal (unconfirmed)
♦ African Confederation of Roller Skating / see World Skate Africa (#21787)
♦ African Confederation of Sports for All (inactive)
♦ African Confederation of Sports of Roller Skating / see World Skate Africa (#21787)

♦ African Confederation of Traditional Wrestling Sports (AFCTWS) ... 00263
Contact address not obtained. E-mail: sztbez@gmail.com.
History 7 Jan 2006, Johannesburg (South Africa).
Members in 4 countries:
Cameroon, Egypt, Mauritius, South Africa.
IGO Relations *UNESCO (#20322).* **NGO Relations** Member of: *International Belt Wrestling Association (#12334).* [2009/XM2374/**D**]

♦ African Confederation of UNESCO Clubs, Centres and Associations (CACU) 00264
Contact Section UNESCO Clubs and New Partnerships, Sector External Relations and Cooperation, 7 place de Fontenoy, 75352 Paris SP, France. T. +33145680954. Fax +33145685854.
History 1999, as a regional branch of *World Federation of UNESCO Clubs, Centres and Associations (WFUCA, #21498).* **Events** *General Assembly* Nairobi (Kenya) 2011.
Members Clubs in 35 countries:
Angola, Benin, Burkina Faso, Burundi, Cameroon, Central African Rep, Chad, Comoros, Congo Brazzaville, Congo DR, Côte d'Ivoire, Equatorial Guinea, Gabon, Gambia, Ghana, Guinea, Guinea-Bissau, Kenya, Lesotho, Liberia, Madagascar, Mali, Mauritania, Mauritius, Mozambique, Niger, Nigeria, Rwanda, Senegal, Sierra Leone, Sudan, Tanzania UR, Togo, Uganda, Zambia. [2011/XJ2058/**E**]

♦ African Conference on the Integrated Family Planning, Nutrition and Parasite Control Project (meeting series)
♦ African Conservation Centre (internationally oriented national body)
♦ African Conservation Foundation (internationally oriented national body)

♦ African Conservation Tillage Network (ACT) 00265
Exec Dir PO Box 10375, Kari-Narl, Waiyaki Way, Nairobi, 00100, Kenya. T. +254208076064. E-mail: info@act-africa.org.
URL: http://www.act-africa.org/
History 1999, Harare (Zimbabwe). Previously also known under the acronym *ACTnet.* **Aims** Promote the adoption of conservation tillage in Africa. **Structure** General Assembly (annual). Board of Directors, comprising Chairman, Executive Director and 9 members. Secretariat. **Finance** Donations. **Activities** Promotes formation of national conservation tillage networks; identifies and promotes effective technology transfer techniques; links promoters and practitioners in and between countries; assists funding for cross-visits in Africa and between Africa and South America. **Events** *African Congress on Conservation Agriculture* Lusaka (Zambia) 2014, *World congress on conservation agriculture* Nairobi (Kenya) 2005, *Small-scale equipment workshop* Zambia 2001. **Publications** *Act info* (12 a year) – online newsletter.
Members Full in 20 countries:
Botswana, Brazil, Burkina Faso, Eswatini, Ethiopia, Germany, Ghana, Italy, Kenya, Lesotho, Malawi, Mozambique, Namibia, Senegal, South Africa, Sudan, Tanzania UR, Tunisia, Uganda, Zambia.
IGO Relations Partner of: *Global Soil Partnership (GSP, #10608).* [2013/XF5577/**F**]

♦ African Conservation Trust (internationally oriented national body)

♦ African Consortium for Law and Religion Studies (ACLARS) 00266
Secretariat Private Bag X3009, Houghton, 2041, South Africa. E-mail: secretariat@aclars.org.
Registered Address Office of Legal Counsel, 5A Jubilee Road, Parktown, 2193, South Africa.
URL: https://www.aclars.org/
History 2014, Stellenbosch (South Africa). Registration: South Africa. **Aims** Promote the development of studies of law and religion and their interaction in and about Africa. **Structure** General Assembly; Board of Directors; Secretariat. **Finance** Sources: members' dues. **Activities** Events/meetings. **NGO Relations** Cooperates with (1): *G20 Interfaith Forum Association (IF20, #10055).* [2022/AA0115/**D**]

♦ African Continental Free Trade Area (AfCFTA) 00267
SG c/o AU Headquarters, PO Box 3243, Roosvelt STreet, W21K19 Addis Ababa, Ethiopia. T. +251115517700. Fax +251115517844.
URL: https://au.int/en/cfta/
History Announced at Summit, 22 Oct 2008, by *East African Community (EAC, #05181), Southern African Development Community (SADC, #19843)* and *Common Market for Eastern and Southern Africa (COMESA, #04296),* to gather 26 African countries within one zone. May 2012, idea was extended to also *Economic Community of West African States (ECOWAS, #05312), Economic Community of Central African States (ECCAS, #05311)* and *Arab Maghreb Union (AMU, #01004).* At summit of *African Union (AU, #00488),* 2015, negotiations launched to create a free trade zone. *African Continental Free Trade Agreement (AfCFTA)* signed 21 Mar 2018, Kigali (Rwanda) and entered into force, 30 May 2019. Operational phase launched 7 Jul 2019. Secretariat officially commissioned and handed over to African Union, Aug 2020. Former names and other names: *Africa Free Trade Zone (AFTZ)* – former; *African Free Trade Area* – former; *Continental Free Trade Zone (CFTZ)* – former (2015).
Members Signatories to AfCFTA Consolidated Text (54):
Algeria, Angola, Benin, Botswana, Burkina Faso, Burundi, Cameroon, Cape Verde, Central African Rep, Chad, Comoros, Congo Brazzaville, Congo DR, Côte d'Ivoire, Djibouti, Egypt, Equatorial Guinea, Eswatini, Ethiopia, Gabon, Gambia, Ghana, Guinea, Guinea-Bissau, Kenya, Lesotho, Liberia, Libya, Madagascar, Malawi, Mali, Mauritania, Mauritius, Morocco, Mozambique, Namibia, Niger, Nigeria, Rwanda, Sahrawi ADR, Sao Tomé-Principe, Senegal, Seychelles, Sierra Leone, Somalia, South Africa, South Sudan, Sudan, Tanzania UR, Togo, Tunisia, Uganda, Zambia, Zimbabwe.
Ratifications as at Jul 2019 (27):
Burkina Faso, Chad, Congo Brazzaville, Côte d'Ivoire, Djibouti, Egypt, Equatorial Guinea, Eswatini, Ethiopia, Gabon, Gambia, Ghana, Guinea, Kenya, Mali, Mauritania, Namibia, Niger, Rwanda, Sahrawi ADR, Sao Tomé-Principe, Senegal, Sierra Leone, South Africa, Togo, Uganda, Zimbabwe. [2019/XJ1515/t/**E***]

♦ African Continental Korfball Federation (ACKF) 00268
Contact address not obtained. T. +27123353230. Fax +27123353230. E-mail: sakf@mweb.co.za.
History 4 Apr 2009, Pretoria (South Africa). Also referred to as *African Korfball Federation.* **Aims** Promote and enhance the game of Korfball on the African continent. **Structure** Executive Committee. **Languages** English. **Staff** None.
Members Full in 9 countries:
Botswana, Cameroon, Côte d'Ivoire, Ghana, Malawi, Morocco, South Africa, Zambia, Zimbabwe. [2017.03.09/XJ0364/**D**]

♦ African Contingency Operations Training and Assistance (internationally oriented national body)
♦ African Convention on the Conservation of Nature and Natural Resources (1968 treaty)

♦ African Correctional Services Association (ACSA) 00269
Sec Private bad 136 – PTA 0001 SA, Pretoria, South Africa. T. +27123072271. E-mail: acsa.secretariat@dcs.gov.za.
URL: http://www.dcs.gov.za/acsa/

History Sep 2008, Livingstone (Zambia), following resolutions at 2007 conference of CESCA. Replaces *Conference of Eastern, Southern and Central African Heads of Correctional Services (CESCA, inactive).* **Events** *Meeting* Pretoria (South Africa) 2008.
Members Membership countries not specified; members include an organization listed in this Yearbook: *Prisoners Rehabilitation and Welfare Action (PRAWA, #18502).* [2015/XJ8214/y/**D**]

♦ African Cotton Association 00270

Association cotonnière africaine (ACA)

Pres ACA Secretariat, Cotonou, Benin. T. +229337644. Fax +229337644. E-mail: a.c.africaine@gmail.com.
URL: http://www.africotton.org/aca/en/

History 19 Sep 2002, Cotonou (Benin). Registered in accordance with Benin law. **Aims** Increase cooperation between cotton professionals in Africa. **Structure** General Assembly (annual). Management Committee, comprising President, 2 Vice-Presidents, Treasurer and 1 further member. **Events** *Congress* Bamako (Mali) 2019, *Mechanised cotton farming – essential requirement to boost african cotton production* Abuja (Nigeria) 2018, *Congress* Ndjamena (Chad) 2016, *Congress* Cotonou (Benin) 2015, *Congress* Yamoussoukro (Côte d'Ivoire) 2014.
Members in 30 countries:
Algeria, Benin, Botswana, Burkina Faso, Cameroon, Chad, Côte d'Ivoire, Djibouti, Egypt, Ethiopia, Gambia, Guinea, Guinea-Bissau, Kenya, Libya, Madagascar, Mali, Mauritania, Morocco, Namibia, Niger, Nigeria, Senegal, Sierra Leone, South Africa, Sudan, Tanzania UR, Tunisia, Zambia, Zimbabwe.
NGO Relations Member of: *Committee for International Cooperation between Cotton Associations (CICCA, #04265).* [2015/XM2664/**D**]

♦ African Cotton and Textile Industries Federation (ACTIF) 00271

Exec Dir PO Box 1249-00606, TRV Plaza, Muthithi Road, Westlands, Nairobi, Kenya. T. +254205100381. Fax +254202022531.
Facebook: https://www.facebook.com/ACTIFAFRICA/

History Jun 2005. **Aims** Bring the needs of the cotton, textile and apparel sectors into cohesive and consensus driven positions at regional and international trade and development forums. **Structure** General Assembly; Board of Directors; Executive Director. **Languages** English. **Staff** 4.00 FTE, paid. **Finance** Members' dues. Other sources: projects; events. **Activities** Advocacy/lobbying/activism; networking/liaising; events/meetings. **Events** *Origin Africa Conference* Dar es Salaam (Tanzania UR) 2019. **Publications** *Origin Africa* – magazine.
Members in 31 countries:
Benin, Botswana, Burkina Faso, Burundi, Cameroon, Chad, Côte d'Ivoire, Egypt, Eswatini, Ethiopia, Gambia, Ghana, Guinea, Guinea-Bissau, Kenya, Lesotho, Madagascar, Malawi, Mozambique, Namibia, Nigeria, Rwanda, Sierra Leone, South Africa, Sudan, Tanzania UR, Togo, Uganda, Zambia, Zimbabwe.
NGO Relations Member of: *International Textile Manufacturers Federation (ITMF, #15679).* [2019/XM2448/t/**D**]

♦ African Council of AIDS Service Organizations (AfriCASO) 00272

Conseil des organisations d'action contre le SIDA en Afrique – Consejo Africano de Organizaciones al Servicio del SIDA

Communication/Documentation Manager Sicap Liberté 6 Immeuble F11, Appt 6912 2ème étage, BP 28366, Dakar, Senegal. T. +221338593939. Fax +221338673534.
URL: http://www.africaso.net/

History May 1991, Florence (Italy), as one of 5 regional organizations of *ICASO (#11040).* **Aims** Promote and facilitate development of *HIV* and AIDS community response in Africa – through advocacy, networking, development of sustainable organizational systems and capacity building for networks, NGOs, CBOs and PLWHAs groups – so as to improve the quality of life of communities. **Structure** Board of Directors (meets twice a year) comprising Chairperson of each of 5 sub-regional networks: *Central African Network of AIDS Service Organizations (CANASO, see: #00272),* based in Yaoundé (Cameroon); *Eastern African Network of AIDS Service Organizations (EANNASO, see: #00272),* based in Arusha (Tanzania UR); *Northern African Network of AIDS Service Organizations (NANASO, see: #00272),* based in Tunis (Tunisia); *Southern African Network of AIDS Service Organizations (SANASO, see: #00272),* based in Windhoek (Namibia); *Western African Network of AIDS Service Organizations (WANASO, see: #00272),* based in Bamako (Mali). Secretariat. **Languages** English, French. **Staff** 7.00 FTE, paid. **Activities** Events/meetings; advocacy/lobbying/activism; training/education; monitoring/evaluation; networking/liaising. **Events** *Meeting* Dakar (Senegal) 2015, *ICASA : international conference on HIV/AIDS and sexually transmitted infections in Africa* Dakar (Senegal) 2008, *International conference on traditional medicine* Dakar (Senegal) 2004, *International home and community care conference for people living with HIV/AIDS* Dakar (Senegal) 2003, *ICASA : international conference on AIDS and sexually transmitted infections in Africa* Nairobi (Kenya) 2003. **Publications** *AfriCASO News* – bulletin. Directory. **IGO Relations** Principle technical partners and sources of funding include: *African Union (AU, #00488); Canadian International Development Agency (CIDA, inactive); Deutsche Gesellschaft für Internationale Zusammenarbeit (GIZ); Global Fund to Fight AIDS, Tuberculosis and Malaria (Global Fund, #10383); Joint United Nations Programme on HIV/AIDS (UNAIDS, #16149); UNDP (#20292); UNICEF (#20332); WHO (#20950).*
NGO Relations Instrumental in setting up: *African Ethical and Legal Network on HIV/AIDS (no recent information).* Principle technical partners and sources of funding include:
– *AWARE International; Bill and Melinda Gates Foundation (BMGF); Coalition africaine de la société civile contre le SIDA; Ford Foundation (#09858); Frontline AIDS (#10007); Gavi – The Vaccine Alliance (Gavi, #10077); Global Health Action (GHA); Global Interaction (GiA); Global Network of People Living with HIV/AIDS (GNP+, #10494); Humanistisch Instituut voor Ontwikkelingssamenwerking (Hivos); Humanity and Inclusion (HI, #10975); International Community of Women Living with HIV/AIDS (ICW, #12826); Network of African People Living with HIV and AIDS (NAP+, #16986); Open Source Initiative (OSI); Society on AIDS in Africa (SAA, #19518); Society for Women and AIDS in Africa (SWAA International, inactive); Terre sans frontières (TSF); UHC2030 (#20277); WHO European Healthy Cities Network (WHO Healthy Cities, #20936).* [2016.06.01/XE2126/**E**]

♦ African Council for Communication Education (ACCE) 00273

Conseil africain d'enseignement de la communication (CAEC)

Exec Coordinator Univ of Nairobi, Edu Bldg – 3rd Floor, PO Box 47495, Nairobi, Kenya. T. +2542227043 – +2542215270. Fax +2542216135.
URL: http://www.accenigeria.org/

History Dec 1976, Nairobi (Kenya), when constitution formally adopted by heads of 14 training institutions, following initiatives dating back to meeting, 1961, Moshi (Tanzania UR). Mode of operation decided at meeting of directors of communications training schools, 1974. **Aims** Promote *journalism* and communication education and develop communication resources in African countries; promote awareness among African governments, policy-makers and planners of the role of communication and the mass media in national development; improve quality of communication training and subsequently of communication in Africa; offer a forum for trainers to confer and to plan common training strategies; raise awareness on current issues among communication training institutes; assess common needs and generate common solutions. **Structure** General Assembly (every 2 years, at Conference). Executive Committee, consisting of President, 2 Vice-Presidents, Treasurer, 4 other elected members and 2 ex-officio members. Executive Coordinator. National Chapters. Headquarters in Nairobi (Kenya). **Languages** English, French. **Staff** 8.00 FTE, paid. **Finance** Members' annual dues: Institutional US$ 100; Associate US$ 50; Individual US$ 35 (outside Africa), US$ 25 within Africa; Student US$ 10. Budget (annual): US$ 600,000. **Activities** Promotes communication education and development through workshops, seminars, courses and consultations at local, regional and continental levels. Assists in curriculum development at the request of African communication educational institutions and encourages the circulation of the various curricula and course designs among the institutions. Assesses the common needs of educational institutions and generates common solutions to those needs. Evolves a system of accreditation for African communication educational institutions. Facilitates staff and student exchanges. Encourages communication research within Africa. Collects and disseminates information on media development, research and training. Collaborative programmes: Information, Education and Communication (IEC) and advocacy on good governance for poverty eradication, with UNDP and government of Kenya; JourNet, global network for professional education in journalism and the media, with UNESCO. Instrumental in setting up: Jul 1983, *ACCE Institute for Communication Development and Research (ACCE/ICDR, no recent information),* Nairobi (Kenya); Sep 1984, *African Regional Documentation Centre on Communication Research and Policies (ACCE/ICDR Documentation Centre, no recent information),* Nairobi, a major communication resource centre specifically to link with COMNET through *Africa Network of Documentation Centres on Communication Research and Policies (AFRICA-COMNET, no recent information),* set up 1987 as a basis for *ACCE/ICDR Regional Network (no recent information).* **Events** *Annual General Assembly* Abuja (Nigeria) 2019, *Annual General Assembly* Lagos (Nigeria) 2018, *Annual General Assembly* Jos (Nigeria) 2017, *Annual General Assembly* Nsukka (Nigeria) 2014, *Annual General Assembly / Annual General Meeting* Enugu (Nigeria) 2013. **Publications** *Africa Media Review (AMR)* (3 a year) in English – research journal; *Africom* (3 a year) in English, French – newsletter. *Africa Media Monograph Series.* Communication teaching modules and study materials; books; videos; reports; proceedings.
Members Institutional (indicated by); Associate; Individual; Student; Patrons. Members in 33 countries:
Australia, Botswana, Burkina Faso, Burundi, Cameroon, Congo DR, Côte d'Ivoire, Egypt, Eritrea, Ethiopia, Gambia, Germany (*), Ghana, Kenya (*), Lesotho, Liberia, Malawi, Mauritius, Morocco, Mozambique, Namibia, Niger, Nigeria, Sierra Leone, South Africa, Sudan, Tanzania UR, Togo, Tunisia, Uganda, USA, Zambia, Zimbabwe.
Consultative Status Consultative status granted from: *UNEP (#20299).* **IGO Relations** Collaborates with and financial assistance from: *Canadian International Development Agency (CIDA, inactive); International Development Research Centre (IDRC, #13162); Swedish International Development Cooperation Agency (Sida).* **NGO Relations** Member of: *World Journalism Education Council (WJEC, #21602).* Associate member of: *International Association for Media and Communication Research (IAMCR, #12022).* Cooperates with: *African Bureau for the Defence of the Rights of Writers (ABRW, no recent information); Council for the Development of Social Science Research in Africa (CODESRIA, #04879); Fellowship of Christian Communicators in Africa and Madagascar (FOCCAM, no recent information); Friedrich-Ebert-Stiftung (FES); International Institute of Social Studies, The Hague (ISS); Pan African Episcopal Committee for Social Communication (inactive); World Association for Christian Communication (WACC, #21126).* [2015/XD6825/**D**]

♦ African Council for Distance Education (ACDE) 00274

Exec Dir Kenyatta Univ Main Campus – Thika Road, Kenyatta Univ Conference Centre, PO Box 8023, Nairobi, 00100, Kenya. T. +2540208704118. E-mail: info@acde-afri.org – execdirector@acde-afri.org.
URL: https://acde-afri.org/

History Jan 2004, Njoro (Kenya). Registration: Kenya. **Aims** Promote collaboration, research, and quality assurance in open and distance learning (ODL) including e-Learning to increase access to quality education and training in Africa. **Structure** General Assembly (in conjunction with Conference); Board; Secretariat, headed by Executive Director. **Languages** Arabic, English, French, Portuguese, Spanish. **Staff** 2.00 FTE, paid. **Finance** Sources: members' dues; subscriptions. **Activities** Advocacy/lobbying/activism; capacity building; events/meetings; networking/liaising; research/documentation; training/education. **Events** *General Assembly and Conference* Nairobi (Kenya) 2024, *General Assembly and Conference* Accra (Ghana) 2021, *General Assembly and Conference* Khartoum (Sudan) 2017, *General Assembly and Conference* Victoria Falls (Zimbabwe) 2014, *General Assembly and Conference* Dar es Salaam (Tanzania UR) 2011. **Publications** *African Journal of Distance Education* (2 a year); *ACDE Newsletter.*
Members Categories: Institutional – institutions of learning; Associate – national or sub-regional distance learning associations; Individual – educators, researchers, scholars, students. Members in 16 countries:
Botswana, Cameroon, Canada, Eswatini, Ghana, Kenya, Mauritius, Mozambique, Nigeria, Rwanda, South Africa, Sudan, Tanzania UR, UK, Zambia, Zimbabwe.
NGO Relations Member of (1): *International Council for Open and Distance Education (ICDE, #13056)* (Associate). Partner of (1): *Open Educational Resources Africa (OER Africa, #17750).* [2022.05.12/XJ1110/**D**]

♦ African Council of Optometry (AFCO) 00275

Pres ICEE, 272 Umbilo Road, Durban, 4001, South Africa. E-mail: nhnsubuga@yahoo.com.
Events *General Meeting* Victoria Falls (Zimbabwe) 2016, *General Meeting* Dar es Salaam (Tanzania UR) 2009, *General delegates meeting / General Meeting* Kampala (Uganda) 2008, *Workshop on the role of optometry in the prevention of blindness* Gaborone (Botswana) 2004, *General delegates meeting* Midrand (South Africa) 2004. **Members** Membership countries not specified. **NGO Relations** Regional member of: *World Council of Optometry (WCO, #21335).* [2015/XD9263/**D**]

♦ African Council of Organic Associations (no recent information)

♦ African Council of Religious Leaders – Religions for Peace (ACRL-RfP) 00276

Secretary General No 5 Mararo Road, PO Box 6352, Nairobi, 00200, Kenya. T. +254727531170. E-mail: secretariat@acrl-rfp.org.
URL: http://acrl-rfp.org/

History Proposed late 1990s; conceived 2002; inaugurated 2003. A network of *Religions for Peace (RfP, #18831).* **Aims** Mobilize religious leaders and their communities to build peaceful, just, hopeful and harmonious societies in Africa. **Structure** General Assembly; Governing Board; Executive Committee; Secretariat.
Members National Inter-Religious Councils in 26 countries and territories:
Benin, Burundi, Cameroon, Comoros, Congo DR, Côte d'Ivoire, Ethiopia, Ghana, Guinea, Kenya, Liberia, Madagascar, Malawi, Mauritius, Mozambique, Nigeria, Réunion, Rwanda, Seychelles, Sierra Leone, South Africa, South Sudan, Sudan, Tanzania UR, Uganda, Zambia.
General Assembly comprised of individuals of:
African Religious Youth Network; African Women of Faith Network; *All Africa Conference of Churches (AACC, #00640); Baha'i International Community (#03062); General Conference of Seventh-Day Adventists (SDA, #10109);* Hindu Council of Africa; *Organization of African Instituted Churches (OAIC, #17853);* Pan African Islamic Body; *Religions for Peace (RfP, #18831);* Representatives from Muslim Women Leaders in Africa; Representatives from the Indigenous Religions of Africa; *Symposium of Episcopal Conferences of Africa and Madagascar (SECAM, #20077); World Islamic Call Society (WICS, inactive); World Union of Catholic Women's Organisations (WUCWO, #21876).*
Consultative Status Consultative status granted from: *UNEP (#20299).* [2020.06.25/XM8508/**D**]

♦ African Council for Social and Human Sciences (inactive)

♦ African Council for Sustainable Health Development (ACOSHED) ... 00277

Conseil africain pour le développement soutenable de santé

Dir House B Plot 722, Isiyaku Rabiu Estate, Wuse II, Abuja, Federal Capital Territory, Nigeria.
History 1998. Continues the work of World Bank Expert Panel for Better Health in Africa (BHA). **Structure** General Assembly (every 2 years); Executive Board; Advisors. **IGO Relations** Endorsed by: *African Union (AU, #00488).* **NGO Relations** Member of: *Global Health Workforce Alliance (GHWA, inactive).* [2011/XD9385/**D**]

♦ African Council for the Training and Promotion of Health Sciences Teachers and Specialists (inactive)
♦ **African Court Coalition** Coalition for an Effective African Court on Human and Peoples' Rights (#04055)

♦ African Court on Human and Peoples' Rights (AfCHPR) 00278

Main Office Mwalimu Julius Nyere Conservation Centre, Dodoma Road, PO Box 6274, 23100 Arusha, Tanzania UR. T. +255272970430. E-mail: registrar@african-court.org.
URL: http://www.african-court.org/

History Established Jun 1998, Ouagadougou (Burkina Faso), on signature of the Protocol to the African Charter on Human and Peoples' Rights, adopted by Member States of the then *Organization of African Unity (OAU, inactive).* Protocol entered into force 25 Jan 2004. First Judges elected Jan 2006, Khartoum (Sudan); sworn in before the Assembly of Heads of State and Government of *African Union (AU, #00488),* 2 Jul 2006, Banjul (Gambia). Will merge with *Court of Justice of the African Union (#04935),* when Protocol on the Statute of *African Court of Justice and Human Rights* enters into force, merging both courts into a single court. **Aims** Complement the protective mandate of the African Commission on Human and Peoples' Rights; take final and binding decisions on human rights violations. **Structure** Composed of 11 Judges, nationals of Member States of the African Union, elected in their individual capacity by the Assembly of Heads of State and Government of the African Union for a period of 6 years, and may be re-elected once. **Languages** AU languages. **Staff** All Judges except the President, perform their functions on a part-time basis. **Events** *Ordinary Session* Arusha (Tanzania UR) 2020. **Publications** *African Charter on Human and Peoples' Rights; Protocol to the African Charter on Human and Peoples' Rights on the Establishment of an African Court on Human and Peoples' Rights; Rules of the Court.* **IGO Relations** *African Commission on Human and Peoples' Rights (ACHPR, #00255); Deutsche Gesellschaft für Internationale Zusammenarbeit (GIZ); European Court of Human Rights (#06855); European Union (EU, #08967).* [2020/XF6450/**F***]

♦ African Court of Justice and Human Rights (unconfirmed)

♦ African Cricket Association (ACA) 00279

CEO Africa, c/o Cricket-SA, PO Box 55009, Northlands, 2116, South Africa. T. +27118454881. Fax +27118454885.
URL: http://www.africacricket.org/

History Regional council of *International Cricket Council (ICC, #13105)*. Also referred to as *African Cricket Council (ACC)*. **Aims** Develop cricket in Africa from grassroots level. **Structure** Executive Committee, comprising Chairman, Vice-Chairman, Honourable Secretary, Treasurer and Director of Development. **Finance** Members' dues. Sponsorship.
Members Test Playing Nations (2):
South Africa, Zimbabwe.
Associates in 6 countries:
Kenya, Namibia, Nigeria, Tanzania UR, Uganda, Zambia.
Affiliates in xx countries and territories:
Botswana, Gambia, Ghana, Lesotho, Malawi, Morocco, Mozambique, Rwanda, Sierra Leone, St Helena. [2011/XJ0538/**E**]

♦ African Cricket Council / see African Cricket Association (#00279)
♦ African Criminology and Justice Association (internationally oriented national body)
♦ African Crisis Response Initiative / see African Contingency Operations Training and Assistance

♦ African Crop Science Society (ACSS) 00280

Past Pres Dept of Genetics, Fac of Agriculture, Minia Univ, El Minia MINYA, EG-61519, Egypt. T. +20862362182. Fax +20862362182.
URL: http://www.bioline.org.br/cs/

History Founded 1993. **Aims** Promote crop production and *food security* in Africa; foster and promote study of crops in all its facets; foster liaison with other bodies with common or similar interests, both in Africa and abroad; obtain and disseminate knowledge, information and ideas related to crops; promote member works and interests; promote contacts amongst national and regional crop science societies in Africa; encourage scientific training in crop science; promote a general awareness of the environment and use, protect and conserve the environment. **Structure** General Meeting; Council. **Languages** English, French. **Staff** 25.00 FTE, paid. **Finance** Members' dues. Other sources: subscription fees; donations; sales of publications. **Activities** Research/documentation; events/meetings; training/education. **Events** *Biennial Conference* Cape Town (South Africa) 2018, *Biennial Conference* Abuja (Nigeria) 2015, *Biennial Conference / Congress* Entebbe (Uganda) 2013, *International conference for modern agriculture* El Minia (Egypt) 2011, *Biennial conference / Congress* Maputo (Mozambique) 2011. **Publications** *African Crop Science Journal* (4 a year); *ACSS Biweekly News*. Conference proceedings. **Members** Fellow; Honorary; Ordinary; Associate; Student; Institutional. Membership countries not specified. **NGO Relations** Member of: *Global Plant Council (#10550)*. [2017.10.12/XD5908/**D**]

♦ African Crowdfunding Association (unconfirmed)
♦ African Cultural Institute (internationally oriented national body)
♦ African Cultural Institute (inactive)
♦ African Cultural Institute – Association for promoting understanding between people / see Afrika Kulturinstitut
♦ African Curriculum Organization (no recent information)
♦ African Deaf Sports Federation / see Confederation of Africa Deaf Sports (#04498)
♦ **AfricanDefenders** Pan-African Human Rights Defenders Network (#18052)

♦ African Democracy Forum (ADF) 00281

Secretariat c/o Never Again Rwanda, KG 268 St 9 Avenue, PO Box 4969, Kigali, Rwanda. T. +250738302821. E-mail: info@africademocracyforum.org.
URL: http://www.africademocracyforum.org/

History Oct 2000, Abuja (Nigeria). Regional network of *World Movement for Democracy (#21661)*. **Aims** Be an active advocate for democracy, defense and promotion of human rights, good governance and the rule of law. **Structure** General Assembly (annual); Management Committee; Secretariat, headed by Coordinator. **Languages** English, French. **Staff** 2.00 FTE, paid. **Finance** Funding from National Endowment for Democracy. **Activities** Events/meetings; training/education. **Events** *Conference on Democracy in Africa* Kigali (Rwanda) 2018, *Annual Meeting* Monrovia (Liberia) 2007, *Annual meeting* Istanbul (Turkey) 2006, *Annual meeting* Lagos (Nigeria) 2005, *Annual meeting* Durban (South Africa) 2004. **Publications** *ADF Newsletter*. Annual Report. **Members** Individuals and organizations in 54 countries. Membership countries not specified. [2018.06.01/XM1809/**F**]

♦ African Dental Education Association (AfDEA) 00282

Exec Sec Dept of Dentistry, Fac of Medicine/Pharmacy/Dentistry, Univ Cheikh Anta Diop, Dakar, Senegal.
URL: http://ifdea.org/associations/africa.html

History Inaugural meeting, 2007, Dublin (Ireland). Constitution adopted, Sep 2007. **Aims** Promote advancement in dental education, training and research so as to improve oral and general health, especially in the African region. **Structure** General Assembly. Executive Committee. [2009/XJ0001/**D**]

♦ African Dermatovenereology Officers Association (unconfirmed)
♦ African Development Aid Association (internationally oriented national body)
♦ African Development Assistance Consult (internationally oriented national body)

♦ African Development Bank (ADB) 00283

Banque africaine de développement (BAD) – Banco Africano de Desarrollo

SG ADB Headquarters – Immeuble du CCIA, Avenue Jean-Paul II, 01 BP 1387, Abidjan 01, Côte d'Ivoire. T. +22520204444. Fax +22520204959. E-mail: afdb@afdb.org.
Temp Relocation Agency 15 Avenue du Ghana, PO Box 323-1002, Belvedere, Tunis, Tunisia. T. +216171103626. Fax +216171103751.
URL: http://www.afdb.org/

History 4 Aug 1963, Khartoum (Sudan), on adoption of *'Agreement Establishing the African Development Bank'*, signed by African governments and entered into force 10 Sep 1964. First meeting of Board of Governors held 4-7 Nov 1964, Lagos (Nigeria). The Bank began operations on 1 Jul 1966. Initially only independent African state were eligible to become ADB members. Following amendment of the establishment agreement, 7 May 1982, Lusaka (Zambia), membership was opened to non-regional countries. ADB is also known by English initials *AfDB*. Statutes registered in *'UNTS 1/21052'*. Under Article 8 of the agreement establishing ADB, the Bank is authorized to establish or be entrusted with the administering and managing special funds which are consistent with its purposes and functions. In conformity with these provisions, *African Development Fund (ADF, #00285)* was established with non-African states, 29 Nov 1972, Abidjan (Côte d'Ivoire), and *Nigeria Trust Fund (NTF)*, with the Nigerian Government, Feb 1976. The *African Development Bank Group (ADB Group, #00284)* was set up 29 Nov 1972, Abidjan; it currently comprises ADB, ADF and NTF. **Aims** Promote sustainable economic development and social progress in Africa by mobilizing and allocating resources for investment in Member Countries and providing policy advice and technical assistance to support development efforts, particularly for projects that have the strongest poverty reduction impact on the economies and can improve the living conditions of the population.
Structure Annual Meeting, always in May. Board of Governors of the Bank, comprising a Governor and an Alternate Governor representing each member country (usually Ministers of Finance and Planning and high level officials). Board of Directors, consisting of 18 Executive Directors who are neither Governors nor Alternate Governors (12 members elected by Governors of regional member countries and 6 by Governors of non-regional member countries). Field offices (25): Algeria; Angola; Burkina Faso; Cameroon; Chad; Congo DR; Egypt; Gabon; Ghana; Kenya; Madagascar; Malawi; Morocco; Mozambique; Mali; Nigeria; Rwanda; Senegal; Sudan; Sierra Leone; South Africa; Tanzania UR; Uganda; Zimbabwe. Also includes: *African Development Institute (ADI, #00286)*.
Organizational structure as of Dec 2009:
- Presidency, includes: Office of the President and Chief Operation Officer; Departments General Secretariat; Legal Counsel and Legal; Office of the Auditor General with Units (3) – Ombudsman; Security; External Relations and Communication.
- Chief Economist, includes: Departments (2) – Development Research; Statistics.
- Vice-Presidency Operation I – Country and Regional Programmes and Policy, includes Departments (12) – Results and Quality Assurance; Procurement and Fiduciary Services; Operational Resources and Policies; Regional West 1; Regional West 2; Regional East 1; Regional East 2; Regional Center; Regional North 1; Regional North 2; Regional South 1; Regional South 2.
- Unit – Partnerships and Cooperation. Vice-Presidency Operation II – Sector Operations, includes: Departments (3) – Agriculture and Agro Industry; Human Development; Governance, Economic and Financial Reforms; Units (2) – Fragile States; Gender, Climate and Sustainable Development.
- Vice-Presidency Operations III – Infrastructure, Private Sector and Regional Integration, includes: Departments (4) – Infrastructure; Private Sector; Water and Sanitation; NEPAD, Regional Integration and Trade.
- Vice-Presidency Corporate Services, includes: Departments (4) – General Services; Information Management; Human Resources Management; Language Services.
- Vice-Presidency Finance, includes: Departments (3) – Financial Control; Treasury; Financial Management.

Languages English, French. **Staff** 1491.00 FTE, paid. Staff negotiations through *Staff Council of the African Development Bank (#19943)*. **Finance** Authorized capital subscribed to by 77 member countries (53 independent African countries and 24 non-African countries).
Activities Grants non-concessional loans to finance projects and programmes in African member countries, financial charges reflecting the direct cost of funds. Maturities range from 12 to 20 years, including grace periods of up to 5 years. Projects, programmes and studies normally concern several member States or are designed to make their economies increasingly complementary and to bring about an orderly expansion of their foreign trade, namely agricultural, public utilities, transport and communication, industry or social sectors. Non-project lending includes provision of structural adjustment and policy-based loans and various forms of technical assistance and advice.
Current operational priorities:
- *'Infrastructure'* – make investments, especially for transport, power and ICT; secure demonstrable public benefit by improving growth, productivity, employment and access to market opportunities and essential services, particularly where required to accelerate progress toward the MDGs; exercise leadership in the continental initiatives (NEPAD, ICA); accelerate access to improved rural water and sanitation services while addressing the needs of Africa's growing peri-urban and urban populations;
- *'Governance'* – strengthen governance in key areas linked directly to core operational priorities, particularly strengthening transparency and accountability in the management of public resources, at country, sector and regional levels, with special attention to fragile states and natural resources management; choice and mix of instruments are tailored to country circumstances, combining budget support, institution strengthening projects, non-lending operations, and analytical and advisory work;
- *'Private Sector Development'* – effectively seek to utilize its integrated structure by having sovereign, sub-sovereign and non-sovereign instruments at its disposal, including concessionary resources under ADF, to promote private sector led growth; strengthen the articulation of the "development case" and expected results for specific transactions and will develop a model to ensure appropriate assessment of development impact; operational focus on infrastructure, industry and services, financial intermediation and microfinance/SMEs;
- *'Higher Education, Technology and Vocational Training'* – invest to upgrade and rehabilitate existing facilities including national and regional centres of excellence to provide quality tertiary level training to improve the conditions for scientific and technological innovations; develop partnerships with the private sector to design and implement projects to sustain economic and social growth in the RMCs; support technical and vocational education and training operations to build skills to address chronic high unemployment.

ADB administers: *Arab Oil Fund (no recent information)* and Nigeria Trust Fund, set up by Algeria and Nigeria respectively in their roles as members of *Organization of the Petroleum Exporting Countries (OPEC, #17881)*; *Special Emergency Assistance Fund for Drought and Famine in Africa (SEAF, #19908)*; Special Relief Fund. It was instrumental in setting up:
- *Africa Project Development Facility (APDF, inactive)*;
- *African Business Roundtable (ABR, #00232)*;
- *The African Capacity Building Foundation (ACBF, #00233)*;
- *African Export-Import Bank (Afreximbank, #00305)*;
- *African Industrial Development Fund (AIDF)* (with OAU);
- *African Management Services Company (AMSCO, #00367)*;
- *African Reinsurance Corporation (AFRICA RE, #00438)* (with OAU);
- *Association of African Development Finance Institutions (AADFI, #02353)*;
- *Association of African Trading Enterprises (ASATRADE, inactive)*;
- *Company for Habitat and Housing in Africa (Shelter-Afrique, #04408)* (ADB is currently a Class 'B' shareholder member);
- *Federation of African Consultants (FEAC, inactive)*;
- *Joint Africa Institute (JAI, inactive)* (with IMF and IBRD);
- *SIFIDA Investment Company (inactive)*.

Events *Solidarity of Women Entrepreneurs in Africa and Japan* Tokyo (Japan) 2022, *Japan-Africa Business Forum* Tokyo (Japan) 2021, *ACRIS – Africa Climate Resilience Infrastructure Summit* Johannesburg (South Africa) 2019, *Africa Investment Roadshow in Asia Forum* Seoul (Korea Rep) 2019, *Smart Urban Solution Joint Workshop* Seoul (Korea Rep) 2019. **Publications** *ADB Bulletin – Bulletin de la BAD* (4 a year); *African Development Review* (2 a year) in English, French; *ADB Quarterly Review*; *Annual Compendium of Statistics*; *Annual Review of Post-Evaluation Reports*. *Economic Research Papers* – series.
Members Independent African (regional) countries (53):
Algeria, Angola, Benin, Botswana, Burkina Faso, Burundi, Cameroon, Cape Verde, Central African Rep, Chad, Comoros, Congo Brazzaville, Congo DR, Côte d'Ivoire, Djibouti, Egypt, Equatorial Guinea, Eritrea, Eswatini, Ethiopia, Gabon, Gambia, Ghana, Guinea, Guinea-Bissau, Kenya, Lesotho, Liberia, Libya, Madagascar, Malawi, Mali, Mauritania, Mauritius, Morocco, Mozambique, Namibia, Niger, Nigeria, Rwanda, Sao Tomé-Principe, Senegal, Seychelles, Sierra Leone, Somalia, South Africa, Sudan, Tanzania UR, Togo, Tunisia, Uganda, Zambia, Zimbabwe.
Non-African (non-regional) countries (24):
Argentina, Austria, Belgium, Brazil, Canada, China, Denmark, Finland, France, Germany, India, Italy, Japan, Korea Rep, Kuwait, Netherlands, Norway, Portugal, Saudi Arabia, Spain, Sweden, Switzerland, UK, USA.
IGO Relations Special links with: *United Nations Economic Commission for Africa (ECA, #20554)*. Observer to: *Agricultural and Land and Water Use Commission for the Near East (ALAWUC, #00570)*; *Global Bioenergy Partnership (GBEP, #10251)*; *Global Forum on Transparency and Exchange of Information for Tax Purposes (#10379)*; *UNEP (#20299)*. Observer to General Assembly of: *United Nations (UN, #20515)*. Special agreement with: *UNESCO (#20322)*; *ECOSOC (#05331)*. Participates in the activities of: *UNCTAD (#20285)*. Representative in Governing Board of: *UNESCO – International Institute for Capacity Building in Africa (IICBA, #20308)*. In the context of interregional cooperation, established relations with: *Asian Development Bank (ADB, #01422)*; *Inter-American Development Bank (IDB, #11427)*; IBRD. International organizational member of: *CGIAR System Organization (CGIAR, #03843)*. Member of: *Committee of International Development Institutions on the Environment (CIDIE, no recent information)*; *Eastern and Southern African Anti-Money Laundering Group (ESAAMLG, #05252)*; *Trade and Development Bank (TDB, #20181)*; *Eurasian Group on Combating Money Laundering and Financing of Terrorism (EAG, #05608)*; *International Rice Research Institute (IRRI, #14754)*. Provides financial assistance to: *African Regional Centre for Agriculture (inactive)*. Collaborative organization of: *Arab Organization for Agricultural Development (AOAD, #01018)*. Accredited to the Conference of the Parties of: *Secretariat of the United Nations Convention to Combat Desertification (Secretariat of the UNCCD, #19208)*. Accredited by: *United Nations Framework Convention on Climate Change – Secretariat (UNFCCC, #20564)*. Invited to sessions of Intergovernmental Council of: *International Programme for the Development of Communication (IPDC, #14651)*. Multilateral donor of: *Consultative Group to Assist the Poor (CGAP, #04768)*. Involved in: *Africa Partnership Forum (APF, #00510)*; *Facilité africaine de l'eau (FAE, #09233)*. Heads: *Infrastructure Consortium for Africa (ICA, #11206)*. Cooperates with: *United Nations Institute for Training and Research (UNITAR, #20576)*. Supports: *UNESCO Regional Bureau for Education in Africa (BREDA, inactive)*. Instrumental in setting up: *African Legal Support Facility (ALSF, #00361)*; *Anti-Corruption Initiative for Asia and the Pacific (#00852)*; *Global Environment Facility (GEF, #10346)*. Adheres to: *Global Partnership for Effective Development Co-operation (GPEDC, #10532)*. Cooperation agreements with:
- *African Union (AU, #00488)*;
- *Arab Bank for Economic Development in Africa (#00904)*;
- *Arab Maghreb Union (AMU, #01004)*;
- *Banque de développement des Etats de l'Afrique centrale (BDEAC, #03168)*;
- *Economic Community of Central African States (ECCAS, #05311)*;
- *Economic Community of West African States (ECOWAS, #05312)*;
- *ILO (#11123)*;
- *International Bank for Reconstruction and Development (IBRD, #12317)*;
- *International Civil Aviation Organization (ICAO, #12581)*;
- *International Fund for Agricultural Development (IFAD, #13692)*;
- *International Telecommunication Union (ITU, #15673)*;
- *Islamic World Educational, Scientific and Cultural Organization (ICESCO, #16058)*;
- *Norwegian Agency for Development Cooperation (Norad)*;
- *Southern African Development Community (SADC, #19843)*;
- *UNDP (#20292)*;

- *UNIDO (#20336)*;
- *United Nations Development and Technical Cooperation Programme (inactive)*;
- *United Nations Population Fund (UNFPA, #20612)*;
- *WHO (#20950)*;
- *World Food Programme (WFP, #21510)*.

NGO Relations Cooperation agreement with: *International Union for Conservation of Nature and Natural Resources (IUCN, #15766)*. Member of: *Association for Human Resources Management in International Organizations (AHRMIO, #02634)*; *Consultative Group to Assist the Poor (CGAP, #04768)*; *Council of Non-Governmental Organizations for Development Support (#04911)*; *Global Road Safety Partnership (GRSP, #10581)*; *International Network for Environmental Compliance and Enforcement (INECE, #14261)*; *Mountain Partnership (MP, #16862)*; *World Water Council (WWC, #21908)*. Library is member of: *International Federation of Library Associations and Institutions (IFLA, #13470)*. Special assistance to: *African Academy of Sciences (AAS, #00193)*; *Association of African Universities (AAU, #02361)*. Regular relations with: *International Social Security Association (ISSA, #14885)*. Joint sponsor of programme for francophone Africa administered by: *Centre for Studies and Research on International Development, Clermont-Ferrand (CERDI)*. Partner of: *Centre d'étude et de prospective stratégique (CEPS, #03739)*. Instrumental in setting up: *African Development Forum (ADF, inactive)*. Supports: *Africare (#00516)*; *African Institute of Management Science (AIMS)*; *African Rice Initiative (ARI, no recent information)*; *Development Training International (DTI)*; *Forum for Agricultural Research in Africa (FARA, #09897)*; *Regional Agricultural Information Network (RAIN, inactive)*; *Union for African Population Studies (UAPS, #20346)*. [2014/XF0018/F*]

♦ African Development Bank Group (ADB Group) 00284

Groupe de la Banque africaine de développement (Groupe BAD)

Headquarters Rue Joseph Anoma, Abidjan 01, Côte d'Ivoire. T. +22520204444. Fax +22520204959. E-mail: afdb@afdb.org.

Temporary Relocation Agency BP 323, Belvedere, 1002 Tunis, Tunisia. T. +216171333511. Fax +216171351933. E-mail: afdb@afdb.org.

URL: http://www.afdb.org/

History 1964. Inaugural meeting of the Board of Governors of the Bank held 4-7 Nov 1964, Lago (Nigeria). Operations commenced 1 Jul 1966. **Aims** Spur sustainable economic development and social progress in Regional Member Countries (RMCs), thus contributing to *poverty* reduction; mobilize and allocate resources for investment in RMCs; provide policy advice and technical assistance to support development effort. **Structure** Comprises 3 distinct entities: *African Development Bank (ADB, #00283)*, parent institution; *African Development Fund (ADF, #00285)*; *Nigeria Trust Fund (NTF)*. Headquarters opened in Abidjan (Côte d'Ivoire), Mar 1965. Since early 2003, operates from Temporary Relocation Agency (TRA), Tunis (Tunisia). Shareholders comprise 53 African countries (RMCs) and 24 non-African countries (non-RMCs). Board of Governors is the highest policy-making organ, comprising one representative from each member country. Board of Directors, elected by Board of Governors, consisting of 20 members, including 13 from RMCs and 7 from non-RMCs, for a 3-year term, once renewable. President, elected by Board of Governors from among RMCs for 5-year term, once renewable, is also the Chair of the Board of Directors, and appoints Vice-Presidents. **Languages** English, French. **Staff** 787.00 FTE, paid.

Activities Operational activities in 2010 reached 4.10 billion Units of Account (UA). In terms of financing from the Bank Group windows: (i) ADB approved UA 2.58 billion (63%) of which UA 1.21 billion was for private sector operations; (ii) ADF approved UA 1.46 billion (35.5%); (iii) NTF approved UA 29.5 million (.7%). Distribution total approvals among various sectors during 2010 reflected the Bank's adherence to its policy of selectivity, project focus and effectiveness. It also aligned rising demand for infrastructure support from RMCs. In line with the Medium-Term Strategy (MTS), infrastructure ranked first, with an approvals allocation of UA 2.6 billion (70.9%), followed by finance, mostly comprising private sector operations, with UA 319.9 million (8.7%), then multisector, which includes support for governance and public sector management, etc, with UA 301.2 million (8.2%). These 3 sectors jointly accounted for 87.8% of total operational loans and grants.

Emphasis on infrastructure reveals the Bank's selectivity in targeting high impact projects that will create an enabling climate for private sector investment, improve competitiveness and productivity in RMCs, enhance employment opportunities, and support sustainable economic growth. Bank Group loan and grant approvals for the 5 subregions (including multinational projects) totalled UA 3.67 billion. Largest share of approvals allocated to North Africa, with UA 1.47 billion (40.1%), followed by West Africa, UA 595.8 million (16.2%), East Africa, UA 560.3 million (15.2%), Southern Africa, UA 492.8 million (13.4%), Central Africa, UA 234.6 million (6.4%), and multinational, UA 319.1 million (8.7%).

In general, loans were used for accelerating economic growth and reducing poverty, while the lines of credit (LOCs) aimed at deepening domestic financial markets for lending to small- and medium-size enterprise (SMEs). Investments in many sizeable multinational projects and programmes took the form of loans, LOCs, and private equity; these supported economic cooperation and regional integration, thereby improving the investment climate on the continent.

Events *AEC : African Economic Conference* Cape Verde 2021, *AEC : African Economic Conference* Addis Ababa (Ethiopia) 2020, *ACF : Africa Carbon Forum* Accra (Ghana) 2019, *AEC : African Economic Conference* Sharm el Sheikh (Egypt) 2019, *AEC : African Economic Conference* Kigali (Rwanda) 2018. **Publications** *African Economic Outlook*. Annual Report.

Members totally 77 Member States. RMCs (53):

Algeria, Angola, Benin, Botswana, Burkina Faso, Burundi, Cameroon, Cape Verde, Central African Rep, Chad, Comoros, Congo Brazzaville, Congo DR, Côte d'Ivoire, Djibouti, Egypt, Equatorial Guinea, Eritrea, Eswatini, Ethiopia, Gabon, Gambia, Ghana, Guinea, Guinea-Bissau, Kenya, Lesotho, Liberia, Libya, Madagascar, Malawi, Mali, Mauritania, Mauritius, Morocco, Mozambique, Namibia, Niger, Nigeria, Rwanda, Sao Tomé-Principe, Senegal, Seychelles, Sierra Leone, Somalia, South Africa, Sudan, Tanzania UR, Togo, Tunisia, Uganda, Zambia, Zimbabwe.

Non RMCs (24):

Argentina, Austria, Brazil, Canada, Chile, China, Denmark, Finland, France, Germany, India, Italy, Japan, Korea Rep, Kuwait, Netherlands, Norway, Portugal, Saudi Arabia, Spain, Sweden, Switzerland, UK, USA.

IGO Relations Formal cooperation with the following multilateral institutions:
- *African Management Services Company (AMSCO, #00367)*;
- *Arab Bank for Economic Development in Africa (#00904)*;
- *ILO (#11123)*;
- *International Bank for Reconstruction and Development (IBRD, #12317)*;
- *International Civil Aviation Organization (ICAO, #12581)*;
- *International Fund for Agricultural Development (IFAD, #13692)*;
- *International Telecommunication Union (ITU, #15673)*;
- *UNEP (#20299)*;
- *UNESCO (#20322)*;
- *UNIDO (#20336)*;
- *United Nations Development and Technical Cooperation Programme (inactive)*;
- *United Nations Economic Commission for Africa (ECA, #20554)*;
- *WHO (#20950)*;
- *World Food Programme (WFP, #21510)*.

Formal cooperation arrangements with the following Africa-based regional organizations:
- *Africa Rice Center (AfricaRice, #00518)*;
- *African Union (AU, #00488)*;
- *Banque de développement des Etats de l'Afrique centrale (BDEAC, #03168)*;
- *Banque ouest africaine de développement (BOAD, #03170)*;
- *East African Development Bank (EADB, #05183)*;
- *Inter-African Coffee Organization (IACO, #11383)*.

Also cooperates with:
- *Organisation of African, Caribbean and Pacific States (OACPS, #17796)*;
- *ECOWAS Bank for Investment and Development (EBID, #05334)*;
- *Intergovernmental Authority on Development (IGAD, #11472)*;
- *International Development Association (IDA, #13155)*;
- *Islamic Development Bank (IsDB, #16044)*;
- *League of Arab States (LAS, #16420)*;
- *Multilateral Investment Guarantee Agency (MIGA, #16888)*;
- *Nordic Development Fund (NDF, #17271)*;
- *OPEC Fund for International Development (OFID, #17745)*;
- *Regional African Satellite Communications Organization (RASCOM, #18748)*.

Technical and economic cooperation and co-financing are implemented with such financial development institutions as:
- World Bank;
- BADEA;
- *Inter-American Development Bank (IDB, #11427)*;
- UNDP;
- *United States Agency for International Development (USAID)*.

Regional integration emphasized through assistance to: *Economic Community of Central African States (ECCAS, #05311)*; *Communauté économique des pays des Grands Lacs (CEPGL, #04375)*; *Economic Community of West African States (ECOWAS, #05312)*; *Mano River Union (MRU, #16566)*; *Southern African Development Community (SADC, #19843)*.

NGO Relations Works closely with: *Association of African Development Finance Institutions (AADFI, #02353)*. [2011.12.08/XF0121/F*]

♦ African Development and Emergency Organization (internationally oriented national body)

♦ African Development Foundation (internationally oriented national body)

♦ African Development Fund (ADF) 00285

Fonds africain de développement (FAD) – Fondo Africano de Desarrollo

Headquarters Rue Joseph Anoma 01, Abidjan 01, Côte d'Ivoire. T. +22520204444. Fax +22520204959. E-mail: afdb@afdb.org.

Temp Relocation Agency 15 Ave du Ghana, PO Box 323-1002, Belvedere, Tunis, Tunisia. T. +21671102805. Fax +21671103751.

URL: http://www.afdb.org/

History 29 Nov 1972, Abidjan (Côte d'Ivoire), on signature of an agreement during a Conference of Plenipotentiaries of *African Development Bank (ADB, #00283)*, with which organization, together with *Nigeria Trust Fund (NTF)*, it comprises *African Development Bank Group (ADB Group, #00284)*. Agreement entered into force 10 Jun 1973. Formally inaugurated at 9th Annual Meeting of ADB, Jul 1973, Lusaka (Zambia). Commenced operations 1 Aug 1973, and first loan granted 16 Jan 1974. Also referred to by English and French initials *AfDF – FAfD*. Statutes registered in *'UNTS/1 19019'*. **Aims** Reduce poverty and promote economic and social development in regional Member Countries, particularly in the 38 least-developed African countries, by providing concessional funding for projects and programmes, as well as technical assistance for studies and capacity-building activities. **Structure** Board of Governors comprises the Governors and Alternate Governors of the Bank, who are *'ex-officio'* Governors and Alternate Governors of the Fund. Board of Directors comprises 12 Directors, of whom 6 are designated by the Bank from among its regional Executive Directors and 6 appointed by state participants. President of the Bank is *'ex-officio'* President of the Fund and Chairman of its Board of Directors. ADB and ADF each have 1,000 votes in the ADB Group. **Finance** Main source: contributions and periodic replenishments by members. Other sources include funds derived from operations or otherwise accruing. Periodic replenishments from participants: ADF-I, about US$ 327 million, covered the operational period 1976-1978; ADF-II, US$ 712 million, covered 1979-1981; ADF-III, about US$ 1,000 million, covered 1982-1984; ADF-IV, about US$ 1,500 million, covered 1985-1987; ADF-V, about US$ 2,800 million, 1988-1990; ADF-VI, about US$ 3,420 million, 1991-1993; ADF-VII, about US$ 3,200 million, 1996-1998; ADF-VIII, about US$ 3,100 million, 1999-2001; ADF-IX, about US$ 3,507 million, 2002-2004; ADF-X, about US$ 4,628 million, 2005-2007; ADJ-XI, about US$ 8,900 million, 2008-2010. **Activities** As the main concessional "window" of the ADB Group, provides loans repayable over 50 years, including a 10-year grace period, carrying a service charge of only 0.75% per annum. Core strategic priorities for ADJ-XI: infrastructure; governance; fragile states; regional integration. Resources are largely directed to the 38 low-income member countries of the Group which do not normally qualify for ADB non-concessional resources and are allocated according to 3 principles: focus on poverty reduction; improvement in development effectiveness; targeting countries with a demonstrable commitment to poverty reduction. Funds are mainly used for project and technical assistance financing and for studies. **Events** *Annual meeting* Busan (Korea Rep) 2018, *Annual meeting* Abidjan (Côte d'Ivoire) 2010, *Annual meeting* Dakar (Senegal) 2009, *Annual meeting* Dakar (Senegal) 2009, *Annual meeting* Maputo (Mozambique) 2008.

Members State participants (25 non-African states):

Argentina, Austria, Belgium, Brazil, Canada, China, Denmark, Finland, France, Germany, India, Italy, Japan, Korea Rep, Kuwait, Netherlands, Norway, Portugal, Saudi Arabia, Spain, Sweden, Switzerland, UK, United Arab Emirates, USA.

Corporate member (1):

African Development Bank.

IGO Relations Together with African Development Bank, has cooperation agreement with: *United Nations Population Fund (UNFPA, #20612)*. **NGO Relations** Member of: *EarthAction (EA, #05159)*. [2013/XF6183/f/F*]

♦ African Development Institute (ADI) 00286

Institut africain de développement

Dir 15 Avenue du Ghana, PO Box 323-1002, Tunis, Tunisia. T. +21671103900 – +21671351933. E-mail: adiinfo@afdb.org.

URL: http://www.afdb.org/en/knowledge/african-development-institute/

History as the training branch of *African Development Bank (ADB, #00283)*. Also referred to as *EADI*. **Aims** Develop the capacity of the African Development Bank's regional member countries officials and national experts to manage their economies. **Activities** Events/meetings; training/education. **Information Services** *Knowledge and Virtual Resources Centre (KVRC)*. **IGO Relations** Organizes training courses with: *World Trade Organization (WTO, #21864)*. Collaborates with: *International Fund for Agricultural Development (IFAD, #13692)*; *OECD (#17693)*. Partner of: *African Management Services Company (AMSCO, #00367)*; *ILO (#11123)*; *International Monetary Fund (IMF, #14180)*; *Islamic Development Bank (IsDB, #16044)*; *United Nations Economic Commission for Africa (ECA, #20554)*; *World Bank Institute (WBI, #21220)*; other organizations in the United Nations system. **NGO Relations** Partner of: *The African Capacity Building Foundation (ACBF, #00233)*; *African Economic Research Consortium (AERC, #00292)*; *Association of African Development Finance Institutions (AADFI, #02353)*. [2015/XE4183/j/E*]

♦ African Development Programme (internationally oriented national body)

♦ African Development Solutions (Adeso) 00287

Headquarters PO Box 70331-00400, Nairobi, Kenya. T. +254208000881. E-mail: info@adesoafrica.org.

USA Office 1875 Connecticut Ave NW, 10th Fl, Washington DC 20009, USA.

UK Office CAN Mezzanine, 49-51 East Road, London, N1 6AH, UK.

URL: http://adesoafrica.org/

History 1991, in the State of Connecticut (USA), as *Horn of Africa Relief and Development Organization*. By 1998, simply known as *Horn Relief*. Current title adopted 2011. Registration: Kenya; 501c3, USA; Charity, No/ID: 1131711, England and Wales. **Aims** Work towards an Africa that is not dependent on aid, but on the *resourcefulness* and capabilities of its people. **Structure** Board. Headquarters in Kenya; Offices in UK and USA. **Consultative Status** Consultative status granted from: *ECOSOC (#05331)* (Special). **NGO Relations** Member of: *InsideNGO (inactive)*; *Start Network (#19969)*. [2020/XJ9887/F]

♦ African Dialogue Group / see Democrat Union of Africa (#05036)

♦ African Diaspora Policy Centre (internationally oriented national body)

♦ African Diaspora Youth Forum in Europe (unconfirmed)

♦ African Diaspora Youth Network in Europe (ADYNE) 00288

Contact Place Gaucheret 10, 1030 Brussels, Belgium.

History Dec 2009, Almada (Portugal), at the conclusion of a workshop. **Aims** Connect organizations and individuals to collaborate and actively participate as global citizens to shape the lives of young people of the African diaspora in Europe. **Structure** Board. **Activities** *African Diaspora Youth Forum in Europe (ADYFE)*. **Events** *Annual Forum* Vienna (Austria) 2017, *Annual Forum* Vienna (Austria) 2016, *Annual Forum* Vienna (Austria) 2015, *Annual Forum* Vienna (Austria) 2014. **Members** Full; Partner; Corporate; Individual (Associate; Affiliate; Professional; Honorary). Membership countries not specified. **NGO Relations** Member of: *European Network against Racism (ENAR, #07862)*. [2018/XJ8277/F]

♦ African Digital Libraries Support Network / see African Digital Library Support Network (#00289)

♦ African Digital Library Support Network (ADLSN) 00289
Contact PO Box 150057, Addis Ababa, Ethiopia. E-mail: info@adlsn.org.
URL: https://adlsn.org/
History Serves as an advanced and expanded version of the *Southern Africa Greenstone Support Network (SAGSN)*, set up 2007. Also referred to as *African Digital Libraries Support Network*. **Aims** Facilitate access to local digital content in Africa. **Structure** Governing Board; National Centres; Local Support Communities. **Languages** English, French. **Staff** 15.00 FTE, voluntary. **Finance** External and self-financing. **Activities** Training/education; advocacy/lobbying/activism.
Members Centres in 13 countries:
Cameroon, Ethiopia, Ghana, Kenya, Lesotho, Malawi, Mauritius, Namibia, Nigeria, Senegal, Tanzania UR, Uganda, Zimbabwe.
IGO Relations *African Union (AU, #00488)*; *UNESCO (#20322)*. **NGO Relations** Digital Divide Data.
[2018/XJ7074/F]

♦ African Dignity Foundation (internationally oriented national body)
♦ African Econometric Society (inactive)

♦ African Economic Community (AEC) 00290
Communauté économique africaine
Contact c/o African Union, PO Box 3243, Roosvelt Street (Old Airport Area) W21K19, Addis Ababa, Ethiopia. T. +251115517700. Fax +251115517844.
History 3 Jun 1991, Abuja (Nigeria), during 27th ordinary session of *Organization of African Unity (OAU, inactive)*, on adoption of *Treaty Establishing the African Economic Community (Abuja treaty, 1991)* by Heads of State and Government. The Treaty came into force in May 1994, following its ratification by the required two-thirds of OAU Member States. Regional economic communities consolidating and acting as engines for integration: CENSAD; *Arab Maghreb Union (AMU, #01004)*; *Common Market for Eastern and Southern Africa (COMESA, #04296)*; *Economic Community of Central African States (ECCAS, #05311)*; *Economic Community of West African States (ECOWAS, #05312)*; *Intergovernmental Authority on Development (IGAD, #11472)*; *Southern African Development Community (SADC, #19843)*. Will be part of the *African Union (AU, #00488)*, which superseded the OAU in Jul 2002. Not yet operational. Has also been referred to as *Continental Common Market*. **Aims** Set up a common market built on the regional economic communities; promote economic, social and cultural development and African economic integration so as to increase self-sufficiency and endogenous development; create a framework for development and human and materials mobilization; promote cooperation and development in all aspects of human activity with a view to raising living standards, maintaining economic stability and establishing close and peaceful relations among member states; coordinate and harmonize policies among existing and future economic communities. **Structure** Bodies: Conference of Heads of State or Government (annual); Council of Ministers – OAU Council of Ministers – (meets twice a year); Pan-African Parliament – election of its members by continental universal suffrage; Economic and Social Commission (that of the OAU); Court of Justice; General Secretariat (that of the OAU); Specialized Technical Committees (7) on: Rural Economy and Agriculture; Monetary and Financial Affairs; Trade, Customs and Immigration; Industry, Science and Technology, Energy, Natural Resources and Environment; Transport, Communications and Tourism; Health, Work and Social Affairs; Education, Culture and Human Resources. **Activities** Regional economic communities are working at economic development and integration and promoting peace through conflict resolution in their regions. They aim to achieve the setting up of the Community by coordination, harmonization and progressive integration over a period of 34 years, taking place progressively in 6 stages: Reinforcement of regional economic communities (5 years); Stabilization of tariffs, and other barriers to intra-community exchanges and reinforcement of sectorial integration (8 years); Creation of free trade area (10 years); Creation of African customs union (2 years); Creation of African common market (4 years); Consolidation of common market (5 years). The final stage (in about 2025) provides for the establishment of a *Pan-African Parliament (PAP, #18058)*. **Events** *Ordinary session* Lusaka (Zambia) 2001, *Ordinary session* Tripoli (Libyan AJ) 2001.
Members Governments of 53 countries:
Algeria, Angola, Benin, Botswana, Burkina Faso, Burundi, Cameroon, Cape Verde, Central African Rep, Chad, Comoros, Congo Brazzaville, Congo DR, Côte d'Ivoire, Djibouti, Egypt, Equatorial Guinea, Eritrea, Eswatini, Ethiopia, Gabon, Gambia, Ghana, Guinea, Guinea-Bissau, Kenya, Lesotho, Liberia, Libya, Madagascar, Malawi, Mali, Mauritania, Mauritius, Mozambique, Namibia, Niger, Nigeria, Rwanda, Sahara West, Sao Tomé-Principe, Senegal, Seychelles, Sierra Leone, Somalia, South Africa, Sudan, Tanzania UR, Togo, Tunisia, Uganda, Zambia, Zimbabwe.
IGO Relations Special links with: *United Nations Economic Commission for Africa (ECA, #20554)*; *African Development Bank (ADB, #00283)*.
[2008/XF2245/F*]

♦ African Economic History Network (AEHN) 00291
Contact address not obtained. E-mail: aehnetwork@gmail.com.
URL: https://www.aehnetwork.org/
History 2011. **Aims** Foster communication, collaboration and research as well as teaching amongst scholars studying the long-term development of sub-Saharan Africa, from the pre-colonial era to the present-day. **Structure** Board. **Finance** Supported by: *European Research Council (ERC, #08364)*; Riksbankens Jubileumsfond; Wageningen University. **Activities** Events/meetings. **Events** *Annual Meeting* Bloemfontein (South Africa) 2020, *Annual Meeting* Barcelona (Spain) 2019. **Publications** *AEHN Newsletter* (6 a year). *AEHN Working Papers. The History of African Development* – online.
[2020/AA0651/F]

♦ African Economic Research Consortium (AERC) 00292
Consortium pour la recherche économique en Afrique (CREA)
Contact 3rd Floor, Middle East Bank Towers Bldg, Milimani Road, PO Box 62882 00200, Nairobi, Kenya. T. +254202734157 – +254202734150. Fax +254202734170. E-mail: exec.dir@aercafrica.org.
URL: http://www.aercafrica.org/
History Aug 1988, following initiatives from 1984, as a consortium of national and international economic researchers supported by donors, lateral governments and international organizations. **Aims** Strengthen local capacity for conducting independent, rigorous enquiry into problems pertinent to the management of economies in *Sub-Saharan Africa*. **Structure** Board of Directors; Advisory Committee; Secretariat. **Finance** Sources: lateral governments; foundations; international development agencies/organizations; donors. **Activities** Research on: poverty, income distribution and labour market issues; trade, regional integration and sectoral policies; macroeconomic policies, stabilization and growth; finance, resource mobilization and investment. Educational activities, including MA and PhD Programmes, conferences, symposia, seminars, technical workshops and visiting scholar programmes. Research workshops; grants, scholarships and institutional support to public universities. **Events** *Senior Policy Seminar* Harare (Zimbabwe) 2019, *Senior Policy Seminar* Entebbe (Uganda) 2018, *Senior Policy Seminar* Abidjan (Côte d'Ivoire) 2017, *Plenary meeting on globalization and Africa* Nairobi (Kenya) 2000, *Symposium on remote sensing and GIS for monitoring soils and geomorphic processes to assist integrated development of mountainous land* Kathmandu (Nepal) 1999. **Publications** *AERC Newsletter* (2 a year); *Research News* (2 a year). Annual Report; research papers; special papers; brochures; abstracts; teaching manuals; workshop proceedings. Maintains a library/resource centre.
Members Includes 13 supporting member organizations listed in this Yearbook:
African Capacity Building Foundation; African Development Bank; *DANIDA*; *Department for International Development (DFID, inactive)*; *European Union (EU, #08967)*; *Ford Foundation (#09858)*; *International Bank for Reconstruction and Development (IBRD, #12317)* (World Bank); *MacArthur Foundation*; *Norwegian Agency for Development Cooperation (Norad)*; *Swedish International Development Cooperation Agency (Sida)*; *Swiss Agency for Development and Cooperation (SDC)*; *The Rockefeller Foundation (#18966)*; *United States Agency for International Development (USAID)*.
IGO Relations Involved in African Capacity Building Initiative of: World Bank, *UNDP (#20292)* and *African Development Bank (ADB, #00283)*. Non-member funding from: *European Commission (EC, #06633)*. Partner of: *African Development Institute (ADI, #00286)*. **NGO Relations** Assists: *African Centre for Monetary Studies (ACMS, inactive)*; African Economics Association (no recent information). Houses: *African Agricultural Economics Education Network (AAEEN, #00198)*. Regional organization: *Eastern and Southern African Economics Association* (no recent information). Founding member of: *Global Research Consortium on Economic Structural Transformation (GReCEST)*. Member of: *International Center for Economic Growth (ICEG, inactive)*; *Organization for Social Science Research in Eastern and Southern Africa (OSSREA, #17888)*. Non-member funding from: *The African Capacity Building Foundation (ACBF, #00233)*. Regional Network of: *Global Development Network (GDN, #10318)*. *International Lawyers and Economists Against Poverty (ILEAP, #14006)*.
[2010/XF2467/y/F]

♦ African Editors' Forum (TAEF) 00293
Chair CNP-RZ, 04 BP 8524, Ouagadougou 04, Burkina Faso.
SG address not obtained.
History 2003, South Africa. Formally launched, Apr 2004, Kinshasa (Congo DR). **Structure** Management Committee, comprising Chairman, Deputy-Chairman, Secretary-General and Treasurer. **Events** *Conference* Chad 2014, *Conference* Kigali (Rwanda) 2012, *Conference* Johannesburg (South Africa) 2005.
[2012/XM1959/F]

♦ African Educational Research Network (AERN) 00294
Managing Editor Department of Teacher Education, Albany State University, Albany GA 31705, USA. T. +12294304737. Fax +12294304993.
URL: http://www.africanresearch.org/
History 1992. **Aims** Support research capacity building in African *universities*; increase access of Northern universities to the information resources dealing with general education and human development issues in and about Africa. **Structure** Senior Academic Officers (2); Managing Editor; Senior Editors (5); Production Editors (4); Corresponding Editor. Consulting Editors and Advisory Committee, comprising 10 members. **Finance** Contribution from member institutions. **Activities** Holds summit (annual, always in April). **Events** *Annual Summit* Nkozi (Uganda) 2009, *Annual Summit* Uganda 2009, *Annual Summit* Botswana 2008, *Annual Summit* Windhoek (Namibia) 2008, *Annual Summit* Athens, OH (USA) 2007. **Publications** *The African Symposium (TAS)* (2 a year) – online journal.
Members Universities (14) in 11 countries:
Canada, Ethiopia, Ghana, Kenya, Lesotho, Namibia, Nigeria, Uganda, UK, USA, Zimbabwe.
NGO Relations African and American universities.
[2008.09.23/XF4548/F]

♦ African Electrotechnical Standardization Commission (AFSEC) 00295
Commission électrotechnique africaine de normalisation
Exec Sec address not obtained. T. +201223272761. E-mail: secretariat@afsec-africa.org – info@afsec-africa.org.
URL: http://www.afsec-africa.org/
History Founded Feb 2008, Accra (Ghana), following collaborative effort among stakeholders since 2005, and underpinned by a Declaration of the Conference of African Ministers of Energy, 17 Feb 2008, Algiers (Algeria). **Aims** Identify existing standards and prioritize needs; harmonize existing standards through either adoption of international standards or – where necessary – their adaptation to African conditions; where necessary, identify draft standards to be developed by members for adoption; recommend harmonized standards for application by the appropriate bodies of the African Union. **Structure** General Assembly/Council; Management Committee. Regions: West Africa; North Africa; East Africa; Southern Africa; Central Africa; *Association of Power Utilities in Africa (APUA, #02867)*; *African Energy Commission (AFREC, #00298)*. Technical Committees; Secretariat. **Languages** Arabic, English, French, Portuguese. **Staff** 0.50 FTE, paid. **Finance** Members' dues. Other sources: sponsorships; voluntary contributions. **Activities** Standards/guidelines. **Events** *Africa Smart Grid Forum* Kigali (Rwanda) 2018, *General Assembly* Cairo (Egypt) 2016, *Joint Conformity Assessment Seminar* Accra (Ghana) 2015, *General Assembly* Kinshasa (Congo DR) 2014, *Joint Conformity Assessment Seminar* Lubumbashi (Congo DR) 2014. **Publications** *AFSEC Newsletter* (3 a year).
Members Statutory in 14 countries:
Benin, Congo DR, Côte d'Ivoire, Egypt, Ghana, Kenya, Libya, Namibia, Nigeria, Rwanda, Senegal, South Africa, Sudan, Zambia.
Affiliate members (6):
African Energy Commission (AFREC, #00298); *Association of Power Utilities in Africa (APUA, #02867)*; *Eastern Africa Power Pool (EAPP, #05226)*; *Power Institute for East and Southern Africa (PIESA, #18474)*; Southern African Development Community Standardization Expert Group (SADCSTAN); *Southern African Power Pool (SAPP, #19858)*.
IGO Relations Cooperates with: *African Union (AU, #00488)* through *Pan African Quality Infrastructure (PAQI)* and Commission for Infrastructure and Energy. Observer member of: *Intra-Africa Metrology System (AFRIMETS, #15992)*. **NGO Relations** Cooperates with: *European Committee for Electrotechnical Standardization (CENELEC, #06647)*; *International Electrotechnical Commission (IEC, #13255)*. [2019/XJ2230/y/D]

♦ African Elephant Coalition (EAC) 00296
Coalition pour l'Éléphant d'Afrique (CEA)
Contact address not obtained. T. +254739085276. E-mail: info@africanelephantcoalition.org.
Facebook: https://www.facebook.com/africanelephantcoalition/
History Established 7 Feb 2008, Bamako (Mali), through Bamako Declaration. **Aims** Have a viable and healthy elephant population free of threats from international ivory trade. **Structure** Council of Elders. **Events** *Summit* Nairobi (Kenya) 2019, *Summit* Addis Ababa (Ethiopia) 2018, *Summit* Montreux (Switzerland) 2016, *Summit* Cotonou (Benin) 2015, *Summit* Gaborone (Botswana) 2013.
Members Countries (32):
Benin, Burkina Faso, Burundi, Cameroon, Central African Rep, Chad, Comoros, Congo Brazzaville, Congo DR, Côte d'Ivoire, Equatorial Guinea, Eritrea, Ethiopia, Gabon, Gambia, Ghana, Guinea, Guinea-Bissau, Kenya, Liberia, Mali, Mauritania, Niger, Nigeria, Rwanda, Senegal, Sierra Leone, Somalia, South Sudan, Sudan, Togo, Uganda.
IGO Relations *African Elephant Fund (AEF, #00297)*; *Convention on International Trade in Endangered Species of Wild Fauna and Flora (CITES, 1973)*. **NGO Relations** Partners include: *David Shepherd Wildlife Foundation*; *Franz Weber Foundation*; *Humane Society International (HSI, #10966)*; *International Fund for Animal Welfare (IFAW, #13693)*.
[2019/XM8473/D*]

♦ African Elephant Fund (AEF) 00297
Contact c/o UN Environment, PO Box Box 30552-00100, Nairobi, Kenya. E-mail: unenvironment-africanelephantfund@un.org.
URL: http://www.africanelephantfund.org/
Aims Ensure a secure future for African elephants and their habitats by reducing poaching incidences, maintaining elephant habitats and influencing relevant policies. **Structure** Steering Committee. **Finance** Donors: Belgium; China; *European Commission (EC, #06633)*; France; Germany; Netherlands; South Africa; UK. **Events** *Meeting* Accra (Ghana) 2019. **Publications** Newsletter (3 a year).
Members Countries having adopted the African Elephant Action Plan (37):
Angola, Benin, Botswana, Burkina Faso, Cameroon, Central African Rep, Chad, Congo Brazzaville, Congo DR, Côte d'Ivoire, Equatorial Guinea, Eritrea, Eswatini, Ethiopia, Gabon, Ghana, Guinea, Guinea-Bissau, Kenya, Liberia, Malawi, Mali, Mozambique, Namibia, Niger, Nigeria, Rwanda, Senegal, Sierra Leone, Somalia, South Africa, Sudan, Tanzania UR, Togo, Uganda, Zambia, Zimbabwe.
Ex-Officio members (3):
Convention on International Trade in Endangered Species of Wild Fauna and Flora (CITES, 1973) (Monitoring the Illegal Killing of Elephants Programme MIKE); *Convention on the Conservation of Migratory Species of Wild Animals (Bonn Convention, 1979)*; *UNEP (#20299)*.
IGO Relations *African Elephant Coalition (EAC, #00296)*; *UNEP (#20299)*.
[2019/XM8474/f/F*]

♦ African Energy Commission (AFREC) 00298
Commission africaine de l'energie
Exec Dir 2 rue Chenoua, BP 791, Hydra, 16035 Algiers, Algeria. T. +21321694868. Fax +21321692083. E-mail: afrec@africa-union.org – afrienergy@yahoo.com.
URL: http://www.afrec-energy.org/
History Officially launched 17 Feb 2008, Algiers (Algeria), following meetings organized by *African Union (AU, #00488)*, dating back to 1980. Previously known under the acronym *AEC*. **Aims** Ensure, coordinate and harmonize protection, preservation, development and national exploitation, marketing and integration of energy *resources* of the African continent. **Structure** Officers: Executive Director; Head of Energy Policy, Planning and Strategy; Principal Policy Officer. **Languages** Arabic, English, French. **Staff** 7.00 FTE, paid. **Finance** Supported by the African Union Commission. Annual Budget: US$ 800,000. **Activities** Knowledge management/information dissemination; networking/liaising; publishing activities; training/education; capacity building. **Events** *Africa Smart Grid Forum* Kigali (Rwanda) 2018. **Publications** *AFREC Newsletter* (2 a year). Information Services: Maintains databases.
Members All 54 African States:

Algeria, Angola, Benin, Botswana, Burkina Faso, Burundi, Cameroon, Cape Verde, Central African Rep, Chad, Comoros, Congo Brazzaville, Congo DR, Côte d'Ivoire, Djibouti, Egypt, Equatorial Guinea, Eritrea, Eswatini, Ethiopia, Gabon, Gambia, Ghana, Guinea, Guinea-Bissau, Kenya, Lesotho, Liberia, Libya, Madagascar, Malawi, Mali, Mauritania, Mauritius, Morocco, Mozambique, Namibia, Niger, Nigeria, Rwanda, Sao Tomé-Principe, Senegal, Seychelles, Sierra Leone, Somalia, South Africa, South Sudan, Sudan, Tanzania UR, Togo, Tunisia, Uganda, Zambia, Zimbabwe.
IGO Relations Member of: *Global Bioenergy Partnership (GBEP, #10251).* Memorandum of Understanding with: *Regional Center for Renewable Energy and Energy Efficiency (RCREEE, #18754).* **NGO Relations** *Association of Power Utilities in Africa (APUA, #02867)* is member. Represented in *African Electrotechnical Standardization Commission (AFSEC, #00295).* [2018.09.23/XJ2251/**E***]

♦ African Engineering Education Association (AEEA) 00299

Pres Univ of Lagos – Dept of Engr/Civil/Envir, Akoka, University Road, Lagos, Nigeria. E-mail: president@aeeaonline.org.
URL: http://www.aeeaonline.org/
History following 3rd African Regional Conference on Engineering Education (ARCEE), Sep 2006, Pretoria (South Africa). **Aims** Enhance engineering education in Africa. **Structure** Officers: President; 4 Vice-Presidents (Central Africa, East Africa, North Africa, Southern Africa); Secretary-General. **Languages** Arabic, English, French. **Finance** Members' dues. **Activities** Training/education; events/meetings. **Events** *International Conference* Lagos (Nigeria) 2019, *African Regional Conference on Engineering Education* Bloemfontein (South Africa) 2016, *Global Education Forum* Dubai (United Arab Emirates) 2016, *Global Education Forum* Dubai (United Arab Emirates) 2015, *Workshop* Lagos (Nigeria) 2015. **Publications** Conference and workshop proceedings.
Members Institutions in 4 countries:
Libya, Nigeria, South Africa, Tanzania UR.
Individuals in 19 countries:
Algeria, Burkina Faso, Cameroon, Canada, Denmark, Egypt, France, Ghana, Kenya, Libya, Malawi, Morocco, Namibia, Nigeria, Sierra Leone, South Africa, Uganda, USA, Zimbabwe.
NGO Relations Member of: *International Federation of Engineering Education Societies (IFEES, #13412).* [2019.02.06/XJ1439/**E**]

♦ African Engineers Forum (AEF) 00300

Contact c/o SAICE, SAICE House, Private Bag X200, Halfway House, Midrand, 1685, South Africa. E-mail: civilinfo@saice.org.za.
URL: http://www.africaengineersforum.org/
History 1995. **Aims** Ensure an appropriate level of efficient human resource capacity in the built environment professions but in particular engineering, so as to enable Africa to ultimately achieve sustainable development for all the people of Africa.
Members Full in 20 countries:
Angola, Botswana, Congo DR, Eswatini, Ghana, Kenya, Lesotho, Malawi, Maldives, Mauritius, Mozambique, Namibia, Nigeria, Seychelles, South Africa, Tanzania UR, Tunisia, Uganda, Zambia, Zimbabwe.
NGO Relations Member of: *World Council of Civil Engineers (WCCE, #21321).* [2013/XJ6404/**F**]

- ♦ African Enterprise Fund (inactive)
- ♦ African Entrepreneur Collective (internationally oriented national body)
- ♦ African Environmental Law and Policy Association (inactive)

♦ Africa Network for Animal Welfare (ANAW) 00301

CEO Ste 2 – 1st Floor, Westend Place Bldg, Mai Mahiu Rd Off Mbagathi, Lang'ata Round About, PO Box 3731, Nairobi, 00506, Kenya. T. +25426006510. Fax +25426006961. E-mail: info@anaw.org.
Exec Dir USA Office Posner Ctr for Intl Development, 1031 33rd St Suite 174, Denver CO 80205, USA. E-mail: info@anaw-usa.org.
URL: http://www.anaw.org/
History 2006. **Aims** Work with communities, governments, partners and other stakeholders across Africa to promote *humane* treatment of all animals. **Activities** Advocacy/lobbying/activism; awareness raising; capacity building; humanitarian/emergency aid; networking/liaising; training/education. **Consultative Status** Consultative status granted from: *ECOSOC (#05331)* (Special); *UNEP (#20299).* [2021.08.31/XM6774/**F**]

♦ Africa Network Campaign on Education for All (ANCEFA) 00302

Réseau Africain de Campagne pour l'Education pour Tous
Regional Office Amitié III Villa 4566 B, BP 3007, Dakar, Senegal. T. +221338242244. Fax +2218241363. E-mail: ancefa@orange.sn.
URL: http://www.ancefa.org/
History 2001. **Aims** Promote, enable and build capacity of African civil society to advocate and campaign for access to free quality education for all.
Members National organizations (27) in 27 countries:
Angola, Benin, Burkina Faso, Burundi, Cameroon, Chad, Congo Brazzaville, Congo DR, Côte d'Ivoire, Egypt, Ethiopia, Gambia, Ghana, Kenya, Liberia, Malawi, Mali, Mozambique, Niger, Nigeria, Senegal, Sierra Leone, Sudan, Tanzania UR, Togo, Uganda, Zambia.
Consultative Status Consultative status granted from: *UNESCO (#20322)* (Associate Status). **IGO Relations** Key partner of: *United Nations Girls' Education Initiative (UNGEI, #20566).* **NGO Relations** Member of: *Global Campaign for Education (GCE, #10264); End Corporal Punishment (#05457); Inter-agency Network for Education in Emergencies (INEE, #11387).* Regional member of: *International Council for Adult Education (ICAE, #12983).* Supported by: *ActionAid (#00087); Oxfam GB.* Supports: *Forum for African Women Educationalists (FAWE, #09896).* Hosts *Global Call for Action Against Poverty (GCAP, #10263)* Office for Africa. [2021/XF7169/**F**]

♦ Africa Network of Young Peace-Builders (ANYP) 00303

Intl Coordinator UNOY, Africa Desk, Laan v Meerdervoort 70, 2517 AN The Hague, Netherlands. T. +317036477990. Fax +31703622633.
URL: http://www.unoy.org/
History 7 Jul 2001, Franschhoek (South Africa), during a conference organized by United Network of Young Peacebuilders (UNOY). **Aims** Develop strategies and actions to empower local capacities of young persons working in fields related to peace-building in Africa as well to link up young people with like-minded individuals around the world. **Languages** Dutch, English, French, Spanish. **Activities** Working Groups (7): African Young Women Building Peace; Youth Advocacy; Peace Education; African Youth Transformation Conflict; Small Arms and Light Weapons; Children and Armed Conflict; HIV/AIDS.
Members Individuals in 35 countries:
Algeria, Angola, Benin, Botswana, Burkina Faso, Burundi, Cameroon, Cape Verde, Chad, Congo DR, Côte d'Ivoire, Ethiopia, Gabon, Ghana, Kenya, Lesotho, Liberia, Madagascar, Malawi, Mauritius, Morocco, Mozambique, Namibia, Nigeria, Rwanda, Sao Tomé-Principe, Senegal, Sierra Leone, South Africa, Tanzania UR, Togo, Tunisia, Uganda, Zambia, Zimbabwe. [2008.07.23/XF7057/**F**]

- ♦ African-Eurasian Migratory /Water Bird/ Agreement (1995 treaty)
- ♦ African-European Radio Astronomy Platform (unconfirmed)

♦ African Evaluation Association (AfrEA) 00304

Association Africaine d'Evaluation
Office 36 Kofi Annan Avenue, North Legon, Accra, Ghana. T. +233307032706. E-mail: info@afrea.org – adkorda@afrea.org.
URL: http://www.afrea.org/
History 17 Sep 1999, Nairobi (Kenya). Formalized 24 Mar 2009, Cairo (Egypt). **Aims** Promote Africa-rooted and Africa-led evaluation through sharing African evaluation perspectives. **Structure** Executive Board; Secretariat. **Languages** English, French. **Staff** 2.00 FTE, paid. Board members voluntary. **Finance** Members' dues. Grants. **Activities** Networking/liaising; events/meetings; standards/guidelines. **Events** *Conference* Addis Ababa (Ethiopia) 2022, *Accelerating Africa's development – strengthening national evaluation ecosystems* Abidjan (Côte d'Ivoire) 2019, *Evaluation of the sustainable development goals – opportunities and challenges for Africa* Kampala (Uganda) 2017, *Evaluation for development – from analysis to impact* Yaoundé (Cameroon) 2014, *Conference* Cairo (Egypt) 2009.
Members National (39) in 12 countries:
Cape Verde, Comoros, Eritrea, Ethiopia, Ghana, Kenya, Madagascar, Niger, Rwanda, South Africa, Zambia, Zimbabwe.
NGO Relations Member of: *International Organisation for Cooperation in Evaluation (IOCE, #14426).* Core partner of: *EvalPartners (#09208).* Instrumental in setting up: *Africa Gender and Development Evaluators Network (AGDEN, #00177).* [2020.03.03/XD8488/**D**]

- ♦ African Evangelical Office / see Association of Evangelicals in Africa (#02587)

♦ African Export-Import Bank (Afreximbank) 00305

Banque africaine d'import-export
Pres PO Box 613, Cairo, 11757, Egypt. T. +2024564100 – +2024564101 – +2024564103. Fax +2024564110 – +2024515008. E-mail: info@afreximbank.com – feedback@afreximbank.com.
Street address 72B El-Maahad Es-Eshteraky Street, Cairo, 11341, Egypt.
URL: http://www.afreximbank.com/
History 7 May 1993, Abidjan (Côte d'Ivoire), at constituent assembly, when Agreement for establishment of Afreximbank and Charter were opened for signature by participating countries. Agreement and Charter adopted at 1st Annual General Meeting, 27 Oct 1993, Abuja. Set up following resolution of Annual Meeting of Board of Governors of *African Development Bank (ADB, #00283),* 1987, Cairo (Egypt), and findings of a multidisciplinary team funded by *UNDP (#20292).* Became operational Sep 1994. **Aims** Stimulate consistent expansion, diversification and development of African trade while operating as a first class, profit-oriented, socially responsible financial institution and a center of excellence in African trade matters. **Structure** General Meeting of Shareholders (annual); Board of Directors, representing 3 classes of shareholder; Executive Committee; Branch Management Committees. Principal officers: President (Chairman of the Board); Executive Vice-President; Deputy Director Operations; Deputy Director Projects and Administrative Services; Assistant Director Finance; Assistant Director Planning and Development and Special Assistant to the President; Assistant Director Credit; Head Board Secretariat; Chief Legal Officer. **Languages** English, French. **Staff** 200.00 FTE, paid. **Finance** Authorized share capital: US$ 5,000,000,000. **Activities** Events/meetings. **Events** *General Meeting* Cairo (Egypt) 1995, *General Meeting* Abuja (Nigeria) 1993. **Publications** *Africa in Figures* (2 a year); *Africa at a Glance* (annual). Annual Report.
Members Government and Institutional Investors in 61 countries:
Angola, Belgium, Benin, Botswana, Brazil, Burkina Faso, Burundi, Cameroon, Cape Verde, Chad, China, Comoros, Congo Brazzaville, Congo DR, Côte d'Ivoire, Czechia, Djibouti, Egypt, Equatorial Guinea, Eritrea, Eswatini, Ethiopia, France, Gabon, Gambia, Ghana, Guinea, Guinea-Bissau, India, Japan, Kenya, Lesotho, Liberia, Luxembourg, Madagascar, Malawi, Mali, Mauritania, Mauritius, Morocco, Mozambique, Namibia, Niger, Nigeria, Russia, Rwanda, Sao Tomé-Principe, Senegal, Seychelles, Sierra Leone, South Africa, South Sudan, Sudan, Tanzania UR, Togo, Tunisia, Uganda, UK, USA, Zambia, Zimbabwe.
IGO Relations Participates in the activities of: *UNCTAD (#20285).* Cooperation Agreement with: *International Fund for Agricultural Development (IFAD, #13692).* Member of: *Global Network of Export-Import Banks and Development Finance Institutions (G-NEXID, #10489).* **NGO Relations** Member of (1): *Aman Union (#00763).* [2022/XF3580/**F***]

- ♦ African Fairtrade Network / see Fairtrade Africa (#09239)
- ♦ African Farmers Association (inactive)
- ♦ African Federalist Association (inactive)
- ♦ African Federation of Clerical Workers / see Fédération panafricaine des employés (#09700)

♦ African Federation of Clinical Chemistry (AFCC) 00306

Sec Box A1877, Avondale, Harare, HARARE, Zimbabwe. T. +2634791631ext2126. Fax +2634705155. E-mail: matarirah@yahoo.com – afccafrica@gmail.com.
URL: http://www.afccafrica.org/
History Founded following workshop, 2008, South Africa. Inaugurated, Oct 2009, Ibadan (Nigeria). A regional society belonging to *International Federation of Clinical Chemistry and Laboratory Medicine (IFCC, #13392).* **Aims** Promote improvement in the health and well-being of the communities it serves through improving development and practice of clinical chemistry through education and scientific excellence. **Structure** Officers. **Languages** English. **Events** *Congress* Lusaka (Zambia) 2021, *Integrating clinical chemistry and laboratory medicine in evidence based laboratory p4 (personalised, preventative, predictive and participatory) medicine* Victoria Falls (Zimbabwe) 2015, *Congress* Cape Town (South Africa) 2013, *Congress* Nairobi (Kenya) 2011.
Members Full in 14 countries:
Botswana, Egypt, Ethiopia, Ghana, Kenya, Morocco, Nigeria, Rwanda, South Africa, Sudan, Tunisia, Uganda, Zambia, Zimbabwe. [2021/XJ0957/**E**]

♦ African Federation for Emergency Medicine (AFEM) 00307

Fédération Africaine de Médecine d'Urgence
Contact Private Bag X24, Belville 7535, Cape Town, South Africa. E-mail: programs@afem.info – admin@afem.info.
Contact address not obtained.
URL: http://www.afem.info/
History Founded 26 Nov 2009, South Africa. Registered in accordance with South African law. **Aims** Be the leading organization supporting development of universal access to quality emergency care in Africa; advocate to all stakeholders for universal access to emergency care; ensure scientifically rigorous, quality emergency care systems by developing clinical and research capacity, provision of technical guidance protocols and frameworks, and building collaborative networks across the continent and beyond. **Structure** General Meeting (annual); Board; Interim Executive Committee. **Languages** English, French. **Staff** 9.00 FTE, voluntary. **Finance** No budget. **Events** *African Conference on Emergency Medicine* Accra (Ghana) 2022, *African Conference on Emergency Medicine* 2020, *African Conference on Emergency Medicine* Kigali (Rwanda) 2018, *African Conference on Emergency Medicine* Cairo (Egypt) 2016, *International Conference on Emergency Medicine and Public Health* Doha (Qatar) 2016. **Publications** *African Journal of Emergency Medicine (AfJEM). African Handbook of Emergency Care* (2013). **Information Services** *African Emergency Care Database.*
Members Individuals; societies; affiliate organizations. Membership and affiliated organizations stands at over 2,000. Members in 7 countries:
Egypt, Ethiopia, Libya, Nigeria, South Africa, Sudan, Tanzania UR.
NGO Relations Member of: *International Federation for Emergency Medicine (IFEM, #13409).* [2015.07.07/XJ5302/**D**]

- ♦ African Federation of Gastroenterology (no recent information)

♦ African Federation for the Gifted and Talented (AFGT) 00308

Contact address not obtained. T. +254731333725 – +254731333728. E-mail: info@giftedafrica.org.
URL: https://giftedafrica.org/
History 20 Mar 2010. **Aims** Provide advocacy for Africa's gifted and talented. **Structure** Executive Federation Secretariat (EFS).
Members Affiliate; Corporate; Individual. Affiliate organizations include:
Africa Youth for Peace and Development (AYPAD); Global Network for Good Governance (GNGG, #10490).
NGO Relations Affiliate federation of: *World Council for Gifted and Talented Children (WCGTC, #21328).* [2021/XJ7376/y/**D**]

- ♦ African Federation of the International College of Surgeons (see: #12650)
- ♦ African Federation of Inventors' Associations (inactive)

♦ African Federation of Obstetrics and Gynaecology (AFOG) 00309

SG PO Box 10026, Khartoum, Sudan. E-mail: info@afog-org.com.
URL: https://afog-org.com/
History Founded 2012, Rome (Italy), during Congress of *Fédération Internationale de Gynécologie et d'Obstétrique (FIGO, #09638),* as its African arm. Registered in accordance with the law of Sudan, 2013. **Aims** Improve the sexual reproductive health and rights of women, neonates, children, adolescents and men in Africa; raise the status of women's health and enable their active participation to achieve their reproductive and sexual rights with access to efficient education and services throughout their life cycle; upgrade the practice of obstetrics and gynaecology; strengthen collaborative partnerships and networks that promote SRHR activities in the African Continent. **Structure** General Assembly; Executive Board. Sub-Groups. **Finance** Members' dues. **Activities** Events/meetings; training/education. **Events** *African and Eastern Mediterranean Regional Congress* Kigali (Rwanda) 2020, *African and Eastern Mediterranean Regional Congress* Dubai (United Arab Emirates) 2018.
Members Full in 44 countries:
Algeria, Benin, Burkina Faso, Burundi, Cameroon, Central African Rep, Chad, Congo Brazzaville, Congo DR, Côte d'Ivoire, Egypt, Eritrea, Ethiopia, Gabon, Ghana, Guinea, Iraq, Jordan, Kenya, Kuwait, Lebanon, Libya, Madagascar, Malawi, Mali, Mauritania, Morocco, Mozambique, Niger, Nigeria, Palestine, Rwanda, Saudi Arabia, Senegal, Sierra Leone, South Africa, Sudan, Syrian AR, Tanzania UR, Tunisia, Uganda, United Arab Emirates, Zambia, Zimbabwe.

NGO Relations Allied regional federation of *Fédération Internationale de Gynécologie et d'Obstétrique (FIGO, #09638).* [2021/XM8082/**D**]

♦ African Federation of Orthopedic Technologists / see Fédération Africaine des Professionnels de la Réadaptation (#09399)
♦ African Federation of Private Schools Associations (internationally oriented national body)

♦ African Federation of Public Health Associations (AFPHA) 00310

Sec c/o Ethiopian Public Health Assn, PO Box 7117, Kirkos Sub City, Addis Ababa, Ethiopia. E-mail: info@etpha.org.
URL: http://www.afphas.org/

History Launched 31 Aug 2011, Yamoussoukro (Côte d'Ivoire), when Constitution and Bylaws were adopted. **Aims** Engage all key stakeholders in Africa and the world to influence policies, strategies and activities that will positively impact the health of all the African people. **Structure** Executive Committee, including President, Vice-President and Secretary. **Events** *Congress* Cape Town (South Africa) 2013. **NGO Relations** Member of: *World Federation of Public Health Associations (WFPHA, #21476).* [2014/XJ7061/**D**]

♦ African Federation of Rehabilitation Professionals (#09399)

♦ African Federation of Science Journalists 00311

Pres address not obtained. E-mail: administrator@sasja.co.za.
Contact House 6, Golden Garden Estate, off Adisa Estate, Durumi, PO Box 5616, Abuja, Federal Capital Territory, Nigeria. T. +23417748397.

History Founded Oct 2004, Montréal (Canada). **Aims** Facilitate networking between science journalists in Africa. **NGO Relations** Member of: *World Federation of Science Journalists (WFSJ, #21479).* [2017/XM0287/**D**]

♦ African Federation for Sexual Health and Rights (AFSHR) 00312

Contact c/o Action Health Incorporated, 17 Lawal Str, Off Oweh St, Jibowu, Lagos, Nigeria. T. +23417743745. E-mail: conference@africasexuality.org.
Office 804 West 180 St, Ste 36, New York NY 10033 10033, USA. E-mail: info@actionhealthinc.org.
URL: http://www.worldsexology.org/

History 2002. Regional continental federation of: *World Association for Sexual Health (WAS, #21187).* **Events** *Conference* Freetown (Sierra Leone) 2022, *Conference* Johannesburg (South Africa) 2018, *Conference* Accra (Ghana) 2016, *Eliminating women and girls sexual and reproductive health vulnerabilities in Africa* Yaoundé (Cameroon) 2014, *Sexual health and rights in Africa, where are we?* Windhoek (Namibia) 2012. **Members** Membership countries not specified. **NGO Relations** *Southern African Sexual Health Association (SASHA); Africa Regional Sexuality Resource Centre, Lagos (ARSRC).* [2014/XD9296/**D**]

♦ African Federation for the Study of Pain (no recent information)
♦ African Federation for Technology in Health Care (no recent information)

♦ African Federation of Women Entrepreneurs (AFWE) 00313

Fédération africaine des femmes entrepreneurs (FAFE)

SG PO Box 7600, Accra, Ghana. T. +233307011413 – +23330(233279955664. Fax +233307011413. E-mail: ghgawe@yahoo.com.
URL: http://www.ghanawomenentrepreneurs.org/

History 3 Jun 1993, Accra (Ghana), following a proposal of *United Nations Economic Commission for Africa (ECA, #20554).* Originally referred to as *Federation of African Women Entrepreneurs (FAWE).* Registered in accordance with Ethiopian law, 4 Apr 1994. Head Office moved to Accra in 1997. **Aims** Enhance the active participation of African Women Entrepreneurs in the national, regional and global economy. **Structure** General Assembly. Executive Committee, comprising; President; 1st and 2nd Vice-Presidents; Secretary-General; Deputy Secretary-General; Treasurer; 2 representatives of each sub-region (Central Africa, East Africa, West Africa, Southern Africa, Northern Africa). **Languages** English, French. **Staff** 4.00 FTE, paid; 2.00 FTE, voluntary. **Finance** Members' dues. Other sources: assistance and aid; loans and grants. **Activities** Conducts research; lobbies governments. Organizes: trade fairs; conferences; seminars; workshops; exhibitions; studies; trade tours, particularly Global Women Entrepreneurs Trade Fair and Investment Forum (every 2 years); exchanges visits; ideas and information. **Events** *Biennial global women entrepreneurs investment forum* Miami, FL (USA) 2000, *Biennial global women entrepreneurs investment forum* Addis Ababa (Ethiopia) 1998. **Publications** *Directory of African Women Entrepreneurs.*

Members Regular – national associations (operating in 30 countries in Africa), whose members are all self-employed women manufacturers and exporters of goods and services; Associate – individuals. National associations in 15 countries:
Burkina Faso, Burundi, Cameroon, Cape Verde, Côte d'Ivoire, Egypt, Mali, Morocco, Namibia, Niger, South Africa, Sudan, Togo, Zambia, Zimbabwe.

IGO Relations Provisional secretariat provided by: *African Centre for Gender (ACG).* **NGO Relations** Agreement signed with: *Foundation for Democracy in Africa.* [2016/XD4104/**D**]

♦ African Fencing Confederation (no recent information)

♦ African Fertilizer and Agribusiness Partnership (AFAP) 00314

Pres/CEO Edenburg Terraces, Third Floor, Block D, 348 Rivonia Boulevard, PO Box 53, Rivonia 2128, Johannesburg, 2128, South Africa. T. +27118447320. E-mail: info@afap-partnership.org.
URL: http://www.afap-partnership.org/

History 2003, as part of *New Partnership for Africa's Development (NEPAD, #17091),* building on the work of *Comprehensive Africa Agriculture Development Programme (CAADP).* **Aims** Eliminate hunger and reduce poverty by growing the agricultural sector in Africa. **Structure** Board of Trustees. Headquarters in Johannesburg (South Africa); Offices in: Accra (Ghana); Maputo (Mozambique); Dar es Salaam (Tanzania UR). **Staff** 17.00 FTE, paid. **IGO Relations** Partner: *New Partnership for Africa's Development (NEPAD, #17091).* **NGO Relations** Partners: *Agricultural Market Development Trust (AGMARK, #00572); Alliance for a Green Revolution in Africa (AGRA, #00685).* Member of: *Global Open Data for Agriculture and Nutrition (GODAN, #10514).* [2014/XJ7794/**E**]

♦ African Fertilizer Development Centre / see African Centre for Fertilizer Development (#00241)

♦ African Field Epidemiology Network (AFENET) 00315

Réseau Africain d'épidémiologie de terrain

Main Office Lugogo House, Ground Floor – Wings B and C – Plot 42, Lugogo By-Pass, PO Box 12874, Kampala, Uganda. T. +256417700650 – +25641(256312700650. E-mail: sec@afenet.net.
URL: http://www.afenet.net/

History 2005. Founded as a networking alliance of African Field Epidemiology (and Laboratory) Training Programmes (FELTPs), and other applied epidemiology training programmes. **Aims** Improve the capacity of health systems in Africa to manage *disease* outbreaks and other priority health problems. **Structure** General Assembly; Board of Directors; Independent Advisory Committee,; Secretariat, based in Kampala (Uganda), including Working Unites (4): Programs; Finance; Administration; Communications and Strategic Information. Country Programmes. **Languages** English, French, Portuguese. **Staff** Secretariat staff led by Executive Director. Within each country in the Network, training programmes are guided by a Program Director, assisted by an Administrator and a Resident Advisor. Together with counterparts from the country's Ministry of Health, the programme staff are responsible for country-level coordination and implementation. **Finance** Mainly funded by the Centers for Disease Control and Prevention (CDC). **Activities** Capacity building; events/meetings; guidance/assistance/consulting; networking/liaising; training/education. Active in: Angola, Benin, Burkina Faso, Cameroon, Congo DR, Côte d'Ivoire, Ethiopia, Gambia, Ghana, Guinea, Guinea-Bissau, Kenya, Mali, Mauritania, Mozambique, Namibia, Niger, Nigeria, Rwanda, Senegal, Sierra Leone, South Africa, South Sudan, Tanzania UR, Togo, Uganda, Zimbabwe. **Events** *Scientific Conference* Maputo (Mozambique) 2018, *Scientific Conference* Abuja (Nigeria) 2016, *Scientific Conference* Addis Ababa (Ethiopia) 2013, *Scientific conference* Dar es Salaam (Tanzania UR) 2011. **Publications** *AFENET Monthly Newsletter.* Annual Report; quarterly programme reports; weekly updates; daily news briefs. **IGO Relations** Cooperates with: *European Union (EU, #08967);* African government agencies; *United States Agency for International Development (USAID); WHO (#20950);* WHO Multi Disease Surveillance Center (MDSC); *WHO Regional Office for Africa (AFRO, #20943).* **NGO Relations** Member of (1): *Consortium for Non-communicable Diseases Prevention and Control in sub-Saharan Africa (CNCD-Africa, #04754).* Cooperates with (4): *African Society for Laboratory Medicine (ASLM, #00463); Global Outbreak Alert and Response Network (GOARN, #10521); Task Force for Global Health (TFGH, #20098); Training Programs in Epidemiology and Public Health Interventions NETwork (TEPHINET, #20198).* Also cooperates with academic institutions; national organizations; private entities. [2021/XJ3741/**F**]

♦ African Finance and Economic Development Association / see African Finance and Economics Association
♦ African Finance and Economics Association (internationally oriented national body)
♦ African Financial Community (#04377)

♦ African Fine Coffees Association (AFCA) 00316

Main Office PO Box 27405, Kampala, Uganda. T. +256414269140. Fax +256414269148. E-mail: secretariat@africanfinecoffees.org.
URL: https://afca.coffee/

History May 2000. Former names and other names: *Eastern African Fine Coffees Association (EAFCA)* – former. **Aims** Establish and promote a network for the coffee production, processing and marketing industry in Eastern Africa and other sub-regions in Africa; increase quality and value of the coffee production; promote production, processing, consumption and export of coffee; promote sustainable production systems involving coffee and other tree crops. **Structure** General Meeting (annual). Board of Directors, including Chairman, Vice-Chairman, Treasurer and Secretary. **Finance** Sources: members' dues. **Events** *African Fine Coffees Conference* Kigali (Rwanda) 2023, *African Fine Coffees Conference* Addis Ababa (Ethiopia) 2021, *Conference* Kigali (Rwanda) 2019, *Conference* Kampala (Uganda) 2018, *Conference* Dar es Salaam (Tanzania UR) 2016.

Members in 7 countries:
Burundi, Ethiopia, Kenya, Rwanda, Tanzania UR, Uganda, Zambia.

IGO Relations *United States Agency for International Development (USAID).* **NGO Relations** Member of: *Finance Alliance for Sustainable Trade (FAST, #09763).* Associate member of: *Global Coffee Platform (GCP, #10298).* [2023/XJ3166/**D**]

♦ African Food Network of Food Data Systems (AFROFOODS) 00317

Coordinator Dept of Biochemistry, Nutrition and Dietetics Unit, Univ of Calabar, Calabar 540271, Cross River, Nigeria. T. +2348036754151. E-mail: nkeneobong@yahoo.com.
URL: http://www.fao.org/infoods/infoods/regional-data-centres/

History as the African arm of *International Network of Food Data Systems (INFOODS, #14271).* **Structure** Sub-regions: ECSAFOODS; WAFOODS; CAFOODS; NAFOODS. **Events** *Regional meeting / Meeting* Accra (Ghana) 1994.

Members Full in 46 countries:
Algeria, Angola, Benin, Botswana, Burkina Faso, Burundi, Cameroon, Central African Rep, Chad, Congo Brazzaville, Congo DR, Côte d'Ivoire, Djibouti, Eritrea, Eswatini, Ethiopia, Gabon, Gambia, Ghana, Kenya, Lesotho, Liberia, Libya, Madagascar, Malawi, Mali, Mauritania, Mauritius, Morocco, Mozambique, Namibia, Niger, Nigeria, Rwanda, Senegal, Seychelles, Sierra Leone, Somalia, South Africa, Sudan, Tanzania UR, Togo, Tunisia, Uganda, Zambia, Zimbabwe. [2015/XU7650/**E**]

♦ African Football Confederation / see Confédération africaine de football (#04500)

♦ African Forest Forum (AFF) 00318

Exec Sec PO Box 30677, Nairobi, 00100, Kenya. T. +254207224000. Fax +254207224001. E-mail: exec.sec@afforum.org.
URL: http://www.afforum.org/

Aims Contribute to the improvement of the livelihoods of the people of Africa and the environment they live in through the sustainable management and use of tree and forest resources on the African continent. **Structure** Members' Forum; Governing Council; Executive Committee. Secretariat. **Activities** Awareness raising; capacity building; knowledge management/information dissemination; events/meetings. **Publications** *AFF Newsletter.* Books; policy briefs; factsheets; reports. **Members** Individuals (over 600). Membership countries not specified. **Consultative Status** Consultative status granted from: *UNEP (#20299).* **IGO Relations** *African Forestry and Wildlife Commission (AFWC, #00319).* Accredited to the Conference of the Parties of: *Secretariat of the United Nations Convention to Combat Desertification (Secretariat of the UNCCD, #19208).* **NGO Relations** Member of: *EverGreen Agriculture Partnership (#09213).* [2019/XJ8468/v/**F**]

♦ African Forestry Commission / see African Forestry and Wildlife Commission (#00319)

♦ African Forestry and Wildlife Commission (AFWC) 00319

Commission des forêts et de la faune sauvage pour l'Afrique (CFFSA) – Comisión Forestal y de la Flora y Fauna Silvestres para Africa (CFFSA)

Mailing Address c/o FAO Regional Office for Africa, PO Box 1628, Accra, Ghana. T. +2333027010930. Fax +233302668427. E-mail: afwc@fao.org.
URL: http://www.fao.org/forestry/afwc/en/

History 1959. Established within the framework of *FAO (#09260),* by Article VI-I of its Constitution, and by resolution 26/59 of 10th Session of FAO Conference. First Session Nov 1960. Rules of procedure adopted 1961; amended 1978. Statutes amended, 2011. Based at *FAO Regional Office for Africa (FAO/RAF, #09265),* Accra (Ghana). Former names and other names: *African Forestry Commission (AFC)* – former; *Commission des forêts pour l'Afrique (CFA)* – former. **Aims** Advise on the formulation of forestry and wildlife policies and programmes; play a key role in the international arrangement on forests; serve as a link between global dialogue at the Committee on Forestry (COFO), The Africa Regional Conference of FAO and the United Nations Forum on Forests (UNFF), and national implementation. **Structure** Executive Committee. Working Party on Wildlife and Protected Area Management. **Languages** English, French. **Staff** Serviced by the FAO through its Regional Office for Africa. **Finance** Meetings of the Committee and its subsidiary bodies financed by *FAO (#09260),* its partners and the host country for the meeting. Members of the Commission pay for their participation at meetings. **Activities** Events/meetings. **Events** *Session* Kinshasa (Congo DR) 2022, *Session* Dakar (Senegal) 2018, *Session* Tanzania UR 2016, *Session* Windhoek (Namibia) 2013, *Session* Cotonou (Benin) 2012. **Publications** *Nature and Faune* (2 a year).

Members Open to all FAO Member Nations and Associate Members whose territories are situated wholly or partly in Africa or who are responsible for the international relations of non-self-governing territories in that region, and who desire to be considered members. Currently governments of 48 countries:
Algeria, Angola, Benin, Botswana, Burkina Faso, Burundi, Cameroon, Cape Verde, Central African Rep, Chad, Congo Brazzaville, Congo DR, Côte d'Ivoire, Egypt, Equatorial Guinea, Eswatini, Ethiopia, France, Gabon, Gambia, Ghana, Guinea, Guinea-Bissau, Kenya, Lesotho, Liberia, Libya, Madagascar, Malawi, Mali, Mauritania, Mauritius, Morocco, Mozambique, Namibia, Niger, Nigeria, Rwanda, Senegal, Sierra Leone, South Africa, Sudan, Tanzania UR, Togo, Tunisia, Uganda, Zambia, Zimbabwe.

Observers from 9 countries:
Comoros, Djibouti, Eritrea, Sao Tomé-Principe, Seychelles, Somalia, Spain, UK, USA. [2022/XE9583/**E***]

♦ African Forum against the Death Penalty (internationally oriented national body)

♦ African Forum for Agricultural Advisory Services (AFAAS) 00320

Contact House No 26 Kigobe Road, Minister's Village-Ntinda, PO Box 34624, Kampala, Uganda. T. +256312313400. E-mail: info@afaas-africa.org.
URL: https://www.afaas-africa.org/

History 11 Oct 2005, Kampala (Uganda). Created at 1st Regional Networking Symposium on Innovations in AAS. Former names and other names: *Sub-Saharan African Network on Agricultural Advisory Services (SSANAAS)* – former (2004 to 2006). Registration: Uganda. **Aims** Strengthen national agricultural extension and advisory services. **Structure** Board. **Activities** Advocacy/lobbying/activism; knowledge management/information dissemination; training/education. **IGO Relations** Partner of (1): *Centre for Coordination of Agricultural Research and Development for Southern Africa (CCARDESA, #03736).* **NGO Relations** Partner of (4): *Access Agriculture (#00047); Association for Strengthening Agricultural Research in Eastern and Central Africa (ASARECA, #02933); Forum for Agricultural Research in Africa (FARA, #09897); West and Central African Council for Agricultural Research and Development (WECARD, #20907).* [2020/AA1255/**F**]

♦ African Forum for Children's Literacy in Science and Technology (internationally oriented national body)
♦ African Forum for Mathematical Ecology (no recent information)

♦ African Forum and Network on Debt and Development (AFRODAD) . 00321

Exec Dir 31 Atkinson Drive, Hillside, PO Box CY1517, Causeway, Harare, HARARE, Zimbabwe. T. +263247785316 – +2632429127514. Fax +26324747878. E-mail: fanwell@afrodad.co.zw – afrodad@afrodad.co.zw.
URL: http://www.afrodad.org/

History Founded Mar 1996, Zimbabwe. Previously referred to as *African Network on Debt* and *African Network on Debt and Development*. **Aims** Secure policy change that will redress and avert Africa's debt crisis based on a human rights value system; enhance efficient and effective management and use of resources by African governments; secure a paradigm shift in the international socio-economic and political world order to a development process that addresses the needs and aspirations of the majority of the people in the world; facilitate dialogue between civil society and governments on issues related to debt and development in Africa and elsewhere. **Structure** Board. **Staff** 19.00 FTE, paid. **Finance** Institutional and project funding from various partners. Annual budget: about US$ 1,460,000. **Activities** Awareness raising; knowledge management/ information dissemination; capacity building; research and development; guidance/assistance/consulting; events/meetings; politics/policy/regulatory. **Events** *Civil society forum* Doha (Qatar) 2008. **Publications** *Debt and Development in Africa* (6 a year) – newsletter. *African Borrowing Charter* in English, French, Portuguese. Annual Report; research reports; policy briefs; infographics; articles. **NGO Relations** Supports: *Global Call for Action Against Poverty (GCAP, #10263)*. Member of: *The Reality Of Aid (ROA, #18626)*; *Tax Justice Network-Africa (TJN-A, #20101)*. Working relationship with: *European Network on Debt and Development (EURODAD, #07891)*. Alliances with like-minded organizations working in other countries. [2019.02.18/XF3375/**F**]

♦ African Forum for Research and Education in Health (AFREhealth) 00322

Secretariat School of Publich Health – College of Health Sciences, Kwame Nkrumah Univ of Science and Technology, Private Mail Bag – Univ Post Office, Kumasi, Ghana. T. +233508351306. E-mail: afrehealth@gmail.com – info@afrehealth.org.
URL: http://afrehealth.org/

History 2 Aug 2016, Nairobi (Kenya). Emerged from the Medical Education Partnership Initiative (MEPI) and Nursing Education Partnership Initiative (NEPI). Registration: Registrar General's Department, No/ID: CG113882017, Start date: 16 Nov 2017, Ghana. **Aims** Establish AFREhealth as a self-sustaining, viable, relevant and impactful institution in addressing Africa's health challenges. **Structure** Annual General Meeting; Governing Council;Executive Committee; Subcommittees; Secretariat. **Languages** English. **Staff** 3.00 FTE, paid. **Finance** Sources: grants. Annual budget: 256,812 USD. **Activities** Capacity building; events/meetings; networking/liaising; research/documentation; training/education. **Events** *Social Justice and Equity for Health in Africa* Kumasi (Ghana) 2021, *Symposium* Addis Ababa (Ethiopia) 2020, *Symposium* Lagos (Nigeria) 2019, *Towards achieving universal health coverage in Africa – creating synergies and capacity through education, research and quality health services* Durban (South Africa) 2018, *Symposium* Accra (Ghana) 2017. **Publications** *AFREhealth Newsletter* (4 a year).
Members Full in 8 countries:
Botswana, Ghana, Kenya, Nigeria, Tanzania UR, Uganda, Zambia, Zimbabwe.
IGO Relations Partners include: *African Union (AU, #00488)*; *United Nations (UN, #20515)*; *West African Health Organization (WAHO, #20881)*; *WHO (#20950)*. **NGO Relations** Accredited by (4): *Consortium of Universities for Global Health (CUGH)*; *Educational Commission for Foreign Medical Graduates (ECFMG)*; *Johns Hopkins Program for International Education in Gynecology and Obstetrics (JHPIEGO)*; *The Network: Towards Unity for Health (The Network: TUFH, #17060)*. Als partnerships with national organizations. [2020.07.07/XM7503/**F**]

♦ African Forum for Urban Security (AFUS) 00323

Forum africain pour la sécurité urbaine (FASU)

Contact address not obtained. T. +221338490811 – +221776504100.
URL: http://fasu.unblog.fr/

History 7 Feb 1998, Dakar (Senegal), at constitutive meeting. Registered in accordance with the law of Senegal. **Aims** Promote local initiatives in Africa concerning prevention and urban safety. **Structure** General Assembly. Executive Council; General Delegation; Technical commissions; Cooperation Consultative Council. **Languages** English, French. **Staff** 6.00 FTE, paid; 2.00 FTE, voluntary. **Finance** Members' dues. Other sources: City of Dakar; subsidies; income from activities; grants and legacies.
Members Mayors in 12 countries:
Benin, Burkina Faso, Cameroon, Côte d'Ivoire, Ethiopia, Gambia, Mali, Mauritania, Niger, Senegal, South Africa, Togo.
NGO Relations Supported by: *European Forum for Urban Security (Efus, #07340)*; *Foro Latinoamericano para la Seguridad Urbana y la Democracia (FLASUD, #09883)*; *International Centre for the Prevention of Crime (ICPC, #12508)*. [2014.06.01/XF4817/**F**]

♦ African Forum for Utility Regulators (AFUR) 00324

Forum africain pour la réglementation des services publics

Exec Sec 526 Madiba Street, Arcadia, Pretoria, 0083, South Africa. T. +27124014740. Fax +27124014763. E-mail: info@afurnet.org.
URL: http://www.afurnet.org/

History Nov 2002. Founded through Clause 110 of *New Partnership for Africa's Development (NEPAD, #17091)* Framework Document. **Aims** Support the development of effective utility regulation in Africa through facilitation, harmonization of regulatory policies, exchange of information and lessons of experience amongst regulators, and capacity building in support of the socio-economic development of the continent. **Structure** General Assembly (annual); Executive Committee; Secretariat. Sectoral Committees (4): Communications; Water and Sanitation; Energy; Transport. **Languages** English, French. **Staff** 3 permanent; 3 seconded experts. **Finance** Members' dues. Other sources: projects funded through donor funding; capacity building workshops. **Activities** Events/meetings; knowledge management/information dissemination; training/education. **Events** *Annual conference* Pretoria (South Africa) 2020, *World Forum on Energy Regulation (WFER)* Istanbul (Turkey) 2015, *Conference* South Africa 2012, *Conference* South Africa 2011, *Conference* Abuja (Nigeria) 2010.
Members Organizations in 23 countries:
Algeria, Burkina Faso, Cameroon, Côte d'Ivoire, Gambia, Ghana, Kenya, Lesotho, Malawi, Mali, Mauritania, Mozambique, Namibia, Niger, Nigeria, Rwanda, Senegal, South Africa, Tanzania UR, Togo, Uganda, Zambia, Zimbabwe.
Observer organizations in 11 countries:
Angola, Benin, Botswana, Cameroon, Eswatini, Ethiopia, Madagascar, Mauritius, Niger, South Africa, Sudan.
IGO Relations Mandate partners: *African Union (AU, #00488)*; *New Partnership for Africa's Development (NEPAD, #17091)*. Strategic partners: *African Development Bank (ADB, #00283)*; *Deutsche Gesellschaft für Internationale Zusammenarbeit (GIZ)*; *ECOWAS Regional Electricity Regulatory Authority (ERERA, #05337)*; *International Bank for Reconstruction and Development (IBRD, #12317)*. Support from: *Commonwealth Telecommunications Organisation (CTO, #04365)*. **NGO Relations** Regional partner: *Regional Electricity Regulators Association of Southern Africa (RERA, #18779)*. Member of: *International Confederation of Energy Regulators (ICER, #12859)*. [2020/XJ2868/**F**]

♦ African Foundation for Development (internationally oriented national body)
♦ African Foundation For Human Advancement (internationally oriented national body)

♦ African Foundation for International Law (AFIL) 00325

Fondation Africaine pour le Droit International (FADI)

Contact Laan van Meerdervoort 70, 2517 AN The Hague, Netherlands. T. +31653435291 – +31684712549. E-mail: secretariat@afil-fadi.org.
URL: http://www.afil-fadi.org/

History Dec 2003, The Hague (Netherlands). Registered in accordance with Dutch law: 27264619. **Aims** Promote study, research and analysis on international legal matters of particular interest and relevance to African countries and foster the teaching and dissemination of international law in Africa; encourage and promote intellectual debate and exchanges on international legal issues of particular interest to Africa and its peoples and foment establishment of networks among African international lawyers as well as between the latter and scholars of other continents; contribute actively to the promotion and building of the rule of law in Africa, in general. **Structure** Governing Board; Executive Committee. **Publications** *African Yearbook of International Law*. **NGO Relations** *African Association of International Law (AAIL, #00208)*; *African Institute of International Law (AIIL, #00341)*. [2013/XJ6553/t/**F**]

♦ African Foundation for Research and Development (no recent information)
♦ African Foundation for Urban Management (internationally oriented national body)
♦ African Freedom of Expression Exchange (unconfirmed)
♦ African Free Trade Area / see African Continental Free Trade Area (#00267)

♦ African Fund for Guarantee and Economic Cooperation 00326

Fonds africain de garantie et de coopération économique (FAGACE)

Gen Dir 01 BP 2045 RP, Cotonou, Benin. T. +22921300877 – +22921300376 – +22921300521. Fax +22921300284. E-mail: fagace_dg@yahoo.fr – courriel.fagace@le-fagace.org.
URL: http://www.le-fagace.org/

History 10 Feb 1977, Kigali (Rwanda), under the title *Fonds de garantie et de coopération de l'OCAM*, as a joint venture of the then *'Afro-Malagasy Union for Economic Cooperation'*, subsequently (until its dissolution in 1985), *African and Mauritian Common Organization (OCAM, inactive)*. Commenced operations 1981, following ratification of Convention. Also referred to as *Guaranty and Cooperation Fund of AMCO*. **Aims** Contribute to the economic and social development of member states, individually and collectively, either in taking part in the financing of their development projects or in facilitating their achievements through accompanying measures like interest rate subsidy or extension of credit's duration (a special interest is paid to the most economically underprivileged countries, given either to their geographical situation or further to disasters or natural calamities). **Structure** General Assembly of Shareholders. Board of Directors, comprising the Finance Minister of each member state and one representative per member institution. Administrative Council, consisting of 2 Administrators per member state, one Administrator for each non-regional member state and one Administrator per member institution. Director General, elected by the General Assembly of Shareholder, manages the Fund. **Languages** French. **Staff** 29.00 FTE, paid. **Finance** Members' dues. Other sources: release of subscribed capital; loans; subsidies; gifts; legacies; income from investments; earnings from lending operations; other proceeds from activities. Authorized capital (at 31 Dec 2004): FCFA 30,000 million; capital prone to call: FCFA 22,263.16 million. **Activities** Guarantees productive loans destined to the financially and economically viable projects; grants interest rate subsidies and extensions to loan repayment periods in respect of loans granted for economic ventures where terms make profitability doubtful; provides loans and grants for specific operations, notably relating to the fight against poverty and protection of the environment; subscribes to social capital of national or regional enterprises; manages funds on behalf of third parties. Main areas of intervention: industries aiming at developing local natural resources or import of substitution products; rural development, including agriculture and livestock breeding; infrastructure; small and medium-scale enterprises producing goods and services. Beneficiaries include: member states or their agencies; individual and collectively-owned private or joint-venture enterprises, newly created or expanding private and state owned enterprises having their headquarters or main field of action in member states; national finance institutions; regional institutions working towards integration of member states' economies. **Publications** Annual Report in French/English.
Members Governments of both African and non-African states; financial institutions. Governments of 9 countries:
Benin, Burkina Faso, Central African Rep, Côte d'Ivoire, Mali, Niger, Rwanda, Senegal, Togo.
IGO Relations Member of: *Association of Regional and Sub-regional Development Finance Institutions in West Africa (AIRFD, no recent information)*. Cooperates with: *Agence française de développement (AFD)*; *Banque ouest africaine de développement (BOAD, #03170)*; *Community of Sahel-Saharan States (CEN-SAD, #04406)*; *Trade and Development Bank (TDB, #20181)*; *ECOWAS Bank for Investment and Development (EBID, #05334)*; *Fonds de solidarité africain (FSA, #09838)*; *Islamic Corporation for the Insurance of Investment and Export Credit (ICIEC, #16041)*; *Mutual Aid and Loan Guaranty Fund of the Entente Council (EC-Fund, no recent information)*. **NGO Relations** Member of: *Association of African Development Finance Institutions (AADFI, #02353)*. Cooperates with: *Fonds de garantie des investissements privés en Afrique de l'Ouest (Fonds GARI, see: #03170)*. [2018/XF9108/f/**F***]

♦ African Futures Institute (AFI) 00327

Institut des futurs africains

Contact PO Box 13953, The Tramshed, Pretoria, 0126, South Africa. T. +27124511254 – +27123524107. Fax +27123226699. E-mail: info@africanfutures.org.
Street Address 1st Floor, Vudec Bldg, 360 Cnr Van der Walt and Skinner Street, Pretoria, 0003, South Africa.
URL: http://africanfutures.org/

History 2004, to sustain prospective thinking in Africa by optimizing on the achievements of the African Futures project, set up 2002, by *UNDP (#20292)*. Registered in accordance with South African law. **Aims** Contribute to the development of prospective studies and thinking in Africa; secure individual and institutional capacity-building; assist Africans to implement their programmes and initiatives based on truly shared visions of the long term development process. **Structure** Board of Trustees. **IGO Relations** Close links with a large number of organizations and governments, including: *African Development Bank (ADB, #00283)*; *International Bank for Reconstruction and Development (IBRD, #12317)*; *New Partnership for Africa's Development (NEPAD, #17091)*; UNDP. **NGO Relations** Close links with: *The African Capacity Building Foundation (ACBF, #00233)*. [2014/XM1962/j/**E**]

♦ African Gamebird Research, Education and Development Trust (internationally oriented national body)
♦ African Gender Institute (internationally oriented national body)
♦ African Gender and Media Initiative (internationally oriented national body)
♦ African Geographers' Association (no recent information)

♦ African Geoparks Network (AGN) 00328

Contact Fac of Sciences, BO 20, Geology Dept, 24000 El Jadida, Morocco. T. +212668038116. Fax +212523342187.
URL: http://www.africangeoparksnetwork.org/

History May 2009, Abidjan (Côte d'Ivoire), during pre-congress of 5th conference of *African Association of Women in Geosciences (AAWG, #00219)*. **Aims** Identify, promote, and advise on the importance and preservation of geological sites in Africa in collaboration with other stakeholders. **Structure** Executive Committee. **Finance** Support from: *UNESCO (#20322)*; *International Union of Geological Sciences (IUGS, #15777)*; *Geological Society of Africa (GSAf, #10135)*. **Events** *International Conference on Geoparks in Africa and Middle East* El Jadida (Morocco) 2018, *Biennial Assembly* Arusha (Tanzania UR) 2015, *International Conference on Geoparks in Africa and Middle East* Dakar (Senegal) 2014, *International conference on African and Arabian geoparks* El Jadida (Morocco) 2011. [2017/XJ4840/**F**]

♦ African Gerontological Society (inactive)

♦ African Golf Confederation 00329

Confédération africaine de golf (CAG)

Office PO Box 2122, Windhoek, Namibia. T. +26464405644. E-mail: prado@iway.na.
Pres c/o Zambia Golf Union, PO Box 71869, Ndola, Zambia. T. +260977787037. Fax +2602655155. E-mail: mwanzac@indeni.com.zm.
Vice Pres c/o FGCI, 26 BP 411, Abidjan 26, Côte d'Ivoire. E-mail: fgolfci@gmail.com.

History Founded Dec 1986, Algiers (Algeria). **Members** in 10 countries. Membership countries not specified. [2015/XD3840/**D**]

♦ African Graduate Nutrition Students Network 00330

Réseau des étudiants africains en nutrition

Coordinator Dept of Community Nutrition/Food and Nutrition Security Unit, Univ for Development Studies, Tamale, Ghana. T. +2337126717. E-mail: jm324@cornell.edu.
URL: http://agsnet.human.cornell.edu/

Aims Provide a forum for collaboration among professionals and African graduate students in nutrition worldwide. **Structure** Steering Committee. **Events** *Conference* Nairobi (Kenya) 2010, *Inaugural conference / Conference* Durban (South Africa) 2005.
Members Individuals in 19 countries:
Algeria, Angola, Benin, Botswana, Burkina Faso, Burundi, Cameroon, Cape Verde, Central African Rep, Chad, Comoros, Congo Brazzaville, Congo DR, Côte d'Ivoire, Djibouti, Egypt, Equatorial Guinea, Eritrea, Ethiopia.
NGO Relations *International Union of Nutritional Sciences (IUNS, #15796)*. [2010/XJ4358/**F**]

♦ African Grantmakers Network / see Africa Philanthropy Network (#00512)

♦ African Graphics Association (internationally oriented national body)
♦ African Green Foundation International (unconfirmed)
♦ African Greens – Coalition of Green Parties and political movements in Africa / see African Greens Federation (#00331)

♦ African Greens Federation (AGF) 00331

Fédération des Verts Africains (FEVA)

Pres c/o DGPR, Kigali, Rwanda. T. +250788563039. E-mail: info@rwandagreendemocrats.org.
SG Univ Gaston Berger, Sci Juridique, Saint Louis, Senegal.
URL: http://www.africangreens.org/

History 17 Apr 2010, Kampala (Uganda). Full title: *African Greens – Coalition of Green Parties and political movements in Africa.* **Aims** Facilitate coordination of diverse African Green's voices to influence governments and African Union.
Members National political parties (30) in 29 countries:
Angola, Benin, Burkina Faso, Burundi, Central African Rep, Chad, Congo DR, Côte d'Ivoire, Egypt, Gabon, Ghana, Guinea, Kenya, Madagascar, Mali, Mauritius, Morocco, Mozambique, Niger, Nigeria, Rwanda, Senegal, Sierra Leone, Somalia, South Africa, Togo, Tunisia, Uganda, Zambia.
NGO Relations Through *Global Greens (#10394)*, links with: *Asia-Pacific Greens Federation (APGF, #01919); Federación de Partidos Verdes de las Américas (FPVA, #09385).* [2022/XM3989/**D**]

♦ African Groundnut Council (AGC) 00332

Conseil africain de l'arachide (CAA) – Afrikaanse Aardnootraad

Headquarters Plot C43, Rijiyar Zaki, Gwarzo Road, Opposite NYSC Secretariat, Wase Satellite Town, PO Box 14695, Kano, Nigeria. T. +23464978890.
Liaison Office PO Box 3025, Lagos, Nigeria. T. +2348033030520.

History 18 Jun 1964, Dakar (Senegal), on signing of Governmental Convention following Agreement, 1962, between governments of Nigeria and Senegal. Statutes revised 27 Oct 1968, Niamey (Niger). **Aims** Ensure remunerative prices for groundnut and its by-products in the world market; promote groundnut consumption; organize exchange of technical and scientific information on research relating to the production, marketing and possible uses of groundnuts; promote solidarity among member States. **Structure** Annual Council of Ministers (supreme body); Council of Representatives (meets annually). Specialized Committees (6), each meeting at least annually: Finance and Administrative; Economic and Commercial; Scientific and Technical; Permanent Structure. Executive Secretariat, headed by Executive Secretary. Departments (3): Economic and Commercial; Scientific and Technical; Finance and Administrative. **Languages** English, French. **Staff** 19.00 FTE, paid. **Finance** Annual contributions by member governments in proportion to their level of groundnut production. Subsidies and other funds. **Activities** Multiplication and distribution of groundnut seeds in West and Central Africa. **Events** *Annual Ministerial Meeting* Mali 2006, *Annual ministerial meeting* Bamako (Mali) 2003, *Annual ministerial meeting* Kano (Nigeria) 2002, *Annual ministerial meeting* Senegal 1991, *Annual ministerial meeting* Gambia 1990. **Publications** *Groundnut Newsletter*; *Groundnut Review*; *Statistical Bulletin*. Leaflets; information; brochures.
Members Governments of 6 countries:
Gambia, Mali, Niger, Nigeria, Senegal, Sudan.
IGO Relations Participates in activities of: *UNCTAD (#20285).* Participates as observer in the activities of: *Codex Alimentarius Commission (CAC, #04081).* [2011/XD0020/**D***]

♦ African Growth and Opportunity Act (internationally oriented national body)

♦ African Guarantee Fund 00333

CEO 7th Floor Mayfair Ctr, Ralph Bunche Road, Nairobi, Kenya. T. +254732148000. Fax +2542721517.
URL: http://www.africanguaranteefund.com/

History Launched 2 Jun 2012, Arusha (Tanzania UR). Full title: *African Guarantee Fund for Small and Medium Sized Enterprises.* Set up as a company limited by shares, incorporated under the business laws of Mauritius. **Aims** Assist financial institutions increase their financing to African Small and Medium Sized Enterprises (SMEs) through the provision of partial financial guarantees and capacity development assistance. **Structure** Board of Directors; Management Team. **Finance** Owned by: Government of Denmark through *DANIDA*; Government of Spain through *Agencia Española de Cooperación Internacional para el Desarrollo (AECID)*; *African Development Bank (ADB, #00283)*; *Nordic Development Fund (NDF, #17271).* **Activities** Financial and/or material support. **Events** *Africa SME Champions Forum* Abidjan (Côte d'Ivoire) 2016, *Africa SME Champions Forum* Nairobi (Kenya) 2015. **IGO Relations** Development partners: *Swedish International Development Cooperation Agency (Sida)*; *United States Agency for International Development (USAID).* [2016/XM5073/**F***]

♦ African Guarantee Fund for Small and Medium Sized Enterprises / see African Guarantee Fund (#00333)
♦ African Gulf Society of Sexual Medicine (inactive)

♦ African Gymnastic Union 00334

Union africaine de gymnastique (UAG)

Pres c/o BP 561, El Biar, 16000 Algiers, Algeria.
URL: http://www.uagym.org/

History 1990, Algiers (Algeria). **Aims** Study all questions concerned with gymnastics in Africa; reinforce and develop *sporting* and friendly relations between members and safeguard their interests; promote gymnastics in all facets expedient for members. **Structure** Congress (every 2 years); Executive Committee; Management Committee; Appeal and Inspection Committee; Technical Committees (4); Regional Zones (3). **Languages** Arabic, English, French. **Finance** Members' dues. **Activities** Events/meetings; training/education; sporting activities. **Events** *General Assembly* Congo Brazzaville 2015, *General Assembly* Algiers (Algeria) 2013, *General Assembly* Cape Town (South Africa) 2006, *General Assembly* Thiès (Senegal) 2004, *Congress* Algiers (Algeria) 1993. **Publications** *UAG Bulletin*.
Members Affiliate (national federations, must also be affiliates of IGF); Honorary; Patron, in 18 countries:
Algeria, Angola, Burkina Faso, Cape Verde, Côte d'Ivoire, Egypt, Eswatini, Kenya, Libya, Morocco, Namibia, Nigeria, Senegal, Seychelles, South Africa, Sudan, Tunisia, Zimbabwe.
NGO Relations *Fédération internationale de gymnastique (FIG, #09636); European Gymnastics (#07442).* [2016.11.23/XD3099/**D**]

♦ African Health Economics and Policy Association (AfHEA) 00335

Association Africaine d'Economie et Politique de la Santé

Office Peach Bldg, No 8 Blohum Street, Dzorwulu, PO Box 8629, Cantonments, Accra, Ghana. T. +233302797109 – +233547347035. E-mail: afhea08@gmail.com.
URL: http://afhea.org/

History 17 Sep 2008. Initially registered in accordance with UK law. Registration: Start date: Apr 2010, Ghana. **Aims** Contribute to promotion and strengthening of the use of health economics and health policy analysis in achieving equitable and efficient health systems, as well as improved health outcomes in Africa, especially for the most vulnerable populations. **Structure** General Assembly; Board of Trustees; Executive Committee; sub-regional Advisors. **Languages** English, French. **Staff** 5.50 FTE, paid; 12.00 FTE, voluntary. **Finance** Sources: meeting proceeds; members' dues. Other sources: funding from partners. **Activities** Events/meetings; projects/programmes. **Events** *International Scientific Conference* 2022, *International Scientific Conference* Accra (Ghana) 2019, *International Scientific Conference* Rabat (Morocco) 2016, *International Scientific Conference* Nairobi (Kenya) 2014, *International Scientific Conference* Saly (Senegal) 2011. **Publications** *Afya Newsletter*. Policy brief.
Members Full in 27 countries:
Benin, Botswana, Burkina Faso, Burundi, Cameroon, Congo DR, Côte d'Ivoire, England, Ethiopia, Ghana, Kenya, Liberia, Mali, Mauritania, Morocco, Mozambique, Namibia, Nigeria, Rwanda, Senegal, Sierra Leone, South Africa, Tanzania UR, Togo, Uganda, Zambia, Zimbabwe.
IGO Relations Strategic relationships with: *African Union (AU, #00488); East, Central and Southern African Health Community (ECSA-HC, #05216); West African Health Organization (WAHO, #20881).* Collaborates with: *International Development Research Centre (IDRC, #13162); United States Agency for International Development (USAID); WHO Regional Office for Africa (AFRO, #20943).* **NGO Relations** Member of: *Gavi – The Vaccine Alliance (Gavi, #10077)* CSO Constituency; *Sustainable Development Solutions Network (SDSN, #20054); UHC2030 (#20277).* Strategic relationship with: *African Economic Research Consortium (AERC, #00292).* Collaborates with: *Bill and Melinda Gates Foundation (BMGF); The Rockefeller Foundation (#18966).* [2022.02.15/XJ7856/**D**]

♦ African Health Policy Network (internationally oriented national body)

♦ African Heart Network (AHN) 00336

Sec Unit 5B Graphic Centre, 5 Buiten Street, Cape Town, 8001, South Africa. T. +27214221586. E-mail: africanheartnetwork@gmail.com.
URL: http://www.ahnetwork.org/

History 2001. **Aims** Prevent and reduce *cardiovascular diseases* as the major causes of premature death and disability throughout Africa. **Structure** General Meeting (annual). Officers: President; President Emeritus; Vice-President; Secretary-Treasurer; Executive Secretary. **Languages** English, French. **Staff** 0.50 FTE, paid. **Activities** Areas: hypertension; salt reduction. Organizes: World Heart Day; World No Tobacco Day. **Events** *WHF African Summit on Best Practices and Access to Care* Khartoum (Sudan) 2017, *Annual General Meeting* Kampala (Uganda) 2011, *Annual General Meeting* Beijing (China) 2010, *Annual general meeting / Annual Meeting* Abuja (Nigeria) 2009, *Annual general meeting / Annual Meeting* Maputo (Mozambique) 2008. **Publications** *AHN Newsletter*.
Members National organizations (13) in 13 countries:
Cameroon, Congo Brazzaville, Congo DR, Ghana, Kenya, Mozambique, Nigeria, Rwanda, South Africa, Sudan, Tunisia, Uganda, Zambia.
NGO Relations Member of: *International Union for Health Promotion and Education (IUHPE, #15778); The NCD Alliance (NCDA, #16963); World Action on Salt, Sugar & Health (WASSH, #21070); World Heart Federation (WHF, #21562).* [2019/XM1520/**F**]

♦ African Heritage Research Library / see African Heritage Research Library and Cultural Center (#00337)

♦ African Heritage Research Library and Cultural Center (AHRLC) 00337

Founder/Dir PO Box 36330 Agodi, Ibadan 20001, Oyo, Nigeria. E-mail: africanheritagelibrary@yahoo.com.
Street Address Adeyipo Village, On Bashorun/Akobo-Ojurin, Idi-Igba, Kufi 1 road, Lagelu Local Gov't, Ibadan, Oyo, Nigeria.
Chief Librarian address not obtained.
URL: http://www.myspace.com/heritagelibrary

History 1988, Ila Orangun (Nigeria), as *African Heritage Research Library (AHRL).* **Aims** Serve the educational needs of rural dwellers, students, researchers, scholars, documentalists and archivists in Africa and worldwide. **Languages** English. **Staff** 10.00 FTE, paid. **Finance** Donations. **Activities** Commissioning of Afe Babalola Rural Community Service Building; African Writers Enclave. **Publications** Information Services: Library currently contains over 100,000 volumes. **IGO Relations** *UNESCO (#20322).* **NGO Relations** Member of: *UNESCO Network of Associated Libraries (UNAL, #20311).* [2012.06.01/XF5460/**F**]

♦ African HIV Policy Network / see African Health Policy Network

♦ African Hockey Federation (AfHF) 00338

Vice-Pres PO Box NG 160, Nungua, Accra, Ghana. T. +233244268333 – +233208184730. Fax +23321761805. E-mail: degangs@yahoo.com.
Pres 693 Al Horrya Rd, Lauran, Alexandria, Egypt. T. +2035766146. Fax +2035736360.
URL: http://www.africahockey.org/

History 1966, Nairobi (Kenya). Formally founded 29 Mar 1970, Nairobi. Constitution amended, 16 Sep 1995, Harare (Zimbabwe); 16 Sep 1999, Johannesburg (South Africa); 30 Jun 2002, Cairo (Egypt); 29 Mar 2003, Pretoria (South Africa); 8 Oct 2005, Pretoria (South Africa); 21 Jul 2007, Nairobi (Kenya). **Aims** Introduce, develop, advance, promote, organize and generally encourage hockey for both men and women, youth, juniors and seniors, in Africa; promote relations and cooperation amongst the members of the federation and other *sport* bodies. **Structure** Congress (every 2 years), comprising 1 or 2 delegates from each affiliated national association. Executive Board (meets at least annually), comprising President, 1st and 2nd Vice-Presidents, Honorary Secretary General, Honorary Treasurer and 2 members. Committees (5), meet at least annually. Office Manager. **Languages** English. **Staff** 1.00 FTE, paid. Voluntary. **Finance** Members' dues. Other sources: entry fees; contribution from *International Hockey Federation (#13802)*; Sponsors. Budget (annual): pounds15,000. **Activities** Organizes: Africa Cup for Nations for Seniors; Africa Cup of Nations for Juniors (21 years; Boys and Girls – up to 18 years); Africa Cup for Club Champions Men and Women; Africa Hockey Federation Presidents' Cup; hockey event included in all Africa Games programmes; occasional qualifying competitions; courses for African umpires, coaches and technical officials. Committees (5): Umpires; Event and Competitions; Coaching and Development; Marketing; Special Projects. **Events** *Biennial Congress* Accra (Ghana) 2009, *Biennial Congress* Nairobi (Kenya) 2007, *Biennial Congress* Pretoria (South Africa) 2005, *Africa forum* Leipzig (Germany) 2004, *Biennial Congress* Pretoria (South Africa) 2003. **Publications** *History of African Hockey Federation* (2000) by Gamal Shirazi.
Members National associations in 17 countries:
Botswana, Egypt, Ghana, Kenya, Libya, Malawi, Morocco, Namibia, Nigeria, Seychelles, South Africa, Sudan, Tanzania UR, Togo, Uganda, Zambia, Zimbabwe.
NGO Relations Recognized by: *Association of African Sports Confederations (AASC, #02360); Association of National Olympic Committees of Africa (ANOCA, #02820).* Under the authority of: *International Hockey Federation (#13802).* [2017/XD3372/**D**]

♦ African Humanitarian Aid and Development Agency (internationally oriented national body)
♦ African Human Resource Confederation (unconfirmed)
♦ African Human Rights Heritage (internationally oriented national body)
♦ African Human Rights Organization (inactive)
♦ African Hungarian Union (internationally oriented national body)
♦ African Indigenous and Minority Peoples Organization / see African Initiative For Mankind Progress Organization
♦ African Indigenous Women's Organization (no recent information)
♦ African Industrial Development Fund (unconfirmed)
♦ African Information Society Initiative (inactive)
♦ African Initiative For Mankind Progress Organization (internationally oriented national body)
♦ African Initiatives (internationally oriented national body)

♦ African Initiatives for Relief and Development (AIRD) 00339

Head Office Plot 42 Lugogo By-Pass, Lugogo House Block C First Floor, PO Box 32225, Kampala, Uganda. T. +256414289452. Fax +256414286956. E-mail: info@airdinternational.org.
URL: http://airdinternational.org/

History 2006. **Aims** Deliver world class humanitarian support for those displaced by conflict and other disasters. **Structure** General Assembly; Board of Directors. **Languages** English, French. **Staff** National staff: 1,722; expatriate: 59. **Finance** Funded by UN organizations and other donors. Annual budget: 35,000,000 USD (2022). **Activities** Capacity building; humanitarian/emergency aid; projects/programmes. Active in: Burkina Faso, Burundi, Cameroon, Central African Rep, Chad, Congo DR, Liberia, Niger, Tanzania UR, Uganda. **Publications** Annual Report. https://airdinternational.org/wp-content/uploads/2021/06/Annual-Report-ENGLISH-2020-.pdf **IGO Relations** *Australian Aid (inactive); Irish Aid; UNDP (#20292); UNHCR (#20327); UNICEF (#20332); World Food Programme (WFP, #21510).* **NGO Relations** Member of: *International Council of Voluntary Agencies (ICVA, #13092).* [2022.05.05/XM4447/**F**]

♦ African Innovation Foundation (internationally oriented national body)
♦ African Institute / see Instytut Studiów Regionalnych i Globalnych
♦ African Institute for Applied Economics (internationally oriented national body)
♦ African Institute for Capacity Development (internationally oriented national body)

♦ African Institute for Community-Driven Development (Khanya-aicdd) **00340**

Contact 1st Floor Maths Ctr, 28 Juta Street, Braamfontein, Johannesburg, South Africa. T. +27114039844. Fax +27113396361.
URL: http://www.khanya.org/

History 1998. Former names and other names: *Khanya-managing rural change (Khanya-mrc)* – former (1998 to Feb 2006). **Aims** Work with partners to transform development systems to support the livelihoods of poor people in Africa. **Structure** Board of Directors. [2012/XJ5820/j/**D**]

♦ African Institute of Corporate Citizenship (internationally oriented national body)
♦ African Institute for Development Policy Research and Dialogue (internationally oriented national body)
♦ African Institute for Economic and Social Development / see Center of Research and Action for Peace (#03651)
♦ African Institute for Economic and Social Development – African Training Centre (#11233)
♦ African Institute for Health and Development (internationally oriented national body)
♦ African Institute of Informatics (#11235)

♦ African Institute of International Law (AIIL) **00341**
Institut africain de droit international (IADI)

Contact PO Box 561, Arusha, Tanzania UR. T. +255785079573. E-mail: info@aiil-iadi.org.
Streed address 3rd Floor Serengeti Wing, Arusha Intl, Conference Ctr, Arusha, Tanzania UR.
URL: http://aiil-iadi.org/

History Set up by *Latin America-Caribbean Privatization Network (inactive)* in close collaboration with Tanzanian Government, 2012. Endorsed by Assembly of Heads of States and Governments of *African Union (AU, #00488)*, Jan 2012, Addis Ababa (Ethiopia). Seat Agreement signed 12 Mar 2013, Dar es Salaam (Senegal). **Structure** Project Implementation Committee (PIC). **Staff** 4.00 FTE, paid. **Activities** Training/education. **NGO Relations** *African Association of International Law (AAIL, #00208)*; *African Foundation for International Law (AFIL, #00325)*; *International Association of Law Schools (IALS, #11993)*. [2015/XJ9580/**D**]

♦ African Institute of Management Science (internationally oriented national body)

♦ African Institute for Mathematical Sciences (AIMS) **00342**

Admin Office 6-8 Melrose Road, Muizenberg, 7945, South Africa. T. +27217879320. Fax +27217879321. E-mail: info@aims.ac.za – contact@nexteinstein.org.
AIMS-NEI Secretariat Rue KG590 ST, Cellule Kamatamu, Secteur Kacyiru, Kigali, Rwanda.
URL: http://aims.ac.za/

History Sep 2003, Cape Town (South Africa). Founded on the initiative of Neil Turok and others, in an attempt to implement a new programme for training top African talent. Expanded to *AIMS Next Einstein Initiative* in 2008 to build new centres on the AIMS model across the continent. A partnership project of the Universities of Cambridge, Cape Town, Oxford, Paris Sud XI, Stellenbosch and the Western Cape. **Aims** Promote mathematics and science in Africa; recruit and train students and teachers; build capacity for African initiatives in education, research, and technology. **Structure** Council, comprising representatives from partner universities. International Board, based in UK. Independent institutions registered in South Africa, Senegal and Ghana working as part of the linked network. **Languages** English, French. **Staff** 23.00 FTE, paid. **Finance** Funded mainly by governments (Canada, South Africa, Senegal, Ghana, France) as well as private companies and universities. **Activities** Training/education; financial and/or material support; events/meetings. **Members** Centres of excellence in mathematical sciences throughout Africa. Membership countries not specified. **NGO Relations** Partner of: *UNLEASH*. [2021/XM7124/j/**E**]

♦ African Institute for the Prevention of Crime and the Treatment of Offenders / see United Nations African Institute for the Prevention of Crime and the Treatment of Offenders (#20519)
♦ African Institute of Private International Law (#11234)
♦ African Institute for Remittances (unconfirmed)
♦ African Institute for Strategic Research Governance and Development (internationally oriented national body)

♦ African Insurance Organization (AIO) **00343**
Organisation des assurances africaines (OAA)

SG PO Box 5860, Douala, Cameroon. T. +237233420163 – +237233429496. Fax +237233432008. E-mail: aio@africaninsurance.net.
Street address 30 Avenue de Gaulle, AIO Bldg, Douala, Cameroon.
URL: http://www.african-insurance.org/

History 9 Jun 1972, Mauritius. Founded by delegates attending 1st African Insurance Conference. **Aims** Promote development and expansion of a healthy insurance and reinsurance industry in Africa; promote cooperation between different insurance markets; promote and encourage professional training of insurance staff in Africa. **Structure** Conference (annual); Executive Committee; Technical Committees. **Languages** English, French. **Staff** Secretariat: full-time. **Finance** Members' dues. Other sources: grants; special income. **Activities** Events/meetings; networking/liaising. **Events** *Conference and General Assembly* Lagos (Nigeria) 2021, *Conference* Johannesburg (South Africa) 2019, *Conference* Accra (Ghana) 2018, *Conference* Kampala (Uganda) 2017, *Conference* Marrakech (Morocco) 2016. **Publications** *AIO Annual Review*; *AIO Bulletin*. Conference documents.
Members Insurance Industry; Regulatory/supervisory authorities; Training centres; national and regional associations. Members in 49 countries:
Algeria, Angola, Australia, Bahrain, Benin, Botswana, Burkina Faso, Burundi, Cameroon, Cape Verde, Chad, Congo Brazzaville, Congo DR, Côte d'Ivoire, Djibouti, Egypt, Eritrea, Eswatini, Ethiopia, Gabon, Germany, Ghana, Guinea, India, Kenya, Lesotho, Liberia, Libya, Madagascar, Malawi, Mali, Mauritania, Mauritius, Morocco, Mozambique, Namibia, Nigeria, Rwanda, Senegal, Seychelles, Sierra Leone, South Africa, Sudan, Tanzania UR, Togo, Tunisia, Uganda, UK, Zambia, Zimbabwe.
Consultative Status Consultative status granted from: *UNCTAD (#20285)* (General Category). **IGO Relations** Partner of: *Inter-African Conference on Insurance Markets (#11385)*. **NGO Relations** Instrumental in setting up: *African Insurance Clearing House (no recent information)*; *Association of African Insurance Brokers (AAIB, #02358)*; *Association of African Insurance Supervisory Authorities (AAISA, no recent information)*. [2021/XD5298/**D**]

♦ African Intellectual Property Organization **00344**
Organisation africaine de la propriété intellectuelle (OAPI)

Contact Rue Hyppodrome, 158 Place de la Prefecture, Yaoundé, Cameroon. T. +2372205700. Fax +2372205727. E-mail: oapi@oapi.int.
URL: http://www.oapi.int/

History 13 Sep 1962, Libreville (Gabon), to succeed the *African and Malagasy Industrial Property Office (AMIUPO) – Office africain et malgache de la propriété industrielle (OAMPI)*, on signature of an Agreement by the members of the then *African and Malagasy Union (Brazzaville Group, inactive)*, subsequently (until its dissolution in 1985) *African and Mauritian Common Organization (OCAM, inactive)*. Agreement entered into force 1 Jan 1964, having been ratified by all signatories. Agreement revised and present title adopted 2 Mar 1977, Bangui (Central African Rep); revised again 24 Feb 1999 and revised Agreement came into force 28 Feb 2002. Previously also referred to in French as *Association pour la promotion de la propriété intellectuelle en Afrique (APPIA)* and under the English acronym *AIPO*. **Aims** Contribute to achievement of industrial development policy objectives of member states by: ensuring protection and publication of intellectual property rights; encouraging creativity and technology transfer through use of intellectual property systems; providing regulatory conditions attractive to private investment through creation of favourable conditions and effective application of intellectual property principles; setting in motion effective training programmes to improve the capacity of the OAPI system to offer quality services; creating favourable conditions for national enterprises to enhance research results and exploit new technology. **Structure** Administrative Council; High Commission of Appeal; Directorate General; Directorates (6); Cabinet. **Languages** English, French. **Staff** 87.00 FTE, paid. **Finance** Fees for services rendered. **Activities** Events/meetings; training/education; awards/prizes/competitions; guidance/assistance/consulting. **Publications** *Bulletin officiel de la propriété intellectuelle (BOPI)* (4 a year); *Revue OAPI-Magazine* (4 a year); *Scientific Review* (4 a year). Annual Report; guides; collections of texts, in French; CD-ROM. Information Services: Instrumental in setting up *Centre africain de documentation et d'information en matière de brevets (CADIB, inactive)*. Maintains collection of texts, including all provisions relating to the Office. **Information Services** *DOCU Database*; *RESOLU Database*.
Members Governments of 17 countries:
Benin, Burkina Faso, Cameroon, Central African Rep, Chad, Comoros, Congo Brazzaville, Côte d'Ivoire, Equatorial Guinea, Gabon, Guinea, Guinea-Bissau, Mali, Mauritania, Niger, Senegal, Togo.
Consultative Status Consultative status granted from: *World Intellectual Property Organization (WIPO, #21593)* (Observer Status). **IGO Relations** Cooperation agreements with: *African Regional Intellectual Property Organization (ARIPO, #00434)*; *European Patent Office (EPO, #08166)*; *UNESCO (#20322)*; *UNIDO (#20336)*; *United Nations Economic Commission for Africa (ECA, #20554)*. Member of: *Intergovernmental Organizations Conference (IGO Conference, #11498)*. Close working relations with: *Agency for International Trade Information and Cooperation (AITIC, #00553)*. Contracting party to: *The Hague Agreement Concerning the International Deposit of Industrial Designs (1925)*, *Geneva Act of the The Hague Agreement Concerning the International Registration of Industrial Designs (1999)* *Protocol to the Madrid Agreement Concerning the International Registration of Marks (1989)* and *Singapore Treaty on the Law of Trademarks (Singapore Treaty, 2006)*. Partner of: *Organisation pour l'Harmonisation en Afrique du Droit des Affaires (OHADA, #17806)*. Cooperates with: *Eurasian Patent Office (EAPO, #05612)*. **NGO Relations** Memorandum of Understanding with: *International Trademark Association (INTA, #15706)*. [2019/XD0013/**D***]

♦ African International Association (inactive)

♦ African International Institute for Peace (AFIIP) **00345**

Dir-Gen Avenue Louise 209A box 7, 1050 Brussels, Belgium. T. +3222340257. E-mail: afiip1971@gmail.com.
Facebook: https://www.facebook.com/afiipd.org/

History 2013. Founded by a group of African intellectuals. Registration: Banque-Carrefour des Entreprises, No/ID: 0651.918.291, Start date: 14 Apr 2016, Belgium. **Aims** Work towards a world without violent conflict. **Structure** Administrative Office; President; General Secretary. **Languages** Dutch, English, French. **Finance** Funding from Belgian government and charities and friends. **Activities** Training/education; capacity building; networking/liaising; events/meetings; research/documentation; monitoring/evaluation; guidance/assistance/consulting.
Members Representatives in 12 countries:
Belgium, Egypt, Finland, France, Libya, Malawi, Morocco, Netherlands, Nigeria, Senegal, Sudan, Tunisia.
NGO Relations Member of: *European Network against Racism (ENAR, #07862)*. [2022/XM8422/**E**]

♦ African Investment Bank (unconfirmed)

♦ African Iron and Steel Association (AISA) **00346**
Association africaine du fer et de l'acier (AAFA)

SG FNMS, 19b Suez Crescent – Wuse Zone 4, PMB 268, Garki, Abuja, Federal Capital Territory, Nigeria. T. +23495233275. Fax +23495233275.
London Liaison Office 74D Adelaide Road, London, NW3 3PX, UK. T. +442075866895. Fax +442075866895.
URL: http://www.afristeel.org/

History 18 Dec 1991, Algiers (Algeria), when Statutes adopted, under the auspices of *UNIDO (#20336)*; Statutes approved by General Assembly, 20 Nov 1992, Abuja (Nigeria). **Aims** Promote and stimulate in all African countries the development of iron ore mining and processing industries as well as the metallurgical, iron and steel industries on one hand and the processing, distribution and consumption of iron and steel products and sub-products on the other hand. **Structure** General Assembly (annual). Board of Directors, consisting of 14 Active members, 4 Associate members, President of the Board of Directors, 2 Vice-Presidents and Secretary-General from the Bureau. General Secretariat, headed by Executive Secretary-General. **Languages** Arabic, English, French. **Staff** 50.00 FTE, paid. **Finance** Members' dues. Other sources: contributions; periodical subscriptions; revenues generated by services rendered; symposium, seminar and conference participation fees. **Activities** Knowledge management/information dissemination; research/documentation; training/education. **Events** *General Assembly* Abuja (Nigeria) 2004, *International conference* Bamako (Mali) 2004, *General Assembly* Abuja (Nigeria) 2002, *General Assembly* Abuja (Nigeria) 1992. **Publications** *African Steel* (4 a year).
Members Active; Associate: states/governments, national organizations and individuals in 53 countries:
Algeria, Angola, Benin, Botswana, Burkina Faso, Burundi, Cameroon, Cape Verde, Central African Rep, Chad, Comoros, Congo Brazzaville, Congo DR, Côte d'Ivoire, Djibouti, Egypt, Equatorial Guinea, Eritrea, Eswatini, Ethiopia, Gabon, Gambia, Ghana, Guinea, Guinea-Bissau, Kenya, Lesotho, Liberia, Libya, Madagascar, Malawi, Mali, Mauritania, Mauritius, Morocco, Mozambique, Namibia, Niger, Nigeria, Rwanda, Sao Tomé-Principe, Senegal, Seychelles, Sierra Leone, Somalia, South Africa, Sudan, Tanzania UR, Togo, Tunisia, Uganda, Zambia, Zimbabwe.
IGO Relations Associate member: *African Union (AU, #00488)*. [2012/XD3456/**D**]

♦ African Islamic Network of Associations and Organizations for Population and Development / see African Islamic Organization on Population and Development (#00347)

♦ African Islamic Organization on Population and Development **00347**

Pres PO Box 411, Medina Baye, Kaolack, Senegal. T. +2219412353. Fax +2219411786.
History 14 Mar 2005, Abuja (Nigeria). 14-18 Mar 2005, Abuja (Nigeria), during a workshop organized by *Centre for African Family Studies (CAFS, #03726)*. Also referred to as *African Islamic Network of Associations and Organizations for Population and Development*. **NGO Relations** *African-American Islamic Institute*. [2007.08.16/XM1305/**F**]

♦ African Israel Nineveh Church (internationally oriented national body)

♦ African Jesuit AIDS Network (AJAN) **00348**
Réseau jésuite africain contre le SIDA – Rede Jesuita Africana contra a SIDA

Dir Box 571 Sarit, Nairobi, 00606, Kenya. T. +254202013541. Fax +254203877971. E-mail: info@ajan.africa.
URL: https://ajan.africa/

History 2002, within the framework of *Society of Jesus (SJ)*. **Aims** Encourage and assist the Society of Jesus to respond to *HIV*/AIDS in Africa. **Structure** Functions in nearly 30 countries of sub-saharan Africa, wherever Jesuits are present. AJAN House, Nairobi (Kenya), serves and supports the network. **Languages** English, French, Portuguese, Swahili. **Staff** 3-4 senior staff; 1 FTE; 6 support. **Activities** Religious activities; events/meetings. **Events** *General Assembly* Nairobi (Kenya) 2007, *General Assembly* Nairobi (Kenya) 2003. **Publications** *AJANews* (12 a year) in English, French, Portuguese – electronic newsletter. Annual Report. Books. **Members** Functioning in 29 countries of Sub-Saharan Africa. Membership countries not specified. [2020/XJ3992/**F**]

♦ African Jewish Congress (AJC) **00349**

Spiritual Leader PO Box 51663, Raedene, 2124, South Africa. T. +27824402621. Fax +27866146724. E-mail: rabbiajc@gmail.com.
URL: http://www.africanjewishcongress.com/

History 29 May 1994, Harare (Zimbabwe), at the founding meeting. **Aims** Ensure survival of the Jewish people and foster their unity; enable smaller Jewish communities to establish and maintain contact with larger Jewish communities, which in turn would provide them with access to various facilities; give Africa and African Jews a voice in international Jewry through a proper forum. **Structure** Officers: President; 2 Vice-Presidents; Spiritual Leader. **Activities** Organizes annual conference. **Events** *Annual meeting* Swaziland 2002, *Annual Meeting* Johannesburg (South Africa) 1999. **Publications** Annual Report.
Members Covers 15 countries:
Botswana, Congo DR, Eswatini, Kenya, Lesotho, Madagascar, Malawi, Mauritius, Mozambique, Namibia, South Africa, Tanzania UR, Uganda, Zambia, Zimbabwe.
NGO Relations Affiliated to: *World Jewish Congress (WJC, #21599)*. [2008/XF3157/**F**]

♦ African Judo Union (AJU) **00350**
Union africaine de judo (UAJ) – Unión Africana de Judo

Gen Sec FGJ, BP 14238, Libreville, Gabon. T. +2416267973.
Pres address not obtained. T. +33686074195. Fax +33145755093.
URL: http://www.judoafrica.org/

History 1961, Dakar (Senegal).
Members National Federations in 33 countries:
Algeria, Angola, Benin, Burkina Faso, Cameroon, Central African Rep, Chad, Comoros, Congo Brazzaville, Congo DR, Côte d'Ivoire, Djibouti, Egypt, Gabon, Guinea, Kenya, Libya, Madagascar, Mali, Mauritania, Mauritius, Morocco, Mozambique, Niger, Nigeria, Senegal, South Africa, Sudan, Togo, Tunisia, Uganda, Zambia, Zimbabwe.
NGO Relations Continental Union of: *International Judo Federation (IJF, #13975)*. [2010/XD5282/**D**]

♦ African Jurists' Association (AJA) 00351

Association des juristes africains

Contact 8 Rue Abdou Karim Bourgi, BP 9053, 10 065 Dakar, Senegal. T. +221211948. Fax +221217557.

History 1979, as *Association des jeunes juristes africains*. Also referred to as *International Society for African Jurists*. Current name adopted 1983. **Aims** Instigate reflection from which would emerge *juridical* systems adapted to socio-economic and cultural realities of Africa; favour development of a current of opinion serving to promote and protect the *rights* of man, and individual and collective *freedom*, a necessary condition for autocentric and integral development of the African peoples. Given the critical situation of human rights in Africa, oppose in general: the *death penalty*, *imprisonment* for offences of opinion; *torture*, *ill-treatment* and *arbitrary arrest*. **Structure** International Bureau of 5; regional delegations (5); national representatives (one per country). **Languages** Arabic, English, French, Portuguese. **Events** *Annual General Assembly* Saint-Malo (France) 2002.

Members Professionals and specialists with a high level of competence – lawyers, magistrates and persons active in defence and promotion of human rights. Individuals in 20 countries:
Algeria, Angola, Benin, Burkina Faso, Cameroon, Congo Brazzaville, Congo DR, Côte d'Ivoire, Equatorial Guinea, Gabon, Guinea, Mali, Morocco, Nigeria, Senegal, Sierra Leone, Sudan, Togo, Tunisia, Zimbabwe.

Consultative Status Consultative status granted from: *African Commission on Human and Peoples' Rights (ACHPR, #00255)* (Observer). **NGO Relations** Member of: *International Association of Democratic Lawyers (IADL, #11837)*. [2011/XD5730/v/**D**]

♦ African Kickboxing Federation / see WKF Africa (#20972)
♦ African Korfball Federation / see African Continental Korfball Federation (#00268)

♦ African Kurash Union (AKU) 00352

Pres 31 George Greyst Street, Vanderbijlpark, 1911, South Africa. T. +27828591905.
URL: http://www.kurash-africa.com/

History Founded 2001. Continental federation of *International Kurash Association (IKA, #13993)*. **Aims** Promote and protect the interests of Kurash and its values on the African continent. **Structure** Congress (annual, during Continental Championship); Directing Committee; Commissions. **Languages** English, French, Portuguese. **Finance** Members' dues. Other sources: donations; sponsorship; official events; financial support from World Foundation on Kurash Development. **Activities** Events/meetings. **Events** *African Kurash Championship* Mbabane (Swaziland) 2014, *African Kurash Championship* Johannesburg (South Africa) 2013, *African Kurash Championship* Brazzaville (Congo Brazzaville) 2012, *African Kurash Championship* Maputo (Mozambique) 2010, *African Kurash Championship* Lusaka (Zambia) 2009.

Members National federations in 21 countries:
Angola, Botswana, Cameroon, Central African Rep, Congo Brazzaville, Congo DR, Eswatini, Kenya, Libya, Madagascar, Mauritius, Morocco, Mozambique, Namibia, Niger, Nigeria, Senegal, South Africa, Tanzania UR, Zambia, Zimbabwe. [2020.03.03/XM0858/**D**]

♦ African Laboratory for Natural Products (ALNAP) 00353

Coordinator Dept of Chemistry, Addis Ababa Univ, PO Box 30270, Addis Ababa, Ethiopia. T. +2511553499. Fax +2511551244.
URL: http://alnapnetwork.com/

History 1997. **Members** Membership countries not specified. **NGO Relations** Member of: *AFASSA (no recent information)*. [2012/XF6993/**F**]

♦ African Labour Law Society (ALLS) 00354

Secretariat address not obtained.
URL: https://www.africanlabourlawsociety.org/

History 2017. Current constitution adopted Sep 2018. **Aims** Advance and promote labour law and social security law as legal and academic disciplines in Africa. **Structure** Management Committee; Secretariat. **Languages** English. **Activities** Events/meetings; knowledge management/information dissemination; networking/liaising. **Events** *Conference* Grand-Baie (Mauritius) 2023, *Conference* Nairobi (Kenya) 2021, *Conference* Gaborone (Botswana) 2020, *Conference* Cape Town (South Africa) 2018, *Conference* Sun City (South Africa) 2017.

Members Full in 18 countries:
Angola, Botswana, Burkina Faso, Eswatini, Kenya, Lesotho, Malawi, Mauritius, Morocco, Namibia, Nigeria, Somalia, South Africa, Tanzania UR, Togo, Uganda, Zambia, Zimbabwe. [2021.07.05/XM8852/**D**]

♦ African Labour Sports Organisation / see Organisation du Sport Africain Travailliste et Amateur (#17827)

♦ African Language Association of Southern Africa (ALASA) 00355

Treas Dept of African Languages, PO Box 392, Pretoria, 0003, South Africa. T. +27124298038. Fax +27124298038. E-mail: mojapml@unisa.ac.za.
URL: http://www.alasa.org.za/

History Founded 1979, Unisa (South Africa). **Aims** Promote and coordinate research, study and teaching of African languages. **Structure** Executive Board; Regional Committees. **Languages** Afrikaans, English, Irish Gaelic, Ndebele, Sotho, Sotho, Tsonga, Tswana, Xhosa, Zulu. **Staff** Voluntary. **Finance** Members' dues. Other sources: donations; sales of publications. **Activities** Events/meetings; financial and/or material support; awards/prizes/competitions. **Events** *Biennial Conference* Bloemfontein (South Africa) 2019, *Biennial Conference* Grahamstown (South Africa) 2017, *Biennial Conference / Biennial International Conference* Cape Town (South Africa) 2015, *Biennial Conference* Matatiele (South Africa) 2013, *Biennial International Conference* Durban (South Africa) 2011. **Publications** *South African Journal of African Languages* (2 a year); *ALASA Newsletter*.

Members Individuals (about 170) in 21 countries:
Belgium, Botswana, Burundi, Congo DR, Eswatini, Gabon, Germany, Ghana, Italy, Kenya, Lesotho, Malawi, Namibia, Netherlands, Nigeria, Rwanda, South Africa, UK, USA, Zambia, Zimbabwe.

NGO Relations Instrumental in setting up: *African Association for Lexicography (AFRILEX)*. Links with national organizations. [2018/XD3762/**D**]

♦ African Laser, Atomic and Molecular Sciences Network (LAM Network) 00356

Pres Dept de Physique, Fac des Sciences, Univ Cheikh Diop, BP 5005 Dakar-Fann, Dakar, Senegal. T. +221776341961. Fax +221338246318. E-mail: mansourfaye@sunugal.com.
URL: http://www.lamnetwork.org/

History 1991, Dakar (Senegal). **Aims** Stimulate cooperation and exchange of information among African scientists; enhance the awareness of optics and its uses in the African continent. **Finance** Sponsored by *Abdus Salam International Centre for Theoretical Physics (ICTP, #00005)* and International Science Program, Uppsala University (Sweden). **Activities** Organizes workshops. **Events** *International conference on optics and lasers in science and technology for sustainable development* Dakar (Senegal) 2009, *International workshop on the physics and modern applications of lasers* Khartoum (Sudan) 1996. **Publications** *LAM Network Netwsletter*. **NGO Relations** Member of: *International Commission for Optics (ICO, #12710)*. [2013/XF3850/**F**]

♦ African Laser Centre (ALC) 00357

Contact Natl Laser Ctr, CSIR, PO Box 395, Pretoria, South Africa. T. +27128412713. E-mail: kramonyai@csir.co.za.
URL: https://www.africanlasercentre.net/

History Set up 2002, as a virtual centre of excellence. **Aims** Enable African nations to collaborate with each other and play a major role internationally in utilizing light to advance science and technology, thereby contributing to the strengthening of their economies, global competitiveness, education and welfare of their people. **Structure** Board of Directors. **Events** *Annual Workshop* Rabat (Morocco) 2014. **IGO Relations** *New Partnership for Africa's Development (NEPAD, #17091)*. [2019/XJ9940/**D**]

♦ African Law Center (internationally oriented national body)
♦ African Law Foundation (internationally oriented national body)
♦ African Law Students' Association (internationally oriented national body)
♦ African Law Students and Young Lawyers Association (no recent information)

♦ African Leadership Centre (ALC) 00358

Nairobi Office Jacaranda Avenue, PO BOX 25742, Nairobi, 00603, Kenya. E-mail: info@africanleadershipcentre.org.
London Office Global Institutes, Chesham Bldg, King's College London – Room 12B, Strand Campus Strand, London, WC2R 2LS, UK. E-mail: alc@kcl.ac.uk.
URL: http://www.africanleadershipcentre.org/

History 2010, Kenya, as a joint initiative of King's College London (UK) and the University of Nairobi (Kenya). **Aims** Train and mentor young Africans with potential to lead and enable innovative change in their communities and in the region. **Structure** Board of Trustees. **Languages** English. **Staff** 17.00 FTE, paid. **Activities** Training/education; capacity building; research and development; guidance/assistance/consulting. **Publications** *The Journal of Developing Societies*; *The Voice of ALC* – newsletter. Keynote Series; Lecture Series. Monographs; working papers; research reports; policy briefs; opinions. [2016.10.19/XJ6258/**E**]

♦ African Leadership Conference (unconfirmed)

♦ African Leaders Malaria Alliance (ALMA) 00359

Chair address not obtained. E-mail: info@alma2030.org.
URL: http://alma2030.org/

History 1 Feb 2010. Founded by African Heads of State and Government. **Aims** End malaria-related deaths. **Activities** Healthcare. Initiatives include: Mosquito net utilization; Removal of taxes and tariffs; Removal of oral artemisin monotherapies; ALMA Tender; Local manufacture of malaria commodities.

Members Governments (41):
Angola, Benin, Botswana, Burkina Faso, Cameroon, Cape Verde, Comoros, Congo Brazzaville, Congo DR, Djibouti, Egypt, Equatorial Guinea, Ethiopia, Gambia, Ghana, Guinea, Kenya, Lesotho, Liberia, Madagascar, Malawi, Mali, Mauritania, Mauritius, Mozambique, Namibia, Nigeria, Rwanda, Sao Tomé-Principe, Senegal, Seychelles, Sierra Leone, Somalia, South Africa, South Sudan, Sudan, Tanzania UR, Togo, Uganda, Zambia, Zimbabwe.

Regional entity (1):
African Union (AU, #00488). [2023/XJ5050/**D***]

♦ African League Against Rheumatism / see African League of Associations for Rheumatology (#00360)

♦ African League of Associations for Rheumatology (AFLAR) 00360

Ligue Africaine des Associations en Rhumatologie

SG University Hospital of Batna, Route de Tazoult, 05000 Batna, Algeria. E-mail: contact@aflar.net.
Registered Address Rheumatology unit, Lagos State University Teaching Hospital, 1-5 Oba Akinjobi Way, Ikeja 100271, Lagos, Nigeria.
URL: http://www.aflar.net/

History 3 Aug 1989. Former names and other names: *African League Against Rheumatism (AFLAR)* – former (3 Aug 1989); *Ligue africaine contre le rhumatisme* – former (3 Aug 1989). **Aims** Stimulate and promote development of awareness, knowledge and means of prevention, treatment, rehabilitation and relief of rheumatic diseases – that is, diseases of connective tissue and medical disorders of the musculoskeletal or locomotor system. **Structure** General Assembly (every 2 years, at Congress); Executive Committee (meets annually); Standing Committees (5). **Languages** English, French. **Staff** Voluntary. **Finance** Sources: donations; investments; members' dues. **Activities** Events/meetings; research and development. **Events** *Biennial Congress* Flic en Flac (Mauritius) 2019, *Biennial Congress* Algiers (Algeria) 2018, *Biennial Congress* Lagos (Nigeria) 2015, *Quadrennial Congress* Durban (South Africa) 2013, *Quadrennial Congress* Algiers (Algeria) 2011. **Publications** *African Journal of Rheumatology*.

Members National scientific or medical organizations and national community agencies (one federation per country). Members in 19 countries:
Algeria, Cameroon, Congo Brazzaville, Congo DR, Côte d'Ivoire, Egypt, Gabon, Kenya, Libya, Madagascar, Mauritania, Mauritius, Morocco, Nigeria, Senegal, South Africa, Sudan, Togo, Tunisia.

IGO Relations Cooperates with (2): *WHO (#20950)*; *WHO Regional Office for Africa (AFRO, #20943)*. **NGO Relations** Member of (1): *International League of Associations for Rheumatology (ILAR, #14016)* (as regional league). [2020.06.23/XD3125/**D**]

♦ African Leasing Association (inactive)
♦ African Legal Information Institute (unconfirmed)

♦ African Legal Support Facility (ALSF) 00361

Facilité africaine de soutien juridique

Dir Immeuble CCIA, Plateau, 01 BP 1387, Abidjan 01, Côte d'Ivoire. T. +22520263596. E-mail: alsf@afdb.org.
URL: http://www.aflsf.org/

History Established Dec 2008, as an autonomous legal and independent international organization. Constitutive Assembly 29 Jun 2009, Tunis (Tunisia), following Agreement signed as a Treaty by *African Development Bank (ADB, #00283)*, and 29 African States. **Aims** Operate as a legal and technical service provider to regional member countries, allowing them access to sound legal advice and technical assistance on matters relating to creditor litigation, complex commercial transactions, particularly with regard to infrastructure strengthening and extractive resource management and negotiation, debt management and restructuring; focus on capacity building and knowledge management from a technical, legal viewpoint, with a views to strengthening legal capacity throughout Africa. **Structure** Governing Council (meets annually); Management Board; Directorate. **Languages** English, French. **Staff** 12.00 FTE, paid. **Finance** AfDB allocated US$ 10 million to launch Facility in 2010. Grant Agreements with: *Department for International Development (DFID, inactive)*; Norway; Netherlands; Canada; *African Development Bank (ADB, #00283)*; *United States Agency for International Development (USAID)*. **Activities** Conflict resolution; guidance/assistance/consulting; capacity building; events/meetings; training/education; knowledge management/information dissemination. **Events** *Meeting* Busan (Korea Rep) 2018, *Meeting* Busan (Korea Rep) 2018, *Annual Meeting* Kigali (Rwanda) 2014, *Annual Meeting* Marrakech (Morocco) 2013, *Annual Meeting* Arusha (Tanzania UR) 2012. **Publications** *ALSF Bulletin*. Annual Report; Medium Term Strategy 2013-2017.

Members States having signed the Agreement (51):
Belgium, Benin, Brazil, Burkina Faso, Burundi, Cameroon, Central African Rep, Chad, Comoros, Congo Brazzaville, Congo DR, Côte d'Ivoire, Djibouti, Egypt, Eswatini, Ethiopia, France, Gabon, Gambia, Ghana, Guinea, Guinea-Bissau, Kenya, Lesotho, Liberia, Libya, Madagascar, Malawi, Mali, Mauritania, Mauritius, Morocco, Mozambique, Netherlands, Niger, Nigeria, Rwanda, Sao Tomé-Principe, Senegal, Seychelles, Sierra Leone, Somalia, South Sudan, Sudan, Tanzania UR, Togo, Tunisia, Uganda, UK, Zambia, Zimbabwe.

Organizations having signed the Agreement (7):
Africa Finance Corporation; *African Development Bank (ADB, #00283)*; *African Union (AU, #00488)*; *Banque ouest africaine de développement (BOAD, #03170)*; *ECOWAS Bank for Investment and Development (EBID, #05334)*; *Islamic Development Bank (IsDB, #16044)*; *Organisation pour l'Harmonisation en Afrique du Droit des Affaires (OHADA, #17806)*. [2014.11.17/XJ0427/y/**F***]

♦ African Lesbian Alliance / see Coalition of African Lesbians (#04046)

♦ African Liberal Youth (OALY) 00362

Contact address not obtained. T. +27831437508. Fax +27862609193.

History Set up 1997. Relaunched under full title, Feb 2011. Full title: *African Liberal Youth – Liberal Energizing African Democracy (OALY-LEAD)*.

Members Organizations in 16 countries:
Burkina Faso, Burundi, Congo DR, Côte d'Ivoire, Guinea, Madagascar, Malawi, Mali, Senegal, Seychelles, Sierra Leone, South Africa, South Sudan, Sudan, Uganda, Zambia.

NGO Relations Associate member of: *Africa Liberal Network (ALN, #00187)*. [2014/XJ8607/**D**]

♦ African Liberal Youth – Liberal Energizing African Democracy / see African Liberal Youth (#00362)

♦ African Library and Information Associations and Institutions (AfLIA) 00363

Association Africaine des Bibliothèques et des Institutions d'Information – Associação Africana de Bibliotecas e Instituições de Informação

Exec Dir PO Box BC 38 Burma Camp, Accra, Ghana. T. +233544252212. E-mail: info@aflia.net.
URL: https://web.aflia.net

History 2013. Registration: Start date: Oct 2014, Ghana. **Aims** Empower the library and information community in Africa to actively promote the African development agenda through dynamic services that transform livelihoods. **Structure** Governing Council. **Languages** English, French, Portuguese. **Staff** 8.00 FTE, paid. **Finance** Sources: grants; members' dues. **Activities** Advocacy/lobbying/activism; awards/prizes/competitions; awareness raising; capacity building; certification/accreditation; events/meetings; guidance/assistance/consulting; knowledge management/information dissemination; networking/liaising; publishing activities; research/documentation; standards/guidelines; training/education. **Events** *Conference* Accra (Ghana) 2021, *Conference* Nairobi (Kenya) 2019, *Conference* Yaoundé (Cameroon) 2017, *Conference* Accra (Ghana) 2015. **Publications** *AfLIA Monthly e-Newsletter.* News Alerts. **Members** Full in 34 countries. Membership countries not specified. **Consultative Status** Consultative status granted from: *World Intellectual Property Organization (WIPO, #21593)* (Observer Status). **NGO Relations** Partner of (6): *Bill and Melinda Gates Foundation (BMGF); Electronic Information for Libraries (EIFL, #05425)*; figshare; *International Federation of Library Associations and Institutions (IFLA, #13470); International Library and Information Group (CILIP ILIG, #14037); Open Educational Resources Africa (OER Africa, #17750).* [2023.02.22/XM8477/**D**]

- ♦ African Library Project (internationally oriented national body)
- ♦ African Life Cycle Assessment Network (unconfirmed)
- ♦ AfricanLII – African Legal Information Institute (unconfirmed)
- ♦ African Linguistics and Cross-Cultural Studies Association (inactive)
- ♦ African Literature Association (internationally oriented national body)
- ♦ African Lotteries Association (#02791)
- ♦ African and Malagasy Coffee Organization (no recent information)

♦ African and Malagasy Council for Higher Education 00364

Conseil africain et malgache pour l'enseignement supérieur (CAMES)

Mailing Address 01 BP 134, Ouagadougou 01, Burkina Faso. T. +22625368146. Fax +22625368573. E-mail: cames@lecames.org.
URL: http://www.lecames.org/

History 10 Feb 1968, Libreville (Gabon). Founded by *Conférence des ministres de l'éducation des Etats et gouvernements de la Francophonie (CONFEMEN, #04632)*, following Conference, 22 Jan 1966, Niamey (Niger), of Heads of State and Government of the then *'Union africaine et malgache de coopération économique (UAMCE)'*, later, until its dissolution in 1985, *African and Mauritian Common Organization (OCAM, inactive).* Former names and other names: *African and Mauritian Council on Higher Education* – alias; *Conseil africain et mauricien pour l'enseignement supérieur* – alias. **Aims** Promote and favour understanding and solidarity among member states and found a permanent cultural and scientific cooperation among them; collect and disseminate university and research documents (statistics, information on examinations, offers and requests for employment); prepare projects for conventions among the concerned states in the areas of higher education and research, and contribute to the application of these conventions; devise and promote concertation with the aim of pedagogical harmonization among higher education establishments. **Structure** Council of Ministers (meets annually, alternating among member states). Presidency is assured for 2 years by each member state in turn. Secretariat General, comprising financial service and technical services. General Consultative Committee. **Languages** French. **Staff** 11.00 FTE, paid. **Finance** Contributions of member states. **Activities** Organizes: annual conference; colloquia. Programmes: Recognition and equivalence of diplomas; African pharmacopoeia and traditional medicine; Consultative inter-African Committees; competitive examinations for higher qualifications in further education teaching competitive examinations for higher qualifications in secondary school teaching; International Order of Academic Palms; Information and documentation centre project. **Events** *Council Session* Libreville (Gabon) 2011, *Session* Libreville (Gabon) 2006, *Annual conference* Ouagadougou (Burkina Faso) 2005, *Session / Council Session* Ouagadougou (Burkina Faso) 2005, *Session* Abidjan (Côte d'Ivoire) 2004. **Publications** *CAMES Info* – bulletin; *Revue CAMES*; *Revue pharmacopée et médecine traditionnelle africaines.* Proceedings of colloquia on pharmacopoeia and traditional medicine. Information Services: Documentation centre including notes, theses and other publications, open to interested researchers.

Members Governments of 19 countries:
Benin, Burkina Faso, Burundi, Cameroon, Central African Rep, Chad, Congo Brazzaville, Congo DR, Côte d'Ivoire, Equatorial Guinea, Gabon, Guinea, Guinea-Bissau, Madagascar, Mali, Niger, Rwanda, Senegal, Togo.
Friends of CAMES, Governments of 4 countries and territories:
Belgium, Canada, France, Québec.
International Members (7):
AGRHYMET Regional Centre (#00565); Centre international de recherche-développement sur l'élevage en zone subhumide (CIRDES, #03760); Centre international de recherches médicales de Franceville (CIRMF); Institut International d'Ingénierie de l'Eau et de l'Environnement (2iE, #11313); International Higher Institute for IT and Management (ISIG); *Inter-State School of Veterinary Sciences and Medicine (#15982); Multinational Higher School of Telecommunications of Dakar (#16898).*
IGO Relations Partners: CONFEMEN; *Union économique et monétaire Ouest africaine (UEMOA, #20377); UNESCO (#20322); WHO (#20950).* **NGO Relations** Partners: *Agence universitaire de La Francophonie (AUF, #00548); Conférence internationale des doyens des facultés de médecine d'expression française (CIDMEF, #04616); Institut pour le développement de l'enseignement supérieur francophone, Bordeaux (IDESUF).* [2022/XD0012/y/**D***]

- ♦ African and Malagasy Sugar Council (inactive)
- ♦ African and Malagasy Union (inactive)

♦ African Malaria Network Trust (AMANET) 00365

Secretariat Commission for Science and Technology Bldg, PO Box 33207, Dar es Salaam, Tanzania UR. T. +255222700018. Fax +255222700380.

History 24 Feb 1995, Arusha (Tanzania UR). Founded by Prof Wen Kilama. Former names and other names: *African Malaria Vaccine Testing Network (AMVTN)* – former (1995 to 2002). **Aims** Promote and coordinate capacity strengthening of malaria R and D in African institutions; create global awareness of the Africa malaria burden; sponsor clinical and field trials; promote development of African indigenous antimalaria medicines; promote development of appropriate antimalaria medicines; promote good governance, efficient management and networking of malaria institutions. **Structure** General Assembly. Scientific Coordinating Committee of 12 members from African, European and American institutions. Board of 10 members. Secretariat. **Languages** English. **Staff** 12.00 FTE, paid. **Finance** Funding from several organizations, including: *DANIDA; European Community (inactive); European Development Fund (EDF, #06914); Bill and Melinda Gates Foundation (BMGF); Wellcome Trust.* **Activities** Determines the needs and characterization of potential sites for testing malaria interventions in Africa; promotes cooperation and collaboration among stakeholders in the fight against malaria; strengthens infrastructure and provides equipment to prospective trial sites; builds institutional capacities in health research ethics among institutional and national ethics review committees/boards in Sub-Saharan Africa; sponsors clinical and field trials of malaria interventions in Africa; organizes workshops; sponsors the Afro-Immunoassay Network. **Events** *Conference* Nairobi (Kenya) 2009, *Conference* Zanzibar (Tanzania UR) 2007, *Biennial General Assembly* Arusha (Tanzania UR) 2004, *Workshop on good clinical practice for African researchers* Bagamoyo (Tanzania UR) 2004, *Workshop on advanced health research ethics in Africa* Zanzibar (Tanzania UR) 2004. **Publications** *AMANET Newsletter* (2 a year). Annual Report. **Information Services** *Directory of Potential Institutions for Testing Malaria Vaccines* – database.
Members Committee members in 41 countries:
Belgium, Botswana, Burkina Faso, Cameroon, Congo Brazzaville, Côte d'Ivoire, Denmark, Egypt, Eswatini, Ethiopia, Finland, France, Gabon, Gambia, Germany, Ghana, India, Italy, Kenya, Libya, Luxembourg, Malawi, Mali, Mozambique, Netherlands, Nigeria, Norway, Papua New Guinea, Portugal, Senegal, South Africa, Sudan, Sweden, Switzerland, Tanzania UR, Thailand, Uganda, UK, USA, Zambia, Zimbabwe.
IGO Relations *Organization of Coordination for the Control of Endemic Diseases in Central Africa (#17860).*
NGO Relations Host secretariat of: *Multilateral Initiative on Malaria (MIM, #16886).* [2008.06.01/XF4609/**F**]

- ♦ African Malaria Vaccine Testing Network / see African Malaria Network Trust (#00365)

♦ African Management Development Institutes Network (AMDIN) ... 00366

Head of Secretariat Private Bag x 759, Pretoria, 0001, South Africa. T. +27124416179. Fax +27124416040. E-mail: secretariat@africamdin.net.
Street address ZK Matthews Building, 70 Meintjies Street, Sunnyside, Pretoria, 0002, South Africa.
URL: http://www.africamdin.net/

History Founded 2002, within the context of *African Union (AU, #00488)* and its *New Partnership for Africa's Development (NEPAD, #17091).* **Aims** Create for African MDIs a platform that articulates their collective voice and that promotes mutual partnership and collaboration with a view to developing leadership and management capacity in response to the needs of the African people and their governments. **Structure** General Assembly (every 2 years); Council; Secretariat. **Languages** Arabic, English, French, Portuguese. **Staff** 3.00 FTE, paid. **Finance** Members' dues. Donor funded. **Activities** Events/meetings; projects/programmes; publishing activities. **Publications** *Africa Journal of Public Sector Development and Governance (AJPSDG).*
Members Institutions (31) in 31 countries:
Benin, Burkina Faso, Burundi, Cameroon, Chad, Congo DR, Côte d'Ivoire, Ethiopia, Gabon, Gambia, Ghana, Guinea, Guinea-Bissau, Kenya, Lesotho, Liberia, Malawi, Mali, Mauritania, Mozambique, Namibia, Niger, Nigeria, Rwanda, Senegal, Seychelles, Sierra Leone, South Africa, South Sudan, Togo, Uganda. [2017.03.08/XM1740/**D**]

♦ African Management Services Company (AMSCO) 00367

CEO 25 Rudd Road, Illovo, Johannesburg, 2196, South Africa. T. +27112195000. Fax +27112680088. E-mail: info@amscobv.com.
Head Office Dam 5b, Unit A, 1012 JS Amsterdam, Netherlands. T. +31206641916. Fax +31206642959.
URL: http://www.amsco.org/

History 19 Apr 1989, Amsterdam (Netherlands), by *UNDP (#20292), African Development Bank (ADB, #00283)* and *International Finance Corporation (IFC, #13597)*, to serve as the operational unit of UNDP's *African Training and Management Services (ATMS)* Project. A company registered in the Netherlands. **Aims** Help African enterprises become globally competitive, profitable and sustainable through providing professional management and capacity building services to selected African businesses, particularly Small and Medium Enterprises (SMEs). **Structure** Directors (6), including Chairman. Head Office: Amsterdam (Netherlands). Operational headquarters: Johannesburg (South Africa). Regional Offices: East Africa – Nairobi (Kenya); Southern Africa – Johannesburg (South Africa); West Africa – Accra (Ghana). Country offices: Lagos (Nigeria); Yaoundé (Cameroon); Dakar (Senegal). **Finance** Shareholders: *African Development Bank (ADB, #00283)* – 7.52%; *Agence française de développement (AFD)* – 13.59%; Banco de Fomento e Exterior (Portugal) – 7.19 %; *Teollisen Yhteistyön Rahasto (FINNFUND)* – 3.72%; *Investeringsfonden for Udviklingslande (IFU)* 27.09%; *International Finance Corporation (IFC, #13597)* – 23.84%; *Nederlandse Financierings-Maatschappij voor Ontwikkelingslanden (FMO)* – 7.27%; *Norwegian Investment Fund for Developing Countries (Norfund)* – 4.82%; *Swedfund – International* – 4.95%. **Activities** Offers: Interim Management Placement; Capacity Building; Monitoring and Evaluation. Covers 28 African countries. Can apply to the *'ATMS Foundation'* for subsidies for the companies within the AMSCO protocol. **Events** *Annual Congress* Paris (France) 2008, *Annual donor meeting* The Hague (Netherlands) 2006, *African management forum* Harare (Zimbabwe) 1998, *Meeting* Amsterdam (Netherlands) 1993. **Publications** Annual Report; newsletters; operations reports, country activity reports.
Members AMSCO Shareholders – international development finance institutions – (9):
African Development Bank (ADB, #00283); Agence française de développement (AFD); Banco de Fomento e Exterior (Portugal); *International Finance Corporation (IFC, #13597); Investeringsfonden for Udviklingslande (IFU); Nederlandse Financierings-Maatschappij voor Ontwikkelingslanden (FMO); Norwegian Investment Fund for Developing Countries (Norfund); Swedfund – International; Teollisen Yhteistyön Rahasto (FINNFUND).*
IGO Relations Formal cooperation agreement with: *African Development Bank Group (ADB Group, #00284).* Partner of: *African Development Institute (ADI, #00286).* **NGO Relations** Member of: *Aspen Network of Development Entrepreneurs (ANDE, #02310).* [2010.12.17/XF1386/ey/**F***]

- ♦ African Man and Environment Alliance, Congo DR (unconfirmed)
- ♦ African Marine Waste Network (internationally oriented national body)
- ♦ African Maritime Safety and Security Agency (unconfirmed)

♦ African Masters Athletics (AFMA) 00368

Pres address not obtained. T. +23796827306 – +23796(23777759513. E-mail: aaacameroun@yahoo.fr.
URL: https://world-masters-athletics.org/regions/africa/

History 12 May 1994, as *African Veterans Athletic Association (AVAA)*, as a regional body of *World Masters Athletics (WMA, #21640).*
Members Affiliated IAAF countries in 54 countries and territories:
Algeria, Angola, Benin, Botswana, Burkina Faso, Burundi, Cameroon, Cape Verde, Central African Rep, Chad, Comoros, Congo Brazzaville, Congo DR, Côte d'Ivoire, Djibouti, Egypt, Equatorial Guinea, Eritrea, Eswatini, Ethiopia, Gabon, Gambia, Ghana, Guinea, Guinea-Bissau, Kenya, Lesotho, Liberia, Libya, Madagascar, Malawi, Mali, Mauritania, Mauritius, Morocco, Mozambique, Namibia, Niger, Nigeria, Réunion, Rwanda, Sao Tomé-Principe, Senegal, Seychelles, Sierra Leone, Somalia, South Africa, Sudan, Tanzania UR, Togo, Tunisia, Uganda, Zambia, Zimbabwe. [2019.02.14/XD9101/**D**]

♦ African Materials Research Society (African MRS) 00369

Administrator Dept of Materials Science and Engineering, Univ of Ghana, Legon Boundary, Accra, Ghana. T. +233246112530. E-mail: amrsghana@gmail.com.
URL: http://www.africanmrs.org/

History Dec 2002, Dakar (Senegal). **Aims** Promote excellence in all aspects of materials research in Africa. **Structure** Commissions (7): Adhering Body Applications; Awards; Education; Finance; International Networks; Meetings and Conferences; Publications. **Events** *Conference* Dakar (Senegal) 2022, *Conference* Arusha (Tanzania UR) 2019, *Conference* Gaborone (Botswana) 2017, *Conference* Accra (Ghana) 2015, *Western Africa Meeting* Abuja (Nigeria) 2014.
Members National organizations in 4 countries:
Cameroon, Ethiopia, Nigeria, Senegal. [2017/XD9151/**D**]

- ♦ African Mathematical Association (no recent information)

♦ African Mathematical Union (AMU) 00370

Union mathématique africaine (UMA)

SG PO Box 1014, 1409 Quartier de le Grande Delle, Rabat, Morocco. T. +212661300199. Fax +212537775471. E-mail: secretary@africamathunion.org – president@africamathunion.org.
URL: http://www.africamathunion.org/

History Jul 1976, Rabat (Morocco). **Aims** Promote the development of mathematics research and education including their applications to the economic, social and cultural development of the continent; promote an active cooperation among African mathematicians, and favour closer relationships between all scientists and technicians of the continent; promote scientific cooperation between Africa and the other continents in mathematical research and education. **Structure** General Assembly (every 4 years); Executive Committee. Commissions (6): Research & Innovation; Africa Matematica; Maths Education in Africa; Pan African Maths Olympiads; African Women in Maths; History of Mathematics in Africa. Maintains *Mathematical Sciences Network for Africa (no recent information).* **Languages** English, French. **Finance** Sources: donations; gifts, legacies; members' dues; revenue from activities/projects; subsidies. **Activities** Awards/prizes/competitions; events/meetings; networking/liaising; research/documentation. **Events** *PACOM: Pan African Congress of Mathematics* Brazzaville (Congo Brazzaville) 2022, *PACOM: Pan African Congress of Mathematics* Brazzaville (Congo Brazzaville) 2021, *Pan African Congress of Mathematicians* Abuja (Nigeria) 2013, *Pan-African congress / Pan-African Congress of Mathematicians* Tunis (Tunisia) 2004, *Pan-African congress* Cape Town (South Africa) 2000. **Publications** *Afrika Matematika* (annual) in English, French; *African Mathematical Union Information Bulletin.*
Members National sections in 27 countries:
Angola, Benin, Burkina Faso, Burundi, Cameroon, Central African Rep, Congo Brazzaville, Côte d'Ivoire, Egypt, Ethiopia, Gabon, Ghana, Guinea, Kenya, Mali, Mauritania, Morocco, Mozambique, Niger, Nigeria, Senegal, South Africa, Sudan, Tanzania UR, Tunisia, Uganda, Zimbabwe.
Individuals in 35 countries:
Algeria, Angola, Benin, Botswana, Burkina Faso, Burundi, Cameroon, Central African Rep, Congo Brazzaville, Congo DR, Côte d'Ivoire, Egypt, Ethiopia, France, Gabon, Germany, Ghana, Guinea, Kenya, Mali, Mauritania, Morocco, Mozambique, Niger, Nigeria, Senegal, South Africa, Sudan, Tanzania UR, Togo, Tunisia, Uganda, USA, Zambia, Zimbabwe.
NGO Relations Member of (1): *International Mathematical Union (IMU, #14121)* (Affiliate). Represented on International Scientific Council of: *Centre international de mathématiques pures et appliquées (CIMPA, #03758).* [2022/XD8478/**D**]

- ♦ African and Mauritian Common Organization (inactive)

♦ African and Mauritian Council on Higher Education / see African and Malagasy Council for Higher Education (#00364)
♦ African and Mauritian Office for Law Research and Studies (inactive)
♦ African Medical Library Association / see Association for Health Information and Libraries in Africa (#02630)
♦ African Medical and Research Foundation / see Amref Health Africa (#00806)
♦ African Medicines Agency (unconfirmed)

♦ African Membrane Society (AMSIC) 00371

Gen Sec address not obtained.
Pres address not obtained.
URL: http://www.sam-ptf.com/

History 2014. **Aims** Prepare and train experts across Africa in the field of membrane science, water treatment processes and sustainable energy technologies. **Structure** Board; Executive Committee. **Activities** Training/education; events/meetings knowledge management/information dissemination. **Events** *Congress* Dakar (Senegal) 2021, *Membrane and filtration technologies for sustainable development* Dakar (Senegal) 2020, *Economic growth and prosperity in Africa using membrane and filtration technologies* Johannesburg (South Africa) 2018, *Membrane water treatment in small urban and village centers* Sfax (Tunisia) 2016. **Publications** *AMSIC Newsletter*. Proceedings. **NGO Relations** Member of (1): *World Association of Membrane Societies (WA-MS, #21165).* [2021/XM7630/D]

♦ African Meteorological Society (no recent information)
♦ African Methodist Episcopal Church (internationally oriented national body)
♦ African Methodist Episcopal Church Service and Development Agency (internationally oriented national body)
♦ African Methodist Episcopal Zion Church (internationally oriented national body)

♦ African Middle East Association of Gastroenterology (AMAGE) 00372

Pres 17 Etzobat Buildings, Alharam Street, In Front of Giza Province, Giza, 12111, Egypt. T. +27114823010. Fax +27114823143.

History Founded 2000. **Events** *Congress* Calabar (Nigeria) 2012, *Congress* Sharjah (United Arab Emirates) 2006, *Meeting* Johannesburg (South Africa) 2003, *Congress* Amman (Jordan) 2002, *Congress* Cairo (Egypt) 2001. **Members** Membership countries not specified. **NGO Relations** Regional member of: *World Gastroenterology Organisation (WGO, #21536).* [2016/XD9153/D]

♦ African-Middle East Association of Radiologists (unconfirmed)
♦ African Midwives Research Network / see Lugina Africa Midwives Research Network (#16522)
♦ African Minerals Development Centre (unconfirmed)

♦ African Minerals and Geosciences Centre (AMGC) 00373

Centre africain des minéraux et des géosciences

Dir Gen Kundichi Beach Area, PO Box 9573, Dar es Salaam, Tanzania UR. T. +255222650347. Fax +255222650319. E-mail: seamic@seamic.org.
URL: http://www.seamic.org/

History 1977. Established under the auspices of *United Nations Economic Commission for Africa (ECA, #20554)*. Agreement Establishing the Centre and Rules of Procedure amended Jan 1998, Dar es Salaam (Tanzania UR); current mission and objectives adopted by Governing Council, 13 Jun 1997. Former names and other names: *East African Mineral Resources Development Centre (EAMRDC)* – former; *Eastern and Southern African Mineral Resources Development Centre (ESAMRDC)* – former; *Southern and Eastern African Mineral Centre (SEAMIC)* – former (2 Nov 1998); *Centre de mise en valeur des ressources minérales de l'Afrique de l'Est et du Sud* – former (2 Nov 1998). **Aims** Promote socio-economic and environmentally responsible geosciences-mining sector development in Africa. **Structure** Governing Council; Standing Committee of Officials (SCO); Board of Directors. **Languages** English. **Staff** 35.00 FTE, paid. **Finance** Intermittent support from development partners, including: *European Commission (EC, #06633)*; *European Development Fund (EDF, #06914)*; *UNDP (#20292)*; *UNIDO (#20336)*; *United Nations Economic Commission for Africa (ECA, #20554)*; governments of Belgium, China, France, Germany, India, Japan, Korea Rep. Annual operational budget: 60% Member States' contributions; 40% income generating activities. **Activities** Capacity building; events/meetings; guidance/assistance/consulting; knowledge management/information dissemination; research and development; training/education. **Events** *Annual meeting* Maputo (Mozambique) 2007, *Annual meeting* Dar es Salaam (Tanzania UR) 2006, *Annual meeting* Kampala (Uganda) 2005, *Annual meeting* Dar es Salaam (Tanzania UR) 2004, *Annual meeting* Addis Ababa (Ethiopia) 2003. **Publications** *AMGC News* (12 a year). **Information Services** *GEO-Information* – geoscience data management and processing department. **Members** Governments of 8 countries:
Angola, Comoros, Ethiopia, Kenya, Mozambique, Sudan, Tanzania UR, Uganda.
NGO Relations Associated with (1): *Geoscience InfoRmation in AFrica (GIRAF).* [2023/XE9708/E*]

♦ African Ministerial Conference on the Environment (AMCEN) 00374

Conférence ministérielle africaine sur l'environnement

Sec UNEP Regional Office for Africa, PO Box 30552, Nairobi, Kenya. T. +254207624289. E-mail: amcensec@unep.org.
URL: http://www.unep.org/roa/Amcen/

History Also referred to as *Conference of African Ministers on the Environment*. In accordance with recommendations of ECA Executive Secretary, May 1996, includes work of the previous *Conference of African Ministers Responsible for Sustainable Development and the Environment (AMCEN, inactive)*, with activities broadened to include sustainable development. **Structure** Joint Secretariat originally comprised *United Nations Economic Commission for Africa (ECA, #20554)*, *Organization of African Unity (OAU, inactive)* and *UNEP (#20299)*. However, following decision of 8th Session, Apr 2001, Abuja (Nigeria), Secretariat is fully ensured by UNEP. **Events** *Special Session* Cairo (Egypt) 2016, *Session* Cairo (Egypt) 2015, *Special Session* Gaborone (Botswana) 2013, *Session* Arusha (Tanzania UR) 2012, *Special Session* Bamako (Mali) 2011. **NGO Relations** Member of: *Mountain Partnership (MP, #16862).* [2008/XF6186/c/F*]

♦ African Ministerial Conference on Meteorology (AMCOMET) 00375

Conférence Ministérielle Africaine sur la Météorologie

Secretariat c/o WMO, Avenue de la Paix 7bis, PO Box 2300, 1211 Geneva 2, Switzerland. T. +41227308513. E-mail: amcomet@wmo.int.
URL: http://www.wmo.int/amcomet/

History Set up as permanent forum, by *World Meteorological Organization (WMO, #21649)* and *African Union (AU, #00488)*. First Conference organized Apr 2010, Nairobi (Kenya), when AMCOMET as high-level policy mechanism and intergovernmental authority for the development of meteorology and its applications in Africa, through adoption of Nairobi Ministerial Declaration was established. **Aims** Promote political cooperation and streamline policies at a pan-African level; advocate for sound decision-making based on robust science; provide political leadership, policy direction and advocacy in the provision of weather, water and climate information and services that meet sector specific needs. **Structure** Bureau. Secretariat provided by *World Meteorological Organization (WMO, #21649)*. **Activities** Politics/policy/regulatory. **Events** *High-Level Session* Cairo (Egypt) 2019, *Africa Hydromet Forum* Addis Ababa (Ethiopia) 2017. **Publications** *AMCOMET Newsletter.* [2017/XM6424/c/F]

♦ African Ministerial Conference on Water / see African Ministers' Council on Water (#00376)
♦ African Minister's Conference on Water / see African Ministers' Council on Water (#00376)

♦ African Ministers' Council on Water (AMCOW) 00376

Conseil des ministres africains chargés de l'eau

Exec Sec 11 T Y Danjuma Str, Asokoro District, Abuja, Federal Capital Territory, Nigeria. T. +2349096074166. E-mail: info@amcow-online.org.
URL: http://www.amcow-online.org/

History 30 Apr 2002, Abuja (Nigeria), when 'Abuja Ministerial Declaration on Water' was signed. Secretariat in Abuja (Nigeria). Became a Specialized Technical Committee for Water and Sanitation in *African Union (AU, #00488)*. Also referred to as *African Ministerial Conference on Water* and *African Minister's Conference on Water*. **Aims** Provide political leadership, policy direction and advocacy in the provision, use and management of water resources for sustainable social and economic development and maintenance of African ecosystems. **Structure** General Assembly of Ministers; Governing Council; Executive Committee; Technical Advisory Committee; Secretariat, headed by Executive Secretary. **Languages** English, French. **Events** *African Water Week* Dakar (Senegal) 2014, *Symposium on Monitoring Sustainable WASH Service Delivery* Addis Ababa (Ethiopia) 2013, *General Assembly* Cairo (Egypt) 2012, *African regional preparatory process kicked-off meeting for the fifth world water forum* Istanbul (Turkey) 2009, *Session* Johannesburg (South Africa) 2009. **Publications** *2012 Status Report on the Application of Integrated Approaches to Water Resources Management in Africa.* Technical documents; policy documents.
Members Governments of 53 countries:
Algeria, Angola, Benin, Botswana, Burkina Faso, Burundi, Cameroon, Cape Verde, Central African Rep, Chad, Comoros, Congo Brazzaville, Congo DR, Côte d'Ivoire, Djibouti, Egypt, Equatorial Guinea, Eritrea, Eswatini, Ethiopia, Gabon, Gambia, Ghana, Guinea, Guinea-Bissau, Kenya, Lesotho, Liberia, Libya, Madagascar, Malawi, Mali, Mauritania, Mauritius, Morocco, Mozambique, Namibia, Niger, Nigeria, Rwanda, Sao Tomé-Principe, Senegal, Seychelles, Sierra Leone, Somalia, South Africa, Sudan, Tanzania UR, Togo, Tunisia, Uganda, Zambia, Zimbabwe.
IGO Relations Partners:. *African Development Bank (ADB, #00283)*; *African Ministerial Conference on the Environment (AMCEN, #00374)*; *Economic Community of Central African States (ECCAS, #05311)*; *FAO (#09260)*; *Intergovernmental Authority on Development (IGAD, #11472)*; *International Bank for Reconstruction and Development (IBRD, #12317)*; *New Partnership for Africa's Development (NEPAD, #17091)*; *Southern African Development Community (SADC, #19843)*; *UNEP (#20299)*; *UNESCO (#20322)*; *United Nations System-wide Special Initiative on Africa (SIA, inactive)*; *World Meteorological Organization (WMO, #21649)*. Involved in: *Facilité africaine de l'eau (FAE, #09233)*. **NGO Relations** Partner in: *Sanitation and Water for All (SWA, #19051).* [2018.03.12/XE4596/c/E*]

♦ African Model Forest Network (AMFN) 00377

Réseau africain de Forêts Modèles (RAFM) – Red Africana de Bosques Modelo

Address not obtained.
URL: http://www.imfn.net/african-model-forest-network/

History 2009. Founded with support of Canadian government, as a regional network of *International Model Forest Network (IMFN, #14175)*. **Aims** Facilitate development of a pan-African network of model forests representative of the continent's wealth and diversity. **Structure** Regional Secretariat based in Yaoundé (Cameroon). **IGO Relations** Member of: *Congo Basin Forest Partnership (CBFP, #04662)*. **NGO Relations** Cooperates with: *Global Forum on Agricultural Research (GFAR, #10370).* [2017/XJ8363/E]

♦ African Monetary Fund (unconfirmed)
♦ African Monitor (internationally oriented national body)
♦ African Monitoring of the Environment for Sustainable Development (inactive)

♦ African Monsoon Multidisciplinary Analyses (AMMA International) . 00378

Project Office LOCEAN/IPSI, IRD/Univ Pierre et Marie Curie, Boite 100, Couloir 45-55 4ème étage, 4 place Jussieu, 75252 Paris CEDEX 05, France. T. +33144277536. Fax +33144273508.
URL: http://www.amma-international.org/

History 2002, Niamey (Niger). **Aims** Improve knowledge of the West African monsoon and its variability. **Structure** International Governing Board (IGB); International Scientific Steering Committee (ISSC); International Implementation and Coordination Group (ICIG). **Events** *Conference* Toulouse (France) 2012, *Conference* Ouagadougou (Burkina Faso) 2009, *International conference / Conference* Karlsruhe (Germany) 2007, *International conference / Conference* Dakar (Senegal) 2005. **IGO Relations** Cooperates with: *Global Climate Observing System (GCOS, #10289)*; *Global Ocean Observing System (GOOS, #10511)*. **NGO Relations** Endorsed by: *World Climate Research Programme (WCRP, #21279).* [2017.03.09/XM3457/F]

♦ African Mothers Health Initiative (internationally oriented national body)
♦ African Motorcycle Union / see FIM Africa (#09758)
♦ African Mountain Association (inactive)
♦ African Movement of Working Children and Youth (unconfirmed)
♦ **African MRS** African Materials Research Society (#00369)

♦ African Music Council (AMC) 00379

Conseil africain de la musique

Head Office Nabemba Tower, 22nd Floor – Offices 15 and 16, PO Box 14862, Brazzaville, Congo Brazzaville. T. +242010442848 – +242055568728 – +242055858833. E-mail: amc@imc-cim.org.
URL: https://www.facebook.com/African-Music-Council/

History Jul 2007, Brazzaville (Congo Brazzaville), by *International Music Council (IMC, #14199)*. **Aims** Ensure representation and implementation of the International Music Council programmes in Africa; promote *Five Rights to Music*. **Structure** General Assembly; Executive Committee. **Languages** English, French. **Staff** 1.00 FTE, paid. **Finance** Members' dues. Subventions. **Events** *Forum Africain de la Musique* Segou (Mali) 2016, *General Assembly* Brazzaville (Congo Brazzaville) 2012.
Members National Music Councils (7); national and specialized organizations (14). Members in 14 countries:
Benin, Burkina Faso, Cameroon, Congo Brazzaville, Congo DR, Côte d'Ivoire, Ghana, Kenya, Mali, Mozambique, Niger, Nigeria, Uganda, Zimbabwe.
Regional organization:
Pan African Society for Musical Arts Education (PASMAE, #18067).
IGO Relations Bilateral agreement with: government of the Republic of Congo. **NGO Relations** *International Music Council (IMC, #14199).* [2021/XM4247/E]

♦ African Mycological Association (inactive)
♦ African Mycotoxin Network (unconfirmed)
♦ African National Television and Broadcasting Union / see African Union of Broadcasting (#00490)
♦ African and Near East Billiards Confederation (inactive)
♦ The African Network (internationally oriented national body)

♦ African Network for Agriculture, Agroforestry and Natural Resources Education (ANAFE) 00380

Exec Sec c/o Kenyatta Univ, PO Box 43844-00100, School of Environmental Studies, Nairobi, Kenya.
URL: http://www.anafeafrica.net/

History 19 Apr 1993, Nairobi (Kenya). Former names and other names: *African Network for Agroforestry Education* – former. **Aims** Promote and support multidisciplinary approach in the teaching of *agriculture* and *natural resource* management with special focus on agroforestry; strengthen content and delivery of tertiary education; facilitate linkage among education research, extension and local communities. **Structure** General Members Workshop (every 4 years); Steering Committee; Regional Agroforestry Training (RAFTs) and Education Teams (4); Coordination Unit; Head Office in Nairobi (Kenya). **Staff** 1.00 FTE, paid. **Finance** Sources: revenue from activities/projects. **Activities** Events/meetings; knowledge management/information dissemination; training/education. **Events** *Regional Workshop on Developing Learning Materials* Nairobi County (Kenya) 2020, *Regional Workshop on Developing an Innovative Regional Agroforestry Curriculum* Nairobi (Kenya) 2019, *International symposium on building agricultural and natural resources education in Africa* Nairobi (Kenya) 2003. **Publications** *Agroforestry Education News* (2 a year) – newsletter. Workshop proceedings; teaching guides. **Information Services** *ANAFE Database.*
Members Universities and technical colleges (117) in 34 countries:
Benin, Botswana, Burkina Faso, Burundi, Cameroon, Congo Brazzaville, Congo DR, Côte d'Ivoire, Egypt, Eritrea, Eswatini, Ethiopia, Gambia, Ghana, Kenya, Lesotho, Liberia, Madagascar, Malawi, Mali, Mauritius, Mozambique, Namibia, Niger, Nigeria, Rwanda, Senegal, Sierra Leone, South Africa, Sudan, Tanzania UR, Togo, Uganda, Zambia, Zimbabwe.
Focal institutions (2 focal institutions in each of the 4 regions where ANAFE operates) in 8 countries:
Benin, Botswana, Burkina Faso, Ghana, Kenya, Malawi, Mali, Uganda.

African Network Agroforestry
00380

alphabetic sequence excludes
For the complete listing, see Yearbook Online at

NGO Relations Coordinated by: *World Agroforestry Centre (ICRAF, #21072)*. Collaborates with regional programmes, including: *African Academy of Sciences (AAS, #00193)*; *Association for Strengthening Agricultural Research in Eastern and Central Africa (ASARECA, #02933)*; *Comparative and International Education Society (CIES)*; *International Foundation for Science (IFS, #13677)*; *Southeast Asian Network for Agroforestry Education (SEANAFE, #19776)*; *West and Central African Council for Agricultural Research and Development (WECARD, #20907)*. Member of: *Global Confederation of Higher Education Associations for Agriculture and Life Sciences (GCHERA, #10304)*. [2021.06.07/XF4504/**F**]

♦ African Network for Agroforestry Education / see African Network for Agriculture, Agroforestry and Natural Resources Education (#00380)

♦ African Network for Basin Organizations (ANBO) 00381

Réseau africain des organismes de bassin (RAOB)

Secretariat OMVS – Haut Commissariat, 46 rue Carnot, BP 3152, Dakar, Senegal. T. +2218420216. Fax +2218220163. E-mail: amayelsn@yahoo.fr.

Contact RIOB, c/o Office international de l'eau, 21 rue de Madrid, 75008 Paris, France. T. +33144908860. Fax +33140080145. E-mail: riob2@wanadoo.fr – dg@oieau.fr – stp-riob@oieau.fr.

URL: http://www.riob.org/

History 11 Jul 2002, Dakar (Senegal), as a regional network of *International Network of Basin Organizations (INBO, #14235)* on the initiatives of the *Réseau des organismes de bassin de l'Afrique de l'ouest (ROBAO)*. **Aims** Unite African lake, river and aquifer basin organizations. **Structure** General Assembly (every 2 years). **Activities** Events/meetings; capacity building. **Events** *General Assembly* Tunis (Tunisia) 2019, *General Assembly* Kigali (Rwanda) 2016, *General Assembly* Addis Ababa (Ethiopia) 2015, *Atelier sur le Bilan des Expériences des Organismes de Bassin Transfrontaliers* Ouagadougou (Burkina Faso) 2013, *General Assembly* Dakar (Senegal) 2010. **NGO Relations** *Council for World Mission (CWM, #04925)* is member. [2019.12.12/XF6940/**E**]

♦ African Network for Care of Children Affected by HIV/AIDS (ANECCA) 00382

Exec Dir PO Box 7484, Plot 4B Kololo Hill Drive, Kampala, Uganda. T. +256312516266. E-mail: mail@anecca.org.

URL: http://anecca.org/

History 2001. **Aims** Improve access to quality and comprehensive HIV prevention, care, treatment and support services for children, integrated within the broader maternal and child health framework. **Structure** Board of Directors, headed by Chair.

Members Chapters (22) in 22 countries:

Benin, Burkina Faso, Burundi, Cameroon, Central African Rep, Congo Brazzaville, Congo DR, Ethiopia, Ghana, Guinea, Kenya, Malawi, Mali, Niger, Nigeria, Senegal, South Africa, Tanzania UR, Togo, Uganda, Zambia, Zimbabwe.

IGO Relations Partners include: *United States Agency for International Development (USAID)*. **NGO Relations** Member of: *Regional Inter-Agency Task Team on Children and AIDS in Eastern and Southern Africa (RIATT-ESA, #18791)*. Partners include: *Catholic Relief Services (CRS, #03608)*; *Management Sciences for Health (MSH)*; *Regional Centre for Quality of Health Care (RCQHC, inactive)*; *World Vision International (WVI, #21904)*. [2014.04.01/XJ7270/**F**]

♦ African Network of Centres for Investigative Reporting (unconfirmed)

♦ African Network for Chemical Analysis of Pesticides (ANCAP) 00383

Exec Sec Inst Marine Sciences, Univ of Dar es Salaam, PO Box 668, Zanzibar, Zanzibar Urban/ West, Tanzania UR. T. +255242232128. Fax +255242233050. E-mail: mmochi@ims.udsm.ac.tz – avitimmochi@gmail.com.

URL: http://www.ancapnet.org/

History 2001. **Aims** Study, promote and develop the science of all aspects of chemical analysis of pesticides, including residue analyses, degradation and environmental fate with the overall objective of not only safeguarding public health and the environment, but also ensuring the safety of African *agriculture* and *aquatic* products thus making them competitive on the world market, thereby significantly contributing to the region's *poverty* eradication endeavours. **Structure** Coordinating Board, comprising Executive Secretary, Assistant Secretary/Treasurer, all national coordinators of member countries and ex officio representatives of donor agencies. **Finance** Members' dues. **Events** *SETAC Africa meeting* Kampala (Uganda) 2009, *Inaugural conference / Conference* Arusha (Tanzania UR) 2004, *Regional symposium* Nairobi (Kenya) 2003.

Members Full in 6 countries:

Ethiopia, Kenya, Sudan, Tanzania UR, Uganda, Zimbabwe.

IGO Relations *UNESCO (#20322)* International Science Programme. [2019/XF7005/**F**]

♦ African Network of Constitutional Law / see African Network of Constitutional Lawyers (#00384)

♦ African Network of Constitutional Lawyers (ANCL) 00384

Réseau africain de droit constitutionnel (RADC) – Rede Africana de Juristas Constitucionalistas

Secretariat c/o DGRU, Dept of Public Law, Fac of Law, Univ of Cape Town, Private Bag X3, Rondebosch 7701, Cape Town, South Africa. Fax +27116505607. E-mail: vanja.karth@uct.ac.za.

URL: https://ancl-radc.org.za/

History Nov 1999, Senegal, as *African Network of Constitutional Law*, within *International Association of Constitutional Law (IACL, #11811)*. Ceased to exist. Re-launching discussed Apr 2006, Cape Town (South Africa), by a small group of scholars and jurists. **Aims** Contribute to development of democracy and constitutionalism; advance protection of rights and the rule of law in Africa. **Structure** General Assembly (every 2 years); Coordinating Committee. **Languages** Arabic, English, French, Portuguese. **Staff** 2.00 FTE, paid. **Finance** Fundraising. **Activities** Events/meetings. **Events** *Biennial Conference* Nairobi (Kenya) 2021, *Biennial Conference* Nairobi (Kenya) 2020, *Biennial Conference* Gaborone (Botswana) 2018. **Members** Full in 34 countries. Membership countries not specified. **NGO Relations** Member of: *Africa Freedom of Information Centre (AFIC, #00175)*; *Freedom of Information Advocates Network (FOIAnet, #09985)*. [2020.01.10/XF4390/**F**]

♦ African Network on Debt / see African Forum and Network on Debt and Development (#00321)
♦ African Network on Debt and Development / see African Forum and Network on Debt and Development (#00321)
♦ African Network for the Development of Horticulture (no recent information)

♦ African Network for Economics of Learning, Innovation and Competence Building Systems (AFRICALICS) 00385

SG c/o ACTS, Gigiri Court No 49, Off UN Crescent, PO Box 45917, Nairobi, 00100, Kenya. E-mail: secretariat@africalics.org.

URL: http://www.africalics.org/

History Mar 2012, Dar es Salaam (Senegal), during a working session co-organized by *Global Network for Economics of Learning, Innovation and Competence Building Systems (GLOBELICS, #10488)* and STIPRO, Tanzania UR. **Structure** Scientific Board; Secretariat. **Activities** Research/documentation; events/meetings; research/training. **Events** *Conference* Yaoundé (Cameroon) 2022, *Conference* Dar es Salaam (Tanzania UR) 2019, *Conference* Oran (Algeria) 2017, *Unpacking systems of innovations for sustainable development in Africa* Kigali (Rwanda) 2015, *Conference* Maputo (Mozambique) 2013.

Members Scholars from 7 countries:

Algeria, Kenya, Mozambique, Nigeria, Senegal, South Africa, Tanzania UR.

NGO Relations Chapter of: *Global Network for Economics of Learning, Innovation and Competence Building Systems (GLOBELICS, #10488)*. [2015/XJ9674/**F**]

♦ African Network for Environment and Economic Justice (internationally oriented national body)

♦ African Network for Evidence-to-Action in Disability (AFRINEAD) .. 00386

Contact Centre for Disabilities & Rehabilitation Studies, Stellenbosch Univ, PO Box 241, Cape Town, 8000, South Africa. T. +27219389090. E-mail: afrinead@sun.ac.za.

Coordinator address not obtained.

URL: https://blogs.sun.ac.za/afrinead/history-of-afrinead/

History Nov 2007, Stellenbosch (South Africa). Founded by the Centre for Disability and Rehabilitation Studies at Stellenbosch University. **Aims** Promote, facilitate and coordinate implementation of disability research evidence into policy and practice so as to impact real change in the quality of life of people with disabilities in Africa. **Structure** Governing Board; Disability Research Country Working Group. **Languages** English. **Staff** 1.50 FTE, paid. **Finance** Sources: donations; sponsorship. Other sources: registration fees. **Activities** Advocacy/lobbying/activism; events/meetings; knowledge management/information dissemination; research and development. **Events** *AfriNEAD Conference* Cape Town (South Africa) 2023, *AfriNEAD Conference* Cape Town (South Africa) 2020, *AfriNEAD Conference* Accra (Ghana) 2017, *AfriNEAD Conference* Mangochi (Malawi) 2014, *Building communities of trust – evidence-to-action on disability research* Victoria Falls (Zimbabwe) 2011. **Publications** *African Journal on Disability (AJOD)*. *Best Evidence-to-Action Practice Guidelines*.

Members Full in 26 countries:

Botswana, Canada, Eswatini, Ethiopia, Ghana, Ireland, Kenya, Lesotho, Malawi, Mauritius, Mozambique, Namibia, Niger, Nigeria, Norway, Rwanda, Sierra Leone, Somalia, South Africa, Sudan, Tanzania UR, Uganda, UK, USA, Zambia, Zimbabwe. [2023.02.14/XJ2017/**D**]

♦ African Network for Geo-Education (ANGE) 00387

Réseau Africain pour la Geo-Education

Contact Lab of Geodynamic and Variscan Geosciences, Dept of Geology – Fac of Sciences, Chouaïb Doukkali Univ, BP 20 24000, El Jadida, Morocco. E-mail: geoeducation.africa@gmail.com.

Contact Dept of Natural Resources – Geology, Inst of African Research and Studies, Cairo Univ, Giza, Egypt.

URL: http:///sites.google.com/site/geoeducationafrica/home

Aims Promote geoscience education in Africa at all levels; work for enhancement of the quality of geoscience education in Africa and Arabian world; encourage developments raising public awareness of geoscience. **Structure** Board. **Languages** Arabic, English, French. **Activities** Training/education. **Publications** *Geo-education in Egypt between Current and Innovative* (2018) by Kholoud M Abdel Maksoud; *Monitoring and Evaluation For Postgraduate Students In Learning Geo Education In Egypt* (2016) by Kholoud M Abdel Maksoud; *Geo-education in Egypt, ideas, challenges and vision* (2013) by Kholoud M Abdel Maksoud et al.

Members Individuals in 10 countries:

Algeria, Egypt, India, Malawi, Morocco, Nigeria, Norway, Saudi Arabia, South Africa, Tunisia.

NGO Relations *Academic Scientific Research Organization (ASRO, #00023)*; *Arabian Geosciences Union (ArabGU, #00975)*; *International Association for Geoethics (IAGETH, #11915)*; *International Association for Promoting Geoethics (IAPG, #12107)*; *Promoting Earth Science for Society (YES Network, #18541)*. [2019.09.25/XJ9993/v/**F**]

♦ African Network in Global History (ANGH) 00388

Réseau Africain d'Histoire Mondiale (RAHM)

Contact Dept of History, Univ of Ilorin, PMB 1515, Ilorin, Kwara, Nigeria.

History 9 Dec 2009, Ilorin (Nigeria). 9-11 Dec 2009, Ilorin (Nigeria). Also referred to as *African Network of Universal and Global History*. **Aims** Support studies in world and global history that address the African continent and the world as seen from African perspectives. **NGO Relations** Member of: *Network of Global and World History Organizations (NOGWHISTO, #17033)*. [2010/XJ5785/**D**]

♦ African Network on HIV/AIDS – Europe (ANHA-Europe) 00389

Contact Grdr Migrations-Citizenship-Development, 66-72 rue Marceau, 93109 Montreuil, France. T. +33148577580. Fax +33148575975.

History Netherlands, by *European Project AIDS and Mobility (A and M, inactive)*.

Members National organizations (13) in 10 countries:

Belgium, Denmark, France, Italy, Netherlands, Norway, Spain, Sweden, Switzerland, UK.

NGO Relations *Groupe de recherche et de réalisations pour le développement rural dans le Tiers-monde (GRDR)*. [2014.10.31/XF3586/**F**]

♦ African Network Information Centre / see AFRINIC (#00533)

♦ African Network for Integrated Development (ANID) 00390

Réseau africain pour le développement intégré (RADI)

Sec RADI, BP 12085 Colobane, Dakar, Senegal. T. +221338607698. E-mail: radi@orange.sn.

Street address Lot no97 Ngor Virage, face to SV City Dakar, Dakar, Senegal.

URL: https://www.radi-afrique.org/

History Founded Oct 1985, Dakar (Senegal), by a group of African professionals. **Aims** Fight against poverty, injustice and ignorance as part of the individual and collective promotion of African people through implementation of an integrated, participatory, popular and democratic development process that respects their culture and independence. **Structure** General Conference (every 5 years); Orienteering Committee. **Languages** English, French. **Finance** Supported by: *Christian Aid*; Cives Mundi; CONEMUND; Coopération Canaries; Coumba Gold; European Union; Foundation for Just Society; *ICCO – Interchurch Organization for Development Cooperation*; *International Development Research Centre (IDRC, #13162)*; Kumba International; Local Communities; Manos Unidos; MCA-Senegal; *New Field Foundation*; *Pan African Movement (PAM)*; PADEM; *UN Women (#20724)*; *USA for Africa*; *United States Agency for International Development (USAID)*; USC Canada. **Activities** Knowledge management/information dissemination; training/education; capacity building; guidance/assistance/consulting; advocacy/lobbying/activism. Active in: Burkina Faso, Gambia, Guinea, Guinea-Bissau, Mauritania, Niger. **Events** *Annual General Assembly* Dakar (Senegal) 1993, *Conference* Dakar (Senegal) 1987. **Publications** *Jëf-Jël* (12 a year).

Members Organizations and individuals in 13 countries:

Benin, Burkina Faso, Canada, Central African Rep, Congo DR, Guinea, Guinea-Bissau, Mali, Senegal, South Africa, Tanzania UR, Uganda, Zimbabwe.

Consultative Status Consultative status granted from: *African Commission on Human and Peoples' Rights (ACHPR, #00255)* (Observer). **NGO Relations** Member of: *African Network of Micro-Finance and Micro-Enterprise (MICROFIN AFRIC, no recent information)*; *Council of Non-Governmental Organizations for Development Support (#04911)*; *Environment Liaison Centre International (ELCI, no recent information)*. Instrumental in setting up: *Forum of African Voluntary Development Organizations (FAVDO, inactive)*; *Intercontinental Network for the Promotion of the Social Solidarity Economy (INPSSE, #11463)*; *Pan African Agency for Research and Consultation (PARC, no recent information)*. [2019.06.20/XF0543/**F**]

♦ African Network for Internationalization of Education (ANIE) 00391

Exec Dir Margaret Thatcher Library, Moi Univ, PO Box 3900, Eldoret, Kenya. E-mail: director@anienetwork.org – sec@anienetwork.org.

URL: http://www.anienetwork.org/

History Developed out of 'Higher Education in Africa: The International Dimension' – project, concluded 2008. **Aims** Enhance understanding and further development of the international dimension of higher education in Africa. **Structure** Board; Secretariat. **Languages** English. **Staff** 5.00 FTE, paid. **Finance** Members' dues. Other sources: research grants; project funding; in kind support. **Activities** Research and development; capacity building; knowledge management/information dissemination; networking/liaising; advocacy/lobbying/activism. **Events** *Joint Virtual Conference* 2020, *Annual Conference* Kigali (Rwanda) 2017, *Annual Conference* Accra (Ghana) 2016, *Annual Conference* Dar es Salaam (Tanzania UR) 2015, *Annual Conference* Addis Ababa (Ethiopia) 2013. **Publications** *ANIE Newsletter*. Policy briefs; book. **Members** Full (140), mainly from African universities. Membership countries not specified. **NGO Relations** Affiliated with (1): *International Association of Universities (IAU, #12246)*. [2018.10.05/XJ5467/**F**]

♦ African Network of Mathematical Statistics and its Applications (#18866)

♦ African Network Operators Group (AfNOG) 00392

Secretariat 16 Boundary Road, East Legon, PO Box No CT 9086, Accra, Ghana. T. +233277552308 – +23327(233208587222. Fax +233302521696. E-mail: secretariat@afnog.org.

URL: http://www.afnog.org/

History Founded 6 May 2000, Cape Town (South Africa). **Aims** Promote a discussion of implementation issues that require community cooperation through coordinating and cooperation among network service providers to ensure stability of service to end users on the African continent. **Finance** Support from international organizations, including: *Internet Society (ISOC, #15952)*. **Activities** Training/education; events/meetings. **Events** *Africa Internet Summit* Kampala (Uganda) 2019, *Africa Internet Summit* Dakar (Senegal) 2018, *Meeting* Gaborone (Botswana) 2016, *Meeting* Tunis (Tunisia) 2015, *Annual Meeting and Workshop / Meeting* Djibouti (Djibouti) 2014. [2016/XF5969/**F**]

♦ African Network for Prevention and Protection Against Child Abuse and Neglect (ANPPCAN) 00393

Réseau africain pour la prévention et la protection contre l'abus et la négligence de l'enfant (RAPPANE)

Regional Dir Komo Lane, Off Wood Avenue, PO Box 1768, Nairobi, 00200, Kenya. T. +254202140010 – +254202140011-2140013. Fax +254738410690. E-mail: regional@anppcan.org.
URL: http://www.anppcan.org/

History 1986, Enugu (Nigeria), during first African Conference on Child Abuse and Neglect. Registered in Kenya. **Aims** Enhance prevention and protection of children from all forms of maltreatment, ensuring the rights of children are realized. **Structure** General Council/General Meeting (meets every 2 years); National Chapter. Executive Committee/Board (meets annually); National Chapters; Headquarters in Nairobi (Kenya). **Languages** English, French. **Staff** 22.00 FTE, paid. **Finance** Members' dues. Main supporters include: *Anti-Slavery International (#00860)*; *Bernard van Leer Foundation (BvLF)*; *End Child Prostitution, Child Pornography and Trafficking of Children for Sexual Purposes (ECPAT, #05456)*; *European Commission (EC, #06633)* through Save the Children, Finland; *German Catholic Bishops' Organisation for Development Cooperation (MISEREOR)*; *International Programme on the Elimination of Child Labour and Forced Labour (IPEC+, #14652)*; *International Society for Prevention of Child Abuse and Neglect (ISPCAN, #15385)*; national foundations; *Oak Foundation*; *Rädda Barnen – Save the Children Sweden*; *Save the Children International (#19058)*; *Terre des hommes Foundation (Tdh Foundation, #20132)*; *Winrock International*. Annual budget; about US$ 941,115. **Activities** Research/documentation; monitoring/evaluation; networking/liaising; capacity building; guidance/assistance/consulting; events/meetings. **Events** *International Conference* Accra (Ghana) 2012, *African conference on child abuse and neglect* Addis Ababa (Ethiopia) 2009, *International Conference* Nairobi (Kenya) 2007, *African conference on child abuse and neglect* Nairobi (Kenya) 1998, *Continental conference on children in situation of armed conflicts* Addis Ababa (Ethiopia) 1997. **Publications** *Childwatch* – newsletter. Research studies; training manuals/guides; conference reports/proceedings.

Members National Chapters in 26 countries:
Benin, Cameroon, Congo DR, Côte d'Ivoire, Ethiopia, Ghana, Kenya, Lesotho, Liberia, Malawi, Mauritius, Mozambique, Niger, Nigeria, Rwanda, Senegal, Sierra Leone, Somalia, South Africa, Sudan, Tanzania UR, Togo, Tunisia, Uganda, Zambia, Zimbabwe.

Consultative Status Consultative status granted from: *African Commission on Human and Peoples' Rights (ACHPR, #00255)* (Observer). **IGO Relations** Consultative Status with: *African Union (AU, #00488)*. **NGO Relations** Memorandum of Understanding with: *International Day of the African Child and Youth (IDAY, #13140)*. Member of: *CHS Alliance (#03911)*; *International Peace Bureau (IPB, #14535)*.
[2017.06.01/XF0834/**F**]

♦ African Network of Religious Leaders Living with or Personally Affected by HIV and AIDS / see International Network of Religious Leaders Living with or Personally Affected by HIV and AIDS (#14315)

♦ African Network of Research on Bruchids / see African Network of Research on Storage Insects (#00394)

♦ African Network of Research on Storage Insects (ANERSI) 00394

Réseau africain de recherche sur les insectes des stocks (REARIS)

Dir Laboratoire d'Entomologie appliquée, Fac des Sciences, Univ de Lomé, BP 1515, Lomé, Togo. T. +2282255094. Fax +2282258595.

History Aug 1993, Banjul (Gambia), under the auspices of *Inter-African Phytosanitary Council (AU-IAPSC, #11386)*. Original title: *African Network of Research on Bruchids (ANERB) – Réseau africain de recherche sur les bruches (REARB)*. **Aims** Develop *biotechnology* to protect cultures and stocks against infestation of *beetles*; support the joint use throughout Africa of material and human resources in inter-state programmes combating beetles; promote diffusion of results and access of researchers to available data banks; establish relationships with financial organizations with the help of specialized agencies. **Structure** Scientific Committee; Organizing Committee; Coordinators (2). **Languages** English, French. **Staff** Voluntary. **Finance** Financed through: Inter-African Phyto-Sanitary Council; scientific programmes. **Activities** Training/education; knowledge management/information dissemination. **Events** *Colloquium* Lomé (Togo) 2008, *Colloquium* Cotonou (Benin) 2001, *General Assembly* Cotonou (Benin) 2001, *Colloque international* Niamey (Niger) 2000, *Réunion sur la lutte contre les prédateurs des denrées stockées par les agriculteurs en Afrique / Colloquium* Lomé (Togo) 1997. **Publications** *La Bruche*. Colloquium proceedings; guides; articles. **IGO Relations** *African Union (AU, #00488)*; *UNESCO (#20322)*. **NGO Relations** *Association of African Universities (AAU, #02361)*; *West and Central African Council for Agricultural Research and Development (WECARD, #20907)*. [2014.11.12/XF5623/**F**]

♦ African Network on Rural Poultry Development / see International Network on Family Poultry Development (#14267)

♦ African Network of Scientific and Technological Institutions (ANSTI) 00395

Réseau africain d'institutions scientifiques et techniques (RAIST)

Coordinator c/o UNESCO Nairobi, PO Box 30592-00100, Nairobi, Kenya. T. +254207622620. Fax +254207622750. E-mail: j.njoroge@unesco.org.
Facebook: https://www.facebook.com/pages/category/Non-Governmental-Organization – NGO-/ANSTI-1473682402856905/

History 6 Jan 1980, Nairobi (Kenya). Founded following an agreement signed by UNESCO and UNDP in May 1979, with support from the Government of Germany FR. Preparatory meetings had been held, 1976 and 1978, Nairobi, at *UNESCO Office, Nairobi – Regional Bureau for Sciences in Africa (ROSTA, inactive)*, following recommendations, Jan 1974, Dakar (Senegal), of *Conference of Ministers Responsible for the Application of Science and Technology to Development in Africa (CASTAFRICA)*. **Aims** Bring about close and active collaboration among African *engineering*, scientific and technological institutions with regard to *post-graduate training* and research; build high-level *human resources* capacity by pooling resources available in the region. **Structure** Governing Council; Programme Committee, comprising representatives of: coordinating institutions; *UNESCO (#20322)*; *Association of African Universities (AAU, #02361)*; ANSTI funding agencies. Project Coordinator. Subnetworks (5): Biotechnology; Water Resources Engineering and Management; Renewable Energy Resources; Material Science; Environmental Science. **Languages** English, French. **Staff** 4.00 FTE, paid. **Finance** Supported by: UNESCO; *UNDP (#20292)*; *United Nations University (UNU, #20642)*; government of Germany; government of Netherlands. **Activities** Training/education; financial and/or material support; knowledge management/information dissemation; research/documentation; events/meetings. **Events** *African Regional Conference of Vice Chancellors and Deans of Science Engineering and Technology COVIDSET* Enugu (Nigeria) 2015, *COVIDSET : Biennial African Regional Conference of Vice Chancellors and Deans of Science, Engineering and Technology* Gaborone (Botswana) 2013, *COVIDSET : African regional conference of vice chancellors and deans of science, engineering and technology* Abuja (Nigeria) 2011, *COVIDSET: African regional conference of vice chancellors, provosts and deans of science, engineering and technology* Kampala (Uganda) 2009, *COVIDSET: African regional conference of vice chancellors, provosts and deans of science, engineering and technology* Johannesburg (South Africa) 2007. **Publications** *African Journal of Science and Technology*. Directory of Grantees and Fellows. Textbooks, occasional reports.

Members Institutions (147) in 34 countries:
Benin, Botswana, Burkina Faso, Burundi, Cameroon, Congo Brazzaville, Congo DR, Côte d'Ivoire, Eswatini, Ethiopia, Gabon, Ghana, Guinea, Kenya, Lesotho, Liberia, Madagascar, Malawi, Mali, Mauritius, Mozambique, Niger, Nigeria, Rwanda, Senegal, Sierra Leone, Somalia, South Africa, Sudan, Tanzania UR, Togo, Uganda, Zambia, Zimbabwe.

NGO Relations Founding member of: *International Association for Continuing Engineering Education (IACEE, #11817)*. Supports: *African Physical Society (AfPS, #00417)*. [2018/XF0929/**F**]

♦ African Network of Social Entrepreneurship Scholars (unconfirmed)

♦ African Network for Strategic Communication in Health and Development (AfriComNet) 00396

Secretariat Plot 15 Binayomba Road, Bugolobi, PO Box 3495, Kampala, Uganda. T. +25641250183 – +25641237222 – +25641250192. Fax +256414221340.
Youtube: https://www.youtube.com/channel/UCq8otKXQ35DjIVU16YRWF3g

History Oct 2001, Nairobi (Kenya), as *Regional HIV and AIDS Behaviour Change Communication Network (BCC)*. **Aims** Promote strategic communication practices in an African context; increase recognition of strategic communication as critical to effectiveness of health and development; strengthen organizational capacity, credibility and visibility of the organization. **Structure** General Assembly; Steering Committee; Secretariat. **Languages** English, French. **Staff** 2.00 FTE, paid. **Activities** Capacity building in strategic communication – partnership with African universities to develop short courses. Annual award for excellence in HIV/AIDS communication. Information sharing. **Events** *Conference* Johannesburg (South Africa) 2007, *Conference* Addis Ababa (Ethiopia) 2006, *Strategic communication for care, support and treatment* Dar es Salaam (Tanzania UR) 2005, *Inaugural general assembly* Kampala (Uganda) 2003. **Publications** *AfricComnet Newsletter*. News updates. Strategic Plan 2006-2011. **Members** Individuals and organizations (1200) in 49 countries. Membership countries not specified. **NGO Relations** Partnership with African universities.
[2015/XM4510/**F**]

♦ African Network for Support to Women Entrepreneurs (ANSWE) ... 00397

Réseau africain pour le soutien à l'entrepreneuriat féminin (RASEF)

Pres Zone Industrielle Domaine SONEPI, Lot No 71/A, BP 30081, Dakar, Senegal. T. +221338255718.

History 18 Nov 1994, Dakar (Senegal), at a business forum organized in conjunction with 5th African Women's Conference. **Aims** Promote inter-African commerce and South-South commerce; create support structures for women entrepreneurs in both formal and informal sectors; facilitate members' access to bank credit and other sources of finance, in particular through new and original financial structures oriented towards female business; assist members in promoting and developing economic activities bringing in revenue for their operators; ensure follow-up and development of contacts, business relationships and cooperative links among members; promote African products and protection of the environment. **Structure** General Assembly (annual), comprising up to 5 representatives of each national network. International Bureau (meets twice a year), comprising President, 5 Vice-Presidents, Secretary-General, 3 Assistant Secretaries-General, Treasurer-General, 3 Assistant Treasurers-General, Secretary for International Relations, 3 Assistant Secretaries for International Relations, Organization Secretary and 3 Assistant Organization Secretaries. Executive Committee. Executive Secretariat. Technical commissions. **Languages** Arabic, English, French. **Finance** Members' dues. Contributions from institutions and funds. **Activities** Contribution to 4th World Conference, Sep 1995, Beijing (China). Organizes international seminars. Setting up: data base of information on members and their countries; solidarity fund and mutual assistance (and, long-term, a woman's bank); training programmes for SME-SMI women directors. Sectors targeted: industrial and mining; agro-pastoral; commercial and services; craft; marine products. **Events** *International seminar* Yaoundé (Cameroon) 1995.

Members Covers 13 countries:
Benin, Burkina Faso, Cameroon, Chad, Gabon, Guinea, Mali, Mauritius, Morocco, Nigeria, Senegal, Sierra Leone, Tunisia.

IGO Relations *UNIDO (#20336)*. **NGO Relations** Member of *African Network of Micro-Finance and Micro-Enterprise (MICROFIN AFRIC, no recent information)*. [2018/XF2997/**F**]

♦ African Network of Universal and Global History / see African Network in Global History (#00388)

♦ African Network of Women Shelters (ANWS) 00398

Secretariat Rwanda Women's Network, PO Box 3157, Kigali, Rwanda. E-mail: info@africannetworkofwomenshelters.org.
URL: http://www.africannetworkofwomenshelters.org/

History Feb 2012, Washington DC (USA), following a resolution by the African Caucus during 2nd World Conference on Women Shelters. **Aims** Unite to advocate for policy transformation to end violance against women and girls, and provision of shelters, safe spaces and holistic services for women and girls in Africa. **Structure** Interim Executive Committee; Secretariat. **NGO Relations** Represented with: *Global Network of Women's Shelters (GNWS, #10504)*. [2015/XJ9805/**F**]

♦ African Network of Young Leaders for Peace and Sustainable Development (ANYL4PSD) 00399

Gen Sec PO Box 1932, Yaoundé, Cameroon. T. +237695962496. E-mail: info@anyl4psd.org.
Coordinator address not obtained.
URL: http://anyl4psd.org/

History Registered in accordance with the law of Cameroon, 2015. **Aims** Contribute decisively to the emergence of the youth class, its positioning and its effective participation in public policies. **Structure** Convention; Board of Directors; Executive Board; Expanded Board. **Languages** English, French. **Staff** 32.00 FTE, paid; 68.00 FTE, voluntary. **Finance** Members' dues. Other sources: municipal funding; private sector; other NGOs and IGOs; income generated activities. **Activities** Projects/programmes; research and development; capacity building; awareness raising; advocacy/lobbying/activities; guidance/assistance/consulting; events/meetings. **Publications** Articles; memoires.

Members Full in 12 countries:
Benin, Cameroon, Central African Rep, Chad, Congo Brazzaville, Congo DR, Ethiopia, Gabon, Niger, Nigeria, Rwanda, Senegal.
Organizational members include 1 organization listed in this Yearbook:
Union internationale des jeunes écrivains et artistes pour la paix, l'amour et la justice (UNIJEAPAJ).

Consultative Status Consultative status granted from: *ECOSOC (#05331)* (Special); *UNEP (#20299)*. **IGO Relations** *Secretariat of the United Nations Convention to Combat Desertification (Secretariat of the UNCCD, #19208)*; *UNDP (#20292)*; *United Nations Office for Disaster Risk Reduction (UNDRR, #20595)*; *United Nations Population Fund (UNFPA, #20612)*. **NGO Relations** *Global Network of Civil Society Organizations for Disaster Reduction (GNDR, #10485)*; *World Wide Fund for Nature (WWF, #21922)*. [2019.12.23/XM7131/**F**]

♦ African Nuclear-weapon-free-zone Treaty (1996 treaty)

♦ African Nutrition Society (ANS) 00400

Société africaine de nutrition (SAN)

SG PO Box K18, Korle Bu, Accra, Ghana. T. +233244872410. Fax +23321513294. E-mail: info@ansnet.org.
URL: http://www.ansnet.org/

History 2008. Foundedas an umbrella organization, also created to oversee the Africa nutritional Epidemiology conferences (ANEC), organized since 2002. Registration: No/ID: 27604, Ghana. **Aims** Develop and promote the nutrition profession in Africa. **Structure** Council; Board of Trustees; Scientific Committees; Working Groups. **Languages** English, French. **Staff** 9.00 FTE, paid. **Finance** Members' dues. Sponsorship. **Activities** Awards/competitions/prizes; events/meetings. **Events** *African Nutritional Epidemiology Conference* Lusaka (Zambia) 2020, *African Nutritional Epidemiology Conference* Addis Ababa (Ethiopia) 2018, *African Nutritional Epidemiology Conference* Accra (Ghana) 2014, *African nutritional epidemiology conference* Bloemfontein (South Africa) 2012, *Africa nutritional epidemiology conference* Nairobi (Kenya) 2010. **Publications** *African Nutrition Matters* – newsletter. Annual Report. **Members** Full; Student/Graduate; Affiliate; Institutional; Concessionary; Honorary. Membership countries not specified. **NGO Relations** Affiliate of: *International Union of Nutritional Sciences (IUNS, #15796)*. [2020/XM4069/**E**]

♦ African Observatory of Science, Technology and Innovation (AOSTI) 00401

Observatoire Africain pour la science, la technologie et l'innovation (OASTI) – Observatório Africano de Ciência, Tecnologia e Inovação

Contact PO Box 549, Malabo, Equatorial Guinea. E-mail: info@aosti.org.
URL: http://www.aosti.org/

History Decision Assembly/AU/Dec-235 (XII), Feb 2009 of *African Union (AU, #00488)* first proposed establishment of AOSTI. Agreement signed between AU and Equatorial Guinea as host country, 6 Jul 2010. Actual creation through Decision Assembly/AU/Dec-452 (XX), Jan 2013. Statutes adopted 30 Jan 2016, Addis Ababa (Ethiopia). **Aims** Serve as the continental repository for Science, Technology, and Innovation (STI) data and statistics and a source of policy analysis in support of evidence based policy-making in Africa. **Publications** *Policy Brief*. Working Papers; reports. [2019/XM8542/**F***]

♦ African Office for Development and Cooperation (internationally oriented national body)
♦ African Oil Chemists' Society (no recent information)
♦ African Oil Palm Development Association (no recent information)
♦ Africa Nomads Conservation (internationally oriented national body)
♦ African Ombudsman and Mediators Association (#02838)

African Ophthalmology Council
00402

alphabetic sequence excludes
For the complete listing, see Yearbook Online at

♦ African Ophthalmology Council (AOC) 00402

Contact 3 Ribadu Raod, SW Ikoyi, Lagos 23401, Nigeria. T. +2348033061261. E-mail: festusodiley@aocouncil.org – info@aofsite.org.
URL: http://www.aofsite.org/

History Set up Mar 2014, originating in an initiative set up 2009, by *International Council of Ophthalmology (ICO, #13057)* and *Middle East African Council of Ophthalmology (MEACO, #16752)*. Officially launched 3 Apr 2014, Tokyo (Japan), during World Ophthalmology Congress. **Aims** Harness the potentials of ophthalmologists, their training institutions, through their ophthalmological societies, towards promoting a high standard of professional and leadership training, thereby putting them in a position that is well equipped to face the challenges of vision preservation and restoration in Sub Sahara Africa. **Structure** Board; Executive. **Activities** Events/meetings. **Events** *WOC : World Ophthalmology Congress* Geneva (Switzerland) 2020, *Conference on Building a Common Secure and Democratic Future* Brussels (Belgium) 2016.
Members Full in 4 countries:
Ghana, Rwanda, South Africa, South Sudan. [2017/XM5662/**D**]

♦ African Organic Network (unconfirmed)

♦ African Organisation of English-speaking Supreme Audit Institutions (AFROSAI-E) 00403

Communications Manager 3rd Floor – Pegasus 2 Bldg, Menlyn Maine, c/o Jan Masilela Av & Amarand Av Waterkloof Glen Ext 2, Pretoria, 0181, South Africa. T. +27102860104. E-mail: info@afrosai-e.org.za.
URL: http://www.afrosai-e.org.za/

History 1 Jan 2005. Existed as an unnamed informal association of English speaking Auditors General (1998-2004), together with *Southern African Development Cooperation of Supreme Audit Institutions (SADCOSAI)*. Formally set up when SADCOSAI was incorporated into AFROSAI-E. An English language subgroup of *African Organization of Supreme Audit Institutions (AFROSAI, #00406)*. Statutes amended: 10 May 2013; 19 May 2021. **Aims** Cooperate with and support member SAIs to enhance their institutional capacity to successfully fulfil their audit mandates, thereby making a difference to the lives of citizens. **Structure** Governing Board; Executive Secretariat. **Languages** English. **Staff** Staff seconded from other SAIs (South Africa, Sweden, Norway, Uganda, Zambia and Tanzania) and staff appointed and funded directly from AFROSAI-E basket funding. **Activities** Capacity building. Active in all member countries. **Publications** *AFROSAI-E Bulletin* in English. Technical manuals; handbooks; guidelines; reports and research papers.
Members Full in 26 countries:
Angola, Botswana, Eritrea, Eswatini, Ethiopia, Gambia, Ghana, Kenya, Lesotho, Liberia, Malawi, Mauritius, Mozambique, Namibia, Nigeria, Rwanda, Seychelles, Sierra Leone, Somalia, South Africa, South Sudan, Sudan, Tanzania UR, Uganda, Zambia, Zimbabwe.
Associate (2):
African Union Commission; *Pan African Federation of Accountants (PAFA, #18050)*. [2022.10.25/XJ9447/**D**]

♦ African Organisation for Standardisation (ARSO) 00404

Organisation Africaine de Normalisation

SG PO Box 57363-00200, Nairobi, Kenya. T. +25420224561. E-mail: sg@arso-oran.org – arso@arso-oran.org – info@arso-oran.org.
Head Office 3rd Floor, International Life House, Mama Ngina Street, Nairobi, Kenya.
URL: http://www.arso-oran.org/

History Established Jan 1977, Accra (Ghana), as *African Regional Organization for Standardization (ARSO) – Organisation régionale africaine de normalisation (ORAN)*, at the Founding Conference, 10-17 Jan 1977 by African governments under the auspices of *United Nations Economic Commission for Africa (ECA, #20554)* and *Organization of African Unity (OAU, inactive)*, currently *African Union (AU, #00488)*, when the first constitution was adopted. Constitution ratified and signed by 9 African presidents and 8 designated government officials and deposited with ECA. Serves as one of 4 pillars of *Pan African Quality Infrastructure*, set up Aug 2013. **Aims** Facilitate intra-African and global trade through providing harmonized standards and facilitating implementation of standards; act as a standardization centre promoting *trade and industry*. **Structure** General Assembly (annual); Council; Central Secretariat. **Languages** AU languages. **Staff** 4.00 FTE, paid. Also voluntary. **Finance** Members' dues. International partners. **Activities** Standards/guidelines; knowledge management/information dissemination; networking/liaising; events/meetings. **Events** *Annual General Assembly* Durban (South Africa) 2018, *Annual General Assembly* Ouagadougou (Burkina Faso) 2017, *Annual General Assembly* Arusha (Tanzania UR) 2016, *Annual General Assembly* Addis Ababa (Ethiopia) 2015, *Annual General Assembly* Kigali (Rwanda) 2014. **Publications** *African Standardisation Watch: Reflections within Africa* (4 a year) – newsletter. *African Standards Harmonization Models*; *ARSO Foundation from the Beginning*; *Benefits and Advantages of Standardisation*; *Boosting African Trade*; *Establishment and Operationalization of NSBs*; *Mainstreaming African SMEs*; *The ARSO Network of Documentation and Information (ARSO-DISNET)*. Articles. Information Services: ARSO Documentation and Information Centre. **Information Services** *ARSO DISNET Africa Trade Help Web Portal*; *Database of African Experts on Standards and Conformity Assessment*.
Members Governments of 33 countries:
Benin, Burkina Faso, Cameroon, Congo Brazzaville, Congo DR, Côte d'Ivoire, Egypt, Eswatini, Ethiopia, Gabon, Ghana, Guinea, Guinea-Bissau, Kenya, Liberia, Madagascar, Malawi, Mauritius, Namibia, Niger, Nigeria, Rwanda, Senegal, Seychelles, Sierra Leone, South Africa, Sudan, Tanzania UR, Togo, Tunisia, Uganda, Zambia, Zimbabwe.
Founding governments (21):
Burkina Faso, Cameroon, Côte d'Ivoire, Egypt, Ethiopia, Ghana, Guinea-Bissau, Kenya, Liberia, Libya, Malawi, Mauritius, Niger, Nigeria, Sierra Leone, Sudan, Tanzania UR, Togo, Tunisia, Uganda, Zambia.
IGO Relations Represented at Founding Conference: Arab Organization for Standardization and Metrology (ARSM); *International Organization of Legal Metrology (#14451)*; *UNIDO (#20336)*; *Union of African Railways (UAR, #20347)*; *United Nations Economic Commission for Africa (ECA, #20554)*. Relationship agreement signed with: UNIDO. Participates as observer in the activities of: *Codex Alimentarius Commission (CAC, #04081)*. Observer member of: *Intra-Africa Metrology System (AFRIMETS, #15992)*. **NGO Relations** Represented at Founding Conference: *International Electrotechnical Commission (IEC, #13255)*; *International Organization for Standardization (ISO, #14473)*. Member of: *Global Network for Resource Efficient and Cleaner Production (RECPnet, #10497)*. Memorandum of Understanding with: *Comité européen de normalisation (CEN, #04162)*. [2016.12.14/XE6038/**E***]

♦ African Organization of Cartography and Remote Sensing (inactive)
♦ African Organization for Freedom and Democracy (no recent information)
♦ African Organization of Mines, Metal, Energie, Chemical and Allied Trade Unions (no recent information)

♦ African Organization for Research and Training in Cancer (AORTIC) 00405

Organisation africaine pour la recherche et l'enseignement sur le cancer (OAREC)

Managing Dir PO Box 186, Rondebosch, 7701, South Africa. T. +27216895359. Fax +27216895350. E-mail: info@aortic-africa.org.
Treas PO Box 633, Hamilton Grange Station, New York NY 10031, USA.
URL: http://www.aortic-africa.org/

History 12 Sep 1982, Seattle, WA (USA). Founded at 13th International Congress on Cancer. In Jul 1983, Lomé (Togo), an initial meeting was held and AORTIC was officially established as a functioning organization. Reactivated and subsequently incorporated in the State of New York (USA), 25 Oct 2001. Registration: No/ID: 13-419-5653, USA. **Aims** Provide appropriate consultation, and coordinate and facilitate the organization of research aiming at the prevention, early detection and treatment of cancer in Africa; support the management and the funding of training programmes in member and other institutions. **Languages** English, French. **Staff** 1.00 FTE, paid; 17.00 FTE, voluntary. **Finance** Fundraising activities. **Activities** Events/meetings; projects/programmes; training/education. **Events** *Cancer in Africa – Approaches, Collaborations, Impact* Rondebosch (South Africa) 2021, *Conference* Maputo (Mozambique) 2019, *Conference* Kigali (Rwanda) 2017, *AORTIC roadmap to cancer control in Africa* Marrakech (Morocco) 2015, *Cancer in Africa – bridging science and humanity* Durban (South Africa) 2013. **Publications** *AORTIC Bulletin* (4 a year) in English, French. **NGO Relations** Member of: *International Psycho-Oncology Society (IPOS, #14665)*; *The NCD Alliance (NCDA, #16963)*; *Union for International Cancer Control (UICC, #20415)*. [2021/XD1610/**D**]

♦ African Organization of Supreme Audit Institutions (AFROSAI) 00406

Organisation africaine des institutions supérieures de contrôle des finances publiques – Organización de Entidades Fiscalizadoras Superiores de Africa – Afrikanische Organisation der Obersten Rechnungskontrollbehörden

Gen Dir PO Box 376, Yaoundé, Cameroon. T. +237222220182. Fax +237222234403. E-mail: sg.afrosai@afrosai.org.
Communications Dir address not obtained.
URL: https://www.afrosai.org/

History Nov 1976. Founded with the assistance of *Deutsche Stiftung für Internationale Entwicklung (DSE, inactive)*. Current statutes adopted 4-12 Jun 1990, Cairo (Egypt). Proposes setting up: *Institut de perfectionnement de l'AFROSAI (no recent information)*. **Aims** Promote and develop exchange of views and experience among supreme audit institutions at regional level; promote and realize systematic studies in matters of control of public finance; coordinate or enable specific studies on demand; act as regional information centre and support creation of sub-regional groups and subsidiary information and documentation centres; keep members up-to-date on modifications to national legislation, on control of public finance and on changes in the functioning of respective institutions; liaise among higher education institutions and encourage exchange of specialists and experts; promote and direct specialist training of personnel in the field; promote theoretical and practical studies and the creation of study centres, institutes and university chairs; promote unification of principles, procedures and terminology in the African region. **Structure** General Assembly (meets every 3 years); Board of Directors (meets at least once a year); Permanent Secretariat; Technical Commissions; Linguistic Sub-groups including *African Organisation of English-speaking Supreme Audit Institutions (AFROSAI-E, #00403)*. **Languages** Arabic, English, French, Portuguese. **Staff** 10.00 FTE, voluntary. **Finance** Sources: donations; government support; members' dues; sale of publications. Annual budget: 390,000 USD. **Activities** Awards/prizes/competitions; events/meetings; training/education. **Events** *Triennial General Assembly* Dakar (Senegal) 2021, *Triennial General Assembly* Dakar (Senegal) 2020, *Triennial General Assembly* Windhoek (Namibia) 2017, *Triennial General Assembly* Sharm el Sheikh (Egypt) 2014, *Triennial General Assembly* Abidjan (Côte d'Ivoire) 2005. **Publications** *AFROSAI – Circulaire* (2 a year); *Journal africain de vérification intégrée*.
Members Institutions entrusted with auditing public funds in OAU member States. Institutions in 54 countries:
Algeria, Angola, Benin, Botswana, Burkina Faso, Burundi, Cameroon, Cape Verde, Central African Rep, Chad, Comoros, Congo Brazzaville, Congo DR, Côte d'Ivoire, Djibouti, Egypt, Equatorial Guinea, Eritrea, Eswatini, Ethiopia, Gabon, Gambia, Ghana, Guinea, Guinea-Bissau, Kenya, Lesotho, Liberia, Libya, Madagascar, Malawi, Mali, Mauritania, Mauritius, Morocco, Mozambique, Namibia, Niger, Nigeria, Rwanda, Sao Tomé-Principe, Senegal, Seychelles, Sierra Leone, Somalia, South Africa, South Sudan, Sudan, Tanzania UR, Togo, Tunisia, Uganda, Zambia, Zimbabwe. [2021/XD6433/**D**]

♦ African Oriental Federation (inactive)
♦ African Ostomy Association (inactive)
♦ Africa Now (internationally oriented national body)

♦ African Paediatric Nephrology Association (AFPNA) 00407

Sec address not obtained. E-mail: info@afpna.com.
Pres address not obtained.
URL: https://www.afpna.org

History 1999. Official representative of *International Pediatric Nephrology Association (IPNA, #14543)*. Also referred to as *African Pediatric Nephrology Association*. **Finance** Members' dues. **Events** *African Nephrology and Transplantation Summit* Cairo (Egypt) 2023, *Joint Congress* Abidjan (Côte d'Ivoire) 2021, *Joint Congress* Mombasa (Kenya) 2019, *Congress* Yaoundé (Cameroon) 2017, *Congress* Nairobi (Kenya) 2010. **Publications** *African Journal of Paediatric Nephrology* (2 a year). **Members** Full (163) in 29 countries. Membership countries not specified. [2020/XM4683/**D**]

♦ African Paintball Federation (AFPBF) 00408

Contact address not obtained. E-mail: info@afpbf.org.
URL: https://afpbf.org/

Members Full in 5 countries:
Gabon, Ghana, Namibia, Nigeria, South Africa.
NGO Relations Member of (1): *United Paintball Federation (UPBF, #20654)*. [2021/AA1940/**D**]

♦ African Palliative Care Association (APCA) 00409

Exec Dir PO Box 72518, Plot 95, Dr Gibbons Road, Kampala, Uganda. T. +256393264978 – +256393265978. E-mail: info@africanpalliativecare.org.
URL: http://africanpalliativecare.org/

History Formally set up 2004, Tanzania UR. **Aims** Ensure palliative care is widely understood, integrated into health systems at all levels, and underpinned by evidence in order to reduce pain and suffering across Africa. **Structure** Board. **Languages** English, French, Portuguese. **Staff** 21.00 FTE, paid. **Finance** Funding from diverse sources. **Activities** Healthcare; awareness raising; research and development; politics/policy/regulatory; training/education; financial and/or material support; events/meetings; guidance/assistance/consulting. **Events** *International African Palliative Care Conference* Kampala (Uganda) 2022, *International Conference* Kigali (Rwanda) 2019, *International Conference* Kampala (Uganda) 2016, *Meeting* Johannesburg (South Africa) 2013. **Members** Full in over 68 countries. Membership countries not specified. **IGO Relations** *WHO (#20950)*; regional bodies. **NGO Relations** Member of (1): *Worldwide Hospice Palliative Care Alliance (WHPCA, #21924)*. [2020/XJ6371/**D**]

♦ African Paralympic Committee / see African Paralympic Committee (#00410)

♦ African Paralympic Committee (APC) 00410

Pres Rua Cirilo Da Conceicao 13, Luanda, Angola. T. +244222339340. Fax +244222395729.

History 1987, Algeria. Formalized as a legal entity in 1990. Full title: *African Sports Confederation of the Disabled – African Paralympic Committee (ASCOD) – Confédération africaine des sports pour handicapés – Comité paralympique africaine (CASH)*. Also referred to in French as *Confédération africaine des sports pour handicapés et inadaptés (CASHI)*. Also referred to as *African Paralympic Committee – Comite paralympique africaine*. Also referred to as *African Paralympics Committee*. Statutes revised, Cairo (Egypt), 2 Dec 2001. **Aims** Coordinate and promote the sports for persons with disabilities in Africa. **Structure** General Assembly (every 2 years); Executive Council. **Languages** Arabic, English, French. **Finance** Members' dues. **Activities** Training/education. **Events** *African Development Congress for Sports of Disabled* Ismailia (Egypt) 2003.
Members Full (members of IPC); Associate. National Paralympic Committees in 49 countries (" indicates suspended):
Algeria, Angola, Benin, Botswana, Burkina Faso, Burundi, Cameroon, Cape Verde, Central African Rep, Comoros, Congo Brazzaville, Congo DR, Côte d'Ivoire, Djibouti, Egypt, Ethiopia, Gabon, Gambia, Ghana, Guinea, Guinea-Bissau, Kenya, Lesotho, Liberia, Libya, Madagascar, Malawi, Mali, Mauritania (*), Mauritius, Morocco, Mozambique, Namibia, Niger, Nigeria, Rwanda, Sao Tomé-Principe, Senegal, Seychelles, Sierra Leone, Somalia, South Africa, Sudan, Tanzania UR, Togo, Tunisia, Uganda, Zambia, Zimbabwe.
NGO Relations Member of: *International Paralympic Committee (IPC, #14512)*. [2017/XD2249/**D**]

♦ African Paralympics Committee / see African Paralympic Committee (#00410)

♦ African Parks (AP) 00411

Head Office Wickham House, Fairway Office Park, 52 Grosvenor Road, Bryanston, 2191, South Africa. T. +27114650050. Fax +27866624992. E-mail: info@africanparks.org.
Netherlands Office PO Box 313, 3940 AH Doorn, Netherlands. T. +31343565019. E-mail: netherlands@africanparks.org.
URL: https://www.africanparks.org/

History 2000. Registration: South Africa; Handelsregister, No/ID: KVK 30191949, Netherlands; Swiss Civil Code, Switzerland; 501(c)(3) organization, No/ID: EIN: 30-0241904, Start date: 2004, USA, NY; Charity Commission, No/ID: SC050047, Start date: 16 Mar 2020, Scotland. **Aims** Ensure the long-term survival of national parks in Africa. **Structure** Boards (6): African Parks Network, South Africa; Stichting African Parks Foundation, Netherlands; African Parks Foundation, Germany; African Parks Foundation, Switzerland; African Parks Foundation, USA; Asia Pacific Advisory Group; African Parks UK. **Activities** Capacity building; projects/programmes; research and development. **Publications** Reports.
Members Parks (22) in 12 countries:

Angola, Benin, Central African Rep, Chad, Congo Brazzaville, Congo DR, Malawi, Mozambique, Rwanda, South Sudan, Zambia, Zimbabwe.
IGO Relations Accredited by (1): *European Union (EU, #08967)*. **NGO Relations** Member of (1): *Global Rewilding Alliance (GRA, #10579)*. Partner of (3): *Elephant Protection Initiative Foundation (EPI Foundation, #05429)*; *Fondation Segré*, *Save the Elephants (STE)*. [2023.02.17/XM4393/**F**]

♦ African Parliamentarians Network Against Corruption (see: #10518)

♦ African Parliamentary Union (APU) 00412
Union parlementaire africaine (UPA)
SG PO Box V 314, Abidjan, Côte d'Ivoire. T. +22520303970 – +22520303971 – +22520303974. Fax +22520304405 – +22520304409. E-mail: upa1@aviso.ci – upa2@aviso.ci.
URL: http://www.apunion.org
History 13 Feb 1976, Abidjan (Côte d'Ivoire). Founded when statutes were adopted, following signature of a declaration, 27 Jan 1975, and meeting of the Working and Study Committee, Nov 1975, Luxembourg. Statutes modified statutes, Sep 1999, Luanda (Angola). Former names and other names: *Union of African Parliaments (UAP)* – former (1976 to Sep 1999); *Union des parlements africains (UPA)* – former (1976 to Sep 1999). **Aims** Unite parliamentary institutions of African states; favour contacts among parliamentary Africans and with parliamentarians worldwide; contribute to strengthening the institution of parliament in Africa, to promoting democracy and human rights and to realizing of objectives of the Organization of African Unity for establishment of a durable peace. **Structure** Conference of Presidents of National Parliamentary Assemblies (annual); Executive Committee; National Groups; General Secretariat. **Languages** Arabic, English, French, Portuguese. **Staff** 15.00 FTE, paid. **Finance** Members' dues. **Activities** Monitoring/evaluation; events/meetings; training/education. **Events** *Conference* Djibouti 2019, *African Parliamentary Conference on the Contribution of African Migrants to the Development of Countries of Origin and Destination* Djibouti (Djibouti) 2016, *Conference* Algiers (Algeria) 2004, *Session* Algiers (Algeria) 2004, *African parliamentary conference* Cotonou (Benin) 2004. **Publications** Conference proceedings.
Members National groups: parliaments of OAU member States which adhere to APU Statutes. Honorary Members: distinguished African personalities. Members in 41 countries:
Algeria, Angola, Benin, Burkina Faso, Burundi, Cameroon, Central African Rep, Chad, Comoros, Congo Brazzaville, Congo DR, Côte d'Ivoire, Djibouti, Egypt, Equatorial Guinea, Ethiopia, Gabon, Gambia, Ghana, Guinea, Guinea-Bissau, Kenya, Liberia, Libya, Madagascar, Mali, Mauritania, Morocco, Niger, Nigeria, Rwanda, Sao Tomé-Principe, Senegal, Sierra Leone, Somalia, South Sudan, Sudan, Togo, Tunisia, Uganda, Zimbabwe.
Observers: Parliaments of 13 countries:
Botswana, Cape Verde, Eritrea, Lesotho, Malawi, Mauritius, Mozambique, Namibia, Seychelles, South Africa, Sweden, Tanzania UR, Zambia.
IGO Relations Member of: *Parliamentary Union of the OIC Member States (PUIC, #18220)*. **NGO Relations** Privileged relations with: *Arab Inter-Parliamentary Union (Arab IPU, #00995)*. [2020/XD5233/**D**]

♦ African Parliament of Civil Society (#18207)
♦ African Participatory Research Network (inactive)
♦ African Pastors' Fellowship (internationally oriented national body)
♦ African Pastors' Fund / see African Pastors' Fellowship
♦ African Peace Network (internationally oriented national body)
♦ African Peace Research Association / see Africa Peace Research and Education Association (#00511)
♦ African Peace Research Institute / see Africa Peace Research and Education Association (#00511)
♦ African Pediatric Nephrology Association / see African Paediatric Nephrology Association (#00407)

♦ African Peer Review Mechanism Panel of Eminent Persons 00413
CEO APR Secretariat, PO Box 1234, Halfway House, Midrand, 1685, South Africa.
URL: http://www.aprm-au.org/
History A panel of eminent Africans of high moral nature. **Finance** Funded by participating countries. *APRM Implementation Trust Fund* funds operational activities of the Panel and Secretariat. **Activities** Manages the governance review processes under the African Peer Review Mechanism (APRM). Undertakes review and submits reports to the African Peer Review Forum (APR Forum). **Events** *APR forum summit* Addis Ababa (Ethiopia) 2009, *Panel meeting* Addis Ababa (Ethiopia) 2009, *APR forum summit* Sirte (Libyan AJ) 2009, *Panel meeting* Cotonou (Benin) 2008, *Panel meeting* Johannesburg (South Africa) 2008.
Members Individuals (7) in 7 countries:
Algeria, Cameroon, Kenya, Mozambique, Nigeria, Senegal, South Africa.
IGO Relations Partners: *African Development Bank (ADB, #00283)*; *UNDP (#20292)* (Regional Bureau for Africa); *United Nations Economic Commission for Africa (ECA, #20554)*. [2015/XM1625/**F**]

♦ African Penitentiary Association (no recent information)
♦ African Petroleum Producers Association / see African Petroleum Producers's Organization (#00414)

♦ African Petroleum Producers's Organization (APPO) 00414
Organisation des Producteurs de Pétrole Africains (OPPA)
Secretariat 7th Floor BSCA Bldg, Av. de l'Amitié, Brazzaville, Congo Brazzaville. T. +242065349296. E-mail: info@apposecretariat.org.
URL: https://apposecretariat.org/
History 27 Jan 1987, Lagos (Nigeria), as *African Petroleum Producers Association (APPA)* – *Association des producteurs de pétrole africains*. **Aims** Promote common policy initiatives and projects in all facets of the petroleum industry with a view to maximizing developmental and welfare benefits accruable from petroleum exploitation activities in Africa. **Structure** Council of Ministers (meets annually); Committee of Experts (meets 2 times a year); Secretariat; APPA Fund for Technical Cooperation. **Languages** Arabic, English, French, Portuguese, Spanish. **Staff** 16.00 FTE, paid. **Finance** Contributions from member countries. **Activities** Training/education; events/meetings. **Events** *CAPE Conference* Malabo (Equatorial Guinea) 2019, *Ordinary Session* Malabo (Equatorial Guinea) 2019, *Extraordinary Session* Luanda (Angola) 2018, *Ordinary Session* Ndjamena (Chad) 2018, *Ordinary Session* Abidjan (Côte d'Ivoire) 2017. **Publications** *APPA Bulletin* (3 a year).
Members Governments of 18 countries:
Algeria, Angola, Benin, Cameroon, Chad, Congo Brazzaville, Congo DR, Côte d'Ivoire, Egypt, Equatorial Guinea, Gabon, Ghana, Libya, Mauritania, Niger, Nigeria, South Africa, Sudan.
IGO Relations *International Energy Forum (IEF, #13272)*; *Organization of Arab Petroleum Exporting Countries (OAPEC, #17854)*; *Organization of the Petroleum Exporting Countries (OPEC, #17881)*. **NGO Relations** *African Refiners and Distributors Association (ARA, #00429)*; *Centre d'études en administration internationale (CETAI, no recent information)*; *World Energy Council (WEC, #21381)*. [2021/XD1632/**D***]

♦ African Pharmaceutical Students Federation (no recent information)

♦ African Philanthropy Forum (APF) 00415
Exec Dir 14 Chris Maduike Street Lekki Phae 1, Lagos, Nigeria. T. +2348037291889. E-mail: apf@africanpf.org.
Contact Anslow Office Park, 8 Anslow Crescent, Bryanston 2021, Johannesburg, South Africa.
URL: https://africanpf.org/
History Founded 2014, by *Global Philanthropy Forum*. Became and independent affiliate from GPF, 2017. **Aims** Build a learning community of strategic African philanthropists and social investors committed to inclusive and sustainable development throughout the Continent. **Structure** Board. **Activities** Events/meetings; projects/programmes. **NGO Relations** Member of: *Worldwide Initiatives for Grantmaker Support (WINGS, #21926)*.
[2019/XM8800/**F**]

♦ African Physical Activity Network (AFPAN) 00416
Contact UCT/MRC Research Unit for Exercise Science and Sports Medicine, PO Box 115 Newlands, Cape Town, 7725, South Africa.
URL: http://afpan.weebly.com/
History Mar 2007. Functions as the African arm for the Global Advocacy for Physical Activity (GAPA), representing the advocacy council for *International Society for Physical Activity and Health (ISPAH, #15365)*. **Aims** Establish open communication links between most, if not all, physical activity advocates, practitioners, policy makers and inter-sectoral partners throughout Africa; provide member organisations with a platform to build global contacts. **NGO Relations** Regional network of: *Agita Mundo Network (#00560)*.
[2015/XJ8532/**D**]

♦ African Physical Society (AfPS) 00417
Pres c/o Edouard A Bouchet Centre for Science and Technology, PO Box 197, Legon, Accra, Ghana. T. +233302544102. E-mail: president@africanphysicalsociety.org.
URL: http://www.africanphysicalsociety.org/
History 26 Aug 1983, in the framework of *Abdus Salam International Centre for Theoretical Physics (ICTP, #00005)*, as *ICTP Society of African Physicists and Mathematicians (ISAPAM)*; formal inauguration 8 Oct 1984, Trieste (Italy) at Pan African Symposium on the State of Physics and Mathematics in Africa. Subsequently changed title into *Society of African Physicists and Mathematicians (SAPAM) – Société africaine de physiciens et de mathématiciens*. Current title decided upon 24 Jan 2007, South Africa and relaunched under this title Nov 2009, Dakar (Senegal). Existed under current title since 2000 as an email group. Officially launched 2010, Dakar (Senegal). Registered in accordance with the law of Ghana. **Aims** Promote and further education and research in *physical sciences* and their applications, so as to enhance technological, economic, social and cultural development in Africa; promote effective contacts and cooperation among African scientists; collaborate with international organizations in furthering scientific activities in Africa. **Structure** General Assembly (every 4 years). Executive Council, consisting of at-large regional representatives (English-speaking West Africa, French-speaking West Africa, East Africa, Central Africa, North Africa, Southern Africa) and representatives from national physics-related professional societies. Officers: President; 2 Vice-Presidents; Secretary-Treasurer. Technical Groups (16). Since 2007, includes *African Association of Physics Students (AAPS, #00211)*. **Languages** English.
Finance Members' dues. Financial support from governments of Botswana, Burundi, Côte d'Ivoire, Ethiopia, France, Ghana, Italy, Kenya, Liberia, Nigeria and Sierra Leone and from the following institutions:
– *Abdus Salam International Centre for Theoretical Physics (ICTP, #00005)*;
– *African Academy of Sciences (AAS, #00193)*;
– *African Network of Scientific and Technological Institutions (ANSTI, #00395)*;
– *Association of African Universities (AAU, #02361)*;
– *British Council*;
– *Intergovernmental Bureau of Informatics (IBI)*;
– *International Development Research Centre (IDRC, #13162)*;
– *OPEC Fund for International Development (OFID, #17745)*;
– *Swedish International Development Cooperation Agency (Sida)* Department formerly known as Swedish Agency for Research Cooperation with Developing Countries (SAREC);
– *UNEP (#20299)*;
– *UNESCO (#20322)*;
– *United Nations University (UNU, #20642)*;
– *World Meteorological Organization (WMO, #21649)*.
Activities Events/meetings; training/education. **Events** *Workshop on Applicability of Environmental Physics and Meteorology in Africa* Botswana 2006, *Regional workshop for university physics teachers* Cape Coast (Ghana) 2003, *Regional workshop on algebraic combinatorics* Cape Coast (Ghana) 2003, *African regional workshop on VLSI design and techniques* Kumasi (Ghana) 2003, *Biennial workshop on applicability of environmental physics and meteorology in Africa / Workshop on Applicability of Environmental Physics and Meteorology in Africa* Gaborone (Botswana) 1999. **Publications** *SAPAM Handbook* (annual). *Applicability of Environmental Physics and Meteorology in Africa* (1994); *Ultrasound in Medical Practice in Africa* (1990); *Curriculum Development and Design in Mathematics, Physics and Computer Science in Africa* (1986); *State of Physics and Mathematics in Africa* (1985); *Handbook 2004*. Abstracts; conference proceedings (with ICTP).
Members Ordinary: African physicists, mathematicians and related scientists; Associate: non-African or Africans residing outside Africa in the same disciplines; Honorary; Patrons. Members in 30 countries:
Benin, Botswana, Burkina Faso, Burundi, Cameroon, Central African Rep, Côte d'Ivoire, Egypt, Eswatini, Ethiopia, Ghana, Guinea, Kenya, Liberia, Madagascar, Mali, Morocco, Niger, Nigeria, Sao Tomé-Principe, Senegal, Sierra Leone, South Africa, Sudan, Tanzania UR, Togo, Tunisia, Uganda, Zambia, Zimbabwe.
IGO Relations Observer status with: *African Union (AU, #00488)*, formerly the Organization of African Unity. Observer member of: *United Nations Economic Commission for Africa (ECA, #20554)*. **NGO Relations** Observer member of: *Federation of European Societies on Trace Elements and Minerals (FESTEM, #09550)*.
[2013/XD1020/v/**D**]

♦ African Planning Association (no recent information)
♦ African Plant Breeders Association (unconfirmed)

♦ African Plant Nutrition Institute (APNI) 00418
Dir-Gen UM6P Experimental Farm, 41350 Ben Guerir, Morocco.
URL: https://www.apni.net/
History 2019. **Aims** Innovate plant nutrition through evidence-based practices for a resilient and food-secure Africa. **Structure** Scientific Advisory Team. **Activities** Awards/prizes/competitions; awareness raising; capacity building; events/meetings; financial and/or material support; knowledge management/information dissemination; projects/programmes; publishing activities; research and development; research/documentation; training/education. **Events** *African Conference on Precision Agriculture* Nairobi (Kenya) 2022, *African Conference on Precision Agriculture* 2020, *African Conference on Precision Agriculture* Morocco 2020. **IGO Relations** Cooperates with (1): *International Development Research Centre (IDRC, #13162)*. **NGO Relations** Cooperates with (8): *Alliance for a Green Revolution in Africa (AGRA, #00685)*; Cooperative Development Foundation of Canada; International Center for Tropical Agriculture; *International Fertilizer Association (IFA, #13589)*; *International Fertilizer Development Center (IFDC, #13590)*; *International Institute of Tropical Agriculture (IITA, #13933)*; *International Society of Precision Agriculture (ISPA, #15379)*; Mohammed VI Polytechnic University. Instrumental in setting up (1): *African Association for Precision Agriculture (AAPA, #00213)*. [2022/AA2027/**D**]

♦ African Policing Civilian Oversight Forum (APCOF) 00419
Coordinator Ste 103-105A, Building 17, Waverley Business Park, Wyecroft Road, Mowbray, Cape Town, 7925, South Africa. T. +27214471818. Fax +27214470373. E-mail: info@apcof.org.za.
URL: http://www.apcof.org.za/
History 2004. **Aims** Create and sustain public confidence in police; develop a culture of human rights, integrity, transparency and accountability within the police; promote a good working relationships between police and community. **Structure** Directors. **Consultative Status** Consultative status granted from: *African Commission on Human and Peoples' Rights (ACHPR, #00255)* (Observer). **NGO Relations** Member of: *International Centre for the Prevention of Crime (ICPC, #12508)*. [2015/XJ7341/**F**]

♦ African Politics Conference Group (internationally oriented national body)
♦ African Population Advisory Council (inactive)
♦ African Population Conference (meeting series)

♦ African Population and Health Research Center (APHRC) 00420
Exec Dir GPO Box 10787, Nairobi, 00100, Kenya. T. +254204001000. Fax +254204001101. E-mail: smwero@aphrc.org – info@aphrc.org.
URL: https://aphrc.org/
History 1995. Founded within the framework of *Population Council (#18458)*. Became an autonomous institution, 2001. Former names and other names: *African Population Policy Research Centre (APPRC)* – former (1995). Registration: 501(c)3, No/ID: 06-1608361, USA. **Aims** Conduct high quality policy-relevant research on population, health, education, urbanization and related development issues across Africa; engage policymakers and other stakeholders to achieve policy impacts and ensure decision making is informed by rigorous evidence-based research. **Structure** Board of Directors. **Languages** English. **Staff** 180.00 FTE, paid. **Finance** Supported by: Bill and Melinda Gates Foundation (BMGF); Carnegie Corporation of New York; *Comic Relief*; The David and Lucile Packard Foundation; *Ford Foundation (#09858)*; The William and Flora Hewlett Foundation; *International Development Research Centre (IDRC, #13162)*; *International Food Policy Research Institute (IFPRI, #13622)*; MacArthur Foundation; *Swedish International Development Cooperation Agency (Sida)*; United States Agency for International Development (USAID); *Wellcome Trust*. **Activities** Research/documentation; politics/policy/regulatory; capacity building; training/education; events/meetings. **Events** *International Conference on Urban Health* Nairobi (Kenya) 2009, *Urban Health Champions Forum* Nairobi (Kenya) 2009. **Publications** Annual Report; newsletters; working papers; research reports; papers; fact sheets; policy briefs. **Consultative Status** Consultative status granted from: *UNEP (#20299)*. **NGO Relations** Member of: *ORCID (#17790)*; *Planetary Health Alliance (PHA, #18383)*. [2022/XK1934/**E**]

African Population Policy
00420

alphabetic sequence excludes
For the complete listing, see Yearbook Online at

- ♦ African Population Policy Research Centre / see African Population and Health Research Center (#00420)
- ♦ African Postal and Telecommunications Union (inactive)
- ♦ African Postal Union (no recent information)
- ♦ African Posts and Telecommunications Union (inactive)

♦ African Potato Association (APA) 00421

Sec Ethiopian Inst of Agricultural Research, PO Box 2003, Bole, Addis Ababa, Ethiopia.
URL: http://www.africanpotatoassociation.org/

History Founded Sep 1983, Lusaka (Zambia). Launched Sep 1985. Headquarters in Madagascar. **Aims** Promote the interests of potato and sweetpotato workers in Africa; act as a central source of information and resource exchange; facilitate greater inter-country collaboration and horizontal exchange of information and exchange visits by scientists; stimulate development of potato and sweetpotato research, production and utilization in Africa; popularize potato and sweetpotato as important food items in Africa; act as a link between the International Potato Center (CIP) and other relevant associations in the world and members/member countries; monitor training opportunities to members. **Events** *Triennial Congress* Lilongwe (Malawi) 2022, *Triennial Congress* Kigali (Rwanda) 2019, *Triennial Congress* Addis Ababa (Ethiopia) 2016, *Triennial Congress* Naivasha (Kenya) 2013, *Triennial Congress* Cape Town (South Africa) 2010. **Publications** *APA Newsletter*. Reports. **Members** Membership countries not specified. [2015/XD9342/**D**]

♦ African Powerlifting Federation (APF) 00422

Contact PO Box 1180, Sun Valley, 7985, South Africa. Fax +27217830535.
History A regional federation of *International Powerlifting Federation (IPF, #14630)*. [2010/XJ4256/**D**]

♦ African Press Network for the 21st Century (RAP 21) 00423

Réseau africain pour la presse du 21ème siècle

Contact WAN-IFRA, 72 rue d'hauteville, 75010 Paris, France. T. +33687921725. E-mail: info@wan-ifra.org.
URL: http://www.wan-ifra.org/microsites/rap21-african-press-network/

History 28 Sep 2000, by *Union des éditeurs de presse d'Afrique centrale (UEPAC, no recent information)* and *World Association of Newspapers (WAN, inactive)*. An electronic network. Currently operated by: *World Association of Newspapers and News Publishers (WAN-IFRA, #21166)*. **Aims** Provide advice and assistance to *newspapers* in Africa. **Languages** English, French. **Finance** Supported by: World Association of Newspapers (WAN). **Publications** Electronic newsletter.
Members in 51 countries:
Algeria, Angola, Benin, Botswana, Burkina Faso, Burundi, Cameroon, Cape Verde, Central African Rep, Chad, Comoros, Congo Brazzaville, Congo DR, Côte d'Ivoire, Djibouti, Egypt, Equatorial Guinea, Eswatini, Ethiopia, Gabon, Gambia, Ghana, Guinea, Guinea-Bissau, Kenya, Lesotho, Liberia, Madagascar, Malawi, Mali, Mauritania, Mauritius, Morocco, Mozambique, Namibia, Niger, Nigeria, Rwanda, Sao Tomé-Principe, Senegal, Seychelles, Sierra Leone, Somalia, South Africa, Sudan, Tanzania UR, Togo, Tunisia, Uganda, Zambia, Zimbabwe.
IGO Relations Consultative status with: *UNESCO (#20322)*. [2015/XF6361/**F**]

♦ African Press Organization (APO) 00424

Organisation de la presse africaine (OPA)

Headquarters 12 Bd Djily Mbaye, Immeuble Azur 15, BP 50555, Dakar, Senegal. T. +41215474444. E-mail: senegal@apo-opa.org.
Regional Office Europe Voie du Chariot 3, 1003 Lausanne VD, Switzerland. T. +41215474444. E-mail: switzerland@apo-opa.org.
URL: http://www.apo-opa.org/

Aims Provide free services to African journalists; provide innovative communications products to public authorities; support African and international institutions in their strategic communications. **Structure** International Advisory Board. **Publications** Database of 25,000 contacts. [2019/XJ1760/**D**]

- ♦ African Primatological Society (unconfirmed)

♦ African Private Equity and Venture Capital Association (AVCA) 00425

Chair The Banking Hall, Cropthorne Court, 26 Maida Vale, London, W9 1RS, UK. T. +442036320408. E-mail: avca@avca-africa.org.
URL: http://www.avca-africa.org/

History Founded as *International Accountability Project (IAP)*. **Aims** Promote, develop and stimulate private equity and venture capital in Africa. **Structure** Board of Directors, comprising Chairperson, Vice-Chairperson, Treasurer, Managing Director and 7 members. **Languages** English. **Activities** Advocacy/lobbying/activism; research/documentation; training/education; events/meetings. **Events** *Conference* Cairo (Egypt) 2023, *Conference* London (UK) 2022, *Conference* Nairobi (Kenya) 2019, *Conference* Marrakech (Morocco) 2018, *Conference* Abidjan (Côte d'Ivoire) 2017. **Publications** *AVCA Newsletter*. *Africa Investment Activity Report*, *AVCA Members Directory*. **Members** Full and Associate (83), including several international organizations (not specified). [2014/XJ1984/y/**D**]

- ♦ African Professional Statistical Association / see African Statistical Association (#00475)
- ♦ African Programme for Onchocerciasis Control (no recent information)
- ♦ The African Project / see Cohesive Communities Development Initiative
- ♦ African Promise Foundation (internationally oriented national body)
- ♦ African Protestant Church (internationally oriented national body)
- ♦ African Public Relations Association (unconfirmed)

♦ African Publishers Network (APNET) 00426

Réseau des éditeurs africains – Rede Africana de Editores

Acting Executive Director c/o Ghana Publishers Association, Bureau of Ghana Languages Building, Kawukudi Culture, P.O. Box LT 471, Laterbiokorshie, Accra, Ghana. T. +233246946773 – +233302912764. E-mail: info.africanpublishers@gmail.com.
URL: http://www.african-publishers.net/

History Feb 1992, Harare (Zimbabwe). Constitution amended and adopted, May 2002, Abuja (Nigeria). Current constitution adopted, 15 June, 2007. Registration: Registrar General Department, Ghana. **Aims** Strengthen African publishing through networking, training and trade promotion to fully meet Africa's need for quality books relevant to African social, political, economic and cultural reality. **Structure** General Council; Executive Board headed by Chairman; Committees; Secretariat in Accra (Ghana), headed by Executive Director. **Languages** Arabic, English, French. **Staff** 0.00 FTE, paid; 1.00 FTE, voluntary. **Finance** Sources: international organizations; members' dues. Supported by: Kopinor; Quarterfold Printabilities; Sharjah Book Authority. **Activities** Advocacy/lobbying/activism; awareness raising; knowledge management/information dissemination; networking/liaising; publishing activities; research/documentation; training/education. **Events** *Regional Training For Trainers in Africa Workshop* Abidjan (Côte d'Ivoire) / Dar es Salaam (Tanzania UR) 2020. **Publications** *African Publishing Review* in English, French. Annual Report; directories; catalogues; survey reports.
Members Full Members – national publishers' associations and founders Affiliate Members – all those who have a specific commitment to African publishing Associate Members – individuals or organizations with an outstanding record of service to African publishing.
Algeria, Angola, Benin, Botswana, Burkina Faso, Burundi, Cameroon, Central African Rep, Congo DR, Côte d'Ivoire, Egypt, Eritrea, Gabon, Ghana, Guinea, Kenya, Lesotho, Libya, Madagascar, Malawi, Mali, Mauritania, Mauritius, Morocco, Mozambique, Namibia, Niger, Nigeria, Rwanda, Senegal, Sierra Leone, South Africa, Sudan, Tanzania UR, Togo, Tunisia, Uganda, Zambia, Zimbabwe.
NGO Relations Partners include: *African Books Collective (ABC, #00226)*; *Afro-Asian Book Council (AABC, #00535)*; *Association for the Development of Education in Africa (ADEA, #02471)*; *Association internationale des éditeurs africains francophones (AIEAF, no recent information)*; *Book Aid International*; *CODE*; *International Publishers Association (IPA, #14675)*; *Pan African Booksellers Association (PABA, #18041)*; *The Rockefeller Foundation (#18966)*; IFFRO. [2020.05.08/XF2768/**F**]

♦ African Quality Assurance Network (AfriQAN) 00427

Secretariat African Universities House, Trinity Avenue, East Legon, PO Box AN 5744, Accra, Ghana. T. +23321774495 – +23321761588. Fax +23321774821.
Contact address not obtained.
URL: http://www.afriqan.org/

History 2007, Dar es Salaam (Tanzania UR), by *Association of African Universities (AAU, #02361)*. Constitution adopted 2009. **Aims** Provide assistance to institutions concerned with Quality Assurance in higher education in Africa. **Structure** Executive Board. **Languages** English, French. **Finance** Members' dues. Donor funding. **Activities** Training/education; events/meetings. **Events** *International Conference on Quality Assurance in Higher Education in Africa* Abuja (Nigeria) 2019, *International Conference on Quality Assurance in Higher Education in Africa* Yaoundé (Cameroon) 2018, *International Conference on Quality Assurance in Higher Education in Africa* Accra (Ghana) 2017, *Annual General Meeting* Libreville (Gabon) 2013, *Annual General Meeting* Abidjan (Côte d'Ivoire) 2012. **Publications** *The Quality Assurance Situation and Capacity Building Needs of Higher Education in Africa*. Studies. **Members** Full; Associate. Membership countries not specified. **NGO Relations** Cooperation agreement with: *African Quality Assurance Network (AfriQAN, #00427)*; *International Network of Quality Assurance Agencies in Higher Education (INQAAHE, #14312)*. [2017.03.14/XM3688/**E**]

- ♦ African Rabies Expert Bureau (unconfirmed)
- ♦ African Radio Drama Association (internationally oriented national body)
- ♦ African Rainforest Conservancy (internationally oriented national body)

♦ African Real Estate Society (AfRES) 00428

Exec Dir 5th Floor, Western House, 8-10 Broad Street, Lagos, Nigeria. E-mail: afres.info@gmail.com.
Head Office 4 Orchard Road, Orchards, Johannesburg, 2192, South Africa.
URL: http://www.afres.org/

History 1997. **Aims** Promote networking, research and education among property professionals throughout Africa. **Structure** Board of Directors. Officers: President; Vice-Director; Secretary/Treasurer. Regions (3): Southern; Eastern; Western. Executive Director. **Languages** English, French. **Staff** 14.00 FTE, voluntary. **Finance** Members' dues fixed by regional chapters. **Events** *Conference* Lusaka (Zambia) 2021, *Conference* Lusaka (Zambia) 2020, *Conference* Arusha (Tanzania UR) 2019, *Integrating the African real estate market – an agenda* Abeokuta (Nigeria) 2018, *Conference* Johannesburg (South Africa) 2017. **Publications** *Journal of African Real Estate Research (JARER)*.
Members Full in 16 countries:
Botswana, Burkina Faso, Germany, Ghana, Kenya, Malawi, Namibia, Nigeria, Rwanda, South Africa, Tanzania UR, Uganda, UK, USA, Zambia, Zimbabwe.
NGO Relations Member of: *International Real Estate Society (IRES, #14702)*. [2015/XD8523/**D**]

- ♦ African Refiners Association / see African Refiners and Distributors Association (#00429)

♦ African Refiners and Distributors Association (ARA) 00429

Association des Raffineurs Africains

Exec Sec address not obtained. T. +22522446616. Fax +22522484348. E-mail: info@afrra.org.
URL: http://www.afrra.org/

History 23 Mar 2006, Cape Town (South Africa). Previously also known as *African Refiners Association (ARA)*. **Aims** Provide a pan-African voice for the African oil supply, refining and distribution industry. **Structure** Executive Committee. Work Groups. **Events** *Annual General Meeting* Cape Town (South Africa) 2019.
Members Full in 17 countries:
Algeria, Angola, Burkina Faso, Cameroon, Côte d'Ivoire, Egypt, Ethiopia, Gabon, Libya, Morocco, Nigeria, Senegal, South Africa, Sudan, Tanzania UR, Togo, Zambia.
NGO Relations Partner of: *Partnership for Clean Fuels and Vehicles (PCFV, #18231)*. [2020/XM5020/**D**]

- ♦ African Refugee Development Center (internationally oriented national body)

♦ African Refugees Foundation (AREF) 00430

CEO Lagos State Old Secretariat Road, Off Oba Akinjobi Street, PO Box 5051K, Ikeja, Lagos, Nigeria. E-mail: jolusola@yahoo.com – aref24@hotmail.com.
Corporate HQ Plot 49, Babs Animashaun Estate Ext, Surulere, Lagos, Nigeria. T. +2348023548482.

History Sep 1993. Founded by Segun Olusola. **Aims** Be a key player in the relief environment in Africa after all efforts at attaining peace has failed; develop the potential within Africans to activate and provide *humanitarian aid* and longer term *development* solutions to the refugee and returnee problem; anticipate disasters; rehabilitate victims; encourage peace; facilitate development. **Structure** Patrons (7); Board of Trustees of 10 members; Strategy Group of 9 members; Advisory Committee of 16 members. Honorary Consultants. **Languages** English, French, Yoruba. **Staff** 4.00 FTE, paid. **Activities** Research and development; knowledge management/information dissemination; humanitarian/emergency aid; events/meetings; projects/programmes. **Publications** *AREF Newsletter* (4 a year). *A Guide to Peace Education and Peace Promotion Strategies in Africa*; *Alleviating Tensions Associated with Indigene/Settler Dichotomy in Nigeria*.
Members Individuals in 9 countries:
Benin, Ethiopia, Finland, France, Kenya, Nigeria, UK, USA, Zimbabwe.
IGO Relations Cooperates with: *African Union (AU, #00488)*; Nigeria Commission for Refugees; *UNHCR (#20327)*. [2015.07.01/XF3204/f/**F**]

- ♦ African Regional Agricultural Credit Association / see African Rural and Agricultural Credit Association (#00446)
- ♦ African Regional Centre for Engineering Design and Manufacturing (no recent information)
- ♦ African Regional Centre for Solar Energy (no recent information)
- ♦ African Regional Centre for Space Science and Technology Education / see African Regional Centre for Space Science and Technology Education – English (#00431)

♦ African Regional Centre for Space Science and Technology Education – English (ARCSSTE-E) 00431

Exec Dir Obafemi Awolowo Univ Campus, PMB 019 OAU, Post Office, Ile Ife 220282, Osun, Nigeria. T. +2348030705787 – +2348037253958. E-mail: director@arcsstee.org.ng – admin@arcsstee.org.ng.
URL: http://arcsstee.org.ng/

History 24 Nov 1998. Founded as one of the Regional Centres for Space Science and Technology Education Affiliated to the United Nations within the framework of *Committee on the Peaceful Uses of Outer Space (COPUOS, #04277)*, as part of *United Nations Programme on Space Applications (PSA)* within *United Nations Office for Outer Space Affairs (UNOOSA, #20601)*, and in the light of recommendations of *Global Action Plan for Environment and Development in the 21st Century (Agenda 21, inactive)*. **Aims** Develop skills and knowledge of *university educators* and of research and applications *scientists* in *English-speaking* Africa through rigorous theory, research, applications, field exercises and pilot-projects in aspects of space science and technology able to enhance social and economic development in each country, specifically through strengthening *remote sensing* and *geographical* information systems (GIS) capacities, *meteorological satellite* applications, satellite *communications* and global positioning systems and space and *atmospheric* sciences. **Structure** Governing Board of representatives from member countries. Hosted by Obafemi Awolowo University, Ile Ife (Nigeria). **Languages** English. **Finance** Sources: contributions of member/participating states; government support. Supported by: *Committee on the Peaceful Uses of Outer Space (COPUOS, #04277)*. **Activities** Capacity building; events/meetings; knowledge management/information dissemination; research/documentation; training/education. **Events** *Workshop on Global Navigation Satellite Systems* Ile Ife (Nigeria) 2016, *International workshop on satellite meteorology and disaster mitigation* 2001. **Members** Participating governments of 25 countries. Membership countries not specified. **IGO Relations** Partner of (1): *Group on Earth Observations (GEO, #10735)*. **NGO Relations** Member of (1): *International Society for Photogrammetry and Remote Sensing (ISPRS, #15362)*. [2022.12.16/XE3506/**E***]

♦ African Regional Centre of Technology (ARCT) 00432

Centre régional africain de technologie (CRAT)

Exec Dir 17 étage, Immeuble Fahd B A Aziz, BP 2435, Dakar, Senegal. E-mail: arct@orange.sn – crat@crat-arct.org.
URL: http://crat-arct.org/

History Nov 1977, Kaduna (Nigeria), under the aegis of *Organization of African Unity (OAU, inactive)* and *United Nations Economic Commission for Africa (ECA, #20554).*
Aims *'Objectives'*: Contribute to the development and use of technology, stimulate awareness of technological development and strengthen technological capabilities of member States; promote the use of technology suitable for the development objectives of member States and assist in the formulation of technology policies as an integral part of planned *scientific*, technological and *socio-economic development*; encourage research and training in the methodologies of technology planning; improve, for the benefit of member States, the terms and conditions under which technology is imported; promote within member States the diffusion and dissemination of technology, encouraging the collection and use of technological information; promote cooperation among countries of the African region particularly amongst member States; assess social implications of the development, transfer, and adaptation of technology and promote the understanding of such implications.
'Functions': On request from Governments of member States or institutions of technology within such member States, assist in the establishment of national institutions for the development, transfer and adaptation of technology, and identify and supply consultants to advise on matters relating to technology; advise national institutions of members States on the choice of technology, promoting through them effective links between producers and users of technology at the national level within member States; compile and maintain registers in the field of technology of: (i) African research institutions, their programmes and achievements; (ii) institutions outside Africa which are concerned with technologies relevant to the needs of member States; (iii) available specialists in the various fields of technology within the Centre and elsewhere; organize training seminars and workshops in the field of technology; promote the exchange of technical, managerial and research personnel amongst member States; assist in training technical and managerial personnel; identify and provide information on specific opportunities for training in technology; promote and encourage as appropriate the orientation of education, training and curricula towards technological needs of member States; assist Governments of member States in identifying *alternative sources* of technology; assist in training of specialist personnel in: (i) unpackaging of technologies, (ii) evaluation and assessment of technology, (iii) negotiation of contracts and arrangements relating to the development, transfer and adaptation of technology, (iv) problems connected with industrial property rights; provide for member States information and documentation services, in particular in alternative technologies and alternative sources of technologies; cooperate with governmental, public or private institutions engaged in development of methods to be applied in a unified approach to development planning; sponsor, promote and encourage original research in the forecasting, assessment and planning of technology; encourage inclusion of courses in the methodology of technology planning in the education and training of development planners; assist member States in the effective use of the International Code of Conduct for the Transfer of Technology and other relevant international agreements.
Structure Council (every 2 years), consisting of the Ministers responsible for technology in the Government of each member State, the Executive Secretary of ECA and the Secretary General of OAU. Executive Board, consisting of one third of the number of member States, the Executive Secretary of ECA as ex-officio Chairman, a representative of OAU, the Executive Director of the Centre, ex-officio Secretary, and the representatives of the United Nations Agencies desirous of assisting the Centre in its activities and whose activities are relevant to the work of the Centre, as observers. Secretariat, consisting of Executive Director, Deputy Executive Director and Directors of Divisions and professional and support staff. Functional organization of the Centre: Office of the Executive Director; Administration Division; Information and Documentation Division; Technological Consulting Services Division; Training Division. **Languages** English, French. **Staff** 24.00 FTE, paid. **Finance** Initial input from *United Nations Trust Fund for African Development (UNTFAD, #20640).* Annual and special contributions from member States; assistance, aid, loans, gifts, bequests or grant from governments, international organizations, financial institutions, public or private institutions, associations, bodies or individual persons; fees and other charges levied for services rendered under provisions of the Constitution. Supported by: *International Development Research Centre (IDRC, #13162); UNDP (#20292); UNIDO (#20336).* **Activities** The framework is the *'Lagos (Nigeria) Plan of Action for the Implementation of the Monrovia (Liberia) Strategy for the Economic Development of Africa'*, adopted by the Heads of States and Governments of the Organization of African Unity, Apr 1980, Lagos, and its fundamental principle of establishing of self-sustaining development and economic growth based on collective self-reliance. The work programme stresses: development of indigenous technological capabilities; human resources development and utilization; rural development; contributing technologically towards the activation of the priority sectors of socio-economic development; strengthening the information and data base on technological requirements and on natural resources and their exploitation. Current projects include: *'Cassava processing technology development'*; *'Energy development'* (biogas); *'Fish processing'*; *'Enhancing Africa's technological infrastructures'* (Regional Atlas on Food Technologies); *'Human resources inventory and development'*. **Events** *Ministerial forum on frontier environmentally sound technologies for Africa's sustainable development* Accra (Ghana) 2006. **Publications** *African Technodevelopment – Bulletin of the African Regional Centre for Technology*; *Alert Africa* – newsletter, advanced technology information for Africa; *INFONET Bulletin*; *Rice Parboiler Hardware Development in the African Region – A Review of Current Designs*. *Biomass Technology in Africa* in English, French; *Directory of Science and Technology Institutions and Experts in Africa*; *On-Farm Handling, Processing and Storage of Food-Grains in Africa*; *Survey of Major Science and Technology Resources in Africa*; *Technological Consulting and Advisory Services* in English, French; *The Scope for the Development and Promotion of Biomass Energy Technology in Africa* in English, French; *Towards Self-Sufficiency in Food Production: Reduction of Post-Harvest Losses* in English, French. *African Regional Centre for Technology – Brochure* in English, French. **Information Services** *AFDIR Database* – scientific societies and technical associations in Sub-Saharan Africa; *ARCTIS Database* – documentation funds, library; *ERGS Database* – energy; *FORMA Database* – institutes of engineering training; *IDA Database* – industry; *INSEXP Database* – institutes and experts in science and technology in Africa; *REQT Database* – technological requests; *VENT Database* – joint ventures.
Members Governments of 31 countries:
Algeria, Benin, Burkina Faso, Burundi, Cameroon, Cape Verde, Congo DR, Egypt, Equatorial Guinea, Ethiopia, Ghana, Guinea, Guinea-Bissau, Kenya, Liberia, Malawi, Mauritania, Morocco, Mozambique, Niger, Nigeria, Rwanda, Senegal, Sierra Leone, Somalia, Sudan, Tanzania UR, Togo, Uganda, Zambia.
IGO Relations Special agreement with: UNIDO; *ECOSOC (#05331).* Cooperation Agreement with: *International Fund for Agricultural Development (IFAD, #13692).* Permanent observer status with: *World Intellectual Property Organization (WIPO, #21593).* Accredited by: *United Nations Framework Convention on Climate Change – Secretariat (UNFCCC, #20564).* Member of: *Intergovernmental Organizations Conference (IGO Conference, #11498).* [2018/XE8763/**E***]

- ♦ African Regional Computer Confederation (inactive)
- ♦ African Regional Cooperative Agreement for Research, Development and Training Related to Nuclear Science and Technology (treaty)
- ♦ African Regional Industrial Property Organization / see African Regional Intellectual Property Organization (#00434)

♦ African Regional Institute for Geospatial Information Science and Technology (AFRIGIST) 00433

Institut Régional Africain pour la Science et la Technologie de l'Information Géospatiale
Exec Dir Off Road 1, Obafemi Awolowo Univ, PMB 5545, Ile Ife, Osun, Nigeria. T. +2348033840581.
URL: http://afrigist.org/
History 1 Jan 1972, Ile Ife (Nigeria). Established under the auspices of *United Nations Economic Commission for Africa (ECA, #20554).* Formally opened 21 Oct 1972, with 4 governments as founding member states. Normal lectures on photogrammetry started 26 Oct 1972. Former names and other names: *Regional Centre for Training in Aerospace Surveys (RECTAS)* – former; *Centre régional de formation aux techniques des levés aérospatiaux* – former. **Aims** Provide nationals of African countries with theoretical and practical training in the field of aerospace *surveys* and geoinformatics, including *remote sensing, photogrammetry, cartography, geographic* information systems and airborne *geophysical* surveys, so as to meet manpower requirements of *African* countries in the stipulated fields; conduct research and studies with particular reference to peculiarities of the African environment and needs. **Structure** Governing Council; Departments; Units; Executive Director. **Languages** English, French. **Staff** 75.00 FTE, paid. **Finance** Sources: contributions from member countries and donor countries; income from services rendered. **Activities** Training/education; events/meetings; research/documentation. **Events** *Annual meeting* Ile Ife (Nigeria) 1993, *International seminar on remote sensing applications* Ile Ife (Nigeria) 1992, *Annual meeting* Ile Ife (Nigeria) / Dakar (Nigeria) 1988, *Annual meeting* Ile Ife (Nigeria) 1987, *Annual meeting* Ile Ife (Nigeria) 1986. **Publications** *AFRIGIST Newsletter* (annual). Annual Report.
Members Governments of 8 countries:
Benin, Burkina Faso, Cameroon, Ghana, Mali, Niger, Nigeria, Senegal.
IGO Relations Partner of: *Economic Community of West African States (ECOWAS, #05312); Group on Earth Observations (GEO, #10735).* **NGO Relations** Regional member of: *African Association of Remote Sensing of the Environment (AARSE, #00216); International Cartographic Association (ICA, #12446); International Society for Photogrammetry and Remote Sensing (ISPRS, #15362).* Participates in: *International Working Group on Satellite-Based Emergency Mapping (IWG-SEM, #15911).* [2022/XE9638/**E***]

♦ African Regional Intellectual Property Organization (ARIPO) 00434

Secretariat 11 Natal Road, Belgravia, Harare, HARARE, Zimbabwe. T. +2634794065. Fax +2634794072. E-mail: mail@aripo.org.
URL: http://www.aripo.org/
History 9 Dec 1976, Lusaka (Zambia). Established under the auspices of *United Nations Economic Commission for Africa (ECA, #20554)* and *World Intellectual Property Organization (WIPO, #21593)*, on signature of an agreement by delegates of 6 states, following resolutions adopted 1972, Nairobi (Kenya) and 1974, Addis Ababa (Ethiopia), and meeting, Oct 1975, Nairobi. Agreement entered into force 15 Feb 1978. Secretariat established 1 Jun 1981, Harare (Zimbabwe), prior to which ECA and WIPO acted as joint secretariat in Nairobi. Name changed Dec 1985, Harare, to *African Regional Industrial Property Organization*, at 9th session, following amendment to the Lusaka Agreement so as to no longer restrict membership to English-speaking states but to open it to all members of *Organization of African Unity (OAU, inactive)* or ECA.
Protocols to the Lusaka agreement:
- *Protocol on Patents and Industrial Designs within the Framework of ARIPO (Harare Protocol, 1982)*, concluded 10 Dec 1982, Harare, as *'Protocol on patents and industrial designs within the framework of ESARIPO'*.

Revised, 1 Jul 1994, to link with
Patent Cooperation Treaty (PCT, 1970); and again under revision in the light of *Patent Law Treaty (PLT, 2000).* Protocol was amended to incorporate utility model 'Petty Patents', 1999.
- *Banjul Protocol on Marks (1993)*, concluded 1993, Banjul (Gambia).

Revised since 1997, to align with
Trademark Law Treaty (TLT, 1994) and *WTO Agreement on Trade Related Aspects of Intellectual Property Rights (TRIPS, 1994)*;
- *Swakopmund Protocol on the protection of traditional knowledge and expressions of folklore (2010)*, adopted 2010, Swakopmund (Namibia);
- *ARIPO Protocol for the Protection of New Varieties of Plants (2015)*, adopted 6 July 2015, Arusha (Tanzania).
- Kampala Protocol on the Voluntary Registration of Copyright and Related Rights, adopted 28 August 2021, Kampala (Uganda).

Former names and aliases: *Industrial Property Organization for English-Speaking Africa (ESARIPO)* – former; *Organisation de la propriété industrielle de l'Afrique anglophone* – former; *African Regional Industrial Property Organization* – former.
Aims Promote harmonization and development of intellectual property laws, and matters related thereto, appropriate to the needs of members and of the region as a whole; foster establishment of a close relationship between members; establish common services or organs for coordination, harmonization and development of intellectual property activities; establish schemes for training of staff in administration of intellectual property laws; promote exchange of ideas, experience, research and studies; promote and evolve a common view and approach of members; assist members in acquisition and development of technology relating to intellectual property matters; promote, in its members, the development of copyright and related rights. **Structure** Council of Ministers (meets every 2 years); Administrative Council (meets at least once a year); Independent Board of Appeal; Technical and Administrative Committees; Secretariat. Includes: *Patent Documentation and Information Centre (PADIC, see: #00434).* **Languages** English. **Staff** 55.00 FTE, paid. **Finance** Sources: contributions of member/participating states. Fees earned from operations of the Harare Protocol and the Banjul Protocol. Annual budget: 7,000,000 USD. **Activities** Certification/accreditation; events/meetings; guidance/assistance/consulting; knowledge management/information dissemination; research and development; training/education. **Events** *Annual Session* Maputo (Mozambique) 2022, *Annual Session* Victoria (Seychelles) 1998, *Biennial ministerial council session* Harare (Zimbabwe) 1990, *Biennial ministerial council session* 1988, *Annual Session* Harare (Zimbabwe) 1988. **Publications** *ARIPO Journal*; *ARIPO Magazine*. Annual Report; brochures; surveys; guidelines; studies. **Information Services** *Anderson Ray Zikonda Library* – Information and documentation centre; *Patent Documentation and Information Centre (PADIC)* – set up 1978 as 'English-Speaking Africa Patent Documentation and Information Centre (ESAPADIC).
Members Signatory to the agreement – governments of 22 countries:
Botswana, Cape Verde, Eswatini, Gambia, Ghana, Kenya, Lesotho, Liberia, Malawi, Mauritius, Mozambique, Namibia, Rwanda, Sao Tomé-Principe, Seychelles, Sierra Leone, Somalia, Sudan, Tanzania UR, Uganda, Zambia, Zimbabwe.
IGO Relations Working relationship with: *African Union (AU, #00488); United Nations Economic Commission for Africa (ECA, #20554); World Intellectual Property Organization (WIPO, #21593).* Cooperates with: *African Intellectual Property Organization (#00344); Eurasian Patent Office (EAPO, #05612); European Patent Office (EPO, #08166)*; other IGOs. Member of: *Budapest Union for the International Recognition of the Deposit of Microorganisms for the Purposes of Patent Procedure (#03345); Intergovernmental Organizations Conference (IGO Conference, #11498).* Recognized by WIPO as an International Deposit Authority (IDA) for patent deposits under the terms of: *Budapest Treaty on the International Recognition of the Deposit of Microorganisms for the Purposes of Patent Procedure (Budapest Treaty of 1977, 1977).* Signatory organization of: *African Foundation for Research and Development (AFRAND, no recent information).* Cooperation agreements with: *African Organisation for Standardisation (ARSO, #00404); Common Market for Eastern and Southern Africa (COMESA, #04296).* [2022.12.02/XD0023/**D***]

♦ African Regional Labour Administration Centre, Harare (ARLAC) ... 00435

Contact PO Box 6097, Harare, HARARE, Zimbabwe. T. +2632422109191. E-mail: arlac@arlac.co.zw.
Street address Former Salisbury Motel, 16km Peg Bulawayo Road, Snake Park, Harare, HARARE, Zimbabwe.
URL: http://www.arlac.co.zw/
History 1974, as a project of *ILO (#11123)* and *UNDP (#20292)*, for English-speaking countries, the other 2 centres being *African Regional Labour Administration Centre, Yaoundé (#00436)* and *Regional Arab Centre for Labour Administration (RACLA, inactive).* A 'fixed address' was eventually provided for the Centre in Nairobi (Kenya) Kenya, in 1975, but was suspended in late 1976 due to UNDP liquidity crisis; re-established in 1978 with renewed UNDP funding and substantial ILO, EEC and donor-country input. Previously also referred to in French as *Centre régional africain d'administration du travail, Harare.* Became autonomous 1982. **Aims** Strengthen labour administration systems in English speaking African member countries. **Structure** Governing Council; Executive Office; Committee of Senior Officials; Secretariat. **Languages** English. **Staff** 5.00 FTE, paid. **Finance** Members' dues. Support from: *ILO (#11123).* **Activities** Training/education; knowledge management/information dissemination; guidance/assisting/consulting; research/documentation; publishing activities; events/meetings. **Events** *Regional Workshop on Employment Injury Compensation Schemes* Harare (Zimbabwe) 2015, *Regional Workshop on Employment of People with Disabilities* Harare (Zimbabwe) 2015, *Regional Workshop on International Labour Standards* Harare (Zimbabwe) 2015, *Regional Workshop on Labour Inspection and Gender Equality* Harare (Zimbabwe) 2015, *Meeting / Governing Council Meeting* Harare (Zimbabwe) 2013. **Publications** *ARLAC Newsletter*. Workshop reports; training materials.
Members Governments which have ratified the ARLAC Agreement, represented by their respective ministers of labour or employment, from 19 English-speaking African countries:
Botswana, Egypt, Eswatini, Ethiopia, Ghana, Kenya, Lesotho, Liberia, Malawi, Mauritius, Namibia, Nigeria, Sierra Leone, Somalia, South Africa, Sudan, Uganda, Zambia, Zimbabwe.
IGO Relations Relations with, and attends major events organized by (among others): *African Union (AU, #00488); ILO (#11123); International Occupational Safety and Health Knowledge Network (no recent information); Southern African Development Community (SADC, #19843); WHO (#20950).* **NGO Relations** Member of: *International Association of Labour Inspection (IALI, #11983).* Relations with, and attends major events organized by (among others): *International Social Security Association (ISSA, #14885).*
[2019.02.15/XE3207/**E***]

♦ African Regional Labour Administration Centre, Yaoundé 00436
Centre régional africain d'administration du travail, Yaoundé (CRADAT)
Dir BP 1055, Yaoundé, Cameroon. T. +23722233204. Fax +23722222180.
History Established 1965, for the French-speaking countries, as *Centre de perfectionnement des cadres de l'administration du travail (CPCAT)*, the other two centres being *Regional Arab Centre for Labour Administration (RACLA, inactive)* and *African Regional Labour Administration Centre, Harare (ARLAC, #00435)*. Present name adopted in 1969. Since 1972 located on the campus of Yaoundé (Cameroon) University. Set up as a regional intergovernmental body by a convention signed by 13 countries, 8 Jan 1975, Yaoundé. **Aims** Ensure the training, specialization and improvement of: the managerial staff of the civil service and of government services in the fields of labour, professional training, health at work, child labour and human resources; union executives and of company managers; those responsible of professional organizations in member countries, dealing with labour and social issues. Intensify mutual technical cooperation. **Structure** Managing Board; Executive Bureau; Administrative and Technical Services. **Languages** French. **Finance** Sources: member states; UNDP; ILO; government of Belgium; external subsidies; grants; scholarships. **Activities** Studies and documentation. Provides technical assistance. Organizes: conferences; training courses; specialization courses; seminars. **Events** *Labour inspection and the role of social partners* Bamako (Mali) 1992, *Labour inspection and the role of social partners* Bujumbura (Burundi) 1992, *Labour inspection and the role of social partners* Niger 1992, *Labour code and collective agreement* Ouagadougou (Burkina Faso) 1992. **Publications** *Liaisons Sociales Africaines* (4 a year). *Guide pour l'élaboration, la mise en oeuvre et l'évaluation d'une politique nationale du travail, de l'emploi et de la formation professionnelle.*
Members Governments of 18 countries:
Benin, Burkina Faso, Burundi, Cameroon, Central African Rep, Chad, Congo Brazzaville, Congo DR, Côte d'Ivoire, Djibouti, Gabon, Guinea, Mali, Mauritania, Niger, Rwanda, Senegal, Togo.
IGO Relations *African Training and Research Centre in Administration for Development (CAFRAD, #00486); ILO (#11123); UNDP (#20292).* **NGO Relations** *International Social Security Association (ISSA, #14885).*
[2014.01.14/XE4764/E*]

♦ African Regional Organization of the International Federation of Commercial, Clerical, Professional and Technical Employees / see UNI Global Union – Africa Region (#20339)
♦ African Regional Organization for Standardization / see African Organisation for Standardisation (#00404)
♦ African Regional Postgraduate Programme in Insect Science (see: #12499)
♦ African Region Caritas / see Caritas Internationalis – Africa Region (#03581)

♦ African Rehabilitation Institute (ARI) 00437
Institut africain de réadaptation (IAR)
Contact address not obtained. T. +2634759211. Fax +2634759218.
History 22 Jan 1985, Arusha (Tanzania UR). 22-24 Jan 1985, Arusha (Tanzania UR), at International Conference, as a project of *Organization of African Unity (OAU, inactive)*, being developed in cooperation with *ILO (#11123)* and *United Nations Economic Commission for Africa (ECA, #20554)* and deriving from *Southern African Regional Rehabilitation Programme.* Also known as *African Rehabilitation Institute for Disabled Persons.* Achieved full legal status, Jul 1986, on signature of an agreement by ministers of Chad, Comoros, Congo, Côte d'Ivoire, Egypt, Gabon, Lesotho, Malawi, Senegal, Uganda and Zimbabwe. **Aims** Assist Member States of the Organization of African Unity to: (a) develop a unified approach for promoting the development of prevention and rehabilitation services; (b) create facilities such as income generating programmes to satisfy the needs of handicapped African persons who, because of their disabilities, find it difficult to adapt themselves to the rapidly changing world; (c) promote the development of rehabilitation centres in all OAU Member States in the African continent to assist them to harmonize as much as possible their basic conceptual principles and work out strategies in the field of rehabilitation of the disabled persons within the African region; (d) create favourable conditions for inter-African cooperation and mutual assistance as part of rehabilitation and strengthening the already existing rehabilitation institutions in various parts of Africa; and utilizing them for the training of the manpower required for the development of local rehabilitation activities carried out in Africa; (e) provide an appropriate framework for the establishment and launching of training and research programmes in the field of rehabilitation and other special projects to be carried out at regional level with the priorities and demands of those countries willing to participate in these regional programmes; (f) create a structure which would encourage and facilitate coordinated actions, measures and programmes among the African countries and the various international, governmental and nongovernmental donor organizations in all areas of comprehensive rehabilitation development; (g) promote and ensure the exchange of information and experience among African States and other countries of the world; (h) organize special projects in the field of rehabilitation and disability prevention, with a view to developing local teaching and research facilities and material. **Structure** Governing Board, comprising one representative each from OAU (ex officio Chairman), ILO and ECA, and 2 representatives of each of 5 regions of Africa (2-year terms). Technical Advisory Committee. Activities generated from 3 centres: Harare (Zimbabwe) (the seat of ARI); Brazzaville (Congo Brazzaville) (for Central African nations); Dakar (Senegal) (for West Africa). **Languages** Arabic, English, French. **Finance** Contributions of Member States. Donations of intergovernmental and nongovernmental organizations; fund raising activities. **Activities** Training/education; events/meetings. **Events** *United nations standard rules seminar* Harare (Zimbabwe) 1998, *Formal meeting* Harare (Zimbabwe) 1997. **Publications** *African Rehabilitation Journal* (4 a year). *Manual on Evaluation Methodology and Utilization and Processing of Statistical Data Related to Disability.*
Members Open to all members of AU. As at Jun 2017, ratified by 27 governments:
Angola, Benin, Botswana, Burkina Faso, Cameroon, Chad, Congo Brazzaville, Côte d'Ivoire, Eswatini, Ethiopia, Guinea, Kenya, Lesotho, Libya, Malawi, Mali, Mauritania, Mozambique, Namibia, Niger, Nigeria, Rwanda, Senegal, Togo, Uganda, Zambia, Zimbabwe.
IGO Relations *Arab Gulf Programme for United Nations Development Organizations (AGFUND, #00971).*
[2017/XD0333/j/E*]

♦ African Rehabilitation Institute for Disabled Persons / see African Rehabilitation Institute (#00437)

♦ African Reinsurance Corporation (AFRICA RE) 00438
Société africaine de réassurance – Corporación Africana de Reaseguros
Managing Director/CEO Plot 1679 Karimu Kotun Street, Victoria Island, PMB 12765, Lagos, Nigeria. T. +23412800072 – +23414616829. Fax +23412800073. E-mail: info@africa-re.com.
URL: http://www.africa-re.com/
History 24 Feb 1976, Yaoundé (Cameroon), after several years of study and negotiation between governments and their insurers and following recommendations of 1st African Ministerial Conference on Economic Cooperation, Independence and Financial Problems, Abidjan (Côte d'Ivoire); on signature of an agreement which came into force Jan 1977. Started operations 1978. Jointly owned by *African Development Bank (ADB, #00283)*, 41 member states of *African Union (AU, #00488)*, and about 150 insurance and reinsurance companies. Statutes registered in *'UNTS 1/19020'.* **Aims** Foster development of the insurance and reinsurance industry in Africa; promote growth of national, regional and sub-regional underwriting capacities; support African economic development. **Structure** General Assembly (annual); Board of Directors; Management Team; Subsidiaries (2). **Languages** English, French. **Staff** 229.00 FTE, paid. Staff from 26 countries. **Finance** Authorized capital: US$ 500 million. Called and paid-up capital: US$ 300 million. **Events** *Annual General Assembly* Accra (Ghana) 2015, *Annual General Assembly* Cairo (Egypt) 2014, *Annual General Assembly* Dakar (Senegal) 2013, *Annual General Assembly* Rabat (Morocco) 2012, *Annual General Assembly* Addis Ababa (Ethiopia) 2011. **Publications** *The African Reinsurer* (annual). Annual Report.
Members African States (members of the African Union) (39):
Algeria, Angola, Benin, Burkina Faso, Burundi, Cameroon, Central African Rep, Chad, Congo DR, Côte d'Ivoire, Egypt, Eritrea, Eswatini, Ethiopia, Gabon, Gambia, Ghana, Guinea, Kenya, Liberia, Libya, Madagascar, Mali, Mauritania, Mauritius, Morocco, Niger, Nigeria, Rwanda, Senegal, Seychelles, Sierra Leone, Somalia, Sudan, Tanzania UR, Togo, Tunisia, Uganda, Zambia.
Regional intergovernmental organization (1), listed in this Yearbook:
African Development Bank (ADB, #00283).
National insurance and reinsurance companies (about 150). Membership countries not specified.
IGO Relations AU (Observer Status). Member of: *African Trade Insurance Agency (ATI, #00485).* Participates in the activities of: *UNCTAD (#20285).* Partial owner of: *African Export-Import Bank (Afreximbank, #00305); Company for Habitat and Housing in Africa (Shelter-Afrique, #04408);* other private investment funds. **NGO Relations** Member of: *African Insurance Organization (AIO, #00343); Federation of African National Insurance Companies (#09408); Federation of Afro-Asian Insurers and Reinsurers (FAIR, #09413).*
[2015.06.01/XF9774/ey/F*]

♦ African Relief in Action (internationally oriented national body)
♦ African Remote Sensing Council (inactive)

♦ African Renewable Energy Alliance (AREA) 00439
Chair address not obtained. E-mail: info@area-net.org.
URL: http://area-net.org/
History Oct 2009, Ethiopia, by *World Future Council Foundation (WFC, #21533).* Registered in accordance with South African law. **Aims** Exchange information and consult about policies, technologies and financial mechanisms for the accelerated uptake of renewable energies in Africa. **Structure** Steering Committee; Secretariat. **Activities** Knowledge management/information dissemination; guidance/assistance/consulting; events/meetings. **NGO Relations** Supports: *Global 100% RE (#10160).* [2015/XM5637/D]

♦ African Research on Ageing Network (AFRAN) 00440
Secretariat Oxford Inst of Population Ageing, 66 Banbury Road, Oxford, OX2 6PR, UK. T. +441865612800. Fax +441865612801. E-mail: administrator@ageing.ox.ac.uk.
URL: http://www.ageing.ox.ac.uk/research/regions/africa/afran/
History 2005. **Publications** Working papers in English, French; monographs; research reports. **Members** Individuals and national organizations. Membership countries not specified. **NGO Relations** Standing Committee of: *International Association of Gerontology and Geriatrics (IAGG, #11920).* [2023.02.14/XJ8167/F]

♦ African Research and Development Network for the Industrial Production of Drugs of Medicinal Plants (inactive)
♦ African Research Foundation / see Amref Health Africa (#00806)

♦ African Research and Resource Forum (ARRF) 00441
CEO 305 Mountain View Estate, off Waiyaki Way, PO Box 57103 – 00200, Nairobi, Kenya. T. +254203002721. Fax +2542008330457.
URL: http://www.arrforum.org/
History 2002. **Aims** Facilitate and enhance thinking and action on development challenges facing East Africa and the Greater Horn of Africa. **Structure** Board of Directors. Program Staff, comprising Program Officer, Project Officer, Librarian and Project Assistants. Administration Team, including Finance and Administration Officer, Administrative Secretary, Accounts Assistant and other support staff. Secretariat, headed by Executive Director. **Languages** English, Swahili. **Finance** Funded by: *The African Capacity Building Foundation (ACBF, #00233); Heinrich Böll Foundation.* **Activities** Organizes workshops and conferences. Conducts: research; debates; analysis. Disseminates research findings. **Publications** *New Path: African Forum for Intellectual Thought* (4 a year). Books; occasional papers. **IGO Relations** Memorandum of Understanding with: *Intergovernmental Authority on Development (IGAD, #11472).* Partners with: *International Development Research Centre (IDRC, #13162).* **NGO Relations** Member of: *African Books Collective (ABC, #00226).* Partners include: *African Academy of Sciences (AAS, #00193); The African Capacity Building Foundation (ACBF, #00233); Ford Foundation (#09858); Friedrich-Ebert-Stiftung (FES); Hanns Seidel Foundation; Heinrich Böll Foundation; Norwegian People's Aid (NPA).* [2012.08.15/XJ4810/F]

♦ African Resources Watch (internationally oriented national body)
♦ African Rights Initiative International (internationally oriented national body)

♦ African Risk Capacity Agency (ARC) 00442
Institution de la Mutuelle Panfricaine de Gestion de Risques – Agência da Capacidade Africana de Risco
Dir-Gen Bldg 1 – Sunhill Park, 1 Eglin Road, Sunninghill, Johannesburg, 2157, South Africa. T. +27115171535. E-mail: info@arc.int.
CEO address not obtained.
URL: http://www.africanriskcapacity.org/
History Established as a Specialized Agency of *African Union (AU, #00488)*, through Agreement for the Establishment of the African Risk Capacity (ARC) Agency, done 23 Nov 2012, Pretoria (South Africa). **Aims** Assist assist AU Member States to reduce the risk of loss and damage caused by extreme weather events and natural disasters affecting Africa's populations by providing targeted responses to disasters in a more timely, cost-effective, objective and transparent manner. **Structure** Conference of the Parties; Governing Board; Secretariat. **Publications** *ARV Bulletin.*
Members Signatories (33):
Benin, Burkina Faso, Burundi, Central African Rep, Chad, Comoros, Congo Brazzaville, Côte d'Ivoire, Djibouti, Gabon, Gambia, Ghana, Guinea, Guinea-Bissau, Kenya, Liberia, Libya, Madagascar, Malawi, Mali, Mauritania, Mozambique, Niger, Nigeria, Rwanda, Sahrawi ADR, Sao Tomé-Principe, Senegal, Sierra Leone, Sudan, Togo, Zambia, Zimbabwe. [2023/XM6954/E*]

♦ African Road Maintenance Funds Association (ARMFA) 00443
Association des fonds d'entretien routier africains (AFERA)
Secretariat address not obtained. T. +1251114702467 – +1251114702935. Fax +1251114702662. E-mail: armfa.secretariat@gmail.com – tgsernesa@gmail.com – merontad29@gmail.com.
Pres Fairley Road – Plot 33, PO Box 50695, Lusaka, Zambia. T. +260211253145 – +260211255660 – +260211250823. Fax +260211253154 – +260211252731.
URL: http://www.armfahq.org/
History Dec 2003, Libreville (Gabon). **Aims** Promote exchange of information on practices of financing road maintenance in Africa; increase cooperation between road maintenance funds in Africa; ensure sustainability and harmonious development of road maintenance funds. **Structure** General Assembly (annual); Executive Committee; Secretariat. **Finance** Members' dues. **Events** *Annual General Assembly* Swakopmund (Namibia) 2019, *Annual General Assembly* Addis Ababa (Ethiopia) 2018, *General Assembly* Yaoundé (Cameroon) 2009, *General Assembly* Maputo (Mozambique) 2008, *General Assembly* Antananarivo (Madagascar) 2007.
Members Institutions in 32 countries:
Benin, Burkina Faso, Burundi, Cameroon, Central African Rep, Chad, Comoros, Congo Brazzaville, Congo DR, Côte d'Ivoire, Djibouti, Eswatini, Ethiopia, Gabon, Ghana, Guinea, Guinea-Bissau, Kenya, Lesotho, Madagascar, Malawi, Mali, Mozambique, Namibia, Niger, Rwanda, Senegal, Sierra Leone, Tanzania UR, Togo, Uganda, Zambia, Zimbabwe. [2018/XM0517/D]

♦ African Roundtable for Sustainable Consumption and Production (ARSCP) 00444
Pres KNCPC Industrial Research and Development Inst, Popo Road, Nairobi South C/PO Box 1360-00200 City Square, Nairobi, Kenya. T. +254206004870 – +254206004871. Fax +254206004871.
Exec Sec Mahando Str 393, Masaki, PO Box 105581, Dar es Salaam, Tanzania UR. T. +255222602338 – +2552222602242. Fax +255222602339.
History 18 May 2004, Casablanca (Morocco). Registration: Start date: 6 Sep 2004, Tanzania UR. **Aims** Promote development of national and regional capacities for effective promotion and implementation of sustainable consumption and production principles; serve as the regional clearinghouse for sustainable consumption and production activities in the Africa region. **Structure** General Assembly; Executive Board; Secretariat, headed by Executive Secretary. **Languages** English. **Staff** 3.00 FTE, paid. **Finance** Members' dues. Other sources: projects; conferences; sale of publications; special contributions; expert advice services. Annual budget: about US$ 250,000. **Activities** Events/meetings; training/education; projects/programmes; publishing activities. **Events** *Meeting* Ouagadougou (Burkina Faso) 2018, *Meeting* Kampala (Uganda) 2016, *Meeting* Windhoek (Namibia) 2014, *Meeting* Accra (Ghana) 2012, *Meeting* Cairo (Egypt) 2010. **Publications** *ARSCP Newsletter* (2 a year). Reports; meeting reports; manuals; leaflets; brochures; press releases.
Members Individual; Institutional; Corporate. Institutional in 15 countries:
Cape Verde, Egypt, Ethiopia, Ghana, Kenya, Lebanon, Morocco, Mozambique, Namibia, Rwanda, South Africa, Tanzania UR, Tunisia, Uganda, Zimbabwe.
Included in the above, 1 organization listed in this Yearbook:
Consultative Status Consultative status granted from: *UNEP (#20299).* **NGO Relations** Member of: *Global Network for Resource Efficient and Cleaner Production (RECPnet, #10497).* [2019.02.12/XM5068/F]

♦ African Rowing Federation (FASA) 00445
Contact Third Floor Union Bldg, Cairo Stadium, Nasr City, Cairo, Egypt. T. +20222623942. E-mail: african_rowing_fasa@yahoo.com – info@africanrowing.com.
URL: http://africanrowing.com/ [2019/XM1603/D]

♦ African Rugby Football Union / see Rugby Africa (#18996)

♦ African Rural and Agricultural Credit Association (AFRACA) 00446

Association régionale du crédit agricole pour l'Afrique

SG PO Box 41378, Nairobi, 00100, Kenya. E-mail: afraca@africaonline.co.ke.

Secretariat Kenya School of Monetary Studies, Off Thika Super Highway, Nooridin Road, Nairobi, 00100, Kenya. T. +254202715991. Fax +254202710082.

URL: https://www.afraca.org/

History 1977, Nairobi (Kenya). Founded at 1st General Assembly, on recommendations of a regional seminar under the auspices of the FAO, 1973, Accra (Ghana). Former names and other names: *African Regional Agricultural Credit Association* – former. **Aims** Foster cooperation among government and financial institutions in the field of rural and agricultural credit and *banking*; improve planning and management of financial services for rural development; advocate the extension of banking services to small-scale farmers. **Structure** General Assembly of members' representatives (every 2 years); Executive Committee; Secretariat, headed by Secretary General. **Languages** English, French. **Staff** 10.00 FTE, paid. **Finance** Sources: donations; members' dues. Donations from international financial institutions and aid agencies. **Activities** Operates sub-regional peripatetic training centres (3): *East African Centre for Rural and Agricultural Credit Training (EACRACT)*; *Southern African Centre for Rural and Agricultural Credit Training (SACRACT)*; *West African Centre for Rural and Agricultural Credit Training (WACRACT)*. Conducts: regional and national training, workshops, seminars, round tables, courses; in-service training programmes. Supports rural development through: technical assistance for members in conducting feasibility studies, identifying development projects and organizing training programmes; developing products for rural areas which encourage mobilization of savings and credit delivery, including (with GTZ) self-help groups and savings clubs; developing models for implementing credit guarantee schemes (with FAO); developing action-oriented assistance to rural financial services, with emphasis on strengthening existing rural, community or village banks (with IFAD); processing funds from international financial institutions and aid agencies. Organizes 'technical cooperation among developing countries' (TCDC) through training exchanges. **Events** *World Congress on Agricultural and Rural Finance* Morelia (Mexico) 2022, *Biennial General Assembly* Nairobi (Kenya) 2021, *World Congress on Agricultural and Rural Finance* New Delhi (India) 2019, *Biennial General Assembly* Lomé (Togo) 2018, *Biennial General Assembly* Dakar (Senegal) 2016. **Publications** *AFRACA Newsletter* (4 a year) in English, French. *AFRACA Rural Finance Series*. Case studies; reports. Information Services: Secretariat Reference Unit provides members with information.

Members African institutions and government departments in 21 countries:
Burkina Faso, Cameroon, Congo Brazzaville, Congo DR, Ethiopia, Gabon, Gambia, Ghana, Kenya, Lesotho, Liberia, Mali, Namibia, Nigeria, Senegal, Sierra Leone, South Africa, Tanzania UR, Tunisia, Uganda, Zimbabwe.

Consultative Status Consultative status granted from: *ECOSOC (#05331)* (Ros C); *FAO (#09260)* (Liaison Status). [2022.02.15/XD0745/**D**]

♦ African Rural Development Fund (see: #11233)

♦ African Rural Development Movement (ARUDMO) 00447

Mouvement pour le développement rural en Afrique

Pres PO Box 9026 OSU, Accra, Ghana. E-mail: arudmo@gmail.com – community@arudmo.org – info@arudmo.org.

Overseas Coordinator address not obtained.

URL: http://www.arudmo.org/

History 1995, by David Atieku. **Aims** Work with women, youth and rural communities in Africa to provide education, training and resources for economic, political and personal empowerment. **Structure** Headquarters; Country representatives (9). **Languages** English, French. **Staff** 5.00 FTE, paid. **Finance** Donations; foundations. **Activities** Active in 9 countries: Benin, Burkina Faso, Ghana, Kenya, Mali, Niger, Senegal, South Africa, Togo. **NGO Relations** Member of: *End Water Poverty (EWP, #05464)*. [2014.06.01/XM3943/**F**]

♦ African Safari Lodge Foundation (ASL Foundation) 00448

Exec Dir Postnet Ste 117, Private Bag X7, Parkview, 2122, South Africa. T. +27116461391. Fax +27865089673.

URL: http://www.asl-foundation.org/

History Also referred to as *ASLF*. Registered in accordance with South African law. **Aims** Maximize pro-poor impacts of nature *tourism* enterprises by increasing the flow of tangible benefits from these businesses into the households of local residents, via wages, supply contracts, equity agreements and local institutions that encourage fair and equitable distribution of such benefits. **Structure** Board of 7. **Languages** English. **Staff** 5.50 FTE, paid. **Finance** Funders include: *Ford Foundation (#09858)*; *International Union for Conservation of Nature and Natural Resources (IUCN, #15766)*; Critical Ecosystems Partnership Fund; SA Lotto. **Activities** Works on over 30 projects in Namibia, Mozambique and South Africa. **Publications** *ASLF Newsletter*. **NGO Relations** Member of: *Sustainable Tourism Certification Alliance Africa (STCAA, #20068)*. Cooperates with several national NGOs. [2013.11.25/XJ7301/**f**/**F**]

♦ African Sailing Confederation (ASCON) 00449

Gen Sec Ecole Natl de Voile, Alger Plage 31 000, Algiers, Algeria. T. +21321864141.

NGO Relations Continental federation of: *World Sailing (#21760)*. [2015/XJ6295/**D**]

♦ African School of Architecture and Town Planning 00450

Ecole africaine des métiers d'architecture et d'urbanisme (EAMAU)

Dir 422 rue ds Balises, Tokoin Doumassésé, Lomé, Togo. T. +22822216253. E-mail: info.eamau@eamau.org – eamau@tg.refer.org.

URL: http://www.eamau.org/

History 16 Dec 1975, Kigali (Rwanda), under the name *African School of Architecture and Town Planning – Ecole africaine et mauricienne d'architecture et d'urbanisme*, as a joint venture of *African and Mauritian Common Organization (OCAM, inactive)*. New name adopted 1994. **Aims** Provide architectural and town-planning courses, including in-service training, taking into account the present-day African environment. **Structure** Governing Board; Scientific and Education Council; Directorship of the School; Council of Teachers. **Finance** Contributions from member states. Other sources: subventions; grants; donations; private students. **Activities** Seminars; internships; research. **Events** *Quel avenir pour la formation en architecture et en urbanisme ?* Abidjan (Côte d'Ivoire) 1993.

Members Governments of 9 countries:
Benin, Burkina Faso, Cameroon, Central African Rep, Côte d'Ivoire, France, Gabon, Niger, Togo.

IGO Relations *African and Malagasy Council for Higher Education (#00364)*; *Inter-State School of Veterinary Sciences and Medicine (#15982)*. **NGO Relations** Member of: *Agence universitaire de La Francophonie (AUF, #00548)*. [2023/XF7849/**F***]

♦ African School of Meteorology and Civil Aviation (#05295)

♦ African Scientific Technical and Research Innovation Council (ASRIC) 00451

Conseil Africain de la recherche scientifique et de l'innovation (CARSI) – Conselho Africano de Pequisa Cientifica e Inovação

Secretariat c/o AU STRC, PMB 5368 Wuse Zone, Abuja, Federal Capital Territory, Nigeria. T. +2348065891643. E-mail: asric.au@outlook.com – info@asric.africa.

Street Address Plot 114 Yakubu Gowon Crescent, Asokoro, Abuja, Federal Capital Territory, Nigeria.

URL: http://www.asric.africa/

History Creation first proposed Dec 2004, Cairo (Egypt). Statutes reviewed by African Ministerial Conference in charge of Science and Technology (AMCOST), Apr 2014, Congo Brazzaville. Statutes adopted 30 Jan 2016. An organ within *African Union (AU, #00488)* – *African Union Scientific Technical Research Commission (AU STRC, #00493)*. **Aims** Mobilize African research excellence, innovation and provide a platform for dialogue and the voice of the scientific community in building and sustaining continental research-policy nexus with the aim of addressing Africa's socio-economic development challenges. **Structure** Congress; Bureau; Scientific Committee; Secretariat. Committees (3): Science and Innovation; Communication; Resource Mobilization. [2019/XM8543/**E***]

♦ African Scottish Development Organisation (internationally oriented national body)

♦ African Seabird Group (unconfirmed)

♦ African Securities Exchanges Association (ASEA) 00452

Pres c/o Nairobi Securities Exchange, The Exchange, 55 Wetlands Road, PO Box 43633, Nairobi, 00100, Kenya. T. +254202831000. Fax +25420224200. E-mail: aseasecretariat@nse.co.ke.

URL: http://www.african-exchanges.org/

History 13 Nov 1993, Nairobi (Kenya). Founded as *African Stock Exchanges Association*. Registration: Kenya. **Aims** Foster systematic mutual cooperation, exchange of information, materials and persons, mutual assistance and joint programmes between members; promote the establishment of securities exchanges in all African countries. **Structure** Annual General Meeting; Executive Committee. **Languages** English, French. **Staff** 1.00 FTE, paid. **Finance** Members' dues. **Activities** Guidance/assistance/consulting; standards/guidelines; knowledge management/information dissemination; research/documentation; events/meetings. **Events** *Annual Conference* Kasane (Botswana) 2019, *Annual Conference* Lagos (Nigeria) 2018, *Annual Conference* Cairo (Egypt) 2017, *Annual Conference* Kigali (Rwanda) 2016, *Annual Conference* Johannesburg (South Africa) 2015. **Publications** *ASEA Quarterly Newsletter*; *ASEA Yearbook*.

Members Membership open to any stock exchange or nascent stock exchange located in the African region.
Full: stock exchanges (24) representing 32 countries:
Benin, Botswana, Burkina Faso, Cameroon, Cape Verde, Côte d'Ivoire, Egypt, Eswatini, Ghana, Guinea-Bissau, Kenya, Libya, Malawi, Mali, Mauritius, Morocco, Mozambique, Namibia, Niger, Nigeria, Rwanda, Senegal, Seychelles, Sierra Leone, South Africa, Sudan, Tanzania UR, Togo, Tunisia, Uganda, Zambia, Zimbabwe.
Full: regional stock exchange: Bourse Régionale des Valeurs Mobilières de l'Afrique de l'Ouest (BRVM). Affiliate member (1):
Affiliate member (1):
South Asian Federation of Exchanges (SAFE, #19729). [2021/XD4790/**y**/**D**]

♦ African Security Sector Network (ASSN) 00453

Réseau africain du secteur de la sécurité – Rede Africano do Sector da Segurança

Contact 27 Kofi Annan Avenue, North Legon, PO Box AF 2457 – Adenta, Accra, Ghana. T. +233263011501. E-mail: info@africansecuritynetwork.org.

URL: http://www.africansecuritynetwork.org/

History Nov 2003, Elmina (Ghana). Registration: Registrar General Department -Ghana, No/ID: CG183212015, Start date: 29 Sep 2015, Ghana. **Aims** Envision an African owned security sector that is democratically governed, people-centred, rights compliant, well managed, and accountable as well as effective in supporting and sustaining human security. **Structure** Executive Committee (ExCo). **Languages** English, French, Portuguese. **Finance** Sources: grants. **Activities** Guidance/assistance/consulting; knowledge management/information dissemination; networking/liaising; politics/policy/regulatory; research/documentation; training/education. **Publications** *Security Governance in Africa Handbook* in English, French, Portuguese.

Members Institutions; individuals. Membership countries not specified.
Included in the above, one organization listed in this Yearbook:
Prisoners Rehabilitation and Welfare Action (PRAWA, #18502). [2020.06.25/XJ8215/**y**/**D**]

♦ African Seed Trade Association (AFSTA) 00454

Association africaine du commerce des semences

Main Office 7-D Commodore Office Suites, Kindruma Road, Nairobi, Kenya. E-mail: afsta@afsta.org.

URL: http://www.afsta.org/

History 22 Mar 2000, Pretoria (South Africa). **Aims** Provide a forum for interaction and information exchange within the African seed industry; represent interests of the African seed industry; promote development of the seed industry for the betterment of crop production in Africa. **Structure** General Assembly (annual). Board of Directors of max 12 members. Executive Committee, comprising President, Vice-President and Past-Vice-President. Secretariat headed by Secretary-General. **Finance** Members' dues. **Events** *Congress* Dakar (Senegal) 2023, *Congress* Djerba (Tunisia) 2022, *Congress* Nairobi (Kenya) 2021, *Congress* Livingstone (Zambia) 2020, *Congress* Mombasa (Kenya) 2019.

Members Ordinary. Seed associations and enterprises (34) in 17 countries:
Algeria, Cameroon, Côte d'Ivoire, Egypt, Eswatini, Ethiopia, Ghana, Kenya, Madagascar, Malawi, Mozambique, Nigeria, Senegal, South Africa, Tunisia, Zambia, Zimbabwe.
Associate. Government agencies, nongovernmental organizations, product and service providers. Members (8) in 7 countries:
Algeria, Angola, Denmark, France, Mozambique, South Africa, USA.

IGO Relations Observer to: *Union internationale pour la protection des obtentions végétales (UPOV, #20436)*.
NGO Relations Partner of: *Global Horticulture Initiative (GlobalHort, #10412)*. [2020/XD7937/**t**/**D**]

♦ African Services Committee (internationally oriented national body)

♦ African Sex Workers Alliance (ASWA) 00455

Contact PO Box 5986-00200, Nairobi, Kenya. T. +2544403644. E-mail: admin@aswaalliance.org.

URL: http://aswaalliance.org/

History Set up 2009. **Aims** Create a conducive environment of partnerships that enable sex workers to address the complexities, dynamics and diversities within the sex work industry. **Structure** Board. **Languages** English, French, Portuguese. **Publications** *ASWA Newsletter*.

Members Organizations (over 100) in 29 countries:
Angola, Benin, Botswana, Burkina Faso, Burundi, Cameroon, Central African Rep, Congo DR, Côte d'Ivoire, Eswatini, Ethiopia, Gambia, Ghana, Kenya, Lesotho, Liberia, Mali, Mauritius, Mozambique, Nigeria, Rwanda, Senegal, Sierra Leone, South Africa, South Sudan, Tanzania UR, Togo, Uganda, Zambia.

NGO Relations *Aidsfonds*. [2020.03.05/XM6756/**D**]

♦ African Shooting Confederation / see African Shooting Sport Federation (#00456)

♦ African Shooting Sport Federation 00456

Pres Rue el Estad el Bahary Nasr City, PO Box 290, Cairo, 11511, Egypt. T. +2024028904. Fax +2022613992. E-mail: africashooting@gmail.com.

URL: http://www.issf-sports.org/theissf/organisation/cont_confederations.ashx

History 13 Mar 1981, Tunis (Tunisia), as a continental confederation of *International Shooting Sport Federation (ISSF, #14852)*. Previously referred to as *African Shooting Confederation*.

Members National Federations (15) in 14 countries:
Algeria, Congo Brazzaville (suspended), Egypt, Eswatini, Kenya, Malawi (suspended), Namibia, Nigeria, Senegal, South Africa, Sudan, Tunisia, Uganda, Zimbabwe (2). [2015.01.08/XD1126/**D**]

♦ African Slave Trade Mixed Tribunals (inactive)

♦ African Social Forum (ASF) 00457

Forum social africain

Secretariat Enda/Syspro, 73 Rue Carnot, BP 6879, Dakar, Senegal. T. +2218217033. Fax +2218235754.

Contact MWENGO, PO Box HG 817, Highlands, Harare, HARARE, Zimbabwe.

Aims Consolidate the capacities of analysis, proposal and mobilization of the organizations of the African social movement so that they can fully play their part in Africa and within the world social movement; build an African space of concerted development of alternatives to neo-liberal globalization, starting from a diagnosis of its social, economic and political effects; define strategies of social, economic and political rebuilding, including a redefinition of the role of the state, market and organizations; define the methods of control citizen so that political alternation supports the expression and the implementation of alternative answers. **Languages** English, French. **Events** *Forum* Niamey (Niger) 2008, *Forum* Conakry (Guinea) 2005, *Forum* Lusaka (Zambia) 2004, *Forum* Addis Ababa (Ethiopia) 2003, *Forum* Bamako (Mali) 2002. **Publications** *Africa Flames*. **NGO Relations** Observer to: *World Social Forum (WSF, #21797)*. [2010/XG9050/**F**]

♦ African Society of Association Executives (AFSAE) 00458

Pres c/o AAAE, c/o Univ of Nairobi, College of Agriculture and Veterinary Sciences, Upper Kabete Campus, PO Box 63515, Nairobi, 00619, Kenya. T. +254572511300.

Contact Longpoint Office Park, 484 Bradford Drive, corner Monte Casino, Boulevard & Witkoppen Road Fourways, Johannesburg, 2191, South Africa. E-mail: info@afsae.org – support@afsae.org.

URL: http://www.afsae.org/

History Feb 2015. **Aims** Provide a forum for the education, training and sharing of knowledge about the practice of association or not for profit management in Africa. **Structure** Executive Committee; Secretariat. **Languages** English, French. **Finance** Sources: donations; members' dues. **Activities** Events/meetings. **Events** *AfSAE Africa Association Summit* Kigali (Rwanda) 2021, *Annual Africa Associations Summit* Nairobi (Kenya) 2019, *Annual Education Conference* Johannesburg (South Africa) 2018, *Annual Education Conference* Johannesburg (South Africa) 2017, *Meetings Africa* Johannesburg (South Africa) 2016. [2019/XM4396/**D**]

♦ African Society for Bioinformatics and Computational Biology (ASBCB) 00459

Contact Group of Bioinformatics and Mathematical Modelling, Inst Pasteur de Tunis, BP74 1002, Tunis, Tunisia. T. +21622938439. E-mail: info@asbcb.org.
URL: http://www.asbcb.org/

History Set up Feb 2004, Cape Town (South Africa), transforming from *African Bioinformatics Network (ABioNET)*. **Aims** Advance bioinformatics and computational biology in Africa. **Structure** Governing Council. **Languages** English. **Staff** 7.00 FTE, paid. **Finance** Members' dues. **Events** *Africa Conference on Bioinformatics* Entebbe (Uganda) 2017, *Africa Conference on Bioinformatics* Dar es Salaam (Tanzania UR) 2015, *Africa Conference on Bioinformatics / Conference* Casablanca (Morocco) 2013. **Publications** *ASBCB Newsletter*. **NGO Relations** Affiliate organization of: *International Society for Computational Biology (ISCB, #15026)*. Instrumental in setting up: *Global Organisation for Bioinformatics Learning, Education and Training (GOBLET, #10516)*. [2018.09.06/XJ6802/**D**]

♦ African Society for Cell and Developmental Biology (no recent information)

♦ African Society of Dermatology and Venerology (ASDV) 00460

Société de Dermatologie et Vénéréologie

Secretariat Room 121, Dept of Medicine, College of Medicine, Univ of Lagos, Idi-araba, Lagos, Nigeria. T. +2349098880921. E-mail: info@asdvafrica.org.
URL: http://www.asdvafrica.org/

History 2014, Kenya. **Activities** Events/meetings. **Events** *Annual Scientific Meeting* Durban (South Africa) 2018, *Scientific Meeting* Abuja (Nigeria) 2016. **NGO Relations** *African Society of Dermatopathology (#00461)*. [2017/XM4944/**D**]

♦ African Society of Dermatopathology 00461

Sec Dept of Medicine, Lagos State Univ Teaching Hosp, 1-5 Oba Akinjobi Way, Ikeja, Lagos, Nigeria.

History Jan 2016, Moshi (Tanzania UR). **Aims** Advance the sub-speciality of dermatopathology in all its aspects in Africa; promote high quality diagnostic procedures and clinical practice in dermatology, pathology and allied disciplines in Africa; promote high research standards and ethical principles in practice of medicine. **Structure** Executive Committee. **Languages** English. **Staff** Voluntary. **Finance** Members' dues. Grants. **Activities** Events/meetings. **Events** *African Dermatopathology Conference* Moshi (Tanzania UR) 2016. **Members** Full in 8 countries:
Egypt, Kenya, Nigeria, Rwanda, Senegal, South Africa, Tanzania UR, Uganda.
NGO Relations *African Society of Dermatology and Venerology (ASDV, #00460)*; *European Academy of Dermatology and Venereology (EADV, #05788)*; *International Committee for Dermatopathology (ICDP, #12762)*. [2020.03.05/XM5038/**D**]

♦ African Society of Forensic Medicine (unconfirmed)
♦ African Society of Gynaecologists and Obstetricians (#19454)

♦ African Society of Human Genetics (AfSHG) 00462

Pres c/o SBIMB, Private Bag 3, Wits, 2050, South Africa.
URL: http://www.afshg.org/

History 2003. **Events** *Conference* Rabat (Morocco) 2022, *Conference* Dar es Salaam (Tanzania UR) 2021, *Conference* Dar es Salaam (Tanzania UR) 2020, *Conference* Bamako (Mali) 2019, *Conference* Kigali (Rwanda) 2018. **NGO Relations** Full member of: *International Federation of Human Genetics Societies (IFHGS, #13451)*. Cooperates with: *Southern African Society of Human Genetics (SASHG)*. [2017/XM3786/**D**]

♦ African Society of International and Comparative Law (no recent information)

♦ African Society for Laboratory Medicine (ASLM) 00463

CEO Joseph Tito Street, Nega City Mall, Ste 800, PO Box 5487, Kirkos Subcity, Kebele 08, Addis Ababa, Ethiopia. T. +251115571021. Fax +251115571030. E-mail: admina@aslm.org – info@aslm.org.
Chair University of Maryland School of Medicine, 655 W Baltimore St, Baltimore MD 21201, USA. T. +14107061941. Fax +14107061944.
URL: http://www.aslm.org/

History Concept developed, Jan 2008 with Maputo Declaration. Properly set up 2010, with Kampala Statement. Launched Mar 2011, Addis Ababa (Ethiopia) and began functioning Apr 2011. **Aims** Improve diagnostic services and increase patient access to high quality laboratory testing across the continent. **Structure** Board of Directors. **Events** *International Conference* 2021, *International Conference* Abuja (Nigeria) 2018, *International Conference* Cape Town (South Africa) 2016, *International Conference* Cape Town (South Africa) 2014, *International Conference* Cape Town (South Africa) 2012. **Publications** *African Journal of Laboratory Medicine (AJLM)*. **NGO Relations** Member of: *International Federation of Biosafety Associations (IFBA, #13373)*. Stakeholder member in: *African Accreditation Cooperation (AFRAC, #00196)*. Cooperates with: *African Field Epidemiology Network (AFENET, #00315)*. [2017/XJ6239/**D**]

♦ African Society of Mycotoxicology (unconfirmed)
♦ African Society for Nile Basin Studies (inactive)

♦ African Society of Organization Gestosis (ASOG) 00464

SG Ain Shams Univ – Fac of Medicine, Dept of Obstetrics and Gynaecology, CSPP, 28 Asma Fahmi St, Heliopolis, Cairo, Egypt. T. +2026860069. Fax +2024847653 – +2026825344.

History 6 Dec 1996, Cairo (Egypt), as the African regional society of *Organization Gestosis (OG, #17869)*. **Aims** Study the special regional factors in the *aetiology* and *clinical* picture as well as the management of pathophysiology of *pregnancy*. Support, foster, encourage and coordinate all efforts made continent wide in the field of gestosis; foster cooperation with health authorities in African countries. **Structure** Board of Directors; Permanent Secretary General; Representatives from each African country. **Languages** English. **Finance** Members' dues. **Activities** Organizes meetings. **Events** *Biennial Conference* Nairobi (Kenya) 2002, *Biennial Conference* Cape Town (South Africa) 2000, *Biennial Conference* Casablanca (Morocco) 2000, *Biennial Conference* Luxor (Egypt) 1998, *Biennial Conference* Cairo (Egypt) 1996. **Publications** *ASOG Bulletin* (2 a year). **Members** Membership countries not specified. [2010/XD3894/**E**]

♦ African Society for Paediatric and Adolescent Endocrinology (ASPAE) 00465

Secretariat Paediatric Endocrinology Training Ctr, Gertrudes Children Hosp, PO Box 42325-00100, Nairobi, Kenya. T. +254202702600. E-mail: info@aspaed.org.
URL: http://www.aspaed.org/

History Jul 2009. **Aims** Promote the highest levels of knowledge, research, education and clinical practice of paediatric endocrinology and metabolism throughout Africa. **Structure** Executive Committee. **Activities** Events/meetings; training/education. **Events** *Joint Meeting of Paediatric Endocrinology* Buenos Aires (Argentina) 2021, *Annual Scientific Meeting* Nairobi (Kenya) 2021, *Annual Scientific Meeting* Lagos (Nigeria) 2019, *Annual Scientific Meeting* Nairobi (Kenya) 2018, *Joint Meeting of Paediatric Endocrinology* Washington, DC (USA) 2017. **Publications** *ASPAE Newsletter*. **Members** Active/Ordinary; Corresponding; Honorary. Membership countries not specified. **NGO Relations** *Global Pediatric Endocrinology and Diabetes (GPED, #10545)*; *International Society for Pediatric and Adolescent Diabetes (ISPAD, #15344)*. [2019/XJ7297/**D**]

♦ African Society for Paediatric Infectious Diseases (AfSPID) 00466

Contact address not obtained. E-mail: afspid@gmail.com.
Pres address not obtained.

History Nov 2012. Constitution approved Jan 2015. **Aims** Advance the understanding of and exchange of information on paediatric infectious diseases, related medical microbiology, immunology, vaccinology and virology, and in this regard foster greater collaboration between the clinical and laboratory-based disciplines; support the prevention and control of hospital- and community-acquired paediatric infections; forge links with societies representing similar interests throughout the world. **Structure** Executive Committee (EXCO). Regional Representation: North Africa; East Africa; West Africa; Central Africa; Southern Africa. **Languages** English. **Staff** 12.00 FTE, voluntary. **Activities** Events/meetings; guidance/assistance/consulting; knowledge management/information dissemination; networking/liaising; publishing activities; standards/guidelines. Southern Africa, East Africa, Nigeria, the Gambia, North Africa. **Publications** *AfSPID Bulletin* (3 to 4 a year). **Members** Pediatric infectious diseases specialists, fellows (registrars), interested pediatricians, general practitioners, nurses, etc. Membership countries not specified. **NGO Relations** Member of (1): *World Society of Pediatric Infectious Diseases (WSPID, #21810)*. [2023.02.15/XM8957/**D**]

♦ African Society of Pediatric Surgery (unconfirmed)

♦ African Society for Quality in Healthcare (ASQH) 00467

Sec Al Mohandes Tower, Hamadan street 7 – Flat 17 – Box 12211, Giza, Egypt. T. +20121099369.
Founder and Chairman address not obtained.
LinkedIn: https://www.linkedin.com/company/african-society-for-quality-in-healthcare-asqh

Aims Improve quality in health care in Africa by improving quality and reducing errors in patient care; work towards an effective, efficient and equitable healthcare system to ensure wide spread use of effective health measures all over Africa. **Structure** Board of Directors. **Activities** Works to prevent, protect and cure the epidemic spreading diseases in Africa such as HIV/AIDS, TB, Malaria, children's and maternal diseases and all other infectious dangerous diseases. Organizes training courses. [2019/XJ1956/**D**]

♦ African Society of Radiology (ASR) 00468

Pres PO Box 14108-00800, Westlands, Nairobi, Kenya.

History 2007. **Aims** Promote best quality practice for radiology in Africa. **Languages** English, French. **Activities** Events/meetings. **Events** *Conference* Cape Town (South Africa) 2020, *Conference* Cairo (Egypt) 2019, *Conference* Tunis (Tunisia) 2017, *Conference* Mombasa (Kenya) 2015, *International Conference* Alexandria (Egypt) 2012. **NGO Relations** *International Society of Radiology (ISR, #15412)*; *Mediterranean and African Society of Ultrasound (MASU, #16640)*. [2021/XJ8250/**D**]

♦ African Society for Regional Anesthesia (AFSRA) 00469

Pres 35 A Abou-Elfeda Street, Zamalek, Cairo, Egypt. T. +20122160808. E-mail: info@afsra.org.
URL: http://afsra.org/

History 2010. **Aims** Encourage and promote excellence in regional anesthesia education, research and practice. **Structure** Board. **Languages** English. **Staff** 2.00 FTE, paid. **Events** *Annual Conference* Cairo (Egypt) 2019, *Annual Conference* Cairo (Egypt) 2016, *World Congress of Regional Anaesthesia and Pain Therapy* Cape Town (South Africa) 2014, *Conference* Cairo (Egypt) 2013, *World Congress of Regional Anaesthesia and Pain Therapy* Sydney, NSW (Australia) 2013. [2019.02.22/XJ7514/**D**]

♦ African Society for Sexual Medicine (ASSM) 00470

Société Africaine de Medicine Sexuelle

Office PO Box 94, 1520 AB Wormerveer, Netherlands. T. +31756476372. Fax +31756476371. E-mail: office@assmweb.org.
URL: http://www.assmweb.org/

Aims Establish a scientific society to benefit the public by encouraging the highest standards of practice, education and research in the field of human sexuality; develop and assist in developing scientific methods for the diagnosis, prevention and treatment of conditions affecting human sexual function; promote publication and encourage contributions to the medical and scientific literature in the field of sexual function; focus on the African area specific major sexual health problems and explore the potential of the old African remedies. **Structure** Board of Directors; Executive Committee. Committees (3): Administrative and Finance; Constitution By Law; Scientific and Conference. **Finance** Members' dues. **Events** *Biennial Congress* Somone (Senegal) 2018, *Biennial Congress* Durban (South Africa) 2015, *Biennial Meeting* Dakar (Senegal) 2014, *Biennial Meeting* Dakar (Senegal) 2011. **Publications** *ASSM Newsletter*. **Members** Full; Associate; Honorary. Membership countries not specified. [2019/XM4217/**D**]

♦ African Society for Traumatic Stress Studies (AFSTSS) 00471

Contact SA Inst for Traumatic Stress, 18A Gill Street, Observatory, Johannesburg, 2198, South Africa. T. +27114871465. Fax +27116486105.

History Founded 18 May 2000, Pretoria (South Africa). **Aims** Increase the quality of services to survivors of violence in Africa through provision of quality training and support to a range of service providers. **Structure** International Advisory Board; Board of Directors. **Languages** English. **Staff** 3.50 FTE, paid. Voluntary. **Finance** Funded by 2 Dutch organizations. Budget (annual): euro 105,940. **Activities** Organize monthly seminars; provides training and training; conducts research. **Events** *Conference* Johannesburg (South Africa) 1998. **Publications** Newsletter (4 a year).
Members Individuals in 15 countries:
Angola, Botswana, Egypt, Eswatini, Ethiopia, Lesotho, Liberia, Mozambique, Namibia, Rwanda, Somalia, South Africa, Sudan, Uganda, Zimbabwe. [2015/XD7564/v/**D**]

♦ African Softball Confederation 00472

Pres c/o BSA, PO Box 319, Gaborone, Botswana. E-mail: wsb@it.bw.

History Oct 2007. **Events** *Congress* Zambia 2008. **NGO Relations** Regional federation of *International Softball Federation (ISF, inactive)*. [2015/XM4065/**D**]

♦ African Soil Science Society / see Africa Soil Science Society (#00520)
♦ African Solidarity Fund (#09838)
♦ African Solutions to African Problems (internationally oriented national body)
♦ African Space Agency (unconfirmed)

♦ African Sport Management Association (ASMA) 00473

SG PO Box 43844, Nairobi, 00100, Kenya. T. +254208710901ext57209. E-mail: info@asma-online.org.
Organizing Sec address not obtained.
URL: http://www.asma-online.org/

History 8 Jun 2010, Nairobi (Kenya), during 17th Conference of *International Society for Comparative Physical Education and Sport (ISCPES, #15023)*. Registered in accordance with Kenyan law. **Aims** Strengthen sport management in Africa as an academic and a professional engagement as well as a vital contributor to the continental and global social-economic development. **Structure** General Meeting (annual); Executive Committee. **Finance** Members' dues. **Events** *Conference* Nigeria 2015, *Conference* Dar es Salaam (Tanzania UR) 2013, *Conference* Kampala (Uganda) 2011. **Publications** *ASMA Journal*; *ASMA Newsletter*. **Members** Individuals; Groups. Membership countries not specified. **NGO Relations** Regional organization of *World Association for Sport Management (WASM, #21194)*. [2015/XJ9557/**D**]

♦ African Sports Confederation of the Disabled – African Paralympic Committee / see African Paralympic Committee (#00410)
♦ African Sports Journalists Union (inactive)
♦ African Squash Federation / see Squash Federation of Africa (#19933)
♦ African Squash Rackets Federation / see Squash Federation of Africa (#19933)

♦ Africans Rising For Justice, Peace and Dignity 00474

Coordinator address not obtained. T. +2209884761. E-mail: media@africans-rising.org – engagement@africans-rising.org.
URL: http://africans-rising.org/

History Process started as *Africa Civil Society Centre*, Oct 2015. Widened into *Africa Civil Society Initiative*, May 2016. Since 24 Aug 2016, known under current title when Kilimanjaro Declaration was made. Launched 25 May 2017. Also known as *Africans Rising Movement*. **Aims** Foster Africa-wide solidarity and unity of purpose of the Peoples of Africa to build a future which includes right to peace, social inclusion and shared prosperity. **Structure** Decentralized movement with virtual offices. **Languages** Arabic, English, French, Portuguese, Swahili. **Finance** Members' dues. Grants and funds from international organizations, trusts and foundations. **Activities** Events/meetings; advocacy/lobbying/activism. **Members** Membership (6500). Membership countries not specified. [2019.03.25/XM6047/**F**]

♦ Africans Rising Movement / see Africans Rising For Justice, Peace and Dignity (#00474)
♦ African Standing Conference on Bibliographic Control (inactive)
♦ African States of the Casablanca Charter (inactive)

♦ African Statistical Association (AFSA) 00475

Association africaine de statistique

Address not obtained.

History 1960s, as *African Statisticians' Association*. Became inactive and replaced by a new association under current title, 1984. Became inactive late 1980s. Revived 2010. Also known under the acronym *ASA*. Also referred to as *African Professional Statistical Association*. **Structure** Interim Committee, comprising President, Vice-President, Secretary, Treasurer and 3 members. **Finance** Supported by: *African Development Bank (ADB, #00283)*. **IGO Relations** *United Nations Economic Commission for Africa (ECA, #20554)*. [2011/XD2315/**D***]

♦ African Statisticians' Association / see African Statistical Association (#00475)
♦ African Stock Exchanges Association / see African Securities Exchanges Association (#00452)
♦ African Strategic and Peace Research Group / see Pan-African Strategic and Policy Research Group (#18068)

♦ African Strategies for Advancing Pathology (ASAP) 00476

Project Coordinator address not obtained. E-mail: pathologyinafrica@gmail.com.
CEO address not obtained.
Chair address not obtained.
URL: http://www.pathologyinafrica.org/

History 2014. **Aims** Increase and improve access to diagnostic pathology and laboratory medicine in sub-Saharan Africa (SSA) and other regions of the world that currently lack access to these services. **Structure** Board of Directors. **NGO Relations** *Aga Khan University (AKU, #00546)*; *Association of Pathologists of East, Central and Southern Africa (APECSA, #02853)*; *College of Pathologists of East Central and Southern Africa (COPECSA, #04109)*; *International Academy of Pathology (IAP, #11567)*; *International Collaboration on Cancer Reporting (ICCR, #12637)*. [2017/XM5511/**F**]

♦ African Studies Association (internationally oriented national body)
♦ African Studies Association of Australasia and the Pacific (internationally oriented national body)
♦ African Studies Association of Ireland (internationally oriented national body)
♦ African Studies Association of the UK (internationally oriented national body)
♦ African Studies Association of the West Indies (inactive)
♦ African Studies Center, Los Angeles / see James S Coleman African Studies Center, Los Angeles
♦ African Studies Center, Boston (internationally oriented national body)
♦ African Studies Center, Michigan State University (internationally oriented national body)
♦ African Studies Center, Philadelphia PA (internationally oriented national body)
♦ African Studies Centre (internationally oriented national body)
♦ African Studies Centre Leiden (internationally oriented national body)
♦ African Studies Centre, Maputo (internationally oriented national body)
♦ African Studies Program, Bloomington (internationally oriented national body)
♦ African Studies Resource Center, Lawrence KS / see Kansas African Studies Center

♦ African Sumo Union 00477

Continental Dir c/o Egyptian Judo, Aikido and Sumo Federation, Egyptian Olympic Sports Federation Complex, Cairo Stadium, Salah Salem Rd, Nasr City, Cairo, Egypt.

Aims Serve as an umbrella body for national Sumo organizations in Africa; promote the sport of Sumo. **Activities** Guidance/assistance/consulting; sporting activities. **Events** *All African Sumo Championship* Cairo (Egypt) 2001.

Members National Sumo organizations in 11 countries:
Algeria, Congo Brazzaville, Congo DR, Côte d'Ivoire, Egypt, Kenya, Mali, Mauritius, Senegal, South Africa, Zimbabwe.

NGO Relations Member of: *International Sumo Federation (IFS, #15624)*. [2015/XD7598/**D**]

♦ Africans Unite against Child Abuse (internationally oriented national body)
♦ African Sustainable Energy Association (unconfirmed)

♦ African Table Tennis Federation 00478

Fédération africaine de tennis de table

Pres 14 Abdel-Monem Riad St, Dokki GIZA, Egypt. T. +201001484045. Fax +20227538130. E-mail: kes-ittf-africa@hotmail.com.

History 1961, Cairo (Egypt). **Aims** Promote table tennis in Africa. **Structure** Council Board; Executive Committee; Committees; Zonal Sections. **Languages** Arabic, English, French. **Staff** 1.00 FTE, paid. **Finance** Budget (annual): about US$ 100,000. **Events** *Meeting* Khartoum (Sudan) 2014, *Meeting* Johannesburg (South Africa) 1999.

Members National associations in 49 countries:
Algeria, Angola, Benin, Botswana, Burkina Faso, Burundi, Cameroon, Central African Rep, Chad, Comoros, Congo Brazzaville, Congo DR, Côte d'Ivoire, Djibouti, Egypt, Equatorial Guinea, Eswatini, Ethiopia, Gabon, Gambia, Ghana, Guinea, Kenya, Lesotho, Liberia, Libya, Madagascar, Malawi, Mali, Mauritania, Mauritius, Morocco, Mozambique, Namibia, Niger, Nigeria, Rwanda, Senegal, Seychelles, Sierra Leone, Somalia, South Africa, Sudan, Tanzania UR, Togo, Tunisia, Uganda, Zambia, Zimbabwe.

NGO Relations Continental federation of: *International Table Tennis Federation (ITTF, #15650)*. [2014.09.23/XD0024/**D**]

♦ African Taekwondo Union / see World Taekwondo Africa (#21845)

♦ African Tax Administration Forum (ATAF) 00479

Forum sur l'Administration Fiscale Africaine (ATAF) – Fórum Africano das Administrações Tributárias (ATAF)

Executive Secretary 333 Grosvenor Street, Blog G, 2nd Floor, Hatfield Gardens, Pretoria, 0181, South Africa. T. +27124518800 – +27124518814 – +27797902960. E-mail: communication@ataftax.org – lwort@ataftax.org – info@ataftax.org.
Main Website: https://www.ataftax.org

History 19 Nov 2009, Kampala (Uganda). Inspired by a 2008 conference on taxation and state building in Pretoria. **Aims** Create a platform to promote and facilitate mutual cooperation among African Tax Administrations and other relevant and interested stakeholders so as to improve efficiency of their tax legislation and administration. **Structure** General Assembly (meets every 2 years); Council; Secretariat, headed by Executive Secretary. **Languages** English, French, Portuguese. **Staff** 28.00 FTE, paid; 4.00 FTE, voluntary. **Finance** Sources: contributions of member/participating states; donations; fees for services; in-kind support. Supported by: *African Development Bank (ADB, #00283)*; *Austrian Development Agency (ADA)*; *DANIDA*; *Department for International Development (DFID, inactive)*; *Deutsche Gesellschaft für Internationale Zusammenarbeit (GIZ)*; *European Union (EU, #08967)*; Government of Finland; *Irish Aid*; Ministry of Foreign Affairs of the Netherlands; *OECD (#17693)*; Open society Initiative Africa (OSIWA); State Secretariat for economic affairs – Switzerland; *The William and Flora Hewlett Foundation*. **Activities** Events/meetings. Africa. **Events** *General Assembly* Lusaka (Zambia) 2020, *International Conference on Tax in Africa* Kampala (Uganda) 2019.

Members Full in 39 countries:
Angola, Benin, Botswana, Burkina Faso, Burundi, Cameroon, Chad, Comoros, Côte d'Ivoire, Egypt, Eritrea, Eswatini, Gabon, Gambia, Ghana, Kenya, Lesotho, Liberia, Madagascar, Malawi, Mali, Mauritania, Mauritius, Morocco, Mozambique, Namibia, Niger, Nigeria, Rwanda, Senegal, Seychelles, Sierra Leone, South Africa, Sudan, Tanzania UR, Togo, Uganda, Zambia, Zimbabwe.

IGO Relations Observer to: *Global Forum on Transparency and Exchange of Information for Tax Purposes (#10379)*. Partners include:
– *African Development Bank (ADB, #00283)*;
– *Arab Maghreb Union (AMU, #01004)*;
– *Common Market for Eastern and Southern Africa (COMESA, #04296)*;
– *Department for International Development (DFID, inactive)*;
– *Deutsche Gesellschaft für Internationale Zusammenarbeit (GIZ)*;
– *East African Community (EAC, #05181)*;
– *Economic Community of West African States (ECOWAS, #05312)*;
– *Intergovernmental Authority on Development (IGAD, #11472)*;
– *International Monetary Fund (IMF, #14180)*;
– *Irish Aid*;
– *New Partnership for Africa's Development (NEPAD, #17091)*;
– *Norwegian Agency for Development Cooperation (Norad)*;
– *OECD (#17693)*;
– *Southern African Development Community (SADC, #19843)*;
– *Swedish International Development Cooperation Agency (Sida)*.

NGO Relations Member of: *Effective Institutions Platform (EIP, #05384)*. Instrumental in setting up: *African Tax Research Network (ATRN, #00480)*. Partners include: *Centre de rencontres et d'études des dirigeants des administrations fiscales (CREDAF, #03779)*; *Commonwealth Association of Tax Administrators (CATA, #04314)*; *Development Bank of Southern Africa (DBSA)*; *Inter-American Centre for Tax Administrations (#11405)*; *Intra-European Organization of Tax Administrations (IOTA, #15993)*; *International Centre for Tax and Development (ICTD, #12523)*. [2021/XJ9528/**F**]

♦ African Tax Research Network (ATRN) 00480

Contact c/o ATAF, Block G – Hatfield Gardens, Pretoria, South Africa. T. +27124518820. E-mail: atrncongress@ataftax.org.
URL: http://atrnafrica.org/

History Set up following African Academic Forum, Aug 2013, Nairobi (Kenya), convened by *African Tax Administration Forum (ATAF, #00479)*. Steering Committee set up May 2014. **Aims** Facilitate African capacity for credible research in tax policy, administration, law and leadership. **Events** *Annual Congress* 2021, *Annual Congress* Ouagadougou (Burkina Faso) 2019, *Annual Congress* Ifrane (Morocco) 2018, *Annual Congress* Antananarivo (Madagascar) 2017, *Annual Congress* Mahe Is (Seychelles) 2016. [2016/XJ9529/**F**]

♦ African Team Ministries (internationally oriented national body)
♦ African Technical Association (inactive)
♦ African Technology Foundation (internationally oriented national body)

♦ African Technology Policy Studies Network (ATPS) 00481

Réseau d'études sur la politique technologique en Afrique

Exec Dir PO Box 10081-00100, 3rd Floor, The Chancery, Valley Road, Nairobi, Kenya. T. +254202714092. Fax +254202714028. E-mail: executivedirector@atpsnet.org – info@atpsnet.org.
URL: http://atpsnet.org/

History Successor to *Eastern Africa and Southern Africa Policy Studies Network (EATPS)* and *West African Technology Policy Studies Network (WATPS)*. Secretariat originally housed at *International Development Research Centre (IDRC, #13162)*, 1994, with subsequent transition from Focal Points to National Chapters. **Aims** Improve the understanding and functioning of science, technology and innovation (STI) processes and systems to strengthen the learning capacity, social responses and governance of STI for addressing Africa's development challenges, with a specific focus on the Millennium Development Goals. **Structure** Board of Governors. Main sub-regions: Southern Africa; Eastern Africa; Western Africa; Francophone Africa. Board Committees (3): Administrative; Fundraising; Finance. Responsible STI Advisory Committee; Secretariat, led by Secretariat Management Committee (SMC). **Languages** Arabic, English, French. **Staff** 13.00 FTE, paid. **Finance** Donors and sponsors: Dutch Government; *The Rockefeller Foundation (#18966)*; National Universities Commission (NUC); Nigeria through the Raw Materials Research and Development Council (RMRDC); Technical Centre for Agriculture (CTA/Netherlands); UK Parliamentary Office of Science and Cultural Organisation (UK-POST); *European Commission (EC, #06633)*; *UNESCO (#20322)*; *UNEP (#20299)*; Welcome Trust; *DANIDA* (through Forum for Agricultural Research in Africa); University of Palermo; University of Maastricht. Has also been funded by: *African Development Bank (ADB, #00283)*; *International Development Research Centre (IDRC, #13162)*; *Ford Foundation (#09858)*; Coca-Cola, Eastern Africa; *Carnegie Corporation of New York*; *International Bank for Reconstruction and Development (IBRD, #12317)* (World Bank – InfoDev); *United Nations African Institute for Economic Development and Planning (#20518)*; UK Institute of Science and Technology (UK-POST); *International Society for Ecological Economics (ISEE, #15069)*; *OPEC Fund for International Development (OFID, #17745)*; Government of Nigeria; *New Partnership for Africa's Development (NEPAD, #17091)*; *Common Market for Eastern and Southern Africa (COMESA, #04296)*; *International Centre for Trade and Sustainable Development, Geneva (ICTSD, #12524)*; *Swedish International Development Cooperation Agency (Sida)*/SAREC. **Activities** Research/documentation; capacity building; networking/liaising; training/education; knowledge management/information dissemination; monitoring/evaluation; events/meetings. **Events** *Low-Carbon Development in Africa Workshop* Nairobi (Kenya) 2015, *Annual Conference* Cairo (Egypt) 2010.

Members National chapters in 28 countries:
Benin, Botswana, Burkina Faso, Cameroon, Côte d'Ivoire, Egypt, Eswatini, Ethiopia, Gambia, Ghana, Kenya, Lesotho, Liberia, Madagascar, Malawi, Mali, Mozambique, Nigeria, Rwanda, Senegal, Sierra Leone, South Africa, Sudan, Tanzania UR, Tunisia, Uganda, Zambia, Zimbabwe.

IGO Relations Cooperates with: *African Union (AU, #00488)*; *Bioversity International (#03262)*, formerly IPGRI – Sub-Saharan Africa (SSA); *Common Market for Eastern and Southern Africa (COMESA, #04296)*; *International Crops Research Institute for the Semi-Arid Tropics (ICRISAT, #13116)*; *New Partnership for Africa's Development (NEPAD, #17091)*; *UNEP (#20299)*; *UNESCO (#20322)*; *United Nations African Institute for Economic Development and Planning (#20518)*; *United Nations Human Settlements Programme (UN-Habitat, #20572)*. **NGO Relations** Cooperates with: *African Academy of Sciences (AAS, #00193)*; *African Centre for Technology Studies (ACTS, #00243)*; *African Institute for Applied Economics (AIAE)*; *Association of African Universities (AAU, #02361)*; Biotechnology Trust Africa (BTA); *British Council* – Kenya; *Forum for Agricultural Research in Africa (FARA, #09897)*; *International Centre of Insect Physiology and Ecology (ICIPE, #12499)*, *Pan African Agribusiness and Agro-Industry Consortium (PanAAC, #18034)*; national organizations; *Practical Action (#18475)*, formerly Intermediate Technology Development Group, Eastern Africa (ITDG-EA); *World Wide Fund for Nature (WWF, #21922)* – Eastern Africa (WWF-EARPO). [2018/XG9290/**E**]

♦ African Telecommunications Union (ATU) 00482

Union africaine des télécommunications (UAT)

Chairman PO Box 35282, Nairobi, 00200, Kenya. T. +254722203132. E-mail: sg@atuuat.africa.
URL: https://atuuat.africa/

History 7 Dec 1999, at 4th Extraordinary Session of the Conference of Plenipotentiaries of *Pan-African Telecommunication Union (PATU, inactive)*, replacing PATU as specialized agency of *Organization of African Unity (OAU, inactive)* in the field of telecommunications. OAU was replaced by *African Union (AU, #00488)* in 2002. **Aims** Promote rapid development of info-communications in Africa in order to achieve universal service and access, in addition to full inter-country connectivity, so as to make Africa an active participant in the Global Information Society. In particular: promote development and adoption of appropriate African telecommunications policies and regulatory frameworks; promote funding of telecommunications development and of programmes to develop African information society; prepare special programmes for Africa's Least Developed countries and rural telecommunications development; promote human resources development in the field and establishment of info-communications industries; promote regional coordination in value-added services, equipment certification, technical standards and harmonization of tariffs. **Structure** Conference of Plenipotentiaries. Administrative Council. General Secretariat. Regions (5): North Africa; West Africa; Central Africa; East Africa; Southern Africa. **Languages** Arabic, English, French. **Finance** Sources: contributions of member/participating states. **Activities** Capacity building; events/meetings. Core activity programmes: contributing to global decision-making; integrating regional markets; promoting investment in ICT infrastructure; building human and institutional capacity. Coordinates strategies and positions of member states in preparation for and at international meetings; undertakes studies for the benefit of members and associate members; responsible for coordinating *Pan African Telecommunications Network (PANAFTEL, no recent information)*. **Events** *ICTe Africa conference* Nairobi (Kenya) 2006, *Ordinary session* Nairobi (Kenya) 2001. **Publications** *Golden Book*.

Members Full: member states of AU which have acceded to the constitution and convention; non-AU members which have acceded to the constitution and convention and have had their application duly approved by the Union. Associate: entities in Member States of the Union, or in non-member States whose membership is duly approved by the Union. Governments of 46 countries:
Algeria, Angola, Benin, Burkina Faso, Burundi, Cameroon, Central African Rep, Chad, Comoros, Congo Brazzaville, Congo DR, Côte d'Ivoire, Djibouti, Egypt, Equatorial Guinea, Eswatini, Ethiopia, Gabon, Gambia, Ghana, Guinea, Guinea-Bissau, Kenya, Lesotho, Liberia, Libya, Madagascar, Malawi, Mali, Mauritania, Mauritius, Morocco, Niger, Nigeria, Sao Tomé-Principe, Senegal, Sierra Leone, Somalia, South Africa, Sudan, Tanzania UR, Togo, Tunisia, Uganda, Zambia, Zimbabwe.
Associate (18) in 12 countries:
Botswana, Cameroon, Côte d'Ivoire, Egypt, Ghana, Kenya, Lesotho, Mauritius, Nigeria, South Africa, Sudan, Tanzania UR.
IGO Relations Partner of (18): *African Development Bank (ADB, #00283); African Union (AU, #00488); Asia-Pacific Telecommunity (APT, #02064); Comisión Interamericana de Telecomunicaciones (CITEL, #04138); Common Market for Eastern and Southern Africa (COMESA, #04296); Community of Sahel-Saharan States (CEN-SAD, #04406); Conférence européenne des administrations des postes et des télécommunications (CEPT, #04602); Economic Community of West African States (ECOWAS, #05312); Intergovernmental Authority on Development (IGAD, #11472); International Telecommunication Union (ITU, #15673); Multinational Higher School of Telecommunications of Dakar (#16898); New Partnership for Africa's Development (NEPAD, #17091); Pan African Postal Union (PAPU, #18060); Regional African Satellite Communications Organization (RASCOM, #18748); Regional Commonwealth in the Field of Communications (RCC, #18767); Southern African Development Community (SADC, #19843); UNIDO (#20336); United Nations Economic Commission for Africa (ECA, #20554).* **NGO Relations** Partner of (1): *African Advanced Level Telecommunications Institute (AFRALTI, #00197).* [2023/XD6386/**D***]

♦ African Telecommunication Union (inactive)

♦ African Theological Fellowship (ATF) 00483

Fraternité théologique africaine (FTA)
Contact PO Box 76, Akropong-Akuapem, Ghana.
URL: http://atf.acighana.org/
History Jun 1984, Tlayacapan (Mexico), at 2nd international conference of *International Fellowship for Mission as Transformation (INFEMIT, #13584).* **Aims** Serve Churches in Africa and the nations of which they are a part, through excellence in Christian scholarship and research, through rigorous intellectual engagement with the socio-political, cultural and religious realities of the African context, and through concerted effort to apply the fruits of Christian learning in the life of the Christian community and beyond, for the benefit of all. **Structure** Executive Committee; Sub-Regional Programme Coordinators. **Languages** English, French, Portuguese. **Staff** Voluntary. **Finance** Support from: *Akrofi-Christaller Institute of Theology, Mission and Culture (ACI);* partner institutions, churches and other agencies. **Activities** Training/education; research/documentation; events/meetings. **Publications** *Journal of African Christian Thought* (2 a year).
Members African Christian theologians, mission practitioners and Christian intellectuals of evangelical persuasion in 13 countries:
Burkina Faso, Cameroon, Central African Rep, Côte d'Ivoire, Ethiopia, Ghana, Kenya, Mozambique, Nigeria, Sierra Leone, South Africa, Zambia, Zimbabwe. [2016.06.01/XM0461/**D**]

♦ African Timber Organization (no recent information)

♦ African Tobacco Control Alliance (ATCA) 00484

Alliance pour le contrôle du tabac en Afrique (ACTA)
Exec Sec c/o ANCE-Togo, 08 BP 81586, Lomé, Togo. T. +2282513415 – +2282513416. Fax +2282513576.
URL: http://atca-africa.org/
History Constitution adopted 19 Nov 2008, Durban (South Africa). **Aims** Promote development and implementation of international, regional and national legal instruments, policies and activities on tobacco control within the African region. **Structure** General Assembly (annual). Board, comprising Chair, Treasurer and 5 members. Secretariat, headed by Executive Secretary. Working groups (5): Public Education and Communication; Policy Development; Alternative Livelihoods; Environment and Health; Trade and Economy. **Languages** English, French. **Staff** 11.00 FTE, paid; 100.00 FTE, voluntary. **Finance** Grants. Budget (annual): US$ 1 million. **Activities** Promotes and facilitates information sharing on tobacco control in Africa; conducts research on the tobacco epidemic and tobacco control policy in Africa; strengthens the capacities of individuals and civil society organizations involved in tobacco control in Africa; promote and advocate for regional and national legislative and regulatory frameworks favourable for tobacco control; mobilizes and facilitates access to financial, human and technical resources required for tobacco control in Africa. **Publications** *Tax on Tobacco and Illicit Trade; The Smoker's Body; The Truth About the Use of Flavours in Tobacco; Tobacco and Development; Tobacco and Poverty; Tobacco Taxation within ECOWAS Countries; Why Increase Tax on Tobacco?.*
Members Nongovernmental organizations (over 150) and individuals (56), in 29 countries:
Algeria, Benin, Burkina Faso, Cameroon, Central African Rep, Chad, Congo Brazzaville, Congo DR, Côte d'Ivoire, Djibouti, Ethiopia, Gabon, Gambia, Ghana, Guinea, Kenya, Lesotho, Malawi, Mali, Mauritania, Mauritius, Mozambique, Niger, Nigeria, Senegal, Sierra Leone, South Africa, Tanzania UR, Uganda.
IGO Relations *WHO (#20950).* **NGO Relations** Member of: *Consortium for Non-communicable Diseases Prevention and Control in sub-Saharan Africa (CNCD-Africa, #04754).* [2018/XJ1562/**D**]

♦ African Toxicology Society (inactive)
♦ African Trade Center (internationally oriented national body)

♦ African Trade Insurance Agency (ATI) 00485

Agence pour l'Assurance du Commerce en Afrique (ACA)
CEO PO Box 10620, Nairobi, GPO 00100, Kenya. T. +254202726999. Fax +254202719701. E-mail: info@ati-aca.org.
Sec Kenya Re Towers, 5th Floor, Off Ragati Road, Upperhill, Nairobi, Kenya.
URL: http://www.ati-aca.org/
History May 2000. Established following adoption of an agreement by Heads of State and Government of *Common Market for Eastern and Southern Africa (COMESA, #04296).* Officially launched Aug 2001, Kampala (Uganda). Establishment supported by *International Bank for Reconstruction and Development (IBRD, #12317).* Former names and other names: *Agence des assurance et commerce Africain* – former; *ATIA* – former. **Aims** Promote and develop trade and investments for and within African countries by offering insurance services. **Structure** General Meeting; Board of Directors; CEO. **Languages** English, French. **Staff** 48.00 FTE, paid. **Finance** Has an open-ended capital stock based on an initial authorized nominal capital stock of US$ 1,000 million, which is divided into 10,000 shares having a par value of US$ 100,000 each. Equity capital provided by Members: African Member States currently access funds from the *International Development Association (IDA, #13155)* and the *African Development Bank (ADB, #00283).* Total subscribed capital: US$ 256,000,000. **Activities** Financial and/or material support. **Events** *Annual Meeting* Accra (Ghana) 2022, *Annual Meeting* Kampala (Uganda) 2021, *Annual Meeting* Cotonou (Benin) 2019, *Annual Meeting* Abidjan (Côte d'Ivoire) 2018, *Annual Meeting* Nairobi (Kenya) 2015. **Publications** Annual Report; brochures.
Members Government Shareholders (18):
Benin, Burundi, Congo DR, Côte d'Ivoire, Ethiopia, Ghana, Kenya, Madagascar, Malawi, Niger, Nigeria, Rwanda, South Sudan, Tanzania UR, Togo, Uganda, Zambia, Zimbabwe.
Institutional Shareholders include the following 4 organizations listed in this Yearbook:
African Development Bank (ADB, #00283); African Reinsurance Corporation (AFRICA RE, #00438); Common Market for Eastern and Southern Africa (COMESA, #04296); PTA Reinsurance Company (ZEP-RE, #18561); Trade and Development Bank (TDB, #20181).
IGO Relations Partner of (10): *African Development Bank (ADB, #00283); African Export-Import Bank (Afreximbank, #00305); African Reinsurance Corporation (AFRICA RE, #00438); African Union (AU, #00488); Common Market for Eastern and Southern Africa (COMESA, #04296); Economic Community of West African States (ECOWAS, #05312); European Investment Bank (EIB, #07599); PTA Reinsurance Company (ZEP-RE, #18561); The World Bank Group (#21218); Trade and Development Bank (TDB, #20181).* **NGO Relations** Partner of (3): *International Trade and Forfaiting Association (ITFA, #15705); International Union of Credit and Investment Insurers (Bern Union, #15767); Kreditanstalt für Wiederaufbau (KfW).* [2023/XE4132/ty/**E***]

♦ African Trade Union Confederation (inactive)

♦ African Training and Research Centre in Administration for Development (CAFRAD) 00486

Centre Africain de Formation et de Recherche Administratives pour le Développement (CAFRAD)
Dir-Gen BP 1796, 90001 Tangiers, Morocco. T. +212661307269 – +212539322707. Fax +212539325785. E-mail: cafrad@cafrad.org.
URL: http://www.cafrad.org/
History 13 May 1964, by African governments with the support of *UNESCO (#20322).* Permanent multilateral agreement signed by 11 founder member states, 18 Dec 1967, Tangiers (Morocco). **Aims** Serve as a Centre of Excellence to support governments' actions and those of related bodies in capacity development and innovation in public administration for improved service delivery to citizens. **Structure** Governing Board (meets annually); Executive Committee; Scientific Council. **Languages** Arabic, English, French, Portuguese, Spanish. **Staff** 17.00 FTE, paid. **Finance** Members' dues. Other sources: secondment of experts; special grants; gifts and grants; sales of publications; consultancy services; incomes from services rendered. **Activities** Training/education; events/meetings; projects/programmes; research/documentation; guidance/assistance/consulting; knowledge management/information dissemination. **Events** *Annual Session* Fez (Morocco) 2019, *Annual Session* Marrakech (Morocco) 2018, *Annual Session* Rabat (Morocco) 2017, *Annual Session* Marrakech (Morocco) 2015, *Pan-African Forum on the Modernization of Public Service and State Institutions / Annual Session* Marrakech (Morocco) 2015. **Publications** *African Administrative Studies* (2 a year). *Studies and Documents* – research monographs and proceedings of seminars, workshops and conferences. Information Services: CAFRAD Library houses over 35,000 books and bound periodicals and includes subscriptions to 40 journals as well as collections of reference works, government documents, pamphlets, newspapers in many languages, and rare books. *African Network of Administrative Information (ANAI, inactive),* set up Jan 1981. **Information Services** *Online Public Access Catalogue (OPAC)* – for users and all researchers seeking information dealing with administrative sciences and related fields.
Members Membership open to all African States. At present, members in 36 countries:
Algeria, Angola, Benin, Burkina Faso, Burundi, Cameroon, Cape Verde, Central African Rep, Chad, Congo Brazzaville, Congo DR, Côte d'Ivoire, Djibouti, Eswatini, Gabon, Gambia, Ghana, Guinea, Guinea-Bissau, Liberia, Libya, Madagascar, Mali, Mauritania, Morocco, Namibia, Niger, Nigeria, Sao Tomé-Principe, Senegal, Sierra Leone, Somalia, South Africa, Sudan, Togo, Tunisia.
IGO Relations Partner of:
- *African Centre for Applied Research and Training in Social Development (ACARTSOD, #00237);*
- *African Civil Service Observatory (ACSO, #00249);*
- *African Development Bank (ADB, #00283);*
- *African Regional Labour Administration Centre, Yaoundé (#00436);*
- *Arab Administrative Development Organization (ARADO, #00893);*
- *Arab Bank for Economic Development in Africa (#00904);*
- *Arab Planning Institute (API, #01027);*
- *Banque internationale d'information sur les Etats francophones (BIEF, inactive);*
- *Canadian International Development Agency (CIDA, inactive);*
- *Commonwealth Fund for Technical Cooperation (CFTC, #04331);*
- *Deutsche Gesellschaft für Internationale Zusammenarbeit (GIZ);*
- *Eastern and Southern African Management Institute (ESAMI, #05254);*
- *ILO (#11123);*
- *International Bank for Reconstruction and Development (IBRD, #12317)* (World Bank);
- *International Development Research Centre (IDRC, #13162);*
- *Islamic Development Bank (IsDB, #16044);*
- *Islamic World Educational, Scientific and Cultural Organization (ICESCO, #16058);*
- *Maghreb Centre for Administrative Studies and Research (CMERA, no recent information);*
- *Organisation internationale de la Francophonie (OIF, #17809);*
- *UNDP (#20292);*
- *UNESCO (#20322);*
- *UNICEF (#20332);*
- *UNIDO (#20336);*
- *United Nations African Institute for Economic Development and Planning (#20518);*
- *United Nations Committee of Experts on Public Administration (CEPA, #20542);*
- *United Nations Economic Commission for Africa (ECA, #20554);*
- *United Nations Public Administration Network (UNPAN, #20615);*
- *WHO (#20950).*

NGO Relations Instrumental in setting up: *Network of African Consultants (see: #00486).*
[2018.06.27/XD4634/**E***]

♦ African Transformative Leapfrogging Advisory Services (unconfirmed)

♦ African Triathlon Union (ATU) 00487

Vice-Pres c/o Fountain Healthcare, All Seasons Place, 74 Isheri–Ogunnusi Road, Lagos, Nigeria.
URL: http://africa.triathlon.org/
History 1993, Gordon's Bay (South Africa). Regional union of *World Triathlon (#21872).* Former names and other names: *Africa Triathlon* – alias (Oct 2020). **Structure** Executive Board. **Languages** English, French. Official language is English with French as second language. **Activities** Sporting events.
Members Federations in 19 countries:
Burundi, Cameroon, Egypt, Ghana, Kenya, Libya, Madagascar, Mauritius, Morocco, Mozambique, Namibia, Nigeria, Rwanda, Seychelles, South Africa, Togo, Tunisia, Uganda, Zimbabwe. [2020/XM0791/**D**]

♦ African Union (AU) 00488

Union africaine (UA)
Chief of Staff PO Box 3243, Roosvelt Street, Old Airport Area, W21K19 Addis Ababa, Ethiopia. T. +251115517700. Fax +251115517844.
URL: http://www.au.int/
History 8 Jul 2001, Lusaka (Zambia). Established on signature by African Heads of State of a treaty dissolving *Organization of African Unity (OAU, inactive)* and setting up the new organization over a one-year transition period. Constitutive Act signed 11 Jul 2001, Lusaka, came into force 28 Jun 2002. Heads of State and Government meeting/inaugural session of the Assembly, 10 Jul 2002, Durban (South Africa), adopted *African Union Durban Declaration.* Establishment is based on a suggestion in 1999, Sirte (Libyan AJ), by General Moammar Gaddafi, head of Libyan AJ. **Aims** Achieve greater unity and solidarity among African countries and the peoples of Africa; defend the sovereignty, territorial integrity and independence of member states; accelerate political and socio-economic integration of the continent; promote and defend African common positions on issues of interest to the continent and its peoples; encourage international cooperation, taking account of the Charter of the United Nations and the Universal Declaration of Human Rights; promote peace, security and stability on the continent; promote democratic principles and institutions, popular participation, the rule of law and and good governance; promote and protect human and peoples' rights in accordance with the African Charter on Human and Peoples' Rights and other relevant instruments; establish the conditions necessary for the continent to play its rightful role in the global economy and in international negotiations; promote sustainable development on economic, social and cultural levels and the integration of African economies; promote cooperation in all fields of human activity so as to raise living standards of African peoples; coordinate and harmonize policies among existing and future regional economic communities leading to gradual attainment of the Union's objectives; advance the development of the continent by promoting research in all fields, in particular in science and technology; work with relevant international partners in the eradication of preventable diseases and the promotion of good health on the continent.
Structure Assembly of Heads of State and Government; Executive Council; Permanent Representatives Committee (PRC); *Peace and Security Council (PSC);* Specialised Technical Committees; AU Commission; *New Partnership for Africa's Development (NEPAD, #17091)* / AU Development Agency; AU Foundation; Financial Institutions; Judicial, Human Rights and Legal Organs; *Pan-African Parliament (PAP, #18058); Economic, Social and Cultural Council (ECOSOCC);* African Peer Review Mechanism; Regional Economic Communities (RECs); Specialised Agencies and Institutions.
Specialised Technical Committees (13):
Finance, Monetary Affairs, Economic Planning and Integration; Social Development, Labour and Employment; Health, Population and Drug Control; Justice and Legal Affairs; Youth, Culture and Sports; Public Service, Local Government, Urban Development and Decentralisation; Communication and Information Communications Technology; Defence, Safety and Security; Agriculture, Rural Development, Water and Environment; Education, Science and Technology; Gender and Women's Empowerment; Migration, Refugees and Internally Displaced Persons (IDPs); Migration, Refugees and Internally Displaced Persons (IDPs).

Financial Institutions (3): *African Monetary Fund (AMF)*; *African Investment Bank (AIB)*; *African Central Bank (ACB)*.
Judicial, Human Rights and Legal Organs (6): *African Commission on Human and Peoples' Rights (ACHPR, #00255)*; *African Court on Human and Peoples' Rights (AfCHPR, #00278)*; Extraordinary African Chambers (EAC); *African Union Commission on International Law (AUCIL)*; AU Advisory Board on Corruption; *African Committee of Experts on the Rights and Welfare of the Child (ACERWC, #00257)*.
Regional Economic Communities (8) aim to faciliate regional economic integration, through *African Economic Community (AEC, #00290)*: *Arab Maghreb Union (AMU, #01004)*; *Common Market for Eastern and Southern Africa (COMESA, #04296)*; *Community of Sahel-Saharan States (CEN-SAD, #04406)*; *East African Community (EAC, #05181)*; *Economic Community of Central African States (ECCAS, #05311)*; *Economic Community of West African States (ECOWAS, #05312)*; *Intergovernmental Authority on Development (IGAD, #11472)*; *Southern African Development Community (SADC, #19843)*.
Specialised Agencies and Institutions:
- Education, Human Resources, Science and Technology Bodies: *Pan African University (PAU)*; *Pan African Institute for Education for Development (IPED) / African Observatory for Education*; *Centre international pour l'éducation des filles et des femmes en Afrique de l'Union Africaine (UA/CIEFFA, #03752)*; *African Union Scientific Technical Research Commission (AU STRC, #00493)*, including *Pan-African Intellectual Property Organisation (PAIPO)*; *African Scientific Technical and Research Innovation Council (ASRIC, #00451)*; *African Observatory of Science, Technology and Innovation (AOSTI, #00401)*.
- Gender Development: *Fund for African Women*.
- Economic Bodies: *Pan-African Institute for Statistics (STATAFRIC)*; *Pan African Training Centre on Statistics*.
- Energy and Infrastructure Bodies: *African Civil Aviation Commission (AFCAC, #00248)*; *African Airlines Association (AFRAA, #00200)*; *African Telecommunications Union (ATU, #00482)*; *Pan African Postal Union (PAPU, #18060)*; *African Energy Commission (AFREC, #00298)*; *African Commission on Nuclear Energy (AFCONE, #00256)*; *African Minerals Development Centre (AMDC)*.
- Rural Economy and Agricultural Bodies: *Interafrican Bureau for Animal Resources (AU-IBAR, #11382)*; *Inter-African Phytosanitary Council (AU-IAPSC, #11386)*; *Semi-Arid Food Grain Research and Development (AU SAFGRAD, #19226)*; *Pan African Veterinary Vaccine Center of the African Union (AU-PANVAC, #18073)*; Pan African Tsetse and Trypanosomiasis Eradication Campaign (PATTEC); Fouta Djallon Highlands Programme AU Coordination Office; *African Risk Capacity Agency (ARC, #00442)*.
- Security Bodies: *Committee of Intelligence and Security Service of Africa (CISSA, #04263)*; *African Center for the Study and Research on Terrorism (ACSRT, #00236)*; *African Union Mechanism for Police Cooperation (AFRIPOL, #00492)*.
- Social Affairs Bodies: *Africa Centres for Disease Control and Prevention (Africa CDC, #00162)*; *Centre for Linguistic and Historical Studies by Oral Tradition (#03771)*; *African Academy of Languages (ACALAN, #00192)*; *African Institute for Remittances (AIR)*; *African Union Sports Council (AUSC)*; *African Audiovisual and Cinema Commission (AACC)*.
- Other Bodies: *The African Capacity Building Foundation (ACBF, #00233)*; *Pan African Women's Organization (PAWO, #18074)*.

Also includes: *African Medicines Agency*; *African Space Agency (AfSA)*. AfCHPR and *Court of Justice of the African Union (#04935)* will be merged to become *African Court of Justice and Human Rights*.
Languages Arabic, English, French, Portuguese. **Activities** Politics/policy/regulatory. **Events** *International Conference on Public Health in Africa (CPHIA 2022)* Kigali (Rwanda) 2022, *African Forum on Transitional Justice* Lomé (Togo) 2022, *Africa Industrialization Week* Addis Ababa (Ethiopia) 2019, *YES : Youth Entrepreneurship and Self-employment Forum* Addis Ababa (Ethiopia) 2019, *Africa Mining Summit* Gaborone (Botswana) 2019.
Members Member States of AU which had signed, ratified/acceded to the Union (55):
Algeria, Angola, Benin, Botswana, Burkina Faso, Burundi, Cameroon, Cape Verde, Central African Rep, Chad, Comoros, Congo Brazzaville, Congo DR, Côte d'Ivoire, Djibouti, Egypt, Equatorial Guinea, Eritrea, Eswatini, Ethiopia, Gabon, Gambia, Ghana, Guinea, Guinea-Bissau, Kenya, Lesotho, Liberia, Libya, Madagascar, Malawi, Mali, Mauritania, Mauritius, Morocco, Mozambique, Namibia, Niger, Nigeria, Rwanda, Sahara West, Sao Tomé-Principe, Senegal, Seychelles, Sierra Leone, Somalia, South Africa, South Sudan, Sudan, Tanzania UR, Togo, Tunisia, Uganda, Zambia, Zimbabwe.
IGO Relations Accredited to the Conference of the Parties of: *Secretariat of the United Nations Convention to Combat Desertification (Secretariat of the UNCCD, #19208)*. Accredited by: *United Nations Framework Convention on Climate Change – Secretariat (UNFCCC, #20564)*. Entitled to be represented at Sessions of General Conference of *International Atomic Energy Agency (IAEA, #12294)*. Cooperation agreement with: *FAO (#09260)*; *International Maritime Organization (IMO, #14102)*; *UNESCO (#20322)*. Memorandum of Understanding with: *Organisation for the Prohibition of Chemical Weapons (OPCW, #17823)*. Cooperates with: *Union of African Shippers' Councils (UASC, #20348)*; *United Nations Institute for Training and Research (UNITAR, #20576)*. Participates in the activities of: *UNCTAD (#20285)*. Permanent observer status with: *World Intellectual Property Organization (WIPO, #21593)*. Observer to: *Codex Alimentarius Commission (CAC, #04081)*; *International Organization for Migration (IOM, #14454)*; *World Trade Organization (WTO, #21864)*. Observer to General Assembly of: *United Nations (UN, #20515)*. Representative in Governing Board of: *UNESCO – International Institute for Capacity Building in Africa (IICBA, #20308)*. Co-Chairs on an alternating basis with *New Partnership for Africa's Development (NEPAD, #17091)* and G8 and non-G8 member countries of *OECD (#17693)*: *Africa Partnership Forum (APF, #00510)*. Member of: *Common Fund for Commodities (CFC, #04293)*; *International Nuclear Information System (INIS, #14378)*; *Parliamentary Union of the OIC Member States (PUIC, #18220)*; *United Nations Committee on the Exercise of the Inalienable Rights of the Palestinian People (CEIRPP, #20539)*. Invited to sessions of Intergovernmental Council of: *International Programme for the Development of Communication (IPDC, #14651)*. *International Conference on the Great Lakes Region (ICGLR, #12880)* is organized under the auspices of the AU and the United Nations. Supports: *European Development Fund (EDF, #06914)*; *UNHCR (#20327)*. Representatives from: *Unitaid (#20493)*. Instrumental in setting up: *African Organisation for Standardisation (ARSO, #00404)*; *Infrastructure Consortium for Africa (ICA, #11206)*; *African Union/United Nations Hybrid Operation in Darfur (UNAMID, inactive)*; *United Nations Operation in Burundi (ONUB, inactive)*. **NGO Relations** Instrumental in setting up: *African Development Forum (ADF, inactive)*; *Observatory of Cultural Policies in Africa (OCPA, #17644)*. *Council for the Development of Social Science Research in Africa (CODESRIA, #04879)*; *African Physical Society (AfPS, #00417)* and *Association of Power Utilities in Africa (APUA, #02867)* are Observer members. Memorandum of Understanding with: *Council of Africa Political Parties (CAPP, #04856)*; *European Centre for Development Policy Management (ECDPM, #06473)*. Special relationship with: *International Union for Conservation of Nature and Natural Resources (IUCN, #15766)*. Member of: *Forum for Agricultural Research in Africa (FARA, #09897)*. Permanent relations with: *World Family Organization (WFO, #21399)*. Supports: *Afro-Arab Institute for Culture and Strategic Studies (AACI, #00534)*; *Association of African Universities (AAU, #02361)*; *Digital Solidarity Fund (DSF, inactive)*; *Pan African Social Prospects Centre – Albert Tevoedjre Institute (inactive)*; *World Network for Linguistic Diversity (Maaya, #21671)*. Cooperates with: *African Refugees Foundation (AREF, #00430)*; *Global Forum for Media Development (GFMD, #10375)*. Partners: *Africa Governance Institute (AGI, #00178)*. Contact with: *Leonard Cheshire Disability (#16443)*. Instrumental in setting up: *Conference of Directors of the West African National Meteorological and Hydrological Services (AFRIMET, #04589)*. [2022/XD8572/D*]

♦ African Union of the Blind (AFUB) 00489

Union Africaine des Aveugles

Pres Off North Aiport Road, Embakasi, PO Box 72872-00200, Nairobi, Kenya. T. +254202320019. Fax +254206823989. E-mail: info@afub-uafa.org.
URL: http://www.afub-uafa.org/

History Oct 1987, Tunis (Tunisia). **Aims** Protect the rights of blind and partially sighted persons on the African continent. **Structure** General Assembly (every 4 years); Board. Regional (Geographical) Union of the *World Blind Union (WBU, #21234)*. **Languages** English, French, Portuguese. **Staff** 6.00 FTE, paid. **Finance** Annual budget: US$ 500,000. **Activities** Advocacy/lobbying/activism; awareness raising; training/education; projects/programmes. **Events** *Extraordinary General Assembly* Kampala (Uganda) 2014, *General Assembly* Rabat (Morocco) 2008, *IDP Triennial Africa forum / Quadrennial General Assembly* Rabat (Morocco) 2008, *Quadrennial General Assembly* Cape Town (South Africa) 2004, *IDP Triennial Africa forum* Midrand (South Africa) 2004. **Publications** *AFUBNews*. **Members** National associations of the blind (60) in 53 African countries. Membership countries not specified. **Consultative Status** Consultative status granted from: *African Commission on Human and Peoples' Rights (ACHPR, #00255)* (Observer). **IGO Relations** Observer to: *African Committee of Experts on the Rights and Welfare of the Child (ACERWC, #00257)*; *African Union (AU, #00488)*. [2018.06.01/XD1546/D]

♦ African Union of Broadcasting (AUB) 00490

Union Africaine de Radiodiffusion (UAR)

CEO Avenue Carde – Immeuble CSS 1er Etage, BP 3237, 12500 Dakar, Senegal. T. +221338211625 – +221338215970. Fax +221338225113. E-mail: contact@uar-aub.org.
URL: https://www.uar-aub.org/

History Founded with the title *Union of National Radio and Television Organizations of Africa – Union des radiodiffusions et télévisions nationales d'Afrique (URTNA)*, on ratification of statutes which had been first drafted Oct 1960, Tunis (Tunisia). Statutes revised in 1998. Was also sometimes referred to as *African National Television and Broadcasting Union*. Re-launched under listed title, 6 Sep 2007, Nairobi (Kenya) at 1st General Assembly of the transformed organization. **Aims** Support in every field the interests of African *broadcasting* and *television* organizations which adhere to the Statutes; ensure exchange of information on all matters of general interest to such organizations; promote and coordinate consideration of questions relating to broadcasting and television; promote measures designed to assist the development of African radio and television; ensure provision of programmes to enrich the quality of life of viewers and project the true image of Africa. **Structure** General Assembly (annual). Administrative Council, consisting of 15 member organizations (members hosting permanent services are Council members by right, others for 2-year terms). Secretary-General. Specialized Commissions (5): Administrative, Legal and Finance; Programme; Technical; TV News Exchange; Training. **Languages** Arabic, English, French. **Staff** 52.00 FTE, paid. **Finance** Members' subscriptions based on population. Other sources: grants; legacies; donations; subsidies; income from publications. Budget (annual): US$ 2.1 million. **Activities** Research/documentation; knowledge management/ information dissemination; events/meetings; projects/programmes. **Events** *General Assembly* Gaborone (Botswana) 2020, *General Assembly* Marrakech (Morocco) 2019, *General Assembly* Kigali (Rwanda) 2018, *General Assembly* Dakar (Senegal) 2017, *General Assembly* Abuja (Nigeria) 2015. **Publications** *URTNA Review* (4 a year) in English, French. Records; reports.
Members Active: radio and television organizations in 48 African countries (" indicates additional active member):
Algeria, Angola, Benin, Botswana, Burkina Faso, Burundi, Cameroon, Cape Verde, Central African Rep, Chad, Comoros, Congo Brazzaville, Congo DR, Côte d'Ivoire, Djibouti, Egypt, Eswatini, Ethiopia, Gabon (*), Gambia, Ghana, Guinea, Guinea-Bissau, Kenya (*), Liberia, Libya, Madagascar, Malawi, Mali, Mauritania, Mauritius, Morocco, Mozambique, Namibia, Niger, Nigeria, Senegal, Seychelles, Sierra Leone, Somalia, South Africa, Sudan, Tanzania UR, Togo, Tunisia, Uganda, Zambia, Zimbabwe.
Associate: public radio and television organizations in 6 countries outside Africa:
France, Germany, Holy See, Netherlands, Portugal, Switzerland.
Consultative Status Consultative status granted from: *ILO (#11123)* (Special List); *UNESCO (#20322)* (Consultative Status); *World Intellectual Property Organization (WIPO, #21593)* (Permanent Observer Status). **IGO Relations** Observer to: *Intergovernmental Committee of the International Convention of Rome for the Protection of Performers, Producers of Phonograms and Broadcasting Organizations (#11474)*; *Union for the International Registration of Audiovisual Works (#20444)*. Working relations with: *International Telecommunication Union (ITU, #15673)*, including close cooperation with ITU Radiocommunication and Telecommunication Standardization Sectors. Close cooperation with: *Pan African Telecommunications Network (PANAFTEL, no recent information)*. Related union: *Arab States Broadcasting Union (ASBU, #01050)*. Invited to sessions of Intergovernmental Council of: *International Programme for the Development of Communication (IPDC, #14651)*. **NGO Relations** Member Union of: *World Broadcasting Unions (WBU, #21247)*. Member of: *International Council for Film, Television and Audiovisual Communication (IFTC, #13022)*; *Public Media Alliance (PMA, #18568)*. Organizes: *World Conference of Broadcasting Unions*, together with related unions *Asia-Pacific Broadcasting Union (ABU, #01863)*; *Caribbean Broadcasting Union (CBU, #03465)*; *European Broadcasting Union (EBU, #06404)*; *Organización de Telecomunicaciones de Iberoamérica (OTI, #17851)*; *International Association of Broadcasting (IAB, #11738)*; *North American Broadcasters Association (NABA, #17561)*. Partnership on a sustainable programme of assistance for Africa's broadcast community with: *International Federation of Association Football (#13360)*. Member of: *Permanent Conference of Mediterranean Audiovisual Operators (COPEAM, #18320)*. [2020/XD3360/D]

♦ African Union of Building Societies and Housing Finance Institutions / see African Union for Housing Finance (#00491)
♦ African Union Convention on Cross-Border Cooperation (2014 treaty)
♦ African Union Convention on Cyber Security and Personal Data Protection (2014 treaty)
♦ African Union Convention on Preventing and Combating Corruption (2003 treaty)
♦ African Union Convention for the Protection and Assistance of Internally Displaced Persons in Africa (2009 treaty)
♦ African Union for Development Banks (inactive)

♦ African Union for Housing Finance (AUHF) 00491

Chairperson PO Box 72624, Parkview, 2122, South Africa. T. +27114479581. Fax +27866857041. E-mail: kecia@housingfinanceafrica.org.
URL: http://www.auhf.co.za/

History Founded 30 Jun 1983, Nairobi (Kenya), as *African Union of Building Societies and Housing Finance Institutions*, under the auspices of *International Union for Housing Finance (IUHF, #15780)*. Officially inaugurated 14 Jun 1984, Malawi; registered in Kenya shortly thereafter. Initially there were 11 members in 8 countries. South Africa was excluded from membership due to the political situation in the country until 1993. Registered in accordance with South African law. Has changed names 3 times. **Aims** Promote housing finance on the African continent. **Structure** General Meeting and Conference (annual). **Languages** English. **Staff** 15.00 FTE, paid. **Finance** Members' dues. **Activities** Networking/liaising; knowledge management/ information dissemination; advocacy/lobbying/activism; capacity building; training/education. **Events** *Annual Conference* Cape Town (South Africa) 2019, *Annual Conference* Abidjan (Côte d'Ivoire) 2018, *Annual Conference* Kampala (Uganda) 2017, *Annual Conference* Abuja (Nigeria) 2016, *Annual Conference* Nairobi (Kenya) 2014. **Publications** *Financing Housing in Africa* (12 a year) – newsletter.
Members Institutions in the public and private sectors and national associations or institutions, including mortgage banks, building societies, housing corporations and other entities, which mobilize resources for the provision of shelter in Africa. Members (40) in 17 countries:
Botswana, Eswatini, Gambia, Ghana, Kenya, Mauritius, Namibia, Nigeria, Rwanda, Seychelles, South Africa, Tanzania UR, Uganda, UK, USA, Zambia, Zimbabwe. [2019.02.13/XD0329/D]

♦ African Union International Centre for Girls' and Women's Education in Africa (#03752)

♦ African Union Mechanism for Police Cooperation (AFRIPOL) 00492

Mécanism africain de coopération policière – Mecanismo da União Africana para a Cooperação Policial

Address not obtained.

History Established 2017, as a technical institution of *African Union (AU, #00488)*, with Headquarters based in Algiers (Algeria). Statutes adopted 30 Jan 2017, Addis Ababa (Ethiopia). **Structure** General Assembly; Steering Committee; Secretariat; National Liaison Offices. **Finance** Budget is integral part of regular budget of *African Union (AU, #00488)*. **IGO Relations** *International Criminal Police Organization – INTERPOL (ICPO-INTERPOL, #13110)*. [2019/XM8544/F*]

♦ African Union of Physics (inactive)

♦ African Union Scientific Technical Research Commission (AU STRC) 00493

Exec Dir Plot 114 Yakubu Gowon Crescent, Asokoro, PMB 5368 WuseZone 2, Abuja, Federal Capital Territory, Nigeria. T. +2349065891643. E-mail: austrc@africa-union.org – info@austrc.org.
URL: http://www.austrc.org/

History 1 Jan 1965, by decision of the Heads of State and Government of *Organization of African Unity (OAU, inactive)*, to absorb *Commission for Technical Cooperation in Africa South of the Sahara (CTCA, inactive)*, set up Jan 1950, Paris (France), and referred to, from 1962, as *Commission for Technical Cooperation in Africa – Commission de coopération technique en Afrique*. Subsequently referred to as *Scientific, Technical and Research Commission of the Organization of African Unity (OAU/STRC) – Commission scientifique, technique et de la recherche de l'Organisation de l'unité africaine (OUA/CSTR)*. Previously also referred to in French as *Commission de recherches scientifiques et techniques de l'Organisation de l'unité africaine (CRST)*. The Commission serves Africa in all matters relating to science, technology and research by coordinating joint projects as stated in OAU Charter, Lagos (Nigeria) Plan of Action, Africa's Priority Programme for Economic Recovery and Abuja Treaty establishing the African Economic Community. Currently a specialized institution within *African Union (AU, #00488)*. **Aims** Implement the Africa's Science and Technology Policy in coordination with relevant stakeholders; promote the intra-Africa research activates; identify new and comparative priority areas for research; popularize the scientific and technological research culture in Africa. **Structure** Annual Session. Membership open to African governments, subject to approval by all existing

Member Governments. Meetings closed. Secretariat. **Finance** Capital and recurrent budgets: OAU resources. Development projects: technical assistance from international financing and technical institutions such as: *Fonds de solidarité prioritaire (FSP); European Community (inactive); International Development Research Centre (IDRC, #13162); United States Agency for International Development (USAID)*, and from governments of Austria, Japan and Switzerland. **Activities** Research/documentation; guidance/assistance/consulting; advocacy/lobbying/activism; training/education; capacity building. Projects include: African Union Network of Sciences; *Pan-African Intellectual Property Organisation (PAIPO); African Environmental Society (AES); African Scientific Technical and Research Innovation Council (ASRIC, #00451).* **Events** *Interafrican symposium on new, renewable and solar energies in Africa* Bamako (Mali) 1994. **Publications** *OAU/STRC Annual Activities Report; OAU/STRC Newsletter. Animal Genetic Resources in Africa; Distribution Map of Animal Diseases in Africa; Phytosanitary Map of Major Crop Pests and Diseases in Africa; Viral Diseases in Africa Affecting Animals; Viral Diseases in Africa Affecting Man; Viral Diseases in Africa Affecting Plants; Virus Associated Cancers in Africa.* Conference reports; scientific reference works; periodicals issued by technical bureau and committees – all in English and French, obtainable from Publications Bureau.

Members Governments of 54 countries:

Algeria, Angola, Benin, Botswana, Burkina Faso, Burundi, Cameroon, Cape Verde, Central African Rep, Chad, Comoros, Congo Brazzaville, Congo DR, Côte d'Ivoire, Djibouti, Egypt, Equatorial Guinea, Eritrea, Eswatini, Ethiopia, Gabon, Gambia, Ghana, Guinea, Guinea-Bissau, Kenya, Lesotho, Liberia, Libya, Madagascar, Malawi, Mali, Mauritania, Mauritius, Morocco (suspended membership temporarily), Mozambique, Namibia, Niger, Nigeria, Rwanda, Sahara West, Sao Tomé-Principe, Senegal, Seychelles, Sierra Leone, Somalia, South Africa, Sudan, Tanzania UR, Togo, Tunisia, Uganda, Zambia, Zimbabwe.

IGO Relations Collaborative organization of: *Arab Organization for Agricultural Development (AOAD, #01018).* Cooperative Agreement with: *International Fund for Agricultural Development (IFAD, #13692).* Works or has worked closely with:

- *African Development Bank (ADB, #00283);*
- *African Regional Centre for Engineering Design and Manufacturing (ARCEDEM, no recent information);*
- *African Regional Centre of Technology (ARCT, #00432);*
- *CABI (#03393);*
- *Central African Mineral Resources Development Centre (CAMRDC, no recent information);*
- *Centre technique de coopération agricole et rurale (CTA, inactive);*
- *Comité permanent inter-Etats de lutte contre la sécheresse dans le Sahel (CILSS, #04195);*
- *Committee of Intelligence and Security Service of Africa (CISSA, #04263);*
- *Department for International Development (DFID, inactive);*
- *Economic Community of West African States (ECOWAS, #05312);*
- *FAO (#09260);*
- *Fishery Committee for the Eastern Central Atlantic (CECAF, #09784);*
- *Inter-African Phytosanitary Council (AU-IAPSC, #11386);*
- *International Bureau of Education (IBE, #12413);*
- *International Crops Research Institute for the Semi-Arid Tropics (ICRISAT, #13116);*
- *International Livestock Research Institute (ILRI, #14062);*
- *Mediterranean Action Plan (MAP, #16638);*
- *OPEC Fund for International Development (OFID, #17745);*
- *Semi-Arid Food Grain Research and Development (AU SAFGRAD, #19226);*
- *UNEP (#20299);*
- *UNDP (#20292);*
- *UNIDO (#20336);*
- *United Nations Economic and Social Commission for Western Asia (ESCWA, #20558);*
- *West and Central African Action Plan (WACAF, no recent information);*
- *WHO (#20950);*
- *WHO Regional Office for Africa (AFRO, #20943).*

NGO Relations Works or has worked closely with: *International Centre of Insect Physiology and Ecology (ICIPE, #12499); International Fertilizer Development Center (IFDC, #13590); International Scientific Council for Trypanosomiasis Research and Control (ISCTRC, #14809); Pan African Institute for Development (PAID, #18053); Pasteur Institute; World Agroforestry Centre (ICRAF, #21072).* [2018/XE3028/**E***]

♦ African Union Sports Council (unconfirmed)
♦ African Union of Sports Medicine (no recent information)
♦ African Union/United Nations Hybrid Operation in Darfur (inactive)

♦ African University for Cooperative Development (AUCD) 00494

Université africaine de développement coopératif (UADC)

Rector 01 BP 1236, Cotonou, Benin. T. +229330639. Fax +229331506. E-mail: rectoratuadc@yahoo.fr.
URL: http://www.uadc-aucd.org/

History 7 Oct 1967, as *Centre panafricain de formation coopérative (CPFC)*, at the initiative of 1st Pan African Cooperative Conference, representing governments, cooperative movements and trade unions of francophone Africa South of the Sahara. In 1976, the concerned countries decided to sanction the inter-state status of the Centre by adopting, 12 Mar 1976, the *Convention inter-Etats créant le Centre panafricain de formation coopérative.* Name changed to *Institut supérieur panafricain d'économie coopérative (ISPEC)* and privatization of management adopted by the revised Convention, 27 Feb 1993, at 9th Pan African Cooperative Conference. **Aims** Be the means to promote a cooperative and associative movement in the service of the well-being of the African people; support the development of African cooperative movement across training and research in every field of social economy. **Structure** Main authority: Cooperative Pan-African Conference (CPC) uniting representatives of Governments, cooperatives, labour unions and NGOs. Tripartite Board of Directors (cooperatives, labour unions and governments). Departments (3): Cooperative Economics and Management; Financing and Micro-financing; Development Management. **Languages** French. **Finance** Main source: organizations participating to Pan African Cooperative Conference and countries having signed the Convention. Other sources: training scholarships; services; subsidies for activities. **Activities** Research/documentation; training/education; guidance/assistance/consulting. **Events** *Pan African Cooperative Conference* Cotonou (Benin) 2008, *Pan African Cooperative Conference* Cotonou (Benin) 1994, *Conference / Pan African Cooperative Conference* Cotonou (Benin) 1993, *Pan African Cooperative Conference* Ouagadougou (Burkina Faso) 1990, *Pan African Cooperative Conference* Cotonou (Benin) 1988. **Publications** Papers on various subjects.

Members Member countries (20):

Benin, Burkina Faso, Burundi, Cameroon, Cape Verde, Central African Rep, Chad, Comoros, Congo Brazzaville, Congo DR, Côte d'Ivoire, Gabon, Guinea, Guinea-Bissau, Mali, Mauritania, Niger, Rwanda, Senegal, Togo.

NGO Relations Member of: *Support Network for the Capacity Development of Cooperatives (RADEC-COOP, no recent information).* [2017.03.15/XF0448/**F***]

♦ African Venture Philanthropy Alliance (unconfirmed)
♦ African Veterans Athletic Association / see African Masters Athletics (#00368)

♦ African Veterinary Association (AVA) 00495

Association Vétérinaire Africaine

Exec Pres/Founder BP no 267, Cité Mahrajène, 1082 Tunis, Tunisia. T. +21698317601 – +21694604009. E-mail: vetatvac@yahoo.com.
Gen Sec address not obtained. E-mail: associationvetafrique@yahoo.fr – ordrevetmali@yahoo.fr.
Headquarters La Maison du Vétérinaire, La Rabta-Tunis, PO Box 267, 1082 Tunis, Tunisia.

History Nov 2000, Tunis (Tunisia). **Aims** Unite and enhance the role of veterinarians in Africa; reinforce and harmonize veterinary practice; harmonize veterinary education and trainings; participate in the development of animal health; public health, animal welfare, breeding and reinforce veterinary services; represent civil society in Africa and be the voice of the veterinary profession in the continent. **Structure** General Assembly; Executive Board. Technical commissions (5); Advisory groups. **Languages** Arabic, English, French, Portuguese. **Finance** Sources: members' dues; sponsorship. **Activities** Advocacy/lobbying/activism; awareness raising; events/meetings; monitoring/evaluation; politics/policy/regulatory. **Events** *Congress* Tunis (Tunisia) 2022, *Congress* Lubango (Angola) 2013, *Congress* Yaoundé (Cameroon) 2009, *Congress* Bamako (Mali) 2006, *Congress* Tunis (Tunisia) 2002. **Publications** Congress proceedings.

Members Honorary; national and regional associations in 54 countries:

Algeria, Angola, Benin, Botswana, Burkina Faso, Burundi, Cameroon, Cape Verde, Central African Rep, Chad, Comoros, Congo Brazzaville, Congo DR, Côte d'Ivoire, Djibouti, Egypt, Equatorial Guinea, Eritrea, Eswatini, Ethiopia, Gabon, Gambia, Ghana, Guinea, Guinea-Bissau, Kenya, Lesotho, Liberia, Libya, Madagascar, Malawi, Mali, Mauritania, Mauritius, Morocco, Mozambique, Namibia, Niger, Nigeria, Rwanda, Sao Tomé-Principe, Senegal, Seychelles, Sierra Leone, Somalia, South Africa, South Sudan, Sudan, Tanzania UR, Togo, Tunisia, Uganda, Zambia, Zimbabwe.

Observer members in 13 countries:

China, France, Greece, Indonesia, Italy, Korea Rep, Kuwait, Lebanon, Poland, Singapore, Spain, Thailand, Vietnam.

NGO Relations Member of (1): *World Veterinary Association (WVA, #21901).* [2022.03.04/XJ1053/**D**]

♦ African Virtual University (AVU) 00496

Université virtuelle africaine – Universidad Virtual Africana

Rector Cape Office Park (Opp Yaya Ctr), Ring Road Kilimani, PO Box 25405, Nairobi, Kenya. T. +254202528333. E-mail: rector@avu.org – contact@avu.org.
Dakar Regional Office Bureau Régional de l'Afrique de l'Ouest, Sicap Liberté VI Extension, Villa No 8 VDN, BP 50609, Dakar, Senegal. T. +221338670234.
Facebook: https://www.facebook.com/AfricanVirtualUniversity/

History 1997. Founded by *International Bank for Reconstruction and Development (IBRD, #12317).* Transferred to Nairobi (Kenya), 2002, when governments of Kenya, Senegal, Mauritania, Mali, and Côte d'Ivoire signed the Charter. **Aims** Prepare learners, using open distance and eLearning, to better contribute to development of the African continent through provision of high quality tertiary and continuing education. **Structure** Board of Directors. **Languages** English, French, Portuguese. **Staff** 11 permanent; 11 FTE in-house; over 400 external consultants. **Finance** Funding partners; programmes, workshops and consultancies; management fees; contributions and subscriptions. Annual budget: 600,000 USD. **Activities** Events/meetings; knowledge management/information dissemination; training/education. **Events** *International Conference* Nairobi (Kenya) 2015, *International Conference* Nairobi (Kenya) 2013, *International conference on ICT for development education and training* Addis Ababa (Ethiopia) 2006.

Members Participating universities (over 50) in 31 countries (" indicates prospective):

Benin, Burkina Faso, Burundi, Cameroon, Congo DR, Côte d'Ivoire, Djibouti, Egypt (*), Ethiopia, Ghana, Guinea, Guinea-Bissau, Kenya, Libya (*), Madagascar, Malawi, Mali, Mauritania, Mozambique, Namibia, Niger, Nigeria, Rwanda, Senegal, Somalia, Sudan, Tanzania UR, Togo, Uganda, Zambia, Zimbabwe.

IGO Relations Accredited by (8): *African Development Bank (ADB, #00283); African Union (AU, #00488); Canadian International Development Agency (CIDA, inactive); Commonwealth of Learning (COL, #04346); International Development Research Centre (IDRC, #13162); International Institute for Educational Planning (IIEP, #13874); UNDP (#20292)* (Somalia); *UNESCO (#20322).* **NGO Relations** Member of (1): *Open Education Consortium (#17751).* [2020/XF5851/**F***]

♦ African Volleyball Confederation (#04503)
♦ African Voluntary Organization for Child and Maternal Care (inactive)

♦ African Water Association (AfWA) 00497

Association Africaine de l'Eau (AAE)

Exec Dir 25 BP 1174, Abidjan 25, Côte d'Ivoire. T. +2252722499611. E-mail: contact@afwa-hq.org.
URL: http://www.afwa-hq.org/

History 4 Feb 1980, Abidjan (Côte d'Ivoire). Founded at inaugural meeting. Statutes modified: 5-9 Apr 1982, Rabat (Morocco); 31 Jan 1994, Dakar (Senegal); Feb 2008, Cotonou (Benin), 2010 Kampala (Uganda). Former names and other names: *Union of African Water Suppliers (UAWS)* – former; *Union africaine des distributeurs d'eau (UADE)* – former. **Aims** Undertake programmes and support knowledge sharing in sustainable water management – its science, practice and policy – through professional development, networking and advocacy; support members in their efforts to achieve the Millennium Development Goals (MDG) and other near-term targets that have been established for Africa; advocate a balanced approach to utility management, based on corporate governance that is commercially sound, financially self-sustaining and environmentally compliant; foster and promote all actions of cooperation and exchanges in the field of professional training. **Structure** General Assembly; Executive Board; Executive Management; Scientific and Technical Council. **Languages** English, French. **Staff** 12.00 FTE, paid. **Finance** Members' dues based on volume of water sold for utilities and a lump sum for non-utility members. **Activities** Advocacy/lobbying/activism; events/meetings; guidance/assistance/consulting; knowledge management/information dissemination; networking/liaising; training/education. **Events** *Congress* Abidjan (Côte d'Ivoire) 2023, *New Breaking new grounds to accelerate access to water and sanitation for all in Africa* Kampala (Uganda) 2020, *Accelerating access to sanitation and water for all in Africa facing climate change* Bamako (Mali) 2018, *Sustainable access to water and sanitation in africa* Nairobi (Kenya) 2016, *Mobilizing resources and governance of water and sanitation in Africa* Abidjan (Côte d'Ivoire) 2014. **Publications** *AfWA Magazine* (3 a year). Yearbook; reports.

Members Regular: national body in charge of public service; Affiliate: agency/company/research and training institute; Individual; Honorary. Members (over 120) in 45 countries:

Algeria, Angola, Benin, Botswana, Burkina Faso, Burundi, Cameroon, Central African Rep, Chad, Congo Brazzaville, Congo DR, Côte d'Ivoire, Djibouti, Egypt, Equatorial Guinea, Eswatini, Ethiopia, Gabon, Gambia, Ghana, Guinea, Guinea-Bissau, Lesotho, Liberia, Madagascar, Mali, Mauritania, Morocco, Mozambique, Namibia, Niger, Nigeria, Rwanda, Sao Tomé-Principe, Senegal, Sierra Leone, South Africa, South Sudan, Sudan, Tanzania UR, Togo, Tunisia, Uganda, Zambia, Zimbabwe.

NGO Relations Member of (1): *Global Water Operators' Partnerships Alliance (GWOPA, #10652).* Partner of (1): *Africa-EU Innovation Alliance for Water and Climate (AfriAlliance, #00169).* Cooperates with (1): *Sanitation and Water for All (SWA, #19051).* [2022.02.15/XD8744/**D**]

♦ African Water Facility (#09233)
♦ African Widows Organization (no recent information)

♦ African Wildlife Foundation (AWF) 00498

Headquarters Ngong Road, Karen, PO Box 310, Nairobi, 00502, Kenya. Fax +254202765030. E-mail: africanwildlife@awf.org.
URL: http://www.awf.org/

History Founded 1961, as *African Wildlife Leadership Foundation.* Present name adopted 1982. EU Transparency Register: 968063933796-28. **Aims** Ensure the wildlife and wild lands of Africa will endure forever. **Structure** Headquarters in Nairobi (Kenya). International offices in: Washington DC (USA); Livingstone (Zambia); Arusha (Tanzania UR); Kinshasa (Congo DR). **Finance** Contributions from US memberships, multilateral and bilateral donors and foundations, including: *Ford Foundation (#09858); United States Agency for International Development (USAID).* **Activities** Advocacy/lobbying/activism. **Publications** *African Wildlife News* (4 a year). **Members** About 50,000 people, mainly in the USA. Membership countries not specified. **Consultative Status** Consultative status granted from: *ECOSOC (#05331)* (Special); *UNEP (#20299).* **IGO Relations** Member of: *Congo Basin Forest Partnership (CBFP, #04662).* **NGO Relations** Member of: *Africa Biodiversity Collaborative Group (ABCG);* Conservation Council of *The ICCF Group (#11045); Environment Liaison Centre International (ELCI, no recent information); International Union for Conservation of Nature and Natural Resources (IUCN, #15766); World Heritage Watch (WHW).* Partner of: *Elephant Protection Initiative Foundation (EPI Foundation, #05429).* Also links with a number of national organizations active in the field. [2019/XF2063/t/**F**]

♦ African Wildlife Leadership Foundation / see African Wildlife Foundation (#00498)

♦ African Wind Energy Association (AfriWEA) 00499

Pres PO Box 313, Darling, 7345, South Africa. T. +27224923095. Fax +27224923095.

History 2002. **Aims** Promote and support wind energy development on the African continent by facilitating exchange of political and technical information, expertise and experience in the wind energy sector; further wind energy interests of Africa, in particular, and developing countries in general; serve as an influential umbrella organisation representing the sector in Africa and thus assisting interaction and cooperation between all energy players; advance regional cooperation by encouraging communication and collaboration between other African wind energy and renewable energy member committees in Africa to promote renewable energy policy goals which contribute to economic development, alleviation of poverty, protection of the environment and improving quality of life for people in Africa. **Structure** Board, including Executive Committee (President, Vice-President, Secretary General, Director and 5 members). **Languages** English. **Staff** 2.00 FTE, voluntary. **Activities** Stimulates and supports foundation of national and regional wind energy associations in Africa; encourages national governments to set ambitious targets and political frameworks for priority strategies to fast track sustainable development of all renewable energies; attends and organizes international, national and local conferences and workshops; raises awareness of the benefits and desirability of wind energy through a series of training courses and via newsletter; facilitates consultation between the energy industry, national, provincial and local government departments, as well as other organisations on issues of mutual and public interests and creates a channel of industry opinion; collects and circulates relevant information; promotes implementation of cooperative action; publishing activity. Maintains a library, holding some 6,000 volumes. **Events** *Annual Wind Power Africa Conference* Cape Town (South Africa) 2012, *Annual wind power Africa conference* Cape Town (South Africa) 2011, *World wind energy conference / World Wind Energy Conference – WWEC* Cape Town (South Africa) 2003. **Publications** *Fresh Air* (irregular) – electronic newsletter. **Members** Membership countries not specified. **NGO Relations** Member of: *World Wind Energy Association (WWEA, #21937).* [2015/XD9458/D]

♦ African Woman and Child Features Service (internationally oriented national body)
♦ African Women Empowerment Guild (internationally oriented national body)

♦ African Women Jurists Federation 00500

Fédération des juristes africaines

Address not obtained.

History Jul 1978. **Aims** Assist in the harmonization of African legal concepts; promote the progress of African law; further cooperation between states to achieve unity between them; ensure access for women to all careers, particularly legal careers. **Events** *Droit des femmes en Afrique – bilan et perspectives au regard des stratégies prospectives de Nairobi et du programme d'action de Beijing* Dakar (Senegal) 2005. **Publications** *Le message* (irregular). **Members** Full in 21 countries (membership countries not specified). [2010/XD1714/D]

♦ African Women Leaders in Agriculture and the Environment (internationally oriented national body)

♦ African Women in Leadership Organisation (AWLO) 00501

Chief Exec 6 Alhaji Bankole Crescent, Adeniyi Jones, Ikeja, Lagos, Nigeria. T. +2348022473972. E-mail: info@awlo.org.
URL: http://awlo.org/

History Founded 2009. **Aims** Drive women's leadership through gender parity, leadership effectiveness, and global development; bring together female executives, entrepreneurs, professionals and leaders to further enhance their leadership capabilities. **Structure** International Board of Trustees; International Headquarters. Country Vice-Presidents; Coordinator. Chapters; Youth Councils. **Languages** English. **Finance** Members' dues. Other sources: grants; donations. **Activities** Events/meetings; training/education; projects/programmes; capacity building. **Events** *African Women in Leadership Conference (AWLC)* Durban (South Africa) 2022, *Conference* Kigali (Rwanda) 2019, *All Africa/Caribbean First Ladies Summit* Toronto, ON (Canada) 2019. **Publications** *AWLO Magazine. African Women of Worth: 100 Amazons.*
Members Chapters in 11 countries:
Botswana, Cameroon, Gambia, Kenya, Liberia, Nigeria, South Africa, Uganda, UK, USA, Zimbabwe. [2020.03.16/XM6991/D]

♦ African Women's Active Nonviolence Initiatives for Social Change (AWANICh) 00502

Initiatives des Femmes Africaines de la Nonviolence Active pour le changement social

Secretariat PO Box CT 8036, Cantonments, Accra, Ghana. T. +233302733570 – +233302979905.
Street Address C 81/20, Abelemkpe, Accra, Ghana.
Facebook: https://www.facebook.com/African-Womens-Active-Nonviolence-Initiatives-for-Social-Change-AWANICh-297755137038027/

History Jun 2007. Previously hosted by *West Africa Network for Peacebuilding (WANEP, #20878).* Former names and other names: *Women Peacemakers Program-Africa (WPP-Africa)* – former. Registration: Start date: Dec 2011, Ghana. **Aims** Empower African women peacemakers and activists to promote active nonviolence and gender sensitivity within the peace movement as a means of transforming unjust political, social and economic structures in Africa for sustainable peace and development. **Structure** Board; Secretariat.
Members Organizations in 35 countries:
Angola, Benin, Burundi, Cameroon, Central African Rep, Chad, Congo Brazzaville, Congo DR, Côte d'Ivoire, Eritrea, Eswatini, Ethiopia, Gabon, Ghana, Guinea, Guinea-Bissau, Lesotho, Liberia, Madagascar, Malawi, Mali, Mauritania, Niger, Nigeria, Rwanda, Senegal, Seychelles, Sierra Leone, South Africa, South Sudan, Sudan, Togo, Uganda, Zambia, Zimbabwe.
NGO Relations Affiliated with: *International Fellowship of Reconciliation (IFOR, #13586).* [2014/XJ7862/F]

♦ African Women in Science and Engineering (internationally oriented national body)

♦ African Women's Development and Communication Network (FEMNET) 00503

Réseau des femmes africaines pour le développement et la communication

Exec Dir PO Box 54562, Nairobi, 00200, Kenya. T. +254203741301 – +254203741320. Fax +254203742927. E-mail: admin@femnet.or.ke.
URL: http://www.femnet.co/

History Previously, *African Women's Task Force (inactive)* was formed, Oct 1984, Arusha (Tanzania UR), and charged with the responsibility of establishing an institutional means for collective African NGO effort to pursue the implementation of UN Forward Looking Strategies for the Advancement of Women which were the major outcome of the End of the Decade for Women Activities Conference, 1985, Nairobi. At the meeting in Apr 1988, Nairobi, the Task Force fulfilled its mandate by founding FEMNET. Registered in 1991. **Aims** Inform and mobilize African women and *girls* in order to participate and influence policies and processes that affect their lives. **Structure** General Assembly (every 3 years); Board; Secretariat located in Nairobi (Kenya). **Languages** English, French. **Staff** 14.00 FTE, paid. **Finance** Donations. **Activities** Knowledge management/information dissemination; networking/liaising; advocacy/lobbying/activism; capacity building. **Events** *African civil society forum* Addis Ababa (Ethiopia) 2007, *International conference for the reform of international institutions* Geneva (Switzerland) 2006, *Quadrennial conference and general assembly* Nairobi (Kenya) 2003, *Quadrennial conference and general assembly* Nairobi (Kenya) 2001, *Quadrennial conference and general assembly* Nairobi (Kenya) 1996. **Publications** *FEMNET News* (3 a year) in English, French; *Our Rights* (2 a year) in English, French – bulletin.
Members Organizational; individual. Members in 47 countries:
Algeria, Angola, Benin, Botswana, Burkina Faso, Burundi, Cameroon, Central African Rep, Chad, Congo Brazzaville, Congo DR, Côte d'Ivoire, Egypt, Equatorial Guinea, Eswatini, Ethiopia, Gabon, Gambia, Ghana, Guinea, Guinea-Bissau, Kenya, Lesotho, Liberia, Madagascar, Malawi, Mali, Mauritania, Mauritius, Morocco, Mozambique, Namibia, Niger, Nigeria, Rwanda, Senegal, Sierra Leone, Somalia, South Africa, South Sudan, Sudan, Tanzania UR, Togo, Tunisia, Uganda, Zambia, Zimbabwe.
Consultative Status Consultative status granted from: *ECOSOC (#05331)* (Special); *United Nations Population Fund (UNFPA, #20612).* **NGO Relations** Member of: *Association for Women's Rights in Development (AWID, #02980); CIVICUS: World Alliance for Citizen Participation (#03962); Conference of Non-Governmental Organizations in Consultative Relationship with the United Nations (CONGO, #04635); Sudan Consortium (#20031); Freedom of Information Advocates Network (FOIAnet, #09985); International Coalition for the Responsibility to Protect (ICRtoP, #12620); International Council for Adult Education (ICAE, #12983); Women's Working Group on Financing for Development (WWG on FfD, #21036).* Supports: *Global Call for Action Against Poverty (GCAP, #10263).* [2022/XF2166/F]

♦ African Women's Development Fund (AWDF) 00504

Communications Officer PMB CT 89, Cantonments, Accra, Ghana. E-mail: awdf@awdf.org.
URL: http://www.awdf.org/

History Jun 2000. **Aims** As a women led grant-making foundation: support efforts to ensure social justice, equality and respect for women's rights in Africa; mobilize financial, human and material resources to support efforts to develop a strong movement of African women's organizations and networks who can effectively advance gender equality, women's rights and women's leadership. **Structure** Executive Board. **Languages** English, French. **Finance** Funding from private sector, bilateral institutions, individuals, embassies and organizations, including: *ActionAid (#00087); Bill and Melinda Gates Foundation (BMGF); Comic Relief; Norwegian Agency for Development Cooperation (Norad);* Stephen Lewis. **Activities** Financial and/or material support; events/meetings; capacity building; advocacy/lobbying/activism. **Publications** *AWDF Newsletter.* **Members** Women's organizations (over 1,000) in 42 countries. Membership countries not specified. **IGO Relations** Accredited organization of: *Green Climate Fund (GCF, #10714).* **NGO Relations** Member of: *Africa Grantmakers' Affinity Group (AGAG); Africa Philanthropy Network (APN, #00512); Association for Women's Rights in Development (AWID, #02980); Prospera – International Network of Women's Funds (INWF, #18545); Women's Funding Network.* Supports: *African Biodiversity Network (ABN, #00222); International Centre for Reproductive Health and Sexual Rights (INCRESE); Regional Prevention of Maternal Mortality Network (RPMM, inactive); Women in Law and Development in Africa-Afrique de l'Ouest (WiLDAF-AO, #21005).* [2022/XF6982/f/F]

♦ African Women's Economic Policy Network (inactive)
♦ African Women's Network for Community Management of Forests (unconfirmed)
♦ African Women's Organization (internationally oriented national body)
♦ African Women's Organization against female genital mutilation / see African Women's Organization
♦ African Women's Welfare Group (internationally oriented national body)
♦ African Women Unite Against Destructive Extractivism / see WoMin (#21043)
♦ African Workers and Amateurs Sport Organization (#17827)

♦ African World Heritage Fund (AWHF) 00505

Fonds pour le Patrimoine Mondial Africain (FPMA) – Fondo para el Patrimonio Mundial Africano – Fundo para o Património Mundial Africano (FPMA)

Exec Dir DBSA Bldg, 1258 Lever Road, Headway Hill, Midrand, 1685, South Africa. T. +27113133061. Fax +27112063061. E-mail: info@awhf.net.
URL: http://awhf.net/

History 2006. Set up by *African Union (AU, #00488)* and *UNESCO (#20322).* Since Oct 2009, A Category II Centre of UNESCO. **Aims** Support the effective conservation and protection of natural and cultural heritage of outstanding universal value in Africa; develop a strategy to deal with the challenges implementing the 1972 World Heritage Convention. **Structure** Board of Trustees; Secretariat. **Languages** English, French, Portuguese. **Activities** Events/meetings; financial and/or material support; politics/policy/regulatory; projects/programmes. **Events** *Board of Governors Meeting* Johannesburg (South Africa) 2022, *Board of Governors Meeting* Kigali (Rwanda) 2022, *Board of Trustees Meeting* 2021, *Board of Trustees Meeting* Tunis (Tunisia) 2021, *Board of Trustees Meeting* Kinshasa (Congo DR) 2020. **Members** Accessible to all African countries which are member of the World Heritage Convention. Membership countries not specified. **IGO Relations** *Convention Concerning the Protection of the World Cultural and Natural Heritage (World Heritage Convention, 1972).* Observers include: *International Centre for the Study of the Preservation and Restoration of Cultural Property (ICCROM, #12521).* **NGO Relations** Observer: *International Union for Conservation of Nature and Natural Resources (IUCN, #15766).* [2022.11.30/XM5997/F*]

♦ African Wrestling on Belts Alysh Federation (unconfirmed)
♦ African Wrestling Confederation (inactive)
♦ African Young Positives Network (unconfirmed)
♦ African Youth Alliance / see World Youth Alliance – Africa (#21950)
♦ African Youth Foundation (internationally oriented national body)
♦ African Youth Growth Foundation (internationally oriented national body)

♦ African Youth Movement (AYM) 00506

Contact The White House, 9 Ufeh Street, Uyo, Akwa Ibom, Nigeria. T. +2348069563999.
URL: http://www.africanyouthmovement.org/

History Founded 2002. **Aims** Empower Africans, young and old, to work towards a better world through local and global initiatives in disaster risk reduction, poverty eradication, criminal justice and climate change towards the attainment of sustainable development. **Structure** General Assembly; Board of Trustees; Executive Council. **Languages** English. **Staff** 10.00 FTE, paid. **Finance** Contributions from members and partners. Budget (annual): US$ 12,000. **Activities** Advocacy/lobbying/activism. **Events** *Civic responsibility and international governance summit* Uyo (Nigeria) 2006, *Summit* Uyol (Nigeria) 2006. **Publications** *NGO Quarterly.* Article in *Crisis Response Journal.*
Members in 5 countries:
Cameroon, Ghana, Nigeria, Senegal, South Africa.
Consultative Status Consultative status granted from: *ECOSOC (#05331)* (Special). **IGO Relations** Accredited to: Conference of the Parties of the *Secretariat of the United Nations Convention to Combat Desertification (Secretariat of the UNCCD, #19208);* UN Commission against Corruption via *United Nations Office on Drugs and Crime (UNODC, #20596).* Associated with Department of Global Communications of the United Nations. **NGO Relations** Member of: *GEF CSO Network (GCN, #10087);* [2021/XM1883/F]

♦ African Youth in Philanthropy Network (AYPN) 00507

Coordinator Box 40, 00233, Kenyasi, Ghana. E-mail: infoaypn@gmail.com – wapnet@africanyouthphilanthropy.org – eapnet@africanyouthphilanthropy.org.
URL: http://africanyouthphilanthropy.org/

History Founded Jun 2015, Arusha (Tanzania UR). **Aims** Become the platform for shaping an agenda for African youth philanthropy by enhancing policies and practices through coordination, knowledge sharing and capacity building of African Youth philanthropic organizations. **Members** Full (19) in 13 countries. Membership countries not specified. **NGO Relations** Member of: *Worldwide Initiatives for Grantmaker Support (WINGS, #21926).* [2019/XM8801/F]

♦ African Youth Safe Abortion Alliance (AYOSA) 00508

Chair PO Box 748, Mzuzu, Malawi. T. +265995463231. E-mail: abortionyouth@gmail.com.
URL: http://www.ayosa.co/

History 2014, South Africa. **Aims** Work in partnership with youth organizations, civil society to support and advocate for safe abortion in Africa, work collectively to influence policies and practices of African governments through sharing of knowledge, information and experiences. **Structure** Secretariat. **Languages** English. **Staff** 1.00 FTE, paid; 9.00 FTE, voluntary. **Activities** Advocacy/lobbying/activism; awards/prizes/competitions; awareness raising; capacity building; financial and/or material support; guidance/assistance/consulting; knowledge management/information dissemination; events/meetings; networking/liaising; publishing activities; research/documentation; training/education. Active in: Africa.
Members Full in 22 countries:
Angola, Burkina Faso, Burundi, Cameroon, Central African Rep, Côte d'Ivoire, Ethiopia, Gambia, Ghana, Guinea, Kenya, Malawi, Mozambique, Namibia, Nigeria, Rwanda, Senegal, Sierra Leone, South Africa, Tanzania UR, Zambia, Zimbabwe.
NGO Relations *Center for Reproductive Rights; International Campaign for Women's Right to Safe Abortion (#12430); IPAS (#16010)* – Africa Alliance; *PMNCH (#18410); Women Help Women (WHW).* [2016.11.01/XM5271/D]

♦ African Youths Initiative on Crime Prevention (internationally oriented national body)
♦ African Youth for Transparency / see Youth for Transparency International
♦ Africa Parliamentary Knowledge Network (inactive)

♦ Africa Partnership on Climate Change Coalition (APCCC) 00509

Exec Dir PO Box 879, Bukoba, Kagera, Tanzania UR. T. +255768020750. E-mail: edwardbkb@yahoo.com – apccc2007@gmail.com.
Street Address Kemondo Portbay, Bukoba, Kagera, Tanzania UR.
URL: http://envaya.org/apccc/

History Set up by 23 African participants of the International Advanced Training Course, 2007, Sweden. Incorporated in accordance with the laws of Malawi, Tanzania UR and Uganda. **Aims** Facilitate local level climate change awareness and empowerment, disaster risk reduction and sustainable requisite adaptation measures to enable local communities cope with impacts of climate change. **Structure** International Advisory Council; Board of Governors. **NGO Relations** Member of: *Global Alliance for Climate-Smart Agriculture (GACSA, #10189).* Cooperates with: *Global Call for Climate Action (GCCA, inactive).* [2015/XJ9379/F]

♦ Africa Partnership Forum (APF) 00510

Forum pour le Partenariat avec l'Afrique (FPA)

Address not obtained.
URL: http://www.africapartnershipforum.org/

History Established 2003, following the *Group of Eight (G-8, #10745)* Summit, Evian (France). **Aims** Catalyze and support action on both sides of the partnership in support of Africa's *development.* **Structure** Co-Chaired on an alternating basis by representatives of *African Union (AU, #00488)* and *New Partnership for Africa's Development (NEPAD, #17091),* and by G8 and non-G8 member countries of *OECD (#17693).* Forum includes: Heads of State or Government of NEPAD members; Chairperson of African Union Commission; Heads of the African Union 8 Regional Economic Communities; Head of *African Development Bank (ADB, #00283);* Heads of State or Government of Africa's principal industrialized/country development partners; President of *European Commission (EC, #06633);* Heads of selected international institutions, including *United Nations (UN, #20515),*

UNDP (#20292), *United Nations Economic Commission for Africa (ECA, #20554)*, *International Monetary Fund (IMF, #14180)*, and *World Trade Organization (WTO, #21864)* and OECD. **Languages** English, French. **Staff** 5.00 FTE, paid. **Finance** Support Unit is financed by voluntary contributions from G8/OECD APF members. **Activities** Meets twice a year: Africa meeting focuses on monitoring progress; G8 hosted meeting focuses on policy concerns and priorities. **Events** *Meeting* London (UK) 2013, *Illicit financial flows* Paris (France) 2013, *Meeting* Cotonou (Benin) 2012, *Meeting* Paris (France) 2012, *Meeting* Kigali (Rwanda) 2011. **Publications** *Mutual Review of Development Effectiveness in Africa (MRDE)*.

Members African members (21):
Algeria, Benin, Cameroon, Chad, Congo Brazzaville, Egypt, Ethiopia, Gabon, Libya, Malawi, Mali, Mauritania, Nigeria, Rwanda, Senegal, South Africa, Sudan, Tanzania UR, Uganda, Zambia, Zimbabwe.
Regional African members (11):
African Development Bank (ADB, #00283); *African Union (AU, #00488)* (Commission); African Union Presidency; *Arab Maghreb Union (AMU, #01004)*; *Common Market for Eastern and Southern Africa (COMESA, #04296)*; *Community of Sahel-Saharan States (CEN-SAD, #04406)*; *Economic Community of Central African States (ECCAS, #05311)*; *Economic Community of West African States (ECOWAS, #05312)*; *Intergovernmental Authority on Development (IGAD, #11472)*; *New Partnership for Africa's Development (NEPAD, #17091)* (and its Planning and Coordinating Agency (NPCA)); *Southern African Development Community (SADC, #19843)*.
Development partner member governments (19):
Austria, Belgium, Canada, Denmark, Finland, France, Germany, Ireland, Italy, Japan, Netherlands, Norway, Portugal, Russia, Spain, Sweden, Switzerland, UK, USA.
Observers (7):
Australia, Greece, Korea Rep, Luxembourg, Mexico, Poland, Türkiye.
IGO Relations Partners: *African Development Bank (ADB, #00283)*; *European Union (EU, #08967)*; *United Nations Economic Commission for Africa (ECA, #20554)*. [2015/XM3547/y/**E***]

♦ Africa Peace Forum (internationally oriented national body)

♦ Africa Peace Research and Education Association (AFPREA) 00511

Contact 7 Olaide Oshun Close, Ajah, Lagos, Nigeria. T. +2348181315939. E-mail: afreaipra@yahoo.com.
URL: https://www.afprea.com/

History 1985. Aug 2000, Tampere (Finland), current structure was established. Former names and other names: *African Peace Research Association (AFPRA)* – former (1985 to Aug 2000); *African Peace Research Institute (APRI)* – former alias. Registration: Nigeria. **Aims** Advance interdisciplinary research into the conditions of peace and causes of war and other forms of violence. **Structure** General Conference (every 2 year); Executive Committee. Commissions (25): Art and Peace; Conflict Resolution and Peace Building; Development and Peace; Eastern Europe; Ecology and Peace; Forced Migration; Gender and Peace; Global Political Economy; Indigenous Peoples' Rights; Internal Conflicts; International Human Rights; Nonviolence; Peace Culture and Communications; Peace Education; Peace History; Peace Journalism; Peace Movements; Peace Negotiations and Mediation; Peace Theories; Reconciliation and Transitional Justice; Religion and Peace; Security and Disarmament; Sport and Peace; Youth and Peace; Peace Tourism. **Finance** Members' dues. Other sources: sale of publications; grants from foundations. **Activities** Research; advocacy; capacity building; conflict resolution; meetings activities. **Events** *Conference* Juba (South Sudan) 2022, *Conference* Cape Town (South Africa) 2019, *Conference* Abuja (Nigeria) 2015, *Peace Building in the Great Lakes Region in Africa* Kampala (Uganda) 2001, *Inaugural meeting* Lagos (Nigeria) 1990. **Members** Associations; associate; individuals. Membership countries not specified. **IGO Relations** *UNESCO (#20322)*. **NGO Relations** Regional Association of: *International Peace Research Association (IPRA, #14537)*. [2022/XE0747/**D**]

♦ Africa Philanthropy Network (APN) 00512

Main Office Block A, House no 581, Dar es Salaam, Tanzania UR. E-mail: info@africaphilanthropynetwork.org.
URL: http://africaphilanthropynetwork.org/

History 2009, as *African Grantmakers Network (AGN)*, at a meeting led by *African Women's Development Fund (AWDF, #00504)*, Kenya Community Development Foundation (KCDF) and *TrustAfrica (#20251)*. Present name adopted, Jul 2015. **Aims** Facilitate networking and experience sharing among established and emerging African philanthropic institutions. **Structure** General Assembly. Steering Committee. **Events** *General Assembly* Port Louis (Mauritius) 2018, *General Assembly* Johannesburg (South Africa) 2012, *General Assembly* Kenya 2010.

Members Organizations (6):
Akiba Uhaki Foundation, Kenya; Foundation for Civil Society, Tanzania UR; *International Research Network on Organizing by Projects (IRNOP, #14736)*; Kenya Community Development Foundation; *Southern Africa Trust*; *TrustAfrica (#20251)*.
NGO Relations Member of: *Worldwide Initiatives for Grantmaker Support (WINGS, #21926)*. [2020/XJ5876/y/**F**]

♦ Africa Platform (ACP) 00513

Contact Fort Granite, 18 Bishops Road, Nairobi, Kenya. T. +254202055003. E-mail: paul.okumu@africaplatform.org.
URL: http://www.africaplatform.org/

History Jul 2010, as *Africa Civil Society Platform on Principled Partnership (ACP)*. Also previously referred to as *Africa CSO Platform on Principled Partnership*. **Aims** Strengthen active citizen participation in development by creating and supporting an enabling environment for civil society. **Structure** 6. **Activities** Advocacy/lobbying/activism. **Publications** Analysis; reports; videos.
Members Focal points in 23 countries:
Benin, Burundi, Cameroon, Congo DR, Egypt, Equatorial Guinea, Ethiopia, Ghana, Kenya, Liberia, Malawi, Mali, Nigeria, Rwanda, Senegal, Sierra Leone, Somalia, South Sudan, Tanzania UR, Togo, Uganda, Zambia, Zimbabwe. [2017.03.20/XJ6017/**F**]

♦ Africa Platform for Social Protection (APSP) 00514

Contact Hillside Apartments, 4th Floor, Ste 10, Ragati Road PO Box 54305, Nairobi, 00200, Kenya. T. +254202699541.
URL: http://africapsp.org/

Aims Create partnerships with civil society and other organizations to engage with governments and international development agencies (IDAs) to develop and implement innovative social protection strategies and programmes making a difference in people's lives in Africa. **Structure** Board, comprising Chairperson, Vice-Chairperson, Treasurer and 4 members.
Members National platforms in 30 countries:
Burkina Faso, Burundi, Cameroon, Central African Rep, Chad, Congo DR, Egypt, Eswatini, Ethiopia, Gabon, Gambia, Ghana, Kenya, Lesotho, Liberia, Malawi, Mozambique, Namibia, Niger, Nigeria, Rwanda, Senegal, Sierra Leone, South Africa, South Sudan, Tanzania UR, Tunisia, Uganda, Zambia, Zimbabwe.
IGO Relations Partners include: *African Development Bank (ADB, #00283)*; *African Union (AU, #00488)*; *European Commission (EC, #06633)*; *International Bank for Reconstruction and Development (IBRD, #12317)* (World Bank); *Norwegian Agency for Development Cooperation (Norad)*; *Swedish International Development Cooperation Agency (Sida)*. **NGO Relations** Member of: *Regional Inter-Agency Task Team on Children and AIDS in Eastern and Southern Africa (RIATT-ESA, #18791)*. Partners include: *Catholic Organization for Relief and Development (Cordaid)*; *Grow Up Free from Poverty Coalition*; *Privacy International (PI, #18504)*. [2018/XJ7269/**F**]

♦ Africa Project Development Facility (inactive)

♦ Africa Psoriasis Organization (APSO) 00515

Contact PO Box 20548-00100 GPO, Nairobi, Kenya. E-mail: info@psoriasisafrica.org.
URL: http://www.psoriasisafrica.org/

History 27 Mar 2009, Kenya. Registered in accordance with Kenyan law. **Aims** Improve quality of life of people suffering from psoriasis in Africa by enabling them to get appropriate treatment, care and understanding through education, advocacy and research. **Structure** Board of Trustees; Medical Advisory Board. **NGO Relations** Full member of: *International Alliance of Patients' Organizations (IAPO, #11633)*. [2015/XJ7744/**D**]

♦ Africare 00516

Main Office Africare House, 440 R St NW, Washington DC 20001, USA. T. +12024623614. Fax +12023871034.
Twitter: https://twitter.com/Africare

History 1970, State of Hawaii (USA), on the initiative of William Kirker and Barbara Kirker; reincorporated 4 May 1971, Washington DC (USA). Headquarters in Washington DC. Registration: USA. **Aims** Improve the quality of life of people in Africa. **Structure** Headquarters in Washington DC; Offices in Africa (17). **Languages** English, French, Portuguese. **Staff** 1250.00 FTE, paid.
Finance Major donors: corporations, governments, foundations, national and multi-national organizations and individuals, including the following organizations listed in this Yearbook:
- *African Development Bank (ADB, #00283)*;
- *African Methodist Episcopal Church (AME)*;
- *African Programme for Onchocerciasis Control (APOC, no recent information)*;
- *Bill and Melinda Gates Foundation (BMGF)*;
- *CARE International (CI, #03429)*;
- *Catholic Relief Services (CRS, #03608)*;
- *Centre for Development and Population Activities (CEDPA, inactive)*;
- *Christian Relief Services*;
- *Consortium of Christian Relief and Development Association (CCRDA)*;
- *European Development Fund (EDF, #06914)*;
- *FAO (#09260)*;
- *First Voice International (inactive)*;
- *Ford Foundation (#09858)*;
- IFAD;
- *International Centre for Tropical Agriculture (#12527)*;
- *International Finance Corporation (IFC, #13597)*;
- *Plan International (#18386)*;
- *The Rockefeller Foundation (#18966)*;
- *Sabre Foundation (inactive)*;
- *UNDP (#20292)*;
- UNHCR;
- *UNICEF (#20332)*;
- *United Nations Office for the Coordination of Humanitarian Affairs (OCHA, #20593)*;
- *United States Agency for International Development (USAID)*;
- *World Food Programme (WFP, #21510)*;
- *World Vision International (WVI, #21904)*.

Activities Capacity building; events/meetings. Active in: Angola, Benin, Burkina Faso, Chad, Ghana, Liberia, Malawi, Mali, Mozambique, Niger, Nigeria, Senegal, South Africa, Tanzania UR, Uganda, Zambia, Zimbabwe. **Publications** Electronic Newsletter (12 a year). Annual Report. **NGO Relations** Member of: *CORE Group*; *Global Impact*. Partner of: *1,000 Days*. [2018/XG5302/**F**]

♦ **AFRICA RE** African Reinsurance Corporation (#00438)

♦ Africa Regional Centre for Information Science (ARCIS) 00517

Centre régional africain pour la science de l'information

Dir 6 Benue Road, PO Box 22133, University of Ibadan, Ibadan, Oyo, Nigeria. T. +23427517527.
URL: http://www.arcis.ui.edu.ng/

History Nov 1990, Ibadan (Nigeria), by joint collaboration between *International Development Research Centre (IDRC, #13162)*, the General Information Programme Division of *UNESCO (#20322)* and the Federal Government of Nigeria. **Aims** Be a centre of excellence in information science and technology and a major facilitator of information technology training, research, collaboration and advisory services in Africa. **Structure** Governing Board; Headed by Director; International Consultative Committee; Academic Board. **Languages** English. **Staff** 12.00 FTE, paid. **Finance** Financed by Government of Nigeria. Other sources: grants by international development agencies; students' tuition fees; income from consultancies. Annual budget: US$ 190,000. **Activities** Projects/programmes; events/meetings; guidance/assistance/consulting; training/education; research/documentation. **Events** *International conference* Ibadan (Nigeria) 2000, *International conference* Ibadan (Nigeria) 2000, *Inaugural meeting* Ibadan (Nigeria) 1992. **Publications** *ARCIS NewsBulletin* (annual). *ARCIS Readings in Information Science Series*.
Members Full in 7 countries:
Botswana, Cameroon, Gambia, Ghana, Liberia, Nigeria, Sierra Leone, Uganda.
IGO Relations *African Development Bank (ADB, #00283)*; *African Regional Centre of Technology (ARCT, #00432)*; *Commonwealth Secretariat (#04362)*; *Economic Community of West African States (ECOWAS, #05312)*; *United Nations Economic Commission for Africa (ECA, #20554)*. **NGO Relations** *Carnegie Corporation of New York*; *International Institute of Tropical Agriculture (IITA, #13933)*; *Pan African Institute for Development (PAID, #18053)*. Instrumental, with Department for Library and Information Science, University of Botswana; *Ecole des sciences de l'information (ESI, no recent information)*; *School of Information Studies for Africa (SISA, no recent information)*, in setting up: *Consortium of African Schools of Information Science (CASIS, no recent information)*. [2019.05.02/XE2330/**E**]

♦ Africa Regional Sexuality Resource Centre, Lagos (internationally oriented national body)
♦ Africa Research Centre, Leuven / see Institute for Anthropological Research in Africa
♦ Africa for Research in Comparative Education Society (unconfirmed)
♦ Africa Research Institute / see Institute for Development and International Relations
♦ Africa Resources Trust / see Resource Africa
♦ AfriCaribe Microenterprise Network (internationally oriented national body)
♦ **AfricaRice** Africa Rice Center (#00518)

♦ Africa Rice Center (AfricaRice) 00518

Centre du riz pour l'Afrique (AfricaRice)

Dir-Gen 01 BP 4029, Boulevard François Mitterrand, Cocody, Abidjan 01, Côte d'Ivoire. T. +22522480910. E-mail: m.zahui@cgiar.org – africarice@cgiar.org.
URL: http://www.africarice.org/

History 1970, Dakar (Senegal). Established at the Conference of Plenipotentiaries. Acronym adopted 2009. Former names and other names: *West Africa Rice Development Association (WARDA)* – former; *Association pour le développement de la riziculture en Afrique de l'Ouest (ADRAO)* – former. **Aims** Contribute to poverty alleviation and food security in Africa through research, development and partnership activities aimed at increasing productivity and profitability of the rice sector in ways that ensure sustainability of the farming environment. **Structure** Council of Ministers, consisting of one minister from each member State; Board of Trustees; Executive Management Committee (EMC); Office of the Director General; Divisions; Subdivisions; Research Stations; National Experts Committee. **Languages** English, French. **Staff** 230.00 FTE, paid.
Finance Members' dues. Donors include the governments of Belgium, Côte d'Ivoire, Denmark, France, Germany, Japan, Liberia, Netherlands, Norway and Sweden and the following organizations listed in this Yearbook:
- *African Development Bank (ADB, #00283)*;
- *Alliance for a Green Revolution in Africa (AGRA, #00685)*;
- *Arab Bank for Economic Development in Africa (#00904)*;
- *Bill and Melinda Gates Foundation (BMGF)*;
- *Centre technique de coopération agricole et rurale (CTA, inactive)*;
- *CGIAR System Organization (CGIAR, #03843)* and its Generation Challenge Programme (GCP) and Fund;
- *Common Fund for Commodities (CFC, #04293)*;
- *Department for International Development (DFID, inactive)*;
- *Deutsche Gesellschaft für Internationale Zusammenarbeit (GIZ)*;
- *European Commission (EC, #06633)*;
- FAO;
- *Gatsby Charitable Foundation*;
- *Global Crop Diversity Trust (Crop Trust, #10313)*;
- *Institut de recherche pour le développement (IRD)*;
- *International Bank for Reconstruction and Development (IBRD, #12317)* (World Bank);
- *International Fund for Agricultural Development (IFAD, #13692)*;
- *Japan International Cooperation Agency (JICA)*;
- *Japan International Research Centre for Agricultural Sciences (JIRCAS)*;
- *UNDP (#20292)*;

– *Union économique et monétaire Ouest africaine (UEMOA, #20377)*;
– *United States Agency for International Development (USAID)*;
– *West and Central African Council for Agricultural Research and Development (WECARD, #20907)*.
Also support from: governments of Germany and Nigeria; national research and development institutes; universities.
Activities Research and development; training/education; knowledge management/information dissemination; projects/programmes; networking/liaising. **Events** *Meeting* Abidjan (Côte d'Ivoire) 2015, *Meeting* Cotonou (Benin) 2015, *Science Week* Cotonou (Benin) 2015, *Extraordinary Session* Kampala (Uganda) 2015, *Consultative Meeting of the Regional and Country Representatives* Saint Louis (Senegal) 2015. **Publications** *Realizing Africa's Rice Promise*; *Rice Trends in Sub-Saharan Africa*. Annual Report; bibliographies. Information Services: Collects classifies, indexes and publicizes documents relevant to rice production in West Africa; operates advisory service. **Information Services** *West Africa Rice Information System (WARIS)* – uses AfricaRice Library for literature searches, selective dissemination of information and other services.
Members Governments of 26 African countries:
Benin, Burkina Faso, Cameroon, Central African Rep, Chad, Congo Brazzaville, Congo DR, Côte d'Ivoire, Egypt, Ethiopia, Gabon, Gambia, Ghana, Guinea, Guinea-Bissau, Liberia, Madagascar, Mali, Mauritania, Niger, Nigeria, Rwanda, Senegal, Sierra Leone, Togo, Uganda.
Regional Offices in 7 countries:
Benin, Côte d'Ivoire, Liberia, Madagascar, Nigeria, Senegal, Tanzania UR.
IGO Relations Relationship agreement with: *African Union (AU, #00488)*; *Comité permanent inter-Etats de lutte contre la sécheresse dans le Sahel (CILSS, #04195)*; *FAO (#09260)*; *UNIDO (#20336)*. Member of: *Intergovernmental Organizations Conference (IGO Conference, #11498)*. Cooperates with other CGIAR supported centres: *International Livestock Research Institute (ILRI, #14062)*, Nairobi (Kenya); *Bioversity International (#03262)*, Rome (Italy); *International Center for Agricultural Research in the Dry Areas (ICARDA, #12466)*, Aleppo (Syrian AR); *International Crops Research Institute for the Semi-Arid Tropics (ICRISAT, #13116)*, Patancheru (India); *International Rice Research Institute (IRRI, #14754)*, Los Baos (Philippines). Participates as observer in the activities of: *Codex Alimentarius Commission (CAC, #04081)*. **NGO Relations** Cooperates with other CGIAR supported centres: *Center for International Forestry Research (CIFOR, #03646)*, Bogor (Indonesia); *International Centre for Tropical Agriculture (#12527)*, Cali (Colombia): *International Food Policy Research Institute (IFPRI, #13622)*, Washington DC (USA); *International Institute of Tropical Agriculture (IITA, #13933)*, Ibadan (Nigeria); *International Maize and Wheat Improvement Center (#14077)*, Mexico City (Mexico); *International Potato Center (#14627)*, Lima (Peru); *International Water Management Institute (IWMI, #15867)*, Colombo (Sri Lanka); *World Agroforestry Centre (ICRAF, #21072)*, Nairobi (Kenya); *WorldFish (#21507)*, Manila (Philippines). In particular, cooperates with IITA, ICRISAT and ISNAR in: *Agricultural Research Management Training Programme for Sub-Saharan Africa (ARMT, inactive)*. Also cooperates with: *International Fertilizer Development Center (IFDC, #13590)*; *International Centre of Insect Physiology and Ecology (ICIPE, #12499)*. Hosts: *African Rice Initiative (ARI, no recent information)*; *Inland Valley Consortium (IVC, no recent information)*; *Réseau ouest et centre africain du riz (ROCARIZ, no recent information)*. Working relations with: *International Network for Genetic Evaluation of Rice (INGER, see: #14754)*. [2021/XD4477/**D***]

♦ **AfricaRice** Centre du riz pour l'Afrique (#00518)
♦ Africa Safari Club (internationally oriented national body)
♦ Africa Safe Water Foundation (internationally oriented national body)
♦ Africa Seismological Commission (unconfirmed)
♦ **AfricaSIF** Africa Sustainable Investment Forum (#00523)
♦ **AfriCASO** African Council of AIDS Service Organizations (#00272)

♦ Africa Society for Blood Transfusion (AfSBT) 00519

Admin Officer address not obtained. E-mail: info@afsbt.org.
URL: http://www.afsbt.org/
History 9 Dec 1997, Abidjan (Côte d'Ivoire). Registered in accordance with South African law: 2011/008414/08 np. **Aims** Pursue, promote and maintain the highest level of ethical and professional standards so as to achieve safe and cost effective national blood programmes in Africa; contribute to advancement of knowledge; provide opportunities for discussion and presentation of research and development; exchange information among members; act as a resource centre accessible to blood services of national governments; encourage regional collaborative programmes to deal with issues such as manpower development. **Structure** Board of Directors, including President, Past President, President Elect, 5 Vice-Presidents, Treasurer and Secretary-General. **Languages** English, French. **Staff** 5.00 FTE, voluntary. **Finance** Members' dues. Fund raising activities. **Activities** Establishing: Education and Training Programme in Blood Transfusion in Africa; Stepwise Accreditation Scheme for Blood Banks in Africa. **Events** *International Congress* Dakar (Senegal) 2022, *International Congress* Dakar (Senegal) 2020, *International Congress* Arusha (Tanzania UR) 2018, *International Congress* Kigali (Rwanda) 2016, *International Congress / Congress* Victoria Falls (Zimbabwe) 2014. **Publications** *Africa Sanguine* – journal. **Members** Individuals (317) in 39 countries. Membership countries not specified. **IGO Relations** *WHO (#20950)*. [2021/XJ5227/v/**D**]

♦ Africa Soil Science Society (ASSS) 00520

Association africaine de la science du sol (AASS) – Sociedade Africana de Ciência do Solo
Pres IITA Cameroon, BP 2008, Yaoundé, Cameroon. T. +237242015826 – +237694144812 – +237672337437. Fax +237222237437.
SG c/o ICIRSAT CCAFS, BP 320, Bamako, Mali.
URL: http://www.asssonline.org/
History 1986. Previously referred to as *African Soil Science Society*. **Aims** Promote and foster soil science in all its facets. **Structure** General Assembly (every 2 years) during International Conference; Executive Office. **Languages** English, French. **Finance** Members' dues. **Activities** Knowledge management/information dissemination; networking/liaising; advocacy/lobbying/activism; awareness raising; politics/policy/regulatory; guidance/assistance/consulting. **Events** *Conference / Congress* Ouagadougou (Burkina Faso) 2015, *Congress* Nakuru (Kenya) 2013, *Conference / Congress* Yaoundé (Cameroon) 2009, *Conference / Congress* Accra (Ghana) 2007, *Congress* Ibadan (Nigeria) 1995. **Publications** *African Soils*; *Soil Atlas of Africa* in English, French. Administrative and technical documents; conference proceedings; announcements. Information Services: Database. **Members** Full, African scientists working inside or outside of Africa on soil science or related disciplines; Associate, African students or non-African scientists in these fields; Honorary; Life. Membership countries not specified. **IGO Relations** Partner of: *Global Soil Partnership (GSP, #10608)*. [2018.09.05/XD0642/**D**]

♦ Africa Solar Industry Association (AFSIA) 00521

CEO KN 72 street, WAKA Town, Kigali, Rwanda. E-mail: info@afsiasolar.com.
URL: http://afsiasolar.com/
History 24 May 2019, Rwanda. **Aims** Create a solar community in which all stakeholders, from both public and private sectors, can come together and help grow the footprint of solar across the entire African continent. **Languages** Arabic, English, French, Portuguese, Spanish, Swahili. **Staff** 7.00 FTE, paid; 0.00 FTE, voluntary. **Activities** Awards/prizes/competitions; events/meetings; guidance/assistance/consulting; knowledge management/information dissemination; networking/liaising; research/documentation; training/education. Active in all African countries. **Events** *Launch of the Africa Solar Outlook 2022 Report* Abu Dhabi (United Arab Emirates) 2022, *Africa Energy Forum* Brussels (Belgium) 2022, *Africa Renewables Investment Summit* Cape Town (South Africa) 2022. **Publications** *Africa Solar Annual Outlook Report* in English; *AFSIA Newsletter* in English. **Information Services** *Operational Solar Projects* in English.
Members Full in 51 countries:
Algeria, Angola, Benin, Botswana, Burkina Faso, Burundi, Cameroon, Cape Verde, Central African Rep, Chad, Comoros, Congo Brazzaville, Congo DR, Côte d'Ivoire, Djibouti, Egypt, Eritrea, Eswatini, Ethiopia, Gabon, Gambia, Ghana, Guinea, Guinea-Bissau, Kenya, Lesotho, Liberia, Madagascar, Malawi, Mali, Mauritania, Mauritius, Morocco, Mozambique, Namibia, Niger, Nigeria, Rwanda, Sao Tomé-Principe, Senegal, Seychelles, Sierra Leone, Somalia, South Africa, South Sudan, Sudan, Togo, Tunisia, Uganda, Zambia, Zimbabwe. [2023.02.20/AA0346/t/F]

♦ Africa Solidarity and Development (internationally oriented national body)

♦ Africa Solidarity Trust Fund (ASTF) 00522

Contact c/o Regional Office for Africa, PO Box GP 1628, No 2 Gamel Abdul Nasser Road, Accra, Ghana. T. +233302610930. Fax +233302668427. E-mail: raf-adg@fao.org.
URL: http://www.fao.org/africa/perspectives/africa-solidarity-trust-fund/en/
History Officially launched Jun 2013, during 38th Session of the *FAO (#09260)* Conference. Relaunched Apr 2016, at 29th Session of the Regional Conference for Africa. **Aims** Strengthen *food* security across the continent by assisting countries and their regional organizations to eradicate hunger and malnutrition, eliminate rural poverty and manage natural resources in a sustainable manner. **Structure** Fund Assembly; Steering Committee; Programme Management Unit. **Finance** Initial funding from Equatorial Guinea, Angola and a group of civil society organizations in Congo Brazzaville: US$ 40 million. [2016/XM4857/**F***]

♦ Africa's Sustainable Development Council / see ASUDEC

♦ Africa Sustainable Investment Forum (AfricaSIF) 00523

Contact address not obtained. E-mail: africasif@gmail.com.
URL: http://www.africasif.org/
History Feb 2009. Launched Jun 2010. **Aims** Promote sustainable investment that integrates environmental, social and governance factors, across the African continent. **Structure** A virtual network. Steering Committee; Advisory Panel. **Activities** Serves as: a network for practitioners sharing ideas and information on how to approach ESG (environmental, social and governance) in investment in Africa, and collaborating where useful on investment analysis of companies operating or listed in Africa in assessing their ESG performance; a knowledge bank for sustainable investment work in Africa, collecting existing and future work, and conducting a sustainable investment benchmarking survey (every 2 year); an awareness raising and advocacy group that informs policymakers and international organizations what is happening in Africa and promotes Africa as an investment destination for sustainable investors. Organizes annual conference. **Members** Institutions and individuals active in public, private and philanthropy sectors. Membership countries not specified. [2012/XJ2065/**D**]

♦ Africa's Voices Foundation (internationally oriented national body)

♦ Africa Tobacco Control Regional Initiative (ATCRI) 00524

Initiative Régionale pour la Lutte contre le Tabac en Afrique (IRCTA)
Acting Dir c/o ERA/FoEN, No 214 Uselu Lagos Road, Ugbowo, PO Box 10577, Benin City, Edo, Nigeria. T. +23452880619. E-mail: eraction@eraction.org.
URL: http://www.atcri.org/
History as an initiative of UK and US cancer organizations. **Aims** Promote the adoption, implementation and enforcement of comprehensive and effective tobacco control policies, legislation and programs through effective networking and information sharing, capacity development, advocacy and research in sub-Saharan Africa. **NGO Relations** Member of: *Framework Convention Alliance (FCA, #09981)*. [2012/XJ2086/**E**]

♦ Africa Top Level Domain Organization (AfTLD) 00525

Secretariat address not obtained. E-mail: secretariat@aftld.org.
URL: http://www.aftld.org/
Aims Help African country code domain name (ccTLD) managers discuss issues around management of *ccTLDs*; present common positions at global level on key global issues in the Domain Name System (DNS) industry. **Structure** General Assembly; Executive Committee; Working Groups; Secretariat. **Languages** English, French. **Staff** 7.00 FTE, paid. **Activities** Knowledge management/information dissemination; capacity building; training/education; events/meetings. **Events** *Africa Domain Name System (DNS) Forum* Gaborone (Botswana) 2019, *Africa Domain Name System (DNS) Forum* Cotonou (Benin) 2018, *Africa Domain Name System (DNS) Forum* Dar es Salaam (Tanzania UR) 2017, *Africa Domain Name System (DNS) Forum* Marrakech (Morocco) 2016, *Africa Domain Name System (DNS) Forum* Nairobi (Kenya) 2015.
Members Full in 30 countries:
Benin, Botswana, Burundi, Central African Rep, Chad, Comoros, Congo Brazzaville, Congo DR, Côte d'Ivoire, Egypt, Ghana, Kenya, Lesotho, Libya, Madagascar, Malawi, Mali, Mauritania, Mauritius, Mozambique, Nigeria, Rwanda, Senegal, Seychelles, Somalia, South Africa, Sudan, Tanzania UR, Tunisia, Zambia.
NGO Relations *Asia Pacific Top Level Domain Association (APTLD, #02066)*. [2020.03.03/XM5300/**D**]

♦ Africa Trade Network (ATN) 00526

Contact TWN Africa, 9 Ollenu Street, East Legon, PO Box AN 19452, Accra, Ghana. T. +23321503669 – +23321500419. Fax +23321511189. E-mail: twnafrica@twnafrica.org.
URL: http://twnafrica.org/
History 1998, by African section of *Third World Network (TWN, #20151)*. **Events** *Annual Meeting* Dakar (Senegal) 2001. **Members** Organizations (25) in 15 countries. Membership countries not specified. **IGO Relations** Observer status with: *African Union (AU, #00488)*; *United Nations Economic Commission for Africa (ECA, #20554)*. Close links with: *UNCTAD (#20285)*. **NGO Relations** Member of: *World Social Forum (WSF, #21797)*. [2008/XJ4220/t/**F**]

♦ Africa Transport Policy Program (SSATP) 00527

Program Manager SSATP / World Bank, 1818 H St NW, Room J7-700, Washington DC 20433, USA. E-mail: ssatp@worldbank.org.
Communications Officer address not obtained.
Main Website: http://www.ssatp.org/
History 1987. Set up following a meeting under the auspices of *United Nations Economic Commission for Africa (ECA, #20554)* and *The World Bank Group (#21218)*, where program relocated in 1988. Scope and title changed, 1992. Program reviewed 2000. Current Development Plan (DP3) implemented 2016-2021. Expanded activities to North African countries with the addition of Morocco and Tunisia, 2012. Former names and other names: *International Advisory Committee* – former (1987 to 1988); *Sub-Saharan Africa Transport Program* – former (1988 to 1992); *Sub-Saharan Africa Transport Policy Program* – former (1992 to 2012). **Aims** Facilitate policy development and related capacity-building in the transport sector of Africa. **Structure** General Meeting (annual); Executive Committee; Program Management Team; Working Groups. **Languages** English, French. **Staff** 6.00 FTE, paid. **Finance** Sources: international organizations. Supported by: *African Development Bank (ADB, #00283)*; *Agence française de développement (AFD)*; *European Commission (EC, #06633)*; Swiss Secretariat for Economic Affairs; *The World Bank Group (#21218)*. **Activities** Advocacy/lobbying/activism; capacity building; events/meetings; guidance/assistance/consulting; knowledge management/information dissemination; politics/policy/regulatory; projects/programmes; research and development; research/documentation; standards/guidelines. transport policy; urban mobility/accessibility; regional integration; road safety Active in all member countries. **Events** *Annual Meeting* Victoria Falls (Zimbabwe) 2019, *Annual Meeting* Marrakech (Morocco) 2017, *African Road Safety Conference* Addis Ababa (Ethiopia) 2015, *General Assembly* Kenya 2014, *General Assembly* Senegal 2013. **Publications** *SSATP Fourth Development Plan (DP4) – Quatrième plan de développement (DP4) du SSATP* (2022) in English, French – The Africa Transport Policy Program (SSATP) launched its next five-year strategy cycle, the Fourth Development Plan (DP4), at the DP4 Stakeholders Engagement Meetings hosted by the European Commission in Brussels on June 16-17, 2022. Through the DP4, SSATP expects to play a central role in supporting the development and implementation of national, regional, and continental strategic priorities in the African transport sector.. Working papers. **Information Services** *DP3 Publications Brochure: A Wealth of Knowledge* in English – Throughout the Third Development Plan (DP3), a multi-year work program spanning 2016-2021, SSATP focused on supporting member countries with developing sound transport strategies and policies to improve regional integration, urban mobility, and road safety in the continent. The "DP3 Publications Brochure" is a compendium of all the knowledge products produced by the Program during the recently completed DP3 strategy cycle. It includes short summaries of all the publications with linked QR codes for quick access to all the resources..
Members Governments (42):
Angola, Benin, Burkina Faso, Burundi, Cameroon, Cape Verde, Central African Rep, Chad, Comoros, Congo Brazzaville, Congo DR, Côte d'Ivoire, Djibouti, Eswatini, Ethiopia, Gabon, Gambia, Ghana, Guinea, Guinea-Bissau, Kenya, Lesotho, Liberia, Madagascar, Malawi, Mali, Mauritania, Morocco, Mozambique, Namibia, Niger, Nigeria, Rwanda, Senegal, Sierra Leone, South Sudan, Tanzania UR, Togo, Tunisia, Uganda, Zambia, Zimbabwe.
Continental entities (2):
African Union (AU, #00488) (Commission); *United Nations Economic Commission for Africa (ECA, #20554)*.
Regional Economic Communities: [2022.10.11/XK0544/**E***]

♦ Africa Travel Association (ATA) 00528

Association africaine de tourisme

Contact 1100 17th St NW, Ste 1000, Washington DC 20036, USA. T. +12028351115. Fax +12028351117. E-mail: info@africatravelassociation.org.
URL: http://www.africatravelassociation.org/

History 1975, New York NY (USA). **Aims** Promote and foster the growth and development of travel, *tourism* and transport to the African continent in association with the individual African countries, tour and ground operators, incentive, meeting, and convention planners, travel agents, airlines, hoteliers, and all other branches of the travel and *leisure industry* represented in the Association; develop and sponsor public interest in travel and tourism to Africa. **Structure** International Board President; Immediate Past President; 5 Vice Presidents; Treasurer; Secretary; Executive Director; 19 Directors; Founder. Executive Committee, consisting of President, Immediate Past President, 4 Vice Presidents, Treasurer and Secretary. **Languages** English, French. **Staff** 2.00 FTE, paid. Volunteers. **Finance** Members' dues. Proceeds from Congress and awards dinner. **Activities** Provides forums for membership to present their respective products and services. Collects, compiles and publishes information of interest on travel and tourism for and about Africa. Assists membership in practical methods and techniques of marketing and promotion. Plans and implements (annually) an International Congress on African Tourism. Implements, concurrently with the Congress, an annual International Trade Fair. Sponsors an Awards Program. Sponsors monthly chapter meetings. **Events** *Annual International Congress on African Tourism* Johannesburg (South Africa) 2019, *Annual International Congress on African Tourism* Kigali (Rwanda) 2017, *Annual International Congress on African Tourism* Nairobi (Kenya) 2015, *Annual International Congress on African Tourism* Kampala (Uganda) 2014, *Annual US-Africa Tourism Seminar* Washington, DC (USA) 2014. **Publications** *ATA Members' Update* (4 a year); *Africa Travel Magazine*.

Members Active Government Tourism Ministries, Departments, and National Tourism Organizations; Airlines, Cruise Lines, International and Domestic Hotel Chains; Individual Hotels, Wholesalers/Tour Operators, Local Ground Operators, Travel Agencies. Allied Public Relations Firms, Media Organizations, Research and Educational Institutions. Associate (individual travel agents and other persons engaged in the promotion of travel and tourism to Africa). Honorary. Representatives of 22 countries:
Benin, Botswana, Burkina Faso, Burundi, Cameroon, Congo Brazzaville, Côte d'Ivoire, Djibouti, Egypt, Gabon, Gambia, Ghana, Kenya, Lesotho, Malawi, Morocco, Nigeria, Senegal, Togo, Tunisia, Zambia, Zimbabwe.
Chapters (17, mostly in USA) in 9 countries:
Canada, Côte d'Ivoire, Egypt, Ghana, Kenya, Morocco, Senegal, USA (9), Zambia.

NGO Relations Partner of: *International Institute for Peace through Tourism (IIPT)*. [2018/XF6783/**F**]

- ♦ Africa Triathlon / see African Triathlon Union (#00487)

♦ Africa Union of Architects (AUA) 00529

Union des Architectes d'Afrique (UAA)

Contact Rue du Lac Toba, Immeuble Mezgheni, Les Berges du Lac, Tunis, Tunisia. E-mail: africaunionarchitects@gmail.com.
Pres 63B Marine Road, Apapa, Lagos, Nigeria. T. +2348037770011.
URL: http://aua.archi/

History 23 May 1981, Lagos (Nigeria). In English previously also referred to as *Union of African Architects*. **Aims** Create ties based on friendship, understanding and mutual esteem to enable architects to confront their ideas and concepts, share experience, broaden their knowledge and learn from their differences in order to better fulfill their role in improving man's living conditions and environment. **Structure** General Assembly; Executive Committee; Council. **Languages** Arabic, English, French, Portuguese. **Staff** 0.50 FTE, paid. Voluntary. **Finance** Members' dues. Budget (annual): US$ 14,000. **Events** *Triennial Congress* Balaclava (Mauritius) 2018, *Our architecture, our communities, our heritage* Kampala (Uganda) 2015, *Annual General Assembly* Cairo (Egypt) 2014, *Annual General Assembly and Triennial Congress* Kigali (Rwanda) 2013, *Annual General Assembly and Triennial Congress* Tangiers (Morocco) 2013. **Publications** *AUA Newsletter*. *Schools of Architecture in Africa*.

Members National member institutes in 38 countries:
Algeria, Angola, Benin, Botswana, Burkina Faso, Burundi, Cameroon, Central African Rep, Chad, Congo Brazzaville, Congo DR, Côte d'Ivoire, Egypt, Eswatini, Ethiopia, Gabon, Ghana, Kenya, Lesotho, Libya, Malawi, Malaysia, Mauritania, Mauritius, Morocco, Mozambique, Namibia, Niger, Nigeria, Rwanda, Senegal, Somalia, South Africa, Sudan, Togo, Tunisia, Uganda, Zambia.

IGO Relations *UNESCO (#20322)*; *UNIDO (#20336)*; *United Nations Human Settlements Programme (UN-Habitat, #20572)*; *WHO (#20950)*; *World Trade Organization (WTO, #21864)*. **NGO Relations** Partner of: *World Urban Campaign (WUC, #21893)*. [2017/XD9642/**D**]

- ♦ Africa Unite (internationally oriented national body)
- ♦ Africa Unite – Human Rights for Social Cohesion / see Africa Unite
- ♦ Africa University, Mutare (internationally oriented national body)
- ♦ Africa Water Journalist Network (internationally oriented national body)

♦ AfricaWide Movement for Children (AMC) 00530

Contact PO Box 1179, Addis Ababa, Ethiopia. T. +251116628192 – +251116628196 – +251116628197. Fax +251116628200.
Head Office PO Box 10293, Kampala, Uganda.

History May 2008, Addis Ababa (Ethiopia). Founded on the initiative of: *African Child Policy Forum (ACPF, #00246)*; *African Network for Prevention and Protection Against Child Abuse and Neglect (ANPPCAN, #00393)*; Coalition of NGOs Working for Children in Africa (CONAFE); Uganda Child Rights National Network (UCRNN); *Environnement et développement du Tiers-monde (enda, #05510)*; Resources Aimed at the Prevention of Child Abuse and Neglect (RAPCAN); *SOS-Kinderdorf International (#19693)*; *African Movement of Working Children and Youth (AMWCY)*. Constitution adopted Aug 2012. Registration: Uganda. **Aims** Promote and advocate for full realization of the rights and wellbeing of all children in Africa; speak out against child rights violations and facilitate collective action to ensure children's rights are respected and their wellbeing realized. **Structure** General Assembly (every 2 years); Board of Custodians; Secretariat, provided by *African Child Policy Forum (ACPF, #00246)*. **Languages** English, French. **Finance** Members' dues. **Publications** *AMC Newsletter*. **Members** Full; Associate; Honorary. Membership countries not specified. [2016.07.14/XJ2220/**F**]

♦ Africa Women Innovation and Entrepreneurship Forum (AWIEF) . . . 00531

Contact 12 Bell Crescent, Dunrae Bldg, Westlake Business Park, Cape Town, South Africa. T. +27218268878. E-mail: info@awieforum.org.
URL: http://www.awieforum.org/

Aims Foster the economic inclusion, advancement and empowerment of women in Africa through entrepreneurship support and development. **Languages** English. **Staff** 8.00 FTE, paid. **Activities** Events/meetings; awards/prizes/competitions; capacity building; advocacy/lobbying/activism. **Events** *Annual Conference* Cape Town (South Africa) 2019, *Annual Conference* Cape Town (South Africa) 2018, *Annual Conference* Cape Town (South Africa) 2017. [2020.03.16/XM8458/**F**]

- ♦ Africa World Institute (internationally oriented national body)
- ♦ Africa Yoga Federation (internationally oriented national body)
- ♦ Africa Youth Leaders Coordinating Committee for Environmental Education (inactive)
- ♦ Africa Youth for Peace and Development (internationally oriented national body)
- ♦ Africa Youth Trust (internationally oriented national body)
- ♦ AFRICE – Africa for Research in Comparative Education Society (unconfirmed)
- ♦ AFRICGLOT – African Center for Global Trends (unconfirmed)
- ♦ AFRICLEG – Africa Clean Energy Group (internationally oriented national body)
- ♦ AfriCOG – Africa Centre for Open Governance (internationally oriented national body)
- ♦ **AFRICOM** International Council of African Museums (#12986)
- ♦ **AfriComNet** African Network for Strategic Communication in Health and Development (#00396)
- ♦ AFRICSIS – African Center for Science and International Security (internationally oriented national body)
- ♦ **AFRICTIVISTES** League of African Bloggers and Cyber-activists for Democracy (#16476)
- ♦ **AFRICTIVISTES** Ligue Africaine des Blogueurs et Cyber-activistes pour la Démocratie (#16476)
- ♦ **AFRIGIST** African Regional Institute for Geospatial Information Science and Technology (#00433)
- ♦ AFRIGRAPH – African Graphics Association (internationally oriented national body)
- ♦ Afrihealth Optonet Association (internationally oriented national body)
- ♦ Afrikaanse Aardnootraad (#00332)
- ♦ Afrika-Europa Netwerk (internationally oriented national body)
- ♦ Afrikagrupperna i Sverige (internationally oriented national body)
- ♦ Afrikai-Magyar Egyesület (internationally oriented national body)
- ♦ Afrika Instituut / see Netherlands-African Business Council
- ♦ Afrika-Instituut, Tervuren (internationally oriented national body)
- ♦ Afrika Komitee (#00164)
- ♦ Afrika Kulturinstitut (internationally oriented national body)
- ♦ Afrika Kulturinstitut – Verein zur Förderung der Völkerverständigung / see Afrika Kulturinstitut
- ♦ Afrikanisch-Asiatische Studienförderung (internationally oriented national body)
- ♦ Afrikanische Organisation der Obersten Rechnungskontrollbehörden (#00406)
- ♦ Afrikanische Regionalorganisation des IBFG / see International Trade Union Confederation – African Regional Organization (#15709)
- ♦ Afrikanisch-Europäische Institut für die Technologische, Wirtschaftliche und Soziale Entwicklung in Afrika / see Africa Development Solutions
- ♦ Afrika-Studiecentrum Leiden (internationally oriented national body)
- ♦ Afrika Verein, Hamburg (internationally oriented national body)
- ♦ Afrikka Keskus Suomi (internationally oriented national body)
- ♦ AFRILAW – African Law Foundation (internationally oriented national body)
- ♦ AFRILEX – African Association for Lexicography (internationally oriented national body)

♦ AfriMAB Network 00532

Réseau AfriMAB

Secretariat c/o MAB, Div Sciences écologiques et de la Terre, UNESCO, 7 Place de Fontenoy, 75007 Paris, France. T. +33145680557. E-mail: mab@unesco.org.
URL: http://www.unesco.org/mab/

History 9 Oct 1996, Dakar (Senegal), within the framework of *Programme on Man and the Biosphere (MAB, #18526)*. **Aims** Promote regional cooperation in the fields of *biodiversity conservation* and *sustainable development*. **Events** *Regional meeting* Nairobi (Kenya) 2010, *Meeting* Cape Town (South Africa) 2007, *Technical meeting for English-speaking countries* Nairobi (Kenya) 2000.

Members in 31 countries:
Benin, Burkina Faso, Burundi, Cameroon, Congo Brazzaville, Congo DR, Côte d'Ivoire, Equatorial Guinea, Ethiopia, Gabon, Gambia, Ghana, Guinea, Guinea-Bissau, Kenya, Lesotho, Liberia, Madagascar, Malawi, Mali, Niger, Nigeria, Rwanda, Senegal, Sierra Leone, South Africa, Sudan, Tanzania UR, Togo, Uganda, Zimbabwe. [2018.06.26/XE3891/**F**]

- ♦ AFRIMET / see Conference of Directors of the West African National Meteorological and Hydrological Services (#04589)
- ♦ **AFRIMET** Conference of Directors of the West African National Meteorological and Hydrological Services (#04589)
- ♦ **AFRIMETS** Intra-Africa Metrology System (#15992)
- ♦ AFRiMOVE – Africa on the Move (unconfirmed)
- ♦ **AFRINEAD** African Network for Evidence-to-Action in Disability (#00386)

♦ AFRINIC 00533

CEO 11th Floor, Standard Chartered Tower, Cybercity, Ebene 72201, Mauritius. T. +2304035100. Fax +2304666758. E-mail: contact@afrinic.net.
Registered Office 11th Floor Raffles Tower, CyberCity, Ebene, Mauritius.
URL: http://www.afrinic.net/

History Former names and other names: *African Network Information Centre* – full title. Registration: Mauritius. **Aims** Serve the African community by providing professional and efficient management of *Internet* Number Resources, supporting Internet technology usage and development, and promoting Internet self governance. **Structure** General Assembly (annual); Board of 7 primary members and 6 alternates. **Languages** Arabic, English, French, Portuguese. **Finance** Supported by: *Commonwealth Telecommunications Organisation (CTO, #04365)*. **Events** *Africa Internet Summit* Kampala (Uganda) 2019, *Africa Internet Summit* Dakar (Senegal) 2018, *Public Policy Meeting* Dakar (Senegal) 2018, *Public Policy Meeting* Hammamet (Tunisia) 2018, *Public Policy Meeting* Flic en Flac (Mauritius) 2016.

Members Full in 53 countries:
Algeria, Angola, Benin, Botswana, Burkina Faso, Burundi, Cameroon, Cape Verde, Central African Rep, Chad, Comoros, Congo Brazzaville, Congo DR, Côte d'Ivoire, Djibouti, Egypt, Equatorial Guinea, Eritrea, Eswatini, Ethiopia, Gabon, Gambia, Ghana, Guinea, Guinea-Bissau, Kenya, Lesotho, Liberia, Libya, Madagascar, Malawi, Mali, Mauritania, Mauritius, Morocco, Mozambique, Namibia, Niger, Nigeria, Rwanda, Sao Tomé-Principe, Senegal, Seychelles, Sierra Leone, Somalia, South Africa, Sudan, Tanzania UR, Togo, Tunisia, Uganda, Zambia, Zimbabwe.

NGO Relations Member of (2): *Internet Society (ISOC, #15952)*; *Number Resource Organization (NRO, #17625)*. [2021.09.02/XJ0472/**F**]

- ♦ AfriOceans Conservation Alliance (internationally oriented national body)
- ♦ AFRIPA – Association of African Investment Promotion Agencies (no recent information)
- ♦ **AFRIPOL** African Union Mechanism for Police Cooperation (#00492)
- ♦ **AfriQAN** African Quality Assurance Network (#00427)
- ♦ Afrique environnementale – Centre africain de protection environnementale et pour l'assistance (internationally oriented national body)
- ♦ Afrique équatoriale française (inactive)
- ♦ Afrique future (internationally oriented national body)
- ♦ Afrique occidentale française (inactive)
- ♦ Afrique Secours et Assistance (unconfirmed)
- ♦ Les Afriques dans le monde (internationally oriented national body)
- ♦ Afrique verte (internationally oriented national body)
- ♦ **AFRISTAT** Economic and Statistical Observatory for Sub-Saharan Africa (#05321)
- ♦ AFRITERRA – The Cartographic Free Library / see Afriterra Foundation
- ♦ Afriterra Foundation (internationally oriented national body)
- ♦ **AfriWEA** African Wind Energy Association (#00499)
- ♦ **AfroAgEng** Pan African Society for Agricultural Engineering (#18065)
- ♦ Afro-Arab Cultural Institute / see Afro-Arab Institute for Culture and Strategic Studies (#00534)

♦ Afro-Arab Institute for Culture and Strategic Studies (AACI) 00534

Institut Afro-Arabe pour la Culture et les Etudes Stratégiques

Dir Gen Cité du Niger, PO Box E1444, Bamako, Mali. T. +22320215750. Fax +22320215753. E-mail: icaa2002@gmail.com – icaa@afroarab-institute.org.
URL: http://afroarab-institute.org/

History Apr 2002, Bamako (Mali), as *Afro-Arab Cultural Institute*. **Aims** Promote mutual knowledge of African and Arab peoples through their respective cultures; strengthen cultural cooperation and exchange; encourage and facilitate contacts, discussions and dialogue on issues of common interest; promote and encourage cultural exchange between the two regions; contribute to effective implementation of the resolutions, policy decisions and programmes of the African Union (AU) and League of Arab States (LAS). **Structure** Executive Council, comprising: Chairperson of AU; Secretary General of LAS; Director General of ALECSO; African representatives (Senegal, Tunisia, Chad, Kenya, Malawi plus Mali as observer); Arab representatives (Egypt, Jordan, Libyan AJ, Lebanon, Iraq). Scientific Council, comprising from Africa – Burkina Faso, Angola, Zimbabwe and from Arab countries – Libyan AJ, United Arab Emirates, Egypt. Secretariat, comprising Director General, Deputy Director General and 3 departments. **Languages** Arabic, English, French. **Staff** 5.00 FTE, paid. **Finance** Sources: *African Union (AU, #00488)*; *Arab League Educational, Cultural and Scientific Organization (ALECSO, #01003)*; *League of Arab States (LAS, #16420)*; donations from the the Kingdom of Saudi Arabia. **Activities** Events/meetings; research/documentation; awards/prizes/competitions. **Publications** *Yearbook on Afro-Arab Studies and Research*. *Répertoire du Centre Sidi al-Mukhatâr al-Kabîr al-Kuntî pour la documentation et le recherche Gao/Mali* (2011) in French; *Heritage of African Languages – manuscripts in Arabic script*, 1 vol to date. Conference and symposia proceedings. **IGO Relations** Cooperation agreement with: *Arab Fund for Technical Assistance to African Countries (AFTAAC, #00966)*; *Islamic World Educational, Scientific and Cultural Organization (ICESCO, #16058)*; Ministries of Culture of Egypt and Senegal. [2019.02.12/XM1939/j/**E**]

♦ **Afro-Asian Book Council (AABC)** **00535**

SG 4295/3 Ansari Road, Darya Ganj, Delhi 110022, DELHI 110022, India. T. +911145355555. E-mail: aabookcouncil@gmail.com.
URL: https://www.aabookcouncil.org/

History Founded Feb 1990, Delhi (India), during 1st Afro-Asian Publishing Conference. **Aims** Function as a forum for continuing dialogue between authors, academicians, publishers, librarians and policy makers for book development in Africa and Asia through mutual cooperation. **Structure** Executive Committee. **Finance** Members' dues. **Activities** Training/education; events/meetings. **Events** *Afro-Asian Publishing Conference* Delhi (India) 2010, *Afro-Asian Publishing Conference* Delhi (India) 2008, *Afro-Asian Publishing Conference* Delhi (India) 2006, *Afro-Asian Publishing Conference* Delhi (India) 2004, *Afro-Asian Publishing Conference* Delhi (India) 2002. **Publications** *AABC Newsletter* (4 a year). *Formulating the National Book Policy: Need and Guidelines* (1994); *Publishing Cooperation in Afro-Asia Region* (1994); *Literacy and Book Development in South and West Asia* by Abul Hasan. Seminar proceedings.
Members Individual; Corporate organizations and institutions. Members (170) in 25 countries:
Afghanistan, Bangladesh, Bhutan, Cameroon, Fiji, Ghana, India, Indonesia, Iran Islamic Rep, Israel, Japan, Kenya, Malaysia, Mauritius, Nepal, Nigeria, Pakistan, Philippines, Senegal, Singapore, South Africa, Sri Lanka, Tanzania UR, United Arab Emirates, Zimbabwe.
Associate members in 6 countries:
Canada, Germany, Netherlands, Russia, UK, USA.
Consultative Status Consultative status granted from: *World Intellectual Property Organization (WIPO, #21593)* (Permanent Observer Status). **NGO Relations** Member of: *African Publishers Network (APNET, #00426)*. [2022/XF1529/**F**]

♦ Afro-Asian Centre for Maritime Arbitration / see Alexandria Centre for International Maritime Arbitration

♦ **Afro-Asian Council of Ophthalmology (AACO)** **00536**

SG 56 Ramses St, Roxy, Cairo, Egypt. T. +202101615925.
Pres 6 Medan El Falaky-Bab, El Louk, Cairo, Egypt. T. +20227953905. E-mail: prof.emarah@gmail.com.

History 1958. **Aims** Promote scientific and technical developments among participating countries. **Structure** Officers: President; 4 Vice-Presidents; General Secretary; Assistant Secretary; Advocacy Officer to ICO; Treasurer. **Languages** English. **Staff** 18.00 FTE, paid. **Finance** Contributions from Board members; support from medical equipment companies. **Events** *Afro-Asian Congress of Ophthalmology* Xian (China) 2014, *Afro-Asian Congress of Ophthalmology* Istanbul (Turkey) 2012, *Afro-Asian Congress of Ophthalmology* Kolkata (India) 2010, *Afro-Asian congress of ophthalmology* Marrakech (Morocco) 2007, *Afro-Asian congress of ophthalmology* Istanbul (Turkey) 2004.
Members Individuals in 12 countries:
Albania, Egypt, India, Japan, Libya, Morocco, Nigeria, Saudi Arabia, Syrian AR, Tunisia, Türkiye, Ukraine.
[2014/XF5109/v/**F**]

♦ Afro-Asian Federation for Tobacco Producers and Manufacturers (inactive)
♦ Afro-Asian Housing Organization (inactive)
♦ Afro-Asian Islamic Organization (inactive)
♦ Afro-Asian Network on Rural Poultry Development / see International Network on Family Poultry Development (#14267)
♦ Afro-Asian Organization for Economic Cooperation (inactive)

♦ **Afro-Asian Peoples' Solidarity Organization (AAPSO)** **00537**

Organisation de la solidarité des peuples afro-asiatiques (OSPAA) – Organización de Solidaridad de Pueblos Afroasiaticos

Pres 89 Abdel Aziz Al Saoud Street, PO Box 61, 11559 Manial El-Roda, Cairo, 11559, Egypt. T. +2023622946 – +2023636081 – +2023623700. Fax +2023637361. E-mail: aapso@idsc.net.eg.
URL: http://www.aapsorg.org/

History 26 Dec 1957, Cairo (Egypt). Founded as a peoples' organization, following steps taken at the governmental level by Prime Ministers of Burma (currently Myanmar), Ceylon (currently Sri Lanka), India, Indonesia and Pakistan at meetings from 28 Apr to 2 May 1954, Colombo (Sri Lanka), and 28-29 Dec 1954, Bogor (Indonesia), and at Conference of Afro-Asian Nations, 18-24 Apr 1955, Bandung (Indonesia). Originally known as *Organization for Afro-Asian Peoples' Solidarity*. First Constitution, on the basis of a draft prepared by First Council, 1959, Cairo, was adopted by 2nd Conference, Apr 1960, Conakry (Guinea); amended by 11th Council, 1974, Baghdad (Iraq); supplemented by transitional resolution of constitutional character adopted by 13th Council, Mar 1981, Aden (Yemen). Second Constitution adopted May 1988, Delhi. Present Constitution adopted 2008, Hyderabad (India). **Aims** As a non-governmental, pluralist and democratic organization, an integral part of anti-imperialist and peace-loving forces: act for the democratization of *international relations*; establish the New International Economic Order and the New International Information and Communication Order; uphold human rights; protect the environment; promote gender equality and women's rights; complete elimination of nuclear biological and other weapons of mass destruction. **Structure** Congress (every 4 years); Praesidium (meets every 2 years); Bureau (meets annually); Permanent Secretariat. President of AAPSO is President of the Praesidium and is from the country of the Permanent Secretariat. **Languages** Arabic, English, French. **Staff** 35.00 FTE, paid. **Finance** Sources: donations; members' dues. Annual budget: 150,000 USD. **Activities** Events/meetings; financial and/or material support; networking/liaising; research and development. **Events** *Congress* Colombo (Sri Lanka) 2014, *Congress* Delhi (India) 1998, *Meeting* London (UK) 1998, *Meeting* Syrian AR 1998, *Meeting* Cairo (Egypt) 1997. **Publications** *AAPSO Bulletin* (12 a year) in Arabic, English; *Human Rights* (6 a year) in Arabic, English, French – newsletter; *Development and Socio-Economic Progress* (4 a year). *Afro-Asian Publications* – series on issues of topical interest. Books; pamphlets, in Arabic, English, French.
Members National Committees; Affiliated Organizations. Members in 85 countries and territories:
Algeria, Angola, Armenia, Azerbaijan, Bahrain, Bangladesh, Benin, Botswana, Burkina Faso, Burundi, Cambodia, Cape Verde, Chad, China, Congo Brazzaville, Congo DR, Côte d'Ivoire, Cuba, Cyprus, Egypt, Eritrea, Eswatini, Ethiopia, France, Georgia, Germany, Ghana, Greece, Guinea, Guinea-Bissau, Guyana, Hong Kong, India, Indonesia, Iraq, Japan, Jordan, Kazakhstan, Kenya, Korea DPR, Kuwait, Kyrgyzstan, Laos, Lebanon, Libya, Madagascar, Malawi, Malaysia, Mali, Malta, Mauritius, Mongolia, Morocco, Mozambique, Namibia, Nepal, Nicaragua, Nigeria, Pakistan, Palestine, Philippines, Russia, Sao Tomé-Principe, Senegal, Seychelles, Sierra Leone, Somalia, South Africa, Sri Lanka, Sudan, Syrian AR, Tajikistan, Tanzania UR, Thailand, Togo, Tunisia, Turkmenistan, Uganda, UK, Ukraine, Uzbekistan, Vietnam, Yemen, Zambia, Zimbabwe.
Associate members in 8 countries:
Cuba, Cyprus, France, Germany, Greece, Malta, Nicaragua, UK.
Included in the above, 2 organizations listed in this Yearbook:
Greek Committee for International Democratic Solidarity (EEDDA); International Institute for Non-Aligned Studies (IINS, #13904).
Consultative Status Consultative status granted from: *African Commission on Human and Peoples' Rights (ACHPR, #00255)* (Observer); *UNESCO (#20322)* (Consultative Status); *UNCTAD (#20285)* (General Category); *UNIDO (#20336)*. **IGO Relations** *Non-Aligned Movement (NAM, #17146); United Nations Committee on the Exercise of the Inalienable Rights of the Palestinian People (CEIRPP, #20539); United Nations Economic Commission for Africa (ECA, #20554); United Nations Economic and Social Commission for Asia and the Pacific (ESCAP, #20557).* Associated with Department of Global Communications of the United Nations.
NGO Relations Member of:
– *Committee of NGOs on Human Rights, Geneva (#04275);*
– *Conference of Non-Governmental Organizations in Consultative Relationship with the United Nations (CONGO, #04635);*
– *International Coordinating Committee for NGOs on the Question of Palestine (ICCP, inactive);*
– *NGO Committee on Disarmament, Peace and Security, New York NY (#17106)* and *NGO Committee for Disarmament, Geneva (#17105).*
Cooperates with: *Federation of Arab Journalists (FAJ, #09422).* [2020/XC0029/y/**C**]

♦ Afro-Asian Philosophy Association (inactive)
♦ Afro-Asian Psychological Association (unconfirmed)
♦ Afro-Asian Rural Reconstruction Organization / see African-Asian Rural Development Organization (#00203)
♦ Afro-Asian Society of Nematologists (internationally oriented national body)
♦ Afro-Asian Writers' Association (inactive)
♦ Afro-Asia-Oceania Association of Anatomists (no recent information)
♦ Afro-Asiatisches Institut Salzburg (internationally oriented national body)
♦ Afro Centre for Development Peace and Justice (internationally oriented national body)
♦ **AFRODAD** African Forum and Network on Debt and Development (#00321)
♦ AFRODEP – Afro Centre for Development Peace and Justice (internationally oriented national body)
♦ Afro-European Institute of Technological, Economical and Social Development in Africa / see Africa Development Solutions

♦ **Afro-European Medical and Research Network (AEMRN)** **00538**

Pres Jupiterstr 01, 3015 Bern, Switzerland. T. +41319118852. Fax +41319118853. E-mail: contact@aemrnetwork.ch.
Main: http://www.aemrnetwork.ch/

History Founded in Switzerland, by Dr Charles Senessie. **Aims** Improve the quality of life for people from, and living in, resource limited settings. **Structure** International Headquarters, Bern (Switzerland); Country Offices. **Languages** English, French, German. **Staff** 10.00 FTE, paid. **Finance** Members' dues. Other sources: donations; grant applications, other fundraising activities. **Activities** Events/meetings; knowledge management/information dissemination; training/education. Active in: Kenya, Liberia, Sierra Leone, Uganda, Zambia, Zimbabwe. **Events** *Annual Symposium* Bern (Switzerland) 2010, *Congress / Annual Symposium* Amsterdam (Netherlands) 2009, *Annual Symposium* Bern (Switzerland) 2008. **Publications** *Delays in Childhood Immunization in a Conflict Area* – study from Sierra Leone during civil war. **Information Services** *EZcollab* – community based service for exchange of resources, research papers, guidelines and other publications, and to share knowledge, experiences, and lessons learned. **Members** Over 400 members worldwide. Membership countries not specified. **Consultative Status** Consultative status granted from: *ECOSOC (#05331)* (Special). **IGO Relations** *WHO (#20950)*; African Health Ministries. **NGO Relations** Member of: *Global Health Workforce Alliance (GHWA, inactive)*. Board Member of: *Alliance for Health Promotion (A4HP, #00687)*.
[2019/XJ1508/**F**]

♦ Afro-FIET – Organisation régionale africaine de la Fédération internationale des employés techniciens et cadres / see UNI Global Union – Africa Region (#20339)
♦ **AFROFOODS** African Food Network of Food Data Systems (#00317)
♦ AFRO / see International Trade Union Confederation – African Regional Organization (#15709)
♦ AfroLeadership (internationally oriented national body)
♦ Afrolease – African Leasing Association (inactive)
♦ AFROLIT – Society for the Promotion of Adult Literacy in Africa (inactive)

♦ **Afro Middle East Hernia Society (AMEHS)** **00539**

Gen Sec Place Cornavin 16, 1201 Geneva, Switzerland.
URL: http://www.amehs.net/

History 2 Sep 2009. **Aims** Study anatomic, physiologic, pathologic and therapeutic problems relating to the abdominal wall and abdominal hernias. **Structure** Board of Directors. **Languages** English, French. **Staff** 10.00 FTE, paid. **Finance** Members' dues. Donations. **Activities** Publishing activities. **Events** *Congress* Milan (Italy) 2015, *World Conference on Abdominal Wall Hernia Surgery* Milan (Italy) 2015, *Congress* Dakar (Senegal) 2013, *Congress* Niamey (Niger) 2012, *Congress* Tunis (Tunisia) 2010.
Members Individuals in 28 countries:
Algeria, Benin, Burkina Faso, Cameroon, Chad, Congo Brazzaville, Côte d'Ivoire, Egypt, Equatorial Guinea, Gabon, Guinea, Iraq, Italy, Kenya, Kuwait, Libya, Mali, Morocco, Niger, Nigeria, Oman, Rwanda, Saudi Arabia, Senegal, South Africa, Switzerland, Togo, Tunisia. [2015.09.10/XJ7790/v/**D**]

♦ AfrONet – African Organic Network (unconfirmed)
♦ Afronet Trust / see Alliances for Africa
♦ AFRONUS – Africa Council for Food and Nutrition Sciences (no recent information)

♦ **AfroPresencia** **00540**

Mailing Address 47 Duffield St, Brooklyn NY 11201, USA. E-mail: afropresencia88@gmail.com – karenjuanita@gmail.com.
URL: http://www.afropresencia.org/

History Brooklyn, NY (USA). **Aims** Present information about *marginalized* Afro-*descendants* to the global arena; collaborate with other non-governmental organizations; promote the work of activists, organizers and artists currently working on improving the lives of Afro-descendants in the Americas and the Caribbean. **Structure** Board. **Languages** English, Portuguese, Spanish. **Consultative Status** Consultative status granted from: *ECOSOC (#05331)* (Special). [2022.02.11/XM7137/**F**]

♦ AfroREB – African Rabies Expert Bureau (unconfirmed)
♦ **AFROSAI** African Organization of Supreme Audit Institutions (#00406)
♦ **AFROSAI-E** African Organisation of English-speaking Supreme Audit Institutions (#00403)
♦ **AFRO** WHO Regional Office for Africa (#20943)
♦ AFRUCA – Africans Unite against Child Abuse (internationally oriented national body)
♦ AfSA – African Space Agency (unconfirmed)
♦ **AFSA** African Statistical Association (#00475)
♦ **AFSA** Alliance for Food Sovereignty in Africa (#00680)
♦ AfSAAP – African Studies Association of Australasia and the Pacific (internationally oriented national body)
♦ **AFSA** ASEAN Forestry Students Association (#01188)
♦ **AFSA** Asian Farming Systems Association (#01451)
♦ **AFSA** Asian Financial Services Association (#01480)
♦ **AFSA** Asian Food Security Association (#01486)
♦ **AFSAE** African Society of Association Executives (#00458)
♦ AFS / see AFS Intercultural Programs (#00541)
♦ **AFS** AFS Intercultural Programs (#00541)
♦ AFS – American Fisheries Society (internationally oriented national body)
♦ **AFS** Arab Federation of Shipping (#00953)
♦ **AFS** Asian Federation of Speleology (#01474)
♦ **AFS** Asian Fisheries Society (#01483)
♦ AFS / see Asia-Oceania Federation of Sexology (#01798)
♦ AFSAU – Association of Faculties of Science in African Universities (inactive)
♦ **AfSBT** Africa Society for Blood Transfusion (#00519)
♦ AfSC – Africa Seismological Commission (unconfirmed)
♦ AFSC – American Friends Service Committee (internationally oriented national body)
♦ **AFSD** Africa Foundation for Sustainable Development (#00174)
♦ AFSEA – African Sustainable Energy Association (unconfirmed)
♦ **AFSEC** African Electrotechnical Standardization Commission (#00295)
♦ **AfSHG** African Society of Human Genetics (#00462)
♦ **AFSHR** African Federation for Sexual Health and Rights (#00312)
♦ **AFSIA** Africa Solar Industry Association (#00521)

♦ **AFS Intercultural Programs (AFS)** **00541**

Main Office 5 Hanover Sq, Ste 200, 2nd fl, New York NY 10004, USA.
URL: http://www.afs.org/

History Apr 1915, France. Founded by Abram Piatt Andrew (1873-1936), as a humanitarian operation. *AFS Association* was a related entity which operated from May 1920 through 1952. Former names and other names: *American Ambulance Field Service (AAFS)* – former (Apr 1915 to 1917); *American Field Service (AFS)* – former (1917); *AFS International/Intercultural Programs* – former (1978 to 1987); *AFS Programmes interculturels* – former; *AFS Interkulturelle Begegnungen* – former. Registration: USA, New York. **Aims** Provide intercultural learning opportunities to help people develop the knowledge, skills and understanding needed to create a more just and peaceful world; seek to affirm faith in the dignity and worth of every human being and of all nations and cultures; encourage respect for human rights and fundamental freedoms without distinction as to race, sex, language, religion or social status. **Structure** Board of Trustees; International Administration; AFS Network Organizations. **Staff** 40000.00 FTE, voluntary. **Finance** International participant fees; fundraising; grants. **Activities** Networking/liaising; awareness raising; training/education. **Events** *AFS*

Global Conference 2020, *AFS Global Conference* Montréal, QC (Canada) 2019, *AFS Global Conference* Budapest (Hungary) 2018, *World congress* 1993, *Meeting* Vienna (Austria) 1990. **Publications** *The Janus Magazine* (3 a year); *Intercultural Link Newsletter*. Annual Report. **Members** National Offices of affiliated network organizations in over 50 countries and territories (not specified). **Consultative Status** Consultative status granted from: *ECOSOC (#05331)* (Special). **IGO Relations** Associated with Department of Global Communications of the United Nations. **NGO Relations** Cooperates with: *European Federation for Intercultural Learning (EFIL, #07146)*. Member of: *Alliance for International Exchange*. [2021/XF5870/**F**]

- ♦ AFS Interkulturelle Begegnungen / see AFS Intercultural Programs (#00541)
- ♦ AFS International/Intercultural Programs / see AFS Intercultural Programs (#00541)
- ♦ **AFSLAB** Asian Federation of Societies for Lactic Acid Bacteria (#01472)
- ♦ AFSMAS – Association francophone de spectrométrie de masses des solides (no recent information)
- ♦ **AFSM** Asian Federation of Sports Medicine (#01475)
- ♦ **AFSM** Association of Former WHO Staff Members (#02604)
- ♦ **AFSN** Asian Forensic Sciences Network (#01488)
- ♦ AFSOS – Association Francophone pour les Soins Oncologiques de Support (internationally oriented national body)
- ♦ AFSOUTH / see Allied Joint Force Command Naples (#00735)
- ♦ AFSP / see Action on Poverty
- ♦ AFSP – African Federation for the Study of Pain (no recent information)
- ♦ AFSP – Association française de science politique (internationally oriented national body)
- ♦ AFSPC – Association of Financial Supervisors of Pacific Countries (inactive)
- ♦ **AfSPID** African Society for Paediatric Infectious Diseases (#00466)
- ♦ AFS Programmes interculturels / see AFS Intercultural Programs (#00541)
- ♦ **AFSRA** African Society for Regional Anesthesia (#00469)
- ♦ AFSRE / see International Farming Systems Association (#13332)
- ♦ AFSSA – Association for French Studies in Southern Africa (internationally oriented national body)
- ♦ AFSS – Asian Fuzzy Systems Society (inactive)
- ♦ **AFSSRN** Asian Fisheries Social Science Research Network (#01482)
- ♦ **AFSTA** African Seed Trade Association (#00454)
- ♦ **AFSTSS** African Society for Traumatic Stress Studies (#00471)
- ♦ **AFSUMB** Asian Federation of Societies for Ultrasound in Medicine and Biology (#01473)
- ♦ AFSV – Association of French Speaking Veterinarians (no recent information)
- ♦ AFSW – Arab Federation of Social Workers (inactive)
- ♦ AFTAAAC / see Arab Fund for Technical Assistance to African Countries (#00966)
- ♦ AFTAAC / see Arab Fund for Technical Assistance to African Countries (#00966)
- ♦ **AFTAAC** Arab Fund for Technical Assistance to African Countries (#00966)
- ♦ AFTA / see Arab Fund for Technical Assistance to African Countries (#00966)
- ♦ **AFTA** ASEAN Free Trade Area (#01191)
- ♦ AFTA – Association francophone du tourisme d'affaires (internationally oriented national body)
- ♦ AFTA – Association of French Teachers in Africa (no recent information)
- ♦ Aftale om gennemførelse af visse bestemmelser om statsborgerret (2002 treaty)
- ♦ Aftale om kulturelt samarbejde (1971 treaty)
- ♦ Aftale mellem Danmark, Island, Norge og Sverige om samarbejde i konkurrencesager (2001 treaty)
- ♦ **AFTC** Asian Federation of Therapeutic Communities (#01476)
- ♦ AFTCW – Arab Federation of Transport and Communication Workers (no recent information)
- ♦ AFTE – Arab Federation for Technical Education (no recent information)
- ♦ AFTES – Australasian Fluids and Thermal Engineering Society (internationally oriented national body)
- ♦ **AFTEX** ASEAN Federation of Textile Industries (#01185)
- ♦ AFTH – African Federation for Technology in Health Care (no recent information)
- ♦ AFTI – Arab Federation for Textile Industries (inactive)
- ♦ **AfTLD** Africa Top Level Domain Organization (#00525)
- ♦ AFTP – Association Francophone des Types Psychologiques (internationally oriented national body)
- ♦ AFTSC – Association des fédérations de tir sportif de la CE (inactive)
- ♦ AFTU / see World Taekwondo Africa (#21845)
- ♦ AFTW – Arab Federation of Transport Workers (no recent information)
- ♦ AFTZ / see African Continental Free Trade Area (#00267)
- ♦ **AFUB** African Union of the Blind (#00489)
- ♦ **AFUCA** Asian Pacific Federation of UNESCO Clubs and Associations (#01614)
- ♦ AFUL – Association of Finno-Ugric Literatures (unconfirmed)
- ♦ **AFUL** Association francophone des utilisateurs de Linux et des logiciels libres (#02620)
- ♦ **AFUNPI** Association of Former United Nations Personnel in and of India (#02603)
- ♦ **AFUR** African Forum for Utility Regulators (#00324)
- ♦ **AFUS** African Forum for Urban Security (#00323)
- ♦ **AFUS Paris** Association of Former UNESCO Staff Members (#02601)
- ♦ AFVP / see France Volontaires
- ♦ **AfWA** African Water Association (#00497)
- ♦ **AFW Alliance** Asia Floor Wage Alliance (#01278)
- ♦ **AFWC** African Forestry and Wildlife Commission (#00319)

♦ AFWC/EFC/NEFC Committee on Mediterranean Forestry Questions – Silva Mediterranea 00542

Comité CFFSA/CEF/CFPO des questions forestières méditerranéennes – Silva Mediterranea – FAO
Comité CFFSA/CEF/CFCO sobre Cuestiones Forestales del Mediterraneo – Silva Mediterranea

Secretariat FAO Forestry Dept, Viale delle Terme di Caracalla, 00153 Rome RM, Italy. T. +39657055508. Fax +39657055137.
URL: http://www.fao.org/forestry/silvamed/en/

History Established 1948, with the title *Committee of Mediterranean Forestry Questions* by Article VI-1 of the Constitution of *FAO (#09260)* as a subsidiary body of *European Forestry Commission (EFC, #07299)*, evolving from *Silva Mediterranea*, set up 1922, following Mediterranean forestry cooperation since 1911. Became *Joint Sub-Commission on Mediterranean Forestry Problems* by Resolutions of Conference sessions, 1953 and 1961. Present title adopted 1970. Acronyms subsequently altered in line with those of the AFWC. Rules of Procedure adopted at 7th session, 1960; amended at 8th session, 1962. **Aims** Allow Mediterranean countries which are members of the the European Forestry Commission, the Near East Forestry Commission and the African Forestry and *Wildlife* Commission to: meet, share experience and establish cooperative programmes; periodically review trends in use of *forest land* in the Mediterranean area; assess impact of changes implemented in agricultural, industrial and urban sectors; advise member governments on reorientation or improvements necessary to meet changing situations or newly-emerging needs; examine progress in forestry *technology* in *ecological* and regional contexts to assess present forest *land utilization* methods; identify research priorities; determine research projects and recommend measures necessary for their concerted execution by forestry research institutes; conduct technical studies and surveys to assist in implementation of national policies. **Structure** Committee sessions comprise member countries and the European Union, with non-member countries invited as observers. Research networks/working groups (6) active between sessions are the permanent organs: Forest Fire; Cork Oak; Management of Forests and Sustainable Development; Forest Genetic Resources; Mediterranean Forests and Climate Change; Sustainable Financial Mechanisms. Enlarged Executive Committee (meets once a year). FAO Forestry Department is in charge of Secretariat located within FAO Forestry Resources Division. **Languages** Arabic, English, French, Spanish. **Finance** Funding provided through FAO regular programme and trust fund arrangements with donors interested in specific programmes developed by networks/working groups. **Activities** Events/meetings. **Events** *Session* Brummana (Lebanon) 2019, *Mediterranean Forest Week* Agadir (Morocco) 2017, *Session* Agadir (Morocco) 2017, *Mediterranean Forest Week* Tlemcen (Algeria) 2013, *Session* Antalya (Turkey) 2012. **Publications** Ad hoc publications; concent papers.

Members Open to all members of African, European and Near East Forestry Commissions of FAO whose territories are situated wholly or partly in the Mediterranean basin proper or whose forest, agricultural or grazing economies are intimately associated with the Mediterranean Region, and who desire to be members. Currently the governments of 26 countries:

Algeria, Bulgaria, Cyprus, Egypt, France, Greece, Iran Islamic Rep, Iraq, Israel, Italy, Jordan, Lebanon, Libya, Malta, Morocco, Portugal, Romania, Saudi Arabia, Serbia, Slovenia, Spain, Sudan, Syrian AR, Tunisia, Türkiye, Yemen.

Regional intergovernmental member (1):

European Union (EU, #08967).

NGO Relations Member of: *European Forest Institute Mediterranean Facility (EFIMED, #07298)*. [2017.10.25/XE6407/**E***]

- ♦ **AFWE** African Federation of Women Entrepreneurs (#00313)
- ♦ AFXB / see Association François-Xavier Bagnoud
- ♦ **AFYE** Arab Forum for Young Entrepreneur Associations (#00961)
- ♦ AFYL – Asociación de Filosofía y Liberación (internationally oriented national body)
- ♦ AGA – Africa Governance Alert (internationally oriented national body)
- ♦ **AGA** American Galvanizers Association (#00781)
- ♦ **AGA** Arab Geologists' Association (#00967)
- ♦ AGA – Association des géographes africains (no recent information)
- ♦ **AGA** Association de géologues arabes (#00967)
- ♦ AGAC – ASEM Global Aging Center (internationally oriented national body)
- ♦ AGADA – Agir autrement pour le développement en Afrique (internationally oriented national body)
- ♦ AGA / see Fédération Internationale de l'Automobile (#09613)
- ♦ AGAG – Africa Grantmakers' Affinity Group (internationally oriented national body)
- ♦ **AGA** Gesellschaft für Arthroskopie und Gelenkchirurgie (#10141)
- ♦ AGAH – Arbeitsgemeinschaft für Angewandte Humanpharmakologie (internationally oriented national body)

♦ Against Malaria Foundation (AMF) 00543

Contact c/o PwC LLP, 1 Embankment Place, London, WC2N 6RH, UK.
Contact c/o Copilevitz Lam & Raney, 310 W 20th Street, Suite 300, Kansas City MO 64108, USA.
URL: https://www.againstmalaria.com/

History Registration: Australian Company Number ACN, No/ID: 120 213 701, Australia; Australian Business Number (ABN), No/ID: 72 120 213 701, Australia; Banque-Carrefour des Entreprises, No/ID: 0894.651.190, Start date: 4 Jan 2008, Belgium; Charity, No/ID: 834775967RR0001, Canada; CVR, No/ID: 37719242, Denmark; No/ID: W742007982, France; SIREN, No/ID: 917918807, France; No/ID: 333/5913/1072 VST, Germany; Charity, No/ID: CHY 17455, Ireland; CRA Charity, No/ID: 20064969, Ireland; Italy; Handelsregister, No/ID: KVK 34236793, Netherlands; Charities Commission, No/ID: CC 10808, New Zealand; Norway; No/ID: 502085-3775, Sweden; No/ID: CHE-354.091.608, Switzerland; Charity Commission, No/ID: 1105319, England and Wales; 501(c)(3), No/ID: 20-3069841, USA. **Aims** Protect people from malaria. **Structure** Board of Trustees (with separate boards in US, UK, Australia, Belgium, Canada, Germany, Ireland, Italy, Netherlands, New Zealand and South Africa); Malaria Advisory Group; Finance and Audit Committee. **Activities** Financial and/or material support. [2022/AA3088/f/**F**]

♦ Aga Khan Development Network (AKDN) 00544

Head Office Case Postale 2369, 1211 Geneva 2, Switzerland. T. +41229097200. Fax +41229097291. E-mail: info@akdn.org.
URL: http://www.akdn.org/

History 1967, Switzerland. Various AKDN institutions founded at different times since 1967. **Aims** Working in social, economic and cultural development to improve living conditions and opportunities for the *poor*, without regard to their faith, origin or gender. **Structure** A group of 9 private, international, non-denominational development agencies working in environment, health, education, architecture, culture, microfinance, rural development, disaster reduction, promotion of private-sector enterprise and revitalization of historic cities: Agencies (9): Aga Khan Agency for Microfinance (AKAM); *Aga Khan Foundation (AKF, #00545)*; Aga Khan Education Services (AKES); Aga Khan Fund for Economic Development (AKFED); Aga Khan Health Services (AKHS); Aga Khan Agency for Habitat (AKAH); Aga Khan Trust for Culture (AKTC); *Aga Khan University (AKU, #00546)*; University of Central Asia (UCA). Chairman is His Highness the Aga Khan. **Languages** English. **Staff** 96000.00 FTE, paid. Thousands voluntary. **Finance** Funding provided by Imamat, the Ismaili Community and international and local donor agencies. Annual budget: 1,000,000,000 USD (2020). **Activities** Awards/prizes/competitions; networking/liaising; projects/programmes. Active in over 30 countries worldwide. **Events** *International congress on school health* Evora (Portugal) 2009, *International conference on regional cooperation in transboundary river basins* Dushanbe (Tajikistan) 2005, *Dushanbe international fresh water forum* Dushanbe (Tajikistan) 2003. **NGO Relations** Member of (2): *Early Childhood Development Action Network (ECDAN, #05155)*; *PMNCH (#18410)*. [2021.08.31/XF5817/**F**]

♦ Aga Khan Foundation (AKF) 00545

Fondation Aga Khan

Address not obtained.
AKDN: http://www.akdn.org/

History 1967, Geneva (Switzerland). Registered in accordance with Swiss law. Part of the group: *Aga Khan Development Network (AKDN, #00544)*. As of 2006, includes activities of *Bellerive Foundation (inactive)*. **Aims** Seek sustainable solutions to long-term problems of *poverty*, hunger, illiteracy, and ill-health with special emphasis on the needs of *rural* communities in mountainous, coastal and other resource-poor areas. **Structure** Board of Directors; decentralized network of branches and affiliates, each with National or Executive Committee, pursuing common objectives and policies. **Staff** 1500.00 FTE, paid. **Finance** Sources: His Highness the Aga Khan; grants from development agencies; income from the endowment; donations from individuals and corporations. **Activities** Programme priorities: education; rural development; health; civil society; community participation; gender; the environment; pluralism; human resource development. Over 130 projects in selected countries of South and Central Asia, Sub-Saharan Africa and the Middle East. International Scholarship Programme. **Events** *Conference* Lisbon (Portugal) 1995, *Conference* Washington, DC (USA) 1995, *International workshop* Lisbon (Portugal) 1987, *Major conference on the enabling environment for effective private sector contribution to social and economic development* Nairobi (Kenya) 1986. **Publications** Annual Report; reports; training manuals; international strategy; project briefs.

Members Independent affiliates and branches in 15 countries:

Afghanistan, Bangladesh, Canada, India, Kenya, Kyrgyzstan, Mozambique, Pakistan, Portugal, Syrian AR, Tajikistan, Tanzania UR, Uganda, UK, USA.

Consultative Status Consultative status granted from: *WHO (#20950)* (Official Relations).

IGO Relations Cooperating agency of: *UNDP (#20292)*. Invited to Governing Council sessions of: *International Fund for Agricultural Development (IFAD, #13692)*. Associated with Department of Global Communications of the United Nations. Co-funding or cooperating partners include:

- *Asian Development Bank (ADB, #01422)*;
- *Australian Aid (inactive)*;
- *Canadian International Development Agency (CIDA, inactive)*;
- *Department for International Development (DFID, inactive)*;
- *Deutsche Gesellschaft für Technische Zusammenarbeit (GTZ, inactive)*;
- *European Commission (EC, #06633)*;
- *International Bank for Reconstruction and Development (IBRD, #12317)* (World Bank);
- *International Development Research Centre (IDRC, #13162)*;
- *Norwegian Agency for Development Cooperation (Norad)*;
- *Swiss Agency for Development and Cooperation (SDC)*;
- UNDP;
- *UNHCR (#20327)*;
- *UNICEF (#20332)*;
- *United States Agency for International Development (USAID)*;
- *WHO Regional Office for Africa (AFRO, #20943)*.

NGO Relations Accredited by (5): *American Council for Voluntary International Action (InterAction)*; *Aspen Network of Development Entrepreneurs (ANDE, #02310)*; *Inter-agency Network for Education in Emergencies (INEE, #11387)*; *Philanthropy Europe Association (Philea, #18358)*; *Worldwide Initiatives for Grantmaker Support (WINGS, #21926)*.

Works in partnership with:

- *Bernard van Leer Foundation (BvLF)*;
- *British Council*;
- *Bureau international des Médecins sans frontières (MSF International, #03366)*;

- *Calouste Gulbenkian Foundation;*
- *Christian Aid;*
- *Energy 4 Impact (#05465);*
- *Focus Humanitarian Assistance (#09808);*
- *Ford Foundation (#09858);*
- *Global Knowledge Initiative;*
- *ICCO – Interchurch Organization for Development Cooperation;*
- *International Union for Conservation of Nature and Natural Resources (IUCN, #15766);*
- *Kreditanstalt für Wiederaufbau (KfW);*
- *Oxfam Novib;*
- *Oxfam GB;*
- *Pharmaciens sans frontières – Comité international (PSF CI, inactive);*
- *The Rockefeller Foundation (#18966);*
- *UCL Institute for Global Health (IGH);*
- *Voluntary Service Overseas (VSO);*
- *World Learning.*

Canada branch member of: *Ontario Council for International Cooperation (OCIC).* [2018/XF7600/f/F]

♦ Aga Khan University (AKU) 00546

Contact PO Box 3500, Stadium Road, Karachi 74800, Pakistan. T. +922134930051. Fax +922134934294 – +922134932095. E-mail: aku@aku.edu – public.affairs@aku.edu.
URL: http://www.aku.edu/

History 1983, as Pakistan's first private university. Currently 12 teaching sites in 8 countries. Part of *Aga Khan Development Network (AKDN, #00544).* **Aims** Train and educate physicians, nurses and teachers in the *developing world;* conduct research that addresses *health* and *education* problems; upgrade the quality of health and education services by acting as a role model to other institutions; work as a dialogue partner with governments and institutions as an agent of change. **Structure** Academic units or programmes in *'Pakistan':* School of Nursing (AKU-SON); Medical College (AKU-MC); University Hospital (AKUH-K); Institute for Educational Development (AKU-IED); Examination Board (AKU-EB); *'East Africa – Kenya':* Advanced Nursing Studies Programme (AKU-ANS); University Hospital (AKUH-N); Postgraduate Medical Education (PGME); *'Tanzania UR':* Institute for Education Development (AKU-IED); Advanced Nursing Studies Programme (AKU-ANS); Postgraduate Medical Education Programme (PGME); *'Uganda':* Advanced Nursing Studies Programme (AKU-ANS); *'UK':* Institute for the Study of Muslim Civilisations (AKU-ISMC); *'Afghanistan':* Managing French Medical Institute for Children (FMIC). **Languages** English. **Staff** 11216.00 FTE, paid. **Activities** Dissemination of knowledge and service, in an innovative environment equipped with the latest technologies and resources; research; partnerships. **Events** *Regional conference on injury prevention and safety promotion* Cairo (Egypt) 2009. **Publications** *AKU Newsletter.* Biennial progress report; prospectus.
Members Universities in 5 countries:
Kenya, Pakistan, Tanzania UR, Uganda, UK. [2013.08.30/XK1931/E]

♦ **AG** Anatomische Gesellschaft (#00813)
♦ Agape Europe (internationally oriented national body)
♦ Agape International Spiritual Center (internationally oriented national body)
♦ **AG** Australia Group (#03036)
♦ **AGAW** Alliance for Global Water Adaptation (#00683)
♦ AGBA – Arab Gulf Basketball Association (inactive)
♦ AG Bell – Alexander Graham Bell Association for the Deaf and Hard of Hearing (unconfirmed)
♦ **AGBU** Armenian General Benevolent Union (#01110)
♦ **AGC** African Groundnut Council (#00332)
♦ AGC – Artisanal Gold Council (internationally oriented national body)
♦ AGC – Associated General Contractors of America (internationally oriented national body)
♦ **AGC** Association of Global Custodians (#02627)
♦ AGCC / see Gulf Cooperation Council (#10826)
♦ **AGCEI** Asian Group for Civil Engineering Informatics (#01497)
♦ AGC – European Agreement on Main International Railway Lines (1985 treaty)
♦ AGCI – Aspen Global Change Institute (internationally oriented national body)
♦ AG-CNO / see Association of National Olympic Committees (#02819)
♦ AGdD – Arbeitsgemeinschaft der Entwicklungsdienste (internationally oriented national body)
♦ **AGDEN** Africa Gender and Development Evaluators Network (#00177)
♦ AGDF – Aktionsgemeinschaft Dienst für den Frieden (internationally oriented national body)
♦ AGE Africa – Advancing Girls' Education in Africa (internationally oriented national body)
♦ AGEC – Arbeitsgemeinschaft Europäischer Chorverbände (inactive)
♦ AGEDI – Abu Dhabi Global Environmental Data Initiative (internationally oriented national body)
♦ AGEE – Alliance for Gender Equality in Europe (internationally oriented national body)
♦ AGE European Older People's Platform / see AGE Platform Europe (#00557)
♦ **AGEG** Arbeitsgemeinschaft Europäischer Grenzregionen (#02499)
♦ AGEH / see AGIOMONDO
♦ Ageing Asia Alliance (internationally oriented national body)
♦ Age International (internationally oriented national body)
♦ Ageless International Club / see Ageless International Foundation
♦ Ageless International Foundation (internationally oriented national body)
♦ Agence Adventiste d'aide et de développement (#00131)
♦ Agence d'aide à la coopération technique et au développement (internationally oriented national body)
♦ Agence d'approvisionnement d'Euratom (#05617)
♦ Agence des assurance et commerce Africain / see African Trade Insurance Agency (#00485)
♦ Agence pour l'Assurance du Commerce en Afrique (#00485)
♦ Agence belge de développement / see Enabel
♦ Agence de contrôles internationale (#15678)
♦ Agence de coopération et d'information pour le commerce international (#00553)
♦ Agence pour la coopération internationale et le développement local en Méditerranée (inactive)
♦ Agence de coopération et de recherche pour le développement (#00073)
♦ Agence pour la coopération technique industrielle et économique / see Agence française pour le développement international des entreprises
♦ Agence danoise pour le développement international / see DANIDA
♦ Agence pour le développement et la coordination des relations internationales (internationally oriented national body)
♦ Agence pour le Développement Economique et Cultural Nord-Sud (internationally oriented national body)
♦ Agence pour le développement de la littérature chrétienne (inactive)
♦ Agence de développement rural pour les églises chrétiennes en Afrique / see Rural and Urban Resources – Counselling, Outreach and Networking
♦ Agence de diffusion du droit international humanitaire en Afrique centrale (internationally oriented national body)
♦ Agence des droits fondamentaux de l'Union européenne (#08969)
♦ Agence de l'eau Rhin-Meuse (internationally oriented national body)
♦ Agence des Etats-Unis pour le développement international (internationally oriented national body)
♦ Agence européenne de cyber-sécurité (#08971)
♦ Agence européenne pour l'environnement (#06995)
♦ Agence européenne pour l'évaluation des médicaments / see European Medicines Agency (#07767)
♦ Agence européenne pour l'information et le conseil des jeunes (#09142)
♦ Agence européenne des médicaments (#07767)
♦ Agence européenne des produits chimique / see European Chemicals Agency (#06523)
♦ Agence européenne des produits chimiques (#06523)
♦ Agence européenne de reconstruction (inactive)
♦ Agence européenne de la sécurité aérienne (#08978)
♦ Agence européenne pour la sécurité maritime (#07744)
♦ Agence européenne pour la sécurité et la santé au travail (#05843)
♦ Agence finlandaise d'aide au développement / see Department for International Development Cooperation
♦ Agence française de développement (internationally oriented national body)
♦ Agence française pour le développement international des entreprises (internationally oriented national body)
♦ Agence francophone pour l'enseignement supérieur et la recherche / see Agence universitaire de La Francophonie (#00548)
♦ Agence d'information du Golfe (inactive)
♦ Agence interalliée des réparations (inactive)
♦ Agence intergouvernementale de La Francophonie (inactive)
♦ Agence internationale coréenne de coopération (internationally oriented national body)
♦ Agence internationale pour le développement / see Fédération des Agences Internationales pour le Développement (#09414)
♦ Agence internationale pour développement économique (internationally oriented national body)
♦ Agence internationale des églises réformées pour les migrations (inactive)
♦ Agence internationale de l'énergie (#13270)
♦ Agence internationale de l'énergie atomique (#12294)
♦ Agence internationale pour l'industrialisation rurale (no recent information)
♦ Agence internationale ISBN (#13955)
♦ Agence internationale pour la prévention du crime et le droit et la compténence en matière pénale (internationally oriented national body)
♦ Agence islamique internationale de presse / see Union of OIC News AGencies (#20467)
♦ Agence japonaise de coopération internationale (internationally oriented national body)
♦ Agence juive pour Israël (#16111)
♦ Agence luxembourgeoise pour la Coopération au Développement (internationally oriented national body)
♦ Agence marocaine de coopération internationale (internationally oriented national body)
♦ Agence Mondiale Antidopage (#21096)
♦ Agence mondiale de solidarité numérique (#21362)
♦ Agence Monétaire de l'Afrique de l'Ouest (#20887)
♦ Agence multilatérale de garantie des investissements (#16888)
♦ Agence norvégienne d'aide au développement / see Norwegian Agency for Development Cooperation
♦ Agence de l'OCDE pour l'énergie nucléaire (#17615)
♦ Agence OTAN de soutien et de'acquisition (#16948)

♦ Agence Panafricaine de la Grande Muraille Verte (APGMV) 00547

Pan-African Agency of the Great Green Wall (PAGGW)
CEO Lot 414 ilot C Nouakchott RIM, BP 5059, Nouakchott, Mauritania. T. +22245255688.
URL: http://www.grandemurailleverte.org/

History Set up 17 Jun 2010, Ndjamena (Chad), under the auspices of *African Union (AU, #00488),* when convention was signed. **Aims** Fight against *desertification.* **Structure** Conference of Heads of State and Government; Council of Ministers; Executive Secretariat.
Members Governments of 11 countries:
Burkina Faso, Chad, Djibouti, Eritrea, Ethiopia, Mali, Mauritania, Niger, Nigeria, Senegal, Sudan.
IGO Relations Accredited by: *Secretariat of the United Nations Convention to Combat Desertification (Secretariat of the UNCCD, #19208).* [2017/XM6006/D*]

♦ Agence panafricaine d'information (inactive)
♦ Agence de la presse francophone / see Association internationale de la presse francophone
♦ Agence pour la promotion internationale des technologies et des entreprises françaises / see Agence française pour le développement international des entreprises
♦ Agence pour la sécurité de la navigation aérienne en Afrique et à Madagascar (#00556)
♦ Agence pour la Solidarité Internationale, la Culture, le Développement et l'Environnement (internationally oriented national body)
♦ Agence spatiale africaine (unconfirmed)
♦ Agence spatiale européenne (#08798)
♦ Agence suédoise de coopération internationale au développement (internationally oriented national body)

♦ Agence universitaire de La Francophonie (AUF) 00548

Mailing Address BP 49714, Csp du Musée, Montréal QC H3T 2A5, Canada. T. +15143436630. Fax +15143432107. E-mail: rectorat@auf.org.
Paris Office 4 place de la Sorbonne, 75005 Paris, France.
General: http://www.auf.org/

History Founded 13 Sep 1961, Montréal QC (Canada), as *Association des universités partiellement ou entièrement de langue française (AUPELF).* 1990, changes to *Agence francophone pour l'enseignement supérieur et la recherche (AUPELF-UREF),* on modification of the statutes of *Association des universités partiellement ou entièrement de langue française (AUPELF, inactive),* as an umbrella organization to unite formally the activities of AUPELF and *Université des réseaux d'expression française (UREF, inactive),* created Dec 1987, Marrakech (Morocco), the two having worked together since the foundation of UREF. Current title adopted by General Assembly, Apr 1998, Beyrouth (Lebanon). Current Statutes adopted by General Assembly, May 2001, Québec QC (Canada). **Aims** Offer enhanced success to all university and research students wishing to further their work and *French language* skills, through improved mobility and access to the Agency's scientific networks; take part in a worldwide science zone capable of levelling out development inequalities between countries. **Structure** General Assembly (every 4 years). Administrative Council – *'Conseil d'administration'* of 27 members. Associative Council – *'Conseil Associatif'* of 25 members. Scientific Council – *'Conseil scientifique'* of 27 members. *Fonds universitaire de coopération et de développement (no recent information),* under the presidency of the rector of AUF. Head Office in Montréal QC (Canada) is headed by Rector. Regional Offices (10): Asia-Pacific; Caribbean; Central Africa and the Great Lakes; Central and Eastern Europe; Indian Ocean; Maghreb; Middle East; Americas; West Africa; Western Europe and North Africa. Regional Units (65). Institutes (6): *École supérieure de la francophonie pour l'administration et le management (ESFAM, #05298); Institut de la francophonie pour l'entrepreneuriat (IFE); International Francophone Institute (IFI, #13682); Institut de la francophonie pour la médecine tropicale (IFMT, #11308); Institut Aimé Césaire; Institut de la Francophonie pour la gouvernance universitaire (IFGU, #11307).* **Languages** French. **Staff** 427.00 FTE, paid. **Finance** Financed by French-speaking countries.
Activities Programme (2010-2014) aims to: develop higher education and research institutions; strengthen the French-speaking university community on international science; reinforce individual skills and build towards emergence of a new generation of researchers, experts, teachers and students.
Institutional networks within the framework of AUF (12):
- *Association des facultés ou établissements de lettres et sciences humaines des universités d'expression française (AFELSH, #02593);*
- *Association pour la promotion de l'enseignement et de la recherche en aménagement et urbanisme (APERAU, #02875);*
- *Conférence internationale des directeurs et doyens des établissements supérieurs d'expression française des sciences de l'agriculture et de l'alimentation (CIDEFA, #04613);*
- *Conférence internationale des dirigeants des institutions d'enseignements supérieur de gestion d'expression française (CIDEGEF, #04614);*
- *Conférence internationale des doyens des facultés de chirurgie dentaire d'expression totalement ou partiellement française (CIDCDF, #04615);*
- *Conférence internationale des doyens des facultés de médecine d'expression française (CIDMEF, #04616);*
- *Conférence internationale des facultés de droit ayant en commun l'usage du français (CIFDUF, #04618);*
- *Conférence internationale des formations d'ingénieurs et de techniciens d'expression française (CITEF, #04619);*
- *Conférence internationale des responsables des universités et instituts à dominante scientifique et technique d'expression française (CIRUISEF, #04622);*
- *Conférence internationale des doyens des facultés de pharmacie d'expression française (CIDPHARMEF, #04617);*
- *Réseau international francophone des établissements de formation de formateurs (RIFEFF, #18893);*
- *Théophraste Network (#20140).*

Administrator Network (1):
- *Groupement international des secrétaires généraux des universités francophones (GISGUF, #10763).*

Events *Assemblée générale* Marrakech (Morocco) 2017, *ECO-CAMPUS International Colloquium* Paris (France) 2015, *Colloque International sur l'Analyse Contemporaine des Conflits en Afrique* Québec, QC (Canada) 2014, *Assemblée générale* Sao Paulo (Brazil) 2013, *World innovation summit for education* Doha (Qatar) 2010. **Publications** Reviews – online and print; series; dictionaries; CD-ROMs. Information Services: Online library. **Members** French-speaking or partially French-speaking higher education and research institutions (779) in 94 countries. Membership countries not specified. **Consultative Status** Consultative status granted from: *ECOSOC (#05331)* (Ros C); *UNESCO (#20322)* (Associate Status); *United Nations Population Fund (UNFPA, #20612)*. **IGO Relations** Since 1991, operates the higher education and research aspects of: *Conférence au sommet des chefs d'Etat et de gouvernement des pays ayant le français en partage (Sommet de la Francophonie, #04648)*. Carries out relevant programmes of: *Conseil permanent de la Francophonie (CPF, #04697)*. **NGO Relations** Special links with: *Assemblée parlementaire de la Francophonie (APF, #02312)*; *Association Internationale des Maires et responsables des capitales et métropoles partiellement ou entièrement Francophones (AIMF, #02715)*. Associate member of: *International Association of Universities (IAU, #12246)*. [2020/XF3420/y/**C**]

- ♦ Agence des Villes et Territoires Méditerranéens Durables (internationally oriented national body)
- ♦ Agencia de Abasticimiento de Euratom (#05617)
- ♦ Agencia Adventista de Desarrollo y Recursos Asistenciales (#00131)
- ♦ Agência de Aprovisionamento da Euratom (#05617)
- ♦ Agência da Capacidade Africana de Risco (#00442)

♦ Agencia Centroamericana de Acreditación de Programas de Arquitectura y de Ingenieria (ACAAI) 00549

Registered Office Edificio Plaza Aventura, El Dorado, Oficina 431, Panama, Panamá, Panama PANAMá, Panama. T. +5073937607 – +5073937608. E-mail: direccion.ejecutiva@acaai.org.gt – presidencia@acaai.org.gt.
URL: http://acaai.org.gt

History Founded 4 Jul 2006, during 3rd Central American Forum, when statutes were adopted. Registered in accordance with the laws of Panama. **Aims** Accredit academic programmes of architecture and engineering of Central America to contribute to quality assurance, continuous improvement and relevance, thus contributing to regional integration. **Structure** Forum; Accreditation Council; Executive Board; Technical Committees. **Staff** Paid and voluntary. **Finance** Contributions from founding partners; payments for accreditation process. Budget (annual): US$ 152,700. **Activities** Projects/programmes; training/education. Active in: member countries. **Events** *Forum* Granada (Nicaragua) 2016, *Forum* San José (Costa Rica) 2014, *Forum* Honduras 2012, *Forum* Antigua (Guatemala) 2010, *Forum* Panama 2008. **Publications** Books.
Members Full in 6 countries:
Costa Rica, El Salvador, Guatemala, Honduras, Nicaragua, Panama.
NGO Relations Member of: *International Network of Quality Assurance Agencies in Higher Education (INQAAHE, #14312)*; *Red Iberoamericana para el Aseguramiento de la Calidad en la Educación Superior (RIACES, #18657)*. [2016/XJ9843/**D**]

- ♦ Agencia Centroamericana de Navegación Aérea (see: #04837)
- ♦ Agencia Centroamericana de Seguridad Aeronautica (see: #04837)
- ♦ Agencia de los Derechos Fundamentales de la Unión Europea (#08969)
- ♦ Agência Espacial Africana (unconfirmed)
- ♦ Agencia Española de Cooperación Internacional / see Agencia Española de Cooperación Internacional para el Desarrollo
- ♦ Agencia Española de Cooperación Internacional para el Desarrollo (internationally oriented national body)
- ♦ Agencia Europea de Información y Asesoramiento para los Jóvenes (#09142)
- ♦ Agencia Europea de Medio Ambiente (#06995)
- ♦ Agencia Europea de Seguridad Aérea (#08978)
- ♦ Agencia Europea de la Seguridad Maritima (#07744)
- ♦ Agencia Europea para la Seguridad y la Salud en el Trabajo (#05843)
- ♦ Agencia Europea de Sustancias y Mezclas Quimicas (#06523)
- ♦ Agencia Europea de Sustancias y Preparados Quimicos / see European Chemicals Agency (#06523)
- ♦ Agência Europeia do Ambiente (#06995)
- ♦ Agência Europeia dos Produtos Quimicos (#06523)
- ♦ Agência Europeia para a Segurança da Aviação (#08978)
- ♦ Agência Europeia para a Segurança Marítima (#07744)
- ♦ Agência Europeia das Substâncias Quimicas / see European Chemicals Agency (#06523)
- ♦ Agencia de Información y de Cooperación para el Comercio Internacional (#00553)
- ♦ Agencia Interamericana para la Cooperación y el Desarrollo (#11397)
- ♦ Agência Internacional a Industrialização Rural (no recent information)
- ♦ Agencia Internacional para la Industrialización Rural (no recent information)
- ♦ Agencia Internacional ISBN (#13955)
- ♦ Agencia Internacional de Prensa India (internationally oriented national body)
- ♦ Agencia Internacional para la Prevención del Delito, el Derecho Penal y la Jurisdicción (internationally oriented national body)
- ♦ Agência Judaica para Israel (#16111)
- ♦ Agencia Judia para Israel (#16111)

♦ Agencia Latinoamericana y Caribeña de Comunicación 00550

Latin American and Caribbean Agency for Communication

Dir Av Rivadavia 4044, 3o piso, 1205 Buenos Aires, Argentina. T. +541147723123. E-mail: director@alc-noticias.net.
URL: http://www.alc-noticias.net/

History May 1994, Quito (Ecuador). **Aims** Provide information and create avenues of communication through news and other journalistic products that help the mission of the *ecumenical* movement, promote human development and stimulate advocacy. **Structure** General Assembly; Board of Directors. **Languages** English, Portuguese, Spanish. **Staff** 5.00 FTE, paid. **Finance** External financing from cooperating agencies. **Activities** Knowledge management/information dissemination; publishing activities. **NGO Relations** Associated and supporting organizations include: *Alliance of Presbyterian and Reformed Churches in Latin America (#00713)*; *Latin American Council of Churches (LACC, #16309)*; *World Association for Christian Communication (WACC, #21126)*; regional organizations. [2017.07.07/XF3910/**F**]

♦ Agencia Latinoamericana de Información (ALAI) 00551

Head Office Casilla 17-12-877, Quito, Ecuador. T. +59322528716 – +59322505074. Fax +59322505073. E-mail: info@alainet.org.
URL: http://alainet.org/

History 1976, Montréal, QC (Canada). Registration: Start date: 1992, Ecuador. **Aims** Develop and implement responses to the challenges of communication and information, as a strategic area for social action; contribute to democratizing communications. **Languages** English, French, Portuguese, Spanish. **Staff** 5.00 FTE, paid. **Activities** Knowledge management/information dissemination. **Events** *Latin American and Caribbean meeting on human rights* Quito (Ecuador) 1998, *International forum on communication and citizenship* San Salvador (El Salvador) 1998, *Meeting of Latin American popular and alternative media* Quito (Ecuador) 1992. **Publications** *América Latina en Movimiento* (12 a year).
Members Network integrated by alternative media, social organizations, research centres, academic bodies (members and correspondents) and analysts in 20 countries:
Argentina, Bolivia, Brazil, Chile, Colombia, Costa Rica, Cuba, Dominican Rep, Ecuador, El Salvador, Guatemala, Haiti, Honduras, Mexico, Nicaragua, Panama, Paraguay, Peru, Uruguay, Venezuela.
Consultative Status Consultative status granted from: *ECOSOC (#05331)* (Special). **NGO Relations** Member of: International Council of *World Social Forum (WSF, #21797)*; *Just Net Coalition (JNC, #16173)*. [2021/XF0047/**F**]

- ♦ Agência Panafricana da Informação (inactive)
- ♦ Agencia Presidencial de Cooperación Internacional de Colombia (internationally oriented national body)
- ♦ Agencia de Promoción Turistica de Centroamérica (#03674)
- ♦ Agência para a Proscrição de Armas Nucleares na América Latina / see Agency for the Prohibition of Nuclear Weapons in Latin America and the Caribbean (#00554)
- ♦ Agência para a Proscrição de Armas Nucleares na América Latina e no Caribe (#00554)
- ♦ Agencia Suiza para el Desarrollo y la Cooperación (internationally oriented national body)
- ♦ Agencija Euratoma za Opskrbu (#05617)
- ♦ Agencija za Oskrbo Euratom (#05617)
- ♦ Agencja Dostaw Euratomu (#05617)
- ♦ Agency for Christian Literature Development (inactive)

♦ Agency for the Cooperation of Energy Regulators (ACER) 00552

Main Office Trg republike 3, 1000 Ljubljana, Slovenia. T. +38682053400. Fax +38682053412. E-mail: info@acer.europa.eu.
URL: http://www.acer.europa.eu/

History Established 13 Jul 2009, by Regulation (EC) No 713/2009 of *European Parliament (EP, #08146)* and *Council of the European Union (#04895)*. Officially inaugurated 4 Mar 2011, Ljubljana (Slovenia). Took over functions of *European Regulators Group for Electricity and Gas (ERGEG, inactive)*. A decentralized agency of *European Union (EU, #08967)*. **Aims** Complement and coordinate the work of national energy regulators at EU level; work towards completion of the single EU energy market for electricity and natural gas. **Structure** Board of Regulators, consisting of senior representatives of national regulatory authorities (NRAs) for energy of the 28 member states. Administrative Board, appointed by European institutions. Board of Appeal is independent from ACER's administrative and regulatory structure, and deals with complaints lodged against ACER decisions. Departments (5): Director's Office; Administration; Electricity; Gas; Market Monitoring. Working Groups (4): Implementation, Monitoring and Procedures; Monitoring, Integrity and Transparency; Electricity; Gas. Expert Groups. **Staff** Permanent staff and experts seconded by NRAs. **Finance** Financed from: general budget of *European Union (EU, #08967)*. Budget (2014): euro 10,880,000. **Activities** Standards/guidelines; research and development; monitoring/evaluation; events/meetings. **Events** *Workshop on Conditional* Brussels (Belgium) 2018, *Regular Forum* Busan (Korea Rep) 2018, *Joint Conference* Brussels (Belgium) 2017. **Publications** Annual Activity Report.
Members Governments of 27 countries:
Austria, Belgium, Bulgaria, Croatia, Cyprus, Czechia, Denmark, Estonia, Finland, France, Germany, Greece, Hungary, Ireland, Italy, Latvia, Lithuania, Luxembourg, Malta, Netherlands, Poland, Portugal, Romania, Slovakia, Slovenia, Spain, Sweden.
IGO Relations Audited by: *European Court of Auditors (#06854)*. **NGO Relations** Member of (1): *EU Agencies Network (EUAN, #05564)*. [2020/XJ2738/**E***]

- ♦ Agency Coordinating Body for Afghan Relief (internationally oriented national body)
- ♦ Agency for the Development and Coordination of International Relations (internationally oriented national body)
- ♦ Agency for European Integration and Economic Development (internationally oriented national body)
- ♦ Agency for International Cooperation and Local Development in the Mediterranean (inactive)
- ♦ Agency for International Development / see United States Agency for International Development
- ♦ Agency for International Development / see Fédération des Agences Internationales pour le Développement (#09414)
- ♦ Agency for the International Promotion of French Technology and Trade / see Agence française pour le développement international des entreprises

♦ Agency for International Trade Information and Cooperation (AITIC) 00553

Agence de coopération et d'information pour le commerce international (ACICI) – Agencia de Información y de Cooperación para el Comercio Internacional

Contact address not obtained. T. +41229103150. Fax +41229103151.

History 1998. Re-established in 2004, as an intergovernmental organization to assist resource-constrained countries to have more active participation in the Multilateral Trading System and other international trade matters. **Aims** Strengthen the capacity of less-advantaged country missions in Geneva (Switzerland) to lead a more effective trade *diplomacy*; assist the less-advantaged countries (LACs) to benefit from the multilateral trading system through a more active participation in the activities and negotiations of the WTO and other trade-related international organizations; provide trade-related technical assistance to the less-advantages countries (LACs) and countries without permanent representation in Geneva, ie the Non-resident countries. **Structure** Council of Representatives; Executive Board; External Auditors; Secretariat, headed by Executive Director. **Languages** English, French, Spanish. **Staff** 10.00 FTE, paid. **Finance** 7 sponsoring members: Denmark; Finland; Ireland; Netherlands; Sweden; Switzerland; UK. **Activities** Provides assistance to members and other resource-constrained countries, giving priority to the least developed countries. Type of assistance: personalized assistance on demand; organization of (occasionally in collaboration with other institutions) seminars, training sessions, workshops and meetings; preparation on demand of background notes, information briefs and ad-hoc documents on topics relating to international trade and development; support to WTO members and observers without a permanent mission in Geneva through "non-resident" unit. **Publications** *Glossary of Commonly Used International Trade Terminology with Particular Reference to the WTO* in English, French, Macedonian, Portuguese, Russian, Spanish.
Members Sponsoring in 7 countries:
Denmark, Finland, Ireland, Netherlands, Sweden, Switzerland, UK.
Participating in 54 countries:
Afghanistan, Algeria, Antigua-Barbuda, Barbados, Benin, Bhutan, Bolivia, Burundi, Cambodia, Cape Verde, Central African Rep, Chad, Congo Brazzaville, Congo DR, Cuba, Dominica, Dominican Rep, Ecuador, Ethiopia, Gabon, Gambia, Georgia, Guatemala, Guinea, Guyana, Haiti, Honduras, Jamaica, Jordan, Kyrgyzstan, Laos, Madagascar, Mali, Mauritania, Mauritius, Moldova, Mongolia, Montenegro, Morocco, Mozambique, Nicaragua, Nigeria, Rwanda, Samoa, Sri Lanka, St Lucia, Suriname, Togo, Trinidad-Tobago, Tunisia, Uganda, Vanuatu, Yemen, Zambia.
In the process of accession, 6 countries:
Burkina Faso, El Salvador, Nepal, Paraguay, Senegal, Sudan.
IGO Relations Collaborates closely with: *International Trade Centre (ITC, #15703)*; *UNDP (#20292)*; *United Nations Economic Commission for Africa (ECA, #20554)*; *United Nations Economic Commission for Europe (UNECE, #20555)*; *World Intellectual Property Organization (WIPO, #21593)*. Observer status at: *UNCTAD (#20285)*; WIPO Intergovernmental Committee on Intellectual Property and Genetic Resources, Traditional Knowledge and Folklore. Memorandum of Understanding with: *Organisation of Eastern Caribbean States (OECS, #17804)*; *Organisation internationale de la Francophonie (OIF, #17809)*. Close working relations with: *Organisation of African, Caribbean and Pacific States (OACPS, #17796)*; *African Intellectual Property Organization (#00344)*; *Commonwealth Secretariat (#04362)*; *Southern African Customs Union (SACU, #19842)*. *Administrative Tribunal of the International Labour Organization (ILO Tribunal, #00118)* is competent to settle disputes. **NGO Relations** Observer status at: *Inter-Parliamentary Union (IPU, #15961)* Conference on the WTO. Memorandum of understanding with: *Africa Community Technical Service (ACTS)*. Collaborates with: *IDEAS Centre*; *International Centre for Trade and Sustainable Development, Geneva (ICTSD, #12524)*; *Oxfam International (#17922)*. [2019/XG6704/t/**F***]

- ♦ Agency for the Prohibition of Nuclear Weapons in Latin America / see Agency for the Prohibition of Nuclear Weapons in Latin America and the Caribbean (#00554)

♦ Agency for the Prohibition of Nuclear Weapons in Latin America and the Caribbean 00554

Organisme pour l'interdiction des armes nucléaires en Amérique latine et dans les Caraïbes – Organismo para la Proscripción de las Armas Nucleares en la América Latina y el Caribe (OPANAL) – Agência para a Proscrição de Armas Nucleares na América Latina e no Caribe

SG C/ Milton 61, Colonia Anzures, Alcaldía M Hidalgo, 11590 Mexico City CDMX, Mexico. T. +525552552914 – +525552554198. Fax +525552553748. E-mail: adm@opanal.org – info@opanal.org.
URL: https://www.opanal.org/

History 2 Sep 1969, Mexico. Established following depositing of the 11th ratification of *Treaty for the Prohibition of Nuclear Weapons in Latin America and the Caribbean (Treaty of Tlatelolco, 1967)*, 25 Apr 1969, and earlier preparatory meetings: *Preliminary Meeting on Denuclearization of Latin America (REUPRAL)*; *Preparatory Commission for the Denuclearization of Latin America (COPREDAL)*; *Preliminary Meeting of OPANAL (REOPANAL)*.

The Treaty was open for signature by: (a) all the Latin American republics; (b) all other sovereign States situated in their entirety south of latitude 35 degrees north in the Western hemisphere; and all such States which become sovereign, when they have been admitted by the General Conference. In accordance with Article 28 of the Treaty, it enters into force among the States that have ratified it as soon as: (a) all the Latin American Republics have deposited the instruments of ratification; (b) all extra continental States have signed and ratified both Additional Protocols, and (c) Safeguards Agreements are concluded with IAEA by all ratifiers; unless the right to waive these requirements is declared by the ratifier State. On fulfillment of requirements of article 28, paragraph 1, the zone of application will become that area situated in the Western hemisphere within the following limits (except the continental part of the territory of the United States of America and its territorial waters): from a point located at 35 degrees North latitude, 75 degrees West longitude, directly southward to a point at 30 degrees North latitude, 75 degrees West longitude; from there directly eastward to a point at 30 degrees North latitude, 50 degrees West longitude; from there, along a loxodromic line to a point at 5 degrees North latitude, 20 degrees West longitude; from there, directly southward to a point at 60 degrees South latitude, 20 degrees West longitude; from there, directly westward to a point at 60 degrees South latitude, 115 degrees West longitude; from there, directly northward to a point at 0 degree latitude, 115 degrees West longitude; from there, along a loxodromic line to a point at 35 degrees North latitude, 150 degrees West longitude; from there, directly eastward to a point at 35 degrees North latitude 75 degrees West longitude. A number of States have waived Article 28 and currently apply the Treaty within their own territorial limits.
Additional Protocol I has been signed and ratified by France, the Netherlands, United Kingdom, United States. Additional Protocol II has been signed and ratified by China, France, Russia (undertaking obligations of the former USSR), United Kingdom, United States. The following amendments have been made to the Treaty: 1. to amend the legal denomination of the Treaty, giving it its current full title; 2. to make possible the entry to the *System of Tlatelolco* countries previously impeded from doing so; 3. to reassure confidentiality of industrial secrets by requesting the International Atomic Energy Agency to carry out special inspections referred to under the Treaty. Former names and other names: *Agency for the Prohibition of Nuclear Weapons in Latin America* – former (2 Sep 1969 to 1985); *Organisme pour l'interdiction des armes nucléaires en Amérique latine* – former (2 Sep 1969 to 1985); *Organismo para la Proscripción de las Armas Nucleares en la América Latina* – former (2 Sep 1969 to 1985); *Agência para a Proscrição de Armas Nucleares na América Latina* – former (2 Sep 1969 to 1985).
Aims Contribute towards ending the armaments race, especially in the field of nuclear weapons, and towards strengthening a world at peace, based on the sovereign equality of States, mutual respect and good neighbourliness. Promote the total prohibition of the use and manufacture of nuclear weapons and weapons of mass destruction of every type. Assure the principle of an acceptable balance of mutual responsibilities and duties for the nuclear and non-nuclear powers. Strengthen the peace and security of the hemisphere, and make imperative that the legal prohibition of nuclear war should be strictly observed in practice if the survival of civilization and of mankind itself is to be assured. Proclaim that nuclear weapons constitute, through the persistence of the radioactivity they release, an attack on the integrity of the human species and ultimately may even render the whole earth uninhabitable, that general and complete disarmament under effective international control is a vital matter which all the peoples of the world equally demand to assure that nuclear energy should be used in the region exclusively for peaceful purposes and that the Latin American countries should use their right to the greatest and most equitable possible access to this energy in order to expedite the economic and social development of their people.
Ensure compliance with the obligations of the Treaty, be responsible for the electing of periodic or extraordinary consultations among Member States on matters relating to the purposes, measures and procedures set forth in the Treaty and to the supervision of compliance with the obligations arising from the Treaty of Tlatelolco, signed in 1967; ensure the absence of nuclear weapons in the Zone of application set forth in the Treaty; contribute to the movement against proliferation of nuclear weapons; promote general and complete disarmament; prevent the testing, use, manufacture, production or acquisition by any means whatsoever of any nuclear weapons, by the Parties themselves directly or indirectly, on behalf of any one else or in any other way; prevent the receipt, storage, installation, deployment and any form of possession of any nuclear weapons, directly or indirectly, by the Parties themselves, by any one on their behalf or in any other way; refrain from engaging, encouraging or authorizing, directly or indirectly, or in any way participating in the testing, use, manufacture, production, possession or control of any nuclear weapons.
Structure General Conference (meeting every 2 year in regular sessions); Council; Secretariat. Committee on Contributions and Administrative and Budgetary Matters (CCAAP). **Languages** English, French, Portuguese, Spanish. **Staff** 8.00 FTE, paid. **Finance** Apportioned contributions from member States. **Activities** Events/meetings. **Events** *General Conference* Mexico City (Mexico) 2021, *General Conference* Mexico City (Mexico) 2019, *Biennial General Conference* Mexico City (Mexico) 2017, *Biennial General Conference* Mexico City (Mexico) 2015, *Biennial General Conference* Buenos Aires (Argentina) 2013.
Members States having fully ratified the Treaty and waived Article 28 (33):
Antigua-Barbuda, Argentina, Bahamas, Barbados, Belize, Bolivia, Brazil, Chile, Colombia, Costa Rica, Cuba, Dominica, Dominican Rep, Ecuador, El Salvador, Grenada, Guatemala, Guyana, Haiti, Honduras, Jamaica, Mexico, Nicaragua, Panama, Paraguay, Peru, St Kitts-Nevis, St Lucia, St Vincent-Grenadines, Suriname, Trinidad-Tobago, Uruguay, Venezuela.
IGO Relations Observer status with (2): *ECOSOC (#05331)*; *United Nations (UN, #20515)*. Memorandum of Understanding with (1): *African Commission on Nuclear Energy (AFCONE, #00256)*. Cooperates with (7): *Comisión Permanente del Pacífico Sur (CPPS, #04141)*; *Comprehensive Nuclear-Test-Ban Treaty Organization (CTBTO, #04420)*; *International Atomic Energy Agency (IAEA, #12294)*; *Latin American Energy Organization (#16313)*; *Pacific Islands Forum Secretariat (#17970)*; *United Nations Commission on Crime Prevention and Criminal Justice (CCPCJ, #20530)*; *United Nations Regional Centre for Peace, Disarmament and Development in Latin America and the Caribbean (UNLIREC, #20618)*. [2023/XD0031/**D***]

♦ Agency for the Promotion of European Research, Rome (internationally oriented national body)

♦ Agency for Public Health Education Accreditation (APHEA) 00555

Office Av de l'Armée 10, 1040 Brussels, Belgium. T. +3227350890.
URL: http://www.aphea.net/

History Founded by a consortium composed of the following organizations: *Association of Schools of Public Health in the European Region (ASPHER, #02904)*; *European Public Health Association (EUPHA, #08298)*; *EuroHealthNet (#05693)*; *European Public Health Alliance (EPHA, #08297)*; *European Health Management Association (EHMA, #07458)*. Registered in accordance with Belgian law. **Aims** Accredit Master of Public health programmes; contribute to quality assurance and improvement of public health and global health education and training. **Structure** General Assembly; Board of Directors; Appeals Committee; Reviewers' Pool; Board of Accreditation; Review Teams; Secretariat. **Languages** English, French. **Staff** 1.50 FTE, paid. **Finance** Accreditation fees. **Activities** Certification/accreditation; training/education. [2021/XJ8764/**E**]

♦ Agency for the Safety of Aerial Navigation in Africa and Madagascar 00556

Agence pour la sécurité de la navigation aérienne en Afrique et à Madagascar (ASECNA)
Contact 32-38 avenue Jean Jaurés, BP 3144, Dakar, Senegal. T. +221338496600. Fax +221338234654.
General: http://www.asecna.aero/

History 12 Dec 1959, Saint Louis (Senegal), on signature of a a convention, which was subsequently superseded by *Dakar Convention on the Safety of Aerial Navigation in Africa and Madagascar*, signed 25 Oct 1974, Dakar, amended 1987, Dakar. ASECNA was set up in the framework of the previous *African and Mauritian Common Organization (OCAM, inactive)*. **Aims** Provide services necessary to guarantee the regularity and safety of flights of aircraft and of general air traffic in the territories of member states; manage members' airspace and those airspace for which the members have been vested with responsibility for meteorological and air traffic services. **Structure** Supervisory Ministers' Committee, consisting of one representative of each Member State. Governing Council, comprising one representative of each Member State. General Manager. Financial Controller. Agency Representative in each Member State. Audit Committee. **Staff** 7.00 FTE, paid. **Activities** Provides technical and air traffic information, in-flight information, weather forecasts and reports, air traffic control services. Runs Civil Aviation and Meteorology Schools: *Ecole africaine de la météorologie et de l'aviation civile (EAMAC, #05295)* in Niamey (Niger); *Ecole régionale de sécurité incendie (ERSI, no recent information)* in Douala (Cameroon); *Regional School for Aerial Navigation and Management (#18809)* in Dakar (Senegal). Organizes meetings and colloquia. **Events** *Seminar on cost-recovery of aeronautical meteorological service* Dakar (Senegal) 2006, *Forum* Dakar (Senegal) 1998. **Publications** *Sécurité Aviation* (3 a year); *ASECNA Infos* – internal.
Members Governments of 17 countries:
Benin, Burkina Faso, Cameroon, Central African Rep, Chad, Comoros, Congo Brazzaville, Côte d'Ivoire, Equatorial Guinea, Gabon, Guinea-Bissau, Madagascar, Mali, Mauritania, Niger, Senegal, Togo.
IGO Relations Working relations with: *International Telecommunication Union (ITU, #15673)*. Consultative Status with: *International Civil Aviation Organization (ICAO, #12581)*. Close cooperation with: *EUROCONTROL (#05667)*. [2015/XE4873/**D***]

♦ Agency for Technical Cooperation and Development (internationally oriented national body)
♦ Agency for Technical, Industrial and Economic Cooperation / see Agence française pour le développement international des entreprises
♦ Agenda 21 – Global Action Plan for Environment and Development in the 21st Century (inactive)
♦ **AGENDA** Actions for Genuine Democratic Alternatives (#00097)
♦ Agentia de Aprovizionare a Euratom (#05617)
♦ Agentjia Europeanã pentru Produse Chimice (#06523)
♦ Agentur für Europäische Integration und Wirtschaftliche Entwicklung (internationally oriented national body)
♦ Agentur der Europäischen Union für Gründrechte (#08969)
♦ Agenzia di Approvvigionamento dell'Euratom (#05617)
♦ Agenzia Europea dell'Ambiente (#06995)
♦ Agenzia Europea per l'Informazione e la Consulenza dei Giovani (#09142)
♦ Agenzia Europea per la Sicurezza Aerea (#08978)
♦ Agenzia Europea per la Sicurezza Marittima (#07744)
♦ Agenzia Europea delle Sostanze Chimiche / see European Chemicals Agency (#06523)
♦ Agenzia Europea per le Sostanze Chimiche (#06523)
♦ Agenzia per la Promozione della Ricerca Europea, Roma (internationally oriented national body)
♦ Agenzija Ghall-Provvista ta' l-Euratom (#05617)
♦ **AGEPAR** Association des Gestionnaires et Partenaires Africains de la Route (#02626)

♦ AGE Platform Europe 00557

SG Av de Tervuren 168, boite 2, 1150 Brussels, Belgium. T. +3222801470. Fax +3222801522. E-mail: info@age-platform.eu.
URL: https://www.age-platform.eu/

History Jan 2001. Founded by *European Commission (EC, #06633)* in collaboration with *Eurolink Age (inactive)*, *European Platform of Seniors' Organizations (EPSO, no recent information)* and *Fédération internationale des associations de personnes âgées (FIAPA, #09609)*. Former names and other names: *AGE European Older People's Platform* – former; *Plate-forme européenne des personnes agées* – former. Registration: Banque-Carrefour des Entreprises, No/ID: 0475.620.296, Start date: 27 Sep 2001, Belgium; EU Transparency Register, No/ID: 16549972091-86, Start date: 29 Jul 2009. **Aims** Voice and promote the interests of people over 50 in the European Union. **Structure** General Assembly; Executive Committee; Council of Administration; Accreditation Committee; Brussels Section; Task Forces (7); Policy Coordination Groups (2). **Languages** English, French. **Staff** 13.50 FTE, paid. **Finance** Sources: donations; grants; members' dues. Supported by: *European Commission (EC, #06633)*. **Activities** Awareness raising; events/meetings; advocacy/lobbying/activism; training/education. **Events** *European Retirement Week | Pension Adequacy and Value for Money in the Time of Financial Repression* Brussels (Belgium) 2022, *Human rights for All Ages Conference* 2021, *Adapting European Cities to Population Ageing Conference* Brussels (Belgium) 2020, *Joint Online Conference* Brussels (Belgium) 2020, *Annual Conference* Brussels (Belgium) 2018. **Publications** *CoverAGE* (11 a year) in English – online magazine.
Members Full; Observer; European. Full in 26 countries:
Austria, Belgium, Bulgaria, Croatia, Cyprus, Czechia, Denmark, Estonia, Finland, France, Germany, Greece, Hungary, Ireland, Italy, Latvia, Lithuania, Malta, Netherlands, Poland, Portugal, Slovakia, Slovenia, Spain, Sweden, UK.
Observer in 12 countries:
Albania, France, Germany, Ireland, Italy, Japan, Portugal, Spain, Switzerland, Türkiye, UK, USA.
Included in the above, 1 organization listed in this Yearbook:
AARP International.
European Federations (5):
EURAG – European Federation of Older Persons (#05597); *European Senior Organization (ESO, #08465)*; *European Seniors' Union (ESU, #08466)*; *Fédération internationale des associations de personnes âgées (FIAPA, #09609)*; Nordic Older People's Organisation (NOPO).
European Associations (4):
European Ageing Network (EAN, #05841); *Group of European Retired Staff and Pensioners from Savings Banks, Banks and Related Institutions (#10777)*; *Older Women's Network – Europe (OWN Europe, #17716)*; *Seniors of the European Public Service (SEPS, #19229)*.
Consultative Status Consultative status granted from: *Council of Europe (CE, #04881)* (Participatory Status); *ECOSOC (#05331)* (Special). **NGO Relations** Member of (7): *Citizens for Europe (CFEU, #03956)*; *EU Alliance for a democratic, social and sustainable European Semester (EU Semester Alliance, #05565)*; *European Anti-Poverty Network (EAPN, #05908)*; *European Coalition for Vision (ECV)*; *European Public Health Alliance (EPHA, #08297)*; *Global Alliance for the Rights of Older People (#10226)*; *Social Platform (#19344)*. [2022/XF6346/y/**F**]

♦ AGERA – Association des géophysiciens en exploration et recherches en Afrique de l'Ouest (inactive)
♦ AGES – African Gerontological Society (inactive)
♦ **AGES** Arbeitsgemeinschaft Europäischer Stadtmissionen (#06263)
♦ AGES – Australasian Gynaecological Endoscopy and Surgery (internationally oriented national body)
♦ **AGESCO** Arab Geophysical Exploration Services Company (#00968)
♦ Age UK (internationally oriented national body)
♦ **AGF** African Greens Federation (#00331)
♦ **AGF** ASEAN Golf Federation (#01193)
♦ AGF – Asian Games Federation (inactive)
♦ AGFI – African Green Foundation International (unconfirmed)
♦ **AGFUND** Arab Gulf Programme for United Nations Development Organizations (#00971)

♦ Aggregates Europe (UEPG) 00558

Union européenne des producteurs de granulats (UEPG) – Europäischer Verband der Kies-, Sand- und Schotterproduzenten
SG Square de Meeûs 38/40, 1000 Brussels, Belgium. T. +3222335300. E-mail: secretariat@uepg.eu.
Pres address not obtained.
URL: http://www.uepg.eu/

History 24 Sep 1987. Former names and other names: *European Aggregates Association* – former. Registration: Banque-Carrefour des Entreprises, No/ID: 0880.755.545, Start date: 14 Apr 2006, Belgium; EU Transparency Register, No/ID: 15340821653-49, Start date: 7 May 2009. **Aims** Identify EU initiatives and policies that are likely to impact on European aggregates producers; provide information; positively promote the profile and image of the European aggregates industry. **Structure** Delegates Assembly; Board; General Secretariat; Committees (4); Task Forces (7); Working Groups (3). **Languages** English, French, German. **Activities** Awards/prizes/competitions; events/meetings; politics/policy/regulatory. **Events** *Delegates Assembly* Kiel (Germany) 2021, *General Assembly* Barcelona (Spain) 2018, *General Assembly* Vienna (Austria) 2017, *General Assembly* Lisbon (Portugal) 2011, *General Assembly* Oslo (Norway) 2009. **Publications** *UEPG Annual Review.*
Members Organizations in 26 countries:
Austria, Belgium, Cyprus, Denmark, Estonia, Finland, France, Germany, Greece, Hungary, Ireland, Israel, Italy, Luxembourg, Netherlands, Norway, Poland, Portugal, Romania, Slovakia, Spain, Sweden, Switzerland, Türkiye, UK, Ukraine.
NGO Relations Member of (5): *Construction 2050 Alliance (#04760)*; *Construction Products Europe AISBL (#04761)*; *European Network on Silica (NEPSI, #08001)*; *Global Aggregates Information Network (GAIN)*; *Industry4Europe (#11181)*. Cooperates with (1): *Comité européen de normalisation (CEN, #04162)*. [2023.02.28/XD2532/**D**]

♦ **AGI** Africa Governance Institute (#00178)
♦ AGI – African Gender Institute (internationally oriented national body)
♦ **AGI** Alliance graphique internationale (#00684)
♦ AGI – Asian Growth Research Institute (internationally oriented national body)
♦ AGICOA Alliance / see Association for the International Collective Management of Audiovisual Works (#02658)
♦ **AGICOA** Association for the International Collective Management of Audiovisual Works (#02658)
♦ **AGID** Association of Geoscientists for International Development (#02623)
♦ **AGIFORS** Airline Group of IFORS (#00605)

♦ Agile Alliance 00559

Main Office 6525 Idumea Rd, Corryton TN 37721, USA.
URL: http://www.agilealliance.org/

Aims Support individuals and organizations who use Agile approaches to develop *software*. **Finance** Members' dues. **Events** *International Conference on Agile Software Development* Corryton, TN (USA) 2020, *International Conference on Agile Software Development* Montréal, QC (Canada) 2019, *Singapore Conference* Singapore (Singapore) 2013, *Agile conference* Salt Lake City, UT (USA) 2011, *Annual Australian conference on Agile software development* Sydney, NSW (Australia) 2011. **Publications** *Better Software* – newsletter.
Members User groups (67) in 24 countries:
Argentina, Australia, Bangladesh, Belgium, Brazil, Canada, Denmark, France, Germany, India, Ireland, Israel, Italy, Japan, Korea Rep, Luxembourg, Netherlands, New Zealand, Spain, Sri Lanka, Sweden, Switzerland, UK, USA. [2020/XM0313/**F**]

♦ **AGILE** Association of Geographic Information Laboratories for Europe (#02622)
♦ Agile Business Consortium (internationally oriented national body)
♦ Agile International (internationally oriented national body)
♦ AGIOMONDO (internationally oriented national body)
♦ AGIR abcd / see Association générale des intervenants retraités
♦ AGIRabcd – Association générale des intervenants retraités (internationally oriented national body)
♦ Agir autrement pour le développement en Afrique (internationally oriented national body)
♦ Agir ensemble pour les droits de l'homme / see Agir ensemble pour les droits humains
♦ Agir ensemble pour les droits humains (internationally oriented national body)
♦ Agir pour les femmes en situation précaire (internationally oriented national body)
♦ AGIS – Afrikagrupperna i Sverige (internationally oriented national body)
♦ **AGISEE** Association for Geospatial Information in South-East Europe (#02624)
♦ AGI Society – Artificial General Intelligence Society (unconfirmed)
♦ Agita Mundo – Global Physical Activity Promotion Network / see Agita Mundo Network (#00560)

♦ Agita Mundo Network 00560

Central Coordination CELAFISCS, Rua Heloisa Pamplona 279, sala 31, CEP 09520-320, Bairro Fundação, São Caetano do Sul SP, 09520-320, Brazil. T. +551142298980. Fax +551142299643.
Chair address not obtained.
URL: http://www.panh.ch/agitamundo/

History Oct 2002, Sao Paulo (Brazil). Full title: *Agita Mundo – Global Physical Activity Promotion Network*. **Aims** Promote *physical activity* as healthy behaviour for people of all countries; stimulate research; encourage information dissemination on health benefits of physical activity and effective strategies to increase physical activity; advocate for physical activity and health; support development of national and local programmes and networks for physical activity promotion. **Structure** Executive Board. Advisory Board. **Events** *Annual Meeting* Rio de Janeiro (Brazil) 2014, *Annual Meeting* Indianapolis, IN (USA) 2013, *Annual Meeting* Sydney, NSW (Australia) 2012, *Annual Meeting* Amsterdam (Netherlands) 2011, *Annual Meeting* Sao Paulo (Brazil) 2010.
Members Networks in 72 countries. Membership countries not specified. Regional networks (4):
Regional networks (4):
African Physical Activity Network (AFPAN, #00416); Asia Pacific Physical Activity Network (APPAN, no recent information); HEPA Europe (#10909); Physical Activity Network of the Americas (PANA, #18366).
NGO Relations Cooperates with: *International Society for Physical Activity and Health (ISPAH, #15365).* [2015/XJ0673/**F**]

♦ **AGLINET** Agricultural Libraries Network (#00571)

♦ Aglow International 00561

Acting Treas PO Box 1749, Edmonds WA 98020-1749, USA. T. +14252750215 – +14257757282. Fax +14257789615. E-mail: aglow@aglow.org.
Street Address 123 2nd Ave South, Suite 100, Edmonds WA 98020-1749, USA.
URL: http://www.aglow.org/

History 1967. Former names and other names: *Women's Aglow Fellowship International (WAFI)* – former (1967); *Aglow International – A Network of Caring Women* – former; *Aglow International – Every nation touched. Every heart changed* – full title. Registration: 501(c)(3) Charitable Nonprofit, USA. **Aims** Carry the truth of the Kingdom that: restores people to a radiant place of relationship with *God* and one another; breaks the tyranny of oppression; brings freedom and empowerment. **Structure** International Board of Directors; International Regional Committees; National Boards and Committees. **Languages** English, French, Portuguese, Spanish. **Staff** 19.00 FTE, paid. 15,000 volunteers worldwide. **Activities** Networking/liaising; training/education. **Events** *Conference* St Louis, MO (USA) 2022, *International Conference* Jerusalem (Israel) 2019, *Annual Conference* San Diego, CA (USA) 2016, *US Conference* San Diego, CA (USA) 2016, *Annual Conference* Indianapolis, IN (USA) 2015. **Publications** Books; training and resource materials; brochures; CD-ROMs; DVDs; MP3s; social media. **Members** Active groups in 172 countries. Membership countries not specified. [2023.02.15/XF5542/**F**]

♦ Aglow International – Every nation touched. Every heart changed / see Aglow International (#00561)
♦ Aglow International – A Network of Caring Women / see Aglow International (#00561)
♦ AGMA – American Gear Manufacturers Association (internationally oriented national body)
♦ **AGMARK** Agricultural Market Development Trust (#00572)
♦ AGMCD – Arab Group for Muslim-Christian Dialogue (see: #16756)
♦ **AG-MGF** Alliance globale contre les MGF (#10183)
♦ **AGN** African Geoparks Network (#00328)
♦ AGN / see Africa Philanthropy Network (#00512)
♦ **AGN** Arbeitskreis Geschichte der Nachrichtendienste (#13942)
♦ AGN – European Agreement on Main Inland Waterways of International Importance (1996 treaty)

♦ AGN International 00562

International/European Executive Office 6 Hays Lane, London, EC1N 8SS, UK. T. +442079717373. E-mail: info@agn.org.
Regional Dir 13918 E Mississippi Ave, Suite 63308, Aurora CO 80012, USA. T. +13037437880.
Sr Represetnative Unit 36, Level 9, China Central Place, Tower 2, 79 Jianguo Road, Chaoyang District, 100025 Beijing, China. T. +861065800678. E-mail: asia-pacific@agn.org.
URL: http://www.agn.org/

History 1 Jan 1996, on merger of 2 previous international accounting associations. From 2002, includes membership of the former *TAG International (inactive)*. **Aims** Provide the highest level of information and professional services for member *accountancy* and *consultancy* firms and their clients worldwide. **Structure** Regions (5): Asia/Pacific; Central and South America; Europe; North America; West Asia and Africa. **Languages** English. **Staff** 12.00 FTE, paid. **Finance** Members' dues. **Activities** Events/meetings. **Events** *Annual World Congress* Barcelona (Spain) 2019, *North America Regional Meeting* Cleveland, OH (USA) 2019, *Asia-Pacific Regional Meeting* Kuala Lumpur (Malaysia) 2019, *Europe, Middle East and Africa Meeting* Limassol (Cyprus) 2019, *Central and South America Regional Meeting* Quito (Ecuador) 2019. **Publications** *World Directory* (annual). **Members** Firms (202) separate and independent accounting and consulting firms in 94 countries. Membership countries not specified. [2017/XF6635/**F**]

♦ AGOA – African Growth and Opportunity Act (internationally oriented national body)
♦ **AGOCA** Alliance of Central Asian Mountain Communities (#00662)
♦ **AGOL** Alianza Global del Ombudsperson Local (#00629)
♦ Agopuntura Senza Frontiere (#00106)

♦ AGORA Club International 00563

Pres Eyermanstraat 23, 9160 Lokeren, Belgium. T. +3293847753.
URL: http://www.agoraclubinternational.com/

History 1996, Strasbourg (France). **Aims** Link national Agora clubs providing a platform for *women* aged 42 and older to meet in a non-political and non-sectarian setting of *service* and *tolerance*. **Structure** General Meeting. Board, comprising President, Vice-President, Secretary, Treasurer and Past-President. **Languages** English. **Activities** Each individual Agora Club participates in service projects helping people who are less fortunate, especially women and children. **Events** *Conference* Marrakech (Morocco) 2019, *Conference* Ghent (Belgium) 2018. **Publications** *Electronic Newsletter* (1-2 a year).
Members National associations in 10 countries:
Belgium, Cyprus, Estonia, Finland, France, Italy, Netherlands, Romania, South Africa, Switzerland. [2013/XM2479/**E**]

♦ Agostiniani dell'Assunzione (religious order)
♦ Agostiniani – Ordine di Sant'Agostino (religious order)
♦ Agostiniani Recolletti (religious order)
♦ Agostiniani Scalzi (religious order)
♦ Agostiniani Secolari (religious order)
♦ **AGPA** Asian Group for Public Administration (#01498)
♦ **AGPAEA** Association de gestion des ports de l'Afrique de l'Est et australe (#18462)
♦ **AGPAOC** Association de gestion des ports de l'Afrique de l'Ouest et du Centre (#18463)
♦ AG-PDM / see Municipal Development Partnership for West and Central Africa (#16902)
♦ **AGRA** Alliance for a Green Revolution in Africa (#00685)
♦ Agraw Amad'lan Amazigh (internationally oriented national body)
♦ AGRE – Atlantic Gas Research Exchange (inactive)
♦ AGRECOL Afrique: Networking and Information Centre for Sustainable Agriculture in Africa (internationally oriented national body)
♦ AGRECOL Andes (internationally oriented national body)
♦ Agrecol – Association for AgriCulture and Ecology (internationally oriented national body)
♦ AGRED – African Gamebird Research, Education and Development Trust (internationally oriented national body)
♦ Agreed Declaration Relating to Atomic Energy (1945 treaty)
♦ Agreed Measures for the Conservation of Antarctic Fauna and Flora (1964 treaty)
♦ Agreement on the Abolition of Visas, 1974 (1974 treaty)
♦ Agreement on the Abolition of Visas, Apr 1970 (1970 treaty)
♦ Agreement on the Abolition of Visas, Oct 1970 (1970 treaty)
♦ Agreement on the Acceptance of Persons at the Frontier (1965 treaty)
♦ Agreement on the Action Plan for the Environmentally Sound Management of the Common Zambezi River System (1987 treaty)
♦ Agreement on Administrative Arrangements for the Perk Thnot – Cambodia – Power and Irrigation Development Project (1968 treaty)
♦ Agreement on the Adoption of the Inter-American Manual on Traffic Control Devices for Streets and Highways (1979 treaty)
♦ Agreement on Aerial Navigation with a View to the Application of Article 128 of the Treaty of Trianon (1927 treaty)
♦ Agreement on Aerial Navigation with a View to the Application of Article 144 of the Treaty of Saint-Germain-en-Laye (1927 treaty)
♦ Agreement on Aerial Navigation with a View to the Application of Article 198 of the Treaty of Versailles (1926 treaty)
♦ Agreement on Aerial Navigation with a View to the Application of Article 89 of the Treaty of Neuilly (1927 treaty)
♦ Agreement Amending the Nordic Convention of 19 November 1934 Regarding Inheritance and the Settlement of the Devolution of Property (1975 treaty)
♦ Agreement Amending the Nordic Convention of 7 November 1933 Regarding Bankruptcy (1977 treaty)
♦ Agreement on the Application among the Member States of the European Communities of the Council of Europe Convention on the Transfer of Sentenced Persons (1987 treaty)
♦ Agreement on the Application of the Most-favored-nation Clause (1934 treaty)
♦ Agreement for the Application of Safeguards (1970 treaty)
♦ Agreement on ASEAN Preferential Trading Arrangements (1977 treaty)
♦ Agreement for the Avoidance of Double Taxation and the Prevention of Fiscal Evasion with Respect to Taxes on Income and for the Encouragement of International Trade and Investment (1973 treaty)
♦ Agreement to Ban Smoking on International Passenger Flights (1994 treaty)
♦ Agreement of Caracas – Agreement on the Adoption of the Inter-American Manual on Traffic Control Devices for Streets and Highways (1979 treaty)
♦ Agreement between the Central African States Concerning the Creation of a Special Fund for the Conservation of Wild Fauna (1983 treaty)
♦ Agreement on Certain Measures to Facilitate Customs Clearance of Products Covered by the ECSC Treaty Carried by Rail (1962 treaty)
♦ Agreement on Collaboration in the Development and Exploitation of the Gas Centrifuge Process for Producing Enriched Uranium (1970 treaty)
♦ Agreement on Commercial Relations (1911 treaty)
♦ Agreement on the Common Effective Preferential Tariff (1992 treaty)
♦ Agreement on a Comprehensive Political Settlement of the Cambodia Conflict (1991 treaty)
♦ Agreement Concerning the Abolition of the Visa Requirement, Sep 1970 (1970 treaty)
♦ Agreement Concerning Acceptance of Aircraft Pilots' and Navigators' Certificates in Lieu of National Passports (1937 treaty)
♦ Agreement Concerning the Administration of Joint Nordic Assistance Projects in Developing Countries (1968 treaty)
♦ Agreement concerning the Adoption of Harmonized Technical United Nations Regulations for Wheeled Vehicles, Equipment and Parts which can be Fitted and/or be Used on Wheeled Vehicles and the Conditions for Reciprocal Recognition of Approvals Granted on the Basis of these United Nations Regulations (1958 treaty)
♦ Agreement Concerning the Adoption of Uniform Conditions for Periodical Technical Inspections of Wheeled Vehicles and the Reciprocal Recognition of Such Inspections (1997 treaty)
♦ Agreement Concerning Amendments to the Convention Regarding the Collection of Maintenance Allowances (1953 treaty)
♦ Agreement Concerning the Application of the Agreement of 11 February 1977, in the Field of Gas-cooled Reactor Concepts and Technology (1977 treaty)
♦ Agreement Concerning the Application of the European Convention on the Suppression of Terrorism among the Member States of the European Communities (1979 treaty)
♦ Agreement Concerning British Military Cemeteries (1917 treaty)
♦ Agreement Concerning the Carriage of Persons and Goods by Road, 1958 (1958 treaty)
♦ Agreement Concerning the Carriage of Persons and Goods by Road, 1971 (1971 treaty)
♦ Agreement Concerning Cash-on-delivery Items, 1952 (1952 treaty)
♦ Agreement Concerning Cash-on-delivery Items, 1957 (1957 treaty)
♦ Agreement Concerning Cash-on-delivery Items, 1964 (1964 treaty)
♦ Agreement Concerning Cash-on-delivery Items, 1969 (1969 treaty)
♦ Agreement Concerning the Collection of Bills, 1964 (1964 treaty)
♦ Agreement Concerning the Collection of Bills, 1969 (1969 treaty)
♦ Agreement Concerning the Collection of Bills, Drafts, 1952 (1952 treaty)
♦ Agreement Concerning the Collection of Bills, Drafts, 1957 (1957 treaty)
♦ Agreement Concerning a Common Labour Market (1954 treaty)
♦ Agreement Concerning a Common Nordic Labour Market (1982 treaty)
♦ Agreement Concerning a Common Scandinavian Labour Market for Dentists (1966 treaty)

- Agreement Concerning a Common Scandinavian Labour Market for Nurses (1968 treaty)
- Agreement Concerning a Common Scandinavian Labour Market for Pharmacists (1969 treaty)
- Agreement Concerning a Common Scandinavian Labour Market for Physicians (1965 treaty)
- Agreement Concerning the Conditions of Employment of Rhine Boatmen (1954 treaty)
- Agreement Concerning Cooperation (1962 treaty)
- Agreement concerning co-operation between authorities and institutions in the field of vocational rehabilitation and training for the labour market (1982 treaty)
- Agreement Concerning Cooperation to Ensure Compliance with the Regulations for Preventing the Pollution of the Sea by Oil (1967 treaty)
- Agreement Concerning Cooperation in the Field of Veterinary Science (1959 treaty)
- Agreement Concerning Cooperation in Ice-breaking (1961 treaty)
- Agreement Concerning Cooperation at Local Government Levels Across Inter-Nordic National Borders (1977 treaty)
- Agreement Concerning Cooperation in Marine Fishing (1962 treaty)
- Agreement Concerning Cooperation Over the Nordic National Frontiers between Local Authorities (1977 treaty)
- Agreement Concerning Cooperation in the Quarantine of Plants and Their Protection Against Pests and Diseases (1959 treaty)
- Agreement Concerning Cooperation for the Saving of Human Lives and Assistance to Vessels and Aircraft in Distress in the Black Sea (1956 treaty)
- Agreement Concerning Cooperation in Taking Measures Against Pollution of the Sea by Oil (1971 treaty)
- Agreement Concerning Cooperative Research in Reactor Science (1970 treaty)
- Agreement Concerning Cultural Cooperation (1971 treaty)
- Agreement Concerning Economic Development (1952 treaty)
- Agreement Concerning the Establishing of Global Technical Regulations for Wheeled Vehicles, Equipment and Parts Which Can be Fitted And/or be Used on Wheeled Vehicles (1998 treaty)
- Agreement Concerning Giro Transfers (1969 treaty)
- Agreement Concerning Helicopter Pilot Training (1977 treaty)
- Agreement Concerning Higher Education (1960 treaty)
- Agreement Concerning Insured Letters and Boxes, 1952 (1952 treaty)
- Agreement Concerning Insured Letters and Boxes, 1957 (1957 treaty)
- Agreement Concerning Insured Letters and Boxes, 1964 (1964 treaty)
- Agreement Concerning Insured Letters and Boxes and Detailed Regulations (1969 treaty)
- Agreement Concerning Interim Arrangements Relating to Polymetallic Nodules of the Deep Sea Bed (1982 treaty)
- Agreement Concerning International Direct Goods Traffic by Rail and Water (1959 treaty)
- Agreement Concerning the International Savings Bank Service, 1957 (1957 treaty)
- Agreement Concerning the International Savings Bank Service, 1964 (1964 treaty)
- Agreement Concerning the International Savings Bank Service, 1969 (1969 treaty)
- Agreement Concerning the Legal Status and Privileges of International Specialized Organizations for Economic Cooperation (1966 treaty)
- Agreement Concerning the Legal Status of Staff Employed in Nordic Institutions (1974 treaty)
- Agreement Concerning the Liberalization of Trade in Fishing Products (1956 treaty)
- Agreement Concerning Manned Lightships Not on Their Stations (1930 treaty)
- Agreement Concerning Maritime Signals (1930 treaty)
- Agreement Concerning Measures for the Protection of the Stocks of Deep-sea Prawns (1952 treaty)
- Agreement Concerning Nordic Development Assistance Cooperation (1981 treaty)
- Agreement Concerning Population Registration (1968 treaty)
- Agreement Concerning Postal Money Orders and Postal Travellers' Cheques, 1952 (1952 treaty)
- Agreement Concerning Postal Money Orders and Postal Travellers' Cheques, 1964 (1964 treaty)
- Agreement Concerning Postal Money Orders and Postal Travellers' Cheques, 1969 (1969 treaty)
- Agreement Concerning Postal Parcels, 1952 (1952 treaty)
- Agreement Concerning Postal Parcels, 1957 (1957 treaty)
- Agreement Concerning Postal Parcels, 1964 (1964 treaty)
- Agreement Concerning Postal Parcels, 1969 (1969 treaty)
- Agreement Concerning Postal Travellers' Cheques, 1957 (1957 treaty)
- Agreement Concerning the Preparation of a Transit Card for Emigrants (1929 treaty)
- Agreement Concerning the Preservation or the Re-establishment of the Rights of Industrial Property Affected by the World War (1920 treaty)
- Agreement Concerning Protection of the Salmon in the Baltic Sea (1962 treaty)
- Agreement Concerning the Protection of the Waters of the Mediterranean Shores (1976 treaty)
- Agreement Concerning Reciprocal Assistance in the Collection of Taxes (1952 treaty)
- Agreement Concerning the Regulations of Lake Inari by Means of the Kaitakoski Hydro – Electric Power Station and Dam (1959 treaty)
- Agreement Concerning the Relationship between Compulsory Military Service and Nationality (1956 treaty)
- Agreement Concerning Research on the Effects of Radioactivity in the Sea (1961 treaty)
- Agreement Concerning the Residence of Refugees within the Meaning of the Convention Relating to the Status of Refugees (1965 treaty)
- Agreement Concerning Sickness Benefits and Benefits in Respect of Pregnancy and Confinement (1975 treaty)
- Agreement Concerning the Social Security of Rhine Boatmen, 1950 (1950 treaty)
- Agreement Concerning the Social Security of Rhine Boatmen, 1961 (1961 treaty)
- Agreement Concerning the Social Security of Rhine Boatmen, 1979 (1979 treaty)
- Agreement Concerning Specific Stability Requirements for Ro-ro Passenger Ships Undertaking Regular Scheduled International Voyages Between, to or from Designated Ports in North West Europe and the Baltic Sea (1996 treaty)
- Agreement Concerning Subscriptions to Newspapers and Periodicals, 1952 (1952 treaty)
- Agreement Concerning Subscriptions to Newspapers and Periodicals, 1957 (1957 treaty)
- Agreement Concerning Subscriptions to Newspapers and Periodicals, 1964 (1964 treaty)
- Agreement Concerning Subscriptions to Newspapers and Periodicals, 1969 (1969 treaty)
- Agreement Concerning the Suppression of the Manufacture of, Internal Trade in, and Use of, Prepared Opium, 1925 (1925 treaty)
- Agreement Concerning the Suppression of the Manufacture of, Internal Trade in, and Use of, Prepared Opium, 1946 (1946 treaty)
- Agreement Concerning the Suppression of Opium Smoking, 1931 (1931 treaty)
- Agreement Concerning the Suppression of Opium Smoking, 1946 (1946 treaty)
- Agreement Concerning Telegraph and Telephone Circuits between Bujumbura and Kigali (1970 treaty)
- Agreement Concerning Transfers of Persons Insured for Sickness Benefit and Concerning Sickness Benefit During Temporary Residence (1967 treaty)
- Agreement Concerning Transfers to and from Postal Cheque Accounts, 1957 (1957 treaty)
- Agreement Concerning Transfers to and from Postal Cheque Accounts, 1964 (1964 treaty)
- Agreement Concerning Transfers to and from Postal Cheque Accounts and Supplement Dealing with the Negotiation through Postal Cheque Accounts of Securities Made Payable at Postal Cheque Offices (1952 treaty)
- Agreement Concerning Transfers between Sick Funds and Sickness Benefits During Temporary Residence (1956 treaty)
- Agreement Concerning Uniform Rules for the Marking of Navigable Waters (1962 treaty)
- Agreement Concerning the Voluntary Contributions to be Given for the Execution of the Project to Preserve Borobudur (1973 treaty)
- Agreement Concerning the Voluntary Contributions to be Given for the Execution of the Project to Preserve and Develop the Monumental Site of Mohenjodaro (1980 treaty)
- Agreement Concerning the Voluntary Contributions to be Given for the Execution of the Project to Save the Abu Simbel Temples (1963 treaty)
- Agreement Concerning the Voluntary Contributions to be Given for the Execution of the Project to Save the Temples of Philae (1970 treaty)
- Agreement on a Concerted Action Project in the Field of Registration of Congenital Abnormalities (1979 treaty)
- Agreement concluded by Denmark, Finland, Iceland, Norway and Sweden on Admission to Higher Education (1996 treaty)
- Agreement Concluded between the Governments of El Salvador, Honduras and Guatemala, the Inter-American Institute for Cooperation on Agriculture and the OAS General Secretariat Relative to an Extension for the Technical Cooperation for Execution of the Integral Development Plan for the Border Region Shared by the Three Countries (1994 treaty)
- Agreement on the Conservation of Albatrosses and Petrels (2001 treaty)
- Agreement on the Conservation of Cetaceans of the Black Sea, Mediterranean Sea and contiguous Atlantic Area (1996 treaty)
- Agreement on the Conservation of Gorillas and Their Habitats (2007 treaty)
- Agreement on Conservation of Polar Bears (1973 treaty)
- Agreement on the Conservation of Populations of European Bats (1991 treaty)
- Agreement on the Conservation of Seals in the Wadden Sea (1990 treaty)
- Agreement on the Conservation of Small Cetaceans of the Baltic, North East Atlantic, Irish and North Seas (1992 treaty)
- Agreement on Consuls (1911 treaty)
- Agreement on the Conveyance in Transit of Deported Persons (1965 treaty)
- Agreement on Cooperation among Air Traffic Companies (1965 treaty)
- Agreement on Cooperation in Astrophysics (1979 treaty)
- Agreement for Cooperation and Consultation between the Central African States for the Conservation of Wild Fauna (1983 treaty)

◆ Agreement for cooperation in dealing with pollution of the North Sea by oil and other harmful substances (Bonn Agreement) — 00564
Accord de Bonn

Secretariat The Aspect, 12 Finsbury Square, London, EC2A 1AS, UK. T. +442074305200. E-mail: secretariat@bonnagreement.org.
URL: http://www.bonnagreement.org/
History 13 Sep 1983, Bonn (Germany FR), when agreement was signed. In force 1 Sep 1989. **Aims** Offer mutual assistance and cooperation between Member States and the European Community in combating pollution; carry out surveillance as an aid to detecting and combating pollution and preventing violations of anti-pollution regulations. **Structure** Bonn Agreement Meeting of Contracting Parties (Bonn-Germany; annual); Working Group on Operational, Technical and Scientific Questions concerning Counter Pollution Activities (OTSOPA). **Languages** English, French. **Staff** 1.50 FTE, paid. **Finance** Contributions of contracting parties. Budget (2010): pounds85,109. **Activities** Bonn Agreement Working Group on Operational, Technical and Scientific Questions concerning Counter Pollution Activities (OTSOPA) meets every autumn. **Events** Annual meeting of contracting parties Germany 2009, Annual meeting of contracting parties France 2008, Annual meeting of contracting parties Brussels (Belgium) 2007, Annual meeting of contracting parties Ostend (Belgium) 2005, Annual meeting of contracting parties York (UK) 2004. **Publications** Bonn Agreement Aerial Surveillance Handbook; Bonn Agreement Counter-Pollution Manual; North Sea Manual on Maritime Oil Pollution Offences. Annual report on aerial surveillance; ad hoc reports.
Members Signatory governments of 9 countries:
Belgium, Denmark, France, Germany, Ireland, Netherlands, Norway, Sweden, UK.
Signatory regional entity (1):
European Union (EU, #08967).
International Observers (4):
Baltic Marine Environment Protection Commission – Helsinki Commission (HELCOM, #03126); International Maritime Organization (IMO, #14102); OECD (#17693); Regional Marine Pollution Emergency Response Centre for the Mediterranean Sea (REMPEC, #18795).
IGO Relations Administration undertaken by: OSPAR Commission for the Protection of the Marine Environment of the North-East Atlantic (OSPAR Commission, #17905). [2019/XF3000/y/F*]

- Agreement on cooperation in education (treaty)
- Agreement on Cooperation among Maritime Trade Shipping Organizations (1971 treaty)
- Agreement on Cooperation in Monetary, Economic and Financial Matters (1960 treaty)
- Agreement for Cooperation in a Plan of Comprehensive Rural Development in Latin America (1966 treaty)
- Agreement on Cooperation for the Sustainable Development of the Mekong River Basin (1995 treaty)
- Agreement on Cooperation in the Technical Supervision and the Classification of Ships (1961 treaty)
- Agreement on Cooperative Assistance to Kenya (1967 treaty)
- Agreement on Cooperative Enforcement Operations Directed at Illegal Trade in Wild Fauna and Flora (1994 treaty)
- Agreement on the Co-ordination of the Distribution of Channels for Mobile Maritime Service in the Band 2065 to 2107 Khz (1980 treaty)
- Agreement for the Co-ordination, Distribution and Use of Sound Broadcasting FM Channels in the 88-108 MHz Band (1980 treaty)
- Agreement on Co-ordination of Pension Entitlement under State Pension Schemes (1973 treaty)
- Agreement on Cross-border Cooperation (2005 treaty)
- Agreement between Customs Authorities in Order to Facilitate the Procedure in the Case of Undischarged or Lost Triptychs (1931 treaty)
- Agreement Between Denmark, Finland, Iceland, Norway and Sweden on the Implementation of Certain Provisions Concerning Nationality (2002 treaty)
- Agreement between Denmark, Iceland, Norway and Sweden concerning cooperation in matters of competition (2001 treaty)
- Agreement for Dispensing with Bills of Health (1934 treaty)
- Agreement for Dispensing with Consular Visas on Bills of Health (1934 treaty)
- Agreement as to Disposition of Rights in Atomic Energy Inventions (1956 treaty)
- Agreement on Economic and Technical Cooperation (1970 treaty)
- Agreement for an Embargo on Arms for China (1919 treaty)
- Agreement on the Exchange of War Cripples between Member Countries of the Council of Europe with a View to Medical Treatment (1955 treaty)
- Agreement on the Exploitation and Conservation of the Maritime Resources of the South Pacific (1952 treaty)
- Agreement Extending the Territorial Scope of the South Pacific Commission (1951 treaty)
- Agreement on the Extension of Certain Measures Relating to Social Security (1977 treaty)
- Agreement to Facilitate the Sanitary Control of Traffic (1955 treaty)
- Agreement for Facilitating the International Circulation of Visual and Auditory Materials of an Educational, Scientific and Cultural Character (1948 treaty)
- Agreement on General Conditions for the International Carriage of Passengers by Bus (1970 treaty)
- Agreement on a Global System of Trade Preferences among Developing Countries (1988 treaty)
- Agreement on the Global Weather Experiment (1979 treaty)
- Agreement Governing the Activities of States on the Moon and other Celestial Bodies (1979 treaty)
- Agreement on Governmental Supervision of the Operation of the Aeroplanes Involved under Technical Cooperation Agreements between Air France, Lufthansa and Sabena (1976 treaty)
- Agreement on Government Procurement (1979 treaty)
- Agreement between the Governments of the Benelux Countries and the Government of the Republic of Slovenia on the Abolition of the Obligation to Obtain a Visa (1992 treaty)

- ♦ Agreement between the Governments of the Kingdom of Belgium, of the Grand Duchy of Luxembourg and of the Kingdom of the Netherlands, on the One Hand, and the Government of the Republic of Slovenia, on the other Hand, Concerning the Re-admission of Persons Who Have Entered or Resided Illegally (1992 treaty)
- ♦ Agreement between the Governments Represented at the Bermuda Telecommunication Conference (1945 treaty)
- ♦ Agreement on the Harmonisation of Fiscal Incentives to Industry (1973 treaty)
- ♦ Agreement on the History of the Liberator (1911 treaty)
- ♦ Agreement on Illicit Traffic by Sea, Implementing Article 17 of the United Nations Convention Against Illicit Traffic in Narcotic Drugs and Psychotropic Substances (1995 treaty)
- ♦ Agreement on the Implementation of Certain Provisions Concerning Nationality (1969 treaty)
- ♦ Agreement on the Implementation of a European Concerted Action Project in the Field of Metallurgy on the Topic – Materials for Desalination Plants (1971 treaty)
- ♦ Agreement on the Implementation of a European Concerted Action Project in the Field of Metallurgy on the Topic – Materials for Gas Turbines (1971 treaty)
- ♦ Agreement on the Implementation of a European Project on Pollution, on the Topic 'Analysis of Organic Micropollutants in Water' (1971 treaty)
- ♦ Agreement on the Implementation of a European Project on Pollution, on the Topic 'research into Physico-chemical Behaviour of Sulphur Dioxide in the Atmosphere' (1971 treaty)
- ♦ Agreement on the Implementation of a European Project on Pollution, on the Topic 'sewage Sludge Processing' (1971 treaty)
- ♦ Agreement on the Implementation of a European Telecommunications Project on the Topic 'aerial Network with Phase Control' (1972 treaty)
- ♦ Agreement on the Implementation of a European Telecommunications Project on the Topic: Aerials with Reduced First Side-lobes and Maximum G/T Yield (1971 treaty)
- ♦ Agreement for the Implementation of the Provisions of the United Nations Convention on the Law of the Sea Relating to the Conservation and Management of Straddling Fish Stocks and Highly Migratory Fish Stocks (1995 treaty)
- ♦ Agreement on the Importation of Educational, Scientific and Cultural Materials (1950 treaty)
- ♦ Agreement on Import Licensing Procedures (1979 treaty)
- ♦ Agreement on the International Carriage of Passengers by Road by Means of Occasional Coach and Bus Service (1982 treaty)
- ♦ Agreement on the International Carriage of Perishable Foodstuffs and on the Special Equipment to be Used for Such Carriage (1970 treaty)
- ♦ Agreement on an International Energy Program (1974 treaty)
- ♦ Agreement on the Joint Financing of Certain Air Navigation Services in Greenland and the Faeroe Islands (1956 treaty)
- ♦ Agreement on the Joint Financing of Certain Air Navigation Services in Iceland (1956 treaty)
- ♦ Agreement for Joint Financing of North Atlantic Ocean Stations (1974 treaty)
- ♦ Agreement on the Joint Regulations of Fauna and Flora (1977 treaty)
- ♦ Agreement on the Judicial Acts of Aliens (1911 treaty)
- ♦ Agreement on Literary and Artistic Property (1911 treaty)
- ♦ Agreement of Madrid for the International Registration of Trademarks (1957 treaty)
- ♦ Agreement between the Member States of the Council of Europe on the Issue to Military and Civilian War-disabled of an International Book of Vouchers for the Repair of Prosthetic and Orthopaedic Appliances (1962 treaty)
- ♦ Agreement on Minimum Requirements for the Issue and Validity of Driving Permits (1975 treaty)
- ♦ Agreement for the Mutual Safeguarding of Secrecy of Inventions Relating to Defence and for Which Applications for Patents Have Been Made (1960 treaty)
- ♦ Agreement between the Parties to the North Atlantic Treaty for Cooperation Regarding Atomic Information, 1955 (1955 treaty)
- ♦ Agreement between the Parties to the North Atlantic Treaty for Cooperation Regarding Atomic Information, 1964 (1964 treaty)
- ♦ Agreement between the Parties to the North Atlantic Treaty Regarding the Status of Their Forces (1951 treaty)
- ♦ Agreement on Patents and Privileges of Invention (1911 treaty)
- ♦ Agreement on Port State Measures to Prevent, Deter and Eliminate Illegal, Unreported and Unregulated Fishing (2009 treaty)
- ♦ Agreement on the Practical Application of the Provisions of Article 83bis of the Convention on International Civil Aviation (1994 treaty)
- ♦ Agreement on the Preparation of a Tripartite Environmental Management Programme for Lake Victoria (1994 treaty)
- ♦ Agreement on the Preservation of the Confidentiality of Data Concerning Deep Seabed Areas (1986 treaty)
- ♦ Agreement on the Privileges and Immunities of the International Atomic Energy Agency (1959 treaty)
- ♦ Agreement on the Privileges and Immunities of the International Criminal Court (2002 treaty)
- ♦ Agreement on the Privileges and Immunities of the International Tribunal for the Law of the Sea (1997 treaty)
- ♦ Agreement on Privileges and Immunities of the Organization of American States (1949 treaty)
- ♦ Agreement on Products within the Province of the European Coal and Steel Community (treaty)
- ♦ Agreement to Promote Compliance with the International Conservation and Management Measures by Fishing Vessels on the High Seas (1993 treaty)
- ♦ Agreement for the Promotion of Commercial Exchanges (1937 treaty)
- ♦ Agreement for the Prosecution and Punishment of the Major War Criminals of the European Axis (1945 treaty)
- ♦ Agreement on the Protection of Confidentiality of Data Related to Deep Sea-bed Areas for Which Application of Authorisation Has Been Made (1984 treaty)
- ♦ Agreement Providing for the Provisional Application of the Draft International Customs Conventions on Touring, on Commercial Road Vehicles and on the International Transport of Goods by Road (1949 treaty)
- ♦ Agreement for the Readmittance of Aliens Who Have Illegally Entered the Territory of Another Contracting Party (1952 treaty)
- ♦ Agreement on Reciprocal Access to Fishing in the Skagerrak and the Kattegat (1966 treaty)
- ♦ Agreement Regarding British War Cemeteries in Iraq (1935 treaty)
- ♦ Agreement Regarding British War Memorial Cemeteries and Graves in Egypt (1937 treaty)
- ♦ Agreement Regarding Certain Questions Connected with the Regime Applicable to Navigation on the Rhine (1939 treaty)
- ♦ Agreement Regarding Cooperation in the Field of Civil Aviation (1951 treaty)
- ♦ Agreement Regarding Cooperation and Mutual Assistance among National Customs Directorates (1981 treaty)
- ♦ Agreement Regarding Decennial Liability and Insurance of Certain Architects and Contractors (1979 treaty)
- ♦ Agreement Regarding Documents of Identity for Aircraft Personnel, 1938 (1938 treaty)
- ♦ Agreement Regarding Documents of Identity for Aircraft Personnel, 1939 (1939 treaty)
- ♦ Agreement Regarding Documents of Identity for Aircraft Personnel, Brussels (1938 treaty)
- ♦ Agreement Regarding Documents of Identity for Aircraft Personnel, Paris (1938 treaty)
- ♦ Agreement Regarding Financial Guarantees to Certain Airlines, 1951 (1951 treaty)
- ♦ Agreement Regarding Financial Guarantees to Certain Airlines, 1955 (1955 treaty)
- ♦ Agreement Regarding Financial Guarantees to Certain Airlines, 1959 (1959 treaty)
- ♦ Agreement Regarding the Free Right of Passage to Aircraft Over British and French Territories in the Antarctic (1938 treaty)
- ♦ Agreement Regarding Monitoring of the Stratosphere (1976 treaty)
- ♦ Agreement Regarding the Mutual Recognition of Documents of Identity for Aircraft Personnel (1938 treaty)
- ♦ Agreement Regarding Passports and Visas (1922 treaty)
- ♦ Agreement Regarding the Regulation of Plaice and Flounder Fishing in the Baltic Sea (1929 treaty)
- ♦ Agreement Regarding Rules for Recognition of Contribution Periods and Periods of Employment in the Case of Persons Covered by Unemployment Insurance Who Remove from One Country to Another (1959 treaty)
- ♦ Agreement Regarding Rules for Recognition of Qualifying Periods and the Like in Connection with the Right of Persons Covered by Unemployment Insurance to Unemployment Benefits (1976 treaty)
- ♦ Agreement Regarding Tourist Traffic (1938 treaty)
- ♦ Agreement in Regard to War Graves (1935 treaty)
- ♦ Agreement on Regional Cooperation in Combating Pollution of the South-East Pacific by Hydrocarbons or other Harmful Substances in Cases of Emergency (1981 treaty)
- ♦ Agreement on the Regulation of North Pacific Whaling (1970 treaty)
- ♦ Agreement Relating to Application of the European Convention on International Commercial Arbitration (1962 treaty)
- ♦ Agreement Relating to Cereals (1967 treaty)
- ♦ Agreement Relating to the Chinese Courts in the International Settlement at Shanghai (1930 treaty)
- ♦ Agreement Relating to Economic Cooperation (1952 treaty)
- ♦ Agreement Relating to the Establishment of a Reserve of Industrial Diamonds Upon the North American Continent (1943 treaty)
- ♦ Agreement Relating to Governmental Supervision of Airworthiness, Operation and Maintenance of Aeroplanes Involved under the Technical Cooperation Agreements between KLM, SAS, Swissair and UTA (1972 treaty)
- ♦ Agreement Relating to the Implementation of Part XI of the United Nations Convention on the Law of the Sea of 10 December 1982 (1994 treaty)
- ♦ Agreement Relating to the International Convention for Regulating the Police of the North Sea Fisheries (1955 treaty)
- ♦ Agreement Relating to a Joint Ocean Weather Station in the North Atlantic (1949 treaty)
- ♦ Agreement Relating to the Naval and Air Bases Leased to the United States of America (1941 treaty)
- ♦ Agreement Relating to the Provision and Operation of Air Traffic Services and Facilities by EUROC-ONTROL at the Central European Air Traffic Services Upper Area Control Centre (1997 treaty)
- ♦ Agreement Relating to Refugee Seamen (1957 treaty)
- ♦ Agreement Relating to Writs and Letters of Request (1952 treaty)
- ♦ Agreement Relative to the Assignment of Frequencies on the North American Continent (1929 treaty)
- ♦ Agreement Relative to Radiography (1911 treaty)
- ♦ Agreement on the Rescue of Astronauts, the Return of Astronauts and the Return of Objects Launched into Outer Space (1968 treaty)
- ♦ Agreement on Research Participation and Technical Exchange in the In-pile CABRI and Annular Core Pulsed Reactor Research Programs Related to Fast Reactor Safety (1978 treaty)
- ♦ Agreement on the Resolution of Practical Problems with Respect to Deep Seabed Mining Areas (1987 treaty)
- ♦ Agreement with Respect to Corn, Sorghum, Ordinary Wheat, Rice and Poultry (1962 treaty)
- ♦ Agreement Respecting Documents of Identity for Aircraft Personnel, 1940 (1940 treaty)
- ♦ Agreement Respecting Facilities to be Given to Merchant Seamen for the Treatment Venereal Disease (1924 treaty)
- ♦ Agreement Respecting Internal Revolutions and Neutrality (1911 treaty)
- ♦ Agreement Respecting Merchant Shipping (1919 treaty)
- ♦ Agreement Respecting the Peace of the Americas and the Bolivian Congresses (1911 treaty)
- ♦ Agreement Respecting the Publication of Historical Records (1911 treaty)
- ♦ Agreement Respecting the Unification of the Pharmacopoeial Formulas for Potent Drugs (1906 treaty)
- ♦ Agreement Respecting the Whangpoo Conservancy (1905 treaty)
- ♦ Agreement Revising the Agreement Respecting the Unification of Pharmacopoeial Formulas for Potent Drugs (1929 treaty)
- ♦ Agreement on Roads and Waterways (1911 treaty)
- ♦ Agreement on Road Transport (1955 treaty)
- ♦ Agreement on Scientific Cooperation in the Field of Organizational Control, Cybernetics and Operational Research (1972 treaty)
- ♦ Agreement on Signs for Road Works (1955 treaty)
- ♦ Agreement on Simplification of Visa Procedures for the Businessmen of ECO Countries (1995 treaty)
- ♦ Agreement on Social Security (1977 treaty)
- ♦ Agreement on Special Equipment for the Transport of Perishable Foodstuffs and on the Use of Such Equipment for the International Transport of Some of Those Foodstuffs (1962 treaty)
- ♦ Agreement on Special Maritime Border Zone (1954 treaty)
- ♦ Agreements Regarding the Regulation of Beef Imports into the United Kingdom (1939 treaty)
- ♦ Agreement for the Stabilization of Raisin – Sultanas Marketing (1964 treaty)
- ♦ Agreement for the Stabilization of Raisin – Sultanas Markets (1963 treaty)
- ♦ Agreement on the Status of the North Atlantic Treaty Organisation, National Representatives and International Staff (1951 treaty)
- ♦ Agreement Supplementary to the Nyon Arrangement (1937 treaty)
- ♦ Agreement for the Suppression of the Circulation of Obscene Publications, 1949 (1949 treaty)
- ♦ Agreement on the System of Central American Integrated Industries (1958 treaty)
- ♦ Agreement on Tariff of Navigation Dues at the Sulina Mouth of the Danube (1908 treaty)
- ♦ Agreement on Technical Barriers to Trade (1979 treaty)
- ♦ Agreement on Telegraphs (1911 treaty)
- ♦ Agreement on the Temporary Importation, Free of Duty, of Medical, Surgical and Laboratory Equipment for Use on Free Loan in Hospitals and other Medical Institutions for Purposes of Diagnosis or Treatment (1960 treaty)
- ♦ Agreement on Trade in Civil Aircraft (1979 treaty)
- ♦ Agreement on Trade Negotiations among Developing Member Countries (1975 treaty)
- ♦ Agreement on Transboundary Cooperation with a View to Preventing or Limiting Harmful Effects for Human Beings, Property or the Environment in the Event of Accidents (1989 treaty)
- ♦ Agreement on the Transfer of Corpses (1973 treaty)
- ♦ Agreement for the Transfer of a Training Reactor and Enriched Uranium (1970 treaty)
- ♦ Agreement on Unification of Container Transport Systems (1971 treaty)
- ♦ Agreement on the Unification of Requirements with Regard to the Formulation and Filing of Patent Applications (1975 treaty)
- ♦ Agreement on the Unification of Requirements with Regard to the Formulation and Presentation of Patent Applications (1975 treaty)
- ♦ Agreement with a View to the Administrative and Technical Re-organization of the Southern Railway Company's System (1923 treaty)
- ♦ Agreement on the Waiver of Visa Requirements, 1971 (1971 treaty)
- ♦ AGR – European Agreement on Main International Traffic Arteries (1975 treaty)

♦ AGRHYMET Regional Centre 00565

Centre régional AGRHYMET

Dir Gen BP 11011, Niamey, Niger. T. +227733116 – +227732436. Fax +227732435.
URL: http://www.agrhymet.ne/

History Dec 1974. Founded by member countries of *Comité permanent inter-Etats de lutte contre la sécheresse dans le Sahel (CILSS, #04195)*, as a specialized institute of CILSS; commenced operations in Oct 1975. Following a comprehensive restructuring of CILSS, 1993, the Centre's operational activities were recognized into two Major Programmes. Former names and other names: *Centre régional de formation et d'application en agrométéorologie et hydrologie opérationnelle (Centre AGRHYMET)* – former (Dec 1974). **Aims** Ensure harmonious and integrated exploitation of *meteorological*, agrometeorological, pest control, remote sensing and hydrological competences and services in the *Sahel* region; strive to secure food security of member states; ensure increased food production in the management of natural resources in the

Sahel region by applying agrometeorological and hydrological information. **Structure** Directorate General, comprising Management, Marketing and Documentation Centre. Administrative and Financial Management Centre. Marketing Unit. **Finance** Sources: contributions of member/participating states; donations. Sources: CILSS member states; Belgium, France, Italy, Netherlands, Switzerland, USA, UNDP. **Activities** Awards/prizes/competitions; events/meetings; knowledge management/information dissemination; research/documentation; training/education. **Events** *Conférence internationale sur l'alerte précoce et le suivi de l'environnement* Niamey (Niger) 1994, *Annual committee meeting* Geneva (Switzerland) 1986. **Publications** *AGRHYNET Info* (4 a year) – newsletter; *Bulletin de liaison* (2 a year); *Synthèse annuelle des bulletins* (annual); *Bulletin agro-hydro-météorologique décadaire* (every 10 days between May and October); *Bulletin agro-hydro-météorologique mensuel* (monthly between May and October). Annual Report. Information Services: Computerized documentation centre with 25,000 scientific and technical publications. **Information Services** *CLICOM Database* – meteorological information; *CLIMAT Database* – meteorological information; *CLIMBASE Database* – meteorological information; *DBASE Database* – agricultural information; *Geographical Information System (GIS) – Système d'information géographique* – geo-referenced products developed and distributed in the framework of CILSS Early Warning System; *HYDROM Database* – hydrological information; *SRBD/GIS Database* – regional database of meteorological, hydrological, agricultural and satellite information.
Members CILSS Member States (9):
Burkina Faso, Cape Verde, Chad, Gambia, Guinea-Bissau, Mali, Mauritania, Niger, Senegal.
IGO Relations Accredited by (1): *African and Malagasy Council for Higher Education (#00364)*. Partner of (3): *Group on Earth Observations (GEO, #10735)*; *Niger Basin Authority (NBA, #17134)*; *West African Science Service Center on Climate Change and Adapted Land Use (WASCAL, #20897)*. Cooperates with (6): *African Centre of Meteorological Applications for Development (ACMAD, #00242)*; *Centre de coopération internationale en recherche agronomique pour le développement (CIRAD, #03733)*; *Institut de recherche pour le développement (IRD)*; *International Crops Research Institute for the Semi-Arid Tropics (ICRISAT, #13116)*; *Lake Chad Basin Commission (LCBC, #16220)*; *UNESCO (#20322)*. Supported by: *FAO (#09260)*; *UNDP (#20292)*; *United Nations Institute for Training and Research (UNITAR, #20576)*; *United States Agency for International Development (USAID)*; *WHO (#20950)*; *World Meteorological Organization (WMO, #21649)* **NGO Relations** Cooperates with (3): *Helen Keller International (HKI, #10902)*; *Sahel and West Africa Club (SWAC, #19034)*; *World Agroforestry Centre (ICRAF, #21072)*. Instrumental in setting up (1): *Conference of Directors of the West African National Meteorological and Hydrological Services (AFRIMET, #04589)*. [2017/XE2429/**E***]

♦ Agribusiness in Sustainable Natural African Plant Products (ASNAPP) 00566

Exec Dir address not obtained. T. +233302505617. Fax +233302505617.
URL: http://www.asnapp.org.za/
History 1999, South Africa. **Aims** Help create and develop successful African agribusinesses in the natural products sector, providing income, employment and development, through environmentally and socially conscious practices to produce high quality natural products for local, regional and overseas markets. **Structure** Advisory Board of 11 members. University Consortium and Principles Investigators. In-Country Board of Directors. **Finance** Donor funded. Budget (annual): US$ 1 million. **Activities** Scientific research and technology transfer; Market intelligence and market development; Farmer mobilization and enterprise development; Quality control and quality assurance; Capacity building; Policy advocacy. **Publications** *ASNAPP Newsletter*.
Members Full in 4 countries:
Ghana, Rwanda, Senegal, Zambia. [2014/XJ0223/**F**]

♦ AgriCord 00567

Admin Manager Rue de Trèves 61, 1040 Brussels, Belgium. T. +3222392330. E-mail: info@agricord.org.
URL: https://www.agricord.org/
History Informal meetings held since 1997, prior to formal founding. Decisive meeting of Development Cooperation Committee of *International Federation of Agricultural Producers (IFAP, inactive)*, held at *OECD (#17693)*, when intention to set up AgriCord was confirmed. Set up early 2002, after a 5-year period of gestation. Formally created in the beginning of 2003 by eight agri-agencies: AFDI (France), AGRITERRA (Netherlands), DAC (Denmark), IDACA (Japan), IVA (Belgium), FERT (France), NORGES VEL (Norway) and UPA-DI (Canada). Registration: Crossroads Bank for Enterprises, No/ID: 0480.255.611, Start date: 9 Jan 2003, Belgium. **Aims** Foster the economic viability of farming activities, aimed at improving the livelihood conditions of farmers, their families and the rural communities they work and live in; strengthen the contribution of the farming community – through strong farmers' organisations – to tackling the global and local challenges; promote and help to build other farmers' organisations and cooperatives of family farmers- through peer-to-peer approach; organize family farmers in an effective, efficient, inclusive and democratic manner to spur their development. **Structure** General Assembly; Board of Directors; Programme Commission; Audit Commission; Partnerships and Resources Mobilisation Committee. **Languages** English, French, Spanish.
Activities Awareness raising; financial and/or material support; guidance/assistance/consulting; knowledge management/information dissemination; training/education. Four strategic roles of AgriCord alliance:
1. To promote the mutual support amongst farmers organisations worldwide, by advice, training and exchanges, highlighting the added value of this international farmer cooperation in the alliance's communications.
2. To ensure financial support for the activities with farmers' organisations by prospecting, co-designing, negotiating and managing funding contracts, as well as promoting and coordinating a common mobilisation of resources strategy in close coordination with the farmers' organisations and cooperatives.
3. To ensure quality cooperation among agri-agencies, farmers' organisations and cooperatives creating an environment in which joint knowledge production, learning by exchange and improvement by peer support and self-evaluation becomes a natural attitude.
4. To ensure visibility and coordinate information and awareness campaigns on the above strategic roles.

Active in: Benin, Bolivia, Brazil, Burkina Faso, Burundi, Cambodia, Cameroon, Colombia, Congo DR, Côte d'Ivoire, Dominican Rep, Ecuador, Gambia, Ghana, Guinea, Haiti, Honduras, Indonesia, Kenya, Madagascar, Malawi, Mali, Micronesia FS, Paraguay, Peru, Philippines, Polynesia Fr, Senegal, Tanzania UR, Uganda, Vietnam.
Members Agri-agencies mandated by farmers' organisations and cooperatives in 10 countries:
Belgium, Brazil, Canada, Finland, France, Germany, Philippines, Senegal, Spain, Sweden.
https://www.agricord.org/en/our-membership.
IGO Relations Cooperates with (6): *Agence française de développement (AFD)*; *Directorate-General for Development Cooperation (DGDC)*; *European Commission (EC, #06633)*; *FAO (#09260)*; *International Fund for Agricultural Development (IFAD, #13692)*; *Organisation of African, Caribbean and Pacific States (OACPS, #17796)*. **NGO Relations** *AGRINATURA (#00578)*. [2023.02.15/XM8657/**C**]

♦ Agriculteurs français et développement international (internationally oriented national body)
♦ Agricultural Biotechnology International Center / see Agricultural Biotechnology International Conference Foundation (#00568)

♦ Agricultural Biotechnology International Conference Foundation (ABIC Foundation) 00568

Managing Dir 101-111 Research Drive, Saskatoon SK S7N 3R2, Canada. E-mail: abicfoundation@abic.ca.
URL: http://www.abic.ca/
History Founded 12 Jun 1998, Saskatoon SK (Canada), following the first Agricultural Biotechnology International Conference (ABIC), 1996, Saskatoon. Second conference in 1998 resulted in formation of an organization that would oversee the ABIC Concept, and oversee the continued success of the ABIC conference series. Incorporates activities of *Global Agricultural Biotechnology Association (GABA, inactive)*. Also referred to as *Agricultural Biotechnology International Center*. **Aims** Ensure ongoing opportunities for continuous learning and networking within the agricultural biotechnology community through organization of a conference; stimulate and encourage research, development and commercialization of new biotechnologies to improve human health, create a sustainable food supply and foster new energy sources for all nations, including the developing world. **Structure** Meeting (annual). Board. **Languages** English. **Finance** Income from conferences and contributions. **Activities** Organizes Agricultural Biotechnology International Conference (annual) which promotes innovation in bioscience to ensure sustainable food, feed, fibre and fuel security as the climate changes. **Events** *ABIC : Agricultural Biotechnology International Conference / Annual Conference* Melbourne, VIC (Australia) 2015, *ABIC : Agricultural Biotechnology International Conference* Saskatoon, SK (Canada) 2014, *Annual Conference* Saskatoon, SK (Canada) 2014, *ABIC : Agricultural Biotechnology International Conference* Calgary, AB (Canada) 2013, *Annual Conference* Calgary, AB (Canada) 2013.
Members Individuals and organizations in 65 countries and territories:
Argentina, Australia, Austria, Belgium, Bolivia, Brazil, Canada, Cape Verde, Chile, China, Colombia, Costa Rica, Cuba, Czechia, Denmark, Ecuador, Egypt, Eswatini, Fiji, Finland, France, Germany, Guatemala, Hong Kong, Hungary, Iceland, India, Indonesia, Iran Islamic Rep, Iraq, Ireland, Israel, Italy, Japan, Kenya, Korea Rep, Malawi, Malaysia, Mexico, Nepal, Netherlands, New Zealand, Nigeria, Norway, Pakistan, Papua New Guinea, Paraguay, Peru, Philippines, Poland, Russia, Scotland, Singapore, Slovenia, South Africa, Spain, Sweden, Switzerland, Taiwan, Thailand, Türkiye, UK, Uruguay, USA, Venezuela.
Also indicates Tasmania and Scandinavia as members. [2013.06.01/XF5563/**f**/**F**]

♦ Agricultural Economics Society of South East Asia (inactive)

♦ Agricultural and Food Marketing Association for Asia and the Pacific (AFMA) 00569

Main Office FAO Annex, 1 Empire Tower II, 47 Fl 4703 Yannawa, Bangkok, 10120, Thailand. E-mail: info@afmaasia.org.
URL: http://www.afmaasia.org/
History 8 Feb 1983, Bangkok (Thailand). Established 8-10 Feb 1983, Bangkok (Thailand), at the first General Assembly, by national level institutions involved in the marketing of grains, livestock, fruits and vegetables, following recommendations of *Group Consultation on Technical Cooperation among Developing Countries (TCDC)*, 12-14 Jan 1982, Bangkok and meeting, 2-3 Jun 1982, Bangkok when constitution, by-laws and programme of work were drafted. Original title: *Association of Food Marketing Agencies in Asia and the Pacific*. Subsequently changed title to *Association of Food and Agricultural Marketing Agencies in Asia and the Pacific*. Current title adopted in 2006. **Aims** Improve food marketing systems in the countries of the region by stimulating economic and technical cooperation among food marketing institutions; establish machinery for systematic interchange of information and experience on policies, programmes, projects and technologies of food marketing; train senior level policy makers and middle level managerial and technical staff; plan, initiate, implement and evaluate specific policies, programmes and projects. **Structure** General Assembly (every 2 years); Executive Committee; Secretariat. **Languages** English. **Staff** 1.50 FTE, paid. **Finance** Members' dues. Projects and international support. Office space is shared with *FAO Regional Office for Asia and the Pacific (RAP, #09266)*. **Activities** Guidance/assistance/consulting; research and development; politics/policy/regulatory; projects/programmes; training/education; events/meetings; knowledge management/information dissemination. **Events** *Regional Round Table on the World Programme for the Census of Agriculture 2020* Bangkok (Thailand) 2016, *Asian Rice : meeting on modernizing the Asian rice industry* Bangkok (Thailand) 2011, *Grains world summit* Istanbul (Turkey) 2011, *Asian agro-marketing forum / General Assembly* Rangoon (Myanmar) 2010, *General Assembly* Rangoon (Myanmar) 2010. **Publications** *AFMA Newsletter* (4 a year); *Commodity Association Directory* (annual).
Members Governmental ministries and food marketing agencies, apex cooperative associations and private sector food marketing enterprises and associations (16) in 11 countries:
Bangladesh, China, India, Indonesia, Korea Rep, Malaysia, Myanmar, Nepal, Pakistan, Philippines, Sri Lanka.
IGO Relations *FAO Regional Office for Asia and the Pacific (RAP, #09266)*. [2021/XD0718/**D***]

♦ Agricultural Food Marketing Association for the Near East and North Africa Region (no recent information)

♦ Agricultural and Land and Water Use Commission for the Near East (ALAWUC) 00570

Contact c/o FAO Regional Office for the Near East and North Africa, 11 Al-Eslah Al-Zerai St, Dokki, PO Box 2223, Cairo, 12611, Egypt. T. +20233316000. Fax +20237495981. E-mail: fao-rne@fao.org.
URL: http://www.fao.org/neareast/alawuc/en/
History within the framework of *FAO (#09260)*, on merger of *Near East Regional Commission on Agriculture (COAG/NE, inactive)* and *Regional Commission on Land and Water Use in the Near East (LWU, inactive)*, as regional commission of *FAO Regional Office for the Near East and North Africa (#09269)*. **Aims** Provide a forum through which member nations can exchange information and experience and promote joint programmes at regional and sub-regional levels for complementarity of resources; assist FAO and other potential donors with identifying issues, problems and future work programmes in the region. **Structure** Session (every 2 years); Secretariat. **Languages** Arabic, English. **Staff** No permanent staff. **Events** *Biennial Session* Cairo (Egypt) 2008, *Biennial Session* Sanaa (Yemen) 2006, *Session / Biennial Session* Doha (Qatar) 2004, *Session / Biennial Session* Teheran (Iran Islamic Rep) 2002, *Session / Biennial Session* Beirut (Lebanon) 2000. **Publications** Session report.
Members Member Countries; Observer Countries; Observer Organizations. Member Countries (23):
Afghanistan, Bahrain, Cyprus, Egypt, Iran Islamic Rep, Iraq, Jordan, Kuwait, Lebanon, Libya, Mauritania, Morocco, Oman, Pakistan, Qatar, Saudi Arabia, Somalia, Sudan, Syrian AR, Tunisia, Türkiye, United Arab Emirates, Yemen.
Observer countries (13):
Algeria, Azerbaijan, Djibouti, France, Kazakhstan, Kyrgyzstan, Malta, Palestine, Tajikistan, Turkmenistan, UK, USA, Uzbekistan.
Representatives of UN and specialized agencies:
International Fund for Agricultural Development (IFAD, #13692); *UNEP (#20299)* (Regional Office for West Asia); *UNESCO Office, Cairo – Regional Bureau for Sciences in the Arab States (ROSTAS, #20312)*; *World Food Programme (WFP, #21510)*.
Observers from 7 intergovernmental organizations:
African Development Bank (ADB, #00283); *Arab Organization for Agricultural Development (AOAD, #01018)*; *Centre for Environment and Development for the Arab Region and Europe (CEDARE, #03738)*; *Deutsche Gesellschaft für Technische Zusammenarbeit (GTZ, inactive)*; *International Development Research Centre (IDRC, #13162)*; *League of Arab States (LAS, #16420)*; *Saudi Fund for Development (SFD)*.
IGO Relations Instrumental in setting up (1): *Near East Research and Development Network on Treatment and Re-use of Sewage Effluent for Irrigation (inactive)*. [2021/XE2076/**y**/**E***]

♦ Agricultural Libraries Network (AGLINET) 00571

Knowledge and Information Management Officer David Lubin Memorial Library – FAO, Via delle Terme di Caracalla, 00153 Rome RM, Italy. Fax +39657052002.
URL: http://www.fao.org/library/
History 2 Nov 1971, Rome (Italy). 2-4 Nov 1971, Rome (Italy), within the framework of *International Association of Agricultural Information Specialists (IAALD, inactive)*, by participants at symposium on *World Network of Agricultural Libraries*. Statutes revised: Jun 1982; Jun 1984; Jun 1994. **Aims** Improve inter-library *document* provision in all formats in the agricultural sector. **Structure** International Coordinating Centre; Primary Centres; Subject Centres. **Languages** English, French, Italian, Russian, Spanish. **Staff** 2.00 FTE, paid. **Finance** A cooperative; no budget. **Activities** Knowledge management/information dissemination. **Events** *Meeting* Rome (Italy) 1986.
Members Agricultural libraries (68) in 56 countries:
Algeria, Argentina, Australia (2), Belarus, Belgium, Benin, Botswana, Brazil (2), Bulgaria, Canada, China, Colombia, Costa Rica, Czechia, Denmark, Egypt, Estonia, Ethiopia (2), Fiji, Finland, Germany (2), Hungary, India (2), Indonesia, Italy (4), Japan, Jordan, Kenya, Korea DPR, Korea Rep, Latvia, Lithuania, Malawi, Malaysia, Mexico, Moldova, Mozambique, Netherlands, Norway, Philippines (2), Poland, Portugal, Russia (2), Samoa, Slovakia, Slovenia, Spain, Sri Lanka (2), Sweden, Syrian AR, Thailand, Trinidad-Tobago (2), UK, Uruguay, USA, Zambia.
IGO Relations International Centre at: *FAO (#09260)*, Rome (Italy). Includes library of: *Caribbean Agricultural Research and Development Institute (CARDI, #03436)*; FAO; *Inter-American Institute for Cooperation on Agriculture (IICA, #11434)*; *International Crops Research Institute for the Semi-Arid Tropics (ICRISAT, #13116)*; *International Fund for Agricultural Development (IFAD, #13692)*; *International Livestock Research Institute (ILRI, #14062)*; *International Rice Research Institute (IRRI, #14754)*. **NGO Relations** Includes libraries of the following institutes and centres listed in this Yearbook: *International Centre for Tropical Agriculture (#12527)*; *International Institute of Tropical Agriculture (IITA, #13933)*; *International Maize and Wheat Improvement Center (#14077)*; *International Water Management Institute (IWMI, #15867)*. [2016.10.24/XF8416/**F**]

♦ Agricultural Market Development Trust (AGMARK) 00572

Head Office Graceland Court, Ground Fl – Suite G2, Opposite Kenyatta Univ School of Law, Parklands Campus, PO Box 14184 – 00800, Parklands, Nairobi, Kenya. T. +254202661403. E-mail: info@agmark.org.

URL: https://agmark.org/
History 2004, Kenya. **Aims** Improve incomes and food security of *smallholder* farmers by facilitating agricultural *development* in *Africa* through adoption of improved production technologies and effective output marketing in response to identified market opportunities. **Structure** Board of Trustees. **Staff** 6.00 FTE, paid. **Activities** Projects/programmes; training/education. Active in: Burundi, Eswatini, Ethiopia, Ethiopia, Kenya, Malawi, Rwanda, South Sudan, Tanzania UR, Uganda, Zambia. **Publications** *AGMARK Newsletter*. **NGO Relations** Partner of: *African Fertilizer and Agribusiness Partnership (AFAP, #00314).*
[2020.03.19/XJ7795/**F**]

♦ **Agricultural Market Information System (AMIS)** **00573**
Secretariat c/o FAO, Viale delle Terme di Caracalla, 00153 Rome RM, Italy. T. +39657053539. Fax +39657053152. E-mail: amis-secretariat@fao.org.
URL: http://www.amis-outlook.org/
History Set up as an initiative of *Group of Twenty (G20, #10793)*. **Aims** Enhance food market transparency; encourage coordination of policy action in response to market uncertainty. **Structure** Secretariat, comprising *FAO (#09260)*, Group on Earth Observations Global Agricultural Monitoring Initiative (GEOGLAM), *International Food Policy Research Institute (IFPRI, #13622), International Fund for Agricultural Development (IFAD, #13692), International Grains Council (IGC, #13731), OECD (#17693), UNCTAD (#20285), International Bank for Reconstruction and Development (IBRD, #12317), World Food Programme (WFP, #21510)* and *World Trade Organization (WTO, #21864)*. Steering Committee. *Global Food Market Information Group* (meets twice a year). Rapid Response Forum (meets annually). **Languages** English. **Publications** *AMIS Market Monitor* (10 a year).
[2021.10.26/XJ7656/**E***]

♦ Agricultural Missions (internationally oriented national body)

♦ **Agricultural and Rural Convention (ARC2020)** **00574**
Coordinator 38 rue Saint-Sabin, 75011 Paris, France. E-mail: contact@arc2020.eu.
Campaign Coordinator Berlin Office, Marienstr 19-20, 10117 Berlin, Germany. T. +493028242326. E-mail: communication@arc2020.eu.
URL: http://www.arc2020.eu/
History Set up as a multi-NGOs platform (2010-2013). Restructured as an independent NGO. EU Transparency Register: 549022520858-24. **Aims** Offer a space to regenerate public debate in Europe. **Publications** *NewsFlash* (12 a year) – newsletter.
[2017/XM5442/**F**]

♦ **e-Agriculture** **00575**
Contact address not obtained. E-mail: e-agriculture@fao.org – info@e-agriculture.org.
URL: http://www.e-agriculture.org/
History Officially launched 2007, as a Community of Practice, following a get-together of several founding Partners, 2006. **Aims** Serve as a catalyst for institutions and individuals in agricultural and *rural* development to share knowledge, learn from others, and improve decision making about the vital role of information and communication technologies (ICTs) to empower rural communities, improve rural livelihoods, and build sustainable agriculture and *food* security. **Languages** English, French, Spanish. **Staff** 4.00 FTE, paid. **Activities** Events/meetings. **Members** Individuals (over 16,000). Membership countries not specified. **IGO Relations** Founding partners include: *CGIAR System Organization (CGIAR, #03843); Centre technique de coopération agricole et rurale (CTA, inactive); FAO (#09260); Inter-American Institute for Cooperation on Agriculture (IICA, #11434); International Bank for Reconstruction and Development (IBRD, #12317); International Fund for Agricultural Development (IFAD, #13692).* **NGO Relations** Founding partners include: *Global Alliance for ICT and Development (GAID, #10200); Global Forum on Agricultural Research (GFAR, #10370); Global Knowledge Partnership Foundation (GKPF, #10443).*
[2020/XJ2883/**F**]

♦ Agriculture, Nutrition and Health Academy (internationally oriented national body)

♦ **AgriCultures Network** **00576**
Secretariat IED Afrique, 24 Sacré Cour III, Dakar, Senegal. E-mail: agriculturesnetwork2017@gmail.com.
URL: http://www.agriculturesnetwork.org/
Aims Facilitate practice-based knowledge sharing on *sustainable* family farming so it becomes a mainstream *agricultural* practice worldwide. **Structure** Secretariat provided by *ILEIA – Centre for learning on sustainable agriculture (inactive).* **Activities** Knowledge management/information dissemination; advocacy/lobbying/activism; training/education. **Publications** *Farming Matters* – global magazine. Regional and national magazines.
Members Partners in 6 countries:
Brazil, Ethiopia, India, Netherlands, Peru, Senegal.
[2021/XJ4902/**F**]

♦ Agri-Energy Roundtable (internationally oriented national body)

♦ **Agri-Food Chain Coalition (AFCC)** **00577**
Contact address not obtained. E-mail: info@agrifoodchaincoalition.eu.
URL: http://agrifoodchaincoalition.eu/
Aims Unlock the potential of *agriculture* and the food industry in the EU.
Members Associations (13):
AnimalhealthEurope (#00837); Committee of the Trade in Cereals, Oilseeds, Pulses, Olive Oil, Oils and Fats, Animal Feed and Agrosupply of the EU (COCERAL, #04289); COPA – european farmers (COPA, #04829); CropLife Europe (#04965); European Agricultural Machinery Association (CEMA, #05846); European Forum of Farm Animal Breeders (EFFAB, #07310); European Liaison Committee for Agricultural and Agri-Food Trades (#07687); Euroseeds (#09179); Fédération européenne des fabricants d'aliments composés pour animaux (FEFAC, #09566); FEFANA – EU Association of Specialty Feed Ingredients and their Mixtures (#09720); Fertilizers Europe (#09738); FoodDrinkEurope (#09841); General Confederation of Agricultural Cooperatives in the European Union (#10107).
[2018/XM6313/y/**D**]

♦ **AGRIMBA** International Network for the MBA in Agribusiness and Commerce (#14295)

♦ **AGRINATURA** **00578**
SG Czech University of Life Sciences Prague, Kamycka 129, 165 21 Prague, Czechia. T. +420224382011. Fax +420224382012. E-mail: secretariat@agrinatura-eu.eu.
AGRINATURA-EEIG 42 rue Scheffer, 75116 Paris, France. T. +33153702264. Fax +33153702156.
URL: http://www.agrinatura-eu.eu/
History 2009. Established by merger of *Network of European Agricultural – Tropically and Subtropically Oriented – Universities and Scientific Complexes Related with Agricultural Development (NATURA, inactive)* and *European Consortium for Agricultural Research in the Tropics (ECART, inactive)*. AGRINATURA – *European Economic Interest Grouping (EEIG, #06960)* functions as its operational arm. A Standing Committee of *Association for European Life Science Universities (ICA, #02519)*. Former names and other names: *AGRINATURA – European Alliance on Agricultural Knowledge for Development* – former. **Aims** Support agricultural development in a sustainable manner in order to improve people's lives. **Structure** General Assembly; Board of Directors. **Languages** English, French. **Staff** 1.00 FTE, paid. **Finance** Sources: members' dues. **Events** *General Assembly* Cork (Ireland) 2022, *General Assembly* Vienna (Austria) 2014. **Publications** *Agris Mundus Master of Science in Sustainable Development in Agriculture – Book of Abstracts; Building Competence and Confidence in Agricultural Innovation – Stories of Change CDAIS.*
Members Organizations and universities in 16 countries:
Austria, Belgium, Czechia, Denmark, Finland, France, Germany, Hungary, Ireland, Italy, Netherlands, Portugal, Spain, Sweden, Switzerland, UK.
Included in the above, 3 organizations listed in this Yearbook:
Centre de coopération internationale en recherche agronomique pour le développement (CIRAD, #03733); Institut de recherche pour le développement (IRD); International Centre for Development Oriented Research in Agriculture (ICRA).
[2023/XJ1712/y/**F**]

♦ AGRINATURA – European Alliance on Agricultural Knowledge for Development / see AGRINATURA (#00578)
♦ AgriProFocus / see Netherlands Food Partnership
♦ **AGRIS** International Information System for the Agricultural Sciences and Technology (#13848)
♦ AGRISUD – Institut international d'appui au développement (internationally oriented national body)
♦ AGRISUD International / see Institut international d'appui au développement
♦ Agriterra (internationally oriented national body)
♦ AGRM – Association of Gospel Rescue Missions (internationally oriented national body)
♦ Agro-action allemande / see Welthungerhilfe

♦ **AgroBioMediterraneao (ABM)** **00579**
Permanent Secretariat Derigny 49, 104 34 Athens, Greece. E-mail: cm@organizationearth.org.
Pres address not obtained.
URL: http://abm.ifoam.bio/
History 1990, Vignola (Italy), as a regional initiative. As of 1997, an official regional group of *IFOAM – Organics International (IFOAM, #11105).* **Aims** Promote, develop and disseminate information, knowledge and expertise related to *Mediterranean organic agriculture* and *food* production. **Structure** General Assembly; Regional Board; Permanent Secretariat.
Members Full (146) in 16 countries and territories:
Albania, Bosnia-Herzegovina, Croatia, Cyprus, Egypt, France, Greece, Israel, Italy, Palestine, Portugal, Serbia, Slovenia, Spain, Tunisia, Türkiye.
NGO Relations Member of: *TP Organics – European Technology Platform (TP Organics, #20180).*
[2020/XJ0640/**E**]

♦ **AgroCare** **00580**
Contact Weverstr 18, 1761 Borchtlombeek, Belgium. T. +32476824364. E-mail: secretary@agrocare.org.
Registered Office Ridderstr 14, 1050 Brussels, Belgium.
URL: http://www.agro-care.org/
History Founded 28 Apr 2008, Brussels (Belgium). Registered in accordance with Belgian law. **Aims** Represent the independent post-patent *crop protection industry*. **Structure** Annual Meeting; Board of Directors.
Members Associations (4):
AgroCare Latinoamérica (#00581); China Crop Protection Industry Association; *European Crop Care Association (ECCA, #06865);* Pesticides Manufacturers and Formulators Association of India.
NGO Relations Participates as observer in the activities of: *Codex Alimentarius Commission (CAC, #04081).*
[2018/XM7039/y/**C**]

♦ **AgroCare Latinoamérica** **00581**
Contact address not obtained. T. +50622712752. Fax +50622714184. E-mail: info@agrocarelatinoamerica.org.
URL: http://www.agrocarelatinoamerica.org/
History Registered in accordance with the law of Costa Rica. **Structure** Board of Directors.
Members Full in 8 countries:
Argentina, Brazil, Costa Rica, Ecuador, Guatemala, Mexico, Paraguay, Peru.
NGO Relations *AgroCare (#00580).*
[2018/XM7040/**D**]

♦ Agroecologia Europa (#00582)

♦ **Agroecology Europe** **00582**
Agroecologia Europa
SG Rue C Warichet 4, Box 22, 1425 Corbais, Belgium.
URL: http://agroecology-europe.org/
History Set up 27 Jan 2016, Gaurain-Ramecroix (Belgium). **Aims** Analyse, design, develop and promote the transition towards agroecology-based farming and food systems. **Structure** General Assembly; Board; Advisory Committee; Working Groups. **Languages** English. **Staff** 1.00 FTE, paid. **Finance** Members' dues. **Activities** Events/meetings; training/education; publishing activities; networking/liaising; research and development; knowledge management/information dissemination; politics/policy/regulatory. **Events** *Forum* Barcelona (Spain) 2021, *Forum* Heraklion (Greece) 2019, *Forum* Lyon (France) 2017.
[2019.12.11/XM6349/**D**]

♦ **Agroecology Fund (AEF)** **00583**
Co-Dir address not obtained. E-mail: contact@agroecologyfund.org.
Main Website: http://www.agroecologyfund.org/
History Jan 2012. Launched by four founding donors: *Christensen Fund (TCF), New Field Foundation*, the Swift Foundation and one anonymous foundation. **Aims** Mobilize resources to build power that transforms food systems and fosters the well-being of people and the planet. **Structure** Advisory Board. **Languages** English, French, Portuguese, Spanish. **Finance** Sources: donations; international organizations; private foundations. Supported by: *American Jewish World Service (AJWS); Christensen Fund (TCF); David and Lucile Packard Foundation; Fondation Charles Léopold Mayer pour le progrès de l'homme (FPH, #09815); Franciscan Sisters of Mary (FSM); Grassroots International (GI); McKnight Foundation; New Field Foundation; Open Society Foundations (OSF, #17763); Synchronicity Earth; Wallace Global Fund; W K Kellogg Foundation (WKKF).* **Activities** Financial and/or material support; networking/liaising. **Publications** *Strategic Plan 2022-2026* (2022). **NGO Relations** Also links with dozens of organizations and networks to amplify agroecological solutions across the globe.
[2023.02.13/XM6801/f/**F**]

♦ Agro-forestry Coordinating Association of Indigenous Peoples and Farmers (#02120)
♦ Agromash – International Association for Vine, Fruit, and Vegetable-Growing Mechanization (inactive)
♦ Agro Nature Protection / see Centre Africain de Recherches Forestières Appliquées et de Développement
♦ Agronomes et vétérinaires sans frontières (internationally oriented national body)
♦ Agropolis – Complexe international de recherche et d'enseignement supérieur agronomique / see Agropolis International
♦ Agropolis International (internationally oriented national body)
♦ Agrupación Europea de Cajas de Ahorros (#08426)
♦ Agrupación Europea de Jubilados de las Cajas de Ahorro, Bancos e Instituciones Afines / see Group of European Retired Staff and Pensioners from Savings Banks, Banks and Related Institutions (#10777)
♦ Agrupación Europea de Jubilados y Pensionistas de Cajas de Ahorros, Bancos e Instituciones Afines (#10777)
♦ Agrupación de Jubilados y Pensionistas de las Cajas de Ahorros Europeas / see Group of European Retired Staff and Pensioners from Savings Banks, Banks and Related Institutions (#10777)
♦ Agrupación Mundial de Ex Boxeadores (inactive)
♦ Agrupación Mundial del Judaismo Marroqui (unconfirmed)
♦ Agrupación Rotarios Naciones Unidas / see United Nations Friends in Rotary
♦ Agrupación de Trabajadores Latinoamericanos Sindicalistas (inactive)
♦ AGS – Africa Groups of Sweden (internationally oriented national body)
♦ AGS – ASIAN Geographic Society (unconfirmed)
♦ AGSI – Association for Global Strategic Information (inactive)
♦ **AGSSEA** Association of Geotechnical Societies in Southeast Asia (#02625)
♦ AGSSM – African Gulf Society of Sexual Medicine (inactive)
♦ AGST / see Asia Graduate School of Theology – Malaysia/Singapore/Thailand
♦ AGST-MST – Asia Graduate School of Theology – Malaysia/Singapore/Thailand (internationally oriented national body)
♦ AGTA – Australasian Genomic Technologies Association (internationally oriented national body)
♦ AGTC – European Agreement on Important International Combined Transport Lines and Related Installations (1991 treaty)
♦ AGTO – Alliance of Global Talent Organizations (unconfirmed)
♦ **AguaJaring** South East Asia Regional Network for Capacity Building in IWRM (#19796)
♦ AGU – American Geophysical Union (internationally oriented national body)
♦ Agua Potable para el Mundo (internationally oriented national body)
♦ **AGU** Arabian Gulf University (#00976)

♦ **AGU** Asian Gymnastics Union (#01499)

♦ Agudath Israel World Organization (AIWO) 00584

Organisation mondiale Agudath Israel (OMAI) – Organización Mundial Agudath Israel – Welt-Organisation Agudath Israel

Exec Office Davidka Square, POB 326, Jerusalem, Israel. T. +97225384357. Fax +97225383634.
Joint SG 18 Zvi Yehuda Street, Jerusalem, Israel.
Joint SG 42 Yechezkel Street, Jerusalem, Israel.

History 1912, Katowice (Poland). Founded at a Congress of orthodox Jewry. Before World War II this organization was officially represented in the Polish, Romanian and Lithuanian Parliaments. Now represented in the Israeli Parliament. **Aims** In the spirit of *traditional Judaism*, solve problems which periodically confront the Jewish people as a whole by coordinating Orthodox Jewish effort worldwide, especially among Jews of Eastern and Western Europe; work in and for Israel, amelioration of economic position of Jews in lands of need, creation of a Jewish press and literature inspired by Jewish tradition, systematic furthering of religious education and representation and protection of the interests of *Torah*-true Jewish communities and of the Jewish people. **Structure** Congress (every 5 years). Two Chairmen (Jerusalem and New York). World Rabbinical Council, consisting of members of national rabbinical councils, responsible for religious matters. International Central Council (annual), composed of 100 members nominated by affiliated organizations. World Executive. Special sections (4): Youth Education; Adult Education; Boys; Girls. **Languages** English, French, German, Hebrew. **Finance** Members' dues. Funds for education, colonization, relief, youth work. Annual budget: 5,000,000 USD. **Activities** Financial and/or material support; religious activities. **Events** *Executive Meeting* Jerusalem (Israel) 2003, *Executive Meeting* Bournemouth (UK) 2000, *Executive Meeting* Bournemouth (UK) 1999, *Executive Meeting* Jerusalem (Israel) 1997, *Executive Meeting* New York, NY (USA) 1996. **Publications** *Hamodia* (daily) in English, Hebrew; *Hamodia* (weekly) in English; *Coalition* (12 a year) in English; *Jedion* (12 a year) – Antwerp; *Jedion Jerusalem* (12 a year) in Hebrew; *Jewish Observer* (12 a year) in English; *Jüdische Stimme* (12 a year) in German; *La Voz Judia* (12 a year) in Spanish, Yiddish; *Perspective* (12 a year) – Toronto; *Yiddishe Wort* (12 a year) in Yiddish.

Members Affiliated organizations, totalling 500,000 members, in 17 countries:
Argentina, Austria, Belgium, Brazil, Canada, Chile, Denmark, France, Germany, Israel, Italy, Mexico, Netherlands, South Africa, Switzerland, UK, USA.

Consultative Status Consultative status granted from: *UNICEF (#20332)*. **IGO Relations** Accredited by: *United Nations Office at Vienna (UNOV, #20604)*. Associated with Department of Global Communications of the United Nations. **NGO Relations** Member of: *World Jewish Restitution Organization (WJRO, #21601)*.
[2016/XF0032/**F**]

♦ Agustinos – Orden de San Agustin (religious order)
♦ Agustinos Recoletos (religious order)
♦ Agustinos Seculares (religious order)
♦ **AGW-NET** Africa Groundwater Network (#00179)
♦ AHA – Africa Humanitarian Action (internationally oriented national body)
♦ **AHA** Asian Hematology Association (#01503)
♦ **AHA** Association des historiens africains (#02357)
♦ **AHA Centre** ASEAN Coordinating Centre for Humanitarian Assistance on disaster management (#01161)
♦ AHADA – African Humanitarian Aid and Development Agency (internationally oriented national body)
♦ AHAPRO – Asociación Habitat Pro (internationally oriented national body)
♦ AHBN – Africa Health Budget Network (unconfirmed)
♦ AHBx – Asociación de Hispanistas del Benelux (internationally oriented national body)
♦ AHCE / see Historical Archives of the European Union (#10927)
♦ **AHCFE** AHC Federation of Europe (#00585)

♦ AHC Federation of Europe (AHCFE) 00585

Contact address not obtained. E-mail: info@ahcfe.eu.
URL: http://www.ahcfe.eu/

History Founded 2013. **Aims** Find a treatment for the *neurological* disorder *Alternating Hemiplegia of Childhood* (AHC). **Structure** Board. **Activities** Events/meetings.

Members Founding members in 10 countries:
Denmark, France, Germany, Iceland, Ireland, Italy, Netherlands, Poland, Spain, UK.

NGO Relations Associate member of: *EURORDIS – Rare Diseases Europe (#09175)*. [2022/XM7449/**D**]

♦ AHCIET / see Asociación Interamericana de Empresas de Telecomunicaciones (#02160)
♦ AHC – International Association for History and Computing (no recent information)
♦ **AHCTA** Alliance for Harmonisation of Cellular Therapy Accreditation (#00686)
♦ AHDA – Association for Human Rights and Democracy in Africa (internationally oriented national body)
♦ AHDA – Australasian Human Development Association (internationally oriented national body)
♦ **AHDMA** Asian Hyperbaric and Diving Medical Association (#01508)
♦ AHEAD Energy (internationally oriented national body)
♦ **AHEAD Network** Applied Health, Equity and Development Research Network (#00880)
♦ **AHFA** Adventist Health Food Association (#00132)
♦ AHF – AIDS Healthcare Foundation (internationally oriented national body)
♦ **AHF** Americas Health Foundation (#00794)
♦ **AHF** Arab Hospitals Federation (#00973)
♦ **AHF** Asian Handball Federation (#01500)
♦ **AHF** Asian Hockey Federation (#01505)
♦ **AHF** Asian Hospital Federation (#01506)
♦ AHFE International – International Conference on Applied Human Factors and Ergonomics (meeting series)
♦ AHI – Africa Hepatitis Initiative (unconfirmed)
♦ **AHI** Asian Health Institute (#01502)
♦ **AHILA** Asociación de Historiadores Latinoamericanistas Europeos (#02517)
♦ **AHILA** Association for Health Information and Libraries in Africa (#02630)

♦ Ahimsa Fund 00586

Pres 20 rue Ernest Fabrègue, 69009 Lyon, France. T. +33620721755. E-mail: contact@ahimsa-fund.com.
URL: http://www.ahimsa-fund.com/

History 2011, France, Former names and other names: *Accelerator, HomeMaker, Incubator, MatchMaker, SenseMaker, Art ambassador* – full title. **Aims** Focus on the most *underprivileged* populations of the world; advise realistic, innovative, cost-effective and replicable public *health* initiatives. **Structure** Strategic Committee. **Activities** Events/meetings; projects/programmes. **Events** *Fostering a New Movement for Health Access for the Most Vulnerable People* Lyon (France) 2021, *Innovation in global health* Annecy (France) 2019, *Global health, social entrepreneurship and faith-inspired communities* Annecy (France) 2017, *Global health and faith-inspired communities* Cape Town (South Africa) 2015, *Forum* Annecy (France) 2013. **Publications** *AHIMSA Newsletter*. **IGO Relations** Partner of (2): *Joint United Nations Programme on HIV/AIDS (UNAIDS, #16149)*; *UNICEF/UNDP/World Bank/WHO Special Programme for Research and Training in Tropical Diseases (TDR, #20331)*. **NGO Relations** Member of (1): *International Partnership on Religion and Sustainable Development (PaRD, #14524)*. Partner of (6): *Ecumenical Foundation of Southern Africa (EFSA)*; *Gavi – The Vaccine Alliance (Gavi, #10077)*; *Handa Foundation*; *Religions for Peace (RfP, #18831)*; *Rotary International (RI, #18975)*; *World Faiths Development Dialogue (WFDD)*. [2021.05.19/XM7712/**f**/**F**]

♦ **AHJUCAF** Association des hautes juridictions de cassation des pays ayant en partage l'usage du Français (#02629)
♦ AHK debelux – Deutsch-Belgisch-Luxemburgische Handelskammer (internationally oriented national body)
♦ **AHLE** Asociación de Historia de la Lengua Española (#02132)
♦ Ahl-Ul-Bait World Assembly (internationally oriented national body)
♦ Ahlul-Bayt World Assembly / see Ahl-Ul-Bait World Assembly
♦ Ahmadiyya Anjuman-i-Ishaat-i-Islam Lahore / see Lahore Ahmadiyya Society (#16219)
♦ Ahmadiyya Anjuman Lahore (#16219)
♦ Ahmadiyya Society for the Propagation of Islam / see Lahore Ahmadiyya Society (#16219)
♦ **AHN** African Heart Network (#00336)
♦ AHNS – Association for the History of the Northern Seas (no recent information)
♦ AHO – Africa Health Organisation (internationally oriented national body)
♦ AHO – Association of Holocaust Organizations (internationally oriented national body)
♦ **AHPADA** ASEAN Handicraft Promotion and Development Association (#01194)
♦ **AHP** Association for Humanistic Psychology (#02633)
♦ AHPN – African Health Policy Network (internationally oriented national body)
♦ **AHRA** ASEAN Hotel and Restaurant Association (#01195)
♦ Al Ahram Centre for Political and Strategic Studies (internationally oriented national body)
♦ AHRC – African Human Resource Confederation (unconfirmed)
♦ **AHRC** Asian Human Rights Commission (#01507)
♦ **AHRD** Academy of Human Resource Development (#00038)
♦ AHRF – Arab Human Rights Foundation (internationally oriented national body)
♦ AHRH – African Human Rights Heritage (internationally oriented national body)
♦ **AHRI** Africa Health Research Institute (#00180)
♦ **AHRI** Association of Human Rights Institutes (#02635)
♦ AHRL / see African Heritage Research Library and Cultural Center (#00337)
♦ **AHRLC** African Heritage Research Library and Cultural Center (#00337)
♦ **AHRMIO** Association for Human Resources Management in International Organizations (#02634)
♦ **AHRN** Asian Harm Reduction Network (#01501)
♦ **AHS** AsiaHaptics Society (#01281)
♦ AHS – Australasian Hydrographic Society (internationally oriented national body)
♦ AHSF – Abdul Hameed Shoman Foundation (see: #00903)
♦ AHSN – Arab Human Security Network (unconfirmed)
♦ AHTIPC – Asian Horological Trade and Industry Promotion Conference (meeting series)
♦ AHU – African Hungarian Union (internationally oriented national body)
♦ **AHUE** Archives historiques de l'Union européenne (#10927)
♦ Ahvenanmaan Pohjola-instituutti (internationally oriented national body)
♦ AHWP / see Global Harmonization Working Party (#10399)
♦ AIA – Acupuncture International Association (inactive)
♦ AIA – Aleut International Association (internationally oriented national body)
♦ **AIA** Arab International Association for Tourism and Automobile Clubs (#00991)
♦ AIA – ASEAN Investment Area (see: #01141)
♦ AIA – Asociación Iberoamericana de Atletismo (inactive)
♦ **AIA** Association of International Accountants (#02654)
♦ **AIA** Association for International Arbitration (#02655)
♦ **AIA** Association internationale aphasie (#02668)
♦ **AIA** Association internationale de l'asphalte (#14119)
♦ **AIA** Athletes in Action International (#03005)
♦ AIACA – Association internationale pour l'automation de la chimie analytique (inactive)
♦ **AIAC** Asociación Internacional de Arqueologia del Caribe (#11756)
♦ **AIAC** Association internationale d'archéologie de la Caraïbe (#11756)
♦ AIAC – Association internationale des auteurs de comics et de cartoons (inactive)
♦ **AIAC** Associazione Internazionale di Archeologia Classica (#02988)
♦ AIACC – Association internationale des armateurs et commanditaires de compétitions (no recent information)
♦ AIACE / see Association internationale des anciens de l'Union Européenne (#02667)
♦ **AIACE** Association internationale des anciens de l'Union Européenne (#02667)
♦ AIACE – Associazione Internazionale di Archeologia Computazionale (no recent information)
♦ AIA Continental European Chapter – American Institute of Architects – Continental European Chapter (internationally oriented national body)
♦ AIACR / see Fédération Internationale de l'Automobile (#09613)
♦ **AIACT** Asociación Iberoamericana de Cirugia Toracica (#02135)
♦ AIAD – Association internationale des avocats de la défense (inactive)
♦ **AIADR** Asian Institute of Alternative Dispute Resolutions (#01514)
♦ **AIADTSS** Academia Iberoamericana de Derecho del Trabajo y de la Seguridad Social (#00013)
♦ AIAE – African Institute for Applied Economics (internationally oriented national body)
♦ **AIAE** Association internationale des anciens d'EUROCONTROL (#02666)
♦ AIAE / see Autism-Europe (#03040)
♦ **AIAF** Association internationale des archives francophones (#02669)
♦ **AIAF** Association Internationale des Avocats du Football (#02672)
♦ **AIAFD** Association des institutions africaines de financement du développement (#02353)
♦ AIAG / see Association internationale des assureurs de la production agricole (#02671)
♦ **AIAG** Association internationale des assureurs de la production agricole (#02671)
♦ AIAH – Asociación Interamericana de Hoteles (no recent information)
♦ AIA – International Association of Water Polo Referees (inactive)
♦ AIA / see International Chrysotile Association (#12570)
♦ AIAL – Académie internationale des arts et des lettres, Paris (internationally oriented national body)
♦ **AI** Altrusa International (#00757)
♦ AIAM / see Association of Global Automakers
♦ **AIAM5** Alianza Global de Promoción al Consumo de Frutas y Hortalizas "5 al dia" (#10221)
♦ AIAM5 / see Global Alliance to Promote Fruits and Vegetable Consumption "5 a day" (#10221)
♦ **AIAM5** Global Alliance to Promote Fruits and Vegetable Consumption "5 a day" (#10221)
♦ AIAMA – Abacusking International Abacus Mental-Arithmetic Alliance (unconfirmed)
♦ AIAMA – Association internationale pour l'art et les moyens audio-visuels (inactive)
♦ AIAM – Accademia Internazionale d'Arte Moderna (internationally oriented national body)
♦ **AI** Amnesty International (#00801)
♦ **AIAMP** Asociación Iberoamericana de Ministerios Públicos (#02149)
♦ AIAO / see Pan-Iberican Association of Olympic Academies (#18181)
♦ AIAP – Asociación Internacional de Abogacia Preventiva (no recent information)
♦ **AIAP** Association internationale des arts plastiques (#11710)
♦ AI – Appraisal Institute (internationally oriented national body)
♦ AIARD – Association for International Agriculture and Rural Development (internationally oriented national body)
♦ AIAREF – Association internationale des anesthésistes-réanimateurs d'expression française (inactive)
♦ AiArthritis – International Foundation for Autoimmune & Autoinflammatory Arthritis (internationally oriented national body)
♦ AI – Asian Institute, University of Toronto (internationally oriented national body)
♦ **AIAS** International Association of Independent Art and Design Schools (#11957)
♦ AIAT / see Conseil français des investisseurs en Afrique
♦ AIAT – Association internationale – Art-thérapie (no recent information)
♦ AIAWP – Association internationale des arbitres de water polo (inactive)
♦ **AIB** Academy of International Business (#00040)
♦ AIBADA – Asociación Iberoamericana para el Derecho Alimentario (internationally oriented national body)
♦ AIB – African Investment Bank (unconfirmed)
♦ **AIB** Arab International Bank (#00992)
♦ **AIB** Association for International Broadcasting (#02656)
♦ AIB – Association internationale de bibliologie (inactive)
♦ **AIB** Association internationale de bibliophilie (#02673)

AIB Association Issuing
00586
alphabetic sequence excludes
For the complete listing, see Yearbook Online at

♦ **AIB** Association of Issuing Bodies (#02768)
♦ **AIBC** Association internationale Blaise Cendrars (#03279)
♦ AIBDA – Asociación Interamericana de Bibliotecarios, Documentalistas y Especialistas en Información Agricola (no recent information)
♦ **AIBD** Asia-Pacific Institute for Broadcasting Development (#01934)
♦ AIBD / see International Capital Market Association (#12438)
♦ AIBF / see Financial Services Institute of Australasia
♦ AIBI – Association internationale Bible et informatique (inactive)
♦ **AIBI** Association internationale de la boulangerie industrielle (#02674)
♦ AiBi – Associazione Amici dei Bambini (internationally oriented national body)
♦ AIB International (internationally oriented national body)
♦ **AIBIS** Asia Islet Biology and Incretin Research Association (#01286)
♦ **AIBM** Association internationale des bibliothèques, archives et centres de documentation musicaux (#12042)
♦ AIBOFA – Asociación Iberoamericana de Odontologia Familiar (inactive)
♦ AIBR – Antropólogos Iberoamericanos en Red (unconfirmed)
♦ **AIBSA** Association pour l'information et les bibliothèques de santé en Afrique (#02630)
♦ AIBS / see International Association of School Librarianship (#12146)
♦ AIC / see Ageless International Foundation
♦ AIC / see Arab Investment Company (#00996)
♦ **AICA** Alliance of International Corporate Advisors (#00692)
♦ **AICA** Association internationale des contrôleurs des assurances (#11966)
♦ **AICA** Association internationale des critiques d'art (#02680)
♦ AICA – Associazione Internazionale per la Comunicazione Ambientale (internationally oriented national body)
♦ **AIC** Académie Internationale de la Céramique (#11540)
♦ AICAD – African Institute for Capacity Development (internationally oriented national body)
♦ AICAF / see Japan Association for International Collaboration of Agriculture and Forestry
♦ AICA / see International Association for Mathematics and Computers in Simulation (#12019)
♦ AICAR – Association internationale de coopération et d'animation régionales (inactive)
♦ AICARDES – Association of Arab Institutes and Centres for Economic and Social Research (inactive)
♦ **AIC** ASEAN Insurance Council (#01201)
♦ **AIC** Asociación Interamericana de Contabilidad (#11395)
♦ **AIC** Asociación Internacional de Camineria (#02162)
♦ **AIC** Associação Internacional de Caprinos (#13725)
♦ AIC – Association internationale cardijn (internationally oriented national body)
♦ **AIC** Association Internationale des Charités (#02675)
♦ **AIC** Association internationale du chrysotile (#12570)
♦ **AIC** Association internationale de climatologie (#02676)
♦ AIC – Association internationale du Congo (inactive)
♦ AIC – Association internationale de cybernétique (inactive)
♦ AICBA – Association of International Customs and Border Agencies (internationally oriented national body)
♦ AICBH / see Institute of International Harmonization for Building and Housing
♦ AICC / see Ibero-American Association of Chambers of Commerce (#11014)
♦ AICC – African Institute of Corporate Citizenship (internationally oriented national body)
♦ **AICCAT** Asociación Iberoamericana Contra el Cancer de Tiroides (#02136)
♦ AICCF – Association internationale du congrès des chemins de fer (inactive)
♦ **AICD** Agencia Interamericana para la Cooperación y el Desarrollo (#11397)
♦ **AICE** Associació Internacional de Ciutats Educadores (#11860)
♦ **AICEF** Academia Iberoamericana de Criminalistica y Estudios Forenses (#00012)
♦ **AICEME** Association of International Churches in Europe and the Middle East (#02657)
♦ AICE / see Network of European Foundations (#17019)
♦ **AICEP** Associação dos Operadores de Correios e Telecomunicações dos Paises e Territórios de Lingua Oficial Portuguesa (#02333)
♦ aicep Portugal Global – Trade and Investment Agency (internationally oriented national body)
♦ **AICESIS** Association internationale des conseils économiques et sociaux et institutions similaires (#11858)
♦ AICF – Académie internationale de culture française (inactive)
♦ AICF / see Action Against Hunger (#00086)
♦ AICF – AMAR International Charitable Foundation (internationally oriented national body)
♦ **AIC FORUM** Forum of the Adriatic and Ionian Chambers of Commerce (#09891)
♦ AICGS – American Institute for Contemporary German Studies (internationally oriented national body)
♦ **AICH** Association internationale des capitaines au long cours 'cap-horniers' (#11755)
♦ **AICHE** Association internationale d'histoire contemporaine de l'Europe (#02705)
♦ AICI / see Centre de Solidarité Internationale Corcovado
♦ **AIC** International Colour Association (#12655)
♦ AICK – Association internationale pour la conscience de Krishna (religious order)
♦ AICLA – Australasian Institute of Chartered Loss Adjusters (internationally oriented national body)
♦ AICL / see Association internationale de la critique littéraire (#02679)
♦ **AICL** Association internationale de la critique littéraire (#02679)
♦ **AICLF** Association internationale des criminologues de langue française (#02678)
♦ AICLST – Asia International Conference of Leather Science and Technology (meeting series)
♦ AICMR – Association internationale des constructeurs de matériel roulant (inactive)
♦ AICO – Arab Organization for International Cooperation (unconfirmed)
♦ **AICO** Asociación Iberoamericana de Camaras de Comercio (#11014)
♦ **AICO** Association Internationale des Collectionneurs Olympiques (#02677)
♦ AICPA – Association of International Certified Professional Accountants (internationally oriented national body)
♦ **AICP** Asociación Iberoamericana de Cirugia Pediatrica (#02134)
♦ **AICP** Association internationale des circuits permanents (#03934)
♦ AICP / see Association internationale villes et ports – réseau mondial des villes portuaires (#02751)
♦ AICPF – Association Internationale des Conférenciers Professionnels de la Francophonie (internationally oriented national body)
♦ AICP / see International Academy of Collaborative Professionals (#11541)
♦ AICPR / see Alliance for Peacebuilding
♦ AICPRO – Association internationale des cyclistes professionnels (inactive)
♦ AICR / see Alliance for Peacebuilding
♦ **AICR** Amicale internationale des sous-directeurs et chefs de réception des grands hôtels (#00798)
♦ AICS / see International Federation of Cardio HIIT BodyWeight Exercise
♦ AICS – Alliance internationale de coopération scolaire (inactive)
♦ AICS – Association internationale du cinéma scientifique (inactive)
♦ AICT – Association internationale contre la torture (no recent information)
♦ **AICT** Association internationale des critiques de théâtre (#12226)
♦ **AICTO** Arab Information and Communication Technologies Organization (#00982)
♦ AICTO – Asia Information Communication Technology Organization (no recent information)
♦ AICU / see Association of American International Colleges and Universities
♦ **AICV** Association des Industries des Cidres et Vins de Fruits de l'UE (#02643)
♦ **AICVD** Asian College of Veterinary Dermatology (#01388)
♦ **AiCVIM** Asian College of Veterinary Internal Medicine (#01389)
♦ AICVS – Association internationale pour un sport sans violence (no recent information)
♦ AID / see United States Agency for International Development
♦ AIDA (unconfirmed)
♦ AIDAA – Association internationale des auteurs de l'audiovisuel (no recent information)
♦ **AIDA** Asociación Interamericana para la Defensa del Ambiente (#11398)
♦ **AIDA** Asociación Internacional de Derecho de Aguas (#12263)
♦ AIDA – Association interculturelle pour le Développement Artistique (unconfirmed)
♦ AIDA – Association internationale de défense des artistes (inactive)
♦ AIDA – Association internationale pour le développement de l'apnée / see International Association for the Development of Freediving (#11845)
♦ **AIDA** Association internationale de dialectologie arabe (#02683)
♦ **AIDA** Association internationale de la distribution (#11851)
♦ AIDA – Association internationale de droit africain (inactive)
♦ **AIDA** Association Internationale de Droit des Assurances (#02684)
♦ AIDA – Azerbaijan International Development Agency (internationally oriented national body)
♦ AIDAC / see International Association for Community Development (#11793)
♦ **AID-Afrique** Association internationale pour la démocratie en Afrique (#11836)
♦ **AIDA International** International Association for the Development of Freediving (#11845)
♦ **AIDAP** Associação Iberoamericana de Diagnóstico e Avaliação Psicológica (#02138)
♦ AIDAS – Asociación Iberoamericana de Derecho a la Salud (no recent information)
♦ AID – Association for International Development (inactive)
♦ **AID** Association internationale de développement (#13155)
♦ AID – Association internationale des documentalistes et techniciens de l'information (inactive)
♦ AID – Association internationale des documentaristes (inactive)
♦ AIDBA – Association internationale pour le développement de la documentation, des bibliothèques et des archives en Afrique (inactive)
♦ Aid to Believers in the Soviet Union / see ACER-Russie
♦ **AIDC** Académie internationale de droit comparé (#00027)
♦ AIDC – Alternative Information and Development Centre (internationally oriented national body)
♦ AIDC – Appui International Durable aux Communautés (internationally oriented national body)
♦ AIDC – Asian Industrial Development Council (inactive)
♦ **AIDC** Association internationale de droit constitutionnel (#11811)

♦ Aid to the Church in Need 00587

Aide à l'Eglise en détresse – Ayuda a la Iglesia Necesitada – Kirche in Not/Ostpriesterhilfe – Aiuto alla Chiesa che Soffre – Kerk in Nood/Oostpriesterhulp – Ajuda à Igreja que Sofre – Pomoc Kosciolowi w Potrzebie

SG Postfach 1209, 61452 Königstein, Germany. T. +4961742910. Fax +4961743423. E-mail: info@acn-intl.org – projects@acn-intl.org.
Executive Pres address not obtained.
URL: https://acninternational.org/

History 1947. Founded on the initiative of Fr Werenfried van Straaten. **Aims** Help poor and *persecuted* churches through prayer, pastoral relief and material assistance. **Structure** International headquarters located in Königstein (Germany). National Offices (21). **Languages** English, French, German, Italian, Polish, Portuguese, Spanish. **Finance** Sources: donations. No public or official church monies received. **Activities** Events/meetings; financial and/or material support. **Events** *Congrès Mission* Paris (France) 2018, *International congress* Königstein (Germany FR) 1986. **Publications** *Religious Freedom Report* (2 a year); *Aid to the Church in Need Newsletter* (8 a year) in Dutch, English, French, German, Italian, Polish, Portuguese, Spanish.
Members National offices in 21 countries:
Australia, Austria, Belgium, Brazil, Canada, Chile, Colombia, France, Germany, Ireland, Italy, Korea Rep, Malta, Mexico, Netherlands, Poland, Portugal, Spain, Switzerland, UK, USA.
NGO Relations Member of (2): *Forum of Catholic Inspired NGOs (#09905)*; *Riunione delle Opere per l'Aiuto alle Chiese Orientali (ROACO, see: #04672).* [2022.02.11/XF0401/F]

♦ AIDCO – EuropeAid Cooperation Office (inactive)
♦ **Aidcom** Asian Institute for Development Communication (#01515)
♦ AIDD / see International Association of Sports Law (#12180)
♦ AIDE / see International Association for Water Law (#12263)
♦ AIDEA – Asociación Iberoamericana de Educación Acuatica Especial e Hidroterapia (internationally oriented national body)
♦ Aide et action / see ActionAid (#00087)
♦ Aide et action France (internationally oriented national body)

♦ Aide et action International 00588

Dir Gen Route des Morillons 15, Grand-Saconnex, 1218 Geneva, Switzerland. T. +41225442980. E-mail: info@aide-et-action.org.
URL: http://www.aide-et-action.org/

History 2007, by *Aide et action France.* **Aims** Bring together actors from several continents, working in solidarity with each other to advance the cause of development through education across the world. **Structure** Congress (every 2 years); International Board; International Directors' Committee. **Activities** Advocacy/lobbying/activism. **Consultative Status** Consultative status granted from: *ECOSOC (#05331)* (Special). **NGO Relations** *Aide et Action International Afrique (#00589).* [2017/XM5533/F]

♦ Aide et Action International Afrique 00589

Contact Immeuble Gruntisky Akofala, Aflao Gakly – Quartier Djidjolé, BP 2998, Lomé, Togo. T. +22822507479. Fax +22822502849. E-mail: aeaiafrique.dra@aide-et-action.org.
URL: http://afrique.aide-et-action.org/

History Constituent assembly, Jun 2010. **Aims** Advance the cause of Education for All for vulnerable populations whose fundamental right to quality education is endangered or not applied, in order to enable to choose their future freely. **Structure** Administrative Council; Regional and National Networks. **Languages** English, French, Spanish. **Staff** 140.00 FTE, paid. **Finance** Annual budget: about euro 1,300,000. **Activities** Projects/programmes; research and development; training/education; events/meetings. **Publications** *Newsletter* (4 a year); *Le Magazine.* Annual activity report; project reports. [2017.09.14/XM5534/F]

♦ AIDE – Aide internationale au développement et à l'enfance (internationally oriented national body)
♦ Aide allemande au développement de l'habitat social (internationally oriented national body)
♦ AIDE – Asociación Interamericana de Educación (inactive)
♦ AIDE – Association internationale de droit économique (inactive)
♦ AIDE / see Association mondiale de dispacheurs (#02809)
♦ AIDEC / see Elevages sans frontières
♦ AIDEC – Association internationale d'expertise chimique (inactive)
♦ Aide catholique nordique au développement (inactive)
♦ Aide au développement international (internationally oriented national body)
♦ AIDEDS – Association Internationale des Droits de l'enfant en difficulté et dans la souffrance (internationally oriented national body)
♦ Aide à l'Eglise en détresse (#00587)
♦ Aide de l'Eglise norvégienne (internationally oriented national body)
♦ Aide à l'enfant réfugié / see Avenir pour l'Enfant des Rizières
♦ Aide aux enfants en détresse (internationally oriented national body)
♦ Aide à l'équipement médical dans le Tiers-Monde / see Aide médicale et développement
♦ Aide à l'équipement scolaire et culturelle (internationally oriented national body)
♦ **AIDEF** Asociación Interamericana de Defensorias Públicas (#02159)
♦ AIDE / see Fédération des Agences Internationales pour le Développement (#09414)
♦ **AIDE Fédération** Fédération des Agences Internationales pour le Développement (#09414)
♦ Aide à l'implantation monastique / see Alliance inter-monastères (#00691)
♦ Aide inter-monastères / see Alliance inter-monastères (#00691)
♦ Aide internationale au développement et à l'enfance (internationally oriented national body)
♦ Aide internationale pour l'enfance (internationally oriented national body)
♦ Aide internationale des travailleurs, 1925 (inactive)
♦ AIDELA – Association internationale d'éditeurs de linguistique appliquée (inactive)
♦ Aide aux lépreux Emmaüs / see FAIRMED

♦ Aide aux lépreux Emmaüs Suisse / see FAIRMED
♦ **AIDELF** Association internationale des démographes de langue française (#02682)
♦ Aide médicale et développement (internationally oriented national body)
♦ Aide médicale internationale / see Première Urgence Internationale
♦ Aide médicale internationale à l'enfance (internationally oriented national body)
♦ Aide médical à l'équipement / see Aide médicale et développement
♦ Aide aux missions / see Association Aide au Tiers-Monde
♦ Aide mondiale pour les enfants et les familles (inactive)
♦ **AIDEO** Association of International Dressage Event Organizers (#02663)
♦ Aide odontologique internationale (internationally oriented national body)
♦ **AIDEP** Asociación Iberoamericana de Diagnóstico y Evaluación Psicológica (#02138)
♦ Aide à la réalisation de projects africains (internationally oriented national body)
♦ Aide de Saint-André au Tiers-monde (internationally oriented national body)
♦ AIDES – Association de lutte contre le sida (internationally oriented national body)
♦ Aide – Solidarité / see Fédération des Agences Internationales pour le Développement (#09414)
♦ Aide de Solidarité Internationale / see Actions de Solidarité Internationale
♦ Aides sans frontières, Benin (internationally oriented national body)
♦ AIDF – African Industrial Development Fund (unconfirmed)
♦ AIDF – Aid and International Development Forum (unconfirmed)
♦ AID FOR AIDS International (internationally oriented national body)
♦ AID / see GIGAEurope AISBL (#10151)
♦ **AIDGUM** Association for International Development of Natural Gums (#02662)
♦ AIDH – Association Internationale des Droits de l'Homme (internationally oriented national body)
♦ AIDHRO / see Association for International Development of Natural Gums (#02662)
♦ **AIDIA** Asia Interior Design Institute Association (#01284)
♦ Aid and International Development Forum (unconfirmed)
♦ **AIDIS** Asociación Interamericana de Ingenieria Sanitaria y Ambiental (#11400)
♦ **AIDL** Académie internationale de droit linguistique (#11556)
♦ AIDLAIT – Association internationale de défense des producteurs de lait, des agriculteurs et des industries de transformation connexes (inactive)
♦ AIDL – Alliance Internationale pour la défense des Droits et des Libertés (internationally oriented national body)
♦ AIDL – Asociación Interamericana pro Democracia y Libertad (inactive)
♦ AIDLC – Association internationale pour le développement de logements coopératifs (inactive)
♦ AIDLCM / see Association pour les Langues et Cultures Européennes Menacées (#02782)
♦ Aidlink (internationally oriented national body)
♦ **AIDLR** Association internationale pour la défense de la liberté religieuse (#02681)
♦ AIDMAT – ASEED International Institute of Development Management Technology (internationally oriented national body)
♦ AIDMO / see Arab Industrial Development, Standardization and Mining Organization (#00981)
♦ **AIDN** Association internationale du droit nucléaire (#14379)
♦ AIDOAO / see Federation of European Art Galleries Associations (#09492)
♦ AIDO – Arab Industrial Development Organization (inactive)
♦ AIDO – Association internationale des directeurs d'opéra (inactive)
♦ AIDOS – Association italienne des femmes pour le développement ONLUS (internationally oriented national body)
♦ AIDOS – Associazione Italiana Donne per lo Sviluppo ONLUS (internationally oriented national body)
♦ AIDOS – Italian Association for Women in Development ONLUS (internationally oriented national body)
♦ AIDOT – Association internationale pour le développement de l'odonto-stomatologie tropicale (no recent information)
♦ Aid to Pakistan Club / see Pakistan Development Forum (#18028)
♦ Aid-to-Pakistan Consortium / see Pakistan Development Forum (#18028)
♦ **AIDP** Association internationale de droit pénal (#12074)
♦ AIDP / see International Association of Paediatric Dentistry (#12064)
♦ AIDR – Association internationale de développement rural (inactive)
♦ **AIDROM** Asociación Iberoamericana de Derecho Romano (#11016)
♦ Aid to Russian Christians / see ChildAid
♦ Aid to the Russian Church / see ChildAid
♦ Aid to Russia and the Republics / see ChildAid
♦ AIDSA – Association internationale de défense du saumon atlantique (internationally oriented national body)
♦ AIDS Accountability International / see Accountability International (#00059)

♦ AIDS Action Europe 00590

Secretariat Wilhelmstr 138, 10963 Berlin, Germany. T. +49306900870. Fax +493069008742.
General: http://www.aidsactioneurope.org/

History 23 Mar 2004, Brussels (Belgium), during the Open Forum on AIDS Action in Europe. **Aims** Unite civil society to work towards a more effective response to the *HIV* epidemic in Europe and Central Asia; strive for best standards of human rights protection and universal access to prevention, treatment, care and support; reduce health inequalities focusing on most at risk populations and the epidemic. **Structure** Steering Committee; Secretariat located in Berlin (Germany). **Languages** English, German, Russian. **Staff** 3.00 FTE, paid. **Finance** Contributions from: *European Commission (EC, #06633)*; companies; national organizations. **Activities** Advocacy/lobbying/activism. **Events** *HIV in Europe conference* Stockholm (Sweden) 2009, *Conference on HIV in Europe 2007* Brussels (Belgium) 2007, *European gay health seminar* Paris (France) 2007. **Publications** *AIDS Action Europe Network News* (12 a year); *Clearinghouse Up-Dates* (12 a year). Reports; manuals. Information Services: Online Clearinghouse.
Members Organizations (over 400) in 46 countries:
Albania, Armenia, Austria, Azerbaijan, Belarus, Belgium, Bosnia-Herzegovina, Bulgaria, Croatia, Cyprus, Czechia, Denmark, Estonia, Finland, France, Georgia, Germany, Greece, Hungary, Ireland, Israel, Italy, Kazakhstan, Kyrgyzstan, Latvia, Lithuania, Malta, Moldova, Montenegro, Netherlands, North Macedonia, Norway, Poland, Portugal, Romania, Russia, Serbia, Slovakia, Slovenia, Spain, Sweden, Switzerland, Tajikistan, UK, Ukraine, Uzbekistan.
IGO Relations Cooperates with: *European Commission (EC, #06633)*. **NGO Relations** Member and co-chair of: *European Civil Society Forum on HIV/AIDS (CSF, #06568)*. Cooperates with: Deutsche AIDS-Hilfe eV; *European AIDS Treatment Group (EATG, #05850)*. Member of: *European Alliance for Responsible R and D and Affordable Medicines (#05879)*. [2015.08.26/XM0864/**E**]

♦ **AIDS** Asociación Iberoamericana de Derecho Sanitario (#02137)
♦ AIDS Care Education and Training International / see ACET International
♦ AIDSEGA / see International Scout and Guide Fellowship (#14812)
♦ AIDS Empowerment and Treatment International (no recent information)
♦ AIDSETI – AIDS Empowerment and Treatment International (no recent information)
♦ Aidsfonds (internationally oriented national body)
♦ AIDS Foundation East-West (internationally oriented national body)
♦ AIDS Healthcare Foundation (internationally oriented national body)
♦ AIDS Health Foundation / see AIDS Healthcare Foundation

♦ AIDS Impact 00591

Contact c/o UCL Centre for Gender and Global Health, 30 Guilford Street, London, WC1N 1EH, UK.
URL: http://www.aidsimpact.com/

Structure Board; Scientific Board; Secretariat in The Netherlands. **Events** *International conference* London (UK) 2019, *International conference / Conference* Santa Fe, NM (USA) 2011, *International conference / Conference* Gaborone (Botswana) 2009, *International conference / Conference* Marseille (France) 2007, *International conference / Conference* Cape Town (South Africa) 2005. **NGO Relations** *Sahara Resource Network*. [2019.02.13/XJ4194/**F**]

♦ **AIDSMO** Arab Industrial Development, Standardization and Mining Organization (#00981)
♦ Aid To Southeast Asia (internationally oriented national body)
♦ Aidspan (internationally oriented national body)
♦ AIDS and Rights Alliance for Southern Africa (unconfirmed)

♦ AIDS Society for Asia and the Pacific (ASAP) 00592

Société de lutte contre le SIDA pour l'Asie et le Pacifique

Secretariat 420/1, Research Ctr for Health Economics and Evaluation, Bldg 7 – 8th Floor, Fac of Public Health, Toong Phayathai, Ratchathewi Disctrict, Bangkok, 10400, Thailand. T. +6626409853. Fax +6626409853.

History 1990, Canberra (Australia). Previously registered in accordance with Australian law. Since 2013, registered in accordance with Thai law. **Aims** Promote opportunities for the discussion of HIV/AIDS issues and the exchange of relevant information and technologies; influence HIV/AIDS policy development in the region and awareness of the gravity of the regional epidemic internationally; work with different regional sectors and stakeholders in Asia and the Pacific towards collective advocacy efforts. **Structure** Executive Committee; Secretariat. Vice-Presidents, Acting Treasurer, Immediate Past President, Public Officer, Representatives of UNAIDS and IAS, one or more PLHIV member and up to 11 additional members. Secretariat, comprising Executive Director, Manager Operations and Assistant to the President. **Languages** English. **Staff** 2.00 FTE, paid. **Finance** Members'dues: US$ 50-200. Other sources: donors; local fund raising; pharmaceutical companies. Annual budget: US$ 200,000. **Activities** Events/meetings; advocacy/lobbying/activism. **Events** *ICAAP: International Congress on AIDS in Asia and the Pacific / International Conference on AIDS in Asia and the Pacific – ICAAP* Dhaka (Bangladesh) 2015, *ICAAP: International Congress on AIDS in Asia and the Pacific / International Conference on AIDS in Asia and the Pacific – ICAAP* Bangkok (Thailand) 2013, *ICAAP: international congress on AIDS in Asia and the Pacific / International Conference on AIDS in Asia and the Pacific – ICAAP* Busan (Korea Rep) 2011, *International Conference on AIDS in Asia and the Pacific – ICAAP* Bali (Indonesia) 2009, *ICAAP: international congress on AIDS in Asia and the Pacific* Nusa Dua (Indonesia) 2009. **Publications** *ASAP Newsletter* (4 a year); *e-ASAP* (4 a year) – online. Information Services: Extensive database related to projects, programmes and government policies on AIDS in the region.
Members Organizational members in 11 countries and territories:
Australia, Bangladesh, Fiji, Hong Kong, India, Japan, Malaysia, Pakistan, Philippines, Singapore, Thailand.
Included in the above, 2 organizations listed in this Yearbook:
Asian Forum of Parliamentarians on Population and Development (AFPPD, #01493); ICDDR,B (#11051).
IGO Relations Collaborates with: *Joint United Nations Programme on HIV/AIDS (UNAIDS, #16149); UNDP (#20292); WHO (#20950)*. **NGO Relations** Collaborates with: *Coalition of Asia Pacific Regional Networks on HIV/AIDS (Seven Sisters, #04051).* [2015/XD4794/v/**D**]

♦ Aids Vaccine Advocacy Coalition / see Global Advocacy for HIV Prevention (#10172)
♦ AIDT – Association internationale de développement de tontines (internationally oriented national body)
♦ Aiducation International (internationally oriented national body)
♦ AIDUIM – Association internationale pour le développement des universités internationales et mondiales (no recent information)
♦ **AIDV** Association internationale des juristes du droit de la vigne et du vin (#15891)
♦ AID/WATCH (internationally oriented national body)
♦ AIEA2 – Asociación Internacional de Economia Alimentaria y Agroindustrial (inactive)
♦ AIEA2 – Association internationale d'économie alimentaire et agro-industrielle (inactive)
♦ **AIEA** Agence internationale de l'énergie atomique (#12294)
♦ **AIEA** Asian Innovation and Entrepreneurship Association (#01513)
♦ AIEA – Association of International Education Administrators (internationally oriented national body)
♦ **AIEA** Association internationale des économistes agronomiques (#11695)
♦ **AIEA** Association internationale des études arméniennes (#11709)
♦ **AIE** Adriatic Ionian Euroregion (#00120)
♦ AIEAF – Association internationale des éditeurs africains francophones (no recent information)
♦ **AIE** Agence internationale de l'énergie (#13270)
♦ AIEA / see International Association of Students in Agricultural and Related Sciences (#12191)
♦ AIE – Alliance for International Education (internationally oriented national body)
♦ AIEAS – Association internationale des études de l'Asie du Sud-Est (inactive)
♦ AIE – Asociación Iberoamericana de Ergonomia (inactive)
♦ **AIE** Association Internationale pour les Edulcorants (#15639)
♦ **AIE** Association internationale d'esthétique (#11692)
♦ **AIEB** Association internationale des études byzantines (#11751)
♦ **AIEC** Association internationale des étudiants cavaliers (#02694)
♦ **AIECE** Association d'instituts européens de conjoncture économique (#02506)
♦ AIECM2 / see Association Internationale pour l'Étude des Céramiques Médiévales et Modernes en Méditerranée (#02711)
♦ **AIECM3** Association Internationale pour l'Étude des Céramiques Médiévales et Modernes en Méditerranée (#02711)
♦ AIECM – Association internationale d'étude des civilisations méditerranéennes (inactive)
♦ **AIEDE** Association internationale pour l'échange de droits d'émission (#13262)
♦ AIEDRI – Association for International Egg Donation Research and Information (no recent information)
♦ AIEE – Association des instituts d'études européennes (inactive)
♦ **AIEE** Association internationale d'esthétique expérimentale (#11867)
♦ **AIEE** Association internationale pour l'évaluation éducative (#11861)
♦ AIEE / see International Association for Energy Economics (#11869)
♦ AIE / see European Waterproofing Association (#09084)
♦ AIE / see EuropeOn (#09166)
♦ AIEF – Association internationale pour l'égalité des femmes (unconfirmed)
♦ **AIEF** Association internationale des études françaises (#02690)
♦ **AIEFFA** Association internationale des établissements francophones de formation à l'assurance (#02687)
♦ **AIEFSB** Internationella Föreningen för Betonghåltagare (#11806)
♦ **AIEG** Asociación Internacional de Estudios Galegos (#02164)
♦ **AIEGL** Association internationale d'épigraphie Grecque et Latine (#11924)
♦ **AIEIA** Association internationale des écoles et instituts d'administration (#12147)
♦ AIEI – Association internationale pour l'éducation intégrative (inactive)
♦ **AIEI** Association internationale pour l'éducation interculturelle (#11969)
♦ **AIEI** Association internationale pour l'évaluation d'impacts (#11956)
♦ AIEID – Asociación Internacional de Estudio Integral del Deporte (inactive)
♦ **AIEJI** Association internationale des éducateurs sociaux (#12167)
♦ **AIEL** Asociación Internacional de Estructuras Laminares y Espaciales (#12162)
♦ **AIEL** Association of Independent European Lawyers (#02640)
♦ **AIELF** Association Internationale des Economistes de Langue Française (#02686)
♦ AIEL / see International Association for Greek and Latin Epigraphy (#11924)
♦ **AIEMA** Association internationale pour l'étude de la mosaïque antique (#02689)
♦ AIEM – Association internationale pour l'essai des matériaux (inactive)
♦ AIEM – Association internationale des études sur la mécanographie (inactive)
♦ AIEMCA – Australasian Institute for Ethnomethodology and Conversation Analysis (internationally oriented national body)
♦ **AIEMPR** Association internationale d'études medico-psychologiques et religieuses (#12028)
♦ AIEMPR / see International Association for Medico-Psychological and Religious Studies (#12028)
♦ **AIEN** Association of International Energy Negotiators (#02722)
♦ **AIENL** Association Internationale d'Études néo-latines (#12048)
♦ **AIEO** Association internationale d'études occitanes (#02691)
♦ AIEPAD – Asociación Iberoamericana de Estudio de los Problemas del Alcohol y la Droga (no recent information)

♦ **AIEP** Asociación Internacional de Escritores Policiacos (#11825)
♦ AIEP – Association internationale des éducateurs à la paix (internationally oriented national body)
♦ **AIEP** Association internationale d'études patristiques (#02692)
♦ **AIEP** Association internationale des experts en philatélie (#02696)
♦ AIEP / see Cargo Rail Europe (#03431)
♦ AIEPELF – Association internationale des écoles partiellement ou entièrement de langue française (inactive)
♦ AIEPM – Association internationale des éducateurs pour la paix du monde (internationally oriented national body)
♦ AIEQ – Association internationale des études québécoises (internationally oriented national body)
♦ **AIERI** Association internationale des études et recherches sur l'information (#12022)
♦ **AIERTI** Association internationale pour l'étude des rapports entre texte et image (#12276)
♦ **AIESAD** Asociación Iberoamericana de Educación Superior a Distancia (#11015)
♦ **AIES** Association internationale pour l'enseignement statistique (#12184)

♦ AIESEC 00593

Secretariat 5605 Ave De Gaspé, Suite 208, Montréal QC H2T 2A4, Canada.
URL: http://aiesec.org/

History 1949, Stockholm (Sweden). Founded following a meeting, 1948, of students from 12 European universities in 7 countries. Informal activities started 1946. Former names and other names: *AIESEC – International Association of Students in Economics and Management* – former; *AIESEC – Association internationale des étudiants en sciences économiques et commerciales* – former; *AIESEC – The Global Youth Network impacting the world through leadership development experiences* – full title; *Stichting AIESEC International* – legal name. Registration: Handelsregister, No/ID: KVK 24280781, Netherlands; No/ID: 1055154-6, Start date: 2018, Canada. **Aims** Achieve peace and fulfillment of humankind's potential by activating *leadership* qualities in *youth* through learning from practical experiences in challenging environments. **Structure** Executive Body; National Offices; Global Headquarters in Rotterdam (Netherlands). *AIESEC Alumni International (AAI, #00594)* set up 1986. **Languages** English. **Staff** 25.00 FTE, paid. **Finance** Sources: sponsoring; international internships; membership fees from member National Committees. **Activities** Training/education. **Events** *International Congress* 2022, *YouthSpeak Forum Middle East Africa* Dubai (United Arab Emirates) 2021, *International Congress* Montréal, QC (Canada) 2021, *Annual Congress* Rotterdam (Netherlands) 2020, *Asia Pacific YouthSpeak Forum* Singapore (Singapore) 2020. **Publications** *The Power of Youth* – annual report. **Members** Young people (about 50,000) in over 2,400 universities in 122 countries and territories. Membership countries not specified. **Consultative Status** Consultative status granted from: *ECOSOC (#05331)* (Special and Ros C); *UNESCO (#20322)* (Consultative Status); *ILO (#11123)* (Special List); *UNIDO (#20336)*; *Council of Europe (CE, #04881)* (Participatory Status). **NGO Relations** Member of (5): *EarthAction (EA, #05159)*; *Junior Chamber International (JCI, #16168)*; *The European Law Students' Association (ELSA, #07660)*; *Transparency, Accountability and Participation Network (TAP Network, #20222)*; *United Nations Global Compact (#20567)*. Partner of (1): *UNLEASH*. Participates in: *Global Meeting of Generations (GMG)*. [2021/XB1349/**B**]

♦ AIESEC Alumni International (AAI) 00594

Main Office Rigiweg 13, 6343 Holzhäusern, Switzerland. E-mail: info@aiesec-alumni.org.
URL: http://www.aiesec-alumni.org/

History 1986. Founded as the alumni association of *AIESEC (#00593)*. Registration: Switzerland; Belgium. **Aims** Contribute to international understanding; assist members in their personal development; provide opportunities for continuing, close and cordial relations among members; assist members in developing their *professional* ability and widening their cultural horizons; maintain cooperative relations with AIESEC. **Structure** General Assembly (annual, at international congress); Executive Board. **Languages** English. **Staff** No professional staff. **Finance** Members' dues. Donations; contributions. **Activities** Personal and business networking; international study tours. **Events** *International Congress* Accra (Ghana) 2023, *International Congress* Hurghada (Egypt) 2018, *Asia Pacific Conference* Subang Jaya (Malaysia) 2018, *International Congress* Porto (Portugal) 2015, *International Symposium* Chiba (Japan) 2012. **Publications** Central communication centre for members through website. **Members** Individuals. Membership countries not specified. **NGO Relations** Member of: *Society for International Development (SID, #19581)*. [2022/XE2501/v/**E**]

♦ AIESEC – Association internationale des étudiants en sciences économiques et commerciales / see AIESEC (#00593)
♦ AIESEC – The Global Youth Network impacting the world through leadership development experiences / see AIESEC (#00593)
♦ AIESEC – International Association of Students in Economics and Management / see AIESEC (#00593)
♦ **AIESEE** Association internationale d'études du Sud-Est européen (#02693)
♦ **AIESEP** Association internationale des écoles supérieures d'éducation physique (#02685)
♦ **AIEST** Association internationale d'experts scientifiques du tourisme (#02697)
♦ **AIETAO** Association des Institutions d'Enseignement Theologique en Afrique Occidentale (#02953)
♦ AIETI – Asociación Ibérica de Estudios de Traducción e Interpretación (internationally oriented national body)
♦ AIETI – Asociación de Investigación y Especialización sobre Temas Iberoamericanos (internationally oriented national body)
♦ **AIETS** Association internationale des écoles de travail social (#12149)
♦ AIEV / see International Association for Vegetation Science (#12253)
♦ **AIFA** Association internationale francophone des aînés (#02702)
♦ AIF – African Innovation Foundation (internationally oriented national body)
♦ AIF – Ageless International Foundation (internationally oriented national body)
♦ **AIF** Alliance internationale des femmes (#11639)
♦ AIF – Asian Institute of Finance (internationally oriented national body)
♦ **AIF** Asociación Internacional de Fomento (#13155)
♦ **AIFBD** Association internationale francophone des bibliothécaires et documentalistes (#02703)
♦ AIFC – Association internationale des fabricants de confiserie (inactive)
♦ AIFE – Association internationale des femmes écrivains (inactive)
♦ AIFF – Association internationale des femmes francophones (no recent information)
♦ AIF / see Futuribles International (#10052)
♦ **AIFI** Académie internationale du Fiqh islamique (#13960)
♦ **AIFI** Association internationale francophone des intervenants auprès des familles séparées (#02704)
♦ AIF / see International Islamic Fiqh Academy (#13960)
♦ **AIFM** Association internationale des femmes médecins (#16630)
♦ **AIFM** Association internationale forêts méditerranéennes (#02699)
♦ **AIFMC** Association internationale des facultés de médecine catholiques (#11759)
♦ AIFME – Association Internationale de la Femme Marocaine à l'Étranger (internationally oriented national body)
♦ AIFO – Italian Association Amici di Raoul Follereau (internationally oriented national body)
♦ **AIFP** Asociación Iberoamericana de Filosofia Politica (#02141)
♦ **AIFP** Asociación Iberoamericana de Filosofia Practica (#02142)
♦ AIFP – Association internationale de la fonction publique (no recent information)
♦ AIFPAUR – Association internationale pour la formation professionnelle en aménagement urbain et régional (inactive)
♦ AIFR – Arab Institute for Forestry and Range (no recent information)
♦ **AIFREF** Association internationale de formation et de recherche en éducation familiale (#02700)
♦ AIFRF / see Raoul Follereau International Union (#18618)
♦ **AIFRIS** Association Internationale pour la Formation, la Recherche et l'Intervention Sociale (#02701)
♦ AIFRO – Association internationale francophone de recherche odontologique (no recent information)
♦ **AIFT** International Association of Free Thought (#11906)
♦ **AIGA** Alleanza Internazionale Giovanna d'Arco (#19992)
♦ **AIGA** Asia Industrial Gases Association (#01283)
♦ **AIGA** Association internationale de géomagnetisme et d'aéronomie (#11916)
♦ AIG – Académie internationale de la gastronomie (unconfirmed)
♦ **AIG** Académie internationale de généalogie (#00028)
♦ **AIG** Advertising Information Group (#00137)
♦ **AIG** Association internationale de géodésie (#11914)
♦ **AIG** Association internationale de gérodontologie (#11919)
♦ **AIG** Association internationale du goudron (#15655)
♦ **AIGAV** Associazione Internazionale dei Giornalisti Accreditati in Vaticano (#02773)
♦ **AIGCC** Asia Investor Group op Climate Change (#01285)
♦ AIGCEV – Association Internationale de Gouvernance du Cachet Electronique Visible (internationally oriented national body)
♦ AIGC / see International Association of GeoChemistry (#11913)
♦ AIGE / see Organización Panamericana de Gastroenterologia (#17847)
♦ AIGHD – Amsterdam Institute for Global Health and Development (internationally oriented national body)
♦ AIGI / see International Association of Engineering Geology and the Environment (#11872)
♦ AIG / see International Association of Gerontology and Geriatrics (#11920)
♦ **AIGLP** Asociación Iberoamericana de Gas Licuado del Petróleo (#02143)
♦ **AIGM** Association internationale de grands magasins (#11842)
♦ **AIGN** Associated International Group of Nurseries (#02340)
♦ AIGP – Association internationale de gérontologie psychanalytique (inactive)
♦ AIGSL – Alleanza Internazionale dei Giornalisti e Scrittori Latini (inactive)
♦ AIGS / see World Glaucoma Association (#21540)
♦ AIHA – American International Health Alliance (internationally oriented national body)
♦ **AIH** Académie internationale d'héraldique (#11549)
♦ **AIH** Asociación Internacional de Hidatidologia (#11949)
♦ **AIH** Asociación Internacional de Hispanistas (#02165)
♦ **AIH** Association internationale des hydrogéologues (#11953)
♦ AIHCA – Associação Internacional de História e Civilização do Açúcar (internationally oriented national body)
♦ AIHD – African Institute for Health and Development (internationally oriented national body)
♦ **AIHD** ASEAN Institute for Health Development (#01197)
♦ AIHDI – Association internationale d'histoire du droit et des institutions (inactive)
♦ AIH / see International Hotel and Restaurant Association (#13813)
♦ **AIHJA** Association internationale des hautes juridictions administratives (#12215)
♦ AIHMM – Azerbaycan Insan Hüquqlarini Mudafie Merkezi (internationally oriented national body)
♦ AIHP / see International Association Interactions of Psychoanalysis (#11968)
♦ **AIHR** Arab Institute for Human Rights (#00983)
♦ AIHR – Asian Institute for Human Rights (internationally oriented national body)
♦ **AIHTC** Assembly for the International Heat Transfer Conferences (#02318)
♦ AIHTI – Association internationale d'histoire des télécommunications et de l'informatique (inactive)
♦ **AIHV** Association internationale pour l'histoire du verre (#02706)
♦ AIIA – Australian Institute of International Affairs (internationally oriented national body)
♦ **AII** Adriatic and Ionian Initiative (#00121)
♦ AIIAF – Association internationale des ingenieurs agronomes francophones (inactive)
♦ AIIAS – Adventist International Institute of Advanced Studies (internationally oriented national body)
♦ **AIIB** Asian Infrastructure Investment Bank (#01512)
♦ AIIBP – Association internationale de l'industrie des bouillons et potages (inactive)
♦ **AIIC** Association internationale des interprètes de conférence (#11807)
♦ **AIICM** Association internationale et interdisciplinaire sur la chaîne des médicaments (#02707)
♦ **AIICS** Asociación Internacional de Investigación sobre la Comunicación Social (#12022)
♦ AIID – Amsterdam Institute for International Development (internationally oriented national body)
♦ AIIDAP – Association internationale d'information et de documentation en administration publique (inactive)
♦ AIIE / see Institute of Industrial and Systems Engineers (#11270)
♦ AIIFL – Asian Institute of International Financial Law (internationally oriented national body)
♦ AIIH / see International Association for Hydro-Environment Engineering and Research (#11950)
♦ AIII – Association internationale d'irradiation industrielle (inactive)
♦ AIII – Association of International Industrial Irradiation (inactive)
♦ **AIIL** African Institute of International Law (#00341)
♦ AIIM / see Association for Intelligent Information Management (#02652)
♦ **AIIM** Association for Intelligent Information Management (#02652)
♦ AIIMB / see International Association of Infant Massage (#11962)
♦ AI / see Inter-Cultural Association (#11465)
♦ AIIRM – Association internationale des intérêts radio-maritimes (inactive)
♦ AIIS – Albanian Institute for International Studies (internationally oriented national body)
♦ AIIS – American Institute for International Steel (internationally oriented national body)
♦ **AIIS** Association internationale pour l'informatique statistique (#12183)
♦ AIISUP – Association internationale d'information scolaire universitaire et professionnelle (inactive)
♦ **AIIT** Association internationale de l'inspection du travail (#11983)
♦ **AIJA** Association internationale des jeunes avocats (#12282)
♦ AIJA – Australasian Institute of Judicial Administration (internationally oriented national body)
♦ AIJ / see Asian Institute of Journalism and Communication (#01517)
♦ **AIJC** Asian Institute of Journalism and Communication (#01517)
♦ **AIJC** Association Internationale des Journalistes de Cyclisme (#02708)
♦ **AIJD** Association internationale des juristes démocrates (#11837)
♦ AIJE – Association des industries du jute européennes (inactive)
♦ AIJE – Association Internationale Jacques Ellul (internationally oriented national body)
♦ AIJF – Association internationale des jeunes francophones (no recent information)
♦ AIJF – Association internationale des journalistes ferroviaires (no recent information)
♦ AIJIC – Asociación Internacional de Jóvenes Investigadores en Comunicación (internationally oriented national body)
♦ AIJM – Asociación Interamericana de Jueces de Menores (inactive)
♦ AIJN / see European Fruit Juice Association (#07362)
♦ **AIJN** European Fruit Juice Association (#07362)
♦ **AIJP** Association internationale des journalistes philatéliques (#02709)
♦ **AIJS** Association internationale des journalistes du ski (#02710)

♦ Aikido Yoshinkai Foundation (AYF) 00595

Chairman Aikido Yoshinkan Hombu Dojo, 2F Toyo Bldg, 4-17-15 Takada-no-baba, Shinjuku-ku, Tokyo, 169-0075 Japan. T. +81333685556. Fax +81333685578.
URL: http://www.yoshinkan.net/

History Founded 1 Jan 1990, as *International Yoshinkan Aikido Federation (IYAF)*. Also known as: *Yoshinkan Aikido*. **Aims** Teach the curriculum of Yoshinkan Aikido; spread its spirit and practice all over the world. **Languages** English, Japanese. **Activities** Training/education; certification/accreditation; events/meetings. **Members** Individuals in 15 countries:
Australia, Brazil, Canada, France, Germany, Japan, Malaysia, New Zealand, Philippines, Poland, Russia, Thailand, UK, Ukraine, USA. [2018/XD5279/t/**F**]

♦ Aikuiskasvatuksen ja Kansansivistystyön Pohjoismainen Yhteistyö (#17504)
♦ Aikuiskasvatuksen ja Sivistystyön Pohjoismainen Yhteistyö / see Nordisk Folkeoplysnings- og Voksenundervisningssamarbejde (#17504)
♦ **AILA** Asociación de Industriales Latinoamericanos (#16341)
♦ **AILA** Associação dos Industriais Latinoamericanos (#16341)
♦ **AILA** Association internationale de linguistique appliquée (#02713)
♦ **AILAC** Asociación Ibero Latinoamericana de Colombofilia (#02156)
♦ AILAE / see Asociación Iberolatinoamericana de Endodoncia (#02157)

♦ **AILAE** Asociación Iberolatinoamericana de Endodoncia (#02157)
♦ AILANCYP – Asociación IberoLatinoAmericana de Neurociencias y Psiquiatría (unconfirmed)
♦ **AILASA** Association of Iberian and Latin American Studies of Australasia (#02637)
♦ **AIL** Associação Internacional de Lusitanistas (#12006)
♦ AIL / see Association of International Librarians and Information Specialists (#02754)
♦ AILA-VDC – Academia Ibero-Latinoamericana de Valoración del Daño Corporal (unconfirmed)
♦ **AILC** Association internationale de littérature comparée (#12829)
♦ **AILCC** Association internationale de lutte contre la cybercriminalité (#02714)
♦ AILCD – Asian Institute of Low Carbon Design (unconfirmed)
♦ AILDC – Academia Ibero-Latinoamericana de Disfunción Craneo-Mandibular y Dolor Facial (internationally oriented national body)
♦ AILE – Association internationale des loteries d'Etat (inactive)
♦ **AILF** Association des informaticiens de langue française (#02644)
♦ **AILF** Association internationale des libraires francophones (#02712)
♦ **AILFN** Association of International Law Firm Networks (#02753)
♦ AIL / see International Literacy Association (#14057)
♦ AIL / see International Society of Limnology (#15232)
♦ **AILIS** Association of International Librarians and Information Specialists (#02754)
♦ AILLS – Association internationale des langues et littératures slaves (inactive)
♦ **AILN** Asian Intense Laser Network (#01522)
♦ **AILO** Association of International Life Offices (#02755)
♦ **AILP** Asociación Internacional de Libre Pensamiento (#11906)
♦ **AILP** Associação Internacional de Linguistica do Português (#02330)
♦ **AILP** Association Internationale de Libre Pensée (#11906)
♦ **AILPcsh** Associação Internacional de Ciências Sociais e Humanas em Língua Portuguesa (#02329)
♦ AIM (internationally oriented national body)
♦ **AIMA** Alternative Investment Management Association (#00752)
♦ **AIMA** Asociación Iberoamericana de Medicina Aerospacial (#02147)
♦ AIMA – Asociación Internacional Mujeres en las Artes (internationally oriented national body)
♦ **AIMA** Association internationale des musées d'agriculture (#02720)
♦ **AIMAC** Association internationale de management de l'art et de la culture (#02716)
♦ AIMAF – Association des institutions de formation et de perfectionnement au management d'Afrique francophone (no recent information)
♦ AIM / see Africa Inland Mission International (#00182)
♦ **AIM** Alliance inter-monastères (#00691)
♦ **AIMAS** Académie internationale de médecine aéronautique et spatiale (#11537)
♦ **AIM** Asian Institute of Management (#01518)
♦ **AIM** Association des industries de marques (#06397)
♦ AIM – Association internationale de la meunerie (inactive)
♦ AIM – Association internationale missionnaire (internationally oriented national body)
♦ **AIM** Association internationale de la mutualité (#02721)
♦ AIMAV – Association internationale pour la communication interculturelle (inactive)
♦ AIMBE – Association internationale de médecine et de biologie de l'environnement (inactive)
♦ **A-IMBN** Asia-Pacific International Molecular Biology Network (#01935)
♦ **AIMC** AI Music Creativity (#00596)
♦ AIMCAL – Association of International Metallizers, Coaters and Laminators (internationally oriented national body)
♦ **AIMC** Arab Interior Ministers' Council (#00990)
♦ **AIMC** Associazione Internazionale Mosaicisti Contemporanei (#11816)
♦ **AIMD** Association internationale des musées des douanes (#11831)
♦ AIMEA – Association internationale des métiers et enseignements d'art (inactive)
♦ AIME – Association of Business and Industrial Marketing for Europe (no recent information)
♦ AIMECA / see International Committee for Insurance Medicine (#12780)
♦ **AIME** European Society for Artificial Intelligence in Medicine (#08524)
♦ **AIMES -AFRIQUE** Association Internationale des Médecins pour la promotion de l'Education et de la Santé en Afrique (#02718)
♦ **AIM** European Academy for Industrial Management (#05796)
♦ AIMF – Aspen International Mountain Foundation (internationally oriented national body)
♦ **AIMF** Association Internationale des Maires et responsables des capitales et métropoles partiellement ou entièrement Francophones (#02715)
♦ **AIMFR** Association internationale des mouvements familiaux de formation rurale (#02719)
♦ AIMG – Association Internationale des Ministères de Guérison (unconfirmed)
♦ **AIMH** Association internationale des musées d'histoire (#12040)
♦ Aim for Human Rights (internationally oriented national body)
♦ AIMI / see AIM
♦ **AIMICT** Arab International Society for Management Technology (#00993)
♦ AIM International / see AIM
♦ **AIM International** Africa Inland Mission International (#00182)
♦ **AIMJF** Association internationale des magistrats de la jeunesse et de la famille (#12283)
♦ AIMJ / see International Association of Youth and Family Judges and Magistrates (#12283)
♦ **AiML** Advances in Modal Logic (#00128)
♦ AIMLC / see Association of Marine Laboratories of the Caribbean (#02794)
♦ AIMO / see International Society for Orthomolecular Medicine (#15334)
♦ AIMPA / see International Association of Meteorology and Atmospheric Sciences (#12031)
♦ AIMPO / see African Initiative For Mankind Progress Organization
♦ AIMPO – African Initiative For Mankind Progress Organization (internationally oriented national body)
♦ AIMR / see CFA Institute
♦ **AIMRI** Alliance of International Market Research Institutes (#00695)
♦ AIMS / see Accelerating International Mission Strategies
♦ **AIMSA** Association internationale de météorologie et de sciences de l'atmosphère (#12031)
♦ AIMS – Accelerating International Mission Strategies (internationally oriented national body)
♦ AIMS – African Institute of Management Science (internationally oriented national body)
♦ **AIMS** African Institute for Mathematical Sciences (#00342)
♦ **AIMS** Alliance of Independent recognised Members of Sport (#00690)
♦ AIMS – American Institute for Maghrib Studies (internationally oriented national body)
♦ **AIMS** Association internationale du management stratégique (#02717)
♦ **AIMS** Association internationale pour les media dans la science (#12024)
♦ **AIMS** Association of International Marathons and Distance Races (#02756)
♦ AIMS International – Amusement Industry Manufacturers and Suppliers International (internationally oriented national body)
♦ AIMS / see International Federation of Sports Medicine (#13554)
♦ AIMS-NEI / see African Institute for Mathematical Sciences (#00342)
♦ AIMS Next Einstein Initiative / see African Institute for Mathematical Sciences (#00342)

♦ AI Music Creativity (AIMC) 00596

Contact address not obtained. E-mail: aimusic-steering@sfu.ca.
URL: https://aimusiccreativity.org/

History 2020. Created on merger of Musical Metacreation (MuMe) and Computer Simulation of Music Creativity (CSMC). **Aims** Bring together scholars and artists interested in the virtual emulation of musical creativity and its use for music creation; provide an interdisciplinary platform to promote, present and discuss their work in scientific and artistic contexts. **Structure** Steering Committee. **Activities** Events/meetings. **Events** *AIMC Conference on AI Music Creativity* 2023, *Conference on AI Music Creativity* Japan 2022, *Joint Conference on AI Music Creativity* Graz (Austria) 2021, *Joint Conference on AI Music Creativity* Stockholm (Sweden) 2020. **Publications** *Journal of Creative Music Systems (JCMS).* [2022/AA1593/**F**]

♦ **AINA** Arctic Institute of North America (#01099)
♦ **AIN** Amicale internationale de Neuengamme (#14347)
♦ **AIN** Andean Information Network (#00819)
♦ **AIN** Applied Improvisation Network (#00881)
♦ **AIN** Arab Institute of Navigation (#00985)
♦ AINC – African Israel Nineveh Church (internationally oriented national body)
♦ **AInCI** Asociación Internacional de la Comunicación Interactiva (#02163)
♦ AINL – AINL: Artificial Intelligence and Natural Language Conference (meeting series)
♦ AINL: Artificial Intelligence and Natural Language Conference (meeting series)
♦ AINLF – Association internationale des navigants de langue française (inactive)
♦ **AINP** Academia Iberoamericana de Neurologia Pediatrica (#11013)
♦ **AINP** Association internationale des numismates professionnels (#12104)
♦ **AIO** Académie internationale olympique (#14406)
♦ **AIO** African Insurance Organization (#00343)
♦ **AIO** Asociación Iberoamericana de Ortodoncistas (#02151)
♦ AIO – Associazione Internazionale di Ontopsicologia (internationally oriented national body)
♦ **AIOB** Association internationale d'océanographie biologique (#11726)
♦ AIOC – Association internationale de l'icône et des objects de culte (no recent information)
♦ AIOCC cross – Association internationale des organisateurs de courses cyclistes (inactive)
♦ AIOD / see Osteosynthesis and Trauma Care Foundation (#17911)
♦ **AIOEP** Asociación Internacional para la Orientación Educativa y Profesional (#11862)
♦ **AIOF** Association Internationale des Orthodontistes Francophones (#02724)
♦ **AIOI** Academia Internacional de Odontologia Integral (#00014)
♦ AIONP – Association internationale pour l'optimisation de la nutrition des plantes (inactive)
♦ AIOP / see International Association for the Physical Sciences of the Oceans (#12082)
♦ AIORMS – Association olympique internationale pour la recherche médico-sportive (no recent information)
♦ **AIOS** Asociación Internacional de Organismos de Supervisión de Fondos de Pensiones (#02167)
♦ **AIOSP** Association internationale d'orientation scolaire et professionnelle (#11862)
♦ **AIOTI** Alliance for Internet of Things Innovation (#00697)
♦ **AIOWF** Association of the International Olympic Winter Sports Federations (#02757)
♦ **AIPA** ASEAN Intellectual Property Association (#01203)
♦ **AIPA** ASEAN Inter-Parliamentary Assembly (#01205)
♦ **AIPA** Association Internationale de la Psychologie Adlérienne (#11960)
♦ **AIPA** Association internationale de psychologie analytique (#11700)
♦ **AIPA** Association internationale de psychologie appliquée (#11705)
♦ **AIP** Académie internationale de la pipe (#00029)
♦ **AIP** Asociación Internacional de Pediatria (#14541)
♦ **AIP** Association internationale de papyrologues (#02725)
♦ **AIP** Association internationale de pédiatrie (#14541)
♦ AIP – Association internationale des pompiers (internationally oriented national body)
♦ **AIP** Association internationale des ports (#12096)
♦ **AIPC** Asociación Iberoamericana de Periodismo Cientifico (#19140)
♦ **AIPC** Association internationale des ponts et charpentes (#11737)
♦ AIPC – Association internationale de prophylaxie de la cécité (inactive)
♦ **AIPCC** Asociación Mundial de Carreteras (#21754)
♦ **AIPCE** Alliance of Independent Press Councils of Europe (#00689)
♦ **AIPCE** Association des industries du poisson de l'Union Européenne (#08989)
♦ **AIPCF** Association Internationale de Psychanalyse de Couple et de Famille (#11822)
♦ AIPC / see International Association of Convention Centres (#11818)
♦ **AIPC** International Association of Convention Centres (#11818)
♦ AIPCN / see PIANC (#18371)
♦ **AIPCR** Association mondiale de la route (#21754)
♦ AIPD-GL – Action internationale pour la paix et le développement dans la région des Grands Lacs, Switzerland (internationally oriented national body)
♦ AIPDIP – Asociación Interamericana de Profesores de Derecho Internacional Privado (inactive)
♦ **AIPEA** Association internationale pour l'étude des argiles (#02688)
♦ AIPE – Aide internationale pour l'enfance (internationally oriented national body)
♦ **AIPE** Association internationale du personnel d'EUROCONTROL (#00597)
♦ AIPE – Association internationale de la presse échiquéenne (inactive)
♦ AIPE – Associazione Internazionale di Psicanalisi Eclettica (inactive)
♦ AIPEC – Associação Iberoamericana de Portas e Costas (inactive)

♦ AIPE-International Association of EUROCONTROL Staff 00597

Association internationale du personnel d'EUROCONTROL (AIPE)

Contact c/o AIPE-EUROCONTROL, Rue de la Fusée 96, 1130 Brussels, Belgium. T. +3227293341.

History within the framework of *EUROCONTROL (#05667).* Also referred to as *International Association of the Staff of the European Organization for the Safety of Air Navigation – Association internationale du personnel de l'Organisation européenne pour la sécurité de la navigation aérienne.* Registered in accordance with Belgian law. **Aims** Strengthen social and cultural relationship between the various nationalities represented among the staff of EUROCONTROL. [2018.02.08/XE3540/v/**E**]

♦ AIPELF / see Association francophone internationale de recherche scientifique en éducation (#02615)
♦ AIPEPO – Association internationale de presse pour l'étude des problèmes d'outre-mer (inactive)
♦ AIPES / see Nuclear Medicine Europe (#17619)
♦ **AIPET Internacional** Asociación Iberoamericana de Periodistas Especializados y Técnicos (#02152)
♦ **AIPF** Association internationale pour la participation financière (#11891)
♦ AIPF – Association internationale de la presse francophone (internationally oriented national body)
♦ **AIPFE** Association internationale pour la promotion de femmes d'Europe (#12109)

♦ AIP Foundation 00598

President 12B Ngoc Khanh Street, Ba Dihn District, Hanoi 00000, Vietnam. T. +84437710700. Fax +84437710701. E-mail: info@aipf-vietnam.org.
CEO 74 Mac Dinh Chi, Da Kao Ward, District 1, Ho Chi Minh City HO CHI MINH 00000, Vietnam. T. +8462991409. E-mail: info@aipf-vietnam.org.
URL: http://www.aip-foundation.org/

History 1999. Former names and other names: *Asia Injury Prevention Foundation* – full title. **Aims** Provide life-saving *road safety* knowledge and skills to low- and middle-income countries with the goal of preventing road crash fatalities and injuries. **Structure** Board of Directors; Advisory Board. **Languages** English, Mon-Khmer languages, Thai, Vietnamese. **Staff** 50.00 FTE, paid. **Finance** Sources: government support; private foundations; sponsorship. **Activities** Advocacy/lobbying/activism; awareness raising; capacity building; knowledge management/information dissemination; monitoring/evaluation; networking/liaising; projects/programmes; standards/guidelines; training/education. **Publications** *AIP Foundation Newsletter* (12 a year); *Impact Report* (annual). Articles; infographics.

Members Programme partners in 6 countries:
Cambodia, Denmark, India, Philippines, Thailand, Vietnam.

Consultative Status Consultative status granted from: *ECOSOC (#05331)* (Special).
[2022.03.08/XF6945/f/**F**]

♦ **AIPFS** Association internationale pour la promotion des fluids supercritiques (#14904)
♦ **AIPG** Association for International Promotion of Gums (#02759)
♦ **AIPH** Association internationale des producteurs de l'horticulture (#11940)
♦ AIPIA – Active and Intelligent Packaging Industry Association (unconfirmed)
♦ **AIPI** Associazione Internazionale dei Professori d'Italiano (#02989)
♦ AIPIN – Agencia Internacional de Prensa India (internationally oriented national body)
♦ AIP / see International Association of Applied Psychology (#11705)

♦ AIP / see International Union of Photobiology (#15798)
♦ AIPISA – Asociación Interamericana de Profesores de Ingenieria Sanitaria y Ambiental (no recent information)
♦ **AIPL** Association Internationale de Psychomécanique du Langage (#02735)
♦ AIPLF / see Assemblée parlementaire de la Francophonie (#02312)
♦ **AIPMAS** Arab Intellectual Property Mediation and Arbitration Society (#00989)
♦ AIPN / see Australasian Injury Prevention Network
♦ AIPN / see Association of International Energy Negotiators (#02722)
♦ AIPN – Australasian Injury Prevention Network (internationally oriented national body)
♦ AIPO / see African Intellectual Property Organization (#00344)
♦ AIPO / see ASEAN Inter-Parliamentary Assembly (#01205)
♦ **AIPP** Asia Indigenous Peoples Pact (#01282)
♦ AIPP – Association of International Property Professionals (internationally oriented national body)
♦ AIPPEN – Australasian Interprofessional Practice and Education Network (internationally oriented national body)
♦ **AIPPF** Asociación Internacional de Psicoanalisis de Pareja y Familia (#11822)
♦ **AIPPF** Association internationale des procureurs et poursuivants francophones (#02730)
♦ **AIPPh** Association internationale des professeurs de philosophie (#02732)
♦ **AIPPI** Association internationale pour la protection de la propriété intellectuelle (#12112)
♦ **AIPPYC** Asociación Internacional de Profesionales de Puertos y Costas (#02169)
♦ AIPR / see Auschwitz Institute for the Prevention of Genocide and Mass Atrocities
♦ **AIPRAL** Alianza de Iglesias Presbiterianas y Reformadas de América Latina (#00713)
♦ AIPRAL / see Alliance of Presbyterian and Reformed Churches in Latin America (#00713)
♦ AIPRES – Asociación Iberoamericana de Información y Promoción Profesional de Seguros (no recent information)
♦ **AIPS** Académie internationale de philosophie des sciences (#11570)

♦ AIPS America 00599

AIPS América

SG Calle Hurtado 467 y Jose Mascote, Guayaquil, Ecuador. T. +59342518276. Fax +59342518276. E-mail: gerardo22ec@gmail.com – info@aipsamerica.com.
URL: http://www.aipsamerica.com/

History 10 Aug 1982, Havana (Cuba), as *Federación Latinoamericanana y del Caribe de Periodistas Deportivos*. 1985, name changed to *Federación de Periodistas Deportivos de América (FEPEDA)*. Previously also referred to by the acronym *FPDA*. 2011, present name adopted. **Structure** Officers: President; 1st Vice-President; General Secretary; Continental Delegate; 5 Vice-Presidents (Panama, Uruguay, Cuba, Honduras, Bolivia); Treasurer; Deputy Treasurer. Members (4). **Members** Sports journalists' associations. Membership countries not specified. **NGO Relations** A continental section of *Association internationale de la presse sportive (AIPS, #02729)*. [2017/XD5525/**D**]

♦ AIPS – Association internationale pour le patrimoine souterrain (no recent information)
♦ **AIPS** Association internationale de la presse sportive (#02729)
♦ **AIPS** Association internationale pour la prévention du suicide et l'intervention en cas de suicide (#12213)
♦ AIPS – Association internationale des professions de la santé (inactive)
♦ AIPS – Association internationale pour le progrès social (inactive)
♦ AIPS – Association internationale de psychiatrie spirituelle (inactive)
♦ **AIPS Europe** European Sports Press Union (#08822)
♦ AIPT – Association internationale pour la promotion du thé (inactive)
♦ **AIPTI** Asociación Internacional de Profesionales de la Traducción y la Interpretación (#12106)
♦ **AIPTLF** Association internationale de psychologie du travail de langue française (#02734)
♦ AIPU / see Arab Inter-Parliamentary Union (#00995)
♦ **AIPU** Association Internationale de Pédagogie Universitaire (#02727)
♦ **AIPU** Association internationale du personnel de l'UNESCO (#15597)
♦ AIPULF – Association internationale des presses universitaires de langue française (inactive)
♦ AIPYC – Asociación Iberoamericana de Puertos y Costas (inactive)
♦ AIPYS – Asociación Internacional de Profesores de Yoga Solar (internationally oriented national body)
♦ AIQE – Association internationale pour la qualité de l'eau (inactive)
♦ AIRA – Asociación Iberoamericana de Reproducción Animal (no recent information)
♦ AIR – African Institute for Remittances (unconfirmed)
♦ **AIRAPT** International Association for the Advancement of High Pressure Science and Technology (#11686)
♦ AirAsia Foundation (internationally oriented national body)
♦ **AIR** Asociación Internacional de Radiodifusión (#11738)
♦ AIR – Association for Institutional Research (internationally oriented national body)
♦ **AIR** Association internationale de radiodiffusion (#11738)
♦ AIR – Autorité internationale de la Ruhr (inactive)

♦ Air Baltic Corporation 00600

Contact Riga International Airport, Marupes district, Riga LV-1053, Latvia.
URL: http://www.airbaltic.com/

History Aug 1995, Riga (Latvia). Previously also referred to as *Baltic International Airlines*. **Staff** 1600.00 FTE, paid. **NGO Relations** Member of: *International Air Transport Association (IATA, #11614)*. [2019.06.26/XF4050/e/**F**]

♦ Airborne Connections (internationally oriented national body)
♦ **AIRCA** Association of International Research and Development Centers for Agriculture (#02760)
♦ **AIRC** Association Internationale des Réparateurs en Carosserie (#02741)
♦ AIRCAT – Association internationale des régies et commissions des accidents du travail (internationally oriented national body)
♦ AirClim – Air Pollution & Climate Secretariat (internationally oriented national body)

♦ Air Conditioning and Refrigeration European Association (AREA) . . 00601

Groupement européen des fédérations et syndicats nationaux d'installateurs frigoristes dans tous les systèmes et applications – Verband der europäischen Hersteller und Verteiler von Kühl- und Klimatisierungsanlagen

SG Diamant Building – 5th Floor, Bd A Reyers 80, 1030 Brussels, Belgium. T. +3227068237. Fax +3227068261. E-mail: info@area-eur.be.
URL: http://www.area-eur.be/

History 1988. Statutes modified: 28 Sep 1995; 2009. Registration: EU Transparency Register, No/ID: 03396347383-49, Start date: 9 Dec 2011; No/ID: 0440.154.920, Start date: 6 Mar 1990, Belgium. **Aims** Represent the refrigeration and air conditioning installation industry, in particular with the European Commission and with UNEP; coordinate education and training in order to harmonize techniques and qualifications; promote technical development of air-conditioning and refrigeration and recommend appropriate techniques; participate in environment protection. **Structure** General Assembly (annual). Board; working bodies; secretariat. **Languages** English, French. **Staff** 1.50 FTE, voluntary. **Finance** Members' dues. **Activities** Organizes 2 meetings a year: one in May in Belgium; General Assembly in Oct/Nov in a member country. Formulates necessary competence, objectives and joint declarations of members. **Events** *General Assembly* Bratislava (Slovakia) 2019, *General Assembly* Vienna (Austria) 2018, *Annual General Assembly* Stockholm (Sweden) 2015, *Annual General Assembly* Padua (Italy) 2014, *Annual General Assembly* Porto (Portugal) 2013. **Publications** *Refrigeration Craftsman* (2005) – available online.
Members Effective; Corresponding; Associate; Honorary. National associations (25) in 21 countries.
Austria, Belgium, Croatia, Czechia, Denmark, Estonia, Finland, France, Germany, Greece, Ireland, Italy, Netherlands, Norway, Poland, Portugal, Slovakia, Spain, Sweden, Türkiye, UK.
IGO Relations Accredited by: *United Nations Framework Convention on Climate Change – Secretariat (UNFCCC, #20564)*. **NGO Relations** Member of: *European Partnership for Energy and the Environment (EPEE, #08157)*; *Federation of European and International Associations Established in Belgium (FAIB, #09508)*. [2020/XD2496/**D**]

♦ Aircraft Engineers International (AEI) 00602

SG Pb 5, 2450 AA Leimuiden, Netherlands. T. +31655930175. Fax +31655930175. E-mail: aei.secgeneral@airengineers.org.
Street Address Luzernestraat 13G, 2153 ME Nieuw Vennep, Netherlands.
URL: http://www.airengineers.org/

History Proposed 1972, by associations in Australia, UK and India. Current structure set up 1976, with headquarters then located in London (UK), when associations of Norway and Sweden joined. EU Transparency Register: 34931206489-95. **Aims** Represent the licensed aircraft maintenance Engineer. **Structure** Executive Board. **Languages** English. **Staff** 10.00 FTE, voluntary. **Finance** Sources: members' dues. **Activities** Events/meetings. **Events** *Annual Congress* Berlin (Germany) 2019, *Annual Congress* Stockholm (Sweden) 2018, *Annual Congress* Lisbon (Portugal) 2017, *Annual Congress* Seattle, WA (USA) 2015, *Annual Congress* Melbourne, VIC (Australia) 2013.
Members Affiliates in 34 countries:
Australia, Bangladesh, Bulgaria, Canada, Cyprus, Czechia, Fiji, Finland, France, Germany, Greece, Iceland, India, Kuwait, Madagascar, Malta, Morocco, Netherlands, New Zealand, Nigeria, Norway, Pakistan, Portugal, Russia, Serbia, Slovenia, Spain, Sri Lanka, Sweden, Tunisia, Türkiye, UK, USA, Zimbabwe. [2021/XJ8461/**C**]

♦ Aircraft Rescue and Fire Fighting Working Group (internationally oriented national body)
♦ AIRDA – Association internationale pour le respect des droits des peuples autochtones (inactive)
♦ **AIRD** African Initiatives for Relief and Development (#00339)
♦ **AIRDC** Association of Insurers and Reinsurers of Developing Countries (#02650)
♦ **AIRDF** Association internationale pour la recherche en didactique du français (#02736)
♦ AIRDOI – Association des institutions de recherche et développement de l'océan Indien (inactive)
♦ AIREA / see Appraisal Institute
♦ **AIRE** Airlines International Representation in Europe (#00608)
♦ **AIRE** Association internationale des ressources en eau (#15871)
♦ AIRE Centre – Advice on Individual Rights in Europe Centre (internationally oriented national body)
♦ **AIREH** Asociación Internacional de Recursos Hidricos (#15871)
♦ **AIREPME** Association internationale de recherche en entrepreneuriat et PME (#02737)
♦ Airey Neave Trust (internationally oriented national body)
♦ **AIRF** Association internationale des régions francophones (#02739)
♦ AIRFD – Association des institutions régionales et sous-régionales de financement du développement en Afrique de l'Ouest (no recent information)
♦ AIRG – Avian Immunology Research Group (meeting series)
♦ **AIRH** Association internationale d'ingénierie et de recherches hydrauliques et environmentales (#11950)
♦ **AIRH** Association internationale Reine Hélène (#02740)
♦ AIRHH – Association internationale pour la recherche en hygiène hospitalière (no recent information)
♦ **AIRHM** Association internationale de recherche scientifique en faveur des personnes handicapées mentales (#02738)

♦ Air Infiltration and Ventilation Centre (AIVC) 00603

Contact INIVE, Lozenberg 7, 1932 Sint-Stevens-Woluwe, Belgium. T. +3226557711. Fax +3226530729. E-mail: info@aivc.org.
URL: http://www.aivc.org/

History 1979, by *International Energy Agency (IEA, #13270)*. **Aims** Provide technical support to the research and development of ventilation technology; promote dissemination of information on related energy and *air quality* issues. **Structure** Board. **Activities** Events/meetings. **Events** *Annual Conference* Athens (Greece) 2022, *Annual Conference* Athens (Greece) 2021, *Annual Conference* Athens (Greece) 2020, *Annual Conference* Ghent (Belgium) 2019, *Annual Conference* Antibes (France) 2018. **Publications** *AIVC Newsletter* (2 a year). *AIVC CD* – bibliographic database.
Members in 17 countries:
Australia, Belgium, China, Denmark, France, Greece, Ireland, Italy, Japan, Korea Rep, Netherlands, New Zealand, Norway, Spain, Sweden, UK, USA.
NGO Relations Member of (1): *Indoor Environmental Quality – Global Alliance (IEQ Global Alliance, #11168)*. Operating agent: *International Network for Information on Ventilation and Energy Performance (INIVE, #14288)*. [2020/XE4301/**E**]

♦ AIR / see International Association of Broadcasting (#11738)
♦ AIRIT – Association internationale de recherche en informatique toxicologique (inactive)
♦ Airline Ambassadors International (internationally oriented national body)

♦ Airline Catering Association (ACA) 00604

Acting Managing Dir Rue du Luxembourg 3, 1000 Brussels, Belgium. T. +3223197067. E-mail: info@aca.catering.
URL: https://www.aca.catering/

History Registration: No/ID: 0688.667.237, Start date: 19 Jan 2018, Belgium. **Aims** Represent, promote, and defend the common interests of its members in particular, and of the airline catering industry in general; monitor relevant regulatory initiatives and inform its members about those. **Structure** Strategic Committee; Board of Directors; Secretariat. **Activities** Events/meetings; knowledge management/information dissemination; monitoring/evaluation. **NGO Relations** Member of (1): *European Tourism Manifesto (#08921)*. [2021.02.24/AA0962/**C**]

♦ Airline Group of IFORS (AGIFORS) 00605

Communications Officer Sabre Holdings, 3150 Sabre Drive, Southlake TX 76092, USA. T. +16826051710.
URL: https://agifors.org/

History Oct 1961, Spring Valley NY (USA), during a Symposium on Operational Research in airlines, as a group within *International Federation of Operational Research Societies (IFORS, #13493)*, of which it is also a kindred society. **Aims** Forward the practice of *operational research* in airlines. **Structure** Council (elected every 3 years); Study Groups. **Languages** English. **Events** *Airline Operations Study Group Conference* Paris (France) 2019, *Annual Symposium* Seattle, WA (USA) 2019, *Annual Symposium* Tokyo (Japan) 2018, *Annual Symposium* London (UK) 2017, *Annual Symposium* Santiago (Chile) 2016.
Members Full operational research workers who are also employed by recognized civil airlines (about 1,200 representing over 100 airlines and related organizations). Correspondents people keenly interested in the application of operational research to aviation problems. Membership covers 60 countries and territories:
Argentina, Australia, Austria, Bahrain, Belgium, Brazil, Canada, Chile, Colombia, Costa Rica, Côte d'Ivoire, Cyprus, Czechia, Denmark, Dominican Rep, Egypt, Fiji, Finland, France, Germany, Greece, Hong Kong, Hungary, Iceland, India, Indonesia, Ireland, Israel, Italy, Jamaica, Japan, Jordan, Kuwait, Lebanon, Macau, Malaysia, Mexico, Netherlands, New Zealand, Norway, Pakistan, Philippines, Poland, Portugal, Saudi Arabia, Singapore, South Africa, Spain, Sweden, Switzerland, Taiwan, Tanzania UR, Thailand, Trinidad-Tobago, Türkiye, UK, United Arab Emirates, USA, Yemen, Zambia. [2018.09.05/XE0817/v/**E**]

♦ Airline Medical Examiners Association / see Civil Aviation Medical Association (#03964)
♦ Air Line Pilots Association, International (internationally oriented national body)
♦ Airlines for America (internationally oriented national body)

♦ Airlines Association of Southern Africa (AASA) 00606

CEO Greenstone Hill Office Park – Bldg 13 – 1st floor, Emerald Blvd, Johannesburg, 1645, South Africa. T. +27116090050. Fax +27116090169. E-mail: aasa@global.co.za – aasa@aasa.za.net.
URL: http://aasa.za.net/

History 16 Apr 2003, Johannesburg (South Africa). **Aims** Protect and enhance the airline's business in Southern Africa and Indian Ocean islands, by participating on a number of committees and forums with other participants in the industry. **Structure** General Meeting (annual). **Languages** English. **Staff** 6.00 FTE, paid; 6.00 FTE, voluntary. **Finance** Annual budget: 3,533 ZAR (2021). **Members** Airlines (16); Associate (33). Membership countries not specified. [2022.02.15/XD8651/**D**]

♦ **Airlines for Europe (A4E)** **00607**

Managing Dir Rond-point Schuman 6, 1040 Brussels, Belgium. T. +3227930911. E-mail: contact@a4e.eu.

URL: https://a4e.eu/

History 2016. Registration: No/ID: 0651.611.257, Start date: 5 Apr 2016, Belgium; EU Transparency Registry, No/ID: 807912421050-91, Start date: 14 Mar 2016. **Aims** Promote long-term solutions to reduce the environmental impact of aviation. **Publications** *A4E News.* **Members** Airlines; Manufacturing; Associate. Membership countries not specified. **NGO Relations** Member of (1): *European Tourism Manifesto (#08921).* [2022.05.12/AA0235/**F**]

♦ **Airlines International Representation in Europe (AIRE)** **00608**

Main Office Rue Belliard 40, BP 5, 1040 Brussels, Belgium. E-mail: aire.hq@aire.aero.

URL: http://aire.aero/

History Jun 1971, Strasbourg (France). Articles modified Jun 1973, permitting scheduled carriers engaged in charter activities or their affiliates to become active members of the Association. Former names and other names: *International Air Carrier Association (IACA)* – former (1971 to Jun 2017); *Association internationale de charter aérien* – former (1971 to Jun 2017); *Asociación Internacional de Charters Aéreos* – former (1971 to Jun 2017). Registration: Banque-Carrefour des Entreprises, Start date: Jun 1983, Belgium; Swiss Civil Code, Start date: Oct 1971, Switzerland; EU Transparency Register, No/ID: 686630315059-63. **Aims** Raise awareness of the specific interests of its airline members and promote their needs to key decision-makers at national, European and international levels. **Structure** General Assembly (annual); Board of Directors; Standing Committees (4); ad hoc Working Groups; Secretariat, headed by Director General. **Languages** English. **Staff** 5.00 FTE, paid. **Finance** Sources: members' dues. **Activities** Advocacy/lobbying/activism; knowledge management/information dissemination. **Events** *Annual General Assembly* 2021, *Annual General Meeting* Palma (Spain) 2014, *Annual General Meeting* Brussels (Belgium) 2010, *General Assembly* Brussels (Belgium) 2006, *Annual General Meeting* 2005. **Publications** Press releases; policy briefs; position papers; statistics.

Members Airlines, both scheduled and non-scheduled, in 11 countries:
Belgium, Denmark, Italy, Norway, Poland, Portugal, Slovakia, Spain, Sweden, Türkiye, UK.

IGO Relations Member of: *World Tourism Organization (UNWTO, #21861).* **NGO Relations** Member of: *Air Transport Action Group (ATAG, #00614); Council for Environmentally Friendly Aviation (CEFA, #04880); International Federation of Air Line Pilots' Associations (IFALPA, #13349); International Federation of Air Traffic Controllers' Associations (IFATCA, #13350).* [2022.05.13/XD4084/**D**]

♦ **Airline Sports and Cultural Association (ASCA)** **00609**

Association sportive et culturelle des agents des compagnies de navigation aérienne

Information Officer Austrian Airlines, Austrian Sports Club, Office Park 2, Schwechat Airport, 1300 Schwechat, Austria.

URL: http://www.asca.cc/

History May 1947, Paris (France). Former names and other names: *Airline Staff International Association (ASIA)* – former (1947 to 1986); *Association internationale des agents des compagnies de navigation aérienne* – former (1947 to 1986). **Aims** Develop friendly relations between persons working in *civil aviation* by facilitating social, cultural, tourist and sporting contacts between the personnel of member companies. **Structure** General Assembly (annual); Executive Committee. Meetings closed. **Languages** English. **Staff** Voluntary. **Events** *Annual General Meeting* Dublin (Ireland) 2020, *Annual General Meeting* Luxembourg (Luxembourg) 2019, *Annual General Meeting* Reykjavik (Iceland) 2018, *Annual General Meeting* Lisbon (Portugal) 2017, *Annual General Assembly* London (UK) 2016.

Members Airlines in 19 countries:
Australia, Austria, Belgium, Denmark, Finland, France, Germany, Iceland, Ireland, Israel, Italy, Luxembourg, Norway, Portugal, Spain, Sweden, Switzerland, UK, United Arab Emirates. [2021/XD0034/**D**]

♦ Airline Staff International Association / see Airline Sports and Cultural Association (#00609)
♦ Airlines Worldwide Telecommunications and Information Services / see SITA (#19299)
♦ Airline Telecommunication and Information Services / see SITA (#19299)
♦ Airlink (internationally oriented national body)
♦ AIRLINK – Disaster Response Delivered / see Airlink
♦ AIRMAP – Association Internationale de Recherche en Management Public (internationally oriented national body)
♦ AIRMEC – Association internationale pour la recherche médicale et les échanges culturels (no recent information)
♦ Airmhean Comhphairteach Taighde (#16147)
♦ Air Movement and Control Association International (internationally oriented national body)
♦ Air Navigation Convention (1919 treaty)
♦ AIRP – Association internationale des receveurs de la poste (inactive)
♦ AIRP / see International Labour and Employment Relations Association (#13997)
♦ AIRP / see International Radiation Protection Association (#14686)
♦ **AIRPOL** European Network of Airport Law Enforcement Organisations (#07866)
♦ Air Pollution & Climate Secretariat (internationally oriented national body)
♦ Air Pollution Control Association / see Air and Waste Management Association
♦ Airport Associations Coordinating Council (inactive)
♦ Airport Regions Conference / see Airport Regions Council (#00610)

♦ **Airport Regions Council (ARC)** **00610**

Dir Gen Rue Montoyer 21, 1000 Brussels, Belgium. T. +3225134885. E-mail: info@airportregions.org.

URL: http://www.airportregions.org/

History 1994. Founded by regional and local authorities which have an international airport situated within or near their territory. Former names and other names: *Airport Regions Conference* – former. Registration: Banque-Carrefour des Entreprises, No/ID: 0472.917.659, Start date: 1 Oct 1999, Belgium; EU Transparency Register, No/ID: 624421515921-72, Start date: 9 Feb 2015. **Aims** Enhance the role of regional and local governments as active partners in development of European air transport policies; cooperate at European level to pursue common interests; undertake common initiatives for the exchange of information and best practice among members. **Languages** English. **Staff** 4.00 FTE, paid. **Events** *Conference on Sustainable Aviation Fuel and the ReFuel EU Aviation* Brussels (Belgium) 2022, *From Recovery to Sustainability: How to Finance the Costs?* Brussels (Belgium) 2022, *No Way Out – Greening Aviation and Airports Together* Brussels (Belgium) 2022, *Urban Air Mobility: Preparing for (very) near future* Brussels (Belgium) 2022, *Meeting on Ultrafine Particles in Airport Regions* Brussels (Belgium) 2017. **Publications** *Regions and Airport Newsletter.*

Members Local authorities (30) in 17 countries:
Austria, Belgium, Czechia, Finland, France, Germany, Hungary, Ireland, Israel, Malta, Netherlands, Norway, Poland, Portugal, Romania, Spain, Sweden. [2022.02.11/XM3715/**F**]

♦ Airports Association Council International / see Airports Council International (#00611)

♦ **Airports Council International (ACI)** **00611**

Dir Gen 800 Rue du Sq Victoria, Suite 1810, PO Box 302, Montréal QC H4Z 1G8, Canada. T. +15143731200. E-mail: aci@aci.aero.

Contact address not obtained.

URL: http://aci.aero/

History Derived from *Airport Associations Coordinating Council (AACC, inactive)*, and resulted from the merger of *International Civil Airports Association (ICAA, inactive)* and *Airports Operators Council International (AOCI, inactive).* Constitution approved by ICAA, Sep 1990, Monte Carlo (Monaco), at 30th World Congress, and by AOCI, Oct 1990, Chicago IL (USA), at 43rd Annual Conference. Constitution became effective, 1 Jan 1991. Former names and other names: *Airports Association Council International (AACI)* – former (1 Jan 1991). **Aims** Advance the collective interests of, and act as the voice of, the world's airports and the communities they serve; promote professional excellence in airport *management* and operations. **Structure** General Assembly (annual); Governing Board; Executive Committee. Standing Committees (6). Regional offices (5), including *ACI Africa (#00069); Airports Council International – European Region (ACI EUROPE, #00612)*, replacing *International Civil Airports Association European Community Bureau (ICAA European Community Bureau, inactive).* **Languages** English, French, Spanish. **Staff** 85.00 FTE, paid. **Finance** Sources: members' dues. **Activities** Events/meetings. **Events** *ACI EUROPE / WORLD Annual General Assembly, Conference (WAGA)* Barcelona (Spain) 2023, *Customer Experience Global Summit* Incheon (Korea Rep) 2023, *Airport Exchange Conference* Krakow (Poland) 2022, *Customer Excellence Global Summit* Krakow (Poland) 2022, *ATAG Global Sustainable Aviation Forum* 2021. **Publications** *ACI World Report* (12 a year); *ACI Airport World* (6 a year). Annual report; specialized publications; position papers.

Members As of Jan 2023, serves 712 members operating 1,925 airports in 175 countries and territories:
Albania, Algeria, Angola, Antigua-Barbuda, Argentina, Armenia, Australia, Austria, Bahrain, Bangladesh, Barbados, Belarus, Belgium, Belize, Benin, Bermuda, Bosnia-Herzegovina, Botswana, Brazil, Brunei Darussalam, Bulgaria, Burkina Faso, Burundi, Cambodia, Cameroon, Canada, Cape Verde, Cayman Is, Central African Rep, Chile, China, Colombia, Comoros, Congo Brazzaville, Congo DR, Cook Is, Costa Rica, Côte d'Ivoire, Croatia, Cuba, Cyprus, Czechia, Denmark, Djibouti, Dominican Rep, Ecuador, Egypt, El Salvador, Equatorial Guinea, Eritrea, Estonia, Ethiopia, Fiji, Finland, France, Gabon, Gambia, Georgia, Germany, Ghana, Gibraltar, Greece, Grenada, Guadeloupe, Guam, Guiana Fr, Guinea, Guyana, Haiti, Honduras, Hong Kong, Hungary, Iceland, India, Indonesia, Iran Islamic Rep, Ireland, Israel, Italy, Jamaica, Japan, Jordan, Kazakhstan, Kenya, Korea Rep, Kuwait, Latvia, Lebanon, Liberia, Lithuania, Luxembourg, Macau, Madagascar, Malawi, Malaysia, Maldives, Mali, Malta, Marshall Is, Martinique, Mauritania, Mauritius, Mexico, Micronesia FS, Moldova, Monaco, Mongolia, Montenegro, Morocco, Mozambique, Namibia, Nepal, Netherlands, New Caledonia, New Zealand, Nicaragua, Niger, Nigeria, North Macedonia, Northern Mariana Is, Norway, Oman, Palestine, Panama, Paraguay, Peru, Philippines, Poland, Polynesia Fr, Portugal, Qatar, Réunion, Romania, Russia, Rwanda, Samoa, Samoa USA, Saudi Arabia, Senegal, Serbia, Sierra Leone, Singapore, Slovakia, Slovenia, South Africa, Spain, Sri Lanka, St Kitts-Nevis, St Lucia, Sudan, Suriname, Sweden, Switzerland, Taiwan, Tanzania UR, Thailand, Togo, Tonga, Trinidad-Tobago, Tunisia, Türkiye, Uganda, UK, Ukraine, United Arab Emirates, Uruguay, USA, Uzbekistan, Vanuatu, Vietnam, Virgin Is USA, Yemen, Zambia, Zimbabwe.
Les Aéroports Francophones (#00145).

Consultative Status Consultative status granted from: *International Civil Aviation Organization (ICAO, #12581)* (Observer Status). **IGO Relations** Accredited by (1): *United Nations Office at Vienna (UNOV, #20604).* Memorandum of Understanding with (1): *World Customs Organization (WCO, #21350).* Cooperates with (2): *EUROCONTROL (#05667); European Aviation Security Training Institute (EASTI, #06304).* Contacts with: *Arab Civil Aviation Organization (ACAO, #00920); European Civil Aviation Conference (ECAC, #06564); International Criminal Police Organization – INTERPOL (ICPO-INTERPOL, #13110); International Transport Forum (ITF, #15725); Latin American Civil Aviation Commission (LACAC, #16297); UNEP (#20299); United Nations Economic Commission for Europe (UNECE, #20555); WHO (#20950); World Meteorological Organization (WMO, #21649); World Tourism Organization (UNWTO, #21861).* Associated with Department of Global Communications of the United Nations. **NGO Relations** Member of (2): *Air Transport Action Group (ATAG, #00614); International Industry Working Group (IIWG, #13841).* In liaison with technical committees of: *International Organization for Standardization (ISO, #14473).* [2023/XB0031/y/**B**]

♦ **Airports Council International – European Region (ACI EUROPE)** ... **00612**

Main Office 37-40 Boulevard du Régent, 5th Floor, 1000 Brussels, Belgium. E-mail: communique@aci-europe.org.

URL: http://www.aci-europe.org/

History 1 Jan 1991. Founded in the framework of *Airports Council International (ACI, #00611).* Replaced *International Civil Airports Association European Community Bureau (ICAA European Community Bureau, inactive)* of *International Civil Airports Association (ICAA, inactive).* Former names and other names: *European Region of the Airports Council International (ACI)* – former. Registration: No/ID: 0431.887.748, Start date: 14 Jun 1987, Belgium; EU Transparency Register, No/ID: 42566063487-73, Start date: 22 Apr 2010. **Aims** Advance the collective interests of Europe's airports; promote professional excellence in airport management and operations. **Structure** Board of Directors. Committees (6): Policy; Aviation Security; Economics; Environmental Strategy; Facilitation and Customer Services; Technical and Operational Safety. Fora (4): Commercial; Digital Communications; Leaders and HR; Regional Airports. Working Groups. **Staff** 19.00 FTE, paid. **Activities** Events/meetings. **Events** *ACI EUROPE / WORLD Annual General Assembly, Conference (WAGA)* Barcelona (Spain) 2023, *Regional Airports' Conference and Exhibition (RACE 2023)* Chania (Greece) 2023, *Airport Exchange Conference* Krakow (Poland) 2022, *Regional Airports Conference (RACE)* Palermo (Italy) 2022, *Airport Exchange Conference* Amsterdam (Netherlands) 2020.

Members Regular in 45 countries:
Albania, Austria, Belarus, Belgium, Bosnia-Herzegovina, Bulgaria, Croatia, Cyprus, Czechia, Denmark, Estonia, Finland, France, Georgia, Germany, Greece, Hungary, Iceland, Ireland, Israel, Italy, Kosovo, Latvia, Lithuania, Luxembourg, Malta, Moldova, Monaco, Montenegro, Netherlands, North Macedonia, Norway, Poland, Portugal, Romania, Russia, Serbia, Slovakia, Slovenia, Spain, Sweden, Switzerland, Türkiye, UK, Ukraine.

Affiliate Regular in 1 territory:
Réunion.

National Airport Associations in 7 countries:
France, Germany, Italy, Romania, Switzerland, UK, Ukraine.

NGO Relations Member of (2): *European Tourism Manifesto (#08921); Federation of European and International Associations Established in Belgium (FAIB, #09508).* [2022/XK0321/**E**]

♦ **Airport Services Association (ASA)** **00613**

Dir Gen Rue du Luxembourg 3, 1000 Brussels, Belgium. T. +441625664500. E-mail: admin@asaworld.aero.

Registered Address c/o Buchhaltungsfabrik, Baselstr 44, 4125 Riehen BS, Switzerland.

URL: https://www.asaworld.aero/

History 1974. Current articles adopted 1 Jan 2019. Former names and other names: *Independent Aviation Handlers Association (IAHA)* – former (1974). Registration: Civil Code, Switzerland. **Aims** Contribute to the improvement of the quality of ground services on airports for the benefit of its operators and passengers. **Structure** General Assembly; Board. **Finance** Sources: members' dues. **Publications** *ASA Newsletter.* **Members** Full; Associate. Membership countries not specified. **IGO Relations** Cooperates with (1): *International Civil Aviation Organization (ICAO, #12581).* **NGO Relations** Member of (1): *European Tourism Manifesto (#08921).* Cooperates with (2): *Airports Council International (ACI, #00611); International Air Transport Association (IATA, #11614).* [2020/AA0970/**C**]

♦ Airports Operators Council International (inactive)
♦ Air Secours International / see Actions de Solidarité Internationale
♦ Air Serv International (internationally oriented national body)
♦ AIRT / see International Labour and Employment Relations Association (#13997)

♦ **Air Transport Action Group (ATAG)** **00614**

Exec Dir Route de l'Aéroport 33, PO Box 49, 1215 Geneva 15, Switzerland. T. +41227702672. Fax +41227702686. E-mail: information@atag.org.

URL: http://www.atag.org/

History 1990. Registration: EU Transparency Register, No/ID: 377462122157-01. **Aims** Promote aviation's sustainable growth for the benefit of global society. **Structure** Board of Directors; Secretariat, located in Geneva (Switzerland). **Languages** English. **Staff** 4.00 FTE, paid. **Finance** Sources: members' dues. **Activities** Advocacy/lobbying/activism; events/meetings; research/documentation. Active in all member countries. **Events** *ATAG Global Sustainable Aviation Forum* 2021, *ATAG Global Sustainable Aviation Forum* 2020, *ATAG Global Sustainable Aviation Forum* Montréal, QC (Canada) 2019, *ATAG Global Sustainable Aviation Summit* Geneva (Switzerland) 2018, *ATAG Global Sustainable Aviation Summit* Geneva (Switzerland) 2017. **Publications** *Aviation: Benefits Beyond Borders* – see also on website: https://www.atag.org/our-publications/latest-publications.html. Brochures; reports; position papers; fact sheets; guides.

Members Funding members (11), including 3 organizations listed in this Yearbook:
Airports Council International (ACI, #00611); Civil Air Navigation Services Organisation (CANSO, #03963); International Air Transport Association (IATA, #11614).

Active members (10), including 5 organizations listed in this Yearbook:
Airlines for Europe (A4E, #00607); Airlines International Representation in Europe (AIRE, #00608); Arab Air Carriers Organization (AACO, #00896); European Regions Airline Association (ERA, #08347); Latin American and Caribbean Air Transport Association (#16263).

Associate members (12), including 6 organizations listed in this Yearbook:
Aerospace and Defence Industries Association of Europe (ASD, #00146); Airlines for America (A4A); Association of Asia Pacific Airlines (AAPA, #02385); European Business Aviation Association (EBAA, #06415); General Aviation Manufacturers Association (GAMA); International Business Aviation Council (IBAC, #12418). [2021.06.24/XF1614/y/**E**]

Air Transport Association
00614

alphabetic sequence excludes
For the complete listing, see Yearbook Online at

♦ Air Transport Association of America / see Airlines for America

♦ **Air Transport Research Society (ATRS)** **00615**
Contact 3433 Van Munching Hall, Robert H Smith School of Business, Univ of Maryland, College Park MD 20742, USA. T. +13014052204. Fax +13013141023. E-mail: atrsmailbox@gmail.com – kun.wang@sauder.ubc.ca.
URL: http://www.atrsworld.org/
History Founded 1995, Sydney (Australia), as a Special Interest Group of *World Conference on Transport Research Society (WCTRS, #21301)*, during its 7th Conference. **Aims** Help organize and expand air transport related sessions at WCTR Conferences and attract more people from airlines, airports, governments, research institutes and academia to the Society and its activities; exchange research ideas and results via more frequent symposia, conferences or regional meetings; enhance research capability for multi-national and multi-disciplinary issues on air transportation; interact with international and national institutions which deal with policy and/or infrastructure issues concerning international aviation; provide forums to facilitate the exchange of ideas for forming multi-national and/or multi-disciplinary research teams to investigate topics of worldwide or continental interest. **Structure** Networking Committee, including President and 3 Vice-President (External and Development; Publications; Scientific and Programs). **Languages** English. **Events** *Annual Conference* Sydney, NSW (Australia) 2021, *Annual Conference* Sydney, NSW (Australia) 2020, *Annual Conference* Amsterdam (Netherlands) 2019, *Annual Conference* Seoul (Korea Rep) 2018, *Annual Conference* Singapore (Singapore) 2015. **Publications** *Global Airport Benchmarking Report* (annual). [2020/XJ1976/E]

♦ AIRT / see Rubber Trade Association of Europe (#18995)
♦ Air and Waste Management Association (internationally oriented national body)
♦ **AISA** Académie internationale des sciences Ararat (#00030)
♦ AISA – Africa Institute of South Africa (internationally oriented national body)
♦ **AISA** African Iron and Steel Association (#00346)
♦ AISA – Association internationale pour la sécurité aérienne (inactive)
♦ AISA – Association Internationale Soufie Alâwiyya (unconfirmed)
♦ **AISA** Association of International Schools in Africa (#02761)
♦ **AISA** Associazione Internazionale per la Storia delle Alpi (#02990)
♦ AISAC – Association internationale des institutions sanitaires catholiques (no recent information)
♦ AISAC – Associazione Internazionale delle Istituzioni Sanitarie Cattoliche (no recent information)
♦ **AISADC** Association of Insurance Supervisory Authorities of Developing Countries (#02649)
♦ AISA / see International Blind Sports Federation (#12363)
♦ **AIS** Akademio Internacia de la Sciencoj, San Marino (#00617)
♦ AIS – Alcohol Interlock Symposium (meeting series)
♦ AISAM – Association internationale des sociétés d'assurance mutuelle (inactive)
♦ AIS – Ambassadors in Sport (internationally oriented national body)
♦ **AIS** Association for Information Systems (#02645)
♦ AIS – Association internationale de la savonnerie et de la détergence (inactive)
♦ **AIS** Association internationale de sémiotique (#12160)
♦ **AIS** Association internationale de sociologie (#15553)
♦ AIS – Association internationale de la soie (inactive)
♦ AIS – Association internationale de somatothérapie (no recent information)
♦ AIS – Association for Iranian Studies (internationally oriented national body)
♦ AIS – Associazione Italiana degli Slavisti (internationally oriented national body)
♦ AISB / see International Alliance for Biological Standardization (#11622)
♦ AISC – Arab Institute for Studies and Communication, Lebanon (internationally oriented national body)
♦ AISC / see ASEAN Iron and Steel Industry Federation (#01206)
♦ **AISC** Association Internationale des Skål Clubs (#02743)
♦ **AISCCUF** Association des institutions supérieures de contrôle ayant en commun l'usage du français (#02647)
♦ **AISCGre** Associazione Internazionale Studi di Canto Gregoriano (#02991)
♦ **AISE** Association internationale de la savonnerie, de la détergence et des produits d'entretien (#12166)
♦ **AISE** Association internationale des sciences économiques (#13222)
♦ AISE – Association internationale des services d'eau (inactive)
♦ **AISE** Association internationale des statisticiens d'enquêtes (#12218)
♦ AISE / see International Association for the Semiotics of Space and Time (#12159)
♦ AISEN – Association internationale de spécialistes en énergie (no recent information)
♦ **AISE + T** Association Internationale de Sémiotique de l'Espace et du Temps (#12159)
♦ AISF – Association internationale de solidarité francophone (inactive)
♦ **AISG** Amitié internationale scoute et guide (#14812)
♦ **AISH** Association internationale des sciences hydrologiques (#11954)
♦ AISI – African Information Society Initiative (inactive)
♦ **AISI** American Iron and Steel Institute (#00784)
♦ AISI – Association internationale des syndicats d'initiative et groupements similaires (inactive)
♦ **AISIF** ASEAN Iron and Steel Industry Federation (#01206)
♦ AISIM / see International Association for Visual Semiotics (#12258)
♦ **AISJ** Association internationale des sciences juridiques (#11997)
♦ **AIS-LAC** Acción Internacional por la Salud – Latinoamérica and Caribe (#00056)
♦ **AISL** Association internationale pour l'oeuvre du docteur Albert Schweitzer de Lambaréné (#02723)
♦ **AISLF** Association internationale des sociologues de langue française (#02744)
♦ **AISLLI** Associazione Internazionale per gli Studi di Lingua e Letteratura Italiana (#12202)
♦ **AISLLI** International Association for the Study of the Italian Language and Literature (#12202)
♦ **AISM** Academia Internacional de Sexologia Médica (#11552)
♦ **AISM** Association internationale de signalisation maritime (#12013)
♦ AISM / see International Union of Microbiological Societies (#15794)
♦ AISO / see Asociación Iberoamericana de Investigación en Sociología de las Organizaciones y Comunicación (#02145)
♦ **AISOC** Asociación Iberoamericana de Investigación en Sociología de las Organizaciones y Comunicación (#02145)
♦ AISP – Association of Information Systems Professionals (inactive)
♦ **AISP** Association internationale de science politique (#14615)
♦ **AISP** Association internationale des soldats de la paix (#19678)
♦ **AISP** Association of International Seafood Professionals (#02762)
♦ **AISPIT** Association internationale de séismologie et de physique de l'intérieur de la Terre (#12157)
♦ **AISPO** Association internationale des sciences physiques de l'océan (#12082)
♦ **AISR** Académie internationale des sciences religieuses (#00031)
♦ AISRGD – African Institute for Strategic Research Governance and Development (internationally oriented national body)
♦ AISRU – Association internationale pour la statistique régionale et urbaine (inactive)
♦ **AISS** Asociación Internacional de la Seguridad Social (#14885)
♦ **AISS** Association internationale de la sécurité sociale (#14885)
♦ **AISS** Association Internationale des Seniors pour la Santé (#19228)
♦ AISSCAP – Asociación de Instituciones de Seguridad Social de Centroamérica y Panama (inactive)
♦ AISS / see International Union of Soil Sciences (#15817)
♦ AIST – Association internationale pour la santé des touristes (no recent information)
♦ **AIST** Association Internationale pour la Sauvegarde de Tyr (#12144)
♦ **AIST** Association internationale pour la sécurité du transport des jeunes (#02742)
♦ AISTATS – International Conference on Artificial Intelligence and Statistics (meeting series)
♦ AISTS – Académie internationale des sciences et techniques du sport (internationally oriented national body)
♦ **AISU** Arab Iron and Steel Union (#00998)
♦ **AISV** Association internationale de sémiotique visuelle (#12258)
♦ **AiSVD** Asian Society of Veterinary Dermatology (#01749)
♦ **AiSVO** Asian Society of Veterinary Ophthalmology (#01750)
♦ **AiSvS** Asian Society of Veterinary Surgery (#01751)
♦ **AITAA** Asian Institute of Technology Alumni Association (#01520)
♦ AITA / see Association of International Travel Agents Network (#02764)
♦ **AITADIS** Asociación Iberoamericana de Tecnologias de Apoyo a la Discapacidad (#02154)
♦ **AITA/IATA** Asociación Internacional del Teatro de Arte (#11647)
♦ **AITA/IATA** Association internationale du théâtre amateur (#11647)
♦ **AITA/IATA** International Amateur Theatre Association (#11647)
♦ AITAL / see Latin American and Caribbean Air Transport Association (#16263)
♦ **AIT** Alliance internationale de tourisme (#00694)
♦ AIT Alumni Association / see Asian Institute of Technology Alumni Association (#01520)
♦ **AITAN** Association of International Travel Agents Network (#02764)
♦ **AIT** Asian Institute of Technology (#01519)
♦ **AIT** Asian Institute of Tourism (#01521)
♦ **AIT** Asociación Internacional de los Trabajadores (#15906)
♦ **AIT** Association of Inhalation Toxicologists (#02646)
♦ **AIT** Association internationale du tournesol (#15625)
♦ AIT – Association internationale des travailleurs, 1864 (inactive)
♦ **AITC** Association internationale des traducteurs de conférence (#02748)
♦ AITD – Asian Institute of Transport Development (internationally oriented national body)
♦ AITEC / see ACCION International
♦ **AITEC** Association internationale de techniciens, experts et chercheurs (#02745)
♦ AITEC – Association internationale de technologie des conférences (inactive)
♦ AITED – Association internationale des télévisions d'éducation et de découverte (no recent information)
♦ **AITES** Association internationale des tunnels et de l'espace souterrain (#15744)
♦ AITES / see International Tunnelling and Underground Space Association (#15744)
♦ AITF – Asociación Iberoamericana de Terapeutas Florales (no recent information)
♦ **AITIC** Agency for International Trade Information and Cooperation (#00553)
♦ AITIT – Association internationale de la teinture et de l'impression textiles (inactive)
♦ AITL – Association internationale du théâtre lyrique (no recent information)
♦ AIT Library / see Regional Energy Resources Information Center (#18780)
♦ **AITO** Association internationale pour les technologies objets (#02746)
♦ **AITRI** ASEAN Insurance Training and Research Institute (#01202)
♦ **AITRS** Arab Institute for Training and Research in Statistics (#00987)
♦ AITS – Association internationale pour le tourisme social (no recent information)
♦ **AITT** Asociación Iberoamericana de Telesalud y Telemedicina (#02155)
♦ **AITT** Associação Iberoamericana de Telessaúde e Telemedicina (#02155)
♦ AITT – Association internationale des techniciens de théâtre (inactive)
♦ AITT – Association internationale de la teinture textile (inactive)
♦ **AITT** Association internationale de traitement thermique et de l'ingénierie des surfaces (#13443)
♦ **AITU** Association internationale du théâtre à l'université (#15831)
♦ **AITVM** Association of Institutions of Tropical Veterinary Medicine (#02648)
♦ **AIU** Alliance israélite universelle (#00698)
♦ AIU – Alliant International University (internationally oriented national body)
♦ AIU – Arab Investors Union (no recent information)
♦ **AIU** Asociación Internacional de Urbanistas (#15012)
♦ **AIU** Association internationale des Universités (#12246)
♦ **AIU** Association internationale des urbanistes (#15012)
♦ AIUEALF – Association internationale des universitaires, écrivains et artistes de langue française (inactive)
♦ AIUE – Asia Institute of Urban Environment (unconfirmed)
♦ AIUFFASS / see Association internationale des utilisateurs de fils de filaments artificiels et synthétiques et de soie naturelle (#02750)
♦ **AIUFFASS** Association internationale des utilisateurs de fils de filaments artificiels et synthétiques et de soie naturelle (#02750)
♦ **AIUL** Asociación Internacional de Universidades La Salle (#12142)
♦ AIULRE – Asociación Internacionala per l'Usança de la Lengas Regionalas a l'Escola (no recent information)
♦ **AIUTA** Association internationale des universités du troisième âge (#02749)
♦ Aiuto alla Chiesa che Soffre (#00587)
♦ AIVA – Association internationale des villes d'avenir (inactive)
♦ AIVAC – Association internationale pour la vidéo dans les arts et la culture (inactive)
♦ **AIVC** Air Infiltration and Ventilation Centre (#00603)
♦ **AIVCIT** Association internationale de volcanologie et de chimie de l'intérieur de la Terre (#12259)
♦ **AIVE** Association internationale des ville éducatrices (#11860)
♦ AIVFC / see Coésio – Destinations Francophone de Congrès (#04082)
♦ **AIVM** Association internationale pour les voiles minces et les voiles spatiaux (#12162)
♦ **AIVMP** Association internationale des villes messagères de la paix (#12073)
♦ AIVN / see International Urban Development Association (#15832)
♦ AIVPA – Asociación Internacional Veterinaria de Producción Animal (inactive)
♦ AIVPA – Association internationale vétérinaire de production animale (inactive)
♦ AIVP / see Association internationale villes et ports – réseau mondial des villes portuaires (#02751)
♦ **AIVP** Association internationale villes et ports – réseau mondial des villes portuaires (#02751)
♦ **AIVS** Association of International Vascular Surgeons (#02765)
♦ AIWA – Armenian International Women's Association (internationally oriented national body)
♦ AIWA – Art International Women Association (internationally oriented national body)
♦ **AIW** American Indian Workshop (#00782)
♦ **AIW** Association internationale Walras (#15862)
♦ **AIWC** All India Women's Conference (#00737)
♦ **AIWCS** Association of Interbalkan Women's Cooperation Societies, Thessaloniki (#02653)
♦ **AIWF** Arab International Women's Forum (#00994)
♦ AIWF / see Association of the International Olympic Winter Sports Federations (#02757)
♦ **AIWM** Association of International Wealth Management (#02766)
♦ **AIWN** Asian Indigenous Women's Network (#01511)
♦ AIWO – African Indigenous Women's Organization (no recent information)
♦ **AIWO** Agudath Israel World Organization (#00584)

♦ **Aix Group** **00616**
Secretariat CEREFI, Univ de Paul Cézanne, Aix-Marseille III, 3 av Robert Schuman, 13628 Aix-en-Provence, France. T. +33442216011. Fax +33442230894. E-mail: info@aix-group.org.
Palestinian Secretariat DATA Studies and Consultation, Antonian Society Street, Bethlehem, West Bank PALESTINE, Via Israel. T. +97222743343. Fax +97222743369. E-mail: data@databethlehem.com.
URL: http://www.aix-group.org/
History 2002. **Aims** Publish and disseminate position papers identifying economic scenarios to promote sustainable and mutually beneficial relations between *Israel* and *Palestine*. **Structure** Steering Committee. **Events** *Meeting* Paris (France) 2008, *Seminar* Paris (France) 2008. **Publications** Position papers. [2016.06.01/XM2930/E]

♦ **AJA** African Jurists' Association (#00351)
♦ **AJA** Asia Journalist Association (#01287)
♦ **AJAN** African Jesuit AIDS Network (#00348)
♦ AJAR – Asia Justice and Rights (internationally oriented national body)
♦ AJC / see American Jewish Committee

♦ **AJC** African Jewish Congress (#00349)
♦ AJC – American Jewish Committee (internationally oriented national body)
♦ **AJCEEQ** Association des Jeunes Chercheurs Européens en études québécoise (#02771)
♦ AJCELQ / see Association des Jeunes Chercheurs Européens en études québécoise (#02771)
♦ AJC – Global Jewish Advocacy / see American Jewish Committee
♦ AJCPP – Asian Joint Conference of Propulsion and Power (meeting series)
♦ AJC PSE – Asian Joint Committee on Plasma Surface Engineering (unconfirmed)
♦ AJC Transatlantic Institute (internationally oriented national body)
♦ **AJCU-AP** Association of Jesuit Colleges and Universities in Asia Pacific (#02770)
♦ AJCU-EAO / see Association of Jesuit Colleges and Universities in Asia Pacific (#02770)
♦ AJCV / see International Association for Vegetation Science (#12253)
♦ **AJDH** Association européenne des juristes pour la démocratie et les droits de l'homme dans le monde (#06105)
♦ **AJE** Association of Japanese Language Teachers in Europe (#02769)
♦ **AJE** Association des journalistes européens (#02516)
♦ AJEL – Asociación Japonesa de Estudios Latinoamericanos (internationally oriented national body)
♦ **AJFE** Association des jeunes fonctionnaires européens (#02772)
♦ Ajia Juihifuka Gakkai (#01749)
♦ Ajia Keisei Zaidan (#01263)
♦ AJI – Alliance internationale de journalistes (internationally oriented national body)
♦ Ajia Seikei Gakkai / see Japan Association for Asian Studies
♦ Ajia-Taiheiyo Seinen Rengo (#01647)
♦ **AJJBWF** Asian Jujitsu Belt Wrestling Federation (#01523)
♦ AJM / see Jean Monnet Association
♦ AJM – Association Jean Monnet (internationally oriented national body)
♦ AJNL – Asociación de Jóvenes Nucleares Latinoamericanos (unconfirmed)
♦ **AJO** Alliance of Jumping Organizers (#00699)
♦ AJP – Association des journalistes du Pacifique (inactive)
♦ AJPF – Association des journalistes de la presse francophone (no recent information)
♦ **AJU** African Judo Union (#00350)
♦ Ajuda à Igreja que Sofre (#00587)
♦ AJVSME – Association des Jeunes Volontaires au Service du Monde Environnemental (internationally oriented national body)
♦ AJWRC – Asia Japan Women's Resource Centre (internationally oriented national body)
♦ AJWS – American Jewish World Service (internationally oriented national body)
♦ Akademie Europäischer Privatrechtswissenschaftler (#00036)
♦ Akademie für multidisziplinäre Neurotraumatologie (#00042)
♦ Akademie für Raumforschung und Landesplanung (internationally oriented national body)
♦ Akademio de Esperanto (#05543)

♦ Akademio Internacia de la Sciencoj, San Marino (AIS) 00617

International Academy of Sciences, San Marino – Académie internationale des sciences, San Marino – Internationale Akademie der Wissenschaften, San Marino – Accademia Internazionale delle Scienze, San Marino

Sec/Information Office Rahel-Straus-Weg 19, 81673 Munich, Germany. E-mail: informo@ais-sanmarino.org.
URL: http://www.ais-sanmarino.org/

History 13 Sep 1985, San Marino. Founded on signature of the founding constitution; definitive constitution signed 2 May 1987. Registration: San Marino. **Aims** Act as a platform for eminent, linguistically progressive scientists worldwide; enhance international communication and *interdisciplinary* cooperation so as to achieve greater efficiency in scientific research and teaching, and closer contact between teaching of arts and technology; promote international scientific collaboration without language discrimination; eventually achieve the human right of communication without language barriers or language discrimination. **Structure** Senate; Sectors (4); Colleges, comprising members appointed by Senate: *International Scientific College (ISK, see: #00617)*; *International College of Technology (ITKanoj)*; *International College of Arts (IAKanoj)*. **Languages** English, Esperanto, French, German, Italian. **Staff** 12.00 FTE, voluntary. **Finance** Material support from sponsors and members of Colleges. Participants' fees. **Activities** Events/meetings; training/education; awards/prizes/competitions. **Events** *Annual Academic Conference / Annual Academy Conference* Warsaw (Poland) 2012, *Annual Academic Conference / Annual Academy Conference* Sibiu (Romania) 2011, *Session / Annual Academy Conference* Karlovo (Bulgaria) 2010, *Annual academic conference / Annual Academy Conference* Rimini (Italy) 2009, *Meeting / Annual Academy Conference* Banja Luka (Bosnia-Herzegovina) 2008. **Publications** *Grundlagenstudien aus Kybernetik und Geisteswissenschaft* (4 a year) in English, Esperanto, French, German, Italian. Conference proceedings; bi- and multi-lingual papers – with publishers, research institutions and academic societies in various countries.
Members Supporting and college members and collaborators, full associated professors and professors in ordinary, associated and other members in 58 countries and territories:
Albania, Algeria, Argentina, Australia, Austria, Belarus, Belgium, Bosnia-Herzegovina, Brazil, Bulgaria, Burkina Faso, Canada, China, Croatia, Czechia, Denmark, El Salvador, Finland, France, Germany, Greece, Guatemala, Hong Kong, Hungary, India, Iran Islamic Rep, Ireland, Israel, Italy, Jamaica, Japan, Kazakhstan, Korea Rep, Lithuania, Malta, Mexico, Moldova, Netherlands, New Zealand, Niger, Norway, Poland, Portugal, Romania, Russia, San Marino, Serbia, Slovakia, Slovenia, South Africa, Spain, Sweden, Switzerland, Taiwan, UK, Ukraine, USA, Venezuela.
NGO Relations Member of: *International Association of University Professors and Lecturers (IAUPL, #12250)*. Associated with: *Universal Esperanto Association (UEA, #20676)*. [2018.08.02/XE6017/**E**]

♦ Akademio Literatura de Esperanto (no recent information)
♦ 'Akademischer Austauschdienst / see Deutscher Akademischer Austauschdienst
♦ Akademisches Forum für Aussenpolitik – Hochschulliga für die Vereinten Nationen (internationally oriented national body)
♦ Akademisches Forum für Aussenpolitik – Österreich / see United Nations Youth and Student Association of Austria – Academic Forum for Foreign Affairs
♦ **AK** Afrika Komitee (#00164)
♦ AKASSA ONG Internationale (see: #12726)
♦ ÄK-BYGG – Nordiska Ämbetsmannakommittén för Samarbete inom Byggsektorn (inactive)
♦ **AKC** ASEAN Kite Council (#01207)
♦ **AKC** ASEAN-Korea Centre (#01208)
♦ Akdeniz Su EnstitüsÜ (#11323)
♦ Akdeniz Gençler Orkestrasi (#17788)
♦ Akdeniz Orman Iletisimcileri Agi (unconfirmed)
♦ Akdeniz Politikalar Merkezi (internationally oriented national body)
♦ **AKDN** Aga Khan Development Network (#00544)
♦ AKEG / see European Hospital and Healthcare Federation (#07501)
♦ AKFA / see Churches' Commission for Migrants in Europe (#03912)
♦ **AKF** Aga Khan Foundation (#00545)
♦ AKF – Asian Karatedo Federation (see: #21608)
♦ AKF / see WKF Africa (#20972)
♦ AKI – Animal-Kind International (internationally oriented national body)
♦ Akkoord van Schengen (1985 treaty)
♦ AKLHÜ / see AKLHÜ – Netzwerk und Fachstelle für internationale Personelle Zusammenarbeit
♦ AKLHÜ – Netzwerk und Fachstelle für internationale Personelle Zusammenarbeit (internationally oriented national body)
♦ ÄK-LIVS / see Committee of Senior Officials of the Nordic Countries, Estonia, Latvia and Lithuania in the Field of Food Issues (#04286)
♦ AKMS / see Arab International Society for Management Technology (#00993)
♦ Akrofi-Christaller Centre for Mission Research and Applied Theology / see Akrofi-Christaller Institute of Theology, Mission and Culture
♦ Akrofi-Christaller Institute of Theology, Mission and Culture (internationally oriented national body)
♦ **AKSE** Association for Korean Studies in Europe (#02776)
♦ **AKSF** Association Kangourou sans Frontières (#02775)
♦ AKSI / see Action in Solidarity with Asia and the Pacific
♦ **AKTEA** European Network of Women's Organisations in Fisheries and Aquaculture (#08035)
♦ akte – Arbeitskreis Tourismus und Entwicklung (internationally oriented national body)
♦ Aktie voor Ontwikkeling (internationally oriented national body)
♦ Aktie Service Europese Staatsburgers / see European Citizen Action Service (#06555)
♦ Aktion Afrika Hilfe (internationally oriented national body)
♦ Aktion für Bergbauregionen / see Association of Europe's Coalfield Regions (#02585)
♦ Aktion Biafra-Hilfe / see Society for Threatened Peoples International (#19654)
♦ Aktion Børnehjaelp (internationally oriented national body)
♦ Aktion für die Entwicklung (internationally oriented national body)
♦ Aktiondienst Europäische Bürger / see European Citizen Action Service (#06555)
♦ Aktion Dritte Welt (internationally oriented national body)
♦ Aktion Europäischer Föderalisten (inactive)
♦ Aktion Fünf Prozent für die Dritte Welt (internationally oriented national body)
♦ Aktion Gesundheitsentwicklung für Südosteuropa (#19807)
♦ Aktion gegen den Hunger (#00086)
♦ Aktion Mission und Leprahilfe Schiefbahn (internationally oriented national body)
♦ Aktion Partnerschaft Dritte Welt / see Aktion Eine Welt
♦ Aktionsgemeinschaft Dienst für den Frieden (internationally oriented national body)
♦ Aktionsgemeinschaft Solidarische Welt (internationally oriented national body)
♦ Aktionskomitee für die Vereinigten Staaten von Europa (inactive)
♦ Aktion Sühnezeichen Friedensdienste (internationally oriented national body)
♦ Aktion Eine Welt (internationally oriented national body)
♦ Aktion Zahnfreudlich International / see Toothfriendly International
♦ AKTIOUN-ABC – Aktioun A B C fir Bildung a Gesondheet am Tiers-Monde (internationally oriented national body)
♦ Aktioun A B C fir Bildung a Gesondheet am Tiers-Monde (internationally oriented national body)
♦ Aktivitetstjeneste Borger i Europa / see European Citizen Action Service (#06555)
♦ **AKU** African Kurash Union (#00352)
♦ **AKU** Aga Khan University (#00546)
♦ Akvo Foundation (internationally oriented national body)
♦ **ALAA** Australasian Law Academics Association (#03025)
♦ ALA – African Literature Association (internationally oriented national body)
♦ ALA – American Library Association (internationally oriented national body)
♦ **ALA** American Literature Association (#00786)
♦ **ALA** ASEAN Law Association (#01209)
♦ **ALA** Asociación Latinoamericana de Acuicultura (#02177)
♦ **ALA** Asociación Latinoamericana de Antropologia (#16234)
♦ **ALA** Asociación Latinoamericana de Archivos (#02183)
♦ **ALA** Asociación Latinoamericana de Avicultura (#02185)
♦ **ALA** Association for Language Awareness (#02778)
♦ **ALA** Association des Loteries d'Afrique (#02791)
♦ ALA – Australasian Lymphology Association (internationally oriented national body)
♦ **ALAB** Asociación Latinoamericana de Antropologia Biológica (#02180)
♦ **ALABAT** Asociación Latinoamericana de Bancos de Tejidos (#02186)
♦ ALABIC – Asociación Latinoamericana de Industrias de Bienes de Capital e Infraestructura (no recent information)
♦ ALABYB – Asociación Latinoamericana de Biotecnologia y Bioingenieria (unconfirmed)
♦ **ALAC** Alianza Latinoamericana Anticontrabando (#00631)
♦ **ALACAT** Federación de Asociaciones Nacionales de Agentes de Carga de América Latina y del Caribe (#16276)
♦ **ALACAURP** Asociación Latinoamericana de Carreras Universitarias de Relaciones Públicas (#02192)
♦ ALACCSA / see Asociación Latino Americana de Cirugia de Catarata, Segmento Anterior y Refractiva (#02194)
♦ **ALACCSA-R** Asociación Latino Americana de Cirugia de Catarata, Segmento Anterior y Refractiva (#02194)
♦ **ALACCTA** Asociación Latinoamericano y del Caribe de Ciencia y Tecnologia de los Alimentos (#02276)
♦ **ALACDE** Asociación Latinoamericana e Ibérica de Derecho y Economia (#16340)
♦ ALACDE / see Latin American and Iberian Law and Economics Association (#16340)
♦ ALACEA – Asociación de Latinoamérica y del Caribe de Economia Agricola (no recent information)
♦ ALACEA – Latin American and Caribbean Association of Agricultural Economy (no recent information)
♦ **ALACE** Asociación Latinoamericana de Cirujanos Endoscópistas (#16239)
♦ **ALACED** Asociación Latinoamericana de Cooperación en Emergencia Médica y Desastres (#02200)
♦ ALACEL – Latin American Wireless Industry Association (no recent information)
♦ ALACEM – Asociación Latinoamericana y del Caribe sobre Estudios de la Mujer (inactive)
♦ **Alacero** Asociación Latinoamericana del Acero (#02176)
♦ **ALACF** Asociación Latino-americana de Ciencias Fisiológicas (#16250)
♦ **ALACI** Asociación Latinoamericana y Caribeña de Inmunologia (#16265)
♦ **ALACI** Associação Latino-Americana e do Caribe de Imunologia (#16265)
♦ **ALACIBU** Asociación Latinoamericana de Cirugia y Traumatologia Bucomaxilofacial (#02195)
♦ **ALACI** Latin American and Caribbean Association of Immunology (#16265)
♦ **ALACIP** Asociación Latinoamericana de Ciencia Politica (#02193)
♦ **ALAC-ITS** Asociación Latinoamericana y Caribeña para el control de las Infecciones de Transmisión (#02191)
♦ ALACODE – Asociación Latinoamericana de Periodistas para el Desarrollo (inactive)
♦ **ALACOP** Asociación Latinoamericana de Consultores Politicos (#02198)
♦ **ALACP** Latin American Association of Coloproctology (#16237)
♦ ALACRED / see Asociación Latinoamericana y del Caribe de Burós de Crédito (#02189)
♦ **ALACRED** Asociación Latinoamericana y del Caribe de Burós de Crédito (#02189)
♦ **ALADAA** Asociación Latinoamericana de Estudios de Asia y Africa (#16236)
♦ **ALADA** Asociación Latinoamericana de Derecho Aeronautico y Espacial (#02202)
♦ ALAD – Asociación Latinoamericana de Adiccionologia (unconfirmed)
♦ **ALAD** Asociación Latinoamericana de Diabetes (#16311)
♦ ALAD – Associação Latinoamericana de Dragages (inactive)
♦ **ALADEE** Asociación Latinoamericana de Economia de la Energia (#02206)
♦ **ALADEFE** Asociación Latinoamericana de Escuelas y Facultades de Enfermeria (#02211)
♦ ALADE / see Latin American and Iberian Law and Economics Association (#16340)
♦ **ALADI** Asociación Latinoamericana de Integración (#16343)
♦ **ALADI** Associação Latino-Americana de Integração (#16343)
♦ **ALADI** Association latinoaméricaine d'intégration (#16343)
♦ ALADI / see Latin American Association of Design (#16238)
♦ **ALADI** Latin American Association of Design (#16238)
♦ ALADIM – Asociación Latinoamericana para el Desarrollo y la Integración de la Mujer (inactive)

♦ ALADIN 00618

Program Manager Fac of Sciences – Dept of Physics and Astronomy, Proeftuinstr 86, 9000 Ghent, Belgium.
URL: http://www.umr-cnrm.fr/aladin/

History Founded 1990, at the initiative of Méteo France. First Memorandum of Understanding (MoU) signed for period 1996-2001; 2nd MoU for 2001-2005; 3rd MoU signed end 2005; 4th MoU signed end 2010; 5th MoU signed early 2016. **Aims** As an interactive sky *atlas* allowing the user to visualize *digitized astronomical* images or full surveys, superimpose entries from astronomical catalogues. **Structure** General Assembly; Bureau; Program Manager; Policy Advisory Committee. **Events** *General Assembly* Istanbul (Turkey) 2019, *Workshop* Madrid (Spain) 2019, *Short Range NWP (SRNWP) EUMETNET Meeting* Vienna (Austria) 2018, *General Assembly* Zagreb (Croatia) 2018. **Publications** *ALADIN-HIRLAM Newsletter.*
Members Partners – National Meteorological Services in 16 countries:
Algeria, Austria, Belgium, Bulgaria, Croatia, Czechia, France, Hungary, Morocco, Poland, Portugal, Romania, Slovakia, Slovenia, Tunisia, Türkiye. [2019/XM7899/**D**]

- ALADO – Asociación Latino Americana de Ostomizados (inactive)
- **ALADYR** Asociación Latinoamericana de Desalación y Reúso del Agua (#02204)
- ALAEH – Asociación Latinoamericana de Educadoras del Hogar (inactive)
- **ALAEITS** Asociación Latinoamericana de Enseñanza e Investigación en Trabajo Social (#02210)
- ALAESP – Asociación Latinoamericana y del Caribe de Educación en Salud Pública (inactive)
- ALAESS – Associação Latinoamericana de Escolas de Serviço Social (inactive)
- **ALAEST** Associação Latino-Americana de Engenharia de Segurança do Trabalho (#16314)
- ALAETS – Asociación Latinoamericana de Escuelas de Trabajo Social (inactive)
- ALAEX – Asociación Latinoamericana de Expositores (unconfirmed)
- **ALAFA** Alianza Latinoamericana para la Familia (#00633)
- ALAFAB – Asociación Latinoamericana de Fabricantes de Alimentos Balanceados (no recent information)
- ALAFACE / see Cerveceros Latinoamericanos (#03836)
- **ALAFAR** Asociación Latinoamericana de Fabricantes de Materiales Refractarios (#16244)
- **ALAF** Asociación Latinoamericana de Antropologia Forense (#02181)
- **ALAF** Asociación Latinoamericana de Ferrocarriles (#16365)
- ALAFATA – Asociación Latinoamericana de Fabricantes de Tableros y Fibras de Maderas y Similares (no recent information)
- ALAFAVE – Asociación Latino Americana de Fabricantes de Velas (unconfirmed)
- **ALaFe** Autismo Latinoamérica Federación (#03042)
- **ALAFEC** Asociación Latinoamericana de Facultades y Escuelas de Contaduria Administración (#02783)
- **ALAFEM** Asociación Latinoamericana de Facultades y Escuelas de Medicina (#16245)
- ALAFO – Asociación Latinoamericana de Facultades de Odontologia (inactive)
- **ALAG** Asociación Latinoamericana de Genética (#02225)
- **ALAGE** Asociación Latinoamericana de Geofísica Espacial (#02226)
- **ALAGO** Associação Latinoamericana de Geoquimica Orgânica (#02331)
- ALAGRAN – Latin American Association on Post-Harvest Grain Technology (inactive)
- ALAHUA – Asociación Latinoamericana para la Promoción del Habitat, del Urbanismo y de la Arquitectura (inactive)
- **ALAI** Agencia Latinoamericana de Información (#00551)
- **ALAI** Asociación Latinoamericana de Internet (#02234)
- **ALAI** Association littéraire et artistique internationale (#14058)
- ALAIC – Asociación Latinoamericana de la Industria Curtidora (inactive)
- **ALAIC** Asociación Latinoamericana de Investigadores de la Comunicación (#02237)
- ALAIC – Latin American Business Credit Reporting Association (no recent information)
- **ALAIL** Asociación Latinoamericana de la Industria del Letrero (#02229)
- ALAI / see Latin American and Caribbean Association of Immunology (#16265)
- **ALAINEE** Asociación Latinoamericana de la Industria Eléctrica, Electrónica y de Gasodomésticos (#02228)
- **ALAIPO** Asociación Latina Interacción Persona-Ordenador (#02174)
- **ALAIST** Asociación Latino-americana de Ingenieros de Seguransa del Trabajo (#16314)
- ALAJO – Asociación Latinoamericana de Jojoba (inactive)
- ALAL – Asociación Latinoamericana de Abogados Laboralistas (unconfirmed)
- ALALC – Asociación Latinoamericana de Libre Comercio (inactive)
- ALALC – Associação Latinoamericana de Livre Comércio (inactive)
- ALALE – Association latinoaméricaine de libre échange (inactive)
- **ALALOG** Asociación Latinoamericana de Logistica (#02239)
- **ALAMAR** Asociación Latinoamericana de Armadores (#16369)
- **ALAM** Asociación Latinoamericana de Malherbologia (#16394)
- **ALAM** Asociación Latinoamericana de Microbiologia (#16247)
- ALAM – Asociación Latinoamericana de Museos (inactive)
- **ALAMCTA** Asociación Latinoamericana de Mutagenesis, Carcinogeneisi y Teratogenesis Ambiental (#16240)
- **ALAMES** Asociación Latinoamericana de Medicina Social (#02241)
- ALAMI – Asociación Latinoamericana de Sistemas Privados de Salud (unconfirmed)
- ALAMO – Associação Latino-Americana de Pesquisa de Mercado e Opinião (no recent information)
- **ALAMOC** Asociación Latinoamericana de Analisis y Modificación del Comportamiento (#02179)
- ALAMPYME – Asociación Latinoamericana de Micro, Pequeños y Medianos Empresarios (no recent information)
- **ALAMYS** Asociación Latinoamericana de Metros y Subterraneos (#02242)
- **ALAN** Acute Leukemia Advocates Network (#00107)
- **ALANAM** Asociación Latinoamericana de Academias Nacionales de Medicina (#02175)
- ALAN – Asociación Latinoamericana de neuropsicologia (unconfirmed)
- Åland Islands Peace Institute (internationally oriented national body)
- Ålands Fredsinstitut (internationally oriented national body)
- **ALANEPE** Asociación Latinoamericana de Nefrologia Pediatrica (#16379)

♦ Alan Walker College of Evangelism (AWCE) 00619

Contact c/o Alan Walker, 16 Masons Drive, Parramatta NSW 2151, Australia.
URL: http://www.awce.org/

History Mar 1989, Sydney (Australia), as *Pacific College for Evangelism.* **Aims** Teach and research effective and responsible evangelism; serve the wider *church* in pacific region by: providing courses and resources in evangelism, mission, aplogetics and leadership; providing consultation services; conducting and publishing research. **Structure** Board. **Languages** English. **Staff** 1.00 FTE, paid. **Finance** Donations; rental of property; fundraising activities. **Activities** Training/education; research/documentation; guidance/assistance/consulting. **Events** *Conference on pastoral care and HIV-AIDS* Sydney, NSW (Australia) 2000, *Conference on women in evangelism* Sydney, NSW (Australia) 2000, *Meeting on reconciliation philosophy and practice* Sydney, NSW (Australia) 2000, *Symposium on leadership in the church at the beginning of the new millennium* Sydney, NSW (Australia) 2000, *Christian leaders symposium* Parramatta, NSW (Australia) 1997.
Members Affiliated Churches (20) in 16 countries and territories:
Australia, Cook Is, Fiji, Indonesia, Kiribati, Korea Rep, Nauru, New Caledonia, New Zealand, Papua New Guinea, Samoa, Samoa USA, Solomon Is, Tonga, Tuvalu, Vanuatu.
Individuals in 3 countries:
India, Philippines, Timor-Leste.
NGO Relations The following international organizations are affiliated and have stakeholding status: Uniting International Mission (Australia); Uniting Mission and Education (Australia); *World Methodist Evangelism Institute (WMEI, see: #21650).* [2019.07.11/XF1044/**E**]

- **ALAPA** Associação Latino Americana de Pneus e Aros (#02332)
- **ALAPAC/ML** Latin American Clinical Pathology and Laboratory Medicine (#16299)
- ALAP – Asociación Latinoamericana de Administración Pública (inactive)
- **ALAP** Asociación Latinoamericana de Agencias de Publicidad (#16235)
- **ALAP** Asociación Latinoamericana de la Papa (#02250)
- **ALAP** Asociación Latinoamericana de Perfusión (#02253)
- **ALAP** Asociación Latinoamericana de Población (#02256)
- **ALAPCCO** Federação Latino-Americana de Psicoterapias Cognitivas e Comportamentais (#09363)
- **ALAPCCO** Federación Latinoamericana de Psicoterapias Cognitivas y Conductuales (#09363)
- **ALAPE** Asociación Latinoamericana de Pediatria (#16360)
- ALAPE – Asociación Latinoamericana de Planificadores Energéticos (inactive)
- ALAPP – Applied Linguistics and Professional Practice Society (meeting series)
- **ALAPP** Asociación Latinoamericana de Piso Pélvico (#02254)
- **ALAPRE** Asociación Latinoamericana de Plantas de Rendimiento (#02255)
- ALAPROVI – Asociación Latinoamericana de Productores de Vidrio (no recent information)
- **ALAPSA** Asociación Latinoamericana de Psicologia de la Salud (#02259)
- **ALAPSI** Asociación Latinoamericana de Psicoterapias Integrativas (#02260)
- ALAPSISEX – Asociación Latinoamericana de Psicólogos Sexólogos (inactive)
- ALAPSO – Asociación Latinoamericana de Psicologia Social (inactive)
- **ALAPT** Asociación Latinoamericana de Patologia Toxicologica (#16387)
- ALAPTER – Asociación Latinoamericana de Pteridologia (inactive)
- **ALAR** Asociación Latinoamericana de Rizobiologia (#02262)
- **ALAR** Asociación Latinoamericana de Rorschach (#02263)
- **ALARB** Asociación Latinoamericana de Arbitraje (#02182)
- ALARC – Latin American Association of Cancer Registries (no recent information)
- **ALARP** Asociación Latinoamericana de Relaciones Públicas (#02261)
- **ALARYS** Asociación Latinoamericano de Administradores de Riesgos y Seguros (#02275)
- **ALASA** African Language Association of Southern Africa (#00355)
- **ALASA** Asociación Latinoamericana para el Desarrollo del Seguro Agropecuario (#02205)
- ALASAG – Alianza Latinoamericana de Salud Global (inactive)
- ALAS – Asociación Latinoamericana de Seguridad (unconfirmed)
- **ALAS** Asociación Latinoamericana de Sistémica (#02266)
- **ALAS** Asociación Latinoamericana de Sociologia (#02267)
- **ALAS** Asociación Latinoamericana de Supermercados (#02269)
- **ALAS** Asociación Latinoamericana de Surfistas Profesionales (#02270)
- **ALASBIMN** Asociación Latinoamericana de Sociedades de Biologia y Medicina Nuclear (#16251)
- **ALASECE** Asociación Latinoamericana de Organismos de Seguros de Crédito a la Exportación (#16241)
- **ALASEHT** Asociación Latinoamericana de Seguridad e Higiene en el Trabajo (#02265)
- **ALAS Foundation** Latin America in Solidarity Action (#16396)
- **ALASRU** Asociación Latinoamericana de Sociologia Rural (#16368)
- **ALASS** Asociación Latina para el Analisis de los Sistemas de Salud (#02171)
- **ALAST** Asociación Latinoamericana de Sociologia del Trabajo (#02268)
- ALATA / see Asociación Latinoamericana del Tórax (#02273)
- ALATAC – Asociación Latinoamericana del Transporte Automotor por Carreteras (inactive)
- ALAT – Asociación Latinoamericana de Analisis Transaccional (no recent information)
- ALAT – Asociación Latinoamericana de Empresas Comercializadoras Internacionales (no recent information)
- **ALAT** Asociación Latinoamericana del Tórax (#02273)
- ALATIR – Asociación Latinoamericana de Tiempo Libre y Recreación (inactive)
- **ALATOX** Asociación Latinoamericana de Toxicologia (#02274)
- ALATPU – Fundación Latinoamericana de Transporte Público y Urbano (unconfirmed)
- ALATRA – Asociación Latinoamericana de Técnicos Radiólogos (unconfirmed)
- **ALATRO** Asociación Latinoamericana de Terapia Radiante Oncológica (#02272)
- Al-Awda – Palestine Right to Return Coalition (internationally oriented national body)
- **ALAWUC** Agricultural and Land and Water Use Commission for the Near East (#00570)
- **ALAyTeC** Asociación Latinoamericana de Aféresis y Terapias celulares (#02178)
- ALB / see Egyptian Arab Land Bank
- ALBA / see Alianza Bolivariana de los Pueblos de Nuestra América (#00627)
- **ALBA** Alianza Bolivariana de los Pueblos de Nuestra América (#00627)
- Albanian Institute for International Studies (internationally oriented national body)
- **ALB** Asociación Latinoamericana de Botanica (#02187)
- Alberta Council for Global Cooperation (internationally oriented national body)

♦ Albertine Rift Conservation Society (ARCOS) 00620

Société de Conservation du Rift Albertine
Exec Dir 40 St Vincent's Close, Girton, Cambridge, CB3 0PE, UK. E-mail: info@arcosnetwork.org.
URL: http://arcosnetwork.org/

History 1995. Registered in accordance with Ugandan law; a UK registered charity. **Aims** Enhance conservation of critical *ecosystems* and promote sustainable development in the Albertine Rift through collaborative actions between various partners in the region. **Structure** Board of Directors, including Bureau, comprising Chairman, Vice-Chairman, Treasurer, Secretary, Executive Secretary and Regional Coordinator. **Events** *African Great Lakes Conference* Entebbe (Uganda) 2017. **Publications** *ARCOS Newsletter.* **IGO Relations** Memorandum of Cooperation with: *Secretariat of the Convention of Wetlands (#19200).* Participant of: *Global Biodiversity Information Facility (GBIF, #10250).* **NGO Relations** Participates in: *Mountain Forum (MF, #16861).* Member of: *Mountain Partnership (MP, #16862).* [2013/XJ7096/**E**]

- Albert Schweitzer Fellowship (internationally oriented national body)
- Albert Schweitzer Institute for the Humanities (internationally oriented national body)

♦ Albinism Europe 00621

Address not obtained.
URL: http://albinism.eu/

Aims Collaborate in spreading proper and correct information on albinism and the best available treatments. **Structure** Scientific Committee. **Events** *Meeting of Young People with Albinism* Hurdal (Norway) 2018, *Meeting of Young People with Albinism* Milan (Italy) 2016, *Meeting of Young People with Albinism* Valencia (Spain) 2014.
Members Associations in 11 countries:
Denmark, Finland, France, Germany, Ireland, Italy, Netherlands, Norway, Spain, Türkiye, UK. [2019/XM8037/**D**]

- ALBOAN (internationally oriented national body)
- **ALBTP** Association africaine des laboratoires du bâtiment et des travaux publics (#02349)
- ALCA / see Asociación Latinoamericana de Carcinologia (#02188)
- ALCA – Asociación Latinoamericana de Ciencias Agricolas (inactive)
- **ALCACJ** Alianza Latinoamericana y del Caribe de Asociaciones Cristianas de Jóvenes (#16264)
- **ALC** African Laser Centre (#00357)
- ALC – African Law Center (internationally oriented national body)
- **ALC** African Leadership Centre (#00358)
- ALC – African Leadership Conference (unconfirmed)
- **ALCAM** Alianza Latinoamericana de Compositores y Autores de Música (#00632)
- ALCANET – African Life Cycle Assessment Network (unconfirmed)
- ALCARCINUS / see Asociación Latinoamericana de Carcinologia (#02188)
- **ALCARCINUS** Asociación Latinoamericana de Carcinologia (#02188)
- ALC – Asia Lighting Conference (meeting series)
- ALC – Asociación Latinoamericana para la Calidad (inactive)
- ALC-COACHING – Asociación Latinoamericana de Coaching (unconfirmed)
- ALCEAPA – Asociación Latinoamericana y del Caribe de Empresas de Agua Potable y Alcantarillado (no recent information)
- ALCECOOP – Asociación Latinoamericana de Centros de Educación Cooperativa (no recent information)
- **ALCEM** Asociación Latinoamericana de Conservatorios y Escuelas de Música (#02197)
- **ALCEM** Association pour les Langues et Cultures Européennes Menacées (#02782)

- ♦ ALCESXXI – Asociación Internacional de Literatura y Cine Españoles Siglo XXI (internationally oriented national body)
- ♦ ALCEU – Association linguistique du Canada et des Etats Unis (internationally oriented national body)
- ♦ ALCIDED – Associação Latino Americana de Ciências do Esporte, Educação Fisica e Dança (unconfirmed)
- ♦ Alcide de Gasperi-Institut für Europäischen Studien (internationally oriented national body)
- ♦ ALC – International Symposium on Atomic Level Characterizations for New Materials and Devices (meeting series)
- ♦ ALCLI – Asociación Latinoamericana de Centros de Lucha contra las Intoxicaciones (inactive)

♦ Alcoa Foundation 00622

Contact address not obtained. E-mail: foundationcontact@alcoa.com.
URL: http://www.alcoa.com/foundation/

History 1952. **Aims** Promote *environmental stewardship*; educate tomorrow's leaders; enable economic and social *sustainability* in communities. **Structure** Board. **Staff** 9.00 FTE, paid. **Finance** Assets (2013): US$ 468 million. **Activities** Financial and/or material support; training/education. **Publications** *Alcoa Foundation Update.* [2014/XJ8707/f/F]

♦ Alcohol and Drugs History Society (ADHS) 00623

Co-Editor-in-Chief 546 Park Hall, North Campus SUNY, Buffalo NY 14222, USA. E-mail: treasurer@alcoholanddrugshistorysociety.org.
URL: http://alcoholanddrugshistorysociety.org/

History 1979. Current constitution amended and ratified Jun 2017. Former names and other names: *Alcohol and Temperance History Group (ATHG)* – former (1979 to 2004). **Aims** Advance, support and encourage the study of any aspect of alcohol and drug use or policy in any society or era; enhance public awareness of the history of alcohol and drugs both licit and illicit. **Structure** General Meeting; Executive Committee. **Finance** Sources: members' dues. **Activities** Events/meetings. **Events** *Biennial Conference* Mexico City (Mexico) 2022, *Biennial Conference* Shanghai (China) 2019, *Biennial Conference* Utrecht (Netherlands) 2017, *Biennial Conference* Bowling Green, OH (USA) 2015, *Biennial Conference* London (UK) 2013. **Publications** *Social History of Alcohol and Drugs* (2 a year) – journal. [2021/XJ9680/v/C]

♦ Alcoholics Anonymous World Services (AAWS) 00624

Contact Grand Central Station, PO Box 459, New York NY 10163, USA. T. +12128703400. Fax +12128703003.
Street address 475 Riverside Drive, 11th Floor, New York NY 10115, USA.
URL: http://www.aa.org/

History 1935, Akron OH (USA). **Aims** As an international fellowship of men and women, share experience, strength and hope with each other to solve their common problem and help others to recover from alcoholism (the only requirement for membership is a desire to stop drinking). Primary purpose of members is to stay sober and help other alcoholics to achieve *sobriety*. **Finance** No dues or fees. Organization is self-supporting through voluntary members' contributions. **Activities** Events/meetings; networking/liaising. **Events** *Quinquennial International Meeting* Vancouver, BC (Canada) 2025, *Quinquennial International Meeting* Detroit, MI (USA) 2020, *Quinquennial International Meeting* Atlanta, GA (USA) 2015, *Quinquennial international meeting* San Antonio, TX (USA) 2010, *Quinquennial international meeting* Toronto, ON (Canada) 2005. **Publications** *About AA: A Newsletter for Professionals.* Pamphlets; books; videos; audio tapes. **Members** Individuals in 170 countries and territories. Membership countries not specified. [2017.07.12/XF5496/F]

- ♦ Alcohol Interlock Symposium (meeting series)
- ♦ Alcohol Policy Youth Network / see International Youth Health Organization (#15933)
- ♦ Alcohol and Temperance History Group / see Alcohol and Drugs History Society (#00623)
- ♦ **ALCONPAT** Asociación Latinoamericana de Control de Calidad, Patologia y Recuperación de la Construcción (#02199)
- ♦ ALCONPAT Internacional / see Asociación Latinoamericana de Control de Calidad, Patologia y Recuperación de la Construcción (#02199)
- ♦ ALCORDES – Asociación Latinoamericana de Corporaciones Regionales de Desarrollo (inactive)
- ♦ **ALCP** Asociación Latinoamericana de Cuidados Paliativos (#02201)
- ♦ **ALCVA** Asociación Latinoamericana de Cirugia Vascular y Angiologia (#02196)
- ♦ ALDA / see European Association for Local Democracy (#06110)
- ♦ **ALDA** European Association for Local Democracy (#06110)
- ♦ **ALDE** Alliance of Liberals and Democrats for Europe (#00702)
- ♦ Aldeas Infantiles-SOS Internacional (#19693)
- ♦ ALDEC – Asociación Latinoamericana de Derecho Constitucional (no recent information)
- ♦ ALDE-CoR / see Renew Europe – Committee of the Regions (#18841)
- ♦ **ALDEFO** Asociación Latinoamericana de Facultades de Optometria (#02220)
- ♦ ALDE Group / see Renew Europe (#18840)
- ♦ ALDENAVE – Asociación Latinoamericana de Derecho de la Navegación y del Mar (no recent information)
- ♦ ALDE-PACE / see Alliance of Liberals and Democrats for Europe (#00702)
- ♦ **ALDE Party** Alliance of Liberals and Democrats for Europe Party (#00703)
- ♦ ALDHEA – Alternativas Latinoamericanas de Desarrollo Humano y Estudios Antropológicos (unconfirmed)
- ♦ **ALDHU** Asociación Latinoamericana para los Derechos Humanos (#16243)
- ♦ ALDMA – Asociación Latinoamericana de Mercadeo de Alimentos (no recent information)
- ♦ ALDO – Asociación Latinoamericana de Desarrollo Organizacional (no recent information)
- ♦ **ALDOO** Asociación Latinoamericana de Optometria y Optica (#02247)
- ♦ ALEA – Accord de libre échange asiatique (1992 treaty)
- ♦ **ALE** Alliance libre européenne (#07356)
- ♦ ALEAR – Asociación Latinoamericana y del Caribe de Economistas Ambientales y de Recursos Naturales (inactive)
- ♦ ALEAS – Asociación Latinoamericana de Educación Agricola Superior (no recent information)
- ♦ **ALE** Autonome Lokomotivführer-Gewerkschaften Europas (#03043)
- ♦ ALEBCI – Asociación Latinoamericana de Escuelas de Biblioteconomia y Ciencias de la Información (inactive)
- ♦ ALEBCI – Associação Latinoamericana de Escolas de Biblioteconomia e Ciências da Informação (inactive)
- ♦ ALEC – Asociación Latinoamericana de Exportadores de Carne (inactive)
- ♦ **ALECIF** Asociación Latinoamericana de Estudiantes de Ciencias Forestales (#02213)
- ♦ **ALECSO** Arab League Educational, Cultural and Scientific Organization (#01003)
- ♦ **ALED** Asociación Latinoamericana de Estudios del Discurso (#02217)
- ♦ ALE / see European Free Alliance (#07356)
- ♦ ALEF – Asociación Latinoamericana de Entrenadores de Fútbol (unconfirmed)
- ♦ **ALEF** Associação Latinoamericana para o Estudo do Figado (#16252)
- ♦ **ALEF** Association latinoaméricaine pour l'étude du foie (#16252)
- ♦ **ALEG** Asociación Latinoamericana de Endocrinologia Ginecológica (#02208)
- ♦ ALEGEO – Asociación Latinoamericana de Editores de Geociencias (inactive)
- ♦ **ALEH** Asociación Latinoamericana para el Estudio del Higado (#16252)
- ♦ ALEIA – Asociación Latinoamericana y del Caribe de Estudiantes de Ingeniería Agrícola (unconfirmed)
- ♦ **ALEIIAF** Asociación Latinoamericana de Estudiantes de Ingenieria Industrial y Afines (#02214)
- ♦ Aleimar (internationally oriented national body)
- ♦ Aleimar – Insieme ai bambini del mondo / see Aleimar
- ♦ **ALEIQ** Asociación Latinoamericana de Estudiantes de Ingenieria Quimica (#02215)
- ♦ **ALENE** Asociación Latinoamericana de Etica en los Negocios y Economia (#16262)
- ♦ ALEP – Asociación Latinoamericana de Evaluadores de Proyectos (inactive)
- ♦ Aleph / see Aum Supreme Truth (#03018)
- ♦ ALEPH – Asociación de Jóvenes Investigadores de la Literatura Hispánica (internationally oriented national body)
- ♦ Aleph Zadik Aleph / see B'nai B'rith Youth Organization (#03291)
- ♦ ALEPRyCS – Asociación Latinoamericana de Especialistas en Pequeños Rumiantes y Camélidos Sudamericanos (unconfirmed)
- ♦ ALER / see Asociación Latinoamericana de Educación y Comunicación Popular (#02207)
- ♦ **ALER** Asociación Latinoamericana de Educación y Comunicación Popular (#02207)
- ♦ **ALER** Asociación Latinoamericana para el Estudio de las Religiones (#02216)
- ♦ ALER – Associação Lusófona de Energias Renovaveis (internationally oriented national body)
- ♦ ALERB – Asociación Latinoamericana de Redactores de Revistas Biológicas (inactive)
- ♦ **ALERT** All Africa Leprosy, Tuberculosis and Rehabilitation Training Centre (#00642)
- ♦ **ALERT** Alliance of Leading Environmental Researchers & Thinkers (#00701)
- ♦ Alerte aux réalités internationales / see Association Réalités et Relations Internationales
- ♦ **ALERT Geomaterials** Alliance of Laboratories in Europe for Education, Research and Technology (#00700)
- ♦ **ALERT Géomatériaux** Alliance de laboratoires européens pour la recherche et la technologie (#00700)
- ♦ Alertis – Fund for Bear and Nature Conservation / see Bears in Mind
- ♦ Alertis – Stichting voor Beer- en Natuurbescherming / see Bears in Mind
- ♦ ALES / see FAIRMED
- ♦ ALES – Asociación Latinoamericana de Energia Solar (inactive)
- ♦ **ALES** Asociación Latinoamericana de Estudios de la Escritura en Educación Superior y Contextos Profesionales (#02218)
- ♦ **ALES** Asociación Latinoamericana de Exportadores de Servicios (#02219)
- ♦ ALETI / see Federación de Asociaciones de América Latina, el Caribe, España y Portugal de Entidades de Tecnologías de Información y Comunicación (#09288)
- ♦ **ALETI** Federación de Asociaciones de América Latina, el Caribe, España y Portugal de Entidades de Tecnologías de Información y Comunicación (#09288)
- ♦ **ALEUP** Asociación Latinoamericana de Escuelas de Urbanismo y Planeación (#02212)
- ♦ Aleut International Association (internationally oriented national body)
- ♦ Alexander Friedmann International Seminar on Gravitation and Cosmology (meeting series)
- ♦ Alexander Graham Bell Association for the Deaf and Hard of Hearing (unconfirmed)
- ♦ Alexander von Humboldt Foundation (internationally oriented national body)
- ♦ Alexander von Humboldt-Stiftung (internationally oriented national body)

♦ Alexander Technique International (ATI) 00625

Mailing Address PO Box 30558, Indianapolis IN 46230, USA. E-mail: office@alexandertechniqueinternational.org.
URL: https://www.alexandertechniqueinternational.com/

History 1992. Statutes ratified May 1992. Statutes revised Nov 1993, Nov 1994. **Aims** Promote and advance the teaching method developed by F Matthias Alexander. **Structure** General Meeting (annual). Executive Board, including Chair, Assistant Chair, Executive Secretary, Corresponding Secretary and Treasurer. Committees (2): Complaints; Ethics. Standing committees (5). Regional offices (9). **Languages** English. **Finance** Members' dues. **Activities** Standing committees (5): Communications; Development; Membership; Nominations; Professional Vision/Mission. **Events** *Annual Conference* Kyoto (Japan) 2018.
Members General; Teaching; Sponsoring. Membership countries not specified. Regional offices (9) in 9 countries:
Regional offices (9) in 9 countries:
Australia, France, Germany, Ireland, Norway, Sweden, Switzerland, UK, USA. [2020/XE3805/E]

- ♦ Alexandria Centre for International Maritime Arbitration (internationally oriented national body)
- ♦ Alexian Brothers – Congregation of Cellites (religious order)
- ♦ Alexiens – Frères Cellites (religious order)
- ♦ ALFA-ACI / see Les Aéroports Francophones (#00145)
- ♦ ALFA / see Asian Financial Services Association (#01480)
- ♦ ALFA – Association for Low Flow Anaesthesia (no recent information)
- ♦ **ALF** Academia Latinitati Fovendae (#00015)
- ♦ **ALF** Africa Leadership Forum (#00183)

♦ ALFA International 00626

CEO 980 North Michigan Ave, Ste 1180, Chicago IL 60611, USA. T. +13126422532. Fax +13126425346.
URL: http://www.alfainternational.com/

History Founded 1980, USA, as American Law Firm Association. Full title: *ALFA International – The Global Legal Network.* **Aims** Provide legal services and legal solutions to business issues worldwide. **Structure** Board of Directors; Executive Committee. **Staff** 10.00 FTE, paid. **Events** *Asia Regional Seminar* Bangkok (Thailand) 2017, *International Law Practice Group Seminar* San José (Costa Rica) 2016, *International Law Practice Group Seminar* Sydney, NSW (Australia) 2011, *International law practice group seminar* Paris (France) 2010. **Publications** Various articles.
Members Firms (about 150) in 61 countries and territories:
Argentina, Australia, Austria, Barbados, Belgium, Brazil, Canada, Chile, China, Colombia, Costa Rica, Cyprus, Ecuador, Egypt, France, Germany, Ghana, Greece, Guam, Guatemala, Hong Kong, Hungary, India, Indonesia, Ireland, Israel, Italy, Japan, Kenya, Korea Rep, Kuwait, Luxembourg, Malaysia, Mexico, Micronesia FS, New Zealand, Nigeria, Northern Mariana Is, Norway, Pakistan, Panama, Paraguay, Peru, Philippines, Poland, Portugal, Puerto Rico, Romania, Samoa USA, Singapore, South Africa, Spain, Taiwan, Türkiye, Uganda, UK, United Arab Emirates, Uruguay, USA, Venezuela, Zambia. [2018/XJ2339/F]

- ♦ ALFA International – The Global Legal Network / see ALFA International (#00626)
- ♦ **ALFAL** Asociación de Lingüistica y Filologia de la América Latina (#02278)
- ♦ Alfalit International (internationally oriented national body)
- ♦ **ALFAn** Asociación Latinoamericana de Filosofia Analitica (#02221)
- ♦ **ALF** Animal Liberation Front (#00838)
- ♦ ALFA Programme (inactive)
- ♦ **ALF** Asian Liturgy Forum (#01530)
- ♦ **ALF** Asociación Latinoamericana de Farmacologia (#16249)
- ♦ **ALF** Asociación Latinoamericana de Fitopatologia (#02223)
- ♦ ALFASOL – Alphabétisation solidaire (internationally oriented national body)
- ♦ ALF – Avenir de la langue française (internationally oriented national body)
- ♦ **ALFE** Asociación Latinoamericana de Filosofia de la Educación (#02222)
- ♦ ALFEDIAM / see Société Francophone du Diabète (#19468)
- ♦ **ALFEPSI** Asociación Latinoamericana para la Formación y Enseñanza de la psicologia (#02224)
- ♦ **ALFEST** Association de la langue française de l'étude du stress et du traumatisme (#02781)
- ♦ **ALFiD** Asociación Latina de Filosofía del Deporte (#02172)
- ♦ **ALFIM** Asociación Latinoamericana de Fisica Médica (#16246)
- ♦ **ALFORJA** Programa Regional Coordinado de Educación Popular (#18456)
- ♦ Alfred Jurzykowski Foundation (internationally oriented national body)
- ♦ Alfried Krupp von Bohlen und Halbach Foundation (internationally oriented national body)
- ♦ Alfried Krupp von Bohlen und Halbach-Stiftung (internationally oriented national body)
- ♦ Al-Fuqra / see Jamaat ul-Fuqra (#16087)
- ♦ Algalita (internationally oriented national body)
- ♦ Algebraic Topology: Methods, Computation, and Science (meeting series)
- ♦ **ALGEDE** Asociación Latinoamericana de Gerencia Deportiva (#02227)
- ♦ Algiers-Lagos Trans-Saharan Coordinating Committee (inactive)
- ♦ AlgorithmWatch (internationally oriented national body)
- ♦ ALGWE – Association of Lesbian and Gay Writers Living in Europe (inactive)
- ♦ **ALHSUD** Asociación Latinoamericana de Hidrologia Subterranea para el Desarrollo (#16242)
- ♦ **ALIA** Asian League of Institutes of the Arts (#01528)
- ♦ **ALIA** Asian Lubricants Industry Association (#01532)
- ♦ **ALIA** Asociación Latinoamericana y del Caribe de Ingeniería Agrícola (#02190)
- ♦ ALIAM / see Alliance des ligues francophones africaines et méditerranéennes (#00704)

- ♦ **ALIAM** Alliance des ligues francophones africaines et méditerranéennes (#00704)
- ♦ ALIAM MNT / see Alliance des ligues francophones africaines et méditerranéennes (#00704)
- ♦ Aliança dos Editores Independentes / see Alliance internationale des éditeurs indépendants
- ♦ Aliança dos Editores Independentes para uma Outra Globalização / see Alliance internationale des éditeurs indépendants
- ♦ Aliança de Gênero e Agua (#10102)
- ♦ Aliança de Igrejas Presbiterianas e Reformadas da América Latina (#00713)
- ♦ Aliança Internacional dos Editores Independentes (internationally oriented national body)
- ♦ Aliança Internacional de Jornalistas (internationally oriented national body)
- ♦ Aliança Latino-Americana para as Doenças Raras (#00630)
- ♦ Aliança Social Continental (#00635)
- ♦ ALIANS / see Studio Globo
- ♦ Alianza Asiatica de ACJs (#01826)
- ♦ Alianza Bautista Mundial (#03176)

♦ Alianza Bolivariana de los Pueblos de Nuestra América (ALBA) ... 00627

Bolivarian Alliance for the Americas

Contact Office of the President, Calle Ayacucho s/n, La Paz, Bolivia. T. +59122202321. Fax +59122202321.
URL: http://www.alianzabolivariana.org/

History 2004, Havana (Cuba), *Alternativa Bolivariana para los Pueblos de Nuestra América (ALBA) – Bolivarian Alternative for Latin America and the Caribbean.* Present name adopted, 24 Jun 2009. Founded in opposition to the FTAA. **Activities** *People's Trade Agreement – Tratado de Comercio de los Pueblos (TCP).*
Members Governments of 9 countries:
Antigua-Barbuda, Bolivia, Cuba, Dominica, Ecuador, Honduras, Nicaragua, St Vincent-Grenadines, Venezuela.
[2015/XJ8059/**E***]

- ♦ Alianza para Bosques (internationally oriented national body)
- ♦ Alianza de Civilizaciones de las Naciones Unidas (#20520)
- ♦ Alianza del Clima (#04005)
- ♦ Alianza del Clima de las Ciudades Europeas con los Pueblos Indigenas de los Bosques Tropicales / see Climate Alliance (#04005)
- ♦ Alianza Clima y Desarrollo (#04012)
- ♦ Alianza Cooperativa Internacional (#12944)
- ♦ Alianza de los Demócratas y Liberales por Europa / see Renew Europe (#18840)
- ♦ Alianza de los Editores Independientes / see Alliance internationale des éditeurs indépendants
- ♦ Alianza de los Editores Independientes para otra Mundialización / see Alliance internationale des éditeurs indépendants
- ♦ Alianza para la Educación LGBT (internationally oriented national body)

♦ Alianza Eurolatinoamericana de Cooperación entre Ciudades (AL-LAs) 00628

Contact Coordinación Gen de Asuntos Int de la Jefature Gob Ciudad México, República de Chile 6 – Ctr Histórico, Delgación Cuauhtémoc CP 06010, Mexico City CDMX, Mexico. T. +525556627926 ext 112.
URL: https://proyectoallas.net/

History 2013. Also referred to as *Alianza Euro Latinomericana de Cooperación entre Ciudades.* **Aims** Strengthen international relations of local governments in Latin America and Europe, their networks and associations so as to improve the quality of their public policies and territorial development.
Members Full in 8 countries:
Brazil, Colombia, Ecuador, France, Mexico, Peru, Spain, Venezuela.
Included in the above, 1 organization listed in this Yearbook:
Fondo Andaluz de Municipios para la Solidaridad Internacional (FAMSI).
NGO Relations Member of: *Global Taskforce of Local and Regional Governments (Global Taskforce, #10622).*
[2019/XM8601/**C**]

- ♦ Alianza Euro Latinomericana de Cooperación entre Ciudades / see Alianza Eurolatinoamericana de Cooperación entre Ciudades (#00628)
- ♦ Alianza Europea de ACJ / see YMCA Europe (#21977)
- ♦ Alianza Europea de la Pequeña y Mediana Empresa (#08494)
- ♦ Alianza sobre evaluación ambiental y desempeño ecológico de la ganadería (#16500)
- ♦ Alianza Evangélica Latina (#16397)
- ♦ Alianza Evangélica Mundial (#21393)
- ♦ Alianza de Género y Agua (#10102)
- ♦ Alianza Global a Favor de la Iniciativa Salarios Dignos Norte y Sur / see Jus Semper Global Alliance

♦ Alianza Global del Ombudsperson Local (AGOL) 00629

Global Alliance of Local Ombudsman

Pres Calle Trinidad 1, 28801 Alcala de Henares, Madrid, Spain. T. +34918855034. E-mail: alianzaagol@gmail.com.
Exec Sec address not obtained.
URL: https://agol.es/

History May 2019, Córdoba (Argentina). Former names and other names: *Global Alliance of the Local Ombudsperson (GOAL)* – alias. **Aims** Strengthen cooperation between local Ombuspersons to generate global impacts; provide a space for the exchange of strategies for the defense of human rights in local communities and areas with a gender perspective and focus on socio-environmental challenges. **Languages** Spanish. **Activities** Advocacy/lobbying/activism; events/meetings; guidance/assistance/consulting; training/education. Active in all member countries. **Events** *Congreso* Madrid (Spain) 2022. **Publications** *MANUAL DE PRACTICAS SOSTENIBLES DE DEFENSORIAS LOCALES* (1ª ed 2022) in Spanish.
Members Organizations in 5 countries:
Argentina, Colombia, Mexico, Spain, Uruguay.
NGO Relations Also links with national institutions. [2022.10.22/AA0950/**D**]

- ♦ Alianza Global de Promoción al Consumo de Frutas y Hortalizas "5 al dia" (#10221)
- ♦ Alianza Global para la Salud de la Mujer (#10233)
- ♦ Alianza para el Goberno Abierto (#17753)

♦ Alianza Iberoamericana de Enfermedades Raras o Poco Frecuentes (ALIBER) 00630

Latin American Alliance for Rare Diseases – Aliança Latino-Americana para as Doenças Raras

Pres C/ San Cristóbal 7, 4,437.31 mi, 30850 Totana, Murcia, Spain. E-mail: aliber@aliber.org – proyectos@aliber.org – direccion@aliber.org.
URL: http://aliber.org/

History 2013, Murcia (Spain). **Aims** Coordinate actions to strengthen the associative movement, give visibility and represent people with rare diseases in Latin America. **Structure** Board. **Languages** Portuguese, Spanish. **Staff** 11.00 FTE, paid. **Activities** Advocacy/lobbying/activism; guidance/assistance/consulting; knowledge management/information dissemination. **Events** *Encuentro Iberoamericano de Enfermedades Raras* 2021, *Meeting* 2020, *Meeting* Murcia (Spain) 2019, *Encuentro Iberoamericano de Enfermedades Raras, Huérfanas, o Poco Frecuentes* Bogota (Colombia) 2018, *Encuentro Iberoamericano de enfermedades raras* 2016. **Publications** *El movimiento asociativo de las enfermedades raras en Iberoamérica* (2018) by Juan Carrión et al.
Members Full in 17 countries:
Argentina, Bolivia, Brazil, Chile, Colombia, Costa Rica, Ecuador, Guatemala, Mexico, Nicaragua, Panama, Paraguay, Peru, Portugal, Spain, Uruguay, Venezuela.
NGO Relations Member of (2): *Rare Diseases International (RDI, #18621); World Patients Alliance (WPA).*
[2022/XM7436/**D**]

- ♦ Alianza de Iglesias Presbiterianas y Reformadas de América Latina (#00713)
- ♦ Alianza Inter-Monasterios (#00691)
- ♦ Alianza Internacional para el Apoyo a la Niñez / see Save the Children International (#19058)
- ♦ Alianza Internacional de Asociaciones y Movimientos "5 al dia" / see Global Alliance to Promote Fruits and Vegetable Consumption "5 a day" (#10221)
- ♦ Alianza Internacional para la Consolidación de la Paz / see Interpeace (#15962)
- ♦ Alianza Internacional pro Derechos Civiles (#12584)
- ♦ Alianza Internacional de los Editores Independientes (internationally oriented national body)
- ♦ Alianza Internacional para el Federación de Desarrollo Juvenil Comunitario (internationally oriented national body)
- ♦ Alianza Internacional para la Gestión del Agua de Lluvia / see International Rainwater Harvesting Alliance (#14695)
- ♦ Alianza Internacional de Mujeres (#11639)
- ♦ Alianza Internacional para la Reforma del Cannabis (inactive)
- ♦ Alianza Internacional "Save the Children" / see Save the Children International (#19058)
- ♦ Alianza International de Organizaciones de Patientes (#11633)
- ♦ Alianza en Jesús por Maria, 1925 (religious order)

♦ Alianza Latinoamericana Anticontrabando (ALAC) 00631

Latin American Alliance against Contraband

Dir ANDI, Calle 73 No 8, 13 Piso 7 Torre A, Bogota, Bogota DC, Colombia.
URL: https://www.andi.com.co/Home/Pagina/26

History 2016. **Aims** Build a joint agenda with the governments of the region so as to reduce smuggling. **Events** *Meeting* San Pedro Sula (Honduras) 2022, *Meeting* Quito (Ecuador) 2021, *Meeting* San José (Costa Rica) 2019, *Meeting* Brasilia (Brazil) 2018, *Meeting* Guatemala (Guatemala) 2017.
Members Full in 14 countries:
Argentina, Bolivia, Brazil, Chile, Colombia, Costa Rica, Ecuador, Guatemala, Honduras, Mexico, Nicaragua, Panama, Peru, Venezuela.
NGO Relations Partner of (1): *Transnational Alliance to Combat Illicit Trade (TRACIT).* [2022/AA3016/**D**]

- ♦ Alianza Latinoamericana y del Caribe de Asociaciones Cristianas de Jóvenes (#16264)

♦ Alianza Latinoamericana de Compositores y Autores de Música (ALCAM) 00632

Address not obtained.
URL: http://www.alcamusica.com/

History Launched Aug 2012, Sao Paulo (Brazil). **Aims** Promote protection, development and recognition of the rights of music authors and composers at local, national, Latin American and international levels. **Structure** Officers.
Members Full in 11 countries:
Argentina, Bolivia, Brazil, Chile, Costa Rica, Ecuador, Guatemala, Mexico, Paraguay, Peru, Uruguay.
NGO Relations Partner of: *International Council of Music Authors (#13052).* [2018/XM6671/**D**]

♦ Alianza Latinoamericana para la Familia (ALAFA) 00633

Latin American Alliance for the Family

CEO Calle Guaicaipuro, Ed Askain, Piso 1 Oficina L, Urb El Rosal Municipio Chacao, Caracas 1060 DF, Venezuela. T. +582129529555. E-mail: wauwatosalife@gmail.com.
Dir 2427 Presidential Way, Suite 602, West Palm Beach FL 33401, USA. T. +15615789400.
URL: https://alafaorg.wordpress.com/

History 1983. Founded as a loose coalition of associations. **Aims** Guide young people to understand, appreciate and try to adopt universal values, skills and habits that lead to a healthy, happy and stable family and community; give a practical method of reducing poverty and violence by forming children and young people in accordance with the realities which cause social problems. **Structure** President; General Manager; Academic Director; Academic Trainers; International Coordinator in USA, Representatives in Latin America, Europe and Kenya. **Languages** English, French, German, Korean, Polish, Portuguese, Romanian, Spanish. **Finance** Sources: donations; fees for services. **Activities** Events/meetings; publishing activities; training/education. **Publications** *Aprendiendo a Querer* in English, Portuguese, Spanish – 12 year curriculum. Student texts; teacher manuals; teacher training courses.
Members in 19 countries:
Argentina, Brazil, Chile, Colombia, Costa Rica, Ecuador, El Salvador, Honduras, Hungary, Korea Rep, Mexico, Panama, Peru, Philippines, Poland, UK, Uruguay, USA, Venezuela. [2020.05.22/XF3211/**F**]

- ♦ Alianza Latinoamericana de Salud Global (inactive)
- ♦ Alianza Libre Europea / see European Free Alliance (#07356)
- ♦ Alianza Marial (see: #21334)
- ♦ Alianza de Mesas Redondas Panamericanas (#00711)
- ♦ Alianza Mesoamericana de Pueblos Bosques (unconfirmed)
- ♦ Alianza para las Migraciones en Centroamérica y México (unconfirmed)
- ♦ Alianza por la Mineria Responsable (#00717)
- ♦ Alianza para las Montañas (#16862)
- ♦ Alianza Mundial de Asociaciones Cristianas de Jóvenes (#21090)
- ♦ Alianza Mundial de Derecho Ambiental (#05503)
- ♦ Alianza Mundial de los Pueblos Indigenas y Tribales de los Bosques Tropicales (#11629)
- ♦ Alianza Mundial por el Suelo (#10608)

♦ Alianza del Mutualismo de América (AMA) 00634

Mutualism Alliance of America – Alliance du mutualisme de l'Amérique

Contact Paysandú 941 – Piso 6 – Oficina 4, 11100 Montevideo, Uruguay. T. +59829001741. E-mail: mutualidad@umu.com.uy.
URL: http://www.amamutualidades.org/

History 16 Jun 1988, Buenos Aires (Argentina). Headquarters in Montevideo (Uruguay) since 2004. Previously also referred to in English as: *Alliance of Mutual Benefit Societies of America.* Registered in accordance with the law of Uruguay, 1 Feb 2006. **Aims** Materialize the principles of integration on which mutual assistance is based; contribute to the development of friendly links between mutual assistance associations in various countries; promote the growth of and defend the mutual assistance system in America. **Structure** General Assembly; Board of Directors; Executive Committee. **Languages** Spanish. **Finance** Members' dues. Other sources: annual contributions; grants; subsidies. **Activities** Training/education; events/meetings. **Events** *General Assembly* Montevideo (Uruguay) 2014, *International meeting / General Assembly* Buenos Aires (Argentina) 2010, *General Assembly* Cartagena de Indias (Colombia) 2009, *General Assembly* Medellin (Colombia) 2008, *General Assembly* Montevideo (Uruguay) 2007.
Members Organizations in 9 countries:
Argentina, Bolivia, Brazil, Chile, Colombia, Costa Rica, Mexico, Paraguay, Uruguay.
IGO Relations Governments of Argentina, Columbia, Uruguay; *Ibero-American Social Security Organization (#11028); Southern Common Market (#19868)* – Specialized Meeting of Cooperatives (RECM); *UNESCO (#20322)*; national associations. **NGO Relations** Member of: *América Cooperativa y Mutual (Red AMEC, #00773).* [2015.06.01/XF5528/**F**]

- ♦ Alianza Panamericana de Médicas / see Pan American Medical Women's Alliance (#18120)
- ♦ Alianza Panamericana de Mujeres Médicas (#18120)
- ♦ Alianza para la Prevención del Cancer Cervical (#00663)
- ♦ Alianza de Productores de Cacao (no recent information)
- ♦ Alianza Reformada Mundial (inactive)

♦ Alianza Social Continental (ASC) 00635

Hemispheric Social Alliance (HSA) – Alliance Sociale Continentale – Aliança Social Continental

Executive Secretariat address not obtained. T. +5712488989.

History Apr 1997, Belo Horizonte (Brazil). **Aims** As a global movement of social organizations, sectoral and thematic networks around the *western hemisphere*, exchange information, define strategies and promote joint action. **Structure** Council. Continental Coordination Group, comprising one representative each of the 4 regional blocs (North America, Central America, Caribbean, Andean and Southern Cone) and one representative each of the social sectors (women, indigenous people, peasants, youth, working people) and representatives of social networks. Executive Secretariat (rotating). **Activities** Organizes 'Summit of the People'. **Events** *Summit* Trinidad-Tobago 2009, *Summit* Mar del Plata (Argentina) 2005, *Summit* Québec, QC (Canada) 2001, *Summit* Santiago (Chile) 1998.
Members Organizations in 19 countries:
Argentina, Bolivia, Brazil, Canada, Chile, Colombia, Costa Rica, Cuba, Ecuador, El Salvador, Guatemala, Haiti, Honduras, Mexico, Nicaragua, Paraguay, Peru, Uruguay, USA.
Regional organizations included in this Yearbook (10):
Consejo Latinoamericano de Ciencias Sociales (CLACSO, #04718); *Convergencia de Movimientos de los Pueblos de las Américas (COMPA, no recent information)*; *Coordinadora Andina de Organizaciones Indígenas (CAOI, #04804)*; *Coordinadora de Centrales Sindicales del Cono Sur (CCSCS, #04805)*; *Coordinadora Latinoamericana de Organizaciones del Campo (CLOC, #04808)*; *International Gender and Trade Network (IGTN, #13707)*; *Jubilee South (#16159)* (Americas); *Latin American Women's Network to Transform the Economy (#16395)*; *Organización Continental Latinoamericana y Caribeña de Estudiantes (OCLAE, #17834)*; *Plataforma Interamericana de Derechos Humanos, Democracia y Desarrollo (PIDHDD, #18395)*.
NGO Relations Member of: *Climate Justice Now ! (CJN!, inactive)*. Supports: *Global Call for Action Against Poverty (GCAP, #10263)*. [2012/XJ2846/y/**D**]

- ♦ Alianza para Sociedades Responsables y Sostenibles (#00718)
- ♦ Alianza de Solidaristas Rusos (internationally oriented national body)
- ♦ Alianza Universal de los Obreros del Diamante (inactive)
- ♦ **ALIBER** Alianza Iberoamericana de Enfermedades Raras o Poco Frecuentes (#00630)
- ♦ ALICA – Asociación Latinoamericana de Industriales y Camaras de la Alimentación (inactive)
- ♦ ALICA – Associação Latinoamericana de Industriais e Camaras da Alimentação (inactive)
- ♦ **ALICC** Asociación Latina e Ibérica Contra el Cancer (#02173)
- ♦ **ALICE** Asociación Latinoamericana de Investigadores en Campañas Electorales (#02236)
- ♦ ALICE / see European Technology Platform ALICE (#08888)
- ♦ **ALICE** European Technology Platform ALICE (#08888)
- ♦ **ALIDA** Asociación Latinoamericana de Investigación y Desarrollo del Algodón (#02235)
- ♦ **ALIDE** Asociación Latinoamericana de Instituciones Financieras para el Desarrollo (#02233)
- ♦ ALIDS – Asociación Latinoiberoamericana de Derecho a la Salud (no recent information)
- ♦ ALIET – Asociación Latinoamericana de Instituciones de Educación Teológica (unconfirmed)
- ♦ **ALIFAR** Asociación Latinoamericana de Industrias Farmacéuticas (#02232)
- ♦ aligned approaches and responses to European research calls (#05874)
- ♦ ALIGNN – Alliance of Global Neonatal Nursing (unconfirmed)

♦ ALIMA 00636

Main Office Route de l'Aéroport, Rue NG 96, BP 15530, Dakar, Senegal. T. +221778554159. E-mail: office@alima.ngo.
France 15 rue des Immeubles Industriels, 75011 Paris, France. T. +33180899939.
USA Office One Whitehall St, 2nd Fl, New York NY 10004, USA.
URL: http://www.alima-ngo.org/
History 2009. ALIMA stands for *The Alliance for International Medical Action*. Registered in accordance with French law. Operational headquarters in Dakar (Senegal). ALIMA-USA is registered as a US 501(c)(3) nonprofit organization. **Aims** Save lives and provide *care* for the most *vulnerable* populations, without any discrimination based on identity, religion or politics, through actions based on proximity, innovation, and the alliance of organizations and individuals. **Structure** General Assembly; Board of Directors; USA Board of Directors. **Activities** Healthcare; networking/liaising; research and development. **NGO Relations** Member of: *Start Network (#19969)*. [2020/XM6949/**C**]

- ♦ ALIM – Asociación Latinoamericana de Industriales Molineros (no recent information)
- ♦ ALIM – Association linguistique interméditerranéenne (inactive)
- ♦ Alimentos Para Los Pobres (internationally oriented national body)
- ♦ **ALINA** Asociación Latinoamericana de la Industria Nacional de Agroquimicos (#02230)
- ♦ **ALIN** Asia Legal Information Network (#01288)
- ♦ **ALIN- East Africa** Arid Lands Information Network – Eastern Africa (#01105)
- ♦ ALINORM / see Codex Alimentarius Commission (#04081)
- ♦ **ALIO** Asociación Latino-Iberoamericana de Investigación Operativa (#16398)
- ♦ ALIPA – European Aliphatic Isocyanates Producers Association (internationally oriented national body)
- ♦ **ALIP** Asociación Latinoamericana de la Industria del Petróleo (#02231)
- ♦ **ALIPH** International Alliance for the Protection of Heritage in Conflict Areas (#11635)
- ♦ ALIPLAST – Asociación Latinoamericana de Industrias Plasticas (no recent information)
- ♦ ALIRH / see Asociación Latinoamericana de Investigadores en Reproducción Humana (#02238)
- ♦ **ALIRH** Asociación Latinoamericana de Investigadores en Reproducción Humana (#02238)
- ♦ ALISEI – Associazione per la Cooperazione Internazionale e l'Aiuto Umanitario (internationally oriented national body)
- ♦ **ALITA** Asia-Pacific Legal Innovation and Technology Association (#01946)
- ♦ Al-Itihad al-Arabi Lil-Ta'Lem al-Tekni (no recent information)
- ♦ Al-Jabhah al-Islamiyyah al-'Alamiyyah li-Qital al-Yahud wal-Salibiyyin (#00748)

♦ Al-Jihad 00637

Address not obtained.
History in the 1970s, Egypt. Other titles: *Jihad Group*; *International Justice Group*; *Islamic Jihad*; *New Jihad Group*; *Talaa' al-Fateh*; *Vanguards of Conquest*; *World Justice Group*. Several factions, including *Vanguards of Conquest – Talaa' al-Fateh*. **Aims** Use any means, *political* or *violent*, including *terrorism*, to overthrow the present Egyptian government and replace it with an *Islamic* state. **Members** Membership countries not available but sympathizers in several countries. [2008/XN7857/s/**F**]

♦ All Africa Anglican-Lutheran Commission (AAALC) 00638

Co-Chairman 5625 Murambi East, Mutare, Manicaland, Mutare MANICALAND, Zimbabwe.
Co-Chairman Evangelical Lutheran Church in Zimbabwe, Dept of Religious Studies, Classics and Philosophy, Univ of Zimbabwe, Harare, HARARE, Zimbabwe.
History by *Anglican Consultative Council (ACC, #00828)* and *The Lutheran World Federation (LWF, #16532)*. [2012.08.16/XE4605/**E**]

♦ All Africa Baptist Fellowship (AABF) 00639

Gen Sec 21 Obafemi Awolowo Way, Okebola, Ibadan, Oyo, Nigeria. E-mail: aabfgs@gmail.com.
URL: https://allafricabaptist.org/
History 10 Jul 1982, Limuru (Kenya). Founded as one of the 6 regional branches of *Baptist World Alliance (BWA, #03176)*. **Aims** Facilitate communication, networking and partnership amongst Baptists in Africa to assist in the *evangelism*, *training* and *leadership* development and strategies for cooperative social action. **Structure** General Assembly (every 5 years); General Council (every 2 years); Executive Committee (annual); Departments (3). Subregions (4): Central, Eastern, Southern, Western. **Languages** English, French. **Staff** 3.00 FTE, paid. **Finance** Members' dues. Other sources: annual grant from Baptist World Alliance; grants from other partners for specified conferences and training programmes. **Activities** Events/meetings; knowledge management/information dissemination; religious activities; training/education. **Events** *General Assembly* Nigeria 2021, *General Assembly* Accra (Ghana) 2016, *Leadership Conference and General Assembly* Douala (Cameroon) 2013, *General Assembly* Nairobi (Kenya) 2006, *Quadrennial General Assembly* 2004. **Publications** *Prayer Bulletin* (12 a year); *All Africa Baptist Newsletter* (4 a year). *AABF Brochure* – revised as necessary.
Members Baptist Conventions/Unions in 31 countries:
Angola, Benin, Botswana, Burkina Faso, Burundi, Cameroon, Central African Rep, Congo Brazzaville, Congo DR, Côte d'Ivoire, Ethiopia, Gambia, Ghana, Kenya, Liberia, Madagascar, Malawi, Mali, Mozambique, Namibia, Nigeria, Rwanda, Senegal, Sierra Leone, South Africa, South Sudan, Tanzania UR, Togo, Uganda, Zambia, Zimbabwe. [2019.10.18/XE3270/**E**]

- ♦ All Africa Church Music Association (inactive)

♦ All Africa Conference of Churches (AACC) 00640

Conférence des Eglises de toute l'Afrique (CETA)
Gen Sec PO Box 14205, 00800 Westlands, Nairobi, Kenya. T. +254204441483 – +254204441338 – +254204441339. E-mail: secretariat@aacc-ceta.org.
Regional Office BP 2268, Lomé, Togo. T. +2285924. Fax +228215266.
URL: http://www.aacc-ceta.org/
History Jan 1958. Founded on initiative of the then *'International Missionary Council (IMC)'*, now *Commission on World Mission and Evangelism of the World Council of Churches (CWME, inactive)*. Constitutional Assembly: Apr 1963, Kampala (Uganda). Former names and other names: *Provisional Committee of the All Africa Church Conference* – former. **Aims** Keep before Churches and national Christian councils the demands of the Gospel on their life and mission, for unity, for evangelism and for their witness and service in society; to this end, promote consultation and action among them; stimulate and promote common programmes, research and experimentation so as to assist Churches, national Christian councils, theological institutions, lay training centres and Christian student organizations in interpreting and responding to the decisive action of God in Jesus Christ in terms of Africa's culture, experience and needs; provide for programmes of study and research to encourage Africa's contribution to worldwide Christian thought, worship and action; assist Churches in finding, training and placing personnel and utilizing other resources for effective pursuit of their common task and in their common work of lay and clerical leadership development for common responsibility in liberation, justice, peace, reconciliation, human development and integrity of creation; act as a regional point of reference in worldwide fellowship of the Christian Church and promote cooperation and coordination with agencies of the World Council of Churches, of the Roman Catholic Church and of similar bodies as mutually agreed. **Structure** Assembly (every 5 years); General Committee; Executive Committee. Sub-regions (5): East Africa; Southern Africa; Northern Africa; West Africa; Central Africa. Registered Trustees (7). Units (3) each with a number of desks and subsidiary agencies. General Secretariat in Nairobi (Kenya); Regional Office in Lomé (Togo). **Languages** English, French, Portuguese. **Staff** 36.00 FTE, paid. **Finance** Members' dues. Grants from Churches and ecumenical organizations. **Activities** Events/meetings; training/education. Includes *Africa Peace Forum (APFO)*. **Events** *Quinquennial Assembly* Abuja (Nigeria) 2023, *Quinquennial Assembly* Kigali (Rwanda) 2018, *Quinquennial Assembly* Kampala (Uganda) 2013, *Quinquennial Assembly* Maputo (Mozambique) 2008, *Quinquennial Assembly* Yaoundé (Cameroon) 2003. **Publications** *AACC Newsletter* (6 a year); *Tam Tam Magazine*. All publications in English, French and Portuguese. Information Services: Documentation Centre.
Members National or regional bodies. Full Churches (138). Associate (30) Christian councils (20), theological institutions, lay training centres, Christian student organizations. Members in 39 countries:
Algeria, Angola, Benin, Botswana, Burundi, Cameroon, Central African Rep, Congo Brazzaville, Congo DR, Côte d'Ivoire, Djibouti, Egypt, Equatorial Guinea, Ethiopia, Gabon, Gambia, Ghana, Kenya, Lesotho, Liberia, Madagascar, Malawi, Mauritius, Morocco, Mozambique, Namibia, Nigeria, Rwanda, Senegal, Seychelles, Sierra Leone, South Africa, Sudan, Sweden, Tanzania UR, Togo, Uganda, Zambia, Zimbabwe.
Consultative Status Consultative status granted from: *African Commission on Human and Peoples' Rights (ACHPR, #00255)* (Observer); *UNEP (#20299)*. **NGO Relations** Member of: *ACT Alliance (#00081)*; *African Council of Religious Leaders – Religions for Peace (ACRL-RfP, #00276)*; *All Africa Leprosy, Tuberculosis and Rehabilitation Training Centre (ALERT, #00642)*; *Ecumenical Advocacy Alliance (EAA, inactive)*; *International Council on Archives (ICA, #12996)*. Theology department is member of: *Conference of African Theological Institutions (CATI, #04580)*. Supports: *Global Call for Action Against Poverty (GCAP, #10263)*. [2023/XD0036/**D**]

♦ All Africa Farmers Network (AaFaNet) 00641

Contact PO Box DD 46, Dodowa, Accra, Ghana. T. +23321766576. Fax +23321227586. [2010/XM3499/**F**]

- ♦ All Africa Foundation (internationally oriented national body)
- ♦ All Africa Leprosy and Rehabilitation Training Centre / see All Africa Leprosy, Tuberculosis and Rehabilitation Training Centre (#00642)
- ♦ All Africa Leprosy, TB, Rehabilitation, Research and Training Centre / see All Africa Leprosy, Tuberculosis and Rehabilitation Training Centre (#00642)

♦ All Africa Leprosy, Tuberculosis and Rehabilitation Training Centre (ALERT) 00642

Training Director PO Box 165, Addis Ababa, Ethiopia. T. +251113211341 – +251113211351. Fax +251113211351. E-mail: leprosytb@ethionet.et.
History 1965, Addis Ababa (Ethiopia), as *All Africa Leprosy and Rehabilitation Training Centre*, based on an agreement between the Ethiopian Government and a number of voluntary organizations worldwide. Also referred to as *All Africa Leprosy, TB, Rehabilitation, Research and Training Centre*. **Aims** Serve as a specialized treatment, research and training resource center for Ethiopia, Africa and beyond, focused on leprosy, TB, HIV/AIDS and other relevant infectious diseases and disabilities bases on acceptable best practices. **Structure** Management Committee of 9 members. Administered by Board of Governors (meets twice a year) of 6 members. **Languages** Amharic, English. **Staff** 754.00 FTE, paid. **Finance** Financed by Ethiopian Government and supported by German leprosy, TB, Relief association and US Center for Disease Prevention and Control (PEPFAR). **Activities** International and national training; general hospital services; supportive services like orthopaedic appliances workshop; medico-social, occupational therapy; physiotherapy; speech therapy. **Events** *Annual General Meeting* Addis Ababa (Ethiopia) 1992, *Annual General Meeting* Addis Ababa (Ethiopia) 1991, *Annual General Meeting* Addis Ababa (Ethiopia) 1990, *Annual General Meeting* Addis Ababa (Ethiopia) 1988, *THELEP workshop* Addis Ababa (Ethiopia) 1987. **Publications** *ALERT* (annual) – report. Annual Report; training materials: videos; training calendar; slides; booklets; brochures.
Members Organizations (18), of which national organizations (16) in 12 countries:
Belgium, Ethiopia, France, Germany, Italy, Luxembourg, Netherlands, Norway, Sweden, Switzerland, UK, USA.
International organizations (2):
All Africa Conference of Churches (AACC, #00640) (and its member organizations); *RI Global (#18948)*; *World Council of Churches (WCC, #21320)*.
IGO Relations *WHO (#20950)*. **NGO Relations** Links with national Leprosy Relief organizations, including: *LEPRA Health in Action (LEPRA)*; *Damien Foundation – Voluntary Organization for Leprosy and TB Control (AF)*; *Leprosy Mission International (TLMI, #16446)*; *Raoul Follereau International Union (#18618)*; Swedish Church Aid; Swedish Red Cross. Also links with national leprosy relief organizations. [2010.06.01/XF2410/y/**E**]

- ♦ All African Credit Union Association / see African Confederation of Cooperative Savings and Credit Associations (#00261)
- ♦ All African Farmers' Union (inactive)
- ♦ All African Peoples' Conference (inactive)
- ♦ All-African People's Organization (internationally oriented national body)
- ♦ All African Trade Union Federation (inactive)
- ♦ All African Travel Agents Association (inactive)
- ♦ All African Women's Conference / see Pan African Women's Organization (#18074)

♦ All Africa Pool Association (AAPA) 00643

Pres 90 Main Road, Kyalami, Johannesburg, South Africa. T. +2784555506. E-mail: info@aapa.co.za.
URL: http://aapa.co.za/
Aims Promote all cue sports in Africa conducted pursuant to the World Pool *Billiard* Association. **Structure** General Meeting (annual). Executive Committee, including President, Vice-President, Secretary and Treasurer.
Members Affiliated national organizations in 15 countries:
Congo DR, Egypt, Ghana, Kenya, Lesotho, Libya, Malawi, Morocco, Nigeria, South Africa, Tanzania UR, Tunisia, Uganda, Zambia, Zimbabwe.
NGO Relations Affiliate member of: *World Pool-Billiard Association (WPA, #21733)*. [2016/XD8484/**D**]

- ♦ All Africa Religious Liberty Council (inactive)

♦ All-Africa Students Union (AASU) **00644**
Union panafricaine des étudiants
SG P. O. Box M 274, Accra – Ghana, Accra, Ghana. T. +233302247128. E-mail: info@aasuonline.org.
Headquarters 7 New Rd, Madina, Ghana, Accra, Ghana.
URL: https://aasuonline.org/
History Jul 1972, Kumasi (Ghana). Amalgamated, 1973, with *Student Movement for African Unity (inactive)*. Former names and other names: *AASU* – alias. Registration: No/ID: CG076882017, Ghana. **Aims** Be a leading organization in mobilizing, coordinating and involving African students in efforts geared towards socio-economic, political and cultural advancement of Afria. **Structure** Congress (every 4 years); Executive Committee; Secretariat. Sub-regional Coordinators (5): Central Africa; East Africa; North Africa; Southern Africa; West Africa. **Languages** Arabic, English, French, Portuguese. **Staff** 30.00 FTE, paid; 15.00 FTE, voluntary. **Finance** Sources: government support; members' dues. **Activities** Financial and/or material support; knowledge management/information dissemination; networking/liaising; projects/programmes; training/education. Active in all member countries. **Events** *Africa Students and Youth Summit* Rabat (Morocco) 2019, *Africa Students and Youth Summit* Kigali (Rwanda) 2018, *Congress* Accra (Ghana) 2011, *Conference on education and sustainable development* Windhoek (Namibia) 1993, *International conference on the role of students in Africa's priority recovery programme* Accra (Ghana) 1991. **Publications** *AASU Newsletter* (4 a year). Press releases.
Members Student unions in 54 countries:
Algeria, Angola, Benin, Botswana, Burkina Faso, Burundi, Cameroon, Cape Verde, Central African Rep, Chad, Comoros, Congo Brazzaville, Congo DR, Côte d'Ivoire, Djibouti, Egypt, Equatorial Guinea, Eritrea, Eswatini, Ethiopia, Gabon, Gambia, Ghana, Guinea, Guinea-Bissau, Kenya, Lesotho, Liberia, Libya, Madagascar, Malawi, Mali, Mauritania, Mauritius, Morocco, Mozambique, Namibia, Niger, Nigeria, Rwanda, Sao Tomé-Principe, Senegal, Seychelles, Sierra Leone, Somalia, South Africa, South Sudan, Sudan, Tanzania UR, Togo, Tunisia, Uganda, Zambia, Zimbabwe.
Consultative Status Consultative status granted from: *UNESCO (#20322)* (Consultative Status). **NGO Relations** Member of (2): *Global Student Forum (GSF, #10614); Informal Consultative Meeting of Regional and International Students Structures.* Partner of (1): *100 Million (#22042).* Working relations with: *Association of African Universities (AAU, #02361).* Affiliate to: *Scholars at Risk (SAR).* [2020.06.24/XD0419/**D**]

♦ All Africa Teachers' Organization (no recent information)
♦ Allard K Lowenstein International Human Rights Project (internationally oriented national body)
♦ **AL-LAs** Alianza Eurolatinoamericana de Cooperación entre Ciudades (#00628)
♦ All Asia Bar Association (inactive)
♦ All Asian Women's Conference (inactive)
♦ Allavida (internationally oriented national body)

♦ All.Can **00645**
Secretariat Rue du Luxembourg 22-24, 1000 Brussels, Belgium. T. +3227616673. E-mail: secretariat@all-can.org.
URL: https://www.all-can.org/
History Former names and other names: *All.Can – Changing cancer care together* – full title; *All.Can International asbl* – legal name. Registration: Banque Carrefour des Entreprises, No/ID: 0746.638.692, Start date: 4 May 2020, Belgium; EU Transparency Register, No/ID: 025568638034-92, Start date: 5 May 2020. **Aims** Identify ways to optimize the use of resources in cancer care to improve patient outcomes. **Structure** General Meeting; Board of Directors; Advisory Council; Working Groups. **Languages** English, French. **Staff** 1.50 FTE, paid. There is no direct employment and support via service providers comes down to 1.5 FTE. **Finance** Sources: members' dues; revenue from activities/projects. Annual budget: 542,500 EUR (2020). **Activities** Events/meetings; research/documentation. **Events** *Global Summit* 2021.
Members Organizations include 6 listed in this Yearbook:
Digestive Cancers Europe (DiCE, #05070); European Cancer Organisation (ECO, #06432); European Cancer Patient Coalition (ECPC, #06433); International Brain Tumour Alliance (IBTA, #12393); Pancreatic Cancer Europe (PCE, #18172); World Bladder Cancer Patient Coalition (WBCPC, #21233).
NGO Relations Member of (1): *EU Health Coalition.* [2021.06.16/AA0087/y/**D**]

♦ All.Can – Changing cancer care together / see All.Can (#00645)
♦ All.Can International asbl / see All.Can (#00645)
♦ ALLC / see European Association for Digital Humanities (#06014)
♦ **AllChemE** Alliance for Chemical Sciences and Technologies in Europe (#00664)

♦ ALL DIGITAL **00646**
Main Office Rue du Commerce 123, 1000 Brussels, Belgium. T. +3228953381. E-mail: info@all-digital.org.
URL: http://all-digital.org/
History Started as an informal network of managers and individuals. Following a meeting in Riga (Latvia), Apr 2008, publicly launched Dec 2008, Vienna (Austria). Formally launched as a non-profit international association, 14 Oct 2010, Budapest (Hungary). Former names and other names: *Telecentre-Europe* – former. Registration: Banque-Carrefour des Entreprises, No/ID: 0830-256-454, Belgium. **Aims** Work to enhance digital skills across Europe. **Structure** General Assembly (annual); Board; Advisory Board. **Languages** English. **Staff** 6.50 FTE, paid. **Finance** Sources: members' dues. **Activities** Advocacy/lobbying/activism; events/meetings; guidance/assistance/consulting; politics/policy/regulatory; training/education. **Events** *Summit* Prague (Czechia) 2022, *General Assembly* Brussels (Belgium) 2021, *Summit* Brussels (Belgium) 2021, *Summit* Bologna (Italy) 2020, *Summit* Bologna (Italy) 2019. **Publications** *Telecentre Europe Newsletter* (12 a year). *Making the Case for Digital Empowerment* (2015); *Newsletter as an Email Marketing Tool in NGOs* (2014); *Survey on eInclusion Actors in the EU27* (2013). Policy papers; opinions.
Members Full in 31 countries:
Albania, Belgium, Bulgaria, Croatia, Cyprus, Czechia, Denmark, Estonia, France, Germany, Greece, Hungary, Ireland, Italy, Latvia, Lithuania, Malta, Moldova, Netherlands, North Macedonia, Norway, Poland, Portugal, Romania, Russia, Serbia, Slovenia, Spain, Sweden, Switzerland, UK.
NGO Relations Cooperates with (4): *Council of European Professional Informatics Societies (CEPIS, #04893); European Association for the Education of Adults (EAEA, #06018); Lifelong Learning Platform – European Civil Society for Education (LLLP, #16466); MEDEA: MEDIA and LEARNING (Media and Learning Association, #16612).* [2022.02.27/XJ5612/**D**]

♦ ALLEA – ALL European Academies **00647**
Exec Dir c/o BBAW, Jaegerstr 22/23, 10117 Berlin, Germany. T. +4930206066500. E-mail: secretariat@allea.org.
URL: http://www.allea.org/
History 22 Mar 1994, Paris (France). Founded following an initiative started in 1990. Former names and other names: *European Federation of Academies of Sciences and Humanities* – former. **Aims** Promote science as a global public good; facilitate scientific collaboration across borders and disciplines. **Structure** General Assembly; Presidency; Board; Working Groups; Task Forces. **Languages** English. **Staff** 7.50 FTE, paid. **Finance** Sources: donations; grants; in-kind support; members' dues. **Activities** Awards/prizes/competitions; capacity building; events/meetings; guidance/assistance/consulting; knowledge management/information dissemination; projects/programmes; research and development; research/documentation. Active in all member countries. **Events** *General Assembly* Brussels (Belgium) 2022, *General Assembly* Helsinki (Finland) 2021, *General Assembly* Bern (Switzerland) 2019, *Migration, Health, and Medicine Conference* Brussels (Belgium) 2019, *General Assembly* Sofia (Bulgaria) 2018. **Publications** *ALLEA Newsletter.* Reports; statements; surveys; conference proceedings.
Members Academies of sciences and humanities (54) in 39 countries and territories:
Albania, Armenia, Austria, Belgium, Bosnia-Herzegovina, Bulgaria, Croatia, Cyprus, Czechia, Denmark, Estonia, Finland, Georgia, Germany, Greece, Hungary, Ireland, Israel, Italy, Kosovo, Latvia, Lithuania, Moldova, Montenegro, Netherlands, North Macedonia, Norway, Poland, Portugal, Romania, Serbia, Slovakia, Slovenia, Spain, Sweden, Switzerland, Türkiye, UK, Ukraine.
NGO Relations Member of (1): *European Academies' Science Advisory Council (EASAC, #05778).* Partner of (2): *European Network of Research Ethics and Research Integrity (ENERI); Global Young Academy (GYA, #10662).* [2022.05.05/XF3430/**F**]

♦ Alleanza Alpe-Adria (#00747)
♦ Alleanza nelle Alpi (#00656)
♦ Alleanza per il Clima (#04005)
♦ Alleanza Europea dell Piccole e Medie Imprese Indipendenti (#08494)
♦ Alleanza in Gesù per Maria, 1925 (religious order)
♦ Alleanza Internazionale dei Giornalisti e Scrittori Latini (inactive)
♦ Alleanza Internazionale Giovanna d'Arco (#19992)
♦ Alleanza Libera Europea (#07356)

♦ Allergic Rhinitis and its Impact on Asthma Initiative (ARIA) **00648**
Exec Dir address not obtained.
Administrator address not obtained.
URL: http://www.whiar.org/
Aims Educate and implement evidence-based management of allergic rhinitis in conjunction with asthma worldwide. **Structure** Executive Committee of 29 members. Board of Directors, comprising Chair, Executive Director, Administrator and 6 members. Committees (2): Scientific; Advisory. **NGO Relations** Participates in: *Global Alliance Against Chronic Respiratory Diseases (GARD, #10182).* [2017/XJ6388/**F**]

♦ All Europe Taekwon-Do Federation (AETF) **00649**
Main Office Milenijna 5/B Street, 20-884 Lublin, Poland. T. +48817431150. E-mail: info@itfeurope.org.
URL: http://www.itfeurope.org/
History Jun 1979, Oslo (Norway), by representatives of national federations, within the framework of *International Taekwon-Do Federation (ITF, #15652).* Also referred to as *All Europe TKD Federation.* **Aims** Develop Korean Art of self-defence in Europe; progress and encourage physical, moral, educational and general cultural education of national European federations; create and cultivate respect, emulation, peace and compassion among European countries; promote TKD *championships* in accordance with the spirit and principles of *amateur athletics*; promote and develop TKD according to the rules and regulations of ITF. **Structure** Board of Directors; Secretariat in Lublin (Poland). **Languages** English. **Staff** Voluntary.
Members National federations in 37 countries:
Armenia, Austria, Azerbaijan, Belarus, Belgium, Bosnia-Herzegovina, Bulgaria, Croatia, Czechia, Denmark, England, Finland, France, Georgia, Germany, Greece, Hungary, Ireland, Israel, Italy, Latvia, Luxembourg, Moldova, Netherlands, Norway, Poland, Portugal, Romania, Russia, Scotland, Slovakia, Slovenia, Spain, Sweden, Switzerland, Ukraine, Wales.
[2018.06.26/XD4449/**D**]

♦ All Europe TKD Federation / see All Europe Taekwon-Do Federation (#00649)
♦ **ALLF** Association des léprologues de langue française (#02787)
♦ Allgemeine Anthroposophische Gesellschaft (#10103)
♦ Allgemeine erklärung der menschenrechte (1948 treaty)
♦ Allgemeiner Ausschuss des Ländlichen Genossenschaftswesens der EU / see General Confederation of Agricultural Cooperatives in the European Union (#10107)
♦ Allgemeiner Ausschuss des Ländlichen Genossenschaftswesens der Europäischen Gemeinschaft / see General Confederation of Agricultural Cooperatives in the European Union (#10107)
♦ Allgemeiner Verband der Frauenvereine (internationally oriented national body)
♦ Allgemeiner Verband der Landwirtschaftlichen Genossenschaften der Europäischen Union (#10107)
♦ Allgemeines abkommen über die vorrechte und befreiungen des Europarats (1949 treaty)
♦ All Hands Volunteers (internationally oriented national body)
♦ ALLi – Alliance of Independent Authors (internationally oriented national body)
♦ Alliance / see Alliance for International Exchange
♦ The Alliance / see Alliance for International Exchange

♦ Alliance2015 . . . . **00650**
Dir Residence Palace, Rue de la Loi 155, 1040 Brussels, Belgium. T. +3222352325. E-mail: info@alliance2015.org.
URL: http://www.alliance2015.org/
History 2000. **Aims** Fight *poverty* more effectively by cooperating on various levels, working together in least developed countries, and influencing and campaigning at EU level. **Structure** A strategic partnership of 7 European NGOs. **Languages** English. **Staff** 4.00 FTE, paid. **Finance** Members' dues. Contributions to joint initiatives. Annual budget (2016): about euro 350,000. **Activities** Advocacy/lobbying/activism; humanitarian/emergency aid; projects/programmes. **Events** *Round Table* Milan (Italy) 2015, *Round Table* Copenhagen (Denmark) 2014, *Round Table* Dublin (Ireland) 2013. **Publications** *2015-Watch Reports* – series. Brochure; reports; campaign publications; DVD.
Members Organizations (7, " indicates Founding member):
Agency for Technical Cooperation and Development (ACTED) (France); *CESVI Fondazione* (Italy); *Concern Worldwide* (Ireland); *HELVETAS Swiss Intercooperation*; *Humanistisch Instituut voor Ontwikkelingssamenwerking (Hivos)*; *People in Need (PIN)*; *Welthungerhilfe* (Germany).
NGO Relations Supports: *Global Call for Action Against Poverty (GCAP, #10263).* [2019/XF6690/y/**F**]

♦ Alliance4Europe (unconfirmed)
♦ Alliance for Accelerating Excellence in Science in Africa (unconfirmed)
♦ Alliance ACT (#00081)

♦ Alliance for Affordable Internet (A4AI) **00651**
Exec Dir 1110 Vermont Ave NW, Ste 500, Washington DC 20005, USA. E-mail: contact@webfoundation.org.
Senior Communnications Adviser address not obtained. T. +442032897261. E-mail: gabe@webfoundation.org.
URL: http://a4ai.org/
History Oct 2013, by *World Wide Web Foundation (#21936).* **Aims** Advance the aim of affordable access to both mobile and fixed-line Internet in developing countries. **Structure** Advisory Council; Team. **Finance** Sponsored by global sponsors: Google; Omidyar Network; *Clearinghouse on Development Communication (CDC, no recent information); Department for International Development (DFID, inactive).* **Activities** Guidance/assistance/consulting; research/documentation; advocacy/lobbying/activism.
Members Full (over 70), including 30 organizations listed in this Yearbook:
- *Africa Information and Communication Technologies Alliance (AfICTA, #00181);*
- *African Technology Foundation (ATF);*
- *Association for Progressive Communications (APC, #02873);*
- *Cherie Blair Foundation for Women;*
- *Collaboration on International ICT Policy-Making for East and Southern Africa (CIPESA);*
- *Commonwealth Telecommunications Organisation (CTO, #04365);*
- *Communications Regulators' Association of Southern Africa (CRASA, #04384);*
- *Consumers International (CI, #04773);*
- *Digital Society Foundation;*
- *Economic Community of West African States (ECOWAS, #05312);*
- *FHI 360;*
- *Grameen Foundation (GF, #10694);*
- *International Research and Exchanges Board (IREX);*
- *Internet Sans Frontières (ISF);*
- *Internet Society (ISOC, #15952);*
- *Internews;*
- *Inveneo;*
- *LIRNEasia (#16489);*
- *Mercy Corps International (MCI);*
- *New Partnership for Africa's Development (NEPAD, #17091);*
- *Regional Dialogue on the Information Society (#18777);*
- *The World Bank Group (#21218);*
- *United Nations University Institute on Computing and Society (UNU-CS, #20644);*
- *United States Agency for International Development (USAID);*
- *UN Women (#20724);*
- *West Africa Telecommunications Regulators Association (WATRA, #20903);*
- *Women in Global Science and Technology Network (WISAT, #20999);*
- *World Pulse;*
- *World Wide Web Foundation (#21936);*
- *Youth for Technology Foundation (YTF).*

NGO Relations Secretariat hosted by: *World Wide Web Foundation (#21936).* [2020/XJ7434/y/**E**]

♦ Alliance africaine pour le commerce électronique (AACE) 00652

African Alliance for e-Commerce

Contact 1 Allée Seydou Nourou TALL, 5ème étage Immeuble Sophie Mbaey Point E, Dakar, Senegal. T. +221338593999. Fax +221338241724.

URL: http://www.african-alliance.org/

Aims Promote the concept of national and regional single window in compliance with recommendations of international institutions. **Structure** General Assembly; Executive Committee. **Activities** Events/meetings.

Members Full in 18 countries:

Benin, Burkina Faso, Cameroon, Congo Brazzaville, Côte d'Ivoire, Egypt, Gabon, Ghana, Kenya, Libya, Madagascar, Mali, Mauritius, Morocco, Mozambique, Nigeria, Senegal, Tunisia.

IGO Relations *United Nations Centre for Trade Facilitation and Electronic Business (UN/CEFACT, #20527).* [2019/XM8457/**D**]

♦ Alliance africaine des UCJG / see Africa Alliance of Young Men's Christian Associations (#00155)
♦ Alliance africaine des unions chrétiennes de jeunes gens (#00155)
♦ Alliance of African and Mediterranean French-speaking Leagues (#00704)
♦ Alliance of African and Mediterranean french speaking Leagues for cancer control / see Alliance des ligues francophones africaines et méditerranéennes (#00704)

♦ Alliance Against Biopiracy 00653

No fixed address address not obtained.

History 18 Feb 2002, Cancún (Mexico), as *Group of Allied Mega-Biodiverse Nations.* An informal grouping.

Members Governments of 13 countries:

Brazil, China, Colombia, Costa Rica, Ecuador, India, Indonesia, Kenya, Mexico, Peru, South Africa, Venezuela.

[2010/XF6627/**F***]

♦ Alliance Against Counterfeit Spirits (AACS) 00654

Sec 21 Holborn Viaduct, London, EC1A 2DY, UK.

URL: https://aacs-global.com/

History Former names and other names: *International Federation of Spirits Producers* – former (23 May 2005 to 31 Mar 2020). Registration: Companies House, No/ID: 05460509, Start date: 23 May 2005, England and Wales. **Aims** Combat the counterfeiting of its members' distilled spirits brands. **Activities** Awareness raising; guidance/assistance/consulting; monitoring/evaluation; training/education. **Members** Spirits producing companies (6). **NGO Relations** Partner of (1): *Asia Pacific International Spirits and Wines Alliance (APISWA).* [2022/AA0952/**C**]

♦ Alliance Against Genocide (AAG) 00655

Alliance contre les génocides

Pres c/o Genocide Watch, 1405 Cola Drive, McLean VA 22101, USA. T. +17034486665. E-mail: communications@genocidewatch.org.

URL: http://www.genocidewatch.com/

History 1999, The Hague (Netherlands), at the *Hague Appeal for Peace (HAP, #10848)*, as *International Campaign to End Genocide (ICEG) – Campagne internationale pour mettre fin aux génocides – Campaña Internacional para Eliminar el Genocidio – Internationale Kampagne zur Beendigung von Völkermord – Campanha Internacional para Eliminar o Genocidio.* Subsequently referred to as *International Alliance to End Genocide (IAEG) – Campagne internationale pour mettre fin aux génocides.* **Aims** Predict, prevent, stop and punish genocide and other forms of mass murder through: consciousness raising; coalition forming; policy advocacy. **Structure** Coordinated by Genocide Watch. **Languages** Afrikaans, Amharic, Arabic, Armenian, Bengali, Burmese, English, French, German, Hebrew, Kurdish, Mon-Khmer languages, Portuguese, Spanish, Swahili. **Staff** 6.00 FTE, paid. **Finance** Private and public donations. **Activities** Events/meetings; awareness raising; networking/liaising; advocacy/lobbying/activism. **Events** *Conference* Kigali (Rwanda) 2012, *Geneva Summit for Human Rights, Tolerance and Democracy* Geneva (Switzerland) 2010, *Geneva Summit for Human Rights, Tolerance and Democracy* Geneva (Switzerland) 2009. **Publications** *Countries at Risk* – reports.

Members National and international anti-genocide organizations (about 70) in 30 countries:

Austria, Belgium, Bosnia-Herzegovina, Cambodia, Canada, Denmark, Ethiopia, Finland, France, Germany, Guatemala, Iraq, Israel, Italy, Kenya, Malaysia, Myanmar, Netherlands, Nigeria, Norway, Rwanda, South Africa, Spain, Sudan, Sweden, Switzerland, Thailand, UK, USA, Zimbabwe.

Included in the above, 10 organizations listed in this Yearbook:

AEGIS Trust; Christian Solidarity International (CSI, #03909); Institute on the Holocaust and Genocide (IHG, #11268); International Alert (#11615); International Crisis Group (Crisis Group, #13111); International Forensic Centre of Excellence for the Investigation of Genocide (Inforce Foundation); Minority Rights Group International (MRG, #16820); Montreal Institute for Genocide and Human Rights Studies (MIGS); Survival International (#20047); TRIAL International.

IGO Relations Contacts with: *European Commission (EC, #06633); Inter-American Commission on Human Rights (IACHR, #11411); OECD (#17693); United Nations (UN, #20515)* and its agencies, especially the Special Advisor to the UN Secretary General for the Prevention of Genocide and *Office of the United Nations High Commissioner for Human Rights (OHCHR, #17697).* Also has contacts with USA, UK and other governments. **NGO Relations** Coordinated by: *Genocide Watch.* Cooperates with: *International Association of Genocide Scholars (IAGS).* [2018.06.01/XF6932/y/**F**]

♦ Alliance Against Traffic in Women Foundation / see Global Alliance Against Traffic in Women (#10184)
♦ **The Alliance** Alliance for Child Protection in Humanitarian Action (#00667)
♦ **ALLIANCE** Alliance of European Voluntary Service Organizations (#00677)
♦ Alliance dans les Alpes (#00656)

♦ Alliance in the Alps 00656

Alliance dans les Alpes – Allianz in den Alpen – Alleanza nelle Alpi – Povezanost v Alpah

Dir Feldwieser Str 27, 83236 Übersee, Germany. T. +4986426531. E-mail: info@alpenallianz.org.

Assistant address not obtained.

Assistant address not obtained.

URL: http://www.alpenallianz.org/

History 1997, Bovec (Slovenia). Proposed by *CIPRA International (#03930)*, in collaboration with other relevant bodies and with the support of DG XI (Environment) of *European Commission (EC, #06633)*, in order to implement *Convention for the Protection of the Alps (Alpine convention, 1991).* Former names and other names: *Gemeinde-Netzwerk – Allianz in den Alpen* – former; *Réseau de communes – Alliance dans les Alpes* – former; *Rete di Comuni – Alleanza nelle Alpi* – former; *Omrezje obcin – Povezanost v Alpah* – former; *Réseau de communes alpines* – full title; *Alliance in the Alps – The Community Network* – full title; *Povezanost v Alpah – Omrezje Obcin* – full title. Registration: Bavaria District court, No/ID: VR 20611, Start date: 18 Nov 1997, Germany, Traunstein. **Aims** Develop the alpine living environment in a *sustainable* way. **Structure** Council; Executive Board. **Languages** French, German, Italian, Slovene. **Finance** Members' dues. National funds. **Activities** Events/meetings; guidance/assistance/consulting; knowledge management/information dissemination; projects/programmes. **Events** *AlpWeek* Brig (Switzerland) 2022. **Publications** Electronic newsletter (4 a year). Annual Report.

Members in 7 countries:

Austria, France, Germany, Italy, Liechtenstein, Slovenia, Switzerland. [2022/XF3855/**F***]

♦ Alliance in the Alps – The Community Network / see Alliance in the Alps (#00656)

♦ Alliance for Arab Women (AAW) 00657

Chairperson 28 Adly St, Downtown, Cairo, Egypt. T. +2023939899 – +2023950911 – +2023928012. Fax +2023936820.

URL: http://www.theallianceforarabwomen.org/

History 1987, Cairo (Egypt). **Aims** Enhance the status of women and mobilize all efforts to enable them to play en effective role in the economic, social and political development of their country. **Structure** General Assembly. Board of Directors, consisting of Chairperson, Vice Chairperson, Secretary, Trustee and 11 members. Secretariat in Cairo (Egypt). **Staff** 20.00 FTE, paid. **Finance** Members' dues. International grants and donations. **Activities** Acts as an umbrella of about 350 NGOs in Egypt. Carries out projects in the following areas: poverty; public participation; violence; health and education. Awareness campaigns; meetings and workshops. **Events** *Seminar on women's health within the CEDAW convention* Cairo (Egypt) 1993. **Publications** *Newsletter. Arab Women Years in Judiciary; Women Status in Iran; Women Status in Tunisia.* Meeting reports.

Members Individuals (about 200) in 6 countries:

Egypt, Kuwait, Lebanon, Sudan, United Arab Emirates, Yemen.

Consultative Status Consultative status granted from: *ECOSOC (#05331)* (Special). **IGO Relations** *Canadian International Development Agency (CIDA, inactive); Deutsche Gesellschaft für Technische Zusammenarbeit (GTZ, inactive); European Commission (EC, #06633); UNDP (#20292); UNICEF (#20332); United Nations Population Fund (UNFPA, #20612); United States Agency for International Development (USAID); WHO (#20950).* **NGO Relations** *Oxfam Novib; Swissaid.* [2014/XD3550/v/**D**]

♦ Alliance asiatique de UCJG (#01826)
♦ Alliance balkanique (inactive)
♦ Alliance baptiste mondiale (#03176)

♦ Alliance for Beverage Cartons and the Environment (ACE) 00658

Alliance Carton et Environnement

Communications Manager Av Louise 250, Bte 106, 1050 Brussels, Belgium. T. +3225040710. Fax +3225040719. E-mail: secretariat@beveragecarton.eu.

URL: http://www.beveragecarton.eu/

History 1995. Registration: Banque-Carrefour des Entreprises, No/ID: 0443.076.402, Start date: 19 Apr 1990, Belgium; EU Transparency Register, No/ID: 57004293853-27, Start date: 12 Jul 2010. **Aims** Act as European ambassador and knowledge hub for beverage carton *manufacturers* and their *paperboard* suppliers; study and communicate the environmental value of cartons as a renewable, *recyclable* and low carbon packaging solution. **Structure** Board of Directors. **Languages** English. **Staff** 5.00 FTE, paid. **Finance** Sources: contributions; members' dues; revenue from activities/projects. **Activities** Guidance/assistance/consulting; knowledge management/information dissemination; politics/policy/regulatory; research/documentation. Active in: Belgium, Czechia, Denmark, Italy, Norway, Portugal, Slovakia, Slovenia, Spain, Sweden. **Events** *The contribution of sustainable resource management to a circular economy* Brussels (Belgium) 2014, *Symposium / Annual Symposium* Brussels (Belgium) 2001, *Annual Symposium* Brussels (Belgium) 1999, *Annual Symposium* Brussels (Belgium) 1998. **Publications** *The Beverage Carton Industry Roadmap to 2030 and Beyond* (2021). Fact sheets; press releases; brochures; position papers; infographics; video; online publications. **Members** Beverage carton producers and paperboard producers with head offices in Europe. Membership countries not specified. **NGO Relations** Member of (3): *European Food Sustainable Consumption and Production Round Table (European Food SCP Roundtable, #07289); European Policy Centre (EPC, #08240); Federation of European and International Associations Established in Belgium (FAIB, #09508).* Signatory to Declaration of: *European Paper Recycling Council (EPRC, #08139).* [2022/XF3538/**F**]

♦ Alliance biblique universelle (#20498)
♦ Alliance for Biomedical Research in Europe / see Biomedical Alliance in Europe (#03251)

♦ Alliance of Blood Operators (ABO) 00659

Contact Australian Red Cross Blood Service, 417 Kilda Road, Melbourne VIC 3004, Australia. E-mail: abosecretariat@redcrossblood.org.au.

URL: https://www.allianceofbloodoperators.org/home.aspx/

History 2004. **Activities** Sub-Group: 'International Blood Emergency Planning Advisory Group'. **Events** *Meeting* San Francisco, CA (USA) 2005.

Members Founding members national organizations (3) in 3 countries:

Australia, Canada, USA.

Regional organization (1):

European Blood Alliance (EBA, #06351). [2016/XM3261/**F**]

♦ Alliance of Business Lawyers (ABL) 00660

Coordinator c/o DGN Avocats, Rue Charles-Bonnet 2, 1206 Geneva, Switzerland. E-mail: info@ ablglobal.net.

URL: https://www.ablglobal.net/

History 2003. Founded on merger of Integra Legal International and Druces International. Registration: Registre du Commerce de Genève, No/ID: CH-660-9461004-8, Start date: 2004, Switzerland. **Structure** General Meeting; Executive Board. **Activities** Events/meetings. **Events** *Conference* London (UK) 2023, *Conference* Chicago, IL (USA) 2022, *Conference* Hamburg (Germany) 2022, *Conference* Tokyo (Japan) 2020, *Conference* San Francisco, CA (USA) 2019.

Members Business law firms in 17 countries and territories:

Belgium, Bermuda, Canada, Cyprus, France, Germany, Israel, Italy, Japan, Malta, Netherlands, Spain, Sweden, Switzerland, UK, USA, Virgin Is UK.

NGO Relations Affiliated with (1): *Council of International Investigators (CII).* [2023.02.23/AA1785/**C**]

♦ Alliance of Business Women International (internationally oriented national body)
♦ Alliance canadienne féministe pour l'action internationale (internationally oriented national body)
♦ Alliance canadienne pour la paix (internationally oriented national body)
♦ Alliance Carton et Environnement (#00658)

♦ Alliance for a Cavity-Free Future (ACFF) 00661

Dir King's College London, Fac of Dentistry/Oral/Craniofacial Sciences, Floor 17 – Tower Wing, Guy's Hosp, London, SE1 9RT, UK. E-mail: admin@acffglobal.org.

URL: http://www.allianceforacavityfreefuture.org/

History Launched 2010. **Aims** Promote integrated clinical and public health action in order to stop the initiation and progression of *dental* caries. **Structure** Chapters (29). **Languages** English, French, Spanish. **Staff** 1.00 FTE, paid. **Finance** Sources: grants. **Activities** Advocacy/lobbying/activism; awareness raising; events/meetings; knowledge management/information dissemination; networking/liaising; politics/policy/regulatory; research and development; training/education.

Members Chapters (29) spanning 54 countries:

Algeria, Australia, Bahrain, Belize, Brazil, Canada, China, Colombia, Costa Rica, Czechia, Denmark, El Salvador, Estonia, Finland, France, Greece, Guatemala, Honduras, Hungary, Iceland, India, Italy, Japan, Jordan, Kuwait, Latvia, Lebanon, Lithuania, Malaysia, Mexico, Morocco, New Zealand, Nicaragua, Nigeria, Norway, Oman, Panama, Philippines, Poland, Qatar, Romania, Russia, Saudi Arabia, Slovakia, South Africa, Spain, Sweden, Thailand, Tunisia, Türkiye, UK, United Arab Emirates, USA, Venezuela. [2022.06.15/XM6468/**C**]

♦ Alliance of Central Asian Mountain Communities (AGOCA) 00662

SG 80 Timiryazeva, 720001 Bishkek, Kyrgyzstan. T. +996312881304. E-mail: agoca.centralasia@ gmail.com – chashmai_nosir08@mail.ru.

URL: http://www.agoca.kg/

History Founded Jun 2003, Dushanbe (Tajikistan), with the support of *CIPRA International (#03930).* **Aims** Work in the field of sustainable development to contribute to poverty alleviation, sustainable use of natural resources, food security, income and opportunities. **Structure** Meeting of Representatives; Board of Management; Revision (Audit) Commission. **Languages** Kazakh, Kirghiz, Russian, Tajik. **Staff** 7.00 FTE, paid. **Finance** Members' dues. Other sources: grants; income from services. **Publications** *Ayil Demi* – newspaper.

Members Full (20) in 3 countries:

Kazakhstan, Kyrgyzstan, Tajikistan.

NGO Relations Member of: *Mountain Partnership (MP, #16862)*; national organizations. [2017.03.09/XJ5118/**D**]

♦ Alliance for Cervical Cancer Prevention (ACCP) 00663

Alliance pour la prévention du cancer du col de l'utérus – Alianza para la Prevención del Cancer Cervical

Contact c/o PATH, PO Box 900922, Seattle WA 98109, USA. T. +12062853500.

History 1999. **Aims** Clarify, promote and implement strategies for preventing cervical cancer in *developing countries.* **Activities** Projects focus on regions in which cervical cancer incidence and mortality are highest (Sub-Saharan Africa, Latin America and South Asia). Works with developing-country partners on the following: exploring new approaches for detection of precancerous lesions; evaluating effectiveness of combined detection and treatment approaches; improving delivery of cervical cancer prevention services; developing the means by which clinicians can be trained in providing quality cervical cancer prevention services; assessing what women and health care providers need to know about cervical cancer prevention; preparing

key information packages for health care decision-makers; providing small grants to local agencies working on cervical cancer prevention in their communities; ensuring that community perspectives and needs are incorporated into programme design; heightening awareness of cervical cancer and effective prevention strategies. **Publications** Fact sheets; presentations; planning guides; training materials; technical reports; conference proceedings; journal articles.
Members Founding members (5):
EngenderHealth; International Agency for Research on Cancer (IARC, #11598); JHPIEGO; *Pan American Health Organization (PAHO, #18108);* PATH.
NGO Relations Coordinated by: *PATH (#18260).* [2012/XF5930/y/**F**]

♦ Alliance for Chemical Sciences and Technologies in Europe (AllChemE) 00664

Contact c/o CEFIC, Avenue E van Nieuwenhuyse 4 – Bte 1, 1160 Brussels, Belgium. T. +3226767387. Fax +3226767347.
History 1995. **Aims** Promote chemistry and chemical engineering in Europe; influence the future strategies of the European Commission, other European groupings and national bodies; provide Europe with a highly effective and reliable single voice on matters of mutual importance to industry, academia and government; identify and promote fruitful avenues of research that will ultimately lead to a more *sustainable* world; seek innovation in chemical sciences by promoting interaction with other branches of science and technology; provide input in the development of a European R and TD policy; stimulate a more innovative approach to scientific education and training; attract high quality human resources and funding for molecular sciences and related technologies throughout the enlarged Europe; promote public understanding of the benefits of molecular sciences and technologies; promote public awareness of chemistry and the chemical industry as major contributors to health, wealth and employment; promote creation of infrastructure that will sustain a chemical industry that is capable of meeting the needs of people throughout an enlarged Europe. **Activities** Knowledge management/information dissemination; networking/liaising; events/meetings. **Publications** Reports.
Members International organizations (4), listed in this Yearbook:
Chairmen of the European Research Councils' Chemistry Committees (CERC3, #03846); Conseil européen de l'industrie chimique (CEFIC, #04687); European Cooperation in Science and Technology (COST, #06784); European Federation of Chemical Engineering (EFCE, #07074). [2016/XD6952/y/**F**]

♦ Alliance for Childhood 00665

Dir Troonstraat 194, 1050 Brussels, Belgium. T. +32473895179. E-mail: info@allianceforchildhood.org.uk.
Netherlands Office Amsterdamseweg 4D, 3812 RS Amersfoort, Netherlands. T. +31332852470.
URL: http://www.alliancechildhood.org/
History 1998. **Aims** Increase respect for childhood as a basis for human development; develop solutions to problems which could endanger the good quality of childhood; provide a platform to unite all people that influence children's lives. **Structure** Network with office support. **Languages** Dutch, English. **Staff** Voluntary. **Finance** Contributions; loans. Annual budget: euro 15,000. **Events** *The Voice of Children Conference* Brussels (Belgium) 2015, *Unfolding Conference* Brussels (Belgium) 2013, *Conference* Budapest (Hungary) 2010, *Conference* Aarhus (Denmark) 2009, *Conference* Edinburgh (UK) 2009. **Publications** *A Critical Look at Computers in Childhood; Tech Tonic Towards a New Literacy of Technology; The Genius of Play Celebrating the Spirit of Childhood* by Sally Jenkinson. Conference proceedings. **IGO Relations** Working Group on the Quality of Childhood in *European Parliament (EP, #08146).* [2021/XF4745/**F**]

♦ Alliance for Childhood European Network Foundation / see Alliance for Childhood European Network Group (#00666)

♦ Alliance for Childhood European Network Group (AFC-ENG) 00666

Contact Troonstraat 194, 1050 Brussels, Belgium.
Chairman address not obtained.
URL: http://www.allianceforchildhood.eu/
History 21 Mar 2006, Brussels (Belgium). Former names and other names: *Alliance for Childhood European Network Foundation* – alias. Registration: Crossroads Bank for Enterprises, No/ID: 0880.102.675, Start date: 21 Mar 2006, Belgium; EU Transparency Register, No/ID: 805062413338-50, Start date: 26 Mar 2014. **Aims** Advocate for the good quality of childhood in EU member states and beyond. **Structure** Steered by *Alliance for Childhood European Network Foundation.* **Languages** English. **Staff** 1.00 FTE, voluntary. **Finance** Sources: members' dues. Annual budget: 15,000 EUR. **Activities** Advocacy/lobbying/activism; events/meetings; publishing activities. **Events** *The unfolding conference nurturing a culture that allows each and every child to unfold their unique potential and to engage in society* Brussels (Belgium) 2013, *Child in the balance* Budapest (Hungary) 2010, *How children learn* Salzburg (Austria) 2005, *The heart and soul of learning* Zeist (Netherlands) 2002, *Rights to children – a bridge to the future* Brussels (Belgium) 2000. **Publications** *Improving the Quality of Childhood in Europe* (2010-2016) – vols 2-6; *Improving the Quality of Childhood in the European Union – Current Perspectives* (2009).
Members Full (29) in 9 countries:
Austria, Belgium, Denmark, Finland, France, Germany, Italy, Netherlands, Sweden.
Included in the above, 5 organizations listed in this Yearbook:
Alliance ELIANT (#00672); Children of Prisoners Europe (COPE, #03875); European Council for Steiner Waldorf Education (ECSWE, #06844); European Foundation for the Care of Newborn Infants (EFCNI, #07344); European Parents' Association (EPA, #08142). [2022/XJ2419/y/**E**]

♦ Alliance for Child Protection in Humanitarian Action (The Alliance) 00667

Coordinator UNICEF, 3 UN Plaza, New York NY 10017, USA.
URL: http://alliancecpha.org/
History Nov 2016, Geneva (Switzerland), evolving from the *Child Protection Working Group (CPWG)* (2006-2016), led by *UNICEF (#20332).* **Aims** Support efforts of humanitarian actors to achieve high quality and effective child protection interventions in humanitarian settings. **Structure** Steering Committee; Working Groups; Task Forces; Secretariat. **Languages** Arabic, English, French, Spanish. **Staff** 3.00 FTE, paid. **Finance** Donor financing; member agencies contribute to staff time. **Activities** Standards/guidelines; guidance/assistance/consulting; capacity building; knowledge management/information dissemination; advocacy/lobbying/activism; events/meetings. **Events** *Annual Meeting for Child Protection in Humanitarian Action* Geneva (Switzerland) 2019, *Round Table* Nairobi (Kenya) 2018, *Annual Meeting for Child Protection in Humanitarian Action* Kampala (Uganda) 2017, *Annual Meeting for Child Protection in Humanitarian Action* Geneva (Switzerland) 2016. **Publications** *Alliance Newsletter* (6 a year).
Members General; Associate; Core. Core members (15) include the following 12 organizations listed in this Yearbook:
ChildFund Alliance (#03868); Danish Refugee Council (DRC); International Federation of Red Cross and Red Crescent Societies (#13526); International Islamic Relief Organization (IIRO); International Organization for Migration (IOM, #14454); International Rescue Committee (IRC, #14717); Plan International (#18386); Save the Children International (#19058); Terre des Hommes International Federation (TDHIF, #20133); UNHCR (#20327); UNICEF (#20332); World Vision International (WVI, #21904).
IGO Relations *ILO (#11123); International Organization for Migration (IOM, #14454); UNHCR (#20327); UNICEF (#20332).* [2018/XM5571/y/**E**]

♦ Alliance des civilisations des Nations Unies (#20520)
♦ Alliance pour le Climat (#04005)
♦ Alliance pour le Climat entre les Villes Européennes et les Peuples Indigènes des Forêts Tropicales / see Climate Alliance (#04005)
♦ Alliance of Cocoa Producing Countries (no recent information)

♦ Alliance for Commodity Trade in Eastern and Southern Africa (ACTESA) 00668

Acting CEO Ben Bella Road, PO Box 30051, Lusaka, Zambia.
URL: https://www.comesa.int/industry-agriculture/
History Launched 24 Sep 2008, by *Common Market for Eastern and Southern Africa (COMESA, #04296)* Ministers of Agriculture. Established as a Specialized Agency of COMESA, by COMESA Heads of State, 9 Jun 2009. **Aims** Increase *farmer* productivity and incomes in the Eastern and Southern Africa region through trade in strategic agricultural commodities. **Finance** Financial partners include: *United States Agency for International Development (USAID); Department for International Development (DFID, inactive); World Food Programme (WFP, #21510); Alliance for a Green Revolution in Africa (AGRA, #00685); Australian Aid (inactive); European Commission (EC, #06633).* **Events** *Africa rice outlook conference* Cape Town (South Africa) 2010. **Publications** *ACTESA Newsletter.* [2020/XJ2975/t/**E***]

♦ Alliance of Communicators for Sustainable Development (COMplus) 00669

Global Communications Officer c/o IUCN, AP 146-2150 Moravia, San José, San José, San José, Costa Rica. T. +50622410101.
URL: http://www.complusalliance.org/
History 2003. **Aims** Provide a communications platform on issues related to sustainable development and communications. **Structure** Secretariat in Costa Rica. **IGO Relations** Partners include: *CGIAR System Organization (CGIAR, #03843); Global Environment Facility (GEF, #10346); International Bank for Reconstruction and Development (IBRD, #12317)* (World Bank). **NGO Relations** Partners include: *BBC Media Action; International Federation of Environmental Journalists (IFEJ, inactive); International Union for Conservation of Nature and Natural Resources (IUCN, #15766); IPS – Inter Press Service International Association (#16013); Thomson Reuters Foundation (TRF).* [2015/XM1364/**F**]

♦ Alliance for a Competitive European Industry (ACEI) 00670

Chair c/o Cembureau, Rue d'Arlon 55, 1040 Brussels, Belgium. T. +3222341011. E-mail: main@businesseurope.eu.
URL: https://www.businesseurope.eu/alliance-competitive-european-industry
History 2004. Founded by 11 major European industry sector associations and *BUSINESSEUROPE (#03381).* **Aims** Promote the competitiveness of European industry on a global scale. **Languages** English.
Members European industry sector associations representing about 6,000 large companies and 1.7 million SMEs. Included in the above, 12 organizations listed in this Yearbook:
Association européenne des métaux (EUROMETAUX, #02578); BUSINESSEUROPE (#03381); CEMBUREAU – The European Cement Association (CEMBUREAU, #03634); Confederation of European Paper Industries (CEPI, #04529); Conseil européen de l'industrie chimique (CEFIC, #04687); EURATEX – The European Apparel and Textile Confederation (EURATEX, #05616); European Automobile Manufacturers' Association (ACEA, #06300); European Steel Association (EUROFER, #08835); FoodDrinkEurope (#09841); FuelsEurope (#10014); Orgalim – Europe's Technology Industries (#17794); Union of the Electricity Industry – Eurelectric (#20379). [2021.05.26/XJ0648/ty/**E**]

♦ Alliance of Conservatives and Reformists in Europe / see European Conservatives and Reformists Party (#06747)
♦ Alliance for Consumer Fire Safety in Europe (internationally oriented national body)
♦ Alliance contre les génocides (#00655)
♦ Alliance pour le contrôle du tabac en Afrique (#00484)
♦ Alliance coopérative internationale (#12944)
♦ Alliance culturelle européenne (inactive)
♦ Alliance Defending Freedom International / see ADF International (#00112)
♦ Alliance of Democracies Foundation (internationally oriented national body)
♦ Alliance des démocrates et des libéraux pour l'Europe / see Renew Europe (#18840)

♦ Alliance of Digital Humanities Organizations (ADHO) 00671

Main Office address not obtained. E-mail: communications@digitalhumanities.org – adho@adho.org.
URL: http://adho.org/
History 2006, Victoria, BC (Canada). Founded following a proposal during a joint conference organized by *European Association for Digital Humanities (EADH, #06014)* and *Association for Computers and the Humanities (ACH, #02446),* Tübingen (Germany), 2002. Registration: Netherlands. **Aims** Promote and support digital research and teaching across arts and humanities disciplines, drawing together humanists engaged in digital and computer-assisted research, teaching, creation, dissemination and beyond; support initiatives for publication, presentation, collaboration and training; recognize and support excellence in these endeavours; act as an community-based consultative and advisory force. **Structure** Steering Committee. Committees (8). **Activities** Awards/prizes/competitions; events/meetings; financial and/or material support; guidance/assistance/consulting; knowledge management/information dissemination. **Events** *Digital Humanities Conference* Graz (Austria) 2023, *Digital Humanities Conference* Graz (Austria) 2022, *Digital Humanities Conference* Tokyo (Japan) 2022, *Digital Humanities Conference* Tokyo (Japan) 2021, *Digital Humanities Conference* Ottawa, ON (Canada) 2020. **Publications** *Digital Scholarship in the Humanities (DSH)* – peer reviewed journal. **Information Services** *Humanist Discussion Forum* – international digital seminar.
Members Organizations in 7 countries, including 6 listed in this Yearbook:
Australia, Canada, Germany, Japan, Mexico, Taiwan, USA.
Association for Computers and the Humanities (ACH, #02446); Australasian Association for Digital Humanities (aaDH); centerNet; Digital Humanities im deutschsprachigen Raum (DHd, #05079); European Association for Digital Humanities (EADH, #06014); Humanistica (#10971). [2021/XM3170/y/**C**]

♦ Alliance for Earth Sciences, Engineering and Development in Africa (internationally oriented national body)
♦ Alliance des éditeurs (inactive)
♦ Alliance des éditeurs indépendants / see Alliance internationale des éditeurs indépendants
♦ Alliance des éditeurs indépendants pour une autre mondialisation / see Alliance internationale des éditeurs indépendants
♦ Alliance pour l'éducation LGBT (internationally oriented national body)

♦ Alliance ELIANT 00672

Office Rue du Trône 194, 1050 Brussels, Belgium. T. +3216843334. E-mail: info@eliant.eu.
URL: http://www.eliant.eu/
History 2006. Full title: *European Alliance of Initiatives for Applied Anthroposophy – Alliance européenne des initiatives issues de l'anthroposophie – Europäische Allianz von Initiativen Angewandter Anthroposophie – Europese Alliantie van Initiatieven voor Toegepaste Antroposofie.* **Aims** Work with other organizations to create a regulatory framework of environmentally sound and value-based objectives which allow parents to decide how they want their children to be educated, enable individuals to choose medicines in which they have confidence, and introduce, maintain and develop products which are produced in a way that sustains the earth and environment. **Structure** Management Board. **Languages** English. **Staff** 2.50 FTE, paid. **Finance** Members' dues. Donations. **Activities** Publishing activities; events/meetings. **Events** *Conference on Soul of Europe* Brussels (Belgium) 2019, *Conference on Digitalization and Childhood* Brussels (Belgium) 2017, *Conference on Freedom of choice under threat* Brussels (Belgium) 2016, *Unfolding Conference* Brussels (Belgium) 2013. **Publications** *ELIANT Newsletter* (12 a year).
Members Members include 7 organizations listed in this Yearbook:
Demeter International (#05029); European Cooperation in Anthroposophical Curative Education and Social Therapy (ECCE, #06783); European Council for Steiner Waldorf Education (ECSWE, #06844); European Federation of Patients' Associations for Anthroposophic Medicine (EFPAM, #07189); International Association for Steiner/Waldorf Early Childhood Education (IASWECE, #12185); International BioDynamic Association (IBDA, #12346); Internationale Vereinigung Anthroposophischer Ärztegesellschaften (IVAA, #13314).
NGO Relations Member of: *Alliance for Childhood European Network Group (AFC-ENG, #00666).* [2017.04.11/XM3379/y/**F**]

♦ Alliance to End Hunger (internationally oriented national body)

♦ Alliance to End Plastic Waste (AEPW) 00673

CEO 160 Greentree Dr, Ste 101, Dover DE 19904, USA. T. +12022496134. E-mail: info@endplasticwaste.org.
URL: http://endplasticwaste.org/

History 2019. Registration: EU Transparency Register, No/ID: 614241333938-75, Start date: 12 Feb 2019; 501(c)3, USA, Delaware. **Aims** Develop, deploy and bring to scale solutions that will minimize and manage plastic waste; promote solutions for used plastics, including reuse, recovery and *recycling* plastic to keep it out of the *environment*. **Finance** Sources: members' dues. **Activities** Advocacy/lobbying/activism; training/education. **Events** *Packaging Committee Meeting Introducing of the Alliance to End Plastic Waste* Singapore (Singapore) 2020. **Members** Companies (over 40). Membership countries not specified. [2021/XM7464/**C**]

- ♦ Alliance of Euro-Mediterranean Cultural Cities (#00726)
- ♦ Alliance of European Conservatives and Reformists / see European Conservatives and Reformists Party (#06747)
- ♦ Alliance of European Cultural Cities / see Alliance de Villes Euro-méditerranéennes de Culture (#00726)

♦ Alliance of European Football Coaches' Associations (AEFCA) 00674

Contact Daimlerring 4, Nordenstadt, 65205 Wiesbaden, Germany. T. +491726735253. E-mail: info@aefca.eu.
URL: http://www.aefca.eu/

History Founded 12 Jan 1980, as *UEF*. **Structure** Board; Executive Committee.
Members Full in 44 countries an territories:
Austria, Belarus, Belgium, Bosnia-Herzegovina, Bulgaria, Croatia, Cyprus, Czechia, Denmark, England, Faeroe Is, Finland, France, Germany, Greece, Iceland, Ireland, Israel, Italy, Kosovo, Latvia, Lithuania, Luxembourg, Malta, Montenegro, Netherlands, North Macedonia, Northern Ireland, Norway, Poland, Portugal, Romania, Russia, San Marino, Scotland, Serbia, Slovakia, Slovenia, Spain, Sweden, Switzerland, Türkiye, Ukraine, Wales.
NGO Relations Member of: *Sport Integrity Global Alliance (SIGA, #19925).* [2020/XM8978/**D**]

♦ Alliance for European Logistics (AEL) 00675

Main Office Rue Defacqz 52, 1050 Brussels, Belgium. T. +3225368667. E-mail: contact@logistics-alliance.eu.
URL: http://logistics-alliance.eu/

History 2008. Registration: EU Transparency Register, No/ID: 38033128051-39. **Aims** Raise the profile and understanding of the logistics industry amongst European policymakers. **Events** *Summit* Brussels (Belgium) 2017, *Summit* Brussels (Belgium) 2016, *Summit* Brussels (Belgium) 2015, *Summit* Brussels (Belgium) 2013, *Summit* Brussels (Belgium) 2012. [2018/XM7127/**D**]

♦ Alliance of European Republican Movements (AERM) 00676

Contact address not obtained. E-mail: secretary@aerm.org.
URL: http://aerm.org/

History Set up Jun 2010, Stockholm (Sweden). **Aims** Create a network of cross-party republican movements in all the countries in Europe that continue to have a monarch as their head of state. **Languages** English. **Finance** Ad hoc funding by member organizations. **Events** *Conventions* Utrecht (Netherlands) 2020, *Annual Conference* Copenhagen (Denmark) 2019, *Annual Conference* London (UK) 2018, *Annual Conference* Madrid (Spain) 2016.
Members Full in 7 countries:
Belgium, Denmark, Netherlands, Norway, Spain, Sweden, UK. [2020.03.03/XM5694/**D**]

♦ Alliance of European Voluntary Service Organizations (ALLIANCE) 00677

Alliance des organisations de service volontaire de l'Europe

Secretary Asmalı Mescit, İstiklal Cd, No108 Beyoglu, 34430 Istanbul/Istanbul, Türkiye. T. +902122446230. E-mail: alliance@alliance-network.eu.
Pres c/o MS/Action Aid Denmark, Faelledvej 12, 2200 Copenhagen, Denmark. E-mail: president@alliance-network.eu.
URL: http://www.alliance-network.eu/

History 1982. Founded by MS Denmark, Concordia France, IJGD Germany, SIW Netherlands, SVI Spain, QISP United Kingdom and UNA Exchange United Kingdom. Former names and other names: *Alliance of Western European Voluntary Service Organisations* – former. **Aims** Promote intercultural dialogue, peace, inclusion and participation through International Voluntary Service. **Structure** Annual General Assembly; President; General Secretary; Treasurer; Teams; Necessary Action Groups; Communities of Interest. **Languages** English. **Staff** 2.00 FTE, paid. Several voluntary. **Finance** Sources: grants; members' dues. Supported by: *European Commission (EC, #06633)*; *European Youth Foundation (EYF, #09141)*. **Activities** Events/meetings; projects/programmes; training/education. **Events** *General Conference* Alicante (Spain) 2018, *General Conference* Petnica (Serbia) 2016, *Alliance Congress* Grosseto (Italy) 2014, *General Conference* Mozet (Belgium) 2012, *General Conference* Ankara (Turkey) 2010. **Publications** Annual Report; annual statistics report.
Members Full, Associate and candidate Member Organizations (MOs), 49 in total. Members in 30 countries and territories, among which 34 members based in 19 Erasmus+ programme countries*.
Armenia, Austria (*), Belarus, Belgium (*), Canada, Catalunya, Czechia (*), Denmark (*), Estonia (*), Finland (*), France (*), Germany (*), Greece (*), Hungary (*), India, Italy (*), Japan, Latvia (*), Lithuania (*), Mexico, Nepal, Netherlands (*), Poland (*), Russia, Serbia (*), Slovakia (*), Spain (*), Türkiye (*), UK, Ukraine.
Included in the above, 5 organizations listed in this Yearbook:
Concordia; *ELIX – Conservation Volunteers Greece (ELIX-CVG)*; *Internationale Begegnung in Gemeinschaftsdiensten (IBG)*; *International Workcamps (IJGD)*; *Mellemfolkeligt Samvirke (MS)*.
Associate (6) in 5 countries:
Canada, Japan, Korea Rep, Mexico, Nepal.
NGO Relations Member of (2): *Coordinating Committee for International Voluntary Service (CCIVS, #04819)*; *European Youth Forum (#09140)*. Cooperates with (5): *International Cultural Youth Exchange (ICYE Federation, #13122)*; *Network for Voluntary Development in Asia (NVDA, #17063)*; *Service Civil International (SCI, #19238)*; *South East European Youth Network (SEEYN, #19821)*; *Youth of European Nationalities (YEN, #22013)*. [2023.02.28/XF1211/y/**F**]

♦ Alliance for a Europe of Democracies (EUDemocrats) 00678

Alliance pour une europe des démocraties

Contact address not obtained. T. +3225030514.
URL: http://eudemocrats.org/

History 2005. **Finance** Partly funded by: *European Parliament (EP, #08146)*. **Events** *Conference on the future of Europe / Conference* Berlin (Germany) 2007. **Publications** *EUD Newsletter* (12 a year). [2013/XM3127/**F**]

- ♦ Alliance pour une europe des démocraties (#00678)
- ♦ Alliance européenne des agences de presse / see European Alliance of News Agencies (#05877)
- ♦ Alliance européenne des associations de myopathes (#05876)
- ♦ Alliance Européenne des Consultantes en Lactation (#07638)
- ♦ Alliance européenne pour l'éthique en publicité (#05829)
- ♦ Alliance européenne de la grande distribution (inactive)
- ♦ Alliance européenne des initiatives issues de l'anthroposophie / see Alliance ELIANT (#00672)
- ♦ Alliance Européenne Numismatique (internationally oriented national body)
- ♦ Alliance européenne d'organisations féminines catholiques (#05864)
- ♦ Alliance européenne des pêcheurs à la ligne (#05900)
- ♦ Alliance européenne des PMI/PME (#08494)
- ♦ Alliance européenne pour la santé publique (#08297)
- ♦ Alliance européenne pour la télévision et la culture (#05888)
- ♦ Alliance européenne des UCJG / see YMCA Europe (#21977)
- ♦ Alliance européenne des unions chrétiennes féminines / see European Young Women's Christian Association (#09135)
- ♦ Alliance évangélique européenne (#07010)
- ♦ Alliance évangélique universelle (#21393)
- ♦ Alliance des femmes pour la démocratie (#21013)
- ♦ Alliance des Femmes Evangeliques en Afrique (#18043)

♦ Alliance for Financial Inclusion (AFI) 00679

Alliance pour l'Inclusion Financière

Exec Dir Sasana Kijang 2, Jalan Dato' Onn, 50480 Kuala Lumpur, Malaysia. T. +60327769000. E-mail: communication@afi-global.org.
Head Communications address not obtained.
URL: http://www.afi-global.org/

History 2008. Founded as the first global knowledge sharing network designed exclusively for financial inclusion policymakers from developing countries. **Aims** Empower policymakers to increase access to quality financial services to the poorest populations. **Structure** Steering Committee; Management Unit. **Languages** English, French, Spanish. **Staff** 70.00 FTE, paid. **Finance** Sources: donations; members' dues; revenue from activities/projects. **Activities** Capacity building; events/meetings; knowledge management/information dissemination; projects/programmes; training/education. **Events** *Annual General Meeting* 2021, *Financial Inclusion Beyond the Pandemic – A Policy Leadership Dialogue* 2021, *Working Group Convergence Meeting* 2021, *Asia Pacific Regional Workshop on Fintech and Risk-Based Approach* Seoul (Korea Rep) 2017, *Annual Global Policy Forum* Sharm el Sheikh (Egypt) 2017. **Publications** Publications and multimedia pieces for policymakers. Members make their financial inclusion publications accessible either through the AFI library or by providing links directly to their own websites. **Information Services** *AFI Library*. **Members** Central banks and other financial regulatory institutions from over 90 developing countries. Membership countries not specified. [2021.09.01/XJ5270/y/**F**]

- ♦ Alliance for Food Aid (internationally oriented national body)

♦ Alliance for Food Sovereignty in Africa (AFSA) 00680

Coordinator PO Box 571, Kampala, Uganda. E-mail: afsa@afsafrica.org.
URL: https://afsafrica.org/

History 2008, Durban (South Africa). Launched at *United Nations Framework Convention on Climate Change (UNFCCC, 1992)* Conference of Parties 17 (COP 17). **Aims** Influence policies and promote African solutions for food sovereignty. **Structure** General Assembly; Board of Directors.
Members Core; Associate. Core includes 19 organizations listed in this Yearbook:
African Biodiversity Network (ABN, #00222); *African Centre for Biodiversity (ACB)*; *Coalition pour la Protection du Patrimoine Génétique Africain (COPAGEN, #04065)*; *Comité Ouest-Africain des Semences Paysannes (COASP)*; *Eastern and Southern Africa small scale Farmers' Forum (ESAFF, #05256)*; *Fahamu*; *Fellowship of Christian Councils and Churches in West Africa (FECCIWA, #09724)*; *Groundswell International (#10731)* (West Africa); *Health of Mother Earth Foundation (HOMEF)*; *Indigenous Peoples of Africa Coordinating Committee (IPACC, #11163)*; *Institut Africain pour le Développement Economique et Social – Centre Africain de Formation (INADES-Formation, #11233)*; *La Via Campesina (#20765)* (Africa); *Participatory Ecological Land Use Management (PELUM Association, #18225)*; *Plateforme Régionale des Organisations Paysannes d'Afrique Centrale (PROPAC)*; *Regional Schools and Colleges Permaculture Programme (ReSCOPE Programme, #18812)*; *Southern African Faith Communities' Environment Institute (SAFCEI)*; *West African Association for the Development of Artisanal Fisheries (WADAF, #20867)*; *West African Network of Farmers' Organizations and Agricultural Producers (#20891)*; *World Neighbors (WN)*. [2020/AA1173/**D**]

- ♦ Alliance française / see Fondation des Alliances Françaises (#09814)

♦ Alliance francophone 00681

Pres 24-26 avenue Perrichont, 75016 Paris, France. T. +33142307800. Fax +33142307810.
SG address not obtained.
URL: http://www.alliance-francophone.org/

History 6 Feb 1992. **Aims** Promote, in France and abroad, the influence of *Francophonie*, its potential and values. **Structure** General Assembly. Administrative Council. Bureau. **Finance** Members' dues. **Activities** Supports various projects: *'Le passeport étudiant francophone'*; *'Le musée de la presse'*. Awards prizes: Prix international de poésie francophone; Django d'or du jazz. **Publications** *La lettre Francophone* (4 a year).
Members Individuals and associations in 85 countries and territories:
Afghanistan, Algeria, Argentina, Australia, Austria, Bangladesh, Belgium, Benin, Brazil, Bulgaria, Burkina Faso, Cambodia, Cameroon, Central African Rep, Chad, Colombia, Congo Brazzaville, Congo DR, Côte d'Ivoire, Cuba, Djibouti, Dominican Rep, Egypt, France, Gabon, Germany, Greece, Guinea, Guinea-Bissau, Haiti, Hong Kong, Hungary, India, Indonesia, Iran Islamic Rep, Iraq, Ireland, Italy, Japan, Jordan, Korea Rep, Laos, Lebanon, Liberia, Libya, Luxembourg, Madagascar, Malaysia, Mali, Mauritania, Mexico, Morocco, Namibia, Netherlands, Niger, Nigeria, Pakistan, Palestine, Panama, Poland, Portugal, Québec, Romania, Russia, Rwanda, Saudi Arabia, Scotland, Senegal, Singapore, Somalia, South Africa, Spain, Sri Lanka, Sudan, Switzerland, Syrian AR, Taiwan, Thailand, Togo, Tunisia, United Arab Emirates, Uruguay, USA, Venezuela, Vietnam.
NGO Relations Member of: *Association francophone d'amitié et de liaison (AFAL, #02605).* [2022/XF0767/**F**]

- ♦ Alliance of Francophone Youth Movements (inactive)

♦ Alliance for the Freedom of Car Repair in the EU (AFCAR) 00682

Secretariat c/o FIGIEFA, Bd de la Woluwe 42, Bte 5, 1200 Brussels, Belgium. T. +3227619510. Fax +3227621255.
URL: http://www.figiefa.eu/alliances/

History as an alliance of European associations representing the interests of independent automotive aftermarket operators in the field of access to technical information.
Members Organizations (5):
Association Internationale des Réparateurs en Carosserie (AIRC, #02741); *European Council for Motor Trades and Repairs (#06832)*; *European Garage Equipment Association (EGEA, #07377)*; *Fédération Internationale de l'Automobile (FIA, #09613)*; *Fédération internationale des grossistes importateurs et exportateurs en fournitures automobiles (FIGIEFA, #09635).* [2019.09.27/XM7429/y/**E**]

- ♦ Alliance for Gender Equality in Europe (internationally oriented national body)
- ♦ Alliance Genève ACP pour les Droits de l'Homme (internationally oriented national body)
- ♦ Alliance Genève – Afrique Caraïbes Pacifique pour les Droits de l'Homme / see Alliance Genève ACP pour les Droits de l'Homme
- ♦ Alliance Genre et Eau (#10102)
- ♦ **the Alliance** Global Alliance for Trade Facilitation (#10232)
- ♦ Alliance globale contre les MGF (#10183)
- ♦ Alliance for Global Justice (internationally oriented national body)
- ♦ Alliance of Global Neonatal Nursing (unconfirmed)
- ♦ **The Alliance** Global Research Alliance for Sustainable Finance and Investment (#10571)
- ♦ Alliance of Global Talent Organizations (unconfirmed)

♦ Alliance for Global Water Adaptation (AGAW) 00683

Secretariat c/o SIWI, Linnégatan 87 A, Box 101 87, SE-100 55 Stockholm, Sweden. T. +46812136071.
URL: http://alliance4water.org/

History Sep 2010. An informal network organized through a charter. **Aims** Provide tools, partnerships, guidance and technical assistance to improve effective decision making, action, governance and analytical processes in water resources management, focusing on climate adaptation and mitigation. **Structure** Annual General Meeting; Steering Committee. Co-Chaired by *International Bank for Reconstruction and Development (IBRD, #12317)* (World Bank) and *Stockholm International Water Institute (SIWI)*. Secretariat currently hosted by SIWI. **Publications** *AGWA Updates* (12 a year) – internal electronic newsletter. Guides; reports. **Members** Regional and global development banks; government agencies and ministries; non-governmental organizations; private sector. Members (over 1,100) in over 100 countries. Membership countries not specified. [2018.01.11/XM5941/**E**]

♦ Alliance graphique internationale (AGI) 00684

Address not obtained.
URL: http://www.a-g-i.org/

History 3 Nov 1951, Paris (France). Registration: Switzerland. **Aims** Promote graphic design in lectures, education and publishing; encourage knowledge and understanding among the young and foster contact with other institutions, organizations and companies involved in graphic design. **Structure** General Assembly (annual); Presiding International Executive Committee. **Languages** English. **Finance** Sources: members' dues. **Activities** Events/meetings; networking/liaising. **Events** *Congress* Trieste (Italy) 2022, *Congress* Sydney, NSW (Australia) 2020, *Congress* Rotterdam (Netherlands) 2019, *Congress* Mexico City (Mexico) 2018, *Congress* Paris (France) 2017. **Publications** *AGI Members Newsletter. AGI Graphic Design.*
Members Individuals in 32 countries:
Australia, Austria, Belgium, Brazil, Canada, China, Czechia, Denmark, Finland, France, Germany, Greece, Hungary, Iran Islamic Rep, Israel, Italy, Japan, Korea Rep, Mexico, Netherlands, Norway, Poland, Portugal, Russia, South Africa, Spain, Sweden, Switzerland, Türkiye, UK, USA, Venezuela.
NGO Relations Member of: *International Council of Design (ICoD, #13013).* [2019/XC2083/v/**C**]

♦ Alliance for a Green Revolution in Africa (AGRA) 00685

Pres PO Box 66773, Westlands, Nairobi, 00800, Kenya. T. +254203675000. Fax +254203675401. E-mail: info@agra.org.
URL: http://agra.org/
History 12 Sep 2006. Founded by *Bill and Melinda Gates Foundation (BMGF)* and *The Rockefeller Foundation (#18966).* **Aims** Improve agricultural development in Africa by addressing both farming and relevant economic issues, including soil fertility and irrigation, farmer management practices and farmer access to markets and financing. **Structure** Board of Directors. Hosts: *Africa Enterprise Challenge Fund (AECF, #00168).* **Finance** Budget: US$ 85 million. **Events** *AGRF : Africa's Food Systems Forum* Kigali (Rwanda) 2022, *AGRF : Africa's Food Systems Forum* Kigali (Rwanda) 2021, *AGRF : African Green Revolution Forum* 2020, *AGRF : African Green Revolution Forum* Accra (Ghana) 2019, *All Africa Postharvest Congress* Addis Ababa (Ethiopia) 2019. **IGO Relations** Memorandum of Understanding with: *International Fund for Agricultural Development (IFAD, #13692).* Supports: *Africa Rice Center (AfricaRice, #00518); Alliance for Commodity Trade in Eastern and Southern Africa (ACTESA, #00668); Regional Centre for Mapping of Resources for Development (RCMRD, #18757).* Partner of: *West African Science Service Center on Climate Change and Adapted Land Use (WASCAL, #20897).* **NGO Relations** Memorandum of Understanding with (1): *PanAfrican Farmers' Organization (PAFO, #18049).* Member of (2): *Global Open Data for Agriculture and Nutrition (GODAN, #10514); InsideNGO (inactive).* Partner of (1): *Food and Land Use Coalition (FOLU).* Cooperates with (2): *African Fertilizer and Agribusiness Partnership (AFAP, #00314); International Fertilizer Development Center (IFDC, #13590).*
[2021/XM2842/**F**]

♦ Alliance for Harmonisation of Cellular Therapy Accreditation (AHCTA) 00686

Contact c/o Blutspende SRK Schweiz AG, Laupenstr 37, 3001 Bern, Switzerland. E-mail: wbmt_admin@wmda.info – mail@wbmt.org.
URL: https://www.wbmt.org/professionals/ahcta/
History 2009. A committee of *Worldwide Network for Blood and Marrow Transplantation (WBMT, #21929).* **Aims** Recommend policies, programs, and actions pertaining to regulatory matters, practices, and codes with both national and international implicationsto the WBMT Executive Committee. **Staff** 1.00 FTE, paid. **Activities** Guidance/assistance/consulting; healthcare; management of treaties and agreements; monitoring/evaluation; networking/liaising; projects/programmes; publishing activities; research and development; standards/guidelines. **Information Services** *Training practices of cell processing laboratory staff* in English.
Members Organizations (13):
AABB; American Society for Blood and Marrow Transplantation; *Center for International Blood and Marrow Transplant Research (CIBMTR, #03645); Eastern Mediterranean Blood and Marrow Transplantation Group (EMBMT, #05242); European Federation for Immunogenetics (EFI, #07141); European Society for Blood and Marrow Transplantation (EBMT, #08533); Foundation for the Accreditation of Cellular Therapy (FACT); International Society for Cell & Gene Therapy (ISCT, #15000)* (Europe); *International Society of Blood Transfusion (ISBT, #14979);* Joint Accreditation Committee ISCT (Europe)- EBMT; *Latin American Bone Marrow Transplantation Group (LABMT, #16257);* National Marrow Donor Program; *World Marrow Donor Association (WMDA, #21635).*
NGO Relations *Worldwide Network for Blood and Marrow Transplantation (WBMT, #21929).*
[2021.05.26/XM4436/y/**E**]

♦ Alliance for Health Promotion (A4HP) 00687

Sec Grand-Montfleury 48, 1290 Versoix GE, Switzerland. T. +41227555456. E-mail: secretariat@alliance4healthpromotion.org.
URL: https://allianceforhealthpromotion.org/
History Founded 1997, Jakarta (Indonesia), as *NGO Advisory Group on Health Promotion.* Current title adopted 22 Aug 2008, Geneva (Switzerland), when statutes were adopted. Statutes amended and approved 12 Nov 2010; most recently amended 2012. Registered in accordance with Swiss Civil Code. **Aims** Facilitate and support the work of NGOs and Civil Society for health promotion, at the international, regional, national and community levels; catalyze and coordinate NGOs and Civil Society in the promotion of health; partner with the World Health Organization building on the past contributions to promote the Jakarta and Bangkok Declarations and subsequent Conference Declarations. **Structure** Annual General Meeting; Board of 12 members. **Finance** Sources: donations; members' dues; sponsorship. Other sources: project overheads. **Events** *Global Forum on Health Promotion* Geneva (Switzerland) 2022, *Global Forum on Health Promotion* Ottawa, ON (Canada) 2020, *Annual General Meeting* Geneva (Switzerland) 2019, *Annual General Meeting* Geneva (Switzerland) 2017, *Annual General Meeting* Geneva (Switzerland) 2015.
Members Organizations, including the following 8 listed in this Yearbook:
Afro-European Medical and Research Network (AEMRN, #00538); Associated Country Women of the World (ACWW, #02338); Global Alliance for Women's Health (GAWH, #10233); Inter-African Committee on Traditional Practices Affecting the Health of Women and Children (IAC, #11384); International Council on Social Welfare (ICSW, #13076); International Federation of Medical Students' Associations (IFMSA, #13478); International Pharmaceutical Federation (#14566); International Pharmaceutical Students' Federation (IPSF, #14568); World Federation for Mental Health (WFMH, #21455).
Consultative Status Consultative status granted from: *ECOSOC (#05331)* (Special); *WHO (#20950)* (Official).
NGO Relations Cooperates with (1): *International Federation for Home Economics (IFHE, #13447).*
[2020/XJ2398/y/**A**]

♦ Alliance for Healthy Cities 00688

Secretariat c/o Promotion Committee for Healthy Cities, Kanda-surugadai 2-1-19-1112 Chiyoda-ku, Tokyo, 101-0062 Japan. T. +81355776780. Fax +81355776780. E-mail: alliance.ith@tmd.ac.jp.
URL: http://www.alliance-healthycities.com/
History Founded 17 Oct 2003, Manila (Philippines). **Aims** Protect and enhance the health of city dwellers. **Structure** General Assembly; Steering Committee; Secretariat. Working Committees; Committee on Awards. Chapters (4): Japan; China; Korean; China Hong Kong; Australian. **Finance** Members' dues. **Activities** Events/meetings. **Events** *Global Conference* Hong Kong (Hong Kong) 2020, *International Forum* Seoul (Korea Rep) 2020, *International Forum* Seoul (Korea Rep) 2019, *Global Conference* Kuching (Malaysia) 2018, *Global Conference* Wonju (Korea Rep) 2016.
Members Full: cities; provinces; governmental agencies. Associate: NGOs; academic institutions; national agencies; private sector; international agencies. Full in 10 countries and territories:
Australia, Cambodia, China, Hong Kong, Japan, Korea Rep, Malaysia, Mongolia, Philippines, Vietnam.
Associate in 8 countries and territories:
Australia, Hong Kong, Japan, Korea Rep, Malaysia, Philippines, Singapore, Taiwan.
Included in the above, 1 organization listed in this Yearbook: [2017/XM6256/**D**]

- ♦ Alliance hindoue mondiale (#21569)
- ♦ Alliance homme-environnement d'Afrique, Congo DR (unconfirmed)
- ♦ Alliance pour l'Inclusion Financière (#00679)
- ♦ Alliance of Independent Authors (internationally oriented national body)

♦ Alliance of Independent Press Councils of Europe (AIPCE) 00689

Contact c/o IPSO Gate House, 1 Farringdon Street, London, EC4M 7LG, UK.
URL: http://www.aipce.net/
History 1999. Founded as a informal group of self-regulation bodies. **Aims** Serve as a forum for exchanging ideas and sharing experience among press councils in Europe. **Languages** English. **Staff** None. **Finance** None. **Events** *Annual Meeting* Helsinki (Finland) 2018, *Annual Meeting* Budapest (Hungary) 2017, *Annual Meeting* Stockholm (Sweden) 2016, *Annual Meeting* Vienna (Austria) 2015, *Annual Meeting* Brussels (Belgium) 2014.
Members National organizations (34) in 34 countries and territories:
Albania, Armenia, Azerbaijan, Belgium, Bosnia-Herzegovina, Bulgaria, Croatia, Cyprus, Denmark, Estonia, Finland, France, Georgia, Germany, Hungary, Ireland, Israel, Kazakhstan, Kosovo, Luxembourg, Malta, Moldova, Montenegro, Netherlands, North Macedonia, Norway, Russia, Serbia, Slovenia, Spain, Sweden, Switzerland, UK, Ukraine.
NGO Relations Member of (1): *Ethical Journalism Network (EJN, #05554).* [2016.10.19/XJ3814/**F**]

- ♦ Alliance of Independent Publishers / see Alliance internationale des éditeurs indépendants
- ♦ Alliance of Independent Publishers for Another Globalization / see Alliance internationale des éditeurs indépendants

♦ Alliance of Independent recognised Members of Sport (AIMS) 00690

Contact c/o Maison du Sport Int, Ave de Rhodanie 54, 1007 Lausanne VD, Switzerland. E-mail: admin@aims.sport.
URL: https://aims.sport/
History 2009. Founded by 21 non-IOC recognized members of *Global Association of International Sport Federations (GAISF, inactive),* of which it was the 4th group. Current statutes adopted Nov 2021. **Aims** Strengthen each individual sport, combine expertise, share knowledge and maintain close cooperation with the International Olympic Committee (IOC), so that the individual sport will achieve official recognition from the IOC. **Structure** General Assembly; Council; Executive Board. **Languages** English.
Members Full: International Federations that are not members of ASOIF, AIOWF or ARISF (20):
Confédération internationale de la pêche sportive (CIPS, #04562); Fédération Internationale de Savate (FISav, #09656); Fédération Internationale de Teqball (FITEQ, #09663); Fédération Mondiale du Jeu de Dames (FMJD, #09690); International Aikido Federation (IAF, #11605); International Casting Sport Federation (ICSF, #12447); International Dragon Boat Federation (IDBF, #13197); International Federation of Sleddog Sports (IFSS, #13541); International Fistball Association (IFA, #13609); International Fitness and Bodybuilding Federation (IFBB, #13610); International Go Federation (IGF, #13726); International Kendo Federation (FIK, #13982); International Powerlifting Federation (IPF, #14630); International Practical Shooting Confederation (IPSC, #14631); International Sepaktakraw Federation (ISTAF, #14835); International Soft Tennis Federation (ISTF, #15555); Ju-Jitsu International Federation (JJIF, #16164); World Armwrestling Federation (WAF, #21110); World Darts Federation (WDF, #21355); World Minigolf Sport Federation (WMF, #21653).
Associate: federations currently members of ASOIF, AIOWF or ARISF (9):
Fédération internationale de SAMBO (FIAS, #09655); International Cheer Union (ICU, #12539); International Federation Icestocksport (IFI, #13455); International Federation of American Football (IFAF, #13354); International Federation of Muaythai Associations (IFMA, #13482); International Ski Mountaineering Federation (ISMF, #14871); World Association of Kickboxing Organizations (WAKO, #21151); World Flying Disc Federation (WFDF, #21509); World Lacrosse (#21616).
Observer (11):
Federation for International FootGolf (FIFG, #09672); International Federation of Match Poker (IFMP); International Jump Rope Union (IJRU, #13978); International Padel Federation (FIP, #14496); International Pole Sports Federation (IPSF, #14611); International Rafting Federation (IRF, #14691); International Rugby League (IRL, #14773); International Table Soccer Federation (ITSF, #15649); International Union of Kettlebell Lifting (IUKL, #15786); World Dodgeball Association (WDA, #21365); WORLD OBSTACLE (#21679).
NGO Relations Member of (1): *Olympic Movement (#17719).* Cooperates with (5): *Association of Summer Olympic International Federations (ASOIF, #02943); Association of the International Olympic Winter Sports Federations (AIOWF, #02757); Association of the IOC Recognized International Sports Federations (ARISF, #02767); Commonwealth Games Federation (CGF, #04332); The Association for International Sport for All (TAFISA, #02763).*
Recognized by: *International Olympic Committee (IOC, #14408).* Former membes which have received official recognition from IOC:
- *Union internationale des associations d'alpinisme (UIAA, #20420);*
- *World Flying Disc Federation (WFDF, #21509);*
- *International Federation of American Football (IFAF, #13354);*
- *International Cheer Union (ICU, #12539);*
- *International Federation of Muaythai Associations (IFMA, #13482);*
- *World Association of Kickboxing Organizations (WAKO, #21151);*
- *Fédération internationale de SAMBO (FIAS, #09655);*
- *World Lacrosse (#21616);*
- *International Federation Icestocksport (IFI, #13455).* [2022/XM4778/y/**C**]

♦ Alliance inter-monastères (AIM) 00691

Alliance for International Monasticism – Alianza Inter-Monasterios
SG 7 rue d'Issy, 92170 Vanves, France. T. +33146447957. E-mail: aim.vanves@wanadoo.fr.
USA Section Saint Benedict Center, 345 East Ninth St, Erie PA 16503, USA. T. +18144597199. Fax +18144598066.
URL: http://www.aimintl.org/
History 1961. Founded as a 'Secretariat for Mission', within the framework of *Benedictine Confederation.* Former names and other names: *Aide à l'implantation monastique* – former (1966 to 1976); *Aide inter-monastères* – former (1976 to 1997). **Aims** Promote human, cultural and religious development of *benedictine monasteries* throughout the world and of their surrounding populations. **Structure** Comes under the authority of the Abbot Primate in Rome (Italy). International Council; Executive Committee; Secretariats in France, Italy, UK and USA. **Languages** English, French, German, Spanish. **Staff** France: 2 (1 monk and 1 nun); UK: 2 (monks); USA: 2 (sisters); Germany: 1 (monk); Brazil: 1 (monk). **Finance** Financed by monasteries of the Western world. Annual budget: 600,000 EUR. **Activities** Financial and/or material support; guidance/assistance/consulting; religious activities. **Publications** *Bulletin de l'AIM* (2 a year) in English, French, German, Italian, Portuguese, Spanish. *So Far Yet so Near – Monasticism for a New World* (2012); *Annuaire des Monastères bénédictins et cisterciens dans les jeunes Eglises* (1996). Books; brochures.
Members Communities in 58 countries and territories:
Angola, Argentina, Bahamas, Belize, Benin, Bolivia, Brazil, Burkina Faso, Cameroon, Central African Rep, Chile, Colombia, Congo Brazzaville, Congo DR, Costa Rica, Côte d'Ivoire, Dominican Rep, Ecuador, Ethiopia, Ghana, Guatemala, Guinea, Guyana, Haiti, Hong Kong, India, Indonesia, Israel, Japan, Kenya, Korea Rep, Lebanon, Madagascar, Mali, Mexico, Morocco, Namibia, Nicaragua, Nigeria, Paraguay, Peru, Philippines, Puerto Rico, Rwanda, Senegal, South Africa, Sri Lanka, St Lucia, Taiwan, Tanzania UR, Togo, Trinidad-Tobago, Uganda, Uruguay, Venezuela, Vietnam, Zambia, Zimbabwe.
NGO Relations Instrumental in setting up (2): *Monastic Interreligious Dialogue (#16849); Monastic Interreligious Dialogue – North America (MID).* [2022.10.20/XF2924/**F**]

- ♦ Alliance for International Conflict Prevention and Resolution / see Alliance for Peacebuilding
- ♦ Alliance for International Conflict Resolution / see Alliance for Peacebuilding

♦ Alliance of International Corporate Advisors (AICA) 00692

Exec Dir Hoogheimstraplein 82, 3514 AX Utrecht, Netherlands.
URL: https://aicanetwork.com/
History 2009. **Aims** Provide investors and middle market companies with access to proven investment banking expertise and resources on an international basis. **Structure** Board of Directors. **Activities** Events/meetings. **Events** *Annual Global Meeting* Dublin (Ireland) 2023, *Annual Global Meeting* Vancouver, BC (Canada) 2022, *Annual Global Meeting* Singapore (Singapore) 2019.
Members Firms (over 40) in 29 countries:
Australia, Belgium, Brazil, Canada, China, Czechia, Denmark, Finland, France, Germany, India, Ireland, Israel, Italy, Japan, Korea Rep, Mexico, Netherlands, Norway, Poland, Singapore, South Africa, Spain, Switzerland, Thailand, Türkiye, UK, USA, Vietnam.
[2022.10.12/AA0180/**C**]

- ♦ Alliance internationale des administrateurs de biens immobiliers / see Fédération internationale des professions immobilières (#09653)
- ♦ Alliance internationale pour une agriculture viable (internationally oriented national body)

♦ Alliance internationale d'aide à l'enfance / see Save the Children International (#19058)

♦ Alliance Internationale – Association des anciens et amis de la Cité internationale universitaire de Paris 00693

International Alliance – Association of Former Students of the Cité internationale universitaire de Paris

Pres 21 boulevard Jourdan, 75014 Paris CEDEX 14, France. T. +33144166550. Fax +33153620257. E-mail: contact@allianceinternationale.org.
URL: http://www.allianceinternationale.org/

History 1948, Paris (France). Also referred to as *Association des anciens résidents et amis de la Cité internationale universitaire de Paris*. **Aims** Serve the work of international comprehension and friendship by continuing contacts and friendship created by residents during their stay at the Cité Internationale of the University of Paris (CIUP). **Structure** Annual General Assembly; Administrative Council. **Languages** French. **Staff** 1.00 FTE, paid. **Finance** Members' dues. **Activities** Networking/liaising; knowledge management/ information dissemination; guidance/assistance/consulting; events/meetings. **Events** *General Assembly* Paris (France) 1993, *General Assembly* Paris (France) 1986. **Publications** Online newsletter (10 a year). Information Services: Alumni directory (database) of more than 65,000 former residents now living all over the world.
Members Individuals in 74 countries and territories:
Algeria, Argentina, Australia, Austria, Belgium, Benin, Bolivia, Brazil, Burkina Faso, Cambodia, Cameroon, Canada, Chile, China, Colombia, Comoros, Congo DR, Costa Rica, Côte d'Ivoire, Cuba, Czechia, Denmark, Egypt, Finland, France, Gabon, Germany, Greece, Guiana Fr, Honduras, Hong Kong, Hungary, India, Ireland, Israel, Italy, Japan, Korea DPR, Korea Rep, Lebanon, Luxembourg, Madagascar, Mauritius, Mexico, Monaco, Morocco, Myanmar, Netherlands, New Zealand, Norway, Pakistan, Poland, Portugal, Romania, Russia, Saudi Arabia, Senegal, Serbia, Slovakia, South Africa, Spain, Sri Lanka, Sweden, Switzerland, Taiwan, Thailand, Togo, Tunisia, Türkiye, UK, Uruguay, USA, Venezuela, Vietnam.
IGO Relations *Council of Europe (CE, #04881); UNESCO (#20322); WHO (#20950).* [2017.08.13/XE4220/v/E]

♦ Alliance internationale pour la consolidation de la paix / see Interpeace (#15962)
♦ Alliance internationale contre le VIH/SIDA / see Frontline AIDS (#10007)
♦ Alliance internationale de coopération scolaire (inactive)
♦ Alliance internationale corcovado / see Centre de Solidarité Internationale Corcovado
♦ Alliance Internationale pour la défense des Droits et des Libertés (internationally oriented national body)
♦ Alliance internationale de la distribution par câble / see GIGAEurope AISBL (#10151)
♦ Alliance for International Education (internationally oriented national body)
♦ Alliance for International Educational and Cultural Exchange / see Alliance for International Exchange
♦ Alliance internationale des éditeurs indépendants (internationally oriented national body)
♦ Alliance internationale pour l'entreprise digitalisée (#13175)
♦ Alliance internationale des femmes (#11639)
♦ Alliance Internationale des Femmes pour le Café (internationally oriented national body)
♦ Alliance internationale pour la gestion de l'eau de pluie (#14695)
♦ Alliance internationale de l'hôtellerie (inactive)
♦ Alliance internationale de journalistes (internationally oriented national body)
♦ Alliance internationale de journalistes et écrivains latins (inactive)
♦ Alliance internationale des juifs chrétiens / see International Messianic Jewish Alliance (#14148)
♦ Alliance internationale des organisateurs équestres (#13289)
♦ Alliance internationale des organisations de patients (#11633)
♦ Alliance internationale des peuples autochtones-tribaux des forêts tropicales (#11629)
♦ Alliance internationale des peuples indigènes des forêts tropicales / see International Alliance of the Indigenous Tribal Peoples of the Tropical Forests (#11629)
♦ Alliance internationale pour la protection du patrimoine dans les zones en conflit (#11635)
♦ Alliance internationale pour la réforme du chanvre (inactive)
♦ Alliance Internationale Sainte Jeanne d'Arc / see St Joan's International Alliance (#19992)
♦ Alliance internationale "Save the Children" / see Save the Children International (#19058)
♦ Alliance internationale pour le suffrage et l'action civique et politique des femmes / see International Alliance of Women (#11639)
♦ Alliance internationale pour le suffrage des femmes / see International Alliance of Women (#11639)

♦ Alliance internationale de tourisme (AIT) 00694

International Touring Alliance

Pres Chemin de Blandonnet 2, 1215 Geneva 15, Switzerland. T. +41225444400. Fax +41225444450. E-mail: ait-admin@fia.com.
Admin Services c/o FIA, 8 place de la Concorde, 75008 Paris, France. T. +33143124455. Fax +33143124466. E-mail: ait-admin@fia.com.
URL: http://www.ait-touringalliance.com/information

History 4 Aug 1898, Luxembourg. Statutes adjusted 1975 to new regional structure. Former names and other names: *Ligue internationale des associations touristes (LIAT)* – former (4 Aug 1898 to May 1919). Registration: Switzerland. **Aims** Represent the interests of national *automobile* associations and touring clubs; represent the interests of *cyclists* at an international level. **Structure** General Assembly (annual); Committee, comprising President, Vice-President and Treasurer. **Languages** English. **Finance** Sources: members' dues. Other sources: contributions from the production of documents. **Activities** Knowledge management/information dissemination; research/documentation. **Events** *Annual General Assembly* Paris (France) 2015, *Annual General Assembly* Doha (Qatar) 2014, *Annual General Assembly* Paris (France) 2013, *Annual General Assembly* Istanbul (Turkey) 2012, *Annual General Assembly* Delhi (India) 2011. **Publications** Assembly reports. **Members** Automobile associations, touring clubs, organizations involved in open-air tourism and national tourist organizations. Total membership comprises over 120 affiliates grouping over 100 million individual members in 97 countries. Membership countries not specified. **IGO Relations** Participates in the work of: *United Nations Economic Commission for Europe (UNECE, #20555).* Accredited by: *United Nations Office at Vienna (UNOV, #20604).* Associated with Department of Global Communications of the United Nations. **NGO Relations** Member of: *Fédération des Institutions Internationales établies à Genève (FIIG, #09599).* Close cooperation with: *Fédération Internationale de l'Automobile (FIA, #09613).* Joint organizations with FIA: *AIT and FIA Information Centre (no recent information).* In liaison with technical committees of: *International Organization for Standardization (ISO, #14473).* [2019/XB2636/B]

♦ Alliance for International Exchange (internationally oriented national body)

♦ Alliance of International Market Research Institutes (AIMRI) 00695

Sec 26 Granard Avenue, London, SW15 6HJ, UK. T. +442087803343. Fax +442082466893.
URL: http://www.aimri.net/

History 1991, Bruges (Belgium), as *Association of European Market Research Institutes (AEMRI)*, by 32 independent research agencies. **Aims** Represent the corporate and business interests of international market research agencies with the aim to help them win more business. **Structure** Council, comprising Chairman and 12 international members. **Languages** English. **Staff** 2.00 FTE, paid. **Finance** Members' dues. **Activities** Organizes conferences; promotes business interests of members. **Events** *Conference* Limassol (Cyprus) 2012, *Conference* New York, NY (USA) 2012, *Conference* Prague (Czech Rep) 2012, *Conference* London (UK) 2011, *Conference* Munich (Germany) 2011. **Publications** *AIMRI Newsletter* (12 a year); *Synergie* (4 a year).
Members Full (80) in 30 countries and territories:
Austria, Belgium, Brazil, Canada, China, Denmark, Egypt, France, Germany, Greece, Hong Kong, India, Iran Islamic Rep, Ireland, Italy, Japan, Korea Rep, Netherlands, Nigeria, Pakistan, Portugal, Romania, Russia, South Africa, Spain, Sweden, Switzerland, UK, United Arab Emirates, USA. [2012.06.06/XD7762/D]

♦ The Alliance for International Medical Action / see ALIMA (#00636)
♦ Alliance for International Monasticism (#00691)

♦ Alliance of International Science Organizations (ANSO) 00696

Exec Dir No 16 Lincui Road, Chaoyang District, 100101 Beijing, China. T. +861084249454. E-mail: anso-public@anso.org.cn.
URL: http://www.anso.org.cn/

History 4 Nov 2018, Beijing (China). Former names and other names: *Alliance of International Science Organizations in the Belt and Road Region* – alias. **Aims** Become an international science organization of global impact in catalyzing and implementing concrete innovative programs, initiatives and actions in Science, Technology, Innovation and Capacity Building (STIC) for the promotion of shared-development and the advancement of the UN Sustainable Development Goals (SDGs). **Structure** General Assembly; Governing Board; Secretariat. **Activities** Awards/prizes/competitions; guidance/assistance/consulting; projects/programmes; training/education. **Publications** *ANSO Update.* Brochure; reports.
Members Full in 31 countries and territories:
Armenia, Bangladesh, Belarus, Belgium, Brazil, Bulgaria, Chile, China, Egypt, Hong Kong, Hungary, Iran Islamic Rep, Kazakhstan, Kenya, Kyrgyzstan, Macau, Mexico, Mongolia, Morocco, Nepal, New Zealand, Pakistan, Poland, Romania, Russia, Slovenia, Sri Lanka, Tajikistan, Thailand, Türkiye, Uzbekistan.
European Academy of Sciences and Arts (EASA, #05814); International Centre for Integrated Mountain Development (ICIMOD, #12500); TWAS (#20270); UNESCO (#20322). [2020/AA1154/y/C]

♦ Alliance of International Science Organizations in the Belt and Road Region / see Alliance of International Science Organizations (#00696)

♦ Alliance for Internet of Things Innovation (AIOTI) 00697

SG Avenue Louise 87, 1050 Brussels, Belgium. E-mail: info@aioti.eu.
URL: https://aioti.eu/

History Registration: No/ID: 0663.895.516, Start date: 26 Jul 2016, Belgium; EU Transparency Register, No/ID: 380738729287-22, Start date: 12 Dec 2017. **Aims** Enhance innovation and economic development in the Internet of Things in Europe. **Structure** General Assembly; Management Board; Steering Board; Working Gropus; Secretariat. **Events** *Signature Event* Brussels (Belgium) 2022, *Signature Event* Brussels (Belgium) 2021. **Publications** *AIOTI Monthly Newsletter* (12 a year).
Members Full; Associate. Membership countries not specified.
Committee for European Construction Equipment (CECE, #04254); COPA – european farmers (COPA, #04829); ERTICO ITS Europe (#05532); European Agricultural Machinery Association (CEMA, #05846); European Association of the Machine tool Industries and related Manufacturing Technologies (CECIMO, #06113); European Construction Technology Platform (ECTP, #06768); European Digital SME Alliance (#06925); European Telecommunications Standards Institute (ETSI, #08897); European Ventilation Industry Association (EVIA, #09052); General Confederation of Agricultural Cooperatives in the European Union (#10107); GS1 (#10809); LightingEurope (#16472); Mandat International; SINTEF; Toy Industries of Europe (TIE, #20179).
NGO Relations Memorandum of Understanding with (1): *European Technology Platform for High Performance Computing (ETP4HPC, #08889).* [2020/AA0081/y/D]

♦ Alliance interreligieuse interculturelle de Genève (internationally oriented national body)

♦ Alliance israélite universelle (AIU) 00698

Dir 27 av de Ségur, 75007 Paris, France. T. +33153328855. E-mail: info@aiu.org.
Pres address not obtained.
URL: http://www.aiu.org/

History Founded 1860, Paris (France). **Aims** Contribute to development of *Jewish* education and culture. **Structure** Haut Conseil de l'Alliance (High Council); Administrative Council. **Languages** English, French, Hebrew. **Staff** 30.00 FTE, paid; 5.00 FTE, voluntary. **Finance** Subscriptions; donations; grants. Annual budget: euro 5,000,000. **Activities** Events/meetings; training/education; knowledge management/information dissemination. Active in: Belgium, Canada, France, Israel, Morocco, Spain. **Events** *Colloquium* Paris (France) 2005, *Colloquium* Paris (France) 2004, *Colloquium* Paris (France) 2003, *Colloquium* Paris (France) 2002, *Colloquium* Paris (France) 2001.
Members Committees, chapters or branches totalling 8,000 members in 9 countries:
Belgium, Canada, France, Israel, Morocco, Spain, Switzerland, UK, USA.
NGO Relations Member of: *Association francophone d'amitié et de liaison (AFAL, #02605); Consultative Council of Jewish Organizations (CCJO, no recent information).* Instrumental in setting up: *Collège des études juives (CEJ); European Institute Emmanuel Levinas (IEEL).* [2019.02.12/XF3405/F]

♦ Alliance in Jesus through Mary, 1925 (religious order)

♦ Alliance of Jumping Organizers (AJO) 00699

SG address not obtained. T. +31653472520.
URL: http://www.equestrianorganizers.com/_html/main_ajo.php

History 1 Dec 2000, Amsterdam (Netherlands). **Aims** Promote *equestrian* sport worldwide; observe and protect equine rights and ethical behaviour in equestrian sport; promote fair-play in sports. **Structure** General Assembly. Executive Board, comprising President, Vice-President, Secretary-General and 7 further members. **Finance** Members' dues. **Activities** Sportinng activities. **Events** *Meeting* Aachen (Germany) 2015, *Meeting* Paris (France) 2004, *Meeting* Madrid (Spain) 2001. **Members** Organizers of international show-jumping events (70). Membership countries not specified. **NGO Relations** Member of: *International Equestrian Organisers' Alliance (IEOA, #13289).* [2015/XF6664/F]

♦ Alliance de laboratoires européens pour la recherche et la technologie (#00700)

♦ Alliance of Laboratories in Europe for Education, Research and Technology (ALERT Geomaterials) 00700

Alliance de laboratoires européens pour la recherche et la technologie (ALERT Géomatériaux)

Contact Laboratoire 3SR / Bât Galilée, CS 40700, 38058 Grenoble, France. E-mail: director@alertgeomaterials.eu.

History 1989. Registration: Start date: 2006, France. **Aims** Develop a European School of Thinking in the field of the Mechanics of Geomaterials. **Structure** Board of Directors; Bureau. **Activities** Awards/prizes/competitions; events/meetings; training/education.
Members Universities and organizations in 13 countries:
Austria, Belgium, Czechia, France, Germany, Greece, Italy, Netherlands, Norway, Spain, Sweden, Switzerland, UK.
Associate in 3 countries:
Australia, France, USA. [2021/AA1839/D]

♦ Alliance to Lay New Foundations for Governance in Africa / see Alliance for Rebuilding Governance in Africa (#00715)

♦ Alliance of Leading Environmental Researchers & Thinkers (ALERT) 00701

Dir address not obtained. E-mail: alert@alert-conservation.org.
URL: http://alert-conservation.org/

Aims Help world-class scientists to influence key environmental decisions; help scientists to communicate dynamically via the growing power of social media with journalists and the general public; promote and disseminate cutting-edge environmental research; help journalists to connect with leading environmental experts. **Activities** Guidance/assistance/consulting; knowledge management/information dissemination; research/documentation. **NGO Relations** Partner of (1): *Re:wild.* [2021/AA2218/v/C]

♦ Alliance of Liberals and Democrats for Europe / see Renew Europe (#18840)

♦ Alliance of Liberals and Democrats for Europe (ALDE) 00702

Secretariat Room 5.081, Council of Europe, 67075 Strasbourg CEDEX, France. T. +33388412682. Fax +33388413761.
URL: http://www.alde-pace.org/

History Founded 1974, as *Liberal Group.* Changed title to *Liberal, Democratic and Reformers' Group (LDR) – Groupe libéral, démocrate et réformateur (LDR)*, mid-1980s, as a political group of the *Parliamentary Assembly of the Council of Europe (PACE, #18211).* Current title adopted, 2005, to reinforce cooperation with *Renew Europe (#18840).* **Aims** Guard Council of Europe values, through enhanced *political* action inside and outside the Parliamentary Assembly. **Structure** General Assembly; Bureau. **Languages** English, French, German, Italian, Russian. **Finance** Annual budget: euro 100,000. **Activities** Events/meetings. **Publications** Annual bulletin; newsletters; reports.
Members Parliamentarians (76) in 30 countries:
Andorra, Armenia, Azerbaijan, Belgium, Bulgaria, Croatia, Czechia, Denmark, Estonia, Finland, Georgia, Germany, Iceland, Ireland, Italy, Latvia, Liechtenstein, Lithuania, Luxembourg, Moldova, Monaco, Netherlands, North Macedonia, Norway, Serbia, Slovenia, Spain, Sweden, Switzerland, Ukraine. [2018.07.23/XF3609/v/F]

♦ Alliance of Liberals and Democrats for Europe – Committee of the Regions / see Renew Europe – Committee of the Regions (#18841)
♦ Alliance of Liberals and Democrats for Europe of the Parliamentary Assembly of the Council of Europe / see Alliance of Liberals and Democrats for Europe (#00702)

♦ Alliance of Liberals and Democrats for Europe Party (ALDE Party) . 00703

Parti de l'Alliance des Démocrates et des Libéraus pour l'Europe – Partido de la Alianza de los Demócratas y Liberales por Europa – Europäische Liberale, Demokratische und Reformpartei – Partido Aliança dos Democratas e Liberais pela Europa – Partito dell'Alleanza dei Democratici e dei Liberali per l'Europa – Partij van de Alliantie van Liberalen en Democraten voor Europa – Partiet Alliansen Liberaler och Demorater för Europa – Alliancen af Liberale og Demokrater for Europa – Euroopan Liberaalidemokraattisten Puolueiden Liitto – Pairti Chomhghuailliocht na Liobralaithe agus na nDaonlathaithe don Eoraip – Strana Aliance Liberalu a Demokratu pro Evropu – Strana Aliancie liberalov Demokratov za Európu – A Liberalisok és Demokratak Szövetsége Európaért Part – Partia Porozumienia Liberałów Demokratów na rzecz Europy – Stranka Zaveznistva Liberalcev in Demokratov za Evropo – Euroopa Demokraatide ja Liberaalide Liidu Erakond – Partija "Eiropas Liberalu un Demokratu Apvieniba – Liberalu ir Demokratu Aljanso uz Europa Partija – Partidul Alianta Liberalilor si Democratilor pentru Europa – Avrupa Icin Liberaller ve Demokratlar Ittifaki Partisi

SG Rue d'Idalie 11, 1050 Brussels, Belgium. T. +3222370140. Fax +3222311907. E-mail: info@aldeparty.eu.
URL: http://www.aldeparty.eu/

History Constituent Congress, 26-27 Mar 1976, Stuttgart (Germany) when statutes adopted; most recently revised Apr 2004, Brussels (Belgium). Former names and other names: *Federation of Liberal and Democratic Parties in the European Community* – former (1976 to 1986); *Fédération des partis libéraux et démocratiques de la Communauté européenne* – former (1976 to 1986); *Federation of Liberal, Democrat and Reform Parties of the European Community* – former (1986); *Fédération des partis libéraux, démocratiques et réformateurs de la Communauté européenne* – former (1986); *Federation of European Liberal, Democrat and Reform Parties* – former (1993); *Fédération des partis libéraux, démocratiques et réformateurs européens* – former (1993); *European Liberal, Democrat and Reform Party (ELDR)* – former (8 Dec 1993 to 8 Nov 2012); *Parti européen des libéraux, démocrates et réformateurs* – former; *Partido Europeo de los Liberales, Demócratas y Reformistas* – former; *Europäische Liberale, Demokratische und Reformpartei* – former; *Partido Europeu dos Liberais, Democratas e Reformistas* – former; *Partito Europeo dei Liberali, Democratici e Riformatori* – former; *Europese Liberale en Democratische Partij* – former; *Europeiska Liberala och Demokratiska Partiet* – former; *Europaeiske Liberal Demokratiske og Reform Parti* – former; *Euroopan liberaali demokraattinen puolue* – former; *Evropska liberalne democraticka a reformni strana* – former; *Európska liberalna, demokraticka a reformna strana* – former; *Európai Liberalis, Demokrata és Reformpart* – former; *Europejska Partia Liberalnych Demokratów Partia* – former; *Stranka Evropskih liberalcev, demokratov in reformistov* – former; *Euroopa Liberaalide, Demokraatide ja Reformistide Partei* – former; *Eiropas Liberaldemoratiska reformu partija* – former; *Europos liberalu democratu ir reformu partija* – former; *El Partit Liberal, Demòcrata i Reformista Europeu* – former; *Pairti Daonlathach Liobralach agus Athchóiriú Eorpach* – former; *Partidul European al Liberalilor, Democratilor si Reformistilor* – former; *Avrupa Liberal, Demokrat ve Reform Partisi* – former. Registration: Belgium. **Aims** Bring together political parties and individuals in Europe who, within the framework of liberal, democratic and reformist ideals, wish to contribute to the *European Union*. **Structure** Congress (annual); Council; Bureau; Leaders and Ministers Meetings. Registered Office and Secretariat located in Brussels (Belgium). **Languages** English, French. **Staff** 25.00 FTE, paid. **Finance** Sources: contributions; members' dues. European Parliament subvention (linked to election result). **Activities** Awareness raising; networking/liaising; politics/policy/regulatory. **Events** *Congress* Brussels (Belgium) 2021, *Congress* Athens (Greece) 2019, *Congress* Madrid (Spain) 2018, *Congress* Amsterdam (Netherlands) 2017, *Congress* Warsaw (Poland) 2016. **Publications** *Liberal Insider* (weekly) in English – newsletter; *Liberal Insider Pro* (10 a year) in English – Newsletter; *ALDE Party Liberal Bulletin* (2 a year) in English – ALDE Party's magazine. Congress proceedings; election manifesto; brochures. **Members** Individuals (1,100); Parties (70) in 44 countries, of which 27 EU Member States. Membership countries not specified. **NGO Relations** Member of (1): *European Movement International (EMI, #07825)*. Cooperates with (2): *European Liberal Forum (ELF, #07689)*; *Liberal International (LI, #16454)*. [2021.10.25/XE5355/**E**]

♦ Alliance libre européenne (#07356)

♦ Alliance des ligues francophones africaines et méditerranéennes (ALIAM) 00704

Alliance of African and Mediterranean French-speaking Leagues

Contact 14 rue Corvisart, 75013 Paris, France. T. +33153552889. Fax +33153552549.
URL: http://www.aliam.org/

History Oct 2009. Former names and other names: *Alliance des Ligues francophones, africaines et méditerranéennes contre le cancer (ALIAM)* – full title; *Alliance of African and Mediterranean french speaking Leagues for cancer control* – full title; *ALIAM MNT* – alias. Registration: France. **Aims** Cooperate with patients, their relatives and health professionals and institutions; develop the fights against cancer through promotion of North-South and South-South cooperation between leagues, associations and NGOs. **Structure** Committee. **Activities** Events/meetings. **Events** *Meeting* Paris (France) 2013, *Congrès francophone international de stomatologie et de chirurgie maxillo-faciale* Marrakech (Morocco) 2012, *Rencontres africaines francophones de diabétologie* Brazzaville (Congo Brazzaville) 2011, *Meeting* Monastir (Tunisia) 2011, *Prévention des risques communs aux maladies non transmissibles* Tunis (Tunisia) 2011.
Members Full in 26 countries:
Algeria, Benin, Burkina Faso, Burundi, Cameroon, Chad, Comoros, Congo Brazzaville, Congo DR, Côte d'Ivoire, Djibouti, Egypt, France, Gabon, Guinea, Israel, Lebanon, Madagascar, Mali, Mauritania, Mauritius, Morocco, Nigeria, Senegal, Syrian AR, Tunisia, Türkiye.
IGO Relations Partner of (1): *Organisation internationale de la Francophonie (OIF, #17809)*. **NGO Relations** Partner of (2): *Agence universitaire de La Francophonie (AUF, #00548)*; *Conférence internationale des doyens des facultés de médecine d'expression française (CIDMEF, #04616)*. [2017/XJ4546/**C**]

♦ Alliance des Ligues francophones, africaines et méditerranéennes contre le cancer / see Alliance des ligues francophones africaines et méditerranéennes (#00704)

♦ Alliance for Lobbying Transparency and Ethics Regulation (ALTER-EU) 00705

Coordinator c/o Mundo B, Rue d'Edimbourg 26, 1050 Brussels, Belgium. T. +3228931062. E-mail: info@alter-eu.org.
URL: http://www.alter-eu.org/

History 19 Jul 2005, Brussels (Belgium). Registration: Banque-Carrefour des Entreprises, No/ID: 0545.919.562, Start date: 10 Feb 2014, Belgium; EU Transparency Register, No/ID: 2694372574-63, Start date: 29 Oct 2008. **Aims** Provide a cohesive and consolidated approach to campaigning in Europe on curbing the influence of corporations on the political agenda in Europe, the resulting loss of democracy in EU decision-making and the postponement, weakening or blockage of urgently needed progress on social, environmental and consumer-protection reforms. **Structure** Steering Committee.
Members EU Civil Society Organizations; Academic Supporters; Law firms; Consultancies; Member organizations outside the EU. Members (over 200). EU Civil Society Organizations in 23 countries:
Austria, Belgium, Bosnia-Herzegovina, Czechia, Denmark, Estonia, Finland, France, Germany, Greece, Hungary, Ireland, Italy, Luxembourg, Malta, Netherlands, Poland, Portugal, Romania, Slovakia, Spain, Sweden, UK.
Included in the above, 28 organizations listed in this Yearbook:
- *Action for Solidarity, Equality, Environment and Diversity (A SEED, #00098)*;
- *Association for the Taxation of Financial Transactions for the Aid of Citizens (#02947)*;
- *Both ENDS (#03307)*;
- *CEE Bankwatch Network (#03624)*;
- *Comhlamh*;
- *Corporate Europe Observatory (CEO, #04839)*;
- *European Centre of the International Council of Women (ECICW, #06485)*;
- *European Citizen Action Service (ECAS, #06555)*;
- *European Coalition for Corporate Justice (ECCJ, #06591)*;
- *European Federation of Journalists (EFJ, #07152)*;
- *European Federation of Public Service Unions (EPSU, #07202)*;
- *European Network on Debt and Development (EURODAD, #07891)*;
- *Fern (#09736)*;
- *Friends of the Earth Europe (FoEE, #10001)*;
- *Greenpeace International (#10727)* (European Office);
- *Health Action International (HAI, #10868)* (European Office);
- *International Baby Food Action Network (IBFAN, #12305)* (European Office);
- *Kairos-Europe*;
- *Leave it in the Ground Coalition (LINGO)*;
- *Mani Tese (MT)*;
- *Nonviolent Peaceforce (NP, #17153)*;
- *Pesticide Action Network Europe (#18338)*;
- *Pesticide Action Network (PAN, #18336)*;
- *Privacy International (PI, #18504)*;
- *Public Services International (PSI, #18572)*;
- *Quaker Council for European Affairs (QCEA, #18587)*;
- *Sciences Citoyennes*;
- *SERVAS International (#19234)*.

Organizations outside the EU in 7 countries:
Andorra, Bangladesh, Brazil, Iraq, Lebanon, Mexico, USA.
Included in the above, 1 organization listed in this Yearbook:
International Gender and Trade Network (IGTN, #13707).
NGO Relations Member of (1): *Citizens for Europe (CFEU, #03956)*. [2020/XM0434/**F**]

♦ Alliance for Logistics Innovation through Collaboration in Europe / see European Technology Platform ALICE (#08888)
♦ Alliance Maghreb-Machrek pour l'eau (#16544)
♦ Alliance des maires et des responsables municipaux sur le VIH/SIDA en Afrique (#00707)

♦ Alliance for Malaria Prevention (AMP) 00706

Administrative Coordinator address not obtained. E-mail: allianceformalariaprevention@gmail.com.
URL: http://allianceformalariaprevention.com/

Aims Promote malaria prevention with long lasting insecticide treated nets (LLINs), both through mass distribution campaigns and through continuous distribution channels. **Structure** Core Group.
Members Partners (over 40) government agencies; private sector businesses; public sector organizations; faith-based organizations; humanitarian organizations. Included in the above, 21 listed in this Yearbook:
- *Catholic Relief Services (CRS, #03608)*;
- *FHI 360*;
- *Global Fund to Fight AIDS, Tuberculosis and Malaria (Global Fund, #10383)*;
- *Global Health Advocates (#10400)*;
- *His Nets*;
- *International Federation of Red Cross and Red Crescent Societies (#13526)*;
- *Lutheran World Relief (LWR)*;
- *Malaria Consortium*;
- *Malaria No More*;
- *Medical Care Development International (MCDI)*;
- *MENTOR Initiative*;
- *NetsforLife*;
- *PATH (#18260)* (MACEPA);
- *PSI (#18555)*;
- *RTI International*;
- *UNICEF (#20332)*;
- *United Methodist Committee on Relief (UMCOR)*;
- *United Nations Foundation (UNF, #20563)*;
- *United States Agency for International Development (USAID)*;
- *World Vision International (WVI, #21904)*;
- *Y's Men International (#19326)*. [2015/XJ8622/y/**E**]

♦ Alliance Mariale (see: #21334)
♦ Alliance of Marine Mammal Parks and Aquariums (internationally oriented national body)

♦ Alliance of Mayors and Municipal Leaders on HIV/AIDS in Africa (AMICAALL) 00707

Alliance des maires et des responsables municipaux sur le VIH/SIDA en Afrique

Country Dir Alliance of Mayors Secretariat, PO Box 60401, Katutura, Windhoek, Namibia. T. +26461300754. Fax +26461300798. E-mail: cd@amicaall-namibia.org.
URL: http://www.amicaall.org/

History Jan 1998, Abidjan (Côte d'Ivoire). **Structure** Coordinating Committee; Secretariat in Namibia. **Activities** Projects/programmes. **Publications** *AMICAALL Bulletin*.
Members National chapters in 10 countries:
Burkina Faso, Côte d'Ivoire, Eswatini, Malawi, Mali, Namibia, South Africa, Tanzania UR, Uganda, Zambia.
IGO Relations *Joint United Nations Programme on HIV/AIDS (UNAIDS, #16149)*; *UNDP (#20292)*. [2019.10.03/XF7158/**F**]

♦ Alliance pour un mécanisme mondial d'observation sur l'eau (#20831)
♦ Alliance médicale internationale (inactive)

♦ Alliance of Mediterranean News Agencies (AMAN) 00708

SG Cyprus News Agency, 21 Akadimias Avenue, 2107 Aglantzia, PO Box 23947, CY-1687 Nicosia, Cyprus. T. +35722556009. Fax +35722556103. E-mail: amannews@aman-alliance.org.
URL: http://www.aman-alliance.org/

History 21 Nov 1991, Tunis (Tunisia). **Structure** General Assembly (annual). Officers: President; 2 Vice-Presidents; Secretary General. Follow-up Committee. **Finance** Sources: members' dues. **Events** *General Assembly* Ramallah (Palestine) 2013, *General Assembly* Rome (Italy) 2012, *General Assembly* Rome (Italy) 2012, *General Assembly* Tangiers (Morocco) 2011, *General Assembly* Marseille (France) 2010.
Members Agencies (19) in 19 countries and territories:
Albania, Algeria, Croatia, Cyprus, Egypt, France, Greece, Italy, Lebanon, Libya, Mauritania, Morocco, Palestine, Portugal, Serbia, Spain, Syrian AR, Tunisia, Türkiye.
NGO Relations Partner of (1): *Fédération Atlantique des Agences de Presse Africaines (FAAPA, #09462)*. [2022/XF5918/**F**]

♦ Alliance for Middle East Peace (internationally oriented national body)
♦ Alliance pour la Migration, le Leadership et le Développement (unconfirmed)
♦ Alliance mondiale pour l'allaitement maternel (#21079)
♦ Alliance mondiale pour les bâtiments et la construction (#10187)
♦ Alliance mondiale contre le changement climatique (inactive)
♦ Alliance mondiale pour la sécurité des patients / see WHO Patient Safety (#20940)
♦ Alliance Mondiale des Terres Arides (#10326)
♦ Alliance mondiale des unions chrétiennes féminines (#21947)
♦ Alliance mondiale des villes contre la pauvreté (#21080)
♦ Alliance Mondiale pour les Villes Intelligentes en Afrique (unconfirmed)
♦ Alliance des mouvements de jeunesse de La Francophonie (inactive)
♦ Alliance for Multilateralism (unconfirmed)
♦ Alliance pour le multilatéralisme (unconfirmed)
♦ Alliance of Mutual Benefit Societies of America / see Alianza del Mutualismo de América (#00634)
♦ Alliance du mutualisme de l'Amérique (#00634)

♦ Alliance of NGOs on Crime Prevention and Criminal Justice 00709

Alliance d'organisations non gouvernementales pour la prévention du crime et la justice criminelle

Sec Wagramer Str 5, 1400 Vienna, Austria. E-mail: info@crimealliance.org.
URL: https://crimealliance.org/

History 1972. Comes within the framework of *Conference of Non-Governmental Organizations in Consultative Relationship with the United Nations (CONGO, #04635).* Branches in New York NY (USA) and Vienna (Austria). Former names and other names: *Alliance des ONG* – alias. **Aims** Facilitate planning for international *policy* in crime prevention and criminal justice by providing for an institutionalized two-way conduit of information and consultation between the UN Secretariat and the international NGO community; assist the *United Nations* in identifying issues, providing research studies, recommending action and technical assistance in specific areas of Alliance interest; strengthen collective services by facilitating exchange of information and cooperation among member organizations regarding programs, research projects, publications and other matters of mutual interest. **Structure** Board. **Finance** Members' dues. Donations. **Activities** Politics/policy/regulatory. **Events** *Regular Meeting* New York, NY (USA) 2015, *Regular Meeting* New York, NY (USA) 2014, *Regular Meeting* New York, NY (USA) 2014, *Regular Meeting* New York, NY (USA) 2014, *Regular Meeting* New York, NY (USA) 2014.
Members Classes of affiliation Member; Observer. Members NGOs in consultative status with the UN which have a substantial interest in some aspects of crime prevention, criminal justice administration or treatment of offenders, including 26 organizations listed in this Yearbook:
- *Academy of Criminal Justice Sciences (ACJS);*
- *Amnesty International (AI, #00801);*
- *Defence for Children International (DCI, #05025);*
- *Friends World Committee for Consultation (FWCC, #10004);*
- *Howard League for Penal Reform;*
- *International Association for Forensic Psychotherapy (IAFP, #11899);*
- *International Association of Chiefs of Police (IACP, #11765);*
- *International Association of Judges (IAJ, #11978);*
- *International Association of Penal Law (IAPL, #12074);*
- *International Association of Youth and Family Judges and Magistrates (IAYFJM, #12283);*
- *International Center for Religion and Diplomacy (ICRD);*
- *International Commission of Jurists (ICJ, #12695);*
- *International Community Corrections Association (ICCA, #12822);*
- *International Corrections and Prisons Association for the Advancement of Professional Corrections (ICPA, #12970);*
- *International Council of Prison Medical Services (ICPMS, no recent information);*
- *International Council on Alcohol and Addictions (ICAA, #12989);*
- *International Narcotic Enforcement Officers Association (INEOA);*
- *International Society for Traumatic Stress Studies (ISTSS, #15518);*
- *International Society of Criminology (ISC, #15038);*
- *International Society of Social Defence and Humane Criminal Policy (ISSD, #15447);*
- *Junior Chamber International (JCI, #16168);*
- *Prison Fellowship International (PFI, #18503);*
- *Salvation Army (#19041);*
- *Women's Federation for World Peace International (WFWPI);*
- *World Federation for Mental Health (WFMH, #21455);*
- *World Psychiatric Association (WPA, #21741).*

Observers NGOs with some interest in the subject, including 10 organizations listed in this Yearbook: *Foundation for International Probation and Parole Practices (no recent information); Human Rights Watch (HRW, #10990); International Legal Defense Counsel (ILDC); International Penal and Penitentiary Foundation (IPPF, #14553); International Police Association (IPA, #14612)* (US Section); *International Probation Organization (INTERPRO, no recent information); International Social Service (ISS, #14886); Society for Psychological Study of Social Issues (SPSSI); World Peace Academy; World Union of Catholic Women's Organisations (WUCWO, #21876).*
IGO Relations Memorandum of Understanding with (1): *United Nations Office on Drugs and Crime (UNODC, #20596).* [2021/XE9969/y/**E**]

- ♦ Alliance of NGOs and CSOs for South-South Cooperation (unconfirmed)
- ♦ Alliancen af Liberale og Demokrater for Europa (#00703)
- ♦ Alliance nordique pour la protection des enfants et de la jeunesse (inactive)
- ♦ Alliance oecuménique des communautés et des associations de diaconesses / see World Federation of Diaconal Associations and Diaconal Communities (#21429)
- ♦ Alliance de l'OMS pour l'elimination du trachoma (#20935)
- ♦ Alliance des ONG / see Alliance of NGOs on Crime Prevention and Criminal Justice (#00709)

♦ Alliance for Oral Health Across Borders 00710

Chairman Temple Kornberg School, 3223 North Broad St, Philadelphia PA 19140, USA. T. +12157072799. E-mail: info@alliancefororalhealthacrossborders.org.
URL: http://alliancefororalhealthacrossborders.org/
History Charter signed, 3 Aug 2011, Philadelphia PA (USA). **Aims** Promote peace and understanding through oral health projects. **Structure** Board, comprising Chairman, Vice Chairman, Secretary, Treasurer and 23 members. **Languages** English. **Staff** 1.00 FTE, paid. **Finance** Sources: donations; members' dues. Annual budget: 50,000 USD. **Activities** Organizes annual workshop. **Publications** None.
Members Schools; Dental industry; NGOs; Individuals. Schools in 16 countries and territories:
Australia, Bulgaria, Canada, China, India, Israel, Italy, Japan, Kuwait, Palestine, Russia, Tanzania UR, Thailand, Türkiye, UK, USA.
NGO Relations Dental schools; dental organizations. [2013.09.28/XJ2980/**C**]

- ♦ Alliance of the Orders of St John of Jerusalem (religious order)
- ♦ Alliance d'organisations non gouvernementales pour la prévention du crime et la justice criminelle (#00709)
- ♦ Alliance des organisations de service volontaire de l'Europe (#00677)
- ♦ Alliance of Organizers Concours Complet International / see Eventing Organisers Association (#09211)
- ♦ Alliance of Overseas Filipinos in Asia, Pacific and Middle East / see MIGRANTE International (#16797)
- ♦ Alliance du Pacifique des fédérations nationales de gymnastique (#17925)
- ♦ Alliance panaméricaine des femmes médecins (#18120)

♦ Alliance of Pan American Round Tables 00711

Alianza de Mesas Redondas Panamericanas (AMRP)
Dir Gen address not obtained. E-mail: directorageneralamrp@gmail.com – webalianzamrp@gmail.com.
Corresponding Sec address not obtained. E-mail: alianzacorrsec@gmail.com.
URL: http://alianzademrp.org/
History 1944, following activities begun in 1916 by Florence Terry Griswold which gave rise to the Pan American Round Table movement. **Structure** Directorate. Consultative Council. **Events** *Biennial Convention* Buenos Aires (Argentina) 2012. **IGO Relations** Links with *OAS (#17629).* [2014/XU2508/**D**]

- ♦ Alliance des pays producteurs de cacao (no recent information)
- ♦ Alliance for Peacebuilding (internationally oriented national body)

♦ Alliance for Permanent Access 00712

Contact 2 High Street, Yetminster, DT9 6LF, UK. T. +441935872660.
URL: http://www.alliancepermanentaccess.org/
History 2005, as *Task Force on Permanent Access.* Current title adopted 2007. Also referred to as *Alliance for Permanent Access to the Records of Science.* **Aims** Develop a shared vision and framework for a sustainable organizational infrastructure for permanent access to *scientific information.* **Events** *Annual Conference* Budapest (Hungary) 2008.
Members Full in 4 countries:
Germany, Netherlands, UK, USA.
International organizations (3):
European Organization for Nuclear Research (CERN, #08108); European Space Agency (ESA, #08798); International Association of Scientific, Technical and Medical Publishers (STM, #12154).
NGO Relations Partner of: *euroCRIS (#05672).* [2013.07.16/XM3484/y/**F**]

- ♦ Alliance for Permanent Access to the Records of Science / see Alliance for Permanent Access (#00712)
- ♦ Alliance des petits Etats insulaires (#00721)
- ♦ Alliance of Popular Composer Organisations in Europe (inactive)

♦ Alliance of Presbyterian and Reformed Churches in Latin America . 00713

Alianza de Iglesias Presbiterianas y Reformadas de América Latina (AIPRAL) – Aliança de Igrejas Presbiterianas e Reformadas da América Latina
Exec Sec Rivadavia 575, 70000 Colonia del Sacramento, Colonia, Uruguay. T. +598098664969. E-mail: secretaria@aipral.net – comunicaciones@aipral.net.
URL: http://www.aipral.net/
History Jun 1966, Mexico City (Mexico). Replaced *Comisión de Cooperación Presbiteriana en América Latina (CCPAL)*, set up during its 1st Congress, Jul 1955, Campinas (Brazil). New statutes and present name adopted by 8th General Assembly, Nov 1997, Mexico City. Former names and other names: *Association of Presbyterian and Reformed Churches in Latin America* – former; *Asociación de Iglesias Presbiterianas y Reformadas de América Latina* – former; *Comisión de Cooperación Presbiteriana en América Latina (CCPAL)* – former; *Aliança de Igrejas Presbiterianas e Reformadas da América Latina (AIPRAL)* – alias. **Aims** Create a space of unity, encounter, reflection and solidarity of the reformed family in Latin America and Caribbean region. **Structure** General Assembly (every 7 years); Executive Committee; Departments (4). **Languages** Portuguese, Spanish. **Staff** 0.50 FTE, paid. **Finance** Sources: members' dues. Financial assistance from: Fondation pour l'aide au protestantisme Réformé (FAP); Presbyterian Church in USA; *World Communion of Reformed Churches (WCRC, #21289)*; other Protestant institutions. **Activities** Advocacy/lobbying/activism; networking/liaising; religious activities; training/education. Active in: Caribbean; Central America; South America. **Events** *General Assembly* Sao Paulo (Brazil) 2016, *General Assembly* Guatemala (Guatemala) 2011, *General Assembly* Cartagena de Indias (Colombia) 2006, *General Assembly* Sao Paulo (Brazil) 2002, *General Assembly* Mexico City (Mexico) 1997. **Publications** *La Voz* (bimensual). Books.
Members Churches (22) in 15 countries:
Argentina, Brazil, Chile, Colombia, Costa Rica, Cuba, Dominican Rep, El Salvador, Honduras, Mexico, Nicaragua, Paraguay, Puerto Rico, Uruguay, Venezuela.
NGO Relations Member of (1): *Agencia Latinoamericana y Caribeña de Comunicación (#00550).* Partner of (2): *Council for World Mission (CWM, #04925); World Council of Churches (WCC, #21320).* Cooperates with (1): *G20 Interfaith Forum Association (IF20, #10055).* Affiliated with (1): *World Communion of Reformed Churches (WCRC, #21289).* Also partnership with other Ecumenical organizations. [2021.10.05/XD6252/**D**]

- ♦ Alliance for the Preservation of Forests (internationally oriented national body)
- ♦ Alliance pour la Préservation des Forêts (internationally oriented national body)
- ♦ Alliance pour la prévention du cancer du col de l'utérus (#00663)
- ♦ Alliance for the Prudent Use of Antibiotics (internationally oriented national body)
- ♦ Alliance Publishing Trust (internationally oriented national body)
- ♦ Alliance for Rabies Control / see Global Alliance for Rabies Control

♦ Alliance of Rail New Entrants (ALLRAIL) 00714

SG Rue Washington 40, 1000 Brussels, Belgium. T. +32479070806. E-mail: info@allrail.eu.
URL: http://allrail.eu/
History Apr 2017, Brussels (Belgium). Set up by several rail companies and independent ticket vendors. Registration: Banque-Carrefour des Entreprises, No/ID: 0675.784.944, Start date: 17 May 2017, Belgium; EU Transparency Register, No/ID: 828617341174-24, Start date: 1 Feb 2021. **Aims** Call for a more open *market* for European passenger rail services. **Structure** Board of Directors; Secretariat. **Languages** English, French. **Staff** 3.00 FTE, paid. **Activities** Advocacy/lobbying/activism; awareness raising; events/meetings; knowledge management/information dissemination; monitoring/evaluation; networking/liaising; politics/policy/regulatory; projects/programmes; publishing activities. Active in: Austria, Belgium, Czechia, Denmark, France, Germany, Hungary, Italy, Netherlands, Norway, Poland, Spain, Sweden, Switzerland, UK. **Members** Full (14); Associate (3). Membership countries not specified. **NGO Relations** Member of (2): *Federation of European and International Associations Established in Belgium (FAIB, #09508); Rail Working Group (RWG, #18610).* [2022.10.19/XM7161/**D**]

♦ Alliance for Rebuilding Governance in Africa (ARGA) 00715

Alliance pour Refonder la Gouvernance en Afrique
Head Office Ouest Foire-Cité Douanes, Villa n°13- 2F, 10200 Dakar, Senegal. T. +221338201581. E-mail: arga-regional@forums.afrique-gouvernance.net.
Mali Office BPE 867, Rue 816 porte 1350, Bamako, Mali. T. +22376288113 – +22376498879. E-mail: arga.mali@forums.afrique-gouvernance.net.
URL: http://www.afrique-gouvernance.net/
History 2003. Incorporates continuation of the network *Dialogues on governance in Africa: decentralization and regional integration*, set up 1999. Former names and other names: *Alliance to Lay New Foundations for Governance in Africa* – alias. **Aims** As an alliance of African and non-African actors, contribute to the development of an African way of thinking and an African governance project. **Structure** Council; Resource Centre. **Languages** French. **Staff** 2.00 FTE, paid. **Activities** Events/meetings; projects/programmes. **Events** *Annual Meeting* Abidjan (Côte d'Ivoire) 2020, *Global forum on reinventing government* Vienna (Austria) 2007. **Publications** Books and booklets about governance, inclding national and continental governance, local governance, conflict and governance, justice and governance, and land and governance.
Members Members in 10 countries:
Algeria, Benin, Burkina Faso, Cameroon, Congo DR, Guinea, Mali, Morocco, Senegal, Togo.
NGO Relations Also links with many NGO's, universities and grassroots organizations in Africa. [2020/XJ5931/**D**]

- ♦ Alliance pour Refonder la Gouvernance en Afrique (#00715)

♦ Alliance for Reform and Democracy in Asia (ARDA) 00716

Address not obtained.
URL: http://www.asiademocracy.org/
History 8 Oct 2000, Bangkok (Thailand). **Aims** Offer Asian democrats and reformers a network to provide information, support and non-violent intervention during times of political crises; serve as a catalyst for new ideas and initiatives to promote democracy and freedom throughout Asia.
Members Individuals in 24 countries and territories:
Bangladesh, Bhutan, Brunei Darussalam, Cambodia, China, Hong Kong, India, Indonesia, Japan, Korea DPR, Korea Rep, Laos, Malaysia, Mongolia, Myanmar, Nepal, Pakistan, Philippines, Singapore, Taiwan, Thailand, Tibet, Timor-Leste, Vietnam.
NGO Relations Instrumental in setting up: *World Forum for Democratization in Asia (WFDA, #21515).* [2014/XM0816/**F**]

- ♦ Alliance réformée mondiale (inactive)
- ♦ Alliance for Regenerative Medicine (internationally oriented national body)

♦ Alliance for Responsible Mining (ARM) 00717

Alianza por la Mineria Responsable
Exec Dir Calle 32 B Sur 44 A 61, Medellin, Antioquia, Colombia. T. +5743324711. E-mail: arm@responsiblemines.org.
URL: http://www.responsiblemines.org/
History 2004. **Aims** Work for sustainable development of artisanal and small-scale mining (ASM), and for social justice and environmental responsibility as the values driving the transformation of ASM. **Structure** Board of Directors; Executive Committee; Stakeholder Alliance; Executive Director. **Languages** English, Spanish. **Staff** 37.00 FTE, paid. **Finance** Support from various organizations, including: *Inter-American Development Bank (IDB, #11427); UNIDO (#20336); Global Environment Facility (GEF, #10346); Fonds français pour l'environnement mondial (FFEM); Oxfam International (#17922); Stichting DOEN.* **Activities** Standards/guidelines; certification/accreditation; research and development; advocacy/lobbying/activism; projects/programmes. Active in: Bolivia, Brazil, Burkina Faso, Cameroon, Colombia, Congo DR, Ecuador, Gabon, Kenya, Mali, Peru, Rwanda, Senegal, Uganda. **Publications** Annual Report; Toolkit; case studies; comics; research papers; position papers. **IGO Relations** *UNIDO (#20336).* **NGO Relations** Partner of (1): *Global Battery Alliance (GBA, #10249).* Subscriber to: *ISEAL (#16026).* [2022/XJ2184/**D**]

♦ Alliance for Responsible and Sustainable Societies 00718

Alliance pour des sociétés responsables et durables – Alianza para Sociedades Responsables y Sostenibles

Contact c/o Response Trust, PO Box 12-090, Thorndon, Wellington 6144, New Zealand. E-mail: info@alliance-respons.net.
URL: http://www.alliance-respons.net/
History Originated in *Vézelay Group (inactive)*, set up 1987. Developed out of *Forum on Ethics and Responsibility*, within *Fondation Charles Léopold Mayer pour le progrès de l'homme (FPH, #09815)*, founded 2002. Became an independent organization under current title, 2015. **Aims** Catalyze responsibility as a theme for transitions to low carbon economies involving renewable energy, wealth sharing, and people taking care of the planet. **Structure** Assembly; Consultative Committee. **Finance** Funding from *Fondation Charles Léopold Mayer pour le progrès de l'homme (FPH, #09815)*. **Activities** Knowledge management/information dissemination; research/documentation. **Publications** Newsletter.
Members Organizations; individuals. Organizations include 3 organizations listed in this Yearbook:
Asian Solidarity Economy Coalition (ASEC, #01754); *Education and Solidarity Network (#05374)*; *Globethics.net Foundation (#10669)*. [2019/XM8598/**E**]

♦ Alliance for Rural Electrification (ARE) 00719

SG Rue d'Arlon 69-71, 1040 Brussels, Belgium. T. +3227095542. E-mail: j.jaeger@ruralelec.org – are@ruralelec.org.
URL: http://www.ruralelec.org/
History 2006, by *European Biomass Industry Association (EUBIA, #06339)*, *SolarPower Europe (#19676)*, *European Small Hydropower Association (ESHA, #08495)*, *WindEurope (#20965)* and *Global Wind Energy Council (GWEC, #10656)*. **Aims** Represent the decentralized energy sector working towards integration of renewables into rural electrification markets in developing and emerging countries; enable improved energy access through business development support along the whole value chain for off-grid technologies. **Structure** General Assembly; Board of Directors; Secretariat. **Languages** English. **Staff** 3.00 FTE, paid. **Finance** Members' dues. Other sources: project acquisitions; sponsorship. Budget (annual): euro 300,000. **Activities** Networking/liaising. **Events** *Energy Access Investment Forum* Lusaka (Zambia) 2021, *International Off-Grid Renewable Energy Conference* Singapore (Singapore) 2018, *Annual General Meeting* Lisbon (Portugal) 2017, *Energy Access Workshop* Madrid (Spain) 2015, *Meeting on Accessing Africa's Renewable Energy Markets* Brussels (Belgium) 2014. **Publications** *ARE Newsletter*. Best practices; position papers; technology papers; market briefs.
Members Organizations (over 90) in 31 countries:
Australia, Austria, Bangladesh, Belgium, Burkina Faso, China, Congo DR, Denmark, Finland, France, Germany, Ghana, India, Italy, Kenya, Laos, Luxembourg, Mali, Mauritania, Mexico, Mozambique, Netherlands, Nigeria, Philippines, Portugal, Somalia, Spain, Switzerland, UK, United Arab Emirates, USA.
NGO Relations Founding member of: *Global Energy Storage Alliance (GESA, #10343)*. Cooperates with: *International Electrotechnical Commission (IEC, #13255)*; *OPEC Fund for International Development (OFID, #17745)*; *Practical Action (#18475)*; *REN21 (#18836)*; *Sustainable Energy for All (SEforALL, #20056)*; *United Nations Foundation (UNF, #20563)*. [2020/XM0983/**E**]

- ♦ Alliance of Russian Solidarists (internationally oriented national body)
- ♦ Alliance for Safe Online Pharmacies (internationally oriented national body)

♦ Alliance for Safe Online Pharmacy – EU (ASOP EU) 00720

Contact address not obtained.
URL: http://www.asop.eu/
History 2011. Founded as a loose coalition of patient groups, companies, organizations and individuals. **Aims** Make buying *medicines* online safer, in countries where it is permitted by law. **Activities** Advocacy/lobbying/activism; awareness raising; research/documentation.
Members Full members include 13 organizations listed in this Yearbook:
Affordable Medicines Europe (#00150); *Alliance for Safe Online Pharmacies (ASOP Global)*; *Digestive Cancers Europe (DiCE, #05070)*; *European Alliance for Access to Safe Medicines (EAASM, #05859)*; *European Depression Association (EDA, #06905)*; *European Federation of Neurological Associations (EFNA, #07177)*; *European Federation of Pharmaceutical Industries and Associations (EFPIA, #07191)*; *European Men's Health Forum (EMHF, #07783)*; *European Parkinson's Disease Association (EPDA, #08145)*; *European Society for Sexual Medicine (ESSM, #08733)*; *Groupement International de la Répartition Pharmaceutique (GIRP, #10762)*; *Institute of Research Against Counterfeit Medicines (IRACM)*; *International Federation of Pharmaceutical Manufacturers and Associations (IFPMA, #13505)*.
Observers include 8 organizations listed in this Yearbook:
European Patients' Forum (EPF, #08172); *European Police Office (Europol, #08239)*; *GS1 (#10809)*; *International Alliance of Patients' Organizations (IAPO, #11633)*; *International Pharmaceutical Federation (#14566)*; *Medicines for Europe (#16633)*; *Pharmaceutical Group of the European Union (PGEU, #18352)*; *RIPE Network Coordination Centre (RIPE NCC, #18951)*.
NGO Relations Member of (1): *EU Health Coalition*. Partner of (2): *Fight the Fakes (#09755)*; *Transnational Alliance to Combat Illicit Trade (TRACIT)*. [2016/XM5028/y/**D**]

- ♦ Alliances for Africa (internationally oriented national body)
- ♦ Alliance to Save Energy (internationally oriented national body)
- ♦ Alliance scandinave des juifs et des chrétiens (inactive)
- ♦ **Alliance** Science and Technology Alliance for Global Sustainability (#19143)
- ♦ Alliance scientifique universelle (inactive)
- ♦ the Alliance – Scotland's International Development Alliance (internationally oriented national body)
- ♦ Alliance for Securing Democracy (internationally oriented national body)
- ♦ Alliance de singe (#00871)

♦ Alliance of Small Island States (AOSIS) 00721

Alliance des petits Etats insulaires
Chair Perm Mission – Maldives, 801 Second Ave, Ste 202-E, New York NY 10017, USA. T. +12125996794 – +12125996195. Fax +12126616405.
URL: http://aosis.org/
History Nov 1990, Geneva (Switzerland), at 2nd World Climate Conference, as an ad hoc coalition of Small Island Developing States (SIDS). **Aims** Focus attention on the special problems faced by small islands and low-lying coastal developing states, particularly the serious threats of sea-level rise and coral bleaching resulting from global warming and climate change; emphasize the importance of information and information technology in the process of achieving sustainable development. **Structure** Bureau. **Activities** Implementation of *Barbados Programme of Action for the Sustainable Development of Small Island Developing States*, 1994, containing measures over the short, medium and long terms in 14 priority areas: Climate change; Natural and environmental disasters; Management of wastes; Coastal and marine resources; Freshwater resources; Land resources; Energy resources; Tourism resources; Biodiversity resources; National institutions and administrative capacity; Regional institutions and technical cooperation; Transport and communication; Science and technology; Human resource development. Also includes actions and policies related to environmental and development planning. Instrumental in setting up: *International Climate Fund (no recent information)*; *International Insurance Pooling System (no recent information)*; *Small Island Developing States Network (SIDSnet, #19315)*. **Events** *Ministerial Conference on Climate Change* Victoria (Seychelles) 2014, *International meeting for the 10-year review of the Barbados Programme of Action (BPoA + 10) for the sustainable development of small islands developing states* Port Louis (Mauritius) 2005, *Inter-regional preparatory meeting for the 10-year review of the Barbados Programme of Action (BPoA + 10)* Nassau (Bahamas) 2004, *Preparatory meeting for the 10-year review of the Barbados Programme of Action (BPoA + 10)* New York, NY (USA) 2004, *Caribbean regional preparatory meeting for the 10-year review of the Barbados Programme of Action (BPoA + 10)* Apia (Samoa) 2003.
Members Island nations (39):
Antigua-Barbuda, Bahamas, Barbados, Belize, Cape Verde, Comoros, Cook Is, Cuba, Dominica, Dominican Rep, Fiji, Grenada, Guinea-Bissau, Guyana, Haiti, Jamaica, Kiribati, Maldives, Marshall Is, Mauritius, Micronesia FS, Nauru, Niue, Palau, Papua New Guinea, Samoa, Sao Tomé-Principe, Seychelles, Singapore, Solomon Is, St Kitts-Nevis, St Lucia, St Vincent-Grenadines, Suriname, Timor-Leste, Tonga, Trinidad-Tobago, Tuvalu, Vanuatu.
Observers (5):
Guam, Neth Antilles, Puerto Rico, Samoa USA, Virgin Is USA.
IGO Relations Instrumental in setting up: *Small Island Developing States – Island Energy for Island Life (SIDS DOCK, #19314)*. **NGO Relations** Participates in: *Global Island Partnership (GLISPA, #10436)*. [2017/XF5450/**F***]

- ♦ Alliances Mondiales pour l'Eau et le Climat (#10230)

♦ Alliance for Social and Ecological Consumer Organisations (ASECO) 00722

Contact address not obtained. T. +4535372030.
Aims Promote sustainable consumption in Europe. **Structure** Steering Committee of 4.
Members Organizations (14) in 13 countries:
Belgium, Bulgaria, Czechia, Denmark, Finland, France, Germany, Greece, Italy, Lithuania, Netherlands, Sweden, UK.
IGO Relations *Council of Europe (CE, #04881)*. **NGO Relations** Member of: *European Inter-Network of Ethical and Responsible Initiatives (#07593)*. [2008/XM1506/**D**]

- ♦ Alliance Sociale Continentale (#00635)
- ♦ Alliance pour des sociétés responsables et durables (#00718)
- ♦ Alliance solaire internationale (#15563)
- ♦ Alliance pour la Solidarité and le Partage en Afrique-Jeunesse pour l'Intégration Culturelle et Sociale-Humanitarian Focus Foundation / see ASPAFRIQUE-JICS-HFFUN
- ♦ Alliance Sud, Arbeitsgemeinschaft Swissaid – Fastenopfer – Brot für Alle – Helvetas – Caritas – Heks (internationally oriented national body)
- ♦ Alliance Sud, Communauté de travail Swissaid – Action de carême – Pain pour le prochain – Helvetas – Caritas – Eper (internationally oriented national body)
- ♦ Alliance Sud, Swiss Alliance of Development Organisations Swissaid – Catholic Lenten Fund – Bread for All – Helvetas – Caritas – Interchurch Aid (internationally oriented national body)

♦ Alliance for Surgery and Anesthesia Presence (ASAP) 00723

Contact c/o ISS, Seefeldstrasse 88, 8008 Zurich ZH, Switzerland. T. +41445337650. Fax +41445337659. E-mail: asaptoday@gmail.com.
URL: https://www.asaptoday.org/
History 2007. Since 2013, an integrated society of *International Society of Surgery (ISS, #15496)*. Registration: USA. **Aims** Provide the evidence base to effectively advocate for access to safe, quality, timely surgery and anesthesia as an essential component of universal health care. **Structure** Board. **Activities** Advocacy/lobbying/activism; events/meetings; research/documentation. [2022/AA2962/**C**]

- ♦ Alliance for Sustainability (internationally oriented national body)
- ♦ Alliances for Voluntary Initiatives and Development / see Allavida

♦ Alliance for Synthetic Fuels in Europe (ASFE) 00724

Secretariat c/o Weber Shandwick, Av de Cortenbergh 100, 1000 Brussels, Belgium. T. +3228949000. Fax +3228949069.
URL: https://syntheticfuels.org/
History 2006. Founded by leading car manufacturers and fuel producers; endorsement of *European Commission (EC, #06633)*. **Aims** Promote synthetic fuels and their contribution to *motor vehicle emission* reduction; raise public awareness on the multiple benefits of synthetic fuels, and their role in making European transport sustainable; create a favourable policy environment at both EU and national level to stimulate introduction and market penetration of different types of alternative fuel. **Publications** Press releases; brochure; position papers. **Members** Leading automotive and fuel supply companies (5). [2021/XJ0790/**F**]

- ♦ Alliance of Technology Transfer Professionals / see ATTP (#03012)
- ♦ L'Alliance terre des femmes (#19992)
- ♦ Alliance touristique de l'Océan Indien (inactive)
- ♦ Alliance Toward Harnessing Global Opportunities Corporation (internationally oriented national body)
- ♦ Alliance and Union Treaty (1745 treaty)
- ♦ Alliance universelle (#20671)
- ♦ Alliance universelle pour l'amitié universelle par la religion (inactive)
- ♦ Alliance universelle évangélique (inactive)
- ♦ Alliance universelle des femmes pour la paix par l'éducation (inactive)
- ♦ Alliance universelle de l'ordre et de la civilisation (inactive)
- ♦ Alliance universelle des ouvriers diamantaires (inactive)
- ♦ Alliance universelle des unions chrétiennes de jeunes gens (#21090)

♦ Alliance of Universities for Democracy (AUDEM) 00725

Pres State Univ of New York, State University Plaza, Albany NY 12246, USA. T. +15183201410. Fax +15184435042.
European Office Office of International Relations, Univ of Pecs, Pécs 7633, Hungary.
URL: http://www.audem.org/
History Nov 1990, Budapest (Hungary), when Charter was adopted. **Aims** Enhance the role of education in promoting democratic institutions and economic development. **Structure** Board of Directors. Executive Committee, comprising President, 2 Vice-Presidents, Treasurer. **Languages** English. **Staff** 1.00 FTE, paid. **Finance** Members' dues. Conference proceeds. **Activities** University Partnership in Social Work. **Events** *Annual Conference* Pécs (Hungary) 2010, *Annual conference* Bursa (Turkey) 2009, *Annual Conference* Baku (Azerbaijan) 2008, *Annual Conference* Cluj-Napoca (Romania) 2007, *Annual conference* Katowice (Poland) 2006. **Publications** *AUDEM: International Journal of Higher Education and Democracy* (annual).
Members Associate; Supporting; Individual; Honorary; Cooperating. Universities (125) in 19 countries:
Albania, Azerbaijan, Belarus, Bosnia-Herzegovina, Bulgaria, Czechia, Hungary, Lithuania, Moldova, North Macedonia, Poland, Romania, Russia, Slovakia, Slovenia, Switzerland, UK, Ukraine, USA. [2010.06.01/XF4619/**F**]

- ♦ Alliance verte alternative européenne / see Group of the Greens – European Free Alliance (#10781)
- ♦ Alliance verte européenne / see European Green Party (#07409)
- ♦ Alliance Vietnam liberté (#09990)

♦ Alliance de Villes Euro-méditerranéennes de Culture (AVEC) 00726

Alliance of Euro-Mediterranean Cultural Cities
General Delegate Service patrimoine – Marie d'Arles, BP 196, 13637 Arles CEDEX, France. T. +33490493521.
Registered Seat Marie de Tours, 1-3 rue des Minimes BP 3215, 37032 Tours CEDEX 01, France.
Facebook: https://facebook.com/reseau.avec/
History 1997. Current statutes approved 16 Feb 2004, Cosenza (Italy). Former names and other names: *European Network of Historical Cities and Territories* – former (1997); *Alliance of European Cultural Cities* – former; *Alliance de Villes Européennes de Culture (AVEC)* – former; *Európai Kulturalis Varosok Halózata* – former. Registration: France. **Aims** Position local heritage as a motor for sustainable development; give international visibility to the network; integrate innovation into existing structures as harmoniously as possible; contribute to economic success and international development of member cities and territories. **Structure** General Assembly; Bureau. **Languages** English, French, Italian, Spanish. **Activities** Projects/programmes; events/meetings; publishing activities; networking/liaising. **Events** *Workshop for the management of the Mediterranean heritage* Paris (France) 2010.
Members Active; Associate; Honorary. Members in 11 countries:
Belgium, Bulgaria, Croatia, France, Hungary, Italy, Malta, Portugal, Romania, Serbia, Spain.
Consultative Status Consultative status granted from: *UNESCO (#20322)* (Consultative Status). **NGO Relations** Member of (2): *Europa Nostra (#05767)*; *Union internationale des associations et organismes scientifiques et techniques (UATI, #20421)*. [2020/XJ2299/**D**]

- ♦ Alliance de Villes Européennes de Culture / see Alliance de Villes Euro-méditerranéennes de Culture (#00726)

♦ Alliance for Water Stewardship (AWS) 00727

Main Office 2 Quality Street, North Berwick, EH39 4HW, UK.
URL: http://allianceforwaterstewardship.org/
History Registration: Charity, No/ID: SC045894, Scotland. **Aims** Promote responsible use of freshwater that is socially and economically beneficial as well as environmentally sustainable. **Structure** Board of Directors. **Events** *European River Symposium* Vienna (Austria) 2021.
Members Board Organizations (10):

CDP (#03621); CEO Water Mandate; *European Water Partnership (EWP, #09083)*; *International Water Management Institute (IWMI, #15867)*; *Pacific Institute*; *The Nature Conservancy (TNC)*; *Water Environment Federation (WEF)*; Water Stewardship Australia; *Water Witness International*; *World Wide Fund for Nature (WWF, #21922)*.
IGO Relations Partner of: *Global Alliances for Water and Climate (GAfWaC, #10230)*. **NGO Relations** Member of (3): *Better Cotton Initiative (BCI, #03218)*; *ISEAL (#16026)* (Affiliate); *Natural Capital Coalition (NCC, #16952)*. Partner of (2): *European Water Stewardship (EWS)*; *Global Resilience Partnership (GRP, #10577)*.
[2019/XJ6094/y/**C**]

♦ Alliance of Western European Voluntary Service Organisations / see Alliance of European Voluntary Service Organizations (#00677)

♦ Alliance World Fellowship (AWF) 00728

Pres Rua Doutor Rui Batista Pereira 90, Sao Paulo SP, 05517-080, Brazil. T. +5511975877806.
URL: http://www.awf.world/

History 1975, as the international fellowship of national churches and ministries related to the *Christian and Missionary Alliance (CMA)*. **Aims** Facilitate cooperation among members as they work for fulfilment of the Great Commission. **Structure** Quadrennial Convocation; Executive Committee. **Languages** English, French, Spanish. **Finance** Members' dues. **Events** *Quadrennial Conference* Thailand 2016, *Quadrennial Conference* Toronto, ON (Canada) 2012, *Quadrennial Convocation* Toronto, ON (Canada) 2012, *Quadrennial conference / Quadrennial Convocation* Santiago (Chile) 2008, *Quadrennial conference / Quadrennial Convocation* Dalfsen (Netherlands) 2004.
Members National churches and ministries in 52 countries and territories:
Angola, Argentina, Australia, Bolivia, Brazil, Burkina Faso, Cambodia, Canada, Chile, China, Colombia, Congo Brazzaville, Congo DR, Costa Rica, Côte d'Ivoire, Cuba, Dominican Rep, Ecuador, France, Gabon, Germany, Guatemala, Guinea, Hong Kong, India, Indonesia, Iraq, Israel, Italy, Japan, Jordan, Lebanon, Liberia, Mali, Mexico, Mongolia, Myanmar, Netherlands, New Zealand, Palestine, Peru, Philippines, Russia, Spain, Syrian AR, Taiwan, Thailand, UK, Uruguay, USA, Venezuela, Vietnam.
[2018.06.01/XE4554/**E**]

♦ Alliance of Young Nurse Leaders and Advocates International (internationally oriented national body)

♦ Alliance for Youth Movements 00729

Co-Founder c/o Howcast Media Inc, 518 Broadway, 2nd Floor, New York NY 10012, USA. E-mail: info@movements.org.
URL: http://www.movements.org/

History Dec 2008, during summit that brought together experts in social media with pioneering grassroots mouvement leaders. **Aims** Promote, connect and support *digital activists* from around the world. **Finance** Sponsorship from global industry leaders and public entities. **Activities** Hosts annual summit, events and trainings that link influential leaders in technology, media, private and public sectors with the some of the world's most promising digital activists. Website serves as a hub for discussion, resources and news about digital activism around the world. **Events** *Summit / Annual Summit* London (UK) 2010, *Annual Summit* Mexico City (Mexico) 2009, *Annual Summit* New York, NY (USA) 2008. [2014/XJ2071/**F**]

♦ Alliance for Zero Extinction (AZE) 00730

Secretariat PO Box 249, 4249 Loudoun Ave, The Plains VA 20198-2237, USA. E-mail: aupgren@abcbirds.org.
URL: http://www.zeroextinction.org/

History Launched 2005. **Aims** Designate and effectively conserve the most important sites for global *biodiversity conservation*. **Structure** Steering Committee.
Members Partners include 28 organizations listed in this Yearbook:
- *African Conservation Foundation (ACF)*;
- *Amphibian Survival Alliance (ASA, #00804)*;
- *Asociación de Conservación de los Ecosistemas Andinos (ECOAN)*;
- *Bat Conservation International (BCI)*;
- *BirdLife International (#03266)*;
- *BirdsCaribbean (#03267)*;
- *Charles Darwin Foundation for the Galapagos Islands (CDF, #03852)*;
- *Durrell Wildlife Conservation Trust*;
- *EcoHealth Alliance*;
- *Endangered Wildlife Trust (EWT)*;
- *Fauna & Flora International (FFI, #09277)*;
- *Global Society for Ecology and Sound Economy (ECO2TERRA International)*;
- *Humane Society International (HSI, #10966)*;
- *International Association of Communication Activists (IACACT, #11791)*;
- *International Crane Foundation (ICF, #13102)*;
- *International Iguana Foundation (IIF)*;
- *International Union for Conservation of Nature and Natural Resources (IUCN, #15766)*;
- *Latin American Center of Social Ecology (#16292)*;
- *Rainforest Trust*;
- *Rare*;
- *Re:wild*;
- *Synchronicity Earth*;
- *The Nature Conservancy (TNC)*;
- *Turtle Conservation Fund (TCF, #20263)*;
- *Turtle Survival Alliance (TSA, #20264)*;
- *Wildlife Conservation Society (WCS)*;
- *World Parrot Trust (WPT, #21713)*;
- *World Pheasant Association (WPA, #21724)*.

NGO Relations Memorandum of Understanding signed with: *Conservation International (CI)*; *World Wide Fund for Nature (WWF, #21922)*. [2018/XJ4297/y/**C**]

♦ Alliantie van Liberalen en Democraten voor Europa Fractie / see Renew Europe (#18840)
♦ Alliant International University (internationally oriented national body)
♦ Allianz in den Alpen (#00656)
♦ Allianz Cultural Foundation (internationally oriented national body)
♦ Allianzhilfe Schweiz / see TearFund, Schweiz
♦ Allianz Kulturstiftung (internationally oriented national body)
♦ Allied Command Europe / see Allied Command Operations (#00731)
♦ Allied Command Europe Rapid Reaction Corps / see Allied Rapid Reaction Corps (#00736)

♦ Allied Command Operations (ACO) 00731

Headquarters c/o SHAPE, Avenue de Berlin, 7010 Shape, Belgium. T. +3265443872. E-mail: shapepao@shape.nato.int.
URL: http://www.aco.nato.int/

History 1951, as *Allied Command Europe (ACE) – Commandement allié en Europe (CAE) – Alliierter Kommandobereich Europa* as one of the originally 4, now 2, commands of *NATO (#16945)*. Current title adopted 1 Sep 2003. **Aims** /Task of ACO/: focus on planning and executing NATO operations. /Task of Supreme Allied Commander Europe (SACEUR): contribute to preserving the peace, *security* and *territorial integrity* of *NATO* member nations; contribute to *crisis* management and provide effective *defence* of NATO territory and forces; should aggression occur, execute all *military* measures within capability and authority of the command to demonstrate the solidarity of the Alliance and the preparedness to maintain the integrity of Alliance territory, to safeguard freedom of the seas and of economic lifelines and to preserve or restore the security of the NATO area of responsibility. **Structure** *Supreme Allied Commander Europe (SACEUR)* assisted by political and scientific advisers in addition to military staff, with headquarters *Supreme Headquarters Allied Powers Europe (SHAPE, #20039)*. National Military Representatives (NMRs) from member countries provide military liaison. Subordinate commands on operational level within ACO responsible to the Supreme Allied Commander Europe: *Allied Joint Force Command Brunssum (JFC Brunssum, #00734)*, based at Joint Force Command Headquarters North, Brunssum (Netherlands); *Allied Joint Force Command Naples (JFC Naples, #00735)*, based at Joint Force Command Headquarter, Naples (Italy). Single Component Commands on the tactical level are located in Germany (Air Force), Turkey (Army) and UK (Navy). **Languages** English. **Finance** Financed by NATO military budget. Peacetime facilities and operation and maintenance costs are generally funded nationally. **Activities** Politics/policy/regulatory; conflict resolution.
Members Governments of 29 countries:
Albania, Belgium, Bulgaria, Canada, Croatia, Czechia, Denmark, Estonia, France, Germany, Greece, Hungary, Iceland, Italy, Latvia, Lithuania, Luxembourg, Montenegro, Netherlands, Norway, Poland, Portugal, Romania, Slovakia, Slovenia, Spain, Türkiye, UK, USA.
[2017.10.12/XE2231/**E***]

♦ Allied Command Transformation (ACT) 00732

Headquarters 7857 Blandy Rd, Ste 100, Norfolk VA 23551-2490, USA. T. +17577473600. Fax +17577473234. E-mail: pao@act.nato.int.
URL: http://www.act.nato.int/

History Comes within the framework of *NATO (#16945)*, apparently replacing *NATO Allied Command Atlantic (ACLANT, inactive)* and responsible to Supreme Allied Commander Atlantic (SACLANT) or his replacement. One of two Strategic Commands (SCs) in NATO, the other being Allied Command Operations (ACO). The primary function of the NATO Command Structure (NCS) is first and foremost to provide the command and control needed to contribute to the deterrence of aggression and the preservation of peace, security and the territorial integrity of the Alliance. Ultimately, the NCS plays an essential role in preserving cohesion and solidarity within the Alliance. It helps maintain and strengthen the vital transatlantic link between Europe and North America and promotes the principle of equitable sharing of roles, risks and responsibilities among the Allies, as well as the sharing of collective defence benefits. Also referred to as *Supreme Allied Command Transformation*. **Aims** Promote and lead initiatives designed to transform NATO's military structure, its forces, capabilities and doctrine. **Structure** Headquarters, located in Norfolk VA (USA), is the only permanent NATO Headquarters outside of Europe and sole NATO Headquarters in North America. It directs ACT's various subordinate commands: Joint Warfare Centre (JWC) in Norway; Joint Forces Training Centre (JFTC) in Poland; Joint Analysis and Lessons Learned Centre (JALLC) in Portugal. It also has strong links with the Pentagon and other US military entities, national headquarters and NATO-accredited Centres of Excellence, Academia and 'Think Tanks' as well as the NATO Force Structure in general. The Supreme Allied Commander Transformation (SACT) is a four-star level flag or general officer who is responsible to the Military Committee (MC) for the transformation and development of the Alliance. The MC is the senior military authority in NATO and it is under the overall political authority of the North Atlantic Council (NAC). **Activities** Training/education; research and development; networking/liaising. **Events** *Resource Conference* Paris (France) 2018.
[2016.06.01/XE4740/**E***]

♦ Allied Commission for Austria (inactive)
♦ Allied Control Authority for Germany (inactive)

♦ Allied Coordination Committee (ACC) 00733

Address not obtained.

History Dec 1944, by civilian and military security services of participating nations. *Treaty for Collaboration in Economic, Social and Cultural Matters and for Collective Self-defence (Brussels Treaty, 1948)*, signed 1948, created *Clandestine Committee of the Western Union (CCWU)*, which became, by 1951, *Clandestine Planning Committee (CPC)*, based in Paris. CPC created, 1957, 2 sub-committees, one of which went on to become ACC. Also known as: *Stay Behind Network*; *GLADIO Network*. Current level of activity, if any, is unclear. **Aims** In the event of a Soviet attack on western Europe: function as a *resistance network*; evacuate VIPs; remove *security service* secret documents; maintain contact with government ministers. **Activities** Coordination of 'Stay Behind' networks. In peacetime: elaboration of directives for the network; development of its clandestine capability; organization of bases in UK and USA. In wartime: planning of stay behind operations in conjunction with SHAPE; activation of clandestine bases. Between 1980 and 1986, arranged triennial international exercises to test radiocommunications network and the collation of information. *Joint Meetings of CPC and ACC* recorded 1986. Last known meeting, Oct 1990, purportedly discussed re-orientation of ACC.
Members Purported involvement of 10 governments:
Belgium, Denmark, France, Germany, Italy, Luxembourg, Netherlands, Norway, UK, USA.
IGO Relations Purported links, through CPC, with *Supreme Headquarters Allied Powers Europe (SHAPE)*.
[2008/XF1722/**F**]

♦ Allied Council for Japan (inactive)
♦ Allied Forces Central Europe / see Allied Joint Force Command Brunssum (#00734)
♦ Allied Forces North Europe / see Allied Joint Force Command Brunssum (#00734)
♦ Allied Forces Southern Europe / see Allied Joint Force Command Naples (#00735)
♦ Allied High Commission for Germany (inactive)

♦ Allied Joint Force Command Brunssum (JFC Brunssum) 00734

Public Information Office Post Box 270, 6440 AG Brunssum, Netherlands. T. +31455262409. Fax +31455263095. E-mail: pao@jfcbs.nato.int – pio@jfcbs.nato.int.
Street address Rimburgerweg 30, 6445 PA Brunssum, Netherlands.
URL: http://www.jfcbs.nato.int/

History Established 1951, Fontainebleau (France), as *Allied Forces Central Europe (AFCENT)*, within the framework of *Allied Command Operations (ACO, #00731)* of *NATO (#16945)*. Moved to Brunssum (Netherlands), Mar 1967. Name changed to *Allied Forces North Europe (AFNORTH) – Forces alliées du Nord Europe*, Mar 2000, with NATO HQ restructuring. Previously also referred to as *Joint Force Command North*. Current title adopted following ongoing NATO Headquarters restructuring, 2004. Responsible to the Supreme Allied Commander Europe (SACEUR). **Aims** Participate in the International Security Assistance Force (ISAF) mission in Afghanistan; contribute to deterrence of aggression; preserve peace, security and territorial integrity of *NATO* member states; contribute to overall stability beyond NATO's area of responsibility by promoting peace through cooperation and dialogue, and, every second year, act as the Standby Operational Command for the NATO Response Force; seeks to generate increasingly better relationship, at the operational level, with military and civilian actors engaged in security throughout NATO's northern region (northern Regional Focus). **Structure** Responsible to the Supreme Allied Commander Europe. Based at JFC HQ, Brunssum (Netherlands), headed by COM JFC Brunssum. **Languages** English. **Staff** 800.00 FTE, paid. **Finance** by Member States. **Activities** Operations. **Publications** *Northern Star* (10 a year) – magazine. **IGO Relations** *United Nations (UN, #20515)*. **NGO Relations** *International Committee of the Red Cross (ICRC, #12799)*. [2019.04.30/XK0384/**F***]

♦ Allied Joint Force Command Naples (JFC Naples) 00735

Public Affairs Office Via Madonna del Pantano, Lago Patria, Giugliana in Campania, 80014 Naples NA, Italy. T. +39817212752 – +39817213838. E-mail: jfcnppaogroup@jfcnp.nato.int.
URL: http://www.jfcnaples.nato.int/

History Jun 1951, Naples (Italy), as *Allied Forces Southern Europe (AFSOUTH)* within the framework of *Allied Command Operations (ACO, #00731)* of *NATO (#16945)*. Name changed to *Joint Force Command South* following ongoing NATO Headquarters restructuring, 2004. **Aims** Prepare for, plan and conduct military operations in order to preserve the peace, security and territorial integrity of Alliance member states and freedom of the seas and economic lifelines throughout SACEUR's Area of Responsibility (AOR) and beyond; contribute to crisis management and *deterrence* by ensuring that assigned headquarters and forces are at the designated state of readiness for the conduct and support of operations, and conduct prudent operational level military analysis and planning that includes the identification of required forces. **Structure** Headed by Commander Joint Force. Responsible to the Supreme Allied Commander Europe. Comprises: Component Command Air South based at Headquarters Air South, Izmir (Turkey); Component Command Land South based at Headquarters Land South, Madrid (Spain); Component Command Navy South based at Headquarters Nav South, Naples (Italy). **Staff** Commands at 2nd level about 1,800 officers, enlisted and civilian personnel at its headquarters in Naples (Italy), and about 4,500 personnel within its entire command structure (excluding component forces).
Members Military and civilian personnel provided by 15 countries:
Canada, Czechia, Denmark, Germany, Greece, Hungary, Italy, Netherlands, Norway, Poland, Portugal, Spain, Türkiye, UK, USA.
[2016/XK0389/**F***]

♦ Allied Rapid Reaction Corps (ARRC) 00736

Contact Imjin Barracks, Innsworth, Gloucester, GL3 1HW, UK. T. +441452718007. E-mail: contact@arrc.nato.int.
URL: https://arrc.nato.int/

History 2 Oct 1992. Established under the command of Supreme Allied Commander Europe (SACEUR), on official recognition by *Supreme Headquarters Allied Powers Europe (SHAPE, #20039)*, to whom it reports in peacetime. Comes within the framework of *Allied Command Operations (ACO, #00731)*, as a rapid reaction force of *NATO (#16945)*. Former names and other names: *Allied Command Europe Rapid Reaction Corps* – former; *ACE Rapid Reaction Corps* – former. **Aims** In order to meet NATO, EU, national or multi-national requirements, be prepared to deploy: as a Corps HQ; as a Land Component HQ; as a Theatre-level Joint Task Force HQ. **Structure** Multinational Headquarters in Gloucester (UK), with personnel from 20 NATO countries. **Languages** English. **Staff** Headquarters (peacetime): over 400. **Finance** The UK Ministry of Defence are the framework nation for the headquarters and contribute the majority of funding. Other NATO contributing countries contribute to a shared fund with contributions proportional to the number of personnel in the peacetime establishment. Share fund contributes towards cost of training and pays for transport and movements for official business. Contributing countries are responsible for their own costs. During operations, NATO common funds become available to replace both framework and shared fund expenditures, while personnel costs remain a national responsibility. **Publications** *Imjin Magazine* (2 a year) in English.
Members Personnel from 20 NATO countries:
Albania, Canada, Croatia, Czechia, Denmark, Estonia, France, Germany, Greece, Italy, Latvia, Lithuania, Netherlands, Poland, Portugal, Romania, Spain, Türkiye, UK, USA. [2023.02.17/XK0535/**F***]

- Alliierter Kommandobereich Europa / see Allied Command Operations (#00731)
- All India Boy Scouts Association (internationally oriented national body)

♦ All India Women's Conference (AIWC) 00737

Conférence des femmes de l'Inde – Conferencia Panindia de Mujeres

Pres c/o Sarojini House, 6 Baghwan Dass Road, Delhi 110001, DELHI 110001, India. T. +911123389680 – +911123384314. Fax +911123384092 – +911123388567. E-mail: aiwcsarojini@gmail.com – info@aiwc.org.in.
URL: http://www.aiwc.org.in/

History 1926. First conference: 1927, Pune (India). Liaison group established in London (UK), 1934. Registered in India, 18 Jul 1930. Constitution amended: 1951, Bangalore (India); 1973, Delhi (India); Oct 1986, Delhi; Oct 1994, Delhi. Constitution adopted: Dec 1983, Delhi; Jan 1987, Delhi; Jan 1995, Delhi. **Aims** Work for a society based on the principles of social *justice*, personal integrity and equal *rights* and opportunities for all; work for general progress and welfare of women and children and help women to utilize to the fullest the fundamental rights conferred on them by the constitution of the Indian Union. **Structure** Session (twice a year); Standing Committee; Executive Committee. **Languages** English, Hindi. **Staff** 69.00 FTE, paid. **Finance** Members' dues. Other sources: sales of publications; Government grants; donations; income from exhibitions; rent from tenants. **Activities** Advocacy/lobbying/activism; awareness raising; training/education; events/meetings. **Events** *South Asian conference on women in environment* Delhi (India) 1992. **Publications** *Roshni* (4 a year) in English. Annual Report; tracts; pamphlets. **Members** Branches (530) and individuals (1,500,000). Membership countries not specified. **Consultative Status** Consultative status granted from: *ECOSOC (#05331)* (Special); *UNICEF (#20332)*. **IGO Relations** *FAO (#09260)*. Accredited by: *United Nations Office at Vienna (UNOV, #20604)*. Observer to: *United Nations Framework Convention on Climate Change – Secretariat (UNFCCC, #20564)*. Associated with Department of Global Communications of the United Nations. **NGO Relations** Board member of: *Conference of Non-Governmental Organizations in Consultative Relationship with the United Nations (CONGO, #04635)*. Member of: *NGO Committee on the Status of Women, Geneva (#17117)*; *NGO Committee on UNICEF (#17120)*. Affiliated to: *International Alliance of Women (IAW, #11639)*; *Pan Pacific and South East Asia Women's Association (PPSEAWA, #18186)*. [2018/XE0038/**E**]

♦ Alliott Group 00738

Head Office Imperial House, 8 Kean Street, London, WC2B 4AS, UK. T. +442033300110.
Registered Office Lyndum House, 12-14 High St, Petersfield, GU32 3JG, UK.
URL: https://www.alliottgroup.net/

History 1979, UK. **Aims** Provide a global solution; ensure clients have access to the combined expertise of accountants and lawyers; provide a collaborative, cost efficient alternative to an international 'network'. **Structure** Worldwide Board; Regional Advisory Committees; Executive Office. **Activities** Events/meetings; training/education. **Events** *EMEA Regional Conference* Dubai (United Arab Emirates) 2019, *Annual Conference* Madrid (Spain) 2019, *EMEA Regional Conference* Prague (Czechia) 2018. **Members** Accounting and law firms (about 170) in 70 countries. Membership countries not specified. [2020/AA0470/**F**]

- Allmän förklaring om de mänskliga rättigheterna (1948 treaty)
- ALLMEP – Alliance for Middle East Peace (internationally oriented national body)
- All Nations Christian College (internationally oriented national body)
- All Nations Generating Equal Love (internationally oriented national body)
- Alloy Phase Diagram International Commission (unconfirmed)
- All Pakistan Women's Association (internationally oriented national body)
- All Party Working Group on the Separation of Religion and Politics / see European Parliament Platform for Secularism in Politics (#08152)
- **ALLPI** Africa Leather and Leather Products Institute (#00185)
- **ALLRAIL** Alliance of Rail New Entrants (#00714)
- All-Russia Market Research Institute (internationally oriented national body)
- **ALLS** African Labour Law Society (#00354)
- All Slavic Beekeeping Union / see Federacia Vcelarskych Organizacii (#09287)

♦ All Terrain Vehicle Industry European Association (ATVEA) 00739

SG c/o LOGOS, Bvd du Souverain 280, 1160 Brussels, Belgium. T. +3228999662. E-mail: secretariat@atvea.org.
URL: http://www.atvea.org/

History 2003. EU Transparency Register; 37135513916-07. **Aims** Promote the correct and responsible use of All Terrain Vehicles (ATV) in Europe; enable members to work more closely together on issues of mutual interest. **Structure** General Assembly; Council; Secretariat. Committees (2): Education and Communication; Technical. **NGO Relations** In liaison with technical committees of: *Comité européen de normalisation (CEN, #04162)*. [2016/XJ4952/t/**D**]

- All-Union Aeronautical Society (inactive)
- All Union Theriological Society (internationally oriented national body)
- All Union Znanie Society / see International Association 'Znanie'
- All We Can (internationally oriented national body)
- **ALMA** African Leaders Malaria Alliance (#00359)
- ALMACA / see International Employee Assistance Professionals Association (#13264)
- **ALM** Adults Learning Mathematics: International Research Forum (#00125)
- **ALMAE** Alliance Maghreb-Machrek pour l'eau (#16544)
- **ALM** Asociación Latinoamericana de Micologia (#16248)
- ALM – Association of Lactose Manufacturers (inactive)
- ALM – Associazione Laicale Missionaria (internationally oriented national body)
- Alment Praktiserende Laegers Europaeiske Organisation / see European Union of General Practitioners / Family Physicians (#08993)
- **ALMER** Asociación Latinoamericana de Medicina Reproductiva (#02240)
- **ALMID** Academia Latinoamericana de Médicos Intervencionistas en Dolor (#00016)
- ALM / see Inter-Cultural Association (#11465)
- ALM International / see Inter-Cultural Association (#11465)
- ALM International – American Leprosy Missions (internationally oriented national body)
- ALMU / see Asian Lubricants Industry Association (#01532)

♦ ALN 00740

Communications Manager PO Box 200-00606, Sarit Centre, Nairobi, 00606, Kenya. E-mail: info@aln.africa.
Communications Manager ALN House, Eldama Ravine Close, Off Eldama Ravine Road, Westlands, Nairobi, 00606, Kenya.
URL: https://aln.africa

History 2004, Ebene (Mauritius). Former names and other names: *Africa Legal Network (ALN)* – former. **Aims** Bring global expertise, continental reach and deep local know-how to help clients navigate the multitude of opportunities and risks in Africa, holistically combining legal, tax, regulatory and commercial advice. **Languages** English. **Activities** Networking/liaising. Legal services Active in all member countries. **Events** *Africa Investment Conference* Dubai (United Arab Emirates) 2018, *Africa Investment Conference* Dubai (United Arab Emirates) 2017, *Africa Investment Conference* Dubai (United Arab Emirates) 2016. **Publications** *Africa Bulletin* in English. Legal notes; investment guides. **Information Services** *Legal Alerts* in English.
Members Full in 16 countries:
Algeria, Côte d'Ivoire, Ethiopia, Guinea, Kenya, Madagascar, Malawi, Mauritius, Morocco, Nigeria, Rwanda, Sudan, Tanzania UR, Uganda, United Arab Emirates, Zambia. [2022.05.12/XM5661/**F**]

- **ALN** Africa Liberal Network (#00187)
- ALN – Africa Logistics Network (unconfirmed)
- **ALNAP** Active Learning Network for Accountability and Performance in Humanitarian Action (#00101)
- **ALNAP** African Laboratory for Natural Products (#00353)
- Alnoor Institute for the Arabian Gulf / see Saudi Bahraini Institute for the Blind
- **ALO** Arab Labour Organization (#01001)
- **ALOAS** Asociación Latinoamericana de Operadores de Agua y Saneamiento (#02246)
- **ALODYB** Asociación Latinoamericana de Odontologia Restauradora y Biomateriales (#02244)
- **ALOGIA** Asociación Latinoamericana de Obstetricia y Ginecologia Infantil y de la Adolescencia (#02243)
- **ALOOH** Asociación Latinoamericana Out of Home (#02248)
- **ALOP** Asociación Latinoamericana de Odontopediatría (#02245)
- ALOP – Asociación Latinoamericana de Organizaciones de Promoción (inactive)
- **ALPA** Asociación Latinoamericana para la Producción Animal (#02257)
- ALPAI – Air Line Pilots Association, International (internationally oriented national body)
- ALPAR / see Asociación Latinoamericana de Parques Cementerios y Servicios Funderarios (#02251)
- **ALPAR** Asociación Latinoamericana de Parques Cementerios y Servicios Funderarios (#02251)

♦ AlpArray 00741

Contact address not obtained.
URL: http://www.alparray.ethz.ch/

Aims Advance the understanding of orogenesis and its relationship to mantle dynamics, plate reorganizations, surface processes and seismic hazard in the Alps-Apennines-Carpathians-Dinarides orogenic system. **Structure** Steering Committee; Project Coordination; Science Council; Working Groups. **Activities** Events/meetings; research/documentation; training/education. **Events** *Scientific Meeting* Prague (Czechia) 2022, *Scientific Meeting* Prague (Czechia) 2021, *Scientific Meeting* 2020, *Science Meeting* Frankfurt-Main (Germany) 2019, *Science Meeting* Zurich (Switzerland) 2018. **NGO Relations** Cooperates with (1): *European Geosciences Union (EGU, #07390)*. [2022.10.25/AA0615/**F**]

- **ALP** Association of Logic Programming (#02790)
- ALPCA – Automobile License Plate Collectors Association (internationally oriented national body)
- ALPCyT – Asociación Latinoamericana de Politica Cientifica y Tecnológica (inactive)
- Alpe-Adria / see Alps-Adriatic-Alliance (#00747)

♦ Alpe Adria Association for Perinatal Medicine 00742

Contact Dept Gynecology and Obstetrics, Perinatal Ctr, Klinikum Klagenfurt am Wörthersee, Feschnigstr 11, 9020 Klagenfurt am Wörthersee, Austria. T. +4346353839603. Fax +4346353839607.
Contact Dept of Obstetrics and Gynecology, Medizinische Uni Graz, Auenbruggerplatz 14, 8036 Graz, Austria. T. +4331638517069. Fax +4331638514197. E-mail: obstet.obgyn@medunigraz.at.
URL: http://www.alpeadria2014.eu/

Structure Scientific Committee. **Events** *Meeting* Graz (Austria) 2019, *Meeting* Ljubljana (Slovenia) 2018, *Meeting* Tapolca (Hungary) 2017, *Meeting* Zagreb (Croatia) 2016, *Meeting* Bassano del Grappa (Italy) 2015.
Members Full in 5 countries:
Austria, Croatia, Hungary, Italy, Slovenia. [2019.02.13/XJ9639/**D**]

- ALPEC – Asociación Latinoamericana de Derecho Penal y Criminologia (unconfirmed)
- Alpen-Adria-Allianz (#00747)
- Alpen-Adria / see Alps-Adriatic-Alliance (#00747)
- Alpen-Initiative (internationally oriented national body)
- Alphabétisation solidaire (internationally oriented national body)
- Alpha Delta Kappa (internationally oriented national body)
- Alpha Europe Federation – European Federation for Alpha1 Antitrypsin Deficiency (inactive)
- Alpha Omega International Dental Fraternity (internationally oriented national body)

♦ Alpha – Scientists in Reproductive Medicine 00743

Admin 19 Mayis Mah, 19 Mayis Cad, Nova Baran Center No 4, 34360 Istanbul/Istanbul, Türkiye. T. +905444419766.
Chairperson London Bridge Fertility/Gynaecology/Genetics Centre, First Direct Bank, 40 Wakefield Road, 1 St Thomas Street, London, SE1 9RY, UK.
URL: http://www.alphascientists.org/

History 1994. **Aims** Advance the art and science of clinical embryology for the benefit of the public worldwide, through international promotion of education, communication and collaboration. **Languages** English. **Events** *Biennial Conference* Copenhagen (Denmark) 2016, *Biennial Conference* Antalya (Turkey) 2014, *Biennial Conference* London (UK) 2012, *Biennial Conference* Budapest (Hungary) 2010, *Biennial Conference* Istanbul (Turkey) 2008. **Publications** *RBMOnline* – journal.
Members Full in 38 countries and territories:
Afghanistan, Australia, Austria, Belgium, Canada, China, Croatia, Cyprus, Czechia, Denmark, Finland, France, Germany, Greece, Hungary, India, Ireland, Israel, Italy, Japan, Jordan, Mexico, Netherlands, New Zealand, Norway, Poland, Portugal, Russia, Serbia, Singapore, Spain, Sweden, Switzerland, Taiwan, Thailand, Türkiye, UK, USA.
Also members in West Indies. Membership countries not specified. [2021/XF5788/**F**]

- ALPI – Africa Liaison Program Initiative (internationally oriented national body)
- Alpine convention – Convention for the Protection of the Alps (1991 treaty)
- Alpine Ibex European Specialist Group / see Alpine Ibex European Specialist Group (#00744)

♦ Alpine Ibex European Specialist Group (GSE-AIESG) 00744

Gruppo Stambecco Europa (GSE)

Sec Parco Nazionale Gran Paradiso, Via Pio VII 9, 10135 Turin TO, Italy. T. +39118606211. E-mail: segreteria@pngp.it – info@pngp.it.
URL: http://www.pngp.it/gse

History Jul 1988. Founded as a work of the Sanitary Service of the Gran Paradiso National Park (GPNP). Former names and other names: *Alpine Ibex European Specialist Group (GSE-AIESG)* – former; *GSE-European Alpine Ibex Specialist Group* – former. **Aims** Collect information relative to the state of *conservation* of Alpine ibex on the whole Alpine Arc. **Structure** Secretariat at Gran Paradiso National Park, Turin (Italy). **Languages** English, French, Italian. **Activities** Knowledge management/information dissemination; monitoring/evaluation; projects/programmes; research/documentation; standards/guidelines. **Events** *World Conference on Mountain Ungulates* Cogne (Italy) 2022, *Meeting* Pont du Fossé (France) 2019, *Meeting* Kals am Grossglockner (Austria) 2015, *Meeting* Zernez (Switzerland) 2012, *Meeting* Turin (Italy) 2008.
Members Full in 6 countries:
Austria, France, Germany, Italy, Slovenia, Switzerland. [2022.05.04/XD6470/**E**]

♦ Alpine Tourist Commission (ATC) 00745

Touristische Gemeinschaft der Alpenländer (TGA)

Address not obtained.

History 1954. Previously referred to in French as *Commission de propagande touristique des pays alpins*. **Aims** Organize joint promotional campaigns, mainly on the American market. **Structure** Board of Directors, comprising heads of national tourist offices in member countries and of working group in North America (which comprises 1 representative of each member country). **Languages** English, German. **Activities** Annual *Walk My Alps* campaign in USA. **Publications** *The Alps – The Great Outdoors* (1996); *The Grand Tour of the Alps* (1991, 1994, 1995); *The United States of the Alps* (1990); *The Alps – A Sporting Life* (1989).
Members National tourist offices of 5 countries:
Austria, France, Germany, Italy, Switzerland. [2010.08.24/XD5518/**D**]

- ♦ Alpine Town of the Year Association (#20753)
- ♦ ALPJF – Asociación Latinoamericana de Psicologia Juridica y Forense (unconfirmed)
- ♦ **ALPMF** Asociación Latinoamericana de Profesores de Medicina Familiar (#02258)
- ♦ Alpok-Adria Munkaközösség / see Alps-Adriatic-Alliance (#00747)
- ♦ Alpok-Adria Szötvetség (#00747)
- ♦ ALPO – Latin American OTC Association / see Asociación Latinoamericana de Autocuidado Responsable (#02184)
- ♦ **ALPP** Asociación Latinoamericana de Paleobotanica y Palinologia (#02249)
- ♦ ALPRODI – Asociación Latinoamericana de Promotores de Desarrollo Institucional (inactive)

♦ Alps-Adria Acoustics Association (AAAA) 00746

Address not obtained.
URL: https://www.alpsadriaacoustics.eu/

History Sep 2002, Portoroz (Slovenia). **Aims** Promote all fields of research in acoustics in the whole Alps-Adria region and beyond; improve cooperation between national acoustical societies of the countries in this region. **Structure** General Assembly; Board; President; Chairperson. **Languages** Croatian, English, German, Slovene. **Staff** None. **Finance** None. **Activities** Events/meetings. **Events** *Congress* Budapest (Hungary) 2021, *Congress* Zagreb (Croatia) 2018, *Congress* Ljubljana (Slovenia) 2016, *Congress* Graz (Austria) 2014, *Congress* Zadar (Croatia) 2012.
Members Full in 3 countries:
Austria, Croatia, Slovenia. [2021/XD9149/**D**]

♦ Alps-Adriatic-Alliance 00747

Alpen-Adria-Allianz – Alleanza Alpe-Adria – Savez Alpe-Jadran – Zveza Alpe-Jadran – Alpok-Adria Szötvetség

General Secretariat Miesstaler Strasse 1, 9021 Klagenfurt am Wörthersee, Austria. T. +435053610134. Fax +435053610130. E-mail: abt1.alpeadria@ktn.gv.at.
URL: http://www.alps-adriatic-alliance.org

History 20 Nov 1978, Venice (Italy). Founded upon signing of a 'Joint Declaration'. Current title adopted when reorganized as a successor to original Community. Former names and other names: *Working Community of Cantons, Länder, Counties, Regions and Republics of the Eastern Alpine Regions* – former; *Arbeitsgemeinschaft von Ländern, Komitaten Regionen und Republiken des Ostalpengebiete* – former; *Comunità di Lavoro dei Länder, dei Comitati, delle Regioni e delle Repubbliche delle Alpi Orientali* – former; *Delovna Skupnost Dezel, Zupanij, Regij in Republik Vzhodnoalpskega Obmocja* – former; *Radna Zajednica Pokrajina, Zupanija Regija i Republika Istocnoalpskog Podrucja* – former; *A Keleti-Alpok Térsége Tartomanyainak, Megyéinek, Régióinak es Köztarsasagainak Munkaközössége* – former; *Association of the Eastern Alps* – former; *Association des régions des Alpes orientales* – former; *Asociación de las Regiones de los Alpes Orientales* – former; *Arbeitsgemeinschaft der Regionen der Ostalpen (Alpen-Adria)* – former; *Associazione delle Regioni delle Alpi Orientali (Alpe-Adria)* – former; *Alps-Adriatic Working Community* – former; *Communauté de travail Alpes-Adriatique* – former; *Arbeitsgemeinschaft Alpen-Adria* – former; *Comunità di Lavoro Alpe-Adria* – former; *Delovna Skupnost Alpe-Jadran* – former; *Radna Zajednica Alpe-Jadran* – former; *Alpok-Adria Munkaközösség* – former. **Aims** Strengthen *peace* and good-neighbourly relations; deepen knowledge of one another; exchange experience in common problems; cooperate in all spheres of common interest; search for new common interests and cultivate old common *traditions*; support south-eastern integration. **Structure** Alps-Adriatic Council; Steering Committee; Alps-Adriatic Contact Points; Thematic Coordination Points. **Languages** Croatian, German, Hungarian, Slovene. **Staff** 1.00 FTE, paid. **Finance** Sources: members' dues. **Activities** Networking/liaising. **Events** *Meeting* Klagenfurt am Wörthersee (Austria) 2020, *Meeting* Klagenfurt am Wörthersee (Austria) 2020, *Meeting* Varazdin (Croatia) 2019, *Meeting* Klagenfurt am Wörthersee (Austria) 2017, *Meeting* Klagenfurt am Wörthersee (Austria) 2015.
Members Länder, counties and republics (11) in 4 countries:
Austria (3), Croatia (6), Hungary (1), Slovenia (1).
IGO Relations Cooperates with (1): *Working Community of the Danube Regions (#21056)*. **NGO Relations** Instrumental in setting up (1): *Assembly of European Regions (AER, #02316)*. [2021.09.07/XE0414/**E**]

- ♦ Alps-Adriatic Working Community / see Alps-Adriatic-Alliance (#00747)
- ♦ **ALPS** Association for Law, Property and Society (#02785)
- ♦ **ALPSP** Association of Learned and Professional Society Publishers (#02786)
- ♦ ALPZA / see Asociación Latinoamericana de Parques Zoológicos y Acuarios (#02252)
- ♦ **ALPZA** Asociación Latinoamericana de Parques Zoológicos y Acuarios (#02252)

♦ Al-Qa'ida 00748

International Islamic Front for Jihad Against the Jews and Crusaders – Al-Jabhah al-Islamiyyah al-'Alamiyyah li-Qital al-Yahud wal-Salibiyyin

Address not obtained.

History late 1980s, by Osama bin Laden – also referred to as Usama Ibn Ladin – as an Islamic terrorist organization. Other titles: *The Base*; *Islamic Army for the Liberation of the Holy Places*; *Islamic Salvation Foundation*; *Qa'idat al-Jihad*; *Al Qaeda*. Commonly associated with the terrorist attack on the USA, 11 Sep 2001. Founded following splits within the *Maktab al-Khidamat (MAK) – Services Office*, co-founded by Osama bin Laden and Abdallah Azzam, mid-1980's, to coordinate and supply foreign material and human resources to the 'Mujahedeen' fighting the Soviet occupation of Afghanistan. **Aims** Unite the Muslim population and establish a government based on the rule of the Caliphs; eliminate opposition and impediments to the establishment of a Caliphate. **Structure** Consultative Council – 'shura al-majlis'. **Activities** Material, financial and training assistance to Muslim individuals and groups. **Members** A global network of individuals (approx 50,000) and groups (65). Membership countries not specified. **NGO Relations** Linked organizations: *Abu Hafs al-Masri Brigade (#00009)*; *Islamic Information Observatory (inactive)*; *Jemaah Islamiya (JI, #16097)*; *Islamic International Peacekeeping Brigade (IIPB, no recent information)*; *Rejection of Sins and Exodus (#18829)*; *Yemen Islamic Jihad (#21973)*. Possible links with: *Benevolence International Foundation (BIF, no recent information)*. [2009/XG9119/s/**F**]

♦ Al-Quds Committee 00749

Comité d'Al-Quds

Main Office c/o OIC, PO Box 178, Jeddah 21411, Saudi Arabia.
URL: http://www.oicun.org/6/37/

History Jun 1975, Jeddah (Saudi Arabia), as a Specialized Committee of *Organisation of Islamic Cooperation (OIC, #17813)*, on recommendation of the 6th *Council of Foreign Ministers (CFM, see: #17813)*. At the 10th Conference of Islamic Foreign Ministers, 1979, Fez (Morocco), King Hassan II of Morocco accepted the Chairmanship. Reconstituted 1981. Has also been referred to as *Jerusalem Committee – Comité de Jérusalem*. **Aims** Study the situation *Al-Quds* – Jerusalem (Israel); follow the implementation of related resolutions by OIC; follow the implementation of resolutions adopted by various international bodies on Jerusalem; put forward proposals to Member States and concerned bodies on measures to ensure implementation of these resolutions and cope with new situations. **Structure** Representatives of 16 countries elected for 3-year terms by OIC. **Activities** Maintains *Al-Quds Fund (no recent information)*. **Events** *International symposium* Fez (Morocco) 1998.
Members Foreign Ministers of 16 countries:
Bangladesh, Egypt, Guinea, Indonesia, Iran Islamic Rep, Iraq, Jordan, Lebanon, Mauritania, Morocco, Niger, Pakistan, Palestine, Saudi Arabia, Senegal, Syrian AR. [2015/XE8294/**E***]

- ♦ **ALRC** Asian Legal Resource Centre (#01529)
- ♦ ALSA – African Law Students' Association (internationally oriented national body)
- ♦ **ALSA** Asian Law & Society Association (#01526)
- ♦ **ALSA** Asian Law Students' Association (#01527)
- ♦ ALSA – Australasian Law Students' Association (internationally oriented national body)
- ♦ ALSEV – Asociación Latinoamericana de Seguridad Vial (internationally oriented national body)
- ♦ **ALSF** African Legal Support Facility (#00361)
- ♦ **ALSFAL** Asociación de Lingüística Sistémico Funcional de América Latina (#02279)
- ♦ **ALSMA** Asian Local Search and Media Association (#01531)
- ♦ **ALSO** Asociación Latinoamericana de Salud Ocupacional (#02264)
- ♦ ALSO / see Organisation du Sport Africain Travailliste et Amateur (#17827)

♦ Alström Syndrome International (ASI) 00750

Secretariat 14 Whitney Farm Rd, Mount Desert ME 04660, USA. E-mail: robin.marshall@alstrom.org – heather.cox@alstrom.org – info@alstrom.org.
URL: http://www.alstrom.org/

History Founded Aug 1995, Yarmouth NS (Canada), as *International Society for Alström Syndrome Families (SASF)*. **Aims** Provide resources, networking and emotional support among individuals and their families afflicted with Alström Syndrome; promote and encourage genetic and clinical research on the syndrome. **Structure** Board of Directors. **Languages** English, French, German, Italian, Japanese, Portuguese, Spanish, Turkish. **Staff** 6.00 FTE, voluntary. **Finance** Grants; donations. Budget (annual): US$ 200,000. **Activities** Research/documentation; training/education. **Events** *Family and Medical Conference* Galveston, TX (USA) 2019, *Family and Medical Conference* Plymouth, MA (USA) 2016, *Family and Medical Conference* Plymouth, MA (USA) 2013, *Family and medical conference* Bar Harbor, ME (USA) 2010, *International Belgian family conference* Ghent (Belgium) 2008. **Members** Individuals in 56 countries and territories (not specified). **NGO Relations** Member of: *EURORDIS – Rare Diseases Europe (#09175)*. [2017/XD7506/**D**]

- ♦ **ALTA** Asociación Latinoamericana y del Caribe de Transporte Aéreo (#16263)
- ♦ ALTA / see Australasian Law Academics Association (#03025)
- ♦ ALTAC – Asociación Latinoamericana de Transportadores Aéreos de Carga (inactive)
- ♦ Altadeva (unconfirmed)
- ♦ **ALT** Association for Linguistic Typology (#02788)
- ♦ **ALTE** Asociación Latino Americana de Teoria Económica (#02271)
- ♦ **ALTE** Association of Language Testers in Europe (#02779)
- ♦ ALTEC / see Asociación Latino-Iberoamericana de Gestión Tecnológica y de la Innovación (#02277)
- ♦ **ALTEC** Asociación Latino-Iberoamericana de Gestión Tecnológica y de la Innovación (#02277)
- ♦ **ALTER ESDR** ALTER – European Society for Disability Research (#00751)
- ♦ **ALTER-EU** Alliance for Lobbying Transparency and Ethics Regulation (#00705)

♦ ALTER – European Society for Disability Research (ALTER ESDR) .. 00751

Société Européenne de Recherche sur le Handicap

Contact PHS-EHESS, 190 avenue de France, 75013 Paris, France.
URL: http://www.alter-asso.org/

Aims Advance interdisciplinary research in social sciences and humanities in the area of disabilities. **Structure** Board. **Activities** Events/meetings. **Events** *Annual International Conference* Cologne (Germany) 2019, *Annual International Conference* Lille (France) 2018, *Annual International Conference* Lausanne (Switzerland) 2017, *Annual International Conference* Stockholm (Sweden) 2016, *Annual International Conference* Paris (France) 2015. **Publications** *Alter – European Journal of Disability Research*. [2019/XM4965/**D**]

- ♦ AlterInter / see Alternatives International (#00753)
- ♦ **Alter-Inter** Alternatives International (#00753)
- ♦ Alternativa Bolivariana para los Pueblos de Nuestra América / see Alianza Bolivariana de los Pueblos de Nuestra América (#00627)
- ♦ alterNativa – Intercanvi amb Pobles Indigenes (internationally oriented national body)
- ♦ Alternativas Latinoamericanas de Desarrollo Humano y Estudios Antropológicos (unconfirmed)
- ♦ Alternativa Solidaria – PLENTY / see alterNativa – Intercanvi amb Pobles Indigenes
- ♦ Alternativas Sostenibles de Desarrollo (internationally oriented national body)
- ♦ Alternative Action for African Development (internationally oriented national body)
- ♦ Alternative ASEAN Network on Burma (internationally oriented national body)
- ♦ Alternative Information and Development Centre (internationally oriented national body)

♦ Alternative Investment Management Association (AIMA) 00752

CEO 2nd floor, 167 Fleet Street, London, EC4A 2EA, UK. T. +442078228380. Fax +442078228381. E-mail: info@aima.org.
URL: http://www.aima.org/

History 1990. Former names and other names: *European Managed Futures Association (EMFA)* – former (1990 to 1997). Registration: Companies House, No/ID: 4437037, England and Wales. **Aims** Provide an interactive and professional forum for members and act as a catalyst and promoter of the global *hedge fund* industry; provide leadership to the industry and be its pre-eminent voice; develop sound practices, enhance industry transparency and education, and liaise with the wider financial community, institutional investors, the media, regulators, governments and other policy makers. **Structure** Governing Council; National Groups; Global Offices (8). **Languages** Czech, English, French, German, Mandarin Chinese, Spanish. **Staff** 38.00 FTE, paid. **Finance** Sources: members' dues. **Activities** Advocacy/lobbying/activism; events/meetings; networking/liaising; publishing activities; research/documentation; training/education. **Events** *Next Generation Manager Forum* London (UK) 2023, *Digital Assets Conference* New York, NY (USA) 2023, *Singapore Annual Forum* Singapore (Singapore) 2023, *APAC Annual Forum* Hong Kong (Hong Kong) 2022, *Global Policy & Regulatory Forum* Paris (France) 2022. **Publications** *AIMA Journal* (4 a year). Research papers; sound practice guides. Information Services: Online Regulatory and Tax Resource. **Members** Corporate members (over 2,100) in over 60 countries. Membership countries not specified. **NGO Relations** Instrumental in setting up (1): *Chartered Alternative Investment Analyst Association (CAIA Association)*. [2023.02.24/XD3407/**D**]

- ♦ Alternatives – Action and Communication Network for International Development (internationally oriented national body)
- ♦ Alternatives au développement / see Society for Development Alternatives
- ♦ Alternatives de développement durable (internationally oriented national body)

♦ Alternatives International (Alter-Inter) 00753

SG c/o Alternatives CA, 3720 ave du Parc, Ste 300, Montréal QC H2X 2J1, Canada. T. +15149826635.
URL: http://alternatives-international.net/

History Also referred to as *AlterInter*. **Publications** *Alternatives International Journal*.
Members Organizations in 9 countries and territories:
Canada, France, India, Israel, Morocco, Niger, Palestine, South Africa.
NGO Relations *Agence pour la Solidarité Internationale, la Culture, le Développement et l'Environnement (AMORCES)*. [2010/XM4639/**F**]

♦ Alternatives to Neo-Liberalism in Southern Africa (ANSA) 00754

Secretariat 78 East Road, Avondale, Harare, HARARE, Zimbabwe. T. +2634308846. Fax +2634339833. E-mail: timothy@ledriz.co.zw – ngoni@ledriz.co.zw – godfrey@ledriz.co.zw.
URL: http://www.ansa-africa.org/

History 2003. **Aims** Stimulate a process of building a critical mass than can organize, mobilize and lead a regional process aimed at: creating participatory radical democracy; scrutinizing and questioning neo-liberalism; advocating for implementation of an anti-neo-liberal, pro-poor, sustainable, people-driven and human-centres alternative development model for Southern Africa. **Structure** Coordinating Committee. **Languages** English. **Staff** 4.00 FTE, paid. **Finance** Funded by cooperating partners and stakeholders organizations. Budget (annual): US$ 500,000. **Activities** Research/documentation; knowledge management/information dissemination. **IGO Relations** *Southern African Development Community (SADC, #19843)*. [2014.09.22/XJ8669/**D**]

- ♦ Alternatives – Réseau d'action et de communication pour le développement international (internationally oriented national body)
- ♦ Alternatives for Sustainable Development (internationally oriented national body)

♦ Alternatives to Violence Project International (AVP International) .. 00755

Pres address not obtained. E-mail: president@avp.international.
URL: http://avp.international/

Alternative Trade Mandate
00755

History 1975, New York, NY (USA). Originally a US workshop programme; became international early 1990's. **Aims** Support local AVP groups, programmes and facilitators by providing workshop materials, creating networks and organising events for facilitators to learn from each other and share their experiences. **Structure** A volunteer-based Committee structure. **Languages** English. Conferences are held in 15 languages; materials in 18 languages. **Staff** 2.00 FTE, paid. Over 70 volunteers from 25 countries. **Finance** Sources: donations. **Activities** Events/meetings; training/education. Active in: Angola, Argentina, Armenia, Australia, Azerbaijan, Belize, Bolivia, Bosnia-Herzegovina, Brazil, Burundi, Canada, Colombia, Congo DR, Costa Rica, Croatia, Cuba, Dominican Rep, Ecuador, El Salvador, Estonia, Ethiopia, France, Georgia, Germany, Guatemala, Haiti, Honduras, Hungary, India, Indonesia, Iraq, Ireland, Israel, Jordan, Kenya, Korea Rep, Lebanon, Liberia, Malaysia, Mexico, Namibia, Nepal, New Zealand, Nicaragua, Nigeria, Norway, Palestine, Panama, Peru, Philippines, Portugal, Romania, Russia, Rwanda, Samoa, Singapore, South Africa, South Sudan, Sudan, Uganda, UK, USA, Virgin Is USA, Zimbabwe. **Events** *Biennial Conference* USA 2006, *Biennial Conference* Auckland (New Zealand) 2004, *Biennial Conference* Papakura (New Zealand) 2004, *Biennial Conference* Lagos (Nigeria) 2002, *Biennial Conference* Nigeria 2002.
Members Formally recognised member AVP groups in 17 countries:
Australia, Bolivia, Canada, Ecuador, El Salvador, Germany, Ireland, Kenya, Liberia, Namibia, Nepal, Palestine, Romania, South Africa, Uganda, Ukraine, Zimbabwe.
[2023.02.14/XF5771/**F**]

♦ Alternative Trade Mandate Alliance (unconfirmed)
♦ Alternativs Européennes (#05891)
♦ ALTER-Net / see Alternet (#00756)

♦ Alternet
00756
Council Chair INBO, Havenlaan 88, bus 73, 1000 Brussels, Belgium.
Management Board Chair NINA, Høgskoleringen 9, 7034 Trondheim, Norway.
URL: http://alterneteurope.eu/

History Brussels (Belgium). Set up as an EU Network of Excellence (2004-2009). Since 2009 an independent consortium of institutional partners. Former names and other names: *A Long-Term Biodiversity, Ecosystem and Ecosystem Services Research and Awareness Network (ALTer Network)* – former; *ALTER-Net* – former. Registration: Federale Overheidsdienst Justitie, No/ID: 0755472622, Start date: 22 Aug 2020, Belgium. **Aims** Provide sound scientific evidence to international, European, national, and regional policymakers and businesses and people aimed at or involved in actively improving sustainable use, management, conservation and restoration of biodiversity, ecosystems, ecosystem services, and social involvement, through integration of European interdisciplinary research capacity, knowledge integration and communication. **Structure** Association Council (AC); Management Board. **Languages** English. **Staff** 0.50 FTE, paid; 10.00 FTE, voluntary. **Finance** Sources: in-kind support; members' dues. **Activities** Events/meetings; networking/liaising; projects/programmes; research/documentation; training/education. **Events** *Conference* Ghent (Belgium) 2022, *Conference on Synergies, Conflicts and Trade-Offs in the Relationship between Nature and Society* Ghent (Belgium) 2017, *Conference on Nature Based Solutions and Health in Urban Contexts* Ghent (Belgium) 2015, *Conference on Science Underpinning the EU 2020 Biodiversity Strategy* Ghent (Belgium) 2013.
Members Institutions (27) in 19 countries:
Austria, Belgium, Czechia, Estonia, Finland, France, Germany, Greece, Hungary, Italy, Luxembourg, Netherlands, Poland, Romania, Slovakia, Spain, Sweden, UK.
Included in the above, 3 institutes listed in this Yearbook:
ECNC – European Centre for Nature Conservation (#05289); European Regional Centre for Ecohydrology of the Polish Academy of Sciences, Lodz (ERCE PAS, #08341); Potsdam Institute for Climate Impact Research (PIK).
NGO Relations Instrumental in setting up (1): *European Long-Term Ecosystem Research Network (LTER-Europe, #07712)*.
[2022.12.02/XJ7481/y/**F**]

♦ ALTer Network / see Alternet (#00756)
♦ Alter Summit (unconfirmed)
♦ Altiero Spinelli Institute for Federalist Studies (internationally oriented national body)
♦ **ALTO** Association of Language Travel Organizations (#02780)

♦ Altrusa International (AI)
00757
Main Office One North LaSalle St, Ste 1955, Chicago IL 60602, USA. T. +13124274410. E-mail: altrusa@altrusa.org.
Pres address not obtained. E-mail: president@altrusa.org.
URL: http://www.altrusa.org/

History 1917, Nashville TN (USA), as (US) National Association of Altrusa Clubs. Became *International Association of Altrusa Clubs* in 1935. Present title adopted 1947. Originally exclusively for women is now open to both sexes. **Aims** Provide opportunities by which *executives* and professionals may join forces and work for community and world improvement, and become established in careers; take part in community and public affairs on a non-partisan basis; promote better race relations and mutual understanding between peoples of all nations. **Structure** Convention (every 2 years); Board of Directors (meets annually). Committees (6): Communications; Leadership Development; Membership Development; Service Development; United Nations; Clubs at Large. Membership is exclusively for outstanding representatives of each particular business or profession and by invitation only. **Languages** English. **Staff** 8.00 FTE, paid. **Finance** Dues on a per capita basis. Special contributions to Altrusa International Foundation. **Activities** Carries on a diversity of community projects; supports charities; holds career conferences in schools; helps older workers prepare for jobs. Clubs are guided by 2-year planned programme. **Events** *Biennial Convention* Reno, NV (USA) 2019, *Biennial Convention* Nashville, TN (USA) 2017, *Biennial Convention* Kansas City, MO (USA) 2015, *Biennial Convention* Rapid City, SD (USA) 2011, *Biennial Convention* Indianapolis, IN (USA) 2009. **Publications** *Altrusa Accent* (4 a year); *International Altrusan* (annual).
Members Clubs, totalling over 17,000 individuals, in 15 countries and territories:
Bahamas, Bermuda, Canada, Chile, Dominican Rep, Ecuador, Guatemala, India, Ireland, Mexico, Puerto Rico, Russia, Ukraine, USA.
Consultative Status Consultative status granted from: *ECOSOC (#05331)* (Ros A). **IGO Relations** Accredited by: *United Nations Office at Vienna (UNOV, #20604)*. Associated with Department of Global Communications of the United Nations. **NGO Relations** Member of: *Conference of Non-Governmental Organizations in Consultative Relationship with the United Nations (CONGO, #04635)*.
[2019/XC0045/v/**D**]

♦ ALTSEAN Burma – Alternative ASEAN Network on Burma (internationally oriented national body)
♦ **ALU** Arab Lawyers' Union (#01002)
♦ Aluminium Foil Conference (inactive)

♦ Aluminium Stewardship Initiative (ASI)
00758
CEO address not obtained.
URL: http://aluminium-stewardship.org/

History Global group of stakeholders got together to initiate ASI, 2009. Incorporated as a non-profit entity, Jun 2015. **Aims** Define globally applicable standards for sustainability performance and material chain-of-custody for the aluminium value chain; promote measurable and continual improvements in the key environmental, social and governance impacts of aluminium production, use and recycling; develop a credible assurance and certification system that both mitigates the risks of non-conformity with ASI standards and minimizes barriers to broad scale implementation. **Structure** Board. **Activities** Standards/guidelines; knowledge management/information dissemination; events/meetings. **Events** *World Aluminium Conference* London (UK) 2023.
Members Associations; Civil Society; Downstream Supporters; General Supporters; Industrial Users; Production and Transformation. Members (55). Membership countries not specified. Included in the above, 9 organizations listed in this Yearbook:
European Aluminium (#05893); European Outdoor Group (EOG, #08122); Fauna & Flora International (FFI, #09277); Global Aluminium Foil Roller Initiative (GLAFRI, #10234); Gulf Aluminium Council (GAC); IndustriALL Global Union (IndustriALL, #11177); Institute for Human Rights and Business (IHRB); International Union for Conservation of Nature and Natural Resources (IUCN, #15766); World Wide Fund for Nature (WWF, #21922).
NGO Relations Full member of: *ISEAL (#16026)*.
[2021/XM6205/**F**]

♦ Alumni Association of the Inter-American School of Librarianship
00759
Association des anciens élèves de l'Ecole interaméricaine de bibliothéconomie – Asociación de Egresados de la Escuela Interamericana de Bibliotecología (ASEIBI)
Main Office Univ de Antioquia, Edif TEQUENDAMA – Carr 49 No 52, 61 Of 704, Medellin, Antioquia, Colombia. Fax +5742512116. E-mail: aseibi.org@gmail.com.
URL: http://www.aseibi.org.co/

History Nov 1982, Medellin (Colombia). Officially recognized Jun 1983. **Aims** Represent, defend and protect *professional* interests of members; monitor professional ethics fulfilment; stimulate research in library science, documentation and information science; promote professional training and continuing education among affiliates; offer technical and consultative advice to the public and private sector, for the planning, organization and development of its information units. **Structure** General Assembly. Management Board, consisting of President, Vice-President, Secretary, Treasurer, 4 additional members and Auditor. **Activities** Organizes Alumni Meeting every other year. Training; formal courses; 'ASEIBI Thursdays' (specific subject conferences held every 2 months). Grants the Luis Florén Lozano Award (annually). **Publications** *Boletin de ASEIBI* (6 a year).
[2011/XE1116/**E**]

♦ Alumni Europae (AE)
00760
Contact Av Huart-Hamoir 48, 1030 Brussels, Belgium. E-mail: admin@alumnieuropae.org.
URL: http://www.alumnieuropae.org/

History 2011. *euresco.org (inactive)* merged into Alumni Europae, 2013. **Aims** Unite and reunite former students, as well as parents, teachers and staff from all European Schools, by putting like-minded people in touch on a social and professional level. **Structure** Annual General Meeting; Board. **Languages** All European languages. **Finance** Sources: donations. **Activities** Events/meetings; networking/liaising; training/education.
Members Individuals (over 5,000) mainly in Europe. Membership countries not specified. **IGO Relations** *European Commission (EC, #06633)*. **NGO Relations** European Schools General Secretariat.
[2021.06.07/XM6616/**E**]

♦ **ALUS** – Association for Literary Urban Studies (internationally oriented national body)
♦ **ALVAO** – Association des langues vivantes pour l'Afrique occidentale (inactive)
♦ **ALVEFAS** – Asociación Latinoamericana de Veterinarios de Fauna Silvestre (unconfirmed)
♦ **ALVEFAS** – Associação Latinoamericana de Veterinarios de Fauna Silvestre (unconfirmed)
♦ **ALVO** – Asociación Latinoamericana de Volcanologia (unconfirmed)
♦ Al-Wifaq Al Watani Al-Iraqi (internationally oriented national body)

♦ Alzheimer Europe (AE)
00761
Exec Dir Rue Dicks 14, L-1417 Luxembourg, Luxembourg. T. +352297970. Fax +352297972. E-mail: info@alzheimer-europe.org.
Events Manager address not obtained.
URL: http://www.alzheimer-europe.org/

History 2 Mar 1992, Brussels (Belgium). Founded on adoption of statutes, following initial moves, 3 Sep 1990, Leuven (Belgium) and inaugural meeting, Jan 1991, Nordbergum (Netherlands). Statutes amended and adopted at Annual Meeting on 1 Oct 1997, Helsinki (Finland), when seat transferred to Luxembourg. Most recent statutes adopted, Jul 1999, London (UK). Registration: Luxembourg; EU Transparency Register, No/ID: 37399753690-65, Start date: 1 Jun 2010. **Aims** Support patients suffering from Alzheimer's disease, or related disorders, and their care providers; raise awareness of Alzheimer's disease among medical practitioners, paramedical organizations, social workers and other European institutions; develop models for improved care of Alzheimer patients and promote training of care personnel; increase political advocacy in each member country; encourage and support research and the advance of knowledge into the cause, early diagnosis, treatment and prevention of the disease; promote worldwide cooperation with other organizations having the same or similar objectives. **Structure** General Meeting (annual); Board of Directors; Secretariat, headed by Executive Director. **Languages** English. **Staff** 4.00 FTE, paid. **Finance** Members' dues. Other sources: European Commission; donations; corporate sponsorship. **Activities** Events/meetings; projects/programmes. **Events** *Alzheimer Europe Conference* Helsinki (Finland) 2023, *Alzheimer Europe Conference* Bucharest (Romania) 2022, *Alzheimer Europe Conference* 2021, *Annual Conference* 2020, *Annual Conference* The Hague (Netherlands) 2019. **Publications** *Dementia in Europe* (3 a year); *Alzheimer Europe Quarterly Newsletter*. *Alzheimer Care Manual*; *Alzheimer Self Help Manual* – in the 12 EU languages; *Alzheimer Telephone Helpline Manual*. Annual Report; children's books. Information Services: Databases of publications, member organizations and meetings.
Members Full organizations (28) in 24 countries:
Austria, Belgium, Czechia, Denmark, Finland, France, Germany, Greece, Iceland, Ireland, Italy, Luxembourg, Malta, Netherlands, Norway, Poland, Portugal, Romania, Slovakia, Spain, Sweden, Switzerland, Türkiye, UK.
Provisional members (2) in 1 country:
Bulgaria.
Consultative Status Consultative status granted from: *Council of Europe (CE, #04881)* (Participatory Status). **NGO Relations** Member of (2): *European Institute for Innovation through Health Data (i-HD, #07561); European Patients' Forum (EPF, #08172)*. Cooperates with (3): *Alzheimer's Disease International (ADI, #00762); European Institute of Women's Health (EIWH, #07574); Mental Health Europe (MHE, #16715)*. Participates in: *European Prevention of Alzheimer's Dementia Consortium (EPAD, #08271)*.
[2021/XD2168/**D**]

♦ Alzheimer's Disease International (ADI)
00762
CEO 57 Great Suffolk Street, London, SE1 0BL, UK. T. +442079810880. E-mail: info@alzint.org.
URL: https://www.alzint.org/

History 1984, Chicago, IL (USA). Located in London (UK) since 1995. Former names and other names: *Alzheimer's Disease International – International Federation of Alzheimer's Disease and Related Disorders Societies* – full title. Registration: USA. **Aims** Strengthen and support Alzheimer associations; raise awareness about dementia worldwide; make dementia a global health priority; empower people with dementia and their care partners; increase investment in dementia research. **Structure** Council; Board; Medical and Scientific Advisory Panel. **Languages** English. **Staff** 13.00 FTE, paid. **Finance** Sources: donations; members' dues. **Activities** Advocacy/lobbying/activism; awareness raising; events/meetings; knowledge management/information dissemination. **Events** *Annual International Conference* Amsterdam (Netherlands) 2023, *Annual International Conference* London (UK) 2022, *Asia Pacific Regional Conference* Taipei (Taiwan) 2022, *Annual International Conference* Singapore (Singapore) 2020, *Annual International Conference* Singapore (Singapore) 2020. **Publications** *Global Perspective* (2 a year); *World Alzheimer Report* (annual). Booklets; factsheets.
Members Full: national organizations representing people with dementia and their families and related disorders in 127 countries and territories:
Albania, Argentina, Armenia, Aruba, Australia, Austria, Azerbaijan, Bahamas, Bangladesh, Barbados, Belgium, Bermuda, Bolivia, Bonaire Is, Bosnia-Herzegovina, Brazil, Brunei Darussalam, Bulgaria, Burundi, Cameroon, Canada, Cayman Is, Chile, China, Colombia, Costa Rica, Croatia, Cuba, Curaçao, Cyprus, Czechia, Denmark, Dominica, Dominican Rep, Ecuador, Egypt, El Salvador, Estonia, Ethiopia, Finland, France, Georgia, Germany, Ghana, Gibraltar, Greece, Grenada, Guatemala, Honduras, Hong Kong, India, Indonesia, Iran Islamic Rep, Ireland, Israel, Italy, Jamaica, Japan, Jordan, Kenya, Korea Rep, Lebanon, Lesotho, Lithuania, Macau, Madagascar, Malaysia, Maldives, Mali, Malta, Mauritius, Mexico, Montenegro, Morocco, Myanmar, Nepal, Netherlands, New Zealand, Nicaragua, Nigeria, North Macedonia, Norway, Oman, Pakistan, Panama, Peru, Philippines, Portugal, Puerto Rico, Qatar, Romania, Russia, Saudi Arabia, Scotland, Senegal, Seychelles, Singapore, Slovakia, Slovenia, South Africa, Spain, Sri Lanka, St Kitts-Nevis, St Maarten, Suriname, Sweden, Switzerland, Taiwan, Tanzania UR, Thailand, Tonga, Trinidad-Tobago, Tunisia, Türkiye, Uganda, UK, Ukraine, United Arab Emirates, Uruguay, USA, Venezuela, Vietnam, Virgin Is UK, Virgin Is USA, Yemen, Zambia, Zimbabwe.
Associate: organizations with similar interests; individuals; corporate bodies. Membership countries not specified.
Consultative Status Consultative status granted from: *WHO (#20950)* (Official Relations). **NGO Relations** Member of (2): *International Alliance of Patients' Organizations (IAPO, #11633); Philanthropy Impact*.
[2022.10.20/XF1543/**F**]

♦ Alzheimer's Disease International – International Federation of Alzheimer's Disease and Related Disorders Societies / see Alzheimer's Disease International (#00762)
♦ **AMAAC** Arab Medical Association Against Cancer (#01006)
♦ **AMA** – African Mountain Association (inactive)
♦ **AMA** – African Mycological Association (inactive)
♦ **AMA** Agence Mondiale Antidopage (#21096)

♦ **AMA** Alianza del Mutualismo de América (#00634)
♦ **AMA** American Management Association International (#00787)
♦ AMA – Andean Mountain Association (inactive)
♦ **AMA** Art Moves Africa (#01124)
♦ **AMA** Asia Masters Athletics (#01291)
♦ AMA – Asia Missions Association (internationally oriented national body)
♦ **AMA** Asian Magic Association (#01533)
♦ **AMA** Asian Mycological Association (#01545)
♦ AMA – Asociación de Montañas Andinas (inactive)
♦ AMA – Association méditerranéenne d'andrologie (inactive)
♦ AMAC / see World Business Associates (#21253)
♦ **AMACZOOA** Asociación Mesoamericana y del Caribe de Zoológicos y Acuarios (#16730)
♦ **AMADE** Association Mondiale des Amis de l'Enfance (#02808)
♦ AMADE MONDIALE / see Association Mondiale des Amis de l'Enfance (#02808)
♦ AMAEA – Asia Medical Aesthetic Exchange Association (unconfirmed)
♦ AMAFE – Association of Manufacturers of Animal-Derived Food Enzymes (no recent information)
♦ AM – African Monitor (internationally oriented national body)
♦ **AMAGE** African Middle East Association of Gastroenterology (#00372)
♦ AMA/I / see American Management Association International (#00787)
♦ AMA International / see American Management Association International (#00787)
♦ Amalgamated Sheet Metal Worker's International Association / see International Association of Sheet Metal, Air, Rail and Transportation Workers
♦ AM – Alliance Mariale (see: #21334)
♦ AMALTA – Asociación de Mujeres de América Latina para el Control del Tabaquismo (inactive)
♦ **AMaMeF** Advanced Mathematical Methods for Finance (#00127)
♦ AMAMS – Asian Meeting of Animal Medicine Specialties (meeting series)
♦ **AMAN** Alliance of Mediterranean News Agencies (#00708)
♦ AM / see Ananda Marga Pracaraka Samgha (#00810)
♦ AMAN – Arab Regional Resource Center on Violence Against Women (internationally oriented national body)
♦ **AMAN** Asian Muslim Action Network (#01544)
♦ **AMANET** African Malaria Network Trust (#00365)
♦ **Amani Forum** Great Lakes Parliamentary Forum on Peace (#10705)
♦ Amani Institute (internationally oriented national body)

♦ Aman Union 00763

Secretariat General c/o ICIEC, Kingdom of Saudi Arabia, PO Box 15722, Jeddah 21454, Saudi Arabia. T. +966126467591. Fax +966126443447. E-mail: mmizouri@isdb.org.
URL: http://amanunion.net/

History Founded 28 Oct 2008, following an agreement between *Arab Investment and Export Credit Guarantee Corporation (DHAMAN, #00997)* and *Islamic Corporation for the Insurance of Investment and Export Credit (ICIEC, #16041).* **Aims** Promote and develop the *commercial* and non-commercial *risk insurance* industry in member countries; strengthen the mutual relationships among members. **Structure** General Assembly; Executive Council of 7 members; General Secretariat. **Activities** Events/meetings; training/education. **Events** *Annual Meeting* 2022, *Annual Meeting* 2020, *Annual Meeting* Muscat (Oman) 2019, *Annual Meeting* Cairo (Egypt) 2018, *Annual Meeting* Istanbul (Turkey) 2017.
Members Full (19) in 15 countries:
Algeria, Egypt, Indonesia, Iran Islamic Rep, Jordan, Lebanon, Malaysia, Oman, Qatar, Saudi Arabia, Senegal, Sudan, Tunisia, Türkiye, United Arab Emirates.
Included in the above, 2 multilateral members:
Arab Investment and Export Credit Guarantee Corporation (DHAMAN, #00997); Islamic Corporation for the Insurance of Investment and Export Credit (ICIEC, #16041).
Associate (8) in 4 countries:
Indonesia, Sudan, United Arab Emirates, Uzbekistan.
Observer (12) in 8 countries:
Austria, Cyprus, Egypt, France, Germany, Lebanon, Netherlands, UK.
Included in the above, 2 organizations listed in this Yearbook:
African Export-Import Bank (Afreximbank, #00305); Multilateral Investment Guarantee Agency (MIGA, #16888). [2022.05.08/XJ2307/y/**E**]

♦ **AMAO** Agence Monétaire de l'Afrique de l'Ouest (#20887)
♦ **AMAP** Arctic Monitoring and Assessment Programme (#01100)
♦ **AMARC** Association mondiale des radiodiffuseurs communautaires (#02810)

♦ AMARC Europe 00764

Pres Rue de la Linière 11, 1060 Brussels, Belgium. T. +326094440. E-mail: contact@amarceurope.eu.
URL: https://amarceurope.eu/

History A section of *Association mondiale des radiodiffuseurs communautaires (AMARC, #02810).* Registration: Banque-Carrefour des Entreprises, No/ID: 0812.054.603, Start date: 3 Jun 2009, Belgium. **Structure** General Assembly; Board. **Finance** Sources: members' dues. **Activities** Advocacy/lobbying/activism; events/meetings. **Publications** *AMARC Europe Newsletter.*
Members Regular; Associate. Members in 22 countries:
Armenia, Austria, Belgium, Czechia, Denmark, Finland, France, Germany, Greece, Hungary, Ireland, Italy, Netherlands, North Macedonia, Norway, Romania, Serbia, Slovenia, Spain, Sweden, Switzerland, UK.
Community Media Forum Europe (CMFE, #04402). [2020/AA1272/y/**E**]

♦ AMARC International / see Association mondiale des radiodiffuseurs communautaires (#02810)
♦ AMAR International Charitable Foundation (internationally oriented national body)
♦ **AMAS** Area Maritima del Atlantico Sur (#19750)
♦ AMAS – ASEAN Meeting of Aesthetic Surgery and Medicine (meeting series)
♦ AMAS – Association de médecine aéronautique et spatiale (internationally oriented national body)
♦ **AMASC** Association mondiale des anciennes et anciens du Sacré Coeur (#21116)
♦ AMATA / see Australasian Genomic Technologies Association

♦ Amateo 00765

Gen Sec Galerie Ravenstein 50, 1000 Brussels, Belgium. E-mail: info@amateo.org.
Communications Officer address not obtained.
Pres address not obtained.
URL: https://www.amateo.org

History 21 Jun 2008, Ljubljana (Slovenia). Former names and other names: *NAPCA* – former; *The European Network for Active Participation in Cultural Activities (Amateo)* – full title. Registration: Banque-Carrefour des Entreprises, Start date: 2 Oct 2008, Belgium. **Aims** Promote intercultural dialogue; enhance the information flow, especially in the domain of socio-cultural activities among participating organizations; promote political acknowledgement of the importance of active participation in cultural activities; exchange information and practical demonstration among participants; enhance the realization of mutual cultural projects such as festivals, exhibitions, exchanges, touring, etc; enhance mobility of artists; gather initiatives for cultural projects, exchanges and touring as well as offer help in finding relevant partners in participating countries; promote joint research in the field of active participation in cultural activities. **Structure** Board; Secretariat, headed by General Secretary. **Languages** Croatian, Danish, Dutch, English, German, Serbian, Slovene. Many other languages spoken among the team and the wider network. **Staff** 0.60 FTE, paid. **Finance** Sources: contributions of member/participating states; grants; private foundations. Supported by: Creative Europe (Programme of the European Union); *European Cultural Foundation (ECF, #06868); European Union (EU, #08967).* **Activities** Advocacy/lobbying/activism; awards/prizes/competitions; capacity building; events/meetings; knowledge management/information dissemination; networking/liaising; projects/programmes; research/documentation; training/education. **Events** *General Assembly* 2021, *Annual Conference* Milan (Italy) 2021, *General Assembly* 2020, *Annual Conference* Vienna (Austria) 2020, *Annual General Meeting and Conference* Novi Sad (Serbia) 2019.
Members Individuals (over 50) from 23 countries:
Austria, Belgium, Bosnia-Herzegovina, Croatia, Cyprus, Czechia, Denmark, Estonia, Finland, France, Germany, Greece, Ireland, Italy, Montenegro, Netherlands, North Macedonia, Portugal, Serbia, Slovakia, Slovenia, Spain, Sweden, UK.
NGO Relations Member of (1): *Culture Action Europe (CAE, #04981).* [2023.02.14/XM1540/**F**]

♦ Amateur Chamber Music Players / see ACMP – The Chamber Music Network (#00072)
♦ Amateur Softball Association – Asia (no recent information)
♦ Amateur Swimming Union of the Americas / see PanAm Aquatics (#18077)
♦ **AMAV** Asociación Mundial de Anatomistas Veterinarios (#21202)
♦ **AMAV** Association mondiale des anatomistes vétérinaires (#21202)
♦ Amazigh World Congress (internationally oriented national body)
♦ Amazon Center for Environmental Education and Research (internationally oriented national body)
♦ Amazon Conservation Association (internationally oriented national body)
♦ Amazon Conservation Team (internationally oriented national body)

♦ Amazon Cooperation Treaty Organization (ACTO) 00766

Organización del Tratado de Cooperación Amazónica (OTCA) – Organização do Tratado de Cooperação Amazônica (OTCA)

SG SEPN 510, Bloco A 3º andar, Asa Norte, Brasilia DF, 70750-521, Brazil. E-mail: secretaria.permanente@otca.org.br – contato@otca.org.br.
URL: http://www.otca.info/

History 3 Jul 1978, Brasilia (Brazil). Established on ratification by governments of 8 countries of the *Treaty for Amazonian Cooperation (Amazon Pact, 1978).* Former names and other names: *Amazonian Cooperation Council (OTCA)* – former. **Aims** Establish closer cooperation among the eight Latin American countries within the Amazonian areas in order to promote: harmonious development; preservation of the environment; national use of the region's natural resources; full integration of the Amazonian territories in respective national economies. **Structure** Meeting of Ministers of Foreign Affairs; Amazon Cooperation Council (CCA); Coordination Commission of the Amazon Cooperation Council (CCOOR); Permanent National Commissions. **Languages** Dutch, English, Portuguese, Spanish.
Members Governments of 8 countries:
Bolivia, Brazil, Colombia, Ecuador, Guyana, Peru, Suriname, Venezuela.
IGO Relations Accredited by: *United Nations Framework Convention on Climate Change – Secretariat (UNFCCC, #20564).* [2021/XD8970/**D***]

♦ Amazon Environmental Research Institute (internationally oriented national body)
♦ Amazonian Cooperation Council / see Amazon Cooperation Treaty Organization (#00766)

♦ Amazonian Parliament 00767

Parlamento Amazónico

Exec Sec Av Universidad, Esq La Bolsa, Edif Antigua Corte Suprema, Piso 2, El Silencio, Caracas DF, Venezuela. T. +582124849321. E-mail: parlamentoamazonicovenezolano@gmail.com.

History 1989. **Structure** General Assembly (annual). Board of Directors, comprising President, a Vice-President per member country, Secretary General. Executive Secretariat. Commissions (4). **Activities** Commissions (4): Sustainable Development, Ecology and Biodiversity; Juridical, Legislative, of International Cooperation and Integration Matters; Political, Women, Human Rights, Peoples and Ethnic Groups of the Amazon; Cultural, Scientific, Technological and Educational Matters. Set up *Pan-Amazonian University, Manaos (no recent information),* Nov 1991. **Events** *Annual assembly / General Assembly* Lima (Peru) 2000, *General Assembly* Santa Cruz (Bolivia) 1996, *General Assembly* Quito (Ecuador) 1994, *General Assembly* Brasilia (Brazil) 1993, *General Assembly* Caraballeda (Venezuela) 1991. **Publications** *Informative Bulletin.*
Members Members of Parliaments of 8 countries:
Bolivia, Brazil, Colombia, Ecuador, Guyana, Peru, Suriname, Venezuela.
IGO Relations Formal agreement with: *UNESCO (#20322).* [2009/XF5444/**F***]

♦ Amazonia Working Group (internationally oriented national body)
♦ Amazon Pact – Treaty for Amazonian Cooperation (1978 treaty)
♦ Amazon Watch (internationally oriented national body)
♦ AMAZOO / see Meso-American and Caribbean Zoo and Aquarium Association (#16730)
♦ **AMBA** Association of MBAs (#02795)
♦ Ambasadori Odrzivog Razvoja i Zivotne Sredine (internationally oriented national body)
♦ Ambasadori Zivotne Sredine – Ambasadori Odrzivog Razvoja i Zivotne Sredine (internationally oriented national body)
♦ **AMB** Asociación Mundial de Boxeo (#21241)
♦ **AMB** Asociación Mundial de Buiatria (#21122)
♦ Ambassadors for Children (internationally oriented national body)

♦ Ambassadors for Christ International (AFCI) 00768

Main Office PO Box 470, Tucker GA 30085, USA. T. +17709214705. E-mail: info@afciworld.org.
URL: http://www.afciworld.org/

History 1948, as 'Australian Institute of Evangelism', by John Ridley and Alf Davey, Sydney (Australia). Present name adopted 1958. **Aims** Accelerate the spread of the *Gospel* through local churches worldwide; support local church efforts in evangelism, leadership training and church planting. **Structure** International Board; National Boards. **Activities** Networking/liaising. **Events** *General Conference* Valencia (Spain) 2002, *Conference* Singapore (Singapore) 1990. **Members** Individuals (101) in 23 countries. Membership countries not specified. [2018.09.24/XN1729/**F**]

♦ Ambassadors in Sport (internationally oriented national body)
♦ **AMBC** American Boxing Confederation (#00776)
♦ **AMBC** Confederación Americana de Boxeo (#00776)

♦ Ambedkar Center for Justice and Peace (ACJP) 00769

Gen Sec Gokuldas Pasta lane Dadar (East), Mumbai, Nagpur, Maharashtra 400 014, Nagpur MAHARASHTRA 400 014, India. T. +912224156697. Fax +912224156697.
URL: http://acjpindia.org/

History 1991, Toronto (Canada). Registered in accordance with Canadian law. **Aims** Make known internationally the problems of *untouchables* in *South Asia*; *empower* them through education and economic *self-dependence.* **Structure** International Board of Directors; International Board of Advisors. President, Vice-President, General Secretary-Treasurer. **Finance** Donations. **Activities** Creating a documentation and research centre; organizes meetings, conferences and seminars.
Members Covers 12 countries:
Austria, Canada, Chile, Denmark, Germany, Guatemala, India, Malaysia, Sri Lanka, Switzerland, UK, USA.
NGO Relations *Conference of Non-Governmental Organizations in Consultative Relationship with the United Nations (CONGO, #04635); International Human Rights Association of American Minorities (IHRAAM).* [2016/XE2155/**E**]

♦ **AMBER Alert Europe** European Child Rescue Alert and Police Network on Missing Children (#06533)

♦ Ambient Assisted Living Association (AAL Assocation) 00770

Dir Rue du Luxembourg 3, 1000 Brussels, Belgium. E-mail: info@aal-europe.eu.
URL: http://www.aal-europe.eu/

History Founded 19 Sep 2007, Brussels (Belgium). Registered in accordance with Belgian law. **Aims** Foster emergence of innovative ICT-based products, services and systems for *ageing* well at home, in the community and at work, thus increasing the quality of life, autonomy, participation in social life, skills and employability of the *elderly*, and reducing costs of health and *social care.* **Structure** General Assembly; Executive Board. **Languages** English. **Staff** 6.00 FTE, paid. **Finance** Budget (2013-2020): about euro 700 million. **Activities** Projects/programmes; events/meetings. **Events** *Forum* Trieste (Italy) 2021, *Forum* Aarhus (Denmark) 2019, *Forum* Bilbao (Spain) 2018, *Forum* Coimbra (Portugal) 2017, *Forum* St Gallen (Switzerland) 2016. **Publications** *AAL Newsletter.* Catalogue; forum proceedings.
Members National funding bodies in 19 countries:
Austria, Belgium, Cyprus, Denmark, Finland, Hungary, Israel, Italy, Luxembourg, Netherlands, Norway, Poland, Portugal, Romania, Slovenia, Spain, Sweden, Switzerland, UK.
IGO Relations *European Commission (EC, #06633)* – DG CONNECT. **NGO Relations** *AGE Platform Europe (#00557).* [2020/XJ1367/**D**]

- **AMB** Société mondiale de buiatrie (#21122)
- Ambulances animaux sans frontières (internationally oriented national body)
- Ambulances animaux sans frontières – SAVU / see Ambulances animaux sans frontières
- Ambulances ASF – Ambulances animaux sans frontières (internationally oriented national body)
- Ambulances ASF-SAVU / see Ambulances animaux sans frontières
- Ambulances Dieren Zonder Grenzen (internationally oriented national body)
- Ambulances Dieren Zonder Grenzen – SAVU / see Ambulances animaux sans frontières
- Ambulances DZG – Ambulances Dieren Zonder Grenzen (internationally oriented national body)
- Ambulances DZG-SAVU / see Ambulances animaux sans frontières
- AMCA – Asian Marine Conservation Association (internationally oriented national body)
- **AMC** African Music Council (#00379)
- **AMC** AfricaWide Movement for Children (#00530)
- AMCA International – Air Movement and Control Association International (internationally oriented national body)
- **AMC** Asian Methodist Council (#01539)
- AMC – Asian Migrant Centre (internationally oriented national body)
- **AMC** Asian Minifootball Confederation (#01541)
- AMC / see Association of World Citizens (#02982)
- **AMCB** Asian Migrants Coordinating Body (#01540)
- AMCB – Asian Migrants' Coordinating Body (internationally oriented national body)
- AMCC – Alliance mondiale contre le changement climatique (inactive)
- **AMCC** Asociación Mundial para la Comunicación Cristiana (#21126)
- **AMCC** Association mondiale pour la communication chrétienne (#21126)
- **AMCE** Asociación Mondial de Ciencias de la Educación (#02811)
- **AMCEN** African Ministerial Conference on the Environment (#00374)
- AMCEN – Conference of African Ministers Responsible for Sustainable Development and the Environment (inactive)
- AMCF – Association of Military Christian Fellowships (internationally oriented national body)
- AmChams in Europe / see European Council of American Chambers of Commerce (#06803)
- AMCHC / see Council of Arab Ministers for Housing and Reconstruction (#04862)
- AMCI – Agence marocaine de coopération internationale (internationally oriented national body)
- AMC Institute (internationally oriented national body)
- AMC – Latin-Ibero American Society for Computational Methods in Engineering (inactive)
- **AMCOMET** African Ministerial Conference on Meteorology (#00375)
- **AMCOW** African Ministers' Council on Water (#00376)
- **AMCPCP** Associação Mundial de Counselling e Psicoterapia Centrados-na-Pessoa (#21172)
- AMDA – Association of Medical Doctors of Asia (internationally oriented national body)
- AMD – Aide médicale et développement (internationally oriented national body)
- **AMD** Association mondiale de dispacheurs (#02809)
- AMDC – African Minerals Development Centre (unconfirmed)
- AMDE / see Association of Medical Schools in Europe (#02799)
- **AMDIN** African Management Development Institutes Network (#00366)
- **AMDISA** Association of Management Development Institutions in South Asia (#02792)
- **AMDP** Association mondiale pour le développement de la philatélie (#21132)
- AMDS – International Conference on Algebraic Methods in Dynamical Systems (meeting series)
- AME / see AME World Ecology Foundation
- AME / see Aide médicale et développement
- AMEA – Alliance homme-environnement d'Afrique, Congo DR (unconfirmed)
- **AMEA** Asian Medical Education Association (#01537)
- AMEA – Associazione Mediterranea di Educazione degli Adulti (inactive)
- AME – African Methodist Episcopal Church (internationally oriented national body)
- **AME** Anti-Money Laundering Europe (#00857)
- **AME** Association for Moral Education (#02813)
- AMEB – Agrupación Mundial de Ex Boxeadores (inactive)
- AMECA – Asociación Médica del Caribe (internationally oriented national body)
- AMECA – Associação de Medicina Chinesa e Acupuntura da América do Sul (no recent information)
- **AMEC** Alliances Mondiales pour l'Eau et le Climat (#10230)
- AMEC – Asociación Mexicana de Estudios del Caribe (internationally oriented national body)
- **AMECEA** Association of Member Episcopal Conferences in Eastern Africa (#02805)

♦ AMECEA Pastoral Institute (API/Gaba) 00771

Institut pastoral de l'AMECEA

Pastoral Department PO Box 21191, Nairobi, 00505, Kenya. T. +254202444935. E-mail: pastoral@amecea.org.

URL: https://www.cuea.edu/?page_id=7221

History 1967, Gaba (Uganda). Founded by *Association of Member Episcopal Conferences in Eastern Africa (AMECEA, #02805).* In 1976, moved to Eldoret (Kenya). As of 2008, considered a campus of *Catholic University of Eastern Africa, The (CUEA, #03610).* Former names and other names: *API* – former. **Aims** As a *Catholic* pastoral institute, provide ongoing training and renewal of pastoral leaders and agents of *evangelization* in a supportive setting enriched by dialogue among *lay* persons, *religious* men, women and *clergy.* **Structure** Plenary Assembly. **Staff** 14.00 FTE, paid. **Finance** Members' dues. Scholarships from funding bodies in Germany, Italy, Netherlands. Budget (annual): about Kenyan Shillings 12 million. **Activities** Conducts research; offers one-year residential courses; provides pastoral training and spiritual renewal opportunities in the region. Core courses in the following areas: Pastoral Theology; Pastoral Communication; Pastoral Counselling; Religious Education/Catechesis; Spirituality; Liturgy; Scripture; Pastoral Anthropology; Development Studies. Organizes workshops. **Publications** *African Ecclesial Review (AFER)* (6 a year). *Spearhead Monograph Series.*

Members Full in 8 countries:
Eritrea, Ethiopia, Kenya, Malawi, Sudan, Tanzania UR, Uganda, Zambia.
Associate in 1 country:
Seychelles. [2019/XE5117/**E**]

- **AMEC** International Association for Measurement and Evaluation of Communication (#12020)
- **AMEDA** Africa and Middle East Depositories Association (#00190)
- AMED – Asia-Middle East Dialogue (meeting series)
- AMED – Association for Management Education and Development (internationally oriented national body)
- AMED – Association méditerranéenne de dermato-vénéréologie (inactive)
- **AMEE** Asociación Mundial de Educación Especial (#21193)
- **AMEE** Association for Medical Education in Europe (#02797)
- **AMEEMR** Association for Medical Education in the Eastern Mediterranean Region (#02796)

♦ L'âme de L'Europe 00772

The Soul of Europe

Pres Rue d'Arlon 53, 1000 Brussels, Belgium.

URL: http://www.lamedeleurope.eu/

History Registration: Banque-Carrefour des Entreprises, No/ID: 0780.609.280, Start date: 18 Jan 2002, Belgium; EU Transparency Register, No/ID: 686344047807-33, Start date: 30 Sep 2022. **Aims** Celebrate the founding fathers of Europe; highlight the rotating Presidencies of the European Union through culture and the environment; enhance cultural innovations and ecosystems, human well-being in the environment, air and food quality. [2022/AA2981/**E**]

- AME-Fundação Mundial de Ecologia (internationally oriented national body)
- AMEG – Arctic Methane Emergency Group (unconfirmed)
- **AMEHS** Afro Middle East Hernia Society (#00539)
- AMEI – Asociación Mexicana de Estudios Internacionales (internationally oriented national body)
- **AMEI-WAECE** Asociación Mundial de Educadores Infantiles (#21136)
- **AMEI-WAECE** Associação Mundial de Educadores Infantis (#21136)
- **AMEI-WAECE** World Association of Early Childhood Educators (#21136)
- **AMEM** Missão AMEM (#20850)
- AMEN – AfriCaribe Microenterprise Network (internationally oriented national body)
- Amendement à la Convention de Bâle sur le contrôle des mouvements transfrontières de déchets dangereux et de leur élimination (1995 treaty)
- Amendement au Protocole de Montréal relatif à des substances qui appauvrissant la couche d'ozone (2016 treaty)
- Amendement au Protocole de Montréal relatif à des substances qui appauvrissant la couche d'ozone (1999 treaty)
- Amendement au Protocole de Montréal relatif à des substances qui appauvrissent la couche d'ozone (1992 treaty)
- Amendement au Protocole de Montréal relatif à des substances qui appauvrissent la couche d'ozone (1990 treaty)
- Amendement au Protocole de Montréal relatif à des substances qui appauvrissent la couche d'ozone, 1997 (1997 treaty)
- Amendements à la Convention pour la protection de la mer Méditerranée contre la pollution (1995 treaty)
- Amendements au Protocole relatif à la prévention de la pollution de la mer Méditerranée par les opérations d'immersion effectuées par les navires et aéronefs (1995 treaty)
- Amendement du Traité visant l' interdiction des armes nucléaires en Amérique latine (1990 treaty)
- Amendment of Article Seven of the Inter-American Amateur Radio Service Convention (1988 treaty)
- Amendment to the Basel Convention on the Control of Transboundary Movements of Hazardous Wastes and their Disposal (1995 treaty)
- Amendment to the Convention on Access to Information, Public Participation in Decision-Making and Access to Justice in Environmental Matters (2005 treaty)
- Amendment to the Montreal Protocol on Substances That Deplete the Ozone Layer, 1990 (1990 treaty)
- Amendment to the Montreal Protocol on Substances That Deplete the Ozone Layer, 1992 (1992 treaty)
- Amendment to the Montreal Protocol on Substances That Deplete the Ozone Layer, 1997 (1997 treaty)
- Amendment to the Montreal Protocol on Substances That Deplete the Ozone Layer, 1999 (1999 treaty)
- Amendment to the Montreal Protocol on Substances that Deplete the Ozone Layer, 2016 (2016 treaty)
- Amendments to the Convention for the Protection of the Mediterranean Sea Against Pollution (1995 treaty)
- Amendments to the Protocol for the Prevention of Pollution of the Mediterranean Sea by Dumping from Ships and Aircraft (1995 treaty)
- Amendments to the Protocol for the Protection of the Mediterranean Sea Against Pollution from Land-based Sources and Activities (1996 treaty)
- Amendment to the Treaty for the Prohibition on Nuclear Weapons in Latin America (1990 treaty)
- Amendment to the Treaty for the Prohibition of Nuclear Weapons in Latin America, 1992 (1992 treaty)
- **AMEPPA** Association for Middle Eastern Public Policy and Administration (#02807)
- **AMEPS** Asian Manufacturers of Expanded Polystyrene (#01534)
- AMERA / see AMERA International
- AMERA International (internationally oriented national body)

♦ América Cooperativa y Mutual (Red AMEC) 00773

Address not obtained.

URL: http://www.acym.net/

History 11 Oct 2006, with the support of the 'Strategies and Tools against social Exclusion and Poverty (STEP)' programme of *ILO (#11123).* Also referred to with the abbreviation *ACYM* and *Red ACYM.* Members sign or agree to the 'Protocol of Collaboration' for the network. **Aims** Provide a platform for the exchange and development of the technical capacities of organizations involved in cooperative and mutual assistance activities for social protection across the continent.

Members Permanent; Associate. Included in the above, 2 organizations listed in this Yearbook:
Alianza del Mutualismo de América (AMA, #00634); Confederación Latinoamericana de Cooperativas y Mutuales de Trabajadores (COLACOT, #04456). [2009/XJ0332/y/**E**]

- América Latina en Acción Solidaria (#16396)
- America-Mideast Educational and Training Services (internationally oriented national body)
- American Ambulance Field Service / see AFS Intercultural Programs (#00541)
- American Anaplastology Association / see International Anaplastology Association (#11651)
- American Anti-Slavery Group (internationally oriented national body)
- American Apparel Contractors Association / see Americas Apparel Producers Network
- American Apparel Producers Network / see Americas Apparel Producers Network
- American-Arab Anti-Discrimination Committee (internationally oriented national body)
- American Association for Accreditation of Laboratory Animal Care / see AAALAC International
- American Association for the Advancement of Science (internationally oriented national body)
- American Association for the Advancement of Slavic Studies / see Association for Slavic, East European, and Eurasian Studies
- American Association for the Advancement of Tension Control / see International Stress Management Association (#15611)
- American Association for Artificial Intelligence / see Association for the Advancement of Artificial Intelligence
- American Association of Bible Colleges / see Association for Biblical Higher Education
- American Association of Blood Banks / see AABB
- American Association of Cereal Chemists / see Cereals and Grains Association (#03830)
- American Association of Collegiate Schools of Business / see AACSB International – Association to Advance Collegiate Schools of Business
- American Association of Cost Engineers / see AACE International (#00001)
- American Association of Fund-Raising Counsel / see Giving Institute: Leading Consultants to Non-Profits
- American Association of Gynecologic Laparoscopists / see Advancing Minimally Invasive Gynecology Worldwide (#00130)
- American Association of Jurists (#02110)

♦ American Association of Language Specialists (TAALS) 00774

Association américaine des spécialistes en langues

Contact 3051 Idaho Ave NW, Ste 425, Washington DC 20016, USA. T. +16506197625. E-mail: info@taals.net.

URL: http://www.taals.net/

History 1957, Washington DC (USA). Statutes adopted 16 Jun 1958; revised 14 Dec 1970; 2007; Dec 2016. **Aims** Define and represent the profession of language specialist; safeguard legitimate interests of members – highly qualified *interpreters* and *translators.* **Structure** Assembly of Members (annual); Council; Admissions Committee. **Languages** Arabic, Dutch, English, French, German, Greek, Haitian, Hebrew, Hungarian, Indonesian, Italian, Japanese, Latvian, Malay, Mandarin Chinese, Polish, Portuguese, Romanian, Russian, Serbo-Croatian, Spanish, Ukrainian, Yiddish. **Finance** Members' dues. **Publications** *TAALS Yearbook.*

Members Active; Associate; Honorary. Individuals (155), mainly in the American continent, in 23 countries and territories:
Argentina, Australia, Canada, Chile, China, Colombia, Costa Rica, Côte d'Ivoire, France, Germany, Honduras, Hong Kong, Italy, Japan, Lebanon, Malaysia, Mexico, Panama, Spain, Switzerland, Trinidad-Tobago, USA, Venezuela. [2022/XD0166/v/**D**]

♦ American Association of Oilwell Drilling Contractors / see International Association of Drilling Contractors
♦ American Association of Petroleum Geologists (internationally oriented national body)

♦ American Association of Port Authorities (AAPA) 00775

Association américaine des autorités portuaires

Pres 1010 Duke St, Alexandria VA 22314-3589, USA. T. +17036845700. Fax +17036846321. E-mail: info@aapa-ports.org.
URL: http://www.aapa-ports.org/

History Founded 1912. Registered as non-profit corporation in 1930. **Aims** Provide an organizational resource to ports of the Western Hemisphere; secure orderly promotion and development of ports and harbours in the region; ensure professionalism of port managers; promote the image and prestige of ports as a discrete industry, providing essential transportation services to the communities and nations they serve. **Structure** Board of Directors; Standing Committees (16). **Languages** English, Portuguese, Spanish. **Staff** 15.00 FTE, paid. **Finance** Members' dues. Other sources: programmes; conventions; publications. Annual budget: US$ 2,000,000. **Activities** Research/documentation; networking/liaising; events/meetings; advocacy/lobbying/activism. **Events** *Annual Convention* Orlando, FL (USA) 2022, *Annual Convention* Austin, TX (USA) 2021, *Latin American Ports Congress* Cartagena de Indias (Colombia) 2021, *Annual Convention* Québec, QC (Canada) 2020, *Latin American Ports Congress* Miami, FL (USA) 2019. **Publications** *AAPA Advisory Newsletter* (weekly) in English, Spanish; *AAPA Directory, Seaports of the Americas* (annual); *US Legislative Alert*. Manuals; books; booklets; reports; proceedings.
Members Full Ports and port systems in the USA, Canada, the Caribbean, Central America and South America. Firms and Individuals interested in the port industry. Corporate members (157 public port agencies) in 27 countries and territories:
Argentina, Bahamas, Barbados, Bolivia, Brazil, Canada, Cayman Is, Chile, Colombia, Costa Rica, Ecuador, Guatemala, Honduras, Israel, Jamaica, Mexico, Neth Antilles, Panama, Peru, Puerto Rico, St Lucia, St Vincent-Grenadines, Trinidad-Tobago, Uruguay, USA, Venezuela, Virgin Is UK. [2020.03.04/XD0046/**D**]

♦ American Association of Private International Law (#02109)
♦ American Association of Public Employment Offices / see International Association of Workforce Professionals (#12278)
♦ American Association of Railway Surgeons (inactive)
♦ American Association of Retired Persons / see AARP International
♦ American Association for the Study of Liver Diseases (internationally oriented national body)
♦ American Association of Women Ministers / see International Association of Women Ministers (#12268)
♦ American Baptist Foreign Mission Society / see American Baptist International Ministries
♦ American Baptist International Ministries (internationally oriented national body)
♦ American Baptist Missionary Union / see American Baptist International Ministries
♦ American Bar Association Rule of Law Initiative (internationally oriented national body)

♦ American Boxing Confederation (AMBC) 00776

Confederación Americana de Boxeo (AMBC)

Pres Av Castro Barros 75, Caba, CP 1178 Buenos Aires, Argentina. T. +5491149818615. E-mail: osrabi@gmail.com.
URL: http://www.americanbc.org/index.php

History Set up as a continental boxing federation of *World Boxing Council (WBC, #21242)* under the title *Federación Centroamericana de Boxeo (FECARBOX)*. Previously referred to as *Central American and Caribbean Boxing Federation – Federación Centroamericana y del Caribe de Boxeo*. Current title adopted, 31 Jan 2009, when merged with the American Office of *International Boxing Association (IBA, #12385)* during an Extraordinary Assembly in Sao Paulo (Brazil); a regional confederation of AIBA. **Structure** Executive Committee of 11 members; Board of 5 members.
Members Boxing federations in 21 countries and territories:
Aruba, Bahamas, Barbados, Belize, Colombia, Costa Rica, Curaçao, Dominican Rep, El Salvador, Guyana, Haiti, Honduras, Jamaica, Mexico, Nicaragua, Panama, Puerto Rico, Suriname, Trinidad-Tobago, Venezuela, Virgin Is USA.
NGO Relations Member of (1): *Asociación de Confederaciones Deportivas Panamericanas (ACODEPA, #02119)*. [2020/XE2390/**E**]

♦ American Braille Press for War and Civilian Blind / see Helen Keller International (#10902)
♦ American Business Communication Association / see Association for Business Communication
♦ American Business Women International / see Alliance of Business Women International
♦ American Business Writing Association / see Association for Business Communication
♦ American Center for International Labor Solidarity / see Solidarity Center
♦ American Center of Oriental Research, Amman (internationally oriented national body)
♦ American Citizens Abroad (internationally oriented national body)

♦ American Coal Ash Association (ACAA) 00777

Exec Dir 38800 Country Club Dr, Farmington Hills MI 48331, USA. E-mail: info@acaa-usa.org.
URL: http://www.acaa-usa.org/

History Mar 1968, Washington DC (USA). **Aims** Advance management and use of coal combustion products in ways that are environmentally responsible, technically sound, commercially competitive, and more supportive of a sustainable global community. **Structure** Executive Director; Communications Coordinator; Member Liaison; Special Assistant; Adviser. **Languages** English. **Staff** 3.00 FTE, paid. **Finance** Members' dues. Annual budget: about US$ 450,000. **Activities** Events/meetings; publishing activities; advocacy/lobbying/activism. **Events** *Winter Meeting* Houston, TX (USA) 2019, *WOCA : World of Coal Ash Conference* St Louis, MO (USA) 2019, *WOCA : World of Coal Ash Conference* Lexington, KY (USA) 2017, *WOCA : World of Coal Ash Conference* Nashville, TN (USA) 2015, *WOCA : World of Coal Ash Conference* Lexington, KY (USA) 2013. **Publications** *Soil Sabilization Manual* (2007); *Fly Ash Facts for Highway Engineers*. Symposium proceedings; fact sheets; resource bulletins.
Members Mainly North American membership, but members in a total of 8 countries:
Australia, Canada, India, Israel, Japan, Poland, South Africa, USA.
Regional organization (1), listed in this Yearbook:
European Coal Combustion Products Association (ECOBA, #06588). [2018.06.19/XF4796/**F**]

♦ American College of Chest Physicians (CHEST) 00778

Collège américain de médecine thoracique

Pres 2595 Patriot Blvd, Glenview IL 60026, USA. T. +12245219601. Fax +12245219801. E-mail: chestcustomersupport@chestnet.org.
URL: http://www.chestnet.org/

History Founded 1935, Albuquerque NM (USA), as *Federation of American Sanatoria*. Reorganized and present name adopted in 1937. Currently includes the previous *International Academy of Chest Physicians and Surgeons (inactive)*. **Aims** Promote the prevention and treatment of diseases of the chest through leadership, education, research and communication. **Events** *World Congress* Bologna (Italy) 2021, *World Congress* Bologna (Italy) 2020, *Annual Meeting* Glenview, IL (USA) 2020, *Annual Meeting* New Orleans, LA (USA) 2019, *World Congress* Shanghai (China) 2016. **Publications** *Chest* (12 a year) – journal; *Pulmonary Perspectives* (4 a year); *ACCP-SEEK* (annual).
Members Members (mostly in USA) in 97 countries and territories:
Albania, Angola, Argentina, Australia, Austria, Bahamas, Bangladesh, Barbados, Belgium, Bolivia, Bosnia-Herzegovina, Brazil, Bulgaria, Canada, Chile, China, Colombia, Costa Rica, Cyprus, Czechia, Denmark, Dominican Rep, Ecuador, Egypt, El Salvador, Estonia, Finland, France, Germany, Greece, Guatemala, Honduras, Hong Kong, Hungary, Iceland, India, Indonesia, Iran Islamic Rep, Iraq, Ireland, Israel, Italy, Jamaica, Japan, Jordan, Korea Rep, Kuwait, Lebanon, Lithuania, Luxembourg, Macau, Malaysia, Malta, Mexico, Myanmar, Nepal, Netherlands, New Zealand, Nicaragua, Nigeria, North Macedonia, Norway, Oman, Pakistan, Panama, Paraguay, Peru, Philippines, Poland, Portugal, Puerto Rico, Qatar, Romania, Saudi Arabia, Serbia, Singapore, Slovakia, Slovenia, South Africa, Spain, Sri Lanka, Sudan, Sweden, Switzerland, Syrian AR, Tahiti Is, Taiwan, Thailand, Trinidad-Tobago, Türkiye, UK, United Arab Emirates, Uruguay, USA, Venezuela, Vietnam.
Also members in the Caribbean. Membership countries not specified. [2014.12.12/XF0295/**F**]

♦ American College of International Physicians (internationally oriented national body)
♦ American Committee for Armenian and Syrian Relief / see Near East Foundation
♦ American Committee on Dependent Territories (inactive)
♦ American Committee for the Evangelization of Greeks / see Advancing the Ministries of the Gospel International
♦ American Committee for KEEP (internationally oriented national body)
♦ American Committee for Relief in the Near East / see Near East Foundation
♦ American Concrete Institute (internationally oriented national body)
♦ American Confederation of Bank Employees (inactive)
♦ American Conference of Undenominational Churches / see IFCA International
♦ American Council for Nationalities Service / see US Committee for Refugees and Immigrants
♦ American Council of Parent Cooperatives / see Parent Cooperative Preschools International
♦ American Councils for International Education (internationally oriented national body)
♦ American Council of Teachers of Russian / see American Councils for International Education
♦ American Council for Voluntary International Action (internationally oriented national body)
♦ American Critical Incident Stress Foundation / see International Critical Incident Stress Foundation

♦ American Dental Society of Europe (ADSE) 00779

Société dentaire américaine de l'Europe

Address not obtained.
URL: http://www.ads-eu.org/

History 1873, Rigi-Lucerne (Switzerland). **Aims** Afford graduates of *North American* dental schools practising in Europe the benefits of an organization devoted to a furtherance of dental knowledge. **Languages** English. **Events** *Annual Meeting* Switzerland 2020, *Annual Meeting* Prague (Czechia) 2019, *Annual Meeting* Biarritz (France) 2018, *Annual Meeting* Berlin (Germany) 2017, *Annual Meeting* Florence (Italy) 2016.
Members Individuals in 15 countries:
Belgium, Denmark, France, Germany, Greece, Ireland, Italy, Monaco, Netherlands, Norway, Portugal, Sweden, Switzerland, UK, USA. [2019/XE0049/v/**E**]

♦ American Enterprise Association / see American Enterprise Institute
♦ American Enterprise Institute (internationally oriented national body)
♦ American Enterprise Institute for Public Policy Research / see American Enterprise Institute
♦ American European Community Association (internationally oriented national body)

♦ American-European Congress of Ophthalmic Surgery (AECOS) 00780

Exec Dir address not obtained.
URL: https://aecosurgery.org/

History 2011, USA. Originally a congress of American thought leaders. Registration: non-profit 501(c)(6), USA. **Aims** Foster communication and cooperation between leading anterior segment surgeons, ophthalmic industry executives, select venture capitalists, and technology entrepreneurs. **Structure** American Executive Committee; European Executive Committee. Management Team. **Activities** Advocacy/lobbying/activism; events/meetings. **Events** *AECOS European Symposium* Antwerp (Belgium) 2022, *AECOS European Symposium* Florence (Italy) 2021, *AECOS European Symposium* 2020, *AECOS European Symposium* Barcelona (Spain) 2019, *AECOS European Symposium* Berlin (Germany) 2018. **Members** Individuals. Membership countries not specified. [2022/AA0636/v/**F**]

♦ American Express Foundation (internationally oriented national body)
♦ American Family Foundation / see International Cultic Studies Association (#13121)
♦ American Federation of Jews from Central Europe (internationally oriented national body)
♦ American Federation of Soroptimist Clubs / see Soroptimist International of the Americas (#19688)
♦ American Field Service / see AFS Intercultural Programs (#00541)
♦ American Film Institute (internationally oriented national body)
♦ American Film Marketing Association / see Independent Film and Television Alliance
♦ American Fish Culturist's Association / see American Fisheries Society
♦ American Fisheries Society (internationally oriented national body)
♦ American Foreign Law Association (internationally oriented national body)
♦ American Foreign Policy Council (internationally oriented national body)
♦ American Forum for Global Education (internationally oriented national body)
♦ American Foundation for Overseas Blind / see Helen Keller International (#10902)
♦ American Friends of the Middle East / see America-Mideast Educational and Training Services
♦ American Friends Service Committee (internationally oriented national body)

♦ American Galvanizers Association (AGA) 00781

Contact 6881 South Holly Circle, Ste 108, Centennial CO 80112, USA. T. +17205540900. Fax +17205540909. E-mail: aga@galvanizeit.org.
URL: http://www.galvanizeit.org/

History 1935. **Aims** Serve the needs of specifiers, engineers, contractors and fabricators throughout North America; provide information on the most innovative applications and state-of-the-art technological developments in hot-dip galvanizing for corrosion protection. **Structure** Departments (3): Technical; Marketing; Administrative. **Languages** English. **Staff** 7.00 FTE, paid. **Finance** Members' dues. **Activities** Maintains a technical library; distributes numerous industry publications; offers free educational seminars; provides toll-free technical support to the specifying community. Organizes annual conference. **Publications** *American Galvanizer* (6 a year) – newsletter; *Galvazing Insights* (4 a year) – electronic newsletter.
Members Companies in 3 countries:
Canada, Mexico, USA.
Affiliate members throughout the world. Membership countries not specified.
NGO Relations Member of: *International Zinc Association (IZA, #15942)*. [2010/XD6786/**D**]

♦ American Gear Manufacturers Association (internationally oriented national body)
♦ American Geophysical Union (internationally oriented national body)
♦ American Graduate School of International Management / see Thunderbird – The Garvin School of International Management

♦ American Indian Workshop (AIW) 00782

Address not obtained.
URL: http://www.american-indian-workshop.org/

History Founded 1980, Amsterdam (Netherlands), at Meeting of *International Sea Cadet Association (ISCA, #14814)*. **Aims** Provide a platform for established academics and young scholars to share their expertise and experiences as well as to benefit from one another's critical engagement. **Finance** Donations. **Activities** Events/meetings. **Events** *Annual Conference* Pardubice (Czechia) 2024, *Annual Conference* Budapest (Hungary) 2023, *Annual Conference* Luxembourg (Luxembourg) 2022, *Annual Conference* Nicosia (Cyprus) 2021, *Annual Conference* Munich (Germany) 2020. [2019/XM7885/c/**E**]

♦ American Indigenous Parliament (#18202)
♦ American Industrial Arts Association / see International Technology and Engineering Educators Association
♦ American Institute of Architects – Continental European Chapter (internationally oriented national body)
♦ American Institute of Collaborative Professionals / see International Academy of Collaborative Professionals (#11541)
♦ American Institute for Contemporary German Studies (internationally oriented national body)
♦ American Institute for the Decision Sciences / see Decision Sciences Institute
♦ American Institute for Foreign Trade / see Thunderbird – The Garvin School of International Management
♦ American Institute of Industrial Engineers / see Institute of Industrial and Systems Engineers (#11270)
♦ American Institute for International Steel (internationally oriented national body)
♦ American Institute for Maghrib Studies (internationally oriented national body)
♦ American Institute of Real Estate Appraisers / see Appraisal Institute

♦ **American International Consortium of Academic Libraries (AMICAL)** **00783**
Contact c/o University Library, American Univ of Paris, 9 rue de Monttessuy, 75007 Paris, France. T. +33140620557. Fax +33145569289.
URL: http://www.amicalnet.org/
History May 2004, Paris (France). **Aims** Advance learning, teaching and research through collaborative development of library and *information services* and of curricular resources at member institutions; share information and technology across national and linguistic borders, using English as primary language. **Structure** Coordinating Committee; Small Grant Committee. Working Groups. **Finance** Support from: *Andrew W Mellon Foundation.* **Events** *Annual Meeting* Blagoevgrad (Bulgaria) 2015, *Annual Meeting* Athens (Greece) 2014, *Annual Meeting* Rome (Italy) 2013, *Annual Meeting* Sharjah (United Arab Emirates) 2012, *Annual Meeting* Beirut (Lebanon) 2011.
Members Full; Affiliate; Consortial. Full (17) in 14 countries:
Armenia, Bulgaria, Egypt, France, Greece, Hungary, Italy, Kyrgyzstan, Lebanon, Morocco, Russia, Spain, Switzerland, United Arab Emirates.
Affiliate (5) in 5 countries:
Afghanistan, Kosovo, Lebanon, Nigeria, Pakistan.
Consortial (3) in 3 countries:
France, Kuwait, UK.
NGO Relations Member of: *International Coalition of Library Consortia (ICOLC, #12615).* Partner of: *Online Computer Library Center (OCLC, #17740).* [2015/XJ2703/E]

♦ American International Health Alliance (internationally oriented national body)
♦ American International Institute for the Protection of Childhood / see Inter-American Children's Institute (#11406)
♦ American International Schools in the Americas (internationally oriented national body)

♦ **American Iron and Steel Institute (AISI)** **00784**
Contact 25 Massachusetts Ave NW, Ste 800, Washington DC 200001, USA. T. +12024527100.
URL: http://www.steel.org/
History 1908. Takes over activities American Iran and Steel Association, founded 1855. **Events** *Annual General Meeting* Scottsdale, AZ (USA) 2014, *Annual General Meeting* Scottsdale, AZ (USA) 2008, *Annual General Meeting* Las Vegas, NV (USA) 2007, *Annual General Meeting* Boca Raton, FL (USA) 2006, *European Continuous Casting Conference* Nice (France) 2005. **Publications** *AISI e-news* (6 a year) – online E-J journal.
Members Full; Associate. Companies in 3 countries:
Canada, Mexico, USA. [2015/XE3499/j/E]

♦ American Jesuit Missionary Association / see Jesuit Missions
♦ American Jewish Committee (internationally oriented national body)

♦ **American Jewish Joint Distribution Committee (JDC)** **00785**
Exec Vice-Pres/CEO 220 E 42nd St, New York NY 10017, USA. T. +12126876200. E-mail: info@jdc.org.
URL: http://www.jdc.org/
History 1914, USA, on the merger of *Central Relief Committee for the Relief of Jews* and the *American Jewish Relief Committee,* to give global expression to the principle that all Jews are responsible for one another. **Aims** Act on behalf of North America's Jewish communities and others to rescue Jews in danger, provide relief to those in distress, revitalize overseas Jewish communities, and help Israel overcome the social challenges of its citizens. **Structure** International Council; Board; Executive Committee; Officers. **Activities** Humanitarian/emergency aid; training/education. **Events** *European conference of Jewish community centers* Bucharest (Romania) 2008, *Conference on communities in transition* Jerusalem (Israel) 2008, *International conference* Moscow (Russia) 2002. **Publications** Annual report; pamphlets; newsletters; studies; books; website. **Members** Not a membership organization. Works in over 70 countries worldwide (countries not specified). **IGO Relations** Observer to: *International Organization for Migration (IOM, #14454).* **NGO Relations** Member of: *American Council for Voluntary International Action (InterAction); Consortium of Christian Relief and Development Association (CCRDA); Interfaith Hunger Appeal (IHA, no recent information); International Council on Jewish Social and Welfare Services (INTERCO, #13035); International Council on Social Welfare (ICSW, #13076); JDC International Centre for Community Development (JDC-ICCD); World Jewish Restitution Organization (WJRO, #21601).* Instrumental in setting up: *European Centre for Jewish Leadership (Le'atid Europe); European Council of Jewish Communities (ECJC, #06825).* [2018.06.01/XF0251/E]

♦ American Jewish World Service (internationally oriented national body)
♦ American Leprosy Missions (internationally oriented national body)
♦ American Library Association (internationally oriented national body)

♦ **American Literature Association (ALA)** **00786**
Exec Dir Princeton Univ, Program in Gender and Sexuality Studies, Princeton NJ 08544, USA. E-mail: ab23@princeton.edu.
URL: https://americanliteratureassociation.org/
History Jun 1989, San Diego, CA (USA). **Aims** Advance humanistic learning by encouraging the study of American authors and their works. **Structure** Executive Board; Council of American Authors Societies. **Activities** Events/meetings; knowledge management/information dissemination. **Events** *Annual Conference* Boston, MA (USA) 2025, *Annual Conference* Chicago, IL (USA) 2024, *Annual Conference* Boston, MA (USA) 2023, *Annual Conference* Chicago, IL (USA) 2022, *Annual Conference* Boston, MA (USA) 2021.
Members Individuals; Institutions, including 6 organizations listed in this Yearbook:
Emily Dickinson International Society (#05441); International Raymond Carver Society (IRCS, #14700); International Vladimir Nabokov Society (IVNS); Kate Chopin International Society; Poe Studies Association (PSA); Society for the History of Authorship, Reading and Publishing (SHARP, #19570). [2022/AA1646/y/E]

♦ **American Management Association International (AMA)** **00787**
Contact 1601 Broadway, New York NY 10019, USA. E-mail: customerservice@amanet.org.
URL: http://www.amanet.org/
History 1923, when 'parent' organization, *American Management Association,* was set up. Also referred to as *AMA International (AMA/I).* **Aims** Provide professional development training. **Structure** Includes: American Management Association (Atlanta, New York, Chicago, Washington DC, San Francisco); AMA China (Shanghai, Beijing, Guangzhou); *Management Centre Europe (MCE, #16561)* (Brussels); Canadian Management Centre (Toronto); Management Center de Mexico (Mexico City). Affiliates and licensing partners provide training in Australia, Korea Rep, Malaysia, Philippines, Singapore, Thailand and other locations worldwide. **Events** *Asia conference on using R and D to create business growth* Singapore (Singapore) 1997, *Human resources development Asia conference* Singapore (Singapore) 1996, *Global conference on management innovation* Tokyo (Japan) 1990. **Publications** *AMA Quarterly* – journal. E-newsletters.
Members Managers and executives (over 100,000) in 65 countries and territories:
Antigua-Barbuda, Argentina, Australia, Bahamas, Bangladesh, Barbados, Belize, Bermuda, Bolivia, Botswana, Brazil, Brunei Darussalam, Canada, Chile, China, Colombia, Costa Rica, Dominica, Dominican Rep, Ecuador, El Salvador, Ethiopia, Fiji, Ghana, Guatemala, Guyana, Honduras, India, Indonesia, Iran Islamic Rep, Jamaica, Jordan, Kenya, Korea Rep, Malaysia, Mauritius, Mexico, Morocco, Nepal, Neth Antilles, New Zealand, Niger, Oman, Pakistan, Panama, Paraguay, Peru, Philippines, Puerto Rico, Seychelles, Singapore, South Africa, Sri Lanka, Syrian AR, Taiwan, Tanzania UR, Thailand, Trinidad-Tobago, Uganda, Uruguay, USA, Venezuela, Yemen, Zambia, Zimbabwe. [2014.12.03/XF1855/F]

♦ American Mission to Greeks / see Advancing the Ministries of the Gospel International
♦ American Mission to Lepers / see American Leprosy Missions
♦ American Near East Refugee Aid (internationally oriented national body)
♦ American Nuclear Society (internationally oriented national body)
♦ American Oil Chemists' Society (internationally oriented national body)

♦ **American Outlaws Association (AOA)** **00788**
Address not obtained.
URL: http://www.outlawsmcworld.com/
History 1935, USA. 1935, McCook IL (USA), as *Outlaws Motorcycle Club.* Incorporated under current name, 1965. A 'one-percenter' motorcycle gang.
Members Chapters in 18 countries and territories:
Australia, Austria, Belgium, Canada, France, Germany, Ireland, Italy, Japan, Norway, Philippines, Poland, Russia, Spain, Sweden, Thailand, UK, USA. [2010/XM3950/s/F]

♦ American Peace Corps / see Peace Corps

♦ **American Peptide Society (APS)** **00789**
Manager address not obtained. T. +16143005887. E-mail: apsoffice17@gmail.com.
URL: https://www.americanpeptidesociety.org/
History 1990. **Aims** Provide a forum for advancing and promoting knowledge of the chemistry and biology of peptides. **Structure** General Assembly (every 2 years). Board of Directors; Committees (9). **Activities** Awards/prizes/competitions; events/meetings. **Events** *American Peptide Symposium* Whistler, BC (Canada) 2022, *American Peptide Symposium* Monterey, CA (USA) 2019, *American Peptide Symposium* Whistler, BC (Canada) 2017, *American Peptide Symposium* Orlando, FL (USA) 2015, *American Peptide Symposium* Waikoloa, HI (USA) 2013. **Publications** *Peptide Science* – journal. **Members** Active; Student; Life; Sustaining; Corporate; Emeritus; Honorary. Members (mainly in North America) in over 30 countries. Membership countries not specified. [2018.06.01/XM3422/D]

♦ American Petroleum Credit Association / see International Energy Credit Association (#13271)
♦ American Political Science Association (internationally oriented national body)
♦ American Psychological Society / see Association for Psychological Science (#02879)
♦ American Red Cross Overseas Association (internationally oriented national body)
♦ American Refugee Committee (internationally oriented national body)
♦ American Refugee Committee International / see American Refugee Committee
♦ American Relief Agency for the Horn of Africa (internationally oriented national body)
♦ American Rescue Team International (internationally oriented national body)
♦ American Road Builders Association / see American Road and Transportation Builders Association
♦ American Road Makers / see American Road and Transportation Builders Association
♦ American Road and Transportation Builders Association (internationally oriented national body)
♦ American-Scandinavian Foundation (internationally oriented national body)
♦ American Scandinavian Student Exchange / see International Student Exchange Programs
♦ American Schools of Oriental Research (internationally oriented national body)
♦ Americans for Democratic Action (internationally oriented national body)
♦ American Shooting Confederation / see Confederación Americana de Tiro (#04439)
♦ Americans for Middle East Understanding (internationally oriented national body)
♦ American Society of Agricultural and Biological Engineers (internationally oriented national body)
♦ American Society of Association Executives / see ASAE
♦ American Society for Chemotherapy of Tuberculosis (inactive)

♦ **American Society for Engineering Education (ASEE)** **00790**
Société américaine pour la formation des ingénieurs – Sociedad Estadounidense de Estudios de Ingenieria
Main Office 1818 N St NW, Ste 600, Washington DC 20036, USA. T. +12023313545. Fax +12022658504.
URL: http://www.asee.org/
History 1893, USA. Former names and other names: *Society for Promotion of Engineering Education (SPEE)* – former (1893 to 1947). **Aims** Further education in engineering and engineering *technology* by promoting excellence in instruction, research, public service and practice; exercise worldwide leadership; foster technological education of society. **Structure** Board of Directors (Executive Committee); Councils (4); Standing and Ad Hoc Committees. **Languages** English. **Staff** 60.00 FTE, paid. **Finance** Members' dues. Proceeds from publications, advertising and projects. **Activities** Politics/policy/regulatory; advocacy/lobbying/activism; events/meetings; networking/liaising. **Events** *Annual Conference* Baltimore, MD (USA) 2023, *Annual Conference* Minneapolis, MN (USA) 2022, *Frontiers in Education Conference* Uppsala (Sweden) 2022, *Frontiers in Education Conference* Lincoln, NE (USA) 2021, *Annual Conference* Long Beach, CA (USA) 2021. **Publications** *Prism* (10 a year); *Journal of Engineering Education* (4 a year); *Advances in Engineering Education* (3 a year); *Engineering Go For It* (every 2-3 years). **Members** Corporate corporations, government agencies and associations; Academic Institutional. Members in 16 countries. Membership countries not specified. **Consultative Status** Consultative status granted from: *ECOSOC (#05331)* (Ros A). **IGO Relations** Associated with Department of Global Communications of the United Nations. **NGO Relations** Member of: *Engineering for the Americas (EftA, no recent information); Global Engineering Deans Council (GEDC, #10344); International Association for Continuing Engineering Education (IACEE, #11817); International Federation of Engineering Education Societies (IFEES, #13412).* [2021/XF1413/F]

♦ American Society for Horticultural Science – Tropical Region / see InterAmerican Society of Tropical Horticulture (#11451)
♦ American Society for Industrial Security / see ASIS International
♦ American Society of International Law (internationally oriented national body)
♦ American Society of Limnology and Oceanography / see Association for the Sciences of Limnology and Oceanography
♦ American Society of Mechanical Engineers (internationally oriented national body)
♦ American Society for Metals / see ASM International
♦ American Society of Parasitologists (internationally oriented national body)
♦ American Society for Personnel Administration / see Society for Human Resource Management
♦ American Society of Plant Taxonomists (internationally oriented national body)
♦ American Society for Quality (internationally oriented national body)
♦ American Society for Quality Control / see American Society for Quality
♦ American Society for Steel Treating / see ASM International
♦ American Society for Testing and Materials / see ASTM International (#02994)
♦ American Society of Tool Engineers / see SME
♦ American Society of Tool and Manufacturing Engineers / see SME
♦ American Society of Travel Advisors (internationally oriented national body)
♦ American Society of Travel Agents / see American Society of Travel Advisors
♦ American Society of Tropical Medicine and Hygiene (internationally oriented national body)
♦ American Society for Tropical Veterinary Medicine / see Society for Tropical Veterinary Medicine (#19656)
♦ Americans for Peace Now (internationally oriented national body)
♦ American Steamship and Tourist Agents Association / see American Society of Travel Advisors
♦ American Steel Treaters Society / see ASM International
♦ American Studies Foundation (internationally oriented national body)
♦ Americans for UNESCO (internationally oriented national body)
♦ Americans for the Universality of UNESCO / see Americans for UNESCO
♦ American Thoracic Society (internationally oriented national body)
♦ American Toll Bridge Association / see International Bridge, Tunnel and Turnpike Association (#12400)
♦ American Trade Association Executives / see ASAE
♦ American Treaty on Pacific Settlement (1948 treaty)
♦ American Triathlon Confederation / see Americas Triathlon (#00795)

♦ **American Water Works Association (AWWA)** **00791**
CEO 6666 West Quincy Ave, Denver CO 80235, USA. T. +13033476135. Fax +13033470804. E-mail: pmacilwaine@awwa.org – janderson@awwa.org.
URL: http://www.awwa.org/
History 1881. A North American water supply organization of *International Water Services Association (IWSA, inactive),* since 1999 active within *International Water Association (IWA, #15865).* **Aims** Provide solutions to improve public health, protect the environment, strengthen the economy and enhance our quality of life. **Structure** Board of Directors (meets twice a year); Executive Committee; Councils (7); Divisions (8); Sections (43); Committees (250). **Languages** English. **Staff** 140.00 FTE, paid. **Finance** Annual budget: about US$ 30,000,000. **Activities** Events/meetings; training/education; advocacy/lobbying/activism; knowledge management/information dissemination; standards/guidelines. **Events** *Annual Conference* Anaheim, CA (USA) 2015, *Annual Conference* Boston, MA (USA) 2014, *Annual Conference* Denver, CO (USA) 2013, *Annual Conference* Dallas, TX (USA) 2012, *Americas Business Forum* Singapore (Singapore) 2012. **Publications**

Waterweek (weekly) – online newsletter; *Journal AWWA* (12 a year); *Opflow* (12 a year); *Main Stream* (4 a year) – newspaper. *Officers and Committee Directory*; *Reservoir*; *Sourcebook*. Proceedings of conferences and seminars. Information Services: Teleconferences. **Information Services** *Waternet* – bibliographic database of 60,000 entries on CD-ROM; *WATERSTATS* – database of North American Water Utilities Operations (in preparation). **Members** Members in 103 countries. Membership countries not specified.
[2016.12.14/XE0467/**E**]

♦ American Welding Society (internationally oriented national body)
♦ American West African Freight Conference (meeting series)
♦ American Youth Understanding Diabetes Abroad (internationally oriented national body)
♦ Americares Foundation (internationally oriented national body)
♦ Americas Aerospace Quality Group (internationally oriented national body)
♦ Americas Apparel Producers Network (internationally oriented national body)
♦ Americas Association of Cooperative / Mutual Insurance Societies / see International Cooperative and Mutual Insurance Federation / Regional Association for The Americas (#12949)

♦ Americas' Central Securities Depositories Association (ACSDA) . . . 00792

Asociación de Depósitos Centrales de Valores de América

Sec c/o CAVALI ICLV SA, Pasaje Acuña 191, 1, Lima, Peru.
Exec Dir address not obtained.
URL: http://www.acsda.org/

History 1999. Former names and other names: *Asociación de Centros de Depósito de América* – former. Registration: Peru. **Aims** Create a forum for exchange of information and experience between members. **Structure** General Assembly (annual); Executive Committee; Executive Director. **Languages** English, Spanish. **Staff** 0.50 FTE, paid. **Finance** Members' dues (annual). **Activities** Knowledge management/information dissemination; events/meetings. **Events** *Annual General Assembly* Nassau (Bahamas) 2018, *Annual General Assembly* La Paz (Bolivia) 2017, *Annual General Assembly* Buenos Aires (Argentina) 2016, *Annual General Assembly* Cancún (Mexico) 2015, *General Assembly* Santiago (Chile) 2014. **Publications** *ACSDA Member Profiles*.
Members Central Securities Depositories and Clearing Houses (28) in 23 countries:
Argentina, Barbados, Bermuda, Bolivia, Brazil, Canada, Chile, Colombia, Dominican Rep, Ecuador, El Salvador, Guatemala, Jamaica, Mexico, Nicaragua, Panama, Paraguay, Peru, South Africa, Trinidad-Tobago, Uruguay, USA, Venezuela.
Also members in Eastern Caribbean. Membership countries not specified.
NGO Relations Cooperates with (1): *Ibero-American Federation of Exchanges (#11022)*. [2021/XD9216/**D**]

♦ Americas Communication Research Network / see Communication Policy Research Latin America (#04382)
♦ Americas Democrat Union / see Union of Latin American Parties (#20448)
♦ Americas Democrat Union (no recent information)
♦ America's Development Foundation (internationally oriented national body)

♦ Americas Federation of Netball Associations (AFNA) 00793

Sec 33 Sunny Meadows, Nursery 2, St Philip, ST PHILIP, Barbados. T. +12464307725. Fax +12464296182.

Structure General Meeting (annual). Executive Committee, comprising President, Immediate Past-President, 2 Vice-Presidents, Treasurer and Honorary Secretary. **Activities** Organizes championships. **NGO Relations** *Caribbean Netball Association (CNA, #03526)*. [2016/XD8628/**D**]

♦ Americas Health Foundation (AHF) 00794

Contact 909 New Jersey Avenue SE, Suite 1101, Washington DC 20003, USA. T. +12026507080. E-mail: getinfo.ahf@gmail.com.
URL: https://americashealthfoundation.org/

History 2010. Registration: 501(c)(3) non-profit foundation, No/ID: EIN: 45-3048929, Start date: 2015, USA, Washington DC. **Aims** Promote increased access to quality healthcare and treatments throughout the Americas. **Structure** Board; International Advisors. **Activities** Events/meetings. [2021/AA1219/**f/F**]

♦ Americas Indigenous Encounter (unconfirmed)
♦ Americas Network on Nationality and Statelessness (unconfirmed)
♦ Americas Research Industry Alliance (unconfirmed)
♦ Americas Society (internationally oriented national body)

♦ Americas Triathlon (AT) 00795

Pres Canelones 982, 11 100 Montevideo, Uruguay. T. +59822042839.
URL: http://americas.triathlon.org/

History 9 May 1992, San Andrés (Colombia). Regional confederation of *World Triathlon (#21872)*. Former names and other names: *Pan American Triathlon Confederation (PATCO)* – former; *Confederación Panamericana de Triathlon* – former; *American Triathlon Confederation* – former; *Confederación Americana de Triatlón (CAMTRI)* – former. **Aims** Promote and generally advance the sport of triathlon to a Panamerican level; develop a friendly and supportive cooperation by all organizations, and their leaders and athletes who participate in this sport, thus contributing to the creation of a more peaceful world. **Structure** Congress (annual); Executive Board. Standing Commissions: Technical; Medical; Constitution; Women; Duathlon; Information; Audit; Credential; Athletes; Youth. **Languages** English, Portuguese, Spanish. **Finance** Sources: members' dues. **Activities** Sporting activities.
Members National Federations in 40 countries and territories:
Antigua-Barbuda, Argentina, Aruba, Bahamas, Barbados, Belize, Bermuda, Bolivia, Brazil, Canada, Cayman Is, Chile, Colombia, Costa Rica, Cuba, Dominican Rep, Ecuador, El Salvador, Grenada, Guatemala, Haiti, Honduras, Jamaica, Mexico, Neth Antilles, Nicaragua, Panama, Paraguay, Peru, Puerto Rico, St Kitts-Nevis, St Lucia, Suriname, Trinidad-Tobago, Turks-Caicos, Uruguay, USA, Venezuela, Virgin Is UK, Virgin Is USA.
NGO Relations Member of (2): *Asociación de Confederaciones Deportivas Panamericanas (ACODEPA, #02119)*; *Asociación de Confederaciones Deportivas Sudamericanas (ACODESU, no recent information)*.
[2023/XD5072/**D**]

♦ AmeriGEOSS 00796

Contact address not obtained. E-mail: amerigeoss@gmail.com.
URL: http://www.amerigeoss.org/

History A regional initiative of *Group on Earth Observations (GEO, #10735)*. **Aims** Promote collaboration and coordination among *GEO* members in the American continent, "to realize a future wherein decisions and actions, for the benefit of the region, are informed by coordinated, comprehensive and sustained *Earth observations* and information". **Structure** America's Caucus; Regional Coordination Working Group. **Activities** Research/documentation; capacity building; training/education. *Comunidad para la Información Espacial e Hidrografica en Latinoamérica y el Caribe (CIEHLYC) – Centre of Hydrologic and Spatial Information for Latin America and the Caribbean*. **Events** *AmeriGEOSS Week* Lima (Peru) 2019, *AmeriGEOSS Week* São José dos Campos (Brazil) 2018, *AmeriGEOSS Week* San José (Costa Rica) 2017, *AmeriGEOSS Week* Bogota (Colombia) 2016, *GEO-CIEHLYC Water Cycle Capacity-Building Workshop* Cartagena de Indias (Colombia) 2015.
Members Governments (16):
Argentina, Bahamas, Belize, Brazil, Canada, Chile, Colombia, Costa Rica, Ecuador, Honduras, Mexico, Panama, Paraguay, Peru, Uruguay, USA.
Participating organizations include:
Comisión Centroamericana de Ambiente y Desarrollo (CCAD, #04129); *Committee on Earth Observation Satellites (CEOS, #04249)*; *Water Center for the Humid Tropics of Latin America and the Caribbean (#20824)*.
[2018/XM6835/**E***]

♦ Amerika Kankyu Shinkokh (internationally oriented national body)
♦ AME-SADA – African Methodist Episcopal Church Service and Development Agency (internationally oriented national body)
♦ AMESD – African Monitoring of the Environment for Sustainable Development (inactive)
♦ AMETIAP / see Global Maritime Education and Training Association (#10464)
♦ **AMETOS** Association médicale européenne tabac ou santé (#07762)
♦ AMEU – Americans for Middle East Understanding (internationally oriented national body)
♦ AMEWG / see CropLife Africa Middle East (#04963)
♦ AME World Ecology Foundation (internationally oriented national body)
♦ AMEWPR / see Western Pacific Association for Medical Education (#20917)
♦ AME Zion – African Methodist Episcopal Zion Church (internationally oriented national body)
♦ AMFA – Affordable Medicines for Africa (internationally oriented national body)
♦ AMF – African Monetary Fund (unconfirmed)
♦ **AMF** Against Malaria Foundation (#00543)
♦ **AMF** Arab Monetary Fund (#01009)
♦ **AMF** Asia Marketing Federation (#01290)
♦ **AMF** Asian Mayors Forum (#01535)
♦ AMF – Asian Monetary Fund (unconfirmed)
♦ **AMF** Asociación Mundial de Futsal (#21532)
♦ **AMFEP** Association of Manufacturers and Formulators of Enzyme Products (#02793)
♦ AMFET – Association for Modelling and Forecasting Economies in Transition (unconfirmed)
♦ AMFFBTV – Asociación Mundial de Fisiólogos, Farmacólogos, Bioquimicos y Toxicólogos Veterinarios (no recent information)
♦ **AMFI** Association mutuelle des fonctionnaires internationaux (#12585)
♦ AMFIE / see Association coopérative financière des fonctionnaires internationaux (#02455)
♦ **AMFIE** Association coopérative financière des fonctionnaires internationaux (#02455)
♦ **AMFIE** Financial Cooperative Association of International Civil Servants (#02455)
♦ **AMFMEG** Arab Maternal – Fetal Medicine Expert Group (#01005)
♦ AM/FM-GIS Nordic Region / see Nordic Network for Geographic Information (#17355)
♦ AMFM / see World Federalist Movement – Movement for a Just World Order through a Strengthened United Nations (#21404)
♦ **AMFN** African Model Forest Network (#00377)
♦ **AMFORHT** Association mondiale pour la formation hôtelière et touristique (#21144)

♦ amfori 00797

Pres Av de Tervuren 270„ Woluwe-Saint-Pierre, 1150 Brussels, Belgium. T. +3227620551. Fax +3227627506. E-mail: info@amfori.org.
URL: http://www.amfori.org/

History 1977. Former names and other names: *Foreign Trade Association (FTA)* – former (1977 to 2017); *amfori – Trade with purpose* – full title. Registration: No/ID: 0427.557.786, Start date: 29 Jul 1985, Belgium; EU Transparency Register, No/ID: 84768556104-35, Start date: 28 Jun 2011. **Aims** Promote the values of international trade and *sustainable* supply chains. **Structure** General Assembly; Board of Directors; Committees and Councils; Secretariat. **Languages** English. **Staff** 50.00 FTE, paid. **Finance** Sources: members' dues. **Activities** Advocacy/lobbying/activism; knowledge management/information dissemination. Initiatives: *Business Social Compliance Initiative (BSCI)*; *Business Environmental Performance Initiative (amfori BEPI)*. **Events** *Unleash Opportunity Conference* Brussels (Belgium) 2019, *Unleash Opportunity Conference* Amsterdam (Netherlands) 2018, *Conference* Brussels (Belgium) 2017, *Conference on the Power of Collaboration* Brussels (Belgium) 2016, *Sustainability Conference* Paris (France) 2016. **Publications** Annual report; corporate brochures. **Members** Members (over 2400) in 46 countries. Membership countries not specified.
IGO Relations Recognized by: *European Commission (EC, #06633)*. Collaborates with: *Deutsche Gesellschaft für Internationale Zusammenarbeit (GIZ)*; *ILO (#11123)*; *International Organization for Migration (IOM, #14454)*; *OECD (#17693)*; *Office of the United Nations High Commissioner for Human Rights (OHCHR, #17697)*; *UNCTAD (#20285)*; *UNDP (#20292)*; *UNIDO (#20336)*; *United Nations (UN, #20515)* – Working Group on Business and Human Rights; *World Trade Organization (WTO, #21864)*. **NGO Relations** Member of (4): *European Business Ethics Network (EBEN, #06418)*; *European Services Forum (ESF, #08469)*; *Federation of European and International Associations Established in Belgium (FAIB, #09508)*; *The Consumer Goods Forum (CGF, #04772)*. Collaborates with: *ASEAN CSR Network (#01166)*; *Business for Social Responsibility (BSR)*; *Ethical Trading Initiative (ETI)*; *Fair Labor Association (FLA)*; *Fairfood International (#09237)*; *GLOBALG.A.P (#10386)*; *Humanistisch Instituut voor Ontwikkelingssamenwerking (Hivos)*; national organizations; *Rainforest Alliance*; *Save the Children International (#19058)*; *Sedex (#19211)*; *Social Accountability Accreditation Services (SAAS, #19332)*; *Social Accountability International (SAI)*; *SOLIDARIDAD Network (#19681)*; *United Nations Global Compact (#20567)*. [2021.02.18/XD9929/**D**]

♦ amfori – Trade with purpose / see amfori (#00797)
♦ AMFORT / see World Association for Hospitality and Tourism Education and Training (#21144)
♦ **AMFUF** Asia Maritime & Fisheries Universities Forum (#01289)
♦ AMG – Associazione Mondo Giusto (internationally oriented national body)
♦ **AMGC** African Minerals and Geosciences Centre (#00373)
♦ **AMGE** Association mondiale des guides et des éclaireuses (#21142)
♦ AMGI / see Multilateral Investment Guarantee Agency (#16888)
♦ AMG International – Advancing the Ministries of the Gospel International (internationally oriented national body)
♦ **AMGK Network** Ananda Marga Gurukula (#00809)
♦ **AMGS** Asociación Mundial de las Guias Scouts (#21142)
♦ AMHI – African Mothers Health Initiative (internationally oriented national body)
♦ **AMHMV** Asociación Mundial de Historia de la Medicina Veterinaria (#21143)
♦ **AMHMV** Association mondiale de l'histoire de la médecine vétérinaire (#21143)
♦ AMI / see Première Urgence Internationale
♦ **AMIA** ASEAN Music Industry Association (#01212)
♦ **AMIA** Asociación Mundial de Ingenieros Agrónomos (#21115)
♦ AMIA – Association of Moving Image Archivists (internationally oriented national body)
♦ AMI – Alliance médicale internationale (inactive)
♦ AMI – Apostolat Militaire International (religious order)
♦ **AMI** Asociación Miraismo Internacional (#02282)
♦ AMI – Association maçonnique internationale (inactive)
♦ **AMI** Association Montessori Internationale (#02812)
♦ **AMICAALL** Alliance of Mayors and Municipal Leaders on HIV/AIDS in Africa (#00707)
♦ **AMICAL** American International Consortium of Academic Libraries (#00783)
♦ Amicale internationale des capitaines au long cours Cap Horniers / see International Association of Cape Horners (#11755)

♦ Amicale internationale des sous-directeurs et chefs de réception des grands hôtels (AICR) 00798

International Association of Deputy Managers and Reception Heads of Luxury Hotels

Contact c/o Le Meurice, 228 Rue de Rivoli, 75001 Paris, France.
URL: http://www.aicr-int.com/

History 2 Feb 1973, Lausanne (Switzerland). Foundation followed a national (French) body having been created in 1965, Nice (France). **Aims** Provide contact between member associations; preserve and foster fraternal sentiments among members; supervise and arbitrate any important decisions of the member associations; facilitate and strengthen the professional relationships between members and promote and publicize the importance of their profession. **Structure** International Committee, consisting of Chairman, Vice Chairman, General Secretary, Treasurer, Auditor, Assistant Secretary and Public Relations Executive. Membership Meeting (regular or special). **Finance** Sources: percentages of dues paid by member associations; gifts; subsidies. **Activities** General Assembly held biannually with congress. **Events** *AICR International Congress and General Assembly* Warsaw (Poland) 2020, *Congress and General Assembly* London (UK) 2019, *Congress and General Assembly* Zurich (Switzerland) 2018, *Congress and General Assembly* Paris (France) 2017, *Congress and General Assembly* Vienna (Austria) 2016.
Members Associations; Individuals (mostly in France) Active, Benefactor, Honorary, Retired. Members in 7 countries:
Austria, Belgium, France, Germany, Italy, Switzerland, UK. [2021/XD8655/**D**]

♦ Amicale Internationale KZ Neuengamme / see International Neuengamme Committee (#14347)
♦ Amicale internationale de Neuengamme (#14347)

♦ Amicale rotarienne internationale des espérantistes (#18973)
♦ **AMIC** Asian Media Information and Communication Centre (#01536)
♦ **AMICE** Association of Mutual Insurers and Insurance Cooperatives in Europe (#02816)
♦ Amici delle Isole di Pace (internationally oriented national body)
♦ Amici delle Isole di Pace e dell'Azione Pane della Pace / see Friends of the Islands of Peace
♦ Amici della Rilegatura d'Arte / see ARA International (#01080)

♦ Amici Thomae Mori (ATM) 00799

Sec 5 rue des Flots Bleus, 34140 Bouzigues, France.
Pres address not obtained.
URL: http://www.amici-thomae-mori.com/

History 29 Dec 1962, Brussels (Belgium). Also known as *Société des Amici Thomae Mori – Friends of Thomas More Association*. **Aims** Disseminate research and popularize the thought and works of *Thomas More* as well as humanists of his time. **Structure** Board of Directors; Editorial Committee; Scientific Committee. **Languages** English, French, German, Italian, Spanish. **Staff** 2.00 FTE, voluntary. **Finance** Members' dues. Other sources: subscriptions; donations; royalties. **Activities** Events/meetings; publishing activities. **Events** *Conference* Berlin (Germany) 2015, *Conference* New York, NY (USA) 2014, *Conference* Washington, DC (USA) 2014, *Triennial conference / Conference* Paris (France) 2012, *Conference* Montréal, QC (Canada) 2011. **Publications** *Gazette Thomas More* (2 a year); *Moreana* (2 a year) in English, French – journal. **Members** Individuals (90). Membership countries not specified. [2016.10.19/XE7458/**E**]

♦ Amicus Curiae (unconfirmed)
♦ AMIDEAST – America-Mideast Educational and Training Services (internationally oriented national body)
♦ L'AMIE – Aide médicale internationale à l'enfance (internationally oriented national body)
♦ AMIEV – Association médicale internationale pour l'étude des conditions de vie et de santé (inactive)
♦ AMI – Fundação Assistência Médica Internacional (internationally oriented national body)
♦ **AMIGO** Asociación Medioambiental Internacional de Gestores del Olor (#02281)
♦ AMIGO FRIEND – Caribbean Mesoamerica FRIEND (see: #13826)
♦ Amigonianos – Terciarios Capuchinos de Nuestra Señora de los Dolores (religious order)
♦ Amigos de las Américas (internationally oriented national body)
♦ Amigos Anonimos CVV / see Samaritans
♦ Amigos de Honduras / see Amigos de las Américas
♦ Amigos da Ilhas de Paz (internationally oriented national body)
♦ Amigos da Ilhas de Paz e da Acção Pão da Paz / see Friends of the Islands of Peace
♦ Amigos Internacionales (inactive)
♦ Amigos de Islas de Paz (internationally oriented national body)
♦ Amigos de las Islas de Paz de la Acción Pan de la Paz / see Friends of the Islands of Peace
♦ Amigos del Orden Budista Occidental / see Triratna Buddhist Community (#20243)
♦ Amigos do Protocolo de Kyoto (internationally oriented national body)
♦ Amigos de la Tierra Europa (#10001)
♦ Amigos de la Tierra Internacional (#10002)
♦ Amika Rondo de Esperantaj-Kolektantoj / see Esperanto-Ligo Filatelista (#05545)
♦ Amilcar Cabral Centre of Information and Documentation (internationally oriented national body)
♦ AMINA – Association mondiale des inventeurs et chercheurs scientifiques (inactive)
♦ AMISA – American International Schools in the Americas (internationally oriented national body)
♦ **AMIS** Agricultural Market Information System (#00573)
♦ Les Amis d'un coin de l'Inde et du monde (internationally oriented national body)
♦ Les Amis d'Elvis / see Treat Me Nice Fan Club (#20230)
♦ Amis de l'Europe, les (#10003)
♦ Amis du Fonds mondial Europe (internationally oriented national body)
♦ Amis d'Iles de Paix (internationally oriented national body)
♦ Amis des îles de paix et de l'action pain de la paix / see Friends of the Islands of Peace
♦ Amis internationaux (inactive)
♦ Amis de la reliure d'art, Les / see ARA International (#01080)
♦ Amis du Sahel / see Sahel and West Africa Club (#19034)
♦ Amistades Cristianas Europeas (inactive)
♦ Amis de la Terre International (#10002)
♦ Amitié internationale judéo-chrétienne (#13006)
♦ Amitié internationale scoute et guide (#14812)
♦ Amitié internationale des scouts et guides adultes / see International Scout and Guide Fellowship (#14812)
♦ Amitié oecuménique internationale (#13226)
♦ Amitié rotarienne pour les Nations Unies / see United Nations Friends in Rotary
♦ Amitiés acadiennes (internationally oriented national body)
♦ Amitiés catholiques françaises dans le mondes (internationally oriented national body)
♦ Amitiés chrétiennes européennes (inactive)
♦ **AMITOM** Association méditerranéenne internationale de la tomate transformée (#16659)
♦ Amizade (internationally oriented national body)
♦ **AMJ** Asamblea Mundial de la Juventud (#21113)
♦ **AMJ** Assemblée mondiale de la jeunesse (#21113)
♦ AMJ – Association mondiale des journaux (inactive)
♦ AMJF – Alliance des mouvements de jeunesse de La Francophonie (inactive)
♦ AMLA / see Association for Health Information and Libraries in Africa (#02630)
♦ AMLaP – Architectures and Mechanisms for Language Processing (meeting series)
♦ **AMLAR** Asociación Médica Latinoamericana de Rehabilitación (#02280)
♦ AMLATFEDOP / see Coordinadora Latinoamericana de Trabajadores de los Servicios Públicos (#04809)
♦ **AMLC** Association of Marine Laboratories of the Caribbean (#02794)
♦ AMLD – Alliance pour la Migration, le Leadership et le Développement (unconfirmed)

♦ Amma – Europe 00800

Amma Belgium Broekstraat 6, 9140 Tielrode, Belgium. T. +3237715227. Fax +3237715034. E-mail: vriendenvanamma@telenet.be – webmaster@amma-europe.org.
URL: http://www.amma-europe.org/

History Set up by disciples of Mata Amritanandamayi (Amma).
Members Full in 22 countries:
Austria, Belgium, Czechia, Denmark, Finland, France, Germany, Greece, Hungary, Ireland, Italy, Luxembourg, Netherlands, Norway, Poland, Portugal, Russia, Slovenia, Spain, Sweden, Switzerland, UK. [2015/XE4268/**E**]

♦ **AMMA International** African Monsoon Multidisciplinary Analyses (#00378)
♦ Amman Center for Peace and Development (internationally oriented national body)
♦ Amman Declaration / see International Civil Defence Organization (#12582)
♦ Ammariyyah (religious order)
♦ **AMM** Asociación Médica Mundial (#21646)
♦ **AMM** Association médicale mondiale (#21646)
♦ AMM – Association méditerranéenne de motocyclisme (no recent information)
♦ AMMF – Association mondiale des médecins francophones (no recent information)
♦ **AMMM** Asociación de Museos Marítimos del Mediterráneo (#02801)
♦ **AMMM** Association of Mediterranean Maritime Museums (#02801)
♦ AMMPA – Alliance of Marine Mammal Parks and Aquariums (internationally oriented national body)
♦ **AMMPE** Asociación Mundial de Mujeres Periodistas y Escritoras (#21206)
♦ **AMN** Africa Mining Network (#00191)

♦ Amnesty International (AI) 00801

SG Peter Benenson House, 1 Easton Street, London, WC1X 0DW, UK. T. +442074135598 – +442074135500. Fax +442074135727. E-mail: secgen@amnesty.org – contactus@amnesty.org.
URL: http://www.amnesty.org/

History 28 May 1961, London (UK), when launched by British lawyer Peter Benenson. Statutes most recently amended 2001, Dakar (Senegal). **Aims** Undertake research and action focused on preventing and ending grave *abuses* of the rights to physical and mental integrity, *freedom* of conscience and expression and freedom from discrimination within the context of work to promote *human rights*; oppose abuses by opposing groups, including hostage-taking, torture and killing of *prisoners* and other deliberate and arbitrary killings. **Structure** International Council (meeting every 2 years). International Board (IB) of 9 members elected every 2 years. Sections; Local Groups. International Secretariat. Regional organization: *Amnesty International – European Institutions Office (#00802)*. **Languages** Arabic, English, French, Spanish. **Staff** 186.00 FTE, paid; 75.00 FTE, voluntary. **Finance** Sources: donations; fundraising; members' dues.
Activities Assists asylum-seekers who are at risk of being returned to a country where they will be at risk of violations of basic and fundamental human rights; cooperates with other non-governmental organizations, the United Nations (UN) and with regional intergovernmental organizations; campaigns to increase accountability in international military, security and police relations; organizes human rights education and awareness-raising programmes. Oct 2002, launched worldwide campaign to highlight discrepancy between human rights protection which those living in the Russian Federation have in international and national law and the reality of widespread human rights abuses committed in a climate of impunity. During 2003, delegates visited dozens of countries and territories to meet victims of human rights violations, observe trial and interview local human rights activists and officials. Together with Oxfam International and IANSA, launched an arms control campaign calling for a Global arms trade treaty' – a draft resolution for *Arms Trade Treaty (ATT, 2013)* approved by the United nations in 2006 – and for local action to protect civilians from armed violence. Launched 'Demand Dignity Campaign', 2009 – to stop and prevent the human rights abuses that drive and deepen poverty. Mainstream activities include both opposition to and denouncing of violations of civil and political human rights and also preventative human rights work such as human rights awareness and human rights education programmes. Approaches have included: lobbying to ensure incorporation of human rights into official training and education curricula of schools, universities, military and police academies, civil service and other professional training programmes; advice on curricula; workshops and training programmes for target groups.
Highlights:
– Conference for the Abolition of Torture, 1973.
– Conference for the Abolition of the Death Penalty, 1977.
– International Conference on Extrajudicial Executions 1982.
– International Conference on Disappearances and Political Killings, 1992.
– appeal for the establishment of an *International Criminal Court (ICC, #13108)* by the year 2000, launched Oct 1996.
– In 1977, received the Nobel Peace Prize for its contribution to "securing the journal for freedom, for justice, and thereby also for peace in the world".
– In 1978, on the 30th anniversary of the Universal Declaration of Human Rights, awarded the United Nations Human Rights Prize for "outstanding achievements in the field of human rights".
Events *Human Rights Defenders World Summit* Paris (France) 2018, *Directors Forum* Barcelona (Spain) 2016, *Nordic Youth Conference* Helsinki (Finland) 2016, *Directors Forum* The Hague (Netherlands) 2015, *Directors Forum* Vienna (Austria) 2013. **Publications** *Wire* (6 a year); *Amnesty International Report* (annual). Country reports; background briefing papers on a range of countries in all regions; other major reports; training materials in several languages.
Members Groups and individuals in 167 countries and territories:
Albania, Algeria, Angola, Argentina, Armenia, Aruba, Australia, Austria, Azerbaijan, Bahamas, Bahrain, Bangladesh, Barbados, Belarus, Belgium, Belize, Benin, Bermuda, Bolivia, Bosnia-Herzegovina, Botswana, Brazil, Brunei Darussalam, Bulgaria, Burkina Faso, Burundi, Cameroon, Canada, Cape Verde, Central African Rep, Chad, Chile, Colombia, Comoros, Congo Brazzaville, Congo DR, Costa Rica, Côte d'Ivoire, Croatia, Cuba, Curaçao, Cyprus, Czechia, Denmark, Djibouti, Dominica, Dominican Rep, Ecuador, Egypt, El Salvador, Equatorial Guinea, Estonia, Eswatini, Ethiopia, Faeroe Is, Finland, France, Gabon, Gambia, Georgia, Germany, Ghana, Greece, Grenada, Guatemala, Guinea, Guinea-Bissau, Guyana, Haiti, Honduras, Hong Kong, Hungary, Iceland, India, Indonesia, Ireland, Israel, Italy, Jamaica, Japan, Jordan, Kazakhstan, Kenya, Korea Rep, Kuwait, Kyrgyzstan, Laos, Latvia, Lebanon, Lesotho, Liberia, Lithuania, Luxembourg, Macau, Madagascar, Malawi, Malaysia, Mali, Malta, Mauritius, Mexico, Moldova, Mongolia, Morocco, Mozambique, Namibia, Nepal, Netherlands, New Zealand, Nicaragua, Niger, Nigeria, North Macedonia, Norway, Pakistan, Palestine, Panama, Papua New Guinea, Paraguay, Peru, Philippines, Poland, Portugal, Puerto Rico, Romania, Russia, Rwanda, Samoa, Sao Tomé-Principe, Senegal, Serbia, Seychelles, Sierra Leone, Singapore, Slovakia, Slovenia, Solomon Is, Somalia, South Africa, Spain, St Vincent-Grenadines, Suriname, Sweden, Switzerland, Taiwan, Tanzania UR, Thailand, Togo, Tonga, Trinidad-Tobago, Tunisia, Türkiye, Turkmenistan, Tuvalu, Uganda, UK, Ukraine, Uruguay, USA, Uzbekistan, Vanuatu, Venezuela, Vietnam, West Bank-Gaza, Yemen, Zambia, Zimbabwe.
Consultative Status Consultative status granted from: *African Commission on Human and Peoples' Rights (ACHPR, #00255)* (Observer); *ECOSOC (#05331)* (Special); *UNESCO (#20322)* (Associate Status); *ILO (#11123)* (Special List); *Council of Europe (CE, #04881)* (Participatory Status); *UNEP (#20299)*. **IGO Relations** Observer status with: *International Organization for Migration (IOM, #14454)*. Special guest at General Assembly of: *OAS (#17629)*. Partner of: *UNHCR (#20327)*. Accredited by: *United Nations Office at Vienna (UNOV, #20604)*. Associated with Department of Global Communications of the United Nations.
NGO Relations Member of:
– *Campaign to Stop Killer Robots (#03405)*;
– *CHS Alliance (#03911)*;
– *Control Arms (#04782)*;
– *EarthAction (EA, #05159)*;
– *European Roma Policy Coalition (ERPC, no recent information)*;
– *Fédération des Institutions Internationales établies à Genève (FIIG, #09599)*;
– *Global Call for Climate Action (GCCA, inactive)*;
– *International Action Network on Small Arms (IANSA, #11585)*;
– *International NGO Platform on the Migrant Workers' Convention (IPMWC, #14367)*;
– *NGO Working Group on the Security Council (#17128)*;
– *Alliance of NGOs on Crime Prevention and Criminal Justice (#00709)*;
– *NGO Committee on UNICEF (#17120)*;
– *Transparency, Accountability and Participation Network (TAP Network, #20222)*;
– *UNITED for Intercultural Action – European Network Against Nationalism, Racism, Fascism and in Support of Migrants and Refugees (UNITED, #20511)*;
– *World Coalition Against the Death Penalty (#21281)*.
Observer member of: *Consortium for Street Children (CSC)*; *International Federation of Health and Human Rights Organisations (IFHHRO, #13440)*. Steering Committee member of: *International Corporate Accountability Roundtable (ICAR, #12968)*. Instrumental in setting up and member of: *International Coalition to Stop Crimes Against Humanity in North Korea (ICNK, #12622)*. Represented on the Organizing Committee of: *Hague Appeal for Peace (HAP, #10848)*. Signatory to the 'Publish What You Pay' appeal of: *Publish What You Pay Coalition (PWYP, #18573)*. [2019/XB0054/**B**]

♦ Amnesty International – Association européenne / see Amnesty International – European Institutions Office (#00802)
♦ Amnesty International – Association de l'Union européenne / see Amnesty International – European Institutions Office (#00802)
♦ Amnesty International – European Association / see Amnesty International – European Institutions Office (#00802)
♦ Amnesty International – European Community Project / see Amnesty International – European Institutions Office (#00802)

♦ Amnesty International – European Institutions Office 00802

Main Office Ave de Cortenbergh 71, 4th fl, 1000 Brussels, Belgium. T. +3225021499. E-mail: eio@amnesty.org.
URL: http://www.amnesty.eu/

History Dec 1992, Brussels (Belgium). Founded as *Amnesty International – European Community Project*, within the framework of *Amnesty International (AI, #00801)*. Previously also referred to as *Amnesty International – European Union Association – Amnesty International – Association de l'Union européenne* and subsequently *Amnesty International – European Association – Amnesty International – Association européenne*. Registration: No/ID: 0447.121.696, Start date: 31 Mar 1992, Belgium; EU Transparency Register, No/ID: 11063928073-34, Start date: 29 Feb 2012. **Aims** Strive for the adherence to and observance of the United Nations Universal Declaration of Human Rights (1948) by promoting *human rights* education and

awareness and by demanding ratification of international human rights instruments; prevent and end grave abuses of the rights to physical and mental integrity, freedom of conscience and expression and freedom from discrimination. **Structure** General Assembly (annual); Executive Board. **Languages** English, French. **Staff** 18.00 FTE, paid. **Finance** Financed by sections in the European Union member states. No funds are sought or accepted from governments. **Activities** Research/documentation; advocacy/lobbying/activism; capacity building. **Events** *Meeting* Brussels (Belgium) 1994, *Meeting* Brussels (Belgium) 1993. **Publications** Annual Report; recommendations.
Members Membership open to sections and structures of Amnesty International in Europe. Members in 23 countries:
Austria, Belgium, Czechia, Denmark, Finland, France, Germany, Greece, Hungary, Ireland, Italy, Luxembourg, Moldova, Netherlands, Norway, Poland, Portugal, Slovakia, Slovenia, Spain, Sweden, UK, Ukraine.
IGO Relations *Council of Europe (CE, #04881)*; European Union institutions; United Nations. Participant in Fundamental Rights Platform of *European Union Agency for Fundamental Rights (FRA, #08969)*. Member of Consultative Forum of: *Frontex, the European Border and Coast Guard Agency (#10005)*. **NGO Relations** *European NGO Platform Asylum and Migration (EPAM, #08051)*. [2020/XE3084/**E**]

♦ Amnesty International – European Union Association / see Amnesty International – European Institutions Office (#00802)
♦ **AMO** Association mondiale des olympiens (#21682)
♦ Amoco Foundation / see BP Foundation
♦ AMOI – Association of Museums of the Indian Ocean (inactive)
♦ **AMOR** Asia-Oceania Meeting of Religious (#01802)
♦ AMORCES – Agence pour la Solidarité Internationale, la Culture, le Développement et l'Environnement (internationally oriented national body)
♦ **AMPA** Asociación Mundial para la Producción Animal (#21117)
♦ **AMPAI** Association mondiale de patinage artistique sur patins en ligne (#21584)
♦ **AMP** Alliance for Malaria Prevention (#00706)
♦ AMP – Association méditerranéenne de psychiatrie (no recent information)
♦ AMP – Association mondiale de phytothérapie (inactive)
♦ **AMP** Association mondiale de psychanalyse (#21177)
♦ **AMP** Association mondiale de psychiatrie (#21741)
♦ AMPB – Alianza Mesoamericana de Pueblos Bosques (unconfirmed)
♦ **AMPC** Asian Modern Pentathlon Confederation (#01542)
♦ AMPEF – Association of Manufacturers of Polyester Film (inactive)
♦ AMPEI – Asociación Mexicana para la Educación Internacional (internationally oriented national body)
♦ **AMPERE Europe** Association for Microwave Power in Europe for Research and Education (#02806)
♦ AMP Global – Global Congress on Molecular Pathology (meeting series)

♦ Amphibian Ark (AArk) 00803

Exec Dir c/o Conservation Breeding Specialist Group, 12101 Johnny Cake Ridge Rd, Apple Valley MN 55124-8151, USA. T. +19529979800. Fax +19529979803.
URL: http://www.amphibianark.org/
History Set up by *World Association of Zoos and Aquariums (WAZA, #21208)*, *International Union for Conservation of Nature and Natural Resources (IUCN, #15766)* – SSC Conservation Breeding Specialist Group (CBSG) and *IUCN/SSC Amphibian Specialist Group (ASG)*. Constitution adopted Feb 2007. **Aims** Ensure *survival* and diversity of amphibian species focusing on those that cannot currently be safeguarded in their natural environments. **Structure** Steering Committee; Executive Co-Chairs; Advisory Committees (3). **Languages** English, Spanish. **Staff** 2.00 FTE, paid; 2.00 FTE, voluntary. **Activities** Awareness raising; financial and/or material support; monitoring/evaluation; training/education. **Publications** *AArk Newsletter*.
Members Members include 10 international organizations listed in this Yearbook:
Asociación Latinoamericana de Parques Zoológicos y Acuarios (ALPZA, #02252); *Botanic Gardens Conservation International (BGCI, #03306)*; *Eurasian Regional Association of Zoos and Aquariums (EARAZA, #05614)*; *European Association of Zoos and Aquaria (EAZA, #06283)*; *Meso-American and Caribbean Zoo and Aquarium Association (#16730)*; *Pan-African Association of Zoos and Aquaria (PAAZA, #18039)*; *South Asian Zoo Association for Regional Cooperation (SAZARC, #19746)*; *Southeast Asian Zoos and Aquariums Association (SEAZA, #19788)*; *Species360 (#19915)*; *Zoo and Aquarium Association Australasia (#22039)*.
NGO Relations Member of (1): *International Association of Communication Activists (IACACT, #11791)*. Partner of (2): *Amphibian Survival Alliance (ASA, #00804)*; *Re:wild*. [2021/XJ8564/y/**E**]

♦ Amphibian Survival Alliance (ASA) 00804

Exec Dir c/o Global Wildlife Conservation, PO Box 129, Austin TX 78767-0129, USA. T. +15125378951. E-mail: info@amphibiansurvivalalliance.org.
URL: http://www.amphibians.org/
History Proposed at Amphibian Mini Summit, Aug 2009, London (UK). **Aims** Protect amphibians and their habitats through dynamic partnerships worldwide. **Structure** Global Council. Secretariat. **NGO Relations** Strategic partners include: *1% for the Planet*; *Alliance for Zero Extinction (AZE, #00730)*; *Conservation International (CI)*; *Endangered Wildlife Trust (EWT)*; *European Association of Zoos and Aquaria (EAZA, #06283)*; *European Herpetological Society (#07481)*; *Re:wild*; *International Union for Conservation of Nature and Natural Resources (IUCN, #15766)* and its Species Survival Commission (SSC); *World Association of Zoos and Aquariums (WAZA, #21208)*. [2017/XJ0458/**C**]

♦ AM Platform / see European Technology Platform in Additive Manufacturing (#08886)
♦ **AM Platform** European Technology Platform in Additive Manufacturing (#08886)

♦ Amplify 00805

Address not obtained.
URL: https://www.amplifyyouth.org/
History Derived from 'International Youth Summit for Nuclear Abolition', Aug 2015, Hiroshima (Japan). **Aims** As an international *youth* network, work towards *nuclear abolition* and a world without nuclear *weapons*. **Structure** Steering Committee. **Activities** Events/meetings; advocacy/lobbying/activism. **NGO Relations** Partner of: *International Campaign to Abolish Nuclear Weapons (ICAN, #12426)*. [2020/XM8973/**E**]

♦ Amplio (internationally oriented national body)
♦ AMPM / see Archive of Maori and Pacific Sound
♦ AMPPBTV – Association mondiale de physiologistes, pharmacologistes, biochimistes et toxicologistes vétérinaires (no recent information)
♦ AMP / see Peoples' Global Action Against Free Trade and the WTO (#18304)
♦ AMPSAD / see Australasian Professional Society on Alcohol and Other Drugs
♦ **AMPS** Ananda Marga Pracaraka Samgha (#00810)
♦ AMPS – Archive of Maori and Pacific Sound (internationally oriented national body)
♦ AMPS – Association mondiale de prospective sociale (inactive)
♦ AMPTC – Arab Maritime Petroleum Transport Company (see: #17854)
♦ AMPV – Asociación Mundial de Patólogos Veterinarios (no recent information)
♦ AMPV – Association mondiale des pathologistes vétérinaires (no recent information)
♦ AMP – WMO Applications of Meteorology Programme (see: #21649)
♦ AMRA – Association of Maize Researchers in Africa (no recent information)
♦ e-amracom (inactive)
♦ AMR – Africa Ministry Resources (internationally oriented national body)
♦ AMRC – Asia Monitor Resource Centre (internationally oriented national body)
♦ AMRDI – Arctic and Mountain Regions Development Institute (internationally oriented national body)
♦ AMREF / see Amref Health Africa (#00806)

♦ Amref Health Africa 00806

Group CEO PO Box 27691, Langata Road, Nairobi, 00506, Kenya. T. +254206993000. Fax +25420609518. E-mail: info@amref.org.
URL: http://www.amref.org/
History 7 Aug 1957, Nairobi (Kenya). Field operations registered 27 Jan 1961, Kenya. Former names and other names: *Flying Doctors Service* – former; *African Research Foundation* – former; *African Medical and Research Foundation (AMREF)* – former (Mar 1962); *Fondation pour la médecine et la recherche en Afrique* – former (Mar 1962); *Gesellschaft für Medizin und Forschung in Afrika* – former (Mar 1962). Registration: Start date: 1957, USA, New York; England and Wales. **Aims** Improve the health of people in Africa by partnering with, and empowering, communities; strengthen health systems. **Structure** Board of Directors; Executive Committee; Senior Management Team; Country Directors. **Languages** Dutch, English, French, Spanish. **Staff** 1050.00 FTE, paid. **Finance** Donors: bilateral and multilateral institutions; private corporations; private charities; international organizations; individuals. **Activities** Capacity building; healthcare; research/documentation; advocacy/lobbying/activism; projects; programmes; training/education. Maintains the *'AMREF Mahler Library'* and *Network for Water and Sanitation International (NETWAS International, #17064)*. **Events** *Africa Health Agenda International Conference (AHAIC)* Kigali (Rwanda) 2023, *Africa Health Agenda International Conference (AHAIC)* Nairobi (Kenya) 2021, *Meeting* Salzburg (Austria) 2012, *Meeting on African health* London (UK) 1998, *Workshop on health promotion and education* Arusha (Tanzania UR) 1997. **Publications** *AFYA* (6 a year); *AMREF News* (4 a year); *Defender* (4 a year); *Helper* (4 a year); *The COBASHECA Newsletter* (4 a year); *AMREF in Action* (annual). *Rural Health Series Manuals* – series. Annual report; books on primary health care; reference works.
Members Country offices in 4 countries:
Kenya, South Africa, Tanzania UR, Uganda.
International offices in 11 countries:
Austria, Canada, Denmark, France, Germany, Italy, Netherlands, Spain, Sweden, UK, USA.
Consultative Status Consultative status granted from: *ECOSOC (#05331)* (Ros A); *WHO (#20950)* (Official Relations); *UNICEF (#20332)*; *United Nations Population Fund (UNFPA, #20612)*.
IGO Relations Special links with: *Commonwealth Secretariat (#04362)*; *International Fund for Agricultural Development (IFAD, #13692)*; *UNDP (#20292)*; *United Nations Volunteers (UNV, #20650)*. Associated with Department of Global Communications of the United Nations. Supported by:
- *Canadian International Development Agency (CIDA, inactive)*;
- *Centre for Environment and Development for the Arab Region and Europe (CEDARE, #03738)*;
- *DANIDA*;
- *Department for International Development (DFID, inactive)*;
- *Deutsche Gesellschaft für Technische Zusammenarbeit (GTZ, inactive)*;
- *Deutsche Stiftung für Internationale Entwicklung (DSE, inactive)*;
- *European Commission (EC, #06633)*;
- *International Development Research Centre (IDRC, #13162)*;
- *Norwegian Agency for Development Cooperation (Norad)*;
- *Swedish International Development Cooperation Agency (Sida)*;
- *UNHCR (#20327)*;
- *United States Agency for International Development (USAID)*.

NGO Relations Member of (15): *Africa Capacity Alliance (ACA, #00160)*; *American Council for Voluntary International Action (InterAction)*; *Consortium of Christian Relief and Development Association (CCRDA)*; *CORE Group*; *Gavi – The Vaccine Alliance (Gavi, #10077)* (CSO Constituency); *Global Health Council (GHC, #10402)*; *Global Health Workforce Alliance (GHWA, inactive)*; *Global Impact*; *InsideNGO (inactive)*; *International Coalition for Trachoma Control (ICTC, #12624)*; *Neglected Tropical Diseased NGO Network (NNN, #16969)*; *NGO Committee on UNICEF (#17120)*; *PMNCH (#18410)*; *UHC2030 (#20277)*; *UK Consortium on AIDS and International Development*.
AMREF-Canada is member of: *Ontario Council for International Cooperation (OCIC)*. AMREF-Germany is member of: *Bensheim Circle (no recent information)*. AMREF-UK is full member of: *British Overseas NGO's for Development (BOND)*. Partner of: *International Confederation of Midwives (ICM, #12863)*; *Stop TB Partnership (#19999)*; *UNLEASH*. Supported by:
- *ActionAid (#00087)*;
- *Aide et action France*;
- *Atkinson Foundation (no recent information)*;
- *Brot für die Welt*;
- *Centre for International Migration and Development (CIM)*;
- *ChildFund International (#03869)*;
- *Comitato Internazionale per lo Sviluppo dei Popoli (CISP)*;
- *Episcopal Migration Ministries (EMM)*;
- *Ford Foundation (#09858)*;
- *The William and Flora Hewlett Foundation*;
- *IMPACT (#11136)*;
- *London School of Hygiene and Tropical Medicine (LSHTM)*;
- *Lutheran World Relief (LWR)*;
- *Norwegian Church Aid*;
- *Oxfam GB*;
- *Pharmaciens sans frontières – Comité international (PSF CI, inactive)*;
- *Population Council (#18458)*;
- *Refugee Council (#18739)*;
- *The Rockefeller Foundation (#18966)*;
- *Save the Children UK (SC UK)*;
- *Terre des Hommes International Federation (TDHIF, #20133)*;
- *Welthungerhilfe*;
- *World Council of Churches (WCC, #21320)*.

Links also with: *African Population and Health Research Center (APHRC, #00420)*; *Aga Khan Foundation (AKF, #00545)*; *Canadian Physicians for Aid and Relief (CPAR)*; *East African School of Library and Information Science (EASLIS, #05188)*; *Flying Doctors' Society of Africa (FDSA)*; *International Community for the Relief of Starvation and Suffering (ICROSS)*; *International Society of Radiographers and Radiological Technologists (ISRRT, #15410)*; *Network of AIDS Researchers of Eastern and Southern Africa (NARESA, #16990)*; *PRONTO International*. [2020/XF4288/f/**F**]

♦ AMR – International Workshop on Adaptive Multimedia Retrieval (meeting series)
♦ AMRN / see Lugina Africa Midwives Research Network (#16522)
♦ **AMRO** ASEAN+3 Macroeconomic Research Office (#01134)
♦ AMRO / see Pan American Sanitary Bureau (#18129)
♦ **AMROP** Association mondiale de recherches sur l'opinion publique (#21180)
♦ **AMRP** Alianza de Mesas Redondas Panamericanas (#00711)
♦ **AMRP** Association mondiale pour la réadaptation psychosociale (#21178)
♦ **AMSA** Association of Medical Schools in Africa (#02798)
♦ AMSAD / see Australasian Professional Society on Alcohol and Other Drugs
♦ **AMS** Aesthetic Multispecialty Society (#00147)
♦ AMS / see African Membrane Society (#00371)
♦ **AMSA International** Asian Medical Students' Association International (#01538)
♦ AMS / see Arab International Society for Management Technology (#00993)
♦ **AMS** Aseanian Membrane Society (#01196)
♦ **AMS** Asian Musculoskeletal Society (#01543)
♦ **AMSAT** Radio Amateur Satellite Corporation (#18601)
♦ **AMS** Australasian Menopause Society (#03026)
♦ AMS – Australasian Mycological Society (internationally oriented national body)
♦ **AMSC** Asociación Mundial de Sociedades de Cocineros (#21124)
♦ **AMSCO** African Management Services Company (#00367)
♦ **AMSE** Association of Medical Schools in Europe (#02799)
♦ **AMSE** Association mondiale des sciences de l'éducation (#02811)
♦ AMSEE – Association méditerranéenne des sciences de l'environnement et de l'espace (inactive)
♦ **AMSE** International Association for the Advancement of Modelling and Simulation Techniques in Enterprises (#11688)
♦ **AMSEP** Association mondiale des services d'emploi publics (#21179)
♦ **AMSIC** African Membrane Society (#00371)
♦ AMSIG – Australasian Musculoskeletal Imaging Group (internationally oriented national body)
♦ AMS – International Conference on Accelerator Mass Spectrometry (meeting series)
♦ AMSME / see Association for Medical Education in the Eastern Mediterranean Region (#02796)

AMSP
00806

alphabetic sequence excludes
For the complete listing, see Yearbook Online at

♦ AMSP – Association médico-sociale protestante de langue française (no recent information)
♦ **AMSPE** Asociación Mundial de Servicios Públicos de Empleo (#21179)
♦ AMSSA – African Maritime Safety and Security Agency (unconfirmed)
♦ AMSS UK – Association of Muslim Social Scientists, UK (internationally oriented national body)
♦ Amsterdam Center for International Law (internationally oriented national body)
♦ Amsterdam Institute for Global Health and Development (internationally oriented national body)
♦ Amsterdam Institute for International Development (internationally oriented national body)
♦ Amsterdam School of International Relations (internationally oriented national body)
♦ **AMSTS** ASEAN Membrane Science and Technology Society (#01211)
♦ AMTA / see Arab Academy for Science, Technology and Maritime Transport (#00891)
♦ AMTA – Association for Machine Translation in the Americas (internationally oriented national body)
♦ AMTA – Association mondiale pour l'union du troisième âge (inactive)
♦ AMTC – Asia Pacific MSME Trade Coalition (unconfirmed)
♦ Amt der Europäischen Union für Geistiges Eigentum (#08996)
♦ AMTIESA – Association of Management Training Institutions of Eastern and Southern Africa (no recent information)
♦ Amt für Veröffentlichungen der Europäischen Union (#18562)
♦ **AMU** African Mathematical Union (#00370)
♦ **AMU** Arab Maghreb Union (#01004)
♦ AMU – Associazione Azione per un Mondo Unito (internationally oriented national body)
♦ **AMUE** Association des Magistrats de l'Union Européenne (#07614)
♦ AMU / see FIM Africa (#09758)
♦ **AMURT** Ananda Marga Universal Relief Team (#00811)
♦ Amusement Industry Manufacturers and Suppliers International (internationally oriented national body)
♦ **AMVA** Asociación Mundial Veterinaria de Avicultura (#21902)
♦ **AMVA** Association mondiale vétérinaire d'aviculture (#21902)
♦ **AMV** Asociación Mundial Veterinaria (#21901)
♦ **AMV** Association mondiale vétérinaire (#21901)
♦ **AMVCP** Alliance mondiale des villes contre la pauvreté (#21080)
♦ **AMVHA** Asociación Mundial de Veterinarios Higienistas de los Alimentos (#21204)
♦ AMVMI – Asociación Mundial de los Veterinarios Microbiológios y Especialistas en Enfermedades Infecciosas (no recent information)
♦ AMVMI – Association mondiale des vétérinaires microbiologistes, immunologistes et spécialistes des maladies infectieuses (no recent information)
♦ **AMVPA** Asociación Mundial Veterinaria de Pequeños Animales (#21795)
♦ AMVR – Asociación Mundial de Vivienda Rural (inactive)
♦ AMVTN / see African Malaria Network Trust (#00365)
♦ AMWCY – African Movement of Working Children and Youth (unconfirmed)
♦ AMWN – African Marine Waste Network (internationally oriented national body)
♦ **AMZ** Association mondiale de zootechnie (#21117)
♦ AMZFI / see World Economic Processing Zones Association (#21368)
♦ AMZIE / see World Economic Processing Zones Association (#21368)
♦ ANA – Association of Nordic Aeroclubs (no recent information)
♦ **ANAC** Asian Network of Analytical Chemistry (#01546)
♦ **AnaEE** Analysis and Experimentation on Ecosystems (#00808)

♦ Anaerobe Society of the Americas (ASA) 00807

Exec Dir PO Box 452058, Los Angeles CA 90045, USA. T. +13102169265. E-mail: asa@anaerobe.org.
URL: http://www.anaerobe.org/

History Founded 1992, Los Angeles CA (USA). Registered in the State of California. **Aims** Stimulate interest in anaerobes; encourage and facilitate interchange among anaerobists from all disciplines, including medical, dental, veterinary, environmental and basic sciences. **Languages** English. **Staff** 0.50 FTE, paid. **Finance** Members' dues. Grants. **Events** *Biennial Conference* Los Angeles, CA (USA) 2020, *Biennial Conference* Las Vegas, NV (USA) 2018, *Biennial Conference* Nashville, TN (USA) 2016, *Biennial Conference / Biennial Congress* Chicago, IL (USA) 2014, *Biennial Conference / Biennial Congress* San Francisco, CA (USA) 2012. **Publications** *ASA News* – online. Conference' proceedings.
Members Individuals in 53 countries and territories:
Argentina, Australia, Barbados, Belgium, Brazil, Bulgaria, Canada, Chile, China, Colombia, Costa Rica, Cuba, Czechia, Denmark, Ecuador, Egypt, El Salvador, Estonia, Finland, France, Germany, Greece, Guatemala, Hungary, India, Iran Islamic Rep, Italy, Japan, Korea Rep, Kuwait, Mexico, Netherlands, New Zealand, Nigeria, Norway, Oman, Peru, Poland, Romania, Russia, Singapore, Slovenia, South Africa, Spain, Sweden, Switzerland, Taiwan, Thailand, Türkiye, UK, Ukraine, USA, Venezuela.
[2021/XD6853/v/**D**]

♦ **ANAFE** African Network for Agriculture, Agroforestry and Natural Resources Education (#00380)
♦ ANAIC / see Asian Network of Analytical Chemistry (#01546)

♦ Analysis and Experimentation on Ecosystems (AnaEE) 00808

Contact address not obtained.
Coordination INRA, UMR GABI, Domaine de Vilvert, 78352 Jouy-en-Josas CEDEX, France. T. +33134652178.
URL: http://www.anaee.com/

Aims Act as a research infrastructure for experimental manipulation of managed and unmanaged terrestrial and aquatic ecosystems. **Structure** Steering Committee; Scientific Advisory Board. **Finance** Funders: *European Commission (EC, #06633)*; national funding from institutions in Belgium, France, UK, Italy and Finland. **Activities** Capacity building; knowledge management/information dissemination. **Events** *International Conference* Paris (France) 2016.
Members Partners in 10 countries:
Belgium, Czechia, Denmark, Finland, France, Italy, Norway, Sweden, Türkiye, UK. [2018/XM5825/**F**]

♦ Analytical Centre on Globalization and Regional Cooperation (internationally oriented national body)
♦ Ananda Marga / see Ananda Marga Pracaraka Samgha (#00810)

♦ Ananda Marga Gurukula (AMGK Network) 00809

Acting Sec AMGK Cakradhuri, Gopal Anandanagar, PO Chitmu Dist Purulia, Anandanagar, West Bengal 723215, Anandanagar WEST BENGAL 723215, India. T. +919953101378. E-mail: kulapati@gurukul.edu.
Liaison Office 146 Honness Lane, Ithaca NY 14850, USA. E-mail: amgk.glo@gurukul.edu.
European Office Aprikosgatan B 1 Lgh 1001, SE-165 60 Hasselby, Sweden. T. +46734127337. E-mail: satishkohli1@gmail.com.
URL: http://www.gurukul.edu/

History 7 Sep 1990. Founded by Shrii P R Sarkar, as an international network of educational institutes engaged in teaching, research and service. **Aims** Advent a society in which there is love, peace, understanding, inspiration, justice and health for all; establish and support initiatives that further the cause of neohumanism; promote establishment of new curricula addressing *holistic* development of individuals and creating a sustainable progressive society. **Structure** Steering Body; Academic Council. **Languages** English. **Staff** 10.00 FTE, voluntary. **Finance** Sources: donations. Annual budget: 50,000 USD. **Activities** Events/meetings; projects/programmes; training/education. **Events** *Meeting* Caracas (Venezuela) 2014, *Meeting* Sweden 2013, *Meeting* Ydrefors (Sweden) 2013, *Meeting* Bhubaneswar (India) 2012, *Meeting* Denpasar (Indonesia) 2011. **Publications** *Gurukula Network* (2 a year).
Members Institutions in 60 countries and territories:
Albania, Argentina, Australia, Brazil, Burkina Faso, Cambodia, Chile, Colombia, Congo DR, Costa Rica, Côte d'Ivoire, Croatia, Cyprus, Denmark, Dominican Rep, Egypt, El Salvador, Finland, Ghana, Guatemala, Guyana, Haiti, Iceland, India, Indonesia, Ireland, Israel, Italy, Jamaica, Japan, Jordan, Kenya, Korea Rep, Laos, Malaysia, Malta, Mexico, Moldova, Mongolia, Myanmar, Nepal, Netherlands, Norway, Paraguay, Philippines, Romania, Russia, South Africa, Sweden, Switzerland, Syrian AR, Taiwan, Tanzania UR, Thailand, Togo, Uganda, UK, USA, Venezuela, Vietnam.
NGO Relations *Ananda Marga Pracaraka Samgha (AMPS, #00810).* [2022.05.04/XM0488/**F**]

♦ Ananda Marga Pracaraka Samgha (AMPS) 00810

Headquarters Anandanagar, PO Baglata, Purulia, West Bengal DIST 723 213, Purulia WEST BENGAL DIST 723 213, India. T. +91325460203.
European Office Weisenauer Weg 4, 55129 Mainz, Germany. T. +493161832995. Fax +493161834628. E-mail: europe@anandamarga.org.
URL: http://www.amps.org/

History 1955. Follows the socio-spiritual ideology of Shri *Anandamurtiji* also known as Prabhat Ranjan Sarkar, believing in the emergence of *One Human Society – Ek Manav Samaj (EMS)*. Also known as *Ananda Marga (AM)*. Full title translates as 'Organization to Propagate the Path of Bliss'. **Aims** Promote common *spiritual* ideology, universal moral code, spirituality in family life, socio-economic equality and security of all human beings, and abolition of caste, states, communal, racial, national, geographical, linguistic and cultural barriers; propagate neo-*humanism*, with a subjective approach to life through objective adjustment; support and strengthen international organizations in order to build a well-knit social order and all factors that encourage fundamental human ties; encourage and organize common social functions and festivals and use of common systems. **Structure** Regional sectors (6); sectorial offices (9). *Renaissance Universal (RU)* aims to bring about intellectual-intuitional renaissance; *Renaissance Artists and Writers (RAWA)* is the cultural wing; Women's Welfare Department (WWD); Prevention of Cruelty to Animals and Plants and Cheap Literature (PCAP-CL); Ananda Marga University. **Finance** Decentralized: each country chapter raises its own funds from sympathizers, members or through charitable donations, sale of publications, etc; each country has its own annual budget. Funding from several European governments for social service activities in developing countries. **Activities** Provides free instruction in meditation and yoga; organizes clubs for discussion and debate. Education, Relief and Welfare Section (ERAWS) runs educational institutions in more than 180 countries and islands, works for social welfare of underprivileged groups. **Events** *Summer Conference* Wendelsheim (Germany) 2003, *Spiritual Conference* Pundag (India) 2002, *Sectorial conference* Milkow (Poland) 2001, *Spiritual conference* Pundag (India) 2001, *Summer conference* Wendelsheim (Germany) 2001. **Publications** *New Renaissance* (4 a year) – journal. Monographs; pamphlets; brochures. Publications cover spiritual philosophy, yogic health and the science of meditation, social history and development neo-humanism.
Members Individuals in 117 countries and territories:
Albania, Argentina, Australia, Austria, Bangladesh, Barbados, Belarus, Belgium, Belize, Bolivia, Bosnia-Herzegovina, Brazil, Burkina Faso, Burundi, Cambodia, Cameroon, Canada, Chile, China, Colombia, Congo Brazzaville, Costa Rica, Côte d'Ivoire, Croatia, Cuba, Cyprus, Czechia, Denmark, Djibouti, Dominican Rep, Ecuador, Egypt, El Salvador, Eritrea, Ethiopia, Fiji, Finland, France, Germany, Ghana, Greece, Guatemala, Guinea, Guyana, Haiti, Honduras, Hong Kong, Hungary, Iceland, India, Indonesia, Ireland, Israel, Italy, Jamaica, Japan, Jordan, Kenya, Korea Rep, Laos, Lebanon, Madagascar, Malaysia, Malta, Mauritania, Mexico, Moldova, Mongolia, Mozambique, Myanmar, Nepal, Netherlands, New Zealand, Nicaragua, Nigeria, North Macedonia, Norway, Oman, Pakistan, Panama, Papua New Guinea, Paraguay, Peru, Philippines, Poland, Portugal, Puerto Rico, Romania, Russia, Rwanda, Serbia, Singapore, Slovakia, Slovenia, Solomon Is, South Africa, Spain, Sri Lanka, Sudan, Sweden, Switzerland, Syrian AR, Taiwan, Tanzania UR, Thailand, Togo, Trinidad-Tobago, Türkiye, Uganda, UK, Ukraine, Uruguay, USA, Venezuela, Vietnam, Zambia, Zimbabwe.
NGO Relations Cooperates with a large number of relief organizations, including: *International Committee of the Red Cross (ICRC, #12799); International Federation of Red Cross and Red Crescent Societies (#13526).* [2014/XF6353/v/**F**]

♦ Ananda Marga Universal Relief Team (AMURT) 00811

Main Office 2502 Lindley Terrace, Rockville MD 20850, USA. T. +13017387122. Fax +13017387123. E-mail: info@amurt.net.
URL: http://www.amurt.net/

History 1955, India. A registered charity in UK. **Aims** Help improve the quality of life for the poor and disadvantaged people of the world, and those affected by calamity and conflict. **Structure** A team within the framework of *Ananda Marga Yoga Society*. **Staff** Voluntary. **Finance** Sources: fundraising; grants. **Activities** Guidance/assistance/consulting; humanitarian/emergency aid; training/education. **Events** *Conference* Córdoba (Argentina) 1995, *Disaster relief management* India 1995, *Conference* India 1990, *Conference* India 1989.
Members Full in 50 countries and territories:
Albania, Australia, Brazil, Burkina Faso, Canada, Côte d'Ivoire, Cyprus, Denmark, Dominican Rep, Fiji, Finland, Germany, Ghana, Greece, Guatemala, Haiti, Iceland, India, Indonesia, Italy, Jamaica, Kenya, Malaysia, Malta, Mexico, Moldova, Mongolia, Mozambique, Netherlands, New Zealand, Norway, Papua New Guinea, Paraguay, Peru, Philippines, Portugal, Romania, Singapore, South Africa, Spain, Sweden, Switzerland, Taiwan, Thailand, Uganda, UK, USA, Venezuela, Zambia, Zimbabwe.
IGO Relations Associated with Department of Global Communications of the United Nations. **NGO Relations** Member of (2): *American Council for Voluntary International Action (InterAction); Conference of Non-Governmental Organizations in Consultative Relationship with the United Nations (CONGO, #04635)* (associate member). Cooperates with (1): *Alliance Against Hunger and Malnutrition (AAHM, no recent information).* Supports (1): *Global Call for Action Against Poverty (GCAP, #10263).* [2021.08.31/XF0973/**F**]

♦ Ananda Marga Yoga Society (religious order)

♦ Anarchist Black Cross Network 00812

Address not obtained.

History 2001. The Anarchist Black Cross (ABC) originated in Russia, as *Red Cross*. Became *Black Cross* during the Russian Civil War and moved to Berlin (Germany) after the Civil War, where it continued to aid prisoners of the Bolshevik regime as well as victims of Italian fascism and others. Activities ceased circa 1940. Restarted circa 1967, UK, to aid prisoners of the Spanish fascist regime. **Aims** Recognize, expose and support the struggles of *prisoners* in general and *political prisoners* and prisoners of war in particular. **Structure** No central secretariat.
Members Prisoner groups in 21 countries:
Argentina, Australia, Austria, Belarus, Bulgaria, Canada, Colombia, Czechia, Finland, France, Germany, Mexico, Netherlands, Peru, Poland, Russia, Spain, Sweden, Switzerland, UK, USA. [2008/XF5755/**F**]

♦ Anarchist International (inactive)
♦ **ANARLF** Association de neuro-anesthésie-réanimation de langue française (#02824)
♦ **ANASE** Association des nations de l'Asie du Sud-Est (#01141)
♦ Anatomical Society (#00813)
♦ Anatomical Society of Southern Africa (internationally oriented national body)
♦ Anatomical Society of West Africa (no recent information)
♦ Anatomiese Vereniging van Suider Afrika (internationally oriented national body)

♦ Anatomische Gesellschaft (AG) 00813

Anatomical Society (AS)
Contact Inst für Anatomie LST II, Friedrich-Alexander-Univ Erlangen, Universitätsstr 19, 91054 Erlangen, Germany.
URL: http://www.anatomische-gesellschaft.de/

History 23 Sep 1886, having existed since 29 Sep 1822 as a section in the *'Gesellschaft Deutscher Naturforscher und Ärzte'*. Refounded 26 Apr 1949. Has been referred to as *Society of German-Speaking Anatomists*. **Aims** Advance anatomical science to its fullest extent. **Structure** General Assembly; Executive Board of 4. Secretary. **Languages** English, German. **Staff** 2.50 FTE, voluntary. **Finance** Members' dues: euro 40. **Activities** Annual scientific meeting and annual scientific workshop, focusing on primary subjects. **Events** *Annual Meeting* Innsbruck (Austria) 2021, *Annual Meeting* Innsbruck (Austria) 2020, *Annual Meeting* Würzburg (Germany) 2019, *Annual Meeting* Rostock (Germany) 2018, *Annual Meeting* Würzburg (Germany) 2017. **Publications** *Annals of Anatomy* – official journal.
Members Although based in Germany, huge amount of members come from other countries. Individuals (about 800) in 42 countries and territories:
Austria, Belarus, Belgium, Brazil, Bulgaria, Canada, Cayman Is, Croatia, Czechia, Denmark, Egypt, Estonia, Finland, France, Germany, Hungary, India, Ireland, Italy, Japan, Korea Rep, Latvia, Lebanon, Lithuania, Mexico, Netherlands, New Zealand, Poland, Portugal, Romania, Russia, Serbia, Singapore, Slovakia, Spain, Switzerland, Türkiye, UK, Ukraine, United Arab Emirates, USA, Venezuela.
NGO Relations Member of: *European Federation for Experimental Morphology (EFEM, #07115); International Federation of Associations of Anatomists (IFAA, #13361).* [2020/XD0336/v/**C**]

♦ **ANAW** Africa Network for Animal Welfare (#00301)
♦ **ANBD** Asia Network Beyond Design (#01442)
♦ **ANBD** Asian Network of Bipolar Disorder (#01547)

♦ **ANBO** African Network for Basin Organizations (#00381)
♦ ANCAD – Asian Network for Culture and Development (internationally oriented national body)
♦ ANC – Africa Nomads Conservation (internationally oriented national body)
♦ **ANCAP** African Network for Chemical Analysis of Pesticides (#00383)
♦ ANCARA – Advanced Networked Cities and Regions Association (no recent information)
♦ ANCBS – Association of National Committees of the Blue Shield (inactive)
♦ ANCBS / see Blue Shield International (#03286)
♦ **ANCEFA** Africa Network Campaign on Education for All (#00302)
♦ Ancelle della Carità (religious order)
♦ Ancelle del Cuore di Gesù (religious order)
♦ Ancelle della Divina Misericordia (religious order)
♦ Ancelle di Maria (religious order)
♦ Ancelle Mater Misericordiae (religious order)
♦ Ancelle Missionarie della Santissima Trinità (religious order)
♦ Ancelle dei Poveri di Jeanne Delanoue (religious order)
♦ Ancelle del Sacro Cuore di Gesù (religious order)
♦ Ancelle del Sacro Cuore di Gesù (religious order)
♦ Ancelle del San Sacramento (religious order)
♦ Ancelles de la Charité (religious order)
♦ Ancelle dello Spirito Santo dell'Adorazione Perpetua (religious order)
♦ Ancelles du Sacré-Coeur (religious order)
♦ ANCER – Asia Pacific Network for Cultural Education and Research (unconfirmed)
♦ **ANCG** Arab Neonatal Care Group (#01010)
♦ Ancien et Mystique Ordre Rosae Crucis (religious order)

♦ Anciens Association of the NATO Defense College 00814

Sec c/o NATO Defense College, Via Giorgio Pelosi 1, 00143 Rome RM, Italy. T. +39650525240. Fax +39650525786.
URL: http://www.ndc.nato.int/

History 1955, for former members of *NATO Defense College (NDC, #16944)*. **Aims** Preserve and develop the associations and friendships made while serving with the NATO Defense College; encourage formation of national and headquarters associations further the objectives of the Association; enable Anciens to study and to be informed about the Alliance and about activities of the NATO Defense College; provide an influential and informed body of opinion to support the Alliance. **Structure** General Meeting (annual), headed by President. Executive Committee, comprising Chairman (Vice-President of the Association), Executive Secretary, Administrator, Members' Secretary, Secretary of the Anciens' Association, Treasurer, Chief, Public Affairs Office, 3 College and 2 outside members. **Finance** Members' dues. **Activities** Maintains official register of all members of the Association. **Publications** *SPOTLIGHT*. **Members** Ordinary; Honorary. Membership countries not specified. [2018/XE6755/**E**]

♦ Anciens de la fonction publique européenne / see Seniors of the European Public Service (#19229)
♦ Ancient Arabic Order of the Nobles of the Mystic Shrine / see Shriners International
♦ Ancient Forest International (internationally oriented national body)

♦ Ancient and Primitive Rite of Memphis-Misraïm 00815

Rite ancien et primitif de Memphis-Misraïm

Grand Master address not obtained. E-mail: info.nss@memphis-misraim.us.
URL: http://www.iss-ic-memphis-misraim.com/

History 1881. Founded under the influence of General Garibaldi, on merger of two rites: *Rite of Misraïm*, first referred to in 1738, developed by Joseph Balsamo, called Cagliostro, who gave a patent to this Rite in 1788; *Rite of Memphis*, constituted by Jacques Etienne Marconis de Nègre in 1838 as a variant of the Rite of Misraïm. Merger came into effect in 1889. Former names and other names: *Egyptian Freemasonry* – alias; *Ordre International du Rite Ancien et Primitif de Memphis-Misraïm (OIRAPMM)* – alias. **Aims** As a *Masonic* rite that is traditional, symbolic and spiritual, be associated with the principles of tolerance and liberty. Follow an initiatic quest founded on: a spiritual and deist orientation; a vocation to preserve and transmit philosophical reflection on symbols of Ancient Egypt and on the Hermetic, Gnostic, Kabbalistic, Templar and Rosicrucian currents that have marked Western civilization. **Activities** Events/meetings. Freemasons of the Rite follow an apprenticeship and methodology founded on the knowledge of symbols and that call into question all that has been acquired, always refining perception and developing discernment. As perceptions and vision of the world evolve the Mason has begun the conquest of the self. **Events** *Annual meeting* Paris (France) 1987, *Annual meeting* Paris (France) 1986.
Members Individual adherents in 12 countries:
Argentina, Brazil, Chile, France, Martinique, Mauritius, New Caledonia, Spain, Switzerland, Uruguay, USA, Venezuela.
Also in Scandinavia (countries not specified). [2022/XF2396/v/**F**]

♦ Ancillae A Caritate (religious order)
♦ Ancillae Sacri Cordis Jesu (religious order)
♦ Ancillae Sanctae Ecclesiae (religious order)
♦ ANCIR – African Network of Centres for Investigative Reporting (unconfirmed)
♦ **ANCL** African Network of Constitutional Lawyers (#00384)
♦ **ANCLS** Asian Network on Standardization and Harmonization in Laboratory Medicine (#01559)
♦ ANCOPI – Association des négociateurs-conseils en propriété industrielle (inactive)
♦ **ANCR** Association of Nordic Cancer Registries (#02826)
♦ ANCSSC – Alliance of NGOs and CSOs for South-South Cooperation (unconfirmed)
♦ **ANCST** Asian Network on Climate Science and Technology (#01548)
♦ ANCT / see Association nationale cultures du monde
♦ ANCT – Association nationale cultures du monde (internationally oriented national body)
♦ Andalusian Association for Peace and Solidarity (internationally oriented national body)
♦ **ANDANTE** European Alliance of Catholic Women's Organisations (#05864)
♦ AND – Association for the Study of Neurons and Diseases (internationally oriented national body)
♦ Andean Action (internationally oriented national body)
♦ Andean Airlines Association (no recent information)
♦ Andean Alliance for Sustainable Development (internationally oriented national body)
♦ Andean Association of International Road Transportation (no recent information)
♦ Andean Association of Shipowners (no recent information)
♦ Andean Business Advisory Council (see: #00817)
♦ Andean Center of Popular Action (internationally oriented national body)
♦ Andean Children's Foundation / see Center for Humanitarian Outreach and Intercultural Exchange

♦ Andean Commission of Jurists (ACJ) 00816

Commission andine des juristes – Comisión Andina de Juristas (CAJ)

Dir Gen Los Sauces 285, 36274, Lima, Peru. T. +5114407907. E-mail: cajpe@cajpe.org.pe.
URL: http://www.cajpe.org.pe/

History 1980, Bogota (Colombia). Headquarters moved to Lima (Peru) in 1982. **Aims** Encourage institutional reform favourable to continuity of constitutional order and reinforcement of democracy; reform administration of justice, establishing an independent and efficient system with a spirit of democracy, increasing legitimacy of the judiciary and public confidence in it, and ensuring integrity of judges; promote recognition and observance of the rights of indigenous peoples in Andean countries so that legislation reflects the multi-ethnic and pluri-cultural nature of society in the region and the value and identity of the indigenous population; protect and work towards observance of human rights in the region, encouraging greater use and efficacy of mechanisms designed for this purpose nationally and throughout the region. **Structure** Governing Council. President; Director General; Executive Director; Administrative Director. **Languages** English, Spanish. **Staff** 32.00 FTE, paid. **Finance** Sources: international cooperation; grants. **Activities** Research/documentation; knowledge management/information dissemination. **Events** *International justice from an Andean perspective* 2000, *Women human rights* Lima (Peru) 2000, *Public services (electricity and telecommunications) in the Andean region* Quito (Ecuador) 2000, *Pacification in Colombia and Peru* Bogota (Colombia) 1987. **Publications** *Andean Newsletter* (12 a year); *Lecturas sobre Temas Constitucionales* (2 a year); *Regional Report* (annual). *Democratic Charter Series*. Monographs; studies; conference proceedings.

Members Individuals in 6 countries:
Bolivia, Chile, Colombia, Ecuador, Peru, Venezuela.
Consultative Status Consultative status granted from: *ECOSOC (#05331)* (Special). **IGO Relations** Cooperation with: *OAS (#17629)*. Accredited by: *United Nations Office at Vienna (UNOV, #20604)*. **NGO Relations** Affiliated to: *International Commission of Jurists (ICJ, #12695)*. Supports: *International Campaign Against Mass Surveillance (ICAMS, no recent information)*. [2012/XD1792/v/**D**]

♦ Andean Committee of Maritime Transport Authorities (#04147)

♦ Andean Community 00817

Communauté andine – Comunidad Andina

SG Av Paseo de la República 3895, San Isidro, 27, Lima, Peru. T. +5117106400. Fax +5112213329. E-mail: correspondencia@comunidadandina.org.
URL: http://www.comunidadandina.org/

History 9 Mar 1996, Trujillo (Peru). Established by the *Acta de Trujillo*, during 8th Congress of the Andean Presidential Council. Commenced operations on 1 Aug 1997, with General Secretariat headquarters in Lima (Peru), and is sometimes referred to as the *Andean Community of Nations (ACN)*. Establishment followed a history of Andean cooperation, formalized in the *Andean Subregional Integration Agreement (Cartagena Agreement, 1969)*, signed 26 May 1969, Bogota (Colombia), by representatives of Bolivia, Chile, Colombia, Ecuador and Peru. The Agreement aimed to establish a customs union within a period of 10 years. Although actually signed in Bogota, the Cartagena Agreement is officially named in honour of the city where the conclusive negotiations took place. The Cartagena Agreement is often referred to as *'Andean Pact – Pacte andin – Pacto Andino'*, and the nations signatory to it as *Andean Group – Groupe andin – Grupo Andino*. The Cartagena Agreement came into force in Oct 1969. Venezuela acceded to the Agreement in Feb 1973. Chile withdrew in Oct 1976.

The basically closed conception of inward-looking integration based on the import substitution model gradually gave way to a scheme of open regionalism: *Protocol of Quito*, adopted 12 May 1987, Quito, came into effect 25 May 1988, adjusted principal policies, instruments and mechanisms to prevailing conditions and allowed greater freedom for countries to establish their own rules on foreign investment; objectives and instruments were extended to economic and social cooperation. *Declaration of Caracas*, Feb 1989, marked an agreement of the Andean Presidents to promote and deepen subregional integration by taking over direct leadership of the process. The Community is the result of the progress of integration and emergence of new challenges stemming from global economic change which gave rise to a need for both institutional and policy reforms in the Cartagena Agreement, accomplished through Protocols of Trujillo and Sucre respectively. While the Community was set up through institutional reforms, policy reforms extended the scope of integration beyond purely trade and economic areas. The Council of Presidents and the Council of Foreign Ministers were formally established under the Act as new policy-making and membership bodies and the legislative role of the Commission of the Andean Community, originally comprising the trade ministers, was broadened by including ministers of other sectors. Expected to merge with *Southern Common Market (#19868)*; complete integration expected by Summit, Colombia, Dec 2007.

Aims Promote balanced and harmonious development of member countries under equitable conditions; accelerate their growth through integration and economic and social development; enhance participation in the regional integration process with a view to progressive formation of a Latin American common market; strive for a steady improvement in living conditions of member countries' inhabitants.

Structure The Community is a subregional organization with international legal status, comprising Bolivia, Colombia, Ecuador, Peru and Venezuela and the bodies and institutions of the *Sistema Andino de Integración (SAI, #19292)*.

– *Andean Presidential Council (see: #00817)* (meets annually plus special sessions as necessary), is the highest-level body of the Andean Integration System and comprises Presidents of the member countries. It is responsible for issuing guidelines on different spheres of Andean subregional integration, which are then implemented by the bodies and institutions of the System in accordance with the spheres of responsibility and mechanisms established in their respective treaties and instruments. It also: defines subregional integration policy; orients and promotes actions on matters of interest to the subregion; evaluates the course and results of the integration process; examines all issues and matters connected with the progress of integration and its relations with the world; and considers and makes pronouncements on reports and recommendations put forward by other organs and institutions of the SAI. The Council's Chairmanship rotates annually among members, the Chairman representing the Andean Community at the highest political level.

– *Andean Council of Foreign Ministers (#00818)*, the political leadership body, consists of the Ministers of Foreign Affairs of member countries. It ensures that the objectives of Andean subregional integration are attained and makes and carries out the Andean Community's foreign policy. The Council: signs conventions and agreements on global foreign policy and cooperation issues with third countries or groups of countries and with international organizations; coordinates the joint position of member countries in international fora and negotiations on matters within its sphere of responsibility. It expresses its will through *'Declarations'* (statements that are non-binding) and *'Decisions'* (legally binding and governed by the Charter the Court of Justice of the Cartagena Agreement); both must be adopted by consensus.

– *Commission of the Andean Community (#04203)*, the main policy-making body, consists of a plenipotentiary representative from each member country of the Andean Community. It shares its legislative role, expressed through the adoption of Decisions, with the Andean Council of Foreign Ministers. The Commission makes, implements and evaluates Andean subregional integration policy in the areas of trade and investment; adopts the necessary measures for attaining the objectives of the Cartagena Agreement and for implementing the Guidelines of the Andean Presidential Council; and coordinates the joint position of member countries in international fora and negotiations within its area of responsibility.

– *General Secretariat of the Andean Community – Secrétariat général de la Communauté andine – Secretaria General de la Comunidad Andina*, is the executive body and is headed by the Secretary General of the Andean Community. It commenced operations on 1 Aug 1997, taking on, among other tasks, the functions of the Board of the Cartagena Agreement. It has the power to draw up Draft Decisions and propose them to the Andean Council of Foreign Ministers and to the Commission and to pass on initiatives and suggestions to the Council of Foreign Ministers meeting in enlarged session so as to contribute to or hasten compliance with the Cartagena Agreement. Other functions: managing the subregional integration process; resolving issues submitted for its consideration; ensuring that Community commitments are fulfilled; maintaining on-going links with member countries and working relations with the executive bodies of other regional integration and cooperation organizations.

– *Andean Parliament (#00820)*, established 25 Oct 1979, La Paz (Bolivia), is the joint deliberative body of the System, representing the peoples of the Andean Community. It puts forward draft provisions of common interest to the bodies of the System and promotes harmonization of member countries' legislation. Its recommendations about the integration process are adopted by a two-thirds majority.

– *Court of Justice of the Andean Community (#04936)* was created as a principal organ of the Cartagena Agreement on signature of a treaty by member countries, 28 May 1979. It consists of 5 judges, one for each country, who assume the presidency in rotation. The Court interprets Andean Community law to ensure it is applied uniformly in the territories of member countries; and settles disputes that may arise in its application.

– *Development Bank of Latin America (CAF, #05055)*, set up 7 Feb 1968, is a financial institution with Latin American and Caribbean shareholders. It aims to support the sustainable development of shareholder countries and of integration by efficiently raising funds for timely delivery of financial services.

– *Latin American Reserve Fund (#16367)*, established in Jan 1977 as *'Andean Reserve Fund (ARF)'*, commenced operations in Jul 1978, and was restructured under present title in Mar 1991. It provides balance of payments assistance to member countries by granting credits or guaranteeing loans to third parties. It also helps harmonize Andean countries' exchange, monetary and financial policies and improves the terms of investment of international reserves made by them.

– *Universidad Andina Simón Bolivar (UASB, #20687)*, set up 11-16 Dec 1985, La Paz, during 5th Session of the Andean Parliament.

– *'Social Agreements'* – intergovernmental institutions created to complement integration efforts in the economic and trade sectors with action in other fields:

– For health: *Hipólito Unanue Agreement (#10921)*, formed 18 Dec 1971, includes annual sessions of *Meeting of Ministers of Health in the Andean Region (REMSAA)*;
– For social security: *Convenio andino de seguridad social (CONASS, no recent information)*;

– For labour affairs: *Simón Rodriguez Agreement (#19284)*, set up 22 Oct 1973, currently being revitalized.
– *'Advisory Institutions'* These comprise top-level delegates chosen directly by representative organizations in the relevant sectors of each member country. They were set up, 26 Jul 1998, on approval of Decisions 441 and 442 by the Commission of the Andean Community -
– *Consejo Consultivo Empresarial Andino (CCEA, see: #00817)*;
– *Andean Labor Advisory Council (CCLA, see: #00817)*.

Languages Spanish. **Staff** 150.00 FTE, paid. **Finance** General Secretariat financed by member countries' contributions. Annual budget: about US$ 7.8 million.

Activities *'Trade in Goods'* – a Customs Union is partially in place, in that trade in goods among member countries is now deregulated and a common external tariff covers imports from non-member countries. Current efforts aim at perfecting the enlarged market in line with ensuring transparent and proper operation of customs instruments, technical and health provisions and provisions on origin and competition.
'Deregulation of Trade in Services' – general framework on deregulation principles and provisions, approved by Decision 439 of CAN Council, 11 Jun 1998, is to be accomplished by 2005 through progressive elimination of restrictive measures affecting national treatment and access to the market. Advances in specific sectors include approval of provisions for transportation, telecommunications and tourism, while Decisions on financial services, recognition of professional degrees and authorization and licences to provide services in the sub-region are in the pipeline.
'Foreign Relations' – strategy of open regionalism has led to: signature of a framework agreement for the creation of a free trade zone with MERCOSUR, Apr 1998; signature of an economic complementation agreement with Brazil, Aug 1999, and with Argentina, as first steps towards creation of a free trade zone; setting up of *Trade and Investment Council (no recent information)* – also referred to as *'Council on Trade and Investment'* and as *'Council on Trade Relations between the Andean Community and the United States'* – 30 Oct 1998, Washington DC (USA); a '4-pillar' relationship with the European Union, covering political dialogue, preferential access to the European market (Drug GSP), the Framework Cooperation Agreement and specialized dialogue on war against drugs; other international relationships, including negotiating as a single voice on the proposed *Free Trade Area of the Americas (FTAA, no recent information)* and exploring closer relations, including possible trade relations, with Russia.
'Social Agenda' – Andean presidential summit, 1999, Cartagena de Indias (Colombia) agreed to carry out a multidimensional social agenda to make the Community more aware of citizens' expectations, centering on creation of jobs, education, health and housing. The agenda incorporates the basis for policies on migration, on protecting basic rights of workers, on safeguarding and promoting the Andean identity (educational, cultural, scientific and technological policy) and an Andean strategy on sustainable development.
'Common Market' – A free-trade zone was established, 1 Jan 1992, following signature of the *Caracas Declaration*, 18 May 1991, by Presidents of the 5 Andean countries. Community countries are committed to establishing the *Andean Common Market (ANCOM, no recent information)* by 2005 at latest. Having deregulated trade in goods and set in motion liberalization of trade in services, current efforts focus on free circulation of capital and persons. A draft protocol to the Cartagena Agreement so as to establish the Common Market is being considered by member countries.

Events *Regional Plant Protection Organizations (RPPOs) Annual Technical Consultation* London (UK) 2022, *Regional Plant Protection Organizations (RPPOs) Annual Technical Consultation* Rome (Italy) 2021, *Regional Plant Protection Organizations (RPPOs) Annual Technical Consultation* Rome (Italy) 2020, *Regional Plant Protection Organizations (RPPOs) Annual Technical Consultation* Abuja (Nigeria) 2019, *Regional Plant Protection Organizations (RPPOs) Annual Technical Consultation* Lima (Peru) 2018. **Publications** *Informativo Andino* (occasional); *Gaceta Oficial del Acuerdo de Cartagena* (occasional); *Boletin Diario de Noticias*. *Estadisticas Comercio* – series; *Estudios* – series; *Instrumentos* – series.

Members Representatives of National Congresses of 4 countries:
Bolivia, Colombia, Ecuador, Peru.
Partner countries (5):
Argentina, Brazil, Chile, Paraguay, Uruguay.
Observer countries (2):
Morocco, Spain.

IGO Relations Observer status with (2): *World Intellectual Property Organization (WIPO, #21593)*; *World Trade Organization (WTO, #21864)*. Permanent Observer to: *ECOSOC (#05331)*. Relationship agreement with: *FAO (#09260)*. Participates in the activities of: *UNCTAD (#20285)*. Observer to: *Sistema Económico Latinoamericano (SELA, #19294)*. Serves as one of 10 Regional Plant Protection Organizations (RPPOs) of *International Plant Protection Convention, 1951 (IPPC, 1951)*. Close cooperation/negotiation with: *Caribbean Community (CARICOM, #03476)*. Related treaty: *Convenio Andrés Bello de integración educativa, científica y cultural de América Latina y España (Convenio Andrés Bello, #04785)*. [2020/XD0055/**F***]

- ♦ Andean Community of Nations / see Andean Community (#00817)
- ♦ Andean Convention on Social Security (no recent information)
- ♦ Andean Cooperation in Health (no recent information)
- ♦ Andean Council of Engineers (inactive)

♦ Andean Council of Foreign Ministers 00818

Consejo Andino de Ministros de Relaciones Exteriores

Chairman c/o Comunidad Andina, Av Paseo de la República 3895, San Isidro, 27, Lima, Peru. T. +5117106400. Fax +5112213329. E-mail: correspondencia@comunidadandina.org.
URL: http://www.comunidadandina.org/

History within the framework of *Andean Community (#00817)*, as the political leadership body of *Sistema Andino de Integración (SAI, #19292)*. **Aims** Ensure that the objectives of Andean subregional integration are attained; make and carry out the Andean Community's *foreign policy*. **Structure** Council comprises the Ministers of Foreign Affairs of Andean Community member countries. **Activities** The Council: signs conventions and agreements on global foreign policy and cooperation issues with third countries or groups of countries and with international organizations; coordinates the joint position of member countries in international fora and negotiations on matters within its sphere of responsibility. It expresses its will through *'Declarations'* (statements that are non-binding) and *'Decisions'* (legally binding and governed by the Charter the Court of Justice of the Cartagena Agreement); both must be adopted by consensus. Meeting in Enlarged Session, it makes preparations for the meetings of the Andean Presidents, elects and, when appropriate, removes the Secretary General, evaluates the performance of the General Secretariat and considers the initiatives and proposals submitted to it by member countries or the General Secretariat. **IGO Relations** Relevant treaty: *Andean Subregional Integration Agreement (Cartagena Agreement, 1969)*. Shares its legislative role, expressed through the adoption of Decisions, with the *Commission of the Andean Community (#04203)*. **NGO Relations** *Consejo Consultivo Empresarial Andino (CCEA, see: #00817)*; *Andean Labor Advisory Council (CCLA, see: #00817)*. [2015/XE3582/**E***]

- ♦ Andean Development Corporation / see Development Bank of Latin America (#05055)
- ♦ Andean Federation of the Crop Protection Industry (no recent information)
- ♦ Andean Federation for Pharmacy and Biochemistry (inactive)

♦ Andean Information Network (AIN) 00819

Red Andina de Información (RAI)

Director Casilla 4817, Cochabamba, Bolivia. T. +59144486137. Fax +59144486137.
URL: http://www.ain-bolivia.org/

History Founded 1992. **Aims** Change US anti-drug policy in the Andean region by seeking to replace them with policies that address the underlying economic, social, political and cultural needs in the region; change *drug* policy by strengthening the fluid rapport with victims of human rights abuses and by promoting the identification and prosecution of perpetrators of human rights violations in coca-growing regions in the civilian and not military court system. **Languages** English, Spanish. **Activities** Research/documentation; training/education. **Publications** *Children of the Law 1008* (1997); *Violaciones a los Derechos Humanos Civiles bajo la Ley 1008* (1996); *The Weight of the Law 1008* (1995); *Human Rights Violations Stemming from the War on Drugs in Bolivia* (1993). *Mujeres y Niños en las Carceles de Bolivia* (1997) – video; *The Historic March* (1995) – video.

Members Individuals in 7 countries:
Belgium, Bolivia, Canada, Italy, Netherlands, UK, USA.

NGO Relations Cooperates with: *Amnesty International (AI, #00801)*; *Andean Action*; *Human Rights Watch (HRW, #10990)*, Americas Division; *Maryknoll Sisters of Saint Dominic*; *Progressio (inactive)*; *School for International Training (SIT)*; *Washington Office on Latin America (WOLA)*. Also close contacts with national organizations interested in the field. [2016/XF3247/v/**F**]

- ♦ Andean Institute of Ecology and Development (internationally oriented national body)
- ♦ Andean Institute of Popular Arts (no recent information)
- ♦ Andean Institute of Systems (internationally oriented national body)
- ♦ Andean Integration System (#19292)
- ♦ Andean Labor Advisory Council (see: #00817)
- ♦ Andean Mountain Association (inactive)

♦ Andean Parliament 00820

Parlement andin – Parlamento Andino

SG AK 14 No 70A – 61, Avenida Caracas, Bogota, Bogota DC, Colombia. E-mail: info@parlamentoandino.org.
URL: http://www.parlamentoandino.org/

History 25 Oct 1979, La Paz (Bolivia). Established on signature of a Treaty by representatives of the member countries of the *Andean Community (#00817)*. First regular session held Aug 1980, Bogota. Became a Principal Organ of the *Andean Subregional Integration Agreement (Cartagena Agreement, 1969)*, in accordance with the Protocol of Quito (Ecuador), which entered into force 25 May 1989. A Protocol modifying the charter and additional protocol on direct and universal elections of the representatives, signed Apr 1997, will enable consolidation as joint deliberative body of the *Sistema Andino de Integración (SAI, #19292)* representing the peoples of the Andean Community. **Aims** Participate in the legislative process by putting forward draft provisions of common interest to the bodies of the System; promote harmonization of member country legislation and the growth of cooperative and coordinated relations with parliaments of the Andean countries and of third countries; promote and guide the Andean subregional integration process; promote popular participation in the Andean integration process; encourage development of an Andean community spirit; maintain the full rule of freedom, social justice and democracy in which all in the Andean subregion participate; ensure that human rights are respected within the framework of the international instruments in force on the subject for all contracting parties; promote among the peoples of the Andean subregion awareness and extensive dissemination of the guiding principles and rules for establishing a new international order; encourage development and integration of the Latin American community; help strengthen international peace and justice. **Structure** Parliament meets in 2 annual ordinary sessions in Bogota (except during sessions where authorities of Andean Parliament are chosen, in which case the session takes place in the country that will assume presidency) and may also meet during extraordinary sessions. Board of Directors, comprising President, 4 Vice-Presidents, General Executive Secretariat and members. Other parliaments (20), 4 of each country, with one representative each in each of the 5 Commissions. Commissions (5): Political, Parliamentary, Integration and Foreign Affairs; Juridical Problems, Legal Development, Harmonization, Culture, Education, Science and Technology; Human Development, Sustainable Development, Environment, Agriculture and Fight Against Illicit Trafficking of Drugs; Economics, Budget and Audit of the Andean Integration System and Tourism; Women, Childhood, Family, Indians, Afro-Americans and Defence of Human Rights. **Finance** Member countries' annual contributions. Secretariat supported by annual contributions of Colombian Ministry of Foreign Affairs. **Activities** Recommends and promulgates decisions, resolutions, recommendations, declarations and agreements about the integration process through recommendations adopted by a two-thirds majority. Organizes: symposia on border problems; seminars on different affairs of the Andean Community; integration observatories; legislative assemblies; electoral observation missions. **Events** *Europe-Latin America interparliamentary conference* Lima (Peru) 2005, *Europe-Latin America interparliamentary conference* Brussels (Belgium) 2003, *Europe-Latin America interparliamentary conference* Valparaiso (Chile) 2001, *Europe-Latin America interparliamentary conference* Brussels (Belgium) 1999, *Extraordinary Session* Caracas (Venezuela) 1996. **Publications** *Carta Social Andina*; *Cumbre Andina de Lucha Andina Contra las Drogas y sus Delitos Conexos*; *Instrumentos Basicos del Parlamento Andino Sistemas Electorales Plan de Desarrollo Institucional Memorias de los Periodos Ordinarios y Extraordinarios de Sesiones*; *Organismos del Sistema Andino de Integración – Estructura Normativa*; *Racismo, Xenofobia, Intlerancia y Otros Delitos*; *Segunda Cumbre Social Andina*. **Information Services** *El Centro de Documentación del Parlamento Andino Simón Rodriguez* – library and digital repository.

Members With the exception of Venezuela, currently comprises representatives of National Congresses. From 8 Nov 1998, in accordance with the Additional Protocol of Apr 1997, representatives of Venezuela and Ecuador are elected by direct and universal vote; this mechanism will in future be put in practice by other member countries. Representatives of the people of 5 countries:
Bolivia, Colombia, Ecuador, Peru, Venezuela.

IGO Relations Formal agreement with: *UNESCO (#20322)*. Relationship agreement signed with: *UNIDO (#20336)*. Member of: *Euro-Latin American Parliamentary Assembly (EUROLAT, #05700)*; *Intergovernmental Organizations Conference (IGO Conference, #11498)*. Set up: *Universidad Andina Simón Bolivar (UASB, #20687)*. Observer to: *Sistema Económico Latinoamericano (SELA, #19294)*. **NGO Relations** Member of: *Inter-Parliamentary Union (IPU, #15961)*. [2022/XF9018/**F***]

- ♦ Andean-Patagonian Forestry Research and Advisory Centre (internationally oriented national body)
- ♦ Andean Patagonian Naturalist Society (internationally oriented national body)
- ♦ Andean Presidential Council (see: #00817)
- ♦ Andean Reserve Fund / see Latin American Reserve Fund (#16367)
- ♦ Andean Subregional Integration Agreement (1969 treaty)
- ♦ Andean Timber Laboratory (no recent information)
- ♦ Andean Tribunal of Justice / see Court of Justice of the Andean Community (#04936)
- ♦ ANDE – Arab Network for Democratic Elections (unconfirmed)
- ♦ **ANDE** Aspen Network of Development Entrepreneurs (#02310)
- ♦ Änderungsprotokoll zu dem Europäischen übereinkommen zum schutz von tieren in landwirtschaftlichen tierhaltungen (1992 treaty)
- ♦ Änderungsprotokoll zu dem Europäischen übereinkommen zum schutz der für versuche und andere wissenschaftliche zwecke verwendeten wirbeltiere (1998 treaty)
- ♦ Änderungsprotokoll zu dem Europäischen übereinkommen über das grenzüberschreitende fernsehen (1998 treaty)
- ♦ **ANDESAPA** Asociación Andina de Empresas e Instituciones de Servicio de Agua Potable y Saneamiento (#02111)
- ♦ Andes University (internationally oriented national body)
- ♦ ANDF – Asian Network on Debris Flow (unconfirmed)
- ♦ Andheri-Hilfe, Bonn (internationally oriented national body)
- ♦ ANDINATIC – Asociación Andina de Transportistas Internacionales por Carretera (no recent information)
- ♦ Andragogium / see Europäische Bildungs-und Begegnungszentren (#05750)
- ♦ André Ryckmans Foundation (internationally oriented national body)
- ♦ **Andrés Bello Convention** Andrés Bello convention for the educational, scientific and cultural integration of Latin America and Spain (#04785)
- ♦ Andrés Bello convention for the educational, scientific and cultural integration of Latin America and Spain (#04785)
- ♦ Andrés Bello Convention Organization for Educational, Scientific, Technological and Cultural Integration (no recent information)
- ♦ Andrew W Mellon Foundation (internationally oriented national body)
- ♦ Andrew Young Center For International Affairs (internationally oriented national body)
- ♦ **ANDRO** Asociación de Sociedades Iberoamericanas de Andrologia (#02298)

♦ Androgen Excess and PCOS Society (AE-PCOS) 00821

Main Office 12520 W Magnolia Blvd, Ste 212, North Hollywood CA 91607, USA.
URL: http://www.ae-society.org/

History Jun 2001, USA. Founding plans developed during meetings of the Endocrine Society. Former names and other names: *Androgen Excess Society* – former (2001 to 2007). **Aims** Promote knowledge, and original clinical and basic research, in every aspect of androgen excess *disorders* so as to improve understanding, diagnosis, treatment, and prevention of these disorders. **Structure** Board of Directors. **Events** *Annual Meeting* North Hollywood, CA (USA) 2021, *Annual Meeting* Lorne, NSW (Australia) 2016, *Annual Meeting* Siracusa (Italy) 2015, *Annual Meeting* Kauai Is (USA) 2014, *Annual Meeting* Newport Beach, CA (USA) 2013. **Publications** *AEPCOS Newsletter*. **Members** Regular; Associate; Corporate. Membership countries not specified. [2016/XM5052/**C**]

♦ Androgen Excess Society / see Androgen Excess and PCOS Society (#00821)
♦ **ANE** Association of Nordic Engineers (#02828)
♦ **ANEC** Association européenne pour la coordination de la représentation des consommateurs pour la normalisation (#02561)
♦ **ANEC** Association nordique des études canadiennes (#17181)
♦ **ANECCA** African Network for Care of Children Affected by HIV/AIDS (#00382)
♦ **ANEC** European Association for the Coordination of Consumer Representation in Standardization (#02561)
♦ ANEEJ – African Network for Environment and Economic Justice (internationally oriented national body)
♦ **ANENT** Asian Network for Education in Nuclear Technology (#01549)
♦ ANERA – American Near East Refugee Aid (internationally oriented national body)
♦ ANERB / see African Network of Research on Storage Insects (#00394)
♦ ANERELA+ / see International Network of Religious Leaders Living with or Personally Affected by HIV and AIDS (#14315)
♦ **A.NERGY** Asian iNstitute for Environmental Research and enerGY (#01516)
♦ **ANERSI** African Network of Research on Storage Insects (#00394)
♦ ANESMICA – Association of Independent Electronic Mass Media Organization of Central Asia (no recent information)
♦ ANESVAD – Acción Sanitaria y Desarrollo Social (internationally oriented national body)
♦ ANESVAD Foundation (internationally oriented national body)
♦ **ANEW** African Civil Society Network on Water and Sanitation (#00250)
♦ **ANFA** Asian Nonwoven Fabric Association (#01569)
♦ **ANF** Asia Network Forum (#01443)
♦ **ANF** Association du notariat francophone (#02836)
♦ **ANFN** Asia-Pacific Network for Food and Nutrition (#01964)
♦ ANF / see Netball Asia (#16977)
♦ **ANFREL** Asian Network for Free Elections (#01550)
♦ **ANGE** African Network for Geo-Education (#00387)
♦ ANGEL – All Nations Generating Equal Love (internationally oriented national body)
♦ Los Angeles University of International Relations / see School of International Relations, Los Angeles
♦ **ANGH** African Network in Global History (#00388)
♦ **ANGI** Association for the Nordic Game Industry (#02829)

♦ Anglican Alliance 00822

Exec Dir Anglican Communion Office, 16 Tavistock Crescent, London, W11 1AP, UK. T. +442073133922. E-mail: anglicanalliance@aco.org.
URL: http://www.anglicanalliance.com/

History Subtitle: *Development – Relief – Advocacy*. **Aims** Bring together development, relief and advocacy work across the Communion. **Structure** Board of Trustees; Advisory Council. **Activities** Advocacy/lobbying/activism. **NGO Relations** *Anglican Communion (#00827)*. Member of: *Joint Learning Initiative on Faith and Local Communities (JLI, #16139)*; *Side by Side (#19265)*; *We Will Speak Out (WWSO)*. [2019/XM7723/**E**]

♦ Anglican Association of Biblical Scholars (internationally oriented national body)

♦ Anglican Church in Aotearoa, New Zealand and Polynesia 00823

Gen Sec Anglican Church General Synod Office, PO Box 87188 Meadowbank, Auckland 1742, New Zealand. T. +6495214439. E-mail: gensec@anglicanchurch.org.nz.
URL: http://www.anglican.org.nz/

History Established as an autonomous member Church of the *Anglican Communion (#00827)*. Former names and other names: *Church of the Province of New Zealand* – former (1991). **Languages** English, Fijian, Hindi, Maori, Samoan, Tongan. **Staff** 3.00 FTE, paid. **Activities** Events/meetings. **Events** *General Synod* Nelson (New Zealand) 2022, *General Synod* Auckland (New Zealand) 2020, *General Synod* Nelson (New Zealand) 2020, *General Synod* New Plymouth (New Zealand) 2018, *General Synod* Napier (New Zealand) 2016. **Publications** *A New Zealand Prayer Book – He Karakia Mihinare o Aotearoa*.
Members Parishes (405) in 5 countries and territories:
Cook Is, Fiji, New Zealand, Samoa USA, Tonga.
NGO Relations Member of (2): *Christian Conference of Asia (CCA, #03898)*; *World Council of Churches (WCC, #21320)*. Represented on the: *Anglican Consultative Council (ACC, #00828)*. Every diocese represented at the: *Lambeth Conference of Bishops of the Anglican Communion (#16224)*. Primates meet at: *Primates Meeting of the Anglican Communion (#18497)*. [2023.02.14/XE2130/**E**]

♦ Anglican Church of Central America (#11108)

♦ Anglican Church of the Province of the Indian Ocean 00824

Province ecclésiastique de l'Océan indien – Provansa Eklesiastikan'ny Ranomasimbe Indiana
Contact Bishop's House, Nalletamby Road, Vacoas-Phoenix, Mauritius. T. +2306865158. Fax +2306971096. E-mail: dioang@intnet.mu.
URL: http://www.anglicancommunion.org/

History 1973, as an autonomous member Church of *Anglican Communion (#00827)*, the Anglican mission having first begun in 1810 in Mauritius. **Aims** Continue the *mission* of *God* in the Indian Ocean region. **Structure** Archbishop elected for 5-year term; Province; Standing Committee; Woman Network; Dioceses (8). **Languages** English, French. **Finance** Participation in dioceses; partners-in-mission, under the form of subventions. **Activities** Training/education; events/meetings. **Publications** *Le Cordage* – newsletter; *Le Phare* – newsletter. Diocesan magazines.
Members Individual Anglicans (513,000) in 144 parishes in 8 dioceses in 4 countries and territories:
Madagascar, Mauritius, Réunion, Seychelles.
NGO Relations Member of: *Council of Anglican Provinces of Africa (CAPA, #04857)*; *Lambeth Conference of Bishops of the Anglican Communion (#16224)*; *Primates Meeting of the Anglican Communion (#18497)*. [2014.06.01/XE2133/**E**]

♦ Anglican Church of the Province of Melanesia / see Church of the Province of Melanesia (#03918)

♦ The Anglican Church of South America 00825

Provincial Sec Capricornio s/n, Casa La Cabaña, esquina Tucán,, 20000 Maldonado, Uruguay.
URL: http://www.anglicancommunion.org/

History 1983. Founded as an autonomous member Church of *Anglican Communion (#00827)*. Former names and other names: *Anglican Church of the Southern Cone of America* – former; *Iglesia Anglicana del Cono Sur de América* – former. **Activities** Missionary work carried out through *South American Mission Society (SAMS International, #19705)*.
Members Individual Anglicans (27,000) in 6 dioceses comprising 265 Churches in 6 countries:
Argentina, Bolivia, Chile, Paraguay, Peru, Uruguay.
NGO Relations Represented on the: *Anglican Consultative Council (ACC, #00828)*. Every diocese represented at the: *Lambeth Conference of Bishops of the Anglican Communion (#16224)*. Primates meet at: *Primates Meeting of the Anglican Communion (#18497)*. [2022/XE2134/**E**]

♦ Anglican Church of Southern Africa (ACSA) 00826

Archbishop 20 Bishopscourt Drive, Claremont, 7708, South Africa. T. +27217631320. Fax +27217614193. E-mail: chaplain@anglicanchurchsa.org.za.
URL: http://www.anglicanchurchsa.org/

History 1870, as an autonomous member church of *Anglican Communion (#00827)*, British Anglicans having first met for worship in Cape Town (South Africa) in 1806 and first bishop appointed 1847. Original title: *Church of the Province of Southern Africa (CPSA)*. Current title adopted 30 Sep 2006. **Aims** Honour God in worship that feeds and empowers us for faithful witness and service; embody and proclaim the message of God's redemptive hope and healing for people and creation; grow communities of faith that form, inform and transform those who follow Christ. **Structure** Provincial Synod (every 3 years); Provincial Standing Committee (meets annually between Provincial Synods); Synod of Bishops (twice a year). **Finance** Parishioners' pledges. Annual budget: South African Rand 9,300,000. **Activities** Projects/programmes; religious activities. **Events** *Triennial synod* 1995. **Publications** *Southern Anglican* – newspaper. Booklets; documents.
Members Individual Anglicans (6 million) in 1,000 churches, 28 dioceses, in 7 countries and territories:
Angola, Eswatini, Lesotho, Mozambique, Namibia, South Africa, St Helena.
NGO Relations Member of: *All Africa Conference of Churches (AACC, #00640)*; *Council of Anglican Provinces of Africa (CAPA, #04857)*; *South African Council of Churches (SACC, #19699)*; *World Council of Churches (WCC, #21320)*. Represented on the: *Anglican Consultative Council (ACC, #00828)*. Every diocese represented at the: *Lambeth Conference of Bishops of the Anglican Communion (#16224)*. Primates meet at: *Primates Meeting of the Anglican Communion (#18497)*. Programmes carried out through: Publishing Committee; *Southern African Anglican Theological Commission (SAATC, inactive)*. [2021/XF3239/**F**]

♦ Anglican Church of the Southern Cone of America / see The Anglican Church of South America (#00825)

♦ Anglican Communion 00827

SG Anglican Communion Office, St Andrews's House, 16 Tavistock Crescent, London, W11 1AP, UK. T. +442073133900. Fax +442073133999. E-mail: aco@anglicancommunion.org.
Exec Officer 815 Second Avenue, New York NY 100017, USA. T. +12129225268. Fax +12126871336.
URL: http://www.anglicancommunion.org/

History Set up during the post-Reformation expansion of the *Church of England* and other Episcopal or Anglican Churches. From the 17th Century established alongside colonialization in USA, Australia, Canada, New Zealand, South Africa. From 18th Century established through missionary work in Asia, Africa and Latin America. **Aims** Uphold and proclaim the Catholic and Apostolic faith, based on the creeds and scripture, interpreted in the light of Christian tradition, scholarship and reason. Following the teachings of Jesus Christ, the Churches are committed to the proclamation of the Good News of the Gospel to the whole creation. **Structure** No central legislative body, but a practice of consultation and acknowledged interdependence assures its identity as a worldwide family of autonomous Churches and Provinces in communion with the See of Canterbury. *Anglican Consultative Council (ACC, #00828)*, comprising up to 3 representatives of each Province of the Communion, is presided over by the Archbishop of Canterbury, who is also Chairman of the *Primates Meeting of the Anglican Communion (#18497)* and President of *Lambeth Conference of Bishops of the Anglican Communion (#16224)*. *International Anglican Family Network (IAFN, see: #00827)* and *International Anglican Women's Network (IAWN, see: #00827)* were set up by the ACC. **Finance** Contributions of member Churches. Special appeals and projects; other income. *Inter Anglican Finance Committee* draws up core budget. Separate funding for special projects. **Activities** Religious activities; training/education; networking/liaising, among others through: *Anglican-Roman Catholic International Commission (ARCIC, #00831)*. **Events** *International old catholic and anglican theological conference* 2011, *Meeting* Germany 2010, *Meeting* Oxford (UK) 2010, *Meeting* Canterbury (UK) 2009, *Meeting* Chania (Greece) 2009. **Publications** *Anglican Communion News Service (ACNS)* (12 a year) – by electronic mail; *Anglican World* (4 a year). *Anglican Communion Essential Guide*; *Book of Common Prayer*; *Common Worship*.
Members Individuals in 45 Member Churches/Provinces and Extra Provincials. Member churches in 134 countries and territories:
Angola, Argentina, Aruba, Australia, Austria, Bahamas, Bahrain, Bangladesh, Barbados, Belgium, Belize, Bermuda, Bolivia, Botswana, Brazil, Burundi, Canada, Chile, China, Colombia, Congo Brazzaville, Congo DR, Cook Is, Costa Rica, Cuba, Cyprus, Czechia, Denmark, Dominican Rep, Ecuador, Egypt, El Salvador, England, Eswatini, Ethiopia, Falklands/Malvinas, Fiji, Finland, France, Gambia, Germany, Ghana, Gibraltar, Greece, Guatemala, Guinea, Guyana, Haiti, Honduras, Hong Kong, Hungary, India, Indonesia, Iran Islamic Rep, Iraq, Ireland, Israel, Italy, Jamaica, Japan, Jordan, Kenya, Korea Rep, Kuwait, Latvia, Lesotho, Liberia, Libya, Luxembourg, Madagascar, Malawi, Malaysia, Malta, Mauritius, Mexico, Monaco, Mozambique, Myanmar, Namibia, Netherlands, New Caledonia, New Zealand, Nicaragua, Nigeria, Norway, Oman, Pakistan, Panama, Papua New Guinea, Paraguay, Peru, Philippines, Poland, Polynesia Fr, Portugal, Puerto Rico, Qatar, Romania, Russia, Rwanda, Samoa, Scotland, Serbia, Seychelles, Sierra Leone, Singapore, Solomon Is, South Africa, South Sudan, Spain, Sri Lanka, St Helena, St Kitts-Nevis, Sudan, Sweden, Switzerland, Taiwan, Tanzania UR, Thailand, Tonga, Trinidad-Tobago, Türkiye, Uganda, United Arab Emirates, Uruguay, USA, Vanuatu, Venezuela, Virgin Is UK, Wales, Windward Is, Yemen, Zambia, Zimbabwe.
Regional Provincial Churches (11):
Anglican Church in Aotearoa, New Zealand and Polynesia (#00823); *Anglican Church of Southern Africa (ACSA, #00826)*; *Anglican Church of the Province of the Indian Ocean (#00824)*; *Church in the Province of the West Indies (CPWI, #03921)*; *Church of the Province of Central Africa (#03917)*; *Church of the Province of Melanesia (#03918)*; *Church of the Province of South East Asia (#03919)*; *Church of the Province of West Africa (CPWA, #03920)*; *Episcopal Church in Jerusalem and the Middle East (#05513)*; *Iglesia Anglicana de la Region Central de América (IARCA, #11108)*; *The Anglican Church of South America (#00825)*.
Regional council (1) including representatives of East Asia member churches and of the Philippine Episcopal Church, Church in Myanmar and Church in Australia (autonomous Churches):
Council of Churches of East Asia (CCEA, #04877).
IGO Relations Appoints an observer to the United Nations. **NGO Relations** Special relationship with: *Communion of Evangelical Episcopal Churches (CEEC, #04385)*. Other Churches in Communion: Old Catholic Churches; Philippine Independent Church; Mat Thoma Syrian Church of Malabar (India). Instrumental in setting up: *Fellowship of Confessing Anglicans (FCA, #09725)*; *Five Talents International*. UN Office is full member of: *NGO Committee on Financing for Development, New York (#17108)*. [2018/XF5079/y/**F**]

♦ Anglican Communion Catholic Anglicans in West Africa (unconfirmed)

♦ Anglican Consultative Council (ACC) 00828

SG Anglican Communion Office, St Andrews House, 16 Tavistock Crescent, London, W11 1AP, UK. T. +442073133900. Fax +442073133999. E-mail: aco@anglicancommunion.org.
Exec Officer address not obtained.
URL: https://www.anglicancommunion.org/structures/instruments-of-communion/acc.aspx

History 1969, London (UK). Founded within the *Anglican Communion (#00827)*, pursuant to a resolution of a Conference, 1968, London, of the *Lambeth Conference of Bishops of the Anglican Communion (#16224)*. New constitution adopted 2010. **Aims** Function as an advisory body to follow up *Lambeth Conference* resolutions and provide continuity and policy guidance within the Anglican Communion; share information about developments with other parts of the Communion; serve as an instrument of common action; develop as far as possible agreed Anglican policies in the world *mission* of the *Church*; encourage national and regional Churches to engage together in developing and implementing such policies by sharing their resources to the advantage of all; encourage and guide Anglican participation in the *ecumenical* movement and in ecumenical organizations. **Structure** Council comprises up to 3 representatives of each Province of the Communion. President is the Archbishop of Canterbury. Chairman; Vice-Chairman; Secretary-General. Anglican Communion Office (ACO). Communications Office. **Languages** English, Spanish. **Staff** 16.00 FTE, paid. **Finance** Contributions from member churches. Small 'Personal Emergency Fund', set up 1980. **Activities** I. *'Mission'*, especially the *Decade of Evangelism*, 1991-2000. This includes: encouraging exchange of resources, people and ideas through 'Partnership in Mission (PIM)'; 'Mission Issues and Strategy Advisory Group (MISAG)'; 'Mission Agencies Working Group (MAWG)'. II. *'Communication'*, especially through: 'Anglican Cycle of Prayer'; *Inter Anglican Publishing Network* in 12 member Churches, which can publish Anglican books simultaneously in different parts of the world; *Inter-Anglican Information Network (IAIN, no recent information)* which enables electronic transfer of news and information. III. *'Liturgy'*, coordinating the work of *Inter Anglican Liturgical Network* and the Anglican Liturgical Officer. IV. *'Social Concerns/Networks'*, networks (4) coordinated by the Council: Peace and Justice; Family and Community; Youth; Refugee. V. *'Church Unity'*, bilateral dialogue with: Lutheran World Communion; Oriental Orthodox, Orthodox and Roman Catholic Churches; discussions with World Alliance of Reformed Churches; planned dialogue with Methodist,

Baptist and Pentecostal Churches; multilateral dialogue through Faith and Order Commission of the World Council of Churches. Funds the *Anglican Centre*, Rome (Italy), promoting Anglican/Roman Catholic Dialogue. Joint Commission: *All Africa Anglican-Lutheran Commission (AAALC, #00638)*. Instrumental in setting up and administers: *International Anglican Family Network (IAFN, see: #00827)*; *International Anglican Women's Network (IAWN, see: #00827)*. **Events** *Anglican Consultative Council Meeting* Hong Kong 2019, *Anglican Consultative Council Meeting* Lusaka (Zambia) 2016, *Anglican Consultative Council Meeting* Auckland (New Zealand) 2012, *Anglican Consultative Council Meeting* Kingston (Jamaica) 2009, *Anglican Consultative Council Meeting* Nottingham (UK) 2005. **Publications** *Anglican Communion News Service (ACNS)* (12 a year) – electronic mail and by post; *Anglican World* (4 a year). Anglican Communion Guide. **Members** Bishops, priests and lay people. Members comprise those countries represented at the most recent meeting. **Consultative Status** Consultative status granted from: *ECOSOC (#05331)* (Special); *UNICEF (#20332)*; *UNEP (#20299)*. **IGO Relations** Accredited by: *United Nations Office at Vienna (UNOV, #20604)*. Associated with Department of Global Communications of the United Nations. **NGO Relations** Member of: *Conference of Non-Governmental Organizations in Consultative Relationship with the United Nations (CONGO, #04635)*; *NGO Committee on Disarmament, Peace and Security, New York NY (#17106)*. Cooperates with: *Christian Conference of Asia (CCA, #03898)*; *World Council of Churches (WCC, #21320)*; *International Old Catholic Bishops' Conference (IBC, #14403)*. Acts as secretariat of: *Primates Meeting of the Anglican Communion (#18497)*.
[2019/XD5454/E]

♦ Anglican and Eastern Churches Association (A and ECA) 00829

Chair St John's Vicarage, 25 Ladbroke Road, London, W11 3PD, UK. T. +442077273439.
URL: http://www.aeca.org.uk/

History 1864. Currently *Eastern Churches Association*. **Aims** Advance the *Christian religion* particularly by teaching members of the Anglican and *Orthodox* Churches about each other, in order to prepare the way for an ultimate union between them, in accordance with our Lord's prayer that 'all may be one'. **Structure** Officers: Orthodox Patron, Anglican Patron, Anglican President, Orthodox President, Chairman of the Committee, Secretary General, Treasurer, Editor of the Journal. **Publications** *The Journal of the Anglican and Eastern Churches Association (ECNL)*.
Members Churches in 53 countries and territories:
Armenia, Australia, Bahamas, Belgium, Bermuda, Bosnia-Herzegovina, Brazil, Bulgaria, Canada, Croatia, Cyprus, Denmark, Egypt, Ethiopia, Fiji, Finland, France, Gambia, Georgia, Germany, Ghana, Greece, Holy See, Hungary, India, Ireland, Israel, Italy, Jamaica, Japan, Kenya, Lithuania, Luxembourg, Mexico, Netherlands, New Zealand, Norway, Papua New Guinea, Poland, Romania, Russia, Seychelles, South Africa, Spain, Sudan, Sweden, Switzerland, Tunisia, Türkiye, UK, Ukraine, USA, Zimbabwe.
[2011/XF5486/F]

♦ Anglican Frontier Missions (internationally oriented national body)
♦ Anglican Overseas Aid (internationally oriented national body)

♦ Anglican Pacifist Fellowship (APF) 00830

Hon Sec 11 Weavers End, Hanslope, Milton Keynes, MK19 7PA, UK. T. +441908510642.
URL: http://www.anglicanpeacemaker.org.uk/

History 1937. **Aims** Promote Christianity, especially by the study and application of the Christian gospel in its relation to modern war and allied social evils. **Structure** General Meeting (annual). Governing Body, comprising Chairperson, Vice Chairperson, Honorary Secretary, Honorary Treasurer, Commissioning Editor, Membership Secretary and 15 members. Counsellors (up to 10); Area Secretaries. **Finance** Members' dues. Other sources: donations, legacies. Budget (annual): pounds13,000. **Activities** Lectures schools; organizes and maintains corporate work of mercy, both in war and in peace, with opportunities for applying the Christian faith by relieving suffering; organizes annual conference (always in the UK); publishing activity. **Events** *Annual Conference* Leicester (UK) 2004, *Annual Conference* Aylesford (UK) 1998, *Annual Conference* Ely (UK) 1997, *Annual conference* Ely (UK) 1996, *Annual conference* Ely (UK) 1995. **Publications** *The Anglican Peacemaker* (4 a year). Books; pamphlets; Album of Songs; peace prayer cards.
Members Full in 30 countries and territories:
Australia, Belgium, Botswana, Canada, Denmark, Fiji, Gambia, Germany, Ghana, Guyana, India, Ireland, Israel, Italy, Japan, Kenya, Lesotho, Malawi, Malta, New Zealand, Nigeria, Pakistan, Palestine, Sierra Leone, South Africa, Spain, Tanzania UR, UK, USA, Zimbabwe.
NGO Relations Member of: *Church and Peace (#03916)*; *International Peace Bureau (IPB, #14535)*.
[2010.09.02/XF1335/F]

♦ The Anglican Patriarchate (religious order)

♦ Anglican-Roman Catholic International Commission (ARCIC) 00831

Commission internationale anglicane – catholique romaine
Address not obtained.
URL: http://www.anglicancommunion.org/

History 1970. After *ARCIC I* completed its work, *ARCIC II* was created in 1982 and completed in 2005. *ARCIC III* started 2011. Also referred to in French as *Commission mixte internationale du dialogue entre l'Eglise catholique et la Communion anglicane*. Ceased to exist prior to 2012. **Aims** Seek to resolve outstanding *doctrinal* differences between the two *Churches*; study all that hinders recognition of *ministries*; recommend practical steps which reflect the present degree of unity between Catholics and Anglicans. **Activities** Networking/liaising. **Events** *Annual Plenary Meeting* Rome (Italy) 2015, *Annual Plenary Meeting* Durban (South Africa) 2014, *Annual Plenary Meeting* Rio de Janeiro (Brazil) 2013, *Annual Plenary Meeting* Hong Kong (Hong Kong) 2012, *Annual Plenary Meeting* Bose (Italy) 2011.
Members Full in 8 countries:
Australia, Belgium, Brazil, Canada, Holy See, Switzerland, UK, USA. [2015/XF7825/E]

♦ Anglican Women's Fellowship 00832

Contact c/o ACSA, 20 Bishopscourt Drive, Claremont, 7708, South Africa.
URL: http://www.anglicanwomensfellowship.co.za/

History 1965, as part of *Anglican Church of Southern Africa (ACSA, #00826)*.
Members Individuals in 5 countries:
Botswana, Eswatini, Lesotho, Namibia, South Africa. [2010/XF2821/F]

♦ AngliCORD / see Anglican Overseas Aid
♦ Anglo-American Real Property Institute / see Association for Real Property and Infrastructure
♦ Anglo-European College of Chiropractic / see AECC University College
♦ Anglo-Israelism / see British Israel World Federation (#03331)
♦ ANGMA – Australasian Neurogastroenterology and Motility Association (internationally oriented national body)
♦ **ANGOC** Asian NGO Coalition for Agrarian Reform and Rural Development (#01566)
♦ **ANGVA** Asia Pacific Natural Gas Vehicles Association (#01963)
♦ ANH Academy – Agriculture, Nutrition and Health Academy (internationally oriented national body)
♦ **ANHA-Europe** African Network on HIV/AIDS – Europe (#00389)
♦ **ANHN** Asian New Humanities Net (#01565)
♦ ANHRE / see Arab Network for Civic Education (#01011)
♦ **ANHRE** Arab Network for Civic Education (#01011)
♦ **ANHRI** Arabic Network for Human Rights Information (#00979)
♦ ANHS – Asian Narcolepsy & Hypersomnolence Society (unconfirmed)
♦ **ANI** Academia de Negocios Internacionales (#00040)
♦ ANI / see Academy of International Business (#00040)
♦ **ANI** Autism Network International (#03041)
♦ **ANID** African Network for Integrated Development (#00390)
♦ **ANIE** African Network for Internationalization of Education (#00391)

♦ ANIMA Investment Network 00833

General Delegate 11 bis rue St-Ferréol, 13001 Marseille, France. T. +33496116760. Fax +33496116761. E-mail: contact@anima.coop.
URL: http://www.anima.coop/

History Statutes adopted May 2006; amended Sep 2006, 20 Nov 2006, May 2007 and Apr 2009. Registration: SIREN, No/ID: 493470579, France; RNA, No/ID: W133001504, France. **Aims** Promote economies of Mediterranean countries; contribute and favour networking and cooperation between economic actors from European and Mediterranean countries. **Structure** General Assembly (meets as necessary, at least once a year); Board of Directors. **Languages** English, French. **Staff** 15.00 FTE, paid. **Finance** Sources: members' dues. Supported by: *European Commission (EC, #06633)*. **Activities** Capacity building; monitoring/evaluation; networking/liaising; projects/programmes; research/documentation; training/education. **Events** *Covid Crisis Investment Opportunities – Attracting New Projects while Protecting your Economy from Predators* 2021, *Impact Conference* 2021, *Annual Meeting* Cairo (Egypt) 2019, *Mediterranean economic leaders summit* Barcelona (Spain) 2010. **Publications** *ANIMA Newsletter* (24 a year). Reports; white papers; studies. Other publications.
Members Governmental agencies and international organizations (about 70). Members in 18 countries and territories:
Algeria, Andorra, Belgium, Cyprus, Egypt, France, Greece, Italy, Jordan, Lebanon, Malta, Morocco, Palestine, Spain, Syrian AR, Tunisia, Türkiye, UK.
Included in the above, 12 organizations listed in this Yearbook:
Agence française de développement (AFD); *Association of Organisations of Mediterranean Businesswomen (#02840)*; *Euromed Capital (#05714)*; *European Association of Regional Development Agencies (EURADA, #06187)*; *European Business and Innovation Centre Network (EBN, #06420)*; *European Trade Association for Business Angels, Seed Funds, and other Early Stage Market Players (EBAN, #08923)*; *Institut de Prospective économique du Monde Méditerranéen (IPEMED, #11352)*; *Institut de recherche pour le développement (IRD)*; *International Network for Small and Medium Sized Enterprises (INSME, #14325)*; *OECD (#17693)* (FDI-MENA Programme); *Réseau méditerranéen des écoles d'ingénieurs (RMEI, #18899)*; *World Association of Investment Promotion Agencies (WAIPA, #21149)*.
NGO Relations Member of (1): *United Nations Global Compact (#20567)*. [2021.09.24/XJ2249/y/F]

♦ Animal Air Transportation Association / see Animal Transportation Association (#00844)

♦ Animal Assisted Intervention International (AAII) 00834

Sec Koningin Wilhelminaweg 18, 6562 KZ Groesbeek, Netherlands.
URL: http://www.aai-int.org/

History 2013, growing out of discussions within *Assistance Dogs International (ADI, #02323)*. Registered in accordance with Dutch law. **Aims** Establish and promote standards of excellence in all areas of animal assisted intervention work; facilitate communication and learning amongst members and their staff and volunteers; disseminate information. **Structure** Annual General Meeting; Board. **Activities** Certification/accreditation; events/meetings; knowledge management/information dissemination; standards/guidelines. **Events** *Conference* Prague (Czech Rep) 2016, *Annual General Meeting* Spa (Belgium) 2013. **Publications** *AAII Newsletter*.
Members Full in 14 countries:
Argentina, Australia, Belgium, Chile, Croatia, Finland, Germany, Italy, Netherlands, New Zealand, Spain, Sweden, UK, USA.
Affiliate in 5 countries:
Belgium, Brazil, Italy, Sweden, USA.
Regional affiliate members (2):
Assistance Dogs Europe (ADEu, #02322); *Assistance Dogs International (ADI, #02323)*.
NGO Relations *Assistance Dogs Europe (ADEu, #02322)*; *Assistance Dogs International (ADI, #02323)*.
[2016/XM4719/y/C]

♦ Animal Cell Technology Industrial Platform (ACTIP) 00835

Exec Sec PO Box 256, 03580 La Nucia, Castellón, Spain. T. +34687967080. E-mail: secretariat@actip.org – exec.secr@actip.org.
URL: http://www.actip.org/

History 1990. **Aims** Promote the use of animal cell technology in development and production of biopharmaceuticals, vaccines and other preventative or therapeutic approaches. **Structure** Steering Committee; Secretariat. **Languages** English. **Activities** Events/meetings; networking/liaising; research/documentation. **Events** *Meeting* 2021, *Meeting* 2021, *Meeting* 2020, *Meeting* Darmstadt (Germany) 2019, *Meeting* Nijmegen (Netherlands) 2019. **Publications** *ACTIP Newsletter*.
Members Companies in 12 countries and territories:
Belgium, Denmark, France, Germany, Ireland, Netherlands, Poland, Portugal, Scotland, Sweden, Switzerland, UK.
[2021.09.01/XM7776/t/F]

♦ Animal Defenders International (internationally oriented national body)

♦ Animal Equality 00836

Exec Vice-Pres 8581 Santa Monica Blvd, Ste 350, Los Angeles CA 90069, USA. T. +14242506236. E-mail: info@animalequality.org.
URL: https://animalequality.org/

History 2006. Registration: 501(c)(3) non-profit, No/ID: EIN 47-2420444, USA. **Aims** Work with society, governments and companies to end cruelty to farmed animals. **Activities** Advocacy/lobbying/activism; knowledge management/information dissemination; monitoring/evaluation; research/documentation; training/education. **Publications** *Their Voice*.
Members Offices in 8 countries:
Brazil, Germany, India, Italy, Mexico, Spain, UK, USA.
NGO Relations Member of (1): *Open Wing Alliance*. [2023.02.17/AA2038/F]

♦ AnimalhealthEurope 00837

Contact Avenue de Tervuren 168, Boîte 8, 1150 Brussels, Belgium. T. +3225437560. E-mail: info@animalhealtheurope.eu.
URL: http://www.animalhealtheurope.eu/

History Former names and other names: *International Federation for Animal Health Europe (IFAH-Europe)* – former. Registration: EU Transparency Register, No/ID: 63322037415-37. **Aims** Represent manufacturers of veterinary *medicines*, vaccines and other animal health products in Europe. **Structure** Board. **Staff** 10.00 FTE, paid. **Activities** Advocacy/lobbying/activism; politics/policy/regulatory. **Events** *Annual Conference* 2021, *Meeting on Preventing Animal Diseases in Europe* Brussels (Belgium) 2019, *Meeting on Innovation in Animal Health and Sustainable Livestock Production in Europe* Brussels (Belgium) 2018, *Conference on Availability of Animal Health Solutions for the Future of Livestock in Europe* Brussels (Belgium) 2017, *Annual Conference* Brussels (Belgium) 2014.
Members Corporate. Membership countries not specified.
National animal health associations in 19 countries:
Belgium, Czechia, Denmark, Finland, France, Germany, Greece, Hungary, Ireland, Italy, Netherlands, Norway, Poland, Portugal, Slovakia, Spain, Sweden, Switzerland, UK.
NGO Relations Member of (8): *Agri-Food Chain Coalition (AFCC, #00577)*; *European Animal Research Association (EARA, #05903)*; *European Food Sustainable Consumption and Production Round Table (European Food SCP Roundtable, #07289)* (Founding); European Livestock Voice; *European Platform for the Responsible Use of Medicines in Animals (EPRUMA, #08231)*; *GLOBALG.A.P (#10386)* (Associate); *Health for Animals (#10870)*; *Industry4Europe (#11181)*. Partner of (1): *European Partnership for Alternative Approaches to Animal Testing (EPAA, #08155)*. Cooperates with (1): *Fédération européenne de l'industrie des aliments pour animaux familiers (FEDIAF, #09571)*. Instrumental in setting up (1): *Pet Alliance Europe (PetPower)*.
[2023.02.14/XM2942/E]

♦ Animal-Kind International (internationally oriented national body)

♦ Animal Liberation Front (ALF) 00838

Contact North American Press Office, 3371 Glendale Blvd, Ste 107, Los Angeles CA 90039, USA. T. +12136405048. E-mail: press@animalliberationpressoffice.org.
URL: http://www.animalliberationfront.com/

History 1976, UK. **Aims** Liberate animals from laboratories, factory farms, fur farms, etc; inflict economic damage to those who profit from the misery and exploitation of animals; reveal the horror and atrocities committed against animals behind locked doors, take all necessary precautions against harming any animal, human and non-human. **Structure** Composed of small autonomous groups adhering to ALF guidelines. Includes *ALF Supporters Group*. **Finance** Donations. **Publications** *Underground* (3-4 a year) – magazine.
Members Not a membership organization. [2008.06.01/XF4706/F]

♦ Animal Production and Health Commission for Asia and the Pacific (APHCA) 00839

Commission de la production et de la santé animales pour l'Asie, l'Extrême-Orient et le Pacifique Sud-Ouest – Comisión de Producción y Sanidad Pecuarias para Asia, el Lejano Oriente y el Sudoeste del Pacifico

Sec FAO/RAP, 39 Phra Atit Road, Bangkok, 10200, Thailand. T. +6626974326.
URL: http://www.aphca.org/

History 29 Dec 1975, Bangkok (Thailand), within the framework of *FAO (#09260)*, as *Regional Animal Production and Health Commission for Asia, the Far East and the South-West Pacific*, by Article XIV of FAO Constitution, following approval of 60th session of FAO Council, 1973, Rome (Italy), (Resolution 1/60). First session Jun 1976. Agreement amended: 1978 and 1979, at 76th session of FAO Council, Resolution 1/76. Statutes registered in *'UNTS 1/14604'*. Current title adopted 1986. Also referred to as *FAO Regional Animal Production and Health Commission for Asia and the Pacific (APHCA) – Commission régionale FAO de la production et de la santé animales pour l'Asie, l'Extrême-Orient et le Pacifique Sud-Ouest – Comisión Regional de la FAO de Producción y Sanidad Pecuarias para Asia, el Lejano Oriente y el Sudoeste del Pacifico.* **Aims** Promote general development and national and international action and technical capacity building in animal *husbandry* and health problems; build up regional and national *livestock* programmes based on collective self-reliance and mutual assistance within the region; promote livestock production as an industry and as part of the *farming* system on the basis of self-reliance at the farm level; improve rural livestock agriculture and resource development through disease eradication, enhanced services and inputs, organizational efficiency, diversification of farm production and rural cooperation; raise nutrition levels and living standards of small farmers and rural communities through the optimal exploitation of potential resources for livestock development; develop livestock as an integral part of agriculture through programmes relevant to Asia's farming systems; in this regard, focus on small farmers and the harmonious integration of crop, livestock, poultry and fish production so as to maximize agricultural production in smallholdings; in general enhance livestock industry and trade so as to bring direct benefit to rural communities and improve their quality of life. **Structure** Commission Sessions (annual). Executive Committee, consisting of Chairman, Vice-Chairman, 3 members elected by the members annually from among themselves and (ex officio) immediate Past Chairman. Senior Animal Production and Health Officer of *FAO Regional Office for Asia and the Pacific (RAP, #09266)* is Secretary of both the Commission and the Executive Committee. **Languages** English. **Staff** 1.00 FTE, paid. 5 based at FAO Regional Office, Bangkok (Thailand). **Finance** Members' dues to Commission's Trust Fund. **Activities** Advocacy/lobbying/activism; events/meetings; knowledge management/information dissemination; training/education. **Events** *Dairy Asia Meeting* Bangkok (Thailand) 2014, *Regional Workshop on Brucellosis* Chiang Mai (Thailand) 2014, *Session* Thimphu (Bhutan) 2013, *Session* Negombo (Sri Lanka) 2012, *Session* Cebu City (Philippines) 2011. **Publications** Technical publications; proceedings; manuals.
Members Governments of 19 countries:
Australia, Bangladesh, Bhutan, India, Indonesia, Iran Islamic Rep, Korea DPR, Laos, Malaysia, Mongolia, Myanmar, Nepal, Pakistan, Papua New Guinea, Philippines, Samoa, Singapore, Sri Lanka, Thailand. [2018.06.01/XE9649/**E***]

♦ Animal Research Tomorrow 00840

Managing Dir -, 4000 Basel BS, Switzerland. E-mail: contact@animalresearchtomorrow.org.
URL: https://animalresearchtomorrow.org/

History 2010. Founded on signing the Basel Declaration. Former names and other names: *Basel Declaration Society* – former. **Aims** Promote ethically responsible and transparent animal research as outlined in the Basel Declaration. **Structure** Board. **NGO Relations** Member of (1): *European Animal Research Association (EARA, #05903).* [2020/AA1335/**E**]

♦ Animals Asia 00841

CEO Room 1501, Tung Hip Commercial Bldg, 244-252 Des Voeux Road Central, Sheung Wan, Hong Kong. T. +85227912225. Fax +85227912320. E-mail: info@animalsasia.org.
UK 17 Mary Seacole Road, The Millfields, Plymouth, PL1 3JY, UK. T. +441752224424. Fax +441752601215.
URL: http://www.animalsasia.org/

History 1998. Active since 1994. Registration: Hong Kong; Charity Commission, No/ID: 1086903, England and Wales. **Aims** Promote compassion and respect for all animals and work to bring about long-term change. **Structure** Board of Directors. Offices: Australia; Germany; Hong Kong; Italy; UK; USA. **Languages** English, German, Italian, Mandarin Chinese, Vietnamese. **Activities** Advocacy/lobbying/activism; humanitarian/emergency aid; research/documentation. Active in: China, Vietnam. **Publications** *China Cat and Dog Welfare* (6 a year) – review. Manuals; guidebooks.
Members Full in 7 countries and territories:
Australia, Germany, Hong Kong, Italy, Luxembourg, UK, USA.
NGO Relations Member of (2): *Asia Canine Protection Alliance (ACPA, #01257); Asia for Animals Coalition (AfA, #01250).* [2022.02.09/XJ9552/**F**]

♦ Animals Asia Foundation (AAF) 00842

Head Office Tung Hip Commercial Bldg, Room 1501, 244-252 Des Voeux Road, Central, Sheung Wan, Hong Kong. T. +85227912225. Fax +85227912320. E-mail: info@animalsasia.org.
URL: http://www.animalsasia.org/

History 1998. Government-registered charity in Hong Kong, UK, USA, Italy and Germany. Registered charity in Australia, Germany, Hong Kong, Italy, UK and USA. **Aims** End cruelty and restore respect for animals throughout Asia. **Languages** English, German, Italian, Mandarin Chinese, Vietnamese. **Staff** 270.00 FTE, paid. **Activities** Awareness raising; projects/programmes, capacity building. **Events** *Asia for Animals Conference* Singapore (Singapore) 2014. **Publications** *The Paw Print* – newsletter. **NGO Relations** Member of: *Asia for Animals Coalition (AfA, #01250); International Tiger Coalition (ITC); Species Survival Network (SSN, #19916).* Partner of: *1% for the Planet.* [2018.09.11/XG7121/f/**F**]

♦ Animals without Frontiers / see Animals without Frontiers – International
♦ Animals without Frontiers – International (internationally oriented national body)

♦ Animal Traction Network for Eastern and Southern Africa (ATNESA) 00843

Chair PO Box 11316-00100 GPO, Nairobi, Kenya. T. +254206769939. Fax +254206769939.
URL: http://www.animaltraction.net/

History 1990. **Aims** Improve information exchange and regional cooperation relating to animal draft power; unite researchers, manufacturers, development workers, institutions and users of animal traction. **Structure** General Assembly (every 3 years, during major workshops). Steering Committee (meets at least annually) comprising: specialists from 6 African countries; representatives of 2 supporting organizations; invited resource persons. National networks. **Languages** English. **Staff** No full-time staff. **Activities** Organizes workshops and other activities through national networks/members in different countries. Conducts studies, surveys and research. **Events** *Workshop* Alice (South Africa) 2003, *Workshop* Jinja (Uganda) 2002, *Workshop* Jinja (Uganda) 2001, *Workshop* Chimoio (Mozambique) 2000, *International workshop / Workshop* Loskopdam (South Africa) 1999. **Publications** Workshop proceedings; discussion papers; extension manuals; books.
Members National networks (), organizations, individuals and contacts in 15 countries:
Botswana, Eritrea, Eswatini, Ethiopia (*), Kenya (*), Lesotho, Malawi, Mozambique, Namibia, South Africa (*), Sudan, Tanzania UR (*), Uganda, Zambia, Zimbabwe.
NGO Relations Collaborates with: *International Forum for Rural Transport and Development (IFRTD, #13650); Southern and Eastern Africa Society of Agricultural Engineers (SEASAE, no recent information); Western African Animal Traction Network (WAATN, no recent information).* [2008/XF3848/**F**]

♦ Animal Transportation Association (ATA) 00844

Main Office 678 Bluebell Dr, Terra Alta WV 26764, USA. T. +12026767077. Fax +12029623939. E-mail: info@animaltransportationassociation.org.
URL: http://www.animaltransportationassociation.org/

History 1975, as *Animal Air Transportation Association (AATA).* **Aims** Promote improved management, health and welfare in transport of animals worldwide. **Structure** Board of Directors. **Finance** Members' dues. Subscriptions. **Activities** Guidance/assistance/consulting; training/education. **Events** *Annual Conference* Mérida (Mexico) 2023, *Annual Conference* Terra Alta, WV (USA) 2022, *Annual Conference* Terra Alta, WV (USA) 2021, *Annual Conference* Abu Dhabi (United Arab Emirates) 2020, *Annual Conference* Budapest (Hungary) 2019. **Publications** *Migrations* (weekly) – e-newsletter. **Members** Company; Individual; Government/Academic/Research organizations; Library/Museum/Press. Individuals and organizations in 35 countries. Membership countries not specified. **IGO Relations** Observer statuts with: *Council of Europe (CE, #04881); Secretariat of the Convention on International Trade in Endangered Species of Wild Fauna and Flora (CITES Secretariat, #19199).* [2021/XF4329/**F**]

♦ Animatie Wereldsolidariteit / see WSM
♦ Animation solidarité mondiale / see WSM
♦ Animaux sans Frontières – International (internationally oriented national body)
♦ Anir Foundation (internationally oriented national body)

♦ Aniridia Europe 00845

Sec Laskenveien 79A, 3214 Sandefjord, Norway. T. +34646718142. E-mail: post@aniridia.eu.
URL: http://www.aniridia.eu/

History 25 Sep 2011. Current statutes adopted Sep 2011 and modified Aug 2016. Former names and other names: *European Federation of Aniridia Associations (Aniridia Europe)* – former. Registration: No/ID: 997 986 156, Norway. **Aims** Promote research and knowledge exchange on aniridia; empower patients with aniridia throughout Europe. **Structure** General Assembly; Board of Directors; Scientific Committee; Nominating Committee. **Events** *European Aniridia Conference* Alicante (Spain) 2022, *European Aniridia Conference* 2021, *European Aniridia Conference* Paris (France) 2018, *European Aniridia Conference* Duisburg (Germany) 2016, *European Conference on Aniridia* Venice (Italy) 2014.
Members Full; Affiliated; Honorary. National associations in 8 countries:
Finland, France, Germany, Italy, Norway, Spain, Sweden, UK.
NGO Relations Member of (1): *EURORDIS – Rare Diseases Europe (#09175).* [2022/XJ5341/**D**]

♦ ANIRIDIA-NET 00846

Chair Univ Hosp Cologne – Ctr for Ophthalmology, COST 18116, Kerpener Str 62, 50937 Cologne, Germany. E-mail: management@aniridia-net.eu.
URL: https://aniridia-net.eu/

Aims Improve aniridia clinical management; promote innovative research and development of new alternatives for its diagnosis and treatment of this ocular disease. **Structure** Steering Committee; Action Leadership. **Finance** Supported by: *European Cooperation in Science and Technology (COST, #06784).* **Activities** Knowledge management/information dissemination; research and development; research/documentation; standards/guidelines.
Members Members in 26 countries:
Austria, Belgium, Bulgaria, Cyprus, Denmark, Estonia, Finland, France, Germany, Greece, Hungary, Ireland, Israel, Italy, Latvia, Malta, Netherlands, Norway, Poland, Portugal, Serbia, Slovenia, Spain, Sweden, Türkiye, UK.
NGO Relations Member of (1): *European Alliance for Vision Research and Ophthalmology (EU-EYE, #05890).* [2020/AA1480/**F**]

♦ Anjoman-e Beynolmelali-e Ghaadjaarshenassi (#14677)
♦ Ankara Centre / see Statistical, Economic and Social Research and Training Centre for Islamic Countries (#19971)
♦ Ankylosing Spondylitis International Federation / see Axial Spondyloarthritis International Federation (#03052)
♦ ANLE – Academia Norteamericana de la Lengua Española (internationally oriented national body)
♦ **ANMA** Asian Neurogastroenterology and Motility Association (#01563)
♦ **ANMA** Association of Nordic Music Academies (#02830)
♦ ANMAP – Asian Network on Medical and Aromatic Plants (inactive)
♦ **ANMB** Asian Nuclear Medicine Board (#01570)
♦ **ANMC 21** Asian Network of Major Cities 21 (#01552)
♦ ANME – Association of Natural Medicine in Europe (internationally oriented national body)
♦ **ANMSA** African Network of Mathematical Statistics and its Applications (#18866)
♦ **ANNA** Association of National Numbering Agencies (#02818)
♦ ANNA – Australasian Neuroscience Nurses' Association (internationally oriented national body)

♦ Anna Lindh Euro-Mediterranean Foundation for the Dialogue between Cultures (Anna Lindh Foundation) 00847

Fondation euro-méditerranéenne Anna Lindh pour le dialogue entre les cultures

Exec Dir c/o Bibliotheca Alexandrina, 3rd floor conference Ctr, Alexandria, 21111, Egypt. T. +2034820342 – +2034820343. Fax +2034820471. E-mail: info@annalindhfoundation.org – secretariat@euromedalex.org.
EU Office c/o Friends of Europe, Sq De Meeûs 5-6, 1000 Brussels, Belgium.
URL: http://www.annalindhfoundation.org/

History 30 Nov 2004, The Hague (Netherlands). Established by *Union for the Mediterranean (UfM, #20457).* Current title in honour of former Swedish Foreign Minister Anna Lindh (1957-2003). Alexandria headquarters inaugurated Apr 2005. Former names and other names: *Euro-Mediterranean Foundation for Dialogue between Cultures* – former. **Aims** Promote dialogue between cultures through cooperation between civil society partners in education, culture, science and communication; strengthen intellectual cooperation and capacity-building in fields such as human rights, democratic citizenship, sustainable development, learning, knowledge and information society, gender and youth; contribute to shaping the Euro-Mediterranean space as an area of cooperation, exchange, mobility, mutual understanding and peace. **Structure** Board of Governors; President; Executive Director. Jointly co-hosted by the Bibliotheca Alexandrina and the Swedish Institute in Alexandria (Egypt). **Languages** Arabic, English, French. **Staff** 15-20. **Finance** Co-financed by EUROMED members and *European Commission (EC, #06633).* **Activities** Awards/prizes/competitions; events/meetings; training/education. **Events** *Forum* Valletta (Malta) 2016, *Forum* Marseille (France) 2013, *Forum* Barcelona (Spain) 2010, *Meeting* Brussels (Belgium) 2010, *Conference on education for intercultural understanding and dialogue* Copenhagen (Denmark) 2008. **Publications** *Euro Med Dialogue* (6 a year) – newsletter.
Members Governments of the 43 EU and Mediterranean Partner Countries (MPCs) of EUROMED:
Albania, Algeria, Austria, Belgium, Bosnia-Herzegovina, Bulgaria, Croatia, Cyprus, Czechia, Denmark, Egypt, Estonia, Finland, France, Germany, Greece, Hungary, Ireland, Israel, Italy, Jordan, Latvia, Lebanon, Lithuania, Luxembourg, Malta, Mauritania, Monaco, Montenegro, Morocco, Netherlands, Palestine, Poland, Portugal, Romania, Slovakia, Slovenia, Spain, Sweden, Tunisia, Türkiye, UK.
IGO Relations Agreement with: *Council of Europe (CE, #04881).* Conference centre at: *Bibliotheca Alexandrina Council of Patrons (#03227).* **NGO Relations** Memorandum of Understanding with (1): *Euro-Mediterranean University (EMUNI, #05728).* Member of (1): *EuroMed Permanent University Forum (EPUF, #05731).* Cooperates with (3): *Association of Organisations of Mediterranean Businesswomen (#02840); European Association of History Educators (EUROCLIO, #06069); International Association of Music Information Centres (IAMIC, #12041).* Supports (3): *Fonds Roberto Cimetta (FRC, #09837); Programme for Palestinian-European-American Cooperation in Education (PEACE Programme, #18527); United Network of Young Peacebuilders (UNOY, #20653).* Instrumental in setting up (1): *APS Europeo Istituto Pegaso (#00883).* Declaration with: *Arco Latino (#01094).* Network members include: *Council for MENA Affairs (ForMENA).* [2022/XM0839/f/**E***]

♦ **Anna Lindh Foundation** Anna Lindh Euro-Mediterranean Foundation for the Dialogue between Cultures (#00847)
♦ Annals of Public and Cooperative Economics / see Centre international de recherches et d'information sur l'économie publique, sociale et coopérative (#03764)
♦ **ANN** Asia News Network (#01447)
♦ ANN – Australasian Neuromuscular Network (internationally oriented national body)
♦ **ANND** Arab NGO Network for Development (#01016)

♦ Les Anneaux de la Mémoire 00848

Coordinator 18 rue Scribe – espace Cosmopolis, 44000 Nantes, France. T. +33240696852. E-mail: contact@anneauxdelamemoire.org.
URL: https://www.anneauxdelamemoire.org/

History 1991, Nantes (France). Registration: RNA, No/ID: W442016507, Start date: 2016, France. **Aims** Implement cultural projects on the themes of memory, history of the transatlantic slave trade and its legacies. **Activities** Events/meetings. **IGO Relations** Accredited by (1): *Organisation internationale de la Francophonie (OIF, #17809).* [2021/AA2373/**F**]

♦ Anne Cocuk Egitim Vakfi (internationally oriented national body)
♦ Année francophone Internationale / see Centre international de documentation et d'échanges de la Francophonie – L'Agora francophone internationale
♦ Anne Frank Fonds (internationally oriented national body)
♦ **ANNI** Asian NGO Network on National Human Rights Institutions (#01567)
♦ ANNIC – Applied Nanotechnology and Nanoscience International Conference (meeting series)
♦ Annonciades Célestes (religious order)
♦ ANNS – Asian Nephrology Nursing Symposium (meeting series)
♦ Annual Conference of Experimental Sociology (meeting series)
♦ Annual Conference of Pastors and Wives Serving English Speaking Churches in Europe and the Middle East / see Association of International Churches in Europe and the Middle East (#02657)
♦ Annual Conference on Theory and Applications of Models of Computation (meeting series)
♦ Annual Congress on Controversies in Ophthalmology: Europe (meeting series)
♦ Annual Environmental Politics and Governance Conference (meeting series)
♦ Annual European E-Commerce Conference (meeting series)
♦ Annual Latin American Forum on Informatics and the Information Industry (meeting series)
♦ Annual Meeting in Conservation Genetics (meeting series)
♦ Annual Nordic Cyber in Finance Conference (meeting series)
♦ Annual Symposium on the Analytical Chemistry of Pollutants / see International Association of Environmental Analytical Chemistry (#11876)
♦ Annual Symposium on ATP1A3 in Disease (meeting series)
♦ Annual Symposium on Combinatorial Pattern Matching (meeting series)
♦ Annual Symposium on Environmental Analytical Chemistry / see International Association of Environmental Analytical Chemistry (#11876)
♦ Annual Symposium on Self-Monitoring of Blood Glucose (meeting series)
♦ Annunciades – Order of the Annunciation (religious order)
♦ **ANNuR** Arab Network of Nuclear Regulators (#01013)
♦ **ANOCA** Association of National Olympic Committees of Africa (#02820)
♦ **ANOC** Association of National Olympic Committees (#02819)
♦ ANOM – Archives nationales d'Outre mer (internationally oriented national body)
♦ **ANOR** Asia Network of Organics Recycling (#01444)
♦ ANP / see Centre Africain de Recherches Forestières Appliquées et de Développement
♦ **ANPhA** Asian Nuclear Physics Association (#01571)
♦ **ANPOR** Asian Network for Public Opinion Research (#01555)
♦ **ANPPCAN** African Network for Prevention and Protection Against Child Abuse and Neglect (#00393)
♦ **ANPUD** Asian Network of People Who Use Drugs (#01553)
♦ **ANQAHE** Arab Network for Quality Assurance in Higher Education (#01014)
♦ **ANQ** Asian Network for Quality (#01556)
♦ **ANRA** Advances in Neuroblastoma Research Association (#00129)
♦ ANRA – Professional Association of Natural Rubber in Africa (no recent information)
♦ **ANREV** Asian Association for Investors in Non-Listed Real Estate Vehicles (#01327)
♦ ANROAV / see Asian Network for the Rights Of Occupational and Environmental Victims (#01558)
♦ **ANROEV** Asian Network for the Rights Of Occupational and Environmental Victims (#01558)
♦ **ANRPC** Association of Natural Rubber Producing Countries (#02822)
♦ ANRPD / see International Network on Family Poultry Development (#14267)
♦ **ANRRC** Asian Network of Research Resource Centers (#01557)
♦ **ANSA** Alternatives to Neo-Liberalism in Southern Africa (#00754)
♦ ANSA – Applied Neuroscience Society of Australasia (internationally oriented national body)
♦ **ANSAB** Asia Network for Sustainable Agriculture and Bioresources (#01445)
♦ **ANS** African Nutrition Society (#00400)
♦ ANS – American Nuclear Society (internationally oriented national body)
♦ Ansar as-Salam (internationally oriented national body)
♦ **ANSE** Association of National Organisations for Supervision in Europe (#02821)
♦ **ANSER** Academic Network for Sexual and Reproductive Health and Rights Policy (#00022)
♦ ANSES – African Network of Social Entrepreneurship Scholars (unconfirmed)
♦ **ANSN** Asian Nuclear Safety Network (#01572)
♦ **ANSO** Alliance of International Science Organizations (#00696)
♦ **ANSO** Association of Nordic and Pol-Balt LGBTQ Student Organizations (#02832)
♦ ANSORP / see Asian Network for Surveillance of Resistant Pathogens (#01560)
♦ **ANSORP** Asian Network for Surveillance of Resistant Pathogens (#01560)
♦ ANSR / see Asian College of Schizophrenia Research (#01387)
♦ **ANSSH** Asian Nutrition Society for Sports and Health (#01573)
♦ **ANSTI** African Network of Scientific and Technological Institutions (#00395)
♦ **ANSWE** African Network for Support to Women Entrepreneurs (#00397)

♦ Antarctic and Southern Ocean Coalition (ASOC) 00849

Exec Dir 1320 19th St NW, 5th Floor, Washington DC 20036, USA. T. +12022342480. E-mail: secretariat@asoc.org.
URL: http://www.asoc.org/

History 1978. Incorporated in Washington DC (USA). **Aims** Serve as the main voice devoted solely to *conservation* and environmental protection in the Antarctic Treaty System which governs Antarctica. **Structure** Council; Board. **Languages** English, French, Korean, Portuguese, Russian, Spanish. **Staff** 15.00 FTE, paid. **Finance** Members' dues. Other sources: individual donations; foundation grants. **Activities** Politics/policy/regulatory; networking/liaising; knowledge management/information dissemination; projects/programmes; events/meetings. **Events** *ATCM Meeting* Rio de Janeiro (Brazil) 1987. **Publications** *Eco Newsletter* (4-6 a year). *ASOC Briefing and Information Documents* – series. Educational posters; educational resources.
Members Environmental groups and other organizations (150) in 36 countries:
Argentina, Australia, Austria, Belgium, Brazil, Canada, Chile, China, Denmark, Ecuador, Estonia, Finland, France, Germany, Ghana, India, Indonesia, Ireland, Italy, Japan, Korea Rep, Luxembourg, Malaysia, Netherlands, New Zealand, Norway, Peru, Poland, Russia, South Africa, Spain, Sweden, Switzerland, UK, Uruguay, USA.
Included in the above, 10 organizations listed in this Yearbook:
BirdLife International (#03266); Cetacean Society International (CSI); Earth Island Institute (EII); Friends of the Earth International (FoEI, #10002); Global 2000 Environmental Organization (Global 2000, no recent information); Greenpeace International (#10727); International Fund for Animal Welfare (IFAW, #13693); Sierra Club International Program (#19266); Wilderness Society; World Wide Fund for Nature (WWF, #21922).
IGO Relations Accredited by: *International Whaling Commission (IWC, #15879).* Observer at meetings of: *Antarctic Treaty (AT, #00850).* **NGO Relations** Member of: *Deep Sea Conservation Coalition (DSCC, #05024); High Seas Alliance (HSA, #10918); International Union for Conservation of Nature and Natural Resources (IUCN, #15766).* Partner of: *1% for the Planet.* [2017.06.27/XF9411/y/F]

♦ Antarctic Treaty (AT) 00850

Traité sur l'Antarctique (TA) – Tratado Antártico (TA)

Information Officer c/o Antarctic Treaty Secretariat, Maipú 757 – 4th Floor, C1006ACI Buenos Aires, Argentina. T. +541139914256. Fax +541139914253. E-mail: ats@ats.aq.
Exec Sec address not obtained. E-mail: executive.secretary@ats.aq.
URL: https://www.ats.aq/

History 1 Dec 1959, Washington, DC (USA). Established on signature of the Treaty by representatives of 12 countries. In force 23 Jun 1961. Statutes registered in *'UNTS 1/5778'.* **Aims** Ensure "in the interest of all mankind that Antarctica shall continue for ever to be used exclusively for peaceful purposes and shall not become the scene or object of international discord". **Structure** Meeting of representatives of consultative member nations (annual). **Languages** English, French, Russian, Spanish. **Staff** 9.00 FTE, paid. **Finance** Budget provided by Consultative Parties in A- E scales. Parties pay their own expenses. Annual budget: 1,380,097 USD (2019). **Activities** Events/meetings; management of treaties and agreements. Also manages: *Agreed Measures for the Conservation of Antarctic Fauna and Flora (1964),* later incorporated into *Protocol to the Antarctic Treaty on Environmental Protection (1991).* Protocol on Environmental Protection, which entered into force on 14 Jan 1998, includes 6 specific annexes covering: marine pollution; fauna and flora; environmental impact assessment; waste management; protected area management; liability for damage caused by environmental emergencies. It prohibits all activities relating to mineral resources except scientific research. *Convention on the Regulation of Antarctic Mineral Resource Activities (CRAMRA, 1988),* signed 1988, Wellington (New Zealand), which did not enter into force. Manages the following treaties/agreements: *Convention for the Conservation of Antarctic Seals (CCAS, 1972); Convention on the Conservation of Antarctic Marine Living Resources (CCAMLR, 1980).* **Events** *Consultative Meeting* Helsinki (Finland) 2023, *Consultative Meeting* Berlin (Germany) 2022, *Consultative Meeting* Paris (France) 2021, *Consultative Meeting* Prague (Czechia) 2019, *Consultative Meeting* Buenos Aires (Argentina) 2018. **Publications** *Rules of Procedure of the ATCM and the CEP.* Compilation of key documents of the Antarctic Treaty System; Reports of the Antarctic Treaty Consultative Meetings (2005 onward).
Members Consultative (voting) members – 29, original signatories marked " include 7 nations (marked ") claiming portions of Antarctica as national territory, the remainder followed by their year of accession to the Treaty:
Argentina (**), Australia (**), Belgium (*), Brazil (1983), Bulgaria (1998), Chile (**), China (1985), Czechia (2014), Ecuador (1990), Finland (1989), France (**), Germany (1981), India (1983), Italy (1987), Japan (*), Korea Rep (1989), Netherlands (1990), New Zealand (**), Norway (**), Peru (1989), Poland (1977), Russia (* – as USSR), South Africa (*), Spain (1988), Sweden (1988), UK (**), Ukraine (2004), Uruguay (1985), USA (*).
Non-consultative (non-voting) members – 26, followed by year of accession to the Treaty:
Austria (1987), Belarus (2006), Canada (1988), Colombia (1989), Costa Rica (2022), Cuba (1984), Denmark (1965), Estonia (2001), Greece (1987), Guatemala (1991), Hungary (1984), Iceland (2015), Kazakhstan (2015), Korea DPR (1987), Malaysia (2011), Monaco (2008), Mongolia (2015), Pakistan (2012), Papua New Guinea (1981), Portugal (2010), Romania (1971), Slovakia (1993), Slovenia (2019), Switzerland (1990), Türkiye (1995), Venezuela (1999).
IGO Relations Member of (1): *Hydrographic Commission on Antarctica (HCA, see: #13825).* Invited to participate in consultative meetings: *International Civil Aviation Organization (ICAO, #12581); Intergovernmental Oceanographic Commission (IOC, #11496); International Group of P and I Clubs (#13751); International Hydrographic Organization (IHO, #13825); International Maritime Organization (IMO, #14102); International Oil Pollution Compensation Funds (IOPC Funds, #14402); UNEP (#20299); United Nations Framework Convention on Climate Change – Secretariat (UNFCCC, #20564); World Meteorological Organization (WMO, #21649); World Tourism Organization (UNWTO, #21861).* **NGO Relations** Invited to participate in consultative meetings: *Antarctic and Southern Ocean Coalition (ASOC, #00849); International Association of Antarctica Tour Operators (IAATO, #11702); International Union for Conservation of Nature and Natural Resources (IUCN, #15766).*
[2022.10.11/XF0711/**F***]

♦ Antenna International (internationally oriented national body)
♦ Antenna internationale (internationally oriented national body)
♦ Antenna technologie (internationally oriented national body)
♦ Antenna Technology (internationally oriented national body)

♦ Anthropology Southern Africa 00851

Pres c/o FHISER, 4 Hill Street, East London, 5201, South Africa.
URL: http://www.asnahome.org/

History Founded 2001, on merger of *Association for Anthropology in Southern Africa (AASA) – Vereniging vir Antropologie in Suider-Afrika (VASA),* founded 1987, with South African Society of Cultural Anthropologists (SASCA), founded 1980. **Aims** Support anthropological work in southern Africa. **Structure** Regional Executive Board. **Languages** English. **Staff** Voluntary. **Finance** Members' dues. **Activities** Organizes: annual conference; exchange programme among African countries. **Events** *Annual Conference* Windhoek (Namibia) 2020, *Annual Conference* Port Elizabeth (South Africa) 2019, *Annual Conference* Gaborone (Botswana) 2018, *Annual Conference* Zomba (Malawi) 2017, *Annual Conference* Thohoyandou (South Africa) 2016. **Publications** *Anthropology Southern Africa* (4 a year) – journal.
Members Full in 13 countries:
Angola, Botswana, Cameroon, Czechia, Germany, Lesotho, Namibia, Norway, South Africa, UK, USA, Zambia, Zimbabwe.
NGO Relations Member of: *World Council of Anthropological Associations (WCAA, #21317).*
[2015/XD4586/**D**]

♦ Anthroposophical Society (inactive)
♦ Anthroposophische Gesellschaft (inactive)
♦ Anti-Atom-International (internationally oriented national body)
♦ Anti-Comintern Pact (1936 treaty)
♦ Anti-Communist International Union (inactive)
♦ Anti-Conterfeiting Trade Agreement (2011 treaty)

♦ Anti-Corruption Initiative for Asia and the Pacific 00852

Contact Dir Poverty Reduction, Social Development and Governance Div, Regional and Sustainable Development Dept, ADB, 6 ADB Avenue, Mandaluyong City, 1550 METRO Manila, Philippines. T. +63263252931. Fax +6326362193.
URL: http://www.oecd.org/

History 1999, as a joint initiative of *African Development Bank (ADB, #00283)* and *OECD (#17693).* **Aims** Develop and implement the Anti-Corruption Action Plan for Asia and the Pacific. **Activities** Fosters policy dialogue; provides policy analysis; promote capacity building.
Members Governments of 28 countries and territories:
Australia, Bangladesh, Bhutan, Cambodia, China, Cook Is, Fiji, Hong Kong, India, Indonesia, Japan, Kazakhstan, Korea Rep, Kyrgyzstan, Macau, Malaysia, Mongolia, Nepal, Pakistan, Palau, Papua New Guinea, Philippines, Samoa, Singapore, Sri Lanka, Thailand, Vanuatu, Vietnam.
IGO Relations Partner of: *Australian Aid (inactive); Deutsche Gesellschaft für Technische Zusammenarbeit (GTZ, inactive); International Bank for Reconstruction and Development (IBRD, #12317); Swedish International Development Cooperation Agency (Sida); UNDP (#20292).* **NGO Relations** Partner of: *Basel Institute on Governance; American Bar Association Rule of Law Initiative (ABI ROLI); Pacific Basin Economic Council (PBEC, #17938); Transparency International (TI, #20223).* [2019/XJ0278/**E***]

♦ Anti-Corruption Network for Eastern Europe and Central Asia (ACN) 00853

Manager Directorate for Financial and Enterprise Affairs, OECD, 2 rue André Pascal, 75775 Paris CEDEX 16, France. T. +33145241319. Fax +33144306307.
URL: http://www.oecd.org/corruption/acn/

History Oct 1998, Istanbul (Turkey), as *Anti-Corruption Network for Transition Economies.* A regional outreach programme of *OECD (#17693)* Working Group on Bribery. **Aims** Support member countries in their fight against corruption by providing a regional forum for promotion of anti-corruption activities, information exchange, elaboration of best practices and donor coordination. **Structure** Steering Group composed of representatives from: *Council of Europe (CE, #04881); European Bank for Reconstruction and Development (EBRD, #06315); European Commission (EC, #06633); International Bank for Reconstruction and Development (IBRD, #12317); International Chamber of Commerce (ICC, #12534); International Monetary Fund (IMF, #14180);* OECD; *Transparency International (TI, #20223);* United Nations; *United States Agency for International Development (USAID).* Also represented are *Business and Industry Advisory Committee to the OECD (BIAC, #03385)* and *Trade Union Advisory Committee to the OECD (TUAC, #20186).* Secretariat based at Anti-Corruption Division of OECD Directorate for Financial and Enterprise Affairs. **Languages** Croatian, English, Russian, Serbian. **Staff** 1-3. **Finance** Supported by: OECD. Voluntary contributions provided by OECD member states and other donors. **Activities** Organizes general meetings, conferences, thematic activities, sub-regional initiatives and country specific projects. **Events** *General Meeting* Tbilisi (Georgia) 2008, *General Meeting* Istanbul (Turkey) 2007, *Annual meeting / General Meeting* Istanbul (Turkey) 1999. **Publications** *Fighting Corruption in Transition Economies* – report series. *Istanbul Anti-Corruption Action Plan – Progress and Challenges* (2008); *Glossary of International Anti-Corruption Standards with Examples of National Legal Practice* (2006); *Specialized Anti-Corruption Institutions* (2006).
Members Participating countries (23):
Albania, Armenia, Azerbaijan, Belarus, Bosnia-Herzegovina, Bulgaria, Croatia, Estonia, Georgia, Kazakhstan, Kyrgyzstan, Latvia, Lithuania, Moldova, Montenegro, North Macedonia, Romania, Russia, Serbia, Tajikistan, Turkmenistan, Ukraine, Uzbekistan.
[2018/XF5655/**F***]

♦ Anti-Corruption Network for Transition Economies / see Anti-Corruption Network for Eastern Europe and Central Asia (#00853)

- ♦ Anti-Corruption Student Network / see Anti-Corruption Student Network in South East Europe (#00854)
- ♦ Anti-Corruption Student Network in SEE / see Anti-Corruption Student Network in South East Europe (#00854)

♦ Anti-Corruption Student Network in South East Europe (ACSN SEE) 00854

Address not obtained.
URL: http://see-corruption.net/

History Also referred to as *Anti-Corruption Student Network (ACSN)* and *Anti-Corruption Student Network in SEE.* **Aims** Lower the level of corruption at universities; create transparent higher education environment in the region.
Members Organizations in 6 countries:
Albania, Bulgaria, Croatia, Moldova, North Macedonia, Serbia. [2011/XJ8242/**F**]

- ♦ Anti-Death Penalty Asia Network (unconfirmed)
- ♦ Anti-Defamation League of B'nai B'rith (internationally oriented national body)
- ♦ Anti-doping Convention (1989 treaty)

♦ Antidote Europe 00855

Contact Boîte 1 – 5 rue Perrée, 75003 Paris, France.
URL: https://antidote-europe.eu/

History Registered in accordance with French law. **Aims** Promote sound scientific methods of research and campaigns on issues of *consumer* safety. **Structure** Scientific Committee. **Activities** Awareness raising; knowledge management/information dissemination. [2022/XM6940/**D**]

- ♦ Antigonish Movement (internationally oriented national body)
- ♦ Antikrebs Weltbewegung (#21095)
- ♦ Antikrebs Weltbewegung "21 Jahrhundert: Menschheit gegen Krebs" / see World Anticancer Movement (#21095)

♦ Antilles Episcopal Conference (AEC) 00856

Conférence épiscopale des Antilles

Contact 9a Gray Street, Port-of-Spain, Trinidad-Tobago. T. +18686222932. Fax +18686283688.
URL: http://www.aecrc.org/

History 24 Apr 1975. **Aims** Promote *Catholic faith.* **Structure** Composed of 21 ecclesiastical territories; Permanent Board of 8 members. Commissions (11); Executive Committee of Bishops. **Languages** English. **Staff** 1.50 FTE, paid. **Finance** Self-financing. **Activities** Religious activites. **Events** *Annual Plenary Meeting* Port-of-Spain (Trinidad-Tobago) 2016, *Annual Plenary Meeting* Montego Bay (Jamaica) 2015, *Annual Plenary Meeting* Mandeville (Jamaica) 2014, *Annual Plenary Meeting* Pointe-à-Pitre (Guadeloupe) 2013, *Annual Plenary Meeting* Georgetown (Guyana) 2012. **Publications** *Caring forthe Earth – Our Responsibility*; *Pastoral Letter of the Gift of Life*; *Pastoral Letter on Capital Punishment.*
Members Covers 28 countries and territories:
Anguilla, Antigua-Barbuda, Aruba, Bahamas, Barbados, Belize, Bermuda, Bonaire Is, Cayman Is, Curaçao, Dominica, Grenada, Guadeloupe, Guiana Fr, Guyana, Jamaica, Martinique, Montserrat, Saba, St Eustatius, St Kitts-Nevis, St Lucia, St Maarten, St Vincent-Grenadines, Suriname, Trinidad-Tobago, Turks-Caicos, Virgin Is UK.
NGO Relations Member of: *Caribbean Conference of Churches (CCC, #03479)*; *Catholic Biblical Federation (CBF, #03600).* [2016.06.01/XD8682/**F**]

- ♦ Antimilitaristiska Prästers och Predikanters Internationella Union (inactive)

♦ Anti-Money Laundering Europe (AME) 00857

Contact Schuman Associates, Rue Archimède 5, 1000 Brussels, Belgium. T. +3222307439. E-mail: info@schumanassociates.com.
URL: http://www.amleurope.com/

History Jun 2004. **Aims** Serve as an interactive public/private sector forum on EU financial *crime* issues such as money laundering, *fraud* and *terrorist* financing. **Languages** English. **Staff** 2.00 FTE, paid. **Finance** Sources: members' dues. **Activities** Events/meetings; networking/liaising; politics/policy/regulatory.
Members Membership is exclusive and drawn form the main sectors most impacted by EU AML policy and legislation. Members are senior executives in their respective organizations. Companies and organizations (11), including 3 organizations listed in this Yearbook:
European Corporate Security Association (ECSA); *European Gaming and Betting Association (EGBA, #07375)*; *Society for Worldwide Interbank Financial Telecommunication (SWIFT, #19661).* [2022/XJ2022/y/**F**]

- ♦ Anti-Persoonsmijnen Ontmijnende Productontwikkeling (internationally oriented national body)
- ♦ Anti-Phishing Working Group (internationally oriented national body)

♦ AntiPhospholipid Syndrome Alliance For Clinical Trials and InternatiOnal Networking (APS ACTION) 00858

Coordinator Hosp for Special Surgery, 535 E 70th St, New York NY 10021, USA. T. +12127742795.
URL: https://apsaction.com/

History Nov 2010, Miami FL (USA), resulting from the 13th *International Congress on Antiphospholipid Antibodies.* **Aims** Prevent, treat, and cure antiphospholipid antibody (aPL) associated clinical manifestations through high-quality, multicenter, and multidisciplinary clinical research. **Structure** Steering Committee; Executive Committee. **Activities** Events/meetings; awards/prizes/competitions; research and development. **Events** *International Congress on Antiphospholipid Antibodies* Istanbul (Turkey) 2016, *Annual Summit* Boston, MA (USA) 2014, *Working Meeting* Paris (France) 2014, *Working Meeting* Madrid (Spain) 2013, *Annual Summit / Congress* Rio de Janeiro (Brazil) 2013.
Members Individuals in 14 countries:
Australia, Brazil, Canada, China, France, Greece, Italy, Jamaica, Japan, Lebanon, Netherlands, Spain, UK, USA. [2021/XJ9276/v/**E**]

- ♦ Antiqui Societatis Jesus Alumni (#21877)

♦ Anti-Seismic Systems International Society (ASSISi) 00859

Head Office c/o Ente Naz per le Nuove Tecnologie – ENEA, Via Martiri di Monte Sole 4, 40129 Bologna BO, Italy.
URL: http://assisisociety.com/

History Founded 5 Oct 2001, Assisi (Italy), during the Closing Panel of the 7th International Seminar on Seismic Isolation, Passive Energy Dissipation and Active Control of Seismic Vibrations of Structures. Registered in accordance with Italian law. **Aims** Disseminate the results of research programmes, application examples and basic training material to foster further development and acceptance of seismic protection solutions and techniques. **Structure** General Assembly; Foundation Committee; Executive Committee. **Finance** Sources: members' dues. **Activities** Events/meetings. **Events** *World Conference on Seismic Isolation, Energy Dissipation and Active Vibration Control of Structures* St Petersburg (Russia) 2019, *World Conference on Seismic Isolation, Energy Dissipation and Active Vibration Control of Structures* Sendai (Japan) 2013. [2020/XM8733/**C**]

♦ Anti-Slavery International 00860

Communications Manager Thomas Clarkson House, The Stableyard, Broomgrove Road, London, SW9 9TL, UK. E-mail: supporter@antislavery.org.
URL: http://www.antislavery.org/

History 17 Apr 1839, London (UK). Amalgamated, 1909, with *Aborigines Protection Society*, set up 1837. Former names and other names: *British and Foreign Anti-Slavery Society* – former; *Anti-Slavery Society for the Protection of Human Rights* – former; *Société anti-esclavagiste pour la protection des droits de l'homme* – former; *Liga contra la Esclavitud* – former; *Anti-Slavery Society* – former; *Anti-Slavery International for the Protection of Human Rights* – former. Registration: Charity Commission, No/ID: 1049160, England and Wales. **Aims** Work to eliminate all forms of slavery and slavery like practices throughout the world; deal with the root causes of slavery and its consequences to achieve sustainable change. **Structure** Annual General Meeting; Board. **Languages** Arabic, English, French, Spanish. **Staff** 32.00 FTE, paid; 5.00 FTE, voluntary. **Finance** Sources: donations; fundraising; gifts, legacies; government support; international organizations; members' dues; private foundations. Supported by: *Comic Relief*; *Department for International Development (DFID, inactive)*; *Norwegian Agency for Development Cooperation (Norad)*; *The Freedom Fund.* Annual budget: 3,100,000 GBP. **Activities** Advocacy/lobbying/activism; awareness raising; events/meetings; knowledge management/information dissemination; management of treaties and agreements; networking/liaising; research/documentation. Manages the following treaties/agreements: *Supplementary Convention on the Abolition of Slavery, the Slave Trade, and Institutions and Practices Similar to Slavery (1956).* **Publications** *The Reporter* (2 a year) – supporter magazine; *Impact Report* (annual). Annual Review; educational videos and packs; reports on slavery issues. **Members** Subscribing members (about 1,800) and supporters (over 10,000). Membership countries not specified. **Consultative Status** Consultative status granted from: *ECOSOC (#05331)* (Special); *ILO (#11123)* (Special List); *Council of Europe (CE, #04881)* (Participatory Status); *African Commission on Human and Peoples' Rights (ACHPR, #00255)* (Observer). **IGO Relations** Makes submissions to United Nations bodies, including: *Committee on the Rights of the Child (#04283)*; *United Nations Commission on Human Rights (inactive).* Accredited by: *United Nations Office at Vienna (UNOV, #20604).* Contacts with: *Commonwealth Secretariat (#04362)* Associated with Department of Global Communications of the United Nations. **NGO Relations** Member of (16): *Child Rights Connect (#03884)*; *Child Rights International Network (CRIN, #03885)*; *Coalition for an Effective African Court on Human and Peoples' Rights (African Court Coalition, #04055)*; *Conference of Non-Governmental Organizations in Consultative Relationship with the United Nations (CONGO, #04635)*; *Crisis Action (#04957)*; *EarthAction (EA, #05159)*; *Ethical Trading Initiative (ETI)*; *Girls not Brides (#10154)*; *International Dalit Solidarity Network (IDSN, #13129)*; *International NGO Platform on the Migrant Workers' Convention (IPMWC, #14367)*; *NGO Committee on UNICEF (#17120)*; *Platform for International Cooperation on Undocumented Migrants (PICUM, #18401)*; *Religious in Europe Networking Against Trafficking and Exploitation (RENATE, #18833)*; *Sudan Consortium (#20031)*; *UNCAC Coalition (#20283)*; *World Organisation Against Torture (OMCT, #21685).* Observer member of: *Consortium for Street Children (CSC).* Together with: *Netherlands Centre for Indigenous Peoples (NCIV)*; *Vlaamse Steungroep voor Inheemse Volken (KWIA, inactive)*, set up *Human Rights Fund for Indigenous Peoples (HRFIP, inactive).* Supports: *African Network for Prevention and Protection Against Child Abuse and Neglect (ANPPCAN, #00393)*; *GoodWeave International (#10681).* [2022.06.15/XD0058/v/**C**]

- ♦ Anti-Slavery International for the Protection of Human Rights / see Anti-Slavery International (#00860)
- ♦ Anti-Slavery Society / see Anti-Slavery International (#00860)
- ♦ Anti-Slavery Society for the Protection of Human Rights / see Anti-Slavery International (#00860)

♦ Anti-Smoking International Alliance (ASIA) 00861

SG 45 Brookscroft, Linton Glade, Croydon, CR0 9NA, UK. T. +442086515436. Fax +442086513428.
URL: http://antismokingalliance.org/

History Founded 1 Oct 1991, London (UK), at 2nd seminar, as *International Network Towards Smokefree Hospitals (INTSH)* – *Réseau international pour les hôpitaux sans tabac* – *Red Internacional pro Hospitales sin Fumar* – *Internationales Netz zur Förderung von Rauchfreien Krankenhäusern* – *Internacia Reto por Senfumigi Hospitalojn.* UK Registered Charity: 1004061. **Aims** Protect, preserve and improve the *health* of patients, visitors and persons working in *hospitals* or in connection with health services, particularly nurses, by helping to protect them from *risks* and injurious consequences of *tobacco* smoking, including fire risks, and including all areas where smoking affects users and those *inhaling* smoke produced by smokers. **Structure** Meeting (annual); Officers. **Languages** English. **Finance** Members' dues. Donations. **Activities** Awards/prizes/competitions. **Events** *Global Conference* Kuwait (Kuwait) 2017. **Publications** *Smoke-free Hospitals International* – newsletter. Information leaflets; seminar reports.
Members Individuals and organizations in 5 countries:
France, Switzerland, UK, United Arab Emirates, USA. [2018.06.01/XF3244/**F**]

- ♦ Anti-war Treaty of Non-aggression and Conciliation (1933 treaty)
- ♦ ANTLER – Asia-Pacific Network of Transport and Logistics Education and Research (unconfirmed)
- ♦ Antoniani (religious order)
- ♦ Antonines (religious order)
- ♦ Antonio Bana's Foundation for Research on Ornithological Migration and Environmental Protection / see European Foundation Il Nibbio
- ♦ **ANTRIEP** Asian Network of Training and Research Institutions in Educational Planning (#01561)
- ♦ Antropólogos Iberoamericanos en Red (unconfirmed)
- ♦ **ANTS** Association for Nordic Theatre Scholars (#02833)
- ♦ ANU Centre for European Studies (internationally oriented national body)
- ♦ ANUCES – ANU Centre for European Studies (internationally oriented national body)
- ♦ ANUVIBHA – Anuvrat Visha Bharati (internationally oriented national body)
- ♦ Anuvrat Global Organization (internationally oriented national body)
- ♦ Anuvrat Visha Bharati (internationally oriented national body)
- ♦ Anwälte Ohne Grenzen (#03050)
- ♦ ANWIST / see Arab Network for Women in Science and Technology (#01015)
- ♦ **ANWS** African Network of Women Shelters (#00398)
- ♦ **ANWS** Asian Network of Women's Shelters (#01562)
- ♦ **ANWST** Arab Network for Women in Science and Technology (#01015)
- ♦ **ANWUNMV** Association of Nordic War and UN Military Veterans (#02834)
- ♦ **ANYL4PSD** African Network of Young Leaders for Peace and Sustainable Development (#00399)
- ♦ **ANYP** Africa Network of Young Peace-Builders (#00303)
- ♦ ANZAHPE – Australian and New Zealand Association for Health Professional Educators (internationally oriented national body)
- ♦ ANZAME / see Australian and New Zealand Association for Health Professional Educators
- ♦ ANZAME – Association for Health Professional Education, The / see Australian and New Zealand Association for Health Professional Educators
- ♦ ANZAScA – Architectural Science Association (internationally oriented national body)
- ♦ ANZCCART – Australian and New Zealand Council for the Care of Animals in Research and Teaching (internationally oriented national body)
- ♦ ANZCIES / see Oceania Comparative and International Education Society
- ♦ ANZOS – Australian and New Zealand Obesity Society (internationally oriented national body)
- ♦ ANZSIL – Australian and New Zealand Society of International Law (internationally oriented national body)
- ♦ ANZUPJ / see Union for Progressive Judaism

♦ ANZUS Council 00862

Conseil de l'ANZUS

Address not obtained.

History 1 Sep 1951, San Francisco CA (USA), under Article VII of *Security Treaty (1951)*, also referred to as the *ANZUS Treaty*, signed by Australia, New Zealand and USA, which entered into force on 29 Apr 1952. The Treaty in the English language and the instruments of ratification are deposited with the Government of Australia, Canberra (Australia). Following a dispute in 1985 over USA access to New Zealand ports and airfields, meetings of the full Anzus Council have not taken place since 1984. On 11 Aug 1986 the USA suspended security obligations to New Zealand. Commitments between the USA and Australia were mutually reaffirmed the same day and thus remain unaltered. Currently, Anzus continues to govern security relations between (a) Australia and the USA, (b) Australia and New Zealand. **Aims** Declare publicly and formally the sense of unity among members and coordinate their efforts for collective *defence* for the preservation of peace and security in the *Pacific* area; consult together whenever in the opinion of any party the territorial integrity, political independence or security of any of the parties is threatened in the Pacific; act to meet the common danger according to constitutional processes. **Structure** Council (up to 1985, met annually), consisting of the Foreign Ministers (or their Deputies) of signatory Powers. Since 1985 bilateral Australia/USA meetings have been held annually. There are no formally designated headquarters and no permanent staff; arrangements for meetings are made among the governments concerned. Meetings closed. **Languages** English. **Activities** Military cooperation includes exchange of technical information and strategic intelligence, together with a program of exercises, exchanges and visits involving armed forces. Although such contacts between the USA and New Zealand have been curtailed, contacts continue between Australia and USA, including free access to Australian ports by US naval vessels. Defence cooperation programs are arranged on a bilateral basis with other countries of the region.

ANZUS Treaty
00862

alphabetic sequence excludes
For the complete listing, see Yearbook Online at

Members Foreign Ministers (or their Deputies) of Signatory Powers (3):
Australia, New Zealand, USA.
IGO Relations *Commonwealth Secretariat (#04362).* [2010/XD0059/**D***]

- ♦ ANZUS Treaty / see ANZUS Council (#00862)
- ♦ **AOAA** Association ouest africaine d'archéologie (#20866)
- ♦ **AOA** American Outlaws Association (#00788)
- ♦ **AOA** ASEAN Orthopaedic Association (#01217)
- ♦ **AOA** Asian Ombudsman Association (#01589)
- ♦ AOA / see Asian and South Pacific Ostomy Association (#01756)
- ♦ AOA – Asia and Oceania Association of the ICMIF (see: #12948)
- ♦ AOA – Asia Offshore Association (unconfirmed)
- ♦ AOAC / see AOAC INTERNATIONAL (#00863)

♦ AOAC INTERNATIONAL 00863

Exec Dir 2275 Research Blvd, Ste 300, Rockville MD 20850-3250, USA. T. +13019247077.
URL: http://www.aoac.org/

History 1884, Philadelphia, PA (USA). Former names and other names: *Association of Official Agricultural Chemists* – former (1884 to 1965); *Association of Official Analytical Chemists (AOAC)* – former (1965 to 1991); *Association des chimistes analytiques officiels* – former (1965 to 1991); *Asociación de Quimicos Analíticos Oficiales* – former (1965 to 1991); *Association of Official Analytical Collaboration (AOAC)* – full title (2020). **Aims** Advance the global food and agricultural *chemistry* and *microbiology* analytical community by promoting methods validation and quality measurements. **Structure** Board of Directors; Committees. **Languages** English. **Staff** 25.00 FTE, paid. **Finance** Sources: grants; members' dues; revenue from activities/projects; sale of publications. Annual budget: 7,000,000 USD (2022). **Activities** Certification/accreditation; events/meetings; monitoring/evaluation; training/education. **Events** *Annual Meeting* Toronto, ON (Canada) 2027, *Annual Meeting* Indianapolis, IN (USA) 2026, *Annual Meeting* San Diego, CA (USA) 2025, *Annual Meeting* Baltimore, MD (USA) 2024, *Annual Meeting* New Orleans, LA (USA) 2023. **Publications** *Inside Laboratory Management* (6 a year) – magazine; *Journal of AOAC INTERNATIONAL* (6 a year). *Official Methods of Analysis of AOAC INTERNATIONAL*. Handbooks; manuals; monographs; pamphlets.
Members Individual; Honorary; Sustaining Member Organization. Members (mainly in USA) in 98 countries and territories:
Albania, Andorra, Argentina, Australia, Austria, Bahamas, Bangladesh, Barbados, Belgium, Belize, Bermuda, Botswana, Brazil, Bulgaria, Canada, Chile, China, Colombia, Costa Rica, Croatia, Cyprus, Czechia, Denmark, Dominican Rep, Ecuador, Egypt, El Salvador, Estonia, Finland, France, Germany, Ghana, Greece, Guatemala, Guyana, Honduras, Hong Kong, Hungary, Iceland, India, Indonesia, Ireland, Israel, Italy, Jamaica, Japan, Jordan, Kenya, Korea Rep, Kuwait, Lebanon, Lithuania, Malawi, Malaysia, Malta, Mexico, Netherlands, New Zealand, Nicaragua, North Macedonia (former Yugoslav Rep of), Norway, Oman, Pakistan, Panama, Paraguay, Peru, Philippines, Poland, Portugal, Puerto Rico, Qatar, Romania, Russia, Saudi Arabia, Serbia, Seychelles, Singapore, Slovakia, Slovenia, South Africa, Spain, Sri Lanka, Sweden, Switzerland, Syrian AR, Taiwan, Thailand, Trinidad-Tobago, Türkiye, UK, United Arab Emirates, Uruguay, USA, Venezuela, Vietnam, Virgin Is USA, Zambia, Zimbabwe.
Consultative Status Consultative status granted from: *ECOSOC (#05331)* (Ros C); *FAO (#09260)* (Special Status). **IGO Relations** Participates as observer in the activities of: *Codex Alimentarius Commission (CAC, #04081)*. **NGO Relations** Member of (2): *Cooperation on International Traceability in Analytical Chemistry (CITAC, #04797); International Laboratory Accreditation Cooperation (ILAC, #13995).* Associated organization of: *International Union of Pure and Applied Chemistry (IUPAC, #15809).* Observer to: *EURACHEM (#05595).* In liaison with technical committees of: *International Organization for Standardization (ISO, #14473).* Liaison with: *Collaborative International Pesticides Analytical Council (CIPAC, #04099); ICC – International Association for Cereal Science and Technology (#11048); International Commission on Microbiological Specifications for Foods (ICMSF, #12703); International Confectionery Association (ICA, #12840); Cereals and Grains Association (#03830); International Commission for Uniform Methods of Sugar Analysis (ICUMSA, #12736).* [2023/XF1837/**B**]

- ♦ **AOAD** Arab Organization for Agricultural Development (#01018)

♦ AO Alliance 00864

Acting Managing Dir Clavadelerstr 8, 7270 Davos-Platz, Switzerland. E-mail: info@ao-alliance.org.
URL: https://ao-alliance.org/

History Jan 2015. Set up, building on the AO Socio-Economic Committee (AO SEC), set up by *AO Foundation (#00866)*. Alliance set up as an independent organization. **Aims** Improve the care of the injured in low- and middle-income countries (LMICs). **Structure** Board of Directors. **Activities** Advocacy/lobbying/activism; politics/policy/regulatory; training/education. [2021/AA2265/**E**]

- ♦ **AOAN** Asian and Oceanian Association of Neurology (#01574)
- ♦ AOAPC – Association des organisations africaines de promotion commerciale (no recent information)
- ♦ **AOAPO** Asia Oceania Agricultural Proteomics Organization (#01791)
- ♦ **AOARP** Asian and Oceanic Association for Radiation Protection (#01586)
- ♦ AOAS / see Arab Administrative Development Organization (#00893)
- ♦ **AOASO** Asia-Oceania Association for the Study of Obesity (#01793)
- ♦ AOAV – Action on Armed Violence (internationally oriented national body)
- ♦ AOBO / see Triratna Buddhist Community (#20243)
- ♦ AOCA – AfriOceans Conservation Alliance (internationally oriented national body)
- ♦ **AOC** African Ophthalmology Council (#00402)
- ♦ AOCASS – Association ouest et centre africaine de la science du sol (no recent information)
- ♦ AOC – Association of Old Crows (internationally oriented national body)
- ♦ **AOCC** Asian Organization for Crohn's & Colitis (#01592)
- ♦ AOCCI / see Eventing Organisers Association (#09211)
- ♦ AOCE – Asia-Oceania Congress of Endocrinology (meeting series)
- ♦ **AOCF** Asia-Oceania Ceramic Federation (#01794)
- ♦ AOCFI / see Association of Career Firms International (#02400)
- ♦ AOCI – Airports Operators Council International (inactive)
- ♦ AOCL – Asian and Oceanian Cyclodextrin League (unconfirmed)

♦ AO CMF 00865

Dir Clavadelerstr 8, 7270 Davos-Platz, Switzerland. T. +41814142111. Fax +41814142280. E-mail: info@aocmf.org.
URL: https://aocmf.aofoundation.org/

History 2008. CMF recognized as a specialty area, 1974. A clinical division of *AO Foundation (#00866).* **Aims** Promote excellence in patient care and outcomes in trauma and musculoskeletal disorders. **Structure** International Board; Regional Boards (Asia Pacific, Europe and Southern Africa, Middle East and Northern Africa, Latin America, and North America); Commissions. **Activities** Events/meetings; research and development; training/education. **Publications** *Craniomaxillofacial Trauma & Reconstruction.* [2022/AA2262/**E**]

- ♦ **AOCNA** Asian Oceanian Child Neurology Association (#01575)
- ♦ AOCRS – African Organization of Cartography and Remote Sensing (inactive)
- ♦ AOCS – American Oil Chemists' Society (internationally oriented national body)
- ♦ AOCT / see Association of Overseas Countries and Territories of the European Union (#02843)
- ♦ AOCTS – Assemblée des Ordinaires Catholiques de Terre Sainte (religious order)
- ♦ AODC / see IMCA International Marine Contractors Association (#11127)
- ♦ AODC International Association of Underwater Engineering Contractors / see IMCA International Marine Contractors Association (#11127)
- ♦ **AODES** Academy of Operative Dentistry – European Section (#00043)
- ♦ **AODP** Arab Organization of Disabled People (#01019)
- ♦ **AOEA** Asian and Oceanian Epilepsy Association (#01577)
- ♦ **AOECS** Association of European Coeliac Societies (#02504)
- ♦ **AOEE** Association ouest africaine pour l'évaluation environnementale (#20868)
- ♦ AOEMA – Asia Oceania E-Business Marketplace Alliance (inactive)
- ♦ AOEO – Asian-Oceanian Epilepsy Organization (inactive)
- ♦ AOFAAM – Asia-Oceania Federation of Anti-Aging Medicine (no recent information)
- ♦ AOF – African Oriental Federation (inactive)
- ♦ AOF – Afrique occidentale française (inactive)
- ♦ **AOFCD** Asian-Oceanian Federation of Conservative Dentistry (#01578)
- ♦ AOFD – African Organization for Freedom and Democracy (no recent information)
- ♦ AOF i Norden / see Nordic Organization of Workers' Educational Associations (#17377)
- ♦ **AOFNMB** Asia and Oceania Federation of Nuclear Medicine and Biology (#01795)
- ♦ **AOFOG** Asia & Oceania Federation of Obstetrics and Gynaecology (#01796)

♦ AO Foundation 00866

CEO Clavadelerstr 8, 7270 Davos GR, Switzerland. T. +41814142801. Fax +41814142280. E-mail: info@aofoundation.org – foundation@aofoundation.org.
URL: http://www.aofoundation.org/

History 1958, Biel (Switzerland). Founded by 13 surgeons. Charter signed, 1984. Former names and other names: *Arbeitsgemeinschaft für Osteosynthesefragen* – former; *Association for the Study of Internal Fixation* – former. Registration: Switzerland. **Aims** Promote excellence in patient care and outcomes in *trauma* and *musculoskeletal disorders*. **Structure** Assembly of Trustees; Board; Executive Committee; Ethics and Compliance Committee. Institutes; Clinical Divisions; Clinical Unit; Business Partners. Groups (5): *AO Trauma International (AO Trauma, #00869); AO Spine (#00868); AO CMF (#00865); AO VET (#00870); AO Recon (#00867).* **Activities** Events/meetings; research/documentation; training/education. **Events** *FACE AHEAD – Young Surgeons CMF Summit* Barcelona (Spain) 2022, *FACE AHEAD – Young Surgeons CMF Summit* Barcelona (Spain) 2021, *FACE AHEAD – Young Surgeons CMF Summit* Barcelona (Spain) 2020, *World Meeting* Madrid (Spain) 2019, *Trauma Symposium* Seoul (Korea Rep) 2017. **Publications** *CMF Trauma and Reconstruction Journal* (4 a year); *AOTK Innovations News* (annual) – Magazine; *Global Spine Journal* (8 a year). Medical books; course materials and presentations. **Members** Surgeons and operating room personnel (over 18,000). Network of over 385,000 health care professionals in 124 countries. Membership countries not specified. **NGO Relations** Supports (1): *AO Alliance (#00864).* Instrumental in setting up (1): *Global Neuro (#10505).* Associate Scientific member of: *International Combined Orthopaedic Research Societies (I-CORS, #12657).* [2021/XF6685/f/**F**]

- ♦ **AOFS** Asia-Oceania Federation of Sexology (#01798)
- ♦ **AOFS** Asociación de Odontólogos Forenses de Sudamérica (#02283)
- ♦ **AOGEOSS** Asia-Oceania GEOSS (#01800)
- ♦ **AOGIN** Asia-Oceania Research Organization in Genital Infection and Neoplasia (#01805)
- ♦ AOGS – Asian-Oceanic Glaucoma Society (inactive)
- ♦ **AOGS** Asia Oceania Geosciences Society (#01799)
- ♦ AoG World Ministries – Assemblies of God World Ministry (see: #10110)
- ♦ AOHE – Association of European Horticultural Breeders (no recent information)
- ♦ **AOHR** Arab Organization for Human Rights (#01020)
- ♦ **AOHUPO** Asia Oceania Human Proteome Organization (#01801)
- ♦ AOI / see Associazione delle organizzazioni italiane di cooperazione e solidarietà internazionale
- ♦ AOIA – Asian Oral Implant Academy (inactive)
- ♦ **AOI** Academia Ophthalmologica Internationalis (#00017)
- ♦ AOI – Aide odontologique internationale (internationally oriented national body)
- ♦ AOI – Associazione delle organizzazioni italiane di cooperazione e solidarietà internazionale (internationally oriented national body)
- ♦ AOIFE – Association of Institutions for Feminist Education and Research in Europe (inactive)
- ♦ AOI / see SOLIDAR (#19680)
- ♦ A-OKMCnet – Asia and Oceania Kangaroo Mother Care Network (unconfirmed)
- ♦ **AOLF** Association des orthopédistes de langue française (#02842)
- ♦ AOM / see International Association of Operative Millers
- ♦ **AOMA** Association des ombudsmans et médiateurs africains (#02838)
- ♦ **AOM** Asian Organization for Mycoplasmology (#01593)
- ♦ **AOM** Association des Ombudsmans de la Méditerranée (#02802)
- ♦ **AOMC** Asian and Oceanian Myology Centre (#01579)
- ♦ **AOMF** Association des ombudsmans et médiateurs de la Francophonie (#02839)
- ♦ **AOMG** ASEAN Oleochemical Manufacturers Group (#01216)
- ♦ AOMR – Arab Organization for Mineral Resources (inactive)
- ♦ **AOMS** Association des anciens de l'OMS (#02604)
- ♦ AONBP / see European Confederation of National Bakery and Confectionery Organizations (#06714)
- ♦ **AONSA** Asia-Oceania Neutron Scattering Association (#01803)
- ♦ **AONS** Asian Oncology Nursing Society (#01590)
- ♦ AOOS / see Asia-Oceania Association of Otolaryngology – Head and Neck Surgery Societies (#01792)
- ♦ AOPA – Asian Oceanic Pancreatic Association (unconfirmed)
- ♦ AOP – Action on Poverty (internationally oriented national body)
- ♦ AOPJ – Asociace Ochrôncz Zivotniho Prostedi pro Jadernou Energii (internationally oriented national body)
- ♦ AOPTS / see Asian-Pacific Postal College (#01624)
- ♦ AOPU / see Asian-Pacific Postal Union (#01625)
- ♦ AORC – Association of Official Racing Chemists (unconfirmed)

♦ AO Recon 00867

Manager Clavadelerstrasse 8, 7270 Davos-Platz, Switzerland.
URL: https://aorecon.aofoundation.org/

History 2014. A specialty of *AO Foundation (#00866).* **Aims** Disseminate arthroplasty knowledge globally to empower orthopedic surgeons around the world to provide best patient care. **Structure** Steering Board. **Activities** Research and development; training/education. [2021/AA2264/**E**]

- ♦ **AORTIC** African Organization for Research and Training in Cancer (#00405)
- ♦ **AOSA** Aspect-Oriented Software Association (#02308)
- ♦ AOS – Apostleship of the Sea – Stella Maris (religious order)
- ♦ **AOS** Arab Orthodontic Society (#01022)
- ♦ **AOS** Asian Oncology Society (#01591)
- ♦ **AOSBS** Asian-Oceanian Skull Base Society (#01581)
- ♦ **AOSCA** Association of Official Seed Certifying Agencies (#02837)
- ♦ **AOSCE** Asia and Oceania Society for Comparative Endocrinology (#01806)
- ♦ AOSDAC – Asia Oceania Soap and Detergent Association Conference (meeting series)
- ♦ AOSD – Arab Organization for Social Defence Against Crime (inactive)
- ♦ AOSD – Asia-Oceania Steel Drum Manufacturers (no recent information)
- ♦ **AOSEF** Asian and Oceanian Stock Exchanges Federation (#01585)
- ♦ AOSF – Asian O-Sport Federation (unconfirmed)
- ♦ **AOSIS** Alliance of Small Island States (#00721)
- ♦ AOSIVA – Asian and Oceanic Society for Intravenous Anaesthesia (no recent information)
- ♦ **AOSNHNR** Asian and Oceanian Society of Neuroradiology and Head and Neck Radiology (#01582)
- ♦ **AOSP** Asia and Oceania Society for Photobiology (#01807)

♦ AO Spine 00868

Dir Clavadelerstrasse 8, 7270 Davos GR, Switzerland. T. +41442002425. E-mail: info@aospine.org.
URL: https://aospine.aofoundation.org/

History Jun 2003. Evolved from an *AO Speciality Board for Spine Surgery*, 2000, within *AO Foundation (#00866).* Former names and other names: *AO Spine International* – former. **Aims** Create, disseminate and exchange knowledge to promote excellence in patient care and outcomes. **Structure** International Board; Global Commissions; Regional Boards (5); Country Councils. **Activities** Events/meetings; knowledge management/information dissemination; networking/liaising; publishing activities; research/documentation; standards/guidelines; training/education. **Events** *Global Spine Congress* Las Vegas, NV (USA) 2022, *Global Spine Congress* Paris (France) 2021, *Global Spine Congress* Rio de Janeiro (Brazil) 2020, *Global Spine Congress* Toronto, ON (Canada) 2019, *Global Spine Congress* Singapore (Singapore) 2018. **Publications** *Global Spine Journal* – open access and peer-reviewed journal. **Members** Individuals (about 6,000) surgeons, researchers, allied spine professionals. Membership countries not specified. [2022.05.04/XM0586/**E**]

♦ AO Spine International / see AO Spine (#00868)
♦ **AOSPR** Asian and Oceanic Society for Pediatric Radiology (#01587)
♦ AOSPRM / see Asia Oceanian Society of Physical and Rehabilitation Medicine (#01804)
♦ **AOSPRM** Asia Oceanian Society of Physical and Rehabilitation Medicine (#01804)
♦ AOSRA / see Asian and Oceanic Society of Regional Anaesthesia and Pain Medicine (#01588)
♦ **AOSRA-PM** Asian and Oceanic Society of Regional Anaesthesia and Pain Medicine (#01588)
♦ **AOSR** Asian Oceanian Society of Radiology (#01583)
♦ **AOSSG** Asian-Oceanian Standard-Setters Group (#01584)
♦ **AOSTI** African Observatory of Science, Technology and Innovation (#00401)
♦ **AOSWA** Asia Oceania Space Weather Alliance (#01808)
♦ **AOTA** Asia and Oceania Thyroid Association (#01810)
♦ AOTA – Association oecuménique des théologiens africains (no recent information)
♦ **AOTCA** Asia-Oceania Tax Consultants' Association (#01809)
♦ Aotearoa New Zealand International Development Studies Network (internationally oriented national body)
♦ **AO Trauma** AO Trauma International (#00869)

♦ AO Trauma International (AO Trauma) 00869

Exec Dir Clavadelerstr 8, 7270 Davos-Platz, Switzerland. T. +41814142111. Fax +41814142280. E-mail: info@aotrauma.org.
URL: https://aotrauma.aofoundation.org/

History 2008. A group within *AO Foundation (#00866).* **Aims** Promote excellence in patient care and outcomes in trauma and musculoskeletal disorders. **Structure** International Board; Regional Boards; Global Commissions. Regions (5): Asia Pacific (TAP); Europe and Southern Africa (TESA); Latin America (TLA); Middle East and Northern Africa (TMENA); North America (TNA). **Activities** Research and development; training/education. [2022/AA2261/**E**]

♦ AOTS / see Association for Overseas Technical Cooperation and Sustainable Partnerships
♦ AOTS – Association for Overseas Technical Cooperation and Sustainable Partnerships (internationally oriented national body)
♦ AOU – Arab Open University (internationally oriented national body)
♦ AOVET / see AO VET (#00870)

♦ AO VET 00870

Dir Clavadelerstr 8, 7270 Davos-Platz, Switzerland. T. +41814142111. Fax +41814142280. E-mail: info@aovet.org.
URL: https://aovet.aofoundation.org/

History 1969. Recognized as a specialty area of *AO Foundation (#00866)*, 2007. Former names and other names: *AOVET* – alias. **Aims** Advance the practice of veterinary surgery to improve patient outcomes. **Structure** International Board; Regional Boards (Asia Pacific; European; Latin American; North American); Commissions. **Activities** Research and development; training/education. [2021/AA2263/**E**]

♦ AOYE – Arab Office for Youth and Environment (internationally oriented national body)
♦ AP6 / see Asia-Pacific Partnership for Clean Development and Climate (#01990)
♦ **APAAACI** Asia Pacific Association of Allergy, Asthma and Clinical Immunology (#01831)
♦ APAA / see ASEAN Ports Association (#01223)
♦ **APAA** Asian Patent Attorneys Association (#01655)
♦ APAA – Associacija Pisatelej Azii i Afriki (inactive)
♦ **APAA** Association pan-américaine d'aérobiologie (#18078)
♦ APAACI / see Asia Pacific Association of Allergy, Asthma and Clinical Immunology (#01831)
♦ **APA** African Potato Association (#00421)
♦ **APA** Arab Publishers' Association (#01032)
♦ **APAARI** Asia-Pacific Association of Agricultural Research Institutions (#01830)
♦ **APA** Aromatics Producers' Association (#01113)
♦ **APAAS** Asia Pacific Anti-Aging Society (#01827)
♦ **APA** ASEAN Ports Association (#01223)
♦ **APA** Asian and Oceanian Photochemistry Association (#01580)
♦ **APA** Asian Palaeolithic Association (#01650)
♦ **APA** Asian Parliamentary Assembly (#01653)
♦ **APA** Asian Population Association (#01670)
♦ **APA** Asia Pacific Alliance for Sexual and Reproductive Health and Rights (#01825)
♦ **APA** Asociación Panamericana de Atletismo (#02284)
♦ **APA** Association pan-africaine d'anthropologie (#18036)
♦ **APA** Association of Panamerican Athletics (#02284)
♦ APA – Association pénitentiaire africaine (no recent information)
♦ APA – Association des psychiatres en Afrique (inactive)
♦ APA – Association of Psychiatrists in Africa (inactive)
♦ APA – Australasian Pool Association (no recent information)
♦ **APAB** Asian-Pacific Association for Biomechanics (#01595)
♦ APABE – Asociación Panamericana de Bioética (no recent information)
♦ APABIS – Asia Pacific Academy of Business in Society (inactive)
♦ **APABO** Asociación Pan Americana de Bancos de Ojos (#02285)
♦ **APAC** Abortion and Postabortion Care Consortium (#00007)
♦ APAC – African Population Advisory Council (inactive)
♦ **APACALL** Asia-Pacific Association for Computer-Assisted Language Learning (#01836)
♦ **APAC** Asia Pacific Accreditation Cooperation (#01816)
♦ APAC – Asia Pacific Activities Conference (unconfirmed)
♦ **APAC** Asia Pacific Alliance of Coaches (#01821)
♦ APAC – Asia Partnership Conference of Pharmaceutical Associations (unconfirmed)
♦ APAC – Association des professionnelles africaines de la communication (no recent information)
♦ **APACC** Asia Pacific Accreditation and Certification Commission (#01815)
♦ AP – Accession Partnership (inactive)
♦ **APACCM** Asia Pacific Association of Critical Care Medicine (#01838)
♦ **APACD** Asia-Pacific Association of Communication Directors (#01835)
♦ **APACE** Asia-Pacific Association of Chemical Ecologists (#01834)
♦ **APACI** Asia-Pacific Alliance for the Control of Influenza (#01822)
♦ APACL / see Asian-Pacific League for Freedom and Democracy (#01617)
♦ **APACM** Asian Pacific Association for Computational Mechanics (#01596)
♦ **APACMed** Asia Pacific Medical Technology Association (#01953)
♦ **APACPH** Asia-Pacific Academic Consortium for Public Health (#01811)
♦ **APACRS** Asia-Pacific Association of Cataract and Refractive Surgeons (#01833)
♦ APACS – Asian Pacific Academy of Cosmetic Surgery (no recent information)
♦ **APACS** Asia-Pacific Association of Catalysis Societies (#01832)
♦ **APACT** Asia Pacific Association for the Control of Tobacco (#01837)
♦ **A-PAD** Asia Pacific Alliance for Disaster Management (#01823)
♦ APAD – Asia Pacific Association of Derivatives (unconfirmed)
♦ **APAD** Association pour l'anthropologie du changement social et du développement (#02369)
♦ APAD – Euro-African Association for the Anthropology of Social Change and Development / see Association pour l'anthropologie du changement social et du développement (#02369)
♦ **APAEA** Asia-Pacific Applied Economics Association (#01828)
♦ APAEA – Asia-Pacific Association for Educational Assessment (no recent information)
♦ APAED – Association panafricaine des étudiants en droit (no recent information)
♦ **APAFRI** Asia-Pacific Association of Forestry Research Institutions (#01841)
♦ **AP** African Parks (#00411)
♦ **APAFS** Asia Pacific Association for Fiduciary Studies (#01840)
♦ APAFTI – Association panafricaine des femmes professionnelles des télécommunications et des Technologies de l'information (no recent information)
♦ APAG – Association pour l'Appel de Genève (internationally oriented national body)
♦ **APAGE** Asian Pacific Association of Gastroenterology (#01598)
♦ **APAGE** Asia Pacific Association for Gynecologic Endoscopy and Minimally Invasive Therapy (#01842)
♦ APAG / see European Oleochemicals and Allied Products Group (#08081)
♦ **APAG** European Oleochemicals and Allied Products Group (#08081)
♦ APAI – Association of Paroling Authorities International (internationally oriented national body)
♦ APAI – Associazione Patologie Autoimmuni Internazionale (internationally oriented national body)
♦ APA/ICPD / see Asia Pacific Alliance for Sexual and Reproductive Health and Rights (#01825)
♦ **APAiD** Asia Pacific Academy of Implant Dentistry (#01812)
♦ **APAIE** Asia-Pacific Association for International Education (#01844)
♦ **APAL** Asociación Psiquiatría de América Latina (#16363)
♦ **APALMS** Asian Pacific Association for Lasers in Medicine and Surgery (#01599)
♦ **APAM** Asia Pacific Academy of Materials (#01813)
♦ **APAME** Asia Pacific Association of Medical Journal Editors (#01846)
♦ **APAMEI** Asia-Pacific Association of Methodist-related Educational Institutions (#01848)
♦ **APAMI** Asian Pacific Association for Medical Informatics (#01600)
♦ **APAMT** Asia Pacific Association of Medical Toxicology (#01847)
♦ **APAN** Asia Pacific Adaptation Network (#01818)
♦ **APAN** Asia-Pacific Advanced Network (#01819)
♦ **APANF** Association des pédiatres d'Afrique noire francophone (#02854)
♦ **APAO** Asia-Pacific Academy of Ophthalmology (#01814)
♦ **APAO** Asociación Panibérica de Academias Olimpica (#18181)
♦ APAPA – Asia Pacific Alcohol Policy Alliance (internationally oriented national body)
♦ **APAPARI** Asia Pacific Association of Pediatric Allergy, Respirology and Immunology (#01849)
♦ APA – A Partnership with Africa (internationally oriented national body)
♦ **APAP** Asia-Pacific Association of Psychotherapists (#01852)
♦ **APA-PHS** Asia-Pacific Association On Problem-based Learning In Health Sciences (#01851)
♦ **APAPU** Asia Pacific Association of Pediatric Urologists (#01850)
♦ **APAQG** Asia Pacific Aerospace Quality Group (#01820)
♦ APARA – Asia Pacific Assistive Robotics Association (internationally oriented national body)
♦ A/PARC / see Walter H Shorenstein Asia-Pacific Research Center
♦ APARC – Asia-Pacific Association for Respiratory Care (inactive)
♦ **APARDO** Asia Pacific Alliance for Rare Disease Organisations (#01824)
♦ **APARS** Asia Pacific Association of Robotic Surgeons (#01853)
♦ **A-PART** International Association of Private Assisted Reproductive Technology Clinics and Laboratories (#12100)
♦ **APAS** Asia-Pacific Arthroplasty Society (#01829)
♦ **APAS** Asociación Panamericana de Surf (#18135)
♦ **APASL** Asian Pacific Association for the Study of the Liver (#01602)
♦ APASP – Asia Pacific Association of Societies of Pathologists (no recent information)
♦ APAST – Association africaine pour l'avancement des sciences et technique (no recent information)
♦ **APASTB** Asia Pacific Association of Surgical Tissue Banking (#01854)
♦ **APASWE** Asian and Pacific Association for Social Work Education (#01601)
♦ APATAP – Asia Pacific Association of Threat Assessment Professionals (internationally oriented national body)
♦ APATAS – Asia Pacific Association of Technology and Society (unconfirmed)
♦ **APATCC** Asia-Pacific Association of Theoretical & Computational Chemists (#01855)
♦ **APAY** Asia and Pacific Alliance of YMCAs (#01826)
♦ APBA – African Plant Breeders Association (unconfirmed)
♦ **A-PBA** Asia Pacific Biosafety Association (#01859)
♦ **APBA** Asia Pacific Burn Association (#01864)
♦ APBA – Asia-Pacific Business Association (no recent information)
♦ APBC – Australasian Plant Breeding Conference (meeting series)
♦ **APBDA** Asia and Pacific Band Directors' Association (#01856)
♦ **APBF** Asia Pacific Baptist Federation (#01857)
♦ **APBF** Asia Pacific Bridge Federation (#01862)
♦ **APBioNet** Asia Pacific Bioinformatics Network (#01858)
♦ **APBMT** Asia Pacific Blood and Marrow Transplantation Group (#01860)
♦ **APBN** Asia Pacific Blood Network (#01861)
♦ APBP – Asociación Panamericana de Bolsas de Productos (no recent information)
♦ **APBREBES** Association for Plant Breeding for the Benefit of Society (#02861)
♦ APBSEA – Asia-Pacific Biomedical Science Educators Association (unconfirmed)
♦ APBSG / see Asia-Pacific Metabolic & Bariatric Surgery Society (#01956)
♦ **APBSLG** Asia Pacific Business School Librarians' Group (#01865)
♦ **APBU** Asian Pocket Billiards Union (#01668)
♦ APBY – Asia Pacific Baptist Youth (unconfirmed)
♦ APCA / see Asian Professional Counselling and Psychology Association
♦ **APCA** African Palliative Care Association (#00409)
♦ **APCA** Asia Pacific Craniofacial Association (#01878)
♦ APCA – Association des palais de congrès africains (inactive)
♦ APCAEM / see Centre for Sustainable Agricultural Mechanization (#03789)
♦ **APC** African Paralympic Committee (#00410)
♦ APC – Agreement on Minimum Requirements for the Issue and Validity of Driving Permits (1975 treaty)
♦ **APC** Arab Potash Company (#01029)
♦ **APCAS** Asia and Pacific Commission on Agricultural Statistics (#01873)
♦ APC / see Asian Paralympic Committee (#01652)
♦ **APC** Asian Paralympic Committee (#01652)
♦ **APC** Asian Peasant Coalition (#01658)
♦ **APCASO** Asia-Pacific Council of AIDS Service Organizations (#01875)
♦ **APC** Association for Progressive Communications (#02873)
♦ **APCB** Association de pilotage des conférences B (#12328)
♦ **APCCA** Asian and Pacific Conference of Correctional Administrators (#01606)
♦ APCCAL – Asia Pacific Contact Centre Association Leaders (unconfirmed)
♦ APCC – APEC Climate Center (internationally oriented national body)
♦ **APCCC** Africa Partnership on Climate Change Coalition (#00509)
♦ APCCC – Asia Pacific Corrosion Control Conference (meeting series)
♦ **APCChE** Asian Pacific Confederation of Chemical Engineering (#01605)
♦ APCC / see International Coconut Community (#12628)
♦ APC-Colombia – Colombian Presidential Agency of International Cooperation (internationally oriented national body)
♦ APCCRPR – Asia-Pacific Centre for Complex Real Property Rights (internationally oriented national body)
♦ APCD – Asia-Pacific College of Diplomacy (internationally oriented national body)
♦ APCDF – Asia Pacific Chiropractic Doctors' Federation (inactive)
♦ **APCD Foundation** Foundation of Asia-Pacific Development Centre on Disability (#09941)
♦ APCDM – Asia Pacific Conference on Disaster Medicine (meeting series)
♦ **APCEA** Asia-Pacific Centre for Environmental Accountability (#01867)
♦ **APCEA** Association parlementaire pour la coopération euro-arabe (#18217)
♦ APCEAS – Asia-Pacific Conference on Engineering Applied Sciences (meeting series)
♦ APCEIU – Asia-Pacific Centre of Education for International Understanding (internationally oriented national body)

♦ APCEL – Asia-Pacific Centre for Environmental Law, Singapore (internationally oriented national body)
♦ APCELSQ / see Asia Pacific Centre for Leadership and Change
♦ **APCEO** Asia-Pacific CEO Association (#01870)
♦ **APCERT** Asia Pacific Computer Emergency Response Team (#01874)
♦ APCG – African Politics Conference Group (internationally oriented national body)
♦ APCG – Australasian Personal Construct Group (internationally oriented national body)
♦ **APCHT** Asociación Panamericana y Caribeña de Hipnosis Terapéutica (#02286)
♦ **APCICT** Asian and Pacific Training Centre for Information and Communication Technology for Development (#01645)
♦ APCIMS-EASD (inactive)
♦ APCIO – Asia-Pacific Society of Interventional Oncology (unconfirmed)
♦ APCLA – Asia Pacific Corpus Linguistics Association (unconfirmed)
♦ APCLC – Asia Pacific Centre for Leadership and Change (internationally oriented national body)
♦ APCMB – Asia-Pacific Conference on Management and Business (meeting series)
♦ **APCNS** Asia Pacific Clinical Nutrition Society (#01871)
♦ APCO – Asian Parasite Control Organization (inactive)
♦ **APCO** Asia Pacific Council of Optometry (#01876)
♦ APCOC – Asia Pacific Council on Contraception (inactive)
♦ APCOE – Alliance of Popular Composer Organisations in Europe (inactive)
♦ **APCOF** African Policing Civilian Oversight Forum (#00419)
♦ **APCOM** Asia Pacific Coalition on Male Sexual Health (#01872)
♦ **APCosPA** Asia Pacific Organization for Cosmology and Particle Astrophysics (#01985)
♦ APCPA – Asian Professional Counselling and Psychology Association (internationally oriented national body)
♦ **APCP** Association pan-africaine de coopération portuaire (#18038)
♦ APCPC – Asian-Pacific Christian Peace Conference (no recent information)
♦ **AP-CPLP** Assembleia Parlamentar da Comunidade dos Países de Língua Portuguesa (#02315)
♦ APCPZ – Asian-Pacific Congress for Parasitic Zoonoses (meeting series)
♦ APCRA – Asian-Pacific Cardiothoracic-Renal Association (no recent information)
♦ APCRF / see Corporate Registers Forum (#04841)
♦ APCRSHR – Asia Pacific Conference on Reproductive and Sexual Health and Rights (meeting series)
♦ **APCS** African Parliament of Civil Society (#18207)
♦ APCS – Asia Pacific Cities Summit (meeting series)
♦ APCSC – Asia Pacific Customer Service Consortium (unconfirmed)
♦ APCSIP – Asia-Pacific Centre for Social Investment and and Philanthropy (internationally oriented national body)
♦ APCSS – Asia-Pacific Center for Security Studies (internationally oriented national body)
♦ APCTP – Asia-Pacific Centre for Theoretical Physics (internationally oriented national body)
♦ **APCTT** Asian and Pacific Centre for Transfer of Technology (#01603)
♦ APCV – Asia Pacific Conference on Vision (meeting series)
♦ APCWD – Asian and Pacific Centre for Women and Development (inactive)
♦ **APCWT** Asia-Pacific Centre for Women and Technology (#01869)
♦ APDA – Asian People's Disability Alliance (internationally oriented national body)
♦ APDA – Asian Population and Development Association (internationally oriented national body)
♦ APDA – Asia-Pacific Dairy Association (no recent information)
♦ **APDA** Asia Pacific Desalination Association (#01883)
♦ APDAC – Asian and Pacific Development Administration Centre (inactive)
♦ **APDBN** Asia-Pacific Developmental Biology Network (#01884)
♦ **APDC** Asian and Pacific Development Centre (#01608)
♦ APDC – Asia Pacific Design Centre (unconfirmed)
♦ APDEC – Asia Pacific Education Conference (meeting series)
♦ APDF – Africa Project Development Facility (inactive)
♦ **APDF-APRO** Asia Pacific Dental Federation/Asian Pacific Regional Organization of the Fédération Dentaire Internationale (#01882)
♦ APDF / see Asia Pacific Dental Federation/Asian Pacific Regional Organization of the Fédération Dentaire Internationale (#01882)
♦ **APDF** Asia-Pacific Disability Forum (#01885)
♦ APD – Fondation Damien – Mouvement de lutte contre la lèpre (internationally oriented national body)
♦ APDH / see Asociación pro Derechos Humanos
♦ APDHAC – Association pour la promotion des droits de l'homme en Afrique centrale (internationally oriented national body)
♦ APDIA – Asia-Pacific Dental Industry Association (no recent information)
♦ APDI – Asian and Pacific Development Institute (inactive)
♦ APDIC – Alloy Phase Diagram International Commission (unconfirmed)
♦ APDMHN – Asia Pacific Disaster Mental Health Network (unconfirmed)
♦ APDRA – Association pisciculture et développement rural en Afrique tropicale humide (internationally oriented national body)
♦ APDRC – Asia Pacific Disaster Resilience Centre (internationally oriented national body)
♦ **APDSA** Asian Pacific Dental Students Association (#01607)
♦ **APDSC** Asia Pacific Deaf Sports Confederation (#01880)
♦ APDSF / see Asia Pacific Federation of Down Syndrome (#01898)
♦ **APDSF** Asia Pacific Federation of Down Syndrome (#01898)
♦ **APDU** Asia Pacific Democrat Union (#01881)
♦ APDW / see Aktion Eine Welt
♦ **APDWF** Asian Pacific Digestive Week Federation (#01609)
♦ APEA – Arab Private Equity Association (unconfirmed)
♦ **APEA** Asia-Pacific Economic Association (#01886)
♦ **APEA** Asia-Pacific Evaluation Association (#01894)
♦ APEA – Association des producteurs européens d'azote (inactive)
♦ **APE** Accord partiel élargi sur les Itinéraires culturels (#05486)
♦ **APEAEN** Asia Pacific Association of Educators in Agriculture and Environment (#01839)
♦ **APEAL** Association professionelle des producteurs européens d'aciers pour emballage (#06167)

♦ Ape Alliance 00871

Alliance de singe

Coordinator 30 Landsdown, Stroud, GL5 1BG, UK. E-mail: coordinator@4apes.com – katy@4apes.com.
URL: http://www.4apes.com/

History 1996. **Aims** Provide a forum for discussion of issues relating to apes. **Finance** Members' dues. Grants from: *Born Free Foundation*. **Activities** Advocacy/lobbying/activism; publishing activities; projects/programmes; knowledge management/information dissemination. **Publications** Position papers.
Members Corresponding; contributing; supporting. National and international organizations in 13 countries:
Australia, Cameroon, Congo DR, France, Gambia, Germany, Indonesia, Nigeria, Sierra Leone, Switzerland, Uganda, UK, USA.
Included in the above, 12 organizations listed in this Yearbook:
Born Free Foundation; Dian Fossey Gorilla Fund International; Humane Society International (HSI, #10966); International Fund for Animal Welfare (IFAW, #13693); International Primate Protection League (IPPL, #14641); Jane Goodall Institute (JGI, #16089); Mountain Gorilla and Rainforest Direct Aid (BRD); Orangutan Foundation International (OFI, #17784); Pan African Sanctuary Alliance (PASA, #18064); Primate Conservation (PCI, no recent information); Rettet den Regenwald (RdR); World Animal Protection (#21092).
NGO Relations *Great Apes Survival Project (GRASP, #10699).* [2019/XF6800/y/**F**]

♦ APE / see Aqua Publica Europea (#00887)
♦ **APE** Aqua Publica Europea (#00887)
♦ **APEAR** Asia Pacific Employee Assistance Roundtable (#01891)
♦ APE – Artists Project Earth (internationally oriented national body)
♦ APE – Association parlementaire européenne (internationally oriented national body)
♦ APECA / see Association of Psychological and Educational Counsellors of Asia (#02878)
♦ **APEC** Asian Pacific Endodontic Confederation (#01610)
♦ **APEC** Asia-Pacific Economic Cooperation (#01887)
♦ APEC – Association of Private European Cable Operators (inactive)
♦ APECC – Asia Pacific Exhibition and Convention Council (inactive)
♦ APEC Centre for Technology Foresight (internationally oriented national body)
♦ APEC Climate Center (internationally oriented national body)
♦ APECCO – Association européenne des promoteurs de centres commerciaux (inactive)
♦ APEC EINet / see Asia Pacific Emerging Infections Network (#01890)
♦ APEC Emerging Infections Network / see Asia Pacific Emerging Infections Network (#01890)

♦ APEC Port Services Network (APSN) 00872

Secretariat No 8 Xitucheng Road, Haidian District, 100088 Beijing, China. T. +861065290569. Fax +861065290554. E-mail: info@apecpsn.org.
URL: http://www.apecpsn.org/

History 28 Jan 2008, Beijing (China), following recommendations made by Chinese President Hu Jintao, Nov 2006, during 14th *Asia-Pacific Economic Cooperation (APEC, #01887)* Economic Leaders Summit. Also referred to as *Asia-Pacific Economic Cooperation Port Services Network (APSN)*. Constitution adopted 17 Apr 2008, Manila (Philippines) and entered into force 18 May 2008. **Aims** Promote liberalization and facilitation of trade and investment; enhance supply chain security. **Structure** Council; Advisory Board. **Languages** English. **Activities** Networking/liaising; capacity building; knowledge management/information dissemination. **Events** *Meeting* Cusco (Peru) 2019, *Meeting* Singapore (Singapore) 2018, *Meeting* Singapore (Singapore) 2018, *Workshop* Singapore (Singapore) 2018. **Publications** *APSN Newsletter*; *The Apec Port Development Report*. **Information Services** *APSN Port database*. **Members** Corporate; Associate. Members from port, shipping, logistics, trade, finance and other related industries in the APEC region. Membership countries not specified. [2019.02.17/XM3940/**E**]

♦ **APECSA** Association of Pathologists of East, Central and Southern Africa (#02853)
♦ **APECS** Association of Polar Early Career Scientists (#02864)

♦ APEC SME Innovation Center (SMEIC) 00873

Main Office 430 Dongjin-ro, 6th floor, Jinj-si, Gyeongsan NORTH GYEONGSANG 52851, Korea Rep. T. +82557519734. Fax +82557519729.
URL: http://www.apec-smeic.org/

History Dec 2004. **Aims** Help APEC member economies exchange information on SME innovation; establish cooperative networks among APEC members for SME innovation. **Structure** Business Advisory Council; Secretariat. **Activities** Events/meetings; research/documentation; guidance/assistance/consulting. **Events** *Workshop on BCP with Crisis Management for SMEs* Jinju (Korea Rep) 2021. **IGO Relations** *Asia-Pacific Economic Cooperation (APEC, #01887).* **NGO Relations** Member of: *International Network for Small and Medium Sized Enterprises (INSME, #14325).* [2020/XM5531/**E**]

♦ APECTF – APEC Centre for Technology Foresight (internationally oriented national body)
♦ APEDAC – Action positive pour l'environnement et le développement en Afrique centrale (internationally oriented national body)
♦ APED – Arbeitsgemeinschaft Privater Entwicklungsdienste (internationally oriented national body)
♦ **APEDNN** Asia Pacific Emergency and Disaster Nursing Network (#01889)
♦ **APEE** Association for Paediatric Education in Europe (#02847)
♦ **APEF** Archives Portal Europe Foundation (#01090)
♦ APEF – Association des pays exportateurs de minerai de fer (inactive)
♦ APEFE – Association pour la promotion de l'éducation et de la formation à l'étranger (internationally oriented national body)
♦ APEG – Australasian Paediatric Endocrine Group (internationally oriented national body)
♦ APEID / see Asia-Pacific Programme of Educational Innovation for Development (#02001)
♦ **APEID** Asia-Pacific Programme of Educational Innovation for Development (#02001)
♦ **AP-EINet** Asia Pacific Emerging Infections Network (#01890)
♦ APEN – Asian Pacific Environmental Network (internationally oriented national body)
♦ **APEN** Australasia Pacific Extension Network (#03035)
♦ **APEOD** Asia-Pacific Environmental and Occupational Dermatology Group (#01892)
♦ **APEP** Association des producteurs européens de potasse (#02872)
♦ **APERA** Asia-Pacific Educational Research Association (#01888)
♦ **APERAU** Association pour la promotion de l'enseignement et de la recherche en aménagement et urbanisme (#02875)
♦ APERAU-Internationale / see Association pour la promotion de l'enseignement et de la recherche en aménagement et urbanisme (#02875)
♦ APERC – Asia-Pacific Energy Research Centre (internationally oriented national body)
♦ Apereo Foundation (unconfirmed)
♦ **APES** Accord partiel élargi sur le sport (#05487)
♦ **APES** Asian Pavement Engineering Society (#01656)
♦ APES – Asia Pacific Ecotourism Society (unconfirmed)
♦ **APES** Asia-Pacific EPR/ESR Society (#01893)
♦ **APET** Association for Public Economic Theory (#02881)
♦ **APETIT** Network of Asia-Pacific Education and Training Institutes in Tourism (#16994)
♦ APETNA – Asia Pacific Enterostomal Therapy Nurses Association (see: #21327)
♦ APEX / see Earth Economics
♦ **APEx** Association of Power Exchanges (#02866)
♦ APF / see Association internationale de la presse francophone
♦ **APFA** Asia Plasma and Fusion Association (#02080)
♦ APFA – Association des professeurs de français en Afrique (no recent information)
♦ APF – African Pastors' Fellowship (internationally oriented national body)
♦ **APF** African Philanthropy Forum (#00415)
♦ **APF** African Powerlifting Federation (#00422)
♦ **APF** Africa Partnership Forum (#00510)
♦ APF – Alliance pour la Préservation des Forêts (internationally oriented national body)
♦ APFAMA – Asia Pacific Federation of Aerospace Medicine Associations (unconfirmed)
♦ **APFAN** Asia Pacific Food Analysis Network (#01908)
♦ **APF** Anglican Pacifist Fellowship (#00830)
♦ **APFAO** Asia-Pacific Federation of Association Organizations (#01895)
♦ **APF** ASEAN Pediatric Federation (#01220)
♦ **APF** Asian Packaging Federation (#01648)
♦ **APF** Asian Pickleball Federation (#01665)
♦ **APF** Asian Powerlifting Federation (#01671)
♦ APF – Asia Pacific Forum for Graduate Students' Research in Tourism (meeting series)
♦ **APF** Asia Pacific Forum of National Human Rights Institutions (#01911)
♦ **APF** Asociación Panamericana de Fianzas (#18134)
♦ **APF** Assemblée parlementaire de la Francophonie (#02312)
♦ APFB – Asia-Pacific Conference on Few-Body Problems in Physics (meeting series)
♦ APF Canada – Asia Pacific Foundation of Canada (internationally oriented national body)
♦ **APFC** Asia-Pacific Forestry Commission (#01909)
♦ **APFC** Asia Pacific Franchise Confederation (#01913)
♦ APFCB / see Asia Pacific Federation for Clinical Biochemistry and Laboratory Medicine (#01896)
♦ **APFCB** Asia Pacific Federation for Clinical Biochemistry and Laboratory Medicine (#01896)
♦ APFCCN – Asia Pacific Federation of Critical Care Nurses (no recent information)
♦ **APFCP** Asia Pacific Federation of Coloproctology (#01897)
♦ APFE / see GlassFibreEurope (#10158)

♦ **APFEJ** Asia-Pacific Forum of Environmental Journalists (#01910)
♦ **APFG** Asia-Pacific Federation on Giftedness (#01899)
♦ **APFHRM** Asian Pacific Federation of Human Resource Management (#01611)
♦ **APFIC** Asia-Pacific Fishery Commission (#01907)
♦ APFID – Asia Pacific Foundation for Infectious Diseases (internationally oriented national body)
♦ **APFinSA** Asia Pacific Financial Services Association (#01906)
♦ **APFITA** Asia-Pacific Federation for Information Technology in Agriculture (#01900)
♦ **APFLS** Asia Pacific Federation of Logistics and SCM Systems (#01901)
♦ APFM – Arctic Pelvic Floor Meeting (meeting series)
♦ **APFMMA** Asia Pacific Free Methodist Missions Association (#01914)
♦ **APFNDT** Asia Pacific Federation for Non Destructive Testing (#01902)
♦ **APFNet** Asia-Pacific Network for Sustainable Forest Management and Rehabilitation (#01977)
♦ APFO – Africa Peace Forum (internationally oriented national body)
♦ APFOCC – Asian and Pacific Federation of Organizations for Cancer Research and Control (inactive)
♦ APFO / see Organization of the Families of Asia and the Pacific (#17867)
♦ **APFP** Asia Pacific Federation of Pharmacologists (#01903)
♦ **APFPM** Asia Pacific Federation of Project Management (#01904)
♦ **APFSHT** Asia Pacific Federation for Societies for Hand Therapy (#01905)
♦ **APFSRM** Asian Pacific Federation of Societies for Reconstructive Microsurgery (#01612)
♦ **APFSSH** Asian Pacific Federation of Societies for Surgery of the Hand (#01613)
♦ APFT – Asian-Pacific Federation of Thermology (no recent information)
♦ APFTC / see Asian Federation of Therapeutic Communities (#01476)
♦ **APFW** Arab Press Freedom Watch (#01030)
♦ **APG** Asia/Pacific Group on Money Laundering (#01921)
♦ **APGC** Asia Pacific Golf Confederation (#01918)
♦ APGCS – Asia-Pacific Gastroenterology Cancer Summit (meeting series)
♦ **APGDS** Association internationale des Praticiens de la méthode GDS (#02728)
♦ **APGF** Asia-Pacific Greens Federation (#01919)
♦ **APGGA** Asia Pacific General Galvanizing Association (#01915)
♦ **APGMV** Agence Panafricaine de la Grande Muraille Verte (#00547)
♦ **APGN** Asia Pacific Geoparks Network (#01916)
♦ APGN / see Asia-Pacific Greens Federation (#01919)
♦ **APGS** Asia-Pacific Glaucoma Society (#01917)
♦ APGTC – Asia-Pacific Gene Therapy Consortium (unconfirmed)
♦ APHA – Asia Pacific Heart Association (unconfirmed)
♦ Aphasia International / see Association internationale aphasie (#02668)
♦ Aphasia United (unconfirmed)
♦ APHCA / see Animal Production and Health Commission for Asia and the Pacific (#00839)
♦ **APHCA** Animal Production and Health Commission for Asia and the Pacific (#00839)
♦ **APHCON** Asia Pacific Hematology Consortium (#01925)
♦ APHD / see Caritas Asia (#03578)
♦ **APHEA** Agency for Public Health Education Accreditation (#00555)
♦ APHEDA / see Union Aid Abroad-APHEDA

♦ APHELEIA – Humanities International Association For Cultural Integrated Landscape Management 00874

Contact ITM – Museu, Lg Infante D Henrique, 6120-750 Mação, Portugal. T. +351249346363. E-mail: itm.macao@gmail.com.
URL: http://www.apheleiaproject.org

History Founded as a continuation of a project 'Apheleia – Cultural Integrated Landscape Management', which ran 2014-2017. Became an European organization, 2017 and an International Association, 2019. **Aims** Structure a convergent set of strategies based in the methodology of the Humanities that will foster the need for a properly Integrated Cultural Landscape Management human understandings. **Structure** General Assembly; Board. **Languages** English, French, Portuguese, Spanish. **Finance** Sources: members' dues. **Publications** *Arkeos* – in 2 vols. Books; reports; videos. **Members** Full; Correspondent; Honorary; Institutional; Observer. Membership countries not specified. **NGO Relations** Member of (1): *International Council for Philosophy and Human Sciences (CIPSH, #13061).* [2021.05.25/XM8678/**E**]

♦ APHEN – Association africaine des professionnels de l'hygiène et de l'environnement (inactive)
♦ **APHIA** Asia Pacific Histocompatibility and Immunogenetics Association (#01927)
♦ **APHN** Asia-Pacific Heart Network (#01923)
♦ **APHN** Asia Pacific Hospice Palliative Care Network (#01928)
♦ **APHoMSA** Asia-Pacific Heads of Maritime Safety Agencies (#01922)
♦ **A-PHPBA** Asian-Pacific Hepato-Pancreato-Biliary Association (#01616)
♦ APHRA – Arab Programme for Human Rights Activists (internationally oriented national body)
♦ **APHR** ASEAN Parliamentarians for Human Rights (#01219)
♦ **APHRC** African Population and Health Research Center (#00420)
♦ **APHRS** Asia Pacific Heart Rhythm Society (#01924)
♦ **APHS** Asia Pacific Hernia Society (#01926)
♦ **APHW** Asia Pacific Association of Hydrology and Water Resources (#01843)
♦ API / see AMECEA Pastoral Institute (#00771)
♦ **APIA** Asia and Pacific Internet Association (#01936)
♦ **APIA** Asociación Panamericana de Ingenieros Agrónomos (#02289)
♦ **API** Arab Planning Institute (#01027)
♦ **API** Asociación Panamericana de Infectologia (#02288)
♦ **API** Association de la presse internationale (#02868)
♦ APICA – Asia Pacific International Congress of Anatomists (meeting series)
♦ **APICA** Association pour la promotion des initiatives communautaires africaines (#02874)
♦ **APIC** Active Pharmaceutical Ingredients Committee (#00102)
♦ APIC – Agreement on the Privileges and Immunities of the International Criminal Court (2002 treaty)
♦ **APIC** Asian Paint Industry Council (#01649)
♦ APIC – Asia Petrochemical Industry Conference (meeting series)
♦ APIC – Association for Promotion of International Cooperation (internationally oriented national body)
♦ APIC-DENT – Asociación Panamericana de Industria y Comercio Dentales (inactive)
♦ **APICE** Asociación Panamericana de Instituciones de Crédito Educativo (#18084)
♦ APICE / see Pan American Association of Student Loan Institutions (#18084)
♦ **APICES** Association paléographique internationale – culture, écriture, société (#02848)
♦ **APICORP** Arab Petroleum Investments Corporation (#01026)

♦ ApiCOWplexa 00875

Address not obtained.
URL: http://www.apicowplexa.net/

History 2012. An informal network. **Aims** Bring together scientists, veterinarians, students and others that are interested in apicomplexan parasites causing disease in farm animals. **Activities** Events/meetings. **Events** *International Meeting on Apicomplexan Parasites in Farm Animals (ApiCOWplexa)* Berlin (Germany) 2019, *International Meeting on Apicomplexan Parasites in Farm Animals (ApiCOWplexa)* Madrid (Spain) 2017, *International Meeting on Apicomplexan Parasites in Farm Animals (ApiCOWplexa)* Edinburgh (UK) 2015, *International Meeting on Apicomplexan Parasites in Farm Animals (ApiCOWplexa)* Kusadasi (Turkey) 2013, *International Meeting on Apicomplexan Parasites in Farm Animals (ApiCOWplexa)* Lisbon (Portugal) 2012. [2019/AA0752/v/**F**]

♦ **APICSA** Asociación Psicológica Iberoamericana de Clinica y Salud (#02295)
♦ APIDD – Asia Pacific Institute for Democratization and Development (internationally oriented national body)
♦ APIDEP – Association protestante internationale de prêt (inactive)
♦ **APIEMS** Asia Pacific Industrial Engineering and Management Society (#01930)
♦ APIFIS – Asian and Pacific International Fluid Inclusion Society (no recent information)
♦ **API/Gaba** AMECEA Pastoral Institute (#00771)
♦ APIIA / see Asia-Pacific Association of Cataract and Refractive Surgeons (#01833)
♦ **APIL** Association of Pacific Island Legislatures (#02844)
♦ **APIMED** Association internationale des producteurs indépendants de la méditerranée (#02731)
♦ Apimondia Foundation / see Fundatia Institutul International de Tehnologie si Economie Apicola
♦ **APIMONDIA** International Federation of Beekeepers' Associations (#13370)
♦ Apimondia International Institute of Beekeeping Technology and Economy / see Fundatia Institutul International de Tehnologie si Economie Apicola
♦ APIMTIMA / see Pacific Islands Maritime Association (#17974)
♦ **APIN** Asia Pacific Information Network (#01931)
♦ **AP-IN** Asia Pacific Innovation Network (#01933)
♦ APINMAP – Asian-Pacific Information Network on Medicinal and Aromatic Plants (no recent information)
♦ APIPA – Asian Pediatric Interventional Pulmonology Association (unconfirmed)
♦ **APIPNM** Asia Pacific Network on Integrated Plant Nutrient Management (#01969)
♦ **APIRAS** Asia-Pacific Islands Rural Advisory Services Network (#01937)
♦ **APISA** Asian Political and International Studies Association (#01669)
♦ **APIS** Asia-Pacific Implant Society (#01929)
♦ APISAT – Asia-Pacific International Symposium on Aerospace Technology (meeting series)
♦ **Apislavia** Federacia Vcelarskych Organizacii (#09287)
♦ APISWA – Asia Pacific International Spirits and Wines Alliance (unconfirmed)
♦ APITA – Asian Pancreas and Islet Transplant Association (unconfirmed)

♦ ApiTrade Africa 00876

Sec/CEO Plot 2117, Ntinda Town, Velocity Mansions, 2nd Floor, PO Box 23441, Kampala, Uganda. T. +256414667845.
Chairperson address not obtained.
Twitter: https://twitter.com/apitradeafrica

History 2008, Uganda. Established following discussions initiated in 2005. A member based non-profit company. **Aims** Promote trade in African bee products by addressing market access constraints and coordinating marketing initiatives. **Structure** Board of Directors; Secretariat; Departments (3): Promotion & Publicity; Finance & Administration; Technical Services. **Activities** Events/meetings. **Events** *ApiExpo Africa* Addis Ababa (Ethiopia) 2021, *ApiExpo Africa* Abuja (Nigeria) 2018, *Conference* Addis Ababa (Ethiopia) 2012. **Publications** *African Honey Magazine* (periodical).
Members Core; Associate; Honorary. Members in 8 countries:
Belgium, Ethiopia, Kenya, Rwanda, Tanzania UR, Uganda, UK, Zambia.
NGO Relations Member of (1): *International Federation of Beekeepers' Associations (APIMONDIA, #13370).* [2021/XM4005/t/**D**]

♦ APIYN – Asia Pacific Indigenous Youth Network (unconfirmed)
♦ APJA – Asia Pacific Jurist Association (internationally oriented national body)
♦ APJC – Asia Pacific Journalism Centre (internationally oriented national body)
♦ **APJE** Association of Philosophy Journal Editors (#02858)
♦ **APJRF** Asia and Pacific Jump Rope Federation (#01938)
♦ **APJSA** Association of Principals of Jewish Schools of Australasia (#02870)
♦ APK – Amigos do Protocolo de Kyoto (internationally oriented national body)
♦ **APKASS** Asia-Pacific Knee, Arthroscopy and Sports Medicine Society (#01939)
♦ APKN – Africa Parliamentary Knowledge Network (inactive)
♦ APLA – Asia-Pacific Lawyers Association (no recent information)
♦ APLA / see Asia Pacific Lottery Association Limited (#01949)
♦ **APLA** Asia Pacific Lottery Association Limited (#01949)
♦ **APLA** Asociación Petroquimica y Quimica Latinoamericana (#02294)
♦ APLA – Association of Parliamentary Libraries of Australasia (internationally oriented national body)
♦ **APLAES** Association européenne de professeurs de langues anciennes de l'enseignement supérieur (#06260)
♦ **APLAP** Association of Parliamentary Librarians of Asia and the Pacific (#02851)
♦ **APLAR** Asia Pacific League of Associations for Rheumatology (#01945)
♦ Aplastic Anemia and MDS International Foundation (unconfirmed)
♦ APLE – Asociación de Palinólogos de Lengua Española (internationally oriented national body)
♦ **APLESA** Association of Parliamentary Libraries of Eastern and Southern Africa (#02852)
♦ **APLF** Asian-Pacific Logistics Federation (#01618)
♦ **APLF** Asia Pacific Leadership Forum on HIV/AIDS and Development (#01942)
♦ **APLF** Association des palynologues de langue française (#02849)
♦ **APLF** Association des pédiatres de langue française (#02855)
♦ APLF – Association des planétariums de langue française (internationally oriented national body)
♦ **APLFD** Asian-Pacific League for Freedom and Democracy (#01617)
♦ APLI – Asia Pacific Laser Institute (unconfirmed)
♦ APLIC / see Asia Pacific Financial Services Association (#01906)
♦ APLIC-I / see Association for Population / Family Planning Libraries and Information Centers – International
♦ APLIC International – Association for Population / Family Planning Libraries and Information Centers – International (internationally oriented national body)
♦ APLiN – ASEAN Public Libraries Information Network (unconfirmed)
♦ **APLL** Austronesian and Papuan Languages and Linguistics research group (#03039)
♦ **APLMA** Asia Pacific Leaders Malaria Alliance (#01944)
♦ **APLMA** Asia Pacific Loan Market Association (#01948)
♦ **APLMF** Asia-Pacific Legal Metrology Forum (#01947)
♦ **APLN** Asia-Pacific Leadership Network for Nuclear Non-Proliferation and Disarmament (#01943)
♦ APLN – ITUC Asia-Pacific Labour Network
♦ **APLS** Association for Politics and the Life Sciences (#02865)
♦ **APLU** Asia Pacific Lacrosse Union (#01941)
♦ **APMAA** Asia-Pacific Management Accounting Association (#01951)
♦ **APMA** Asia-Pacific Music Creators' Alliance (#01960)
♦ APM / see ASEAN Inter-Parliamentary Assembly (#01205)
♦ **APM** Assemblée parlementaire de la Méditerranée (#18212)
♦ APMA Worldwide / see Marketing Agencies Association Worldwide (#16585)
♦ **APMBSS** Asia-Pacific Metabolic & Bariatric Surgery Society (#01956)
♦ AP-MCSTA / see Asia-Pacific Space Cooperation Organization (#02051)
♦ APME / see Association of Plastics Manufacturers in Europe (#02862)
♦ APMEC – Asia Pacific Medical Education Conference (meeting series)
♦ APMEC – Asia Pacific Medical Education Network (unconfirmed)
♦ **APMEN** Asia Pacific Malaria Elimination Network (#01950)
♦ APMF / see Asia Marketing Federation (#01290)
♦ **APMF** Asia Pacific Mediation Forum (#01952)
♦ **APMF** Asia Pacific Menopause Federation (#01955)
♦ **APM International** Association pour les peuples menacés international (#19654)
♦ APM – International Conference on Automated People Movers (meeting series)
♦ **APM Internazionale** Associazione per i Popoli Minacciati Internazionale (#19654)
♦ **APMLA** Asia-Pacific Medico-Legal Association (#01954)
♦ APMM – Asia Pacific Mission for Migrants (internationally oriented national body)
♦ **APMM** Asociación de Poblaciones de Montaña del Mundo (#21658)
♦ **APMM** Association des populations des montagnes du monde (#21658)
♦ **APMM** Associazione delle Popolazioni delle Montagne del Mondo (#21658)

- ♦ APMMC – Asia Pacific Military Medicine Conference (meeting series)
- ♦ APMMF / see Asia Pacific Mission for Migrants
- ♦ **APMN** Asia Pacific Mountain Network (#01958)
- ♦ APMNF – Asian Conference on Plant-Microbe Symbiosis and Nitrogen Fixation (meeting series)
- ♦ **APMP** Asia Pacific Metrology Programme (#01957)
- ♦ **APMP** Association for the Philosophy of Mathematical Practice (#02859)
- ♦ **APMSTS** Asia Pacific Musculo Skeletal Tumour Society (#01959)
- ♦ APNAC – African Parliamentarians Network Against Corruption (see: #10518)
- ♦ **APN** Africa Philanthropy Network (#00512)
- ♦ APN – Americans for Peace Now (internationally oriented national body)
- ♦ **APNAN** Asia Pacific Natural Agriculture Network (#01962)
- ♦ **APN** Arab Group for the Protection of Nature (#00970)
- ♦ **APN** Arab Press Network (#01031)
- ♦ **APN** Asia-Pacific Network for Global Change Research (#01966)
- ♦ **APN+** Asia-Pacific Network of People Living with HIV/AIDS (#01973)
- ♦ APN – Asia Pacific Privatization Network (unconfirmed)
- ♦ **APN** Asia-Pacific Producers Network (#02000)
- ♦ **APN** Asociación Panamericana Nikkei (#02290)
- ♦ APN – Ayuda Popular Noruega (internationally oriented national body)
- ♦ Apne Aap International / see Apne Aap Women Worldwide
- ♦ Apne Aap Women Worldwide (internationally oriented national body)
- ♦ APNET – African Peace Network (internationally oriented national body)
- ♦ **APNET** African Publishers Network (#00426)
- ♦ **APNETS** Asia Pacific Neuroendocrine Tumour Society (#01979)
- ♦ **APNFS** Asia Pacific Network on Food Sovereignty (#01965)
- ♦ **APNG** Asia-Pacific Networking Group (#01968)
- ♦ **APNHAN** Asia-Pacific National Health Accounts Network (#01961)
- ♦ APNHE – Asia-Pacific Network for Holistic Education (unconfirmed)
- ♦ APNHI / see Asian Peace and History Education Association
- ♦ **APNHR** Asia-Pacific Network for Housing Research (#01967)
- ♦ **APNI** African Plant Nutrition Institute (#00418)
- ♦ APNIC – Asian-Pacific Network Information Centre (internationally oriented national body)
- ♦ **APNIEVE** Asia-Pacific Network for International Education and Values Education (#01970)
- ♦ **APNME** Asia-Pacific Network of Moral Education (#01971)
- ♦ APNMR – Asia Pacific NMR Symposium (meeting series)
- ♦ APNNA / see Asia Pacific Neural Network Society (#01978)
- ♦ **APNNO** Asia-Pacific Nutrigenomics and Nutrigenetics Organisation (#01980)
- ♦ **APNNS** Asia Pacific Neural Network Society (#01978)
- ♦ **APNOG** Asia Pacific Network Operators Group (#01972)
- ♦ APNOMS – Asia-Pacific Network Operation and Management Symposium (meeting series)
- ♦ **APNSW** Asia Pacific Network of Sex Workers (#01975)
- ♦ APNSWP / see Asia Pacific Network of Sex Workers (#01975)
- ♦ **APNU** Administration postale des Nations Unies (#20613)
- ♦ APOA / see Asia Pacific Orchid Conference Trust (#01984)
- ♦ **APOA** Asia Pacific Orthopaedic Association (#01987)
- ♦ **APO** African Press Organization (#00424)
- ♦ **APO** Asian Productivity Organization (#01674)
- ♦ APOC – African Programme for Onchocerciasis Control (no recent information)
- ♦ **APOC** Asia Pacific Orchid Conference Trust (#01984)
- ♦ **APOCB** Asian-Pacific Organization for Cell Biology (#01619)
- ♦ APOCP – Asian Pacific Organization for Cancer Prevention (internationally oriented national body)
- ♦ APodC – Australasian Podiatry Council (internationally oriented national body)
- ♦ **APOIS** Asia-Pacific Ocular Imaging Society (#01983)
- ♦ APOME – Association de Promotion de l'Organisation Mondiale de l'Environnement (unconfirmed)
- ♦ APOPO – Anti-Persoonsmijnen Ontmijnende Productontwikkeling (internationally oriented national body)
- ♦ APOR / see International Society for Pharmacoeconomics and Outcomes Research (#15354)
- ♦ **APORS** Association of Asian-Pacific Operational Research Societies within IFORS (#02381)
- ♦ **APOS** Asia Pacific Orthodontic Society (#01986)
- ♦ **APOSHO** Asia Pacific Occupational Safety and Health Organization (#01981)
- ♦ APOSSM / see Asia-Pacific Knee, Arthroscopy and Sports Medicine Society (#01939)
- ♦ Apostleship of Prayer (religious order)
- ♦ Apostleship of the Sea – Stella Maris (religious order)
- ♦ Apostles of the Sacred Heart (religious order)
- ♦ Apostolado del Mar (religious order)
- ♦ Apostolado Militar Internacional (religious order)
- ♦ Apostolado de la Oración (religious order)
- ♦ Apostolat des Meeres (religious order)
- ♦ Apostolat de la Mer (religious order)
- ♦ Apostolat Militaire International (religious order)
- ♦ Apostolat mondial de Fatima (religious order)
- ♦ Apostolato della Preghiera (religious order)
- ♦ Apostolat de la Prière (religious order)
- ♦ Apostolatus Maris (religious order)
- ♦ Apostolatus Orationis (religious order)
- ♦ Apostole del Sacro Cuore (religious order)
- ♦ Apostole del Sacro Cuore di Gesù (religious order)
- ♦ Apóstoles del Sagrado Corazón de Jesús (religious order)
- ♦ Apostolic and Lay Cooperative Action in Latin America (internationally oriented national body)
- ♦ Apostolic Union of Clergy / see International Confederation Apostolic Union of Clergy (#12844)
- ♦ Apostolic Union of Diocesan Presbyters / see International Confederation Apostolic Union of Clergy (#12844)
- ♦ Apostolic Union of Secular Presbyters / see International Confederation Apostolic Union of Clergy (#12844)
- ♦ Apostolic World Christian Fellowship (internationally oriented national body)
- ♦ **AP OTAN** Assemblée parlementaire de l'OTAN (#16946)
- ♦ APOT – Asia-Pacific Onboard Travel (unconfirmed)
- ♦ Apôtres du Sacré-Coeur de Jésus (religious order)
- ♦ **APOTRG** Asia Pacific Occupational Therapists Regional Group (#01982)
- ♦ APOTS – Asia-Pacific Ophthalmic Trauma Society (unconfirmed)
- ♦ APOYO / see Association for Heritage Preservation of the Americas
- ♦ APOYOnline – Association for Heritage Preservation of the Americas (internationally oriented national body)
- ♦ APPA / see APPA-Leadership in Educational Facilities
- ♦ APPA – Action for Peace through Prayer and Aid (internationally oriented national body)
- ♦ APPA / see African Petroleum Producers's Organization (#00414)
- ♦ **APPA** Arab Pediatric Pulmonology Association (#01024)
- ♦ **APPA** Asian and Pacific Parkinsons Association (#01620)
- ♦ **APPA** Asian Pacific Phycological Association (#01623)
- ♦ **APPA** Asian Pacific Publishers Association (#01627)
- ♦ APPA / see Asia Pacific Pediatric Association (#01992)
- ♦ **APPA** Asia Pacific Pediatric Association (#01992)
- ♦ **APPA** Asia Pacific Privacy Authorities (#01999)
- ♦ **APPA** Asia Pacific Protein Association (#02003)
- ♦ APPA-Leadership in Educational Facilities (internationally oriented national body)
- ♦ **APPAN** Asia-Pacific Performing Arts Network (#01994)
- ♦ APPAN – Asia Pacific Physical Activity Network (no recent information)
- ♦ **APP** Asian Producers' Platform (#01673)
- ♦ **APP** Asia Pacific Photoforum (#01996)
- ♦ **APP** Association of Pacific Ports (#02845)
- ♦ **APPAT** Asociación Panamericana de Profesionales de la Agrimensura y Topografia (#02291)
- ♦ **APPC** Arab Permanent Postal Commission (#01025)
- ♦ **APPC** Asian-Pacific Postal College (#01624)
- ♦ APPC – Asia-Pacific Productivity Conference (meeting series)
- ♦ APPC – Asociación Panamericana para la Conservación (internationally oriented national body)
- ♦ **APPCDC** Asia-Pacific Partnership for Clean Development and Climate (#01990)
- ♦ **APPCED** Asian-Pacific Parliamentarians' Conference on Environment and Development (#01621)
- ♦ APPCE – Du pain pour chaque enfant (internationally oriented national body)
- ♦ **APPCS** Asia Pacific Pediatric Cardiac Society (#01993)
- ♦ APPDA / see Asian and Pacific Parkinsons Association (#01620)
- ♦ **APPDE** Association of Physiotherapists in Parkinson's Disease Europe (#02860)
- ♦ **APPEAL** Asia-Pacific Programme of Education for All (#02002)
- ♦ **APPEC** Astroparticle Physics European Consortium (#02998)
- ♦ L'appel / see Appel aide aux enfants victimes de conflits
- ♦ Appel aide aux enfants victimes de conflits (internationally oriented national body)
- ♦ Appel aide aux enfants victimes de la guerre / see Appel aide aux enfants victimes de conflits
- ♦ Appel de Genève (internationally oriented national body)
- ♦ **APPEND** Asia-Pacific Philosophy Education Network for Democracy (#01995)
- ♦ APPE / see Petrochemicals Europe (#18342)
- ♦ **APPES** Asia Pacific Paediatric Endocrine Society (#01988)
- ♦ **APPF** Asia Pacific Parliamentary Forum (#01989)
- ♦ APPF – Association de la presse philatélique francophone (inactive)
- ♦ APPFI – Asia Pacific Pathways to Progress Foundation (internationally oriented national body)
- ♦ APPIA / see African Intellectual Property Organization (#00344)
- ♦ **APPIMAF** Association pour la protection de la propriété industrielle dans le monde arabe (#02877)
- ♦ APPITA / see Appita – Australia and New Zealand Pulp and Paper Industry Technical Association
- ♦ Appita – Australia and New Zealand Pulp and Paper Industry Technical Association (internationally oriented national body)
- ♦ **APPLE** Asia-Pacific Primary Liver Cancer Expert Association (#01998)

♦ APPLiA – Home Appliance Europe 00877

Dir Gen Bd Brand Whitlock 114, 1200 Brussels, Belgium. T. +3227387810. Fax +3224030841. E-mail: hello@applia-europe.eu.
URL: http://www.applia-europe.eu/

History 1959. Most recent statutes adopted Jul 2007. Former names and other names: *Conseil européen des constructeurs d'appareillage électro-domestique* – former; *Federation of European Domestic Appliance Manufacturers (CECED)* – former; *European Committee of Domestic Equipment Manufacturers* – former; *Conseil européen des constructeurs d'appareils domestiques (CECED)* – former; *Europäischer Verband der Hersteller von Hausgeräten* – former; *Consiglio Europeo dei Costruttori di Apparecchi Domestici* – former. Registration: No/ID: 0460.033.584, Start date: 22 Jan 1997, Belgium; EU Transparency Register, No/ID: 04201463642-88, Start date: 21 May 2010. **Aims** Represent and defend the interests of the European industry of domestic appliance manufacturers. **Structure** General Assembly (annual); Steering Committee. Task forces and working groups. National delegations (one per country). Permanent Secretariat in Brussels (Belgium). **Languages** English, French. **Staff** 10.00 FTE, paid. **Finance** Sources: members' dues. **Activities** Events/meetings; knowledge management/information dissemination; networking/liaising. **Events** *Conference on smart cities need smart consumers* Brussels (Belgium) 2010, *EUSEW : EU sustainable energy week* Brussels (Belgium) 2007, *General Assembly* Vienna (Austria) 2007, *Annual international appliance technical conference* Lexington, KY (USA) 2004. **Members** Direct (21); National Associations (25). Members in 24 countries. Membership countries not specified. **IGO Relations** Recognized by: *European Commission (EC, #06633)*. **NGO Relations** Partner organization: *European Committee for Electrotechnical Standardization (CENELEC, #06647)*. In liaison with technical committees of: *Comité européen de normalisation (CEN, #04162)*; *International Organization for Standardization (ISO, #14473)*. Member of: *Coalition for Energy Savings (#04056)*; *Energy Efficiency Industrial Forum (EEIF, #05470)*. [2020/XD3570/**D**]

- ♦ Application of Safeguards on Implementation of Article III 1 and 4 of the Treaty on the Non-proliferation of Nuclear Weapons (1973 treaty)

♦ Applications of Computer Algebra Working Group (ACA WG) 00878

Contact address not obtained. E-mail: eroanes@mat.ucm.es – wester@math.unm.edu – stanly@math.unm.edu.
URL: https://math.unm.edu/aca.html

History 1995. Conferences organized originally as *International Association for Mathematics and Computers in Simulation (IMACS, #12019)* – ACA. Since 1998 held under ACA alone. **Aims** Organize the Applications of Computer Algebra (ACA) activities. **Languages** English. **Staff** None paid. **Finance** Sources: donations; fees for services. **Activities** Events/meetings. **Events** *Conference* Warsaw (Poland) 2023, *Conference* Gebze (Turkey) 2022, *Conference* 2021, *Conference* Athens (Greece) 2020, *Conference* Montréal, QC (Canada) 2019. **Members** Individuals in 11 countries:
Austria, Bulgaria, Canada, Czechia, Germany, Greece, Israel, Japan, Russia, Spain, USA. [2022.11.07/XM8764/cv/**E**]

- ♦ Application of the Theory of Probability to Telecommunication Research, Engineering and Administration / see International Teletraffic Congress (#15674)

♦ Applied Computational Electromagnetics Society (ACES) 00879

Pres Colorado School of Mines, 1500 Illinois St, Golden CO 80401, USA. E-mail: newsletter@aces-society.org.
URL: http://aces-society.org/

History 1985, USA. **Aims** Advance the theory and practice of electrical and electronics engineering and allied arts and sciences. **Structure** Board of Directors; Executive Committee; Committees (13). **Languages** English. **Staff** 0.50 FTE, paid. **Finance** Members' dues. Conference surplus revenues; sale of publications. **Activities** Networking/liaising; knowledge management/information dissemination. **Events** *International Symposium* Monterey, CA (USA) 2023, *International Symposium* Xuzhou (China) 2022, *International Symposium* Miami, FL (USA) 2019, *International Symposium* Nanjing (China) 2019, *International Symposium* Beijing (China) 2018. **Publications** *ACES Express Journal* (12 a year); *ACES Journal* (12 a year); *ACES Newsletter* (4 a year). **Members** Full (954) in 44 countries and territories:
Algeria, Australia, Austria, Belgium, Brazil, Canada, China, Colombia, Croatia, Egypt, Finland, France, Germany, Greece, Hong Kong, Iceland, India, Indonesia, Iran Islamic Rep, Israel, Italy, Japan, Korea Rep, Kuwait, Malaysia, Mexico, Netherlands, Nigeria, Pakistan, Poland, Saudi Arabia, Serbia, Singapore, South Africa, Spain, Sweden, Taiwan, Thailand, Türkiye, UK, Ukraine, United Arab Emirates, USA, Vietnam.
International organizational members (9) in 8 countries and territories:
China, Germany, Hong Kong, Italy, Japan, Taiwan, UK, USA. [2022/XW0118/**D**]

- ♦ Applied Conflict Resolution Organizations Network / see Alliance for Peacebuilding
- ♦ Applied Diamond Conference (meeting series)

♦ Applied Health, Equity and Development Research Network (AHEAD Network) 00880

Réseau de Recherche Appliquée en Équité, Santé et Développement

Coordinator Aix-Marseille School of Economics, 5-9 boulevard Bourdet, CS 50498, 13205 Marseille CEDEX 1, France. E-mail: contactus.ahead@gmail.com.
URL: http://www.ahead-network.org/

History Founded 2015, as part of the SANTEMED project. Registered in accordance with French law. **Aims** Facilitate scientific exchange between researchers and help pool together existing knowledge on questions relating to health and development. **Structure** Steering Committee; Advisory Board. **Activities** Events/meetings. **Events** *The quest for universal health coverage in the Mediterranean developing countries* Casablanca (Morocco) 2018, *Symposium* Marseille (France) 2017, *Symposium* Marseille (France) 2016, *Symposium* Tunis (Tunisia) 2015, *Symposium* Beirut (Lebanon) 2014. **Publications** *AHEAD Working Paper Series.* [2018/XM7517/F]

♦ Applied Improvisation Network (AIN) 00881

Address not obtained.
URL: http://appliedimprovisation.network/

History Founded 2002. **Aims** Promote the practice of applied improvisation; develop methods of practice. **Structure** Board of Directors. **Staff** Voluntary. **Activities** Guidance/assistance/consulting; networking/liaising; events/meetings. **Events** *Communicating beyond borders and barriers* New York, NY (USA) 2019, *Conference* Paris (France) 2018, *Conference* Irvine, CA (USA) 2017, *Conference* Oxford (UK) 2016, *Conference* Montréal, QC (Canada) 2015. [2019/XM8429/F]

- ♦ Applied Linguistics and Professional Practice Society (meeting series)
- ♦ Applied Nanotechnology and Nanoscience International Conference (meeting series)
- ♦ Applied Neuroscience Society of Australasia (internationally oriented national body)

♦ Applied Stochastic Models and Data Analysis International Society (ASMDA International Society) 00882

Contact Data Analysis and Forecasting Lab, Technical Univof Crete, 731 00 Chania, Greece.
URL: http://www.asmda.com/

Aims Serve as an interface between Stochastic Modeling and Data Analysis and their real life applications such as business, finance and insurance, management, production and reliability, biology and medicine and other scientific fields. **Structure** Scientific Committee. **Activities** Events/meetings; awards/prizes/competitions. **Events** *Stochastic Modeling Techniques and Data Analysis International Conference* Barcelona (Spain) 2020, *QQML : Qualitative and Quantitative Methods in Libraries International Conference* Chania (Greece) 2020, *Conference* Florence (Italy) 2019, *QQML : Qualitative and Quantitative Methods in Libraries International Conference* Florence (Italy) 2019, *QQML : Qualitative and Quantitative Methods in Libraries International Conference* Chania (Greece) 2018. **Publications** Conference proceedings. [2015/XM8189/F]

- ♦ **APPM** Académie des professeurs pour la paix mondiale (#18520)
- ♦ APPN / see Asia-Pacific Producers Network (#02000)
- ♦ APPN / see AME World Ecology Foundation
- ♦ **APPO** African Petroleum Producers's Organization (#00414)
- ♦ APP / see Pacific Maritime Transport Alliance (#17982)
- ♦ APPPAH – Association for Pre- and Perinatal Psychology and Health (internationally oriented national body)
- ♦ **APPPC** Asia and Pacific Plant Protection Commission (#01997)
- ♦ APPPI – Association internationale pour la promotion et la protection des investissements privés en territoires étrangers (inactive)
- ♦ **APPRA** Asia Pacific Peace Research Association (#01991)
- ♦ Appraisal Institute (internationally oriented national body)
- ♦ APPRC / see African Population and Health Research Center (#00420)
- ♦ Appropriate Technology Asia (internationally oriented national body)
- ♦ **APPROTECH ASIA** Asian Alliance of Appropriate Technology Practitioners (#01306)
- ♦ APPSA – Asian-Pacific Political Science Association (inactive)
- ♦ APPSAM – Asia Pacific Society of Precision Anti-Aging Medicine (unconfirmed)
- ♦ **APPS** Asian Pacific Prostate Society (#01626)
- ♦ APPS – Asian Paediatric Pulmonology Society (unconfirmed)
- ♦ APPS – Association pour la promotion des publications scientifiques en langue française (inactive)
- ♦ APPS – Australasian Plant Pathology Society (internationally oriented national body)
- ♦ APPSC – Association of Plant Physiologists of SAARC Countries (no recent information)
- ♦ APPSPGAN / see Asian Pan-Pacific Society for Paediatric Gastroenterology, Hepatology, and Nutrition (#01651)
- ♦ **APPSPGHAN** Asian Pan-Pacific Society for Paediatric Gastroenterology, Hepatology, and Nutrition (#01651)
- ♦ APPTC / see Asian-Pacific Postal College (#01624)
- ♦ APPTEA – Asia Pacific Physics Teachers and Educators Association (inactive)
- ♦ **APPU** Asian-Pacific Parliamentarians' Union (#01622)
- ♦ **APPU** Asian-Pacific Postal Union (#01625)
- ♦ Appui au Développement Autonome / see ADA Microfinance
- ♦ Appui International Durable aux Communautés (internationally oriented national body)
- ♦ APQCO / see Asia Pacific Quality Organization (#02005)
- ♦ **APQN** Asia-Pacific Quality Network (#02004)
- ♦ **APQO** Asia Pacific Quality Organization (#02005)
- ♦ APRA / see Automotive Parts Remanufacturers Association
- ♦ APRA – African Public Relations Association (unconfirmed)
- ♦ APRA / see Asia Pacific Peace Research Association (#01991)
- ♦ APRA – Australasian Philosophy of Religion Association (internationally oriented national body)
- ♦ APRA – Automotive Parts Remanufacturers Association (internationally oriented national body)
- ♦ **APRACA** Asia Pacific Rural and Agricultural Credit Association (#02019)
- ♦ APRACA Consultancy Services (see: #02019)
- ♦ APRAD – Association pluridisciplinaire pour la recherche et l'action en matière de développement (internationally oriented national body)
- ♦ **APRAG** Asia Pacific Regional Arbitration Group (#02008)
- ♦ APRAM – Association des Praticiens du Droit des Marques et des Modèles (internationally oriented national body)
- ♦ **APRC** Asian Peace and Reconciliation Council (#01657)
- ♦ **APRC** Asia Pacific Research Committee (#02011)
- ♦ **APRCC** Asia Pacific Rim Confederation of Counsellors (#02015)
- ♦ APRCP / see Asia Pacific Roundtable on Sustainable Consumption and Production (#02017)
- ♦ APRD / see International Association of Parkinsonism and Related Disorders (#12068)
- ♦ APRDO – Asia Pacific Resort Development Organisation (unconfirmed)
- ♦ APREA / see Asia Pacific Real Assets Association (#02006)
- ♦ **APREA** Asia Pacific Real Assets Association (#02006)
- ♦ APRE – Agenzia per la Promozione della Ricerca Europea, Roma (internationally oriented national body)
- ♦ APRI / see Instituto Português de Relações Internacionais e Segurança
- ♦ APRI / see Austrian Study Centre for Peace and Conflict Resolution
- ♦ **APRIA** Asia-Pacific Risk and Insurance Association (#02016)
- ♦ APRI / see Africa Peace Research and Education Association (#00511)
- ♦ APRIM – Asia-Pacific Research Institute (internationally oriented national body)
- ♦ **APRI Network** Asia Pacific Research Integrity Network (#02012)
- ♦ APRIS – Asia Pacific Retinal Imaging Society (unconfirmed)
- ♦ **APRL** Asia-Pacific Rugby League (#02018)
- ♦ **APRN** ASEAN Public Relations Network (#01226)
- ♦ **APRN** Asia-Pacific Research Network (#02013)
- ♦ APRO – Arab Penal Reform Organization (unconfirmed)
- ♦ APRO / see Asia Pacific Dental Federation/Asian Pacific Regional Organization of the Fédération Dentaire Internationale (#01882)
- ♦ APRO – Asia Pacific Responsible Care Organization (unconfirmed)
- ♦ APRODEH – Asociación pro Derechos Humanos (internationally oriented national body)
- ♦ APRODEV / see ACT Alliance EU (#00082)
- ♦ APROFONO – Asociación Centroamericana de Productores Fonograficos (no recent information)
- ♦ APRO / see ITUC – Asia Pacific (#16076)
- ♦ APROS – Asia-Pacific Researchers in Organization Studies (inactive)
- ♦ **APRRN** Asia Pacific Refugee Rights Network (#02007)
- ♦ **APRSAF** Asia-Pacific Regional Space Agency Forum (#02010)
- ♦ **APRSCP** Asia Pacific Roundtable on Sustainable Consumption and Production (#02017)
- ♦ APRSSA – Association of Plastic and Reconstructive Surgeons of Southern Africa (internationally oriented national body)
- ♦ **APRU** Association of Pacific Rim Universities (#02846)
- ♦ **APSAA** Asia-Pacific Student Accommodation Association (#02058)
- ♦ APSA – American Political Science Association (internationally oriented national body)
- ♦ **APSAAR** Asia-Pacific Society for Alcohol and Addiction Research (#02028)
- ♦ **APSA** Asian Planning Schools Association (#01667)
- ♦ **APSA** Asian Professional Security Association (#01675)
- ♦ **APSA** Asia and Pacific Seed Association (#02023)
- ♦ **APSA** Asia Pacific Sociological Association (#02049)
- ♦ **APSA** Asia-Pacific Structured Finance Association (#02057)
- ♦ **APSA** Asia-Pacific Superyacht Association (#02060)
- ♦ APSA – Australasian Pharmaceutical Science Association (internationally oriented national body)
- ♦ APSA – Australasian Political Studies Association (internationally oriented national body)
- ♦ **APSACHD** Asia-Pacific Society for Adult Congenital Heart Disease (#02027)
- ♦ **APS ACTION** AntiPhospholipid Syndrome Alliance For Clinical Trials and InternatiOnal Networking (#00858)
- ♦ APSAD / see Australasian Professional Society on Alcohol and Other Drugs
- ♦ APSAD – Australasian Professional Society on Alcohol and Other Drugs (internationally oriented national body)
- ♦ APS – African Primatological Society (unconfirmed)
- ♦ APSAI / see Asia Pacific Association of Allergy, Asthma and Clinical Immunology (#01831)
- ♦ **APS** American Peptide Society (#00789)
- ♦ **APSAO** Asia-Pacific Society for Artificial Organs (#02030)
- ♦ **APSAP** Asia-Pacific Society for Applied Phycology (#02029)
- ♦ **APS** Asian Pentecostal Society (#01661)
- ♦ APS – Association of Pacific Systematists (no recent information)
- ♦ **APS** Association for Psychological Science (#02879)
- ♦ APS – Australasian Planetarium Society (internationally oriented national body)
- ♦ **APSAVD** Asian-Pacific Society of Atherosclerosis and Vascular Diseases (#01630)
- ♦ APSBF – Asia Pacific Snooker & Billiards Federation (internationally oriented national body)
- ♦ **APSCA** Asia Pacific Smart Card Association (#02026)
- ♦ **APSC** Asian Pacific Society of Cardiology (#01631)
- ♦ **APSCC** Asia-Pacific Satellite Communications Council (#02021)
- ♦ **APSCE** Asia-Pacific Society for Computers in Education (#02034)
- ♦ APSCI – Asia Pacific Symposium on Cochlear Implant and Related Sciences (meeting series)
- ♦ **APSCIT** Asia Pacific Society for Computing and Information Technology (#02035)
- ♦ **APSCMI** Asia-Pacific Society of Clinical Microbiology and Infection (#02032)
- ♦ APSCO – Arab Petroleum Services Company (see: #17854)
- ♦ **APSCO** Asia-Pacific Space Cooperation Organization (#02051)
- ♦ **APSCOM** Asia-Pacific Society for the Cognitive Sciences of Music (#02033)
- ♦ APSCRS – Asia-Pacific Society of Cornea and Refractive Surgery (inactive)
- ♦ **APSCVIR** Asia Pacific Society of Cardiovascular and Interventional Radiology (#02031)
- ♦ **APSDA** Asian Pacific Society of Dialysis Access (#01632)
- ♦ **APSDA** Asia Pacific Space Designers' Alliance (#02052)
- ♦ **APSDE** Asian-Pacific Society for Digestive Endoscopy (#01633)
- ♦ APSDEP – Asian and Pacific Skill Development Programme (no recent information)
- ♦ **APSE** Asia-Pacific Society for Ethnomusicology (#02036)
- ♦ APSEC – Asia-Pacific Software Engineering Conference (meeting series)
- ♦ APSEG / see Crawford School of Economics and Government
- ♦ APSEG – Asia Pacific Society of Eye Genetics (unconfirmed)
- ♦ APSEM / see Crawford School of Economics and Government
- ♦ APSEM – Asian and Pacific Shipbuilding Experts Meeting (meeting series)
- ♦ APSERI – Asia Pacific Socio-Economic Research Institute (internationally oriented national body)

♦ APS Europeo Istituto Pegaso 00883

Contact Corso Matteotti 86, 71121 Foggia FG, Italy. T. +39881709102. Fax +39881723359.

History Founded 25 Sep 2007, on the initiative of *European Commission (EC, #06633)* and *Anna Lindh Euro-Mediterranean Foundation for the Dialogue between Cultures (Anna Lindh Foundation, #00847)*, following an evaluation of the European educational system in the environment field. An ISO 9001:2008 certified institution. **Aims** Provide training and informational support to the activities of the European Commissions and Anna Lindh Euro-Mediterranean Foundation for the Dialogue between Cultures. **Structure** Scientific Committee of 9 members. Legal and administrative office, Foggia (Italy); training center, Florence (Italy); territorial headquarters, Rome (Italy); social development centre, Bari (Italy); educational farm for hippotherapy and music therapy and education activities for health food, Cassano delle Murge (Italy). Branches (5): Bratislava (Slovakia); Bucharest (Romania); Split (Croatia); Almaty (Kazakhstan); Malaytia Region (Turkey). **Activities** Training/education. **Publications** *European News Report* – journal in print in Italian/English, online in English, Italian, Spanish. **IGO Relations** Accredited to: *United Nations (UN, #20515)*. **NGO Relations** Member of: *United Nations Academic Impact (UNAI, #20516).* [2019/XJ1025/j/E]

- ♦ APSEV – Asian Pacific Societies for Extracellular Vesicles (unconfirmed)
- ♦ APSF – African Pharmaceutical Students Federation (no recent information)
- ♦ APSF – Asean Para Sports Federation (unconfirmed)
- ♦ **APSF** Association of Pension and Social Funds of the CIS (#02856)
- ♦ **APSHG** Asia Pacific Society of Human Genetics (#02038)
- ♦ **APSHQ** Asia Pacific Society for Healthcare Quality (#02037)
- ♦ APSIA – Association of Professional Schools of International Affairs (internationally oriented national body)
- ♦ **APSIC** Asian Pacific Society of Interventional Cardiology (#01636)
- ♦ **APSIC** Asia Pacific Society of Infection Control (#02039)
- ♦ **APSIF** Asian Pencak Silat Federation (#01660)
- ♦ **APSIGO** Asian-Pacific Society for Infections in GYN/OB (#01635)
- ♦ **APSIPA** Asia-Pacific Signal and Information Processing Association (#02025)
- ♦ APSIR / see Asia Pacific Society for Sexual Medicine (#02045)
- ♦ APSJ – Action for Post-Soviet Jewry (internationally oriented national body)
- ♦ APSLF – Association de psychologie scientifique de langue française (no recent information)
- ♦ **APSMB** Asian-Pacific Society of Marine Biotechnology (#01637)
- ♦ **APSMI** Asia-Pacific Self-Medication Industry (#02024)
- ♦ **APSMM** Asian Pacific Society for Medical Mycology (#01638)
- ♦ **APSMR** Asia Pacific Society for Materials Research (#02040)
- ♦ **APSMV** Asian-Pacific Society for Medical Virology (#01639)
- ♦ APSN / see APEC Port Services Network (#00872)
- ♦ **APSN** APEC Port Services Network (#00872)
- ♦ **APSN** Asian-Pacific Society of Nephrology (#01640)
- ♦ **APSN** Asian Pacific Society for Neurochemistry (#01641)
- ♦ **APSN** Asian Privacy Scholars Network (#01672)
- ♦ **APSN** Asia-Pacific Safeguards Network (#02020)

- ♦ APSN – Asia Pacific Solidarity Network (internationally oriented national body)
- ♦ APSNC – Asian Pacific Society of Nuclear Cardiology (no recent information)
- ♦ **APSO** Africa Psoriasis Organization (#00515)
- ♦ APSO – Asia-Pacific Socialist Organization (inactive)
- ♦ **APSO** Asia Pacific Society of Osseointegration (#02042)
- ♦ **APSO** Asia Pacific Stroke Organization (#02056)
- ♦ **APSO** Association of Paralympic Sports Organisations (#02850)
- ♦ **APSOC** Asia Pacific Solidarity Coalition (#02050)
- ♦ APSOCPIS – Asia-Pacific Society for Process Intensification and Sustainability (unconfirmed)
- ♦ APSOOP – Asia-Pacific Society of Ocular Oncology and Pathology (unconfirmed)
- ♦ **APSOPRS** Asia Pacific Society of Ophthalmic Plastic and Reconstructive Surgery (#02041)
- ♦ APSOT – Asia-Pacific Symposium on Tritium Science (meeting series)
- ♦ **APSPA** Asia Pacific Society for Public Affairs (#02044)
- ♦ **APSP** Africa Platform for Social Protection (#00514)
- ♦ APSPG – Asian Pacific Society for Paediatric Gastroenterology (inactive)
- ♦ **APSPOS** Asia-Pacific Strabismus and Paediatric Ophthalmology Society (#02055)
- ♦ **APSPR** Asian Pacific Society of Prion Research (#01642)
- ♦ APSPT – Asia-Pacific International Symposium on the Basics and Applications of Plasma Technology (meeting series)
- ♦ **APSR** Asian Pacific Society of Respirology (#01643)
- ♦ APSRC – Asia Pacific Symposium on Radiation Chemistry (meeting series)
- ♦ **APSSA** Asia Pacific Student Services Association (#02059)
- ♦ **APSSAM** Asia Pacific Society for the Study of the Aging Male (#02047)
- ♦ **APSS** Asia Pacific Spine Society (#02054)
- ♦ APSSEAR / see Asia Pacific Pediatric Association (#01992)
- ♦ APSSIR / see Asia Pacific Society for Sexual Medicine (#02045)
- ♦ **APSSLH** Asia Pacific Society of Speech, Language and Hearing (#02046)
- ♦ **APSSM** Asia Pacific Society for Sexual Medicine (#02045)
- ♦ APSSRA – Asian-Pacific Symposium on Structural Reliability and Its Applications (meeting series)
- ♦ **APSTH** Asian-Pacific Society on Thrombosis and Hemostasis (#01644)
- ♦ **APSTSN** Asia-Pacific Science, Technology and Society Network (#02022)
- ♦ **APSU** Asian Society of Uro-Oncology (#01746)
- ♦ **APSWC** Asia-Pacific Spa and Wellness Coalition (#02053)
- ♦ **APsyA** Asian Psychological Association (#01676)
- ♦ APTA – Asia Pacific Theological Association (see: #10110)
- ♦ **APTA** Asia Pacific Tourism Association (#02067)
- ♦ APT Action on Poverty (internationally oriented national body)
- ♦ APT – Alliance Publishing Trust (internationally oriented national body)
- ♦ **APT** ASEAN Plus Three Financial Grouping (#01222)
- ♦ **APT** Asia-Pacific Telecommunity (#02064)
- ♦ **APT** Association for the Prevention of Torture (#02869)
- ♦ **APTBF** Asia Pacific Tchoukball Federation (#02063)
- ♦ APTCCN – ASEAN Plus Three Cultural Cooperation Network (unconfirmed)
- ♦ APT Design and Development / see APT Action on Poverty
- ♦ APTEC – Asia-Pacific Tourism Exchange Centre (internationally oriented national body)
- ♦ APT Enterprise Development / see APT Action on Poverty
- ♦ **APTF** Asia-Pacific Tax Forum (#02061)
- ♦ **APTHS** Asia Pacific Travel Health Society (#02070)
- ♦ APTI – Arab Petroleum Training Institute (no recent information)
- ♦ **APTi** Association for Psychological Type International (#02880)
- ♦ APT International – Association for Preservation Technology International (internationally oriented national body)
- ♦ APTIRC – Asian-Pacific Tax and Investment Research Centre (inactive)
- ♦ **APTLD** Asia Pacific Top Level Domain Association (#02066)
- ♦ APTLF / see Association internationale de psychologie du travail de langue française (#02734)
- ♦ **APTM** Asociación Panamericana de Tecnólogos Médicos (#02292)
- ♦ **APTN** Asia and Pacific Transgender Network (#02069)
- ♦ **APTO** Asociación Panamericana de Trauma Ocular (#02293)
- ♦ **APTOS** Asia Pacific Tele-Ophthalmology Society (#02065)
- ♦ **APTRA** Asia Pacific Travel Retail Association (#02071)
- ♦ APTS – Asian Pacific Theological Seminary (internationally oriented national body)
- ♦ **APTS** Asia-Pacific Society of Thyroid Surgery (#02048)
- ♦ **APTS** Asia Pacific Trade Seminars (#02068)
- ♦ APTS – Australasian Particle Technology Society (internationally oriented national body)
- ♦ APTTA – Australasian Piano Tuners and Technicians Association (internationally oriented national body)
- ♦ APTU – African Posts and Telecommunications Union (inactive)
- ♦ **APTU** Asia Pacific Taxpayers Union (#02062)
- ♦ APUA – Alliance for the Prudent Use of Antibiotics (internationally oriented national body)
- ♦ **APUA** Association of Power Utilities in Africa (#02867)
- ♦ **APU** African Parliamentary Union (#00412)
- ♦ APU – African Postal Union (no recent information)
- ♦ APU / see Arab Inter-Parliamentary Union (#00995)
- ♦ APU / see Arab Permanent Postal Commission (#01025)
- ♦ APU / see Asian-Pacific Parliamentarians' Union (#01622)
- ♦ APU/ATU – African Postal and Telecommunications Union (inactive)
- ♦ **APUCEN** Asia-Pacific University – Community Engagement Network (#02072)
- ♦ **APUEA** Asia Pacific Urban Energy Association (#02073)
- ♦ APUME – Association for Peace and Understanding in the Middle East (internationally oriented national body)
- ♦ **AP – UpM** Assemblée Parlementaire – Union pour la Méditerranée (#18216)
- ♦ **APURE** Association for European Rural Universities (#02541)
- ♦ **APURE** Association pour les universités rurales européennes (#02967)
- ♦ APU – Ritsumeikan Asia Pacific University (internationally oriented national body)
- ♦ **APV** Arbeitsgemeinschaft für Pharmazeutische Verfahrenstechnik (#01082)
- ♦ APVC – Asia-Pacific Vibration Conference (meeting series)
- ♦ **APVIA** Asian Photovoltaic Industry Association (#01663)
- ♦ **APVRS** Asia-Pacific Vitreo-retina Society (#02075)
- ♦ **APVS** Asian Pig Veterinary Society (#01666)
- ♦ APVS – Asia Pacific Vascular Society (internationally oriented national body)
- ♦ **APVU** Asia Pacific Vegetarian Union (#02074)
- ♦ APWA – All Pakistan Women's Association (internationally oriented national body)
- ♦ **APWA** Asia Pacific Wrist Association (#02079)
- ♦ **APWF** Asia-Pacific Water Forum (#02076)
- ♦ APWG – Anti-Phishing Working Group (internationally oriented national body)
- ♦ APWINC – Asian Pacific Women's Information Network Center (internationally oriented national body)
- ♦ **APWLD** Asia Pacific Forum on Women, Law and Development (#01912)
- ♦ APWM – Asia-Pacific Worm Meeting (meeting series)
- ♦ **APWSL** Asia Pacific Workers Solidarity Link (#02078)
- ♦ **APWSS** Asian Pacific Weed Science Society (#01646)
- ♦ **APWW** Asia Pacific Women's Watch (#02077)
- ♦ APYEF – Asia-Pacific Youth Environmental Federation (inactive)
- ♦ **APYF** Asian Pacific Youth Forum (#01647)
- ♦ APYN / see International Youth Health Organization (#15933)
- ♦ APYO – Asia-Pacific Youth Organisation (internationally oriented national body)
- ♦ AQAAIW / see Association of Quality Assurance Agencies of the Islamic World (#02882)
- ♦ **AQAN** Asean Quality Assurance Network (#01227)
- ♦ AQC – Adiabatic Quantum Computing Conference (meeting series)
- ♦ **AQI** Access Quality International (#00053)
- ♦ AQIS – Asian Quantum Information Science Conference (meeting series)
- ♦ AQL – International Conference on Advances in Quantitative Laryngology, Voice and Speech Research (meeting series)
- ♦ AQOCI – Association québécoise des organismes de coopération internationale (internationally oriented national body)
- ♦ AQUA-AFRICA (internationally oriented national body)
- ♦ Aqua for All (internationally oriented national body)
- ♦ AQUA / see Association européenne de fabricants de compteurs d'eau et d'énergie thermique (#02567)
- ♦ **AQUA** Association européenne de fabricants de compteurs d'eau et d'énergie thermique (#02567)
- ♦ AquaConSoil (meeting series)

♦ Aquacultural Engineering Society (AES) 00884

Pres P.O. Box 2974, Riverview FL 33578, USA. E-mail: info@aesweb.org.
URL: http://www.aesweb.org/

History 1993. **Aims** Serve as a forum for the discussion of engineering problems related to aquaculture. **Structure** Board of Directors. Officers: President, 2 Vice-Presidents, Secretary-Treasurer, Past-President. **Activities** Events/meetings. **Events** *Conference* New Orleans, LA (USA) 2019, *Conference* Roanoke, VA (USA) 2006. **Publications** *AES Newsletter* (4 a year); *Aquacultural Engineering* (8 a year) – journal. Proceedings. **Information Services** *Fishbase*; *Fish Protein*; *Netfish*. [2021/XD6762/**D**]

♦ Aquaculture Stewardship Council (ASC) 00885

Contact Daalseplein 101, 3511 SX Utrecht, Netherlands. T. +31302303110. E-mail: info@asc-aqua.org.
UK Office 27 Old Gloucester Street, London, WC1N 3AX, UK.
URL: http://www.asc-aqua.org/

History 2010. Founded by *World Wide Fund for Nature (WWF, #21922)* and Dutch Sustainable Trade Initiative (IDH). Registration: Handelsregister, No/ID: 34389683, Netherlands; Charity Commission, No/ID: 1150418, England and Wales. **Aims** Transform aquaculture towards environmental sustainability and social responsibility using efficient market mechanisms that create value across the chain. **Structure** Supervisory Board; Technical Advisory Group; Technical Working Groups; Steering Committees. **Languages** English. **Activities** Certification/accreditation; standards/guidelines. **NGO Relations** Memorandum of Understanding with (1): *HCV Network Ltd (HCV Network, #10865)*. Member of (2): *High Level Panel for a Sustainable Ocean Economy (Panel, #10917)* (Advisory Network); *ISEAL (#16026)*. Participates in: *Global Partnership for Oceans (GPO, #10537)*. [2022.02.10/XJ6774/**F**]

- ♦ AQUA EUROPA / see European Water and Wastewater Industry Association (#09087)
- ♦ **Aqua Europa** European Water and Wastewater Industry Association (#09087)
- ♦ **AquaFed** International Federation of Private Water Operators (#13517)
- ♦ **AquaForMed** Mediterranean Network of Water Training Centers (#16666)

♦ Aquapol 00886

Address not obtained.
URL: http://www.aquapol-police.com/

History Feb 2002, by Dutch, German and Belgian water police. Full title: *AQUAPOL – international police cooperation on the water*. **Aims** Establish high-quality international cooperation among members, *police* forces and inland *shipping inspectorates*; be a qualified advisor for European legislative and regulatory bodies in relevant areas of responsibility. **Structure** Assembly. Council, comprising one representative of each member. Working Groups (4): Inland Shipping Affairs; Maritime Affairs; Security/Criminality; Support/Coordination. Secretariat. President; Vice-President; Secretary; Director. **Finance** Support from *European Commission (EC, #06633)*. **Activities** Carries out international control operations. **Events** *Assembly* Antwerp (Belgium) 2010. **Publications** *Aquapol Magazine*.
Members Police forces (14) from 10 countries:
Austria, Belgium, Bulgaria, Czechia, France, Germany, Hungary, Italy, Netherlands, Romania, Slovakia, Switzerland.
[2018/XJ2450/**D***]

- ♦ AQUAPOL – international police cooperation on the water / see Aquapol (#00886)

♦ Aqua Publica Europea (APE) 00887

Exec Dir Blvd de l'Impératrice 17/19, 1000 Brussels, Belgium. T. +3225188655. E-mail: info@aquapublica.eu.
URL: http://www.aquapublica.eu/

History 2008. Full title *Aqua Publica Europea – The European Association of Public Water Operators (APE)*. EU Transparency Register: 81643548590-64. **Aims** Promote public *water management* at European and international level. **Structure** General Assembly; Management Board; Strategic Committee. Secretariat. Working Groups. **Staff** 2.00 FTE, paid. **Activities** Knowledge management/information dissemination; politics/policy/regulatory; events/meetings; research/documentation. **Events** *Meeting on the Role of Public Water Operators in Ensuring Adequate Information and in Contributing to Stakeholder Engagement* Brussels (Belgium) 2018, *Conference on Empowering Public Procurement for Innovation in the EU Water Sector* Saragossa (Spain) 2016, *General Assembly* Bari (Italy) 2014, *General Assembly* Paris (France) 2013.
Members Publicly owned water and sanitation services, and their national and regional associations. Members in 7 countries:
Belgium, France, Germany, Italy, Portugal, Spain, Switzerland. [2017/XJ8572/**D**]

- ♦ Aqua Publica Europea – The European Association of Public Water Operators / see Aqua Publica Europea (#00887)

♦ Aquarian Tabernacle Church (ATC) 00888

Archpriest c/o ATC World Headquarters, PO Box 409, Index WA 98256-0409, USA. T. +13607931945. Fax +13607933537. E-mail: atc@aquatabch.org.
Street Address 48631 River Park Drive, Index WA 98256, USA.
Main: http://www.aquatabch.org/

History 31 Oct 1979. **Aims** Provide *religious* services and support to the larger *Wiccan* community; sponsor Wiccan scouting programmes worldwide. **Structure** Core group of about 55 people. Archpriestess and Archpriest. Congregations worldwide, mainly in USA, Canada, Australia, New Zealand, South Africa and Ireland. **Languages** English. **Staff** 55.00 FTE, voluntary. **Finance** Fundraising. No worldwide budget; national units are fiscally independent. **Activities** Organizes 2 annual Pagan religious festivals: Hekatee's Sickle Festival; Spring Mysteries Festival. Provides open public workshop rituals following lunar calendar. Operates college level seminary programme and awards Associate through Doctorate degree in Ministry; participates in Interfaith Councils at local, state, national and international levels; provides consultancy services; operates prison and hospital ministry programmes. **Publications** *Panegyria – The Official Voice of the Aquarian Tabernacle Church* (8 a year) – online.
Members Affiliated churches in many countries, including the following 9 countries:
Australia, Canada, France, Ireland, Mexico, New Zealand, South Africa, UK, USA.
NGO Relations Founding member of: *North American Interfaith Network (NAIN)*. Member of: *United Religions Initiative (URI, #20658)*. [2010.08.09/XF6810/**F**]

♦ Aquatic Ecosystem Health and Management Society (AEHMS) 00889

Sec address not obtained. E-mail: info@aehms.org.
URL: http://www.aehms.org/

History 1989. Inaugural meeting was held in 1990. **Aims** Encourage and promote ecosystem-based science approaches to the health, management, conservation and restoration of marine and fresh waters of the world. **Structure** Executive Committee; Editorial Board; Working Groups; International Chapters (4): South and South-East Asia, Africa, Latin America, and China. **Languages** English. **Staff** 3.00 FTE, paid. **Finance** Sources: sale of publications. **Activities** Events/meetings; publishing activities. **Events** *Ecosystem Health and Fisheries of Indian Inland Waters* Pantnagar (India) 2021, *Emerging frontiers for African Great Lakes* Kisumu (Kenya) 2019, *Managing the health of the Gulf Ecosystem* Al Ain (United Arab Emirates) 2018, *Marine and Freshwater Invasive Species: Solutions for water security (MFIS-China)* Beijing (China) 2018, *Restoring Great Lakes Areas of Concern* Detroit, MI (USA) 2017. **Publications** *Aquatic Ecosystem Health and Management* – journal. *Ecovision World Monograph Series.* **NGO Relations** Universities and research organizations worldwide.
[2022.06.26/XJ6652/**C**]

♦ Aquatic Entomological Societies in East Asia / see Benthological Society of Asia (#03208)
♦ Aquaverde (internationally oriented national body)
♦ ARA / see African Refiners and Distributors Association (#00429)
♦ **ARA** African Refiners and Distributors Association (#00429)
♦ ARA / see ARA International (#01080)
♦ ARA – Arbeitsgemeinschaft Regenwald und Artenschutz (internationally oriented national body)
♦ ARA – Asian Recycling Association (inactive)
♦ ARA – Asian Renal Association (unconfirmed)
♦ Arab Academy of Banking and Financial Sciences (internationally oriented national body)
♦ Arab Academy of Banking and Financial Studies / see Arab Academy of Banking and Financial Sciences
♦ Arab Academy of Dermatology and Aesthetics (unconfirmed)

♦ Arab Academy of Music (AAM) 00890

Académie arabe pour la musique

SG PO Box 3361, Amman 11181, Jordan. T. +96265929726. Fax +96265929727. E-mail: info@arabmusicacademy.org.

Street Address Flat 4 – Building 46, Khaled Shoman Street, Zahran District, Amman, Jordan.

URL: http://arabmusicacademy.com/

History 1971, as a specialized body acting in the framework of *League of Arab States (LAS, #16420).* Also known as: *Academy of Arab Music; Arab Music Academy.* **Aims** Develop teaching and diffusion of musical culture; collect Arab music publications and preserve them; take care of Arab music and *singing* production and their development. **Structure** General Assembly; Executive Council; Academic Commission; Artistic Committees (5). **Languages** Arabic. **Staff** 7.00 FTE, paid. **Finance** Financed by LAS. Individual membership fees; donations, contributions and others. **Activities** Awards/prizes/competitions; events/meetings. **Events** *General Assembly* Algeria 2015, *General Assembly* Amman (Jordan) 2015, *General Assembly* Qatar 2013, *General Assembly* Jordan 2011, *General Assembly* Amman (Jordan) 2009. **Publications** *Electronic Arab Music Magazine* (12 a year); *Research Journal of Arab Music* (2 a year).

Members Governments of 22 countries:
Algeria, Bahrain, Comoros, Djibouti, Egypt, Iraq, Jordan, Kuwait, Lebanon, Libya, Mauritania, Morocco, Oman, Palestine, Qatar, Saudi Arabia, Somalia, Sudan, Syrian AR, Tunisia, United Arab Emirates, Yemen. [2014.12.03/XE3291/**E***]

♦ Arab Academy of Pharmacy (no recent information)
♦ Arab Academy for Science and Technology / see Arab Academy for Science, Technology and Maritime Transport (#00891)

♦ Arab Academy for Science, Technology and Maritime Transport (AASTMT) 00891

Académie arabe des sciences, des technologies et des transports maritimes

Pres Gamal Abdel Naser St, PO Box 1029, Miami, Alexandria, Egypt. T. +2035622366 – +2035622388 – +2035610950. Fax +2035622525 – +2035610950. E-mail: ismail.ghafar@aast.edu.

URL: http://www.aast.edu/

History 1972, Alexandria, as *Arab Maritime Transport Academy, Alexandria (AMTA).* In accordance with a resolution of *Council of Arab Ministers of Transport (no recent information),* 7 Nov 1989, amalgamated with *Arab Maritime Transport Academy, Sharjah (AMTA, inactive),* to form one Academy. Current title adopted 1995. Also referred to as: *Arab Academy for Science and Technology; Arab Science and Technology Academy (ASTA).* A specialized agency of *League of Arab States (LAS, #16420).* **Aims** Provide quality educational services in maritime specialization in compliance with the international standards of education, scientific research, innovation and training; promote cooperation with research teams at national and international levels; contribute to the social and economic development of the Arab region. **Structure** Colleges (9); Graduate School of Business (1). **Activities** Training/education. **Events** *ITS Europe, Middle East, North African Regional Conference* Aswan (Egypt) 2019, *International maritime safety conference* Alexandria (Egypt) 2011, *International conference on coastal zone management of river deltas and low land coastlines* Alexandria (Egypt) 2010, *Global meeting on sharing quality higher education across borders* Alexandria (Egypt) 2005, *Arab international conference for management in the context of globalization* Alexandria (Egypt) 1998. **Publications** *Maritime Research Bulletin* (12 a year); *Journal of Arab Academy for Science, Technology and Maritime Transport* (2 a year) in Arabic, English. **IGO Relations** Joint courses with: *Japan International Cooperation Agency (JICA).* **NGO Relations** Member of: *Association of Arab Universities (AARU, #02374); International Association of Maritime Universities (IAMU, #12016); International Association of Universities (IAU, #12246).* Located within the premises of AASTMT: *Alexandria Centre for International Maritime Arbitration (ACIMA); Arab Institute of Navigation (AIN, #00985).* Associate Member of: *International Association of Ports and Harbors (IAPH, #12096).* Agreement with: *Arab International Society for Management Technology (AIMICT, #00993).*
[2018.06.01/XF1625/**F***]

♦ Arab Accreditation Cooperation (ARAC) 00892

Contact address not obtained. T. +212600785678. E-mail: m.barrak@arabarac.org – secretariat@arabarac.org.

URL: http://arac-accreditation.org/

History Set up Jun 2008, by Ministerial Decree of *Arab Industrial Development, Standardization and Mining Organization (AIDSMO, #00981).* Launched 12 Jun 2011. **Aims** Coordinate and develop the accreditation infrastructure in the Arab region so as to be internationally recognized. **Structure** General Assembly; Executive Committee; Secretariat. Committees (3): Technical; MLA; Communications and Marketing. **Activities** Certification/accreditation.

Members Governments of 17 countries:
Algeria, Bahrain, Egypt, Iraq, Jordan, Kuwait, Libya, Mauritania, Morocco, Oman, Palestine, Qatar, Saudi Arabia, Sudan, Tunisia, United Arab Emirates, Yemen.

IGO Relations Recognized by: *League of Arab States (LAS, #16420).* **NGO Relations** Regional cooperation body of: *International Laboratory Accreditation Cooperation (ILAC, #13995).* Member of: *International Accreditation Forum (IAF, #11584).* Memorandum of Understanding with: *Asia Pacific Accreditation Cooperation (APAC, #01816).* [2017/XM5877/**E***]

♦ Arab Administrative Development Organization (ARADO) 00893

Organisation arabe pour le développement administratif (OADA)

Dir Gen PO Box 2692, Alhorria, Heliopolis, Cairo, Egypt. T. +20222580006 – +20222581144. Fax +20222580077. E-mail: arado@arado.org.

URL: http://www.arado.org

History 1 Apr 1961, as *Arab Organization of Administrative Sciences (AOAS) – Organisation arabe des sciences administratives (OASA).* Commenced activities, 1 Jan 1969, within the framework of the Human and Administrative Development Sector of *League of Arab States (LAS, #16420),* of which it is a specialized agency and for whom it serves as an official consultative house in the field of administration for its Arab member states. Charter amended 1982. Current title adopted 1990. **Aims** Contribute to administrative development in Arab States in a way that serves overall Arab comprehensive development issues. **Structure** General Assembly (every 2 years); Executive Council; Directorate General, headed by Director General. **Languages** Arabic, English. **Staff** 154.00 FTE, paid. **Finance** Member States' contributions. Other sources: capital investments; income generated from activities (such as training, research and studies, consultancy services and private activities); donations, grants and other assistance. **Activities** Knowledge management/information dissemination; networking/liaising; guidance/assistance/consulting; training/education; events/meetings. **Events** *Meeting on new frontiers for strengthening administrative integrity, transparency and accountability* Cairo (Egypt) 1999, *Regional ministerial seminar on good governance for private sector development and investment* Amman (Jordan) 1996, *Ministerial meeting* Cairo (Egypt) 1992, *Strategic management for government organizations* Cairo (Egypt) / Riyadh (Saudi Arabia) / Rabat (Morocco) / Amman (Jordan) 1992, *Scientific conference of administrative development* Amman (Jordan) 1988. **Publications** *Management Today* (12 a year); *The Arab Journal of Administration* (4 a year). *Management Research and Studies Series.* Information Services: Maintains digital library.

Members Membership is open to Arab states accredited by the League of Arab States. Member States and Focal Points (22):
Algeria, Bahrain, Comoros, Djibouti, Egypt, Iraq, Jordan, Kuwait, Lebanon, Libya, Mauritania, Morocco, Oman, Palestine, Qatar, Saudi Arabia, Somalia, Sudan, Syrian AR, Tunisia, United Arab Emirates, Yemen.

NGO Relations Member of: *International Association of Schools and Institutes of Administration (IASIA, #12147); International Institute of Administrative Sciences (IIAS, #13859).* [2017.09.13/XD5290/**D***]

♦ Arab Aeronautical Federation (inactive)
♦ Arab Aerospace Educational Organization (inactive)
♦ Arab African Institute for Culture and Strategic Studies (unconfirmed)
♦ Arab and African Research Centre (internationally oriented national body)

♦ Arab African Youth Council (AAYC) 00894

Conseil de la Jeunesse Arabe et Africaine

SG House No 30, Amarat Street, Khartoum, Sudan. T. +24983562819. Fax +24983562820. E-mail: info@aayouthc.org.

URL: http://www.aayouthc.org/

History 2004, following recommendations from the Afro-Arab Youth Festival, Sudan. **Aims** Determine values of collaboration and solidarity; strengthen awareness of youth issues; support youth activities in voluntary work, science, arts and sports and encourage and protect youth initiatives in the field; cooperate with national and international organizations; increase cooperation of girls in Arab and African countries in decision-making. **Structure** General Assembly. General Council (meets annually), consisting of 3 Committees: Executive; Advisory; Auditing. Executive Committee, comprising President, Vice-President, Secretary-General, Regional Coordinators and one representative of the Diaspora. General Council. Regional offices (7): South Africa; North Africa (Morocco); West Africa (Senegal); Central Africa; Arab Gulf and Yemen (Yemen); Arabic East (Syria); Diaspora (Finland). **Languages** Arabic, English, French. **Finance** Members' dues. Additional donations. **Activities** Organizes: festivals; seminars; youth camps; workshops. **Publications** *AFRABIA YOUTH* – magazine. Books. **Members** Active; Associate; Honorary. Membership countries not specified. **IGO Relations** *African Union (AU, #00488); League of Arab States (LAS, #16420).* **NGO Relations** Consultative member of: *World Assembly of Youth (WAY, #21113).* [2011.02.28/XJ2216/**E**]

♦ Arab Agricultural Cooperative Federation (inactive)

♦ Arab Agricultural Engineers Union (AAEU) 00895

Chair PO Box 3800, Damascus, Syrian AR.

History Also referred to as *Federation of Arab Agricultural Engineers.* **Activities** Events/meetings. **Events** *Arab symposium for planning and promoting fish culture and crustaceans* Damascus (Syrian AR) 1993. **Members** Membership countries not specified. **IGO Relations** Specialized Agency of: *League of Arab States (LAS, #16420).* [2017/XD2411/**D**]

♦ Arab Agronomists Union (no recent information)

♦ Arab Air Carriers Organization (AACO) 00896

Organisation Régionale des Compagnies Aériennes Arabes

SG Beirut Harbor, Saifi Area, Downtown, PO Box 13-5468, Beirut, Lebanon. T. +9611989250 – +9611989251 – +9611989252. Fax +9611989253. E-mail: sgoffice@aaco.org – ext.aff@aaco.org – info@aaco.org.

Regional Training Centre – Jordan 12 Abdallah Ben Omar Street, Shmeisani, PO Box 930039, Amman 11193, Jordan. T. +96265683381 – +96265683382. Fax +96265683383. E-mail: rtc@aacortc.com.

URL: http://www.aaco.org/

History 1965. Founded under the auspices of *League of Arab States (LAS, #16420),* following a decision taken at Conference of Arab Ministers of Transport, 1964, Beirut (Lebanon). Former names and other names: *Regional Organization of Arab Airlines* – alias; *Organisation Arabe du Transport Aérien* – former. **Aims** Serve Arab airlines, represent their common interests and facilitate, in a manner consistent with all applicable competition and other laws, cooperation so as to improve operational efficiencies and better serve the travelling public. **Structure** General Assembly (annual); Executive Committee; Steering Boards; Task Forces; Secretariat General. **Languages** Arabic, English. **Staff** 32.00 FTE, paid. **Finance** Sources: members' dues. **Activities** Events/meetings; projects/programmes; training/education. **Events** *Annual General Assembly* Abu Dhabi (United Arab Emirates) 2022, *Annual General Assembly* Doha (Qatar) 2021, *Annual General Assembly* 2020, *Annual General Assembly* Amsterdam (Netherlands) 2020, *Annual General Assembly* Kuwait (Kuwait) 2019. **Publications** *3D Bulletin; Arab Air Transport Statistics; Fuel Bulletin; Regulatory Update; Safe and Level; The Ground Handling Update; The Nashra; TopView; Weekly Web News.* Annual Report; economic review; RTC catalogue.

Members Arab airline companies, bearing the nationality of a country member of the League of Arab States and of which majority capital is Arab. Airlines (33) of 19 countries and territories:
Algeria, Bahrain, Egypt, Iraq, Jordan, Kuwait, Lebanon, Libya, Mauritania, Morocco, Oman, Palestine, Qatar, Saudi Arabia, Sudan, Syrian AR, Tunisia, United Arab Emirates, Yemen.

IGO Relations All governmental bodies related to aviation. [2022.05.11/XD4017/**D**]

♦ Arab Airline Pilot Association (inactive)

♦ Arab Air Sports Federation 00897

Contact PO Box 8220, Nasr City, Cairo, 11371, Egypt. T. +201115110533. E-mail: arabairsportsfed@gmail.com.

Street Address 57 Madint Nasr, Rabaa, Cairo, Egypt.

URL: http://arabairsports.org/

History 26 Jan 1994. [2022.10.19/XM4419/**D**]

♦ ARABAL – International Arab Aluminium Conference (meeting series)
♦ Arab Amateur Athletic Federation (inactive)
♦ Arab Angling Federation (inactive)
♦ Arab Anti-Corruption Organization (no recent information)
♦ Arab Aquaculture Society / see Arabian Aquaculture Society (#00974)
♦ Arab Archery Federation (no recent information)

♦ Arab Architects Organization 00898

Organisation des Architectes Arabes

Pres c/o Order of Engineers, PO Box 11-3118, Beirut, Lebanon.

Vice Pres address not obtained. E-mail: bitar@so.com.jo.

URL: http://www.arabarchitect.org/

History 1994. Also referred to as *Organization of Arab Architects.* **Aims** Promote the ethics of the *profession;* facilitate exchanges of knowledge and experiences between architects from different countries; elaborate standards in the field and supervise the training of architects; preserve and safeguard the Arab architectural heritage. **Structure** General Assembly, comprising the member countries of the founder organization *Federation of Arab Engineers (FAE, #09420).* Executive Committee, consisting of the representatives of 7 member countries and one observer (Palestine), includes President. **Finance** Annual members' dues: US$ 3,000 per member country. Donations. **Events** *General Assembly* Amman (Jordan) 1999, *International congress* Beirut (Lebanon) 1999. **Publications** *AAO Bulletin* (4 a year).

Members Members countries (8):
Egypt, Iraq, Jordan, Lebanon, Libya, Palestine, Sudan, Syrian AR. [2010/XF3557/**F**]

♦ Arab Archives Institute (internationally oriented national body)

♦ Arab Association of Cardiothoracic Surgery (unconfirmed)
♦ Arab Association for Comparative Literature (inactive)
♦ Arab Association for Democracy (unconfirmed)

♦ Arab Association of Engineering Consultants 00899

Contact c/o FAE, Po Box 9, Faggala, Cairo, Egypt. E-mail: arabengs@hotmail.com – arabengs@arabfedeng.org.

Aims Organize engineering consultancy works on Arab world level; introduce the capabilities of Arab engineering offices, associations and expert engineers and encourage experience collaboration between them and with foreign compagnies; unify design supervision, construction, standards and specifications in the Arab world; build an information centre. **Structure** General Council; Executive Committee. **Finance** Members' dues. **Activities** Organizes conferences, symposia, engineering workshops and training courses. **Publications** Annual Report; annual agenda; pocket book; brochures; periodic scientific and cultural issues.
Members Full in 13 countries and territories:
Algeria, Bahrain, Egypt, Iraq, Jordan, Kuwait, Lebanon, Libya, Morocco, Palestine, Sudan, Syrian AR, Tunisia.
[2020/XD4725/**D**]

♦ Arab Association for Information and Technology Systems (no recent information)
♦ Arab Association of International Arbitration / see Arab Union of International Arbitration (#01068)
♦ Arab Association of Obstetrics and Gynaecology Societies / see Federation of Arab Gynecology Obstetric Societies (#09421)
♦ Arab Association of Petroleum Professionals (unconfirmed)
♦ Arab Association of Political Science (inactive)
♦ Arab Association of Science Journalists / see Arab Science Journalists Association (#01038)
♦ Arab Association for Sports Journalism / see Arab Federation of Sports Journalists (#00954)

♦ Arab Association of Urology (AAU) 00900

Manager c/o MCI, PO Box 124752, Dubai, United Arab Emirates.
URL: https://www.araburology.org/

Events *AAU Annual Conference* Kuwait (Kuwait) 2021, *AAU Annual Conference* Dubai (United Arab Emirates) 2020, *Annual Congress* Casablanca (Morocco) 2019, *Annual Congress* Dubai (United Arab Emirates) 2018, *EUSC : Emirates International Urological Conference* Dubai (United Arab Emirates) 2018. **Publications** *Arab Journal of Urology.*
Members Individuals in 21 countries:
Algeria, Bahrain, Djibouti, Egypt, Iraq, Jordan, Kuwait, Lebanon, Libya, Mauritania, Morocco, Oman, Palestine, Qatar, Saudi Arabia, Somalia, Sudan, Syrian AR, Tunisia, United Arab Emirates, Yemen. [2020/XM4209/**D**]

♦ Arab Association of Veterinary Medical Faculties (inactive)

♦ Arab Atomic Energy Agency (AAEA) 00901

Contact 7 Rue de l'assistance, Cité el Khadhra, 1003 Tunis, Tunisia. T. +21671808400. Fax +21671808450. E-mail: aaea@aaea.org.tn – aaea_org@yahoo.com.
URL: http://www.aaea.org.tn/

History 17 Aug 1988. Founded within the framework of *League of Arab States (LAS, #16420).* Former names and other names: *Joint Arab Scientific Council for the Utilization of Atomic Energy* – former; *Arab Commission for Nuclear Energy* – former. **Aims** Among member states: coordinate activities in peaceful applications of atomic energy for improvement of overall economic development; assist in capacity building and scientific information transfer; focus on training and support Arab scientists to attend relevant conferences related to peaceful uses of atomic energy; set up harmonized regulations on radiation protection, nuclear safety and security and safe handling of radioactive materials; develop an emergency response system; coordinate scientific and technical activities with concerned regional and international organizations; organize and sponsor relevant regional conferences; create scientific and technical awareness towards nuclear sciences through publication of scientific documents and translation of related rules and regulations. **Structure** General Conference (annual); Executive Council (meeting twice a year); Director-General; DG Office, supervising 3 Units; Department of Scientific Affairs; Department of Administrative and Financial Affairs. **Languages** Arabic, English, French. **Staff** 21.00 FTE, paid. **Finance** Sources: contributions of member/participating states. Annual budget: 2,000,000 USD. **Activities** Capacity building; events/meetings; knowledge management/information dissemination; networking/liaising; publishing activities; training/education. **Events** *Arab Conference on the Peaceful Uses of Atomic Energy* Aswan (Egypt) 2021, *Arab Conference on the Peaceful Uses of Atomic Energy* Cairo (Egypt) 2020, *Arab Forum on the Prospects of Nuclear Power for Electricity Generation and Seawater Desalination* Cairo (Egypt) 2019, *Arab Conference on the Peaceful Uses of Atomic Energy* Sharm el Sheikh (Egypt) 2018, *Arab Forum on the Prospects of Nuclear Power for Electricity Generation and Seawater Desalination* Amman (Jordan) 2017. **Publications** *Alzarra wa Attanmyah – Atom and Development* (4 a year). Specialized books.
Members Membership open to all Arab States. Current membership: governments of 14 countries and territories:
Bahrain, Egypt, Iraq, Jordan, Kuwait, Lebanon, Libya, Mauritania, Palestine, Saudi Arabia, Sudan, Syrian AR, Tunisia, Yemen.
IGO Relations Memorandum of Understanding with (4): China National Nuclear Corporation; *Joint Institute for Nuclear Research (JINR, #16134)*; Korean Atomic Energy Research Institute (KAERI); Korean Institute for Nuclear Safety (KINS). Member of (2): *International Nuclear Information System (INIS, #14378)*; *League of Arab States (LAS, #16420).* Cooperates with (2): *International Atomic Energy Agency (IAEA, #12294)*; Lawrence Livermore National Laboratory (USA). [2022.10.13/XD2901/**D***]

♦ Arab Authority for Agricultural Investment and Development (AAAID) 00902

Autorité arabe pour les investissements et le développement agricoles – Organismo Arabe para Inversiones y Desarrollo Agricolas

Head Office Cnr Osman Digna Street & Al Baladia Street, PO Box 2102, 11111, Khartoum, Sudan. T. +249187096100. Fax +249183794350 – +249183772600. E-mail: info@aaaid.org.
Regional Office PO Box 51250, Deira, Dubai, United Arab Emirates. T. +97144161555 – +97142566222. Fax +97142566656 – +97142566657.
URL: http://www.aaaid.org/

History 1 Nov 1976, Khartoum (Sudan). Established under the auspices of *Arab Fund for Economic and Social Development (AFESD, #00965)*, on signature of 3 agreements which came into force 22 Mar 1977, for a period of 30 years. Commenced operations, May 1978. **Aims** Contribute to food security in the Arab World; maximize return on agricultural investments; promote concepts of innovation and governance in the work environment; leverage resources to diversify and increase revenues; provide support services efficiently and effectively. **Structure** General Assembly (annual) of Board of Shareholders, consisting of ministers of finance representing member states. Board of Directors, comprising President and 9 members. Executive Committee. **Languages** Arabic, English. **Staff** 202.00 FTE, paid. **Finance** Capital subscription by member countries. Subscribed capital (as at 31 Dec 2020): Kuwaiti Dinars 336 million; paid-in capital: about Kuwaiti Dinars 221.1 million (US$ 729.1 million). Distributed profits: US$ 502.6 million (represent 69% of paid capital). URL: https://www.aaaid.org/wp-content/uploads/2021/05/Annual-Report-2020-English.pdf **Activities** Capacity building; guidance/assistance/consulting; research and development; training/education. Plant production; animal production; agricultural processing; marketing; inter-Arab trade. **Events** *Annual Investment Meeting* Dubai (United Arab Emirates) 2020, *Meeting on the Promotion of the Great Lakes Investment and Trade Conference* Dubai (United Arab Emirates) 2020, *Annual Joint Meeting of Arab Financial Institutions* Kuwait (Kuwait) 2019, *Annual Meeting* Amman (Jordan) / Rabat (Morocco) 2018, *Annual Affiliate Meeting* Dubai (United Arab Emirates) 2018. **Publications** *Reports and Studies* (annual); *Newsletter* (Every 6 Month). Annual Report;sStudies and research and development activities; investment opportunities.
Members Shareholders (21 Arab States):
Algeria, Bahrain, Comoros, Djibouti, Egypt, Iraq, Jordan, Kuwait, Lebanon, Morocco, Mauritania, Oman, Palestine, Qatar, Saudi Arabia, Somalia, Sudan, Syrian AR, Tunisia, United Arab Emirates, Yemen. [2021.11.07/XF8668/**F***]

♦ Arab Bank 00903

Chairman PO Box 950545, Amman 11195, Jordan. T. +96265664104 – +96265600000. Fax +96265606793 – +96265606830.
URL: http://www.arabbank.com/

History 1930, Jerusalem, on the initiative of Abdel Hameed Shoman (1890 – 1974). **Activities** Founded: *Abdul Hameed Shoman Foundation (AHSF, see: #00903)*, in memory of the Bank's founder; *Arab Bank Centre for Scientific Research (ABCSR, see: #00903).* **Events** *International conference on women health* Reykjavik (Iceland) 1998. **IGO Relations** Shareholder in: *Arab Trade Financing Programme (ATFP, #01060).*
[2015/XF3549/e/**F**]

♦ Arab Bank Centre for Scientific Research (see: #00903)

♦ Arab Bank for Economic Development in Africa 00904

Banque arabe pour le développement économique en Afrique (BADEA) – Banco Arabe para el Desarrollo de Africa – El Masraf el Arabi Lel Tanmia el Ectesadia fi Afriqya

Dir Gen PO Box 2640, 11111, Khartoum, Sudan. T. +249183773646 – +249183773709. Fax +249183770600 – +249183770498. E-mail: badea@badea.org.
Cairo Office 82 Al-Merghani Street, No 7 – Second Floor, Misr Al Jadida, Cairo, Egypt. T. +2024175501. Fax +2024175501.
URL: http://www.badea.org/

History 18 Feb 1974, as a specialized agency of *League of Arab States (LAS, #16420)*, on signature of establishment agreement by a number of LAS member states and pursuant to decision of 6th Arab Summit, 28 Nov 1973, Algiers (Algeria). Commenced operations in Mar 1975. Financial resources of *Special Arab Aid Fund for Africa (SAAFA, inactive)*, established concurrently with BADEA in Jan 1974, were incorporated into BADEA in 1977. **Aims** Strengthen economic, financial and technical cooperation between Arab and African countries and the embodiment of Arab-African solidarity based on equality and friendship. **Structure** Board of Governors (meets annually); Board of Directors; Director General. **Languages** Arabic, English, French. **Staff** 163.00 FTE, paid. **Finance** Funded by governments of member states. Balance of capital at 31 Dec 2016: US$ 3,797,700. **Activities** Financial and/or material support; projects/programmes. **Events** *Meeting on the Promotion of the Great Lakes Investment and Trade Conference* Dubai (United Arab Emirates) 2020, *Annual Joint Meeting of Arab Financial Institutions* Kuwait (Kuwait) 2019, *Annual meeting* Kuwait (Kuwait) 2019, *Forum International pour l'Investissement au Tchad* Ndjamena (Chad) 2019, *Annual meeting* Sweimeh (Jordan) 2018. **Publications** Annual Report; brochures; research reports.
Members Governments of 18 Arab states:
Algeria, Bahrain, Egypt, Iraq, Jordan, Kuwait, Lebanon, Libya, Mauritania, Morocco, Oman, Palestine, Qatar, Saudi Arabia, Sudan, Syrian AR, Tunisia, United Arab Emirates.
IGO Relations Formal agreement with: *UNESCO (#20322).* Observer to: *UNEP (#20299).* Participates in the activities of: *UNCTAD (#20285).* Formal cooperation agreement with: *African Development Bank (ADB, #00283)*; *African Development Bank Group (ADB Group, #00284)*; *Islamic World Educational, Scientific and Cultural Organization (ICESCO, #16058).* Cooperates with: *Mediterranean Action Plan (MAP, #16638).* A multilateral aid institution of: *Organization of the Petroleum Exporting Countries (OPEC, #17881).* Member of: *Committee of International Development Institutions on the Environment (CIDIE, no recent information).* **NGO Relations** Special member of: *Association of African Development Finance Institutions (AADFI, #02353).* Multilateral agency of: *Coordination Group of Arab National and Regional Development Institutions (#04826).*
[2019/XF3515/**F***]

♦ Arab Bankers Association 00905

Association des banquiers arabes

Main Office 43 Upper Grosvenor Street, London, W1K 2NJ, UK. T. +442076594889 – +44204892. Fax +442076594868. E-mail: office@arab-bankers.co.uk.
URL: http://www.arab-bankers.co.uk/

History 1980, London (UK). In Jul 1984, reorganized in UK as a private company limited by guarantee. **Aims** Promote the professional interests of Arab bankers; provide services to the international Arab banking community and to Arab banking and financial institutions. **Structure** General Assembly; Board of Directors; Administrative Committee. **Languages** Arabic, English. **Staff** 3.00 FTE, paid. **Finance** Members' dues. Donations. **Activities** Conferences and seminars; monthly gatherings; training courses. Building a documentation centre. Publications. **Events** *Annual general meeting / Meeting* London (UK) 2010, *Seminar / Meeting* London (UK) 1988, *Meeting* Sharjah (United Arab Emirates) 1987, *Meeting* London (UK) 1986, *Meeting* London (UK) 1985. **Publications** *The Arab Banker* (6 a year).
Members Active; Honorary; Associate (Institutional). Members in 25 countries:
Algeria, Austria, Bahrain, Belgium, Canada, Egypt, France, Germany, Iraq, Italy, Jordan, Kuwait, Lebanon, Morocco, Oman, Qatar, Saudi Arabia, Spain, Sudan, Switzerland, Syrian AR, Tunisia, United Arab Emirates, USA, Yemen.
IGO Relations *International Bank for Reconstruction and Development (IBRD, #12317)*; *International Monetary Fund (IMF, #14180).* **NGO Relations** *Union of Arab Banks (UAB, #20349).* [2014/XD6486/**D**]

♦ Arab Banking Corporation (ABC) 00906

Group CEO Bank ABC, PO Box 5698, Manama, Bahrain. T. +97317543200 – +97317543000. Fax +97317533163. E-mail: webmaster@bank-abc.com.
URL: http://www.arabbanking.com/

History 17 Jan 1980, when incorporated in the State of Bahrain. Incorporated as *Arab Banking Corporation BSC.* **Aims** Act as issuing and distribution agent in various international *capital markets.* **Structure** Board of Directors, consisting of Chairman, 2 Deputy Chairmen, 10 Directors and Secretary to the Board. Senior Management, comprising President/Chief Executive and Managers of Support Groups (4): Banking; Treasury; Administration; Credit. Branch Offices (4): Baghdad (Iraq); Cayman Is; New York NY (USA); Tunisia. Representative Offices (4): Iran Islamic Rep; Libyan AJ; Singapore (Singapore); United Arab Emirates. Subsidiaries (7): Algeria; Bahrain; Brazil; Egypt; Jordan; Tunisia; UK (with Subsidiary offices in Paris (France), Frankfurt-Main (Germany) and Milan). **Finance** Principal shareholders: Kuwait (29.7%); Libyan AJ (29.5%); Abu Dhabi (27.6%). Authorized capital: US$ 3,500,000,000. million; subscribed and fully paid-up capital: US$ 3,110,000,000. 2,000 million. Total assets at 31 Dec 2017: US$ 29,499,000,000. Stockholders' Equity: US$ 3,930,000,000. **Activities** cover commercial, merchant and investment banking.
Members Subsidiaries in 21 countries:
Algeria, Bahrain, Brazil, Cayman Is, Egypt, France, Germany, Iran Islamic Rep, Iraq, Italy, Jordan, Lebanon, Libya, Singapore, Spain, Sweden, Tunisia, Türkiye, UK, United Arab Emirates, USA.
IGO Relations Shareholder in: *Arab Trade Financing Programme (ATFP, #01060).* **NGO Relations** Member of: *International Capital Market Association (ICMA, #12438).* [2018/XF5046/e/**F***]

♦ Arab Banking Corporation BSC / see Arab Banking Corporation (#00906)
♦ Arab Basketball Confederation (inactive)
♦ Arab Beekeeping Association (unconfirmed)

♦ Arab-Belgian-Luxembourg Chamber of Commerce (ABLCC) 00907

Chambre de commerce Belgique-Luxembourg-Pays arabes (CCBLA) – Kamer van Koophandel Belgie-Luxemburg-Arabische Landen (KvKBLA)

SG Rue Mignot Delstanche 60, 1050 Brussels, Belgium. T. +3223448204. Fax +3223475764. E-mail: info@ablcc.org.
URL: http://www.ablcc.org/

History Founded 1961, Brussels (Belgium). Transformed into a Chamber of Commerce, 1978. Registered in accordance with Belgian law. **Aims** Favour and develop the *economic*, commercial and *industrial* relations between Belgium, Luxemburg and the Arab countries. **Structure** Board of Directors. **Languages** Arabic, Dutch, English, French. **Staff** 6.00 FTE, paid. **Activities** Advocacy/lobbying/activism; guidance/assistance/consulting; events/meetings. **Publications** *ABLCC Newsletter* – electronic.
Members Covers 24 countries and territories:
Algeria, Bahrain, Belgium, Comoros, Djibouti, Egypt, Iraq, Jordan, Kuwait, Lebanon, Libya, Luxembourg, Mauritania, Morocco, Oman, Palestine, Qatar, Saudi Arabia, Somalia, Sudan, Syrian AR, Tunisia, United Arab Emirates, Yemen.
NGO Relations Member of: *Union of Arab Chambers (UAC, #20350).* [2014.10.03/XE2127/**E**]

♦ Arab Beverage Association (ABA) 00908

SG Chtoura, Main Road, Mansour Center 2 , 2nd floor Bekaa', Beirut, Lebanon. T. +9618542604. Fax +9618542605.
URL: https://arabbeverages.org/

Aims Provide consultancy and research services to the beverage industry. **Structure** Executive Committee. **Events** *Conference / Arab Beverages Conference* Amman (Jordan) 2015. **Members** Founder; Ordinary; Individual; Governmental and other organizations; Honorary. Membership countries not specified. **NGO Relations** Member of (1): *Arab Federation for Food Industries (AFFI, #00946).* [2019/XJ9851/**D**]

♦ Arab Body Building Federation (inactive)
♦ Arab Boxing Confederation (inactive)

♦ Arab Bridge Maritime Company 00909

Admin Manager PO Box 989, Aqaba 77110, Jordan. T. +96232092000. Fax +96232092001.
URL: http://www.abmaritime.com.jo/
History 1987. **Activities** Sea transport of passengers and goods, shipping agencies, forwarding and land transport.
Members Governments of 3 countries:
Egypt, Iraq, Jordan. [2018/XF3193/e/**F***]

♦ Arab-British Centre (internationally oriented national body)
♦ Arab Bureau for Consultation and Implementation of Agricultural Projects (no recent information)

♦ Arab Bureau of Education for the Gulf States (ABEGS) 00910

Bureau arabe de l'éducation pour les Etats du Golfe – Oficina Arabe de Educación para los Estados del Golfo
Dir Gen PO Box 94693, Riyadh 11614, Saudi Arabia. T. +96614800555. Fax +96614802839. E-mail: abegs@abegs.org.
URL: http://www.abegs.org/
History 1975, Riyadh (Saudi Arabia). Was awarded, Nov 1993, an international medal by UNESCO on the occasion of 400th anniversary of the birth of Jan Amos Comenius. **Aims** Coordinate, integrate and whenever possible unify the efforts of member states in the fields of education, *culture* and *science*; reinforce unity among the Gulf peoples; establish a system of education on firm scientific basis with clearly stated goals; create joint educational centres and institutions; improve the Arab *Islamic* image of the region and strengthen cultural ties and links. **Structure** General Assembly (every 2 years), consisting of Ministers of Education of member states. Executive Council (meeting twice a year), comprising Deputy Ministers/Under-secretaries of Education of member states. Director General. Executive Officer. Main Departments (3): Programmes; Informations; Financial and Administrative Affairs. Sections and Units (7): Computer; Relations with Foreign Organizations; Library; Council's Secretarianship; Studies and Publications; Printing Office; Public Relations and Media. Specialized organs (4): *Arabian Gulf University (AGU, #00976)*; *Gulf Arab States Educational Research Centre (GASERC, #10822)*, Kuwait; *Arab Educational Training Centre for Gulf States*; *Educational Centre for Arabic Language (ECAL)*. **Languages** Arabic. **Staff** 63.00 FTE, paid. **Finance** Contributions by member states in fixed percentages. Biennial budget: about US$ 10,000,000. **Activities** Main Programmes: Development of special curricula and textbooks for the education of handicapped and of gifted students. Unification of educational goals and curricula. Popularization of science. Publishing Directories of: Faculty members of the Gulf universities; Academic specializations in the Gulf universities; Archaeology in the Gulf region; Educational books and documents in the Gulf region libraries. Regional conferences and seminars on educational problems of the Gulf Region. Tries to enrich the Arabic Library of Pedagogical Sources through translations and original works in the fields of educational methodology and curriculum development. Following the work of the *Experts' Commission for Preparing a Future Plan for Education in the Arab States of the Gulf*, ABEGS has set up a new specialized commission *Commission for Previewing the Future of Education in the Gulf States* in which thinkers and scholars of the region highlight the outlook for education in the Gulf. **Events** *Global Education Forum* Dubai (United Arab Emirates) 2016, *Global Education Forum* Dubai (United Arab Emirates) 2015. **Publications** *Risalat Ul-Khaleej Al-Arabi* (4 a year). Directories; education books and documents.
Members Governments of 7 countries:
Bahrain, Kuwait, Oman, Qatar, Saudi Arabia, United Arab Emirates, Yemen.
IGO Relations Cooperation agreement with: *Islamic World Educational, Scientific and Cultural Organization (ICESCO, #16058)*; *UNESCO (#20322)*. Member of: *Abdus Salam International Centre for Theoretical Physics (ICTP, #00005)*. Invited to sessions of Intergovernmental Council of: *International Programme for the Development of Communication (IPDC, #14651)*. **NGO Relations** Member of: *Consortium on Science, Technology and Innovation for the South (COSTIS, no recent information)*. [2018.06.01/XE7283/**E***]

♦ Arab Businessmen Confederation / see Federation of Arab Businessmen (#09418)
♦ Arab Businessmen and Investors Conference (meeting series)

♦ Arab Campaign for Education for All (ACEA) 00911

Headquarters PO Box 1948, Ramallah, West Bank PALESTINE, Via Israel. T. +97022959960. Fax +97022966481.
URL: http://www.arabcampaignforeducation.org/index-en.html
History Announced 27 May 2009. Comes within the framework of *Global Campaign for Education (GCE, #10264)*. **Aims** Guarantee that all children, youth, vulnerable, marginalized, and disadvantaged groups can access quality, free, and safe education.
Members Full in 11 countries:
Egypt, Iraq, Jordan, Lebanon, Mauritania, Morocco, Palestine, Somalia, Sudan, Tunisia, Yemen.
Included in the above, 1 organization listed in this Yearbook:
Arab Network for Civic Education (ANHRE, #01011). [2019/XM7611/**F**]

♦ Arab Cardiac Society (no recent information)

♦ Arab Center for the Development of the Rule of Law and Integrity (ACRLI) 00912

Head – RND Unit SIWAR Complex, Zouk Mosbeh, Lebanon. T. +9619221527. Fax +9619221527. E-mail: info@arabruleoflaw.org.
URL: http://www.arabruleoflaw.org/
History 2003. **Aims** Enhance the Rule of Law and promote good governance in the Middle East and North Africa (MENA) region. **Structure** Board of Trustees. **Languages** Arabic, English, French. **Finance** Sources: donations; international organizations. **Activities** Advocacy/lobbying/activism; capacity building; politics/policy/regulatory; projects/programmes; research and development.
Members Representatives in 13 countries:
Bahrain, Egypt, Iraq, Kuwait, Libya, Morocco, Qatar, Saudi Arabia, Sudan, Syrian AR, Tunisia, United Arab Emirates, Yemen.
NGO Relations Member of (2): *Coalition for the International Criminal Court (CICC, #04062)*; MEPI-LAA. Partner of (1): *Global Forum on Law, Justice and Development (GFLJD, #10373)*. [2021/XJ6248/**D**]

♦ Arab Center for Research and Policy Studies (ACRPS) 00913

Exec Dir PO Box 10277, Al Tarfa Street, Zone 70, Wadi Al Banat, Al Daayen, Qatar. T. +97440356888. E-mail: research@dohainstitute.org – office@dohainstitute.org.
Beirut Office PO Box 11-4965, Bldg 174 Mar Maroun Street, Saifi District Bvd, General Fouad Chehab, Beirut, Lebanon. T. +9611991837. E-mail: beirutoffice@dohainstitute.org.
URL: https://www.dohainstitute.org/en/
History 2010, Doha (Qatar). **Aims** Foster communication between Arab intellectuals and specialists in social sciences and humanities; establish synergies between these groups; unify priorities; build a network of Arab and international research centers. **Structure** Executive Board; Administrative Team; Research Teams. **Languages** Arabic, English. **Activities** Awards/prizes/competitions; events/meetings; projects/programmes; publishing activities. **Events** *Annual Palestine Forum* Doha (Qatar) 2023, *Strategic Studies Unit Annual Conference* Doha (Qatar) 2023, *Arab Graduate Students Conference* 2022, *The Iranian Studies Unit Conference* Al Daayen (Qatar) 2022, *Annual Conference on Democracy and Democratic Transition* Al Daayen (Qatar) 2021. **Publications** *ACRPS Newsletter*. Journals; research papers; policy analysis; case analysis; reports; dossiers; books; book reviews. https://www.dohainstitute.org/en/BooksAndJournals/Pages/index.aspx **NGO Relations** Cooperative Agreement with: *Arab Thought Forum (ATF, #01055)*. Links with: *Arab Educational Information Network (Shamaa, #00938)* [2023.02.20/XJ7713/**D**]

♦ Arab Central Bank Governors Council / see Council of Arab Central Banks and Monetary Agencies' Governors (#04858)
♦ Arab Central Bureau of Statistics and Documentation (see: #04859)
♦ Arab Centre for Administration and Training of Education Personnel / see UNESCO Regional Office for Education in the Arab States (#20320)
♦ Arab Centre for Agricultural Documentation (no recent information)

♦ Arab Centre for Arabization, Translation, Authorship and Publication (ACATAP) 00914

Centre arabe d'arabisation, de traduction, de production et d'édition
Address not obtained.
URL: http://www.acatap.org/
History 1990. Currently an affiliated body adopting programmes supported by *Arab League Educational, Cultural and Scientific Organization (ALECSO, #01003)*. Former names and other names: *Centre arabe pour l'arabisation, la traduction, la création et la publication* – alias. **Aims** Assist the process of arabization of higher education in Arab countries; introduce Arabic language translations of academic texts into educational systems. **Structure** Board; Scientific Council. **Languages** English. **Staff** 12.00 FTE, paid. **Finance** Sources: ALECSO; subsidies from Arabic countries. **Activities** Events/meetings; publishing activities; training/education. Concerns: equivalence of credentials; expertise for Arab universities. **Events** *Seminar* Syrian AR 2020, *Conférence sur l'arabisation de l'enseignement supérieur dans les universités arabes* Beirut (Lebanon) 1995. **Publications** *Arabization* (2 a year) – journal. **NGO Relations** Links with Arabic language academies (not specified). [2022.03.01/XE2035/**E***]

♦ Arab Centre for Human Resources Development (see: #01001)
♦ Arab Centre for the Independence of the Judiciary and the Legal Profession (internationally oriented national body)
♦ Arab Centre for Information and Early Warning (no recent information)

♦ Arab Centre for International Humanitarian Law and Human Right Education (ACIHL) 00915

Centre arabe pour l'éducation au droit international humanitaire et aux droits humains
Pres 6 avenue Charles de Gaulle, 67800 Bischheim, France. T. +33388629984. Fax +33388629984. E-mail: contact@acihl.org.
URL: http://www.acihl.org/
History 2000. **Structure** Bureau, comprising President, Executive Director, Treasurer and Coordinator. Regional offices (6): Algeria; Egypt; Jordan; Kuwait; Lebanon; Yemen. Committees (5): Finance; Information and Public Relations; Publishing and Documentation; Research and Studies; Training and Education. [2013/XE4608/**E**]

♦ Arab Centre for Labour Administration and Employment (internationally oriented national body)
♦ Arab Centre for Legal and Judicial Research, Beirut (unconfirmed)

♦ Arab Centre for Media Studies 00916

Contact 22 Talat Harb St, Information Dept Bldg, Cairo, Egypt. T. +20225795121 – +20225795123 – +20225795126. Fax +20225795165 – +20225795103. [2008/XJ0213/**D**]

♦ Arab Centre for Mediation and Arbitration (ACMA) 00917

Contact PO Box 6367, Amman 11118, Jordan. T. +96264651989. Fax +96264649636.
URL: http://www.aipmas.org/
History 13 Aug 2003, Amman (Jordan), by *Arab Intellectual Property Mediation and Arbitration Society (AIPMAS, #00989)*. **Structure** Executive Committee. **Activities** Conflict resolution. [2010/XJ4263/**E**]

♦ Arab Centre for Medical Literature (no recent information)
♦ Arab Centre for Security Studies and Training / see Naif Arab University for Security Sciences (#16929)
♦ Arab Centre for Security and Training Studies / see Naif Arab University for Security Sciences (#16929)
♦ Arab Centre for Social Insurance, Khartoum (see: #01001)

♦ Arab Centre for the Studies of Arid Zones and Dry Lands (ACSAD) 00918

Centre arabe pour l'étude des zones arides et des terres sèches – Centro Arabe para el Estudio de las Zonas y Tierras Aridas
Chairman Almuhafaza Street, Great Billal Hotal Bldg, Damascus, Syrian AR. T. +963112266250 – +963112266251. Fax +963112264707.
URL: http://www.acsad.org/
History 1968, Damascus (Syrian AR), as a specialized Arab intergovernmental organization, by decision of the Council of *League of Arab States (LAS, #16420)*. **Aims** Unify the Arab efforts which aim to develop the scientific *agricultural* research in the arid and semi-arid areas and help in the exchange of information and experiences in a way that allows to make use of the scientific progress conduct and encourages the transfer, development and establishment of the modern agricultural techniques in order to increase the agricultural production in these areas and improve the livelihood of their residents. **Structure** General Assembly, comprising Arab ministers of agriculture from Arab member countries. Executive Council, consisting of 7 representatives of 7 member states. Specialized Departments (6): Land and Water Uses; Water Resources; Animal Wealth; Plant Resources; Economy and Planning; Administrative and the Financial Affairs. **Finance** Contributions from Arab Member States; grants from Arab and international organizations. **Activities** Assumes responsibility for the agricultural development and the exploration of the means of achieving water and food security through: production of new and high-yielding varieties of cereals which are tolerant of drought; provision of reliable genetic resources of fruit trees and range plants and production of animal breeds which suit Arab arid conditions; realization of the integrated management of water resources and the rational use of these resources; sound management of the use of saline, waste and treated waste water in agriculture; conservation of the environment and the biodiversity; combating desertification; rehabilitation of desertified lands and establishment of databases of water and soil resources and plant and animal health. Makes surveys of the renewable natural resources and prepares maps of their distribution and uses through the use of remote sensing and Geographic Information System techniques. Disseminates results of research and studies through cooperation and scientific conferences, training courses, seminars and workshops. **Events** *International conference on wadi hydrology* Muscat (Oman) 2007, *WATMED : international conference on water resources in Mediterranean basin* Tripoli (Lebanon) 2006, *Meeting on land degration management in the Arab countries* Amman (Jordan) 2005, *International conference on wadi hydrology* Sanaa (Yemen) 2005, *Seminar on Arab water security* Tripoli (Libyan AJ) 1993. **Publications** Annual report; progress and project reports; papers. Information Services: Database for the available and improved feedstuffs for the different animal species in each of the Arab countries in the Middle East and North Africa. **Information Services** *Arab Database for Arid Zones Plants (ADAP)*; *Bibliographic Database for ACSAD's Publications*; *Climatic Database for Arab Countries*; *Water Resources Database in Arab Countries*.
Members National organizations in 18 countries and territories:
Algeria, Comoros, Egypt, Iraq, Jordan, Kuwait, Lebanon, Libya, Mauritania, Morocco, Palestine, Qatar, Saudi Arabia, Somalia, Sudan, Syrian AR, Tunisia, Yemen.
IGO Relations Formal agreement with: *UNESCO (#20322)*. Relationship agreement with: *FAO (#09260)*. Member of: *International Information System for the Agricultural Sciences and Technology (AGRIS, #13848)*. Accredited to the Conference of the Parties of: *Secretariat of the United Nations Convention to Combat Desertification (Secretariat of the UNCCD, #19208)*. Cooperative relationship with:
- *Arab Bank for Economic Development in Africa (#00904)*;
- *Arab Fund for Economic and Social Development (AFESD, #00965)*;
- *Arab League Educational, Cultural and Scientific Organization (ALECSO, #01003)*;
- *Arab Organization for Agricultural Development (AOAD, #01018)*;
- *Arab Permanent Committee for Meteorology (see: #16420)*;
- *Association of Agricultural Research Institutions in the Near East and North Africa (AARINENA, #02364)*;
- *Bioversity International (#03262)*;
- *Centre for Environment and Development for the Arab Region and Europe (CEDARE, #03738)*;
- *CIHEAM – International Centre for Advanced Mediterranean Agronomic Studies (CIHEAM, #03927)*;
- *Convention on Biological Diversity (Biodiversity convention, 1992)*;
- *Deutsche Gesellschaft für Technische Zusammenarbeit (GTZ, inactive)*;
- *Federation of Arab Scientific Research Councils (FASRC, no recent information)*;
- *International Atomic Energy Agency (IAEA, #12294)*;
- *International Center for Agricultural Research in the Dry Areas (ICARDA, #12466)*;
- *International Development Research Centre (IDRC, #13162)*;
- *International Fund for Agricultural Development (IFAD, #13692)*;

- *Islamic Development Bank (IsDB, #16044);*
- League of Arab States;
- *Observatoire du Sahara et du Sahel (OSS, #17636);*
- *UNEP (#20299);*
- *UNDP (#20292);*
- *United Nations Convention to Combat Desertification (UNCCD, 1994);*
- *United Nations Economic and Social Commission for Western Asia (ESCWA, #20558);*
- *World Meteorological Organization (WMO, #21649).*

NGO Relations Member of: *Arab Geologists' Association (AGA, #00967); Date Palm Global Network (DPGN, #05013); Femise Network (#09731); International Network of Feed Information Centres (INFIC, no recent information).* Participates in *Global Terrestrial Observing Network (GT-Net, no recent information).* Supports: *Climate Institute.* Partner of: *Rainwater Partnership (no recent information).* Cooperative relationship with: *Arab Agricultural Engineers Union (AAEU, #00895); ArabMAB Network (no recent information); Federation of Arab Engineers (FAE, #09420); Inter-Regional Cooperative Research Network on Olives (#15969); International Association of Hydrogeologists (IAH, #11953); International Union for Conservation of Nature and Natural Resources (IUCN, #15766); International Union of Nutritional Sciences (IUNS, #15796).* [2014/XE5527/**E***]

♦ Arab Chess Confederation / see Arab Chess Federation (#00919)

♦ Arab Chess Federation (ACF) 00919

Headquarters c/o Sharjah Cultural & Chess Club, PO Box 6277, Sharjah, United Arab Emirates. E-mail: arabchessfederation@gmail.com.
URL: https://arabchessfederation.com/

History 1975, Damascus (Syrian AR). Previously referred to as *Arab Chess Confederation* and *Arab Chess Union (ACU).* **Structure** General Assembly.
Members Organizations in 17 countries:
Algeria, Bahrain, Egypt, Iraq, Kuwait, Lebanon, Libya, Mauritania, Morocco, Palestine, Qatar, Somalia, Sudan, Syrian AR, Tunisia, United Arab Emirates, Yemen.
NGO Relations *Arab Sports Confederation (ASC, inactive); Fédération internationale des échecs (FIDE, #09627).* [2020/XD0943/**D**]

♦ Arab Chess Union / see Arab Chess Federation (#00919)
♦ Arab Chinese Forum (no recent information)
♦ Arab Cities Organization / see Arab Towns Organization (#01059)

♦ Arab Civil Aviation Organization (ACAO) 00920

Dir Gen PO Box 5052, Souissi, 10105 Rabat, Morocco. T. +212537658323 – +212537658340. Fax +212537658154 – +212537658111. E-mail: acac@acac.org.ma.
Street Address 20 rue Ait Ba'amrane, 5052 Rabat, Morocco.
URL: http://www.acac.org.ma/

History Jun 1996, as *Arab Civil Aviation Commission (ACAC),* on signature of a treaty by Arab countries, replacing the previous *Civil Aviation Council of Arab States (CACAS) – Conseil de l'aviation civile des Etats arabes* or *Arab Civil Aviation Council – Conseil arabe de l'aviation civile,* set up 6 Nov 1967, which ceased to exist in Nov 1989. The Council was a specialized agency of LAS. ACAO also carries out the work of the previous *Arab Civil Aviation Committee,* set up under the auspices of LAS in May 1991, jointly by *Arab Air Carriers Organization (AACO, #00896)* and representatives of Arab air carriers. **Aims** Enhance cooperation and coordination among Arab countries in the field of civil aviation; set a general plan for developing civil aviation in Arab countries and ensuring its safety; develop Arab civil aviation in order to meet the needs of Arab countries for a safe, secure and regular air transport. **Structure** General Assembly (every 2 years). Executive Council (meets twice a year), comprising Chairman and 4 further members. Directorate General, headed by Director-General. Permanent experts. Committees comprising additional experts representing member states: Air Transport; Air Safety; Aviation Security; Air Navigation; Financial Control. **Languages** Arabic, English, French. **Staff** 18.00 FTE, paid. **Finance** Member states' annual contributions. **Activities** Major fields: Air Safety; Air Navigation; Air Transport. Organizes major international seminars and symposia; sets up trainings; conducts studies. **Events** *General Assembly* Marrakech (Morocco) 2006, *Seminar on airdrome certification* Marrakech (Morocco) 2003. **Publications** *Aviation Arab* (4 a year); *ACAO training catalogue* (annual); *Arab Civil Aviation* (periodical). Guid of Arab Airlines.
Members Governments of 22 Arab countries and territories:
Algeria, Bahrain, Comoros, Djibouti, Egypt, Iraq, Jordan, Kuwait, Lebanon, Libya, Mauritania, Morocco, Oman, Palestine, Qatar, Saudi Arabia, Somalia, Sudan, Syrian AR, Tunisia, United Arab Emirates, Yemen.
IGO Relations Consultative Status with: *League of Arab States (LAS, #16420).* Memorandum of Understanding with: *African Civil Aviation Commission (AFCAC, #00248); European Civil Aviation Conference (ECAC, #06564); EUROCONTROL (#05667); International Civil Aviation Organization (ICAO, #12581); Latin American Civil Aviation Commission (LACAC, #16297).* Formal relations of cooperation with: *European Commission (EC, #06633).*
NGO Relations Major partner: AACO. Formal relations of cooperation with: *African Airlines Association (AFRAA, #00200); Airports Council International (ACI, #00611); Airlines Association of Southern Africa (AASA, #00606); European Regions Airline Association (ERA, #08347); Airlines International Representation in Europe (AIRE, #00608); International Air Transport Association (IATA, #11614).* [2019.03.04/XD4166/**D***]

♦ Arab Coalition Against the Death Penalty (Arab Coalition) 00921

Coordinator Al Abdali, Al Sharaf Buidling, 4th Floor, Amman 212524, Jordan. T. +96264655045. Fax +96264655043. E-mail: achrs@achrs.org.
History 2007. **Members** Membership countries not specified. **NGO Relations** Member of: *World Coalition Against the Death Penalty (#21281).* [2019/XJ0726/**F**]

♦ **Arab Coalition** Arab Coalition Against the Death Penalty (#00921)

♦ Arab Coalition for the International Criminal Court (ACICC) 00922

Contact ACIJLP, 8/10 Mathaf El-Manial St, 11th Floor, Manial El-Roda, Cairo, 11451, Egypt. T. +20225310027 – +20223620732. E-mail: acijlp@thewayout.net.
URL: http://www.acicc.org/

History Jun 1999. Founded to work for the setting up of *International Criminal Court (ICC, #13108).* **Aims** Call upon Arab governments to ratify Rome Statute; coordinate between efforts of Arab non-governmental organizations in order to create a supportive public opinion of the International Criminal Court. **Finance** Funded through annual budget of *Arab Centre for the Independence of the Judiciary and the Legal Profession (ACIJLP);* grants; projects. Annual budget: 1,200,000 GBP. **Activities** Events/meetings; knowledge management/ information dissemination; publishing activities.
Members NGOs (61) in 15 countries and territories:
Algeria, Bahrain, Egypt, Iraq, Jordan, Kuwait, Lebanon, Libya, Morocco, Palestine, Saudi Arabia, Sudan, Syrian AR, Tunisia, Yemen.
Included in the above, 7 organizations listed in this Yearbook:
Arab Archives Institute; Arab Centre for the Independence of the Judiciary and the Legal Profession (ACIJLP); Arab Commission for Human Rights (ACHR, #00924); Arab Lawyers' Union (ALU, #01002); Arab Organization for Human Rights (AOHR, #01020); Cairo Institute for Human Rights Studies (CIHRS, #03397); Egyptian Organization for Human Rights (EOHR).
NGO Relations Located at: *Arab Centre for the Independence of the Judiciary and the Legal Profession (ACIJLP).* [2022.10.24/XM2495/y/**F**]

♦ Arab College of Neurosurgery 00923

Address not obtained.
URL: http://www.panarabneurosurgery.org.sa/

History by *Pan Arab Neurosurgical Society (PANS, #18151).* **Structure** Executive Committee, comprising Dean, Vice-Dean and Executive Dean Assistant. **Finance** Sponsored by: *European Association of Neurosurgical Societies (EANS, #06134);* PANS; *World Association of Lebanese Neurosurgeons (WALN, #21156).* [2010/XE4656/**E**]

♦ Arab Commission for Human Rights (ACHR) 00924

Commission arabe des droits humains

Pres 5 rue Gambetta, 92240 Malakoff, France. T. +33140921588. Fax +33146541913.
URL: http://www.achr.eu/

History 17 Jan 1998. Registered in accordance with French law. **Aims** Promote protection of human rights and fundamental freedoms throughout the Arab world. **Structure** Board of Directors, comprising President and 17 members. **Finance** 90% self-financed. **Activities** Organizes seminars, congresses and training courses. **Publications** Books; reports.
Members Full in 15 countries and territories:
Algeria, Bahrain, Egypt, Iraq, Lebanon, Mauritania, Morocco, Oman, Palestine, Qatar, Saudi Arabia, Sudan, Syrian AR, Tunisia, USA.
Also members in Europe. Membership countries not specified.
IGO Relations Special Consultative Status with: *ECOSOC (#05331).* **NGO Relations** Member of: *Arab Coalition for the International Criminal Court (ACICC, #00922).* Links with about 300 organizations worldwide. [2015/XJ3974/**E**]

♦ Arab Commission for Nuclear Energy / see Arab Atomic Energy Agency (#00901)

♦ Arab Committee on Banking Supervision (ACBS) 00925

Secretariat c/o AMF, PO Box 2818, Abu Dhabi, United Arab Emirates. T. +97126215000. Fax +97126391255. E-mail: acbs@amfad.org.ae – cog-acbma@amfad.org.ae.
URL: http://www.amf.org.ae/en/acbs/

History Aug 1991, by *Council of Arab Central Banks and Monetary Agencies' Governors (CGACB, #04858)* to study the decisions of *Basel Committee on Banking Supervision (BCBS, #03183),* specifically those concerning international convergence of capital measurement and capital adequacy requirements, to determine and assess both short and long-term impact of their implementation on the Arab financial and banking sector and to recommend a coordinated and pragmatic approach towards the issues involved. Established as a permanent committee with wider objectives, 1992. **Aims** Follow progress made by Arab banks in implementation of the capital adequacy standard set by the Basel Committee; inform member countries of latest developments in the banking sector and concurrent supervisory requirements for enhancement of its soundness and directives issued by the Basel Committee; review methods and procedures of banking supervision practised in Arab countries with the aim of their standardization; harmonize between accounting systems adopted by Arab countries and work towards their future unification in a way that fully conforms with the International Accounting Standards; review and harmonize banking legislation in Arab countries; strengthen the role of banking supervision in the Arab countries and facilitate and mobilize technical aid and training to supervisory authorities; liaise and coordinate with supervisory groups. **Structure** Committee meets at least annually. Task Force, comprising members from Algeria, Bahrain, Egypt, Lebanon, Qatar, Saudi Arabia, Tunisia and the United Arab Emirates. **Activities** Politics/policy/regulatory; standards/guidelines. **Events** *Annual Meeting* Abu Dhabi (United Arab Emirates) 2022, *Annual Meeting* Abu Dhabi (United Arab Emirates) 2015, *Annual Meeting* Abu Dhabi (United Arab Emirates) 2015, *Annual Meeting* Casablanca (Morocco) 2014, *Annual Meeting* Abu Dhabi (United Arab Emirates) 2013.
Members Bank supervising directors in 21 countries:
Algeria, Bahrain, Djibouti, Egypt, Iraq, Jordan, Kuwait, Lebanon, Libya, Mauritania, Morocco, Oman, Palestine, Qatar, Saudi Arabia, Somalia, Sudan, Syrian AR, Tunisia, United Arab Emirates, Yemen.
IGO Relations *Arab Monetary Fund (AMF, #01009)* acts as secretariat. [2015/XE1874/y/**E***]

♦ Arab Committee of Seven (no recent information)
♦ Arab Committee of Sports Journalism / see Arab Federation of Sports Journalists (#00954)
♦ Arab Company for Detergent Chemicals (see: #17854)
♦ Arab Company for Development of Animal Resources / see Arab Company for Livestock Development (#00927)
♦ Arab Company for the Development of Animal Wealth / see Arab Company for Livestock Development (#00927)
♦ Arab Company for the Development of Livestock / see Arab Company for Livestock Development (#00927)

♦ Arab Company for Drug Industries and Medical Appliances (ACDIMA) 00926

Société arabe des industries des produits pharmaceutiques et instruments médicaux

Headquarters PO Box 925161, Amman 11190, Jordan. T. +96265821618. Fax +96265821649.
URL: http://www.acdima.com/

History Mar 1976, Cairo (Egypt). Established within the framework of *Council of Arab Economic Unity (CAEU, #04859).* Since 1979, headquartered in Amman (Jordan). **Aims** Build a *pharmaceutical* industrial base as a pillar of economic growth and social development; establish *pharmacological* security; provide medical appliances. **Structure** Board of Directors. **Languages** Arabic, English. **Finance** Sources: members' dues. Annual budget: 60,000,000 KWD. **Activities** Events/meetings; research and development. **Events** *Symposium* Tunis (Tunisia) 2000, *Symposium* Amman (Jordan) 1999, *Symposium* Amman (Jordan) 1997, *Symposium* Amman (Jordan) 1993, *Symposium* Amman (Jordan) 1992. **Publications** *Al-Dawa' Al-Arabi* (2 a year).
Members Governments of 16 countries:
Algeria, Bahrain, Egypt, Iraq, Jordan, Kuwait, Libya, Oman, Palestine, Qatar, Saudi Arabia, Sudan, Syrian AR, Tunisia, United Arab Emirates, Yemen. [2016.07.24/XM1029/et/**F***]

♦ Arab Company for Livestock Development (ACOLID) 00927

Regional Office PO Box 75026, Riyadh 11578, Saudi Arabia. T. +96614625445. Fax +96614651497. E-mail: reg@acolid.com.
URL: http://www.acolid.com/

History 10 Jun 1974, by Resolution No 661 of *Council of Arab Economic Unity (CAEU, #04859),* adopted at its 23rd ordinary session. Memorandum and Articles of the Association signed, 4 Apr 1975, by the member countries. Constituent general meeting: 5 Aug 1975. Operations began in 1977. Also known as: *Arab Company for the Development of Livestock; Arab Livestock Development Corporation; Arab Company for Development of Animal Resources (ACDAR); Arab Company for the Development of Animal Wealth – Société arabe de développement des richesses animales.* **Aims** In agreement with the Governments and other institutions concerned: undertake all agricultural, industrial, commercial and technical operations connected with the production, processing, transport and marketing of animal products and fodder, as well as materials, machinery, tools and equipment necessary for its activities. **Structure** General Assembly (annual). Board of Directors, consisting of 10-12 members. Director General. **Activities** Carries out projects. Instrumental in setting up such joint ventures as: *Arab Company for Animal Production, Ras Al Khaima (no recent information); Arab Company for Poultry Production, Al Fujairah (no recent information).*
Members Governments of 11 countries:
Egypt, Iraq, Jordan, Kuwait, Qatar, Saudi Arabia, Somalia, Sudan, Syrian AR, United Arab Emirates, Yemen.
International company:
Arab Investment Company (TAIC, #00996).
IGO Relations A collaborative Arab organization of: *Arab Organization for Agricultural Development (AOAD, #01018).* [2021/XM1028/e/**F***]

♦ Arab Computer Society (ACS) 00928

Contact address not obtained. E-mail: info@arabcomputersociety.org.
URL: http://www.arabcomputersociety.org/

Aims Advance theory and practice of information science and technology. **Events** *International Conference on Computer Systems and Applications* Abu Dhabi (United Arab Emirates) 2022, *International Conference on Computer Systems and Applications* Tangiers (Morocco) 2021, *International Conference on Computer Systems and Applications* 2020, *International Conference on Computer Systems and Applications* Abu Dhabi (United Arab Emirates) 2019, *International Conference on Computer Systems Applications* Tunis (Tunisia) 2017. **Publications** *ACS Newsletter.* [2013/XM2306/**D**]

♦ Arab Confederation of Employees of Banks, Insurances and Financial Affairs (inactive)
♦ Arab Convention on the Suppression of Terrorism (1998 treaty)
♦ Arab Cooperation Council (inactive)
♦ Arab Cooperative Union (inactive)

♦ Arab Council for Childhood and Development (ACCD) 00929

Conseil arabe de l'enfance et le développement

SG Intersection of Makram Ebeid and WHO Streets, PO Box 7537, 8th District, Nasr City, Cairo, 11762, Egypt. T. +20223492024. Fax +20223492030. E-mail: accd@arabccd.org.
URL: http://www.arabccd.org/

History Founded Apr 1987, Cairo (Egypt). **Aims** Be a leading organization in the field of child rights in the Arab world. **Structure** Board of Trustees; General Secretariat, headed by Secretary General. **Languages** Arabic, English, French. **Staff** 30.00 FTE, paid. **Finance** Members' dues. Other sources: private donations; organizations' donations; fund raising. **Activities** Knowledge management/information dissemination; awareness raising; networking/liaising; guidance/assistance/consulting; capacity building; events/meetings. **Events** *Regional conference* Lebanon 1994, *Meeting on community day for the pre-school children* Cairo (Egypt) 1991, *Meeting on pre-school education in the Arab region* Cairo (Egypt) 1991, *Seminar on facing the effects of the Gulf war on the Arab child* Cairo (Egypt) 1991, *Workshop on human health and reproduction in the Arab region* Cairo (Egypt) 1991. **Publications** *Childhood and Development.* Reports; studies; training manuals; guides; handbooks.

Members Full (individuals and associations); Associate (economic, financial and developmental companies and institutions); Honorary (physical persons). Members in 19 countries:
Algeria, Bahrain, Egypt, Iraq, Jordan, Kuwait, Lebanon, Libya, Mauritania, Morocco, Oman, Qatar, Saudi Arabia, Somalia, Sudan, Syrian AR, Tunisia, United Arab Emirates, Yemen.
Included in the above, 3 organizations listed in this Yearbook:
Abu Dhabi Fund for Development (Abu Dhabi Fund); Arab Labour Organization (ALO, #01001); International Planned Parenthood Federation (IPPF, #14589).

Consultative Status Consultative status granted from: *UNESCO (#20322)* (Consultative Status). **NGO Relations** Member of: *Conference of Non-Governmental Organizations in Consultative Relationship with the United Nations (CONGO, #04635).* [2019.02.28/XF0712/y/**D**]

♦ Arab Council for Communication, Information Research and Documentation (inactive)

♦ Arab Council for Graduate Studies and Scientific Research (ACGSSR) 00930

Headquarters Cairo Univ, Giza, Egypt. T. +20235676048 – +20235676032. Fax +20237484423. E-mail: training.acgssr@gmail.com.

History Jul 1992, Alexandria (Egypt), by *Association of Arab Universities (AARU, #02374).* **Aims** Establish an accurate database of graduate studies groups and scientific research centres in Arab universities; set scientific measures for accrediting graduate studies programmes in Arab universities; encourage basic and applied research relating to existing problems in the Arab world so as to build self-sufficiency in advanced technologies; collaborate with Arab universities; plan for continuous training. **Structure** Board of Directors.

Members Full in 13 countries and territories:
Bahrain, Egypt, Iraq, Kuwait, Lebanon, Libya, Oman, Palestine, Saudi Arabia, Sudan, Syrian AR, Tunisia, Yemen.
[2017.03.09/XJ2939/**E**]

♦ Arab Council of Ministers for Telecommunication and Information / see Arab Telecommunication and Information Council of Ministers (#01054)

♦ Arab Council of Operations and Maintenance (OMAINTEC) 00931

Contact PO Box 14/6647, 1105 2140, Beirut, Lebanon. T. +9611821421. Fax +9611821482. E-mail: info@omaintec.org.
Riyadh PO Box 88819, Riyadh, Saudi Arabia. T. +966114602332 – +966114608822. Fax +966114608282.
URL: http://omaintec.org/en/

History Founded Jun 2004, Beirut (Lebanon). Previously also referred to as *Arab Institute for Operation and Management.* **Aims** Raise the operations and maintenance (O and M) standards; best practices and procedures/norms in Arab countries to global levels by setting benchmarks. **Structure** Board. **Activities** Training/education; awards/prizes/competitions. **Events** *International Operations and Maintenance Conference in the Arab Countries* Dubai (United Arab Emirates) 2019. **Publications** *OMAINTEC Journal.* **NGO Relations** *International Maintenance Association (IMA, #14076); Middle East Facility Management Association (MEFMA, #16763).* [2018/XM8591/**D**]

♦ Arab Council for the Social Sciences (ACSS) 00932

Conseil Arabe pour les Sciences Sociales (CASS)

Dir Gen Alamuddin Bldg – 2nd floor, John Kennedy Street, Ras Beirut, Beirut, Lebanon. T. +9611370214. Fax +9611370215. E-mail: dg@theacss.org – info@theacss.org.
URL: http://www.theacss.org/

History Oct 2010. Founded through collaboration with Arab NGO Network for Development (ANND), based in Beirut (Lebanon), and which provides space, facilities, financial services and specialized staff. Registration: Start date: 6 Oct 2010, Lebanon, Beirut. **Aims** Identify and address the needs of social scientists and social science communities in the Arab countries; enhance social science capacities of individual researchers, as well as academic and research institutions; encourage production of independent, high quality research in the Arab region; provide forums for exchange and communication among social scientists in the Arab region; articulate and support the role of the social sciences in promoting the public interest; support effective networks among research, academic, policy and practitioners' communities as well as with the public and the media. **Structure** General Assembly; Board of Trustees; Secretariat, headed by Director General. **Languages** Arabic, English, French. **Staff** 18.00 FTE, paid. **Finance** Sources: international organizations. Annual budget: 5,000,000 USD (2021). **Activities** Events/meetings; financial and/or material support; training/education. **Events** *Conference* Beirut (Lebanon) 2023, *Conference* Beirut (Lebanon) 2021, *Biennial Conference* Beirut (Lebanon) 2019, *Biennial Conference* Beirut (Lebanon) 2017, *Biennial Conference* Beirut (Lebanon) 2015.

Members Institutional; Individual. Members in 28 countries and territories:
Algeria, Belgium, Canada, Denmark, Egypt, France, Germany, Iraq, Italy, Jordan, Kuwait, Lebanon, Libya, Mauritania, Morocco, Netherlands, Palestine, Qatar, Saudi Arabia, Sudan, Sweden, Syrian AR, Tunisia, Türkiye, UK, United Arab Emirates, USA, Yemen.

NGO Relations Member of (3): *Arab Foundations Forum (AFF, #00963); International Science Council (ISC, #14796); Middle East Studies Association (MESA).* [2021.09.16/XJ5099/**D**]

♦ Arab Council for Supporting Fair Trial (unconfirmed)

♦ Arab Council for the Training of Students of Arab Universities (ACTSAU) 00933

Contact address not obtained. T. +96265355000. Fax +9626536747.
URL: http://fetweb.ju.edu.jo/actsau/

Aims Encourage member universities and various Arab organizations to provide training opportunities for students of Arab universities. **Structure** Board of Directors. [2011/XJ2938/**D**]

♦ Arab Countries Water Utilities Association (ACWUA) 00934

SG Umm Umarah Street 19 A, Alrasheed Area, PO Box 962449, Amman 11196, Jordan. T. +96265161700. Fax +96265161800. E-mail: acwua_secretariat@acwua.org.
URL: http://www.acwua.org/

History 2006. Officially launched, 30 Jul 2009, Amman (Jordan). **Aims** Bring together active water experts and utilities in the Arab region; represent and promote common technical managerial, legal, scientific and economic interest of water utilities in the Arab region; participation in the propagation of relevant water industry standards; support members and other regional professionals in various water science and management fields according to their needs; collaborate with governmental and nongovernmental organizations on both national and international levels. **Structure** General Assembly; Board of Directors; Specialized Committees (6); Secretariat, headed by Secretary General. **Languages** Arabic, English. **Staff** 13.00 FTE, paid. **Finance** Sources: fees for services; meeting proceeds; members' dues. **Activities** Capacity building; certification/accreditation; events/meetings; guidance/assistance/consulting; knowledge management/information dissemination; monitoring/evaluation; networking/liaising; publishing activities; research/documentation; standards/guidelines; training/education. **Events** *Arab Water Week International Conference* Amman (Jordan) 2023, *Arab Water Week International Conference* Sweimeh (Jordan) 2019, *Arab Water Week International Conference* Sweimeh (Jordan) 2017, *Arab Water Week International Conference* Sweimeh (Jordan) 2015, *Best Practices Conference* Algiers (Algeria) 2013. **Publications** *ACWUA Newsletter.* Guidelines; reports; manuals; operational guides.

Members Full in 22 countries and territories:
Algeria, Bahrain, Canada, Egypt, Germany, Iraq, Jordan, Kuwait, Lebanon, Libya, Mauritania, Morocco, Oman, Palestine, Saudi Arabia, Sri Lanka, Sudan, Syrian AR, Tunisia, United Arab Emirates, USA, Yemen.

NGO Relations Member of (5): *Euro-Mediterranean-Arab Association (EMA, #05717); Global Water Operators' Partnerships Alliance (GWOPA, #10652); Global Water Partnership (GWP, #10653); International Water Association (IWA, #15865); World Water Council (WWC, #21908).* Member of: national associations. [2022.04.01/XJ6906/**D**]

♦ Arab Court of Justice (unconfirmed)

♦ Arab Cycling Federation 00935

Chairman PO Box 69666, Sharjah, United Arab Emirates. T. +97165665554. Fax +97165675151. E-mail: arab.cyc.fed@gmail.com.
URL: http://www.arabcycling.com/

Languages Arabic. **Staff** 3.00 FTE, paid. **Events** *High-Level International Conference on Water Cooperation* Dushanbe (Tajikistan) 2013. [2016.06.01/XD0947/**D**]

♦ Arab Demographers' Association (no recent information)

♦ Arab Dental Federation (ADF) 00936

Fédération dentaire arabe

Pres Kuwait Dental Association, Jabriya, Kuwait. E-mail: kda.org.kw@gmail.com.

History 1969. **Events** *Afro-Arab Conference* Khartoum (Sudan) 2007, *Congress* Khartoum (Sudan) 2005, *Congress* Amman (Jordan) 1988. **Members** Membership countries not specified. [2014/XD0203/**D**]

♦ Arab Development Fund (no recent information)
♦ Arab Distributors' Union (inactive)
♦ Arab Drilling and Workover Company (see: #17854)

♦ Arab Economic and Social Council (AESC) 00937

Conseil économique et social arabe (CESA)

Assistant SG c/o LAS, Midan el Tahrir, PO Box 11642, Cairo, Egypt. T. +202750511. Fax +202740331.

History Apr 1950, within the framework of *League of Arab States (LAS, #16420),* according to article VIII of the *Joint Arab Defence and Economic Cooperation Treaty,* signed in 1950. **Aims** Ensure a climate of well-being and prosperity in Arab countries; raise *living standards,* cooperate in promoting their economies; explore their natural assets; facilitate the *trading* of their national *agriculture* and *industrial* product; and in general do everything possible to organize economic activity, to standardize it and to conclude the agreements necessary to attain such aims. **Structure** Council is composed of Ministers of Economic Affairs or their representatives and meets twice a year on ministerial level of the ministries concerned. Preparatory Commissions (3): Economic Commission; Social Commission; Organizations Commission for coordination and follow-up. **Languages** Arabic. **Finance** Annual budget of the General Department for Economic Affairs. **Activities** Draws up general Arab economic policies and framework strategy for Joint Arab Action; implements economic plans based on this strategy. Supervises the work of Arab specialized organizations affiliated to the LAS and coordinates the work of the Coordination Committee between the League and these organizations. Provides these organizations with compulsory advice regarding their budgets and makes requests to them on implementation of Arab joint ventures in accordance with Council conditions. Instrumental in setting up: *Arab Fisheries Company (AFC, #00959); Council of Arab Ministers of Tourism (#04865); Arab Satellite Communications Institute (no recent information); Société arabe de navigation maritime (inactive); Société arabe de potassium (inactive).* **Events** *Session* Cairo (Egypt) 2009, *Session* Cairo (Egypt) 2009, *Session* Aden (Yemen) 2005, *Session* Cairo (Egypt) 2004, *Session* Cairo (Egypt) 2004. **Publications** *Joint Arab Economic Report* (annual). Treaties; studies; reports, mainly on Arab States economic integration.

Members Ministers in charge of economic affairs, or their representatives, in 21 countries:
Algeria, Bahrain, Djibouti, Egypt, Iraq, Jordan, Kuwait, Lebanon, Libya, Mauritania, Morocco, Oman, Palestine, Qatar, Saudi Arabia, Somalia, Sudan, Syrian AR, Tunisia, United Arab Emirates, Yemen.

IGO Relations *Arab Trade Financing Programme (ATFP, #01060).* [2008/XE5263/**E***]

♦ Arab Economic and Social Development Fund / see Arab Fund for Economic and Social Development (#00965)

♦ Arab Educational Information Network (Shamaa) 00938

Exec Dir Point A Tower, 10th Floor, Marguerite Marie Street, Mathaf, Achrafieh, Beirut, Lebanon. T. +9611611560. E-mail: shamaa@shamaa.org.
URL: http://www.shamaa.org/

History 2010, Beirut (Lebanon). **Aims** Acts as a main reference for researchers and others concerned with educational knowledge, in its capacity as a database that documents all sorts of scholarly work on education produced in the Arab countries and by Arab researchers. **Structure** Board of Trustees; Executive Committee. **Languages** Arabic, English, French. **Staff** 10.00 FTE, paid. **Activities** Capacity building; events/meetings; knowledge management/information dissemination. **Consultative Status** Consultative status granted from: *UNESCO (#20322)* (Consultative Status). **NGO Relations** Also links with national organizations. [2022.04.25/AA0003/**F**]

♦ Arab Educational Training Centre for Gulf States (internationally oriented national body)
♦ Arab Endodontic Society / see Arab Endodontic Society (#00939)

♦ Arab Endodontic Society (AES) 00939

Pres Lab of Dento-Facial/Clinical/Biological Approach, Fac of Dental Medicine, Univ of Monastir, Avicenne Avenue 5019, Monastir, Tunisia. E-mail: hediabgna@yahoo.fr – hedia@psm.rnu.tn.

History Proposed 2007, Dubai (United Arab Emirates). Officially announced 2008, Amman (Jordan). Former names and other names: *Arab Endodontic Society (AES)* – former; *Pan Arab Endodontic Society* – former. **Aims** Be a leading provider of evidence-based continuing endodontic education. **Structure** Board; Endodontic Board Committee. **Languages** Arabic, English, French. **Finance** Sources: members' dues; sponsorship. **Activities** Events/meetings. **Events** *Pan Arab Endodontic Conference* Dubai (United Arab Emirates) 2021, *Conference* Marrakech (Morocco) 2020, *Conference* Cairo (Egypt) 2017, *Pan Arab Endodontic Conference* Hammamet (Tunisia) 2015, *Pan Arab Endodontic Conference* Lebanon 2013. **Publications** Articles.

Members Full in 14 countries:
Algeria, Egypt, Iraq, Jordan, Lebanon, Libya, Morocco, Palestine, Qatar, Saudi Arabia, Sudan, Syrian AR, Tunisia, United Arab Emirates. [2021/XJ8567/**D**]

♦ Arab Engineering Industries Company (inactive)
♦ Arab Engineering Union / see Federation of Arab Engineers (#09420)
♦ Arab Equestrian Federation (inactive)
♦ Arab Federation of Automobile Clubs and Tourist Societies (inactive)
♦ Arab Federation of Building and Wood Workers (no recent information)

♦ Arab Federation of Chambers of Shipping 00940

Exec Sec 584 El-Horreya Street, Gleem, Alexandria, 21619, Egypt. T. +2035840346 – +201553422424. Fax +2035838266. E-mail: info@arabfcs.org – secretary@arabfcs.org.
Exec Assistant address not obtained.
URL: http://www.arabfcs.org/

History 24 Jul 2002, Alexandria (Egypt). Founded within the framework of *Council of Arab Economic Unity (CAEU, #04859).* **Aims** Provide support and assistance in the fields of maritime transport and its services. **Structure** Board. **Languages** Arabic, English. **Staff** 5.50 FTE, paid. **Finance** Sources: members' dues. **Activities** Events/meetings. **Publications** *Newsletter* (12 a year).

Members Affiliated; Operating. Organizations and companies in 8 countries:
Egypt, Jordan, Lebanon, Morocco, Sudan, Syrian AR, United Arab Emirates, Yemen. [2022.02.16/XM1481/**D**]

♦ Arab Federation of Chemical Fertilizer Producers / see Arab Fertilizer Association (#00958)
♦ Arab Federation of Chemical and Petrochemical Industries (no recent information)

♦ **Arab Federation of Clinical Biology (AFCB)** **00941**
Pres address not obtained.
History 1974, Egypt. Status revised 1991. **Aims** Enhance laboratory medicine practice in the region. **Structure** Executive Board. **Languages** Arabic, English, French. **Staff** 4.00 FTE, paid. **Finance** Sources: members' dues. Annual budget: 5,000 USD. **Activities** Events/meetings. **Events** *Congress* Beirut (Lebanon) 2021, *Triennial Congress* Khartoum (Sudan) 2015, *Triennial Congress* Marrakech (Morocco) 2012, *Triennial Congress* Beirut (Lebanon) 2009, *Triennial Congress* Damascus (Syrian AR) 2006. **Publications** Journals.
Members Full in 12 countries:
Algeria, Egypt, Jordan, Lebanon, Libya, Morocco, Palestine, Saudi Arabia, Sudan, Syrian AR, Tunisia, Yemen.
IGO Relations *WHO (#20950)*. **NGO Relations** Member of: *International Federation of Clinical Chemistry and Laboratory Medicine (IFCC, #13392)*. [2021/XM2814/**D**]

♦ Arab Federation of Construction, Wood and Building Materials (inactive)

♦ **Arab Federation for the Consumer (AFC)** **00942**
Pres PO Box 926692, Amman 11190, Jordan. T. +96265153211. Fax +96265156983. E-mail: consumer@go.com.jo.
History Founded by *Council of Arab Economic Unity (CAEU, #04859)*. Also referred to as *Arab Federation for Consumers*. **Aims** Defend consumer rights. **Structure** General Assembly; Board of Directors. **Languages** Arabic, English. **Staff** 3.50 FTE, paid. Voluntary. **Finance** Funding from: national institutions; grants from individuals; governments. Budget (annual): about US$ 35,000. **Activities** Research/documentation; advocacy/lobbying/activism; training/education; conflict resolution. **Events** *Meeting* Muscat (Oman) 2010, *Meeting* Amman (Jordan) 1998. **Publications** Weekly letter for prices; price index letters.
Members Societies in 14 countries and territories:
Algeria, Bahrain, Egypt, Iraq, Jordan, Lebanon, Morocco, Oman, Palestine, Saudi Arabia, Sudan, Syrian AR, United Arab Emirates, Yemen.
IGO Relations Observer status with: *League of Arab States (LAS, #16420)*. **NGO Relations** Observer status with: *Consumers International (CI, #04773)*; *International Organization for Standardization (ISO, #14473)*. [2014.10.01/XJ3402/**D**]

♦ Arab Federation for Consumers / see Arab Federation for the Consumer (#00942)
♦ Arab Federation for Democracy and Workers Education Associations (no recent information)
♦ Arab Federation for Drug Industries and Medical Appliances / see Arab Union of Manufacturers of Pharmaceuticals and Medical Appliances (#01070)

♦ **Arab Federation for Engineering Industries (AFEI)** **00943**
Fédération arabe pour les industries d'ingénierie
General Secretariat Daraa HWY, Sahnaya, PO Box 14429, Damascus, Syrian AR. T. +963116712311. Fax +963116712319. E-mail: afei.sy@gmail.com.
URL: http://www.arabengineeringindustries.org/
History 28 Dec 1975, Baghdad (Iraq), on the initiative of *Arab Industrial Development Organization (AIDO, inactive)* and *Council of Arab Economic Unity (CAEU, #04859)*. **Aims** Assist members in marketing their products in Arab markets and in dealing with international markets as a cooperative group; assist in procuring raw and intermediate materials and in production requirements at best terms, and facilitate exchange of these materials among Arab countries; furnish members with statistics and commercial, economic and technical information relating to engineering *industries*; improve vocational, technical and professional capabilities of staff in engineering industries; carry out technical and economic feasibility studies, alone or in cooperation with other parties; assist in acquiring 'know-how rights' from all over the industrial world and encourage exchange of know-how among members for the benefit of Arab countries; act as conciliator and arbitrator in disputes between members and non-members when required. **Structure** General Assembly. Board of Directors, consisting of a number of full active members which does not exceed 1.5 times the number of countries represented. General Secretariat, headed by Secretary General. Regional Offices in Tunis (Tunisia) and Cairo (Egypt). **Languages** Arabic. **Staff** 10.50 FTE, paid. **Finance** Members' dues. Budget (annual): US$ 250,000. **Events** *EuroArab Conference on SMEs* Damascus (Syrian AR) 2010.
Members Full Active; Participant; Associate; Observer. Members in 13 countries:
Algeria, Egypt, Iraq, Jordan, Kuwait, Lebanon, Libya, Morocco, Qatar, Saudi Arabia, Syrian AR, Tunisia, Yemen.
Consultative Status Consultative status granted from: *ECOSOC (#05331)* (Ros C); *UNCTAD (#20285)* (General Category). **IGO Relations** One of the specialized unions within: *League of Arab States (LAS, #16420)*. Collaborative Arab organization of: *Arab Organization for Agricultural Development (AOAD, #01018)*. **NGO Relations** *Arab Iron and Steel Union (AISU, #00998)*. [2017/XD9858/t/**D**]

♦ **Arab Federation of Exchanges (AFE)** **00944**
SG Bechara El Khoury Street, Ghanaga Bldg – 5th Floor, PO Box 11-9696 Riad el Solh, Beirut, Lebanon. T. +9611643749. Fax +9611643436. E-mail: info@arab-exchanges.org.
URL: http://www.arab-exchanges.org/
History 1978. Previously also referred to as *Union of Arab Stock Exchanges (UASE) – Union arabe des bourses de valeur (UAB)* and *Union of Arab Stock Exchanges and Securities Commissions*. **Aims** Create a transparent and developed environment for Arab Capital Markets in order to reduce barriers of securities trading across countries, enhance communication among members and coordinate activities with regional and international partners. **Structure** Board; Chairman; Executive Committee; Secretariat, headed by Secretary General. **Languages** Arabic, English. **Publications** *AFE Newsletter* (4 a year). Quarterly Report. Annual Report; studies; surveys; guides.
Members Regulated Stock Exchanges (18), Clearing Settlement and Depository Companies (4), and affiliated Brokerage Firms (13) in 17 countries and territories:
Bahrain, Egypt, Iraq, Jordan, Kurdish area, Kuwait, Lebanon, Libya, Morocco, Oman, Palestine, Qatar, Saudi Arabia, Sudan, Syrian AR, Tunisia, United Arab Emirates.
Stock Exchanges of 16 countries and territories:
Bahrain, Egypt, Iraq, Jordan, Kuwait, Lebanon, Libya, Morocco, Oman, Palestine, Qatar, Saudi Arabia, Sudan, Syrian AR, Tunisia, United Arab Emirates.
Clearing houses in 7 countries:
Egypt, Jordan, Kuwait, Lebanon, Morocco, Oman, Tunisia.
Brokerage firms in 3 countries:
Kuwait, Lebanon, United Arab Emirates.
IGO Relations *Arab Monetary Fund (AMF, #01009)*. **NGO Relations** Associate member of: *Union of Arab Securities Authorities (UASA, #20357)*. [2015.02.18/XD1413/**D**]

♦ **Arab Federation of Fish Producers (AFFP)** **00945**
Fédération arabe des industries de la pêche (FAIP) – Federación Arabe de Productores Pesqueros (FAPP)
Tunisia Regional Office Dir Gén de la Pêche et de l'aquaculture, 30 rue Alain Savary, 1002 Tunis, Tunisia. T. +21671782635. Fax +21671799401.
Egypt Regional Office General Authority for Fish Resources Development, 4 Tayaran Street, Nasr City, Cairo, Egypt. T. +2022620118 – +2022620119.
Jordan Regional Office Jordan Cooperative Organization, PO Box 1343 – 6240, Amman, Jordan. T. +9626665170 – +9626665176.
History 2 Oct 1976, Baghdad (Iraq), as a Specialized Arab Federation within the framework of *Council of Arab Economic Unity (CAEU, #04859)*. Also referred to as *Arab Union of Fish Producers – Union arabe des produits de la pêche (UAPP)*. **Aims** Promote development of *fisheries* in Arab countries. **Structure** Plenary Assembly (annual); Council; Officers. **Languages** Arabic. **Staff** 11.00 FTE, paid. **Finance** Members' dues. **Activities** Knowledge management/information dissemination; events/meetings; training/education; networking/liaising. **Events** *Arab symposium for planning and promoting fish culture and crustaceans* Damascus (Syrian AR) 1993. **Publications** *AFFP Quarterly Journal*. *The Arab Fisheries Guide* in Arabic. Studies.
Members Governments of 14 countries:
Algeria, Djibouti, Egypt, Iraq, Jordan, Libya, Mauritania, Morocco, Palestine, Somalia, Sudan, Syrian AR, Tunisia, Yemen.
Bodies (1) in 1 country:
Saudi Arabia.
IGO Relations Special links with: *FAO (#09260)*. Participates in the activities of: *UNCTAD (#20285)*. One of the specialized unions within: *League of Arab States (LAS, #16420)*. Collaborative Arab organization of: *Arab Organization for Agricultural Development (AOAD, #01018)*. Observer to: *Regional Commission for Fisheries (RECOFI, #18763)*. [2015.12.16/XD0361/t/**D***]

♦ **Arab Federation for Food Industries (AFFI)** **00946**
Fédération arabe des industries alimentaires (FAIA)
Pres PO Box 10088, Damascus, Syrian AR. E-mail: president@arabffi.org.
Gen Sec PO Box 470, Amman 11118, Jordan. E-mail: arabfood3@gmail.com.
Facebook: https://www.facebook.com/arabfood/
History 27 Jul 1977, Cairo (Egypt). Founded following recommendations of a meeting of LAS, 7 Oct 1976, Baghdad (Iraq). Statutes amended 25 Feb 1980, Baghdad. A specialized union within *Council of Arab Economic Unity (CAEU, #04859)*. Former names and other names: *Arab Union for Foodstuff Industries* – former. **Aims** Strengthen the Arab food industry by developing commercial, industrial, administrative and technical relations related to industrial food and beverages and regional integration projects from raw materials to production and marketing. **Structure** General Assembly (annual); Board of Directors; Secretariat General; Coordinating Offices; Regional Offices. Sectoral Committees (13): *Pan Arab Committee for Dairy Products (no recent information)*; *Pan Arab Committee for Feed Industries (no recent information)*; *Pan Arab Committee for Grains (no recent information)*; Pan Arab Committee for Investment; *Pan Arab Committee for Oil Seeds and Vegetable Oils (no recent information)*; *Pan Arab Committee for Packing and Packaging (no recent information)*; *Pan Arab Committee for Poultry (no recent information)*; Pan Arab Committee for Soaps, Detergents, and Cosmetics; *Pan Arab Committee for Soft Drinks, Juices and Mineral Waters (no recent information)*; *Pan Arab Committee for Standardization and Quality Control (no recent information)*; Pan Arab Committee for Sugar; Pan Arab Committee for Sugar Confectionery; *Pan Arab Committee for Tomato Products (no recent information)*. **Languages** Arabic, English. **Staff** 12.00 FTE, paid; 22.00 FTE, voluntary. **Finance** Sources: government support; grants; international organizations; members' dues. **Activities** Capacity building; events/meetings; knowledge management/information dissemination; monitoring/evaluation; research/documentation; training/education. **Events** *Arab Bread Day Annual Conference* Amman (Jordan) 2021, *Arab Food Industries Forum on Food Safety and Trade Facilitation* Amman (Jordan) 2019, *Conference for Poultry and Feed* Amman (Jordan) 2014, *International seminar on children, nutrition and food industries* Baghdad (Iraq) 1996, *Pan Arab seminar on raw materials of soap and detergents industry* Tripoli (Libyan AJ) 1996. **Publications** *Arab Food Industries Journal* (4 a year); *Arab Meat Industry Journal* (4 a year); *Food Statistics* (annual). Directories; reports.
Members Working and Associate: companies (private and governmental) in 19 countries and territories:
Algeria, Bahrain, Egypt, Iraq, Jordan, Kuwait, Lebanon, Libya, Mauritania, Morocco, Oman, Palestine, Qatar, Saudi Arabia, Sudan, Syrian AR, Tunisia, United Arab Emirates, Yemen.
Contacts with organizations outside the region in 7 countries:
Canada, Finland, France, Germany, Italy, Spain, USA.
Consultative Status Consultative status granted from: *ECOSOC (#05331)* (Ros C); *UNIDO (#20336)*. **IGO Relations** Member of (1): *League of Arab States (LAS, #16420)* (Hunger Eradication Committee). Cooperates in related fields with: *FAO (#09260)*; *International Olive Council (IOC, #14405)*. Collaborative Arab organization of: *Arab Organization for Agricultural Development (AOAD, #01018)*. [2022.05.12/XD4223/t/**D**]

♦ Arab Federation of Food Workers (inactive)
♦ Arab Federation of Health Workers' Unions (inactive)
♦ Arab Federation of Leather Industries (inactive)

♦ **Arab Federation for Libraries and Information (AFLI)** **00947**
Union arabe des bibliothèques et de l'information (FABI)
Pres PO Box 80202, Jeddah 21589, Saudi Arabia.
URL: http://www.arab-afli.org/
History 19 Jan 1986, Kairouan (Tunisia). Previously also referred to in French as *Fédération arabe des bibliothèques et centres d'information*. **Aims** Conserve and make known the Arab heritage everywhere in both written or audiovisual form. **Structure** Executive Bureau, consisting of President, Vice-President, Secretary-General, Treasurer and 3 members. **Languages** Arabic. **Staff** 2.00 FTE, paid. **Finance** Member's dues. **Activities** Organizes: Arab Information Congress with FTERSI and Arab universities; other congresses; manifestations; national remembrance days. **Events** *Congress* Hammamet (Tunisia) 2014, *Congress* Medina (Saudi Arabia) 2013, *Congress* Khartoum (Sudan) 2011, *Congress* Beirut (Lebanon) 2010, *Congress* Casablanca (Morocco) 2009. **Publications** *Sada El-Ittihad – Echo de l'AFLI* (12 a year) in Arabic, French – bulletin. Meeting proceedings; studies.
Members Individuals in 21 countries and territories:
Algeria, Bahrain, Djibouti, Egypt, France, Iraq, Jordan, Kuwait, Lebanon, Libya, Mauritania, Morocco, Oman, Palestine, Qatar, Saudi Arabia, Sudan, Tunisia, United Arab Emirates, USA, Yemen.
IGO Relations Agreement with: *Arab League Educational, Cultural and Scientific Organization (ALECSO, #01003)*. [2014/XD0977/v/**D**]

♦ Arab Federation for Metrology (unconfirmed)
♦ Arab Federation of Municipality Workers (inactive)

♦ **Arab Federation of NGOs for Drug Abuse Prevention (AFNDA)** **00948**
Contact PO Box 8180, Nasr City, Cairo, 11371, Egypt. T. +2024013976 – +2024013977 – +2024015741. Fax +2022600541 – +2024015741.
NGO Relations Member of: *International Federation of Non-Government Organizations for the Prevention of Drug and Substance Abuse (IFNGO, #13490)*. [2008/XM1587/**D**]

♦ Arab Federation of the Organizations of the Deaf / see Arab Federation of Organizations Working with the Deaf (#00949)

♦ **Arab Federation of Organizations Working with the Deaf (AFOWD)** . **00949**
Contact PO Box 4230, Damascus, Syrian AR. Fax +963112217401.
History 1972, Damascus (Syrian AR), as *Arab Federation of the Organizations of the Deaf (AFOD)*. Later known as *Arab Federation of the Organs of the Deaf (AFOD) – Fédération arabe des organismes au service des sourds*. Also referred to as *AFOOD*. **Aims** Coordinate efforts of medical, educational and social agencies working for the deaf; provide *care*, education and *rehabilitation* of the deaf throughout the Arab world. **Structure** General Conference (every 4 years). **Languages** Arabic. **Staff** 3.00 FTE, paid; 3.00 FTE, voluntary. **Finance** Members' contributions. Grants. Budget (annual): Syrian Pounds 450,000. **Activities** Supports programmes and scientific surveys; organizes conferences (every 4 years), scientific symposia (every 4 years) and enables exchange of experience among Arab countries on problems related to the deaf; develops education and rehabilitation programmes; unifies sign terms and sign alphabet of the deaf. Sections (4): Scientific; Medical; Social; Educational-Psychological. Rehabilitation courses for teachers of the deaf. Works on ability assessment and adjustment of tests to be suitable for the deaf. Annual celebration of the Week of the Deaf Child. **Events** *Biennial Scientific Symposium* Riyadh (Saudi Arabia) 2008, *Biennial Scientific Symposium* Riyadh (Saudi Arabia) 2007, *Biennial Scientific Symposium* Sharjah (United Arab Emirates) 1990, *Biennial scientific symposium* Sharjah (United Arab Emirates) 1990, *Scientific symposium / Biennial Scientific Symposium* Damascus (Syrian AR) 1988. **Publications** *AFOD Newsletters* (occasional). Symposium proceedings.
Members Governmental and private institutions in 13 countries:
Algeria, Egypt, Iraq, Jordan, Kuwait, Lebanon, Libya, Oman, Palestine, Saudi Arabia, Sudan, Syrian AR, Tunisia.
IGO Relations Formal relations with: *Arab League Educational, Cultural and Scientific Organization (ALECSO, #01003)*. [2015/XD7806/**D**]

♦ Arab Federation of the Organs of the Deaf / see Arab Federation of Organizations Working with the Deaf (#00949)
♦ Arab Federation of Paper Industries and Printing / see Arab Federation for Paper, Printing and Packaging Industries (#00950)

♦ **Arab Federation for Paper, Printing and Packaging Industries (AFPPPI)** **00950**
Union arabe des industries papetières et de l'imprimerie
Office Sin El Fil-Beirut Hall Area, Wadih ammoun Str, Farid Tourma Bldg Bloc B 2nd Floor, Beirut, Lebanon. T. +9611510179. E-mail: info@afpppi.com.
URL: http://www.afpppi.com/

History 29 Mar 1977, Cairo (Egypt). Founded as a specialized federation of *Council of Arab Economic Unity (CAEU, #04859)*. Former names and other names: *Arab Union for Paper and Printing Industries* – former; *Arab Federation of Paper Industries and Printing* – former; *Union arabe de papeterie et des imprimeurs* – former; *Société arabe d'imprimerie* – former. **Aims** Assist Arab paper industries to cooperate and coordinate so as to serve all members in their different activities of production, marketing, technical assistance and exchange of *raw materials*. **Structure** General Assembly. Board of Directors. **Finance** Members' dues. Other sources: government assistance; donations. **Activities** Events/meetings. **Events** *International conference / Conference* Cairo (Egypt) 2000, *International conference / Conference* Tunis (Tunisia) 1999. **Publications** *Al Warak* (3 a year) in Arabic.
Members Paper companies, printers and converters in 16 countries:
Algeria, Bahrain, Egypt, Iraq, Jordan, Kuwait, Lebanon, Libya, Morocco, Palestine, Saudi Arabia, Sudan, Syrian AR, Tunisia, United Arab Emirates, Yemen.
IGO Relations A specialized union within: *League of Arab States (LAS, #16420)*. [2020/XD5048/t/**D**]

♦ Arab Federation of Petroleum, Miners, Metal, Chemical and Allied Industries Workers (no recent information)
♦ Arab Federation of Posts, Telegram and Telephone Workers (inactive)
♦ Arab Federation for Producers of Drugs and Medical Appliances / see Arab Union of Manufacturers of Pharmaceuticals and Medical Appliances (#01070)

♦ Arab Federation for the Protection of Intellectual Property Rights (AFPIPR) 00951

Contact al Nil Tower, 7th floor, 97-B Corniche Al Niel, Cairo, Egypt. T. +202584070. Fax +202584070.
URL: http://afpipr.com/
Consultative Status Consultative status granted from: *UNCTAD (#20285)* (Special Category); *World Intellectual Property Organization (WIPO, #21593)* (Permanent Observer Status). [2019/XJ0941/**D**]

♦ Arab Federation of Psychiatrists (AFP) 00952

Fédération arabe de psychiatrie
Pres Service de Psychiatrie, Hospital Razi, La Manousa, 2010 Tunis, Tunisia. E-mail: sarhan34@gmail.com.
URL: http://www.arabpsynet.com/Associations/AFP.ass.htm
Events *Conference* Cairo (Egypt) 2015, *Conference* Amman (Jordan) 2014, *Pan Arab Psychiatric Conference* Beirut (Lebanon) 2014, *Conference* Doha (Qatar) 2013, *International conference on psychiatry* Jeddah (Saudi Arabia) 2011. **NGO Relations** Affiliate member of: *World Psychiatric Association (WPA, #21741)*. [2016/XD6669/**D**]

♦ Arab Federation of Shipping (AFS) 00953

Fédération arabe des transporteurs maritime
SG Talet El Khayat – Canal 7 Street, PO Box 11, Beirut, Lebanon. T. +9611738620. Fax +9611738620. E-mail: info@afos-shipping.com.
Chairman address not obtained.
URL: http://www.afos-shipping.com/
History 10 Apr 1979. Established pursuant resolution taken by *Council of Arab Economic Unity (CAEU, #04859)*. Expanded from *'Arab Maritime Transport Academy, Abou-Keir Region Alexandria (AMTA)'*, set up Apr 1975, as a specialized agency acting in the framework of the Transport and Communications sector of *League of Arab States (LAS, #16420)*, which in its turn had been expanded from the *Arab Academy for Maritime Transport (AAMT)*, formed 26 May 1972. Former names and other names: *AFOS* – former; *Union arabe des transporteurs maritime* – former; *Fédération arabe des armateurs* – former. **Aims** Coordinate member states efforts in order to develop Arab *maritime transport*; participate in the elaboration of Arab *economic* common action and economic integration. **Languages** Arabic, English, French. **Staff** 4.00 FTE, paid. **Finance** Sources: members' dues. Annual budget: 30,000 USD. **Activities** Events/meetings; research and development. **Events** *General Meeting* Egypt 2015, *General Meeting* Egypt 2014, *General Meeting* Beirut (Lebanon) 2013, *General Meeting* Damascus (Syrian AR) 2007, *General assembly / General Meeting* Damascus (Syrian AR) 2000. **Publications** *Maritime Industry* (6 a year).
Members Arab shipping companies of 17 Arab countries:
Algeria, Bahrain, Egypt, Iraq, Jordan, Kuwait, Lebanon, Libya, Morocco, Oman, Palestine, Qatar, Saudi Arabia, Sudan, Syrian AR, Tunisia, United Arab Emirates.
IGO Relations Cooperation agreement with and Member of: *International Maritime Organization (IMO, #14102)*. Participates in the activities of and Member of: *UNCTAD (#20285)*. **NGO Relations** Instrumental in setting up (1): *Association of African Maritime Training Institutes (AAMTI, no recent information)*. [2020.09.01/XF6002/**F***]

♦ Arab Federation of Social Workers (inactive)
♦ Arab Federation for Sports Journalism / see Arab Federation of Sports Journalists (#00954)

♦ Arab Federation of Sports Journalists 00954

Association arabe des journalistes sportifs
Contact address not obtained. T. +96415413877.
History An Autonomous Special Panel of *Federation of Arab Journalists (FAJ, #09422)*. Also referred to as: *Arab Sports Journalism Confederation*; *Arab Sports Journalism Federation* and *Arab Association for Sports Journalism*; *Arab Committee of Sports Journalism*; *Arab Federation for Sports Journalism*. **Members** Individuals. Membership countries not specified. **NGO Relations** Member of: *Arab Sports Confederation (ASC, inactive)*. [2014/XD8060/v/**D**]

♦ Arab Federation of Sports Medicine (inactive)

♦ Arab Federation of Surveyors 00955

Fédération arabe des géomètres
Pres Bechara El Khoury Street, Ghanaga Bldg, 4th Floor, Beirut, Lebanon. T. +9611659141. E-mail: u.a.g.t.dr.s@gmail.com – info@auog.org.
History Oct 2002, Beirut (Lebanon). Former names and other names: *Arab Union of Surveyors (AUS)* – alias. **Aims** Promote cooperation, coordination and communication among surveyors in the Arab countries. **Activities** Events/meetings. **Events** *Symposium on land administration in the Arab world* Jordan 2005, *International scientific congress on the surveying sciences and their role in economic and social development plans* Beirut (Lebanon) 2004, *FIG regional conference for the Arab countries and francophone Africa* Marrakech (Morocco) 2003. **NGO Relations** *Global Land Tool Network (GLTN, #10452)*; *Union Méditerranéenne des Géomètres (UMG, #20460)*. [2019.09.24/XJ1008/**D**]

♦ Arab Federation for Technical Education (no recent information)
♦ Arab Federation for Textile Industries (inactive)
♦ Arab Federation of Textile Workers (inactive)

♦ Arab Federation of Tire and Rubber Industries 00956

Contact address not obtained. T. +2034294376.
URL: http://af-tri.org/
History 1993, Alexandria (Egypt). **Activities** Conferences; technical meetings. **IGO Relations** *Council of Arab Economic Unity (CAEU, #04859)*. [2015/XD8817/t/**D**]

♦ Arab Federation of Transport and Communication Workers (no recent information)
♦ Arab Federation of Transport Workers (no recent information)
♦ Arab Federation of Workers in Metal, Mechanical and Electrical Industries (no recent information)

♦ Arab Fencing Confederation 00957

Pres address not obtained.
History Also referred to as *Arab Fencing Federation*. [2014/XD0931/**D**]

♦ Arab Fencing Federation / see Arab Fencing Confederation (#00957)

♦ Arab Fertilizer Association (AFA) 00958

SG 9 Ramo Buildings, Omar Ibn El-Khattab St, AL-Nasr Road, PO Box 8109,Nasr City, Cairo, 11371, Egypt. T. +20223054464. Fax +20223054465. E-mail: afa@arabfertilizer.org.
URL: http://www.arabfertilizer.org/
History 1 Mar 1975, Kuwait, as *Arab Federation of Chemical Fertilizer Producers (AFCFP)* – *Fédération arabe des producteurs des engrais chimiques*, when Articles of Association were signed following first meeting called by Secretary General of *Council of Arab Economic Unity (CAEU, #04859)*. Commenced operations, 4 Jun 1976. Current title adopted in 1992, after moving to Egypt. **Aims** Promote best utilization of available natural resources, to accomplish highest achievement of added value together with effective contribution in economic development. **Structure** General Assembly (annual). Board of Directors. General Secretariat. Committees (3). **Languages** Arabic, English. **Staff** 13.00 FTE, paid. **Finance** Members' dues. Other sources: proceeds from events. **Activities** Events/meetings; training/education. Information bank provides network of assistance with members' questions. **Events** *Annual International Conference* Cairo (Egypt) 2019, *Annual Technical International Conference* Casablanca (Morocco) 2018, *Annual International Conference* Sharm el Sheikh (Egypt) 2018, *Annual Technical International Conference* Amman (Jordan) 2017, *Annual International Conference* Cairo (Egypt) 2017. **Publications** *AFA Fertilizer Journal* (3 a year). Statistical Annual Report; Annual Report; membership directory; proceedings.
Members Ordinary Arab companies, state-owned or private; Associate Arab companies, chambers of industry, unions; Observer. Ordinary (44) in 14 countries:
Algeria, Bahrain, Egypt, Iraq, Jordan, Kuwait, Libya, Morocco, Oman, Qatar, Saudi Arabia, Syrian AR, Tunisia, United Arab Emirates.
Associate (13) in 3 countries:
Egypt, Jordan, Saudi Arabia.
Observer (17) in 11 countries:
Bahrain, Czechia, Denmark, Egypt, Germany, India, Netherlands, Pakistan, Russia, UK.
Supporting (105) in 21 countries and territories:
Australia, Belgium, Canada, Egypt, Germany, Gibraltar, India, Jordan, Kenya, Lebanon, Libya, Oman, Qatar, Saudi Arabia, Sudan, Syrian AR, Tunisia, Türkiye, UK, United Arab Emirates, USA.
Regional members (2):
Arab Mining Company (ARMICO, #01008); *Arab Petroleum Investments Corporation (APICORP, #01026)*.
Consultative Status Consultative status granted from: *ECOSOC (#05331)* (Ros C); *UNIDO (#20336)*; *FAO (#09260)* (Liaison Status). **IGO Relations** One of the specialized unions within: *League of Arab States (LAS, #16420)*. Collaborative Arab organization of: *Arab Organization for Agricultural Development (AOAD, #01018)*. [2017.03.08/XD4015/y/**D**]

♦ Arab Fisheries Company (AFC) 00959

Société arabe des pêches
Contact address not obtained. T. +966126081881. Fax +966126080150. E-mail: info@arabfisheries.com – arabfiscom@arabfisheries.com – sb-gm@arabfisheries.com.
URL: http://www.arabfisheries.com/
History 22 Feb 1978, Jeddah (Saudi Arabia), by Resolution No (718), under the framework of *Arab Economic and Social Council (AESC, #00937)*. An Affiliate of *League of Arab States (LAS, #16420)*. Also referred to as *Arab Fishing Company*; *Arab Fisheries Group*; *Arab Fisheries Company Group (AFCG)*. **Aims** Develop fish resources of the region and an *aquaculture* system; further consultancy, *trading* and cooperation in the field, especially with Arab countries. **Structure** Board of Directors of 7 members rotates every 3 years. Head Office: Jeddah (Saudi Arabia). Branches (2): Cairo (Egypt), Amman (Jordan). **Finance** Budget (annual): about SR 8 million. **Activities** Aquaculture projects: fish farm project in Khulais (Saudi Arabia); fish farm project in Berseik (Egypt); fish hatchery projects in Abbassah (Egypt); shrimp project in Ras Jalajel (Saudi Arabia) (under negotiation); fish farm project in Omloj (Saudi Arabia). Administration of Pan Arab importing and exporting trade projects. Research. Specialized scientific symposia and conferences. **Publications** Activity Report. Research papers. Information Services: Library.
Members Governments of 12 countries and territories:
Comoros, Iraq, Jordan, Kuwait, Libya, Mauritania, Palestine, Qatar, Saudi Arabia, Sudan, Tunisia, Yemen.
IGO Relations A collaborative Arab organization of: *Arab Organization for Agricultural Development (AOAD, #01018)*. [2014/XE0771/e/**E***]

♦ Arab Fisheries Company Group / see Arab Fisheries Company (#00959)
♦ Arab Fisheries Group / see Arab Fisheries Company (#00959)
♦ Arab Fishing Company / see Arab Fisheries Company (#00959)
♦ Arab Forensic Pathologists and Physicians Union (unconfirmed)
♦ Arab Forum for Alternatives (unconfirmed)

♦ Arab Forum for Environment and Development (AFED) 00960

Secretariat PO Box 113-5474, Beirut, Lebanon. T. +9611321800. Fax +9611321900. E-mail: info@afedonline.org.
Street Address Eshmoun bldg, Rue de Damas, Beirut, Lebanon.
URL: http://www.afedonline.org/
History 17 Jun 2006, Beirut (Lebanon). **Aims** Promote prudent environmental policies and programmes across the Arab region. **Structure** Board of Trustees. Executive Committee, including President, 2 Vice Presidents, Financial Officer and Secretary General. **Publications** *AFED Newsletter*.
Members Corporate; NGOs; Media; Academic and Research Institutions; Government Agencies (Observer Status). Organizations in 7 countries:
Bahrain, Jordan, Kuwait, Lebanon, Qatar, Syrian AR, Tunisia.
Institutions in 6 countries:
Bahrain, Egypt, Jordan, Kuwait, Lebanon, Palestine.
Included in the above, 2 organizations listed in this Yearbook:
Arabian Gulf University (AGU, #00976); *Beirut Arab University (BAU)*.
Government agencies in 3 countries:
Kuwait, Saudi Arabia, United Arab Emirates.
Included in the above, 4 organizations listed in this Yearbook:
Arab Water Academy (AWA, no recent information); *International Center for Biosaline Agriculture (ICBA, #12468)*; *Kuwait Fund for Arab Economic Development (KFAED)*; *Saudi Fund for Development (SFD)*.
Consultative Status Consultative status granted from: *ECOSOC (#05331)* (Special); *UNEP (#20299)*. **NGO Relations** Partner of: *Green Growth Knowledge Platform (GGKP, #10719)*. [2020/XJ7353/y/**F**]

♦ Arab Forum for Young Entrepreneur Associations (AFYE) 00961

Contact La Maison de l'Entreprise, Avenue principale, Les Berges du Lac 1053, Tunis, Tunisia. T. +21671962331. Fax +21671962516.
Aims Promote entrepreneurship among young arabs.
Members Organizations in 7 countries and territories:
Algeria, Egypt, Lebanon, Libya, Morocco, Palestine, Tunisia.
Included in the above, 2 organizations listed in this Yearbook:
Institut arabe des chefs d'entreprises (IACE, #11236); *Lebanese International Businessmen Associations' Network (LIBAN)*. [2010.06.01/XF7078/**F**]

♦ ARABFOS – Pan Arab Federation of Otolaryngological Societies (unconfirmed)

♦ Arab Foundation for Marine Environment (AFME) 00962

Dir PO Box 264, Sidi Gaber, Alexandria, Egypt. T. +2035432704. Fax +2035435956. E-mail: ecosalex@yahoo.com.
History 1995, as *Environmental Consultants and Operative Studies Group*. Current name adopted, 2003. **Aims** Measure, analyse, treat and recycle environmental *pollutants*; supply specialized consultants and operative studies for specific environmental issues. **Languages** Arabic, English, French. **Staff** 5.00 FTE, paid. Staff may be supplemented by consultants. **Finance** Budget (annual): varies, but about US$ 20,000. **Activities** focusing on measurement, analysis, treatment and recycling of environmental pollutants cover: emitted, discharged and accumulated industrial wastes; sewage and urban wastes; oil release and tanker waste; noise, thermal and light intensity levels; water eutrophication; water acidity; wet-lands and soil degradation; ground water contamination. Members are involved in projects and programmes, and in some cases act as consultants for

operating agencies for specific environmental issues, including: measurement of depth and fixing postillions of submerged features such as reefs, rocks, banks, wrecks, etc; carrying out of hydrographic and environmental surveys comprising complex monitoring (eg, tidal rise and fall, mean sea level determination), as well as mathematical and statistical elaboration (including application of numerical models); carrying out of marine meteorological surveys and atmospheric mathematical model application; preparing oceanographic and limnological environmental reports; preparing of operative studies and applied plants for management of coastal zone areas. Projects to date: physical oceanographic and marine meteorological studies and surveys in the Mediterranean sea, Arabian Gulf and Red Sea; evaluation of the South-Eastern Mediterranean productivity; application of numerical hydrodynamics and ecosystem 3D models on the Mediterranean coastal area off Egypt; forecasting information system of the Mediterranean ecosystem and meteorology; management of Lake Manzalah ecosystem and fisheries; Alexandria sewage discharge and its impact on marine and coastal zones; geophysical surveys for pipe-lines extension Western Petroleum Company. Organizes: international conferences; regional and other training courses. **Events** *International conference on tourism development in Arab world* Alexandria (Egypt) 2009, *International conference on essential principles of tourism strategy in Arab world and their impact on national economics* Alexandria (Egypt) 2006, *International conference on marine pollution in the Arab region* Alexandria (Egypt) 2006, *International conference on marine pollution in the Arab region* Alexandria (Egypt) 2005. **Publications** *Arab Journal of Limnology and Oceanography* (2 a year). [2011.06.01/XJ0254/f/**F**]

♦ Arab Foundations Forum (AFF) 00963

Contact PO Box 840888, Amman 11184, Jordan. T. +96267767809. Fax +96265938017. E-mail: info@arabfoundationsforum.org.
URL: http://www.arabfoundationsforum.org/

History 2006. **Aims** Foster dialogue, networking, learning and collaborating among themselves and with partners so as to strengthen the capacity of Arab *philanthropy*. **Structure** General Assembly. Board of Directors, comprising Chairman, Vice-Chairman, Treasurer and 4 members. **Languages** Arabic, English. **Staff** 2.00 FTE, paid. **Activities** Organizes: Annual Meeting; Members' Platform. **Events** *Meeting on corporate philanthropy* Dubai (United Arab Emirates) 2010. **Publications** *Arab Encyclopedia on Philanthropy* – online.
Members Full; Associate; Fellow. Full in 7 countries and territories:
Egypt, Jordan, Lebanon, Palestine, Saudi Arabia, UK, United Arab Emirates.
Included in the above, 3 organizations listed in this Yearbook:
Arab Council for the Social Sciences (ACSS, #00932); Arab Fund for Arts and Culture (AFAC, #00964); Arab Human Rights Foundation (AHRF).
Associate in 4 countries:
Egypt, Jordan, Lebanon, UK.
NGO Relations Member of: *Worldwide Initiatives for Grantmaker Support (WINGS, #21926).* [2018/XJ0645/y/**F**]

- ♦ Arab-French Chamber of Commerce / see Chambre de commerce franco-arabe
- ♦ Arab Fund / see Arab Fund for Economic and Social Development (#00965)

♦ Arab Fund for Arts and Culture (AFAC) 00964

Exec Dir 5th Floor – Gardenia Bldg, Sourati Street, Hamra, PO Box Beirut 13-5290, Beirut, Lebanon. T. +9611747761 – +9611747762. Fax +9611747762. E-mail: info@arabculturefund.org.
URL: http://www.arabculturefund.org/

History 2007. Registered in accordance with Swiss Civil Code. **Aims** Enhance Arab public awareness of modern contemporary artistic production. **Structure** Board. **Languages** Arabic, English, French. **Finance** Sources: grants; donations. Budget (annual): US$ 3 million. **Activities** Awareness raising; events/meetings; financial and/or material support. **Publications** *Grantee Stories* (12 a year); *AFAC Newsletter* (4 a year). Annual Report. **NGO Relations** Member of: *Arab Foundations Forum (AFF, #00963).* [2014.06.01/XJ4983/f/**F**]

♦ Arab Fund for Economic and Social Development (AFESD) 00965

Fonds Arabe pour le Développement Economique et Social (FADES) – Fondo Arabe para el Desarrollo Económico y Social

Dir Gen/Chairman, Board of Directors PO Box 21923, Safat, 13080 Kuwait, Kuwait. T. +96524959000. Fax +96524959390 – +96524959391. E-mail: admin@arabfund.org – hq@arabfund.org.
URL: http://www.arabfund.org/

History 16 May 1968. Established following agreement by the Economic and Social Council of *League of Arab States (LAS, #16420).* Agreement entered into force, 18 Dec 1971. Commenced full operations in 1974. Establishment Agreement amended by Board of Governors in 1997 in response to the need to enhance the developmental role of the private sector in member countries; now authorized to finance private sector development projects in Arab countries. Former names and other names: *Arab Economic and Social Development Fund (Arab Fund)* – former. **Aims** Contribute to financing of economic and social development projects in Arab countries by extending loans, on concessionary terms, to governments and public corporations and enterprises of member states, giving preference to projects which are vital to the Arab world and to joint Arab projects; serve as a catalyst for encouraging direct or indirect *investment* of public and private capital in a manner conducive to development of the Arab economy; provide expertise and technical support in various spheres of economic development. **Structure** Board of Governors (meets at least annually); Board of Directors. **Languages** Arabic, English, French. **Staff** 78.00 FTE, paid. **Finance** Activities funded by financial resources comprising paid-up capital and reserves allocated from retained earnings. **Activities** Events/meetings; financial and/or material support; projects/programmes. **Events** *Arab Energy Conference* Qatar 2023, *Annual Joint Meeting of Arab Financial Institutions* Kuwait (Kuwait) 2019, *Annual Meeting* Amman (Jordan) 2018, *Quadrennial Arab Energy Conference* Marrakech (Morocco) 2018, *Annual Meeting* Rabat (Morocco) 2017. **Publications** *Report* (annual). *Agreement Establishing the Arab Fund for Economic and Social Development* in Arabic, English; *Joint Arab Economic Report* in Arabic, English; *Policy Guidelines and Rules for Financing Public Sector Projects* in Arabic; *Policy Guidelines and Rules for Private Sector* in Arabic; *Policy Guidelines and Rules for Special Account* in Arabic; *Unified Guide for Environmental Requirements for Development Projects* in Arabic.
Members Governments of 22 countries and territories, members of LAS:
Algeria, Bahrain, Comoros, Djibouti, Egypt, Iraq, Jordan, Kuwait, Lebanon, Libya, Mauritania, Morocco, Oman, Palestine, Qatar, Saudi Arabia, Somalia (suspended since 1993), Sudan, Syrian AR, Tunisia, United Arab Emirates, Yemen.
IGO Relations Member of (1): *International Rice Research Institute (IRRI, #14754).* Partner of (1): *Global Alliance to Eliminate Lymphatic Filariasis (GAELF, #10195).* Cooperates with (1): *International Fund for Agricultural Development (IFAD, #13692).* Supports (1): *Centre for Environment and Development for the Arab Region and Europe (CEDARE, #03738).* Participates in the activities of: *UNCTAD (#20285).* Joint studies, research activities and meetings with: *Arab Authority for Agricultural Investment and Development (AAAID, #00902).* Publishes *'Joint Arab Economic Report'* in cooperation with: *Arab Monetary Fund (AMF, #01009);* LAS; *Organization of Arab Petroleum Exporting Countries (OAPEC, #17854).* Shareholder in: *Arab Trade Financing Programme (ATFP, #01060).* Adheres to: *Global Partnership for Effective Development Co-operation (GPEDC, #10532).* **NGO Relations** Provides secretariat for: *Coordination Group of Arab National and Regional Development Institutions (#04826).* [2022.10.12/XF4228/f/**F***]

- ♦ Arab Fund for Technical Assistance / see Arab Fund for Technical Assistance to African Countries (#00966)
- ♦ Arab Fund for Technical Assistance to African and Arab Countries / see Arab Fund for Technical Assistance to African Countries (#00966)
- ♦ Arab Fund for Technical Assistance to African Countries / see Arab Fund for Technical Assistance to African Countries (#00966)

♦ Arab Fund for Technical Assistance to African Countries (AFTAAC) . 00966

Contact address not obtained. T. +2023590322. Fax +2023592099.

History Oct 1974, as *Arab Fund for Technical Assistance to African Countries (AFTAAC),* on approval of the statutes by 7th Arab Summit Conference, following Resolution 588 of Economic Council of the *League of Arab States (LAS, #16420),* Dec 1973. Operations commenced May 1975. Also referred to originally as *Arab Fund for Technical Assistance (AFTA).* Changed name to *Arab Fund for Technical Assistance to African and Arab Countries (AFTAAAC),* 1992. Subsequently changed name back to original title. **Aims** Coordinate and finance technical assistance programmes to African and Arab countries arranged by the League of Arab States and other Arab specialized agencies; prepare surveys of *development projects* in African and Arab countries; provide consultancy services and experts; organize their exchange between Arab and African countries; coordinate scientific and technological development and the development of the means and modes of production between those same countries. **Structure** Board of Directors, consisting of 7 experts appointed for a 3-year term by the Council of the League on the nominations by its members. The Secretary General of LAS is ex officio Chairman of the Board and the Directors-General of *Arab Bank for Economic Development in Africa (#00904)* and ALECSO are ex officio members. The Fund is an organ of the LAS, but enjoys autonomy in the performance of its functions. **Finance** Capital is US$ 25 million, which may be supplemented from other sources. **Activities** Provides technical assistance for the development of human resources through the supply of Arab and African experts, the provision of scholarships and grants for training in the Arab States and the organization of training programmes.
Members Member Governments (all LAS member governments) (21):
Algeria, Bahrain, Djibouti, Egypt, Iraq, Jordan, Kuwait, Lebanon, Libya, Mauritania, Morocco, Oman, Palestine, Qatar, Saudi Arabia, Somalia, Sudan, Syrian AR, Tunisia, United Arab Emirates, Yemen.
IGO Relations Participates in the activities of: *UNCTAD (#20285).* Memorandum of Understanding with: *Arab Women Organization (AWO, #01078).* [2010/XF4654/f/**F***]

♦ Arab Geologists' Association (AGA) 00967

Association de géologues arabes (AGA)

Pres PO Box 941792, Amman 11194, Jordan. T. +96265652310. Fax +96265652312.
Facebook: https://www.facebook.com/Arab-Geologists-Association-478562782175463/

History Aug 1975, Baghdad (Iraq). Former names and other names: *Association of Arab Geologists* – alias. **Aims** Promote the geological profession and raise its scientific standard in order to meet requirements of the Arab world; study geological problems and matters of common interest among Arab countries and exchange information and experts in vocational and technical fields; support geological commissions in Arab countries and assist geologists in forming such commissions where they do not yet exist; raise the standard of Arab geologists morally and materially and promote their scientific, practical and professional backgrounds. **Structure** General Conference (every 4 years), comprising delegations of geological commissions of member countries. Supreme Council. Executive Bureau, consisting of Chairman, Secretary-General and the Supreme Council representative of the Geological Commission of the next country to take up Chairmanship. **Languages** Arabic, English. **Staff** Part-time. **Finance** Members' dues. Sale of publications. **Activities** Organizes conferences, seminars and training courses. **Events** *Geological conference on the Middle East / Congress* Al Ain (United Arab Emirates) 2006, *Symposium on geological correlation between Arab countries / Congress* Sanaa (Yemen) 1999, *Geological conference on the Middle East / Congress* Beirut (Lebanon) 1998, *Symposium on geological correlation between Arab countries* Beirut (Lebanon) 1998, *Arab gas conference / Congress* Amman (Jordan) 1997. **Publications** *Geoscience and Arab Development* (4 a year). Congress proceedings.
Members Full national geological commissions; Associate commercial companies and other interested organizations. Members in 13 countries and territories:
Canada, China, Egypt, Iraq, Jordan, Lebanon, Libya, Morocco, Palestine, Sudan, Syrian AR, Tunisia, Yemen.
Included in the above 4 organizations listed in this Yearbook:
Arab Centre for the Studies of Arid Zones and Dry Lands (ACSAD, #00918); Arab Drilling and Workover Company (ADWOC, see: #17854); Arab Mining Company (ARMICO, #01008); Arab Well Logging Company (AWLCO, see: #17854).
NGO Relations Affiliated member of: *International Union of Geological Sciences (IUGS, #15777).* [2013.10.07/XD2799/y/**D**]

♦ Arab Geophysical Exploration Services Company (AGESCO) 00968

Contact Suani Road, Sidi Mousa Street, PO Box 84224, Tripoli, Libya. T. +218214804863. Fax +218214803199. E-mail: agesco@agesco-ly.com.
URL: http://agesco-ly.com/

History 1984, Tripoli (Libyan AJ), as a joint undertaking of *Organization of Arab Petroleum Exporting Countries (OAPEC, #17854).* A subsidiary of *Arab Petroleum Services Company (APSCO, see: #17854).* Shareholder companies: *Arab Petroleum Investments Corporation (APICORP, #01026);* Arab Petroleum Services Company. **Aims** Carry out exploration programmes in *geophysical surveying.* **Finance** Authorized capital: Libyan dinars: about 12 million. **Activities** Specialized training programmes and hands-on courses for seismic crews give priority to Arabization of personnel. [2018/XF2377/e/**F***]

- ♦ Arab Golf Confederation / see Arab Golf Federation (#00969)

♦ Arab Golf Federation 00969

SG EGF Office, Dubai Creek Golf and Yacht Club, Dubai, United Arab Emirates. T. +97142952277. E-mail: info@arabgolffederation.org.
Pres address not obtained.
URL: http://arabgolffederation.org/

History Also referred to as *Arab Golf Confederation.*
Members Federations in 14 countries and territories:
Algeria, Bahrain, Egypt, Jordan, Kuwait, Lebanon, Libya, Morocco, Oman, Palestine, Qatar, Saudi Arabia, Tunisia, United Arab Emirates. [2020/XD0918/**D**]

- ♦ Arab Group for Muslim-Christian Dialogue (see: #16756)

♦ Arab Group for the Protection of Nature (APN) 00970

Pres PO Box 811815, Amman 11181, Jordan. T. +96265673331. Fax +96265699777. E-mail: info@apnature.org – operations@apnature.org.
URL: http://www.apnature.org/

History Founded Apr 2003. **Aims** Strengthen the capacity of the Arab peoples to sustain the region's *natural resources* and gain sovereignty over them, particularly in areas suffering from war and occupation. **Structure** General Assembly; Board of Directors. **Languages** Arabic, English. **Staff** 4.00 FTE, paid. **Finance** Financed by private institutions and multilateral organizations. **Activities** Awareness raising; research/documentation; advocacy/lobbying/activism; events/meetings. **Consultative Status** Consultative status granted from: *ECOSOC (#05331)* (Special); *UNEP (#20299).* **NGO Relations** Member of: *International NGO/CSO Planning Committee for Food Sovereignty (IPC, #14365); International Union for Conservation of Nature and Natural Resources (IUCN, #15766).* [2014.06.01/XJ3953/**E**]

- ♦ **ArabGU** Arabian Geosciences Union (#00975)
- ♦ Arab Guides' Union (inactive)
- ♦ Arab Gulf Basketball Association (inactive)
- ♦ Arab Gulf Cooperation Council / see Gulf Cooperation Council (#10826)
- ♦ Arab Gulf Fund (see: #00971)
- ♦ Arab Gulf Programme / see Arab Gulf Programme for United Nations Development Organizations (#00971)

♦ Arab Gulf Programme for United Nations Development Organizations (AGFUND) 00971

Programme du Golfe arabe pour les organisations de développement des Nations Unies

Mailing Address PO Box 18371, Riyadh 11415, Saudi Arabia. T. +96614418888 – +96614416240 – +96614416257. Fax +96614412963. E-mail: director@agfund.org – info@agfund.org.
Pres address not obtained. T. +96614416240 – +96614416257 – +96614413218. Fax +96614412963.
URL: http://www.agfund.org/

History 18 Apr 1981. A multilateral aid institution of *Organization of the Petroleum Exporting Countries (OPEC, #17881).* Former names and other names: *Arab Gulf Programme* – alias. **Aims** Finance *humanitarian* aspects of development; support programmes to benefit women and children in *developing countries* through financial contributions to projects of UN development organizations; participate in projects of other IGOs and international and Arab NGOs, particularly with respect to motherhood and childhood; establish institutions specialized in providing services to women and children; support training and education efforts to help women acquire skills and gain self-reliance; contribute to social, economic, health, nutrition, environmental protection programmes and to emergency *relief.* **Structure** Board of Directors, composed of one representative and

one deputy representative from each Member State, chaired by President. Vice-President. President's Office, consisting of Office Manager and 3 Department Directors. Includes *Arab Gulf Fund (see: #00971)*. **Languages** Arabic, English. **Staff** 30.00 FTE, paid. **Finance** Basic resources financed by OPEC member countries. Other sources: voluntary contributions from governments; fundraising revenue from public and private organizations in member states and worldwide. **Activities** Contributes up to 25% of external financing for projects prepared and carried out in cooperation with UN agencies; coordinates Arab Gulf assistance offered to UN bodies; provides assistance to a number of non-governmental Arab organizations; launches fund-raising campaigns for specific causes. Total commitments from commencement of operations to end 1996: US$ 188 million to the benefit of 125 countries, of which US$ 166 million has been disbursed. Projects have been in the fields of: basic services to mothers and children; combating disease; human resources development. **Events** *Microcredit Summit* Abu Dhabi (United Arab Emirates) 2016, *Symposium on Microfinance* Vienna (Austria) 2012.
Members Governments of 6 countries:
Bahrain, Kuwait, Oman, Qatar, Saudi Arabia, United Arab Emirates.
IGO Relations Invited to sessions of Intergovernmental Council of: *International Programme for the Development of Communication (IPDC, #14651)*. Finances projects in cooperation with:
- *FAO (#09260)*;
- *ILO (#11123)*;
- *International Fund for Agricultural Development (IFAD, #13692)*;
- *International Training Centre of the ILO (ITC, #15717)*;
- *UNEP (#20299)*;
- *UNDP (#20292)*;
- *UNESCO (#20322)*;
- *UNHCR (#20327)*;
- *UNICEF (#20332)*;
- *United Nations Economic and Social Commission for Western Asia (ESCWA, #20558)*;
- *United Nations Office for the Coordination of Humanitarian Affairs (OCHA, #20593)*;
- *United Nations Population Fund (UNFPA, #20612)*;
- *United Nations Relief and Works Agency for Palestine Refugees in the Near East (UNRWA, #20622)*;
- *United Nations University (UNU, #20642)*;
- *United Nations Volunteers (UNV, #20650)*;
- *WHO (#20950)*.

NGO Relations Multilateral agency of: *Coordination Group of Arab National and Regional Development Institutions (#04826)*. Finances projects in cooperation with: *International Committee of the Red Cross (ICRC, #12799)*. Instrumental in setting up: *Arab Open University (AOU)*. Provides assistance to a number of Arab nongovernmental organizations, including *Programme for Palestinian-European-American Cooperation in Education (PEACE Programme, #18527)*. Stakeholder in: *Child and Youth Finance International (CYFI, inactive)*. [2020/XE4484/f/**F***]

♦ Arab Gulf Psychiatric Association 00972

Contact address not obtained.
NGO Relations Member of: *World Psychiatric Association (WPA, #21741)*. [2016/XD6718/**D**]

♦ Arab Gulf States Folklore Centre (no recent information)
♦ Arab Gymnastics Confederation (inactive)
♦ Arab Handball Confederation (inactive)

♦ Arab Hospitals Federation (AHF) 00973

Main Office PO Box 2914, Jounieh MOUNT LEBANON, Lebanon. T. +9619900111. Fax +9619900110. E-mail: ahfonline@ahfonline.net.
URL: http://www.ahfonline.net/
History 2002, Lebanon. **Aims** Reach an Arab world of healthy communities served by well managed hospitals and excellent health services. **Structure** General Assembly; Board; Committees. **Languages** Arabic, English. **Activities** Advocacy/lobbying/activism; events/meetings; healthcare; knowledge management/information dissemination; research and development; training/education. **Events** *Medhealth Congress* Cairo (Egypt) 2020, *Congress* Cairo (Egypt) 2019, *Arab Healthcare Development Annual Forum* Muscat (Oman) 2018, *Medhealth Congress* Cairo (Egypt) 2017, *Medhealth Congress* Cairo (Egypt) 2016.
Members Full in 22 countries:
Algeria, Bahrain, Comoros, Djibouti, Egypt, Iraq, Jordan, Kuwait, Lebanon, Libya, Mauritania, Morocco, Oman, Palestine, Qatar, Saudi Arabia, Somalia, Sudan, Syrian AR, Tunisia, United Arab Emirates, Yemen. [2021.09.01/XM8252/**D**]

♦ Arab Human Rights Foundation (internationally oriented national body)
♦ Arab Human Security Network (unconfirmed)

♦ Arabian Aquaculture Society 00974

Contact Animal and Fish Production Dept, Fac of Agriculture (Saba Basha) Alexandria Univ, PO Box 21531 Bolkly, Alexandria, Egypt. T. +2035820016. Fax +2035832008. E-mail: arabaquasoc@gmail.com – aldahhar@hotmail.com.
URL: http://arabaqs.org/
History Also referred to as *Arab Aquaculture Society*. **Aims** Promote the development of aquaculture education and scientific technologies of aquatic animal production. **Events** *Arab aquaculture conference* Cairo (Egypt) 2010, *Global fisheries and aquaculture research conference* Cairo (Egypt) 2010. **Members** Individuals (approx 360). Membership countries not specified. [2014/XJ2369/**D**]

♦ Arabian Centre for Educational Leaders Training in the Arab Gulf States / see Arab Educational Training Centre for Gulf States

♦ Arabian Geosciences Union (ArabGU) 00975

Pres Geology Dept, Fac of Science, Benha Univ, Qalyubia Governorate, Benha QALYUBIA, 13518, Egypt.
URL: http://arabgu.com/
History Founded Jun 2013. **Structure** Founding Team, comprising President, 6 Vice-Presidents and Webmaster. **Events** *WMESS : World Multidisciplinary Earth Sciences Symposium* Prague (Czechia) 2022, *WMESS : World Multidisciplinary Earth Sciences Symposium* Prague (Czechia) 2019, *International Conference on Geoparks in Africa and Middle East* El Jadida (Morocco) 2018, *International Conference* El Jadida (Morocco) 2018, *WMESS : World Multidisciplinary Earth Sciences Symposium* Prague (Czechia) 2018. **Publications** *Arabian Geo-Frontiers (AGF)* – scientific journal.
Members Individuals in 13 countries:
Algeria, Egypt, Japan, Jordan, Libya, Morocco, Saudi Arabia, Sri Lanka, Sudan, UK, United Arab Emirates, USA, Yemen.
NGO Relations Supported by: *International Association for Geoethics (IAGETH, #11915)*. [2019.12.07/XJ7090/**D**]

♦ Arabian Gulf Rugby Football Union (inactive)
♦ Arabian Gulf States Joint Programme Production Institution (inactive)

♦ Arabian Gulf University (AGU) 00976

Pres PO Box 26671, Manama 329, Bahrain. T. +973239801. Fax +973272555. E-mail: president@agu.edu.bh.
URL: http://www.agu.edu.bh/
History Apr 1981, Baghdad (Iraq), at meeting of the General Conference of Ministers of Education in the Arab Gulf States – members of *Arab Bureau of Education for the Gulf States (ABEGS, #00910)*. **Aims** Address developmental issues of the Gulf Cooperation Council countries through innovative and effective educational and research programs with relevance to Arabian Gulf regional issues. **Structure** Board of Trustees; University Council. **Activities** Training/education; research/documentation. **Events** *Middle East Energy Management Conference* Manama (Bahrain) 2013. **Publications** *Bulletin of the Arabian Gulf University* (annual); *Arabian Gulf University Catalogue*.
Members States of the Arabian Gulf (7):
Bahrain, Iraq, Kuwait, Oman, Qatar, Saudi Arabia, United Arab Emirates.
NGO Relations Member of: *Arab Forum for Environment and Development (AFED, #00960)*; *Federation of the Universities of the Islamic World (FUIW, #09710)*. [2021/XF4170/**F***]

♦ Arabian Scientific Research Organization / see Academic Scientific Research Organization (#00023)

♦ Arabian Society for Human Resource Management (ASHRM) 00977

Contact Marcom – Dubai Office, PO Box 336467, Dubai, United Arab Emirates.
URL: http://www.ashrm.com/
History 1991, Dhahran (Saudi Arabia). **Aims** Provide a forum for the exchange of information and expertise in the area of human resource management and related fields. **Structure** Council of Trustees. **Languages** Arabic, English. **Staff** 25.00 FTE, voluntary. **Finance** Member' dues. **Activities** Organizes: presentations; international conferences and exhibitions; workshops. **Events** *Conference* Dubai (United Arab Emirates) 2018, *International Conference* Dubai (United Arab Emirates) 2017, *International Conference* Dubai (United Arab Emirates) 2016, *International Conference / Conference* Dubai (United Arab Emirates) 2014, *International Conference* Abu Dhabi (United Arab Emirates) 2012. **Publications** *ASHRM Magazine* – electronic. **Members** Active; Honorary. Membership countries not specified. [2016/XD7901/**D**]

♦ Arabic Alliance for Freedom and Democracy (unconfirmed)

♦ Arabic Language International Council 00978

Mailing Address PO Box 6888, Beirut, Lebanon. T. +9611364611. E-mail: info@alarabiah.org.
URL: http://www.alarabiah.org/
History Former names and other names: *International Council of the Arabic Language* – alias. **Aims** Serve the Arabic language; support institutions and individuals who have interest in improving Arabic language learning and *teaching*. **Structure** General Assembly; Board of Directors; General Secretariat. Includes: International Association of Arabic Departments; International Conference on the Arabic Language; International Federation of the Arabic Language; International Federation of Translation. **Events** *International Conference on Arabic Language* Dubai (United Arab Emirates) 2020, *International Conference on Arabic Language* Dubai (United Arab Emirates) 2018, *International Conference on Arabic Language* Dubai (United Arab Emirates) 2017. **Consultative Status** Consultative status granted from: *UNESCO (#20322)* (Consultative Status). [2022/XM6606/**D**]

♦ Arabic Network for Human Rights Information (ANHRI) 00979

Contact 2 Behlar Passage, off Kasr El Nil St, 5th floor – flat 39, Down Town, Cairo, Egypt. E-mail: info@anhri.net.
URL: http://www.anhri.net/
History Oct 2003, with initial funding of *Open Society Foundations (OSF, #17763)*. **Aims** Make available Middle East and North African human rights organizations' reports and statements to Arabic readers worldwide; provide resources about human rights issues to the media, activists, and the general public; increase access to information about specific human rights issues or abuses. **Publications** *Weekly Bulletin*. **NGO Relations** Regional member of: *EuroMed Rights (#05733)*. Partner of: *Crisis Action (#04957)*. [2019/XJ4726/**F**]

♦ Arab ICT Organization / see Arab Information and Communication Technologies Organization (#00982)

♦ Arab India Cooperation Forum 00980

Address not obtained.
History Dec 2008, on initiative of *League of Arab States (LAS, #16420)*. **Aims** Increase and strengthen political, social, cultural, economic ties between India and the Arab world. [2010/XJ1561/**F***]

♦ Arab Industrial Development and Mining Organization / see Arab Industrial Development, Standardization and Mining Organization (#00981)
♦ Arab Industrial Development Organization (inactive)

♦ Arab Industrial Development, Standardization and Mining Organization (AIDSMO) 00981

Dir Gen PO Box 8019, United Nations 10102, Agdal, 10102 Rabat, Morocco. T. +212537274500. Fax +212537772188. E-mail: aidsmo@aidsmo.org.
URL: http://www.aidsmo.org/
History Esteblished on merger of *Arab Industrial Development Organization (AIDO, inactive)*, *Arab Organization for Mineral Resources (AOMR, inactive)* and *Arab Organization for Standardization and Metrology (ASMO, inactive)*. Former names and other names: *Arab Industrial Development and Mining Organization (AIDMO)* – former. **Aims** Uphold inclusive and sustainable industrial development in the Arab countries; keepsabreast of ongoing advancements at global level in the fields of industry, standardization and mining. **Structure** General Assembly (every 2 years); Executive Board; Administration. **Languages** Arabic, English, French. **Finance** Sources: contributions; contributions of member/participating states; donations; grants; international organizations; sponsorship. **Activities** Events/meetings; knowledge management/information dissemination; networking/liaising; projects/programmes; publishing activities; research/documentation; standards/guidelines; training/education. **Events** *Arab Energy Conference* Qatar 2023, *Quadrennial Arab Energy Conference* Marrakech (Morocco) 2018, *Quadrennial Arab Energy Conference* Abu Dhabi (United Arab Emirates) 2014, *EuroArab Conference on SMEs* Damascus (Syrian AR) 2010, *Quadrennial Arab energy conference* Doha (Qatar) 2010. **Publications** *Arab Industry Report*. Studies; guides; reports.
Members Member States (21):
Algeria, Bahrain, Djibouti, Egypt, Iraq, Jordan, Kuwait, Lebanon, Libya, Mauritania, Morocco, Oman, Palestine, Qatar, Saudi Arabia, Somalia, Sudan, Syrian AR, Tunisia, United Arab Emirates, Yemen.
IGO Relations Cooperates with (14): *Arab Administrative Development Organization (ARADO, #00893)*; *Arab Atomic Energy Agency (AAEA, #00901)*; *Arab Bank for Economic Development in Africa (#00904)*; *Arab Fund for Economic and Social Development (AFESD, #00965)*; *GCC Standardization Organization (GSO, #10084)*; *Gulf Organization for Industrial Consulting (GOIC, #10837)*; *Islamic Development Bank (IsDB, #16044)*; *Islamic World Educational, Scientific and Cultural Organization (ICESCO, #16058)*; *League of Arab States (LAS, #16420)*; *Swedish International Development Cooperation Agency (Sida)*; *UNEP (#20299)*; *UNIDO (#20336)*; *United Nations Economic and Social Commission for Western Asia (ESCWA, #20558)*; *United Nations Economic Commission for Africa (ECA, #20554)*. **NGO Relations** Member of (1): *Arab Union of Electricity (AUE, #01066)* (Observing). Cooperates with (8): *ASTM International (#02994)*; *Comité européen de normalisation (CEN, #04162)*; Global Food Regulatory Science Society; *International Electrotechnical Commission (IEC, #13255)*; *International Organization for Standardization (ISO, #14473)*; Saudi Mining Services Company; Talal Abu Ghazaleh; *Union of Arab Chambers (UAC, #20350)*. [2022.10.28/XD1444/t/**D***]

♦ Arab Information and Communication Technologies Organization (AICTO) 00982

Organisation arabe des technologies de l'information et de la communication
SG 12 Rue d'Angleterre, 1000 Tunis, Tunisia. T. +21671320713. Fax +21671320719. E-mail: contact@aicto.org.
URL: http://www.aicto.org/
History 29 Oct 2001, Tunis (Tunisia). Set up by Tunis Declaration, issued by meeting of Arab Communications Ministers, working under the aegis of *League of Arab States (LAS, #16420)*. Also referred to as *Arab ICT Organization*. **Aims** Develop ICTs throughout the Arab region; provide the necessary mechanisms to support cooperation and complementarity between members, promote and enrich common policies and strategies to develop vital technological domains. **Structure** General Assembly (annually); Council; Secretarial General, headed by Secretary-General. **Activities** Research and development; events/meetings; capacity building; awards/prizes/competitions. **Events** *Arab Cybersecurity Forum* Gammarth (Tunisia) 2021, *ICT 4 all forum – Tunis +5* Tunis (Tunisia) 2010.
Members Governments (17):
Algeria, Comoros, Djibouti, Egypt, Iraq, Jordan, Lebanon, Libya, Mauritania, Morocco, Oman, Palestine, Somalia, Sudan, Syrian AR, Tunisia, Yemen.
Associate: private and public companies active in ICT sector. Members in 9 countries:
China, Egypt, Iraq, Lebanon, Mauritania, Oman, Qatar, Tunisia, United Arab Emirates. [2021/XJ0935/**E***]

♦ Arab Institute of Business Managers (#11236)
♦ Arab Institute for Forestry and Range (no recent information)

♦ Arab Institute for Human Rights (AIHR) 00983
Institut arabe des droits de l'homme (IADH)
Main Office 2 avenue 9 Avril, 1009 Tunis, Tunisia. T. +21671483683. Fax +21671483725. E-mail: aihr.iadh@gmail.com – chehbi.hajer@gmail.com.
URL: http://www.aihr-iadh.org/
History 20 Mar 1989. Founded by *Arab Organization for Human Rights (AOHR, #01020)*, *Arab Lawyers' Union (ALU, #01002)* and Tunisian League for Human Rights, with the coordination and support of *Office of the United Nations High Commissioner for Human Rights (OHCHR, #17697)*. **Aims** Raise awareness of civil, political, cultural, social and economic human rights as proclaimed in the Universal Declaration for Human Rights and the related international instruments; disseminate the culture of human rights and democracy in the Arab region. **Structure** Board of Directors (meets at least once a year), consisting of President and 3 representatives of each of the 3 founding parties, one representative each of UNESCO, OHCHR, *UNICEF (#20332)* and *UNDP (#20292)* and a representative of the Institute Scientific Committee. Executive Board, comprising Chairman and 2 Vice-Chairmen. Consultative Scientific Committee. Liaison Offices (3): Lebanon; Egypt; Morocco. **Languages** Arabic, English, French. **Staff** Permanent. **Finance** Sources: contributions of member/participating states; grants; sale of publications; subsidies. Also revenue from charitable activities. Annual budget: 1,000,000 USD. **Activities** Knowledge management/information dissemination; research/documentation; training/education. **Events** *Arab NGOs workshop* Tunis (Tunisia) 1993, *Conférence arabe sur l'éducation aux droits de l'homme et à la démocratie dans le monde arabe* Tunis (Tunisia) 1993. **Publications** *Arab Review for Human Rights* – online scientific review. *NGOs, Political Parties and Trade Unions* (2009) in Arabic, English. Collection of documents and lectures from training sessions; conference proceedings; pamphlets. Information Services: Specialized library. **Information Services** AHRINET – *Arab Human Rights Information and Documentation Network*. **Members** Membership countries not specified. **Consultative Status** Consultative status granted from: *African Commission on Human and Peoples' Rights (ACHPR, #00255)* (Observer); *ECOSOC (#05331)* (Special); *UNESCO (#20322)* (Associate Status). **IGO Relations** Observer status with (1): *League of Arab States (LAS, #16420)* (Permanent Committee of Human Rights). Associated with Department of Global Communications of the United Nations. **NGO Relations** Member of (2): *EuroMed Non-Governmental Platform (#05730)*; *EuroMed Rights (#05733)*. Serves as secretariat for: *Arab Human Rights Documentation and Information Network (AHRINET, no recent information)*.
[2021.05.26/XE0182/j/E]

♦ Arab Institute for Labour Administration and Employment / see Arab Centre for Labour Administration and Employment

♦ Arab Institute for Labour Education and Research 00984
Institut arabe d'éducation ouvrière et de recherches sur le travail
Dir Family Cntr, Ben-Aknoun, Algiers, Algeria. Fax +21323384214 – +21323384216. E-mail: institut.arabe@gmail.com.
URL: http://www.institut-arabe.org/
History 1974, within the framework of *Arab Labour Organization (ALO, #01001)*. **Aims** Carry out ALO policies and objectives in the field. **Languages** Arabic, French. **Activities** Training/education; research/documentation; financial and/or material support; events/meetings. **IGO Relations** *Arab Labour Organization (ALO, #01001)*; League of Arab States (LAS, #16420).
[2015.12.28/XE2008/j/E]

♦ Arab Institute of Navigation (AIN) 00985
Institution Arabe de Navigation
Pres Cross Road of Sebaei Str and 45 Str, Miami, Alexandria, Egypt. T. +2035509824. Fax +2035509686.
URL: http://www.ainegypt.org/
History 30 Aug 1978, Alexandria (Egypt), within the premises of *Arab Academy for Science, Technology and Maritime Transport (AASTMT, #00891)*, which provided the necessary administrative support. Registered in accordance with Egyptian law. **Aims** Develop a scientific community for all those interested in *maritime*, *air* or *land* navigation; follow up the latest technologies and the latest achievements in general navigation, *electronic* navigation, *satellite* navigation and communications, VTS, etc; collect information on scientific and technological development in fields directly related to navigation, such as astronomy, charts, oceanography, electronics and communications; conduct research into *safety* navigation developments and safety of off-shore units such as mobile and fixed off-shore drilling units and related service marine units; keep up with the latest trends in fire fighting equipments and pollution prevention on board maritime units. **Structure** General Assembly; Board; Administrative Secretariat. **Languages** Arabic, English. **Staff** 3.00 FTE, paid. **Finance** Members' dues. Other sources: donations; grants. **Activities** Knowledge management/information dissemination; events/meetings; training/education. **Events** *Biennial Conference* Cairo (Egypt) 2012, *Biennial Conference* Cairo (Egypt) 2010, *Biennial Conference* Hurghada (Egypt) 2008, *Biennial Conference* Cairo (Egypt) 2004, *Symposium* Alexandria (Egypt) 1994. **Publications** *El Mallah* (4 a year) – newsletter; *Year Book of Lectures*.
Members Individuals Full (700); Associate (723). Associate Companies (45). Members in 6 countries: Egypt, Kuwait, Libya, Saudi Arabia, Sudan, United Arab Emirates.
IGO Relations Observer member of: *International Committee on Global Navigation Satellite Systems (ICG, #12775)*. **NGO Relations** Member of: *International Association of Institutes of Navigation (IAIN, #11965)*.
[2018/XE0067/j/E]

♦ Arab Institute for Operation and Management / see Arab Council of Operations and Maintenance (#00931)

♦ Arab Institute for Security Studies 00986
Dir PO Box 141939, Amman, Jordan. T. +96265818062. Fax +962795569317. E-mail: info@acsis.org.
URL: http://www.acsis.org/
History 1995. **Aims** Maintain global security, non-proliferation of WMD, nuclear security; promote establishment of a Middle East free from all weapons of mass destruction. **Structure** Board of Trustees. **Languages** Arabic, English. **Staff** 12.00 FTE, paid. **Finance** Self-financing.
[2018.06.01/XJ1721/j/D]

♦ Arab Institute for Studies and Communication, Lebanon (internationally oriented national body)

♦ Arab Institute for Training and Research in Statistics (AITRS) 00987
Institut arabe de formation et de recherches statistiques
Dir PO Box 851104, 164 Macaa Street Office 308, Amman 11185, Jordan. T. +96265549805. Fax +96265549804. E-mail: info@aitrs.org.
URL: http://www.aitrs.org/
History 1971, Baghdad (Iraq). Founded under the auspices of UN and *UNDP (#20292)*. Former names and other names: *Regional Institute for Training and Research in Statistics for the Near East* – former; *Arab Institute for Training and Statistical Research* – former. **Aims** Increase quantity and enhance skills of statisticians in the Arab World; assist Arab countries to strengthen their national statistical offices and systems; provide guidance and support for research on statistical methodologies and problems of particular importance and interest to the region. **Structure** Board of Trustees; Headquarters. **Languages** Arabic, English. **Staff** 12.00 FTE, paid. **Finance** Sources: donations; fees for services; members' dues. Annual budget: 600,000 USD. **Activities** Guidance/assistance/consulting; knowledge management/information dissemination; research/documentation; training/education. **Events** *Arab statistical conference* Doha (Qatar) 2007. **Members** National Statistical Offices in 22 Arab countries. Membership countries not specified. **IGO Relations** Cooperates with (8): *Arab Labour Organization (ALO, #01001)*; *Arab Organization for Agricultural Development (AOAD, #01018)*; *FAO (#09260)*; *ILO (#11123)*; *OECD (#17693)*; *Statistical, Economic and Social Research and Training Centre for Islamic Countries (SESRIC, #19971)*; *United Nations Economic and Social Commission for Western Asia (ESCWA, #20558)*; United Nations Statistical Division (UNSD).
[2020.11.17/XE1368/j/E]

♦ Arab Institute for Training and Statistical Research / see Arab Institute for Training and Research in Statistics (#00987)

♦ Arab Insurance Group (ARIG) 00988
Gen Mgr PO Box 26992, Manama, Bahrain. T. +973544444. Fax +973531155 – +973530289. E-mail: info@arig.com.bh.
URL: http://www.arig.com.bh/
History 1980. **Aims** Support the expansion and development of the Arab insurance *industry*, participate in regional initiatives to increase insurance awareness and provide training and development to enhance the level of insurance expertise in the region. **Structure** Board of Directors, consisting of Chairman, 2 Vice Chairmen and 7 Directors. Management, comprising Chief Executive, General Manager – Insurance Investments, General Manager – Reinsurance, General Manager – Financial Services and Business Support. **Staff** 730.00 FTE, paid. **Activities** Main activities: insurance, reinsurance, investments, financial services. **Publications** Annual Report.
Members Governmental shareholders (3):
Kuwait, Libya, United Arab Emirates.
Subsidiary companies in 6 countries:
Bahrain, Egypt, Jordan (*), Lebanon, Morocco, Tunisia.
[2018/XF3194/e/F*]

♦ Arab Intellectual Property Mediation and Arbitration Society (AIPMAS) 00989
Contact PO Box 11192, Amman 921100, Jordan. T. +96265100900. Fax +96265100902. E-mail: info@aspip.org.
URL: http://www.aipmas.org/
History Developed out of *Arab Society for Intellectual Property (ASIP, #01046)*. When registered in accordance with the law of Jordan, current title adopted. **Aims** Reinforce and develop the systems of protecting intellectual property through education and raising awareness, explaining the nature of intellectual property and its role in and impact on the local and the international economy. **Finance** Members' dues. **Publications** *AIPMAS Newsletter*. **NGO Relations** Instrumental in setting up: *Arab Centre for Mediation and Arbitration (ACMA, #00917)*.
[2018/XJ4262/D]

♦ Arab Interior Ministers' Council (AIMC) 00990
Conseil des ministres de l'intérieur arabes
SG Impasse du Lac Windermere, BP 4, 1053 les berges du lac, Tunis, Tunisia. T. +21671656656. Fax +21671656222. E-mail: aimc@planet.tn.
URL: http://www.aim-council.org/
History Dec 1982, as part of the *League of Arab States (LAS, #16420)*. Previously also referred to as: *Council of Arab Ministers of the Interior (CAMI)*; *Council of Ministers of Interior of Arab Countries (CMIA)*. **Aims** Develop and strengthen cooperation and coordinating efforts among Arab States in the field of internal security and *prevention* of *crime*. **Structure** Council meets annually in January. Meeting is attended by Interior Ministers, LAS Secretary General (or one of his assistants) and Chairman of *Naif Arab University for Security Sciences (NAUSS, #16929)*. Chairmanship rotates among Interior Ministers in alphabetical order of the Arab States; Vice-Chairman is the Interior Minister of the state which alphabetically follows the state holding the chairmanship. Secretariat General in Tunis (Tunisia), headed by Secretary General, includes 5 specialized offices: *Arab Office for Intellectual Security*, Casablanca (Morocco); *Arab Office for Combating Crime*, Baghdad (Iraq); *Arab Office for Combating Crime*, Riyadh (Saudi Arabia); *Pan Arab Bureau for Narcotics Affairs*; Amman (Jordan); *Arab Office for Security Information*, Cairo (Egypt). *Arab Police Sports Confederation (#01028)*, Cairo (Egypt), is also attached to the Secretariat General. One specialized body in each member states liaises with the Secretariat General, specialized offices and other bodies of the Council, and with similar offices in the other member states. **Languages** Arabic. **Staff** 70.00 FTE, paid. **Activities** Politics/policy/regulatory; events/meetings.
Members Governments of 22 countries:
Algeria, Bahrain, Comoros, Djibouti, Egypt, Iraq, Jordan, Kuwait, Lebanon, Libya, Mauritania, Morocco, Oman, Palestine, Qatar, Saudi Arabia, Somalia, Sudan, Syrian AR, Tunisia, United Arab Emirates, Yemen.
IGO Relations Special agreement with: *ECOSOC (#05331)*; *International Criminal Police Organization – INTERPOL (ICPO-INTERPOL, #13110)*.
[2015.10.28/XE0798/E*]

♦ Arab International Association for Tourism and Automobile Clubs (AIA) 00991
Sec 960 Capability Green, Luton, LU1 3PE, UK.
Contact 24 Chiswell Street, London, EC1Y 4YX, UK. T. +441582635077. E-mail: general@theaia.org.uk.
URL: http://theaia.wordpress.com/
History 1988, London (UK). Incorporated as a company limited by guarantee in England and Wales: 2414704. **Aims** Spread awareness and information to the public about the safety and dangers of the roads and how to be more cautious to prevent accidents. **Publications** *AIA Newsletter* (4 a year). **Members** Membership countries not specified. **IGO Relations** Associated with Department of Global Communications of the United Nations.
[2019/XD3399/D]

♦ Arab International Bank (AIB) 00992
Banque arabe et internationale
Chairman-Managing Dir 35 Abdel Khalek Sarwat Street, Cairo, Egypt. T. +2023918794 – +2023916391 – +2023916492. Fax +2023916233.
URL: http://www.aib.com.eg/
History 1974, by international treaty, following transformation of *Egyptian International Bank*, 15 Sep 1972, Cairo (Egypt), with the assistance of *European Arab Holding (EURAB, inactive)*. **Aims** Undertake: *commercial* banking operations; financing of foreign *trade* of Arab countries and of Arab *development* programmes. **Structure** Board of Directors, comprising Chairman/Managing Director, 4 Deputy Chairmen, 2 Managing Directors and 10 members. All offices and branches in Egypt: Head Office – Cairo (Egypt); Main Branch – Cairo; Other branches (6): Alexandria, Port Said, El Tharir, Heliopolis, Mohandessin, Nasr City. 2 General and 7 Branch Managers. **Staff** 1294.00 FTE, paid. **Finance** Authorized capital: US$ 300 million. Subscribed and fully paid up capital: US$ 278 million. Total assets and liabilities as at 30 Jun 2003: US$ 3,418 million. **Activities** For year end 30 Jun 2002: syndicated international loans – US$ 127 million, of which US$ 13 million to governments and US$ 114 million to financial and industrial institutions; short and medium-term loans – US$ 361 million, financing productive activity and meeting working capital requirements of individuals, companies and organizations operating in the local market. Special Unit for preparation and appraisal of projects. **Publications** Annual Report in English/Arabic.
Members Shareholders governments of 5 countries:
Egypt, Libya, Oman, Qatar, United Arab Emirates.
Private Arab participants (not specified).
IGO Relations Shareholder in: *Arab Trade Financing Programme (ATFP, #01060)*. **NGO Relations** Member of: *International Capital Market Association (ICMA, #12438)*.
[2008/XF1924/e/F*]

♦ Arab International Society for Management Technology (AIMICT) .. 00993
Chairman PO Box 921951, Amman 11192, Jordan. E-mail: akms@akms.org.
URL: http://aimict.org/
History 10 Jul 1990, Amman (Jordan), as as *Arab Management Society (AMS)*, following meeting, 29 Aug 1989, New York NY (USA). Later known as *Arab Knowledge Management Society (AKMS)*. 2015, present name adopted. **Aims** Utilize modern management and technology to effectively develop Arab capabilities; derive social and economic value from organization knowledge resources; increase ability of organizations to efficiently harness the tacit and explicit knowledge in its organization for economic benefit; disseminate information useful to this pursuit; seek development of the Arab "Knowledge Society" at large. **Structure** General Meeting (annual); Board of Trustees; Executive Committee, comprising Chairman, 3 Deputy Chairman, Secretary, Treasurer and 19 members. Committees (4): Membership; Education, Institutes and Academic Institutions; Finance; Media and Publishing. **Languages** Arabic, English. **Finance** Members' dues. Donations. **Activities** Organizes conferences; conducts several seminars a year to disseminate modern management techniques and principles to members; collaborates with management associations in different countries so as to exchange ideas and gain recognition for members. **Events** *Regional conference on quality and integrated management in the Mediterranean and Gulf countries* Beirut (Lebanon) 2001, *Arab international accounting conference* Abu Dhabi (United Arab Emirates) 2000, *Conference on electronic commerce* Muscat

(Oman) 2000, *Arab international conference for management in the context of globalization* Alexandria (Egypt) 1998, *Conference for Arab and international businessmen and policy makers* United Arab Emirates 1998. **Publications** *AKMS Monthly Bulletin*; *Al-Inma Wal Idar'a*. *The Arab World in the New World Order* (1991); *Abu-Ghazaleh Business and Accounting Dictionary*; *Business Circles Guide to Global Trade System*. Annual report; information booklet; books; journals; video cassettes; film-strips; tapes.
Members Individual; Company. Selected managers, professors, businessmen, industrialists, educational organizations and institutions operating in various economic sectors in 19 countries and territories:
Algeria, Bahrain, Egypt, France, Iraq, Jordan, Kuwait, Lebanon, Morocco, Oman, Palestine, Qatar, Saudi Arabia, Syrian AR, Tunisia, UK, United Arab Emirates, USA, Yemen.
IGO Relations Agreement with: *Arab Academy for Science, Technology and Maritime Transport (AASTMT, #00891)*. **NGO Relations** Member of: *Multilingual Internet Names Consortium (MINC)*. In liaison with technical committees of: *International Organization for Standardization (ISO, #14473)*. [2017/XD2467/**D**]

♦ Arab International Tourist Union / see Arab Tourism Organization (#01057)

♦ Arab International Women's Forum (AIWF) 00994

Chairperson Berkeley Square House, Berkeley Square, London, W1J 6BD, UK. T. +442078877630. Fax +442078876001. E-mail: info@aiwfonline.com.
URL: http://www.aiwfonline.com/
History 2001, London (UK). **Aims** Serve as a network of knowledge for Arab and international business women; improve development of their economic and business activities worldwide. **Structure** Board of Trustees. **Finance** Members' dues. **Activities** Events/meetings. **Events** *Young Arab women leaders – the voice of the future* Kuwait (Kuwait) 2016, *Conference* Paris (France) 2009, *Conference* Cairo (Egypt) 2005. **Publications** *AIWF Newsletter*. **NGO Relations** Member of: *Association of Organisations of Mediterranean Businesswomen (#02840)*; *United Nations Global Compact (#20567)*. [2016/XF7171/**F**]

♦ Arab Inter-Parliamentary Union (Arab IPU) 00995

Union interparlementaire arabe (UIPA)
Contact Bldg 201 Unit 1B Maarad Street, Marfaa' Area, Beirut, Lebanon. T. +9611985960 – +9611985961 – +9611985962. Fax +9611985963. E-mail: info@arabipu.org – arab.ipu@gmail.com.
URL: http://www.arabipu.org/
History 21 Jun 1974, Damascus (Syrian AR). Former names and other names: *Arab Parliamentary Union (APU)* – former. **Aims** Strengthen Arab parliamentary cooperation as an essential foundation for Arab solidarity; represent the Arab popular will through representatives of Arab parliaments to voice the ambitions and causes of the Arab citizen; coordinate and cooperate with the Arab parliaments in the face of dangers and challenges that threaten Arab national security in various spheres; communicate with the representatives of the executive branch of the Arab countries through the President of the Union and the Speakers of Arab Parliaments to implement the decisions of the Union concerning support for Arab solidarity; advance cooperation, coordination, and agreement on issues, topics, problems and dangers faced by the Arab world in various regional and international parliamentary forums, and at international organizations in which the Union participates as an observer; support the rights of Arab youth, women, and children by strengthening the legislative and regulatory roles of Arab parliaments to highlight thereof in inter-parliamentary and intergovernmental forums regionally and internationally; strengthen communication and cooperation with civil society organizations and all other Arab institutions to achieve the purposes of this Charter; promote dialogue and hold joint parliamentary events to coordinate Arab efforts in various areas of Arab solidarity and cooperation; deepen the culture of human rights and promote the concepts of representative democracy. **Structure** Conference (annual); Executive Committee; General Secretariat. **Languages** Arabic. **Staff** 10.00 FTE, paid. **Finance** Member parliaments' contributions according to percentage determined by Conference. **Activities** Events/meetings; knowledge management/information dissemination; networking/liaising. **Events** *Biennial Conference* Damascus (Syrian AR) 2004, *Afro-Arab parliamentary conference* Addis Ababa (Ethiopia) 2003, *Extraordinary session / Council Session – ordinary and extraordinary* Baghdad (Iraq) 2002, *Euro-Arab parliamentary dialogue / Annual Meeting of Euro-Arab Parliamentary Dialogue (jointly with PAEAC) / Euro-Arab Parliamentary Dialogue – with the Arab Inter-Parliamentary Union* Brussels (Belgium) 2002, *Extraordinary session / Council Session – ordinary and extraordinary* Cairo (Egypt) 2002. **Publications** *Arab Parliamentary Prospects* (2 a year); *Parliament* (periodical). Information bulletins; pamphlets; monographs; studies.
Members Parliaments of 22 countries and territories:
Algeria, Bahrain, Comoros, Djibouti, Egypt, Iraq, Jordan, Kuwait, Lebanon, Libya, Mauritania, Morocco, Oman, Palestine, Qatar, Saudi Arabia, Somalia, Sudan, Syrian AR, Tunisia, United Arab Emirates, Yemen.
IGO Relations Observer status with (9): *Arab Parliament (#01023)*; *European Parliament (EP, #08146)*; *Inter-parliamentary Assembly of Member Nations of the Commonwealth of Independent States (IPA CIS, #15958)*; *League of Arab States (LAS, #16420)*; *Parlamento Latinoamericano (PARLATINO, #18203)*; *Parliamentary Assembly of the Council of Europe (PACE, #18211)*; *Parliamentary Assembly of the Mediterranean (PAM, #18212)*; *Parliamentary Union of the OIC Member States (PUIC, #18220)*; *UNESCO (#20322)*. **NGO Relations** Observer status with (12): *African Parliamentary Union (APU, #00412)*; *Arabic Language International Council (#00978)*; *Arab Lawyers' Union (ALU, #01002)*; *Asian Parliamentary Assembly (APA, #01653)*; *Assemblée parlementaire de la Francophonie (APF, #02312)*; *Consultative Council of the Arab Maghreb Union (#04765)*; *General Union of Arab Writers (no recent information)*; *International Confederation of Arab Trade Unions (ICATU, #12845)*; *Inter-Parliamentary Union (IPU, #15961)*; *Parliamentary Association for Euro-Arab Cooperation (PAEAC, #18217)*; *Permanent Forum of Arab-African Dialogue (PFAAD, inactive)*; *Union of Arab Jurists (UAJ, #20354)*. [2022.05.18/XD3423/**D**]

♦ Arab Intrusive and Therapeutic Radiology Association (inactive)

♦ Arab Investment Company (TAIC) 00996

Société arabe d'investissement
CEO PO Box 4009, Riyadh 11491, Saudi Arabia. T. +96614760601. Fax +96614760514. E-mail: taic@taic.com – feedback@taic.com.
URL: http://www.taic.com/
History 16 Jul 1974, Riyadh (Saudi Arabia), by a special agreement signed by 7 Arab countries (Bahrain, Egypt, Kuwait, Qatar, Saudi Arabia, Sudan and United Arab Emirates). Other Arab States joined the Company in 1975 (Iraq, Jordan, Libyan AJ, Morocco, Oman, Qatar, Syrian AR, Tunisia) and in 1977 (Yemen). Later Lebanon and Algeria joined. Commenced operations in 1975. Previously also known under the acronyms *AIC – SAI*. **Aims** Invest Arab funds to develop Arab resources in different economic sectors by initiating investment projects in different economic sectors based on sound economic and *commercial* criteria, in a manner that would support and develop the Arab *economy*. **Structure** General Assembly (annual). Board of Directors, consisting of Chairman, Vice Chairman and 13 members. Chairman of the Board is Company's legal representative. Offshore Banking Unit (OBU) in Bahrain. **Staff** 131.00 FTE, paid. **Finance** Authorized capital: US$ 450 million. **Activities** Main activities: *'Equity Participation in Projects'* – the company acts as a catalyst and a promoter for investment; *'Banking Services'* – Commercial Banking Services, Investment Banking Services, Islamic Banking Services. **Publications** Annual Report.
Members Governmental shareholding enterprises in 17 countries:
Algeria, Bahrain, Egypt, Iraq, Jordan, Kuwait, Lebanon, Libya, Morocco, Oman, Qatar, Saudi Arabia, Sudan, Syrian AR, Tunisia, United Arab Emirates, Yemen.
IGO Relations Collaborative Arab organization of: *Arab Organization for Agricultural Development (AOAD, #01018)*. Member of: *Arab Company for Livestock Development (ACOLID, #00927)*. Shareholder in: *Arab Trade Financing Programme (ATFP, #01060)*; *Kenana Sugar Company (KSC, no recent information)*. [2018/XM1025/e/**F***]

♦ Arab Investment and Export Credit Guarantee Corporation (DHAMAN) 00997

Dir-Gen PO Box 23568, 13096 Safat, Kuwait. T. +96524959555. Fax +96524959596 – +96524959597. E-mail: operations@dhaman.org.
Regional Office PO Box 25166, Riyadh 11466, Saudi Arabia. T. +966114789270 – +966114789280. Fax +966114781195. E-mail: riadhoffice@dhaman.org.
URL: http://www.dhaman.org/
History 1974. Established by Inter-Arab Governmental Convention as the first multilateral credit and political risk insurer in the world. Original title: *Inter-Arab Investment Guarantee Corporation (IAIGC) – Compagnie inter-arabe pour la garantie des investissements (CIAGI)*. Commenced activities 1975. Rated AA by Standard and Poor's since 2008. **Aims** Participate in Member Countries' industrial, agricultural and infrastructure development, food security and trade. **Structure** Shareholder Council; Board of Directors; Director General. **Languages** Arabic, English, French. **Staff** 65.00 FTE, paid. **Finance** As at 14 Dec 2016: Subscribed capital: US$ 322,000,000; paid-up capital: US$ 284,000,000; general reserves: US$ 145,000,000. **Activities** Events/meetings; financial and/or material support; guidance/assistance/consulting; training/education. **Events** *Annual Meeting* Amman (Jordan) 2018, *Annual Meeting* Rabat (Morocco) 2017, *Annual Meeting* Manama (Bahrain) 2016, *Arab Investment Forum* Kuwait 2013, *Annual Meeting* Riyadh (Saudi Arabia) 2001. **Publications** *Dhaman al Istithmar* (12 a year) – newsletter; *Report on Investment Climate in Arab Countries* (annual). *Capsule Series*. Annual report; legal encyclopaedias.
Members Governments of 21 countries and territories:
Algeria, Bahrain, Djibouti, Egypt, Iraq, Jordan, Kuwait, Lebanon, Libya, Mauritania, Morocco, Oman, Palestine, Qatar, Saudi Arabia, Somalia, Sudan, Syrian AR, Tunisia, United Arab Emirates, Yemen.
IGO Relations Cooperates with (4): *Arab Bank for Economic Development in Africa (#00904)*; *Arab Fund for Economic and Social Development (AFESD, #00965)*; *Arab Monetary Fund (AMF, #01009)*; *Arab Organization for Agricultural Development (AOAD, #01018)*. **NGO Relations** Member of (1): *International Union of Credit and Investment Insurers (Bern Union, #15767)* (as Multilateral member of). Together with *Islamic Corporation for the Insurance of Investment and Export Credit (ICIEC, #16041)*, instrumental in setting up: *Aman Union (#00763)*. [2022/XF2177/e/**F***]

♦ Arab Investors Union (no recent information)
♦ **Arab IPU** Arab Inter-Parliamentary Union (#00995)

♦ Arab Iron and Steel Union (AISU) 00998

Union arabe du fer et de l'acier (UAFA)
SG Hai El Bina 81, Dely Ibrahim, PO Box 04 Cheraga, 16027 Algiers, Algeria. T. +21323304221 – +21323304239. Fax +2132304254. E-mail: relex@solbarab.org – aisucairo@solbarab.org.
URL: https://aisusteel.org/en/
History 17 Jan 1972, Cairo (Egypt). Founded by *Council of Arab Economic Unity (CAEU, #04859)*, following recommendations of meeting of *League of Arab States (LAS, #16420)*, 29 Apr 1971, Algiers (Algeria). New Statutes adopted 28 Apr 1976. **Aims** Encourage development of iron and steel *industries* in Arab countries. **Structure** General Assembly (annual); Board of Directors; Technical Committee on Steel Production; Departments (4). **Languages** Arabic, English, French. **Staff** 25.00 FTE, paid. **Finance** Members' dues. **Activities** Networking/liaising; knowledge management/information dissemination; training/education; events/meetings; standards/guidelines. **Events** *Arab Steel Summit* Manama (Bahrain) 2020, *Arab Steel Summit* Tunis (Tunisia) 2019, *Arab Steel Summit* Amman (Jordan) 2018, *Arab Steel Summit* Casablanca (Morocco) 2017, *Arab Steel Summit* Dubai (United Arab Emirates) 2016. **Publications** *Arab Steel Review* (6 a year); *AISU Directory* (annual).
Members Mining and metallurgical companies (90) in 15 countries:
Algeria, Bahrain, Egypt, Iraq, Jordan, Kuwait, Lebanon, Libya, Mauritania, Morocco, Qatar, Saudi Arabia, Syrian AR, Tunisia, United Arab Emirates.
Consultative Status Consultative status granted from: *ECOSOC (#05331)* (Ros C); *UNIDO (#20336)*. **NGO Relations** Working relationship with: *International Iron Metallics Association (IIMA, #13953)*. [2020/XD4018/**D**]

♦ Arabization Coordination Bureau 00999

Bureau de coordination de l'arabisation (BCA)
Dir BP 290, 82 rue Oued Ziz Agdal, 10000 Rabat, Morocco. T. +21237772422 – +21237772423. Fax +21237772426. E-mail: bca@arabization.org.ma.
URL: http://www.arabization.org.ma/
History Established 1961, on the initiative of Morocco; subsequently sponsored by *League of Arab States (LAS, #16420)* and a subsidiary agency of *Arab League Educational, Cultural and Scientific Organization (ALECSO, #01003)* since 1970. Also referred to as: *Bureau of Coordination of Arabization*; *Permanent Bureau for Arabization – Bureau permanent pour l'arabisation*; *Bureau permanent de coordination de l'arabisation dans le monde arabe*. **Aims** Coordinate efforts on *Arabic* teaching and encourage its use as a language of instruction at all levels of education and in all disciplines; harmonize efforts to enrich the *Arabic language* with new *terminology* in all areas of knowledge; follow up the above in scientific and cultural contexts at national and international levels; coordinate efforts with language academies, specialized scientific bodies and other language institutions. **Staff** 16.00 FTE, paid. **Activities** Organizes congresses, conferences and seminars; carries out research. **Events** *Congrès d'arabisation* 1996, *Conférence sur le perfectionnement de la terminologie scientifique arabe* United Arab Emirates 1995. **Publications** *Al-Lisan El-Arabi Magazine* (annual). *Translations of Distinguished Books on Science and Technology* – series. Lexicons approved by Arabization Conference; specialized dictionaries. Information Services: Scientific terminology database. [2014.01.09/XE9545/**E***]

♦ Arab Judo Confederation 01000

Chairman address not obtained. E-mail: yemenjf@yahoo.com.
URL: http://www.arabjudo.com/
History 1977, Cairo (Egypt). Also referred to as *Arab Judo Federation*. [2014/XD0948/**D**]

♦ Arab Judo Federation / see Arab Judo Confederation (#01000)
♦ Arab Jurists Union / see Union of Arab Jurists (#20354)
♦ Arab Karate Confederation (inactive)
♦ Arab Knowledge Management Society / see Arab International Society for Management Technology (#00993)
♦ Arab Labour Federation of Printing and Information Workers (inactive)

♦ Arab Labour Organization (ALO) 01001

Organisation arabe du travail (OAT) – Organización Arabe del Trabajo
Contact 7 Al-Mesaha Squarre, Dokki, Cairo, Egypt. T. +202333362719. Fax +20237484902. E-mail: alo@alolabor.org.
Permanent Office in Geneva PO Box 578, 1211 Geneva, Switzerland.
URL: https://alolabor.org/
History 12 Jan 1965, Baghdad (Iraq). Founded according to resolution No 1 passed at 1st Conference of Arab Ministers of Labour, approved by resolution No 2102 d/43, dated 21 Mar 1965, of the Council of *League of Arab States (LAS, #16420)* On 8 Jan 1970, the 5th Arab Labour Ministers' Conference issued a resolution to establish the "ALO" as a specialized agency on labour and workers. Commenced activities: 25 Sep 1972. **Aims** Coordinate efforts in work and workers' fields at the Arab and international levels; develop and maintain trade unions rights and freedom of association; provide technical assistance in all fields of labor to the tripartite in the Member States; develop labor legislation in the Member States and working on standardization; improve work conditions in the Member States; develop Arab human resources to take advantage of its full capacities in economic and social development; develop the Arab workforce and raise productivity efficiency; prepare a guide and lay the foundations for occupational classification and characterization; translate into Arabic the labor and vocational training terms. **Structure** General Conference (Arab Labor Conference – annual): Member States represented by a delegation composed of two government delegates, an employer delegate, a worker delegate, and their respective advisers. International and regional organizations also attend but as observers. Board of Directors (2 a year), composed of 8 titular members (4 Governments, 2 Employers, and 2 Workers) and 3 deputy members (one representing each group). Arab Labor Office: permanent secretariat, located in Cairo (Egypt), and headed by Director General. **Languages** Arabic. **Finance** Sources: members' dues. **Activities** Events/meetings; guidance/assistance/consulting; knowledge management/information dissemination; research/documentation; training/education. Active in all member countries. **Events** *Annual general conference* Marrakech (Morocco) 2006, *Annual general conference* Algeria 2005, *Annual general conference* Syrian AR 2004, *Annual general conference* Tunisia 2003, *Annual general conference* Cairo (Egypt) 2002. **Publications** *ALO Bulletin* (12 a year); *Arab Labour Review* (4 a year); *Legislative Bulletin* (4 a year).

Members Governments, employers, and workers of 21 Member States:
Algeria, Bahrain, Djibouti, Egypt, Iraq, Jordan, Kuwait, Lebanon, Libya, Mauritania, Morocco, Oman, Palestine, Qatar, Saudi Arabia, Somalia, Sudan, Syrian AR, Tunisia, United Arab Emirates, Yemen.
Affiliates:
Arab Centre for Human Resources Development (see: #01001); *Arab Centre for Labour Administration and Employment (ACLAE)*; *Arab Centre for Social Insurance, Khartoum (see: #01001)*; *Arab Institute for Labour Education and Research (#00984)*; *Arab Institute for Vocational Health and Safety (no recent information)*.
IGO Relations Memorandum of Understanding with (1): *Arab Women Organization (AWO, #01078)*. Participates in all activities of the Secretariat-General of the LAS, especially those related to socio-economic development in the Arab homeland. Cooperation and coordination agreements with: *ILO (#11123)* (and participates in all activities of the ILO Asian regional group); *United Nations Economic and Social Commission for Western Asia (ESCWA, #20558)*. Participates in the activities of: *UNCTAD (#20285)*. Collaborative Arab organization of: *Arab Organization for Agricultural Development (AOAD, #01018)*. Links with Arab and other international institutions and specialized organizations. **NGO Relations** Participate as observers: *International Confederation of Arab Trade Unions (ICATU, #12845)*; *Union of Arab Chambers (UAC, #20350)*.
[2022.11.30/XD0063/**D***]

♦ Arab Land Bank / see Egyptian Arab Land Bank

♦ Arab Lawyers' Union (ALU) 01002

Union des avocats arabes (UAA)

SG 13 Itehad El-Mohameen El-Arab St, Garden City, Cairo, Egypt. T. +2027952486. Fax +2027947719. E-mail: alu@intouch.com.

History 1958, Cairo (Egypt). Former names and other names: *Federation of Arab Lawyers* – alias. **Aims** Act in the interests of the Arab Nation to achieve its national objectives; facilitate contacts between Arab lawyers; safeguard and develop legislative and judiciary language; assure the freedom of lawyers in their work and the independence of magistrates; allow all Arab lawyers to take cases in any Arab country; harmonize the conditions of the legal profession; establish and harmonize links with international legal organizations; restore the study of Muslim law as a basis for law; promote and protect human rights. **Structure** Congress; Permanent Bureau; General Secretariat, consisting of Secretary General, Assistant Secretary General, Technical Secretary. **Finance** Membership paid by Bars of Arab countries. **Activities** Commissions (9): Arab Affairs; Palestine; Unification of Law in Arab Countries; Defence of Civil Liberties and Rule of Law in Arab Countries; Harmonization of Legal Terminology; Rules on the Legal Profession; Socialization; Support of the Palestine Liberation Movement; Defence of Palestinian Resistance Workers. Engaged in founding an *Arab Organization for Human Rights (AOHR, #01020)*. Decolonization action against racism, racial discrimination and apartheid. **Events** *Congress* Kuwait 1987, *Congress* Tunis (Tunisia) 1984, *Congress* Rabat (Morocco) 1980, *Congress* Cairo (Egypt) 1973, *Congress* Algiers (Algeria) 1970. **Publications** *Al Hakk (The Law)* in Arabic – with French and English sections. Documents; studies.
Members Bar associations (15) in 15 countries:
Algeria, Bahrain, Egypt, Iraq, Jordan, Kuwait, Lebanon, Libya, Mauritania, Morocco, Palestine, Sudan, Syrian AR, Tunisia, Yemen.
Consultative Status Consultative status granted from: *African Commission on Human and Peoples' Rights (ACHPR, #00255)* (Observer); *ECOSOC (#05331)* (Special); *UNESCO (#20322)* (Consultative Status); *ILO (#11123)* (Special List). **IGO Relations** *UNHCR (#20327)*. Accredited by: *United Nations Office at Vienna (UNOV, #20604)*.
NGO Relations Board member of: *Conference of Non-Governmental Organizations in Consultative Relationship with the United Nations (CONGO, #04635)*. Member of:
- *Afro-Asian Peoples' Solidarity Organization (AAPSO, #00537)*;
- *Arab Coalition for the International Criminal Court (ACICC, #00922)*;
- *Committee of NGOs on Human Rights, Geneva (#04275)*;
- *International Association of Democratic Lawyers (IADL, #11837)*;
- *International Centre for Trade Union Rights (ICTUR, #12525)*;
- *International Commission of Jurists (ICJ, #12695)*;
- *International Criminal Bar (ICB, #13107)*;
- *International Legal Assistance Consortium (ILAC, #14025)*;
- *NGO Committee for Disarmament, Geneva (#17105)*;
- *NGO Committee on Disarmament, Peace and Security, New York NY (#17106)*;
- *World Organisation Against Torture (OMCT, #21685)*;
- *World Peace Council (WPC, #21717)*.

Together with: *African Institute of Human Rights (inactive)*, *African Bar Association (AFBA, #00220)* and *Conférence des avocats francophones (inactive)*, instrumental in setting up, 1980, *Inter-African Union of Lawyers (IAUL, inactive)*, of which it is a member. Together with: *Arab Institute for Human Rights (AIHR, #00983)*, Arab Organization for Human Rights and *Human Rights Information and Documentation Systems, International (HURIDOCS, #10985)*, set up *Arab Human Rights Documentation and Information Network (AHRINET, no recent information)*. Represented on the Organizing Committee of: *Hague Appeal for Peace (HAP, #10848)*. Close cooperation with: *Arab Inter-Parliamentary Union (Arab IPU, #00995)*; *Inter-African Committee on Traditional Practices Affecting the Health of Women and Children (IAC, #11384)*; *International Federation for Human Rights (#13452)*.
[2018/XD4247/**D**]

♦ Arab League / see League of Arab States (#16420)

♦ Arab League Educational, Cultural and Scientific Organization (ALECSO) 01003

Organisation arabe pour l'éducation, la culture et la science – Organización Arabe para la Educación, la Cultura y la Ciencia

Contact PO Box 1120, 1000 Tunis, Tunisia. T. +2161784466. Fax +2161784965. E-mail: alecso@alecso.org.tn.
URL: http://www.alecso.org.tn/

History 25 May 1964, Cairo (Egypt). Established when Charter was approved by the Council of *League of Arab States (LAS, #16420)*, at its 41st Session. Officially established under Article 3 of the Charter for Arab Cultural Unity; creation officially announced 25 Jul 1970, Cairo (Egypt). **Aims** Empower intellectual unity between Arab countries through education, culture and science; enhance the level of culture in the region in order to keep up with and contribute to universal civilization.
Structure /Constitutional Structure/: General Conference (every 2 years), consists of 5 representatives per member state, headed by Minister with responsibility for each state's national commission to ALECSO (usually the Minister of Education). Executive Board (meeting twice a year), comprises one representative from each member state, plus Chairman of General Conference as consultant; meetings may be attended by an aide of the Director General. /Executive Structure/: Director General; Deputy Director General.
/Technical and Administrative Structure/:
1. *'Programme Supporting Services'*, all in Tunis (Tunisia):
- Secretariat of Executive Board and General Conference, headed by Secretary General;
- Office of the Director General;
- Department of Administrative and Financial Affairs;
- Department of Communication and Information (including Farabi Data Bank, ALECSO Printing Press and Publication, Distribution Unit and Central Library);
- Department of Culture;
- Department of Education;
- Department of Science and Scientific Research.

2. *'ALECSO Affiliate External Bodies'*:
- *Arab Centre for Arabization, Translation, Authorship and Publication (ACATAP, #00914)*, Damascus (Syrian AR);
- *Arabization Coordination Bureau (#00999)*, Rabat (Morocco);
- *Institute of Arab Manuscripts (no recent information)*, Cairo (Egypt);
- *Institute of Arab Research and Studies (no recent information)*, Cairo (Egypt);
- *Khartoum International Institute for the Arabic Language (no recent information)*, Khartoum (Sudan).

Languages Arabic, English, French. **Staff** 100.00 FTE, paid. About 85 non-permanent and casual experts. **Finance** Shares of member states calculated on the basis of each country's share in the budget of the League of Arab States. Other sources: grants; donations. Budget (biannual): US$ 17 million. **Activities** Technical assistance; training; education; projects. **Events** *Conference of Arab Culture Ministers* Dubai (United Arab Emirates) 2021, *Conference of Arab Culture Ministers* Cairo (Egypt) 2018, *Conference on education for intercultural understanding and dialogue* Copenhagen (Denmark) 2008, *International conference on wadi hydrology* Muscat (Oman) 2007, *International conference on wadi hydrology* Sanaa (Yemen) 2005. **Publications** *ALECSO News – Les nouvelles de l'ALECSO* (12 a year) in Arabic, English, French; *Arab Journal of Culture* (2 a year); *Arab Journal of Education* (2 a year); *Arab Journal of Information* (2 a year); *Arab Journal of Science* (2 a year); *Journal for Arab Research and Studies* (2 a year); *Youth Arab Scientific Magazine* (2 a year); *Arab Bulletin of Publications* (annual); *Arab Lexicographical Journal* (annual); *Journal of Education for Masses* (annual); *ALECSO Newsletter*, *Fadha'at Newsletter*, *Spaces* – bulletin for distance education. *Arab Encyclopaedia for Animal Resources* – series; *Arabic Paintings* – series; *Arab-Islamic Art* – series; *Learning Arabic for the Children of Arab Emigrants* – series; *Palestinian Town Stories* – series. *Arabization of Dewey's Decimal Classification* (12th ed 1998); *Radiation Solar Atlas for the Arab World* (1997); *Reference Book on the Integrated Subjects for the Basic Level of Education* (1996); *ALECSO's Trilingual Thesaurus* (1995) in Arabic, English, French; *Palestinian Encyclopaedia* (1990); *Basic Arab Dictionary* (1988); *Reference Book on Environmental Education* (1984); *Basic Learning Books for Non-Arab Speakers* (1983 -1993) – 3 vols. Books; guides; monographs; translations. **Information Services** *ALECSO Data Bank (FARABI Data Bank)* – includes 10 documentation databases and 2 statistics databases, with published and online information and training courses.
Members Governments of 22 Arab countries and territories:
Algeria, Bahrain, Comoros, Djibouti, Egypt, Iraq, Jordan, Kuwait, Lebanon, Libya, Mauritania, Morocco, Oman, Palestine, Qatar, Saudi Arabia, Somalia, Sudan, Syrian AR, Tunisia, United Arab Emirates, Yemen.
IGO Relations Formal agreement with: *Council of Europe (CE, #04881)*; *UNESCO (#20322)*. Permanent observer status with: *World Intellectual Property Organization (WIPO, #21593)*. Participates in the activities of: *UNCTAD (#20285)*. Working arrangement with: *World Meteorological Organization (WMO, #21649)*. Cooperation agreement with: *Islamic World Educational, Scientific and Cultural Organization (ICESCO, #16058)*; *Organisation internationale de la Francophonie (OIF, #17809)*; *UNIDO (#20336)*. Memorandum of Understanding with: *Arab Women Organization (AWO, #01078)*. Member of: *Regional Remote Sensing Centre for North African States (#18807)*. Cooperation under discussion with: *Arab States Broadcasting Union (ASBU, #01050)*. Participates in administration of: *African Bureau of Educational Sciences (BASE, no recent information)*. Invited to sessions of Intergovernmental Council of: *International Programme for the Development of Communication (IPDC, #14651)*.
NGO Relations In liaison with technical committees of: *International Organization for Standardization (ISO, #14473)*. Member of Permanent Council of: *International Congress of African Studies (ICAF, inactive)*. Regional member of: *International Council for Adult Education (ICAE, #12983)*. Supports: *Afro-Arab Institute for Culture and Strategic Studies (AACI, #00534)*. Agreement with: *International Council of Museums (ICOM, #13051)*. Formal contacts with:
- *Arab Federation for Libraries and Information (AFLI, #00947)*;
- *Asia South Pacific Association for Basic and Adult Education (ASPBAE, #02098)*;
- Canadian Regional Council for Adult Education;
- *European Association for the Education of Adults (EAEA, #06018)*;
- *International Council on Archives (ICA, #12996)*;
- *International Federation of Library Associations and Institutions (IFLA, #13470)*.

[2021/XD4163/**D***]

♦ Arab Livestock Development Corporation / see Arab Company for Livestock Development (#00927)

♦ Arab Maghreb Union (AMU) 01004

Union du Maghreb arabe (UMA)

SG 73 Rue Tensift, Agdal, 10080 Rabat, Morocco. T. +212537681371 – +212537681372 – +212537681376. Fax +212537681377. E-mail: sg.uma@maghrebarabe.org.
URL: http://www.maghrebarabe.org/

History 17 Feb 1989, Marrakech (Morocco). Established as a project adopted by a Maghreb Summit. Former names and other names: *Maghreb Union* – former; *Union of the Arab Maghreb (UAM)* – former. **Aims** Define the means and tools to realize integration of the five states of the Maghreb Arabe (Libyan AJ, Tunisia, Algeria, Morocco and Mauritania) through continuation of a common policy in different areas and progressive fulfillment of free mouvement of persons, services, goods and capital; safeguard Maghrebian economic interests; foster and promote economic and cultural cooperation among member states; intensify mutual commercial exchanges as a necessary precursor for integration and the creation of a Maghreb Economic Space. **Structure** Supreme Council of the Heads of State (chaired in succession on a yearly basis) – also referred to as Presidential Council; Consultative Assembly; Council of Ministers of Foreign Affairs; Committees; Judiciary Body; Permanent General Secretariat; Maghreb Academy of Sciences and Maghreb University in Tripoli (Libyan AJ); Maghreb Bank for Investment and Foreign Commerce Tunis (Tunisia). **Languages** Arabic. **Staff** 60.00 FTE, paid. **Finance** Sources: contributions of member/participating states. **Activities** Working towards creation of a *Maghreb Economic Space*. Aims to create: a free market in energy products; free movement of citizens within the region; joint transport undertakings, including a joint airline and road railway improvements; formation of Maghreb union of textile and leather industries; creation of a customs union. Instrumental in setting up *Consultative Council of the Arab Maghreb Union (#04765)*; *Maghreb sans frontières (inactive)*. **Events** *EU troika – Arab Magreb Union meeting* Rabat (Morocco) 2008, *Summit Meeting* Tunis (Tunisia) 1994, *Joint Meeting* Brussels (Belgium) 1992, *Summit conference / Summit Meeting* Nouakchott (Mauritania) 1992, *Summit Meeting* Ras Lanuf (Libyan AJ) 1991.
Members Governments of 5 countries:
Algeria, Libya, Mauritania, Morocco, Tunisia.
IGO Relations Member of: *Africa Partnership Forum (APF, #00510)*; *Regional Remote Sensing Centre for North African States (#18807)*. Observer to: *International Organization for Migration (IOM, #14454)*; *World Trade Organization (WTO, #21864)*. Cooperation agreement with: *UNCTAD (#20285)*; *UNIDO (#20336)*. Collaborative Arab organization of: *Arab Organization for Agricultural Development (AOAD, #01018)*. Accredited to the Conference of the Parties of: *Secretariat of the United Nations Convention to Combat Desertification (Secretariat of the UNCCD, #19208)*. Regional Economic Community of: *African Union (AU, #00488)*. Accredited by: *United Nations Framework Convention on Climate Change – Secretariat (UNFCCC, #20564)*.
[2022.03.08/XF1048/**F***]

♦ Arab Management Society / see Arab International Society for Management Technology (#00993)
♦ Arab Maritime Petroleum Transport Company (see: #17854)
♦ Arab Maritime Transport Academy, Alexandria / see Arab Academy for Science, Technology and Maritime Transport (#00891)

♦ Arab Maternal – Fetal Medicine Expert Group (AMFMEG) 01005

Address not obtained.

History 2005, Lebanon. **Aims** Exchange knowledge and expertise; write protocols and guidelines related to MFM application in the Arab world; launch and conduct research; establish collaborative communication between Arab or international organizations to help promote the health of the mother and the foetus. **Structure** Executive Board. **Activities** Events/meetings; networking/liaising; research/documentation; standards/guidelines; training/education. **Events** *Congress* Jeddah (Saudi Arabia) 2018, *Congress* Dubai (United Arab Emirates) 2017.
[2018/XM6815/**F**]

♦ Arab Medical Association Against Cancer (AMAAC) 01006

SG KHIBC, 162 Mecca St, 6th Floor, Amman 11814, Jordan.
URL: http://www.amaac.org/

History Founded 2001, as part of *'Arab Medical Association'*, and as a continuation of *'Arab Council against Cancer'*, founded in 1995. **Aims** Raise awareness of cancer prevention and control; improve the level of knowledge of cancer professionals; raise efficacy of cancer treatment in Arab countries. **Structure** General Assembly; Administrative Council; Executive Board; Office in Cairo (Egypt). Includes: *Junior Arab Medical Association Against Cancer (JAMAAC)*. **Languages** Arabic, English. **Staff** 1.00 FTE, paid. **Finance** Members' dues. Other sources: donations; conferences. **Activities** Events/meetings; financial and/or material support. **Events** *Annual Pan Arab Cancer Congress* Amman (Jordan) 2019, *Annual Pan Arab Cancer Congress* Tunis (Tunisia) 2018, *Annual Pan Arab Cancer Congress* Algiers (Algeria) 2017, *Pan Arab Cancer Congress* Cairo (Egypt) 2016, *Pan Arab Cancer Congress* Beirut (Lebanon) 2015. **Publications** *Pan Arab Journal of Oncology (PAJO)* (4 a year).
Members in 18 countries and territories:
Algeria, Bahrain, Egypt, Iraq, Jordan, Kuwait, Lebanon, Libya, Mauritania, Morocco, Oman, Palestine, Saudi Arabia, Sudan, Syrian AR, Tunisia, United Arab Emirates, Yemen.
NGO Relations Member of: *Consortium for Non-communicable Diseases Prevention and Control in sub-Saharan Africa (CNCD-Africa, #04754)*; *The NCD Alliance (NCDA, #16963)*; *Union for International Cancer Control (UICC, #20415)*.
[2017.04.08/XJ4586/**D**]

♦ Arab Medical Federation / see Arab Medical Union (#01007)

♦ Arab Medical Union 01007

Union des médecins arabes (UMA)

SG Al-Aini Palace, Dar Al-Hikma, Cairo, Egypt. T. +20227958681. E-mail: media@arabmu.com.
URL: https://www.arabmu.com/

History 28 May 1961, Cairo (Egypt). Also referred to as *Arab Medical Federation – Fédération médicale arabe*. **Aims** Promote medicine and medical research in Arab countries; facilitate contacts between Arab *physicians* in various countries; establish friendly contacts with other medical bodies. **Structure** Higher Council (meets once a year, on the occasion of the Arab Medical Congress), consisting of 2 representatives of every member country. General Secretariat, consisting of Secretary-General and 6 Assistant Secretaries-General. **Languages** Arabic, English, French. **Staff** Voluntary. **Finance** Annual members' dues. **Events** *Annual Arab Medical Congress* Algiers (Algeria) 2011, *Annual Arab medical congress* London (UK) 2002, *Annual congress / Annual Arab Medical Congress* Beirut (Lebanon) 2001, *Annual congress* Abu Dhabi (United Arab Emirates) 2000, *International telemedicine symposium for the Arab world, Africa and Europe* Tunis (Tunisia) 1998. **Publications** *Revue médicale de l'Union des médecins arabes* (4 a year) in Arabic.
Members Arab medical associations and medical trade unions in 16 countries:
Algeria, Bahrain, Iraq, Jordan, Kuwait, Lebanon, Libya, Mauritania, Morocco, Oman, Palestine, Qatar, Syrian AR, Tunisia, United Arab Emirates, Yemen.
IGO Relations Member of: *Council of Arab Ministers of Health (#04861)*. **NGO Relations** Co-founder, together with: *Balkan Medical Union (#03078)* and *Surgery Society of the Latin Mediterranean (#20042)*, of *Entente médicale méditerranéenne (EMM, no recent information)*. [2018/XD8699/**D**]

♦ Arab Medical Union in Europe / see Union of Arab Doctors in Europe (#20352)
♦ **ARABMED** Union Arabischer Mediziner in Europa (#20352)

♦ Arab Mining Company (ARMICO) 01008

Contact PO Box 20198, Amman 11118, Jordan. T. +96265663146 – +96265663148 – +96265663149. Fax +96265684114. E-mail: info@armico.com.
URL: http://www.armico.com/

History 1 Feb 1975, Amman (Jordan). Established within the framework of *Council of Arab Economic Unity (CAEU, #04859)*. Activities started 10 Jun 1976. The Governments of Morocco, Tunisia and Mauritania decided to become participant shareholders in the Company in 1977, 1978 and 1981 respectively. **Aims** Ensure optimal returns from investments that drive growth in the mining sector in the Arab world. **Structure** General Assembly (annual); Board of Directors. **Finance** Financed by its own capital and retained earnings. Authorized capital: Kuwaiti Dinars 54.470.000. **Activities** Pan-Arab projects listed in this Yearbook in which the Company participates: *Arab Company for Detergent Chemicals (ARADET, see: #17854)*; *Arab Iron and Steel Union (AISU, #00998)*; *Société arabe des mines de l'Inchiri (SAMIN, no recent information)*. **Publications** *Arab Mining Journal*. Annual Report.
Members Governments of 14 countries:
Egypt, Iraq, Jordan, Kuwait, Libya, Mauritania, Morocco, Saudi Arabia, Somalia, Sudan, Syrian AR, Tunisia, United Arab Emirates, Yemen.
Regional shareholder:
Arab Investment Company (TAIC, #00996).
IGO Relations *Arab Petroleum Investments Corporation (APICORP, #01026)*; *Islamic Development Bank (IsDB, #16044)*. Member of: *Arab Potash Company (APC, #01029)*. **NGO Relations** Member of: *Arab Fertilizer Association (AFA, #00958)*; *Arab Geologists' Association (AGA, #00967)*; *Arab Union for Cement and Building Materials (AUCBM, #01065)*. [2021/XM1056/e/**F***]

♦ Arab Modern Pentathlon and Biathlon Union (inactive)

♦ Arab Monetary Fund (AMF) 01009

Fonds Monétaire Arabe (FMA)

Dir Gen PO Box 2818, Abu Dhabi, United Arab Emirates. T. +97126171400. Fax +97126326454. E-mail: centralmail@amfad.org.ae.
URL: http://www.amf.org.ae/

History Established 27 Apr 1976, Rabat (Morocco), on signature of 'Arab Monetary Fund Agreement' by Economy and Finance Ministers of Arab States, following approval, 14 Dec 1975, of *Council of Arab Economic Unity (CAEU, #04859)* and, 8 Dec 1975, of the Economic Council of *League of Arab States (LAS, #16420)*. Commenced operations 13 Feb 1977, when Agreement came into force. A multilateral aid institution. **Aims** Promote *monetary* and *economic* integration development among Arab countries. *'Main Objectives'*: (1) Correcting disequilibria in the balance of payments of member states. (2) Promoting the stability of exchange rates among Arab *currencies*, rendering them mutually convertible, and assisting in the elimination of restrictions on current payments between member states. (3) Promoting the development of Arab *financial* markets. (4) Studying ways to promote the use of the Arab dinar as a unit of account and paving the way for the creation of a unified Arab currency. (5) Coordinating the position of member states in dealing with international monetary and economic problems with the aim of realizing their common interest while, at the same time, contributing to the settlement of world monetary problems. (6) Settling current payments between member states in order to promote trade among them. **Structure** Board of Governors; (meets annually, normally in April); Board of Executive Directors. Departments (currently 6): Economics and Technical; Economic Policy Institute; Investment; Finance and Computer; Legal; Administration. Internal Audit Bureau; Bureau of Director General; *Arab Trade Financing Programme (ATFP, #01060)*. Serves as secretariat for: *Arab Committee on Banking Supervision (ACBS, #00925)*; Arab Committee on Payment and Settlement Systems (ACPSS); Council of Arab Finance Ministers; *Council of Arab Central Banks and Monetary Agencies' Governors (CGACB, #04858)*. **Languages** Arabic, English, French. **Staff** 153.00 FTE, paid.
Finance Activities financed through contributions by member countries. Unit of account is the Arab Accounting Dinar (AAD), equivalent to 3 units of Special Drawing Rights (SDR).
Provides 4 types of loan to member states in support of economic adjustment programmes: Automatic (3 years), under which members may draw unconditionally up to 75% of paid-in capital in convertible currencies to finance balance-of-payment deficits; Ordinary (5 years) for loans in excess of the Automatic 75% limit, subject to a financial adjustment programme; Extended (up to 7 years), similar to Ordinary loans but subject to a structural reform programme approved by AMF; Compensatory (3 years) to accommodate balance-of-payment deficits arising from unforeseeable factors. In addition, there are few facilities that are extended in support of sectorial reforms (Structural Adjustment Facility, Trade Reform Facility, Oil Facility, Short term Liquidity Facility). Loans approved in 2014: AAD 56.5 million; disbursements in 2014: AAD 59.3 million. Total loans approved to end 2014: AAD 1.75 billion; total repayments: AAD 651,622,000.
Activities Financial and/or material support; training/education; events/meetings. **Events** *Conference on the Role of Cross-Border Payments in Fostering Regional Financial Integration* Abu Dhabi (United Arab Emirates) 2019, *Annual World Government Summit* Dubai (United Arab Emirates) 2019, *Annual Joint Meeting of Arab Financial Institutions* Kuwait (Kuwait) 2019, *Annual Meeting* Amman (Jordan) 2018, *Annual World Government summit* Dubai (United Arab Emirates) 2018. **Publications** *Arab Countries Selected Economics Indicators* (annual); *Arab Financial Markets Performance* (annual); *Arab Governments Finance* (annual); *Balance of Payments and External Public Debt for Arab Countries* (annual); *Cross Exchange Rates of Currencies of Arab Countries* (annual); *Foreign Trade of Arab Countries* (annual); *Joint Arab Economic Report* (annual); *National Accounts of Arab Countries* (annual); *Statistics of Inter and Intra Arab Trade Competitiveness* (annual).
Members Members of the Arab League, governments of 22 countries and territories:
Algeria, Bahrain, Comoros, Djibouti, Egypt, Iraq, Jordan, Kuwait, Lebanon, Libya, Mauritania, Morocco, Oman, Palestine, Qatar, Saudi Arabia, Somalia, Sudan, Syrian AR, Tunisia, United Arab Emirates, Yemen.
IGO Relations Cooperates with: *UNCTAD (#20285)*. Member of: *Islamic Development Bank (IsDB, #16044)*; *OPEC Fund for International Development (OFID, #17745)*. [2015.03.01/XF5515/f/**F***]

♦ Arab Music Academy / see Arab Academy of Music (#00890)

♦ Arab Neonatal Care Group (ANCG) 01010

Address not obtained.
URL: https://anccdubai.com/

History Founded 2010. **Aims** Help neonatologist in the Arab world to bridge the gap with international healthcare professionals to promote research and adapt evidence based care. **Structure** Board. **Activities** Training/education; events/meetings. **Events** *International Arab Neonatal Care Conference* Dubai (United Arab Emirates) 2022, *International Arab Neonatal Care Conference* Dubai (United Arab Emirates) 2021, *International Arab Neonatal Care Conference* Dubai (United Arab Emirates) 2019, *International Arab Neonatal Care Conference* Dubai (United Arab Emirates) 2018. [2022/XM8084/**D**]

♦ Arab Network for Civic Education (ANHRE) 01011

Exec Dir Sharef Nasser Bin Jameel St, Wadi-Saqra complex no 47, 6th Floor – Office no 603, PO Box 4799, Amman 11953, Jordan. T. +96265560497. Fax +96265560913. E-mail: fotouh.younes@gmail.com – info@anhre.org.
URL: http://www.anhre.org/

History Founded 2009, as *Arab Network for Human Rights and Citizenship Education (ANHRE)*. **Aims** Enhance cooperation, exchange and sharing as well as dissemination of a culture of human rights and citizenship education in the Arab World according to scientific and educational methodologies at promoting and strengthening human rights and concepts of citizenships through making available relevant information, effective methodologies and capacity building for improvement of performance of members. **Structure** General Assembly; Coordination Committee. **Finance** Funding from: *Canadian International Development Agency (CIDA, inactive)*; *Equitas – International Centre for Human Rights Education*. **Publications** *ANHRE Newsletter*.
Members Organizations (45) in 9 countries:
Algeria, Egypt, Iraq, Jordan, Lebanon, Morocco, Palestine, Tunisia, Yemen.
IGO Relations *Anna Lindh Euro-Mediterranean Foundation for the Dialogue between Cultures (Anna Lindh Foundation, #00847)*. **NGO Relations** Member of: *Arab Campaign for Education for All (ACEA, #00911)*; *Global Campaign for Education (GCE, #10264)*; *International Council fpr Adult Education (ICAE, #12983)*. [2019/XJ1998/**D**]

♦ Arab Network for Democratic Elections (unconfirmed)
♦ Arab Network for Human Rights and Citizenship Education / see Arab Network for Civic Education (#01011)

♦ Arab Network on Nanotechnology (ArNano) 01012

Contact address not obtained. T. +4687908158. Fax +4687909072. E-mail: mamoun@kth.se.
History A network functioning under the umbrella of *Arab Science and Technology Foundation (ASTF, #01039)*. **Aims** Increase cooperation between research centres and institutions in the Arab world working on nanotechnology. **Structure** Advisory Board. Coordinator. **Languages** Arabic, English. [2009.06.01/XM3281/**F**]

♦ Arab Network of Nuclear Regulators (ANNuR) 01013

Contact c/o IAEA – VIC, PO Box 100, 1400 Vienna, Austria. E-mail: y.chaari@iaea.org – annur.contact-point@iaea.org.
URL: http://gnssn.iaea.org/main/ANNuR/

History 2010. Functions within *Global Nuclear Safety and Security Network (GNSSN, #10509)* of *International Atomic Energy Agency (IAEA, #12294)*. **Aims** Strengthen and harmonize the regulatory infrastructure in Arab countries; exchange regulatory knowledge and experiences with other international and regional networks. **Structure** Plenary; Steering Committee; Thematic Working Groups.
Members Active Member States (22):
Algeria, Bahrain, Comoros, Djibouti, Egypt, Iraq, Jordan, Kuwait, Lebanon, Libya, Mauritania, Morocco, Oman, Palestine, Qatar, Saudi Arabia, Somalia, Sudan, Syrian AR, Tunisia, United Arab Emirates, Yemen.
IGO Relations *Arab Atomic Energy Agency (AAEA, #00901)*. [2016/XM6493/**F***]

♦ Arab Network for Quality Assurance in Higher Education (ANQAHE) 01014

Secretariat c/o National Authority, PO Box 30347, Manama, Bahrain. T. +97317562313. Fax +97317589296.
URL: http://anqahe.org/

History Dec 2005, Cairo (Egypt). Former names and other names: *Arab Society for Quality Assurance in Education* – former. **Aims** Create a mechanism between the Arab countries to: exchange information about quality assurance; construct new quality assurance agencies or organizations; develop standards to establish new quality assurance agencies or support the already present one; disseminate good practice in quality assurance; strengthen liaison between quality assurance bodies in the different countries. **Structure** Board. **Events** *Conference* Abu Dhabi (United Arab Emirates) 2009. **Publications** Annual Report; reports; guidelines.
Members Full in 14 countries and territories:
Bahrain, Egypt, Jordan, Kuwait, Lebanon, Libya, Morocco, Oman, Palestine, Qatar, Saudi Arabia, Sudan, United Arab Emirates, Yemen.
IGO Relations Support from: *International Bank for Reconstruction and Development (IBRD, #12317)* (World Bank); *UNESCO (#20322)*. **NGO Relations** Regional member of: *International Network of Quality Assurance Agencies in Higher Education (INQAAHE, #14312)*. [2020/XM3354/**D**]

♦ Arab Network for Women in Science and Technology (ANWST) 01015

Contact Bibliotheca Alexandrina, PO Box 138, El Shatby, Alexandria, 21526, Egypt. T. +2034839999. Fax +2034820450. E-mail: secretariat@bibalex.org.
URL: http://www.bibalex.org/anwst/

History Also referred to as *ANWIST*. **Aims** Stimulate effective participation of women in science and technology; build a scientific society capable of facing the challenges of sustainable development in the Arab World. **Structure** Board of Directors, comprising Chairperson and 15 members. **IGO Relations** Housed at: *Bibliotheca Alexandrina Council of Patrons (#03227)*. [2011/XJ2436/**F**]

♦ Arab NGO Network for Development (ANND) 01016

Contact PO Box 5792/14, Al-Mazra'a, Beirut, Lebanon. T. +9611319366. Fax +9611815363.
URL: http://www.annd.org/

History Founded Jun 1996. EU Transparency Register: 235474015095-10. **Aims** Strengthen civil society; enhance the values of democracy, respect for human rights and sustainable development in the Arab region. **Structure** General Assembly (every 2 years); Coordination Committee. **Languages** Arabic, English. **Staff** 14.50 FTE, paid; 3.00 FTE, voluntary. **Finance** Budget (annual): US$ 650,000-750,000. **Activities** Capacity building; advocacy/lobbying/activism; events/meetings. **Events** *Civil society forum* Doha (Qatar) 2008. **Publications** *ANND Newsletter*. Publications on: Islamic Development Bank, Euro Mediterranean Partnership; role of civil society in democratic changes in the Arab region; social and economic conditions in the Arab region; MDGs in the region; tax policies in 6 arab countries; austerity policies (IMF); subsidies (IMF); right to work and right to education; social protection politics. Manuals; other publications.
Members Full in 11 countries and territories:
Bahrain, Egypt, Iraq, Jordan, Lebanon, Mauritania, Morocco, Palestine, Sudan, Tunisia, Yemen.
Consultative Status Consultative status granted from: *ECOSOC (#05331)* (Ros A); *UNCTAD (#20285)* (General Category). **IGO Relations** Cooperates with: *International Institute for Democracy and Electoral Assistance (International IDEA, #13872)*. Associated with Department of Global Communications of the United Nations. **NGO Relations** Member of: *Asia-Pacific Research Network (APRN, #02013)*; *CIVICUS: World Alliance for Citizen Participation (#03962)*; *ETO Consortium (ETOs, #05560)*; *EuroMed Non-Governmental Platform (#05730)*; *Global Call for Action Against Poverty (GCAP, #10263)*; *International Network for Economic, Social and Cultural Rights (ESCR-Net, #14255)*; *Just Net Coalition (JNC, #16173)*; *Social Watch (#19350)*; *Our World is Not for Sale (OWINFS, #17917)*; *The Reality Of Aid (ROA, #18626)*. Cooperates with: *FIM-Forum for Democratic Global Governance (FIM, #09761)*; *International Center for Not-for-Profit Law (ICNL, #12471)*; *Third World Network (TWN, #20151)*. [2020/XJ4304/**F**]

♦ Arab NGO Network for Environment and Development (RAED) 01017

Réseau arabe des ONG pour l'environnement et le développement

Contact 3A Masr lel-Tameer bldgs, Zahraa el Maadi St, Elmaadi, Cairo, Egypt. T. +20225161519. E-mail: info@raednetwork.org.
URL: http://www.raednetwork.org/

History 1990, Cairo (Egypt), following Arab NGOs Consultancy Conference. **Aims** Stimulate: national resources and cultural *heritage* protection; sound *sustainable* development management guiding human behaviour towards achieving peace and a safe environment in the Arab region; livelihood enhancement. **Structure** General Assembly. National Coordinators Council. Executive Board. General Secretariat, managed by General Coordinator. **Languages** Arabic, English, French. **Staff** 5.00 FTE, paid. **Finance** In addition to *European Commission (EC, #06633)*, financed through: various funding agencies; *Mediterranean Action Plan (MAP, #16638)*; *UNDP (#20292)*; other UN agencies; embassies. **Activities** In charge of South Mediterranean actions in cooperation with *Mediterranean Information Office for Environment, Culture and Sustainable Development (MIO-ECSDE, #16657)*; convenes meetings in cooperation with Technical General Secretariat of Council of Arab Ministers Responsible for the Environment (CAMRE). With experience in climate change, forest fire fighting and environmental degradation, activities include: strategic planning for management of water resources and water conservation on the domestic level and in the industrial and agricultural sectors; designing a model for community awareness-raising and education in the field of water and energy; projects in the fields of solid waste management, desertification and international waters. **Events** *Regional consultation for North Africa and the Middle East* Lebanon 1996. **Publications** *Montada Al Biah* (12 a year) – newsletter.
Members NGOs (about 250) in 19 countries:
Algeria, Bahrain, Egypt, Iraq, Jordan, Kuwait, Lebanon, Libya, Mauritania, Morocco, Oman, Palestine, Qatar, Saudi Arabia, Sudan, Syrian AR, Tunisia, United Arab Emirates, Yemen.
Consultative Status Consultative status granted from: *ECOSOC (#05331)* (Special). **IGO Relations** Recognised, 1995, by: *League of Arab States (LAS, #16420)* (formal contacts). Official observer status in: *Council of Arab Ministers Responsible for the Environment (CAMRE, #04863)*. **NGO Relations** Member of: *CIVICUS: World Alliance for Citizen Participation (#03962)*; *GEF CSO Network (GCN, #10087)*; *International NGO Forum (INGOF, no recent information)*; *International Union for Conservation of Nature and Natural Resources (IUCN, #15766)*; *Mediterranean Information Office for Environment, Culture and Sustainable Development (MIO-ECSDE, #16657)*; *Mediterranean Social-Ecological Youth Network (MARE, no recent information)*; *World Social Forum (WSF, #21797)*. [2018/XF2657/**F**]

- ♦ Arabo-African Summit (meeting series)
- ♦ Arabo-African Union of Ageing, Pensioners and of Intergenerational Alliance (no recent information)
- ♦ Arab Office for Youth and Environment (internationally oriented national body)
- ♦ Arab Open University (internationally oriented national body)
- ♦ Arab Organization of Administrative Sciences / see Arab Administrative Development Organization (#00893)

♦ Arab Organization for Agricultural Development (AOAD) 01018
Organisation Arabe du Développement Agricole
Dir-Gen Almarat St 7, PO Box 474, 11111, Khartoum, Sudan. T. +249183472176 – +249183472174. Fax +249183471050. E-mail: info@aoad.org.
URL: http://www.aoad.org/
History 11 Mar 1970. Established on approval of an agreement by the Council of *League of Arab States (LAS, #16420)*, following meeting of Arab Ministers of Agriculture, 1969, Cairo (Egypt). Commenced operations Sep 1972, Khartoum (Sudan). **Aims** Identify and develop linkages between Arab countries and coordinate all agricultural and agricultural related activities among them in order to attain full regional integration in the sector. **Structure** General Assembly; Executive Council; General Administration; Units (4); Departments and Specialized Centers (8); Regional Offices (4). **Languages** Arabic, English. **Staff** 109.00 FTE, paid. **Finance** Sources: contributions of member/participating states. Target funding by member states or as part of cooperation agreements with development and financing organizations for joint activities. **Activities** Capacity building; guidance/assistance/consulting; knowledge management/information dissemination; monitoring/evaluation; projects/programmes; publishing activities; research/documentation; training/education. **Events** *Arab Agriculture Day Meeting* Khartoum (Sudan) 2021, *Enhancing the Resilience and Sustainability of the Agricultural Sector in the Arab Region* Khartoum (Sudan) 2021, *General Assembly* Khartoum (Sudan) 2020, *The 2030 Agenda for Sustainable Development in the Arab Region Meeting* Khartoum (Sudan) 2020, *Regional Smart Agriculture Forum* Khartoum (Sudan) 2018. **Publications** *Arab Fishery Statistics Yearbooks* (annual); *Arab Agricultural Statistics Yearbook* (annual); *Arab Food Security Report* (annual); *AOAD Annual Report*. Information Services: Agricultural information databases.
Members Governments of 22 countries and territories:
Algeria, Bahrain, Comoros, Djibouti, Egypt, Iraq, Jordan, Kuwait, Lebanon, Libya, Mauritania, Morocco, Oman, Palestine, Qatar, Saudi Arabia, Somalia, Sudan, Syrian AR, Tunisia, United Arab Emirates, Yemen.
IGO Relations Close working and cooperation relations with IGOs and international and regional agencies, not specified. **NGO Relations** Close working and cooperation relations with NGOs and international and regional agencies, not specified. [2021.12.05/XD5526/**D***]

♦ Arab Organization of Disabled People (AODP) 01019
Gen Dir Toufic Tabbara Center, Zarief, Beirut, Lebanon. T. +9611738296. Fax +9611738297. E-mail: aodp@cyberia.net.lb.
URL: http://www.aodp-lb.net/
History 1998, Egypt. **Aims** Provide presentation of disabled people in the Arab world. **Members** in 15 countries. Membership countries not specified. **NGO Relations** Member of: *International Disability Alliance (IDA, #13176)*. Participates in: *Global Partnership on Children with Disabilities (GPcwd, #10529)*. [2018/XM1768/**D**]

♦ Arab Organization for Human Rights (AOHR) 01020
Organisation arabe des droits de l'homme – Organización Arabe de Derechos Humanos
SG 91 Merghani Street, Heliopolis, Cairo, 11341, Egypt. T. +20224181396. Fax +20224185346. E-mail: info@aohr.net – aohrarab@gmail.com.
Exec Dir address not obtained.
URL: https://aohr.net/en/
History 12 Dec 1983, Limassol (Cyprus). Founded when Statutes were adopted, following resolution of a meeting, Apr 1983, Hammamet (Tunisia). **Aims** Call for respect of human rights and fundamental freedoms of all citizens and individuals in Arab countries in accordance with provisions of international human rights instruments; defend any individual or group whose human rights are subjected to violations which are contrary to the Universal Declaration of Human Rights, the International Covenant on Economic, Social and Cultural Rights and the International Covenant on Civil and Political Rights, as well al the other international human rights instruments; endeavour, regardless of political considerations, to obtain release of detained or imprisoned persons, and provide relief and assistance for persons whose freedom is restricted in any way or who are subject to coercion of any kind because of their beliefs and political convictions, or for reasons of race, sex, colour or language; protest in cases where a fair trial is not guaranteed; provide legal assistance where necessary and possible; call for improvements in conditions of prisoners of conscience; work for amnesty of persons sentenced for political reasons. **Structure** General Assembly (every 3 years); Board of Trustees (meets annually); Executive Committee; General Secretariat. **Languages** Arabic, English. **Staff** 21.00 FTE, paid. **Finance** Members' dues. Sales of publications; unconditional, non-governmental donations; interests of foundation deposit. **Activities** Carries out fact finding missions to verify the human rights developments in the Arab region, and field missions in an effort to release political prisoners, in some cases as an observer and in other as a member of the defence panel. Receives complaints from individuals, groups and organizations and contacts the concerned authorities. In addition to the offering of legal assistance in several cases, the Organization provides financial assistance to families of victims. In coordination with Arab Lawyers' Union launched a campaign for 'Freedom for Prisoners of Conscience in the Arab World'. Conferences and seminars. Instrumental in setting up: *Arab Human Rights Documentation and Information Network (AHRINET, no recent information)*; *Arab Institute for Human Rights (AIHR, #00983)*. **Events** *Triennial General Assembly* Cairo (Egypt) 2011, *Triennial General Assembly* Cairo (Egypt) 2008, *Triennial General Assembly* Cairo (Egypt) 2004, *Triennial General Assembly* Cairo (Egypt) 2000, *Triennial General Assembly* Morocco 1997. **Publications** *Arab Organization for Human Rights Newsletter* (6 a year) in Arabic, English; *Human Rights Issues* in Arabic. Annual Report. Reports on specific human rights issues; workshop and seminar reports.
Members Branches (22), represented by Arab NGOs working at national level in 19 countries and territories:
Algeria, Austria, Bahrain, Egypt, Germany, Iraq, Jordan, Kuwait, Lebanon, Mauritania, Morocco, Palestine, Sudan, Syrian AR, Tunisia, UK, United Arab Emirates, Yemen.
Individuals (about 1,700) in 39 countries worldwide. Membership countries not specified.
Consultative Status Consultative status granted from: *African Commission on Human and Peoples' Rights (ACHPR, #00255)* (Observer); *ECOSOC (#05331)* (Special); *UNESCO (#20322)* (Consultative Status). **NGO Relations** Member of: *Abolition 2000 – Global Network to Eliminate Nuclear Weapons (Abolition 2000, #00006)*; *Arab Coalition for the International Criminal Court (ACICC, #00922)*; *EarthAction (EA, #05159)*; *Habitat International Coalition (HIC, #10845)*; *International Criminal Bar (ICB, #13107)*; *International Legal Assistance Consortium (ILAC, #14025)*. [2020/XD9700/**D**]

- ♦ Arab Organization for International Cooperation (unconfirmed)
- ♦ Arab Organization for Mineral Resources (inactive)
- ♦ Arab Organization for Social Defence Against Crime (inactive)
- ♦ Arab Organization for Standardization and Metrology (inactive)

♦ Arab Organization of Supreme Audit Institutions (ARABOSAI) 01021
Groupe arabe des institutions supérieures de contrôle des finances publiques
General Secretariat Tayeb M'hiri Avenue, No 87, 1002 Belvedere, Tunis, Tunisia. T. +21671780040. Fax +21671780029. E-mail: rajahleli@yahoo.fr.
SG address not obtained. E-mail: secretaire.general@courdescomptes.nat.tn.
URL: http://www.arabosai.org/
History 1976, Cairo (Egypt), at constitutional congress. Current Charter approved 1983, Tunis (Tunisia), at 3rd Congress. **Aims** Regulate and develop various forms of cooperation among members, strengthening relations between them, and with specialized agencies of the League of Arab States, with INTOSAI and with other international and regional organizations; encourage exchange of opinion, ideas, experience, study and research among members while raising their standards in members' institutions both scientifically and practically; provide assistance to Arab countries wishing to establish or extend supreme audit institutions; unify scientific terminology; support the role of institutions by spreading 'audit consciousness' in the Arab region; promote the entrusting of ARABOSAI with nomination of audit commissions reviewing accounts of the Arab League and its affiliated organizations, and those financed by the League or by Arab states, endeavouring to raise the standard of auditing in them. **Structure** General Assembly (every 3 years). Executive Council, comprising President, 1st and 2nd Vice-Chairmen and 8 members. General Secretariat, headed by Secretary-General. **Languages** Arabic. **Staff** 8.00 FTE, paid; 0.50 FTE, voluntary. **Finance** Members' dues. Budget (annual): US$ 162,000. **Activities** Holds conferences and seminars; sets up committees to study specific subjects and to submit proposals and recommendations, and joint scientific research commissions; organizes exchange of experts. **Events** *Joint Conference* Doha (Qatar) 2015, *Joint Conference* Baku (Azerbaijan) 2013, *General Assembly* Riyadh (Saudi Arabia) 2010, *Joint conference* France 2009, *General Assembly* Cairo (Egypt) 1998. **Publications** *Al Raqaba Al Malia* (2 a year).
Members Supreme Audit Institutions of 22 countries:
Algeria, Bahrain, Comoros, Djibouti, Egypt, Iraq, Jordan, Kuwait, Lebanon, Libya, Mauritania, Morocco, Oman, Palestine, Qatar, Saudi Arabia, Somalia, Sudan, Syrian AR, Tunisia, United Arab Emirates, Yemen.
IGO Relations *League of Arab States (LAS, #16420)*. **NGO Relations** *African Organization of Supreme Audit Institutions (AFROSAI, #00406)*; *Asian Organization of Supreme Audit Institutions (ASOSAI, #01594)*; *European Organization of Supreme Audit Institutions (EUROSAI, #08115)*; *International Organization of Supreme Audit Institutions (INTOSAI, #14478)*. [2013/XD1062/**D**]

♦ Arab Orthodontic Society (AOS) 01022
Société arabe d'orthodontie
SG 180 Prt Said Str, Alexandria, Egypt. T. +2035919144. E-mail: info@arabortho.org.
URL: http://www.arabortho.org/
History 29 Apr 1993, Amman (Jordan), at the first Arab Orthodontic Congress. **Aims** Promote and encourage orthodontic research in the Arab world; raise standards of orthodontic teaching in Arab universities and institutions; encourage continued education. **Structure** High Council, comprising up to 3 representatives (one vote) of each member society, including President. Executive Council, comprising Past President, President Elect and elected scientific member of Congress and Journal. President (rotating every 2 years, to body hosting Arab Orthodontic Congress). Head Office, headed by Secretary General. Treasurer. **Staff** Part-time, voluntary. **Finance** Members' dues. Donations from NGOs. **Activities** Currently working to establish the *'Arab Orthodontic Board Council'* for clinical orthodontic training and certification. Organizes Arab Orthodontic Congress (at least every 2 years). **Events** *Congress* Dubai (United Arab Emirates) 2011, *Congress* Hammamet (Tunisia) 2009, *Congress* Damascus (Syrian AR) 2007, *Congress* Amman (Jordan) 2005, *Congress* Jeddah (Saudi Arabia) 2003.
Members Active national societies, clubs and associations of qualified Arab orthodontists; individuals in countries where no such association as yet exists. Associate Arab orthodontists practising outside Arab countries. Societies in 11 countries and territories:
Egypt, Iraq, Jordan, Lebanon, Morocco, Palestine, Saudi Arabia, Sudan, Syrian AR, Tunisia, United Arab Emirates.
Individual members (470) from all Arab countries. Membership countries not specified.
NGO Relations Affiliated with: *World Federation of Orthodontists (#21469)*. Member of: *Mediterranean Orthodontic Integration Project (MOIP, #16671)*. [2014/XD7939/**D**]

- ♦ **ARABOSAI** Arab Organization of Supreme Audit Institutions (#01021)
- ♦ Arab Paint and Coating Producers Association (unconfirmed)

♦ Arab Parliament 01023
Contact 84 104 street Maadi, Cairo, Egypt. T. +20225243044. Fax +20225245017. E-mail: sg@ar-pr.org.
URL: http://ar-pr.org/
History Idea of establishing the organization traced to 1955 when the Secretariat of the *League of Arab States (LAS, #16420)* put forward proposals to amend the League Charter. The League cooperated with *Arab Inter-Parliamentary Union (Arab IPU, #00995)* to develop common rules for establishing the proposed Arab Parliament, which served as the basis for the Leagues Charter amendments including adding Article IXX by summit Resolution (290) of the 7th Ordinary Session of the Council of the League, 23 Mar 2005, Algeria, to establish the Arab Parliament. Activities commenced 26 Dec 2005 as the Transitional Arab Parliament. Term extended by 2 years by Resolution No 501 adopted 28 Mar 2010 at the 22nd Ordinary Session, Surt (Libyan AJ). Became permanent, 29 Mar 2012, following adopting of Resolution No 559 at the 23rd Ordinary Session, Baghdad (Iraq). **Aims** Establish an Arab system whereby the principles of Shura and *democracy* are practised, freedom and human rights are respected, and an all-embracing framework for parliamentary representation of the people in the Arab world is formed; participate in the making of common Arab policy, and establishing an integrated Arab system to achieve social justice, face challenges and enhance the developments taking place in the Arab nation; participate in the promotion of the Arab peoples' awareness of joint Arab action, and contribute to the reinforcement of peace, security and stability in the Arab region; achieve economic integration, social cohesion and sustainable development with a view to realizing Arab unity. **Structure** Comprises 4 representatives of each member state. Speaker; Bureau. Committees (4): Foreign and Political Affairs and National Security; Economic and Financial Affairs; Legislative and Legal Affairs and Human Rights; Social, Educational, Cultural, Women and Youth Affairs. May establish other standing, temporary, special or joint committees or sub-committees. Secretariat. **Languages** Arabic, English, French. **Finance** Equal annual quotas paid by member states; voluntary donation of member states of the League; donations by national, regional and international parliaments; gifts and bequests; donations by non-member state and civil society organizations; returns of Parliament assets. **Activities** Legislative terms are 4 years, beginning in October and ending in Jun of the following year. Holds session and may convene extraordinary sessions. Sittings are public. Works to strengthen inter-Arab relations, develop forms of joint Arab action and strengthen mechanisms thereof, ensure Arab national security and promote human rights, and may make recommendations to achievement of the above. Follows up the process of joint Arab action, holds hearings with heads of ministerial councils, the Secretary-General of the League, Speakers or general managers of specialized Arab organizations. Approves unified draft laws and collective Arab agreements referred to it before approval by the League Council.
Members Governments of 22 countries:
Algeria, Bahrain, Comoros, Djibouti, Egypt, Iraq, Jordan, Kuwait, Lebanon, Libya, Mauritania, Morocco, Oman, Palestine, Qatar, Saudi Arabia, Somalia, Sudan, Syrian AR, Tunisia, United Arab Emirates, Yemen.

IGO Relations Observer member of: *Pan-African Parliament (PAP, #18058)*; *Parliamentary Union of the OIC Member States (PUIC, #18220)*. **NGO Relations** Observer member of: *Arab Inter-Parliamentary Union (Arab IPU, #00995)*; *Consultative Council of the Arab Maghreb Union (#04765)*; IOM; *Parliamentary Assembly of the Mediterranean (PAM, #18212)*; Parliamentary Assembly Union for the Mediterranean (PA-UFM). Associate member of: *Inter-Parliamentary Union (IPU, #15961)*. [2022/XM1176/**E***]

♦ Arab Parliamentary Union / see Arab Inter-Parliamentary Union (#00995)
♦ Arab Peace and Security Council (see: #16420)

♦ Arab Pediatric Pulmonology Association (APPA) 01024

Treas Sultan Qaboos Univ Hospital, Dept Child Health, PO Box 1490, 112, Ruwi, Oman. T. +96899889624. E-mail: husseink30@yahoo.com.

Aims Promote and improve education and research on paediatric pulmonary diseases and related health care issues in Arab countries; find field practice of clinical work in this area of specialty, and create an environment of close cooperation and exchange of clinical experiences; encourage and assist the foundation of new paediatric pulmonary centers in the Arab countries especially where does not have one; study the causes of common pulmonary diseases and methods of treatment and prevention. **Structure** Executive Board, comprising President, Vice-President, General Secretary, Treasurer and 5 members. **Activities** Organizes: Annual Congress; meetings. **Events** *Congress* Doha (Qatar) 2016, *Congress* Dubai (United Arab Emirates) 2014, *Annual Congress* Abu Dhabi (United Arab Emirates) 2012, *Gulf thoracic congress* Abu Dhabi (United Arab Emirates) 2011, *Annual Congress* Luxor (Egypt) 2011. [2010/XJ2117/**D**]

♦ Arab Penal Reform Organization (unconfirmed)
♦ Arab Permanent Committee for Meteorology (see: #16420)
♦ Arab Permanent Military Commission (no recent information)

♦ Arab Permanent Postal Commission (APPC) 01025

Commission arabe permanente des postes (CAPP) – Comisión Arabe Permanente de Correos

Contact League of Arab States General Secretariat, Place Al Tahrir, PO Box 11642, Cairo, Egypt. T. +2025750511. Fax +2025740331.

History 12 Apr 1952, Syrian AR. 12 Apr 1952, Damascus (Syria), as *Arab Postal Union (APU) – Union postale arabe (UPA) – Unión Postal Arabe*, following: recommendations of postal conference, 9 Dec 1946, Sofar (Lebanon); work of Communications Commission of *League of Arab States (LAS, #16420)*. Activities commenced 1 Apr 1954. Present name adopted 1989. A Restricted Union of *Universal Postal Union (UPU, #20682)*. **Aims** Organize, develop, and unify postal services and bring to a high level the postal service in the Arab region; study and improve inter-Arab and international postal relations; reinforce pan-Arab action through the post. **Structure** Congress (every 5 years); Executive Council (meets annually); Consultative Council for Postal Studies; General Secretariat. Special Committees. Instrumental in setting up the previous *Arab Postal Faculty, Damascus (inactive)*. **Languages** Arabic. **Finance** Members' contributions. **Events** *Congress* Damascus (Syrian AR) 1985, *Congress* Baghdad (Iraq) 1980, *Congress* Algiers (Algeria) 1975, *Congress* Cairo (Egypt) 1971, *Congress* Beirut (Lebanon) 1966. **Publications** *APU Bulletin* (12 a year); *APU Review* (4 a year); *APU News* (annual). Occasional studies.

Members Postal administrations in 22 countries:
Algeria, Bahrain, Comoros, Djibouti, Egypt, Iraq, Jordan, Kuwait, Lebanon, Libya, Mauritania, Morocco, Oman, Palestine, Qatar, Saudi Arabia, Somalia, Sudan, Syrian AR, Tunisia, United Arab Emirates, Yemen.

IGO Relations Close links with: *UNESCO (#20322)*. Links with the other Restricted Unions: *African Postal Union (APU, no recent information)*; *Associação dos Operadores de Correios e Telecomunicações dos Países e Territórios de Língua Oficial Portuguesa (AICEP, #02333)*; *Association of European Public Postal Operators (PostEurop, #02534)*; *Baltic Postal Union (BPU, #03137)*; *Caribbean Postal Union (CPU, #03541)*; *Conférence européenne des administrations des postes et des télécommunications (CEPT, #04602)*; *Conference of Posts and Telecommunications of Central Africa (#04642)*; *Nordic Postal Union (NPU, #17391)*; *Postal Union of the Americas, Spain and Portugal (PUASP, #18466)*. [2019/XD0065/**D***]

♦ Arab Petroleum Investments Corporation (APICORP) 01026

Société arabe d'investissements pétroliers

CEO Ahmad Bin Hamad Al-Nuaimi, PO Box 9599, Dammam 31423, Saudi Arabia. T. +96638470444. Fax +96638470011 – +96638470022.
URL: http://www.apicorp-arabia.com/

History 23 Nov 1975, Khobar (Saudi Arabia), as a joint undertaking of member states of *Organization of Arab Petroleum Exporting Countries (OAPEC, #17854)*. Operations commenced officially in 1976. **Aims** Finance projects in petroleum and related industries with priority to Arab joint ventures. **Structure** General Assembly (annual). Board of Directors, consisting of 10 members representing share-holding states and including Chairman and Deputy Chairman. General Manager heads 7 Departments: Projects; Projects and Trade Finance; Treasury and Capital Markets; Financial Control; Legal; Administrative Services; Human Resources. **Finance** Authorized capital: US$ 1,200 million. **Activities** Operations concentrate on: Arab oil trade finance; gas liquefaction; petrochemicals; oil refining; pipelines; tankers; fertilizers; drilling; detergents and synthetic rubber; catalysts; synthetic fibres; pesticides; paints and plastics. Major subsidiary: *Arab Company for Detergent Chemicals (ARADET, see: #17854)*. Also a shareholding company in: *Arab Drilling and Workover Company (ADWOC, see: #17854)*; *Arab Engineered Systems and Controls Company, Bahrain (ABB ARESCON EC, no recent information)*; *Arab Geophysical Exploration Services Company (AGESCO, #00968)*; Bahrain National Gas Company (BANAGAS); Paktank Méditerranée (PAKMED), Tunisia; *Saudi European Petrochemical Company, Saudi Arabia (IBN ZAHR, no recent information)*. **Events** *Annual Energy Forum* Manama (Bahrain) 2015, *Annual General Assembly* Cairo (Egypt) 2005, *Annual general assembly / General Assembly* Cairo (Egypt) 2003, *Annual General Assembly* Cairo (Egypt) 1999, *Annual General Assembly* Cairo (Egypt) 1997. **Publications** Annual Report in English/Arabic. Information Services: Maintains a Library and Documentation Centre.

Members Member states of OAPEC (10):
Algeria, Bahrain, Egypt, Iraq, Kuwait, Libya, Qatar, Saudi Arabia, Syrian AR, United Arab Emirates.

IGO Relations *Arab Mining Company (ARMICO, #01008)*. **NGO Relations** Member of: *Arab Fertilizer Association (AFA, #00958)*. [2018/XM1038/e/**F***]

♦ Arab Petroleum Services Company (see: #17854)
♦ Arab Petroleum Training Institute (no recent information)
♦ Arab Pharmacists Union / see Union of Arab Pharmacists (#20356)
♦ Arab Philosophical Society (no recent information)
♦ Arab Physical Education and Sport Confederation (inactive)

♦ Arab Planning Institute (API) 01027

Institut arabe de planification

Dir Gen PO Box 5834, 13059 Safat, Kuwait. T. +9654843130 – +9654846215 – +9654848754. Fax +9654842935. E-mail: api@api.org.kw.
URL: http://www.arab-api.org/

History Established 1972, Kuwait, with participation of originally 15 Arab states, following setting up, Jan 1966, with assistance of *UNDP (#20292)*, of a national Kuwaiti institute, the *Kuwait Institute for Economic and Social Planning in the Middle East*. **Aims** Concentrate on fundamental *socio-economic* problems in Arab countries; train government employees to utilize and implement qualitative and quantitative development techniques in planning and economic management. **Structure** Board of Trustees; Higher Consultative Council. **Languages** Arabic, English. **Staff** 53.00 FTE, paid. **Finance** Contributions of member States. Budget (annual): about US$ 3 million. **Activities** Conferences; seminars; expert group meetings; discussion circles; courses; programmes; research studies; consultation and advisory services; economic management; development policies; new trade agenda; project management; structural adjustment; environment; social policies; national projects; planning techniques; human resources development. **Events** *Arab Investment Forum* Kuwait 2013, *Regional Forum on the "Economics of the Arab Spring"* Jordan 2012, *Conference* Kuwait 2012, *SMEs and their role in sustainable development in the Arab region* Safat (Kuwait) 2012, *New trends in financing for development* Beirut (Lebanon) 2011. **Publications** *Development Bridge* (12 a year) in Arabic; *Journal of Development and Economic Policies* (2 a year) in Arabic, English; *Arab Competitiveness Report* (every 2 years) in Arabic. *Expert Group Meeting* in Arabic – series; *Working Paper* in Arabic, English – series. Research papers; seminar reports; study materials.

Members Governments of 15 countries and territories:
Bahrain, Egypt, Iraq, Jordan, Kuwait, Lebanon, Libya, Mauritania, Oman, Palestine, Qatar, Sudan, Syrian AR, Tunisia, United Arab Emirates, Yemen.

IGO Relations
- *African Training and Research Centre in Administration for Development (CAFRAD, #00486)*;
- *Arab Administrative Development Organization (ARADO, #00893)*;
- *Arab Centre for Energy Studies (ACES, no recent information)*;
- *Arab Federation for Technical Education (AFTE, no recent information)*;
- *Arab Fund for Economic and Social Development (AFESD, #00965)*;
- *Arab Labour Organization (ALO, #01001)*;
- *Arab Organization for Agricultural Development (AOAD, #01018)*;
- *FAO (#09260)*;
- *Gulf Organization for Industrial Consulting (GOIC, #10837)*;
- *ILO (#11123)*;
- *Kuwait Fund for Arab Economic Development (KFAED)*;
- *League of Arab States (LAS, #16420)*;
- *Mediterranean Development Forum (MDF, no recent information)*;
- *Organization of Arab Petroleum Exporting Countries (OAPEC, #17854)*;
- *Regional Centre for Adult Education (ASFEC, no recent information)*;
- *Statistical, Economic and Social Research and Training Centre for Islamic Countries (SESRIC, #19971)*;
- *United Nations Economic and Social Commission for Western Asia (ESCWA, #20558)*.

NGO Relations *International Center for Economic Growth (ICEG, inactive)*. [2013.09.08/XE7392/j/**E***]

♦ Arab Police Sports Confederation 01028

Contact 24 Sakk El Ommlah, El Darrasah, Cairo, Egypt. E-mail: bo7a44@yahoo.com.

History 5 Aug 1975, Baghdad (Iraq). Also referred to as *Arab Police Sports Federation*. **Aims** Enhance the Arab sports movement and unify Arab position in Police Sports Conference; spread sports activities among police and security personnel for development of their physical and mental potential; cooperate and coordinate among members in unifying and developing sports rules and regulations, enhancing and enforcing rules of international sports federations; support members in raising standards of staff, provision of supplies, equipment and materials and construction of sports facilities; organize events based on the principle of *amateurism*. **Structure** Executive Board, consisting of President, Vice-President and Secretary-General and 4 members. Technical Commission (7 members); Information Commission (6 members). Attached to the Secretariat General of *Arab Interior Ministers' Council (AIMC, #00990)*. **Languages** Arabic. **Staff** Several full-time, paid. **Finance** Members' dues. **Activities** Organizes clinics, championships, tournaments and festivals in sports including: shooting, football, volleyball, handball, basketball, athletics, boxing, cross-country, tennis, judo, equestrian, cycling and table-tennis. Honours distinguished athletes. **Publications** *Arab Police Sports Magazine*. Brochures.

Members Governments of 22 countries:
Algeria, Bahrain, Comoros, Djibouti, Egypt, Iraq, Jordan, Kuwait, Lebanon, Libya, Mauritania, Morocco, Oman, Palestine, Qatar, Saudi Arabia, Somalia, Sudan, Syrian AR, Tunisia, United Arab Emirates, Yemen. [2013/XD0916/**D***]

♦ Arab Police Sports Federation / see Arab Police Sports Confederation (#01028)
♦ Arab Postal Union / see Arab Permanent Postal Commission (#01025)

♦ Arab Potash Company (APC) 01029

Main Office PO Box 1470, Amman 11118, Jordan. T. +96265674376. Fax +96265674416. E-mail: info@arabpotash.com.
URL: http://www.arabpotash.com/

History 7 Jul 1956, by *League of Arab States (LAS, #16420)*. Was granted, 1958, by the Jordanian Government a concession to exploit the minerals and salts of the Dead Sea Brine. Currently the company produces and market potassium chloride only and trade it in the international market. **Aims** Exploit *minerals* contained in *Dead Sea* brine. **Structure** General Assembly (annual). Board of Directors, including Chairman and Deputy Chairman. Executive Officers: Chairman; General Manager; Deputy General Manager/ Marketing Manager; Deputy Manager for Technical Affairs; Deputy General Manager for Financial Affairs/ Financial Manager. Departments. **Staff** 5.00 FTE, paid. **Finance** Authorized capital: Jordanian Dinars (JD) 83,317,500; issued and outstanding capital: JD 79,695,000. **Activities** Departments (11): Projects; Civil Works; Operations, including Training Center, Safety and Environment Department, Production Department, Maintenance Department, Technical Department; Research and Studies; Procurement; Medical Services; Housing and Utilities; Administration; Marketing; Quality Control; Finance and Computer. **Events** *International meeting on the promotion of local music heritage in the age of globalization / General Assembly* Amman (Jordan) 2000. **Publications** Annual Report.

Members Governmental shareholding enterprises in 4 countries:
Iraq, Jordan, Kuwait, Libya.
International organizations (2):
Arab Mining Company (ARMICO, #01008); *Islamic Development Bank (IsDB, #16044)*. [2009/XF3187/e/**F***]

♦ Arab Press Freedom Watch (APFW) 01030

Contact address not obtained. T. +447821120158. Fax +44879126253 – +4487(442025780643.

History Registered in accordance with UK law. **Aims** Defend freedom of expression in the arab world; promote human rights and democracy. **Events** *Annual Conference* Cairo (Egypt) 2006, *Annual Conference* Rabat (Morocco) 2004, *Annual Conference* Cairo (Egypt) 2003, *Annual Conference* London (UK) 2002. [2007/XM0626/**F**]

♦ Arab Press Network (APN) 01031

Contact Andrew Heslop, WAN-IFRA Secretariat, 96 bis rue Beaubourg, 75003 Paris, France. T. +33147428500. Fax +33142789233. E-mail: andrew.heslop@wan-ifra.org – info@wan-ifra.org.
URL: http://www.wan-ifra.org/microsites/apn-arab-press-network/

History by *World Association of Newspapers (WAN, inactive)*, as a digital network. Currently operated by: *World Association of Newspapers and News Publishers (WAN-IFRA, #21166)*. **Aims** Support the development of a stronger independent press in the Arab world by facilitating the exchange of ideas and experiences between newspaper publishers and editors. [2015/XJ2033/**E**]

♦ Arab Private Equity Association (unconfirmed)
♦ Arab Programme for Human Rights Activists (internationally oriented national body)

♦ Arab Publishers' Association (APA) 01032

Executive Office 92 Tahrir St, Saridar Tower – 2nd Floor, Dokki, Giza, Egypt. T. +20237622058. Fax +20237622058 – +2023748082. E-mail: info@arab-pa.org.
General Secretariat Beer Hassan, Chadia Bldg – 1st Floor, PO Box 8843, Beirut, Lebanon. T. +9611840372. E-mail: arabpa@cyberia.net.lb.
URL: http://www.arab-pa.org/

History Apr 1995, Beirut (Lebanon), at General Conference for Arab Publishers. **Aims** Defend and develop the Arab publishing industry and protect intellectual property rights, and defense of Arab Culture in all its components. **Structure** General Assembly; Board. **Activities** Events/meetings. **Events** *Conference* Giza (Egypt) 2020, *Horizons and challenges of the digital age for the publishing industry* Sharjah (United Arab Emirates) 2015, *Conference* Egypt 2014, *Conference* Egypt 2013, *Conference* Saudi Arabia 2012. **Publications** *APA Magazine*.

Members Publishers in 22 countries and territories:
Algeria, Bahrain, Egypt, France, Iraq, Jordan, Kuwait, Lebanon, Libya, Morocco, Oman, Palestine, Qatar, Saudi Arabia, Somalia, Sudan, Syrian AR, Tunisia, Türkiye, UK, United Arab Emirates, Yemen. [2020/XD8167/**D**]

♦ Arab Red Crescent and Red Cross Organization (ARCO) 01033

Admin Dir Bin a-mojdi, St Diplomatic Quarter, PO Box 94729, Riyadh 11 614, Saudi Arabia. T. +966114881479 – +966114881439. Fax +966114881856. E-mail: info@arabrcrc.org.
URL: http://www.arabrcrc.org/

History 1975, Riyadh (Saudi Arabia), as *General Secretariat of Arab Red Crescent and Red Cross Societies*, in the framework of *International Federation of Red Cross and Red Crescent Societies (#13526)*, following proposals dating back to 1965. Also referred to as *Federation of Arab Red Crescent and Red Cross Societies*, *Federation of Arab Red Crescent Societies*. Permanent headquarters first set up in Jeddah (Saudi Arabia) and subsequently moved to Riyadh. **Aims** Strengthen cooperation and coordinate efforts amongst national

societies on regional and international levels in order to achieve the mission of the Red Crescent and Red Cross according to the fundamental principles of the international movement. **Structure** General Assembly. Executive Committee. Consultative Board. General Secretariat. **Languages** Arabic. **Staff** 20.00 FTE, paid. **Finance** Members' dues. Annual contribution from Saudi government. **Activities** Humanitarian/emergency aid; events/meetings; projects/programmes; capacity building. **Events** *Conference* Kuwait 2011, *Conference* Sudan 2009, *Conference* Amman (Jordan) 1996, *Conference* Geneva (Switzerland) 1989, *Conference* Cairo (Egypt) 1988. **Publications** *International Humanitarian Law in Islamic Heritage.*
Members Organizations in 19 countries:
Algeria, Bahrain, Comoros, Djibouti, Egypt, Iraq, Jordan, Kuwait, Lebanon, Libya, Mauritania, Morocco, Palestine, Qatar, Saudi Arabia, Somalia, Sudan, Syrian AR, Tunisia, United Arab Emirates, Yemen.
Consultative Status Consultative status granted from: *ECOSOC (#05331)* (Special). **IGO Relations** Observer Status with: *League of Arab States (LAS, #16420).* [2019.02.25/XD8760/**E**]

♦ Arab Reform Initiative (ARI) 01034
Exec Dir 10 rue des Bluets, 75011 Paris, France. E-mail: contact@arab-reform.net – ari-communications@arab-reform.net.
URL: http://www.arab-reform.net/
History 2006, France. Formed through the collaboration between policy research centres from ten Arab countries, four European think tanks, and one from the United States to set the agenda for political and social reforms in the region based on the priorities that the region's societies themselves formulated. ARI became a think tank in its own right with 20 peer partners across the region, acting as resources for exclusive knowledge on their respective governments and societies. ARI's strategy has evolved over the years, reflecting changes in the avenues for achieving democratic reform. **Aims** As a think tank of the 2011 political generation, articulate a home-grown agenda for democratic change and social justice in the Arab world, guided by the principles of impartiality, gender equality and diversity; conduct policy analysis and research that draws on exclusive insider knowledge; provide a platform for inspirational voices and create new forums for exchange; empower young and emerging actors of change. **Structure** Board; Team; hubs in Beirut (Lebanon), Paris (France), Tunis (Tunisia). **Languages** Arabic, English, French. **Finance** Sources: government support; private foundations. **Activities** Advocacy/lobbying/activism; awareness raising; capacity building; networking/liaising; research/documentation. **Events** *The Future of Human Rights Action in the Arab Region* Amman (Jordan) 2020, *Political Participation in Egypt: How Activists Confront Closing Spaces* Berlin (Germany) 2020. **Publications** *The Rugged Road: The Emergence, Evolution and Challenges of Human Rights Action in Arab Countries* (2019). Annual Report; Arab Reform Briefs; country reports; thematic studies; public opinion surveys; policy recommendations. **NGO Relations** Member of (1): *Euro-Mediterranean Study Commission (EuroMeSCo, #05727).* [2021.09.01/XM3472/y/**F**]

♦ Arab Regional Branch of the International Council on Archives (see: #12996)

♦ Arab Regional Centre for World Heritage (ARC-WH) 01035
Secretarita Bldg 465, Road 2209, Block 319, Manama, Bahrain. T. +97317003213.
URL: http://arcwh.org/
History Established 5 Feb 2010. A Category II Centre of *UNESCO (#20322).* **Aims** Strengthen the implementation of the 1972 World Heritage Convention in the Arab States Region, by strengthening application of the decisions and recommendations of the World Heritage Committee for the benefit of World Heritage properties in the region. **Structure** Governing Board; Advisory Committee; Advisory Bodies.
Members States Parties (19):
Algeria, Bahrain, Egypt, Iraq, Jordan, Kuwait, Lebanon, Libya, Mauritania, Morocco, Oman, Palestine, Qatar, Saudi Arabia, Sudan, Syrian AR, Tunisia, United Arab Emirates, Yemen. [2017/XM6128/**E***]

♦ Arab Regional Literacy Organization (inactive)
♦ Arab Regional Resource Center on Violence Against Women (internationally oriented national body)
♦ Arab Region Ecotechnie Network (see: #05333)
♦ Arab Region Parliamentarians Against Corruption (see: #10518)
♦ Arab Regulators Network (unconfirmed)
♦ Arab Renaissance for Democracy and Development (internationally oriented national body)

♦ Arab Reporters for Investigative Journalism (ARIJ) 01036
Dir-Gen Bldg No 4 – 3rd floor, Abdallah Alasbah St, Al-Shemisani, Amman 11194, Jordan. T. +96264640411. Fax +96264640406. E-mail: info@arij.net.
URL: http://www.arij.net/
History 2005, Amman (Jordan). Founded as the first media organization in the region dedicated to promoting investigative journalism in Arab newsrooms. Was the initiative of several leading Arab journalists, editors, media activists and professionals who came together with a like-minded group of Danes driven by commitment to professional in-depth reporting for the benefit of local communities. They held several meetings in Copenhagen (Denmark), Damascus (Syrian AR), Beirut (Lebanon) and Amman (Jordan). **Aims** Enhance excellence in investigative journalism, which is essential in a free society and remains key to ensure transparency, accountability and a diversity of views and opinions based on documented facts, research and multiple sources. **Structure** Annual Conference; Board of Directors. **Languages** Arabic, English. **Staff** 14.00 FTE, paid. **Finance** Set up with funds from Danish Parliament, disbursed through *International Media Support (IMS, #14128)*; the Danish Association for Investigative Journalism (FUJ) provided technical support. Subsequent financial support from: *Open Society Foundations (OSF, #17763)*; *UNESCO (#20322)*; *International Center for Journalists (ICFJ)*; *Swedish International Development Cooperation Agency (Sida)*; Norwegian Foreign Ministry; Embassy of the Kingdom of the Netherlands, Amman (Jordan); CFI (France). **Activities** Financial and/or material support; training/education; guidance/assistance/consulting; research/documentation; event/meetings; projects/programmes; knowledge management/information dissemination; events/meetings. **Events** *Annual Regional Forum* Amman (Jordan) 2020, *Annual Regional Forum* Amman (Jordan) 2019, *Annual Conference* Amman (Jordan) 2015, *Annual Conference* Egypt 2013, *Annual Conference* Tunisia 2012. **Publications** *Story-based Inquiry: a manual for investigative journalism* in Arabic, Bosnian, Chinese, English, French, Japanese, Macedonian, Mongolian, Portuguese, Russian, Spanish, Turkmen. *Best Practices: A Collection of Arab Investigative Stories* (2011) – electronic and print.
Members Full in 9 countries and territories:
Bahrain, Egypt, Iraq, Jordan, Lebanon, Palestine, Syrian AR, Tunisia, Yemen.
NGO Relations Member of (2): *Ethical Journalism Network (EJN, #05554)*; *Global Forum for Media Development (GFMD, #10375).* [2022/XJ0606/**F**]

♦ Arab Research Centre for Arab African Studies and Documentation / see Arab and African Research Centre
♦ Arab Resource Collective (internationally oriented national body)
♦ Arab Roads Association (inactive)
♦ Arab Rowing Federation (inactive)
♦ Arab Sailing Federation (inactive)
♦ **ARABSAT** Arab Satellite Communications Organization (#01037)

♦ Arab Satellite Communications Organization (ARABSAT) 01037
Organisation arabe des communication par satellites – Organización Arabe de Comunicación por Satélites
Pres – CEO C-6 Public Pension Agency Complex, Alfazari Square, Diplomatic Quarters, PO Box 1038, Riyadh 11431, Saudi Arabia. T. +96614820000. Fax +96614887999. E-mail: info@arabsat.com.
URL: http://www.arabsat.com/
History 14 Apr 1976, Riyadh (Saudi Arabia), by the 21 Member States of the Arab League, as a specialized agency acting in the framework of *League of Arab States (LAS, #16420).* Also known as *Arab Space Communications Organization (ASCO).* **Aims** Develop, establish and operate a regional *telecommunications* satellite system; provide a wide range of space telecommunication services, such as digital and analogue direct-to-Home television broadcasting, Internet, regional and domestic TV program exchange, regional and domestic telephony, ARABSAT business services (ABS) and VSAT services among various parts of Arab world and countries within coverage of its satellites. **Structure** General Assembly (annual); Board of Directors. Headquarters staff operating under Director General. **Languages** Arabic, English. **Staff** 126.00 FTE, paid. **Finance** Funding provided by member countries. Current paid capital: US$ 163,141,262. **Activities** Currently owns and operates 3 satellites: *'ARABSAT2A'*, launched 1996; *'ARABSAT3A'*, launched 1999, co-located and dedicated to Digital and Analogue Direct-to-Home TV Broadcasting and Internet services; *'ARABSAT2B'*, launched 1996, used for other telecommunications services. **Publications** Annual Report. Brochures.
Members Governments of 21 countries and territories:
Algeria, Bahrain, Djibouti, Egypt, Iraq, Jordan, Kuwait, Lebanon, Libya, Mauritania, Morocco, Oman, Palestine, Qatar, Saudi Arabia, Somalia, Sudan, Syrian AR, Tunisia, United Arab Emirates, Yemen.
IGO Relations Working relations with: *International Telecommunication Union (ITU, #15673)*, especially its Radiocommunication Sector. Invited to sessions of Intergovernmental Council of: *International Programme for the Development of Communication (IPDC, #14651).* Collaborates with: *Arab Centre for the Studies of Arid Zones and Dry Lands (ACSAD, #00918).* Formal agreement with: *International Telecommunications Satellite Organization (ITSO, #15670).* **NGO Relations** Member of: *GVF (#10842).* [2019.02.13/XD7395/**D***]

♦ Arab School of Science and Technology (internationally oriented national body)

♦ Arab Science Journalists Association (ASJA) 01038
Vice Chairperson 45A 10th District, Giza, Sheikh Zayed GIZA, 12588, Egypt. T. +20237619722. Fax +20237616284.
History Dec 2006, Cairo (Egypt). A network functioning under the umbrella of *Arab Science and Technology Foundation (ASTF, #01039).* Former names and other names: *Arab Association of Science Journalists* – former. **Aims** Develop the field of science and technology in the Arab world through developing scientific Arabic mass media and its role in the field of technology and science. **Structure** Board of Directors. **Languages** Arabic. **Staff** None. **Finance** Projects have separate budgets. Funding through international and Arab donors. **Activities** Awards/prizes/competitions; events/meetings; projects/programmes; training/education.
Members in 16 countries and territories:
Algeria, Egypt, Iraq, Jordan, Kuwait, Lebanon, Libya, Morocco, Oman, Palestine, Qatar, Saudi Arabia, Sudan, Syrian AR, United Arab Emirates, Yemen.
NGO Relations Member of: *World Federation of Science Journalists (WFSJ, #21479).* [2020.08.04/XM0288/**D**]

♦ Arab Science and Technology Academy / see Arab Academy for Science, Technology and Maritime Transport (#00891)

♦ Arab Science and Technology Foundation (ASTF) 01039
Pres PO Box 2668, Sharjah, United Arab Emirates. T. +971504622626. Fax +97165584331.
Facebook: https://www.facebook.com/ASTF2000/
History Apr 2000. Founded upon recommendation during a symposium organized by the University of Sharjah. Statutes adopted Dec 2000. **Aims** Identify and support outstanding scientific research conducted in the fields of science, technology and innovation in the Arab world; defend the region's interests in scientific and technological progress. **Structure** Board of Directors; Executive Board; Branches (6); Networks (7), include: *Arab Network on Nanotechnology (ArNano, #01012)*; *Arab Science Journalists Association (ASJA, #01038).* Headquarters in Sharjah (UAE) and Cairo (Egypt). **Languages** Arabic, English. **Staff** 27.00 FTE, paid. **Finance** Fundraising; activities; donations. **Activities** Networking/liaising; knowledge management/information dissemination; research and development; awards/prizes/competitions; financial and/or material support; training/education. **Events** *International conference on metamaterials photonic crystals and plasmonics* Cairo (Egypt) 2010, *Conference on water-resources, technologies and management in the Arab world* Sharjah (United Arab Emirates) 2005, *Symposium on scientific research outlook in the Arab world* Riyadh (Saudi Arabia) 2004, *Arab conference on solar energy* Sharjah (United Arab Emirates) 2001. **Publications** *ASTF News*; *ASTF Newsletter. Research and Innovation Towards a Knowledge Economy* (2015); *11 Years of Giving* (2012). **Members** Individuals (about 37,000). Membership countries not specified. [2019.02.24/XN9672/f/**F**]

♦ Arab Sea Ports Federation (ASPF) 01040
Head Office PO Box 21514, El-Shalat Gardens, Alexandria, Egypt. T. +2034818791. Fax +2034818791. E-mail: arabport@yahoo.com.
URL: http://www.aspf.org.eg/
History 7 Jun 1976, according to Resolution 748-Session 27 of *Council of Arab Economic Unity (CAEU, #04859).* **Aims** Establish cooperation among Arab seaports; assist them in overcoming obstacles.
Members Representatives of 7 countries:
Iraq, Jordan, Kuwait, Libya, Sudan, Tunisia, Yemen.
NGO Relations Working relations with: *North African Port Management Association (NAPMA, #17556).* Associate Member of: *International Association of Ports and Harbors (IAPH, #12096).* [2017/XD8650/**D***]

♦ Arab Security Studies and Training Centre / see Naif Arab University for Security Sciences (#16929)
♦ Arab Shipbuilding and Repair Yard Company (see: #17854)

♦ Arab Shooting Confederation 01041
Pres c/o KSSF, PO Box 8, 13085 Dasma, Kuwait. E-mail: kssf@kssf.com.kw.
URL: http://www.arab-shooting.org/
History Also referred to as *Arab Shooting Federation.* [2014/XD0917/**D**]

♦ Arab Shooting Federation / see Arab Shooting Confederation (#01041)
♦ Arab Social Democratic Forum (unconfirmed)
♦ Arab Social Science Council (inactive)
♦ Arab Society for Academic Freedom (unconfirmed)

♦ Arab Society for Academic Freedoms (ASAF) 01042
Contact Level 4 – Sharif Complex, Umayah Bin Abd Shams Street 6, Amman, Jordan. E-mail: nizam@arsaf.org.
URL: http://www.arsaf.org/
History Set up Apr 2008. **Aims** Safeguard academic freedom for the higher education and scientific research institutes in the Arab countries in accordance with the international declaration issued in this connection. **Structure** General Assembly; Board of Directors; Executive Committee. **Consultative Status** Consultative status granted from: *ECOSOC (#05331)* (Special). [2018/XM7140/**D**]

♦ The Arab Society of Certified Accountants / see International Arab Society of Certified Accountants (#11665)

♦ Arab Society of Chemotherapy, Microbiology and Infectious Diseases 01043
Vice-Pres King Saud Univ, Riyadh 12372, Saudi Arabia. T. +96614678042. Fax +96614683813.
Events *ISAAR : international symposium on antimicrobial agents and resistance* Singapore (Singapore) 2007, *Arab symposium on prudent use of antimicrobials / Congress* Tunis (Tunisia) 2006, *Congress* Egypt 2005, *Congress* Riyadh (Saudi Arabia) 2000. **NGO Relations** Member of: *International Society of Antimicrobial Chemotherapy (ISAC, #14925).* [2016/XD6637/**D**]

♦ Arab Society for Computer Aided Architectural Design (ASCAAD) . . 01044
Communication Officer address not obtained. E-mail: communication@ascaad.org.
URL: http://www.ascaad.org/
History 16 May 2001, Jordan. **Aims** Facilitate communication and information exchange regarding the use of computers and information technology in architecture, planning and building science. **Structure** Board of Directors, comprising President, Vice-President and 8 members. **Events** *Conference* Beirut (Lebanon) 2022, *Conference* Amman (Jordan) 2018, *Conference* London (UK) 2016, *Digital crafting – virtualizing architecture and delivering real built environment* Jeddah (Saudi Arabia) 2013, *Conference* Manama (Bahrain) 2012. **Publications** *ASCAAD Newsletter* – electronic. Conference proceedings.
Members Individuals in 22 countries and territories:
Algeria, Austria, Bahrain, Canada, Chad, Egypt, France, Germany, Greece, Hong Kong, Jordan, Malaysia, Morocco, Oman, Pakistan, Qatar, Saudi Arabia, Sudan, Tunisia, UK, United Arab Emirates, USA.
NGO Relations Related organizations: *Association for Computer Aided Design in Architecture (ACADIA)*; *International Heavy Haul Association (IHHA, #13787)*; *Education and research in Computer Aided Architectural Design in Europe (eCAADe, #05373)*; *Sociedad Iberoamericana de Grafica Digital (SIGraDI, #19370).* [2016/XJ6630/**D**]

♦ Arab Society of Environmental Health and Safety (no recent information)
♦ Arab Society for Ethics in Science and Technology (internationally oriented national body)

♦ Arab Society for Forensic Sciences and Forensic Medicine (ASFSFM) 01045

SG Naif Arab Univ for Security Sciences, Riyadh 11452, Saudi Arabia. T. +9661124634441600. Fax +9661124634441601. E-mail: asfsfm@nauss.edu.sa.
URL: http://asfsfm.nauss.edu.sa/

History 2008, Riyadh (Saudi Arabia), when formation was approved. Officially launched 4 Jun 2013. **Aims** Establish a scientific platform for forensic scientists, medico-legal experts, academics, jurists and security related professionals to simultaneously communicate, collaborate and lead a joint scientific effort to improve the quality of forensic science education, research and practice in the world. **Structure** Assembly; Board of Directors; Advisory Board; Team of Managing Assistants; Scientific and Management and Organizing Committees. **Languages** Arabic, English. **Staff** 8.00 FTE, paid; 25.00 FTE, voluntary. **Finance** Through Naif Arab University for Security Sciences. **Activities** Events/meetings; publishing activities; research and development; research/documentation; standards/guidelines; training/education. **Events** *International Arab Forensic Sciences and Forensic Medicine Conference* Riyadh (Saudi Arabia) 2018, *International Arab Forensic Science and Forensic Medicine Conference* Riyadh (Saudi Arabia) 2015, *International Arab Forensic Science and Forensic Medicine Conference / Conference* Riyadh (Saudi Arabia) 2014. **Publications** *Arab Journal of Forensic Sciences and Forensic Medicine (AJFSMFM).*
Members Individuals (about 250) in 24 countries:
Algeria, Austria, Bahrain, Egypt, Germany, India, Iraq, Jordan, Kuwait, Lebanon, Libya, Malaysia, Mauritania, Morocco, Nigeria, Oman, Pakistan, Palestine, Qatar, Saudi Arabia, Syrian AR, Tunisia, Türkiye, Yemen. [2015.12.09/XJ9942/**D**]

♦ Arab Society for Fungal Conservation (internationally oriented national body)
♦ Arab Society of Industrial Property / see Arab Society for Intellectual Property (#01046)

♦ Arab Society for Intellectual Property (ASIP) 01046

Contact Bldg No 46, Abdel Raheem Al-Waked Street, Amman 921199, Amman 11192, Jordan. T. +96265100900 ext 1529. E-mail: info@aspip.org.
URL: http://www.aspip.org/

History 23 Feb 1987, Munich (Germany FR), as *Arab Society of Industrial Property*, by *Council of Arab Economic Unity (CAEU, #04859)*. Changed name to *Arab Society for the Protection of Intellectual Property (ASPIP)*, 1993. Current title adopted, 2000. **Aims** Establish, develop and modernize intellectual property disciplines; spread awareness in IP issues and capacity building among professionals and practitioners; assist in the advancement of IP systems and enhance Arab IP law; represent and bring to light the regional interest in developing international legal instruments and technical standards. **Structure** General Meeting (annual); Board of Directors. **Languages** Arabic, English. **Finance** Members' dues. Donations. **Activities** Training/education. **Events** *Annual General Meeting* Amman (Jordan) 2006, *Annual General Meeting* Amman (Jordan) 2005, *Annual General Meeting* Amman (Jordan) 2004, *Annual General Meeting* Beirut (Lebanon) 2003, *Annual General Meeting* Damascus (Syrian AR) 2002. **Publications** *AIPMAS Monthly Bulletin. Abu-Ghazaleh Intellectual Property Dictionary*; *Guide to the Intellectual Property Expert Program.*
Members Leaders in the field of industrial property protection, and leading attorneys, scholars and government officers. Individuals in 20 countries and territories:
Algeria, Bahrain, Canada, Egypt, India, Iraq, Jordan, Kuwait, Lebanon, Libya, Morocco, Oman, Palestine, Qatar, Saudi Arabia, Sudan, Syrian AR, Tunisia, United Arab Emirates, Yemen.
Consultative Status Consultative status granted from: *ECOSOC (#05331)* (Ros C); *World Intellectual Property Organization (WIPO, #21593)* (Permanent Observer Status). **IGO Relations** Accredited by: *United Nations Office at Vienna (UNOV, #20604)*. Cooperates with: *European Union Intellectual Property Office (EUIPO, #08996)*. Associated with Department of Global Communications of the United Nations.
[2020.03.03/XD2537/v/**D**]

♦ Arab Society of Nephrology and Renal Transplantation (ASNRT) ... 01047

Société arabe de néphrologie et de transplantation rénale

SG Misr Kidney Center, 9 Okba St from Tahrir St, Dokki, Giza, Egypt. T. +2023358723. Fax +2023389288 – +2024530494.
URL: https://asnrt-online.org/

History 1986. Registered in accordance with Egyptian law, Mar 2006. **Languages** Arabic, English. **Staff** 2.00 FTE, paid. **Finance** Members' dues. Congress proceeds. **Activities** Organizes meetings. **Events** *Congress* Kuwait 2022, *Congress* Amman (Jordan) 2019, *Congress* Cairo (Egypt) 2017, *Managing kidney diseases – quality, perfection versus outcome* Alexandria (Egypt) 2014, *Congress* Damascus (Syrian AR) 2010. **Publications** *Journal of Nephrology and Transplantation (AJNT)* – official journal.
Members Full (over 800) in 22 countries and territories:
Algeria, Bahrain, Comoros, Djibouti, Egypt, Iraq, Jordan, Kuwait, Lebanon, Libya, Mauritania, Morocco, Oman, Palestine, Qatar, Saudi Arabia, Somalia, Sudan, Syrian AR, Tunisia, United Arab Emirates, Yemen.
NGO Relations Member of: *International Society of Nephrology (ISN, #15294).* [2021/XD3523/**D**]

♦ Arab Society for Paediatric Endocrinology and Diabetes (ASPED) .. 01048

Contact Office Ste No 902, Level 9, Dubai World Trade Ctr, PO Box 124752, Dubai, United Arab Emirates. T. +97143116364. E-mail: adeeb@seha.ae.
URL: http://www.asped.org/

Aims Ensure a high standard of care and development in the field of paediatric endocrinology and diabetes in the Arab region. **Structure** Board of Directors. Committees (3): Research; Education; Clinical Guidelines. Gulf through the Northern African countries. **Activities** Training/education; events/meetings; standards/guidelines.
Members Full in 15 countries:
Algeria, Bahrain, Egypt, Jordan, Kuwait, Lebanon, Libya, Morocco, Oman, Palestine, Qatar, Saudi Arabia, Sudan, Tunisia, United Arab Emirates.
NGO Relations Member of: *Global Pediatric Endocrinology and Diabetes (GPED, #10545).*
[2020/XM5410/**D**]

♦ Arab Society for Plant Nutrition and Fertilization (inactive)

♦ Arab Society for Plant Protection (ASPP) 01049

Main Office PO Box 113-6057, Beirut, Lebanon. T. +9611809173. Fax +9611809173. E-mail: aspp@terra.net.lb.
URL: http://www.asplantprotection.org/

History 1981, Beirut (Lebanon). Founded following activities initiated in 1977. Registration: Lebanon. **Aims** Promote scientific activities and enhance interaction among plant protection scientists in the Arab world. **Structure** Executive Committee. National representatives in each Arab member country. **Languages** Arabic, English. **Staff** 2.00 FTE, paid. **Finance** Sources: donations; members' dues. Annual budget: 13,000 USD. **Activities** Events/meetings. **Events** *Triennial Congress* Hammamet (Tunisia) 2021, *Triennial Congress* Hammamet (Tunisia) 2020, *Triennial Congress* Cairo (Egypt) 2017, *Triennial Congress* Amman (Jordan) 2014, *Triennial Congress* Beirut (Lebanon) 2009. **Publications** *Arab and Near East Plant Protection Newsletter* (2 a year); *Arab Journal of Plant Protection* (2 a year).
Members Individuals (1,500) in 29 countries and territories:
Afghanistan, Algeria, Bahrain, Belgium, Egypt, France, Germany, Greece, Iraq, Jordan, Lebanon, Libya, Morocco, Netherlands, Oman, Pakistan, Palestine, Poland, Qatar, Saudi Arabia, Sudan, Sweden, Switzerland, Syrian AR, Tunisia, UK, United Arab Emirates, USA, Yemen. [2022.03.04/XD3121/v/**D**]

♦ Arab Society for the Protection of Intellectual Property / see Arab Society for Intellectual Property (#01046)
♦ Arab Society for Quality (inactive)
♦ Arab Society for Quality Assurance in Education / see Arab Network for Quality Assurance in Higher Education (#01014)
♦ Arab Space Communications Organization / see Arab Satellite Communications Organization (#01037)
♦ Arab Sports Confederation (inactive)
♦ Arab Sports Federation for Special Groups (inactive)
♦ Arab Sports Journalism Confederation / see Arab Federation of Sports Journalists (#00954)
♦ Arab Sports Journalism Federation / see Arab Federation of Sports Journalists (#00954)

♦ ARABSSCO – Arab Social Science Council (inactive)

♦ Arab States Broadcasting Union (ASBU) 01050

Union de radiodiffusion des Etats arabes – Unión de Radiodifusión de los Estados Arabes

Dir-Gen PO Box 250, Centre urbain nord, CEDEX, 1080 Tunis, Tunisia. T. +21671849000 – +21671841445 – +21671841420. Fax +21671843101 – +21671843505. E-mail: asbu.fx@asbu.net – asbu@asbu.intl.tn.
URL: http://www.asbu.net/

History 9 Feb 1969, Khartoum (Sudan). Set up at 1st General Assembly, following ratification by 7 member governments of *League of Arab States (LAS, #16420)* of a convention drawn up Oct 1955. New Charter ratified Jun 1994 by General Assembly, effective Jan 1996, allows private Arab broadcasters to act as participating members. Also referred to in French as *Union des radios arabes*. **Aims** Serve as the umbrella under which Arab government-owned radio and TV channels can work together harmoniously; provide the appropriate framework within which issues of Arab audiovisual production are discussed. **Structure** General Assembly (annual). Executive Council (meeting at least twice a year). General Directorate in Tunis (Tunisia), headed by Director General. *Arab Centre for News and Programme Exchanges (no recent information)*; *Arab Training Centre for Radio and Television (no recent information)*; ASBU Training Academy. **Languages** Arabic, English, French. **Staff** 54.00 FTE, paid. **Finance** Members' contributions. Payments from associate members for services rendered. New Charter, 1996, leading to a system of self-financing. **Activities** Main basic services: organizing and coordinating exchange of information; programmes and sport coverage; technical assistance; covering major events within and outside the Arab region; programmes broadcast to the world; training staff from member corporations; from 2008, enabling news and programme exchange among members; negotiating broadcasting rights of major international sporting events on behalf of member corporations; training of Arab radio and television professionals. *'ASBU-Multimedia Exchange Network Over Satellite (ASBU-MENOS)'* establishes exchange among members and other users. *'Arab Unified Bouquet'* – allows Arab satellite channels, technological, economic and strategic benefits while providing best services to Arab viewers worldwide. In Nov 2011, ITU and WBU declared support for establishing a satellite broadcast network for TV and radio contribution and exchange services for members of AUB, and adopted ASBU-MENOS to implement it. **Events** *Arab Media Congress* Jeddah (Saudi Arabia) 2023, *Annual General Assembly* Jeddah (Saudi Arabia) 2009, *Joint meeting* Jeddah (Saudi Arabia) 2009, *Meeting* Jeddah (Saudi Arabia) 2009, *Symposium on modern TV news rooms* Tunis (Tunisia) 2008. **Publications** *ASBU Review* (4 a year) in Arabic. *Broadcasting Studies and Research* – series; *Satellite Broadcasting Report* – (annual) series. Regular publications related to seminar and symposia themes.
Members Active: Broadcasting organizations in the 22 LAS countries and territories:
Algeria, Bahrain, Comoros, Djibouti, Egypt, Iraq, Jordan, Kuwait, Lebanon, Libya, Mauritania, Morocco, Oman, Palestine, Qatar, Saudi Arabia, Somalia, Sudan, Syrian AR, Tunisia, United Arab Emirates, Yemen.
Participating: Private Arab radio and television institutions which broadcast partly or totally in Arabic, in 5 countries:
Egypt, Kuwait, Lebanon, Qatar, United Arab Emirates.
Associate: Broadcasting organizations in 7 countries:
China, France, Italy, Lebanon, Russia, Sudan, United Arab Emirates.
IGO Relations Formal agreement with: *UNESCO (#20322)*. Working relations with: *International Telecommunication Union (ITU, #15673)* and observer member of its Radiocommunication Sector. Active Invited to sessions of Intergovernmental Council of: *International Programme for the Development of Communication (IPDC, #14651)*. Permanent observer status with: *World Intellectual Property Organization (WIPO, #21593)*. Close relationship with: *Arab Satellite Communications Organization (ARABSAT, #01037)*. **NGO Relations** Member of: *Digital Radio Mondiale Consortium (DRM, #05082)*; *Permanent Conference of Mediterranean Audiovisual Operators (COPEAM, #18320)*; *World Broadcasting Unions (WBU, #21247)*. Organizes: *World Conference of Broadcasting Unions*, together with related unions: *African Union of Broadcasting (AUB, #00490)*; *Asia-Pacific Broadcasting Union (ABU, #01863)*; *Caribbean Broadcasting Union (CBU, #03465)*; *European Broadcasting Union (EBU, #06404)*; *International Association of Broadcasting (IAB, #11738)*; *North American Broadcasters Association (NABA, #17561)*; *Organización de Telecomunicaciones de Iberoamérica (OTI, #17851)*.
[2023/XD3875/**D***]

♦ Arab States Military Organization (inactive)

♦ Arab States Research and Education Network (ASREN) 01051

Managing Dir PO Box 921100, Amman 11192, Jordan. T. +96265100900. Fax +96265100901. E-mail: info@asrenorg.net.
URL: http://www.asrenorg.net/

History Set up under the umbrella of *League of Arab States (LAS, #16420)*. Registered in accordance with German law, 3 Jun 2011. **Aims** Implement, manage and extend sustainable Pan-Arab e-Infrastructures dedicated for the research and education communities; boost scientific research and cooperation in member countries through the provision of world-class e-Infrastructures and e-services. **Events** *International Conference* Abu Dhabi (United Arab Emirates) 2019. **Publications** *ASREN Monthly Newsletter.*
Members Shareholders; Partners; Arab NRENs (Arab region National Research and Education Networks). Members in 22 countries:
Algeria, Bahrain, Comoros, Djibouti, Egypt, Iraq, Jordan, Kuwait, Lebanon, Libya, Mauritania, Morocco, Oman, Palestine, Qatar, Saudi Arabia, Somalia, Sudan, Syrian AR, Tunisia, United Arab Emirates, Yemen.
IGO Relations Partner of: *Group on Earth Observations (GEO, #10735).* [2019.03.03/XM6272/**F**]

♦ Arab Student Aid International (ASAI) 01052

Pres PO Box 3546, Dublin OH 43016, USA. T. +16148899420. Fax +16148899430.
URL: http://www.arabstudentaid.org/

History 1977. Founded as an educational, non-political, non-religious, tax exempt, and independent foundation. Until 2005, registered in the State of New Jersey (USA); now registered in the State of Ohio (USA). Registration: Start date: 1977, USA; Start date: 2005, USA. **Aims** Promote human resource development and capacity building for decision and policy makers of NGOs about advanced management. **Structure** Board of Trustees; Board of Directors; Executive Committee; Main office located in USA; Groups of Trustees; National Representatives; Independent Entities. **Languages** Arabic, English. **Staff** 2.00 FTE, paid. Several voluntary. **Finance** Sources: contributions; grants; international organizations; investments. Repayment of student loans; funds from Zakat and Waqf are accepted. **Activities** Capacity building; financial and/or material support; projects/programmes; training/education. **Events** *Annual meeting* Jeddah (Saudi Arabia) 1990, *Meeting* Jeddah (Saudi Arabia) 1988. **Publications** *Arab Student Aid Newsletter* (2 a year) in Arabic, English. *35th Anniversary Report (1977-2011)*. Annual Report; leaflets.
Members Trustee members in 9 countries and territories:
Jordan, Kuwait, Lebanon, Morocco, Palestine, Saudi Arabia, UK, United Arab Emirates, USA. [2022/XF0384/**F**]

♦ Arab Sugar Federation (inactive)
♦ Arab Swimming Confederation (inactive)

♦ Arab-Swiss Chamber of Commerce and Industry (CASCI) 01053

Contact Rue de Lausanne 63, 1202 Geneva, Switzerland. T. +41223473202. Fax +41223473870. E-mail: arabswisscham@casci.ch.
URL: http://www.casci.ch/

History 1974. **Aims** Promote economic and cultural relations between Switzerland and the Arab countries. **Structure** Executive Board, comprising President, Secretary General, Secretary General of *Union of Arab Chambers (UAC, #20350)*, Treasurer, 1st Vice President and 3 members. **Publications** *Arab Swiss Cooperation Magazine*; *Monthly Bulletin*. Annual Directory.
Members Chambers in 23 countries:
Algeria, Bahrain, Comoros, Djibouti, Egypt, Iraq, Jordan, Kuwait, Lebanon, Libya, Mauritania, Morocco, Oman, Palestine, Qatar, Saudi Arabia, Somalia, Sudan, Switzerland, Syrian AR, Tunisia, United Arab Emirates, Yemen.
Consultative Status Consultative status granted from: *UNCTAD (#20285)* (General Category). **IGO Relations** *League of Arab States (LAS, #16420).* [2017.06.01/XJ6082/t/**D**]

♦ Arab Table Tennis Federation (inactive)
♦ Arab Taekwondo Confederation (inactive)

♦ **Arab Telecommunication and Information Council of Ministers** **01054**
Contact address not obtained. E-mail: info@mcit.gov.sa.
History As *Council of Arab Telecom Ministers*, in the framework of *League of Arab States (LAS, #16420)*. Also referred to as *Arab Council of Ministers for Telecommunication and Information*. **Events** *Session* Beirut (Lebanon) 2015.
Members Full in 22 countries:
Algeria, Bahrain, Comoros, Djibouti, Egypt, Iraq, Jordan, Kuwait, Lebanon, Libya, Mauritania, Morocco, Oman, Palestine, Qatar, Saudi Arabia, Somalia, Sudan, Syrian AR, Tunisia, United Arab Emirates, Yemen.
IGO Relations Agreement with: *Conférence européenne des administrations des postes et des télécommunications (CEPT, #04602)*. [2015/XE2353/**E***]

♦ Arab Telecommunication Union (inactive)
♦ Arab Tennis Confederation (inactive)
♦ Arab Theatre Institute (internationally oriented national body)
♦ Arab Thoracic Association (no recent information)

♦ **Arab Thought Forum (ATF)** **01055**
Al Muntada
Main Office PO Box 1541, Amman 11941, Jordan. T. +96265333261. Fax +96265331197. E-mail: atf@atf.org.jo.
URL: http://www.atf.org.jo/
History Founded Mar 1981. **Aims** Develop contemporary Arab thought with regard to basic issues facing the Arab world; intensify public awareness of and concern with these issues; pay particular attention to Arab unity and a framework that synthesizes Arab *cultural heritage* and modern values; study economic, social and cultural links within the Arab Nation and with other developing regions, with the object of strengthening dialogue, promoting cooperation and serving common interests; formulate an Arab point-of-view on international development issues addressed by international fora, in particular on efforts to establish new relations on just and equitable bases and foster close economic complementarity; build bridges of communication between *intellectuals* and *decision-makers* in the Arab Nation so as to ensure that public policies are based on sound grounds and facilitate popular participation in implementing these policies; conduct studies and projects that would lead to practical solutions and viable options on issues such as unity, security, social and economic development, good governance, freedom, human dignity, human security, women empowerment, youth, and intercultural and intellectual dialogue. **Structure** General Assembly. Board of Trustees, consisting of Chairman, Vice Chairman, Secretary General and 18 members. Administrative Committee, comprising 5 members from the Board of Trustees and Secretary General. General Secretariat, headed by Secretary General and Executive Organs. **Languages** Arabic, English. **Staff** 15.00 FTE, paid. **Finance** Members' dues. Other sources: subscription for publications; donations from individuals; donations from Arab and international non-governmental bodies, in addition to modest endowment income. **Activities** Arab-International Dialogues – comprise conferences, seminars and workshops. Inter-Arab Dialogues – comprise workshops and symposia. Strategic Research – research projects are conducted by teams of qualified Arab specialists addressing current and future issues facing the Arab world. Publishing Activity. Organizes conferences, round tables, seminars, symposia and rounds of dialogue on specific issues related to the region. **Events** *Korea-Middle East Cooperation Forum* Seoul (Korea Rep) 2015, *Joint meeting* Amman (Jordan) 1997, *Conference on mass movement of population* Amman (Jordan) 1992. **Publications** *Al Mutanda* (4 a year) in Arabic; *ATF News* (annual) in English. *Series of Arab-International Dialogues and Seminars*; *Series of Arab Studies* in Arabic; *Series of Regional-Arab Dialogues, Meetings and Seminars*; *Series of Strategic Studies* in Arabic; *Series of Translated International Works*.
Members Active members individuals in 22 countries and territories:
Algeria, Bahrain, Egypt, Iraq, Jordan, Kuwait, Lebanon, Libya, Mauritania, Morocco, Oman, Palestine, Qatar, Saudi Arabia, Sudan, Switzerland, Syrian AR, Tunisia, UK, United Arab Emirates, USA, Yemen.
Supportive members banks, corporations, foundations, funds and other bodies in different Arab countries (not specified).
IGO Relations Cooperative agreement with: *Islamic World Educational, Scientific and Cultural Organization (ICESCO, #16058)*. **NGO Relations** Member of: Arab Forum for Security and Nuclear Non-proliferation; *UNCAC Coalition (#20283)*. Cooperative agreement with: *Arab Center for Research and Policy Studies (ACRPS, #00913)*; national organizations and other research and policy studies centres and universities in Turkey, India, pakistan and China. [2013.07.29/XF2904/**F**]

♦ **Arab Thought Foundation (ATF)** **01056**
Fondation de la Pensée Arabe
Contact Akoury Street, Arab Thought Foundation Bldg, Behind the Omari Mosque, Downtown – Solidère, Beirut, Lebanon. T. +9611997100. Fax +9611997101. E-mail: info@arabthought.org.
URL: http://www.arabthought.org/
History 29 May 2000, Beirut (Lebanon). Founded as an initiative by His Royal Highness Prince Khalid Al-Faisal. **Aims** Uphold the importance of objective and critical thinking and calling for a constantly renewed Arab thought; highlight the importance of reason and science, stimulating creativity and innovation; highlight Arab achievements and emphasizing the Pan-Arab identity; promote the Arabic language; providing youth with skills to develop their energies and competencies; adopt a culture of cooperation, partnership, and integration and strive to consolidate the approach of joint Arab action, broadening its scope and capacity. **Structure** General Assembly; Board of Trustees; Board of Directors; General Management; Advisors; Advisory Committees. **Languages** Arabic. **Staff** 30.00 FTE, paid. Voluntary. **Finance** Sources: contributions. Return on endowment money of memberships. **Activities** Awards/prizes/competitions; awareness raising; capacity building; events/meetings; knowledge management/information dissemination; networking/liaising; projects/programmes; publishing activities; research and development; research/documentation; training/education. **Events** *Annual Conference* Dhahran (Saudi Arabia) 2019, *Stabilization Challenges amidst Regional Turmoil* Dubai (United Arab Emirates) 2018, *Annual Conference* Abu Dhabi (United Arab Emirates) 2016, *Arab Integration: Challenges and Prospects"* Cairo (Egypt) 2015, *The Arab Integration: The Dream of Unity and the Reality of Division* Skhirat (Morocco) 2014. **Publications** *Ofoq* (bi-weekly) in Arabic; *Arab Report on Cultural Development* (annual) in Arabic. *One Civilization – Hadara Wahida* in Arabic – A selection of the most important and distinguished books from French, Spanish, Chinese and Hindi translated into Arabic.. **Consultative Status** Consultative status granted from: *UNESCO (#20322)* (Foundations). [2022.12.05/XM0966/f/**D**]

♦ Arab Tour Guides Federation (no recent information)

♦ **Arab Tourism Organization (ATO)** **01057**
Organisation arabe de tourisme
Chairman Prince Sultan Road, The Orchards, Jeddah 23717, Saudi Arabia. T. +966226393369. Fax +96622757292. E-mail: at_organization@yahoo.com – segeato@gmail.com – info@atoorg.org.
URL: http://www.arab-tourismorg.org/
History 1954, Cairo (Egypt), as *Arab International Tourist Union*, by member States of *League of Arab States (LAS, #16420)*. Subsequently known as *Arab Tourism Union (ATU) – Union arabe de tourisme*. Present name adopted 1969. **Aims** Promote tourism in the Arab area, and to this end coordinate all efforts to draw up a unified Arab tourist policy, providing members with all possible services and assisting them to acquire professionalism by supplying them with relevant studies and information; remove obstacles to the expansion of tourism. **Structure** General Assembly; Executive Committee; Secretariat General. **Finance** Administrative budget; Programmes budget. **Activities** Organizes: conferences of Arab Ministers of Tourism; seminars. Offers scholarships. **Events** *General conference* Tangiers (Morocco) 1990. **Publications** *Press Bulletin* (12 a year) in Arabic, English; *Arab Tourism* (6 a year) in Arabic. *Arab Tourism: Rules and Methods*; *Arab Tourism: Rules and Principals*; *International Associations*; *Role of International Tourism on the Economic Development of Developing Countries* – a UN Study; *Therapy Tourism*; *Tourism and Youth*; *Tourism Statistics*. **IGO Relations** Participates in the work of: *UNCTAD (#20285)*. [2017/XD3619/**D***]

♦ Arab Tourism Union / see Arab Tourism Organization (#01057)

♦ **Arab Towns Development Fund (ATDF)** **01058**
Fonds de développement des villes arabes
Secretariat c/o ATO General Secretariat, PO Box 68160, 71962 Kaifan, Kuwait. T. +96524849705 – +96524849706. Fax +96524849319 – +9654849322. E-mail: ato@arabtowns.org.
URL: http://www.arabtowns.org/
History Founded 1979, as part of *Arab Towns Organization (ATO, #01059)* but with its own legal personality. **Aims** Provide loans for member towns as a means of helping to implement projects designed to raise the standard of *municipal services* and *utilities*. **Structure** Board of Directors, comprising Secretary General and Director General of ATO and 5 further members of ATO Permanent Bureau. Executive Body, headed by Secretary General. **Finance** Member towns' contributions. Other sources: government allocations; contributions from non member towns, financial bodies and institutions; loans from Arab and international institutions. **Activities** Finances municipal projects of member towns through medium-term soft loans. **Events** *Meeting* 1993.
Members Member towns in 22 countries and territories:
Algeria, Bahrain, Comoros, Djibouti, Egypt, Iraq, Jordan, Kuwait, Lebanon, Libya, Mauritania, Morocco, Oman, Palestine, Qatar, Saudi Arabia, Somalia, Sudan, Syrian AR, Tunisia, United Arab Emirates, Yemen. [2007/XF0219/f/**F**]

♦ **Arab Towns Organization (ATO)** **01059**
Organisation des villes arabes (OVA)
SG ATO General Secretariat, PO Box 68160, 71962 Kaifan, Kuwait. T. +9654849603 – +9654849705 – +9654849706. Fax +9654849264 – +9654849319.
URL: http://www.arabtowns.org/
History 15 Mar 1967, Kuwait (Kuwait). Founded on approval of statutes, following conference, 11 Mar 1967, Kuwait City. Former names and other names: *Arab Cities Organization (ACO)* – former. **Aims** In relation to Arab towns: preserve identity and heritage; support development and modernization of municipal and local authorities; improve and boost services and utilities; support member towns development schemes through providing loans and assistance; maintain cooperation with member towns in the process of planning and coordination of development activities and services, accordingly with each economic, social, cultural and environmental capacities; facilitate exchange of service-related achievements and expertise among member towns; coordinate efforts to modernize and standardize municipal regulations and codes; maintain liaison and cooperation working in ATO-related fields. **Structure** General Conference (every 3 years); Permanent Bureau (meets annually), serves as Board of Executives; General Secretariat, headed by Secretary General. ATO institutions: *Arab Towns Development Fund (ATDF, #01058)*; *Arab Urban Development Institute (AUDI, #01071)*; *'Arab Urban Environment Centre'*; *'Arab Forum on Information Systems'*; *'Heritage and Arab Historic City Foundation'*; *'Arab Urban Observatory'*. **Languages** Arabic. **Activities** Awards/prizes/competitions; events/meetings; networking/liaising; research/documentation; training/education. **Events** *General Conference* Amman (Jordan) 2019, *General Conference* Manama (Bahrain) 2016, *General conference* Doha (Qatar) 2013, *General Conference* Kuwait (Kuwait) 2010, *General Conference* Marrakech (Morocco) 2007. **Publications** *Arab City Magazine*.
Members Arab towns. Municipalities or local authorities of over 500 Arab towns and cities in 22 countries and territories:
Algeria, Bahrain, Comoros, Djibouti, Egypt, Iraq, Jordan, Kuwait, Lebanon, Libya, Mauritania, Morocco, Oman, Palestine, Qatar, Saudi Arabia, Somalia, Sudan, Syrian AR, Tunisia, United Arab Emirates, Yemen.
IGO Relations Specialized Agency of: *League of Arab States (LAS, #16420)*. Cooperates with various regional and international bodies and institutes working in the same field. Consultative Status with: *European Economic and Social Committee (EESC, #06963)*. **NGO Relations** Member of (2): *Global Taskforce of Local and Regional Governments (Global Taskforce, #10622)*; *World Organization of United Cities and Local Governments (UCLG, #21695)*. Cooperates with various regional and international bodies and institutes working in the same field. [2020.12.09/XD2765/**D**]

♦ **Arab Trade Financing Programme (ATFP)** **01060**
CEO and Chairman of the Board PO Box 26799, Abu Dhabi, United Arab Emirates. T. +97126316999. Fax +97126316793 – +97126316299. E-mail: ceo@atfp.org.ae – finadmin@atfp.org.ae.
Street address AMF Bldg, Corniche Street, Abu Dhabi, United Arab Emirates.
URL: https://www.atfp.org.ae/
History 16 Mar 1989, in accordance with resolution No 4/1989 of the Board of Governors of *Arab Monetary Fund (AMF, #01009)*, as a specialized financing institution. Enjoys privileges and immunities granted by the United Arab Emirates, where it is domiciled, pursuant to the Protocol of Privileges and Immunities issued as Federal Decree No 3 of 1990. **Aims** Promote Arab trade and the realization of the objectives of the Agreement for the Facilitation and the Development of Trade between Arab Countries and the Arab Free Trade Zone. **Structure** General Assembly; Board of Directors; Executive Panel, headed by Chief Executive and Chairman of the Board of Directors; Departments (3); National Agencies designated by monetary authorities of Arab countries. **Languages** Arabic, English. **Staff** 25.00 FTE, paid. **Finance** Shareholders (53): *'Category A'* – Arab Monetary Fund (AMF), multilateral Arab financing institutions and public financial and banking institutions (19), of which 6 included in this Yearbook: *Arab Authority for Agricultural Investment and Development (AAAID, #00902)*; *Arab Banking Corporation (ABC, #00906)*; *Arab Fund for Economic and Social Development (AFESD, #00965)*; *Arab Investment Company (TAIC, #00996)*; *Gulf International Bank (GIB, #10832)*; *Arab Investment and Export Credit Guarantee Corporation (DHAMAN, #00997)*. *'Category B'* – Private financial and banking institutions (33), of which 2 included in this Yearbook: *Arab Bank (#00903)*; *Arab International Bank (AIB, #00992)*. *'Category C'* – Joint Arab-foreign financial and banking institutions (1). Authorized capital comprises 200,000 shares at par value US$ 5,000 per share. Resources as at 31 Dec 2015: issued and fully paid-up capital – US$ 987,000,000; retained earnings and reserves – US$ 126,000,000. **Activities** Financial and/or material support; knowledge management/information dissemination; events/meetings. **Events** *Buyers sellers meeting* Lebanon 2003, *Buyers sellers meeting* United Arab Emirates 2003, *Buyers sellers meeting* Algeria 2002, *Buyers sellers meeting* Egypt 2002, *Buyers sellers meeting* Lebanon 2002. **Publications** *Arab Trade Financing Programme – Articles of Association* in Arabic, English; *ATFP General Features – Objectives and Activities* in Arabic, English; *Protocol of Immunities and Privileges signed with the UAE* in Arabic. Annual Report in Arabic, English. **Information Services** *Arab Integrated Trade Information Network (AITIN)*.
Members Governments of 22 countries and territories:
Algeria, Bahrain, Comoros, Djibouti, Egypt, Iraq, Jordan, Kuwait, Lebanon, Libya, Mauritania, Morocco, Oman, Palestine, Qatar, Saudi Arabia, Somalia, Sudan, Syrian AR, Tunisia, United Arab Emirates, Yemen.
National Agencies (206) in the above 22 and the following 5 non-Arab countries:
Belgium, Brazil, France, Malta, UK.
IGO Relations *League of Arab States (LAS, #16420)*; *UNDP (#20292)*. Special links with: *Arab Economic and Social Council (AESC, #00937)* of the League of Arab States. [2018.09.09/XF5173/et/**F***]

♦ **Arab Transfusion Medicine Forum (ATMF)** **01061**
Pres address not obtained.
URL: http://www.atmfweb.org/
History 2004, as Arab Transfusion Medicine Course (ATMC). Current title adopted 2012. **Aims** Educate professionals in transfusion medicine at all levels regarding significant and updating professional issues; establish a professional forum for training, staff development and sharing experience a structured manner on a regular basis; provide regional opportunities for individual development. **Structure** Steering Committee; Executive Committee. **Events** *Annual Meeting* Cairo (Egypt) 2015, *Annual Meeting* Agadir (Morocco) 2014, *Annual Meeting* Kuwait (Kuwait) 2012, *Annual Meeting* Doha (Qatar) 2011, *Annual Meeting* Cairo (Egypt) 2010. **NGO Relations** *European School of Transfusion Medicine (ESTM, #08437)*; *International Society of Blood Transfusion (ISBT, #14979)*. [2015/XJ9976/**F**]

♦ **Arab Translators Network – Arab Professional Translators Society (ATN-APTS)** **01062**
Pres PO Box 25/122, Beirut, Lebanon.
Contact address not obtained. E-mail: maburisha@arabtranslators.org.
URL: http://www.arabtranslators.net/
History May 2000. Registered in accordance with Swiss Civil Code. **Aims** Facilitate interaction between Arab freelance translators, translation agencies and their clients. **Languages** Arabic. **Publications** *ATN-APTS Magazine*. **Members** Membership countries not specified. [2017.06.01/XJ8054/t/**F**]

♦ Arab Union (inactive)

♦ **Arab Union for Astronomy and Space Sciences (AUASS)** **01063**

Pres Univ of Sharjah, PO BOX 27272, Sharjah, United Arab Emirates. T. +97165050200. Fax +97165050489. E-mail: alnaimiy@sharjah.ac.ae.
SG PO Box 782, Amman 11941, Jordan. T. +962777745204. Fax +96265534826.

History Founded 30 Aug 1998, Amman (Jordan). **Aims** Raise the profile of astronomy and the space sciences to a level that that these fields may play a major role in the scientific and technological progress and development of the Arab society; preserve the Arab/Islamic scientific heritage and raise its profile in the advancement of human civilization; study scientific issues of common interest among Arab countries and promote exchange information and experience in the various basic and applied scientific fields of astronomy and the space sciences; promote interest in astronomy and the space sciences in Arab countries, support scientific institutions and associations in the Arab/Islamic nation, and contribute to helping astronomers and Arab specialists in astronomy and the space sciences to form scientific institutions and associations in Arab countries that do not yet have such authorities or associations; raise the level of the scientific and technical performance of specialists and those interested in the fields of astronomy and space sciences in the Arab nation; seek to identify the beginning of the lunar months by scientific means and using observational methods to substantiate findings; work to standardize scientific terms in the fields of astronomy and the space sciences in the Arab nations; promote research, publishing, writing books and translating scientific material into and out of the Arabic language; provide consultation to institutions, authorities and individuals in relationship to astronomy and the space sciences. **Structure** Higher Council; Headquarters in Amman (Jordan); regional offices throughout the Middle East. **Languages** Arabic, English. **Finance** Support from: governments of Jordan; member organizations such as *International Astronomical Union (IAU, #12287)*; private and governmental entities with an interest in furthering astronomy and the space sciences in the Middle East region. **Activities** Research and development; events/meetings; knowledge management/information dissemination; guidance/assistance/consulting. **Events** *Conference* Amman (Jordan) 2002, *Conference* Amman (Jordan) 2000. **Publications** *ALKAWN Journal*.

Members Founding astronomy and space science institutions and associations and those that might join later in the Arab nations; naturalists in these specializations in countries that do not yet have Arab astronomy or space science institutions or associations; Arab scientific institutions such as institutes, universities and others, which offer astronomy and space science programmes; any party that the Higher Council approves. Members (over 500). Membership countries not specified. Included in the above, one organization listed in this Yearbook:
Included in the above, one organization listed in this Yearbook:
International Astronomical Union (IAU, #12287).

IGO Relations Member of: *Council of Arab Economic Unity (CAEU, #04859)*; *League of Arab States (LAS, #16420)*. Cooperates with: National Aeronautics and Space Administration (NASA); *Regional Centre for Space Science and Technology Education for Western Asia (see: #04277)*. **NGO Relations** Member of: *International Astronomical Union (IAU, #12287)*. [2020.03.05/XM1482/y/**D**]

♦ Arab Union of Bank, Insurance and Finance Employees (inactive)

♦ **Arab Union for the Blind** **01064**

Pres PO Box 45525, Doha, Qatar. T. +974558328. Fax +97444503330. E-mail: arub_07@yahoo.com.

History Aug 2007. **Aims** Protect the rights of people with *disabilities*; promote rehabilitation of the visually impaired; work on the application of international conventions for the disabled. **Structure** Executive Board. **Languages** Arabic. **Staff** 6.00 FTE, voluntary. **Finance** Donations. Budget (annual): US$ 150,000. **Activities** Events/meetings. **Publications** Newspapers. [2019/XJ5041/**D**]

♦ **Arab Union for Cement and Building Materials (AUCBM)** **01065**

Union arabe du ciment et des matériaux de construction (UACMC)

SG PO Box 9015, Damascus, Syrian AR. T. +963116118598 – +963116115412. Fax +963116121731. E-mail: aucbm@scs-net.org – aucbm1977@gmail.com.
URL: http://www.aucbm.net/

History 27 Mar 1977, Cairo (Egypt). Founded at 1st meeting, in response to decree 745/27,1976, of *Council of Arab Economic Unity (CAEU, #04859)*, in cooperation with the previous *Arab Industrial Development Organization (AIDO, inactive)*, now merged into *Arab Industrial Development, Standardization and Mining Organization (AIDSMO, #00981)*. A specialized union within: *League of Arab States (LAS, #16420)*. **Aims** Coordinate, on technical and economic levels, and encourage cooperation and development of Arab member companies operating in the field of cement and building materials. **Structure** General Assembly; Board of Directors; Arab Training Committee. **Languages** Arabic, English, French. **Staff** 12.00 FTE, paid. **Finance** Sources: fees for services; meeting proceeds; members' dues; sale of publications. **Activities** Events/meetings; guidance/assistance/consulting; knowledge management/information dissemination; networking/liaising; research/documentation; standards/guidelines; training/education. **Events** *Arab International Cement Conference* Amman (Jordan) 2022, *Arab International Cement Conference* Riyadh (Saudi Arabia) 2020, *Arab International Cement Conference* Cairo (Egypt) 2019, *Arab International Cement Conference* Amman (Jordan) 2018, *Arab International Cement Conference* Sharm el Sheikh (Egypt) 2017. **Publications** *Cement and Building Materials Review* (4 a year) in Arabic, English; *Statistical Cement Report* (annual); *Directory of Arab Cement Plants* (every 5 years). *Report of the Union's Activities 1984-2015*; *Statistical Studies of Cement*. Studies; reports; monographs; statistical bulletins; glossaries; dictionaries.

Members Full: Arab companies, enterprises and plants in production or marketing of cement and building materials (88); Associate: marketing and consultancy organizations in the same field (24); Observer: Arab organizations, scientific and research bodies and training centres (13). Members in 22 countries and territories:
Algeria, Bahrain, Comoros, Djibouti, Egypt, Iraq, Jordan, Kuwait, Lebanon, Libya, Mauritania, Morocco, Oman, Palestine, Qatar, Saudi Arabia, Somalia, Sudan, Syrian AR, Tunisia, United Arab Emirates, Yemen.
Included in the above, one organization listed in the Yearbook:
Arab Mining Company (ARMICO, #01008).

NGO Relations Also links with Arab research centres, universities and unions that are under the umbrella of CAEU; national associations. [2022.05.17/XD5001/y/**D**]

♦ Arab Union for Dealers in the Financial Markets (unconfirmed)
♦ Arab Union for Economy and Business Forum (unconfirmed)

♦ **Arab Union of Electricity (AUE)** **01066**

Union arabe d'électricité (UAE)

SG Natl Electric Power Company (NEPCO), PO Box 2310, Amman 11181, Jordan. T. +96265819164. Fax +96265859403. E-mail: contact-us@auptde.org.
URL: http://www.auptde.org/

History Current name adopted, Tunis (Tunisia), at a General Assembly. Statutes adopted 30 Nov – 1 Dec 1987, Tunis (Tunisia). Headquarters in Amman (Jordan). Former names and other names: *Arab Union of Producers, Transporters and Distributors of Electricity (AUPTDE)* – former; *Union arabe des producteurs, transporteurs et distributeurs d'électricité (UAPTDE)* – former. **Aims** Improve and develop production, transport and distribution of electrical energy in the Arab world, improve and coordinate areas of interest of members, and strengthen relationships among them. **Structure** General Assembly (annnual); Board of Directors (meets at least every 6 months); Committees (6); Secretariat. **Languages** Arabic, English. **Staff** 3.00 FTE, paid. **Finance** Sources: meeting proceeds; members' dues; sponsorship. **Activities** Events/meetings; networking/liaising; research/documentation. **Events** *General Conference* Doha (Qatar) 2022, *General Conference* Amman (Jordan) 2018, *Arab Forum on the Prospects of Nuclear Power for Electricity Generation and Seawater Desalination* Amman (Jordan) 2017, *General Conference* Marrakech (Morocco) 2016, *Arab Forum on the Prospects of Nuclear Power for Electricity Generation and Seawater Desalination* Manama (Bahrain) 2015. **Publications** *Arab Electricity* (annual) – magazine. *Dictionary of Technical Terms* in Arabic, English, French; *Manual of Arab Manufacturing Companies of Electricity*; *Manual of Power Stations in the Arab Countries*; *Maps of Electrical Interconnection in the Arab Countries*; *Tariffs in the Arab Countries*. Annual statistical bulletin; meeting reports.

Members Active: Arab companies directly responsible for production, transport and distribution of electrical energy. Associate: establishments and professional organizations working in one of the electricity industry fields, and supporting the activities of the Union. Observers: international organizations and associations. Active in 18 countries:
Algeria, Bahrain, Egypt, Iraq, Jordan, Kuwait, Lebanon, Libya, Mauritania, Morocco, Palestine, Qatar, Saudi Arabia, Sudan, Syrian AR, Tunisia, United Arab Emirates, Yemen.
Associate in countries:
Egypt, Saudi Arabia.

NGO Relations Member of (1): *MEDELEC (#16614)*. [2022.10.24/XD1838/**D**]

♦ Arab Union of Fish Producers / see Arab Federation of Fish Producers (#00945)
♦ Arab Union for Foodstuff Industries / see Arab Federation for Food Industries (#00946)
♦ Arab Union of Forensic Physicians (unconfirmed)

♦ **Arab Union of Information Technology** **01067**

Contact 115 Ismail ELfangry, Cairo, Egypt. T. +20201008103652.
URL: http://aucit.blogspot.be/2016/02/contact-us.html

History by *Council of Arab Economic Unity (CAEU, #04859)*. **Aims** Establish a market position in the field of information technology; make the benefits of information technology available, accessible and easy to use for Arab citizens; minimize the digital divide gap between developed and developing countries; empower the IT field to boost economic and social development; build a team of professionals. [2016/XM1480/**D**]

♦ **Arab Union of International Arbitration (AUIA)** **01068**

SG 1 Al Saleh Ayoub Street, Zamalek, Cairo, Egypt. T. +2027351333. Fax +2027351336. E-mail: yahia.rashwan@crcica.org.
URL: http://au-ia.org/

History Nov 1997, Cairo (Egypt), under the auspices of *Cairo Regional Centre for International Commercial Arbitration (CRCICA, #03398)*, following recommendations of the First Arab Arbitrations Institutions Conference. Previously also referred to as *Arab Association of International Arbitration*. **Aims** Develop, modernize and unify arbitral trends in the Arab world; enhance means of inter-Arab cooperation in the field of ADR techniques. **Structure** General Secretariat. **Languages** Arabic, English. **Activities** Awareness raising; conflict resolution; events/meetings; guidance/assistance/consulting; knowledge management/information dissemination; monitoring/evaluation; networking/liaising; publishing activities; research/documentation; training/education. **Events** *Sharm El Sheikh Conference* Sharm el Sheikh (Egypt) 2016, *Biennial Conference* Rabat (Morocco) 2004, *Biennial conference* Sanaa (Yemen) 2002, *Biennial Conference* Tunis (Tunisia) 2001, *Biennial Conference* Jeddah (Saudi Arabia) 1999. **Publications** *Journal of Arab Arbitration*.

Members Full in 23 countries:
Algeria, Bahrain, Djibouti, Egypt, Iraq, Jordan, Kuwait, Lebanon, Libya, Madagascar, Mauritania, Morocco, Oman, Palestine, Qatar, Saudi Arabia, Somalia, South Sudan, Sudan, Syrian AR, Tunisia, United Arab Emirates, Yemen.
Included in the above, 1 organization listed in the above: [2018.09.17/XD0568/y/**E**]

♦ Arab Union for International Exhibitions and Conferences, Cairo (no recent information)
♦ Arab Union of Journalists / see Federation of Arab Journalists (#09422)

♦ **Arab Union of Land Transport (AULT)** **01069**

Union arabe des transports routiers

Contact PO Box 926324, Amman 11190, Jordan. T. +96265663153. Fax +96265664232. E-mail: ault@auolt.org – membership@auolt.com.
URL: http://www.auolt.org/

History 20 Nov 1978. Pursuant to a resolution of *Council of Arab Economic Unity (CAEU, #04859)*. Former names and other names: *Société arabe et internationale de transport terrestre* – former. **Aims** Coordinate Arab member States efforts in order to develop land transport in the Arab region; facilitate transport of passengers and goods; coordinate and link between Arab fleets. **Structure** General Assembly (annual); Governing Board; Secretariat General. **Languages** Arabic. **Staff** 10.00 FTE, paid. **Finance** Contributions of members. **Events** *Annual General Assembly* Dubai (United Arab Emirates) 2014, *Euro-Asian bus and coach forum* Istanbul (Turkey) 2010, *Seminar on Arab and international road transport agreements and their role in developing Arab foreign trade / IRU-LAS-AULT International Seminar* Cairo (Egypt) 2009, *Arab transportation symposium* Bahrain 2003. **Publications** *Arab Land Transport* (4 a year); *Public Transport Magazine* (4 a year). *Arab World Route Map*. Studies on land transport.

Members Land transport regulatory bodies, national and private land transport companies, in 16 countries and territories:
Algeria, Bahrain, Egypt, Iraq, Jordan, Kuwait, Lebanon, Libya, Morocco, Palestine, Saudi Arabia, Sudan, Syrian AR, Tunisia, United Arab Emirates, Yemen.

NGO Relations Member of: *International Association of Public Transport (#12118)*. Memorandum of Understanding with: *International Road Transport Union (IRU, #14761)*. [2015/XD7593/**D**]

♦ **Arab Union of Manufacturers of Pharmaceuticals and Medical Appliances (AUPAM)** **01070**

Contact address not obtained. T. +962795616375. E-mail: info@aupam.org.
URL: http://www.aupam.org/

History Feb 1986, Amman (Jordan). Also referred to as: *Arab Federation for Drug Industries and Medical Appliances*; *Arab Federation for Producers of Drugs and Medical Appliances*; *Arab Union of Pharmaceutical Manufacturers and Medical Appliance Manufacturers*. **Aims** Develop the Arab pharmaceutical *industry* so that high quality *drugs* are available at reasonable cost; establish cooperation among Arab pharmaceutical manufacturing companies; work towards establishing an Arab pharmaceutical common market; cooperate with international bodies in matters related to the pharmaceutical industry. **Structure** General Assembly of representatives of Arab pharmaceutical industries (one per company). Board of Directors, comprising one representative per country and 4 elected members. President who also serves as Chairman. Secretary-General. **Languages** Arabic, English. **Staff** 3.00 FTE, paid; 3.00 FTE, voluntary. **Finance** Members' dues. **Activities** Organizes seminars, workshops. **Events** *Annual seminar* Cairo (Egypt) 1996, *Annual seminar* Baghdad (Iraq) 1995, *Auditing for compliance with GMP guidelines* Amman (Jordan) 1994, *Annual seminar* Cairo (Egypt) 1994, *Annual seminar* Damascus (Syrian AR) 1994. **Publications** *Arab Guidelines on Good Manufacturing Practices for Pharmaceutical Products* (1995); *Index of Arab Pharmaceuticals* (1995); *Arab Guidelines on Stability Testing of Pharmaceutical Products*.

Members Pharmaceutical companies (27) in 9 countries:
Egypt, Iraq, Jordan, Libya, Morocco, Palestine, Sudan, Syrian AR, Yemen.

IGO Relations Specialized union of: *Council of Arab Economic Unity (CAEU, #04859)*. **NGO Relations** *Union of Arab Pharmacists (UAP, #20356)*. [2014/XD1600/**D**]

♦ Arab Union for Paper and Printing Industries / see Arab Federation for Paper, Printing and Packaging Industries (#00950)
♦ Arab Union of Pharmaceutical Manufacturers and Medical Appliance Manufacturers / see Arab Union of Manufacturers of Pharmaceuticals and Medical Appliances (#01070)
♦ Arab Union of Producers, Transporters and Distributors of Electricity / see Arab Union of Electricity (#01066)
♦ Arab Union of Railways (inactive)
♦ Arab Union for Small Enterprises (inactive)
♦ Arab Union of Sport Information Centers (no recent information)
♦ Arab Union of Surveyors / see Arab Federation of Surveyors (#00955)
♦ Arab Union of Veterinary Surgeons (inactive)
♦ Arab Union of Youth Hostels Associations (no recent information)
♦ Arab Union of Youth Scientific Clubs (no recent information)

♦ **Arab Urban Development Institute (AUDI)** **01071**

Institut arabe pour le développement urbain

Dir Gen 8144 Abd Ibn Hudhafah As Sahmi, As Safarat Unit 1, AR Riyadh 12521-3803, PO Box 6892, Riyadh 11452, Saudi Arabia. T. +96614802555. Fax +96614802666. E-mail: info@araburban.org.
Pres/Mayor of Riyadh address not obtained.
URL: http://www.araburban.org/

History 1979, Riyadh (Saudi Arabia), acting as the technical and scientific arm of *Arab Towns Organization (ATO, #01059)*. **Aims** Support the urban development efforts of Arab *cities* and *municipalities* through specialized programs for which it solicits partnerships with local, regional and international organizations. **Structure** Executive Board; Departments; Programs. **Languages** Arabic, English. **Staff** 25.00 FTE, paid. **Finance** Sources: specially created fund; returns from exchange of services. Annual budget: about US$ 2,000,000 – 3,000,000. **Activities** Projects/programmes; capacity building; events/meetings; research/documentation; guidance/assistance/consulting; training/education. **Events** *Global city forum* Abu Dhabi (United Arab Emirates) 2011, *Global city forum* Abu Dhabi (United Arab Emirates) 2009, *Symposium on the role of training, legislations, regulations and mechanisms for their implementation in urban sustainable development / International Symposium on Knowledge Cities* Wad Medani (Sudan) 2009, *International Symposium on Knowledge Cities* Istanbul (Turkey) 2008, *International Symposium on Knowledge Cities* Shah Alam (Malaysia) 2007. **Publications** Symposium and conference proceedings; seminar reports; books; monographs. Information Services: Data centre for compilation of municipal documents, information and legislation. **Information Services** *Arab City Information Centre*; *Data centre for compilation of municipal documents, information and legislation.*
Members Covers over 550 Arab cities and towns in 22 countries and territories:
Algeria, Bahrain, Comoros, Djibouti, Egypt, Iraq, Jordan, Kuwait, Lebanon, Libya, Mauritania, Morocco, Oman, Palestine, Qatar, Saudi Arabia, Somalia, Sudan, Syrian AR, Tunisia, United Arab Emirates, Yemen.
Consultative Status Consultative status granted from: *ECOSOC (#05331)* (Ros A). **IGO Relations** Cooperates with: *International Bank for Reconstruction and Development (IBRD, #12317)*; *United Nations Human Settlements Programme (UN-Habitat, #20572)*; *United Nations Population Fund (UNFPA, #20612)*.
NGO Relations Member of:
- *Commonwealth Association for Public Administration and Management (CAPAM, #04310)*;
- *International City / County Management Association (ICMA, #12579)*;
- *International Environmetrics Society (TIES, #13284)*;
- *International Federation for Housing and Planning (IFHP, #13450)*;
- *International Road Federation (IRF Global, #14759)*;
- *International Solid Waste Association (ISWA, #15567)*;
- *International Urban Development Association (INTA, #15832)*;
- *Middle East Studies Association (MESA)*. [2019.06.20/XE2780/j/**E**]

♦ Arab-US Association for Communication Educators (AUSACE) 01072
Pres CSS Building – Office 152, Rollins College, 1000 Holt Avenue, Winter Park FL 32789, USA.
URL: https://ausace.org/
History 4 May 1995. Founded on adoption of the AUSACE Charter. **Aims** Develop professional relationships and educational exchanges among Arab and American university faculty and media professionals. **Structure** Board of Directors (meets at least annually); National Branches; Working Committees (12). **Languages** Arabic, English. **Finance** Members' dues. Other sources: grants; contributions. **Activities** Networking/liaising; projects/programmes; training/education; research/documentation; events/meetings; knowledge management/information dissemination. **Events** *Annual Conference* Lafayette, LA (USA) 2018, *Conference* Cairo (Egypt) 2017, *Annual Conference* Tangiers (Morocco) 2016, *Annual Conference* Doha (Qatar) 2015, *Annual Conference* Irbid (Jordan) 2014. **Publications** *Journal of Middle East Media (JMEM)*.
Members Full; Affiliate; Student. Individuals in 19 countries and territories:
Bahrain, Canada, Czechia, Egypt, Germany, Jordan, Kuwait, Lebanon, Libya, Morocco, Oman, Palestine, Qatar, Saudi Arabia, Syrian AR, Tunisia, UK, United Arab Emirates, USA.
NGO Relations Member of: *World Journalism Education Council (WJEC, #21602)*. [2021/XD7653/**D**]

♦ Arab Volleyball Association 01073
Contact PO Box 5176, Manama, Bahrain. Fax +97317122003. E-mail: arabvolley@gmail.com.
URL: http://www.arabvolleyball.org/
History Founded 1975, as *Arab Volleyball Confederation*. Also referred to as *Arab Volleyball Federation*.
Members in 18 countries and territories:
Algeria, Bahrain, Egypt, Iraq, Jordan, Kuwait, Lebanon, Libya, Morocco, Oman, Palestine, Qatar, Saudi Arabia, Sudan, Syrian AR, Tunisia, United Arab Emirates, Yemen. [2015/XD0941/**D**]

- ♦ Arab Volleyball Confederation / see Arab Volleyball Association (#01073)
- ♦ Arab Volleyball Federation / see Arab Volleyball Association (#01073)

♦ Arab Watch Coalition (AWC) 01074
Sec address not obtained. E-mail: info@arabwatchcoalition.org.
URL: https://arabwatchcoalition.org/
History Apr 2018. **Aims** Watchthe operations of international financial institutions in the MENA region to make sure that the development processes are inclusive, participatory, just and sustainable for all. **Structure** Board of Directors. **Activities** Advocacy/lobbying/activism; projects/programmes.
Members Full in 7 countries:
Egypt, Iraq, Jordan, Lebanon, Morocco, Tunisia, Yemen.
NGO Relations Member of (1): *Coalition for Human Rights in Development (#04061)*. Partner of (9): *Accountability Counsel*; *Bank Information Center (BIC)*; *Bretton Woods Project*; *CEE Bankwatch Network (#03624)*; *Inclusive Development International (IDI)*; *International Accountability Project (IAP)*; *Recourse (#18630)*; *Stichting Onderzoek Multinationale Ondernemingen (SOMO)*; *Urgewald*. [2023.02.20/AA2842/**D**]

♦ Arab Water Council (AWC) 01075
Contact 9 al-Mokhayam Al-Da'em St, Al-Hay Al-Sades, Nasr City, Cairo, Egypt. T. +20224023253 – +20224023276. Fax +20222600218. E-mail: awc@arabwatercouncil.org.
URL: http://arabwatercouncil.org/
History 14 Apr 2004, Cairo (Egypt). **Aims** Promote better understanding and management of *water resources* in Arab countries. **Structure** General Assembly. Governing Board. Executive Committee, comprising President, Vice-President, Treasurer, Secretary-General and 4 members. **Events** *Arab Water Reuse Convention* Dubai (United Arab Emirates) 2022, *Arab Water Forum* Dubai (United Arab Emirates) 2021, *Middle East and North Africa Business Forum* Singapore (Singapore) 2012, *Arab water forum* Cairo (Egypt) 2011, *Middle East and North Africa Business Forum* Singapore (Singapore) 2011. **Publications** *Arab Water Journal* (2 a year); *AWC Newsletter*. **IGO Relations** Member of: *Regional Remote Sensing Centre for North African States (#18807)*. **NGO Relations** Member of: *World Water Council (WWC, #21908)*. Partner of: *Sanitation and Water for All (SWA, #19051)*. [2022/XJ3156/**D**]

♦ Arab Water Network for Capacity Building (Awarenet) 01076
Contact c/o ESCWA, PO Box 11-8575, Riad el-Solh Square, Beirut, Lebanon. T. +9611981301 – +9611978802. Fax +9611981510.
NGO Relations Member of: *Network for Capacity Building in Integrated Water Resources Management (CAP-Net, #17000)*. [2011/XJ2392/**F**]

- ♦ Arab Water Ski Federation (inactive)
- ♦ Arab Weightlifting Federation (inactive)
- ♦ Arab Well Logging Company (see: #17854)
- ♦ Arab West Foundation (internationally oriented national body)
- ♦ Arab Women Centre for Training and Research, Tunis / see Center of Arab Women for Training and Research, Tunis (#03637)

♦ Arab Women Investors Union (AWIU) 01077
Main Office 55 H Hadek, El Ahram second gate, Giza, Egypt. E-mail: info@awiu.net.
URL: http://awiu.net/
History 2005, within the framework of *Council of Arab Economic Unity (CAEU, #04859)*. [2014/XM1485/**D**]

- ♦ Arab Women in Maritime Association (unconfirmed)

♦ Arab Women Organization (AWO) 01078
Dir Gen 25 Ramses Street, Korba, Heliopolis, Cairo, Egypt. T. +20224183301 – +20224183101. Fax +20224183110. E-mail: info@arabwomenorg.net.
URL: http://english.arabwomenorg.org/
History Set up when agreement came into effect, Mar 2003, under the umbrella of *League of Arab States (LAS, #16420)*, emerging from the Cairo Declaration, issued by the 1st Arab Women Summit, Nov 2000, Cairo (Egypt). **Aims** Empower Arab women and build capacities to promote progress of Arab societies; raise awareness of the necessity of engaging women as equal partners in *societal development*; coordinate Arab efforts so as to foster women *empowerment* and elevate awareness of their vital role in society. **Structure** Supreme Council; Executive Council; Advisory Committees; General Administration. **Activities** Knowledge management/information dissemination; research/documentation; events/meetings. **Events** *Conference* Cairo (Egypt) 2016, *Conference* Algeria 2013, *Conference* Tunisia 2010, *Conference* United Arab Emirates 2008, *Conference* Bahrain 2006.
Members States (16):
Algeria, Bahrain, Egypt, Iraq, Jordan, Lebanon, Libya, Mauritania, Morocco, Oman, Palestine, Sudan, Syrian AR, Tunisia, United Arab Emirates, Yemen.
IGO Relations Memorandum of Understanding with: *Arab Fund for Technical Assistance to African Countries (AFTAAC, #00966)*; *Arab Labour Organization (ALO, #01001)*; *Arab League Educational, Cultural and Scientific Organization (ALECSO, #01003)*; *Arab Organization for Agricultural Development (AOAD, #01018)*; *Islamic World Educational, Scientific and Cultural Organization (ICESCO, #16058)*; *UNEP (#20299)*; *UN Women (#20724)*; *United Nations Economic and Social Commission for Western Asia (ESCWA, #20558)*. **NGO Relations** Memorandum of Understanding with: *Center of Arab Women for Training and Research, Tunis (CAWTAR, #03637)*. [2015/XJ9297/**D***]

- ♦ Arab Women's Habitat Network (internationally oriented national body)
- ♦ Arab Women's Solidarity Association (inactive)
- ♦ Arab World Evangelical Ministers Association (internationally oriented national body)
- ♦ Arab World Evangelical Ministries Association / see Arab World Evangelical Ministers Association
- ♦ Arab World Institute (#11324)

♦ Arab World Internet Institute (AW2I) 01079
Contact 3421 University Boulevard, Ste 304, Kensington MD 20895, USA. T. +13014760910. E-mail: info@awii.org.
Regional Office 16 Avenue Tarek Ibn Zied, Menzeh 5, Tunis, Tunisia.
URL: http://www.awii.org/
Aims Conduct independent conduct research on the Internet in the Arab world. **Structure** Management Team; Advisory Board. **NGO Relations** Member of: *International Governance Forum Support Association (IGFSA, #13730)*; *Network of Internet and Society Research Centers (NoC, #17045)*. [2012/XJ5817/j/**D**]

- ♦ Arab World Ministries (internationally oriented national body)
- ♦ Arab World Regional EC Network (unconfirmed)
- ♦ Arab Wrestling Federation (inactive)
- ♦ Arab Youth Movement (see: #13327)
- ♦ Arab Youth Union (no recent information)
- ♦ **ARAC** Arab Accreditation Cooperation (#00892)
- ♦ **ARAC** Asia Regional Adhesive Council (#02083)
- ♦ **ARACD** Asian Regional Association for Career Development (#01681)
- ♦ ARACON – Asian Rabies Control Network (unconfirmed)
- ♦ ARADET – Arab Company for Detergent Chemicals (see: #17854)
- ♦ **ARADO** Arab Administrative Development Organization (#00893)
- ♦ ARAHA – American Relief Agency for the Horn of Africa (internationally oriented national body)
- ♦ **ARAHE** Asian Regional Association for Home Economics (#01682)

♦ ARA International 01080
Pres c/o ARA-CANADA, CP 47 171, Succ Sheppard, Québec QC G1S 4X1, Canada. E-mail: admin@aracanada.org.
URL: http://www.ara-international.lu/
History Jul 1982, Toulouse (France), as *Friends of Art Bookbinding, The – Amis de la reliure d'art, Les (ARA) – Freunde der Kunstbuchbinderei, Die – Amici della Rilegatura d'Arte*. Also referred to as previously as *Association internationale Les amis de la reliure d'art*. Present name and new statutes adopted at 5th International Forum, 27 Sep 1996, Montréal (Canada). Registered in accordance with Luxembourg law. **Aims** Disseminate knowledge about the *art* of *bookbinding*; encourage and help members of the profession. **Structure** General Assembly (every 2 years). Bureau, comprising International President, Treasurer, Secretary General, Treasurer and 5 members elected by General Assembly. **Languages** English, French, German, Italian. **Finance** Members' dues. **Activities** Promotes and encourages various public showings such as exhibitions, contests and fairs. Organizes *Forum international de la reliure d'art (FIRA)* (every 2-3 years). **Events** *Biennial Forum* Bruges (Belgium) 2011, *Biennial Forum* Fribourg (Switzerland) 2007, *Biennial Forum* Limoges (France) 2005, *Biennial Forum* Athens (Greece) 2002, *Biennial Forum* Venice (Italy) 1999. **Publications** *Reliure d'art* (2 a year) – bulletin. Monographs; exhibition catalogues; documents of the 'Forum international de la reliure d'art'; conference proceedings.
Members National and Regional Sections in 7 countries and territories:
Belgium, Canada, Catalunya, France, Greece, Italy, Switzerland.
National Delegates in 7 countries:
Australia, Brazil, Israel, Japan, Netherlands, Russia, USA. [2019/XF0468/**F**]

- ♦ Aram Society for Syro-Mesopotamian Studies (internationally oriented national body)
- ♦ **ARAPE** Association pour le rayonnement de l'art pariétal européen (#02886)
- ♦ Ararat International Academy of Sciences (#00030)
- ♦ ARASA – AIDS and Rights Alliance for Southern Africa (unconfirmed)
- ♦ ARASIA – Cooperative Agreement for Arab States in Asia for Research, Development and Training Related to Nuclear Science and Technology (2002 treaty)
- ♦ ARASWE / see Asian and Pacific Association for Social Work Education (#01601)
- ♦ ARAVEG / see Asian Regional Association for Career Development (#01681)
- ♦ **ARAWA** Association of Radiologists of West Africa (#02884)
- ♦ ARAZPA / see Zoo and Aquarium Association Australasia (#22039)
- ♦ ARBA / see American Road and Transportation Builders Association
- ♦ **ARBC** ASEAN Rubber Business Council (#01232)
- ♦ Arbeiter-Jugend-Internationale (inactive)
- ♦ Arbeiter Radio Internationale (inactive)
- ♦ Arbeiterwohlfahrt International (internationally oriented national body)
- ♦ Arbeitsgemeinschaft Alpen-Adria / see Alps-Adriatic-Alliance (#00747)

♦ Arbeitsgemeinschaft Alpenländer (ARGE ALP) 01081
Association des Régions des Alpes centrales – Asociación de las Regiones de los Alpes Centrales – Association of the Central Alps – Comunità di Lavoro delle Regioni Alpine
Secretariat Amt der Tiroler Landesregierung, Eduard-Wallnöfer-Platz 3, 6020 Innsbruck, Austria. T. +435125082340. Fax +43512508742345. E-mail: info@argealp.org.
URL: https://www.argealp.org/de
History 12 Oct 1972, Mösern (Austria). **Aims** Tackle common problems and concerns of member countries in ecological, cultural, social and economic fields through transfrontier *cooperation*; promote mutual understanding and European integration. **Structure** Annual Governors' Conference; Project Groups. **Languages** German, Italian. **Finance** Members participate in covering costs. **Activities** Events/meetings; awards/prizes/competitions. **Events** *Annual Governors Conference / Annual Governors' Conference* Galtür (Austria) 2013, *Annual Governors' Conference* Salzburg (Austria) 2011, *Annual governors conference* Appiano sulla Strada del Vino (Italy) 2010, *Annual governors conference / Annual Governors' Conference* Flims (Switzerland) 2009, *Annual governors conference / Annual Governors' Conference* Prien am Chiemsee (Germany) 2008. **Publications** Studies.
Members Regions (10): Bavaria, Bozen/South Tyrol, Grisons, Lombardy, Salzburg, St Gall, Ticino, Tyrol, Trento and Vorarlberg in 4 countries:
Austria, Germany, Italy, Switzerland.
NGO Relations Instrumental in setting up: *Centro di Ecologia Alpina (CEA)*. [2022/XE0411/**E**]

- ♦ Arbeitsgemeinschaft für Angewandte Humanpharmakologie (internationally oriented national body)

- Arbeitsgemeinschaft der Archivrestauratoren / see International Association of Book and Paper Conservators (#11729)
- Arbeitsgemeinschaft Deutschsprachiger Myriapodologen (unconfirmed)
- Arbeitsgemeinschaft Donauländer (#21056)
- Arbeitsgemeinschaft der Entwicklungsdienste (internationally oriented national body)
- Arbeitsgemeinschaft für Entwicklungshilfe / see AGIOMONDO
- Arbeitsgemeinschaft Entwicklungspolitische Friedensarbeit / see Arbeitsgemeinschaft Frieden und Entwicklung
- Arbeitsgemeinschaft der Europäischen Anerkannten Sachverständigen (#02538)
- Arbeitsgemeinschaft der Europäischen Gipsindustrie / see European Association of Plaster and Plaster Product Manufacturers (#06152)
- Arbeitsgemeinschaft Europäischer Berufsphotographen (inactive)
- Arbeitsgemeinschaft Europäischer Chorverbände (inactive)
- Arbeitsgemeinschaft Europäischer Grenzregionen (#02499)
- Arbeitsgemeinschaft Europäischer Junggärtner (#04376)
- Arbeitsgemeinschaft Europäischer Stadtmissionen (#06263)
- Arbeitsgemeinschaft Europäischer Trocknungsbetriebe (#06896)
- Arbeitsgemeinschaft Evangelikaler Missionen (internationally oriented national body)
- Arbeitsgemeinschaft Frieden und Entwicklung (internationally oriented national body)
- Arbeitsgemeinschaft für Friedens-und Konfliktforschung (internationally oriented national body)
- Arbeitsgemeinschaft fur Veterinärpathologen / see European Society of Veterinary Pathology (#08785)
- Arbeitsgemeinschaft des Jura / see Conférence TransJurassience
- Arbeitsgemeinschaft der Katholischen Familienorganisationen in Europa / see Federation of Catholic Family Associations in Europe (#09468)
- Arbeitsgemeinschaft von Ländern, Komitaten Regionen und Republiken des Ostalpengebiete / see Alps-Adriatic-Alliance (#00747)
- Arbeitsgemeinschaft für Osteosynthesefragen / see AO Foundation (#00866)
- Arbeitsgemeinschaft Österreichische Lateinamerikaforschung / see Lateinamerikaforschung Austria

♦ Arbeitsgemeinschaft für Pharmazeutische Verfahrenstechnik (APV) 01082

International Association for Pharmaceutical Technology – Association internationale pour la technologie pharmaceutique

Pres Inst für Pharmazeutische Technologie, Heinrich-Heide-univ Düsseldorf, Geb 26, 22 Universitätstr 1, 40225 Düsseldorf, Germany.
URL: http://www.apv-mainz.de/

History 1954. Registered in accordance with German law. **Aims** Promote international scientific cooperation; promote further education of qualified pharmaceutical personnel; encourage exchange of scientific information, results, etc; provide working guidelines for the pharmaceutical industry. **Structure** Executive Board; Headquarters; Working Groups (11). **Languages** English, German. **Staff** 10.00 FTE, voluntary. **Finance** Members' dues. Proceeds from seminars, conferences, trade fairs and consulting. **Activities** Events/meetings; awards/prizes/competitions; knowledge management/information dissemination; standards/guidelines. **Events** *World Meeting on Pharmaceutics, Biopharmaceutics and Pharmaceutical Technology* Düsseldorf (Germany) 2021, *Conference* Frankfurt-Main (Germany) 2021, *World Meeting on Pharmaceutics, Biopharmaceutics and Pharmaceutical Technology* Vienna (Austria) 2020, *Conference* Vienna (Austria) 2019, *Conference* Cologne (Germany) 2018. **Publications** *European Journal of Pharmaceutics and Biopharmaceutics* (9 a year) – official journal; *APVbasics*; *APV Pharma Reflexions*. APV paperback; guidelines.
Members Individuals in 49 countries:
Australia, Austria, Belgium, Bosnia-Herzegovina, Brazil, Bulgaria, Cameroon, Canada, Chile, China, Croatia, Czechia, Denmark, Egypt, Finland, France, Germany, Greece, Guinea, Hungary, India, Indonesia, Israel, Italy, Japan, Korea Rep, Luxembourg, Malaysia, Malta, Mexico, Namibia, Netherlands, New Zealand, Norway, Poland, Portugal, Romania, Russia, Serbia, Slovenia, South Africa, Spain, Sweden, Switzerland, Thailand, Tunisia, Türkiye, UK, USA. [2020/XD5600/v/**D**]

- Arbeitsgemeinschaft Privater Entwicklungsdienste (internationally oriented national body)
- Arbeitsgemeinschaft Regenwald und Artenschutz (internationally oriented national body)
- Arbeitsgemeinschaft der Regionen der Ostalpen / see Alps-Adriatic-Alliance (#00747)
- Arbeitsgemeinschaft der Rhein- und Maaswasserwerke / see Association of River Water Companies (#02895)
- Arbeitsgemeinschaft für Sachsenforschung / see Internationales Sachsensymposion – Arbeitsgemeinschaft zur Archäologie der Sachsen und ihrer Nachbarvölker in Nordwesteuropa (#13305)
- Arbeitsgemeinschaft von Sammlungen von Judaica und Hebraica in Europa (inactive)

♦ Arbeitsgemeinschaft Simulation (ASIM) 01083

Contact PF 1210, 23952 Wismar, Germany. T. +4938417537204. E-mail: info@asim-gi.org.
URL: http://www.asim-gi.org/

History 1981. **Aims** Act as an association for simulation in the *German-speaking* area of Europe. **Structure** Board; Gesellschaft für Informatik (GI) – unit of organization of German associations for computer science; Working Groups (4). **Languages** English, German. **Staff** None. **Finance** Sources: members' dues. **Activities** Events/meetings; knowledge management/information dissemination. **Events** *Symposium on Simulation Techniques* Bayreuth (Germany) 2020, *Symposium on Simulation Techniques* Hamburg (Germany) 2018, *Symposium on Simulation Techniques* Dresden (Germany) 2016, *Symposium on Simulation Techniques* Berlin (Germany) 2014, *Symposium on Simulation Techniques* Winterthur (Switzerland) 2011. **Publications** *Simulation Notes Europe (SNE)*. *Fortschritte in der Simulationstechnik*. *ASIM-Mitteilungen* – working group reports. Conference proceedings.
Members Individuals; companies; institutions. Members (about 680) in 3 countries:
Austria, Germany, Switzerland. [2021/XD1942/v/**D**]

- Arbeitsgemeinschaft Swissaid – Fastenopfer – Brot für Alle – Helvetas / see Alliance Sud, Swiss Alliance of Development Organisations Swissaid – Catholic Lenten Fund – Bread for All – Helvetas – Caritas – Interchurch Aid
- Arbeitsgemeinschaft Swissaid – Fastenopfer – Brot für Alle – Helvetas – Caritas / see Alliance Sud, Swiss Alliance of Development Organisations Swissaid – Catholic Lenten Fund – Bread for All – Helvetas – Caritas – Interchurch Aid
- Arbeitsgemeinschaft für Tropenpädiatrie / see Gesellschaft für Tropenpädiatrie und Internationale Kindergesundheit
- Arbeitsgemeinschaft Tropische und Subtropische Agrarforschung (internationally oriented national body)
- Arbeitsgemeinschaft der Verbände der Europäischen Schloss- und Beschlagindustrie (#07054)
- Arbeitsgemeinschaft für Werbung, Markt- und Meinungsforschung (inactive)
- Arbeitsgemeinschaft für Wissenschaft und Politik (internationally oriented national body)
- Arbeitsgruppe Alternative Wirtschaftspolitik für Europa (#06964)
- Arbeitsgruppe Friedensforschung und Europäische Sicherheitspolitik (internationally oriented national body)
- Arbeitsgruppe Naturwissenschaft und Internationale Sicherheit (internationally oriented national body)
- Arbeitskomitee der Mälzereien in der EU (#21055)
- Arbeitskomitee der Mälzereien in der EWG / see Working Committee of the Malting Industry of the EU (#21055)
- Arbeitskreis Geschichte der Nachrichtendienste (#13942)
- Arbeitskreis Historische Friedensforschung / see Arbeitskreis Historische Friedens- und Konfliktforschung
- Arbeitskreis Historische Friedens- und Konfliktforschung (internationally oriented national body)
- Arbeitskreis Lernen und Helfen in Übersee / see AKLHÜ – Netzwerk und Fachstelle für internationale Personelle Zusammenarbeit
- Arbeitskreis Telemetrie eV, The European Society of Telemetering / see The European Society of Telemetry
- Arbeitskreis Tourismus und Entwicklung (internationally oriented national body)
- Arbeitsstelle Ferntourismus im EED (internationally oriented national body)
- Arbeitsstelle Transnationale Beziehungen, Aussen- und Sicherheitspolitik (internationally oriented national body)
- Arbejdskomiten for Malterier i EU (#21055)
- Arbejkomiteen for EU Malterier / see Working Committee of the Malting Industry of the EU (#21055)
- Arbetarnas Bildningsförbund i Norden (#17377)

♦ Arbetarrörelsens Barnorganisationer i Norden (ABN) 01084

Contact c/o Sunderby Folkhögskola, Kråkbergsvägen 7, SE-954 42 Södra Sunderbyn, Sweden. E-mail: info@sunderbyfolkhogskola.se.
Facebook: https://www.facebook.com/Arbetarr%C3%B6relsens-Barnorganisation-i-Norden-534132543390829/

History 1960. Former names and other names: *Joint Committee of Scandinavian Falcon Organizations* – former; *Comité mixte des organisations scandinaves de jeunes faucons* – former. **Aims** Work with and for *children* and *youngsters*. **Structure** Congress (every 3 years). Secretariat held by the organization which has the chairmanship. **Languages** Swedish. **Staff** 0.50 FTE, paid. **Activities** Events/meetings; networking/liaising. **Events** *Triennial Congress* Oslo (Norway) 1999.
Members Representatives (2) for each of the following 5 countries and territories:
Denmark, Finland, Greenland, Norway, Sweden. [2020/XD2846/**D**]

- Arbetsgruppen för Mälterier i EU (#21055)
- ARBICA – Arab Regional Branch of the International Council on Archives (see: #12996)
- Arbitration Court of the China Chamber of International Commerce / see China International Economic and Trade Arbitration Commission
- **ARBS** Asia Reproductive Biotechnology Society (#02087)
- ARC / see Global Alliance for Rabies Control
- ARC / see Arab and African Research Centre
- **ARC2020** Agricultural and Rural Convention (#00574)
- Arca Foundation (internationally oriented national body)
- ARC – African Rainforest Conservancy (internationally oriented national body)
- **ARC** African Risk Capacity Agency (#00442)
- **ARC** Airport Regions Council (#00610)
- **ARCAL** Acuerdo Regional de Cooperación para la Promoción de la Ciencia y Tecnologia Nucleares en América Latina y el Caribe (#18772)
- **ARCAL Agreement** Regional Cooperation Agreement for the Promotion of Nuclear Science and Technology in Latin America and the Caribbean (#18772)
- ARC – American Refugee Committee (internationally oriented national body)
- ARC – Arab Resource Collective (internationally oriented national body)
- **ARCASIA** Architects Regional Council Asia (#01087)
- **ARC** Asian Research Center for Religion and Social Communication (#01686)
- ARCBC / see ASEAN Centre for Biodiversity (#01149)
- ARCB-CD – Association des Rotary clubs belges pour la coopération au développement (internationally oriented national body)
- ARCC – African Regional Computer Confederation (inactive)
- **ARCC** Architectural Research Centers Consortium (#01088)
- **ARCCNM** Asian Regional Cooperative Council for Nuclear Medicine (#01683)
- ARCCS – Asian Robotic Camp for Colorectal Surgeons (meeting series)
- **ARCEA** Association pour la route Centre Europe-Atlantique (#02899)
- ARCEDEM – African Regional Centre for Engineering Design and Manufacturing (no recent information)
- ARCH – Asian Regional Consortium for Headache (unconfirmed)
- Archbishop's Appeals Unit / see Archbishop of Sydney's Anglican Aid
- Archbishop of Sydney's Anglican Aid (internationally oriented national body)
- Archbishop of Sydney's Overseas Relief and Aid Fund / see Archbishop of Sydney's Anglican Aid
- Archconfraternity of Christian Mothers (religious order)
- Archconfraternity of the Cincture of Our Mother of Consolation, St Augustine and St Monica (religious order)
- Archconfraternity of the Mass of Reparation (religious order)

♦ L'Arche International 01085

L'Arche Internationale

Contact 25 rue Rosenwald, 75015 Paris, France. T. +33153680800. E-mail: international@larche.org.
URL: http://www.larche.org/

History 1964, France. Founded by Jean Vanier. The community comprises Christians and people of other or no faith. Former names and other names: *Fédération internationale des communautés de l'Arche* – alias. **Aims** Enable men and women with *intellectual disability* to play their full roles as citizens of the world by discovering how their unique talents can be shared to improve the quality of life of local society. **Structure** General Assembly. International Stewardship Board; International Leadership Team. A Federation of communities. **Languages** Dutch, English, French, German, Polish, Spanish. **Staff** 48.00 FTE, paid. **Finance** Sources: donations. Annual budget: 3,287 EUR (2014). **Activities** Establishes and maintains houses in neighbourhoods and towns where people with mental disabilities live together with people without disabilities. **Events** *General Assembly* Atlanta, GA (USA) 2012, *Colloque Gandhi* Montpellier (France) 1998. **Publications** *Letters of L'Arche* (3 a year) in English, French. Annual Report. **Members** Communities (157) in 37 countries. Membership countries not specified. [2022.02.04/XE3470/**E**]

- L'Arche Internationale (#01085)
- Archery Association of Europe (internationally oriented national body)
- Arche Verte / see Green Ark Committee (#10712)
- Archiconfrérie des Mères Chrétiennes (religious order)
- ARCH – International Conference on Architecture, Research, Care and Health (meeting series)
- **ARCHIPEL** Réseau européen – Théâtre contemporain pour le jeune public (#18879)
- Architectes de l'urgence (internationally oriented national body)
- Architects' Council of Central and Eastern Europe (no recent information)

♦ Architects Council of Europe (ACE) 01086

Conseil des Architectes d'Europe (CAE)

SG Rue Paul Emile Janson 29, 1050 Brussels, Belgium. T. +3225431140. Fax +3225431141. E-mail: info@ace-cae.eu.
URL: http://www.ace-cae.eu/

History 11 May 1990, Treviso (Italy). Founded by 17 organizations representing the architectural profession in the 15 countries of the European Community. Replaces *Liaison Committee of the Architects of the United Europe (inactive)*. Registration: Banque-Carrefour des Entreprises, No/ID: 0464.884.970, Start date: 1 Jan 1998, Belgium; EU Transparency Register, No/ID: 15914681331-83, Start date: 10 Mar 2009, Belgium. **Aims** Anticipate and monitor relevant policy and legislative developments at EU level so as to: architectural quality in the built environment; support sustainable development in the construction sector; ensure high standards of qualifications for architects; advocate quality in architectural practice; take full account of users needs; foster cross-border practice; enhance the image of the profession; promote architecture in Europe. **Structure** General Assembly (2 a year); Executive Board; Secretariat. **Languages** English, French. **Staff** 8.00 FTE, paid. **Finance** Members' dues. **Activities** Advocacy/lobbying/activism; standards/guidelines; events/meetings. **Events** *Climate Change And Built Heritage* Brussels (Belgium) 2021, *Workshop on Co Design for New Forms of Urban Living* Brussels (Belgium) 2020, *Conference on Quality Architecture for Sustainable and High- Performing Buildings* Brussels (Belgium) 2019, *General Assembly* Brussels (Belgium) 2018, *Workshop on Smart and Smart-Er* Brussels (Belgium) 2018. **Publications** *ACE Info* (6 a year) – newsletter. Studies; guides. **Members** Organizations, representing about 561,000 architects, in 45 Countries. Membership countries not specified. **IGO Relations** *European Commission (EC, #06633)*; *European Economic and Social Committee (EESC, #06963)*; *European Parliament (EP, #08146)*. **NGO Relations** Member of (4): *European Business Services Alliance (EBSA, #06426)*; *European Heritage Alliance 3.3 (#07477)*; *Federation of European and International Associations Established in Belgium (FAIB, #09508)*; *Global Alliance for Buildings and Construction (GlobalABC, #10187)*. Partner of (1): *European Federation of Fortified Sites (EFFORTS, #07127)*. [2020.03.03/XD2305/**D**]

Architects Regional Council
01087

alphabetic sequence excludes
For the complete listing, see Yearbook Online at

♦ Architects Regional Council Asia (ARCASIA) 01087

Conseil régional des architectes d'Asie

Registered Address 26 Eng Hoon Street, Singapore 169776, Singapore. E-mail: info@arcasia.net.
URL: http://www.arcasia.org/

History 16 Sep 1979, Jakarta (Indonesia). Founded at Inaugural Meeting, when Constitution was adopted, the ARCASIA Executive Committee having been set up during 1st Asian Regional Conference of *Commonwealth Association of Architects (CAA, #04301)*, Dec 1967, Singapore (Singapore) and Kuala Lumpur (Malaysia). Registration: Accounting and Corporate Regulatory Authority (ACRA), No/ID: 202018266H, Singapore, Singapore. **Aims** Foster and maintain professional contact, mutual cooperation and assistance among member institutes; present architects of member institutes at national and international levels; promote recognition of the architect's role in society; promote development and education of architects to serve society; promote research and technical advancement in the field of *built environment*. **Structure** Annual Meeting; Council. **Languages** English. **Staff** 2.00 FTE, voluntary. **Finance** Sources: members' dues; sponsorship. **Activities** Awards/prizes/competitions; events/meetings. Active in all member countries. **Events** *Biennial Congress* Shanghai (China) 2021, *Forum* Dhaka (Bangladesh) 2019, *Biennial Congress* Tokyo (Japan) 2018, *Biennial Congress* Hong Kong (Hong Kong) 2016, *Forum* Ayutthaya (Thailand) 2015. **Publications** *Architecture Asia Magazine (AA)* (4 a year). *13 ACGs- ARCASIA COVID-19 Guidelines* (2020) by Thana Chirapiwat and Norwina Mohd Nawawi et al – Co-authors: Manguesh Prabhugaonker, Tony S.F. Wong; *Celebrating 50 Years of ARCASIA 1969-2019* (2019) by Szue Hann Tan; *ARCASIA History Book* (2014).
Members Institutes of architects and architectural organizations in 21 countries and territories:
Bangladesh, Bhutan, Brunei Darussalam, China, Hong Kong, India, Indonesia, Japan, Korea Rep, Laos, Macau, Malaysia, Mongolia, Myanmar, Nepal, Pakistan, Philippines, Singapore, Sri Lanka, Thailand, Vietnam.
NGO Relations Cooperates with (5): *Africa Union of Architects (AUA, #00529)*; American Institute of Architects (AIA); *Architects Council of Europe (ACE, #01086)*; *International Association of Unions of Architects (IAUA, #12245)*; *Union internationale des architectes (UIA, #20419)*. [2021.09.01/XF2920/**F**]

♦ Architectural Research Centers Consortium (ARCC) 01088

Pres College of Architecture and Planning, Ball State Univ, Muncie IN 47306, USA. T. +17652855859. Fax +17652853726. E-mail: mmounaya@bsu.edu.
URL: http://www.arccweb.org/

History 1976. **Aims** Promote research in architecture and related disciplines. **Structure** Board of Directors, comprising President, Vice-President, Treasurer, Secretary, Past-President and 4 members at large. **Languages** English. **Finance** Members' dues. **Activities** Organizes: annual meeting; topical research conferences and theme sessions. Grants annual research awards: James Haecker; King Student Medal; ARCC Incentive Fund; ARCC New Researcher. **Events** *EAAE-ARCC International Conference* Miami, FL (USA) 2022, *EAAE – ARCC International Conference* Valencia (Spain) 2020, *EAAE – ARCC International Conference* Philadelphia, PA (USA) 2018, *EAAE-ARCC International Conference* Lisbon (Portugal) 2016, *EAAE-ARCC International Conference* Manoa, HI (USA) 2014. **Publications** *ARCC Newsletter* (2 a year); *ARCC Journal*.
Members Full institutes and universities; Associate individuals. Members in 5 countries:
Australia, Canada, Spain, United Arab Emirates, USA. [2008.06.01/XF4658/**F**]

♦ Architectural Research European Network Association / see Architectural Research Network (#01089)

♦ Architectural Research Network (ARENA) 01089

Contact The Bartlett School of Architecture, UCL Fac of the Built Environment, Wates House, 22 Gordon Street, London, WC1H 0QB, UK. E-mail: webmaster@arena-architecture.eu.
URL: http://www.arena-architecture.eu/

History 4 May 2013, London (UK). Former names and other names: *Architectural Research European Network Association* – alias. **Aims** Disseminate all forms of architectural research. **Activities** Events/meetings; knowledge management/information dissemination; networking/liaising. **Events** *Conference for Artistic and Architectural (Doctoral) Research* Lisbon (Portugal) 2019. **Publications** *ARENA Journal of Architectural Research (AJAR)* in English.
Members Research centre representatives from 33 institutions in 13 countries:
Austria, Belgium, Czechia, France, Ireland, Netherlands, Portugal, Serbia, Slovenia, Spain, Sweden, Switzerland, UK.
[2020.06.26/AA0367/v/**F**]

♦ Architectural Science Association (internationally oriented national body)
♦ Architecture and Development (internationally oriented national body)
♦ Architecture and Développement (internationally oriented national body)
♦ Architectures and Mechanisms for Language Processing (meeting series)
♦ Archive of Maori and Pacific Sound (internationally oriented national body)
♦ Archiveros Sin Fronteras (#01091)
♦ Archives historiques des Communautés européennes / see Historical Archives of the European Union (#10927)
♦ Archives historiques de l'Union européenne (#10927)
♦ Archives nationales d'Outre mer (internationally oriented national body)

♦ Archives Portal Europe Foundation (APEF) 01090

Registered Address Prins Willem-Alexanderhof 20, 2595 BE The Hague, Netherlands. E-mail: info@archivesportaleurope.net.
URL: https://www.archivesportaleurope.net/

History 1 Oct 2015. Former names and other names: *Stichting Archives Portal Europe Foundation* – legal name. Registration: Handelsregister, No/ID: KVK 61771767, Netherlands; EU Transparency Register, No/ID: 393578247967-97, Start date: 24 Oct 2022. **Aims** Promote the integration of the European archival heritage through digital technologies, maintaining together new standards, and collaborating to ensure the digital future of our archival institutions. **Structure** Assembly of Associates; Governing Board. Country Managers. **Activities** Research/documentation. [2022/AA2982/f/**F**]

♦ Archivistes sans Frontières (#01091)

♦ Archivists without Borders International (AwB International) 01091

Arxivers sense Fronteres – Archiveros Sin Fronteras – Archivistes sans Frontières

Contact address not obtained. E-mail: secretaria.asf@gmail.com.
URL: https://arxivers.org/

History 1998, Barcelona (Spain). **Aims** Cooperate in the sphere of archives work in countries whose documentary *heritage* is in danger of disappearing or of suffering irreversible damage, with particular emphasis on the protection of human *rights*. **Structure** International Coordination Council; Executive Committee, comprising President, Vice-President and Secretary-General.
Members Associations/entities in 11 countries:
Argentina, Bolivia, Brazil, Chile, Colombia, Ecuador, France, Mexico, Peru, Spain, Uruguay. [2023.02.21/XJ7667/**F**]

♦ Archiv der Zukunft – Netzwerk 01092

Contact Eppendorfer Landstr 46, 20249 Hamburg, Germany. T. +494046774497. Fax +494046774496. E-mail: geschaeftsstelle@adz-netzwerk.de.
URL: http://www.adz-netzwerk.de/

History 15 Jun 2007, Hamburg (Germany). Statutes adopted 15 Jun 2007; amended 5 Oct 2008, 15 Jun 2009 and 24 Mar 2012. Registered in accordance with German law. [2014/XJ8335/**F**]

♦ ARCHumankind 01093

Pres Av Paul Hymans 124/5, 1200 Brussels, Belgium.
URL: http://www.archumankind.com/

History Founded Brussels (Belgium). Full title: *ARCHumankind – Alliance to Renew Co-operation among Humankind*. Registered in accordance with Belgian law. **Aims** Gather people of diverse geographical, professional and cultural upbringing, united in their will to advance *cooperation* and *understanding*. **Structure** General Assembly; Board of Directors; Board of Advisors; Executive Director. **Languages** English, Portuguese. **Staff** 2.00 FTE, paid. **Activities** Networking/liaising. Active in Europe. **Publications** Policy briefs; reports; commentaries. **Members** Membership countries not specified. [2019.12.11/XJ2889/**F**]

♦ ARCHumankind – Alliance to Renew Co-operation among Humankind / see ARCHumankind (#01093)
♦ **ARCIC** Anglican-Roman Catholic International Commission (#00831)
♦ ARCIC I / see Anglican-Roman Catholic International Commission (#00831)
♦ ARCIC II / see Anglican-Roman Catholic International Commission (#00831)
♦ ARCIC III / see Anglican-Roman Catholic International Commission (#00831)
♦ ARC International (internationally oriented national body)
♦ ARCI RAGAZZI – Associazione Europea per il Progresso Sociale e Culturale (inactive)
♦ **ARCIS** Africa Regional Centre for Information Science (#00517)
♦ Arc Latin (#01094)
♦ Arc Llati (#01094)
♦ ARCM – Asian Research Centre for Migration (internationally oriented national body)
♦ ARCMED (internationally oriented national body)
♦ ARCOA – American Red Cross Overseas Association (internationally oriented national body)
♦ **ARCO** Arab Red Crescent and Red Cross Organization (#01033)

♦ Arco Latino 01094

Arc Latin – Arc Llati

Secretariat C/ Londres 55, Altillo, 08036 Barcelona, Spain. E-mail: secretariat@arcolatino.org.
URL: http://www.arcolatino.org/

History Founded 2002, Montpellier (France), based on the territorial cooperation experience gathered during the 1990s. Registered in accordance with Spanish law. **Aims** Defend the interests and needs of the western *Mediterranean* region and its citizens to European institutions; value and strengthen capacities and help internationalize actions and strategies of members in favour of common objectives. **Structure** General Assembly; Executive Board. Wise Committee, comprising Euro-Mediterranean experts. Permanent Secretariat, located in Barcelona (Spain). Work commissions. **Languages** Catalan, French, Italian, Spanish. **Activities** Works at political and technical level through 4 thematic commissions. *Social Cohesion* – Artistic and cultural, material and immaterial Mediterranean heritage as a vector for common values. Fields include: equal opportunities; demographic changes and migrations; intercultural and intergenerational dialogue; health and welfare; active citizenship and the rights of citizens. *Economic Cohesion* – Promotes the region, including: competitiveness, innovation and sustainable economy; promotion and internationalization of small and medium-sized business. *Territorial Cohesion* – Issues include: multilevel governance; territorial planning; local development and infrastructures connecting the Arco Latino space; climate change and adaptation to its effects; research and use of renewable energies; protection of natural areas and biodiversity; agricultural policies. Establishes institutional relations and decentralized public cooperation actions between members and other local administrations from the Mediterranean basin; participates in Euro-Mediterranean forums; collaborates with several networks of local Euro-Mediterranean governments and European institutions. **Events** *General Assembly* Barcelona (Spain) 2010, *Meeting* Barcelona (Spain) 2010, *General Assembly* Palma (Spain) 2008, *International seminar on immigration and social cohesion in Mediterranean* Palma (Spain) 2008, *Seminar / Conference* Stockholm (Sweden) 2007. **Publications** *Arc Latin Horizons* – magazine; *Enquêtes Journalistiques*; *L'Arc Latin et ses Municipalités* – local bulletin. *Etudes et Recherches*. **Members** Mediterranean local authorities including Spanish provincial councils and insular councils; French departments; Italian provinces. Membership countries not specified. **IGO Relations** Adriatic Arc; *Anna Lindh Euro-Mediterranean Foundation for the Dialogue between Cultures (Anna Lindh Foundation, #00847)*; *European Committee of the Regions (CoR, #06665)*; *European Commission (EC, #06633)*; Subsidiarity Monitoring Network (SMN). *European Confederation of Local Intermediate Authorities (#06710)*. **NGO Relations** *Agropolis International*; Governance Empowerment Mediterranean Model (GEMM); Covenant of Mayor – *Conference of Peripheral Maritime Regions of Europe (CPMR, #04638)*; *International Mediterranean Women's Forum (IMWF, #14143)*; *International Movement for the Defence of and the Right to Pleasure (Slow Food, #14194)*; national organizations. [2017/XM3666/**F**]

♦ **ARCOS** Albertine Rift Conservation Society (#00620)
♦ **ARC-PEACE** International Architects, Designers, Planners for Social Responsibility (#11666)
♦ ARCSA – Association for Rhetoric and Communication in Southern Africa (internationally oriented national body)
♦ ARCSE – African Regional Centre for Solar Energy (no recent information)
♦ ARCS – International Conference on Architecture of Computing Systems (meeting series)
♦ **ARCSSTE-E** African Regional Centre for Space Science and Technology Education – English (#00431)
♦ **ARCT** African Regional Centre of Technology (#00432)
♦ Arctic and Antarctic Research Institute (internationally oriented national body)
♦ Arctic Athabaskan Council (internationally oriented national body)
♦ Arctic Centre, Groningen (internationally oriented national body)
♦ Arctic Centre, Rovaniemi (internationally oriented national body)

♦ Arctic Circle 01095

CEO Menntavegur 1, 101 Reykjavik, Iceland. E-mail: secretariat@arcticcircle.org.
URL: http://www.arcticcircle.org/

Aims Act as a network of international dialogue and cooperation on the future of the Arctic. **Structure** Board; Secretariat. **Languages** English. **Activities** Events/meetings. **Events** *Annual Assembly* Reykjavik (Iceland) 2023, *Annual Assembly* Reykjavik (Iceland) 2022, *Annual Assembly* Reykjavik (Iceland) 2021, *Annual Assembly* Reykjavik (Iceland) 2020, *Annual Assembly* Reykjavik (Iceland) 2019. **NGO Relations** Partner of (8): *Bloomberg Philanthropies*; *Carnegie Corporation of New York*; *Conservation International (CI)*; *Eco Forum Global (EFG)*; *European Climate Foundation (ECF, #06574)*; *MacArthur Foundation*; *Rockefeller Brothers Fund (RBF)*; *World Wide Fund for Nature (WWF, #21922)*. [2021.08.31/XM8586/**F**]

♦ Arctic Coast Guard Forum (ACGF) 01096

Chair address not obtained. E-mail: acgf@lhg.is.
URL: http://www.arcticcoastguardforum.com/

History An independent, informal organization. **Aims** Foster safe, secure, and environmentally responsible *maritime* activity in the Arctic. **Structure** Chairmanship rotates in accordance with that of *Arctic Council (#01097)*. Chair; Secretariat; Working Groups. **Activities** Politics/policy/regulatory; events/meetings. **Events** *Meeting* Helsinki (Finland) 2018.
Members Countries (8):
Canada, Denmark, Finland, Iceland, Norway, Russia, Sweden, USA. [2019/XM7918/**F***]

♦ Arctic Contaminants Action Program (see: #01097)

♦ Arctic Council 01097

Secretariat Framsenteret, Postboks 6606, Stakkevollan, 9296 Tromsø, Norway. T. +4777750140. Fax +4777750501. E-mail: acs@arctic-council.org – ac-chair@arctic-council.org.
URL: http://www.arctic-council.org/

History 19 Sep 1996, Ottawa, ON (Canada). Established through Ottawa Declaration. Took over the activities of *Arctic Environmental Protection Strategy (AEPS, inactive)*. As of May 2022, Council and subsidiary body events are suspended due to the Russian invasion of Ukraine. **Aims** Provide a mechanism to address common concerns and challenges of Arctic governments and the people of the Arctic; protect the Arctic *environment* and *sustainable development* as a means of improving the economic, social and cultural well-being of the north. **Structure** Meetings of Foreign Ministers of member states and political leaders of the Permanent Participants (every 2 years). Committee of Senior Arctic Officials (SAOs). Includes *Arctic Council Indigenous Peoples' Secretariat (IPS, #01098)*. Rotating Chairmanship. Permanent Secretariat in Tromsø (Norway). Working Groups (6): *Arctic Contaminants Action Program (ACAP, see: #01097)*; *Arctic Monitoring and Assessment Programme (AMAP, #01100)*; *Conservation of Arctic Flora and Fauna (CAFF, #04728)*, including *Circumpolar Biodiversity Monitoring Program (CBMP, #03941)*; *Emergency, Prevention, Preparedness and Response (EPPR, #05437)*; *Protection of the Arctic Marine Environment (PAME, #18547)*, including *Regional Programme of Action for the Protection of the Arctic Marine Environment from Land-based Activities (RPA, #18806)*; *Working Group on Sustainable Development (SDWG, #21061)*. **Languages** English, Russian. **Staff** 12.00 FTE, paid. **Finance** Programmes are funded voluntarily by individual Arctic states. **Events** *International Symposium on the Threat of Plastics to the Arctic and Sub-Arctic Marine Environment* Reykjavik (Iceland) 2021, *International Symposium on the Threat of Plastics to the Arctic and Sub-Arctic Marine Environment* Reykjavik (Iceland) 2020, *Science and Policy Conference* Bergen (Norway) 2019, *Ministerial Meeting* Rovaniemi (Finland) 2019, *Senior Arctic Officials Plenary Meeting* Rukatunturi (Finland) 2019. **Publications** Documents; working group, task force and expert group reports and assessments.

Members Governments of 8 circumpolar countries:
Canada, Denmark, Finland, Iceland, Norway, Russia, Sweden, USA.
Permanent participants (6):
Aleut International Association (AIA); Arctic Athabaskan Council (AAC); Gwich'in Council International (GCI); Inuit Circumpolar Council (ICC, #15995); Russian Association of Indigenous Peoples of the North (RAIPON); Saami Council (#19012).
Observing Governments (13):
China, France, Germany, India, Italy, Japan, Korea Rep, Netherlands, Poland, Singapore, Spain, Switzerland, UK.
Observing organizations (23):
- *Advisory Committee on Protection of the Sea (ACOPS, #00139);*
- *Arctic Institute of North America (AINA, #01099);*
- *Association of World Reindeer Herders (WRH, #02985);*
- *Circumpolar Conservation Union (CCU);*
- *International Arctic Science Committee (IASC, #11668);*
- *International Arctic Social Sciences Association (IASSA, #11669);*
- *International Council for the Exploration of the Sea (ICES, #13021);*
- *International Federation of Red Cross and Red Crescent Societies (#13526);*
- *International Maritime Organization (IMO, #14102);*
- *International Union for Circumpolar Health (IUCH, #15764);*
- *International Union for Conservation of Nature and Natural Resources (IUCN, #15766);*
- *International Work Group for Indigenous Affairs (IWGIA, #15907);*
- *Nordic Council of Ministers (NCM, #17260);*
- *Nordic Environment Finance Corporation (NEFCO, #17281);*
- *North Atlantic Marine Mammal Commission (NAMMCO, #17573);*
- *Northern Forum, The (#17592);*
- *Oceana;*
- *OSPAR Commission for the Protection of the Marine Environment of the North-East Atlantic (OSPAR Commission, #17905);*
- *Standing Committee of Parliamentarians of the Arctic Region (SCPAR, #19958);*
- *UNDP (#20292);*
- *UNEP (#20299);*
- *United Nations Economic Commission for Europe (UNECE, #20555);*
- *University of the Arctic (UArctic, #20696);*
- *West Nordic Council (#20925);*
- *World Meteorological Organization (WMO, #21649);*
- *World Wide Fund for Nature (WWF, #21922).* [2022/XD5969/y/**D***]

♦ Arctic Council Indigenous Peoples' Secretariat (IPS) 01098

Exec Sec Fram Centre, Postboks 6606 Langnes, 9296 Tromsø, Norway. T. +4777750158. E-mail: elle.merete@arctic-council.org.
URL: http://www.arcticpeoples.org/

History Founded as *AEPS Indigenous Peoples' Secretariat.* Integrates activities of *Arctic Environmental Protection Strategy (AEPS, inactive)* within *Arctic Council (#01097).* Operations commenced 1994. **Aims** Provide support to 6 Indigenous Peoples Organizations with permanent status in the Arctic Council, particularly on issues of sustainable development and *environmental* protection in the *Arctic.* **Structure** Governing Board; Secretariat. **Languages** English. **Staff** 2.00 FTE, paid. **Finance** Contributions from authorities of Denmark, Greenland, Finland, Norway and Canada. [2017/XE3856/**E**]

- ♦ Arctic Council – Protection Arctic Marine Environment / see Protection of the Arctic Marine Environment (#18547)
- ♦ Arctic Council Working Group on Protection of the Arctic Marine Environment / see Protection of the Arctic Marine Environment (#18547)
- ♦ Arctic Frontiers (internationally oriented national body)
- ♦ The Arctic Institute (internationally oriented national body)
- ♦ The Arctic Institute – Center for Circumpolar Security Studies / see The Arctic Institute

♦ Arctic Institute of North America (AINA) 01099

Exec Dir Univ of Calgary, 2500 University Drive NW, Calgary AB T2N 1N4, Canada. T. +14032207515. Fax +14032824609. E-mail: arctic@ucalgary.ca.
URL: https://www.arctic.ucalgary.ca/

History 1945, Montréal, QC (Canada). Founded at McGill University. Moved, 1976, to University of Calgary (Canada). **Aims** Operate in the fields of natural and social sciences and the humanities in the Arctic, Subarctic, Alpine and cold regions; contribute to understanding of the North through research, teaching and information dissemination. **Structure** Board of Directors. **Languages** English. **Staff** 10.00 FTE, paid. **Finance** Sources: government support; members' dues. Government of Canada; Government of Alberta. **Activities** Awards/prizes/competitions; events/meetings; research and development. **Events** *Inuit studies conference* 2004. **Publications** *Arctic* (4 a year). *Northern Lights.* Annual Report; books; technical and research papers; proceedings of conferences and symposia.
Members Individual regular; retired; student; life. Organizational subscribing; corporate associate. Members in 22 countries and territories:
Australia, Belgium, Canada, China, Denmark, Finland, France, Germany, Hong Kong, Iceland, India, Israel, Italy, Japan, Mexico, Netherlands, Norway, Russia, Sweden, Switzerland, UK, USA.
IGO Relations Observer status with (1): *Arctic Council (#01097).* **NGO Relations** Partner of (1): *INTERACT – International Network for Terrestrial Research and Monitoring in the Arctic (INTERACT, #11377).* [2023.02.24/XE3971/j/**E**]

- ♦ Arctic Marine Ecosystem Research Network (internationally oriented national body)
- ♦ Arctic Methane Emergency Group (unconfirmed)

♦ Arctic Monitoring and Assessment Programme (AMAP) 01100

AMAP Secretariat The Fram Centre, PO Box 6606 Langnes, 9296 Tromsø, Norway. T. +4721080480. E-mail: amap@amap.no.
Street address Hjalmar Johansens gate 14, 9007 Tromsø, Norway.
URL: http://www.amap.no/

History Jun 1991, Rovaniemi (Finland). Established at 1st Arctic Ministerial Conference, to implement parts of the *Arctic Environmental Protection Strategy (AEPS, inactive),* adopted by governments of the eight circumpolar nations (Canada, Denmark, Finland, Iceland, Norway, Russian Federation, Sweden and USA). AEPS and its programme groups, including AMAP, were incorporated, 1997, within the responsibility of the *Arctic Council (#01097).* May take up some of the activities of the former *Arctic Climate Impact Assessment (ACIA, inactive).* **Aims** Monitor and assess the status of the Arctic region with respect to pollution and climate change issues; document levels and trends, pathways and processes, and effects on ecosystems and humans, and propose actions to reduce associated threats for consideration by governments; produce sound science-based, policy-relevant assessments and public outreach products to inform policy and decision-making processes. **Languages** English. **Finance** Much of the implementation of AMAP monitoring and assessment work is funded at national level within participating countries. AMAP is additionally financed by voluntary contributions from some of its members, cooperating/observer countries and international organizations. Voluntary contributions mainly provided to fund specific projects and cover some costs related to Programmes's monitoring and assessment work. Secretariat financed mainly by the Norwegian Government. **Activities** Monitoring/evaluation. **Events** *Meeting* Helsinki (Finland) 2018, *Snow, Water, Ice and Permafrost in the Arctic Workshop* Helsinki (Finland) 2018, *Working Group Meeting* Kiruna (Sweden) 2018, *Meeting on the Environmental Scientific Work of the Arctic Council* Helsinki (Finland) 2017, *Meeting* Helsinki (Finland) 2017. **NGO Relations** Partner of (1): *INTERACT – International Network for Terrestrial Research and Monitoring in the Arctic (INTERACT, #11377).* Participates in: *Global Terrestrial Observing Network (GT-Net, no recent information).* [2020.09.10/XE2315/y/**E***]

- ♦ Arctic and Mountain Regions Development Institute (internationally oriented national body)
- ♦ ArcticNet Student Association (internationally oriented national body)
- ♦ Arctic Pelvic Floor Meeting (meeting series)

♦ Arctic Regional Hydrographic Commission (ARHC) 01101

Commission hydrographique régionale de l'Arctique (CHRA)

Vice-Chair Canadian Hydrographic Services, Fisheries and Oceans Canada, 200 Kent Street, 13th Fl – Station 13E228, Ottawa ON K1A 0E6, Canada. E-mail: info@iho.int.
URL: http://www.iho.int/

History Oct 2010, Ottawa ON (Canada), as regional hydrographic commission of *International Hydrographic Organization (IHO, #13825).* **Aims** Promote technical cooperation in the domain of hydrographic surveying, marine cartography and nautical information; examine the implications in the Arctic Ocean Region of matters of general interest; stimulate the widening of hydrographic activity in the Arctic Ocean Region and encourage seeking technical advice and assistance in establishing and strengthening hydrographic capabilities; define the needs for new hydrographic products and services; facilitate information exchange and aid in the planning and organization of hydrographic activities. **Structure** Plenary Conference. Chair; Vice-Chair. Secretariat. **Languages** English. **Events** *Meeting* St Petersburg (Russia) 2015, *Special Meeting* Monte Carlo (Monaco) 2014, *Meeting* Portsmouth, NH (USA) 2014, *Meeting* Tromsø (Norway) 2012, *Meeting* Copenhagen (Denmark) 2011.
Members Governments (5):
Canada, Denmark, Norway, Russia, USA.
Observers (2):
Finland, Iceland. [2014/XJ5154/**E***]

- ♦ Arctic Region Foundation of Vocational Training / see Arctic Vocational Foundation (#01102)
- ♦ Arctic Science Ministerial (meeting series)

♦ Arctic Vocational Foundation 01102

Stiftelsen Utbildning Nordkalotten – Utbildning Nord

Postal Address Stiftelsen Utbildning Nord, Box 42, SE-957 21 Övertorneå, Sweden. T. +4692775100. Fax +4692775120. E-mail: info@utbnord.se.
URL: http://www.utbnord.se/

History 1991. Has also been referred to as *Arctic Region Foundation of Vocational Training* and *Education North.* **Aims** Promote *labour market* education, especially in the north of the *Nordic* countries. **Languages** English, Finnish, Norwegian, Swedish. **Finance** Budget (annual): Swedish Kr 70 million. **Activities** Training/education.
Members A common institution of 3 countries:
Finland, Norway, Sweden.
IGO Relations *Nordic Council of Ministers (NCM, #17260).* [2016.06.01/XF5113/f/**F**]

- ♦ Arctisch Centrum, Groningen (internationally oriented national body)
- ♦ ARCTOS Research Network – Arctic Marine Ecosystem Research Network (internationally oriented national body)
- ♦ **ARC-WH** Arab Regional Centre for World Heritage (#01035)
- ♦ ARDA – African Radio Drama Association (internationally oriented national body)
- ♦ **ARDA** Alliance for Reform and Democracy in Asia (#00716)
- ♦ ARDA Development Communication Inc / see African Radio Drama Association
- ♦ ARDA / see HAI – Asia-Pacific (#10852)
- ♦ ARDC – African Refugee Development Center (internationally oriented national body)
- ♦ ARDD – Arab Renaissance for Democracy and Development (internationally oriented national body)
- ♦ ARDIFLE – Association pour la recherche didactique du français langue étrangère (internationally oriented national body)
- ♦ **ARDIN** Association for Research in Digital Interactive Narratives (#02892)
- ♦ **AREA** African Renewable Energy Alliance (#00439)
- ♦ **AREA** Air Conditioning and Refrigeration European Association (#00601)
- ♦ AREA – Augmented Reality for Enterprise Alliance (internationally oriented national body)
- ♦ **ARE** Alliance for Rural Electrification (#00719)
- ♦ Area Maritima del Atlantico Sur (#19750)
- ♦ **ARE** Asamblea de las Regiones de Europa (#02316)
- ♦ **ARE** Assemblea delle Regioni d'Europa (#02316)
- ♦ **ARE** Assemblée des régions d'Europe (#02316)
- ♦ Area Study Centre for Africa, North and South America (internationally oriented national body)
- ♦ Area Study Centre for Europe, Karachi (internationally oriented national body)
- ♦ **AREC** Adriatic Region Employers' Centre (#00122)
- ♦ **ARECOP** Asia Regional Cookstove Programme (#02084)
- ♦ **AREF** African Refugees Foundation (#00430)
- ♦ **AREFLH** Assemblée des Régions Européennes Fruitières, Légumières et Horticoles (#02314)
- ♦ AREGNET – Arab Regulators Network (unconfirmed)
- ♦ AREK / see Esperanto-Ligo Filatelista (#05545)
- ♦ ARELA – Asociación de Reaseguradores Latinoamericanos (no recent information)
- ♦ ARELAP – Asociación Regional Latinoamericana de Puertos de Pacifico (inactive)
- ♦ **ARENA** Architectural Research Network (#01089)
- ♦ **ARENA** Asian Regional Exchange for New Alternatives (#01684)
- ♦ AREN – Arab Region Ecotechnie Network (see: #05333)
- ♦ **ARENOTECH** Association européen art éducation – nouvelles technologies (#02553)
- ♦ **AREPO** Association des Régions Européennes des Produits d'Origine (#02890)
- ♦ AREP – WMO Atmospheric Research and Environment Programme (see: #21649)
- ♦ **ARERT** Association du Réseau Européen des Registres Testamentaires (#07984)
- ♦ ARES Conference – International Conference on Availability, Reliability and Security (meeting series)
- ♦ ARES Group – Armament Industry European Research Group (unconfirmed)
- ♦ **AREV** Asamblea de las Regiones Europeas Vitícolas (#02317)
- ♦ **AREV** Assemblea delle Regioni Europee Viticole (#02317)
- ♦ **AREV** Assemblée des régions européennes viticoles (#02317)
- ♦ **AREV** Assembleia das Regiões Européias Viticolas (#02317)
- ♦ **AREV** Assembly of European Wine Regions (#02317)
- ♦ **AREV** Sinelevsi Evropaikon Ampeloinikon Periohon (#02317)
- ♦ **AREV** Versammlung der Europäischen Weinbauregionen (#02317)
- ♦ **ARF** ASEAN Regional Forum (#01228)
- ♦ ARF – Asian Resource Foundation (internationally oriented national body)
- ♦ **ARF** Asian Rowing Federation (#01687)
- ♦ **ARF** Asia Racquetball Federation (#02082)
- ♦ **ARFE** Asociación de Regiones Fronterizas Europeas (#02499)
- ♦ **ARFE** Associação das Regiões Fronteiriças Europaias (#02499)
- ♦ **ARFE** Association des Régions Frontalières Européennes (#02499)
- ♦ ARFFWG – Aircraft Rescue and Fire Fighting Working Group (internationally oriented national body)
- ♦ ARFID / see Asia Pacific Foundation for Infectious Diseases
- ♦ **ARFIE** Association de recherche et de formation sur l'insertion en Europe (#02887)
- ♦ ARF / see Latin American Reserve Fund (#16367)
- ♦ ARFO – ASEAN-ROK Film Cooperation Organisation (unconfirmed)
- ♦ ARFU / see Asia Rugby (#02089)
- ♦ **ARGA** Alliance for Rebuilding Governance in Africa (#00715)
- ♦ ARG / see ASEAN Rhinology Society (#01231)
- ♦ **ARGE ALP** Arbeitsgemeinschaft Alpenländer (#01081)
- ♦ **ARGE** Arbeitsgemeinschaft Donauländer (#21056)
- ♦ **ARGE** Europäische ARGE Landenentwicklung und Dorferneuerung (#05748)
- ♦ **ARGE** European Federation of Associations of Locks and Builders Hardware Manufacturers (#07054)
- ♦ Argentine Council for International Relations (internationally oriented national body)
- ♦ Argidius Foundation (internationally oriented national body)
- ♦ **ARHC** Arctic Regional Hydrographic Commission (#01101)
- ♦ ARHC – Asia Remote Health Committee (unconfirmed)
- ♦ ARHRP / see Hydrocarbon and Rosin Resins Producers Association (#10996)
- ♦ Århus Convention – Convention on Access to Information, Public Participation in Decision-making and Access to Justice in Environmental Matters (1998 treaty)

ARI
01102
alphabetic sequence excludes
For the complete listing, see Yearbook Online at

- ARI / see Association Réalités et Relations Internationales
- **ARIA** Allergic Rhinitis and its Impact on Asthma Initiative (#00648)
- ARIA – Americas Research Industry Alliance (unconfirmed)
- **ARIACO** Asia Region International Association of Cooperating Organizations (#02085)
- Ariadne / see Ariadne – European Funders for Social Change and Human Rights (#01103)
- **Ariadne** Ariadne – European Funders for Social Change and Human Rights (#01103)

♦ Ariadne – European Funders for Social Change and Human Rights (Ariadne) 01103

Dir 17 Oval Way, London, SE11 5RR, UK.
URL: http://ariadne-network.eu/

History 2009, by European donors, as *European Human Rights Funders Network (Ariadne)*. A project of *Global Dialogue*. **Aims** Strengthen *philanthropy*, help funders act strategically and encourage new donors to enter the field with maximum impact. **Structure** Offices in London (UK) and Brussels (Belgium). **Languages** English. **Staff** 4.00 FTE, paid. **Finance** Support from several donors, including: *American Jewish World Service (AJWS); Charles Stewart Mott Foundation; Fondation Charles Léopold Mayer pour le progrès de l'homme (FPH, #09815); Oak Foundation; Open Society Foundations (OSF, #17763); Sigrid Rausing Trust*; Zennström Philanthropies. **Activities** Networking/liaising; training/education; events/meetings. **Publications** *Ariadne Forecast* (annual). Studies; guides; knowledge tools. **Members** Donors (582) from 22 countries. Membership countries not specified. [2019.04.25/XJ6865/F]

- **ARIAE** Asociación Iberoamericana de Entidades Reguladoras de la Energia (#02139)
- **ARI** African Rehabilitation Institute (#00437)
- ARIA International – African Relief in Action (internationally oriented national body)
- **ARI** Arab Reform Initiative (#01034)
- Arias Foundation for Peace and Human Progress (internationally oriented national body)
- **ARI** Asian Rural Institute – Rural Leaders Training Center (#01688)
- ARI – Asia Research Institute (internationally oriented national body)
- ARI – Aussie Rules International (internationally oriented national body)

♦ Arica Institute 01104

Office Manager PO Box 645, Kent CT 06757, USA. T. +18609271006. Fax +18609271007. E-mail: contact@arica.org – orders@arica.org – admin@arica.org.
Street Address 10 Landmark Lane, Kent Green, Kent CT 06757-1526, USA.
URL: https://www.arica.org/

History 1971, New York, NY (USA). Founded by Oscar Ichazo. Former names and other names: *The Arica School* – alias; *Arica Institute in America* – former. Registration: USA. **Aims** Foster harmonious *social transformation* through harmonious *personal transformation*. **Structure** Arica Institute and a worldwide network of independent organizers and sponsors. **Activities** Training/education. **Publications** *Arica Day of Unity Report* (12 a year). Training manuals; visual aids; audiocassettes.
Members Training centers (37, mainly in USA) in 20 countries:
Argentina, Australia, Brazil, Canada, Chile, France, Germany, Greece, Ireland, Israel, Netherlands, Puerto Rico, South Africa, Spain, Sweden, Switzerland, Thailand, UK, Uruguay, USA. [2022.10.20/XF0314/j/F]

- Arica Institute in America / see Arica Institute (#01104)
- The Arica School / see Arica Institute (#01104)
- **ARIC** Association pour la recherche interculturelle (#02888)
- ARICEA – Association of Regulators of Information and Communications for Eastern and Southern Africa (no recent information)
- ARICSA – Association of Retired International Civil Servants, Austria (internationally oriented national body)
- **ARID** Association Régionale pour l'Irrigation et le Drainage en Afrique de l'Ouest et du Centre (#02889)

♦ Arid Lands Information Network – Eastern Africa (ALIN- East Africa) 01105

Réseau d'information des terres arides de l'Afrique de l'est (RITA-Afrique de l'est)
Regional Dir PO Box 10098-00100 GPO, Nairobi, Kenya. T. +254202731557. Fax +254202737813. E-mail: info@alin.net.
Street Address AAYMCA Bldg, State House Crecent, off State House Avenue, Nairobi, Kenya.
URL: http://www.alin.net/

History 1988, Dakar (Senegal). **Aims** Improve livelihoods of arid land communities in East Africa through delivery of practical information using modern technologies. **Structure** Regional organizations throughout Africa. Headquarters in Nairobi (Kenya); Country office in Uganda. **Languages** English. **Staff** 25.00 FTE, paid. **Finance** Donations; legacies. Budget (annual): over US$ 1 million. **Activities** Knowledge management/information dissemination; training/education; events/meetings; networking/liaising. Disseminates information on best development practice. **Publications** *Baobab* – newsletter; *Joto Africa* – newsletter.
Members Individuals in 3 countries:
Kenya, Tanzania UR, Uganda. [2016/XF3626/v/F]

- ARIE – Association des régions industrielles européennes (inactive)

♦ Ariel Foundation International (AFI) 01106

CEO Chemin des Papillons 4, 1216 Geneva, Switzerland. T. +41225349441.
URL: http://arielfoundation.org/

History Registered in accordance with US, Swiss, French and Lithuanian laws. **Aims** Promote participation and partnerships, peace and prosperity through *entrepreneurship*. **Structure** Board of Directors; Executive Management; International Advisory Board. **Languages** English, French. **Staff** 2.00 FTE, paid. **Finance** Donations. **Activities** Training/education; networking/liaising; events/meetings. **Publications** Reports; videos. **Consultative Status** Consultative status granted from: *ECOSOC (#05331)* (Special). **NGO Relations** Member of: *Eurochild (#05657)*. Links with national associations. [2021/XM4946/f/F]

- **ARIG** Arab Insurance Group (#00988)
- Arigatou Foundation / see Arigatou International
- Arigatou International (internationally oriented national body)
- ARII – African Rights Initiative International (internationally oriented national body)
- **ARIJ** Arab Reporters for Investigative Journalism (#01036)
- ARiMI – Asia Risk Management Institute (internationally oriented national body)
- **ARIN-AP** Asset Recovery Interagency Network – Asia Pacific (#02320)
- **ARIN-CARIB** Asset Recovery Inter-Agency Network for the Caribbean (#02321)

♦ ARINSA 01107

Contact 1059 Francis Baard Street, Hatfield, Pretoria, 0028, South Africa. T. +27124320820. E-mail: fitz-roy.drayton@un.org.
URL: https://new.arinsa.org/

History Founded 2009, as an informal network. Full title: *Asset Recovery Inter-Agency Network for Southern Africa*. **Aims** Increase the effectiveness of members' efforts, on a multi-agency basis, in depriving criminals of instrumentalities of crime and illicit profits. **Activities** Knowledge management/information dissemination.
Members Participating countries (16):
Angola, Botswana, Eswatini, Kenya, Lesotho, Madagascar, Malawi, Mauritius, Mozambique, Namibia, Seychelles, South Africa, Tanzania UR, Uganda, Zambia, Zimbabwe.
IGO Relations *United Nations Office on Drugs and Crime (UNODC, #20596)*. **NGO Relations** Observer to: *Asset Recovery Interagency Network – Asia Pacific (ARIN-AP, #02320)*. [2019/XM8743/F]

- ARIN-WA – Asset Recovery Inter-Agency Network for West Africa (unconfirmed)
- ARIN-WCA – Asset Recovery Inter-Agency Network in West and Central Asia (unconfirmed)
- **ARIPO** African Regional Intellectual Property Organization (#00434)
- ARIPO Protocol for the Protection of New Varieties of Plants (2015 treaty)

♦ ARISE 01108

Address not obtained.
URL: https://www.ariseglobalnetwork.org/

History 2015. Founded by *United Nations Office for Disaster Risk Reduction (UNDRR, #20595)*. Former names and other names: *ARISE – the Private Sector Alliance for Disaster Resilient Societies (ARISE)* – full title. **Aims** Support the private sector to become a key partner in reducing disaster risk. **Structure** Led by *United Nations Office for Disaster Risk Reduction (UNDRR, #20595)*. Board; National Networks. **Members** Private sector companies (over 300). Membership countries not specified. **NGO Relations** Member of (1): *Coalition for Disaster Resilient Infrastructure (CDRI)*. [2021/AA2166/E]

- ARISE – the Private Sector Alliance for Disaster Resilient Societies / see ARISE (#01108)
- **ARISF** Association of the IOC Recognized International Sports Federations (#02767)
- **ARISI** Association Rorschach Internationale pour le Système Intégré (#04421)
- Aristides Calvani Institute / see Instituto de Formación Demócrata Cristiana

♦ Aristotelian Society (AS) 01109

Managing Editor Univ of London, Senate House, Malet Street, London, WC1 7HU, UK. E-mail: mail@aristoteliansociety.org.uk.
Hon Dir c/o Univ College London, Dept of Philosophy, Fac of Arts and Humanities, Room 402, 4th Floor, 19 Gordon Square, London, WC1H 0AW, UK. T. +442079793069.
URL: http://www.aristoteliansociety.org.uk/

History 1880. UK Registered Charity. **Aims** Advance public education in the field of *philosophy* and publish proceedings to this end. **Structure** Council; Executive Committee. **Languages** English. **Staff** 1.00 FTE, paid. **Finance** Members' dues. Sale of publications. **Activities** Events/meetings; publishing activities. **Events** *Annual Philosophy Joint Session* Warwick (UK) 2015, *Conference* Exeter (UK) 2013, *Conference* Stirling (UK) 2012, *Conference* UK 2011, *Annual philosophy joint session / Conference* Dublin (Ireland) 2010. **Publications** *Aristotelian Society Proceedings* – journal; *Supplementary Volume* – journal. Series of books.
Members 5 categories of membership. Individuals in 41 countries:
Antigua-Barbuda, Argentina, Australia, Bahamas, Bangladesh, Barbados, Belgium, Brazil, Bulgaria, Canada, Denmark, Finland, France, Germany, Greece, Hungary, India, Iran Islamic Rep, Ireland, Israel, Italy, Japan, Lesotho, Malaysia, Mexico, Netherlands, New Zealand, Norway, Philippines, Poland, Portugal, Saudi Arabia, Singapore, South Africa, Spain, Sweden, Switzerland, Trinidad-Tobago, Türkiye, UK, USA. [2018.06.01/XE3316/E]

- ARJORA – Association des réalisateurs de journaux ruraux africains (inactive)
- Ark Foundation of Africa (internationally oriented national body)
- Arko Cooperation (internationally oriented national body)
- ARKO-Samarbeidet (internationally oriented national body)
- Arko-Samarbetet (internationally oriented national body)
- Arktinen keskus (internationally oriented national body)
- Arktisen Lääketieteen Pohjoismainen Yhteistyökomitea (inactive)
- Arktiswissenschaftsministerkonferenz (meeting series)
- **ARLAC** African Regional Labour Administration Centre, Harare (#00435)
- ARLAC – Asociación de Refugiados de Latinoamérica y del Caribe (internationally oriented national body)
- ARL – Akademie für Raumforschung und Landesplanung (internationally oriented national body)
- ARLE / see Europe plurilingue
- **ARLE** International Association for Research in L1 Education (#12135)
- **ARLEM** Assemblée Régionale et Locale Euro-Méditerranéenne (#02313)
- ARLIS NORDEN (internationally oriented national body)
- ARLO – Arab Regional Literacy Organization (inactive)
- **ARMA** ASEAN Rehabilitation Medicine Association (#01230)
- ARMA – Association of Rotational Moulders Australasia (internationally oriented national body)
- ARMA International (internationally oriented national body)
- ARM – Alliance réformée mondiale (inactive)
- ARM – Alliance for Regenerative Medicine (internationally oriented national body)
- **ARM** Alliance for Responsible Mining (#00717)
- Armament Industry European Research Group (unconfirmed)
- Armaments and Research Agency / see European Defence Agency (#06895)
- ARMAO – Association pour la recherche médicale en Afrique de l'Ouest (inactive)
- ARM – Association routière maghrébine (no recent information)
- ARM-CE – Association of Rotational Moulding – Central Europe (internationally oriented national body)
- Armed Conflict Location & Event Data Project (internationally oriented national body)
- Armed Forces Communications and Electronics Association International (internationally oriented national body)
- Arme Dienstmägde Jesu Christi (religious order)
- Armée du salut (#19041)
- Armen-Brüder vom Heiligen Franziskus Seraphikus (religious order)

♦ Armenian General Benevolent Union (AGBU) 01110

Pres 55 E 59th St, New York NY 10022-1112, USA. T. +12123196383. Fax +12123196507. E-mail: agbuny@agbu.org.
URL: http://www.agbu.org/

History 1906, Cairo (Egypt). **Aims** Preserve and promote the Armenian identity and *heritage* through educational, cultural and humanitarian programs. **Structure** General Assembly (every 2 years). Central Board of Directors. *AGBU Europe*. **Languages** Armenian, English, French. **Staff** 27.00 FTE, paid. **Finance** Sources: endowment; general contributions; tuition income; portfolio investment income. Annual budget: US$ 46,000,000. **Activities** Training/education; events/meetings. **Events** *World chapters and members meeting* Los Angeles, CA (USA) 1996. **Publications** *Desilk* (12 a year); *Mioutune* (12 a year); *Ararat* (4 a year) – literary and arts magazine; *Deghegadou* (4 a year); *Khosnag* (4 a year); *Generación* (3 a year); *Hoosharar* (2 a year); *Revue Arménienne des Questions Contemporaines* (2 a year); *AGBU News Magazine* (2-3 a year). Books.
Members Individuals (about 22,000) in 24 countries:
Argentina, Armenia, Australia, Austria, Belgium, Brazil, Bulgaria, Canada, Cyprus, Egypt, Ethiopia, France, Greece, Iran Islamic Rep, Iraq, Italy, Lebanon, Netherlands, South Africa, Switzerland, Syrian AR, UK, Uruguay, USA.
IGO Relations Associated with DPI of United Nations. [2017.03.09/XF3517/v/F]

- Armenian International Women's Association (internationally oriented national body)

♦ Armenian Relief Society (ARS) 01111

Exec Dir 80 Bigelow Ave, Suite 300, Watertown MA 02472, USA. T. +16179265892. Fax +16179264855. E-mail: ceb@ars1910.org – execdirector@ars1910.org.
URL: http://ars1910.org/

History 1910, New York, NY (USA). Founded by the union of numerous relief and aid groups formed to assisting their compatriots throughout the world. Registration: Department of Corporations and Taxation, No/ID: 04-2219512, Start date: 29 May 1939, USA, MA. **Aims** Preserve the *cultural identity* of the Armenian people worldwide; serve the *humanitarian* needs of all communities that may require emergency aid, regardless of ethnic origin or religious affiliation; promote the educational, social, health and welfare of communities; encourage participation in local organizations engaged in community activities and social services compatible with the principle of the Society. **Structure** International Convention (every 4 years), elects Central Executive Board of Directors. **Languages** Arabic, Armenian, English, French, Irish Gaelic, Spanish. **Staff** 1.00 FTE, paid. **Finance** Sources: contributions; donations; gifts, legacies; government support; grants; members' dues. Supported by: *Norwegian Refugee Council (NRC); United States Agency for International Development (USAID); World Food Programme (WFP, #21510)*. Annual budget: 1,250,000 USD. **Activities** Financial and/or material support; projects/programmes; training/education. **Events** *International Convention* Montréal, QC (Canada) 2019, *International Convention* Yerevan (Armenia) 2015, *International Convention* Athens (Greece) 2011, *International Convention* Yerevan (Armenia) 2008, *International Convention* Canada 2005. **Publications** *Hai Sird* – international multilingual periodical. News bulletins; brochures.
Members Organizations, totaling about 15,000 members, in 26 countries:
Argentina, Armenia, Australia, Belgium, Brazil, Bulgaria, Canada, Cyprus, Egypt, France, Georgia, Germany, Greece, Israel, Jordan, Kuwait, Lebanon, Palestine, Russia, Sweden, Switzerland, Syrian AR, UK, United Arab Emirates, Uruguay, USA.

Consultative Status Consultative status granted from: *ECOSOC (#05331)* (Ros A). **IGO Relations** Accredited by (2): *UNICEF (#20332)*; *WHO (#20950)*. Associated with Department of Global Communications of the United Nations. [2021.06.03/XE6142/**E**]

♦ Armen Schwestern vom Heiligen Franziskus (religious order)
♦ Armenseelenschwestern (religious order)
♦ Arme Schulschwestern von Unserer Lieben Frau (religious order)
♦ **ARMFA** African Road Maintenance Funds Association (#00443)
♦ **ARMICO** Arab Mining Company (#01008)
♦ ARMIF – Asociación Regional para las Migraciones Forzadas (no recent information)
♦ **ARM International** Association of Rotational Molders International (#02897)
♦ **ARMO** Affiliation of Rotational Moulding Organisations (#00149)
♦ ARMSA – Association of Rotational Moulders of Southern Africa (internationally oriented national body)
♦ **ARMS** Australasian Research Management Society (#03027)
♦ ARMS – Australian Relief and Mercy Services (internationally oriented national body)
♦ Arms Trade Treaty (2013 treaty)
♦ **ARNA** Action Research Network of the Americas (#00096)
♦ **ArNano** Arab Network on Nanotechnology (#01012)
♦ ARN – Association pour la recherche en neuroéducation (internationally oriented national body)
♦ ARN – Association for Research in Neuroeducation (internationally oriented national body)
♦ **ARNEC** Asia-Pacific Regional Network for Early Childhood (#02009)
♦ Arnold Bergstraesser Institute pour les recherches socio-culturelles (internationally oriented national body)
♦ Arnold Bergstraesser Institute for Social-Cultural Research (internationally oriented national body)
♦ Arnold Bergstraesser Institut für Kulturwissenschaftliche Forschung (internationally oriented national body)
♦ ARNOVA – Association for Research on Nonprofit Organizations and Voluntary Action (internationally oriented national body)
♦ **ARNS** International Association of Retired NATO Civilian Staff and their Dependents (#02665)
♦ **AROA** Asian Railway Operators Association (#01678)
♦ AROA – Association de recherche ouest africaine (internationally oriented national body)
♦ ARO – Asian Relations Organization (inactive)
♦ **ARO** Association internationale des anciens agents, retraités de l'OTAN et de leurs ayants-droits (#02665)
♦ ARO / see Association for Research in Vision and Ophthalmology (#02894)
♦ AROCSA – Association for Research on Civil Society in Africa (internationally oriented national body)
♦ **ARO** FDI African Regional Organization (#09280)
♦ Arogya World (internationally oriented national body)
♦ ARO / see ITUC – Asia Pacific (#16076)

♦ Arolsen Archives – International Center on Nazi Persecution 01112

Dir Grosse Allee 5-9, 34454 Bad Arolsen, Germany. T. +4956916290. Fax +495691629501. E-mail: info@arolsen-archives.org.
URL: https://arolsen-archives.org/

History Established 1943, London (UK), on the initiative of the Allied Forces Headquarters at the British Red Cross, London (UK), when Department of International Affairs was transformed into a Tracing Bureau. Tasks subsequently undertaken by *Supreme Headquarters of the Allied Expeditionary Forces (SHAEF, inactive)*, which set up *Central Tracing Bureau*, 15 Feb 1944. Location of the bureau moved along with the Front to Versailles (France), and then to Frankfurt-Main (Germany FR). Then taken over by the *United Nations Relief and Rehabilitation Administration (UNRRA, inactive)*, until 30 Jun 1947. Relocated Jan 1946, Arolsen (Germany FR). Taken over by *International Refugee Organization (IRO, inactive)*, 1 Jul 1947. 1 Jan 1948, name changed to *International Tracing Service (ITS) – Service International de Recherches – Internationaler Suchdienst*. Placed under management of *Allied High Commission for Germany (HICOG, inactive)*, Apr 1951. Direction and administration assumed by the *International Committee of the Red Cross (ICRC, #12799)* in Geneva (Switzerland), 1955. Archive opened to research pursuant to new agreement concluded between member states of the International Commission. ICRC withdrew from ITS management, Dec 2012. Commission signed 2 new agreements on both the future and administration of the ITS, replacing all previous ones, Jan 2013, when German Federal Archives became the new institutional partner. **Aims** Based on the unique collection on the victims of Nazi persecution, honor the legacy by engaging with today's society to preserve historical truth and stand up for respect, diversity and democracy. **Structure** International Commission of 11 member governments. Legally based on the Berlin agreements which came into force Jan 2013, replacing the Bonn agreements from 1955. **Languages** English, French, German, Polish, Russian. **Staff** 220.00 FTE, paid. **Finance** German Federal Budget. Annual budget: 16,475,000 EUR (2022). **Activities** Knowledge management/information dissemination; publishing activities; research/documentation; training/education. **Events** *Annual meeting* 1992. **Publications** Annual Report; pedagogical materials; scholarly publications; leaflets; yearbooks. Information Services: UNESCO has inscribed the original documents (30 million documents) and the Central Name Index of the Arolsen Archives into the Memory of the World Register. **Information Services** *Online Archive*.
Members Governments of 11 countries:
Belgium, France, Germany, Greece, Israel, Italy, Luxembourg, Netherlands, Poland, UK, USA.
IGO Relations Cooperates with (1): *International Holocaust Remembrance Alliance (IHRA, #13803)*. [2022.10.18/XF2637/**F***]

♦ Aromatics Producers' Association (APA) 01113

Contact c/o CEFIC, Rue Belliard 40, bte 15, 1040 Brussels, Belgium. T. +3224369300. E-mail: info@petrochemistry.eu.
URL: https://www.aromaticsonline.eu/

History as a sector group of *Conseil européen de l'industrie chimique (CEFIC, #04687)*. **Aims** Develop a co-ordinated approach to health, safety, environment, distribution and technical issues, whilst promoting competitiveness of the industry. **Structure** General Assembly; Steering Committee; Task Forces. **Languages** English. [2021.09.09/XK1192/**E**]

♦ AROW / see Independent Retail Europe (#11154)
♦ ARPA – Aide à la réalisation de projects africains (internationally oriented national body)
♦ ARPA – Asia Regulatory Professionals Association (unconfirmed)
♦ ARPA – Association for Research on Periodontal Diseases (inactive)
♦ ARPAC – Arab Region Parliamentarians Against Corruption (see: #10518)
♦ ARP – Association of Reformers in Psychiatry (no recent information)
♦ ARPEDAC – Association pour la Recherche et la Promotion de l'Energie Durable en Afrique Centrale (unconfirmed)
♦ ARPEL / see Asociación Regional de Empresas del Sector Petróleo, Gas y Biocombustibles en Latinoamérica y el Caribe (#02296)
♦ **ARPEL** Asociación Regional de Empresas del Sector Petróleo, Gas y Biocombustibles en Latinoamérica y el Caribe (#02296)
♦ ARPE / see Nuclear Medicine Europe (#17619)
♦ ARPES / see Nuclear Medicine Europe (#17619)
♦ ARPI – Association for Real Property and Infrastructure (internationally oriented national body)
♦ ARPI – Association of Retired Persons International (inactive)
♦ ARPPIS – African Regional Postgraduate Programme in Insect Science (see: #12499)
♦ ARPS – Australasian Radiation Protection Society (internationally oriented national body)
♦ **ARQUISUR** Asociación de Facultades de Arquitectura del Sur del MERCOSUR (#02128)
♦ Arrangement pour l'application de l'Accord européen du 17 octobre 1980 concernant l'octroi des soins médicaux aux personnes en séjour temporaire (1988 treaty)
♦ Arrangement for the Application of the European Agreement of 17 October 1980 Concerning the Provision of Medical Care to Persons During Temporary Residence (1988 treaty)
♦ Arrangement entre autorités douanières pour faciliter l'apurement des triptyques non déchargés ou perdus (1931 treaty)
♦ Arrangement dans le but de reviser l'Arrangement pour l'unification de la formule des médicaments héroïques (1929 treaty)
♦ Arrangement between Certain Member States of the European Space Research Organisation and the European Space Research Organisation Concerning the Execution of a Meteorological Satellite Programme (1972 treaty)
♦ Arrangement entre certains Etats membres de l'Organisation européenne de recherches spatiales et l'Organisation européenne de recherches spatiales concernant l'exécution d'un programme de satellite météorologique (1972 treaty)
♦ Arrangement concernant les abonnements aux journaux et écrits périodiques (1984 treaty)
♦ Arrangement concernant les abonnements aux journaux et écrits périodiques, 1952 (1952 treaty)
♦ Arrangement concernant les abonnements aux journaux et écrits périodiques, 1957 (1957 treaty)
♦ Arrangement concernant les abonnements aux journaux et écrits périodiques, 1964 (1964 treaty)
♦ Arrangement concernant les colis postaux, 1952 (1952 treaty)
♦ Arrangement concernant les colis postaux, 1957 (1957 treaty)
♦ Arrangement concernant les colis postaux, 1964 (1964 treaty)
♦ Arrangement concernant les colis postaux, 1984 (1984 treaty)
♦ Arrangement concernant le commerce international des textiles (1973 treaty)
♦ Arrangement concernant la conservation ou le rétablissement des droits de propriété industrielle (1920 treaty)
♦ Arrangement concernant le dépôt international des dessins et modèles industriels (1925 treaty)
♦ Arrangement concernant les envois contre remboursement (1984 treaty)
♦ Arrangement concernant les envois contre remboursement, 1952 (1952 treaty)
♦ Arrangement concernant les envois contre remboursement, 1957 (1957 treaty)
♦ Arrangement concernant les envois contre remboursement, 1964 (1964 treaty)
♦ Arrangement concernant les lettres et les boîtes avec valeur déclarée, 1952 (1952 treaty)
♦ Arrangement concernant les lettres et les boîtes avec valeur déclarée, 1957 (1957 treaty)
♦ Arrangement concernant les lettres et les boîtes avec valeur déclarée, 1964 (1964 treaty)
♦ Arrangement concernant les mandats de poste et les bons postaux de voyage, 1952 (1952 treaty)
♦ Arrangement concernant les mandats de poste et les bons postaux de voyage, 1957 (1957 treaty)
♦ Arrangement concernant les mandats de poste et les bons postaux de voyage, 1964 (1964 treaty)
♦ Arrangement concernant les mandats de poste et les bons postaux de voyage, 1984 (1984 treaty)
♦ Arrangement concernant les recouvrements (1984 treaty)
♦ Arrangement concernant les recouvrements, 1952 (1952 treaty)
♦ Arrangement concernant les recouvrements, 1957 (1957 treaty)
♦ Arrangement concernant les recouvrements, 1964 (1964 treaty)
♦ Arrangement concernant le service des chèques postaux, 1984 (1984 treaty)
♦ Arrangement concernant le service international de l'épargne (1984 treaty)
♦ Arrangement concernant le service international de l'épargne, 1957 (1957 treaty)
♦ Arrangement concernant le service international de l'épargne, 1964 (1964 treaty)
♦ Arrangement concernant la suppression des patentes de santé (1934 treaty)
♦ Arrangement concernant la suppression des visas consulaires sur les patentes de santé (1934 treaty)
♦ Arrangement concernant les virements postaux, 1957 (1957 treaty)
♦ Arrangement concernant les virements postaux, 1964 (1964 treaty)
♦ Arrangement concernant les virements postaux et supplément visant le règlement par virement postal des valeurs domiciliées dans les bureaux de chèques postaux (1952 treaty)
♦ Arrangement Concerning Consultations Prior to the Installation in the Vicinity of the Frontiers of Permanent Stores of Explosive Substances for Civil Use (1950 treaty)
♦ Arrangement Concerning the Extension to other Categories of Refugees of Certain Measures Taken in Favour of Russian and Armenian Refugees (1928 treaty)
♦ Arrangement pour le développement des échanges commerciaux (1937 treaty)
♦ Arrangement européen sur l'échange des programmes au moyen de films de télévision (1958 treaty)
♦ Arrangement européen pour la protection des émissions de télévision (1960 treaty)
♦ Arrangement interaméricain de radiocommunications, 1937 (1937 treaty)
♦ Arrangement international sur les céréales, 1967 (1967 treaty)
♦ Arrangement international concernant le transport des corps (1937 treaty)
♦ Arrangement international relatif à l'exportation des os (1929 treaty)
♦ Arrangement international relatif à l'exportation des peaux (1928 treaty)
♦ Arrangement international relatif à la répression de la circulation des publications obscènes, 1910 (1910 treaty)
♦ Arrangement international relatif aux statistiques des causes de décès (1934 treaty)
♦ Arrangement international en vue d'assurer une protection efficace contre le trafic criminel connu sous le nom de traite des blanches (1904 treaty)
♦ Arrangement on the Joint Financing of a North Atlantic Height Monitoring System (1995 treaty)
♦ Arrangement de Lisbonne concernant la protection des appellations d'origine et leur enregistrement international (1958 treaty)
♦ Arrangement de Locarno instituant une classification internationale pour les dessins et modèles industriels (1968 treaty)
♦ Arrangement de Madrid concernant l'enregistrement international des marques, 1891 (1891 treaty)
♦ Arrangement de Madrid concernant l'enregistrement international des marques de fabrique (1957 treaty)
♦ Arrangement de Madrid concernant la répression des indications de provenance fausses ou fallacieuses, 1891 (1891 treaty)
♦ Arrangement de Nice concernant la classification internationale des produits et des produits et des services aux fins de l'enregistrement des marques (1957 treaty)
♦ Arrangement de Nyon (1937 treaty)
♦ Arrangement provisoire concernant l'enregistrement et le licenciement de marins à Memel et à Dantzig (1922 treaty)
♦ Arrangement provisoire concernant les questions relatives aux grands fonds marins (1984 treaty)
♦ Arrangement provisoire concernant le statut des réfugiés provenant d'Allemagne (1936 treaty)
♦ Arrangement Regarding Bovine Meat (1979 treaty)
♦ Arrangement Regarding International Trade in Textiles (1973 treaty)
♦ Arrangement relatif à l'application de la Convention européenne sur l'arbitrage commercial international (1962 treaty)
♦ Arrangement relatif à la délivrance des certificats d'identité aux réfugiés russes et arméniens (1926 treaty)
♦ Arrangement relatif aux documents d'identité pour le personnel des aéronefs, 1938 (1938 treaty)
♦ Arrangement relatif aux documents d'identité pour le personnel des aéronefs, 1939 (1939 treaty)
♦ Arrangement relatif à l'établissement d'une carte de transit pour émigrants (1929 treaty)
♦ Arrangement relatif à l'extension à d'autres catégories de réfugiés de certaines mesures prises en faveur des réfugiés russes et arméniens (1928 treaty)
♦ Arrangement relatif aux facilités à donner aux marins du commerce pour le traitement des maladies vénériennes (1924 treaty)
♦ Arrangement relatif aux marins réfugiés (1957 treaty)
♦ Arrangement relatif au secteur laitier (1979 treaty)
♦ Arrangement relatif au statut juridique des réfugiés russes et arméniens (1928 treaty)
♦ Arrangement relatif à la viande bovine (1979 treaty)
♦ Arrangement Relating to the Issue of Identity Certificates to Russian and Armenian Refugees (1926 treaty)
♦ Arrangement Relating to the Legal Status of Russian and Armenian Refugees (1928 treaty)
♦ Arrangement Respecting the Chinese Import Tariffs (1902 treaty)
♦ Arrangement spécial concernant les relations télégraphiques (1921 treaty)

- ♦ Arrangements pour la réglementation de la chasse pélagique à la baleine dans l'Antarctique (1962 treaty)
- ♦ Arrangements for the Regulation of Antarctic Pelagic Whaling (1962 treaty)
- ♦ Arrangements supplémentaires pour la réglementation de la chasse pélagique à la baleine dans l'Antarctique (1962 treaty)
- ♦ Arrangement de Strasbourg concernant la classification internationale des brevets (1971 treaty)
- ♦ Arrangement au sujet des consultations préalables à l'installation à proximité des frontières de dépôts permanents de substances explosives à usage civil (1950 treaty)
- ♦ Arrangement de Vienne instituant une classification internationale des éléments figuratifs des marques (1973 treaty)
- ♦ Arrangement de Wassenaar sur le contrôle des exportations d'armes conventionnelles et de biens et technologies à double usage (#20819)
- ♦ ARRC / see ChildAid
- ♦ **ARRC** Allied Rapid Reaction Corps (#00736)
- ♦ ARRC – Asian Regional Resource Centre for Human Rights Education (internationally oriented national body)
- ♦ **ARRCN** Asian Raptor Research and Conservation Network (#01679)
- ♦ Arreglo a cobros (1984 treaty)
- ♦ Arreglo de La Haya relativo al depósito internacional de dibujos y modelos industriales (1925 treaty)
- ♦ Arreglo interamericano sobre radiocomunicaciones, 1937 (1937 treaty)
- ♦ Arreglo de Lisboa relativo a la protección de denominaciones de origen y su registro internacional (1958 treaty)
- ♦ Arreglo de Locarno que establece una clasificación internacional para los dibujos y modelos industriales (1968 treaty)
- ♦ Arreglo de Niza relativo a la clasificación internacional de productos y servicios para el registro de las marcas (1957 treaty)
- ♦ Arreglo de los productos lacteos (1979 treaty)
- ♦ Arreglo relativo a abonos de periódicos (1984 treaty)
- ♦ Arreglo relativo a la carne de bovino (1979 treaty)
- ♦ Arreglo relativo al comercio internacional de textiles (1973 treaty)
- ♦ Arreglo relativo a envios contra reembolso (1984 treaty)
- ♦ Arreglo relativo a los mandatos postales y bonos postales de viaje, 1984 (1984 treaty)
- ♦ Arreglo Relativo a paquetos postales, 1984 (1984 treaty)
- ♦ Arreglo relativo al servicio internacional del ahorro (1984 treaty)
- ♦ Arreglo relativo a servicios de cheques postales, 1984 (1984 treaty)
- ♦ Arreglo de Wassenaar Sobre Control de Exportaciones de Armas Convencionales y Productos y Tecnología de Doble Uso (#20819)
- ♦ **ARRF** African Research and Resource Forum (#00441)
- ♦ ARRI / see Association Réalités et Relations Internationales
- ♦ ARRI – Association Réalités et Relations Internationales (internationally oriented national body)
- ♦ ARRICOD – Association nationale des directeurs et responsables des relations internationales et de la coopération décentralisée des collectivités territoriales (internationally oriented national body)
- ♦ ARRO – Australasian Road Rescue Organisation (internationally oriented national body)
- ♦ **ARROW** Asian-Pacific Resource and Research Centre for Women (#01629)
- ♦ **ARSA** Asian Rural Sociology Association (#01689)
- ♦ **ARSA** Asia Region SUZUKI Association (#02086)
- ♦ **ARS** Armenian Relief Society (#01111)
- ♦ **ARS** ASEAN Rhinology Society (#01231)
- ♦ ARS – Asian Research Service (internationally oriented national body)

♦ ARS BALTICA 01114

Dir Nordkolleg Rendsburg, Am Gerhardshain 44, 24768 Rendsburg, Germany. E-mail: info@nordkolleg.de.
URL: http://www.ars-baltica.net/

History Nov 1990, Kiel (Germany). Founded on initiative of Prime Minister of Schleswig-Holstein (Germany), at first meeting of the organizing committee, 1988. **Aims** Promote multilateral *cultural* cooperation with an emphasis on common projects of quality in the *Baltic Sea* Region, so as to provide the region with a profile of its own and strengthen its cultural identity; act as a bridge and messenger of Baltic cultural expression to the rest of *Europe*. **Structure** Organizing Committee (Board); Rotating Chairmanship and Secretariat. Includes: *Bibliotheca Baltica (#03228)*. **Languages** English. **Staff** 2.00 FTE, paid. **Finance** No joint pool for funding. **Activities** Events/meetings; guidance/assistance/consulting; knowledge management/information dissemination; networking/liaising. **Events** *Ars Baltica Forum* Rendsburg (Germany) 2011, *Half-Yearly Meeting* Rendsburg (Germany) 2011, *Half-Yearly Meeting* Turku (Finland) 2011, *Half-Yearly Meeting* Salzau (Germany) 2010, *Ars Baltica Forum* Copenhagen (Denmark) 2007. **Publications** *ARS BALTICA e-newsletter*.
Members Participants in 10 countries:
Denmark, Estonia, Finland, Germany, Latvia, Lithuania, Norway, Poland, Russia, Sweden.
NGO Relations Member of: *On the Move (OTM, #16868)*. [2021/XF3951/F]

- ♦ ARSC – African Remote Sensing Council (inactive)
- ♦ **ARSCP** African Roundtable for Sustainable Consumption and Production (#00444)
- ♦ **A-RSF** Restauradores Sin Fronteras (#18922)
- ♦ ARSO / see African Organisation for Standardisation (#00404)
- ♦ **ARSO** African Organisation for Standardisation (#00404)
- ♦ ARSOM – Académie royale des sciences d'outre-mer (internationally oriented national body)
- ♦ ARSP – Action Reconciliation Services for Peace (internationally oriented national body)
- ♦ ARSPC – Australasian Remote Sensing and Photogrammetry Conference (meeting series)
- ♦ ARSR – Asian Research Symposium in Rhinology (meeting series)
- ♦ ARSRC – Africa Regional Sexuality Resource Centre, Lagos (internationally oriented national body)
- ♦ ART / see Resource Africa
- ♦ ARTA – Autorité de la route transafricaine Mombasa-Lagos (inactive)
- ♦ Art Accord – Association des écoles engagées dans des échanges internationaux (no recent information)
- ♦ ARTAG / see Round Table Arabian Gulf (#18979)
- ♦ ARTBA – American Road and Transportation Builders Association (internationally oriented national body)
- ♦ Art Cities in Europe (internationally oriented national body)

♦ Art Directors Club of Europe (ADCE) 01115

Exec Dir Plaça de les Glories 37-38, 08018 Barcelona, Spain. T. +34932566766. E-mail: office@adceurope.org.
URL: http://www.adceurope.org/

History Founded 1990. **Aims** Foster and reward creative excellence in European design and advertising; raise the standards of creativity throughout Europ; encourage people to embrace the value of creativity for society, culture and economy. **Structure** Board (meets 3 times a year). **Languages** English. **Staff** 3.00 FTE, paid. **Finance** Members' dues. Other sources: registrations for awards and festival; funds from the EU – Culture Program which co-finances some projects; private sponsors; other public funds. **Activities** Awards/prizes/competitions; events/meetings. **Events** *European Creativity Festival* Barcelona (Spain) 2015, *European Creativity Festival* Barcelona (Spain) 2014. **Publications** *The Annual of Annuals*.
Members National associations of art directors and advertising creative directors in 20 countries:
Austria, Croatia, Cyprus, Czechia, Estonia, Finland, Georgia, Germany, Iceland, Italy, Latvia, Portugal, Romania, Russia, Slovakia, Slovenia, Spain, Switzerland, UK, Ukraine. [2019/XF2622/F]

- ♦ ARTDO / see ARTDO International (#01117)

♦ ARTDO Asia-Pacific Human Resources Development Centre 01116

Exec Dir ARTDO, c/o ITD Consulting Group Inc, Unit 1108, 11/F88 Corporate Center, 141 Valero Street – Salcedo Village, Makati 1227, 1227 Manila, Philippines. T. +6328877428.
URL: http://www.artdointernational.com/

History Penang (Malaysia), within the framework of *ARTDO International (#01117)*. **Aims** Upgrade standards and practice of human resource development in the region; develop training methods which take into account the unique learning conditions in Asian countries; make training technology available and affordable, particularly to *developing countries* in the Asia-Pacific region. **Structure** Executive Management Committee, comprising Chairman, President, 2 Vice Presidents, 5 Directors, Executive Director and Honorary Secretary. International Board of Advisers. **Activities** Organizes workshops. Develops and conducts diploma courses. **Publications** *HRD Focus* (periodical).
Members Organizations; Individual. Members in 42 countries and territories:
Australia, Bahrain, Bangladesh, Brunei Darussalam, Cambodia, Canada, China, Denmark, Egypt, Fiji, France, Germany, Ghana, Hong Kong, India, Indonesia, Japan, Jordan, Kenya, Korea Rep, Kuwait, Laos, Malaysia, Myanmar, Nepal, New Zealand, Nigeria, Pakistan, Papua New Guinea, Philippines, Saudi Arabia, Singapore, Spain, Sri Lanka, Sudan, Switzerland, Taiwan, Thailand, UK, United Arab Emirates, USA, Vietnam. [2012.09.12/XE1678/E]

♦ ARTDO International 01117

SG c/o ITD Consulting Group Inc, Unit 1108, 11/F88 Corporate Center, 141 Valero Street – Salcedo Village, Makati 1227, 1227 Manila, Philippines. T. +6328877428. E-mail: itdmanila@itdworld.com.
URL: http://www.artdointernational.org/

History Developed from the First Asian Regional Training and Development Conference convened on 9 Nov 1974. Former names and other names: *Asian Regional Training and Development Organization (ARTDO)* – former. **Aims** Encourage a unified approach to common problems and concerns in *human resource* development; assist in the formation and growth of training and development organizations; cooperate with international organizations and with private and government institutions working in the field of human resource development; encourage and sponsor research and publications designed to meet the training and development needs; serve as a resource centre. **Structure** Executive Board, consisting of President, President-Elect, Senior Vice-President, 4 Vice-Presidents, immediate Past President (ex officio), Secretary General (ex officio), 6 Directors and 4 Regional Directors. 6 Council Representatives. Secretariat General, headed by Secretary General. **Languages** English. **Staff** 3.00 FTE, voluntary. **Finance** Members' dues. Donations. **Activities** International and inter-regional conferences. Distribution and exchange of documents. Establishment of continuing committees for research and documentation on special problems related to human resources development and other services. Training seminars; courses or institutes on particular subjects. Organization of professional training centres. Exchange of trainers, students and experts in human resources development. Annual HRD Awards. Maintains *ARTDO Asia-Pacific Human Resources Development Centre (#01116)*, which serves as the research and professional development arm. **Events** *Annual Conference* Manila (Philippines) 2020, *Annual Conference* Colombo (Sri Lanka) 2019, *Annual Conference* Taipei (Taiwan) 2018, *Annual Conference* George Town (Malaysia) 2017, *Conference* Malaysia 2017. **Publications** *ARTDO International Journal* (2 a year); *HRD Focus* (2 a year). Occasional paper series.
Members Organizations Regular; Associate; Affiliate; Individual lifetime membership. Members in 42 countries and territories:
Australia, Bahrain, Bangladesh, Brunei Darussalam, Cambodia, Canada, China, Denmark, Egypt, Fiji, France, Germany, Ghana, Hong Kong, India, Indonesia, Japan, Jordan, Kenya, Korea Rep, Kuwait, Laos, Malaysia, Nepal, New Zealand, Nigeria, Pakistan, Papua New Guinea, Philippines, Qatar, Saudi Arabia, Singapore, Spain, Sri Lanka, Sudan, Switzerland, Taiwan, Thailand, UK, United Arab Emirates, USA, Vietnam.
IGO Relations *Asian and Pacific Skill Development Programme (APSDEP, no recent information); Asian Productivity Organization (APO, #01674)* (Observer Status); *ILO (#11123)*. **NGO Relations** *United Nations Global Compact (#20567)*. [2020/XE4949/D]

- ♦ **ARTEA** Association of Round Tables in Eastern Africa (#02898)
- ♦ ARTEA – Autorité de la Route trans-est-africaine Le Caire-Gaborone (inactive)
- ♦ Art Education for the Blind (internationally oriented national body)
- ♦ Art Education – New Technologies in Europe (#02553)
- ♦ Arte Educación – Nuevas Tecnologias en Europa (#02553)
- ♦ Arte Educazione – Nuove Technologie in Europa (#02553)
- ♦ Artefact – Centre for Appropriate Technology and International Development Cooperation / see Artefact – Centre for Energy, Appropriate Technology and International Development Cooperation
- ♦ Artefact – Centre for Energy, Appropriate Technology and International Development Cooperation (internationally oriented national body)
- ♦ Artefact – Zentrum für Angepasste Technik und Internationale Entwicklungszusammenarbeit / see Artefact – Centre for Energy, Appropriate Technology and International Development Cooperation
- ♦ Artefact – Zentrum für Energie, Angepasste Technik und Internationale Entwicklungszusammenarbeit (internationally oriented national body)
- ♦ ARTE G.E.I.E. – Association Relative à la Télévision Européenne (internationally oriented national body)
- ♦ Arte-Magna International (internationally oriented national body)
- ♦ Arte-Magna International-ASBL / see Arte-Magna International
- ♦ ARTEMIS European Technology Platform / see Inside Industry Association (#11230)
- ♦ ARTEMIS Industry Association / see Inside Industry Association (#11230)

♦ ARTerial Network 01118

Main Office c/o DG du MASA, Plateau, 17 Blvd Roume, Abidjan, Côte d'Ivoire. E-mail: info@arterialnetwork.org.
URL: http://www.arterialnetwork.org/

History Founded Mar 2007, Dakar (Senegal). Constitutional framework adopted Sep 2009, Johannesburg (South Africa). Full constitution adopted, Nov 2010, Morocco. **Aims** Build and/or further develop effective, sustainable national, regional and continental networks within and across *arts* disciplines to play advocacy and lobbying roles within countries, regions, on the continent and internationally as appropriate, and in support of the *African* creative sector. **Structure** Conference (annual); General Council; Steering Committee; Secretariat, located in Cape Town (South Africa); Regional Secretariat in Kenya (for East Africa); National Steering Committees. **Events** *Forum Africain de la Musique* Segou (Mali) 2016, *Biennial Meeting* Johannesburg (South Africa) 2009. **Publications** *ARTerial Network Newsletter*.
Members Full; Associate; Honorary. Chapters in 34 countries:
Algeria, Benin, Burkina Faso, Cameroon, Cape Verde, Central African Rep, Chad, Congo DR, Côte d'Ivoire, Egypt, Eswatini, Ghana, Kenya, Liberia, Malawi, Mali, Mauritania, Morocco, Mozambique, Namibia, Niger, Nigeria, Rwanda, Senegal, Seychelles, Sierra Leone, South Africa, Sudan, Tanzania UR, Togo, Tunisia, Uganda, Zambia, Zimbabwe.
Consultative Status Consultative status granted from: *UNESCO (#20322)* (Consultative Status). **IGO Relations** Cooperates with: *Commonwealth Foundation (CF, #04330); European Commission (EC, #06633)*. **NGO Relations** Cooperates with: *Africalia; Centre for Culture and Development (MIMETA); Humanistisch Instituut voor Ontwikkelingssamenwerking (Hivos); Stichting DOEN; Strømme Foundation (SF)*. [2020/XJ5203/F]

- ♦ **ARTERY** Association for Research into Arterial Structure and Physiology (#02891)
- ♦ **ARTES RENASCENTES** Association Internationale Artes Renascentes (#02670)
- ♦ Art En Exil (internationally oriented national body)
- ♦ Artfactories – International Resource Platform for Independent Art Spaces (internationally oriented national body)
- ♦ **ARTGLACE** Confédération des associations des artisans glaciers de la Communauté européenne (#04514)

♦ Arthroplasty Society in Asia (ASIA) 01119

Secretariat No 1605 Tianxingjian Office Bldg, 47 Fuxing Rd, Haidian District, 100036 Beijing, China. T. +861059007165. E-mail: secretariat@asiaarthroplasty.org.
URL: https://www.arthroplastyonline.asia/

History 4 Sep 2012, Hong Kong (Hong Kong). **Aims** Increase orthopaedic academy collaboration so as to achieve regional health reform and quality of patient life; advance orthopaedic treatment outcomes across the region, professional education, clinical research, travelling fellowship and subspecialty symposium need to be systematically advocated and organized in Asian countries. **Structure** Steering Committee; Board; Committees (2); Officers. **Languages** English. **Staff** 25.00 FTE, paid. **Finance** Financed by private corporation.

Annual budget: 200,000 USD. **Activities** Financial and/or material support; networking/liaising. **Events** *Annual Meeting* Seoul (Korea Rep) 2019, *Annual Meeting* Shanghai (China) 2018, *Annual Meeting* Tokyo (Japan) 2017, *Annual Meeting* Guangzhou (China) 2016, *Annual Conference* Seoul (Korea Rep) 2014. **Publications** *ASIA Newsletter*.
Members Full in 11 countries and territories:
Australia, China, India, Indonesia, Japan, Korea Rep, Malaysia, Singapore, Taiwan, Thailand, USA. [2021/XJ7838/**D**]

♦ Arthroscopy Association of North America (internationally oriented national body)

♦ Arthur Rubinstein International Music Society 01120

Société internationale de musique Arthur Rubinstein

Office Manager 9 Bilu Street, 6522214 Tel Aviv, Israel. T. +97236856684. Fax +97236854924. E-mail: competition@arims.org.il.
URL: http://www.arims.org.il/

History 1980. **Aims** Maintain and perpetuate the *artistic* and *spiritual* heritage of Arthur Rubinstein. **Structure** Public Council, consisting of Chairman of the Board, Chairman of the Executive Committee, Treasurer, Founder/Director and Secretariat. **Staff** 3.00 FTE, paid; 100.00 FTE, voluntary. **Finance** Sources: government support; sale of publications; sponsorship. Support from: Culture Authority of the Ministry of Education and Culture of Israel; Tel Aviv-Yafo Municipality. Other sources: competition benefactors and friends; concerts; financing fund. **Activities** Awards/prizes/competitions; events/meetings; training/education. Holds the *Arthur Rubinstein International Piano Master Competition* (every 3 years). Initiated and organized: a worldwide series of concerts 'Hommage à Rubinstein'; Arthur Rubinstein international festivals in the great art of the keyboard; documentary exhibitions and lectures on Arthur Rubinstein's life and art. **Publications** *Arthur Rubinstein International Music Society Bulletin* (annual). Competition brochure and prospectus; CD's and videos. **Members** Individuals in 35 countries. Membership countries not specified. **NGO Relations** Member of (1): *International Music Council (IMC, #14199)*. [2022.02.15/XE0597/v/**E**]

♦ ARTI – American Rescue Team International (internationally oriented national body)

♦ ARTICLE 19 01121

Exec Dir Free Word Ctr, 60 Farringdon Rd, London, EC1R 3GA, UK. T. +442073242500. E-mail: info@article19.org.
URL: http://www.article19.org/

History 1986. Takes its name from 19th article of the Universal Declaration of Human Rights which states that everyone has the right to freedom of opinion and expression. Former names and other names: *ARTICLE 19, International Centre Against Censorship* – former; *Centre international contre la censure* – former; *International Centre Against Censorship – Article 19* – former; *ARTICLE 19, Global Campaign for Free Expression* – former. Registration: Charities Commission, No/ID: 327421, England and Wales. **Aims** Promote, protect and develop freedom of expression, including access to information and the means of communication. **Structure** International Board of 12 members; Executive Director. Offices in: Bangladesh; Brazil; Kenya; Mexico, Senegal; Tunisia; UK. **Staff** 70.00 FTE, paid. **Finance** Individual donations. Also supported by foundations and organizations, including the following listed in this Yearbook: *Council of Europe (CE, #04881)*; *Department for International Development (DFID, inactive)*; *European Commission (EC, #06633)*; *International Media Support (IMS, #14128)*; *Organization for Security and Cooperation in Europe (OSCE, #17887)*; *Swedish International Development Cooperation Agency (Sida)*; *UNESCO (#20322)* (ROCILAC). **Activities** Advocacy/lobbying/activism; capacity building; awareness raising; conflict resolution. **Events** *Forum on how regional human rights mechanisms can strengthen freedom of expression* Banjul (Gambia) 2006, *Annual seminar for chairpersons and members of parliamentary human rights bodies* Geneva (Switzerland) 2005, *International seminar on the right to know* Oxford (UK) 2000, *Réunion sur la liberté d'expression* Montréal, QC (Canada) 1992. **Publications** All online: Analyses; briefings; thematic publications; standards; books; handbooks; manuals; papers; guidelines. **Members** Not a membership organization. **Consultative Status** Consultative status granted from: *African Commission on Human and Peoples' Rights (ACHPR, #00255)* (Observer); *ECOSOC (#05331)* (Ros A). **IGO Relations** Associated with Department of Global Communications of the United Nations. Accredited by: *United Nations Office at Vienna (UNOV, #20604)*. **NGO Relations** Member of (9): *Accountable Now (#00060)*; *CHS Alliance (#03911)*; *Ethical Journalism Network (EJN, #05554)*; *European Digital Rights (EDRi, #06924)*; *Freedom of Information Advocates Network (FOIAnet, #09985)*; *Global Net Neutrality Coalition (#10480)*; *Global Transparency Initiative (GTI, #10634)*; *Transparency, Accountability and Participation Network (TAP Network, #20222)*; *UNCAC Coalition (#20283)*. Cooperates with (2): *Financial Transparency Coalition (FTC, #09772)*; *Global Call for Climate Action (GCCA, inactive)*. [2021/XF0012/**E**]

♦ ARTICLE 19, Global Campaign for Free Expression / see ARTICLE 19 (#01121)
♦ ARTICLE 19, International Centre Against Censorship / see ARTICLE 19 (#01121)
♦ Article 36 (internationally oriented national body)
♦ Articulación Feminista Marcosur (#09730)
♦ ARTIDEA / see International Institute of Gastronomy, Culture, Arts and Tourism (#13883)
♦ Artificial General Intelligence Society (unconfirmed)
♦ Art International Women Association (internationally oriented national body)
♦ Artisanal Gold Council (internationally oriented national body)

♦ Artistes sans frontières 01122

Contact 7 impasse du Rouet, 75014 Paris, France. T. +33140447741. E-mail: bureau.asso@artistes-sf.org.
Contact 9 rue de la Douane, 34200 Sète, France. T. +33467785609. E-mail: contact@artistes-sf.org.
URL: http://www.artistes-sf.org/

History in Brussels (Belgium). Originally registered in accordance with Belgian law, 1992. When headquarters transferred to Paris (France), registered in accordance with French law, 2006. **Aims** Study, preserve and upgrade artistic and cultural heritage; promote contemporary art and defend artists' rights in the framework of a real understanding of their social role; respond to the need for a better definition of the role of the creative artist, especially as catalyst in the dynamics of socio-economic development; promote artistic expression as a universal language in the service of peace and understanding; mobilize professionals and specialists at both individual and institutional level in different fields of competence; assist social, commercial and craft education in cultural artistic expression; resist marginalization and assist cultural integration of specific groups such as the handicapped; promote use of new technology in the artistic arena; encourage greater access to cultural property. **Structure** Administrative Council, including President, 2 Vice-Presidents, Treasurer and Secretary-General. **Languages** English, French. **Staff** 1.50 FTE, paid. **Finance** Private and public sources. **Activities** Projects: Training in arts and crafts in Lebanon; Tools of training in cooperation for development; training and socio-economic integration of Palestinian refugee women in Jordan; INFODEV-CULTURE. Organizes workshop and questionnaire: 'situation des artistes en Europe et en Méditerranée'. **Events** *Forum interrégional* Amman (Jordan) 2000. [2019/XF2753/**F**]

♦ Artists Against Racism (AAR) 01123

Exec Dir 1500 Avenue Rd, Box 1382, Toronto ON M5M 0A1, Canada. T. +16477832403. E-mail: aarcharity@gmail.com.
URL: http://www.artistsagainstracism.org/

History 1993, Canada. **Aims** Combat racial and religious prejudice. **Structure** Board of Directors. Advisory Board. **Languages** English. **Staff** 1.00 FTE, voluntary. **Finance** Support from foundations, artists, etc. **Activities** Organizes public education campaigns. **Publications** *One People* (annual) – newsletter.
Members Individuals in 8 countries:
Argentina, Australia, Canada, Germany, Italy, Japan, UK, USA. [2014/XD6179/v/**D**]

♦ Artists chrétiens européennes (internationally oriented national body)
♦ Artists for Conservation (internationally oriented national body)
♦ Artists for Peace Association (inactive)
♦ Artists Project Earth (internationally oriented national body)
♦ Art Library Societies Norden (internationally oriented national body)
♦ Art of Living Foundation (internationally oriented national body)

♦ Art Moves Africa (AMA) 01124

Coordinator 98 rue Antoine Dansaert, 1000 Brussels, Belgium. E-mail: communication@artmovesafrica.org.
URL: http://artmovesafrica.org/

History Former names and other names: *Art Moves Africa: the Mobility Fund of Artists and Cultural Operators within Africa* – full title. **Aims** Facilitate cultural and artistic exchanges within the African continent. **Structure** Board of Directors. **Languages** English, French. **Staff** 1.00 FTE, voluntary. **Finance** Financed by private foundation and international NGOs (not specified). **Activities** Financial and/or material support; events/meetings. **Publications** *Mobility and Touring in East Africa* (2011).
Members in 10 countries:
Cameroon, Chad, Egypt, Kenya, Malawi, Morocco, Senegal, South Africa, Tanzania UR, Zimbabwe. [2021/XJ6128/f/**F**]

♦ Art Moves Africa: the Mobility Fund of Artists and Cultural Operators within Africa / see Art Moves Africa (#01124)
♦ Art Museum of the Americas, OAS (see: #17629)
♦ **ARTNeT** Asia-Pacific Research and Training Network on Trade (#02014)

♦ Art Nouveau European Route 01125

Route européenne del Modernisme – Ruta Europea del Modernisme

Permanent Secretariat Inst del Paisatge Urbà i la Qualitat de Vida, Av Drassanes 6-8, 21st floor, 08001 Barcelona, Spain. T. +34932562509. Fax +34932178750. E-mail: coupdefouet@coupdefouet.eu.
URL: http://www.artnouveau.eu/

History 2000, Barcelona (Spain). Current statutes adopted Feb 2007. **Aims** Develop useful and efficient mechanisms for international promotion and protection of Art Nouveau *heritage*; foster communication and exchange to share experience in *restoration* of monuments, public awareness programmes, fundraising strategies and development of sustainable tourism. **Structure** Plenary Meeting; Honorary Council; Permanent Secretariat. **Languages** Catalan, English, French, Spanish. **Staff** 2.00 FTE, paid. **Finance** Barcelona City Council budget; income from Art Nouveau Club subscribers. **Activities** Events/meetings. **Events** *Coup De Fouet International Congress* Barcelona (Spain) 2018, *Coup De Fouet International Congress* Barcelona (Spain) 2015, *Congress* Barcelona (Spain) 2013, *Plenary Meeting* Barcelona (Spain) 2007, *Plenary Meeting* Barcelona (Spain) 2000. **Publications** *coupDefouet* (2 a year) – magazine; *Art Nouveau Calendar* (annual). *Art Nouveau European Route*.
Members Local governments; non-governmental institutions. Cities in 25 countries:
Argentina, Austria, Belgium, Chile, Croatia, Cuba, Finland, France, Georgia, Germany, Hungary, Italy, Latvia, Mexico, Namibia, Norway, Portugal, Puerto Rico, Romania, Russia, Serbia, Slovenia, Spain, Switzerland, UK.
Institutions include 3 organizations listed in this Yearbook:
Centre international pour la ville, l'architecture et le paysage (CIVA); *Charles Rennie Mackintosh Society (CRM Society, #03853)*; *Raymond Lemaire International Centre for the Conservation of Historic Towns and Buildings (RLICC)*. [2017.06.26/XM4465/y/**F**]

♦ Art Nouveau Network / see Réseau Art Nouveau Network (#18867)
♦ **ARTOF** Association for the Rational Treatment of Fractures (#02885)
♦ ARTSA / see Round Table Southern Africa (#18984)

♦ Arts-Based Research Global Consortium (ABR) 01126

Contact address not obtained.
Contact address not obtained.
URL: https://www.abrglobalconsotium.org/

History Former names and other names: *ABR Global Consortium* – alias. **Aims** Raise the visibility of arts-based research; highlight its contribution to social consciousness central to the quality of human life, empathy, social justice and discourse. **Activities** Research/documentation.
Members Individuals in 20 countries:
Australia, Belgium, Brazil, Canada, Colombia, Denmark, France, Germany, Greece, Ireland, Israel, Italy, Malta, Netherlands, Poland, Russia, South Africa, Spain, UK, USA.
NGO Relations Partner of (1): *European Network for Qualitative Inquiry (ENQI, #07980)*. [2020/AA2069/**C**]

♦ Arts Council of the African Studies Association (internationally oriented national body)
♦ Arts Cultural Management Conference (meeting series)
♦ Artsen Zonder Grenzen (#03366)
♦ Artsen Zonder Vakantie (internationally oriented national body)
♦ Arts for Global Development (internationally oriented national body)
♦ Arts International (internationally oriented national body)

♦ Arts Schools Network 01127

Address not obtained.
URL: http://www.artsschoolsnetwork.org/

History 1983, as *International Network of Performing and Visual Arts Schools*. Name subsequently changed to *International Network of Schools for the Advancement of Arts Education*. **Aims** Promote excellence in arts education by inspiring and serving arts leaders, institutions and organizations. **Structure** Governing Board. Executive Committee, comprising President, 1st and 2nd Vice-Presidents, Secretary, Treasurer and Immediate Past President. Executive Director. Committees (16). **Finance** Members' dues. Sponsorship. **Activities** Committees: College and Career; Best Practices; Leadership; Elementary and Middle Arts Schools, Arts Integration; Awards; Current Conference; Future Conferences (2): Finance; Membership; Nominations, Board and Slate; Past Presidents; Research; Sponsorship; Master Series – Life in the Arts; Student Recognition – On Your Way. Offers programmes, including: international conferences (in USA or Canada); leadership retreats; arts schools evaluation; exemplary schools; ife in the arts video series; on your say student recognition programme; awards and recognition; regional workshops and institutes; consulting services; Arts Education Career Center. **Events** *Annual Conference* Seattle, WA (USA) 2015, *Annual Conference* Denver, CO (USA) 2014, *Annual Conference* New York, NY (USA) 2013, *Annual Conference* Chicago, IL (USA) 2012, *Annual Conference* Pittsburgh, PA (USA) 2005. **Publications** *Network News* (24 a year) – electronic. Membership directory.
Members Public and private K-12 schools, School District Offices, Post-secondary schools, Associations related to arts instruction, corporations and individuals. Schools in 4 countries:
Canada, Italy, UK, USA. [2016/XF4724/**F**]

♦ Arts in Society Research Network (unconfirmed)

♦ ART for The World 01128

Main Office 7 rue Monnier, 1206 Geneva, Switzerland. T. +41227891557. Fax +41223466960. E-mail: projects@artfortheworld.net.
ART for the World Europa Corso Matteotti 37, 10100 Turin TO, Italy. T. +39236524881.
URL: http://www.artfortheworld.net/

History Founded 1995, as a loose structure operating on a global scale, inspired by Article 27 of the Universal Declaration of Human Rights. **Aims** Create, through the universal language of art a meaningful and enduring dialogue among diverse peoples, cultures, and world views in order to encourage tolerance and solidarity and foster education as a human right. **Structure** Board. **IGO Relations** Associated with Department of Global Communications of the United Nations. [2018/XQ0160/**F**]

♦ **ARUDMO** African Rural Development Movement (#00447)
♦ **ARUPS** ASEAN Regional Union of Psychological Societies (#01229)
♦ ARUSIA – Association pour la Recherche de l'Unité, la Solidarité et l'Identité Africaine (unconfirmed)
♦ **ARVO** Association for Research in Vision and Ophthalmology (#02894)
♦ **ARWA** International Association for Archaeological Research in Western & Central Asia (#11708)
♦ **ARWC** Asian Rural Women's Coalition (#01690)
♦ ARW / see Internationale Arbeitsgemeinschaft der Wasserwerke im Rheineinzugsgebiet (#13215)
♦ Arxivers sense Fronteres (#01091)
♦ **ARZENU** ARZENU – International Federation of Reform and Progressive Religious Zionists (#01129)

♦ ARZENU – International Federation of Reform and Progressive Religious Zionists (ARZENU) 01129

Exec Dir Mercaz Shimshon, Eliyahu Shama St 6, 9410806 Jerusalem, Israel.
URL: https://www.arzenu.org/

History Founded 1980, as a constituent of *World Zionist Organization (WZO, #21961)*. **Aims** Represent, support, develop and stimulate Zionist interest and activities in Reform and Progressive communities worldwide; encourage adherence to WZO Jerusalem Program; foster development of Progressive Judaism in Israel; work for authentic Jewish pluralism within the state through introduction of legislation and other measures to support equal rights for all religious streams. **Activities** Advocacy/lobbying/activism.
Members National groups in 11 countries:
Argentina, Australia, Brazil, Canada, Germany, Israel, Netherlands, South Africa, Switzerland, UK, USA.
NGO Relations Official affiliate: *Netzer Olami – International Progressive Zionist Youth Movement (Netzer Olami, #17068)*. Cooperates with: *World Union for Progressive Judaism (WUPJ, #21883)*. [2018/XD4165/**D**]

- ♦ Ärzte für die Dritte Welt / see German Doctors
- ♦ ASA / see African Statistical Association (#00475)
- ♦ ASAA – Asian Studies Association of Australia (internationally oriented national body)
- ♦ ASA – African Studies Association (internationally oriented national body)
- ♦ ASA – Afrique Secours et Assistance (unconfirmed)
- ♦ ASA – Aid To Southeast Asia (internationally oriented national body)
- ♦ **ASA** Airport Services Association (#00613)
- ♦ **ASA** Amphibian Survival Alliance (#00804)
- ♦ **ASA** Anaerobe Society of the Americas (#00807)
- ♦ ASA – ArcticNet Student Association (internationally oriented national body)
- ♦ ASA-Asia – Amateur Softball Association – Asia (no recent information)
- ♦ **ASA** Asian Shakespeare Association (#01696)
- ♦ **ASA** Asian Shipowners Association (#01697)
- ♦ **ASA** Asian Society of Andrology (#01706)
- ♦ ASA – Asian Society of Arachnology (unconfirmed)
- ♦ **ASA** Asian Sponsorship Association (#01758)
- ♦ ASA – Asia Students Association (no recent information)
- ♦ **ASA** Association of Secretaries and Administrative Professionals in Asia Pacific (#02910)
- ♦ **ASA** Association of Social Anthropologists of the UK (#02917)
- ♦ ASA – Association of South-East Asia (inactive)
- ♦ ASA – Association of Subscription Agents and Intermediaries (inactive)
- ♦ ASA – Australasian Sleep Association (internationally oriented national body)
- ♦ **ASAB** Association for the Study of Animal Behaviour (#02935)
- ♦ ASABE – American Society of Agricultural and Biological Engineers (internationally oriented national body)
- ♦ AsACA – Asian Association of Clinical Anatomists (unconfirmed)
- ♦ ASAC / see Asian Securities and Investments Federation (#01695)
- ♦ ASACP – Australasian Society for Asian and Comparative Philosophy (no recent information)
- ♦ **ASACR** Association sud-asiatique de coopération régionale (#19721)
- ♦ **ASAD** Asian Society Against Dementia (#01704)
- ♦ ASADHO – Association africaine de défense des droits de l'homme (internationally oriented national body)
- ♦ **ASADIP** Asociación Americana de Derecho Internacional Privado (#02109)
- ♦ ASAE (internationally oriented national body)
- ♦ **ASAE** Asian Society of Agricultural Economists (#01705)
- ♦ ASAE – The Center for Association Leadership / see ASAE
- ♦ **ASAEE** Associação Sul Americana de Engenharia Estrutural (#02336)
- ♦ ASAEE – Association for Small Animal Endoscopy and Endosurgery (unconfirmed)
- ♦ **AsAES** Asian Association of Endocrine Surgeons (#01321)
- ♦ **AS** Aetherius Society (#00148)
- ♦ **ASAF** Arab Society for Academic Freedoms (#01042)
- ♦ ASAFAS – Graduate School of Asian and African Area Studies (internationally oriented national body)
- ♦ **ASAF** Asian Sailing Federation (#01691)
- ♦ ASAF / see Asian Securities and Investments Federation (#01695)
- ♦ ASAFED – Association africaine d'éducation pour le développement (no recent information)
- ♦ ASAFFAD – Association africaine francophone de formation à distance (no recent information)
- ♦ Asahi Foundation for Chemical Industry Promotion / see Asahi Glass Foundation
- ♦ Asahi Glass Foundation (internationally oriented national body)
- ♦ Asahi Glass Foundation for Industrial Technology / see Asahi Glass Foundation
- ♦ ASAI – African Studies Association of Ireland (internationally oriented national body)
- ♦ **ASAI** Arab Student Aid International (#01052)
- ♦ ASAI – Association of Spiritual Academies International (internationally oriented national body)
- ♦ **ASAIHL** Association of Southeast Asian Institutions of Higher Learning (#02920)
- ♦ ASAJA – Asociación Sudamericana de Jueces de Atletismo (inactive)
- ♦ **ASALE** Asociación de Academias de la Lengua Española (#02108)
- ♦ ASALH / see Association for the Study of African American Life and History
- ♦ ASALH – Association for the Study of African American Life and History (internationally oriented national body)
- ♦ ASAM – Australasian Society of Aerospace Medicine (internationally oriented national body)
- ♦ Asamblea de las Camaras de Comercio e Industria del Mediterraneo / see Asociación de las Camaras de Comercio e Industria del Mediterraneo (#02112)
- ♦ Asamblea de Cooperación por la Paz (internationally oriented national body)
- ♦ Asamblea General de los Comités Nacionales Olimpicos / see Association of National Olympic Committees (#02819)
- ♦ Asamblea Hispano-Luso-Americano-Filipina de Turismo (inactive)
- ♦ Asamblea Internacional de Parlamentarios de Lengua Francesa / see Assemblée parlementaire de la Francophonie (#02312)
- ♦ Asamblea Mundial de Empresas Pequeñas y Medianas / see World Association for Small and Medium Enterprises (#21189)
- ♦ Asamblea Mundial de Estudiantes (#20019)
- ♦ Asamblea Mundial de la Juventud (#21113)
- ♦ Asamblea Parlamentaria Euro-Latinoamericana (#05700)
- ♦ Asamblea Parlamentaria de la Francofonia (#02312)
- ♦ Asamblea Permanente por los Derechos Humanos (internationally oriented national body)
- ♦ Asamblea de las Regiones de Europa (#02316)
- ♦ Asamblea de las Regiones Europeas Vitícolas (#02317)
- ♦ AS – Americas Society (internationally oriented national body)
- ♦ ASANAL – Asian Association of National Languages (inactive)
- ♦ **AS** Anatomical Society (#00813)
- ♦ **ASANRA** Association of Southern African National Road Agencies (#02924)
- ♦ ASAO – Association for Social Anthropology in Oceania (internationally oriented national body)
- ♦ ASAP / see Asia-Pacific Society for Applied Phycology (#02029)
- ♦ ASAP – Action in Solidarity with Asia and the Pacific (internationally oriented national body)
- ♦ ASAP – African Solutions to African Problems (internationally oriented national body)
- ♦ **ASAP** African Strategies for Advancing Pathology (#00476)
- ♦ **ASAP** AIDS Society for Asia and the Pacific (#00592)
- ♦ **ASAP** Alliance for Surgery and Anesthesia Presence (#00723)
- ♦ **ASAP** Asian Strategic Alliance for Pneumococcal Disease Prevention (#01761)
- ♦ **ASAP** Asia Safe Abortion Partnership (#02090)
- ♦ **ASAPE** Asian Society for Adapted Physical Education and Exercise (#01703)
- ♦ **ASAPRA** Asociación de Agentes Profesionales de Aduana de las Américas (#18512)
- ♦ ASAPRA / see Professional Customs Brokers Association of the Americas (#18512)
- ♦ ASAPS – Australasian Society of Aesthetic Plastic Surgeons (internationally oriented national body)
- ♦ **ASAR** Asian Society of Abdominal Radiology (#01702)
- ♦ ASAR – Asian Society for Aging Research (unconfirmed)
- ♦ ASARC – Australia South Asia Research Centre (internationally oriented national body)
- ♦ **ASARECA** Association for Strengthening Agricultural Research in Eastern and Central Africa (#02933)
- ♦ **AS** Aristotelian Society (#01109)
- ♦ **ASARP** Association for the Study of the Art of Record Production (#02936)
- ♦ ASAS – Agustinos Seculares (religious order)
- ♦ **ASAS** Assessment of SpondyloArthritis International Society (#02319)
- ♦ ASAS – Association of Southern African States (inactive)
- ♦ **ASASP** Association of Synthetic Amorphous Silica Producers (#02946)
- ♦ ASATA – Association of Southern African Travel Agents (now national)
- ♦ ASATRADE – Association of African Trading Enterprises (inactive)
- ♦ ASAUK – African Studies Association of the UK (internationally oriented national body)
- ♦ ASAWA – Association for the Advancement of Women in Africa (no recent information)
- ♦ ASAWI – African Studies Association of the West Indies (inactive)
- ♦ ASB / see Australasian Society for for Biomaterials and Tissue Engineering
- ♦ **AsBAA** Asian Business Aviation Association (#01370)
- ♦ **ASBA** Asian Synthetic Biology Association (#01764)
- ♦ **ASBA** Association of Supervisors of Banks of the Americas (#02944)
- ♦ ASBALC / see Association of Supervisors of Banks of the Americas (#02944)
- ♦ **ASBC** Asian Boxing Confederation (#01363)
- ♦ **ASBCB** African Society for Bioinformatics and Computational Biology (#00459)
- ♦ ASBD / see Australasian Society for Bipolar and Depressive Disorders
- ♦ ASBDA – Asia Society of Basic Design and Art (unconfirmed)
- ♦ ASBD – Australasian Society for Bipolar and Depressive Disorders (internationally oriented national body)
- ♦ ASBD – Australasian Society for Breast Disease (internationally oriented national body)
- ♦ Asbestos International Association / see International Chrysotile Association (#12570)
- ♦ AsBIC – Asian Biological Inorganic Chemistry Conference (meeting series)
- ♦ ASBTE – Australasian Society for for Biomaterials and Tissue Engineering (internationally oriented national body)
- ♦ **ASBU** Arab States Broadcasting Union (#01050)
- ♦ **ASCAAD** Arab Society for Computer Aided Architectural Design (#01044)
- ♦ **ASCA** Airline Sports and Cultural Association (#00609)
- ♦ **AsCA** Asian Crystallographic Association (#01416)
- ♦ **ASCA** Asian Society of Cardiothoracic Anaesthesia (#01707)
- ♦ ASCA – Association for Science Cooperation in Asia (no recent information)
- ♦ ASCAC – Association for the Study of Classical African Civilizations (internationally oriented national body)
- ♦ ASCAD – Asian Cities Against Drugs (unconfirmed)
- ♦ ASC – African Services Committee (internationally oriented national body)
- ♦ ASC – African Studies Center, Boston (internationally oriented national body)
- ♦ ASCA / see International Arab Society of Certified Accountants (#11665)
- ♦ **ASC** Alianza Social Continental (#00635)
- ♦ **ASCAME** Asociación de las Camaras de Comercio e Industria del Mediterraneo (#02112)
- ♦ **ASCAPAP** Asian Society for Child and Adolescent Psychiatry and Allied Professions (#01710)
- ♦ ASCAP / see Asian Society for Child and Adolescent Psychiatry and Allied Professions (#01710)
- ♦ **ASC** Aquaculture Stewardship Council (#00885)
- ♦ ASC – Arab Sports Confederation (inactive)
- ♦ ASCAS – Asian Society of Computer Aided Surgery (unconfirmed)
- ♦ ASC – Asian Seismological Commission (see: #12157)
- ♦ **ASC** Asian Shippers' Council (#01698)
- ♦ **ASC** Asian Shooting Confederation (#01699)
- ♦ ASC – Asian Socialist Conference (inactive)
- ♦ **ASC** Asian Society of Cryosurgery (#01716)
- ♦ **ASCASS** Asian Society for Colloid and Surface Science (#01712)
- ♦ ASCAT – Association internationale des éditeurs de catalogues de timbres-poste d'albums et de publications philatéliques (#01130)
- ♦ ASCAT – Association internationale des éditeurs de catalogues de timbres-poste et de publications philatéliques / see ASCAT – International Association of Stamp Catalogue, Stamp Album and Philatelic Magazine Publishers (#01130)
- ♦ ASCATEP / see UNESCO Regional Office for Education in the Arab States (#20320)
- ♦ ASCAT – International Association of Publishers of Stamp Catalogues and Philatelic Magazines / see ASCAT – International Association of Stamp Catalogue, Stamp Album and Philatelic Magazine Publishers (#01130)

♦ ASCAT – International Association of Stamp Catalogue, Stamp Album and Philatelic Magazine Publishers 01130

ASCAT – Association internationale des éditeurs de catalogues de timbres-poste d'albums et de publications philatéliques

Pres Schwaneberger Verlag GmbH Ohmstrasse 1, 85716 Unterschleissheim, Germany. E-mail: sekretariat@michel.de.
URL: http://ascat-org.com/

History 12 Oct 1977, Barcelona (Spain), as *International Association of Publishers of Postage Stamp Catalogues – Association internationale des éditeurs de catalogues de timbres-poste*. Subsequently changed title to *ASCAT – International Association of Publishers of Stamp Catalogues and Philatelic Magazines – ASCAT – Association internationale des éditeurs de catalogues de timbres-poste et de publications philatéliques*. **Aims** Defend the professional interests of its members and serve as a link between postal services, UPU, international organizations, experts, journalists and dealers. **Structure** General Assembly (annual). Executive Committee, consisting of President, 3 Vice-Presidents, Secretary-General, Treasurer and 2-4 members. **Languages** English, French. **Finance** Members' dues. **Activities** Awards the biennial *'Grand Prix de la Philatélie ASCAT'*. **Events** *Annual General Assembly* Verona (Italy) 2005, *Annual General Assembly* Valencia (Spain) 2004, *Annual General Assembly* Monte Carlo (Monaco) 2003, *Annual General Assembly* Monte Carlo (Monaco) 2002, *Annual General Assembly* Brussels (Belgium) 2001.
Members Companies in 22 countries:
Armenia, Austria, Belgium, Czechia, Denmark, Finland, France, Germany, Greece, Hungary, Italy, Japan, Luxembourg, Netherlands, Norway, Russia, Slovenia, South Africa, Spain, Sweden, Switzerland, UK.
NGO Relations *Association internationale des journalistes philatéliques (AIJP, #02709)*; *International Federation of Stamp Dealers' Associations (IFSDA, #13557)*; *World Association for the Development of Philately (WADP, #21132)*. [2014/XD7940/**D**]

- ♦ **ASCCI** Association of SADC Chambers of Commerce and Industry (#02901)
- ♦ **ASCCS** Association for International Cooperation and Research in Steel-Concrete Composite Structures (#02659)
- ♦ ASCDB – African Society for Cell and Developmental Biology (no recent information)
- ♦ ASCDi / see AscdiNatd (#01131)

♦ AscdiNatd 01131

Office Manager 131 NW First Avenue, Delray Beach FL 33444, USA. T. +15612669016.
European Dir PO Box 74, 9320 Hjallerup, Denmark. T. +4598283311. Fax +4599472005. E-mail: bl@danecomputer.dk.
URL: http://www.ascdi.com/

History 1994, by merger of American Society of Computer Dealers and *European Society of Computer Dealers (ESCD, inactive)*. 2000, took over activities of *European Computer Leasing and Trading Association (ECLAT, inactive)* and merged with Computer Dealers Association (CDLA), Digital Dealers Association (DDA) and Information Technology Resellers Association (ITRA), and adopted the title *Association of Service and Computer Dealers International (ASCD International) – ASCDi*. Current title adopted on merger with North American Association of Telecom Dealers (NATD), 2012. **Aims** Represent interests of users, owners, buyers, sellers and maintainers of mid-range and mainframe *computer equipment* worldwide; promote and enforce high ethical standards of *business* conduct within the industry; provide a forum which promotes the exchange of industry ideas among membership and industry *suppliers*; assist members in becoming the vendor of choice for their customers and the business partner of choice for manufacturers, developers and distributors; provide educational and promotional assistance to enable the membership to grow its customer base. **Structure** Board. Committees (16): Charity Foundation; CISCO; Convention; Finance; HP/DEC/Compaq; IBM; Membership; Network; Sun Microsystems; Technical Services; Industry Relations; ATN; Vendor Relations; Nominating; Ethics; Storage Products. **Activities** Events/meetings. **Events** *Annual European Conference* Rome (Italy) 2019, *Annual European Conference* Amsterdam (Netherlands) 2018, *Fall Meeting* Las Vegas, NV (USA) 2018, *Annual European Conference* Copenhagen (Denmark) 2017, *Annual European Conference* Berlin (Germany) 2016.
Members Full: companies in 23 countries:
Australia, Austria, Belgium, Brazil, Canada, Cayman Is, Chile, China, Czechia, Denmark, France, Germany, Israel, Japan, Malaysia, Netherlands, Saudi Arabia, Singapore, Spain, Switzerland, Thailand, UK, USA. [2018/XD5297/**D**]

- ♦ ASCD International / see AscdiNatd (#01131)
- ♦ ASCE – Area Study Centre for Europe, Karachi (internationally oriented national body)
- ♦ **ASCE** Association of Significant Cemeteries in Europe (#02915)
- ♦ ASCECE – Association of Scientific Centres in a Changing Europe (inactive)
- ♦ ASCE / see Comparative Education Society of Asia (#04409)
- ♦ ASCEP / see Australasian Society of Clinical and Experimental Pharmacology and Toxicology
- ♦ ASCEPT – Australasian Society of Clinical and Experimental Pharmacology and Toxicology (internationally oriented national body)
- ♦ ASCHT – Asian Symposium on Computational Heat Transfer and Fluid Flow (meeting series)
- ♦ ASCIA – Australasian Society of Clinical Immunology and Allergy (internationally oriented national body)
- ♦ **ASCI** Asian Society of Cardiovascular Imaging (#01708)
- ♦ ASCI – Association of Sport Climbers International (inactive)
- ♦ ASCILITE – Australasian Society for Computers in Learning in Tertiary Education (internationally oriented national body)
- ♦ ASCL – African Studies Centre Leiden (internationally oriented national body)
- ♦ **ASCM** Asian Society of Conservation Medicine (#01714)
- ♦ **AsCNP** Asian College of Neuropsychopharmacology (#01385)
- ♦ ASCO / see Arab Satellite Communications Organization (#01037)
- ♦ ASCOBANS – Agreement on the Conservation of Small Cetaceans of the Baltic, North East Atlantic, Irish and North Seas (1992 treaty)
- ♦ ASCOBIC – African Standing Conference on Bibliographic Control (inactive)
- ♦ ASCOD / see African Paralympic Committee (#00410)
- ♦ ASCOFAM – Association mondiale de lutte contre la faim (inactive)
- ♦ **ASCOJA** ASEAN Council of Japan Alumni (#01163)
- ♦ **ASCON** African Sailing Confederation (#00449)
- ♦ **ASCoN** Asian Spinal Cord Network (#01757)
- ♦ **ASCOPE** ASEAN Council on Petroleum (#01164)
- ♦ **ASCPaLM** Asian Society for Clinical Pathology and Laboratory Medicine (#01711)
- ♦ ASCS – ASEAN Society of Colorectal Surgeons (unconfirmed)
- ♦ **ASCS** Asian Society of Cosmetic Scientists (#01715)
- ♦ ASCS – Australasian Society for Classical Studies (internationally oriented national body)
- ♦ ASC Sisters – Adorers of the Blood of Christ (religious order)
- ♦ ASCTS – Australasian Society of Cardiac and Thoracic Surgeons (internationally oriented national body)
- ♦ ASCVS / see Asian Society for Cardiovascular and Thoracic Surgery (#01709)
- ♦ **ASCVTS** Asian Society for Cardiovascular and Thoracic Surgery (#01709)
- ♦ **ASD** Aerospace and Defence Industries Association of Europe (#00146)
- ♦ **ASD** Asian Society of Dermatopathology (#01717)
- ♦ ASDE – Alternativas Sostenibles de Desarrollo (internationally oriented national body)
- ♦ ASDF – Arab Social Democratic Forum (unconfirmed)
- ♦ Asdi – Agence suédoise de coopération internationale au développement (internationally oriented national body)
- ♦ ASDIFLE – Association de didactique du français langue étrangère (internationally oriented national body)
- ♦ ASDO – African Scottish Development Organisation (internationally oriented national body)
- ♦ ASDR – Australasian Society for Dermatology Research (internationally oriented national body)
- ♦ **ASD-STAN** ASD-STAN Standardization (#01132)

♦ ASD-STAN Standardization (ASD-STAN) 01132

Dir Rue Belliard 40, 1040 Brussels, Belgium. T. +327863128. E-mail: contact@asd-stan.org.
URL: http://www.asd-stan.org/
History 1970. Founded by former members of *European Association of Aerospace Industries (AECMA, inactive)*. **Aims** Develop and maintain European standards for the European *aerospace* and *defence* industry. **Structure** General Assembly; Board; Technical Authority. **Languages** English. **Staff** 3.00 FTE, paid. Over 100 experts involved. **Finance** Sources: members' dues; sale of products. Standard sales. **Activities** Knowledge management/information dissemination; standards/guidelines. **Publications** *ASD-STAN Newsletter*. Standards; technical reports.
Members Full in 6 countries:
France, Germany, Italy, Spain, Sweden, UK.
European organizations (2):
Aerospace and Defence Industries Association of Europe (ASD, #00146); *European Union Aviation Safety Agency (EASA, #08978)*.
NGO Relations Associated body of: *Comité européen de normalisation (CEN, #04162)*. [2022/XM4795/**E**]

- ♦ **ASDV** African Society of Dermatology and Venerology (#00460)
- ♦ **ASEA** African Securities Exchanges Association (#00452)
- ♦ **ASEA** Association des Sociétés d'Electricité d'Afrique (#02867)
- ♦ ASEA – Association of Surgeons of East Africa (inactive)
- ♦ ASEAC – Association of Southeast Asian Cinemas (unconfirmed)
- ♦ **ASEACCU** Association of Southeast and East Asian Catholic Colleges and Universities (#02923)
- ♦ ASEACU / see Association of Southeast and East Asian Catholic Colleges and Universities (#02923)
- ♦ ASE – Alliance to Save Energy (internationally oriented national body)
- ♦ ASEAMS – Association of Southeast Asian Marine Scientists (no recent information)

♦ ASEAN+3 Bond Market Forum (ABMF) 01133

Address not obtained.
URL: https://wpqr4.adb.org/asean3abmf/
History Founded Sep 2010, and operating under the ambit of ASEAN+3. **Aims** Foster standardization of market practices and harmonization of regulations relating to cross-border bond transactions in the region. **Events** *Meeting* Fukuoka (Japan) 2018, *Meeting* Jakarta (Indonesia) 2018, *Meeting* Tokyo (Japan) 2013. **Members** National members; national experts; international experts. Membership countries not specified. **IGO Relations** *Asian Development Bank (ADB, #01422)*. [2019/XM7884/**F**]

♦ ASEAN+3 Macroeconomic Research Office (AMRO) 01134

Dir 10 Shenton Way, 15-08 MAS Bldg, Singapore 079117, Singapore. T. +6563239844. Fax +6562238187. E-mail: enquiry@amro-asia.org.
URL: https://www.amro-asia.org/
History Jul 2011, Singapore. Originally established as a company. On signing of the AMRO Agreement, Oct 2014, established as an International Organization. Registration: Start date: Apr 2011, End date: Oct 2014, Singapore. **Aims** Contribute to securing the macroeconomic and financial stability in the ASEAN+3 region. **Structure** Executive Committee; Advisory Panel; Senior Management; Group Heads. **Languages** English. **Activities** Events/meetings; guidance/assistance/consulting; monitoring/evaluation.
Members Governments (14):
Brunei Darussalam, Cambodia, China, Hong Kong, Indonesia, Japan, Korea Rep, Laos, Malaysia, Myanmar, Philippines, Singapore, Thailand, Vietnam.
IGO Relations Observer status with (1): *United Nations (UN, #20515)* (General Assembly). Memorandum of Understanding with (5): *Asian Development Bank (ADB, #01422)*; *European Stability Mechanism (ESM, #08829)*; *International Monetary Fund (IMF, #14180)*; *Latin American Reserve Fund (#16367)*; *Trilateral Cooperation Secretariat (TCS, #20239)*. [2020.08.27/AA1013/**F***]

♦ ASEAN Academy of Engineering and Technology (AAET) 01135

Secretariat No 40-2 Jalan 2/109E, Desa Business Park, Taman Desa, 58100 Kuala Lumpur, Malaysia. T. +60379838088. Fax +60379809390. E-mail: kbchoo@yahoo.com.
Contact No 17 Jalan Kenari 4, Bandar Puchong Jaya, 47100 Puchong, Selangor, Malaysia.
URL: https://aaet-asean.org/
History Registration: Registry of Societies, Singapore, Start date: 23 Jul 2007. **Aims** Promote, enhance and apply engineering sciences, technology and innovation for the advancement of economy, society and humanity or the realization thereof in the ASEAN communities in particular and the World communities in general. **Structure** Council.
Members Fellows (320) in 20 countries and territories:
Australia, Brunei Darussalam, Cambodia, China, India, Indonesia, Korea Rep, Laos, Malaysia, Myanmar, Nigeria, Pakistan, Philippines, Rwanda, Singapore, Taiwan, Thailand, USA, Vietnam, Zimbabwe.
Consultative Status Consultative status granted from: *ASEAN (#01141)*. [2021.02.17/XJ9840/**D**]

♦ ASEAN Academy of Neurotology Otology and Audiology (AANOA) . . 01136

Pres Fac of Medicine, Univ Kebangsaan Malaysia, Medical Centre, 43600 UKM SELANGOR Bangi, Selangor, Malaysia. E-mail: aanoamalaysia@yahoo.com.
Events *Congress* Singapore (Singapore) 2016, *Congress* Kuala Lumpur (Malaysia) 2012, *Congress* Bangkok (Thailand) 2009, *Congress* Manila (Philippines) 2008. **IGO Relations** *ASEAN (#01141)*. [2012/XJ0666/**E**]

- ♦ ASEAN Agreement on the Conservation of Nature and Natural Resources (1985 treaty)
- ♦ ASEAN Agreement on Customs (1997 treaty)
- ♦ ASEAN Agreement on Disaster Management and Emergency Response (2005 treaty)
- ♦ ASEAN Agreement on Transboundary Haze Pollution (2002 treaty)
- ♦ ASEAN Airlines Association (no recent information)

♦ ASEAN Alliance of Health Supplement Associations (AAHSA) 01137

Secretariat 18 Cross Street No 12-01/08, China Square Central, Singapore 048423, Singapore. T. +6567827630. Fax +6567899067. E-mail: info@aahsa.org.sg.
URL: http://www.aahsa.org.sg/
History 2006. **Aims** Develop the ASEAN health supplements sector. **Structure** Executive Committee, comprising Chairman, 2 Vice-Chairmen, Honorary Secretary, Assistant Honorary Secretary, Honorary Treasurer, Assistant Honorary Treasurer and 6 members. **Languages** English. **Events** *Traditional Medicine and Health Supplements Products Working Group Meeting* Singapore (Singapore) 2012.
Members Full in 7 countries:
Brunei Darussalam, Indonesia, Malaysia, Philippines, Singapore, Thailand, Vietnam.
IGO Relations *ASEAN (#01141)*. [2020/XJ6825/**D**]

- ♦ ASEANAM – ASEAN Association of Museums (inactive)

♦ ASEANAPOL 01138

Permanent Secretariat Level 1 Tower 2, Royal Malaysia Police HQ, Bukit Aman, 50560 Kuala Lumpur, Malaysia. T. +60322668821 – +60322668822. Fax +60322668825. E-mail: aseanapolsec@aseanapol.org.
URL: http://www.aseanapol.org/
History First formal meeting, Oct 1981, Manila (Philippines), organizes as *ASEAN Chiefs of Police Conference*. Originally a rotating secretariat. Permanent Secretariat operational since 1 Jan 2010. Full title: *ASEAN National Police*. Also referred to as *ASEAN National Police Chiefs*. **Aims** Enhance police professionalism; forge stronger regional cooperation in policing; promote lasting friendship among police officers of member countries. **Structure** Conference (annual); Executive Committee; Permanent Secretariat, headed by Executive Director. **Languages** English. **Staff** 24.00 FTE, paid. **Finance** Members' dues. **Events** *Annual Conference* Jakarta (Indonesia) 2015, *Annual Conference* Manila (Philippines) 2014, *Annual Conference* Pattaya (Thailand) 2013, *Annual Conference* Nay Pyi Taw (Myanmar) 2012, *Annual Conference* Vientiane (Laos) 2011. **Publications** *ASEANAPOL Bulletin* (2 a year).
Members Police forces of 10 countries:
Brunei Darussalam, Cambodia, Indonesia, Laos, Malaysia, Myanmar, Philippines, Singapore, Thailand, Vietnam.
Observer forces (2):
Timor-Leste, UK.
Regional Observer force:
European Police Office (Europol, #08239).
International organizations (2):
ASEAN Wildlife Enforcement Network (ASEAN-WEN, #01246); *International Committee of the Red Cross (ICRC, #12799)*.
Dialogue partners (7):
Australia, China, Japan, Korea Rep, New Zealand, Russia, Türkiye.
International dialogue partners (2):
ASEAN (#01141); *International Criminal Police Organization – INTERPOL (ICPO-INTERPOL, #13110)*. [2017/XS0004/c/**E***]

♦ ASEAN Association for Clinical Laboratory Sciences (AACLS) 01139

Sec address not obtained. E-mail: prolab96@yahoo.com.ph.
Contact MIMLS, c/o Inst for Medical Research, Jalan Pahang, 50588 Kuala Lumpur, Malaysia.
URL: http://www.aacls.net/
History 5 Apr 1985, as *ASEAN Association of Medical Laboratory Technologists (AAMLT)*. Present name adopted, 2006, when constitution was amended. **Aims** Foster all aspects of medical laboratory sciences in the ASEAN region; promote cooperation in scientific exchange among ASEAN countries; establish a closer professional and personal rapport amongst members; help establish and formulate policies for attaining the highest possible level of the practice of Laboratory Medicine for the people of ASEAN. **Structure** Council. **Events** *ASEAN Conference* Pattaya (Thailand) 2016, *ASEAN Conference* Singapore (Singapore) 2015, *Conference* Kuala Lumpur (Malaysia) 2010, *ASEAN conference / Conference* Yogyakarta (Indonesia) 2006, *ASEAN conference* Chiang Mai (Thailand) 2004.
Members National associations in 6 countries:
Brunei Darussalam, Indonesia, Malaysia, Philippines, Singapore, Thailand.
Consultative Status Consultative status granted from: *ASEAN (#01141)*. [2015/XE4215/**E**]

- ♦ ASEAN Association of Maritime Education and Training Institutions (no recent information)
- ♦ ASEAN Association of Medical Laboratory Technologists / see ASEAN Association for Clinical Laboratory Sciences (#01139)
- ♦ ASEAN Association of Museums (inactive)

♦ ASEAN Association of Radiology (AAR) 01140

Congress Secretariat Kantor PDSRI Pusat, Menteng Square, 3rd Floor, Tower A/AO-07, Jl Matraman No 30E, Skybridge, Jakarta PUSAT 10510, Indonesia. T. +62213913656. Fax +62213913656. E-mail: aar2015.indonesia@gmail.com.
URL: http://aar2017.com/

History 1986. **Aims** Foster all aspects of *medical* radiological sciences and *imaging* techniques, particularly in the ASEAN region; promote cooperation in scientific exchange of knowledge among ASEAN countries. **Finance** Members' dues. **Events** *Congress* Singapore (Singapore) 2019, *Congress* Kuala Lumpur (Malaysia) 2017, *Congress / Biennial Congress* Bali (Indonesia) 2015, *Congress / Biennial Congress* Bangkok (Thailand) 2013, *Congress* Singapore (Singapore) 2011. **Publications** *ASEAN Journal of Radiology* (4 a year).
Members National radiological societies, associations or colleges in 8 countries:
Brunei Darussalam, Indonesia, Malaysia, Myanmar, Philippines, Singapore, Thailand, Vietnam.
Consultative Status Consultative status granted from: *ASEAN (#01141).* [2020/XE0263/**E**]

♦ ASEAN – Association of South East Asian Nations 01141

Association des nations de l'Asie du Sud-Est (ANASE) – Asociación de Naciones del Asia Sudoriental

SG ASEAN Secretariat, 70 A Jalan Sisingamangaraja, Jakarta 12110, Indonesia. T. +62217262991 – +62217243372. Fax +62217398234 – +62217243504. E-mail: public@asean.org.
URL: http://www.asean.org/

History 8 Aug 1967, Bangkok (Thailand), at a meeting of the Foreign Ministers of the five founding Member States (Indonesia, Malaysia, Philippines, Singapore (Singapore) and Thailand), on signature of the *ASEAN Declaration (Bangkok Declaration).* Previous regional organizations *Association of South-East Asia (ASA, inactive)* and *Maphilindo (inactive)* subsequently amalgamated with ASEAN. Brunei Darussalam adhered on 1 Jan 1984, Vietnam on 28 Jul 1995, Laos and Myanmar on 23 Jul 1997 and Cambodia on 30 Apr 1999. *Treaty of Amity and Cooperation in Southeast Asia (TAC, 1976)* and *Declaration of ASEAN Concord* were signed by member governments at first Summit, 24 Feb 1976, Bali (Indonesia). A second Summit was held in Aug 1977, Kuala Lumpur (Malaysia) and the third Summit, Dec 1987, Manila (Philippines), resulting in the *Manila Declaration. 'Protocol Amending the Treaty of Amity and Cooperation'* enabled countries outside the ASEAN region to accede. At 4th Summit, 27-29 Jan 1992, Singapore, Heads of Government signed the *Singapore Declaration* and a *Framework Agreement on Enhancing ASEAN Economic Cooperation (1992)*; member countries also signed the *Agreement on the Common Effective Preferential Tariff (CEPT, 1992)*, the main tool to establish *ASEAN Free Trade Area (AFTA, #01191).* Agreement on the establishment of a permanent Secretariat (in Jakarta) concluded 24 Feb 1976. *Agreement on ASEAN Preferential Trading Arrangements (PTA, 1977)* signed Feb 1977. Statutes registered in *'1/UNTS 22341'.* Agreement on the establishment of ASEAN Secretariat registered in *'1/UNTS 22342'.* Current Charter signed, 20 Nov 2007, and entered into force 15 Dec 2008, following which ASEAN operates under a new legal framework with new organs. **Aims** Accelerate economic growth, social progress and cultural development in the region through joint endeavours in the spirit of equality and partnership in order to strengthen the foundation for a prosperous and peaceful community of Southeast Asian Nations; promote regional peace and stability through abiding respect for justice and the rule of law in the relationship among countries of the region and adherence to the principles of the United Nations Charter; promote active collaboration and mutual assistance on matters of common interest in economic, social, cultural, technical, scientific and administrative fields; provide assistance to each other in the form of training and research facilities in educational, professional, technical and administrative spheres; collaborate more effectively for the greater utilization of agriculture and industries, expansion of trade, including the study of problems of international commodity trade, improvement of transportation and communications facilities and raising of living standards; promote Southeast Asian studies; maintain close and beneficial cooperation with existing international and regional organizations with similar aims and purposes and explore all avenues for even closer cooperation.
Structure *ASEAN Summit* of Heads of State or Government (originally every 3 years, now biannual). *'ASEAN Coordinating Council'* consisting of ASEAN Foreign Ministers (meets biannually). *'ASEAN Community Councils'* (3): ASEAN Political-Security Community; ASEAN Economic Community; ASEAN Socio-Cultural Community. *'ASEAN Sectoral Ministerial Bodies'* organized under above-mentioned pillars.
I. *'ASEAN Political Security Community'*:
1. ASEAN Foreign Ministers Meeting (AMM), including: ASEAN Senior Political Officials Meeting; ASEAN Standing Committee (ASC); Senior Officials Meeting on Development Planning (SOMDP).
2. Commission on the Southeast Asia Nuclear Weapon-Free Zone (SEANWFZ Commission), including: Executive Committee of the SEANWFZ Commission.
3. ASEAN Defence Ministers Meeting (ADMM), including: ASEAN Defence Senior Officials Meeting (ADSOM).
4. ASEAN Law Ministers Meeting (ALAWMM), including: ASEAN Senior Law Officials Meeting (ASLOM).
5. ASEAN Ministerial Meeting on Transnational Crime (AMMTC); including: ASEAN Senior Officials Meeting on Transnational Crime (SOMTC); ASEAN Senior Officials on Drug Matters (ASOD); Directors-General of Immigration Departments and Heads of Consular Affairs Divisions of Ministries of Foreign Affairs Meetings (DGICM).
6. *ASEAN Regional Forum (ARF, #01228),* including ASEAN Regional Forum Senior Officials Meeting (ARF SOM).
II. *'ASEAN Economic Community'*:
1. ASEAN Economic Ministers (AEM), including: High Level Task Force on ASEAN Economic Integration (HLTF-EI); ASEAN Senior Economic Officials Meeting (SEOM).
2. *ASEAN Free Trade Area (AFTA, #01191)* Council.
3. *ASEAN Investment Area (AIA, see: #01141)* Council.
4. ASEAN Finance Ministers Meeting (AFMM), including: ASEAN Finance and Central Bank Deputies Meeting (AFDM); ASEAN Directors-General of Customs Meeting (Customs DG).
5. ASEAN Ministers on Agriculture and Forestry (AMAF), including: Senior Officials Meeting of the Asean Ministers on Agriculture and Forestry (SOM-AMAF); ASEAN Senior Officials on Forestry (ASOF).
6. ASEAN Ministers on Energy Meeting (AMEM), including: ASEAN Senior Officials Meeting on Energy (SOME).
7. ASEAN Ministerial Meeting on Minerals (AMMin), including ASEAN Senior Officials Meeting on Minerals (ASOMM).
8. ASEAN Ministerial Meeting on Science and Technology (AMMST), including: Committee on Science and Technology (COST).
9. ASEAN Telecommunications and Information Technology Ministers Meeting (TELMIN), including: ASEAN Telecommunications Senior Officials Meeting (TELSOM); ASEAN Telecommunication Regulators' Council (ATRC).
10. ASEAN Transport Ministers Meeting (ATM), including: ASEAN Senior Transport Officials Meeting (STOM).
11. ASEAN Tourism Ministers Meeting (M-ATM), including Meeting of the ASEAN National Tourism Organisations (ASEAN NTOs).
12. ASEAN Mekong Basin Development Cooperation (AMBDC), including: ASEAN Mekong Basin Development Cooperation Steering Committee (AMBDC SC); High Level Finance Committee (HLFC).
13. *ASEAN Centre for Energy (ACE, #01150).*
14. *ASEAN Promotion Centre on Trade, Investment and Tourism (ASEAN-JAPAN CENTRE, #01225).*
III. *'ASEAN Socio-Cultural Community'*:
1. Conference of the ASEAN Ministers Responsible for Information (AMRI), including: Senior Officials Meeting Responsible for Information (SOMRI).
2. ASEAN Ministers Responsible for Culture and Arts (AMCA), including: Senior Officials Meeting for Culture and Arts (SOMCA).
3. ASEAN Education Ministers Meeting (ASED), including: Senior Officials Meeting on Education (SOM-ED).
4. ASEAN Ministerial Meeting on Disaster Management (AMMDM), including: ASEAN Committee on Disaster Management (ACDM).
5. ASEAN Ministerial Meeting on the Environment (AMME), including: ASEAN Senior Officials on the Environment (ASOEN).
6. Conference of the Parties to the *ASEAN Agreement on Transboundary Haze Pollution (2002),* including: Committee (COM) under the COP to the ASEAN Agreement on Transboundary Haze Pollution.
7. ASEAN Health Ministers' Meeting (AHMM), including ASEAN Senior Officials' Meeting on Health Development (SOMHD).
8. ASEAN Labour Ministers Meeting (ALMM), including: ASEAN Senior Labour Officials Meeting (SLOM); ASEAN Committee on the Implementation of the ASEAN Declaration on the Protection and Promotion of the Rights of Migrant Workers.
9. ASEAN Ministers on Rural Development and Poverty Eradication (AMRDPE), including: ASEAN Senior Officials on Rural Development and Poverty Eradication (SOMRDPE).
10. ASEAN Ministerial Meeting for Social Welfare and Development (AMMWSD), including: ASEAN Senior Official's Meeting on Social Welfare and Development (SOMSWD).
11. ASEAN Ministerial Meeting on Youth (AMMY), including: ASEAN Senior Officials' Meeting on Youth (SOMY).
12. ASEAN Conference on Civil Service Matters (ACCSM).
13. *ASEAN Centre for Biodiversity (ACB, #01149).*
14. *ASEAN Coordinating Centre for Humanitarian Assistance on disaster management (AHA Centre, #01161)* – functioning under *ASEAN Agreement on Disaster Management and Emergency Response (AADMER, 2005).*
15. *ASEAN Earthquake Information Centre (AEIC, #01169).*
16. ASEAN Specialised Meteorological Centre (ASMC).
17. *ASEAN University Network (AUN, #01243).*
'Committee of Permanent Representatives'. 'National Secretariats', in the Foreign Ministry of each ASEAN member country, each headed by a Director-General. Committees Abroad. ASEAN Chair; ASEAN Secretariat, headed by Secretary-General.
Also includes: *ASEAN Foundation (#01190).*
Other ASEAN Centres and Facilities not mentioned above:
- ASEAN Centre for the Development of Agricultural Cooperatives (ACEDAC);
- ASEAN Coordinating Centre for Transboundary Haze Pollution;
- *ASEAN Council on Petroleum (ASCOPE, #01164)*;
- ASEAN-EC Management Centre (AEMC);
- *ASEAN Insurance Training and Research Institute (AITRI, #01202)*;
- *South East Asian Central Banks Research and Training Centre (SEACEN Centre, #19760).*

Instrumental in setting up: *Southeast Asian Nuclear Weapon-Free Zone (SEANWFZ, see: #01141).*
Languages English, Filipino, Indonesian, Laotian, Malay, Mon-Khmer languages, Tamil, Thai, Vietnamese. **Staff** Professional staff (open recruitment) at Secretariat: 50 paid. **Finance** *ASEAN Development Fund (ADF, #01167)*, set up 2005 to support activities of the 3 pillars of *ASEAN Community.*
Activities *'ASEAN Vision 2020'* adopted 1997. At 9th Summit, 2003, resolved to set up *ASEAN Community.* Commitment affirmed at 12th ASEAN Summit, 2007, when *'Cebu Declaration of the Establishment of an ASEAN Community by 2015'* was signed. ASEAN Community is comprised of 3 pillars, each with its own Blueprint: *ASEAN Political-Security Community (APSC); ASEAN Economic Community (AEC); ASEAN Socio-Cultural Community (ASCC).*
At 10th Summit, the *'Vientiane Action Programme (VAP)'* was also adopted, a 6-year plan to realize the end goals of the ASEAN Vision 2020 and the Declaration of ASEAN Concord II. The VAP focuses on deepening regional integration and narrowing the development gap within ASEAN, particularly the least developed Member Countries.*ASEAN Development Fund (ADF, #01167)* was established to support the implementation of the VAP and future action programmes.
I: *'ASEAN Political-Security Community (APSC)'*
Blueprint adopted at 14th ASEAN Summit, 1 Mar 2009, Cha-Am (Thailand). Aims to ensure that countries in the region live at peace with one another and with the world in a just, democratic and harmonious environment. Key characteristics: A Rules-based Community of shared values and norms; A Cohesive, Peace, Stable and Resilient Region with shared responsibility for comprehensive security; A Dynamic and Outward-looking Region in an increasingly integrated and interdependent world. Actions include: *ASEAN Intergovernmental Commission on Human Rights (AICHR)*; upholding existing political instruments such as *Treaty of Amity and Cooperation in Southeast Asia (TAC, 1976),Treaty on the Southeast Asia Nuclear Weapon-free Zone (Bangkok Treaty, 1995),* Declaration on Zone of Peace, Freedom and Neutrality (ZOPFAN) and Declaration on the Conduct of Parties (DOC) in the South China Sea;*ASEAN Regional Forum (ARF, #01228).*
II: *'ASEAN Economic Community (AEC)'*
Blueprint adopted at 13th ASEAN Summit, 20 Nov 2007, Vientiane (Laos). Aims for economic integration, bases on a convergence of interests of ASEAN Member Countries to deepen and broaden economic integration through existing and new initiatives with clear timelines. Key elements (4): Single Market and Production Base; Competitive Economic Region; Equitable Economic Development; Integration into the Global Economy. Treaties and actions include:*ASEAN Free Trade Area (AFTA, #01191)* and its *Agreement on the Common Effective Preferential Tariff (CEPT, 1992);ASEAN Investment Area (AIA, see: #01141);ASEAN Agreement on Customs (1997);ASEAN Framework Agreement on Intellectual Property Cooperation (1995);ASEAN Framework Agreement on Services (AFAS, 1995);ASEAN Framework Agreement on the Facilitation of Goods in Transit (1998);ASEAN Framework Agreement on Multimodal Transport (2005);ASEAN Framework Agreement on the Facilitation of Inter-state Transport (1998); ASEAN Single Aviation Market;ASEAN Power Grid (#01224)* – overlooked by *Forum of Heads of ASEAN Power Utilities/Authorities (HAPUA, #09917),* and *Trans-ASEAN Gas Pipeline (TAGP);E-ASEAN Framework Agreement (2000).*
III: *'ASEAN Socio-Cultural Community (ASSC)'*
Blueprint adopted at 14th ASEAN Summit, 1 Mar 2009, Cha-Am (Thailand). Aims to contribute to realizing an ASEAN Community that is people-centred and socially responsible so as to achieve enduring solidarity and unity, by forging a common identity and building a caring and sharing society inclusive and harmonious where well-being, livelihood and welfare are enhanced. Key characteristics: Human Development; Social Welfare and Protection; Social Justice and Rights; Ensuring Environmental Sustainability; Building the ASEAN Identity; Narrowing the Development Gap. Actions and Treaties include:*ASEAN Occupational Safety and Health Network (ASEAN-OSHNET, #01215);ASEAN Agreement on Transboundary Haze Pollution (2002);ASEAN Agreement on the Conservation of Nature and Natural Resources (1985).*
Events *ASEAN Food Conference* Bali (Indonesia) 2023, *ASEAN-Japan Smart Cities Network High-Level Meeting* Aizu-Wakamatsu (Japan) 2022, *Japan-ASEAN Multi-Stakeholder Strategic Consultancy Forum* Tokyo (Japan) 2022, *ASEAN-Korea Frontier Forum* Busan (Korea Rep) 2021, *ASEAN-Japan Social Security High-Level Meeting* Tokyo (Japan) 2021. **Publications** *ASEAN Journal on Science and Technology for Development.* Guidelines; yearbooks; studies; chartbooks; directories; reports.
Members Governments of 10 countries:
Brunei Darussalam, Cambodia, Indonesia, Laos, Malaysia, Myanmar, Philippines, Singapore, Thailand, Vietnam.
IGO Relations *United Nations (UN, #20515)* – ASEAN supports the central role of the United Nations in the maintenance of international peace and security. Memorandum of Understanding signed with: *UNESCO (#20322); UNEP (#20299).* Relationship agreement with: *FAO (#09260).* Dialogue relationship with: *UNDP (#20292).* Permanent observer status with: *World Intellectual Property Organization (WIPO, #21593).* Permanent Observer to: *ECOSOC (#05331).* Cooperates with: *United Nations Institute for Training and Research (UNITAR, #20576).* Relations with: *Asian Development Bank (ADB, #01422).* Takes joint approaches and coordinates in various regional and international fora, especially: *Asia-Pacific Economic Cooperation (APEC, #01887)* (observer status); *Secretariat of the Convention on International Trade in Endangered Species of Wild Fauna and Flora (CITES Secretariat, #19199); Pacific Islands Forum (#17968).* Participates as observer in the activities of: *Codex Alimentarius Commission (CAC, #04081).* Accredited by: *United Nations Framework Convention on Climate Change – Secretariat (UNFCCC, #20564).* Together with: *AVRDC – The World Vegetable Center (#03051)*, set up: *ASEAN-AVRDC Regional Network on Vegetable Research and Development (AARNET, #01143).* Member of: *Asia/Pacific Group on Money Laundering (APG, #01921).* Associated entities: *ASEAN Supreme Audit Institutions (ASEANSAI, #01237); Southeast Asian Fisheries Development Center (SEAFDEC, #19767).*
NGO Relations Associated entitites (72) subdivided into 5 categories:
- Parliamentarians and Judiciary: *ASEAN Inter-Parliamentary Assembly (AIPA, #01205)*;
- Council of ASEAN Chief Justices (CACJ).

Business Organisations:
- *ASEAN Automotive Federation (AAF, #01142)*;
- *ASEAN Bankers Association (ABA, #01144)*;
- *ASEAN Business Advisory Council (ASEAN BAC, #01146)*;
- *ASEAN Chemical Industries Council (ACIC, #01152)*;
- *ASEAN Cosmetic Association (ACA, #01162)*;
- *ASEAN Federation of Textile Industries (AFTEX, #01185)*;
- *ASEAN Furniture Industries Council (AFIC, #01192)*;
- *ASEAN Insurance Council (AIC, #01201)*;

- *ASEAN Intellectual Property Association (AIPA, #01203);*
- *ASEAN Iron and Steel Industry Federation (AISIF, #01206);*
- *ASEAN Ports Association (APA, #01223);*
- *ASEAN Tourism Association (ASEANTA, #01238);*
- *EU-ASEAN Business Council (EU-ABC, #05566);*
- *Federation of ASEAN Economic Associations (FAEA, #09425);*
- *US-ASEAN Business Council.*

Think Tank and Academic Institutions:
- *ASEAN Institute for Peace and Reconciliation (ASEAN-IPR, #01198);*
- *ASEAN Institutes for Strategic and International Studies (ASEAN-ISIS, #01200).*

Civil Society Organisations (CSOs):
- *AirAsia Foundation;*
- *ASEAN Academy of Engineering and Technology (AAET, #01135);*
- *ASEAN Alliance of Health Supplement Associations (AAHSA, #01137);*
- *ASEAN Association of Radiology (AAR, #01140);*
- *ASEAN Chess Confederation (ACC, #01153);*
- *ASEAN Confederation of Employers (ACE, #01158);*
- *ASEAN Confederation of Women's Organizations (ACWO, #01159);*
- *ASEAN Constructors Federation (ACF, #01160);*
- *ASEAN Council of Japan Alumni (ASCOJA, #01163);*
- *ASEAN Council of Teachers (ACT, #01165);*
- *ASEAN CSR Network (#01166);*
- *ASEAN Disability Forum (ADF, #01168);*
- *ASEAN Federation of Accountants (AFA, #01171);*
- *ASEAN Federation of Electrical Engineering Contractors (AFEEC, #01174);*
- *ASEAN Federation of Engineering Organizations (AFEO, #01176);*
- *ASEAN Federation of Forwarders Associations (AFFA, #01177);*
- *ASEAN Federation of Land Surveying and Geomatics (AFLAG, #01180);*
- *ASEAN Federation of Mining Associations (AFMA, #01181);*
- *ASEAN Football Federation (AFF, #01187);*
- *ASEAN Handicraft Promotion and Development Association (AHPADA, #01194);*
- *ASEAN Kite Council (AKC, #01207);*
- *ASEAN Law Association (ALA, #01209);*
- *ASEAN Music Industry Association (AMIA, #01212);*
- *ASEAN Neurological Association (ASNA, #01214);*
- *ASEAN Oleochemical Manufacturers Group (AOMG, #01216);*
- *ASEAN Orthopaedic Association (AOA, #01217);*
- *Asean Para Sports Federation (APSF);*
- *ASEAN Pediatric Federation (APF, #01220);*
- *ASEAN Thalassaemia Society (ATS, no recent information);*
- *ASEAN Tourism Research Association (ATRA, #01239);*
- *ASEAN Valuers Association (AVA, #01245);*
- *Asian Partnership for the Development of Human Resources in Rural Asia (AsiaDHRRA, #01654);*
- *Committee for ASEAN Youth Cooperation (CAYC, #04242);*
- *Federation of ASEAN Consulting Engineers (FACE, #09424);*
- *Federation of ASEAN Shipowners Associations (FASA, #09427);*
- *International Federation of Non-Government Organizations for the Prevention of Drug and Substance Abuse (IFNGO, #13490);*
- *Medical Association of South East Asian Nations (MASEAN, #16623);*
- *Southeast Asia Regional Initiatives for Community Empowerment (SEARICE, #19795);*
- *Southeast Asia School Principals Forum (SEASPF);*
- *Southeast Asian Directors of Music (SEADOM, #19763);*
- *Southeast Asian Studies Regional Exchange Program Foundation (SEASREP Foundation, #19784);*
- *Traditional Textile Arts Society of South East Asia (TTASSEA, #20194);*
- *Veterans Confederation of ASEAN Countries (VECONAC, #20759).*

Other Stakeholders include:
- *Federation of Institutes of Food Science and Technology of ASEAN (FIFSTA, #09598).*

Other organizations linked to ASEAN:
- *ASEAN Academies of Science, Engineering and Technology (ASEANCASE, no recent information);*
- *ASEAN Association for Clinical Laboratory Sciences (AACLS, #01139);*
- *ASEAN Association for Planning and Housing (AAPH, no recent information);*
- *ASEAN Book Publishers Association (ABPA, #01145);*
- *ASEAN Business Forum (ABF, #01147);*
- *ASEAN Chambers of Commerce and Industry (ASEAN-CCI, #01151);*
- *ASEAN College of Surgeons (ACS, no recent information);*
- *ASEAN Federation of Cardiology (#01172);*
- *ASEAN Federation of Cement Manufacturers (AFCM, #01173);*
- *ASEAN Federation of Endocrine Societies (AFES, #01175);*
- *ASEAN Federation of Flying Clubs (AFFC, inactive);*
- *ASEAN Federation of Glass Manufacturers (AFGM, #01178);*
- *ASEAN Federation of Heart Foundations (AFHF, no recent information);*
- *ASEAN Federation of Plastic Industries (AFPI, #01182);*
- *ASEAN Federation of Plastic Surgeons (#01183);*
- *ASEAN Federation for Psychiatry and Mental Health (AFPMH, #01184);*
- *ASEAN Finance Corporation (#01186);*
- *ASEAN Fisheries Federation (AFF, no recent information);*
- *ASEAN Forestry Students Association (AFSA, #01188);*
- *ASEAN Forum on Coal (AFOC, #01189);*
- *ASEAN Hotel and Restaurant Association (AHRA, #01195);*
- *ASEAN International Airports Association (AAA, #01204);*
- *ASEAN Motion Picture Producers Association (AMPPA, no recent information);*
- *ASEAN NGOs for the Prevention of Drugs and Substance Abuse, Malaysia (no recent information);*
- *ASEAN Otorhinolaryngological – Head and Neck Federation (ASEAN ORL HNS Federation, #01218);*
- *ASEAN Patent Attorney Association (no recent information);*
- *ASEAN Pharmaceutical Industry Club (#01221);*
- *ASEAN Public Relations Network (APRN, #01226);*
- *ASEAN Telecommunication Regulators' Council (ATRC);*
- *ASEAN Trade Union Council (ATUC, #01240);*
- *ASEAN University Sports Council (AUSC, #01244);*
- *ASEAN Women's Circle (AWC, no recent information);*
- *Asian Bankers Association (ABA, #01355);*
- *Asian Institute of Technology (AIT, #01519);*
- *Asian Law Students' Association (ALSA, #01527);*
- *Confederation of ASEAN Journalists (CAJ, #04509);*
- *Federation of ASEAN Shippers' Councils (FASC, no recent information);*
- *Isis Women's International Cross Cultural Exchange (ISIS-WICCE, #16031);*
- *Orchid Society of South East Asia (OSSEA, #17789);*
- *Rheumatism Association of ASEAN (RAA, #18935).*

Regular consultation with: *International Trademark Association (INTA, #15706).* Provided input or influence on aspects of development or regulation of: *Internet (#15948).* Member of: *Asia-Pacific Regional Space Agency Forum (APRSAF, #02010).* [2020/XD0165/**D***]

♦ ASEAN Automotive Federation (AAF) 01142

Pres c/o Automotive Federation Malaysia, F-1-47, Block F, Jalan PJU 1A/3, Taipan Damansar 2, Parcel 1, 47301 Petaling Jaya, Selangor, Malaysia. T. +60378439947. E-mail: secretariat@asean-autofed.com.
URL: http://www.asean-autofed.com/

History Founded 1976, as *ASEAN Federation of Automotive Associations (AFAA).* Activities ceased, 1983, when national automotive associations in each ASEAN country focused their efforts to develop their respective national automotive industry. Revived, 1996, with the implementation of AFTA and its schemes. A regional industry club of *ASEAN Chambers of Commerce and Industry (ASEAN-CCI, #01151)* within the framework of *ASEAN (#01141).* **Aims** Promote automotive market integration and growth, cooperation and investments in the ASEAN region. **Structure** Membership Meeting (at least twice a year); Council (meeting twice a year); Technical Committees. **Languages** English. **Staff** 4.00 FTE, voluntary. **Finance** Initial contributions from member economies.
Members National associations within the automotive business community representing constituent members in 10 countries:
Brunei Darussalam, Cambodia, Indonesia, Laos, Malaysia, Myanmar, Philippines, Singapore, Thailand, Vietnam.
[2016/XE0012/**D**]

♦ ASEAN-AVRDC Regional Network on Vegetable Research and Development (AARNET) 01143

Contact c/o AVRDC – The World Vegetable Center, PO Box 42, Shanhua, Tainan 74199, Taiwan. T. +66294286867. Fax +6629428688.
URL: http://avrdc.org/aarnet/

History Established 1999, Singapore (Singapore), within the framework of *AVRDC – The World Vegetable Center (#03051)* and *ASEAN (#01141).* **Aims** Coordinate and facilitate development and implementation of R and D projects on vegetables in ASEAN member countries; facilitate information exchange, technology transfer and training on vegetable production related fields. **Structure** Steering Committee. **Finance** Donor funding for projects. **Activities** Projects/programmes. **Events** *Meeting* Tagaytay (Philippines) 2018, *Meeting* Shanhua (Taiwan) 2017, *Meeting* Kuala Lumpur (Malaysia) 2016, *Meeting* Pakse (Laos) 2015, *Meeting* Bandung (Indonesia) 2014.
Members Countries covered (10):
Brunei Darussalam, Cambodia, Indonesia, Laos, Malaysia, Myanmar, Philippines, Singapore, Thailand, Vietnam.
[2015/XE4670/**E***]

♦ **ASEAN BAC** ASEAN Business Advisory Council (#01146)

♦ ASEAN Bankers Association (ABA) 01144

SG 10 Shenton Way, 12-08 MAS Building, Singapore 079117, Singapore. T. +6562207842. Fax +6562227482.
Chairman address not obtained.
URL: http://www.aseanbankers.org/

History 25 Aug 1976. Current Statutes signed 27 Jul 1985. Previously referred to as *ASEAN Banking Association.* **Aims** Accelerate *economic growth* of ASEAN countries; promote the development of the banking and *financial* system and *profession* in the ASEAN countries; identify growth opportunities for ASEAN banks and promote their common interests. **Structure** Conference (every 2 years). Council (executive arm – meets annually), consisting of Chairman, 1 to 5 Delegates nominated by each Member and Secretary-General. Permanent Committees (3): Cooperation in Finance, Investment and Trade (COFIT); Banking Education; ASEAN Inter-Regional Relations. **Languages** English. **Activities** Organizes courses; co-organizes and supports other events. **Events** *Biennial Conference* Phnom Penh (Cambodia) 2019, *Meeting* Phnom Penh (Cambodia) 2019, *Meeting* Bandar Seri Begawan (Brunei Darussalam) 2018, *Annual ASEAN Regulatory Summit* Singapore (Singapore) 2018, *International Workshop on Deepening Comprehension on Safety Case on Deep Geological Repository (DGR) and Public Confidence on Japan's DGR Programme* Tokyo (Japan) 2018. **Publications** *ASEAN Banker* (4 a year) – newsletter.
Members National associations of banks in the 10 ASEAN countries:
Brunei Darussalam, Cambodia, Indonesia, Laos, Malaysia, Myanmar, Philippines, Singapore, Thailand, Vietnam.
IGO Relations Affiliated with: *ASEAN (#01141).* [2020/XE0815/**E**]

♦ ASEAN Banking Association / see ASEAN Bankers Association (#01144)

♦ ASEAN Book Publishers Association (ABPA) 01145

SG Block 86, Marine Parade Central 03-213, Singapore 44008, Singapore. T. +6563447801. Fax +6564470897.
URL: https://sites.google.com/site/aseanbookpublishersassociation/

History 31 Aug 2005, Philippines, among 6 national book publishers associations of the ASEAN countries, namely Indonesia, Malaysia, Philippines, Singapore, Thailand and Vietnam. Previously referred to as *Publishers and Booksellers Association of ASEAN.* **Aims** Produce a catalogue of English-language books of interest to ASEAN countries; seek economic cooperation in the form of loans for ASEAN publishers from the World Bank or other sources; approach Book Development Councils in each country to request the removal of restrictions impeding development and availability. **Events** *Conference* Vietnam 2006.
Members National associations and government offices in 8 countries:
Brunei Darussalam, Indonesia, Laos, Malaysia, Philippines, Singapore, Thailand, Vietnam.
IGO Relations *ASEAN (#01141).* [2014/XE4428/**E**]

♦ ASEAN Business Advisory Council (ASEAN BAC) 01146

Contact 70 A, Jl Sisingamangaraja, Jakarta 12110, Indonesia. T. +62217220539. E-mail: aseanbac@asean.org.
URL: https://www.asean-bac.org/

History Nov 2001, Bandar Seri Begawan (Brunei Darussalam). Established by *ASEAN (#01141)* Heads of State and Government (HOSGs), at 7th ASEAN Summit. Launched Apr 2003. **Aims** Provide private sector feedback and guidance to boost ASEAN's efforts towards economic integration. **Activities** Awards/prizes/competitions; events/meetings. **Events** *ASEAN Tourism Summit* Manila (Philippines) 2019.
Members High-level companies of 10 countries:
Brunei Darussalam, Cambodia, Indonesia, Laos, Malaysia, Myanmar, Philippines, Singapore, Thailand, Vietnam.
[2019/AA0056/**E**]

♦ ASEAN Business Forum (ABF) 01147

SG c/o Farlim Group, No 2-8, Bangunan Farlim, Jalan PJS 10/32, Bandar Sri Subang, 46000 Petaling Jaya, Selangor, Malaysia.
Contact 302 Orchard Road, 11-01 Tong Building, Singapore 238862, Singapore. T. +6568363517. Fax +6568363516.
URL: http://abf.tma.or.th/index.php

History Founded Nov 1991, under the name *ASEAN Institute,* as a private sector initiative. Present name adopted 24 Mar 1994. **Aims** Promote closer economic, cultural and social ties between member countries of ASEAN; generate closer business ties between ASEAN companies through *joint-ventures,* technical agreements, etc; facilitate inquiries and provide assistance to companies seeking to invest in a specific country. **Structure** Board of Governors, consisting of President, Deputy President, 6 Vice Presidents, Secretary, Treasurer and Executive Director. **Activities** Events/meetings; awards/prizes/competitions; training/education. **Events** *Annual Forum* Bangkok (Thailand) 2015, *ASEAN women business summit* Petaling Jaya (Malaysia) 2005, *Asia young leaders forum* Philippines 1994, *Asia young leaders forum* Kuala Lumpur (Malaysia) 1993.
Members ASEAN-based companies in 6 countries:
Brunei Darussalam, India, Malaysia, Philippines, Singapore, Thailand.
IGO Relations Affiliated with: *ASEAN (#01141).* [2015/XF3812/**F**]

♦ ASEAN Cardiologists' Federation / see ASEAN Federation of Cardiology (#01172)
♦ **ASEAN-CCI** ASEAN Chambers of Commerce and Industry (#01151)

♦ ASEAN Central Bank Forum (ACBF) 01148

Address not obtained.

History 5 Nov 1997, within the framework of *ASEAN (#01141).* **Aims** Evaluate economic and financial risks of member countries; minimize impact of risks through early action and policy options. **Structure** Includes: *ASEAN Central Bank Governors' Meeting (ACGM)* and *ASEAN Finance and Central Bank Deputies Meeting (AFDM).* **Events** *Meeting* Bandar Seri Begawan (Brunei Darussalam) 2013, *Meeting* Phnom Penh (Cambodia) 2012, *Meeting* Nha Trang (Vietnam) 2010, *Meeting* Pattaya (Thailand) 2009. [2012/XF6845/**F***]

♦ ASEAN Centre for Biodiversity (ACB) 01149

Exec Dir Domingo M Lantican Avenue, 4031 Los Baños LAG, Philippines. T. +63495362865. Fax +6325844210. E-mail: contact.us@aseanbiodiversity.org.
Contact c/o ASEAN Secretariat, 70 A Jalan Sisingamangaraja, Jakarta 12110, Indonesia.
URL: http://www.aseanbiodiversity.org/

History Feb 1999, within *ASEAN (#01141),* with the signing of *'ASEAN Agreement for the Establishment of the ASEAN Centre for Biodiversity'* by the 10 ASEAN Member Countries. Officially launched 27 Sep 2005 during the 9th Informal ASEAN Ministerial Meeting on the Environment, held in Makati City (Philippines). Original title: *ASEAN Regional Centre for Biodiversity Conservation (ARCBC).* **Aims** Intensify biodiversity conservation through improved cooperation in a comprehensive regional context by assisting in setting up a network of institutional links among ASEAN countries and between ASEAN and EU partner organizations. **Structure** Governing Board; Executive Director. **Finance** Initial funding from the European Union; ASEAN provides counterpart funding. **Activities** Knowledge management/information dissemination; networking/liaising; research/documentation; events/meetings. **Events** *Meeting* Bangkok (Thailand) 2019, *Meeting* Singapore (Singapore) 2018, *ASEAN Conference on Biodiversity* Bangkok (Thailand) 2016, *International Conference on Conservation Financing in Southeast Asia* Manila (Philippines) 2015, *Meeting* Manila (Philippines) 2010. **IGO Relations** Member of: *Global Biodiversity Information Facility (GBIF, #10250)*. Non-Country partner of: *Partnerships in Environmental Management for the Seas of East Asia (PEMSEA, #18242)*. Memorandum of Cooperation with: *Secretariat of the Convention of Wetlands (#19200)*. **NGO Relations** Member of: *East Asian – Australasian Flyway Partnership (EAAFP, #05198)*. Affiliate partner of: *Biodiversity Indicators Partnership (BIP, #03242)*. Supports: *Wetlands International (#20928)*. [2017/XK2082/**E**]

♦ ASEAN Centre for Energy (ACE) 01150

Exec Dir Jl HR Rasuna Said Blok X-2, Kav 07-08, Kuningan, Jakarta 12950, Indonesia. T. +62215279332. Fax +62215279350. E-mail: secretariat@aseanenergy.org.
URL: http://www.aseanenergy.org/

History 4 Jan 1999, by *ASEAN (#01141)*, taking over activities of the previous *ASEAN-EC Energy Management and Research Training Centre (AEEMTRC, inactive)*. **Structure** Governing Council, comprising Senior Officials on energy and representative from the ASEAN Secretariat. Includes: *Promotion of Renewable Energy Sources in Southeast Asia (PRESSEA)*. **Events** *ASEAN-Korea Energy Safety Management Policy Forum* Incheon (Korea Rep) 2021, *ASEAN Energy Business Forum* Sejong (Korea Rep) 2020, *ASEAN Plan of Action for Energy Cooperation Drafting Committee Meeting* Singapore (Singapore) 2019, *Meeting* Singapore (Singapore) 2019, *ASEAN Energy Business Forum* Singapore (Singapore) 2018. **Publications** *ASEAN Energy Bulletin*. **IGO Relations** *International Energy Agency (IEA, #13270)*. [2020/XE4112/**E***]

♦ ASEAN Centre for Preventive Drug Education / see ASEAN Training Center for Preventive Drug Education (#01241)

♦ ASEAN Chambers of Commerce and Industry (ASEAN-CCI) 01151

Chambres de commerce et de l'industrie de l'ANASE

Pres c/o Fed of Thailand Industries, Queen Sirkit Natl Convention Center, Zone C, 4th Floor, 60 New Rachadapisek Rd Klongtoey, Bangkok, 10110, Thailand. T. +6623451000. Fax +662345129699. E-mail: information@off.fti.or.th.

History 1972. Current constitution adopted, 9 Dec 2005. **Aims** Support the objectives of ASEAN in its pursuit of effective measures for regional economic cooperation and integration; accelerate economic growth and progress in the region through joint approaches, endeavours and action in order to strengthen the foundation and coordination for the enhancement of the communities of ASEAN; foster closer relations and cooperation between and among the constituent members through mutual assistance in matters of common interest in the solution of economic problems in the area; maintain closer relations and cooperation with regional and international organizations having similar aims and objectives. **Structure** Council (meets twice a year), consisting of President/Chairman of Executive Committee, 10 Vice-Presidents, Deputy Chairman of Executive Committee/President-Elect, Treasurer, Secretary-General, Assistant Secretary-General, Executive Director and at least 5 persons from each of the constituent members. Executive Committee, comprising Chairman, Deputy Chairman, committee chairmen and representatives from each member. Committees (9); Regional Industry Clubs; Business Councils with dialogue partners. Permanent Secretariat, located at ASEAN Secretariat in Jakarta (Indonesia). **Languages** English. **Staff** No permanent staff. **Finance** Members' dues: US$ 1,000 a year, plus additional US$ 500 as development fee from constituent members and additional US$ 500 as development fee from constituent members from CLMV.

Activities Works through working committees and business partners. Committees (9): Airlines, Tourism; Automotive; e-ASEAN; Electronics; Food, agriculture, forestry, rubber-based products, wood-based products, fisheries and agro-based products; Healthcare; Textiles/Apparel; Trade Environment, WTO, NTMs; Finance. Regional Industry Clubs include:
- *ASEAN Aluminium Industry Club (AAIC, inactive)*;
- *ASEAN Chemical Industries Council (ACIC, #01152)*;
- *ASEAN Federation of Agricultural Machinery Manufacturers (AFAMM, inactive)*;
- *ASEAN Automotive Federation (AAF, #01142)*;
- *ASEAN Federation of Cement Manufacturers (AFCM, #01173)*;
- *ASEAN Federation of Electrical, Electronics and Allied Industries (AFEEA, inactive)*;
- *ASEAN Federation of Food Processing Industries (AFFPI-ASEAN-CCI, inactive)*;
- *ASEAN Furniture Industries Council (AFIC, #01192)*;
- *ASEAN Federation of Glass Manufacturers (AFGM, #01178)*;
- *ASEAN Federation of Plastic Industries (AFPI, #01182)*;
- *ASEAN Federation of Textile Industries (AFTEX, #01185)*;
- *ASEAN Iron and Steel Industry Federation (AISIF, #01206)*;
- *ASEAN Panel Products Federation (APPF, inactive)*;
- *ASEAN Pharmaceutical Industry Club (#01221)*;
- *Rubber Industries Association of Southeast Asian Nations (RIASEAN, inactive)*.

Organizes ASEAN Business Summits of world business leaders and government officials.
Events *ASEAN-EU Business Summit* Hanoi (Vietnam) 2013, *ASEAN-EU Business Summit* Phnom Penh (Cambodia) 2012, *ASEAN-EU Business Summit* Jakarta (Indonesia) 2011, *Meeting* Chiang Mai (Thailand) 2007, *Meeting* Kuala Lumpur (Malaysia) 2007.
Members National chambers of commerce and industry of 10 ASEAN countries:
Brunei Darussalam, Cambodia, Indonesia, Laos, Malaysia, Myanmar, Philippines, Singapore, Thailand, Vietnam.
IGO Relations *ASEAN (#01141)*; *World Trade Organization (WTO, #21864)*. **NGO Relations** Memorandum of Understanding with: *World Chambers Federation (WCF, #21269)*. [2011/XE8063/t/**E**]

♦ ASEAN Chemical Industries Club / see ASEAN Chemical Industries Council (#01152)

♦ ASEAN Chemical Industries Council (ACIC) 01152

Contact address not obtained. E-mail: secretariat@scic.sg – secretariat@cicm.org.my.
History Original title: *ASEAN Chemical Industries Club*. A regional industry club of *ASEAN Chambers of Commerce and Industry (ASEAN-CCI, #01151)*. **Events** *Conference* Singapore (Singapore) 1998. **IGO Relations** *ASEAN (#01141)*. [2018/XD5193/t/**E**]

♦ ASEAN Chess Confederation (ACC) 01153

Secretariat 170 Upper Bukit Timah Road 10-04, Bukit Timah Shopping Centre, Singapore 588179, Singapore.
URL: http://www.aseanchess.org/

History Founded 28 May 2000, Vung Tau (Vietnam). **Aims** Further the interests of chess in ASEAN, as well as interests of member federations. **Structure** General Meeting; Board. **Languages** English. **Finance** Members' dues. Sponsorship. **Activities** Sporting activities. **Events** *ASEAN+ Age-Group Championships* Singapore (Singapore) 2015.
Members National federations in 10 countries:
Brunei Darussalam, Cambodia, Indonesia, Laos, Malaysia, Myanmar, Philippines, Singapore, Thailand, Vietnam.
Consultative Status Consultative status granted from: *ASEAN (#01141)*. [2016.10.20/XD8991/**D**]

♦ ASEAN-China Alliance of Private Higher Education Institutions (unconfirmed)

♦ ASEAN-China Centre (ACC) 01154

Secretariat No 43 Liang maqiao Road, Chaoyang District, 100600 Beijing, China. T. +861065321660 ext 655. Fax +861085322527. E-mail: iprd@asean-china-centre.org.
URL: http://www.asean-china-center.org/

History Established on Memorandum of Understanding between Governments of the Member States of the Association of Southeast Asian Nations and the Government of the People's Republic of China, with headquarters in China. Inaugurated Nov 2011. **Structure** Joint Council; Joint Executive Board; Secretariat. Divisions (4): General Affairs and Coordination; Trade and Investment; Education, Culture and Tourism; Information and Public Relations. **Publications** *ACC Newsletter*.
Members States (11):
Brunei Darussalam, Cambodia, China, Indonesia, Laos, Malaysia, Myanmar, Philippines, Singapore, Thailand, Vietnam.
[2022.10.11/XM7772/**E***]

♦ ASEAN Cocoa Club (ACC) 01155

Dir-Gen c/o Malaysian Cocoa Board, 5th-7th Floor, Wisma SEDCO, Lorong Plaza Wawasan, Off Coastal Highway, Locked Bag 211, 88999 Kota Kinabalu, Sabah, Malaysia. T. +6088234477 – +6088234472 – +6088234473. Fax +6088256912 – +6088239575. E-mail: mhazlan@koko.gov.my.
URL: http://www.koko.gov.my/acc/

History Founded at inaugural meeting of 2-3 Jul 1996, Kota Kinabalu (Malaysia). **Aims** Strengthen the objective bargaining position of ASEAN on matters affecting *agriculture* and *forest products* trade in the world market; expand agriculture and forest products export through product diversification of downstream processing and higher value added activity; continue upgrading the quality of ASEAN agriculture and forest products; lay down the foundation for bigger and closer economic ties between ASEAN member countries. **Languages** English. **Finance** Sources: government support. Supported by government of Malaysia. **Activities** Politics/policy/regulatory. **Events** *Meeting* Putrajaya (Malaysia) 2019, *Meeting* Ho Chi Minh City (Vietnam) 2018, *Meeting* Manila (Philippines) 2017, *Meeting* Yogyakarta (Indonesia) 2016, *Meeting* Bangkok (Thailand) 2015.
Members Representatives from government and private sector of 10 countries:
Brunei Darussalam, Cambodia, Indonesia, Laos, Malaysia, Myanmar, Philippines, Singapore, Thailand, Vietnam.
IGO Relations Ministry of Plantation Industries and Commodities, Malaysia. [2021.05.20/XF6465/**F**]

♦ ASEAN Coffee Federation (ACF) 01156

CEO 18 Sin Ming Lane, Suite 02-08, Midview City, Singapore 573960, Singapore. T. +6569779848. E-mail: info@aseancoffee.org.
URL: http://aseancoffee.org/

History 14 Mar 2013. Inaugural meeting held 2010, Pattaya (Thailand). Officially founded, 2013, when constitution was adopted. **Aims** Promote ASEAN coffee worldwide. **Structure** Board. **Languages** English. **Activities** Certification/accreditation; events/meetings; knowledge management/information dissemination; training/education. **Events** *Annual General Meeting* Singapore (Singapore) 2019.
Members Full in 8 countries:
Indonesia, Laos, Malaysia, Myanmar, Philippines, Singapore, Thailand, Vietnam. [2021.02.17/XM5326/**D**]

♦ ASEAN Colorectal Forum (meeting series)

♦ ASEAN Committee on Consumer Protection (ACCP) 01157

Contact CCPID – Market Integration Directorate, ASEAN Economic Community Dept, ASEAN Secretariat, Jl Sisingamangaraja 70A, Kebayoran Baru, Jakarta 12110, Indonesia. T. +6221726991 – +62217243372. Fax +62217398234 – +62217243504.
URL: http://www.aseanconsumer.org/

History Aug 2007, as *ASEAN Coordinating Committee on Consumer Protection (ACCCP)*. Initiated under the *ASEAN (#01141)* Economic Community (EAC) Blueprint. **Aims** Provide a channel or facility for ASEAN consumers to complain or claim for any loss incurred in a less cumbersome, speedy manner and at a minimal cost. **Structure** Chair; Working Groups (3). **Events** *Meeting* Bangkok (Thailand) 2019, *Meeting* Manila (Philippines) 2018, *Meeting* Singapore (Singapore) 2018, *Meeting* Manila (Philippines) 2014.
Members ASEAN governments (10):
Brunei Darussalam, Cambodia, Indonesia, Laos, Malaysia, Myanmar, Philippines, Singapore, Thailand, Vietnam.
[2016/XM5895/**E***]

♦ ASEAN Community (unconfirmed)

♦ ASEAN Confederation of Employers (ACE) 01158

Confédération des employeurs de l'ANASE

Contact ECOT, 3th floor – Global Electrics Bldg, 888/8 Srinakarin Road, Samut Prakan, 10270, Thailand. T. +6623857177 – +6623857117 – +6623857777. Fax +6623857116 – +6623857117. E-mail: ecot@ecot.or.th – toecot@gmail.com.
URL: http://www.aseanemployers.org/

History 25 Nov 1978, Singapore (Singapore), when Constitution was adopted. Constitution amended by 11th Meeting of the Board of Directors, 3 Aug 1985, Bangkok (Thailand). **Aims** Foster solidarity and development of employers' organizations in the region; safeguard and promote the interests of ASEAN employers; collate and disseminate information on legislative changes and general developments in the fields of labour, social and economic matters, which are likely to affect the interests of employers. **Structure** Board of Directors (meets once a year). Secretariat, headed by Executive Secretary. **Finance** Annual members' contributions: US$ 1,000. **Activities** Events/meetings. **Events** *CEOs and BODs Meeting* Makati (Philippines) 2019, *Joint Meeting* Manila (Philippines) 2019, *ASEAN Regional Tripartite Social Dialogue Conference* Singapore (Singapore) 2018, *CEOs and BODs Meeting* Kuala Lumpur (Malaysia) 2015, *CEOs and BODs Meeting* Kuala Lumpur (Malaysia) 2014. **Publications** *ACE Bulletin* (2 a year).
Members Employers' organizations in 6 countries:
Cambodia, Indonesia, Malaysia, Philippines, Singapore, Thailand.
Consultative Status Consultative status granted from: *ASEAN (#01141)*; *ILO (#11123)* (Regional). **NGO Relations** *International Organisation of Employers (IOE, #14428)*. [2015/XE0583/**E**]

♦ ASEAN Confederation of Women's Organizations (ACWO) 01159

Exec Dir 46 jalan 14/29, 46100 Petaling Jaya, Selangor, Malaysia. T. +60379543008.
URL: http://acwo.org/

History 20 Nov 1981, Jakarta (Indonesia). **Aims** Bring together women's organizations in the Asean region to work in concerted efforts towards the full integration of women in *development*. Coordinate and act as a confederation for national women organizations of the ASEAN member countries in order to: secure all such reforms as necessary to give full meaning to *equality* in *human rights*, status and opportunities; urge women to realize and accept their responsibilities in the exercise of their rights and influence in public and private life to ensure respect for human dignity; promote cooperation, peace and understanding and increase mutual support among women through international contacts. **Structure** General Assembly. Conference Council, consisting of 2 confederate members of each national organization. Board of Directors, comprising President, Vice-President, Secretary General, Treasurer, Immediate Past President, Past President and 5 Directors. **Finance** Members' dues. Other sources: sponsors; sale of publications. **Activities** Projects/programmes. **Events** *Bord Meeting* Bangkok (Thailand) 2016, *General Assembly* Kuala Lumpur (Malaysia) 2014, *General Assembly* Jakarta (Indonesia) 2012, *Southeast Asia Women Entrepreneur Conference* Kuching (Malaysia) 2012, *General Assembly* Hanoi (Vietnam) 2010. **Publications** *ACWO echo* – newsletter. *Daughters of Asia* (2002).
Members National committees of women in 10 countries:
Brunei Darussalam, Cambodia, Indonesia, Laos, Malaysia, Myanmar, Philippines, Singapore, Thailand, Vietnam.
Consultative Status Consultative status granted from: *ASEAN (#01141)*. **IGO Relations** Associated with Department of Global Communications of the United Nations. [2019/XE6116/**E**]

♦ ASEAN Constructors Federation (ACF) 01160

Secretariat c/o Indonesia Contractors Assoc, Jl Darmawangsa Raya No 2, Jakarta 12160, Indonesia.
URL: http://www.aseanconstructorsfederation.org/

History 30 May 1985, Jakarta (Indonesia), when Constitution was adopted. **Aims** Provide a forum for dialogues, foster cooperation and promote mutual consultation among construction *contractors* in the AESAN region; unify efforts of the construction contractors in the ASEAN region with a will to promote export of construction services to countries outside the region, and to pool resources, if necessary and desirable, to attain the goal. **Structure** Council (meets once a year). Chairman; Secretary General. **Finance** Members' dues. **Activities** Promotes joint ventures and joint operations for enhancement of their construction contracting capabilities through complementation and/or supplementation. Encourages exchange of information and know-how for improvement of construction technology and management, upgrading of construction labour skills and standards, and, ultimately, achieving rapid advancement of the construction industry in the ASEAN region. Organizes symposia and meetings. **Events** *Meeting* Taipei (Taiwan) 1992, *ASEAN international symposium on construction and development* Kuala Lumpur (Malaysia) 1990.
Members National associations of construction contractors in 7 countries:
Cambodia, Indonesia, Malaysia, Philippines, Singapore, Thailand, Vietnam.
Consultative Status Consultative status granted from: *ASEAN (#01141)*. [2018/XD1844/**E**]

♦ ASEAN Coordinating Centre for Humanitarian Assistance on disaster management (AHA Centre) **01161**

Contact Gedung Graha BNPB, 13 Floor, Jalan Pramuka Raya Kav 38, Jakarta 13120, Indonesia. T. +622121012278. Fax +622121012287. E-mail: info@ahacentre.org.
URL: http://www.ahacentre.org/

History Set up 17 Nov 2011, Bali (Indonesia), on signature of *Agreement on the Establishment of the ASEAN Coordinating Centre for Humanitarian Assistance on disaster management*, by all *ASEAN (#01141)* Member States. Hosted by Government of Indonesia. Functions under *ASEAN Agreement on Disaster Management and Emergency Response (AADMER, 2005)*. **Aims** Facilitate cooperation and coordination among ASEAN Member States and with the UN and international organizations for disaster management and emergency response in the ASEAN region. **Structure** Governed by *ASEAN Committee on Disaster Management (ACDM)*. **Staff** 23.00 FTE, paid. **Activities** Monitoring/evaluation; humanitarian/emergency aid. **Events** *Humanitarian Assistance in Southeast Asia during COVID-19* Singapore (Singapore) 2020, *Meeting* Mandalay (Myanmar) 2019, *Meeting* Nay Pyi Taw (Myanmar) 2019, *Seminar* Singapore (Singapore) 2018.
Members Governments of 10 countries:
Brunei Darussalam, Cambodia, Indonesia, Laos, Malaysia, Myanmar, Philippines, Singapore, Thailand, Vietnam.
[2020/XM5351/**E***]

♦ ASEAN Coordinating Committee on Consumer Protection / see ASEAN Committee on Consumer Protection (#01157)

♦ ASEAN Cosmetic Association (ACA) **01162**

Office Room 306, Parc 15th Ave Condomium, 226 15th Avenue, Barangay San Roque, Cubao, 1109 Quezon City, Philippines. E-mail: susan.neo@aseancosmetics.org.
URL: http://www.aseancosmetics.org/

History Feb 2001. Also referred to as *ASEAN Cosmetics Association*. **Aims** Help, develop and maintain a sustainable and trusted cosmetic industry association in ASEAN by advocating best ethical practices, proactively partnering with local associations, creating a forum where talented people are inspired to create innovative cosmetics products and services. **Structure** Board. **Events** *Leaders Forum* Singapore (Singapore) 2019, *Conference on Safety Assessment of Cosmetics* Seoul (Korea Rep) 2016, *Cosmetics Leaders Forum* Jakarta (Indonesia) 2015, *Meeting* Kuala Lumpur (Malaysia) 2013, *Conference* Tokyo (Japan) 2013.
Members National organizations in 10 countries:
Brunei Darussalam, Cambodia, Indonesia, Laos, Malaysia, Myanmar, Philippines, Singapore, Thailand, Vietnam.
Consultative Status Consultative status granted from: *ASEAN (#01141)*. [2020/XD8995/**D**]

♦ ASEAN Cosmetics Association / see ASEAN Cosmetic Association (#01162)

♦ ASEAN Council of Japan Alumni (ASCOJA) **01163**

Secretariat c/o OJSAT, 408 Phaholyothin Place 16th Floor, Room No 408/65, Phaholyothin Road, Samsen-nai, Phyathai, Bangkok, 10400, Thailand. T. +6623571241 – +6623571242 – +6623571245. Fax +6623571246. E-mail: admin@ojsat.or.th.
URL: http://www.ascoja.org/

History Jun 1977, Japan. **Aims** Serve as a centre for a continuing exchange of information and experience; undertake projects designed to foster closer ties. **Structure** Board, including Chairman, Vice-Chairman, Secretary-General and Treasurer. Secretariat in Manila (Philippines). **Events** *Conference* Singapore (Singapore) 2020, *Conference* Vientiane (Laos) 2019, *Conference* Siem Reap (Cambodia) 2018, *Conference* Bandar Seri Begawan (Brunei Darussalam) 2017, *Conference* Subang Jaya (Malaysia) 2016.
Members Associations in 9 countries:
Brunei Darussalam, Cambodia, Indonesia, Malaysia, Myanmar, Philippines, Singapore, Thailand, Vietnam.
Consultative Status Consultative status granted from: *ASEAN (#01141)*. [2020/XJ5697/**D**]

♦ ASEAN Council on Petroleum (ASCOPE) **01164**

Sec PTT Public Company Limited, 20th Floor, Building 1, 555 Vibhavadi Rangsit Road, Chatuchak, Bangkok, 10900, Thailand. T. +6625373941. Fax +6625372978.
URL: http://ascope.org/

History Established 15 Oct 1975, Jakarta (Indonesia). Brunei Darussalam joined in 1985, Cambodia and Myanmar in 2001. **Aims** Promote active collaboration and mutual assistance in the development of *petroleum resources* in the region; collaborate in the efficient *utilization* of petroleum; provide mutual assistance in personnel training and the use of facilities and services in all phases of petroleum *industry*. **Structure** Council (meets once a year, usually in October); National Committees (meet twice a year); Working Committees (3): Technical; Economic; Legal; ASCOPE Secretariat. **Languages** English. **Staff** 3.00 FTE, paid. **Finance** Contributions and commitments from members. **Activities** Interest focuses on all fields of the oil and gas industry. Drawing up a Memorandum of Understanding to expedite the *Trans-ASEAN Gas Pipeline (TAGP)*. TAGP Task Force, set up Nov 1999, identifies possible new gas interconnections and addresses such cross-border issues as: energy/gas market reserves; supply and demand; economic feasibility and energy pricing; technical scheduling and gas pipeline and power grid routing; institutional, legal, financial/commercial and management frameworks. **Events** *Meeting* Hanoi (Vietnam) 2019, *Meeting* Bangkok (Thailand) 2018, *Annual Meeting* Singapore (Singapore) 2017, *Meeting* Singapore (Singapore) 2017, *Meeting* Siem Reap (Cambodia) 2016.
Members National oil companies of 10 ASEAN countries:
Brunei Darussalam, Cambodia, Indonesia, Laos, Malaysia, Myanmar, Philippines, Singapore, Thailand, Vietnam.
[2020/XE0014/**E***]

♦ ASEAN Council of Physical Education and Sport (unconfirmed)

♦ ASEAN Council of Teachers (ACT) **01165**

Address not obtained.

History 23 Nov 1978, Singapore (Singapore). **Aims** Strengthen ties of friendship, brotherhood and solidarity among teachers of the region; enhance their participation in regional and national development efforts; improve their status, conditions of work and professional competence. **Structure** Convention (annual); Board of Directors, consisting of one representative from each country. Secretariat rotates (changes annually, located in the town of the last convention). **Activities** Events/meetings; training/education. **Events** *Annual Convention* Seoul (Korea Rep) 2016, *Annual Convention* Singapore (Singapore) 2014, *Annual Convention* Singapore (Singapore) 2014, *Annual Convention* Kuala Lumpur (Malaysia) 2013, *Annual Convention* Melaka (Malaysia) 2013.
Members Teachers' organizations in 6 countries:
Brunei Darussalam, Indonesia, Malaysia, Philippines, Singapore, Thailand.
Consultative Status Consultative status granted from: *ASEAN (#01141)*. [2015/XD2077/**D**]

♦ ASEAN CSR Network **01166**

CEO 803 King George's Avenue, #02-144, Singapore 200803, Singapore. E-mail: info@asean-csr-network.org.
URL: http://www.asean-csr-network.org/

History Incorporated Dec 2010 and launched 11 Jan 2011. Registration: Accounting and Corporate Regulatory Authority, No/ID: UEN201025962K, Start date: 18 Dec 2010, Singapore. **Aims** Promote and enable responsible business conduct in ASEAN to achieve sustainable, equitable and inclusive social, environmental and economic development. **Structure** Board of Trustees; Advisory Council; Secretariat. **Languages** English. **Events** *ASEAN Responsible Business Forum* Singapore (Singapore) 2020, *ASEAN Responsible Business Forum* Singapore (Singapore) 2019, *ASEAN Responsible Business Forum* Singapore (Singapore) 2018, *Forum on Sustainability Reporting in ASEAN and Singapore* Singapore (Singapore) 2018, *Plans for SCOPE Seminar* Singapore (Singapore) 2018.
Members Organizations (7) in 7 countries:
Indonesia, Malaysia, Myanmar, Philippines, Singapore, Thailand, Vietnam.
Regional association (1):
ASEAN Foundation (#01190).
Consultative Status Consultative status granted from: *ASEAN (#01141)*. [2020.05.05/XJ9491/**F**]

♦ ASEANCUPS – Association of South-East Asian Nation Countries' Union of Polymer Science (inactive)

♦ ASEAN Development Fund (ADF) **01167**

Contact ASEAN Secretariat, 70 A Jalan Sisingamangaraja, Jakarta 12110, Indonesia.
URL: http://www.asean.org/

History 26 Jul 2005, Vientiane (Laos), by *ASEAN (#01141)*, to realize ASEAN Vision 2020 and support setting up of *ASEAN Community*, as articulated in the *Declaration of ASEAN Concord II*. Takes over activities of *Fund for the Association of South-East Asian Nations (ASEAN Fund, inactive)*. **Finance** Initial contribution of each member state: US$ 1 million.
Members Governments of 10 countries:
Brunei Darussalam, Cambodia, Indonesia, Laos, Malaysia, Myanmar, Philippines, Singapore, Thailand, Vietnam.
[2005/XM1087/f/**F***]

♦ ASEAN Disability Forum (ADF) **01168**

Secretariat Menteng Square Office – Appartment Tower A Lt 2, Unit AR-01, Jl Matraman Raya No 30E, Jakarta, Indonesia. T. +622129614294. Fax +622129614294. E-mail: secretariat@aseandisabilityforum.org – adfsecretariat9@gmail.com.
URL: http://aseandisabilityforum.org/

History Founded 2009. **Aims** Promote full participation and equal opportunity to people with disabilities in the ASEAN community. **Structure** Advisory Board; Executive Board.
Members Full in 10 countries:
Brunei Darussalam, Cambodia, Indonesia, Laos, Malaysia, Myanmar, Philippines, Singapore, Thailand, Vietnam.
Consultative Status Consultative status granted from: *ASEAN (#01141)*. [2018/XM8410/**F**]

♦ ASEAN Earthquake Information Centre (AEIC) **01169**

Main Office Jalan Angkasa I no 2, Kemayoran, Jakarta 10720, Indonesia. T. +62214209103. Fax +62216546316.
URL: http://aeic.bmkg.go.id/

History 2000, following a proposal by the National Meteorological Services of *ASEAN (#01141)*, Aug 1990. **Aims** Disseminate information on big/strong earthquakes as early as possible occurring in the territories of ASEAN countries; provide scientific and technical training of seismologists from members of ASEAN. **Activities** Knowledge management/information dissemination. [2016/XG4384/**E**]

♦ ASEAN-EC Management Centre (internationally oriented national body)

♦ ASEAN-European Academic University Network (ASEA UNINET) . . . **01170**

Head Office c/o OeAD GmbH, Service Ctr for European and Intl Mobility and Cooperation, Ebendorferstrasse 7, 1010 Vienna, Austria. T. +43153480409. E-mail: asea-uninet@oead.at.
URL: http://www.asea-uninet.org/

History 1994, as *Austrian South-East Asian University Partnership Network*. Subsequently changed title to *Asean-European University Network*, 1999. **Aims** Encourage and facilitate cooperation between academic institutions. **Structure** Plenary; University Coordinators; National Coordinators; Coordinators and Vice-Coordinators for Europe and South-East Asia; Chairperson. **Languages** English. **Staff** 6.00 FTE, paid. **Finance** Government and university contributions. **Activities** Networking/liaising; research/documentation; events/meetings; financial and/or material support; training/education. **Events** *National Coordinators Meeting / Meeting* Bratislava (Slovakia) 2015, *Plenary Meeting* Innsbruck (Austria) 2015, *Plenary Meeting / Meeting* Innsbruck (Austria) 2014, *National Coordinators Meeting / Meeting* Ioannina (Greece) 2013, *Plenary Meeting / Meeting* Kuala Lumpur (Malaysia) 2013.
Members Full: universities (84) in 17 countries:
Austria, Cambodia, Czechia, Germany, Greece, Indonesia, Iran Islamic Rep, Italy, Malaysia, Myanmar, Pakistan, Philippines, Portugal, Slovakia, Spain, Thailand, Vietnam.
[2020/XM0520/**F**]

♦ Asean-European University Network / see ASEAN-European Academic University Network (#01170)

♦ ASEAN Federation of Accountants (AFA) **01171**

Secretariat Inst of Indonesia Chartered Accountants, Graha Akuntan, Singdanglaya street 1, Menteng, Jakarta 10310, Indonesia. T. +622131904232. Fax +62217245078. E-mail: afa@afa-accountants.org.
URL: http://www.afa-accountants.org/home

History Mar 1977. **Aims** Provide an organization for ASEAN accountants to further advance the profession in the region so as to establish an ASEAN philosophy on the accounting profession; establish a medium for closer relations, regional cooperation, and assistance among ASEAN accountants; enhance the continuous development of the profession in the region through joint endeavours; identify and highlight vital problems affecting the profession in the region and formulate proposals towards their solution; provide accountants with a venue for information exchange; represent accountants in their collective dealings with international accounting and other organizations; cooperate with ASEAN business regional groupings whose economic development efforts may be complemented by ASEAN accountants. **Structure** Council, consisting of up to 4 official representatives from each primary member body. **Finance** Members' dues. **Events** *Conference* Singapore (Singapore) 2019, *Making ASEAN the voice of global accounting profession* Bangkok (Thailand) 2003, *Conference* Singapore (Singapore) 2001, *Conference* Davao (Philippines) 1999, *Conference* Davao (Philippines) 1999. **Publications** *Easy Guide to Setting Up Accountancy Practices in ASEAN Countries*. Annual Report. Survey Report.
Members Primary members national organizations of accounting professionals representing counties within the territorial jurisdiction of ASEAN. Members in 10 countries:
Brunei Darussalam, Cambodia, Indonesia, Laos, Malaysia, Myanmar, Philippines, Singapore, Thailand, Vietnam.
Associate members internationally recognized bodies of accounting professionals of any country supportive of ASEAN, regardless of territorial jurisdiction of ASEAN. Members in 2 countries:
Australia, UK.
Included in the above, 1 organization listed in this Yearbook:
Association of Chartered Certified Accountants (ACCA).
Consultative Status Consultative status granted from: *ASEAN (#01141)*. [2020/XE7299/**E**]

♦ ASEAN Federation of Automotive Associations / see ASEAN Automotive Federation (#01142)

♦ ASEAN Federation of Cardiology **01172**

Contact 5th Fl, Royal Golden Jubilee Building, No 2, Soi Soonvijai, New Petchburi Road, Bangkapi, Bangkok, 10320, Thailand. T. +6627180067. Fax +6627180068.
URL: http://www.afccmyanmar2016.com/

History 1973, Jakarta (Indonesia). Previously referred to as *ASEAN Cardiologists' Federation (ACF)*. **Aims** Promote cooperation in cardiology research. **Events** *Towards Cardiovascular Health – Cradle of Life* Siem Reap (Cambodia) 2021, *Congress* Siem Reap (Cambodia) 2020, *Congress* Jakarta (Indonesia) 2019, *ESC Asia Meeting* Singapore (Singapore) 2019, *Congress* Bangkok (Thailand) 2018. **Publications** *ASEAN Heart Journal*.
Members Representatives in 6 countries:
Indonesia, Malaysia, Philippines, Singapore, Thailand, Vietnam.
IGO Relations *ASEAN (#01141)*. **NGO Relations** *Asian Pacific Society of Cardiology (APSC, #01631)*. Member of: *World Heart Federation (WHF, #21562)*. [2014/XE8261/**E**]

♦ ASEAN Federation of Cement Manufacturers (AFCM) **01173**

Pres c/o Vietnam Natl Cement Association, 37 Le Dai Hanh Street, Hai Ba Trung District, Hanoi, Vietnam. E-mail: julia.limsoomyin@heidelbergcement.com – info@afcm-org.com.
URL: http://afcm-org.com/

History 1977, as a regional industry club of *ASEAN Chambers of Commerce and Industry (ASEAN-CCI, #01151)*. Previously also known under the acronym *AFCM-ASEAN-CCI*. **Aims** Promote cooperation and coordination among cement manufacturers in the ASEAN region; initiate and coordinate programmes that will accelerate the orderly development of the cement *industry* in the ASEAN region; promote closer relation and cooperation between and among the cement manufacturing business communities in the member countries and with other regional and international organizations with similar aims and objectives. **Structure** Council (meets once a year). Office bearers: President, Vice President, Secretary-General, Deputy Secretary-General and the Coordinators of the 3 Standing Committees on: Marketing Cooperation, Technical Cooperation and Human Resources Development. **Activities** Events/meetings. **Events** *Technical Symposium* Bandung (Indonesia) 2018, *Conference* Penang (Malaysia) 2017, *Technical Symposium* Hanoi (Vietnam) 2015, *Biennial Technical Symposium* Malaysia 2012, *Technical Symposium* Petaling Jaya (Malaysia) 2012.
Members Associations in 7 countries:
Brunei Darussalam, Indonesia, Malaysia, Philippines, Singapore, Thailand, Vietnam.
IGO Relations *ASEAN (#01141)*. [2018/XE6115/**E**]

♦ ASEAN Federation of Electrical Engineering Contractors (AFEEC) .. 01174
Fédération des entrepreneurs de l'électromécanique de l'ANASE
Secretariat Soc of Philippine Electrotechnical Constructors and Suppliers, 2nd Floor IIEE Bldg, No 41 Monte De Piedad Street, Brgy Immaculate Concepcion Cubao, Quezon City, Philippines. T. +6327224725. Fax +6324130994. E-mail: specsphils.68@gmail.com.
URL: http://www.afeec.org/
History 5 Aug 1979, Manila (Philippines). **Aims** Standardize the regulations for electrical installations in the ASEAN region; promote joint venture. **Structure** Council. **Finance** Members' dues. Other sources: sale of publications; small commission from conference organizer. **Activities** Events/meetings. **Events** *Joint Conference* Gwangju (Korea Rep) 2019, *Joint Conference* Manila (Philippines) 2018, *Joint Conference* Kuala Lumpur (Malaysia) 2017, *Joint Conference* Singapore (Singapore) 2016, *Joint Conference* Taipei (Taiwan) 2014. **Publications** *ASEAN Currents* (2 a year). Reports.
Members Electrical engineering contractors in 5 countries:
Indonesia, Malaysia, Philippines, Singapore, Thailand.
Consultative Status Consultative status granted from: *ASEAN (#01141)*. **NGO Relations** Closely affiliated with: *Federation of Asian and Pacific Electrical Contractors Associations (FAPECA, #09443)*.
[2019.03.01/XE8550/**E**]

♦ ASEAN Federation of Endocrine Societies (AFES) 01175
Congress Chairman c/o Queen Sirikit National Convn Cnt, 60 New Radchadapisek Road, Klongtoey, Bangkok, 10110, Thailand. T. +6622293332. Fax +6622293346.
URL: http://www.asean-endocrinejournal.org/
Events *AFES Congress* Manila (Philippines) 2019, *Advancing the frontiers of endocrinology in Southeast Asia* Kuala Lumpur (Malaysia) 2015, *Congress* Jakarta (Indonesia) 2013, *Translating endocrinology research into clinical care* Ho Chi Minh City (Vietnam) 2011, *Congress* Bangkok (Thailand) 2009. **Publications** *Journal of AFES*.
Members Societies in 6 countries:
Indonesia, Malaysia, Philippines, Singapore, Thailand, Vietnam.
IGO Relations *ASEAN (#01141)*. **NGO Relations** Cooperates with: *Asia and Oceania Thyroid Association (AOTA, #01810)*; *International Society of Endocrinology (ISE, #15086)*. [2014/XE0095/**E**]

♦ ASEAN Federation of Engineering Organizations (AFEO) 01176
Contact c/o Bangunan Ingenieur, Lots 60/62, Jalan 52/4, PO Box 223 Jalan Sultan, 46720 Petaling Jaya, Selangor, Malaysia. T. +60379684010. Fax +60379577678. E-mail: aer@iem.org.my.
URL: http://www.afeo.org/
History Founded 1980, Manila (Philippines). **Aims** Promote opportunity in the field of education, research and practice; exchange ideas and experience; discuss problems of common interest; and promote understanding, goodwill and cooperation amongst national engineering organizations and their members. **Structure** Governing Board (annual); Secretariat, located in Petaling Jaya (Malaysia). Includes: *Young Engineers of ASEAN Federation of Engineering Organisations (YEAFEO, no recent information)*. **Languages** English. **Staff** 3.00 FTE, paid. **Finance** Members' dues. **Activities** Events/meetings. **Events** *Conference* Jakarta (Indonesia) 2019, *Engineering rail connectivity and fostering excellence in engineering education* Singapore (Singapore) 2018, *Conference* Bangkok (Thailand) 2017, *Conference* Puerto Princesa (Philippines) 2016, *The lights to bytes – ASEAN engineering evolution and future challenges* Penang (Malaysia) 2015. **Publications** Conference proceedings.
Members National engineering organizations within South East Asia in 10 countries:
Brunei Darussalam, Cambodia, Indonesia, Laos, Malaysia, Myanmar, Philippines, Singapore, Thailand, Vietnam.
Consultative Status Consultative status granted from: *ASEAN (#01141)*. **IGO Relations** *ASEAN Coordinating Centre for Humanitarian Assistance on disaster management (AHA Centre, #01161)*; *ASEAN (#01141)* Secretariat; Ministry of Foreign Affairs and Ministry of International Trade of respective ASEAN Countries. **NGO Relations** *International Engineering Alliance (#13275)*; *World Federation of Engineering Organizations (WFEO, #21433)*. [2019.12.12/XE0013/**E**]

♦ ASEAN Federation of Flying Clubs (inactive)

♦ ASEAN Federation of Forwarders Associations (AFFA) 01177
Chairman Cargo Village Complex Bldg A, NAIA Ave cor Multinational Ave, 1700 Parañaque METRO MANILA, Philippines. T. +6328523445. Fax +6328526821 – +6328522857.
History Dec 1991, Singapore. Constitution adopted March 1992, Jakarta (Indonesia). **Aims** Foster, promote, develop and maintain close cooperation between and among the freight forwarders in the ASEAN region. **Events** *Annual Meeting* Jakarta (Indonesia) 2005, *General Meeting* Singapore (Singapore) 2002, *Annual Meeting* Bali (Indonesia) 1996, *Annual Meeting* Penang (Malaysia) 1995, *Annual Meeting* Singapore (Singapore) 1994. **Consultative Status** Consultative status granted from: *ASEAN (#01141)*. [2010/XD7829/**D**]

♦ ASEAN Federation of Furniture Manufacturers Association / see ASEAN Furniture Industries Council (#01192)

♦ ASEAN Federation of Glass Manufacturers (AFGM) 01178
Contact c/o ASEAN-CCI, 3rd Floor, ASEAN Secretariat Bldg, 70A Jalan Sisingamangaraja, Jakarta 12110, Indonesia. T. +62217267325 – +62217262991 – +62217243372ext198. Fax +62217267326. E-mail: info.afgm@gmail.com.
URL: http://www.aseanglass.org/
History 1977, Manila (Philippines). Constitution and bye-laws ratified, 31 Oct 1977, Manila. Previously also known under the acronym *AFFPI-ASEAN-CCI*. **Structure** Council. Officers: Chairman; Vice-Chairman; Secretary General. Working Groups (3). **Activities** Events/meetings. **Events** *Conference* Cebu (Philippines) 2019, *Annual Conference* Hua Hin (Thailand) 2016, *Annual Conference / ASEAN Glass Conference of the ASEAN Federation of Glass Manufacturer* Cebu City (Philippines) 2015, *Annual Conference* Penang (Malaysia) 2014, *Annual Conference / ASEAN Glass Conference of the ASEAN Federation of Glass Manufacturer* Hanoi (Vietnam) 2012.
Members Glass federations in 5 countries:
Indonesia, Malaysia, Philippines, Thailand, Vietnam.
IGO Relations *ASEAN (#01141)*. **NGO Relations** Since 26 Jul 1978, member of Working Group on Industrial Complementation of: *ASEAN Chambers of Commerce and Industry (ASEAN-CCI, #01151)*. [2016/XD5308/**E**]

♦ ASEAN Federation of Haematology (AFH) 01179
Pres c/o Medicomms Asia Pte Ltd, 27 Foch Road No 02-08, Hoa Nam Building, Singapore 209264, Singapore. T. +6562938220. Fax +6562938230.
History Inaugural meeting, Apr 2010, Kuala Lumpur (Malaysia). **Events** *Congress* Manila (Philippines) 2016, *Congress* Bangkok (Thailand) 2014, *Congress* Singapore (Singapore) 2012, *Congress* Kuala Lumpur (Malaysia) 2010. [2016/XJ1314/**D**]

♦ ASEAN Federation of Heart Foundations (no recent information)

♦ ASEAN Federation of Land Surveying and Geomatics (AFLAG) 01180
Contact c/o Assn of Authorised Land Surveyors Malaysia, 2735A Jalan Permata 4, Tmn Permata, Ulu Kelang, 53300 Kuala Lumpur, Malaysia. T. +60341088540. Fax +60341081140. E-mail: secretariat.pejuta@gmail.com.
URL: http://www.aseanflag.org/
History 15 Mar 1995. Former names and other names: *ASEAN FLAG* – alias. Registration: Malaysia. **Aims** Promote and advance science, practice and application of land surveying and geomatics; encourage communication between persons charged with technical responsibility for planning, design and execution of land surveying and geomatics; educate and seek to improve, extend and elevate technical and general knowledge of members and persons concerned with land surveying and geomatics; serve as a focal point for exchange of ideas in the ASEAN region; disseminate information on land surveying and geomatics in the region. **Structure** General Meeting; Council. **Languages** English. **Staff** 2.50 FTE, paid. Voluntary. **Finance** Members' dues (annual): RM 250. Other sources: donations; subscriptions. **Activities** Events/meetings; research/documentation; knowledge management/information dissemination. **Events** *South East Asia Survey Congress (SEASC)* Bandung (Indonesia) 2022, *South East Asia Survey Congress* Darwin, NT (Australia) 2019, *South East Asia Survey Congress* Singapore (Singapore) 2015, *South East Asia Survey Congress* Singapore (Singapore) 2015, *South East Asian Survey Congress* Manila (Philippines) 2013. **Publications** *ASEAN Flag Newsletter*.
Members Institutional; Corporate; Honorary; Sustaining individuals and organizations 7 countries:
Brunei Darussalam, Indonesia, Malaysia, Philippines, Singapore, Thailand, Vietnam.
Observers in 3 countries:
Cambodia, Laos, Myanmar.
Consultative Status Consultative status granted from: *ASEAN (#01141)*. **NGO Relations** *International Federation of Surveyors (FIG, #13561)*. Also links with a large number of national organizations in the ASEAN region. [2022/XD7903/**D**]

♦ ASEAN Federation of Mining Associations (AFMA) 01181
SG c/o Malaysian Chamber of Mines, 8th Floor, West Block, Wisma Selangor Dredging, 142-C Jalan Ampang, 50450 Kuala Lumpur, Malaysia. T. +60321616171. Fax +60321616179. E-mail: muhd_nor@mcom.com.my – mcom@mcom.com.my.
URL: http://www.mcom.com.my/index.php/afma
History 1984. **Aims** Promote *mineral development* in South-East Asia through regional cooperation; monitor changes in the industry and promote harmonious development of mineral wealth in the region, thus optimizing the contribution of minerals to *economic development*. **Languages** English. **Finance** Budget (annual): US$ 20,000. **Activities** Events/meetings. **Events** *Asia Pacific Mineral Resource Conference* Kuala Lumpur (Malaysia) 2016, *Private Sector Forum* Kuala Lumpur (Malaysia) 2016, *Asia-Pacific Conference* Jakarta (Indonesia) 2014, *Asia Pacific conference* Manila (Philippines) 2007, *Private Sector Forum* Manila (Philippines) 2006. **Publications** Proceedings of conferences and seminars.
Members Mining associations in 6 ASEAN countries:
Cambodia, Indonesia, Malaysia, Myanmar, Philippines, Thailand.
Consultative Status Consultative status granted from: *ASEAN (#01141)*. **NGO Relations** *Association of Geoscientists for International Development (AGID, #02623)*. Instrumental in setting up the currently inactive: *Forum for International Mineral Development (FIMD, inactive)*. [2016.06.28/XE0577/**E**]

♦ ASEAN Federation of Plastic Industries (AFPI) 01182
Secretariat c/o SPIA, 15-B Lorong 4, Geylang, Singapore 399272, Singapore. T. +6567435571. Fax +6567433309. E-mail: info@ftiplastic.com – spia@spia.org.sg.
URL: http://www.aseanplastic.com/
History 5 Dec 1981, Manila (Philippines). A regional industry club of *ASEAN Chambers of Commerce and Industry (ASEAN-CCI, #01151)*. **Aims** Promote economic cooperation and coordination of efforts by plastic industries in the region; undertake, coordinate and encourage research and studies to identify opportunities, projects and products; serve as a channel of communication and clearinghouse for information; facilitate exchange of views among members and their governments; initiate, encourage and coordinate harmonization; act as a common institution in dealings with public and private sectors. **Structure** Council of national delegations each comprising a Chief Delegate, 2 other persons and 2 alternates. **Activities** Events/meetings; awards/prizes/competitions. Database with contributions from every member country. **Events** *Asia Plastics Forum* Bangkok (Thailand) 2016, *Asia plastics forum* Kuala Lumpur (Malaysia) 2007, *Term conference* Kuala Lumpur (Malaysia) 2007, *Asia plastics forum* Manila (Philippines) 2006, *Term conference* Singapore (Singapore) 2005. **Publications** *AFPI Manufacturers Directory*. Information Services: ASEAN plastics industries database.
Members National organizations of the plastics industry in 7 countries:
Indonesia, Malaysia, Myanmar, Philippines, Singapore, Thailand, Vietnam.
IGO Relations *ASEAN (#01141)*. [2014/XD4028/t/**D**]

♦ ASEAN Federation of Plastic Surgeons 01183
Fédération de spécialistes en chirurgie plastique de l'ANASE
Contact G-1 Medical Academies of Malaysia, 210 Jalan Tun Razak, 50400 Kuala Lumpur, Malaysia. T. +60340234700 – +60340254700 – +60340253700. Fax +60340238100.
History 1982, Singapore (Singapore). Also referred to as *ASEAN Federation of Plastic Surgery*. **Activities** *ASEAN Congress of Plastic Surgery (ACPS)*. **Events** *Biennial Congress* Boracay Is (Philippines) 2012, *International Conference* Philippines 2012, *Biennial Congress* Kuching (Malaysia) 2010, *Biennial Congress* Singapore (Singapore) 2002, *Biennial Congress* Singapore (Singapore) 2000.
Members Full in 6 countries:
Indonesia, Malaysia, Philippines, Singapore, Thailand, USA.
IGO Relations *ASEAN (#01141)*. [2010/XD2399/**D**]

♦ ASEAN Federation of Plastic Surgery / see ASEAN Federation of Plastic Surgeons (#01183)

♦ ASEAN Federation for Psychiatry and Mental Health (AFPMH) 01184
Pres Fac of Medicine, University of Indonesia, Salemba Raya 6, PO Box 1358, Jakarta 10430, Indonesia.
URL: http://www.aseanjournalofpsychiatry.org/
History 11 Feb 1981, Bangkok (Thailand). **Structure** Council (meets once a year), consisting of presidents of the member national psychiatric associations of ASEAN countries. **Languages** English. **Events** *Biennial Congress* Singapore (Singapore) 2012, *ASEAN Congress on Psychiatry and Mental Health* Kuala Lumpur (Malaysia) 2010, *ANBD conference* Bangkok (Thailand) 2008, *Biennial Congress* Bangkok (Thailand) 2008, *ASEAN Congress on Psychiatry and Mental Health* Indonesia 2006. **Publications** *ASEAN Mental Health Bulletin*.
Members National Psychiatric Associations of the 6 ASEAN countries:
Brunei Darussalam, Indonesia, Malaysia, Philippines, Singapore, Thailand.
Consultative Status Consultative status granted from: *ASEAN (#01141)*. **NGO Relations** Founder member of: *Asian Federation of Psychiatric Associations (AFPA, #01470)*. [2015/XD1658/**E**]

♦ ASEAN Federation of Textile Industries (AFTEX) 01185
Permanent Sec 58 Lorong Kuang Bulan, Taman Kepong, 52100 Kuala Lumpur, Malaysia.
History Founded in 1977. Incorporated as a nonprofit organization, 2011. A regional industry club of *ASEAN Chambers of Commerce and Industry (ASEAN-CCI, #01151)*. **Events** *Asia Apparel and Textile Machinery Seminar* Singapore (Singapore) 2014. **IGO Relations** *ASEAN (#01141)*. [2018/XD5304/t/**E**]

♦ ASEAN Finance Corporation 01186
Société financière de l'ANASE
Address not obtained.
URL: http://www.afcmerchantbank.com/
History 1981, Singapore (Singapore), on the initiative of the Asean Bankers Association (ABA), the current *ASEAN Bankers Association (ABA, #01144)*, with headquarters in Singapore. Business name of *AFC Merchant Bank* used since 1991. **Aims** Mobilize financial resources to finance projects and assist in promotion of industrialization and overall economic development in the ASEAN region. **Structure** President/CEO is Secretary General of ABA. Members are associations of banks in ASEAN countries. **Languages** English. **Staff** 25.00 FTE, paid. **Activities** Project financing; capital markets syndication; loans; corporate finance advisory services.
Members Privately and publicly-owned banks and financial institutions in the 5 original ASEAN countries:
Indonesia, Malaysia, Philippines, Singapore, Thailand.
IGO Relations *ASEAN (#01141)*. [2012.08.06/XF6943/e/**F**]

♦ ASEAN FLAG / see ASEAN Federation of Land Surveying and Geomatics (#01180)
♦ **ASEANFOODS** Association of Southeast Asian Networks of Food Data Systems (#02921)

♦ ASEAN Football Federation (AFF) 01187
Persekutuan Bolasepak Asean
Gen Sec 33 Jalan SS 3/76, 47300 Petaling Jaya, Selangor, Malaysia. T. +60378755515. Fax +60378755376. E-mail: gensec@aseanfootball.org.
URL: http://www.aseanfootball.org/
History 31 Jan 1984. **Aims** Develop football in ASEAN. **Structure** Congress (annual); Council; Ad hoc Committees; General Secretariat. **Languages** English. **Staff** 5.00 FTE, paid. **Finance** Members' dues. Other sources: donations; sponsorship. **Activities** Events/meetings; sporting activities; training/education. **Publications** Annual Report.
Members National football associations of 12 countries:

Australia, Brunei Darussalam, Cambodia, Indonesia, Laos, Malaysia, Myanmar, Philippines, Singapore, Thailand, Timor-Leste, Vietnam.
NGO Relations Under supervision and jurisdiction of: *Asian Football Confederation (AFC, #01487)* and *International Federation of Association Football (#13360).* [2019.12.20/XE0265/**E**]

♦ ASEAN Forestry Students Association (AFSA) 01188

Main Office Fac of Forestry – Kasetsart Univ, Ladyao Subdistrict, Jatujak District, Bangkok, 10900, Thailand. T. +6625790170. E-mail: fforpwd@ku.ac.th.
Contact Fac of Forestry, Bogor Agricultural University, JL Dermaga, Bogor 16680, Indonesia. T. +62251622202.
History Founded 24 Sep 1993, following discussions initiated in 1991. **Aims** Increase cooperation between ASEAN forestry students. **Structure** General Assembly; Executive Committee. **Events** *Meeting* Thailand 2008, *Conference* Vietnam 2002. **Consultative Status** Consultative status granted from: *ASEAN (#01141).* [2015/XD7911/**D**]

♦ ASEAN Forum on Child and Adolescent Psychiatry (meeting series)

♦ ASEAN Forum on Coal (AFOC) 01189

Contact ASEAN Centre for Energy, ACE Bldg 6th Fl, Jalan HR Rasuna Said Bloc X2, Kav 07-08 Kuningan, Jakarta 12950, Indonesia.
URL: http://www.aseanenergy.org/
History May 2000, Jakarta (Indonesia), on signature of a charter. **Structure** National Committees. **Events** *Meeting* Kuala Lumpur (Malaysia) 2019, *Meeting* Ha Long City (Vietnam) 2008, *Meeting* Makati (Philippines) 2005, *Meeting* Jakarta (Indonesia) 2003, *Meeting* Petaling Jaya (Malaysia) 2002.
Members Companies and institutions involved in the coal business in the ASEAN region and ASEAN government agencies concerned with the sector. Members in 10 countries (" indicates national committee):
Brunei Darussalam, Cambodia, Indonesia (*), Laos, Malaysia (*), Myanmar (*), Philippines (*), Singapore, Thailand (*), Vietnam.
IGO Relations *ASEAN (#01141).* [2008/XF6500/**F**]

♦ ASEAN Foundation 01190

Exec Dir Heritage Bldg 1st Floor, Jl Sisingamangaraja N. 70A, Jakarta 12110, Indonesia. T. +622127091702. Fax +622127091700. E-mail: secretariat@aseanfoundation.org.
URL: http://www.aseanfoundation.org/
History 15 Dec 1997, Kuala Lumpur (Malaysia). Established when a Memorandum of Understanding was signed between Foreign Ministers of *ASEAN (#01141).* **Aims** Build a cohesive and prosperous ASEAN Community. **Structure** Board of Trustees; Executive Director. **Languages** English. **Staff** 18.00 FTE, paid. **Finance** Sources: contributions; donations; grants. **Activities** Awareness raising; events/meetings; financial and/or material support; networking/liaising; projects/programmes; training/education. **Events** *Climate Smart and Disaster Resilience ASEAN International Conference (CSDRA)* Shah Alam (Malaysia) 2020, *Model ASEAN Meeting* Bangkok (Thailand) 2019, *Climate Smart and Disaster Resilience ASEAN International Conference (CSDRA)* Manila (Philippines) 2019, *Model ASEAN Meeting* Singapore (Singapore) 2018, *ASEAN Community Forum* Singapore (Singapore) 2017. **Publications** *ASEAN Foundation Model*; *ASEAN Meeting Guidebook*. Annual Report.
Members ASEAN governments (10):
Brunei Darussalam, Cambodia, Indonesia, Laos, Malaysia, Myanmar, Philippines, Singapore, Thailand, Vietnam.
NGO Relations Instrumental in setting up (1): *ASEAN CSR Network (#01166).* Collaborates with: ASEAN sectoral bodies; *Asian Farmers'Association for Sustainable Rural Development (AFA, #01450)*; *Asian Partnership for the Development of Human Resources in Rural Asia (AsiaDHRRA, #01654).* [2021.02.25/XF5831/f/**F***]

♦ ASEAN Framework Agreement on the Facilitation of Goods in Transit (1998 treaty)
♦ ASEAN Framework Agreement on the Facilitation of Inter-state Transport (1998 treaty)
♦ ASEAN Framework Agreement on Intellectual Property Cooperation (1995 treaty)
♦ ASEAN Framework Agreement on Multimodal Transport (2005 treaty)
♦ ASEAN Framework Agreement on Services (1995 treaty)

♦ ASEAN Free Trade Area (AFTA) 01191

Contact c/o ASEAN Secretariat, 70A Jalan Sisingamangaraja, Jakarta 12110, Indonesia. T. +62217262991 – +62217243372. Fax +62217398234 – +62217243504.
URL: http://www.asean.org/communities/asean-economic-community/
History 28 Jan 1992, Singapore (Singapore), at 4th Summit of *ASEAN (#01141)*, on signature of *Agreement on the Common Effective Preferential Tariff (CEPT, 1992)* by Economic Ministers of ASEAN member countries. CEPT Scheme commenced 1 Jan 1993 and is expected to be completed in 2003. Subsequently: Vietnam became a member of ASEAN in Jul 1995 and started to implement CEPT on 1 Jan 1996; Laos and Myanmar became members in Jul 1997 and started to implement CEPT on 1 Jan 1998; Cambodia became a member in Apr 1999 and started to implement CEPT on 1 Jan 2000. CEPT was replaced by *ASEAN Trade in Goods Agreement (ATIGA, 2009)*, which entered into force May 2010. **Aims** Create an integrated market and production base with a free flow of goods. **Structure** Council, inaugurated 11 Sep 1992, reports to meetings of ASEAN Economic Ministers (AEM) and comprises Ministers of ASEAN member states and ASEAN Secretary General. *'Coordinating Committee on the Implementation of the CEPT Scheme for AFTA'* meets frequently. AFTA Unit at ASEAN Secretariat (currently functioning within the Bureau of Trade and Industry and Services) and national AFTA Units in ASEAN member countries were set up by 26th meeting of ASEAN Economics Ministers, Sep 1994, to support implementation of the CEPT Scheme. Subordinate bodies responsible for AFTA implementation, customs harmonization and harmonization of product standards report to AFTA Council. **Activities** Politics/policy/regulatory. **Events** *ASEAN Economic Ministers Meeting* Bangkok (Thailand) 2019, *Meeting* Singapore (Singapore) 2018, *Meeting* Bandar Seri Begawan (Brunei Darussalam) 2002, *Symposium* Jakarta (Indonesia) 2002. **Publications** *Tariff Reduction Programmes under the Common Effective Preferential Tariff Scheme (CEPT)* (2001) – tariff reduction schedules and MFN tariff rates for each country, printed and diskette versions; *AFTA Reader* – in 5 vols; *AICO Reader*, *ASEAN Handbook on Customs Procedures*.
Members Governments of 10 countries:
Brunei Darussalam, Cambodia, Indonesia, Laos, Malaysia, Myanmar, Philippines, Singapore, Thailand, Vietnam.
IGO Relations Complementary schemes: *ASEAN Industrial Cooperation Scheme (AICO)*; *ASEAN Investment Area (AIA, see: #01141).* **NGO Relations** Harmonizes national standards with those of: *International Organization for Standardization (ISO, #14473).* [2014/XF5151/t/**F***]

♦ ASEAN Furniture Industries Council (AFIC) 01192

Main Office Jurong Town Hall Road, Trade Association Hub, #03-01, Singapore 609431, Singapore. E-mail: afic@aseanfurnitures.org.
URL: https://www.aseanfurniture.org/
History 1978. Founded as a regional industry club of *ASEAN Chambers of Commerce and Industry (ASEAN-CCI, #01151).* Former names and other names: *ASEAN Federation of Furniture Manufacturers Association (AFFMA)* – former alias. **Structure** Officers: Chairman; Secretary-General; 4 Vice-Chairmen. **Events** *Conference* Singapore (Singapore) 1996.
Members Full in 7 countries:
Indonesia, Malaysia, Myanmar, Philippines, Singapore, Thailand, Vietnam.
Consultative Status Consultative status granted from: *ASEAN (#01141).* [2021/XE0271/t/**E**]

♦ ASEAN Golf Federation (AGF) 01193

SG c/o Malaysian Golf Assoc, 14 Jalan 4/76C, Desa Pandan, 55100 Kuala Lumpur, Malaysia. T. +60392837300. Fax +60392839300.
URL: http://www.mgaonline.com.my/index.php/asean-golf-federation/
Structure Annual General Meeting. **Languages** English. **Staff** 1.00 FTE, paid. **Finance** Members' dues. Sponsors. **Activities** Sporting activities. **Events** *South East Asia Amateur Golf Team Championship* Khon Kaen (Thailand) 2015, *Annual General Meeting* Singapore (Singapore) 2008.
Members National golf associations in 10 countries:
Brunei Darussalam, Cambodia, Indonesia, Laos, Malaysia, Myanmar, Philippines, Singapore, Thailand, Vietnam. [2019.07.09/XJ0310/**D**]

♦ ASEAN Handicraft Promotion and Development Association (AHPADA) 01194

Regional Secretariat c/o Society Atelier Sarawak, 1 Rumah Mesra, Jalan Taman Budaya, 93000 Kuching, Malaysia.
URL: http://www.ahpadaexpo.com/
History following the Handicraft Export Workshop, Feb 1981, Bangkok (Thailand). Formally inaugurated, Jakarta (Indonesia). **Aims** Ensure a common approach is taken to develop, promote and market *crafts* within and beyond the ASEAN region; strengthen and improve the status of craftspeople in the region, including the number of employment opportunities and the preservation of traditional craft skills as a crucial part of *cultural heritage*. **Structure** Board of Directors, including President, Immediate Past President and Honorary Chairman. Rotating Presidency. **Finance** Funded by projects in collaboration support form various NGOs. **Activities** Projects/programmes; events/meetings.
Members Full in 10 countries:
Brunei Darussalam, Cambodia, Indonesia, Laos, Malaysia, Myanmar, Philippines, Singapore, Thailand, Vietnam.
Consultative Status Consultative status granted from: *ASEAN (#01141).* **IGO Relations** Cooperates with: *UNESCO (#20322).* **NGO Relations** Partner of: *Development Innovations and Networks (#05057).* [2019/XE0264/**E**]

♦ ASEAN Hotel and Restaurant Association (AHRA) 01195

Co-Dir c/o SHA, 21 Bukit Batok Street, Singapore 659589, Singapore. E-mail: ahra@sha.org.sg – secretariat@sha.org.sg.
History 1970. **Finance** Members' dues. Sponsorship; seminar/workshop programmes. **Events** *Food and Hotel Asia Conference* Singapore (Singapore) 2018, *Conference* Bangkok (Thailand) 2015, *Hotel GM forum* Singapore (Singapore) 2008, *Conference* Manila (Philippines) 1996, *Convention* Manila (Philippines) 1990. **Publications** *AHRA Newsletter* (6 a year).
Members Hotel and restaurant groups in 5 countries:
Indonesia, Malaysia, Philippines, Singapore, Thailand.
IGO Relations *ASEAN (#01141).* **NGO Relations** Member of: *ASEAN Tourism Association (ASEANTA, #01238)*; *International Hotel and Restaurant Association (IH&RA, #13813).* [2021/XE2761/**E**]

♦ Aseanian Membrane Society (AMS) 01196

Sec address not obtained.
URL: http://www.ams-membrane.net/
History 2002. Name derives from a combination of "Asian" with "Oceanian". **Structure** Council; Advisory Board. **Events** *AMS Conference* Singapore (Singapore) 2021, *Conference* Jeju (Korea Rep) 2019, *Conference* Brisbane, QLD (Australia) 2018, *Conference* Nara (Japan) 2016, *Conference* Taipei (Taiwan) 2015.
Members Societies in 5 countries and territories:
Australia, China, Japan, Korea Rep, Singapore.
NGO Relations Member of (1): *World Association of Membrane Societies (WA-MS, #21165).* Co-organizer of: *International Congress on Membranes and Membrane Processes (ICOM).* [2021/XD9257/**D**]

♦ ASEAN Institute / see ASEAN Business Forum (#01147)

♦ ASEAN Institute for Health Development (AIHD) 01197

Public Relations Officer Mahidol Univ – Salaya Campus, 25-5 Phutthamonthon 4 Rd, Nakhon Pathom, 73170, Thailand. T. +6624419040. Fax +6624419044.
Dir address not obtained. E-mail: directad@mahidol.ac.th.
URL: https://aihd.mahidol.ac.th/
History 1982. Recognized as an institute, 11 Oct 1988. Former names and other names: *ASEAN Training Centre for Primary Health Care Development (ATC/PHC)* – former. **Aims** Provide transformative education for graduates to become proficient leaders in health system management and sustainability. **Structure** Offices (3): Academic Cluster; Office of the Director; Office of Academic Services. **Languages** English, Thai. **Staff** 80.00 FTE, paid. **Finance** Support from the Thai government for administrative costs; institutional income from training courses, education, research, other activities. At present, key sponsors include: *Japan International Cooperation Agency (JICA)*; *Korea International Cooperation Agency (KOICA)*; *United States Agency for International Development (USAID)*; *WHO (#20950).* **Activities** Events/meetings; knowledge management/information dissemination; research and development; training/education. **Events** *International Graduate Students Conference on Population and Public Health Sciences* Bangkok (Thailand) 2020, *International Graduate Students Conference on Population and Public Health Sciences* Bangkok (Thailand) 2019, *International Graduate Students Conference on Population and Public Health Sciences* Bangkok (Thailand) 2018, *International Graduate Students Conference on Population and Public Health Sciences* Bangkok (Thailand) 2017, *International Conference on Population and Public Health Sciences* Bangkok (Thailand) 2014. **Publications** *Journal of Public Health Development* (3 a year). Maintains: library; Information on HIV/AIDS. **Members** Not a membership institute. [2021.06.09/XE6022/j/**E**]

♦ ASEAN Institute for Peace and Reconciliation (ASEAN-IPR) 01198

Exec Dir Mission of Indonesia to ASEAN Bldg – 3rd floor, Training Ctr MoFA Rep of Indonesia, Jl Sisingamangaraja bi 73, Kebayoran Baru, Jakarta SELETAN 12120, Indonesia. E-mail: admin@asean-aipr.org – aipr.secretariat@gmail.com.
URL: https://asean-aipr.org/
History Established 8 May 2011, when *ASEAN (#01141)* Leaders adopted a Joint Statement on the Establishment of an ASEAN Institute for Peace and Reconciliation. Terms of Reference adopted Jul 2012; launched 18 Nov 2012. **Aims** Serve as the ASEAN institution for research and capacity building activities on peace, conflict management and conflict resolution in the region as requested by ASEAN Member States. **Structure** Governing Council; Advisory Board; Secretariat. **Activities** Research/documentation; capacity building; networking/liaising knowledge management/information dissemination. **Events** *Meeting* Jakarta (Indonesia) 2020, *Symposium on Non-Traditional Threat on Human Security* Bangkok (Thailand) 2019, *Meeting* Jakarta (Indonesia) 2019, *Meeting* Jakarta (Indonesia) 2019, *Retreat* Jakarta (Indonesia) 2019. **Consultative Status** Consultative status granted from: *Conseil européen de l'industrie chimique (CEFIC, #04687).* [2023/XM8409/**E**]

♦ ASEAN Institute of Physics (ASEANIP) 01199

Pres Physics Dept, Fac of Science, Chulalongkorn Univ, Bangkok, 10330, Thailand. T. +6622517300 – +6622185113. Fax +6622552775. E-mail: svirulh@chula.ac.th.
Contact Dept of Physics, Univ Kebangsaan Malaysia, Selangor, Bangi, Selangor, Malaysia. T. +6038292890. Fax +6038292880.
History 1980. Constitution adopted 26 Jul 1989, at Meeting of ASEANIP Council. Regional network of *UNESCO Office, Jakarta – Regional Bureau for Sciences in Asia and the Pacific (#20313).* **Aims** Promote the advancement and status of physics in ASEAN countries; facilitate cooperation among physicists in ASEAN countries. **Structure** Council, consisting of Chairman, Vice-Chairman and 4 ordinary members. Secretariat, including Honorary Secretary and Honorary Treasurer. **Events** *Conference* Penang (Malaysia) 1993, *Asia-Pacific physics conference / Conference / Conference* Kuala Lumpur (Malaysia) 1992, *Laser and plasma technology* Kuala Lumpur (Malaysia) 1990, *Conference* Bangkok (Thailand) 1989.
Members Ordinary societies of physics in 5 countries:
Indonesia, Malaysia, Philippines, Singapore, Thailand.
NGO Relations Member of: *Association of Asia Pacific Physical Societies (AAPPS, #02388).* [2010/XE5904/j/**E**]

♦ ASEAN Institutes for Strategic and International Studies (ASEAN-ISIS) 01200

Secretariat CSIS, Jakarta Post Bldg, 3rd Floor, Jl Palmerah Barat 142-143, Jakarta 10270, Indonesia. T. +622153654601. Fax +622153654607. E-mail: csis@csis.or.id.
URL: http://www.isis.org.my/index.php/networks/asean-isis
History Jun 1988. Founded within the framework of *ASEAN (#01141).* A network of think-tanks. Former names and other names: *Institutes for Strategic and International Studies (ISIS)* – alias. **Aims** Ensure regular exchange of views on enhancing enduring regional *peace, stability* and *security* outside the intergovernmental framework. **Activities** Organizes *ASEAN ISIS Colloquium on Human Rights (AICOHR)*, always held in

Manila (Philippines) from 1993 to the present. **Events** *Colloquium on human rights* Singapore (Singapore) 2010, *Latin Asia business forum* Singapore (Singapore) 2010, *Global diaspora business summit* Singapore (Singapore) 2009, *Latin Asia business forum* Singapore (Singapore) 2009, *Meeting on EU-ASEAN cooperation in sustainable tourism* Singapore (Singapore) 2009. **Publications** *ASEAN-ISIS Monitor.*
Members Institutes (10) in 9 ASEAN countries:
Brunei Darussalam, Cambodia, Indonesia, Laos, Malaysia, Myanmar, Philippines, Singapore, Thailand, Vietnam.
Asia Pacific Pathways to Progress Foundation (APPFI); Cambodian Institute for Cooperation and Peace (CICP); Centre for Strategic and International Studies, Jakarta (CSIS); Diplomatic Academy of Vietnam (DAV); Institute of Security and International Studies, Bangkok (ISIS); Institute of Strategic and International Studies, Malaysia (ISIS); Singapore Institute of International Affairs (SIIA).
NGO Relations Instrumental in setting up: *ASEAN People's Assembly (APA, no recent information).*
[2020/XD4867/jy/**E**]

♦ ASEAN Insurance Council (AIC) 01201
Operation Office Permanent Secretariat, Permata Kuningan Bldg, 2nd Floor, Jl Kuningan Mulia 9C Jakarta Selatan, Jakarta 12980, Indonesia. T. +622129069760. Fax +622129069759. E-mail: secretariat@aicsec.org.
URL: http://www.aseaninsurancecouncil.org/
History Founded 1978, by the insurance industry for strictly commercial purposes. Also known as *Insurance Council of the ASEAN Countries.* **Aims** Promote development of insurance and reinsurance in the region. **Structure** Council; Secretariat. **Languages** English. **Finance** Members' dues. **Activities** Events/meetings; knowledge management/information dissemination; networking/liaising. **Events** *Meeting* Kuala Lumpur (Malaysia) 2018, *The fourth industrial revolution ans its impact on the ASEAN insurance industry* Kuala Lumpur (Malaysia) 2018, *Meeting* Vientiane (Laos) 2017, *Summit* Yogyakarta (Indonesia) 2016, *Meeting* Phnom Penh (Cambodia) 2015. **Publications** *ASEAN Insurance Quarterly E-Magazine.* Journals; magazines. Statistical report.
Members Representatives of the insurance industry in 8 countries:
Brunei Darussalam, Cambodia, Indonesia, Malaysia, Philippines, Singapore, Thailand, Vietnam.
IGO Relations *ASEAN (#01141).* **NGO Relations** Cooperates with associations and organizations having similar objectives. [2019/XE9814/**E**]

♦ ASEAN Insurance Training and Research Institute (AITRI) 01202
CEO 6th Floor, Wisma FGV, Jalan Raja Laut, 50350 Kuala Lumpur, Malaysia. T. +60327128882. E-mail: aitrisecretariat@mii.org.my.
Sec address not obtained.
URL: http://www.aitri.org/
History Sep 2000. Founded by ASEAN insurance regulators. Operational since 2001; officially incorporated 1 Dec 2004, Malaysia. **Aims** Promote rapid and equitable development of intellectual capital in the ASEAN insurance market. **Structure** Board of Trustees; Management Board; Secretariat. **Languages** English. **Staff** 3.00 FTE, paid. **Finance** Sources: donations. Supported by: *Financial Sector Reform and Strengthening Initiative (FIRST Initiative, #09769); Give2Asia; International Association of Insurance Supervisors (IAIS, #11966); OECD (#17693).* **Activities** Awards/prizes/competitions; events/meetings. **Events** *ASEAN Insurance Congress* 2021, *ASEAN Insurance Congress* Bali (Indonesia) 2019, *ASEAN Insurance Congress* Vientiane (Laos) 2017, *ASEAN Insurance Congress* Danang (Vietnam) 2014, *Regional Seminar on Enterprise Risk Management for Solvency Purposes* Singapore (Singapore) 2014. **Publications** Research studies.
Members Full in 10 countries:
Brunei Darussalam, Cambodia, Indonesia, Laos, Malaysia, Myanmar, Philippines, Singapore, Thailand, Vietnam.
[2021/XJ7714/j/**E**]

♦ ASEAN Intellectual Property Association (AIPA) 01203
Pres c/o Vision and Associates – Attorneys, Unit 308-310 3rd Floor, Hanoi Towers, 49 Hai Ba Trung Street, Hanoi, Vietnam. T. +84439340629. Fax +84439340631.
Hon Sec address not obtained.
URL: http://www.aseanipa.org/
History Founded 1 Dec 1996. **Aims** Foster ties of mutual friendship, cooperation and understanding among those who are concerned with intellectual property in ASEAN countries; promote development and protection of intellectual property in ASEAN. **Structure** Annual General Meeting; Council. **Languages** English, Vietnamese. **Staff** 100.00 FTE, paid. **Finance** Members' dues. Conference fees. Annual budget: US$ 10,000. **Events** *Annual Conference* Singapore (Singapore) 2019, *Annual Conference* Phnom Penh (Cambodia) 2018, *Annual Conference* Manila (Philippines) 2017, *Annual Conference* Kuala Lumpur (Malaysia) 2016, *Annual Conference* Bangkok (Thailand) 2015.
Members Full in 10 countries:
Brunei Darussalam, Cambodia, Indonesia, Laos, Malaysia, Myanmar, Philippines, Singapore, Thailand, Vietnam.
Consultative Status Consultative status granted from: *World Intellectual Property Organization (WIPO, #21593)* (Permanent Observer Status). **IGO Relations** *ASEAN (#01141).* **NGO Relations** *Asian Patent Attorneys Association (APAA, #01655); Fédération Internationale des Conseils en Propriété Intellectuelle (FICPI, #09624); International Association for the Protection of Intellectual Property (#12112); International Trademark Association (INTA, #15706).* [2020/XD6266/**D**]

♦ ASEAN International Airports Association (AAA) 01204
Secretariat Dept of Civil Aviation, Ministry of Communications, Brunei Int Airport, Bandar Seri Begawan, Brunei-Muara BB2513, Bandar Seri Begawan BRUNEI-MUARA BB2513, Brunei Darussalam. Fax +6732331706.
History 1982. **Aims** Foster regional cooperation among international airport operators in terms of airport management, operations and developments; promote mutual interests of members. **Structure** Chairmanship rotates annually among members; chairing member also hosts the annual meeting. **Finance** Members' dues. Operating costs borne by host country. **Events** *Annual Meeting* Manila (Philippines) 2010, *Annual Meeting* Brunei Darussalam 2004, *Regional meeting* Bangkok (Thailand) 2002, *Annual meeting* Brunei Darussalam 1993, *Annual meeting* Singapore (Singapore) 1990.
Members Airport operators in 10 countries:
Brunei Darussalam, Cambodia, Indonesia, Laos, Malaysia, Myanmar, Philippines, Singapore, Thailand, Vietnam.
IGO Relations *ASEAN (#01141).* [2013.07.30/XE1633/**E**]

♦ ASEAN Inter-Parliamentary Assembly (AIPA) 01205
Secretariat 6th Fl, Nusantara 3 Bldg, DPR RI Compound, Jalan Gatot Subroto, Senayan, Jakarta 10270, Indonesia. T. +62215715511 – +62215715691. Fax +62215731319. E-mail: aipa@aipasecretariat.org.
URL: https://aipasecretariat.org/
History Proposed 1975, at *ASEAN Parliamentary Meeting (APM).* Established 2 Sep 1977, Manila (Philippines), as *ASEAN Inter-Parliamentary Organization (AIPO),* at 3rd ARM, upon agreement of draft Statues. Statutes amended 1997, 2007 and 2013. Present name and new structure adopted, 2006, Cebu (Philippines), at 27th General Assembly. New organizational chart approved at 34th General Assembly, 2013, Brunei Darussalam. **Aims** Promote solidarity, understanding, cooperation and close relations among Parliaments of ASEAN Member States, AIPA Special Observers, Observers and other parliamentary organizations; facilitate the achievement of ASEAN's goals as constituted in ASEAN Declaration of August 1967, as well as ASEAN Vision 2020 taking into account Bali Concord II 2003 leading to the realization of an ASEAN Community; study, discuss and suggest solutions to problems of common interest and express its views on such issues with the aim of bringing about action and timely response by AIPA's members; promote principles of human rights, democracy, peace, security and prosperity in ASEAN. **Structure** General Assembly; Presidency; Executive Committee; Committees; Secretariat. **Languages** English. **Finance** Members' dues. Expenses for meetings borne by host country. **Activities** Knowledge management/information dissemination; networking/liaising. **Events** *General Assembly* Hanoi (Vietnam) 2020, *General Assembly* Bangkok (Thailand) 2019, *General Assembly* Singapore (Singapore) 2018, *Meeting* Singapore (Singapore) 2018, *General Assembly* Malaysia 2015. **Publications** *AIPO Newsletter* (2 a year).
Members National Parliaments of 10 countries:
Brunei Darussalam, Cambodia, Indonesia, Laos, Malaysia, Myanmar, Philippines, Singapore, Thailand, Vietnam.
Observer Parliaments of 11 countries:
Australia, Belarus, Canada, China, India, Japan, Korea Rep, New Zealand, Papua New Guinea, Russia, Timor-Leste.
Included in the above, 1 regional Parliament:
European Parliament (EP, #08146). [2021/XE0372/c/**E**]

- ♦ ASEAN Inter-Parliamentary Organization / see ASEAN Inter-Parliamentary Assembly (#01205)
- ♦ ASEAN Investment Area (see: #01141)
- ♦ **ASEANIP** ASEAN Institute of Physics (#01199)
- ♦ **ASEAN-IPR** ASEAN Institute for Peace and Reconciliation (#01198)
- ♦ ASEAN Iron and Steel Council / see ASEAN Iron and Steel Industry Federation (#01206)

♦ ASEAN Iron and Steel Industry Federation (AISIF) 01206
SG c/o The Malaysian Iron and Steel Industry Federation, 5th Floor, Block 2, Worldwide Business Park, Jalan Tinju 13/50, Section 13, 40675 Shah Alam, Selangor, Malaysia. T. +60355133970. Fax +60355133891.
History 1977, as a Regional Industry Club under the aegis the Working Group on Industrial Cooperation of *ASEAN Chambers of Commerce and Industry (ASEAN-CCI, #01151).* Also referred to as *ASEAN Iron and Steel Council (AISC).* **Aims** Promote economic cooperation among the iron and steel industries in the ASEAN region in areas such as intra-ASEAN trade, the establishment of joint ventures and the exchange of technology and information; initiate, encourage and coordinate the preparation and implementation of programmes, plans and projects to accelerate and harmonize growth and progress of iron and steel industries in the region; compile and disseminate information of common concern; provide facilities for consultation and exchange of views between and among members; serve as a sole body representing the private sector to implement and deal with problems of ASEAN cooperation in iron and steel industries; develop and initiate preparation and implementation of plans, programmes and projects to promote and advance intra-regional trade and the trading of exportable iron and steel and related products; formulate and develop recommendations on investment incentive, tariffs, non-tariff benefits and other measures of protection for iron and steel projects and products for complementation. **Structure** General Conference (at least every 2 years). Council (meets at least once a year), consisting of President, 5 Vice Presidents and a maximum of 3 representatives from each constituent member. Committees. **Finance** Members' contributions. **Activities** Conferences and Seminars in cooperation with SEAISI. **Publications** *AISIF Directory.*
Members Iron and steel industry clubs in 5 ASEAN countries:
Indonesia, Malaysia, Philippines, Singapore, Thailand.
IGO Relations *ASEAN (#01141).* **NGO Relations** Cooperates with: *South East Asia Iron and Steel Institute (SEAISI, #19756).* [2010/XE1335/t/**E**]

- ♦ **ASEAN-ISIS** ASEAN Institutes for Strategic and International Studies (#01200)
- ♦ ASEAN-Japan Centre / see ASEAN Promotion Centre on Trade, Investment and Tourism (#01225)
- ♦ **ASEAN-JAPAN CENTRE** ASEAN Promotion Centre on Trade, Investment and Tourism (#01225)

♦ ASEAN Kite Council (AKC) 01207
Dep Pres 297 Boni Serrano Avenue, Quezon City, Philippines. E-mail: kiteasia@yahoo.com.
History Jun 2004, Pasir Gudang (Malaysia). **Aims** Revive and promote the cultural/traditional as well as the modern kite aspects of each member country at domestic and international levels. **Structure** Officers. **Languages** English. **Staff** Voluntary. **Finance** Minimal contributions. No annual budget. **Activities** Sporting activities.
Members Organizations in 9 countries:
Brunei Darussalam, Cambodia, Indonesia, Malaysia, Myanmar, Philippines, Singapore, Thailand, Vietnam.
Affiliate members in 5 countries:
Australia, India, Japan, Korea Rep, New Zealand.
Consultative Status Consultative status granted from: *ASEAN (#01141).* [2016.10.18/XJ9839/**D**]

♦ ASEAN-Korea Centre (AKC) 01208
SG 8th fl – 124 Sejong-daero, Jung-gu, Seoul 100-750, Korea Rep. T. +82222871115. Fax +82222871160.
URL: http://www.aseankorea.org/
History Inaugurated 13 Mar 2009. **Aims** Promote economic and socio-cultural *cooperation* between the ASEAN Member States and Korea. **Structure** Council; Executive Board; Secretariat. Units (4). **Events** *Annual Council Meeting* Seoul (Korea Rep) 2022, *ASEAN Connectivity Forum* Seoul (Korea Rep) 2021, *Meeting* Seoul (Korea Rep) 2021, *KOREAN-ASEAN COVID-19 Response Seminar* Seoul (Korea Rep) 2020, *Seminar on ASEAN-Korea Tourism* Seoul (Korea Rep) 2020. **Publications** *ASEAN-Korea Centre Newsletter.*
Members Member States (11):
Brunei Darussalam, Cambodia, Indonesia, Korea Rep, Laos, Malaysia, Myanmar, Philippines, Singapore, Thailand, Vietnam.
[2019/XM8385/**E***]

♦ ASEAN Law Association (ALA) 01209
Pres c/o Law Firm Swandy Halim and Partners, Jalan H R Rasuna Said Blok X-5 Kav 2-3 – 19th floor, Jakarta 12950, Indonesia. T. +622157903666. Fax +622157903787. E-mail: ala_asean@yahoo.com.
URL: http://www.aseanlawassociation.org/
History 10 Feb 1979, Jakarta (Indonesia), at a conference of ASEAN lawyers. Constitution adopted at 1st General Assembly, Nov 1980, Manila (Philippines). **Aims** Promote closer relations, cooperation and mutual understanding among lawyers in ASEAN countries; provide an organizational framework for regional cooperations; provide organizational facilities for ASEAN cooperation in conflict avoidance, in the arbitration of legal disputes and in transnational contacts within the ASEAN region; cooperate with similar organizations. **Structure** General Assembly (every 3 years). Governing Council, consisting of 5 representatives from each member country. Standing Committees (7): Judicial Cooperation; International Law; Legal Profession; Business Law; Legal Education; Legal Information; Alternative Dispute Resolution. **Languages** English. **Finance** Members' dues. Donations. **Activities** Works on harmonizing laws and developing regional laws. **Events** *Conference* Singapore (Singapore) 2018, *General Assembly* Singapore (Singapore) 2018, *Meeting* Singapore (Singapore) 2018, *Meeting* Kuala Lumpur (Malaysia) 2014, *Meeting of Chief of Justices of ASEAN* Singapore (Singapore) 2013. **Publications** *ALA Newsletter, ASEAN Law Journal. ASEAN Comparative Law Series. ALA: 25 years and beyond* (2005); *Legal Systems in ASEAN* (2005).
Members Individuals and institutions involved in a branch of law in 8 countries:
Brunei Darussalam, Indonesia, Laos, Malaysia, Philippines, Singapore, Thailand, Vietnam.
Consultative Status Consultative status granted from: *ASEAN (#01141).* [2015/XD5625/**D**]

♦ ASEAN Medical Education Alliance 01210
Contact address not obtained. E-mail: contact@aseanmeded.org.
URL: https://aseanmeded.org/
History 18 May 2017. **Aims** Promote the development of medical education, thereby improving medical education at all levels. **Structure** General Assembly; Executive Committee. **Events** *ASEAN Medical Education Conference* 2021, *ASEAN Medical Education Conference* Nakhon Pathom (Thailand) 2019, *ASEAN Medical Education Conference* Bangkok (Thailand) 2017. [2021/AA2879/**D**]

- ♦ ASEAN Meeting of Aesthetic Surgery and Medicine (meeting series)

♦ ASEAN Membrane Science and Technology Society (AMSTS) 01211
Contact N29a Advanced Membrane Tech Research Centre, Univ Teknologi Malaysia, 81310 Johor Bahru, Johor, Malaysia.
URL: http://amtec.utm.my/
History 2002, Johor Bahru (Malaysia), at Universiti Teknologi Malaysia. **Aims** Promote growth of knowledge in membrane science and technology; promote collaborative efforts of membrane researchers and end-users. **Structure** Committee. **Languages** English. **Staff** 80.00 FTE, voluntary. **Finance** Sources: meeting proceeds; members' dues. **Activities** Events/meetings. **Events** *Conference* Singapore (Singapore) 2019, *Conference* Teheran (Iran Islamic Rep) 2015, *Conference* Kuala Lumpur (Malaysia) 2013, *Conference* Bangkok (Thailand) 2012, *Conference* Singapore (Singapore) 2011. **Publications** Books; articles.
Members Institutions in 6 countries:
Australia, Indonesia, Iran Islamic Rep, Malaysia, Singapore, Thailand.
IGO Relations None. **NGO Relations** None. [2020.03.23/XM3085/**D**]

♦ **ASEAN Music Industry Association (AMIA)** **01212**
Contact c/o IFPI (South East Asia), 22/F Shanghai Industrial Investment Bldg, No 48-62 Hennessy Rd, Wan Chai, Wanchai, Hong Kong.
Members ASEAN Member States (5 of 10):
Indonesia, Malaysia, Philippines, Singapore, Thailand.
IGO Relations Member of: *ASEAN (#01141).* [2019/XE0262/t/**E**]

♦ **ASEAN-NARCO** ASEAN Narcotics Cooperation Center (#01213)

♦ **ASEAN Narcotics Cooperation Center (ASEAN-NARCO)** **01213**
Main Office 5 Din Daeng Road, Phyathai District, Bangkok, 10400, Thailand. E-mail: aseannarco@oncb.go.th.
Contact address not obtained.
URL: https://aseannarco.oncb.go.th/
History 2014. **Structure** Narcotics Control Board. [2020/AA0055/**E***]

♦ ASEAN National Police / see ASEANAPOL (#01138)
♦ ASEAN National Police Chiefs / see ASEANAPOL (#01138)
♦ **ASEAN NCAP** New Car Assessment Program for Southeast Asian Countries (#17078)

♦ **ASEAN Neurological Association (ASNA)** **01214**
Contact c/o NNI, 11 Jalan Tan Tock Seng, Singapore 308433, Singapore.
URL: https://www.neurology-asia.org
History 17 Nov 1994, Philippines. 17 Nov 1994, Laoag City (Philippines). Previously referred to as *ASEAN Neurological Society.* **Events** *Biennial Convention* Bangkok (Thailand) 2021, *Biennial Convention* Yangon (Myanmar) 2019, *Biennial Convention* Manila (Philippines) 2017, *Biennial Convention* Singapore (Singapore) 2015, *Biennial Convention* Bandar Seri Begawan (Brunei Darussalam) 2013. **Publications** *Neurology Asia.*
Members Full in 5 countries:
Indonesia, Malaysia, Philippines, Singapore, Thailand.
Consultative Status Consultative status granted from: *ASEAN (#01141).* [2020/XD2911/**D**]

♦ ASEAN Neurological Society / see ASEAN Neurological Association (#01214)
♦ ASEAN Neurosurgical Society (no recent information)
♦ ASEAN NGO Coalition on Ageing (inactive)

♦ **ASEAN Occupational Safety and Health Network (ASEAN-OSHNET)** . **01215**
Coordinator Ministry of Labor Pangkham Rd, PO Box 347, Vientiane, Laos. T. +85621213247. Fax +85621213287.
Dir Gen address not obtained.
URL: http://www.aseanoshnet.org/
History Oct 1996, Quezon City, by *ASEAN (#01141).* Also referred to as *Occupational Safety and Health Network (OSHNET).* Inaugural Ceremony: 16 Feb 2001, Jakarta (Indonesia). **Aims** Foster a safe and healthy *working environment*; promote cooperation and solidarity among national occupational safety and health (OSH) centres of ASEAN countries; enhance the capability of these centres in OSH promotion, training and research; facilitate and promote exchange of relevant OSH information and the sharing of training expertise; facilitate and promote development and harmonization of ASEAN OSH *standards* and guidelines. **Structure** Coordinating Board, comprising one representative from each ASEAN member country, a representative of the Secretary-General of ASEAN, and Executive Director. Secretariat. **Finance** Members' dues. **Activities** Knowledge management/information dissemination; training/education; standards/guidelines; research/documentation; events/meetings. **Events** *Conference* Yogyakarta (Indonesia) 2019, *Meeting* Yogyakarta (Indonesia) 2019, *Policy Dialogue to Develop a New Work Plan* Singapore (Singapore) 2016, *Conference* Bangkok (Thailand) 2015, *Policy Dialogue on Revitalisation of ASEAN-OSHNET* Singapore (Singapore) 2011.
Members Covers 10 countries:
Brunei Darussalam, Cambodia, Indonesia, Laos, Malaysia, Myanmar, Philippines, Singapore, Thailand, Vietnam.
[2014/XF4237/**F**]

♦ **ASEAN Oleochemical Manufacturers Group (AOMG)** **01216**
Secretariat Wisma FMM, 3 Persiaran Dagang, PJU 9, Bandar Sri Damansara, 52200 Kuala Lumpur, Malaysia. T. +61362761211. Fax +61362776714. E-mail: ksqua@aomg.org.my.
URL: http://www.aomg.org.my/
History Aug 1986, Manila (Philippines). **Aims** Promote cooperation and coordination among oleochemical manufacturers in the ASEAN region. **Structure** Board; Committees; Secretariat. **Languages** English. **Events** *World conference on global oleochemicals* Barcelona (Spain) 2002.
Members Full in 3 countries:
Indonesia, Malaysia, Philippines.
Consultative Status Consultative status granted from: *ASEAN (#01141).* [2015/XD7907/**D**]

♦ ASEAN Orchid Society / see Orchid Society of South East Asia (#17789)
♦ **ASEAN ORL HNS Federation** ASEAN Otorhinolaryngological – Head and Neck Federation (#01218)

♦ **ASEAN Orthopaedic Association (AOA)** **01217**
Contact c/o Orthopaedic Clinic Pte Ltd, 3 Mt Elizabeth, 05-07/08 Mt Elizabeth Medical Centre, Singapore 228510, Singapore. T. +6567342244. Fax +6567331485. E-mail: orthopod@singnet.com.sg.
Events *Annual Congress* Manila (Philippines) 2021, *Annual Congress* Petaling Jaya (Malaysia) 2021, *Annual Congress* Jakarta (Indonesia) 2019, *Annual Congress* Yangon (Myanmar) 2018, *Annual Congress* Hanoi (Vietnam) 2017.
Members Full in 5 countries:
Indonesia, Malaysia, Philippines, Singapore, Thailand.
Consultative Status Consultative status granted from: *ASEAN (#01141).* **NGO Relations** *Asia Pacific Orthopaedic Association (APOA, #01987).* [2014/XD1657/**E**]

♦ **ASEAN-OSHNET** ASEAN Occupational Safety and Health Network (#01215)
♦ ASEAN Otorhinolaryngological Federation / see ASEAN Otorhinolaryngological – Head and Neck Federation (#01218)

♦ **ASEAN Otorhinolaryngological – Head and Neck Federation (ASEAN ORL HNS Federation)** **01218**
SG Consultant Rhinologists and Otolaryngologists, Hosp Raja Permaisuri Bainun Ipoh, Ipoh, Perak, Malaysia.
URL: http://www.aseanorl.org/
History 2 Jul 1980, Medan (Indonesia), at 6th National Congress of the Indonesian Otorhinolaryngological Society, as *ASEAN Otorhinolaryngological Federation.* **Aims** Foster study and dissemination of all aspects of otorhinolaryngological knowledge, particularly in the region of ASEAN; promote cooperation in scientific exchange amongst member, and establish closer personal and *professional* contacts amongst those interested and working in this field. **Structure** Executive Council. **Languages** English. **Finance** Members' dues. **Activities** Events/meetings. **Events** *Southeast Asian Congress on Otorhinolaryngology and Head-Neck Surgery (ASEAN ORL-HNS Congress)* Hanoi (Vietnam) 2023, *Biennial Congress* Singapore (Singapore) 2019, *Biennial Congress* Chiang Mai (Thailand) 2015, *Biennial Congress* Cebu City (Philippines) 2013, *Biennial Congress* Kuching (Malaysia) 2011.
Members National associations in the 10 ASEAN countries:
Brunei Darussalam, Cambodia, Indonesia, Laos, Malaysia, Myanmar, Philippines, Singapore, Thailand, Vietnam.
IGO Relations *ASEAN (#01141).* **NGO Relations** Formal contacts with: *International Federation of Oto-Rhino-Laryngological Societies (IFOS, #13496).* [2022/XE0811/**E**]

♦ **ASEAN Parliamentarians for Human Rights (APHR)** **01219**
Contact address not obtained. E-mail: info@aseanmp.org.
URL: https://aseanmp.org/
History Jun 2013. **Aims** Promote democracy and human rights across Southeast Asia. **Structure** Board. **Finance** Also support from Norwegian Ministry of Foreign Affairs. Supported by: *International Center for Not-for-Profit Law (ICNL, #12471); International Panel of Parliamentarians for Freedom of Religion or Belief (IPPFoRB, #14506); Open Society Foundations (OSF, #17763); Swedish International Development Cooperation Agency (Sida).*
Members Parliamentarians in:
Cambodia, Indonesia, Malaysia, Myanmar, Philippines, Singapore, Thailand, Timor-Leste.
NGO Relations Partner of (1): *International Parliamentary Alliance for the Recognition of Ecocide (Ecocide Alliance, #14517).* [2022/AA2675/v/**F**]

♦ ASEAN Parliamentary Meeting / see ASEAN Inter-Parliamentary Assembly (#01205)

♦ **ASEAN Pediatric Federation (APF)** **01220**
Pres APF Secretariat, c/o Dept of Paediatrics – Yangon Children Hosp, 2 Pyidaungsu Yeiktha Street, Dagon Township, Yangon 11191, Myanmar. E-mail: secretariat@sps.org.sg.
Sec address not obtained.
URL: http://apf-online.webs.com/
History 3 Aug 1976, Jakarta (Indonesia). **Events** *Congress* Hanoi (Vietnam) 2020, *Congress* Hanoi (Vietnam) 2020, *Ensuring healthy lives and promoting well-being of ASEAN children* Yangon (Myanmar) 2017, *Congress* Penang (Malaysia) 2014, *Trends, Issues, Priorities in Paediatrics* Singapore (Singapore) 2011.
Members Full in 10 countries:
Brunei Darussalam, Cambodia, Indonesia, Laos, Malaysia, Myanmar, Philippines, Singapore, Thailand, Vietnam.
Consultative Status Consultative status granted from: *ASEAN (#01141).* **NGO Relations** *Asia Pacific Pediatric Association (APPA, #01992).* [2019.12.11/XE9857/**E**]

♦ ASEAN Pharmaceutical Club / see ASEAN Pharmaceutical Industry Club (#01221)

♦ **ASEAN Pharmaceutical Industry Club** **01221**
Contact c/o ASEAN-CCI, 3rd Floor, ASEAN Secretariat Building, 70A Jalan Sisingamangaraja, Jakarta 12110, Indonesia. T. +62217267325 – +62217262991 – +62217243372ext198. Fax +62217267326.
History A regional industry club of *ASEAN Chambers of Commerce and Industry (ASEAN-CCI, #01151).* Also referred to as *ASEAN Pharmaceutical Club.* **IGO Relations** *ASEAN (#01141).* [2011/XD5216/t/**E**]

♦ ASEAN Plus Three Cultural Cooperation Network (unconfirmed)

♦ **ASEAN Plus Three Financial Grouping (APT)** **01222**
Contact ASEAN Secretariat, 70 A Jalan Sisingamangaraja, Jakarta 12110, Indonesia. T. +62217262991 – +62217243372. Fax +62217398234 – +62217243504.
History 1997, by *ASEAN (#01141)* and the Governments of China, Japan and Korea Rep. **Aims** Protect the economies in the member countries by enabling them to swap reserves in the event their currencies are targeted by speculators as they were in 1997 during the Asian financial crises. [2011/XM3243/**E***]

♦ ASEAN Port Authorities Association / see ASEAN Ports Association (#01223)

♦ **ASEAN Ports Association (APA)** **01223**
Chairman c/o Phnom Penh Autonomous Port, 185 St 450, Phnom Penh 120908, Cambodia. T. +85512309309. Fax +85512309309.
Permanent Secretariat Philippine Ports Authority, Bonifacio Drive, Port Area, 1018 Manila, Philippines. T. +635274856. Fax +63527485. E-mail: ogm@ppa.com.ph.
URL: https://apaport.org/
History Sep 1975, Manila (Philippines). Conceived during a sports festival held in Sabah (Malaysia), 1974 by R Geotina of the Philippines and J E Habibie of Indonesia. Former names and other names: *ASEAN Port Authorities Association (APAA)* – former (1975 to 1997). **Aims** Provide ASEAN ports with a vehicle for regional cooperation in port development, operations and management; promote and protect the interest of member ports. **Structure** Main Meeting; Working Committee; Sports Committee; Technical Committee. **Languages** English. **Staff** 11.00 FTE, paid. Permanent Secretariat staff. **Finance** Sources: members' dues. Annual budget: 45,000 USD. **Activities** Capacity building; events/meetings; projects/programmes; sporting activities. **Events** *Executive Meeting* Manila (Philippines) 2021, *Executive Meeting* Manila (Philippines) 2020, *Working Committee Meeting* Bohol (Philippines) 2019, *Annual Meeting* Siem Reap (Cambodia) 2019, *Main Meeting* Singapore (Singapore) 2018. **Publications** *APA Newsletter.*
Members ASEAN Ports Association member countries (9):
Brunei Darussalam, Cambodia, Indonesia, Malaysia, Myanmar, Philippines, Singapore, Thailand, Vietnam.
Consultative Status Consultative status granted from: *ASEAN (#01141).* **IGO Relations** Accredited by (1): *ASEAN (#01141).* [2022.03.02/XE0266/**E**]

♦ **ASEAN Power Grid** **01224**
Information Centre Electricity Generating Authority of Thailand, Bang Kruai, Nonthaburi, 11130, Thailand. T. +6624363500. E-mail: patrapong.t@egat.co.th.
URL: http://www2.egat.co.th/apg/
History Initiated at 2nd *ASEAN (#01141)* Informal Summit, as part of the ASEAN Vision 2020, 15 Dec 1997, Kuala Lumpur (Malaysia). *Forum of Heads of ASEAN Power Utilities/Authorities (HAPUA, #09917)* is responsible for its implementation. Comes under ASEAN Ministries of Energy Meeting (AMEM). **Aims** Promote efficient use of power; develop new permanent power sources for future use. **Structure** Council; Working Committee; ASEAN Power Grid Consultative Committee (APGCC); Secretariat. Working Groups (5) under the Working Committee: Generation; APG/Transmission; Distribution and Power Reliability and Quality; Policy and Commercial Development; Human Resources. **Languages** English. **Staff** Personnel from relevant utilities. **Finance** Sponsored by relevant utilities. **Activities** Meetings; conferences; seminars; workshops; studies; site visits. **Events** *Meeting* Cambodia 2014. **Publications** Reports.
Members Utilities authorities in 10 countries:
Brunei Darussalam, Cambodia, Indonesia, Laos, Malaysia, Myanmar, Philippines, Singapore, Thailand, Vietnam.
[2014.01.28/XJ2757/**E***]

♦ **ASEAN Promotion Centre on Trade, Investment and Tourism (ASEAN-JAPAN CENTRE)** **01225**
Centre pour la promotion du commerce, des investissements et du tourisme en Asie du Sud-Est – Centro para la Promoción del Comercio, las Inversiones y el Turismo en Asia Sudoriental
SG Shin Onarimon Bldg, 6-17-19 Shimbashi, Minato-ku, Tokyo, 105-0004 Japan. T. +81354028001. Fax +81354028003. E-mail: toiawase_ga@asean.or.jp.
URL: http://www.asean.or.jp/en/
History 25 May 1981, Japan. Established by the Agreement signed by the Governments of *ASEAN (#01141)* Member States and Japan. Former names and other names: *ASEAN-Japan Centre* – alias. Registration: Japan. **Aims** Enhance the economic partnership between ASEAN Member States and Japan through: promotion of export; acceleration of flow of investment; vitalization of tourist traffic; expansion of exchanges of persons. **Structure** Council (meets annually); Executive Board; Secretariat, headed by Secretary-General and comprising Planning and Coordination Office and 2 Divisions. **Languages** English, Japanese. **Staff** 23.00 FTE, paid. **Finance** Funded by governments of Japan and ASEAN Member States. **Activities** Events/meetings; capacity building; research/documentation; knowledge management/information dissemination; publishing activities. **Events** *ASEAN-Japan Business Week Seminar* Tokyo (Japan) 2022, *Seminar with Myanmar CEOs* Tokyo (Japan) 2020, *Meeting on the Development of Kuala Tanjung Port and Voluntary Pilotage Service in Water of Malacca Strait and Singapore Strait* Tokyo (Japan) 2018, *Myanmar Investment Forum* Tokyo (Japan) 2018, *Symposium on ASEAN 50th Anniversary* Tokyo (Japan) 2018. **Publications** *ASEAN-Japan Centre* (annual) – online and brochure. *ASEAN Information Map* – online and brochure; *ASEAN Tourism Map* – online and brochure. Brochures; posters; DVDs; photographs.
Members Governments of Japan and ASEAN Member States (11):
Brunei Darussalam, Cambodia, Indonesia, Japan, Laos, Malaysia, Myanmar, Philippines, Singapore, Thailand, Vietnam.
NGO Relations Links with national organizations. [2020/XF2483/t/**E***]

♦ ASEAN Public Libraries Information Network (unconfirmed)

♦ **ASEAN Public Relations Network (APRN)** **01226**
Headquarters London School of Public Relations Jakarta, Ctr for ASEAN Public Relations, Sudirman Park Complex Jl KH Mas Mansyur Kav 35, Jakarta 10220, Indonesia. T. +622157943802. E-mail: secretariat@aseanprnetwork.org.
URL: http://www.aseanprnetwork.org/

History Founded 2 Jun 2014. **Aims** Champion connectivity, friendship and mutual understanding among ASEAN member countries, gaining skills and strength from each others PR best practices. **Structure** Honorary Council; Board of Experts; Officers. **Activities** Standards/guidelines; events/meetings; research/documentation; awards/prizes/competitions.
Members Associations in 5 countries:
Indonesia, Malaysia, Philippines, Thailand, Vietnam.
IGO Relations *ASEAN (#01141).* **NGO Relations** Member of: *Global Alliance for Public Relations and Communication Management (GA, #10223).* [2020.01.16/XM8413/F]

♦ Asean Quality Assurance Network (AQAN) 01227

Secretariat c/o Malaysian Qualifications Agency, 13th Floor – Block B, Menara PKNS-PJ, Jalan Yong Shook Lin, 46050 Petaling Jaya, Selangor, Malaysia. T. +60379569209. E-mail: aqan@mqa.gov.my.
URL: https://aqan.org/
History 8 Jul 2008, Kuala Lumpur (Malaysia). Founded through adoption of Kuala Lumpur Declaration. **Aims** Promote and share good practices of quality assurance in higher education in the Southeast Asia region; collaborate on capacity building of quality assurance in higher education in the region; share information on higher education and facilitate mutual recognition of qualifications throughout the region; develop a regional quality assurance framework for Southeast Asia. **Structure** Executive Committee. President; Vice-President; Executive Secretary; 3 members. **Languages** English. **Finance** Sources: members' dues. **Activities** Events/meetings. Organizes AQAN Seminar and Roundtable Meeting. **Events** *Seminar and Round Table* Ho Chi Minh City (Vietnam) 2013, *Seminar and Round Table* Kuala Lumpur (Malaysia) 2012, *Seminar and Round Table* Jakarta (Indonesia) 2010, *Seminar and Round Table* Bangkok (Thailand) 2009.
Members Full (17) in 10 countries:
Brunei Darussalam, Cambodia, Indonesia, Laos, Malaysia, Myanmar, Philippines, Singapore, Thailand, Vietnam.
Associate (3) in 2 country:
Thailand, Vietnam.
Regional associations (3):
ASEAN University Network (AUN, #01243); SEAMEO Regional Centre for Higher Education and Development (RIHED, #19174); SEAMEO Regional Training Centre.
NGO Relations Cooperates with (2): *European Association for Quality Assurance in Higher Education (ENQA, #06183); International Network of Quality Assurance Agencies in Higher Education (INQAAHE, #14312).* [2022/XJ4641/E*]

♦ ASEAN Regional Centre for Biodiversity Conservation / see ASEAN Centre for Biodiversity (#01149)

♦ ASEAN Regional Forum (ARF) 01228

Forum régional de l'ASEAN
ARF Unit ASEAN Secretariat, 70A Jl Sisingamangaraja, Jakarta 12110, Indonesia. T. +62217262991. Fax +62217398234. E-mail: arfunit@asean.org.
URL: http://aseanregionalforum.asean.org/
History Agreement to establish ARF among 17 Pacific Rim countries at 26th *ASEAN (#01141)* Ministerial Meeting and Post Ministerial Conference, 23-25 Jul 1993, Singapore (Singapore), following previous policy decisions of *'Singapore Declaration'*, 28 Jan 1992, Singapore. Inaugural meeting, 25 Jul 1994, Bangkok (Thailand). Forum participants initially included ASEAN members, Southeast Asian states that were not yet ASEAN members, ASEAN's then 7 dialogue partners, Papua New Guinea (an ASEAN observer) and China and Russia, then still 'consultative partners' of ASEAN. India became a participant on becoming a dialogue partner in 1996. Mongolia and Korea DPR were admitted in 1999 and 2000. Former names and other names: *Association of South-East Asian Nations Regional Forum* – alias; *Asia Regional Forum* – alias. **Aims** Foster constructive dialogue and consultation on *political* and *security* issues of common interest and concern; make significant contributions to efforts towards confidence-building and preventive diplomacy in the Asia-Pacific region; promote open dialogue on political and security operation in the region. **Structure** Ministerial Meetings (annually), chaired by Chairman of ASEAN Standing Committee. Senior Officials meet annually before Ministerial Meeting. Secretary. **Languages** English. **Staff** 4.00 FTE, paid. **Finance** Unit is run by ASEAN Secretariat's management, which is financed by ASEAN Member Countries' annual contributions. **Activities** An average of 15 ARF activities convened within one inter-sessional year. Meetings and ad-hoc activities are held on various areas of cooperation, including counter-terrorism, non-proliferation, demining, small-arms and light weapons, peacekeeping, disaster relief, maritime security, energy security, and other non-traditional security issues. **Events** *Inter-Sessional Meeting on Non-Proliferation and Disarmament* 2021, *ARF Senior Officials Meeting* Brunei Darussalam 2021, *ASEAN Regional Forum* Brunei Darussalam 2021, *Workshop on Implementing UNCLOS and other International Instruments to Address Emerging Maritime Issues* Hanoi (Vietnam) 2021, *Experts and Eminent Persons Meeting* Jakarta (Indonesia) 2021. **Publications** *ARF Document Series* (1994-2006).
Members ASEAN Member Countries (10) and non-ASEAN Member Countries (15):
Australia, Bangladesh, Brunei Darussalam, Cambodia, Canada, China, India, Indonesia, Japan, Korea DPR, Korea Rep, Laos, Malaysia, Mongolia, Myanmar, New Zealand, Pakistan, Papua New Guinea, Philippines, Russia, Singapore, Thailand, Timor-Leste, USA, Vietnam.
Non-ASEAN partner (1):
European Union (EU, #08967). [2020/XF3004/F*]

♦ ASEAN Regional Union of Psychological Societies (ARUPS) 01229

Address not obtained.
URL: http://www.arups.org/
History Registered in accordance with Indonesian law, 1 Aug 2006. **Aims** Promote psychology and the professional status of psychologists. **Events** *Congress* Gelugor (Malaysia) 2019, *Driving mental revolution in the psychological century – enhacing psychological services for a better future* Denpasar (Indonesia) 2017, *Professionalising psychology – raising the standards of psychology for nation building* Singapore (Singapore) 2015, *Building hope and resilience – the role of ASEAN psychologists* Manila (Philippines) 2013, *Understanding minds, empowering lives – psychology's role in the future of South East Asia* Kuala Lumpur (Malaysia) 2010.
Members in 10 countries:
Brunei Darussalam, Cambodia, Indonesia, Laos, Malaysia, Myanmar, Philippines, Singapore, Thailand, Vietnam.
IGO Relations *ASEAN (#01141).* **NGO Relations** Affiliated to: *International Union of Psychological Science (IUPsyS, #15807).* [2015/XM1839/D]

♦ ASEAN Rehabilitation Medicine Association (ARMA) 01230

Contact address not obtained. E-mail: arma2013@yahoo.com.
Events *SYNERGY: Cutting-Edge Practices in Rehabilitation Medicine* Manila (Philippines) 2013, *Congress* Bangkok (Thailand) 2009, *Congress* Chiang Mai (Thailand) 1998.
Members Full in 8 countries:
Indonesia, Laos, Malaysia, Myanmar, Philippines, Singapore, Thailand, Vietnam. [2017/XJ2811/E]

♦ ASEAN Research and Training Centre for Land and Forest Fire Management (no recent information)
♦ ASEAN Rhinology Group / see ASEAN Rhinology Society (#01231)

♦ ASEAN Rhinology Society (ARS) 01231

Address not obtained.
History 10 Oct 1993, Jakarta (Indonesia). Founded during 12th ASEAN ORL Congress. Former names and other names: *ASEAN Rhinology Group (ARG)* – former (1993 to 1998); *The Society of ASEAN Rhinologists (STAR)* – former (1998 to 2004). **Events** *Asian Research Symposium in Rhinology* Singapore (Singapore) 2012. [2020/AA0179/E]

♦ ASEAN-ROK Film Cooperation Organisation (unconfirmed)
♦ ASEAN Rubber Business Club / see ASEAN Rubber Business Council (#01232)

♦ ASEAN Rubber Business Council (ARBC) 01232

SG c/o Malaysian Rubber Exchange, Malaysian Rubber Board, 4th Floor, Bangunan Getah Asli (Menara), 148 Jalan Ampang, 50450 Kuala Lumpur, Malaysia. T. +60392062108 – +60392062091 – +60392062092. Fax +60321616586. E-mail: csang@lgm.gov.my – baizurah@lgm.gov.my.
URL: http://www.aseanrubber.net/
History Founded 23 Oct 1992, Jakarta (Indonesia). Previously known as *ASEAN Rubber Business Club*, until upgraded into a Council under current title, 1 Jan 2005. **Aims** Establish closer rapport through exchanges of market information; consult and discuss common trade practices; monitor progress and development of the industry in member countries; foster closer coordination, cooperation and goodwill between private sector amongst member organizations. **Structure** Assembly (twice a year); Executive Committee; Rotating Chairmanship (every 2 years); Committees (5); Permanent Secretariat in Malaysia, headed by Secretary-General. **Languages** English. **Staff** 4.00 FTE, paid. **Finance** Members' dues. Annual budget: Malaysian Ringgit about 24,000. **Events** *General Assembly* Bali (Indonesia) 2018, *General Assembly* Penang (Malaysia) 2017, *General Assembly* Jakarta (Indonesia) 2016, *General Assembly* Kuala Lumpur (Malaysia) 2015, *Meeting* Bangkok (Thailand) 2013. **Publications** None.
Members Rubber Trade Associations in 6 countries:
Cambodia, Indonesia, Malaysia, Singapore, Thailand, Vietnam.
NGO Relations Has assumed the activities of: *Tripartite Rubber Business Alliance (TRBA, inactive).* [2017.06.01/XE4705/E]

♦ **ASEANSAI** ASEAN Supreme Audit Institutions (#01237)

♦ ASEAN Sleep Surgical Society 01233

Pres Orchad Paragon Medical Ctr, 290 Orchard Rd, 18-04, Paragon, Singapore 238859, Singapore. T. +6568360060. Fax +6568360030.
URL: http://www.aseansleepsurgicalsociety.com/
History Mar 2008, on the initiative of Dr Kenny Peter Pang. **Activities** Organizes training courses. **Events** *Congress* Taipei (Taiwan) 2015, *Meeting* Singapore (Singapore) 2010. **Members** Membership countries not specified. [2015/XJ8085/E]

♦ ASEAN Social Security Association (ASSA) 01234

Acting Gen Dir address not obtained.
URL: http://www.asean-ssa.org/
History 13 Feb 1998, Bangkok (Thailand). Founded upon signing of a Memorandum of Understanding. Comes within *ASEAN (#01141).* **Aims** Provide a forum for member institutions to exchange views and experiences on social security issues. **Structure** Board (meets annually). **Languages** English. **Activities** Events/meetings. **Events** *Board Meeting* Thailand 2026, *Board Meeting* Singapore (Singapore) 2025, *Board Meeting* Philippines 2024, *Board Meeting* Malaysia 2023, *Board Meeting* Luang Prabang (Laos) 2022. **Publications** *ASSA News* (annual).
Members Institutions (21) in 10 countries:
Brunei Darussalam, Cambodia, Indonesia, Laos, Malaysia, Myanmar, Philippines, Singapore, Thailand, Vietnam. [2022.11.11/XM3016/D]

♦ ASEAN Society of Colorectal Surgeons (unconfirmed)
♦ ASEAN Society of Oto-Rhino-Laryngology (inactive)

♦ ASEAN Society for Sports Medicine and Arthroscopy (ASSA) 01235

SG c/o The Philippine Orthopaedic Assn, W2106-B Philippine Stock Exchange Ctr, Exchange Rd, Ortigas Ctr, 1605 Pasig City RIZ, Philippines. T. +6326673926. Fax +6326379842. E-mail: rich@aseanorthosports.com.
Pres address not obtained.
Facebook: https://www.facebook.com/aseanorthosports
Activities Events/meetings. **Events** *Annual Meeting* Manila (Philippines) 2021, *Annual Meeting* Manila (Philippines) 2020, *Annual Meeting* Kuala Lumpur (Malaysia) 2019, *Annual Meeting* Semarang (Indonesia) 2018, *Annual Meeting* Bali (Indonesia) 2017. [2022/AA1903/D]

♦ ASEAN Society of Tropical Medicine and Parasitology (unconfirmed)

♦ ASEAN Specialized Meteorological Centre (ASMC) 01236

Mailing Address ASEAN Specialised Meteorological Centre, PO Box 8, Changi Airport, Singapore 918141, Singapore. E-mail: asmc_enquiries@nea.gov.sg – media@nea.gov.sg.
Street address Room 048-033, 4th storey, Changi Airport Terminal 2, Singapore 819643, Singapore.
URL: http://asmc.asean.org/home/
History 2 Jan 1993, Singapore (Singapore). **Aims** Undertake research and development to improve scientific understanding and prediction of weather and climate systems of significance to the region; serve as the regional centre for monitoring land/forest fires and haze for ASEAN, including provision of an operational service for early warning of transboundary haze; conduct regional capability development programmes to help ASEAN NMSs benefit from advances in science and technology and enhance the effectiveness of meteorological services in ASEAN. **Structure** Director. **Languages** English. **Activities** Events/meetings; knowledge management/information dissemination; monitoring/evaluation. **Events** *Workshop on Subseasonal to Seasonal Predictions for South-East Asia* Singapore (Singapore) 2019, *Workshop on Subseasonal to Seasonal Predictions for South-East Asia* Singapore (Singapore) 2018. **Publications** *Monthly Weather and Haze Review.*
Members Services 10 countries:
Brunei Darussalam, Cambodia, Indonesia, Laos, Malaysia, Myanmar, Philippines, Singapore, Thailand, Vietnam. [2021.09.01/XE2061/E]

♦ Asean Para Sports Federation (unconfirmed)

♦ ASEAN Supreme Audit Institutions (ASEANSAI) 01237

Secretariat Jl Gatot Subroto Kav 31, Gedung Baru BPK RI 5th Floor, Jakarta CENTRAL 10210, Indonesia. T. +622125549OO ext 1212. Fax +622157953198. E-mail: international@bpk.go.id – aseansai@bpk.go.id.
URL: http://www.aseansai.org/home/
History Agreement signed 16 Nov 2011, Bali (Indonesia); agreement amended 8 Dec 2016, Abu Dhabi (United Arab Emirates). **Aims** Build capacity and promote cooperation and understanding through the exchange and sharing of knowledge and experiences in the field of public sector auditing so as to strengthen the audit institutions; provide a conducive environment and facilities to promote research, training, and continuous education through the sharing of best practices and exchange of lessons learned; serve as a centre of information and as a link with other international organizations and institutions in the field of public sector auditing. **Structure** Assembly; Committees (5): Strategic Planning; Rules and Procedure; Executive; Knowledge Sharing; Training. Secretariat, headed by Secretary General. **Events** *General Assembly* Brunei Darussalam 2013, *General Assembly* Bali (Indonesia) 2011. **Publications** *ASEANSAI Newsletter.*
Members Supreme Audit Institutions of 10 countries:
Brunei Darussalam, Cambodia, Indonesia, Laos, Malaysia, Myanmar, Philippines, Singapore, Thailand, Vietnam.
IGO Relations *ASEAN (#01141).* [2019/XJ9835/D*]

♦ **ASEANTA** ASEAN Tourism Association (#01238)
♦ ASEAN Thalassaemia Society (no recent information)

♦ ASEAN Tourism Association (ASEANTA) 01238

Pres Jalan P5/6 Precint 5, 6th Tower 1 No 2, Ministry of Tourism Arts Culture, 62200 Putrajaya, Malaysia. T. +60102874611. E-mail: aseanta.secretariat@gmail.com.
URL: https://aseanta.org/
History 27 Mar 1971, Putrajaya (Malaysia). Took over activities of *ASEAN Tourism Information Centre (ATIC, inactive).* **Aims** Influence the ASEAN tourism landscape, shaping tourism development growth and policies in the region. **Structure** Board. Officers: President; Vice-President; Treasurer; Secretary General. **Languages** English. **Events** *ATF : ASEAN Tourism Forum* Sihanoukville (Cambodia) 2022, *ATF : ASEAN Tourism Forum* Phnom Penh (Cambodia) 2021, *ATF : ASEAN Tourism Forum* Bandar Seri Begawan (Brunei Darussalam) 2020, *ATF : ASEAN Tourism Forum* Ha Long City (Vietnam) 2019, *ATF : ASEAN Tourism Forum* Chiang Mai (Thailand) 2018. **Publications** *Dateline ASEAN* (4 a year); *SPARK* (4 a year).
Members National airlines, hotel associations, travel agent associations and national tourism organizations in 9 countries:
Brunei Darussalam, Cambodia, Indonesia, Laos, Malaysia, Philippines, Singapore, Thailand, Vietnam.
IGO Relations Cooperates with (1): *ASEAN (#01141).* [2021.06.16/XE2760/E]

♦ **ASEAN Tourism Research Association (ATRA)** **01239**
Persatuan Kajian Pelancongan ASEAN
Contact CRiT, Taylor's Univ, No 1 n in Tourism Jalan Taylor's, 47500 Subang Jaya, Selangor, Malaysia. T. +60356295588. Fax +60356295522. E-mail: atra.secretariat@gmail.com.
URL: http://www.atrasecretariat.com/
History Officially established Nov 2013. Registered in accordance with the laws of Malaysia. **Aims** Support the ASEAN integration policies through tourism research and innovation. **Structure** Annual General Meeting; Board of Directors; Secretariat. **Languages** English. **Finance** Members' dues. Other sources: consultancy fees; research grants; endowments; revenue through advertisement and events. **Activities** Research/documentation; events/meetings; knowledge management/information dissemination. **Consultative Status** Consultative status granted from: *ASEAN (#01141).* [2020.03.19/XM7869/**D**]

♦ ASEAN Tourism Training and Education Network (no recent information)
♦ ASEAN Trade in Goods Agreement (2009 treaty)

♦ **ASEAN Trade Union Council (ATUC)** **01240**
SG c/o TUCP-PGEA Compound, Masaya and Maharlika Streets, Diliman 1101, Quezon City, Philippines. T. +6329247551. Fax +6329219758. E-mail: tucpgensec.grs@gmail.com – r_certeza_11@yahoo.com.
URL: http://www.aseantuc.org/
Aims Represent collective interests of workers in ASEAN countries. **Structure** Officers: President; Secretary-General. **Events** *Joint Meeting* Manila (Philippines) 2019, *Leaders Meeting* Singapore (Singapore) 2011, *Plenary Meeting* Singapore (Singapore) 2011, *Meeting and Conference* Hanoi (Vietnam) 2010, *Meeting and Conference* Cebu City (Philippines) 2009. **IGO Relations** *ASEAN (#01141).* [2014.06.01/XE4761/t/**E**]

♦ ASEAN Traditional Textile Arts Community / see Traditional Textile Arts Society of South East Asia (#20194)

♦ **ASEAN Training Center for Preventive Drug Education (ATCPDE)** ... **01241**
Dir College of Education, Univ of the Philippines, Diliman, 1101 Quezon City, Philippines. Fax +6329289756. E-mail: atcpde@gmail.com.
URL: http://archives.pia.gov.ph/atcpde/
History 30 Nov 1979, Kuala Lumpur (Malaysia), during 4th Meeting of the *ASEAN (#01141)* Drug Experts, through a Memorandum of Understanding adapted and approved by ASEAN member countries (Indonesia, Malaysia, Philippines, Singapore and Thailand). Quezon City (Philippines) as site formalized 1980. Also referred to previously as *ASEAN Centre for Preventive Drug Education.* **Aims** Conduct training in preventive drug education for ASEAN Member States; conduct research on training programs, new approaches, content and instructional materials in preventive drug education; provide technical assistance in preventive drug education; maintain links with ASEAN Member States and other international agencies on matters related to preventive drug education. **Structure** Foreign Ministries of ASEAN Member States through ASEAN Offices. Dangerous Drugs Board of the Philippines. Drug Education Committee, headed by Director. Executive Secretary. Members from different government agencies (6): Education; Social Welfare and Development; Philippine Information Agency; Health; Commission on Higher Education; University of the Philippines. **Languages** English, Filipino. **Staff** 1.00 FTE, paid. **Finance** Funding from Philippine Government through Dangerous Drugs Board. Annual budget: Pesos 1,000,000. **Activities** Advocacy/lobbying/activism; training/education; events/meetings; network/liaising; guidance/assistance/consulting; research/documentation. **Events** *ASEAN-EC seminar workshop on the development and validation of evaluation instruments for drug abuse prevention education programs* Manila (Philippines) 1992. **Publications** *ATCPDE Bulletin* (annual). *ASEAN Adoption of the Drug Use Prevention International Standards* (2017).
Members Full in 10 countries:
Brunei Darussalam, Cambodia, Indonesia, Laos, Malaysia, Myanmar, Philippines, Singapore, Thailand, Vietnam.
IGO Relations *ASEAN (#01141)*; national agencies. [2018.09.21/XE1638/**E***]

♦ ASEAN Training Centre for Primary Health Care Development / see ASEAN Institute for Health Development (#01197)

♦ **ASEAN Troika** **01242**
Contact ASEAN Secretariat, 70 A Jalan Sisingamangaraja, Jakarta 12110, Indonesia. T. +62217262991 – +62217243372. Fax +62217398234 – +62217243504.
URL: http://www.aseansec.org/3637.htm
History 25 Jul 2000, Bangkok (Thailand), within *ASEAN (#01141).* **Aims** Address urgent and important regional *political* and *security* issues. **Structure** Comprises Foreign Ministers of present, past and future chairmen of the ASEAN Standing Committee of Foreign Ministers. [2010/XJ3174/**F***]

♦ ASEAN TTAC / see Traditional Textile Arts Society of South East Asia (#20194)
♦ ASEAN-United States Business Council / see US-ASEAN Business Council

♦ **ASEAN University Network (AUN)** **01243**
Exec Dir Room 210 – Jamjuree I Building, Chulalongkorn University, Phyathai Road, Bangkok, 10330, Thailand. T. +6622153640 – +6622183256 – +6622183257. Fax +6622168808.
URL: http://www.aunsec.org/
History Nov 1995, within *ASEAN (#01141)*, on signature of *'AUN Charter'* by ASEAN Ministers responsible for higher education and of *'Agreement on the establishment of AUN'* by the Presidents/Rectors/Vice-Chancellors of the 11 Participating Universities. Set up following recommendations of ASEAN Heads of State/Government at 4th ASEAN Summit, Jan 1992, Singapore (Singapore), and adoption of both Charter and Memorandum of Agreement at 3rd Meeting of *'ASEAN Sub-Committee on Education (ASCOE)'*, 20-22 Jun 1995, Manila (Philippines). **Aims** Strengthen the existing network of cooperation among universities in the region by promoting collaborative study and research programmes on the priority areas identified by ASEAN; promote cooperation and solidarity among scientists and scholars in ASEAN member countries; develop academic and professional human resources in the region; produce and transmit scientific and scholarly knowledge and information to achieve ASEAN goals; promote information dissemination including electronic networking of libraries, exchanges and sharing of appropriate information among members of the academic community, policy-makers, students and other relevant users. **Structure** *'ASEAN University Network Board of Trustees (AUN BOT)'* (meeting at least twice a year), comprises a representative of each ASEAN country, designated by the respective government, plus (ex officio) ASEAN Secretary-General and Executive Director of the Network. Secretariat, headed by Executive Director, hosted by Thailand's Commission on Higher Education. Includes *Southeast Asia Engineering Education Development Network (SEED-Net, see: #01243).* **Languages** English. **Staff** 11.00 FTE, paid. **Finance** Annual budget and 3-year plan approved by Board of Trustees. **Activities** Training/education; meeting activities. **Events** *ASEAN + Three Rectors Conference* Kanazawa (Japan) 2021, *ASEAN Science Diplomats Assembly (SDA)* Makati (Philippines) 2019, *AUN Quality Assurance International Conference* Makati (Philippines) 2019, *ASEAN Science Diplomats Assembly (SDA)* Manila (Philippines) 2019, *Regional Conference on Geological and Geo-Resources Engeeniring (RC GeoE)* Quezon City (Philippines) 2019. **Publications** *AUN Newsletter* (2 a year). Books; proceedings. **Information Services** *Inter-Library Online (AUNILO).*
Members Participating universities (21) in 10 countries:
Brunei Darussalam, Cambodia, Indonesia, Laos, Malaysia, Myanmar, Philippines, Singapore, Thailand, Vietnam.
IGO Relations Cooperation agreement with: *Asean Quality Assurance Network (AQAN, #01227).* **NGO Relations** Observer of: *Asia-Pacific Quality Network (APQN, #02004).* [2020/XF4054/**F***]

♦ **ASEAN University Sports Council (AUSC)** **01244**
Contact c/o Sports Div (Higher Education Sector), Ministry of Education – Tower 2 – Level 2 – no2, Jalan P5/6, Precint 5, 62200 WP Putrajaya, Malaysia. T. +60388706146. Fax +60388706214.
URL: http://www.ausc.my/
Activities Organizes 'ASEAN University Games' (every 2 years). **Events** *Meeting* Bandung (Indonesia) 1990, *Meeting* Pattaya (Thailand) 1988, *Conference* Singapore (Singapore) 1986. **Members** Membership countries not specified. **IGO Relations** Affiliated with: *ASEAN (#01141).* **NGO Relations** Cooperates with: *Asian University Sports Federation (AUSF, #01775).* [2017/XE0272/**E**]

♦ **ASEAN Valuers Association (AVA)** **01245**
Main Office 18 Office Park, 3rd Floor, Jalan TB Simatupang Kav 18, Jakarta, Indonesia. E-mail: secretariat@asean-valuers.org.
URL: https://asean-valuers.org/
History Jun 1981, Kuala Lumpur (Malaysia). **Events** *Congress* Bali (Indonesia) 2022, *Congress* Cambodia 2021, *Congress* Pattaya (Thailand) 2019, *Congress* Yogyakarta (Indonesia) 2018, *Congress* Singapore (Singapore) 2017.
Members Full in 5 countries:
Indonesia, Malaysia, Philippines, Singapore, Thailand.
Consultative Status Consultative status granted from: *ASEAN (#01141).* [2012/XE0268/**E**]

♦ **ASEAN-WEN** ASEAN Wildlife Enforcement Network (#01246)

♦ **ASEAN Wildlife Enforcement Network (ASEAN-WEN)** **01246**
Contact Sisingamangaraja 70A, Kebayoran Baru, Jakarta 12110, Indonesia. T. +62217243372.
URL: https://environment.asean.org/the-asean-wildlife-enforcement-network-asean-wen/
History Dec 2005. **Aims** Combat illegal wildlife trade. **Activities** Events/meetings; training/education.
Members ASEAN governments (10):
Brunei Darussalam, Cambodia, Indonesia, Laos, Malaysia, Myanmar, Philippines, Singapore, Thailand, Vietnam.
IGO Relations Member of: *ASEANAPOL (#01138).* **NGO Relations** *Global Tiger Initiative (GTI, #10629).* [2021/XJ9706/**F***]

♦ **ASEAN Working Group on Social Forestry (AWG SF)** **01247**
Main Office Ministry of Forestry, 14th Fl – Block I, Manggala Wanabhakti Bldg, Jalan Gatot Subroto, Jakarta 10270, Indonesia. T. +62215703246ext710. Fax +62215730136.
URL: http://www.awg-sf.org/
History Proposed Mar 2005, Madiun (Indonesia). Endorsed Aug 2005, Phnom Penh (Cambodia), during 8th Meeting of *ASEAN Senior Officials on Forestry (ASOF).* Originally known as *ASEAN Social Forestry Network (ASFN).* Present name adopted, 2016. **Aims** Strengthen ASEAN cooperation in social forestry through the sharing of information and knowledge. **Events** *Annual Meeting* Chiang Mai (Thailand) 2017, *Annual Meeting* Puerto Princesa (Philippines) 2016, *Annual Meeting* Myanmar 2015, *Annual Meeting* Kota Kinabalu (Malaysia) 2014, *Annual Meeting* Luang Prabang (Laos) 2013.
Members Governments (10):
Brunei Darussalam, Cambodia, Indonesia, Laos, Malaysia, Myanmar, Philippines, Singapore, Thailand, Vietnam.
IGO Relations *ASEAN (#01141).* **NGO Relations** Partner organizations: *Center for International Forestry Research (CIFOR, #03646); Non-Timber Forest Products Exchange Programme for South and Southeast Asia (NTFP-EN, #17151); RECOFTC – The Center for People and Forests (RECOFTC, #18628).* [2017/XJ7913/**E***]

♦ ASEAN Young Professionals Volunteers Corps (unconfirmed)
♦ ASEAP – Association of South East Asian Publishers (inactive)
♦ **ASEAPS** Association of South-East Asian Pain Societies (#02922)
♦ **ASE** Asian Society of Endourology (#01719)
♦ **ASE** Association of Space Explorers (#02927)
♦ ASEAS(UK) – Association of Southeast Asian Studies (UK) (internationally oriented national body)
♦ ASEATTA / see Asia Pacific Histocompatibility and Immunogenetics Association (#01927)
♦ **ASEA UNINET** ASEAN-European Academic University Network (#01170)
♦ **ASECAP** Association Européenne des Concessionnaires d'Autoroutes et d'Ouvrages à Péage (#02559)
♦ **ASEC** Asian Solidarity Economy Coalition (#01754)
♦ ASEC / see Confederation of European Senior Expert Services (#04533)
♦ **ASECNA** Agence pour la sécurité de la navigation aérienne en Afrique et à Madagascar (#00556)
♦ **ASECO** Alliance for Social and Ecological Consumer Organisations (#00722)
♦ ASECU / see Association of Economic Universities of South and Eastern Europe and the Black Sea Region (#02479)
♦ **ASECU** Association of Economic Universities of South and Eastern Europe and the Black Sea Region (#02479)
♦ **ASEE** American Society for Engineering Education (#00790)
♦ **A SEED** Action for Solidarity, Equality, Environment and Diversity (#00098)
♦ ASEED – Asian Society for Entrepreneurship Education and Development (no recent information)
♦ Aseed-IDMAT / see ASEED International Institute of Development Management Technology
♦ ASEED International Institute of Development Management Technology (internationally oriented national body)
♦ ASEEES – Association for Slavic, East European, and Eurasian Studies (internationally oriented national body)
♦ **ASEES** Association scientifique européenne pour l'eau et la santé (#02908)
♦ **ASEF** Active Shipbuilding Experts' Federation (#00103)
♦ **ASEF** Asia-Europe Foundation (#01270)
♦ **ASEFUAN** Asia-Europe Foundation University Alumni Network (#01271)
♦ ASEF University Alumni Network / see Asia-Europe Foundation University Alumni Network (#01271)
♦ ASEG – Asian Society for Environmental Geotechnology (inactive)
♦ **ASEIBI** Asociación de Egresados de la Escuela Interamericana de Bibliotecologia (#00759)
♦ ASEKO – Association for Environmental Education (no recent information)
♦ ASELACMAR – Asociación de Especialistas Latinoamericanos en Ciencias del Mar (inactive)
♦ **ASELE** Asociación para la Enseñanza del Español como Lengua Extranjera (#02123)
♦ ASELT – Association européenne pour l'échange de la littérature technique dans le domaine de la sidérurgie (inactive)
♦ **ASEM** Asia-Europe Meeting (#01272)
♦ **ASEM** Asian Society for Emergency Medicine (#01718)
♦ ASEM – Asian Society of Experimental Mechanics (unconfirmed)
♦ ASEM – Australasian Society for Emergency Medicine (internationally oriented national body)
♦ ASEM-CCSTI – ASEM Cooperation Centre for Science Technology and Innovation (unconfirmed)
♦ ASEM Cooperation Centre for Science Technology and Innovation (unconfirmed)
♦ ASEM Global Aging Center (internationally oriented national body)
♦ **ASEMUS** Asia-Europe Museum Network (#01273)
♦ ASEN – Association for the Study of Ethnicity and Nationalism (internationally oriented national body)
♦ **ASEPA** Asian Epilepsy Academy (#01439)
♦ ASEP – Asian Society for Environmental Protection (inactive)
♦ ASEP – Austrian Senior Experts Pool (internationally oriented national body)
♦ ASEPELT – European Scientific Association of Applied Economics (no recent information)
♦ ASEP – Secretaria Permanente del Acuerdo Sudamericano sobre Estupefacientes y Psicotrópicos (inactive)
♦ ASEQUA – Association scientifique pour l'étude du quaternaire africain (inactive)
♦ ASERA – Australasian Science Education Research Association (internationally oriented national body)
♦ ASER – Asociación Sudamericana de Endoscopia Respiratoria (unconfirmed)
♦ ASER – Association for Ethnic and Regional Studies (internationally oriented national body)
♦ ASERCOM / see Association of European Refrigeration Component Manufacturers (#02537)
♦ **ASERCOM** Association of European Refrigeration Component Manufacturers (#02537)
♦ ASERIC – Asian Soils and Environment Research Information Center (unconfirmed)
♦ ASEST – Arab Society for Ethics in Science and Technology (internationally oriented national body)
♦ **ASETA** Asociación de Empresas de Telecomunicaciones de la Comunidad Andina (#02951)
♦ **ASFAA** Asiania Sport For All Association (#01510)
♦ **ASFA** Association of Special Fares Agents (#02928)
♦ ASF / see Acupuncture sans frontières International (#00106)
♦ **ASF** African Social Forum (#00457)
♦ ASF – Aktion Sühnezeichen Friedensdienste (internationally oriented national body)
♦ ASF – American-Scandinavian Foundation (internationally oriented national body)
♦ ASF – Arab Sugar Federation (inactive)

Asfari Foundation
01247
alphabetic sequence excludes
For the complete listing, see Yearbook Online at

- ♦ The Asfari Foundation (internationally oriented national body)
- ♦ ASF / see Asian Shipowners Association (#01697)
- ♦ **ASF** Asian Silambam Federation (#01700)
- ♦ **ASF** Asian Squash Federation (#01760)
- ♦ ASF – Asian Stroke Forum (meeting series)
- ♦ **ASF** Asia Securities Forum (#02093)
- ♦ ASF – Association Apprentissages Sans Frontières (internationally oriented national body)
- ♦ ASF – Atlantic Salmon Federation (internationally oriented national body)
- ♦ **ASF** Avocats Sans Frontières (#03050)
- ♦ ASF Belgium – Aviation sans frontières, Belgique (internationally oriented national body)
- ♦ ASFC – Arab Society for Fungal Conservation (internationally oriented national body)
- ♦ **ASFE** Alliance for Synthetic Fuels in Europe (#00724)
- ♦ ASFEC – Regional Centre for Adult Education (no recent information)
- ♦ ASF France – Aviation sans frontières, France (internationally oriented national body)
- ♦ **ASF International** Acupuncture sans frontières International (#00106)
- ♦ ASF-International – Animaux sans Frontières – International (internationally oriented national body)
- ♦ ASF International – Aviation Sans Frontières (unconfirmed)
- ♦ ASFM – African Society of Forensic Medicine (unconfirmed)
- ♦ **ASFSFM** Arab Society for Forensic Sciences and Forensic Medicine (#01045)
- ♦ **ASF** A Soul for Europe (#19697)
- ♦ ASGA – Association des services géologiques africains (inactive)
- ♦ ASG – African Seabird Group (unconfirmed)
- ♦ ASG – Australasian Seabird Group (internationally oriented national body)
- ♦ ASGC – Australasian Society of Genetic Counsellors (internationally oriented national body)
- ♦ ASGD – Australasian Society of Diagnostic Genomics (internationally oriented national body)
- ♦ ASGFMOF / see Administration universitaire francophone et européenne en médecine et odontologie (#00115)
- ♦ **ASGMI** Asociación de Servicios de Geologia y Mineria Iberoamericanos (#02297)
- ♦ **ASGO** Asian Society of Gynecologic Oncology (#01720)
- ♦ **ASGP** Association of Secretaries General of Parliaments (#02911)
- ♦ ASGP / see International Association for the Study of German Politics (#12200)
- ♦ **ASG-PLP** Associação de Secretários-Gerais dos Parlamentos de Língua Portuguesa (#02334)
- ♦ **ASGRG** Australasian Society for General Relativity and Gravitation (#03028)
- ♦ **ASGRS** Asian Society for Gynecologic Robotic Surgery (#01721)
- ♦ ASHA – Asia Society of Hip Arthroscopy & Preservation (unconfirmed)
- ♦ ASHA – Australasian Sexual Health Alliance (internationally oriented national body)
- ♦ ASHAD – African-American Society for Humanitarian Aid and Development (internationally oriented national body)
- ♦ ASHBPS / see Asian-Pacific Hepato-Pancreato-Biliary Association (#01616)
- ♦ ASHCS – Association for Security in HealthCare Information Systems (unconfirmed)
- ♦ ASHHNA – Australasian Sexual Health and HIV Nurses Association (internationally oriented national body)
- ♦ Ashinaga (internationally oriented national body)
- ♦ ASHM / see Australasian Society for HIV, Viral Hepatitis and Sexual Health Medicine
- ♦ ASHM – Australasian Society for HIV, Viral Hepatitis and Sexual Health Medicine (internationally oriented national body)
- ♦ ASHNA / see Australasian Sexual Health and HIV Nurses Association
- ♦ ASHNA – Assistance to Support Humanity and Need for Aid Organization (internationally oriented national body)
- ♦ **ASHNO** Asian Society of Head and Neck Oncology (#01722)
- ♦ ASHO – Asian Society for Hyperthermic Oncology (internationally oriented national body)
- ♦ Ashoka Fellowship International / see Ashoka – Innovators for the Public (#01248)

♦ Ashoka – Innovators for the Public 01248

Global Headquarters 1700 North Moore St, Ste 2000, Arlington VA 22209, USA. T. +17035278300. Fax +17035278383.
Contact Rue Joseph II 20, 1000 Brussels, Belgium. T. +3226752219. E-mail: ashokabelgium@ashoka.org.
URL: http://www.ashoka.org/

History 1980. Founded by Bill Drayton. Former names and other names: *Ashoka Fellowship International* – former (1980). **Aims** Develop the profession of social entrepreneurship around the world; seek out and support innovative social *entrepreneurs* worldwide – individuals who have practical, unique ideas for the public good, in the fields of learning/youth development, environment, health, human rights, civic participation and economic development. **Activities** Financial and/or material support. Active in: Argentina, Austria, Brazil, Canada, China, Egypt, France, Germany, Hungary, India, Indonesia, Ireland, Israel, Japan, Kenya, Korea Rep, Mexico, Nigeria, Pakistan, Philippines, Poland, Portugal, Senegal, Singapore, South Africa, Spain, Sri Lanka, Sweden, Switzerland, Thailand, Türkiye, Uganda, UK, USA, Venezuela. **Events** *Ashoka Changemaker Summit* Turin (Italy) 2021, *Conference on Advancing Women Social Entrepreneurship in ASEAN* Singapore (Singapore) 2020, *European Changemaker Summit* Barcelona (Spain) 2019, *Changemaker Xchange Conference* Singapore (Singapore) 2019, *Global youth enterprise conference* Washington, DC (USA) 2009. **Publications** *The Changemakers Review* (4 a year) – magazine; *Leading Social Entrepreneurs* (annual). **Members** Ashoka Fellows (about 3,000) in 70 countries. Membership countries not specified. **NGO Relations** Participates in: *Global Meeting of Generations (GMG)*. Member of: *Asian Venture Philanthropy Network (AVPN, #01778)*; *NetHope (#16979)*. Stakeholder in: *Child and Youth Finance International (CYFI, inactive)*. Supports: *SEED (#19213)*. Ashoka – Youth Venture is member of the Advisory Committee of: *Making Cents International*. Partner of: *UNLEASH*. [2021/XF0091/**F**]

- ♦ **ASHRM** Arabian Society for Human Resource Management (#00977)
- ♦ ASHS – Asian Society of Human Services (internationally oriented national body)
- ♦ ASHS / see InterAmerican Society of Tropical Horticulture (#11451)
- ♦ ASI / see Actions de Solidarité Internationale
- ♦ Asia 2000 Foundation / see Asia New Zealand Foundation
- ♦ Asia 2000 Foundation of New Zealand / see Asia New Zealand Foundation
- ♦ Asia AAOH / see Asian Association of Occupational and Environmental Health (#01330)

♦ Asia Academy of Management (AAM) 01249

Contact Fac of Business Administration, Chinese Univ of Hong Kong, Shatin, Hong Kong. Fax +85226036840. E-mail: asia-aom@cuhk.edu.hk.
URL: http://www.baf.cuhk.edu.hk/asia-aom/

History Aug 1997. Inaugural conference in 1998. **Events** *Biennial Conference* Bali (Indonesia) 2019, *Biennial Conference* Kitakyushu (Japan) 2017, *Biennial Conference* Hong Kong (Hong Kong) 2015, *Summer Research Forum for Young Scholars* Hong Kong (Hong Kong) 2013, *Biennial Conference* Seoul (Korea Rep) 2012. **Publications** *Asia Pacific Journal of Management* (4 a year).
Members Universities (11) in 8 countries and territories:
China, Hong Kong, India, Japan, Korea Rep, Singapore, Taiwan, USA. [2013/XD6596/**D**]

- ♦ ASIA / see Airline Sports and Cultural Association (#00609)
- ♦ Asia Alliance of YMCAs / see Asia and Pacific Alliance of YMCAs (#01826)

♦ Asia for Animals Coalition (AfA) 01250

Co-Founder Animals Asia Foundation, Room 1501, Tung Hip Commercial Bldg, 244-252 Des Voeux Road Central, Sheung Wan, Hong Kong. E-mail: afacoalition@gmail.com.
URL: http://www.asiaforanimals.com/

History 2011. Founded by *Animals Asia (#00841)*, Animal People, ACRES, Animal Guardians, *Humane Society International (HSI, #10966)*, *International Animal Rescue (IAR)*, *International Fund for Animal Welfare (IFAW, #13693)*, Philippine Animal Welfare Society, Royal Society for the Prevention of Cruelty to Animal, (Hong Kong) Society for the Prevention of Cruelty to Animals and *World Animal Protection (#21092)*. **Aims** Provide support to organizations working throughout the Asia region to to tackle some of the most pressing animal welfare concerns. **Structure** Coordinator; one representative per membership organization. **Languages** English. **Staff** 2.00 FTE, paid. **Finance** Members' dues. **Activities** Advocacy/lobbying/activism; events/meetings. **Events** *Conference* Sheung Wan (Hong Kong) 2021, *Conference* Kuching (Malaysia) 2015, *Asia For Animals Conference* Singapore (Singapore) 2014, *Asia For Animals Conference* Chengdu (China) 2011, *Asia For Animals Conference* Bali (Indonesia) 2009.
Members Organizations (22), including the following 12 listed in this Yearbook:
Animals Asia (#00841); *Animals Asia Foundation (AAF, #00842)*; *Born Free Foundation*; *Change For Animals Foundation (CFAF)*; *Donkey Sanctuary, The (#05120)*; *Earth Island Institute (EII)*; *Humane Society International (HSI, #10966)*; *International Animal Rescue (IAR)*; *International Fund for Animal Welfare (IFAW, #13693)*; *Jane Goodall Institute (JGI, #16089)*; *Vier Pfoten International (#20776)*; *World Animal Protection (#21092)*.
IGO Relations None. **NGO Relations** Links with nearly 150 international animal protection groups. [2021/XJ9550/y/**D**]

- ♦ **ASIA** Antiqui Societatis Jesus Alumni (#21877)
- ♦ **ASIA** Anti-Smoking International Alliance (#00861)
- ♦ Asia Archipelago Cruise Alliance (unconfirmed)

♦ Asia Arsenic Network (AAN) 01251

Dhaka Office House No 46 Apt No 4b, Road No 13/C Block-E, Banani, Dhaka 1213, Bangladesh. T. +88029894493. E-mail: aandhaka@citech-bd.com – sayedsunny@ymail.com.
Jessore Office Krishnabati casino en ligne bonus sans depot, Pulerhat, Jessore Benapole Road, Jessore, Bangladesh. T. +88042168663. E-mail: aan.jessore@gmail.com.
Miyazaki Office Miyazaki NPO House, Room 208 2-9-6, Tsurunoshima, Miyazaki, 880-014 Japan. T. +81985202201. E-mail: aanm2201@miyazaki-catv.ne.jp.
URL: http://www.aan-bangladesh.org/

History Apr 1994. **Aims** Provide a positive and meaningful response to arsenic contamination in Asia. **Activities** Organizes annual *'Forum of Asian Underground Water Contaminated by Arsenic'*. Research and study; mitigation. **Publications** *AAN Newsletter*. [2020/XF6705/**F**]

- ♦ **ASIA** Arthroplasty Society in Asia (#01119)
- ♦ Asia Arthroscopy Congress (meeting series)

♦ Asia Association of Coaching Science (AACS) 01252

Gen Sec Room 701A, No 20 Chu-Lun Str, Taipei 104, Taiwan. T. +886287711808. Fax +886287711960. E-mail: shihchung@gmail.com – coach.twn@gmail.com.
URL: http://www.coachingscience.asia/

History 2012. **Aims** Promote and maintain the highest possible values in *sport* and the coaching profession; collaborate for the development of theory and practice of sport coaching in Asian regions. **Structure** Board of Directors; Executive Committee. **Languages** English. **Finance** Members' dues. **Activities** Events/meetings; awards/prizes/competitions. **Events** *Asia-Pacific Conference* Shanghai (China) 2016, *Asia-Pacific Conference / Asia pacific Conference of Coaching Science – APCOCS* Sapporo (Japan) 2014. **Publications** *Asian Journal of Coaching Science*. [2016.06.01/XJ9494/**D**]

♦ Asia Association for Global Studies (AAGS) 01253

Dir address not obtained. E-mail: president@aags.org.
URL: http://www.aags.org/

History 2005. Current constitution adopted 1 Apr 2007. Registered in accordance with Japanese law. **Aims** Promote innovative research and alternatives perspectives on issues of international significance. **Structure** Board. **Events** *Annual Conference* Kyoto (Japan) 2018, *Annual Conference* Mitaka (Japan) 2015, *Annual Conference* Shantou (China) 2014, *International Conference / Annual Conference* Bangkok (Thailand) 2013, *Conference / Annual Conference* Tokyo (Japan) 2012. **Publications** *Asia Journal of Global Studies* (2 a year). Books; conference proceedings. [2015/XJ6364/**D**]

♦ Asia Association of Medical Laboratory Scientists (AAMLS) 01254

Pres Clinical Chemistry FAHS, 154 Rama 1 Road, Pathumwan, Bangkok, 10330, Thailand. E-mail: rachana.s@chula.ac.th.

History 14 May 1997, Nagoya (Japan). **Aims** Elevate status of medical laboratory science in Asia and its neighbouring countries; offer opportunities for exchange of information between countries; enhance mutual understanding among scientists in the field from various countries and work for mutual assistance and improvement of expertise technologies; improve reliability on accuracy of medical laboratory tests through cooperation between countries. **Structure** Board, comprising President, 2 Vice-Presidents, Treasurer/Secretary and 8 Directors. **Languages** English. **Staff** None. **Finance** Members' dues. **Activities** Photo survey programme; information exchange (since 2004); organizes conferences. **Events** *Congress* Pattaya (Thailand) 2019, *Scientific reunification – from basis to cutting-edge medical laboratory sciences* Busan (Korea Rep) 2017, *Congress* Singapore (Singapore) 2013, *Congress* Yokohama (Japan) 2009, *Congress* Shanghai (China) 2005.
Members National organizations in 12 countries and territories:
Brunei Darussalam, China, Hong Kong, India, Indonesia, Japan, Korea Rep, Malaysia, Philippines, Singapore, Thailand, Vietnam. [2013.06.27/XD7831/**D**]

- ♦ ASIA – Association scientifique internationale d'auriculothérapie (inactive)
- ♦ **ASIA** Association of Sports Institutes in Asia (#02931)
- ♦ Asia and Australasia Hotel and Restaurant Association (inactive)

♦ Asia Baptist Graduate Theological Seminary (ABGTS) 01255

Philippines Branch c/o PBTS, 19 Tacay Road, Guisad, 2600 Baguio BEN, Philippines. Fax +63744423294. E-mail: abgts@pbts.net.ph.
URL: http://www.abgts.org/

History 1959, under the sponsorship of the (USA) Southern Baptist Convention and eight Baptist theological seminaries in the region. **Aims** Provide graduate training for God-called men and women preparing for vocational *Christian* ministry, primarily within the Asian Baptist context. **Structure** Board of Trustees.
Members Partner schools in 9 countries and territories:
Hong Kong, Indonesia, Japan, Korea Rep, Philippines, Singapore, Taiwan, Thailand, USA. [2019/XN1418/**F**]

♦ Asia Business Trade Association (ABTA) 01256

SG 41A Ann Siang Road, Singapore 069717, Singapore. T. +6565363414. E-mail: info@asiabusiness.trade.
URL: http://www.asiabusiness.trade/

History Registered in accordance with the law of Singapore. **Aims** Promote regional trade issues in cooperation with governments. **Structure** Executive Committee; Secretariat, provided by *Asian Trade Centre (ATC)*. Working Groups. Includes: *Asia Pacific MSME Trade Coalition (AMTC)*. **Activities** Capacity building; advocacy/lobbying/activism; knowledge management/information dissemination. **Events** *Asia Trade Summit* Hong Kong (Hong Kong) 2019, *Comprehensive and Progressive Agreement for Trans-Pacific Partnership (CPTPP) Forum* Singapore (Singapore) 2019, *SME Digital Economy Summit* Singapore (Singapore) 2019. [2019/XM7597/t/**D**]

♦ Asia Canine Protection Alliance (ACPA) 01257

Coordinator Room 301, No 97 Tran Quoc Toan Str, Hoan Kiem District, Hanoi, Vietnam. T. +84439289264. Fax +84439289265. E-mail: acpa.vietnam@gmail.com.
URL: http://www.acpagroup.org/

History May 2013, by *Animals Asia (#00841)*, Change for Animals Foundation, *Humane Society International (HSI, #10966)* and Soi Dog Foundation. **Aims** Provide the people and governments of Asia with the required support and expertise to eliminate rabies and other communicable diseases, by ending trade in dogs for human consumption and providing humane and sustainable dog population management solutions. **Languages** English, Vietnamese. **Staff** 5.00 FTE, paid. **Finance** Costs shared between members. No fixed budget. **Activities** Awareness raising; events/meetings. **Publications** No regular publications.

Members Organizations (4):
Animals Asia (#00841); Change For Animals Foundation (CFAF); Humane Society International (HSI, #10966); Soi Dog Foundation. [2015.07.22/XJ9672/y/**D**]

- ♦ Asia Center for Theological Studies and Mission (internationally oriented national body)
- ♦ Asia Centre (internationally oriented national body)
- ♦ Asia Centre of the Commonwealth Youth Programme (see: #04362)
- ♦ Asia Centre for Social Entrepreneurship and Philanthropy (internationally oriented national body)
- ♦ Asia Christian Evangelistic Society (inactive)

♦ Asia Cloud Computing Association (ACCA) 01258

Exec Dir address not obtained. E-mail: info@asiacloudcomputing.org.
URL: http://asiacloudcomputing.org/

History 2010. **Aims** Establish collaboration among cloud stakeholders in Asia to accelerate the growth of the cloud market. **Structure** Board; Executive Committee; Working Groups. **Activities** Research/documentation; training/education; events/meetings. **Events** *Big Data and AI Leaders Summit* Singapore (Singapore) 2019, *Digital Marketing Leaders Summit* Singapore (Singapore) 2019, *Internet of Things Asia Conference* Singapore (Singapore) 2019. **Publications** *The Cumulus* – newsletter. [2020/XM4095/**D**]

♦ Asia Cohort Consortium (ACC) 01259

Contact Natl Cancer Ctr, 5-1-1 Tsukiji, Chuo-ku, Tokyo, 104-0045 Japan. E-mail: cc@asiacohort.org.
URL: http://www.asiacohort.org/

History First proposed 2004, Seoul (Korea Rep). **Aims** Understand the relationship between genetics, environmental exposures, and the etiology of *disease*; serve as a platform for cross-cohort collaborative projects and combined analysis; act as an incubator for new cohorts. **Structure** Executive Committee; Coordinating Center. **Languages** English. **Activities** Events/meetings; research and development. **Events** *Working Group Meeting* Tokyo (Japan) 2022, *General Membership Meeting* Tokyo (Japan) 2021, *Working Group Meeting* Kyoto (Japan) 2020, *General Membership Meeting* Tokyo (Japan) 2020, *Online Meeting* Tokyo (Japan) 2020.
Members Full in 10 countries and territories:
Bangladesh, China, India, Iran Islamic Rep, Japan, Korea Rep, Malaysia, Mongolia, Singapore, Taiwan.
[2022.02.15/XM8295/**D**]

- ♦ Asia Color Association (unconfirmed)

♦ Asia Competition Association (ACA) 01260

Secretariat Sookmyung Women's Univ, 100 Cheongpa-ro 47-gil, Yongsan-gu, Seoul 04310, Korea Rep. T. +82220777091. Fax +82220777969. E-mail: asia.competition@gmail.com.
URL: http://asiacompetition.org/

History 4 Sep 2008. Founded by 16 founding members from China, Japan and Korea Rep. **Aims** Contribute to expansion and enhancement of competition culture in Asia by enhancing international exchange and cooperation on competition *laws* and *policies* in Asia at non-governmental level. **Structure** Council; Steering Committee. **Events** *Annual Conference* Kyoto (Japan) 2021, *Annual Conference* Seoul (Korea Rep) 2020, *Annual Conference* Seoul (Korea Rep) 2019, *Annual Conference* Guangzhou (China) 2018, *Annual Conference* Sapporo (Japan) 2017.
Members Full in 6 countries and territories:
China, India, Japan, Korea Rep, Singapore, Taiwan. [2019.02.18/XJ2054/**D**]

- ♦ AsiaConstruct (unconfirmed)

♦ Asia Cooperation Dialogue (ACD) 01261

SG Al Salam, Block 7, Street no 27, House no 14, Kuwait, Kuwait. E-mail: narisara.bahalayothin@gmail.com – acd.secretariat@gmail.com.
URL: http://www.acd-dialogue.org/

History Jun 2002, Cha-Am (Thailand), by *ASEAN (#01141)* and 3 member countries, with a membership of 18 countries. **Aims** Constitute the missing link in Asia by incorporating every Asian country and building an Asian Community without duplicating other organizations or creating a bloc against others. **Structure** Ministerial Meeting; Summit; Provisional Secretariat. **Activities** Events/meetings; poltics/policy/regulatory. **Events** *Meeting on Inclusive and Sustainable Development* Kuwait (Kuwait) 2018, *Ministerial Meeting* Teheran (Iran Islamic Rep) 2018, *Ministerial Meeting* Abu Dhabi (United Arab Emirates) 2017, *Meeting on Promoting Approaches to Inclusive and Sustainable Development* Bangkok (Thailand) 2017, *Ministerial Meeting* Bangkok (Thailand) 2016. **Publications** *ACD E-News* (4 a year).
Members Participating countries (34):
Afghanistan, Bahrain, Bangladesh, Bhutan, Brunei Darussalam, Cambodia, China, India, Indonesia, Iran Islamic Rep, Japan, Kazakhstan, Korea Rep, Kuwait, Kyrgyzstan, Laos, Malaysia, Mongolia, Myanmar, Nepal, Oman, Pakistan, Philippines, Qatar, Russia, Saudi Arabia, Singapore, Sri Lanka, Tajikistan, Thailand, Türkiye, United Arab Emirates, Uzbekistan, Vietnam.
[2020/XF6784/**F***]

- ♦ **AsiaCORD** Network of Cord Blood Banks in Asia (#17002)

♦ Asia Cornea Society (ACS) 01262

Secretariat One Orchard Boulevard 13-03, Camden Medical Ctr, Singapore 248649, Singapore.
URL: http://www.asiacorneasociety.org/

History 2007, following the activities of *Asia-Pacific Society of Cornea and Refractive Surgery (APSCRS, inactive)*. **Aims** Provide a forum for regional interaction so as to advance the development of these fields of ophthalmology in Asia; contribute to international development in this arena, with the ultimate aim of alleviation of corneal blindness. **Structure** Council; Board; Secretariat. **Events** *Biennial Scientific Meeting* Bangkok (Thailand) 2022, *Biennial Scientific Meeting* Osaka (Japan) 2021, *Biennial Scientific Meeting* Osaka (Japan) 2020, *Biennial Scientific Meeting* Qingdao (China) 2018, *Biennial Scientific Meeting* Seoul (Korea Rep) 2016. **Members** Individuals. Membership countries not specified. **NGO Relations** *European Society of Cornea and Ocular Surface Disease Specialists (EuCornea, #08569)*. Instrumental in setting up: *Association of Eye Banks of Asia (AEBA, #02591)*. Member of: *Asia-Pacific Academy of Ophthalmology (APAO, #01814)*.
[2019/XM8240/v/**D**]

♦ Asia Crime Prevention Foundation (ACPF) 01263

Fondation asiatique pour la prévention du crime – Ajia Keisei Zaidan

Contact c/o UNAFEI, 2-1-18 Mokusei-no-mori, Akishima-shi, Tokyo, 196-0035 Japan. T. +81425437725. Fax +81425437726. E-mail: info@acpf.org.
URL: http://www.acpf.org/

History Founded 17 Feb 1982, under the aegis of *United Nations Asia and Far East Institute for the Prevention of Crime and the Treatment of Offenders (UNAFEI, #20521)*. **Aims** Offer moral and financial support to UNAFEI alumni associations and in the region; encourage activities of UNAFEI, its alumni members and other crime prevention agencies; support research, training and field work enhancing effective administration of governmental and non-governmental crime prevention policies and activities, and policies contributing to Asian peace and safety. **Structure** President, elected by and among the Directors. Board of Directors, consisting of not less than 15 and not more than 25 Directors (currently 20 members). Executive Director, serving as Chairman of the Board of Directors. Auditor. **Languages** English, Japanese. **Finance** Financial sources: dues and occasional donations by persons and organizations of the membership; donations by associations and corporates; contributions by the Japanese Government regularly through *Japan International Cooperation Agency (JICA)* and occasionally through Management of Coordination Agency in regard to ad hoc research projects; interests gained on the capital of the Foundation. **Activities** Organizes or assists in organizing international training programme of criminal justice personnel in the Asian region. Promotes regional and interregional cooperation in studying, devising and implementing effective crime prevention strategies both at governmental and non-governmental levels. Establishes, maintains and strengthens cooperative ties among various agencies and individuals serving in crime and justice field in the Asian region. Organizes or assists in organizing symposia, workshops or seminars, both at regional and national levels. Sends and invites or assists in sending and inviting researchers or experts in the field of crime prevention and criminal justice. Evaluates or assists in evaluating the effectiveness of training programmes and undertakes or assists in undertaking research and survey for identifying measures to improve the training programme. Publishes, exchanges and disseminates relevant views, data and information. **Events** *Meeting on criminal policy* Tokyo (Japan) 2007, *Symposium on home without crime* Tokyo (Japan) 2007, *World Conference* Macau 2004, *World Conference* Tokyo (Japan) 2002, *World Conference* Beijing (China) 2000. **Publications** *ACPF TODAY*; *The Asian Journal of Crime Prevention and Criminal Justice / Newsletter of Asia Crime Prevention Foundation.*
Members Membership open to individuals, associations and corporates. Members in 60 countries and territories:
Argentina, Australia, Bangladesh, Barbados, Brazil, Brunei Darussalam, Chile, China, Colombia, Costa Rica, Cuba, Ecuador, Egypt, Ethiopia, Fiji, Ghana, Guatemala, Guinea, Honduras, Hong Kong, India, Indonesia, Iraq, Jamaica, Japan, Kenya, Korea Rep, Lesotho, Liberia, Malaysia, Marshall Is, Mauritius, Micronesia FS, Mongolia, Morocco, Mozambique, Myanmar, Nepal, New Zealand, Nigeria, Pakistan, Panama, Papua New Guinea, Paraguay, Peru, Philippines, Samoa, Saudi Arabia, Singapore, Solomon Is, Sri Lanka, St Lucia, Sudan, Tanzania UR, Thailand, Tonga, United Arab Emirates, USA, Venezuela, Zambia.
Consultative Status Consultative status granted from: *ECOSOC (#05331)* (General). **IGO Relations** Accredited by (1): *United Nations Office at Vienna (UNOV, #20604)*. **NGO Relations** Member of (1): *International Centre for the Prevention of Crime (ICPC, #12508)*. [2018/XF8604/f/**F**]

- ♦ Asia Cruise Leaders Network (unconfirmed)

♦ Asia Cruise Terminal Association (ACTA) 01264

Secretariat 1 Maritime Square, No 07-01, Singapore 099253, Singapore. T. +6565132200. E-mail: enquiry@asiacruiseterminal.org.
URL: https://www.asiacruiseterminal.org/

History 15 Nov 2011, Singapore. **Aims** Provide: a cruise-friendly environment; a vehicle for regional cooperation in terminal development, operations and management. Increase awareness of cruise terminal facilities and services internationally. **Structure** General Meeting (annual); Council; Secretariat. **Finance** Sources: members' dues. **Events** *Asia Cruise Forum* Jeju (Korea Rep) 2019, *Asia Cruise Forum* Jeju (Korea Rep) 2018, *Asia Cruise Forum* Jeju (Korea Rep) 2017, *Asia Cruise Forum* Jeju (Korea Rep) 2015, *Annual Meeting* Shanghai (China) 2013.
Members Ordinary; Associate; Honorary; Affiliate. Members in 7 countries and territories:
China, Japan, Korea Rep, Malaysia, Philippines, Singapore, Taiwan. [2019/XM4334/**D**]

- ♦ **ASI** Action santé internationale (#10868)
- ♦ ASI – Actions de Solidarité Internationale (internationally oriented national body)
- ♦ Asia Dance Association (inactive)
- ♦ Asia Darshana (internationally oriented national body)

♦ Asia Democracy Network (ADN) 01265

Secretary General Signature Tower West Wing, 10F – PO1026, Cheonggyecheon-ro, Jung-gu, Seoul 04542, Korea Rep.
Senior Program Manager address not obtained.
URL: http://www.adnasia.org/

History Oct 2013, Seoul (Korea Rep). Launched following meetings held 2012 and 2013. **Aims** Promote and advance democratization and democratic governance at all levels of society through effective solidarity and cooperation among civil society organizations and democracy advocates in Asia. **Structure** Governing Council; Secretariat. **Activities** Advocacy/lobbying/activism; awareness raising; capacity building; knowledge management/information dissemination; networking/liaising; projects/programmes; research and development; training/education. (1) Democracy Unity and solidarity: Regional convening and consolidation of the pro-democratic actors; extend solidarity in the country under democratic crisis. (2) Promote local democracy. (3) Nurture youth and next generation democracy advocate. Active in all member countries. **Events** *Asia Democracy Assembly* Bali (Indonesia) 2022, *Tokyo Democracy Forum* Tokyo (Japan) 2022, *Asia Democracy Assembly* Seoul (Korea Rep) 2021, *Human Rights in Cambodia* Seoul (Korea Rep) 2021, *Role of Journalists in Fighting for Democracy and Freedom of Expression* Seoul (Korea Rep) 2021.
Members Organizations involved include the following organizations:
Asia Democracy Research Network (ADRN); *Asia Development Alliance (ADA, #01266); Asian Forum for Human Rights and Development (FORUM-ASIA, #01491); Asian Network for Free Elections (ANFREL, #01550); East Asia Institute, Seoul (EAI); Global Partnership for the Prevention of Armed Conflict (GPPAC, #10538); Migrant Forum in Asia (MFA, #16798)*; Northeast Asia Democracy Forum (NEADF); *People's SAARC (#18308); Society for Participatory Research in Asia (PRIA); Transparency International (TI, #20223)* (Asia).
[2022.05.11/XJ9567/**D**]

♦ Asia Development Alliance (ADA) 01266

Secretariat KoFID, 4/F – World Cup-ro 12-gil, Mapo-gu, Seoul 04004, Korea Rep. T. +82269256589. Fax +825051153682. E-mail: ada2030.secretariat@gmail.com.
URL: http://www.ada2030.org/

History Feb 2013, Bangkok (Thailand), as a joint regional platform of members of *Forus (#09934)* and *CIVICUS: World Alliance for Citizen Participation (#03962)* Affinity Group of National Associations (AGNA). **Aims** Enhance effectiveness and impact of civic engagement and advocacy in implementing the UN 2030 Agenda for Sustainable Development and Sustainable Development Goals (SDGs) at national and international levels. **Structure** Annual Conference; Steering Committee; Coordination Committee. Working Groups. **Activities** Events/meetings. **Events** *Tokyo Democracy Forum* Tokyo (Japan) 2022, *Busan Democracy Forum* Busan (Korea Rep) 2019, *Busan Democracy Forum* Busan (Korea Rep) 2018, *Asian Youth Leadership Forum for Democracy* Seoul (Korea Rep) 2017, *Asian Civil Society Forum on Sustainable Development Goals* Bangkok (Thailand) 2016. **Publications** *ADA Newsletter*.
Members Organizations (24) in 16 countries and territories:
Afghanistan, Bangladesh, Cambodia, China, India, Indonesia, Japan, Korea Rep, Malaysia, Mongolia, Nepal, Pakistan, Philippines, Singapore, Taiwan, Timor-Leste.
NGO Relations Member of: *Asia Democracy Network (ADN, #01265); Forus (#09934)*.
[2017.06.01/XM5446/**D**]

♦ Asia Development Dialogue 01267

Contact Oxfam Asia Regional Ctr, 4AB Fl, Q House Convent Bldg, 38 Convent Rd, Silom, Bangrak, Bangkok, 10500, Thailand. T. +6626320033.
Facebook: https://www.facebook.com/asiadialogue/

History A collaboration between *Oxfam International (#17922)*, Chulangongkorn University (Thailand), Lee Kuan Yew School of Public Policy (Singapore) with support of *The Rockefeller Foundation (#18966)*. **Aims** Initiate multi-sector dialogue on urban challenges for government leaders, senior civil servants, NGOs, private sector, and academics; enable innovative, process driven analyses of urban governance challenges; promote knowledge sharing and partnership on inclusive local economic development, urban resilience, and citizen participation with a special focus on secondary cities in Asia. **Structure** Advisory Committee. **Activities** Events/meetings. [2017/XJ9862/**E**]

- ♦ Asia Development and Training Centre for Small Hydro-Power Generation / see International Network on Small Hydro Power (#14324)
- ♦ **AsiaDHRRA** Asian Partnership for the Development of Human Resources in Rural Asia (#01654)
- ♦ Asia Diabolo Association (unconfirmed)
- ♦ Asia Disability Institute (internationally oriented national body)
- ♦ Asia Dyestuff Industry Federation (unconfirmed)
- ♦ Asia EDIFACT Board / see Asia Pacific Council for Trade Facilitation and Electronic Business (#01877)

♦ Asia eHealth Information Network (AeHIN) 01268

Secretariat Natl Telehealth Ctr, National Institutes of Health, Univ of the Philippines, 3rd Floor IT Complex, General Hospital Taft Ave, Ermita, Manila, Philippines. E-mail: webmaster@aehin.net.
Secretariat address not obtained.
URL: http://www.aehin.org/

History Set up 11 Dec 2011, Bangkok (Thailand). Officially launched 7 Aug 2012, Bangkok (Thailand) during 1st meeting. **Aims** Promote better use of information communication technology (ICT) to achieve better health through peer-to-peer assistance and knowledge sharing and learning through a regional approach for greater country-level impacts across South and Southeast Asia. **Structure** General Meeting; Chair; Executive Director; Secretariat; Satellite Secretariat. **Languages** English. **Staff** 3.00 FTE, paid. **Finance** Development partners. **Activities** Training/education; events/meetings. **Events** *ASEAN-Japan healthcare ICT Forum* Tokyo (Japan) 2017, *Annual General Meeting* Bali (Indonesia) 2015, *Global Forum on Research and Innovation for Health* Manila (Philippines) 2015, *Annual General Meeting* Manila (Philippines) 2014, *Annual General Meeting* Manila (Philippines) 2013. **Publications** Position papers.

Members Full in 54 countries and territories:
Afghanistan, Albania, Australia, Bangladesh, Belgium, Bhutan, Cambodia, Canada, China, Denmark, Egypt, Fiji, France, Germany, Ghana, Hong Kong, India, Indonesia, Japan, Kenya, Kiribati, Korea Rep, Laos, Malaysia, Maldives, Mali, Mongolia, Myanmar, Nepal, Netherlands, New Zealand, Nigeria, Norway, Pakistan, Philippines, Portugal, Qatar, Russia, Samoa, Singapore, Somalia, South Africa, Sri Lanka, Switzerland, Taiwan, Tajikistan, Tanzania UR, Thailand, Timor-Leste, Tonga, UK, USA, Vietnam, Zambia. [2019/XJ9793/**F**]

♦ Asia Electronics and Info-Communications Union (no recent information)

♦ Asia Europe Economic Forum (AEEF) 01269

Contact Bruegel, Rue de la Charité 33, 1210 Brussels, Belgium. T. +3222274274.
URL: http://bruegel.org/asia-europe-economic-forum-aeef/

History Founded 2006, by *Asian Development Bank Institute (ADB Institute, #01423), Bruegel, Kiel Institute for the World Economy (IfW), French Leading Center for International Economic Studies, Paris (CEPII),* Chinese Academy of Social Sciences, Keio University (Japan), Korea University and "Politics, Economics and Global Governance: The European Dimensions" (PEGGED). **Aims** Serve as a high-level forum to give Asian and European policy experts an occasion for in-depth research-based exchanges on global issues of mutual interest. **Events** *Conference* Berlin (Germany) 2019, *Conference* Brussels (Belgium) 2018, *Conference* Seoul (Korea Rep) 2017, *Conference* Beijing (China) 2016, *Global governance of public goods – Asian and European perspectives* Paris (France) 2015. **IGO Relations** Cooperates with: *Asia-Europe Foundation (ASEF, #01270).* **NGO Relations** Cooperates with: *Asian Development Bank Institute (ADB Institute, #01423); Bertelsmann Foundation; Bruegel;* Chinese Academy of Social Sciences; *French Leading Center for International Economic Studies, Paris (CEPII);* Korea University. [2015.10.20/XJ5309/c/**F**]

♦ Asia-Europe Environmental Technology Centre (inactive)

♦ Asia-Europe Foundation (ASEF) 01270

Exec Dir 31 Heng Mui Keng Terrace, Singapore 119595, Singapore. T. +6568749700. Fax +6568721135. E-mail: info@asef.org.
URL: http://www.asef.org/

History 15 Feb 1997. Established following first summit of Asia-Europe Heads of State – *Asia-Europe Meeting (ASEM, #01272)* – 1-2 Mar 1996, Bangkok (Thailand). Comprises the 4th "pillar" of a Euro-Asian "House", representing the engagement between civil societies of the two regions; the only permanent physical institution of ASEM process. **Aims** Advance mutual understanding and collaboration between Asia and Europe through intellectual, cultural and people-to-people exchanges in areas of common interest to both regions. Act as an interface between *civil society* and ASEM governments by: operating as the civil society outreach of ASEM; creating permanent networks aiming to reinforce bi-regional relations; injecting civil society inputs into the ASEM process. **Structure** Board of Governors appointed by all ASEM partners. Executive Office in Singapore. Programme Departments (4): Cultural; Education; Political and Economic; Public Affairs. Other departments (2): Finance; Administration. **Languages** English. **Staff** About 40-50, including interns and contract staff. **Finance** Voluntary contributions from ASEM partners. Most projects supported by civil society organizations, public institutions and private enterprises. **Activities** Training/education; networking/ liaising; events/meetings. **Events** *Informal ASEM Seminar on Human Rights (ASEMHRS21)* Luxembourg (Luxembourg) 2022, *Informal ASEM Seminar on Human Rights (ASEMHRS20)* Sangju (Korea Rep) 2021, *Forum on Combatting Substandard and Falsified Medicines (SFMs)* Singapore (Singapore) 2020, *Informal Seminar on Human Rights* Singapore (Singapore) 2020, *WAHED24 (World Access to Higher Education Day) Asia Conference* Singapore (Singapore) 2020. **Publications** Annual Report.
Members Participating countries (49):
Australia, Austria, Bangladesh, Belgium, Brunei Darussalam, Bulgaria, Cambodia, China, Cyprus, Czechia, Denmark, Estonia, Finland, France, Germany, Greece, Hungary, India, Indonesia, Ireland, Italy, Japan, Korea Rep, Laos, Latvia, Lithuania, Luxembourg, Malaysia, Malta, Mongolia, Myanmar, Netherlands, New Zealand, Norway, Pakistan, Philippines, Poland, Portugal, Romania, Russia, Singapore, Slovakia, Slovenia, Spain, Sweden, Switzerland, Thailand, UK, Vietnam.
Regional participating organizations (2):
ASEAN (#01141) (Secretariat); *European Union (EU, #08967).*
NGO Relations Member of (2): *International Network of Observatories in Cultural Policies (#14299); On the Move (OTM, #16868).* Cooperates with (1): *Asia Europe Economic Forum (AEEF, #01269).* Supports (1): *Asia-Europe Museum Network (ASEMUS, #01273).* [2020/XF4712/f/**F***]

♦ Asia-Europe Foundation University Alumni Network (ASEFUAN) . . . 01271

Main Office Avenue Louise 146, Bte 9, 1050 Brussels, Belgium.
Facebook: https://www.facebook.com/ASEFUAN-317951321662161/

History Set up 2002, as an association of former participants of *Asia-Europe Foundation (ASEF, #01270)* University. Registered in accordance with Belgian law, 6 Aug 2006. Also referred to as *ASEF University Alumni Network.* **Aims** Strengthen cross-cultural ties and promote excellence; foster Asia-Europe relaetions at a grass roots or local community level. **Structure** General Assembly; Executive Committee. **Activities** Training/ education; events/meetings. **Events** *Annual General Meeting* Yangon (Myanmar) 2016, *Annual General Meeting* Hangzhou (China) 2014, *Annual General Meeting* Dublin (Ireland) 2013, *Annual General Meeting* Manila (Philippines) 2012, *Annual General Meeting* Amsterdam (Netherlands) 2011. **IGO Relations** *Asia-Europe Meeting (ASEM, #01272).* [2016/XM5304/**E**]

♦ Asia-Europe Heads of State Meeting / see Asia-Europe Meeting (#01272)

♦ Asia-Europe Meeting (ASEM) 01272

Communications Dir ASEM InfoBoard, c/o Asia-Europe Foundation, 31 Heng Mui Keng Terrace, Singapore 119595, Singapore. T. +6568749700. Fax +6568721135. E-mail: admin@ aseminfoboard.org.
URL: http://www.aseminfoboard.org/

History 1 Mar 1996, Bangkok (Thailand). Proposed Nov 1994, by Singapore and France. 1-2 Mar 1996, Bangkok (Thailand), at first meeting, when country leaders of of the *European Union (EU, #08967)* met ASEAN country leaders plus China, Japan and Korea Rep. Former names and other names: *Asia-Europe Heads of State Meeting* – alias; *Asia-Europe Summit* – alias; *Sommet euro-asiatique* – former. **Languages** English. **Finance** *European Union (EU, #08967).* **Activities** Events/meetings. **Events** *Education Intermediate Senior Officials Meeting* St Julian's (Malta) 2022, *Education Ministers Meeting* Bangkok (Thailand) 2021, *Asia-Europe Parliamentary Partnership Meeting* Phnom Penh (Cambodia) 2021, *Biennial Summit* Phnom Penh (Cambodia) 2021, *Elderly Human Rights Forum* Seoul (Korea Rep) 2021. **Publications** *ASEM InfoBoard (AIB)* (12 a year) – newsletter.
Members Partners (53):
Australia, Austria, Bangladesh, Belgium, Brunei Darussalam, Bulgaria, Cambodia, China, Croatia, Cyprus, Czechia, Denmark, Estonia, Finland, France, Germany, Greece, Hungary, India, Indonesia, Ireland, Italy, Japan, Kazakhstan, Korea Rep, Laos, Latvia, Lithuania, Luxembourg, Malaysia, Malta, Mongolia, Myanmar, Netherlands, New Zealand, Norway, Pakistan, Philippines, Poland, Portugal, Romania, Russia, Singapore, Slovakia, Slovenia, Spain, Sweden, Switzerland, Thailand, UK, Vietnam.
ASEAN (#01141) (Secretariat); *European Union (EU, #08967).*
IGO Relations Instrumental in setting up: *Asia-Europe Foundation (ASEF, #01270).* **NGO Relations** Instrumental in setting up: *Asia-Europe People's Forum (AEPF, #01274).* [2022.12.08/XF4191/c/**F***]

♦ Asia-Europe Museum Network (ASEMUS) 01273

Sec National Museum of World Culture, PO Box 5306, SE-402 27 Gothenburg, Sweden. T. +4631632711. Fax +4631632710.
URL: https://culture360.asef.org/asemus-culture360/

History 9 Sep 2000, Stockholm (Sweden), during the Asia-Europe Conference on Museums. **Aims** Increase cooperation between museums in Asia and Europe. **Structure** Executive Committee. **Finance** Supported by: *Asia-Europe Foundation (ASEF, #01270).* **Events** *General Conference* Kuching (Malaysia) 2018, *General Conference* New Delhi (India) 2017, *General Conference* Vienna (Austria) 2014, *General Conference* Seoul (Korea Rep) 2012, *Meeting* Seoul (Korea Rep) 2012.
Members Full Museums (61) in 25 countries:
Austria, Belgium, Brunei Darussalam, China, Denmark, Finland, France, Germany, Greece, Hong Kong, Indonesia, Ireland, Italy, Japan, Korea Rep, Malaysia, Netherlands, Philippines, Portugal, Singapore, Spain, Sweden, Thailand, UK, Vietnam.
Associate museums (4) in 3 countries:
Australia, Laos, Norway. [2017/XF6721/**F**]

♦ Asia-Europe People's Forum (AEPF) 01274

Coordinator c/o Transnational Inst, PO Box 14656, 1001 LD Amsterdam, Netherlands.
Asia Coordinator address not obtained.
URL: http://www.aepf.info/

History 1996, to monitor meetings of *Asia-Europe Meeting (ASEM, #01272).* **Aims** Make the ASEM process more accountable, transparent and open to civil society. **Structure** International Organizing Committee. **Languages** English. **Finance** *European Commission (EC, #06633)* – DG DEVCO. **Activities** Events/meetings. **Events** *Forum* Amsterdam (Netherlands) 2021, *Workshop ON Challenges of a Common Security Policy in Eurasia* Berlin (Germany) 2019, *Building new solidarities – working for inclusive, just and equal alternatives in Asia and Europe* Ghent (Belgium) 2018, *Meeting* Vientiane (Laos) 2012, *Challenging and eroding corporate power – building states of citizens for citizens* Brussels (Belgium) 2010.
Members Organizations, including the following 4 listed in this Yearbook:
Asian Forum for Human Rights and Development (FORUM-ASIA, #01491); Centre international LEBRET-IRFED; Focus on the Global South (Focus, #09807); Transnational Institute (TNI, #20219).
NGO Relations *Coalition of the Flemish North South Movement – 11 11 11.* [2021/XM1942/cy/**F**]

♦ Asia-Europe Summit / see Asia-Europe Meeting (#01272)

♦ Asia Evangelical Alliance (AEA) 01275

SG 805/92 Deepali Bldg, Nehru Place, Delhi 110019, DELHI 110019, India.
Chairman 55 Yangjae-Dong, Sucho-Gu, Seoul 137-130, Korea Rep. T. +8225707007. Fax +8225707379.
URL: http://www.asiaevangelicals.org/

History 1 Jul 1983, Seoul (Korea Rep), as *Evangelical Fellowship of Asia (EFA),* following Asian Conference on Church Renewal, 18-22 Aug 1982. Officially inaugurated 12 Aug 1983, Hong Kong. Based in Delhi (India), 1983-1989; office moved to Singapore (Singapore), Jan 1990. Present office in Sri Lanka. **Aims** Advance the Kingdom of God in Asia by building up networking and partnering among the National Evangelical Fellowships and Asia-wide Evangelical Agencies; motivate and assist the Churches to be more effectively involved in the mission of the Church. **Structure** General Assembly. Executive Council, comprising Chairman, General Secretary, Associate General Secretary South East Asia, Associate General Secretary North East Asia, Treasurer, Honorary Secretary and 4 members. Commissions (7): Missions; Church Renewal; Theological; Religious Liberty; Social Concern; Women's; Youths. **Languages** English. **Staff** 2.00 FTE, paid. **Finance** Members' dues. Other sources: donations from individuals, Churches and Christian organizations. **Events** *Engage with neighbours to share the good news* Seongnam (Korea Rep) 2011, *General Assembly* Delhi (India) 2008, *General Assembly* India 2004, *Asian Church Congress* Korea Rep 2004, *Asian church congress* Sil Lim (Korea Rep) 2004. **Publications** *Asian Church Today* (4 a year). Asia Missions Congress and Asia Church Consultation Compendiums.
Members Evangelical organizations and Christian organizations in 16 countries:
Australia, Bangladesh, Cambodia, India, Indonesia, Japan, Korea Rep, Malaysia, Mongolia, Myanmar, Nepal, Pakistan, Philippines, Singapore, Sri Lanka, Thailand.
NGO Relations Member of: *World Evangelical Alliance (WEA, #21393).* [2015/XD9071/**D**]

♦ AsiaEvo Conference (meeting series)
♦ Asia Exchange Association (unconfirmed)
♦ Asia and Far East Commission on Agricultural Statistics / see Asia and Pacific Commission on Agricultural Statistics (#01873)
♦ Asia and Far East Institute for the Prevention of Crime and the Treatment of Offenders / see United Nations Asia and Far East Institute for the Prevention of Crime and the Treatment of Offenders (#20521)

♦ Asia Fashion Federation (AFF) 01276

Contact address not obtained. E-mail: aff@fashion.org.cn.
Contact address not obtained. E-mail: ysjung@koreafashion.org.
URL: http://www.asiafashionfederation.org/

History 22 Nov 2002, Beijing (China). **Aims** Advance lifestyles and fashion of each member country; promote fashion businesses; export fashion to European countries under mutual trust and cooperation. **Events** *Conference* Singapore (Singapore) 2016, *Rising Asian Fashion* Bangkok (Thailand) 2014, *Conference* Singapore (Singapore) 2013, *Conference* Singapore (Singapore) 2013, *Conference* Tokyo (Japan) 2012.
Members Full in 6 countries:
China, Japan, Korea Rep, Singapore, Thailand, Vietnam. [2014/XJ8345/**D**]

♦ Asia Federation of the International College of Surgeons (see: #12650)
♦ Asia-FIET / see UNI Global Union – Asia and Pacific Regional Office (#20341)

♦ Asia Fire Protection Inspection Council (AFIC) 01277

Contact 331 Jisam-ro, Giheung-gu, Yongin-si, Gyeonggi-do, Yongin GYEONGGI 17088, Korea Rep. E-mail: afric@kfi.or.kr.
URL: http://www.aficfire.org/

Aims Represent the Asian field of fire protection; promote collaboration for mutual benefit and technical exchange based on each country's industry and technology and development of Asia's fire protection technology to be shared with the rest of the world; enable the region to secure its position in the world in the field of fire protection technology. **Structure** Office; Sub-Committees; Working Groups; Secretariat. **Activities** Events/meetings. **Events** *Meeting* Daegu (Korea Rep) 2019, *Meeting* Ho Chi Minh City (Vietnam) 2017, *Meeting* Daegu (Korea Rep) 2015.
Members Full in 10 countries:
China, India, Indonesia, Japan, Korea Rep, Malaysia, Philippines, Singapore, Thailand, Vietnam. [2019/XM8421/**D**]

♦ Asia Floor Wage Alliance (AFW Alliance) 01278

International Secretariat c/o Soc for Labour and Development, C-23 (First Floor), Haus Khas, Delhi 110016, DELHI 110016, India. E-mail: anannya48@gmail.com – asiafloorwage@gmail.com.
URL: http://asia.floorwage.org/

History 2007, following International Planning Meeting. **Aims** Fight for a basic wage for *garment workers* in Asia. **Structure** Steering Committee; International Coordinating Office. Regional Coordinating Offices (6). **Activities** Runs the *Asia Floor Wage Campaign.*
Members Organizations in 18 countries and territories:
Bangladesh, Belgium, Bulgaria, Cambodia, Canada, China, Hong Kong, India, Indonesia, Malaysia, Netherlands, Pakistan, Philippines, Sri Lanka, Thailand, Türkiye, UK, USA.
Included in the above, 5 organizations listed in this Yearbook:
Clean Clothes Campaign (CCC, #03986); Coalition of the Flemish North South Movement – 11 11 11; Grassroots Global Justice Alliance (GGJ); International Brotherhood of Teamsters (IBT); War on Want. [2022/XJ4711/y/**F**]

♦ Asia Florists' Association (no recent information)

♦ AsiaFlux 01279

Office 16-2 Onogawa, Tsukuba, Ibaraki OSAKA, 305-8506 Japan. T. +81298502971. Fax +81298582645. E-mail: secretary@asiaflux.net – tsukuba@asiaflux.net.
URL: http://asiaflux.net/

History Sep 1999. **Aims** Bring Asia's key ecosystems under observation to develop and transfer scientific knowledge to ensure quality and sustainability of life in Asia. **Structure** Advisory Committee; Science Steering Committee; Secretariat. **Finance** Supported by: *Asia-Pacific Network for Global Change Research (APN, #01966).* **Activities** Events/meetings; training/education. **Events** *Asiaflux Conference* Kuching (Malaysia) 2022, *Workshop* Kuching (Malaysia) 2021, *Workshop* Kuching (Malaysia) 2020, *Workshop* Takayama (Japan) 2019, *AsiaFlux Workshop* Darwin, NT (Australia) 2018. **Publications** *AsiaFlux Newsletter.* **NGO Relations** Cooperates with (1): *FLUXNET (#09803).* [2022/AA0094/**F**]

♦ Asia Forest Network (internationally oriented national body)
♦ Asia Foundation (internationally oriented national body)
♦ Asia Freerunning Parkour Union (unconfirmed)
♦ Asia Fukushi Kyoiku Zaidan (internationally oriented national body)
♦ Asia Fund for Credit Union Development (see: #02377)

♦ Asia Fund for Human Development / see Caritas Asia (#03578)

♦ Asia Geographic Information System Association (Asia GIS) 01280

SG Center of Urban Studies, Univ of Hong Kong, Pokfulam Road, Hong Kong, Central and Western, Hong Kong. T. +85228592721. Fax +85225590468. E-mail: hdxugoy@hku.hk.
URL: http://www.asiagis.org/

History Oct 2003. **Aims** Provide a forum to promote teaching, research, development and applications of Geographic Information System (GIS) and its related technology in Asia; encourage the conduct of collaborative research and dissemination of its results by researchers and professionals, and the development of and provision for the dissemination of information on new and improved methods, in GIS in Asia. **Structure** General Assembly (every 2 years). Council, comprising country and region representatives and members of the Executive Committee (President, Vice-President, Secretary, Past President and 3-5 members). **Activities** Organizes International Conference (every 2 years). **Events** *Asia GIS Conference* Hong Kong (Hong Kong) 2017, *Asia GIS Conference* Chiang Mai (Thailand) 2014, *Asia GIS Conference / International Conference* Ulaanbaatar (Mongolia) 2012, *Asia GIS conference / International Conference* Kaohsiung (Taiwan) 2010, *Asia GIS conference / International Conference* Busan (Korea Rep) 2008. **Members** Full – associations, societies, research institutes, university and government department, and companies in Asia; Corresponding – same as Full members, but outside Asia; Individual. Membership countries not specified. [2017/XJ0497/**D**]

♦ **Asia GIS** Asia Geographic Information System Association (#01280)
♦ Asia Graduate School of Theology / see Asia Graduate School of Theology – Malaysia/Singapore/Thailand
♦ Asia Graduate School of Theology – Malaysia/Singapore/Thailand (internationally oriented national body)
♦ Asia Gymnastics Federation / see Asian Gymnastics Union (#01499)

♦ AsiaHaptics Society (AHS) 01281

Contact address not obtained.
URL: http://asiahaptics.org/

History 2020. **Aims** Facilitate communication and cooperation among researchers, developers, creators, system integrators, and users of haptics. **Structure** Steering Committee. **Activities** Events/meetings. **Events** *Asia Haptics Conference* Beijing (China) 2022, *Asia Haptics Conference* Beijing (China) 2020, *Asia Haptics Conference* Incheon (Korea Rep) 2018, *Asia Haptics Conference* Kashiwa (Japan) 2016, *Asia Haptics Conference* Tsukuba (Japan) 2014. [2020/AA1198/**D**]

♦ Asia Harvest (internationally oriented national body)

♦ Asia Indigenous Peoples Pact (AIPP) 01282

SG 108 Moo 5, Tambon Sanpranate, Amphur San Sai, Chiang Mai, 50210, Thailand. T. +6653380168. Fax +6653380752. E-mail: robie@aippnet.org – aippmail@aippnet.org.
URL: http://www.aippnet.org/

History 1988, by indigenous peoples' movements. Operational subsequent to 1st General Assembly, Apr 1992. Registered as a Foundation in accordance with the law of Thailand, 2002. **Aims** Promote and defend indigenous peoples' rights and *human rights*; articulate issues of relevance to indigenous peoples. **Structure** General Assembly (every 4 years); Executive Council; Advisory Board. Programme Committees. Secretariat. Sub-Regional Formations: South Asia; South East Asia; Mekong; East Asia. **Languages** English. **Staff** 16.00 FTE, paid. **Finance** Core activities funded by: *International Work Group for Indigenous Affairs (IWGIA, #15907)*; Tamalpais Trust Fund; Oxfam Australia. Programme donors include: *European Instrument for Democracy and for Human Rights (EIDHR, #07576)*; *German Catholic Bishops' Organisation for Development Cooperation (MISEREOR)*; *Christensen Fund (TCF)*; *Norwegian Agency for Development Cooperation (Norad)*; *Oxfam Novib*; *UN Women (#20724)*; national organizations. Budget (annual): about US$ 950,000. **Activities** Research and development; politics/policy/regulatory; advocacy/lobbying/activism; capacity building. **Events** *Quadrennial General Assembly* Chiang Mai (Thailand) 2016, *Quadrennial General Assembly* Chiang Mai (Thailand) 2012, *Quadrennial General Assembly* Chiang Mai (Thailand) 2008, *Asian regional meeting on the composite report on traditional knowledge* Baguio (Philippines) 2005, *Asia regional conference on indigenous development* Philippines 2005. **Publications** Annual Report; posters; briefing papers; case studies; manuals; reports; comic books.

Members Full (47) in 14 countries and territories:
Bangladesh, Cambodia, India, Indonesia, Japan, Laos, Malaysia, Myanmar, Nepal, Philippines, Taiwan, Thailand, Timor-Leste, Vietnam.

Consultative Status Consultative status granted from: *ECOSOC (#05331) (Special)*; *UNEP (#20299)*. **IGO Relations** Accredited by: *Green Climate Fund (GCF, #10714)*. **NGO Relations** Member of: *Forest Peoples Programme (FPP, #09865)*; *GEF CSO Network (GCN, #10087)*. [2014.06.01/XF3410/**F**]

♦ Asia Industrial Gases Association (AIGA) 01283

Registered Office 52 Jurong Gateway Road, JEM, 15-02, Singapore 608550, Singapore. T. +6562760160.
URL: http://www.asiaiga.org/

History 2002. Registration: Singapore. **Aims** Foster exchange of technical information in the safe handling and use of industrial, speciality and medical gases; liaise with national authorities, so as to work towards the highest level of safety and environmental care across Asian countries. **Structure** Board; Technical Committee; Secretariat. Technical Work Groups. **Events** *Meeting* Bangalore (India) 2020, *Meeting* Bangkok (Thailand) 2019, *Meeting* Kuala Lumpur (Malaysia) 2019, *Meeting* Singapore (Singapore) 2018, *Meeting* Taipei (Taiwan) 2018. **Publications** *AIGA Newsletter*. Technical literature. **NGO Relations** Member of (1): *International Harmonization Council (IHC, #13775)*. Cooperates with (1): *European Industrial Gases Association (EIGA, #07525)*. [2020/XM5396/t/**D**]

♦ Asia Information Communication Technology Organization (no recent information)
♦ Asia Injury Prevention Foundation / see AIP Foundation (#00598)
♦ Asia Institute of Urban Environment (unconfirmed)

♦ Asia Interior Design Institute Association (AIDIA) 01284

Secretariat Ste 1107, Korea Science and Technology Center, 635-4 Yeogsam-Dong, Kangnam-Gu, Seoul 135-703, Korea Rep. E-mail: aidia@globalaidia.org – aidia2019@piid.org.ph.
URL: http://www.globalaidia.org/

History 1998. **Structure** General Assembly. **Events** *International Student Workshop* Cebu City (Philippines) 2019, *Board Meeting* Seoul (Korea Rep) 2017, *Future Building Forum* Seoul (Korea Rep) 2017, *Korean Interior Design Seminar* Seoul (Korea Rep) 2017, *Urban Renewal Seminar* Seoul (Korea Rep) 2017. **Publications** *AIDIA Journal*.

Members Founding members in 3 countries:
China, Japan, Korea Rep. [2019/XM2896/j/**D**]

♦ Asia International Conference of Leather Science and Technology (meeting series)

♦ Asia Investor Group op Climate Change (AIGCC) 01285

Exec Dir address not obtained. E-mail: info@aigcc.net.
URL: https://www.aigcc.net/

History 2011. Founded as an initiative by *Association for Sustainable and Responsible Investment in Asia (ASrIA, inactive)*. Launched under current structure, Sep 2016, Singapore. **Aims** Create awareness among Asia's asset owners and financial institutions about the risks and opportunities associated with climate change and low carbon investing. **Structure** Operates under the governance and as part of the structure of *Investor Group on Climate Change (IGCC)*. Board; Secretariat. **NGO Relations** Member of (1): *Global Investor Coalition on Climate Change (GIC, #10434)*. [2022/AA1117/**E**]

♦ Asia IRP – Asian Association of Independent Research Providers (internationally oriented national body)

♦ Asia Islet Biology and Incretin Research Association (AIBIS) 01286

Pres 10 Bamgogae-ro 1-gil, Suseo-dong, Gangnam-gu, Seoul 06349, Korea Rep. T. +8224598236. Fax +8224598256. E-mail: 2017aibis@gmail.com.
URL: http://www.aibis.org/

Structure Scientific Committee. **Activities** Events/meetings. **Events** *Symposium* Seoul (Korea Rep) 2021, *Symposium* Seoul (Korea Rep) 2020, *Symposium* Seoul (Korea Rep) 2019, *Symposium* Seoul (Korea Rep) 2018. [XM8214/c/**D**]

♦ Asia Japan Women's Resource Centre (internationally oriented national body)
♦ Asia Josei Kooryuu Kenkyuu Forum (internationally oriented national body)

♦ Asia Journalist Association (AJA) 01287

Chairman 207 33-90 Myeongnyun-dong 1-ga, Jongno-gu, Seoul 110-521, Korea Rep. T. +8227124111. E-mail: aja@ajanews.asia – ajanews@ajanews.asia.
URL: https://www.ajanews.asia/

History 2005. **Aims** Promote press freedom, democratic ideas and world peace. **Structure** General Assembly; Executive Board; Sub-Committees (3); Secretariat. **Languages** Arabic, English, Irish Gaelic, Korean. **Activities** Awards/prizes/competitions; events/meetings; projects/programmes. **Events** *General Assembly* Seoul (Korea Rep) 2018, *General Assembly* Korea Rep 2017, *General Assembly* Seoul (Korea Rep) 2016, *Conference* Seoul (Korea Rep) 2010, *General Assembly* Seoul (Korea Rep) 2009. **Publications** *The Magazine N* (12 a year); *The AsiaN Newsletter*. Books.

Members Full in 20 countries and territories:
Bangladesh, Cambodia, China, Hong Kong, India, Indonesia, Israel, Japan, Laos, Malaysia, Mongolia, Myanmar, Nepal, Pakistan, Philippines, Singapore, Sri Lanka, Taiwan, Thailand, Vietnam.

Observers in 4 countries:
Germany, Russia, South Africa, Switzerland.

NGO Relations Supports (1): *World Journalists Conference (WJC)*. [2022/XJ1250/**D**]

♦ Asia Justice and Rights (internationally oriented national body)
♦ ASIALEASE / see Asian Financial Services Association (#01480)

♦ Asia Legal Information Network (ALIN) 01288

Contact 15 Gukchaegyeonguwon-ro, Sejong 30147, Korea Rep. T. +82448610300. Fax +82448689913. E-mail: alin@klri.re.kr.
URL: https://www.e-alin.org/

History 2005. **Aims** Provide a collaborative platform for exchange of legal information among Asian countries, building institutional capacity to foster better law in Asia. **Structure** General Meeting; Secretariat. **Activities** Events/meetings; knowledge management/information dissemination; research/documentation. **Events** *International Conference* Seoul (Korea Rep) 2021, *International Conference* Seoul (Korea Rep) 2020, *International Conference* Bangkok (Thailand) 2019, *International Conference* Ulaanbaatar (Mongolia) 2018, *International Conference* Kathmandu (Nepal) 2017.

Members Full in 18 countries and territories:
Bangladesh, Cambodia, China, India, Indonesia, Japan, Kazakhstan, Korea Rep, Malaysia, Mongolia, Myanmar, Nepal, Philippines, Russia, Taiwan, Thailand, Uzbekistan, Vietnam. [2022/AA2753/**F**]

♦ **ASIALEX** Asian Association for Lexicography (#01328)
♦ **ASIALICS** Asian Network for Learning, Innovation and Competence Building Systems (#01551)
♦ Asia Lighting Conference (meeting series)
♦ AsiaLink (internationally oriented national body)
♦ **ASI** Alliance solaire internationale (#15563)
♦ **ASI** Alström Syndrome International (#00750)
♦ **ASI** Aluminium Stewardship Initiative (#00758)

♦ Asia Maritime & Fisheries Universities Forum (AMFUF) 01289

SG Ctr for Intl Affairs – Korea Maritime & Ocean Univ, 727 Taejong-ro, Yeongdo-gu, Busan 49112, Korea Rep. T. +82514104771. Fax +82514040701. E-mail: cofa@kmou.ac.kr.
URL: https://www.kmou.ac.kr/amfuf/main.do

History 7 Nov 2002, Busan (Korea Rep). **Aims** Promote the academic exchange among the Asian Maritime & Fisheries Education Institutes; foster international cooperation on the education and research for the maritime & fisheries experts. **Structure** Representative Committee; Secretariat. **Activities** Events/meetings; knowledge management/information dissemination; research/documentation; training/education. **Events** *Asia Maritime and Fisheries Universities Forum (AMFUF)* Mokpo (Korea Rep) 2022, *Asia Maritime and Fisheries Universities Forum (AMFUF)* Gyeongju (Korea Rep) 2021, *Asia Maritime and Fisheries Universities Forum (AMFUF)* Gyeongju (Korea Rep) 2020, *Asia Maritime and Fisheries Universities Forum (AMFUF)* Hai Phong (Vietnam) 2019, *Asia Maritime and Fisheries Universities Forum (AMFUF)* Zhanjiang (China) 2018.

Members Full in 12 countries and territories:
China, Indonesia, Japan, Korea Rep, Myanmar, Philippines, Russia, Sri Lanka, Taiwan, Thailand, Türkiye, Vietnam. [2021/AA2752/c/**F**]

♦ Asia Marketing Federation (AMF) 01290

Contact c/o Japan Marketing Assn, 9th Floor, Roppongi Yamada Bldg, 3-5-27 Roppingi, Minato-ku, Tokyo, 1060032 Japan. E-mail: info@asiamarketingfederation.org.
URL: http://asiamarketingfederation.org/

History 1991, *Asia Pacific Marketing Federation (APMF)*. Current title adopted 2007. **Aims** Further *economic development* and contribute to *living standards* of consumers in countries of the region through professional cooperation, information exchange on new marketing ideas, experience, techniques and technology and through collaborative research. **Languages** English. **Events** *Conference* Seoul (Korea Rep) 2016, *Annual General Meeting* Foshan (China) 2015, *Annual General Meeting* Manila (Philippines) 2014, *Conference* Manila (Philippines) 2014, *Annual General Meeting* Bangkok (Thailand) 2013.

Members National marketing bodies in 12 countries and territories:
Hong Kong, Indonesia, Japan, Korea Rep, Malaysia, Mongolia, Philippines, Singapore, Sri Lanka, Taiwan, Thailand, Vietnam. [2015/XD5478/**D**]

♦ Asia Masters Athletics (AMA) 01291

Gen Sec 185D Rivervale Crescent 04-149, Singapore 544185, Singapore. T. +6568814684. Fax +6562441454.
URL: http://www.world-masters-athletics.org/regions/asia/

History 1986, Jakarta (Indonesia), as *Asian Veteran Athletes Association (AVAA)* as a regional body of *World Masters Athletics (WMA, #21640)*. **Aims** Promote athletics (track and field) amongst Asians above the age of 35. **Structure** General Assembly (at least every 2 years). Council. Executive Board, comprising President, 3 Vice-Presidents (Stadia; Non-Stadia; General Affairs), General Secretary, Treasurer and Women's Representative. **Finance** Main sponsor: *World Athletics (#21209)*. Other sources: championship fees. **Events** *Asian Championship* Bangalore (India) 2006, *Asian Championship* Bangkok (Thailand) 2004, *Asian Championship* Dahlan (China) 2002, *Asian Championship* Bangalore (India) 2000, *Asian Championship* Naha (Japan) 1998. **Publications** *Asia Masters Athletics Handbook*.

Members Affiliate in 24 countries and territories:
Brunei Darussalam, China, Hong Kong, India, Indonesia, Iran Islamic Rep, Japan, Kazakhstan, Korea Rep, Kyrgyzstan, Lebanon, Malaysia, Mongolia, Myanmar, Nepal, Pakistan, Philippines, Singapore, Sri Lanka, Taiwan, Tajikistan, Thailand, Turkmenistan, United Arab Emirates. [2012/XD7231/**D**]

♦ Asia Medical Aesthetic Exchange Association (unconfirmed)
♦ Asia Middle East Bottled Water Association (inactive)
♦ Asia-Middle East Dialogue (meeting series)
♦ Asia Missions Association (internationally oriented national body)
♦ Asia Monitor Resource Centre (internationally oriented national body)

♦ Asian Academic Accounting Association (FourA) 01292

Secretariat School of Accountancy, UUM College of Business, Univ Utara Malaysia, Kedah, 06010 Sintok, Kedah, Malaysia. T. +6049287222. E-mail: admin@foura.org.
URL: http://www.foura.org/

History Founded following 2 meetings in Jun 1998, Hong Kong and Oct 1998, Hawaii (USA). **Aims** Provide a forum for persons with a professional interest in accounting education and research and their impact on practice; enhance communication and cooperation among members; provide a framework for better dissemination of information on accounting pedagogy and research; provide input and represent the interests and views of members on matters relating to accounting education, research and practice. **Finance** Sources: members' dues. **Events** *Annual Conference* Khon Kaen (Thailand) 2021, *Annual Conference* Khon Kaen (Thailand) 2020, *Annual Conference* Seoul (Korea Rep) 2019, *Annual Conference* Bali (Indonesia) 2017, *Annual Conference* Kuching (Malaysia) 2016. [2021/XD7946/D]

♦ Asian Academic Society for Vocational Education and Training (unconfirmed)

♦ Asian Academy of Aesthetic Dentistry 01293

Contact 166-4 Joongkok Dong, Kwangin Gu, Seoul 04908, Korea Rep. T. +821062604829. E-mail: kmj5671@gmail.com – kimchonghwa@hotmail.com.
URL: http://asia-aad.org/

History 1990. **Aims** Promote aesthetic dentistry. **Structure** Executive Committee. **Languages** English. **Staff** 0.50 FTE, paid. **Finance** Members' dues. **Events** *Biennial Meeting* Seoul (Korea Rep) 2021, *Biennial Meeting* Seoul (Korea Rep) 2020, *Biennial Meeting* Singapore (Singapore) 2018, *Meeting* Foshan (China) 2014, *Meeting* Sapporo (Japan) 2012. **Publications** *Asian Journal of Aesthetic Dentistry* (annual).
Members Individuals in 13 countries and territories:
China, Hong Kong, India, Indonesia, Israel, Japan, Korea Rep, Maldives, Nepal, Philippines, Singapore, Taiwan, Thailand.
NGO Relations Member of: *International Federation of Esthetic Dentistry (IFED, #13417).* [2021/XD2947/v/D]

♦ Asian Academy of Dermatology and Venereology (unconfirmed)
♦ Asian Academy of Family Therapy (unconfirmed)

♦ Asian Academy for Heritage Management (AAHM) 01294

Programme Specialist Regional Advisor for Culture, UNESCO Office 5th Floor, 920 Sukhumvit Road, Bangkok, 10110, Thailand. T. +6623910577 ext 513. Fax +6623910866.
URL: https://bangkok.unesco.org/

History Nov 2001, Bangkok (Thailand), during a seminar organized by *UNESCO (#20322)* and *International Centre for the Study of the Preservation and Restoration of Cultural Property (ICCROM, #12521).* **Aims** Strengthen professional capacity to sustainably manage heritage resources by providing a regional platform for institutional cooperation in training, research, and exchange; promote integrated, holistic and multi-disciplinary management of heritage resources, including both tangible and intangible expressions of culture. **Structure** Central Secretariat. **Activities** Organizes 'Asian Academy Field School'. Certifying in-field practitioners; Executive development for decision-maker; Training-of-trainers programmes; Student internship programme; Cross-registration of students and exchange of faculty members; Research programmes; Awards programme for outstanding student work. Online database for heritage management experts. **Events** *Asia-Pacific regional conference on underwater cultural heritage* Manila (Philippines) 2011, *Strategy Meeting* Bangkok (Thailand) 2006, *Strategy Meeting* Macau 2004. **Publications** *Asian Academy Newsletter.* Information Services: Online database for heritage management experts. Online virtual library for heritage management resources.
Members Institutional; Individual; Associate; Provisional. Institutional (43) in 17 countries:
Australia, Bangladesh, China, India, Indonesia, Japan, Laos, Malaysia, Mongolia, Nepal, New Zealand, Philippines, Sri Lanka, Thailand, USA, Uzbekistan, Vietnam.
Included in the above, 4 organizations listed in this Yearbook:
Centre for Nepal and Asian Studies (CNAS); Cultural Heritage Asia Pacific Network (CHAP); Institute of International Culture, Tokyo; Research School of Pacific and Asian Studies, Canberra (RSPAS).
Individual Affiliates in 14 countries:
Australia, Cambodia, Canada, China, Indonesia, Malaysia, Mongolia, Morocco, Philippines, Singapore, Sri Lanka, Thailand, UK, USA.
Institutional Affiliates (5) in 3 countries:
Cambodia, Japan, Vietnam.
Included in the above, 2 organizations listed in this Yearbook:
Global Development Research Centre (GDRC); Modern Asian Architecture Network (mAAN, #16841).
Associate members (2) in 2 countries:
Sweden, United Arab Emirates.
IGO Relations Secretariat provided by: *UNESCO Asia and Pacific Regional Bureau for Education (#20301).* [2019/XM0898/y/E]

♦ Asian Academy of Minimally Invasive Spinal Surgery (AAMISS) 01295

General Office Ste 1, 36 Bayswater Road, Potts Point NSW 2011, Australia. T. +61293583244. Fax +61293583255.

Aims Educate, promote and standardize the rapidly evolving Asian minimally invasive spine market. **Structure** Executive Board, comprising President, Secretary General, Treasurer, Commercial Director and 3 members. **Activities** *Asian Board of Minimally Invasive Spine Surgery (ABMISS).* **Events** *Annual Meeting* Honolulu, HI (USA) 2008, *Annual Meeting* Seoul (Korea Rep) 2004. [2010/XJ1492/E]

♦ Asian Academy of Orofacial Pain and Temporomandibular Disorders (AAOT) 01296

Contact address not obtained. E-mail: ctreet@gmail.com.
URL: http://www.kaop.org/intro-eng/aaot.html

History 1985. **Structure** Officers: President (2-year term); President-Elect; Vice-President; Secretary (2-year term); Treasurer. Council, comprising Immediate Past President, 4 Country Representatives, 6 Academic Affairs Representatives, 4 International Liaison Representatives and 6 Membership Promotion Representatives. National Chapter Academies in Korea Rep and Japan (holding annual meetings). **Languages** English. **Staff** All voluntary. **Finance** Members' dues. **Activities** Organizes biannual meeting; also co-organizes International Conference on Orofacial Pain and Temporomandibular Disorders (ICOT), a joint meeting with EACD, Ibero-Latin American Academy of Craniomandibular Disorders, Australian and New Zealand Academy of Craniomandibular Disorder and American Academy of Orofacial Pain (every 4 years). **Events** *Scientific Meeting* Goyang (Korea Rep) 2021, *Scientific Meeting* Manila (Philippines) 2019, *International Congress on Orofacial Pain* Yokohama (Japan) 2016, *Scientific Meeting* Yokohama (Japan) 2016, *Scientific Meeting* Daegu (Korea Rep) 2015. **Publications** *Journal of Orofacial Pain* (4 a year) – journal.
Members Individuals in 5 countries and territories:
Indonesia, Japan, Korea Rep, Philippines, Taiwan.
NGO Relations *European Academy of Craniomandibular Disorders (EACD, #05785); Ibero-Latin American Academy of Craniomandibular Disorders (ILADC);* national academies. [2019/XD5131/v/D]

♦ Asian Academy of Osseointegration (AAO) 01297

Secretariat c/o SNU Dentistry – Prosthodontics, 101 Daehak-ro, Jongro-gu, Seoul 03080, Korea Rep.
URL: http://www.aao-org.com/

History 2004, Seoul (Korea Rep). **Aims** Promote communication and collaboration between Asian implantologists; achieve better treatment outcome for Asian *dental implant* patients. **Structure** Board of Councillors. Officers (6). **Languages** English. **Events** *Congress* Taipei (Taiwan) 2022, *Congress* 2021, *Congress* Seoul (Korea Rep) 2018, *Congress* Bangkok (Thailand) 2016, *Congress* Sapporo (Japan) 2014.
Members Full in 10 countries and territories:
China, India, Indonesia, Japan, Korea Rep, Malaysia, Mongolia, Singapore, Taiwan, Thailand. [2022/XJ2646/D]

♦ Asian Academy of Preventive Dentistry (AAPD) 01298

Contact c/o SPDHK Room 3B26, Prince Philip Dental Hospital, 34 Hospital Road, Sai Ying Pun, Central and Western, Hong Kong.
URL: https://aapdasia.com/

Aims Gather and disseminate information on *oral health* among members. **Languages** English. **Finance** Congress registration fees. **Events** *International Congress* Hong Kong (Hong Kong) 2023, *Congress* Daegu (Korea Rep) 2021, *Congress* Daegu (Korea Rep) 2020, *Congress* Khon Kaen (Thailand) 2018, *Congress* Tokyo (Japan) 2016. **Publications** *AAPD Newsletter.* Proceedings.
Members Individuals in 23 countries:
Australia, Bangladesh, China, Denmark, Hong Kong, India, Indonesia, Japan, Korea Rep, Malaysia, Netherlands, New Zealand, Norway, Philippines, Singapore, Sri Lanka, Sweden, Switzerland, Taiwan, Thailand, UK, USA, Vietnam. [2022/XD6374/v/D]

♦ Asian Academy of Prosthodontics (AAP) 01299

Sec Shanghai Ninth People's Hospital, School of Medicine, Shanghai Jiao Tong Univ, 639 Zhizaoju Road, 200011 Shanghai, China. T. +862123271699ext5276. Fax +862163135412.
URL: http://aap-org.com/

History Founded 1994. **Aims** Promote the speciality of prosthodontics in Asia through international exchange. **Structure** Members' Business Meeting and Scientific Meeting (every 2 years). Executive Council, comprising President, President-Elect, Immediate Past President, 3 Vice-Presidents, 2 Secretaries, 2 Treasurers, 2 Information technology officers, 2 editors, 9 Councillors and Regional Representatives. **Languages** English. **Staff** 2.00 FTE, voluntary. **Finance** Members' dues and initiation fee. Contributions. **Activities** Events/meetings; awards/prizes/competitions. **Events** *Biennial Congress* Bali (Indonesia) 2021, *Biennial Congress* Bali (Indonesia) 2020, *Biennial Congress* Kuala Lumpur (Malaysia) 2018, *Biennial Congress* Pattaya (Thailand) 2016, *Biennial Congress* Taipei (Taiwan) 2014.
Members Categories Active; Affiliate; Honorary. Members in 11 countries and territories:
China, India, Indonesia, Japan, Korea Rep, Malaysia, Mongolia, Philippines, Singapore, Taiwan, Thailand. [2014/XD8248/D]

♦ Asian Aerosol Federation (AAF) 01300

Contact address not obtained. E-mail: info@aerosol-asia.org.
URL: http://www.aerosol-asia.org/

History Oct 2011, Zhongshan (China), when Rules and Constitution were agreed. Registered in accordance with the law of Hong Kong. **Aims** Promote the growth of a prosperous, safe and environmentally responsible aerosol industry across the region. **Structure** President; Vice-President. **Languages** English. **Activities** Events/meetings; knowledge management/information; standards/guidelines; awareness raising. **Events** *Meeting* Sydney, NSW (Australia) 2014, *Meeting* Tokyo (Japan) 2012.
Members Associations in 6 countries:
Australia, China, India, Japan, New Zealand, Thailand. [2015/XJ9163/D]

♦ Asian Aerosol Research Assembly (AARA) 01301

Pres address not obtained.
Sec address not obtained.
URL: http://www.aaraonline.org/

Aims Provide an international forum among Asian countries for the planning and organization of the continuing series of the Asian Aerosol Conferences. **Structure** Assembly (every 2 years, at Conference). Officers. **Languages** English. **Finance** Conference proceeds. **Activities** Meeting activities; awards. **Events** *Conference* Taipei (Taiwan) 2022, *Conference* Taipei (Taiwan) 2021, *Conference* Hong Kong (Hong Kong) 2019, *Conference* Jeju (Korea Rep) 2017, *Conference* Kanazawa (Japan) 2015.
Members National organizations (6) in 6 countries and territories:
China, India, Japan, Korea Rep, Taiwan, Thailand. [2013/XM2024/F]

♦ Asian African Association for Plasma Training (AAAPT) 01302

Pres c/o NSSE-NIE, Nanyang TU, 1 Nanyang Walk, Singapore 637616, Singapore.
URL: http://www.aaapt.org/

History 18 Jun 1988, Kuala Lumpur (Malaysia), with the support of *Abdus Salam International Centre for Theoretical Physics (ICTP, #00005).* **Aims** Initiate and strengthen plasma physics research among smaller groups in Asia and Africa. **Structure** Council; Secretariat. **Languages** English. **Events** *International Conference on Plasma Science and Applications* Nakhon Si Thammarat (Thailand) 2017, *International Conference on Plasma Science and Applications ICPSA2016* Pulau Langkawi (Malaysia) 2016, *International Conference on Plasma Science and Applications* Singapore (Singapore) 2013, *International meeting on frontiers of physics* Kuala Lumpur (Malaysia) 1998. **Members** Institutes (34) in 21 countries. Membership countries not specified.
IGO Relations *UNESCO (#20322).* [2018/XD8564/D]

♦ Asian-African Legal Consultative Committee / see Asian-African Legal Consultative Organization (#01303)

♦ Asian-African Legal Consultative Organization (AALCO) 01303

Organisation consultatif juridique Afrique-Asie

SG 29-C Rizal Marg, Diplomatic Enclave, Chanakyapuri, Delhi 110021, DELHI 110021, India. T. +911124197000 – +911126117641. Fax +911126117640. E-mail: mail@aalco.int.
Permanent Observer to the UN – New York 7 Barn Hill Road, Greenwich CT 06831, USA. T. +12035959800.
Permanent Observer to the UN – Vienna Steinmülargasse 31, 1160 Vienna, Austria. T. +4314605484.
URL: http://www.aalco.int/

History 15 Nov 1956. Former names and other names: *Asian Legal Consultative Committee* – former (1956 to 1958); *Asian-African Legal Consultative Committee (AALCC)* – former (1958 to 2001); *Comité consultatif juridique Afrique-Asie* – former (1958 to 2001). **Aims** Serve as an Advisory Body of Legal Experts to participating countries; examine matters before the International Law Commission and other United Nations agencies in the field of international and commercial *law*; place views on legal issues before the International Law Commission; consider legal problems referred by member countries; exchange views and information on other legal matters of common concern. **Structure** Sessions (normally annual) in member countries by rotation. Secretary General, elected by Member States for a renewable term of 4 years, on a rotational basis from the 2 regions. Seconded senior officers of member governments act as Deputy Secretaries General and Assistant Secretaries General. Secretariat in Delhi (India) acts as permanent consultative body with Liaison Officers of member countries. **Languages** Arabic, English. **Staff** 25.00 FTE, paid. **Finance** General budget: members' contributions, minimum US$ 5,500. voluntary contributions. Special budgets for specific purposes such as Arabic Division. Expenses connected with meetings normally borne by country in which meeting is held.

Activities Works closely with member governments at ministerial and official levels; assists them to prepare themselves on major international questions before the United Nations, in particular the subjects of Plenipotentiary Conferences; considers international law problems referred by member governments; renders advice, on request, on a confidential basis on any question of interest to a member states – recent emphasis has been on economic relations and trade law; prepares standard model contract forms and model bilateral agreements suited to the needs of the Asian-African region; provides facilities for training of officials of member states engaged in international law matters; trains officers of member states in techniques of research and handling of international legal questions; extends legal assistance to member states in drafting Model Legislation, draft Constitutions or Bilateral Agreements.

Organizes seminars and workshops. Pursuant to *'Integrated Scheme for Settlement of Disputes in the Economic and Commercial Transaction'*, launched 1978, established and maintains 4 Regional Arbitration Centres to promote international commercial arbitration in the Asian-African regions and provide for conducting international arbitrations: *Kuala Lumpur Regional Centre for Arbitration (KLRCA, #16210); Cairo Regional Centre for International Commercial Arbitration (CRCICA, #03398); Regional Centre for International Commercial Arbitration, Lagos (LRCICA, #18756); Regional Centre for Arbitration, Teheran; Nairobi Centre for International Arbitration.*

Events *Annual Session* Arusha (Tanzania UR) 2019, *Annual Session* Tokyo (Japan) 2018, *Annual Session* Nairobi (Kenya) 2017, *Annual Session* Delhi (India) 2016, *Annual Session* Beijing (China) 2015. **Publications** *AALCO Journal of International Law; AALCO Newsletter; Yearbook of the AALCO.*
Members Governments of 48 countries:
Bahrain, Bangladesh, Brunei Darussalam, Cameroon, China, Cyprus, Egypt, Gambia, Ghana, India, Indonesia, Iran Islamic Rep, Iraq, Japan, Jordan, Kenya, Korea DPR, Korea Rep, Kuwait, Lebanon, Libya, Malaysia, Mauritius, Mongolia, Myanmar, Nepal, Nigeria, Oman, Pakistan, Palestine, Philippines, Qatar, Saudi Arabia, Senegal, Sierra Leone, Singapore, Somalia, South Africa, Sri Lanka, Sudan, Syrian AR, Tanzania UR, Thailand, Türkiye, Uganda, United Arab Emirates, Vietnam, Yemen.
Permanent Observers (2):
Australia, New Zealand.
IGO Relations Permanent Observer Status with the United Nations and close collaboration with the UN through inter-secretariat consultations and participation in plenipotentiary conferences. Relations with: *UNESCO (#20322).* Participates in the activities of: *UNCTAD (#20285).* Member of: *Intergovernmental Organizations Conference (IGO Conference, #11498).* Permanent observer status with: *World Intellectual Property Organization (WIPO, #21593).* Observer to: *International Organization for Migration (IOM, #14454).* Observer to General Assembly of: *United Nations (UN, #20515).* Close cooperation with: *International Law Commission (ILC, #14004).* Accredited to the Conference of the Parties of: *Secretariat of the United Nations Convention to Combat Desertification (Secretariat of the UNCCD, #19208).* Accredited by: *United Nations Framework Convention on Climate Change – Secretariat (UNFCCC, #20564).* Agreement with:

- *Commonwealth Secretariat (#04362)*;
- *ECOSOC (#05331)*;
- *FAO (#09260)*;
- *The Hague Conference on Private International Law (HCCH, #10850)*;
- *International Atomic Energy Agency (IAEA, #12294)*;
- *International Institute for the Unification of Private Law (UNIDROIT, #13934)*;
- *International Maritime Organization (IMO, #14102)*;
- *League of Arab States (LAS, #16420)*;
- *Office of the United Nations High Commissioner for Human Rights (OHCHR, #17697)*;
- *Sistema Económico Latinoamericano (SELA, #19294)*;
- *UNEP (#20299)*;
- *UNHCR (#20327)*;
- *UNIDO (#20336)*;
- *United Nations Commission on Crime Prevention and Criminal Justice (CCPCJ, #20530)*;
- *United Nations Commission on International Trade Law (UNCITRAL, #20531)*;
- *United Nations Economic Commission for Africa (ECA, #20554)*;
- *United Nations Economic and Social Commission for Asia and the Pacific (ESCAP, #20557)*;
- *United Nations Economic and Social Commission for Western Asia (ESCWA, #20558)*;
- *United Nations University (UNU, #20642)*. [2021.02.25/XC0069/**C***]

♦ Asian-African Society of Mycobacteriology (AASM) 01304

Co-Chair and Admin Dir Mycobacteriology Research Center , (NRITLD), Shahid Beheshti University of Medical Sciences, PO 19575-154, Teheran, 1956944413, Iran Islamic Rep. T. +9826109505. Fax +9826109505.
Pres address not obtained.
URL: http://theaasm.org/

History 2008. **Aims** As a non-profit,scientific organization, establish unilateral,bilateral and multilateral networks of scientific research and training among experts from AASM countries; make a network of laboratories whose aim is to increase the quality control and quality assurance within and between AASM countries; improve diagnosis, treatment and prevention of mycobacterial disease; advise,cooperate and participate with governmental and non-governmental agencies in matters of common interest; establish and maintain a close link with those agencies who work to prevent mycobacterial diseases worldwide (e.g.,WHO,CDC,ASM,IUATLD,etc.). **Structure** Leadership; Scientific Board; Advisory Board. **Languages** Arabic, English, Persian. **Staff** 10.00 FTE, paid; 250.00 FTE, voluntary. 4000 academic -researchers in Mycobacteriology field , all over the world. **Finance** Sources: members' dues. **Activities** Awards/prizes/competitions; events/meetings; financial and/or material support; knowledge management/information dissemination; networking/liaising; publishing activities; research and development; training/education. Active in Asian and African countries. **Events** *Congress* Iran Islamic Rep 2021, *Congress* Delhi (India) 2017, *Congress* Isfahan (Iran Islamic Rep) 2017, *Congress* Isfahan (Iran Islamic Rep) 2015. **Publications** *International Journal of Mycobacteriology (IJMYCO)* (4 a year).
Members Scientific Members (16) in 20 countries:
Algeria, Armenia, Belarus, China, India, Iran Islamic Rep, Iraq, Italy, Japan, Kenya, Lebanon, Niger, Nigeria, Pakistan, Russia, Saudi Arabia, South Africa, Sudan, Sweden, UK.
For a full description of the Members: https://www.theaasm.org/constituent-members/.
IGO Relations none. **NGO Relations** Research institutions; medical universities. [2023/XJ8952/**D**]

- ♦ Asian Agricultural Journalists and Writers Association (inactive)
- ♦ Asian Agricultural Remote Sensing Symposium (meeting series)
- ♦ Asian Aid Organization (internationally oriented national body)
- ♦ Asian Airline Association / see Association of Asia Pacific Airlines (#02385)

♦ Asian Allelopathy Society (AAS) 01305

Pres Inst Tropical and Subtropical Ecology, South China Agric Univ, Guangzhou, Wushan, 510642 Guangdong, China.
URL: http://www.asian-allelopathy-society.org/

History 2009, Guangzhou (China), during the first International Conference. **Aims** Promote the cooperation and collaboration in the field of allelopathy between Asian scientists and those from the other parts of the world. **Structure** Officers: President; Secretary; Vice-President; Treasurer; Joint Secretary. **Languages** English. **Finance** Members' dues (every 3 years). **Events** *Conference* Chandigarh (India) 2012, *Conference* Guangzhou (China) 2009. **Members** Individuals. Membership countries not specified. **NGO Relations** *International Allelopathy Society (IAS, #11618)*. [2015/XM3864/v/**D**]

- ♦ Asian Allergy and Asthma Foundation (internationally oriented national body)

♦ Asian Alliance of Appropriate Technology Practitioners (APPROTECH ASIA) 01306

Contact address not obtained. T. +6325847888. Fax +6326355026. E-mail: fglumampao@approtech.org – info@approtech.org.
URL: http://approtech.org/

History Founded 1980, Bangkok (Thailand). Also referred to as under the acronym *AAATP*. **Aims** Increase the access of Asia's poor to technologies and processes appropriate and relevant to their needs and expanding capacities; promote and facilitate exchange and transfer of appropriate technology; stimulate and facilitate discussion and promotion of sustainable development issues and policies among policy-makers and social development practitioners; strengthen and develop networking strategies and mechanisms for international cooperation and sharing. **Structure** Council. **Languages** English. **Staff** 6.00 FTE, paid; 10.00 FTE, voluntary. **Finance** Budget (annual): operating/administrative expenses – about US$ 50,000; programme expenses – euro 100,000. Grants from: *Asia Regional Cookstove Programme (ARECOP, #02084)*; *Department for International Development (DFID, inactive)*; *International Network on Gender and Sustainable Energy (ENERGIA, #14272)*; *Japan International Cooperation Agency (JICA)* Perez-Guerrero Trust Fund. **Activities** Research and development; training/education; events/meetings; knowledge management/information dissemination; guidance/assistance/consulting. Library on trade and industry in West Africa; information unit. **Events** *Conference* Bangkok (Thailand) 1996, *International symposium on women in science and technology development and transfer* Bangkok (Thailand) 1992, *Conference on appropriate technology and sustainable development* Delhi (India) 1992, *Conference* Bangkok (Thailand) 1988. **Publications** *The Management of NGOs: Case Studies of Asian NGOs* (1991) by Ernesto D Garilao et al. Technology manuals; pamphlets; series.
Members Full (17), Associate (24), Honorary (1) in 10 countries:
Bangladesh, India, Indonesia, Nepal, Pakistan, Philippines, Singapore, Sri Lanka, Thailand, Vietnam.
Partners in 6 countries:
Cambodia, China, Kyrgyzstan, Mongolia, Myanmar, Pakistan.
IGO Relations Cooperates with: *UNESCO Office, Jakarta – Regional Bureau for Sciences in Asia and the Pacific (#20313)*. **NGO Relations** Cooperates with: *International Network for Sustainable Energy (INFORSE, #14331)*. Member of: *Freshwater Action Network (FAN, inactive)*; *Global Gender and Climate Alliance (GGCA, no recent information)*. [2015/XD0486/y/**D**]

- ♦ Asian Amateur Athletic Association / see Asian Athletics Association (#01348)
- ♦ Asian Amateur Kabaddi Federation (inactive)
- ♦ Asian Amateur Swimming Federation / see Asia Swimming Federation (#02099)
- ♦ Asian Amateur Wrestling Committee / see Asian Associated Wrestling Committee (#01311)
- ♦ Asian Amateur Wrestling Federation / see Asian Associated Wrestling Committee (#01311)
- ♦ Asian America MultiTechnology Association (internationally oriented national body)
- ♦ Asian American Center for Theology and Strategies / see Pacific and Asian American Center for Theology and Strategies, USA
- ♦ Asian American Manufacturers Association / see Asian America MultiTechnology Association

♦ Asian Angle-Closure Glaucoma Club (AACGC) 01307

Secretariat Room 8607, Seoul Natl Univ Hosp, 101 Daehak-ro, Jongo-gu, Seoul 03080, Korea Rep. T. +82220722438. Fax +8227413187. E-mail: kihopark@snu.ac.kr.
URL: http://www.aacgc.org/

History 2001. Since 2012, serves as umbrella society of *Asia-Pacific Glaucoma Society (APGS, #01917)*, founded on merger of *South East Asia Glaucoma Interest Group (SEAGIG, inactive)* and *Asian-Oceanic Glaucoma Society (AOGS, inactive)* and AACGC. **Aims** Establish a scientific network for the Asian glaucomatologists who are interested in angle-closure glaucoma in exchange of knowledge about angle-closure glaucoma. **Structure** Executive Committee. **Activities** Events/meetings. **Events** *Meeting* Seoul (Korea Rep) 2019, *Meeting* Ulaanbaatar (Mongolia) 2018, *Annual Meeting* Boao (China) 2017, *Meeting* Yangon (Myanmar) 2016, *Meeting* Hanoi (Vietnam) 2015. [XM3713/**F**]

- ♦ Asian Animal Protection Network (internationally oriented national body)

♦ Asian Anti-Counterfeit Association (AAA) 01308

Contact address not obtained. T. +85223806896. Fax +85223806893.

History Founded 2004, Shenzhen (China). Registered in accordance with Hong Kong law. Also referred to as *Asian Anti-Counterfeiting Association (AAA)*. **Aims** Be a link and bridge between enterprises and institutions and users in different member countries; strengthen international communication and coordination; promote the level of technique and management of anti-counterfeit of every member; promote technological development of the anti-counterfeit industry and the quality of products. **Structure** General Assembly. **Events** *Conference* Kochi (India) 2011, *Conference* Singapore (Singapore) 2006, *Conference* Singapore (Singapore) 2006. **NGO Relations** Member of: *Global Security Industry Alliance (GSIA, #10587)*. [2015/XM3259/**D**]

- ♦ Asian Anti-Counterfeiting Association / see Asian Anti-Counterfeit Association (#01308)

♦ Asian Apicultural Association (AAA) 01309

SG ASAC, Xiang shan, 100093 Beijing, China. E-mail: china-apiculture@263.net.
Pres Graduate School, Maejo Univ, Sansai, Chiang Mai, 50290, Thailand.
URL: http://www.asianapiculture.org/index.asp

History 1992. Current statutes revised Nov 2010. **Aims** Save the rich diversity of honey bee fauna in Asia; promote beekeeping through encouragement of friendly information exchange between beekeepers and bee scientists in the area. **Structure** Council; Executive Committee. **Languages** English. **Finance** Sources: members' dues. **Events** *Biennial Conference* Hanoi (Vietnam) 2021, *International Meliponine Conference* Los Baños (Philippines) 2020, *Biennial Conference* Abu Dhabi (United Arab Emirates) 2019, *Biennial Conference* Jeddah (Saudi Arabia) 2016, *Biennial Conference* Antalya (Turkey) 2014. **Publications** *Asian Bee Journal*.
Members Chapters in 21 countries and territories:
Australia, Bangladesh, Brunei Darussalam, China, India, Indonesia, Israel, Japan, Korea Rep, Malaysia, Nepal, New Zealand, Oman, Pakistan, Philippines, Saudi Arabia, Sri Lanka, Taiwan, Thailand, Türkiye, Vietnam. [2021/XD5362/**D**]

♦ Asian Aquaculture Network (AAN) 01310

Coordination Office 599/27 Ratchadapisek Road, Jatujak, Bangkok, 10900, Thailand. T. +6621921787. Fax +6621921733. E-mail: info@asianaquaculturenetwork.com.
Headquarters 8 Temasek Boulevard, Suntec Tower 3, Penthouse Level, Singapore 038983, Singapore. Fax +6568663636.
URL: http://asianaquaculturenetwork.com/

History 2009. **Aims** Inspire new generations through the sharing of knowledge, education initiatives and practical resources for the ecological sustainability of aquaculture in order to feed the world. **Activities** Advocacy/lobbying/activism; events/meetings; knowledge management/information dissemination; training/education. **Events** *Singapore Aquaculture Conference* Singapore (Singapore) 2018. **Publications** *AQUA Practical* (4 a year). [2021/AA2252/**F**]

- ♦ Asian Archery Federation / see World Archery Asia (#21107)
- ♦ Asian Associated Wrestling Committee / see Asian Associated Wrestling Committee (#01311)

♦ Asian Associated Wrestling Committee (AAWC) 01311

Pres c/o Korea Wrestling Federation, 604 Olympic Center, 88 Oryundong, Seoul 138-749, Korea Rep. T. +82312618587. Fax +8224204254.

History 1973, Baghdad (Iraq), as *Asian Associated Wrestling Committee (AAWC)*. Previously also referred to as *Asian Amateur Wrestling Committee* and as *Asian Amateur Wrestling Federation*. Current Constitution revised during 11th Asian Championships, 30 Jun 1995, Manila (Philippines). Current By-Law revised, 30 Apr 2009, Pattaya (Thailand). **Aims** Promote friendship and peace between the people of Asia; promote the wrestling through Asian countries. **Structure** Congress, consisting of delegates of each of the affiliated federations and members of the Executive Council. Executive Council, comprising 7 elected members and Asian FILA Bureau members. **Languages** English. **Finance** Members' dues: US$ 200. FILA subsidies. **Activities** Organizes continental championships in Greco-Roman, Freestyle and Women Wrestling. **Events** *Conference* Pattaya (Thailand) 2009, *Conference* Manila (Philippines) 2007, *Conference* Wuhan (China) 2005, *Conference* Busan (Korea Rep) 2002, *Congress / Conference* Bangkok (Thailand) 1998.
Members National wrestling federations or associations in 36 countries and territories:
Afghanistan, Bangladesh, Cambodia, China, Hong Kong, India, Indonesia, Iran Islamic Rep, Iraq, Japan, Jordan, Kazakhstan, Korea DPR, Korea Rep, Kyrgyzstan, Laos, Lebanon, Mongolia, Myanmar, Nepal, Pakistan, Palestine, Philippines, Qatar, Saudi Arabia, Singapore, Sri Lanka, Syrian AR, Taiwan, Tajikistan, Thailand, Turkmenistan, United Arab Emirates, Uzbekistan, Vietnam, Yemen. [2012/XD8320/**D**]

♦ Asian Association of Agricultural Colleges and Universities (AAACU) 01312

Association des instituts et universités agronomiques d'Asie

Exec Sec College of Agriculture Dean's Office, Univ of the Philippines Los Banos, College Laguna, 4031 Los Baños LAG, Philippines. T. +63495363535.

History 1 May 1972, Baguio City (Philippines), during 2nd Agricultural College and University Seminar. Constitution adopted by 17 Asian institutions of higher learning in agriculture from 9 countries: Indonesia; Thailand; the Philippines; China; Malaysia; Korea Rep; South Vietnam; Turkey; Iran. **Aims** Advance the study, teaching and practice of agricultural studies and related sciences; enhance effectiveness of programmes in agricultural instruction, research and extension; formulate plans, programmes and policies on areas of mutual interest to member institutions; determine ways and means by which member institutions may be able to build strong linkages with institutions and agencies serving agriculture; exchange experiences among members as to the means by which they can contribute more effectively to the advancement of human welfare in Asia. **Structure** General Assembly. Governing Council (meeting every 2 years at the biennial convention), comprising the CEO of each member institution or their representative. Executive Board (meets annually), comprising President, 1st and 2nd Vice-Presidents, Immediate Past President, Executive Secretary/Treasurer and 2 board members. Permanent Secretariat located at College of Agriculture Dean's Office, University of the Philippines, Los Baños, (Philippines). **Languages** English. **Staff** 2.00 FTE, paid. **Finance** Members' dues (annual) for full members. Member universities serving as hosts are also co-sponsors; contributions from Affiliate members and donor agencies, including: *FAO (#09260)*; *International Development Research Centre (IDRC, #13162)*; *UNESCO (#20322)*. **Activities** Programmes: Faculty and Administrator Exchange; Student Exchange; Study Tours; International Symposium; Information Drive; Curriculum Development; Textbook Writing. Technical Committee works for integration of nutrition into agriculture and rural development. Conducts: Biennial Convention; seminars and workshops. Organizes training programmes; carries out fund raising activities. **Events** *Biennial Convention* Tokyo (Japan) 2016, *Biennial Convention* Nakhon Pathom (Thailand) 2014, *Biennial Convention* Seoul (Korea Rep) 2012, *Biennial Conference / Biennial Convention* Mangilao (Guam) 2010, *Biennial convention* Manila (Philippines) 2008. **Publications** *AAACU Newsletter*. *Restructuring Agricultural Colleges and Universities for the 21st Century* (2002); *Global Agribusiness: The Role of Asian Agricultural Academic Institutions* (2002); *Application of Information Technology in Agriculture Education* (1999); *Training Agriculture and Rural Development Personnel for Agroforestry Education* (1984); *Nutrition Considerations in Agriculture and Rural Development* (1982); *Integration of Postharvest Technology in Higher Education in Agriculture* (1981); *Postharvest Technology and Food Processing* (1980); *Role on the AAACU-FAO Member Institutions* (1978); *Involvement of Agricultural Colleges and Universities in Population Education-Rural Development Programs* (1977); *Asian Agricultural Colleges and Universities: Facts and Figures* (1976); *Facilitating Academic Interchange Among Graduate Schools of Agriculture in Asia* (1976); *Strengthening the Linkage Between Research and Extension* (1976); *The Role of Agricultural Colleges and Universities in Small Farmer Education* (1976); *Increasing the Influence of Agricultural Universities in National Policy Making* (1974); *Non-Formal Education as a Responsibility of Agricultural Colleges and Universities* (1974); *Organizing Various Schools/Colleges of Agricultural Colleges and Universities* (1974); *Organizing Various Schools/Colleges of Agricultural Sciences Into An Efficient National System* (1974); *Linkage of Institutions and Services Supporting Agricultural Development* (1972). Books; proceedings; reports.

Members Regular; Affiliate agricultural universities and colleges. Regular members (46) in 16 countries and territories:
Bangladesh, Guam, India, Indonesia, Iran Islamic Rep, Japan, Korea Rep, Malaysia, Nepal, Pakistan, Philippines, Saudi Arabia, Taiwan, Thailand, Türkiye, Vietnam.
Affiliate members (4) in 3 countries:
Japan, Korea Rep, Philippines.
Included in the above, one organization listed in this Yearbook:
Southeast Asian Regional Center for Graduate Study and Research in Agriculture (SEARCA, #19781).
NGO Relations Member of: *Global Confederation of Higher Education Associations for Agriculture and Life Sciences (GCHERA, #10304).* [2016/XD7336/**D**]

♦ Asian Association for Agricultural Engineering (AAAE) 01313

SG Room B206, No 31 Bldg/No 1 Beishatan, Deshengmen Wai, CAAMS, 100083 Beijing, China. T. +861064882358 – +861064882214. Fax +861064883508 – +861064882284. E-mail: iaejeditor@yahoo.com – iaejeditor@aliyun.com.
Pres Flat S-2, Rajhans Apartment Tarabai Park, Kolhapur, Maharashtra 416003, Kolhapur MAHARASHTRA 416003, India.
URL: https://aaae.in/

History 5 Dec 1990, Bangkok (Thailand), during International Agricultural Engineering Conference of *Asian Institute of Technology (AIT, #01519).* **Aims** Advance the profession and practice of agricultural engineering internationally; promote information exchange, improve communications, minimize duplication of effort and optimize use of resources; formulate, establish and promote voluntary academic, professional and technical standards; support at international level the activities of national societies and maintain liaison among them. **Structure** Executive Committee. **Languages** English. **Staff** Voluntary. **Finance** Members' dues. **Events** *International Agricultural Engineering Conference* Beijing (China) 2014, *Conference* Beijing (China) 2013, *International Agricultural Engineering Conference* Muscat (Oman) 2013, *International Symposium on Actual Tasks on Agricultural Engineering* Opatija (Croatia) 2013, *International Agricultural Engineering Conference / Conference* Hangzhou (China) 2012. **Publications** *AAAE Newsletter* (4 a year); *International Agricultural Engineering Journal* (4 a year).
Members Foundation; Life; Regular; Corporate. Individuals in 37 countries and territories:
Australia, Bangladesh, Belgium, Brazil, Canada, China, Croatia, Egypt, France, Germany, Hong Kong, India, Indonesia, Iran Islamic Rep, Israel, Italy, Japan, Jordan, Kenya, Korea Rep, Malaysia, Nepal, Netherlands, New Zealand, Norway, Oman, Pakistan, Philippines, Poland, Saudi Arabia, Sri Lanka, Sweden, Taiwan, Tanzania UR, Thailand, UK, USA.
NGO Relations Member of: *International Commission of Agricultural and Biosystems Engineering (#12661).* [2021/XD3344/v/**D**]

♦ Asian Association for Algorithms and Computation (AAAC) 01314

Contact address not obtained.
URL: http://www.aa-ac.org/

History 2007. **Aims** Promote collaborations in theoretical computer science within the region. **Structure** Board. **Activities** Events/meetings. **Events** *Annual Meeting* Tainan (Taiwan) 2021, *Annual Meeting* Nara (Japan) 2020, *Annual Meeting* Seoul (Korea Rep) 2019, *Annual Meeting* Beijing (China) 2018, *AAAC 2017* Hong Kong (Hong Kong) 2017. [2021/AA0220/**D**]

♦ Asian Association for Biology Education (AABE) 01315

Sec-Treas BIOTA-Philippines, PSHS System, Agham Road, Diliman, Quezon City, Manila, Philippines. T. +632984276.

History 1966, following a planning Conference held in 1965, Sri Lanka. **Aims** Improve the teaching of and promote research in biology in Asian countries; bring together biology teachers and educators of Asian countries at conferences held periodically; establish an agency in Asia to serve as a centre for the exchange of teaching materials, journals and research papers, specialists and teachers in biological science, and open channels of communication between this agency and agencies in different countries doing similar work; promote the creation of biological teaching centres in each Asian country; promote the use of local resources for the teaching of biology. **Structure** General Meeting. Executive Committee, consisting of elected Executive Director and elected members (Secretary is an ex-officio member). Organizing Committee of at least 4 members including Executive Director. **Languages** English. **Finance** Members' dues: US$ 10. **Activities** A loosely organized association, meeting for Biennial Conferences and occasional regional meetings, remaining in contact in between through newsletter. **Events** *Biennial Conference* Goa (India) 2016, *Biennial Conference* Korea Rep 2014, *Biennial Conference* Kuala Lumpur (Malaysia) 2014, *Biennial Conference* Indonesia 2012, *Biennial Conference* Singapore (Singapore) 2010. **Publications** *AABE Newsletter.* Conference proceedings.
Members Individual and institutional membership. Biologists and interested parties attend conferences but are not permanent members. There are official country representatives in 12 countries and territories:
Australia, Hong Kong, India, Indonesia, Israel, Japan, Jordan, Korea Rep, Malaysia, Philippines, Singapore, Thailand. [2018/XD5310/**D**]

♦ Asian Association of Business Incubation 01316

Coordinator 100 Qin Zhou Road, Xuhui District, 200235 Shanghai, China. T. +862164839009. Fax +862164833567. E-mail: stic@stn.sh.cn.
URL: http://www.aabi.info/

History 30 Apr 2002, Toronto ON (Canada). **Aims** Promote business incubation activities by facilitating information exchange among Asian incubators, incubator clients and related organizations. **Structure** General Assembly; Officers; Secretariat. **Languages** English. **Staff** 2.00 FTE, paid; 2.00 FTE, voluntary. **Finance** Members' dues. Outside funding. **Activities** Advocacy/lobbying/activism; guidance/assistance/consulting; research/documentation; knowledge management/information dissemination; awareness raising; events/meetings. **Events** *General Assembly* Daegu (Korea Rep) 2015, *International Conference* Seoul (Korea Rep) 2012. **Publications** *AABI Newsletter, Asia Pacific Journal of Innovation and Entrepreneurship.*
Members Full in 8 countries and territories:
China, Hong Kong, India, Korea Rep, New Zealand, Taiwan, Thailand, Vietnam.
Other organizations (140) in 18 countries and territories:
Australia, China, Hong Kong, India, Indonesia, Japan, Kazakhstan, Korea Rep, Kyrgyzstan, Malaysia, New Zealand, Pakistan, Philippines, Singapore, Taiwan, Thailand, Uzbekistan, Vietnam. [2015.08.11/XJ9906/**D**]

♦ Asian Association of Carbon Groups (unconfirmed)

♦ Asian Association of Career Management Professionals (AACMP) . 01317

Contact c/o 10 Anson Road No 14-I4, Intl Plaza, Singapore 079903, Singapore. T. +6583014080. Fax +6562221829.

History Founded Dec 2001, Singapore (Singapore). **Aims** Promote career management and career development as a profession in Asia; serve as a source of professional development and networking of career management professionals; build and foster international links and relationships; define and maintain standards of practice for services relating to career management professionals; provide benchmarking of practice and credentialing. **Structure** General Meeting (annual); Board. **Events** *Career management regional conference / Annual Meeting* Singapore (Singapore) 2006. **Publications** *The Voice* (6 a year). *Navigate Your Career 2005: starting out* (2005). [2008/XM3084/t/**D**]

♦ Asian Association of Catholic Philosophers / see Asian Association of Christian Philosophers (#01318)

♦ Asian Association of Christian Philosophers (AACP) 01318

Contact Dept of Philosophy, College of Liberal Arts, National Taiwan Univ, No 1, Sec 4, Roosevelt Rd, Taipei 10617, Taiwan. T. +886233663366. Fax +886223627651. E-mail: tran@ntu.edu.tw.
Contact Assumption Univ, Graduate School of Philosophy and Religion, Hua Mak, Bang Kapi, Bangkok, 10240, Thailand. T. +6623004543ext1325. Fax +6623004543.

History 1991, Choung Chou Island (Hong Kong), as *Asian Association of Catholic Philosophers (AACP).* Constitution approved, 1992. Current title adopted, Dec 2008. **Aims** Promote teaching, learning and research in philosophy and religion; disseminate philosophical and religious knowledge to society; exchange and share ideas among Christian philosophers and other scholars; promote the understanding of one's own culture and other cultures; promote mutual understanding, peace and cooperation on both a regional and global scale. **Structure** Board of Directors of 11 members. President; Secretary-General/Treasurer; 2 Honorary Presidents. Honorary members. **Languages** English. **Staff** Voluntary. **Finance** Private sponsoring; donations from country members, individual members and friends. **Events** *Conference* Shanghai (China) 2010, *The role of Asian christian thinkers in the global age* Chung Li (Taiwan) 2008, *Conference* Taiwan 2008, *Conference* Bandung (Indonesia) 2006, *Conference* Bangkok (Thailand) 2004. **Publications** Journals; Conference Proceedings.
Members Full country members and individuals in 20 countries and territories:
Austria, Belgium, Canada, China, France, Germany, Hong Kong, India, Indonesia, Italy, Japan, Korea Rep, Lebanon, Malaysia, Philippines, Switzerland, Taiwan, Thailand, USA, Vietnam. [2018/XJ2012/**D**]

♦ Asian Association of Clinical Anatomists (unconfirmed)

♦ Asian Association of Convention and Visitor Bureaus (AACVB) 01319

Contact c/o TCEB, Siam Tower, 12 Bth and 26th Floor, Rama I Road, Pathumwan, Bangkok, 10330, Thailand. T. +6626946000. Fax +6626581411.

History Founded 5 Feb 1983, Manila (Philippines), on the initiative of Philippine Ministry of Tourism. Statutes most recently amended, 5-9 Apr 1988, Kuala Lumpur (Malaysia). Re-established by eight members, 2009. **Aims** Increase Asia's share of the international convention and incentive *travel* market; promote regional cooperation in developing Asia's convention potential and promoting the region as a convention destination; stimulate intra-regional conventions; encourage the formation of city or nation-wide convention organizations; develop and promote sound professional practices in the soliciting and servicing of meetings and conventions; initiate training programmes to achieve these objectives; facilitate exchange of information through establishing a comprehensive Asian convention data bank; serve as a clearing house of information on the Asian convention industry. **Structure** General Meeting (annual); Board of Directors (meets annually). **Languages** English. **Staff** 1.00 FTE, paid. **Finance** Members; dues. Other sources: funds contributed by founding members; registration fees. Budget (annual): US$ 50,000. **Activities** Projects/programmes; networking/liaising; events/meetings; training/education. **Events** *Asia for Asia Meetings Industry Leaders Summit* Daejeon (Korea Rep) 2012, *Asia for Asia Summit* Singapore (Singapore) 2011, *Joint seminar on professional congress organisation* Busan (Korea Rep) 2002, *Annual Conference* Hong Kong (Hong Kong) 2002, *Planning meeting* Singapore (Singapore) 2002. **Publications** *AACVB Information Exchange Program Manual. AACVB Information Brochures.* Information Services: Databank on past conferences.
Members Full CVB; Associate CVB; Associate Industry. National tourism organizations, convention bureaux, convention industry members, international or regional organizations and media with interest in the Asian Convention industry, in 10 countries and territories:
China, Hong Kong, Indonesia, Japan, Korea Rep, Macau, Malaysia, Philippines, Singapore, Thailand.
Individuals in 5 countries:
Australia, France, Germany, UK, USA.
NGO Relations Member of: *Joint Meetings Industry Council (JMIC, #16140).* [2014/XD2752/**D**]

♦ Asian Association for Dynamic Osteosynthesis (AADO) 01320

Contact c/o Orthopaedic Learning Centre, 1/F Li Ka Shing Specialist Clinics, Prince of Wales Hosp, Shatin, Hong Kong. T. +85226323482. Fax +85226477432. E-mail: secretariat@aado.org – info@aado.org.
URL: http://www.aado.org/

History 1992. **Activities** Organizes workshops, symposia and conferences. **Events** *Biennial Orthopaedic Nursing Conference* Hong Kong (Hong Kong) 2016, *Meeting on science of intramedullary reaming* Hong Kong (Hong Kong) 1995, *International conference on musculo-skeletal trauma* Hong Kong (Hong Kong) 1994. [2018/XD3817/**D**]

♦ Asian Association of Endocrine Surgeons (AsAES) 01321

Contact Unit 1-6 – Level 1, Enterprise 3B, Jalan Innovasi 1, Technology Park Malaysia, Lebuhraya Puchng – Sungei Besi, Bukit Jalil, 57000 Kuala Lumpur, Malaysia. T. +60389960700. Fax +60386694700. E-mail: secretariat@asianaes.org.
URL: http://www.asianaes.org/

History 1988. **Aims** Promote the exchange of knowledge and advancements in endocrine surgery. **Activities** Events/meetings. **Events** *Congress* Tokyo (Japan) 2023, *Biennial Congress* Melbourne, VIC (Australia) 2020, *Biennial Congress* Delhi (India) 2018, *Biennial Congress* Seoul (Korea Rep) 2016, *Biennial Congress* Negombo (Sri Lanka) 2014. **Publications** *World Journal of Endocrine Surgery.*
Members Individuals in 25 countries and territories:
Australia, China, Egypt, Hong Kong, India, Indonesia, Iran Islamic Rep, Japan, Korea Rep, Malaysia, New Zealand, Oman, Pakistan, Philippines, Saudi Arabia, Serbia, Singapore, Sri Lanka, Taiwan, Thailand, Türkiye, UK, United Arab Emirates, USA, Vietnam.
NGO Relations *International Association of Endocrine Surgeons (IAES, #11868); International Coalition for Organizations Supporting Endocrine Patients (ICOSEP, #12618).* [2019/XD7179/**D**]

♦ Asian Association of Environmental and Resource Economics (AAERE) 01322

SG c/o Environmental Planning Center, 14 Yoshida Kawaramachi, Sakyo-ku, Kyoto, 606-8314 Japan. E-mail: eaaere.secretariat@gmail.com – aaere.president@hotmail.com.
URL: https://aaere.org/

History 2010, Sapporo (Japan), during 5th Symposium. Registered in accordance with Japanese law. Former names and other names: *East Asian Association of Environmental and Resource Economics (EAAERE)* – former (2010 to 2019). **Aims** Encourage exchange of ideas, research and other professional activities that are of an interdisciplinary nature relating to economics and management of environment and natural resources in East Asia. **Structure** Council; Board of Directors. **Languages** English. **Staff** None. **Finance** Members' dues. **Events** *Congress* Seoul (Korea Rep) 2021, *Congress* Seoul (Korea Rep) 2020, *World Congress of Environmental and Resource Economists* Gothenburg (Sweden) 2018, *Congress* Singapore (Singapore) 2017, *EAAERE Congress* Fukuoka (Japan) 2016. **Publications** *EAAERE Newsletter, Environmental Economics and Policy Studies (EEPS)* – official journal.
Members Individual; Institutional. Members in 12 countries and territories:
Australia, China, Indonesia, Japan, Korea Rep, Malaysia, Philippines, Singapore, Taiwan, Thailand, USA, Vietnam.
NGO Relations Cooperates with (1): *Economy and Environment Programme for Southeast Asia (EEPSEA, #05324).* [2020/XJ8990/**D**]

♦ Asian Association for Foundation of Software (AAFS) 01323

Co-Chair Dept of Computer Science, School of Computing, National Univof Singapore, 13 Computing Drive, Singapore 117417, Singapore. T. +6565166228. Fax +6567794580. E-mail: chinwn@comp.nus.edu.sg.
Co-Chair Programming Research Lab, Information Systems Architecture Research Div, National Inst of Informatics, 2-1-2 Hitotsubashi, Chiyoda-ku, Tokyo, 101-8430 Japan.
URL: http://logic.cs.tsukuba.ac.jp/AAFS/

Aims Support research in computer software and related fields. **Structure** Executive Committee. **Activities** Events/meetings. **Events** *Asian Symposium on Programming Languages and Systems* Chicago, IL (USA) 2021, *Asian Symposium on Programming Languages and Systems* Fukuoka (Japan) 2020, *Asian Symposium on Programming Languages and Systems* Nusa Dua (Indonesia) 2019, *Asian Symposium on Programming Languages and Systems* Auckland (New Zealand) 2018, *Asian Symposium on Programming Languages and Systems* Suzhou (China) 2017. [2015/XM8127/f/**D**]

♦ Asian Association for Frailty and Sarcopenia (AAFS) 01324

SG c/o KHU School of Medicine, Kyungheedae-ro 26, Dongdaemun-gu, Seoul 02447, Korea Rep.
URL: https://aafs-asia.org/

History 2017. **Aims** Promote awareness of frailty and sarcopenia; share experience and skills, and create knowledge of frailty and sarcopenia; promote research collaboration in the field; promote diagnostic criteria, practice guidelines, and other recommendations. **Structure** Executive Board. **Events** *Asian Conference for Frailty and Sarcopenia (ACFS)* Nagoya (Japan) 2022, *Asian Conference for Frailty and Sarcopenia (ACFS)* Suwon (Korea Rep) 2021. **Publications** *Aging Medicine and Healthcare* (4 a year).
Members Full in 3 countries and territories:
Japan, Korea Rep, Taiwan. [2022/AA3179/**D**]

♦ Asian Association of Hair Restoration Surgeons (AAHRS) 01325

Contact 4th Fl, 513-1, Shinsadong, Gangnamgu, Seoul 135-887, Korea Rep. T. +8225455824. Fax +8225455829. E-mail: aahrs2010@gmail.com.
URL: http://aahrs.asia/

History 2010. **Aims** Promote continuing quality improvement and education for professionals in the field of medical hair restoration surgery for Asian people. **Structure** Board of Governors. Officers: Founder President; Secretary/Treasurer; Immediate Past President. Committees (5): Website; By laws; Membership; Finance/fund-raising; Annual meeting chair. **Events** *Annual Scientific Meeting* Bangkok (Thailand) 2017, *Annual Scientific Meeting* Seoul (Korea Rep) 2012, *Annual Scientific Meeting* Bangkok (Thailand) 2011. [2013/XJ6473/**D**]

♦ Asian Association of Independent Research Providers (internationally oriented national body)

♦ Asian Association of Indigenous and Cultural Psychology (AAICP) . 01326

Address not obtained.
URL: http://aaicp.wg.ugm.ac.id/

History Founded Jul 2010. **Structure** Council; Committee; Board of Advisors. **Activities** Events/meetings. **Events** *International Conference* Kota Kinabalu (Malaysia) 2018. [2018/XM8339/**D**]

♦ Asian Association for Investors in Non-Listed Real Estate Vehicles (ANREV) 01327

CEO 1701 17/F Kinwick Ctr, 32 Hollywood Rd, Central, Hong Kong, Central and Western, Hong Kong. E-mail: info@anrev.org.
URL: http://www.anrev.org/

Aims Serve as a platform for institutional investors; address key issues facing the Asian non-listed real estate funds industry. **Structure** Management Board; Executive Board; Investor Advisory Board; Executive Office. **Activities** Events/meetings; training/education. **Events** *Korea Conference* Seoul (Korea Rep) 2022, *Annual Conference* Singapore (Singapore) 2022, *Korea Conference* Seoul (Korea Rep) 2021, *Annual Conference* Hong Kong (Hong Kong) 2020, *Young Professionals Conference* Singapore (Singapore) 2020.
Members Full in 19 countries and territories:
Australia, Canada, China, Denmark, France, Germany, Hong Kong, India, Japan, Korea Rep, Luxembourg, Malaysia, Netherlands, Singapore, Switzerland, UK, United Arab Emirates, USA, Vietnam.
NGO Relations Member of: *International Ethics Standards Coalition (IES Coalition, #13307)*; *International Property Measurement Standards Coalition (IPMSC, #14656)*. [2022/XM4445/**D**]

♦ Asian Association for Lexicography (ASIALEX) 01328

Sec address not obtained.
URL: http://www.asialex.org/

History 29 Mar 1997, Hong Kong. **Aims** Foster scholarly and professional activities in the fields of lexicography and dictionaries in and for Asia. **Structure** Executive Committee, including President, Vice-President, Secretary and Treasurer. **Languages** English. **Staff** None. **Activities** Organizes symposia, courses. **Events** *Conference* Seoul (Korea Rep) 2023, *Conference* Nanning (China) 2022, *Conference* Yogyakarta (Indonesia) 2021, *Conference* Yogyakarta (Indonesia) 2020, *Conference* Istanbul (Turkey) 2019. **Publications** *ASIALEX Newsletter*.
Members Individuals in 26 countries and territories:
Australia, Austria, Belgium, Brazil, Canada, China, Czechia, Finland, France, Germany, Hong Kong, India, Indonesia, Iran Islamic Rep, Israel, Japan, Jordan, Korea Rep, Malaysia, Mongolia, Singapore, South Africa, Taiwan, Thailand, UK, USA.
NGO Relations *African Association for Lexicography (AFRILEX)*; *Australasian Association for Lexicography (AUSTRALEX)*; *Dictionary Society of North America (DSNA)*; *European Association for Lexicography (EURALEX, #06107)*. [2014/XD6642/**D**]

♦ Asian Association of Management Organizations (AAMO) 01329

Association des organisations de gestion d'Asie

Secretariat c/o All India Management Assn, Management House, 14 Institutional Area, Lodhi Road, Delhi 110003, DELHI 110003, India. T. +911124645100. E-mail: aamo.secretariat@aima.in.
Pres address not obtained.
URL: http://www.aamo.network/

History 1960, as a Regional Group of *World Council of Management (CIOS, inactive)*. Previous name: *Asian Association of Management Organizations – World Council of Management (AAMOCIOS)*. **Aims** Improve social and economic well-being by promoting better managerial performance in private, public and community services; encourage management research, education, training and development. **Structure** Assembly (every 3 years); Council; Sub-Groups on specific issues; Presidency and Secretariat rotate among member organizations every 3 years. **Languages** English. **Finance** Members' dues. Other sources: conference fees, occasional grants. **Activities** Events/meetings; training/education; research/documentation. **Events** *Triennial Conference* Macau 2013, *Triennial International Management Conference* Macau (Macau) 2013, *Triennial Conference* Hong Kong (Hong Kong) 2010, *Triennial international management conference* Hong Kong (Hong Kong) 2010, *Triennial international management conference / Triennial Conference* Kolkata (India) 2007. **Publications** *AAMO Newsletter* in English.
Members National Management Organizations (NMOs) in 11 countries and territories:
Australia, Hong Kong, India, Korea Rep, Macau, Malaysia, Nepal, New Zealand, Pakistan, Philippines, Sri Lanka.
NGO Relations *Association of World Economic Studies (AWES)*. [2019.11.06/XD6856/**D**]

♦ Asian Association of Management Organizations – World Council of Management / see Asian Association of Management Organizations (#01329)
♦ Asian Association of National Languages (inactive)

♦ Asian Association of Occupational and Environmental Health (AAOEH) 01330

Vice Pres 20 Lower Kent Ridge Road, Singapore 119080, Singapore. Fax +6567746979.

History 3 Nov 1964, Indonesia. Founded at 4th Asian Conference on Occupational Health, in compliance with Tokyo (Japan) proclamation of 3 Nov 1956. Constitution adopted 1973. Most recently amended 23 Oct 1979, Seoul (Korea Rep), when bylaws adopted. Former names and other names: *Asian Association of Occupational Health (AAOH)* – former (3 Nov 1964); *Asia AAOH* – former alias. **Aims** Improve health, welfare and safety of the working population in Asia and the Pacific through development of occupational health activities in industry and agriculture; establish and promote permanent relations among individuals working in the field; improve the standards of living and help eliminate the social factors leading to poverty and backwardness of the working population; promote research. **Structure** General Committee (meets at least every 3 years); Council. Technical Committees: Education; International Liaison; Occupational Health Services; Agricultural and Plantation Health; Ergonomics; Research; Occupational Mental Health. **Languages** English. **Staff** Voluntary. **Finance** Members' dues and admission fees. **Activities** Events/meetings. **Events** *Asian Conference on Occupational Health (ACOH)* Daegu (Korea Rep) 2023, *Asian Conference on Occupational Health* Daegu (Korea Rep) 2020, *Asian Conference on Occupational Health* Kaohsiung (Taiwan) 2017, *Asian Conference on Occupational Health* Fukuoka (Japan) 2014, *Asian Conference on Occupational Health* Bangkok (Thailand) 2011. **Publications** Reports. Conference Proceedings.
Members National bodies and individuals in 14 countries and territories:
Australia, Bahrain, China, Hong Kong, India, Indonesia, Japan, Korea Rep, Malaysia, New Zealand, Papua New Guinea, Philippines, Singapore, Thailand. [2022/XD5503/**D**]

♦ Asian Association of Occupational Health / see Asian Association of Occupational and Environmental Health (#01330)

♦ Asian Association of Open Universities (AAOU) 01331

SG AAOU Secretariat, Office of the Chancellor, Univ of the Philippines Open Univ, Los Baños, Santa Cruz LAG, Philippines. T. +63495366001 – +63495366002 – +63495366006. Fax +63495366015. E-mail: aaou@upou.edu.ph.
URL: http://www.aaou.org/

History Founded 18 Nov 1987, Thailand, at inaugural meeting, by open universities in the Asian region. Statutes amended: 21 Sep 1992, Seoul (Korea Rep); Feb 1995, Delhi (India); 14 Oct 1999, Beijing (China); Jan 2015, Hong Kong. **Aims** Strive to widen educational opportunities available to all people in Asia; improve the quality of the institutions in terms of their educational management, teaching and research; promote education by distance teaching systems, as well as professional and ethical standards; develop potentialities of open and distance education; cooperate with official bodies and others directly or indirectly interested in open education; facilitate cooperation with other similar regional and international bodies. **Structure** Executive Committee. **Languages** English. **Staff** 3.00 FTE, paid. **Finance** Members' dues. **Activities** Events/meetings. **Events** *Annual Conference* Seogwipo (Korea Rep) 2022, *Annual Conference* Colombo (Sri Lanka) 2021, *Annual Conference* Kuala Lumpur (Malaysia) 2015, *Annual Conference* Hong Kong (Hong Kong) 2014, *Annual Conference* Islamabad (Pakistan) 2013. **Publications** *AAOU Journal* (2 a year). **Members** Full (45); Associate (18). Members in 25 countries. Membership countries not specified. [2018.08.15/XD2505/**D**]

♦ Asian Association of Oral and Maxillo Facial Surgeons / see Asian Association of Oral and Maxillofacial Surgeons (#01332)

♦ Asian Association of Oral and Maxillofacial Surgeons 01332

Exec Dir c/o Japanese Society of Oral Surgeons, Mita SS Building 3F, 5-27-1, Shiba, Minato-ku, Tokyo, 108-0014 Japan.
URL: http://www.asianaoms.org/

History Former names and other names: *Asian Association of Oral and Maxillo Facial Surgeons (AAOMFS)* – alias. **Aims** Improve the quality and standards of the specialty of oral and maxillofacial surgery in the region. **Structure** Governing Council. **Events** *Asian Congress on Oral and Maxillofacial Surgery* Seoul (Korea Rep) 2022, *Asian Congress on Oral and Maxillofacial Surgery* Manila (Philippines) 2021, *Asian Congress on Oral and Maxillofacial Surgery* Taipei (Taiwan) 2018, *Asian Congress on Oral and Maxillofacial Surgery* Manila (Philippines) 2016, *Asian Congress on Oral and Maxillofacial Surgery* Xian (China) 2014. **Publications** *Journal of Oral and Maxillofacial Surgery, Medicine, and Pathology*. [2022/XD4249/**D**]

♦ Asian Association of Paediatric Dentistry / see Pediatric Dentistry Association of Asia (#18286)

♦ Asian Association of Pediatric Surgeons (AAPS) 01333

Association asiatique des chirurgiens pédiatres

SG c/o KKH, 100 Bukit Timah Road, Singapore 229899, Singapore. E-mail: secretariat_aaps@hotmail.com.
URL: http://www.aaps-asia.com/

History 25 Jun 1972. **Aims** Make and renew contacts among pediatric surgeons in the region; exchange ideas and information beneficial to children in need of surgical care. **Structure** Board. **Languages** English. **Finance** Members' dues. Meeting proceeds. **Activities** Events/meetings. **Events** *Congress* Ho Chi Minh City (Vietnam) 2021, *Congress* Ho Chi Minh City (Vietnam) 2020, *Congress* Dubai (United Arab Emirates) 2018, *Congress* Fukuoka (Japan) 2016, *Congress* Hanoi (Vietnam) 2014.
Members Individuals (about 300) in 17 countries:
Bahrain, Bangladesh, China, India, Indonesia, Japan, Korea Rep, Malaysia, Myanmar, Pakistan, Philippines, Singapore, Sri Lanka, Taiwan, Thailand, Türkiye, United Arab Emirates. [2021/XD4019/v/**D**]

♦ Asian Association of Personnel Management / see Asian Pacific Federation of Human Resource Management (#01611)

♦ Asian Association for Public Administration (AAPA) 01334

Exec Sec Room 423, Law School Bldg, Sungkyunkwan Univ, Sungkyunkwan-ro, Jongro-gu, Seoul 03063, Korea Rep. T. +8227401880. Fax +8227401880. E-mail: aapa@skku.edu.
URL: http://www.aapa.asia/

History Jan 2010, Tokyo (Japan). Formally established at final meeting of Asian Public Management Forum. **Aims** Expand and improve research and academic exchange on public administration and public policy in the Asian region. **Structure** Board of Directors. **Activities** Awards/prizes/competitions; events/meetings; networking/liaising. **Events** *Annual Conference* Shanghai (China) 2022, *Annual Conference* Moscow (Russia) 2021, *Annual Conference* 2020, *Annual Conference* Shanghai (China) 2020, *Annual Conference* Manila (Philippines) 2019. **Consultative Status** Consultative status granted from: *ECOSOC (#05331)* (Special). **NGO Relations** Memorandum of Understanding with (3): *African Association for Public Administration and Management (AAPAM, #00215)*; *International Public Policy Association (IPPA, #14669)*; *Network of Institutes and Schools of Public Administration in Central and Eastern Europe (NISPAcee, #17039)*. [2021/AA1771/v/**F**]

♦ Asian Association for Radiation Research (AARR) 01335

Pres c/o SSR, ACRO Nanavati Hosp, Swami Vivekanand Road, Vile Parle West, Mumbai, Maharashtra 400056, Mumbai MAHARASHTRA 400056, India.
Sec Bhabha Atomic Research Center, Trombay, Mumbai, Maharashtra 400085, Mumbai MAHARASHTRA 400085, India. T. +912225595043. E-mail: badrinarayan@yahoo.co.in.
URL: https://sites.google.com/site/aarrinfo/

History 2005, Hiroshima (Japan). **Aims** Promote basic radiation research and applications related to environment and human health. **Structure** Council; Secretariat in Mumbai (India). **Languages** English. **Finance** Members' dues. **Activities** Research and development; guidance/assistance/consulting; events/meetings; knowledge management/information dissemination. **Events** *Congress* Mumbai (India) 2021, *Congress* Beijing (China) 2013, *Congress* Seoul (Korea Rep) 2009, *Congress* Hiroshima (Japan) 2005. **Publications** *Biolocal Response, Monitoring and Protection from Radiation Exposure*.
Members Representatives from 10 countries:
China, India, Indonesia, Japan, Kazakhstan, Korea Rep, Philippines, Singapore, Thailand, Vietnam.
NGO Relations Member of: *International Association for Radiation Research (IARR, #12119)*. [2020.03.03/XJ1317/**D**]

♦ Asian Association on Remote Sensing (AARS) 01336

Sec Sokuryo Kaikan 5F, Room 505, 1-3-4 Koishikawa, Bunkyoku, Tokyo, 112-0002 Japan.
Gen Sec Research and Information Center, Takanawa Campus, Tokai Univ, 2-3-23 Takanawa, Minato-Ku, Tokyo, 108-8619 Japan.
URL: https://a-a-r-s.org/

History Statutes adopted: 2 Nov 1981, Beijing, and amended: 24 Oct 1986, Seoul (Korea Rep); 28 Nov 1988, Bangkok (Thailand); 19 Nov 1990, Guangzhou (China); 4 Nov 1991, Singapore (Singapore). **Aims** Promote remote sensing through exchange of information, mutual cooperation, international understanding and goodwill amongst members. **Structure** General Conference (annual); Council. **Languages** English. **Staff** 1.00 FTE, voluntary. **Finance** Members' dues. Budget (annual) US$ 5,850. **Activities** Events/meetings; training/education. **Events** *Asian Conference on Remote Sensing (ACRS)* Taipei (Taiwan) 2023, *Asian Conference on Remote Sensing (ACRS)* Ulaanbaatar (Mongolia) 2022, *Asian Conference on Remote Sensing (ACRS)* Can Tho (Vietnam) 2021, *Conference* Deqing (China) 2020, *Conference* Daejeon (Korea Rep) 2019. **Publications** *Application of Remote Sensing in Asia and Oceania* (1991).
Members Ordinary (only one membership for each country) in 20 countries and territories:
Australia, Bangladesh, Bhutan, China, Hong Kong, India, Indonesia, Japan, Jordan, Korea Rep, Malaysia, Mongolia, Myanmar, Nepal, Philippines, Singapore, Sri Lanka, Taiwan, Thailand, Vietnam.
Associate (9) in 8 countries:
Canada, France, Germany, Japan, Netherlands, Switzerland, UK, USA.
Included in the above, 1 organization listed in this Yearbook:
European Space Agency (ESA, #08798).
Sustaining (11) in 7 countries and territories:
Australia, Canada, China, India, Japan, Korea Rep, UK.
NGO Relations Member of: *International Society for Photogrammetry and Remote Sensing (ISPRS, #15362)*. [2023/XD2452/**D**]

♦ Asian Association of Scholarly Publishers (inactive)

♦ Asian Association of Schools of Pharmacy (AASP) 01337

Pres Kyoto Pharmaceutical Univ, Misasagi, Yamashina-ku, Kyoto, 607-8414 Japan. E-mail: aasp.sec@outlook.com.
URL: https://www.aaspnet.org/

History Apr 2001. **Aims** Promote cooperative advancement of pharmacy education and research amongst pharmacy schools in Asia. **Structure** Board of Directors. **Activities** Events/meetings; knowledge management/information dissemination; networking/liaising. **Events** *Conference* Kuala Lumpur (Malaysia) 2022, *Asian Association of Schools of Pharmacy Conference* Gyeonggi (Korea Rep) 2019, *Asian Association of Schools of Pharmacy Conference* Mysore (India) 2017, *Asian Association of Schools of Pharmacy Conference* Taipei (Taiwan) 2015, *Pharmacy Deans Forum* Tokyo (Japan) 2014. **Publications** *Journal of the Asian Association of Schools of Pharmacy (JAASP)*.

Members Institutional members in 10 countries and territories:
Australia, Cambodia, Hong Kong, Indonesia, Korea Rep, Malaysia, Philippines, Singapore, Taiwan, Thailand.
[2022/AA0257/**D**]

♦ Asian Association of Social Psychology (AASP) 01338

Pres Elect Corner High Rd/Willeri Dr, Riverton, Perth WA 6148, Australia.
SG Fac of Psychology, Beijing Normal Univ, Beijing, China.
URL: http://www.asiansocialpsych.org/

History Founded 1995. **Aims** Promote the development of social psychological research and its application in Asia-Pacific; provide opportunities for students to pursue their education and careers in social psychology; provide a forum for social psychologists in Asia-Pacific, in order to promote research and education. **Structure** General Meeting (annual); Executive Committee; Publication and Research Committee; Education and Training Committee. Regions (4): East Asia; South East Asia; South Asia; Insular Pacific. **Languages** English. **Staff** None. **Finance** Members' dues. Donations. **Activities** Events/meetings; research/documentation; training/ education. **Events** *Biennial Conference* Seoul (Korea Rep) 2021, *Biennial Conference* Taipei (Taiwan) 2019, *Biennial Conference* Auckland (New Zealand) 2017, *Biennial Conference* Cebu City (Philippines) 2015, *Biennial Conference* Yogyakarta (Indonesia) 2013. **Publications** *Asian Journal of Social Psychology* (4 a year); *AASP Newsletter* (2 a year) – electronic. Conference proceedings.
Members Member; Student. Individuals in 26 countries and territories:
Australia, Austria, Bangladesh, Canada, China, Denmark, Germany, Hong Kong, India, Indonesia, Iran Islamic Rep, Iraq, Japan, Korea Rep, Malaysia, Nepal, New Zealand, Pakistan, Philippines, Singapore, Taiwan, Thailand, Türkiye, UK, USA, Vietnam.
[2021/XD6095/v/**D**]

♦ Asian Association of Societies for Plant Pathology (AASPP) 01339

Sec Plant Pathology – China Agri Univ, Yuanmingyuan Xilu, Haidian District, Beijing, China. T. +861062731629. Fax +861062813785.
Pres address not obtained.
URL: http://www.isppweb.org/aaspp/

History Aug 2000. **Events** *Conference* Chiang Mai (Thailand) 2014, *New frontiers in plant pathology for Asia and Oceania* Darwin, NT (Australia) 2011, *The role of plant pathology in rapidly globalizing economies of Asia* Yogyakarta (Indonesia) 2007, *Conference* Singapore (Singapore) 2005, *Conference* Beijing (China) 2000. **NGO Relations** Member of: *International Society for Plant Pathology (ISPP, #15371).* [2017/XJ1065/**D**]

♦ Asian Association for Sport Management (AASM) 01340

Secretariat Ctr for Research on Women & Sport, 2-1-1 Hongo, Bunkyo-ku, Tokyo, 113-8401 Japan. E-mail: aasmsecretariat@juntendo.ac.jp.
Permanent Office 250 Wen-Hua 1st Road, Kueishan, Taoyuan 33301, Taiwan.
URL: http://asiansportmanagement.com/

History Formally set up Sep 2002, Korea Rep. **Aims** Encourage and promote original research in both theoretical and applied aspects of sport management theory and practice. **Structure** Committee. **Events** *Conference* Taipei (Taiwan) 2022, *Conference* Bangkok (Thailand) 2021, *Conference* Tokyo (Japan) 2019, *Conference* Manila (Philippines) 2018, *Conference* Pyeongchang (Korea Rep) 2017. **Publications** *AASM News Letter*; *Asian Sport Management Review (ASMR).*
Members Full in 12 countries and territories:
China, Hong Kong, India, Japan, Korea Rep, Malaysia, Mongolia, Philippines, Singapore, Taiwan, Thailand, Vietnam.
NGO Relations Regional organization of: *World Association for Sport Management (WASM, #21194).*
[2021/XJ9556/**D**]

♦ Asian Association for the Study of Australia / see Association for the Study of Australasia in Asia (#02937)

♦ Asian Association for the Study of Diabetes (AASD) 01341

Office 2-2-4 Kojimachi, Chiyoda-ku, Tokyo, 102-0083 Japan. T. +81335141721. Fax +81335141725. E-mail: office@aa-sd.org.
Registered Office 5-25-18 Hongo, Bunkyo-ku, Tokyo, 113-0033 Japan.
URL: http://www.aa-sd.org/

History 2009, Osaka (Japan). Registered in accordance with Japanese law. **Aims** Facilitate discussion on various issues concerning diabetes mellitus; upgrade the level of diabetes research in the region. **Structure** Executive Board, including Chair, 2 Vice-Chairs and Editor-in-Chief. **Finance** Members' dues. **Events** *Annual Meeting* Seoul (Korea Rep) 2021, *Annual Meeting* Sendai (Japan) 2019, *Annual Meeting* Kuala Lumpur (Malaysia) 2018, *Annual Meeting* Nagoya (Japan) 2017, *Annual Meeting* Taipei (Taiwan) 2016. **Publications** *Journal of Diabetes Investigation* (6 a year).
Members Affiliated societies/organizations (20) in 17 countries and territories:
Cambodia, China, Hong Kong, India, Indonesia, Japan, Korea Rep, Macau, Malaysia, Mongolia, Myanmar, Philippines, Singapore, Sri Lanka, Taiwan, Thailand, Vietnam. [2018/XJ6695/**D**]

♦ Asian Association of Teachers of English as a Foreign Language (Asia TEFL) 01342

Gen Sec address not obtained.
URL: http://www.asiatefl.org/

History 6 Dec 2002, Seoul (Korea Rep). **Aims** Promote scholarship, disseminate information and facilitate cross-cultural understanding among persons concerned with the teaching and learning of English in Asia. **Structure** Council; Executive Director; Advisory Board. **Languages** English. **Finance** Donations. **Activities** Events/meetings. **Events** *International Conference* Delhi (India) 2021, *International Conference* Goyang (Korea Rep) 2020, *International Conference* Bangkok (Thailand) 2019, *International Conference* Macau (Macau) 2018, *International Conference* Yogyakarta (Indonesia) 2017. **Publications** *Asia TEFL Journal*. Books series.
Members Individual; Institutional/Corporate. Membership countries not specified. [2021/XM0124/**D**]

♦ Asian Association of Track and Field Statisticians (inactive)
♦ Asian Association of UTI and STD / see Asian Association of UTI and STI (#01343)

♦ Asian Association of UTI and STI (AAUS) 01343

Contact Dept of Urology, School of Medicine, Univ of Occupational and Environmental Health, 1-1 Iseigaoka, Yahatanishi-ku, Kitakyushu FUKUOKA, 807-8555 Japan. T. +81936917446. Fax +81936038724. E-mail: hamaryo@med.uoeh-u.ac.jp.
Contact Dept of Urology, School of Medicine, Catholic Univ of Korea, St Vincent's Hospital, 93 Jungbu-daero, Paldal-gu, Suwon GYEONGGI 442-723, Korea Rep. T. +821059107278. Fax +8210312530949.
URL: http://www.aaus.info/

History Founded 1 Jul 2003, Kitakyushu (Japan), as *Asian Association of UTI and STD (AAUS)*. Current name adopted 2010. **Aims** Clarify etiology and pathology, treatment and prevention of *urinary* tract infections (UTIs) and sexually transmitted infections (STIs); develop research of causative organisms and surveillance of drug susceptibility and attempt to publish these. **Structure** Organizing Committee, comprising President, Vice-President, Immediate Past President, 4 Secretaries, 2 Treasurers, International Advisory Team of 2 members and 14 additional members. **Languages** English. **Staff** Voluntary. **Finance** Individual funds as necessary. **Events** *Forum* Seoul (Korea Rep) 2017, *Forum* Yokohama (Japan) 2013, *Forum* Beijing (China) 2012, *Congress* Nagasaki (Japan) 2012, *Congress* Pattaya (Thailand) 2012.
Members Organizing Committee members in 13 countries and territories:
China, Germany, Hong Kong, Indonesia, Japan, Korea Rep, Pakistan, Russia, Singapore, Taiwan, Thailand, USA, Vietnam.
NGO Relations Member of: *International Society of Antimicrobial Chemotherapy (ISAC, #14925)*; *Urological Association of Asia (UAA, #20733).* [2022/XM2661/**D**]

♦ Asian Association of Veterinary Anatomists (Asian AVA) 01344

SG Faculty of Veterinary Medicine, Kita 18, Nishi 9, Kita-ku, Sapporo HOKKAIDO, 060-0818 Japan.
URL: http://www.jpn-ava.com/aava/

History 2006. Asian-regional branch of *World Association of Veterinary Anatomists (WAVA, #21202).* **Structure** Council; Executive Board. **Finance** Sources: members' dues. **Activities** Events/meetings. **Events** *Congress* Chittagong (Bangladesh) 2021, *Congress* Jeju (Korea Rep) 2019, *Congress* Kuching (Malaysia) 2017, *Congress* Bali (Indonesia) 2015, *Congress* Phuket (Thailand) 2012. [2022.02.15/XJ9326/**D**]

♦ Asian Association of Veterinary Schools (AAVS) 01345

Office Dept of Veterinary Medical Sciences, Graduate School of Agricultural and Life Sciences, Univ of Tokyo, 1-1- Yayoi, Bunkyo-ku, Tokyo, 113-8657 Japan. E-mail: anakaya@mail.ecc.u-tokyo.ac.jp.
URL: http://www.aavs.jpn.org/

History 2001. Registered office based in Japan. Bylaws approved Aug 2003; Revised Oct 2007, Sep 2013 and Dec 2015. **Aims** Advance and enhance education, research and public services in veterinary sciences. **Structure** Assembly; Executive Committee. **Finance** Members' dues. **Activities** Events/meetings; knowledge management/information dissemination. **Events** *Meeting on Veterinary Education in the Time of COVID-19* Tokyo (Japan) 2022, *Annual Assembly Meeting* Tokyo (Japan) 2021, *Meeting on Veterinary Education in the Time of COVID-19* Tokyo (Japan) 2021, *Meeting* Putrajaya (Malaysia) 2019, *Meeting* Tokyo (Japan) 2018.
Members Full; Associate. Full in 14 countries and territories:
Cambodia, Hong Kong, Indonesia, Japan, Korea Rep, Laos, Malaysia, Mongolia, Myanmar, Pakistan, Philippines, Taiwan, Thailand, Vietnam.
Associate in 3 countries:
Canada, Japan, USA.
Included in the above, 1 organization listed in this Yearbook: [2018/XJ5352/y/**D**]

♦ Asian Association of Women's Studies (AAWS) 01346

SG Ewha Women's Univ, 52, Ewhayeodae-gil, Seodaemun-gu, Seoul 03760, Korea Rep. T. +82232774241. Fax +82232772577. E-mail: aaws07@gmail.com.
URL: https://www.aaws07.org/

History Nov 2007. Promotional Committee constituted by feminist scholars from different Asian regions. **Aims** Establish an institutional basis for feminist education and research on Asia, linking associations of women's studies, research institutions, resource centers, as well as individual scholars and practitioners in the region, so as to address issues of common interest in Asia. **Structure** Council; Executive Committee; Secretariat. **Activities** Events/meetings; research/documentation. **Events** *Locating/Centering Women and Gender (Post) Pandemic in The Era of Advanced-Technology* 2023, *Psychology From the East, Psychology from the West International Conference* Depok (Indonesia) 2022, *Facing new challenges for Feminisms in Asia* Seoul (Korea Rep) 2019, *Congress* Hanoi (Vietnam) 2016, *Congress* Quezon City (Philippines) 2013.
Members Institutional (24); Individual (over 670). Members in 44 countries and territories:
Afghanistan, Aruba, Australia, Bangladesh, Bhutan, Brunei Darussalam, Cambodia, Cameroon, Canada, China, Croatia, Ethiopia, France, Germany, Ghana, Hong Kong, India, Indonesia, Iran Islamic Rep, Iraq, Japan, Jordan, Korea Rep, Laos, Malawi, Malaysia, Mongolia, Myanmar, Nepal, Pakistan, Philippines, Romania, Singapore, Sri Lanka, Sweden, Taiwan, Tanzania UR, Thailand, Türkiye, UK, USA, Vietnam, Yemen, Zimbabwe. [2019/AA1196/**D**]

♦ Asian Association for World Historians (AAWH) 01347

Exec Sec c/o Inst of World and Global History, Ewha Woman's Univ, no 622, Ewha-Samsung Education and Culture Bld, 26 Ewhayeodai-gil, Seodaemun-gu, Seoul 120-750, Korea Rep. T. +82232776926. E-mail: aawh.korea@gmail.com.
URL: http://www.theaawh.org/

History Statutes adopted 4 May 2008; ratified 29 May 2009. **Aims** Advance research, teaching, and public discussion on world historical studies in or for the Asian region. **Structure** General Assembly. Board of Directors. Secretariat, headed by Executive Secretary. **Finance** Members' dues. Grants. **Events** *Congress / Triennial Conference* Singapore (Singapore) 2015, *Congress / Triennial Conference* Seoul (Korea Rep) 2012, *Congress / Triennial Conference* Osaka (Japan) 2009. **Publications** *Asian Review of World Histories*. **Members** Individual; Institutional. Membership countries not specified. **NGO Relations** Member of: *Network of Global and World History Organizations (NOGWHISTO, #17033).* [2014/XJ5064/**D**]

♦ Asian Athletic Association of the IAAF / see Asian Athletics Association (#01348)

♦ Asian Athletics Association (AAA) 01348

SG Room 134 TUSC, Chiangrak Rd, Rangsit, Khlong Luang, Pathum Thani, 12121, Thailand. E-mail: sec@asianathleticsassociation.org.
Pres PO Box 2626, Doha, Qatar. E-mail: president@asianathleticsassociation.org.
URL: http://athleticsasia.org/

History 21 Nov 1973, Manila (Philippines). Founded on ratification of constitution at first Asian Athletic Championships, an *'Asian Athletic Association of the IAAF'* having existed since 1958, Tokyo (Japan), having been set up within the framework of *World Athletics (#21209)* at the 3rd Asian Games; and a constitutional committee having been set up 14 Dec 1970, Bangkok (Thailand). Original title: *Asian Amateur Athletic Association (AAAA) – Association d'athlétisme amateur d'Asie*. Current title adopted Aug 2002, Colombo (Sri Lanka). Constitution approved, 29-31 Aug 1974, Rome (Italy), at IAAF Congress. Has taken over activities of *Asian Track and Field Coaches Association (ATFCA, inactive).* **Aims** Establish friendly and loyal cooperation among national governing bodies of athletics for promotion and development of amateur athletics; strive to ensure there is no hindrance to participation of any country or individual in international athletic competitions in Asia on social, religious or political grounds; frame rules governing Asian championships and establishment and recognition of Asian records; crystallize the Asian stand and viewpoint in solution of disputes and other difficulties; represent Asia and work to form an Asian team to participate in international events. **Structure** Congress (every 2 years); Council. **Languages** English. **Activities** Sporting activities. **Events** *Congress* 2021, *Congress* Doha (Qatar) 2019, *Congress* Ranchi (India) 2017, *Meeting* Doha (Qatar) 2016, *Meeting* Manila (Philippines) 2015. **Publications** *Asian Track and Field News* (4 a year). Handbook.
Members National associations in 45 countries and territories:
Afghanistan, Azerbaijan, Bahrain, Bangladesh, Bhutan, Brunei Darussalam, Cambodia, China, Hong Kong, India, Indonesia, Iran Islamic Rep, Iraq, Japan, Jordan, Kazakhstan, Korea DPR, Korea Rep, Kuwait, Kyrgyzstan, Laos, Lebanon, Macau, Malaysia, Maldives, Mongolia, Myanmar, Nepal, Oman, Pakistan, Palestine, Philippines, Qatar, Saudi Arabia, Singapore, Sri Lanka, Syrian AR, Taiwan, Tajikistan, Thailand, Turkmenistan, United Arab Emirates, Uzbekistan, Vietnam, Yemen.
NGO Relations Continental association of IAAF, representing Asia in IAAF Council. [2021/XD3939/**D**]

♦ Asian-Australasian Association of Animal Production Societies (AAAP) 01349

Secretariat Room 708 Sammo Sporex 23, Sillim-ro 59-gil, Gwanak-gu, Seoul 08776, Korea Rep.
Pres address not obtained.
URL: http://www.ajas.info/

History Sep 1980, as *Asian-Australian Association of Animal Production Societies (AAAP)*. **Aims** Promote animal production in the Asian-Australasian region. **Structure** Officers – Past President, President, Vice Presidents (2), Secretary General – and 19 Council members. **Languages** English. **Staff** 2.00 FTE, paid. **Finance** Page charge; advertisement donations. **Activities** Awards/prizes/competitions; events/meetings. **Events** *Animal Science Congress* Seogwipo (Korea Rep) 2022, *Animal Science Congress* Cebu City (Philippines) 2020, *Animal Science Congress* Kuching (Malaysia) 2018, *Animal Science Congress* Fukuoka (Japan) 2016, *Animal Science Congress* Yogyakarta (Indonesia) 2014. **Publications** *Asian-Australasian Journal of Animal Science* (12 a year).
Members Full in 19 countries and territories:
Australia, Bangladesh, China, India, Indonesia, Iran Islamic Rep, Japan, Korea Rep, Malaysia, Mongolia, Nepal, New Zealand, Pakistan, Papua New Guinea, Philippines, Sri Lanka, Taiwan, Thailand, Vietnam.
IGO Relations *FAO (#09260).* **NGO Relations** Instrumental in setting up: *Asian Buffalo Association (ABA, #01367).* [2020.03.05/XD1589/**D**]

♦ Asian-Australasian Association for Composite Materials (unconfirmed)

♦ Asian-Australasian Federation of Interventional and Therapeutic Neuroradiology (AAFITN) 01350

SG Xuanwu Hosp, Capital Medical Univ, 100053 Beijing, China. E-mail: info@aafitn2014.com.
URL: http://www.aafitn2014.com/

History Founded 1994. **Aims** Promote the practice and share the knowledge of interventional and therapeutic neuroradiology in the Asian-Australasian region through meetings. **Events** *Meeting* Seoul (Korea Rep) 2020, *Meeting* Kota Kinabalu (Malaysia) 2018, *Meeting* Bali (Indonesia) 2016, *Meeting* Danang (Vietnam) 2014, *Meeting / Forum* Nagoya (Japan) 2012. [2014/XJ0027/**D**]

♦ **Asian Australasian Federation of Pain Societies (AAFPS)** **01351**
Contact c/o Kenes Asia, Level 5, PICO Creative Ctr, Level 2, 20 Kallang Avenue, Singapore 339411, Singapore. T. +6562920723. Fax +6562924721.
URL: http://aafps.org/
History Founded Dec 2011, as an umbrella organization. **Aims** Establish a pan-Asian network for pain management education that reaches beyond anesthesiology. **Structure** Executive Board. **Languages** English. **Staff** 1.00 FTE, paid. **Finance** Congress proceeds. **Events** *Relieving pain beyond borders* Taipei (Taiwan) 2014, *Congress* Taiwan 2013. **Members** National and regional organizations. Membership countries not specified. [2014.09.24/XJ6227/**D**]

♦ Asian and Australasian Society of Labour Economics (unconfirmed)

♦ **Asian-Australasian Society of Neurological Surgeons (AASNS)** **01352**
Association de neurologie d'Asie et d'Océanie
Manager Kenes Asia / PICO Creative Ctr, 20 Kallang Avenue, Singapore 339411, Singapore. T. +6563896642. Fax +6562924721. E-mail: ongj@kenes.com.
SG address not obtained. E-mail: secretary.aasns@gmail.com.
URL: http://www.aasns.org/
History 1964, Canberra (Australia). **Aims** Facilitate the personal association of neurological surgeons in Asia and Australasia; develop training programmes for neurological surgeons; provide neurosurgical services in developing countries within the scope of this organization; foster and aid research in neurological surgery and allied sciences. **Structure** Congress (every 4 years); Management Committee; Congress Committee; Board. **Languages** English. **Staff** Voluntary. **Finance** Donations, grants. **Events** *Asian Australasian Congress of Neurological Surgeons* Jerusalem (Israel) 2022, *Quadrennial Congress* Mumbai (India) 2019, *Quadrennial Congress* Jeju (Korea Rep) 2015, *Quadrennial Congress* Taipei (Taiwan) 2011, *Quadrennial Congress* Nagoya (Japan) 2007. **Publications** Congress proceedings – in national journals.
Members National neurological societies (18) in 16 countries and territories:
Australia, Bangladesh, China, Hong Kong, India, Indonesia, Japan, Korea Rep, Malaysia, New Zealand, Pakistan, Philippines, Singapore, Sri Lanka, Taiwan, Thailand. [2019/XC0070/**D**]

♦ **Asian-Australasian Society for Pediatric Neurosurgery (AASPN)** . . . **01353**
Central Office Manager c/o The Plan Co, 3F – JUNG E and C Bldg, 31-5 Seocho-daero 58-gil, Seocho-gu, Seoul 06632, Korea Rep. T. +8225382042 – +8225382043. Fax +8225381540. E-mail: info@aaspn.org.
URL: http://www.aaspn.org/
History 2013. **Aims** Advance pediatric neurosurgery in Asia and Australasia. **Structure** Executive Officers; Chairs. **Languages** English. **Staff** 1.00 FTE, paid. **Activities** Events/meetings; networking/liaising; research and development; training/education. **Events** *Congress* Yokohama (Japan) 2023, *Neurooncology Symposium* 2021, *Congress* Sendai (Japan) 2021, *Congress* Incheon (Korea Rep) 2019, *Congress* Mumbai (India) 2017.
Members Full in 5 countries and territories:
China, India, Japan, Korea Rep, Taiwan.
NGO Relations Also links with regional pediatric neurosurgical societies. [2021.06.30/XM4154/**D**]

♦ **Asian-Australasian Society for Stereotactic and Functional Neurosurgery (AASSFN)** **01354**
Sec Neurological Surgery, Nihon Univ School of Medicine, 30-1 Ohyaguchi Kamimachi, Itabashi-ku, Tokyo, 173- 8610 Japan. E-mail: nusmyama@med.nihon-u.ac.jp.
URL: http://www.aassfn.com/
History as *Asian Society for Stereotactic Functional and Computer Assisted Neurosurgery (ASSFCN)*. Regional chapter of *World Society for Stereotactic and Functional Neurosurgery (WSSFN, #21812)*. **Structure** Loosely formed organization without formal constitution. Board, comprising, Honorary President, President, Secretary and 4 members. **Events** *Congress* Osaka (Japan) 2023, *Congress* Gyeongju (Korea Rep) 2020, *Congress* Taichung (Taiwan) 2018, *Congress* Cairns, QLD (Australia) 2016, *Congress* Shanghai (China) 2014. **Publications** Meeting proceedings published in Stereotactic and Functional Neurosurgery, the official journal of WSSFN. **Members** Individuals (about 300) in Asian countries. Membership countries not specified. [2013/XD5576/v/**D**]

♦ Asian-Australian Association of Animal Production Societies / see Asian-Australasian Association of Animal Production Societies (#01349)
♦ Asian-Australian Association for the Study of Australasia / see Association for the Study of Australasia in Asia (#02937)
♦ **Asian AVA** Asian Association of Veterinary Anatomists (#01344)
♦ Asian Badminton Confederation / see Badminton Asia (#03056)
♦ Asian Band Directors' Association / see Asia and Pacific Band Directors' Association (#01856)

♦ **Asian Bankers Association (ABA)** **01355**
Sec-Treas 7F-2 No 760, Section 4, Bade Road, Songshan District, Taipei 10567, Taiwan. T. +886227601139. Fax +886227607569. E-mail: aba@aba.org.tw.
URL: http://www.aba.org.tw/
History 29 Oct 1981. Founded under the auspice of *Confederation of Asia-Pacific Chambers of Commerce and Industry (CACCI, #04512)*, a United Nations recognized non-governmental organization with consultative status. **Aims** Provide a forum for advancing the cause of the banking and finance industry in the region and promoting regional economic cooperation. **Structure** Board of Directors; Advisory Council; Secretariat. **Languages** English. **Finance** Sources: donations; meeting proceeds; members' dues. **Activities** Events/meetings; knowledge management/information dissemination; networking/liaising; publishing activities; training/education. **Events** *Annual General Meeting and Conference* 2022, *Annual General Meeting and Conference* Negombo (Sri Lanka) 2020, *Annual General Meeting and Conference* Makati (Philippines) 2019, *Annual General Meeting and Conference* Maldives 2018, *Annual General Meeting and Conference* Mumbai (India) 2017. **Publications** *ABA Newsletter* (12 a year); *Journal of Banking and Finance* (2 a year). **Members** Regular; Special; Associate; Honorary. Membership countries not specified. [2023.02.14/XD2242/y/**E**]

♦ Asian Baptist Federation / see Asia Pacific Baptist Federation (#01857)
♦ Asian Baptist Fellowship / see Asia Pacific Baptist Federation (#01857)

♦ **Asian Baptist Women's Union (ABWU)** **01356**
Pres 135 Middle Road, 02-12 Bylands Bdlg, Singapore 188975, Singapore. E-mail: vernette@asiabwu.org – info@asiabwu.org.
Sec address not obtained.
URL: https://www.asiabwu.org/
History 1958, India. within *Baptist World Alliance (BWA, #03176)*. **Aims** See women in Asia empowered for leadership; confidently engage in traditional and creative ministries; bring the Gospel to the lost. **Activities** Awareness raising; capacity building; events/meetings; networking/liaising; religious activities; training/education. Active in all member countries. **Events** *President Summit* Seoul (Korea Rep) 2019, *General Assembly* George Town (Malaysia) 2018, *General Assembly* Seoul (Korea Rep) 2013, *Assembly* Okinawa (Japan) 2004, *Assembly* Seoul (Korea Rep) 1977. **Publications** *ABWU ECHOES* (2 a year).
Members Full in 17 countries and territories:
Bangladesh, Bhutan, Cambodia, India, Indonesia, Japan, Korea Rep, Malaysia, Myanmar, Nepal, Pakistan, Philippines, Singapore, Sri Lanka, Taiwan, Thailand, Vietnam. [2020.05.06/XD8138/**E**]

♦ Asian Baseball Federation / see Baseball Federation of Asia (#03181)
♦ Asian Basketball Confederation / see FIBA-Asia (#09746)
♦ Asian Battery Conference (meeting series)
♦ Asian Billiards Confederation (inactive)
♦ Asian Billiards and Snooker Federation / see Asian Confederation of Billiards Sports (#01396)

♦ **Asian Bioethics Association** **01357**
Sec c/o Center for Ethics of Science and Technology, Fac of Arts, Chulalongkorn Univ, 254 Phayathai Road, Bangkok, 10330, Thailand. E-mail: office@eubios.info – asianbioethics@yahoo.co.nz.
Contact c/o Eubios Ethics Inst, I-BOX Phasi Charoen, Bangkok, 10160, Thailand. T. +66941982464.
URL: http://www.eubios.info/asian_bioethics_assn/
History as *East Asian Association for Bioethics*. Present name adopted 5 Nov 1997, Kobe (Japan). **Aims** Promote scientific research in bioethics in Asia and the Pacific; network individuals and institutions interested in bioethics across the region. **Structure** Board of Directors. **Languages** English. **Staff** 2.00 FTE, voluntary. **Finance** Members' dues. Occasional grants. **Activities** Events/meetings; training/education. **Events** *Conference* Kuala Lumpur (Malaysia) 2022, *Conference* Kuala Lumpur (Malaysia) 2021, *Conference* Dhaka (Bangladesh) 2019, *Conference* Kaohsiung (Taiwan) / Pingtung City (Taiwan) 2018, *Joint Conference* Gangneung (Korea Rep) 2017. **Publications** *Eubios Journal of Asian and International Bioethics*.
Members Individuals in 57 countries and territories:
Australia, Bangladesh, Belgium, Brazil, Cambodia, Canada, Chile, China, Colombia, Croatia, Egypt, Ethiopia, Fiji, France, Germany, Greece, Hong Kong, Hungary, India, Indonesia, Iran Islamic Rep, Israel, Italy, Jamaica, Japan, Jordan, Korea Rep, Laos, Lebanon, Malaysia, Mexico, Micronesia FS, Mozambique, Nepal, Netherlands, New Zealand, Pakistan, Philippines, Poland, Portugal, Romania, Russia, Samoa, Saudi Arabia, Singapore, Slovakia, South Africa, Spain, Sri Lanka, Switzerland, Taiwan, Thailand, Türkiye, UK, United Arab Emirates, USA, Vietnam. [2018.06.01/XD7181/v/**D**]

♦ Asian Biological Inorganic Chemistry Conference (meeting series)
♦ Asian Biomaterials Confederation (unconfirmed)

♦ **Asian Biophysics Association (ABA)** **01358**
Chief of Secretariat Convener – 7th ABA, Dept of NMR and MRI Facility, All India Inst of Medical Sciences, Delhi 110 029, DELHI 110 029, India. T. +911126593253 – +911126588533. Fax +911126862663 – +911126588641. E-mail: aba72011@gmail.com.
URL: http://www.aba-bp.com/
History Founded as *East Asian Biophysics Symposium (EABS)*. Current name adopted 14 Nov 2006. **Aims** Promote biophysics in the Asia and Pacific region. **Structure** Steering Committee comprising 7 members. International Advisory Board of 14 members. **Languages** English. **Staff** None. **Finance** Budget (annual): euro 1,000. **Activities** Symposium (held every 2 years) organized by a member society. **Events** *Symposium* Jeju (Korea Rep) 2013, *Symposium* Delhi (India) 2011, *Symposium* Hong Kong (Hong Kong) 2009, *East Asian symposium on biophysics / Symposium* Okinawa (Japan) 2006, *East Asian symposium on biophysics / Symposium* Taipei (Taiwan) 2003.
Members in 7 countries and territories:
Australia, China, Hong Kong, India, Japan, Korea Rep, Taiwan.
NGO Relations Member of: *International Union for Pure and Applied Biophysics (IUPAB, #15808)*. [2010.11.12/XM3717/**D**]

♦ **Asian Bird Fair Network (ABF)** **01359**
Contact 2F No 24, ZhongYang 6th Street, Xindien District, New Taipei City, Taiwan. E-mail: abirdfair@gmail.com.
URL: http://asianbirdfair.org/
History Founded 2010, Malaysia. **Aims** Promote protection of birds and their habitats; encourage birdwatching and other ecotourism activities. **Structure** Executive Committee. **Activities** Events/meetings. **Events** *Forum* Kuching (Malaysia) 2019, *Forum* Chiayi City (Taiwan) 2018, *Forum* Ulsan (Korea Rep) 2017, *Forum* Beijing (China) 2016, *Forum* Singapore (Singapore) 2015.
Members Founding organizations in 6 countries and territories:
China, Malaysia, Philippines, Singapore, Taiwan, Thailand. [2018/XM7509/**F**]

♦ **Asian Blind Union** **01360**
Union asiatique des aveugles
SG c/o Youth Association of the Blind, PO Box 113 5487, Beirut, Lebanon. T. +9611364259. Fax +9611368221. E-mail: nfbsec.g@gmail.com – abusecretariat@yablb.org.
URL: http://wbuap.org/
History Regional Union of the *World Blind Union (WBU, #21234)*. Took over activities of *Regional Committee for the Middle East of the World Blind Union (inactive)*. **Events** *Quadrennial General Assembly* Delhi (India) 2012, *General Assembly* Kuala Lumpur (Malaysia) 1996, *General assembly / Quadrennial General Assembly* Colombo (Sri Lanka) 1995, *Work for the blind* Karachi (Pakistan) 1994, *Quadrennial General Assembly* Karachi (Pakistan) 1989. **Members** Associations of the blind. Membership countries not specified. [2016/XD6500/**D**]

♦ Asian Bodybuilding and Fitness Federation / see Asian Bodybuilding and Physique Sports Federation (#01361)

♦ **Asian Bodybuilding and Physique Sports Federation (ABBF)** **01361**
SG 97/287 Soi Phokaew, Nawamin Road, Klongkum, Bangkok, 10240, Thailand. T. +6681915003. E-mail: abbf.secretary@yahoo.com.
URL: http://www.abbf.asia/
History 1959, as *Asian Bodybuilding and Fitness Federation (ABBF)*. Subsequently changed title to *Asian Federation of Bodybuilding and Fitness (AFBF)*. **Aims** Promote, control and develop bodybuilding, fitness and physical culture in the continent of Asia; promote interest in and a dedication to better fitness and health through physical culture, proper nutrition and weight training; develop and intensify friendship and cooperation among national associations and bodybuilders from all countries; conduct drug testing at all regional and continental levels. **Structure** Congress; Executive. Standing Committees (7): Judges; Women's; Technical; Legal; Rules; Medical; Patrons and Honorary Life Members. Other committees as necessary. Secretariat. **Languages** English. **Staff** 4.00 FTE, voluntary. **Finance** Members' dues: 1st year, US$300; subsequent annual due for remaining years, US$250. Fees for Championships. **Activities** Awards/prizes/competitions; certification/accreditation; networking/liaising; standards/guidelines. **Events** *Annual Congress* Beijing (China) 2016, *Annual Congress* Kitakyushu (Japan) 2015. **Publications** *ABBF News* (periodic). Bulletin (periodic); Calandar of Events (periodic); handbook (periodic).
Members National amateur federations governing bodybuilding for men and women, one federation per country, in 36 countries and territories:
Bahrain, Bangladesh, Brunei Darussalam, Cambodia, China, Hong Kong, India, Indonesia, Iran Islamic Rep, Iraq, Japan, Jordan, Kazakhstan, Korea Rep, Kuwait, Kyrgyzstan, Lebanon, Macau, Malaysia, Maldives, Mongolia, Myanmar, Nepal, Pakistan, Palestine, Philippines, Qatar, Saudi Arabia, Singapore, Sri Lanka, Syrian AR, Taiwan, Thailand, United Arab Emirates, Vietnam, Yemen.
NGO Relations Collaborates with: *International Federation of Sports Medicine (#13554)*; *International Game Council (no recent information)*; *International Olympic Committee (IOC, #14408)*; *Olympic Council of Asia (OCA, #17718)*; *South Pacific Bodybuilding Federation (SPBBF, #19883)*; *Global Association of International Sport Federations (GAISF, inactive)*; *World Bodybuilding and Physique Sports Federation (WBPF, #21237)*. Member of: *General Association of Asia Pacific Sports Federations (GAAPSF, #10106)*. [2018/XD8270/**D**]

♦ Asian Borderlands Research Network (internationally oriented national body)

♦ **Asian Bowling Federation (ABF)** **01362**
Honorary SG Hong Kong Tenpin Bowling Congress, Rm 2004, Olympic House, 1 Stadium Path, So Kon Po, Causeway Bay, Hong Kong. T. +85228936039. Fax +85228936290. E-mail: hktbc@netvigator.com.
URL: http://www.abf-online.org/
History Set up as Asian geographical zone of *World Tenpin Bowling Association (WTBA, inactive)*. Formerly known as *FIQ-WTBA Asian Zone*. Current name adopted in 2000. Currently a zone of *International Bowling Federation (IBF, #12384)*. **Aims** Promote and foster interest in *amateur* tenpin bowling tournaments and competitions in Asia. **Structure** General Assembly (every 2 years); Executive Committee. **Languages** English. **Staff** 1.50 FTE, paid. **Finance** Members' dues. Other sources: sanctioning fees; Asian Ranking fees. **Activities** Sporting events. **Events** *General Assembly* Hong Kong (Hong Kong) 2021, *General Assembly* Kuwait 2019, *Executive Committee Meeting* Hong Kong (Hong Kong) 2012, *General Assembly* Hong Kong (Hong Kong) 2012, *General Assembly* Abu Dhabi (United Arab Emirates) 2011.
Members National federations in 38 countries and territories:
Afghanistan, Australia, Bahrain, Brunei Darussalam, China, Egypt, Guam, Hong Kong, India, Indonesia, Iran Islamic Rep, Iraq, Japan, Jordan, Kazakhstan, Korea DPR, Korea Rep, Kuwait, Macau, Malaysia, Mongolia, Nepal, New Zealand, Northern Mariana Is, Oman, Pakistan, Philippines, Qatar, Saudi Arabia, Singapore, Syrian AR, Taiwan, Thailand, Tunisia, Turkmenistan, United Arab Emirates, Uzbekistan, Vietnam. [2016.12.30/XM3248/**D**]

♦ Asian Boxing Confederation (ASBC) **01363**
Pres Diplomat Business Center, Kunayev str 29/1, Office 1702 – 17th Floor, Nur-Sultan, Kazakhstan, 010000. T. +77172280482. Fax +77172280482. E-mail: info@asiaboxing.org.
URL: http://www.boxingasia.org/
History Founded 1962, Jakarta (Indonesia), as *Federation of Asian Amateur Boxing (FAAB)*. A regional confederation of *International Boxing Association (IBA, #12385)*. **Structure** Executive Committee; Commissions (5): Coaches; Competition; Refereeing and judging; Medical; Women's. **Activities** Sporting activities.
Members National organizations in 41 countries and territories:
Afghanistan, Bangladesh, Bhutan, Brunei Darussalam, Cambodia, China, Hong Kong, India, Indonesia, Iran Islamic Rep, Iraq, Israel, Japan, Jordan, Kazakhstan, Korea Rep, Kuwait, Kyrgyzstan, Laos, Lebanon, Macau, Malaysia, Mongolia, Myanmar, Nepal, Oman, Pakistan, Palestine, Philippines, Qatar, Saudi Arabia, Singapore, Sri Lanka, Syrian AR, Taiwan, Tajikistan, Thailand, Turkmenistan, Uzbekistan, Vietnam, Yemen. [2016/XD9335/**D**]

♦ Asian Boxing Council **01364**
Contact 29 Pahonyothin Road SOI 3, Samsennai Phayathai, Bangkok, 10400, Thailand. T. +6622723008. Fax +6622723007. E-mail: info@asianboxingcouncil.com.
URL: http://www.asianboxingcouncil.com/
History as a continental boxing federation of *World Boxing Council (WBC, #21242)*. **Structure** Executive, comprising: President; 3 Vice-Presidents; Secretary; Treasurer; 4 members.
Members Boxing federations of 16 countries:
Bahrain, Bangladesh, Bhutan, India, Iraq, Kuwait, Malaysia, Maldives, Myanmar, Nepal, Pakistan, Qatar, Sri Lanka, Taiwan, Thailand, United Arab Emirates. [2015/XE6019/**E**]

♦ Asian Breast Cancer Society (no recent information)

♦ Asian Breast Diseases Association (ABDA) **01365**
Pres Dept of Pathology, Singapore General Hospital, Outram Rd, Singapore 169608, Singapore. E-mail: abda.secretariat@gmail.com.
History 2002. Registration: Hong Kong. **Aims** Improve detection, diagnosis and management of patients with diseases of the breast. **Activities** Organizes teaching courses. **Events** *Scientific Meeting* Jakarta (Indonesia) 2021, *Annual Scientific Meeting* Hong Kong (Hong Kong) 2020, *Scientific Meeting* Jakarta (Indonesia) 2020, *Annual Scientific Meeting* Yogyakarta (Indonesia) 2018, *Annual Scientific Meeting* Singapore (Singapore) 2017. **NGO Relations** Scientific Center of: *Senologic International Society (SIS, #19230)*. [2020/XM3726/**D**]

♦ Asian Brotherhood of Clerical Workers (ABCW) **01366**
Pres Mezzanine Floor Haji Abdul Rehman Manzil, Soldier Bazar No 1, Karachi, Pakistan. T. +922132253715. Fax +922132254756. E-mail: presidentabcw@yahoo.com.
History 27 Aug 1992, Bangkok (Thailand), at constitutive conference, by *Brotherhood of Asian Trade Unionists (BATU, inactive)*, as a regional federation of *World Organization of Workers (WOW, #21697)*. Statutes amended 21-24 May 1995, Bangkok. Has also been referred to as: *Asian Trade Federation of Clerical Workers*; *BROTHERHOOD*; *Asian Brotherhood of White Collar Workers (ABWCW)*. **Aims** Unite white collar workers in the region, including banking financing and commercial sectors, insurance, trade and other clerical professions. **Structure** Governing Board (meets annually), composed of: President; Secretary-General; one member from each member country. Other Officers: Vice-President for NICs; Vice-President for ASEAN; Vice-President for South Asia; Treasurer. Committees: Accreditation; Resolutions and Statutes; Policy and Programme; Election. **Finance** Members' dues: US$ 200 for each 1,000 members. Grants from: BATU; Christelijk Nationaal Vakverbond (the Netherlands); WFC. Budget (annual): US$ 46,800. **Activities** Congresses; conferences; seminars; mission visits to affiliates; research; training programmes. **Events** *Congress* Bangkok (Thailand) 2007, *Congress* Bangkok (Thailand) 1995. **Publications** *Flexibilization and its Impact to Workers in Asia*.
Members Full in 11 countries and territories:
Bangladesh, Hong Kong, India, Indonesia, Malaysia, Pakistan, Philippines, Singapore, Sri Lanka, Taiwan, Thailand. [2012/XD5031/**D**]

♦ Asian Brotherhood of White Collar Workers / see Asian Brotherhood of Clerical Workers (#01366)

♦ Asian Buffalo Association (ABA) **01367**
Address not obtained.
URL: http://www.asianbuffaloassociation.org/
History 23 Nov 1992, Bangkok (Thailand), at 6th Animal Science Congress of *Asian-Australasian Association of Animal Production Societies (AAAP, #01349)*. **Aims** Foster research and development on buffaloes in the Asian region. **Structure** Assembly; Executive Committee. **Languages** English. **Staff** Voluntary. **Finance** Members' dues. **Activities** Research and development; events/meetings. **Events** *Sustainable production in the global economic world* Istanbul (Turkey) 2015, *Congress* Phuket (Thailand) 2013, *Congress* Lahore (Pakistan) 2009, *Congress* Nanning (China) 2006, *Congress* Delhi (India) 2003.
Members Regular; Sustaining; Individual, in 15 countries and territories:
Bangladesh, China, India, Indonesia, Iran Islamic Rep, Japan, Laos, Malaysia, Nepal, Pakistan, Philippines, Sri Lanka, Taiwan, Thailand, Vietnam. [2015.01.13/XD4020/**D**]

♦ Asian Building Maintenance Association (ABMA) **01368**
Pres Japan Building Maintenance Assoc, 5-12-5 Nishi-Nippori, Arakawa-ku, Tokyo, 116-0013 Japan. T. +81338057560. Fax +81338057581. E-mail: kokusai@j-bma.or.jp.
History Founded following the 16th Congress of *World Federation of Building Service Contractors (WFBSC, #21416)* 16-19 Oct 2006, Seoul (Korea Rep). **Aims** Raise skills and spread knowledge on building maintenance; secure the global recognition on the value and the role of building maintenance skills. **Events** *Congress* Seoul (Korea Rep) 2017, *Congress* Sapporo (Japan) 2015, *Congress* Shanghai (China) 2013, *Congress* Taipei (Taiwan) 2011, *Congress* Seoul (Korea Rep) 2009.
Members National Associations in 8 countries and territories:
China, Indonesia, Japan, Korea Rep, Mongolia, Singapore, Taiwan, Vietnam. [2015/XJ0122/**D**]

♦ Asian Bukido Federation (unconfirmed)

♦ Asian Bureau of Finance and Economic Research (ABFER) **01369**
Senior Manager c/o NUS Business School, BIZ 2 Storey 4, 04-05, 1 Business Link, Singapore 118592, Singapore. T. +6566013558. E-mail: info@abfer.org.
URL: http://abfer.org/
History Registration: Singapore. **Aims** Create a virtual and independent network of high-quality academics. **Structure** Council; Executive Committee. Secretariat. **Events** *Annual Conference* Singapore (Singapore) 2022, *Asian Monetary Policy Forum* Singapore (Singapore) 2022, *Annual Conference* Singapore (Singapore) 2021, *Asian Monetary Policy Forum* Singapore (Singapore) 2021, *Specialty Conference* Singapore (Singapore) 2020. **Publications** *Research Digest*. Working Papers. **NGO Relations** Cooperates with (1): *Productivity Research Network (PRN)*. [2022/XJ9641/**D**]

♦ Asian Business Aviation Association (AsBAA) **01370**
CEO Suite 405, 4/F, Lee Garden 3, 1 Sunning Road, Causeway Bay, Hong Kong. E-mail: info@asbaa.org.
URL: https://asbaa.org/
Aims Provide a platform for communication and action relating to key issues such as: airport access, regulation and policy, safety, professional development and training, public awareness and the industry's contribution to the economy. **Structure** Board of Governors; Board of Directors; Executive Management. Chapter Heads. **Activities** Advocacy/lobbying/activism; events/meetings; training/education. **Events** *South East Asia Operator Committee Meeting* Singapore (Singapore) 2013. **NGO Relations** Member of (1): *International Business Aviation Council (IBAC, #12418)*. [2021/AA1952/**D**]

♦ Asian Canoe Confederation (internationally oriented national body)
♦ Asian Carom Billiard Federation / see Asian Carombole Sports Confederation (#01371)

♦ Asian Carombole Sports Confederation (ACSC) **01371**
Pres Room 115, 424 Olympic-ro, Songpa-gu, Seoul 05540, Korea Rep. T. +822220346746. Fax +82222034652. E-mail: hyunhyun2709@hanmail.net.
History 1999. Also referred to as *Asian Carom Billiard Federation*. **Members** Founding members in 5 countries. Membership countries not specified. [2019/XJ3822/**D**]

♦ Asian Cartilage Repair Society (unconfirmed)

♦ Asian Cellular Therapy Organization (ACTO) **01372**
Chairperson B101, 2-11-4 Kami-Osaki, Shinagawa-ku, Tokyo, 141-0021 Japan.
URL: http://asianct.org/
Aims Promote scientific research so as to deliver innovative cellular therapies to *patients*. **Structure** Committee. **Finance** Members' dues. **Activities** Events/meetings. **Events** *Annual Meeting* Chiang Mai (Thailand) 2018, *Annual Meeting* Gwangju (Korea Rep) 2015, *Annual Meeting / Meeting* Osaka (Japan) 2014. [2020.02.12/XJ9435/**D**]

♦ Asian Center for Population and Community Development (internationally oriented national body)
♦ Asian Center for the Progress of Peoples (internationally oriented national body)
♦ Asian Center for Research on Remote Sensing / see Geoinformatics Center
♦ Asian Center for Women's Studies (internationally oriented national body)
♦ Asian Centre for Corporate Governance and Sustainability (internationally oriented national body)
♦ Asian Centre for Engineering Computations and Software (internationally oriented national body)
♦ Asian Centre for Human Rights (internationally oriented national body)

♦ Asian Centre of International Parasite Control (ACIPAC) **01373**
Coordinating Office Office of Int'l Cooperation, Fac of Tropical Medicine, Mahidol University, 420/6 Ratchawithi Rd, Ratchathewi, Bangkok, 10400, Thailand. T. +662354910019ext1327 – +662354910019ext1318. Fax +6623549141. E-mail: tmirunit@diamond.mahidol.ac.th – tmjwk@mahidol.ac.th.
URL: http://www.tm.mahidol.ac.th/
History Founded 23 Mar 2000, Bangkok (Thailand), under the Hashimoto Initiative based on the agreement of the Government of the Kingdom of Thailand and the Government of Japan, as a technical cooperation project with a region-wide cooperation scheme of *Japan International Cooperation Agency (JICA)* in collaboration with Mahidol University and the Ministry of Public Health, Thailand. **Aims** Provide the basis for strengthening of parasite control programmes in South-East Asia in terms of human resources and information system development. **Languages** English, Thai. **Staff** 5.00 FTE, paid. **Finance** Staff paid by Faculty of Tropical Medicine, Mahidol University, merging responsibility in Office of International Cooperation. No other funding. **Activities** Capacity building; training/education; networking/liaising; events/meetings. **Events** *Joint International Tropical Medicine Meeting* Bangkok (Thailand) 2014, *Joint international tropical medicine meeting* Nakhon Pathom (Thailand) 2002. **Publications** *Avian Influenza (Bird Flu)* (2008); *Additional Text Book for Primary School Students on Malaria* (2003); *Do You Know About Worms* (2003); *Malaria* (2003); *Soil-Transmitted Helminthiasis* (2003).
Members in 6 countries:
Cambodia, Japan, Laos, Myanmar, Thailand, Vietnam. [2014.06.01/XQ2862/**E**]

♦ Asian Centre for Organisation Research and Development (ACORD) . **01374**
Contact 166 – Pocket II, Lower Ground Floor, Jasola, Delhi 1100025, DELHI 1100025, India. T. +919810082948 – +919899548086.
History Founded 1981, Delhi (India). Registered in accordance with Indian Law. **Aims** Promote participatory change, social and socio-economic development, poverty alleviation and development of good governance through the partnership of civil society and government, public awareness and public education programmes; develop and make available information services, training aids and other cross-cultural exchange services than enhance sustainable change. **Structure** Governing Body; Chairman; Executive Director; Directors; Senior Consultants; Administrative Staff. **Languages** English, Hindi. **Staff** 10.00 FTE, paid. **Finance** Sources: projects; professional fees; contributions. **Activities** *'Development Sector'* – Development through training; Communication material for developmental work; Research; Human resource development; Training and public education; Organizational development; Participatory Change (Urban and Rural); Development of Citizens Participation in Urban Democracy; Bhagidari Project. Designs and conducts Future Search Workshop for state governments, cities and non-profit organizations to build up ownership to change the future and help discover common ground to achieve their improvement goals. **Events** *Séminaire sur les opérations forestières de demain* Bordeaux (France) 1999. **Publications** *Building a Citizens' Partnership in Democratic Governance: the Delhi 'Bhagidari' Process through Large-group Dynamics*; *Empowering Rural Women: Micro-enterprise Through Achievement Motivation*. Audio-visuals. **Members** Organizations; associations; public authorities in South Asian countries. Membership countries not specified. **Consultative Status** Consultative status granted from: *ECOSOC (#05331)* (Special). **IGO Relations** *UNDP (#20292)*; *UNICEF (#20332)*; *Commonwealth Youth Programme (CYP, #04372)*; *DANIDA*. **NGO Relations** *Aide et action France*; *All India Women's Conference (AIWC, #00737)*; *Asian Institute of Christian Communication (AICC, no recent information)*; *Caritas Internationalis (CI, #03580)*; *Catholic Relief Services (CRS, #03608)*; *ChildFund International (#03869)*; *Plan International (#18386)*. [2013.06.12/XE0971/**E**]

♦ Asian Centre for Soil Improvement and Geosynthetics (internationally oriented national body)
♦ Asian Centre, University of the Philippines (internationally oriented national body)

♦ Asian Chemical Editorial Society (ACES) **01375**
Address not obtained.
History 2005. **Activities** Publishing activities. **Publications** *ACES Newsletter* (annual); *Asian Journal of Organic Chemistry*; *Chemistry – An Asian Journal*; *ChemNanoMat* – journal.
Members Participating societies in 13 countries and territories:
Australia, China, Hong Kong, India, Indonesia, Japan, Korea Rep, Malaysia, New Zealand, Singapore, Taiwan, Thailand, Vietnam.
NGO Relations *Federation of Asian Chemical Societies (FACS, #09431)*. [2015/XM5850/**D**]

♦ Asian Chemical Fiber Industries Federation (no recent information)

♦ Asian Chess Federation (ACF) **01376**
SG PO Box 66511, Al Ain, Abu Dhabi, United Arab Emirates.
Street Address Building No 1 Alley, No 9 Mohammed Bin Zayed Alawal Street, Sheikh Shakhboot Road, Al-Markhaneeya, Al-Khabisi Area, Al Ain, United Arab Emirates.
URL: http://www.asianchess.com/
Structure Continental Assembly; Executive Board. **Languages** English. **Activities** Sporting activities.
Members National associations in 50 countries and territories:
Afghanistan, Australia, Bahrain, Bangladesh, Bhutan, Brunei Darussalam, Cambodia, China, Fiji, Guam, Hong Kong, India, Indonesia, Iran Islamic Rep, Iraq, Japan, Jordan, Kazakhstan, Korea Rep, Kuwait, Kyrgyzstan, Laos, Lebanon, Malaysia, Moldova, Mongolia, Myanmar, Nepal, New Zealand, North Macedonia, Pakistan, Palau, Palestine, Papua New Guinea, Philippines, Qatar, Saudi Arabia, Singapore, Solomon Is, Sri Lanka, Syrian AR, Taiwan, Tajikistan, Thailand, Timor-Leste, Turkmenistan, United Arab Emirates, Uzbekistan, Vietnam, Yemen. [2021/XM8102/**D**]

♦ Asian Children's Literature Society (unconfirmed)
♦ Asian Christian Art Association (internationally oriented national body)
♦ Asian Christian Association (no recent information)
♦ Asian Christian Higher Education Institute (internationally oriented national body)

♦ Asian Church Women's Conference (ACWC) **01377**
Conférence des femmes de l'Eglise d'Asie
Contact address not obtained. E-mail: acwc2011@gmail.com.
URL: http://acwc.blogspot.com/
History 12 Nov 1958, Hong Kong. **Aims** As an advocate of women's *rights* and *welfare*, work beyond the boundaries of culture and creed, colour and race so that a stronger regional network of women leaders and organizations may emerge and enable a greater role and responsibility in the family, society and the *church*. **Structure** General Meeting (every 4 years); General Committee (meets every 2 years); Executive Committee (meets annually). **Activities** Offers scholarships; organizes Prayer Partnership, where member countries support each other in prayer; supports member countries to develop Christian Education and Nurture Programme; carries out Signature Campaign, an act of solidarity with women involved in the mission and ministry of the Asian Church Women's Conference; promotes *Fellowship of the Least Coin (FLC, #09728)*; organizes conference (every 4 years). **Events** *Quadrennial general assembly / Conference* Bogor (Indonesia) 2010, *Quadrennial General Assembly* Kuala Lumpur (Malaysia) 2006, *Conference* Malaysia 2003, *Quadrennial general assembly / Conference* Korea Rep 2002, *Quadrennial general assembly / Conference* Thailand 1998. **Publications** *ACWC Newsletter* (4 a year).

Members in 19 countries and territories:
Australia, Bangladesh, Cambodia, Hong Kong, India, Indonesia, Japan, Korea Rep, Malaysia, Mongolia, Myanmar, Nepal, New Zealand, Pakistan, Philippines, Singapore, Sri Lanka, Taiwan, Thailand. [2013/XF2499/**F**]

♦ Asian Cities Against Drugs (unconfirmed)

♦ Asian Civil Engineering Coordinating Council (ACECC) 01378

SG c/o JSCE Headquarters, Yotsuya, 1-chome, Shinjuku-ku, Tokyo, 160-0004 Japan. T. +81333553452. Fax +81353792769.
URL: http://www.acecc-world.org/

History Founded 27 Sep 1999, Tokyo (Japan). **Aims** Promote the acquisition and transfer of civil engineering knowledge for advancing the design and construction practices that ultimately improve the quality of life of all citizens from member countries. **Structure** Executive Committee; Sub-Committees; Secretariat. **Activities** Events/meetings; awards/prizes/competitions. **Events** *CECAR Triennial Conference* Tokyo (Japan) 2019, *CECAR Triennial Conference* Honolulu, HI (USA) 2016, *Global Session* Jeju (Korea Rep) 2016, *International Round Table Meeting* Jeju (Korea Rep) 2016, *Meeting* Jeju (Korea Rep) 2016. **Publications** *ACECC Outlook* (4 a year) – newsletter.
Members National organizations in 12 countries:
Australia, Bangladesh, China, India, Indonesia, Japan, Korea Rep, Mongolia, Pakistan, Philippines, USA, Vietnam. [2015/XM0010/**D**]

♦ Asian Clean Fuels Association (ACFA) 01379

Exec Dir 17 – 17 Republic Plaza II, 9 Raffles Place, Singapore 048619, Singapore. T. +6568238026. E-mail: info@acfa.org.sg.
URL: http://www.acfa.org.sg/

History Founded Aug 2000, Singapore. **Aims** Working closely with fuel policymakers, regulators and stakeholders in the fuel industry, promote and advance the use of cleaner transport fuels based on principles of sound science, cost efficiency and sustainability of the environment. **Structure** Board of Directors. **Languages** English. **Staff** 3.00 FTE, paid. **Finance** Members' dues. **Publications** *ACFA News*.
Members Companies involved in clean fuels business in 7 countries:
China, Germany, Italy, Netherlands, Qatar, Saudi Arabia, USA.
NGO Relations Member of: *Partnership for Clean Fuels and Vehicles (PCFV, #18231).* [2020/XJ7833/**D**]

♦ Asian Clearing Union (ACU) 01380

SG 47-7th Negarestan Alley, Pasdaran Avenue, PO Box 15875-7177, Teheran, 1664645951, Iran Islamic Rep. T. +982122842076. Fax +982129957677. E-mail: acusecret@cbi.ir.
URL: http://www.asianclearingunion.org/

History 9 Dec 1974, Bangkok (Thailand). Established on entry into force of an agreement, under the auspices of *United Nations Economic and Social Commission for Asia and the Pacific (ESCAP, #20557).* Operations commenced 1 Nov 1975. **Aims** Provide a facility for member countries in the Region to settle *payments* for intra-regional transactions among participating central banks on a multilateral basis; economize on the use of foreign exchange reserves and transfer costs; promote trade among participating countries. **Structure** Board of Directors; Secretary General. **Languages** English. **Staff** 11.00 FTE, paid. **Finance** Accounts kept in Asian Monetary Units (AMUs), which are denominated as "ACU dollar", "ACU euro" and "ACU yen". **Activities** Events/meetings; networking/liaising; politics/policy/regulatory. **Events** *Annual Board Meeting* Islamabad (Pakistan) 2022, *Annual Board Meeting* Mumbai (India) 2021, *Annual Board Meeting* Paro (Bhutan) 2019, *Annual Board Meeting* Kathmandu (Nepal) 2018, *Annual Board Meeting* Colombo (Sri Lanka) 2017. **Publications** *ACU Monthly Newsletter* (12 a year). Annual Report; brochure.
Members Central banks or monetary authorities of 9 countries which are members of ESCAP:
Bangladesh, Bhutan, India, Iran Islamic Rep, Maldives, Myanmar, Nepal, Pakistan, Sri Lanka. [2023.02.14/XF6577/**F***]

♦ Asian Clinical Oncology Society (inactive)
♦ Asian CNS / see Asian Congress of Neurological Surgeons (#01401)
♦ Asian Coalition for Housing Finance (no recent information)

♦ Asian Coalition for Housing Rights (ACHR) 01381

Réseau asiatique pour l'habitat
Secretariat 73 Soi Sonthiwattana 4, Ladprao 110, Ladprao Road, Bangkok, 10310, Thailand. T. +6625380919. Fax +6625399950. E-mail: contact@achr.net.
URL: http://www.achr.net/

History Jun 1988, Bangkok (Thailand). Registration: No/ID: No. BKK-287, Start date: 8 Jun 1994, Thailand. **Aims** Articulate and promote access of Asia's *urban poor* to decent, secure housing and basic services; assist in developing alternatives to *eviction*; negotiate with local governments and stakeholders to make alternative housing models happen; help urban poor communities strengthen financial, managerial and networking strength, and share experiences and knowledge to build a region-wide network of mutually supporting urban poor community organizations and networks. **Structure** Regional gathering (every 2 years). Secretariat based in Bangkok (Thailand). **Languages** English. **Staff** 7.00 FTE, paid. **Finance** Budget (annual): about US$ 100,000 – 150,000. **Activities** Programmes include: *Urban Poor Coalition Asia (UPCA)*; *Asian Coalition for Community Action Program (ACCA).* **Events** *Asia-Pacific urban forum* Bangkok (Thailand) 2011, *Asia-Pacific urban forum* Bangkok (Thailand) 1996. **Publications** *E-News Bulletin* (6 a year); *Housing by People in Asia* – newsletter. Special issue publications; community architecture manuals; project reports.
Members Coalition groups in 23 countries and territories:
Afghanistan, Bangladesh, Bhutan, Cambodia, China, Fiji, Hong Kong, India, Indonesia, Japan, Kazakhstan, Korea Rep, Laos, Malaysia, Mongolia, Myanmar, Nepal, Pakistan, Philippines, Sri Lanka, Thailand, Timor-Leste, Vietnam.
NGO Relations Member of: *Global Land Tool Network (GLTN, #10452)*; *Regional Network of Local Authorities for the Management of Human Settlements (CITYNET, #18799).* Close ties with: *Shack-Slum Dwellers International (SDI, #19255).* [2023/XF1171/**F**]

♦ Asian Coalition of Human Rights Organizations (inactive)

♦ Asian Co-Benefits Partnership (ACP) 01382

Program Officer c/o IGES, 2108-11 Kamiyamaguchi, Hayama KANAGAWA, 240-0115 Japan. T. +81468553815. Fax +81468553809. E-mail: acp@iges.or.jp.
URL: http://www.cobenefit.org/

History Proposed Jun 2009, Hayama (Japan), at 1st International Forum for a Sustainable Asia and the Pacific (ISAP), with further meetings to further define organization. Formally launched 2010, Singapore, at Better Air Quality conference. **Aims** Support mainstreaming of co-benefits into sectoral development plans, policies and projects in Asia. **Structure** Advisory Group; Secretariat. **Languages** English. **Staff** Voluntary. **Finance** Support from the Ministry of the Environment, Japan. **Activities** Events/meetings; knowledge management/information dissemination; projects/programmes; networking/liaising. **Events** *International Seminar* Hayama (Japan) 2022. **Publications** *The Co-Benefits Corner Newsletter. ACP White Paper.* Factsheets; reports. **IGO Relations** Members of Advisory Group include: *Regional Resource Centre for Asia and the Pacific (RRC AP)*; *United Nations Economic and Social Commission for Asia and the Pacific (ESCAP, #20557).* Other partners include: *Asian Development Bank (ADB, #01422)*; *UNEP (#20299)*; *United Nations University Institute for the Advanced Study of Sustainability (UNU-IAS, #20643).* **NGO Relations** Secretariat provided by: *Institute for Global Environmental Strategies (IGES, #11266).* Members of Advisory Group include: *Clean Air Asia (#03983).* [2015.08.27/XJ7854/**F**]

♦ Asian Coconut Community / see International Coconut Community (#12628)

♦ Asian Cognitive Behaviour Therapy Association (ACBTA) 01383

Contact Dept of Psychology – Korea Univ, 1, 5-Ka, Anam-Dong, Sungbuk-ku, Seoul 136-701, Korea Rep. T. +82232902067.
URL: https://asiancbt.weebly.com/

Aims Advance the theory and practice of cognitive behaviour therapy in Asia. **Structure** General Meeting; Executive Committee; Board of Governors. **Languages** English. **Activities** Events/meetings. **Events** *World Congress of Cognitive and Behavioral Therapies* Seoul (Korea Rep) 2023.
Members Societies in 8 countries and territories:
Bangladesh, China, India, Japan, Korea Rep, Malaysia, Pakistan, Taiwan.
NGO Relations Member of (1): *World Confederation of Cognitive and Behavioural Therapies (WCCBT, #21292).* [2018/AA0742/**D**]

♦ Asian Collaborative Training Network for Malaria (ACTMalaria) . . . 01384

Exec Coordinator 11/f Ramon Magsaysay Centre, 1680 Roxas Blvd, Malate, Manila, Philippines. Fax +6325360971. E-mail: infonetwork@actmalaria.net.
URL: http://www.actmalaria.net/

History Nov 1996, Chiang Mai (Thailand). **Aims** Provide collaborative training for member countries to meet the needs of malaria control in *Southeast Asia* and *Mekong* valley; improve communication among member countries on malaria problems affecting common borders; facilitate a venue where countries affected by malaria and other mosquito borne diseases can share information; make information accessible to its users and pool resources from member countries to strengthen information exchange. **Structure** Executive Board (meets annually), chaired by Coordinating Country Director (CCD – position rotates among member countries every 2 years) and comprising Directors of National Malaria Control Programmes. Secretariat Office registered as a Foundation: Executive Coordinator; Executive Assistant; IT Assistant; Information Resource Officer. **Languages** English. **Staff** 4.50 FTE, paid. **Finance** Grants and donations from international organizations and private agencies. Technical support from partner organizations and national institutions. No membership fee. Budget (annual): US$ 300,000. **Activities** Knowledge management/information dissemination; training/education. **Publications** *ACTMalaria News* (6 a year). Symposium proceedings; manuals. **Information Services** *ACTMalaria Information Resource Center (AIRC).*
Members National Malaria Control Programmes in 11 countries:
Bangladesh, Cambodia, China, Indonesia, Laos, Malaysia, Myanmar, Philippines, Thailand, Timor-Leste, Vietnam. [2014.12.04/XF4637/**F**]

♦ Asian College of Neuropsychopharmacology (AsCNP) 01385

Main Office c/o A & E Planning Co, Hitotsubashi Bekkan 4F, 2-4-4 Hitotsubashi, Tokyo, 101-0003 Japan. E-mail: secretariat@ascnp.org.
URL: http://ascnp.org/

History 1 Oct 2008, Tokyo (Japan). **Events** *Congress* Xian (China) 2023, *Congress* Singapore (Singapore) 2021, *Congress* Fukuoka (Japan) 2019, *Congress* Nusa Dua (Indonesia) 2017, *Congress* Taipei (Taiwan) 2015. [2022/XJ1494/**D**]

♦ Asian College of Psychosomatic Medicine (ACPM) 01386

Pres address not obtained.

History Founded 12 Apr 1982, Tokyo (Japan), as Asian Chapter of *International College of Psychosomatic Medicine (ICPM, #12649).* Current title adopted, Sep 2002, at 10th congress. **Activities** Events/meetings. **Events** *Congress* Irkutsk (Russia) 2022, *Congress* Seoul (Korea Rep) 2018, *Congress* Fukuoka (Japan) 2016, *Congress* Jakarta (Indonesia) 2014, *Congress* Ulaanbaatar (Mongolia) 2012. [2019/XM8650/**E**]

♦ Asian College of Schizophrenia Research (ACSR) 01387

Pres Faculty of Medicine, Prince of Songkla Univ, 15 Karnjanavanich Rd, Hat Yai, Songkhla, 90110, Thailand. E-mail: upichet@medicine.psu.ac.th – info@acsr2017.com.
URL: http://www.acsr2009.com/

History 2011, Seoul (Korea Rep), at 2nd Congress on Schizophrenia Research. Previously also referred to as *Asian Network for Schizophrenia Research (ANSR).* **Aims** Bring together researchers and clinicians in Asian region so as to encourage and promote scientific exchange and scientific study on schizophrenia and broadly provide current information on schizophrenia to the public. **Structure** General Assembly; Executive Committee. **Languages** English. **Activities** Events/meetings. **Events** *Asian Congress of Schizophrenia Research* Nanjing (China) 2019, *Asian Congress of Schizophrenia Research* Bangkok (Thailand) 2017, *Asian Congress of Schizophrenia Research* Taipei (Taiwan) 2015, *Asian Congress on Schizophrenia Research* Bali (Indonesia) 2013, *Asian Congress of Schizophrenia Research* Seoul (Korea Rep) 2011. **Members** Full; Corporate; Supporting. Membership countries not specified. **NGO Relations** *European Scientific Association on Schizophrenia and other Psychoses (ESAS, #08443).* [2018/XJ6263/**D**]

♦ Asian College of Veterinary Dermatology (AiCVD) 01388

Contact 4-12-45 Nishinomiya-hama, Nishinomiya TOYAMA, 662-0934 Japan.
URL: http://www.aicvd.org/

History 2005. Set up by members of *Asian Society of Veterinary Dermatology (AiSVD, #01749).* **Aims** Advance veterinary dermatology in Asia; increase the competence of those who practice in the field. **Structure** General Assembly (every 2 years). Executive Committee. **Languages** English. **Staff** 8.00 FTE, voluntary. **Finance** Members' dues. Other sources: meeting proceeds; donations. **Activities** Events/meetings. **Publications** None.
Members Full in 4 countries and territories:
China, Japan, Korea Rep, Taiwan.
IGO Relations None. **NGO Relations** Co-organizes: *Asian Meeting of Animal Medicine Specialties (AMAMS).* Instrumental in setting up: *Asian Board of Veterinary Specialists (AiBVS).* [2019/XJ7945/**E**]

♦ Asian College of Veterinary Internal Medicine (AiCVIM) 01389

Address not obtained.
URL: http://www.aicvim.org/

Aims Improve the lives of companion animals and people by advancing the field of veterinary internal medicine in Asia. **Structure** Board. **Finance** Sources: members' dues. **Activities** Events/meetings; research/documentation; training/education.
Members Individuals in 5 countries and territories:
Indonesia, Japan, Korea Rep, Taiwan, Thailand.
NGO Relations Organizes: *Asian Meeting of Animal Medicine Specialties (AMAMS).* [2020/AA1052/**D**]

♦ Asian Committee for Future Accelerators (ACFA) 01390

Sec c/o IHEP, 19B YuquanLu, Shijingshan District, 100049 Beijing, China. E-mail: tangjy@ihep.ac.cn.
URL: http://www.acfa-forum.net/

History 9 Apr 1996, Pohang (Korea Rep). **Events** *Accelerators and Detectors Asian Forum* Daejeon (Korea Rep) 2018, *Global Design Effort Meeting on Linear Collider* Daegu (Korea Rep) 2012, *Physics and Detector Workshop* Daegu (Korea Rep) 2012, *Global design effort meeting on international linear collider* Tsukuba (Japan) 2009, *Physics and detector workshop* Tsukuba (Japan) 2009. **Members** Membership countries not specified. **NGO Relations** *International Committee for Future Accelerators (ICFA, #12774).* [2016/XE4579/**E**]

♦ Asian Committee for People's Organization (inactive)
♦ Asian Committee for Standardization of Physical Fitness Tests (inactive)

♦ Asian Communication Network (ACN) 01391

Sec Public Media Agency, 717 Menara Mutiara Majestic, Jalan Othman, 46000 Petaling Jaya, Selangor, Malaysia. T. +60374962246. Fax +60374962246.

History Jul 2001, Bangkok (Thailand). **Aims** An inter-disciplinary inter-faith communication network aiming at: serving as a catalyst; creating and sustaining communities that promote justice, peace, compassion and dialogue. **Structure** Board of Directors. **Publications** *Going Beyond* – newsletter. **NGO Relations** Member of: *World Catholic Association for Communication (SIGNIS, #21264).* [2013.07.19/XM0278/**F**]

♦ Asian Communications of Glycobiology and Glycotechnology / see Asian Community of Glycoscience and Glycotechnology (#01392)

♦ Asian Community of Glycoscience and Glycotechnology (ACGG) . . . 01392

Administrative Office AIST, 1-1-1 Umezono, Tsukuba, Ibaraki OSAKA, 305-8568 Japan. T. +81298613200. Fax +81298613201. E-mail: acgg_office@aist.go.jp.
URL: https://acgg.asia/

History Former names and other names: *Asian Communications of Glycobiology and Glycotechnology* – former (2009 to 2013). **Aims** Serve as a platform of collaboration of researchers in Asian countries through sharing the technologies, resources, and information toward further advancement of glycoscience. **Structure** Steering Committee; Administrative Office. **Activities** Events/meetings; knowledge management/information dissemination. **Events** *Asian Community of Glycoscience and Glycotechnology Conference* Busan (Korea Rep) 2019, *ACGG Conference* Tainan (Taiwan) 2018, *ACGG Conference* Hong Kong 2017, *ACGG Conference* Wuxi (China) 2016, *ACGG Conference* Miyagi (Japan) 2015. [2019/AA0266/**D**]

♦ **Asian Community Health Action Network (ACHAN)** **01393**
Coordinator 10 32nd Cross Street, Besant Nagar, Chennai, Tamil Nadu 600 090, Chennai TAMIL NADU 600 090, India. T. +914424919 89.
ACHAN Sub Office 303 B Shivalaya, Ethiraj Salai, Chennai, Tamil Nadu 600 008, Chennai TAMIL NADU 600 008, India. T. +914428252702. Fax +914428216705.
History 1980, Bangkok (Thailand). **Aims** Provide a support network for people working in community health; foster exchange of material information and personnel among Asian NGOs in the field. **Structure** Executive Trustees (7); Trustees (11); Coordinator; Coordinating team and Secretariat. **Languages** English. **Staff** 12.00 FTE, paid. **Finance** Sources: *Brot für die Welt*; *Niwano Peace Foundation*; Mainichi Foundation (Japan). **Activities** Main areas: Training: with its emphasis on participatory methodologies, concentrating on the 'Effects of Globalization on the Health of the Poor'; Networking: to form national coalitions of voluntary organizations who will act as a pressure group on national governments; Advocacy: campaigning on the theme 'Primary Health Care is State Responsibility'. Organizes meetings and workshops. Instrumental in setting up: *HAI – Asia-Pacific (HAIAP, #10852)*. **Events** *People's health assembly* Dhaka (Bangladesh) 2000, *Meeting* Dhaka (Bangladesh) 1989, *Meeting* Bangkok (Thailand) 1988, *Meeting* Penang (Malaysia) 1988, *Chinese workshop* Nisshin (Japan) 1987. **Publications** *ACHANEWS* (12 a year); *Linklet* (6 a year); *Link Newsletter* (4 a year).
Members Associations 'Friends'; Individuals. Membership covers 17 countries and territories:
Bangladesh, Cambodia, Hong Kong, India, Indonesia, Japan, Korea DPR, Korea Rep, Malaysia, Myanmar, Nepal, Pakistan, Philippines, Singapore, Sri Lanka, Thailand, Vietnam.
NGO Relations Member of: *People's Health Movement (PHM, #18305)*. [2010.06.01/XF4250/**F**]

♦ Asian Community Trust (internationally oriented national body)
♦ Asian Competition Forum (unconfirmed)
♦ Asian Composer's Conference (meeting series)

♦ **Asian Composers League (ACL)** **01394**
Contact Dept of Music, Univ of Hong Kong, Pokfulam Road, Hong Kong, Central and Western, Hong Kong. E-mail: info@asiancomposersleague.org.
URL: https://www.asiancomposersleague.org/
History 1973, after a Preliminary Meeting in 1971, Taipei (Taiwan). **Aims** Promote, preserve and develop *music* in Asia; further the interests of Asian composers in the region. **Structure** Executive Committee. **Languages** English. **Staff** Voluntary. **Finance** Members' dues. Donations. **Activities** Events/meetings; awards/prizes/competitions. **Events** *Festival and General Assembly* Christchurch (New Zealand) 2022, *Conference* Christchurch (New Zealand) 2020, *Conference* Taipei (Taiwan) 2018, *Conference* Hanoi (Vietnam) / Yen Vinh (Vietnam) 2016, *Conference* Manila (Philippines) / Quezon City (Philippines) / San Juan (Philippines) 2015. **Publications** *Asian Newsletter* (each Festival). Conference reports.
Members Categories (4): Honorary; Country; Individual; Associate. Country members in 15 countries and territories:
Australia, Hong Kong, Indonesia, Israel, Japan, Korea Rep, Malaysia, New Zealand, Philippines, Singapore, Taiwan, Tatarstan, Thailand, Türkiye, Vietnam. [2022/XD9624/**D**]

♦ **Asian Concrete Federation (ACF)** **01395**
SG Edutivity Bldg 3F, Sirindhorn Intl Inst of Technology, Thammasat Univ – Rangsit Campus, 99 Moo 18, Klong Nueng, Klong Luang, Pathum Thani, 12120, Thailand. T. +6629869009ext3408. E-mail: secretary@asianconcretefederation.org.
URL: http://www.asianconcretefederation.org/
History Officially inaugurated at 1st ACF International Conference organized by Thailand Concrete Association, Oct 2004, Chiang Mai (Thailand). **Aims** Promote understanding of concrete structures and provide services to Asian society. **Structure** General Assembly. Executive Council, comprising President, 2 Vice-Presidents (Policy, Technical), Treasurer, Immediate Past President, 5 members and one ex-officio member. **Events** *Symposium* Sapporo (Japan) 2019, *International Conference* Fuzhou (China) 2018, *Symposium* Chiang Mai (Thailand) 2017, *SCESCM : International Conference on Sustainable Civil Engineering Structures and Construction Materials* Bali (Indonesia) 2016, *International Conference* Seoul (Korea Rep) 2014. **Publications** *ACF Newsletter*.
Members Representative; Individual; Corporate. Institutions in 10 countries and territories:
Australia, India, Indonesia, Japan, Korea Rep, Mongolia, Singapore, Taiwan, Thailand, Vietnam. [2013/XJ7737/**D**]

♦ **Asian Confederation of Billiards Sports (ACBS)** **01396**
Pres Al-Mansoura, Al-Muntazah Str, PO Box 8996, Doha, Qatar. T. +97444356099. Fax +97444356099. E-mail: mubarak@acbs.qa – admin@acbs.qa.
SG address not obtained.
URL: http://www.acbs.qa/
History Founded 1984, as *Asian Billiards and Snooker Federation*. **Aims** Promote billiards sports in the Asian region and in the Asian games; provide coaches and other assistance so as to improve standards. **Structure** General Meeting (annual). Regional federation of: *International Billiards and Snooker Federation (IBSF, #12340)*. **Languages** English. **Staff** 2.00 FTE, paid; 4.00 FTE, voluntary. **Finance** Members' dues. Other sources: sponsorship; grants. **Activities** Events/meetings; sporting activities.
Members National organizations in 34 countries and territories:
Afghanistan, Bahrain, Bangladesh, Brunei Darussalam, China, Hong Kong, India, Indonesia, Iran Islamic Rep, Iraq, Japan, Jordan, Korea Rep, Kuwait, Kyrgyzstan, Macau, Malaysia, Maldives, Mongolia, Myanmar, Nepal, Pakistan, Palestine, Philippines, Qatar, Saudi Arabia, Singapore, Sri Lanka, Syrian AR, Taiwan, Thailand, Turkmenistan, United Arab Emirates, Yemen.
NGO Relations Member of: *World Professional Billiards and Snooker Association (WPBSA, #21740)*. [2017.03.09/XD4625/**D**]

♦ **Asian Confederation of Institutes of Internal Auditors (ACIIA)** **01397**
Secretariat address not obtained. T. +60321818008. Fax +60321811717. E-mail: general@aciia.asia.
URL: http://www.theiia.org/chapters/index.cfm
History Mar 1999. Registered in accordance with Malaysian law, 24 Feb 2006. **Aims** Provide dynamic leadership for the profession of internal auditing; coordinate the development, enhancement and promotion of the internal auditing profession in the Asian Region; enhance the standards and practices of the profession through certification and the adoption of international and regional best practices in internal auditing; assist in the growth and development of the Institutes of Internal Auditors affiliates to the Institute of Internal Auditors incorporated in the USA through networking, marketing, education and research and information sharing; foster a strong and cohesive profession by providing leadership on emerging issues and coordinating with IIA Global and other IIA Affiliates to achieve appropriate strategic objectives; Enhance the image and interests of the internal auditing profession regionally through the promotion of its role and achievements. **Structure** Executive Committee, comprising President, Deputy President, Honorary Secretary and Honorary Treasurer. **Events** *Conference* Bangkok (Thailand) 2022, *Audit Committee Forum* Seoul (Korea Rep) 2021, *Conference* Incheon (Korea Rep) 2020, *Leadership Forum* Taipei (Taiwan) 2020, *Towards sustainable management in a new era* Tokyo (Japan) 2019.
Members Affiliates in 10 countries and territories:
Australia, China, Hong Kong, Indonesia, Japan, Korea Rep, Malaysia, Philippines, Taiwan, Thailand.
NGO Relations Associated with: *Institute of Internal Auditors (IIA, #11272)*. [2018/XM1342/**D**]

♦ Asian Confederation of Medical Associations / see Confederation of Medical Associations in Asia and Oceania (#04566)
♦ Asian Confederation of Orthopaedic Manipulative Physical Therapy (unconfirmed)

♦ **Asian Confederation of Physical Therapy (ACPT)** **01398**
Confédération asiatique de thérapie physique
SG Dept Physical Therapy, China Medical Univ, No 91 Hsueh-Shih Road, Taichung 40402, Taiwan.
URL: https://www.acpt-physicaltherapy.org/
History 28 Apr 1980, Taipei (Taiwan). **Structure** Address changes with Secretariat. **Events** *Congress* Macau (Macau) 2020, *Congress* Cebu City (Philippines) 2018, *Congress* Kuala Lumpur (Malaysia) 2016, *Health promotion through physical therapy* Taichung (Taiwan) 2013, *Congress* Bali (Indonesia) 2010.
Members National organizations in 7 countries and territories:
Indonesia, Japan, Korea Rep, Malaysia, Philippines, Taiwan, Thailand.
NGO Relations *World Confederation for Physical Therapy (WCPT, #21293)*. [2021/XD0132/**D**]

♦ Asian Confederation of Teachers (no recent information)

♦ **Asian Conference on Clinical Pharmacy (ACCP)** **01399**
Contact 7102 – 101 – Daehak-ro, Jongno-gu, Seoul 03080, Korea Rep. T. +8227417529. E-mail: kccpgoal@gmail.com.
URL: http://asianccp.org/
History 1997, USA. Former names and other names: *ast Asia Conference on Developing Clinical Pharmacy Practice and Clinical Pharmacy Education (EACDCPPE)* – former (1997 to 2002). **Aims** Improve health care by providing leadership,advocacy, education, and resources to clinical pharmacy practitioners inorder to promote excellence in clinical pharmacy. **Activities** Events/meetings. **Events** *Conference* Nagoya (Japan) 2022, *Conference* Singapore (Singapore) 2021, *Conference* Singapore (Singapore) 2020, *Conference* Manila (Philippines) 2019, *Conference* Teheran (Iran Islamic Rep) 2018. **Publications** *Research in Clinical Pharmacy (RCP)*.
Members Full in 13 countries:
Canada, China, India, Indonesia, Iran Islamic Rep, Japan, Korea Rep, Malaysia, Philippines, Singapore, Thailand, USA, Vietnam. [2021/AA1534/c/**E**]

♦ Asian Conference on Coordination Chemistry (meeting series)
♦ Asian Conference of Correctional Facilities and Planners (meeting series)
♦ Asian Conference of Criminal and Operations Psychology (meeting series)
♦ Asian Conference of Deafness (meeting series)
♦ Asian Conference on Machine Learning (meeting series)
♦ Asian Conference of Neurological Surgeons / see Asian Congress of Neurological Surgeons (#01401)
♦ Asian Conference on Plant-Microbe Symbiosis and Nitrogen Fixation (meeting series)
♦ Asian Conference on Religion and Peace / see Asian Conference of Religions for Peace (#01400)

♦ **Asian Conference of Religions for Peace (ACRP)** **01400**
Conférence d'Asie pour la religion et la paix
Main Office 2-7-1 Wada, Suginami-ku, Tokyo, 166-0012 Japan. T. +81353422381. E-mail: tokyo@rfpasia.net.
URL: https://rfpasia.org/
History 1976, Singapore (Singapore). Founded following suggestions 1974, Leuven (Belgium), of *Religions for Peace (RfP, #18831)*. Former names and other names: *Religions for Peace Asia* – alias; *Asian Conference on Religion and Peace (ACRP)* – former alias. **Aims** Bring peace in the world through religion; understand and appreciate the process of political, economic, social and cultural change and the aspirations for dignity and equality among the peoples of Asia and communicate the same to all religious communities. **Languages** English. **Staff** 2.00 FTE, paid. **Finance** Budget (annual): US$ 75,000. **Events** *Assembly* Incheon (Korea Rep) 2014, *Assembly* Manila (Philippines) 2008, *Assembly* Jakarta (Indonesia) 2002, *Assembly* Yogyakarta (Indonesia) 2002, *Assembly* Ayutthaya (Thailand) 1996. **Publications** *ACRP Newsletter* (6 a year).
Members National Chapters in 16 countries:
Australia, Bangladesh, China, India, Indonesia, Japan, Korea DPR, Korea Rep, Mongolia, Nepal, New Zealand, Pakistan, Philippines, Singapore, Sri Lanka, Thailand.
NGO Relations Close affiliation with WCRP; national chapters also belong to WCRP. [2022/XD6692/**D**]

♦ Asian Conference on Safety and Education in Laboratory (meeting series)
♦ Asian Congress of Health Promotion (meeting series)

♦ **Asian Congress of Neurological Surgeons (ACNS)** **01401**
Secretariat Dept of Neurosurgery, Fujita HU School of Medicine, 1-98 Dengakugakubo, Kutsukake, Toyoake-shi, Aichi, 470-1192 Japan.
URL: http://asiancns.org/
History 1997. Also referred to as *Asian Conference of Neurological Surgeons* and *Asian CNS*. **Structure** Executive Committee. **Activities** Created *Asian Women's Neurosurgical Association (AWNA, #01784)*. **Events** *Congress* Shanghai (China) 2022, *Congress* Kazan (Russia) 2020, *Congress* Dubai (United Arab Emirates) 2018, *Congress* Surabaya (Indonesia) 2016, *Unique science – unique city – let's meet in the heart of Eurasia* Astana (Kazakhstan) 2014.
Members Full in 36 countries and territories:
Afghanistan, Australia, Austria, Bangladesh, Brunei Darussalam, Cambodia, China, Egypt, Hong Kong, India, Indonesia, Iran Islamic Rep, Iraq, Japan, Kazakhstan, Korea DPR, Korea Rep, Malaysia, Mongolia, Myanmar, Nepal, Netherlands, Oman, Pakistan, Philippines, Qatar, Russia, Saudi Arabia, Singapore, Sri Lanka, Syrian AR, Taiwan, Thailand, Türkiye, Uzbekistan, Vietnam. [2015/XM4011/c/**E**]

♦ **Asian Consortium for Computational Materials Science (ACCMS)** .. **01402**
Contact New Industry Creation Hatchery Ctr, Tohoku Univ, Aramaki aza Aobo 4-4-6, Aoba-ku, Sendai MIYAGI, 980-8579 Japan.
URL: http://accms.mobility.niche.tohoku.ac.jp/
History 2000, Sendai (Japan). **Aims** Undertake and actively support research, development and innovations in computational materials science in Asia. **Structure** Virtual General Meeting (annual); Advisory Council; Executive; Secretaries. **Languages** English. **Staff** 2.00 FTE, paid. **Finance** Basic funding from: Tohoku University (Japan). Members provide conference funding. **Activities** Awards/prizes/competitions; events/meetings; research and development; guidance/assistance/consulting; training/education. **Events** *General Meeting* Kuala Lumpur (Malaysia) 2017, *Conference* Nakhon Ratchasima (Thailand) 2013, *Conference* Thailand 2013, *Annual Meeting* Sendai (Japan) 2012, *General Meeting* Sendai (Japan) 2012. **Publications** Conference papers; booklets.
Members Full in 16 countries and territories:
China, Hong Kong, India, Indonesia, Iran Islamic Rep, Japan, Kazakhstan, Korea Rep, Macau, Malaysia, Philippines, Russia, Singapore, Taiwan, Thailand, Vietnam.
Associate in 10 countries:
Argentina, Australia, Brazil, Canada, France, Germany, Italy, Mexico, South Africa, USA. [2018.07.25/XM0011/**F**]

♦ **Asian Consortium for the Conservation and Sustainable Use of Microbial Resources (ACM)** **01403**
Secretariat Biological Resource Ctr – NBRC, 2-49-10, Nishihara, Shibuya-ku, Tokyo, 151-0066 Japan. E-mail: acm_desk@nite.go.jp.
URL: http://www.acm-mrc.asia/
History Founded 2004, Tsukuba (Japan). **Aims** Promote collaboration among government or public organizations in Asian countries so as to enhance conservation and sustainable use of microbial resources in Asia. **Activities** Networking/liaising; research and development; awareness raising; knowledge management/information dissemination; events/meetings. **Events** *Annual Meeting* Bangkok (Thailand) 2021, *Annual Meeting* Tokyo (Japan) 2020, *Annual Meeting* Seri Kembangan (Malaysia) 2019, *Annual Meeting* Ulaanbaatar (Mongolia) 2018, *Annual Meeting* Taipei (Taiwan) 2017.
Members Organizations in 15 countries and territories:
Cambodia, China, India, Indonesia, Iran Islamic Rep, Japan, Korea Rep, Laos, Malaysia, Mongolia, Myanmar, Philippines, Taiwan, Thailand, Vietnam. [2020/XM7504/**D**]

♦ Asian Consultancy on Tobacco Control (internationally oriented national body)

♦ **Asian Consumer and Family Economics Association (ACFEA)** **01404**
Pres c/o The School of Economics and Management, Fuzhou Univ, 2 Xue Yuan Road, University Town, Fuzhou, 350108 Fujian, China. T. +8613799996065. E-mail: asiancfea@gmail.com.
SG address not obtained. E-mail: edouard831@gmail.com.
URL: http://www.asiancfea.org/
History 1995, Malaysia. **Aims** Provide a forum for people involved in Asian consumer and/or family economics research, teaching, business and government policy. **Structure** Officers: President; Treasurer; Secretary; Editor; Outgoing President. **Events** *Biennial Conference* Fujian (China) 2022, *Biennial Conference* Fujian (China) 2020, *Biennial Conference* Fuzhou (China) 2018, *Biennial Conference* Hong Kong (Hong Kong) 2016, *Biennial Conference* Taipei (Taiwan) 2014. **Publications** Conference proceedings.
Members in 10 countries and territories:
Bangladesh, China, India, Japan, Korea Rep, Malaysia, Nepal, Singapore, Taiwan, USA. [2023.02.14/XD6400/**D**]

♦ Asian Control Association (ACA) 01405

Office Bucheon Techno Park 401-1506, 193 Yakdae-dong, Wonmi-gu, Bucheon GYEONGGI 420-734, Korea Rep. T. +82322345801. Fax +82322345807.
Gen Sec Chungnam Natl Univ, 79 Daehangno, Yuseong-gu, Daejeon 305-764, Korea Rep. T. +82428216876. Fax +82428234919.
URL: http://acacontrol.org/

History Proposed during 5th Asian Control Conference, Jul 2004, Melbourne (Australia). Set up, Mar 2006. Successor to *Asian Control Professors Association (ACPA)*, set up 1996. **Aims** Promote control science and *engineering* in Asia. **Structure** Steering Committee. Executive Board, comprising President, 3 Vice-Presidents (Technical Activities; Publications; Education) and General Secretary. Secretariat. **Activities** Organizes biennial 'Asian Control Conference (ASCC)'. **Events** *Asian Control Conference* Jeju (Korea Rep) 2022, *Asian Control Conference* Jeju (Korea Rep) 2021, *Asian Control Conference* Kitakyushu (Japan) 2019, *Asian Control Conference* Gold Coast, QLD (Australia) 2017, *Workshop* Kitakyushu (Japan) 2016. **Publications** *Asian Journal of Control (AJC).* [2017/XJ1309/**E**]

♦ Asian Corporate Governance Association (ACGA) 01406

Office Mgr Rm 1801 18th Fl, Wilson House, 19-27 Wyndham St, Hong Kong, Central and Western, Hong Kong. T. +85221601788. Fax +85221473818.
URL: http://www.acga-asia.org/

History 1999, Hong Kong. **Aims** Promote implementation of effective corporate governance practices throughout Asia. **Structure** Council. **Languages** English. **Staff** 6.50 FTE, paid. **Finance** Members' dues. **Activities** Events/meetings. **Events** *Annual Conference* London (UK) 2022, *Annual Conference* Hong Kong (Hong Kong) 2021, *Annual Conference* Hong Kong (Hong Kong) 2020, *Annual Conference* Beijing (China) 2018, *Annual Conference* Mumbai (India) 2017. **Publications** *CG Watch* (every 2 years) – report. *China Corporate Governance Report.*
Members Full in 18 countries and territories:
Australia, Belgium, Canada, China, France, Hong Kong, India, Japan, Malaysia, Netherlands, Norway, Philippines, Singapore, Sweden, Taiwan, UK, USA, Vietnam. [2020/XM0188/**D**]

♦ Asian Corrugated Carton Association / see Asian Corrugated Case Association (#01407)

♦ Asian Corrugated Case Association (ACCA) 01407

Contact Jl Alam Segar XI 11, Jakarta 12310, Indonesia. Fax +62217657695.
URL: http://www.acca-website.org/

History Founded 1997. Also referred to as *Asian Corrugated Carton Association.* Registered in accordance with Singapore law. **Structure** General Meeting; Management Committee.
Members Ordinary Affiliate/Associate. Associations and companies. Ordinary members in 9 countries and territories:
China, Hong Kong, India, Indonesia, Malaysia, Philippines, Singapore, Taiwan, Thailand.
Affiliate/Associate members in 12 countries and territories:
Belgium, China, Hong Kong, India, Indonesia, Japan, Korea Rep, Malaysia, Singapore, Taiwan, Thailand, USA.
NGO Relations Member of: *International Corrugated Case Association (ICCA, #12974).* [2014/XD8956/**D**]

♦ Asian Cotton Research and Development Network 01408

Address not obtained.
URL: https://staging.icac.org/tech/Regional-Networks/Asian-Cotton-Research-and-Development-Network

History Jun 1999, Multan (Pakistan). Founded at a consultation organized by *International Cotton Advisory Committee (ICAC, #12979).* **Events** *Meeting* Tashkent (Uzbekistan) 2019, *Meeting* Nagpur (India) 2017, *Meeting* Dhaka (Bangladesh) 2014, *Meeting* Lahore (Pakistan) 2011, *Meeting* Anyang (China) 2008. [2019/XJ2704/**E**]

♦ Asian Council on Ergonomics and Design (unconfirmed)

♦ Asian Council of Exercise and Sports Science (ACESS) 01409

Headquarters Exercise Physiology Lab, Dept of Physical Education, Seoul National Univ, San 56-1, Shilim-dong, Kwanak-gu, Seoul 151-742, Korea Rep. T. +8228807804. Fax +8228721900. E-mail: gardenkil@naver.com.
URL: http://www.acess.asia/

History 6 Jul 2001, Seoul (Korea Rep), following a series of informal meetings. **Aims** Promote communication and cooperation between exercise and sports science professionals and students in educational, scientific and research institutions, in particular in the Asian region. **Structure** General Assembly (every 2 years). Executive Board. **Finance** Members' dues. **Events** *Asia-Pacific Conference on Exercise and Sports Science* Mabalacat City (Philippines) 2019, *Asia-Pacific Conference on Exercise and Sports Science* Bangkok (Thailand) 2017, *Asia-Pacific Conference on Exercise and Sports Science* Faridabad (India) 2015, *Asia-Pacific Conference on Exercise and Sports Science* Beijing (China) 2013, *Asia-Pacific Conference on Exercise and Sports Science* Kuala Lumpur (Malaysia) 2011. **Members** Professional; Student. Membership countries not specified. **NGO Relations** Member of: *International Council of Sport Science and Physical Education (ICSSPE, #13077).* [2014/XD9243/**D**]

♦ Asian Council of Peace Research (inactive)
♦ Asian Council for People's Culture (no recent information)

♦ Asian Couture Federation (ACF) 01410

Contact 217 East Coast Road, No 04-01 TIDES, Singapore 428915, Singapore. E-mail: admin@asiancouturefederation.com.
URL: http://asiancouturefederation.com/

Aims Inspire, support, and promote the highest levels of Asia-based *fashion* design artistry to the Asian and global markets. **Structure** Governors Committee; Executive Board. Includes *MENA Couture Council (MCC).* **Members** Individuals. Membership countries not specified. [2015/XM4382/**D**]

♦ Asian Credit Supplementation Institution Confederation (ACSIC) ... 01411

Contact 4th Fl – No 6 – Sec 1, Roosevelt Rd, Zhongzheng District, Taipei 10066, Taiwan. T. +886223214261. Fax +886223947317. E-mail: acsic30@smeg.org.tw.
URL: http://www.acsic2017.tw/

History Founded 17 Oct 1988. **Aims** Promote the sound development of the credit supplementation systems for small and medium enterprises in the region of Asia, excluding areas to the west and north of Pakistan, through exchange of information, personnel and discussions among the institutions. **Activities** Events/meetings. **Events** *Annual Conference* Colombo (Sri Lanka) 2019, *Annual Conference* Udaipur (India) 2018, *Annual Conference* Taipei (Taiwan) 2017, *Annual Conference* Bangkok (Thailand) 2016, *Annual Conference* Bali (Indonesia) 2015.
Members Credit Guarantee Institutions (17) in 12 countries and territories:
India, Indonesia, Japan, Korea Rep, Malaysia, Mongolia, Nepal, Papua New Guinea, Philippines, Sri Lanka, Taiwan, Thailand. [2017/XN4605/**D**]

♦ Asian Cricket Conference / see Asian Cricket Council (#01412)

♦ Asian Cricket Council (ACC) 01412

Pres 8th Fl, Wisma Antah, Off Jalan Semantan, Damansara Heights, 50490 Kuala Lumpur, Malaysia. T. +60320959594. E-mail: acc@asiancricket.org.
URL: http://www.asiancricket.org/

History Founded 19 Sep 1983, as *Asian Cricket Conference.* Regional council of *International Cricket Council (ICC, #13105).* **Events** *Annual Meeting* London (UK) 2003. [2016/XE4616/**E**]

♦ Asian Criminological Association / see Asian Criminological Society (#01413)

♦ Asian Criminological Society (ACS) 01413

Secretariat Block 2 B402, Univy Of Macau, Av Padre Tomas Pereira Taipa, Macau, Macau. T. +85383978552. Fax +85383978559. E-mail: asiancriminologist@gmail.com.
URL: http://acs002.com/

History Registered with the laws of Macau. Former names and other names: *Asian Criminological Association (ACS)* – alias. **Aims** Promote the study of criminology and criminal justice across Asia; enhance cooperation in the fields of criminology and criminal justice by scholars and practitioners; encourage communication between criminologists and criminal justice practitioners in Asia and the world; foster training and research in criminology and criminal justice in institutions of learning, and in criminal justice agencies. **Structure** General Assembly (annual). Executive Board, including President, Vice-Presidents, Secretary-General, Treasurer and Directors. Supervisory Board. **Languages** Chinese, English, Portuguese. **Finance** Members' dues. Donations. **Events** *Annual Conference* Kyoto (Japan) 2021, *Annual Conference* Kyoto (Japan) 2020, *Annual Conference* Cebu City (Philippines) 2019, *Annual Conference* George Town (Malaysia) 2018, *Annual Conference* Cairns, QLD (Australia) 2017. **Publications** *Asian Journal of Criminology (AJOC).*
Members Individuals in 11 countries and territories:
Australia, China, Hong Kong, India, Japan, Korea Rep, Macau, Malaysia, Pakistan, Singapore, Taiwan. [2020/XJ6828/**D**]

♦ Asian Crop Science Association (ACSA) 01414

Past SG The University of Queensland, Hermitage Research Facility, 604 Yangan Road, Warwick QLD 4370, Australia.
Pres Natl Cntr for Genetic Engineering and Biotechnology (BIOTEC), 113 Thailand Science Park, Phahonyothin Road, Klong 1, Khlong Luang, Pathum Thani, 12120, Thailand. T. +6625646700. Fax +6625646701 – +6625646705.
SG address not obtained.

History 1990, Kyoto (Japan), when charter drafted and signed. **Aims** Use crop science to promote human welfare in Asia. **Structure** Conference (also regular meeting). International Committee, including President, Vice-President, Immediate Past-President, Secretary-General and Immediate Past Secretary-General. **Languages** English. **Staff** 2.00 FTE, paid. Voluntary (International Committee). **Events** *Triennial Conference* Nagoya (Japan) 2020, *Triennial Conference* Jeju (Korea Rep) 2017, *Triennial Conference* Hanoi (Vietnam) 2014, *Triennial Conference* Bogor (Indonesia) 2011, *Triennial Conference* Bangkok (Thailand) 2007. **Publications** Articles and papers in journals.
Members Crop science societies in 13 countries and territories:
Australia, Bangladesh, Cambodia, Indonesia, Japan, Korea Rep, Laos, Malaysia, Nepal, Pakistan, Philippines, Taiwan, Thailand. [2012.08.06/XJ2215/**D**]

♦ Asian Crystallization Technology Society (ACTS) 01415

Contact Rm 470 – Dept of Chemical Engineering, Kyung Hee Univ, Seochun-dong 1, Giheung-gu, Yongin GYEONGGI 499-701, Korea Rep. T. +82312012576. Fax +82312732971.
URL: http://www.asiancrystal.org/

History 2011. **Aims** Promote the crystallization technology at Asian as well as global levels. **Languages** English. **Activities** Events/meetings. **Events** *International Symposium* Singapore (Singapore) 2018, *International Symposium* Tianjin (China) 2016, *International symposium* Nara (Japan) 2014, *Congress* La Paz (Bolivia) 2013, *International Symposium* Seoul (Korea Rep) 2012. [2015.10.08/XJ6471/**D**]

♦ Asian Crystallographic Association (AsCA) 01416

Pres School of Life Sciences, Peking Univ, Summer Palace Rd 5, Golden Life Sciences Bldg, Haidian, 100871 Beijing, China.
Sec-Treas School of Chemistry, Univ of Sydney, Eastern Avenue, Sydney NSW 2006, Australia.
URL: http://asca.iucr.org/

History Aug 1987, Perth, WA (Australia). **Aims** Contribute to, and promote advancement of, crystallography and allied subjects. **Structure** Council. **Languages** English. **Staff** Voluntary. **Finance** Sources: donations; members' dues. Annual budget: 1,080 AUD. **Activities** Events/meetings. **Events** *Conference* Malaysia 2024, *Conference* Jeju (Korea Rep) 2022, *Conference* Singapore (Singapore) 2019, *Conference* Auckland (New Zealand) 2018, *Conference* Hanoi (Vietnam) 2016. **Publications** *AsCA Newsletter* (irregular) – electronic.
Members Full in 18 countries and territories:
Australia, Bangladesh, Cambodia, China, India, Indonesia, Japan, Korea Rep, Malaysia, Mongolia, New Zealand, Pakistan, Philippines, Singapore, Sri Lanka, Taipei, Thailand, Vietnam.
NGO Relations Regional Associate of: *International Union of Crystallography (IUCr, #15768).* [2022.02.15/XD2128/**D**]

♦ Asian Cultural Centre for UNESCO / see Asia/Pacific Cultural Centre for UNESCO (#01879)
♦ Asian Cultural Council (internationally oriented national body)

♦ Asian Cycling Confederation (ACC) 01417

Pres 10th Floor MB Gldg, Seongsui-Ro 89, Seongdong-Ku, Seoul, Korea Rep. T. +8224671313. Fax +8224671323. E-mail: acccycling@yahoo.co.kr.
URL: http://www.asiancycling.com/

Aims Promote and develop the sport of cycling in all its forms and levels in Asia. **Structure** Management Committee; Executive Committee; Committees (10). **Activities** Sporting activities; awards/prizes/competitions. **Events** *Congress* Tokyo (Japan) 2016, *Congress* Nakhon Ratchasima (Thailand) 2015, *Congress* Astana (Kazakhstan) 2014, *Congress* Delhi (India) 2013, *Congress* Seoul (Korea Rep) 1986.
Members National cycling organizations (41) in 41 countries and territories:
Afghanistan, Bahrain, Bangladesh, Brunei Darussalam, Cambodia, China, Hong Kong, India, Indonesia, Iran Islamic Rep, Iraq, Japan, Jordan, Kazakhstan, Korea DPR, Korea Rep, Kuwait, Kyrgyzstan, Laos, Lebanon, Macau, Malaysia, Mongolia, Myanmar, Nepal, Oman, Pakistan, Philippines, Qatar, Saudi Arabia, Singapore, Sri Lanka, Syrian AR, Taiwan, Thailand, Timor-Leste, Turkmenistan, United Arab Emirates, Uzbekistan, Vietnam, Yemen.
NGO Relations Continental confederation of: *Union Cycliste Internationale (UCI, #20375).* [2016.06.01/XD6359/**D**]

♦ Asian Cycling Federation (inactive)

♦ Asian Dance Council (ADC) 01418

Sec Chateau Gay, 119 Jalan York, 10450 George Town, Penang, Malaysia. T. +6042615497. E-mail: secretary@asiandancecouncil.com.
URL: https://www.asiandancecouncil.com/

History 2005. **Aims** Educate about, enhance and promote ballroom dancing in Asia. **Structure** President; Secretary General; Assistant Secretary. **Languages** English. **Staff** 2.00 FTE, paid. **Activities** Organizes: annual Asian Ranking Series championships; Asian Open Dance Tour.
Members Full in 12 countries and territories:
China, Hong Kong, Indonesia, Japan, Korea Rep, Macau, Malaysia, Philippines, Singapore, Sri Lanka, Taiwan, Thailand.
Associate in 4 countries and territories:
Hong Kong, Macau, Malaysia, Taiwan.
NGO Relations Member of: *World Dance Council (WDC, #21353).* [2020/XM1161/**E**]

♦ Asian Dance Organisation / see Asian Dance Organisers (#01419)

♦ Asian Dance Organisers (ADO) 01419

Pres address not obtained.
URL: http://www.asiandanceorganisers.org/

History Founded Feb 2016. Also referred to as *Asian Dance Organisation.* **Structure** Board of Directors. **Activities** Sporting activities.
Members Full in 10 countries and territories:
China, Hong Kong, Indonesia, Japan, Korea Rep, Macau, Philippines, Singapore, Taiwan, Thailand.
Included in the above, 1 organization listed in this Yearbook:
Asia Starlight Dance Association. [2020.02.05/XM8839/y/**D**]

♦ Asian Dance Sport Federation (ADSF) 01420

Pres 2-18 Nishikomeno, Makamura, Nagoya AICHI, 453-0812 Japan. T. +81524615345. Fax +81524615345.
Gen Sec Room 806 – 8F, 20 Chu-Lun Street, Taipei, Taiwan. T. +886223627221 – +886287711501. Fax +886223923960. E-mail: ctdsary@ms7.hinet.net.
URL: http://www.asiandancesport.org/

History 2 Nov 1996, Taipei (Taiwan). **Aims** Develop and promote dance sport in the Asian region. **Languages** English. **Staff** Voluntary. **Finance** Sources: members' dues. **Activities** Sporting activities.
Members Full; Associate; Provisional. National associations in 19 countries and territories:
China, Hong Kong, India, Indonesia, Japan, Kazakhstan, Korea Rep, Kyrgyzstan, Lebanon, Macau, Malaysia, Mongolia, Philippines, Singapore, Sri Lanka, Taiwan, Thailand, Turkmenistan, Uzbekistan.
NGO Relations Close relations with: *International Olympic Committee (IOC, #14408)*; *Olympic Council of Asia (OCA, #17718).* [2022.05.11/XD9425/**D**]

♦ Asian Dendrochronology Association (unconfirmed)

♦ Asian Dermatological Association (ADA) 01421

Contact c/o Fed of Medical Societies of Hong Kong, 4th Floor – Duke of Windsor Social Service Bldg, 15 Hennessy Road, Wan Chai, Wanchai, Hong Kong. T. +85225278898. Fax +85228650345. E-mail: info@fmshk.org.
URL: http://www.medicine.org.hk/ada/

History 21 Nov 1986, Hong Kong. **Aims** Promote the study of dermatology. **Events** *Congress* Tokyo (Japan) 2022, *Congress* Dubai (United Arab Emirates) 2018, *Congress* Mumbai (India) 2016, *Congress* Hong Kong (Hong Kong) 2013, *Congress* Seoul (Korea Rep) 2008. **Publications** *Journal of Dermatology* (12 a year).
Members Ordinary; associate; honorary. Members in 28 countries and territories:
Algeria, Australia, China, Egypt, Hong Kong, India, Indonesia, Iran Islamic Rep, Japan, Jordan, Korea Rep, Kuwait, Libya, Malaysia, Oman, Pakistan, Philippines, Saudi Arabia, Singapore, Sudan, Syrian AR, Taiwan, Thailand, Tunisia, UK, United Arab Emirates, USA, Yemen.
NGO Relations Member of: *International League of Dermatological Societies (ILDS, #14018).*
[2017.11.28/XD1163/**D**]

♦ Asian Desk of the International Federation of Catholic Universities / see Association of Southeast and East Asian Catholic Colleges and Universities (#02923)

♦ Asian Development Bank (ADB) 01422

Banque asiatique de développement (BAD) – Banco Asiatico de Desarrollo – Asiatische Entwicklungsbank (AEB)

Headquarters 6 ADB Avenue, Mandaluyong City, 1550 Manila, Philippines. T. +6326324444. Fax +6326362444.
URL: http://www.adb.org/

History 24 Nov 1966, Manila (Philippines), at Inaugural Meeting of the Board of Governors. Establishment followed recommendations of 1st Ministerial Conference on Asian Economic Cooperation, Dec 1963, Manila, under the auspices of the then United Nations Economic Commission for Asia and the Far East (ECAFE), currently *United Nations Economic and Social Commission for Asia and the Pacific (ESCAP, #20557)*, which set up a Working Group of Experts. A Consultative Committee was set up during 21st Session of ECAFE, Mar 1965, Wellington (New Zealand), to prepare a draft agreement. Articles of Agreement were adopted at 2nd Ministerial Conference on Asian Economic Cooperation, Nov-Dec 1965, Manila, and entered into force with the ratification or acceptance by 15 Signatories on 22 Aug 1966. Bank commenced operations on 19 Dec 1966 in Manila with 31 members. **Aims** Five strategic objectives in the Medium-Term Strategic Framework: catalyzing investment; strengthening inclusiveness; promoting regional cooperation and integration; encouraging effective environmental management; improving governance and preventing corruption.
Structure Board of Governors (meets annually), consisting of one Governor and one Alternate Governor appointed by each member country, elects President. Board of Directors, composed of 12 Directors (each with an Alternate) and elected by Board of Governors, 8 representing regional countries and 4 representing non-regional countries. Four Vice-Presidents (Operations 1 and 2, Knowledge Management, Sustainable Development) appointed by Board of Directors on the recommendation of President.
Vice-Presidents (4) oversee:
- Operations 1, including 3 departments/offices: South Asia; Central and West Asia; Private Sector Operations;
- Operations 2, including 4 departments/offices: East Asia; Southeast Asia; Pacific; Central Operations Services;
- Knowledge Management and Sustainable Development, including 3 departments/offices: Regional and Sustainable Development; Economics and Research; Co-financing Operations;
- Finance and Administration, including 7 departments/offices: Secretary; General Counsel; Budget, Personnel and Management Systems; Administrative Services; Controller; Treasury; Information Systems and Technology.

Headquarters in Manila (Philippines). Field offices (26), including representative offices for North America, Europe and Japan.
Languages English. **Staff** Professional staff: 856; support staff: 1,544. Staff represented by *Asian Development Bank Staff Association and Staff Council (#01424).* **Finance** As of 31 Dec 2006, authorized and subscribed capital stock amounted to US$ 53,200 million. ADB raised funds totalling US$ 5,600 million, of which US$ 1,100 million was raised through a global public offering as of 31 Dec 2006. Gross income, which includes revenue and net realized gains, amounted to US$ 1,900 million, US$ 1,200 million of which was generated from the loan portfolio, US$ 573.1 million from the investment portfolio, and US $ 136.4 million from other sources, of which US$ 105 million came from equity investment operations. ADB's Special Funds are: the *Asian Development Fund (ADF, #01425)* with 2006 committed resources amounting to US$ 1,300 million; Technical Assistance Special Fund with US$ 89.4 million; Japan Special Fund with US$ 35.2 million; ADB Institute Special Fund with US$ 11.3 million; Asian Tsunami Fund with US$ 15.3 million; Pakistan Earthquake Fund with US$ 28.5 million. About 73 percent of cumulative lending is from ordinary capital resources (OCR). Funding from the OCR comes from three distinct sources: private placements and capital markets in the form of borrowing; paid-in capital provided by shareholders; accumulated retained income (reserves), which provides a buffer for risks.
Activities are dedicated to poverty reduction in Asia and the Pacific, a region that is home to two thirds of the world's poor. ADB is owned and financed by its 67 member countries, of which 48 are from the region and 19 are from other parts of the globe. Contributes low interest loans, guarantees, grants, private sector investments and knowledge and advice to help build infrastructure and improve essential services such as health and education to boost quality of life, particularly for the nearly 1.9 billion people in the region still living on US$ 2 or less a day. Focus is on encouraging economic growth, social development and good governance, while promoting regional cooperation and integration in partnership with governments, the private sector, and nongovernment and international organizations. Although most lending is in the public sector – and to governments – ADB also provides direct assistance to private enterprises of developing countries through equity investments, and loans. In addition, its triple-A credit rating helps mobilize funds for development.
ADB approved 80 loans (67 projects) for US$ 7,400 million, 14 equity investments for US$ 260.5 million, 3 guarantees for US$ 124.8 million, 5 syndication operations for US$ 530 million, 43 grant projects for US$ 538.4 million, 260 technical assistance projects for US$ 241.6 million, and 8 multi-tranche financing facilities for US$ 3,800 million. ADB approved 43 grant projects for US$ 538.4 million in 2006. Of this amount: US$ 274.9 million was funded from the ADF IX; US$ 28.5 million from the Asian Tsunami Fund and Pakistan Earthquake Fund; US$ 235 million from external sources with full or partial administration by ADB, comprising US$ 67.9 million from the Japan Fund for Poverty Reduction, US$ 1 million from the Japan Fund for Information and Communication Technology, and US$ 166.1 million from other bilateral and multilateral sources (Australia, Canada, Finland, Republic of Korea, the Netherlands, New Zealand, Norway, Sweden, Switzerland, and UK).
Events *Conference on Water Resource Management for Achieving Food Security in Asia Under Climate Change* Tokyo (Japan) 2022, *Joint Conference on Development and Innovative Finance* Tokyo (Japan) 2022, *Joint Forum on Elderly Care System Development* Tokyo (Japan) 2022, *Workshop on Hydrogen in Decarbonization Strategies in Asia and the Pacific* Tokyo (Japan) 2022, *Workshop on Sustainable Approaches to Post-Disaster Reconstruction* Tokyo (Japan) 2022. **Publications** *ADB Business Opportunities* (12 a year); *Asian Development Outlook* (2 a year); *Key Indicators* (annual). Annual report; summaries of proceedings; regional surveys, studies and reports; case studies; occasional papers; economic staff papers; ADB theme papers; statistical publications; sector papers; information brochures; DVDs.
Members Governments of 67 countries and territories:
Afghanistan, Armenia, Australia, Austria, Azerbaijan, Bangladesh, Belgium, Bhutan, Brunei Darussalam, Cambodia, Canada, China, Cook Is, Denmark, Fiji, Finland, France, Georgia, Germany, Hong Kong, India, Indonesia, Ireland, Italy, Japan, Kazakhstan, Kiribati, Korea Rep, Kyrgyzstan, Laos, Luxembourg, Malaysia, Maldives, Marshall Is, Micronesia FS, Mongolia, Myanmar, Nauru, Nepal, Netherlands, New Zealand, Norway, Pakistan, Palau, Papua New Guinea, Philippines, Portugal, Samoa, Singapore, Solomon Is, Spain, Sri Lanka, Sweden, Switzerland, Taiwan, Tajikistan, Thailand, Timor-Leste, Tonga, Türkiye, Turkmenistan, Tuvalu, UK, USA, Uzbekistan, Vanuatu, Vietnam.
[2020/XF0077/**F***]

♦ Asian Development Bank Institute (ADB Institute) 01423

Dean Kasumigaseki Bldg 8F, 3-2-5 Kasumigaseki, Chiyoda-ku, Tokyo, 100-6008 Japan. T. +81335935500. Fax +81335935571. E-mail: info@adbi.org.
URL: http://www.adbi.org/

History Dec 1997, Tokyo (Japan), as a subsidiary organ of *Asian Development Bank (ADB, #01422).* **Aims** Identify effective development strategies; improve development management in ADB's developing member countries; support long-term growth and competitiveness in developing economies in the Asia-Pacific region.
Structure Departments (3): Research; Capacity Building and Training; Administration, Management and Coordination. Head office in Tokyo (Japan). **Languages** English. **Staff** 50.00 FTE, paid. **Activities** Research/documentation; politics/policy/regulatory; capacity building; training/education. **Events** *Asian Regional Round Table on Macroeconomic and Structural Policy Challenges* 2022, *Annual Conference* Tokyo (Japan) 2022, *Conference on Digital Finance and Sustainability* Tokyo (Japan) 2022, *Joint Conference on Development and Innovative Finance* Tokyo (Japan) 2022, *Joint Forum on Elderly Care System Development* Tokyo (Japan) 2022. **Publications** *ADBI News* (4 a year) – newsletter. Books; research papers; working papers; research policy briefs; conference and seminar proceedings; course proceedings. **NGO Relations** Member of: *Council for Global Problem-Solving (CGP, #04898).*
[2021/XK1975/j/**E***]

♦ Asian Development Bank Staff Association and Staff Council 01424

Contact c/o ADB, PO Box 789, 0980 METRO Manila, Philippines.

History Founded in 24 Sep 1975, to represent staff of *Asian Development Bank (ADB, #01422).* Constitution last amended 31 Mar 1982. **Aims** Promote the aims and objectives of the Asian Development Bank; foster and safeguard the rights, interests and welfare of members. **Structure** General Meeting (annual). Staff Council is the executive organ Chairman, Secretary, Treasurer. **Finance** Members' dues. **Activities** Maintains a channel of communication between the staff and the Bank; keeps members informed about developments affecting their interests; identifies and studies problems and difficulties of members and recommends appropriate solutions; makes studies of critical areas in management-staff relations, with a view to recommend solutions; formulates schemes or proposals to promote general staff welfare.
Members Full in 63 countries and territories:
Afghanistan, Australia, Austria, Azerbaijan, Bangladesh, Belgium, Bhutan, Cambodia, Canada, China, Cook Is, Denmark, Fiji, Finland, France, Germany, Hong Kong, India, Indonesia, Italy, Japan, Kazakhstan, Kiribati, Korea Rep, Kyrgyzstan, Laos, Luxembourg, Malaysia, Maldives, Marshall Is, Micronesia FS, Mongolia, Myanmar, Nauru, Nepal, Netherlands, New Zealand, Norway, Pakistan, Palau, Papua New Guinea, Philippines, Portugal, Samoa, Singapore, Solomon Is, Spain, Sri Lanka, Sweden, Switzerland, Taiwan, Tajikistan, Thailand, Timor-Leste, Tonga, Türkiye, Turkmenistan, Tuvalu, UK, USA, Uzbekistan, Vanuatu, Vietnam.
NGO Relations Consultative status with: *Federation of International Civil Servants' Associations (FICSA, #09603).*
[2012/XE1515/v/**E**]

♦ Asian Development Fund (ADF) 01425

Fonds asiatique de développement – Fondo Asiatico de Desarrollo

Head Office c/o ADB Strategy / Policy Dept, 6 ADB Avenue, Mandaluyong City, 1550 METRO Manila, Philippines. T. +6326324444. E-mail: adf-mailbox@adb.org.
URL: http://www.adb.org/ADF/

History Jun 1974, Manila (Philippines), by *Asian Development Bank (ADB, #01422)*, taking over, by 31 Dec 1979, all contributions previously administered by *'Multi-Purpose Special Fund (MPSF)'* (set up 1968, wound up 1980), including those administered by *'Agricultural Special Fund (ASF)'* which was wound up in 1973. **Aims** Provide a systematic mechanism for mobilizing and administering resources for the Asian Development *Bank* to lend on concessional terms to member countries with low per capita gross national product and limited debt repayment capacity. **Structure** Together with *ADB Technical Assistance Special Fund (TASF, inactive)* and, since Mar 1988, the *'Japan Special Fund (JSF)'*, supplements *'Ordinary Capital Resources (OCR)'* of ADB. No separate offices, board, management or staff. **Finance** Prior to 1987, funded entirely by voluntary contributions of member countries. Total resources 31 Dec 1993: US$ 16,648.1 million.
Activities Eligibility for access to loans of ADB developing member countries is based on country economic considerations, particularly per capita GNP and debt repayment capacity. Group A (mainly least developed) countries are normally fully eligible; Groups B and C, countries in more favourable economic positions, are not normally eligible. Loans carry service charge of 1 percent per annum with repayments extending over 40 years, including a grace period of 10 years. **Events** *Annual meeting* Osaka (Japan) 1987.
Members Contributions from 24 countries – all 19 developed member countries of ADB and 5 () developing member countries and territories:
Australia, Austria, Belgium, Canada, Denmark, Finland, France, Germany, Hong Kong (*), Indonesia (*), Italy, Japan, Korea Rep (*), Nauru, Netherlands, New Zealand, Norway, Spain, Sweden, Switzerland, Taiwan (*), Türkiye (*), UK, USA.
[2012/XF5780/f/**F***]

♦ Asian Development Technology Centre (internationally oriented national body)
♦ Asian Directory Publishers Association / see Asian Local Search and Media Association (#01531)

♦ Asian Disaster Preparedness Center (ADPC) 01426

Exec Dir SM Tower – 24th Fl, 979/69 Paholyothin Road, Samsen Nai Phayathai, Bangkok, 10400, Thailand. T. +6622980681 – +6622980682 – +6622980692. Fax +6622980012 – +6622980013. E-mail: adpc@adpc.net.
URL: http://www.adpc.net/

History Founded 30 Jan 1986, at the recommendation of *Office of the United Nations Disaster Relief Coordinator (UNDRO, inactive)* – currently *United Nations Office for the Coordination of Humanitarian Affairs (OCHA, #20593), UNDP (#20292)* and *World Meteorological Organization (WMO, #21649)*, as an outreach activity of *Asian Institute of Technology (AIT, #01519).* **Aims** Support the advancement of safer communities and sustainable development, through programmes and projects that reduce the impact of disasters upon countries and communities in Asia and the Pacific, by: developing and enhancing sustainable institutional disaster risk management capacities, frameworks and mechanisms, and supporting the development and implementation of government policies; facilitating the dissemination and exchange of disaster risk management expertise, experience and information; raising awareness and enhancing disaster risk management knowledge and skills; promoting regional cooperation. **Structure** International Advisory Council; Regional Consultative Committee on Disaster Management; Board of Trustees; Office of Executive Director (OED) includes: Information and Knowledge Management (IKM); OED Support; Finance and Human Resources. **Languages** Burmese, English, Finnish, Hindi, Laotian, Mon-Khmer languages, Nepali, Pashto, Sinhala, Swedish, Tagalog, Thai, Urdu, Vietnamese. **Staff** 103.00 FTE, paid. Interns. **Finance** Sources include: donor governments; foundations; international organizations; UN agencies; training fees; consultancy income. **Activities** Knowledge management/information dissemination; awareness raising; advocacy/lobbying/activism; capacity building; training/education; events/meetings. **Events** *Regional Consultative Committee on Disaster Management Meeting* Bangkok (Thailand) 2020, *Regional Consultative Committee on Disaster Management Meeting* Kathmandu (Nepal) 2018, *International Conference on Building Resilience* Bangkok (Thailand) 2017, *Regional Science meeting in South/Southeast Asia on Land Cover/Land Use Change* Chiang Mai (Thailand) 2017, *Regional Consultative Committee on Disaster Management Meeting* Islamabad (Pakistan) 2016. **Publications** *ADPC Newsletter.* Books; disaster training, various projects and public information materials. Information Services: Maintains a library.
Members Participating entities in 46 countries and territories:
Afghanistan, Australia, Bangladesh, Bhutan, Brunei Darussalam, Cambodia, Canada, China, Fiji, Georgia, Germany, Hong Kong, India, Indonesia, Iran Islamic Rep, Japan, Jordan, Kazakhstan, Kiribati, Korea Rep, Laos, Lebanon, Malaysia, Maldives, Marshall Is, Mongolia, Myanmar, Nepal, New Zealand, Pakistan, Papua New Guinea, Philippines, Samoa, Singapore, Solomon Is, Sri Lanka, Switzerland, Tajikistan, Thailand, Timor-Leste, Tonga, Tuvalu, UK, USA, Vanuatu, Vietnam.
Consultative Status Consultative status granted from: *ECOSOC (#05331)* (Special).
IGO Relations Cooperates with:
- *Australian Aid (inactive);*
- *Canadian International Development Agency (CIDA, inactive);*
- *DANIDA;*
- *Department for International Development (DFID, inactive);*
- *ECHO (inactive);*
- *FAO (#09260);*
- *Japan International Cooperation Agency (JICA);*
- *Swedish International Development Cooperation Agency (Sida);*
- *UNEP (#20299);*
- *UNDP (#20292);*
- *UNESCO (#20322);*
- *UNHCR (#20327);*
- *UNICEF (#20332);*

- *United Nations Framework Convention on Climate Change – Secretariat (UNFCCC, #20564)*;
- *United States Agency for International Development (USAID)*;
- *WHO (#20950)*;
- *WMO/ESCAP Panel on Tropical Cyclones (PTC, #20976)*;
- *World Meteorological Organization (WMO, #21649)*.

NGO Relations Member of: *Asian Disaster Reduction Center (ADRC, #01427); International Campaign to Ban Landmines – Cluster Munition Coalition (ICBL-CMC, #12427); South Asian Initiative on Disaster Migration (Duryog Nivaran, #19734)*. Partner of: *Group on Earth Observations (GEO, #10735)*. [2018/XF0542/E]

♦ **Asian Disaster Reduction Center (ADRC)** 01427
Chairperson 5F 1-5-2 Wakinohamakaigan-dori, Chuo-ku, Kobe HYOGO, 651-0073 Japan. T. +81782625540. Fax +81782625546. E-mail: rep@adrc.asia.
URL: https://www.adrc.asia/
History Jul 1998, Kobe (Japan). **Aims** Act as a centre for promotion of multinational disaster reduction cooperation, through promotion of exchange of disaster reduction experts from each country and concerned bodies, accumulation and provision of disaster reduction information, human resource development and building communities' capabilities. **Structure** Chairman; Executive Director; Research Department; Administrative Department. **Languages** English, Japanese. **Activities** Capacity building; guidance/assistance/consulting; knowledge management/information dissemination; networking/liaising; projects/programmes; research and development; training/education. Active in all member countries. **Events** *Asian Conference on Disaster Reduction* Sendai (Japan) 2023, *International Recovery Forum* Kobe (Japan) 2022, *Asian Conference on Disaster Reduction* Kobe (Japan) 2020, *International Recovery Forum* Kobe (Japan) 2020, *International Recovery Forum* Kobe (Japan) 2019. **Publications** *ADRC Highlights* (12 a year) – newsletter; *The Latest Disaster Information. Tsunami awareness educational materials* (2005) in English; *Glossary on Natural Disasters*; *Natural Disasters Data Book*; *Total Disaster Risk Management: Good Practices*.
Members Full in 31 countries:
Armenia, Azerbaijan, Bangladesh, Bhutan, Cambodia, China, India, Indonesia, Iran Islamic Rep, Japan, Kazakhstan, Korea Rep, Kyrgyzstan, Laos, Malaysia, Maldives, Mongolia, Myanmar, Nepal, Pakistan, Papua New Guinea, Philippines, Russia, Singapore, Sri Lanka, Tajikistan, Thailand, Türkiye, Uzbekistan, Vietnam, Yemen.
Advisory countries (5):
Australia, France, New Zealand, Switzerland, USA.
Observer organization (1):
Asian Disaster Preparedness Center (ADPC, #01426).
IGO Relations Cooperates with (12): *ASEAN (#01141); Asian Development Bank Institute (ADB Institute, #01423); Haut conseil de La Francophonie (HCF, inactive); South Asian Association for Regional Cooperation (SAARC, #19721); UNESCO (#20322); United Nations Economic and Social Commission for Asia and the Pacific (ESCAP, #20557); United Nations Institute for Training and Research (UNITAR, #20576); United Nations Office for Disaster Risk Reduction (UNDRR, #20595); United Nations Office for Outer Space Affairs (UNOOSA, #20601); United Nations Office for the Coordination of Humanitarian Affairs (OCHA, #20593); United Nations University (UNU, #20642); World Meteorological Organization (WMO, #21649)*. **NGO Relations** Member of (3): *Asia-Pacific Regional Space Agency Forum (APRSAF, #02010); Global Alliance of Disaster Research Institutes (GADRI, #10194); International Recovery Platform (IRP, #14704)*. Instrumental in setting up (1): *Asian Disaster Reduction and Response Network (ADRRN, #01428)*. [2023.02.16/XE4260/y/E]

♦ **Asian Disaster Reduction and Response Network (ADRRN)** 01428
Coordinator Level 2, Podium Block, City Point, Kompleks Dayabumi, Jalan Sultan Hishamuddin, PO Box 11216, 50050 Kuala Lumpur, Malaysia. T. +60322733999 – +603(6012215751. Fax +60322723812. E-mail: mihir@seedsindia.org
URL: http://www.adrrn.net/index.html
History Jun 2004, following a meeting in Kobe (Japan) of 30 NGOs from all over Asia organized by *Asian Disaster Reduction Center (ADRC, #01427)*, Kobe, and *United Nations Office for the Coordination of Humanitarian Assistance to Afghanistan (UNOCHA, inactive)*, with the assistance of *ASEAN Foundation (#01190)*. **Aims** Promote coordination and collaboration among NGOs and other stakeholders for effective and efficient disaster reduction and response in the Asia-Pacific region. **Activities** Networking/liaising; awareness raising; capacity building; events/meetings. **Events** *International Conference of Disaster Reduction* Suwon (Korea Rep) 2015, *Asian Ministerial Conference on Disaster Risk Reduction* Bangkok (Thailand) 2014.
Members Organizations in 12 countries:
Afghanistan, Australia, Bangladesh, Cambodia, India, Indonesia, Malaysia, Maldives, Nepal, Pakistan, Philippines, Sri Lanka.
Included in the above, 2 organizations listed in this Yearbook:
Community and Family Services International (CFSI); Community World Service Asia (#04407).
NGO Relations Member of: *International Group for Wind-Related Disaster Risk Reduction (IG-WRDRR, #13760); New World Hope Organization (NWHO)*. Observers status with: *Asian University Network of Environment and Disaster Risk Management (AUEDM, #01774)*. [2010/XJ0997/F]

♦ **Asian Domain Name Dispute Resolution Centre (ADNDRC)** 01429
Secretariat c/o AIAC, Bangunan Sulaiman, Jalan Sultan Hishamuddin, 50000 Kuala Lumpur, Malaysia. T. +60322711000. Fax +60322711010. E-mail: aiac@adndrc.org – diana@aiac.world – aditya@aiac.world.
Hong Kong Office Domain Name Case Administrator, 38/F Two Exchange Square, 8 Connaught Place Central, Hong Kong, Central and Western, Hong Kong. T. +85225252381. Fax +85221995999. E-mail: hkiac@adndrc.org.
URL: http://www.adndrc.org/
Aims Provide dispute resolution services in regard to disputed generic top level domain names approved by ICANN. **NGO Relations** Located at: *China International Economic and Trade Arbitration Commission (CIETAC)* and *Hong Kong International Arbitration Centre (HKIAC)*. [2019/XM0714/E]

♦ **Asian Domestic Workers Network (ADWN)** 01430
Contact c/o CAW, 386/58 Ratchadaphisek 42, Ratchadaphisek Rd, Jakasam, Chatujak, Bangkok, 10900, Thailand. T. +6629305634. Fax +6629305633.
History 2005, following an Exchange workshop of Asian Domestic Workers, 2004, Hong Kong, organized by *Committee for Asian Women (CAW, #04243)*. **Aims** Work towards a society that affirms domestic work as decent and dignified work. **Structure** Secretariat, provided by *Committee for Asian Women (CAW, #04243)*. **Activities** Capacity building; networking/liaising.
Members Regular; Associate. Regular in 5 countries and territories:
Hong Kong, India, Indonesia, Nepal, Sri Lanka.
Associate in 4 countries:
India, Indonesia, Nepal, Pakistan.
NGO Relations Cooperates with: *International Domestic Workers Federation (IDWF, #13190)*. [2015/XJ8447/E]

♦ Asian Domestic Workers' Union (no recent information)
♦ Asian Domestic Workers' Union (unconfirmed)

♦ **Asian Dragon Boat Federation** 01431
Contact 9 Tiyuguan Road, Dongcheng District, 100763 Beijing, China. T. +861067128832. Fax +861067133577. E-mail: adbfdragon@126.com.
History 1992, Beijing (China). **Aims** Encourage development of Dragon Boat racing; spread the Dragon Boat culture in Asia. **Events** *Congress* Busan (Korea Rep) 2012. **NGO Relations** *International Dragon Boat Federation (IDBF, #13197)*. [2017.07.07/XD9449/D]

♦ **Asian Draughts Confederation (ADC)** 01432
President 38-77, 13 horoolol, Bayanzurkh, Ulaanbaatar 13371, Mongolia. T. +97699103339. Fax +97611454340. E-mail: office@asiadraughts.org – president@asiadraughts.org.
URL: http://asiadraughts.org/
History 2000, Tashkent (Uzbekistan). **Structure** Executive Committee. **Languages** English, Russian. **Activities** Awards/prizes/competitions.
Members Full in 18 countries:
China, India, Indonesia, Iran Islamic Rep, Japan, Kazakhstan, Kuwait, Kyrgyzstan, Lebanon, Malaysia, Mongolia, Pakistan, Qatar, Singapore, Tajikistan, Thailand, Turkmenistan, Uzbekistan.
NGO Relations Member of (1): *General Association of Asia Pacific Sports Federations (GAAPSF, #10106)*. Continental federation of: *Fédération Mondiale du Jeu de Dames (FMJD, #09690)*. [2022.10.25/AA1109/D]

♦ Asian Dynamics Initiative (internationally oriented national body)
♦ Asian Ecological Society (inactive)

♦ **Asian Ecotourism Network (AEN)** 01433
Head Office 594/6 Asoke Dindaeng Road, Dindaeng, Bangkok, 10400, Thailand. T. +6626416063 – +6626416064 – +6626416065. E-mail: asianecotourismnetwork@gmail.com.
URL: http://www.asianecotourism.org/
History A regional initiative of *Global Ecotourism Network (GEN, #10330)*. **Aims** Connect stakeholders for knowledge transfer, consulting, marketing, and business development to achieve sustainability. **Structure** Board. **Languages** English, Thai. **Events** *International Ecotourism Forum* Cavite (Philippines) 2022, *International Ecotourism Forum* Cavite (Philippines) 2020, *AEN Semi-Annual General Meeting / Forum* Chengdu (China) 2020, *AEN Ecotourism Conference and Technical Visits* Chiayi City (Taiwan) 2019.
Members Full in 16 countries and territories:
Australia, China, India, Indonesia, Japan, Korea Rep, Laos, Malaysia, Mongolia, Nepal, New Zealand, Pakistan, Philippines, Singapore, Sri Lanka, Taiwan.
NGO Relations Member of: *Global Sustainable Tourism Council (GSTC, #10619)*. [2021/XM7025/F]

♦ **Asian Electroceramics Association (AECA)** 01434
Contact c/o NTUT, 1 Sec 3, Zhongxiao E Rd, Taipei 10608, Taiwan.
Activities *Asia Meeting on Electroceramics (AMEC)*. **Events** *Asian Meeting on Electroceramics* Hiroshima (Japan) 2018, *Meeting* Taipei (Taiwan) 2016, *Meeting* Shanghai (China) 2014, *Asian Meeting on Electroceramics* Penang (Malaysia) 2012, *Meeting* Jeju (Korea Rep) 2010. [2018/XM3060/D]

♦ Asian Electronics Forum (meeting series)

♦ **Asian Electronic Sports Federation (AESF)** 01435
Secretariat Units 801-803, Level 8, Core C, Cyberport 3, No 100 Cyberport Road, Hong Kong, Central and Western, Hong Kong. T. +85264615555. E-mail: secretariat@aesf.com – info@aesf.com.
URL: https://www.aesf.com/
Aims Enhance the quality and professional governance of esports; support and oversee the development of esports in the Asia region; and nurture the development of world-class athletes for success in the international arena. **Structure** General Assembly; Executive Board; President; Committees; Judicial Body; Secretariat. **Languages** Chinese, English. **Activities** Sporting activities. **Events** *Game Rating and Administration Committee Meeting* Busan (Korea Rep) 2021, *Meeting* Busan (Korea Rep) 2020.
Members Full in 45 countries and territories:
Afghanistan, Bahrain, Bangladesh, Bhutan, Brunei Darussalam, Cambodia, China, Hong Kong, India, Indonesia, Iran Islamic Rep, Iraq, Japan, Jordan, Kazakhstan, Korea DPR, Korea Rep, Kuwait, Kyrgyzstan, Laos, Lebanon, Macau, Malaysia, Maldives, Mongolia, Myanmar, Nepal, Oman, Pakistan, Palestine, Philippines, Qatar, Saudi Arabia, Singapore, Sri Lanka, Syrian AR, Taiwan, Tajikistan, Thailand, Timor-Leste, Turkmenistan, United Arab Emirates, Uzbekistan, Vietnam, Yemen.
NGO Relations Memorandum of Understanding with (1): *International Esports Federation (IESF, #13304)*. Member of (1): *World Esports Consortium (WESCO, #21391)*. Recognized by: *Olympic Council of Asia (OCA, #17718)*. [2020.08.27/AA1028/D]

♦ Asian Endoscopic Ultrasound Group / see Asian EUS Group (#01446)

♦ **Asian Energy Institute (AEI)** 01436
Sec c/o TERI, Darbari Seth Block, IHC Complex, Lodhi Road, Delhi 11 0003, DELHI 11 0003, India. T. +911124682100 – +911124682111ext2318. E-mail: mailbox@teri.res.in.
URL: http://www.aeinetwork.org/
History Aug 1989, India, by *Energy and Resources Institute (TERI)*. **Aims** Promote greater information exchange; facilitate sharing and dissemination of knowledge; undertake research and training activities of common interest to members; analyse global energy developments and their implications, in particular energy security, energy and technology cooperation, *climate change* and *environmental* security. **Structure** Steering Committee. Governing Council, comprising one representative per energy institute in the network. Officers: Honorary Chairman; Chairman Emeritus; President; 2 Vice-Presidents; Secretary; Treasurer. **Languages** English. **Staff** 1.50 FTE, paid. **Finance** Sources: members' in-kind contribution; core funds; bilateral and multilateral funding for projects. **Activities** Research/documentation; events/meetings. **Events** *Meeting on energy transformations for Asia* Delhi (India) 2009, *Workshop* Delhi (India) 2000, *Conference on energy security in Asia and its implications* 1999, *Workshop* Delhi (India) 1995, *Workshop on national energy policies / Workshop* Bangalore (India) 1993. **Publications** *AEI Newsletter* (2 a year). *Review of Natural Gas Markets in Asia* (2003); *Sustainable Energy: Perspective for Asia* (2002); *Climate Change in Asia and Brazil: The Role of Technology Transfer*; *Global Warming: Collaborative Study on Strategies to Limit Carbon Dioxide Emissions in Asia and Brazil*; *Global Warming: Mitigation Strategies and Perspectives from Asia and Brazil*.
Members Full Members institutes in 14 countries:
Bangladesh, China, India, Indonesia, Iran Islamic Rep, Japan, Jordan, Korea Rep, Kuwait, Malaysia, Pakistan, Philippines, Sri Lanka, Thailand.
Included in the above, 1 organization listed in this Yearbook:
Institute for Political and International Studies, Teheran (IPIS).
Associate members in 13 countries:
Austria, Brazil, Canada, Italy, Japan, Netherlands, Norway, Sierra Leone, South Africa, Sweden, Switzerland, Thailand, USA.
Included in the above, 4 organizations listed in this Yearbook:
Centre for International Climate and Environmental Research, Oslo (CICERO); International Institute for Applied Systems Analysis (IIASA, #13861); Stockholm Environment Institute (SEI, #19993); World Resources Institute (WRI, #21753). [2016/XE3081/jy/E]

♦ **Asian Environmental Compliance and Enforcement Network (AECEN)** 01437
Secretariat SG Tower 6th Fl Unit 604, 161/1 Soi Mahadlek Luang 3, Rajdamri Road, Patumwan, Bangkok, 10330, Thailand. T. +6626518797. Fax +6626518798.
History 2005. **Aims** Promote improved compliance with environmental legal requirements in Asia through regional exchange of innovative policies and practices. **Structure** Executive Committee of up to 9 members. Secretariat. **Events** *Regional Conference on Next Generation Compliance in Asia* Bangkok (Thailand) 2015, *Regional forum* Kyoto (Japan) 2010.
Members National and sub-national agencies in 16 countries:
Cambodia, China, India, Indonesia, Japan, Korea Rep, Laos, Malaysia, Maldives, Nepal, Pakistan, Philippines, Singapore, Sri Lanka, Thailand, Vietnam.
IGO Relations Partners include: *Asian Development Bank (ADB, #01422); International Bank for Reconstruction and Development (IBRD, #12317)* (World Bank); *OECD (#17693); UNEP (#20299); United States Agency for International Development (USAID)*. **NGO Relations** Partners include: *Asia Pacific Jurist Association (APJA); Australasian Environmental Law Enforcement and Regulators Network (AELERT); International Network for Environmental Compliance and Enforcement (INECE, #14261)*. [2019/XJ4818/F]

♦ Asian Environmental Council (no recent information)

♦ **Asian Environmental Society (AES)** 01438
Secretariat U-112 3rd Floor, Vidhata House Vikas Marg, Shakarpur, Delhi 110092, DELHI 110092, India.
History Founded 1972, Manila (Philippines). **Aims** Serve as a forum for discussion and exchange of ideas and collect and disseminate information on problems that confront the Asian environment; promote research and monitor programmes concerning environmental pollutants; alert Asian governments and people regarding possible hazards and dangers to the environment; provide the people, especially public policy-makers, educators and scientists, with information and factual assessment of the degree and nature of man's polluting activities; formulate specific recommendations and measures regarding the whole environmental and developmental problem; cooperate with bodies and individuals concerned. **Structure** Executive Committee; Board of Trustees, serving as advisory board. **Languages** English. **Staff** 6.00 FTE, paid. **Activities** Research/documentation; training/education; events/meetings. **Events** *Meeting* Singapore (Singapore) 1996, *Asia-Pacific NGO environmental conference* Kyoto (Japan) 1994, *Global forum on environmental and development education* Delhi (India) 1993, *International conference on global atmosphere change* Jaipur (India) 1992, *Asian environments* Rio de Janeiro (Brazil) 1992.

Members Organizations (60) and individuals concerned with environmental problems in 10 countries and territories:
Hong Kong, India, Indonesia, Japan, Korea Rep, Malaysia, Nepal, Philippines, Taiwan, Thailand.
Consultative Status Consultative status granted from: *ECOSOC (#05331)* (Ros B); *UNEP (#20299)*. **NGO Relations** Member of: *Conference of Non-Governmental Organizations in Consultative Relationship with the United Nations (CONGO, #04635)*; *Environment Liaison Centre International (ELCI, no recent information)*.
[2015/XD4291/**D**]

♦ Asian Epilepsy Academy (ASEPA) 01439

Contact Dept of Neurology, Royal Perth Hosp, 197 Wellington St, Perth WA 6847, Australia. Fax +61892247020.
History 2002, as the educational arm of Commission of Asian and Ocean Affairs, within *International League Against Epilepsy (ILAE, #14013)*. **Aims** Provide healthcare workers with the education and training necessary for optimal epilepsy care. **Activities** Training/education; events/meetings; certification/accreditation. **Events** *Asian and Oceanian epilepsy congress* Melbourne, VIC (Australia) 2010, *Workshop on epilepsy surgery* Delhi (India) 2009. [2019.02.13/XJ0679/**E**]

♦ Asian Epilepsy Surgery Society (AESC) 01440

Chairman Rm 7 6th Fl, CN Centre – AIIMS, Delhi 110029, DELHI 110029, India.
URL: http://www2.convention.co.jp/aesc2014/
Activities Events/meetings. **Events** *Congress / Asian Epilepsy Surgery Congress – AESC* Tokyo (Japan) 2014, *Asian Epilepsy Surgery Congress – AESC* Beijing (China) 2013, *Congress* Busan (Korea Rep) 2012, *Asian Epilepsy Surgery Congress – AESC* Hong Kong (Hong Kong) 2011, *Asian Epilepsy Surgery Congress – AESC* Taipei (Taiwan) 2010. [2014/XM0428/c/**E**]

♦ Asian Equestrian Federation (AEF) 01441

Pres Room 603, Olympic Centre, 88 Oryun-Dong, Songpa-Gu, Seoul 138-749, Korea Rep. T. +8224244063. Fax +8224204264. E-mail: aef.secretariat@yahoo.com.
Aims Encourage and develop equestrian sport in the Asian region. **Structure** General Assembly. Executive Committee. Regional Groups. **Languages** English. [2013.10.08/XD9337/**D**]

♦ Asia Network / see Institute of Asian Worlds

♦ Asia Network Beyond Design (ANBD) 01442

Seoul Office address not obtained. E-mail: jeehyun0208@hanmail.net.
URL: http://anbd.info/
Aims Promote exchanges; perform Asian identity through networking over various boundaries. **Structure** Boards in: Seoul (Korea Rep); Taipei (Taiwan); Tianjin (China); Tokyo (Japan). **Activities** Networking/liaising. **Events** *Meeting* Kyoto (Japan) 2019. [2020/AA0100/**F**]

♦ Asia Network Forum (ANF) 01443

Contact PSB Corporation, 1 Science Park Drive, Singapore 118221, Singapore. T. +657729620. Fax +657759725. E-mail: klee@ktl.re.kr.
URL: http://www.theanf.org/
History 26 Oct 2000, Tokyo (Japan). **Aims** Promote mutual understanding and friendship among Asian *testing* and *certification* organizations; increase mutual business development; enhance technical competence and capabilities. **Structure** General Assembly (annual). Officers: President; Secretary General. **Languages** English. **Finance** Members' dues. **Events** *General Assembly* Busan (Korea Rep) 2019, *Seminar on Technical Regulation* Busan (Korea Rep) 2019, *Meeting* Daegu (Korea Rep) 2013, *Annual Meeting / General Assembly* Taipei (Taiwan) 2013, *General Assembly* Taipei (Taiwan) 2012.
Members Organizations (5) in 5 countries:
China, Japan, Korea Rep, Singapore, Taiwan. [2013/XM3059/**F**]

♦ Asia Network of Organics Recycling (ANOR) 01444

Contact Japan Organics Recycling Assn, Bajichikusan-kaikan 401, 2-6-16 Shinkawa, Chuo-ku, Tokyo, 104-0033 Japan. T. +81332975618. Fax +81332975619.
URL: http://www.jora.jp/anor/
History 24 Jun 2002, Tokyo (Japan). **Aims** Reduce organic *waste*; promote maximum diversion of organic materials from *landfill* and *incineration* to utilization as organic resources. **Structure** General Meeting (every 2 years). Steering Committee, comprising Chairman, Vice-Chairman and 3 members. Secretariat located at the organization to which the Chairperson of the Steering Committee belongs. **Languages** English. **Staff** Voluntary. **Finance** Members cover expenses for regional activities; donations; subsidies. **Activities** With regard to the present situation and future challenges of organics recycling and environmental conservation activities, exchanges information and opinions based on science among members, deepens mutual understanding to develop friendship and promotes recycling of organic resources; facilitates support and cooperation among members in promoting awareness of and developing human resources for organic resource recycling; sets standards for smooth distribution of products made from recycled resources in the region and develops these standards in stages into international standards; works to strengthen links to and cooperation with organizations engaged in similar activities in other areas of the world. **Publications** *ANOR Newsletter*.
Members Organizations, colleges and institutes (31) in 16 countries and territories:
Australia, Cambodia, China, Hong Kong, Indonesia, Japan, Korea Rep, Malaysia, Nepal, New Zealand, Pakistan, Philippines, Sri Lanka, Taiwan, Thailand, Vietnam. [2010.06.01/XF7052/**F**]

♦ Asia Network for Small-Scale Agricultural Biotechnologies / see Asia Network for Sustainable Agriculture and Bioresources (#01445)

♦ Asia Network for Sustainable Agriculture and Bioresources (ANSAB) 01445

Contact PO Box 11035, Baneshwor, Kathmandu, Nepal. T. +97714497547 – +97714478412. Fax +97714476586. E-mail: ansab@ansab.org.np.
URL: https://ansab.org.np/
History 1992, Kathmandu (Nepal). Former names and other names: *Asia Network for Small-Scale Agricultural Biotechnologies* – former alias. **Aims** Generate and implement community-based, enterprise-oriented solutions that conserve biodiversity and improve the livelihoods of the poorest while bolstering national economic development and addressing climate change. **Structure** Board of Directors. **Languages** English, Nepali. **Staff** 60.00 FTE, paid.
Finance Sources: international government and non-governmental donor organizations, including:
- *Blue Moon Fund*;
- *Department for International Development (DFID, inactive)*;
- *Entreprise Works / VITA*;
- *European Commission (EC, #06633)*;
- *FAO (#09260)*;
- *Ford Foundation (#09858)*;
- *Global Environment Facility (GEF, #10346)*;
- *ICCO – Interchurch Organization for Development Cooperation*;
- *International Bank for Reconstruction and Development (IBRD, #12317)* (World Bank);
- *International Development Research Centre (IDRC, #13162)*;
- *International Fund for Agricultural Development (IFAD, #13692)*;
- *International Institute for Environment and Development (IIED, #13877)*;
- *MacArthur Foundation*;
- *Manfred-Hermsen-Stiftung for Nature Conservation and Environmental Protection*;
- *SNV Netherlands Development Organisation (SNV)*;
- *Norwegian Agency for Development Cooperation (Norad)*;
- *The Rockefeller Foundation (#18966)*;
- *Swiss Agency for Development and Cooperation (SDC)*;
- *United States Agency for International Development (USAID)*;
- *World Agroforestry Centre (ICRAF, #21072)*;
- *World Resources Institute (WRI, #21753)*;
- *World Wide Fund for Nature (WWF, #21922)*.

Activities Research and development; politics/policy/regulatory; networking/liaising; capacity building. **Publications** *The Himalayan Bioresources* (3 a year) – newsletter. *ANSAB Rural Development Toolkit Series – vols 1-8* (2010). Video documentaries; practical books; manuals; guidelines; price lists.
Members Nepal Non-Timber Forest Products Network (NNN). Organizational (50) and individual (250) members in 5 countries:
Bangladesh, India, Nepal, Sri Lanka, USA.
IGO Relations Partner: *UNEP (#20299)*. **NGO Relations** Partners: *ActionAid (#00087)*; *Canadian Centre for International Studies and Cooperation (CECI)*; *Forest Stewardship Council (FSC, #09869)*; *Future Generations*; *International Centre for Integrated Mountain Development (ICIMOD, #12500)*; *International Development Enterprises (IDE, #13156)*; *International Union for Conservation of Nature and Natural Resources (IUCN, #15766)*; *Mission East*; *Practical Action (#18475)*; *RECOFTC – The Center for People and Forests (RECOFTC, #18628)*; *Relief International*; *Rights and Resources Initiative (RRI, #18947)*; *Winrock International*.
[2023/XF4806/**F**]

♦ Asian-Eurasian Human Rights Forum (internationally oriented national body)

♦ Asian EUS Group (AEG) 01446

Contact address not obtained. E-mail: secretariat@asianeus.org.
URL: https://asianeus.org/
History Aug 2012. Former names and other names: *Asian Endoscopic Ultrasound Group* – alias. **Events** *Asian EUS Congress* Hong Kong (Hong Kong) 2023, *Asian EUS Congress* Hong Kong (Hong Kong) 2021, *Summit* Seoul (Korea Rep) 2020, *Congress* Tokyo (Japan) 2019, *Congress* Mumbai (India) 2017. **NGO Relations** *World Endoscopy Organization (WEO, #21380)*. [2021/XJ9941/**D**]

♦ Asia News Network (ANN) 01447

Contact 1858/127-128, 31st Floor, Bangna-Trad Road, Bangkok, 10260, Thailand. T. +6623383188. E-mail: info@asianews.network.
URL: https://asianews.network/
History Mar 1999. **Aims** Enhance and improve news coverage of Asian affairs; provide member newspapers with reliable access to news sources in Asia; help promote the professional development of journalism in the region. **Finance** Supported by: *Konrad Adenauer Foundation (KAF)*. **Publications** *Changing Asia* (2006).
Members Newspapers (16) in 14 countries:
Bangladesh, China, India, Indonesia, Japan, Korea Rep, Laos, Malaysia, Nepal, Philippines, Singapore, Sri Lanka, Thailand, Vietnam. [2007.08.06/XM0113/**F**]

♦ Asia New Zealand Foundation (internationally oriented national body)

♦ Asian Exim Banks Forum (AEBF) 01448

Address not obtained.
URL: https://www.asianeximbanks.org/
History 1996, India. **Aims** Share the expertise and knowledge gained by Asian ECAs amongst members and explore possible areas of cooperation. **Activities** Events/meetings; knowledge management/information dissemination; networking/liaising; training/education. **Events** *Annual Meeting* Jeju (Korea Rep) 2019.
Members Export Credit Agencies in 11 countries:
Australia, China, India, Indonesia, Japan, Korea Rep, Malaysia, Philippines, Thailand, Türkiye, Vietnam.
Permanent Observer:
Asian Development Bank (ADB, #01422). [2020/AA0265/**F**]

♦ Asian Eye Care (internationally oriented national body)
♦ Asian Eye Care – Association for Eye Care Development in Asia / see Asian Eye Care

♦ Asian Facial Plastic Surgery Society (AFPSS) 01449

Contact Dept of ORL-HNS, Seoul Natl Univ Boramea Medical Ctr, 39 Boramae Road, Dongjak-gu, Seoul 156-707, Korea Rep. T. +8228702454. Fax +8228703866.
URL: http://www.afpss.org/
History 20 Jun 2009, Seoul (Korea Rep). **Aims** Represent the specialty of facial plastic and reconstructive surgery in Asia. **Structure** Board; Executive Board. **Activities** Events/meetings. **Events** *Asian Facial Plastic Surgery Society Congress (AFPSS)* Seoul (Korea Rep) 2019, *Congress* Bangkok (Thailand) 2017, *AFPSS Congress* 2015, *AFPSS Congress* Thailand 2014, *AFPSS Congress* Korea Rep 2013. [2019/AA0225/**D**]

♦ Asian Farmers'Association for Sustainable Rural Development (AFA) 01450

SG Room 206 Parnership Center, No 59 C Salvador St, Loyola Heights, 1108 Quezon City, Philippines. T. +6324364640. Fax +6324364640. E-mail: afaesther@asianfarmers.org – afa@asianfarmers.org.
URL: http://www.asianfarmers.org/
History Founded May 2002. **Aims** Be a strong and influential voice of small men and women farmers in Asia; be a strong lobby and advocacy group for farmers' rights and development, genuine *agrarian* reform and mainstreaming of sustainable agriculture in regional and national policies and programmes; be a facilitator for members' commercial activities in trading and marketing of sustainable agricultural products; be a venue for solidarity and information exchange on agriculture and farmers'development among members. **Structure** General Assembly. Executive Committee; Secretariat. **Languages** English. **Staff** 3.50 FTE, paid. **Finance** Grants. **Activities** Politics/policy/regulatory; capacity building; events/meetings. **Events** *General Assembly* Bali (Indonesia) 2014, *General Assembly* Hanoi (Vietnam) 2012. **Publications** Annual Report; books; monographs; issue papers.
Members Organizations (12) in 11 countries and territories:
Bangladesh, Cambodia, Indonesia, Japan, Korea DPR, Korea Rep, Nepal, Philippines, Taiwan, Thailand, Vietnam.
NGO Relations Member of: *Global Alliance for Climate-Smart Agriculture (GACSA, #10189)*. Cooperates with: *Global Forum on Agricultural Research (GFAR, #10370)*. [2016/XF7189/**F**]

♦ Asian Farming Systems Association (AFSA) 01451

Contact address not obtained.
History Founded 1988. Formally incorporated, 1992. **Aims** Promote and foster improvements in the efficiency and effectiveness of farming systems research and extension through information sharing. **Structure** Governing Board. **Events** *Symposium* Manila (Philippines) 1994, *Symposium* Sri Lanka 1992, *Symposium* Bangkok (Thailand) 1990. **Publications** *AFSA Journal* (4 a year). [2015/XD6043/**D**]

♦ Asian Federation of Advertising Associations (AFAA) 01452

Fédération d'Asie des associations de publicité
Chairman 2-96 Jalan Prima SG 3/2, Taman Prima Sri Gombak, Batu Caves, 68100 Gombak, Selangor, Malaysia. T. +60361868006. Fax +60361862066. E-mail: jameselva@brandequity.com.my.
URL: http://www.afaaglobal.org/
History Founded Jul 1978. **Aims** Unify all Asian associations involved in advertising; upgrade standards, ethics and practices of advertising and bring a more meaningful contribution from advertising activities to both regional and national socio-economic development; foster self-regulation. **Structure** General Body; Executive Committee. **Languages** English. **Staff** Administered by a management company. **Finance** Members' dues. **Activities** Training/education; events/meetings. **Events** *Biennial Asian Advertising Congress* Macau (Macau) 2021, *Forum* Busan (Korea Rep) 2019, *Biennial Asian Advertising Congress* Lahore (Pakistan) 2019, *Biennial Asian Advertising Congress* Bali (Indonesia) 2017, *Biennial Asian Advertising Congress* Taipei (Taiwan) 2015. **Publications** *AFAA Gold Gook* (8th ed 2011); *Advertising Trends of Asia Pacific* (4th ed 2009).
Members Advertising associations in 11 countries and territories:
India, Indonesia, Japan, Korea Rep, Malaysia, Pakistan, Philippines, Taiwan, Thailand, United Arab Emirates, Vietnam.
NGO Relations Member of: *International Advertising Association (IAA, #11590)*. [2019.09.21/XE7500/**E**]

♦ Asian Federation Against Involuntary Disappearances (AFAD) 01453

Federación Asiatica contra la Desaparición Involuntaria
SG Rms 310-311 Philippine Social Science Center Bldg, Commonwealth Avenue, Diliman, 1103 Quezon City, Philippines. T. +6324566434. Fax +6324546759. E-mail: afad@surfshop.net.ph.
URL: http://www.afad-online.org/

History 30 May 2000, Quezon City (Philippines), at founding congress, when constitution was adopted. **Aims** Work for attainment of truth, justice, redress and reconstruction of the historical memory of the *disappeared*; actively participate in the overall struggle for social transformation which is a necessary requirement to realize a world without *desaparecidos*. **Structure** Congress (every 3 years); Council; Secretariat. **Languages** English, Italian, Spanish. **Staff** 9.00 FTE, paid. **Finance** Members' dues. **Activities** Research/documentation; advocacy/lobbying/activism; capacity building. **Events** *Triennial Congress* Philippines 2014, *Triennial Congress* Quezon City (Philippines) 2000. **Publications** *AFAD News Bulletin. From Grief to Courage: Best Practices in Advocating Legislation Against Enforced Disappearances* (2015); *Beyond Tears and Borders* (2013); *Reclaiming Stolen Lives* (2008); *Healing Wounds, Mending Scars* (2005). Annual Report.
Members Organizations in 10 countries:
Bangladesh, India, Indonesia, Korea Rep, Nepal, Pakistan, Philippines, Sri Lanka, Thailand, Timor-Leste.
IGO Relations Adheres to the following human rights instruments: *Universal Declaration of Human Rights (UDHR, 1948)*; *International Covenant on Civil and Political Rights (ICCPR, 1966)*; *International Covenant on Economic, Social and Cultural Rights (ICESCR, 1966)*; *Convention Against Torture and other Cruel, Inhuman or Degrading Treatment or Punishment (1984)*; United Nations Declaration on the Protection of All Persons from Enforced Disappearance (UNDPAPFEID) (1992). Adheres to and promotes approval of: *International Convention for the Protection of all Persons from Enforced Disappearance (2006)*. **NGO Relations** Member of: *Conference of Non-Governmental Organizations in Consultative Relationship with the United Nations (CONGO, #04635)*; *EarthAction (EA, #05159)*; *International Coalition against Enforced Disappearances (ICAED, #12605)*; *International Coalition to Stop Crimes Against Humanity in North Korea (ICNK, #12622)*. [2019/XD7855/**D**]

♦ Asian Federation of American Football (inactive)

♦ Asian Federation of Biotechnology (AFOB) 01454

SG 403, c12, Gaetbeol-ro, Yeonsu-gu, Incheon 21999, Korea Rep. T. +82322600066. E-mail: afob@afob.org.
URL: http://www.afob.org/

History Founded following agreement for its establishment by delegates from Asian countries during the IBS 2008 conference, 12-17 Oct 2008, Dalian (China). Preparative meetings for the formation of AFOB had been held in meetings prior to its official establishment: KSBB National Spring Meeting, Apr 27 2007, Incheon (Korea Rep); APBioChEC Meeting, Nov 5-7 2007, Taipei (Taiwan); KSBB National Spring Meeting, Apr 18 2008, Jeonju (Korea Rep). Registration: Start date: 2008, Korea Rep. **Aims** Promote cooperation, on scientific grounds, between scientists from *academia* and *industry* in the Asian region, for general advancement of biotechnology as an interdisciplinary field of research and as a means of bringing scientific development to industrial level. **Structure** General Assembly; Executive Board; Advisory Board. Committees (4): Financial; Public Relations and Policy; Publication; Academic (with Scientific Divisions). *Young Asian Biological Engineers' Community (YABEC)* functions under its umbrella. **Languages** English. **Staff** 1.00 FTE, paid. **Finance** Supported by city of Incheon (Korea Rep). **Activities** Awareness raising; events/meetings; knowledge management/information dissemination; networking/liaising; publishing activities; research/documentation; training/education. **Events** *AFOB Regional Symposium* Jinning (Taiwan) 2022, *Bioindustrial Forum on Biotechnology for Adding Values of Farm Products* Incheon (Korea Rep) 2021, *Conference* Incheon (Korea Rep) 2021, *Innovations of Science and Technology for Sustainable Development of Green Energy and Cleaner Environment* Incheon (Korea Rep) 2021, *International Symposium on Biomedical Engineering* Incheon (Korea Rep) 2021. **Publications** *Biotechnology Journal – AFOB Special Issue* (2 a year).
Members Individual (3,250); Institutional (11); Regional (13). Members in 14 countries and territories:
Bangladesh, China, India, Indonesia, Japan, Korea Rep, Malaysia, Mongolia, Nepal, Philippines, Singapore, Taiwan, Thailand, Vietnam. [2022/XJ0779/**D**]

♦ Asian Federation of Bodybuilding and Fitness / see Asian Bodybuilding and Physique Sports Federation (#01361)

♦ Asian Federation of Catholic Medical Associations (AFCMA) 01455

Fédération asiatique des associations médicales catholiques – Federación Asiatica de Asociaciones Médicas Católicas

Sec Catholic Doctors Association of Malaysia, Assunta Hospital, Jln Templer, 46000 Petaling Jaya, Selangor, Malaysia. E-mail: cdamail@yahoo.com.
URL: http://www.afcma.blogspot.com/

History 1960, as the Asian Regional Federation of *International Federation of Catholic Medical Associations (#13378)*. 1st Congress: 1960, Manila (Philippines). **Aims** Coordinate efforts of Catholic medical associations in the study and spread of Christian principles throughout the medical profession in general; encourage development of such associations in all countries of Asia to assist Catholic physicians in moral and spiritual development and in academic advancement; take part in general development of the medical profession and promote health and social work in accordance with Christian principles; study and report on problems confronting Catholic medical professionals in Asia. **Structure** General Council (meets at least every 4 years). Officers: President, 2 Vice-Presidents, Secretary-General/Treasurer. Executive Committee (meets at least once a year), comprising officers and one representative of each member Asian country. Ecclesiastical Advisor appointed by *Federation of Asian Bishops' Conferences (FABC, #09430)*. **Languages** English. **Staff** 0.50 FTE, paid. **Finance** Members' dues. Donations. **Activities** Organizes medical congresses. Exchange of research workers, doctors and medical students between various countries. **Events** *Quadrennial Congress* Kyoto (Japan) 2016, *Quadrennial Congress* Bali (Indonesia) 2012, *Quadrennial Congress / Congress* Hong Kong (Hong Kong) 2008, *Congress* Taipei (Taiwan) 2004, *Quadrennial congress / Congress* Kuala Lumpur (Malaysia) 2000. **Publications** *AFCMA Newsletter*.
Members Catholic medical associations in 11 countries and territories:
Hong Kong, India, Indonesia, Japan, Korea Rep, Malaysia, Pakistan, Philippines, Singapore, Taiwan, Thailand. [2010/XD6430/**D**]

♦ Asian Federation of Cheerleading (AFC) 01456

Contact 7F Aoyama Success Bldg, 2-11-13 Minami-Aoyama, Minato-ku, Tokyo, 107-0062 Japan. T. +81334047808. Fax +81334042227.
Facebook: https://www.facebook.com/afc.cheer/

History 2007.
Members National federations in 12 countries and territories:
Cambodia, Hong Kong, India, Indonesia, Japan, Kazakhstan, Korea Rep, Laos, Philippines, Singapore, Taiwan, Thailand.
NGO Relations Continental federation of: *International Federation of Cheerleading (IFC, #13386)*. [2020/XJ6339/**D**]

♦ Asian Federation of Coloproctology / see Asia Pacific Federation of Coloproctology (#01897)

♦ Asian Federation of Computer Vision Societies 01457

Secretariat Rm 505 Taeyang BLGD 44-2, Yoido-dong, Yongdeungpo-gu, Seoul 150-890, Korea Rep. T. +822778334734. Fax +8227833475.

Aims Form a loose federation of Computer Vision, IP and related societies in Asia. **Activities** *Asian Conference on Computer Vision (ACCV)*. **Events** *Asian Conference on Computer Vision* Macau (Macau) 2022, *Asian Conference on Computer Vision* Kyoto (Japan) 2020, *Asian Conference on Computer Vision* Perth, WA (Australia) 2018, *Asian Conference on Computer Vision* Taipei (Taiwan) 2016, *Asian Conference on Computer Vision* Singapore (Singapore) 2014. [2020/XM0430/**D**]

♦ Asian Federation of Corporate Football (unconfirmed)

♦ Asian Federation of Dietetic Associations (AFDA) 01458

SG address not obtained. E-mail: secretary@afda-dietitians.org – president@afda-dietitians.org.
URL: http://www.afda-dietitians.org/

History 1991, Kuala Lumpur (Malaysia), at 6th Asian Congress of Nutrition. Original title: *Asian Federation of Dietetic Professionals (AFDP)*. **Structure** Council. **Activities** Events/meetings; awards/prizes/competitions. **Events** *Asian Congress of Dietetics* Yokohama (Japan) 2022, *Asian Congress of Dietetics* Taipei (Taiwan) 2014, *Asian Congress of Dietetics* Bangkok (Thailand) 2010, *Asian Congress of Dietetics* Manila (Philippines) 2006, *Asian Congress of Dietetics* Kuala Lumpur (Malaysia) 2002.
Members Organizations in 10 countries and territories:
China, Hong Kong, Indonesia, Japan, Korea Rep, Malaysia, Pakistan, Philippines, Singapore, Thailand.
Affiliate in 1 country:
Australia.
NGO Relations *International Confederation of Dietetic Associations (ICDA, #12856)*. [2020/XM4384/**D**]

♦ Asian Federation of Dietetic Professionals / see Asian Federation of Dietetic Associations (#01458)
♦ Asian Federation of Electronic Circuits (unconfirmed)

♦ Asian Federation of Exhibition and Convention Associations (AFECA) 01459

Secretariat c/o EPC, 1003 Bukit Merah Central, Inno Ctr 02-10, Singapore 159836, Singapore. E-mail: secretariat@afeca.asia.
URL: http://afeca.asia/

History 21 Sep 2004, Singapore (Singapore). Registration: Singapore. **Aims** Promote growth and development of the exhibition and convention industry in Asia. **Structure** General Meeting (annual). **Languages** English, Mandarin Chinese. **Finance** Members' dues. **Events** *Annual General Meeting* Manila (Philippines) 2019, *Annual General Meeting* Goyang (Korea Rep) 2018, *Joint Meeting* Goyang (Korea Rep) 2018, *Annual General Meeting* Seoul (Korea Rep) 2015, *Asia Forum* Seoul (Korea Rep) 2015.
Members Associations in 13 countries and territories:
Australia, Bahrain, China, India, Indonesia, Japan, Korea Rep, Macau, Malaysia, Philippines, Singapore, Taiwan, Thailand. [2020/XM4560/**D**]

♦ Asian Federation of Foot and Ankle Societies / see Asian Federation of Foot and Ankle Surgeons (#01460)

♦ Asian Federation of Foot and Ankle Surgeons (AFFAS) 01460

Gen Sec Dept of Orthopedic Surgery, Nara Medical Univ, Shijo-cho 840, Kashihara NARA, 634-8522 Japan. T. +81744223051. Fax +81744294902. E-mail: affas@naramed-u.ac.jp.
URL: https://www.affas.org/

History 1993, Nara (Japan). Regional organization of *International Federation of Foot and Ankle Societies (IFFAS, #13431)*. Former names and other names: *Asian Symposium on Foot Surgery* – former; *Asian Federation of Foot and Ankle Societies* – alias. **Aims** Facilitate exchange of ideas, information and research in the field of foot and ankle surgery and its related musculo-skeletal science among both foot and ankle societies and individual orthopaedic foot and ankle surgeons in Asia. **Structure** Board. **Events** *Annual Meeting* Kaohsiung (Taiwan) 2023, *Annual Meeting* Shanghai (China) 2021, *Triennial Scientific Meeting* Bangkok (Thailand) 2019, *Triennial Scientific Meeting* Nara (Japan) 2016, *Triennial Scientific Meeting* Hong Kong (Hong Kong) 2013.
Members Societies in 12 countries and territories:
China, Hong Kong, India, Indonesia, Japan, Korea Rep, Malaysia, Philippines, Russia, Singapore, Taiwan, Thailand. [2022.05.11/XJ2507/**D**]

♦ Asian Federation for Information Technology in Agriculture / see Asia-Pacific Federation for Information Technology in Agriculture (#01900)

♦ Asian Federation on Intellectual Disabilities 01461

Secretariat Managed by KAIDD, 4F E-room, 22 Uisadangro, Yeongdeungpo-gu, Seoul 150-917, Korea Rep. T. +8225925923. Fax +8225925026. E-mail: kaidd@hanmail.net.
URL: http://www.afid73.org/

History 1973, Manila (Philippines), as *Asian Federation for Persons with Mental Handicap*. Subsequently changed title to *Asian Federation for the Mentally Retarded (AFMR)* and later *Asian Federation on Mental Retardation (AFMR)*. Current title adopted, Nov 2007. **Aims** Provide for better opportunities for mentally retarded in Asia; improve their quality of life; promote better interaction and cooperation amongst the various national NGOs which cater for the needs of intellectually disabled. **Structure** General Assembly (every 2 years); Executive Board (meets annually); Secretariat in Singapore (Singapore). **Languages** English. **Staff** 4.00 FTE, paid. **Finance** Members' dues; donations. **Activities** Organizes regional seminars. **Events** *Biennial Conference* Delhi (India) 2013, *Biennial conference* Jeju (Korea Rep) 2011, *Biennial conference* Singapore (Singapore) 2009, *Biennial Conference* Taipei (Taiwan) 2007, *Biennial Conference* Yogyakarta (Indonesia) 2005. **Publications** Conference proceedings.
Members Affiliate members in 15 countries and territories:
Bangladesh, Hong Kong, India, Indonesia, Iran Islamic Rep, Japan, Korea Rep, Malaysia, Nepal, Pakistan, Philippines, Singapore, Sri Lanka, Taiwan, Thailand.
NGO Relations Associate regional member of: *Inclusion International (#11145)*. [2013/XD6936/**D**]

♦ Asian Federation of Kickboxing / see WKF Asia (#20973)

♦ Asian Federation of Laboratory Animal Science Associations (AFLAS) 01462

SG Laboratory Animal Medicine, Tohoku Univ School of Medicine, Seiryo-machi, Sendai MIYAGI, 980-8575 Japan. T. +81227178174. Fax +81227178180.
URL: http://www.aflas-office.org/

History 29 Nov 2003, Tokyo (Japan). **Structure** Council, including President, 2 Vice-Presidents, Secretary-General and Auditor. **Events** *Congress* Chiang Mai (Thailand) 2021, *Congress* Chiang Mai (Thailand) 2020, *Congress* Bangalore (India) 2018, *Congress* Singapore (Singapore) 2016, *Congress* Kuala Lumpur (Malaysia) 2014.
Members in 5 countries:
Japan, Korea Rep, Philippines, Taiwan, Thailand. [2020/XM2894/**D**]

♦ Asian Federation of Laryngectomees' Associations (AFLA) 01463

Contact c/o GINNREIKAI, 901 Bureau Shinbashi, 5-7-13 Shinbashi, Minato-Ku, Tokyo, 105-0004 Japan. T. +81334361820. Fax +81334363497. E-mail: office@ginreikai.or.jp.
URL: http://www.ginreikai.or.jp/

History Founded 1984, following adoption of project plan at 3rd International Laryngectomees Congress, 1982, Tokyo (Japan). Also referred to as *GINREIKA*. **Aims** Train instructors for esophageal speech rehabilitation; create a basis for the promotion of full social participation by laryngectomees in Asian countries. **Structure** Standing Committee (meets annually); AFLA Esophageal Speech Training Center, established in Bangkok (Thailand), 2001. **Languages** Japanese. **Finance** Support from public and private sectors. **Activities** Training/education. **Events** *Overseas Training* Dhaka (Bangladesh) 2012.
Members Regular members (192) in 14 countries and territories:
Bangladesh, China, Hong Kong, India, Indonesia, Japan, Korea Rep, Malaysia, Nepal, Pakistan, Philippines, Singapore, Taiwan, Thailand. [2015.11.10/XD6748/**D**]

♦ Asian Federation of Library Associations (inactive)
♦ Asian Federation for Medical Chemistry / see Asian Federation of Medicinal Chemistry (#01464)
♦ Asian Federation of Medical Microbiology and Infectious Diseases (inactive)

♦ Asian Federation of Medicinal Chemistry (AFMC) 01464

Secretariat 4F, No 20, Ln 128, Jingye 1st Road, Taipei 10462, Taiwan. Fax +886285297025. E-mail: aimecs.service@elitepco.com.tw.
URL: http://www.aimecs13.tw/

History 1992, Japan. Previously referred to as *Asian Federation for Medical Chemistry*. **Activities** Organizes AIMECS Symposium. **Events** *Symposium* Tokyo (Japan) 2021, *Symposium* Istanbul (Turkey) 2019, *Symposium* Melbourne, VIC (Australia) 2017, *Symposium* Jeju (Korea Rep) 2015, *International Medicinal Chemistry Symposium* Taipei (Taiwan) 2013.
Members National organizations (11) in 4 countries:
Australia, China, Japan, Korea Rep.
NGO Relations *European Federation for Medicinal Chemistry (EFMC, #07165)*; *International Union of Pure and Applied Chemistry (IUPAC, #15809)*. [2013/XD6119/**D**]

♦ Asian Federation of Mediterranean Studies Institutes (AFOMEDI) . . 01465

SG BUFS 65, Geumsaem-ro 485 beon-gil, Geumjeong-gu, Busan 46234, Korea Rep. T. +82515096632. Fax +82515096631.
URL: http://afomedi.org/

History Founded Mar 2016, Busan (Korea Rep). **Aims** Promote international assistance, fellowship and cooperation; encourage exchange of information and knowledge and promote Mediterranean studies in general on political science, social science, archaeology, economics, linguistics, literature, religion; history, technology, culture, etc; develop and strengthen relationships with related institutions; promote and assist in the formation of regional associations. **Structure** Council; Secretariat. **Languages** English. **Activities** Events/meetings. **Events** *International Conference* Busan (Korea Rep) 2022, *International Conference* Taipei (Taiwan) 2020, *International Conference* Tokyo (Japan) 2018, *International Conference* Busan (Korea Rep) 2017. **Publications** *Mediterranean Review (MR)* (2 a year). Proceedings.
Members Institutions (6) in 5 countries and territories:
China, Japan, Korea Rep, Taiwan, Türkiye. [2017/XM6621/j/**D**]

- Asian Federation for the Mentally Retarded / see Asian Federation on Intellectual Disabilities (#01461)
- Asian Federation on Mental Retardation / see Asian Federation on Intellectual Disabilities (#01461)
- Asian Federation of Middle Eastern Studies Associations / see Asian Federation of Middle East Studies Associations (#01466)

♦ Asian Federation of Middle East Studies Associations (AFMA) 01466

Contact PO Box 46A/109, Ulaanbaatar, Mongolia.
URL: http://mideast.site90.com/afma/

History Oct 1995, Seoul (Korea Rep), by *Chinese Association for Middle East Studies (CAMES)*; *Japan Association for Middle East Studies (JAMES)* and *Korean Association of Middle East Studies (KAMES)*. Previously also referred to as *Asian Federation of Middle Eastern Studies Associations*. **Events** *Conference* Seoul (Korea Rep) 2020, *Conference* Beijing (China) 2018, *Conference* Ulaanbaatar (Mongolia) 2016, *Conference* Kyoto (Japan) 2014, *Conference* Busan (Korea Rep) 2012.
Members National associations in (4) countries:
China, Japan, Korea Rep, Mongolia. [2019/XD8001/**D**]

♦ Asian Federation of Natural Language Processing (AFNLP) 01467

Contact address not obtained.
URL: http://www.afnlp.org/

Aims Promote and enhance research and development relating to computational analysis and the automatic processing of all languages of importance to the Asian region without regard to differences in race, gender, language, religious belief or political stand. **Structure** Board, comprising representative of *Asia-Pacific Association for Machine Translation (AAMT, #01845)*, International Conference Members (AIRS; ICCPOL; PACLIC; PACLING), 8 regional association members and 7 regional members. Executive Committee, including President, Vice-Presidents/Chair Conference Coordinating Committee, Secretary General, Honorary Treasurer and Committee Chairs (Asian Language Resources; Communications and Liaison). **Events** *International Joint Conference on Natural Language Processing* 2021, *International Joint Conference on Natural Language Processing* 2020, *International Conference* Beijing (China) 2015, *International Joint Conference on Natural Language Processing – IJCNLP* Chiang Mai (Thailand) 2011, *International Joint Conference on Natural Language Processing – IJCNLP* Singapore (Singapore) 2009. **NGO Relations** Founding member and represented on Board: *Chinese and Oriental Languages Information Processing Society (COLIPS, #03891)*.
[2022/XJ6812/**D**]

- Asian Federation of Netball Associations / see Netball Asia (#16977)
- Asian Federation of Obstetrics and Gynaecology / see Asia & Oceania Federation of Obstetrics and Gynaecology (#01796)

♦ Asian Federation of Osteoporosis Societies (AFOS) 01468

Contact address not obtained. E-mail: info@asianfos.org.
URL: http://asianfos.org/

History Inaugurated 17 May 2008. **Aims** Promote, foster, develop and assist medical and allied profession in the study of and acquisition, dissemination and application of knowledge and information concerning the causes, diagnosis, prevention and treatment of osteoporosis so as to reduce morbidity and mortality in the Asian region. **Structure** Council, comprising President, Vice-President, Secretary-General, Treasurer and 7 members. **Events** *Scientific Meeting* Manila (Philippines) 2019, *Scientific Meeting* Kuala Lumpur (Malaysia) 2017, *Scientific Meeting / Scientific Conference* Seoul (Korea Rep) 2013, *Scientific Conference* Kobe (Japan) 2011, *Scientific Conference* Guangzhou (China) 2009.
Members Societies in 11 countries and territories:
China, Hong Kong, Indonesia, Japan, Korea Rep, Macau, Malaysia, Philippines, Singapore, Taiwan, Thailand.
[2013/XJ7383/**D**]

- Asian Federation for Persons with Mental Handicap / see Asian Federation on Intellectual Disabilities (#01461)

♦ Asian Federation for Pharmaceutical Sciences (AFPS) 01469

Secretariat Dept of Pharmaceutics, Fac of Pharmacy, Keio Univ, 1-5-30 Shiba-koen, Minato-ku, Tokyo, 105-8512 Japan.
Membership office c/o ASAS, 4F, 5-3-13 Otuka, Bunkyo-ku, Tokyo, 112-0012 Japan. T. +81359816011. Fax +81359816012. E-mail: afps@asas-mail.jp.
URL: http://www.afps2007.org/

History Current statutes effective since 26 Oct 2007. Registered in accordance with Japanese law. **Aims** Advance research in pharmaceutical sciences in Asia. **Structure** Executive Committee. **Languages** English. **Finance** Members' dues. **Activities** Grants awards: AFPS Nagai Distinguished Scientist Award; AFPS Nagai-Shukri Pre-doctoral Best Paper Award. **Events** *Conference* Hanoi (Vietnam) 2022, *Conference* Hanoi (Vietnam) 2021, *Biennial Conference* Bali (Indonesia) 2019, *Biennial Conference* Xiamen (China) 2017, *Meeting / Congress* Bangkok (Thailand) 2015. **Publications** *Asian Journal of Pharmaceutical Sciences (AJPS)*.
Members Ordinary; Supporting. Membership countries not specified. [2021/XJ1530/**D**]

♦ Asian Federation of Psychiatric Associations (AFPA) 01470

Pres Fountain House, Lower Mall, Lahore, Pakistan.
URL: http://afpa.asia/

History 2005, Lahore (Pakistan). Founded Feb 2007, Lahore (Pakistan), following proposal by leading Asian psychiatrists and WPA Board Members at the WPA World Congress, Yokohama (Japan) 2002, and agreement at 13th World Congress, Cairo (Egypt), Sep 2005. **Aims** Achieve excellence in psychiatry and mental health services in Asia. **Structure** Council; Executive Committee. **Languages** English. **Staff** Voluntary. **Finance** Donations from: national societies that have organized WCAP, RCAP and other AFPA scientific meetings; corporate supporters; individuals; societies; governments and aid agencies. Other sources: royalties and revenues from publications. **Activities** Events/meetings; networking/liaising; publishing activities; research and development; training/education; standards/guidelines. **Events** *World Congress* Sydney, NSW (Australia) 2019, *International Congress* Manila (Philippines) 2018, *World Congress* Abu Dhabi (United Arab Emirates) 2017, *International Congress* Colombo (Sri Lanka) 2016, *World Congress* Fukuoka (Japan) 2015. **Publications** *Bulletin of AFPA* (2 a year).
Members National psychiatric societies and associations in 21 countries and territories:
Armenia, Australia, Bangladesh, Cambodia, China, Hong Kong, India, Indonesia, Iran Islamic Rep, Japan, Korea Rep, Malaysia, Myanmar, Pakistan, Papua New Guinea, Philippines, Singapore, Sri Lanka, Taiwan, Thailand, Vietnam.
NGO Relations Consultative status with: *World Association for Psychosocial Rehabilitation (WAPR, #21178)*; *World Federation for Mental Health (WFMH, #21455)*; *World Psychiatric Association (WPA, #21741)*.
[2017.10.25/XM3194/**D**]

♦ Asian Federation for Psychotherapy (AFP) 01471

Pres HOD Dept of Yoga Education, Dr Harisingh Gour Univ, Sagar, Madhya Pradesh 47003, Sagar MADHYA PRADESH 47003, India. T. +917582265802. Fax +917582265802.
Contact Arbat Street, House 20 – building 1, Entrance 4 – Studio 45, Moscow MOSKVA, Russia, 119002. T. +79165075810. E-mail: kmoppl@mail.ru.
URL: http://asianpsyche.org/

History Founded 2001. A continental federation of *World Council for Psychotherapy (WCP, #21337)*. Registered in accordance with Indian law. **Aims** Unite all psychotherapists and counsellors, psychotherapeutic and counselling institutes and research in Asia; promote psychotherapy and counselling in Asia; enhance the conditions for patients and clients in Asia; cooperate with national and international organizations; support members. **Structure** General Assembly (annual); Board; Executive Committee. **Languages** English. **Staff** Voluntary. **Finance** Supported by *World Council for Psychotherapy (WCP, #21337)*. **Activities** Events/meetings; standards/guidelines; guidance/assistance/consulting. **Events** *World Congress on Mental Health* Moscow (Russia) 2016, *Congress* Teheran (Iran Islamic Rep) 2016, *Congress / Conference* Kuching (Malaysia) 2015, *Congress / Conference* Moscow (Russia) 2013, *Congress* Delhi (India) 2012. **Publications** Books.
Members Ordinary; Extraordinary; Honorary. Members in 7 countries:
China, India, Iran Islamic Rep, Japan, Kazakhstan, Malaysia, Russia. [2016/XM1263/**D**]

- Asian Federation of Sexology / see Asia-Oceania Federation of Sexology (#01798)

♦ Asian Federation of Societies for Lactic Acid Bacteria (AFSLAB) ... 01472

Pres address not obtained.
Gen Sec address not obtained.
URL: http://www.afslab.asia/

Aims Encourage research, communication, and education in lactic acid bacteria (LAB) and related sciences. **Structure** General Assembly (every 2 years); International Executive Board Committee. Standing Committees (3): Membership; Publication; Awards and Finance. **Activities** Events/meetings. **Events** *Asian Conference on Lactic Acid Bacteria (ACLAB)* Kuching (Malaysia) 2022, *Asian Conference for Lactic Acid Bacteria (ACLAB)* Tokyo (Japan) 2021, *Asian Conference on Lactic Acid Bacteria (ACLAB)* Bangkok (Thailand) 2020, *Conference* Yogyakarta (Indonesia) 2019, *Conference* Gwangju (Korea Rep) 2017.
Members Regular; Individual; Corporate/sponsor; Honorary/fellow. Organizations in 10 countries:
China, India, Indonesia, Iran Islamic Rep, Japan, Korea Rep, Malaysia, Mongolia, Philippines, Singapore. [2020/XM4383/**D**]

♦ Asian Federation of Societies for Ultrasound in Medicine and Biology (AFSUMB) 01473

Sec c/o CTSUM, 8F-1 No 207 Sec 2 Chongqing N Rd, Datong, Taipei 103, Taiwan. T. +886228757598. Fax +886228710848.
URL: http://www.afsumb.org/

History 1986. **Aims** Exchange scientific research and *education*. **Structure** General Assembly; Administrative Council; Executive Board. **Languages** English. **Staff** 17.00 FTE, voluntary. **Finance** Members' dues. **Activities** Events/meetings; training/education. **Events** *Asia Pacific international Symposium on Advances in Medical Ultrasound* Taipei (Taiwan) 2021, *Congress* Zhuhai (China) 2021, *Biennial Congress* Beijing (China) 2020, *Asia Pacific international Symposium on Advances in Medical Ultrasound* New Taipei City (Taiwan) 2019, *Biennial Congress* Seoul (Korea Rep) 2018. **Publications** *Journal of Medical Ultrasound* (4 a year). Annual Report.
Members Affiliated societies, representing over 18,825 physician, scientists, engineers and sonographers, in 16 countries and territories:
Bangladesh, Cambodia, Chad, Hong Kong, India, Indonesia, Japan, Korea Rep, Malaysia, Mongolia, Nepal, Pakistan, Philippines, Singapore, Taiwan, Thailand. [2021/XD2593/**D**]

♦ Asian Federation of Speleology (AFS) 01474

Contact Dept of Geology, Kangwon Nat Univ, Chuncheon GANGWON 200-701, Korea Rep. T. +82332508556. Fax +82332448556.
URL: http://www.asiankarst.com/asian-federation-speleology/

History 2010. Since 2013, a regional of *International Union of Speleology (#15818)*. **Structure** General Assembly; Bureau; Executive Committee. **Events** *General Assembly* Lichuan (China) 2015.
[2016/XM4365/**D**]

♦ Asian Federation of Sports Medicine (AFSM) 01475

SG Room 74029, 5/F Lui Chi Woo Clinical Sciences Bldg, Prince of Wales Hosp, Shatin, Hong Kong. T. +85226464555. E-mail: wancylo@cuhk.edu.hk – afsm.membership@gmail.com.
URL: https://www.afsmsportsmed.org/

History Sep 1990, Beijing (China). Inaugurated at 11th Asian Games. **Aims** Foster development of sports medicine in Asia for sporting excellence and health for all. **Structure** Advisory Board; Executive Committee; Standing Commissions. **Languages** English. **Staff** Voluntary. **Activities** Events/meetings; training/education. **Events** *Tripartite Conference* Kuching (Malaysia) 2022, *Congress* Riyadh (Saudi Arabia) 2019, *Congress* Hong Kong (Hong Kong) 2018, *Towards excellence in sports medicine and sports science* Kuala Lumpur (Malaysia) 2013, *World congress of science and medicine in cricket* Chandigarh (India) 2011.
Members Organizations in 31 countries and territories:
Brunei Darussalam, China, Hong Kong, India, Iran Islamic Rep, Japan, Jordan, Korea Rep, Macau, Malaysia, Maldives, Mongolia, Oman, Philippines, Qatar, Saudi Arabia, Singapore, Sri Lanka, Taiwan, Thailand, United Arab Emirates.
NGO Relations Affiliated with (1): *International Federation of Sports Medicine (#13554)*.
[2022.02.28/XD3319/**D**]

♦ Asian Federation of Therapeutic Communities (AFTC) 01476

Pres Unit 504 Park Trade Ctr, 1716 Investment Drive, Madrigal NBusiness Park, Ayala Alabang, Muntinlupa City METRO MANILA, Philippines. T. +6328094847. Fax +6328098776.
URL: http://www.asianfedtc.org/

History 1984, Rome (Italy), as a regional group of *World Federation of Therapeutic Communities (WFTC, #21491)*. Original title: *Asian-Pacific Federation of Therapeutic Communities (APFTC)*. **Aims** Share knowledge and experience of the therapeutic community movements in *Asia*; enhance the therapeutic community movement in the Asian Region and increase understanding of it as a tool in *drug treatment*. **Structure** General Assembly (every 2 years); Executive Council. **Languages** English. **Finance** Sources: activities of the Federation; donations; contributions; bequests; subscriptions; grants. **Activities** Provides a forum and a means of communication among member organizations and individuals. Provides training opportunities for professionals and volunteers in the therapeutic community. Encourages international and national support, both governmental and non-governmental, for concepts and operations of therapeutic communities. Raises funds for the activity of the Federation. **Events** *International Conference* Pasay City (Philippines) 2010, *International Conference* Philippines 2010, *International Conference* Kunming (China) 1999, *International Conference* Bangkok (Thailand) 1996, *International Conference* Bangkok (Thailand) 1994. **Publications** *AFTC Newsletter* (4 a year). Meeting reports.
Members Organizations, institutions and individuals Full; Associate; Honorary. Members in 13 countries and territories:
China, Hong Kong, India, Indonesia, Korea Rep, Malaysia, Nepal, Pakistan, Philippines, Singapore, Sri Lanka, Thailand, Vietnam.
NGO Relations Member of: *International Federation of Non-Government Organizations for the Prevention of Drug and Substance Abuse (IFNGO, #13490)*. [2013/XE6040/**E**]

- Asian Federation of the Toxicological Sciences / see Asian Society of Toxicology (#01744)
- Asian Federation of UNESCO Clubs and Associations / see Asian Pacific Federation of UNESCO Clubs and Associations (#01614)
- Asian Fencing Confederation / see Fencing Confederation of Asia (#09735)

♦ Asian Ferroelectric Association (AFA) 01477

Chair Shanghai Inst of Ceramics, Chinese Academy of Sciences, 1295 Dingxi Rd, 200050 Shanghai, China. T. +862152411066. Fax +862152413122.
Contact School of Electrical and Electronic Engineering, Div of Microelectrics, Office S2-B2a-03, Nanyang Technological Univ, 50 Nanyang Avenue, Singapore 639798, Singapore.

Structure Board. **Events** *Asian Meeting on Ferroelectrics* Hiroshima (Japan) 2018, *Joint Conference on Applications of Ferroelectrics* Hiroshima (Japan) 2018, *Asian Meeting on Ferroelectrics* Delhi (India) 2016, *Asian Meeting on Ferroelectrics – AMF* Shanghai (China) 2014, *Asian Meeting on Ferroelectrics* Pattaya (Thailand) 2012. [2018/XJ3698/**D**]

♦ Asian Film Commissions Network (AFCNet) 01478

Acting Managing Dir Busan Film Commission, 8th Floor, 39 Centum seo-ro, Haeundae-gu, Busan 48058, Korea Rep. T. +82517200349. Fax +82517200340. E-mail: afcnet.bfc@gmail.com.
URL: http://www.afcnet.org/

Aims Improve and complement a current location supporting system; increase information sharing on film related laws, customs and cultures; contribute to development of the Asian film industry. **Structure** Board of Directors, comprising President, 2 Vice-Presidents and 7 Directors; Advisory Board; ASEAN Committee. **Staff** 3.00 FTE, paid. **Events** *General Assembly* Busan (Korea Rep) 2020, *Asian Film Forum* Busan (Korea Rep) 2019, *General Assembly* Busan (Korea Rep) 2019, *International Film Education Symposium* Busan (Korea Rep) 2019, *Virtual Reality Conference* Busan (Korea Rep) 2019. **Publications** *AFCNet Newsletter* (12 a year); *Location Scope* (6 a year).
Members Film commissions and government agencies. Regular (47) in 18 countries and territories:
Australia, Cambodia, China, Indonesia, Japan, Jordan, Korea Rep, Malaysia, Myanmar, Nepal, New Zealand, Philippines, Russia, Singapore, Taiwan, Thailand, United Arab Emirates, USA.
Associate (7) in 5 countries:
France, Japan, Korea Rep, Malaysia, Singapore. [2023.02.14/XM2895/**F**]

♦ Asian Finance Association 01479

Sec Finace Dept NCCU, No 64 Sec 2, ZhiNan Rd, Wenshan District, Taipei 11605, Taiwan.
URL: http://www.asian-fa.org/
History Founded in 1993, by merger of *Asia Pacific Finance Association (inactive)* and *Pacific Basin Financial Management Society (inactive)*. **Aims** Foster education and advance standards in the discipline of finance in the Asia Pacific region. **Structure** General Meeting (annual, during Conference); Board of Directors; Executive Committee; Standing Committees (3). **Finance** Members' dues. **Events** *Conference* Jinan (China) 2021, *Conference* Tokyo (Japan) 2018, *Conference* Seoul (Korea Rep) 2017, *Conference* Bangkok (Thailand) 2016, *Conference* Changsha (China) 2015. **Members** Ordinary; Student; Institutional. Membership countries not specified. [2018/XD9018/**D**]

♦ Asian Finance and Investment Corporation (inactive)
♦ Asian Financial Cooperation Association (internationally oriented national body)

♦ Asian Financial Services Association (AFSA) 01480

Secretariat Plaza Sentral Building, 14th Floor, Jl Jend Surdiman 47, Jakarta 12930, Indonesia. T. +622152880113 – +622152880124. Fax +622152880114. E-mail: secretariat@afsaworld.org.
URL: http://www.afsaworld.org/
History 1984, Singapore (Singapore). Dissolved 25 Apr 1997, Singapore, when secretariat moved to Jakarta (Indonesia). Similar association with similar name set up in Jakarta (Indonesia), 25 Apr 1997. Registered in accordance with Indonesian law. Originally known as *Asian Leasing Association (ASIALEASE)*. 2005, name changed to *Asian Leasing and Finance Association (ALFA)*. Present name adopted, 2010. **Aims** Increase close cooperation and mutual understanding in order to promote leasing as a medium of finance in Asia. **Structure** General Assembly (annual); Council; Secretariat. Officers: President; Vice-President; Secretary-General. **Events** *General Assembly* Dubai (United Arab Emirates) 2019, *General Assembly* Makati (Philippines) 2012, *Lease financing conference* Manila (Philippines) 1991, *World convention* Singapore (Singapore) 1990, *Lease financing conference* Singapore (Singapore) 1989.
Members Companies and associations in 19 countries and territories:
Australia, Bangladesh, Egypt, India, Indonesia, Japan, Korea Rep, Kuwait, Malaysia, Maldives, Oman, Pakistan, Philippines, Sri Lanka, Taiwan, Thailand, UK, United Arab Emirates, USA. [2019/XD3975/**D**]

♦ Asian Fisheries Acoustics Society (AFAS) 01481

Main Office Fac of Fisheries Sciences, 3-1-1 Minato-cho, Hokkaido Univ, Hakodate HOKKAIDO, 041-8611 Japan. T. +81138408852. Fax +81138408854. E-mail: afas@afas-acoustic.org – nankyokun-eko@gmail.com.
URL: http://www.afas-acoustic.org/
History 2007, Dalian (China). Current statutes enacted Nov 2016. **Aims** Promote progress and popularization of science and technologies on fisheries acoustics in Asia. **Structure** General Meeting; Secretariat. **Finance** Donations. **Activities** Events/meetings; research/documentation; training/education. **Events** *International Conference on Underwater Acoustics for Sustainable Fisheries in Asia* Busan (Korea Rep) 2022, *International Conference on Underwater Acoustics for Sustainable Fisheries in Asia (AFAS2021)* Bogor (Indonesia) 2021, *International Conference on Underwater Acoustics for Sustainable Fisheries in Asia* Keelung (Taiwan) 2019, *International Conference on Underwater Acoustics for Sustainable Fisheries in Asia (AFAS2018)* Jeju (Korea Rep) 2018, *International Conference on Underwater Acoustics for Sustainable Fisheries in Asia (AFAS2013)* Guangzhou (China) 2017. [2022/XM8094/**D**]

♦ Asian Fisheries Social Science Research Network (AFSSRN) 01482

Contact c/o Asian Fisheries Soc, Lab of Marine Science and Aquaculture, Univ Putra Malaysia, 43400 UPM Serdang, Selangor, Malaysia. T. +60389472216. Fax +60389472217.
History 1983, by *WorldFish (#21507)*. Accepted as a section of *Asian Fisheries Society (AFS, #01483)* in 1997. **Aims** Enhance domestic social science research capabilities relating to captive fisheries, *coastal resource* management and *aquaculture* in Asia; develop social science research capacity as a partner to fisheries, biological and engineering sciences in policymaking, planning and implementation processes. **Finance** Source: WorldFish Center. **Activities** Sponsors workshops, training courses and seminars to enhance professional capacities of members; supports collaborative research programmes previously submitted for peer review; disseminates and promotes use of research results. **Events** *Meeting on environmental assessment and management of aquaculture development* Manila (Philippines) 1994. **Publications** *AFSSRNews* – in the WorldFish Center quarterly 'Naga'. Research Report series.
Members Researchers (over 100) in universities, research institutions and government fisheries agencies (14) in 5 countries:
Indonesia, Malaysia, Philippines, Thailand, Vietnam. [2011.06.01/XF3324/**F**]

♦ Asian Fisheries Society (AFS) 01483

Exec Officer c/o Lab of Marine Biotechnology, Int of Bioscience, Univ Putra Malasyia, 43400 UPM Serdang, Selangor, Malaysia. T. +60389472216. Fax +60389472217. E-mail: info@asianfisheriessociety.org.
URL: http://www.asianfisheriessociety.org/
History 2 May 1984, Los Baños (Philippines). Founded when Constitution was adopted, following recommendations of a meeting 23-24 May 1983, Manila (Philippines), organized by *WorldFish (#21507)*. Registration: Start date: 1987, Philippines. **Aims** Promote interaction and cooperation among scientists and technicians involved in fisheries research and development in Asia with a view to encouraging and facilitating complementation, sharing of information and publication of research results; create and propagate awareness of the importance and ways of sound utilization, cultivation, conservation and development of aquatic resources in the region; promote establishment of national fisheries societies and seek affiliation and cooperation with societies, organizations and institutions having similar objectives. **Structure** General Assembly; Council; Executive Committee (meets twice a year in Manila, Philippines). Includes: *Asian Fisheries Social Science Research Network (AFSSRN, #01482)*; *Fish Health Section of the Asian Fisheries Society (FHS, see: #01483)*. Branches (3): Indian; Japan; Taiwan. **Languages** English. **Staff** 3.00 FTE, paid.
Finance Members' dues (US$ 10 – US$ 15 – US$ 25) and entry fee (US$ 10). Other sources: sale of publications; support from a number of national and international organizations, in particular *International Development Research Centre (IDRC, #13162)*. Other support organizations also listed in this Yearbook are:
- *Asian Development Bank (ADB, #01422)*;
- *Asian Network for Biological Sciences (ANBS, no recent information)*;
- *Australian Aid (inactive)*;
- *British Council*;
- *Canadian International Development Agency (CIDA, inactive)*;
- *European Aquaculture Society (EAS, #05909)*;
- ICLARM;
- *International Foundation for Science (IFS, #13677)*;
- *Japan International Cooperation Agency (JICA)*;
- *Southeast Asian Fisheries Development Center (SEAFDEC, #19767)*;
- *UNIDO (#20336)*;
- *United States Agency for International Development (USAID)*;
- *World Aquaculture Society (WAS, #21099)*.

Activities Organizes: Triennial Asian Fisheries Forum; meetings; symposia; workshops; conferences; other gatherings. Helps promote and organize the *'World Fisheries Congress'*; provides financial and technical support to young fisheries scientists from developing countries in order to conduct quality research through research fellowship awards. **Events** *Asian Fisheries and Aquaculture Forum (AFAF)* Tainan (Taiwan) 2022, *Global Conference on Gender in Aquaculture and Fisheries (GAF)* 2021, *Symposium on Diseases in Asian Aquaculture* Kuching (Malaysia) 2021, *Symposium on Diseases in Asian Aquaculture* Kuching (Malaysia) 2020, *Asian Fisheries and Aquaculture Forum (AFAF)* Iloilo (Philippines) 2019. **Publications** *Asian Fisheries Science e-Journal* (4 a year). Reports; documents; directories; books; forum, meeting and workshop proceedings.
Members Full (individuals); Student; Institutional; Honorary. Members (over 3,200) in 76 countries and territories:
Australia, Austria, Bahrain, Bangladesh, Belgium, Belize, Brazil, Brunei Darussalam, Cambodia, Canada, Chile, China, Costa Rica, Côte d'Ivoire, Cuba, Denmark, Fiji, Finland, France, Germany, Ghana, Greece, Honduras, Hong Kong, Hungary, India, Indonesia, Iran Islamic Rep, Iraq, Ireland, Israel, Italy, Japan, Kenya, Kiribati, Korea DPR, Korea Rep, Kuwait, Laos, Madagascar, Malaysia, Mauritius, Mexico, Myanmar, Nepal, Netherlands, New Caledonia, New Zealand, Nigeria, Norway, Oman, Pakistan, Panama, Papua New Guinea, Philippines, Poland, Puerto Rico, Qatar, Saudi Arabia, Singapore, Solomon Is, South Africa, Spain, Sri Lanka, Sweden, Tahiti Is, Taiwan, Tanzania UR, Thailand, Türkiye, UK, USA, Venezuela, Vietnam, Virgin Is UK, Zimbabwe.
Members also in West Africa. Membership countries not specified.
IGO Relations *Asia-Pacific Fishery Commission (APFIC, #01907)*. **NGO Relations** *International Institute of Fisheries Economics & Trade (IIFET, #13880)*. [2020/XD1790/**D**]

♦ Asian Fluid Mechanics Committee (AFMC) 01484

Main Office c/o CSTAM Office, 15 Beisihuanxi Road, 100190 Beijing, China. T. +861062559209. Fax +861062559588. E-mail: office@cstam.org.cn.
URL: http://www.afmc.org.cn/
History 1980, India. Former names and other names: *International Scientific Committee of Asian Congresses of Fluid Mechanics* – alias. **Aims** Advance research in fluid mechanics in Asia through interaction and exchange of information between workers in this field. **Structure** Chairman, 2 Vice-Chairmen and 18 members. **Languages** English. **Events** *Asian International Conference on Fluid Machinery (AICFM)* Yokohama (Japan) 2021, *Congress* Bangalore (India) 2019, *Asian International Conference on Fluid Machinery* Busan (Korea Rep) 2019, *Congress / Asian Congress of Fluid Mechanics – ACFM* Hanoi (Vietnam) 2013, *Congress / Asian Congress of Fluid Mechanics – ACFM* Dhaka (Bangladesh) 2010. **Publications** Proceedings; abstracts.
Members Individuals in 16 countries and territories:
Australia, Bangladesh, China, Hong Kong, India, Indonesia, Iran Islamic Rep, Japan, Korea Rep, Malaysia, Pakistan, Singapore, Sri Lanka, Thailand, USA, Vietnam.
NGO Relations Affiliated organization of: *International Union of Theoretical and Applied Mechanics (IUTAM, #15823)*. [2020/XE1173/v/**E**]

♦ Asian Food and Agriculture Cooperation Initiative (AFACI) 01485

Secretariat c/o Intl Technology Cooperation Ctr, Rural Development Admin, 300 Nongsaengmyeong-ro, Wansan-gu, Jeonju NORTH JEOLLA 54875, Korea Rep. T. +82632381134. Fax +82632381790. E-mail: afaci@korea.kr.
URL: http://www.afaci.org/
History Nov 2009, Seoul (Korea Rep). **Aims** Promote sustainable agricultural growth in the Asian region; contribute to consistent economic development of member countries through technological cooperation in agricultural and food sectors. **Structure** General Assembly (every 2 years); Chair Group; Advisory Committee on Science and Technology; Secretariat. **Languages** English. **Staff** 8.00 FTE, paid. **Activities** Knowledge management/information dissemination; networking/liaising; research and development; events/meetings; projects/programmes. **Events** *High Level Meeting* Seoul (Korea Rep) 2019, *High Level Symposium* Daegu (Korea Rep) 2017, *Principal Investigators Meeting on New Pan-Asian and Regional Projects* Suwon (Korea Rep) 2012, *General Assembly* Philippines 2010. **Publications** *AFACI Newsletter* (2 a year). *Make a Difference*.
Members Governments of 14 countries:
Bangladesh, Bhutan, Cambodia, Indonesia, Korea Rep, Kyrgyzstan, Laos, Mongolia, Myanmar, Nepal, Philippines, Sri Lanka, Thailand, Vietnam. [2016.11.25/XJ5569/**D***]

♦ Asian Food Federation (inactive)
♦ Asian Food Information Council (no recent information)

♦ Asian Food Security Association (AFSA) 01486

Secretariat Food Analysis and Research Lab, Ctr for Advanced Research in Sciences, Univ of Dhaka, Dhaka 1000, Bangladesh. T. +8802966192059ext4721. Fax +88028615583. E-mail: afsa.secretariat@gmail.com.
URL: http://www.afsahome.com/
History Set up 2010, at 5th annual general meeting of Bangladesh-Japan Association for Science and Technology (BJAST). **Aims** Forge effective cooperation among member countries in areas including climate change, food safety and food security. **Structure** Executive Committee; Advisory Committee; Scientific Committee; Country Coordinator. **Languages** English. **Staff** 3.00 FTE, voluntary. **Finance** Members' dues. Donations. **Activities** Knowledge management/information dissemination; events/meetings. **Events** *Conference* Bhubaneswar (India) 2016, *Conference* Bien Hoa (Vietnam) 2014, *Conference on Food Safety and Food Security* Ivato (Japan) 2012. **Publications** *Asian Journal of Food Safety and Security*. Conference proceedings.
IGO Relations *AVRDC – The World Vegetable Center (#03051)*; *FAO Regional Office for Asia and the Pacific (RAP, #09266)*. **NGO Relations** *International Committee on Food Microbiology and Hygiene (ICFMH, #12770)*; *TWAS (#20270)*; national organizations. [2016.06.01/XJ6744/**D**]

♦ Asian Football Confederation (AFC) 01487

Confédération asiatique de football
SG AFC House, Jalan 1/155B, Bukit Jalil, 57000 Kuala Lumpur, Malaysia. T. +60389943388 – +60389942689.
URL: http://www.the-afc.com/
History Founded 8 May 1954, Manila (Philippines). Statutes adopted 31 Aug 1962, Jakarta (Indonesia). Revised statutes adopted 2 Dec 1982, Delhi (India). Continental confederation of: *International Federation of Association Football (#13360)*. **Aims** Promote football in Asia. **Structure** Congress; Executive Committee; Standing Committees; Secretariat. **Languages** Arabic, English. **Staff** 31.00 FTE, paid. **Finance** Members' dues. **Activities** Awards/prizes/competitions. **Events** *Committee Meeting* Kuala Lumpur (Malaysia) 2012, *Congress* Doha (Qatar) 2011, *Conference on science and football medicine* Kuala Lumpur (Malaysia) 2011, *Executive and standing committee meeting* 1986, *Executive committee and standing committee meeting* 1986. **Publications** *Footballasia Magazine* (12 a year).
Members National associations subdivided into 5 zones:
ASEAN Football Federation (AFF, #01187); *Central Asian Football Association (CAFA, #03681)*; *East Asian Football Federation (EAFF, #05204)*; *South Asian Football Federation (SAFF)*; *West Asian Football Federation (WAFF, #20904)*.
National associations in 44 countries and territories:
Afghanistan, Bahrain, Bangladesh, Bhutan, Brunei Darussalam, Cambodia, China, Guam, Hong Kong, India, Indonesia, Iran Islamic Rep, Iraq, Japan, Jordan, Korea DPR, Korea Rep, Kuwait, Kyrgyzstan, Laos, Lebanon, Macau, Malaysia, Maldives, Mongolia, Myanmar, Nepal, Oman, Pakistan, Palestine, Philippines, Qatar, Saudi Arabia, Singapore, Sri Lanka, Syrian AR, Taiwan, Tajikistan, Thailand, Turkmenistan, United Arab Emirates, Uzbekistan, Vietnam, Yemen. [2019/XD0079/**D**]

♦ Asian Forensic Sciences Network (AFSN) 01488

Secretariat Dept of Chemistry Malaysia, Jalan Sultan, 46661 Petaling Jaya, Selangor, Malaysia. E-mail: dora@kimia.gov.my.
URL: http://www.asianforensic.net/
History Oct 2008. **Aims** Provide a forum for forensic science institutes in Asia for discussion on issues relating to forensic services; enhance the quality of forensic services in Asia. **Structure** Board, comprising President, Vice-President, International Liaison Officer and 2 members. **Activities** Expert working groups; training; collaborative studies; proficiency tests and accreditation. **Events** *Annual Meeting* Singapore (Singapore) 2017, *Annual Meeting* Bangkok (Thailand) 2016, *Annual Meeting* Kuala Lumpur (Malaysia) 2015, *Annual Meeting* Seoul (Korea Rep) 2014, *Annual Meeting* Singapore (Singapore) 2013. **Publications** *ForensicAsia Newsletter*.
Members Institutes in 11 countries:
Brunei Darussalam, China, Indonesia, Korea Rep, Laos, Malaysia, Mongolia, Philippines, Singapore, Thailand, Vietnam.
NGO Relations Member of: *International Forensic Strategic Alliance (IFSA, #13626)*. [2014/XJ4591/**D**]

♦ Asian Forest Cooperation Organization (AFoCO) 01489

Secretariat 8th floor, 9 Gukhoedaero 62-gil, Yeongdeungpo-gu, Seoul 07269, Korea Rep. E-mail: contact@afocosec.org.
URL: http://www.afocosec.org/

History Proposed Jun 2009, by Jun 2009, set up following proposal by Korea Rep and ASEAN-ROK Commemorative Summit. Agreement between Governments of *ASEAN (#01141)* and the Republic of Korea on Forest Cooperation signed 18 Nov 2011, Bali (Indonesia) and entered in force 5 Aug 2012. ASEAN-ROK Forest Cooperation initiated as 1st step towards establishment of current AFoCO, which agreement was adopted Sep 2015 and entered into force Apr 2018. **Aims** Strengthen regional forest cooperation by transforming proven technology and policies into concrete actions in the context of sustainable forest management to address the impact of climate change. **Structure** Assembly; Divisions (2); Teams (4); Secretariat. **Languages** English. **Staff** 20.00 FTE, paid. **Finance** Contributions from Parties. **Activities** Events/meetings; projects/programmes; training/education. **Events** *Annual Technical Workshop for Project Management and Performance Review* Seoul (Korea Rep) 2021, *Session* Seoul (Korea Rep) 2021, *Session* Gyeongju (Korea Rep) 2019, *International Wild Plant Seeds Conference* Incheon (Korea Rep) 2019, *Ministerial Meeting* Seoul (Korea Rep) 2019. **Publications** *AFoCO Landmark Program Annual Report.* Annual Report; workshop/event proceedings.
Members Governments (14):
Bhutan, Brunei Darussalam, Cambodia, Indonesia, Kazakhstan, Korea Rep, Laos, Mongolia, Myanmar, Philippines, Singapore, Thailand, Timor-Leste, Vietnam.
IGO Relations Cooperates with: *FAO (#09260)*; *International Tropical Timber Organization (ITTO, #15737).*
NGO Relations Cooperates with: *RECOFTC – The Center for People and Forests (RECOFTC, #18628).*
[2019/XJ6217/**E***]

♦ Asian Forum on Business Education (AFBE) 01490

Pres 6 Malcolm Street, Fremantle WA 6160, Australia.
Facebook: https://www.facebook.com/Asian-Forum-on-Business-Education-AFBE-260071398689/

History 1992, Bangkok (Thailand). **Aims** Improve the quality of business education and research in the region. **Structure** Executive Committee. **Languages** English. **Activities** Research/documentation; events/meetings; certification/accreditation. **Events** *Conference* Bali (Indonesia) 2019, *Annual Conference* Bali (Indonesia) 2015, *Annual Conference* Bangkok (Thailand) 2014, *Annual Conference* Kolkata (India) 2013, *Annual Conference* Putrajaya (Malaysia) 2012. **Publications** *AFBE Journal* (2 a year) – online.
Members Individuals in 6 countries:
Australia, Cambodia, China, Indonesia, Thailand, USA.
NGO Relations Member of: *Asia-Pacific Quality Network (APQN, #02004)*; *United Nations Academic Impact (UNAI, #20516).*
[2019.12.16/XJ8441/v/**F**]

♦ Asian Forum of Environmental Journalists / see Asia-Pacific Forum of Environmental Journalists (#01910)

♦ Asian Forum for Human Rights and Development (FORUM-ASIA) . . 01491

Forum asiatique sur les droits humains et le développement

Regional Secretariat SPD Bldg 3rd Floor, 79/2 Krungthonburi Road, Khlong Ton Sai, Khlong San, Bangkok, 10600, Thailand. T. +6621082643. Fax +6621082646. E-mail: info@forum-asia.org.
Geneva Office Rue de Varembé 1, 2nd Floor, 1202 Geneva, Switzerland. E-mail: una@forum-asia.org.
URL: http://www.forum-asia.org/

History Dec 1991, Manila (Philippines). **Aims** Promote and protect all human rights, including the right to development through cooperation and collaboration among *civil society* organizations working on human right development in Asia; empower people by advocating social justice, sustainable human development, participatory democracy, gender equality, peace and human security. **Structure** General Assembly (every 3 years); Executive Committee; Secretariat. **Languages** English. **Staff** 29.00 FTE, paid. **Finance** Donor agencies provide about US$ 1.5 million. **Activities** Advocacy/lobbying/activism; capacity building; monitoring/evaluation; networking/liaising; research/documentation; training/education. **Events** *CSOs Regional Dialogue* Bangkok (Thailand) 2019, *International Conference on Protection of Rohingya Survivors and Accountability for Genocide* Seoul (Korea Rep) 2019, *Regional Conference on Role of NHRIs in the Context of Democratic Space and Fundamental Freedoms* Seoul (Korea Rep) 2019, *Asian Regional Human Rights Defenders Forum* Bali (Indonesia) 2018, *Asian Regional Human Rights Defenders Forum* Colombo (Sri Lanka) 2016. **Publications** *FORUM-ASIA Newsletter* – electronic. *Working Paper Series.* Annual Human Rights Report; thematic related reports.
Members Organizations in 21 countries:
Afghanistan, Bangladesh, Cambodia, India, Indonesia, Kazakhstan, Korea Rep, Kyrgyzstan, Malaysia, Maldives, Mongolia, Myanmar, Nepal, Pakistan, Philippines, Singapore, Sri Lanka, Taiwan, Thailand, Timor-Leste, Vietnam.
Consultative Status Consultative status granted from: *ECOSOC (#05331)* (Special). **NGO Relations** Member of (8): *Asia Democracy Network (ADN, #01265)*; *Asia-Europe People's Forum (AEPF, #01274)*; *Coalition for the International Criminal Court (CICC, #04062)*; *Conference of Non-Governmental Organizations in Consultative Relationship with the United Nations (CONGO, #04635)*; *International Dalit Solidarity Network (IDSN, #13129)* (Associate); *International Network for Economic, Social and Cultural Rights (ESCR-Net, #14255)*; *Nonviolent Peaceforce (NP, #17153)*; *ProtectDefenders.eu (#18546).* Involved in: *Solidarity for ASEAN People's Advocacy (SAPA, #19683).* Affiliated with: *Alternative ASEAN Network on Burma (ALTSEAN Burma).* Provides secretariat for: *Asian NGO Network on National Human Rights Institutions (ANNI, #01567).* Supports: *Global Call for Action Against Poverty (GCAP, #10263)*; *Global Partnership for the Prevention of Armed Conflict (GPPAC, #10538).*
[2022/XF3262/**F**]

♦ Asian Forum of Insurance Regulators (AFIR) 01492

Secretariat 15 Financial Street, Beijing, China. T. +861066288128. E-mail: secretariat@afirweb.org.
URL: http://www.afirweb.org/

History Proposed 2006, by China Insurance Regulatory Commission (CIRC). **Aims** Facilitate information exchange, cooperation, and mutual understanding among Asian insurance regulators; strengthen regulatory cooperation in the insurance industry, prevent and mitigate cross-border risks, and enhance the stability of Asian insurance market. **Structure** Secretariat. **Languages** English. **Staff** 1.00 FTE, paid; 2.00 FTE, voluntary. **Finance** Costs covered by CIRC. **Activities** Events/meetings. **Events** *Annual Meeting* Macau (Macau) 2019, *Annual Meeting* Hong Kong (Hong Kong) 2018, *Annual Meeting* Singapore (Singapore) 2017, *Annual Meeting* Taipei (Taiwan) 2016, *Annual Meeting* Colombo (Sri Lanka) 2015. **Publications** *AFIR Newsletter.*
Members Governments (20):
Afghanistan, Australia, China, Hong Kong, India, Japan, Korea Rep, Macau, Malaysia, Maldives, Myanmar, Nepal, New Zealand, Papua New Guinea, Philippines, Singapore, Sri Lanka, Taiwan, Thailand, United Arab Emirates.
Regional organization:
IGO Relations *Asian Development Bank (ADB, #01422)*; *OECD (#17693).* **NGO Relations** *Basel Committee on Banking Supervision (BCBS, #03183)*; *International Association of Insurance Supervisors (IAIS, #11966)*; *International Organization of Securities Commissions (IOSCO, #14470).*
[2017.09.28/XM5878/**F***]

♦ Asian Forum of Parliamentarians on Population and Development (AFPPD) 01493

Secretariat c/o APDA, 2-19-5 Nishi-Shinbashi, Minato-ku, Tokyo, 105-0003 Japan. T. +81354058844. Fax +81354058845. E-mail: afppd@afppd.net.
URL: https://afppd.net/

History 1981, Beijing (China). Deriving from *Asian Conference of Parliamentarians on Population and Development*, on the initiative of *United Nations Population Fund (UNFPA, #20612).* Operations and permanent secretariat moved from Delhi (India) to Bangkok (Thailand), 1991. Constitution amended: 1996, Canberra (Australia); 1999, Niigata (Japan); 2002, Beijing (China); 2005, Jakarta (Indonesia); 2008, Hanoi (Vietnam). Registration: Start date: 20 Oct 1994, Thailand. **Aims** Increase awareness and promote the understanding of the interrelationship between population and development issues; initiate, promote and support exchanges and exchange programmes among the parliamentarians of Asia and outside the region, so as to encourage new and effective ideas and approaches to population and development issues. **Structure** General Conference (every 3 years); Executive Committee. **Languages** English. **Finance** Basic financial support from: UNFPA; *International Planned Parenthood Federation (IPPF, #14589)*; Japan Trust Fund for Parliamentarians. Additional funding from: *Australian Aid (inactive)*; *The William and Flora Hewlett Foundation*; *Joint United Nations Programme on HIV/AIDS (UNAIDS, #16149)*; *Japan International Corporation of Welfare Services (JICWELS)*; Ministry of Health and Social Welfare (Japan). Special projects received additional support. National parliaments and governments support national events and activities. Supported provided by: *Asian Population and Development Association (APDA).* **Activities** Training/education; events/meetings. **Events** *International Conference on ICPD25 Commitments* Tokyo (Japan) 2022, *Meeting on the Impact of COVID-19 on Declining Birthrate* Tokyo (Japan) 2021, *Asian Women Ministers and Parliamentarians Conference* Bangkok (Thailand) 2016, *Global Conference of Parliamentarians on Population and Development* Tokyo (Japan) 2016, *Meeting on Proposed Teenage Pregnancy Bill* Bangkok (Thailand) 2015. **Publications** *AFPPD E-mail Information Service* (12 a year); *Asian Forum Newsletter* (every 4 months) in English, Russian.
Members National Committees in 25 countries:
Australia, Bangladesh, Bhutan, Cambodia, China, India, Indonesia, Iran Islamic Rep, Japan, Kazakhstan, Korea Rep, Kyrgyzstan, Laos, Malaysia, Maldives, Mongolia, Nepal, New Zealand, Pakistan, Papua New Guinea, Philippines, Sri Lanka, Tajikistan, Thailand, Vietnam.
Pacific Committee:
Pacific Parliamentary Assembly on Population and Development (PPAPD, #17987).
Consultative Status Consultative status granted from: *ECOSOC (#05331)* (General); *United Nations Population Fund (UNFPA, #20612).* **IGO Relations** Cooperates with: *International Bank for Reconstruction and Development (IBRD, #12317)* (World Bank); *Joint United Nations Programme on HIV/AIDS (UNAIDS, #16149)*; *UNDP (#20292)*; *UNESCO (#20322)*; *UNICEF (#20332)*; *United Nations Economic and Social Commission for Asia and the Pacific (ESCAP, #20557)*; *WHO (#20950)*; Euro Parliamentarian working groups. **NGO Relations** Member of: *AIDS Society for Asia and the Pacific (ASAP, #00592)*; *Asia Pacific Alliance for Sexual and Reproductive Health and Rights (APA, #01825)*; *Conference of Non-Governmental Organizations in Consultative Relationship with the United Nations (CONGO, #04635).* Supports: *Pacific Parliamentary Assembly on Population and Development (PPAPD, #17987).* Cooperates with: *Inter-American Parliamentary Group on Population and Development (IAPG, inactive)*; *European Parliamentary Forum for Sexual & Reproductive Rights (EPF, #08149)*; *International Medical Parliamentarians Organization (IMPO, #14137)*; *International Planned Parenthood Federation (IPPF, #14589)*; *Parliamentarians for Global Action (PGA, #18208).*
[2022/XF0286/y/**F**]

♦ Asian Forum for Polar Sciences (AFoPS) 01494

Secretariat 902-4, Jalan Tun Ismail, 50480 Kuala Lumpur, Malaysia. T. +60326910561. E-mail: secretariat.afops@ypasm.my.
URL: https://afops.org/

History 2004. **Aims** Encourage and facilitate cooperation for the advance of polar sciences among countries in the Asian region. **Structure** Annual General Meeting; Committee; Working Groups/Action Groups. **Events** *Annual General Meeting* 2021, *Annual General Meeting* 2020, *Annual General Meeting* Tachikawa (Japan) 2019, *Annual General Meeting* Xiamen (China) 2018.
Members National polar research institutions of 6 countries:
China, India, Japan, Korea Rep, Malaysia, Thailand.
Observers in 4 countries:
Indonesia, Philippines, Sri Lanka, Vietnam.
NGO Relations Memorandum of Understanding with (2): *International Arctic Science Committee (IASC, #11668)*; *Scientific Committee on Antarctic Research (SCAR, #19147).*
[2021/AA2448/**F**]

♦ Asian Foundation for the Advancement of Veterinary and Animal Science (AFAVAS) 01495

Pres College of Veterinary Medicine, Chonnam National University, 77 Yongbong-ro, Buk-gu, Gwangju 500-757, Korea Rep. T. +82625302843.

History Gwangju (Korea Rep). **Aims** Advance veterinary and animal science education in the developing Asian countries. **Structure** Board of Directors, headed by President and including 12 Advisory Members. **Activities** Events/meetings. **Events** *International symposium* Gwangju (Korea Rep) 2010, *International symposium* Gwangju (Korea Rep) 2009.
[2011.10.05/XJ2724/f/**D**]

♦ Asian Foundation for the Prevention of Blindness (AFPB) 01496

Fondation asiatique pour la prévention de la cécité

CEO Block A3, 10/F, Yee Lim Industrial Centre, 2-28 Kwai Lok Street, Kwai Chung, Tsuen Wan, Hong Kong. T. +85227893331. Fax +85230054401.
URL: http://www.afpb.org.hk/

History 23 Feb 1981, Hong Kong (Hong Kong). **Aims** Support prevention of blindness projects in the region; assist in training *ophthalmic* and multidisciplinary staff. **Structure** Board of Directors. **Finance** Annual budget: Hong Kong $ 10,000,000. **Activities** Healthcare; financial and/or material support; events/meetings; training/education. **Events** *Regional seminar* China 1998.
[2019.02.19/XF1717/f/**F**]

♦ Asian Fuzzy Systems Society (inactive)
♦ Asian Games Federation (inactive)
♦ ASIAN Geographic Society (unconfirmed)

♦ Asian Group for Civil Engineering Informatics (AGCEI) 01497

Pres Div Sustainable Energy and Environmental Engineering, Osaka Univ, 2-1 Yamadaoka, Suita OSAKA, 565-0871 Japan.
URL: http://www.iccbei.com/AGCEI/

History Founded 2012, Tokyo (Japan). Organization involved in the Group's foundation: Japan Construction Information Center (JACIC). **Aims** Organize the biannual International Conference on Civil and Building Engineering Informatics (ICCBEI). **Structure** Board of Directors. **Languages** English. **Staff** None. **Finance** No funding for the Group; ICCBEI conference independently organized for each conference. **Events** *International Conference on Civil and Building Engineering Informatics* Taipei (Taiwan) 2017, *International Conference on Civil and Building Engineering Informatics* Tokyo (Japan) 2015, *International Conference on Civil and Building Engineering Informatics* Tokyo (Japan) 2013. **Publications** Conference proceedings.
Members in 7 countries and territories:
Australia, China, Hong Kong, Japan, Korea Rep, Singapore, Taiwan.
NGO Relations *European Group for Intelligent Computing in Engineering (EG-ICE, #07425)*; *International Society for Computing in Civil and Building Engineering (ISCCBE, #15030)*; Japan Construction Information Center (JACIC).
[2016.06.01/XM4287/c/**D**]

♦ Asian Group for Public Administration (AGPA) 01498

Executive Office Bei Huqu No 15 Street, 3rd Bldg, Chaoyang District, Beijing, China. T. +861059762625. Fax +861057962625. E-mail: iiasagpa@163.com.
Facebook: https://www.facebook.com/pg/iias.agpa

History Set up as a regional group affiliated to *International Institute of Administrative Sciences (IIAS, #13859).* **Aims** Attract and convene institutions and organizations in the field of public administration in Asia through academic activities and events; promote the development of administrative science in Asia. **Structure** Steering Committee. **Events** *Annual Conference* Bali (Indonesia) 2019, *Annual Conference* Quezon City (Philippines) 2018, *Annual Conference* Xiamen (China) 2017, *Annual Conference* Seoul (Korea Rep) 2015, *Annual Conference* Jakarta (Indonesia) 2014. **Publications** *AGPA Newsletter.*
Members Full in 13 countries:
Brunei Darussalam, China, India, Indonesia, Japan, Korea Rep, Malaysia, Maldives, Mongolia, Nepal, Philippines, Thailand, Vietnam.
NGO Relations *European Group for Public Administration (EGPA, #07430)*; *International Association of Schools and Institutes of Administration (IASIA, #12147).*
[2020/XJ7967/**E**]

♦ Asian Group for Rapid Viral Diagnosis / see Asian-Pacific Society for Medical Virology (#01639)
♦ Asian Growth Research Institute (internationally oriented national body)

♦ Asian Gymnastics Union (AGU) 01499

Union asiatique de gymnastique

SG Tornado Tower, 10th Floor, Al Cournich Street, Doha, Qatar. Fax +97444944131. E-mail: info@agu-gymnastics.com.
URL: http://www.agu-gymnastics.com/

History Founded 1964. Also referred to as *Asia Gymnastics Federation* and as *Asiatic Union of Gymnastics – Union asiatique de gymnastique (UASG)*. **Aims** Govern the sport of gymnastics in Asia. **Structure** Executive Committee; Technical Committees (7). **Languages** English. **Staff** 2.00 FTE, paid. **Activities** Sporting activities. **Events** *Congress* Incheon (Korea Rep) 2016, *General Assembly* Seoul (Korea Rep) 2016, *General Assembly* Bangkok (Thailand) 2015, *Scientific Symposium* Doha (Qatar) 2015, *Meeting* Manila (Philippines) 2015.
Members Affiliated federations in 37 countries and territories:
Afghanistan, Bahrain, Bangladesh, Cambodia, China, Hong Kong, India, Indonesia, Iran Islamic Rep, Iraq, Japan, Jordan, Kazakhstan, Korea DPR, Korea Rep, Kuwait, Kyrgyzstan, Lebanon, Macau, Malaysia, Mongolia, Myanmar, Nepal, Pakistan, Palestine, Philippines, Qatar, Saudi Arabia, Singapore, Sri Lanka, Syrian AR, Taiwan, Thailand, Turkmenistan, Uzbekistan, Vietnam, Yemen. [2017.03.08/XD1111/**D**]

♦ Asian Handball Federation (AHF) 01500

Contact PO Box 26312, 13124 Safat, Kuwait. T. +96525219961. Fax +96525219962. E-mail: office@asianhandball.com.
Street address South Surrah, Al-Salam Area Block 7, Street No 705 Villa 508, 13124 Safat, Kuwait.
URL: http://www.asianhandball.org/
History 1974, Teheran (Iran Islamic Rep). **Aims** Develop handball in Asian countries. **Languages** Arabic, English. **Finance** Members' dues. Supported by the Government of Kuwait. Annual budget: US$ 90,000. **Activities** Sporting activities; training/education; events/meetings. **Events** *Ordinary congress* Atlanta, GA (USA) 1996, *Congress* Seoul (Korea Rep) 1986. **Publications** *Asian Handball Magazine* (4 a year).
Members National associations in 42 countries and territories:
Afghanistan, Bahrain, Bangladesh, Bhutan, Brunei Darussalam, Cambodia, China, Hong Kong, India, Indonesia, Iran Islamic Rep, Iraq, Japan, Jordan, Kazakhstan, Korea DPR, Korea Rep, Kuwait, Kyrgyzstan, Lebanon, Macau, Malaysia, Maldives, Mongolia, Nepal, Oman, Pakistan, Palestine, Philippines, Qatar, Saudi Arabia, Singapore, Syrian AR, Taiwan, Tajikistan, Thailand, Timor-Leste, Turkmenistan, United Arab Emirates, Uzbekistan, Vietnam, Yemen.
NGO Relations Regional federation of: *International Handball Federation (IHF, #13771)*.
[2019.02.12/XD7333/**E**]

♦ Asian Harmonization Working Party / see Global Harmonization Working Party (#10399)

♦ Asian Harm Reduction Network (AHRN) 01501

Contact c/o NSAC, 6th Floor Graduate Bldg, Fac of Medicine, Chiang Mai Univ, Intawaroros Road, Muang, Chiang Mai, 50200, Thailand. T. +6653289291. Fax +6653945114.
URL: http://new.ahrn.net/
History 1996. **Aims** Advocate and support harm reduction enabling policies, networking, information sharing and training. **Structure** Executive Committee of 5 members, including Chairman, Vice-Chairman, one Foundation member and Executive Director. Secretariat. **Staff** 13.00 FTE, paid. **Finance** Supported by Dutch Government. **Activities** Organizes a discussion group through daily compilation of news, topic specific in-depths studies or opinion pieces and a weekly bulletin on AHRN activities. **Events** *Annual international harm reduction conferences / International Conference on the Reduction of Drug Related Harm* Bangkok (Thailand) 2009, *ICAAP: international congress on AIDS in Asia and the Pacific / International Conference on AIDS in Asia and the Pacific / International Conference on AIDS in Asia and the Pacific – ICAAP* Kobe (Japan) 2005, *ICAAP : international congress on AIDS in Asia and the Pacific / International Conference on AIDS in Asia and the Pacific / International Conference on AIDS in Asia and the Pacific – ICAAP* Melbourne, VIC (Australia) 2001. **Publications** *Network Bulletin* (weekly); *AHRN Newsletter* (4 a year). *Revisiting the Hidden Epidemic* (2002); *Manual for Reducing Drug Related Harm in Asia* (1999); *The Hidden Epidemic* (1998); *Situation Assessment of Injecting Drug Use in South East and East Asia in the context of HIV* (1997). **Information Services** *AHRN Information Sharing Facility* – online resource archives. **NGO Relations** Member of: *Coalition of Asia Pacific Regional Networks on HIV/AIDS (Seven Sisters, #04051)*. Instrumental in setting up: *Access Quality International (AQI, #00053)*. [2013.08.07/XF4728/**F**]

♦ Asian Health Institute (AHI) 01502

SG 987-30 Minamiyama, Komenoki, Nisshin, Aichi, 470-0111 Japan. T. +81561731950. Fax +81561731990. E-mail: info@ahi-japan.jp.
URL: http://www.ahi-japan.sakura.ne.jp/english/html
History 22 Dec 1980. **Aims** Support development of well-being and well-doing of marginalized people in Asia. **Structure** Board of Directors; Board of Trustees. **Languages** English, Japanese. **Staff** 10.00 FTE, paid. **Finance** Members' dues. Donations. **Activities** Training/education; networking/liaising. **Events** *Meeting on fostering multiculturalism among Asians* Nisshin (Japan) 2009, *International consultation* Bangkok (Thailand) 1992, *Chinese workshop* Nisshin (Japan) 1987. **Publications** *AHI Newsletter* (5 a year) in Japanese – also (2 a year) in English; *Children in Asia* (2 a year). Annual Report; training course proceedings; reports; case studies. **Members** Individuals and organizations, mainly in Japan. Membership countries not specified. **IGO Relations** *Japan International Cooperation Agency (JICA)*. [2018.07.23/XF1861/j/**E**]

♦ Asian Hematology Association (AHA) 01503

Pres Public Health Research Ctr, 1-1-7 Nishiwaseda, Shinjuku-ku, Tokyo, 169-0051 Japan. T. +81432373435. Fax +81433065664. E-mail: info@crmsa.or.jp.
History 2003. **Aims** Provide young hematologists a collaborative platform for promoting scientific exchange and cooperation in Asia for progress in advanced hematology in Asia; develop and promote Asian harmonization properly by integrating the emerging advances in science and technology; cooperate with hematology societies in Asia. **Structure** Committee, comprising President, 2 Vice-Presidents and Secretary General/Treasurer. Board. **Activities** General Assembly with Symposium. **Events** *Symposium* Kobe (Japan) 2015, *Symposium* Kobe (Japan) 2009, *Symposium* Bangkok (Thailand) 2007, *Symposium* Jeju (Korea Rep) 2005, *Symposium* Beijing (China) 2004. [2014/XM3991/**D**]

♦ Asian Hemophiliacs Rescue Association (inactive)

♦ Asian Highway Network 01504

Contact UNESCAP, United Nations Building, Rajadamnern Nok Avenue, Bangkok, 10200, Thailand.
URL: http://www.unescap.org/our-work/transport/asian-highway/about/
History 18 Nov 2003, Bangkok (Thailand), by intergovernmental agreement under the auspices of *United Nations Economic and Social Commission for Asia and the Pacific (ESCAP, #20557)*. Asian Highway Project was initiated in 1959. **Aims** Promote the development of international road transport in the region.
Members Governments of 32 countries:
Afghanistan, Armenia, Azerbaijan, Bangladesh, Bhutan, Cambodia, China, Georgia, India, Indonesia, Iran Islamic Rep, Japan, Kazakhstan, Korea DPR, Korea Rep, Kyrgyzstan, Laos, Malaysia, Mongolia, Myanmar, Nepal, Pakistan, Philippines, Russia, Singapore, Sri Lanka, Tajikistan, Thailand, Türkiye, Turkmenistan, Uzbekistan, Vietnam. [2017/XM0928/**F***]

♦ Asian Hockey Federation (AHF) 01505

Secretariat 47 Jalan Sultan Ismail, 50250 Kuala Lumpur, Malaysia. T. +60321442773. Fax +60321428075. E-mail: secgenahf@gmail.com.
URL: http://www.asiahockey.org/
History Founded 1956. Under the authority of: *International Hockey Federation (#13802)*. **Aims** Regulate and control hockey activity in the region; organize hockey *competitions*. **Structure** Congress (every 2 years); Council (meets annually); Executive Board. Committees (8): Competitions; Development and Coaching; Disciplinary; Finance and Marketing; Media and Public Relations; Medical; Umpiring; Women's. **Languages** English. **Staff** 3.00 FTE, paid. **Finance** Members' dues. Grants from International Hockey Federation and sponsorships. **Activities** Training/education; sporting activities. **Events** *Biennial General Council Meeting* Bangkok (Thailand) 1998, *Biennial meeting / Biennial General Council Meeting* Hiroshima (Japan) 1994, *Biennial meeting / Biennial General Council Meeting* Kuala Lumpur (Malaysia) 1992, *Biennial meeting / Biennial General Council Meeting* Beijing (China) 1990, *General council meeting* Ipoh (Malaysia) 1989.
Members Full; Provisional. National associations (26) in 24 countries and territories:
Bangladesh, Brunei Darussalam, China, Hong Kong, India (2), Indonesia, Iran Islamic Rep, Japan, Kazakhstan, Korea DPR, Korea Rep, Malaysia (2), Nepal, Oman, Pakistan, Philippines, Singapore, Sri Lanka, Taiwan, Tajikistan, Thailand, Turkmenistan, United Arab Emirates, Uzbekistan. [2015/XD7090/**D**]

♦ Asian Horological Trade and Industry Promotion Conference (meeting series)
♦ Asian Horse Racing Conference / see Asian Racing Federation (#01677)

♦ Asian Hospital Federation (AHF) 01506

Secretariat Korean Hosp Association, 13-15F Hyundai Bldg, 15 Mapodaero, Mapo-gu, Seoul, Korea Rep. T. +8227059246. E-mail: ose@kha.or.kr – ahf2018secretariat@gmail.com.
Facebook: https://www.facebook.com/AsianHospitalFederation/
History Founded 26 Sep 1971, when constitution was adopted; declaration of principles, 22 May 1982, Seoul (Korea Rep). Constitution most recently revised, Jun 1999. **Aims** Maintain efficient liaison among member countries and other hospital associations in the region; coordinate activities of hospital associations in the region for the attainment of quality healthcare; establish and promote a system for information exchange on every aspect of hospital and healthcare services and on the latest advances and developments in medical sciences and technology; obtain the highest attainable standards of hospital management and administration; promote and maintain friendly relations and mutual assistance. **Structure** Board of Governors (meets at least twice a year); Secretariat in country of Presidency, currently Malaysia. **Languages** English. **Staff** None. **Finance** Members' dues. Contributions from publishing companies. **Activities** Politics/policy/regulatory; standards/guidelines. **Events** *Regional Conference* Manila (Philippines) 2014, *Annual hospital management Asia conference* Singapore (Singapore) 2011, *Annual hospital management Asia conference* Seoul (Korea Rep) 2010, *Annual Conference* Bangkok (Thailand) 2004, *Forum* Japan 2004. **Publications** *Asian Hospital and Healthcare Management* (annual).
Members Category A national hospital associations; Category B hospitals in countries where there are as yet no national associations; Category C national organizations in allied areas of activity. Members in 14 countries and territories:
Australia, Hong Kong, India, Indonesia, Japan, Korea Rep, Malaysia, Mongolia, New Zealand, Philippines, Taiwan, Thailand, United Arab Emirates, Vietnam. [2020/XD3214/**D**]

♦ Asian Human Rights Commission (AHRC) 01507

Chairperson G/F, 52 Princess Margaret Road, Ho Man Tin, Kowloon, Hong Kong, Central and Western, Hong Kong. T. +85226986339. Fax +85226986367. E-mail: info@ahrc.asia.
URL: http://www.humanrights.asia/
History 10 Dec 1984. Registration: Start date: Apr 1986, Hong Kong. **Aims** Protect and promote human rights; work towards social equality; develop a speedy communication system using modern communication techniques to encourage quicker actions to protect human rights, redress wrongs and prevent *violations* in future; develop appropriate modes of human rights education; promote appropriate legal and administrative reforms; develop close links with *victims* of human rights violations; participate in peace making, reconciliation, conflict resolution, truth commissions and international tribunals; develop cultural and religious programmes; encourage ratification of UN instruments and development of local legislation, law enforcement and judicial practices in keeping with such instruments, and assist the formation and functioning of national human rights commissions; work towards the development of regional human rights mechanisms and encourage people's participation in this process by promoting the Asian Human Rights Charter. **Structure** Advisory Board; Board of Directors. **Staff** 10.00 FTE, paid. **Activities** Projects/programmes; research/documentation; training/education. **Publications** *Human Rights SOLIDARITY* (6 a year). Reports; books; brochures. **Members** Represented in 16 countries. Not a membership organization. **NGO Relations** Member of (1): *International Network for Economic, Social and Cultural Rights (ESCR-Net, #14255)*. Partner of (1): *International Dalit Solidarity Network (IDSN, #13129)*. Affiliated with (1): *Asian Legal Resource Centre (ALRC, #01529)*.
[2020.11.17/XD5100/**E**]

♦ Asian Hyperbaric and Diving Medical Association (AHDMA) 01508

Pres Singapore General Hosp, Dept of Anaesthesiology, 5 Outram Rd, Singapore 169608, Singapore. T. +6563213220.
Sec address not obtained. E-mail: dryusof@ymail.com.
URL: http://www.ahdma.org/
History 2005. Registered in accordance with Australian law. **Events** *Annual Scientific Meeting* Panglao Is (Philippines) 2019, *Annual Scientific Meeting* Kuala Lumpur (Malaysia) 2014, *Annual Scientific Meeting* Singapore (Singapore) 2013, *Annual Scientific Meeting* Phuket (Thailand) 2012, *Annual Scientific Meeting* Jakarta (Indonesia) 2011. [2015/XJ8299/**D**]

♦ Asiania Parachute Federation 01509

Contact PO Box 433, 22 Pacific Terrace – 1st floor, Coolum QLD 4573, Australia. T. +61754465743. E-mail: asiania@bigpond.com.
URL: http://www.asiania.org/
History 1994, Chengdu (China). **Aims** Promote, develop and increase standards in international competition, skills, technical knowledge, training, safety, friendships and better relations in the sport of parachuting and skydiving between member countries; provide a supportive role in promoting the values and benefits of FAI membership; reach safe and most successful parachuting and skydiving for all members and jumpers around the world. **Structure** Board. Committees. **Languages** English. **Staff** part-time, voluntary. **Finance** Members' dues. Sponsorship. **Activities** Awards/prizes/competitions; events/meetings; training/education. **Events** *Annual General Meeting* Jingmen (China) 2019, *Annual General Meeting* Ji'an (China) 2017, *Annual General Meeting* Incheon (Korea Rep) 2009, *Annual General Meeting* United Arab Emirates 2008.
Members Full in 30 countries and territories:
Australia, Bahrain, Brunei Darussalam, China, Egypt, Hong Kong, India, Indonesia, Iran Islamic Rep, Iraq, Japan, Jordan, Kazakhstan, Korea DPR, Korea Rep, Lebanon, Malaysia, Mongolia, New Zealand, Oman, Philippines, Qatar, Saudi Arabia, Singapore, Syrian AR, Taiwan, Thailand, United Arab Emirates, Uzbekistan, Yemen. [2017.03.08/XJ0928/**D**]

♦ Asiania Sport For All Association (ASFAA) 01510

Secretariat Av Dr Rodrigo Rodrigues No 818, Macau, Macau. T. +85328343708. E-mail: secretariat@asfaa.org.
Pres address not obtained. E-mail: info@sport.gov.mo.
URL: http://www.asfaa.org/
History 27 Apr 1991, Seoul (Korea Rep). Regional association of *The Association for International Sport for All (TAFISA, #02763)*. **Aims** Promote sports for all in the Asia and Oceania region. **Structure** General Assembly (annual); Board of Directors; Secretariat. **Languages** English. **Staff** 3.00 FTE, paid. **Finance** Sources: members' dues. **Activities** Events/meetings; knowledge management/information dissemination. **Events** *Biennial Congress* Seoul (Korea Rep) 2021, *Biennial Congress* Seoul (Korea Rep) 2020, *International Workshop* Ulsan (Korea Rep) 2019, *Biennial Congress* Hong Kong (Hong Kong) 2018, *Biennial Congress* Macau (Macau) 2016. **Publications** *What's New?* (2 a year) – newsletter; *JASFA Journal* (annual).
Members Organizations in 27 countries and territories:
Australia, Bangladesh, Cambodia, China, Fiji, Hong Kong, India, Indonesia, Iran Islamic Rep, Iraq, Israel, Japan, Korea Rep, Macau, Malaysia, Maldives, Mauritius, New Zealand, Pakistan, Philippines, Qatar, Saudi Arabia, Singapore, Sri Lanka, Taiwan, Thailand, Vietnam. [2020/XD7788/**D**]

♦ Asian Indigenous Women's Network (AIWN) 01511

Secretariat Tebtebba Foundation, 1 Roman Ayson Rd 2600, Baguio BEN, Philippines. T. +63744447703. Fax +63744439459. E-mail: ellen@tebtebba.org.
History 1993. **Aims** Support, sustain and help consolidate various efforts of indigenous women in Asia to organize, education and mobilize themselves. **Activities** Lobbying and advocacy. **Publications** *AIWN Newsletter*.
Members Organizations in 10 countries and territories:
Bangladesh, China, India, Indonesia, Japan, Mongolia, Myanmar, Philippines, Taiwan, Thailand.
NGO Relations Secretariat at: *Indigenous Peoples' International Centre for Policy Research and Education (Tebtebba Foundation)*. [2010/XF3633/**F**]

♦ Asian Industrial Development Council (inactive)

♦ Asian Infrastructure Investment Bank (AIIB) 01512

Headquarters Tower A, Asia Financial Center, Tianchen East Road 1, Chaoyang District, 100101 Beijing, China. T. +861083580920.
URL: http://www.aiib.org/

History Oct 2014. Memorandum of Understanding signed by 22 Asian countries to set up AIIB. Signing Ceremony of Articles of Agreement 29 Jun 2015, Beijing (China). **Aims** Foster sustainable economic development, create wealth and improve infrastructure connectivity in Asia by investing in infrastructure and other productive sectors; promote regional cooperation and partnership in addressing development challenges by working in close collaboration with other multilateral and bilateral development institutions. **Structure** Chief Negotiators' Meeting (CNM); Multilateral Interim Secretariat. **Languages** Chinese, English, French. **Events** *Legal Seminar* Singapore (Singapore) 2019, *Annual Meeting* Jeju (Korea Rep) 2017.
Members Founding members (57):
Australia, Austria, Azerbaijan, Bangladesh, Brazil, Brunei Darussalam, Cambodia, China, Denmark, Egypt, Finland, France, Georgia, Germany, Iceland, India, Indonesia, Iran Islamic Rep, Israel, Italy, Jordan, Kazakhstan, Korea Rep, Kuwait, Kyrgyzstan, Laos, Luxembourg, Malaysia, Maldives, Malta, Mongolia, Myanmar, Nepal, Netherlands, New Zealand, Norway, Oman, Pakistan, Philippines, Poland, Portugal, Qatar, Russia, Saudi Arabia, Singapore, South Africa, Spain, Sri Lanka, Sweden, Switzerland, Tajikistan, Thailand, Türkiye, UK, United Arab Emirates, Uzbekistan, Vietnam.
IGO Relations Observer status with (1): *United Nations (UN, #20515)* (General Assembly). **NGO Relations** Member of (1): *Global Infrastructure Connectivity Alliance (GICA, #10419).* [2021/XJ9944/**F***]

♦ Asian Innovation and Entrepreneurship Association (AIEA) 01513

SG Dept of Economics and Management of Innovation, Univ of Tokyo, 7-3-1 Hongo, Bunkyo, Tokyo, 113-8654 Japan. E-mail: admin@aiea.org.
URL: http://aiea.kaist.ac.kr/

Aims Advance economic growth and quality of life in Asian countries by stimulating and disseminating innovation in diverse areas of Asian society. **Structure** Executive Board; Advisory Committee. **Activities** Events/meetings; networking/liaising. **Events** *Conference* Seoul (Korea Rep) 2022, *AIEA-NBER Conference* Hsinchu (Taiwan) 2021, *Conference on Innovation and Entrepreneurship* Singapore (Singapore) 2019, *Conference* Tokyo (Japan) 2015, *Conference on Innovation and Entrepreneurship* Daejeon (Korea Rep) 2014.
Members Founding in 3 countries:
China, Japan, Korea Rep. [2021/XJ9544/**D**]

♦ Asian Institute of Alternative Dispute Resolutions (AIADR) 01514

Officer No 28-1, Medan Setia 2, Bukat Damansara, 50490 Kuala Lumpur, Malaysia. T. +60323006032. E-mail: thesecretariat@aiadr.world.
URL: https://aiadr.world/

History 17 Apr 2018, Malaysia. Registration: Suruhanjaya Syarikat Malaysia, No/ID: 1276994-P, Start date: 17 Apr 2018, Malaysia. **Aims** Promote the practice of Alternative Dispute Resolutions (ADR). **Structure** Council; Executive Board. Committees; Sub-Committees. **Languages** English. **Activities** Advocacy/lobbying/activism; knowledge management/information dissemination; training/education. **Events** *COVID-19 Asian Mediation Forum* Kuala Lumpur (Malaysia) 2020. **Publications** *ADR Centurion* (6 a year); *AIADR Journal of International ADR Forum* (4 a year) in Chinese, English, Indonesian, Korean, Malay. [2022/AA1156/**D**]

♦ Asian Institute for Development Communication (Aidcom) 01515

Exec Dir Univ Selangor (UNISEL), Fac of Communication / Visual Arts and Computing, Jalan Zirkon A 7/A, Section 7, 40000 Shah Alam, Selangor, Malaysia. E-mail: aidcom@unisel.edu.my.
URL: http://aidcom.unisel.edu.my/

History 1986, as *Asian Institute for Development Communication and Management.* **Aims** Contribute to equitable human development in the Asia Pacific region through the implementation of development communication programmes. **Structure** Board of Directors. **Languages** English, Malay. **Staff** 4.00 FTE, paid. **Finance** Grant from University of Selangor; projects; programmes. **Activities** Events/meetings; training/education; research/documentation; knowledge management/information dissemination. **Events** *Malaysia international conference on communications and IEEE international conference on networks* Kuala Lumpur (Malaysia) 2005, *ASEAN regional consultative workshop on building knowledge societies* Kuala Lumpur (Malaysia) 1999, *Regional meeting* Singapore (Singapore) 1991. **Publications** *The Journal of Development Communication* (2 a year); *AIDCOM Information.* Reports; case studies.
Members Full members and sister organizations in 13 countries:
Bangladesh, Brunei Darussalam, China, India, Indonesia, Malaysia, Maldives, Nepal, Pakistan, Philippines, Singapore, Sri Lanka, Thailand.
Consultative Status Consultative status granted from: *United Nations Population Fund (UNFPA, #20612).*
IGO Relations Consultation Status with: *Asian and Pacific Training Centre for Information and Communication Technology for Development (APCICT, #01645).* **NGO Relations** Member of: *GEF CSO Network (GCN, #10087); International Federation of Communication Associations.* Associate of: *Asia-Pacific Forum of Environmental Journalists (APFEJ, #01910); Confederation of ASEAN Journalists (CAJ, #04509);* Cornell University.
[2017.10.25/XE1064/j/**E**]

♦ Asian Institute for Development Communication and Management / see Asian Institute for Development Communication (#01515)

♦ Asian iNstitute for Environmental Research and enerGY (A.NERGY) 01516

Dir 12-1 Songdo-dong, Yeonsu-gu, Incheon 406-840, Korea Rep. T. +82328358468. Fax +82327778468. E-mail: anergy@ianergy.org.
URL: http://anergy.org/

History 15 Feb 2012. **Activities** Events/meetings; research/documentation; training/education. **Events** *Symposium* Incheon (Korea Rep) 2022, *Symposium* Incheon (Korea Rep) 2019, *Symposium* Incheon (Korea Rep) 2018.
Members Full in 18 countries and territories:
Bangladesh, Cambodia, Egypt, Indonesia, Kuwait, Kyrgyzstan, Laos, Malaysia, Mongolia, Nepal, Pakistan, Philippines, Saudi Arabia, Sri Lanka, Taiwan, Thailand, Türkiye, Vietnam. [2019/AA0251/**D**]

♦ Asian Institute of Finance (internationally oriented national body)
♦ Asian Institute for Human Rights (internationally oriented national body)
♦ Asian Institute of Insurance / see Insurance Institute for Asia and the Pacific
♦ Asian Institute of International Financial Law (internationally oriented national body)
♦ Asian Institute of Journalism / see Asian Institute of Journalism and Communication (#01517)

♦ Asian Institute of Journalism and Communication (AIJC) 01517

Pres ICTV Bldg, 2244 Espana Boulevard, Manila, Philippines. T. +6327434321 – +6327400396. E-mail: info@aijc.com.ph – gs@aijc.com.ph.
URL: http://www.aijc.com.ph/

History 1980, Manila (Philippines), as *Asian Institute of Journalism (AIJ).* **Aims** Promote *professional* communication development through research, capacity development and graduate studies; provide higher education opportunities to media practitioners; cater to communicators in government, corporate and academic organizations. **Structure** Board of Trustees; Executive Officers. **Languages** English, Filipino. **Finance** Income from: graduate school; research and consultancy projects; training courses; multimedia productions; publications; professoral chairs; grants. **Activities** Training/education; research and development; publishing activities; knowledge management/information dissemination. **Publications** *AIJourn-Com* – journal; *Paghahabi – AIJC Newsletter.* Self-learning modules; books; monographs. Information Services: Virtual Museum on Communication; library. **IGO Relations** Has implemented research and development consultancy projects for: *Asian Development Bank (ADB, #01422); Canadian International Development Agency (CIDA, inactive); FAO (#09260); ILO (#11123); International Bank for Reconstruction and Development (IBRD, #12317)* (World Bank); *UNDP (#20292); UNESCO (#20322); UNICEF (#20332); United States Agency for International Development (USAID).* [2015.06.01/XE0874/j/**E**]

♦ Asian Institute of Low Carbon Design (unconfirmed)

♦ Asian Institute of Management (AIM) 01518

Pres/Dean 123 Paseo de Roxas, Legazpi Village, Makati City 1229, Manila, Philippines. T. +6328924011 – +6328924012 – +6328924023. Fax +6328672114. E-mail: president@aim.edu – strategic.initiatives@aim.edu – admission@aim.edu.
URL: http://www.aim.edu/

History Feb 1968. Registered in accordance with the law of the Philippines. **Aims** Make a difference in promoting sustainable development of Asian societies by developing professional, entrepreneurial and socially responsible leaders and managers. **Structure** International Board of Governors (meets annually). Board of Trustees. Presidents serves as CEO; Dean serves as COO. Composed of 3 schools, each led by a Dean: W SyCip Graduate School of Business; Centre for Development Management; Executive Education and Lifelong Learning Centre. **Languages** English. **Staff** 38 core faculty members; 29 adjunct faculty members. **Finance** Program revenue; donations from domestic and international social investors. **Activities** Degree Programmes (5): 16-month Master in Business Administration (MBA); 11-month Master in Management (MM); 11-month Master in Development Management (MDM); 18-month Executive MBA for Entrepreneurship and Corporate Innovation; 20-month Evening Executive MBA. Offers Executive Education and Development Executive Programs; customized programs; training workshops; seminars; other conferences. **Events** *Asian Forum on Corporate Social Responsibility* Bangkok (Thailand) 2015, *Annual Asian Forum on Corporate Social Responsibility* Bangkok (Thailand) 2012, *Annual Asian Forum on Corporate Social Responsibility* Manila (Philippines) 2011, *Annual Asian Forum on Corporate Social Responsibility* Kuala Lumpur (Malaysia) 2010, *Annual Asian forum on corporate social responsibility* Manila (Philippines) 2009. **Publications** *AIM Leader* – magazine; *Journal of Asian Business* – published jointly with University of Michigan. *AIM Working Paper Series.* Books; cases; journal research papers; policy papers; studies; surveys; primers. **Members** Not a membership institute. **IGO Relations** Projects with: *Asia-Europe Foundation (ASEF, #01270); Asia-Pacific Economic Cooperation (APEC, #01887); Asian Development Bank (ADB, #01422); Australian Aid (inactive); Canadian International Development Agency (CIDA, inactive); Deutsche Gesellschaft für Internationale Zusammenarbeit (GIZ); International Bank for Reconstruction and Development (IBRD, #12317); International Development Research Centre (IDRC, #13162); International Finance Corporation (IFC, #13597); International Monetary Fund (IMF, #14180); Japan International Cooperation Agency (JICA); United Nations (UN, #20515); United States Agency for International Development (USAID); World Bank Institute (WBI, #21220).*
NGO Relations Member of:
- *Association of Asia-Pacific Business Schools (AAPBS, #02386);*
- *EFMD – The Management Development Network (#05387);*
- *Global Development Learning Network (GDLN, #10317);*
- *Global Network for Advanced Management (GNAM);*
- *Globally Responsible Leadership Initiative (GRLI, #10462);*
- *International Management Development Network (INTERMAN, no recent information);*
- *International University Consortium for Executive Education (UNICON);*
- *Pacific Asian Consortium for International Business Education and Research (PACIBER, #17930);*
- Partnership in International Management. [2020/XE0862/j/**E**]

♦ Asian Institute of Technology (AIT) 01519

Institut asiatique de technologie

Dir PO Box 4, Klong Luang, Pathum Thani, 12120, Thailand. T. +662516012044 – +6625245000. Fax +6625162126. E-mail: opa@ait.ac.th.
URL: https://ait.ac.th/

History Nov 1967, Bangkok (Thailand). Founded under an independent charter approved by the then *South-East Asia Treaty Organization (SEATO, inactive),* having functioned since 1959 as *SEATO Graduate School of Engineering.* **Aims** As an international institution of higher learning, engage in instruction, research and outreach activities in *engineering, sciences, management,* and closely-related fields to serve the changing needs of the region. **Structure** Board of Trustees, consisting of about 40 members from Asia, Australia, Europe and North America. Comprises 4 schools and the AIT Extension. Alumni: *Asian Institute of Technology Alumni Association (AITAA, #01520).* Academic Centres, include: *Geoinformatics Center (GIC); Asian Centre for Engineering Computations and Software (ACECOMS); Asian Center for Transportation Studies (ACTS, no recent information); Asian Centre for Soil Improvement and Geosynthetics (ACSIG).* **Languages** English. **Staff** 1,108 staff; 149 faculty. **Finance** Support from governments, foundations, industry, international organizations, endowment, research and outreach contracts, tuition and fees. **Activities** Events/meetings; research/documentation; training/education. **Events** *AINTEC: Asian Internet Engineering Conference* Hiroshima (Japan) 2022, *OHOW: International Symposium on ONE HEALTH, ONE WORLD* Pattaya (Thailand) 2022, *Water Security and Climate Change conference (WSCC)* Hanoi (Vietnam) 2021, *NIES International Forum on Sustainable Future in Asia* Tokyo (Japan) 2021, *Giant Prawn Conference* Shanghai (China) 2019. **Publications** *AIT Newsletter* (12 a year). Annual Report; annual research report; other reports and studies; doctoral theses. **Information Services** *AIT Library.* **Members** Not a membership organization. **IGO Relations** Accredited by (1): *Green Climate Fund (GCF, #10714).* Hosts: *Regional Integrated Multi-Hazard Early Warning System for Africa and Asia (RIMES, #18790).* Links with a large number of organizations (not specified). **NGO Relations** Member of (5): *Asian University Network of Environment and Disaster Risk Management (AUEDM, #01774); Clean Air Asia (#03983); Higher Education Sustainability Initiative (HESI); International Association of Universities (IAU, #12246); United Nations Academic Impact (UNAI, #20516).* Partner of (1): *EFMD – The Management Development Network (#05387).* Links with a large number of organizations (not specified).
[2022/XF4954/j/**F**]

♦ Asian Institute of Technology Alumni Association (AITAA) 01520

Pres c/o AIT, PO Box 4, Klong Luang, Pathum Thani, 12120, Thailand. T. +6625245058. Fax +6625245058. E-mail: aitaa@ait.asia.
URL: https://www.ait.ac.th/alumni/

History Jan 1969, Bangkok (Thailand). Founded by a core group of alumni of *Asian Institute of Technology (AIT, #01519).* Former names and other names: *AIT Alumni Association* – alias. **Aims** Serve the interest of all members, with a firm commitment to harnessing cooperation among all alumni, and between them and AIT. **Structure** Governing Board; Executive Committee; National and Regional Chapters Sub-Chapters; Headquarters based in Pathum Thani (Thailand). **Languages** English. **Staff** 1.00 FTE, paid. **Finance** Sources: members' dues. Annual budget: 10,200 USD. **Activities** Events/meetings. Active in all member countries. **Events** *Annual meeting* Ho Chi Minh City (Vietnam) 2021, *Annual meeting* Ho Chi Minh City (Vietnam) 2020, *Annual meeting* Bangkok (Thailand) 2019, *Annual meeting* Jakarta (Indonesia) 2018, *Annual meeting* Taipei (Taiwan) 2017. **Publications** *AITAA Gazette; AITAA Highlights; Directory of AIT Alumni.* Studies. **Information Services** *AITAA Projects Database.*
Members Regular; Honorary; Affiliate. National Chapters in 28 countries and territories:
Afghanistan, Australia, Bangladesh, Bhutan, Brunei Darussalam, Cambodia, Canada, China, Hong Kong, India, Indonesia, Japan, Kazakhstan (Central Asia), Korea Rep, Laos, Macau, Malaysia, Mongolia, Myanmar, Nepal, Pakistan, Philippines, Singapore, Sri Lanka, Taiwan, Thailand, USA, Vietnam.
Also Regional Chapters in Central Asia and South East Asia (countries not specified). [2022/XD9632/j/**E**]

♦ Asian Institute of Tourism (AIT) 01521

Institut du tourisme asiatique

Dean Commonwealth Ave, Diliman, 1101 Quezon City, Philippines. T. +6329818500.
URL: https://aitupd.wordpress.com/

History 26 Feb 1976, Manila (Philippines), as an academic unit of the University of the Philippines (UP). **Aims** Develop entrepreneurs, managers and qualified staff personnel for the tourism industry in Asia and the *Pacific* area; assist in the development, growth and professionalization of tourism in the *developing countries* of the region; provide a place for the conduct of *professional* and technical programs for *hospitality industry* in Asia and the Pacific area. **Languages** English. **Finance** Receives annual allotments from UP. Budget (annual): US$ 138,000. **Activities** Training/education; research/documentation; networking/liaising. **Publications** UP AIT Newsbriefs. Reports; reference works; manuals; monographs.
Members Membership covers 4 countries:
Korea Rep, Philippines, Thailand, Vietnam.
NGO Relations Member of: *Network of Asia-Pacific Education and Training Institutes in Tourism (APETIT, #16994).* [2019.07.30/XE7096/j/**E**]

♦ Asian Institute of Transport Development (internationally oriented national body)
♦ Asian Institute, University of Toronto (internationally oriented national body)

♦ Asian Intense Laser Network (AILN) 01522

Chair Shanghai Inst of Optics and Fine Mechanics, Chinese Ac of Sciences, No 390 Qinghe Road, Jiading District, 201800 Shanghai, China. T. +862169919005. Fax +862169918006.

Sec RIKEN Center for Advanced Photonics, 2-1 Hirosawa, Wako-shi, Saitama, 351 0198 Japan. T. +81484679492. Fax +81484624682. E-mail: kmidori@riken.jp.

History 17 Jun 2004, Tokyo (Japan). **Aims** Promote collaboration in the areas of intense laser science and technology among research groups in Asian countries and regions. **Structure** Board. **Languages** English. **Staff** 1.00 FTE, paid. **Finance** Proceeds through projects. **Activities** Events/meetings; training/education. **Events** *Asian Symposium on Intense Laser Science (ASILS)* Singapore (Singapore) 2022, *Asian Symposium on Intense Laser Science* Sharjah (United Arab Emirates) 2018, *Asian Symposium on Intense Laser Science (ASILS)* Ninh Binh (Vietnam) 2016, *Asia Pacific Laser Symposium* Huangshan (China) 2012, *Asian Symposium on Intense Laser Science / Symposium – ASILS* Tokyo (Japan) 2012.

Members Full in 9 countries and territories:
Canada, China, India, Japan, Korea Rep, Malaysia, Taiwan, USA, Vietnam. [2021/XJ0238/**D**]

♦ Asian Joint Committee on Plasma Surface Engineering (unconfirmed)
♦ Asian Joint Conference of Propulsion and Power (meeting series)

♦ Asian Jujitsu Belt Wrestling Federation (AJJBWF) 01523

Pres 21-Munawar Chambers 1, Mozang Road, Lahore, Pakistan. T. +92427313383. Fax +92427237875. E-mail: president@ajjbwf.org.

Aims Promote the sport of ju-jitsu and belt wrestling in Asia; increase friendship between member organizations. **Structure** Congress (annual); Board. Zones: Central Asia; East Asia; South Central Asia; West Asia. **Languages** English. **Activities** Sporting activities. **Events** *Asian Open Championship* Istanbul (Turkey) 2014.

Members National federations (22) in 19 countries and territories:
Bangladesh, India, Iran Islamic Rep, Iraq, Japan, Kazakhstan, Korea Rep, Kuwait, Kyrgyzstan, Lebanon, Malaysia, Nepal, Pakistan, Singapore, Taiwan, Tajikistan, Turkmenistan, United Arab Emirates, Uzbekistan.

NGO Relations Member of: *International Belt Wrestling Association (#12334)*; *Ju-Jitsu International Federation (JJIF, #16164).* [2014/XM2364/**D**]

♦ Asian Karatedo Federation (see: #21608)
♦ Asian Kickboxing Federation / see WKF Asia (#20973)

♦ Asian Law and Economics Association (AsLEA) 01524

Sec address not obtained. E-mail: lawecon@gmail.com.
URL: http://aslea.org/

Structure General Assembly. Officers: President; Secretary; Treasurer. **Events** *Annual Meeting* Seoul (Korea Rep) 2022, *Annual Meeting* Kuala Lumpur (Malaysia) 2020, *Annual Meeting* Bangkok (Thailand) 2019, *Annual Meeting* Singapore (Singapore) 2018, *Annual Meeting* Seoul (Korea Rep) 2016. **Publications** *AsLEA Journal.* [2014/XJ1417/**D**]

♦ Asian Law Institute (ASLI) 01525

Secretariat c/o Natl Univ of Singapore, Fac of Law, 469G Bukit Timah Road, Eu Tong Sen Bldg, Singapore 259776, Singapore. T. +6566013573. Fax +6567790979. E-mail: asli@nus.edu.sg.
URL: http://law.nus.edu.sg/asli/

History Founded 21 Mar 2003, Singapore (Singapore). **Aims** Facilitate research, academic exchanges and collaboration between the member institutes. **Structure** Board of 4 members; Secretariat. **Languages** English. **Activities** Events/meetings; networking/liaising. **Events** *Annual Conference* Tokyo (Japan) 2022, *Annual Conference* Singapore (Singapore) 2019, *Seminar on Designing an Evaluation Programme for the Court-Annexed Mediation in India* Singapore (Singapore) 2018, *Seminar on India's Proposed Amendment Bill 2018* Singapore (Singapore) 2018, *Seminar on the Patent Eligibility of Medical Technologies from the Perceptive of Comparative Law* Singapore (Singapore) 2018. **Publications** *Asian Journal of Comparative Law (AsJCL)* (2 a year). *Working Paper Series.*

Members Founding (13) Institutions in 11 countries and territories:
China, Hong Kong, India, Indonesia, Japan, Korea Rep, Malaysia, Philippines, Singapore, Taiwan, Thailand.
Other (70) Institutions in 20 countries and territories:
Australia, Canada, China, Hong Kong, India, Indonesia, Italy, Japan, Korea Rep, Malaysia, Mongolia, Myanmar, Pakistan, Russia, Singapore, Taiwan, Thailand, United Arab Emirates, USA, Vietnam. [2016.06.21/XM0107/j/**E**]

♦ Asian Law & Society Association (ALSA) 01526

Exec Officer 8-901 Waseda Law School, 1-6-1 Nishiwaseda, Shinjuku, Tokyo, 169-8050 Japan. E-mail: alsa_office@yahoo.co.jp.
URL: http://alsa.sakura.ne.jp/

Aims Foster socio-legal scholarship on Asia; disseminate its findings to the broader community of socio-legal scholars. **Structure** Board of Trustees; Executive Office. **Finance** Sources: members' dues. **Activities** Events/meetings. **Events** *Annual Conference* Hanoi (Vietnam) 2022, *Annual Conference* Bangkok (Thailand) 2021, *Annual Conference* Toyonaka (Japan) 2019, *Annual Conference* Gold Coast, QLD (Australia) 2018, *Annual Conference* Taipei (Taiwan) 2017. **Publications** *Asian Journal of Law and Society.* [2020/AA0165/**D**]

♦ Asian Law Students' Association (ALSA) 01527

Contact Student Ctr, Fac of Law Universitas Indonesia, Jl Prof Mr Djokosoetono, Pondok Cina, Kecamatan Beji, Kota Depok, Depok 16424, Indonesia. E-mail: scontact@alsainternational.org.
URL: https://alsainternational.org/

History 7 Sep 2020. Founded on merger of *ASEAN Law Students' Association (ALSA, inactive)* and East Asian Law Students Association, under the 'Tokyo Agreement'. **Aims** Promote development of law and justice in Asia by facilitating communication of young law students in the region. **Structure** General Assembly; Governing Council; International Board; Directors; National Chapters; Local Chapters. **Languages** English. **Finance** Sponsorship; merchandizing. **Activities** Awards/prizes/competitions; training/education. Events/meetings. **Events** *Conference* Seoul (Korea Rep) 2020, *Asian Law Students Association Forum* Cebu City (Philippines) 2019, *Law Students Pro Bono Conference* Singapore (Singapore) 2019, *Forum* Singapore (Singapore) 2017, *Annual Conference* Bangkok (Thailand) 2016. **Publications** *ALSA Magazine.*

Members National chapters in 14 countries and territories:
Brunei Darussalam, China, Hong Kong, Indonesia, Japan, Korea Rep, Laos, Macau, Malaysia, Myanmar, Philippines, Singapore, Sri Lanka, Taiwan, Thailand, Vietnam.
Observers in 3 countries:
Bangladesh, India, Nepal.

Consultative Status Consultative status granted from: *ASEAN (#01141).* **IGO Relations** *ECOSOC (#05331).* [2020/XJ0915/**D**]

♦ Asian League of Institutes of the Arts (ALIA) 01528

Headquarters Taipei Natl Univ of the Arts, No 1 XueYuan Rd,, Beitou District, Taipei 11257, Taiwan. T. +886228938704. Fax +886228948405. E-mail: alia.taipei@tnua.edu.tw – aliaschools14@gmail.com.
URL: https://alia-artschools.com/

History 6 Oct 2012, Seoul (Korea Rep). **Aims** Create art and peace through all forms of dialogues that inspire to understand and learn from each other despite diverse cultures, different educational practices and the vastness of Asia. **Structure** General Assembly; Board. **Events** *Creating a Global Network Symposium* Seoul (Korea Rep) 2012.

Members Full in 12 countries and territories:
Indonesia, Japan, Kazakhstan, Korea Rep, Malaysia, Mongolia, Philippines, Singapore, Switzerland, Taiwan, Thailand, Türkiye. [2020/AA2253/**D**]

♦ Asian Leasing Association / see Asian Financial Services Association (#01480)
♦ Asian Leasing and Finance Association / see Asian Financial Services Association (#01480)
♦ Asian Legal Consultative Committee / see Asian-African Legal Consultative Organization (#01303)

♦ Asian Legal Resource Centre (ALRC) 01529

Exec dir G/F 52 Princess Mararet Road, Ho Man Tin, Kowloon, Hong Kong, Central and Western, Hong Kong. T. +85226986339. Fax +85226986367.
URL: http://alrc.asia/

History Inaugurated 10 Dec 1984. Registered in accordance with the law of Hong Kong, Apr 1986. **Aims** Promote radical changes to the human rights landscape in Asia through structural re-engineering of justice institutions. **Structure** Board; Management; Staff. Head Office in Hong Kong. **Languages** English. **Staff** 22.00 FTE, paid. **Activities** Research/documentation; training/education; knowledge management/information dissemination. Active in: Bangladesh, Burma, Cambodia, China, India, Indonesia, Korea Rep, Malaysia, Nepal, Pakistan, Philippines, Singapore, Sri Lanka, Thailand. **Publications** *Article 2.* Journals; magazines; books; human rights reports; special reports; press releases. **Members** Not a membership organization. **Consultative Status** Consultative status granted from: *ECOSOC (#05331)* (General). **IGO Relations** Works closely with: *European Union (EU, #08967)*; *United Nations (UN, #20515).* **NGO Relations** Sister organization: *Asian Human Rights Commission (AHRC, #01507).* [2017.07.04/XE3613/v/**E**]

♦ Asian Legal Studies Centre, Vancouver / see Centre for Asian Legal Studies, Vancouver
♦ Asian Licensing Association (internationally oriented national body)

♦ Asian Liturgy Forum (ALF) 01530

Forum asiatique pour la liturgie

Contact Kristu Jyoti College, Bangalore, Karnataka 560036, Bangalore KARNATAKA 560036, India.
URL: https://www.facebook.com/asianliturgyforum/

History following a proposal Apr 1995, during a conference organized by and under the auspices of *Federation of Asian Bishops' Conferences (FABC, #09430).* Currently inactive. **Aims** Animate liturgical renewal through continuing training of clergy and lay leaders of Asia in the spirit of Vatican II's liturgical reform; promote research in topical themes; promote exchange of experience between liturgists; facilitate exchange of liturgical resources; make the Asian experience of God enrich the catholicity of the universal Church. **Structure** Plenary Assembly (annual). Executive Committee, consisting of Chairman (a bishop well versed in liturgical matters, appointed by FABC), Executive Secretary and Regional Secretaries. **Finance** Members' dues: US$ 30. **Activities** Instigates research. Organizes annual sub-regional meetings (South, East and North Asia), and meetings of regional representatives (every 2 or 3 years). Encourages exchange of liturgy professors and researchers. **Events** *South East Asian regional meeting* 1997, *Plenary Assembly* Malaybalay (Philippines) 1996. **Publications** Liturgical bulletin. Information Services: Establishing documentation centres in strategic Asian locations.

Members Individuals in 19 countries and territories:
Bangladesh, Brunei Darussalam, China, India, Indonesia, Japan, Korea Rep, Laos, Malaysia, Mongolia, Myanmar, Nepal, Pakistan, Philippines, Singapore, Sri Lanka, Taiwan, Thailand, Vietnam.

NGO Relations Cooperates with FABC. [2018/XF3654/v/**F**]

♦ Asian Local Search and Media Association (ALSMA) 01531

Sec address not obtained. T. +85328517520. Fax +85328517523.
URL: http://www.alsma.org/

History 1997, as *Asian Directory Publishers Association (ADPAI).* Current title adopted 2013. **Aims** Establish a forum for members – those involved in "Local Search" in Asia – to exchange knowledge, experiences, *information* and ideas. **Structure** Board of Trustees. Officers. **Events** *Annual Conference* Hua Hin (Thailand) 2018, *Annual Conference* Siem Reap (Cambodia) 2017, *Annual Conference* Phuket (Thailand) 2016, *Annual Conference* Bangkok (Thailand) 2014, *Annual Conference* Shanghai (China) 2013.

Members Charter members in 17 countries and territories:
Australia, Brunei Darussalam, China, Hong Kong, India, Indonesia, Japan, Macau, Malaysia, Mongolia, Myanmar, Philippines, Singapore, Taiwan, Thailand, United Arab Emirates, Vietnam.
Regular members in 12 countries and territories:
Cyprus, Fiji, Germany, Hong Kong, India, Mauritius, Papua New Guinea, Singapore, Sri Lanka, Thailand, United Arab Emirates, USA.
Lifetime in 5 countries:
Indonesia, Japan, Malaysia, Singapore, Sri Lanka.

NGO Relations Member of: *Search and Information Industry Association (Siinda, #19188).* [2014.09.03/XJ8658/**D**]

♦ Asian Lubricant Manufacturers Union / see Asian Lubricants Industry Association (#01532)

♦ Asian Lubricants Industry Association (ALIA) 01532

Chief Exec The Gateway West, Level 35, 150 Beach Road, Singapore 189720, Singapore. E-mail: secretariat@asianlubricants.org.
URL: https://asianlubricants.org/

History Former names and other names: *Asian Lubricant Manufacturers Union (ALMU)* – former (2001). Registration: Singapore. **Aims** Offer practical support and advice to Members; be the effective and authoritative voice of the Asian lubricants industry; further lubricants business interests in the Asia Pacific region. **Structure** Council.Subcommittees. **Activities** Advocacy/lobbying/activism; events/meetings; knowledge management/information dissemination; networking/liaising; training/education. **Events** *Annual Meeting* Kuala Lumpur (Malaysia) 2023, *Annual Meeting* Bangkok (Thailand) 2022. [2023/AA3198/t/**D**]

♦ Asian Magic Association (AMA) 01533

Gen Sec D7 – 12/F, Hang Cheung Factory Bldg, 1 Wing Ming Str, Lai Chi Kok, Kowloon, Hong Kong. T. +85294837100.
Contact address not obtained. T. +60182048157 – +60193690063. E-mail: kyrglobal@gmail.com – amac12th@gmail.com.
URL: http://www.amac2015.com/

History 28 Apr 2003, Hong Kong, at the International Magic Convention. **Structure** Board. **Events** *Convention* Kuala Lumpur (Malaysia) 2015, *Convention* Korea Rep 2014, *Convention* Davao (Philippines) 2009, *Convention* Hong Kong (Hong Kong) 2007, *Convention* Shenzhen (China) 2004. **NGO Relations** *International Federation of Magic Societies (#13473).* [2016/XM4484/**D**]

♦ Asian Manufacturers of Expanded Polystyrene (AMEPS) 01534

Secretariat address not obtained. E-mail: admin@epsa.org.au.
URL: https://ameps.net/

History 1994. **Aims** Increase the recycling of expanded polystyrene across Asia. **Events** *Annual Conference* Kiev (Ukraine) 2019.

Members Full (16) in 15 countries and territories:
Australia, China, Hong Kong, India, Indonesia, Japan, Korea Rep, Malaysia, New Zealand, Philippines, Russia, Taiwan, Thailand, Ukraine, USA.
European Manufacturers of Expanded Polystyrene (EUMEPS, #07732). [2019/AA2884/y/**F**]

♦ Asian Marine Conservation Association (internationally oriented national body)
♦ Asian Mass Communication Research and Information Centre / see Asian Media Information and Communication Centre (#01536)

♦ Asian Mayors Forum (AMF) 01535

SG Ghalamestan Park, Baq-e-Ferdows, Vali-e-Asr St, Teheran, 1961813355, Iran Islamic Rep. T. +982122708842. Fax +982122708839. E-mail: tehran.amf@gmail.com – secretariat@asianmayors.org.
URL: http://www.mayors.asia

History 2007. Based on Article 63 of the Asian Parliamentary Assembly (APA) Final Declaration. Secretariat launched Nov 2008, Teheran (Iran Islamic Rep). **Aims** Elevate levels of cooperation and partnerships among municipalities; create better environments for balanced *urgan* development with special emphasis on dignity of citizens, cultural and social integrity; offer better solutions for resource allocation towards optimization of urban development. **Structure** General Assembly; Executive Board. **Languages** English. **Staff** 10.00 FTE, paid. **Activities** Events/meetings. **Events** *Meeting* Qazvin (Iran Islamic Rep) / Teheran (Iran Islamic Rep) 2015, *General Assembly* Haikou City (China) 2014, *Meeting* Haikou City (China) 2014, *Meeting* Gaziantep (Turkey) 2013, *General Assembly* Bangkok (Thailand) 2012.

Members Full in 29 countries and territories:
Afghanistan, Bangladesh, Bhutan, China, Hong Kong, Indonesia, Iran Islamic Rep, Iraq, Japan, Korea Rep, Kuwait, Kyrgyzstan, Lebanon, Malaysia, Mongolia, Oman, Palestine, Philippines, Qatar, Saudi Arabia, Singapore, Sri Lanka, Syrian AR, Tajikistan, Thailand, Turkmenistan, United Arab Emirates, Uzbekistan, Vietnam. [2023.01.29/XJ9961/**F**]

♦ Asian Media Information and Communication Centre (AMIC) 01536
Centre asiatique d'information sur les recherches en communication de masse
SG 2F – PWU Annex, Philippine Women's Univ, 1743 Taft Ave, Malate, Manila, Philippines.
URL: http://www.amic.asia/
History Feb 1971. 1st General Meeting held Jun 1972, Kuala Lumpur (Malaysia). Previously also referred to as: *Asian Mass Communication Research and Information Centre.* Secretariat transferred to Manila (Philippines), Jul 2015. **Aims** Encourage ethical and social responsibility of the media to support democratic access and participation in media development and production; provide opportunities for empowerment of disadvantaged sectors in the communication/media environments in developing countries in Asia. **Structure** General Assembly (annual); Board of Directors; Main Departments (3): Publications; Research and Capacity Building; Conferences. **Languages** English. **Finance** Members' dues. Other sources: conference fees; subscriptions and sales of publications; project funding; programme contributions. **Activities** Events/meetings; publishing activities; research/documentation; training/education; knowledge management/information dissemination. **Events** *Annual Conference* Bangkok (Thailand) 2019, *Annual Conference* Manipal (India) 2018, *Annual Conference* Manila (Philippines) 2017, *Annual Conference* Manila (Philippines) 2016, *Annual Conference* Dubai (United Arab Emirates) 2015. **Publications** *Asian Journal of Communication* (6 a year); *AMIC Newsletter* (4 a year); *Media Asia* (4 a year). *Asian Communication Handbook* (6th ed 2013). Edited volumes; media books; conference papers; occasional papers.
Members Individual; Institutional. Members in 27 countries and territories:
Australia, Bangladesh, Bhutan, Canada, China, France, Germany, Hong Kong, India, Indonesia, Japan, Korea Rep, Macau, Malaysia, Nepal, New Zealand, Oman, Pakistan, Papua New Guinea, Philippines, Singapore, Sri Lanka, Taiwan, Thailand, UK, United Arab Emirates, USA.
Consultative Status Consultative status granted from: *ECOSOC (#05331)* (Ros C); *UNESCO (#20322)* (Consultative Status). **IGO Relations** Cooperates with: *UNEP (#20299)*; *UNESCO (#20322)*; *UNICEF (#20332)*; *WHO (#20950).* Invited to sessions of Intergovernmental Council of: *International Programme for the Development of Communication (IPDC, #14651).* Regular relationship with: *Asia-Pacific Institute for Broadcasting Development (AIBD, #01934).* **NGO Relations** Member of: *Asian Pacific Regional Coordinating Committee (no recent information)*; *Commonwealth Environmental Journalists Association (CEJA, #04326)*; *Environment Liaison Centre International (ELCI, no recent information)*; *World Journalism Education Council (WJEC, #21602).* Associate member of: *International Association for Media and Communication Research (IAMCR, #12022).* Regular relationship with: *Asia-Pacific Broadcasting Union (ABU, #01863)*; *Friedrich-Ebert-Stiftung (FES).* [2019.12.11/XE3991/E]

♦ Asian Medical Education Association (AMEA) 01537
Secretariat Univ Hong Kong, Li Ka Shing Fac Medicine, 2/F William MW Mong Block, Fac Medicine Bldg, 21 Sassoon Road, Pokfulam, Hong Kong, Central and Western, Hong Kong. T. +85239179296. E-mail: amea@hku.hk.
URL: http://www.med.hku.hk/amea/
History 2001. **Aims** Recognize that medicine is globalized; identify and enhance the characteristic features and strengths of Asian medical education; share information and experience about medical education; strengthen and promote good pedagogy and research on medical education. **Structure** Management Committee. **Events** *Symposium* Kuala Lumpur (Malaysia) 2019, *Symposium* Hong Kong (Hong Kong) 2017, *Joint Conference* Newcastle, NSW (Australia) 2015, *Symposium* Newcastle, NSW (Australia) 2015, *Symposium* Ulaanbaatar (Mongolia) 2013. **Publications** *AMEA Newsletter.*
Members Medical universities (165) in 28 countries and territories:
Australia, Bangladesh, Cambodia, Canada, China, Hong Kong, India, Indonesia, Iran Islamic Rep, Japan, Kazakhstan, Korea Rep, Laos, Malaysia, Mongolia, Myanmar, Nepal, Netherlands, Pakistan, Philippines, Singapore, South Africa, Sri Lanka, Taiwan, Thailand, UK, USA, Vietnam.
Included in the above, 1 university listed in this Yearbook:
China International Medical University (CIMU, no recent information). [2020/XM1722/D]

♦ Asian Medical Students' Association International (AMSA International) 01538
Chairperson 91 Xueshi Road, Taichung 404, Taiwan. E-mail: chair@amsa-international.org.
URL: https://amsa-international.org/
History 1985. Founded at the 6th Asian Medical Students' Conference (AMSC). **Aims** Promote the interest and welfare of medical students in the Asia-Pacific region and beyond. **Structure** International Executive Board (I-EB), comprising Senior Officers and Executive Committee; Regional Chapters. **Languages** English. **Finance** Sources: members' dues. **Activities** Capacity building; events/meetings; healthcare; publishing activities; research and development; training/education. **Events** *East Asian Medical Students Conference* Bangkok (Thailand) 2019, *Annual Conference* Singapore (Singapore) 2019, *East Asian Medical Students Conference* Kathmandu (Nepal) 2018, *Annual Conference* Kuala Lumpur (Malaysia) 2018, *Annual Conference* Seoul (Korea Rep) 2017. **Publications** *AMSA International eNewsletter*, *Journal of Asian Medical Students' Association (JAMSA).* Conference proceedings.
Members Chapters in 27 countries and territories:
Australia, Bangladesh, China, Egypt, England, Hong Kong, India, Indonesia, Japan, Kazakhstan, Macau, Malaysia, Mongolia, Myanmar, Nepal, New Zealand, Northern Ireland, Pakistan, Palestine, Philippines, Scotland, Singapore, Taiwan, Thailand, Ukraine, Uzbekistan, Vietnam.
NGO Relations Partner of (1): *International Student One Health Alliance (ISOHA).* [2021.02.17/XF2740/D]

- ♦ Asian Meeting of Animal Medicine Specialties (meeting series)
- ♦ Asian Meeting of Religions / see Asia-Oceania Meeting of Religious (#01802)
- ♦ Asian MetaCentre for Population and Sustainable Development Analysis (internationally oriented national body)

♦ Asian Methodist Council (AMC) 01539
Address not obtained.
History 15 Jun 2002, Seoul (Korea Rep). **Structure** General Assembly. Executive Committee. **Events** *Conference* Hong Kong (Hong Kong) 2011. **NGO Relations** Organization involved: *Fellowship of Asian Methodist Bishops (#09722).* [2011/XE4684/E]

- ♦ Asian Migrant Centre (internationally oriented national body)

♦ Asian Migrants Coordinating Body (AMCB) 01540
Contact c/o APMM, G/F, No 2 Jordan Road, Kowloon, Hong Kong. T. +85227237536. Fax +85227354559. E-mail: apmm@apmigrants.org.
URL: http://www.apmigrants.org/
History 1996. **Aims** Unite, educate and mobilize the broadest formations of migrants grassroots organizations for the protection and promotion of migrant *rights.* **Languages** English. **Staff** None. **Finance** Donations. **Activities** Projects/programmes. **Events** *International Migrants Assembly* Manila (Philippines) 2011. **Publications** *APMM News Digest* (12 a year); *Migrant Monitor* (2 a year). Studies.
Members Organizations of migrant workers and foreign domestic helpers in 10 countries and territories:
Australia, Hong Kong, Indonesia, Japan, Korea Rep, New Zealand, Philippines, Saudi Arabia, Taiwan, United Arab Emirates.
NGO Relations *Asia Pacific Mission for Migrants (APMM)*; *International Migrants Alliance (IMA, #14161).* [2017.03.10/XD8653/D]

- ♦ Asian Migrants' Coordinating Body (internationally oriented national body)

♦ Asian Minifootball Confederation (AMC) 01541
Pres Alnoor Way, As Sulymaniyah, Riyadh 12222, Saudi Arabia. T. +966567504060. E-mail: info@asianmf.com.
URL: https://asianmf.com/
History 2014, India. **Aims** Promote, supervise and direct Minifootball in Asia, as a means to contribute to the positive development of society. **Structure** Board. Regional federation of *World Minifootball Federation (WMF, #21652).* **Activities** Sporting activities.
Members Federations in 8 countries:
India, Iran Islamic Rep, Iraq, Malaysia, Nepal, Pakistan, Sri Lanka, United Arab Emirates. [2022/XJ9004/D]

- ♦ Asian Minorities Outreach / see Asia Harvest

♦ Asian Modern Pentathlon Confederation (AMPC) 01542
President's Office 4F Weight Lifting Stadium, 424 Olympicro Songpagu, Seoul 05540, Korea Rep. T. +8224233056. Fax +8224233056. E-mail: ampcpenta@naver.com.
Twitter: https://twitter.com/TheAMPC
History 1987. **Structure** Executive Board. **Events** *Congress* Wuhan (China) 2019, *Annual Congress* Bishkek (Kyrgyzstan) 2008.
Members National federations in 34 countries and territories:
Afghanistan, Bahrain, Bangladesh, China, Hong Kong, India, Indonesia, Iran Islamic Rep, Iraq, Japan, Kazakhstan, Korea DPR, Korea Rep, Kuwait, Kyrgyzstan, Lebanon, Malaysia, Mongolia, Nepal, Pakistan, Palestine, Philippines, Qatar, Saudi Arabia, Singapore, Sri Lanka, Syrian AR, Taiwan, Tajikistan, Thailand, Timor-Leste, Turkmenistan, United Arab Emirates, Uzbekistan.
NGO Relations *World Penthathlon (UIPM, #21720).* [2021/AA2271/D]

- ♦ Asian Monetary Fund (unconfirmed)
- ♦ Asian Motorcycle Union / see FIM Asia (#09759)

♦ Asian Musculoskeletal Society (AMS) 01543
Sec Dept of Radiology, Dr Soetomo General Hospital, May Jen Prof Dr Moestono 6-8, Surabaya 60286, Indonesia. E-mail: ams.secretary1@gmail.com.
URL: http://www.asianmsk.org/
History Founded 17 Sep 1998, Kuala Lumpur (Malaysia), during inaugural meeting. **Aims** Promote all aspects of musculoskeletal radiology in Asia. **Structure** General Assembly (annual); Executive Committee. **Events** *Annual Meeting* Visakhapatnam (India) 2021, *Annual Meeting* Hong Kong (Hong Kong) 2020, *Annual Meeting* Riyadh (Saudi Arabia) 2019, *Annual Meeting* Chennai (India) 2018, *Annual Meeting* Tokyo (Japan) 2017.
Members Radiologists, pathologists, orthopaedic surgeons, rheumatologists, sports physicians, veterinarians, and other individuals with a special interest in musculoskeletal radiology and related fields. Members in 16 countries:
Cambodia, China, India, Indonesia, Japan, Korea Rep, Malaysia, Myanmar, Netherlands, Oman, Philippines, Singapore, South Africa, Sri Lanka, Thailand, USA. [2015/XD8449/v/D]

♦ Asian Muslim Action Network (AMAN) 01544
SG 1562/113 Soi 1/1 Mooban Pibul, Pracharaj Road, Bangkok, 10800, Thailand. T. +6629130196. Fax +6629130197.
URL: http://www.arf-int.org/about-us-aman/
History 16 Oct 1990, Chiang Mai (Thailand). **Aims** Build understanding and solidarity among Muslims and other faith communities in Asia; develop programs that lead to empowerment, upholding human rights, justice and peace. **Structure** Assembly (every 3 years); Council. Currently housed by *Asian Resource Foundation (ARF).* **Languages** English, Thai. **Staff** 3.00 FTE, paid. **Finance** Members' dues. Supported by ecumenical organizations. Budget (annual): US$ 50,000 – 100,000. **Activities** Training/education; awareness raising; research/documentation; networking/liaising; advocacy/lobbying/activism; events/meetings. **Events** *Interfaith peace education conference* Bangkok (Thailand) 2001, *Interfaith conference on culture of peace* Bangkok (Thailand) 2000. **Publications** Conference' reports; training manuals on peace and development; case studies. **Members** Individuals (500) and organizations (60) in 17 countries. Membership countries not specified. **NGO Relations** Instrumental in setting up: *International Institute of Peace and Development Studies (IIPDS, #13908).* [2014.06.01/XF6362/F]

♦ Asian Mycological Association (AMA) 01545
Sec CAS Inst of Microbiology, No 3 1st Beichen West Rd, Haoyang Dist, 100101 Beijing, China. E-mail: msc93@im.ac.cn.
Chair address not obtained.
Chief-Sec address not obtained.
URL: http://www.amcfungi.org/
History Founded 2 Sep 1977, during 2nd International Mycological Congress, under the name *Committee for the Development of Mycology in Asian Countries (CDMAC)*, as a committee of *International Mycological Association (IMA, #14203).* Current constitution adopted, 1998, Goa (India). Subsequently referred to as *International Mycological Association Committee for Asia (IMACA)* and later as *IMA Committee for Asia* and *Asian Mycological Committee.* **Aims** Promote development of *mycology* in countries and regions of Asia. **Languages** English. **Finance** Fundraising; support from parent body for some activities. **Activities** Training/education; research/documentation; events/meetings. **Events** *AMC : Asian Mycological Congress* Busan (Korea Rep) 2023, *AMC : Asian Mycological Congress* Pathum Thani (Thailand) 2022, *AMC : Asian Mycological Congress* Pathum Thani (Thailand) 2021, *AMC : Asian Mycological Congress* Tsu (Japan) 2019, *AMC : Asian Mycological Congress* Ho Chi Minh City (Vietnam) 2017. **Publications** *NAMC – Newsletter of the Asian Mycological.*
Members National representatives from 26 countries and territories:
Australia, Bangladesh, Cambodia, China, Hong Kong, India, Indonesia, Iran Islamic Rep, Israel, Japan, Korea Rep, Kuwait, Laos, Malaysia, Mongolia, Myanmar, Nepal, New Zealand, Philippines, Russia, Saudi Arabia, Singapore, Sri Lanka, Taiwan, Thailand, Vietnam. [2014.09.24/XE7513/v/D]

- ♦ Asian Mycological Committee / see Asian Mycological Association (#01545)
- ♦ Asian Narcolepsy & Hypersomnolence Society (unconfirmed)
- ♦ Asian Nephrology Nursing Symposium (meeting series)
- ♦ Asian Netball Federation / see Netball Asia (#16977)

♦ Asian Network of Analytical Chemistry (ANAC) 01546
Dir Chemistry Dept – Saga Univ, 1 Honjo-machi, Saga, 840-8502 Japan. T. +81952288560.
Co-Dir Chemistry Dept, Seoul National Univ, Seoul 151-742, Korea Rep. T. +8228806638. Fax +8228891568.
URL: http://www.facs-as.org/
History Apr 1984, Kuala Lumpur (Malaysia), as a collaborative network for *Federation of Asian Chemical Societies (FACS, #09431)* and *UNESCO (#20322)*, under the auspices of *UNESCO Asia-Pacific Regional Bureau for Communication and Information (#20300).* Inaugural meeting of the network: Apr 1985, Singapore (Singapore). Previously known as *Asian Network for Analytical and Inorganic Chemistry (ANAIC).* **Aims** Facilitate cooperative research and training programmes in Asia in analytical and inorganic chemistry; in particular, promote activities to strengthen research directed to resource and *industrial development* and *environmental pollution.* **Structure** Coordinating Board appointed by FACS; national contact points (member chemical societies of FACS). **Finance** Project grants from UNESCO. **Activities** Technician and field-oriented training courses; scientific research seminars; workshops; conferences on relevant topics; standardization of reference materials; information collection and services (primarily through FACS Newsletter); small research grants. Priority areas: Analytical standardization and reference materials in tropical agriculture and industry; Chemical analysis of environmental effluents; Chemical analysis and quality control of consumer products; Instrument maintenance and technician training; mineral resource development, particularly chemistry of low-cost and low-energy beneficiation of mineral resources; Bioinorganic chelate chemistry for the treatment of metal toxicity, particularly from iron overload which is a widespread regional problem in health care; photoinorganic chemistry related to solar energy research and development; Catalysis in both homogenous and heterogenous chemical systems for efficient processing of industrial raw materials. **Events** *International conference / Conference* Kuala Lumpur (Malaysia) 1993, *International conference on applied bioinorganic chemistry* China 1992, *Regional seminar on chemical instrumentation* Ho Chi Minh City (Vietnam) 1992, *Research seminar on chemistry and ecology* Tashkent (Uzbekistan) 1992, *International symposium on technician education and training for research and development* Kuala Lumpur (Malaysia) 1991. **Publications** *Network News.*
Members Network research centres in 19 countries and territories:
Australia, Bangladesh, Cambodia, China, Fiji, Hong Kong, India, Indonesia, Iraq, Japan, Korea Rep, Kuwait, Malaysia, Nepal, Papua New Guinea, Philippines, Singapore, Thailand, Vietnam.
NGO Relations Member of: *Asian Coordinating Group for Chemistry (ACGC, no recent information).* [2008/XF2109/F]

- ♦ Asian Network for Analytical and Inorganic Chemistry / see Asian Network of Analytical Chemistry (#01546)

♦ Asian Network of Bipolar Disorder (ANBD) 01547

Contact Fac of Medicine, PO Box 5, Khohong, Hat Yai, Songkhla, 90112, Thailand. E-mail: upichet@medicine.psu.ac.th.

History Registered in accordance with Hong Kong law. **Aims** Promote and advance the awareness and treatment of bipolar disorder in the Asia Pacific region. **Structure** Council. **Events** *Meeting* Kuala Lumpur (Malaysia) 2011, *IRBD Asia Pacific conference* Kochi (India) 2009, *ANBD conference* Bangkok (Thailand) 2008, *Meeting* Kunming (China) 2007, *Meeting* Jeju (Korea Rep) 2006. **NGO Relations** Affiliated to: *International Society for Bipolar Disorders (ISBD, #14977).* [2010/XJ1371/**D**]

♦ Asian Network on Climate Science and Technology (ANCST) 01548

Communications Manager SEADPRI-UKM, Level 6 Block 1, Keris Mas, Univ Kebangsaan Malaysia, 43600 Bangi, Selangor, Malaysia. Fax +60389275629. E-mail: syarnissa@gmail.com – ancst@ancst.org.

URL: http://www.ancst.org/

History Officially launched 19 Nov 2013, following signing of the agreement between Cambridge Malaysian Education and Development Trust (CMEDT), Malaysian Commonwealth Studies Centre (MCSC) and the Universiti Kebangsaan Malaysia (UKM). Resulted from 2 regional meetings held in India (2011) and Malaysia (2012). **Aims** Provide information and develop research coordination projects led by Asian researchers, focusing on particular aspects of climate and disaster resilience specific to Asian conditions and phenomena. **Structure** International Scientific Advisory Committee; International Steering Committee. Implementation coordinated by ANCST Local Administration Committee and *Advisory Committee on Protection of the Sea (ACOPS, #00139).* **Languages** English. **Staff** 2.00 FTE, paid. **Finance** Funded by CMEDT and MCSC for administration and capacity building support for junior staff over the next 3 years. **Activities** Knowledge management/information dissemination; networking/liaising; events/meetings. **Events** *Workshop on Climate Change and Urban Environment / Session* Beijing (China) 2015, *Workshop on Climate Change and Disaster Resilience / Session* Manila (Philippines) 2015, *Session* Sendai (Japan) 2015, *Session* Kuala Lumpur (Malaysia) 2014, *Workshop on Atmospheric Chemistry and Climate Change / Session* Kuala Lumpur (Malaysia) 2014. **Publications** Articles.

Members in 18 countries and territories:
Bangladesh, Brunei Darussalam, Cambodia, China, Hong Kong, India, Indonesia, Japan, Laos, Malaysia, Myanmar, Philippines, Singapore, Sri Lanka, Taiwan, Thailand, UK, Vietnam. [2015.09.06/XJ7706/**F**]

♦ Asian Network for Culture and Development (internationally oriented national body)
♦ Asian Network on Debris Flow (unconfirmed)

♦ Asian Network for Education in Nuclear Technology (ANENT) 01549

Scientific Sec IAEA, c/o VIC, PO Box 100, 1400 Vienna, Austria. T. +431260026579. E-mail: sprho@kaeri.re.kr.

URL: http://www.anent-iaea.org/

History 2004, Malaysia, by *International Atomic Energy Agency (IAEA, #12294).* **Aims** Promote, manage and preserve nuclear knowledge to ensure continued availability of qualified human resources in the region for the sustainability of nuclear technology and to prepare newcomer countries to commence nuclear power programmes. **Structure** Coordination Committee; Scientific Secretary. **Activities** Training/education; events/meetings.

Members States (19):
Australia, Bangladesh, China, India, Indonesia, Japan, Jordan, Korea Rep, Lebanon, Malaysia, Mongolia, Pakistan, Philippines, Sri Lanka, Syrian AR, Thailand, United Arab Emirates, Vietnam, Yemen.

NGO Relations *Latin American Network for Education in Nuclear Technology (LANENT, #16353).* [2017/XM5412/**F***]

♦ Asian Network for Free Elections (ANFREL) 01550

Exec Dir 109 Suthisarnwinichai Road, Huaykwang, Bangkok, 10310, Thailand. T. +6622773627. Fax +6622762183. E-mail: chandanie@anfrel.org – anfrel@anfrel.org.

Chair C52b Gueventville II Libertad St, 1550 Mandaluyong METRO MANILA, Philippines. T. +3225352997 – +3225314428. Fax +3225352997.

URL: http://www.anfrel.org/

History Nov 1997. Previously also referred to as *Asian Network for Free and Fair Elections.* **Aims** Promote and support democratization at national and regional levels in Asia. **Structure** Board of Directors; Advisors; Secretariat. **Languages** English. **Staff** 8.00 FTE, paid. **Activities** Advocacy/lobbying/activism; information dissemination; publishing activities; research/documentation; training/education; politics/policy/regulatory. **Publications** Annual Report; Declaration; mission reports; brochures.

Members Founding members in 6 countries:
Bangladesh, Cambodia, Indonesia, Philippines, Sri Lanka, Thailand.
Organizations (22) in 14 countries:
Afghanistan, Bangladesh, Cambodia, India, Indonesia, Japan, Korea Rep, Mongolia, Nepal, Pakistan, Philippines, Sri Lanka, Thailand, Timor-Leste.

NGO Relations Member of: *Asia Democracy Network (ADN, #01265).* [2014.06.01/XF6134/y/**F**]

♦ Asian Network for Free and Fair Elections / see Asian Network for Free Elections (#01550)

♦ Asian Network for Learning, Innovation and Competence Building Systems (ASIALICS) 01551

Contact School of Economics and Management, Tongji Univ, 200092 Shanghai, China. T. +862165981787. Fax +862165983540.

Aims Explore and develop the concept of learning, innovation and competence building as an analytical framework in Asia. **Events** *ASIALICS Conference* Seoul (Korea Rep) 2019, *Biseul Forum* Daegu (Korea Rep) 2018, *Biseul Forum* Daegu (Korea Rep) 2018, *Biseul Forum* Daegu (Korea Rep) 2017, *ASIALICS Conference* Teheran (Iran Islamic Rep) 2017. **NGO Relations** Chapter of: *Global Network for Economics of Learning, Innovation and Competence Building Systems (GLOBELICS, #10488).* [2010/XM2525/**F**]

♦ Asian Network of Major Cities 21 (ANMC 21) 01552

Contact Intl Affairs Section, HQ Governor of Tokyo, Tokyo Metropolitan Government, 2-8-1 Nishi-shinjuku Shinjuku-ku, Tokyo, 163-8001 Japan. E-mail: s0000573@section.metro.tokyo.jp – s0014504@section.metro.tokyo.jp.

History 18 Oct 2001, Tokyo (Japan). Since 2015, inactive. **Aims** Provide a framework for cooperation among Asian cities in order to strengthen Asian identity and enhance importance of Asia in the international community. **Structure** Plenary Meeting (annual); Secretariat in Tokyo (Japan). **Languages** English. **Staff** 13.00 FTE, paid. **Activities** Networking/liaising; capacity building; research and development. **Events** *Annual Plenary Meeting / Plenary Meeting* Tomsk (Russia) 2014, *Annual Plenary Meeting / Plenary Meeting* Hanoi (Vietnam) 2013, *Annual Plenary Meeting / Plenary Meeting* Singapore (Singapore) 2012, *Annual Plenary Meeting / Plenary Meeting* Seoul (Korea Rep) 2011, *Plenary Meeting* Tokyo (Japan) 2010. **Publications** *ANMC21 Info* – leaflet.

Members Participating cities (13) in 13 countries and territories:
India (Delhi), Indonesia (Jakarta), Japan (Tokyo), Korea Rep (Seoul), Malaysia (Kuala Lumpur), Mongolia (Ulaanbaatar), Myanmar (Yangon), Philippines (Manila), Russia (Tomsk), Singapore (Singapore), Taiwan (Taipei), Thailand (Bangkok), Vietnam (Hanoi). [2016.12.28/XF6214/d/**F**]

♦ Asian Network on Medical and Aromatic Plants (inactive)

♦ Asian Network of People Who Use Drugs (ANPUD) 01553

Chairman Interchange 21, 399 Sukhumvit Rd, Bangkok, 10110, Thailand. T. +66939714847. E-mail: contact@anpud.org.

URL: http://anpud.org/

History 2008, Hong Kong. Registered in 2010. **Aims** Ensure the voices of people who use drugs are represented in regional forums; support development of country networks in the region. **Structure** Executive Board; Secretariat. **Languages** English. **Activities** Advocacy/lobbying/activism; capacity building; guidance/assistance/consulting; events/meetings; networking/liaising; research and development; research/documentation; training/education.

Members Organizations in 9 countries:
Australia, Cambodia, India, Indonesia, Malaysia, Myanmar, Nepal, Thailand, Vietnam.

IGO Relations *Joint United Nations Programme on HIV/AIDS (UNAIDS, #16149); United Nations Office on Drugs and Crime (UNODC, #20596); WHO (#20950).* **NGO Relations** *Asia-Pacific Network of People Living with HIV/AIDS (APN+, #01973); International Drug Policy Consortium (IDPC, #13205); International Network of People who Use Drugs (INPUD, #14301);* national organizations. [2015.06.12/XJ9402/**F**]

♦ Asian Network for Prevention of Illegal Transboundary Movement of Hazardous Wastes 01554

Secretariat Industrial & Hazardous Waste Management Div, Environment, Regeneration & Resource Circulation Bur, Min Environment, 1-2-2 Kasumigaseki, Chiyoda-ku, Tokyo, 100-8975 Japan. T. +81355013157. Fax +81335938264. E-mail: env-basel@env.go.jp.

URL: http://www.env.go.jp/en/recycle/asian_net/index.html

History 2003, Japan. Established as an informal network among the Competent Authorities to the *Basel Convention on the Control of Transboundary Movements of Hazardous Wastes and Their Disposal (UNCRTD, 1989)* in Asia. **Aims** Facilitate exchange and dissemination of information on transboundary movements of hazardous wastes; assist countries in implementing the Basel Convention under each country's system. **Activities** Events/meetings; research/documentation. **Events** *Workshop* Tokyo (Japan) 2021, *Workshop* Tokyo (Japan) 2020, *Workshop* Kuala Lumpur (Malaysia) 2019, *Workshop* Akita (Japan) 2018, *Workshop* Hanoi (Vietnam) 2017.

Members Competent Authorities and Focal Points to the Basel Convention of 13 countries and territories:
Brunei Darussalam, Cambodia, China, Hong Kong, Indonesia, Japan, Laos, Malaysia, Myanmar, Philippines, Singapore, Thailand, Vietnam.

IGO Relations Partner of (4): *Basel Convention on the Control of Transboundary Movements of Hazardous Wastes and Their Disposal (UNCRTD, 1989); International Criminal Police Organization – INTERPOL (ICPO-INTERPOL, #13110)* (Liaison Office for Asia and South Pacific Region); *UNEP (#20299)* (Regional Office for Asia and the Pacific (UNEP/ROAP)); *World Customs Organization (WCO, #21350).* **NGO Relations** Partner of (2): *European Union Network for the Implementation and Enforcement of Environmental Law (IMPEL, #09005); International Network for Environmental Compliance and Enforcement (INECE, #14261).* [2020/AA1920/**F***]

♦ Asian Network for Public Opinion Research (ANPOR) 01555

Gen Sec Room 706 – 7/F, The Jockey Club Tower, Centennial Campus, Univ of Hong Kong, Pokfulam, Hong Kong. T. +85239177700. Fax +85225460561. E-mail: secretariat.anpor@gmail.com.

URL: http://anpor.org/

History Set up 28 Nov 2012, when constitution was adopted. **Aims** Promote in each country or region in Asia the right to conduct and publish scientific research on what the people and its groups think and how this thinking is influenced by various factors; promote knowledge and application of scientific methods in this objective; assist and promote the development and publication of public opinion research in Asia; promote worldwide the publication of public opinion research on Asia; promote international cooperation and exchange among academic and commercial researchers, journalists and political actors, as well as between the representatives of the different scientific disciplines. **Structure** Council; Executive Committee. **Languages** English. **Staff** Voluntary. **Finance** Members' dues. Budget (2014): about US$ 4,000. **Activities** Events/meetings. **Events** *Annual Conference* Bangkok (Thailand) 2015, *Annual Conference* Niigata (Japan) 2014, *Annual Conference* Seoul (Korea Rep) 2013, *Annual Conference* Seoul (Korea Rep) 2013, *Annual Conference* Bangkok (Thailand) 2012. **Publications** *Asian Journal for Public Opinion Research (AJPOR)* (4 a year).

Members Individual; Corporate; Academic; Affiliate. Members in 15 countries and territories:
Bangladesh, China, Hong Kong, India, Indonesia, Japan, Korea Rep, Macau, Malaysia, Nepal, Pakistan, Philippines, Sri Lanka, Taiwan, Thailand. [2015.06.01/XJ9497/**F**]

♦ Asian Network for Quality (ANQ) 01556

Chairperson Singapore Quality Inst, No 1 Sophia Road 05-06/07, Peace Centre Bldg, Singapore 228149, Singapore. E-mail: ken_lwy@yahoo.com.

URL: http://anforq.org/

History Inaugurated Sep 2003, Beijing. **Aims** Improve quality of human life by contributing to the progress of science and technology, and to the development of industry through promotional activities for the research and development of philosophy, theory, methodology and application in the field of quality and quality management. **Structure** Board. **Activities** Training/education. **Events** *Congress* Seoul (Korea Rep) 2020, *Board Meeting* Seoul (Korea Rep) 2017, *Congress* Taipei (Taiwan) 2015, *Congress* Singapore (Singapore) 2014, *International Conference on Quality* Tokyo (Japan) 2014. **Publications** *ANQ News Letter.*

Members Organizations in 17 countries and territories:
Bangladesh, China, Hong Kong, India, Indonesia, Iran Islamic Rep, Japan, Kazakhstan, Korea Rep, Nepal, Pakistan, Russia, Singapore, Taiwan, Thailand, United Arab Emirates, Vietnam. [2015.11.19/XJ1261/**D**]

♦ Asian Network of Research Resource Centers (ANRRC) 01557

Contact 3-1-1 Koyadai, Tsukuba-shi, Ibaraki OSAKA, 305-0074 Japan. T. +81298369044. Fax +81298369144. E-mail: brc-front@brc.riken.jp.

URL: http://www.anrrc.org/

History Sep 2009. **Aims** Accelerate science and technology in Asia for health and wealth of Asian people. **Structure** Executive Board, comprising President, 2 Vice-Presidents, 12 members and one ex-officio member. Committees (9): Information Technology; Biobanking; Regulation; International Affairs; Scientific Affairs; Education and Training; Microorganism; Plant; Animal. **Events** *International Meeting* Tsukuba (Japan) 2022, *International Meeting* Tsukuba (Japan) 2020, *International Meeting* Los Baños (Philippines) 2019, *International Meeting* Seoul (Korea Rep) 2018, *International Meeting* Beijing (China) 2017.

Members Full in 15 countries:
Australia, Azerbaijan, China, India, Indonesia, Japan, Korea Rep, Malaysia, Mongolia, New Zealand, Pakistan, Philippines, Singapore, Thailand, Vietnam.

NGO Relations Memorandum of Understanding with: *European, Middle Eastern and African Society for Biopreservation and Biobanking (ESBB, #07798).* Affiliated with: *International Society for Biological and Environmental Repositories (ISBER, #14964).* [2013/XJ6431/**F**]

♦ Asian Network for the Rights of Occupational Accident Victims / see Asian Network for the Rights Of Occupational and Environmental Victims (#01558)

♦ Asian Network for the Rights Of Occupational and Environmental Victims (ANROEV) 01558

Contact Center for Public Health and Environmental Development (CEPHED), Mahalaxmi Municipality 2, Lalitpur, Kathmandu, Nepal. T. +97715201786. E-mail: anroev@gmail.com.

URL: http://www.anroev.org/

History 1997, as *Asian Network for the Rights of Occupational Accident Victims (ANROAV).* **Publications** *OSH Rights* – newsletter.

Members Organizations in 14 countries and territories:
Bangladesh, China, Hong Kong, India, Indonesia, Japan, Korea Rep, Macau, Malaysia, Nepal, Pakistan, Philippines, Taiwan, Thailand.
Included in the above, 1 organization listed in this Yearbook:
Asia Monitor Resource Centre (AMRC). [2020.03.21/XJ0002/y/**D**]

♦ Asian Network for Schizophrenia Research / see Asian College of Schizophrenia Research (#01387)

♦ Asian Network on Standardization and Harmonization in Laboratory Medicine (ANCLS) 01559

Contact Dept of Lab Medicine, Kangbuk Samsung Hosp, Sungkyunkwan Univ, School of Medicine, 108 Pyung-Dong, Jongro-Ku, Seoul 110-746, Korea Rep. T. +82220012368. Fax +8227230447. E-mail: hspcp@naver.com.

Contact Dept of Lab Medicine, Chung-Ang Univ Hosp, 102 Heukseok-ro, Dongjak-Gu, Seoul 06973, Korea Rep. E-mail: chayoung@cau.ac.kr.

URL: http://www.ancls.org/

History Feb 1999, Jakarta (Indonesia), at 1st Colloquium on Standardization and Harmonization in Laboratory Medicine. Registered in accordance with Korean law. **Aims** Foster the highest standards and harmonization in education, research and practice of laboratory medicine. **Structure** President; 2 Vice-Presidents; Country Coordinators. International Advisory Committee. **Events** *Congress* Seoul (Korea Rep) 2019, *Congress* Seoul (Korea Rep) 2016, *Diagnosis and treatment – improving and challenging* Ho Chi Minh City (Vietnam) 2013, *Congress* Bangkok (Thailand) 2012, *Congress* Bangkok (Thailand) 2011. **Publications** *ANCLS Journal*. **Members** Individuals (97) in 14 countries. Membership countries not specified. [2016.10.19/XJ6985/**F**]

♦ Asian Network for Surveillance of Resistant Pathogens / see Asian Network for Surveillance of Resistant Pathogens (#01560)

♦ Asian Network for Surveillance of Resistant Pathogens (ANSORP) . 01560

Project Manager Ste 1712, Rosedale Officetel, Suseo-dong, Gangnam-gu, Seoul 135-744, Korea Rep. T. +82234106826. Fax +82234106667. E-mail: ansorp@apfid.org.

Chair Div of Infectious Diseases, Samsung Medical Center, Sungkyunkwan Univ School of Medicine, 50 Ilwon-dong, Gangnam-gu, Seoul 135-710, Korea Rep. T. +82234100320. Fax +82234100328. E-mail: ansorp@gmail.com.

URL: http://www.ansorp.org/

History Jan 1996, as *Asian Network for Surveillance of Resistant Pathogens (ANSORP)*. Current title adopted 8 Dec 1999, and officially launched under this title Jan 2000. **Aims** Prevent and control *antimicrobial resistance* (AMR) in the Asian region. **Structure** Advisory Board; Executive Committee; Headquarters; Local ANSORP Networks (17). **Languages** English. **Staff** 10.00 FTE, paid. **Finance** Supported by: *Asia Pacific Foundation for Infectious Diseases (APFID)*; Korean Government; international organizations; pharmaceutical companies. **Activities** Research/documentation. **Events** *Investigator Workshop* Busan (Korea Rep) 2017, *ISAAR : international symposium on antimicrobial agents and resistance* Seoul (Korea Rep) 2003.

Members Hospitals (120) in 14 countries and territories:
China, Hong Kong, India, Indonesia, Japan, Korea Rep, Malaysia, Philippines, Saudi Arabia, Singapore, Sri Lanka, Taiwan, Thailand, Vietnam.

IGO Relations Korea Centers for Disease Control and Prevention (Korea CDC). **NGO Relations** *Asia Pacific Foundation for Infectious Diseases (APFID).* [2014.06.01/XF2148/**F**]

♦ Asian Network of Training and Research Institutions in Educational Planning (ANTRIEP) 01561

Réseau asiatique d'institutions de formation et de recherche en planification de l'éducation – Red Asiatica de Instituciones de Formación e Investigación en Planificación de la Educación

Contact Natl Inst of Educational Planning and Admin, 17-B Aurobindo Marg, Delhi 110016, DELHI 110016, India. T. +911126511996. Fax +911126853041.

URL: http://www.antriep.org/

History Dec 1995. **Aims** Create synergy between participating institutions in order to reinforce their capacities to respond to growing and increasingly diversified needs for skill development in educational planning and management in the region. **Languages** English. **Staff** None. **Finance** Supported by: *International Institute for Educational Planning (IIEP, #13874)*. **Activities** Events/meetings; research/documentation. **Events** *Annual Conference* 2004, *Annual Conference* Kuala Lumpur (Malaysia) 2002. **Publications** *ANTRIEP Newsletter* (2 a year).

Members National institutions (22) in 14 countries:
Australia, Bangladesh, Cambodia, China, France, India, Indonesia, Korea Rep, Malaysia, Nepal, Pakistan, Philippines, Sri Lanka, Vietnam. [2022/XF6000/**F**]

♦ Asian Network of Women's Shelters (ANWS) 01562

Secretariat c/o Garden of Hope Foundation, 1F No 2-1 Shun-an St, Xindian Dist, New Taipei City 23143, Taiwan. T. +886289115595 ext 507. Fax +886289115695. E-mail: secretariat@shelterasia.org.

URL: http://shelterasia.org/

History Feb 2012, Washington, DC (USA). Set up at the 2nd World Conference of Women's Shelters. Former names and other names: *Shelter Asia* – alias. **Aims** Unite, promote and strengthen the women's shelter movement in Asia to end all forms of gender-based violence. **Structure** Steering Committee. **Languages** English. **Activities** Events/meetings. **Events** *Annual Conference* Taipei (Taiwan) 2022, *Asian Conference of Women's Shelters* The Hague (Netherlands) 2015, *Asian Conference of Women's Shelters* Kaohsiung (Taiwan) 2013, *Asian Conference of Women's Shelters* Taipei (Taiwan) 2012.

Members Institutions in 20 countries and territories:
Afghanistan, Bangladesh, Cambodia, Hong Kong, India, Indonesia, Japan, Korea Rep, Macau, Malaysia, Mongolia, Nepal, Pakistan, Singapore, Sri Lanka, Taiwan, Tajikistan, Timor-Leste, USA, Vietnam.

NGO Relations Represented with: *Global Network of Women's Shelters (GNWS, #10504).* [2023.02.14/XJ9806/**F**]

♦ Asian Neurogastroenterology and Motility Association (ANMA) 01563

SG School of Medicine NUS, 1E Kent Ridge Road, Singapore 119228, Singapore.

URL: http://e-anma.inforang.com/

History Founded 21 Mar 2008, Bangkok (Thailand). Registered in accordance with Thai law. **Aims** Pursue a standardized care of *patients* suffering from gastrointestinal motility and functional disorders in Asia; conduct research in the field; exchange knowledge; encourage and advance knowledge in gastrointestinal motility and functional diseases in Asia in all possible ways. **Structure** Steering Committee, including officers and 12-14 Governing Council members. **Languages** English. **Staff** 1.20 FTE, paid. **Finance** Funding from governmental and non-governmental organizations. **Activities** Advocacy/lobbying/activism. **Events** *Biennial Congress* Taipei (Taiwan) 2023, *Biennial Congress* Bangkok (Thailand) 2022, *Biennial Congress* Bangkok (Thailand) 2021, *Biennial Congress* Seoul (Korea Rep) 2019, *Joint International Neurogastroenterology and Motility Meeting* Amsterdam (Netherlands) 2018. **Publications** *Journal of Neurogastroenterology and Motility* (4 a year) – online and print.

Members Full in 11 countries and territories:
China, Hong Kong, India, Japan, Korea Rep, Malaysia, Saudi Arabia, Singapore, Taiwan, Thailand, United Arab Emirates.

NGO Relations Member of: *Federation of Neurogastroenterology and Motility (FNM, #09696).* [2020/XJ1322/**D**]

♦ Asian Neuro-Ophthalmology Society (ASNOS) 01564

Contact Dept Orthoptics and Visual Science, Kitasato Univ, School of Allied Health Sciences, 5 Chome-9-1 Shirokane, Minato, Tokyo, 108-0072 Japan. T. +81427789416. Fax +81427789417. E-mail: asnos@kitasato-u.ac.jp.

Languages English. **Activities** Events/meetings. **Events** *Asian Neuro-Ophthalmology Society Congress* Bangkok (Thailand) 2022, *Asian Neuro-Ophthalmology Society Congress* Manila (Philippines) 2019, *Meeting* Seoul (Korea Rep) 2017, *Meeting* Kobe (Japan) 2011, *Meeting* Tokyo (Japan) 2009. **Publications** *ASNOS Newsletter*. **NGO Relations** Member of: *Asia-Pacific Academy of Ophthalmology (APAO, #01814).* [2019/XM3610/**D**]

♦ Asian New Humanities Net (ANHN) 01565

Pres address not obtained. E-mail: mhpch@arts.cuhk.edu.hk.

URL: http://www.cuhk.edu.hk/rih/ANHN/

History Founded 2004. **Aims** Serve as a regional network for the sharing of humanities *resources* in Asia; enhance academic and research excellence in humanities through the promotion of cooperation among Asian universities and research institutes. **Structure** Steering Committee; Secretariat. **Members** Institutional. Membership countries not specified. **NGO Relations** Member of: *International Council for Philosophy and Human Sciences (CIPSH, #13061).* Affiliate member of: *Consortium of Humanities Centers and Institutes (CHCI).* [2017/XM8677/**D**]

♦ Asian NGO Coalition / see Asian NGO Coalition for Agrarian Reform and Rural Development (#01566)

♦ Asian NGO Coalition for Agrarian Reform and Rural Development (ANGOC) 01566

Coalition asiatique des ONG pour la réforme agraire et le développement rural

Contact 33 Mapagsangguni Str, Sikatuna Village, Diliman, 1101 Quezon City, Philippines. T. +6323510581 – +6323510011. E-mail: angoc@angoc.org.

URL: http://www.angoc.org/

History 14 Feb 1979, Bangkok (Thailand), following a CIDA Programme in 1978-1979 in preparation for *World Conference on Agrarian Reform and Rural Development (WCARRD)* organized by FAO, Jul 1979, Rome (Italy). Incorporation formally registered in Hong Kong, 19 Aug 1983. Registered as a non-profit foundation in Manila (Philippines), 1989. Regional Secretariat based in Bangkok from 1979-1982; since 1983, based in Manila. Memorandum and Articles of Also referred to simply as *Asian NGO Coalition*. **Aims** Catalyze, consolidate and enhance the energies and capacities of Asian NGOs in addressing issues and reforming institutions that impact significantly on Asian rural communities by developing, disseminating and mainstreaming innovative, people-centred development agenda and experiences. **Structure** General Membership Meeting (every 2 years). Board of Directors (meets once a year), consisting of 2 regional representatives, 2 institutional representatives and a representative of each member country. Executive Committee, comprising Chairman, Vice-Chairman and a Board member. Regional Secretariat, managed by Executive Director and Deputy Executive Director. **Languages** English. **Staff** 7.00 FTE, paid. **Finance** Members' dues. Contributions from various organizations, including: *International Fund for Agricultural Development (IFAD, #13692)*; *International Land Coalition (ILC, #13999)*; *German Catholic Bishops' Organisation for Development Cooperation (MISEREOR)*; *Oxfam Novib*. **Activities** Advocacy/lobbying/activism; events/meetings; knowledge management/information dissemination; awareness raising; training/education; research/documentation. **Events** *Asia and Pacific regional FAO/NGO consultation on the world food summit* Bangkok (Thailand) 1996, *Asian Development Forum* Bangkok (Thailand) 1996, *Asian development forum* Kuala Lumpur (Malaysia) 1995, *Asian and the Pacific regional workshop* Kuala Lumpur (Malaysia) 1994, *Conference on sustainable integrated area development* Quezon City (Philippines) 1994. **Publications** *Gotong Royong* – newsletter; *Land Watch* – newsletter; *Lok Niti* – journal. *Enhancing Access of the Poor to Land and Common Property Resources*; *In Search of Common Ground: Forging Land Partnerships in the Philippines*; *Securing the Right to Land: A CSO Overview on Access to Land in Asia*. Discussion papers; workshop proceedings.

Members Regional members (2):
South Asia Rural Reconstruction Association (SARRA, #19748); *Southeast Asia Rural Social Leadership Institute (SEARSOLIN, #19797).*

Institutional members in 4 countries:
India, Indonesia, Nepal, Sri Lanka.

National networks and NGOs in 8 countries:
Bangladesh, Cambodia, China, India, Indonesia, Nepal, Pakistan, Philippines.

Included in the above, 3 organizations listed in this Yearbook:
Association of Voluntary Agencies for Rural Development (AVARD); *Gandhi Peace Foundation (no recent information)*; *Rural Development Foundation of Pakistan (RDF, inactive).*

Consultative Status Consultative status granted from: *ECOSOC (#05331)* (Special); *FAO (#09260)* (Liaison Status). **IGO Relations** Working relations with: *Centre on Integrated Rural Development for Asia and the Pacific (CIRDAP, #03750)*; *International Fund for Agricultural Development (IFAD, #13692)*. Accredited by: *United Nations Office at Vienna (UNOV, #20604)*. Associated with Department of Global Communications of the United Nations. **NGO Relations** Member of: *International Land Coalition (ILC, #13999)*; *International NGO/CSO Planning Committee for Food Sovereignty (IPC, #14365)*; *Global Land Tool Network (GLTN, #10452)*; Philippine Development Assistance Programme (PDAP); *Social Watch (#19350)*. Cooperates with: *ActionAid (#00087)* Asia; *Alliance Against Hunger and Malnutrition (AAHM, no recent information)*; *German Catholic Bishops' Organisation for Development Cooperation (MISEREOR)*; *Global Forum on Agricultural Research (GFAR, #10370)*; *NGO Forum on Cambodia (#17124)*; *Oxfam Novib*; *Oxfam GB*; *Society for Conservation and Protection of Environment (SCOPE)*; national organizations. [2018/XD0374/y/**D**]

♦ Asian NGO Network on National Human Rights Institutions (ANNI) . 01567

Secretariat c/o FORUM-ASIA, 66/2 Pan Road, Silom, Bang Rak, Bangkok, 10500, Thailand. T. +6626532942ext402. E-mail: anni-sec@forum-asia.org.

URL: http://nhriwatch.wordpress.com/

History Set up Dec 2006, Bangkok (Thailand), at 1st Regional Consultation on Cooperation between NHRIs and NGOs in Asia, organized by *Asian Forum for Human Rights and Development (FORUM-ASIA, #01491)*. Also referred to as *Asian NGO Network on NHRIs*. **Aims** Help establish and develop accountable, independent, effective, and transparent national human rights institutions in Asia. **Structure** Secretariat organized by *Asian Forum for Human Rights and Development (FORUM-ASIA, #01491)*. **Events** *Regional Conference* Mongolia 2015, *Regional Conference* Ulaanbaatar (Mongolia) 2015, *Regional Consultation / Regional Conference* Goa (India) 2011, *Regional Consultation on Cooperation between NHRIs and NGOs in Asia / Triennial General Assembly* Bangkok (Thailand) 2006. [2015/XM3932/**F**]

♦ Asian NGO Network on NHRIs / see Asian NGO Network on National Human Rights Institutions (#01567)

♦ Asian NIR Consortium 01568

Sec National Food Research Institute, 2-1-12 Kannondai, Tsukuba IBARAKI, 305-8642 Japan. T. +81298388088. Fax +81298387996.

URL: http://nir.ac.affrc.go.jp/Web-ANC/ANC-index.html

History 28 Jun 2006, Seoul (Korea Rep), during joint summit on NIRS. Constitution amended 9 Nov 2008. **Aims** advance the study and development of near *infrared spectroscopy* in the region. **Events** *Near Infrared Spectroscopy Symposium* Kagoshima (Japan) 2016, *Symposium* Daegu (Korea Rep) 2014, *Near infrared spectroscopy symposium* Bangkok (Thailand) 2012, *Symposium* Thailand 2012, *Near infrared spectroscopy symposium / Symposium* Shanghai (China) 2010. **Members** Membership countries not specified. **NGO Relations** *International Council for Near Infrared Spectroscopy (ICNIRS, #13053).* [2010/XJ8133/**F**]

♦ Asian Nonwoven Fabric Association (ANFA) 01569

Main Office Mengyokaikan Honkan 4F, 5-8 Bingomachi 2-Chome, Chuo-Ku, Osaka, 541-0051 Japan. T. +81662330842. Fax +81662330843. E-mail: info@asianonwovens.com.

URL: http://www.asianonwovens.org/

History Also referred to as *Asia Nonwoven Fabric Association*. **Activities** Exhibition held with congress. **Events** *ANEX : Asia Nonwovens Exhibtion and Conference* Taipei (Taiwan) 2024, *ANEX : Asia Nonwovens Exhibtion and Conference* Shanghai (China) 2021, *Triennial Conference* Tokyo (Japan) 2018, *Regular Meeting* Seoul (Korea Rep) 2017, *Triennial Conference* Shanghai (China) 2015. [2019/XD8804/**D**]

♦ Asian Nuclear Medicine Board (ANMB) 01570

Main Office Multan Ultrasound Service, Distt Jail Road, Multan 60550, Pakistan. E-mail: dsabih@yahoo.com – anmb.aofnmb@gmail.com.

URL: https://www.anmboard.org/

History Proposed 2010. Founded by *Asian Regional Cooperative Council for Nuclear Medicine (ARCCNM, #01683)*. **Aims** Address concerns on the inhomogeneity of training and practice of Nuclear Medicine in Asia. **Structure** Core Committee. **Activities** Certification/accreditation; training/education. [2020/AA0990/**E**]

♦ Asian Nuclear Physics Association (ANPhA) 01571

Sec RIKEN Nishina Ctr, 2-1 Hirosawa, Wako SAITAMA, Japan. E-mail: motobaya@riken.jp – anpha-office@ribf.riken.jp.

Sec address not obtained.

URL: http://ribf.riken.jp/ANPhA/index.html

History 18 Jul 2009. **Aims** Strengthen collaboration among Asian nuclear research scientists through promotion of nuclear physics and its transdisciplinary use and applications; promote education in Asian nuclear science through mutual exchange and coordination in the Asian nuclear science communities; encourage coordination among Asian nuclear scientists by actively utilizing existing research facilities. **Structure** Steering Board. **Languages** English. **Staff** 0.50 FTE, paid. **Finance** No regular financing. **Events** *Symposium* Jeju (Korea Rep) 2019, *Symposium* Beijing (China) 2018, *Symposium* Sendai (Japan) 2016, *Symposium* Gyeongju (Korea Rep) 2015, *Symposium* Kolkata (India) 2014. **Publications** None.

Members Full in 8 countries and territories:
Australia, China, India, Japan, Korea Rep, Mongolia, Taiwan, Vietnam. [2017.03.08/XJ7195/c/**D**]

♦ **Asian Nuclear Safety Network (ANSN)** **01572**
Contact c/o IAEA, PO Box 100, Wagramerstrasse 5, 1400 Vienna, Austria. T. +43126000. Fax +43126007. E-mail: ansn.contact-point@iaea.org.
URL: https://ansn.iaea.org/
History 2002. Functions within *Global Nuclear Safety and Security Network (GNSSN, #10509)* of *International Atomic Energy Agency (IAEA, #12294)*. **Aims** Pool, analyse and share nuclear safety information, existing and new knowledge and practical experience among countries. **Structure** Plenary; Steering Committee. Topical Groups. **Events** *Joint International Workshop* Daejeon (Korea Rep) 2018, *Meeting* Vienna (Austria) 2017, *Regional Workshop on Radiation Safety and Emergency Preparedness* Daejeon (Korea Rep) 2016, *Regional Workshop on Safety Assessment* Daejeon (Korea Rep) 2016, *Global Export Competitiveness Seminar* Seoul (Korea Rep) 2016. **Publications** *ANSN Newsletter* (24 a year).
Members Participating countries (11):
Bangladesh, China, Indonesia, Japan, Kazakhstan, Korea Rep, Malaysia, Philippines, Singapore, Thailand, Vietnam.
Supporting countries (4):
Australia, France, Germany, USA.
Associate country:
Pakistan.
IGO Relations *International Atomic Energy Agency (IAEA, #12294).* [2018/XJ6749/**F***]

♦ **Asian Nutrition Society for Sports and Health (ANSSH)** **01573**
Dir address not obtained.
URL: http://www.anssh.org/
History 2015, by academic leaders from 7 Asian regions. **Aims** Develop and advance scientific research, personnel training and product innovation to provide educational and practical platforms of sports nutrition and public health. **Structure** Executive Committee; President; Secretary-General. **Languages** English. **Staff** 1.00 FTE, paid. **Finance** Members' dues. Industrial sponsorship. **Events** *International Conference on Adaptations and Nutrition in Sports* Taipei (Taiwan) 2021, *International Conference on Adaptations and Nutrition in Sports* Taipei (Taiwan) 2020, *International Conference on Adaptations and Nutrition in Sports* Chonburi (Thailand) 2018, *International Congress* Beijing (China) 2016, *Inaugural Meeting* Taipei (Taiwan) 2015. **Publications** Conference book.
Members Individuals in 7 countries and territories:
China, Japan, Korea Rep, Malaysia, Singapore, Taiwan, Thailand.
IGO Relations None. [2021/XM4282/**D**]

♦ Asian and Oceanian Association of Neurologists / see Asian and Oceanian Association of Neurology (#01574)

♦ **Asian and Oceanian Association of Neurology (AOAN)** **01574**
Past Pres Dept Neurology, Janakpuri Super Speciality Hosp, C-2/B, Delhi, DELHI, India. T. +911125552023. Fax +911125502023. E-mail: mmehndi@hotmail.com – aoanpresident@gmail.com.
URL: http://www.aoaneurology.org/
History 1961. Regional organization of *World Federation of Neurology (WFN, #21461)*. Also referred to as *Asian and Oceanian Association of Neurologists*. **Aims** Promote and foster on an international scale, advancement, exchange and diffusion of information and ideas relating to the nervous system; promote education and research in neurology; promote prevention and treatment of neurological disorders. **Structure** Officers: President; Vice President; Secretary-General/Treasurer. **Languages** English. **Activities** *Asian and Oceanian Congress of Neurology (AOCN)*. **Events** *Biennial Congress* Tokyo (Japan) 2024, *Biennial Congress* Taipei (Taiwan) 2021, *Biennial Congress* Taipei (Taiwan) 2020, *Biennial Congress* Seoul (Korea Rep) 2018, *Biennial Congress* Kuala Lumpur (Malaysia) 2016.
Members National associations in 20 countries and territories:
Afghanistan, Australia, Hong Kong, India, Indonesia, Israel, Japan, Korea Rep, Malaysia, Mongolia, Myanmar, New Zealand, Pakistan, Philippines, Saudi Arabia, Singapore, Sri Lanka, Taiwan, Thailand, Vietnam. [2018.07.31/XJ2485/**D**]

♦ Asian and Oceanian Bureau for Epilepsy / see Asian and Oceanian Epilepsy Association (#01577)

♦ **Asian Oceanian Child Neurology Association (AOCNA)** **01575**
Sec Pediatrics Dept St Marianna, 2-16-1 Sugao, Miyamae-ku, Kawasaki FUKUOKA, 216-8511 Japan. E-mail: h3yama@marianna-u.ac.jp.
URL: http://www.aocna.org/
History 1983. **Activities** *Asian and Oceanian Congress of Child Neurology (AOCCN)*. **Events** *Harmonizing the Diversity in Child Neurology* Bangkok (Thailand) 2021, *Synergy to challenge boundaries in child neurology* Kuala Lumpur (Malaysia) 2019, *Congress* Fukuoka (Japan) 2017, *Congress* Taipei (Taiwan) 2015, *Congress* Riyadh (Saudi Arabia) 2013. **NGO Relations** Cooperates and joint meetings with *International Child Neurology Association (ICNA, #12550)*. [2015/XM3972/**D**]

♦ **Asian-Oceanian Computing Industry Organisation (ASOCIO)** **01576**
Secretariat 6F, No 239, Sec 2, Chengde Rd, New Taipei City, Taiwan. T. +886225533988. Fax +886225533988. E-mail: secretariat@asocio.org.
URL: http://www.asocio.org/
History 4 Jun 1984, Tokyo (Japan). **Aims** Promote, encourage and foster *trade* between members; develop the industry in the Asian and Oceanian region. **Languages** English. **Finance** Members' dues. **Activities** Encourages members to formulate, maintain and establish codes of conduct; promotes the industry's interests through the press, literature, exhibitions, competitions and public fora; works on model legislative and other measures; promotes related service and other industries. Current concerns include unauthorized duplication of computer software. **Events** *Smart City Summit* Taipei (Taiwan) / Kaohsiung (Taiwan) 2023, *General Assembly and Digital Summit* Singapore (Singapore) 2022, *General Assembly and Digital Summit* Dhaka (Bangladesh) 2021, *Smart City Summit* Bangkok (Thailand) 2019, *Digital Masters Summit* Tokyo (Japan) 2018. **Publications** *ASOCIO News* (6 a year); *ASOCIO Bulletin*; *ASOCIO Vision 2020*.
Members Full (21) in 21 countries and territories:
Australia, Bangladesh, Cambodia, Hong Kong, India, Indonesia, Japan, Korea Rep, Laos, Malaysia, Mongolia, Myanmar, Nepal, New Zealand, Pakistan, Philippines, Singapore, Sri Lanka, Taiwan, Thailand, Vietnam.
Guest members (7) in 7 countries:
Canada, France, Kenya, Russia, Spain, UK, USA. [2023/XD2047/t/**D**]

♦ Asian and Oceanian Congress of Obstetricians and Gynecologists (meeting series)
♦ Asian and Oceanian Cyclodextrin League (unconfirmed)

♦ **Asian and Oceanian Epilepsy Association (AOEA)** **01577**
Chairman Neurology Lab, Univ Malaya Medical Centre, 59100 Kuala Lumpur, Malaysia. Fax +60379502968.
History Founded 8 Nov 1998, Taipei (Taiwan), during inaugural congress, as *Asian and Oceanian Bureau for Epilepsy*. **Aims** Improve the quality of life of all persons with epilepsy; promote formation of organisations of persons with epilepsy, their relatives and their friends; promote exchange of information among organisations concerned with epilepsy; bring together, from all sources and countries, information about social and medicare for people with epilepsy and disseminate such information throughout the Asian and Oceanian region; represent epilepsy in relation to national and international organisations concerned with human welfare; encourage education and training with respect to all aspects of epilepsy; stimulate research into the social aspects of epilepsy. **Structure** General Assembly; Executive Committee; Headquarters in Delhi (India). **Languages** English. **Staff** None. **Finance** Members' dues. **Events** *Congress* Kuala Lumpur (Malaysia) 2021, *Congress* Bali (Indonesia) 2018, *Congress* Hong Kong (Hong Kong) 2016, *Congress* Singapore (Singapore) 2014, *Congress* Philippines 2012. **Publications** *AOEA Newsletter*.
Members Chapters and individuals in countries where no chapter exists (1 per country) in 23 countries and territories:
Australia, Bangladesh, Cambodia, China, Hong Kong, India, Indonesia, Iran Islamic Rep, Israel, Japan, Korea Rep, Lithuania, Malaysia, Mongolia, Nepal, New Zealand, Pakistan, Philippines, Singapore, Sri Lanka, Taiwan, Thailand, Vietnam. [2014/XD8541/**D**]

♦ Asian-Oceanian Epilepsy Organization (inactive)

♦ **Asian-Oceanian Federation of Conservative Dentistry (AOFCD)** **01578**
Pres B163 – Seoul Natl Univ Dental Hosp, 101 Daehak-ro, Jongno-gu, Seoul, Korea Rep. T. +8227633818. E-mail: consasia2019@gmail.com.
URL: http://www.aofcd.org/
History First preparatory meeting held 21 Oct 2016, Seoul (Korea Rep). Officially constituted 22 Jan 2018, Seoul (Korea Rep). Registered in accordance with Korean law. **Aims** Contribute to the promotion of oral health in the public interest; facilitate communication and cooperation amongst members in the Asian and Oceanian regions by encouraging excellence in the clinical practice, teaching and research pertinent to the scope of Conservative Dentistry. **Structure** General Assembly; Executive Committee; Standing Committees. **Languages** English. **Finance** Members' dues. **Activities** Events/meetings. **Events** *General Meeting* Taipei (Taiwan) 2023, *Conference* 2022, *General Meeting* Kochi (India) 2021, *General Meeting* Seoul (Korea Rep) 2019, *Congress* Sharjah (United Arab Emirates) 2018.
Members Societies in 4 countries and territories:
India, Iran Islamic Rep, Korea Rep, Taiwan.
Advisory Board Societies in 3 countries:
Korea Rep, Nepal, Türkiye.
Included in the above, 1 organization listed in this Yearbook:
International Federation of Dental Educators and Associations (IFDEA, #13404).
NGO Relations *European Federation of Conservative Dentistry (EFCD, #07087).* [2020/XM8925/**D**]

♦ **Asian and Oceanian Myology Centre (AOMC)** **01579**
Assistant Sec Dept of Neurology, Royal Children's Hosp, Parkville VIC 3052, Australia. T. +61393455641. Fax +61393455977.
Pres Nat'l Inst of Neuroscience, Nat'l Ctr of Neurology and Psychiatry, 4-1-1 Ogawa-Higashi, Kodaira, Tokyo, 187-8502 Japan.
URL: http://www.aomc.info/
History Jan 2001, Tokyo (Japan). **Aims** Advance research into *neuromuscular* disorders. **Structure** Executive Board. **Events** *Annual Scientific Meeting* Busan (Korea Rep) 2021, *Annual Scientific Meeting* Busan (Korea Rep) 2020, *Annual Scientific Meeting* Mumbai (India) 2019, *Annual Scientific Meeting* Kuala Lumpur (Malaysia) 2018, *Annual Scientific Meeting* Singapore (Singapore) 2017. [2017/XM0104/**D**]

♦ **Asian and Oceanian Photochemistry Association (APA)** **01580**
Sec address not obtained. E-mail: apa-st@ms.naist.jp.
URL: http://asianphotochem.com/
History Current constitution revised Nov 2012. **Aims** Promote and encourage the international development of photochemistry and related subjects with special reference to Asian and Oceanian countries. **Structure** Council; Executive Committee. **Finance** Sources: members' dues. **Activities** Awards/prizes/competitions; events/meetings. **Events** *Asian Photochemistry Conference* Daejeon (Korea Rep) 2021, *Asian Photochemistry Conference* Seoul (Korea Rep) 2020, *Asian Photochemistry Conference* Taipei (Taiwan) 2018, *Asian Photochemistry Conference* Singapore (Singapore) 2016, *Asian Photochemistry Conference* Kovalam (India) 2014. [2021/AA2256/**D**]

♦ **Asian-Oceanian Skull Base Society (AOSBS)** **01581**
No fixed address address not obtained.
History Founded 1989, Japan. **Aims** Promote information dissemination about the anatomy, physiology, pathology, and clinical management of diseases involving the skull base. **Structure** Executive Members taken from country organizing the next Congress. **Events** *Asian-Oceanian International Congress on Skull Base Surgery* Fukushima (Japan) 2020, *Asian-Oceanian International Congress on Skull Base Surgery / Congress* Jeju (Korea Rep) 2015, *Asian-Oceanian International Congress on Skull Base Surgery* Mumbai (India) 2015, *Asian-Oceanian International Congress on Skull Base Surgery / Congress* Beijing (China) 2012, *Asian-Oceanian international congress on skull base surgery / Congress* Bali (Indonesia) 2010. [2020/XN9796/**D**]

♦ **Asian and Oceanian Society of Neuroradiology and Head and Neck Radiology (AOSNHNR)** **01582**
Secretariat Radiology Kyoto Prefectural Univ of Medicine, 465 Kajii-cho, Kawaramachi-Hirokoji, Kamigyo-ku, Kyoto, 602-8566 Japan. E-mail: aosnhnr@koto.kpu-m.ac.jp.
URL: http://www.aosnhnr.org/
History 1994, Kumamoto (Japan). **Aims** Promote science, art and best practice in diagnosis and treatment of brain and spine diseases in the region. **Languages** English. **Activities** Events/meetings. **Events** *Asian-Oceanian Congress of Neuroradiology* Singapore (Singapore) 2023, *Asian-Oceanian Congress of Neuroradiology* Seoul (Korea Rep) 2021, *Asian-Oceanian Congress of Neuroradiology* Taipei (Taiwan) 2018, *Asian-Oceanian Congress of Neuroradiology* Beijing (China) 2017, *Asian-Oceanian Congress of Neuroradiology* Fukuoka (Japan) 2015.
Members Full in 20 countries and territories:
Australia, China, Hong Kong, India, Indonesia, Iran Islamic Rep, Japan, Korea Rep, Malaysia, Myanmar, New Zealand, Pakistan, Philippines, Saudi Arabia, Singapore, Sri Lanka, Taiwan, Thailand, Türkiye, Vietnam.
NGO Relations Member of (1): *World Federation of Neuroradiological Societies (WFNRS, #21463).* [2023.02.24/XD4869/**D**]

♦ Asian and Oceanian Society of Radiology / see Asian Oceanian Society of Radiology (#01583)

♦ **Asian Oceanian Society of Radiology (AOSR)** **01583**
Contact 71 Yangjaecheon-ro, Seocho-Gu, Seoul 137-891, Korea Rep. T. +8225785766. Fax +8225297113. E-mail: office@aosr.kr.
URL: http://www.theaosr.org/
History 1971, Melbourne, VIC (Australia). Former names and other names: *Asian and Oceanian Society of Radiology* – alias. **Aims** Stimulate basic and clinical research to advance development of radiology; improve the quality and technique of radiological procedures and improve members' skills in this respect; stimulate interest in, and provide guidelines for, the practice, teaching and post-graduate training in radiology; facilitate exchange of scientific information. **Structure** Executive Council. **Languages** English. **Staff** 1.00 FTE, paid. **Finance** Members' dues. **Activities** Events/meetings; training/education; networking/liaising. **Events** *Asian Oceanian Congress of Radiology (AOCR)* Bangkok (Thailand) 2023, *Asian Oceanian Congress of Radiology (AOCR)* Seoul (Korea Rep) 2022, *Asian Oceanian Congress of Radiology (AOCR)* Kuala Lumpur (Malaysia) 2021, *Asian Oceanian Congress of Radiology (AOCR)* Yokohama (Japan) 2021, *Asian Oceanian Congress of Radiology (AOCR)* Yokohama (Japan) 2020.
Members National societies of radiology, colleges, and government ministries of health in 27 countries and territories:
Australia, Bangladesh, China, Fiji, Hong Kong, India, Indonesia, Japan, Kazakhstan, Korea Rep, Macau, Malaysia, Mongolia, Myanmar, Nepal, New Zealand, Pakistan, Philippines, Samoa, Singapore, Sri Lanka, Taiwan, Thailand, Tonga, United Arab Emirates, Uzbekistan, Vietnam. [2022/XD6597/**D**]

♦ **Asian-Oceanian Standard-Setters Group (AOSSG)** **01584**
Admin Dir c/o ICAI, Indraprastha Marg, PO Box 7100, New Delhi, Delhi 110002, New Delhi DELHI 110002, India.
URL: http://www.aossg.org/
Aims Promote adoption of, and convergence with, International Financial Reporting Standards (IFRS) by jurisdictions in the region; promote consistent application of IFRSs by jurisdictions in the region; coordinate input from the region to the technical activities of the International Accounting Standards Board (IASB); cooperates with governments and regulators and other regional and international organizations to improve the quality of financial reporting in the region. **Structure** Chairman's Advisory Committee; Secretariat; Working Groups. **Languages** English. **Events** *Meeting* 2020, *Meeting* Goa (India) 2019, *Meeting* Singapore (Singapore) 2018, *Meeting* Hangzhou (China) 2017, *Meeting* Wellington (New Zealand) 2016.
Members Full in 26 countries and territories:
Australia, Brunei Darussalam, Cambodia, China, Hong Kong, India, Indonesia, Iraq, Japan, Kazakhstan, Korea Rep, Macau, Malaysia, Mongolia, Nepal, New Zealand, Pakistan, Philippines, Saudi Arabia, Singapore, Sri Lanka, Syrian AR, Thailand, United Arab Emirates, Uzbekistan, Vietnam. [2021/XJ5353/**D**]

♦ **Asian and Oceanian Stock Exchanges Federation (AOSEF)** **01585**
Secretariat Japan Exchange Group, 2-1 Nihombashi Kabuto-Cho, Chuo-Ku, Tokyo, 103-8224 Japan. T. +815033778896. E-mail: secretariat@aosef.org.
URL: http://www.aosef.org/

History 1982, Tokyo (Japan), as *East Asian Stock Exchange Conference (EASEC)*. Name changed to *East Asian and Oceanian Stock Exchanges Federation (EAOSEF)*, 1990, Manila (Philippines), on adoption of Charter. Current title adopted, 2005, with admission of exchanges in India. **Aims** Develop the *securities* markets in the region. **Structure** General Assembly (annual); Working Committee; Secretariat. **Languages** English. **Staff** 3.00 FTE, paid. **Finance** Members' dues. **Activities** Events/meetings; knowledge management/information dissemination; guidance/assistance/consulting. **Events** *Annual Meeting* Singapore (Singapore) 2019, *Annual Meeting* Bangkok (Thailand) 2016, *General Assembly* Tokyo (Japan) 2015, *Annual Meeting* Mumbai (India) 2014, *Annual Meeting* Shenzhen (China) 2013.
Members Stock exchanges (19) in 13 countries and territories:
Australia, China, Hong Kong, Indonesia, Japan, Korea Rep, Malaysia, Mongolia, Philippines, Singapore, Taiwan, Thailand, Vietnam. [2019/XD3729/**D**]

♦ Asian Oceania Society of Physical and Rehabilitation Medicine / see Asia Oceanian Society of Physical and Rehabilitation Medicine (#01804)
♦ Asian Oceania Society of Regional Anaesthesia / see Asian and Oceanic Society of Regional Anaesthesia and Pain Medicine (#01588)

♦ **Asian and Oceanic Association for Radiation Protection (AOARP)** .. **01586**
SG address not obtained.
URL: http://www.jhps.or.jp/AOARP/Executive_Committee.html/

Aims Encourage and stimulate exchange of information between the members; assist in the formation of national radiation protection societies in the region. **Structure** Executive Committee of 5 members. Officers: Chairperson; General-Secretary. **Events** *Asian and Oceanic Regional Congress* Kuala Lumpur (Malaysia) 2014, *Asian and Oceanic regional congress / Congress* Tokyo (Japan) 2010, *Congress* Beijing (China) 2006, *Asian Oceanic regional congress / Congress* Seoul (Korea Rep) 2002.
Members Organizations (5) in 5 countries:
Australia, China, India, Japan, Korea Rep.
Included in the above, 1 organization listed in this Yearbook:
Australasian Radiation Protection Society (ARPS). [2019/XD8372/**D**]

♦ Asian-Oceanic Glaucoma Society (inactive)
♦ Asian Oceanic Pancreatic Association (unconfirmed)
♦ Asian-Oceanic Postal Convention (1961 treaty)
♦ Asian and Oceanic Postal Training School / see Asian-Pacific Postal College (#01624)
♦ Asian-Oceanic Postal Union / see Asian-Pacific Postal Union (#01625)
♦ Asian and Oceanic Society for Intravenous Anaesthesia (no recent information)
♦ Asian and Oceanic Society for Paediatric Radiology / see Asian and Oceanic Society for Pediatric Radiology (#01587)

♦ **Asian and Oceanic Society for Pediatric Radiology (AOSPR)** **01587**
Secretariat address not obtained. E-mail: aospr1@gmail.com.
URL: http://www.aospr.com/

History 13 Jun 2000, Tokyo (Japan). Founded during inaugural meeting. Former names and other names: *Asian and Oceanic Society for Paediatric Radiology* – alias. **Aims** Improve the health of children by improving access of children to specialist paediatric imaging services and improving quality of paediatric imaging services provided. **Structure** General Assembly; Board of Directors; Executive Committee; Admissions Committee. **Languages** English. **Activities** Events/meetings. **Events** *Annual Scientific Meeting* Hong Kong 2023, *Annual Scientific Meeting* Manila (Philippines) 2022, *Meeting* Seoul (Korea Rep) 2019, *Annual Scientific Meeting* Chandigarh (India) 2018, *Meeting* Kuching (Malaysia) 2016. **Publications** *Pediatric Radiology Journal.* **Members** Medical imaging specialists. Membership countries not specified. **NGO Relations** Founding member of: *World Federation of Pediatric Imaging (WFPI, #21472).* [2022/XM4575/**D**]

♦ **Asian and Oceanic Society of Regional Anaesthesia and Pain Medicine (AOSRA-PM)** **01588**
Pres c/o Ganga Medical Centre, 313 Mettupalayam Road, Saibaba Koil, Coimbatore, Tamil Nadu 641043, Coimbatore TAMIL NADU 641043, India.
URL: https://aosrapm.org/

History Founded 29 Nov 1989. Previously the regional section of *World Federation of Societies of Anaesthesiologists (WFSA, #21482).* Also referred to as *Asian Oceania Society of Regional Anaesthesia (AOSRA).* **Aims** Promote study and research into problems in regional anaesthesia and pain relief. **Structure** Board of Directors. **Finance** Members' dues. **Events** *Biennial Congress* Mumbai (India) 2021, *Biennial Congress* Kochi (Japan) 2019, *Biennial Congress* Manila (Philippines) 2017, *Biennial Congress* Bangkok (Thailand) 2015, *World Congress of Regional Anaesthesia and Pain Therapy* Cape Town (South Africa) 2014. **Publications** *AOSRA-PM Newsletter.* [2021/XD4887/**D**]

♦ **Asian Ombudsman Association (AOA)** **01589**
Secretariat Wafaqi Mohtasib Secretariat, Plot 36 – Sector G-5/1, Constitution Avenue, Islamabad, Pakistan. T. +92519252178. Fax +92519252178. E-mail: aoasecretariat@gmail.com.
URL: http://www.asianombudsman.com/

History 16 Apr 1996, Islamabad (Pakistan), following the 1st Conference of the Asian Ombudsmen and the office holders of ombudsman like institutions representing 18 countries on the continent, 1996, Pakistan. **Aims** Promote the concepts of Ombudsmanship and encourage its development in Asia; develop professionalism in discharge of the functions as Ombudsman; encourage and support study and research regarding the institution of Ombudsman. **Structure** General Assembly and Conference (every 2 years). Board of Directors (meets annually), comprising President, Vice-President, Secretary, Treasurer and 5 additional members, elected for 4-year terms. **Languages** English. **Staff** provided by Wafaqi Mohtasib (Federal Ombudsman) Pakistan Secretariat: their Secretary serving as Ex-officio Executive Secretary; their Director (Coordinator) serving as Ex-officio Administrator. **Finance** Members' dues (annual). **Activities** Provides a platform for Ombudsman and similar institutions of accountability and grievance redress working in the Asian region; sponsors training and educational programmes for Ombudsman institutions in the region; provides scholarships, fellowships, grants and other types of financial support to individuals; collects, stores and disseminates information and research data; facilitates exchange of information and experiences among the Ombudsman of the region; plans, arranges and supervises periodic conferences. RETA Project 6465, approved by the Board of Directors of ADB, 24 Jun 2008, envisaged an overall grant of US$.9 million to carry out the following components of its work plan: prepare a survey report entitled *'Assessing the Capacity Development Needs of the Asian Ombudsman Association and its Members'*; capacity building activities; development of knowledge products; strengthening AOA's online resources centre. The survey report (2009) highlighted best practices in ombudsmanship among AOA members and identified their training needs, and has served as a reference point for RETA's activities. Capacity building activities include study tours, training, secondment and retreats. **Events** *Conference* Pyeongchang (Korea Rep) 2017, *Board of Directors Meeting* Seoul (Korea Rep) 2014, *Conference* Tokyo (Japan) 2011, *Annual meeting* Bangkok (Thailand) 2009, *Conference* Bangkok (Thailand) 2009. **Publications** *News Bulletin* (4 a year). Conference reports.
Members are part of their respective governments' structure and enjoy judicial/quasi judicial status. Members in 19 countries and territories:
Azerbaijan, China, Hong Kong, India, Indonesia, Iran Islamic Rep, Japan, Korea Rep, Kyrgyzstan, Macau, Malaysia, Pakistan, Philippines, Sri Lanka, Tatarstan, Thailand, Uzbekistan, Vietnam, Yemen. [2014/XJ8249/**D**]

♦ **Asian Oncology Nursing Society (AONS)** **01590**
Secretariat College of Nursing, Seoul Natl Univ, 103 Daehak-ro, Jongno-gu, Seoul 110-799, Korea Rep. T. +8227408460. E-mail: aons.staff@gmail.com – office@aons.asia.
URL: http://www.aons.asia/

History 2013. **Aims** Contribute to *cancer* nursing. **Structure** Executive Board. Committees (5): Conference; Education; Research; Publication; Communication. **Finance** Members' dues. **Activities** Knowledge base of addresses and advice. **Events** *Conference* Mumbai (India) 2019, *Winter Conference* Seoul (Korea Rep) 2018, *Conference* Beijing (China) 2017, *Conference* Seoul (Korea Rep) 2015. **Publications** *Asia-Pacific Journal of Oncology Nursing (APJON)* (4 a year) – official journal. **Members** Full; Individual; Associate. Membership countries not specified. **NGO Relations** Memorandum of Understanding with: *International Society for Nurses in Cancer Care (ISNCC, #15312).* [2015/XM4310/**D**]

♦ **Asian Oncology Society (AOS)** **01591**
SG Room 1824, Gwanghwamun Officia, 92 Saemunan-ro, Jongno-gu, Seoul 03186, Korea Rep. T. +827088500311. Fax +8227921410. E-mail: aos@aos-asia.org.
URL: http://www.aos-asia.org/

History 2018. Founded on merger of *Asian Clinical Oncology Society (ACOS, inactive)* and *Asian and Pacific Federation of Organizations for Cancer Research and Control (APFOCC, inactive).* Inauguration ceremony, 25 Oct 2019, Fukuoka (Japan). **Aims** Bring together, on a common platform, clinical oncologists from Asian countries; mutually encourage, strengthen and improve facilities for cancer research, diagnosis and management in countries in the region where such help is needed. **Structure** Council; Executive Board; Advisory Board; Scientific Committee. **Events** *International Congress* Yokohama (Japan) 2023, *International Congress* Seoul (Korea Rep) 2022, *International Conference* Manila (Philippines) 2020, *International Conference* Manila (Philippines) 2020.
Members Societies in 13 countries and territories:
China, Hong Kong, India, Indonesia, Iran Islamic Rep, Japan, Korea Rep, Nepal, Pakistan, Philippines, Singapore, Thailand, Vietnam. [2023.02.16/AA1794/**D**]

♦ Asia Nonwoven Fabric Association / see Asian Nonwoven Fabric Association (#01569)
♦ Asian Oral Implant Academy (inactive)

♦ **Asian Organization for Crohn's & Colitis (AOCC)** **01592**
Office 2-12-1-502 Kagurazaka, Shinjuku-Ku, Tokyo, 162-0825 Japan. T. +81332686430. Fax +81362807483. E-mail: aocc_office@aocc-ibd.jp.
URL: https://aocc-ibd.org/

History Current statutes enacted Jan 2013; amended June 2015 and June 2017. **Aims** Support research, education and medical treatment in the field of inflammatory bowel diseases, so as to improve the quality of life of inflammatory bowel disease patients in Asia. **Structure** General Meeting; Governing Board. Standing Committees. **Finance** Sources: members' dues. **Activities** Events/meetings. **Events** *Annual Meeting* Busan (Korea Rep) 2023, *Annual Meeting* Tokyo (Japan) 2022, *Annual Meeting* Guangzhou (China) 2021, *Annual Meeting* Busan (Korea Rep) 2020, *Annual Meeting* Taipei (Taiwan) 2019. **Publications** *Intestinal Research* – online. [2022/AA2276/**D**]

♦ **Asian Organization for Mycoplasmology (AOM)** **01593**
Chairman Pathogenic Biology Inst, School of Medicine, Univ of South China Hengyang, ZhenJiang, Jiangsu, China. T. +867348282913. Fax +867348282913.
URL: http://square.umin.ac.jp/aom/

Aims Conduct basic and applied research on the properties of mycoplasmas and related microorganisms in order to develop this academic field in Asia. **Structure** Board of Directors. **Languages** English. **Activities** Events/meetings; publishing activities; networking/liaising. **Events** *Meeting* Tokyo (Japan) 2018, *Meeting* Zhangjiajie (China) 2014, *Meeting* Nagasaki (Japan) 2011, *Meeting* Taiwan 2009, *Meeting* Korea Rep 2007. **Publications** *Asian Journal of Mycoplasmology.*
Members Universities and research institutes in 4 countries and territories:
China, Japan, Korea Rep, Taiwan.
NGO Relations Affiliated to: *International Organization for Mycoplasmology (IOM, #14456).* [2018/XJ5526/**D**]

♦ **Asian Organization of Supreme Audit Institutions (ASOSAI)** **01594**
Organisation asiatique des institutions supérieures de contrôle des finances publiques – Organización de Entidades Fiscalizadoras Superiores de Asia – Asiatische Organisation der Obersten Rechnungskontrollbehörden
Secretariat National Audit Office of the People's Republic of China, 17 Jinzhongdu Nan Jie, Fengtai District, Beijing, China. E-mail: gs@asosai.org.
URL: https://www.asosai.org/

History Founded by 11 members. Proposed during 9th INTOSAI Congress, 1977, Lima (Peru), by Mr Tantuico, then Chairman of the SAI Philippines. Charter adopted and signed, Sep 1978, by Heads of 9 Asian SAIs who attended a seminar hosted by the Deutsche Stiftung für Internationale Enwicklung (DSE), Berlin (Germany). First Assembly and Governing Board meeting held May 1979, Delhi (India), when Rules and Regulations were approved. One of 7 regional groups of: *International Organization of Supreme Audit Institutions (INTOSAI, #14478).* **Aims** Promote understanding and cooperation among member institutions through the exchange of ideas and experiences in the field of *public audit*; provide facilities for training and continuing education for government auditors with a view to improving the quality of their performance; serve as a centre of information and as a regional link with organizations and institutions in other parts of the world in the field of public audit; promote closer collaboration and brotherhood among auditors in the service of the government of the respective member institutions and among regional groups. **Structure** General Assembly (every 3 years); Governing Board (meets once a year); Audit Committee, elected by the Assembly. **Languages** English. **Staff** Secretariat selection and term determined by the Assembly. Capacity Development Administrator appointed by the Governing Board (ex-officio member). **Finance** Members' admission fee and annual contribution (equal to annual contribution to INTOSAI). **Activities** Capacity building; events/meetings; projects/programmes. **Events** *General Assembly* Bangkok (Thailand) 2021, *Governing Board Meeting* Bangkok (Thailand) 2021, *Governing Board Meeting* Bangkok (Thailand) 2021, *Symposium* Bangkok (Thailand) 2021, *Governing Board Meeting* Dhaka (Bangladesh) 2020. **Publications** *Asian Journal of Government Audit* (2 a year) in English. *10th Research Project on Audit to Detect Fraud and Corruption: Evaluation of the Fight against Corruption and Money Laundering*; *11th Research Project on Methods for Developing Risk-based Audit Plans and Audit of Public-Private Partnership Arrangements*; *12th Research Project on Audit on Implementation of SDGs*; *1st ASOSAI Research Project on Accountability and Control of Public Enterprises*; *2nd ASOSAI Research Project on Financial Accountability and Management in Government*; *3rd ASOSAI Research Project on Audit of Public Works and Projects*; *4th ASOSAI Research Project on Government Revenues – Accountability and Audit*; *5th ASOSAI Research Project on Performance Auditing Guidelines* – PDF; *6th ASOSAI Research Project on IT Audit Guidelines* – PDF; *7th ASOSAI Research Project Guidelines on Audit Quality Management Systems*; *8th ASOSAI Research Project Guidelines on Conducting Environment Audit*; *9th Research Project on Evaluation and Improvement of Internal Audit Systems and the Relationship between the Internal Audit Units and SAIs.* Books; guidelines.
Members Supreme Audit Institutions – SAIs in 47 countries and territories:
Afghanistan, Armenia, Australia, Azerbaijan, Bahrain, Bangladesh, Bhutan, Brunei Darussalam, Cambodia, China, Cyprus, Georgia, India, Indonesia, Iran Islamic Rep, Iraq, Israel, Japan, Jordan, Kazakhstan, Korea Rep, Kuwait, Kyrgyzstan, Laos, Malaysia, Maldives, Mauritius, Mongolia, Myanmar, Nepal, New Zealand, Oman, Pakistan, Palestine, Papua New Guinea, Philippines, Qatar, Russia, Saudi Arabia, Singapore, Sri Lanka, Tajikistan, Thailand, Türkiye, United Arab Emirates, Vietnam, Yemen.
NGO Relations NGOs occasionally invited as special guest to ASOSAI Assembly of Symposium to make presentations on certain subjects. [2022.05.11/XD1585/**D**]

♦ Asian O-Sport Federation (unconfirmed)
♦ Asian Ostomy Association / see Asian and South Pacific Ostomy Association (#01756)
♦ Asian Pacific Academy of Cosmetic Surgery (no recent information)
♦ Asian Pacific Anti-Communist League / see Asian-Pacific League for Freedom and Democracy (#01617)
♦ Asian and Pacific Area Medico-Legal Society / see Indo-Pacific Association of Law, Medicine and Science (#11169)

♦ Asian-Pacific Association for Biomechanics (APAB) 01595

Secretariat Biomechanics Lab, Dept of Mechanical Engineering, Nagoya Univ, Furo-cho, Chikusa-ku, Nagoya AICHI, 464-8603 Japan. T. +81527892721. E-mail: secretary@apbiomech.org.
URL: http://www.apbiomech.org/

History Nov 2005, Taipei (Taiwan). **Aims** Encourage, foster, and promote research in the field of biomechanics in Asian-Pacific region; strengthen presence in the biomechanics community. **Structure** Executive Committee. **Languages** English. **Staff** None. **Finance** Sources: grants; members' dues. **Activities** Awards/prizes/competitions; events/meetings. **Events** *Asian Pacific Conference on Biomechanics* Kyoto (Japan) 2021, *Asian Pacific Conference on Biomechanics* Taipei (Taiwan) 2019, *Asian Pacific Conference on Biomechanics* Brisbane, QLD (Australia) 2017, *Asian-Pacific Conference on Biomechanics* Sapporo (Japan) 2015, *Asian Pacific Conference on Biomechanics* Seoul (Korea Rep) 2013. **Publications** Conference proceedings.
Members Societies in 9 countries:
Australia, China, Hong Kong, Japan, Korea Rep, New Zealand, Singapore, Taiwan, Thailand. [2021/XM3734/**D**]

♦ Asian Pacific Association for Computational Mechanics (APACM) . . 01596

Contact No 1 Section 4, Roosevelt Road, Taipei 10617, Taiwan. E-mail: dchen@ntu.edu.tw.
URL: http://apacm-association.org/

History 1999. **Aims** Promote advances in computational mechanics. **Structure** General Council; Executive Council. **Activities** Meeting activities; awards/prizes/competitions. **Events** *Asian Pacific Congress on Computational Mechanics* Yokohama (Japan) 2022, *COMPSAFE : International Conference on Computational Engineering and Science for Safety and Environmental Problems* Kobe (Japan) 2020, *Asian Pacific Congress on Computational Mechanics* Taipei (Taiwan) 2019, *Asian Pacific Congress on Computational Mechanics* Seoul (Korea Rep) 2016, *COMPSAFE : International Conference on Computational Engineering and Science for Safety and Environmental Problems* Sendai (Japan) 2014.
Members Associations in 12 countries and territories:
Australia, China, Hong Kong, India, Indonesia, Japan, Korea Rep, Malaysia, Singapore, Taiwan, Thailand, Vietnam.
NGO Relations *Australasian Association for Computational Mechanics (no recent information).* [2018/XD7447/**D**]

♦ Asian-Pacific Association of Echocardiography (AAE) 01597

Contact 2nd Fl, Heewon B / D 65-5, Nonhyeon-dong, Gangnam-gu, Seoul 135-816, Korea Rep. E-mail: info@aaecho.org.
URL: https://aaecho.org/

Aims Provide a forum for Asian-Pacific association members to be engaged in the cutting-edge practice, research and education in Echocardiography and to collaborate with others interested in cardiovascular imaging. **Structure** Board; Executive Council. **Finance** Members' dues. **Activities** Events/meetings; training/education. **Events** *Congress* Hong Kong (Hong Kong) 2021, *Congress* Hong Kong (Hong Kong) 2020, *Congress* Brisbane, QLD (Australia) 2019, *Congress* Jeju (Korea Rep) 2018.
Members Full in 11 countries and territories:
Australia, China, Hong Kong, India, Indonesia, Japan, Korea Rep, New Zealand, Philippines, Taiwan, Thailand. [2019/XM8098/**D**]

♦ Asian-Pacific Association of Gastroenterology / see Asian Pan-Pacific Society for Paediatric Gastroenterology, Hepatology, and Nutrition (#01651)

♦ Asian Pacific Association of Gastroenterology (APAGE) 01598

Exec Dir Room C 7th Floor, Thomson Commercial Bldg, 8 Thomson Road, Wan Chai, Wanchai, Hong Kong. T. +85228695933. Fax +85228699533. E-mail: apage@apage.org.
URL: http://www.apage.org/

History 30 Mar 1961, Tokyo (Japan). Incorporated, 15 Jun 2001, Hong Kong. **Aims** Promote excellence in clinical practice/education and research towards the improvement of digestive health in the region and the world. **Structure** General Meeting; Council. JGH Trust. Committees (6): Programme Advisory; Awards; APDW Steering; Journal of Gastroenterology and Hepatology (JGH); International Liaison; Nominations; Education and Research; Past Presidents. **Activities** Events/meetings; training/education; research/documentation. **Events** *Asia Pacific Digestive Week* Xian (China) 2022, *Asia Pacific Digestive Week* Kuala Lumpur (Malaysia) 2021, *Asia Pacific Digestive Week* Kuala Lumpur (Malaysia) 2020, *Asia Pacific Digestive Week* Kolkata (India) 2019, *Asia Pacific Digestive Week* Seoul (Korea Rep) 2018. **Publications** *Asian Pacific Digestive News (APDN)*; *Journal of Gastroenterology and Hepatology* – official publication.
Members Societies in 21 countries and territories:
Afghanistan, Australia, Bangladesh, China, Hong Kong, India, Indonesia, Japan, Korea Rep, Macau, Malaysia, Myanmar, Nepal, New Zealand, Pakistan, Philippines, Singapore, Sri Lanka, Taiwan, Thailand, Vietnam.
NGO Relations Regional member of: *World Gastroenterology Organisation (WGO, #21536).* Member of: *Asian Pacific Digestive Week Federation (APDWF, #01609).* [2020/XD7608/**D**]

♦ Asian Pacific Association for Laser Medicine and Surgery / see Asian Pacific Association for Lasers in Medicine and Surgery (#01599)

♦ Asian Pacific Association for Lasers in Medicine and Surgery (APALMS) 01599

SG Kang Nam Gu Sin Sa Dong 638-5, Best Well Inst, Seoul 135-110, Korea Rep. T. +8225113713. Fax +8225173713. E-mail: khg000@unitel.co.kr.
Pres address not obtained.

History 1985. Also referred to as *Asian Pacific Society for Laser Medicine and Surgery* and as *Asian Pacific Association for Laser Medicine and Surgery.* **Aims** Deliver academic information; present technological, industrial and social innovation. **Structure** Scientific Committee. President; Secretary-General. **Languages** English. **Staff** 105.00 FTE, paid; 10.00 FTE, voluntary. **Finance** Members' dues. Other sources: national academic support; booth; government support; support from NGOs. **Activities** Laser supply to underdeveloped countries; campaigns; charitable work; education. **Events** *Surgical Practice Amidst Global Crisis* Bangkok (Thailand) 2021, *Congress* Bangkok (Thailand) 2018, *Congress* Singapore (Singapore) 2014, *Congress* Taipei (Taiwan) 2012, *Congress* Suwa City (Japan) 2010. **Publications** *Journal of Laser Therapy.* Books. **Members** Doctors and allied professionals who are users of lasers (3,000). Membership countries not specified. [2016/XD2272/v/**D**]

♦ Asian Pacific Association for Medical Informatics (APAMI) 01600

Pres address not obtained. E-mail: secretary@apami.org – webmaster@apami.org.
Sec address not obtained.
URL: http://www.apami.org/

History 12 Nov 1986, Singapore (Singapore). Mooted, 1993, as the Asia Pacific Regional Affiliate of *International Medical Informatics Association (IMIA, #14134).* Inaugural conference, 1994, Singapore. **Aims** Promote Information and Communications Technologies (ICT) in health in the Asia-Pacific region. **Structure** General Assembly (annual); Executive. **Languages** English. **Staff** Voluntary. **Finance** No operating budget. **Activities** Events/meetings; networking/liaising; financial and/or material support. **Events** *Conference* 2024, *Conference* Taipei (Taiwan) 2022, *Informatics of Patient Engagement* Hamamatsu (Japan) 2020, *Conference* Colombo (Sri Lanka) 2018, *Conference* Seoul (Korea Rep) 2016. **Publications** *Healthcare Informatics Research*; *Indian Journal for Medical Informatics.*
Members Full in 12 countries and territories:
Australia, China, Hong Kong, India, Japan, Korea Rep, New Zealand, Philippines, Singapore, Sri Lanka, Taiwan, Thailand.
Corresponding in 6 countries:
Bangladesh, Bhutan, Indonesia, Malaysia, Nepal, Vietnam. [2022/XD4022/**D**]

♦ Asian and Pacific Association for Social Work Education (APASWE) . 01601

Sec address not obtained. E-mail: apaswe.official@gmail.com.
Pres address not obtained.
URL: http://www.apaswe.com/

History 1974, Nairobi (Kenya), as *Asian Regional Association for Social Work Education (ARASWE)*, during 17th International Congress of Schools of Social Work. **Aims** Promote inter-school exchange of bibliographies, teaching materials and curricula, faculty and students and such other activities that might enhance the further development of social work education in the region; serve as a clearing house for communication, planning and implementation of special projects, field research and pilot projects; function as a body through which resources may be channelled to the region; promote inter-regional cooperation. **Structure** General Body (meets every 2 years, during biennial Conference). Executive Board, consisting of President, Vice President, Honorary Secretary, Honorary Treasurer and 4 members. In addition, the Executive Body includes (ex-officio): Immediate Past President; the presidents (or their representatives) of each of the national associations of schools of social work; the representative of ESCAP (without voting powers); and the representatives of 3 NGOs: IASSW, ICSW (Asia and Pacific Region), IFSW (Asia and Pacific Region) (without voting rights). **Languages** English. **Finance** Members' dues. **Activities** Meeting activities; information dissemination. **Events** *APASWE : Asia-Pacific Social Work Conference* Brisbane, QLD (Australia) 2021, *APASWE : Asia-Pacific Social Work Conference* Bangalore (India) 2019, *APASWE : Asia-Pacific Social Work Conference* Shenzhen (China) 2017, *APASWE : Asia-Pacific Social Work Conference* Bangkok (Thailand) 2015, *APASWE : Asia-Pacific Social Work Cconference* Manila (Philippines) 2013. **Publications** *APASWE Post* – newsletter; *Asian Pacific Journal of Social Work and Development* – jointly with the National University of Singapore. Conference papers; studies.
Members Full schools of social work in the region which are members of IASSW; trained social workers or those resident in the region who are interested in social work education (individual membership). Affiliate organizations/agencies which promote training and/or research directly related to social work. Friends of APASWE faculty of schools of social work interested in the problems and concerns of the region. Honorary members (individual membership). Members in 23 countries and territories:
Australia, Bangladesh, Cambodia, China, Fiji, Hong Kong, India, Indonesia, Iran Islamic Rep, Japan, Korea Rep, Kuwait, Malaysia, Nepal, New Zealand, Pakistan, Papua New Guinea, Philippines, Saudi Arabia, Singapore, Sri Lanka, Taiwan, Thailand.
IGO Relations Collaborates with: *UNICEF (#20332)*; *United Nations Economic and Social Commission for Asia and the Pacific (ESCAP, #20557).* **NGO Relations** Affiliated to: *International Association of Schools of Social Work (IASSW, #12149)*; *International Council on Social Welfare (ICSW, #13076)*; *International Federation of Social Workers (IFSW, #13544).* [2013/XE8776/**D**]

♦ Asian Pacific Association for the Study of the Liver (APASL) 01602

Exec Dir 1-24-7-920 Shinjuku, Shinjuku-ku, Tokyo, 160-0022 Japan. T. +81353127686. Fax +81353127687. E-mail: apasl_secretariat@apasl.info.
SG/Treas address not obtained.
URL: http://apasl.info/

History Aug 1978, Singapore (Singapore). **Aims** Promote scientific advancement and education of hepatology in the Asia Pacific region, including the exchange of information and the development of consensus in the field of hepatology. **Structure** Executive Council, comprising President, Immediate Past President, President Elect, Secretary-General-cum-Treasurer and 12 members. Committees (6): Education; Scientific Programme; Ethics and Guidelines; Financial; Data Collection; International Liaison. Working Parties (5). **Activities** Meeting activities. **Events** *Conference* Kyoto (Japan) 2024, *Single Topic Conference* Busan (Korea Rep) 2023, *Single Topic Conference on Oncology* Sendai (Japan) 2023, *Conference* Taipei (Taiwan) 2023, *Single Topic Conference on Oncology* Takamatsu (Japan) 2022. **Publications** *Hepatology International* (4 a year). **NGO Relations** Member of: *Asian Pacific Digestive Week Federation (APDWF, #01609)*; *International Association for the Study of the Liver (IASL, #12203).* [2022/XD4718/**D**]

♦ Asian Pacific Atherosclerosis Society (inactive)
♦ Asian-Pacific Cardiothoracic-Renal Association (no recent information)
♦ Asian and Pacific Centre for Agricultural Engineering and Machinery / see Centre for Sustainable Agricultural Mechanization (#03789)

♦ Asian and Pacific Centre for Transfer of Technology (APCTT) 01603

Centre d'Asie et du Pacifique de transfert de technologie

Dir APCTT Building, C-2 Qutab Institutional Area, PO Box 4575, Delhi 110 016, DELHI 110 016, India. T. +911126966509 – +911126856255. Fax +911126856274. E-mail: postmaster.apctt@un.org.
URL: http://www.apctt.org/

History 16 Jul 1977, Bangalore (India), under the name of *Regional Centre for Technology Transfer (RCTT)*, as an institution of *United Nations (UN, #20515)* under the auspices of *United Nations Economic and Social Commission for Asia and the Pacific (ESCAP, #20557).* Present name adopted Apr 1985. Also referred to as *United Nations Asian and Pacific Centre for Transfer of Technology – Centre d'Asie et du Pacifique de transfert de technologie des Nations Unies.* **Aims** Assist ESCAP members by strengthening their capabilities to develop and manage national innovation systems; develop, transfer, adapt and apply technology improve the terms of transfer of technology; identify and promote the development and transfer of technology relevant to the region. **Structure** Governing Board, elected by ESCAP, receives policy directions from annual ESCAP Sessions and from Consultative Meetings of the 16 designated governmental APCTT Focal Points. Technical Advisory Committee (TAC). Centre headed by Director. **Languages** English. **Staff** 36.00 FTE, paid. **Finance** Contributions from: UN; governments of Bangladesh, China, India, Indonesia, Iran Islamic Rep, Korea Rep, Malaysia, Mongolia, Nepal, Pakistan, Philippines, Russia, Sri Lanka and Thailand and Vietnam. **Activities** (a) Research and analysis of trends, conditions and opportunities; (b) Advisory services; (c) Dissemination of information and good practices; (d) Networking and partnership with international organizations and key stakeholders; (e) Training of national personnel, particularly national scientists and policy analysts. **Events** *Workshop on value addition in fruit and vegetables* Agartala (India) 2001, *Regional consultative meeting on strengthening technology incubation system for creating high-technology based enterprises* Seoul (Korea Rep) 2001, *Product development workshop on laminated bamboo boards* Ahmedabad (India) 2000, *Regional workshop on technology management, technology evaluation and pricing* Hanoi (Vietnam) 2000, *International forum on technology and industry of Chinese herbal medicine* Wuhan (China) 2000. **Publications** *Asia-Pacific Tech Monitor* (6 a year); *VATIS Update* (6 a year) – in each of the following areas: Waste Management. Books; monographs; reports of meetings, seminars, workshops and study tours.
Members Asian and Pacific Governments which have designated focal points (15):
Bangladesh, China, Fiji, India, Indonesia, Iran Islamic Rep, Korea Rep, Malaysia, Mongolia, Nepal, Pakistan, Philippines, Sri Lanka, Thailand, Vanuatu, Vietnam.
IGO Relations Working relations with: *Commission on Science and Technology for Sustainable Development in the South (COMSATS, #04239).* [2020/XE9937/**E***]

♦ Asian and Pacific Centre for Women and Development (inactive)
♦ Asian and Pacific Cerebral Palsy Association (no recent information)

♦ Asian-Pacific Chemical Education Network (ACEN) 01604

Dir address not obtained. E-mail: masahirok@nifty.com.
Co-Dir Dir – Research Ctr for the Natural Sciences, College of Science, Univ of Santo Tomas, Espana Bd, 1015 Manila, Philippines.
URL: http://www.facs-as.org/

History under the auspices of *Federation of Asian Chemical Societies (FACS, #09431).* **Aims** Contribute to the advancement of chemical education in the Asia-Pacific region. **Languages** English. **Finance** by FACS and other organizations. **Activities** Disseminates information on chemical education on the international basis and encourages information dissemination; organizes symposia and panel discussions; provides travel scholarships to young scholars and graduate students. **Publications** *Chemical Education in Asia-Pacific*; *Chemical Education Journal.*
Members Societies (with FACS member societies). Members 27 in countries:
Australia, Bangladesh, Brunei Darussalam, China, Fiji, Hong Kong, India, Indonesia, Iraq, Israel, Japan, Jordan, Korea Rep, Kuwait, Malaysia, Mongolia, Nepal, New Zealand, Pakistan, Papua New Guinea, Philippines, Russia, Singapore, Sri Lanka, Taiwan, Thailand, Vietnam.
Individuals in 6 countries:
Canada, Iran Islamic Rep, Kazakhstan, Saudi Arabia, South Africa, USA. [2019/XF5649/**F**]

♦ Asian-Pacific Christian Peace Conference (no recent information)
♦ Asian-Pacific City Summit (meeting series)
♦ Asian and Pacific Coconut Community / see International Coconut Community (#12628)
♦ Asian Pacific Confederation for Arts Education (no recent information)

♦ Asian Pacific Confederation of Chemical Engineering (APCChE) . . . 01605

Confédération d'Asie et du Pacifique du génie chimique

Secretariat Level 31, 600 Bourke Street, Melbourne VIC 3000, Australia. T. +61393211791.

Pres Director – Yamaguchi University Biomedical Engineering Center (YUBEC), 2-16-1 Tokiwadai, Ube City YAMAGUCHI, 755-8611 Japan.
URL: http://www.apcche.org/

History 1975, Australia. **Aims** Foster the development of chemical engineering in the developing countries of South East Asia and Pacific region. **Languages** English. **Staff** Secretariat: Institution of Engineers Australia. **Finance** Members' dues: US$ 0.10 per member in each society represented. **Events** *Biennial Congress* Beijing (China) 2025, *Biennial Congress* Manila (Philippines) 2023, *Biennial Congress* Kuala Lumpur (Malaysia) 2021, *Biennial Congress* Sapporo (Japan) 2019, *Biennial Congress* Hong Kong (Hong Kong) 2017. **Publications** *APCChE Newsletter*. Proceedings of Congresses.
Members Societies in 13 countries and territories:
Australia, China, Hong Kong, India, Indonesia, Japan, Korea Rep, Malaysia, New Zealand, Philippines, Singapore, Taiwan, Thailand.
Correspondent members in 2 countries and territories:
UK, USA.
NGO Relations Associated organization of: *International Union of Pure and Applied Chemistry (IUPAC, #15809)*. Member of: *World Chemical Engineering Council (WCEC, #21271)*. [2018/XD9745/**D**]

♦ Asian and Pacific Conference of Correctional Administrators (APCCA) 01606

Co-Secretariat HK Correctional Services, 24/F Wanchai Tower, 12 Harbour Road, Wan Chai, Wanchai, Hong Kong. E-mail: secretariat@apcca.org.
Co-Secretariat Singapore Prison Service, 407 Upper Changi Road North, Singapore 507658, Singapore.
URL: http://www.apcca.org/

History First meeting held 1980, Hong Kong. New Framework established 2001-2002 with APCCA Joint Declaration signed 2002, Indonesia. **Structure** Governing Board; Secretariat. **Events** *Annual Conference* Singapore (Singapore) 2020, *Annual Conference* Ulaanbaatar (Mongolia) 2019, *Annual Conference* Melaka (Malaysia) 2018, *Annual Conference* Bangkok (Thailand) 2015, *Annual Conference* Delhi (India) 2013. **Publications** *APCCA Newsletter*.
Members Governmental agencies in 26 countries and territories:
Australia, Bangladesh, Brunei Darussalam, Cambodia, Canada, China, Fiji, Hong Kong, India, Indonesia, Japan, Kiribati, Korea Rep, Macau, Malaysia, Mongolia, New Zealand, Papua New Guinea, Philippines, Singapore, Solomon Is, Sri Lanka, Thailand, Tonga, Vanuatu, Vietnam. [2020/XF2240/c/**F**]

- ♦ Asian Pacific Congress of Allergology and Immunology (meeting series)
- ♦ Asian-Pacific Congress for Parasitic Zoonoses (meeting series)
- ♦ Asian and Pacific Council (inactive)
- ♦ Asian Pacific Dental Federation / see Asia Pacific Dental Federation/Asian Pacific Regional Organization of the Fédération Dentaire Internationale (#01882)

♦ Asian Pacific Dental Students Association (APDSA) 01607

Association des étudiants dentaires de l'Asie et du Pacifique

Main Office Faculty of Dentistry – NMDC, No 161, Sec 6, Mincyuan E Rd, Neihu Dist, Taipei 114201, Taiwan. E-mail: apdsaexco@gmail.com.
URL: https://www.apdsa.org/

History 1968. **Aims** Promote dental health, research and science in the region; promote closer regional and international cooperation and contact among dental students, protecting their interests in the region. **Structure** Congress (annual). Executive Committee. **Languages** English. **Staff** None. **Finance** Sources: meeting proceeds. **Events** *Annual Congress* Taipei (Taiwan) 2022, *Annual Congress* Siem Reap (Cambodia) 2021, *Annual Congress* Siem Reap (Cambodia) 2020, *Annual Congress* Bangkok (Thailand) 2019, *Annual Congress* Kuala Lumpur (Malaysia) 2018. **Publications** *APDSJ*.
Members Organizations (active and corresponding); Individuals (honorary and supporting). Active members in 12 countries and territories:
Australia, Cambodia, Hong Kong, Indonesia, Japan, Korea Rep, Malaysia, New Zealand, Philippines, Singapore, Taiwan, Thailand.
NGO Relations Affiliated to: *Asia Pacific Dental Federation/Asian Pacific Regional Organization of the Fédération Dentaire Internationale (APDF-APRO, #01882)*. [2020/XD3778/**D**]

- ♦ Asian and Pacific Development Administration Centre (inactive)

♦ Asian and Pacific Development Centre (APDC) 01608

Centre de développement pour l'Asie et le Pacifique (CDAP)

Headquarters 1537 Alton St, Aurora CO 80010, USA. T. +13039232920. E-mail: info@apdc.org.
URL: http://www.apdc.org/

History 1 Jul 1980, Kuala Lumpur (Malaysia), under the aegis of *United Nations Economic and Social Commission for Asia and the Pacific (ESCAP, #20557)*, as the product of an evolutionary process in restructuring four previous regional centres for research and training: *Asian and Pacific Centre for Women and Development (APCWD, inactive)*; *Asian and Pacific Development Administration Centre (APDAC, inactive)*; *Asian and Pacific Development Institute (APDI, inactive)*; and *Social Welfare and Development Centre for Asia and the Pacific (SWDCAP, inactive)*. The process began in Nov 1978 with the convening of ESCAP/UNDP Task Force and culminated when the Commission, at its 36th Session, Mar 1980, Bangkok (Thailand), formally decided to establish APDC. An autonomous inter-governmental organization from 1 Jul 1983. Statutes registered in *'UNTS 1/22028'*. **Aims** Help member countries enhance innovative development research and training through both governmental and nongovernmental organizations; provide a regional focus to development issues and promote research and training activities on a collaborative basis by fostering establishment of a network of researchers, administrators and research institutions; promote economic cooperation among countries of the region; identify existing and emerging needs and problems with a view to increasing the awareness of governments of the long-term impact upon the structure of the economy and institutions; undertake studies of development problems, find solutions and help to implement them; promote cooperation among countries of the region by strengthening links with regional networks; act as a catalyst in strengthening the capabilities of national research and training institutions; foster programmes to develop *human resources* to meet the changing needs of the region; in cooperation with national institutions, offer consultancy services to countries of the region; serve as a clearing-house for information on development. **Structure** General Council (meets annually), consisting of member governments. Programme Advisory Board (PAC) (meets annually), comprising 3 government representatives of member governments (one from private sector, one academic and one from an NGO). UNDP and ESCAP are permanent invitees to meetings of the Centre's General Council and PAC. Director appointed by the Council on the basis of the Board's recommendation. **Languages** English. **Staff** 50.00 FTE, paid. **Finance** Supported by: Member Governments; Associate Member Governments; national donor agencies; international or internationally-oriented donor agencies and organizations. **Activities** Programme areas (7): Energy and environment; Trade and information technology; Gender and development; Poverty alleviation/Rural development; Economic/financial management; Public management and human resource development; Urban development. Instrumental in setting up: *Asian Network on Women and International Migration (ANWIM, no recent information)*; *Gender and Human Development Network for Asia and the Pacific (GADNET, no recent information)*. **Events** *ASEAN regional consultative workshop on building knowledge societies* Kuala Lumpur (Malaysia) 1999, *Regional workshop for Western and Central Africa on the operationalisation of the principles of the Tokyo Declaration on African Development* Côte d'Ivoire 1996, *BANK POOR : regional workshop on microfinance for the poor in Asia-Pacific* Kuala Lumpur (Malaysia) 1996, *Biennial Meeting* Kuala Lumpur (Malaysia) 1996, *Seminar on supply and demand of social science information* Kuala Lumpur (Malaysia) 1996. **Publications** *APDC Newsletter* (2 a year); *Asia Pacific Development Monitor* (2 a year); *Asia Pacific Implementation Monitor* (annual); *Issues in Gender and Development* (periodical). *Asian and Pacific Women's Resources and Action Series*. Annual Report; monographs; studies; guidelines; reports. Information Services: Maintains a library and information centre. **Information Services** *Bibliographical Database*; *Energy Database*; *Institutions, Projects and Expertise Database*; *Women Resources Network Database*.
Members Member countries and territories (21):
Bangladesh, Brunei Darussalam, China, Cook Is, Fiji, Hong Kong, India, Indonesia, Japan, Korea Rep, Laos, Macau, Malaysia, Maldives, Nepal, Pakistan, Papua New Guinea, Philippines, Sri Lanka, Thailand, Vietnam.
Members with observer status (2):
UNDP (#20292). [2015/XE9559/y/**E***]

- ♦ Asian and Pacific Development Institute (inactive)

♦ Asian Pacific Digestive Week Federation (APDWF) 01609

Main Office The Meeting Lab Pte Ltd, 695E East Coast Road, Singapore 459059, Singapore. T. +6563464402. Fax +6563464403. E-mail: apdwf_secretariat@apdwcongress.org.
URL: http://www.apdwcongress.org/

History 2003. **Aims** Advance science and education in *gastroenterology*, *hepatology*, *endoscopy* and *surgery* for the benefit of public health; promote and co-ordinate, throughout Asia-Pacific countries and beyond, discussion and exchange of ideas and results relating to the diagnosis, treatment, research and prevention of digestive diseases; provide a suitable medium for the dissemination and discussions of the latest results in the field. **Structure** Board of Directors; Executive Committee. **Activities** Events/meetings. **Events** *Asia Pacific Digestive Week* Xian (China) 2022, *Asia Pacific Digestive Week* Kuala Lumpur (Malaysia) 2021, *Asia Pacific Digestive Week* Kuala Lumpur (Malaysia) 2020, *Asia Pacific Digestive Week* Kolkata (India) 2019, *Asia Pacific Digestive Week* Seoul (Korea Rep) 2018.
Members Organizations (4):
Asian Pacific Association for the Study of the Liver (APASL, #01602); *Asian Pacific Association of Gastroenterology (APAGE, #01598)*; *Asian-Pacific Society for Digestive Endoscopy (APSDE, #01633)*; *International Society for Digestive Surgery (ISDS, #15060)* (Asian Pacific Section). [2019/XM4483/y/**D**]

- ♦ Asian Pacific Economic Council Forum / see Asia-Pacific Economic Cooperation (#01887)

♦ Asian Pacific Endodontic Confederation (APEC) 01610

Pres c/o PNU School of Dentistry, Geumo-ro 20, Mulgeum, Yangsan SOUTH GYEONGSANG 50612, Korea Rep.
Pres-Elect address not obtained. E-mail: sanjaymig@yahoo.com.
URL: http://www.apeconweb.org/

History Established following 2 organizational meetings Dec 1985, Bangkok (Thailand) and Nov 1986, Manila (Philippines). Constitution ratified during 1st Scientific Congress, Jan 1988, Delhi (India). Constitution revised, 1998 and ratified Apr 1999, Singapore (Singapore). Registration: Start date: Nov 1989, Hong Kong. **Aims** Promote, develop and maintain high standards of endodontic research, teaching and clinical practice on the Asian Pacific region; cultivate and foster closer professional relationships of endodontic practitioners within the Asian Pacific region. **Structure** General Assembly (biennial); Council. **Languages** English. **Finance** Sources: members' dues. **Activities** Events/meetings; training/education. **Events** *Scientific Conference* Beirut (Lebanon) 2021, *Scientific Conference* Istanbul (Turkey) 2019, *Scientific Conference* New Delhi (India) 2017, *Scientific Conference* Amman (Jordan) 2015, *Scientific Conference* Seoul (Korea Rep) 2013. **Publications** *APEC Newsletter*, *Australian Endodontic Journal*.
Members Individual; Affiliate; Student; Honorary; Retired. Endodontic Societies and Associations in 13 countries and territories:
Australia, Hong Kong, India, Indonesia, Iran Islamic Rep, Japan, Jordan, Korea Rep, Malaysia, Philippines, Singapore, Taiwan, USA.
NGO Relations Also links with national societies. [2021/XD4901/**D**]

- ♦ Asian Pacific Environmental Network (internationally oriented national body)
- ♦ Asian-Pacific Federation of Clinical Biochemistry / see Asia Pacific Federation for Clinical Biochemistry and Laboratory Medicine (#01896)

♦ Asian Pacific Federation of Human Resource Management (APFHRM) 01611

Sec-Treas c/o AHRI, Level 13, 565 Bourke St, Melbourne VIC 3000, Australia. E-mail: apfhrm@ahri.com.au.
Pres Fujitsu Computer Products Corp, Special Export Processing Zone, Carmelray Industrial Park I, Canlubang, Calamba, Los Baños LAG, Philippines. T. +6328787031. Fax +6328787075.
URL: http://www.apfhrm.com/

History 5 Nov 1968, as *Asian Pacific Federation of Personnel Management Associations* (APFPMA). Also previously referred to as *Asian Association of Personnel Management (AAPM)*. Current title adopted Sep 1991, Manila (Philippines). **Aims** Improve the quality and effectiveness of professional human resource management, as well as the importance of its role in all employing organizations, both public and private, at national and international levels. **Structure** Delegates Assembly. Council (meets at least once a year), consisting of President, 3 Vice-Presidents, Secretary and Treasurer. Second Delegate to the WFPA. Regional Groups: Asean; Indian Sub-continent; East Asia; Australasia. **Languages** English. **Finance** Members' dues. **Events** *Regional Conference* Singapore (Singapore) 2015, *Annual Regional Conference* Goa (India) 2013. **Publications** *APFHRM Newsletter*.
Members Associations in 15 countries and territories:
Australia, Bangladesh, Hong Kong, India, Indonesia, Japan, Korea Rep, Malaysia, New Zealand, Papua New Guinea, Philippines, Singapore, Sri Lanka, Taiwan, Thailand.
NGO Relations Regional member of: *World Federation of People Management Associations (WFPMA, #21474)*. [2012/XD4287/**D**]

- ♦ Asian and Pacific Federation of Organizations for Cancer Research and Control (inactive)
- ♦ Asian Pacific Federation of Personnel Management Associations / see Asian Pacific Federation of Human Resource Management (#01611)
- ♦ Asian Pacific Federation of Societies of Hand Therapists / see Asia Pacific Federation for Societies for Hand Therapy (#01905)

♦ Asian Pacific Federation of Societies for Reconstructive Microsurgery (APFSRM) 01612

SG Ogori Daiichi General Hosp, 862-3 Shimogo Ogori, Yamaguchi, 7540002 Japan. E-mail: office-apfsrm@ogoridaiichi.jp.
Pres Shanghai Inst for Microsurgery of Extremities, No 600 Yishan Road, 200233 Shanghai, China.
URL: http://www.apfsrm.org/

History 2012. **Structure** Council. **Events** *Meeting* Buyeo (Korea Rep) 2014, *Congress* Korea Rep 2014, *Congress* Singapore (Singapore) 2012.
Members Full in 19 countries and territories:
Australia, China, Hong Kong, India, Indonesia, Japan, Kazakhstan, Korea Rep, Kyrgyzstan, Lebanon, Malaysia, Philippines, Singapore, Sri Lanka, Taiwan, Tajikistan, Türkiye, Uzbekistan, Vietnam. [2015/XJ9651/**D**]

♦ Asian Pacific Federation of Societies for Surgery of the Hand (APFSSH) 01613

SG Dept of Plastic and Reconstructive Surgery, Ganga Hospital 313, Mettupalayam Road, Coimbatore, Tamil Nadu 641043, Coimbatore TAMIL NADU 641043, India. T. +914222485000. E-mail: rajahand@gmail.com.
URL: http://www.apfssh.net/

History Mar 1997, Perth (Australia). **Aims** Promote the practice of hand surgery; coordinate the activities of the various societies for surgery of the hand in the Asia-Pacific region. **Structure** Executive Committee. **Activities** Events/meetings; grants/prizes/competitions. **Events** *Congress* Singapore (Singapore) 2023, *Congress* Melbourne, VIC (Australia) 2020, *Congress* Cebu City (Philippines) 2017, *Congress* Kuala Lumpur (Malaysia) 2014, *Congress* Bali (Indonesia) 2012. **Publications** *The Journal of Hand Surgery*. **NGO Relations** *Asia Pacific Federation for Societies for Hand Therapy (APFSHT, #01905)*; *International Federation of Societies for Surgery of the Hand (IFSSH, #13551)*. [2017/XD5898/**D**]

- ♦ Asian-Pacific Federation of Therapeutic Communities / see Asian Federation of Therapeutic Communities (#01476)
- ♦ Asian-Pacific Federation of Thermology (no recent information)

♦ Asian Pacific Federation of UNESCO Clubs and Associations (AFUCA) 01614

Fédération des associations et clubs UNESCO d'Asie et du Pacifique

SG Natl Fed of UNESCO Assns in Japan, Asahi Seimei Ebisu Bldg, 12F, 1-3-1, Ebisu, Shibuya-ku, Tokyo, 150-0013 Japan. T. +81354241121. Fax +81354241126.

URL: http://www.unesco.or.jp/en/afuca.html
History 15 Jul 1974, Kyoto (Japan), as *Asian Federation of UNESCO Clubs and Associations*, at General Conference of UNESCO Associations and Clubs in the Asian region. A regional branch of *World Federation of UNESCO Clubs, Centres and Associations (WFUCA, #21498)*. **Aims** Promote collaboration among UNESCO associations and clubs in the Asia Pacific region and elsewhere; develop and promote activities in the various fields of UNESCO. **Structure** Executive Board (meets every 2 years). **Languages** English. **Finance** Members' dues. Contributions from members. **Events** *Biennial Session* Nara (Japan) 2010, *Regional seminar* Nara (Japan) 2010, *Biennial session / Executive Board Meeting* Beijing (China) 2004, *Biennial session / Executive Board Meeting* Hanoi (Vietnam) 2001, *Biennial session / Executive Board Meeting* Sri Lanka 1999.
Members UNESCO federations in 11 countries:
Bangladesh, China, India, Japan, Korea Rep, Mongolia, Nepal, Russia, Sri Lanka, Thailand, Vietnam.
Observers (5):
Laos, Malaysia, Myanmar, New Zealand, Philippines.
Consultative Status Consultative status granted from: *UNESCO (#20322)* (Formal associate relations through parent body). [2019.01.01/XE4131/E]

♦ Asian Pacific Federation of the World's Poultry Science Association Branches 01615

Sec-Treas Massey Univ, Poultry Research Unit, Private Bag 11 222, Palmerston North, New Zealand.
Pres 60/4 Senanivate Soi 117/4, Senanikom 1 Road, Jorrakaebua, Ladphraeo, Bangkok, 1023, Thailand. T. +66819006028.
URL: http://www.asiapacificpoultry.com/
History 1981, as *Far East and South Pacific Federation of Branches of the World's Poultry Science Association*, within the framework of *World's Poultry Science Association (WPSA, #21825)*. Also referred to as *Federation of Asian Pacific Branches of the World's Poultry Science Association*. **Aims** Advance and disseminate knowledge on all aspects of poultry science and the *poultry industry* in the region; institute regional conventions. **Structure** General Meeting (every 4 years). Executive Committee, comprising one representative of each Branch represented in the Federation. Officers: President, Senior Vice-President, Junior Vice-President, Secretary-Treasurer. **Languages** English. **Finance** Members' dues. Sponsorship. **Activities** Working Groups (3): Small Scale Family Poultry Farming; Waterfowl; Ratites. **Events** *Conference* Bangkok (Thailand) 2018, *Conference / Asian Pacific Poultry Conference* Jeju (Korea Rep) 2014, *World Waterfowl Conference* Hanoi (Vietnam) 2013, *Conference / Asian Pacific Poultry Conference* Taipei (Taiwan) 2011, *World Waterfowl Conference* Thrissur (India) 2009. **Publications** *World's Poultry Science Journal* – electronic.
Members Branches of WPSA and affiliations in 20 countries and territories:
Australia, Bangladesh, China, Fiji, India, Indonesia, Iran Islamic Rep, Japan, Korea Rep, Malaysia, Nepal, New Zealand, Pakistan, Papua New Guinea, Philippines, Singapore, Sri Lanka, Taiwan, Thailand, Vietnam. [2019/XE1509/E]

♦ Asian-Pacific Hepato-Pancreato-Biliary Association (A-PHPBA) . . . 01616

Exec Officer c/o Prince of Wales Hosp, Room 94005, 7/F, Clinical Sciences Bldg, 30-32 Ngan Shing St, Shatin, Hong Kong. T. +85226322626. Fax +85226325459. E-mail: info@a-phpba.org.
URL: http://www.a-phpba.org/
History Regional society of *International Hepato-Pancreato-Biliary Association (IHPBA, #13790)*. Former names and other names: *Asian Society of Hepato-Biliary-Pancreatic Surgery (ASHBPS)* – former (2005). **Aims** Promote the study of liver and pancreatic diseases. **Structure** Council, comprising President, President-elect, Chairman of Nominating Committee, Secretary, Secretary-elect, Treasurer, Chairman and Vice-Chairman of Scientific Committee and 8 members-at-Large. **Languages** English. **Finance** Through private foundations. **Events** *Biennial Congress* Bangkok (Thailand) 2025, *Biennial Congress* Bangalore (India) 2023, *Biennial Congress* Bali (Indonesia) 2021, *Biennial Congress* Seoul (Korea Rep) 2019, *Biennial Asian Pacific Congress* Yokohama (Japan) 2017. **Publications** *Journal of Hepto-Biliary-Pancreatic Surgery*. **Members** Membership countries not specified. [2021/XD5016/E]

♦ Asian-Pacific Information Network on Medicinal and Aromatic Plants (no recent information)
♦ Asian and Pacific International Fluid Inclusion Society (no recent information)

♦ Asian-Pacific League for Freedom and Democracy (APLFD) 01617

Address not obtained.
History 15 Jun 1954, Korea Rep. 15 Jun 1954, Chinhae (Korea Rep), as *Asian Peoples' Anti-Communist League*. Name changed, 1984, to *Asian Pacific Anti-Communist League (APACL)*. Present name adopted 1990. **Aims** Help unite peoples of Asia and the Pacific in promoting freedom, democracy and *human rights* and also in enhancing friendly cooperation for the economic and social wellbeing and security of the peoples of Asia and the Pacific region. **Structure** General Conference (every year); Executive Committee; permanent Secretariat. **Languages** English. **Events** *Annual General Conference* Berlin (Germany) 2015, *Conference* Incheon (Korea Rep) 2010, *Annual General Conference* Manila (Philippines) 2009, *Annual General Conference* Auckland (New Zealand) 2005, *Annual General Conference* Santa Clara, CA (USA) 2004.
Members Full in 32 countries and territories:
Australia, Bahrain, Bangladesh, Cambodia, China, Fiji, Guam, Hong Kong, India, Indonesia, Iran Islamic Rep, Japan, Jordan, Kachinland, Korea Rep, Laos, Lebanon, Macau, Malaysia, Nepal, New Zealand, Oman, Pakistan, Palau, Philippines, Samoa USA, Saudi Arabia, Singapore, Solomon Is, Thailand, Tonga, Vietnam.
NGO Relations Regional Organization of: *World League for Freedom and Democracy (WLFD, #21621)*. [2009/XF1841/F]

♦ Asian Pacific League of Physical Medicine and Rehabilitation (inactive)

♦ Asian-Pacific Logistics Federation (APLF) 01618

Vice Chair c/o SIMM, 9 Ah Hood Road, 04-06 EASB Bldg, Singapore 329975, Singapore. T. +6566531233. Fax +6562540704. E-mail: info@aplf.net.
URL: http://www.aplf.net/
History Nov 1995, Tokyo (Japan). **Aims** Promote efficient functioning of logistics in the Asia-Pacific region. **Structure** General Assembly. **Events** *Biennial general assembly and conference / General Assembly* Tokyo (Japan) 2005, *Biennial general assembly and conference / General Assembly* Seoul (Korea Rep) 2003, *Biennial general assembly and conference / General Assembly* Singapore (Singapore) 2001, *Biennial general assembly and conference / General Assembly* Sydney, NSW (Australia) 1999, *Biennial general assembly and conference / General Assembly* Beijing (China) 1997.
Members in 11 countries:
Australia, China, India, Indonesia, Japan, Korea Rep, Malaysia, New Zealand, Philippines, Sri Lanka, Thailand. [2020/XD9330/D]

♦ Asian-Pacific Meeting of Religious / see Asia-Oceania Meeting of Religious (#01802)
♦ Asian-Pacific Network Information Centre (internationally oriented national body)
♦ Asian Pacific Neural Network Assembly / see Asia Pacific Neural Network Society (#01978)
♦ Asian Pacific Organization for Cancer Prevention (internationally oriented national body)

♦ Asian-Pacific Organization for Cell Biology (APOCB) 01619

SG Inst of Biochemistry and Cell Biology, Shanghai Inst for Biological Sciences, Chinese Ac of Sciences, 320 Yue Yang Road, 200031 Shanghai, China. T. +862154921411. Fax +862154922891.
Pres c/o NCBS – Tata Inst, GKVK, Bellary Road, Bangalore, Karnataka 560065, Bangalore KARNATAKA 560065, India.
URL: http://www.apocb.org/
History 14 Aug 1988, Montréal, QC (Canada). Constitution and by-laws adopted at founding meeting. **Aims** Promote communication among cell biologists in the region; contribute to advancement of cell biology in all its aspects and of related topics. **Structure** General Assembly (every 2 years, at International or APOCB Congress); Executive Committee. **Languages** English. **Staff** 0.50 FTE, voluntary. **Finance** Members' dues. Contributions. **Activities** Events/meetings; projects/programmes. **Events** *Quadrennial Congress* Taipei (Taiwan) 2022, *Quadrennial Congress* Hyderabad (India) 2018, *Quadrennial Congress* Singapore (Singapore) 2014, *Quadrennial Congress* Mandaluyong (Philippines) 2011, *Quadrennial Congress* Beijing (China) 2006.
Members Cell biology organizations and groups in 18 countries and territories:
Australia, Bangladesh, China, Hong Kong, India, Iran Islamic Rep, Iraq, Japan, Korea Rep, Malaysia, Nepal, New Zealand, Palestine, Philippines, Singapore, Taiwan, Thailand, Vietnam.
NGO Relations Close cooperation with: *International Federation for Cell Biology (IFCB, #13382)*. [2020/XD2297/D]

♦ Asian Pacific Paediatric Gastro-Enterology Group / see Asian Pan-Pacific Society for Paediatric Gastroenterology, Hepatology, and Nutrition (#01651)

♦ Asian and Pacific Parkinsons Association (APPA) 01620

Pres Dept of Neurology, All India Inst of Medical Science, Delhi D3/9 Vasant Vihar, Delhi 110057, DELHI 110057, India. T. +91116147730 – +91116148971. Fax +91116569007.
History 1997, Malaysia, as *Asian and Pacific Parkinson's Disease Association (APPDA)*. **Aims** Raise awareness of Parkinson's disease in the region; improve *care* of *patients* with Parkinson's disease. **Structure** APPA Meeting (every 2 years). Loosely structured organization. President rotates and is usually organizer of next APPA Meeting. **Languages** English. **Staff** Usually Symposium Secretariat staff. **Finance** Member country hosting APPA meeting responsible to raise funds for the meeting. **Events** *International Symposium* Hangzhou (China) 2019, *International Symposium* Manila (Philippines) 2016, *International Symposium* Taipei (Taiwan) 2011, *International Symposium* Delhi (India) 2009, *International symposium* Singapore (Singapore) 2007.
Members in 14 countries and territories:
Australia, China, Hong Kong, India, Indonesia, Japan, Korea Rep, Malaysia, New Zealand, Philippines, Singapore, Taiwan, Thailand, Vietnam. [2008.06.01/XE3393/E]

♦ Asian and Pacific Parkinson's Disease Association / see Asian and Pacific Parkinsons Association (#01620)

♦ Asian-Pacific Parliamentarians' Conference on Environment and Development (APPCED) 01621

Conferencia de Parlamentarios de Asia-Pacifico sobre Medio Ambiente y Desarrollo
Dir-Gen Nat'l Assembly Members' Bldg 541-1, 1 Yeuido-dong, Youngdeungpo-ku, Seoul, Korea Rep. T. +8227861109 – +8227845107. Fax +8227852809. E-mail: cpe@assembly.go.kr.
Pres address not obtained.
History 8 Jun 1993, Seoul (Korea Rep), by the National Assembly of the Republic of Korea. **Aims** Form a forum for parliamentarians of the Asia Pacific region with a common concern for environmental and developmental issues. **Structure** General Assembly (annual). Executive Committee (meets at least annually), comprising President, 2 Vice-Presidents, Secretary-General and one parliamentarian from each member country (elected by the member country). **Activities** Supports mutual efforts among governments through policy development as well as collaboration at the parliamentary level. Members adopted the Palau Declaration at the 2009 Assembly in Palau as guidelines for further parliamentary endeavours in respect of climate change. **Events** *General Assembly* Seoul (Korea Rep) 2019, *General Assembly* Seoul (Korea Rep) 2016, *General Assembly* Kuala Lumpur (Malaysia) 2011, *General Assembly* Koror (Palau) 2009, *General Assembly* Korolevu (Fiji) 2004.
Members Governments of 46 countries:
Austria, Bangladesh, Bhutan, Cambodia, Canada, Chile, China, Cook Is, Fiji, India, Indonesia, Iran Islamic Rep, Iraq, Japan, Kazakhstan, Kiribati, Korea Rep, Kyrgyzstan, Laos, Malaysia, Marshall Is, Mexico, Mongolia, Nauru, Nepal, New Zealand, Nicaragua, Norfolk Is, Northern Mariana Is, Pakistan, Palau, Papua New Guinea, Peru, Philippines, Russia, Samoa, Singapore, Solomon Is, Sri Lanka, Syrian AR, Thailand, Tonga, Tuvalu, USA, Vanuatu, Vietnam.
IGO Relations Accredited by: *United Nations Framework Convention on Climate Change – Secretariat (UNFCCC, #20564)*. [2019.11.14/XF6544/c/F*]

♦ Asian-Pacific Parliamentarians' Union (APPU) 01622

Union de parlementaires de l'Asie et du Pacifique
SG Central Secretariat, 701 Azabudai Royal Plaza 3-4-12 Azabudai Minato-ku, Tokyo, 106-0041 Japan. T. +81355715805. Fax +81355734881. E-mail: office@mail.appu-cs.org.
URL: http://www.appu-cs.org/
History 1965, Tokyo (Japan), on the initiative of parliamentarians from 5 Asian nations: Republic of China (Taiwan), Japan, Republic of Korea, Philippines and Thailand, as *Asian Parliamentarians' Union (APU) – Union parlementaire d'Asie*. Present name adopted 9 Oct 1980. **Aims** Achieve and preserve freedom and *democracy*, so as to secure enduring peace and prosperity in Asia and the Pacific; strengthen mutual understanding and unity of all nations and peoples in Asia and the Pacific; promote economic cooperation and exchanges of culture and technology so as to enhance common welfare on a humanitarian basis; discuss all matters affecting peace and security in Asia and the Pacific and carry out decisions that may be agreed upon; respect principles of sovereignty and territorial integrity of all nations, and principles of non-interference in the international affairs of other countries. **Structure** General Assembly (annual); Council; Central Secretariat. **Languages** English. **Staff** 1.50 FTE, paid. **Finance** Members' contributions. President's expenses borne by his member group; meetings borne by host member; travel expenses borne by participants. **Events** *General Assembly* Taipei (Taiwan) 2019, *General Assembly* Nauru 2018, *General Assembly* Beppu (Japan) 2017, *General Assembly* Ngerulmud (Palau) 2016, *General Assembly* Majuro (Marshall Is) 2015. **Publications** Proceedings.
Members National Groups in 21 countries and territories:
Cook Is, Fiji, Japan, Kiribati, Korea Rep, Laos, Malaysia, Marshall Is, Micronesia FS, Mongolia, Nauru, Palau, Papua New Guinea, Philippines, Samoa, Solomon Is, Taiwan, Thailand, Tonga, Tuvalu, Vanuatu.
Associate Groups in 2 territories:
Guam, Northern Mariana Is.
Observer in 1 country:
Vietnam. [2019.12.19/XD0088/D]

♦ Asian Pacific Pediatric Association / see Asia Pacific Pediatric Association (#01992)

♦ Asian Pacific Phycological Association (APPA) 01623

Sec address not obtained.
URL: http://apphycology.org/
History 1993. **Aims** Develop phycology in the Asian Pacific region; serve as the venue for exchange of information related to phycology; promote international cooperation among phycologists and phycology societies in the region. **Structure** Executive Committee; International Advisory Council; Office comprises President, Secretary and Treasurer. **Languages** English. **Finance** No members' dues. **Activities** Events/meetings; knowledge management/information dissemination. **Events** *Triennial Forum* Sapporo (Japan) 2021, *Triennial Forum* Sapporo (Japan) 2020, *Triennial Forum* Kuala Lumpur (Malaysia) 2017, *Triennial Forum* Wuhan (China) 2014, *Triennial Forum* Yeosu (Korea Rep) 2011. **Publications** *APPA Newsletter*.
Members All participants who attend the Asian Pacific Phycological Forum become members for the following 6 years. Members in 16 countries and territories:
Australia, Canada, China, Hong Kong, India, Indonesia, Japan, Korea Rep, Malaysia, Myanmar, New Zealand, Philippines, Taiwan, Thailand, USA, Vietnam. [2020/XD7992/D]

♦ Asian-Pacific Political Science Association (inactive)

♦ Asian-Pacific Postal College (APPC) 01624

SG PO Box 1 Laksi Post Office, 111 Chaeng Wattana Road, Bangkok, 10210, Thailand. T. +6625733831 – +6625737282. Fax +6625731161. E-mail: admin@appu-bureau.org.
URL: http://www.appu-bureau.org/appc_web_pages/intro.htm
History 10 Sep 1970, Bangkok (Thailand), as *Asian and Oceanic Postal Training School (AOPTS)*. Name changed to *Asian-Pacific Postal Training Centre (APPTC) – Centre de formation postale pour l'Asie et le Pacifique*. Became an autonomous organ of the then *'Asian-Oceanic Postal Union (AOPU)'*, currently, since Mar 1981, *Asian-Pacific Postal Union (APPU, #01625)*. **Aims** Provide training facilities to improve postal services within Asia and the Pacific. **Structure** Governing Board (meeting at least once a year); Executive Council. **Languages** English. **Staff** 18.00 FTE, paid. **Finance** Supported by participating/donor countries in cash (cash contributions, fellowship grants) and/or kind (provision of postal consultants, donation of equipment and materials). Annual budget: US$ 838,710. **Activities** Training/education; events/meetings. **Events** *Annual governing board meeting* Singapore (Singapore) 1995, *Annual governing board meeting* Surfers Paradise, QLD (Australia) 1994, *Annual governing board meeting* Kobe (Japan) 1993, *Annual Governing Board Meeting* Delhi (India) 1992, *Annual Governing Board Meeting* Bandar Seri Begawan (Brunei Darussalam) 1991. **Publications** *APPC Newsletter* (6 a year).
Members Postal Administrations, members of the Governing Board, in 10 countries:
Australia, China, India, Indonesia, Japan, Korea Rep, New Zealand, Philippines, Sri Lanka, Thailand.
Beneficiary countries and territories – sending students – (37):
Afghanistan, Australia, Bangladesh, Bhutan, Brunei Darussalam, China, Cook Is, Fiji, India, Indonesia, Iran Islamic Rep, Japan, Kiribati, Korea DPR, Korea Rep, Laos, Malaysia, Maldives, Mongolia, Myanmar, Nauru, Nepal, New Zealand, Niue, Pakistan, Papua New Guinea, Philippines, Qatar, Samoa, Singapore, Solomon Is, Sri Lanka, Thailand, Tonga, Tuvalu, Vanuatu, Vietnam.
IGO Relations *UNDP (#20292)*; *Universal Postal Union (UPU, #20682)*. [2018.06.01/XF3763/F*]

Asian Pacific Postal
01624

alphabetic sequence excludes
For the complete listing, see Yearbook Online at

♦ Asian-Pacific Postal Training Centre / see Asian-Pacific Postal College (#01624)

♦ **Asian-Pacific Postal Union (APPU)** **01625**
Union postale de l'Asie et du Pacifique
SG PO Box 1, Laksi Post Office, 111 Chaeng Wattana Road, Bangkok, 10210, Thailand. T. +6625738331. Fax +6625731161. E-mail: admin@appu-bureau.org.
URL: http://www.appu-bureau.org/
History Established 1 Apr 1962, as *Asian-Oceanic Postal Union (AOPU) – Union postale de l'Asie et de l'Océanie (UPAO)*, on ratification of *Asian-Oceanic Postal Convention (1961)*, drawn up at Manila (Philippines) Postal Conference, 10-23 Jan 1961. Convention revised: 1965; 1970; 1975; 1981, 1985. Last revision: 26 Nov – 6 Dec 1990, Rotorua (New Zealand). Convention concluded and present name adopted, Mar 1981, Yogyakarta (Indonesia). A Restricted Union of *Universal Postal Union (UPU, #20682)*. **Aims** Extend, facilitate and improve postal relations among member countries; promote cooperation in the field of postal services. **Structure** Congress (not more than 2 years after each Universal Postal Congress); Executive Council; *Asian-Pacific Postal College (APPC, #01624)*, administered by Governing Board; Bureau, headed by Secretary General. **Languages** English. **Staff** 12.00 FTE, paid. **Finance** Expenses shared among member countries. Annual budget: 170,000 USD. **Activities** Events/meetings; guidance/assistance/consulting; networking/liaising; projects/programmes; training/education. **Events** *Postal Business Forum* Bangkok (Thailand) 2019, *Meeting* Tokyo (Japan) 2019, *Postal Business Forum* Bangkok (Thailand) 2018, *Meeting* Danang (Vietnam) 2018, *Forum* Bangkok (Thailand) 2017. **Publications** *APPU Newsletter*. Reports.
Members Governments of 31 countries:
Afghanistan, Australia, Bangladesh, Bhutan, Brunei Darussalam, Cambodia, China, Fiji, India, Indonesia, Iran Islamic Rep, Japan, Korea Rep, Laos, Malaysia, Maldives, Mongolia, Myanmar, Nauru, Nepal, New Zealand, Pakistan, Papua New Guinea, Philippines, Singapore, Solomon Is, Sri Lanka, Thailand, Tonga, Vanuatu, Vietnam.
IGO Relations Formal contact with: *United Nations Economic and Social Commission for Asia and the Pacific (ESCAP, #20557)*. Links with the other Restricted Unions: *African Postal Union (APU, no recent information); Associação dos Operadores de Correios e Telecomunicações dos Países e Territórios de Língua Oficial Portuguesa (AICEP, #02333); Association of European Public Postal Operators (PostEurop, #02534); Pan African Postal Union (PAPU, #18060); Postal Union of the Americas, Spain and Portugal (PUASP, #18466); Regional Commonwealth in the Field of Communications (RCC, #18767)*. [2017.10.12/XC0082/**C***]

♦ **Asian Pacific Prostate Society (APPS)** **01626**
SG Dept of Urology, Cath Univ of Korea, Seoul St Mary's Hosp, 505 Banpo-dong Seocho-gu, Seoul 137-701, Korea Rep. T. +82222587638. E-mail: apps@approstate.org.
URL: http://approstate.org/
History Founded 2011, by a gathering of renowned urologists on prostate health and disease factors from 11 countries worldwide. **Aims** Share the latest information; discuss important issues in-depth with practising urologists in the Asia-Pacific region. **Structure** Annual Meeting; Council; Board. Standing Committees (3): Scientific Program; Local Organizing; Finance. **Languages** English. **Finance** Members' dues. **Activities** Networking/liaising; research/documentation; events/meetings. **Events** *Congress* Tokyo (Japan) 2022, *Congress* Shanghai (China) 2019, *Congress* Wailea, HI (USA) 2018, *Congress* Chiang Mai (Thailand) 2017, *Symposium* Seoul (Korea Rep) 2017. **Publications** *Prostate International* – journal.
Members Regular; Associate; Special; Honorary. Individuals in 11 countries and territories:
Australia, China, Hong Kong, Indonesia, Japan, Korea Rep, Malaysia, Philippines, Singapore, Taiwan, Thailand.
[2015/XJ5522/v/**D**]

♦ **Asian Pacific Publishers Association (APPA)** **01627**
Contact KPA, 105-2 Sagan-dong, Jongno-gu, Seoul 110-190, Korea Rep. T. +8227352701. Fax +8227385414.
History Founded 1 Nov 1992, Tokyo (Japan), at the Mutual Cooperation for Publishing in Asia Forum. **Aims** Advance and develop publishing in the Asia Pacific region; improve mutual cooperation between members; improve active exchange of publishing expertise; promote study opportunities for the youth of member countries in the fields of publishing, *printing*, binding and distribution. **Structure** Council; Working Level Committee. Sub Committees (5): Co-publishing; Copyright; CJK Code Research; Digital Contents; Internet Publishing. **Languages** English. **Staff** 3.00 FTE, paid. **Finance** Members' dues. Budget: US$ 30,000. **Events** *Annual General Assembly* Colombo (Sri Lanka) 2012, *Annual general assembly* Seoul (Korea Rep) 2008, *Annual general assembly / Annual General Meeting* Ho Chi Minh City (Vietnam) 2007, *Annual general assembly / Annual General Meeting* Bali (Indonesia) 2006, *Annual general assembly / Annual General Meeting* Islamabad (Pakistan) 2005.
Members Representatives from national publishing organizations in 16 countries:
Australia, Bangladesh, Brunei Darussalam, China, India, Indonesia, Japan, Korea Rep, Malaysia, Mongolia, Pakistan, Philippines, Singapore, Sri Lanka, Thailand, Vietnam.
NGO Relations Member of: *International Publishers Association (IPA, #14675)*. [2018/XD4908/**D**]

♦ Asian and Pacific Regional Agricultural Credit Association / see Asia Pacific Rural and Agricultural Credit Association (#02019)
♦ Asian-Pacific Regional Network on Occupational Safety and Health / see Asia Pacific Occupational Safety and Health Organization (#01981)
♦ Asian Pacific Regional Organization / see Asian Pacific Dental Federation/Asian Pacific Regional Organization of the Fédération Dentaire Internationale (#01882)
♦ Asian and Pacific Regional Organization of the International Federation of Commercial, Clerical, Professional and Technical Employees / see UNI Global Union – Asia and Pacific Regional Office (#20341)

♦ **Asian-Pacific Regional Research and Training Centre for Integrated Fish Farming (IFFC)** **01628**
Main Office No 9 East Shanshui Rd, Wuxi, 214081 Jiangsu, China. T. +8651085555796. Fax +8651085555796 – +8651085553304.
History 1978, by Chinese Government and *UNDP (#20292)*. **Aims** Carry out research and a training programme on sustainable *aquaculture* development; improve the livelihood in rural areas, helping people in *poverty* alleviation and sharing experiences. **Structure** General Office; Research and Development Unit; Training and Education Unit; Support Unit; Experimental Farms. **Languages** Chinese, English, French, Russian. **Staff** 325.00 FTE, paid. **Finance** Sources: Chinese Government; projects; programs; technical dissemination. **Activities** Undertakes research on hydrobiology and aquaculture. Organizes: international technical training course; training workshops. Provides educational program. **Events** *Forum on China Fishery Science and Technology / Forum* Shanghai (China) 2012, *Forum* Wuxi (China) 2010, *International workshop on integrated fish farming* Wuxi (China) 1994. **Publications** *Scientific Fish Farming* (12 a year) in Chinese; *Fish Today* (4 a year) in English – newsletter. **IGO Relations** Operates as the 'Regional Lead Center in China' of *Network of Aquaculture Centres in Asia-Pacific (NACA, #16991)*. **NGO Relations** Instrumental in setting up: *Committee on Earth Observation Satellites (CEOS, #04249)*. [2014.06.01/XE2036/**E**]

♦ Asian-Pacific Research Foundation for Infectious Diseases / see Asia Pacific Foundation for Infectious Diseases

♦ **Asian-Pacific Resource and Research Centre for Women (ARROW)** . **01629**
Exec Dir No 1 and 2, Jalan Scott, Brickfields, 504 70 Kuala Lumpur, Malaysia. T. +60322739913 – +60322729914. Fax +60322739916. E-mail: arrow@arrow.org.my.
URL: http://www.arrow.org.my/
History Jan 1993. **Aims** Provide information and resource materials that will help re-orient policies and programmes to greater sensitivity and responsiveness to women's needs and perspectives; facilitate generation and utilization of new research findings and analysis of policies, programmes and organizations; exchange and disseminate information and research findings through a regional and global network of organizations. **Structure** Steering Committee. Executive Director; Administration and Finance Manager; 2 Programme Managers; 5 Programme Officers; 3 Assistant Programme Officers; Finance Officer; Administrative Assistant; Executive Assistant. **Staff** 17.00 FTE, paid. **Finance** Funded by: *DANIDA*; *Ford Foundation (#09858)*; *Oxfam Novib*; *Swedish International Development Cooperation Agency (Sida)*. **Activities** Knowledge management/information dissemination; research/documentation; publishing activities; guidance/assistance/consulting. **Publications** *Women's Health Bulletin* (3 a year); *Arrows for Change (AFC)* – bulletin. *Reclaiming and Redefining Rights: Status of Sexual Reproductive Health and Rights in Asia*. Annotated Bibliography; Framework and Tools; Resource Kit; information packages. Information Services: Reference/Information Requests; CD-Rom Searches; Internet Searches; Network Searches; Subject Bibliography; Inter-Library Loan Facility; accession lists; selected titles list. **Information Services** *ARROW Database* – Search.
Members Individuals and organizations in 94 countries and territories:
Argentina, Australia, Austria, Azerbaijan, Bangladesh, Barbados, Belgium, Benin, Bhutan, Brazil, Brunei Darussalam, Cambodia, Canada, Chile, China, Colombia, Congo DR, Costa Rica, Denmark, Dominican Rep, Ecuador, Egypt, Ethiopia, Fiji, Finland, France, Gambia, Germany, Ghana, Hong Kong, India, Indonesia, Iran Islamic Rep, Ireland, Italy, Jamaica, Japan, Jordan, Kenya, Kiribati, Korea Rep, Laos, Liberia, Luxembourg, Malaysia, Maldives, Mali, Marshall Is, Mauritius, Mexico, Micronesia FS, Mongolia, Morocco, Myanmar, Nauru, Nepal, Netherlands, New Zealand, Nicaragua, Nigeria, Norway, Pakistan, Palau, Papua New Guinea, Peru, Philippines, Poland, Samoa, Senegal, Seychelles, Sierra Leone, Singapore, Solomon Is, South Africa, Spain, Sri Lanka, Sudan, Sweden, Switzerland, Taiwan, Tajikistan, Tanzania UR, Thailand, Tonga, Tunisia, Tuvalu, Uganda, UK, Uruguay, USA, Vanuatu, Venezuela, Vietnam, Zimbabwe.
Consultative Status Consultative status granted from: *ECOSOC (#05331)* (Special); *United Nations Population Fund (UNFPA, #20612)*. **NGO Relations** Member of: *Asian Women's Resource Exchange (AWORC, no recent information); Conference of Non-Governmental Organizations in Consultative Relationship with the United Nations (CONGO, #04635); Coalition for Sexual and Bodily Rights in Muslim Societies (CSBR, #04068); International AIDS Women's Caucus (IAWC, #11603); Red Internacional de Centros de Documentación Mujer y Salud (no recent information); WomenAction 2000 (no recent information)*. [2010.06.01/XF3657/**E**]

♦ Asian and Pacific Shipbuilding Experts Meeting (meeting series)
♦ Asian and Pacific Skill Development Programme (no recent information)
♦ Asian Pacific Societies for Extracellular Vesicles (unconfirmed)
♦ Asian Pacific Society of Allergy and Immunology / see Asia Pacific Association of Allergy, Asthma and Clinical Immunology (#01831)

♦ **Asian-Pacific Society of Atherosclerosis and Vascular Diseases (APSAVD)** **01630**
Sec-Treas PO Box 5436, Chittaway Bay NSW 2261, Australia. T. +61243560007. E-mail: admin@yoursecretariat.com.au.
URL: http://www.apsavd.org/
History 1996. Registration: Consumer Affairs Victoria. **Aims** Provide a forum for scientists and clinicians interested in Atherosclerosis to meet regularly and share updates on the subject; highlight similarities and differences of the disease as seen in the region compared to that seen in the western world. **Structure** Executive. **Languages** English. **Events** *International Congress on Lipid and Atherosclerosis* Seoul (Korea Rep) 2022, *Congress* Kyoto (Japan) 2021, *Congress* Kuala Lumpur (Malaysia) 2020, *Congress* Taipei (Taiwan) 2019, *Congress* Iloilo (Philippines) 2018.
Members Full in 13 countries and territories:
Australia, Hong Kong, India, Indonesia, Japan, Korea Rep, Malaysia, New Zealand, Philippines, Singapore, Taiwan, Thailand, UK.
NGO Relations Member of (1): *International Atherosclerosis Society (IAS, #12288)*. [2023.02.20/XD6311/**D**]

♦ **Asian Pacific Society of Cardiology (APSC)** **01631**
Société cardiologique Asie-Pacifique
Permanent Secretariat c/o National Heart Association of Malaysia, D-13A-06, Menara Suezcap 1, KL Gateway 2, Jalan Kerinchi, 59200 Kuala Lumpur, Malaysia. T. +60340231500. E-mail: secretariat@apscardio.org.
URL: http://www.apscardio.org/
History 18 Apr 1956, Manila (Philippines), following recommendations of 2nd World Congress on Cardiology, 1954. By-laws revised 1976, Honolulu HI (USA); 1991, Seoul (Korea Rep). **Aims** Foster the study and dissemination of knowledge of diseases of the cardiovascular system in the region of Asia and Oceania, and promote scientific exchange and professional contacts among workers in this field; organize a regional congress every 4 years. **Structure** General Assembly (every 4 years) elects President and Secretary-Treasurer who, together with immediate Past-President and Zone Vice-Presidents, comprise Executive Council. Zones (5): Northeast Asia; Southeast Asia; Pacific; South Asia; West Asia. Scientific Committees (7): Research; Education; Rehabilitation; Prevention; Clinical Cardiology; Paediatric Cardiology; Cardiac Surgery. **Languages** English. **Staff** 1.00 FTE, paid. Voluntary. **Finance** Members' dues (National Societies and individuals). **Activities** Research on epidemiology of cardiovascular diseases in the Asian-Pacific area, including standardization of clinical laboratory techniques, education of members in this area, and promotion of preventative and rehabilitation programmes. **Events** *Annual Congress* Busan (Korea Rep) 2025, *Annual Congress* Dubai (United Arab Emirates) 2024, *Annual Congress* Singapore (Singapore) 2023, *Annual Congress* Osaka (Japan) 2022, *Annual Congress* Bangkok (Thailand) 2021. **Publications** *APSC Newsletter* (annual).
Members National societies in 17 countries and territories:
Australia, Bangladesh, Hong Kong, India, Indonesia, Israel, Japan, Korea Rep, Malaysia, New Zealand, Pakistan, Philippines, Singapore, Sri Lanka, Taiwan, Thailand, USA.
Individual members. Membership countries not specified.
NGO Relations Member of: *The NCD Alliance (NCDA, #16963); World Heart Federation (WHF, #21562)*.
[2020/XC0085/**D**]

♦ **Asian Pacific Society of Dialysis Access (APSDA)** **01632**
Secretariat Catholic Univ of Korea Seoul St Mary's Hosp, 222 Banpo-Daero, Seocho-gu, Seoul 06591, Korea Rep. T. +821030614678. Fax +82105371416. E-mail: secretariat@apsda.info.
URL: https://apsda.info/
History 2017, Nagoya (Japan). **Aims** Improve the quality of dialysis patient care by the advancement of research, education, collaboration and clinical practice standards regarding dialysis access. **Structure** Council; Executive Committee; Council of National Representatives. **Languages** English. **Finance** Members' dues. Other sources: subsidies; gifts. **Activities** Events/meetings; research/documentation; training/education. **Events** *Congress* Delhi (India) 2022, *Congress* Kuala Lumpur (Malaysia) 2019, *Congress* Zhengzhou (China) 2018, *Congress* Nagoya (Japan) 2017, *Congress* Seoul (Korea Rep) 2015. **Members** Active; Associate; Supporting. Membership countries not specified. [2019/XM7861/**D**]

♦ **Asian-Pacific Society for Digestive Endoscopy (APSDE)** **01633**
Pres Room 3702B – Tower 2, Lippo Centre, 89 Queensway, Hong Kong, Central and Western, Hong Kong. T. +85225238248. Fax +85228681919.
Vice-Pres Dept Gastroenterological/Pediatric Surgery, Oita Univ, Fac of Medicine, Hasama-machi, Yufu, Oita, 8795593 Japan. T. +81975865840. Fax +81975496039.
History 1966, Tokyo (Japan). Current statutes adopted, 2002, Hong Kong. **Aims** Promote and foster the exchange and diffusion of information and ideas relating to digestive endoscopy; encourage research and study to this speciality; standardize, on an international scale, endoscopy methods and nomenclature. **Structure** Governing Council; Board. **Languages** English. **Staff** Voluntary. **Finance** Members' dues. **Activities** Training/education. **Events** *Asia Pacific Digestive Week* Kuala Lumpur (Malaysia) 2021, *Asia Pacific Digestive Week* Kuala Lumpur (Malaysia) 2020, *Asia Pacific Digestive Week* Kolkata (India) 2019, *Asia Pacific Digestive Week* Seoul (Korea Rep) 2018, *Asia Pacific Digestive Week* Hong Kong (Hong Kong) 2017. **Publications** *Asian-Pacific Society for Digestive Endoscopy Bulletin*; *Digestive Endoscopy* – journal.
Members Fellows, Honorary, Associate and Supporting members. National societies (18) and fellows (17) in 17 countries and territories:
Afghanistan, Australia, China, Hong Kong, India, Indonesia, Japan, Korea Rep, Macau, Malaysia, New Zealand, Pakistan, Philippines, Singapore, Sri Lanka, Taiwan, Thailand, Vietnam.
NGO Relations Member of: *Asian Pacific Digestive Week Federation (APDWF, #01609); World Endoscopy Organization (WEO, #21380)*. Endorses: *International Symposium on Endoscopic Ultrasonography*.
[2014.06.20/XD6498/**D**]

♦ Asian and Pacific Society of Hematology (inactive)

♦ **Asian-Pacific Society of Hypertension** **01634**
SG Dept of Physiology, Univ of Melbourne, Melbourne VIC 3010, Australia. T. +61439866946. E-mail: secretary@apsh.org.
URL: http://www.apsh.org/

History 1997. **Aims** Advance clinical and scientific understanding of hypertension; improve treatment of hypertension and related vascular disorders in the community; train and educate future leaders in hypertension. **Structure** Council; Executive. **Languages** English. **Events** *Congress* Kyoto (Japan) 2022, *Congress* Hyderabad (India) 2021, *Congress* Brisbane, QLD (Australia) 2019, *Congress* Beijing (China) 2018, *Congress* Singapore (Singapore) 2017.
Members Full in 19 countries and territories:
Australia, Bangladesh, China, Hong Kong, India, Indonesia, Japan, Korea Rep, Malaysia, Mongolia, Nepal, New Zealand, Pakistan, Philippines, Singapore, Sri Lanka, Taiwan, Thailand, Vietnam.
NGO Relations Official affiliate of: *International Society of Hypertension (ISH, #15189).*
[2019.02.18/XD7559/**D**]

♦ Asian-Pacific Society for Infections in GYN/OB (APSIGO) 01635
SG OGSM, Ste C-07-02, Plaza Mont Kiara, No 2 Jalan Mont Kiara, 50480 Kuala Lumpur, Malaysia. E-mail: ogsm@myjaring.net.
History 19 Nov 2010, Singapore (Singapore). 19-21 Nov 2010, Singapore (Singapore), by 66 representatives from 27 countries. **Events** *Foundation meeting* Singapore (Singapore) 2010. **NGO Relations** Joint meeting with: *European Society for Infectious Diseases in Obstetrics and Gynaecology (ESIDOG, no recent information).*
[2010/XJ2125/**D**]

♦ Asian Pacific Society of Interventional Cardiology (APSIC) 01636
Exec Sec Unit C & D, 5/F, Unison Industrial Building, 27-31 Au Pui Wan Street, Fo Tan, Hong Kong, Central and Western, Hong Kong. T. +85231097233. Fax +85225073532. E-mail: secretariat@apsic.net.
URL: http://www.apsic.net/
History 17 Nov 2000. **Aims** Promote interventional cardiology, particularly in the field of coronary intervention, in the Asia Pacific region. **Structure** Advisory Board (meets annually). **Events** *AICT-AsiaPCR* Singapore (Singapore) 2021, *Meeting on complex cardiovascular therapeutics* Kobe (Japan) 2010, *Meeting on complex cardiovascular therapeutics* Kobe (Japan) 2009, *Asian Interventional Cardiovascular Therapeutics Conference* Bangkok (Thailand) 2008, *Asian interventional cardiovascular therapeutics conference (AICT)* Singapore (Singapore) 2005.
Members in 20 countries and territories:
Australia, Austria, Bangladesh, Brunei Darussalam, China, Hong Kong, India, Indonesia, Japan, Korea DPR, Korea Rep, Malaysia, Myanmar, Pakistan, Philippines, Singapore, Sri Lanka, Taiwan, Thailand, Vietnam. [2020/XM1679/**D**]

♦ Asian Pacific Society for Laser Medicine and Surgery / see Asian Pacific Association for Lasers in Medicine and Surgery (#01599)

♦ Asian-Pacific Society of Marine Biotechnology (APSMB) 01637
Contact Zoology Marine Lab, 128 Sec 2 Academia Rd, Nankang, Taipei 11529, Taiwan.
Chair National Institute of Oceanography, Dona Paula, Goa, Goa, India.
History 1995, Japan. **Activities** Events/meetings. **Events** *Asia Pacific Marine Biotechnology Conference* Adelaide, SA (Australia) 2023, *Asia Pacific Marine Biotechnology Conference* Adelaide, SA (Australia) 2021, *Asia Pacific Marine Biotechnology Conference* Shizuoka (Japan) 2019, *Asia-Pacific Marine Biotechnology Conference (APMBC)* Manoa, HI (USA) 2017, *Asia Pacific Marine Biotechnology Conference* Taipei (Taiwan) 2014. [2020/XD5546/**D**]

♦ Asian Pacific Society for Medical Mycology (APSMM) 01638
Pres Dept of Dermatology and Venerology, Peking Univ First Hosp, No 8 Xishiku St, 100034 Beijing, China. E-mail: mycolab@126.com.
History 1997. **Aims** Promote professional and social exchange among medical professionals in the Asia-Pacific region who are interested in medical mycology. **Languages** English. **Activities** Events/meetings. **Events** *Congress* Guangzhou (China) 2019, *Medical mycology in Asia Pacific – towards one health* Bali (Indonesia) 2016, *Congress* Chengdu (China) 2013, *Meeting / Congress* Seoul (Korea Rep) 2008, *Congress* Bangkok (Thailand) 2005. **NGO Relations** Member of: *International Society for Human and Animal Mycology (ISHAM, #15181).* [2019.07.20/XD7962/**D**]

♦ Asian-Pacific Society for Medical Virology (APSMV) 01639
Pres Dept of Microbiology, Univ of Hong Kong, Univ Pathology Bldg, Pokfulam Road, Hong Kong, Central and Western, Hong Kong. T. +85222554897. Fax +85228551241.
History 1982, Sendai (Japan), as *Asian Group for Rapid Viral Diagnosis.* Present name adopted 1988. **Aims** Promote medical virology in the Asia-Pacific region. **Structure** Executive Committee, including President, President-Elect, Immediate Past-President, Secretary and Treasurer. **Languages** English. **Staff** 5.00 FTE, paid. **Finance** Congress subscriptions. **Activities** Knowledge management/information dissemination; publishing activites; guidance/assistance/consulting. **Events** *Triennial Congress* Taipei (Taiwan) 2015, *Triennial congress* Hong Kong (Hong Kong) 2009, *Triennial Congress* Delhi (India) 2006, *Triennial congress* Kuala Lumpur (Malaysia) 2003, *Triennial Congress* Denpasar (Indonesia) 2000.
Members Full; Associate. Members (525) in 37 countries and territories:
Australia, Bangladesh, Belgium, Canada, China, Cuba, Finland, France, Germany, Hong Kong, India, Indonesia, Iran Islamic Rep, Japan, Korea Rep, Kuwait, Malaysia, Myanmar, Netherlands, New Caledonia, New Zealand, Oman, Pakistan, Philippines, Portugal, Russia, Saudi Arabia, Singapore, Sri Lanka, Sweden, Switzerland, Taiwan, Thailand, UK, USA, Venezuela, Vietnam.
NGO Relations Sister organizations: *Pan American Society for Clinical Virology (PASCV); European Society for Clinical Virology (ESCV, #08552).* Member of: *International Society of Antimicrobial Chemotherapy (ISAC, #14925).* [2016/XD9253/**D**]

♦ Asian-Pacific Society for Mountain Medicine (unconfirmed)

♦ Asian-Pacific Society of Nephrology (APSN) 01640
Pres MIMS (Hong Kong) Ltd, 37th Floor, Citicorp Centre, 18 Whitfield Road, Causeway Bay, Hong Kong. T. +85221164320. E-mail: enquiries@apsneph.org – apsn@icc.com.hk.
URL: http://www.apsneph.org/
Aims Promote and encourage the advancement of scientific knowledge and research in all aspects of nephrology; promote the exchange and dissemination of this knowledge in the Asian-Pacific area. **Structure** Council; Executive Committee. **Languages** English. **Staff** None. **Finance** Sources: members' dues. **Activities** Awards/prizes/competitions; events/meetings; research and development; training/education. **Events** *Congress* Bangkok (Thailand) 2023, *Congress* Bangkok (Thailand) 2021, *Congress* Hong Kong (Hong Kong) 2020, *Congress* Beijing (China) 2018, *Congress* Perth, WA (Australia) 2016. **Publications** *Nephrology* (12 a year) – journal. **Members** Affiliated or sponsoring national societies; individuals. Membership countries not specified.
[2022/XD4504/**D**]

♦ Asian Pacific Society for Neurochemistry (APSN) 01641
Contact address not obtained. E-mail: apsn2020@gmail.com.
URL: https://www.apsn-neurochemistry.org/
History 1991. Founded during meeting of *International Society for Neurochemistry (ISN, #15295).* **Aims** Promote research in neurochemistry and related disciplines, particularly through information dissemination and meetings. **Structure** Executive Council, comprising President, Secretary, Treasurer, Past President and 9 members. **Languages** English. **Activities** Runs special training schools. **Events** *ISN-APSN Meeting* Honolulu, HI (USA) 2022, *Biennial Meeting* Singapore (Singapore) 2021, *Biennial Meeting* Singapore (Singapore) 2020, *Biennial Meeting* Macau (Macau) 2018, *International Conference on the Glycobiology of Nervous System* Seoul (Korea Rep) 2017. **Publications** Proceedings.
Members Regular, student and corporate. Members (about 290) in 14 countries and territories:
Australia, Bangladesh, China, Hong Kong, India, Japan, Korea Rep, Malaysia, New Zealand, Pakistan, Singapore, Sri Lanka, Taiwan, Thailand. [2020/XD5852/**D**]

♦ Asian Pacific Society of Nuclear Cardiology (no recent information)
♦ Asian Pacific Society for Paediatric Gastroenterology (inactive)

♦ Asian Pacific Society of Prion Research (APSPR) 01642
Secretariat Dept of Neurochemistry, Tohoku Univ Graduate School of Medicine, 2-1 Seiryo-machi, Aoba-ku, Sendai MIYAGI, 980-8575 Japan. Fax +81227177656. E-mail: info@apspr.org.
URL: http://apspr.org/
History 11 Jul 2011, originating in the Prion Symposium, set up 2004. **Aims** Advance and improve prion and *prion disease* researches, education, and medical care; promote the health of the general public. **Structure** Board of Trustees. **Finance** Members' dues. **Events** *Symposium* Tokyo (Japan) 2016, *Symposium* Kanazawa (Japan) 2015, *Symposium* Jeju (Korea Rep) 2014, *Symposium* Nagasaki (Japan) 2013, *Symposium* Yokohama (Japan) 2012. [2016/XJ9490/**D**]

♦ Asian Pacific Society of Respirology (APSR) 01643
Pres 2F UKs Bldg, 2-29-3 Hongo, Bunkyo-ku, Tokyo, 113-0033 Japan. T. +81356843370. Fax +81356843382. E-mail: apsrinfo@theapsr.org.
URL: http://www.apsresp.org/
History 1986, Tokyo (Japan). **Aims** Promote advances in knowledge of the respiratory system in health and disease; promote exchange of knowledge among respirologists in the Asian and Pacific region. **Structure** Executive Committee; Steering Committee; Finance Committee; Strategic Planning Committee; Research Committee; Education Committee; Membership Committee; Nomination Committee; Ethics and Disclosure Committee; Central Congress Committee; Local Congress Committee; Assemblies (16). **Languages** English. **Staff** 6.00 FTE, paid. **Finance** Members' dues. **Events** *Congress* Singapore (Singapore) 2023, *Congress* Seoul (Korea Rep) 2022, *Congress* Kyoto (Japan) 2021, *Congress* Kyoto (Japan) 2020, *Congress* Hanoi (Vietnam) 2019. **Publications** *Respiratory Update* (12 a year); *ASPR Bulletin* (12 a year); *APSR Newsletter* (2 a year). *Respirology; Respirology Case Reports.*
Members National thoracic societies of 14 countries and territories:
Australia, Bangladesh, Hong Kong, Indonesia, Japan, Korea Rep, Malaysia, Mongolia, New Zealand, Philippines, Singapore, Sri Lanka, Taiwan, Vietnam.
Individuals in 33 countries and territories:
Australia, Bangladesh, Bermuda, Cambodia, Canada, China, Hong Kong, India, Indonesia, Israel, Japan, Korea Rep, Kuwait, Kyrgyzstan, Malaysia, Maldives, Mexico, Mongolia, Myanmar, Nepal, New Zealand, Pakistan, Peru, Philippines, Saudi Arabia, Singapore, Sri Lanka, Taiwan, Tanzania UR, Thailand, United Arab Emirates, USA, Vietnam.
NGO Relations Member of: *Global Alliance Against Chronic Respiratory Diseases (GARD, #10182); International COPD Coalition (ICC, #12961).* Represented in Executive Committee of: *Global Initiative for Chronic Obstructive Lung Disease (GOLD, #10423).* Instrumental in setting up: *Forum of International Respiratory Societies (FIRS, #09922).* [2020/XD2926/**D**]

♦ Asian-Pacific Society on Thrombosis and Hemostasis (APSTH) 01644
Chair Medical Laboratory and Transfusion Service, Hokkaido University Hospital, N14 W5 Kita-ku, Sapporo HOKKAIDO, 060-8648 Japan. E-mail: info@jsth.org.
URL: http://www.apsth.org
History 2000. **Aims** Foster and advance science relating to the important issues of thrombosis, haemostasis and vascular biology in Asia and Pacific regions; promote scientific exchange and cooperation through scientific meetings and publications; promote international harmonization in clinical studies, standardization of nomenclature and methods in Asian and Pacific regions. **Structure** Assembly of Representatives; Management Board. **Languages** English. **Staff** 1.00 FTE, voluntary. **Finance** Sources: members' dues. **Activities** Events/meetings. **Events** *Biennial Congress* Gwangju (Korea Rep) 2021, *Biennial Congress* Gwangju (Korea Rep) 2020, *Biennial Congress* Sapporo (Japan) 2018, *Workshop on Thrombosis and Hemostasis* Bangkok (Thailand) 2017, *Biennial Congress* Taipei (Taiwan) 2016. **Publications** *APSTH Newsletter* (twice a year).
Members Active; Retired. Membership countries not specified. [2022.10.20/XM2578/**D**]

♦ Asian Pacific Society of Uro-Oncology / see Asian Society of Uro-Oncology (#01746)
♦ Asian and Pacific Studies Institute, Beijing / see Institute of Asia-Pacific Studies, Beijing
♦ Asian-Pacific Symposium on Structural Reliability and Its Applications (meeting series)
♦ Asian-Pacific Tax and Investment Research Centre (inactive)
♦ Asian Pacific Theological Seminary (internationally oriented national body)

♦ Asian and Pacific Training Centre for Information and Communication Technology for Development (APCICT) 01645
Main Office G-Tower 5th Floor, 175 Art center-daero, Yeonsu-gu, 24-4 Songo-Dong, Incheon 22004, Korea Rep. T. +82324586650. Fax +82324586691. E-mail: apcict@un.org.
URL: http://www.unapcict.org/
History Inaugurated 16 Jun 2006, as a regional institute of *United Nations Economic and Social Commission for Asia and the Pacific (ESCAP, #20557).* **Aims** Strengthen the efforts of ESCAP member countries to use ICT in heir socio-economic development through human and institutional capacity building. **Structure** Governing Council, consisting of a representative nominated by the Government of Korea Rep and 8 representatives of members and associate members of ESCAP. **Activities** Training/education; Research/documentation; guidance/assistance/consulting. **Events** *Session* Incheon (Korea Rep) 2021, *Meeting on ICT for Disaster Risk Management for Local Government* Incheon (Korea Rep) / Seoul (Korea Rep) 2021, *How the Republic of Korea turned the tide on COVID-19 using ICT* Incheon (Korea Rep) 2020, *Seminar on Digital Technologies for Disaster Risk Management* Incheon (Korea Rep) 2020, *Session* Incheon (Korea Rep) 2019. [2021/XJ2652/**E***]

♦ Asian Pacific Weed Science Society (APWSS) 01646
Société pour l'Asie et du Pacifique de malherbologie
Pres Dept of Agriculture, Ministry of Agriculture and Cooperative, 50 Phaholyothin Rd, Bangkok, Thailand.
SG c/o Plot: 1294A, Road: 63A, Jubilee Hills, Hyderabad, Telangana 500033, Hyderabad TELANGANA 500033, India. T. +919492932165.
Editor-in-Chief address not obtained.
URL: http://www.apwss.org.in
History 22 Jun 1967, Honolulu, HI (USA). Founded under the auspices of *East-West Center (EWC, #05263).* **Aims** Promote weed science in the Asian-Pacific area by pooling and exchanging information; foster weed control programmes, including training programmes, best suited to the circumstances of emerging countries. **Structure** Executive Committee. **Languages** English. **Staff** Voluntary. **Finance** Sources: members' dues. **Activities** Events/meetings; knowledge management/information dissemination; training/education. Active in all member countries. **Events** *Biennial Conference* Kuching (Malaysia) 2019, *Biennial Conference* Kyoto (Japan) 2017, *Biennial Conference* Hyderabad (India) 2015, *Biennial Conference / Conference* Bandung (Indonesia) 2013, *Biennial conference / Conference* Cairns, QLD (Australia) 2011. **Publications** *APWSS Newsletter* (2 a year); *WEEDS – Journal of the Asian-Pacific Weed Science Society* (2 a year) – Official journal – online. *Weed management in rice in the Asian-Pacific region. Asian-Pacific Weed Science Society (APWSS)* (2017) by Dr Nimal Chandrasena and Dr NARAYANA RAO (A N Rao) ADUSUMILLI; *Weed management in rice in the Asian-Pacific region.* (2017) by Dr NARAYANA RAO (A N Rao) ADUSUMILLI and Dr Matsumoto Hiroshi in English; *APWSS History Book. Commemorating 50 Years (1967-2017). 50th Anniversary Celebratory Volume.* (2017) by Dr Chandrasena, N. and Dr A.N. Rao – Asian-Pacific Weed Science Society (APWSS); Indian Society of Weed Science (ISWS); The Weed Science Society of Japan (WSSJ). Conference proceedings.
Members National societies. Individuals (over 500), in 28 countries and territories:
Australia, Bangladesh, China, Fiji, Germany, Hong Kong, India, Indonesia, Iran Islamic Rep, Japan, Korea Rep, Laos, Malaysia, Micronesia FS, Nepal, New Zealand, Pakistan, Philippines, Samoa, Singapore, Solomon Is, Sri Lanka, Taiwan, Thailand, UK, USA, Vanuatu, Vietnam. [2022.06.15/XC0086/**C**]

♦ Asian Pacific Women's Information Network Center (internationally oriented national body)

♦ Asian Pacific Youth Forum (APYF) 01647
Forum de la jeunesse d'Asie et du Pacifique – Ajia-Taiheiyo Seinen Rengo
Sec 17-5 Izumi 2-chome, Suginami-ku, Tokyo, 168-0063 Japan. T. +81333225161. Fax +81333247111.
History Jul 1979, Fukuoka (Japan), following a series of regional youth meetings, started in Dec 1976, by *Organization for Industrial, Spiritual and Cultural Advancement International (OISCA International, #17872).* Also referred to as *Asia-Pacific Youth Forum.* **Aims** Promote coordinated action in national development among youth within the context of regional cooperation. **Structure** Permanent body: *Consultative Committee*

of the *Asian Pacific Youth Forum*, which first met in Jan 1980. **Languages** English, Japanese. **Staff** 4.00 FTE, paid. **Activities** Events/meetings; guidance/assistance/consulting. **Events** *Youth Forum* Cambodia 2003, *Youth Forum* Bangkok (Thailand) 2001, *Youth forum* Pakistan 1999, *Youth Forum* Nepal 1996, *Youth Forum* Taipei (Taiwan) 1995.
Members Youth organizations in 21 countries and territories:
Bangladesh, Cambodia, Fiji, Hong Kong, India, Indonesia, Japan, Korea Rep, Laos, Malaysia, Mongolia, Myanmar, Pakistan, Palau, Papua New Guinea, Philippines, Solomon Is, Sri Lanka, Thailand, Timor-Leste, Tonga.
Consultative Status Consultative status granted from: *ECOSOC (#05331)* (Ros A). [2018.07.03/XD8322/**D**]

♦ Asian Packaging Federation (APF) 01648
Fédération asiatique de l'emballage
SG c/o DIP, 86/6 Industrial Design Bldg, Soi Treemitr, Rama IV Rd, Klongtoey, Bangkok, 10110, Thailand. T. +6623811603.
URL: http://www.asianpackaging.org/
History Founded 26 Sep 1966, Tokyo (Japan). Inaugural meeting 7 Jul 1967, Kyoto (Japan), when statutes were adopted; most recently revised Oct 2009. Registered in Japan. **Aims** Enhance cross country cooperation among all packaging-related bodies, covering a gamut of subjects like training and education, package development, environmental aspects, law and regulations. **Structure** General Assembly (annual); Board of Administration (meeting once a year); Secretariat Office located in Thailand. **Languages** English. **Staff** 1.00 FTE, paid. **Finance** Members' dues. AsiaStar Awards entry fees. **Activities** Awards/prizes/competitions; events/meetings; training/education; knowledge management/information dissemination. **Events** *Annual Congress* Dhaka (Bangladesh) 2012, *Annual Congress* Goyang (Korea Rep) 2012, *Annual Congress* Korea Rep 2012, *Annual Congress* Tokyo (Japan) 2010, *Package design global summit* Tokyo (Japan) 2010. **Publications** *Asian Packaging E-Bulletin* (4 a year).
Members Executive; Ordinary; Affiliate; Honorary. Executive – national associations in 15 countries:
Australia, Bangladesh, China, India, Indonesia, Japan, Korea Rep, Malaysia, Pakistan, Philippines, Russia, Singapore, Sri Lanka, Thailand, Vietnam.
NGO Relations Member of: *World Packaging Organisation (WPO, #21705).* Cooperates with: *International Organization for Standardization (ISO, #14473).* [2019/XD0087/**D**]

♦ Asian Paediatric Pulmonology Society (unconfirmed)

♦ Asian Paint Industry Council (APIC) 01649
Contact c/o Japan Paint Manufacturers Assoc, 1F Tokyo Toryo Kaikan, 3-12-8 Ebisu, Shibuya-ku, Tokyo, 150-0013 Japan. Fax +81334433599. E-mail: info@toryo.or.jp.
URL: http://www.apic-paint.asia/
History Founded 1985. **Aims** Serve as a forum for trade associations representing the paint and coatings industry. **Events** *Meeting* Tokyo (Japan) 2016, *Meeting* Manila (Philippines) 2014, *Meeting* Singapore (Singapore) 2013, *Meeting* Pattaya (Thailand) 2012, *Meeting* Suzhou (China) 2010.
Members Organizations in 12 countries and territories:
Australia, Bangladesh, China, India, Japan, Korea Rep, Malaysia, Philippines, Singapore, Taiwan, Thailand, Vietnam.
[2014/XD8417/t/**D**]

♦ Asian Palaeolithic Association (APA) 01650
Pres address not obtained.
History Jul 2008, Russia. **Events** *Annual Meeting* Gongju (Korea Rep) 2014, *Annual Meeting* Tokyo (Japan) 2011, *Annual Meeting* Gongju (Korea Rep) 2010, *Annual Meeting* China 2009, *Annual Meeting* Russia 2008.
Members Full in 4 countries:
China, Japan, Korea Rep, Russia. [2015/XJ5500/**D**]

♦ Asian Pancreas and Islet Transplant Association (unconfirmed)
♦ Asian Pan-Pacific Association of Gastroenterology and Nutrition / see Asian Pan-Pacific Society for Paediatric Gastroenterology, Hepatology, and Nutrition (#01651)

♦ Asian Pan-Pacific Society for Paediatric Gastroenterology, 01651
Hepatology, and Nutrition (APPSPGHAN)
Pres NTUH – Hepatitis, No 1 Changde St, Zhongzheng Dist, Taipei 100, Taiwan.
History Aug 1976, at 2nd Asian Congress of Paediatrics, superseding *Asian Pacific Society for Paediatric Gastroenterology (APSPG, inactive).* Original title: *Asian Pan-Pacific Society for Paediatric Gastroenterology and Nutrition (APPSPGAN).* Also referred to as: *Asian-Pacific Association of Gastroenterology – Association de gastroentérologie de l'Asie et du Pacifique; Asian Pacific Paediatric Gastro-Enterology Group; Asian Pan-Pacific Association of Gastroenterology and Nutrition.* **Aims** Address problems of gastrointestinal, hepatobiliary, pancreatic, and nutritional disorders of children, in the Asia-Pacific Region. **Structure** Officers: President; Secretary; Treasurer; President-elect; Executive councillors. **Languages** English. **Staff** 0.50 FTE, paid. **Finance** Members' dues. Conference registration fee. **Activities** Organizes quadrennial world congress, biennial teaching workshop, biennial society congress. **Events** *Congress* Kota Kinabalu (Malaysia) 2022, *Biennial Meeting* Bangkok (Thailand) 2018, *Biennial Meeting* Manila (Philippines) 2015, *Biennial Meeting* Tokyo (Japan) 2013, *Biennial meeting* Seoul (Korea Rep) 2009. **Publications** *APPSPGAN Newsletter* (2 a year).
Members Societies in 18 countries and territories:
Australia, Bangladesh, Canada, Hong Kong, India, Indonesia, Japan, Korea Rep, Malaysia, New Zealand, Pakistan, Philippines, Singapore, Sri Lanka, Tahiti Is, Taiwan, Thailand, USA.
NGO Relations Member of: *Federation of International Societies for Pediatric Gastroenterology, Hepatology and Nutrition (FISPGHAN, #09678).* [2014/XD3990/**D**]

♦ Asian Pan-Pacific Society for Paediatric Gastroenterology and Nutrition / see Asian Pan-Pacific Society for Paediatric Gastroenterology, Hepatology, and Nutrition (#01651)

♦ Asian Paralympic Committee (APC) 01652
CEO/ PO Box 232111, Dubai, United Arab Emirates. T. +971506767368. E-mail: info@asianparalympic.org.
Street address Dubai Club for People of Determination, near Stadium metro station, behind LULU Hypermarket, Dubai, United Arab Emirates.
URL: https://asianparalympic.org/
History 30 Oct 2002, Busan (Korea Rep). Founded as a regional organization of *International Paralympic Committee (IPC, #14512).* Merged, 2003, with *Far East and South Pacific Games Federation for the Disabled (FESPIC Federation, inactive).* Former names and other names: *East Asia Paralympic Committee* – former (30 Oct 2002); *Asian Paralympic Council (APC)* – former (2003). **Aims** Support the aims and objectives of the International Paralympic Committee in the region. **Structure** General Assembly (every 2 years); Executive Board; Standing Committees; Management Committee; Secretariat. **Languages** Chinese, English, Russian. Translation available during major events to Arabic. **Staff** 9.00 FTE, paid. **Finance** Sources: members' dues. Rights Fees paid by hosting city of APC Games. **Activities** Sporting activities. **Events** *Coordination Commission Meeting* Incheon (Korea Rep) 2014, *Coordination Commission Meeting* Incheon (Korea Rep) 2014.
Members National Paralympic Committees in 44 countries and territories:
Afghanistan, Bahrain, Bangladesh, Bhutan, Cambodia, China, Hong Kong, India, Indonesia, Iran Islamic Rep, Iraq, Japan, Jordan, Kazakhstan, Korea DPR, Korea Rep, Kuwait, Kyrgyzstan, Laos, Lebanon, Macau, Malaysia, Maldives, Mongolia, Myanmar, Nepal, Oman, Pakistan, Palestine, Philippines, Qatar, Saudi Arabia, Singapore, Sri Lanka, Syrian AR, Taiwan, Tajikistan, Thailand, Timor-Leste, Turkmenistan, United Arab Emirates, Uzbekistan, Vietnam, Yemen. [2021/XM8259/**D**]

♦ Asian Paralympic Council / see Asian Paralympic Committee (#01652)
♦ Asian Parasite Control Organization (inactive)
♦ Asian Parliamentarians' Union / see Asian-Pacific Parliamentarians' Union (#01622)

♦ Asian Parliamentary Assembly (APA) 01653
Secretariat No 4 Golha Alley, Mojahedin Eslam St, Teheran, 1154947411, Iran Islamic Rep. T. +982126118827 – +982126118829. Fax +982126118809. E-mail: secretariat@asianparliament.org.
URL: http://www.asianparliament.org/

History Sep 1999, Dhaka (Bangladesh). Charter adopted 14 Nov 2006. Former names and other names: *Association of Asian Parliaments for Peace (AAPP)* – former (1999 to 2006). **Aims** Promote freedom, social justice, peace, security and friendship; share access to up-to-date knowledge in various areas and promote such knowledge among members so as to promote the progress and equality of its members; exploit cooperatively vast human and natural resources and secure the interests of all members and recognize their permanent authority on their natural resources; provide welfare facilities for the health and nutrition of members' populations; contribute to integration among Asian nations so as to utilize the potential of the region. **Structure** Plenary; Executive Council; Bureau of the Assembly; Committees; Secretariat. **Languages** Arabic, English. **Staff** 10.50 FTE, paid. **Finance** Financed by Islamic Parliament of Iran Islamic Rep. **Activities** Networking/liaising; events/meetings. **Events** *Meeting of the APA Standing Committee on Social & Cultural Affairs* Bangkok (Thailand) 2019, *Plenary Session* Siem Reap (Cambodia) 2016, *Plenary Meeting* Lahore (Pakistan) 2014, *Plenary Meeting* Islamabad (Pakistan) 2013, *Meeting* Seoul (Korea Rep) 2011.
Members Parliaments in 42 countries and territories:
Afghanistan, Azerbaijan, Bahrain, Bangladesh, Bhutan, Cambodia, China, Cyprus, India, Indonesia, Iran Islamic Rep, Iraq, Jordan, Kazakhstan, Kiribati, Korea DPR, Korea Rep, Kuwait, Kyrgyzstan, Laos, Lebanon, Malaysia, Maldives, Mongolia, Nepal, Pakistan, Palau, Palestine, Philippines, Russia, Saudi Arabia, Singapore, Sri Lanka, Syrian AR, Tajikistan, Thailand, Tonga, Türkiye, United Arab Emirates, Uzbekistan, Vietnam, Yemen.
Observers in 16 countries:
Australia, Fiji, Japan, Kazakhstan, Marshall Is, Micronesia FS, Nauru, New Zealand, Oman, Papua New Guinea, Samoa, Solomon Is, Timor-Leste, Turkmenistan, Tuvalu, Vanuatu. [2021/XD8778/**D**]

♦ Asian Partnership for the Development of Human Resources in 01654
Rural Asia (AsiaDHRRA)
Secretariat Room 201, Partnership Center, 59 C Salvador St, Loyala Heights, 1108 Quezon City, Philippines. T. +6324364706 – +6324266739. Fax +6324266739. E-mail: asiadhrra@asiadhrra.org.
URL: http://www.asiadhrra.org/
History Feb 1994, Tagaytay (Philippines). Derives from *Socio-Economic Life in Asia (SELA)*, an informal group set up at 'Development of the Human Resources in Asia Workshop (DHRRAW)', 1974, Swanganivas (Thailand); *Centre for the Development of Human Resources in Rural Asia (CENDHRRA, inactive)* was set up at the same time as support structure to DHRRAW and commenced operations 29 Apr 1975, Manila (Philippines). Secretariat located in Jakarta (Indonesia) from Apr 1994 to Jun 1998, when relocated to current address in the Philippines. Registration: EU Transparency Register, No/ID: 963001335226-19. **Aims** Promote partnerships among DHRRAs – *social development* networks and organizations involved in 'Development of Human Resources in Rural Areas'; develop concepts of self-directed rural development and *self-management* among *small farmers, fishing* populations and rural communities; secure information and resource exchange; strengthen local and regional capabilities; ensure resource accessing and network programmes. **Structure** General Assembly (every 2 years). Standing Board, consisting of Chairperson, Vice (Sub Regional for South East Asia), Vice (Sub Regional for Indo China), Vice (Sub Regional for North Asia), Executive Director and 3 Advisors. Executive Committee, comprising Chairperson and 3 Vice Chairpersons (2 for South Asia and 1 for North Asia) and ex-officio member. *Asian Secretariat for the Development of Human Resources in Rural Areas.* **Staff** 6.00 FTE, paid. **Finance** DHRRA family contributions; contributions from *German Catholic Bishops' Organisation for Development Cooperation (MISEREOR).* Budget (annual): US$ 300,000. **Activities** Programmes respond to specific and regional needs of DHRRA family and partner-communities: *'Institutional Services'* focus on internal programmes for institutional development of DHRRAs – NGDO management development; NGO sustainable development; research and publication. *'Networking'* is directed at promotion and development of the people's economy/movement – economic and technical cooperation, research and documentation, exposure/dialogue programme – and at Asian NGO representation and advocacy, people's employment and development of rural areas, North-South partnership/dialogue/conference, research and publication. **Events** *General Assembly* Santa Cruz (Philippines) 1998, *Biennial conference* Suwon (Korea Rep) 1998, *Workshop on economic initiatives for Asian farmers* Taipei (Taiwan) 1997. **Publications** *AsiaDHRRA Newsletter* (4 a year).
Members Social development networks and organizations (11) in 10 countries and territories:
Cambodia, Indonesia, Japan, Korea Rep, Malaysia, Nepal, Philippines (2), Taiwan, Thailand, Vietnam.
Consultative Status Consultative status granted from: *ASEAN (#01141).* **NGO Relations** Member of (3): *Asia Caucus (no recent information); Conference of Non-Governmental Organizations in Consultative Relationship with the United Nations (CONGO, #04635); South East Asian Committee for Advocacy (SEACA, #19761).* Involved in: *Solidarity for ASEAN People's Advocacy (SAPA, #19683).* [2002.01.28/XK1389/**E**]

♦ Asian Patent Attorneys Association (APAA) 01655
Association asiatique d'experts juridiques en brevets
SG c/o Asamura Patent Office – Tennoz Central Tower 2-2-24, Higashi-Shinagawa, Shinagawa-Ku, Tokyo, 140-0002 Japan. T. +81357158651. Fax +81354606310. E-mail: tokuda@asamura.jp.
URL: http://www.apaaonline.org/
History 26 Dec 1969, Tokyo (Japan). Most recent regulations adopted: 15 Oct 1988; amended: 29 Oct 1994, Niigata (Japan); 14 Nov 2000, Cebu City (Philippines); 21 Oct 2003, Kota Kinabalu (Malaysia); 8 Nov 2006, Kaohsiung (Taiwan); 22 Nov 2009, Hong Kong (Hong Kong). **Aims** Foster ties of mutual friendship and understanding among those practising the profession of patent attorney in Asia; improve and coordinate international and national laws and regulations concerning industrial property and promote protection of industrial property. **Structure** General Assembly (every 3 years); Council. **Languages** English. **Finance** Members' dues: Individual – Yen 11,000; Organization – Yen 33,000. **Activities** Knowledge management/information dissemination; events/meetings. **Events** *Council Meeting* Busan (Korea Rep) 2022, *Council Meeting* Gold Coast, QLD (Australia) 2021, *Council Meeting* Gold Coast, QLD (Australia) 2021, *Triennial General Assembly* Gold Coast, QLD (Australia) 2021, *Council Meeting* Taipei (Taiwan) 2019. **Publications** *APAA News* (annual); *Minutes of General Assemblies and Council Meetings* (annual); *APAA Roster* (every 3 years).
Members Recognized groups (18) and individuals (2,265) in 24 countries and territories:
Australia, Bangladesh, Bhutan, Brunei Darussalam, Cambodia, Hong Kong, India, Indonesia, Japan, Korea Rep, Laos, Macau, Malaysia, Mongolia, Myanmar, Nepal, New Zealand, Pakistan, Philippines, Singapore, Sri Lanka, Taiwan, Thailand, Vietnam.
Consultative Status Consultative status granted from: *World Intellectual Property Organization (WIPO, #21593)* (Permanent Observer Status). [2015/XD4599/**D**]

♦ Asian Pavement Engineering Society (APES) 01656
Sec address not obtained. E-mail: secretary@asian-pes.org.
URL: https://asian-pes.org/
History Initiated 2017. Officially registered in Singapore, May 2019. **Aims** Promote the exchange of ideas, information and cooperation among pavement professionals in the Asia Pacific region. **Structure** Council. **Activities** Events/meetings. **NGO Relations** *International Committee on Pavement Technology (ICPT, #12794).* [2019/XM8865/**D**]

♦ Asian Peace and History Education Association (internationally oriented national body)
♦ Asian Peace and History Institute / see Asian Peace and History Education Association

♦ Asian Peace and Reconciliation Council (APRC) 01657
SG Eastern Asia Univ, 200 Rangsit-Nakorn Nayok Roak (Klong 5), Rangsit, Tanyaburi, Pathum Thani, 12110, Thailand. T. +6625771188. Fax +6625771188. E-mail: info@aprcasia.com.
URL: http://aprcasia.com/
History Feb 2012, Bangkok (Thailand). **Aims** Create a network of experienced individuals from within and outside of Asia, whose expertise and contacts can help in promoting peace and reconciliation in the region. **Structure** Council; Secretariat.
Members Individuals in 19 countries:
Austria, Bhutan, Chile, China, Finland, India, Indonesia, Italy, Japan, Kazakhstan, Korea Rep, Malaysia, Pakistan, Philippines, Poland, Singapore, Thailand, Timor-Leste, USA.
NGO Relations Member of (1): *Silk Road Think Tank Network (SiLKS, #19280).* [2017/AA1153/v/**C**]

♦ Asian Peace Research Association / see Asia Pacific Peace Research Association (#01991)

♦ Asian Peasant Coalition (APC) 01658
Office 217-B Alley 1, Road 7, Project 6, 1100 Quezon City, Philippines. T. +6324565727. Fax +6324565727. E-mail: apcrisingonline@gmail.com.

Facebook: https://www.facebook.com/asianpeasantcoalition/
History Set up following conference organized Mar 2003, Philippines. **Aims** Strengthen and further consolidate peasant movements throughout Asia. **Structure** General Assembly; Coordinating Council; Executive Committee; Secretariat, headed by Secretary General. **Events** *General Assembly* Sri Lanka 2011, *General Assembly* Indonesia 2006, *General Assembly* Bangladesh 2004.
Members Organizations (33) in 9 countries:
Bangladesh, India, Indonesia, Malaysia, Mongolia, Nepal, Pakistan, Philippines, Sri Lanka.
NGO Relations *International League of Peoples' Struggle (ILPS, #14021).* [2020/XM4748/**D**]

♦ Asian Pediatric Interventional Pulmonology Association (unconfirmed)

♦ Asian Pediatric Nephrology Association (AsPNA) 01659

Main Office Unit of Hope Bldg, Sarjapur Road, John Nagar, Koramangala, Bangalore, Karnataka 560034, Bangalore KARNATAKA 560034, India. T. +918022065455. E-mail: contact@aspna-online.org.
URL: http://www.aspna-online.org/
History 1989. Former names and other names: *Asian Society of Pediatric Nephrology* – former. **Aims** Promote the science and art of Pediatric Nephrology in Asia; maintain the highest level of professional skills and ethics in the practice of the subspecialty; foster regional camaraderie and cooperation among member nations; represent AsPNA in IPNA and other international/regional nephrology endeavours. **Structure** Executive Council. **Events** *Congress* Taipei (Taiwan) 2021, *Congress* Taipei (Taiwan) 2020, *Congress* Kuala Lumpur (Malaysia) 2017, *Congress* Delhi (India) 2014, *Congress* Fukuoka (Japan) 2011. **Publications** *AsPNA Chronicle.* [2021/XD7005/**D**]

♦ Asian Pencak Silat Federation (APSIF) 01660

Head Office No 7 Bedok North Street 2, Suite 02-01, Singapore 469646, Singapore. T. +6567418837. E-mail: asianpencaksilat@yahoo.com.sg.
URL: http://apsif.com/
History Officially founded Mar 2009, Singapore. Launched 16 Apr 2011. **Aims** Educate and provide Silat playing opportunities to individuals of all cultures and religions to enhance their *sporting* experience. **Structure** Committee. **Activities** Sporting activities.
Members Full in 27 countries and territories:
Afghanistan, Bangladesh, Brunei Darussalam, Cambodia, India, Indonesia, Iran Islamic Rep, Japan, Kazakhstan, Korea Rep, Kyrgyzstan, Laos, Malaysia, Myanmar, Nepal, Pakistan, Philippines, Saudi Arabia, Singapore, Sri Lanka, Tajikistan, Thailand, Timor-Leste, Turkmenistan, Uzbekistan, Vietnam, Yemen.
NGO Relations Member of (2): *General Association of Asia Pacific Sports Federations (GAAPSF, #10106); International Council of Traditional Sports and Games (ICTSG, #13088).* [XM8621/**D**]

♦ Asian Pentecostal Society (APS) 01661

Vice Chair AG-Malaysia, PO Box 499, Jalan Sultan, 46760 Petaling Jaya, Selangor, Malaysia. E-mail: limyc1@gmail.com.
History 21 Sep 1998, during the 18th *Pentecostal World Fellowship (#18295).* **Events** *Spiritual warfare – revisited* Kuala Lumpur (Malaysia) 2009, *Meeting* Surabaya (Indonesia) 2007, *Meeting* Petaling Jaya (Malaysia) 2006, *Meeting* Baguio (Philippines) 2005, *Meeting* Johannesburg (South Africa) 2004. [2010/XD7895/**D**]

♦ Asian Peoples' Anti-Communist League / see Asian-Pacific League for Freedom and Democracy (#01617)

♦ Asian People's Disability Alliance (internationally oriented national body)

♦ Asian periOpeRative Nurses Association (ASIORNA) 01662

Pres address not obtained.
URL: http://www.asiorna.org/
Aims Improve Asian peri-operative standards. **Structure** Board. **Events** *Conference* Beijing (China) 2022, *Conference* Adelaide, SA (Australia) 2018, *Conference* Hong Kong (Hong Kong) 2016.
Members Full in 9 countries and territories:
Australia, China, Hong Kong, Japan, Korea Rep, Malaysia, New Zealand, Singapore, Thailand. [2016/XM5612/**D**]

♦ Asian Philosophical Association (unconfirmed)

♦ Asian Photovoltaic Industry Association (APVIA) 01663

Secretariat 146 Robinson Road, Suite 07-01, Singapore 068909, Singapore. T. +6531563688. E-mail: office@apvia.org.
Office – Shanghai Room 905-907, No 425 Yishan Road, 200235 Shanghai, China. T. +862133683167.
URL: http://www.apvia.org/
History 16 Jan 2009, Singapore (Singapore). Founded 16 Jan 2009; formally launched 1 Nov 2011, Singapore (Singapore). **Aims** Develop the Asian photovoltaic (PV) industry. **Structure** Board of Directors; Steering Committee; Executive Committee. **Events** *Global Green Energy Associations Meeting* Shanghai (China) 2019, *Global Solar Associations Meeting* Shanghai (China) 2018, *International Photovoltaic Power Generation Conference* Shanghai (China) 2018, *International Photovoltaic Power Generation Conference* Shanghai (China) 2017, *International Photovoltaic Power Generation Conference* Shanghai (China) 2016. **NGO Relations** Member of: *Global Solar Council (GSC, #10609).* [2020/XJ5393/t/**D**]

♦ Asian Physics Education Network (ASPEN) 01664

Réseau asien d'enseignement de la physique

Exec Sec 6th Fl Rm 609 Mahamakut Bldg, Phyathai Rd, Patumwan, Bangkok, 10330, Thailand.
Contact UNESCO/ROSTSEA, Jl M H Thamrin 14, PO Box 1273/JKT, Jakarta 10002, Indonesia. T. +62213141308. Fax +62213150382.
History 1981, Khon Kaen (Thailand). Founded as a regional cooperative programme supported by *UNESCO (#20322).* Regional network of *UNESCO Office, Jakarta – Regional Bureau for Sciences in Asia and the Pacific (#20313).* **Aims** Contribute towards the overall development of *university* physics education in the Asian region; establish a programme of cooperation amongst members in physics education and related areas; establish effective channels of communication; disseminate information. **Structure** General Assembly/Conference (every 5 years). Executive Board, consisting of Chairman, Vice-Chairman, Executive Secretary and 3 members. National Points of Contact (NPCs). **Finance** Sources: members' dues. Supported by: *UNESCO (#20322).* **Activities** Events/meetings; training/education. **Events** *World Conference on Physics Education* Hanoi (Vietnam) 2021, *World Conference on Physics Education* Hanoi (Vietnam) 2020, *World Conference on Physics Education* Sao Paulo (Brazil) 2016, *World Conference on Physics Education* Istanbul (Turkey) 2012, *General Assembly* Shah Alam (Malaysia) 1997. **Publications** Country reports.
Members Participating countries (18):
Afghanistan, Australia, Bangladesh, Bhutan, China, India, Indonesia, Iran Islamic Rep, Korea Rep, Malaysia, New Zealand, Pakistan, Papua New Guinea, Philippines, Russia, Sri Lanka, Thailand, Vietnam. [2013/XF2101/**F***]

♦ Asian Pickleball Federation (APF) 01665

Head Office Shop No.65 (Royals Plaza) Khatipura, Khatipura Road, Chand Bihari Nagar, Khatipura,, Jaipur, Rajasthan 302012, Jaipur RAJASTHAN 302012, India. T. +919829242145. E-mail: apfdirector1@gmail.com.
Office Grassroot Sports Academy & Hotels, Malukawala Vikas Nagar, Dehradun, Uttarakhand 248198, Dehradun UTTARAKHAND 248198, India.
URL: http://www.asianpickleball.org/
History 2018. **Aims** Stimulate the development and growth of the sport throughout Asia.
Members Federations in 9 countries and territories:
Bangladesh, Basque Country, India, Indonesia, Iran Islamic Rep, Nepal, Pakistan, Sri Lanka, Tanzania UR.
NGO Relations Member of (1): *General Association of Asia Pacific Sports Federations (GAAPSF, #10106).* [2020/AA1112/**D**]

♦ Asian Pig Veterinary Society (APVS) 01666

Congress Secretariat 42 Castello St Casa Milan, North Fairview, 1121 Quezon City, Philippines. T. +639175200627. E-mail: zmlapus@yahoo.com.
URL: http://www.apvs2019.com/
History 2001. **Aims** Give people concerned with the pig farming industry in the Asian region opportunities to meet, present research works and exchange information. **Structure** Executive Committee. **Events** *Congress* Seoul (Korea Rep) 2019, *Congress* Wuhan (China) 2017, *Congress* Manila (Philippines) 2015, *Congress* Ho Chi Minh City (Vietnam) 2013, *Congress* Pattaya (Thailand) 2011. [2018/XM1093/**E**]

♦ Asian Planning Schools Association (APSA) 01667

SG c/o Dep Urban Planning and Design, Univ of, Pofulam Road, Hong Kong, Central and Western, Hong Kong. T. +85228592721. Fax +85225590468. E-mail: hdxugoy@hkucc.hku.hk.
URL: http://www.apsaweb.org/
History Aug 1993, Hong Kong, at 2nd International Congress of Asian Planning Schools. **Aims** Provide opportunities for scholars and planners to discuss issues related to planning, exchange opinions and understand problems of planning in Asian countries and foster new generations of academics and professional planners in Asia. **Structure** Officers: President; Vice-President; Secretary General; Executive Committee members. **Languages** English. **Staff** Mainly voluntary. **Finance** Members' dues. **Events** *Congress* Bali (Indonesia) 2022, *Congress* Bali (Indonesia) 2021, *Congress* Seoul (Korea Rep) 2019, *Congress* Beijing (China) 2017, *Congress* Kuala Lumpur (Malaysia) 2015. **Publications** *APSA Monographs.*
Members Full; Associate; Corresponding; Individual. Planning schools (19) in 15 countries and territories:
Bangladesh, China, Hong Kong, India, Indonesia, Japan, Korea Rep, Malaysia, Pakistan, Philippines, Singapore, Sri Lanka, Taiwan, Thailand, Vietnam.
NGO Relations Member of: *Global Planning Education Association Network (GPEAN, #10549).* [2013/XD4304/**D**]

♦ Asian Pocket Billiards Union (APBU) 01668

Contact 29 Alley 1, Lane 524, Sec 5, Chung-Hsiao East Road, Taipei, Taiwan. T. +886227281993. Fax +886227261130. E-mail: apbu@ms68.hinet.net.
URL: http://www.apbucuesports.org/
History Aug 1989, Taipei (Taiwan). Most recent statutes adopted Jun 1999, Taipei. **Aims** Promote and develop pool billiard games under the influence of the WPA. **Structure** General Meeting (annual, during Asian 9-Ball Pool Championship); Board. **Languages** Chinese, English. **Activities** Events/meetings.
Members Full; Founding () members in 24 countries and territories:
Bahrain, Bangladesh, Brunei Darussalam, China, Hong Kong (*), India, Indonesia (*), Iran Islamic Rep, Iraq, Japan (*), Korea Rep (*), Kuwait, Lebanon, Macau, Malaysia, Maldives, Pakistan, Philippines (*), Qatar, Singapore, Sri Lanka (*), Thailand, United Arab Emirates, Vietnam.
NGO Relations Member of: *World Pool-Billiard Association (WPA, #21733)*, through which links with *World Confederation of Billiards Sports (WCBS, #21291).* [2015.01.05/XD4620/**D**]

♦ Asian Political and International Studies Association (APISA) 01669

Exec Sec Fac of Social Sciences, Naresuan Univ, 99 Tha Pho Sub-District, Phitsanulok, 65000, Thailand. T. +6655961999. Fax +6655961900. E-mail: secretariat@apisa.org.
URL: http://www.apisa.org/
History Founded Nov 2001, Kuala Lumpur (Malaysia). Founding congress, 2003, Singapore (Singapore). **Aims** Serve as an academic community for scholars working on Asia as a focus of study. **Structure** Congress; Executive Committee (ExCo); Secretariat based at Naresuan University (Thailand) since 2018. **Languages** English. **Staff** 5.00 FTE, paid. **Finance** Members'dues. **Activities** Events/meetings; awards/prizes/competitions; capacity building. **Events** *Congress* Seoul (Korea Rep) 2021, *Congress* Seoul (Korea Rep) 2020, *Congress* Bangkok (Thailand) 2019, *Congress* Bandung (Indonesia) 2018, *Congress* Phitsanulok (Thailand) 2017. **Publications** *Asian Journal of Peace-building; Asia Pacific Social Science Review; International Studies Review; Philippine Political Science Journal. Asian Public Policy; Development Cooperation and Non-traditional Security in the Asia-Pacific* – series; *Security, Development, and Human Rights in East Asia* – series; *Studies in the Political Economy of Public Policy* – series. **Members** Full (150) in 20 countries. Membership countries not specified. [2019.10.08/XD9281/**D**]

♦ Asian Population Association (APA) 01670

Exec Sec Mahidol Univ, Inst for Population and Social Research, Salaya, Phutthamonthon, Nakhon Pathom, 73170, Thailand.
SG Population Council, Zone 5A Ground Floor, India Habitat Centre, Lodi Road, Delhi 10003, DELHI 10003, India.
URL: http://www.asianpa.org/
History 2007. **Aims** Draw the attention of governments, IGOs, NGOs and the general public to population issues in Asia; promote *demography* as a science. **Structure** Council. **Languages** English. **Staff** 4.00 FTE, paid. **Activities** Knowledge management/information dissemination; awareness raising; capacity building; events/meetings; training/education; networking/liaising; publishing activities. **Events** *Conference* Nakhon Pathom (Thailand) 2021, *Conference* Yogyakarta (Indonesia) 2020, *Conference* Shanghai (China) 2018, *Conference* Kuala Lumpur (Malaysia) 2015, *Conference* Bangkok (Thailand) 2012. **Publications** *APA Newsletter* (1-2 a year).
Members Individuals in 59 countries and territories:
Afghanistan, Algeria, Australia, Austria, Bangladesh, Benin, Bhutan, Brazil, Brunei Darussalam, Burkina Faso, Cambodia, Cameroon, Canada, China, Costa Rica, Côte d'Ivoire, Czechia, Finland, France, Georgia, Germany, Ghana, Hong Kong, India, Indonesia, Iran Islamic Rep, Iraq, Italy, Japan, Korea Rep, Kuwait, Lebanon, Malaysia, Mexico, Mongolia, Morocco, Nepal, Netherlands, New Zealand, Nigeria, Pakistan, Paraguay, Philippines, Poland, Russia, Saudi Arabia, Singapore, South Africa, Spain, Sri Lanka, Switzerland, Taiwan, Thailand, Tunisia, Türkiye, UK, United Arab Emirates, USA, Vietnam.
NGO Relations Links with *International Union for the Scientific Study of Population (IUSSP, #15814).* [2020/XJ6117/**D**]

♦ Asian Population and Development Association (internationally oriented national body)

♦ Asian Powerlifting Federation (APF) 01671

Gen Sec Apt 86, M Road, Bistupur Jamshedpur, Bihar, 831 001, Bihar 831 001, India. T. +91657425531 – +91657425383. Fax +9165723346691.
URL: http://www.powerlifting.jp/asia/
History 1984, Indonesia, during 1st Asian Powerlifting Championships. A regional federation of *International Powerlifting Federation (IPF, #14630).* **Aims** Develop friendship, cooperation and understanding among national powerlifting associations in Asia; promote powerlifting competitions in the area. **Structure** Congress (annual). Board, comprising President, 5 Vice-Presidents, General Secretary/Treasurer, Assistant General Secretary and 4 further members. Committees (3): Medical; Statistical; Technical. **Languages** English. **Finance** Subscriptions. **Activities** Organizes championships. **Events** *Congress* Zarafshan (Uzbekistan) 2004. **Publications** *APF Newsletter.*
Members National organizations (14) in 14 countries and territories:
Hong Kong, India, Indonesia, Iran Islamic Rep, Japan, Kazakhstan, Korea Rep, Mongolia, Pakistan, Philippines, Sri Lanka, Taiwan, Turkmenistan, Uzbekistan.
Provisional members in 6 countries:
Iraq, Kyrgyzstan, Malaysia, Nepal, Tajikistan, United Arab Emirates. [2011/XJ4255/**D**]

♦ Asian Privacy Scholars Network (APSN) 01672

Sec address not obtained.
Exec Officer address not obtained.
URL: https://asianprivacy.org/
History 2010. Created following collaborative links between scholars in the Asian Pacific Region built with the help of UNSW Law Faculty Cyberspace Law and Policy Community's Asia-Pacific Privacy Charter and Interpreting Privacy Principles projects. **Aims** Further the study of personal data protection, privacy, and surveillance in countries of the Asia-Pacific region. **Structure** Secretrariat **Languages** English. **Activities** Events/meetings; networking/liaising. **Events** *Conference* Singapore (Singapore) 2019.
Members Individuals in 23 countries and territories:
Australia, Belgium, Canada, China, Germany, Hong Kong, India, Indonesia, Israel, Japan, Korea Rep, Malaysia, Netherlands, New Zealand, Norway, Philippines, Singapore, South Africa, Taiwan, Thailand, Türkiye, UK, USA. [2023.02.14/AA0206/v/**F**]

♦ Asian Producers' Platform (APP) 01673

Contact address not obtained. E-mail: asiaproducerscamp@gmail.com.
URL: http://www.asianproducersplatform.com/
History 2014. Set up as a long-term public-private partnership. **Aims** Create a strongly linked network of Asian *performing arts* producers who can work effectively across the region, sharing and developing artistic works, professional skills and cultural practices. **Languages** English. **Activities** Events/meetings.
Members Individuals (94) in 10 countries and territories:
Australia, Hong Kong, Indonesia, Japan, Korea Rep, Macau, Malaysia, New Zealand, Singapore, Taiwan. [2019.02.14/XM4605/**F**]

♦ Asian Productivity Organization (APO) 01674

SG UNIZO Hongo 1-Chome Bldg 2F, 1-24-1 Hongo, Bunkyo-ku, Tokyo, 113-0033 Japan. T. +81338300411. Fax +81358405322. E-mail: apo@apo-tokyo.org.
URL: https://www.apo-tokyo.org/

History 11 May 1961. Established 1961, by a Convention, following the First Asian Round Table Productivity Conference, Mar 1959, Tokyo (Japan). **Aims** Contribute to socio-economic development of member countries through productivity enhancement in the spirit of mutual cooperation among members. **Structure** Governing Body; Workshop Meeting of Heads of NPOs (annual); Secretariat. **Languages** English. **Staff** 47.00 FTE, paid. **Finance** Sources: grants; members' dues; revenue from activities/projects. Annual budget: 15,000,000 USD. **Activities** Events/meetings; knowledge management/information dissemination; networking/liaising; research and development. **Events** *Conference on Agrifood Evolution* Tokyo (Japan) 2022, *Workshop on Inclusive Rural Development* Tokyo (Japan) 2022, *Workshop on Service Quality and Productivity Gainsharing* Tokyo (Japan) 2022, *Workshop on the Internet of Things in Agriculture and Food Supply Chain Management* Tokyo (Japan) 2022, *Seminar on Strengthening the Programs of the Center of Excellence on Business Excellence* Singapore (Singapore) 2019. **Publications** *APO News* (12 a year) in English. *APO Productivity Databook*. Annual Report; technical publications; conference proceedings; reports.

Members Open to all Asian and Pacific governments which are members of ESCAP. Governments outside the region may become Associate members. Governments, signatory to the Convention, of 21 countries and territories:
Bangladesh, Cambodia, Fiji, Hong Kong, India, Indonesia, Iran Islamic Rep, Japan, Korea Rep, Laos, Malaysia, Mongolia, Nepal, Pakistan, Philippines, Singapore, Sri Lanka, Taiwan, Thailand, Türkiye, Vietnam.

IGO Relations *African-Asian Rural Development Organization (AARDO, #00203); Centre on Integrated Rural Development for Asia and the Pacific (CIRDAP, #03750); ILO (#11123); OECD (#17693); Southeast Asian Regional Center for Graduate Study and Research in Agriculture (SEARCA, #19781); UNIDO (#20336); United Nations Economic and Social Commission for Asia and the Pacific (ESCAP, #20557).* **NGO Relations** *Regional Institute of Environmental Technology (RIET, no recent information).* [2020.08.27/XD0090/**D***]

♦ Asian Professional Counselling Association / see Asian Professional Counselling and Psychology Association
♦ Asian Professional Counselling and Psychology Association (internationally oriented national body)

♦ Asian Professional Security Association (APSA) 01675

Contact c/o Asian Professional Security Ass, No 5, Jalan Sejat 8/10, Section 8, 40000 Shah Alam, Petaling Jaya, Selangor, Malaysia. T. +60355100944. Fax +60355100945. E-mail: info@apsa-malaysia.com.my.
URL: http://www.apsa-malaysia.com.my/

History Mar 1994, Bangkok (Thailand). **Events** *Annual Conference* Bangkok (Thailand) 2018, *Annual General Meeting* Singapore (Singapore) 2013, *Singapore Seminar on Productivity Gains through Security Innovations* Singapore (Singapore) 2013, *Annual Conference* Kuala Lumpur (Malaysia) 2012, *Global Terrorism and Threat to South and Southeast Asia Meeting* Singapore (Singapore) 2012. [2020/XD8874/t/**D**]

♦ Asian Programme of Educational Innovation for Development / see Asia-Pacific Programme of Educational Innovation for Development (#02001)

♦ Asian Psychological Association (APsyA) 01676

SG address not obtained. T. +628164296384. E-mail: secgen@apsya.org.
URL: http://www.apsya.org/

History 16 Aug 2005, Jakarta (Indonesia). **Aims** Advance psychology and the application of its scientific findings throughout Asia. **Structure** Board of Directors. **Finance** Members' dues. **Activities** Events/meetings. **Events** *Biennial Conference* 2019, *Biennial Conference* Malang (Indonesia) 2017, *Biennial Conference* Jakarta (Indonesia) 2012, *Biennial Conference* Darwin, NT (Australia) 2010, *Biennial Conference* Kuala Lumpur (Malaysia) 2008. **Publications** *Asian Psychology Journal.* **NGO Relations** *European Federation of Psychologists Associations (EFPA, #07199); Inter-American Society of Psychology (ISP, #11450).* [2017/XM1840/**D**]

♦ Asian Public Real Estate Association / see Asia Pacific Real Assets Association (#02006)
♦ Asian Quantum Information Science Conference (meeting series)
♦ Asian Rabies Control Network (unconfirmed)
♦ Asian Racing Conference / see Asian Racing Federation (#01677)

♦ Asian Racing Federation 01677

SG c/o Hong Kong Jockey Club, One Sports Road, Happy Valley, Hong Kong, Central and Western, Hong Kong. T. +85229660345. Fax +85229661098. E-mail: arf@hkjc.org.hk.
URL: http://www.asianracing.org/

History 1960, as *Asian Racing Conference*. Also referred to as *Asian Horse Racing Conference*. **Aims** Meet and foster goodwill and mutual understanding in member countries; promote *horseracing* and breeding; develop mutually beneficial objectives and strategies between racing organizations; exchange ideas and information; encourage, promote and support international competition for jockeys and horses. **Structure** Executive Council (meets three times a year); Central Secretariat. **Finance** Members' dues. **Activities** Sporting activities; monitoring/evaluation; events/meetings. **Events** *Conference* Seoul (Korea Rep) 2018, *Conference* Mumbai (India) 2016, *Conference* Hong Kong (Hong Kong) 2014, *Conference* Turkey 2012, *Conference* Sydney, NSW (Australia) 2010.

Members Full in 20 countries and territories:
Australia, Bahrain, Hong Kong, India, Japan, Korea Rep, Macau, Malaysia, Mauritius, New Zealand, Oman, Pakistan, Philippines, Qatar, Saudi Arabia, Singapore, South Africa, Thailand, Türkiye, United Arab Emirates.
Associate in 1 country:
Mongolia.
Affiliate in 2 countries:
Indonesia, Turkmenistan.

NGO Relations Member of: *International Federation of Horseracing Authorities (IFHA, #13449).* [2017.06.29/XF6541/c/**F**]

♦ Asian Railway Operators Association (AROA) 01678

Contact TDH Exhibitions, PO Box 139, Cranleigh, GU6 7WD, UK. T. +441483548290. Fax +441483548302.
URL: http://www.tdhrail.co.uk/aroa/

Aims Provide a forum for exchange of ideas and information; promote awareness of new technologies; highlight, address and respond to challenges facing rail-bound *transportation* in the *Asia Pacific* region. **Activities** Organizes Rail Solutions Asia (during Annual Congress). **Events** *Annual Congress* Kuala Lumpur (Malaysia) 2014, *Annual Congress* Kuala Lumpur (Malaysia) 2011, *Annual Congress* Taipei (Taiwan) 2010, *Annual Congress* Bangkok (Thailand) 2009, *Annual Congress* Kuala Lumpur (Malaysia) 2008. **Publications** *rdhrail* (4 a year) – official journal.

Members Full in 9 countries and territories:
China, Hong Kong, Korea Rep, Malaysia, Philippines, Singapore, Taiwan, Thailand, Vietnam. [2014/XJ0629/**D**]

♦ Asian Raptor Research and Conservation Network (ARRCN) 01679

Secretariat 1-6-7 Yukihata, Yasu SHIGA, 520 2341 Japan. E-mail: arrc-n@mwa.biglobe.ne.jp.
URL: http://www5b.biglobe.ne.jp/~raptor/

History Dec 1998, Shiga (Japan), during 1st Symposium of Asian Raptor Research and Conservation. **Aims** Promote research and conservation of raptors in Asia. **Finance** Members' dues. **Events** *Symposium* Kuching (Malaysia) 2021, *Symposium* Bali (Indonesia) 2019, *Symposium* Davao (Philippines) 2017, *Symposium* Chumphon (Thailand) 2015, *Symposium* Pune (India) 2014.

Members in 20 countries and territories:
China, Estonia, Germany, India, Indonesia, Iran Islamic Rep, Japan, Kazakhstan, Malaysia, Mongolia, Netherlands, Norway, Philippines, Russia, Saudi Arabia, Singapore, Taiwan, UK, USA, Vietnam. [2020/XM0776/**F**]

♦ Asian Real Estate Society (AsRES) 01680

Secretariat 51 Monroe St, Ste 1100, Rockville MD 20850, USA. E-mail: secretary@asres.org.
URL: http://www.asres.org

History 1996. **Aims** Produce and disseminate real estate related knowledge throughout Asia. **Events** *Annual Conference* Tokyo (Japan) 2022, *Joint Real Eastate Conference* Singapore (Singapore) 2021, *Annual Conference* Shenzhen (China) 2019, *Annual Conference* Incheon (Korea Rep) 2018, *Annual Conference* Taichung (Taiwan) 2017. **Publications** *International Real Estate Review.* **NGO Relations** Member of: *International Real Estate Society (IRES, #14702).* [2021/XD7369/**D**]

♦ **Asian Re** Asian Reinsurance Corporation (#01685)
♦ Asian Recycling Association (inactive)

♦ Asian Regional Association for Career Development (ARACD) 01681

Secretariat Fac of Sociology, Sapporo Otani Univ, 1-1 East 9, North 16, Higashi-ku, Sapporo HOKKAIDO, 065-8567 Japan. T. +81117421965. E-mail: office@aracd.asia.
URL: http://www.aracd.asia/

History 12 Nov 1970, Taipei (Taiwan), as *Asian Regional Association for Vocational and Educational Guidance (ARAVEG).* Current title adopted, Nov 1997, Taipei. **Aims** Strengthen the understanding and cooperation of the people concerned through mutual assistance and exchange of information and experiences among the various organizations and individuals in educational, business and industries, government sector promoting career development and human resource development in member countries, and thus contributing to the prosperity, welfare and peace of the Asian region as a whole. **Structure** General Assembly (every 3 years, at Regional Conference); Executive Committee; Board of Directors. **Languages** English. **Finance** Members' dues. **Activities** Events/meetings. **Events** *Conference* Kuala Lumpur (Malaysia) 2020, *Conference* Seoul (Korea Rep) 2017, *Conference* Tokyo (Japan) 2015, *Conference* Surabaya (Indonesia) 2013, *Integrating living and learning in work* Singapore (Singapore) 2001. **Members** Full; Patron; Honorary. Membership countries not specified. [2021/XD7674/**D**]

♦ Asian Regional Association for Home Economics (ARAHE) 01682

Association pour l'économie familiale de la région d'Asie – Asiatischer Regionalverband für Hauswirtschaft

SG Univ Putra Malaysia, Po Box UPM 280, 43 409 UPM Serdang, Selangor, Malaysia. T. +60389468126. Fax +60389468246. E-mail: blengsoo@gmail.com – hapsahenator@gmail.com.
URL: http://arahe.asia/

History Founded 1983, Tokyo (Japan). Regional organization of *International Federation for Home Economics (IFHE, #13447).* **Aims** Promote development of home economics in Asian nations through research and education related to individual, family and communal living. **Structure** Council (meets every 2 years, at Conference); Executive Committee. **Languages** English. **Staff** Voluntary. **Finance** Members' dues: organization/institution/library. **Events** *Biennial Conference* Kuala Lumpur (Malaysia) 2023, *Biennial Conference* Hangzhou (China) 2019, *Biennial Conference* Tokyo (Japan) 2017, *Biennial Conference* Hong Kong (Hong Kong) 2015, *Biennial Conference* Singapore (Singapore) 2013. **Publications** *Journal of the Asian Regional Association for Home Economics* (4 a year). Conference proceedings.

Members Organizational; Individual; Life; Library members in 18 countries and territories:
Australia, Bangladesh, China, Hong Kong, India, Indonesia, Japan, Jordan, Korea Rep, Malaysia, Nepal, New Zealand, Pakistan, Philippines, Singapore, Sri Lanka, Taiwan, Thailand. [2016/XD6130/**D**]

♦ Asian Regional Association for Social Work Education / see Asian and Pacific Association for Social Work Education (#01601)
♦ Asian Regional Association for Vocational and Educational Guidance / see Asian Regional Association for Career Development (#01681)
♦ Asian Regional Consortium for Headache (unconfirmed)

♦ Asian Regional Cooperative Council for Nuclear Medicine (ARCCNM) 01683

Contact address not obtained. T. +8227657996. Fax +8230334417996. E-mail: arccnm@arccnm.org.
URL: http://www.arccnm.org/

History Feb 2001, Hong Kong. **Aims** Promote nuclear medicine in Asian countries; encourage cooperation and research in the field. **Structure** General Meeting (annual). Board, including Chairman, 3 Vice-Chairmen, Secretary-General and Treasurer. Working Groups; Task Force Groups (6). **Languages** English. **Staff** 1.00 FTE, voluntary. **Finance** Sponsorship from companies. **Events** *Annual General Meeting* Shenyang (China) 2016, *Annual General Meeting* Osaka (Japan) 2014, *Annual General Meeting* Seoul (Korea Rep) 2012, *Annual General Meeting* Ho Chi Minh City (Vietnam) 2011, *Annual General Meeting* Dhaka (Bangladesh) 2010. **Publications** *ARCCNM Newsletter.*

Members Full in 18 countries and territories:
Bangladesh, China, Hong Kong, India, Indonesia, Japan, Korea Rep, Malaysia, Mongolia, Myanmar, Nepal, Pakistan, Philippines, Singapore, Sri Lanka, Taiwan, Thailand, Vietnam.

NGO Relations Member of (1): *World Council of Isotopes (WCI, #21331).* Instrumental in setting up (2): *Asian Nuclear Medicine Board (ANMB, #01570); Asian School of Nuclear Medicine (ASNM, #01692).* [2017/XE4499/**E**]

♦ Asian Regional Cooperative Project on Food Irradiation (inactive)

♦ Asian Regional Exchange for New Alternatives (ARENA) 01684

Contact address not obtained. E-mail: arenafellows@gmail.com.
URL: http://arena-council.org/arenac/en/

History 1983, Hong Kong. Founded at founding consultation of Asian social activists and researchers. **Aims** Build and sustain a community of concerned Asian scholars, intellectuals and activists who will contribute to the process of genuine participatory and sustainable development and social transformation in Asia. **Structure** Council of Fellows (ACF) (meeting every 3 years at Congress), comprises fellows from East Asia, Southeast Asia and South Asia. Executive Board, consists of members representing each of these sub-regions together with Chairperson and former Chairperson. Secretariat in Hong Kong, headed by Coordinator. **Languages** English. **Activities** Events/meetings; research/documentation. **Events** *International workshop* Colombo (Sri Lanka) 2000, *International workshop* Indonesia 1999, *International workshop* Manila (Philippines) 1993, *Joint workshop on alternative development perspectives in Asia* Bali (Indonesia) 1986. **Publications** *Asian Exchange* (2 a year) – journal; *Communiqué* (occasional) – newsletter. *ARENA Press* – ARENA Book Publishing Programme.

Members Council Fellows (41) in 13 countries and territories:
Belgium, China, Hong Kong, India, Indonesia, Japan, Korea Rep, Malaysia, Nepal, Philippines, Thailand, USA, Vietnam.

NGO Relations Member of (3): *Asia Civil Society Forum (ACSF, no recent information); World Forum for Alternatives (WFA, #21513); World Social Forum (WSF, #21797).* Partner of (1): *Development Innovations and Networks (#05057).* Instrumental in setting up (1): *International Coalition for Justice in Bhopal (ICJIB, no recent information).* [2021/XF0264/**F**]

♦ Asian Regional Organization / see ITUC – Asia Pacific (#16076)
♦ Asian Regional Resource Centre for Human Rights Education (internationally oriented national body)
♦ Asian Regional Training and Development Organization / see ARTDO International (#01117)

♦ Asian Reinsurance Corporation (Asian Re) 01685

Société asiatique de réassurance – Corporación Asiatica de Reaseguros

Pres/CEO 17th Floor – Tower B, Chamman Phenjati Business Center, 65 Rama 9 Road, Huaykwang, Bangkok, 10320, Thailand. T. +6622452169 – +6622452197 – +6622452199. Fax +6622488011 – +6622481377. E-mail: asianre@asianrecorp.com.
URL: http://www.asianrecorp.com/

History 28 May 1979, Bangkok (Thailand), as a joint project of *UNCTAD (#20285)* and *United Nations Economic and Social Commission for Asia and the Pacific (ESCAP, #20557).* Commenced operations in 1980. **Aims** Operate as a professional reinsurer accepting business from insurance markets in member States as well as other markets of the region or elsewhere, and retrocede its surpluses after net retention with priority given to national insurance and reinsurance markets of member States; invest a sizeable

proportion of its funds within the region, provided that such investments meet with the requirements of sound insurance techniques; serve as a regional centre for collection of insurance information and development of expertise in insurance and reinsurance to be put at the disposal of national insurance markets of member States; provide technical assistance to national insurance markets of member States. **Structure** Council of Members (usually meets once a year), each member government nominating one member on the Council. Management Board, consisting of Chairman, Vice-Chairman, President/CEO, Executive Vice-President and 2 elected representatives of Associate Members. Senior Management consists of President/CEO, Executive Vice-President, Senior Vice-President, Vice-President and 3 Administrative Officers. **Languages** English. **Staff** 26.00 FTE, paid. **Finance** Authorized capital: US$ 100 million; Subscribed and paid up capital: US$ 50,900,000. **Activities** Training programmes in insurance and reinsurance; advisory services; technical assistance to companies and markets. Organizes: Regional Reinsurance Seminar; Country Specific Seminar; seminars on subjects of topical relevance. Organizes and manages pools.
Members Regular; Associate. Regular members in 10 countries:
Afghanistan, Bangladesh, Bhutan, China, India, Iran Islamic Rep, Korea Rep, Philippines, Sri Lanka, Thailand.
Associate members (10) in 6 countries:
Bangladesh, India, Iran Islamic Rep, Japan, Thailand, United Arab Emirates.
IGO Relations Cooperates with ESCAP and UNCTAD. [2013.09.05/XF9736/e/**F***]

♦ Asian Relations Organization (inactive)
♦ Asian Renal Association (unconfirmed)

♦ Asian Research Center for Religion and Social Communication (ARC) 01686

Contact Saint John's Univ, Ladprao, Bangkok, 10900, Thailand. T. +66293807087. Fax +66293807087. E-mail: arc@stjohn.ac.th – arccat@stjohn.ac.th.
URL: http://www.stjohn.ac.th/arc/
History Apr 1999, Bangkok (Thailand), under the auspices of *Federation of Asian Bishops' Conferences (FABC, #09430)*. **Structure** Board of Trustees. **Staff** 2.00 FTE, paid. [2013/XJ7242/**D**]

♦ Asian Research Centre for Migration (internationally oriented national body)
♦ Asian Research Service (internationally oriented national body)
♦ Asian Research Symposium in Rhinology (meeting series)
♦ Asian Resource Foundation (internationally oriented national body)
♦ Asian Robotic Camp for Colorectal Surgeons (meeting series)

♦ Asian Rowing Federation (ARF) 01687

Secretariat Olympic Center Room 410, Oryundong, Songpagu, Seoul, Korea Rep. T. +8224204275. E-mail: arf@arfrowing.org.
URL: https://www.facebook.com/pages/ARFROWINGORG/141378702619927/
History 23 Nov 1982, Jaipur (India). **Aims** Promote the *sport* of rowing and raise the standard of rowing in Asia; strengthen the bond of friendship among those who practice rowing. **Structure** Executive, consisting of President, 3 Vice-Presidents, General Secretary, Honorary President, Honorary Adviser and Special Adviser. Umpires' Panel, comprising President and 5 members. Chairmen of Umpires Committee, Regatta Committee, Lightweight Committee and Competitive Rowing Committee. **Languages** English. **Staff** 1.00 FTE, paid. **Finance** Members' dues. Championships expenses borne by host country Association. **Events** *Annual Congress* Palembang (Indonesia) 2018, *Annual Congress* Pattaya (Thailand) 2017, *Annual Congress* Gifu (Japan) 2004, *Annual Congress* Guangzhou (China) 2003, *Annual Congress* Busan (Korea Rep) 2002.
Members General; Associate. National rowing federations or associations in 27 countries and territories:
Bangladesh, China, Hong Kong, India, Indonesia, Iran Islamic Rep, Iraq, Japan, Kazakhstan, Korea DPR, Korea Rep, Kuwait, Kyrgyzstan, Macau, Malaysia, Myanmar, Pakistan, Palestine, Philippines, Qatar, Singapore, Sri Lanka, Taiwan, Thailand, Turkmenistan, Uzbekistan, Vietnam.
NGO Relations *World Rowing (#21756)*; *Olympic Council of Asia (OCA, #17718)*. [2019/XD7230/**D**]

♦ Asian Rugby Football Union / see Asia Rugby (#02089)

♦ Asian Rural Institute – Rural Leaders Training Center (ARI) 01688

Dir 442-1 Tsukinokizawa, Nasushiobara TOCHIGI, 329-2703 Japan. T. +81287363111. Fax +81287375833. E-mail: info@ari-edu.org.
URL: http://www.ari-edu.org/
History 1973, Tochigi (Japan), following initiative, 1959, Kuala Lumpur (Malaysia), of *East Asia Christian Conference (EACC)*, currently *Christian Conference of Asia (CCA, #03898)*, and creation, 1960, of a training programme at Tsurukawa Rural Theological Seminary, Tokyo (Japan). Registered in accordance with Japanese law. **Aims** In the love of Jesus *Christ*, nurture and train rural *community* leaders; facilitate *development* of people in the *Third World* at *grassroots* level to achieve a *just* and *peaceful society* in which each can live to the fullest potential, sharing resources and abilities for the common good. **Structure** Board of Trustees; Standing Committee; Board of Councillors. Also maintains office near Tokyo (Japan). **Languages** English, Japanese. **Staff** 20.00 FTE, paid. **Finance** Private donations; grants. **Activities** Training/education. **Events** *Community based women meeting* Moshi (Tanzania UR) 1998. **Publications** *Ajia no Tsuchi* – Japanese newsletter; *ARI Network Bulletin* – newsletter for ARI graduates; *Take my Hand* – newsletter for ARI friends and supporters. Annual Report. **NGO Relations** Participates actively in the NGO network in Japan, Asia and elsewhere, including: Christian Conference of Asia (CCA); *Church World Service (CWS)*; *Japanese NGO Center for International Cooperation (JANIC)*; *World Council of Churches (WCC, #21320)*. [2019.05.20/XF2580/j/**E**]

♦ Asian Rural Sociology Association (ARSA) 01689

Pres WorldFish Philippines Office, c/o SEARCA, College Los Baños, 4031 Santa Cruz LAG, Philippines. E-mail: asiaruralsociology@gmail.com.
URL: http://www.arsa1996.org/html/index.php
History 1992. **Events** *Conference* Vientiane (Laos) 2014, *The multidimensionality of economy, energy and environmental crises and their implications to rural livelihoods* Legazpi City (Philippines) 2010, *Conference* Cixi City (China) 2007, *Conference* Lombok (Indonesia) 2004, *Globalization and rural social change* Bangkok (Thailand) 1999. **NGO Relations** Member of: *International Rural Sociology Association (IRSA, #14774)*. [2015/XJ0089/**D**]

♦ Asian Rural Women's Coalition (ARWC) 01690

Contact PO Box 1170, 10850 Penang, Malaysia. T. +6046570271. Fax +6046560381. E-mail: arwc-secretariat@asianruralwomen.net.
URL: http://asianruralwomen.net/
History Mar 2008. **Aims** Put forward the struggle for rights and interests of rural women in Asia. **Structure** Steering Committee. **Activities** Advocacy/lobbying/activism; events/meetings. **NGO Relations** Member of (1): *Coalition of Agricultural Workers International (CAWI, #04050)*. [2020/AA1209/**D**]

♦ Asian Sailing Federation (ASAF) 01691

SG 1500 East Coast Parkway, Natl Sailing Centre, Singapore 468963, Singapore. T. +6564444555. Fax +6564480485. E-mail: sec_gen@asiansailing.org.
URL: http://www.asiansailing.org/
History Founded 28 Nov 1981, Mumbai (India), at founding meeting attended by founding members. **Aims** Coordinate and develop the sport of sailing by exchange of information and decisions on matters of mutually agreed common interest. **Languages** English. **Staff** 1.00 FTE, paid; 2.00 FTE, voluntary. **Finance** Members' dues. Other sources: sponsorship; event proceeds. **Activities** Awards/prizes/competitions; training/education; sporting activities; events/meetings.
Members Membership open to all recognized national bodies in countries affiliated to the Olympic Council of Asia and who are members of the International Sailing Federation. Members in 26 countries and territories:
Azerbaijan, China, Hong Kong, India, Indonesia, Iran Islamic Rep, Japan, Kazakhstan, Korea DPR, Korea Rep, Kuwait, Kyrgyzstan, Libya, Malaysia, Myanmar, Oman, Pakistan, Palestine, Philippines, Qatar, Singapore, Sri Lanka, Taiwan, Thailand, United Arab Emirates, Vietnam.
NGO Relations Member of: *World Sailing (#21760)*; *Olympic Council of Asia (OCA, #17718)*. [2019/XM2790/**D**]

♦ Asian School of Nuclear Medicine (ASNM) 01692

Secretariat 3rd Fl – Bldg 12, No 470 Guiping Road, Xuhui District, 200025 Shanghai, China. T. +862164959951.
History Set up Feb 2003, with *Asian Regional Cooperative Council for Nuclear Medicine (ARCCNM, #01683)* as parent body. **Aims** Transfer knowledge in nuclear medicine from the more developed countries to the less developed ARCCNM Member States within the region. **Structure** Dean; Regional Vice Deans; Regional Principal; Executive Director. **Activities** Events/meetings; training/education. **Events** *Asian Nuclear Medicine Academic Forum* Melbourne, VIC (Australia) 2018, *Asian Nuclear Medicine Academic Forum* Shanghai (China) 2017, *Asian Nuclear Medicine Academic Forum* Shanghai (China) 2016, *Asian Nuclear Medicine Academic Forum* Shanghai (China) 2015. **NGO Relations** Member of: *World Council of Isotopes (WCI, #21331)*. [2017.07.06/XM4816/**E**]

♦ Asian School of Urology (see: #20733)

♦ Asian Science Park Association (ASPA) 01693

Coordinator 2F Daegu Knowledge Service Center, 481 Dongdaegu-ro, Dong-gu, Daegu 41256, Korea Rep. T. +82532184103. Fax +82532184108. E-mail: aspa@cyberaspa.org.
URL: http://cyberaspa.org/
History 1997, Japan. Founded at first East Asian Science Park Conference; permanent secretariat established 2005, Daegu (Korea Rep). Former names and other names: *East Asia Science Parks Council* – former (1997 to 2000). Registration: Ministry of Trade, Industry and Energy, No/ID: 2003-51, Start date: 24 Nov 2003, Korea Rep, Daegu; Dongdaegu District Tax Office, No/ID: 5345-529-5108-680, Start date: 14 Mar 2018, Korea Rep, Daegu. **Aims** Accomplish joint development in the fields of scientific technology, industry and economy. **Structure** Board of Directors; Advisory Committee; President; Secretariat, headed by Secretary-General. **Languages** English, Japanese, Korean. **Activities** Awards/prizes/competitions; awareness raising; events/meetings; knowledge management/information dissemination; networking/liaising; research/documentation; training/education. **Events** *ASPA LEADERS Meeting* Gyeongju (Korea Rep) 2023, *Sciencepark Innofair Forum* Gyeongju (Korea Rep) 2023, *ASPA Annual Conference* Istanbul (Türkiye) 2023, *ASPA Annual Conference* Jeju (Korea Rep) 2022, *ASPA Annual Conference* Kuala Lumpur (Malaysia) 2021. **Publications** *ASPA Webzine* (12 a year). *Asian Science and Technology Park Directory*. **Members** 170 in 21 countries. Membership countries not specified. **Consultative Status** Consultative status granted from: *ECOSOC (#05331)* (Special). **NGO Relations** Member of (1): *World Alliance for Innovation (WAINOVA, #21082)*. [2022.12.15/XM3615/**D**]

♦ Asian Seafarers Summit Meeting (meeting series)

♦ Asian Secondary Mortgage Market Association (ASMMA) 01694

Address not obtained.
URL: https://asmma.asia/
Aims Provide a basis and a platform for exchange of ideas, views and experiences so as to promote housing finance market to enable citizens in member economies to have better access to home financing support, leading or having better quality of life ultimately. **Events** *Asian Fixed Income Summit* Busan (Korea Rep) 2019, *Asian Fixed Income Summit* Ulaanbaatar (Mongolia) 2018, *Asian Fixed Income Summit* Bali (Indonesia) 2017, *Asian Fixed Income Summit* Bangkok (Thailand) 2016, *Asian Fixed Income Summit* 2015.
Members Organizations in 9 countries:
Indonesia, Japan, Kazakhstan, Korea Rep, Malaysia, Mongolia, Pakistan, Philippines, Thailand. [2019/AA1947/**D**]

♦ Asian Secretariat for the Development of Human Resources in Rural Area / see Asian Partnership for the Development of Human Resources in Rural Asia (#01654)
♦ Asian Securities Analysts Council / see Asian Securities and Investments Federation (#01695)
♦ Asian Securities Analysts Federation / see Asian Securities and Investments Federation (#01695)

♦ Asian Securities and Investments Federation (ASIF) 01695

Manager c/o Security Analysts Association, 5th Floor – Tokyo Stock Exchange Bldg 2-1, Nihonbashi Kabutocho, Chuo-Ku, Tokyo, 103-0026 Japan. T. +81336661515. Fax +81336665843.
Registered Office c/o C D King Chartered Accountant, 6 Wexford Place, Killarney Heights NSW 2087, Australia.
URL: http://www.asif.org.au/
History 2 Nov 1979, Hong Kong (Hong Kong). Former names and other names: *Asian Securities Analysts Council (ASAC)* – former (2 Nov 1979 to 1995); *Conseil asiatique d'analystes financiers* – former (2 Nov 1979 to 1995); *Asian Securities Analysts Federation (ASAF)* – former (1995 to 25 Oct 2008); *Fédération asiatique d'analystes financiers* – former (1995 to 25 Oct 2008). Registration: Australia. **Aims** Promote interchange of security analysis and fund management expertise and collaboration among individual societies. Consult, facilitate exchange of ideas and documentation, and make suggestions on coordination of policy in: development and regulation of securities analysts; corporate disclosure and reporting practices; standardization on analytical techniques and accounting practices; education and qualification of analysts; professional ethics; liaison with international business and professional associations in related fields; exchange of information among societies. **Structure** General Meeting (annual). Council, comprising up to 3 official delegates from each member society. Chairmanship rotates among constituent bodies (2-year term). Executive Committee, comprising Chairman, Deputy Chairman, 4 Directors, Treasurer and Public Officer/Manager. Standing Committees (3): Advocacy; Education; Communications. **Languages** English. **Staff** 0.50 FTE, paid. **Finance** Members' dues. **Activities** Education programme: Certified International Investment Analysts Exam and Designation. **Events** *Indian Pacific Finance Forum* Singapore (Singapore) 2015, *Annual Conference* Tokyo (Japan) 2012, *Annual Conference* Taipei (Taiwan) 2010, *Annual Conference* Sydney, NSW (Australia) 2008, *Annual conference* Delhi (India) 2007. **Publications** *ASAF Newsletter* (4 a year); *ASAF Journal* (2 a year) – electronic; *ASAF Yearbook*.
Members Full Investment analysts societies; Associate Organizations related to investment community in countries without formal securities societies. Members group 37,000 individuals in 11 countries and territories:
Australia, China, Hong Kong, India, Iran Islamic Rep, Japan, Korea Rep, Malaysia, New Zealand, Taiwan, Thailand.
Included in the above, 1 organization listed in this Yearbook:
Financial Services Institute of Australasia (FINSIA).
NGO Relations One Co-Chairman and 5 delegates to: *International Council of Investment Associations (ICIA, #13034)*. [2021/XD6423/**D**]

♦ Asian Seismological Commission (see: #12157)
♦ Asian Sepak Takraw Federation (inactive)

♦ Asian Shakespeare Association (ASA) 01696

Contact Dept of English and Comparative Literature, College of Arts and Letters, Univ of the Philippines, Diliman, 1101 Quezon City, Philippines. E-mail: admin@asianshakespeare.org.
URL: http://asianshakespeare.org/
History Constition ratified Dec 2012, Tokyo (Japan); revised Sep 2017. **Aims** Research, produce, teach, translate and promote Shakespeare from an Asian perspective. **Structure** Executive Committee. **Languages** English. **Finance** Sources: members' dues. **Activities** Events/meetings; research/documentation. **Events** *Conference* Seoul (Korea Rep) 2020, *Conference* Manila (Philippines) 2018, *Conference* New Delhi (India) 2016, *Conference* Taipei (Taiwan) 2014. [2021/AA1951/v/**D**]

♦ Asian Shipowners Association (ASA) 01697

SG 10 Anson Road, 16-18 International Plaza, Singapore 079903, Singapore. T. +6563254737. Fax +6563254451. E-mail: information@asa.org.sg.
URL: http://asianshipowners.org/
History 1992, as *Asian Shipowners Forum (ASF)*. Present name adopted, 2016. **Aims** Promote the interests of the Asian shipping industry. **Structure** General Meeting (annual). Secretariat and Chairman rotates among member associations. **Activities** Standing Committees (5): Seafarers; Ship Insurance and Liability; Safe Navigation and Environment; Ship Recycling; Shipping Economics Review. Represents an estimated 50% of world's cargo carrying fleet. **Events** *Annual General Meeting* Bangkok (Thailand) 2019, *Meeting* Singapore (Singapore) 2019, *Safe Navigation and Environment Committee Meeting* Singapore (Singapore) 2019, *Ship Recycling Committee Meeting* Singapore (Singapore) 2019, *Shipping Insurance and Liability Committee Meeting* Singapore (Singapore) 2019.
Members Shipowner associations in 7 countries and territories:

Australia, China, Hong Kong, India, Japan, Korea Rep, Taiwan.
Included in the above, one regional organization:
Federation of ASEAN Shipowners Associations (FASA, #09427).
IGO Relations Memorandum of Understanding with: *Regional Cooperation Agreement on Combating Piracy and Armed Robbery against Ships in Asia – Information Sharing Centre (ReCAAP ISC, #18771).* [2020/XF6204/F]

♦ Asian Shipowners Forum / see Asian Shipowners Association (#01697)

♦ Asian Shippers' Council (ASC) 01698

Contact Sri Lanka Shippers' Council, c/o The Ceylon Chamber of Commerce, 50 Nawam Mawatha, Colombo, 2, Sri Lanka. T. +94112392840 – +94115588871. Fax +94112449352. E-mail: slsc@chamber.lk.
URL: http://www.asianshippers.org/
History Founded 13 Sep 2004. **Aims** Integrate shippers' councils in Asia into a single entity. **Structure** Permanent Secretariat. Regions (5): China Area; Indian Sub-Continent; North East Asia; Oceania; South East Asia. **Events** *Annual Meeting* Shenzhen (China) 2013, *Annual Meeting* Hong Kong (Hong Kong) 2012, *Annual Meeting* Atlanta, GA (USA) 2011, *Annual Meeting* Macau 2010, *Annual Meeting* Colombo (Sri Lanka) 2009.
Members Shippers' Councils (19) in 17 countries and territories:
Australia, Bangladesh, China, Hong Kong, India, Indonesia, Korea Rep, Macau, Malaysia, New Zealand, Pakistan, Philippines, Singapore, Sri Lanka, Taiwan, Thailand, Vietnam.
NGO Relations Member of: *Global Shippers' Alliance (GSA, #10595).* [2014/XJ0932/D]

♦ Asian Shooting Confederation (ASC) 01699

Pres PO Box 195, 32002 Hawalli, Kuwait. T. +9654713551 – +9654713552. Fax +96524676303. E-mail: asc@asia-shooting.org.
SG A3 – Futiansi, Shijingshan District, PC 100041 Beijing, China. T. +8610888960365. Fax +861088960365.
URL: http://www.asia-shooting.org/
History Founded 1966, as a continental federation of *International Shooting Sport Federation (ISSF, #14852).* Constitution amended at General Assembly, 17 Sep 1991, Beijing (China). **Aims** Promote and guide the sound development of Olympic shooting *sports* throughout Asia; conduct communications among national shooting associations for exchange of ideas on development and perfection of the sport of shooting under the supervision of ISSF. **Structure** General Assembly (every 2 years); Executive Committee; Judges Committee; Medical Committee; Planning and Development Committee. **Languages** English. **Staff** 5.00 FTE, paid. **Activities** Organizes: Asian Airgun Championships; Asian Shotgun Championships; Asian Shooting Competitions. Encourages and supervises regional and other international competitions in Asia; organizes educational and training programme, in cooperation with the Judges Committee of UIT; awards orders of merit to for contribution to development of shooting sports. **Publications** *ASC Bulletin.*
Members National shooting associations or federations recognized by their National Olympic Committees (42) in 42 countries and territories:
Afghanistan, Bahrain, Bangladesh, Bhutan, Brunei Darussalam, China, Hong Kong, India, Indonesia, Iran Islamic Rep, Iraq, Japan (2), Jordan, Kazakhstan, Korea DPR, Korea Rep, Kuwait, Kyrgyzstan, Laos, Lebanon, Macau, Malaysia, Maldives, Mongolia, Myanmar, Nepal, Oman, Pakistan, Philippines, Qatar, Saudi Arabia, Singapore, Sri Lanka, Syrian AR, Taiwan, Tajikistan, Thailand (2), Turkmenistan, United Arab Emirates, Uzbekistan, Vietnam, Yemen. [2013.08.22/XE1053/D]

♦ Asian Shoulder Association (inactive)

♦ Asian Silambam Federation (ASF) 01700

Gen Sec No 16 Taman Nilai, 71800 Nilai, Malaysia. T. +60126700449 – +60123467861. E-mail: silambamasia@gmail.com.
URL: http://silambamasia.org/
History 2009, India. **Structure** Executive Committee. **Activities** Sporting activities.
Members Full in 12 countries:
China, India, Indonesia, Iran Islamic Rep, Iraq, Malaysia, Nepal, Pakistan, Philippines, Singapore, Sri Lanka, Uzbekistan.
IGO Relations *UNESCO (#20322).* **NGO Relations** Instrumental in setting up: *World Silambam Federation (WSF).* [2015/XM4920/D]

♦ **AsianSIL** Asian Society of International Law (#01725)
♦ Asian Silicon Symposium (meeting series)

♦ Asian Sleep Research Society (ASRS) 01701

SG c/o Neuropsychiatry Inst, 5-10-10 SY Building, Yoyogi, Shibuya-ku, Tokyo, 151-0053 Japan.
URL: http://www.asrsonline.org/
History 1994, Tokyo (Japan). Founded during founding congress, following activities initiated in Delhi (India) in 1992. **Aims** Promote all aspects of sleep research. **Structure** Governing Council (meets at least every 3 years). Officers: President; Past-President, Secretary-General; 2 Vice-Presidents; Treasurer; Chair of Scientific Committee; Congress Chair. **Languages** English. **Activities** Awards/prizes/competitions; events/meetings; knowledge management/information dissemination; training/education. **Events** *Congress* Istanbul (Türkiye) 2023, *Congress* Istanbul (Turkey) 2021, *Congress* Istanbul (Turkey) 2020, *Congress* Thiruvananthapuram (India) 2014, *Symposium of Asia Oceania research and sleep medicine* Nago (Japan) 2009. **Publications** *Sleep and Biological Rhythm* – official journal.
Members Groups (15); individuals (5) in 16 countries and territories:
China, Germany, Hong Kong, India, Indonesia, Israel, Japan, Korea Rep, Malaysia, Pakistan, Singapore, Sri Lanka, Taiwan, Thailand, Türkiye, USA.
NGO Relations Member of (1): *World Sleep Society (#21793).* [2022.10.17/XD7469/D]

♦ Asian Social Institute (internationally oriented national body)
♦ Asian Social Institute-Family Centre / see Asian Social Institute
♦ Asian Socialist Conference (inactive)

♦ Asian Society of Abdominal Radiology (ASAR) 01702

Secretariat 12-1 Yamanote-machi, Beppu OITA, 874-0828 Japan. E-mail: asar@secretariat.ne.jp.
Main Office Hasama-machi, Yufu-shi, Oita, 879-5593 Japan.
History 2007. **Aims** Advance the study of abdominal imaging and intervention, in Asia, by encouraging radiological and clinical excellence, teaching, research and further education in the subspeciality; strengthen Asian radiology; reinforce competitiveness compared to American or European radiology. **Structure** Executive Council. **Activities** *Asian Congress of Abdominal Radiology (ACAR).* **Events** *Asian Congress of Abdominal Radiology (ACAR)* Bali (Indonesia) 2023, *Asian Congress of Abdominal Radiology (ACAR)* Taipei (Taiwan) 2022, *Asian Congress of Abdominal Radiology (ACAR)* Singapore (Singapore) 2021, *Asian Congress of Abdominal Radiology (ACAR)* Singapore (Singapore) 2020, *Asian Congress of Abdominal Radiology (ACAR)* Chengdu (China) 2019. [2021/XJ1305/D]

♦ Asian Society for Adapted Physical Education and Exercise (ASAPE) 01703

Pres G06 Kwok Sports Bldg, The Chinese Univ of Hong Kong, Shatin – NT, Hong Kong, Central and Western, Hong Kong.
URL: http://www.asape.net/
History 1986, Korea Rep. Founded as the Asian branch of *International Federation of Adapted Physical Activity (IFAPA, #13338).* Statutes adopted 23 Dec 1989. **Aims** Contribute to development of research and study for adapted physical education and exercise of *children* and *adults* with special needs or *disabilities.* **Structure** General Meeting (every 2 years) elects Chairperson, Advisors (3), Vice-Presidents (5), Directors (15), Treasurer, Office Worker and Secretary-General. **Languages** English. **Staff** 2.00 FTE, paid. **Finance** Sources: members' dues. **Activities** Events/meetings. **Events** *Biennial International Congress* Hong Kong (Hong Kong) 2022, *Biennial International Congress* Hong Kong (Hong Kong) 2020, *Biennial International Congress* Kuala Lumpur (Malaysia) 2018, *Biennial international congress* Seoul (Korea Rep) 2008, *Biennial international congress* Nagasaki (Japan) 2006. **Publications** *Korean Journal of Korean Society of Adapted Physical Activity and Exercise* (4 a year); *ASAPE Newsletter* (2 a year); *Japanese Journal of Adapted Sport Science* (annual).
Members Full (300) in 10 countries an territories:
Bahrain, China, Indonesia, Iraq, Israel, Japan, Korea Rep, Philippines, Thailand, USA. [2021.09.02/XD2365/E]

♦ Asian Society Against Dementia (ASAD) 01704

SG Dept of Pharmacology, Yong Loo Lin School of Medicine, Natl Univ of Singapore, Clinical Research Ctr – MD11, Level 5 Number 05-9, 10 Medical Drive, Singapore 117597, Singapore. T. +6565163264 – +6565163265. Fax +6567730579. E-mail: phccclh@nus.edu.sg.
URL: http://www.asiandementia.org/
Aims Promote and encourage the advancement of scientific knowledge, research and practice in all aspects of dementia, and coordination of the exchange and dissemination of this knowledge and expertise throughout Asia. **Structure** Executive Committee, comprising President, Secretary-General, Treasurer and Chair of Continuing Medical Education (CME). **Events** *International Congress* Sendai (Japan) 2021, *International Congress* Singapore (Singapore) 2019, *International Congress* Bangkok (Thailand) 2017, *International Congress* Kumamoto (Japan) 2015, *International Congress* Kuala Lumpur (Malaysia) 2012. [2013/XJ6700/D]

♦ Asian Society for Aging Research (unconfirmed)

♦ Asian Society of Agricultural Economists (ASAE) 01705

SG address not obtained. E-mail: mercyson@yahoo.com – asae.secretariat@gmail.com – asae2020@pku.edu.cn.
Events – Conference Sec Director for Subcontinent Research Institute, University of Sistan and Baluchestan, Zahedan SISTAN AND BALUCHESTAN, Iran Islamic Rep.
URL: http://asaeweb.org/
Aims Foster the application of the science of agriculture economics conditions of Asian rural people and their associated communities; advance knowledge of agricultural processes and economic organization of Asian agriculture, food, resources and environment; facilitate communication and exchange of information among those concerned with rural welfare throughout Asia. **Structure** Executive Committee. **Events** *International Conference* Tokyo (Japan) 2023, *International Conference* Beijing (China) 2021, *International Conference* Beijing (China) 2020, *International Conference* Bangkok (Thailand) 2017, *International Conference* Bangladesh 2014. **Members** Individuals agricultural economists and other professionals with special interest in agricultural economic issues and affairs. Membership countries not specified. [2021/XD2328/v/D]

♦ Asian Society of Andrology (ASA) 01706

Sec Room 302, Building 16, 294 Taiyuan Rd, 200031 Shanghai, China. T. +862154922824. Fax +862154922825. E-mail: aja@sibs.ac.cn.
URL: http://www.asiaandro.com/
History 8 Nov 1992, Nanjing (China), when statutes were adopted. Statutes modified Mar 2001. **Aims** Advance and promote the knowledge of the male reproductive system and andrology. **Structure** General Assembly (at least every 4 years). Executive Council, comprising 5 officers (President; Vice-President; Secretary; Treasurer; Editor-in-Chief) Immediate Past President and members. **Languages** English. **Staff** 1.50 FTE, paid. **Finance** Members' dues (annual). Other sources: donations; fees; grants. **Activities** Organizes Asia-Pacific Forum on Andrology. **Events** *Asia-Pacific forum / Asia-Pacific Forum on Andrology* Melbourne, VIC (Australia) 2013, *Asia-Pacific forum* Nanjing (China) 2009, *Asia-Pacific Forum on Andrology* Shanghai (China) 2009, *Asia-Pacific forum / Asia-Pacific Forum on Andrology* Shanghai (China) 2006, *Quadrennial Asian and Oceanic congress of andrology* Penang (Malaysia) 2004. **Publications** *Asian Journal of Andrology* (6 a year) in English.
Members Honorary; Regular; Life. Individuals and societies involved in the field of andrology. Individuals in 13 countries and territories:
Australia, Bangladesh, China, Germany, Hong Kong, India, Indonesia, Israel, Jordan, Malaysia, Pakistan, Taiwan, USA. [2014/XD8603/D]

♦ Asian Society of Arachnology (unconfirmed)

♦ Asian Society of Cardiothoracic Anaesthesia (ASCA) 01707

Contact address not obtained. T. +81352518322. Fax +81352518321.
URL: http://www.asca.ac/
History 22 Nov 1995, Singapore (Singapore), during inaugural meeting. **Events** *Meeting* Chiang Mai (Thailand) 2022, *Meeting* Seoul (Korea Rep) 2019, *Meeting* Hong Kong (Hong Kong) 2017, *Meeting* Hangzhou (China) 2015, *Meeting* Singapore (Singapore) 2013. **Members** Membership countries not specified. [2013/XD4679/D]

♦ Asian Society of Cardiovascular Imaging (ASCI) 01708

Main Office 7 Angol-ro 11beon-gil, #202, Bundang-gu, Seongnam GYEONGGI 13572, Korea Rep. E-mail: office@asci-heart.org.
URL: http://www.asci-heart.org/
History 29 Apr 2006. Constitution approved Apr 2007, Seoul (Korea Rep). **Aims** Advance the science and art of cardiovascular imaging. **Structure** General Assembly; Executive Committee; Advisory Committee. **Finance** Sources: members' dues. **Activities** Events/meetings; training/education. **Events** *Congress* Hong Kong (Hong Kong) 2022, *Congress of Asian Society of Cardiovascular Imaging* Danang (Vietnam) 2021, *Congress* Danang (Vietnam) 2020, *Cardiovascular Imaging in Computed Tomography Summit* Seoul (Korea Rep) 2020, *Cardiovascular Imaging in Computed Tomography Summit* Seoul (Korea Rep) 2019. **Publications** *ASCI Journal.* **Members** Ordinary; Honorary; Associate; Junior; International; Founding. Membership countries not specified. [2022/XM3577/v/D]

♦ Asian Society for Cardiovascular Surgery / see Asian Society for Cardiovascular and Thoracic Surgery (#01709)

♦ Asian Society for Cardiovascular and Thoracic Surgery (ASCVTS) .. 01709

Main Office c/o Dept Cardiac Surgery, Univ Tokyo, 7-3-1 Hongo, Bunkyo-ku, Tokyo, 113-8655 Japan. Fax +81358008854.
URL: http://www.ascvts.org/
History 1993. Activities began in 1973 as the Asia Chapter of then then *International Society for Cardiovascular Surgery (International Society for Vascular Specialists (ISVS, inactive)).* 2004, became independent. Former names and other names: *Asian Society for Cardiovascular Surgery (ASCVS)* – former (1992 to 2008). **Aims** Promote study of the art, science and practice of cardiovascular and thoracic surgery; facilitate exchange of ideas in the field through scientific meetings and by personal contact between cardiovascular and thoracic specialists. **Structure** General Assembly (annual); Council; Executive Committee; Committees (3); Secretariat, headed by Secretary General. **Languages** English. **Staff** 0.50 FTE, paid. **Finance** Members' dues. **Activities** Projects/programmes; training/education. **Events** *Annual Meeting 2024, Annual Meeting* Busan (Korea Rep) 2023, *Annual Meeting* Nara (Japan) 2022, *Annual Meeting* Japan 2021, *ASCVTS 2021 Online Conference* Seoul (Korea Rep) 2021. **Publications** *Asian Cardiovascular and Thoracic Annals* – official journal. **Members** Active (784); Senior (175); Honorary; Supporting. Individual physicians in 28 countries. Membership countries not specified. [2021/XD4062/v/D]

♦ Asian Society for Child and Adolescent Psychiatrists and Allied Professions / see Asian Society for Child and Adolescent Psychiatry and Allied Professions (#01710)

♦ Asian Society for Child and Adolescent Psychiatry and Allied Professions (ASCAPAP) 01710

SG Hakuai Research Inst of Developmental Diosorders, Kobe Hakuai Hosp, Dept Child and Adolescent Psychiatry, 1-17 Motomachi-Dori, 7-Chome, Chuo-Ku, Kobe HYOGO, 650-0022 Japan. T. +81783625010. Fax +81783625030. E-mail: s.shiratak@gmail.com.
History 1996, Tokyo (Japan). Former names and other names: *Asian Society for Child and Adolescent Psychiatrists and Allied Professions (ASCAP)* – alias. **Aims** Study scientifically all matters concerning the mental health and development of children and adolescents in Asia; promote professional standards in their mental health care. **Structure** Executive Committee. President. Secretariat. **Languages** English. **Staff** Non-permanent. **Finance** Congress proceeds. **Activities** Events/meetings; knowledge management/information dissemination. **Events** *Congress* Kyoto (Japan) 2023, *Congress* Kyoto (Japan) 2021, *Congress* Chiang Mai (Thailand) 2019, *Congress* Yogyakarta (Indonesia) 2017, *Embracing challenges, providing solutions* Kuala Lumpur (Malaysia) 2015.
Members Full; Affiliate; Corporate; Corresponding; Honorary. Members in 16 countries and territories:
Bangladesh, Cambodia, China, Hong Kong, India, Indonesia, Iran Islamic Rep, Japan, Korea Rep, Malaysia, Nepal, Pakistan, Philippines, Singapore, Taiwan, Thailand. [2020/XD7963/t/D]

♦ Asian Society for Clinical Pathology and Laboratory Medicine (ASCPaLM) **01711**

Pres address not obtained.
Coordinating Chairman address not obtained. E-mail: kohkoh@yuhs.ac.
URL: http://www.ascpalm.org/

History 7 Dec 2002, Kaohsiung (Taiwan) at 7th Asian Conference of Clinical Pathology. **Events** *Laboratory medicine – new frontiers and future realms* Taipei (Taiwan) 2016, *Congress* Seoul (Korea Rep) 2014, *Congress / Conference* Kyoto (Japan) 2012, *Congress / Conference* Jakarta (Indonesia) 2010, *Congress / Conference* Ulaanbaatar (Mongolia) 2009. [2016/XM3854/**D**]

♦ Asian Society for Colloid and Surface Science (ASCASS) **01712**

Pres Graduate Inst of Applied Science and Technology, Jing-Cheng Honors College, Natl Taiwan Univ, 43 Keelung Road, Section 4, Taipei 10607, Taiwan. T. +886227303627.

History 2004, Kolkata (India). **Aims** Promote the exchange of scientific knowledge by and between scientists and professionals from different countries in Asia, encouraging a profitable regional cooperation. **Activities** Events/meetings; knowledge management/information dissemination. **Events** *Asian Conference on Colloid & Interface Science* Kathmandu (Nepal) 2019, *Asian Conference on Colloid and Interface Science* Kuala Lumpur (Malaysia) 2017, *Asian Conference on Colloid and Interface Science* Nagasaki (Japan) 2015, *Asian Conference on Colloid and Interface Science* Darjeeling (India) 2013, *Asian Conference on Colloid and Interface Science* Tainan (Taiwan) 2011.
Members Full in 11 countries and territories:
China, Hong Kong, India, Japan, Korea Rep, Malaysia, Nepal, Pakistan, Russia, Taiwan, Thailand. [2019/AA1950/**D**]

- ♦ Asian Society of Colorectal Surgery (inactive)
- ♦ Asian Society for Comparative Education / see Comparative Education Society of Asia (#04409)
- ♦ Asian Society of Computer Aided Surgery (unconfirmed)
- ♦ Asian Society for Computer Assisted Orthopaedic Surgery / see Asian Society for Computer Assisted Surgery (#01713)

♦ Asian Society for Computer Assisted Surgery (CAOS Asia) **01713**

Founder Pres Doctor's Garden, Gandhinagar, Kottayam, Kerala 686 008, Kottayam KERALA 686 008, India. T. +914812597376.

History 28 Mar 2004, Cochin (India). Founded at the First Asian Meeting for Computer Assisted Orthopaedic Surgery. Regional organization of *International Society for Computer Assisted Orthopaedic Surgery (CAOS-International, #15029)*. Former names and other names: *Asian Society for Computer Assisted Orthopaedic Surgery* – former alias. **Aims** Provide a platform for surgeons and engineers interested in Computer Assisted Orthopaedic Surgery from Asian countries to exchange ideas and to popularize the technology in Asian countries. **Structure** Executive Committee, comprising President, Immediate Past-President, Vice-President, Secretary and Treasurer. Programme and Award Committee. **Languages** English. **Staff** None. **Finance** Members' dues (first 5 years membership is free of cost). **Events** *Annual Meeting* Pattaya (Thailand) 2016, *Annual Meeting* Krabi (Thailand) 2010, *Annual meeting* Osaka (Japan) 2009, *Annual Meeting* Hong Kong (Hong Kong) 2008, *Annual meeting* Hong Kong (Hong Kong) 2008.
Members in 8 countries and territories:
China, Hong Kong, India, Japan, Korea Rep, Singapore, Sri Lanka, Taiwan. [2010/XM0510/**E**]

♦ Asian Society of Conservation Medicine (ASCM) **01714**

SG address not obtained. E-mail: contact@ascminfo.org.
URL: http://www.ascminfo.org/

History 2005. Former names and other names: *Asian Society of Zoo and Wildlife Medicine (ASZWM)* – former (2005 to 2014). **Aims** Bring together students, practitioners, professionals and academics to advance and disseminate knowledge and skills in the field of conservation medicine in Asia. **Structure** Senior Board; Board. **Languages** English. **Activities** Events/meetings; knowledge management/information dissemination; networking/liaising. **Events** *Conference* Chiang Mai (Thailand) 2022, *Conference* Sapporo (Japan) 2021, *Conference* 2020, *Conference* Phnom Penh (Cambodia) 2019, *International Meeting* Kuching (Malaysia) 2017. **Publications** Conference proceedings. **NGO Relations** Member of (2): *Asian Association of Veterinary Schools (AAVS, #01345)* (associate); *Federation of Asian Veterinary Associations (FAVA, #09451)* (associate). [2021.06.11/XJ5351/**D**]

♦ Asian Society of Cosmetic Scientists (ASCS) **01715**

Contact Symrise Asia Pacific, 190 Pandan Loop, Singapore 128379, Singapore. T. +6567794551. Fax +6567781890.

Events *Biennial Conference* Cairns, QLD (Australia) 2015, *Biennial Conference* Bali (Indonesia) 2013, *Biennial Conference* Seoul (Korea Rep) 2011, *Biennial Conference* Yokohama (Japan) 2009, *Biennial Conference* Singapore (Singapore) 2007.
Members in 10 countries:
Australia, Hong Kong, India, Indonesia, Japan, Korea Rep, Philippines, Singapore, Taiwan, Thailand.
NGO Relations *International Federation of Societies of Cosmetic Chemists (IFSCC, #13545)*. [2017.06.29/XU4911/**D**]

♦ Asian Society of Cryosurgery (ASC) **01716**

Secretariat No 2 Tangde Xi Lu, Guangzhou, Tianhe District, 510665 Guangdong, China. Fax +682570152. E-mail: asiansocietyofcryosurgery@gmail.com.
URL: http://www.cryosurgery.asia/

History Sep 2011. Formation meeting, 25 May 2012, Guangzhou (China). **Aims** Enhance the development and the promotion of cryosurgery in Asia. **Structure** Board of Directors. **Events** *Conference* Kuching (Malaysia) 2018, *Conference* Jinan (China) 2017. **NGO Relations** *International Society of Cryosurgery (ISC, #15040)*. [2014/XJ8464/**D**]

♦ Asian Society of Dermatopathology (ASD) **01717**

Contact No 1-2, 4F Section 1, Wuchang Street, Taipei 10046, Taiwan. T. +886223880595 ext 12. Fax +886223880597. E-mail: asian.dermpath@gmail.com.
URL: https://www.asdermpath.org/

History 2016. Registration: Taiwan. **Aims** Enhance the quality of the practice of dermatopathology; promote the development and advancement of dermatopathology as a subspecialty; promote the collaboration and exchange of knowledge, and encourage research in dermatopathology and allied disciplines in Asia. **Structure** Executive Committee; Board of Directors. **Languages** English. **Activities** Awards/prizes/competitions; events/meetings. **Events** *Annual Meeting* Manila (Philippines) 2022, *Annual Meeting* Singapore (Singapore) 2021, *Annual Meeting* Kaohsiung (Taiwan) 2020, *Annual Meeting* New Delhi (India) 2019. **NGO Relations** Member of (1): *International League of Dermatological Societies (ILDS, #14018)*. [2022.12.04/AA2132/**D**]

♦ Asian Society for Emergency Medicine (ASEM) **01718**

Pres Room 809, Hong Kong Ac of Medicine, 99 Wong Chuk Hang Road, Aberdeen, Aberdeen, Southern, Hong Kong. T. +85228708874. Fax +85225542913. E-mail: asiansocietyem@gmail.com.
URL: http://www.asiansem.org/

History 24 Oct 1998, Singapore (Singapore). Founded during first conference, following activities begun in 1995 at 2nd South East Asia Conference on Emergency Medical Care. **Structure** Board. **Events** *Asian Conference on Emergency Medicine* Dubai (United Arab Emirates) 2025, *Asian Conference on Emergency Medicine* Manila (Philippines) 2023, *Asian Conference* Hong Kong (Hong Kong) 2021, *Asian Conference* Seoul (Korea Rep) 2016, *Forum on Human Rights of Older Persons* Seoul (Korea Rep) 2016.
Members National Societies in 12 countries and territories:
Hong Kong, India, Japan, Korea Rep, Malaysia, Myanmar, Philippines, Singapore, Taiwan, Thailand, Türkiye, United Arab Emirates.
NGO Relations Ex-officio member of: *International Federation for Emergency Medicine (IFEM, #13409)*. [2022/XM8104/**D**]

♦ Asian Society of Endourology (ASE) **01719**

Pres Singapore Urology / Fertility Ctr, 3 Mount Elizabeth Road, Ste 10-09, Mount Elizabeth Medical Ctr, Singapore 228510, Singapore.

History Aug 1998. **Aims** Promote training and education in endourology in Asia. **Events** *Asia-Pacific congress on uro-oncology* Manila (Philippines) 2007, *Asia-Pacific congress on uro-oncology* Sydney, NSW (Australia) 2005, *Asia-Pacific congress of uro-oncology* Hong Kong (Hong Kong) 2003, *Asia-Pacific congress on uro-oncology* Singapore (Singapore) 2002. **NGO Relations** Affiliated member of: *Urological Association of Asia (UAA, #20733)*. [2008/XM1296/**D**]

- ♦ Asian Society for Entrepreneurship Education and Development (no recent information)
- ♦ Asian Society for Environmental Geotechnology (inactive)
- ♦ Asian Society for Environmental Protection (inactive)
- ♦ Asian Society of Experimental Mechanics (unconfirmed)
- ♦ Asian Society for Female Urology (no recent information)

♦ Asian Society of Gynecologic Oncology (ASGO) **01720**

Secretariat 35 Shinanomachi, Shinjuku, Tokyo, 160-8582 Japan. E-mail: info@asiansgo.org.
URL: http://asiansgo.org/

History 2009. **Aims** Contribute to development of gynecologic *cancer* science through research and exchange of information in the medical science and friendship among members. **Structure** Council; Board; Committees (8). **Languages** English. **Finance** Sources: contributions; members' dues. **Events** *Biennial Meeting* Bangkok (Thailand) 2021, *International Workshop on Gynecologic Oncology* Taipei (Taiwan) 2020, *Biennial Meeting* Incheon (Korea Rep) 2019, *Workshop on Gynecologic Oncology* Suwon (Korea Rep) 2018, *Biennial Meeting* Tokyo (Japan) 2017. **Publications** *Journal of Gynecologic Oncology.*; *Journal of Gynecologic Oncology.*
Members Regular; Associate; Special; Honorary. Cancer specialists in 10 countries and territories:
China, Hong Kong, India, Indonesia, Japan, Korea Rep, Philippines, Singapore, Taiwan, Thailand. [2021/XJ2978/v/**D**]

♦ Asian Society for Gynecologic Robotic Surgery (ASGRS) **01721**

Secretariat address not obtained. E-mail: secretariat@asgrs.org.
URL: http://www.asgrs.org/

History Aug 2015. Registration: Start date: Jun 2016, Singapore. **Aims** Raise the bar on women's surgical healthcare in Asia with robot-assisted surgery through research, innovation and leadership. **Structure** Board; Executive Board. **Finance** Sources: members' dues. **Events** *Annual Meeting* Jeju (Korea Rep) 2022, *Annual Meeting* Daegu (Korea Rep) 2021, *Annual Meeting* Taipei (Taiwan) 2020. **Publications** *GRS Gynecologic Robotic Surgery Journal.*
Members Full in 6 countries and territories:
Hong Kong, Indonesia, Korea Rep, Malaysia, Singapore, Taiwan.
NGO Relations Affiliated with (1): *Advancing Minimally Invasive Gynecology Worldwide (AAGL, #00130)*. [2021/AA2119/**D**]

♦ Asian Society of Head and Neck Oncology (ASHNO) **01722**

Contact B1, No 95, Wunchang Rd, Shihlin Dist, Taipei 00111, Taiwan. T. +886228332211 ext 2556.
URL: https://www.ashno.org/

History 21 Jul 2008, San Francisco, CA (USA). **Aims** Promote and advance knowledge of prevention, diagnosis, treatment and rehabilitation of *neoplasms* and related diseases of the head and neck; promote highest professional and ethical standards; interact with other organizations interested in neoplasms and other diseases of the head and neck. **Languages** English, Mandarin Chinese. **Events** *Conference* Bangkok (Thailand) 2023, *Congress* Kuala Lumpur (Malaysia) 2021, *Congress* Seoul (Korea Rep) 2019, *Congress* Bali (Indonesia) 2017, *Congress* Kobe (Japan) 2015. **Members** Membership countries not specified. **NGO Relations** Member of (1): *International Federation of Head and Neck Oncologic Societies (IFHNOS, #13438)*. [2021.06.09/XJ8086/**D**]

- ♦ Asian Society of Hepato-Biliary-Pancreatic Surgery / see Asian-Pacific Hepato-Pancreato-Biliary Association (#01616)
- ♦ Asian Society of Human Services (internationally oriented national body)
- ♦ Asian Society for Hyperthermic Oncology (internationally oriented national body)

♦ Asian Society for Innovation and Policy (ASIP) **01723**

Contact 245 Hannuri-daero, SR Parkone No709, Sejong 30127, Korea Rep. T. +82448657608. E-mail: asip.society@gmail.com.
URL: http://innovationandpolicy.asia/

History 2012, Dalian (China). Founded following international conference, Daejeon (Korea Rep), 2011. **Structure** Steering Committee; Board; Committees (5): Academic Advisory, Conference, Policy, Innovation, Climate Change. **Activities** Events/meetings. **Events** *Asian Conference on Innovation and Policy* Bangalore (India) 2022, *Asian Conference on Innovation and Policy* Jeju (Korea Rep) 2021, *Asian Conference on Innovation and Policy* Jeju (Korea Rep) 2020. **Publications** *Asian Journal of Innovation and Policy.* [2023.02.16/AA2735/**D**]

♦ Asian Society for Integrity of Nuclear Components (ASINCO) **01724**

Contact address not obtained.

Activities Events/meetings. **Events** *International Workshop on the Integrity of Nuclear Components* Japan 2023, *International Workshop on the Integrity of Nuclear Components* Seoul (Korea Rep) 2021, *International Workshop on the Integrity of Nuclear Components* Taoyuan (Taiwan) 2018, *International Workshop on the Integrity of Nuclear Components* Nagasaki (Japan) 2016, *International Workshop on the Integrity of Nuclear Components* Busan (Korea Rep) 2014. [2022.07.07/AA1948/**D**]

♦ Asian Society of International Law (AsianSIL) **01725**

Secretariat c/o Fac of Law – Natl Univ of Singapore, Eu Tong Sen Bldg, 469G Bukit Timah Rd, Singapore 259776, Singapore. T. +6565161035. Fax +6567790979. E-mail: asiansil-admin@nus.edu.sg.
URL: http://www.asiansil.org/

History Founded 2007. Registered in accordance with Singapore law. **Aims** Promote research, education and practice of international law by serving as a centre of activities among international law scholars and practitioners in Asia and everywhere; foster and encourage Asian perspectives of international law; promote awareness of and respect for international law in Asia. **Structure** Executive Council of 7 officers and other members; Advisory Council; Research and Planning Committee; Secretariat. **Languages** English. **Staff** 1.00 FTE, voluntary. **Finance** Members' dues. Donations. **Activities** Events/meetings; knowledge management/information dissemination. **Events** *Conference* Manila (Philippines) 2019, *Biennial Conference* Seoul (Korea Rep) 2017, *Biennial Conference* Bangkok (Thailand) 2015, *Inter-Sessional Conference* Bangkok (Thailand) 2015, *Annual Conference* Tokyo (Japan) 2014. **Publications** *Asian Journal of International Law. Working Paper Series.* Conference proceedings; monthly e-newsletters.
Members in 48 countries and territories:
Australia, Austria, Azerbaijan, Bahrain, Bangladesh, Belgium, Brazil, Brunei Darussalam, Cambodia, Canada, China, Denmark, Estonia, France, Germany, Greece, Hong Kong, India, Indonesia, Ireland, Italy, Japan, Korea Rep, Luxembourg, Macau, Malaysia, Mongolia, Nepal, Netherlands, New Zealand, Norway, Pakistan, Philippines, Qatar, Romania, Russia, Seychelles, Singapore, Sri Lanka, Sweden, Switzerland, Taiwan, Thailand, Türkiye, UK, USA, Uzbekistan, Vietnam.
IGO Relations None. [2015.07.08/XJ2680/v/**D**]

♦ Asian Society of Kinesiology (ASK) **01726**

Headquarters 10-304 Gangnam Sangga, 303 Hyoryong-ro, Seochogu, Seoul 06643, Korea Rep. T. +8225863813. Fax +8225863819. E-mail: kinesiologyglobal@gmail.com.
URL: http://askannualmeeting.org/

History Set up 2016, Incheon (Korea Rep), during 7th Asia Conference on Kinesiology. **Aims** Research the specialty of kinesiology; develop the integrated kinesiologist qualification system, with special attention to the convergence fields of kinesiology and sports medicine in the 4th industrial revolution. **Structure** Managing Council. **Activities** Research and development; knowledge management/information dissemination; events/meetings. **Events** *Asia Conference on Kinesiology* Yogyakarta (Indonesia) 2021, *Asia Conference on Kinesiology* Chengdu (China) 2019, *Asia Conference on Kinesiology* Taichung (Taiwan) 2018, *Asia Conference on Kinesiology* Daegu (Korea Rep) 2017. **Publications** *Journal of Kinesiology* – official journal. [2019.03.06/XM6192/**D**]

♦ **Asian Society of Lifestyle Medicine (ASLM)** **01727**
Contact Corporate Ltd, Flat/Rm 501 05/F 197, Tsuen King Circuit, Tsuen Wan, Hong Kong. T. +66629362950. E-mail: info@aslm.asia.
URL: https://aslm.asia/
History Registered in accordance with the law of Hong Kong. **Aims** Transform *healthcare* through lifestyle medicine. **Structure** Board of Directors. Committees (5): Administrative; Executive; Education; Finance; IT. **Activities** Events/meetings; training/education; research/documentation. **Events** *Conference* Seoul (Korea Rep) 2019.
Members Full in 9 countries:
China, India, Indonesia, Japan, Korea Rep, Malaysia, Pakistan, Philippines, Thailand.
NGO Relations *European Lifestyle Medicine Organization (ELMO, #07694).* [2020/XM7829/**D**]

♦ **Asian Society for Mitochondrial Research and Medicine (ASMRM)** . **01728**
Main Office Cardiovascular and Metabolic Diseases Ctr, College of Medicine – Inje Univ, Bokji-ro 75, Busanjin-gu, Busan 614 735, Korea Rep. T. +82518908748. Fax +82518948748.
URL: http://asmrm.org/
History Jan 2003. **Structure** Annual Meeting; Council. **Finance** Members' dues (annual). **Activities** Events/meetings. **Events** *Conference* Fukuoka (Japan) 2019, *Conference* Busan (Korea Rep) 2018, *Conference* Xian (China) 2017, *Conference* Tokyo (Japan) 2016, *Conference* Hangzhou (China) 2015. **Publications** *Mitochondrial News in Science.*
Members Full; Associate. Members in 6 countries and territories:
China, India, Japan, Korea Rep, Singapore, Taiwan. [2017/XM0105/v/**D**]

♦ **Asian Society of Natural Products (ASNP)** **01729**
Office Sujeon-gu, Bokjeong-ro 96, 30-0 1st floor, Seongnam GYEONGGI 13112, Korea Rep. T. +82316704830. E-mail: asnpmail@gmail.com.
URL: http://www.webofasnp.org/
Aims Connect with natural products researchers and businesses worldwide. **Structure** General Meeting; Board of Directors. **Finance** Sources: members' dues. **Activities** Events/meetings. **Events** *Joint International Symposium* Chungju (Korea Rep) 2021. [2020/AA0099/**D**]

♦ **Asian Society for Neuroanesthesia and Critical Care (ASNACC)** **01730**
Contact c/o AIIMS, Ansari Nagar, Delhi 110029, DELHI 110029, India.
History 2006. Founded during the 2nd China-Japan-Korea Joint Symposium for Neuroanesthesia, with 7 membership countries: Korea Rep; Japan; China; Indonesia; Singapore; Malaysia; India. Proposed by Dr Haekyu Kim (Korea Rep) following the 1st China-Japan-Korea Joint Symposium for Neuroanesthesia, 2004 (Korea Rep). **Aims** Exchange information in the field of neuroscience; enhance abilities in clinical practice in the field of neuroanesthesia and critical care in Asia; enhance research abilities in the field of neuroscience in Asia; establish a forum for exchange and interchange of views and for enhancing fellowship among members. **Structure** Board of Directors; Executive Committee; Educational Committee. **Languages** English. **Finance** Members' dues. **Activities** Training/education. **Events** *Congress* Kuching (Malaysia) 2025, *Congress* Manila (Philippines) 2023, *Congress* Cebu City (Philippines) 2021, *Congress* Nara (Japan) 2019, *Building bridges across Asia – enhancing care* Singapore (Singapore) 2017. **Publications** *ASNACC Newsletter.*
Members Societies in 9 countries:
China, India, Indonesia, Japan, Korea Rep, Malaysia, Philippines, Singapore, Thailand. [2021/XJ8655/**D**]

♦ **Asian Society for Neuro-Oncology (ASNO)** **01731**
SG Intl Medical Cntr, Saitama Medical Univ, 1397-1 Yamane, Hidaka-shi, Saitama, 350-1298 Japan. T. +81429844111. Fax +81429844699. E-mail: rnishika@saitama-med.ac.jp – jsno@saitama-med.ac.jp.
URL: http://www.asn-o.com/
History Part of: *World Federation of Neuro-Oncology Societies (WFNOS, #21462).* **Languages** English. **Events** *Meeting* Bali (Indonesia) 2023, *Meeting* Seoul (Korea Rep) 2022, *Meeting* Seoul (Korea Rep) 2021, *Meeting* Taipei (Taiwan) 2019, *Meeting* Beijing (China) 2018.
Members Full in 12 countries and territories:
Australia, China, Hong Kong, India, Indonesia, Japan, Korea Rep, Malaysia, Nepal, Philippines, Singapore, Taiwan, Thailand, Türkiye. [2016.06.01/XD8920/**D**]

♦ **Asian Society of Paediatric Anaesthesiologists (ASPA)** **01732**
Secretariat Dept of Paediatric Anaesthesia, KK Women's / Children's Hospital, 100 Bukit Timah Road, Singapore 229899, Singapore. T. +653941091. Fax +652912661.
URL: http://www.aspa-2000.com/
History 1999, Singapore (Singapore). **Aims** Serve as a forum for paediatric anaesthesiologists in the region; promote research and training in paediatric anaesthesiology. **Structure** Executive Committee. **Finance** Joining fee. **Events** *Scientific Meeting* Singapore (Singapore) 2021, *Scientific Meeting* Sendai (Japan) 2020, *Scientific Meeting* Surabaya (Indonesia) 2019, *Scientific Meeting* Bangkok (Thailand) 2018, *Scientific Meeting* Mumbai (India) 2017.
Members Ordinary; associate. Individuals in 13 countries and territories:
Brunei Darussalam, China, Hong Kong, India, Indonesia, Japan, Malaysia, Pakistan, Singapore, Sri Lanka, Thailand, United Arab Emirates, Vietnam. [2021/XD7945/**D**]

♦ **Asian Society of Pediatric Infectious Diseases (ASPID)** **01733**
Exc Sec INTROP, Dept of Pediatrics, Philippine General Hospital, Taft Avenue, 1000 Manila, Philippines. T. +6323543762. Fax +6325240892 – +6323543762. E-mail: aspid@uplink.com.ph.
URL: http://www.asianpids.org/
History 1994, Manila (Philippines). **Aims** Promote advancement of knowledge and expertise in the diagnosis, prevention and treatment of paediatric infectious diseases in Asia; encourage collaborative national and multinational researches on the subject of high priority. **Structure** General Assembly, elects Standing Committee (2 year terms), which elects Executive Committee from among themselves, comprising President, Vice-President (President Elect), Secretary, Treasurer and 3 members. **Languages** English. **Staff** 0.50 FTE, paid. **Finance** Members' dues. Share of registration fees from ACPID, held every 2 years. Budget (annual): US$ 4,000. **Activities** Events/meetings; research and development. **Events** *Biennial Congress* Seoul (Korea Rep) 2022, *Biennial Congress* Seoul (Korea Rep) 2021, *Biennial Congress* Seoul (Korea Rep) 2020, *Biennial Congress* Fukuoka (Japan) 2018, *Biennial Congress* Bangkok (Thailand) 2016. **Publications** *Asian Journal of Pediatric Infectious Diseases.*
Members (160) in 18 countries and territories:
Bangladesh, Brunei Darussalam, Cambodia, China, Hong Kong, India, Indonesia, Japan, Korea Rep, Laos, Malaysia, Pakistan, Philippines, Singapore, Sri Lanka, Taiwan, Thailand, Vietnam.
NGO Relations Member of: *World Society of Pediatric Infectious Diseases (WSPID, #21810).* Lins indicated by: *Asian Strategic Alliance for Pneumococcal Disease Prevention (ASAP, #01761).* [2013.10.02/XD6909/**D**]

♦ Asian Society of Pediatric Nephrology / see Asian Pediatric Nephrology Association (#01659)

♦ **Asian Society for Pediatric Research (ASPR)** **01734**
Pres Dept of Pediatrics, Graduate School of Medical Sciences, Kyushu Univ, Higashi-ku, Fukuoka, 812-8582 Japan. T. +81926425421. Fax +81926425435. E-mail: aspr@congre.co.jp.
URL: http://www.aspr.jp/
Structure Council of 13 members. **Events** *Annual Congress* 2022, *Annual Congress* 2021, *Annual Congress* Manado (Indonesia) 2019, *Annual Congress* Manila (Philippines) 2018, *Annual Congress* Hong Kong (Hong Kong) 2017. [2012/XJ1785/**D**]

♦ **Asian Society for Pigment Cell Research (ASPCR)** **01735**
Main Office c/o 3 Mount Elizabeth, 11-08 Mt Eliz Medical Ctr, Singapore 228510, Singapore. Fax +6535216589. E-mail: aspcr.org@gmail.com.
URL: http://www.aspcr.org/
History 21 May 2004, Beijing (China). **Aims** Promote the exchange of information in clinical pigmentary disorders research in Asia; encourage collaboration between scientists and clinicians active in the field. **Structure** Council; Officers. **Events** *Conference* Manila (Philippines) 2019, *Colours of health and disease* Colombo (Sri Lanka) 2018, *Conference* Kaohsiung (Taiwan) 2016, *Conference* Shanghai (China) 2015, *Joint Meeting* Sydney, NSW (Australia) 2013. **Publications** *ASPCR Bulletin.* **Members** Full (55). Membership countries not specified. **NGO Relations** Member of: *International Federation of Pigment Cell Societies (IFPCS, #13512).* [2018/XM1498/**D**]

♦ **Asian Society for Precision Engineering and Nanotechnology (ASPEN)** **01736**
Pres Keio University, 4-1-1 Hiyoshi, Kohoku-ku, Yokohama-shi, Yokohama KANAGAWA, 223-8521 Japan. T. +81351271541. E-mail: m-pr@adst.keio.ac.jp.
URL: http://www.aspen-soc.org/
Aims Promote network and collaboration of academic societies and researchers in Asia. **Events** *International Conference* Matsue (Japan) 2019, *International Conference* Seoul (Korea Rep) 2017, *International Conference* Harbin (China) 2015, *International Conference* Taipei (Taiwan) 2013, *International Conference* Hong Kong (Hong Kong) 2011.
Members Academic societies (4) in 3 countries:
China, Japan, Korea Rep. [2019/XJ1520/**D**]

♦ Asian Society of Protective Clothing (unconfirmed)

♦ **Asian Society for Quality in Health Care (ASQua)** **01737**
Contact 6th Floor, Menara Wisma Sejarah, 230 Jalan Tun Razak, 50400 Kuala Lumpur, Malaysia. T. +60326812232. Fax +60326813199. E-mail: asqua@asquaa.org.
URL: https://asquaa.org/
History 2008. Registration: Registrar of Societies, Start date: 28 Jun 2016, Malaysia. **Aims** Improve quality in healthcare at national and international levels. **Structure** Board. **Activities** Events/meetings. **Events** *Asia Healtcare Week Meeting* Kuala Lumpur (Malaysia) 2020, *Asia Healtcare Week Meeting* Singapore (Singapore) 2019.
Members Full in 11 countries and territories:
Australia, Bangladesh, India, Indonesia, Japan, Korea Rep, Malaysia, Mongolia, Philippines, Taiwan, Thailand. [2021/AA0178/**D**]

♦ **Asian Society of Sleep Medicine (ASSM)** **01738**
Pres address not obtained. E-mail: asiansleepmedicine@gmail.com.
History Founded 2013. **Aims** Promote all aspects in sleep medicine and research in Asia. **Structure** General Membership Meeting; Starting Committee; Executive Committee. **Finance** Members' dues. **Activities** Knowledge management/information dissemination; training/education; networking/liaising; events/meetings. **Events** *Congress* Beijing (China) 2021, *Congress* Seoul (Korea Rep) 2018, *Congress* Taipei (Taiwan) 2016.
Members Society; Individual; Alliance; Student. Members in 14 countries and territories:
China, Hong Kong, India, Indonesia, Iran Islamic Rep, Israel, Japan, Korea Rep, Malaysia, Oman, Philippines, Saudi Arabia, Singapore, Taiwan, Thailand, Vietnam.
NGO Relations Associate member of: *World Sleep Society (#21793).* [2018/XM8398/**D**]

♦ **Asian Society for Solid State Ionics (ASSSI)** **01739**
Address not obtained.
History Jun 1986, Singapore (Singapore), on the initiative of Takehiko Takahashi. **Aims** Create awareness among Asian scientists of the importance of solid state ionic *materials* and their applications; provide a forum where they can meet counterparts from other regions. **Structure** Executive Council. Officers: President, Vice-President, Secretary and Treasurer. **Languages** English. **Staff** 2.00 FTE, voluntary. **Finance** Members' dues. Donations. **Activities** *Asian Conference on Solid State Ionics (ACSSI).* **Events** *Biennial Conference* Nagoya (Japan) 2022, *Biennial Conference* Singapore (Singapore) 2014, *Biennial Conference* Xian (China) 2010, *Biennial Conference* Coimbatore (India) 2008, *Biennial Conference* Kandy (Sri Lanka) 2006.
Members Full in 8 countries:
China, India, Japan, Korea Rep, Malaysia, Singapore, Sri Lanka, Thailand. [2018/XD3308/**D**]

♦ **Asian Society of Sport Biomechanics (ASSB)** **01740**
Address not obtained.
URL: http://www.assbweb.org/
History Inaugurated 22 Apr 2006, Korea Rep. **Aims** Provide permanence and stability for periodic meetings of the ASSB conference; communicate information about the ASSB conference and any associated satellite meetings, as well as about the scientific priorities in sport biomechanics, to as many people interested in the subject as possible. **Structure** Board of Directors. **Activities** Events/meetings. **Events** *Conference* Bangkok (Thailand) 2023, *Conference* Taoyuan (Taiwan) 2021, *Conference* Taoyuan (Taiwan) 2020, *Conference* Jeju (Korea Rep) 2018, *Conference* Ningbo (China) 2016. [2021/XM8313/**D**]

♦ Asian Society for Stereotactic Functional and Computer Assisted Neurosurgery / see Asian-Australasian Society for Stereotactic and Functional Neurosurgery (#01354)

♦ **Asian Society of Stoma Rehabilitation (ASSR)** **01741**
Contact c/o Congress Corporation, Kohsai-kaikan Bldg, 5-1 Kojimachi, Chiyoda-ku, Tokyo, 102-8481 Japan. T. +81352165318. Fax +81352165552. E-mail: assr@congre.co.jp.
URL: http://www.congre.co.jp/assr/
Aims Promote quality of life of ostomates through exchange of knowledge, techniques and experiences. **Events** *Congress* Sabah (Malaysia) 2025, *Congress* Singapore (Singapore) 2023, *Congress* Taipei (Taiwan) 2021, *Congress* Delhi (India) 2020, *Congress* Osaka (Japan) 2019. [2021/XJ2944/**D**]

♦ **Asian Society of Structural and Multidisciplinary Optimization (ASSMO)** **01742**
SG address not obtained.
Pres address not obtained.
URL: http://assmo.org/
History 1 Dec 2014. **Aims** Bring together Asian researchers and practitioners in the field of structural and multidisciplinary optimization (SMO). **Structure** Council; Executive Council; General Council. **Activities** Awards/prizes/competitions; events/meetings. **Events** *Asian Congress of Structural and Multidisciplinary Optimization* Matsue (Japan) 2022, *Asian Congress of Structural and Multidisciplinary Optimization* Seoul (Korea Rep) 2020, *Asian Congress of Structural and Multidisciplinary Optimization* Dalian (China) 2018, *Asian Congress of Structural and Multidisciplinary Optimization* Nagasaki (Japan) 2016.
Members Full in 3 countries:
China, Japan, Korea Rep. [2022/AA1567/**D**]

♦ **Asian Society of Thoracic Radiology (ASTR)** **01743**
Address not obtained.
History 2006, Seoul (Korea Rep). **Aims** Improve imaging diagnosis and interventional radiology in the field of thoracic imaging; have adequate treatment of thoracic disease; reduce morbidity and mortality and ultimately improve outcome of thoracic *disease* in Asia. **Structure** Steering Committee; Executive Committee. **Languages** English. **Staff** None paid. **Finance** Members' dues. **Activities** Healthcare; events/meetings. Active in: China, Japan, Korea Rep, Taiwan. **Events** *Asian Congress of Thoracic Imaging (ACTI)* Seoul (Korea Rep) 2023, *Asian Congress of Thoracic Imaging (ACTI)* Shanghai (China) 2019, *Asian Congress of Thoracic Imaging (ACTI)* Taipei (Taiwan) 2015, *Congress* Seoul (Korea Rep) 2013, *Asian Congress of Thoracic Radiology* Kyoto (Japan) 2011. **Publications** None.
Members Full in 10 countries and territories:
China, Hong Kong, Indonesia, Japan, Korea Rep, Malaysia, Mongolia, Taiwan, Thailand, Vietnam.
IGO Relations None. **NGO Relations** *Asian Oceanian Society of Radiology (AOSR, #01583).* [2022/XM2892/**D**]

♦ **Asian Society of Toxicology (ASIATOX)** **01744**
SG Fac of Medicine, Univ of Tsukuba, Tsukuba IBARAKI, 305-8575 Japan. T. +81298533133. Fax +81298533259.
URL: http://www.asiatox.com/
History 8 Jun 1994. Originally also referred to as *Asian Federation of the Toxicological Sciences.* **Aims** Foster scientific cooperation and promote progress in toxicological sciences in the Asian region. **Languages** English. **Events** *Congress* Hangzhou (China) 2021, *Congress* Hangzhou (China) 2020, *Congress* Pattaya (Thailand) 2018, *Congress* Jeju (Korea Rep) 2015, *Congress* Sendai (Japan) 2012. **Publications** *ASIATOX Newsletter.*
Members Affiliate; individual. Affiliate national societies in 6 countries and territories:

China, Iran Islamic Rep, Japan, Korea Rep, Taiwan, Thailand.
Individual toxicologists (over 3,000) from industry, academia and regulatory institutes in Asian region. Membership countries not specified.
NGO Relations Member of: *International Union of Toxicology (IUTOX, #15824).* [2020/XD7437/D]

♦ Asian Society of Transplantation (AST) 01745

SG 101 Daehak-ro, Jongno-gu, Seoul 03080, Korea Rep. T. +8227636316. Fax +8227636317. E-mail: astseoul19@gmail.com.
Treas Dept of Medicine, Queen Mary Hosp, Pokfulam Road, Hong Kong, Central and Western, Hong Kong. T. +85228555360. Fax +85222555411. E-mail: makmm@ha.org.hk.
URL: http://myasot.org/
History 1981. **Aims** Endeavour to provide growth of transplantation in the continent of Asia through scientific knowledge, clinical practice and continuing education with emphasis on ethical practice of transplantation. **Structure** Council. **Finance** Members' dues. **Activities** Events/meetings. **Events** *Congress* Hong Kong (Hong Kong) 2023, *Congress* Penang (Malaysia) 2021, *Congress* Delhi (India) 2019, *Congress* Cebu City (Philippines) 2017, *Congress* Singapore (Singapore) 2015.
Members Societies in 7 countries and territories:
Hong Kong, India, Korea Rep, Malaysia, Pakistan, Saudi Arabia, Thailand.
NGO Relations Associate of: *The Transplantation Society (TTS, #20224).* [2020/XD4374/D]

♦ Asian Society of Tumor Ablation (unconfirmed)

♦ Asian Society of Uro-Oncology (APSU) 01746

Contact c/o Dept of Urology, Singapore General Hospital, Outram Road, Singapore 169608, Singapore. T. +6563214693. Fax +6562273787. E-mail: gursan@sgh.com.sg – angie.see.b.g@sgh.com.sg.
History 1988. Also referred to as *Asian Pacific Society of Uro-Oncology.* **Events** *Joint International Symposium* Seoul (Korea Rep) 2019, *Joint International Symposium* Seoul (Korea Rep) 2018, *Joint International Symposium* Seoul (Korea Rep) 2017, *Meeting* Kuala Lumpur (Malaysia) 2011. **NGO Relations** Affiliated member of: *Urological Association of Asia (UAA, #20733).* Member of: *World Uro Oncology Federation (WUOF, #21895).* [2013/XM1295/D]

♦ Asian Society for Vascular Biology (ASVB) 01747

Pres IEC, Dalian Medical University, 9 West Section, Lushun South Road, Dalian, Liaoning, China. T. +8641186110197.
Honorary Pres address not obtained.
History 2004. **Aims** Promote and advance the field of vascular biology and medicine in Asia. **Structure** Council. **Languages** English. **Staff** 1.00 FTE, voluntary. **Finance** Sources: donations; members' dues. Annual budget: 1,000 USD. **Activities** Awards/prizes/competitions; events/meetings. **Events** *Meeting* Shanghai (China) 2018, *Meeting* Hualien (Taiwan) 2016, *Meeting* Kuala Lumpur (Malaysia) 2014, *Meeting* Xian (China) 2012, *Meeting* Hong Kong (Hong Kong) 2010.
Members Full in 9 countries and territories:
Australia, Canada, China, Japan, Korea Rep, Malaysia, Singapore, Taiwan, USA. [2017.06.01/XM8275/D]

♦ Asian Society for Vascular Surgery (ASVS) 01748

Registered Office 2/F Prof Block, Queen Mary Hosp, 102 Pokfulam Road, Pokfulam, Hong Kong. E-mail: meeting@asianvascular.com.
URL: http://www.asianvascular.com/
History 1992. Former names and other names: *Asian Vascular Society* – former (1992). **Aims** Develop vascular surgery in Asia. **Languages** English. **Staff** 1.50 FTE, paid. **Finance** Sources: meeting proceeds; members' dues. **Activities** Events/meetings. **Events** *Annual Congress* Bangkok (Thailand) 2024, *Annual Congress* Antalya (Türkiye) 2023, *Asian Venous Forum* Antalya (Türkiye) 2023, *Annual Congress* Taipei (Taiwan) 2022, *Annual Congress* Sapporo (Japan) 2021. **Publications** *Annals of Vascular Disease.* Congress proceedings.
Members Full in 15 countries and territories:
Bangladesh, China, Hong Kong, India, Indonesia, Japan, Korea Rep, Malaysia, Philippines, Saudi Arabia, Singapore, Taiwan, Thailand, Türkiye, Vietnam. [2021/XD4754/D]

♦ Asian Society of Veterinary Dermatology (AiSVD) 01749

Ajia Juihifuka Gakkai
SG address not obtained. E-mail: aisvd_info@aisvd.asia.
URL: https://aisvd.asia/
History Nov 2003, Seoul (Korea Rep). **Aims** Further scientific progress in veterinary and comparative dermatology. **Structure** Committee; Executive Board. **Finance** Sources: members' dues. **Activities** Training/education; knowledge management/information dissemination. **Events** *Asian Meeting of Animal Medicine Specialties* Fukuoka (Japan) 2022, *Asian Meeting of Animal Medicine Specialties* Shanghai (China) 2019, *Asian Meeting of Animal Medicine Specialties* Daegu (Korea Rep) 2017, *Asian Meeting of Animal Medicine Specialties* Kuala Lumpur (Malaysia) 2015, *Asian Meeting of Animal Medicine Specialties* Bogor (Indonesia) 2013.
Members Full in 11 countries and territories:
China, Hong Kong, India, Indonesia, Japan, Korea Rep, Malaysia, Philippines, Singapore, Taiwan, Thailand.
NGO Relations Member of (1): *World Association for Veterinary Dermatology (WAVD, #21203).* Instrumental in setting up (1): *Asian College of Veterinary Dermatology (AiCVD, #01388).* Co-organizes: *Asian Meeting of Animal Medicine Specialties (AMAMS).* [2020/XJ7846/D]

♦ Asian Society of Veterinary Ophthalmology (AiSVO) 01750

Address not obtained.
URL: http://www.aisvo.org/
History 2006, San Antonio, TX (USA). **Aims** Further scientific progress of veterinary ophthalmology in Asia; promote improved methods of diagnosis, treatment and prevention of diseases in animals. **Structure** Executive Committee. Committees. **Activities** Events/meetings; research/documentation; training/education. **Events** *Annual Conference* Japan 2022, *Annual Conference* Taipei (Taiwan) 2020, *Annual Conference* Shanghai (China) 2019, *Annual Conference* Hong Kong (Hong Kong) 2018, *Annual Conference* Daegu (Korea Rep) 2017. **NGO Relations** Co-organizes: *Asian Meeting of Animal Medicine Specialties (AMAMS).* [2020/XJ7947/D]

♦ Asian Society of Veterinary Surgery (AiSvS) 01751

Sec Joint Fac of Veterinary Medicine, Yamaguchi Univ, 1677-1 Yoshida, Yamaguchi, 753-8511 Japan. T. +81839335908. Fax +81839335908.
Pres Lab of Veterinary Surgery, Grad School of Agricultural and Life Sciences, Univ of Tokyo, 1-1-1 Yayoi, Bunkyo-ku, Tokyo, 113-8657 Japan. T. +81358415473. Fax +81358411132.
URL: http://aisvs.org/
History Founded 8 May 2011, Bangkok (Thailand). **Aims** Advance the art and science of veterinary surgery and anaesthesia, including small and large animals; promote scientific and technological progresses in veterinary surgery; establish and manage the specialization system for veterinary surgery in Asia; promote undergraduate and postgraduate education in veterinary surgery in Asia; promote cooperation with international veterinary associations. **Structure** Meeting (annual); Executive Board; Regents. **Languages** English. **Finance** Members' dues. **Events** *Annual Congress* Shanghai (China) 2019, *Annual Congress* Taichung (Taiwan) 2018, *Annual Congress* Daegu (Korea Rep) 2017, *Annual Congress* Daegu (Korea Rep) 2016, *Annual Congress* Kuala Lumpur (Malaysia) 2015. **Members** Full; Student; Affiliate; Honorary; Life; Patron. Membership countries not specified. [2015/XJ7946/D]

♦ Asian Society of Zoo and Wildlife Medicine / see Asian Society of Conservation Medicine (#01714)

♦ Asian Soft Tennis Federation (ASTF) 01752

Pres c/o Japan Soft Tennis Assn, 1-16-2-201 Ooi, Shinagawa-ku, Tokyo, 140-0014 Japan.
URL: https://astf.asia/
History 1988. **Aims** Establish friendly relations and foster goodwill and understanding among members in accordance with basic principles of the International Olympic Committee (IOC) and the Olympic Council of Asia (OCA) to develop, improve and propagate soft tennis in Asia. **Activities** Sporting activities; networking/liaising. **Events** *Meeting* Kitakyushu (Japan) 2016, *General Assembly* Mungyeong (Korea Rep) 2008. **Members** Members in 23 countries. Membership countries not specified. [2021/XD9340/D]

♦ Asian Software Testing Alliance (ASTA) 01753

Secretariat Malaysian Software Testing Board, Lot G-2, Jalan Kenari 12B, Bandar Puchong Jaya, Puchong, Selangor, 47100 Shah Alam, Selangor, Malaysia. T. +60380766100. Fax +60380750334. E-mail: info@mstb.org – secretariat@mstb.org.
URL: http://www.mstb.org/ASTA.htm/
History 2007, by member organizations of *International Software Testing Qualifications Board (ISTQB, #15559).* **Aims** Promote software testing and quality in Asia. **Events** *International software testing conference* Seoul (Korea Rep) 2010, *International software testing conference* Seoul (Korea Rep) 2007.
Members National associations in 5 countries:
China, Japan, Korea Rep, Malaysia, Vietnam. [2009/XM3617/F]

♦ Asian Soils and Environment Research Information Center (unconfirmed)

♦ Asian Solidarity Economy Coalition (ASEC) 01754

Contact 57 Diamond St Northview 1, Batasan Hills, Quezon City, Philippines. T. +6329327690 – +6329325429.
History Formally set up 1 Nov 2011, Kuala Lumpur (Malaysia), at Asian Solidarity Economy Forum (ASEF). Continental federation of *Intercontinental Network for the Promotion of the Social Solidarity Economy (INPSSE, #11463).* **Aims** Enhance the responsibilities of stakeholders in co-creating a compassionate, solidarity economy. **Events** *Asian Solidarity Forum* Indonesia 2012.
Members National, Regional and Continental Networks (18) covering 21 countries and territories:
Bangladesh, Bhutan, Cambodia, China, India, Indonesia, Japan, Korea Rep, Laos, Malaysia, Mongolia, Myanmar, Nepal, Pakistan, Philippines, Singapore, Sri Lanka, Taiwan, Thailand, Timor-Leste, Vietnam.
Founding members in 5 countries:
China, Indonesia, Japan, Malaysia, Philippines.
Included in the above, 3 organizations listed in this Yearbook:
Ethnos Asia Ministries (#05555); Global Citizens for Sustainable Development (GCSD); Pacific Asia Resource Centre (PARC).
NGO Relations *Alliance for Responsible and Sustainable Societies (#00718).* [2015/XJ5923/y/D]

♦ Asian-South Pacific Association of Sport Psychology (ASPASP) . . . 01755

Pres Dept of Sport Sciences, Seoul Natl Univ of Science and Technology, 172 Gongneung Nowon, Seoul 139743, Korea Rep. E-mail: info@aspasp.org.
Past Pres Fac of Sport Sciences, Beijing Sport Univ, No 48 Information Road, Haidian District, 100084 Beijing, China. T. +861062989565.
URL: http://www.aspasp.org/
History 12 Aug 1989, Singapore (Singapore). Founded at 7th World Congress in Sport Psychology, at the instigation of *International Society of Sport Psychology (ISSP, #15455).* Statutes most recently revised, Dec 2007, Bangkok (Thailand). **Aims** Facilitate development of sport and exercise psychology throughout the Asian-South Pacific region. **Structure** General Assembly; Managing Council; National Representatives Council. **Languages** English. **Activities** Events/meetings; knowledge management/information dissemination. **Events** *International Congress* 2026, *International Congress* Kuching (Malaysia) 2022, *International Congress* Daegu (Korea Rep) 2018, *International Congress of Sports Psychology* Varanasi (India) 2015, *International Congress* Tokyo (Japan) 2014. **Publications** *ASPASP Newsletter. Inside Sport Psychology* (2011); *Judgment, Decision-making and Success in Sport* (2011); *The New Sport and Exercise Psychology Companion.* Congress proceedings.
Members in 26 countries and territories:
Australia, China, Fiji, Hong Kong, India, Indonesia, Iran Islamic Rep, Iraq, Israel, Japan, Korea Rep, Kuwait, Laos, Macau, Malaysia, Mongolia, Nepal, New Zealand, Philippines, Qatar, Saudi Arabia, Singapore, Sri Lanka, Taiwan, Thailand, Vietnam. [2022/XD2257/D]

♦ Asian South Pacific Bureau of Adult Education / see Asia South Pacific Association for Basic and Adult Education (#02098)

♦ Asian and South Pacific Ostomy Association (ASPOA) 01756

Pres 1-1-1-901 Higashi-Shinkoiwa, Katsushika-Ku, Tokyo, 124-0023 Japan. T. +81356707681. Fax +81356707682.
URL: http://www.ostomyinternational.org/
History as *Asian Ostomy Association (AOA).* Current named adopted when merged with *South Pacific Ostomy Association (SPOA, inactive),* to become a regional affiliate association of *International Ostomy Association (IOA, #14491)* following decision by the World Council, Nov 2010. **Structure** Executive Council, including President, Secretary/Treasurer, Member. **Events** *Triennial Conference* Delhi (India) 2020, *Triennial Conference* Seoul (Korea Rep) 2017, *Triennial Conference* Ho Chi Minh City (Vietnam) 2014, *Triennial Conference* Teheran (Iran Islamic Rep) 2011, *Triennial conference / Regional Meeting* Tokyo (Japan) 2008.
Members in 8 countries and territories:
China, Hong Kong, India, Japan, Korea Rep, Malaysia, Singapore, Thailand. [2018/XD5753/D]

♦ Asian Spinal Cord Network (ASCoN) 01757

Sec c/o Livability, Fermanagh House, Broadmeadow Place, Enniskillen, BT74 7HR, UK. T. +442866320091.
Chairperson CRP, Savar, Dhaka, Bangladesh. T. +88027745464 – +88027745465.
URL: http://www.ascon.info/
History Nov 2001, Bangladesh. Founded as a regional spinal injury network. **Aims** Strengthen spinal *injury* services and human resource development for organizations and people working in spinal injury management in the Asia region; share information, ideas and knowledge of best practices in spinal cord injury management among members. **Structure** Annual General Meeting; Executive Committee. **Languages** English. **Staff** None. **Finance** Support from various international organizations. **Activities** Networking/liaising; awareness raising; training/education; capacity building; research/documentation. **Events** *Annual Conference* Philippines 2021, *Annual Conference* Seoul (Korea Rep) 2020, *Annual Conference* Chiang Mai (Thailand) 2017, *Annual Conference* Dhaka (Bangladesh) 2014, *Annual Conference* Coimbatore (India) 2013. **Publications** *ASCoN Guiding principles for Management of Spinal Cord Injuries; ASCoN Prevention Guidelines.*
Members Organizations (74) in 18 countries:
Afghanistan, Bangladesh, Bhutan, Cambodia, China, India, Indonesia, Japan, Korea Rep, Laos, Malaysia, Myanmar, Nepal, Pakistan, Sri Lanka, Thailand, Timor-Leste, Vietnam.
NGO Relations Member of: *International Spinal Cord Society (ISCoS, #15581).* [2019/XM0991/F]

♦ Asian Sponsorship Association (ASA) 01758

Pres 29-05A Intl Plaza, Singapore 079903, Singapore.
URL: http://www.asiansponsorship.org/
History 2014. Registered in accordance with Singapore law. **Aims** Transform sponsorship practices and grow the *business* sector in Asia. **Structure** Board. **Languages** English. **Staff** 2.00 FTE, paid. **Finance** Members' dues. **Activities** Research/documentation; training/education; advocacy/lobbying/activism; networking/liaising. **Events** *All That Matters Conference* Singapore (Singapore) 2016, *Sports Matters Conference* Singapore (Singapore) 2015. [2015.08.26/XJ9809/D]

♦ Asian Sport Jiu-Jitsu Federation (unconfirmed)

♦ Asian Sports Press Union (ASPU) 01759

Pres Olympic Bd 402, Oryun dong 88, Song-pa ku, Seoul, Korea Rep. T. +82220514234. Fax +8225652405. E-mail: windyhillhong@yahoo.co.kr.
SG address not obtained.
URL: http://www.aipsasia.com/
History Continental section of: *Association internationale de la presse sportive (AIPS, #02729).* **Structure** Officers (10). **Events** *Congress* Incheon (Korea Rep) 2014, *Congress* Kuwait 2008. **Members** National sports journalists' associations. Membership countries not specified. [2014/XD7420/D]

♦ Asian Squash Federation (ASF) 01760

SG Pusat Skusay Kompleks, Sukan Negara – Bukit Jalil, Sri Petaling, 57000 Kuala Lumpur, Malaysia. T. +60389963964. Fax +60389969406. E-mail: asiasquash@gmail.com.
Pres address not obtained.
URL: http://www.asiansquash.org/

History Founded 1980. Constitution amended and approved at 14th General Meeting, 1994, Kuala Lumpur (Malaysia). **Aims** Promote the game in Asia; maintain the authority and autonomy of members; coordinate and protect the common interests of members; uphold the WSF rules of the game; ensure observance of these rules in all national and international *competitions* and matches; settle any dispute in which two or more members are involved, and which requires the Federation's mediation. **Structure** General Meeting (annual). Officers: President, 3 Vice Presidents, Secretary-General, Honorary Treasurer, Director Coaching, Director Referees. Secretariat, located in Kuala Lumpur (Malaysia). Committees (5): Major Games; Championship; Junior Affairs; Coaching; Referees. **Languages** English. **Finance** Members' dues. Other sources: fundraising through Handbook advertising; ball adoption fee; voluntary donations. **Activities** Supervises and organizes: Asian Games; Asian Junior Squash Championships; Asian Squash Championships. **Events** *Annual General Meeting* Cheongju (Korea Rep) 2018, *Annual General Meeting* Seoul (Korea Rep) 2013, *Annual General Meeting* Doha (Qatar) 2012, *Annual General Meeting* Colombo (Sri Lanka) 2011, *Annual General Meeting* Chennai (India) 2010. **Publications** *Asian Squash Federation Handbook* (annual).
Members Full; Corporate. National squash associations in 26 countries and territories:
Bahrain, Bangladesh, Brunei Darussalam, China, Hong Kong, India, Indonesia, Iran Islamic Rep, Japan, Jordan, Korea Rep, Kuwait, Lebanon, Macau, Malaysia, Nepal, Oman, Pakistan, Palestine, Philippines, Qatar, Saudi Arabia, Singapore, Sri Lanka, Taiwan, Thailand.
NGO Relations Regional federation of: *World Squash Federation (WSF, #21826).* [2014/XE5891/**E**]

♦ Asian Statistical Institute / see Statistical Institute for Asia and the Pacific (#19972)

♦ Asian Strategic Alliance for Pneumococcal Disease Prevention (ASAP) 01761

Secretariat Ping Healthcare Pte Ltd, No 20 Sin Ming Lane, Midview City No 06-55, Singapore 573 968, Singapore. T. +6567785620. Fax +6567781372. E-mail: info@pingconference.com.
URL: http://www.asap-pneumo.org/

History Launched 14 Dec 2007. **Aims** Highlight the burden of pneumococcal disease in Asia; foster collaboration in the fight against *diseases* caused by Streptococcus pneumonia. **Structure** Executive Committee. **Events** *Symposium* Singapore (Singapore) 2020, *Asian Dengue Vaccination Advocacy Symposium* Bangkok (Thailand) 2016, *Symposium on pneumococcal vaccine 15 years on* Bangkok (Thailand) 2016, *ASVAC : Asian Vaccine Conference* Hanoi (Vietnam) 2015, *Symposium on the Next Phase in Pneumococcal Vaccination* Penang (Malaysia) 2014. **NGO Relations** Affiliated to: *Asian Society of Pediatric Infectious Diseases (ASPID, #01733).* [2017/XM5665/**D**]

♦ Asian Strategy and Leadership Institute (internationally oriented national body)
♦ Asian Stroke Forum (meeting series)
♦ Asian Student Press Bureau (inactive)
♦ Asian Studies Association of Australia (internationally oriented national body)
♦ Asian Studies Center, Michigan (internationally oriented national body)
♦ Asian Studies Center, Pittsburgh (internationally oriented national body)
♦ Asian Studies Program, University of Pittsburgh / see Asian Studies Center, Pittsburgh
♦ Asian Studies Research Institute / see Sinor Research Institute for Inner Asian Studies

♦ Asian Sumo Federation 01762

Pres 1-15-20 Hyakunicho, Shinjuku-ku, Tokyo, 169-0073 Japan. T. +81333603911. Fax +81333604020. E-mail: office2@ifs-sumo.org.
URL: http://www.ifs-sumo.org/

Aims Promote the sport of Sumo among Asian countries. **Languages** English, Japanese.
Members Full in 22 countries and territories:
China, Hong Kong, India, Indonesia, Iran Islamic Rep, Japan, Kazakhstan, Korea Rep, Kyrgyzstan, Malaysia, Mongolia, Pakistan, Philippines, Singapore, Sri Lanka, Syrian AR, Taiwan, Tajikistan, Thailand, Turkmenistan, Uzbekistan, Vietnam.
NGO Relations Member of: *International Sumo Federation (IFS, #15624).* [2017.11.27/XD7596/**D**]

♦ Asian Surgical Association 01763

Association chirurgicale d'Asie

SG Dept of Surgery, School of Clin Medicine, Li Ka Shing Fac of Medicine, Univ of Hong Kong, Queen Mary Hosp, Pokfulam, Hong Kong. T. +85222554837. Fax +85228162094. E-mail: secretariat@asiansurgassoc.org.
Pres address not obtained.
URL: http://www.asiansurgassoc.org/

History 23 May 1976, Singapore (Singapore). Founded 23 May 1976, following preliminary meeting, 21 Aug 1975, Singapore. Former names and other names: *Association of Surgeons of South East Asia (ASSEA)* – former (1976 to 1988); *Asian Surgical Society* – alias. **Aims** Improve standards of surgical care by establishing professional ties between surgeons of South East Asia and providing a forum for dissemination of surgical knowledge throughout the region. **Structure** Council. **Languages** English. **Staff** 1.00 FTE, paid. **Finance** Sources: donations; members' dues. **Activities** Events/meetings; financial and/or material support. **Events** *Asian Congress of Surgery* Hong Kong (Hong Kong) 2021, *Biennial Congress* Kuala Lumpur (Malaysia) 2019, *Biennial Congress* Tokyo (Japan) 2017, *Biennial Congress* Hong Kong (Hong Kong) 2015, *Biennial Congress* Singapore (Singapore) 2013. **Publications** *Asian Journal of Surgery* (4 a year).
Members Surgeons in 26 countries and territories:
Algeria, Australia, Belgium, Canada, Germany, Hong Kong, India, Indonesia, Italy, Japan, Korea Rep, Kuwait, Malaysia, Myanmar, Netherlands, New Zealand, Oman, Pakistan, Philippines, Poland, Singapore, Taiwan, Thailand, UK, United Arab Emirates, USA. [2022.05.14/XD5458/v/**D**]

♦ Asian Surgical Society / see Asian Surgical Association (#01763)
♦ Asian Surgical Ultrasound Society (unconfirmed)
♦ Asian Symposium on Computational Heat Transfer and Fluid Flow (meeting series)
♦ Asian Symposium on Foot Surgery / see Asian Federation of Foot and Ankle Surgeons (#01460)
♦ Asian Symposium on Medicinal Plants, Spices and Other Natural Products (meeting series)
♦ Asian Symposium on Plant Lipids (meeting series)
♦ Asian Symposium on Psychotropic Medication (meeting series)

♦ Asian Synthetic Biology Association (ASBA) 01764

Contact 1068 Xueyuan Boulevard, University Town of Nanshan, Shenzhen, 518055 Guangdong, China. T. +8675526405754. E-mail: asba2019@synbioasia.org.
URL: http://synbioasia.org/

History 2018. **Structure** Steering Committee. **Activities** Events/meetings. **Events** *Meeting* Singapore (Singapore) 2020, *Meeting* Chengdu (China) 2019, *Meeting* Jeju (Korea Rep) 2018.
Members Full in 4 countries:
China, Japan, Korea Rep, Singapore. [2020/XM8309/**D**]

♦ Asian Table Tennis Union (ATTU) 01765

Pres Room 602, No 6 Zuo An Men Nei Ave, Chong Wen Dist, 100061 Beijing, China. T. +861067186928. Fax +861067186928. E-mail: attubj@vip.163.com.
Hon SG Room 2008 Olympic House, 1 Stadium Path, So Kon Po, Causeway Bay, Hong Kong, Central and Western, Hong Kong. T. +85225755330. Fax +85228389233. E-mail: hktta@netvigator.com.
URL: http://www.attu.org/

History 7 May 1972, Beijing (China). Gradually superseded *Table Tennis Federation of Asia (TTFA, inactive)*, set up 9 Feb 1952, Bombay (India), and officially recognized, 1975, by *International Table Tennis Federation (ITTF, #15650)* as its continental body. **Aims** Enhance friendship among the people and table tennis players of the countries and regions in Asia and develop friendly ties between table tennis circles of Asia and those of the others continents; promote popularization, development and advancement of table tennis in Asia. **Structure** Executive Committee; Council; Congress (every 2 years). Committees (4): Technical and Rules; Coaching and Junior; Veteran; Media. **Languages** English. **Staff** Voluntary. **Finance** Members' dues. Contributions. **Activities** Organizes: Asian Table Tennis Championships (every 2 years, in odd years); Asian Cups (annually); Asian Junior Championships (every 2 years, in odd years). ATTU meetings at all levels. **Events** *Biennial Congress* Busan (Korea Rep) 2013, *Biennial Congress and Championships* Doha (Qatar) 2000, *Biennial Congress and Championships* Osaka (Japan) 1998, *Biennial Congress and Championships* Singapore (Singapore) 1996, *Biennial Congress and Championships* Tianjin (China) 1994. **Publications** *ATTU Bulletin* in English.

Members Associations in 41 countries:
Bahrain, Bangladesh, Brunei Darussalam, Cambodia, China, Hong Kong, India, Indonesia, Iran Islamic Rep, Iraq, Japan, Jordan, Kazakhstan, Korea DPR, Korea Rep, Kuwait, Kyrgyzstan, Laos, Lebanon, Macau, Malaysia, Maldives, Mongolia, Nepal, Oman, Pakistan, Palestine, Philippines, Qatar, Saudi Arabia, Singapore, Sri Lanka, Syrian AR, Taiwan, Tajikistan, Thailand, Turkmenistan, United Arab Emirates, Uzbekistan, Vietnam, Yemen.
Associate members in 2 countries:
Australia, New Zealand.
NGO Relations Contacts with: *General Association of Asian Sports Federations (inactive); Olympic Council of Asia (OCA, #17718).* [2018/XD5770/**D**]

♦ Asian Taekwondo Union (ATU) 01766

Pres 1E-3, Tancheon-ro, Bundang-gu, Seongnam GYEONGGI 468839, Korea Rep. T. +82317089994. Fax +82317099994. E-mail: asiantkdunion@gmail.com – admin@wtasia.org.
SG 134 Yongindaehak-ro, Cheoin-gu, Yongin GYEONGGI 449 714, Korea Rep. T. +82317089994. Fax +82317099994. E-mail: jhkatu@gmail.com.
URL: http://www.asiantaekwondounion.org/

History Founded Sep 1978, Hong Kong. A regional union of *World Taekwondo (#21844).* **Aims** Provide effective international governance of taekwondo as an Olympic Sport and Paralympics Sport in Asia; promote, expand and improve the practice of taekwondo in Asia in light of its educational, cultural and sport values; promote fair play, youth development and education; encourage peace and cooperation through participation in sports; promote or sanction international taekwondo competitions. **Structure** General Assembly (annual); Council; Committees (17). Includes *Southeast Asian Taekwondo Union (SEATU, no recent information).* Headquarters located in the nation of nationality of President. **Languages** English, French, Korean, Spanish. **Finance** Members' dues. Other sources: donations; subsidies. **Events** *Extraordinary General Assembly* Muju (Korea Rep) 2017, *Biennial Asian Taekwondo Championship* China 2008, *General Assembly* Luoyang (China) 2008, *Extraordinary general assembly* Amman (Jordan) 2007, *General Assembly* Seoul (Korea Rep) 2004.
Members Full; Demoted; Provisional; Associate; Suspended. National organizations in 41 countries and territories:
Afghanistan, Bahrain, Bangladesh, Bhutan, Brunei Darussalam, Cambodia, China, Hong Kong, India, Indonesia, Iran Islamic Rep, Iraq, Japan, Jordan, Kazakhstan, Korea Rep, Kuwait, Kyrgyzstan, Laos, Lebanon, Macau, Malaysia, Mongolia, Myanmar, Nepal, Pakistan, Palestine, Philippines, Qatar, Saudi Arabia, Singapore, Sri Lanka, Syrian AR, Taiwan, Tajikistan, Thailand, Turkmenistan, United Arab Emirates, Uzbekistan, Vietnam, Yemen. [2022/XD0394/**D**]

♦ Asian Tchouk-Ball Federation / see Asia Pacific Tchoukball Federation (#02063)
♦ Asian Telecom and Information Exchange Forum (unconfirmed)

♦ Asian Tennis Federation (ATF) 01767

Pres RK Khanna Tennis Stadium, No 1 Africa Ave, Safdarjung Enclave, Delhi 110029, DELHI 110029, India. T. +911126176276 – +91112617628385 – +911126176280. Fax +911126173159.
URL: http://www.asiantennis.com/

History Founded 1958. **Aims** Promote the game of tennis throughout the region; upgrade standards through development initiatives in areas such as coaching, officiating, tournament management, seniors and juniors tennis. **Structure** General Meeting (annual); Committee of Management; Board of Directors. Committees (8): Finance; Juniors; Seniors; Professional; Officiating; Marketing and Sponsorship; Media and Communications; Constitution. Head Office in Delhi (India). **Languages** English. **Staff** 3.00 FTE, paid; 9.00 FTE, voluntary. **Finance** Members' dues. Other sources: sponsorship; sanction fees; ATF Tennis Foundation; contributions; assistance by the ITF. **Activities** Sporting activities. **Events** *Annual Meeting* Uzbekistan 2011, *Annual Meeting* Bangkok (Thailand) 2005, *Annual general meeting / Annual Meeting* Tashkent (Uzbekistan) 2000, *Annual General Meeting* 1995, *Annual General Meeting* Seoul (Korea Rep) 1986. **Publications** *ATF Newsletter* (4 a year); *Tennis Asia* (4 a year) – magazine.
Members Tennis Associations in 44 countries and territories:
Afghanistan, Bahrain, Bangladesh, Bhutan, Brunei Darussalam, Cambodia, China, Hong Kong, India, Indonesia, Iran Islamic Rep, Iraq, Japan, Jordan, Kazakhstan, Korea DPR, Korea Rep, Kuwait, Kyrgyzstan, Laos, Lebanon, Macau, Malaysia, Maldives, Mongolia, Myanmar, Nepal, Oman, Pakistan, Palestine, Philippines, Qatar, Saudi Arabia, Singapore, Sri Lanka, Syrian AR, Taiwan, Tajikistan, Thailand, Turkmenistan, United Arab Emirates, Uzbekistan, Vietnam, Yemen.
NGO Relations Member of: *International Tennis Federation (ITF, #15676).* [2015/XD7100/**D**]

♦ Asian Theological Seminary, Metro Manila (internationally oriented national body)

♦ Asian Thermal Spray Society (ATSS) 01768

Contact School of Materials Science and Engineering, Xi'an Jiatong Univ, Xianning West Road 28, Xian, 710049 Shaanxi, China. T. +862982660970. Fax +862982660970.
URL: http://www.asiantss.com/

Aims Promote advancements of research and development and industrial applications of thermal spray technology in Asian countries. **Structure** Committee. **Activities** Events/meetings; knowledge management/information dissemination. **Events** *Asian Thermal Spray Conference* Singapore (Singapore) 2018, *Asian Thermal Spray Conference* Jeju (Korea Rep) 2017. [2017/XM6595/**D**]

♦ Asian Thermophysical Properties Conference (meeting series)
♦ Asian Thoracic Surgical Club (unconfirmed)
♦ Asian Track and Field Coaches Association (inactive)
♦ Asian Trade Centre (unconfirmed)
♦ Asian Trade Federation of Clerical Workers / see Asian Brotherhood of Clerical Workers (#01366)
♦ Asian Trade Federation of Clothing, Leather, Textile and Handloom Workers (inactive)
♦ Asian Trade Federation for the Mixed Industries Group (no recent information)
♦ Asian Trade Federation of Transport Workers, Dhaka (inactive)
♦ Asian Trade Promotion Forum (meeting series)
♦ Asian Traditional Sports and Games Association (unconfirmed)
♦ Asian Triathlon / see Asian Triathlon Confederation (#01769)

♦ Asian Triathlon Confederation (ASTC) 01769

Pres Room 502 Olympic Center, 88 Oryun-dong, Songpa-gu, Seoul 138-749, Korea Rep.
URL: http://astc.triathlon.org/

History Founded 28 Jun 1991, Beijing (China). A regional union of *World Triathlon (#21872).* Former names and other names: *Asian Triathlon* – alias. **Activities** Sporting activities. **Events** *Congress* Gyeongju (Korea Rep) 2019. **Members** National organizations (29). Membership countries not specified. [2020/XM1440/**D**]

♦ Asian Tribology Council (ATC) 01770

Contact Malaysian Tribology Soc, Dept of Mechanical Enginering, Fac of Engineering, Univ of Malaya, 50603 Kuala Lumpur, Malaysia. E-mail: asiatrib2018@gmail.com.

Activities Events/meetings. **Events** *ASIATRIB : Asia International Conference on Tribology* Tianjin (China) 2024, *ASIATRIB : Asia International Conference on Tribology* Tianjin (China) 2022, *ASIATRIB : Asia International Conference on Tribology* Kuching (Malaysia) 2018, *ASIATRIB : Asia International Conference on Tribology* Agra (India) 2014, *ASIATRIB : Asia International Conference on Tribology* Perth, WA (Australia) 2010. **NGO Relations** *International Tribology Council (ITC, #15730).* [2017/XM4391/**D**]

♦ Asian TV Drama Conference (meeting series)

♦ Asian Underwater Federation (AUF) 01771

SG Rm 112, Handball Arena, 424 Olympic-ro, Songpa-Ku, Seoul, Korea Rep. T. +8224204293. Fax +8224218898. E-mail: cmasasia@kua.or.kr.
URL: http://www.cmasasia.org/

History as part of *World Underwater Federation (#21873).* Also referred to as *CMAS ASIA.* **Aims** Promote CMAS activities in the region. **Languages** English. **Activities** Organizes championships and instruction courses. **Events** *Asia Continental Meeting* Seoul (Korea Rep) 2021, *General Assembly* Seoul (Korea Rep) 2021. [2013.10.07/XM8107/**D**]

♦ Asian Union (unconfirmed)

♦ Asian Union of Magnetics Societies (AUMS) 01772

Exec Sec address not obtained. E-mail: aums.secretary@phys.ntu.edu.tw.
URL: http://aums.ntu.edu.tw/p-1.html

History Jan 2009. **Aims** Promote research, education, and application development in magnetism, magnetic materials, and magnetic devices. **Structure** Council, comprising President, 3 Vice-Presidents, Executive Secretary and 4 members. **Events** *International Conference* Okinawa (Japan) 2020, *International Conference* Jeju (Korea Rep) 2018, *International Conference* Tainan (Taiwan) 2016, *International Conference* Haikou City (China) 2014, *International Conference* Nara (Japan) 2012.
Members Full in 4 countries and territories:
China, Japan, Korea Rep, Taiwan. [2013/XJ6724/**D**]

♦ Asian Union for Microcirculation (no recent information)
♦ Asian Union of Pankration Athlima (inactive)

♦ Asian Union of Thermal Science and Engineering (AUTSE) 01773

SG address not obtained.
URL: https://autse-asia.org/

History 2015. **Aims** Promote and foster cooperation among Asian scientists and engineers working in the field of thermal sciences and heat transfer. **Structure** Executive Board; Scientific Council; Honorary Advisory Board. **Activities** Events/meetings; awards/prizes/competitions. **Events** *Asian Conference on Thermal Sciences* 2021, *International Symposium on Oscillating/Pulsating Heat Pipes* Daejeon (Korea Rep) 2019, *Asian Symposium on Computational Heat Transfer and Fluid Flow* Tokyo (Japan) 2019, *Asian Conference on Thermal Sciences* Jeju (Korea Rep) 2017.
Members Full in 4 countries:
China, India, Japan, Korea Rep. [2021/XM6574/**D**]

♦ Asian University Network of Environment and Disaster Risk Management (AUEDM) 01774

Contact address not obtained. E-mail: auedm.net@gmail.com.
URL: http://www.auedm.net/

Aims Share and work together in promoting environment and disaster management in higher *education*; seek possibilities of mutual collaboration on field-based action research; broaden the scope of education and learning in the environment and disaster management field through collaboration with other stakeholders. **Activities** Events/meetings. **Events** *Future Cooperation Meeting* Busan (Korea Rep) 2016, *Republic of Korea – ASEAN Disaster Management Project Kickoff Workshop* Busan (Korea Rep) 2016.
Members Full in 14 countries:
Bangladesh, Cambodia, China, India, Indonesia, Japan, Malaysia, Nepal, Pakistan, Philippines, Sri Lanka, Taiwan, Thailand, Vietnam.
Observers (7), including 3 organizations listed in this Yearbook:
Asian Disaster Reduction and Response Network (ADRRN, #01428); Church World Service (CWS); United Nations University (UNU, #20642). [2014/XJ8575/**F**]

♦ Asian University Sports Federation (AUSF) 01775

General Coordinator Bldg 33, 2 Ronghuiyuan, Yuhua Rd, Shunyi District, 101318 Beijing, China. E-mail: ausf@ausf.org.
URL: http://www.ausf.org/

History 28 Mar 1992, Bangkok (Thailand). **Aims** Provide a platform for university students in Asia so as to exchange and interact through sports. **Structure** General Assembly (every 4 years). Executive Committee, comprising President, Senior Vice-President, 2 Vice-Presidents, Secretary General, Vice Secretary General, Treasurer, 4 members and 2 Auditors. Steering Committee, comprising President, Vice-Presidents, Secretary General and Treasurer.
Members Full in 32 countries and territories:
Bangladesh, Cambodia, China, Hong Kong, India, Indonesia, Iran Islamic Rep, Japan, Jordan, Kazakhstan, Korea Rep, Kyrgyzstan, Lebanon, Macau, Malaysia, Mongolia, Nepal, Oman, Pakistan, Palestine, Philippines, Singapore, Sri Lanka, Syrian AR, Taiwan, Tajikistan, Thailand, Turkmenistan, United Arab Emirates, Uzbekistan, Vietnam, Yemen.
NGO Relations Support from: *International University Sports Federation (FISU, #15830).* Cooperates with: *ASEAN University Sports Council (AUSC, #01244).* [2019/XJ5370/**D**]

♦ Asian University for Women (unconfirmed)
♦ Asian Urban Information Center of Kobe (internationally oriented national body)

♦ Asian Urban Research Association (AURA) 01776

Exec Sec Geog Earth Science Dept, Shippensburg Univ, 1871 Old Main Drive, Shippensburg PA 17257, USA. T. +17174771776. Fax +17174774029.
URL: https://sites.google.com/site/asianurbanization/

History Jan 1986. **Aims** Promote the study of urbanization and urban growth. **Structure** Executive Committee. **Events** *Asian Urbanization Conference* Ho Chi Minh City (Vietnam) 2019, *Asian Urbanization Conference* Bangkok (Thailand) 2018, *Asian Urbanization Conference* Yogyakarta (Indonesia) 2016, *Asian Urbanization Conference / International Asian Urbanization Conference* Varanasi (India) 2013, *Asian Urbanization Conference / International Asian Urbanization Conference* Hyderabad (India) 2011. [2019/XJ7637/**E**]

♦ Asian Urban Research Group (AURG) 01777

Contact address not obtained. E-mail: info@aurghp.com.
URL: http://aurghp.com/

History 1989. **Aims** Contribute suggestions for Asian provincial city planning. **Structure** Board of Directors. **Languages** English. **Activities** Events/meetings. **Events** *International Symposium on City Planning and Environmental Management in Asian Countries* Seoul (Korea Rep) 2019, *International Symposium on City Planning and Environmental Management in Asian Countries* Nanjing (China) 2018, *International Symposium on City Planning and Environmental Management in Asian Countries* Makassar (Indonesia) 2016, *International Symposium on City Planning and Environmental Management in Asian Countries* Oita (Japan) 2014, *International Symposium on City Planning and Environmental Management in Asian Countries* Tianjin (China) 2012. **Publications** Symposium proceedings.
Members Full in 5 countries:
China, Indonesia, Japan, Korea Rep, Singapore. [2022.07.10/AA0218/**F**]

♦ Asian Vascular Society / see Asian Society for Vascular Surgery (#01748)
♦ Asian Vegetable Research and Development Center / see AVRDC – The World Vegetable Center (#03051)

♦ Asian Venture Philanthropy Network (AVPN) 01778

CEO 3 Shenton Way, Shenton House 22-08, Singapore 068805, Singapore. T. +6565361824. E-mail: info@avpn.asia.
URL: http://www.avpn.asia/

History 2011. Inaugural conference, May 2013, Singapore (Singapore). Registration: No/ID: UEN 201016116M, Singapore. **Aims** Increase the flow of financial, human and intellectual capital to the social sector by connecting and empowering key stakeholders from funders to the social purpose organizations they support. **Structure** Board of Directors. **Languages** English. **Staff** 22.00 FTE, paid. **Finance** Pro bono services and financial support from partner foundations and corporations. **Activities** Networking/liaising; research/documentation; advocacy/lobbying/activism; knowledge management/information dissemination; events/meetings. **Events** *Global Conference* Bali (Indonesia) 2022, *Southeast Asia Social Investment Summit* 2021, *Northeast Asia Social Investment Summit* Seoul (Korea Rep) 2021, *Building Philanthropic Collaboratives in Singapore* Singapore (Singapore) 2020, *Investing in Pandemic Proof Solutions Across Asia-Pacific* Singapore (Singapore) 2020. **Publications** Annual Report; guides.
Members Organizations in 28 countries and territories:
Austria, Bangladesh, Belgium, Cambodia, China, France, Germany, Hong Kong, India, Indonesia, Japan, Korea Rep, Malaysia, Monaco, Myanmar, Nepal, Netherlands, New Zealand, Norway, Philippines, Singapore, Switzerland, Taiwan, Thailand, UK, USA, Vietnam, Virgin Is UK.
Included in the above, 7 organizations listed in this Yearbook:
Charities Aid Foundation (CAF); European Venture Philanthropy Association (EVPA, #09053); Give2Asia; Global Fund for Children (GFC); INSEAD (#11228); International Rice Research Institute (IRRI, #14754); Shell Foundation.
NGO Relations *African Venture Philanthropy Alliance (AVPA); European Venture Philanthropy Association (EVPA, #09053); International Venture Philanthropy Center (IVPC, #15843); Worldwide Initiatives for Grantmaker Support (WINGS, #21926).* [2020/XJ6514/y/**F**]

♦ Asian Veteran Athletes Association / see Asia Masters Athletics (#01291)

♦ Asian Volleyball Confederation (AVC) 01779

SG Room No 1-2, 12th Fl Main Bldg, Sports Authority of Thailand, 286 Ramkhamhaeng Road, Huamark, Bangkapi, Bangkok, 10240, Thailand. T. +6621362861. Fax +6621362864. E-mail: avc.bk@asianvolleyball.net.
URL: http://www.asianvolleyball.com

History 5 May 1952. A confederation of *Fédération internationale de volleyball (FIVB, #09670)*. Former names and other names: *Asian Volleyball Federation (AVF)* – former. **Aims** Promote volleyball and beach volleyball in all its modalities in Asia and Oceania. **Structure** General Assembly (every 2 years); Board of Administration; Executive Committee; Technical Committees and Council. **Languages** English. **Staff** 15.00 FTE, paid. **Activities** Events/meetings; sporting activities. **Events** *General Assembly* Bangkok (Thailand) 2020, *General Assembly* Bangkok (Thailand) 2017, *General Assembly* Riyadh (Saudi Arabia) 2015, *General Assembly* Taicang (China) 2005, *General Assembly* Bangkok (Thailand) 2001.
Members National federations in 65 countries and territories:
Afghanistan, Australia, Bahrain, Bangladesh, Bhutan, Brunei Darussalam, Cambodia, China, Cook Is, Fiji, Guam, Hong Kong, India, Indonesia, Iran Islamic Rep, Iraq, Japan, Jordan, Kazakhstan, Kiribati, Korea DPR, Korea Rep, Kuwait, Kyrgyzstan, Laos, Lebanon, Macau, Malaysia, Maldives, Marshall Is, Micronesia FS, Mongolia, Myanmar, Nauru, Nepal, New Zealand, Niue, Northern Mariana Is, Oman, Pakistan, Palau, Palestine, Papua New Guinea, Philippines, Qatar, Samoa, Samoa USA, Saudi Arabia, Singapore, Solomon Is, Sri Lanka, Syrian AR, Tahiti Is, Taiwan, Tajikistan, Thailand, Timor-Leste, Tonga, Turkmenistan, Tuvalu, United Arab Emirates, Uzbekistan, Vanuatu, Vietnam, Yemen. [2020.11.17/XE3782/**E**]

♦ Asian Volleyball Federation / see Asian Volleyball Confederation (#01779)
♦ Asian Waterqual Group / see IWA Asia Pacific Region Grouping (#16083)
♦ Asian Water Ski Federation / see Asian Waterski and Waterboard Federation (#01780)

♦ Asian Waterski and Waterboard Federation 01780

Address not obtained.

History Set as *Asian Water Ski Federation*.
Members Full in 17 countries and territories:
Australia, China, Hong Kong, India, Indonesia, Iran Islamic Rep, Japan, Korea Rep, Kuwait, Lebanon, Malaysia, New Zealand, Philippines, Singapore, Taiwan, Thailand, United Arab Emirates. [2015/XE3919/**E**]

♦ Asian Weightlifting Federation (AWF) 01781

Fédération asiatique haltérophile

Secretariat 20th Floor Chalearmprakiat Bldg 286, Sports Authority of Thailand, Ramkhamhaeng Road, Huamark Bangkapi, Bangkok, 10240, Thailand. T. +6621709461. E-mail: awfederation@yahoo.com.
Main Office PO Box 2473, Doha, Qatar. E-mail: info@awfederation.com.
URL: http://awfederation.com/

History 1958, Tokyo (Japan). Founded at 3rd Asian Games. **Aims** Promote weightlifting in Asia; supervise Asian weightlifting *championships*; establish list of Asian Federation records (including Australia and New Zealand) and Asian Games records; publish and distribute information for the mutual benefit of affiliated associations. **Structure** General Assembly (during Asian Games); Executive Board; Secretariat. Committees; Commissions. **Languages** English. **Finance** Members' dues. Grants from official and private bodies. **Activities** Sporting activities. **Events** *Congress* Pyeongtaek (Korea Rep) 2012, *Congress / Annual Congress* Manila (Philippines) 2003, *Congress* Jeonju (Korea Rep) 2001, *Annual Congress* Busan (Korea Rep) 1995, *Annual meeting* Busan (Korea Rep) 1995. **Publications** Data on weightlifting affairs in Asia and Asian Games.
Members Affiliated national associations in 45 countries and territories:
Afghanistan, Bahrain, Bangladesh, Bhutan, Brunei Darussalam, Cambodia, China, Hong Kong, India, Indonesia, Iran Islamic Rep, Iraq, Japan, Jordan, Kazakhstan, Korea DPR, Korea Rep, Kuwait, Kyrgyzstan, Laos, Lebanon, Macau, Malaysia, Maldives, Mongolia, Myanmar, Nepal, Oman, Pakistan, Palestine, Philippines, Qatar, Saudi Arabia, Singapore, Sri Lanka, Syrian AR, Taiwan, Tajikistan, Thailand, Timor-Leste, Turkmenistan, United Arab Emirates, Uzbekistan, Vietnam, Yemen.
NGO Relations Member of (2): *General Association of Asia Pacific Sports Federations (GAAPSF, #10106); International Sport Network Organization (ISNO, #15592). International Weightlifting Federation (IWF, #15876).* [2020/XD0096/**D**]

♦ Asian Welding Federation (AWF) 01782

Sec 18 Boon Lay Way, Ste 08-112 Tradehub21, Singapore 609966, Singapore. T. +62317430333. Fax +62317341620. E-mail: secretariatawf.id@gmail.com.
URL: https://www.awf-online.org/

History Oct 2004, Manila (Philippines). Preparations for foundation commenced Jul 2004, Osaka (Japan). **Aims** Improve and promote welding technology for the betterment of the welding communities in Asia in terms of economics and technological progress and growth. **Structure** Governing Council. **Activities** Certification/accreditation; events/meetings; standards/guidelines. **Events** *Asian Welding Technology & Application Forum* Ningbo (China) 2021, *East Asia Symposium on Technology of Welding and Joining* Busan (Korea Rep) 2013.
Members Full in 13 countries:
China, India, Indonesia, Iran Islamic Rep, Japan, Korea Rep, Malaysia, Mongolia, Myanmar, Philippines, Singapore, Thailand, Vietnam. [2021/AA1946/**D**]

♦ Asian Wheelchair Sports Federation (inactive)
♦ Asian Women's Association (inactive)
♦ Asian Women's Conference (meeting series)

♦ Asian Women's Human Rights Council (AWHRC) 01783

Address not obtained.

History Dec 1986, during a regional consultation. 1st General Assembly: 9-17 Dec 1991, Seoul (Korea Rep). **Aims** Promote and develop a critical and feminist perspective on human rights and development matters; understand and bring fresh insight into the reality of Asian women's lives of abuse, exploitation and violence which deny women their right to be human; foster unity among Asian women based on a common understanding of this reality and its roots; engender a sense of purpose and need for change through continuing dialogue among Asian women; foster solidarity and concerted action among women's groups, leaders and advocates in the region for effective promotion of women's human rights as integral in the struggle for the collective rights of people; call for reformulation of existing socio-economic, political and patriarchal systems in Asian countries as they continue to engender severe forms of exploitation, inequality and violence towards women. **Structure** General Assembly/Regional Assembly (every 2 years). Council, composed of 15 members. Regional Secretariat, based in Bangalore. Another secretariat based in Manila (Philippines). Working Groups. **Activities** Working Groups: Development; Violence Against Women; Traffic in Women; Women, Wars and Militarism; Religious Violence; Indigenous Women. Sets up courts of women on various issues in different countries. Organizes: Asian consultations on various issues; national, regional and international fact-finding missions; conferences. Also co-sponsors and participates in conferences. **Events** *Biennial General Assembly* Cape Town (South Africa) 2001, *Biennial General Assembly* Auckland (New Zealand) 1999, *Biennial General Assembly* Manila (Philippines) 1998, *Biennial General Assembly* Bali (Indonesia) 1997, *Asian tribunal on nuclearization and violence against Pacific women* 1995. **Publications** *Asian Womenews* (2 a year); *AWHRC Human Rights Journal* (annual); *Quilt – Asian Women Weave*; *STARQUILT*. Reports; special publications.
Members National Sections, human rights centres, programmes, institutions and individuals in 30 countries and territories:
Australia, Bangladesh, Cambodia, Canada, China, Croatia, Fiji, Hong Kong, India, Indonesia, Israel, Japan, Korea Rep, Laos, Malaysia, Myanmar, Nepal, Netherlands, New Zealand, Pakistan, Philippines, Serbia, Singapore, Sri Lanka, Switzerland, Taiwan, Thailand, USA, Vanuatu, Vietnam.
NGO Relations *Women in Black (WIB, #20987).* [2009/XF2632/**F**]

♦ Asian Women's Institute (inactive)

♦ **Asian Women's Neurosurgical Association (AWNA)** **01784**

Chair Neurosurgery Dept, Fujita Health Univ, 1-98 Dengakugakubo, Kutsukake-cho, Toyoake, Aichi, 470-1192 Japan. T. +81562939253. Fax +81562933118.

History Dec 1996, Kolkata (India). Dec 1996, Calcutta (India), by *Asian Congress of Neurological Surgeons (ACNS, #01401).* **Aims** Help young neurosurgeons in Asian developing countries; exchange information with female neurosurgeons in Asian countries. **Languages** English. **Staff** 2-3. **Finance** No membership fees. **Events** *Meeting* Istanbul (Turkey) 2012, *Meeting* Recife (Brazil) 2011, *Meeting* Kuala Lumpur (Malaysia) 2010, *Meeting* Beijing (China) 2008, *Meeting* Mumbai (India) 2006. **NGO Relations** *Women in Neurosurgery (WINS).* [2014/XM4012/**E**]

♦ Asian Women's Resource Centre / see Asian Women's Resource Centre for Culture and Theology (#01785)

♦ **Asian Women's Resource Centre for Culture and Theology (AWRC)** . **01785**

Coordinator No 74 Old 94, 1st Floor, 4th Street, Abhiramapuram, Chennai, Tamil Nadu 600018, Chennai TAMIL NADU 600018, India. T. +914424992645.
URL: http://www.awrc4ct.org/

History 20 Nov 1987, Singapore (Singapore). 20-29 Nov 1987, Singapore (Singapore). Often referred to simply as *Asian Women's Resource Centre.* **Aims** Form a community of Asian women engaged in theology and *ministry* and encourage them to articulate Asian women's contextual theology and critical feminist theology of liberation and transformation. **Structure** Coordinating Team Members (CTM); Advisory and Governing Committee; Working Group. **Languages** English. **Staff** 1.50 FTE, paid. **Finance** Members' dues. Other sources: overseas donations; individual donations; sale of publications; subscriptions. **Activities** Knowledge management/information dissemination; networking/liaising; events/meetings. **Events** *Meeting* Chiang Mai (Thailand) 2008, *Meeting* Tainan (Taiwan) 2007, *Meeting* Kuala Lumpur (Malaysia) 2006, *Meeting* Kuala Lumpur (Malaysia) 2005, *Meeting* Kuala Lumpur (Malaysia) 2001. **Publications** *In God's Image (IGI)* (2 a year) – training manual; *Womenet* (2 a year) – newsletter. Monographs; conference reports; books.
Members Full in 17 countries and territories:
Australia, Bangladesh, Hong Kong, India, Indonesia, Japan, Korea Rep, Malaysia, Myanmar, Nepal, New Zealand, Pakistan, Philippines, Singapore, Sri Lanka, Taiwan, Thailand. [2019/XF2218/**E**]

♦ Asian Wound Care Association (unconfirmed)
♦ Asian Wrestling on Belts Alysh Federation (unconfirmed)
♦ Asian Writers Conference (meeting series)

♦ **Asian Xiangqi Federation (AXF)** **01786**

Secretariat Blk 321, Yishun Central 03-315, Singapore 760321, Singapore. T. +6596156568. Fax +6568520119. E-mail: secretariat@asianxiangqi.org.
URL: http://www.asianxiangqi.org/

History 1978. **Aims** Promote the game of xiangqi – Chinese *chess.* **Activities** Sporting activities.
Members National organizations (15) in 13 countries:
Brunei Darussalam, China, Hong Kong, India, Indonesia, Japan, Lebanon, Malaysia, Philippines, Singapore, Taiwan, Thailand, Vietnam. [2020.06.24/XD6310/**D**]

♦ Asian Yachting Federation (no recent information)
♦ Asian Young Researchers Conference on Computational and Omics Biology (meeting series)

♦ **Asian Youth Centre (AYC)** **01787**

SG 12-13-1183, Street No 10, Ananda Nilayam, Hyderabad, Hyderabad, Telangana 500017, Hyderabad TELANGANA 500017, India. T. +91409440896053. E-mail: aychyd1@gmail.com.
URL: http://www.asianyouthcentre.org/

History 26 Mar 1984, Chennai (India), during Plenary Session of 1st Asian Federalist Youth Congress. **Aims** In partnership with socially and economically *vulnerable* groups, aim towards a *just* social order, ensuring *equitable* ownership of, and decision making on, *global resources.* **Structure** Executive Body (meets once every 3 years). Executive Committee. Officers: President, Vice-President, Chairperson, Vice-Chairperson, Secretary-General, Secretary – International, Secretary – Peace, Secretary – Development Concerns and Treasurer. **Staff** 11.00 FTE, paid. **Finance** Members' dues: organizations outside Asia: US$ 120; organizations within India: Indian Rs 1,200; individuals outside Asia: US$ 50; individuals within India: Indian Rs 50. Other source: donations. Budget (annual): US$ 40,000. **Activities** Seminars, conferences, workshops, public meetings, training in the areas of: disarmament; development; human rights; environment; social policy; research and evaluation. Projects on Young Hotel Workers, Street and Working Children, the Girl Child. **Events** *Rights of the girl child* Kolkata (India) 1990, *Regional conference* Chennai (India) 1989, *Workshop / General Assembly* Colombo (Sri Lanka) 1989, *Workshop for NGOs* Kathmandu (Nepal) 1989, *General Assembly* Dhaka (Bangladesh) 1986. **Publications** *Global Link* (4 a year).
Members National and associate organizations; individuals. Members in 7 countries:
Bangladesh, India, Japan, Nepal, Pakistan, Sri Lanka, Thailand.
NGO Relations Member of: *International Action Network on Small Arms (IANSA, #11585).* Recognized as an international youth organization of: *World Federalist Movement – Movement for a Just World Order through a Strengthened United Nations (WFM, #21404).* Shares some national offices with: *Youth for Development and Cooperation (YDC, inactive).* [2014/XE0926/**E**]

♦ **Asian Youth Council (AYC)** **01788**

Conseil asiatique de la jeunesse

Exec Sec S2 International Youth Center, Jalan Yaacob Latif, Bandar Tun Razak, Cheras, 56000 Kuala Lumpur, Malaysia. T. +60391717373. Fax +60391716700.
URL: http://asianyouthcouncil.com/

History Founded 14 Aug 1972, Kuala Lumpur (Malaysia). **Aims** Promote solidarity and family spirit among young people in Asia; strengthen national youth organizations in the region. **Structure** General Assembly (every 3 years); Executive Committee; Advisory Council; Bureaux (4); Secretariat. **Languages** English. **Staff** 2.50 FTE, paid. **Finance** Members' dues. Grants from Ministry of Youth. Annual budget: US$ 100,000. **Activities** Events/meetings. **Events** *International Youth Forum on Climate Change* Jakarta (Indonesia) 2011, *General Assembly* Manila (Philippines) 2011, *International youth forum* Seoul (Korea Rep) 2010, *Workshop on the use of infocomm technology by youth organisations in Asia and Europe* Shah Alam (Malaysia) 2002, *International youth forum / General Assembly* Seoul (Korea Rep) 1995. **Publications** *AISAYOUTH Bulletin* (4 a year).
Members National committees of youth organizations in 15 countries:
Australia, Bangladesh, Brunei Darussalam, Fiji, India, Indonesia, Japan, Korea Rep, Malaysia, Nepal, Pakistan, Philippines, Singapore, Sri Lanka, Thailand.
Consultative Status Consultative status granted from: *ECOSOC (#05331)* (Ros A). **NGO Relations** Member of: *Geneva Informal Meeting of International Youth Non-Governmental Organizations (GIM, no recent information); World Assembly of Youth (WAY, #21113).* Instrumental in setting up: *International Youth Centre (IYC).* [2019.07.15/XD5947/**D**]

♦ **Asian Youth Forum (AYF)** **01789**

Contact Tottori University, 4-101 Minami, Koyama-cho, Tottori, 680-8551 Japan. E-mail: asianyouth-forum@gmail.com.
URL: http://www.asianyouthforum.org/

History Founded 1999, by Prof Kip Cates with the assistance of *Pan-Asian Consortium of Language Teaching Societies (PAC, #18164).* Also referred to as *AYF International.* **Aims** Bring together college and university students and young people from all over the Asian region to an international convention to meet with other youth and educators and provide them a venue where they can share their ideas, views and knowledge on culture, language, leadership, social and global issues especially those affecting the youth. **Events** *Meeting / Forum* Seoul (Korea Rep) 2010, *Forum* Philippines 2009, *Meeting / Forum* Tokyo (Japan) 2008, *Meeting / Forum* Bangkok (Thailand) 2007, *Meeting* Vladivostok (Russia) 2004.
Members in 7 countries and territories:
Indonesia, Japan, Korea Rep, Philippines, Russia, Taiwan, Thailand.
NGO Relations *Pan-Asian Consortium of Language Teaching Societies (PAC, #18164).* [2016/XM3559/**F**]

♦ **Asian Youth Orchestra (AYO)** **01790**

Gen Manager 15A One Capital Place, 18 Luard Road, Wanchai, Hong Kong, Central and Western, Hong Kong. T. +85228661623. Fax +85228613340. E-mail: ayo@asianyouthorchestra.com.
URL: http://www.asianyouthorchestra.com/

History 1987, Hong Kong. A non-profit company limited by guarantee. **Aims** Gather the best *musicians* in Asia. **Structure** Board of Directors, comprising 15 business men and women in Asia. **Finance** Sources: private donations; corporate sponsorship. Budget (annual): US$ 2 million. **Activities** Organizes an annual 6-week summer program, which brings together 100 of the finest young musicians in Asia, initially in a Rehearsal Camp environment and then on Tour. Since 1990, AYO has performed 291 concerts for over 1 million concert-goers across Asia, Europe and USA.
Members Young musicians from 12 countries and territories:
China, Hong Kong, Indonesia, Japan, Korea Rep, Malaysia, Mongolia, Philippines, Singapore, Taiwan, Thailand, Vietnam. [2019/XF2877/v/**F**]

♦ Asia: NZ / see Asia New Zealand Foundation
♦ Asian Zoo Educators Conference (meeting series)
♦ Asian Zurkhaneh Sports Confederation (unconfirmed)

♦ **Asia Oceania Agricultural Proteomics Organization (AOAPO)** **01791**

Contact Iranian Proteomics Soc, Mahdasht Road, PO Box 31535-1897, Karaj ALBORZ, Iran Islamic Rep. T. +982612702893. Fax +982612704539. E-mail: contact@aoapo.org.
URL: http://www.aoapo.org/

Aims Further cooperation on agricultural proteomics in Asia Oceania region. **Structure** Council; Executive Committee. **Activities** Events/meetings. **Events** *Congress* Singapore (Singapore) 2023, *Congress* Singapore (Singapore) 2020, *International Symposium on Frontiers in Agricultural Proteome Research* Jeonju (Korea Rep) 2015. **Publications** *AOAPO Newsletter* (2 a year). [2020/AA0216/**D**]

♦ Asia and Oceania Association of the ICMIF (see: #12948)
♦ Asia-Oceania Association of Otolaryngological Societies / see Asia-Oceania Association of Otolaryngology – Head and Neck Surgery Societies (#01792)

♦ **Asia-Oceania Association of Otolaryngology – Head and Neck Surgery Societies (Asia Oceania ORL-HNS)** **01792**

Pres c/o ENT Victoria, 28-32 Arnold Street, Suite 1, Box Hill VIC 3128, Australia.
Facebook: https://www.facebook.com/AsiaOceania-Association-of-OtoRhinoLaryngology-Head-Neck-Surgery-Societies-939990449425942/

History Former names and other names: *Asia-Oceania Association of Otolaryngological Societies (AOOS)* – former; *Asia Oceania ORL Head and Neck Association* – former. **Events** *Asia Oceania Otorhinolaryngological Head and Neck Surgery Congress (AO ORL HNS)* Brisbane, QLD (Australia) 2023, *Quadrennial Congress* Hyderabad (India) 2019, *Quadrennial Congress* Taipei (Taiwan) 2015, *Quadrennial Congress* Auckland (New Zealand) 2011, *Quadrennial Congress* Pattaya (Thailand) 2007. [2021/XD0382/**D**]

♦ **Asia-Oceania Association for the Study of Obesity (AOASO)** **01793**

Sec Napier Road No 09-17, Singapore 258449, Singapore. T. +6581251720.
Pres Monash University, Clayton VIC 3800, Australia.
URL: http://www.aoaso.org/

History 31 Aug 1998, Paris (France). Founded during the 8th International Congress on Obesity, where 6 countries were the original signatories to the establishment of the Associations, namely Australia, Indonesia, Japan, Korea Rep, Malaysia and Philippines. **Aims** Foster international fellowship among scientists of the region; promote collaboration in research, education and action programmes; provide a platform to exchange information and experience in obesity research and action programmes; act as a liaison between member countries and WO and relevant UN agencies. **Structure** Executive Council, elected every 4 years; National Representatives; Rotating Secretariat (where Secretary General resides). **Languages** English. **Staff** No permanent staff. All activities carried out by Executive Council on voluntary basis. **Finance** No operational budget. Activities carried out using local association funds. **Activities** Events/meetings; training/education. **Events** *Asia Oceania Congress on Obesity* Kuala Lumpur (Malaysia) 2021, *Conference* Seoul (Korea Rep) 2019, *Conference* Adelaide, SA (Australia) 2017, *Obesity and metabolic syndrome – from science to clinical practice* Nagoya (Japan) 2015, *Conference* Bandung (Indonesia) 2013. **Publications** *Obesity Research and Clinical Practice* – official journal.
Members National Associations in 12 countries and territories:
Australia, Hong Kong, India, Indonesia, Japan, Korea Rep, Malaysia, New Zealand, Philippines, Singapore, Taiwan, Thailand.
Included in the above, 1 organization listed in this Yearbook:
Australian and New Zealand Obesity Society (ANZOS).
IGO Relations Ministries of Health and related Government Agencies. [2021/XD7581/y/**D**]

♦ **Asia-Oceania Ceramic Federation (AOCF)** **01794**

Pres School of Materials Science and Engineering, Tsinghua Univ, 100084 Beijing, China. E-mail: panw@mail.tsinghua.edu.cn.
URL: http://www.ceramic.or.jp/csj/AOCF/

Aims Promote and stimulate understanding and cooperation among persons and societies from Asia-Oceania. **Structure** Council (meets annually); Executive Committee. **Events** *Conference* Jeju (Korea Rep) 2013, *International Symposium on New Frontier of Advanced Si-Based Ceramics and Composites* Seoul (Korea Rep) 2012, *Conference* Osaka (Japan) 2010, *Conference* Lijiang (China) 2008, *Conference* Daegu (Korea Rep) 2006.
Members National organizations (4) in 4 countries:
Australia, China, Japan, Korea Rep. [2015.06.10/XM2860/**D**]

♦ Asia-Oceania Congress of Endocrinology (meeting series)
♦ Asia-Oceania Congress of Otorhinolaryngology (meeting series)
♦ Asia Oceania E-Business Marketplace Alliance (inactive)
♦ Asia-Oceania Federation of Anti-Aging Medicine (no recent information)

♦ **Asia and Oceania Federation of Nuclear Medicine and Biology (AOFNMB)** **01795**

Fédération de médecine nucléaire et de biologie de l'Asie et de l'Océanie

Pres 3-6-303 Mihogaoka, Ibaraki, Osaka, 565-0047 Japan. T. +81668793461. Fax +81668793469. E-mail: aofnmb.osaka@gmail.com – office@aofnmb.org.
URL: http://www.aofnmb.org/

History 1976. Current Charter revised 1992. **Aims** Unite national societies or groups in the field of nuclear medicine and biology throughout Asia and Oceania; promote the development of nuclear medicine and biology; organize committees, set up technical standards and aid in the diffusion of knowledge and exchange of scientific and technical information in the field; prepare and recommend the organization of a unified program of teaching and training in the field; facilitate the exchange of scientists between member societies. **Structure** Assembly (meets during both AOFNMB and *World Federation of Nuclear Medicine and Biology (WFNMB, #21467)* Congresses) elects President and President elect. Secretary-General and Treasurer appointed by the President. **Languages** English. **Activities** Organizes regional Congresses (every 4 years). Colloquia, symposia, courses. **Events** *Asia Oceania Congress of Nuclear Medicine and Biology* Amman (Jordan) 2021, *Asia Oceania Congress of Nuclear Medicine and Biology* Shanghai (China) 2019, *Congress* Yokohama (Japan) 2017, *Congress* Jeju (Korea Rep) 2015, *Congress* Teheran (Iran Islamic Rep) 2012. **Publications** Monographs; papers; Congress reports.
Members National societies or groups in 23 countries and territories:
Australia, Bangladesh, China, Hong Kong, India, Indonesia, Iran Islamic Rep, Israel, Japan, Jordan, Korea Rep, Kuwait, Malaysia, New Zealand, Pakistan, Philippines, Saudi Arabia, Singapore, Taiwan, Thailand, Türkiye, United Arab Emirates, Vietnam.
NGO Relations Member of: *World Council of Isotopes (WCI, #21331).* [2019/XD7520/**D**]

♦ **Asia & Oceania Federation of Obstetrics and Gynaecology (AOFOG)** **01796**

SG SLCOG House No 112, Model Farm Road, Narahenpita, Colombo, 00800, Sri Lanka. T. +94112671209. Fax +94112689036. E-mail: secretariat@aofog.net.
URL: http://www.aofog.net/

History 1957, Tokyo (Japan). Founded during inaugural meeting. Originally conceived in 1954 as the 'Asian Division' of the International Federation of Gynaecology and Obstetrics. Current name adopted 1979, when Australia and New Zealand became Full members. Statutes adopted 1957; new statutes adopted Oct 1979, Tokyo, at 13th General Assembly. Former names and other names: *Asian Federation of Obstetrics and Gynaecology* – former. **Aims** Promote the science and art of obstetrics, gynaecology and reproductive biology; promote total health care in females throughout life; promote intrauterine and neonatal well-being; support study and implementation of population control; promote international cooperation and goodwill particularly in Asia and Oceania. **Structure** General Assembly (every 2 years, at Asia-Oceania Congress); Executive Board; Council; Committees. **Languages** English. **Staff** Voluntary. **Finance** Sources: meeting proceeds; members' dues. **Activities** Awards/prizes/competitions; events/meetings; financial and/or material support; research/documentation. **Events** Biennial Congress and General Assembly Busan (Korea Rep) 2024, *Biennial Congress and General Assembly* Bali (Indonesia) 2022, *Biennial Congress and General Assembly* Manila (Philippines) 2019, *Biennial Congress and General Assembly* Hong Kong (Hong Kong) 2017, *Biennial Congress and General Assembly* Kuching (Malaysia) 2015. **Publications** *Journal of Obstetrics and Gynaecology Research (JOGR)* (12 a year); *AOFOG Newsletter*.
Members National societies in 28 countries and territories:
Australia, Bangladesh, Cambodia, China, Egypt, Fiji, Hong Kong, India, Indonesia, Israel, Japan, Korea Rep, Laos, Macau, Malaysia, Mongolia, Myanmar, Nepal, New Zealand, Pakistan, Papua New Guinea, Philippines, Saudi Arabia, Singapore, Sri Lanka, Taiwan, Thailand, Vietnam.
NGO Relations Allied regional federation of: *Fédération Internationale de Gynécologie et d'Obstétrique (FIGO, #09638)*. [2021/XF1619/**D**]

♦ **Asia-Oceania Federation of Organizations for Medical Physics (AFOMP)** 01797
Vice-Pres Eastern Housing Mirpur, Dhaka 1212, Bangladesh.
URL: http://www.afomp.org/
History 28 May 2000. Initiative discussed at the International Conference on Medical Imaging, Medical Physics and Precision Radiation Therapy, Guangzhou (China), Oct 5, 1999. Name chosen at 2nd Beijing International Congress on Medical Radiation Physics, Beijing (China), May 28, 2000, where decision was unanimously taken to form a regional medical physics federation affiliated to *International Organization for Medical Physics (IOMP, #14453)*. Officially admitted as Regional Chapter of IOMP at first Council Meeting during World Congress in Medical Physics and Biomedical Engineering, Chicago (USA), July 2000, where a new name was also adopted. Former names and other names: *Asia-Oceanic Federation of Medical Physics Organizations (AFMPO)* – former (28 May 2000 to Jul 2000). **Aims** Promote cooperation and communication between medical physics organizations in the region; develop medical physics and related activities in the region; promote the advancement in status and standard of practice of the medical physics profession. **Structure** Council; Officers; Committees (4). **Languages** English. **Staff** None. **Finance** Sources: members' dues. Annual budget: 20,000 USD (2021). **Activities** Awards/prizes/competitions; awareness raising; certification/accreditation; events/meetings; networking/liaising; publishing activities; training/education. Active in all member countries. **Events** *Asia-Oceania Congress on Medical Physics (AOCMP)* 2024, *International Conference on Medical Physics (ICMP)* Mumbai (India) 2023, *Asia-Oceania Congress on Medical Physics (AOCMP)* Taipei (Taiwan) 2022, *Annual Congress* Dhaka (Bangladesh) 2021, *Annual Congress* Phuket (Thailand) 2020. **Publications** *AFOMP Newsletter* (2 a year).
Members Organizations (22) in 20 countries and territories:
Australia, Bangladesh, China, Hong Kong, India, Indonesia, Japan, Korea Rep, Malaysia, Mongolia, Myanmar, Nepal, New Zealand, Pakistan, Philippines, Singapore, Sri Lanka, Taiwan, Thailand, Vietnam.
Included in the above, 1 organization listed in this Yearbook:
Australasian College of Physical Scientists and Engineers in Medicine (ACPSEM).
NGO Relations Member of (1): *International Organization for Medical Physics (IOMP, #14453)* (as Regional member). [2022.05.17/XD8671/**D**]

♦ **Asia-Oceania Federation of Sexology (AOFS)** 01798
Public Officer Level 7, 35 Spring St, Bondi Junction NSW 2022, Australia. T. +612407399466.
URL: http://www.aofs-asia.org/
History Founded 1990, Hong Kong, as *Asian Federation of Sexology (AFS)*. Current title adopted, 2003. Officially registered in Hong Kong, 1992. Incorporated in New South Wales (Australia), 2016. **Aims** Further and extend knowledge in the field of sexology; network with professionals in the region to attain these goals and for professional support. **Structure** Council. **Languages** English. **Staff** Voluntary. **Finance** Members' dues. Other sources: charitable donations; conference income. **Activities** Networking/liaising; research/documentation; advocacy/lobbying/activism; events/meetings. **Events** *Congress* Chennai (India) 2018, *Congress* Busan (Korea Rep) 2016, *Pan-Asian Men's Health Forum* Busan (Korea Rep) 2016, *Congress* Brisbane, QLD (Australia) 2014, *Congress* Matsue (Japan) 2012. **Publications** *Asian Journal of Sexology* (irregular).
Members Individuals and organizations in 14 countries and territories:
Australia, China, Hong Kong, India, Indonesia, Japan, Korea Rep, Malaysia, New Zealand, Pakistan, Singapore, Taiwan, Thailand, Vietnam.
NGO Relations Member of: *World Association for Sexual Health (WAS, #21187)*. [2020.03.03/XD8557/**D**]

♦ **Asia Oceania Geosciences Society (AOGS)** 01799
Managing Dir Meeting Matters International, 1 Commonwealth Lane, 06-23 One Commonwealth, Singapore 149544, Singapore. T. +6564723108. Fax +6564723208. E-mail: info@asiaoceania.org.
URL: http://www.asiaoceania.org/
History 2003, Singapore (Singapore). **Aims** Promote geophysical science and public benefits in Asia and Oceania. **Structure** Council; Executive Committee; Sections (8). **Languages** English. **Staff** 2.00 FTE, paid. **Finance** Income from activities. Annual budget: 750,000 SGD (2023). **Events** *Annual Meeting* Singapore (Singapore) 2023, *Annual Meeting* Singapore (Singapore) 2022, *Annual Meeting* Singapore (Singapore) 2021, *Annual Meeting* Hongcheon (Korea Rep) 2020, *Annual Meeting* Singapore (Singapore) 2019. **Publications** *Advances in Geosciences* (annual) – in 6 vols; *Geoscience Letters* – journal.
Members Full in 71 countries and territories:
Australia, Austria, Bangladesh, Belgium, Bhutan, Bolivia, Brazil, Bulgaria, Canada, Chile, China, Czechia, Denmark, Egypt, Fiji, Finland, France, Georgia, Germany, Greece, Guadeloupe, Guatemala, Hong Kong, Iceland, India, Indonesia, Iran Islamic Rep, Ireland, Israel, Italy, Jamaica, Japan, Korea Rep, Kuwait, Luxembourg, Macau, Malaysia, Mexico, Myanmar, Nepal, Netherlands, New Zealand, Norway, Oman, Philippines, Poland, Polynesia Fr, Portugal, Puerto Rico, Romania, Russia, Samoa, Saudi Arabia, Singapore, Slovenia, South Africa, Spain, Sri Lanka, Sweden, Switzerland, Syrian AR, Taiwan, Thailand, Trinidad-Tobago, Tunisia, Türkiye, UK, United Arab Emirates, USA, Vanuatu, Vietnam.
NGO Relations Partner of (4): *Asia Pacific Association of Hydrology and Water Resources (APHW, #01843)*; *European Geosciences Union (EGU, #07390)*; *International Union of Geodesy and Geophysics (IUGG, #15776)*; *Science Council of Asia (SCA, #19137)*. Links with national societies. [2022.05.17/XJ3068/**D**]

♦ **Asia-Oceania GEOSS (AOGEOSS)** 01800
Secretariat address not obtained.
URL: http://aogeoss.com/
History Launched Nov 2016, St Petersburg (Russia). A regional initiative of *Group on Earth Observations (GEO, #10735)*. **Aims** Strengthen comprehensive ability of *Earth observation* and applications for jointly proposed by the Asia Oceania Caucus members. **Structure** Caucus; Coordination Board; Secretariat. **Events** *Symposium* Canberra, ACT (Australia) 2019, *Asia-Pacific Symposium* Kyoto (Japan) 2018.
Members Governments (9):
Australia, Bangladesh, Cambodia, China, Japan, Korea Rep, Laos, Mongolia, Vietnam.
Participating Organizations include:
Asia-Pacific Space Cooperation Organization (APSCO, #02051); *Committee on Earth Observation Satellites (CEOS, #04249)*; *International Centre for Integrated Mountain Development (ICIMOD, #12500)*; *International Council for Science (ICSU, inactive)*; *International Society for Digital Earth (ISDE, #15061)*; *International Society for Photogrammetry and Remote Sensing (ISPRS, #15362)*; *Partnership for Observation of the Global Oceans (POGO, #18239)*; *UNEP (#20299)*; *UNESCO (#20322)*; *United Nations Economic and Social Commission for Asia and the Pacific (ESCAP, #20557)*; *World Meteorological Organization (WMO, #21649)*. [2018/XM6836/**E***]

♦ **Asia Oceania Human Proteome Organization (AOHUPO)** 01801
SG Health Sciences, Univ of Macau, Avda da Universidade, Taipa, Macau.
URL: http://www.aohupo.org/
Events *Conference* Singapore (Singapore) 2023, *Conference* Busan (Korea Rep) 2021, *Conference* Busan (Korea Rep) 2020, *Conference* Bangkok (Thailand) 2014, *Annual International Proteomics Conference* Seoul (Korea Rep) 2013.
Members in 13 countries and territories:
Australia, China, India, Iran Islamic Rep, Japan, Korea Rep, New Zealand, Pakistan, Philippines, Singapore, Taiwan, Thailand, Vietnam.
NGO Relations Member of: *Human Proteome Organization (HUPO, #10978)*. [2019.07.11/XD9076/**D**]

♦ Asia and Oceania Kangaroo Mother Care Network (unconfirmed)

♦ **Asia-Oceania Meeting of Religious (AMOR)** 01802
Contact 112(A) Bogyoke Street, Latha Township, Yangon, Myanmar. E-mail: amorxvii2017@gmail.com.
URL: https://www.facebook.com/Asia-oceania-Meeting-of-Religious-11005093833 72426/
History Mar 1971, Hong Kong, as *Asian Meeting of Religions*. Secretariat (Asian Service Centre) successively moved from Hong Kong to: Philippines, Nov 1972; Sri Lanka 1980; Kyoto (Japan), 1983; Seoul (Korea Rep), 30 Jan 1992; Taipei (Taiwan); 1 Jul 1997. Subsequently changed to: *Asian-Pacific Meeting of Religious*. **Aims** Function as a general assembly representing religious *women* of Asia-Pacific regions, in a spirit of solidarity, unity and *communion*, addressing common issues according to the *Gospel* message. **Structure** AMOR is a General Assembly of religious women which takes place every 2 or 3 years. Executive Committee consists of Chairperson, Executive Secretary and 2 or 3 members. *Asian Service Centre (ASC)* is the Secretariat of AMOR and carries out the plans that were decided and suggested at AMOR meetings. **Finance** Members' dues. Other sources: support of the host National Conference; free contributions from other religious congregations, friends and funding agencies for important activities. **Events** *Asia Pacific Meeting of Religious – AMOR* Thailand 2009, *Asia Pacific Meeting of Religious – AMOR* Seoul (Korea Rep) 2006, *Meeting / Asia Pacific Meeting of Religious – AMOR* Taiwan 2003, *Asian-Oceanian women in search of true reconciliation bringing forth new life* Hiroshima (Japan) 2000, *Meeting / Asia Pacific Meeting of Religious – AMOR* Bangalore (India) 1997. **Publications** *AMOR Newsletter* (4 a year).
Members National conferences/organizations/associations of religious (22), grouping about 200,000 individual members, in 24 countries and territories:
Australia, Bangladesh, Brunei Darussalam, Cambodia, Fiji, Hong Kong, India, Indonesia, Japan, Korea Rep, Macau, Malaysia, Myanmar, Nepal, New Zealand, Pakistan, Papua New Guinea, Philippines, Singapore, Solomon Is, Sri Lanka, Taiwan, Thailand, Vietnam.
Individuals in 10 not-affiliated countries:
Belgium, China, France, Guatemala, Italy, Netherlands, Switzerland, Timor-Leste, UK, USA. [2017/XF1931/**F**]

♦ **Asia-Oceania Neutron Scattering Association (AONSA)** 01803
Contact c/o MLF Div, J-PARC Center, 2-4 Shirakata, Tokai, Ibaraki OSAKA, 319-1195 Japan. E-mail: jaehc@korea.ac.kr.
URL: http://www.aonsa.org/
History Officially set up 28 Aug 2008, as an affiliation of neutron scattering societies which directly represent users in the Asia-Oceania Region. Articles last revised 22 May 2010. **Aims** Provide a platform for discussion and a focus for action in neutron scattering and related topics in the Asia-Oceania Region. **Structure** Executive Committee. **Languages** English. **Finance** Members' dues. **Activities** Training/education; events/meetings; awards/prizes/competitions. **Events** *Conference on Neutron Scattering* Kaohsiung (Taiwan) 2019, *Executive Committee Meeting* Bangkok (Thailand) 2017, *Conference on Neutron Scattering* Sydney, NSW (Australia) 2015, *Executive Committee Meeting* Sydney, NSW (Australia) 2015, *Executive Committee Meeting* Tokyo (Japan) 2015. **Publications** *AONSA Newsletter* (2 a year).
Members Organizations (6) in 6 countries and territories:
Australia, China, India, Japan, Korea Rep, Taiwan. [2018.09.06/XJ2640/**D**]

♦ **Asia Oceanian Society of Physical and Rehabilitation Medicine (AOSPRM)** 01804
Secretariat Room C, 3/F Worldwide Centre, 123 Tung Chau Street, Kowloon, Hong Kong. T. +85223966261. Fax +85223966465. E-mail: info@aosprm.org.
URL: http://aosprm.org/
History following informal meetings starting at World Congress of *International Rehabilitation Medicine Association (IRMA, inactive)*, 1997, Tokyo (Japan). Officially set up during 4th Congress of *International Society of Physical and Rehabilitation Medicine (ISPRM, #15366)*, 11 Jun 2007, Seoul (Korea Rep). Former names and other names: *Asian Oceania Society of Physical and Rehabilitation Medicine (AOSPRM)* – former. **Structure** Cabinet, comprising Chairman, Secretary-General, Assistant Secretary, Advisor, Education Chair and 10 Executive members. **Events** *Asia-Oceanian Conference of Physical & Rehabilitation Medicine* Malaysia 2024, *Conference* Seoul (Korea Rep) 2020, *Conference* Christchurch (New Zealand) 2018, *Conference* Cebu City (Philippines) 2016, *Conference / Congress* Bangkok (Thailand) 2014. **NGO Relations** *International Society for Restorative Neurology (ISRN, #15426)*. [2020/XJ0719/**E**]

♦ Asia Oceania ORL Head and Neck Association / see Asia-Oceania Association of Otolaryngology – Head and Neck Surgery Societies (#01792)
♦ **Asia Oceania ORL-HNS** Asia-Oceania Association of Otolaryngology – Head and Neck Surgery Societies (#01792)

♦ **Asia-Oceania Research Organization in Genital Infection and Neoplasia (AOGIN)** 01805
Permanent Sec Ste 10 Level 2, Royal Women's Hospital, Flemington Rd, Parkville VIC 3052, Australia.
SG address not obtained.
URL: http://www.aogin.com/
Aims Increase communication, cooperation and information sharing in order to reduce reproductive tract infections, especially human papilloma virus (HPV), in the Asia, Oceania and Pacific region. **Structure** Executive Committee, including president, President Elect, Vice-President, Treasurer, Secretary-General and Permanent Secretary. **Events** *Unmasking The Secrets of Lower Genital Tract Diseases* Bangkok (Thailand) 2022, *Meeting* Beijing (China) 2019, *Meeting* Sydney, NSW (Australia) 2018, *Tokyo Meeting* Tokyo (Japan) 2017, *Conference* Singapore (Singapore) 2016.
Members in 16 countries and territories:
Australia, Bangladesh, China, Hong Kong, India, Indonesia, Japan, Korea Rep, Laos, Nepal, New Zealand, Philippines, Singapore, Sri Lanka, Taiwan, Thailand.
NGO Relations *European Research Organization on Genital Infection and Neoplasia (EUROGIN, #08378)*; *Women Against Cervical Cancer (WACC, #20985)*. [2017.12.15/XM3230/**D**]

♦ Asia Oceania Soap and Detergent Association Conference (meeting series)

♦ **Asia and Oceania Society for Comparative Endocrinology (AOSCE)** 01806
SG School of Marine Biosciences, Kitasato Univ, 1-15-1 Kitasato, Minami-ku, Tokyo, 252-0373 Japan.
Pres Dept of Biology, Waseda Univ, Wakamatsu-cho, Shinjuku, Tokyo, 162-8480 Japan.
URL: http://aosce.ntou.edu.tw/
History 5 Nov 1987, Nagoya (Japan), at 1st Congress, when constitution was approved. **Aims** Provide forums for scientific activities in the field of comparative endocrinology in Asia and Oceania; establish a deep relationship among members. **Structure** Council. **Languages** English. **Finance** Members' dues: Full – US$ 100; Student – US$ 30. **Activities** Events/meetings. **Events** *Quadrennial Congress* Bogor (Indonesia) 2020, *Symposium* Sydney, NSW (Australia) 2018, *Quadrennial Congress* Seoul (Korea Rep) 2016, *Symposium* Keelung (Taiwan) 2014, *Quadrennial Congress* Kuala Lumpur (Malaysia) 2012. **Publications** *General and Comparative Endocrinology*.
Members Honorary; Ordinary; Student. Individuals in 13 countries and territories:
Australia, China, Hong Kong, India, Indonesia, Iraq, Japan, Korea Rep, Malaysia, New Zealand, Philippines, Taiwan, Thailand.
NGO Relations Instrumental in setting up: *International Federation of Comparative Endocrinological Societies (IFCES, #13396)*. [2014.10.06/XD0889/v/**D**]

♦ **Asia and Oceania Society for Photobiology (AOSP)** **01807**

Pres School of Biological Sciences A12 239B, Univ of Sydney, Camperdown, Sydney NSW 2050, Australia. T. +61290365006. Fax +61293514119.
URL: http://aosp.umin.jp/

History Founded in 2001. **Aims** Become the premier international organization for photo-biologists and associated scientific professionals. **Structure** General Assembly; Executive Committee; Board. **Languages** English. **Activities** Events/meetings. **Events** *Asia and Oceania Conference on Photobiology* Qingdao (China) 2019, *Asia and Oceania Conference on Photobiology* Seoul (Korea Rep) 2017, *Asia and Oceania Conference on Photobiology* Taipei (Taiwan) 2015, *Asia and Oceania Conference on Photobiology* Sydney, NSW (Australia) 2013, *Asia and Oceania Conference on Photobiology* Nara (Japan) 2011. **Members** National and sub-national groups, individuals. Membership countries not specified. **NGO Relations** *International Union of Photobiology (IUPB, #15798)*; *European Society for Photobiology (ESP, #08702).* [2015.09.03/XJ8053/**D**]

♦ **Asia Oceania Space Weather Alliance (AOSWA)** **01808**

Dir c/o NICT Applied Electromagnetic Research Inst, Space Weather and Environment Informatics Lab, 4-2-1 Nukui-Kitamachi, Koganei, Tokyo, 184-8795 Japan. E-mail: sw-project-office@ml.nict.go.jp.
URL: http://aoswa.nict.go.jp/

History 2010. **Aims** Encourage cooperation and share information among institutes in the Asia-Oceania region concerned with and interested in space weather. **Structure** Secretariat. **Activities** Events/meetings. **Events** *The risk of space weather – regional action* Jeju (Korea Rep) 2016, *Workshop* Fukuoka (Japan) 2015, *Space environment impacts and space weather forecast models* Kunming (China) 2013, *Workshop* Chiang Mai (Thailand) 2012. **Publications** *AOSWA LINK* – newsletter.
Members Associates in 13 countries and territories:
Australia, China, India, Indonesia, Japan, Korea Rep, Malaysia, Pakistan, Philippines, Russia, Taiwan, Thailand, Vietnam. [2016/XM4845/**D**]

♦ Asia-Oceania Steel Drum Manufacturers (no recent information)

♦ **Asia-Oceania Tax Consultants' Association (AOTCA)** **01809**

Secretariat c/o The Tax Institute, Level 10, 175 Pitt Street, Sydney NSW 2000, Australia. E-mail: aotca@taxinstitute.com.au.
URL: http://www.aotca.org/

History 1 Jan 1993. **Aims** Promote mutual understanding and cooperation among the organizations; contribute to the expansion of the component members' businesses related to taxation and its related areas; promote friendship among members. **Languages** English. **Events** *International Tax Conference* Busan (Korea Rep) 2019, *International Tax Conference* Hong Kong (Hong Kong) 2016, *International Tax Conference* Osaka (Japan) 2015, *International Tax Conference / Meeting* Taipei (Taiwan) 2014, *International Tax Conference / Meeting* Hanoi (Vietnam) 2013. **Publications** *AOTCA Journal*. Technical papers.
Members Full; Associate (indicated by '). Members in 16 countries and territories:
Australia, Bangladesh (*), China, Hong Kong, India, Indonesia, Japan, Korea Rep, Malaysia, Mongolia, Pakistan, Philippines, Singapore, Sri Lanka, Taiwan, Vietnam. [2013/XD5139/**D**]

♦ **Asia and Oceania Thyroid Association (AOTA)** **01810**

Sec/Treas Rm 5009 Medical Arts Bldg, Univ of Santo Tomas Hospital, España, 1008 Manila, Philippines. T. +6327314548. Fax +6327314548. E-mail: aota.sec@gmail.com.
URL: http://aota.kr/

History 1975, Boston, MA (USA). Founded at the International Thyroid Conference. **Aims** Promote thyroidology in Asia and Oceania Region. **Structure** Council, consisting of President, 3 Vice-Presidents, Secretary, 3 standing members of Programme Organizing Committee and 7 members. **Languages** English. **Staff** No full-time staff. **Finance** Members' dues. **Activities** Organizes meetings (once every 5 years) and workshops between the meetings. **Events** *International Thyroid Congress* 2020, *Congress* Sydney, NSW (Australia) 2019, *Congress* Busan (Korea Rep) 2017, *International Thyroid Congress* Orlando, FL (USA) 2015, *Congress* Bali (Indonesia) 2012.
Members Associations in 16 countries and territories:
Australia, Bangladesh, China, India, Indonesia, Iran Islamic Rep, Japan, Korea Rep, Malaysia, New Zealand, Pakistan, Philippines, Singapore, Sri Lanka, Taiwan, Thailand.
NGO Relations Member of: *International Thyroid Congress.* [2021/XD1236/**D**]

♦ Asia-Oceanic Federation of Medical Physics Organizations / see Asia-Oceania Federation of Organizations for Medical Physics (#01797)
♦ Asia Offshore Association (unconfirmed)
♦ ASIA-Onlus – Associazione per la Solidarietà Internazionale in Asia (internationally oriented national body)

♦ **Asia-Pacific Academic Consortium for Public Health (APACPH)** **01811**

SG c/o Curtin Univ, Fac of Health Sciences, School of Public Health, Bentley Campus – 400 316, Kent Street, Perth WA 6102, Australia. T. +61892667947. Fax +61892662958. E-mail: apacph@hotmail.com.
URL: http://www.apacph.org/

History Jan 1984, Honolulu, HI (USA). Jan 1984, at University of Hawaii, Honolulu HI (USA). By-laws adopted, 30 Jun 1987, during 8th Meeting, Seoul (Korea Rep); amended 8 Dec 1988, Jakarta (Indonesia), 9 Jul 1990, Singapore (Singapore), 24 May 1992, Okinawa (Japan), 13 Dec 1992, Perth (Australia), 21 May 1994, Beijing (China), 17 Dec 1997, Perth (Australia); most recent By-laws amended Mar 2000. Registered in accordance with Australian law, 2004. Relocated and registered in Honolulu HI (USA), 2010. **Aims** Improve quality of life and achieve the highest level of health for citizens in the region; raise the quality of professional education in public health and make it more relevant to current needs, with special emphasis on leadership; enhance knowledge, skills and effective methods available to health workers through joint research, training and service projects; devote greater resources to solving health problems by establishing closer links with each other and with Ministries of Health; improve the quality of educational opportunities for students of public health through curriculum development and academic sharing; make child survival a major priority. **Structure** Meeting (annual since 1998). Executive Council (held twice a year), comprising President, President-Elect, 2 Vice-Presidents, Secretary-General, Editor in Chief, Secretary-Treasurer and 5 Regional Directors (Bangkok (Thailand), Tokyo (Japan), Beijing (China), Australia, Honolulu HI (USA)), Secretary-General, Editor in Chief, Secretary-Treasurer and an additional 3 Directors. Management Board, comprising President, President Elect, 2 Vice-Presidents, Secretary General, Treasurer, Secretary. Standing Committees (5): Finance and Development; Publication; Programme and Research; Membership; Training Standards and Accrediting. Ad-hoc Committees (2): Award; Sub-project Review. **Languages** English. **Staff** 21.00 FTE, paid. **Finance** Members' dues. Other sources: grants; research projects. **Activities** Events/meetings; training/education; research/documentation; awards/prizes/competitions. **Events** *Annual Conference* Surabaya (Indonesia) 2021, *Annual Conference* Surabaya (Indonesia) 2020, *Annual Conference* Bangkok (Thailand) 2019, *Annual Conference* Kota Kinabalu (Malaysia) 2018, *Annual Conference* Incheon (Korea Rep) 2017. **Publications** *Asia Pacific Journal of Public Health* (4 a year); *APACPH Newsletter*. Reports; conference proceedings.
Members Regular; Associate; Individual; Personal Emeritus. Institutional (about 80) universities represented by Schools of Medicine and Public Health and National Institutes of Health in 23 countries and territories:
Australia, Bangladesh, Cambodia, China, Fiji, Hong Kong, India, Indonesia, Japan, Kazakhstan, Korea Rep, Laos, Malaysia, Mongolia, Nepal, New Zealand, Philippines, Singapore, Sri Lanka, Taiwan, Thailand, USA, Vietnam.
NGO Relations Member of: *World Federation of Academic Institutions for Global Health (WFAIGH, inactive).* Instrumental in setting up: *International Cyber University for Health (ICUH, #13126).* [2016/XD6905/**D**]

♦ Asia Pacific Academy of Business in Society (inactive)

♦ **Asia Pacific Academy of Implant Dentistry (APAiD)** **01812**

Contact 1F No 6, Ln 83 – Sec 1, Guangfu Rd, Sangchong Dist, New Taipei City 24101, Taiwan. T. +886229959901. Fax +886229956919.
URL: http://www.apaid.asia/

Aims Improve and promote related education and research in oral implantology; upgrade the professional standing of implant dentistry in Asia through proper international academic exchanges. **Structure** Board. **Finance** Sources: members' dues. **Events** *International Congress* Taipei (Taiwan) 2019, *Bangkok International Symposium of Implant Dentistry* Bangkok (Thailand) 2017, *International Congress* Bangkok (Thailand) 2017, *International Congress* Sendai (Japan) 2014, *International Congress* Sendai (Japan) 2014. [2019/XJ9459/**D**]

♦ **Asia Pacific Academy of Materials (APAM)** **01813**

Contact 62 Wencui Road, Shenyang, 110016 Liaoning, China. T. +862423893841. Fax +862423894149.
URL: http://www.apam-mat.net/

History 1992. **Aims** Increase awareness and expertise in scientific and technical knowledge for sustainable development and use of materials in the Asia-Pacific region. **Structure** General Assembly. Executive Committee. National Chapters. **Activities** Organizes seminars. **Events** *Topical Meeting on Electronics, Energy and Environment* Hong Kong (Hong Kong) 2013, *General Assembly* Hsinchu (Taiwan) 2011, *General Assembly* Delhi (India) 2008, *International conference on micro- and nanoelectronics* Zvenigorod (Russia) 2003, *General Assembly* Seoul (Korea Rep) 2000.
Members Individuals specialists in material science and technology who have made significant contributions to cooperation in Asia-Pacific Region, in 11 countries and territories:
Australia, China, Hong Kong, India, Japan, Korea Rep, Mongolia, Russia, Singapore, Taiwan, Uzbekistan. [2020/XJ3108/**E**]

♦ **Asia-Pacific Academy of Ophthalmology (APAO)** **01814**

Académie d'ophtalmologie pour l'Asie et le Pacifique

Hong Kong Secretariat c/o Chinese Univ of Hong Kong, Dept of Ophthalmology and Visual Sciences, Hong Kong Eye Hosp, 4/F – 147K Argyle Str, Kowloon, Hong Kong. T. +85239435827. Fax +85227159490. E-mail: secretariat@apaophth.org.
Congress Manager address not obtained.
Guangzhou Headquarters State Key Lab – Ophthalmology, Zhongshan Ophthalmic Ctr, Sun Yat-Sen Univ, 1/F – No 7 Jinsui Road, Zhujiang New Town, Guangzhou, Dianhe District, Guangdong, China.
URL: http://www.apaophth.org/

History 20 Feb 1957. Statutes modified: Oct 1958, Brussels (Belgium); 14 Mar 1978. Registered under law of Hawaii (USA). **Aims** Foster the study and dissemination of knowledge of diseases of the eye, particularly in Eastern Asia and countries bordering the Western Pacific and Oceania; promote scientific exchange and help establish closer personal and professional contacts among those interested and working in ophthalmology in this region. **Structure** General Assembly; Council; Standing Committees. **Languages** English. **Staff** 3.00 FTE, voluntary. **Finance** Congress fees. **Activities** Events/meetings; awards/prizes/competitions; training/education. **Events** *WOC : World Ophthalmology Congress* Beijing (China) 2022, *Congress* Kuala Lumpur (Malaysia) 2021, *Congress* Xiamen (China) 2020, *Congress* Bangkok (Thailand) 2019, *Congress* Hong Kong (Hong Kong) 2018. **Publications** *Asia-Pacific Journal of Ophthalmology (APJO)*; *Ocular Surgery News*.
Members National societies in 20 countries and territories:
Australia, Bangladesh, Cambodia, China, Hong Kong, India, Indonesia, Iran Islamic Rep, Japan, Korea Rep, Malaysia, Mongolia, Nepal, Pakistan, Philippines, Singapore, Sri Lanka, Taiwan, Thailand, Vietnam.
Subspecialty society members (6):
Asia Cornea Society (ACS, #01262); *Asia-Pacific Glaucoma Society (APGS, #01917)*; *Asia-Pacific Society of Ocular Oncology and Pathology (APSOOP)*; *Asia Pacific Society of Ophthalmic Plastic and Reconstructive Surgery (APSOPRS, #02041)*; *Asia-Pacific Strabismus and Paediatric Ophthalmology Society (APSPOS, #02055)*; *Asia-Pacific Vitreo-retina Society (APVRS, #02075).*
Associate members (4):
Asian Neuro-Ophthalmology Society (ASNOS, #01564); *Asia-Pacific Ocular Imaging Society (APOIS, #01983)*; *Asia-Pacific Ophthalmic Trauma Society (APOTS)*; *Asia Pacific Tele-Ophthalmology Society (APTOS, #02065).*
NGO Relations Associate member of: *Council for International Organizations of Medical Sciences (CIOMS, #04905).* [2019/XC0066/**D**]

♦ **Asia Pacific Accreditation and Certification Commission (APACC)** .. **01815**

Officer Colombo Plan Staff College, Bldg Blk. C, Dept of Education Complex, Meralco Avenue, Pasig City, 1600 Manila, Philippines. T. +63286310991. E-mail: apacc@cpsctech.org.
URL: https://www.apacc4hrd.org/

History Functions as the implementing agency for accreditation under the *Colombo Plan Staff College (CPSC, #04121).* Programme adopted for quality of technical education, 2003, when CPSC Governing Board approved CPSC Corporate Plan (2003-2008). International Conference on Accreditation and Certification convened, Dec 2004, Seoul (Korea Rep), to explore possibility of a regional body. Subseqent Workshop on "Regional Accreditation Modeling and Accrediting the Accreditors", Aug 2005, fortified APACC accreditation criteria and instruments. **Aims** Provide international accreditation and certification services towards quality management system of technical and vocational education and training (TVET) institutions. **Structure** Steering Committee; Board; Secretariat. National Coordinatros for Accreditation/Special Officers. **Activities** Certification/accreditation; training/education.
Members National Coordinators in 13 countries:
Afghanistan, Bangladesh, Bhutan, Fiji, Malaysia, Maldives, Mongolia, Myanmar, Nepal, Pakistan, Philippines, Sri Lanka, Thailand. [2022/AA2620/**E***]

♦ **Asia Pacific Accreditation Cooperation (APAC)** **01816**

Contact PO Box 5154, South Turramurra, Sydney NSW 2074, Australia. T. +61466262372. E-mail: secretariat@apac-accreditation.org.
URL: http://www.apac-accreditation.org/

History Founded 1 Jan 2019, on merger of *Asia Pacific Laboratory Accreditation Cooperation (APLAC, inactive)* and *Pacific Accreditation Cooperation (PAC, inactive).* **Aims** Manage and expand a mutual recognition arrangement (MRA) among accreditation bodies in the Asia Pacific region. **Structure** General Assembly; Executive Committee. MRA Council; MRA Management Committee. Committees (4): Technical (2): Capacity Building; Communication and Promotion. **Events** *Annual Meeting* Singapore (Singapore) 2019.
Members Full – signatories of MRA (45); Associate (21); Affiliate (8). Full in 27 countries and territories:
Australia, Bangladesh, Canada, China, Hong Kong, India, Indonesia, Iran Islamic Rep, Japan, Kazakhstan, Korea Rep, Malaysia, Mexico, Mongolia, New Zealand, Pakistan, Papua New Guinea, Philippines, Russia, Saudi Arabia, Singapore, Sri Lanka, Taiwan, Thailand, United Arab Emirates, USA, Vietnam.
Included in the above, 2 organizations listed in this Yearbook:
GCC Accreditation Center (GAC, #10082); *IOAS (#16001).*
Associate in 19 countries:
Australia, Brunei Darussalam, Cambodia, Canada, India, Iran Islamic Rep, Korea Rep, Kuwait, Kyrgyzstan, Nepal, Peru, Russia, Saudi Arabia, Tajikistan, Türkiye, United Arab Emirates, USA, Uzbekistan, Vietnam.
Affiliate in 6 countries and territories:
Bhutan, Brunei Darussalam, Korea Rep, Netherlands, Taiwan, Thailand.
Included in the above, 2 organizations listed in this Yearbook:
FHI 360 (Thailand Office); *Union internationale des laboratoires indépendants (UILI, #20429).*
IGO Relations Recognized as a *Asia-Pacific Economic Cooperation (APEC, #01887)* – Special Regional Body (SRB). Memorandum of Understanding with: *Arab Accreditation Cooperation (ARAC, #00892).* **NGO Relations** Memorandum of Understanding with: *African Accreditation Cooperation (AFRAC, #00196)*; *Asia Pacific Metrology Programme (APMP, #01957)*; *Inter-American Accreditation Cooperation (IAAC, #11396)* [2019/XM7466/y/**D**]

♦ **Asia Pacific Action Alliance on Human Resources for Health (AAAH)** **01817**

Secretariat Intl Health Policy Program Thailand, Ministry of Public Health, Tivanond Road, Muang, Nonthaburi, 1100, Thailand. T. +6625902366 – +6625902367. Fax +6625902385. E-mail: secretariat@aaahrh.net.
URL: http://aaahrh.net/

History Aug 2005, Bangkok (Thailand). **Aims** Generate and collate necessary evidence for effective human resource planning and management; develop the capacity within the region under a broader framework of overall health systems strengthening; increase access to effective health services, particularly for the poor; enable accelerated progress towards the Millennium Development Goals. **Structure** Steering Committee of up to 15 members, including Chair. Secretariat. **Publications** *AAAH Newsletter* (6 a year).

Members Governments (15):
Bangladesh, Cambodia, China, Fiji, India, Indonesia, Laos, Myanmar, Nepal, Papua New Guinea, Philippines, Samoa, Sri Lanka, Thailand, Vietnam.
NGO Relations Member of: *Global Health Workforce Alliance (GHWA, inactive).* [2016/XJ1579/E*]

♦ Asia Pacific Activities Conference (unconfirmed)

♦ Asia Pacific Adaptation Network (APAN) 01818

Regional Hub c/o UNEP, 2nd Floor, Block A, UN Building, Rajdamnern Avenue, Bangkok, 10200, Thailand. E-mail: apan.secretariat@un.org.
URL: http://www.asiapacificadapt.net/

History Oct 2009, as a regional network of *Global Adaptation Network (GAN, #10170).* **Aims** Build *climate change* resilient and sustainable human systems, ecosystems and economies. **Structure** Regional hub in Bangkok (Thailand) with *UNEP (#20299)* ROAP acting as secretariat in charge of Steering Committee. Sub-regional nodes and thematic nodes: Central – *Regional Environmental Centre for Central Asia (CAREC)*; South – *Climate Action Network South Asia (CANSA, #04003)*; Southeast – *Local Governments for Sustainability (ICLEI, #16507)*; Northeast – Research Centre for Climate Change Adaptation, Keio University; Pacific – *Secretariat of the Pacific Regional Environment Programme (SPREP, #19205).* Thematic Nodes (3): Water – *Global Water Partnership (GWP, #10653)* South Asia; Mountains – *International Centre for Integrated Mountain Development (ICIMOD, #12500)*; Agriculture – *Southeast Asian Regional Center for Graduate Study and Research in Agriculture (SEARCA, #19781).* **Activities** Knowledge management/information dissemination; events/meetings; training/education; capacity building. **Events** *Asia-Pacific Climate Change Adaptation Forum* Tokyo (Japan) 2021, *Asia-Pacific Climate Change Adaptation Forum* Tokyo (Japan) 2020, *Asia-Pacific Climate Change Adaptation Forum* Colombo (Sri Lanka) 2016, *International Symposium on Climate Change Adaptation* Seoul (Korea Rep) 2016. **Publications** *APAN e-communique* (12 a year) – newsletter. **IGO Relations** Partners include: *Asian Development Bank (ADB, #01422)*; *UNEP (#20299)*; *United States Agency for International Development (USAID).* **NGO Relations** Core partners: *Asian Institute of Technology (AIT, #01519)* – Regional Resource Centre for Asia and the Pacific (RRC.AP); *Institute for Global Environmental Strategies (IGES, #11266)*; *Stockholm Environment Institute (SEI, #19993).* [2020/XJ7849/F]

♦ Asia-Pacific Advanced Network (APAN) 01819

Mailing Address c/o Spectrum IT, C28 Marrs Hill, University Park, Peradeniya, 20400, Sri Lanka. E-mail: sec@apan.net.
Registered Office Room 101, Level 1, Block B, Cyberport 4, 100 Cyberport Road, Hong Kong, Central and Western, Hong Kong.
URL: http://apan.net/

History 3 Jun 1997. Former names and other names: *Asia-Pacific Advanced Network Consortium* – former alias. Registration: Company, Hong Kong. **Aims** Promote research in networking *technologies* and the development of high-performance broadband applications. **Events** *Meeting* Jinan (China) 2022, *Meeting* Daejeon (Korea Rep) 2019, *Meeting* Kuala Lumpur (Malaysia) 2019, *Meeting* Auckland (New Zealand) 2018, *Meeting* Singapore (Singapore) 2018. **Publications** *APAN Monthly Update.*
Members Primary; Associate; Liaison. Individuals, national and international organizations in 18 countries and territories:
Australia, China, Hong Kong, India, Indonesia, Japan, Korea Rep, Malaysia, Nepal, New Zealand, Pakistan, Philippines, Singapore, Sri Lanka, Taiwan, Thailand, USA, Vietnam.
NGO Relations Member of: *Coordinating Committee for Intercontinental Research Networking (CCIRN, #04817)*; *Pacific Rim Applications and Grid Middleware Assembly (PRAGMA, #17996).* [2019/XF4846/F]

♦ Asia-Pacific Advanced Network Consortium / see Asia-Pacific Advanced Network (#01819)
♦ Asia-Pacific Advisory Committee on Influenza / see Asia-Pacific Alliance for the Control of Influenza (#01822)

♦ Asia Pacific Aerospace Quality Group (APAQG) 01820

Secreariat c/o Soc of Japanese Aerospace Companies, NOF Tamieke Bldg, 2F 1-1-14 Akasaka Minatu-ku, Tokyo, 107-0052 Japan. E-mail: info@apaqg.org.
URL: http://www.apaqg.org/

History A cooperative organization serving as the Asia Pacific sector of *International Aerospace Quality Group (IAQG, #11594).* **Aims** Implement initiatives that make significant improvements in quality and reductions in cost throughout the value stream by establishing and maintaining dynamic cooperation, based on trust, between Asia Pacific Region aerospace organizations. **Events** *Meeting* Tokyo (Japan) 2021, *Meeting* Guangzhou (China) 2020, *Joint Forum* Singapore (Singapore) 2019, *Meeting* Singapore (Singapore) 2019, *Meeting* Jeju (Korea Rep) 2018.
Members Full; Associate. Full in 6 countries and territories:
China, Indonesia, Japan, Korea Rep, Singapore, Taiwan.
Associate in 4 countries:
Japan, Philippines, Singapore, Thailand.
NGO Relations *Americas Aerospace Quality Group (AAQG)*; *European Aerospace Quality Group (EAQG, #05838).* [2016/XM4792/E]

♦ Asia Pacific Alcohol Policy Alliance (internationally oriented national body)
♦ Asia-Pacific Alliance: Advancing the ICPD Agenda / see Asia Pacific Alliance for Sexual and Reproductive Health and Rights (#01825)

♦ Asia Pacific Alliance of Coaches (APAC) 01821

Chair c/o Excelsa, 3 Temasek Ave, 34-01 Centennial Tower, Singapore 039190, Singapore.
URL: http://www.apacoaches.org/

History 23 Oct 2007, Singapore. **Aims** Create a forum in the Asia Pacific region for coaches to reach new coaching professionalism and collaborate with one another. **Structure** Executive Committee. **Events** *Asia Pacific Coaching Conference* Mumbai (India) 2019, *Asia Pacific Coaching Conference* Bangkok (Thailand) 2017, *Coaching Conference* Seoul (Korea Rep) 2014, *Asia-Pacific Conference* Singapore (Singapore) 2012, *Asia Pacific coaching conference* Singapore (Singapore) 2010. **Publications** *The Coaching Voice of Asia Pacific* – newsletter. [2012/XJ2698/D]

♦ Asia-Pacific Alliance for the Control of Influenza (APACI) 01822

Exec Dir Business Office, Ste 1222, 1 Queens Road, Melbourne VIC 3004, Australia. T. +61398638650. Fax +61398638652.
Registered Office 1/F Hing Lung Commercial Bldg, 68-74 Bonham Strand, Sheung Wan, Hong Kong.
URL: http://www.apaci.asia/

History Set up 2002, as *Asia-Pacific Advisory Committee on Influenza.* Set up under current title Apr 2011. Registered in accordance with the law of Hong Kong. **Aims** Reduce the burden of influenza in the Asia-Pacific region. **Structure** Executive Council; Board of Directors. **Languages** English. **Staff** 1.00 FTE, paid. **Finance** Industry grants. Annual budget: US$ 200,000. **Activities** Advocacy/lobbying/activism; training/education. **Events** *World Influenza Conference* Beijing (China) 2018, *Workshop* Bhubaneswar (India) 2018, *Symposium on Seasonal Influenza Vaccination Policy Development and Implementation* Beijing (China) 2017, *Workshop* Kuala Lumpur (Malaysia) 2016, *International Influenza Symposium* Seoul (Korea Rep) 2016. **Publications** *APACI Media Bulletin* (weekly); *Journal Alert* (12 a year); *Asia-Pacific Influenza Newsletter* (4 a year).
Members Individuals in 13 countries and territories:
Australia, China, Hong Kong, India, Indonesia, Italy, Japan, Korea Rep, Mongolia, New Zealand, Philippines, Thailand, Vietnam.
NGO Relations Member of: *Developing Countries Vaccine Manufacturers Network (DCVMN, #05052).* Memorandum of Understanding with: DCVMN; *European Scientific Working Group on Influenza (ESWI, #08450)*; Institute of Preventive Medicine and Public Health – Hanoi Medical University; *International Society for Influenza and other Respiratory Virus Diseases (isirv, #15202).* [2020.03.05/XM1674/E]

♦ Asia Pacific Alliance for Disaster Management (A-PAD) 01823

CEO Tomigaya Ogawa Bldg 2F, 2-41-12 Tomigaya, Shibuya-ku, Tokyo, 151-0063 Japan. T. +81357909881. Fax +81357909368. E-mail: info@apadm.org.
URL: http://apadm.org/

History 2012. **Aims** Facilitate cooperation and understanding between governments, private companies and NGOs in the Asia Pacific region. **Structure** General Assembly; Executive Committee; Management Office. **Languages** English, Japanese. **Staff** 18.00 FTE, paid. **Activities** Capacity building; knowledge management/information dissemination; research/documentation; humanitarian/emergency aid.
Members National Platforms; Associate. Members in 6 countries:
Bangladesh, Indonesia, Japan, Korea Rep, Philippines, Sri Lanka.
Consultative Status Consultative status granted from: *ECOSOC (#05331)* (Special). [2019.06.05/XM6178/D]

♦ Asia Pacific Alliance for Rare Disease Organisations (APARDO) 01824

Contact 141 Middle Road No 05-06, GSM Bldg, Singapore 188976, Singapore. T. +6593855053.
URL: https://www.apardo.org/

Aims Help member organizations improve treatment outcomes for those affected by the rare disease (including rare cancers) in the Asia Pacific region. **Structure** Board of Directors. **Events** *Conference* 2021. **Members** Organizations: Ordinary; Affiliate. Membership countries not specified. **NGO Relations** Member of (1): *Rare Diseases International (RDI, #18621).* [2021/AA2323/C]

♦ Asia Pacific Alliance for Sexual and Reproductive Health and Rights (APA) 01825

Reginal Coordinator 18th Floor, Sathorn Thani II, 92 North Sathorn Rd, Bangkok, 10500, Thailand. T. +662365984. E-mail: info@asiapacificalliance.org.
URL: http://www.asiapacificalliance.org/

History 1999, as *Asia-Pacific Alliance: Advancing the ICPD Agenda (APA/ICPD).* **Aims** Ensure everyone's right to health is fully achieved through promotion and inclusion of sexual and reproductive health and rights in development agendas. **Structure** Steering Committee; Secretariat; Working Groups. **Finance** Supported by: Packard Foundation; *The William and Flora Hewlett Foundation.* Budget (biennial): about US$ 350,000. **Events** *Conference* Chiang Mai (Thailand) 2012, *Conference* Bangkok (Thailand) 2010, *Asia Pacific Conference on Reproductive and Sexual Health and Rights* Beijing (China) 2009, *Conference* Bangkok (Thailand) 2006, *Meeting* Bangkok (Thailand) 2005. **Publications** *E-news* (bi-weekly). Annual Report; factsheets; research publications.
Members Organizations (25) in 10 countries:
Australia, Canada, India, Indonesia, Japan, Korea Rep, Malaysia, New Zealand, Thailand, USA.
Included in the above, 6 organizations listed in this Yearbook:
Asian Forum of Parliamentarians on Population and Development (AFPPD, #01493); *International Council on the Management of Population Programs (ICOMP, #13043)*; *Korea International Cooperation Agency (KOICA)*; *Organization for Industrial, Spiritual and Cultural Advancement International (OISCA International, #17872)*; *PAI (#18025)*; *The William and Flora Hewlett Foundation.*
NGO Relations Member of: *Reproductive Health Supplies Coalition (RHSC, #18847).* [2013.10.28/XF6232/y/F]

♦ Asia and Pacific Alliance of YMCAs (APAY) 01826

Alliance asiatique de UCJG – Asiatischer Bund der CVJM – Alianza Asiatica de ACJs
Gen Sec 23 Waterloo Road, 6F, Kowloon, Hong Kong. T. +85227808347. Fax +85223854692. E-mail: office@asiapacificymca.org.
URL: http://www.asiapacificymca.org/

History Founded 1949, Hong Kong, as *Asia Alliance of YMCAs*, within the framework of *World Alliance of Young Men's Christian Associations (YMCA, #21090).* **Aims** Promote, develop and coordinate the work of YMCA movements in Asia and the South *Pacific.* **Structure** Council; Executive Committee; Standing Committees; Task Force. **Languages** English. **Staff** 8.00 FTE, paid. **Finance** Budget (annual): US$ 1,800,000. **Activities** Events/meetings; training/education; projects/programmes. **Events** *General Assembly* Gotemba (Japan) 2019, *Executive meeting* Hong Kong (Hong Kong) 2018, *Conference on Climate Change* Daegu (Korea Rep) 2017, *General Assembly* Daejeon (Korea Rep) 2015, *Regional Youth Conference* Singapore (Singapore) 2012. **Publications** *APAY e-news* (12 a year). Annual Report.
Members National YMCA Councils in 23 countries and territories:
Australia, Bangladesh, China, Fiji, Hong Kong, India, Indonesia, Japan, Korea Rep, Macau, Malaysia, Myanmar, Nepal, New Zealand, Pakistan, Papua New Guinea, Philippines, Samoa, Singapore, Sri Lanka, Tahiti Is, Taiwan, Thailand.
National YMCA Councils in formation in 4 countries:
Cambodia, Mongolia, Timor-Leste, Vietnam. [2015/XE7504/E]

♦ Asia Pacific Anti-Aging Society (APAAS) 01827

Officer 17, Yutongdanji-ro 14-gil, Buk-gu, Daegu 41515, Korea Rep. T. +820533825236. Fax +820533825298. E-mail: apantiaging@gmail.com.
URL: https://www.apantiaging.org/

History 18 Oct 2018, Daegu (Korea Rep). First Foundation Board Meeting and General Assembly held Nov 2018. Registration: Korea National Tax Service, No/ID: 401-82-74171, Start date: 18 Oct 2018, Korea Rep, Daegu. **Aims** Conduct academic research and engage in knowledge exchange related to the anti-aging field; promote amity among members. **Structure** Committees (9): Standing; Program; Bylaws; Industry; International; Publicity; Screening; Finance; National. **Languages** English, Korean. **Staff** 7.00 FTE, paid; 10.00 FTE, voluntary. **Finance** Sources: contributions of member/participating states; government support; international organizations; members' dues; subsidies. Supported by: Daegu Metropolitan City Government; Korea Government. **Activities** Capacity building; certification/accreditation; events/meetings; healthcare; knowledge management/information dissemination; networking/liaising; publishing activities; research and development. Active in: China, Korea Rep, Mongolia, Vietnam. **Events** *Asia-Pacific Anti-Aging Conference* Daegu (Korea Rep) 2022, *Conference on Cooperation for Khazakhstani Medical Technologies and Industries* Daegu (Korea Rep) 2022, *Asia-Pacific Anti-Aging Conference* Daegu (Korea Rep) 2021, *Northeast Asia Import Conference* Daegu (Korea Rep) 2021, *Technology Investment Innovation Conference* Daegu (Korea Rep) 2021. [2022.08.04/AA1921/D]

♦ Asia-Pacific Applied Economics Association (APAEA) 01828

Pres address not obtained. E-mail: contact.apaea@gmail.com – contact@a-paea.org.
URL: https://www.a-paea.org/

History 2016. **Aims** Provide a forum and resource base for developing research capacity of researchers in the Asia-Pacific region, with a particular focus on applied econometrics, economic growth and stability, financial market performance, and energy markets. **Structure** Officers; Advisory Board. **Activities** Events/meetings; financial and/or material support. **Events** *Conference on COVID-19 and Central Banking in Asia and the Pacific* Tokyo (Japan) 2021, *Joint Workshop on Monetary Policy, Banking and Finance, and Central Banking* Tokyo (Japan) 2021, *Regional Workshop on Blue Economy, Disaster Risk Financing and Ocean Infrastructure* Nadi (Fiji) 2019. **Publications** *Asian Economics Letters* (4 a year); *Energy Research Letters* (4 a year); *Islamic Economics & Finance Letters* (4 a year). **Members** Individual; Institutional. Membership countries not specified. [2022/AA2266/D]

♦ Asia-Pacific Arthroplasty Society (APAS) 01829

Sci Chairman 60-A Derby St, Kingswood NSW 2747, Australia.
URL: http://www.apasonline.org/

History 1998, Sanctuary Cove (Australia). **Aims** Foster the art and science of joint replacement surgery in the Asia-Pacific region through education, scientific meetings and industrial facilitation. **Structure** Executive Committee; Officers; Secretariat. **Languages** English. **Staff** 1.00 FTE, paid. **Finance** Members' dues. Meeting proceeds. **Activities** Events/meetings; training/education. **Events** *Meeting* Cebu City (Philippines) 2023, *Annual Conference* Bali (Indonesia) 2021, *Annual Conference* Bali (Indonesia) 2020, *Annual Conference* Xiamen (China) 2019, *Annual Conference* Bangkok (Thailand) 2018. **Publications** *APAS Newsletter.* Abstracts.
Members Full in 13 countries and territories:
Australia, China, Hong Kong, India, Indonesia, Korea Rep, Malaysia, New Zealand, Pakistan, Singapore, Sri Lanka, Thailand, Vietnam. [2022/XD8359/D]

♦ Asia Pacific Assistive Robotics Association (internationally oriented national body)

♦ Asia-Pacific Association of Agricultural Research Institutions (APAARI) 01830

Interim Exec Sec 4th Floor, FAO Annex Bldg, 202/1 Larn Laung Road, Klong Mahanak Sub-District, Pomrab Sattrupai District, Bangkok, 10100, Thailand. T. +6622822918. Fax +6622822919. E-mail: apaari@apaari.org.
URL: http://www.apaari.org/

History 1990, within the framework of *FAO Regional Office for Asia and the Pacific (RAP, #09266)*. **Aims** Promote development of national agricultural research institutions in the Asia-Pacific region through inter-regional and inter-institutional cooperation. **Structure** General Assembly; Executive Committee; Executive Secretary, heading the APAARI Secretariat at FAO Office in Delhi (India). **Languages** English. **Staff** 6.00 FTE, paid. **Finance** Members' dues. Annual budget: about US$ 150,000. **Activities** Events/meetings; guidance/assistance/consulting; knowledge management/information dissemination. **Events** *Asian Maize Conference* Bangkok (Thailand) 2015, *Regional Workshop on Development of Communication Strategies for Adoption of Agri-Biotechnology in Asia* Chiang Rai (Thailand) 2015, *General Assembly* Bangkok (Thailand) 2014, *General Assembly* Delhi (India) 2012, *General Assembly* Tsukuba (Japan) 2008. **Publications** *APAARI Newsletter* (2 a year). *Success Stories* – series on significant research and development in agriculture in NARS. *Agricultural Research Priorities in the Asia-Pacific Region – an APAARI Overview* (1997); *Directory of Agricultural Research Institutions in the Asia-Pacific Region: South Asia* (1995). Forum proceedings; reports of expert consultations; (sub-) regional reports.
Members Research institutions, councils, organizations and universities representing governments of 19 countries and territories:
Australia, Bangladesh, Bhutan, Fiji, India, Iran Islamic Rep, Japan, Korea Rep, Malaysia, Nepal, New Caledonia, Pakistan, Papua New Guinea, Philippines, Samoa, Sri Lanka, Taiwan, Thailand, Vietnam.
Associate members, include 13 organizations listed in this Yearbook:
AVRDC – The World Vegetable Center (#03051); *Bioversity International (#03262)*; *CABI (#03393)*; *International Center for Agricultural Research in the Dry Areas (ICARDA, #12466)*; *International Crops Research Institute for the Semi-Arid Tropics (ICRISAT, #13116)*; *International Food Policy Research Institute (IFPRI, #13622)*; *International Livestock Research Institute (ILRI, #14062)*; *International Maize and Wheat Improvement Center (#14077)*; *International Rice Research Institute (IRRI, #14754)*; *International Torture Documentation Network (ITDN)*; *International Water Management Institute (IWMI, #15867)*; *World Agroforestry Centre (ICRAF, #21072)*; *WorldFish (#21507)*.
IGO Relations *FAO (#09260)* and its regional office RAP; *International Fund for Agricultural Development (IFAD, #13692)*. Cooperates with: *CGIAR System Organization (CGIAR, #03843)* and its supported centres ICARDA, ICRISAT, IRRI and IPGRI. **NGO Relations** Cooperates with CGIAR supported centres: CIMMYT; IWMI; *WorldFish (#21507)*; *International Potato Center (#14627)*; *International Service for National Agricultural Research (ISNAR, inactive)*. Instrumental in setting up: *Banana Asia-Pacific Network (BAPNET, no recent information)*; *Inter-regional Network on Cotton in Asia and North Africa (INCANA, #15972)*. Member of: *Global Confederation of Higher Education Associations for Agriculture and Life Sciences (GCHERA, #10304)*; *Global Forum on Agricultural Research (GFAR, #10370)*; *Global Open Data for Agriculture and Nutrition (GODAN, #10514)*. [2017/XD3559/y/**D***]

♦ Asia Pacific Association of Allergology and Clinical Immunology / see Asia Pacific Association of Allergy, Asthma and Clinical Immunology (#01831)

♦ Asia Pacific Association of Allergy, Asthma and Clinical Immunology (APAAACI) 01831

Secretariat 20 Bendemeer Road, BS Bendemeer Centre, Suite 04-02, Singapore 339914, Singapore. T. +6564116693. E-mail: secretariat@apaaaci.org.
URL: http://www.apaaaci.org/

History 1989, at a regional allergy meeting in Bali (Indonesia), as *Asian Pacific Society of Allergy and Immunology (APSAI)*. Subsequently changed title to *Asia Pacific Association of Allergology and Clinical Immunology (APAACI)*, 2000. Present title adopted, Mar 2007. **Aims** Promote exchange and progress of knowledge on allergy, asthma and clinical immunology in the region. **Structure** House of Delegates (meets during the Congress); Executive Board; Committees (7). **Languages** English. **Staff** 1.00 FTE, paid. **Finance** Sources: members' dues. **Activities** Events/meetings; knowledge management/information dissemination; networking/liaising; research and development; training/education. **Events** *Congress* Kyoto (Japan) 2020, *Joint Congress* Beijing (China) 2019, *Congress* Bangkok (Thailand) 2018, *Joint Congress* Seoul (Korea Rep) 2018, *The era of allergy – local and global insights and intervention* Kuala Lumpur (Malaysia) 2016. **Publications** *APAAACI Newsletter*, *Asia Pacific Allergy*.
Members Full national societies and individuals. Societies in 16 countries and territories (Australia and New Zealand being one association):
Australia, Bangladesh, China, Hong Kong, India, Indonesia, Japan, Korea Rep, Malaysia, Mongolia, New Zealand, Philippines, Singapore, Sri Lanka, Taiwan, Thailand.
Individuals in 2 countries:
Myanmar, Pakistan.
IGO Relations *'Global Alliance Against Chronic Respiratory Disease (GARD)' of WHO (#20950)*. **NGO Relations** Member of: *Global Alliance Against Chronic Respiratory Diseases (GARD, #10182)*; *World Allergy Organization – IAACI (WAO, #21077)*. [2021/XD7563/**D**]

♦ Asia-Pacific Association of Catalysis Societies (APACS) 01832

Secretariat State Key Lab of Catalysis, Dalian Inst of Chemical Physics, Chinese Academy of Sciences, 457 Zhongshan Road, Dalian, 116023 Liaoning, China. T. +8641184379307. Fax +8641184694447. E-mail: apcat@dicp.ac.cn.
URL: http://www.apacs.dicp.ac.cn/

History 14 Jul 2004, Paris (France), during 13th International Congress on Catalysis of *International Association of Catalysis Societies (IACS, #11757)*. **Aims** Promote scientific and technical progress both in the fundamental understanding and the application of catalysis as well as in related scientific disciplines. **Structure** Committee, comprising Chairperson, Vice-Chairperson, Secretary and Treasurer. **Activities** Organizes Asia-Pacific Congress on Catalysis. **Events** *Asia Pacific Congress on Catalysis* Bangkok (Thailand) 2019, *Asia Pacific Congress on Catalysis* Mumbai (India) 2017, *Asia Pacific Congress on Catalysis* Taipei (Taiwan) 2013, *Asia Pacific Congress on Catalysis / Congress* Sapporo (Japan) 2010, *Asia Pacific congress on catalysis* Singapore (Singapore) 2006.
Members Societies in 12 countries and territories:
Australia, China, Hong Kong, India, Japan, Korea Rep, Malaysia, New Zealand, Singapore, Taiwan, Thailand, Vietnam. [2013/XJ7215/**D**]

♦ Asia-Pacific Association of Cataract and Refractive Surgeons (APACRS) 01833

Secretariat c/o Singapore Natl Eye Centre, 11 Third Hospital Ave, Singapore 168751, Singapore. T. +6563227468 – +6563227469. Fax +6563278630. E-mail: apacrs@apacrs.org.
URL: http://www.apacrs.org/

History 1987, Singapore (Singapore). Former names and other names: *Asia Pacific Intraocular Implant Association (APIIA)* – former (1987 to 2000). **Aims** Be the Asia-pacific forum for exchange of knowledge and skills in cataract and refractive surgery; promote research in cataract and refractive surgery; associate with national cataract and/or refractive surgery societies as well as assist them in educational and training issues; collaborate with national associations or organizations to host annual congresses in the region; support and promote the initiative to advance development of cataract and refractive surgery in the Asia-Pacific. **Structure** Board, comprising President, Honorary Life President, Honorary Secretary, Treasurer, 8 members and 6 Honorary Advisors. Secretariat. **Languages** English. **Staff** 3.00 FTE, paid. **Finance** Sponsorship. **Activities** Participates in Combined Symposium of Cataract and Refractive Societies (CSCRS). Annually awards: APACRS LIM Lecture; APACRS Gold Medal; APACRS Certified Educator (ACE) Award. Set up: *World Federation of Cataract and Refractive Surgeons (inactive)*. Annually grants the 'APACRS Educator Award (ACE)'. **Events** *Annual Meeting* Seoul (Korea Rep) 2022, *Annual Meeting* Singapore (Singapore) 2021, *World Cornea Congress* Boston, MA (USA) 2020, *Annual Meeting* Singapore (Singapore) 2020, *Annual Meeting* Kyoto (Japan) 2019. **Publications** *EyeWorld-Asia Pacific* – news magazine, in 3 editions.
Members Individuals in 29 countries and territories:
Aruba, Australia, Belgium, Brunei Darussalam, Canada, China, Germany, Hong Kong, India, Indonesia, Iran Islamic Rep, Israel, Japan, Korea Rep, Malaysia, Mexico, Myanmar, New Zealand, Pakistan, Philippines, Saudi Arabia, Singapore, Spain, Sri Lanka, Taiwan, Thailand, Türkiye, USA, Vietnam.
NGO Relations *Asociación Latino Americana de Cirugia de Catarata, Segmento Anterior y Refractiva (ALACCSA-R, #02194)*; national associations. [2022/XD6284/v/**D**]

♦ Asia-Pacific Association of Chemical Ecologists (APACE) 01834

Vice Pres Ecological Research Center, Kyoto University, 2-509-3 Hirano, Otsu SHIGA, 520-2113 Japan.
Sec Dept of Functional Genomics and Gene Safety, Inst of Plant Protection, Chinese Acad of Agricultural Sciences, No 2 Yuanmingyuan West Road, Haidian District, 100193 Beijing, China.
URL: http://www.newapace.com/

History Founded 21 Nov 1997, Taiwan. **Aims** Promote understanding of interaction between *organisms* and their environment mediated by naturally occurring chemicals. **Structure** Regular Meeting (every 2 years). **Finance** Members' dues. **Events** *Biennial Conference* Kuala Lumpur (Malaysia) 2022, *Joint International Chemical Ecology Conference* Kuala Lumpur (Malaysia) 2022, *Biennial Conference* Hangzhou (China) 2019, *Biennial Conference* Kyoto (Japan) 2017, *Joint International Chemical Ecology Conference* Kyoto (Japan) 2017. **Publications** *APCE Newsletter*.
Members Individuals in 18 countries and territories:
Australia, Brazil, Canada, China, France, Germany, India, Japan, Korea Rep, Malaysia, New Zealand, Pakistan, Romania, South Africa, Taiwan, Thailand, Tunisia, USA. [2016/XM3601/**D**]

♦ Asia-Pacific Association of Communication Directors (APACD) 01835

Contact address not obtained. E-mail: info@apacd.com.
URL: https://apacd.com/

History 2014. **Aims** Facilitate knowledge exchange; advance the profession of communications and public relations directors. **Structure** Annual General Meeting; Board. **Activities** Awards/prizes/competitions; events/meetings. **Events** *Summit* 2021, *Forum* Singapore (Singapore) 2019. [2022.03.04/AA2268/**D**]

♦ Asia-Pacific Association for Computer-Assisted Language Learning (APACALL) 01836

Contact address not obtained. E-mail: webmaster@apacall.org.
URL: https://www.apacall.org/

Aims Provide a mechanism for information exchange on Computer-Assisted Language Learning (CALL); highlight the importance and value of accessibility and professional engagement with CALL for teachers, students, researchers and other interested professionals; promote and support research and good practice in CALL. **Structure** Executive Committee. **Activities** Events/meetings; research/documentation. **Publications** *APACALL Newsletter*. *APACALL Book Series*. [2023.02.15/XM7364/**C**]

♦ Asia Pacific Association for the Control of Tobacco (APACT) 01837

Contact 12F-3 No 57, Fu-Shin North Rd, 105 ROC, Taipei, Taiwan. T. +888227766133. Fax +888227527247. E-mail: service104@jtf.org.tw.
URL: http://www.jtf.org.tw/smokefreeasia/bout-apact.htm/

History 12 Jun 1989, Taipei (Taiwan). **Aims** Create a smoke-free Asia by the year 2001. Assist Asian countries to implement immediately aggressive tobacco control programmes, including bans on all *cigarette* advertising, restrictions on smoking in public places and comprehensive educational and intervention programmes. **Structure** Executive Committee comprising: President; Honorary Life President; President-Elect; Vice-President; Honorary Vice-President; Executive Secretary; Chairman of Nominating Committee. **Languages** English. **Events** *Asia Pacific Conference on Tobacco or Health* Bangkok (Thailand) 2021, *Asia Pacific Conference on Tobacco or Health* Bangkok (Thailand) 2020, *Asia Pacific Conference on Tobacco or Health* Bali (Indonesia) 2018, *Asia Pacific Conference on Tobacco or Health* Beijing (China) 2016, *Asia Pacific Conference on Tobacco or Health* Chiba (Japan) 2013. **Publications** *APACT Newsletter*. **Members** Full in more than 16 countries. Membership countries not specified. [2013/XD2587/**D**]

♦ Asia Pacific Association of Critical Care Medicine (APACCM) 01838

SG Tata Memorial Hospital, Dr Ernest Borges Road, Parel, Mumbai, Maharashtra 400 012, Mumbai MAHARASHTRA 400 012, India. E-mail: kaivalyaak@yahoo.co.in.
URL: http://www.apaccm.org/

History 1977, as *Western Pacific Association of Critical Care Medicine (WPACCM)*. 2004, present name adopted. **Events** *Congress* Mumbai (India) 2019, *Congress* Hong Kong (Hong Kong) 2018, *Conference* Bangkok (Thailand) 2017, *Congress* Bangkok (Thailand) 2016, *Congress* Jaipur (India) 2014. **Publications** *Critical Care and Shock* (periodical). [2019/XN1988/**D**]

♦ Asia Pacific Association of Derivatives (unconfirmed)
♦ Asia-Pacific Association for Educational Assessment (no recent information)

♦ Asia Pacific Association of Educators in Agriculture and Environment (APEAEN) 01839

Exec Dir Central Bicol State Univ of Agriculture, San Jose, Pili CAS, Philippines.
URL: https://apeaen.net/

History 5 Aug 1997, Tokyo (Japan). Founded when constitution and by-laws signed by founding members. Registration: Securities and Exchange Commission, Philippines. **Aims** Serve as an international alliance for identification and dissemination of new developments and best practices in the fields of agriculture and environmental education. **Structure** Board of Directors. **Languages** English. **Staff** 3.00 FTE, voluntary. **Finance** Sources: contributions; donations; grants; members' dues. Annual budget: 200,000 PHP (2023). **Activities** Awareness raising; capacity building; events/meetings; training/education. **Events** *International Conference* Fiji 2016, *International Conference* Naga (Philippines) 2014, *International Conference* Naga (Philippines) 2014, *International conference* Nakhon Pathom (Thailand) 2012, *International Conference* Bangkok (Thailand) 2011. **Publications** *APEAEN Agri-vironment Educator* (2 a year) – official publication. Books; proceedings.
Members Regular; Life; Institutional; Honorary – organizations and individuals. Members in 22 countries and territories:
Bangladesh, Denmark, Fiji, Germany, India, Indonesia, Iran Islamic Rep, Japan, Korea Rep, Laos, Malaysia, Mongolia, Nepal, Netherlands, Pakistan, Philippines, Samoa, Sri Lanka, Taiwan, Thailand, USA, Vietnam. [2023.02.15/XD6783/**D**]

♦ Asia Pacific Association for Fiduciary Studies (APAFS) 01840

Dir of Admin 120 Father Duenas Ave, Ste 102, Hagatna GU 96910, USA. T. +16714770808. Fax +16714770818. E-mail: admin@apafs.org.
URL: http://www.apafs.org/

History 2000. A 501(c)3 non-profit educational and charitable association. **Aims** Raise the level of understanding and standards of practice among fiduciaries in the region by providing educational programmes and opportunities to provide the most prudent stewardship of funds entrusted to their care. **Structure** Board of Governors. **Staff** 1.00 FTE, paid. 1. **Finance** Members' dues. **Activities** Training/education; events/meetings. **Events** *Annual Pacific Region Investment Conference* Manila (Philippines) 2022, *Annual Pacific Region Investment Conference* Makati (Philippines) 2019, *Annual Pacific Region Investment Conference* Makati (Philippines) 2018, *Annual Pacific Region Investment Conference* Manila (Philippines) 2017, *Conference* Manila (Philippines) 2017. **Members** Members throughout 8 jurisdictions in Asia Pacific region. Membership countries not specified. [2017.10.11/XM1695/**D**]

♦ Asia-Pacific Association of Forestry Research Institutions (APAFRI) 01841

Exec Sec Forest Research Inst, Kepong 52109, Kuala Lumpur, Malaysia. T. +6060362722516. E-mail: secretariat@apafri.org – sim@apafri.org.
URL: http://www.apafri.org/

History 20 Feb 1995, Bogor (Indonesia). 20-23 Feb 1995, Bogor (Indonesia). **Aims** Foster development of research on sustainable forest management in the Asia-Pacific region by promoting exchange of scientific and technical know-how and information; promote cooperative research and training programmes; strengthen links among national, regional and international research centres and organizations. **Structure** General Assembly (every 3 years). Executive Committee, comprising Chairman, Vice-Chairman and 4 members (including immediate Past-Chairman). Regional representatives for: South Asia (India, Pakistan, Sri Lanka, Bangladesh, Nepal and Bhutan); China; Japan, Korea and Taiwan; Oceania (Australia, Fiji, Papua New Guinea, Solomon Is, Samoa and Hawaii). Secretariat headed by Executive Secretary. **Languages** English. **Staff** 4.00 FTE, paid. **Finance** Members' dues. Other sources: grants; donations; sale of publications; fees. Support from: ACIAR; *Canadian International Development Agency (CIDA, inactive)*; *Deutsche Gesellschaft für Technische Zusammenarbeit (GTZ, inactive)*; *Southeast Asian Regional Center for Graduate Study and Research in Agriculture (SEARCA, #19781)*; USDA Forest Service; *FAO (#09260)*. **Activities** Training/education; awards/

prizes/competitions; events/meetings. **Events** *General Assembly* Guangzhou (China) 2012, *Asia and Pacific forest products workshop* Colombo (Sri Lanka) 2009, *General Assembly* Kuala Lumpur (Malaysia) 2009, *General Assembly* Kuala Lumpur (Malaysia) 2006, *General Assembly* Manila (Philippines) 2003. **Publications** *APAFRI Newsletter* (2 a year). *Continuing Professional Education* – series, on CD-ROM. Journals, including electronic; scientific case studies; training programmes on CD-ROM; series of research results; proceedings. **Information Services** *ATIS* – APAFRI-Tree Link Information System: online information exchange service.
Members Institutions (63) in 22 countries and territories:
Australia, Bangladesh, Bhutan, Cambodia, China, Fiji, India, Indonesia, Japan, Korea Rep, Laos, Malaysia, Nepal, Pakistan, Papua New Guinea, Philippines, Solomon Is, Sri Lanka, Taiwan, Thailand, USA, Vietnam.
Included in the above, 7 organizations listed in this Yearbook:
ASEAN Forest Tree Seed Centre Project (no recent information); Australian Centre for International Agricultural Research (ACIAR); Bioversity International (#03262); CABI (#03393); Center for International Forestry Research (CIFOR, #03646); International Network for Bamboo and Rattan (INBAR, #14234); Japan International Research Centre for Agricultural Sciences (JIRCAS).
IGO Relations Participates in: *United Nations Forum on Forests (UNFF, #20562).* **NGO Relations** Asian Pacific Chapter of: *International Union of Forest Research Organizations (IUFRO, #15774).* [2017/XD6001/y/D]

♦ Asia Pacific Association for Gynecologic Endoscopy and Minimally Invasive Therapy (APAGE) 01842

Office c/o Dept of OB/GYN, Chang Gung Memorial Hosp, No 5 Fuxing Str, Guishan District, Taoyuan 33305, Taiwan. T. +88633281200 ext 8253. Fax +88633960356. E-mail: gynendowebcontact@gmail.com – mit.apage@gmail.com.
URL: http://www.apagemit.com/

History 2003. **Aims** Stimulate research and knowledge dissemination of all aspects of gynecologic endoscopy and minimally invasive therapy; contribute to standardization of terminology and evaluation of diagnostic and therapeutic procedures; promote cooperation between organizations active in the field. **Structure** General Assembly (annual); Board of Trustees; Executive Board. Committees (6): Scientific; Research; Nominating; Membership; Training; Editorial. **Languages** English. **Activities** Events/meetings. **Events** *Annual Congress* Korea Rep 2026, *Annual Congress* Shanghai (China) 2025, *Annual Congress* Chennai (India) 2024, *Annual Congress* Singapore (Singapore) 2023, *Annual Congress* Taipei (Taiwan) 2022.
Members Societies in 14 countries and territories:
Australia, China, Hong Kong, India, Indonesia, Japan, Korea Rep, Macau, Malaysia, Philippines, Singapore, Taiwan, Thailand, USA. [2022/XM0696/D]

♦ Asia Pacific Association of Hydrology and Water Resources (APHW) 01843

Contact WRRC, Gokasho, Uji, Kyoto, 611-0011 Japan.
URL: http://rwes.dnri.kyoto-u.ac.jp/~tanaka/APHW/APHW.html

History 1 Sep 2002. **Aims** Promote in an appropriate framework for the Asia Pacific region: the exchange of operational knowledge and experience in water resources management; research activities and education. **Languages** English. **Staff** Voluntary. **Finance** Voluntary contributions. **Activities** Promotion of hydrological studies in Asia Pacific region; research on water utilization and management methodologies; organization of conferences and workshops. **Events** *Conference* Roorkee (India) 2019, *Conference* Singapore (Singapore) 2015, *Conference* Seoul (Korea Rep) 2013, *Conference* Hanoi (Vietnam) 2010, *Conference* Beijing (China) 2008. **Publications** *APHW Journal.*
Members Organizations; Individuals. Organizations in 6 countries:
Albania, India, Japan, Nepal, New Zealand, Thailand.
Individuals in 33 countries and territories:
Albania, Australia, Bangladesh, Belarus, Cambodia, Canada, China, Egypt, Finland, Germany, Ghana, Hong Kong, India, Indonesia, Iran Islamic Rep, Japan, Korea Rep, Laos, Malaysia, Mexico, Micronesia FS, Nepal, New Zealand, Norway, Philippines, Singapore, South Africa, Sri Lanka, Taiwan, Thailand, Türkiye, Uzbekistan, Vietnam.
NGO Relations Member of: *Network of Asian River Basin Organizations (NARBO, #16993).* Partner of: *Asia Oceania Geosciences Society (AOGS, #01799).* [2014/XJ3069/D]

♦ Asia-Pacific Association for International Education (APAIE) 01844

Admin Dir address not obtained. E-mail: secretariat@apaie.net.
Main Website: http://www.apaie.net/

History 3 Dec 2004, Seoul (Korea Rep). Founded by a committee of 13 university representatives from countries and regions in Asia-Pacific. **Aims** Enable greater cooperation among higher education institutions in the Asia-Pacific region. **Structure** Board of Directors; Advisory Council; Executive Committee; Secretariat. **Staff** 1.50 FTE, paid. **Activities** Events/meetings; networking/liaising. **Events** *Annual Conference* Bangkok (Thailand) 2023, *Annual Conference* Vancouver, BC (Canada) 2022, *APAIE Update Meeting* 2021, *Annual Conference* Vancouver, BC (Canada) 2020, *Annual Conference* Kuala Lumpur (Malaysia) 2019.
Members Institutions (17) in 10 countries and territories:
Australia, China, Hong Kong, Japan, Korea Rep, New Zealand, Singapore, Taiwan, Thailand, USA. [2022.10.25/XM2542/D]

♦ Asia-Pacific Association for Machine Translation (AAMT) 01845

Pres c/o Japan System Application Co Ltd, Suzuki Bldg 3F, 2-55-2 Ikebukuro, Toshima-ku, Tokyo, 171-0014 Japan. E-mail: aamt-info@aamt.info.
URL: http://www.aamt.info/

History Founded 17 Apr 1991, as Japan Association for Machine Translation. **Structure** Board of Directors; Editorial Committee; Committee for Seeking Future Direction of MT; Internet Working Group. **Activities** Research/documentation; events/meetings; training/education; awards/prizes/competitions. **Events** *Biennial Machine Translation Summit* Nagoya (Japan) 2017, *Biennial Machine Translation Summit* Miami, FL (USA) 2015, *Annual Conference* Tokyo (Japan) 2013, *Annual Conference* Tokyo (Japan) 2012, *Biennial Machine Translation Summit* Tokyo (Japan) 2011. **Publications** *AAMT Journal.* **Members** Corporate (22) machine translation (MT) system manufacturers, T-related software and tool developers, MT system distributors, MT research institutes, and other organizations. Individual (over 50) scholars, researchs, engineers, developers, distributors, document handlers, translation technicians, and translators. Membership countries not specified.
NGO Relations Member of: *International Association for Machine Translation (IAMT, #12008).* [2014/XD6346/D]

♦ Asia Pacific Association of Medical Journal Editors (APAME) 01846

Contact WHO Western Pacific Regional Office, PO Box 2932, 1000 Manila, Philippines. E-mail: apame2008@gmail.com – apame@wpro.who.int.
Facebook: https://www.facebook.com/apameeditors/

History Conceived Nov 2007, Seoul (Korea Rep); formally set up May 2008, Seoul (Korea Rep). Current constitution amended 2 Nov 2010. **Aims** Promote *health care* through dissemination of high-quality knowledge and information on medicine in the Asia Pacific Region. **Structure** General Assembly; Board of Directors. **Events** *Convention* Xian (China) 2019, *Convention* Bangkok (Thailand) 2016, *Advancing access to health information and publication – shifting paradigms, trends and innovation* Manila (Philippines) 2015, *Convention* Ulaanbaatar (Mongolia) 2014, *Convention* Tokyo (Japan) 2013.
Members Individual; Associate. Individuals in 22 countries:
Australia, Bangladesh, Bhutan, Brunei Darussalam, Cambodia, China, Fiji, India, Indonesia, Japan, Korea Rep, Laos, Malaysia, Mongolia, Myanmar, Nepal, New Zealand, Philippines, Singapore, Sri Lanka, Thailand, Vietnam.
Associate in 1 country:
Canada.
IGO Relations Closely affiliated with: *WHO Regional Office for the Western Pacific (WPRO, #20947).* **NGO Relations** Cooperates with: *Eastern Mediterranean Association of Medical Editors (EMAME, #05241); European Association of Science Editors (EASE, #06201); Forum for African Medical Editors (FAME); World Association of Medical Editors (WAME, #21162).* [2019/XJ7780/D]

♦ Asia Pacific Association of Medical Toxicology (APAMT) 01847

Pres Faculty of Medicine, University of Peradeniya, Peradeniya, Sri Lanka. T. +94812384556.
URL: http://www.asiatox.org/

History 1989. **Aims** Promote chemical safety, poison control and treatment within the Asia Pacific region. **Structure** General Assembly (every 2 years). Governing Body, comprising President, 3 Vice-Presidents, Secretary-General, Treasurer and 4 further members. **Events** *Annual Congress* Thiruvananthapuram (India) 2020, *Annual Congress* Putrajaya (Malaysia) 2019, *Annual Congress* Bali (Indonesia) 2018, *Annual Congress* Kandy (Sri Lanka) 2017, *Annual Congress* Singapore (Singapore) 2016.
Members Individuals in 8 countries and territories:
Australia, Bangladesh, India, Iran Islamic Rep, Malaysia, Taiwan, Türkiye, Yemen. [2013/XD9240/D]

♦ Asia-Pacific Association of Methodist-related Educational Institutions (APAMEI) 01848

Gen Sec Yonsei Univ – Yonsei Intl Campus, 85 Songdogwahak-ro, Yeonsu-gu, Incheon 21982, Korea Rep.
URL: http://www.apamei.org/

History Feb 2012. **Aims** Foster solidarity , networking, and development of visionary, dynamic, and holistic, Christian Leadership in Asia and Pacific. **Structure** Board of Directors. **Events** *Joint International Forum* Tokyo (Japan) 2022, *Spirituality in Law and Education* Incheon (Korea Rep) 2021, *Spirituality of Money* Incheon (Korea Rep) 2021, *The Secularity of God* Incheon (Korea Rep) 2021, *Scientific Truth and Christian Faith in Methodist Education* Tokyo (Japan) 2021.
Members Methodist-related institutions (over 50) in 11 countries and territories:
China, India, Japan, Korea Rep, Malaysia, Mongolia, Myanmar, Philippines, Singapore, Sri Lanka, Vietnam.
NGO Relations A regional association of: *International Association of Methodist Schools, Colleges and Universities (IAMSCU).* [2021/AA1772/D]

♦ Asia-Pacific Association on PBL in Health Sciences / see Asia-Pacific Association On Problem-based Learning In Health Sciences (#01851)

♦ Asia Pacific Association of Pediatric Allergy, Respirology and Immunology (APAPARI) 01849

Secretariat c/o Research Center for Allergy, 18-1 Sakuradai, Minamiku, Sagamihara KANAGAWA, 252-0392 Japan. E-mail: info@apapari.org.
URL: http://www.apapari.org/

History 13 May 1998, Bangkok (Thailand). Founded following a 1st meeting in Seoul (Korea Rep), 12 Apr 1997. **Aims** Improve quality of patient care in allergy, respirology and immunology; maintain and advance the diagnostic and therapeutic skills of members and foster their appropriate application; develop and disseminate educational information in the field. **Structure** Council. Board of Directors, comprising President, Vice-President, Honorary Secretary, Treasurer and 3 further members. **Events** *JSPACI-APAPARI Joint Congress* Okinawa (Japan) 2022, *Joint Congress* Seoul (Korea Rep) 2021, *Congress* Bali (Indonesia) 2019, *Novel therapies, prevention and integrated action – towards improved patient care* Bangkok (Thailand) 2018, *The era of allergy – local and global insights and intervention* Kuala Lumpur (Malaysia) 2016. **NGO Relations** Member ofl *European Academy of Allergy and Clinical Immunology (EAACI, #05779).* [2022/XM1653/D]

♦ Asia Pacific Association of Pediatric Urologists (APAPU) 01850

Pres c/o Asan Med Ctr, 88 Olympic-ro, 43-gil, Songpa-gu, Seoul 05505, Korea Rep.
URL: http://www.apapu.net/

History 1998. Current constitution adopted 2014. Registration: Hong Kong. **Structure** Annual Meeting; Board. **Languages** English. **Staff** 1.00 FTE, paid. **Finance** Self-funding. **Activities** Events/meetings; training/education. **Events** *Annual Congress* Karachi (Pakistan) 2023, *Annual Congress* Karachi (Pakistan) 2021, *Annual Congress* Karachi (Pakistan) 2020, *Conference* Perth, WA (Australia) 2019, *Annual Congress* Yogyakarta (Indonesia) 2017.
Members Individuals in 16 countries and territories:
Australia, Cambodia, China, Hong Kong, India, Indonesia, Iran Islamic Rep, Japan, Korea Rep, Malaysia, Myanmar, Pakistan, Philippines, Singapore, Taiwan, USA.
NGO Relations *East Asian Society of Endourology (EASE, #05208); European Society for Paediatric Urology (ESPU, #08688); International Children's Continence Society (ICCS, #12552).* [2022/XJ3592/D]

♦ Asia-Pacific Association On Problem-based Learning In Health Sciences (APA-PHS) 01851

Contact address not obtained. E-mail: apa.pbl.hs@gmail.com.
URL: https://sites.google.com/site/apaphs/

History 2000. Former names and other names: *Asia-Pacific Association on PBL in Health Sciences* – alias. Registration: Start date: 2003, Malaysia. **Structure** Council; Executive Committee. **Activities** Events/meetings. **Events** *Asia Pacific Conference on Problem Based Learning in the Health Sciences and Higher Education* Cebu City (Philippines) 2021, *Asia Pacific Conference on Problem Based Learning in the Health Sciences and Higher Education* Cebu City (Philippines) 2020, *Asia Pacific Conference on Problem Based Learning in Health Sciences and Higher Education* Surabaya (Indonesia) 2018, *Asia-Pacific Joint Conference on PBL* Daegu (Korea Rep) 2016. [2020/AA2269/D]

♦ Asia-Pacific Association of Psychotherapists (APAP) 01852

Secretariat 39 Grosvenor Street, Woollahra NSW 2025, Australia. T. +61293691918. Fax +61293695058.

History 30 Oct 1996, Bali, at inaugural conference. A chapter of *International Federation for Psychotherapy (IFP, #13523).* **Aims** Unite associations, societies and groupings of psychotherapists in member countries to promote and improve the exchange between cultures, professional societies and psychotherapy schools and to encourage and support an appropriate standard in the practice of psychotherapy. **Structure** Assembly. Board, composed of a delegate for each member country. Executive Committee, consisting of Honorary President, President, 2 Vice Presidents, Treasurer and Secretary. **Finance** Members' dues. **Activities** Organizes regional workshops. **Events** *Congress* Mandaluyong (Philippines) 2011, *Congress* Jakarta (Indonesia) 2008, *Congress* Singapore (Singapore) 2003, *Congress* Langkawi (Malaysia) 2000, *Regional workshop* Malaysia 1997.
Members Individuals in 14 countries:
Australia, Canada, Germany, India, Indonesia, Japan, Korea Rep, Malaysia, Netherlands, New Zealand, Switzerland, Thailand, USA, Vietnam. [2013/XE2574/v/E]

♦ Asia-Pacific Association for Respiratory Care (inactive)

♦ Asia Pacific Association of Robotic Surgeons (APARS) 01853

Representative 528 – Hyundaiventurevill 10, Bamgogae-ro 1-gil, Gangnam-gu, Seoul 06349, Korea Rep. T. +822024598236. Fax +8224598256. E-mail: apars.secretariat@gmail.com.
URL: http://www.apars-surgery.org/

Structure Board of Governors. **Activities** Events/meetings. **Events** *Asian Congress of Robotic and Laparoscopic Surgery* Nagoya (Japan) 2022, *Asian Congress of Robotic and Laparoscopic Surgery* Nagoya (Japan) 2021, *Asian Congress of Robotic and Laparoscopic Surgery* Seoul (Korea Rep) 2020, *Asian Congress of Robotic and Laparoscopic Surgery* Singapore (Singapore) 2019, *Asian Congress of Robotic and Laparoscopic Surgery* Shanghai (China) 2018. [2021/AA0205/D]

♦ Asia Pacific Association of Societies of Pathologists (no recent information)

♦ Asia Pacific Association of Surgical Tissue Banking (APASTB) 01854

Asst SG Thai Assoc of Tissue Banking, 14th Floor, Chalermphrakiat Bldg, Fac of Med Siriraj Hosp, Mahidol Univ, Prannok Road, Bangkok-Noi, Bangkok, 10700, Thailand. T. +6624197000ext4507. Fax +6624112506. E-mail: siyvj@mahidol.ac.th.

History Oct 1988, Bangkok (Thailand). Originally referred to as *Pan Asiatic Tissue Association.* **Structure** Officers: President; Past President; 3 Vice-Presidents; Secretary-General; Assistant Secretary-General; Treasurer. **Activities** Organizes international conferences. **Events** *Biennial Conference* Bangkok (Thailand) 2021, *Biennial Conference* Surabaya (Indonesia) 2020, *Biennial Conference* Bangi (Malaysia) 2018, *Biennial Conference* Seoul (Korea Rep) 2016, *Biennial Conference* Gifu (Japan) 2014.
Members in 15 countries and territories:
Australia, Bangladesh, China, Hong Kong, India, Indonesia, Japan, Korea Rep, Malaysia, Pakistan, Philippines, Singapore, Sri Lanka, Thailand, Vietnam.
NGO Relations Member of (1): *World Union of Tissue Banking Associations (WUTBA, #21888).* [2018/XD6462/D]

♦ Asia Pacific Association of Technology and Society (unconfirmed)

♦ Asia-Pacific Association of Theoretical & Computational Chemists (APATCC) 01855

Address not obtained.
URL: http://www.apatcc.org/

History 2004. **Aims** Encourage the development of theoretical/computational chemistry in Asia and Pacific countries. **Structure** Committee. **Activities** Awards/prizes/competitions; events/meetings. **Events** *Asia Pacific Conference on Theoretical and Computational Chemistry (APCTCC)* Sydney, NSW (Australia) 2019. [2020/AA0818/**D**]

♦ Asia Pacific Association of Threat Assessment Professionals (internationally oriented national body)

♦ Asia and Pacific Band Directors' Association (APBDA) 01856

Contact c/o ABDA, PO Box 189, Port Macquarie NSW 2443, Australia.

History 1978, as *Asian Band Directors' Association.* Present name adopted, 1988. **Aims** Provide development and improvement of band and band *music* in the culture of Asia and Pacific. **Structure** Board of Directors; National Representatives. **Languages** Chinese, English, Japanese, Korean. **Staff** Voluntary. **Finance** Members' dues. **Activities** Knowledge management/information dissemination; networking/liaising; training/education; events/meetings. **Events** *Conference* Tainan (Taiwan) 2021, *Conference* Tainan (Taiwan) 2020, *Conference* Hamamatsu (Japan) 2018, *Conference* Sydney, NSW (Australia) 2016, *Conference / Biennial Conference* Jeju (Korea Rep) 2014.

Members National associations and other organizations in 15 countries and territories:
Australia, China, Hong Kong, Indonesia, Japan, Kazakhstan, Korea Rep, Macau, Malaysia, New Zealand, Philippines, Singapore, Taiwan, Thailand, USA.
Associate membership open to individuals, institutions and musical industries interested in band and band activities. Membership countries not specified. [2020.03.05/XD3210/**D**]

♦ Asia Pacific Baptist Federation (APBF) 01857

Fédération des baptistes d'Asie et Pacifique

Main Office Goya 3-22-5, Okinawa, 904-0021 Japan.
URL: http://www.apbf.info/

History 14 Nov 1972, as *Asian Baptist Federation (ABF)*, during a Planning Conference, as *Asian Baptist Fellowship*; formally constituted Mar 1973; Constitution and Bylaws adopted 9 Jul 1975. Regional Secretariat moved, 1988, from Sydney (Australia) to Manila (Philippines). Currently functions as a Region of *Baptist World Alliance (BWA, #03176).* **Aims** Promote fellowship, cooperation and service among Baptists; function as a region of the Baptist World Alliance; assist in uniting and promoting activities of special groups (men, women, youth, etc); stimulate and coordinate evangelism; assist in consultation on and planning of relief and aid programmes; consult with other Christian organizations. **Structure** General Meeting (every 5 years). Executive Committee, consisting of President, 3 Vice Presidents, Secretary, Treasurer, Past Presidents and Past Secretary; members appointed by member organizations; one member nominated by each department (Men, Women, Youth) and of any department that may be established by the Federation. **Languages** English. **Staff** 4.00 FTE, paid. Several volunteers. **Finance** Members' contributions. **Activities** Special groups; evangelism; consultation and planning relief and development aid programmes; international seminars; quinquennial congress. Takes part in UNHCR-related Programme to Refugees in Puerto Princesa (Palawan, Philippines). **Events** *Congress* Seoul (Korea Rep) 2022, *Youth Conference* Bangkok (Thailand) 2015, *Theological Educators Forum* Rangoon (Myanmar) 2014, *Congress* Kuala Lumpur (Malaysia) 2012, *Congress* Chiang Mai (Thailand) 2007. **Publications** *Asian Baptist Digest* (4 a year).

Members Conventions/Unions (55) in 20 countries and territories:
Australia, Bangladesh (3), Cambodia, Fiji, Hong Kong, India (22), Indonesia (3), Japan (3), Korea Rep, Macau, Malaysia, Myanmar, New Zealand, North Macedonia, Papua New Guinea, Philippines (5), Singapore, Sri Lanka, Taiwan, Thailand (4). [2022/XD4336/**D**]

♦ Asia Pacific Baptist Youth (unconfirmed)

♦ Asia-Pacific Bariatric Surgery Group / see Asia-Pacific Metabolic & Bariatric Surgery Society (#01956)

♦ Asia Pacific Bioinformatics Network (APBioNet) 01858

Secretariat Dept Biochemistry, Yong Loo Lin School of Medicine, Natl Univ of Singapore, MD7 8 Medical Drive, Singapore 117596, Singapore. T. +6565167150. Fax +6567777936. E-mail: apbionet.incob@gmail.com – sec@apbionet.org.
Pres 10 Kent Ridge Drive, Singapore 119242, Singapore.
URL: http://www.apbionet.org/

History Jan 1998, Hawaii (USA). **Aims** Foster the growth of bioinformatics and allied disciplines in the Asia-Pacific. **Activities** Events/meetings. **Events** *Asia Pacific Bioinformatics Joint Congress* Okinawa (Japan) 2024, *inCob Annual International Conference* Singapore (Singapore) 2016, *Incob Annual International Conference / International Conference on Bioinformatics (InCoB)* Tokyo (Japan) 2015, *Incob Annual International Conference / International Conference on Bioinformatics (InCoB)* Sydney, NSW (Australia) 2014, *Incob Annual International Conference / International Conference on Bioinformatics (InCoB)* Shanghai (China) / Taicang (China) 2013. **Publications** Conference proceedings; journal supplements.

Members Over 2,000 individuals and organizations in 20 countries and territories. Membership countries not specified. International organization (1); listed in this Yearbook:
International organization (1), listed in this Yearbook:
International Rice Research Institute (IRRI, #14754).

NGO Relations Official affiliation with: *International Society for Computational Biology (ISCB, #15026).* Instrumental in setting up: *Global Organisation for Bioinformatics Learning, Education and Training (GOBLET, #10516).* [2019.12.18/XF5806/**F**]

♦ Asia-Pacific Biomedical Science Educators Association (unconfirmed)

♦ Asia Pacific Biosafety Association (A-PBA) 01859

Contact c/o Temasek Life Sciences Lab, 1 Research Link, National Univ of, Singapore 117604, Singapore. T. +6568727068.

History 22 Feb 2005. **Aims** Foster recognition of *biological safety* as a distinct scientific discipline. **Structure** Committee. **Finance** Members' dues. **Events** *Biosafety and biosecurity – for sustainable development in health and agriculture* Dhaka (Bangladesh) 2019, *Conference* Beijing (China) 2018, *Conference* Ho Chi Minh City (Vietnam) 2017, *Conference* Bangkok (Thailand) 2014, *Annual General Meeting* Singapore (Singapore) 2014.

Members Full in 9 countries and territories:
Brunei Darussalam, China, Hong Kong, Indonesia, Malaysia, Myanmar, Philippines, Singapore, Thailand.

NGO Relations Member of: *International Federation of Biosafety Associations (IFBA, #13373).* [2014/XM3708/**D**]

♦ Asia Pacific Blood and Marrow Transplantation Group (APBMT) 01860

Secretariat Dept Promotion for Blood Marrow Transplantation, Aichi Medical Univ, School of Medicine, 1-1 Yazakokarimata, Nagakute, Aichi, 480-1195 Japan. T. +81561623311 ext 12375. Fax +81561613180. E-mail: office@apbmt.org.
URL: http://www.apbmt.org/

History 1990. **Aims** Share information and cooperate with basic and clinical research in *hematological stem cell* transplantation and cell therapies in the Asia-Pacific countries. **Structure** Chairman; Executive Board; Scientific Committee; Committees (6); Working Groups (10); Editorial Board. **Languages** English. **Staff** 2.00 FTE, paid; 3.00 FTE, voluntary. **Finance** Sources: contributions; members' dues. **Activities** Events/meetings. Active in all member countries. **Events** *Annual Meeting* Kochi (India) 2022, *Annual Meeting* Chiang Mai (Thailand) 2021, *Annual Meeting* Vellore (India) 2020, *Annual Meeting* Busan (Korea Rep) 2019, *Annual Meeting* Taipei (Taiwan) 2018. **Publications** *Blood Cell Therapy* – official journal.

Members Regular; supporting. Members in 22 countries and territories:
Australia, Bangladesh, Cambodia, China, Hong Kong, India, Indonesia, Iran Islamic Rep, Japan, Korea Rep, Malaysia, Mongolia, Myanmar, Nepal, New Zealand, Pakistan, Philippines, Singapore, Sri Lanka, Taiwan, Thailand, Vietnam.

NGO Relations Member of (1): *Worldwide Network for Blood and Marrow Transplantation (WBMT, #21929).* Instrumental in setting up (1): *Worldwide Network for Blood and Marrow Transplantation (WBMT, #21929).* [2022.05.04/XJ8076/**E**]

♦ Asia Pacific Blood Network (APBN) 01861

Secretariat Level 1, 69 Walters Drive, Osborne Park WA 6017, Australia. T. +61862135904. Fax +61862135949. E-mail: apbn@arcbs.redcross.org.au.
URL: http://apbnonline.com/

History 2006. **Aims** Promote blood *safety* through global and regional cooperation, information sharing and collaboration with international and other relevant organizations. **Events** *Workshop on safety and supply of blood and plasma products in the Asia Pacific region* Kyoto (Japan) 2007.

Members National organizations in 9 countries and territories:
Australia, China, Hong Kong, Japan, Korea Rep, New Zealand, Singapore, Taiwan, Thailand. [2010/XJ0060/**F**]

♦ Asia Pacific Bridge Federation (APBF) 01862

Sec Japan Contract Bridge, TJK Yotsuy Bldg, 1-13 Yotsuya, Shinjuku-ku, Tokyo, 160-0004 Japan. T. +81333573741. Fax +81333577444. E-mail: apbfsecretariat@jcbl.or.jp.
Pres 319/1 Soi Sukhumvit 31 (Sawasdee), Sukhumvit Road, Klongton Nur, Watana, Bangkok, 10110, Thailand.
URL: http://www.apbf.net/

History 1957. A zone of *World Bridge Federation (WBF, #21246).* Current constitution most recently revised 28 Aug 2003. Former names and other names: *Far East Bridge Federation* – former (1957 to 1995); *Pacific Asia Bridge Federation* – former (1995 to 2010). **Aims** Promote, foster and promulgate the game of contract bridge through the regions. **Structure** Council. **Languages** English. **Finance** Sources: members' dues. **Activities** Sporting activities. **Events** *Congress* Perth, WA (Australia) 2020, *Congress* Beijing (China) 2016, *Congress* Fukuoka (Japan) 2012, *Congress* Surfers Paradise, QLD (Australia) 2008, *Congress* Taipei (Taiwan) 2004. **Publications** *APBF TD Newsletter.*

Members National bridge organizations in 27 countries and territories:
Australia, Bahrain, Bangladesh, China, Hong Kong, India, Indonesia, Japan, Jordan, Korea Rep, Kuwait, Macau, Malaysia, New Caledonia, New Zealand, Pakistan, Palestine, Philippines, Qatar, Saudi Arabia, Singapore, Sri Lanka, Syrian AR, Taiwan, Thailand, Timor-Leste, Vietnam. [2021.06.10/AA0988/**D**]

♦ Asia-Pacific Broadcasting Union (ABU) 01863

Union de radiodiffusion pour l'Asie et le Pacifique

SG PO Box 12287, 50772 Kuala Lumpur, Malaysia. T. +60322823592. Fax +60322824606. E-mail: natalia@abu.org.my – info@abu.org.my.
Street Address 2nd floor IPPTAR Bldg, Angkasapuri, 50614 Kuala Lumpur, Malaysia.
URL: http://www.abu.org.my/

History 1 Jul 1964, Tokyo (Japan). Founded following 5 Asian Broadcasters' Conferences between 1957 and 1963. Statutes adopted at the last of these Conferences, 30 Sep-5 Oct 1963, Seoul (Korea Rep). **Aims** Assist in development of broadcasting *media* in the Asia/Pacific region; foster the use of these media in the cause of international understanding. **Structure** General Assembly (annual); Administrative Council; Standing Committees (2); Study Groups and Working Parties; Secretariat. Maintains and operates: *Asiavision (AVN, #02104).* **Languages** English. **Staff** 30.00 FTE, paid. **Finance** Members' dues, in proportion to their operational budgets. **Activities** Awards/prizes/competitions; events/meetings; guidance/assistance/consulting; knowledge management/information dissemination. **Events** *General Assembly* Kuala Lumpur (Malaysia) 2021, *General Assembly* Kuala Lumpur (Malaysia) 2020, *International Radio Forum* Seoul (Korea Rep) 2019, *General Assembly* Tokyo (Japan) 2019, *Sports Group conference* Tokyo (Japan) 2019. **Publications** *ABU News* (6 a year); *ABU Technical Review* (6 a year). Annual members' directory.

Members Full national broadcasting organizations operating in independent countries in the Asia/Pacific region (2 full members in each country). Full members (51) in 36 countries:
Afghanistan, Australia, Bangladesh, Bhutan, Brunei Darussalam, Cambodia, China, Egypt, Fiji, India, Indonesia, Iran Islamic Rep, Japan, Jordan, Kazakhstan, Kiribati, Korea Rep, Kyrgyzstan, Laos, Malaysia, Maldives, Mongolia, Nepal, New Zealand, Pakistan, Papua New Guinea, Philippines, Qatar, Saudi Arabia, Singapore, Sri Lanka, Thailand, Timor-Leste, Türkiye, Uzbekistan, Vietnam.
Additional Full broadcasting organizations in the region not eligible to be Full members. Additional Full members (29) in 13 countries and territories:
Australia, Hong Kong, Indonesia, Japan, Korea DPR, Korea Rep, Macau, Malaysia, Mongolia, Norfolk Is, Pakistan, Philippines, Sri Lanka.
Associate broadcasting organizations in countries outside the region, or those in the region not eligible to be full members. Associate members (31) in 22 countries and territories:
Australia, Canada, France, Germany, Hong Kong, India, Indonesia, Japan, Malaysia, Mauritius, Micronesia FS, Netherlands, New Zealand, Norway, Pakistan, Philippines, Polynesia Fr, Russia, Singapore, Switzerland, UK, USA.
Affiliate non-broadcaster, regulators, satellite operators, related industry service provides and other corporate bodies interested in maintaining a close relationship with the broadcasting industry. Affiliate members (49) in 24 countries and territories:
Australia, Canada, France, Hong Kong, India, Indonesia, Japan, Jordan, Kazakhstan, Korea Rep, Malaysia, Mauritius, Myanmar, New Zealand, Pakistan, Singapore, South Africa, Sri Lanka, Sweden, Switzerland, Thailand, Türkiye, UK, USA.
Institutional organizations (5):
Association for International Broadcasting (AIB, #02656); Digital Radio Mondiale Consortium (DRM, #05082); International Academy of Television Arts and Sciences (IATAS); Prix Jeunesse; WorldDAB (#21351).

Consultative Status Consultative status granted from: *ECOSOC (#05331)* (Ros C); *UNESCO (#20322)* (Associate Status); *FAO (#09260)* (Special Status); *World Intellectual Property Organization (WIPO, #21593)* (Permanent Observer Status). **IGO Relations** Observer to: *Intergovernmental Committee of the International Convention of Rome for the Protection of Performers, Producers of Phonograms and Broadcasting Organizations (#11474); Union for the International Registration of Audiovisual Works (#20444).* Working relations with: *International Telecommunication Union (ITU, #15673).* Sister union: *Arab States Broadcasting Union (ASBU, #01050)*; Invited to sessions of Intergovernmental Council of: *International Programme for the Development of Communication (IPDC, #14651).* Together with UNESCO, instrumental in setting up *Asia-Pacific Institute for Broadcasting Development (AIBD, #01934).* **NGO Relations** Member of (4): Digital Radio Mondial; *Ethical Journalism Network (EJN, #05554); World Broadcasting Unions (WBU, #21247); WorldDAB (#21351).* Organizes: *World Conference of Broadcasting Unions* together with sister unions: *Caribbean Broadcasting Union (CBU, #03465); European Broadcasting Union (EBU, #06404); International Association of Broadcasting (IAB, #11738); North American Broadcasters Association (NABA, #17561); Organización de Telecomunicaciones de Iberoamérica (OTI, #17851); African Union of Broadcasting (AUB, #00490).* [2022/XD0075/y/**C**]

♦ Asia Pacific Burn Association (APBA) 01864

Hon Sec Dept of Plastic, Reconstructive Surgery and Burns, Seth G S Medical College and KEM Hosp, Parel, Mumbai, Maharashtra 400012, Mumbai MAHARASHTRA 400012, India. E-mail: secretaryapba@gmail.com.
URL: http://www.apburn.org/

History 20 Jan 2009, Delhi (India). Conferences organized since 1993, with 1st meeting to formalize APBA held 2004, Yokohama (Japan). Registration: Indonesia. **Aims** Improve burn care in the Asia Pacific region. **Structure** Executive Committee; Advisors Committee. **Activities** Events/meetings; knowledge management/information dissemination; training/education. **Events** *Asia Pacific Burn Conference* Chongqing (China) 2023, *Asia Pacific Burn Conference* Tokyo (Japan) 2021, *Asia Pacific Burn Conference* Tokyo (Japan) 2021, *Conference* Singapore (Singapore) 2019, *Conference* Taipei (Taiwan) 2017. **Members** Full; Associate; Honorary. Membership countries not specified. [2021/AA0193/**D**]

♦ Asia-Pacific Business Association (no recent information)

♦ Asia Pacific Business School Librarians' Group (APBSLG) 01865

Coordinator c/o INSEAD, 1 Ayer Rajah Ave, Singapore 138676, Singapore.
Chair c/o Curtin Business School, GPO Box U1987, Perth WA 6845, Australia.
URL: https://www.isb.edu/en/apbslg.html

Aims Provide a forum for discussion of matters of mutual interest and work practices; foster and assist collaborative activities; provide mutual support through information exchange; promote ongoing contact between members. **Activities** Events/meetings. **Events** *Annual Meeting* Singapore (Singapore) 2020, *Joint Meeting* Vienna (Austria) 2020, *Annual Meeting* Singapore (Singapore) 2019, *Annual Meeting* Beijing (China) 2018, *Annual Meeting* Ahmedabad (India) 2017.

Members Directors of business school librairies in 7 countries and territories:
Australia, China, Hong Kong, India, Macau, Malaysia, Singapore. [2022.11.10/XM3727/**D**]

♦ Asia-Pacific Center for Security Studies (internationally oriented national body)

♦ **Asia Pacific Central Securities Depository Group (ACG)** **01866**

Secretariat CDC House, 99-B – Block-B, SMCHS, Main Shahra-e-Faisal, Karachi 74400, Pakistan. T. +912134326030. Fax +912134326024. E-mail: acgsecretariat@cdcpak.com.
URL: http://www.acgcsd.org/

History 28 Nov 1997, Hong Kong. **Aims** Facilitate exchange of information; promote mutual assistance among member securities depositories and clearing organizations in the Asia Pacific region. **Structure** Annual General Meeting; Cross Training Seminar. **Languages** English. **Staff** Voluntary. **Finance** No budget. **Activities** Events/ meetings; training/education. **Events** *Annual General Meeting* Busan (Korea Rep) 2020, *Annual General Meeting* Taipei (Taiwan) 2015, *Annual General Meeting* Xian (China) 2014, *Annual General Meeting* Dhaka (Bangladesh) 2013, *Annual General Meeting* Bali (Indonesia) 2012.
Members Full in 24 countries and territories:
Australia, Bangladesh, Bhutan, China, Hong Kong, India, Indonesia, Iran Islamic Rep, Japan, Kazakhstan, Korea Rep, Malaysia, Maldives, Mongolia, Nepal, New Zealand, Pakistan, Philippines, Singapore, Sri Lanka, Taiwan, Thailand, Uzbekistan, Vietnam.
IGO Relations None. **NGO Relations** Member of: *World Forum of CSDs (WFC, #21514).*
[2016.12.15/XD8244/**D**]

♦ Asia-Pacific Centre for Complex Real Property Rights (internationally oriented national body)
♦ Asia-Pacific Centre of Education for International Understanding (internationally oriented national body)
♦ Asia-Pacific Centre for Education Leadership and School Quality / see Asia Pacific Centre for Leadership and Change

♦ **Asia-Pacific Centre for Environmental Accountability (APCEA)** **01867**

Contact address not obtained. T. +61883027048. Fax +61883020992.
URL: http://www.unisa.edu.au/cags/default.asp

History 1996. **Aims** Promote research into environmental accountability, broadly defined to include environmental, social and economic aspects of *corporate* activity. **Publications** *APCEA Journal.*
Members Institutions (20) in 8 countries:
Argentina, Australia, China, Japan, Korea Rep, Malaysia, New Zealand, Peru. [2009/XM1341/**E**]

♦ Asia-Pacific Centre for Environmental Law, Singapore (internationally oriented national body)
♦ Asia Pacific Centre for Leadership and Change (internationally oriented national body)

♦ **Asia-Pacific Centre for the Responsibility to Protect** **01868**

Dir (International) Univ of Queensland, Level 4, Bldg 39A (General Purpose Bldg North), Blair Drive, St Lucia QLD 4072, Australia. T. +61733466435. Fax +61733466445. E-mail: r2pinfo@uq.edu.au.
URL: http://www.r2pasiapacific.org/

History 20 Feb 2008. **Aims** Deepen knowledge and advance policy on the Responsibility to Protect principle and facilitate effective prevention and response mechanisms to mass atrocities in the Asia Pacific region. **Structure** International Advisory Board. **Languages** English. **Staff** 6.00 FTE, paid. **Finance** Sources: government support. Supported by: Australian Department of Foreign Affairs and Trade. **Activities** Capacity building; events/meetings; networking/liaising; politics/policy/regulatory; research/documentation. **Events** *International Conference* Phnom Penh (Cambodia) 2015. **Publications** *Regional Outlooks* in English – Regional Outlooks provide a snapshot of atrocity risk in the Asia Pacific, providing overviews of at-risk countries and developing issues such as gender-based violence and hate speech; *Risk Assessments* in English – Risk Assessments utilize the UN Secretary General's Framework of Analysis for Atrocity Crimes for an in-depth look at atrocity crime risks in countries within the Asia Pacific. **Information Services** *Information Seminars* in English – The Centre hosts seminars, workshops and round tables on issues regarding R2P and atrocity prevention with participants from Australia and across the Asia Pacific region.. **IGO Relations** Partner of (1): *United Nations Office on Genocide Prevention and the Responsibility to Protect (#20598).* **NGO Relations** Member of (4): *Academic Council on the United Nations System (ACUNS, #00020); Consortium of Non-Traditional Security Studies in Asia (NTS-Asia, #04755); Global Centre for the Responsibility to Protect (GCR2P, #10277); International Coalition for the Responsibility to Protect (ICRtoP, #12620).* [2022.06.03/XJ2112/**F**]

♦ Asia-Pacific Centre for Social Investment and and Philanthropy (internationally oriented national body)
♦ Asia-Pacific Centre for Theoretical Physics (internationally oriented national body)

♦ **Asia-Pacific Centre for Women and Technology (APCWT)** **01869**

Contact POP Box W305, Ballarat VIC 3350, Australia.
Contact c/o Thoughtware, PO Box 153, Helensvale QLD 4212, Australia.

History as a regional initiative of *International Taskforce on Women and Information and Communication Technologies (ITF, #15658).* As of 2009, currently under development. [2012.08.24/XM8206/**E**]

♦ **Asia-Pacific CEO Association (APCEO)** **01870**

Secretariat address not obtained. E-mail: secretariat@apceo.us – ceo@apceo.us.
URL: http://www.apceo.us/

History Early 1990s. **Aims** Promote international *economic* communication and *cooperation.* **Structure** Presidium, comprising Chairman, Co-Chairman, Ex-Chairman, 6 Vice-Chairman, Executive Chairman and 2 Honorary Chairmen. **Events** *World Emerging Industries Summit* Zhengzhou (China) 2015. **Members** Enterprises; individuals. Membership countries not specified. [2015/XJ7210/**C**]

♦ Asia-Pacific Child-Friendly Cities Network / see Child Friendly Asia Pacific (#03867)
♦ Asia-Pacific Chiropractic Doctors' Federation (inactive)
♦ Asia Pacific Cities Summit (meeting series)

♦ **Asia Pacific Clinical Nutrition Society (APCNS)** **01871**

Main Office 38 Dengzhou Road, Qingdao, 266021 Shandong, China. E-mail: apcns@163.com.
URL: https://apcns.ac/

History 1992, Melbourne, VIC (Australia). **Aims** Promote education and training of clinical nutritionists in the region; enhance the practice of human nutrition and related disciplines in their application to health and the prevention of disease; develop standards for nutrition assessment and clinical practice; promote graduate education in clinical nutrition, particularly through Internet and World Wide Web; encourage development of clinical nutrition in medical practice. **Structure** Council, consisting of President, Vice-President, Secretary, Treasurer and one member-at-large. Membership Committee. **Languages** English. **Staff** Voluntary. **Finance** Members' dues. Levies on national organizations; sponsorship. Budget (annual): about US$ 27,000. **Activities** Biennial conference; training courses; seminars; meetings; awards. **Events** *Asia Pacific Conference on Clinical Nutrition (APCCN)* 2022, *Asia Pacific Conference on Clinical Nutrition* 2020, *Asia Pacific Conference on Clinical Nutrition* Nanjing (China) 2019, *Biennial Conference* Adelaide, SA (Australia) 2017, *Biennial Conference* Kuala Lumpur (Malaysia) 2015. **Publications** *Asia Pacific Journal of Clinical Nutrition (APJCN)* in English – abstracts in other languages, notably Chinese.
Members Affiliated societies; their members, either directly or indirectly; other individuals. Members in 17 countries and territories:
Australia, China, Germany, Guatemala, Indonesia, Japan, Korea Rep, Malaysia, Netherlands, New Caledonia, New Zealand, Philippines, Singapore, Taiwan, Thailand, UK, Vietnam.
NGO Relations Member of: *International Union of Nutritional Sciences (IUNS, #15796).* Located at: *Asia Pacific Health and Nutrition Centre (APHNC, no recent information).* [2022/XD4144/**D**]

♦ **Asia Pacific Coalition on Male Sexual Health (APCOM)** **01872**

Contact 66/1 Sukhumvit 2 Road, Klongtoey, Bangkok, 10110, Thailand. T. +6622554410. E-mail: apcom@apcom.org.
URL: http://www.apcom.org/

History 25 Jul 2007. **Aims** Improve male sexual health through increased investment, coverage and quality of sexual health services for our communities. **Structure** Governing Board of Directors; Executive Committee; Secretariat. **Languages** English. **Staff** 15.00 FTE, paid. **Finance** Donations; grants from international funders. **Activities** Advocacy/lobbying/activism; awareness raising; guidance/assistance/consulting; healthcare; knowledge management/information dissemination; networking/liaising. **Publications** Strategic plans; highlight series; scoping papers; analysis tools; workshop reports; news.
Members Networks, organizations and individuals in 31 countries and territories:
Afghanistan, Australia, Bangladesh, Bhutan, Brunei Darussalam, Cambodia, China, Cook Is, Hong Kong, India, Indonesia, Japan, Korea Rep, Laos, Malaysia, Mongolia, Myanmar, Nepal, New Zealand, Pakistan, Papua New Guinea, Philippines, Samoa, Singapore, Sri Lanka, Taiwan, Thailand, Timor-Leste, Tonga, Vanuatu, Vietnam.
Included in the above, 2 organizations listed in this Yearbook:
Islands of Southeast Asian Network on Male and Transgender Sexual Health (ISEAN, #16063); Pacific Sexual and Gender Diversity Network (PSGDN).
NGO Relations Member of: *The Commonwealth Equality Network (TCEN, #04327).*
[2017.03.08/XJ9350/y/**D**]

♦ Asia-Pacific College of Diplomacy (internationally oriented national body)

♦ **Asia and Pacific Commission on Agricultural Statistics (APCAS)** ... **01873**

Commission des statistiques agricoles pour l'Asie et le Pacifique

Sec FAO Regional Office for Asia and the Pacific, Maliwan Mansion, 39 Phra Atit Road, Bangkok, 10200, Thailand. T. +6626974250.
URL: http://www.fao.org/asiapacific/apcas/

History 1963, at 12th session of Conference of *FAO (#09260).* 1st session Sep-Oct 1966, Tokyo (Japan). Originally referred to as *Asia and Far East Commission on Agricultural Statistics.* Present name adopted by FAO Council, 1982. Based at *FAO Regional Office for Asia and the Pacific (RAP, #09266).* **Aims** Monitor developments in the field of *food* and agricultural statistics in the Asia-Pacific region; promote exchange of information and experience among member countries; identify new trends in statistical *methodology* to improve knowledge in the region's agricultural sector. **Structure** Session (every 2 years); working parties. **Languages** English, French. **Staff** 1.00 FTE, paid. **Activities** Convenes working parties; reviews national information systems for food and agriculture; monitors FAO data collection programmes. Recent and current concerns: integrated programme of food and agricultural statistics; food balance sheets; analysis of food consumption and household income and expenditure surveys; economic accounts for agriculture and training activities. **Events** *Biennial Session / Biennial Meeting* Hue (Vietnam) 2012, *Biennial Session / Biennial Meeting* Siem Reap (Cambodia) 2010, *Biennial Meeting* Kuala Lumpur (Malaysia) 2008, *Biennial Session* Kuching (Malaysia) 2008, *Biennial session / Biennial Meeting* Phuket (Thailand) 2006. **Publications** Session reports. Information Services: Priority: development of *World Agricultural Information Centre (WAICENT, see: #09260).*
Members Membership open to all members and associate members of FAO whose territories are wholly or partly in the Asia and Pacific region or who are responsible for any non-self-governing territory in the region. Currently governments of 25 countries:
Afghanistan, Australia, Bangladesh, Bhutan, Cambodia, China, Fiji, France, India, Indonesia, Iran Islamic Rep, Japan, Korea Rep, Laos, Malaysia, Myanmar, Nepal, New Zealand, Pakistan, Philippines, Sri Lanka, Thailand, UK, USA, Vietnam.
IGO Relations Entitled to participate in the Commission's sessions: *ASEAN (#01141); Asian Development Bank (ADB, #01422); Asian Productivity Organization (APO, #01674); Centre on Integrated Rural Development for Asia and the Pacific (CIRDAP, #03750); ILO (#11123); International Rice Research Institute (IRRI, #14754); Southeast Asian Fisheries Development Center (SEAFDEC, #19767); UNDP (#20292); United Nations Economic and Social Commission for Asia and the Pacific (ESCAP, #20557).* [2017/XE9186/**E***]

♦ **Asia Pacific Computer Emergency Response Team (APCERT)** **01874**

Contact address not obtained. E-mail: apcert-sec@apcert.org.
URL: http://www.apcert.org/

History 2005. **Aims** Improve the region's awareness and competency in relation to computer security incidents. **Structure** Steering Committee; Chair; Deputy Chair. Secretariat. Working Groups. **Activities** Working Groups (6): TSUBAME; Information Classification; Information Sharing; Membership; Operational Framework. **Events** *Annual Conference* Singapore (Singapore) 2019, *Annual Conference* Tokyo (Japan) 2016, *Annual Conference* Kuala Lumpur (Malaysia) 2015, *Annual Conference* Bali (Indonesia) 2012, *Annual General Meeting / Annual Conference* Jeju (Korea Rep) 2011. **Publications** Annual Report.
Members Full; General. Full in 15 countries and territories:
Australia, Brunei Darussalam, China, Hong Kong, India, Indonesia, Japan, Korea Rep, Malaysia, Philippines, Singapore, Sri Lanka, Taiwan, Thailand, Vietnam.
General in 7 countries:
Bangladesh, Macau, Mongolia, Myanmar, New Zealand, Philippines, Singapore.
NGO Relations *DotAsia Organisation (DotAsia, #05124).* [2012/XJ5636/**D**]

♦ Asia Pacific Conference on Disaster Medicine (meeting series)
♦ Asia-Pacific Conference on Engineering Applied Sciences (meeting series)
♦ Asia-Pacific Conference on Few-Body Problems in Physics (meeting series)
♦ Asia-Pacific Conference on Management and Business (meeting series)
♦ Asia Pacific Conference on Reproductive and Sexual Health and Rights (meeting series)
♦ Asia Pacific Conference on Vision (meeting series)
♦ Asia Pacific Contact Centre Association Leaders (unconfirmed)
♦ Asia Pacific Corporate Registers Forum / see Corporate Registers Forum (#04841)
♦ Asia Pacific Corpus Linguistics Association (unconfirmed)
♦ Asia Pacific Corrosion Control Conference (meeting series)

♦ **Asia-Pacific Council of AIDS Service Organizations (APCASO)** **01875**

Consejo de Asia-Pacifico de Organizaciones al Servicio del SIDA

Main Office 66/5 33 Tower, Sukhumvit 33 Road, Klongtoey Nua, Wattana, Bangkok, 10110, Thailand. E-mail: rdmarte@apcaso.org.
URL: http://www.apcaso.org/

History Nov 1990, as one of 5 Regional Secretariats, set up by *ICASO (#11040),* formally organized in 1992. Incorporated, 2002. **Aims** Increase the capacity of community-based organizations (CBOs) and non-governmental organizations to respond to HIV and AIDS; develop coordinated regional response through: capacity building; advocacy; networking. **Structure** APCASO is facilitated through Council of Representative (COR) Members, National Focal Points (NFPs) and a Regional Secretariat (RS), which exist to develop ways of cooperating on common concern and try to represent the issues of all groups, organizations and communities most affected by the epidemic. Sub-regions (5): South Asia; Southeast Asia; East-Asia; Australia/New Zealand; Pacific Islands. APCASO does not operate within a framework of a 'member' organization. Partnership – rather than membership – to APCASO is non-hierarchical and open to all NGOs and CBOs in the region. Global Secretariat in Toronto (Canada); regional office in Kuala Lumpur (Malaysia). **Languages** Chinese, English, Hindi, Malay, Tamil, Vietnamese. **Staff** 3.00 FTE, paid. **Finance** Funding through ICASO from *Bill and Melinda Gates Foundation (BMGF), Canadian International Development Agency (CIDA, inactive), DANIDA,* and Glaxo-Smith-Kline Positive Action. Other major funders: *Australian Aid (inactive); Joint United Nations Programme on HIV/AIDS (UNAIDS, #16149).* **Activities** Implements regional projects, including training and workshops; undertakes advocacy. **Events** *ICAAP: international congress on AIDS in Asia and the Pacific / International Conference on AIDS in Asia and the Pacific / International Conference on AIDS in Asia and the Pacific – ICAAP* Kobe (Japan) 2005, *ICAAP : international congress on AIDS in Asia and the Pacific / International Conference on AIDS in Asia and the Pacific / International Conference on AIDS in Asia and the Pacific – ICAAP* Melbourne, VIC (Australia) 2001, *ICAAP : international congress on AIDS in Asia and the Pacific / International Conference on AIDS in Asia and the Pacific / International Conference on AIDS in Asia and the Pacific – ICAAP* Kuala Lumpur (Malaysia) 1999, *South Asia workshop on HIV/AIDS human rights issue* Dhaka (Bangladesh) 1998, *ICAAP : international congress on AIDS in Asia and the Pacific / Conference on AIDS in Asia and the Pacific / International Conference on AIDS in Asia and the Pacific – ICAAP* Chiang Mai (Thailand) 1995. **Publications** *APCASO Compact on Human Right (ACT-HR); HIV/AIDS and Human Rights: A Training Manual for NGOs, community groups and people living with HIV/AIDS; Making UNGASS Work* – translated into more than 100 languages and dialects. Books.
Members National Focal Points in 18 countries and territories:
Australia, Bangladesh, Cambodia, China, Fiji, Hong Kong, India, Indonesia, Japan, Korea Rep, Malaysia, New Caledonia, New Zealand, Pakistan, Philippines, Singapore, Sri Lanka, Thailand.
NGO Relations Member of: *Coalition of Asia Pacific Regional Networks on HIV/AIDS (Seven Sisters, #04051); International Treatment Preparedness Coalition (ITPC, #15729).* [2019/XE2112/**E**]

♦ Asia Pacific Council on Contraception (inactive)
♦ Asia Pacific Council for the Facilitation of Procedures and Practices for Administration, Commerce and Transport / see Asia Pacific Council for Trade Facilitation and Electronic Business (#01877)

♦ Asia Pacific Council of Optometry (APCO) 01876

Administrative Officer address not obtained. E-mail: secretariat@asiapacificoptometry.org.
URL: http://www.asiapacificoptometry.org/
History 1978, Manila (Philippines). Former names and other names: *International Federation of Asian and Pacific Associations of Optometrists (IFAPAO)* – former (1978 to 1995). **Aims** Promote advancement of primary eye health and vision care by optometrists in the region. **Structure** Executive Council. **Languages** English. **Staff** Voluntary. **Finance** Sources: fees for services; members' dues; sponsorship. **Activities** Events/meetings. **Events** *Biennial Asian-Pacific Optometric Congress* Manila (Philippines) 2019, *Biennial Asian-Pacific Optometric Congress* Hyderabad (India) 2017, *Global Optometry Conference* Daegu (Korea Rep) 2016, *Global Optometry Conference* Daegu (Korea Rep) 2015, *Biennial Asian-Pacific Optometric Congress* Kuala Lumpur (Malaysia) 2015.
Members Optometric organizations (24) in 17 countries and territories:
Australia, Cambodia, Canada, China, Fiji, Hong Kong, India, Japan, Korea Rep, Malaysia, Nepal, New Zealand, Philippines, Singapore, Sri Lanka, Taiwan, Vietnam.
NGO Relations Member of (1): *World Council of Optometry (WCO, #21335)* (as regional member).
[2022.05.25/XD5568/**D**]

♦ Asia Pacific Council for Trade Facilitation and Electronic Business (AFACT) 01877

Secretariat 7th Floor, No 15 Naderi Street, Keshavarz Boulevard, Teheran, Iran Islamic Rep. T. +982185193892. Fax +982188969315.
URL: http://www.afact.org/
History 1999. Takes over activities of *Asia EDIFACT Board*, within *United Nations Electronic Data Interchange for Administration, Commerce and Transport (EDIFACT, inactive)*. Previously referred to as *Asia Pacific Council for the Facilitation of Procedures and Practices for Administration, Commerce and Transport*. **Aims** Support policies and activities dedicated to stimulate, improve and promote the ability of business, trade and administrative organisations region; promote the exchange of products and relevant service effectively in a non-political environment. **Structure** Plenary session. Steering Committee, comprising Chairman, 2 Vice-Chairmen, Secretary and Advisor from *United Nations Centre for Trade Facilitation and Electronic Business (UN/CEFACT, #20527)*. **Activities** Working Groups (11): Awareness and Education (AEG); Financial (FWG); Transportation (TWG); Customs (CWG); Supply Chain (SCWG); Security (SWG); Air Transportation (ATG); Legal (LWG); Inter-networking Implementation Committee (IIC); Business collaboration Framework (BCFWG); XML (XMLWG). **Events** *Annual Plenary Meeting* Tokyo (Japan) 2016, *Annual Plenary Meeting* Teheran (Iran Islamic Rep) 2015, *Annual Plenary Meeting* Bangkok (Thailand) 2014, *Annual Plenary Meeting* Ho Chi Minh City (Vietnam) 2013, *Annual Plenary Meeting* Teheran (Iran Islamic Rep) 2012.
Members in 17 countries and territories:
Australia, Cambodia, China, India, Indonesia, Iran Islamic Rep, Japan, Korea Rep, Malaysia, Mongolia, Pakistan, Philippines, Singapore, Sri Lanka, Taiwan, Thailand, Vietnam. [2014/XD8455/t/**D**]

♦ Asia Pacific Craniofacial Association (APCA) 01878

Sec address not obtained. E-mail: tcpataiwan@gmail.com.
URL: http://www.apca.asia/
History 1994. **Aims** Update and advance craniofacial *surgery* in the Asia Pacific region. **Structure** Executive Council. **Languages** English. **Activities** Events/meetings. **Events** *Biennial Conference* Taipei (Taiwan) 2021, *Biennial Conference* Taipei (Taiwan) 2020, *Biennial Conference* Seoul (Korea Rep) 2018, *Biennial Conference* Nara (Japan) 2016, *Biennial Conference* Adelaide, SA (Australia) 2014. **Members** Active (over 300) in 19 countries. Membership countries not specified. [2021/XD6791/**D**]

♦ Asia-Pacific Crop Protection Association / see CropLife Asia (#04964)

♦ Asia/Pacific Cultural Centre for UNESCO (ACCU) 01879

Centre culturel de l'Asie-Pacifique pour l'UNESCO

Dir Gen Japan Publishers Bldg, No 6 Fukuromachi, Shinjuku-ku, Tokyo, 162-8484 Japan. T. +81332694435. Fax +81332694510. E-mail: general@accu.or.jp.
URL: http://www.accu.or.jp/
History Apr 1971, Tokyo (Japan), as *Asian Cultural Centre for UNESCO – Centre culturel asiatique pour l'UNESCO – Yunesuko Ajia Bunka Senta*, in line with the principles of *UNESCO (#20322)*. **Aims** Promote mutual *understanding* and cultural cooperation among peoples in Asia and the Pacific through joint programmes in the fields of cultural cooperation, educational cooperation and personnel exchange. **Structure** Board of Councillors; Board of Directors; Advisors; Programme Committees of Experts (3); Secretariat. **Languages** English, Japanese. **Staff** 24.00 FTE, paid. **Finance** Subsidies from: Government of Japan; UNESCO; Supporting Members; private donations. Budget (annual): US$ 7.9 million. **Activities** Networking/liaising; training/education; capacity building. **Events** *International Conference on Human Resources Development for the Transmission of Traditional Skills* Nara (Japan) 2012, *International Seminar on Cultural Heritage* Nara (Japan) 2012, *Asia-Pacific Forum on Educational Cooperation* Tokyo (Japan) 2011, *International conference on human resources development for cultural heritage protection* Nara (Japan) 2010, *Seminar on archaeology in Mongolia* Nara (Japan) 2010. **Publications** *ACCU News* (6 a year) in Japanese; *Bunka Isan News* (2 a year) in Japanese; *Cultural Heritage News* (2 a year) in English. Music, audiovisual and photographic materials; campaign materials for safeguarding the cultural heritage of the region; children's books; reports of meetings, seminars, workshops and training courses; literacy materials: booklets, posters, games, audiovisual kits, guidebooks, reports; reference materials; ACCU Calendar; postcards; greeting cards. **Information Services** *Asia-Pacific Culture Heritage Protection Database*; *Asia-Pacific Database on Intangible Cultural Heritage*; *Asia-Pacific Literacy Database*.
Members Supporting Members (currently over 100 institutions and over 400 individuals worldwide). Countries and territories participating in ACCU programmes (45):
Afghanistan, Australia, Bangladesh, Bhutan, Brunei Darussalam, Cambodia, China, Cook Is, Fiji, India, Indonesia, Iran Islamic Rep, Japan, Kazakhstan, Kiribati, Korea Rep, Kyrgyzstan, Laos, Malaysia, Maldives, Marshall Is, Micronesia FS, Mongolia, Myanmar, Nauru, Nepal, New Zealand, Niue, Pakistan, Palau, Papua New Guinea, Philippines, Samoa, Singapore, Solomon Is, Sri Lanka, Tajikistan, Thailand, Timor-Leste, Tonga, Turkmenistan, Tuvalu, Uzbekistan, Vanuatu, Vietnam.
IGO Relations Regional network of *UNESCO Office, Jakarta – Regional Bureau for Sciences in Asia and the Pacific (#20313)*. Cooperates with: *UNESCO Asia and Pacific Regional Bureau for Education (#20301)* (UNESCO Bangkok). [2014.12.02/XE8250/**E**]

♦ Asia-Pacific Cultural Creative Industry Association (internationally oriented national body)
♦ Asia Pacific Customer Service Consortium (unconfirmed)
♦ Asia-Pacific Dairy Association (no recent information)

♦ Asia Pacific Deaf Sports Confederation (APDSC) 01880

SG d/a 85 Jalan Juble Perak, Perlis Indera Kayangan, 01000 Kangar, Perlis, Malaysia. Fax +6049764702. E-mail: secgen@apdeafsports.org – info@apdeafsports.org.
URL: http://www.apdeafsports.org/
History Apr 1988, Korea Rep. Registration: Registrar of Societies, Start date: 27 Jun 2012, Malaysia. **Aims** Transform lives of people with a deaf/hard of hearing disability through the joy of sport. **Structure** Executive Committee. **Languages** English. **Finance** Sources: members' dues. **Activities** Sporting activities. **Events** *Meeting* Taoyuan (Taiwan) 2015, *Meeting* Taipei (Taiwan) 2000, *Congress / Meeting* Kuala Lumpur (Malaysia) 1996, *Congress / Meeting* Taipei (Taiwan) 1994, *Meeting* Seoul (Korea Rep) 1992. **Members** Full in 32 countries. Membership countries not specified. [2020/XD4974/**D**]

♦ Asia Pacific Democrat Union (APDU) 01881

Union démocratique Asie Pacifique

Exec Sec Liberal Party of Australia, PO Box 6004, Kingston, Canberra ACT 2604, Australia. T. +61262732564. Fax +61262731534.
History Jun 1982, Tokyo (Japan), following preliminary meeting, 1981, Sydney (Australia), of Pacific members of the European Democrat Union. Formerly referred to as *Pacific Democrat Union (PDU) – Union démocratique Pacifique*. 1998, present name adopted. **Aims** Promote freedom and free enterprise by considering matters of political organization and policy of interest to member parties. **Structure** Council; Steering Committee; Ad hoc Groups. **Languages** English. **Activities** Events/meetings; politics/policy/regulatory. **Events** *Meeting / Council Meeting* Seoul (Korea Rep) 2014, *Meeting / Council Meeting* Wellington (New Zealand) 2012, *Meeting / Council Meeting* London (UK) 2011, *Council Meeting* Taipei (Taiwan) 2010, *Council Meeting* Paris (France) 2008.
Members Liberal, Conservative, Centre and like-minded parties in 15 countries:
Australia, Bangladesh, Canada, Chile, El Salvador, Fiji, Korea Rep, Maldives, Mongolia, Nepal, New Zealand, Russia, Sri Lanka, Taiwan, USA.
NGO Relations Co-founder, in 1983, together with: *European Democrat Union (EDU, inactive)*, of *International Democrat Union (IDU, #13147)*. Instrumental in setting up: *Pacific Democrat Youth (PDY, inactive)*.
[2015.01.14/XD6627/**D**]

♦ Asia Pacific Dental Federation / see Asia Pacific Dental Federation/Asian Pacific Regional Organization of the Fédération Dentaire Internationale (#01882)

♦ Asia Pacific Dental Federation/Asian Pacific Regional Organization of the Fédération Dentaire Internationale (APDF-APRO) 01882

Fédération dentaire Asie-Pacifique/Organisation régionale Asie Pacifique de la Fédération dentaire internationale (FDAP-ORAP)

Address not obtained.
History 1955, Tokyo (Japan). Founded during 1st Asia Dental Congress. Constitution and By-Laws adopted at 2nd Congress, 1958, Manila (Philippines). Since Annual World Dental Congress, 1967, Paris (France), admitted as regional organization of *FDI – World Dental Federation (#09281)*, with listed title. Constitution modified: 1960; 1967; 1970; 1974. Former names and other names: *Asia Pacific Dental Federation (APDF)* – former (1955); *Fédération dentaire Asie Pacifique (FDAP)* – former (1955); *Asian Pacific Regional Organization (APRO)* – alias; *Organisation régionale Asie Pacifique (ORAP)* – alias; *Asian Pacific Dental Federation* – former alias. **Aims** Establish closer relations among dental associations in Asian and Pacific countries; further progress in the field of dental and allied sciences; encourage exchange of information and research to improve dental and general health of the region; carry out other functions as may be assigned by FDI. **Structure** Delegates Meeting; Executive Council. Standing Commissions (5). **Languages** English. **Staff** No permanent staff. **Finance** Members' dues. Income from congresses. **Activities** Knowledge management/information dissemination; research/documentation; liaising/networking; events/meetings. **Events** *Asia Pacific Dental Conference (APDC)* Karachi (Pakistan) 2022, *Congress* Colombo (Sri Lanka) 2021, *Congress* Colombo (Sri Lanka) 2020, *Congress* Seoul (Korea Rep) 2019, *Congress* Manila (Philippines) 2018.
Members National associations in 28 countries and territories:
Bahrain, Bangladesh, Cambodia, Fiji, Guam, Hong Kong, India, Indonesia, Iraq, Jordan, Lebanon, Macau, Malaysia, Mongolia, Myanmar, Nepal, Pakistan, Papua New Guinea, Philippines, Saudi Arabia, Singapore, Solomon Is, Sri Lanka, Taiwan, Thailand, Tonga, United Arab Emirates, Vietnam.
NGO Relations *Asian Pacific Dental Students Association (APDSA, #01607)* is an affiliate. [2022/XE0083/**D**]

♦ Asia-Pacific Dental Industry Association (no recent information)

♦ Asia Pacific Desalination Association (APDA) 01883

Secretariat No 1 Keyandong Road, Nankai District, Tianjin, China. T. +862287898186. Fax +862287892732. E-mail: apdasecretariat@outlook.com.
URL: http://www.apda.asia/
Aims Make contributions to the solution of water problems in the Asia-Pacific region. **Structure** Council; Committee; Board; Secretariat. **Languages** English. **Finance** Donations from each affiliate. **Activities** Guidance/assistance/consulting; events/meetings. **Events** *Joint Forum* Busan (Korea Rep) 2017, *Conference on Clean India Technologies and the Role of Desalination and Water Purification* Chennai (India) 2016, *Joint Forum* Beijing (China) 2015, *Joint Forum* Tokyo (Japan) 2015, *Conference* Singapore (Singapore) 2011.
Members Regular; Individual. Regular in 7 countries:
Australia, China, India, Japan, Korea Rep, Pakistan, Singapore.
NGO Relations Affiliate associate of: *International Desalination Association (IDA, #13152)*.
[2015.11.24/XM4289/**D**]

♦ Asia Pacific Design Centre (unconfirmed)

♦ Asia-Pacific Developmental Biology Network (APDBN) 01884

Secretariat c/o RIKEN Center, 2-2-3 Minatojima-minamimachi, Chuo-ku, Kobe HYOGO, 650-0047 Japan. E-mail: info@apdbn.org.
URL: http://www.apdbn.org/
History Nov 2004, with the support of *International Society of Developmental Biologists (ISDB, #15052)*. **Aims** Promote interests, activities and collaboration in the study of developmental biology in the Asia-Pacific region. **Structure** Board, comprising Chairman, Vice-Chairman and Secretary-Treasurer. **Languages** English. **Events** *Annual Meeting* Osaka (Japan) 2019, *Annual Meeting* Tokyo (Japan) 2018, *Annual Meeting* Tsukuba (Japan) 2015, *Annual Meeting* Nagoya (Japan) 2014, *Meeting* Kyoto (Japan) 2011.
Members in 8 countries and territories:
Australia, China, India, Japan, Korea Rep, New Zealand, Singapore, Taiwan. [2020/XM0694/**F**]

♦ Asia-Pacific Development and Communication Centre (internationally oriented national body)

♦ Asia-Pacific Disability Forum (APDF) 01885

Contact address not obtained. T. +82234723508. Fax +82234723592.
URL: http://www.normanet.ne.jp/~apdf/
History 26 Nov 2003, Singapore. **Aims** Promote, participate in and evaluate implementation of the Biwako Millennium Framework for Action Towards an Inclusive, Barrier Free and Rights Based Society for Persons with a Disability in Asia and the Pacific. **Structure** General Assembly; Executive Committee; Working Committees. **Finance** Members' dues. **Activities** Monitoring/evaluation; events/meetings. **Events** *Assembly* Incheon (Korea Rep) 2012, *International Conference on Disability* Incheon (Korea Rep) 2012, *General assembly and conference / Conference* Dhaka (Bangladesh) 2008. [2016.08.24/XM1770/**F**]

♦ Asia Pacific Disaster Mental Health Network (unconfirmed)
♦ Asia Pacific Disaster Resilience Centre (internationally oriented national body)
♦ Asia Pacific Down Syndrome Federation / see Asia Pacific Federation of Down Syndrome (#01898)
♦ Asia-Pacific Early Mobilization Network (unconfirmed)

♦ Asia-Pacific Economic Association (APEA) 01886

Regional Coordinator Univ of Washington, Dept of Economics, 206 Condon Hall, Box 353330, 1100 NE Campus Parkway, Seattle WA 98195-3330, USA. T. +12065436197. Fax +12066857477.
Regional Coordinator Natl Taiwan Univ, No 1 Section 4, Roosevelt Rd, Da'an District, Taipei 10617, Taiwan.
URL: http://apeaweb.org/
History 10 Dec 2003, Chuncheon (Korea Rep). Founded at the "Asian Crisis V" conference. **Aims** Promote interactions among economists in the Asia-Pacific region and in other parts of the world; encourage and disseminate economic research in the region. **Structure** President; 2 Vice-Presidents; Treasurer/Secretary. **Events** *Annual International Conference* Beijing (China) / Qingdao (China) 2020, *Annual International Conference* Fukuoka (Japan) 2019, *Annual International Conference* Los Angeles, CA (USA) 2018, *Annual International Conference* Seoul (Korea Rep) 2017, *Annual International Conference* Kolkata (India) 2016.
[2020/XJ0090/**D**]

♦ Asia-Pacific Economic Cooperation (APEC) 01887

Exec Dir 35 Heng Mui Keng Terrace, Singapore 119616, Singapore. T. +6568919600. Fax +6568919690. E-mail: info@apec.org.
URL: http://www.apec.org/
History 7 Nov 1989, Canberra, ACT (Australia). Established at meeting of ministers and cabinet-level officials. Subsequent informal meetings of economic leaders: outlined APEC's vision, 1993, Seattle WA (USA); planned free and open trade and investment in the region by 2010 for developed economies and by 2020 for developing economies, 1994, Bogor (Indonesia); adopted the *'Osaka Action Agenda (OAA)'*, 1995, Osaka (Japan); adopted the *'Manila Action Plan for APEC (MAPA)'* and first Collective and Individual Action Plans compiled, 1996, Manila (Philippines); endorsed proposal for Early Voluntary Sectoral Liberalization (EVSL), 1997, Vancouver BC (Canada); agreed on first 9 sectors for EVSL and sought EVSL agreement with non-APEC members at World Trade Organization, 1998, Kuala Lumpur (Malaysia); committed to paperless trading by 2005 in developed economies and 2010 in developing economies and APEC Business Travel Card scheme approved and Mutual Recognition Arrangement on Electrical Equipment and a Framework for the Integration of Women in Apec endorsed, 1999, Auckland (New Zealand); established electronic Individual Action Plan (e-IAP) system, 2000,

Bandar Seri Begawan (Brunei Darussalam); adopted Shanghai Accord and the e-APEC Strategy, 2001, Shanghai (China); adopted Trade Facilitation Action Plan, Policies on Trade and the Digital Economy and Transparency Standards, 2002, Los Cabos (Mexico); agreed to re-energize the WTO Doha Development Agenda negotiations, 2003, Bangkok (Thailand); adopted Best Practices for RTAs and FTAs, Santiago Initiative for Expanded Trade and a Data Privacy Framework, 2004 Santiago (Chile); adopted Busan Roadmap, completed Mid-Term Stocktake and APEC Privacy Framework, 2005, Busan, Korea Rep; APEC Economic Leaders endorsed Ha Noi Action Plan, 2006, Hanoi (Vietnam); issued a Declaration on Climate Change, Energy Security and Clean Development, 2007, Sydney (Australia); focused on the social dimensions of trade and on reducing the gap between developing and developed members, 2008, Lima (Peru); resolved to pursue balanced, inclusive an sustainable growth, while leaders agreed to extend their standstill commitment on protectionism until 2010, 2009, Singapore (Singapore); issued the Yokohama Vision to provide a roadmap for members to realize an economically-integrated, robust and secure APEC community, 2010, Yokohama (Japan); issued the Honolulu Declaration in which leaders committed to taking concrete steps towards a seamless regional economy, addressing shared green growth objectives, and advancing regulatory cooperation and convergence, 2011, Honolulu HI (USA); economies endorsed a ground-breaking APEC List of Environmental Goods that directly and positively contribute to green growth and sustainable development objectives, 2012, Vladivostok (Russia); economies provided the push needed to conclude the "Bali Package" at the 9th World Trade Organization Ministerial Conference to boost global trade, 2013, Bali (Indonesia); leaders committed to taking a concrete step towards greater regional economic integration by endorsing a roadmap to translate the vision of the Free Trace Area of the Asia-Pacific (FTAAP) into a reality, 2014, Beijing (China). Also referred to previously as *'Asian Pacific Economic Council Forum'*. **Aims** Work to meet the Bogor Goals of free and open trade and *investment* in the Asia-Pacific region by 2010 for developed economies and 2020 for developing economies. **Structure** Meetings (5): Leaders'; Ministerial; Senior Officials'; Sectoral Ministerial; Finance Deputies'; Senior Finance Officials'; *APEC Business Advisory Council*; Secretariat. Committees (4): Trade and Investment; Budget and Management; Economic; SOM Steering Committee on ECOTECH. Sub-committees/Expert Groups (8): Business Mobility; Electronic Commerce; Services; Investment Experts; Intellectual Property Rights; Market Access; Standards and Conformance; Customs Procedures. Working Groups (13): Agricultural Technical Cooperation; Anti-Corruption and Transparency; Counter Terrorism; Emergency Preparedness; Energy; Illegal Logging and Associated Trade; Health; Human Resource Development; Ocean and Fisheries; Small and Medium Enterprises; Telecommunications and Information; Tourism; Transportation. Steering Councils (2); Task Force on Mining. Includes: *APEC Centre for Technology Foresight (APECTF)*; *Asia Pacific Emerging Infections Network (AP-EINet, #01890)*. **Languages** English. **Staff** 43.00 FTE, paid. **Finance** Annual budget: 11,600,000 USD. **Activities** Events/meetings; networking/liaising; politics/policy/regulatory. **Events** *APEC Climate Symposium* Busan (Korea Rep) 2021, *Climate Forecast Workshop* Busan (Korea Rep) 2021, *Seminar on Abrupt Shift to Hotter and Drier Climate over Inner East-Asia beyonf the Tipping Point* Busan (Korea Rep) 2021, *Workshop on E-commerce Negotiation* Seoul (Korea Rep) 2021, *Future Education Forum* Seoul (Korea Rep) 2020. **Publications** *APEC Economic Outlook* (annual); *Key Documents* (annual). *APEC Document Series*; *APEC Economic Outlook Series*; *APEC Economic Policy Report Series*; *APEC Energy Handbook Series*; *APEC Energy Overview Series*; *APEC Energy Statistical Analysis Tool Series* – CD-Rom; *APEC Energy Statistics Series*; *Report on Economic and Technical Cooperation Series*. *Handbook on Automated Sphygmomanometers* (2007); *APEC Customs-Business Partnership Programmes* (2006); *Handbook on Verification of Non-Automatic Weighing Instruments* (2006); *The Role of Voluntary Initiatives in Sustainable Production, Trade and Consumption in the APEC Region* (2006); *Socio-Economic Disparity in the APEC Region* (2006); *Small and Micro Enterprise Financing: A Tool for Mainstreaming the Informatl Sector ?* (2006); *Potential for Growth of Natural Gas as a Clean Energy Source in APEC Developing Economies* (2006); *Most recent publications: APEC Customs-Business Partnership Programmes* (2006); *Modern Approaches to Linking Exposure to Toxic Compounds and Biological Effects* (2006); *Intellectual Property Rights Enforcement Strategies* (2006); *Handbook on Electricity Meters* (2006); *Handbook on Prepackaged Goods* (2006); *Benchmarking Knowledge Management Technologies and Behaviours* (2006); *Handbook on CNG Fuel Dispensers* (2006); *Franchising Opportunities in China, Japan and Singapore* (2006); *Evaluation of Access to Domestic and International Leased Lines in the APEC Region* (2006); *Enhancing Investment Liberalization and Facilitation in the Asia-Pacific Region (Stage 1): Reducing Barriers to Investment Across APEC to Lift Growth and Lower Poverty* (2006); *Ecosystem Based Approach: A Comparative Assessment of the Institutional Response in Fisheries Management with APEC Economies: The Case of Demersal Fisheries (Phase 1)* (2006); *Driving Forward a Prosperous and Harmonized APEC Community* (2006); *Best Practices in Sustainable Tourism Management Initiatives for APEC Econmies* (2006); *Tourism Occupational Skill Standard Development in the APEC Region, Stage IV* (2006). Annual Report to Ministers; books; guides; directories; documents; reports; surveys; compendia; statistics; seminar and workshops proceedings; corporate brochures; monographs; studies. **Information Services** *APEC Competition Policy and Law Database*; *APEC Labour Market Information Network*; *APEC Network of Minerals and Energy Data (ANMED)*; *APEC Port Database*; *APEC Project Database*; *APEC Tariff Database*. **Members** Member economies (21, listed in accordance with the convention in this Yearbook with Chinese Taipei referred to as Taiwan and Hong Kong-China referred to as Hong Kong): Australia, Brunei Darussalam, Canada, Chile, China, Hong Kong, Indonesia, Japan, Korea Rep, Malaysia, Mexico, New Zealand, Papua New Guinea, Peru, Philippines, Russia, Singapore, Taiwan, Thailand, USA, Vietnam. Observers (3), listed in this Yearbook: *ASEAN (#01141)*; *Pacific Economic Cooperation Council (PECC, #17947)*; *Pacific Islands Forum (#17968)*. **IGO Relations** Observer status with (1): *Asia/Pacific Group on Money Laundering (APG, #01921)*. Cooperates with (1): *United Nations Institute for Training and Research (UNITAR, #20576)*. Supports (1): *CABI (#03393)*. Instrumental in setting up (1): *Asia-Pacific Energy Research Centre (APERC)*. Stakeholder participation. **NGO Relations** Member of (1): *Our World is Not for Sale (OWINFS, #17917)*. Instrumental in setting up (1): *Joint Organisations Data Initiative (JODI, #16143)*. Development monitored by: *ITUC Asia-Pacific Labour Network (APLN)*. Recognized specialized regional bodies: *Asia-Pacific Accreditation Cooperation (APAC, #01816)*; *Asia Pacific Metrology Programme (APMP, #01957)*; *Pacific Area Standards Congress (PASC, #17927)*.

[2023.02.20/XD2469/y/C*]

♦ Asia-Pacific Economic Cooperation Port Services Network / see APEC Port Services Network (#00872)
♦ Asia Pacific Ecotourism Society (unconfirmed)

♦ Asia-Pacific Educational Research Association (APERA) 01888
Exec Dir c/o NIE NTU, 1 Nanyang Walk, Singapore 637616, Singapore.
URL: http://eras.org.sg/apera/
History 13 Dec 2001, Bangkok (Thailand), during a conference organized by *UNESCO (#20322)* and *Asia-Pacific Programme of Educational Innovation for Development (APEID, #02001)*. **Aims** Support and encourage educational research in the Asia-Pacific region; build stronger links between research, policy and practice in education. **Structure** General Meeting (annual); Board of Directors. **Finance** Members' dues. **Events** *HKERA-APERA International Conference* Shatin (Hong Kong) 2023, *HKERA-APERA International Conference* Hong Kong 2021, *Seminar* Singapore (Singapore) 2019, *International Conference* Singapore (Singapore) 2018, *Global Hospitality, Tourism Marketing and Management Conference* Bangkok (Thailand) 2015. **Publications** *Educational Research for Policy and Practice* – journal. *Education in the Asia-Pacific Regions: Issues, Concerns and Prospects* – series. *Asia-Pacific Handbook on Educational Research*.
Members Founding members (17) in 12 countries and territories:
Australia, China, Hong Kong, Indonesia, Japan, Korea DPR, Laos, Malaysia, New Zealand, Sri Lanka, Thailand, Vietnam.
Included in the above, 1 organization listed in this Yearbook:
UNESCO Asia and Pacific Regional Bureau for Education (#20301).

[2022/XM1811/D]

♦ Asia Pacific Education Conference (meeting series)

♦ Asia Pacific Emergency and Disaster Nursing Network (APEDNN) 01889
Contact 44 Wenhua West Rd, Jinan, 250012 Shandong, China. T. +8653188380705. Fax +8653188380705. E-mail: apednn.sdu@gmail.com.
URL: http://www.apednn.org
History Launched 2007, Bangkok (Thailand). **Aims** Build capacities of nurses and *midwives* to fully contribute to coordinated and effective prevention, preparedness and response efforts; improve service delivery; build community resilience during times of emergencies and disasters. **Events** *International Conference on Disaster Nursing* Daejeon (Korea Rep) 2014, *Meeting* Bangkok (Thailand) 2013, *Meeting* Kuala Lumpur (Malaysia) 2012, *Meeting* Seoul (Korea Rep) / Daejeon (Korea Rep) 2011, *Meeting* Auckland (New Zealand) 2010.
Members Individuals in 8 countries:
Australia, China, India, Japan, Korea Rep, Philippines, Samoa, USA.

[2015/XJ9543/v/F]

♦ Asia Pacific Emerging Infections Network (AP-EINet) 01890
Contact 1107 NE 45th St, Ste 400, Box 354809, Seattle WA 98195-4809, USA. T. +12066168155. Fax +12066169415. E-mail: apecein@uw.edu.
URL: http://blogs.uw.edu/apecein/
History Set up within *Asia-Pacific Economic Cooperation (APEC, #01887)*, as *APEC Emerging Infections Network (APEC EINet)*. **Aims** Foster transparency, communication, and collaboration in emerging infections in the Asia-Pacific. **Publications** *EINet Update* (occasional).

[2013/XF6090/F]

♦ Asia Pacific Employee Assistance Roundtable (APEAR) 01891
Sec 1 Orchard Boulevard, 09-04 Camden Medical Centre, Singapore 248649, Singapore. T. +6593582110. Fax +6593582560. E-mail: apearindia@gmail.com.
URL: http://www.apear.org/
History Founded 2003. **Aims** Promote the highest standards of practice and continuing development of Employee Assistance (EA) professionals, providers and services; present the business case for EA and mental health at work programmes to human resource, occupational health and business leaders with a focus on how to maximize employee performance through EAP; promote better understanding of the clinical practice and application of EA provision; develop regional guidelines for EA as well as a Code of Ethics for EA practitioners and provides; continue the professional exchange and dialogue regarding EA in the Asia Pacific and with othe EA organizations. **Structure** General Meeting (annual); Executive Board; Secretariat. **Languages** English. **Activities** Events/meetings. Registrants are industry leaders, line supervisors, health professionals, trainers, uman resource professionals, medical advisors and those interested in employee work performance, productivity and safety. Active in Europe and: Australia, Canada, China, India, Indonesia, Malaysia, Singapore, Thailand, USA. **Events** *EAP in the modern age – employee engagement* Bangalore (India) 2018, *Conference* Manila (Philippines) 2017, *Conference* Seoul (Korea Rep) 2016, *Conference* Goa (India) 2015, *Conference* Melbourne, VIC (Australia) 2014.

[2016.06.01/XJ0136/F]

♦ Asia-Pacific Energy Research Centre (internationally oriented national body)
♦ Asia Pacific Enterostomal Therapy Nurses Association (see: #21327)
♦ Asia Pacific Environmental Exchange / see Earth Economics

♦ Asia-Pacific Environmental and Occupational Dermatology Group (APEOD) 01892
Contact Occupational Dermatology Research and Education Ctr, Skin and Cancer Foundation Vic, 1/80 Drummond St, Carlton VIC 3053, Australia. T. +61396239402. Fax +61396393575.
URL: http://www.apeods.org/
History 1991. **Aims** Further understanding of environmental and occupational contact dermatitis through regional biennial meetings of interested dermatologists. **Structure** An informal collection of dermatologists representing countries in Asia-Pacific, meeting every 2 years. **Languages** English. **Staff** 1.00 FTE, voluntary. **Finance** No budget. **Events** *APEODS Symposium* Manila (Philippines) 2015, *APEODS Symposium* Yogyakarta (Indonesia) 2013, *APEODS Symposium* Chandigarh (India) 2011, *APEODS Symposium* Kyoto (Japan) 2009, *APEODS Symposium* Gold Coast, QLD (Australia) 2007. **Publications** None.
Members Individuals in 10 countries and territories:
Australia, India, Indonesia, Japan, Korea Rep, New Zealand, Philippines, Singapore, Taiwan, Thailand.

[2016.12.14/XJ4852/v/E]

♦ Asia-Pacific EPR/ESR Society (APES) 01893
Pres address not obtained.
URL: http://www.apeprs.org/
History Founded 23 Jan 1997, Hong Kong, during 1st Asia-Pacific EPR/ESR symposium. **Aims** Advance and stimulate knowledge of the principles, recent developments and applications of *electron paramagnetic* resonance (EPR) – *electron spin resonance* (ESR) *spectroscopy* in the Asia-Pacific region; strengthen collaboration among spectroscopists in the region. **Structure** Board; Advisory Council. **Languages** English. **Staff** Voluntary. **Finance** No budget. **Events** *Symposium* Irkutsk (Russia) 2016, *Symposium* Nara (Japan) 2014, *Symposium* Beijing (China) 2012, *Symposium* Jeju (Korea Rep) 2010, *Symposium* Cairns, QLD (Australia) 2008.
Members Full in 8 countries:
Australia, China, India, Japan, Korea Rep, New Zealand, Russia, Vietnam.
NGO Relations *International EPR Society (IES, #13288)*.

[2017/XM0535/D]

♦ Asia-Pacific Evaluation Association (APEA) 01894
Secretariat Guiguinto, 3015 Bulacan, Philippines. E-mail: apea.secretariat@gmail.com – apea.coordinator@gmail.com.
URL: https://www.asiapacificeval.org/
History 14 Sep 2012. **Aims** Improve theory, practice, use and institutions of evaluation. **Structure** Board of Directors. **Finance** Sources: members' dues. **Activities** Capacity building; events/meetings; networking/liaising. **Events** *APEA Conference* Delhi (India) 2022, *APEA Conference* Manila (Philippines) 2019, *APEA Conference* Hanoi (Vietnam) 2016.
Members Institutions in 14 countries:
Afghanistan, Bhutan, Cambodia, India, Indonesia, Japan, Korea Rep, Mongolia, Myanmar, Nepal, Pakistan, Philippines, Sri Lanka, Vietnam.
Voluntary Service Overseas (VSO).
NGO Relations Member of (1): *International Organisation for Cooperation in Evaluation (IOCE, #14426)*. Cooperates with (1): *EvalPartners (#09208)*.

[2022.10.25/XJ8540/D]

♦ Asia Pacific Exhibition and Convention Council (inactive)
♦ Asia and Pacific Family Organization / see Organization of the Families of Asia and the Pacific (#17867)
♦ Asia Pacific Federation / see Asia-Pacific Federation on Giftedness (#01899)
♦ Asia Pacific Federation of Aerospace Medicine Associations (unconfirmed)

♦ Asia-Pacific Federation of Association Organizations (APFAO) 01895
Pres c/o ADFIAP, 2F Skyland Plaza, Sen Puyat Ave, 1200 Makati, Philippines. T. +6328161672. Fax +6328176498. E-mail: obp@adfiap.org – inquiries@adfiap.org.
URL: http://www.apfao.org/
History 24 Mar 2015, Kowloon (Hong Kong). Launched on signing the 'Hong Kong Charter' by (Australian) Associations Forum (AF), *Australasian Society of Association Executives (AuSAE)*, Korean Society of Association Executives (KSAE) and Philippine Council of Associations and Association Executives (PCAAE). **Aims** Be the Asia-Pacific focal point to share knowledge and best practices of the associations' sector and professionals working in these associations. **Structure** General Assembly; Management Council; Secretariat. **Languages** English. **Staff** 3.00 FTE, voluntary. **Finance** Sources: fees for services; meeting proceeds; members' dues; revenue from activities/projects. **Activities** APFAO speaks at ASAE Global Day. **Events** *General Assembly* Seoul (Korea Rep) 2017, *General Assembly* Hong Kong (Hong Kong) 2016.
Members Organizations (4) in 3 countries:
Australia, Korea Rep, Philippines.
Organizations include 1 listed in this Yearbook:
Australasian Society of Association Executives (AuSAE).

[2023/XM4464/y/D]

♦ Asia Pacific Federation for Clinical Biochemistry and Laboratory Medicine (APFCB) 01896
Pres c/o Solid Track Management Pte, 150 Cecil St, Ste 10-06, Singapore 069543, Singapore. T. +6562239118. Fax +6562239131. E-mail: apfcboffical@apfcb.org.
URL: http://www.apfcb.org/
History 22 Sep 1982, Singapore (Singapore). Founded at 2nd *Asian and Pacific Congress of Clinical Biochemistry*, when constitution was adopted and Executive Committee elected, following decision taken at 1st Congress, 17 Oct 1979, Singapore, when Steering Committee was formed. Former names and other names: *Asian-Pacific Federation of Clinical Biochemistry (APFCB)* – former. **Aims** Contribute to the health and well-being of communities it serves through advancing the development and practice of clinical biochemistry. **Structure** Council; Executive Board; Committees (4). **Languages** English. **Staff** Voluntary. **Finance** Sources: members' dues. **Activities** Awards/prizes/competitions; events/meetings; research/documentation; training/

education. **Events** *Congress* Sydney, NSW (Australia) 2024, *Congress* Seoul (Korea Rep) 2022, *Triennial Congress* Seoul (Korea Rep) 2021, *Triennial Congress* Jaipur (India) 2019, *Triennial Congress* Taipei (Taiwan) 2016. **Publications** *APFCB News* (annual); *Clinical Biochemist Reviews* – in association with AACB. Congress proceedings; newsletters.
Members National associations in 18 countries and territories:
Australia, China, Hong Kong, India, Indonesia, Iran Islamic Rep, Japan, Korea Rep, Malaysia, Mongolia, Nepal, Pakistan, Philippines, Singapore, Sri Lanka, Taiwan, Thailand, Vietnam.
Australasian Association for Clinical Biochemistry and Laboratory Medicine (AACB).
Affiliate organizations in laboratory medicine that are not national/area associations of clinical biochemistry. Affiliate in 6 countries and territories:
China, India, Macau, Nepal, Philippines, Sri Lanka.
Corporate in 9 countries and territories:
Australia, China, Germany, Hong Kong, India, Japan, Philippines, Singapore, UK. [2023/XF5502/y/**D**]

♦ Asia Pacific Federation of Coloproctology (APFCP) 01897
Contact c/o STREAMS, Ste 310 Plaza Edogawabashi, 1-23-6 Sekiguchi Bunkyo-ku, Tokyo, 112-0014 Japan. T. +81362281160. Fax +81362281186. E-mail: apfcp@streams.co.jp.
URL: http://www.streams.co.jp/apfcp/
History Founded at 3rd Congress, as *Asian Federation of Coloproctology (AFCP)*; no permanent infrastructure, rather a series of congresses organized by the society of colon and rectal surgeons where the congress is held. A similar organization, *Asian Society of Colorectal Surgery (inactive)*, existed from the 1st Congress 1975, Bombay (India), until after the 2nd congress, 1977, Nara (Japan) and recommenced, 1992, Osaka, at 3rd congress, in order to set up AFCP. Current title adopted, 2009, when Australia and New Zealand joined. **Aims** Promote advancement of coloproctology in the region; maintain active communication with all organizations interested in the field; related with other international associations; coordinate and facilitate the biennial congress of the federation. **Structure** Governing Council; Executive. **Languages** English. **Staff** 1.00 FTE, paid. **Finance** Congress financed by host country. **Activities** Events/meetings. **Events** *Congress* Singapore (Singapore) 2023, *Congress* Taipei (Taiwan) 2021, *Biennial Congress* Kuala Lumpur (Malaysia) 2019, *Biennial Congress* Seoul (Korea Rep) 2017, *Biennial Congress* Melbourne, VIC (Australia) 2015.
Members Organizations in 16 countries and territories:
Australia, China, Hong Kong, India, Indonesia, Iran Islamic Rep, Israel, Japan, Korea Rep, Malaysia, Nepal, New Zealand, Philippines, Singapore, Taiwan, Thailand. [2021/XD3730/c/**F**]

♦ Asia Pacific Federation of Critical Care Nurses (no recent information)

♦ Asia Pacific Federation of Down Syndrome (APDSF) 01898
Main Office 11/6 Justice Sundaram Road, Mylapore, Chennai, Tamil Nadu 600 004, Chennai TAMIL NADU 600 004, India. T. +914424340254. E-mail: info@apdsf.org.
URL: http://apdsf.org/
History 1992. Restructured in 2004. Also referred to as *Asia Pacific Down Syndrome Federation (APDSF)*. Registered in accordance with Indian law, Mar 2017. **Aims** Speak for the rights of people with Down syndrome in the Asia Pacific region; provide support to them. **Activities** Events/meetings. **Events** *Meeting* Singapore (Singapore) 2003, *Meeting* Auckland (New Zealand) 1998.
Members Full in 19 countries and territories:
Australia, Bangladesh, Bhutan, Hong Kong, India, Indonesia, Japan, Malaysia, Maldives, Mongolia, Myanmar, Nepal, New Zealand, Pakistan, Singapore, Sri Lanka, Thailand, United Arab Emirates, Vietnam. [2020/XJ0162/**D**]

♦ Asia-Pacific Federation on Giftedness (APFG) 01899
Main Office NTNU Special Education Dept, 162 Heping East Road, Section 1, Taipei 10610, Taiwan. E-mail: apfg2014gifted@gmail.com – kaykuo@ntnu.edu.tw.
URL: https://www.apfggiftedness.org/
History 1990, Manila (Philippines), as *Asia-Pacific Federation*. Affiliated to *World Council for Gifted and Talented Children (WCGTC, #21328)*, 1994. Became independent under current title 2010. Previously also referred to as *Asia-Pacific Federation of Gifted and Talented Children*. **Aims** Develop and educate gifted and talented children in Asia-Pacific region. **Structure** Committee, comprising President, Vice-President, Immediate Past-President, Treasurer, Secretary, Journal Editor and 2 members. **Events** *Asia-Pacific Conference on Giftedness (APCG)* Taipei (Taiwan) 2022, *Asia-Pacific Conference on Giftedness (APCG)* Daegu (Korea Rep) 2020, *Asia-Pacific Conference on Giftedness (APCG)* Bangkok (Thailand) 2018, *Asia-Pacific Conference on Giftedness (APCG)* Macau 2016, *Asia-Pacific Conference on Giftedness (APCG)* Beijing (China) 2014.
Members Full in 14 countries:
Australia, China, Hong Kong, India, Indonesia, Korea Rep, Malaysia, New Zealand, Philippines, Saudi Arabia, Singapore, Taiwan, Thailand, United Arab Emirates.
NGO Relations Affiliate federation of: *World Council for Gifted and Talented Children (WCGTC, #21328)*. [2021/XD6474/**D**]

♦ Asia-Pacific Federation of Gifted and Talented Children / see Asia-Pacific Federation on Giftedness (#01899)

♦ Asia-Pacific Federation for Information Technology in Agriculture (APFITA) 01900
SG c/o TAITA, 1F No 12, Ln 16 – Sec 3, Chongqing S Rd, Taipei 100, Taiwan. T. +886223017118. Fax +886223015768. E-mail: jimmy@gis.tw.
URL: http://www.apfita.org/APFITA_Home.aspx
History 24 Jan 1998, Japan. 24 Jan 1998, Wakayama City (Japan), as *Asian Federation for Information Technology in Agriculture (AFITA)*, during 1st Asian Conference for Information Technology in Agriculture. Current title adopted 2018. **Aims** Promote agricultural information technology in the region. **Structure** Board. **Events** *Conference* Taichung (Taiwan) 2019, *World Congress on Computers in Agriculture* Mumbai (India) 2018, *World Congress on Computers in Agriculture* Suncheon (Korea Rep) 2016, *Conference* Perth, WA (Australia) 2014, *Applications in agriculture and natural resources* Taipei (Taiwan) 2012.
Members Full; Institutional; Individual. Members in 12 countries and territories:
Bangladesh, China, India, Indonesia, Japan, Korea Rep, Malaysia, Philippines, Taiwan, Thailand, Timor-Leste, Vietnam.
NGO Relations Member of: *International Network for Information Technology in Agriculture (INFITA, #14287)*. [2019.04.25/XD2503/**D**]

♦ Asia-Pacific Federation of the International Atherosclerosis Society / see IAS Asia Pacific Federation (#11007)

♦ Asia Pacific Federation of Logistics and SCM Systems (APFLS) ... 01901
Contact 1-2-1 Izumi-chou, Narashino, Chiba, 275-8575 Japan. T. +81474742633. Fax +81474742633. E-mail: wakabayashi.keizou@nihon-u.ac.jp.
URL: http://ifls-world.jp/
History Mar 2003. **Aims** Enhance logistics and SCM research; exchange technology and science; collaborate research activities concerned; promote and disseminate research results and real cases. **Structure** General Assembly. Board, comprising Chairman, Vice-Chairmen and members. **Events** *International Congress on Logistics and Supply Chain Management Systems* Tokyo (Japan) 2013, *International Congress on Logistics and Supply Chain Management Systems* Seoul (Korea Rep) 2012, *International Congress on Logistics and Supply Chain Management Systems* Kaohsiung (Taiwan) 2011, *International Congress on Logistics and Supply Chain Management Systems* Seoul (Korea Rep) 2009, *International Congress on Logistics and Supply Chain Management Systems* Bangkok (Thailand) 2008. **Publications** *APFLS Newsletter* (4 a year); *APFLS Journal* (annual).
Members Full in 6 countries and territories:
Australia, Japan, Korea Rep, Singapore, Taiwan, Thailand.
NGO Relations *International Federation of Logistics and SCM Systems (IFLS, #13472)*. [2013/XJ7123/**D**]

♦ Asia Pacific Federation for Non Destructive Testing (APFNDT) 01902
Secretariat address not obtained. E-mail: secretariat@apfndt.org.
Pres Japanese Society for Non-Destructive Inspection, 10F Tachibana Annex Bldg, 2-25-14 Kameido, Koto, Tokyo, 136-0071 Japan. E-mail: secretariat@jsndi.or.jp.
URL: https://www.apfndt.org/
History 2009, Yokohama (Japan). Replaces *Asia-Pacific Committee of Non-Destructive Testing (APCNDT, inactive)*. **Structure** General Assembly; Board of Directors; Executive Committee. Regional Groups; Task Groups. **Activities** Events/meetings. **Events** *Asia-Pacific Conference on Non Destructive Testing* Hawaii (USA) 2025, *Asia-Pacific Conference on Non Destructive Testing* Melbourne, VIC (Australia) 2023, *Asia-Pacific Conference on Non Destructive Testing* Melbourne, VIC (Australia) 2021, *Asia-Pacific Conference on Non Destructive Testing* Singapore (Singapore) 2017, *Asia-Pacific Conference on Non Destructive Testing* Mumbai (India) 2013. **Publications** *APFNDT Regional Newsletter* (4 a year).
Members Full in 17 countries and territories:
Australia, Canada, China, India, Japan, Korea Rep, Malaysia, Mongolia, New Zealand, Pakistan, Philippines, Russia, Singapore, Sri Lanka, Taiwan, Thailand, USA.
Associate in 4 countries:
Bangladesh, Indonesia, Myanmar, Vietnam. [2021/AA2236/**D**]

♦ Asia Pacific Federation of Pharmacologists (APFP) 01903
SG c/o CICM Rangsit, 99 Moo 18 Paholyothin Road, Klongnung, Pathum Thani, 12120, Thailand. E-mail: info@apfp.asia.
URL: https://www.apfp.asia/
History 1991, Hong Kong (Hong Kong). Founded at 6th Regional Meeting of Pharmacologists; reaffirmed during 7th Meeting, 1995, Manila (Philippines). Statutes formulated and distributed in 1997. Formal establishment 1999, Taipei (Taiwan), at 8th Meeting. Former names and other names: *South East Asian/Western Pacific Federation of Pharmacologists (SEA/WPFP)* – former; *South East Asian/Western Pacific Regional Federation of Pharmacologists (SEA/WP)* – former. **Aims** Advance research in and teaching of pharmacology; foster cooperation among pharmacologists in the region; encourage formation of special interest groups in areas of pharmacology and *toxicology*. **Structure** Steering Committee, including Chairman and Secretary. Proposed statutes suggest, once launched: Council, consisting of nominees of local societies affiliated with the International Union of Pharmacology; Executive Committee, comprising President, Vice-President, Secretary, Deputy Secretary and Treasurer; Sub-Committees. **Languages** English. **Finance** Members' dues. **Events** *Meeting* Daegu (Korea Rep) 2028, *Meeting* Melbourne, VIC (Australia) 2024, *Quadrennial Regional Meeting* Taipei (Taiwan) 2021, *Regional Meeting* Taipei (Taiwan) 2021, *Quadrennial Regional Meeting* Taipei (Taiwan) 2020.
Members Following launch Society; Individual; Corporate. Currently Steering Committee members and corresponding members nominated by IUPHAR-affiliated pharmacological societies, in 14 countries and territories:
Australia, China, Hong Kong, Indonesia, Japan, Korea DPR, Korea Rep, Malaysia, New Zealand, Philippines, Singapore, Taiwan, Thailand, Vietnam.
NGO Relations *Asian Federation of Clinical Pharmacologists (no recent information)*; *Asian Pacific Society for Neurochemistry (APSN, #01641)*; *Australasian Society of Clinical and Experimental Pharmacology and Toxicology (ASCEPT)*; *Federation of Asian and Oceanian Physiological Societies (FAOPS, #09440)*. Regional member of: *International Union of Basic and Clinical Pharmacology (IUPHAR, #15758)*. [2023/XD5669/**D**]

♦ Asia Pacific Federation of Project Management (APFPM) 01904
Pres address not obtained.
URL: http://apfpm.org/
History Established Mar 2010. A relaunch of *Asia Pacific Forum*, which was founded 1997. Its structure and focus changed, Oct 2002, when current title was adopted. Founded on the initiative of Bill Young. **Aims** Help national Project Management Associations in the Asia Pacific to effectively collaborate in a connected network; strengthen the Project Management competency and capacity across the region so as to bring to the nations involved greater ability to deliver capital effectiveness and improved stakeholder value, both across their private and public sectors. **Structure** Committee. **Activities** Events/meetings; awards/prizes/competitions; capacity building. **Events** *Meeting* Melbourne, VIC (Australia) 2019. **Publications** *apfpm Newsletter* (4 a year).
Members Associations in 19 countries and territories:
Australia, Bangladesh, Canada, Chile, China, Hong Kong, India, Indonesia, Japan, Korea Rep, Malaysia, Mexico, Nepal, Peru, Philippines, Russia, Singapore, Taiwan, USA.
NGO Relations *International Project Management Association (IPMA, #14655)*. [2020/XM6983/**D**]

♦ Asia Pacific Federation for Societies for Hand Therapy (APFSHT) .. 01905
Founding Pres 43 Bruyere St, Rm-273J, Ottawa ON K1N 5C8, Canada. T. +16135626262 ext 4014.
URL: http://www.apfsht.org/
History Also referred to as *Asian Pacific Federation of Societies of Hand Therapists*. **Aims** Enhance and support international cooperation in clinical hand therapy and education; promote communication and knowledge exchange between hand therapists and hand surgeons; improve the quantity and quality of education and research in the field of the hand therapy within the Asia-Pacific region. **Structure** Council; Executive Committee. **Activities** Events/meetings. **Events** *Congress* Singapore (Singapore) 2023, *Congress* Melbourne, VIC (Australia) 2020, *Congress* Cebu City (Philippines) 2017, *Congress* Kuala Lumpur (Malaysia) 2014, *Congress* Bali (Indonesia) 2012. **NGO Relations** *Asian Pacific Federation of Societies for Surgery of the Hand (APFSSH, #01613)*. [2022/XM5540/**D**]

♦ Asia Pacific Finance Association (inactive)
♦ Asia-Pacific Finance and Development Institute (internationally oriented national body)

♦ Asia Pacific Financial Services Association (APFinSA) 01906
Secretariat 420 North Bridge Road, 04-04 North Bridge Centre, Singapore 188727, Singapore. T. +6567202382. Fax +6567202383. E-mail: info@apfinsa.org.
Main: http://www.apfinsa.org/
History Sep 1991. Former names and other names: *Asia Pacific Life Insurance Council (APLIC)* – former (Sep 1991 to Jul 2003). **Aims** Promote friendship and cooperation between life insurance sales professionals in the Asia-Pacific region; encourage enhancement of educational and professional standards. **Structure** Management Committee, comprising Chairman, Vice-Chairman, Immediate Past Chairman, Honorary Secretary and Honorary Treasurer. **Events** *Asia-Pacific Life Insurance Congress* Singapore (Singapore) 2022, *Asia-Pacific Life Insurance Congress* Singapore (Singapore) 2021, *Asia-Pacific Life Insurance Virtual Congress* Singapore (Singapore) 2021, *Work with mission, serve with passion* Hong Kong (Hong Kong) 2019, *Together as one* Malaysia 2017.
Members National organizations (10) in 10 countries and territories:
Australia, Hong Kong, India, Macau, Malaysia, Philippines, Singapore, Taiwan, Thailand. [2020/XE4720/**E**]

♦ Asia-Pacific Fishery Commission (APFIC) 01907
Commission Asie-Pacifique des pêches – Comisión de Pesca para Asia-Pacifico (CPAP)
Contact FAO-RAP, Maliwan Mansion, 39 Phra Athit Road, Bangkok, 10200, Thailand. T. +6626974149. Fax +6626974445. E-mail: fao-rap@fao.org.
URL: https://www.fao.org/apfic/en/
History 9 Nov 1948. Established on coming into force of an agreement formulated 26 Feb 1948, Baguio (Philippines). Establishment approved at 4th Session of the Conference of *FAO (#09260)*, 1948. Agreement amended: 1961, at 9th Session; 1-5 Nov 1976, Colombo (Sri Lanka), at 17th session, changes being approved at 72nd Session of FAO Council, 8-11 Nov 1977, Rome (Italy); Dec 1993, Bangkok (Thailand), at 24th Session, changes being approved at 107th Session of FAO Council, 15-24 Nov 1994, Rome. Rules of Procedure adopted Mar 1949, at first session; revised 1961, at 9th Session; and amended at 12th, 16th, 17th and 18th Sessions. Former names and other names: *Indo-Pacific Fisheries Council (IPFC)* – former; *Conseil Indo-Pacifique des pêches* – former; *Indo-Pacific Fishery Commission* – former (Nov 1976 to 1993); *Commission Indo-Pacifique des pêches (CIPP)* – former (Nov 1976 to 1993); *Comisión de Pesca del Indo-Pacifico* – former (Nov 1976 to 1993). **Aims** Promote full and proper utilization of living aquatic resources by development and management of fishing and culture operations, and by development of related processing and marketing activities in conformity with the objectives of members in the Asia-Pacific area. **Structure** Commission Sessions (every 2 years); Executive Committee. **Languages** English, French. **Staff** Secretariat function provided by FAO. **Finance** Field activities financed by the regular budget of FAO. Expenses for research or development projects undertaken by members of the Commission paid by the respective governments and/or donor contributions. **Activities** Events/meetings; guidance/assistance/consulting; research and development; training/education. **Events** *Biennial Session* Bangkok (Thailand) 2021, *Biennial Session* Hyderabad (India) 2014, *Biennial Session* Danang (Vietnam) 2012, *Regional Consultative Forum / Biennial Session* Danang (Vietnam) 2012, *Session* Nha

Trang (Vietnam) 2011. **Publications** *Regional Fishery Bodies and Arrangements in Asia and the Pacific* (2009). Session reports; symposia and workshop proceedings; technical documents; training courses and resource materials.
Members Member Nations and Associate Members of FAO who accept the Agreement. Other States admitted by decision of the Council. Currently the governments of 21 countries:
Australia, Bangladesh, Cambodia, China, France, India, Indonesia, Japan, Korea Rep, Malaysia, Myanmar, Nepal, New Zealand, Pakistan, Philippines, Sri Lanka, Thailand, Timor-Leste, UK, USA, Vietnam.
IGO Relations Cooperates with (8): *Bay of Bengal Programme Inter-Governmental Organization (BOBP-IGO, #03189)*; *Coordinating Body on the Seas of East Asia (COBSEA, #04814)*; *Indian Ocean Tuna Commission (IOTC, #11162)*; *Intergovernmental Organization for Marketing Information and Technical Advisory Services for Fishery Products in the Asia and Pacific Region (INFOFISH, #11497)*; *Mekong River Commission (MRC, #16703)*; *Network of Aquaculture Centres in Asia-Pacific (NACA, #16991)*; *Southeast Asian Fisheries Development Center (SEAFDEC, #19767)*; *Western and Central Pacific Fisheries Commission (WCPFC, #20912)*. Instrumental in setting up (1): *Tuna Fisheries Development and Management in the Indian Ocean and the Pacific off Southeast Asia (IPTP, inactive)*. Based at: *FAO Regional Office for Asia and the Pacific (RAP, #09266)*.
NGO Relations Cooperates with (4): *Asian Fisheries Society (AFS, #01483)*; *International Collective in Support of Fishworkers (ICSF, #12639)*; *WorldFish (#21507)*; *World Wide Fund for Nature (WWF, #21922)*.
[2023.02.14/XE1023/**E***]

♦ Asia Pacific Food Analysis Network (APFAN) 01908

Contact address not obtained. T. +62222503051 – +62222503240. Fax +62222503240. E-mail: juliakan@indo.net.id.
History 31 Aug 1989, Brisbane (Australia), following discussion at an international chemistry conference called 'Chemistry International'. **Aims** Serve the needs of food analysts and thereby promote food safety and good *nutrition*. **Structure** Coordinator. Organizing Committee, consists of Coordinator and Country Contacts. Ad hoc Committee set up to organize each Conference or Workshop. Country contacts in most of the countries represented. **Finance** Grants for specific functions from agencies, usually aid agencies. **Activities** Holds annual hands-on workshops, conferences, short courses; provides standard food reference materials for developing country food laboratories worldwide. **Events** *Conference on Food Analysis* Indonesia 2001, *Workshop / Workshop on Food Analysis* Brisbane, QLD (Australia) 1999, *Conference / Conference on Food Analysis* Chiang Mai (Thailand) 1998, *Workshop / Workshop on Food Analysis* Brisbane, QLD (Australia) 1997, *Workshop / Workshop on Food Analysis* Brisbane, QLD (Australia) 1996. **Publications** Conference proceedings.
Members Country Contacts and individuals (450) in 34 countries and territories:
Australia, Bangladesh, Brunei Darussalam, Canada, China, Ethiopia, Fiji, Hong Kong, India, Indonesia, Japan, Kenya, Korea DPR, Korea Rep, Macau, Malawi, Malaysia, Mongolia, Morocco, Mozambique, Nepal, New Zealand, Nigeria, Pakistan, Papua New Guinea, Philippines, Saudi Arabia, Singapore, Sri Lanka, Tanzania UR, Thailand, UK, Vietnam, Zimbabwe.
IGO Relations : *Australian Aid (inactive)*; *Australian Centre for International Agricultural Research (ACIAR)*; *Commonwealth Foundation (CF, #04330)*; *Commonwealth Secretariat (#04362)*; *FAO (#09260)*; *UNESCO (#20322)*; *United Nations University (UNU, #20642)*. **NGO Relations** : [2010/XF1685/**F**]

♦ Asia Pacific Foreign Exchange Congress (meeting series)

♦ Asia-Pacific Forestry Commission (APFC) 01909

Commission des forêts pour l'Asie et le Pacifique (CFAP) – Comisión Forestal para Asia y el Pacifico

Secretary Senior Forestry Officer – FAO Regional Office for Asia and the Pacific, 39 Phra Atit Road, Bangkok, 10200, Thailand. T. +6626974139. Fax +6626974445.
URL: http://www.fao.org/forestry/31089/en/
History Mar 1949, Mysore (India), at 5th session of Conference of *FAO (#09260)*, under Article VI-1 of FAO Constitution and in pursuance of a resolution of the *Forestry and Timber Utilization Conference for Asia and the Pacific*, Mar-Apr 1949, Mysore (India). 1st session Oct 1950, Bangkok (Thailand). Rules of Procedure adopted 1960, Delhi (India); amended: 1962, Hong Kong and 1977, Kathmandu (Nepal). Based at *FAO Regional Office for Asia and the Pacific (RAP, #09266)*. **Aims** Provide advice on forest policy formulation; review and coordinate implementation of forest policy at the regional level; exchange information on suitable practices and solutions for technical problems; develop appropriate recommendations on forestry-related issues for member governments and for FAO. **Structure** General Session (every 2 years). Executive Committee, consisting of Chairman, Vice-Chairmen, and Chairmen of subsidiary bodies. **Languages** English. **Activities** Discusses and analyzes forestry issues to promote environmentally sound and economically efficient technologies and to encourage implementation of appropriate policies in line with changing trends in forestry at the regional level; identifies key problems of regional significance; commissions studies of problems; determines strategic priorities; endorses and supports implementation of recommendations. Current major concerns: shift to devolution of forest management; environment and sustainability; financing for sustainable forest management. **Events** *Session* Incheon (Korea Rep) 2019, *Session* Philippines 2016, *Session* Rotorua (New Zealand) 2013, *Session* Beijing (China) 2011, *Session* Thimphu (Bhutan) 2010. **Publications** Studies; reports.
Members Open to all FAO members and associate members whose territories are situated wholly or partly in the Asia-Pacific Region or who are responsible for the international relations of any non-self-governing territory in that region, and who desire to be considered members. Currently governments of 33 countries:
Australia, Bangladesh, Bhutan, Cambodia, China, Fiji, France, India, Indonesia, Japan, Kiribati, Korea Rep, Laos, Malaysia, Maldives, Mongolia, Myanmar, Nepal, New Zealand, Pakistan, Papua New Guinea, Philippines, Russia, Samoa, Solomon Is, Sri Lanka, Thailand, Timor-Leste, Tonga, Tuvalu, USA, Vanuatu, Vietnam.
Observer 1 country:
UK. [2018/XE9622/**E***]

♦ Asia Pacific Forum / see Asia Pacific Federation of Project Management (#01904)

♦ Asia-Pacific Forum of Environmental Journalists (APFEJ) 01910

Secretariat 8K Guoying Apartment, 38 Houguangping Hutong, 100035 Beijing, China. T. +861066503517. Fax +861066503520.
History 23 Jan 1988, Bangkok (Thailand), *Asian Forum of Environmental Journalists (AFEJ)*, at Conference on Media and the Environment held under the auspices of *United Nations Economic and Social Commission for Asia and the Pacific (ESCAP, #20557)*. **Aims** Promote greater awareness of environmental issues among journalists in the Asian region; initiate dialogues with decision makers in the *media* with a view to giving greater emphasis to environmental issues; encourage greater exchange of ideas and information on environmental matters in the region; create a network of journalists in the Asian region to articulate public concern regarding the state of the environment. **Structure** General Body (annual). Executive Body, consisting of Chairman, 2 Vice-Chairmen, Secretary and the Executive Committee of 19 members. **Languages** English. **Staff** 9.00 FTE, paid. **Finance** Different donors support individual programs. Operational budget (annual): US$ 500,000. **Activities** Organizes: regional training workshops; seminars; study tours; journalist exchange programmes. consultancy service. Awards: regional fellowships; award for excellence in environmental reporting on a regional basis. Acts as an information clearing house. **Events** *Annual Congress* Islamabad (Pakistan) 2010, *Annual congress / Annual World Congress* Colombo (Sri Lanka) 2009, *Annual congress / Annual World Congress* Dhaka (Bangladesh) 2006, *Annual congress / Annual World Congress* Shenzhen (China) 2004, *Annual congress / Annual World Congress* Putrajaya (Malaysia) 2003. **Publications** *Conservation Asia* (6 a year). *Guidebook on Environmental Reporting* in Bengali, Chinese, English, Thai. Annual Report. Newsletters, investigative reports; seminar and congress reports. **Members** National fora; Associate members legally constituted international, regional and subregional organizations whose interests coincide with those of APFEJ. National fora, representing about 8,000 members, in 42 countries. Membership countries not specified. **NGO Relations** Member of: *International Union for Conservation of Nature and Natural Resources (IUCN, #15766)*. [2009/XF1305/**F**]

♦ Asia Pacific Forum for Graduate Students' Research in Tourism (meeting series)

♦ Asia Pacific Forum of National Human Rights Institutions (APF) ... 01911

Main Office Level 3, 175 Pitt Street, Sydney NSW 2000, Australia. E-mail: apf@asiapacificforum.net.
URL: http://www.asiapacificforum.net/
History 10 Jul 1996, Darwin (Australia), during the first Asia Pacific Regional Workshop of National Human Rights Institutions. **Aims** Facilitate formation and growth of national human rights institutions by providing training, networking and resource sharing. **Structure** Forum Council; Committees of Councillors; Secretariat, headed by Director. **Languages** Arabic, English. **Staff** 7.00 FTE, paid. **Finance** Major donors include: *European Union (EU, #08967)*; *Swedish International Development Cooperation Agency (Sida)*; Governments of Australia, India, Republic of Korea, Thailand. **Activities** Training/education; capacity building; guidance/assistance/consulting; networking/liaising. **Events** *Annual Meeting* Seoul (Korea Rep) 2019, *Annual Meeting* Hong Kong (Hong Kong) 2018, *Annual Meeting* Bangkok (Thailand) 2017, *Annual Meeting* Bangkok (Thailand) 2016, *Annual Meeting* Ulaanbaatar (Mongolia) 2015. **Publications** *APF Bulletin* (12 a year).
Members Institutions in 22 countries and territories:
Afghanistan, Australia, Bangladesh, India, Indonesia, Jordan, Kazakhstan, Korea Rep, Malaysia, Maldives, Mongolia, Myanmar, Nepal, New Zealand, Oman, Palestine, Philippines, Qatar, Samoa, Sri Lanka, Thailand, Timor-Leste. [2020/XF5675/**F**]

♦ Asia Pacific Forum on Women, Law and Development (APWLD) 01912

Regional Coordinator 189/3 Changklan Road, Amphoe Muang, Chiang Mai, 50100, Thailand. T. +6653284856 – +6653284527. Fax +6653280847. E-mail: apwld@apwld.org.
URL: https://apwld.org/
History Dec 1986. Founded after development from dialogues, beginning at 1985 Third World Forum on Women, Law and Development, Nairobi (Kenya). Formally established, Jan 1987. Secretariat relocated from Kuala Lumpur (Malaysia) to Chiang Mai (Thailand), Oct 1997. **Aims** Enable women in the Asia Pacific region to use law as an instrument of social change for equality, justice and development; promote the basic concept of human rights. **Structure** Regional Council (ReC); Programme and Management Committee (P and M); Organizing Committee; Secretariat. **Languages** English. **Staff** 24.00 FTE, paid. **Finance** Funding from: *European Union (EU, #08967)*; *Ford Foundation (#09858)*; Foundation for a Just Society (FJS); Foundation for a Just Society (FJS); *Norwegian Agency for Development Cooperation (Norad)*; *Swedish International Development Cooperation Agency (Sida)*. **Activities** Advocacy/lobbying/activism. Management of treaties and agreements: *Convention on the Elimination of all Forms of Discrimination Against Women (CEDAW, 1979)*; *United Nations Convention on the Rights of the Child (CRC, 1989)*; *United Nations Declaration on the Elimination of Violence Against Women (1993)*; *United Nations Framework Convention on Climate Change (UNFCCC, 1992)*; *Universal Declaration of Human Rights (UDHR, 1948)*. Instrumental in setting up and hosts: Asia Pacific Regional CSO Engagement Mechanism (APRCEM); Gender and Trade Coalition; *Southeast Asia Women's Caucus on ASEAN (WC, #19800)*. **Events** *Workshop on feminist counselling II* Chiang Mai (Thailand) 1999, *Workshop on women and decision making in Southeast Asia* Chiang Mai (Thailand) 1999, *Asian women conference* Chiang Mai (Thailand) 1998, *Asian rural and indigenous women conference* Chiang Mai (Thailand) 1997, *Regional forum* Bangkok (Thailand) 1996. **Publications** Resource books; proceedings; training programmes; workshop reports; task force reports; briefings; research reports.
Members Participating women from 27 countries and territories:
Bangladesh, Cambodia, China, Cook Is, Fiji, Hong Kong, India, Indonesia, Japan, Kazakhstan, Korea Rep, Kyrgyzstan, Laos, Malaysia, Mongolia, Myanmar, Nepal, Pakistan, Papua New Guinea, Philippines, Solomon Is, Sri Lanka, Tajikistan, Thailand, Timor-Leste, Vanuatu, Vietnam.
Consultative Status Consultative status granted from: *ECOSOC (#05331)* (Special); *UNCTAD (#20285)* (Special). **IGO Relations** *Asian and Pacific Development Centre (APDC, #01608)*; Asia Pacific Forum on Sustainable Development (APFSD); *Green Climate Fund (GCF, #10714)*; *UN Women (#20724)*; *United Nations Commission on Sustainable Development (CSD, inactive)*; *United Nations Framework Convention on Climate Change – Secretariat (UNFCCC, #20564)*; *United Nations Office at Vienna (UNOV, #20604)*; *WomenWatch (#21040)*.
NGO Relations Member of:
- *Asia Japan Women's Resource Centre (AJWRC)*;
- *Asia Pacific Women's Watch (APWW, #02077)*;
- *Asian-Pacific Resource and Research Centre for Women (ARROW, #01629)*;
- *Asian Women's Resource Exchange (AWORC, no recent information)*;
- *Centre for Asia-Pacific Women in Politics (CAPWIP, #03731)*;
- *Center for Women's Global Leadership (CWGL)*;
- *Climate Justice Now ! (CJN!, inactive)*;
- *Coalition Against Trafficking in Women (CATW, #04047)*;
- *Equality Now (#05518)*;
- *Equitas – International Centre for Human Rights Education*;
- *Global Alliance Against Traffic in Women (GAATW, #10184)*;
- *Human Rights Watch (HRW, #10990)*;
- *International Network for Economic, Social and Cultural Rights (ESCR-Net, #14255)*;
- *IO – Facilitating Space for Feminist Conversations (Io, #16005)*;
- *Just Net Coalition (JNC, #16173)*;
- *Latin American and Caribbean Committee for the Defense of Women's Rights (#16268)*;
- *People's Coalition on Food Sovereignty (PCFS, #18303)*;
- *Women in Law and Development in Africa-Afrique de l'Ouest (WiLDAF-AO, #21005)*;
- *Women, Law and Development International (WLDI, inactive)*;
- *Women's Environment and Development Organization (WEDO, #21016)*. [2023/XF0918/v/**F**]

♦ Asia Pacific Foundation of Canada (internationally oriented national body)
♦ Asia Pacific Foundation for Infectious Diseases (internationally oriented national body)

♦ Asia Pacific Franchise Confederation (APFC) 01913

Secretariat c/o PFA, Unit 701 OMM Citra Bldg, San Miguel Avenue, Ortigas Center, Pasig City RIZ, Philippines. E-mail: exec.dir@pfa.org.ph.
URL: http://franchise-apfc.org/
History Founded 24 Sep 1998, Malaysia. Registered under the Registrar of Society Malaysia, 30 Mar 2005. **Aims** Provide a forum with properly constituted national franchise associations in the Asia Pacific region for sharing of experience, information and technical know-how on franchising; establish better communication channels among members; encourage further development of properly constituted national franchise associations in all countries in the region in order to strengthen industry networking regionally; present regional information on franchising and the common views of national franchise associations within the region to international bodies. **Structure** Meeting (annual); secretariat rotates countries. Full membership open to all national franchise associations in the Asia Pacific region, usually one association per country being recognized but exceptions considered on case by case basis. **Languages** English. **Activities** Events/meetings. **Events** *Annual Franchising Meeting* Taipei (Taiwan) 2014, *Meeting* Kuala Lumpur (Malaysia) 2013, *Meeting* Auckland (New Zealand) 2012, *Meeting* Manila (Philippines) 2011, *Meeting* Seoul (Korea Rep) 2010. **Publications** *Asia Pacific Franchise Directory*.
Members Full national franchise associations in 12 countries and territories:
Australia, China, Hong Kong, India, Indonesia, Japan, Korea Rep, Malaysia, New Zealand, Philippines, Singapore, Taiwan.
NGO Relations Member of: *World Franchise Council (WFC, #21529)*. [2020/XM0130/**D**]

♦ Asia Pacific Free Methodist Missions Association (APFMMA) 01914

Main Office Rm 1602, QPL Ind Bldg, 126-140 Texaco Rd, Tsuen Wan, Hong Kong. T. +85227419020.
Structure General Council; Executive Committee. [2016/XM3966/**D**]

♦ Asia-Pacific Gastroenterology Cancer Summit (meeting series)

♦ Asia Pacific General Galvanizing Association (APGGA) 01915

Secretariat Galvanizers Assn of Australia, Level 5/124 Exhibition Str, Melbourne VIC 3000, Australia. T. +61396541266. E-mail: gaa@gaa.com.au.
URL: https://galvanizingasia.com/
Events *Asia Pacific General Galvanizing Conference* Yokohama (Japan) 2023, *Asia Pacific General Galvanizing Conference* Yokohama (Japan) 2022, *Znchronize Asia for the future* Bangkok (Thailand) 2019, *Conference* Bali (Indonesia) 2016, *Conference* Singapore (Singapore) 2013.
Members National associations in 7 countries and territories:
Australia, China, Indonesia, Japan, Malaysia, Taiwan, Thailand.
Associate in 3 countries:
Malaysia, Philippines, Thailand. [2021/XJ6967/**D**]

♦ Asia-Pacific Gene Therapy Consortium (unconfirmed)

♦ **Asia Pacific Geoparks Network (APGN)** **01916**

Secretariat 26 Baiwanzhuang Road, 100037 Beijing, China. E-mail: apgn.office@vip.163.com.
URL: https://asiapacificgeoparks.org/

Aims Provide a networking platform between stakeholders of established geoparks and geosites (for those without a geopark) with stakeholders of geoheritage sites to facilitate the establishment of future geoparks and improve geoheritage and geoparks governance. **Structure** Advisory Committee; Coordination Committee; Secretariat. **Activities** Events/meetings. **Events** *Symposium* Satun (Thailand) 2022, *Geoparks Niigata International Forum* Niigata (Japan) 2016.
Members Global Geoparks in 8 countries:
China, Indonesia, Iran Islamic Rep, Japan, Korea Rep, Malaysia, Thailand, Vietnam.
NGO Relations Regional network of: *Global Geoparks Network (GGN, #10389).* [2023.02.14/XM5462/**F**]

♦ **Asia-Pacific Glaucoma Society (APGS)** **01917**

Exec Office c/o MCI, Level 11, Wickham Terrace, Spring Hill QLD 4000, Australia. T. +61738585400. E-mail: info@apglaucomasociety.org.
URL: https://apglaucomasociety.org/

History Set up, when *South East Asia Glaucoma Interest Group (SEAGIG, inactive), Asian-Oceanic Glaucoma Society (AOGS, inactive)* and *Asian Angle-Closure Glaucoma Club (AACGC, #01307),* joined and signed agreement Mar 2011, Sydney (Australia). AACGC still functions as umbrella society. **Aims** Facilitate contact between glaucoma specialists in the region; encourage collaborative research and service projects; increase opportunities for exchange of skills and knowledge in the field; assist ophthalmological colleagues and other eye care workers (whether medically trained or not) to be up-to-date with advances in all aspects of glaucoma diagnosis and management. **Structure** Annual General Meeting; Board; Executive Committee. **Finance** Members' dues. **Activities** Networking/liaising; awards/prizes/competitions; standards/guidelines; events/meetings; training/education. **Events** *Asia-Pacific Glaucoma Congress (APGC)* Kuala Lumpur (Malaysia) 2022, *Congress* Spring Hill, QLD (Australia) 2021, *Congress* Kuala Lumpur (Malaysia) 2020, *Congress* Busan (Korea Rep) 2018, *Congress* Chiang Mai (Thailand) 2016. **Members** Individuals. Membership countries not specified.
NGO Relations Member of: *Asia-Pacific Academy of Ophthalmology (APAO, #01814); International Council of Ophthalmology (ICO, #13057); World Glaucoma Association (WGA, #21540).* [2020/XJ5967/**D**]

♦ **Asia Pacific Golf Confederation (APGC)** **01918**

Chairman Golf Australia, Level 3, 95 Coventry St, Melbourne VIC 3205, Australia. E-mail: info@golfaustralia.org.au.
Sec address not obtained.
URL: https://www.apgc.online/

History 1963. **Aims** Furhter the bonds of friendship among member associations as well as other represnetative organizations in golf throughout the world through friendly competition in golf. **Publications** *APGC News.*
Members National golf unions in 17 countries:
Australia, Hong Kong, India, Indonesia, Japan, Korea Rep, Malaysia, Myanmar, New Zealand, Pakistan, Papua New Guinea, Philippines, Singapore, Sri Lanka, Taiwan, Thailand, Vietnam. [2016/XD8430/**D**]

♦ **Asia-Pacific Greens Federation (APGF)** **01919**

Sec Coordinating Committee c/o Australian Greens, Victoria, GPO Box 4589, Melbourne VIC 3001, Australia. T. +61396021141 – +613(61412421763. Fax +61396021655.
URL: http://www.asiapacificgreens.org/

History Founded Feb 2005, Kyoto (Japan), as *Asia-Pacific Greens Network (APGN).* **Aims** Strengthen networking of Asia-Pacific Green parties and green-oriented groups; cooperate towards implementation of the Global Greens Charter; participate in Global Greens. **Structure** Network of Green Parties and mouvements in the Asia-Pacific region, and one of the 4 regional federations of the Global Greens. Congress (every 5 years); Coordinating Committee; Working Committees; Action Groups. Regional network of: *Global Geoparks Network (GGN, #10389).* **Languages** English. **Activities** Carries out joint Asia-Pacific wide campaigns on Global Greens Charter related issues; organizations training workshops; issues public statements on current events. **Events** *Congress* Taipei (Taiwan) 2010, *Congress* Kyoto (Japan) 2005.
Members Full Green Parties (14) in 12 countries and territories:
Australia, Hong Kong, India, Japan, Korea Rep, Mongolia, Nepal, New Zealand, Pakistan, Papua New Guinea, Philippines, Taiwan.
Associate Green Parties and political mouvements (4) in 4 countries:
Australia, Nepal, Philippines, Sri Lanka.
Friends Green Parties or political movements in 3 countries:
China, Indonesia, Nepal.
NGO Relations Through *Global Greens (#10394),* links with: *African Greens Federation (AGF, #00331); Federación de Partidos Verdes de las Américas (FPVA, #09385).* Affiliated with: Asia Pacific Young Greens Network (APYGN). Various member groups are NGOs. [2012/XM3183/**F**]

♦ Asia-Pacific Greens Network / see Asia-Pacific Greens Federation (#01919)

♦ **Asia Pacific Grouping of Consulting Engineers (ASPAC)** **01920**

Chair c/o Cheil Engineering Co Ltd, 22-6 Gangnamdaero 16gil, Seocho-gu, Seoul 06779, Korea Rep.
URL: http://www.fidic.org/aspac/

History 1979, as a regional grouping of *International Federation of Consulting Engineers (#13399).* **Aims** Represent the consulting engineering industry in Asia and the Pacific as a regional grouping of FIDIC member associations. **Structure** General Assembly (in conjunction with FIDIC Conference); Executive Committee; Sub-Committees (4); Secretariat, headed by Chairman. **Languages** English. **Staff** 2.00 FTE, paid. **Finance** Members' dues. **Activities** Events/meetings; knowledge management/information dissemination. **Events** *International Seminar on Underwater Tunnels between Korea and the Middle East* Cheonan (Korea Rep) 2018, *Engineering Forum* Seoul (Korea Rep) 2018, *Annual Conference* Queenstown (New Zealand) 2016, *General Assembly* Dubai (United Arab Emirates) 2015, *Annual Conference* Teheran (Iran Islamic Rep) 2015. **Publications** *ASPAC Newsletter* (4 a year).
Members Groups FIDIC member associations in Asia and the Pacific region. Members in 23 countries:
Australia, Azerbaijan, Bangladesh, China, Hong Kong, India, Indonesia, Iran Islamic Rep, Japan, Kazakhstan, Korea Rep, Malaysia, Mongolia, Nepal, New Zealand, Pakistan, Philippines, Singapore, Sri Lanka, Taiwan, Thailand, Uzbekistan, Vietnam.
IGO Relations *Asian Development Bank (ADB, #01422); International Trade Centre (ITC, #15703).* [2015.09.07/XE1455/**E**]

♦ **Asia/Pacific Group on Money Laundering (APG)** **01921**

Groupe anti-blanchiment de l'Asie/Pacifique (GAP)

Exec Sec Asia/Pacific Group Secretariat, Locked Bag A3000, Sydney NSW 2000, Australia. T. +61251269110. E-mail: mail@apgml.org.
Street address 110 Goulburn Street, Sydney NSW 2000, Australia.
URL: http://www.apgml.org/

History Feb 1997. Regional body of *Financial Action Task Force (FATF, #09765).* **Aims** Fight money laundering, financing of terrorism and proliferation financing in the Asia/Pacific region. **Structure** Co-Chairs (2); Governance Committee; Evaluations Committee; Operations Committee; Working Groups; Secretariat. **Languages** English. **Staff** 24.00 FTE, paid. **Finance** Sources: grants; members' dues; revenue from activities/projects. Financial hosting support from Australian government. Annual budget: 5,000,000 AUD. **Activities** Events/meetings; monitoring/evaluation; research/documentation; standards/guidelines; training/education. Active in all member countries. **Events** *Annual Meeting* Kuala Lumpur (Malaysia) 2022, *Annual Meeting* Sydney, NSW (Australia) 2021, *Annual Meeting* Canberra, ACT (Australia) 2019, *Annual Meeting* Kathmandu (Nepal) 2018, *Seoul Workshop* Seoul (Korea Rep) 2018. **Publications** *Typologies Report* (annual). Annual Report.
Members Jurisdictions of 41 countries and territories:
Afghanistan, Australia, Bangladesh, Bhutan, Brunei Darussalam, Cambodia, Canada, China, Cook Is, Fiji, Hong Kong, India, Indonesia, Japan, Korea DPR, Laos, Macau, Malaysia, Maldives, Marshall Is, Mongolia, Myanmar, Nauru, Nepal, New Zealand, Niue, Pakistan, Palau, Papua New Guinea, Philippines, Samoa, Singapore, Solomon Is, Sri Lanka, Taiwan, Thailand, Timor-Leste, Tonga, USA, Vanuatu, Vietnam.
Observer jurisdictions in 8 countries:
France, Germany, Kiribati, Korea Rep, Micronesia FS, Russia, Tuvalu, UK.
International organizations (27):
– ADB/OECD Anti-Corruption Initiative for Asia/Pacific;
– *ASEAN (#01141);*
– *Asian Development Bank (ADB, #01422);*
– *Asia-Pacific Economic Cooperation (APEC, #01887);*
– *Asset Recovery Interagency Network – Asia Pacific (ARIN-AP, #02320);*
– *Committee of Experts on the Evaluation of Anti-Money Laundering Measures and the Financing of Terrorism (MONEYVAL, #04257);*
– *Commonwealth Secretariat (#04362);*
– *Eastern and Southern African Anti-Money Laundering Group (ESAAMLG, #05252);*
– *Egmont Group of Financial Intelligence Units (#05396);*
– *Eurasian Group on Combating Money Laundering and Financing of Terrorism (EAG, #05608);*
– *Financial Action Task Force (FATF, #09765);*
– *Groupe d'Action contre le Blanchiment d'Argent en Afrique Centrale (GABAC);*
– *Group of International Finance Centre Supervisors (GIFCS, #10782);*
– *Grupo de Acción Financiera de Latinoamérica (GAFILAT, #10799);*
– *Intergovernmental Action Group against Money Laundering in West Africa (#11471);*
– *International Bank for Reconstruction and Development (IBRD, #12317)* (World Bank);
– *International Criminal Police Organization – INTERPOL (ICPO-INTERPOL, #13110);*
– *International Monetary Fund (IMF, #14180);*
– *Middle East and North Africa Financial Action Task Force (MENAFATF, #16779);*
– *Oceania Customs Organisation (OCO, #17658);*
– *Pacific Financial Technical Assistance Centre (PFTAC, #17948);*
– *Pacific Islands Chiefs of Police (PICP, #17964);*
– *Pacific Islands Forum Secretariat (#17970);*
– *Pacific Islands Law Officers' Network (PILON, #17972);*
– *United Nations Office on Drugs and Crime (UNODC, #20596);*
– *United Nations (UN, #20515);*
– *World Customs Organization (WCO, #21350).* [2022.11.29/XK1497/y/**E***]

♦ **Asia-Pacific Heads of Maritime Safety Agencies (APHoMSA)** **01922**

Secretariat address not obtained. E-mail: aphomsa@amsa.gov.au.
URL: http://www.amsa.gov.au/aphomsa/

History 1 May 1996, as an informal entity. Since 2014, Cairns (Australia), more structured. **Aims** Promote safe, secure shipping and a clean marine environment within the Asia-Pacific region. **Activities** Events/meetings. **Events** *Session* Seoul (Korea Rep) 2019, *Session* Viña del Mar (Chile) 2018, *Session* Langkawi (Malaysia) 2017, *Session* Queenstown (New Zealand) 2016, *Session* Shenzhen (China) 2015.
Members Heads of maritime agencies of 23 countries and territories:
Australia, Canada, Chile, China, Cook Is, Fiji, Hong Kong, Indonesia, Japan, Kiribati, Korea Rep, Malaysia, Micronesia FS, New Caledonia, New Zealand, Niue, Papua New Guinea, Philippines, Singapore, Solomon Is, Tuvalu, USA, Vietnam.
Observer organizations include:
ILO (#11123); International Association of Marine Aids to Navigation and Lighthouse Authorities (IALA, #12013); International Hydrographic Organization (IHO, #13825); International Maritime Organization (IMO, #14102); Memorandum of Understanding on Port State Control in the Asia-Pacific Region (Tokyo MOU, #16709); Pacific Community (SPC, #17942); Regional Cooperation Agreement on Combating Piracy and Armed Robbery against Ships in Asia – Information Sharing Centre (ReCAAP ISC, #18771); Secretariat of the Pacific Regional Environment Programme (SPREP, #19205). [2016/XM5066/**F**]

♦ Asia Pacific Heart Association (unconfirmed)

♦ **Asia-Pacific Heart Network (APHN)** **01923**

Red Pacifico Asiatica del Corazón

Secretariat Singapore Heart Foundation, 9 Bishan Place, 07-01 Junction 8 – Office Tower, Singapore 579837, Singapore. T. +6563549340. Fax +6562585240. E-mail: aphn@heart.org.sg.
URL: http://www.aphn.info/

History 28 Aug 1998, Singapore (Singapore). **Aims** Promote an environment through the Asia Pacific region conducive to the reduction of morbidity from *cardiovascular* disease; facilitate the growth of heart foundations and associations, their role in public and professional education, public advocacy and fundraising; foster partnership between health professionals and other sectors of society. **Structure** Board of Directors, comprising President, Vice-President, Secretary/Treasurer and 3 members at large. Executive Director. **Languages** English. **Finance** Members' dues: US$ 300. Annual grant from: *World Heart Federation (WHF, #21562).* **Activities** Coordinating role in especially WHF led initiatives. **Events** *Meeting* Mexico City (Mexico) 2016, *Meeting* Beijing (China) 2010, *Meeting* Kyoto (Japan) 2009, *Meeting* Buenos Aires (Argentina) 2008, *Meeting* Taipei (Taiwan) 2007. **Publications** *APHN Newsletter* (4 a year).
Members Full in 19 countries and territories:
Australia, Bangladesh, Hong Kong, India, Indonesia, Japan, Korea Rep, Kuwait, Malaysia, Nepal, New Zealand, Pakistan, Philippines, Saudi Arabia, Singapore, Sri Lanka, Taiwan, Thailand, Vietnam.
NGO Relations Member of: *The NCD Alliance (NCDA, #16963); World Heart Federation (WHF, #21562).* [2018/XF5772/**F**]

♦ **Asia Pacific Heart Rhythm Society (APHRS)** **01924**

Pres 101 Thomson Road, Suite 06-01, United Square, Singapore 307591, Singapore. T. +6568295365. E-mail: office@aphrs.org – admin@aphrs.org.
URL: http://www.aphrs.org/

History Founded 2008. **Aims** Promote scientific exchanges, education and training of medical, paramedical and allied professionals, and technological development in the research of care of heart rhythm disorders. **Languages** English. **Finance** Members' dues. **Events** *Scientific Session* Hong Kong (Hong Kong) 2020, *Scientific Session* Bangkok (Thailand) 2019, *Scientific Session* Taipei (Taiwan) 2018, *Scientific Session* Yokohama (Japan) 2017, *Scientific Session* Seoul (Korea Rep) 2016. **Publications** *Journal of Arrhythmia.* [2021/XJ0315/**D**]

♦ **Asia Pacific Hematology Consortium (APHCON)** **01925**

Exec Dir Inst of Hematology, Peking Univ, 11 Xizhimen South St, 100044 Beijing, China. T. +861088326006. E-mail: xjhrm@medmail.com.cn.
URL: http://aphcon-org.pautus.com/

History Set up 2011, Singapore. **Aims** Advance the field of hematology oncology through continued education, collaboration and fostering innovations. **Structure** Executive Committee. **Finance** Sources: members' dues. **Activities** Awards/prizes/competitions; events/meetings; training/education. **Events** *International Hematologic Malignancies Conference* Fuzhou (China) 2019, *International Hematologic Malignancies Conference* Seoul (Korea Rep) 2018, *International Hematologic Malignancies Conference* Bangkok (Thailand) 2017. **Members** Active; Honorary; Emeritus; Institutional; Corporate. Membership countries not specified. [2019/XM6702/**C**]

♦ **Asia Pacific Hernia Society (APHS)** **01926**

Founder/Pres Minimally Invasive Surgical Ctr, Dept of Surgery, Natl Univ Hosp, 5 Lower Kent Ridge Road, Singapore 119074, Singapore.

History 29 Sep 2004, Bali (Indonesia). Registration: Start date: 2005, Singapore. **Aims** Provide a professional forum for the exchange of information and education regarding current and future methods of diagnosis and treatment of hernia, including hiatal, parastomal, and pelvic hernias. **Structure** General Meeting (annual); Executive Committee. **Finance** Members' dues. **Activities** Events/meetings; training/education; projects/programmes. **Events** *International Congress* Nusa Dua (Indonesia) 2019, *International Congress* Dubai (United Arab Emirates) 2018, *International Congress* Kaohsiung (Taiwan) 2017, *International Congress* Tokyo (Japan) 2016, *International Congress* Milan (Italy) 2015. **Publications** Newsletter.
Members Full; Corporate; Honorary. Full National Hernia Societies in 11 countries and territories:
China, Hong Kong, India, Indonesia, Japan, Korea Rep, Philippines, Singapore, Taiwan, Thailand, United Arab Emirates. [2019/XM3724/**D**]

♦ **Asia Pacific Histocompatibility and Immunogenetics Association (APHIA)** **01927**

Main Office 397 Smith Street, Ste 9, Fitzroy VIC 3065, Australia. T. +61385689530. Fax +61385689531. E-mail: president@aphia.org.au – secretary@aphia.org.au – aphia@asnevents.net.au.
URL: http://www.aphia.org.au/

History 1975. Statutes amended: 2001; 2010. Former names and other names: *Australasian Tissue Typing Association (ATTA)* – former (1975 to 1983); *Australasian and Southeast Asian Tissue Typing Association (ASEATTA)* – former (1983 to 2010). **Aims** Promote, encourage and assist the study of tissue typing, immunogenetics and transplantation immunology; provide research facilities, grants, quality control, standardization and other support for research into the above subjects; educate the public and the medical profession as to the necessity for a coordinated approach to the provision of facilities for the above subjects; establish, encourage and contribute to scholarships, fellowships and travel grants for the purposes of promoting or encouraging any of the objects of the Association; become a member of or subscribe to any other association, whether incorporated or not, having objects wholly, or in part, similar to those of the Association; provide expert opinion to government, private organizations or instrumentalities on matters related to the above subjects and related areas. **Structure** Council. Officers: President; Secretary/Treasurer. **Languages** English. **Staff** Voluntary. **Finance** Members' dues. Proceeds. **Activities** Organizes annual scientific meeting; provides assurance programme in histocompatibility and immunogenetics; runs annual International Summer School; provides support. **Events** *Scientific Conference* Delhi (India) 2021, *Scientific Conference* Delhi (India) 2020, *Annual Scientific Meeting* Sydney, NSW (Australia) 2018, *Annual Scientific Meeting* Bangkok (Thailand) 2015, *Annual Scientific Meeting* Melbourne, VIC (Australia) 2014.
Members Associations in 14 countries and territories:
Australia, Hong Kong, India, Indonesia, Japan, Malaysia, Mongolia, New Zealand, Papua New Guinea, Philippines, Singapore, South Africa, Thailand, USA. [2020/XD1962/**D**]

♦ Asia Pacific Hospice Palliative Care Network (APHN) 01928

Main Office c/o Div of Palliative Care, National Cancer Ctr, 11 Hospital Crescent, Singapore 169610, Singapore. T. +6562355166. Fax +6567250905. E-mail: aphn@aphn.org.
URL: http://www.aphn.org/
History May 2001, Taipei (Taiwan). Founded following a series of meetings since 1995. Registration: No/ID: 01713, Singapore. **Aims** Promote access to quality hospice and palliative care for all in the Asia Pacific region. **Structure** General Meeting (annual); Council. **Languages** English. **Staff** 2.00 FTE, paid. **Activities** Networking/liaising; guidance/assistance/consulting. **Events** *Asia Pacific Hospice Conference (APHC)* Korea Rep 2023, *Asia Pacific Hospice Conference (APHC)* Kobe (Japan) 2021, *Biennial Conference* Surabaya (Indonesia) 2019, *Biennial Conference* Singapore (Singapore) 2017, *Biennial Conference / Annual Meeting* Taipei (Taiwan) 2015.
Members Individual; ordinary organizational; affiliated organizational. Members in 31 countries and territories:
Australia, Bangladesh, Brunei Darussalam, Cambodia, Canada, China, Hong Kong, India, Indonesia, Iran Islamic Rep, Japan, Korea Rep, Macau, Malaysia, Mongolia, Myanmar, Nepal, New Zealand, Pakistan, Papua New Guinea, Philippines, Saudi Arabia, Singapore, Sri Lanka, Taiwan, Thailand, Uganda, UK, United Arab Emirates, USA, Vietnam. [2021/XM1623/**F**]

♦ Asia Pacific Human Rights Information Center (internationally oriented national body)

♦ Asia-Pacific Implant Society (APIS) 01929

Address not obtained.
History 2002. Former names and other names: *Pan-Pacific Implant Society (PPIS)* – former. **Languages** English. **Staff** Part-time, voluntary. **Finance** Members' dues. Donations. **Events** *Annual Meeting* Seoul (Korea Rep) 2022, *Annual Meeting* Taipei (Taiwan) 2020, *Annual Meeting* Tsukuba (Japan) 2019, *Meeting* Seoul (Korea Rep) 2017, *Meeting* Toyama City (Japan) 2017. **Members** Membership countries not specified. [2021/XJ0237/**D**]

♦ Asia Pacific Indigenous Youth Network (unconfirmed)

♦ Asia Pacific Industrial Engineering and Management Society (APIEMS) 01930

Pres address not obtained.
URL: http://www.apiems.org/
History 1999, Kanazawa (Japan) at 2nd conference. **Aims** Foster better professional understanding of industrialization. **Structure** Board; Executive Committee. **Languages** English. **Staff** None. **Finance** Self-financed. **Activities** Awards/prizes/competitions; events/meetings; publishing activities. **Events** *Conference* Kanazawa (Japan) 2019, *Conference* Hong Kong (Hong Kong) 2018, *Conference* Yogyakarta (Indonesia) 2017, *Conference* Taipei (Taiwan) 2016, *Conference* Ho Chi Minh City (Vietnam) 2015. **Publications** *Industrial Engineering and Management Systems (IEMS)* – official journal.
Members Full in 12 countries and territories:
Australia, China, Hong Kong, India, Indonesia, Japan, Korea Rep, Malaysia, Philippines, Taiwan, Thailand, Vietnam.
International organization members include 1 listed in this Yearbook:
IGO Relations None. **NGO Relations** None. [2019/XJ1259/t/**D**]

♦ Asia Pacific Information Network (APIN) 01931

Contact UNESCO Bangkok Office, 920 Sukhumvit Road, Bangkok, 10110, Thailand. T. +6623910577. Fax +6623910866.
URL: http://www.unescobkk.org/communication-and-information/
History 13 Dec 2002, Bangkok (Thailand), by *UNESCO (#20322)*, by merger of *Regional Informatics Network in South and Central Asia (RINSCA, inactive)*, *Regional Informatics Network for Southeast Asia and the Pacific (RINSEAP, inactive)* and *Regional Network for the Exchange of Information and Experience in Science and Technology in Asia and the Pacific (ASTINFO, inactive)*. Guided by *Information for All Programme (IFAP, see: #20322)*, launched 1 Jan 2001, in accordance with APIN's mandate to promote free flow of ideas. **Aims** Support development of technical and organizational infrastructure for the production of local content and sharing of indigenous knowledge; promote information and knowledge networking at local, national and regional levels; support programs on information, media and ICT literacy, including training, continuing education and lifelong learning; develop guidelines of information policies and promote ICT applications in support of national development plans; build consensus on basic principles on the ethical, legal and societal aspects of ICT applications and promote the use of international standards and best practices in communication, information and informatics; develop and promote standards and management tools and support capacity building programs for the preservation of documentary heritage. **Structure** Coordination Committee, including Chairperson. **Languages** English. **Staff** Managed by Communication and Information Unit of UNESCO Bangkok Office. **Finance** Financed by Regular Programme budget of UNESCO. **Activities** Strategies (5): Information Accessibility; Information Literacy; Information for Development; Information Ethics; Information Preservation. **Events** *Session* Manila (Philippines) 2010, *Session* Hanoi (Vietnam) 2008, *Session* Kuala Lumpur (Malaysia) 2006, *Session* Beijing (China) 2004, *Session* Bangkok (Thailand) 2002.
Members Full in 19 countries:
Bhutan, China, Fiji, India, Indonesia, Iran Islamic Rep, Japan, Korea DPR, Korea Rep, Laos, Malaysia, Maldives, Mongolia, Nepal, New Zealand, Philippines, Sri Lanka, Thailand, Vietnam. [2012.08.20/XF6848/**F**]

♦ Asia-Pacific Initiative on Reproduction (ASPIRE) 01932

Main Office 126 Joo Seng Road, Gold Pine Ind Bldg #08-07, Singapore 368355, Singapore. E-mail: secretariat@aspire-reproduction.org.
URL: http://www.aspire-reproduction.org/
History 2001. **Aims** Promote awareness of infertility and assisted reproductive technology; improve quality of infertility-related services in the Asia-Pacific region. **Structure** Management Board; Executive Board; Country Representatives. **Languages** English. **Events** *Congress* Adelaide, SA (Australia) 2023, *Congress* 2022, *Congress* 2021, *Congress* Manila (Philippines) 2020, *Congress* Hong Kong (Hong Kong) 2019. **Publications** *Fertility and Sterility* – Asia-Pacific edition. [2022/XM3575/**F**]

♦ Asia Pacific Innovation Network (AP-IN) 01933

Contact address not obtained. E-mail: apic@swin.edu.au.
URL: http://ap-ic.org/
History Founded Jan 2010. **Aims** Bring together scholars in the Asia Pacific region interested in the legal, managerial and economic aspects of innovation. **Structure** Scientific Committee; Management Committee. **Languages** English. **Staff** 12.00 FTE, paid. **Finance** Source: contracts. **Events** *Asia-Pacific Innovation Conference* ZhenJiang (China) 2021, *Asia-Pacific Innovation Conference* Incheon (Korea Rep) 2020, *Asia-Pacific Innovation Conference* Beijing (China) 2019, *Asia-Pacific Innovation Conference* Delhi (India) 2018, *Asia-Pacific Innovation Conference* Wellington (New Zealand) 2017.
Members Individuals in 7 countries and territories:
Australia, Japan, Korea Rep, New Zealand, Singapore, Taiwan, USA. [2014.06.01/XJ2309/v/**F**]

♦ Asia-Pacific Institute for Broadcasting Development (AIBD) 01934

Institut de l'Asie et du Pacifique pour le développement des émissions radiophoniques
Dir PO Box 12066, 50766 Kuala Lumpur, Malaysia. T. +60322824618 – +60322823719. Fax +60322822761. E-mail: admin@aibd.org.my.
Street adress 2nd Floor, Bangunan IPPTAR Lama, Angkasapuri, Jalan Pantai Dalam, 50614 Kuala Lumpur, Malaysia.
URL: https://aibd.org.my/
History 12 Aug 1977, Kuala Lumpur (Malaysia). Established, under the auspices of UNESCO, on signature of an Agreement by participating countries; Agreement entered into force on 6 Mar 1981. Had previously operated from 1972 with the assistance of UNESCO, UNDP, CFTC, IPDC and a number of funding/aid agencies. **Aims** Achieve a vibrant and cohesive electronic media environment in the Asia Pacific region through policy and resource development. **Structure** General Conference, consisting of 11 member countries with voting rights, *Asia-Pacific Broadcasting Union (ABU, #01863)*, *Commonwealth Fund for Technical Cooperation (CFTC, #04331)*, *International Telecommunication Union (ITU, #15673)*, *UNDP (#20292)*, *UNESCO (#20322)*, and representatives of private or public funding organizations invited to the meetings of the Governing Council without voting rights. **Staff** 18.00 FTE, paid. **Finance** Members' dues (annual, voluntary). Other sources: International Programme Support; fees from services. **Activities** Training/education; events/meetings; research and development; knowledge management/information dissemination; guidance/assistance/consulting. **Events** *Annual Asia Media Summit* Suva (Fiji) 2022, *Regional Seminar on Community Media Centres* Seoul (Korea Rep) 2019, *Annual Asia Media Summit* Siem Reap (Cambodia) 2019, *Annual Asia Media Summit* Seoul (Korea Rep) 2016, *General Conference* Chiang Mai (Thailand) 2015. **Publications** *The Broadcaster Newsletter*. Books; manuals; presentations.
Members Governments of 26 countries:
Afghanistan, Bangladesh, Bhutan, Brunei Darussalam, Cambodia, China, Fiji, France, India, Indonesia, Iran Islamic Rep, Korea Rep, Laos, Malaysia, Maldives, Micronesia FS, Myanmar, Nepal, Pakistan, Papua New Guinea, Philippines, Samoa, Singapore, Sri Lanka, Thailand, Vietnam.
Affiliate members (52) in 32 countries and territories:
Australia, Canada, Fiji, France, Germany, Hong Kong, India, Indonesia, Italy, Kazakhstan, Kyrgyzstan, Macau, Malaysia, Mauritius, Micronesia FS, Mongolia, Netherlands, Pakistan, Palestine, Papua New Guinea, Philippines, Qatar, Russia, Solomon Is, Sri Lanka, Tanzania UR, Timor-Leste, Tonga, Türkiye, UK, USA, Vanuatu.
Included in the above, 9 organizations listed in this Yearbook:
Commonwealth Educational Media Centre for Asia (CEMCA, #04322); *International Academy of Television Arts and Sciences (IATAS)*; *Inter Press Service (IPS, #15964)*; *Pacific Islands News Association (PINA, #17975)*; *Prix Jeunesse*; *Public Media Alliance (PMA, #18568)*; *Radio France internationale (RFI)*; *South Asian Free Media Association (SAFMA, #19731)*; *TV5Monde (TV5, #20269)*.
IGO Relations *Asia-Pacific Telecommunity (APT, #02064)*; *Commonwealth of Learning (COL, #04346)*; *International Programme for the Development of Communication (IPDC, #14651)*. *UNESCO Office, Jakarta – Regional Bureau for Sciences in Asia and the Pacific (#20313)*; *UNESCO Office for the Pacific States (#20315)*. **NGO Relations** *ARTICLE 19 (#01121)*; *Asian Media Information and Communication Centre (AMIC, #01536)*; *International Planned Parenthood Federation (IPPF, #14589)*; *International Radio and Television Union (#14689)*; *Public Broadcasters International (PBI, #18563)*. [2022/XE0470/y/**F***]

♦ Asia Pacific Institute for Democratization and Development (internationally oriented national body)
♦ Asia Pacific International Congress of Anatomists (meeting series)

♦ Asia-Pacific International Molecular Biology Network (A-IMBN) . . . 01935

Contact address not obtained. T. +8228728016. Fax +8228826702. E-mail: hjlee@a-imbn.org.
URL: http://www.a-imbn.org/
History 1997. **Aims** Promote study, research, innovation, development and dissemination of knowledge in molecular biology and genetic engineering and directly related areas of science and technology; undertake facilities and training programmes in the field of molecular biology. **Activities** Organizes conferences, workshops and training courses. **Events** *Conference* Cheonan (Korea Rep) 2015, *Conference* Manila (Philippines) 2014, *Conference* Singapore (Singapore) 2013, *Conference* Bangkok (Thailand) 2012, *Conference* Shanghai (China) 2012.
Members Full (157); Associate (28). Individuals in 15 countries and territories:
Australia, China, Hong Kong, India, Indonesia, Israel, Japan, Korea Rep, Malaysia, New Zealand, Philippines, Singapore, Switzerland, Taiwan, Thailand.
IGO Relations Cooperates with: *Islamic World Educational, Scientific and Cultural Organization (ICESCO, #16058)*. **NGO Relations** *Asia Pacific Bioinformatics Network (APBioNet, #01858)*. [2016/XF5807/**F**]

♦ Asia Pacific International Spirits and Wines Alliance (unconfirmed)
♦ Asia-Pacific International Symposium on Aerospace Technology (meeting series)
♦ Asia-Pacific International Symposium on the Basics and Applications of Plasma Technology (meeting series)

♦ Asia and Pacific Internet Association (APIA) 01936

Chair APIA Secretariat, PO Box 12600, 50784 Kuala Lumpur, Malaysia. E-mail: apiasec@apia.org.
Sec address not obtained.
URL: http://www.apia.org/
History 1997. Between 2004-2018, organized *Asia Pacific Regional Internet Conference on Operational Technology (APRICOT, inactive)*. **Aims** Promote business interest of commercial internet industry in Asia Pacific region. **Structure** General Assembly (annual). Board of Directors. **Events** *APRICOT : Asia Pacific Regional Internet Conference on Operational Technologies* Kathmandu (Nepal) 2018, *EnterpriseIT : International Information Technology for the Enterprise Conference* Singapore (Singapore) 2018, *APRICOT : Asia Pacific Regional Internet Conference on Operational Technologies* Ho Chi Minh City (Vietnam) 2017, *EnterpriseIT : International Information Technology for the Enterprise Conference* Singapore (Singapore) 2017, *EnterpriseIT : International Information Technology for the Enterprise Conference* Singapore (Singapore) 2016. **Publications** *APIA Newsletter* (3 a year). **Consultative Status** Consultative status granted from: *World Intellectual Property Organization (WIPO, #21593)* (Permanent Observer Status). **NGO Relations** Memorandum of Understanding with (1): *South Asian Network Operators Group (SANOG, #19737)*. Cooperates with (1): *Asia Pacific Network Operators Group (APNOG, #01972)*. Member of: *DotAsia Organisation (DotAsia, #05124)*. [2015/XD6522/**D**]

♦ Asia Pacific Intraocular Implant Association / see Asia-Pacific Association of Cataract and Refractive Surgeons (#01833)

♦ Asia-Pacific Islands Rural Advisory Services Network (APIRAS) . . . 01937

Focal Person GFRAS Asia-Pacific Islands, College of Public Affairs and Development, Univ of the Philippines, 4031 Los Baños LAG, Philippines. E-mail: apirasnet2017@gmail.com.
URL: https://www.facebook.com/groups/112822645452033/
History Formally organized Sep 2011, Los Baños (Philippines), during Regional Forum on Strengthening Rural Advisory Services in Asia-Pacific Islands, held at *Southeast Asian Regional Center for Graduate Study and Research in Agriculture (SEARCA, #19781)*. **Aims** Promote models, frameworks and guidance on strengthening public-private partnerships in the delivery of Rural Advisory Services (RAS) that accrue benefits to *farmers*. **Structure** Core Group; Focal Person. **Languages** English. **Staff** Part-time. **Finance** Donations from institutions. **Activities** Research/documentation; events/meetings; knowledge management/information dissemination; publishing activities. **IGO Relations** Links with *FAO (#09260)*; *International Fund for Agricultural Development (IFAD, #13692)*; *Southeast Asian Regional Center for Graduate Study and Research in Agriculture (SEARCA, #19781)*; *Swedish International Development Cooperation Agency (Sida)*. **NGO Relations** *Global Forum for Rural Advisory Services (GFRAS, #10378)*. [2019.02.12/XJ7918/**F**]

♦ Asia Pacific Jewish Association (inactive)
♦ Asia Pacific Journalism Centre (internationally oriented national body)

♦ Asia and Pacific Jump Rope Federation (APJRF) 01938

Secretariat Flat D – 4th Floor, Fu Hop Factory Blg, 209-211 Wai Yip Steet, Kwun Tung, Hong Kong, Central and Western, Hong Kong. T. +85237050357. E-mail: apjrf@hotmail.com.
Facebook: https://www.facebook.com/AsiaandPacificJumpRopeUnion/
Aims Unify the sport of Jump Rope in Asia and Pacific region; facilitate jump rope sustainable development. **Structure** Board; Secretariat. **Activities** Sporting activities; training/education.
Members National organizations in 9 countries and territories:
China, Hong Kong, India, Indonesia, Kazakhstan, Korea Rep, Malaysia, Singapore, Thailand.
NGO Relations Member of (2): *General Association of Asia Pacific Sports Federations (GAAPSF, #10106)*; *International Sport Network Organization (ISNO, #15592)*. [2019/XM7393/**D**]

♦ Asia Pacific Jurist Association (internationally oriented national body)

♦ Asia-Pacific Knee, Arthroscopy and Sports Medicine Society (APKASS) 01939

Coordinator Rm 74029, 5/F Clinical Sci Bldg, Prince of Wales Hospital, Shatin, Hong Kong. E-mail: info@apkass.org.
URL: http://www.apkass.org/
History 1987, Penang (Malaysia). Former names and other names: *Asia Pacific Orthopaedic Society for Sports Medicine (APOSSM)* – former. **Aims** Promote knowledge and continuing medical education in orthopaedic sports medicine in the Asia-Pacific region. **Structure** Sports Medicine Section of: *Asia Pacific Orthopaedic Association (APOA, #01987).* **Languages** English. **Staff** None. **Finance** Sources: grants; meeting proceeds. **Activities** Events/meetings; networking/liaising. **Events** *Congress* Hainan (China) 2024, *Congress* Pattaya (Thailand) 2022, *Congress* Pattaya (Thailand) 2021, *Congress* Pattaya (Thailand) 2020, *Summit* Chengdu (China) 2019. **Publications** *Asia-Pacific Journal of Sports Medicine, Arthroscopy, Rehabilitation and Technology* (4 a year).
Members APOA members in 18 countries and territories:
Australia, Bangladesh, Hong Kong, India, Indonesia, Japan, Korea Rep, Malaysia, Myanmar, New Zealand, Pakistan, Philippines, Singapore, Sri Lanka, Taiwan, Thailand, Türkiye, Vietnam. [2023.02.27/XD8533/**D**]

♦ Asia Pacific Knee Society 01940

Secretariat G-1 Medical Academies of Malaysia, Jalan Tun Razak 210, 50400 Kuala Lumpur, Malaysia. T. +60340234700 – +60340254700 – +60340233700. E-mail: admin@apoaonline.com.
URL: http://www.apoaonline.com/asia-sacific-knee-society-apks.php
History 1987, Penang (Malaysia). Knee section of *Asia Pacific Orthopaedic Association (APOA, #01987).* **Events** *Congress* Gwangju (Korea Rep) 2018, *Congress* Yokohama (Japan) 2016, *Congress* Phuket (Thailand) 2014, *Congress* Phuket (Thailand) 2014, *Congress* Delhi (India) 2012. [2015/XJ1315/**E**]

♦ Asia Pacific Lacrosse Union (APLU) 01941

Pres address not obtained.
URL: http://www.asiapacificlacrosse.org/
History 2004, by organizations in Australia, Hong Kong, Korea Rep and Japan. **Aims** In the Asia-Pacific region: promote and develop lacrosse; provide a means of communication between all lacrosse playing and developing countries; encourage international exchange and friendship through lacrosse; unify both men and women lacrosse organizations so as to better develop the game. **Structure** Executive Board. **Languages** English. **Staff** Voluntary. **Finance** Members' dues. Other sources: registration fees; fund-raising events. **Activities** Sporting activities; events/meetings. **Events** *General Meeting* Seogwipo (Korea Rep) 2017.
Members Full in 7 countries and territories:
Australia, China, Hong Kong, Japan, Korea Rep, New Zealand, Thailand.
Associate in 4 countries and territories:
India, Malaysia, Singapore, Taiwan.
IGO Relations None. **NGO Relations** *World Lacrosse (#21616).* [2019/XM5683/**D**]

♦ Asia Pacific Laser Institute (unconfirmed)
♦ Asia-Pacific Lawyers Association (no recent information)

♦ Asia Pacific Leadership Forum on HIV/AIDS and Development (APLF) 01942

Forum des dirigeants de la région Asie-Pacifique sur le VIH/sida et le développement – Foro de dirigentes de Asia y el Pacifico sobre el VIH/SIDA y el desarrollo
Contact UNAIDS Regional Support Team for Asia and Pacific, 9th Floor – A-Block, UN Bldg, Rajdamnern Nok Avenue, Pranakorn, Bangkok, 10200, Thailand. T. +6622882178. Fax +6622881092.
History 2002, following the Asia Pacific Ministerial Meeting, Oct 2001, Melbourne (Australia). **Aims** Support and strengthen political and civil society leadership at country, sub-regional and regional levels in taking action to reduce the spread and impact of the AIDS epidemic in the region. **Structure** Steering Committee, comprising Manager, 3 Sub-regional Coordinators (South Asia, Southeast Asia, Pacific) and Programme Assistant. Management through *Joint United Nations Programme on HIV/AIDS (UNAIDS, #16149)* Regional Support Team for Asia and Pacific (RST/AP). **Finance** Funding from: *European Commission (EC, #06633)*; governments of Australia, Japan, New Zealand, UK and USA. **Events** *Annual Asia media summit* Macau (Macau) 2009. **IGO Relations** Partners: *Australian Aid (inactive)*; *Department for International Development (DFID, inactive)*; *European Commission (EC, #06633)*; *Japan International Cooperation Agency (JICA)*; *Joint United Nations Programme on HIV/AIDS (UNAIDS, #16149)*; *New Zealand Ministry of Foreign Affairs and Trade – New Zealand Aid Programme*; *United States Agency for International Development (USAID).* [2009/XM2958/**F**]

♦ Asia-Pacific Leadership Network for Nuclear Non-Proliferation and Disarmament (APLN) 01943

Coordinator 4th fl, 116 Pirundae-ro, Jongno-gu, Seoul 03035, Korea Rep. T. +82221352170. E-mail: apln@apln.network.
URL: http://www.apln.network/
History 18 May 2011, Canberra, ACT (Australia). Registration: The ROK Ministry of Foreign Affairs, No/ID: 3788200312, Start date: 19 Sep 2019, Korea Rep, Seoul. **Aims** Inform and energize public opinion, especially high-level policymakers, to take seriously the very real threats posed by nuclear weapons, and work to achieve a world in which they are contained, diminished, and eventually eliminated. **Structure** Board of Directors; Network Members; Secretariat. **Languages** English. **Staff** 8.00 FTE, paid. **Finance** Sources: grants. Supported by: *Asia Research Fund (ARF, no recent information)*; *Carnegie Corporation of New York*; *MacArthur Foundation*; *Nuclear Threat Initiative (NTI, #17622)*; *Open Society Foundations (OSF, #17763).* **Activities** Advocacy/lobbying/activism; awareness raising; events/meetings. Active in all member countries. **Events** *Amended Convention for the Physical Protection of Nuclear Materials* Seoul (Korea Rep) 2021, *Seoul Peace Initiative Conference* Seoul (Korea Rep) 2021, *The NPT and Security Dynamics in Northeast Asia* Seoul (Korea Rep) 2021, *Cooperative Solutions for North Korean Denuclearization* Seoul (Korea Rep) 2020, *Preemptive Nuclear Attacks on the Korean Peninsula-Fact or Fiction* Seoul (Korea Rep) 2020. **Publications** Policy briefs; Commentaries; Special Reports.
Members Individuals (over 100) in 23 countries:
Australia, Bangladesh, Brunei Darussalam, Cambodia, China, India, Indonesia, Japan, Korea DPR, Korea Rep, Laos, Malaysia, Mongolia, Myanmar, New Zealand, Pakistan, Papua New Guinea, Philippines, Singapore, Sri Lanka, Thailand, Timor-Leste, Vietnam.
NGO Relations Collaborates with: *European Leadership Network (ELN, #07666)*; *Latin American and Caribbean Leadership Network for Nuclear Disarmament and Nonproliferation (LALN).* [2022.05.04/XJ8417/v/**F**]

♦ Asia Pacific Leaders Malaria Alliance (APLMA) 01944

CEO 04-01/02 Helios 11 Biopolis Way, Singapore 138667, Singapore. E-mail: admin@aplma.org.
URL: https://www.aplma.org/
History 2013, Brunei Darussalam. Established at East Asia Summit as an affiliation of Asian and Pacific heads of government. Secretariat incorporated as a non-profit entity, Singapore, Oct 2015. **Aims** Support and facilitate the elimination of malaria from the Asia Pacific by 2030. **Structure** Board of Directors; Secretariat. **Activities** Advocacy/lobbying/activism; politics/policy/regulatory. **Events** *Meeting* Sydney, NSW (Australia) 2014. **IGO Relations** Cooperates with (1): *Asia Pacific Malaria Elimination Network (APMEN, #01950).* [2022/XJ9161/**D***]

♦ Asia Pacific League Against Rheumatism / see Asia Pacific League of Associations for Rheumatology (#01945)

♦ Asia Pacific League of Associations for Rheumatology (APLAR) 01945

Ligue de l'Asie Pacifique contre le rhumatisme
SG Ctr for Clinical Trial, Kaohsiung Medical Univ Hosp, Kaohsiung, Taiwan. T. +88673121101. E-mail: d10153@ms14.hinet.net.
Secretariat 1 Scotts Road No 24-10, Shaw Ctr, Singapore 228208, Singapore. E-mail: secretariat.aplar@gmail.com – info@aplar.org.
URL: http://www.aplar.org/
History Founded Sep 1963, Sydney (Australia), as *South East Asia and Pacific League Against Rheumatism (SEAPAL).* Name changed, 1989, to *Asia Pacific League Against Rheumatism.* As a regional league of *International League of Associations for Rheumatology (ILAR, #14016).* Present name adopted 1994. Registered in accordance with the law of Singapore, 2009. **Aims** Stimulate and promote the development of awareness, knowledge, and the means of prevention, treatment, rehabilitation and relief of rheumatic diseases. **Structure** Congress (annual); Executive Committee; Standing Committees (4); Sub-Committees. **Languages** English. **Staff** 1.00 FTE, paid. **Finance** Members' dues. **Activities** Training/education; events/meetings. **Events** *Congress* Fukuoka (Japan) 2025, *Congress* Chiang Mai (Thailand) 2023, *Congress* Hong Kong (Hong Kong) 2022, *Congress* Kaohsiung (Taiwan) 2021, *Congress* Kyoto (Japan) 2020. **Publications** *International Journal of Rheumatic Diseases* (4 a year).
Members National leagues in 29 countries and territories:
Australia, Bangladesh, China, Hong Kong, India, Indonesia, Iran Islamic Rep, Iraq, Japan, Kazakhstan, Korea Rep, Kuwait, Kyrgyzstan, Malaysia, Mongolia, Myanmar, New Zealand, Oman, Pakistan, Philippines, Singapore, Sri Lanka, Syrian AR, Taiwan, Tajikistan, Thailand, United Arab Emirates, Uzbekistan, Vietnam.
NGO Relations Endorses *World Congress on Controversies, Debates and Consensus in Bone, Muscle and Joint Diseases (BMJD).* [2020/XD3255/**D**]

♦ Asia-Pacific Legal Innovation and Technology Association (ALITA) 01946

Address not obtained.
URL: https://alita.legal/
History 6 Sep 2019, Singapore (Singapore). Launched at TechLaw.Fest. **Aims** Facilitate cross-border collaboration in the space of legal innovation and technology; promote the sharing of knowledge. **Structure** Board of Advisors; Steering Committee. **Members** Full in over 10 countries. Membership countries not specified. [2020/XM8653/**D**]

♦ Asia-Pacific Legal Metrology Forum (APLMF) 01947

Pres address not obtained. E-mail: secretariat@aplmf.org – president@aplmf.org.
URL: http://www.aplmf.org/
History Nov 1994. Founded largely due to the efforts of NSC (Australia) as one of the Specialist Regional Bodies working closely with the International Organization of Legal Metrology. Set up for the economies within the Asia-Pacific Economic Cooperation (APEC) region, and was originally comprised 14 economies from the APEC region. **Aims** Promote free and open *trade* in the region through *harmonization* of technical and administrative requirements in the field of legal metrology; encourage member economies, especially *developing* economies, to participate in international activities of legal metrology. **Structure** Executive Committee, comprising President, Executive Secretary, Immediate-Past President, CIML President (elected) and 3 members; Working Groups (8). **Activities** Advocacy/lobbying/activism; events/meetings; knowledge management/information dissemination; networking/liaising; research/documentation. **Events** *Annual Meeting* Langkawi (Malaysia) 2022, *Annual Meeting* Langkawi (Malaysia) 2021, *Annual Meeting* New Zealand 2020, *Annual Meeting* Ha Long City (Vietnam) 2019, *Annual Meeting* Christchurch (New Zealand) 2018. **Publications** *APLMF Circulars* (4 a year). *Directory of Legal Metrology in the Asia Pacific* (2003).
Members Full; Corresponding Legal Metrology Authorities (28) in 23 countries and territories:
Australia, Brunei Darussalam, Cambodia, Canada, China, Hong Kong, Indonesia, Japan, Kiribati, Korea Rep, Laos, Malaysia, Mongolia, New Zealand, Papua New Guinea, Peru, Philippines, Russia, Singapore, Taiwan, Thailand, USA, Vietnam. [2022.11.17/XF4678/**F***]

♦ Asia Pacific Life Insurance Council / see Asia Pacific Financial Services Association (#01906)

♦ Asia Pacific Loan Market Association (APLMA) 01948

CEO 32nd Fl Jardine House, One Connaught Place, Central, Central and Western, Hong Kong. T. +85228263500.
URL: http://www.aplma.com/
History Aug 1998. **Aims** Promote growth and liquidity in the primary and secondary loan markets of the Asia-Pacific region. **Structure** Board of Directors; Executive Committee. **Finance** Members' dues. **Events** *Seminar on Recent Regulatory Changes in India that May Impact Loan Transactions* Singapore (Singapore) 2020, *CLMV (Cambodia, Laos, Myanmar and Vietnam) Projects and Finance Update Seminar* Singapore (Singapore) 2019, *Competition Law Seminar* Singapore (Singapore) 2019, *IBOR Transition Seminar* Singapore (Singapore) 2019, *Leveraged and Acquisition Finance Conference* Singapore (Singapore) 2019. **Publications** *APLMA Weekly Update.* **Members** Full; Associate. Membership countries not specified. [2020/XJ8301/**D**]

♦ Asia Pacific Lottery Association Limited / see Asia Pacific Lottery Association Limited (#01949)

♦ Asia Pacific Lottery Association Limited (APLA) 01949

Executive Director 190 Middle Road, #14-06 Fortune Centre, Singapore 188979, Singapore.
Assistant to the Chairman Tabcorp Holdings Ltd, Level 8, 180 Ann Street, Brisbane QLD 4000, Australia. E-mail: enquiry@apla.org.sg.
URL: http://www.asiapacific-lotteries.com/
History Oct 1999, Oslo (Norway). Founded at meeting of Asia Pacific Interest Association, as a Regional Association of *World Lottery Association (WLA, #21628).* Inaugurated at first Annual General Meeting, Jun 2000, Glasgow (UK). Former names and other names: *Asia Pacific Lottery Association Limited (APLA)* – legal name. Registration: Start date: 30 Oct 2018, Singapore. **Aims** Advance the goals and collective interests of members; enhance capability, common knowledge and status of members. **Structure** Annual General Meeting; Executive Committee. **Languages** English. **Staff** 2.00 FTE, paid; 1.00 FTE, voluntary. **Finance** Sources: meeting proceeds; members' dues. **Activities** Advocacy/lobbying/activism; events/meetings; guidance/assistance/consulting; networking/liaising. **Events** *Regional Conference* Singapore (Singapore) 2022, *Joint Seminar* Singapore (Singapore) 2021, *Annual Regional Conference* Brisbane, QLD (Australia) 2019, *Annual Regional Conference* Kuching (Malaysia) 2018, *Annual Regional Conference* Seoul (Korea Rep) 2015. **Publications** *Good Practice Case Studies.*
Members Full (21) in 13 countries and territories:
Australia, China, Hong Kong, India, Japan, Korea Rep, Malaysia, New Zealand, Philippines, Polynesia Fr, Singapore, Thailand, Vietnam.
Associate (27) in 13 countries and territories:
Australia, Canada, China, Cyprus, Germany, Greece, Hong Kong, Israel, Japan, Philippines, UK, USA, Vietnam. [2021.07.12/XD8418/**D**]

♦ Asia Pacific Malaria Elimination Network (APMEN) 01950

Contact 04-01/02 Helios 11 Biopolis Way, Singapore 138667, Singapore. E-mail: info@apmen.org.
URL: https://www.apmen.org/
History Feb 2009. **Aims** Support and facilitate elimination of malaria across Asia Pacific by 2030.
Members Governments (21):
Afghanistan, Bangladesh, Bhutan, Cambodia, China, India, Indonesia, Korea DPR, Korea Rep, Laos, Malaysia, Myanmar, Nepal, Pakistan, Papua New Guinea, Philippines, Solomon Is, Sri Lanka, Thailand, Vanuatu, Vietnam.
IGO Relations Partner of (1): *ICDDR,B (#11051).* Cooperates with (1): *Asia Pacific Leaders Malaria Alliance (APLMA, #01944).* **NGO Relations** Partner of (9): *Aga Khan University (AKU, #00546)*; *Asian Collaborative Training Network for Malaria (ACTMalaria, #01384)*; *Institute of Tropical Medicine Antwerp (IMT)*; *London School of Hygiene and Tropical Medicine (LSHTM)*; *Malaria Consortium*; *Malaria No More*; *Medicines for Malaria Venture (MMV, #16634)*; *PSI (#18555)*; *WorldWide Antimalarial Resistance Network (WWARN, #21914).* Partners with several national institutions. [2022/AA2874/**F***]

♦ Asia-Pacific Management Accounting Association (APMAA) 01951

Chair 3-7-47 Shinjo-machi, Toyama City TOYAMA, 930-0992 Japan.
URL: http://apmaa.org/APMAA/
History Nov 2004, Malaysia. **Aims** Promote advancement of management accounting theory and practices with particular reference to Asia-Pacific accounting issues. **Structure** Board of Directors; Steering Committee. **Languages** English. **Staff** None. **Finance** Members' dues. Donations. Annual budget: US$ 50,000 – 100,000. **Activities** Awards/prizes/competitions; capacity building; events/meetings; publishing activities; research and development; training/education. **Events** *Annual Conference* Hanoi (Vietnam) 2024, *Annual Conference* Xian (China) 2023, *Annual Conference* Bangkok (Thailand) 2022, *Annual Conference* Jakarta (Indonesia)

2021, *Annual Conference* Shah Alam (Malaysia) 2020. **Publications** *APMAA NEWS*; *Asia-Pacific Management Accounting Journal (APMAJ)*. **Members** Regular; Professional; Associate; Corporate. Membership countries not specified. [2023/XJ5052/**D**]

♦ Asia Pacific Marketing Federation / see Asia Marketing Federation (#01290)

♦ Asia Pacific Mediation Forum (APMF) 01952

Pres 39 Fifth Avenue, St Peters, Adelaide SA 5069, Australia. T. +61408805641.
URL: http://www.asiapacificmediationforum.org/

History 2001, Adelaide, SA (Australia). Founded at inaugural conference. **Aims** Facilitate exchange and development of knowledge, values and skills of mediation and other dispute resolution processes within and between the countries and cultures in the Asia-Pacific region. **Structure** Steering Committee; Executive Committee; Conference Organizing Committee. **Languages** English. **Staff** Voluntary. **Finance** Sources: meeting proceeds. **Activities** Awards/prizes/competitions; events/meetings. **Events** *Conference* Jeju (Korea Rep) 2019, *Conference* Danang (Vietnam) 2017, *Synergizing Eastern and Western constructs of mediation towards better understanding* Jakarta (Indonesia) 2015, *Conference* Manila (Philippines) 2013, *From talk to action* Bangkok (Thailand) 2011. **Publications** Conference papers. **IGO Relations** *UNDP (#20292)*. **NGO Relations** Resolution Institute Australia; *World Mediation Forum (no recent information)*. [2022.10.19/XM3433/**F**]

♦ Asia Pacific Medical Education Conference (meeting series)
♦ Asia Pacific Medical Education Network (unconfirmed)

♦ Asia Pacific Medical Technology Association (APACMed) 01953

CEO 2 Science Park Drive Ascent, Tower A Number 02-07, Science Park 1, Singapore 118222, Singapore. T. +6568163180. E-mail: info@apacmed.org.
URL: http://apacmed.org/

History 2014. **Aims** Improve standards of care for *patients* through innovative collaborations among stakeholders to jointly shape the future of healthcare in Asia Pacific. **Structure** Board of Directors; Secretariat. Functional Committees. **Languages** English. **Activities** Events/meetings. **Events** *Asia Pacific MedTech Forum* Singapore (Singapore) 2022, *Asia Pacific MedTech Forum* Singapore (Singapore) 2021, *Asia Pacific MedTech Forum* Singapore (Singapore) 2020, *Asia Pacific MedTech Forum* Singapore (Singapore) 2019, *MedTech Forum* Singapore (Singapore) 2019. **NGO Relations** Member of: *Global Medical Technology Alliance (GMTA, #10470)*. [2020.03.12/XM8068/**D**]

♦ Asia-Pacific Medico-Legal Association (APMLA) 01954

Sec CIFS Thailand, 8th Floor B Bldg, Ratthaprasasanabhakti Bld, Government Complex, Chaengwatthana Road, Laksi, Bangkok, 10210, Thailand. T. +661423475. Fax +661439068.
URL: http://www.apmla.net/

History Jun 2012. Constitution adopted 2013. **Aims** Enhance forensic medical capacities through cooperative and collaborative activities and projects. **Structure** General Meeting (annual). Management Committee, including Chairperson, Vice-Chairperson, Treasurer and Secretary/Newsletter Editor. **Events** *IALM Intersocietal Symposium* Venice (Italy) 2016, *Meeting* Seoul (Korea Rep) 2014, *Meeting* Melbourne, VIC (Australia) 2008. **Publications** *APMLA Newsletter*. **NGO Relations** *Indo-Pacific Association of Law, Medicine and Science (INPALMS, #11169)*. [2015/XJ7503/**D**]

♦ Asia Pacific Menopause Federation (APMF) 01955

Pres c/o A Clinic for Women, 17 Yuk Tong Avenue (Chun Tin Court), Singapore 596 322, Singapore. E-mail: info@apmf.net.

Aims Promote and assist the study of age-related changes in reproductive hormones and their consequences in adult men for public interest; improve the quality of life of menopausal women and ageing men for public interest; promote free interchange of technology and expertise related to the menopause and ageing; provide a regional base to facilitate conduct of meetings, courses and other educational activities and encourage the conduct of multicentre trials in the field; establish the epidemiology, clinical features and sequelae of the menopause and ageing, and a consensus for management relating to the menopause and ageing in women and in men; recommend common policies on matters relating to the menopause and ageing when so requested by societies, colleges or similar organizations for the benefit of the public. **Structure** General Meeting (annual). **Events** *Scientific Meeting* Manila (Philippines) 2019, *Scientific Meeting* Singapore (Singapore) 2017, *Scientific Meeting* Tokyo (Japan) 2013, *Scientific meeting* Sydney, NSW (Australia) 2010, *World congress on controversies in obstetrics gynecology and infertility* Shanghai (China) 2007.
Members Full in 13 countries and territories:
China, Hong Kong, India, Indonesia, Japan, Korea Rep, Malaysia, Pakistan, Philippines, Singapore, Taiwan, Thailand, Vietnam.
Also members in Australasia. Membership countries not specified. [2019/XD7814/**D**]

♦ Asia-Pacific Metabolic & Bariatric Surgery Society (APMBSS) 01956

Office Minimally Surgical Ctr – Natl Univ Hosp, 5 Lower Kent Ridge Road, Singapore 119074, Singapore. T. +6567722897. Fax +656774677.
URL: https://www.apmbss.org/

History 2004. Former names and other names: *Asia-Pacific Bariatric Surgery Group (APBSG)* – former. **Structure** Committee. **Activities** Events/meetings; research/documentation. **Events** *Conference* Rayong (Thailand) 2023, *Conference* Shatin (Hong Kong) 2021, *International Congress* Singapore (Singapore) 2010. **Publications** *Asia Pacific Bariatric Surgery Society Newsletter*. [2022/AA2257/**D**]

♦ Asia Pacific Metrology Programme (APMP) 01957

Secretariat Natl Metrology Inst of Japan, 1-1-1 Umezono, Tsukuba, Ibaraki OSAKA, 305-8563 Japan. T. +81298615629. E-mail: apmp-secretariat@aist.go.jp.
URL: http://www.apmpweb.org/

History Originated as an initiative of *Commonwealth Science Council (CSC, #04361)*, 1977. Current title adopted on broadening membership outside the Commonwealth, 1980. Since 1997, a regional body of *Asia-Pacific Economic Cooperation (APEC, #01887)*. **Aims** Improve regional metrological capability through sharing of expertise and exchange of technical services among member laboratories. **Structure** General Assembly; Executive Committee; Technical Committees; Developing Economies' Committee; Focus Groups; Secretariat. **Languages** English. **Finance** Members' dues. **Activities** Knowledge management/information dissemination; capacity building; monitoring/evaluation; events/meetings. **Events** *General Assembly* Tokyo (Japan) 2022, *General Assembly* 2021, *General Assembly* 2020, *General Assembly* Sydney, NSW (Australia) 2019, *Symposium – Digital Metrology Forum* Sydney, NSW (Australia) 2019. **Publications** *APMP Newsletter*.
Members Member economies (24):
Australia, Bangladesh, Cambodia, China, Fiji, Hong Kong, India, Indonesia, Japan, Korea DPR, Korea Rep, Malaysia, Mongolia, Nepal, New Zealand, Pakistan, Papua New Guinea, Philippines, Russia, Singapore, Sri Lanka, Taiwan, Thailand, Vietnam.
Associate member economies (10):
Egypt, Iran Islamic Rep, Iraq, Jordan, Kazakhstan, Kenya, South Africa, Syrian AR, United Arab Emirates, USA. [2017.07.17/XE3352/**E**]

♦ Asia Pacific Military Medicine Conference (meeting series)
♦ Asia Pacific Mission for Migrant Filipinos / see Asia Pacific Mission for Migrants
♦ Asia Pacific Mission for Migrants (internationally oriented national body)

♦ Asia Pacific Mountain Network (APMN) 01958

Knowledge Management/Networking Officer c/o ICIMOD, GPO Box 3226, Kathmandu, Nepal. Fax +97715003299 – +9771503277.

History Nov 1995, following the Sustainable Development of Mountain Areas of Asia (SUDEMAA) conference, Dec 1994, Kathmandu (Nepal). **Aims** Focus on generation, aggregation and dissemination of knowledge on issues recommended by SUDEMAA, including: poverty reduction and economic development; sustainable management of natural resources; gender-balanced decision-making in environment and development policies and programmes; preservation of cultural heritage; reducing the vulnerability to mountain disasters. **Structure** Focal points according to 6 subregions: Australasia, Hindu Kush-Himalaya, North and Central Asia, North East Asia, South East Asia, West Asia. **Languages** English. **Staff** 7.50 FTE, paid. **Finance** Support from: *International Centre for Integrated Mountain Development (ICIMOD, #12500)*; *Mountain Forum (MF, #16861)*; *Mountain Partnership (MP, #16862)*; *Swiss Agency for Development and Cooperation (SDC)*. **Activities** Networking/liaising; knowledge management/information dissemination; financial and/or material support; capacity building; events/meetings. **Publications** *APMN Bulletin*. Online reports; conference reports; electronic newsletters and syntheses. **Members** Covers 43 countries. Membership countries not specified. **IGO Relations** *FAO (#09260)*. [2015.08.28/XF3999/**F**]

♦ Asia Pacific MSME Trade Coalition (unconfirmed)
♦ Asia-Pacific Multilateral Cooperation in Space Technology and Applications / see Asia-Pacific Space Cooperation Organization (#02051)

♦ Asia Pacific Musculo Skeletal Tumour Society (APMSTS) 01959

Address not obtained.
URL: http://www.apmsts.com/

History 1995. Proposed 25 Aug 1993, Singapore (Singapore), at 7th International Symposium of *International Society of Limb Salvage (ISOLS, #15231)*. **Aims** Promote education, scientific exchanges and friendship among scientists in musculoskeletal tumour surgery and related research. **Structure** Board; Advisory Board. **Events** *Meeting* Jakarta (Indonesia) 2025, *Meeting* Taipei (Taiwan) 2023, *Meeting* Okayama (Japan) 2021, *Meeting* Okayama (Japan) 2020, *Meeting* Jaipur (India) 2018.
Members in 22 countries and territories:
Australia, Austria, China, Egypt, Hong Kong, India, Israel, Italy, Japan, Korea Rep, Malaysia, Myanmar, Pakistan, Philippines, Russia, Singapore, Taiwan, Thailand, Türkiye, UK, USA, Vietnam.
NGO Relations *International Society of Limb Salvage (ISOLS, #15231)*. [2022/XD8963/**D**]

♦ Asia-Pacific Music Creators' Alliance (APMA) 01960

Contact c/o FCA, 3-6-12 Uehara, Shibuya-ku, Tokyo, 1518540 Japan. E-mail: apma@outlook.jp.
URL: https://apmaciam.wixsite.com/home

Aims Unify music creators' voices to promote the protection, enforcement and expansion of the rights and interests of music creators in the Asia-Pacific region. **Structure** General Assembly; Executive Committee. **NGO Relations** Partner of: *International Council of Music Authors (#13052)*. [2018/XM6670/**D**]

♦ Asia-Pacific National Health Accounts Network (APNHAN) 01961

Contact address not obtained. E-mail: info@apnhan.org.
URL: http://www.apnhan.org/

History Mar 1998, at a meeting convened by *Asia Pacific Health Economics Network (APHEN, no recent information)*, and supported by *United States Agency for International Development (USAID)* and *WHO Regional Office for South-East Asia (SEARO, #20946)*. **Aims** Promote regional collaboration in technical areas related to national health accounts. **Events** *Joint Meeting of Regional Health Accounts Experts* Seoul (Korea Rep) 2015, *Asian-Pacific regional meeting on health account* Seoul (Korea Rep) 2009. [2010/XJ1303/**E**]

♦ Asia Pacific Natural Agriculture Network (APNAN) 01962

Office 2F Kularb Apartment, 29 Soi Supart Phahonyothin Road Samsennai, Phayathai, Bangkok, 10400, Thailand. T. +66830903308. Fax +6626166022.

History Nov 1989, Thailand. **Events** *International conference on Kyusei nature farming / Conference* Christchurch (New Zealand) 2002. **Members** Membership countries not specified. [2015/XF7071/**F**]

♦ Asia Pacific Natural Gas Vehicles Association (ANGVA) 01963

Exec Dir Level 20 Tower 1, Etiqa Twins No 11, Jalan Pinang, 50450 Kuala Lumpur, Malaysia. T. +60321665140. Fax +60321813522. E-mail: leegs@angva.org – angva@angva.org.
Registered Address Level 2 Block A, Lot 3288 and 3289, Off Jalan Ayer Hitam, Kawasan Institusi Bangi, 43000 Kajang, Selangor, Malaysia.
URL: http://www.angva.org/

History 2002, Korea Rep. Registered under Malaysian law, 28 May 2007. **Aims** Lead and promote Asia Pacific Natural Gas Vehicles (NGV) Industry towards sustainable growth. **Structure** General Meeting (every 2 years); Executive Committee (Governing Board); Membership Committee; ANGVA Technology and Learning Centre (ATLC); Secretariat, headed by Executive Director, based in Kuala Lumpur (Malaysia). **Languages** English. **Staff** 2.00 FTE, paid. **Finance** Self-financing. **Activities** Events/meetings; training/education. **Events** *International Conference* Teheran (Iran Islamic Rep) 2017, *International Conference* Delhi (India) 2013, *International Conference* Beijing (China) 2011, *International conference* Donghae City (Korea Rep) 2009, *Conference* Bangkok (Thailand) 2007. **Publications** Proceedings; biennnial reports.
Members Class A (energy companies); Class C (NVG equipment suppliers, refuelling companies, fleet operators, vehicle converters, research and development organizations and consultants); Class D (trade/industry associations, universities, government agencies and individuals). Class A members (19) in 12 countries:
Canada, China, Germany, India, Indonesia, Iran Islamic Rep, Italy, Korea Rep, Malaysia, Thailand, United Arab Emirates, USA.
Class C members (29) in 14 countries and territories:
Bangladesh, China, Germany, Hong Kong, Indonesia, Iran Islamic Rep, Italy, Korea Rep, Malaysia, Myanmar, New Zealand, Singapore, Thailand, USA.
Class D members (10) in 8 countries:
China, Indonesia, Italy, Japan, Korea Rep, Malaysia, Myanmar, Thailand.
NGO Relations Cooperates with international, regional and national NGV associations, not specified. [2019/XJ0516/**D**]

♦ Asia Pacific Network for Cultural Education and Research (unconfirmed)

♦ Asia-Pacific Network for Food and Nutrition (ANFN) 01964

Contact address not obtained. T. +6626974000. Fax +6626974445. E-mail: fao-rap@fao.org.
URL: http://www.fao.org/world/regional/rap/

History 1988. **Aims** Promote measures leading to *nutritional* adequacy in the region. **Events** *Meeting* Bangkok (Thailand) 2001, *Meeting* Colombo (Sri Lanka) 1999, *Meeting* Bangkok (Thailand) 1994. **Publications** *Regional Expert- Consultation of the Asia-Pacific Network for Food and Nutrition on Establishment of Food Insecurity and Vulnerability Information System* (1998). *Regional Expert Consultation of the Asia-Pacific Network for Food and Nutrition on Food based Approaches to prevent Micronutrient Deficiencies* (1997) – report.
Members Experts invited from 10 countries:
Bangladesh, China, India, Indonesia, Malaysia, Nepal, Pakistan, Philippines, Sri Lanka, Thailand. [2008/XF3534/**F***]

♦ Asia Pacific Network on Food Sovereignty (APNFS) 01965

Regional Dir Unit 503 Fil-Garcia Towers, 104 Kalayaan Ave corner Mayaman Street, 1100 Quezon City, Philippines. T. +6329315452.
URL: http://www.apnfs.info/

Aims Promote and assert the people's basic right to adequate, nutritious and safe food as well as their right to sustainable livelihoods. **Activities** Knowledge management/information dissemination; research/documentation. **Members** Social mouvements, farmers' organizations, women's organizations and NGOs. Membership countries not specified. **IGO Relations** Accredited organization of: *Green Climate Fund (GCF, #10714)*. **NGO Relations** Member of: *More and Better (#16855)*; *NGO Forum on ADB (#17123)*. Member of: *Global Call for Action Against Poverty (GCAP, #10263)*. [2019/XJ0881/**F**]

♦ Asia-Pacific Network for Global Change Research (APN) 01966

APN Secretariat 4F East Building, 1-5-2 Wakinohama Kaigan Dori, Chuo-ku, Kobe HYOGO, 651-0073 Japan. T. +81782308017. Fax +81782308018. E-mail: info@apn-gcr.org.
URL: http://www.apn-gcr.org/

History 1996. Established as a result of the 1990 White House Conference on Science and Economics Research Related to Global Change, at which the then US President George H W Bush invited all countries to join the US in creating 3 regional networks to cooperate in global change research. **Aims** Enable investigations of changes in the Earth's life support systems and their implications for sustainable development in the Asia-Pacific region through support for research and science-based response strategies and measures, effective linkages between science and policy, and scientific capacity development. **Structure** Intergovernmental Meeting; Steering Committee; Scientific Planning Group; Capacity Development Committee; Subregional Committees (South Asia, Southeast Asia, Temperate East Asia, the Pacific); Secretariat. **Languages** English. **Finance** Financial contributions from: The Ministry of the Environment, Japan; Hyogo Prefectural Government,

Japan; Ministry of Environment, Republic of Korea; and the Ministry for the Environment, New Zealand. In-kind contributions from member countries, in particular the Hyogo Prefectural Government, Japan. **Activities** Support collaborative regional research and scientific capacity development, and strengthen linkages between science, policy and practitioner communities. **Events** *Joint Intergovernmental Meeting and Scientific Planning Group Meeting* Kobe (Japan) 2021, *Joint Intergovernmental Meeting and Scientific Planning Group Meeting* Bangkok (Thailand) 2018, *Joint Intergovernmental Meeting and Scientific Planning Group Meeting* New Delhi (India) 2017, *Joint Intergovernmental Meeting and Scientific Planning Group Meeting* Zhengzhou (China) 2016, *Joint Intergovernmental Meeting and Scientific Planning Group Meeting* Kathmandu (Nepal) 2015. **Publications** *Annual Report* (annual) in English – ISSN 2185-7628; *APN Science Bulletin* (annual) in English – ISSN 2522-7971; *Proceedings of intergovernmental meetings* (every 2 years) in English. *Peer-reviewed publications* in English; *Policy briefs* in English; *Synthesis reports* in English.
Members Members countries (22):
Australia, Bangladesh, Bhutan, Cambodia, China, Fiji, India, Indonesia, Japan, Korea Rep, Laos, Malaysia, Mongolia, Nepal, New Zealand, Pakistan, Philippines, Russia, Sri Lanka, Thailand, USA, Vietnam. [2021.09.09/XF4133/**F***]

♦ Asia-Pacific Network for Holistic Education (unconfirmed)

♦ Asia-Pacific Network for Housing Research (APNHR) 01967

Chairperson Dept Urban Planning and Design, Room 836 – Knowles Bldg, Univ of Hong Kong, Pokfulam Road, Hong Kong, Central and Western, Hong Kong. T. +85239172727. Fax +85225590468. E-mail: apnhr@hku.hk.
URL: http://fac.arch.hku.hk/upad/apnhr/
History 17 Apr 2001, Hong Kong. **Aims** Promote and enhance housing research in the Asia-Pacific, particularly comparative studies and theory/model construction; strengthen networking among housing researchers, policy makers and practitioners; enhance the exchange and dissemination of research findings and publications; facilitate housing education and training in the region. **Structure** Steering Committee. **Languages** English. **Finance** Members' dues. **Activities** Events/meetings; networking/liaising. **Events** *Housing 2.0 – search for new paradigms for collaborative housing* Gwangju (Korea Rep) 2015, *Global housing dilemmas – the ways forward* Kuala Lumpur (Malaysia) 2013, *Conference* Hong Kong (Hong Kong) 2011, *Neoliberalism and urbanisation in Asia Pacific – challenges and opportunities for housing* Hong Kong (Hong Kong) 2011, *Southeast Asian Housing Forum* Seoul (Korea Rep) 2011. **Publications** *APNHR Newsletter* (2 a year). **Members** Full; Institutional; Student. Membership countries not specified. [2019.02.28/XF7056/**F**]

♦ Asia-Pacific Networking Group (APNG) 01968

Secretariat intERLab, c/o AIT, PO Box 4, Klong Luang, Pathum Thani, 12120, Thailand. Fax +6625246618.
URL: http://www.apng.org/
Structure Working Groups. Secretariat. **Events** *Half-yearly meeting* Seoul (Korea Rep) 2000, *Meeting* San Jose, CA (USA) 1999, *Meeting* Singapore (Singapore) 1999, *Meeting* Geneva (Switzerland) 1998, *Meeting* Manila (Philippines) 1998.
Members Economies of 20 countries and territories:
Australia, Brunei Darussalam, Cambodia, Canada, China, Hong Kong, India, Indonesia, Japan, Korea Rep, Macau, Malaysia, New Zealand, Philippines, Singapore, Sri Lanka, Taiwan, Thailand, USA, Vietnam.
NGO Relations Input or influence on aspects of development or regulation of: *Internet (#15948)*. Member of: *DotAsia Organisation (DotAsia, #05124)*. [2015/XF4088/y/**E**]

♦ Asia Pacific Network on Integrated Plant Nutrient Management (APIPNM) 01969

Contact FAO-RAP Land Mgmt, Maliwan Mansion, 39 Phra Atit Road, Bangkok, 10200, Thailand.
Aims Strengthen exchange of information, experience and knowledge in integrated plant nutrient management (IPNM) between and among scientists and institutions in Asia and the Pacific region; strengthen capacity building in IPNM research and dissemination within both participant countries and Asia and the Pacific region; formulate programmes to support South-South cooperation to improve transfer of knowledge and information to farmers, policy-makers and field extension agents. **Structure** Coordination Unit. Network Consultative Board, comprising National Coordinators. **Publications** *The Contour Newsletter*.
Members National Coordinators in 8 countries:
Bhutan, China, Indonesia, Nepal, Pakistan, Philippines, Thailand, Vietnam.
IGO Relations *FAO (#09260)*; *FAO Regional Office for Asia and the Pacific (RAP, #09266)*. [2010/XM3963/**D**]

♦ Asia-Pacific Network for International Education and Values Education (APNIEVE) 01970

Officer Caritas Hall, Miriam College, Katipunan Avenue, Loyola Heights, 1108 Quezon City, Philippines. E-mail: apnieve.ph@gmail.com.
URL: http://www.apnieve.org.ph/
History 1995, Seoul (Korea Rep). Regional network of *UNESCO Office, Jakarta – Regional Bureau for Sciences in Asia and the Pacific (#20313)*, within *UNESCO (#20322)*. Former names and other names: *UNESCO-APNIEVE* – alias. **Aims** Promote and develop international education and values education for intercultural understanding, peace, human rights, democracy and sustainable development, through cooperation among UNESCO member states in the Asia-Pacific. **Structure** Chapters (2): Australia; Philippines. Secretariat based in Quezon City (Philippines). **Languages** English. **Staff** Voluntary. **Finance** Sources: members' dues. **Activities** Events/meetings; networking/liaising; publishing activities; training/education. **Publications** *Learning to Know for a Peaceful and Sustainable Future – UNESCO-APNIEVE and APCEIU Sourcebook for Educators and Learners* (2009) in English – Sourcebook; *Learning to Be: A Holistic and Integrated Approache to Values Education for Human Development* – sourcebook; *Learning to Do: Values for Learning and Working Together in a Globalised World, A Holistic and Integrated Approach to Technical and Vocational Education and Training*; *Learning to Live Together in Peace and Harmony* – sourcebook. Newsletters.
Members Individuals and institutions (over 200 total) in 2 countries:
Australia, Philippines.
IGO Relations *Asia-Pacific Programme of Educational Innovation for Development (APEID, #02001)*; *UNESCO International Centre for Technical and Vocational Education and Training (UNESCO-UNEVOC, #20307)*. **NGO Relations** *Asia-Pacific Centre of Education for International Understanding (APCEIU)*. [2022.02.24/XF4305/**F***]

♦ Asia-Pacific Network of Moral Education (APNME) 01971

Sec c/o URBINUS, Jl K H Syahdan No 9, Kemanggisan Palmerah, Jakarta 11480, Indonesia. E-mail: info@apnme.org – conference@apnme.org.
URL: http://www.apnme.org/
History 2006, as an informal network. Formally set up 30 May 2008, Hong Kong. **Aims** Foster and strengthen teaching and research into moral education and moral development. **Structure** Committee. **Activities** Events/meetings; awards/prizes/competitions. **Events** *Annual Conference* Jöetsu (Japan) 2023, *Annual Conference* Manchester (UK) 2022, *Conference* Jakarta (Indonesia) 2021, *Annual Conference* Jakarta (Indonesia) 2020, *Annual Conference* Bali (Indonesia) 2019.
Members Full in 18 countries and territories:
Australia, China, Hong Kong, India, Indonesia, Japan, Korea Rep, Latvia, Macau, Malaysia, Mongolia, New Zealand, Philippines, Poland, Taiwan, Thailand, UK, USA. [2020/XM4697/**F**]

♦ Asia-Pacific Network Operation and Management Symposium (meeting series)

♦ Asia Pacific Network Operators Group (APNOG) 01972

Secretariat PO Box 1908, Milton QLD 4064, Australia. E-mail: board@apnog.org.
URL: https://apnog.org/
History Assumed responsibility of *Asia Pacific Regional Internet Conference on Operational Technology (APRICOT, inactive)*, Jul 2019. Registration: No/ID: ACN 633 052 829, Australia. **Aims** Ensure the future and stability of the APRICOT Summit; build human resource infrastructure for the Internet and foster the efficient, stable and sustainable development of the internet in the Asia Pacific region. **Structure** Board. **Events** *APRICOT : Asia Pacific Regional Internet Conference on Operational Technologies* 2026, *APRICOT : Asia Pacific Regional Internet Conference on Operational Technologies* 2025, *APRICOT : Asia Pacific Regional Internet Conference on Operational Technologies* 2024, *APRICOT : Asia Pacific Regional Internet Conference on Operational Technologies* 2023, *APRICOT : Asia Pacific Regional Internet Conference on Operational Technologies* 2022. **NGO Relations** Memorandum of Understanding with (1): *Asian-Pacific Network Information Centre (APNIC)*. Cooperates with (1): *Asia and Pacific Internet Association (APIA, #01936)*. [2021/AA1312/c/**F**]

♦ Asia-Pacific Network of People Living with HIV/AIDS (APN+) 01973

Secretariat 75/12 Ocean Tower II, 15th Floor, Soi Sukhumvit 19, Klong Toey Nua, Wattana, Bangkok, 10110, Thailand. T. +66225974889. Fax +6622597487. E-mail: apnplus.communication@gmail.com.
URL: http://www.apnplus.org/
History Feb 1994, Kuala Lumpur (Malaysia). Regional network of *Global Network of People Living with HIV/AIDS (GNP+, #10494)*. **Aims** Empower people living with HIV to promote the greater involvement of people living with HIV/AIDS in the response; address issues of treatment care and support; lobby on behalf of them and advocate for their rights addressing stigma and discrimination. **Structure** Board, consisting of 2 representatives of each country network. Steering Committee, comprising 2 Co-Chairs, Treasurer and 3 members. Regional Coordinator. **Languages** English, Thai. **Staff** 4.00 FTE, paid; 2.00 FTE, voluntary. **Finance** Donor organizations include: *International Committee of the Red Cross (ICRC, #12799)*; *Levi Strauss Foundation (LSF)*; *United States Agency for International Development (USAID)*. Budget (annual): about US$ 450,000. **Activities** Advocacy/lobbying/activism. **Events** *Strengthened and expanded HIV legal services* Bali (Indonesia) 2009, *ICAAP: international congress on AIDS in Asia and the Pacific / International Conference on AIDS in Asia and the Pacific / International Conference on AIDS in Asia and the Pacific – ICAAP* Kobe (Japan) 2005, *ICAAP : international congress on AIDS in Asia and the Pacific / International Conference on AIDS in Asia and the Pacific / International Conference on AIDS in Asia and the Pacific – ICAAP* Melbourne, VIC (Australia) 2001, *ICAAP : international congress on AIDS in Asia and the Pacific / International Conference on AIDS in Asia and the Pacific / International Conference on AIDS in Asia and the Pacific – ICAAP* Kuala Lumpur (Malaysia) 1999, *Conference* Geneva (Switzerland) 1998. **Publications** *APN+ Newsletter*. Annual Report.
Members Individuals and PWA Groups in 30 countries and territories:
Australia, Bangladesh, Bhutan, Cambodia, China, Fiji, Guam, India, Indonesia, Iran Islamic Rep, Japan, Korea Rep, Laos, Malaysia, Mongolia, Myanmar, Nepal, New Caledonia, New Zealand, Pakistan, Papua New Guinea, Philippines, Samoa, Singapore, Sri Lanka, Taiwan, Thailand, Timor-Leste, Vanuatu, Vietnam.
NGO Relations Member of: *Coalition of Asia Pacific Regional Networks on HIV/AIDS (Seven Sisters, #04051)*; *International Treatment Preparedness Coalition (ITPC, #15729)*. [2015/XF3360/**F**]

♦ Asia-Pacific Network on Research and Development of Teak / see International Teak Information Network (#15665)

♦ Asia Pacific Network of Science and Technology Centres (ASPAC) . 01974

Exec Dir PO Box No 70066, Kowloon Central Post Office, Hong Kong, Central and Western, Hong Kong. T. +85366820125.
URL: http://www.aspacnet.org/
History 1997. **Aims** Encourage communication, information exchange, staff exchanges and collaboration amongst science and technology centres in the Asia Pacific region. **Structure** Executive Council, comprising President, Vice-President, Executive Director, Secretary, Assistant-Secretary, Treasurer, 2 Councillors and appointed convenors or working groups or standing committees. **Languages** English. **Staff** Voluntary. **Finance** Members' dues. **Events** *Conference* Beijing (China) 2016, *Conference* Manila (Philippines) 2015, *Conference* Brunei Darussalam 2014, *Conference* Daejeon (Korea Rep) 2013, *Gift of Nam June Paik Musically Yours International Symposium* Yongin (Korea Rep) 2013. **Publications** *ASPAC News Update* – electronic newsletter.
Members Institutions (over 70) in 23 countries and territories:
Australia, Brunei Darussalam, Canada, China, Finland, Hong Kong, Indonesia, Ireland, Japan, Korea Rep, Macau, Malaysia, Netherlands, New Zealand, Philippines, Singapore, Sri Lanka, Taiwan, Thailand, UK, United Arab Emirates, USA, Yemen. [2017/XJ3610/**F**]

♦ Asia Pacific Network of Sex Workers (APNSW) 01975

Secretariat Room 518, Phyathai Building, 31 Phaya Thai Road, Ratchathewi, Bangkok, 10400, Thailand. E-mail: secretariat@apnsw.info.
URL: https://apnsw.info/
History Also referred to as *Asia Pacific Network of Sex Workers and Sex Work Groups* and as *Asia Pacific Network of Sex Work Projects (APNSWP)*. **Events** *ICAAP: international congress on AIDS in Asia and the Pacific / International Conference on AIDS in Asia and the Pacific / International Conference on AIDS in Asia and the Pacific – ICAAP* Kobe (Japan) 2005, *ICAAP : international congress on AIDS in Asia and the Pacific / International Conference on AIDS in Asia and the Pacific / International Conference on AIDS in Asia and the Pacific – ICAAP* Melbourne, VIC (Australia) 2001. **NGO Relations** Member of: *Coalition of Asia Pacific Regional Networks on HIV/AIDS (Seven Sisters, #04051)*. [2018/XF6364/**F**]

♦ Asia Pacific Network of Sex Workers and Sex Work Groups / see Asia Pacific Network of Sex Workers (#01975)
♦ Asia Pacific Network of Sex Work Projects / see Asia Pacific Network of Sex Workers (#01975)

♦ Asia-Pacific Network for Sustainable Agriculture Food and Energy (SAFE Network) 01976

Coordinator Fac of Agricultural Technology – Andalas Univ, Kampus Unand Limau Manis, Padang 25163, Indonesia. E-mail: rahmat@polinpdg.ac.id – mr.rahmat@gmail.com.
Sec address not obtained.
URL: https://safe-network.org/
Structure Steering Committee; Advisory Committee; Secretariat. **Activities** Events/meetings; training/education. **Events** *Annual International Conference On Sustainable Agriculture, Food and Energy* Jeju (Korea Rep) 2020, *Annual International Conference On Sustainable Agriculture, Food and Energy* Phuket (Thailand) 2019. [2020/AA0397/**F**]

♦ Asia-Pacific Network for Sustainable Forest Management and Rehabilitation (APFNet) 01977

Exec Dir 6th Floor Baoneng Ctr (Bldg A), 12 Futong Dongdajie, Wangjing area, Chaoyang District, 100102 Beijing, China. T. +861084159140. Fax +861084216958. E-mail: apfnet@apfnet.cn.
URL: http://www.apfnet.cn/
History Proposed by China and co-sponsored by Australia and USA; agreed by 15th *Asia-Pacific Economic Cooperation (APEC, #01887)* Economic Leaders' Meeting, Sep 2007, Sydney (Australia). Incorporated in Sydney APEC Leaders' Declaration on Climate Change, Energy Security and Clean Development. Launched 25 Sep 2008, Beijing (China), at International Symposium on Sustainable Forest Management. **Aims** Promote and improve sustainable forest management and rehabilitation in Asia and the Pacific. **Structure** Interim Steering Committee; Project Appraisal Panel; Working Mechanism for APFNet Focal Points. Secretariat, headed by Executive Director. **Languages** Chinese, English. **Staff** 23.50 FTE, paid. 2 part-time consultants. **Finance** Funding mainly from China and international organizations. **Activities** Capacity building; meeting activities; education. **Events** *International Conference on Forest Producer Organizations* Guilin (China) 2013, *Workshop on Forestry Strategic Planning in the Asia-Pacific Region* Rotorua (New Zealand) 2013, *International conference on response of forests and adaptation management to climate change* Yichun (China) 2011. **Publications** Annual Report. Proceedings; reports.
Members Membership open to APEC economies; non-APEC economies; international organizations operating in the Asia-Pacific region; forestry-related academic institutions and civil societies in the Asia-Pacific region; forests and forestry related enterprises operating in the Asia-Pacific region. Focal points in APEC and non-APEC countries and territories (27):
Australia, Bangladesh, Brunei Darussalam, Cambodia, Canada, China, Fiji, Hong Kong, India, Indonesia, Japan, Laos, Malaysia, Mexico, Mongolia, Myanmar, Nepal, New Zealand, Papua New Guinea, Peru, Philippines, Singapore, Sri Lanka, Taiwan, Thailand, USA, Vietnam.
International organizations:
FAO (#09260); *International Model Forest Network (IMFN, #14175)*; *International Tropical Timber Organization (ITTO, #15737)*; *Pacific Community (SPC, #17942)*; *RECOFTC – The Center for People and Forests (RECOFTC, #18628)*; *The Nature Conservancy (TNC)*. [2018/XJ2771/y/**E***]

♦ Asia-Pacific Network of Transport and Logistics Education and Research (unconfirmed)

♦ Asia Pacific Neural Network Society (APNNS) 01978

Pres Univ of Tokyo, Graduate School of Engineering, Dept of Electrical Engineering and Information Systems, 7-3-1 Hongo, Bunkyo-ku, Tokyo, 113-8656 Japan.
URL: http://www.apnns.org/

History 1993, as *Asian Pacific Neural Network Assembly (APNNA)*. Current title adopted when APNNA was transformed from an assembly into a member-based society, Nov 2015. **Aims** Create a scientific and educational forum for students, educators, scientists, engineers, researchers, and the general public to learn about, share, contribute to, and to advance the state of knowledge in the theoretical modelling and analysis of behaviour and brain processes and their applications in technology. **Structure** Board of Governors; Executive Committee. **Finance** Members' dues. **Activities** Events/meetings. **Events** *ICONIP : International Conference on Neural Information Processing* Sydney, NSW (Australia) 2019, *ICONIP : International Conference on Neural Information Processing* Kyoto (Japan) 2016, *International Symposium on Neural Networks* Jeju (Korea Rep) 2015, *ICONIP : International Conference on Neural Information Processing* Kuching (Malaysia) 2014, *ICONIP : International Conference on Neural Information Processing* Daegu (Korea Rep) 2013. **Publications** *APNNS News*. [2017/XF4688/D]

♦ Asia Pacific Neuroendocrine Tumour Society (APNETS) 01979

Congress Secretariat Academy of Medicine Malaysia, G-1 Medical Academies of Malaysia, 210 Jalan Tun Razak, 50400 Kuala Lumpur, Malaysia. T. +60340234700 – +60340254700. Fax +60340238100. E-mail: admin@apnets.org.
URL: http://apnets.org/

History 2012. **Aims** Enhance management of neuroendocrine tumours in the Asia Pacific through networking and international collaboration. **Structure** Council. **Events** *Annual Conference* Melbourne, VIC (Australia) 2018, *Annual Conference* Mumbai (India) 2017, *Annual Conference* George Town (Malaysia) 2016, *Annual Conference* George Town (Malaysia) 2015, *Annual Conference* Kochi (India) 2014. [2014/XJ7835/D]

♦ Asia Pacific NMR Symposium (meeting series)
♦ Asia Pacific Non-Government Organization on Drug and Substance Abuse Prevention (inactive)

♦ Asia-Pacific Nutrigenomics and Nutrigenetics Organisation (APNNO) 01980

Founding Pres CSIRO, Kintore Avenue, Adelaide SA 5000, Australia.
Sec address not obtained.
Pres Elect Cancer Research Inst, Seoul Natl Univ, 103 Daehak-ro, Jongno-gu, Seoul 03080, Korea Rep.
URL: http://www.apnno.com/

History Launched 2014, Gold Coast (Australia), at 8th Asia-Pacific Nutrigenomics Conference. **Aims** Promote the science of nutrigenomics and nutrigenetics in the Asia-Pacific region; facilitate communication among researchers, clinicians and nutrition industry working in the field in the Asia-Pacific region. **Structure** Executive Committee. **Languages** English. **Staff** 2.00 FTE, voluntary. **Finance** Members' dues. Other sources: sponsorship. **Activities** Events/meetings; research/documentation. **Events** *Biennial Conference* Adelaide, SA (Australia) 2020, *Biennial Conference* Tokyo (Japan) 2018, *Biennial Conference* Gyeongju (Korea Rep) 2016. **Publications** *APNNO Newsletter* (2 a year).
Members Full in 12 countries and territories:
Australia, China, India, Indonesia, Japan, Korea Rep, Malaysia, New Zealand, Philippines, Singapore, Taiwan, Thailand.
IGO Relations None. **NGO Relations** *European Nutrigenomics Organisation (NuGO, #08068)*; *International Society of Nutrigenetics / Nutrigenomics (ISNN, #15314)*. [2018/XM5165/D]

♦ Asia Pacific Occupational Safety and Health Organization (APOSHO) 01981

SG c/o NCSA, 6-7 Hartnett Close, Mulgrave VIC 3170, Australia.
URL: http://www.aposho.org/

History Founded by *Department for International Development Cooperation* and *ILO (#11123)*, as *Coordinating Committee of Asia-Pacific National Safety Councils*. Subsequently referred to as *Asian-Pacific Regional Network on Occupational Safety and Health*, 1992. Constitution approved 7 Sep 1993, Jakarta (Indonesia); amended 23 Apr 1998, Seoul (Korea Rep). **Aims** Promote mutual understanding and cooperation among communities in the Asia-Pacific region; contribute to the enhancement of occupational safety and health in these communities through the exchange of information and views among competent people including top-level managers of member organizations. **Structure** Chairperson. Secretariat. Committees (5): Technical; Membership Screening; Management Development; Occupational Health and Safety Management; Education and Training. **Languages** English. **Events** *Conference* Melbourne, VIC (Australia) 2022, *Annual Conference* Tokyo (Japan) 2021, *Annual Conference* Kuala Lumpur (Malaysia) 2020, *Annual Conference* Guiyang (China) 2019, *Annual Conference* Hong Kong (Hong Kong) 2018. **Publications** *Asian Pacific Newsletter on Occupational Safety and Health*.
Members Full; Associate; Affiliate; Honorary. Full (20) in 17 countries and territories:
Australia, Bangladesh, China, Hong Kong, India, Indonesia, Japan, Korea Rep, Malaysia, Mauritius, Papua New Guinea, Philippines, Singapore, Sri Lanka, Taiwan, Thailand, Vietnam.
Associate (5) in 5 countries and territories:
Brunei Darussalam, Macau, Mongolia, New Zealand, Pakistan.
Affiliate (12) in 10 countries:
Australia, Canada, Indonesia, Korea Rep, Malaysia, Mauritius, Philippines, UK, USA, Vietnam.
Honorary (17) in 10 countries and territories:
Australia, China, Hong Kong, Indonesia, Japan, Korea Rep, Malaysia, New Zealand, Singapore, Taiwan. [2021/XD5212/D]

♦ Asia Pacific Occupational Therapists Regional Group (APOTRG) 01982

Sec Taiwan Occupational Therapy Assn, 5F-3, 9 Bo-Ai Road, Taipei 10044, Taiwan. E-mail: apotrg@gmail.com.

History 18 Jul 2006, Newcastle (Australia), by *World Federation of Occupational Therapists (WFOT, #21468)*. **Aims** Unite members to develop and improve standards of practice, and to advance education and academic knowledge of occupational therapy; advance the theory of occupational therapy to consumers. **Events** *Doing well together* Rotorua (New Zealand) 2015, *Embracing cultural diversity through innovative practice* Hong Kong (Hong Kong) 2007, *Congress* Singapore (Singapore) 2003, *Congress* Taipei (Taiwan) 1999, *Congress* Malaysia 1995.
Members in 13 countries and territories:
Australia, Hong Kong, India, Indonesia, Japan, Korea Rep, Malaysia, New Zealand, Pakistan, Philippines, Singapore, Taiwan, Thailand.
NGO Relations Regional member of: *World Federation of Occupational Therapists (WFOT, #21468)*. [2013.09.27/XM2642/D]

♦ Asia-Pacific Ocular Imaging Society (APOIS) 01983

Pres address not obtained.

Aims Facilitate collaboration between ophthalmologists and vision scientists in the region, with a focus on development and application of ocular imaging. **Events** *Congress* Seoul (Korea Rep) 2021, *Congress* Singapore (Singapore) 2020. **NGO Relations** Member of: *Asia-Pacific Academy of Ophthalmology (APAO, #01814)*. [2020/XM7870/D]

♦ Asia-Pacific Onboard Travel (unconfirmed)
♦ Asia-Pacific Ophthalmic Trauma Society (unconfirmed)
♦ Asia-Pacific Orchid Association / see Asia Pacific Orchid Conference Trust (#01984)

♦ Asia Pacific Orchid Conference Trust (APOC) 01984

Chair 1 Imohori, Ushida, Chiryu, Aichi, 472 0007 Japan.
URL: http://www.apoctrust.org/

History 1984, Japan, as *Asia-Pacific Orchid Association (APOA)*. **Activities** triennial Asia Pacific Conference. **Events** *Triennial Conference* Kuching (Malaysia) 2019, *Triennial Conference* Bangkok (Thailand) 2016, *Triennial Conference / Conference* Okinawa (Japan) 2013, *Triennial conference / Conference* Chongqing (China) 2010, *Triennial Conference* Goyang (Korea Rep) 2007. [2012/XD5894/D]

♦ Asia Pacific Organization for Cosmology and Particle Astrophysics (APCosPA) 01985

Contact Dept of Physics, Natl Taiwan Univ, Taipei 10617, Taiwan. T. +886233665189. E-mail: wyhwang@phys.ntu.edu.tw.
URL: http://www.apcospa.org/

History Sep 2010, Tokyo (Japan), at Symposium on Cosmology and Particle Astrophysics. Constitution adopted 2010. **Structure** General Assembly. **Languages** English. **Events** *International Symposium on Cosmology and Particle Astrophysics* Sydney, NSW (Australia) 2016, *COSPA : International Symposium on Cosmology and Particle Astrophysics* Daejeon (Korea Rep) 2015, *Symposium on Cosmology and Particle Astrophysics – CosPA* Seoul (Korea Rep) 2015, *Symposium on Cosmology and Particle Astrophysics* Seoul (Korea Rep) 2015, *Symposium on Cosmology and Particle Astrophysics / Symposium on Cosmology and Particle Astrophysics – CosPA* Auckland (New Zealand) 2014. **Publications** *The Universe* – newsletter/journal.
Members Institutions in 7 countries and territories:
Australia, China, Japan, Korea Rep, New Zealand, Taiwan, USA. [2017.08.02/XJ9547/D]

♦ Asia Pacific Orthodontic Society (APOS) 01986

SG address not obtained. T. +6590466037.
APOS Publications Ground Floor, Mani Mount, 24 Altamount Road, Mumbai, Maharashtra 400 026, Mumbai MAHARASHTRA 400 026, India. E-mail: apospublications@gmail.com.
URL: http://www.apospublications.com/

History 20 Oct 2001, Tokyo (Japan). **Aims** Assist members to promote excellence in orthodontics through education and research in the Asia Pacific region; disseminate scientific and artistic information relating to orthodontics. **Structure** Executive Committee, comprising President, Vice-President, Secretary General, Treasurer, Immediate Past President and 15 members. **Events** *Biennial Congress* Yokohama (Japan) 2020, *Biennial Congress* Nusa Dua (Indonesia) 2016, *Biennial Congress* Kuching (Malaysia) 2014, *Biennial Congress* Delhi (India) 2012, *Biennial Congress* Sydney, NSW (Australia) 2010.
Members Organizations in 16 countries and territories (" indicates founding):
Australia, Bangladesh, China (*), Hong Kong (*), India (*), Indonesia (*), Japan (*), Korea Rep (*), Macau, Malaysia, Nepal, New Zealand, Pakistan, Philippines (*), Singapore (*), Thailand (*). [2014/XJ2454/D]

♦ Asia Pacific Orthopaedic Association (APOA) 01987

Secretariat Unit 1.6 Level 1 Ent 3B, Jalan Innovasi 1, Lebuhraya Puchong – Sungei Besi, 57000 Kuala Lumpur, Malaysia. E-mail: admin@apoaonline.com.
URL: http://www.apoaonline.com/

History Apr 1962, Manila (Philippines). Former names and other names: *Western Pacific Orthopaedic Association (WPOA)* – former (1962 to 9 Apr 2000). **Aims** Enable orthopaedic surgeons of the Western Pacific area to exchange views, discuss new discoveries and new methods of handling orthopaedic problems; promote the advancement of orthopaedics in Asia in particular and the world in general. **Structure** Executive Committee. Sections (10): Hand & Upperlimb; Foot & Ankle; Hip; Infection; Knee – Asia Pacifici Knee Society; Paediatric – Asia Pacific Paediatric Orthopaedic Society; Research – Asia Pacific Orthopaedic Research Society; Spine – *Asia Pacific Spine Society (APSS, #02054)*; Sports; Asia Pacific Trauma Society. **Languages** English. **Staff** Voluntary. **Finance** Sources: members' dues. Annual budget: 15,000 USD. **Activities** Events/meetings. **Events** *Combined Meeting* Kobe (Japan) 2021, *Biennial Congress* Kuala Lumpur (Malaysia) 2021, *Biennial Congress* Kuala Lumpur (Malaysia) 2020, *Combined Meeting* Incheon (Korea Rep) 2019, *Biennial Congress* Antalya (Turkey) 2018. **Publications** *Journal of Orthopaedic Surgery* (3 a year). Information Services: Abstracts in Excerpta Medica. Available in microform from University Microfilms International. Covered by the Excerpta Medica/Electronic Publishing Division Database (Embase).
Members Fellows; Associate; Honorary; Affiliate; Retired Fellows. Members in 19 countries and territories:
Australia, Bangladesh, China, Hong Kong, India, Indonesia, Japan, Korea Rep, Malaysia, Myanmar, Nepal, New Zealand, Pakistan, Philippines, Singapore, Taiwan, Thailand, Türkiye, Vietnam.
Individuals in 8 countries:
Canada, China, Fiji, France, Italy, South Africa, UK, USA.
NGO Relations Member of (1): *International Combined Orthopaedic Research Societies (I-CORS, #12657)*. [2021/XD4186/D]

♦ Asia Pacific Orthopaedic Society for Sports Medicine / see Asia-Pacific Knee, Arthroscopy and Sports Medicine Society (#01939)

♦ Asia Pacific Paediatric Endocrine Society (APPES) 01988

Secretariat PO Box 180, Morisset NSW 2264, Australia. T. +61249736573. Fax +61249736609. E-mail: secretariat@appes.org.
Treas Inst of Endocrinology and Diabetes, Children's Hosp, Locked Bag 4001, Westmead NSW 2145, Australia.
URL: http://www.appes.org/

History 1999. **Aims** Provide a professional forum for those with an interest in paediatric endocrinology in the Asia Pacific region. **Structure** General Meeting; Council; Executive Council. **Activities** Events/meetings; training/education; awards/prizes/competitions. **Events** *Joint Meeting of Paediatric Endocrinology* Buenos Aires (Argentina) 2021, *Scientific Meeting* Kuala Lumpur (Malaysia) 2021, *Scientific Meeting* Kuala Lumpur (Malaysia) 2020, *Scientific Meeting* Chiang Mai (Thailand) 2018, *Joint Meeting of Paediatric Endocrinology* Washington, DC (USA) 2017. **NGO Relations** Member of: *Global Pediatric Endocrinology and Diabetes (GPED, #10545)*. [2017/XJ0236/D]

♦ Asia Pacific Parliamentary Forum (APPF) 01989

Contact address not obtained.
URL: https://appfpresident.org/

History 15 Jan 1993, Tokyo (Japan). Founded as an informal grouping, on the initiative of Hon Yasuhiro Nakasone (died 2019). **Aims** Promote dialogue among parliamentarians of the Asia Pacific region; identify and discuss matters of common concern and interest and highlight them in a global context; deepen their understanding of policy concerns, interests and experiences of the countries of the region; examine the critical political, social and cultural developments resulting from economic growth and integration; encourage and promote regional cooperation at all levels on matters of common concern to the region. **Structure** General Assembly; Executive Committee of 9 members; Presidency. **Languages** English. **Staff** provided by parliamentary members. **Finance** Annual meeting financed by host parliament; other activities financed by parliament members involved. **Events** *Annual Meeting* Seoul (Korea Rep) 2021, *Annual Meeting* Canberra, ACT (Australia) 2020, *Annual Meeting* Siem Reap (Cambodia) 2019, *Annual Meeting* Hanoi (Vietnam) 2018, *Annual Meeting* Nadi (Fiji) 2017.
Members National parliamentarians in 27 countries:
Australia, Cambodia, Canada, Chile, China, Colombia, Costa Rica, Ecuador, Fiji, Indonesia, Japan, Korea Rep, Laos, Malaysia, Marshall Is, Mexico, Micronesia FS, Mongolia, New Zealand, Papua New Guinea, Peru, Philippines, Russia, Singapore, Thailand, USA, Vietnam.
Observer in 1 country:
Brunei Darussalam.
IGO Relations Observer status in meetings of: *Asia-Pacific Economic Cooperation (APEC, #01887)*. [2022.02.10/XF5769/F]

♦ Asia-Pacific Partnership for Clean Development and Climate (APPCDC) 01990

Address not obtained.
URL: http://www.asiapacificpartnership.org/

History 28 Jul 2005, during a regional forum meeting of *ASEAN (#01141)*. Also referred to as *AP6*. Charter adopted Jan 2006. **Aims** Increase cooperation on development and transfer of technology which enables reduction of greenhouse gas emissions consistent with the principles of the United Nations framework convention on *climate change* TUNFCCC and complementing, but not replacing, the Kyoto protocol. **Structure** Policy and Implementation Committee; Administrative Support Group. **Activities** Task Forces (9): Administration; Aluminium; Buildings and Appliances; Cement; Cleaner Fossil Energy; Coal Mining; Power Generation and Transmission; Renewable Energy and Distributed Generation; Steel. **Events** *Meeting* Kobe (Japan) 2010, *International conference* Busan (Korea Rep) 2008, *Ministerial meeting* Berkeley, CA (USA) 2006, *Meeting* Jeju (Korea Rep) 2006, *Inaugural ministerial meeting / Ministerial Meeting* Sydney, NSW (Australia) 2006.
Members Governments of 6 countries:
Australia, China, India, Japan, Korea Rep, USA.
IGO Relations *International Energy Agency (IEA, #13270)*. [2009/XM0866/F*]

♦ Asia Pacific Pathways to Progress Foundation (internationally oriented national body)

♦ Asia Pacific Peace Research Association (APPRA) 01991

Association asiatique de recherche sur la paix

SG Director, Chetanalaya Inst, Post Box No 11992, Kathmandu, Nepal.
SG Fac of Political Science, Thammasat Univ, Prachan, Bangkok, 10200, Thailand. E-mail: jsombutpoonsiri@gmail.com.
URL: http://appra.net/

History Founded 5 Dec 1980, Yokohama (Japan), under the name *Asian Peace Research Association (APRA)*, as a successor body to *Asian Council of Peace Research (ACPR, inactive)*, set up 1974. Present name adopted 4 Feb 1992. Regional Association of: *International Peace Research Association (IPRA, #14537)*. **Aims** Advance interdisciplinary research on the conditions of peace and the causes of war and violence in all their manifestations. Facilitate international collaboration designed to assist the advancement of peace research, education and action, and in particular: promote national and international studies and teaching relating to pursuit of international peace in accordance with the principle of freedom of scientific research; facilitate contacts between peace researchers, educators and advocates as well as specialists in conflict resolution throughout the region; encourage international dissemination of research results, information and documentation of significant developments of actions for peace. **Structure** Council. Commissions and Committees (4): Security Commission; Peace Education Commission; Peace Building Commission; Conference Organizing Committee. **Languages** English. **Staff** 2.00 FTE, voluntary. **Finance** Members' voluntary contributions. Other sources: subventions; proceeds from the sale of publications; fees for special services: ad hoc fund-raising. **Activities** Events/meetings; research/documentation; training/education; advocacy/lobbying/activism; networking/liaising. **Events** *Empowering culture of peace, sustainable development and defending democracy* Jakarta (Indonesia) 2019, *Conference* George Town (Malaysia) 2017, *Pathways towards just peace* Kathmandu (Nepal) 2015, *Conference* Bangkok (Thailand) 2013, *Conference* Tsu (Japan) 2012. **Publications** *APPRA Waves* – electronic newsletter. *Peace and Security in the Asia Pacific Region* (1993) by Kevin Clements. Selected papers of the inaugural conference; scientific studies, conference proceedings; books; journals.

Members Categories Individuals; National or Sub-Regional Associations; Corporates. Individuals in 17 countries and territories:
Australia, Bangladesh, China, Hong Kong, India, Indonesia, Japan, Korea Rep, Malaysia, Nepal, New Zealand, Pakistan, Philippines, Sri Lanka, Taiwan, Thailand, USA.

IGO Relations Cooperates with: *UNESCO (#20322)*; *United Nations Economic and Social Commission for Asia and the Pacific (ESCAP, #20557)*. [2017/XD8521/v/**D**]

♦ Asia Pacific Pediatric Association (APPA) 01992

SG 3rd Floor, Natl Cancer Society Bldg, 66 Jalan Raja Muda Abdul Aziz, 50300 Kuala Lumpur, Malaysia. T. +60326914773. Fax +60326914773. E-mail: appa.kl.secretariat@gmail.com.
URL: http://www.a-p-p-a.org/

History 30 Apr 1974, Manila (Philippines). Founded as *Association of Pediatric Societies of the Southeast Asian Region (APSSEAR)*, in conjunction with the 1st Asian Congress of Pediatrics. Subsequently known as *Asian Pacific Pediatric Association (APPA)*, 2003. Current title adopted 2012. **Aims** Improve the health status of children living in the Asia Pacific region and surrounding areas. **Structure** Council Meeting of National Delegates (every 3 years); Executive Committee; Advisory Board. **Languages** English. **Staff** 1.00 FTE, paid. **Finance** Members' dues. Other sources: congress proceeds; advertising. **Activities** Projects/programmes; events/meetings; training/education; knowledge management/information dissemination; guidance/assistance/consulting. **Events** *Congress* Lahore (Pakistan) 2021, *SDGs and reducing inequalities – how far have we come?* Nusa Dua (Indonesia) 2018, *Child health priorities post MDG world* Hyderabad (India) 2016, *Asia Pacific Congress of Pediatric Nursing* Kuching (Malaysia) 2012, *Congress* Kuching (Malaysia) 2012. **Publications** *Asia Pacific Journal of Pediatrics and Child Health*.

Members National societies in 23 countries and territories:
Australia, Bangladesh, China, Hong Kong, India, Indonesia, Japan, Korea DPR, Korea Rep, Macau, Malaysia, Mongolia, Myanmar, Nepal, New Zealand, Pakistan, Papua New Guinea, Philippines, Singapore, Sri Lanka, Taiwan, Thailand, Vietnam.

NGO Relations Member of: *International Pediatric Association (IPA, #14541)*. [2021/XD4340/**D**]

♦ Asia Pacific Pediatric Cardiac Society (APPCS) 01993

Address not obtained.

History 2006, Bangkok (Thailand). **Aims** Foster the study and dissemination of knowledge of paediatric cardiovascular *disease*, particularly in the region of Asia-Pacific; promote cooperation through scientific exchanges among member countries and professional contacts among those interested and working in this field; encourage evidence based research activities in the field of paediatric cardiovascular disease particularly on cardiovascular problems common to the region; encourage and facilitate exchange of staff and trainees among member countries and other interested organizations worldwide. **Structure** Congress (every 2 years); Council of National Delegates; Executive Board. **Activities** Events/meetings. **Events** *Congress* Taipei (Taiwan) 2021, *Congress* Taipei (Taiwan) 2020, *Congress* Bali (Indonesia) 2018, *Korean-Japan-China Pediatric Heart Forum* Jeju (Korea Rep) 2016, *Congress* Shanghai (China) 2016. **Members** Paediatric cardiologists, cardiovascular surgeons, pathologists and those interested in paediatric cardiovascular disease. Membership countries not specified. [2021/XM2112/**D**]

♦ Asia-Pacific Performing Arts Network (APPAN) 01994

SG 193-1 Pyeongchang-dong 3F, Jongno-gu, Seoul 110-846, Korea Rep. T. +8223916502. E-mail: appankorea@gmail.com – zendance@hotmail.com.
URL: http://www.appan.co.kr/

History 1999, by the Korean National Commission for *UNESCO (#20322)* and *UNESCO Asia and Pacific Regional Bureau for Education (#20301)*. **Aims** Provide a platform for both networking and performances to all *artists*, especially from the field of performing arts in the Asia-Pacific region. **Structure** Board of Directors. **Languages** English. **Staff** 5.00 FTE, voluntary. **Finance** Board members raise resources individually; income from conferences and workshops organized by Board members in their own countries. **Activities** Events/meetings. **Events** *International symposium* Seoul (Korea Rep) 2007, *International symposium* Rishikesh (India) 2003, *Inauguration conference* Seoul (Korea Rep) 2000. **Publications** Books. **Members** Full in 17 countries. Membership countries not specified. **IGO Relations** Consultative Status with: UNESCO. [2020/XF6019/**F**]

♦ Asia-Pacific Philosophy Education Network for Democracy (APPEND) 01995

Pres Graduate Programs Coord, Ateneo de Manila Univ, 307 Katipunan Road, One Burgunday Plaza, Loyala Heights, Quezon City, Philippines.

History Founded Sep 1995, Seoul (Korea Rep). **Aims** Foster democracy through philosophy education in the Asia-Pacific region. **Events** *Conference* Seoul (Korea Rep) 2008, *Biennial conference / Conference* Philippines 2005, *Biennial conference / Conference* Hanoi (Vietnam) 2004, *Biennial conference / Conference* Sydney, NSW (Australia) 2002, *Biennial conference / Conference* Tokyo (Japan) 2000. **Publications** *APPEND Philosophy Series*.

Members Individuals in 11 countries:
Australia, China, India, Indonesia, Japan, Korea Rep, New Zealand, Philippines, Sri Lanka, Thailand, Vietnam.

IGO Relations *UNESCO (#20322)*. [2013.08.22/XJ3551/**F**]

♦ Asia Pacific Photoforum (APP) 01996

Contact PO Box 147095 Ponsonby, Auckland 1144, New Zealand. T. +6493077055.
URL: http://asiapacificphotoforum.com/

History 2010. Founded by 6 photographic festivals. **Aims** Promote exchange of ideas and artists amongst member festivals and nurture development of *photography* across the Asia-Pacific region by supporting member festivals; promote and engage exchange of ideas, values and concepts that support photographers throughout the region. **Structure** Flat. Member festivals have equal standing. **Languages** Chinese, English, Japanese, Spanish. Website available in Bangla. **Staff** None. **Activities** Events/meetings; networking/liaising; projects/programmes.

Members Festivals in 7 countries:
Australia, Bangladesh, China, Colombia, Japan, New Zealand, Singapore. [2021.09.06/XJ4697/**F**]

♦ Asia Pacific Physical Activity Network (no recent information)

♦ Asia Pacific Physics Teachers and Educators Association (inactive)

♦ Asia and Pacific Plant Protection Commission (APPPC) 01997

Commission phytosanitaire pour l'Asie et le Pacifique

Contact c/o FAO_ROAP, Maliwan Mansion, Phra Atit Road, Bangkok, 10200, Thailand. T. +6626974268. Fax +6626974445. E-mail: fao-rap@fao.org.
URL: http://www.fao.org/asiapacific/apppc/

History 21 Nov 1955. Founded within the framework of *FAO (#09260)*, on approval by FAO Council of Article II of *Plant Protection Agreement for the Asia and Pacific Region (1956)*, which came into force 2 Jul 1956. Executed by *FAO Regional Office for Asia and the Pacific (RAP, #09266)*. Former names and other names: *Plant Protection Committee for the South-East Asia and Pacific Region (PPCSEAPR)* – former; *Comité phytosanitaire pour la région de l'Asie du Sud-Est et du Pacifique* – former; *PPC/AP* – alias. **Aims** Strengthen international cooperation in plant protection, particularly with regard to measures for preventing the introduction and spread of plant diseases and pests dangerous to vegetation in the region; provide inter-governmental consultation on action required for protection of plant resources in the region. **Structure** Commission (meets every 2 years) submits reports to member Governments through the Director-General of FAO, who is responsible for convening its meetings. Executive Committee. Consultant Services. Expert Panels. **Languages** English, French. **Staff** FAO provides Secretariat. **Activities** Plant quarantine; integrated pest management; safe and efficient use of pesticides; information exchange programme with member countries. **Events** *Regional Plant Protection Organizations (RPPOs) Annual Technical Consultation* London (UK) 2022, *Regional Plant Protection Organizations (RPPOs) Annual Technical Consultation* Rome (Italy) 2021, *Regional Plant Protection Organizations (RPPOs) Annual Technical Consultation* Rome (Italy) 2020, *Regional Plant Protection Organizations (RPPOs) Annual Technical Consultation* Abuja (Nigeria) 2019, *Regional Workshop on Reviewing Draft International Standards for Phytosanitary Measures* Busan (Korea Rep) 2019. **Publications** *APPPC Quarterly Newsletter*. Technical documents; pest information notes; meeting and session reports.

Members Governments of 26 states party to the Agreement:
Australia, Bangladesh, Cambodia, China, Fiji, France, India, Indonesia, Korea DPR, Korea Rep, Laos, Malaysia, Myanmar, Nepal, New Zealand, Pakistan, Papua New Guinea, Philippines, Portugal, Samoa, Solomon Is, Sri Lanka, Thailand, Tonga, UK (for Hong Kong), Vietnam.

IGO Relations Serves as one of 10 Regional Plant Protection Organizations of *International Plant Protection Convention, 1951 (IPPC, 1951)*. [2020/XE3927/**E***]

♦ Asia and the Pacific Policy Society (unconfirmed)

♦ Asia-Pacific Primary Liver Cancer Expert Association (APPLE) 01998

Contact HB and I – 1711, Hanshin Bldg, 12 Mapo-daero, Mapo-gu, Seoul 04175, Korea Rep. T. +8223731005. Fax +8223731106. E-mail: secretariat@applecongress.org.
URL: http://www.applecongress.org/

History 2013. **Aims** Promote the scientific advancement of, and education in, liver cancer management in the Asia-Pacific region. **Structure** Governing Board; Executive Committee; Council. **Languages** English. **Events** *Asia-Pacific Primary Liver Cancer Expert Meeting* Shanghai (China) 2022, *Asia-Pacific Primary Liver Cancer Expert Meeting* Seoul (Korea Rep) 2021, *Meeting* Yangon (Myanmar) 2020, *Meeting* Sapporo (Japan) 2019, *Meeting* Seoul (Korea Rep) 2018. **Publications** *Liver Cancer* – official journal. [2021.02.18/XM8389/**D**]

♦ Asia-Pacific Printers Federation (inactive)

♦ Asia Pacific Privacy Authorities (APPA) 01999

Secretariat c/o OIPC-BC, PO Box 9038, Stn Prov Govt, Victoria BC V8W 9A4, Canada. E-mail: appasecretariat@oipc.bc.ca.
URL: http://www.appaforum.org/

History 1992. **Aims** Acts as the principal forum for privacy authorities in the Asia Pacific Region to form partnerships and exchange ideas about privacy regulation, new technologies and the management of privacy enquiries and complaints. **Finance** Members' dues. **Events** *Forum* Seoul (Korea Rep) 2021, *Forum* Melbourne, VIC (Australia) 2020, *Forum* Singapore (Singapore) 2020, *Forum* Cebu City (Philippines) 2019, *Forum* Tokyo (Japan) 2019.

Members Information agencies of 9 countries and territories:
Australia, Canada, Colombia, Hong Kong, Korea Rep, Macau, Mexico, Peru, Singapore.

NGO Relations Partner of (1): *Global Privacy Assembly (GPA, #10555)*. [2021/XJ9054/**D**]

♦ Asia Pacific Privatization Network (unconfirmed)

♦ Asia-Pacific Producers Network (APN) 02000

Contact address not obtained. T. +81362263020. Fax +81362263024. E-mail: inquiry@tiffcom.jp.

History 2001, as a network between Japan and Korea. Extended to include China, 2004. Subsequently changed title to *Asia Producers Network*, 2006. Current title adopted 2007. Currently also known under the acronym *APPN*. **Aims** Encourage cooperation in the regional *cinema* industry. **Activities** Annual symposium. **Events** *Symposium* Auckland (New Zealand) 2011. [2016/XJ4314/**F**]

♦ Asia-Pacific Productivity Conference (meeting series)

♦ Asia-Pacific Programme of Educational Innovation for Development (APEID) 02001

Contact UNESCO Bangkok, 920 Sukhumvit Road, Phrakanong, Bangkok, 10110, Thailand. T. +6623910577. Fax +6623910866. E-mail: apeid.bgk@unesco.org.
URL: http://www.unescobkk.org/education/apeid/

History Founded 4 Nov 1973, Bangkok (Thailand), as *Asian Programme of Educational Innovation for Development (APEID)*, within the framework of *UNESCO (#20322)*, as an integral part of UNESCO Regional Office for Education in Asia and the Pacific (ROEAP), currently *UNESCO Asia and Pacific Regional Bureau for Education (#20301)*. *Asian Centre of Educational Innovation for Development (ACEID, inactive)* set up to facilitate implementation of APEID and acted as Secretariat. In 2001, ACEID was fully subsumed into the title of APEID. A regional network of *UNESCO Office, Jakarta – Regional Bureau for Sciences in Asia and the Pacific (#20313)*. **Aims** Contribute to *sustainable* human development, underpinned by tolerance, human rights and a culture of peace, through design and implementation of education programmes and projects, mainly at *post-primary* level, stressing 'educational innovation for development'. **Structure** Standing Committee. Secretariat. Work monitored by *Intergovernmental Regional Committee on Education in Asia and the Pacific (EDCOM, no recent information)*. **Staff** 10.00 FTE, paid. Long/short-term consultants. **Finance** Staff posts financed by UNESCO's Regular Programme funds. Programme activities funded by: UNESCO; voluntary cash contributions made by some UNESCO member states.

Activities Major strategies: Using Technologies for Information and Communication; Educational Innovation for Human Development; Revitalize APEID as a "Network of Networks"; Research and Development; Building on UNESCO's Strengths to Improve Quality; Evaluation, Monitoring and Quality Control; Identification and Dissemination of Innovative Educational Practices; Promote Effective Mobilization and Allocation of Resources. Programmes themes: Curriculum Change; Educational Technology; Higher and Distance Education; Teacher Education and Training; Technical and Vocational Education; Education for Sustainable Development; Mobile Training Team; International, Moral and Value Education. Services the following networks for the Asia-Pacific region, some originating in the region and some in UNESCO Headquarters:
- *Asia-Pacific Network for International Education and Values Education (APNIEVE, #01970)*;
- *Association of Universities of Asia and the Pacific (AUAP, #02968)*;
- *UNITWIN/UNESCO Chairs Programme (#20669)* (university twinning);
- Individual Membership of ACEID (MACEID).

Events *Meeting on Entrepreneurship Education* Hangzhou (China) 2019, *International Conference on Education* Bangkok (Thailand) 2018, *Meeting on Entrepreneurship Education* Trincomalee (Sri Lanka) 2018, *International Conference on Education* Bangkok (Thailand) 2016, *International Congress on Road Safety for the Safety of Life* St Petersburg (Russia) 2016. **Publications** *ACEID News* (3 a year). *APEID Occassional Paper Series*. Books and other publications covering the programme areas.

Members UNESCO members in the Asia-Pacific region, governments of 31 countries:
Afghanistan, Australia, Bangladesh, Bhutan, Cambodia, China, Fiji, India, Indonesia, Iran Islamic Rep, Japan, Kazakhstan, Korea DPR, Korea Rep, Kyrgyzstan, Laos, Malaysia, Maldives, Mongolia, Myanmar, Nepal, New Zealand, Pakistan, Papua New Guinea, Philippines, Samoa, Sri Lanka, Thailand, Tonga, Türkiye, Vietnam.

IGO Relations Through APEID, links with: *UNESCO PROAP Information Programmes and Services (UNESCO-PIPS, no recent information)*. [2014/XE0607/**E***]

♦ Asia-Pacific Programme of Education for All (APPEAL) 02002

Programme d'éducation pour tous en Asie et dans le Pacifique

Education Advisor/Coordinator UNESCO Asia and Pacific Regional Bureau for Education, Mom Luang Pin Malakul Centenary Building, 920 Sukhumvit Rd, Bangkok, 10110, Thailand. T. +6623910577ext315. Fax +6623910866. E-mail: appeal.bgk@unesco.org.
URL: http://www.unescobkk.org/education/appeal/

History May 1986. as a regional cooperative programme implemented by *UNESCO Asia and Pacific Regional Bureau for Education (#20301)* for *UNESCO (#20322)*. Since 1996, work monitored by *Intergovernmental Regional Committee on Education in Asia and the Pacific (EDCOM, no recent information)*. Originated from a recommendation by the 5th Regional Conference of Ministers of Education, 1985, and its subsequent adoption by UNESCO's General Conference. Launched 1987. **Aims** Promote literacy, early childhood care and education (ECCE), primary education, multilingual education and continuing education as integrated components of basic education and lifelong learning under the guiding principle of a human rights based approach to education; offer good quality education, especially to disadvantaged and vulnerable groups. **Finance** Financing from: UNESCO's regular budget; extrabudgetary funds predominantly from Japan and Nordic countries; voluntary contributions from member states. **Activities** Strategies stress gender mainstreaming, community participation, inclusion, networking, utilization of appropriate ICTs and innovations in both formal and non-formal approaches to offer a good quality education, especially to disadvantaged and vulnerable groups. In implementing the programmes, priority is given to reaching out to excluded and under-served or disadvantaged groups such as women and girls, the poor, minorities and the disabled. Assists Member States in the region through cooperative planning, consultation and organization of regional, sub-regional, national and local-level programmes. Main focus of these activities has been in the following areas: assisting Member States in policy development and planning for activities related to Education for All (EFA), including elaboration of gender-responsive EFA plans; promoting inclusion of all in the learning process through formal and non-formal approaches; improving the quality of basic education through resource development and training as well as effective monitoring and evaluation; supporting innovations at the grassroots level through pilot projects; developing regional networks to facilitate sharing of experiences. Instrumental in setting up: *Community Learning Centres (CLC, see: #02002)*. **Events** *Asia-Pacific regional conference on early childhood development* Singapore (Singapore) 2011, *Annual education conference / Annual International Conference on Education* Bangkok (Thailand) 1997. **Publications** *Advocacy Kit for Promoting Multilingual Education: Including the Excluded*; *Transforming Early Childhood Care and Education in the Insular South-East Asia and Mekong Sub-Regions: Implications of the Global Monitoring Report 2007*. Guidebook; handbook; resource pack; toolkits; conference reports.

Members Participating states (47):
Afghanistan, Australia, Bangladesh, Bhutan, Brunei Darussalam, Cambodia, China, Cook Is, Fiji, India, Indonesia, Iran Islamic Rep, Japan, Kazakhstan, Kiribati, Korea DPR, Korea Rep, Kyrgyzstan, Laos, Malaysia, Maldives, Marshall Is, Micronesia FS, Mongolia, Myanmar, Nauru, Nepal, New Zealand, Niue, Pakistan, Palau, Papua New Guinea, Philippines, Samoa, Singapore, Solomon Is, Sri Lanka, Tajikistan, Thailand, Timor-Leste, Tokelau, Tonga, Turkmenistan, Tuvalu, Uzbekistan, Vanuatu, Vietnam.
NGO Relations Supports: *Asia-Pacific Regional Network for Early Childhood (ARNEC, #02009)*; *Gender in Education Network in Asia-Pacific (GENIA)*; Literacy Resource Centre for Girls and Women (LRC).
[2017/XF0499/**F***]

♦ Asia Pacific Protein Association (APPA) 02003

SG Protein Research Foundation, 4-1-2 Ina, Minoh, Osaka, 562-0015 Japan. E-mail: appa@pssj.jp.
Pres address not obtained.
URL: https://www.pssj.jp/APPA

Aims Advance protein science in countries in the Asia Pacific region. **Structure** Council; Office. **Activities** Awards/prizes/competitions; events/meetings. **Events** *World Conference on Protein Science (2020 WCPS)* Sapporo (Japan) 2020, *Conference* Bang Saen (Thailand) 2017, *Conference* Jeju (Korea Rep) 2014, *Conference* Shanghai (China) 2011.

Members Full in 16 countries and territories:
Australia, Bangladesh, China, Hong Kong, India, Indonesia, Japan, Korea Rep, Malaysia, New Zealand, Pakistan, Philippines, Singapore, Taiwan, Thailand, Vietnam.
[2020/AA1892/**D**]

♦ Asia Pacific Public Affairs Forum (internationally oriented national body)
♦ Asia Pacific Public Health Nutrition Association (no recent information)
♦ Asia Pacific Quality Control Organization / see Asia Pacific Quality Organization (#02005)

♦ Asia-Pacific Quality Network (APQN) 02004

Administrator Shanghai Education Evaluation Inst, 202 South ShaanXi Road, 200031 Shanghai, China. T. +862154032285. Fax +862154670198. E-mail: apqnsecretariat@163.com.
Acting Gen Dir Research Inst of Higher Education (RIHE), Yunnan Univ, Kunming, 650091 Yunnan, China. T. +8668326631.
URL: http://www.apqn.org/

History 18 Jan 2003, Hong Kong. Current constitution adopted at Annual General Meeting 2019, Sri Lanka. Registration: No/ID: ABN:11769716226, Start date: 1 Dec 2004, Australia; No/ID: FN200907115, Start date: 18 Jan 2009; No/ID: 52310000575884994B, Start date: 18 Jun 2011, China. **Aims** Enhance the quality of higher education in the Asia-Pacific Region. **Structure** General Council; Board; Project Group; Committee Chairs. **Languages** English. **Staff** 1.00 FTE, paid. **Finance** Annual budget: 30,000 USD (2019). **Activities** Awards/prizes/competitions; capacity building; certification/accreditation; events/meetings; guidance/assistance/consulting; monitoring/evaluation; projects/programmes; research and development; research/documentation; standards/guidelines; training/education. **Events** *Annual Conference and General Meeting* Singapore (Singapore) 2022, *Annual Conference and General Meeting* Singapore (Singapore) 2021, *Annual Conference and General Meeting* Singapore (Singapore) 2020, *Annual Conference and General Meeting* Colombo (Sri Lanka) 2019, *Annual Conference and General Meeting* Nagpur (India) 2018. **Publications** *APQNews* (2 a year). *Academic Anthologies*. Toolkits; surveys. **Information Services** *APQN Consultant Database*.

Members Full; Intermediate; Associate; Institutional; Individual. Members (250) in 47 countries and territories:
Afghanistan, Australia, Austria, Bangladesh, Bhutan, Brunei Darussalam, Cambodia, China, Croatia, Cyprus, Fiji, Germany, Hong Kong, India, Indonesia, Iran Islamic Rep, Iraq, Japan, Kazakhstan, Korea Rep, Kuwait, Kyrgyzstan, Laos, Macau, Malaysia, Maldives, Mexico, Mongolia, Nepal, New Zealand, Pakistan, Papua New Guinea, Philippines, Russia, Samoa, Saudi Arabia, Singapore, Sri Lanka, Syrian AR, Taiwan, Thailand, Timor-Leste, Tonga, Türkiye, UK, Vanuatu, Vietnam.
Included in the above, 9 organizations listed in this Yearbook:
Asian Institute of Finance (AIF); *Asia Theological Association (ATA, #02101)*; *International Centre of Excellence in Tourism and Hospitality Education (THE-ICE, #12491)*; *International Culture University (ICU)*; *International Islamic University, Islamabad*; *International Union of School and University Health and Medicine (IUSUHM, no recent information)*; *International University of Business Agriculture and Technology (IUBAT)*; *Pakistan Institute of Development Economics (PIDE)*; *University of the South Pacific (USP, #20703)*.
Observers (13) in 9 countries:
Austria, Croatia, Germany, Kuwait, Mexico, New Zealand, Saudi Arabia, Thailand, UK.
Included in the above, 3 organizations listed in this Yearbook:
ASEAN University Network (AUN, #01243); *Asian Forum on Business Education (AFBE, #01490)*; *Foundation for International Business Administration Accreditation (FIBAA, #09961)*.
IGO Relations Memorandum of Understanding with (1): *Commonwealth of Learning (COL, #04346)*. Cooperates with (1): *UNESCO (#20322)*. **NGO Relations** Accredited by (1): *UNESCO Mahatma Gandhi Institute of Education for Peace and Sustainable Development (UNESCO MGIEP, #20310)*. Memorandum of Understanding with (1): *International Network of Quality Assurance Agencies in Higher Education (INQAAHE, #14312)*.
[2022.10.26/XJ2286/y/**D**]

♦ Asia Pacific Quality Organization (APQO) 02005

SG Unit 2721-T, Goldland Millenia Tower, 8001 JM Escriva Drive, Ortigas Center, Pasig City RIZ, Philippines.
URL: http://www.apqo.global/

History Conceived Dec 1981, Manila (Philippines), as *Asia Pacific Quality Control Organization (APQCO)*, at 1st Asia Pacific Congress on Quality Control. Officially set up 23 Oct 1985, Beijing (China), when constitution was signed. Present name adopted 1997. Registered in accordance with the laws of the Philippines. **Aims** Promote quality awareness and practice in the Asia Pacific region, through regular scientific and technical conferences. **Structure** Congress. Council (meets annually), comprising Officers: President; 6 Vice-Presidents (Conferences, External Affairs, Projects and Committees, Publication, Finance, Membership) and nominated representatives of each Full member. Executive Board (meets twice a year), consisting of Officers. Secretariat, headed by Secretary General. **Languages** English. **Staff** 2.00 FTE, paid. **Finance** Members' dues. Other sources: donations; income from activities. Budget (annual): US$ 4,500. **Activities** Includes *Walt L Hurd Foundation*. Awards; Meeting activities. **Events** *Conference* Australia 2021, *Conference* Pasig City (Philippines) 2020, *Conference* Perth, WA (Australia) 2020, *Conference* Bali (Indonesia) 2019, *Conference* Abu Dhabi (United Arab Emirates) 2018. **Publications** *APQO Monitor* (4 a year); *Asia Pacific Journal of Quality Management* – incorporated in 'TQM Magazine'. Congress proceedings.

Members Individuals and Council members. Members in 34 countries and territories:
Argentina, Australia, Canada, Chile, China, Cuba, Dominican Rep, Egypt, Guatemala, India, Indonesia, Iran Islamic Rep, Israel, Italy, Japan, Korea Rep, Malaysia, Mauritius, Mexico, Myanmar, Netherlands, New Zealand, Pakistan, Philippines, Saudi Arabia, Singapore, Sri Lanka, Taiwan, Thailand, UK, United Arab Emirates, Uruguay, USA, Vietnam.
[2017/XD2502/v/**D**]

♦ Asia Pacific Real Assets Association (APREA) 02006

CEO 18 Robinson Road, Suite 15-01, Singapore 049371, Singapore. E-mail: enquiries@aprea.asia.
URL: http://aprea.asia/

History 2005. Former names and other names: *Asian Public Real Estate Association* – alias; *Asia Pacific Real Estate Association (APREA)* – former. **Aims** Promote growth in the real assets sector by being the voice in all policy matters, providing access to industry-advancing research and insights and connecting members to business opportunities. **Structure** Council of Governors; Board of Directors. **Activities** Advocacy/lobbying/activism; events/meetings; networking/liaising; research/documentation. **Events** *Asia Pacific Real Assets Leaders Congress* Singapore (Singapore) 2022, *Forum on Resilience and Growth Prospects in Korea Property Markets Beyond COVID-19* Seoul (Korea Rep) 2021, *Asia Pacific Property Leaders' Congress* Singapore (Singapore) 2021, *Asia Pacific Investors Connection Forum* Singapore (Singapore) 2020, *Asia Pacific Property Market Outlook Conference* Singapore (Singapore) 2020. **Publications** Reports; white papers; updates. **NGO Relations** Member of: *International Ethics Standards Coalition (IES Coalition, #13307)*; Real Estate Equity Securization Alliance (REESA).
[2022/XJ0079/**D**]

♦ Asia Pacific Real Estate Association / see Asia Pacific Real Assets Association (#02006)
♦ Asia Pacific Real Estate Federation (inactive)

♦ Asia Pacific Refugee Rights Network (APRRN) 02007

Coordinator 43/7-8 Silom Surawong Bldg, 5th Floor, Soi Anuman Ratchathon, Surawong Rd, Suriyawong, Bangrak, Bangkok, 10500, Thailand. T. +6622342679. E-mail: info@aprrn.org – lars@aprrn.org.
Contact c/o ICVA, 26-28 Avenue Giuseppe Motta, 1202 Geneva, Switzerland.
URL: https://aprrn.org/

History Nov 2008, Kuala Lumpur (Malaysia). Initiated at the first Asia Pacific Consultation on Refugee Rights (APCRR). **Aims** Advance the rights of refugees and other people in need of protection. **Structure** Board; Steering Committee; Working Groups; Advisors; Secretariat. **Languages** English. **Staff** 10.00 FTE, paid. **Finance** Sources: donations. Annual budget: 400,000 USD. **Activities** Advocacy/lobbying/activism; capacity building; events/meetings; guidance/assistance/consulting; knowledge management/information dissemination; networking/liaising; publishing activities; research/documentation; training/education. **Events** *Consultation* Bangkok (Thailand) 2021, *Refugee Work Rights Roundtable* Bangkok (Thailand) 2020, *Consultation* Bangkok (Thailand) 2018, *Consultation* Bangkok (Thailand) 2016, *Consultation* Bangkok (Thailand) 2014. **Members** Organizational; Individual. Members (451) in 29 countries. Membership countries not specified. **NGO Relations** Member of (1): *International Council of Voluntary Agencies (ICVA, #13092)*.
[2021.05.23/XJ5028/**F**]

♦ Asia Pacific Regional Arbitration Group (APRAG) 02008

Contact c/o THAC 26th fl 689 Bhiraj Tower, Sukhumvit Rd, Khlong Tan Nuea, Vadhana, Bangkok, 10110, Thailand. E-mail: secretariat@aprag.org.
URL: http://www.aprag.org/

History Founded 2 Nov 2004, Sydney (Australia), at the initiative of *Australian Centre for International Commercial Arbitration (ACICA)*. **Aims** Raise standards in, and improve the profile of, international arbitration in the Asia Pacific region. **Structure** General Meeting (every 2 years). Officers: President; up to 3 Past Presidents; up to 12 Vice-Presidents. **Languages** English. **Events** *Conference* Bangkok (Thailand) 2020, *Conference* Nusa Dua (Indonesia) 2016, *Conference* Melbourne, VIC (Australia) 2014, *Conference* Beijing (China) 2013, *Conference* Kuala Lumpur (Malaysia) 2011. **Publications** *APRAG Newsletter* (2 a year).

Members Centres and institutes (38) in 19 countries and territories:
Australia, Brunei Darussalam, China, Hong Kong, India, Indonesia, Japan, Kazakhstan, Korea Rep, Malaysia, Mongolia, Nepal, New Zealand, Pakistan, Philippines, Singapore, Taiwan, United Arab Emirates, Vietnam.
Included in the above, 6 organizations listed in this Yearbook:
ACICA; *China International Economic and Trade Arbitration Commission (CIETAC)*; *Hong Kong International Arbitration Centre (HKIAC)*; *International Chamber of Commerce (ICC, #12534)*; *Singapore International Arbitration Centre (SIAC)*; *Vietnam International Arbitration Centre (VIAC)*.
[2021/XM1166/y/**D**]

♦ Asia-Pacific Regional Network for Early Childhood (ARNEC) 02009

Exec Dir 1 Commonwealth Lane, No 03-27, Singapore 149544, Singapore. T. +6566590227. Fax +6566591227. E-mail: secretariat@arnec.net.
URL: http://www.arnec.net/

History Founded Feb 2008, developing out of *UNICEF (#20332)* – *UNESCO (#20322)* Early Childhood Policy Review Project. Initial support in set-up from UNICEF East Asia and the Pacific Regional Office, *Plan International (#18386)* Regional Office for Asia and *UNESCO Asia and Pacific Regional Bureau for Education (#20301)*. **Aims** Build strong partnerships across sectors and different disciplines, organizations, agencies and institutions in the Asia-Pacific region to advance the agenda on and investment in early childhood. **Structure** Steering Committee of 17 members; Executive Committee of 5 members; Board of Directors of 3 members. **Languages** English. **Staff** 3.00 FTE, paid. **Finance** Supported by: *Open Society Foundations (OSF, #17763)*; *Plan International (#18386)*; *Save the Children Federation (SCF)*; *UNESCO (#20322)*; *UNICEF (#20332)*. **Activities** Knowledge management/information dissemination; advocacy/lobbying/activism; capacity building; networking/liaising. **Events** *Conference / Asia-Pacific Regional ECD Conference* Beijing (China) 2015, *Conference / Asia-Pacific Regional ECD Conference* Manila (Philippines) 2014, *Conference / Asia-Pacific Regional ECD Conference* Singapore (Singapore) 2013, *Conference / Asia-Pacific Regional ECD Conference* Jakarta (Indonesia) 2012, *Conference / Asia-Pacific Regional ECD Conference* Singapore (Singapore) 2011. **Publications** *e-News Flash* (12 a year) – electronic; *ARNEC Connections* (annual). *The White Paper* (2013). **Consultative Status** Consultative status granted from: *UNESCO (#20322)* (Consultative Status). **NGO Relations** Member of (1): *Early Childhood Development Action Network (ECDAN, #05155)*. Cooperates with (1): *Hands to Hearts International (HHI)*.
[2015.09.02/XJ4826/**E**]

♦ Asia-Pacific Regional Space Agency Forum (APRSAF) 02010

Secretariat c/o Japan Aerospace Exploration Agency, Ochanomizu Sola City, 4-6 Kandasurugadai, Chiyoda-ku, Tokyo, 101-8008 Japan. E-mail: secretariat@aprsaf.org.
URL: http://www.aprsaf.org/

History 1993, Japan. Founded following recommendation at Asia-Pacific International Space Year Conference, 1992. **Aims** Gather representatives from space agencies, governmental bodies, provate companies, universities, research institutes and international organizations in the region; seek measures to contribute to socio-economic development and preservation of the global environment through space technology and its applications; exchange views, opinions and information on national space programs and resources; discuss possibilities of future cooperation among space technology developers and users for mutual benefit, identify areas of common interest, and assign priorities thereto; review progress and implementation of plans and programs for further cooperation within the Asia-Pacific region. **Structure** Plenary (annual); Executive Committee (ExCom); Working Groups. **Languages** English. **Finance** Financed by co-organizers of annual sessions. **Activities** Events/meetings; standards/guidelines. **Events** *APRSAF Space Education for All Working Group – Higher Education* Hanoi (Vietnam) 2022, *Annual Session* Tokyo (Japan) 2021, *Annual Session* 2020, *Annual Meeting* Tokyo (Japan) 2020, *Annual Session* Nagoya (Japan) 2019. **Publications** *APRSAF News Mail* (12 a year); *APRSAF News Letter* (2 a year).

Members Organizations in 45 countries and territories:

Australia, Bangladesh, Bhutan, Brunei Darussalam, Cambodia, Canada, Chile, China, Colombia, Czechia, France, Germany, India, Indonesia, Iraq, Israel, Italy, Japan, Kazakhstan, Kenya, Korea Rep, Laos, Malaysia, Mongolia, Myanmar, Nepal, Netherlands, New Zealand, Pakistan, Philippines, Romania, Russia, Singapore, South Africa, Spain, Sri Lanka, Taiwan, Thailand, Türkiye, UK, Ukraine, United Arab Emirates, USA, Uzbekistan, Vietnam.
International organizations (27):
- *ASEAN (#01141)*;
- ASEAN Subcommittee on Space Technology and Applications (ASEANSCOSA);
- *Asian Development Bank (ADB, #01422)*;
- *Asian Disaster Reduction Center (ADRC, #01427)*;
- *Asian Institute of Technology (AIT, #01519)*;
- *Asia-Pacific Satellite Communications Council (APSCC, #02021)*;
- *Committee on the Peaceful Uses of Outer Space (COPUOS, #04277)*;
- *European Space Agency (ESA, #08798)*;
- *FAO Regional Office for Asia and the Pacific (RAP, #09266)*;
- *Group on Earth Observations (GEO, #10735)*;
- *International Astronautical Federation (IAF, #12286)*;
- *International Centre for Integrated Mountain Development (ICIMOD, #12500)*;
- *International Rice Research Institute (IRRI, #14754)*;
- *International Space University (ISU, #15575)*;
- *Mekong River Commission (MRC, #16703)*;
- *OECD (#17693)*;
- *Space Generation Advisory Council in Support of the United Nations Programme on Space Applications (SGAC, #19898)*;
- *Statistical Institute for Asia and the Pacific (SIAP, #19972)*;
- *UNESCO (#20322)*;
- *United Nations Economic and Social Commission for Asia and the Pacific (ESCAP, #20557)*;
- *United Nations Human Settlements Programme (UN-Habitat, #20572)*;
- *United Nations Institute for Disarmament Research (UNIDIR, #20575)*;
- United Nations Office for Outer Space Affairs (UNOOSA);
- UN Secretary General's Advisory Board on Water and Sanitation (UNSGAB). [2020.10.20/XF7154/cy/**F**]

♦ Asia-Pacific Research Center, Stanford CA / see Walter H Shorenstein Asia-Pacific Research Center

♦ Asia Pacific Research Committee (APRC) 02011

SG AMSRS, Level 1, 3 Queen Str, Glebe NSW 2037, Australia. T. +61295663100. Fax +61295715944.
URL: http://www.aprc-research.com/

History Apr 2009. **Aims** Further promote the development of Asia-focused marketing research technologies and insights through creating additional opportunities for cross-border exchanges amongst marketing research associations and communities within the Asia Pacific region. **Structure** Executive Board. **Languages** English. **Staff** 2.00 FTE, paid. **Finance** Members' dues. **Events** *Annual Conference / Conference* Auckland (New Zealand) 2015, *Annual Conference / Conference* Kuala Lumpur (Malaysia) 2014, *Annual Conference / Conference* Bangkok (Thailand) 2013, *Conference* Seoul (Korea Rep) 2012, *Conference* Xian (China) 2011. **Publications** *APRC Newsletter* (4 a year).
Members Associations in 11 countries and territories:
Australia, China, India, Japan, Korea Rep, Malaysia, Mongolia, New Zealand, Singapore, Taiwan, Thailand.
NGO Relations *Americas Research Industry Alliance (ARIA)*; *European Federation of Associations of Market Research Organizations (EFAMRO, #07055)*; *Global Research Business Network (GRBN, #10572)*. [2015.06.01/XJ9575/**D**]

♦ Asia-Pacific Researchers in Organization Studies (inactive)
♦ Asia-Pacific Research Institute (internationally oriented national body)

♦ Asia Pacific Research Integrity Network (APRI Network) 02012

Address not obtained.

History Proposed 2013. First meeting held 2016. **Aims** Further multi-national awareness, understanding and opportunities for collaboration. **Structure** Committee. **Activities** Events/meetings. **Events** *Network Meeting* Tokyo (Japan) 2023, *Seoul Conference* Seoul (Korea Rep) 2021, *Network Meeting* Taipei (Taiwan) 2018, *Network Meeting* Hong Kong 2017, *Network Meeting* San Diego, CA (USA) 2016.
Members Committee members in 11 countries and territories:
Australia, China, Hong Kong, India, Korea Rep, New Zealand, Pakistan, Singapore, Taiwan, Thailand, USA. [2022/XM6648/**C**]

♦ Asia Pacific Research Intelligence Conference (meeting series)
♦ Asia Pacific Research Intelligence Conference – Asia Pacific Research Intelligence Conference (meeting series)

♦ Asia-Pacific Research Network (APRN) 02013

Secretariat Lumang IBON Center, 114 Timog Avenue, 1103 Quezon City, Philippines. T. +6329277060 – +6329277061 – +6329277062. Fax +6329276981. E-mail: secretariat@aprnet.org.
URL: http://www.aprnet.org/

History 1998. **Aims** Develop cooperation among alternative research centres of NGOs, and social movements in the Asia-Pacific region; raise capacity in advocacy and education, particularly in the conduct of research, education, information and advocacy related activities. Increase information exchange on international issues, experiences, technologies and methods in research. **Structure** Board of Convenors. **Languages** English, Filipino, Hindi, Indonesian. **Staff** 3.00 FTE, paid. **Finance** Members' dues. Other sources: grants; sales of publications and services. **Activities** Events/meetings; training/education. **Events** *International conference on women resisting crisis and war / Annual Conference* Baguio (Philippines) 2010, *Annual Conference* Bangalore (India) 2008, *Annual Conference* Bangkok (Thailand) 2007, *Annual Conference* Khon Kaen (Thailand) 2006, *Annual Conference* Hong Kong (Hong Kong) 2005. **Publications** *APRN Journal* (2 a year).
Members National and international organizations (53) in 19 countries and territories:
Australia, Bangladesh, Fiji, Hong Kong, India, Indonesia, Japan, Korea Rep, Lebanon, Malaysia, Mongolia, Nepal, New Zealand, Pakistan, Palestine, Philippines, Sri Lanka, Thailand, Vietnam.
Included in the above, 9 organizations listed in this Yearbook:
Arab NGO Network for Development (ANND, #01016); *Asia Monitor Resource Centre (AMRC)*; *Asia Pacific Forum on Women, Law and Development (APWLD, #01912)*; *Asia Pacific Mission for Migrants (APMM)*; *Consumers International (CI, #04773)* (Regional Office for Asia and the Pacific); *Documentation for Action Groups in Asia (DAGA)*; *International NGO Forum on Indonesian Development (INFID, #14366)*; *Pacific Asia Resource Centre (PARC)*; *PAN Asia and the Pacific (PANAP, #18167)*; *Third World Network (TWN, #20151)*.
NGO Relations Member of: *Climate Justice Now! (CJN!, inactive)*; *Our World is Not for Sale (OWINFS, #17917)*; *People's Coalition on Food Sovereignty (PCFS, #18303)*. Secretariat hosted by: *IBON International (#11037)*. [2018.06.01/XM1859/**y/F**]

♦ Asia-Pacific Research and Training Network on Trade (ARTNeT) . . . 02014

Coordinator Trade Policy UNESCAP, UN Bldg, Rajadamnern Nok Avenue, Bangkok, 10200, Thailand. T. +6622881410. Fax +6622881027 – +6622883066. E-mail: artnetontrade@un.org.
URL: http://artnet.unescap.org/

History Founded Apr 2004, as an open regional network composed of leading trade research institutions across the *United Nations Economic and Social Commission for Asia and the Pacific (ESCAP, #20557)*, with the support of *International Development Research Centre (IDRC, #13162)*. Currently in Phase IV. **Aims** Increase the amount of quality and relevant trade research in the region by harnessing the research capacity already available and developing additional capacity. **Structure** Multi-Stakeholder Steering Committee; Institutional Advisory Board; Secretariat. **Staff** 2.00 FTE, paid. **Finance** In cash contribution: *International Development Research Centre (IDRC, #13162)*. In kind contribution: *United Nations Economic and Social Commission for Asia and the Pacific (ESCAP, #20557)*. Contribution (in kind / in cash) from other core/associate partners made on activity-by-activity basis: *World Trade Organization (WTO, #21864)*; *Asian Development Bank Institute (ADB Institute, #01423)*; *UNCTAD (#20285)*; *International Bank for Reconstruction and Development (IBRD, #12317)* (World Bank). **Activities** Research/documentation; capacity building; knowledge management/information dissemination; events/meetings; politics/policy/regulatory. **Events** *International Conference on Selected Outstanding Issues in Services, Trade and Development* Tokyo (Japan) 2011. **Publications** *ARTNeT Newsletter*. *On-line Book Review Series*; *Policy Brief Series*; *Working Paper Series*. Books.
Members Institutional: research and academic institutions (60) in 24 countries:
Australia, Bangladesh, Cambodia, China, Fiji, Hong Kong, India, Indonesia, Iran Islamic Rep, Korea Rep, Kyrgyzstan, Laos, Malaysia, Mongolia, Myanmar, Nepal, New Zealand, Pakistan, Philippines, Russia, Singapore, Sri Lanka, Thailand, Vietnam.
Included in the above, 18 organizations listed in this Yearbook:
Bangladesh Institute of Development Studies (BIDS); *Centre for Strategic and International Studies, Jakarta (CSIS)*; *China-Europe International Business School (CEIBS, #03888)*; *Energy and Resources Institute (TERI)*; *Indian Council for Research on International Economic Relations (ICRIER)*; *Institute for International Trade (IIT)*; *Institute of Malaysian and International Studies (IKMAS)*; *Institute of South Asian Studies (ISAS)*; *International Institute for Trade and Development (ITD)*; *International Islamic University Malaysia (IIUM, #13961)* (Department of Economics); *ISEAS – Yusof Ishak Institute (ISEAS)*; *Korea Institute for International Economic Policy (KIEP)*; *Mekong Institute (MI, #16701)*; *Research and Information System for Developing Countries, India (RIS, India)*; *South Asian Network on Economic Modeling (SANEM, #19736)*; *South Asia Watch on Trade, Economics and Environment (SAWTEE, #19749)*; *University of International Business and Economics (UIBE)* (School of International Trade and Economics); *University of the South Pacific (USP, #20703)*.
IGO Relations Cooperates with:
- *Agence française de développement (AFD)*;
- *Asia-Pacific Economic Cooperation (APEC, #01887)*;
- *Asian Development Bank (ADB, #01422)*;
- *Asian Development Bank Institute (ADB Institute, #01423)*;
- *FAO (#09260)*;
- *International Bank for Reconstruction and Development (IBRD, #12317)* (World Bank);
- *International Development Research Centre (IDRC, #13162)*;
- *International Trade Centre (ITC, #15703)*;
- *Latin American Integration Association (LAIA, #16343)*;
- *OECD (#17693)*;
- *UNCTAD (#20285)*;
- *UNDP (#20292)* Asia-Pacific Regional Centre;
- *United Nations Economic and Social Commission for Asia and the Pacific (ESCAP, #20557)*;
- *United Nations University (UNU, #20642)* – Comparative Regional Integration Studies, Belgium;
- *World Trade Organization (WTO, #21864)*.

NGO Relations Cooperates with: *Association of Pacific Rim Universities (APRU, #02846)*; *Centre for International Trade, Economics and Environment (CITEE)*; *Economic Research Institute for ASEAN and East Asia (ERIA, #05319)*; *European University Institute (EUI, #09034)* – Global Governance Programme; *Global Trade Analysis Project (GTAP, #10631)*; *Institute of South Asian Studies (ISAS)*; *ISEAS – Yusof Ishak Institute (ISEAS)*; *International Centre for Trade and Sustainable Development, Geneva (ICTSD, #12524)*; *International Institute for Sustainable Development (IISD, #13930)*; *South Asian Network on Economic Modeling (SANEM, #19736)*; *UNU Institute on Comparative Regional Integration Studies (UNU-CRIS, #20717)*. [2018.08.12/XJ5310/**y/F**]

♦ Asia Pacific Resort Development Organisation (unconfirmed)
♦ Asia Pacific Responsible Care Organization (unconfirmed)
♦ Asia Pacific Retinal Imaging Society (unconfirmed)

♦ Asia Pacific Rim Confederation of Counsellors (APRCC) 02015

Pres Hong Kong Shue Yan Univ, 10 Wai Tsui Crescent, Braemar Hill Road, North Point, Hong Kong. E-mail: admin@aprcc.net.
URL: http://aprcc.net/

History Set up following a meeting held 2006, Hong Kong. Incorporated, 19 Jun 2008, Hong Kong. **Aims** Provide counsellors and the general community in the Asia Pacific Rim region an association that will help to develop and maintain standards and delivery of counselling services that are culturally appropriate within the region. **Structure** General Assembly; Council; President; Secretary-General. **Activities** Events/meetings. **Events** *Conference* Brisbane, QLD (Australia) 2019, *Conference* Singapore (Singapore) 2017, *Conference* Wuhan (China) 2015, *Conference* Kuching (Malaysia) 2013, *Conference* Hong Kong (Hong Kong) 2011.
Members Full in 3 countries and territories:
Australia, Hong Kong, New Zealand.
NGO Relations *Asian Professional Counselling and Psychology Association (APCPA)*. [2015/XM6127/**D**]

♦ Asia-Pacific Risk and Insurance Association (APRIA) 02016

Secretariat c/o Singapore College of Insurance, 9 Temasek Boulevard, No 14-01/02/03 Suntec Tower 2, Singapore 038989, Singapore. T. +6562212336. Fax +6562206684. E-mail: apria@scidomain.org.sg.
URL: http://www.apria.org/

History 1997, Singapore (Singapore). **Aims** Promote the study of risk and insurance. **Structure** Board of Governors; Executive Committee. **Languages** English. **Staff** 1.00 FTE, paid. **Finance** Members' dues. Corporate contributions. **Events** *Annual Conference* Osaka (Japan) 2023, *Annual Conference* Seoul (Korea Rep) 2019, *Annual Conference* Singapore (Singapore) 2018, *Annual Conference* Poznań (Poland) 2017, *Seminar on the Role of Mun Jae in Care Settlement and Private Health Insurance* Seoul (Korea Rep) 2017. **Publications** *APRIA Newsletter* (2 a year); *Asia-Pacific Journal of Risk and Insurance* (2 a year).
Members Individuals in 21 countries:
Australia, Austria, Bangladesh, Belgium, China, Germany, Hong Kong, India, Indonesia, Japan, Korea Rep, Malaysia, Oman, Philippines, Singapore, South Africa, Taiwan, Thailand, UK, USA, Vietnam.
Institutions in 5 countries and territories:
Hong Kong, India, Japan, Korea Rep, USA.
NGO Relations Cooperates with: *European Group of Risk and Insurance Economists (EGRIE, #07433)*; *Geneva Association (#10119)*. [2017/XD6528/**D**]

♦ Asia Pacific Rodent Control Society (inactive)
♦ Asia Pacific Roundtable for Consumption and Production / see Asia Pacific Roundtable on Sustainable Consumption and Production (#02017)

♦ Asia Pacific Roundtable on Sustainable Consumption and Production (APRSCP) 02017

Secretariat 35 Soi Petkasem 48 Yak 4-3, Tambon Bangduan, Amphoe Pasicharoen, Bangkok, 10160, Thailand. E-mail: aprscp.secretariat@gmail.com.
URL: http://www.aprscp.net/

History 14 Nov 1997, Bangkok (Thailand), as *Asia Pacific Roundtable for Consumption and Production (APRCP)*. Present name adopted 1998. Current charter adopted 4 Nov 2013. **Aims** Provide leadership and support that will enhance information flow and human resources development, and will strengthen public/private partnerships to stimulate the promotion and implementation of sustainable consumption and production policies, strategies and technologies in the region. **Structure** Board of Trustees; Officers; Secretariat. **Finance** Members' dues. **Activities** Events/meetings. **Events** *Round Table* Cebu City (Philippines) 2021, *Enabling sustainable consumption and production towards achieving green growth* Kuala Lumpur (Malaysia) 2017, *Conference* Siem Reap (Cambodia) 2016, *Conference* Bangkok (Thailand) 2014, *Conference* Colombo (Sri Lanka) 2010. **IGO Relations** Memorandum of Understanding with: *UNEP (#20299)*. **NGO Relations** Member of: *Clean Air Asia (#03983)* Partnership; *Global Network for Resource Efficient and Cleaner Production (RECPnet, #10497)*. [2020/XM1938/**F**]

♦ Asia-Pacific Rugby League (APRL) 02018

COO c/o New Zealand Rugby League, 7 Beasley Av, Penrose, Auckland 1642, New Zealand. E-mail: sua@sua-associates.com.
Sec c/o Australian Rugby League Central, Driver Ave, Moore Park, Sydney NSW 2021, Australia.
URL: http://www.asiapacificrl.com/

History 2011. **Aims** Develop the *sport* of rugby in the Pacific Islands. **Structure** Based at New Zealand Rugby League and Australian Rugby League headquarters. **Languages** English. **Staff** 1.50 FTE, paid; 3.00 FTE, voluntary. **Activities** Training/education; events/meetings; sporting activities. **Publications** Annual Report.
Members Full in 8 countries and territories:
Australia, Cook Is, Fiji, New Zealand, Papua New Guinea, Samoa, South Africa, Tonga.
Observers in 12 countries and territories:
Argentina, Brazil, Chile, El Salvador, Hong Kong, Japan, Niue, Philippines, Solomon Is, Thailand, Uruguay, Vanuatu.
NGO Relations Member of (1): *Organisation of Sports Federations of Oceania (OSFO, #17828)*. Grant from Australian Rugby League Commission. Funding from: *International Rugby League (IRL, #14773)*. [2021/XJ5399/**D**]

♦ **Asia Pacific Rural and Agricultural Credit Association (APRACA)** .. **02019**

SG 109 BAAC Chatuchak (4th Floor), Kamphaeng Phet Rd, Lat Yao, Chatuchak, Bangkok, 10900, Thailand. T. +6622820693 – +6622821365. Fax +6621238743. E-mail: sofia@apraca.org – apraca@apraca.org.
URL: http://www.apraca.org/

History 14 Oct 1977, Delhi (India). Founded at 1st General Assembly, in response to recommendations of FAO sponsored Regional Seminar on Agricultural Credit for Small Farmers in Asia, 1974, and World Conference on Credit for Farmers in Developing Countries, 1975, Rome (Italy). Former names and other names: *Asian and Pacific Regional Agricultural Credit Association* – former; *Association régionale du crédit agricole pour l'Asie et le Pacifique* – former; *Asociación Regional de Crédito Agricola para Asia y el Pacifico* – former. Registration: Department of Provincial Admisistration, No/ID: Jor.3389, Start date: 28 Dec 1994, Thailand, Bangkok. **Aims** Promote efficiency and effectiveness of rural finance and improve access to financial services in the region; support global dissemination. **Structure** General Assembly (every 2 years); Executive Committee. *APRACA Consultancy Services (ACS, see: #02019)*, based in Jakarta (Indonesia). APRACA-Centre for Research and Training in Agricultural Banking (APRACA-CENTRAB), based in Manila (Philippines). **Languages** English. **Staff** 5.00 FTE, paid. **Finance** Sources: donations; members' dues; revenue from activities/projects. **Activities** Capacity building; events/meetings; guidance/assistance/consulting; knowledge management/information dissemination; networking/liaising; politics/policy/regulatory; research/documentation; training/education. Active in all member countries. **Events** *Executive Committee Meeting* Hanoi (Vietnam) 2022, *World Congress on Agricultural and Rural Finance* Morelia (Mexico) 2022, *Biennial General Assembly* New Delhi (India) 2021, *Financing Smallholder Agriculture for Rural Transformation (FINSMART)* Bangkok (Thailand) 2020, *World Congress on Agricultural and Rural Finance* New Delhi (India) 2019. **Publications** *APRACA Newsletter* (4 a year); *Asia-Pacific Rural Finance* (2 a year). Research reports; project implementation reports; country profiles; training toolkits.

Members Institutions (87, mostly central banks, agricultural development banks, commercial banks, microfinance institutions; federations of financial institutions, training and research institutions) involved in rural and agricultural finance activities, at both policy level and implementation level. Members in 24 countries:
Azerbaijan, Bangladesh, Bhutan, Cambodia, China, Fiji, India, Indonesia, Iran Islamic Rep, Japan, Korea Rep, Laos, Malaysia, Myanmar, Nepal, Pakistan, Papua New Guinea, Philippines, Russia, Singapore, Sri Lanka, Thailand, Uzbekistan, Vietnam.

Consultative Status Consultative status granted from: *ECOSOC (#05331)* (Ros C); *FAO (#09260)* (Liaison Status). **IGO Relations** Institution Status with: *International Fund for Agricultural Development (IFAD, #13692)*. **NGO Relations** Cooperates with (2): *Foundation for Development Cooperation*; *International Cooperative Banking Association (ICBA, #12945)*. [2022.10.25/XD6828/**D**]

♦ **Asia-Pacific Safeguards Network (APSN)** **02020**

Secretariat c/o MOFA Nuclear Energy Div, 2-2-1 Kasumigaseki, Chiyoda-ku, Tokyo, 100-8901 Japan. T. +81355018226. Fax +81355018225. E-mail: apsnjapanpoc@mofa.go.jp.
URL: http://www.apsn-safeguards.org/

History Operations commenced 1 Oct 2009. **Aims** Improve the quality, effectiveness and efficiency of safeguards implementation in the Asia-Pacific region. **Structure** Rotating Chair. **Activities** Organizes meetings; coordinates and supports training; facilitates collaboration in research and development; provides technical support and assistance. **Events** *Annual Meeting* Busan (Korea Rep) 2017, *Meeting* Tokyo (Japan) 2015, *Annual Meeting* Jeju (Korea Rep) 2011, *Meeting* Singapore (Singapore) 2011, *Meeting* Denpasar (Indonesia) 2010.

Members Governments and government-affiliated organizations (14):
Australia, Canada, China, Indonesia, Japan, Korea Rep, Malaysia, New Zealand, Philippines, Russia, Singapore, Thailand, USA, Vietnam.
Observer status to:
International Atomic Energy Agency (IAEA, #12294). [2015/XJ5566/**F***]

♦ **Asia-Pacific Satellite Communications Council (APSCC)** **02021**

Main Office Suite T-1602, 170 Seohyeon-ro, Budang-gu, Seongnam GYEONGGI 13590, Korea Rep. T. +82317836244. Fax +82317836249. E-mail: apscc@apscc.or.kr.
URL: http://www.apscc.or.kr/

History 25 Oct 1994, Seoul (Korea Rep). Founded at APSCC Inauguration Council Meeting, when constitution was also adopted and officers were elected. Present were 30 representatives from administrations and regional service operators in the region; United Nations Office for Outer Space Affairs (UN-OOSA) and International Telecommunication Union (ITU) officers witnessed the inauguration. **Aims** Promote communications and *broadcasting* via satellite as well as outer space activities in the Asia-Pacific region for the socioeconomic welfare of the region; develop projects of benefit to the satellite/space industries as a whole. **Structure** Plenary Meeting; Advisory Board; Council; Board of Directors; President; Vice-Presidents; Executive Director; Auditor; Secretariat. **Languages** English. **Staff** 4.00 FTE, paid. **Finance** Members' dues. **Activities** Organizes conferences, workshops, summits and exhibitions through regional coordination in order to discuss issues that affect the industries and to promote and accelerate efficient introduction of outer space activities, new services and business via satellites. **Events** *Satellite Conference* Seoul (Korea Rep) 2022, *Satellite Conference* Manila (Philippines) 2020, *Satellite Conference* Bangkok (Thailand) 2019, *International Communications Satellite Systems Conference* Okinawa (Japan) 2019, *Satellite Conference* Jakarta (Indonesia) 2018. **Publications** *APSCC Monthly E-Newsletter* – electronic; *APSCC Quarterly Newsletter* – print; *APSCC Yearbook*. Proceedings; surveys and reports.

Members As of Nov 2008 Platinum (5); Gold (18) Regular (75); Affiliate (10); Individuals (3). Total members (111) in 31 countries and territories:
Australia, Bangladesh, Cambodia, Canada, China, Fiji, France, Hong Kong, India, Indonesia, Iran Islamic Rep, Israel, Japan, Korea Rep, Luxembourg, Malaysia, Marshall Is, Mongolia, Pakistan, Papua New Guinea, Philippines, Polynesia Fr, Russia, Samoa, Singapore, Taiwan, Thailand, UK, United Arab Emirates, USA, Vietnam.

NGO Relations Member of: *Asia-Pacific Regional Space Agency Forum (APRSAF, #02010)*. [2022/XD6615/**D***]

♦ Asia Pacific School of Economics and Government / see Crawford School of Economics and Government

♦ Asia Pacific School of Economics and Management / see Crawford School of Economics and Government

♦ Asia-Pacific School of Logistics (internationally oriented national body)

♦ **Asia-Pacific Science, Technology and Society Network (APSTSN)** .. **02022**

Contact address not obtained.

History 2008. **Aims** Encourage science, technology and society (STS) research, teaching, collaboration and critical discussion on current STS themes and issues in the Asia-Pacific region. **Events** *Biennial Conference* Kaohsiung (Taiwan) 2015, *Biennial Conference* Singapore (Singapore) 2013. **Publications** *APSTSN Newsletter*. [2014/XJ8474/**F**]

♦ Asia-Pacific Securitisation Association / see Asia-Pacific Structured Finance Association (#02057)

♦ **Asia and Pacific Seed Association (APSA)** **02023**

Secretariat PO Box 1030, Kasetsart Post Office, Bangkok, 10903, Thailand. T. +6629405464. Fax +6629405467. E-mail: apsa@apsaseed.org.
URL: http://www.apsaseed.org/

History Sep 1994. **Aims** Improve conditions for production and supply of quality seed and *planting* material in the Asia-Pacific region; strengthen collaboration between public and private enterprises. **Structure** General Assembly; Executive Committee; Office bearers (5); Standing Committees (4); Committees (2); Special Interest Groups (3); Secretariat located in Bangkok (Thailand). **Languages** English. **Staff** 9.00 FTE, paid. **Finance** Members' dues. **Activities** Networking/liaising; knowledge management/information dissemination; training/education. **Events** *Annual Congress* Bangkok (Thailand) 2022, *Annual Congress* Shenzhen (China) 2020, *Annual Congress* Kuala Lumpur (Malaysia) 2019, *Annual Congress* Manila (Philippines) 2018, *Annual Congress* Bangkok (Thailand) 2017. **Publications** *Asian Seed and Planting Material* (6 a year) – magazine. *Seed Import and Exports*. Seed industry reports; technical reports.

Members Public and private sector enterprises and other organizations in 42 countries and territories:
Argentina, Australia, Bangladesh, Belgium, Bolivia, Cambodia, Canada, Chile, China, Czechia, Denmark, Egypt, France, Germany, Greece, Hong Kong, India, Indonesia, Iran Islamic Rep, Israel, Italy, Japan, Kazakhstan, Kenya, Korea Rep, Libya, Malaysia, Nepal, Netherlands, New Zealand, Pakistan, Philippines, Singapore, South Africa, Spain, Sri Lanka, Syrian AR, Taiwan, Thailand, UK, USA, Vietnam.

IGO Relations Observer to: *Union internationale pour la protection des obtentions végétales (UPOV, #20436)*. [2019/XD5809/**D**]

♦ **Asia-Pacific Self-Medication Industry (APSMI)** **02024**

SG ITOHPIA Iwamotocho 1-chome Bldg, 4th Fl, 1-8-15 Iwamotocho, Chiyoda-ku, Tokyo, 101-0032 Japan. T. +81358092356. Fax +81358234974. E-mail: info@apsmi.net.
URL: http://www.apsmi.net/

History Founded 5 Nov 2010, Taipei (Taiwan). Regional association of: *Global Self-Care Federation (GSCF, #10588)*. **Aims** Contribute to development of consumer healthcare industries, especially OTC industries in the Asia-Pacific region; be recognized and act as the official body of, for and by the region; nurture the responsible self-medication environment for consumers, healthcare professionals and health authorities. **Structure** General Assembly (every 2 years); Board of Directors. **Languages** English. **Staff** 1.00 FTE, paid. **Finance** Members' dues. **Activities** Awareness raising; knowledge management/information dissemination; research and development; events/meetings. **Events** *General Assembly* Beijing (China) 2019, *General Assembly* Nagoya (Japan) 2016, *Asia Pacific Regional Conference* Phuket (Thailand) 2014, *General Assembly* Phuket (Thailand) 2014, *General Assembly* Seoul (Korea Rep) 2012. **Publications** *APSMI Country Report* (2016).

Members Societies in 7 countries and territories:
China, Indonesia, Japan, Korea Rep, Philippines, Taiwan, Thailand.

NGO Relations Member of: *Global Self-Care Federation (GSCF, #10588)*. [2018.09.12/XJ7486/t/**D**]

♦ **Asia-Pacific Signal and Information Processing Association (APSIPA)** **02025**

Manager Ctr for Signal Processing, HK Poly Electronic Information Engineering, Hung Hom, Kowloon, Hong Kong.
Sec address not obtained.
URL: http://www.apsipa.org/

History 2009. Registration: Hong Kong. **Aims** Promote a broad spectrum of research and education activities in signal and information processing. **Structure** Steering Committee. Board of Governors of 4. **Events** *Annual Summit and Conference* Chiang Mai (Thailand) 2022, *Annual Summit and Conference* Tokyo (Japan) 2021, *Annual Summit and Conference* Kowloon (Hong Kong) 2020, *Annual Summit and Conference* Lanzhou (China) 2019, *Annual Summit and Conference* Honolulu, HI (USA) 2018. [2021/XJ4884/**D**]

♦ **Asia Pacific Smart Card Association (APSCA)** **02026**

Dir Unit 804 Modern Communication Bldg, 201 Xin Jinqiao Road, Pudong District, 201206 Shanghai, China. T. +862131200321. Fax +862150777112.
URL: http://www.apsca.org/

Aims Deliver information, consultancy, guidance and networking to corporations and government organisations, including smart card scheme operators and suppliers. **Events** *Transport Payments Asia Pacific Conference* Manila (Philippines) 2019, *Next-General Cards Conference* Singapore (Singapore) 2019, *Powered and Next-Generation Cards Meeting* Singapore (Singapore) 2018, *Powered and Next Generation Cards Conference* Singapore (Singapore) 2017, *Visa Technology Partner Forum* Singapore (Singapore) 2017.

Members Full in 8 countries and territories:
China, Hong Kong, Japan, Korea Rep, Malaysia, Singapore, Taiwan, Thailand. [2019/XJ9164/**D**]

♦ Asia Pacific Snooker & Billiards Federation (internationally oriented national body)

♦ Asia-Pacific Socialist Organization (inactive)

♦ **Asia-Pacific Society for Adult Congenital Heart Disease (APSACHD)** **02027**

Office address not obtained. E-mail: info@apsachd.org.
URL: http://www.apsachd.org/

History 29 May 2008, Jeju (Korea Rep). Constitution and bylaws adopted Jul 2010. **Aims** Promote, maintain and pursue excellence in the care of adults with congenital heart disease. **Structure** Board of Directors. **Events** *Symposium* Gyeongju (Korea Rep) 2020, *Symposium* Okayama (Japan) 2019, *Congress of Asia-Pacific Adult CHD* Shanghai (China) 2016, *Congress of Asia-Pacific Adult CHD* New Delhi (India) 2014, *Congress of Asia-Pacific Adult CHD* Bali (Indonesia) 2012. [2020/AA1891/**D**]

♦ **Asia-Pacific Society for Alcohol and Addiction Research (APSAAR)** **02028**

Office 5-3-1 Nobi, Yokosuka KANAGAWA, 239-0841 Japan. T. +81468481550. Fax +81468497743. E-mail: info@apsaar.org.
URL: http://www.apsaar.org/

Aims Promote excellence in research on alcohol, addiction and related phenomena in Asia-Pacific region. **Structure** Board of Directors. Officers: President; 2 Vice-Presidents; Secretary/Treasurer; Assistant Secretary/Treasurer. Committees (2): Membership; Education. **Finance** Members' dues. **Events** *Congress* Malaysia 2019, *Congress* Taipei (Taiwan) 2017, *Congress* Sydney, NSW (Australia) 2015, *Congress* Bangkok (Thailand) 2011, *Congress* Seoul (Korea Rep) 2009. **NGO Relations** Affiliated with: *International Society for Biomedical Research on Alcoholism (ISBRA, #14968)*. [2019/XJ1248/**D**]

♦ **Asia-Pacific Society for Applied Phycology (APSAP)** **02029**

Pres Yantai Inst of Coastal Zone Research, Chinese Academy of Sciences, 17 Chunhui Road, Yantai, 264005 Shandong, China. T. +865352109005.
URL: http://www.apsap.org/

History Founded 1994. Previously also referred to as *ASAP*. **Aims** Promote development of applied phycology; increase cooperation among individuals and organizations with an interest in applied phycology; promote education and training in applied phycology. **Structure** Executive Council. **Finance** Members' dues. **Events** *Asia-Pacific Conference on Algal Biotechnology* Nanchang (China) 2019, *Asia-Pacific Conference on Algal Biotechnology* Bangkok (Thailand) 2016, *Asia-Pacific Conference on Algal Biotechnology* Adelaide, SA (Australia) 2012, *Asia-Pacific conference on algal biotechnology* Delhi (India) 2009, *Asia-Pacific Conference on Algal Biotechnology* Makati (Philippines) 2006. **Publications** *ASAP Newsletter*. [2017/XD8245/**D**]

♦ **Asia-Pacific Society for Artificial Organs (APSAO)** **02030**

Contact c/o Assn for Supporting Academic Societies, Koishikawa Urban 4F, 5-3-13 Otsuka, Bunkyo-ku, Tokyo, 112-0012 Japan. T. +81359816011. Fax +81359846012. E-mail: apsao@asas-mail.jp.
URL: http://www.jsao.org/apsao/

History 2013. **Aims** Promote the study of the art, science and practice of artificial organs in Asia-Pacific region; facilitate the exchange of ideas in the field of artificial organs through scientific meetings and by personal contact between artificial organs specialists in the region. **Structure** Board of Trustees; Council; Executive Committee; Congress Committee. **Finance** Members' dues. **Activities** Events/meetings; knowledge management/information dissemination. **Members** Individuals: Active; Senior; Honorary; Student; Supporting. Membership countries not specified. [2017/XM6292/**D**]

♦ Asia Pacific Society of Bioscientists (inactive)

♦ **Asia Pacific Society of Cardiovascular and Interventional Radiology (APSCVIR)** **02031**

SG Dept of Radiology, Asian Medical Ctr, 83 Asanbyeongwon-gil, Songpa-gu, Seoul 38-733, Korea Rep. T. +82230104388. Fax +82230103845.
URL: http://www.apscvir.com/

History 1991. **Aims** Meet regularly to encourage international exchange of knowledge vital to cardiovascular and interventional radiology among medical doctors in different countries of the Asia Pacific region; bring together interventional radiologists and individuals in related fields to improve the level of clinical practice and research of the subject; support continuing education and training of doctors in each country through the appropriate forum or refresher courses to further define the role of cardiovascular and interventional radiology as a subspecialty of medicine in the Asia Pacific region. **Structure** International Executive Committee (IEC), consisting of Officers and National Delegates. Officers: President; Immediate Past President; President-Elect; Secretary General; Treasurer; 2 Auditors. **Languages** English. **Events** *Congress* Taipei (Taiwan) 2021, *Congress* Bali (Indonesia) 2019, *Congress* Auckland (New Zealand) 2018, *Asia Pacific Cardiovascular Intervention and Surgery Symposium* Seoul (Korea Rep) 2018, *Congress* Suzhou (China) 2016.

Members Full in 12 countries and territories:
Australia, China, Hong Kong, India, Indonesia, Japan, Korea Rep, Malaysia, New Zealand, Singapore, Taiwan, Thailand. [2014/XD4787/**D**]

♦ Asia-Pacific Society of Clinical Microbiology and Infection (APSCMI) 02032

SG National Centre for Infectious Diseases, Infectious Disease Dept and Training Office, 16 Jalan Tan Tock Seng, Singapore 308442, Singapore. E-mail: secretariat@apscmi.net.
Pres Dept of Medicine, NUS, 5 lower Kent Ridge Rd, Singapore 119074, Singapore. T. +6567795555. Fax +6567794112. E-mail: mdcpat@nus.edu.sg.
URL: https://www.apscmi.net/

History 1986, Bangkok (Thailand). Officially inaugurated Feb 1989, Kuala Lumpur (Malaysia). Former names and other names: *Western Pacific Society of Chemotherapy (WPSC)* – former. **Aims** Facilitate the acquisition and dissemination of knowledge in the field of microbial diseases and their treatment. **Structure** Council of representatives elected by national societies or individuals. Executive Committee, consisting of President, General Secretary, Treasurer, Past President/President-Elect and 3 members. **Languages** English. **Staff** None. **Finance** Members' dues. **Events** *Asia Pacific Congress of Clinical Microbiology and Infection (APCCMI 2023)* Seoul (Korea Rep) 2023, *International Congress of Antimicrobial Chemotherapy* Perth, WA (Australia) 2022, *Asia Pacific Congress of Clinical Microbiology and Infection* Singapore (Singapore) 2021, *Asia Pacific Congress of Clinical Microbiology and Infection* Singapore (Singapore) 2020, *Asia Pacific Congress of Clinical Microbiology and Infection* Wan Chai (Hong Kong) 2018. **Publications** *Journal of Infectious Diseases and Antimicrobial Agents* – with Thai national association. Congress proceedings.
Members Associations in 11 countries and territories:
Australia, China, Hong Kong, Indonesia, Japan, Malaysia, New Zealand, Philippines, Singapore, Taiwan, Thailand.
NGO Relations Member of: *International Society of Antimicrobial Chemotherapy (ISAC, #14925).*
[2021/XD2367/**D**]

♦ Asia-Pacific Society for the Cognitive Sciences of Music (APSCOM) 02033

Pres address not obtained.
Founding Pres Kyoto City University of Arts, Faculty of Music, 13-6 Kutsukake-cho, Nishikyo-ku, Kyoto, 610-11 Japan.
URL: http://apscom.weebly.com/

History 1 Jan 2001, Fukuoka (Japan). **Aims** Foster research and collaboration in the cognitive science of music; promote communication and friendship among researchers in the Asia-Pacific region. **Languages** English. **Events** *Conference* Kyoto (Japan) 2017, *Conference* Seoul (Korea Rep) 2014, *Conference* Beijing (China) 2011, *Conference* Sapporo (Japan) 2008, *Conference* Seoul (Korea Rep) 2005.
Members National societies in 4 countries:
Australia, China, Japan, Korea Rep.
NGO Relations Participating organization in: *International Conference on Music Perception and Cognition (ICMPC).*
[2018/XD8239/**D**]

♦ Asia-Pacific Society for Computers in Education (APSCE) 02034

Main Office Center for Science, 300 Jhongda Road, Office E6-B404, Chung Li 32001, Taiwan. E-mail: managingsecretary@apsce.net.
URL: http://www.apsce.net/

History Evolved from Asia-Pacific Chapter of *Association for the Advancement of Computing in Education (AACE).* Statutes adopted 21 Jan 2004. Amended: 8 Dec 2004; 12 Jul 2007; 27 May 2010; 5 Oct 2010; 11 Jan 2012; 1 Jan 2014. **Aims** Promote conduct and communication of research employing the use of computing technologies in education within the Asia-Pacific region and internationally; encourage and support the academic activities of researchers in member countries and nurture a vibrant research community of younger as well as more experienced researches; enhance international awareness of research conducted by researchers in member countries; obtain greater representation of active researchers from the Asia-Pacific region in committees of related leading academic and professional organizations and the editorial boards of reputable journals. **Structure** Executive Committee; Advisory Board; Special Interest Groups. **Activities** Research/documentation; events/meetings; awards/prizes/competitions. **Events** *International Conference on Computers in Education (ICCE 2021)* 2021, *APSCE International Conference on Computational Thinking and STEM Education* Singapore (Singapore) 2021, *International Conference on Computers in Education (ICCE 2020)* 2020, *International Conference on Computers in Education (ICCE 2019)* Hengchun (Taiwan) 2019, *International Conference on Computers in Education (ICCE 2018)* Manila (Philippines) 2018. **Publications** *Research and Practice in Technology Enhanced Learning* (3 a year). Newsletter.
Members Individuals in 27 countries and territories:
Australia, Austria, Canada, China, Croatia, Denmark, Germany, Ghana, Hong Kong, India, Indonesia, Japan, Korea Rep, Malaysia, Netherlands, New Zealand, Norway, Philippines, Qatar, Singapore, Spain, Sweden, Taiwan, Thailand, UK, United Arab Emirates, USA.
[2021/XM1710/**D**]

♦ Asia Pacific Society for Computing and Information Technology (APSCIT) 02035

Office No 2 Beining Rd, Jhongjheng District, Keelung, Taiwan.
URL: http://www.apscit.org/

Structure Boards (3): Academic Advisory; Industrial Advisory; Operating. **Activities** Events/meetings. **Events** *Annual Meeting* Tsukuba (Japan) 2020, *ISACIT : International Symposium for Advanced Computing and Information Technology* Kaohsiung (Taiwan) 2019, *IC-LYCS: International Conference for Leading and Young Computer Scientists* Okinawa (Japan) 2019, *Annual Meeting* Sapporo (Japan) 2019, *CICCAT: Conference on Intelligent Computing, Communication and Applied Technologies* Zhuhai (China) 2018.
Members Full in 6 countries and territories:
China, Hong Kong, Japan, Korea Rep, Singapore, Taiwan.
[2020/XM7868/**D**]

♦ Asia-Pacific Society of Cornea and Refractive Surgery (inactive)

♦ Asia-Pacific Society for Ethnomusicology (APSE) 02036

Secretariat Fujian-Taiwan Research Ctr, Fujian Teachers Univ, 350007 Fujian, China. T. +8659183443674. Fax +8659183443674.
URL: http://www.mtrc99.net/APSE/index.asp

Events *Annual Conference* Maha Sarakham (Thailand) 2014, *Annual Conference* Hangzhou (China) 2009, *Annual Conference* Maha Sarakham (Thailand) 2008, *Annual Conference* Seoul (Korea Rep) 2007, *Annual Conference* Lanzhou (China) 2006. **NGO Relations** Member of: *International Music Council (IMC, #14199).*
[2014/XJ0671/**D**]

♦ Asia-Pacific Society of Eye Genetics (unconfirmed)

♦ Asia Pacific Society for Healthcare Quality (APSHQ) 02037

Pres Room LB04, Patrick Manson Bldg, 7 Sassoon Rd, Pokfulam, Hong Kong.

Events *International conference* Singapore (Singapore) 2008, *International conference* Hong Kong (Hong Kong) 2006.
[2019.08.13/XJ0096/**D**]

♦ Asia Pacific Society of Human Genetics (APSHG) 02038

Past Pres Clinical Genetic Service, Dept of Health, Cheung Sha Wan Jockey Club Clinic, 2 Kwong Lee Road, Sham Shui Po, Kowloon, Hong Kong. E-mail: apshg@apshg.info.
Registered Office 100 Bukit Timah Road, KK Women's and Children's Hospital, Singapore 229899, Singapore.
URL: http://www.apshg.info/

History 2006. Registration: Start date: 17 Feb 2006, Singapore. **Aims** Promote research in basic and applied human and medical genetics; integrate professional and public education in all areas of human genetics; provide a forum where scientists can share their research findings as well as increase or spread knowledge and standing of human and medical genetics among the various professionals including health professionals, health policy makers, legislators and the general public. **Structure** Board of Directors; Executive Committee. Special Interest Group: *Professional Society of Genetic Counselors in Asia (PSGCA, #18516).* **Events** *Conference* Manila (Philippines) 2019, *Meeting on Clinical Sequencing and Genomics* Singapore (Singapore) 2018, *NGS Bioinformatics and Clinical Curation Workshop* Singapore (Singapore) 2018, *Conference* Bangkok (Thailand) 2017, *Genetics and genomics – the path to translational medicine* Hanoi (Vietnam) 2015. **Members** Regular; Junior; Life; Senior; Corporate. Membership countries not specified. **NGO Relations** Member of (1): *International Federation of Human Genetics Societies (IFHGS, #13451).*
[2020/XM3788/**D**]

♦ Asia-Pacific Society for Impotence Research / see Asia Pacific Society for Sexual Medicine (#02045)

♦ Asia Pacific Society of Infection Control (APSIC) 02039

Pres Singapore General Hospital, Outram Road, Singapore 169608, Singapore.
URL: http://apsic-apac.org/

History Mar 1998. **Aims** Build a network of infection control professionals working towards quality healthcare in the Asia Pacific region, facilitate exchange of information and data on infection control principles and practices; formulate recommendations, guidelines or standards; assist in collaborative work of research or investigations of outbreaks. **Structure** Council; Executive Committee. **Languages** English. **Activities** Events/meetings; networking/liaising. **Events** *International Congress* Singapore (Singapore) 2022, *International Congress* Singapore (Singapore) 2021, *International Congress* Danang (Vietnam) 2019, *International Congress* Bangkok (Thailand) 2017, *International Congress* Taipei (Taiwan) 2015. **Publications** *Asian Journal of Infection Control* (2 a year).
Members Full in 15 countries and territories:
Australia, China, Hong Kong, India, Indonesia, Japan, Korea Rep, Macau, Malaysia, Pakistan, Philippines, Singapore, Taiwan, Thailand, Vietnam.
IGO Relations *WHO (#20950).* **NGO Relations** National infection control societies and associations.
[2017.03.08/XD6926/**D**]

♦ Asia-Pacific Society of Interventional Oncology (unconfirmed)

♦ Asia Pacific Society for Materials Research (APSMR) 02040

Hong Kong Branch Ste 618, Hollywood Plaza, 610 Nathan Road, Mongkok, Kowloon, Hong Kong. E-mail: hk@apsmr.com – japan@apsmr.com.
URL: http://www.apsmr.org/

Aims Promote communications and technical information exchange across all aspects of materials science research. **Structure** Advisory Boards (2): Academic; Industrial. Operating Committee; Student Leaders Division. **Activities** Training/education; events/meetings; awards/prizes/competitions. **Events** *Symposium for the Promotion of Applied Research Collaboration in Asia (SPARCA)* Kowloon (Hong Kong) 2022, *Annual Meeting* Singapore (Singapore) 2021, *Annual Meeting* Tsukuba (Japan) 2020, *Annual Meeting* Sapporo (Japan) 2019, *International Conference for Leading and Young Materials Scientists (IC-LYMS)* Shanghai (China) 2019. **Publications** *Acta Materials Science and Technology (AMST)* – journal.
Members Full in 6 countries and territories:
China, Hong Kong, Japan, Korea Rep, Singapore, Taiwan.
[2022/XM6552/**D**]

♦ Asia-Pacific Society of Ocular Oncology and Pathology (unconfirmed)

♦ Asia Pacific Society of Ophthalmic Plastic and Reconstructive Surgery (APSOPRS) 02041

Secretariat CLINICAHENSON, 066 MacArthur Hi-way, 2009 Angeles PAM, Philippines. T. +639053089960. E-mail: info@apsoprs.org.
URL: http://www.apsoprs.org/

History Founded 2000. **Aims** Promote best practice of ophthalmic plastic and reconstructive surgery in the Asia-Pacific region; conduct studies on oculoplastic conditions; increase education in ophthalmic plastic and reconstructive surgery. **Structure** General Meeting (every 2 years); Council; Advisory Board. Committees (8): Ethics; Finance; Legal; Membership; Nominations; Public Relations; Research; Scientific Programme. **Events** *Biennial Meeting* Manila (Philippines) 2021, *Biennial Meeting* Manila (Philippines) 2020, *Biennial Meeting* Hong Kong (Hong Kong) 2018, *Biennial Meeting* Osaka (Japan) 2016, *Biennial Meeting* Delhi (India) 2014. **Publications** *iPlastics Newsletter.*
Members Individuals in 15 countries and territories:
Australia, Bangladesh, China, Hong Kong, India, Indonesia, Iran Islamic Rep, Japan, Korea Rep, Malaysia, Myanmar, Nepal, Philippines, Singapore, Thailand.
NGO Relations Member of: *Asia-Pacific Academy of Ophthalmology (APAO, #01814); International Council of Ophthalmology (ICO, #13057).*
[2018/XM0575/v/**D**]

♦ Asia Pacific Society of Osseointegration (APSO) 02042

Contact address not obtained. E-mail: apacosseo@gmail.com.
URL: https://osseo.asia/

History 2019. **Aims** Bring together dental practitioners and professionals with interests in the field of Osseointegration and its related disciplines to share research and information. **Structure** Executive Board. **Activities** Events/meetings. **Events** *Annual Meeting* Bangkok (Thailand) 2022, *Annual Meeting* Kuala Lumpur (Malaysia) 2020.
[2022/AA2709/**D**]

♦ Asia Pacific Society of Periodontology 02043

Contact CACDRC – Dental School, Univ of Adelaide, Frome Road, Adelaide SA 5005, Australia. T. +61883033435. Fax +61883036429. E-mail: info@apsperio.org.
Honorary Advisor Dept of Periodontology, Osaka Univ Graduate School of Dentistry, 1-8 Yamakaoka, Suita, Osaka, 565-0871 Japan. T. +81668792930. E-mail: ipshinya@dent.osaka-u.ac.jp.
URL: http://www.apsperio.org/

History 15 Oct 1993, Tokyo (Japan). Founded following the 2nd Asian Pacific Periodontal Symposium. **Aims** Serve as a non-profit medium for the exchange, advancement and dissemination of scientific knowledge related to periodontal research and education in the Asian Pacific regions; foster collegiality, friendships and collaborations in the field of periodontology. **Structure** Officers: President; Vice-President; Immediate Past President; Secretary General; Treasurer; Editor of Publications. Counsellors (5). **Languages** English. **Finance** Members' dues. Donations from dental industry. **Activities** Organizes Asia Pacific Periodontal Symposium (every 2 years). **Events** *International Meeting* Bangkok (Thailand) 2022, *International Meeting* Bangkok (Thailand) 2021, *Meeting* Kuala Lumpur (Malaysia) 2019, *Meeting* Seoul (Korea Rep) 2017, *Meeting* Bali (Indonesia) 2015. **Publications** Symposium proceedings. **Members** Individuals possessing a dental, medical or veterinary degree and who have an interest in periodontology. Membership countries not specified.
[2021/XD6117/**D**]

♦ Asia-Pacific Society for Physical Activity / see Australasian Society for Physical Activity
♦ Asia Pacific Society of Precision Anti-Aging Medicine (unconfirmed)
♦ Asia-Pacific Society for Process Intensification and Sustainability (unconfirmed)

♦ Asia Pacific Society for Public Affairs (APSPA) 02044

Contact address not obtained. T. +62274387656. Fax +62274387646. E-mail: apspaorg@gmail.com.
URL: http://www.apspa.org/

History Founded 20 Feb 2013, Bali (Indonesia). **Structure** Executive Committee; Board of Experts. **Activities** Events/meetings. **Events** *ICONPO : International Conference on Public Organization* Yogyakarta (Indonesia) 2021, *ICONPO : International Conference on Public Organization* Yogyakarta (Indonesia) 2020, *ICONPO : International Conference on Public Organization* Khon Kaen (Thailand) 2019, *ICONPO : International Conference on Public Organization* Tamil Nadu (India) 2018, *ICONPO : International Conference on Public Organization* West Java (Indonesia) 2017.
Members Institutions; Individuals. Institutions in 9 countries and territories:
Cambodia, India, Indonesia, Korea Rep, Malaysia, Myanmar, Philippines, Taiwan, Thailand.
[2019/XM7866/**D**]

♦ Asia-Pacific Society for Sexual and Impotence Research / see Asia Pacific Society for Sexual Medicine (#02045)

♦ Asia Pacific Society for Sexual Medicine (APSSM) 02045

SG Urology Division, Dep Surgery Faculty Medicine, Chulalongkorn Univ, Sirinthorn Bldg, Rama IV Road, Bangkok, 10330, Thailand. T. +6622564515.
URL: http://www.apssm.org/

History 1987, Hong Kong, as *Asia-Pacific Society for Impotence Research (APSIR).* Honorary/Founding President: Prof M Shirai. Also referred to as *Asia-Pacific Society for Sexual and Impotence Research (APSSIR).* **Aims** Improve the quality of care for erectile dysfunction patients; promote research in the field of sexual and male aging. **Structure** Meeting of members (every 2 years). Executive Council of 22 members. Executive Board. Secretariat rotates among members. Officers: President; Founding President; Honorary President; Immediate Past President; Secretary General Deputy Secretary General; Treasurer; Deputy Treasurer. **Languages** English. **Staff** 1.00 FTE, paid. **Finance** Members' dues. **Activities** Runs survey on knowledge, attitude and practices related to erectal dysfunction. Cosponsors meetings. **Events** *Biennial Meeting* Kaohsiung (Taiwan) 2021,

Biennial Meeting Brisbane, QLD (Australia) 2019, *Asian-Japan Conference on Men's Health and Aging* Chiang Mai (Thailand) 2017, *Biennial Meeting* Chiang Mai (Thailand) 2017, *Scientific Conference* Busan (Korea Rep) 2016. **Publications** *APSIR Newsbulletin* (2 a year). *APSIR Handbook*. Supplement.
Members Active persons residing or practising in Asia Pacific countries. Honorary. Individuals in 16 countries and territories:
Australia, China, Hong Kong, India, Indonesia, Japan, Korea Rep, Malaysia, Mongolia, Pakistan, Singapore, Sri Lanka, Taiwan, Thailand, Uzbekistan, Vietnam.
NGO Relations Asian-Pacific Chapter of: *International Society for Sexual Medicine (ISSM, #15441)*.
[2014/XD5344/v/**D**]

♦ Asia Pacific Society of Speech, Language and Hearing (APSSLH) .. 02046

Main Office 1013 Shallom Hall, 40 Kangnam-ro, Giheung-gu, Yongin GYEONGGI 16979, Korea Rep. E-mail: info@apsslh.net.
URL: https://apsslh.net
History Set up with the title *Asia Pacific Society for the Study of Speech, Language and Hearing*. **Aims** Provide a forum for exchange of research and clinical ideas relating to all aspects of normal and disordered speech, language and hearing in the Asia Pacific region. **Structure** General Meeting (every 2 years); Steering Committee. **Languages** English. **Events** *Conference* Narita (Japan) 2017, *Conference* Guangzhou (China) 2015, *Conference* Taichung (Taiwan) 2013, *Conference* Christchurch (New Zealand) 2011, *Conference* Honolulu, HI (USA) 2009. **Publications** *Speech, Language and Hearing*. [2021/XM0083/**D**]

♦ Asia Pacific Society for the Study of the Aging Male (APSSAM) ... 02047

SG Subang Jaya Medical Centre, No 1, Jalan SS 12/1A, Subang Jaya, Selangor, Malaysia. T. +60356391777. Fax +60356306571.
History Founded Mar 2001, Kuala Lumpur (Malaysia), during 1st Asian meeting of *International Society for the Study of the Aging Male (ISSAM, #15462)*. **Aims** Improve health, status, longevity and quality of life of the aging male; promote research and development in the field of aging in the male; promote and facilitate the exchange and dissemination of knowledge and information in the field. **Structure** Council; Executive Committee. **Events** *Meeting* Hyderabad (India) 2013, *Biennial Congress* Busan (Korea Rep) 2011, *Biennial congress* Osaka (Japan) 2009, *Biennial Congress* Bali (Indonesia) 2007, *Biennial congress* Chiang Mai (Thailand) 2005. **Members** Membership countries not specified. [2016.07.26/XD9289/**D**]

♦ Asia Pacific Society for the Study of Speech, Language and Hearing / see Asia Pacific Society of Speech, Language and Hearing (#02046)

♦ Asia-Pacific Society of Thyroid Surgery (APTS) 02048

SG Dept of Otolaryngology-Head and Neck Surgery, College of Medicine, Hanyang Univ, 222 Wangsimni-ro, Seongdong-gu, Seoul 04763, Korea Rep. T. +82222908585. Fax +82222933335. E-mail: kytae@hanyang.ac.kr.
Secretariat c/o Keion Co Ltd, 11F Centenia Bldg 219, Gonghang-daero, Gangseo-gu, Seoul, Korea Rep. E-mail: congress@apthyroid.org.
URL: http://apthyroid.org/
History Preparatory meeting held 27 Jul 2014, New York NY (USA), by 19 doctors from 10 countries. **Aims** Provide a common platform for specialists of thyroid surgery to promote science through research, advance knowledge and techniques of thyroid surgery, and develop a spirit of friendship among surgeons and physicians associated with thyroid surgery. **Structure** Council; Executive Committee; Advisory Committee. Committees (2): Scientific; Research. **Languages** English. **Finance** Sources: members' dues. **Activities** Events/meetings. **Events** *Thyroid – controversies to consensus* Kochi (India) 2020, *Congress* Kaohsiung (Taiwan) 2018, *Congress* Okinawa (Japan) 2017, *Congress* Seoul (Korea Rep) 2015, *Congress* Seoul (Korea Rep) 2015.
Members Individuals (about 1260) in 38 countries and territories:
Australia, Bangladesh, Belgium, Brazil, Bulgaria, Canada, Chile, China, Czechia, Finland, Germany, Hong Kong, India, Indonesia, Iran Islamic Rep, Israel, Italy, Japan, Kazakhstan, Korea Rep, Malaysia, Myanmar, New Zealand, Norway, Pakistan, Philippines, Poland, Russia, Saudi Arabia, Singapore, Spain, Taiwan, Thailand, Türkiye, UK, United Arab Emirates, USA, Vietnam.
[2020.03.16/XM7859/v/**C**]

♦ Asia-Pacific Society of Travel Medicine / see Asia Pacific Travel Health Society (#02070)
♦ Asia Pacific Socio-Economic Research Institute (internationally oriented national body)

♦ Asia Pacific Sociological Association (APSA) 02049

Sec Western Avenue, Camperdown Campus, Univ of Sydney, Sydney NSW 2006, Australia.
URL: https://apsasociology.wordpress.com/
History Sep 1997, Kuala Lumpur (Malaysia). **Aims** Promote development of sociology; represent sociologists in the Asia Pacific region regardless of their school of thought, methodological approach or ideological position. **Structure** General Assembly (every 2 years); Executive Committee; Research Networks. **Languages** English. **Staff** 16.00 FTE, voluntary. **Finance** Sources: members' dues. **Events** *Conference* 2020, *Conference* Hakone (Japan) 2018, *Conference* Phnom Penh (Cambodia) 2016, *Conference* Chiang Mai (Thailand) 2014, *Conference* Manila (Philippines) 2012. **Publications** *APSA Newsletter*.
Members Individuals (Regular, Affiliated, Student); Collective (Regular, Affiliated). Members in 19 countries and territories:
Australia, Bangladesh, Cambodia, China, Fiji, Hong Kong, India, Indonesia, Japan, Korea Rep, Malaysia, Nepal, New Zealand, Philippines, Switzerland, Taiwan, Thailand, USA, Vietnam. [2022.02.15/XD6661/**D**]

♦ Asia-Pacific Software Engineering Conference (meeting series)

♦ Asia Pacific Solidarity Coalition (APSOC) 02050

Program Coordinator Galaxy St, SGIS Subdivision, Matina, 8000 Davao DAS, Philippines. T. +6382299257475. Fax +63822992052. E-mail: gus@iidnet.org.
URL: http://www.iidnet.org/
History 1 May 2005, Philippines, developing out of *Asia Pacific Coalition for East Timor (APCET)*, set up 1994, Manila (Philippines). **Aims** Consolidate efforts of the various groups already working on national issues and amplify those efforts in the regional and international arena; advocate human rights in the region; support the right to self-determination of people as laid down in UN principles; prevent and resolve conflicts. **Structure** Conference (every 2 years). Council. Steering Committee, comprising 5 members. Secretariat. Based at: *Initiatives for International Dialogue*. **Activities** Organizes biennial conferences; provides advocacy assistance; builds awareness; lobbying; networking. **Events** *Strengthening APSOC as a platform to promote South-South solidarity, human security and peace* Thailand 2011. **Publications** *Estafeta* – newsletter.
Members Affiliates in 11 countries and territories:
Australia, Hong Kong, Indonesia, Japan, Korea Rep, Malaysia, New Zealand, Philippines, Sri Lanka, Thailand, USA.
Included in the above 3 organizations listed in this Yearbook:
Action in Solidarity with Asia and the Pacific (ASAP); *Asia Students Association (ASA, no recent information)*; *East Timor and Indonesia Action Network (ETAN)*.
NGO Relations Member of: *International Federation for East Timor (IFET, #13408)*. [2011.06.01/XE3828/y/**E**]

♦ Asia Pacific Solidarity Network (internationally oriented national body)

♦ Asia-Pacific Space Cooperation Organization (APSCO) 02051

Secretariat Bldg 13 and 14, Section 3 – No 188, South West Fourth Ring, Fengtai District, 100070 Beijing, China. T. +861063702677. Fax +861063702286. E-mail: secretariat@apsco.int.
URL: http://www.apsco.int/
History 1992, when Memorandum of Understanding was signed between China, Pakistan and Thailand. Original title: *Asia-Pacific Multilateral Cooperation in Space Technology and Applications (AP-MCSTA)*. Following workshops and conferences, the initiative was formalized into a permanent organization, with Convention finalized Nov 2003. Signing Ceremony of Convention 28 Oct 2005, Beijing (China). **Aims** Promote cooperation among Member States for peaceful uses of outer space in the fields of space science, space technology and its applications. **Structure** Council; Secretariat, headed by Secretary-General; Departments (4). **Languages** English. **Staff** 9.00 FTE, paid. **Finance** Member States' contributions. **Events** *United Nations Conference on Space Law and Policy* Istanbul (Turkey) 2019, *Anniversary High-Level Forum* Beijing (China) 2018, *International Symposium* Beijing (China) 2018, *United Nations International Conference on Space-Based Technologies for Disaster Risk Reduction* Beijing (China) 2018, *Meeting* Teheran (Iran Islamic Rep) 2017. **Publications** *NewsAPSCO* (4 a year).
Members Governments of 8 countries:
Bangladesh, China, Iran Islamic Rep, Mongolia, Pakistan, Peru, Thailand, Türkiye.
Signatory State:
Indonesia.
Associate member:
Egypt.
Observer state:
Mexico.
IGO Relations Observer Status with: *Committee on the Peaceful Uses of Outer Space (COPUOS, #04277)*. Observer of: *International Committee on Global Navigation Satellite Systems (ICG, #12775)*. Partner of: *AmeriGEOSS (#00796)*. [2017.03.15/XU2109/**E***]

♦ Asia-Pacific Space Design Association / see Asia Pacific Space Designers' Alliance (#02052)

♦ Asia Pacific Space Designers' Alliance (APSDA) 02052

Secretariat B-3A-23A 10Boulevard, Lebuhraya Sprint, Jalan Cempaka, Kampung Sungai Kayu Ara, 47400 Petaling Jaya, Selangor, Malaysia. E-mail: secretariat@apsda.org.
URL: http://apsda.org/
History 1989, Taipei (Taiwan), by Chinese Society of Interior Designer (CSID), Japanese Society of Commercial Designers (JCD) and Korean Society of Interior Designers (KOSID). Inaugural Assembly, 1991. Previously also referred to as *Asia-Pacific Space Design Association* and *Asia Pacific Space Designers' Association*. **Aims** Promote better understanding of different cultures of member countries; exchange information and knowledge between members through networking; enable members to work closer and better to achieve a better solution for the design community in facing the free trade zone to come. **Activities** Events/meetings; awards/prizes/competitions. **Events** *General Assembly and Congress* Adelaide, SA (Australia) 2016, *Round Table* Singapore (Singapore) 2016, *Conference* Surakarta (Indonesia) / Yogyakarta (Indonesia) 2014, *Congress* Surakarta (Indonesia) / Yogyakarta (Indonesia) 2014, *Congress* Panaji (India) 2012.
Members Societies in 12 countries and territories:
Australia, China, Hong Kong, India, Indonesia, Japan, Korea Rep, Malaysia, New Zealand, Philippines, Singapore, Thailand.
[2022/XJ0304/**D**]

♦ Asia Pacific Space Designers' Association / see Asia Pacific Space Designers' Alliance (#02052)
♦ Asia-Pacific Spa and Wellness Association / see Asia-Pacific Spa and Wellness Coalition (#02053)

♦ Asia-Pacific Spa and Wellness Coalition (APSWC) 02053

Chairman 10 Anson Rd, Suite 13-11, International Plaza, Singapore 079903, Singapore. T. +66811700780. E-mail: chairman@apswc.org.
URL: http://www.apswc.org/
History Mar 2006. Founded as the result of an informal roundtable where 76 industry professionals from across the region gathered in Singapore to map out a development strategy to improve and promote the spa industry for the benefit of all. Launched membership programme, June 2016. Former names and other names: *Asia-Pacific Spa and Wellness Association* – former. Registration: Registry of Societies, No/ID: 2086/2007, Start date: Jul 2007, Singapore. **Aims** Promote, protect, educate and develop the spa and wellness industry in the Asia-Pacific region. **Structure** Board; Executive Board. **Languages** English. **Staff** Voluntary. **Finance** Sources: meeting proceeds; revenue from activities/projects; sponsorship. **Activities** Advocacy/lobbying/activism; events/meetings; guidance/assistance/consulting; knowledge management/information dissemination; networking/liaising; standards/guidelines. Active in: Australia, Cambodia, China, Hong Kong, India, Indonesia, Japan, Korea Rep, Laos, Macau, Malaysia, Maldives, Myanmar, Nepal, New Zealand, Philippines, Singapore, Taiwan, Thailand, Vietnam. **Events** *Round Table* 2022, *Round Table* Kuala Lumpur (Malaysia) 2021, *Round Table* Danang (Vietnam) 2020, *Round Table* Kuala Lumpur (Malaysia) 2019, *Round Table* Singapore (Singapore) 2018. **Publications** *APSWC White Paper*.
Members Membership is open to anyone with an interest in spa and wellness in the Asia-Pacific, in particular: spa owners, operators, and managers; health, wellness, and natural therapy professionals; spa product and equipment suppliers, spa consultants, architects, and designers; spa, health, and beauty training schools; hoteliers and those in the hospitality industry; travel agents, tour operators and others in the travel industry; health and lifestyle media. As of April 2022, the APSWC represents over 650 businesses across 15 countries and territories:
Alberta, Cambodia, Finland, Hong Kong, India, Indonesia, Japan, Malaysia, Maldives, Nepal, North Rhine-Westphalia, Philippines, Singapore, Thailand, Vietnam.
IGO Relations Links with relevant government ministries. **NGO Relations** Supports (3): Global Wellness Day; TERMATALIA; *World Wellness Weekend (WWW)*. Links with spa and wellness industry associations in Asia-Pacific. [2022.05.11/XJ1632/**D**]

♦ Asia Pacific Spine Society (APSS) 02054

Secretariat c/o Affinity Executive Services, Level 3A, Sunway Visio Tower, Lingkaran SV, Sunway Velocity, 55100 Kuala Lumpur, Malaysia. T. +60397712260. Fax +60389964700. E-mail: spine@apssonline.org – admin@apoaonline.com.
URL: https://www.apssonline.org/
History 1979. Serves as the Spine Section of *Asia Pacific Orthopaedic Association (APOA, #01987)*. **Aims** Advance the science, art and practice of spinal surgery in the region. **Structure** Executive Committee; Board. **Activities** Events/meetings; training/education. **Events** *Annual Meeting* Kolkata (India) 2022, *Combined Meeting* Kobe (Japan) 2021, *Annual Meeting* Shanghai (China) 2020, *Combined Meeting* Incheon (Korea Rep) 2019, *Annual Meeting* Taipei (Taiwan) 2018. **Publications** *Asian Spine Journal*; *Journal of Orthopaedic Surgery*.
Members Chapters in 22 countries and territories:
Australia, Bangladesh, Brunei Darussalam, Cambodia, China, Hong Kong, India, Indonesia, Japan, Korea Rep, Malaysia, Myanmar, Nepal, New Zealand, Pakistan, Philippines, Saudi Arabia, Singapore, Sri Lanka, Thailand, Türkiye, Vietnam.
[2021/AA1853/**D**]

♦ Asia-Pacific Strabismus and Paediatric Ophthalmology Society (APSPOS) 02055

Contact 4/F Hong Kong Eye Hosp; 147K Argyle Str, Kowloon, Hong Kong. T. +85239435827.
URL: http://www.apspos.org/
History 2008. **Aims** Assist the development of paediatric ophthalmology in the Asia-Pacific region; provide a platform for good integration of skills and knowledge of clinicians in this subspecialty. **Structure** Council. **Finance** Members' dues. **Activities** Events/meetings; awards/prizes/competitions. **Events** *Joint Meeting* Sydney, NSW (Australia) 2019, *Congress* Hong Kong (Hong Kong) 2017. **NGO Relations** Official paediatric ophthalmology society within *Asia-Pacific Academy of Ophthalmology (APAO, #01814)*. Member of: *International Council of Ophthalmology (ICO, #13057)*; *International Pediatric Ophthalmology and Strabismus Council (IPOSC, #14544)*. [2019/XM5911/**D**]

♦ Asia Pacific Stroke Association / see Asia Pacific Stroke Organization (#02056)

♦ Asia Pacific Stroke Organization (APSO) 02056

Pres Secretariat Office, Unit C 3/F Worldwide Centre, 123 Tung Chau Street, Kowloon, Hong Kong. T. +85232966261. Fax +85232966465. E-mail: president@theapso.com – apsosec@gmail.com.
URL: http://www.theapso.com/
History Original title: *Asia Pacific Stroke Association*. Current title adopted when merged with *Asia Stroke Federation* 2009. **Aims** Promote and encourage advancement of scientific knowledge, research and practice in all aspects of stroke and associated cerebrovascular *diseases*; coordinate exchange and dissemination of this knowledge and expertise throughout the Asia-Pacific Region; assist stroke self-help societies in promoting the welfare of individuals affected by stroke for the relief of sickness. **Activities** Events/meetings; training/education; awareness raising. **Events** *Asia Pacific Stroke Conference* Chennai (India) 2021, *Asia Pacific Stroke Conference* Seoul (Korea Rep) 2020, *Asia Pacific Stroke Conference* Manila (Philippines) 2019, *Asia Pacific Stroke Conference* Jakarta (Indonesia) 2018, *Asia Pacific Stroke Conference* Kuala Lumpur (Malaysia) 2015.
[2020.03.04/XM0416/**D**]

♦ **Asia-Pacific Structured Finance Association (APSA)** **02057**
SG c/o Eversheds, 21st Floor, Gloucester Tower, The Landmark, 15 Queen's Road, Central, Central and Western, Hong Kong. E-mail: info@apsa-asia.com.
URL: http://www.apsa-asia.com/
History 2006, as *Asia-Pacific Securitisation Association*. Current title adopted 8 Dec 2010. **Aims** Promote the efficient growth and continued development of structured finance throughout the Asia-Pacific region; advocate interests and serve the needs of the structured finance industry. **Structure** Executive Committee. **Languages** English. **Staff** 4.00 FTE, voluntary. **Finance** Members' dues. **Activities** Events/meetings. **Events** *Annual Southeast Asia Forum* Singapore (Singapore) 2016, *Annual Southeast Asia Forum* Singapore (Singapore) 2015. **NGO Relations** *Asia Securities Industry and Financial Markets Association (ASIFMA, #02094)*; *Asian Institute of International Financial Law (AIIFL)*; national associations. [2020/XJ9578/**D**]

♦ **Asia-Pacific Student Accommodation Association (APSAA)** **02058**
Pres PO Box 7345, Beaumaris, Melbourne VIC 3193, Australia. T. +61395866055. E-mail: admin@apsaa.org.au – president@apsaa.org.au.
URL: https://www.apsaa.org.au/
History Former names and other names: *Australasian Association of College and University Housing Officers (AACUHO)*.– former. Registration: Australian Securities and Investments Commission, No/ID: ABN 38 558 365 045, Start date: 2017, Australia. **Aims** Support and facilitate quality standards of service delivery in student accommodation; advocate for the sustainable economic and pedagogical benefits of student accommodation; be the leading professional organisation providing our members access to information and resources. **Structure** Annual General Meeting; Board. Committees. **Activities** Awards/prizes/competitions; events/meetings; training/education. **Events** *Annual Conference* Brisbane, QLD (Australia) 2023, *Summit* Christchurch (New Zealand) 2022, *Annual Conference* Sydney, NSW (Australia) 2022, *Annual Conference* Auckland (New Zealand) 2021, *Annual Conference* Adelaide, SA (Australia) 2020.
Members Institution; Corporate; Individual; Industry Affiliate. Members in 4 countries:
Australia, Malaysia, New Zealand, Singapore. [2023/AA1403/**D**]

♦ **Asia Pacific Student Services Association (APSSA)** **02059**
Admin Sec Student Affairs Office, Hong Kong Univ of Science and Technology, Clear Water Bay, Kowloon, Hong Kong. T. +85223586652. Fax +85223580842.
Gen Sec Taylor's Univ, No 1 Jalan Taylor's, 47500 Subang Jaya, Selangor, Malaysia. T. +60356295023. Fax +60356295036.
URL: http://www.apssa.info/
History 1988. Registered in accordance with the law of Hong Kong. **Aims** Enhance liaison and collaboration between staff across the Asia Pacific region; strengthen the cultural understanding and develop inter-cultural skills; assist in developing and raising awareness of student affairs practices to strengthen their role in tertiary education development. **Structure** Executive Committee. Institute of Student Affairs (ISA). **Finance** Members' dues. **Activities** Training/education. **Events** *Conference* Kuala Lumpur (Malaysia) 2018, *Conference* Chiang Mai (Thailand) 2016, *Conference* Kyoto (Japan) 2014, *Biennial Conference / Conference* Manila (Philippines) 2012, *Biennial Conference / Conference* Brisbane, QLD (Australia) 2010. [2014/XN8921/**D**]

♦ **Asia-Pacific Superyacht Association (APSA)** **02060**
Contact Unit G and H, 21/F – COS Centre, 56 Tsun Yip Street, Kwun Tong, Kowloon, Hong Kong. E-mail: radka@apsuperyacht.org.
URL: http://www.apsuperyacht.org/
Aims Actively promote members who are Asian yacht businesses and for worldwide yacht businesses wanting to do business in Asia. **Structure** Committee. **Events** *Asia Pacific Superyacht Conference* Singapore (Singapore) 2019, *Asia Pacific Superyacht Conference* Singapore (Singapore) 2018. **Publications** *APSA Telegraph*. [2020/XM7701/**D**]

♦ Asia Pacific Surgical Infection Society (unconfirmed)
♦ Asia-Pacific Symposium on Cochlear Implant and Related Sciences (meeting series)
♦ Asia-Pacific Symposium on Engineering Plasticity and its Applications (meeting series)
♦ Asia Pacific Symposium on Radiation Chemistry (meeting series)
♦ Asia-Pacific Symposium on Tritium Science (meeting series)
♦ Asia Pacific Taekwondo Federation / see Asia Taekwondo Federation (#02100)

♦ **Asia-Pacific Tax Forum (APTF)** **02061**
Communications ITIC, 1634 Street NW, Ste 500, Washington DC 20006, USA. T. +12025309799. Fax +12025307987. E-mail: info@iticnet.org.
URL: https://www.iticnet.org/reach?rq=Asia-Pacific%20Tax%20Forum/
History 2005, Singapore, at Asia Excise Taxation Conference. Subsequently referred to as *Asia Tax Forum (ATF)*. **Aims** Create a sustainable and continuing dialogue among all interested sectors on latest developments, studies, issues and challenges in taxation. **Structure** Steering Committee; Working Groups. **Events** *Annual Forum / Forum* Manila (Philippines) 2012, *Annual Forum / Forum* Bali (Indonesia) 2011, *Forum* Phnom Penh (Cambodia) 2010, *Annual Forum* Siem Reap (Cambodia) 2010, *Annual forum / Forum* Sydney, NSW (Australia) 2009. **Publications** Special report bulletins. [2019/XJ1283/**F**]

♦ **Asia Pacific Taxpayers Union (APTU)** **02062**
SG Room 902, Unit 4 – Bldg 3, Beihuan East Road, Beijing Economic and Tech Development Zone, Beijing, China. E-mail: caixiaolitery@163.com.
Chair address not obtained. E-mail: btw@worldtaxpayers.org.
History 19 Oct 2005. **Aims** Serve taxpayers and safeguard their rights and interests. **Structure** Chairman; Secretary-General. **Languages** English, Mandarin Chinese. **Staff** 2.50 FTE, voluntary. **Finance** Donations; sale of publications. **Activities** Knowledge management/information dissemination; networking/liaising; events/meetings. **Events** *Meeting* Shenzhen (China) 2007, *Meeting* Seoul (Korea Rep) 2006, *Meeting* Beijing (China) 2005. **Publications** *World Taxpayers Associations and the Development of Chinese Taxpayers' Undertakings* (2016-2018).
Members Full in 12 countries:
Australia, Azerbaijan, China, Hong Kong, India, Japan, Kazakhstan, Korea Rep, Kyrgyzstan, Mongolia, Philippines, Thailand.
NGO Relations Member of: *World Taxpayers Associations (WTA, #21847)*. [2019.02.15/XM2922/**D**]

♦ **Asia Pacific Tchoukball Federation (APTBF)** **02063**
Gen Sec No 2-126 Lane, Zhi Yi St, SeNan Village, Luju-Hsiang, Kaohsiung 82199, Taiwan. T. +88676975784. Fax +88676975784. E-mail: secretary@aptbf.org – mail@aptbf.org.
Main Website: http://www.aptbf.org
History 13 Aug 1999. Re-founded 13 Aug 2005. Former names and other names: *Asian Tchouk-Ball Federation (ATBF)* – former. **Aims** Promote the sport of tchoukball throughout Asia-Pacific. **Structure** Executive Bureau; Executive Committee; Technical Committee. **Languages** Chinese, English. **Staff** 15.00 FTE, voluntary. **Finance** Sources: government support; sponsorship. **Activities** Events/meetings; sporting activities. **Events** *Southeast Asia Championship* Brunei Darussalam 2010, *Asia Pacific Championship* Singapore (Singapore) 2010. **Members** Full (5). Membership countries not specified. **NGO Relations** Also links with national associations. [2021.06.08/XD9258/**D**]

♦ **Asia-Pacific Telecommunity (APT)** **02064**
Télécommunauté Asie-Pacifique
SG No 12/49, Soi 5, Chaeng Watthana Road, Bangkok, 10210, Thailand. T. +6625730044. Fax +6625737479. E-mail: aptmail@apt.int.
URL: http://www.apt.int/
History 27 Mar 1976, Bangkok (Thailand). Established 1976, by resolution 163 (XXXII) of 32nd session of *United Nations Economic and Social Commission for Asia and the Pacific (ESCAP, #20557)*. Constitution entered into force 25 Feb 1979; commenced activities July 1979, Bangkok. Statutes registered in *'UNTS/1 17583'*. **Aims** Spearhead development and innovation programmes in cooperation with telecom service providers, manufacturers of communication equipment and research and development organizations in the field of communications and information technology. **Structure** General Assembly (every 3 years); Management Committee (meets annually); Secretariat; Meetings in Bangkok (Thailand); meetings in other places if host facilities offered by member countries. **Languages** English. **Staff** 25.00 FTE, paid. **Finance** Sources: contributions; contributions of member/participating states. Regular voluntary contributions on a unit basis chosen by Members, Associate Members and Affiliate Members from a scale of unit classes stipulated in the Constitution; extra-budgetary contributions by members. **Activities** Events/meetings. **Events** *Meeting of the APT Preparatory Group for PP-22* Tokyo (Japan) 2022, *APT Preparatory Group for WRC-23 Meeting* Bangkok (Thailand) 2021, *Policy and Regulatory Forum* Bangkok (Thailand) 2021, *Meeting* 2020, *Preparatory Meeting for the World Radiocommunication Conference* Tokyo (Japan) 2019. **Publications** *APT e-Newsletter* (12 a year).
Members Full: member states of ESCAP or the UN – governments of 38 countries:
Afghanistan, Australia, Bangladesh, Bhutan, Brunei Darussalam, Cambodia, China, Fiji, India, Indonesia, Iran Islamic Rep, Japan, Kiribati, Korea DPR, Korea Rep, Laos, Malaysia, Maldives, Marshall Is, Micronesia FS, Mongolia, Myanmar, Nauru, Nepal, New Zealand, Pakistan, Palau, Papua New Guinea, Philippines, Samoa, Singapore, Solomon Is, Sri Lanka, Thailand, Tonga, Tuvalu, Vanuatu, Vietnam.
Associate: associate member states of ESCAP – governments of 4 countries and territories:
Cook Is, Hong Kong, Macau, Niue.
Affiliate: providers of public telecommunication services within the region in 28 countries and territories:
Afghanistan, Australia, Bangladesh, Bhutan, China, Cook Is, Fiji, Hong Kong, India, Indonesia, Iran Islamic Rep, Japan, Korea Rep, Macau, Malaysia, Maldives, Mongolia, Nepal, New Zealand, Pakistan, Papua New Guinea, Philippines, Singapore, Sri Lanka, Thailand, Tonga, Vanuatu, Vietnam.
IGO Relations Close cooperation with all United Nations bodies, international and regional organizations (not specified). Sector member of: *International Telecommunication Union (ITU, #15673)* (ITU-D, ITU-R, ITU-T). Agreement with: *Conférence européenne des administrations des postes et des télécommunications (CEPT, #04602)*. [2022.10.14/XF5942/**F***]

♦ **Asia Pacific Tele-Ophthalmology Society (APTOS)** **02065**
Contact Ctr for Eye Research Australia, Level 7 Peter Howson Wing, 32 Gisborne Street, Melbourne VIC EAST 3002, Australia. T. +61399298175.
URL: https://asiateleophth.org/
History Founded May 2016. **Aims** Bring together clinicians, researchers, technicians, institutes and organisations to form an alliance that promotes communication, exchange and collaboration in tele-ophthalmology. **Structure** Council. **Activities** Events/meetings. **Events** *Symposium* Shenyang (China) 2022, *Symposium* Bangkok (Thailand) 2021, *Symposium* Seoul (Korea Rep) 2020, *Symposium* Chennai (India) 2019, *Symposium* Singapore (Singapore) 2018. **NGO Relations** Member of: *Asia-Pacific Academy of Ophthalmology (APAO, #01814)*. [2021/XM7872/**D**]

♦ Asia-Pacific Textile and Clothing Industry Forum (meeting series)
♦ Asia Pacific Theological Association (see: #10110)
♦ Asia Pacific TKD Federation / see Asia Taekwondo Federation (#02100)

♦ **Asia Pacific Top Level Domain Association (APTLD)** **02066**
General Manager No 1 Bldg, 4 South 4th Street, Zhongguancun, Haidian District, 100190 Beijing, China. T. +861058813181. E-mail: sec@aptld.org.
URL: http://www.aptld.org/
History 1998. Registration: No/ID: 0314-04-5, Start date: 19 Feb 2004, Malaysia. **Aims** Promote skills development and information exchange related to *Internet* domain names among members; provide a forum to discuss policy matters affecting Internet domain name related entities; act as an interface with Internet coordination bodies and other bodies involved in the Internet domain name operation. **Structure** Board. **Languages** English. **Activities** Capacity building; events/meetings. Active in all member countries. **Events** *Meeting* Delhi (India) 2012, *Members Meeting* Busan (Korea Rep) 2011, *Meeting* Melbourne, VIC (Australia) 2011, *Meeting* Amman (Jordan) 2010, *Meeting* Amman (Jordan) 2010. **Publications** *APTLD e-Newsletter* (6 a year).
Members Ordinary; Associate. Ordinary in 45 countries and territories:
Afghanistan, Australia, Azerbaijan, Bangladesh, Cambodia, China, Christmas Is, Cocos-Keeling Is, Georgia, Hong Kong, India, Indonesia, Iran Islamic Rep, Iraq, Japan, Jordan, Kazakhstan, Korea Rep, Kyrgyzstan, Laos, Macau, Mongolia, Nauru, New Zealand, Niue, Palau, Palestine, Papua New Guinea, Philippines, Qatar, Samoa, Samoa USA, Saudi Arabia, Singapore, Solomon Is, Sri Lanka, Thailand, Timor-Leste, Tokelau, Tuvalu, United Arab Emirates, Uzbekistan, Vanuatu, Vietnam, Wallis-Futuna.
Associate in 17 countriesand territories:
Armenia, Belarus, Czechia, Germany, Guernsey, Ireland, Mexico, Montenegro, Norway, Pakistan, Palau, Russia, Serbia, Sweden, UK, Ukraine, USA. [2022.05.12/XM1683/**D**]

♦ **Asia Pacific Tourism Association (APTA)** **02067**
Sec Dept of Intl Tourism, Dong-A Univ, Bumin-dong 2-ga, Seo-gu, Busan 600-760, Korea Rep. Fax +82512008429. E-mail: aptasecretary.a@gmail.com.
URL: https://www.apta.asia/
History 1995, Busan (Korea Rep). Founded at inaugural conference. Former names and other names: *Asia Tourism Association* – former. **Aims** Further facilitate quality tourism research, especially in the Asia-Pacific area; share research achievements; exchange ideas between academics and their counterparts in the business world. **Structure** Executive Board. **Languages** English. **Staff** 9.00 FTE, paid. **Events** *Annual Conference* Chiang Mai (Thailand) 2023, *Annual Conference* Jeju (Korea Rep) 2022, *Annual Conference* 2021, *Annual Conference* Chiang Mai (Thailand) 2020, *Annual Conference* Danang (Vietnam) 2019. **Publications** *Journal of Asia Pacific Tourism Studies* (annual); *Asia Pacific Journal of Tourism Research* (8 a year); *APTA Newsletter*. Annual Proceedings.
Members National/regional representatives in 16 countries and territories:
Australia, Canada, China, Guam, Hong Kong, India, Japan, Korea Rep, Macau, Malaysia, New Zealand, Philippines, Singapore, Taiwan, Thailand, USA. [2023/XD5044/**D**]

♦ Asia-Pacific Tourism Exchange Centre (internationally oriented national body)

♦ **Asia Pacific Trade Seminars (APTS)** **02068**
Contact Univ Tokyo – Economics, 7-3-1 Hongo, Bunkyo-ku, Tokyo, 113-0033 Japan.
URL: http://www.furusawa.e.u-tokyo.ac.jp/APTS/
History 2008. **Aims** Provide the forum for exchanging research ideas in the field of international trade and investment. **Structure** Board of 9 members. **Events** *Annual Meeting* Tokyo (Japan) 2022, *Annual Meeting* Tokyo (Japan) 2021, *Annual Meeting* Tokyo (Japan) 2019, *Annual Meeting* Hong Kong (Hong Kong) 2018, *Annual Meeting* Hanoi (Vietnam) 2017. [2019/XJ0073/ct/**F**]

♦ Asia-Pacific Traditional Medicine Exchange Association (inactive)

♦ **Asia and Pacific Transgender Network (APTN)** **02069**
Exec Dir One Day, 51 Soi Sukhumvit 26, Klong Tan, Klong Toei, Bangkok, Thailand. T. +6621088855. E-mail: info@weareaptn.org.
URL: http://www.weareaptn.org/
History Dec 2009. **Aims** Enable transgender women and men in the Asia and Pacific region to organize and advocate for the improvement of their health, protection of their legal, social and human rights, and enhancement of their social wellbeing and quality of life. **Structure** Foundation Board; Steering Committee; Secretariat. **Publications** Electronic newsletter. **NGO Relations** Member of: *Robert Carr civil society Networks Fund (RCNF, #18956)*. [2023/XM4241/**F**]

♦ Asia Pacific Travel Health Association / see Asia Pacific Travel Health Society (#02070)

♦ **Asia Pacific Travel Health Society (APTHS)** **02070**
Secretariat c/o Target Conf, 65 Derech Menachem Begin, PO Box 51227, 6713818 Tel Aviv, Israel. E-mail: apths@target-conferences.com.
URL: http://www.apths.org/
History Founded 1996, as *Asia Pacific Travel Health Association*. Name changed to *Asia-Pacific Society of Travel Medicine (ASTM)* in Jul 1998. Comes under the supervision of *International Society of Travel Medicine (ISTM, #15519)*. **Aims** Encourage research in travel medicine and provide a scientific focus for those interested in the field; stimulate the practice of travel medicine at a high professional level; facilitate free and rapid exchange of information on related issues; stimulate development and evaluation of safe and effective preventive and curative interventions. **Languages** English. **Staff** 1.00 FTE, paid. **Finance** Members' dues. **Activities** Research/documentation; events/meetings. **Events** *Around VDB* Bangkok (Thailand) 2022, *Introductions to Travel Medicine* Bangkok (Thailand) 2022, *Introduction to Travel Medicine* 2021, *Asia-Pacific Travel Health Conference* Auckland (New Zealand) 2020, *Asia-Pacific Travel Health Conference* Bangkok (Thailand) 2018. **Publications** *ASTM Newsletter*.

Members Individuals – Regular, Nurse or Student; Clinic/Agency. Members in 14 countries and territories:
Australia, Canada, China, Germany, Hong Kong, India, Indonesia, Israel, Japan, Singapore, Switzerland, Taiwan, UK, USA.
[2020/XD4297/D]

♦ Asia Pacific Travel Retail Association (APTRA) 02071

Admin Officer 8 Eu Tong Sen Street, Suite 18-81 The Central, Singapore 059818, Singapore. T. +6588222527. E-mail: admin@aptra.asia.
URL: http://www.aptra.asia/

History Founded 2005. **Aims** Provide services to members in the *duty free* and travel retail industry within the Asia Pacific region. **Structure** Board. **Languages** English. **Staff** 2.00 FTE, paid. **Finance** Members' dues. **Activities** Networking/liaising; events/meetings; knowledge management/information dissemination; advocacy/lobbying/activism; research/documentation. **Events** *Annual General Meeting* Singapore (Singapore) 2020, *Airports Forum* Singapore (Singapore) 2019, *Annual General Meeting* Singapore (Singapore) 2019, *Airports Forum* Singapore (Singapore) 2018, *Insights Seminar* Singapore (Singapore) 2018. **Members** Corporations in the duty free, tax free or travel retail sector, including brand owners; retailers of products (excluding food and beverage and services); landlords (including airports, airlines and cruise shops) and concession holders; duty free, tax free and travel related associations. 84 members in total. Membership countries not specified. **NGO Relations** *Duty Free World Council*; *European Travel Retail Confederation (ETRC, #08945)*; *Tax Free World Association (TFWA)*. [2020/XM0365/D]

♦ Asia-Pacific Tropical Timber Organization (inactive)

♦ Asia-Pacific University – Community Engagement Network (APUCEN) 02072

Exec Dir Div of Industry/Community Network (DICN), Univ Sains Malaysia, 11800 USM, Penang, Malaysia. T. +6046534492 – +6046534491. Fax +6046534490. E-mail: apucen@usm.my.
URL: http://apucen.usm.my/

History Launched Jul 2011, on the initiative of Universiti Sains Malaysia. **Aims** Promote and instill the community-engagement concept and values to staff and students of institutions of higher learning; create capacity building for university community partnerships; disseminate and share information, knowledge, resources and good practices; provide a platform for joint flagship projects. **Structure** Council of 13. **Events** *Summit* Penang (Malaysia) 2014. **Publications** *APUCEN Bulletin*.
Members Institutions in 14 countries and territories:
Australia, Brunei Darussalam, Cambodia, Fiji, Hong Kong, India, Indonesia, Japan, Malaysia, Nepal, Pakistan, Philippines, Taiwan, Thailand.
Affiliate members (2):
Institut für Internationale Zusammenarbeit des Deutschen Volkshochschul-Verbandes (DVV-International); *Living Knowledge – The International Science Shop Network (#16502)*.
Associate members (2) in 2 countries:
Malaysia, Thailand. [2015/XJ9041/F]

♦ Asia Pacific Urban Energy Association (APUEA) 02073

Exec Dir 2 Silom Edge, 11th Floor, Silom Road, Suriyawong, Bangrak, Bangkok, 10500, Thailand. E-mail: info@apuea.org.
URL: https://www.apuea.org/

History Jun 2017, Manila (Philippines). Founded as an initiative of *International Institute for Energy Conservation (IIEC, #13875)*. Officially launched at Asia Clean Energy Forum, hosted by *Asian Development Bank (ADB, #01422)* and *United States Agency for International Development (USAID)*. **Aims** Promote development of sustainable urban energy systems in the Asia Pacific region. **Structure** Annual General Meeting; Executive Committee; Secretariat. **Finance** Supported by: *Asian Development Bank (ADB, #01422)*; Danish Board of District Heating; *Euroheat and Power (EHP, #05694)*; *UNEP (#20299)*. **Activities** Events/meetings; knowledge management/information dissemination. **Events** *Asia Urban Energy Assembly* Bangkok (Thailand) 2022. **Publications** *APUEA Magazine* (4 a year); *Asia Pacific Urban Energy Outlook* (annual).
Members Full. Membership countries not specified. Includes:
Alliance to Save Energy (ASE); *Euroheat and Power (EHP, #05694)*; *International District Energy Association (IDEA)*; *International Institute for Energy Conservation (IIEC, #13875)*; *Overseas Environment Cooperation Centre (OECC)*. [2022/AA3200/ty/D]

♦ Asia Pacific Vascular Society (internationally oriented national body)

♦ Asia Pacific Vegetarian Union (APVU) 02074

SG c/o HK Vegan Association, Unit 2001 20/F Mongkok Centre, 16 Argyle Street, Kowloon, Hong Kong.
URL: http://www.ivu.org/asia-pacific/index.html

History 14 Feb 2000, Chiang Mai (Thailand). Founded by *International Vegetarian Union (IVU, #15842)*, following 33rd World Vegetarian Congress. **Aims** Promote vegetarianism throughout the Asian region. **Events** *Asian Vegetarian Congress (AVC)* Bangkok (Thailand) 2015, *Asian Vegetarian Congress (AVC)* Kuala Lumpur (Malaysia) 2013, *Asian Vegetarian Congress (AVC)* Hangzhou (China) 2011, *Asian Vegetarian Congress (AVC)* Batam (Indonesia) 2009, *The spiritual perspectives on vegetarianism* Kaohsiung (Taiwan) 2007. **Members** Membership countries not specified. [2018/XD9320/D]

♦ Asia-Pacific Vibration Conference (meeting series)

♦ Asia-Pacific Vitreo-retina Society (APVRS) 02075

Secretariat 4/F HK Eye Hosp, 147K Argyle St, Mongkok, Kowloon, Hong Kong. T. +85239967793. Fax +85227159490. E-mail: secretariat@apvrs.org.
URL: http://www.apvrs.org/

History 2006. **Aims** Assist the development of the *vitreoretinal* subspecialty in the Asia-Pacific region; provide a platform for good integration of skills and knowledge of *ophthalmologists* in the vitreoretinal subspecialty; promote and disseminate eye care information for vitreoretinal diseases and related issues among the general public. **Structure** Council. **Activities** Events/meetings. **Events** *Congress* Taipei (Taiwan) 2022, *Beyond all Limits* Hong Kong (Hong Kong) 2021, *Congress* Taipei (Taiwan) 2020, *Congress* Shanghai (China) 2019, *Congress* Seoul (Korea Rep) 2018. **NGO Relations** Member of: *Asia-Pacific Academy of Ophthalmology (APAO, #01814)*. [2020.03.13/XJ8311/D]

♦ Asia-Pacific Water Forum (APWF) 02076

Secretariat c/o Japan Water Forum, 6th Fl, 5-4 Nihonbashi-Hakozaki-cho, Chuo-ku, Tokyo, 103-0015 Japan. T. +81356458040. Fax +81356458041. E-mail: office@apwf.org.
URL: http://www.apwf.org/

History 27 Sep 2006, Manila (Philippines), following ministerial discussions during the 2003 and 2006 World Water Forums. **Aims** Contribute to *sustainable* water management in order to achieve targets of SDGs in Asia and the Pacific region by capitalizing on the region's diversity and experience in dealing with water; enhance investments and cooperation in the water sector on regional level and beyond. **Structure** President; Governing Council. Secretariat, located in Tokyo (Japan). Lead Organizations; Sub-regional Coordinators; Member Organizations. **Languages** English. **Activities** Events/meetings; advocacy/lobbying/activism. **Events** *Asia-Pacific Water Summit* Kumamoto (Japan) 2022, *Seminar on Engaging Industry in Sustainable Water Management through Water Stewardship* Tokyo (Japan) 2021, *Seminar on Operationalizing IWRM to Build Water Security* Tokyo (Japan) 2021, *Seminar on WASH as Entry Point to Reduce COVID-19 Vulnerabilities and other Hazards* Tokyo (Japan) 2021, *Seminar on Water Governance in Asia Pacific* Tokyo (Japan) 2021. **Publications** *Asian Water Development Outlook (AWDO)* (3rd ed 2016) – ADB, APWF, 1st ed 2007, 2nd ed 2013; *Meta-Guidelines for Water and Climate Change: For practitioners in Asia and the Pacific* (2015) – APWF, ADB, GWP; *Framework Document on Water and Climate Change Adaptation For Leaders and Policy-makers in the Asia-Pacific Region* (2012) – APWF. Policy Brief; proceedings; reports. **Members** Organizations. Membership countries not specified. **IGO Relations** *African Development Bank (ADB, #00283)*; *FAO (#09260)*; *International Centre for Integrated Mountain Development (ICIMOD, #12500)*; *International Centre for Water Hazard and Risk Management (ICHARM)*; *UNESCO (#20322)*; *United Nations Economic and Social Commission for Asia and the Pacific (ESCAP, #20557)*; *United Nations Human Settlements Programme (UN-Habitat, #20572)*. [2020/XJ8218/F]

♦ Asia Pacific Women's Watch (APWW) 02077

Chairperson 56/1 Sarasavi Lane, Castle Street, Colombo, 08, Sri Lanka. E-mail: info@apww-slwngof.org.
URL: http://www.apww-slwngof.org/

History Registered in accordance with Philippines' law. **Aims** Advocate and monitor the implementation of the Beijing (China) Platform for Action (BPFA) and the outcome document from the UN General Assembly on Women 2000. **Structure** Steering Committee. **Consultative Status** Consultative status granted from: *ECOSOC (#05331)* (Special). **NGO Relations** Supports: *Global Call for Action Against Poverty (GCAP, #10263)*. [2014/XJ3410/F]

♦ Asia Pacific Workers Solidarity Link (APWSL) 02078

Coordinator 141 Ananda Rajakaruna MW, Colombo, 10, Sri Lanka. T. +9474617711. Fax +9474617711.

History within *Asian Cultural Forum on Development Foundation (ACFOD, no recent information)*. Became independent 1996. Takes over activities of *Asian Labourers Solidarity (ALS, inactive)*. **Structure** Regional Coordinating Committee.
Members National groups (16) in 16 countries and territories:
Australia, Bangladesh, Fiji, Hong Kong, India, Indonesia, Japan, Korea Rep, Malaysia, Nepal, New Zealand, Pakistan, Philippines, Sri Lanka, Taiwan, Thailand.
NGO Relations Supports: *GoodWeave International (#10681)*. [2009/XF2309/F]

♦ Asia-Pacific Worm Meeting (meeting series)

♦ Asia Pacific Wrist Association (APWA) 02079

Contact Room 74034, 5/F, LCW Clinical Sciences Bldg, Prince of Wales Hosp, Shatin, Hong Kong. T. +85235052010.
URL: https://apwa.asia/

History 2015, Hong Kong. **Aims** Encourage the clinical application of wrist surgery and other diagnostic and therapeutic methods; facilitate exchange of clinical and scientific information and advance knowledge, concept and clinical skill in the field; promote research and collaboration bring together doctors and other medical professionals specializing or with special interest in the aforementioned fields. **Structure** General Assembly; Executive Board. Committees (4): IT; Education; Congress; Travelling Fellowship. **Activities** Events/meetings; networking/liaising; training/education. **Events** *Congress* Shanghai (China) 2021, *Congress* Singapore (Singapore) 2020, *Congress* Seoul (Korea Rep) 2019, *Annual Conference* Narita (Japan) 2018, *Annual Conference* Adelaide, SA (Australia) 2017. **Publications** *APWA Bulletin*. [2020/AA0217/D]

♦ Asia-Pacific Youth Environmental Federation (inactive)
♦ Asia-Pacific Youth Forum / see Asian Pacific Youth Forum (#01647)
♦ Asia-Pacific Youth Organisation (internationally oriented national body)
♦ Asia Partnership Conference of Pharmaceutical Associations (unconfirmed)
♦ Asia Partnership for Human Development / see Caritas Asia (#03578)
♦ Asia Peace and History Institute / see Asian Peace and History Education Association
♦ Asia Petrochemical Industry Conference (meeting series)

♦ Asia Plasma and Fusion Association (APFA) 02080

Pres c/o SWIP-Fusion, PO Box 432, Chengdu, 610041 Sichuan, China.
URL: http://www.jspf.or.jp/introduction/APFA/index.html

History 1997. **Aims** Stimulate plasma and fusion research in the region; encourage scientific exchanges; promote education for young scientists. **Structure** General Assembly. Trustees. **Events** *Conference* Shenzhen (China) 2019, *Conference* Toki (Japan) 2017, *Conference* Gandhinagar (India) 2015, *Conference* Gyeongju (Korea Rep) 2013, *Conference* Guilin (China) 2011. [2013/XJ1596/D]

♦ Asia Producers Network / see Asia-Pacific Producers Network (#02000)
♦ Asia QA Forum (unconfirmed)
♦ **Asia QA Forum** Asia Quality Assurance Forum (#02081)

♦ Asia Quality Assurance Forum (Asia QA Forum) 02081

Address not obtained.

History 2013, Kyoto (Japan). Proposed at 3rd *Global Quality Assurance Conference (GQAC)*, by Japan Society of Quality Assurance and Korean Society of Quality Assurance. **Activities** Events/meetings. **Events** *International Conference* Bangalore (India) 2019, *International Conference* Beijing (China) 2017, *International Conference* Seoul (Korea Rep) 2015, *International Conference* Tokyo (Japan) 2013.
Members Societies in 7 countries and territories:
China, India, Japan, Korea Rep, Malaysia, Singapore, Taiwan. [2019/AA2516/F]

♦ Asia Racquetball Federation (ARF) 02082

Main Office 1816 Day Island Blvd, WUniversity Place, Tacoma WA 98466, USA. E-mail: art@asiaracquetball.org.
URL: http://asiaracquetball.org/

Activities Organizes championships. **Members** Membership countries not specified. **NGO Relations** *International Racquetball Federation (IRF, #14683)*. [2022/XM8103/D]

♦ Asia Regional Adhesive Council (ARAC) 02083

Contact 1-10-4 Kamiyamachi Chiyoda, Tokyo, 101-0044 Japan. T. +81332513360. Fax +81332513380. E-mail: admin@jaia.gr.jp.
URL: http://asia-adhesive.org/

Structure Executive Council of 4. **Events** *World Adhesive and Sealant Conference* Chicago, IL (USA) 2022, *World Adhesive and Sealant Conference* Chicago, IL (USA) 2020, *Conference* Shanghai (China) 2018, *Quadrennial World Conference* Tokyo (Japan) 2016, *Conference* Kobe (Japan) 2014.
Members Organizations (4) in 4 countries and territories:
China, Japan, Korea Rep, Taiwan.
NGO Relations Partner of (1): *Fédération européenne des industries de colles et adhésifs (FEICA, #09572)*. [2020/XJ4713/D]

♦ Asia Regional Cookstove Programme (ARECOP) 02084

Contact address not obtained. T. +62274885247. Fax +62274885423.

History 1991. **NGO Relations** Supports: *Asian Alliance of Appropriate Technology Practitioners (APPROTECH ASIA, #01306)*. [2011/XE1768/E]

♦ Asia Regional Forum / see ASEAN Regional Forum (#01228)

♦ Asia Region International Association of Cooperating Organizations (ARIACO) 02085

Secretariat c/o Asian Strategy and Leadership Institute, 1718 Jalan Ledang, Off Jalan Duta, 50480 Kuala Lumpur, Malaysia. T. +60320935393. Fax +60320934178.

History Sep 1994, Melbourne, VIC (Australia). **Aims** Help organizations enhance competitiveness, leadership and strategic capabilities. **Structure** Informal network of participating organizations. Secretariat at *Asian Strategy and Leadership Institute (ASLI)*. **Languages** English. **Staff** Seconded from member organizations as required. **Activities** Public programmes; policy research; business councils; CEO peer groups; conferences. **Events** *Conference* Australia 2004.
Members Organizations in 9 countries and territories:
Australia, China, Hong Kong, Indonesia, Korea Rep, Malaysia, Philippines, Singapore, Thailand. [2013.11.28/XD7577/D]

♦ Asia Region SUZUKI Association (ARSA) 02086

Contact No 1 Missouri St, Greenhills East, 1502 Mandaluyong City, Manila, Philippines. E-mail: asiasuzuki.vp.tw@gmail.com.
URL: https://asiaregionsuzukiassociation.org/

History Bylaws adopted 2014. Developed out of *Asia Suzuki Association (ASA)*. **Aims** Oversee and advance the growth of the Suzuki Method in Asia. **Structure** Board. **Languages** English. **Finance** Members' dues. **Activities** Events/meetings. **Events** *Conference* Bali (Indonesia) 2016, *Asia Suzuki Conference* Taipei (Taiwan) 2014.

Members Organizations in 5 countries and territories:
Indonesia, Korea Rep, Malaysia, Philippines, Taiwan.
IGO Relations None. **NGO Relations** Member of: *International Suzuki Association (ISA, #15637).* [2015.07.31/XJ9810/E]

♦ Asia Regulatory Professionals Association (unconfirmed)
♦ Asia Remote Health Committee (unconfirmed)

♦ Asia Reproductive Biotechnology Society (ARBS) 02087

Organizing Office address not obtained. T. +8224503679. Fax +8224446830. E-mail: admin@arbsociety.org – arbs@arbsociety.org.
URL: http://www.arbsociety.org/

History 2004. **Aims** Promote the educational and scientific interests of the reproductive biotechnology research community throughout Asia. **Structure** Steering Committee. **Finance** Members' dues. **Events** *Annual Meeting* Bangkok (Thailand) 2014, *Annual Meeting* Ho Chi Minh City (Vietnam) 2013, *Annual Meeting* Manila (Philippines) 2012, *Annual Meeting* Guilin (China) 2011, *Annual Meeting* Kuala Lumpur (Malaysia) 2010. **Publications** *Reproductive Biotechnology* – journal.
Members Regular; Student; Association; Emeritus. Members in 17 countries and territories:
Bangladesh, Brunei Darussalam, Cambodia, China, India, Indonesia, Iran Islamic Rep, Japan, Korea Rep, Laos, Malaysia, Mongolia, Singapore, Taiwan, Thailand, United Arab Emirates, Vietnam. [2014/XJ8693/D]

♦ Asia Research Centre, Murdoch University (internationally oriented national body)
♦ Asia Research Centre on Social, Political and Economic Change, Murdoch University / see Asia Research Centre, Murdoch University
♦ Asia Research Institute (internationally oriented national body)
♦ **AsiaRice** Asia Rice Foundation (#02088)

♦ Asia Rice Foundation (AsiaRice) 02088

Exec Dir College, 4031 Los Baños LAG, Philippines. T. +63495362285 – +6309954021715. Fax +63495362285. E-mail: asia_rice@searca.org.
URL: https://asiarice.org/

History Jun 1999, Laguna (Philippines). **Aims** Mobilize and provide support for research, educational, cultural and advocacy movements that promote public appreciation of the role of rice in the diverse culture of Asia. **Structure** Board of Trustees; Secretariat. **Languages** English. **Staff** 1.00 FTE, paid. Voluntary. **Finance** Sources: donations. Project based funding. **Activities** Awareness raising; events/meetings; publishing activities. **Publications** *Water in Agriculture* (2016); *Mechanization in Rice Farming: Status, Challenges and Opportunities* (2015); *Adaptation to Climate Variability in Rice Production* (2011); *Revisiting the Organic Fertilizer Issue in Rice* (2010); *Beyond Boiled Rice: Value-added Products and Entrepreneurship* (2009); *The Adventures of Gabby Ghas* (2009) – children's book on rice, in English, Visayan (2012), Bicolano (2013), Tagalog (2013), and Ilocano (2013); *Rice, Water and Forests* (2008); *Rice in the Seven Arts* (2004).
Members National organizations (5) in 5 countries:
Bangladesh, China, Indonesia, Philippines, Thailand.
Individuals in 21 countries:
Australia, Bangladesh, Canada, China, France, Germany, India, Iran Islamic Rep, Japan, Korea Rep, Laos, Malaysia, Netherlands, Philippines, South Africa, Sudan, Thailand, UK, USA, Vietnam, Zimbabwe. [2021.09.10/XD8797/f/F]

♦ Asia Risk Management Institute (internationally oriented national body)

♦ Asia Rugby 02089

Gen Manager Room 2001, Sports House, 1 Stadium Path, So Kan Po, Causeway Bay, Hong Kong, Central and Western, Hong Kong. T. +85225048636. Fax +85225767237.
URL: http://www.asiarugby.com/

History Founded 1968, as *Asian Rugby Football Union (ARFU).* **Aims** Promote Rugby Union Football throughout the Asian Region. **Structure** Unions are "Members by Guarantee", each with equal rights. **Languages** English. **Staff** 8.00 FTE, paid. **Finance** Grants issued by: *World Rugby (#21757)*; partnership with sponsors. **Activities** Sporting activities; projects/programmes; research and development.
Members Full: Unions (27) in 27 countries and territories:
Bangladesh, Brunei Darussalam, China, Hong Kong, India, Indonesia, Iran Islamic Rep, Japan, Jordan, Kazakhstan, Korea Rep, Kyrgyzstan, Laos, Lebanon, Macau, Malaysia, Mongolia, Nepal, Pakistan, Philippines, Qatar, Singapore, Sri Lanka, Taiwan, Thailand, United Arab Emirates, Uzbekistan.
Associate: Unions (3) in 3 countries:
Afghanistan, Saudi Arabia, Syrian AR.
NGO Relations *World Rugby (#21757).* [2019.12.12/XD9054/D]

♦ Asia Safe Abortion Partnership (ASAP) 02090

Coordinator Dadar Surgical and Maternity Hospital, Gokhale Road North, Dadar West, Mumbai, Maharashtra 400028, Mumbai MAHARASHTRA 400028, India. E-mail: coordinator@asap-asia.org.
URL: http://www.asap-asia.org/

History Mar 2008, Kuala Lumpur (Malaysia), facilitated by *International Consortium for Medical Abortion (ICMA, inactive).* **Aims** Promote, protect and advance women's sexual and reproductive rights and health in Asia by reducing unsafe abortion and its complications and where it is legal, by promoting access to comprehensive safe abortion services. **Structure** Steering Committee. **Events** *Asia Pacific Conference on Reproductive and Sexual Health and Rights* Beijing (China) 2009.
Members Full in 13 countries:
Bangladesh, Cambodia, India, Indonesia, Malaysia, Mongolia, Nepal, Pakistan, Philippines, Sri Lanka, Thailand, Türkiye, Vietnam.
NGO Relations Partner of: *International Campaign for Women's Right to Safe Abortion (#12430).* [2019/XJ1242/E]

♦ Asia Safe Community Network 02091

Office Madar Square, Adib Blvd, 26th Adib St, 2nd Rasti St, Crisis Management Base, Mashhad RAZAVI KHORASAN, 9095110193, Iran Islamic Rep. T. +985132236119.
URL: http://ascn.info/

Aims Meet a demand for information about the safe community concept in Asia. **Structure** Steering Committee. **Activities** Events/meetings; training/education; awards/prizes/competitions. **Events** *Conference* Busan (Korea Rep) 2014. **Publications** *Asia Safe Community News.* [2018/XJ6966/F]

♦ Asia for Safe Handling of Cytotoxic Drugs Interest Group 02092

Contact Pharmacy Dept NUS, Natl Cancer Ctr, 11 Hospital Drive, Singapore 169610, Singapore. T. +6564368137. Fax +6562202573.
URL: http://www.asia4safehandling.org/

History 2004. **Aims** Provide evidence-based guidelines on safe handling procedures for all those working with cytotoxic drugs in Asia and subsequently raise the practice standard. **Structure** Executive Committee. **Languages** English. **Activities** Events/meetings. **Events** *Asia-Pacific Oncology Pharmacy Congress* Singapore (Singapore) 2018.
Members Full in 7 countries:
China, Indonesia, Japan, Korea Rep, Malaysia, Singapore, Thailand. [2018.03.12/XJ7010/D]

♦ Asia Securities Forum (ASF) 02093

Secretariat 1-5-8 Kayabacho, Nihombashi Chuo-Ku, Tokyo, 103-0025 Japan. T. +81336678537. Fax +81336699574.
URL: http://www.asiasecuritiesforum.org/

History 1995. **Aims** Exchange views and information among securities industry in the Asia-Pacific region; contribute to development of securities markets and economic growth in the region. **Structure** General Meeting (annual). **Events** *Tokyo Round Table Seminar* Tokyo (Japan) 2018, *General Meeting* Seoul (Korea Rep) 2015, *General Meeting* Bangkok (Thailand) 2014, *General Meeting* Taiwan 2013, *General Meeting* Mumbai (India) 2012.
Members Full in 15 countries and territories:
Australia, China, Hong Kong, India, Indonesia, Japan, Korea Rep, Malaysia, Mongolia, New Zealand, Philippines, Taiwan, Thailand, Türkiye, Vietnam. [2019/XJ6968/F]

♦ Asia Securities Industry and Financial Markets Association (ASIFMA) 02094

CEO Unit 3603, Tower 2, Lippo Centre, 89 Queensway, Hong Kong, Central and Western, Hong Kong. T. +85225316500 – +85225316515 – +85225316530. E-mail: info@asifma.org.
URL: http://www.asifma.org/

History Registration: EU Transparency Register, No/ID: 595923137195-20. **Aims** Promote development of liquid, efficient and transparent capital markets in Asia; facilitate their orderly integration into the global financial system. **Structure** Board of Directors. Executive Committee. Standing Committees; Working Groups. **Languages** English, Mandarin Chinese. **Activities** Events/meetings; research/documentation. **Events** *Compliance Asia Conference* 2022, *Doing What is Right and Ethical* Singapore (Singapore) 2020, *ESG and Sustainable Finance in Asia – The Fintech and Data Challenge* Singapore (Singapore) 2020, *Evolving Cyber Landscape in Light of COVID-19 – Managing the Impact* Singapore (Singapore) 2020, *Navigating ESG and Sustainable Finance in Asia* Singapore (Singapore) 2020. **Publications** *Asia Regulatory Review* (weekly).
Members Global and regional banks; securities dealers; brokers; asset managers; credit rating agencies; law firms; trading and analytic platforms; clearance and settlement providers. Membership countries not specified. **NGO Relations** Member of: *Global Financial Markets Association (GFMA, #10359)*; *SME Finance Forum (#19323).* [2020/XJ2827/t/D]

♦ Asia Semiconductor Trading Support Association (ASTSA) 02095

Contact address not obtained. T. +81927214900. Fax +81927214908.
History Founded 30 Oct 2006. **Aims** Function as a mediator for semiconductor-related industries; accelerate international business for semiconductor-related industries; contribute to the development of semiconductor-related industries in Asia. **Events** *International workshop on microelectronics assembling and packaging* Fukuoka (Japan) 2009. [2015/XJ1519/D]

♦ Asia's Four Little Dragons / see Four Dragons (#09977)
♦ ASI – Asian Social Institute (internationally oriented national body)
♦ ASIASIM – Federation of Asia Simulation Societies (unconfirmed)

♦ Asia Society 02096

Contact 725 Park Avenue (at 70th Str), New York NY 10021, USA. T. +12122886400. Fax +12125178315. E-mail: info@asiasociety.org.
URL: http://www.asiasociety.org/

History 1956. Founded by John D Rockefeller 3rd. Former names and other names: *Asia Society, New York* – former. **Aims** Navigate shared futures for Asia and the world across policy, arts and culture, education, sustainability, business, and technology. **Structure** Board of Trustees; Global Council. Centers in: New York NY (USA); Hong Kong; Houston TX (USA). Additional offices in: Australia; France; India; Japan; Korea Rep; California (USA); Philippines; Southern California (USA); Switzerland; Washington DC (USA). **Finance** Contributions from foundations, corporations and individuals. **Activities** Events/meetings; projects/programmes; training/education. **Events** *Asia 21 Young Leaders Summit* Tokyo (Japan) 2022, *International Summit on the Teaching Profession* Wellington (New Zealand) 2014, *International Summit on the Teaching Profession* New York, NY (USA) 2011, *Women Leaders of New Asia Summit* Singapore (Singapore) 2011, *Annual corporate conference* Mumbai (India) 2006. **Publications** *Asian Updates* – series. Conference Reports; Study Mission Reports. Special titles.
Members Individual (Full; Senior Citizen; Student; Associate); Asia Circle; Dual/Family; International Associate; Contributing; Sustaining; President's Circle; Friend of Asian Arts. Primarily North American membership. Members in 5 countries:
Australia, China, Hong Kong, Philippines, USA.
IGO Relations Associated with Department of Global Communications of the United Nations. [2022/XN1975/E]

♦ Asia Society of Basic Design and Art (unconfirmed)
♦ Asia Society of Hip Arthroscopy & Preservation (unconfirmed)
♦ Asia Society, New York / see Asia Society (#02096)
♦ Asia Society of Researchers (unconfirmed)

♦ Asia Society for Social Improvement and Sustainable Transformation (ASSIST) 02097

Contact 8/F Montepino Bldg, 138 Adelantado Str cor Gamboa Str, Legaspi Village, 1229 Makati, Philippines. T. +6324038668. Fax +6324038358. E-mail: info@assistasia.org.
URL: http://www.assistasia.org/

History 2003. **Aims** Develop and protect economic, social and environmental conditions of society; leverage on technology as enabler/driver of change; unite and capacitate key stakeholders to address societal and environmental problems; mobilize public and private sectors as well as civil society as equal partners in attaining meaningful change. **Structure** Head office in Makati City (Philippines). Regional Offices with Board of Directors each: Chennai (India); Ho Chi Minh City (Vietnam); Phnom Penh (Cambodia). **Languages** English, Filipino, French, German, Latvian, Polish, Russian, Tamil, Vietnamese. **Staff** 40.00 FTE, paid. Several voluntary. **Finance** Support from: *Deutsche Gesellschaft für Internationale Zusammenarbeit (GIZ)*; *DEG – Deutsche Investitions- und Entwicklungsgesellschaft*; *European Commission (EC, #06633)*; *European Union (EU, #08967)*; *UNEP (#20299)*; *UNIDO (#20336)*; *United States Agency for International Development (USAID)*; *The World Bank Group (#21218).* **Activities** Guidance/assistance/consulting; monitoring/evaluation; projects/programmes; research and development; knowledge management/information dissemination; events/meetings. **Publications** *Impact* – magazine. **IGO Relations** Additional collaborations with: *Asian Development Bank (ADB, #01422)*; *International Finance Corporation (IFC, #13597)*; *UNEP (#20299)*; *UNIDO (#20336).* **NGO Relations** Member of: *Global Network for Resource Efficient and Cleaner Production (RECPnet, #10497)*; Philippine International Nongovernment Organizations Network (PINGON); *Sustainable Sanitation Alliance (SuSanA, #20066).* [2017.10.11/XJ5818/F]

♦ Asia South Pacific Association for Basic and Adult Education (ASPBAE) 02098

Bureau de l'Asie et du Pacifique Sud de l'éducation des adultes

SG Unit 106, Sterten Place Condo, 116 Maginhawa St, Teachers Village East, Diliman, 1101 Quezon City, Philippines. E-mail: aspbae@gmail.com.
URL: http://www.aspbae.org/

History 1964, Sydney, NSW (Australia). Founded as *Asian South Pacific Bureau of Adult Education (ASPBAE)*, at a UNESCO Regional Seminar on Adult and Non formal Education. Most recent constitution 2000, most recently amended Dec 2008. **Aims** Advance and defend the right of all people to learn and have equitable access to relevant and quality education that promotes gender justice, and to learning opportunities throughout their lives. **Structure** General Assembly (every 4 years); Executive Council. Sub-Regions: South and Central Asia; East Asia; South East Asia; South Pacific. Regional arm of: *International Council for Adult Education (ICAE, #12983).* **Languages** English. **Staff** 14.00 FTE, paid. **Finance** Members' dues. Assistance with projects, in particular from: Institute for International Cooperation; *Institut für Internationale Zusammenarbeit des Deutschen Volkshochschul-Verbandes (DVV-International)*; *Global Campaign for Education (GCE, #10264)*; *European Commission (EC, #06633)*; Open Society Foundations (OSF); *Australian Aid (inactive)*; *Asia/Pacific Cultural Centre for UNESCO (ACCU, #01879).* Budget (annual): about US$ 1 million. **Activities** Capacity building; politics/policy/regulatory; advocacy/lobbying/activism; networking/liaising; training/education. **Events** *General Assembly* Tagaytay (Philippines) 2014, *General Assembly* Phnom Penh (Cambodia) 2012, *General Assembly* Kuala Lumpur (Malaysia) 2008, *General Assembly* Yogyakarta (Indonesia) 2004, *General Assembly* Chiang Mai (Thailand) 2000. **Publications** *ASPBAE e-Bulletin* (12 a year); *ASPBAE Ed-Lines* (4 a year) – newsletter. Annual Activity Report; project publications.
Members Individual; Organizational. Members in 36 countries and territories:
Afghanistan, Australia, Bangladesh, Bhutan, Cambodia, China, Cook Is, Fiji, Hong Kong, India, Indonesia, Iran Islamic Rep, Japan, Korea Rep, Kyrgyzstan, Macau, Malaysia, Maldives, Mongolia, Myanmar, Nepal, New Zealand, Pakistan, Papua New Guinea, Philippines, Samoa, Singapore, Solomon Is, Sri Lanka, Tajikistan, Thailand, Timor-Leste, Tonga, Uzbekistan, Vanuatu, Vietnam.

Consultative Status Consultative status granted from: *ECOSOC (#05331)* (Ros C); *UNESCO (#20322)* (Associate Status). **IGO Relations** Cooperates with: *Asia-Pacific Programme of Educational Innovation for Development (APEID, #02001); International Institute for Adult Education Methods (IIAEM, no recent information); Southeast Asian Ministers of Education Organization (SEAMEO, #19774); UNESCO Asia and Pacific Regional Bureau for Education (#20301); United Nations Girls' Education Initiative (UNGEI, #20566).* **NGO Relations** Member of: *Asia Civil Society Forum (ACSF, no recent information); Asian Pacific Regional Coordinating Committee (no recent information); Conference of Non-Governmental Organizations in Consultative Relationship with the United Nations (CONGO, #04635); Global Campaign for Education (GCE, #10264).* Cooperates with: *Development Innovations and Networks (#05057).* Instrumental in setting up: *Climate change Learning Initiative Mobilizing Action Transforming Environments in Asia Pacific (CLIMATE Asia Pacific, #04009).* [2022/XD3993/**D**]

♦ Asia and South Pacific Design Automation Conference (meeting series)
♦ ASI – Association de la sommellerie internationale (internationally oriented national body)
♦ ASI – Association stomatologique internationale (inactive)
♦ **ASI** Assurance Services International (#02993)
♦ Asia Starlight Dance Association (unconfirmed)
♦ Asia Stroke Federation / see Asia Pacific Stroke Organization (#02056)
♦ Asia Students Association (no recent information)
♦ Asia Sustainable Development Fund (inactive)

♦ **Asia Swimming Federation (AASF)** 02099
SG PO Box 743, Muttrah, 112, Muscat, Oman. T. +96824496161. Fax +96824490660. E-mail: aasf@omantel.net.om.
URL: https://asiaswimmingfederation.com/
History Founded 1978, as *Asian Amateur Swimming Federation*. **Aims** Promote and encourage development of Swimming, Open Water Swimming, Diving, Water Polo, Synchronised Swimming and Masters in Asia; adopt necessary regulations and rules; promote and control all approved Asian Championships; promote and encourage development of regional and international sporting relationships; increase the number of facilities for swimming in the region. **Structure** Bureau of 23 members. Committees (9): Swimming; Diving; Water Polo; Synchronised; Open Water; Master; Finance and Marketing; Medical; Solidarity and Development. **Activities** Sporting activities. **Events** *Congress* Seoul (Korea Rep) 1986. **Members** Full in 27 countries (membership countries not specified). [2020/XD7250/**D**]

♦ **Asia Taekwondo Federation (ATF)** 02100
SG The Cradle of Taekwon-Do, Chukjon-dong, Mangyongdae District, Pyongyang, Korea DPR. T. +850218111ext8809. Fax +85023814410. E-mail: atf_tkd65@126.com.
URL: http://www.atftkd.com/
History Founded 1981, within the framework of *International Taekwon-Do Federation (ITF, #15652)*. Also referred to as: *Asia Pacific Taekwondo Federation; Asia Pacific TKD Federation*. Most recent Statutes adopted 25 Apr 2010, Almaty (Kazakhstan), during 5th Congress. **Aims** Represent, govern, promote, expand and develop Taekwondo in Asia. **Structure** Congress (every 2 years); Executive Board. Standing Committees (5): Technical; Tournament; Umpire; Expansion; Publishing and Information. **Languages** English, Korean. **Activities** Sporting activities. **Events** *Congress* Almaty (Kazakhstan) 2010. **Members** Membership countries not specified. [2015/XD4440/**D**]

♦ Asia Tax Forum / see Asia-Pacific Tax Forum (#02061)
♦ **Asia TEFL** Asian Association of Teachers of English as a Foreign Language (#01342)

♦ **Asia Theological Association (ATA)** 02101
Contact 54 Scout Madrinan St, PO Box 1454-1154, 1103 Quezon City, Philippines. T. +6326681906. E-mail: ataasia@gmail.com.
URL: http://www.ataasia.com/
History Jul 1970. Founded as a direct outcome of the Pan-Asia Congress of Evangelism, 1968, Singapore (Singapore). Initial intention was to serve as a coordinating agency for evangelical theological education in Asia. In 1977, began offering accreditation services to evangelical theological institutions in Asia. Asia Graduate School of Theology established as the research and education arm of the association in 1983. Former names and other names: *Asia Theological Association International (ATA)* – alias. **Aims** Promote and support evangelical theological education in Asia and Asian communities worldwide; facilitate quality theological *education* through accreditation by establishing standards and developing criteria and instruments for the evaluation of programmes at various levels for the sake of quality assurance and excellence; encourage the sharing of resources; promote evangelical theological scholarship that is relevant to the Asian context; encourage writing and publication of contextual theological literature and text books. **Structure** Triennial Meeting; Executive Board of 12 persons. Operates *Asia Graduate School of Theology – Malaysia/Singapore/Thailand (AGST-MST)* / Philippines, Japan. **Languages** English. **Staff** 6.00 FTE, paid; 3.00 FTE, voluntary. **Finance** Sources: members' dues. **Activities** Events/meetings; guidance/assistance/consulting; knowledge management/information dissemination; networking/liaising; projects/programmes; standards/guidelines; training/education. **Events** *Triennial General Assembly* Penang (Malaysia) 2022, *Triennial General Assembly* Singapore (Singapore) 2019, *Triennial General Assembly* Gyeonggi (Korea Rep) 2016, *Theological Education Seminar* Bangkok (Thailand) 2015, *Theological Education Seminar* Korea Rep 2014. **Publications** *ATA News* (4 a year); *Journal of Asian Evangelical Theology (JAET)* (2 a year); *Journal of Asian Mission (JAM)* (2 a year). *Asia Bible Commentary Series: Song of Songs* (2002). *Romans* (2013); *Psalms 73-150* (2013); *Psalms 1-72* (2013); *Leadership in an Age of Turmoil* (2012); *Mark* (2011); *Job* (2011); *Hosea* (2010); *Acts* (2007); *Colossians and Philemon* (2005); *Ephesians* (2005); *John* (2002); *Daniel* (2002); *God in Asian Context* (1988); *The Bible and Theology in Asian Contexts* (1983); *New Era New Vision*; *Striving for Excellence: Educational Ministry in the Church*; *Tending the Seedbeds*; *The Church in a Changing World*; *The Pastor and Theological Education*. Monographs. **Members** Members (282) in 32 countries. Membership countries not specified. **NGO Relations** Member of: *International Council for Evangelical Theological Education (ICETE, #13020); World Evangelical Alliance (WEA, #21393).* [2022.05.12/XD1633/**D**]

♦ Asia Theological Association International / see Asia Theological Association (#02101)
♦ Asiatic Society of Bangladesh / see Bangladesh Asiatic Society
♦ Asiatic Society of Japan (internationally oriented national body)
♦ Asiatic Union of Gymnastics / see Asian Gymnastics Union (#01499)
♦ Asiatische Entwicklungsbank (#01422)
♦ Asiatische Organisation der Obersten Rechnungskontrollbehörden (#01594)
♦ Asiatischer Bund der CVJM (#01826)
♦ Asiatischer Regionalverband für Hauswirtschaft (#01682)
♦ Asia Tourism Association / see Asia Pacific Tourism Association (#02067)
♦ **ASIATOX** Asian Society of Toxicology (#01744)

♦ **Asia Trails Network (ATN)** 02102
China address not obtained. E-mail: liuxmwd@sina.com.
Japan address not obtained. E-mail: civic@npo-mirai.net.
Korea Rep address not obtained. E-mail: jejuolle@jejuolle.org.
URL: http://www.worldtrail.org/network/asia_network.php
History Set up Jan 2014, as a regional hub of *World Trails Network (WTN, #21866)*. **Aims** Share trail issues and common values; take the initiative in building a sustainable development of trail industry through knowledge sharing and an effective cross-promotional platform for trails, creation of a healthy *walking travel* culture, protection of natural resources and implementation of corporate marketing. **Events** *Asia Trails Conference* Busan (Korea Rep) 2019.
Members Regular in 3 countries:
China, Japan, Korea Rep. [2017/XM5677/**E**]

♦ Asia Travel Marketing Association (inactive)
♦ Asia Triple Helix Society / see World Association for Triple Helix and Future Strategy Studies
♦ Asia University (internationally oriented national body)
♦ ASI – Australasian Society for Immunology (internationally oriented national body)

♦ **Asia Video Industry Association (AVIA)** 02103
CEO 20/F Leighton Ctr, 77 Leighton Road, Causeway Bay, Hong Kong. T. +85228549913. E-mail: avia@asiavia.org.
Singapore Office 5008 Ang Mo Kio Aven, 5 #04-09, Techplace II, Singapore 569874, Singapore.
URL: http://asiavia.org/
History 28 May 1991, Hong Kong (Hong Kong). Former names and other names: *Cable and Satellite Broadcasting Association of Asia (CASBAA)* – former (1991). **Aims** Make the video industry stronger and healthier. **Structure** Board of Directors. **Finance** Members' dues. **Activities** Advocacy/lobbying/activism; networking/liaising; events/meetings; publishing activities. **Events** *OTT Summit* Singapore (Singapore) 2021, *OTT Summit* Singapore (Singapore) 2020, *Satellite Industry Forum* Singapore (Singapore) 2020, *The State of Piracy Summit* Singapore (Singapore) 2020, *Asia Video Summit* Singapore (Singapore) 2019. **Members** Patron; Corporate; Small Company; Individual. Membership countries not specified. [2022/XD7712/t/**D**]

♦ **Asiavision (AVN)** 02104
Dir of News PO Box 12287, 50772 Kuala Lumpur, Malaysia. T. +60322827033. Fax +60322827562. E-mail: centre@asiavision.org.
URL: http://www.abu.org.my/
History Jan 1984, within the framework of *Asia-Pacific Broadcasting Union (ABU, #01863)*. **Aims** Ensure a daily exchange of *news* items by satellite among *television* stations in Asia. **Structure** Operations Centre in Kuala Lumpur (Malaysia). **Languages** English. **Staff** ABU Secretariat staff. **Finance** Members' dues. **Activities** Knowledge management/information dissemination; awards/prizes/competitions.
Members Broadcasters in 20 countries and territories:
Afghanistan, Bangladesh, Bhutan, Brunei Darussalam, Cambodia, China, Hong Kong, India, Iran Islamic Rep, Japan, Macau, Malaysia, Mongolia, Nepal, Pakistan, Singapore, Sri Lanka, Thailand, Timor-Leste, Türkiye.
NGO Relations Transmits free of charge to members of: *Eurovision*. [2016.06.27/XF0544/**F**]

♦ **Asia Water Council (AWC)** 02105
SG 200 Sintanjin-ro, Daedeok-gu, Daejeon 34350, Korea Rep. T. +826294233. Fax +826294825. E-mail: awc@asiawatercouncil.org.
Exec Dir address not obtained.
URL: http://www.asiawatercouncil.org/
History Mar 2016, Bali (Indonesia). **Aims** Resolve Asian water problems; promote sustainable growth by solving water issues. **Structure** General Assembly; Board of Council; Bureau; Secretariat. Special Committees. **Events** *Board of Council Meeting* Seoul (Korea Rep) 2021, *General Assembly* Manila (Philippines) 2019. **Publications** *AWC Newsletter*.
Members Full in 22 countries:
Australia, Bangladesh, Cambodia, China, France, Georgia, Indonesia, Japan, Korea Rep, Laos, Malaysia, Mongolia, Myanmar, Nepal, Netherlands, Pakistan, Philippines, Singapore, Switzerland, UK, USA, Vietnam.
Action Against Hunger (#00086); Akvo Foundation; APEC Climate Center (APCC); Asian Development Bank (ADB, #01422); Asian Institute of Technology (AIT, #01519); FAO (#09260); Global Institute for Water, Environment and Health (GIWEH, #10429); Global Water Partnership (GWP, #10653) (South East Asia – Central Asia and Caucasus); International Association for Hydro-Environment Engineering and Research (IAHR, #11950); International Bank for Reconstruction and Development (IBRD, #12317); International Commission on Large Dams (ICOLD, #12696); International Fund for Saving the Aral Sea (IFAS, #13694); International Hydrological Programme (IHP, #13826); International Water Resources Association (IWRA, #15871); Korea International Cooperation Agency (KOICA); Mekong River Commission (MRC, #16703); UNESCO International Centre for Water Security and Sustainable Management (i-WSSM). [2021/AA1848/y/**D**]

♦ **Asia Wind Energy Association** 02106
Contact CapitaGreen – Level 24, 138 Market Street, Singapore 048946, Singapore. T. +6566796071. E-mail: info@asiawind.org.
URL: https://www.asiawind.org/
History Dec 2016. **Aims** Develop and communicate conclusive policies to influence the decision-making process of the Asian governments to create a positive investment environment and enable greater deployment of wind energy in the Asia-Pacific region. **Structure** General Meeting; Board of Directors; Secretariat. **Activities** Events/meetings. **Events** *Asia Offshore Wind Meeting* Tokyo (Japan) 2018. **Members** Corporate. Membership countries not specified. **NGO Relations** Partner of (4): *Energy Industries Council (EIC); Energy Institute (EI); IMCA International Marine Contractors Association (IMCA, #11127); World Ocean Council (WOC, #21680)*. [2022/AA1895/**D**]

♦ Asia Women in Motorsport Association (unconfirmed)
♦ Asia Working Dog Support Association (internationally oriented national body)
♦ ASIBEHU – Asociación Iberoamericana Etico-Humanista (no recent information)
♦ **ASIBEI** Asociación Iberoamericana de Instituciones de Enseñanza de la Ingeniería (#02144)
♦ ASICADE – Asociación Iberoamericana de Profesionales para la Calidad y el Desarrollo (unconfirmed)
♦ **ASICAL** Asociación para la Salud Integral y Ciudadanía de América Latina y el Caribe (#02651)
♦ **ASIC** Association pour la science et l'information sur le café (#02905)
♦ ASIC / see Association for the Science and Information on Coffee (#02905)
♦ ASICL – African Society of International and Comparative Law (no recent information)
♦ ASID – Australasian Society for Infectious Diseases (internationally oriented national body)
♦ ASID – Australasian Society for Intellectual Disability (internationally oriented national body)
♦ **ASIDD** Asociación Internacional de Derecho Deportivo (#12180)
♦ Aside World / see International Side-Saddle Organization
♦ **ASIE** Association for Studies in International Education (#02934)
♦ ASIEM – Australasian Society for Inborn Errors of Metabolism (internationally oriented national body)
♦ **ASIER** Asociación Iberoamericana de Estudios de Regulacion (#02140)
♦ ASIER – Associação Ibero-Americana de Estudos Ricoeurianos (unconfirmed)
♦ ASIET / see Action in Solidarity with Asia and the Pacific
♦ **ASIET** Asociación Interamericana de Empresas de Telecomunicaciones (#02160)
♦ **ASIFA** Association internationale du film d'animation (#02698)
♦ **ASIF** Asian Securities and Investments Federation (#01695)
♦ ASIF / see Axial Spondyloarthritis International Federation (#03052)
♦ **ASIF** Axial Spondyloarthritis International Federation (#03052)
♦ ASI-FC / see Asian Social Institute
♦ **ASIFMA** Asia Securities Industry and Financial Markets Association (#02094)
♦ ASIL – American Society of International Law (internationally oriented national body)
♦ **ASIL** Asociación Iberoamericana de Logoterapia (#02146)
♦ **ASIM** Arbeitsgemeinschaft Simulation (#01083)
♦ **ASINCO** Asian Society for Integrity of Nuclear Components (#01724)
♦ **ASIORNA** Asian periOpeRative Nurses Association (#01662)
♦ **ASIP** Arab Society for Intellectual Property (#01046)
♦ **ASIP** Asian Society for Innovation and Policy (#01723)
♦ **ASIP** Asociación Internacional de Presupuesto Público (#18564)
♦ ASIPI / see Asociación Interamericana de la Propiedad Intelectual (#02161)
♦ **ASIPI** Asociación Interamericana de la Propiedad Intelectual (#02161)
♦ ASIR – Amsterdam School of International Relations (internationally oriented national body)
♦ ASIRT – Association for Safe International Road Travel (internationally oriented national body)
♦ ASIS / see ASIS International
♦ ASiS – Asian Silicon Symposium (meeting series)
♦ ASIS – Associazione Internazionale per la Sintesi della Conoscenza (no recent information)
♦ ASIS International (internationally oriented national body)
♦ ASISS / see Association des journalistes accrédités auprès du Vatican (#02773)
♦ ASIS and T – Association for Information Science and Technology (internationally oriented national body)
♦ ASI / see Statistical Institute for Asia and the Pacific (#19972)
♦ Asistencia Recíproca Petrolera Empresarial Latinoamericana / see Asociación Regional de Empresas del Sector Petróleo, Gas y Biocombustibles en Latinoamérica y el Caribe (#02296)

♦ Asistencia Reciproca Petrolera Estatal Latinoamericana / see Asociación Regional de Empresas del Sector Petróleo, Gas y Biocombustibles en Latinoamérica y el Caribe (#02296)
♦ ASISTI – Asocio de Studado Internacia pri Spiritaj kaj Teologiaj Instruoj (inactive)
♦ **ASIT** Asociación de Seminarios e Instituciones Teológicas (#02912)
♦ ASJ / see Action for Post-Soviet Jewry
♦ **ASJA** Arab Science Journalists Association (#01038)
♦ ASJ – Asiatic Society of Japan (internationally oriented national body)
♦ ASJEL – Association of Jesuit Higher Education Institutions in Europe and Lebanon (inactive)
♦ ASJJF – Asian Sport Jiu-Jitsu Federation (unconfirmed)
♦ ASJU – African Sports Journalists Union (inactive)
♦ **ASK** Asian Society of Kinesiology (#01726)
♦ ASKO Europa-Stiftung (internationally oriented national body)
♦ **ASL** Association for Symbolic Logic (#02945)
♦ **AsLEA** Asian Law and Economics Association (#01524)
♦ **ASLERD** Association for Smart Learning Ecosystem and Regional Development (#02916)
♦ ASLF / see African Safari Lodge Foundation (#00448)
♦ ASLF – Atlantic States Legal Foundation (internationally oriented national body)
♦ **ASL Foundation** African Safari Lodge Foundation (#00448)
♦ **ASLI** Asian Law Institute (#01525)
♦ ASLI – Asian Strategy and Leadership Institute (internationally oriented national body)
♦ **ASLIP** Association for the Study of Language In Prehistory (#02938)
♦ **ASLM** African Society for Laboratory Medicine (#00463)
♦ **ASLM** Asian Society of Lifestyle Medicine (#01727)
♦ ASLM – Australasian Society of Lifestyle Medicine (internationally oriented national body)
♦ ASLO / see Association for the Sciences of Limnology and Oceanography
♦ ASLO – Association for the Sciences of Limnology and Oceanography (internationally oriented national body)
♦ ASM / see ASM International
♦ ASMA – Aerospace Medical Association (internationally oriented national body)
♦ **ASMA** African Sport Management Association (#00473)
♦ ASMAE – Association for Social and Medical Action and Education (internationally oriented national body)
♦ ASMAF – Association de soutien des missions des assemblées de France (internationally oriented national body)
♦ ASM – African Society of Mycotoxicology (unconfirmed)
♦ ASM – ASM International (internationally oriented national body)
♦ **ASMC** ASEAN Specialized Meteorological Centre (#01236)
♦ **ASMDA International Society** Applied Stochastic Models and Data Analysis International Society (#00882)
♦ ASME – American Society of Mechanical Engineers (internationally oriented national body)

♦ ASME International Gas Turbine Institute (IGTI) 02107

Events Manager Gas Turbine Segment – GTS, 11757 Katy Freeway, Suite 380, Houston TX 77079-1733, USA. T. +12814933491. Fax +12814933493. E-mail: igti@asme.org.
URL: http://igti.asme.org/

History 1986, USA. Founded to combine the activities of the Gas Turbine Division of *American Society of Mechanical Engineers (ASME)* and the *ASME International Gas Turbine Center (IGTC)*. A technical institute of American Society of Mechanical Engineers (ASME). **Aims** Support the international exchange and development of information to improve the design, application, manufacture, operation and maintenance, and environmental impact of all types of gas turbines, turbomachinery and related equipment. **Structure** Board of Directors; Technical Committees. **Languages** English. **Staff** 14.00 FTE, paid. **Finance** Financed through income from congresses, expositions, home study courses, advertising, paper sales, investment. Annual budget: 2,000,000 USD. **Activities** Events/meetings; training/education; awards/prizes/competitions. **Events** *International Gas Turbine Congress* Kyoto (Japan) 2023, *Turbomachinery Technical Conference & Exposition* Rotterdam (Netherlands) 2022, *Turbomachinery Technical Conference & Exposition* Houston, TX (USA) 2021, *Turbomachinery Technical Conference & Exposition* London (UK) 2020, *Turbomachinery Technical Conference* Oslo (Norway) 2018. **Publications** *Journal of Engineering for Gas Turbines and Power*; *Journal of Turbomachinery*.

Members Committee members (mainly in USA) in 51 countries and territories:
Argentina, Austria, Belgium, Brazil, Canada, Denmark, Egypt, Ethiopia, Finland, France, Georgia, Germany, Ghana, Greece, Hungary, Israel, Italy, Japan, Kenya, Korea Rep, Kuwait, Malaysia, Mexico, Netherlands, Nigeria, Norway, Paraguay, Philippines, Poland, Portugal, Puerto Rico, Qatar, Russia, Saudi Arabia, Serbia, Singapore, Slovakia, Slovenia, Spain, Sweden, Switzerland, Taiwan, Thailand, Trinidad-Tobago, Türkiye, UK, Ukraine, United Arab Emirates, Uruguay, USA, Venezuela.
[2021/XF5531/j/**F**]

♦ ASMER – Association for the Study of Man Environment Relations (inactive)
♦ ASM International (internationally oriented national body)
♦ **ASMMA** Asian Secondary Mortgage Market Association (#01694)
♦ ASMO – Arab Organization for Standardization and Metrology (inactive)
♦ **ASMOSIA** Association for the Study of Marble and Other Stones in Antiquity (#02939)
♦ **ASMRM** Asian Society for Mitochondrial Research and Medicine (#01728)
♦ **ASNA** ASEAN Neurological Association (#01214)
♦ **ASNACC** Asian Society for Neuroanesthesia and Critical Care (#01730)
♦ **ASN** Agence mondiale de solidarité numérique (#21362)
♦ **ASNAPP** Agribusiness in Sustainable Natural African Plant Products (#00566)
♦ ASNEMGE – Association des sociétés nationales européennes et méditerranéennes de gastro-entérologie (inactive)
♦ **ASNM** Asian School of Nuclear Medicine (#01692)
♦ **ASNO** Asian Society for Neuro-Oncology (#01731)
♦ **ASNOS** Asian Neuro-Ophthalmology Society (#01564)
♦ **ASNP** Asian Society of Natural Products (#01729)
♦ **ASNRT** Arab Society of Nephrology and Renal Transplantation (#01047)
♦ ASOA – Association scientifique de l'Ouest africain (no recent information)
♦ ASoC / see Australasian Society of Diagnostic Genomics
♦ ASOCAN – Asociación de Sociedades Centroamericanas de Neurocirugia (unconfirmed)
♦ **ASOC** Antarctic and Southern Ocean Coalition (#00849)
♦ Asocatia Latinâ pentru Analiza Sistemor de Sânàtate (#02171)
♦ Asociace pro Mezinarodni Otaky (internationally oriented national body)
♦ Asociace Ochrõncz Zivotniho Prostedi pro Jadernou Energii (internationally oriented national body)
♦ Asociácia Európskych bojových umení (internationally oriented national body)
♦ Asociación de Abogados Latinoamericanos por la Defensa de los Derechos Humanos (no recent information)

♦ Asociación de Academias de la Lengua Española (ASALE) 02108

SG c/o RAE, Felipe IV 4, 28014 Madrid, Spain. T. +34914201478. Fax +34914200079.
URL: http://asale.org/

History Founded 1951, Mexico, following the First Congress of Spanish Language Academies. **Aims** Promote the unity, integrity and growth of the Spanish language. **Structure** Board. **Events** *Congress* Panama (Panama) 2011, *Congreso internacionale de la Lengua Española* Valparaiso (Chile) 2010, *Congress / Congreso internacionale de la Lengua Española* Cartagena de Indias (Colombia) 2007, *Congreso internacionale de la Lengua Española* Rosario (Argentina) 2004, *Congress* San Juan (Puerto Rico) 2002.

Members Full in 22 countries:
Argentina, Bolivia, Chile, Colombia, Costa Rica, Cuba, Dominica, Ecuador, El Salvador, Guatemala, Honduras, Mexico, Nicaragua, Panama, Paraguay, Peru, Philippines, Puerto Rico, Spain, Uruguay, USA, Venezuela.
Included in the above, 1 organization listed in this Yearbook:
North American Spanish Language Academy (ANLE). [2018/XM3896/y/**D**]

♦ Asociación Actores Intérpretes (no recent information)
♦ Asociación Africana sobre Asentamientos Humanos (inactive)
♦ Asociación Africana de Instituciones Financieras de Desarrollo (#02353)
♦ Asociación de Agentes Profesionales de Aduana de las Américas (#18512)
♦ Asociación de Agregados Culturales de Latinoamérica, España y Portugal (#02462)
♦ Asociación Alemana de Ayuda al Desarrollo de la Vivienda Social (internationally oriented national body)
♦ Asociación Americana de Agentes de Viajes / see American Society of Travel Advisors
♦ Asociación Americana de Constructores de Caminos (internationally oriented national body)

♦ Asociación Americana de Derecho Internacional Privado (ASADIP) . 02109

American Association of Private International Law

SG c/o BORA, Ave Rómulo Gallegos, Tor Poliprima 6o Of 6 Norte, Caracas 1071 DF, Venezuela.
URL: http://www.asadip.org/

History 6 Oct 2007, Asunción (Paraguay). Founded following the work of *Asociación Interamericana de Profesores de Derecho Internacional Privado (AIPDIP, inactive)*. **Aims** Reaffirm the need of including private international law as a mandatory subject in regular courses at law schools; strengthen its teaching in postgraduate courses; promote studies and research aimed towards developing the discipline; promote joint studies with other legal branches; exchange experiences; encourage information exchange; diffuse the labour of international organizations in private international law matters. **Structure** Annual Assembly; Council. **Languages** English, French, Portuguese, Spanish. **Staff** 4.50 FTE, voluntary. **Finance** Members' dues. **Activities** Research and development; networking/liaising. **Events** *Conference* Asunción (Paraguay) 2022, *Latin American Arbitration Conference* La Paz (Bolivia) 2017, *Latin American Arbitration Conference* Buenos Aires (Argentina) 2013, *Latin American Arbitration Conference* Medellin (Colombia) 2012, *Annual Assembly* Costa Rica 2011. **Publications** *BDG 1: Cómo se codifica hoy el derecho comercial internacional?*; *BDG 2: Teoria juridica del arbitraje internacional*; *BDG 3: Consumer Protection in International Private Relationships*; *BDG 4: Derecho Internacional Privado – Derecho de la Libertad y el Respeto Mutuo – Ensayos a la memoria de Tatiana B de Maekelt*; *Las personas frente a la dinamica y las exigencias del mundo globalizado*. Proceedings of Jornadas de la ASADIP.

Members Individuals in 31 countries:
Argentina, Australia, Belgium, Belize, Bolivia, Brazil, Canada, Chile, China, Colombia, Costa Rica, Cuba, Ecuador, El Salvador, Estonia, France, Germany, Guatemala, Italy, Japan, Mexico, Netherlands, Nicaragua, Panama, Paraguay, Peru, Portugal, Spain, Uruguay, USA, Venezuela. [2021/XM8267/v/**D**]

♦ Asociación Americana de Juristas (AAJ) 02110

American Association of Jurists (AAJ) – Association américaine de juristes – Associação Americana de Juristas (AAJ)

Main Office c/o AABA, 3º piso, Uruguay 485, 1015 Buenos Aires, Argentina. E-mail: aajramaargentina@gmail.com.
URL: http://www.asociacionamericanadejuristas.org/

History 1975, Panama. Statutes adopted 13 Sep 1987. **Aims** Fight for self-determination of peoples, full economic independence as well as sovereignty of the State over its wealth and natural resources; struggle against imperialism, fascism, colonialism and the discrimination against women, indigenous people and national minorities; defend real peace based on the principle of peaceful co-existence between States of different social and economic systems; defend and promote human rights and the realization of better and more effective guarantees to their protection; condemn and denounce repressive legislation existing in American States; defend the legal profession and promote solidarity with persecuted jurists who support these principles. **Structure** General Assembly (every 3 years), each member country having one vote. Continental Council, consisting of Executive Committee and Vice-Presidents (whose number is determined by the Assembly) and by a representative of each branch of the Association. Executive Committee, comprising President, 1st, 2nd and 3rd Vice-Presidents, Secretary General and Assistant Secretary General (Finance). Permanent Secretariat. **Languages** English, French, Portuguese, Spanish. **Finance** Members' dues. Budget (annual): about US$ 20,000. Separate budget for specific events. **Activities** Mobilizes jurists of the American countries to develop joint actions to secure the active involvement of juridical science in the process of social and economic changes in their respective countries which are consistent with the principles and objectives. Conferences; investigative missions. **Events** *Triennial General Assembly* Caracas (Venezuela) 2009, *Triennial General Assembly* La Paz (Bolivia) 2007, *Triennial General Assembly* Buenos Aires (Argentina) 2003, *Triennial General Assembly* Havana (Cuba) 2000, *Biennial general assembly / Triennial General Assembly* Guatemala (Guatemala) 1997. **Publications** *AAJ Law Journal*. Book series.

Members National Branches in 20 countries and territories:
Argentina, Bolivia, Brazil, Canada, Chile, Colombia, Costa Rica, Cuba, Dominican Rep, Ecuador, El Salvador, Guatemala, Nicaragua, Panama, Paraguay, Peru, Puerto Rico, Uruguay, USA, Venezuela.
Individuals in 3 countries and territories:
Haiti, Honduras, Mexico.

Consultative Status Consultative status granted from: *ECOSOC (#05331)* (Special). **NGO Relations** Member of: *International Association of Democratic Lawyers (IADL, #11837)*. [2020/XD6590/**D**]

♦ Asociación Americana de Profesionales de Aduana / see Professional Customs Brokers Association of the Americas (#18512)
♦ Asociación Anacional Mundial (#16941)
♦ Asociación Andaluza por la Solidaridad y la Paz (internationally oriented national body)
♦ Asociación Andina de Armadores (no recent information)
♦ Asociación Andina de Empresas e Instituciones de Servicio de Agua Potable y Alcantarillado / see Asociación Andina de Empresas e Instituciones de Servicio de Agua Potable y Saneamiento (#02111)

♦ Asociación Andina de Empresas e Instituciones de Servicio de Agua Potable y Saneamiento (ANDESAPA) 02111

Main Office Murgeón Oe1-31, entre Jorge Juan y Av 10 de Agosto, Edificio Acuario, 2o piso Of 204, Quito, Ecuador. Fax +59322236842.

History Founded 1986. Also referred to as *Asociación Andina de Empresas e Instituciones de Servicio de Agua Potable y Alcantarillado*. Registered in accordance with the laws of Ecuador, 18 Jun 1993. **Aims** Promote strengthening, interaction and institutional improvement of *water* and *sanitation* public service enterprises of *Andean* countries, by improving quality of services in order to contribute to *conservation* of *natural resources* and the *environment*. **Structure** Board of Directors; Presidency rotates annually; Assistant National Directorates; Technical Committees. **Languages** Spanish. **Staff** 6.00 FTE, paid. **Finance** Contributions from active members. The water supply company of Quito (Ecuador) (EMAAP-Q) pays the salaries of staff members. Budget (annual): US$ 100,000. **Events** *Seminar* Santa Cruz (Bolivia) 1998, *Seminar* Maracaibo (Venezuela) 1997, *Seminar* Panama 1997, *Seminar* Quito (Ecuador) 1997, *Seminar* Quito (Ecuador) 1996. **Publications** *ANDESAPA Information Bulletin* (2 a year).

Members Active (5) in 5 countries:
Bolivia, Colombia, Ecuador, Peru, Venezuela.
Adhering (1) in 1 country:
Chile.

IGO Relations Cooperates with: *Andean Community (#00817)*. [2014.11.14/XD3759/**D**]

♦ Asociación Andina de Lineas Aéreas (no recent information)
♦ Asociación Andina de Transportistas Internacionales por Carretera (no recent information)
♦ Asociación para el Aprendizaje sobre el Cambio Climatico de la Iniciativa Una ONU (#17735)
♦ Asociación de Archiveros Eclesiasticos (#05279)
♦ Asociación de las Autoridades de Libertad Condicional Internacionales (internationally oriented national body)
♦ Asociación del Basquetbol Sudamericano / see Confederación Sudamericana de Básquetbol (#04482)
♦ **Asociación BETA** Asociación de Jóvenes Doctores en Hispanismo (#02170)
♦ Asociación de Bibliotecas Internacionales / see Association of International Librarians and Information Specialists (#02754)
♦ Asociación de Bibliotecas Nacionales de Iberoamérica / see Association of Ibero-American States for the Development of National Libraries (#02638)

- ♦ Asociación de Bibliotecas Públicas de América Latina y el Caribe (no recent information)
- ♦ Asociación de Bibliotecas Universitarias, de Investigación e Institucionales del Caribe (#02413)
- ♦ Asociación Boliviana para la Investigación y Conservación de Ecosistemas Andino-Amazónicos (internationally oriented national body)
- ♦ Asociación de Bolsas de Comercio de Centroamérica, Panama y República Dominicana (inactive)
- ♦ Asociación de Bolsas Europeas de Comercio de Cereales / see European Commodities Exchange (#06674)

♦ Asociación de las Camaras de Comercio e Industria del Mediterraneo (ASCAME) 02112

Association des chambres de commerce et d'industrie de la Méditerranée – Association of the Mediterranean Chambers of Commerce and Industry

Gen Sec Chamber of Commerce of Barcelona, Avda Diagonal 452 – 6th floor, 08006 Barcelona, Spain. T. +34934169556. E-mail: secretariat@ascame.org.
URL: http://www.ascame.org/

History 1 Oct 1982, Barcelona (Spain). Founded as an initiative of the Chamber of Commerce of Barcelona and with the support of 5 chambers of commerce in the Mediterranean. Current By-Laws adopted May 1996; modified May 2000. Former names and other names: *Assembly of the Mediterranean Chambers of Commerce and Industry* – former; *Assemblée permanente des chambres de commerce et d'industrie de la Méditerranée* – former; *Asamblea de las Camaras de Comercio e Industria del Mediterraneo* – former; *Association of Chambers of Commerce and Industry of the Mediterranean Countries* – alias. Registration: Spain. **Aims** Contribute to economic development of the region; encourage Euro-Mediterranean integration through the essential role played by the private sector. **Structure** General Assembly (twice a year); Executive Committee; Bureau; Working Commissions (20); General Secretariat. **Languages** Arabic, English, French. **Staff** 8.00 FTE, paid. **Finance** Sources: members' dues; revenue from activities/projects. **Activities** Events/meetings; networking/liaising; projects/programmes; research and development. **Events** *Mediterranean Women Entrepreneurs Forum* Alexandria (Egypt) 2022, *Mediterranean Week of Economic Leaders (MedaWeek)* Barcelona (Spain) 2020, *Mediterranean Week of Economic Leaders* Barcelona (Spain) 2019, *UfM Business Forum* Cairo (Egypt) 2019, *Mediterranean Week of Economic Leaders* Barcelona (Spain) 2018. **Publications** *ASCAME MedaNews* (6 a year). Annual Activity Report.

Members Full; Associate. Mediterranean Chambers of Commerce and Industry and Associate entities (over 300), representing over 25 million enterprises, in 23 countries and territories:
Albania, Algeria, Bosnia-Herzegovina, Croatia, Cyprus, Egypt, France, Germany, Greece, Israel, Italy, Jordan, Lebanon, Libya, Malta, Montenegro, Morocco, Palestine, Serbia, Spain, Syrian AR, Tunisia, Türkiye.

IGO Relations Partner of: *European Investment Bank (EIB, #07599)*; *Union for the Mediterranean (UfM, #20457)*. Memorandum of Understanding with: *Regional Activity Centre for Sustainable Consumption and Production (SCP/RAC, #18747)*; *World Tourism Organization (UNWTO, #21861)*. **NGO Relations** Member of: *Association of the Balkan Chambers (ABC, #02392)*; *International Chamber of Commerce (ICC, #12534)*. Cooperates with: *Association des chambres de commerce et d'industrie européennes (EUROCHAMBRES, #02423)*. Partner of: *Association des chambres de commerce et d'industrie européennes (EUROCHAMBRES, #02423)*; *Association of Organisations of Mediterranean Businesswomen (#02840)*; *Fédération Mondiale des Zones Franches (FEMOZA, #09693)*; *Institut Europeu de la Mediterrània (IEMed)*; *MEDCITIES Network (#16610)*; *Mediterranean Universities Union (UNIMED, #16687)*. Memorandum of Understanding with: *Centre for Cooperation in the Mediterranean (CCM, #03734)*; *Forum of the Adriatic and Ionian Chambers of Commerce (AIC FORUM, #09891)*; *Global Citizenship Education Fund (#10283)*; *Ibero-American Association of Chambers of Commerce (IACC, #11014)*; *Union of Mediterranean Confederations of Enterprises (BUSINESSMED, #20458)*; *World Chambers Federation (WCF, #21269)*; *World Federation of Consuls (FICAC, #21422)*.
[2020/XF0797/t/**F**]

- ♦ Asociación Canadiense de Estudios Latinoamericanos y del Caribe (internationally oriented national body)
- ♦ Asociación Caribeña para la Investigación y Acción Feministas (#03445)
- ♦ Asociación Cartografica Internacional (#12446)
- ♦ Asociación Católica Interamericana de Filosofia (inactive)
- ♦ Asociación Católica Internacional de Estudios Médico-Psicológicos (inactive)
- ♦ Asociación Católica Internacional de Instituciones de Ciencias de la Educación (#12448)
- ♦ Asociación Católica Internacional de Servicios para la Juventud Femenina (#02417)
- ♦ Asociación Católica Latinoamericana y Caribeña de Comunicación (see: #21264)
- ♦ Asociación Católica Latinoamericana para la Radio, la Televisión y los Medios Afines (inactive)
- ♦ Asociación Católica Mundial para la Comunicación (#21264)
- ♦ Asociación de los Cementerios Históricos-Monumentales en Europa (#02915)
- ♦ Asociación Centroamericana de Aeronautica y del Espacio (internationally oriented national body)
- ♦ Asociación Centroamericana de Armadores (no recent information)

♦ Asociación Centroamericana, del Caribe y Mexicana de Animales de Laboratorio (ACCMAL) 02113

Central American, Caribbean and Mexican Association of Laboratory Animals

Sec address not obtained.

History Founded Feb 1992. **Aims** Promote well-being, ethical and national care and use of laboratory animals involved in research; promote laboratory animal science practice among the scientific academic community of member countries through academic, cultural and social activities. **Structure** General Assembly. Governing Board, comprising President, Vice-President, Secretary-General, Treasurer and 2 Trustees. External Auditor. **Languages** Spanish. **Staff** 1.50 FTE, paid; 3.00 FTE, voluntary. **Finance** Members' dues. Other sources: revenues of meetings and exhibitions; occasional grants. **Activities** Co-sponsors *'ICLAS/ACCMAL/PMI Award'*, offering a scholarship; co-sponsors international biannual congress and regional meetings; offers collaborative training programmes. **Events** *Congress* San José (Costa Rica) 2014, *Congress* Mérida (Mexico) 2013, *Congress* Veracruz, CHIS (Mexico) 2011, *Regional meeting / Congress* Montevideo (Uruguay) 2009.

Members Founder; Active; Honorary. Founder members in 8 countries:
Costa Rica, Cuba, El Salvador, Guatemala, Mexico, Nicaragua, Panama, Trinidad-Tobago.

NGO Relations Member of: *International Council for Laboratory Animal Science (ICLAS, #13039)*.
[2015/XD7269/**D**]

- ♦ Asociación Centroamericana de Ciencias Cosméticas (unconfirmed)
- ♦ Asociación Centroamericana para la Economia, la Salud y el Ambiente (internationally oriented national body)
- ♦ Asociación Centroamericana de Facultades de Medicina (no recent information)
- ♦ Asociación Centroamericana de Familiares de Detenidos Desaparecidos (no recent information)

♦ Asociación Centroamericana de Gastroenterologia y Endoscopia Digestiva 02114

Address not obtained.

History Also referred to as *Asociación de Gastroenterologia Centro América y Panama*. **Events** *Congress* Costa Rica 2011, *Congress* San Salvador (El Salvador) 2006. **NGO Relations** Member of: *World Gastroenterology Organisation (WGO, #21536)*.
[2015/XD6516/**D**]

- ♦ Asociación Centroamericana de Productores Fonograficos (no recent information)
- ♦ Asociación Centroamericana de Psiquiatria (no recent information)

♦ Asociación Centroamericana de Sociologia (ACAS) 02115

Contact c/o FLACSO Guatemala, 3a. calle 4-44, zona 10, 01010 Guatemala, Guatemala. T. +150255178393. E-mail: acassociologiacentroamerica@gmail.com – cefem.ecp@gmail.com – acas.2018@gmail.com.
Facebook: https://www.facebook.com/acas.sociologia.centroamerica/

History Apr 1974, San José (Costa Rica). **Aims** Study and participate in *social changes* and developments occurring in the Central American region; promote the scientific and university teaching of sociology in the region; disseminate sociological knowledge about Central American societies through the existing media. **Structure** Secretariat. Representatives in each member country. **Languages** Spanish. **Staff** None. **Finance** Local sources. **Activities** Events/meetings. **Events** *Congreso Centroamericano de Sociología* Heredia (Costa Rica) 2023, *Biennial Congress* El Salvador 2021, *Biennial Congress* Antigua (Guatemala) 2018, *Biennial Congress* Managua (Nicaragua) 2016, *Biennial Congress* San José de David (Panama) 2014.

Members Individuals (about 150) in 8 countries:
Belize, Costa Rica, Dominican Rep, El Salvador, Guatemala, Honduras, Nicaragua, Panama.
[2020.06.30/XD7147/v/**D**]

- ♦ Asociación Centroamericana de Terapeutas Florales (no recent information)
- ♦ Asociación de los Centros del Comercio Mundial (#21862)

♦ Asociación de Centros de Convenciones del Caribe y Latinoamérica (ACCCLATAM) 02116

Contact Av Kennedy s/n y Paraguay, Rotonda de Limache, CP 4400 Salta, Argentina. T. +543874956015.
URL: http://www.accclatam.org/

History 2016, Salta (Argentina). **Structure** Assembly; Executive Committee. **Members** Convention centres (20). Membership countries not specified. **NGO Relations** Member of (1): *Joint Meetings Industry Council (JMIC, #16140)*.
[2019/XM7613/**D**]

- ♦ Asociación de Centros de Depósito de América / see Americas' Central Securities Depositories Association (#00792)

♦ Asociación de Cervantistas (AC) 02117

Sec San Juan s/n, E-28801 Alcala de Henares, Madrid, Spain. E-mail: secretaria@asociaciondecervantistas.org.
Pres address not obtained. E-mail: presidencia@asociaciondecervantistas.org.
URL: http://asociaciondecervantistas.org/

History 1988, Alcala de Henares (Spain). Registration: Spain. **Aims** Study and disseminate the life and work of Miguel de Cervantes while promoting and bringing together Cervantism in the international arena. **Structure** General Assembly; Board of Directors. **Languages** Spanish. **Staff** 4.00 FTE, voluntary. **Finance** Sources: meeting proceeds; members' dues. **Activities** Events/meetings; research/documentation. **Events** *International Congress* Princeton, NJ (USA) 2023, *International Congress* Princeton, NJ (USA) 2022, *International Congress* Princeton, NJ (USA) 2021, *International Colloquium* Venice (Italy) 2019, *International Congress* Madrid (Spain) 2018. **Publications** Proceedings. **Members** Membership countries not specified.
[2022.05.17/XM7676/**E**]

- ♦ Asociación Cientifica Internacional de Esperantistas (#13301)
- ♦ Asociación Científica Mundial de Cunicultura (#21744)
- ♦ Asociación Cientifica del Pacifico (#18003)
- ♦ Asociación de Cientistas Sociales de la Religión en el Cono Sur / see Asociación de Cientistas Sociales de la Religión del MERCOSUR (#02118)

♦ Asociación de Cientistas Sociales de la Religión del MERCOSUR (ACSRM) 02118

Associação de Cientistas Sociais de Religião do MERCOSUR

Pres Saavedra 15 – 4o Piso, C1083ACA Buenos Aires, Argentina. T. +541149527440. E-mail: acsrm@acsrm.org.
URL: http://www.acsrm.org/

History 1994, Montevideo (Uruguay), as *Asociación de Cientistas Sociales de la Religión en el Cono Sur*. Current title adopted when became registered in accordance with Brazilian law, 1997. **Aims** Encourage research and teaching of the social sciences of religion from a Latin American perspective. **Structure** Board of Directors; Council. **Languages** Portuguese, Spanish. **Staff** 25.00 FTE, voluntary. **Finance** Event proceeds. **Activities** Events/meetings; publishing activities; research/documentation; training/education. Active in: Argentina, Brazil, Chile, Uruguay. **Publications** *ACSRM Newsletter*, *Ciencias Sociales y Religión* in Portuguese, Spanish.

Members Individuals (over 700) in 13 countries:
Argentina, Brazil, Canada, Chile, France, Germany, Italy, Mexico, Paraguay, Peru, Spain, Uruguay, USA.

NGO Relations *International Society for the Sociology of Religions (ISSR, #15451)*; national organizations.
[2017.03.07/XM6229/v/**E**]

- ♦ Asociación de Cirugia Plastica de Centroamérica y del Caribe (no recent information)
- ♦ Asociación de Ciudadanos de Europa (inactive)
- ♦ Asociación de Ciudades para el Reciclaje / see Association of Cities and Regions for Sustainable Resource Management (#02433)
- ♦ Asociación de Ciudades y Regiones para el Reciclaje / see Association of Cities and Regions for Sustainable Resource Management (#02433)
- ♦ Asociación de Colectividades Textiles Europeas (#02435)
- ♦ Asociación de Colegios de Defensa Iberoamericanos (unconfirmed)
- ♦ Asociación de Combustibles Eficientes de Latinoamérica (unconfirmed)
- ♦ Asociación de Comités Olimpicos Nacionales (#02819)
- ♦ Asociación de Comités Olimpicos Nacionales de Africa (#02820)
- ♦ Asociación de las Compañias de Aviación de las Regiones de Europa (#08347)
- ♦ Asociación de Conductas Adictivas y Patologia Dual de Iberoamérica (unconfirmed)

♦ Asociación de Confederaciones Deportivas Panamericanas (ACODEPA) 02119

Association of Pan American Sport Confederations

SG 12 Avenida y 27 Calle de la Zona 5, Segundo Nivel, Edificio Polideportivo, Guatemala, Guatemala. T. +50255544643. E-mail: info@acodepa.org.
URL: http://www.acodepa.org/

History Founded at Congress of *Association of National Olympic Committees (ANOC, #02819)*, 1992, Acapulco (Mexico). Constituted 16 Aug 2000, Mexico City (Mexico). Registration: No/ID: 2827, Start date: 5 Sep 2000, Mexico. **Aims** Coordinate efforts to further development of Pan American sports, acting as the forum through which all continental confederations may express their concerns and point of views; assist organizers of Pan American Games in organization and coordination of the Pan American Sports Confederations. **Structure** Ordinary Congress (every 2 years); Executive Committee. **Languages** English, Spanish. **Staff** 1.00 FTE, paid. **Finance** Main income from ticket revenue.

Members Pan American Sporting Confederations (43):
- *American Boxing Confederation (AMBC, #00776)*;
- *Americas Triathlon (AT, #00795)*;
- *Asociación Panamericana de Atletismo (APA, #02284)*;
- *Confederación Americana de Tiro (CAT, #04439)*;
- *Confederación de Sur y Centro America de Balonmano (Coscabal, #04443)*;
- *Confederación de Tenis de Centroamérica y el Caribe (COTECC, #04496)*;
- *Confederación Norte-Centroamericana y del Caribe de Fútbol (CONCACAF, #04465)*;
- *Confederación Panamericana de Badminton (PABC, #04467)*;
- *Confederación Panamericana de Béisbol (COPABE, #04468)*;
- *Confederación Panamericana de Billar (CPB, #04469)*;
- *Confederación Panamericana de Canoas (COPAC, #04471)*;
- *Confederación Panamericana de Esgrima (CPE, #04475)*;
- *Confederación Panamericana de Judo (CPJ, #04476)*;
- Confederación Panamericana de Pantatión Moderno (CPPM);
- *Confederación Panamericana de Pelota Vasca (CPPV)*;
- *Confederación Panamericana de Remo (COPARE, #04478)*;
- *Confederación Sudamericana de Fútbol (CONMEBOL, #04487)*;
- *Federación Panamericana de Karate (#09381)*;
- *Federación Panamericana de Squash (FPS, #09384)*;

- *FIBA Americas (#09745)*;
- *International Fitness and Bodybuilding Federation (IFBB, #13610)*;
- *North America and the Caribbean Handball Confederation (NACHC, #17557)*;
- *North-Central American and Caribbean Volleyball Confederation (#17576)*;
- *PanAm Aquatics (#18077)*;
- *Pan American Bowling Confederation (PABCON, #18085)*;
- *Pan American Cycling Confederation (#18092)*;
- *Pan-American Equestrian Confederation (PAEC, #18097)*;
- *Pan American Hockey Federation (PAHF, #18110)*;
- *Pan American Racquetball Confederation (PARC, #18123)*;
- *Pan American Sailing Federation (PASAF, #18128)*;
- *Pan American Surf Association (PASA, #18135)*;
- *Pan American Taekwondo Union (PATU, #18136)*;
- *Pan American Weightlifting Confederation (PAWC, #18137)*;
- *Rugby Americas North (RAN, #18997)*;
- *South American Tennis Confederation (#19709)*;
- *Sudamérica Rugby (#20030)*;
- *Unión Latinoamericana de Tenis de Mesa (ULTM, #20453)*;
- *Union Panamericana de Gimnasia (UPAG, #20471)*;
- Unión Panamericana de Sambo;
- *United World Wrestling Americas (UWW Americas, #20666)*;
- *WBSC Americas Softball (#20840)*;
- *World Archery Americas (COPARCO, #21106)*;
- *World Skate America (WS America, #21788)*.

NGO Relations Recognized by: *Panam Sports Organization (Panam Sports, #18138)*. [2023/XD3922/**D**]

♦ Asociación de Confederaciones Deportivas Sudamericanas (no recent information)
♦ Asociación del Congreso Panamericano de Ferrocarriles (#18124)
♦ Asociación para la Conservación del Caribe (#03481)
♦ Asociación para la Conservación de la Cuenca Amazónica (internationally oriented national body)
♦ Asociación de Conservación de los Ecosistemas Andinos (internationally oriented national body)
♦ Asociación para la Conservación del Patrimonio Cultural de las Américas / see Association for Heritage Preservation of the Americas
♦ Asociación de Consultantes Internacionales en Derechos Humanos (inactive)
♦ Asociación de Cooperación Empresarial (no recent information)
♦ Asociación para la Cooperación en la Investigación del Banano en el Caribe y la América Tropical (no recent information)
♦ Asociación para la Cooperación con el Sur – Las Segovias (internationally oriented national body)
♦ Asociación de Cooperativas y Mutuales de Seguros de las Américas / see International Cooperative and Mutual Insurance Federation / Regional Association for The Americas (#12949)

♦ Asociación Coordinadora Indigena y Campesina de Agroforesteria Comunitaria (ACICAFOC) 02120

Agro-forestry Coordinating Association of Indigenous Peoples and Farmers

Contact 50 meters S and 50 meters NW, Pizza Hut los Colegios, Moravia, San José, San José, San José, Costa Rica. T. +50622366217. E-mail: oficinaregional@acicafoc.org.
URL: http://www.acicafoc.org/

History Jun 1994. Previously referred to as *Coordinación Indigena Campesina de Agroforesteria Comunitaria (CICAFOC) – Indigenous Peasant Office of Central American Community Forestry*. In English also referred to as *Central American Indigenous and Peasant Coordination Association for Community Agroforestry* and *Central American Indigenous and Peasant Coordinator of Communal Agroforestry*. **Aims** Strengthen development of mechanisms to ensure governance, land tenure and management of natural resources, promoting local empowerment; develop, strengthen and promote processes of organic production through use of environmentally sustainable technologies tending to consolidate self-sufficiency, competitiveness, value chain and marketing towards the fair-trade market; focus on advocacy and cooperation in development of participatory strategies for management of resources, emphasizing on generational change and social equity. **Languages** English, Spanish. **Staff** 10.00 FTE, paid. **Activities** Capacity building; training/education; monitoring/evaluation. **Publications** Guides; manuals; training materials. **IGO Relations** Accredited by: *Secretariat of the United Nations Convention to Combat Desertification (Secretariat of the UNCCD, #19208)*. Member of: Civil Society Advisory Committee (CSAG) of *International Tropical Timber Organization (ITTO, #15737)*; Board of Directors of Social and Environmental Standards for REDD+. Regional interim Organization for: *Forest Carbon Partnership Facility (FCPF, #09862)* Capacity Building Program for Civil Society Organizations in Latin America. **NGO Relations** Instrumental in setting up: *Global Alliance of Community Forestry (GACF, #10190)*.
[2017.08.04/XE4331/**E**]

♦ Asociación Coreana de Estudios Latinoamericanos, Seoul (internationally oriented national body)
♦ Asociación de Corrugadores del Caribe, Centro y Sur América (#02402)
♦ Asociación de Criollos de Base Lexical Portuguesa y Española (#02325)
♦ Asociación Cristiana Femenina Mundial (#21947)
♦ Asociación para la Defensa de los Pueblos Amenazados Internacional (#19654)
♦ Asociación de Demócratas Cristianos Latinoamericanos Residentes en Europa (inactive)
♦ Asociación Pro Deo (inactive)
♦ Asociación de Depósitos Centrales de Valores de América (#00792)
♦ Asociación de Derecho Internacional (#14003)
♦ Asociación pro Derechos Humanos (internationally oriented national body)
♦ Asociación para los Derechos de la Mujer y el Desarrollo (#02980)
♦ Asociación del Desarrollo para America Central (no recent information)
♦ Asociación para el Desarrollo y la Coordinación de Cambios Turisticos Europeos (inactive)
♦ Asociación para el Desarrollo de Intercambios Internacionales de Productos y Técnicas Agricolas y Agro Alimentarias / see Association for the Development of International Exchanges in Agricultural and Agrifood Products and Techniques
♦ Asociación de Deshidratadores Europeos (#06896)
♦ Asociación de Directores de Academias Diplomaticas de América Latina y Estados del Caribe (no recent information)
♦ Asociación de directores de las Instituciones Lasalianas (#02563)
♦ Asociación de Economia de Latinoamérica y el Caribe (#16274)
♦ Asociación de Economistas de América Latina y el Caribe (#02480)
♦ Asociación de Economistas del Caribe (no recent information)
♦ Asociación de Economistas del Tercer Mundo (inactive)
♦ Asociación Ecuménica Internacional (#13226)
♦ Asociación Ecuménica de Teólogos del Tercer Mundo (#05344)
♦ Asociación de Editores para Deficientes Visuales de Ibero-América (inactive)

♦ Asociación de Editoriales Universitarias de América Latina y el Caribe (EULAC) 02121

Pres c/o ASEUC, Carrera 13A, No 38 – 82 Ofic 901, Bogota, Bogota DC, Colombia. E-mail: contacto@eulac.org.
URL: http://eulac.org/

History Founded 26 Aug 1987, Lima (Peru), during the 'Reunión Regional de Editoriales Universitarias', convened and financially supported by *International Association of Scholarly Publishers (IASP, inactive)*; *International Development Research Centre (IDRC, #13162)*; *Regional Centre for the Promotion of Books in Latin America and the Caribbean (#18758)* and Universidad del Pacifico (Lima). **Aims** Integrate and foster the various universities of Latin America and the Caribbean with the purpose of favouring and promoting the generation, *publication*, distribution and wide circulation of its *editorial production*. **Structure** General Assembly (every 2 years); Executive Committee. **Languages** Portuguese, Spanish. **Staff** 2.00 FTE, paid. **Finance** Members' dues. Other sources: financial assistance from different organizations. **Activities** Training/education. **Events** *Congress* Bogota (Colombia) 2009, *Congress* Bogota (Colombia) 2009, *Congress* San José (Costa Rica) 2007, *Meeting* Florianópolis (Brazil) 1991. **Publications** *Economia Urbana y Regional* (1998) by Mario Polèse. Members' Directory.

Members University presses in 36 countries and territories:
Antigua-Barbuda, Argentina, Bahamas, Barbados, Belize, Bermuda, Bolivia, Brazil, Chile, Colombia, Costa Rica, Cuba, Dominica, Dominican Rep, Ecuador, El Salvador, Grenada, Guatemala, Guyana, Haiti, Honduras, Jamaica, Mexico, Neth Antilles, Nicaragua, Panama, Paraguay, Peru, Puerto Rico, St Kitts-Nevis, St Lucia, St Vincent-Grenadines, Suriname, Trinidad-Tobago, Uruguay, Venezuela. [2015/XD1461/**D**]

♦ Asociación de Educación e Investigación en Bibliotecologia, Archivologia, Ciencias de la Información y Documentación de Iberoamérica y el Caribe / see Asociación de Educación e Investigación en Ciencia de la Información de Iberoamérica y el Caribe (#02122)

♦ Asociación de Educación e Investigación en Ciencia de la Información de Iberoamérica y el Caribe (EDICIC) 02122

Association of Education and Research in Information Science of Iberoamerica and the Caribbean – Associação de Educação e Investigação em Ciência da Informação da Iberoamerica e Caribe

Pres Monte Cqseros 3275, CP 11-600, Montevideo, Uruguay. T. +59824810112. Fax +59824085576. E-mail: mgceretta@gmail.com – edicic@edicic.org.
URL: http://www.edicic.org/

History as *Asociación de Educación e Investigación en Bibliotecologia, Archivologia, Ciencias de la Información y Documentación de Iberoamérica y el Caribe (EDIBCIC)*. Current title adopted 13 Nov 2008, Mexico City (Mexico). **Aims** Strengthen and integrate operations of public and private institutions and professionals. **Structure** Officers include: President; Executive Secretary. Regional Groups (5): Andean; Mercosur; Caribbean; Mexico and Central America; Ibero. Thematic Groups (8). **Languages** Portuguese, Spanish. **Staff** 7.00 FTE, voluntary. **Finance** Members' dues. **Events** *Meeting* Belo Horizonte (Brazil) 2016, *Meeting* Madrid (Spain) 2015, *Meeting* Marilia (Brazil) 2011, *Meeting* Salamanca (Spain) 2008, *Meeting* Marilia (Brazil) 2006. **Publications** *Revista EDICIC*. Directory; documents – online. **Members** Membership countries not specified. [2015/XD9315/**D**]

♦ Asociación para la Educación Médica en Europa (#02797)
♦ Asociación para la Educación Mundial (#02983)
♦ Asociación de Educadores de Latinoamérica y del Caribe (unconfirmed)
♦ Asociación de Educadores de Trabajo Social del Caribe (#02410)
♦ Asociación de Egresados de la Escuela Interamericana de Bibliotecologia (#00759)
♦ Asociación de Elevadores del Mercosur (unconfirmed)
♦ Asociación de Empresarios de la Amazonia (inactive)
♦ Asociación de Empresas Estatales de Telecomunicaciones del Acuerdo Subregional Andino / see Association of Telecommunication Enterprises of the Andean Community (#02951)
♦ Asociación de Empresas de Telecomunicaciones del Acuerdo Subregional Andino / see Association of Telecommunication Enterprises of the Andean Community (#02951)
♦ Asociación de Empresas de Telecomunicaciones de la Comunidad Andina (#02951)
♦ Asociación para las Energias Renovables y el Ahorro Energético (#18837)

♦ Asociación para la Enseñanza del Español como Lengua Extranjera (ASELE) 02123

Contact address not obtained. E-mail: comunicacion@aselered.org – gestion@aselered.org.
URL: http://www.aselered.org/

History 1987. **Structure** Board of Directors. **Events** *International Congress* León (Spain) 2021, *International Congress* León (Spain) 2020, *International Congress* Porto (Portugal) 2019, *International Congress* Santiago de Compostela (Spain) 2018, *International Congress* Tarragona (Spain) 2017. **Publications** *Boletín de ASELE* (2 a year). [2021/AA1969/**E**]

♦ Asociación de Entes Reguladores de Agua y Saneamiento de las Americas (ADERASA) 02124

Association of Regulators of Water and Sanitation of the Americas – Associação de Reguladores de Agua e Saneamento das Américas

Exec Sec Captain Walter Gwynn No 930, c/o Testanova, Asunción, Paraguay. T. +59521425937. Fax +59521435630. E-mail: secretaria@aderasa.org.
URL: http://www.aderasa.org/

History Set up 17 Oct 2001, Cartagena de Indias (Colombia). **Aims** Initiate the process integration and cooperation in the regulation of the sector in the Americas. **Structure** General Assembly; Working Groups. **Activities** Knowledge management/information dissemination; training/education; advocacy/lobbying/activism; politics/policy/regulatory; events/meetings.

Members National regulators of 19 countries:
Argentina, Belize, Bolivia, Brazil, Chile, Colombia, Costa Rica, Dominican Rep, Ecuador, El Salvador, Guatemala, Honduras, Mexico, Nicaragua, Panama, Paraguay, Peru, Portugal, Uruguay. [2017/XM5881/**D***]

♦ Asociación Entrepueblos (internationally oriented national body)
♦ Asociación de Escritoras de España y las Américas, (1300-1800) / see Grupo de Estudios sobre la Mujer en España y las Américas (pre-1800)
♦ Asociación de Escuelas y Facultades de Arquitectura de la Région Sur del MERCOSUR / see Asociación de Facultades de Arquitectura del Sur del MERCOSUR (#02128)
♦ Asociación de Escuelas Internacionales (#14789)
♦ Asociación Española de Americanistas (internationally oriented national body)
♦ Asociación Española para el Derecho Internacional de los Derechos Humanos (internationally oriented national body)
♦ Asociación de Especialistas Latinoamericanos en Ciencias del Mar (inactive)
♦ Asociación de Estados del Caribe (#02411)
♦ Asociación de Estados Iberoamericanos para el Desarrollo de las Bibliotecas Nacionales de Iberoamérica (#02638)
♦ Asociación Estadounidense de Derecho Extranjero (internationally oriented national body)
♦ Asociación Estadounidense para el Progreso de la Ciencia (internationally oriented national body)
♦ Asociación para el Estudio de los Exilios y Migraciones Ibéricos Contemporaneos (internationally oriented national body)
♦ Asociación para el Estudio de la Politica Alemana / see International Association for the Study of German Politics (#12200)
♦ Asociación de Estudios del Caribe (#03559)
♦ Asociación de Estudios Caribeños / see Caribbean Studies Association (#03559)
♦ Asociación de Estudios Euro-Americana de Desarrollo Económico (internationally oriented national body)
♦ Asociación de Estudios Latinoamericanos (#16388)
♦ Asociación para los Estudios de los Problemas de Europa (inactive)
♦ Asociación para el Estudio Taxonómico de la Flora del Africa Tropical (#02948)
♦ Asociación Euro-Americana de Desarrollo Económico / see Euro-American Association of Economic Development Studies
♦ Asociación Europa – Tercer Mundo / see eu can aid (#05570)
♦ Asociación Europea de Abogados / see AEA – International Lawyers Network (#00142)
♦ Asociación Europea de Administradores Locales Demócrata Cristianos (no recent information)
♦ Asociación Europea de Alquiler de Coches y Camiones (inactive)
♦ Asociación Europea de Anatomistas Veterinarios (#06268)
♦ Asociación Europea de Asistentes Sociales Hospitalarios y de Salud (inactive)
♦ Asociación Europea de Autoridades Politicas de Regiones de Montaña (#06021)
♦ Asociación Europea de Aves Rurales (#08416)
♦ Asociación Europea de la Carne (inactive)
♦ Asociación Europea de Catedraticos de Ciencias Empresariales (inactive)
♦ Asociación Europea de Caución Mutua / see European Association of Guarantee Institutions (#06061)
♦ Asociación Europea de Centros Nacionales de Productividad (#06130)
♦ Asociación Europea de Ciencias de la Información (no recent information)

♦ Asociación Europea de Coleopterologia (AEC) 02125

Association européenne de coléoptérologie – European Association of Coleopterology

Contact Depto de Biologia Animal, Fac de Biologia, 1578 Santiago de Compostela, La Coruña, Spain. T. +349815631000. Fax +34981596904.

Pres Dept de Biologia Animal – Artropodes, Facultat de Biologia, Universidat de Barcelona, Avda Diagonal 645, 08028 Barcelona, Spain. T. +34934021443. Fax +34934035740. E-mail: aec@ub.edu.

URL: http://www.ub.es/aec/

History Founded 1987, Barcelona (Spain), when the first Statutes were adopted. Current Statutes adopted by Extraordinary General Assembly, 30 Mar 1990, Barcelona. **Aims** Carry out scientific study and further coleopterology in all its aspects by all appropriate means. **Structure** Executive Committee of 10 members; Advisory Board (currently 24 members). **Languages** English, French, German, Italian, Latin, Spanish. **Staff** Voluntary. **Finance** Members' dues. Financial support from governments of Spain and Catalonia to aid journal publication. **Activities** Meetings; publishing activities. **Events** *International congress* Prague (Czech Rep) 2003, *Social meeting* Florence (Italy) 1996, *International congress* Barcelona (Spain) 1989. **Publications** *AEC Newsletter. Elytron – Bulletin of the European Association of Coleopterology* – series. *Advances in Coleopterology* (1991) by M Zunino et al; *Coleopterological Monographs.* Congress proceedings.

Members Coleopterists in 43 countries and territories:

Argentina, Austria, Belarus, Belgium, Brazil, Bulgaria, Canada, Chile, China, Croatia, Czechia, Denmark, France, Georgia, Germany, Greece, Hungary, India, Ireland, Italy, Japan, Kazakhstan, Korea Rep, Luxembourg, Mexico, Netherlands, New Zealand, Poland, Portugal, Romania, Russia, Serbia, Slovakia, South Africa, Spain, Sweden, Switzerland, Taiwan, Thailand, UK, Ukraine, Uruguay, USA.

NGO Relations Member of: *International Union of Biological Sciences (IUBS, #15760).* [2015/XD2428/v/**D**]

- ♦ Asociación Europea del Comercio de Patatas (#08257)
- ♦ Asociación Europea para el Comercio de los Productos del Yute (#06256)
- ♦ Asociación Europea de Concesionarias de Autopistas, Túneles, Puentes y Vias de Peaje (#02559)
- ♦ Asociación Europea para el Derecho Alimentario / see European Food Law Association (#07286)
- ♦ Asociación Europea de Derecho y Gastronomia (internationally oriented national body)
- ♦ Asociación Europea para el Desarrollo de Bases de Datos para la Formación y la Educación (inactive)
- ♦ Asociación Europea para el Desarrollo del Transporte Ferroviario (#06011)
- ♦ Asociación Europea de dirección y Economia de la Empresa / see European Academy of Management and Business Economics (#05801)
- ♦ Asociación Europea de Dirección de Personal / see European Association for People Management (#06146)
- ♦ Asociación Europea de Directores de Escuelas Hoteleras / see International Association of Hotel School Directors (#11942)
- ♦ Asociación Europea para la Educación de Adultos (#06018)
- ♦ Asociación Europea para la Educación Especial (no recent information)
- ♦ Asociación Europea de Educación Pediatrica / see Association for Paediatric Education in Europe (#02847)
- ♦ Asociación Europea de Empresas Frigorificas (inactive)
- ♦ Asociación Europea para la Energia Eólica / see WindEurope (#20965)
- ♦ Asociación Europea de Energia Minihidraulica (#08495)
- ♦ Asociación Europea de Enseñantes (#02565)
- ♦ Asociación Europea de Escuelas de Enseñanza Primaria (inactive)
- ♦ Asociación Europea de Estaciones Termales (#08805)
- ♦ Asociación Europea de Estanqueidad (#08452)
- ♦ Asociación Europea de la Estevia (#08838)
- ♦ Asociación Europea para el Estudio de los Juegos de Azar (#06231)
- ♦ Asociación Europea de Examinadores de Lenguas (#02779)
- ♦ Asociación Europea de Fabricantes de Computadoras / see Ecma International (#05288)
- ♦ Asociación Europea de Ferroviaros (#02558)
- ♦ Asociación Europea para la Formación Profesional de Editores y Libreros (inactive)
- ♦ Asociación Europea de Impresarios de Instalaciones Eléctricas / see EuropeOn (#09166)
- ♦ Asociación Europea para la Información Pública en Televisión (inactive)
- ♦ Asociación Europea de Instituciones de Garantia (#06061)
- ♦ Asociación Europea para Investigación del Cancer (#05962)
- ♦ Asociación Europea para la Investigación de Mercados y de Opinion / see World Association of Research Professionals (#21182)
- ♦ Asociación Europea de Jueces (#06100)
- ♦ Asociación Europea de Juegos y Deportes Tradicionales (#08931)
- ♦ Asociación Europea de los Juristas por la Democracia y los Derechos Humanos en el Mundo (#06105)
- ♦ Asociación Europea de Linguistas y Profesores de Idiomas (no recent information)
- ♦ Asociación Europea de Loterias y Apuestas Deportivas de Estado (#08833)

♦ Asociación Europea de Mayistas (WAYEB) 02126

European Association of Mayanists – Association européenne de Mayanistes

Pres Dept of World Cultures, Univ of Helsinki, Unioninkatu 38 A, FI-00014 Helsinki, Finland. E-mail: president@wayeb.org.

Sec Knorozov Centre for Mesoamerican Studies, Miusskaya sq 6 bld 3, Moscow MOSKVA, Russia, 125047. E-mail: secretary@wayeb.org.

URL: http://www.wayeb.org/

History Registered in accordance with Belgian law. **Aims** Develop and promote research on Maya civilization by associating, uniting and disseminating scientific efforts and actions of European scholars, students and amateurs from various disciplines and sub-disciplines of the field. **Structure** General Assembly (annual). Council of Active Members, comprising Founding and Active Members, including a maximum of 6 elected members, as well as other Active Members and National Coordinators upon invitation. Administrative Council, elected by General Assembly, comprised Council of Europe citizens. WAYEB Board (Executive organ), comprising President, Vice-President, Secretary and Treasurer, elected for one-year term by the Administrative Council. **Languages** English, Spanish. **Staff** 4.00 FTE, voluntary. **Finance** Registration fees. **Events** *European Maya Conference* Krakow (Poland) 2022, *European Maya Conference* Valencia (Spain) 2018, *European Maya Conference* Malmö (Sweden) 2017, *European Maya Conference* Moscow (Russia) 2016, *European Maya Conference* Bonn (Germany) 2015. **Publications** Conference proceedings.

Members Affiliated – Founding Members (6); Statutory – participate in statutory activities; Supporting and Sponsoring – support and benefit from services. Members in 21 countries:

Austria, Belgium, Canada, Denmark, Finland, France, Germany, Italy, Latvia, Mexico, Netherlands, Norway, Poland, Portugal, Russia, Spain, Sweden, Switzerland, UK, Ukraine, USA. [2022/XE4560/**E**]

- ♦ Asociación Europea de Medicamentos Genéricos / see Medicines for Europe (#16633)
- ♦ Asociación Europea de Medicina Naturista Classica (no recent information)
- ♦ Asociación Europea de Médicos de Equipos de Fútbol (inactive)
- ♦ Asociación Europea de Médicos de Hospitales (#02577)
- ♦ Asociación europea de mujeres pra la investigación teológica (#08789)
- ♦ Asociación Europea de Organizaciones de Productores de Pesca (#06041)
- ♦ Asociación Europea de Padres / see European Parents' Association (#08142)
- ♦ Asociación Europea de Paleontólogos de Vertebrados (#06266)
- ♦ Asociación Europea de Pensamiento Libre (#06048)
- ♦ Asociación Europea de Podólogos (inactive)
- ♦ Asociación Europea de Productores de Moluscos (#07818)

♦ Asociación Europea de Profesores de Español (AEPE) 02127

European Association of Teachers of Spanish – Association européenne des professeurs d'espagnol

Pres address not obtained.

Sec address not obtained.

URL: https://aepe.eu/

History Sep 1967, Santander (Spain). Constitution: adopted at 1st General Assembly, 22-25 Mar 1970, Munich (Germany FR); amended 2 Sep 1972, Neuchâtel (Switzerland). **Aims** Develop a spirit of cooperation and exchange among teachers of Spanish in European countries in particular, and in other countries, both at university and secondary education level; promote teaching of Spanish worldwide. **Structure** General Assembly; Executive Committee. **Languages** Spanish. **Staff** Voluntary. **Finance** Sources: members' dues. **Activities** Events/meetings; financial and/or material support. **Events** *International Colloquium* Bratislava (Slovakia) 2023, *Congress* Vigo (Spain) 2023, *Congress* Ubeda (Spain) 2022, *Congress* 2021, *Congress* Ubeda (Spain) 2020. **Publications** *Boletin AEPE* (4 a year). *Revista Español por el mundo* (2019); *Actas de la AEPE.*

Members Individuals in 54 countries and territories:

Algeria, Argentina, Armenia, Austria, Belarus, Belgium, Bolivia, Brazil, Bulgaria, Cameroon, Canada, Chile, China, Colombia, Congo Brazzaville, Croatia, Denmark, Egypt, France, Gabon, Germany, Greece, Guatemala, Hungary, India, Israel, Italy, Japan, Korea Rep, Lithuania, Martinique, Mexico, Morocco, Netherlands, Norway, Peru, Poland, Portugal, Romania, Russia, Serbia, Slovakia, Spain, Sweden, Switzerland, Taiwan, Tunisia, UK, Ukraine, Uruguay, USA, Uzbekistan, Venezuela, Vietnam.

[2023.02.16/XD4584/v/**D**]

- ♦ Asociación Europea de Propietarios de Remolques (#08956)
- ♦ Asociación Europea de Proteinas Vegetales (#09047)
- ♦ Asociación Europea de Psicoterapia Neuro-Lingüistica (#06131)
- ♦ Asociación Europea de Puertos Pesqueros y Lonjas (inactive)
- ♦ Asociación Europea de Siderurgia / see European Steel Association (#08835)
- ♦ Asociación Europea de Siderurgia Associação Européia da Siderurgia (#08835)
- ♦ Asociación Europea de Suministradores de Servicios para Personas con Minusvalias (#06204)
- ♦ Asociación Europea de Teologia Católica (#08540)
- ♦ Asociación Europea de Terminologia (#06252)
- ♦ Asociación Europea para la Transición Digital (unconfirmed)
- ♦ Asociación Europea de Vias Verdes (#07412)
- ♦ Asociación Evangélica del Caribe (#09210)
- ♦ Asociación Evangélica de Educación Teológica en América Latina (#02326)
- ♦ Asociación des los Ex Funcionarios Internacionales – Geneva (#02599)
- ♦ Asociación de ex Funcionarios Públicos Internacionales – New York (#02600)
- ♦ Asociación de Fabricantes Europeos de Calentadores de Agua y Calentadores de Baño Instantaneos con Gas y de Calderas Murales de Gas (inactive)
- ♦ Asociación de Fabricantes de Gelatina de América del Sur (#19703)

♦ Asociación de Facultades de Arquitectura del Sur del MERCOSUR (ARQUISUR) 02128

MERCOSUR Association of Faculties of Architecture of the South – Associação das Escolas e Faculdades de Arquitetura Públicas da América do Sul

Pres address not obtained.

URL: https://arquisur.org/

History Jun 1992, Salto (Uruguay). Statutes adopted at 4th Meeting, Nov 1993, Florianópolis (Brazil). Former names and other names: *Asociación de Escuelas y Facultades de Arquitectura de la Región Sur del MERCOSUR* – alias. **Structure** Assembly of Deans and Directors (twice a year). President; Executive Secretary. **Activities** Basic programs (4): Publications, published and audiovisual documentation; Implementation of regional post-graduate courses; Training and information of university staff; Academic interexchange of professors and students. **Events** *Congress* Santiago (Chile) 2021, *Congress / Half-Yearly Meeting* Córdoba (Argentina) 2013, *Meeting* Córdoba (Argentina) 2013, *Congress / Half-Yearly Meeting* Mar del Plata (Argentina) 2008, *Meeting* Mar del Plata (Argentina) 2008.

Members Faculties (15) in 4 countries:

Argentina, Brazil, Paraguay, Uruguay.

NGO Relations *Association of Universities of the Montevideo Group (AUGM, #02971).* [2021/XD4788/**D**]

- ♦ Asociación de Facultades de Derecho en Europa (#07656)
- ♦ Asociación de Facultades y Escuelas de Contaduria Pública de América Latina / see Association of Latin American Faculties and Schools of Public Accountancy (#02783)

♦ Asociación de Facultades, Escuelas e Institutos de Derecho de América Latina (AFEIDAL) 02129

Association of Latin American Faculties, Schools and Institutes of Law

Pres Facultad de Derecho de la Universidad Nacional Autónoma de México, Saratoga 313 int 8 Col Portales, Del Benito Juarez, 03300 Mexico City CDMX, Mexico. E-mail: maximo_carvajal@yahoo.com.

SG Fac de Derecho de la Univ Politécnica de Nicaragua, Costado sur Colonia Villa Ruben Dario, AP 3595, Managua, Nicaragua. E-mail: derecho@upoli.edu.ni.

URL: http://www.anfade.org.mx/afeidal/

History Santafé (Colombia). **Structure** General Assembly; Executive Committee. **Events** *Congress* Cartagena de Indias (Colombia) 2010, *Congress* Pucón (Chile) 2008, *Congress* Pucón (Chile) 2007, *Congress* Guayaquil (Ecuador) 2006, *Congress* Antigua (Guatemala) 2005.

Members Affiliated institutes in 16 countries and territories:

Argentina, Bolivia, Chile, Colombia, Dominican Rep, Ecuador, El Salvador, Guatemala, Mexico, Nicaragua, Panama, Paraguay, Peru, Puerto Rico, Uruguay, Venezuela.

NGO Relations Instrumental in setting up: *Global Legal Education Associations Consortium (GLEAC, #10456).* [2018/XD7703/**D**]

- ♦ Asociación de Facultades, Escuelas e Institutos de Economia de América Latina (#02784)
- ♦ Asociación de Facultades de Ingenieria de Sistemas de América Latine (inactive)
- ♦ Asociación de Federaciones y Asociaciones de Empresarias del Mediterraneo (#02840)

♦ Asociación de Filosofia e Historia de la Ciencia del Cono Sur (AFHIC) 02130

Associação de Filosofia e História da Ciência do Cone Sul

Sec address not obtained. E-mail: secretaria.ejecutiva.afhic@gmail.com.

URL: http://www.afhic.com/

History Founded 5 May 2000, Quilmes (Argentina). **Aims** Contribute to the development of research on philosophy of science and history of science in America's Southern Cone. **Structure** Directive Committee, comprising President, Vice-President, Secretary, Treasurer and 4 members. Consultative Committee. **Languages** Portuguese, Spanish. **Staff** Voluntary. **Finance** Members' dues. **Events** *Congress* Córdoba (Argentina) 2014, *Congress* Santiago (Chile) 2012, *Congress* Canela (Brazil) 2010, *Congress* Montevideo (Uruguay) 2008, *Congress* Florianópolis (Brazil) 2006. **Publications** *Ciencias da Vida: Estudos Filosóficos e Históricos* (2006); *Fisica: Estudos Filosóficos e Históricos* (2006).

Members Full; Adherent; Students. Members (about 240) in 4 countries:

Argentina, Brazil, Chile, Uruguay. [2015/XD8697/**D**]

- ♦ Asociación de Filosofia y Liberación (internationally oriented national body)
- ♦ Asociación Fiscal Internacional (#13608)
- ♦ Asociación de Floristas Iberoamericanos (unconfirmed)
- ♦ Asociación para el Fomento de los Estudios Históricos en Centroamérica (internationally oriented national body)
- ♦ Asociación Fonética Internacional (#14573)
- ♦ Asociación del Foro Mundial de la Sociedad Civil / see World Civil Society Forum (#21278)
- ♦ Asociación Garapen Bidean (internationally oriented national body)
- ♦ Asociación de Gastroenterologia Centro América y Panama / see Asociación Centroamericana de Gastroenterologia y Endoscopia Digestiva (#02114)
- ♦ Asociación Gay Internacional / see ILGA World (#11120)
- ♦ Asociación General de Adventistas del Séptimo Dia (#10109)
- ♦ Asociación General de Contratistas de América (internationally oriented national body)
- ♦ Asociación General Europea de Galvanizadores (#07383)
- ♦ Asociación de Geógrafos Latinoamericanistas / see Conference of Latin American Geography (#04625)

♦ Asociación de Geoscientificos para el Desarrollo Internacional (#02623)
♦ Asociación Gernika Gogoratuz / see Gernika Gogoratuz – Peace Research Center
♦ Asociación para la Gestión Colectiva Internacional de Obras Audiovisuales (#02658)
♦ Asociación de Ginebra (#10119)
♦ Asociación Grupo de Investigación en Gobierno, Administración y Políticas Públicas (internationally oriented national body)
♦ Asociación Habitat Pro (internationally oriented national body)
♦ Asociación Hispana de Universidades (internationally oriented national body)
♦ Asociación de Hispanistas del Benelux (internationally oriented national body)

♦ Asociación Hispanoamericana de Medicina del Fútbol (HISPAMEF) . 02131

Pres c/o Clinica MEDS, Av Jose Alcalde Delano 10581, Lo Barnechea, La Dehesa, Santiago Metropolitan, Chile.
URL: https://hispamef.com/

History 2008. **Structure** Board of Directors. **Events** *HISPAMEF International Congress* Santiago (Chile) 2022, *Congreso Hispanoamericano de Medicina del Fútbol* Cartagena de Indias (Colombia) 2021, *Congreso Hispanoamericano de Medicina del Fútbol* Cartagena de Indias (Colombia) 2020, *Congreso Hispanoamericano de Medicina del Fútbol* Lima (Peru) 2018, *Congreso Hispanoamericano de Medicina del Fútbol* Quito (Ecuador) 2016.
Members Full in 15 countries:
Argentina, Bolivia, Brazil, Chile, Colombia, Costa Rica, Ecuador, Guatemala, Mexico, Panama, Paraguay, Peru, Spain, Uruguay, Venezuela. [2022/AA2927/**D**]

♦ Asociación de Historiadores del Caribe (#02407)
♦ Asociación de Historiadores Latinoamericanistas Europeos (#02517)
♦ Asociación de Historiadores Latinoamericanos y del Caribe (#02632)

♦ Asociación de Historia de la Lengua Española (AHLE) 02132

Sec Universidad de Salamanca, Departamento de Lengua Española, Facultad de Filologia, Plaza de Anaya 1, 37008 Salamanca, Spain.
URL: http://ahle.es/

History 1987, Badajoz (Spain). Founded during 1st *Congreso Internacional de Historia de la Lengua Española.* Registration: Spain. **Structure** General Assembly; Board of Directors; Executive Committee. **Activities** Events/meetings. **Events** *Congreso Internacional de Historia de la Lengua Española* 2022, *Congreso Internacional de Historia de la Lengua Española* León (Spain) 2021, *Congreso Internacional de Historia de la Lengua Española* Lima (Peru) 2018, *Congreso Internacional de Historia de la Lengua Española* Saragossa (Spain) 2015, *Congreso Internacional de Historia de la Lengua Española* Cadiz (Spain) 2012. **Publications** *Revista de Historia de la Lengua Española* in Spanish. **Members** Individuals. Membership countries not specified. [2021/AA1967/v/**D**]

♦ Asociación Holandesa de Estudios Latinoamericanos y del Caribe (internationally oriented national body)
♦ Asociación de Hormigón Armado de Centroamérica y Panama (inactive)
♦ Asociación de Hoteles del Caribe / see Caribbean Hotel and Tourism Association (#03516)
♦ Asociación Ibérica de Estudios de Traducción e Interpretación (internationally oriented national body)

♦ Asociación Iberoamericana de Academias de Ciencias Veterinarias 02133

Pres address not obtained.

History Founded 2006, Santiago (Chile), following activities begun at a meeting in 2004 at Buenos Aires (Argentina). **Structure** Permanent Secretariat based in Madrid with rotating Presidency. **Activities** Events/meetings. **Events** *Scientific Meeting* Madrid (Spain) 2011. [2014/XJ8012/**D**]

♦ Asociación Iberoamericana de Academias Olimpicas / see Pan-Iberican Association of Olympic Academies (#18181)
♦ Asociación Iberoamericana de Atletismo (inactive)
♦ Asociación Iberoamericana de Camaras de Comercio (#11014)
♦ Asociación Iberoamericana de Centros de Investigación y Empresas de Telecomunicaciones / see Asociación Interamericana de Empresas de Telecomunicaciones (#02160)

♦ Asociación Iberoamericana de Cirugia Pediatrica (AICP) 02134

Iberoamerican Association of Pediatric Surgery

Perm Sec address not obtained. T. +525752412. Fax +525752640.
URL: http://aiberoamericanacirped.org/

History 3 Nov 1966, Mexico City (Mexico), as *Pan American Association of Pediatric Surgery – Association panaméricaine de chirurgie pédiatrique – Asociación Panamericana de Cirugia Pediatrica.* Present name adopted, 2002. Statutes amended 1972. **Aims** Further efficient medical care and treatment for children; promote scientific research and dissemination of knowledge; maintain relations with governments and private organizations. **Structure** Assembly of active members elects Board, consisting of President, Vice-President, Secretary-Treasurer and 5 Counsellors, represents the following regions: Canada or USA; Mexico; Central America and Caribbean; the Guyanas, Venezuela, Columbia, Ecuador. Governing Council, consisting of Board plus a member from each of the Technical Committees: Face and Neck; Chest; Abdomen; Orthopedic Surgery; Neurosurgery; Other Specializations; Teaching; Pediatric Surgery as a Specialized Activity. **Languages** English, Portuguese, Spanish. **Staff** Unpaid. **Finance** Members' annual quotas. **Events** *Congress* Viña del Mar (Chile) 2024, *Congress* Porto (Portugal) 2020, *Congress* Mexico 2018, *Congress* Lima (Peru) 2016, *Congress* Sao Paulo (Brazil) 2014. **Publications** *Panamerican Pediatric Surgery* – journal. **Members** Founding; Active; Foreign (not eligible for office); Honorary. Individuals in 20 countries. Membership countries not specified. [2014/XD3050/v/**D**]

♦ Asociación Iberoamericana de Cirugia Toracica (AIACT) 02135

Address not obtained.

Events *Congress* Asunción (Paraguay) 2014, *Congress* Mexico City (Mexico) 2013, *Congress* Buenos Aires (Argentina) 2012, *Congress* Guayaquil (Ecuador) 2011, *Congress* Seville (Spain) 2009. [2015/XJ4806/**D**]

♦ Asociación Iberoamericana Contra el Cancer de Tiroides (AICCAT) . 02136

Iberoamerican Association Against Thyroid Cancer

Sec San Nicolas 15, 28013 Madrid, Spain. T. +910299953. E-mail: info@aecat.net.
URL: http://www.cancerdetiroides.org/

History 2004. [2015/XM2002/**D**]

♦ Asociación Iberoamericana de Defensa y Protección Civil / see Asociación Iberoamericana de Organismos Gubernamentales de Defensa y Protección Civil (#02150)
♦ Asociación Iberoamericana para el Derecho Alimentario (internationally oriented national body)
♦ Asociación Iberoamericana de Derecho Romano (#11016)
♦ Asociación Iberoamericana de Derecho a la Salud (no recent information)

♦ Asociación Iberoamericana de Derecho Sanitario (AIDS) 02137

SG c/o AEDS, Velázquez 124, 28006 Madrid, Spain. E-mail: aeds@aeds.org.
URL: https://www.iberoamericanaderechosanitario.org/

History Founded by representatives of national associations. **Structure** Executive Board. **Events** *Meeting* Santiago (Chile) 2002, *Meeting* Madrid (Spain) 2001.
Members Organizations in 4 countries:
Argentina, Chile, Portugal, Spain. [2020/XD7928/**D**]

♦ Asociación Iberoamericana de Diagnóstico y Evaluación Psicológica (AIDEP) 02138

Associação Iberoamericana de Diagnóstico e Avaliação Psicológica (AIDAP)

Contact Fac de Psicologia, Alameda de Universidade, 1649-013 Lisbon, Portugal. T. +351217943608. Fax +351217933408. E-mail: associacaoaidap@gmail.com.
URL: http://www.aidep.org/

History 1995. **Aims** Promote and develop the theoretical, technical and applied research areas of psychological diagnosis and assessment. **Structure** General Assembly; Supervisory Board; Board of Directors. **Languages** Portuguese, Spanish. **Staff** 3.00 FTE, paid. **Finance** Members' dues. **Events** *Congresso Iberoamericano de Diagnóstico e Avaliação Psicológica* Coimbra (Portugal) 2018, *Congress* Maceió (Brazil) 2013, *Congress* Lisbon (Portugal) 2011, *Congress* Buenos Aires (Argentina) 2009, *Congress* Mexico City (Mexico) 2007. **Publications** *Revista Iberoamericana de Diagnóstico y Evaluación – e Avaliaçao Psicológica (RIDEP).*
Members in 11 countries:
Argentina, Bolivia, Brazil, Chile, Mexico, Peru, Portugal, Spain, Uruguay, USA, Venezuela. [2017.08.03/XD8693/**D**]

♦ Asociación Iberoamericana de Educación Acuatica Especial e Hidroterapia (internationally oriented national body)
♦ Asociación Iberoamericana de Educación Superior a Distancia (#11015)

♦ Asociación Iberoamericana de Entidades Reguladoras de la Energia (ARIAE) 02139

Associação Iberoamericana de Entidades Reguladoras da Energia

Contact Comisión Nacional de Energia de España, C/ Alcala 47, 28014 Madrid, Spain. T. +34914329600. E-mail: se-ariae@ariae.org.
URL: http://www.ariae.org/

History 17 Mar 2000, Buenos Aires (Argentina). **Structure** General Assembly (annual); Executive Committee. **Languages** Portuguese, Spanish. **Events** *World Forum on Energy Regulation (WFER)* Istanbul (Turkey) 2015, *Meeting* Madrid (Spain) 2011, *Annual meeting* Madrid (Spain) 2007, *World Forum on Energy Regulation* Rome (Italy) 2003.
Members Full in 20 countries:
Argentina, Bolivia, Brazil, Chile, Colombia, Costa Rica, Cuba, Dominican Rep, Ecuador, El Salvador, Guatemala, Honduras, Mexico, Nicaragua, Panama, Peru, Portugal, Spain, Uruguay, Venezuela.
NGO Relations Member of: *International Confederation of Energy Regulators (ICER, #12859).* [2020/XD9078/**D**]

♦ Asociación Iberoamericana de Ergonomia (inactive)
♦ Asociación Iberoamericana de Estudio de los Problemas del Alcohol y la Droga (no recent information)

♦ Asociación Iberoamericana de Estudios de Regulacion (ASIER) . . . 02140

Contact Fac Ciencias Económicas, Univ Nacl de Cuyo, Ctr Univ Parque General San Martin, CP 5-500, Mendoza, Argentina.
URL: http://www.asier.org/

Structure Executive Committee. **Events** *Congress* San José (Costa Rica) 2017, *Congress* Buenos Aires (Argentina) 2016, *Congress* Monterrey (Mexico) 2015, *Congress* Brasilia (Brazil) 2014, *Congress* La Serena (Chile) 2013. [2016/XJ6974/**D**]

♦ Asociación Iberoamericana Etico-Humanista (no recent information)

♦ Asociación Iberoamericana de Filosofia Politica (AIFP) 02141

Address not obtained.
URL: http://xivsimposioaifp.uv.cl/

History 1997, Mexico. **Structure** Executive Committee; Scientific Committee. **Activities** Organizes symposia. **Events** *Symposium* Valparaiso (Chile) 2015, *Symposium* Juiz de Fora (Brazil) 2013, *Symposium* Bogota (Colombia) 2011, *Symposium* Bahia Blanca (Argentina) 2009, *Symposium* Mexico City (Mexico) 2007. [2015/XD9238/**D**]

♦ Asociación Iberoamericana de Filosofia Practica (AIFP) 02142

Pres Filosofia UniCauca, Calle 2 No 3N-100, Popayan, Cauca, Colombia. E-mail: aristides.o@gmail.com – asoibe.fp@gmail.com.
URL: http://aidefp.org/

History Set up Oct 2012. Registered in accordance with Mexican law. **Aims** Provide a forum for the study, strengthening and development of practical *philosophy.* **Structure** Board of Directors. **Languages** Spanish. **Activities** Events/meetings. **Events** *Congress* Popayan (Colombia) 2015, *Congress* Barcelona (Spain) 2013. [2021/XM4111/**D**]

♦ Asociación Iberoamericana de Gas Licuado del Petróleo (AIGLP) . . 02143

Iberoamerican LP Gas Association

Office Rua da Assembléia 66, 19o piso, Centro, Rio de Janeiro RJ, RJ CEP 20011-000, Brazil. T. +552130782850. Fax +552125312621. E-mail: aiglp@aiglp.org.
URL: http://www.aiglp.org/

History 7 May 1986, Buenos Aires (Argentina). **Aims** Promote good practices with regard to security, excellence in provision of services, logistics efficiency, as well as scientific technical development of the LPG sector. **Structure** Council. **Languages** Portuguese, Spanish. **Events** *Congress* Miami, FL (USA) 2014, *Congress* Mexico City (Mexico) 2013, *Congress* Panama (Panama) 2012, *Congress* Santiago (Chile) 2011, *Congress* Madrid (Spain) 2010. **Publications** Regulations; guidelines; manuals. [2019.11.11/XD7751/**D**]

♦ Asociación Iberoamericana de Información Deportiva (no recent information)
♦ Asociación Iberoamericana de Información y Promoción Profesional de Seguros (no recent information)

♦ Asociación Iberoamericana de Instituciones de Enseñanza de la Ingenieria (ASIBEI) 02144

Exec Sec Carrera 77 128A-58, Bogota, Bogota DC, Colombia. E-mail: jsalazarc@unal.edu.co – jaime.salazar@promeduc.org.
URL: http://www.asibei.net/

History 6 Dec 1999, Mar del Plata (Argentina), following activities initiated in 1997. **Structure** General Assembly; Executive Committee. **Languages** Portuguese, Spanish. **Events** *World Engineering Education Forum* Cartagena de Indias (Colombia) 2013, *International Symposium on Project Approaches in Engineering Education* Lisbon (Portugal) 2011, *Meeting* Lisbon (Portugal) 2011, *International conference on engineering and computer education* São Vicente (Brazil) / Santos (Brazil) 2003. **NGO Relations** Member of: *Engineering for the Americas (EftA, no recent information).* [2018/XD8469/**D**]

♦ Asociación Iberoamericana de Investigación en Sociología de las Organizaciones y Comunicación (AISOC) 02145

Pres Univ Complutense, Facultad CC Información, Av Séneca 2, 28040 Madrid, Spain.
URL: http://aisoc.info/

History 1989, Lima (Peru). Founded as a Subcommittee, by the Iberoamerican Subcommittee of *International Sociological Association (ISA, #15553).* Became an independent organization, Jun 2001, San Juan (Argentina). Former names and other names: *Asociación Iberoamericana de Sociología de las Organizaciones (AISO)* – former. **Languages** Portuguese, Spanish. **Events** *Seminar* Madrid (Spain) 2019, *Seminar* Toronto, ON (Canada) 2018, *Seminar* Madrid (Spain) 2013, *Seminar* Buenos Aires (Argentina) 2012, *Seminar* Guanajuato (Mexico) 2011. [2022.02.14/XM0122/**D**]

♦ Asociación Iberoamericana de Logoterapia (ASIL) 02146

Contact address not obtained. T. +34649155426. E-mail: ma_aeslo@yahoo.es.
URL: http://www.asil.com.ar/

Members National organizations in 3 countries:
Argentina, Mexico, Spain. [2010/XM2003/**D**]

♦ Asociación Iberoamericana de Medicina Aerospacial (AIMA) 02147

Ibero-American Association of Aerospace Medicine

Sec PO Box 25082, Oklahoma City OK 73125, USA. T. +14059546131.
URL: http://www.sites.google.com/site/aima1976org/home/

History Founded 10 Nov 1976, Mexico City (Mexico), as *Latin American Association of Aviation and Space Medicine – Asociación Latinoamericana de Medicina de Aviación y del Espacio.* Also formerly known in French as *Association Ibéroaméricaine de Médecine Aérospatiale.* **Aims** Promote, foster, establish and maintain progress in Aviation and Space Medicine through research, education and scientific exchange with other medical, scientific and technical associations. **Structure** Board of Directors; Permanent Committees (5). **Languages** Spanish. **Staff** Voluntary. **Finance** Members' dues. No annual budget. **Activities** Events/meetings. **Events** *Annual Congress* Orlando, FL (USA) 2015, *Annual Congress* Chicago, IL (USA) 2013, *Annual Congress* Atlanta, GA (USA) 2012, *Annual Congress* Anchorage, AK (USA) 2011, *Annual Congress* Phoenix, AZ (USA) 2010. **Publications** *Boletin – Asociación Iberoamericana de Medicina Aerospacial* (2 a year). *Factores Humanos en Aviación* (1989).
Members Active (20-50); Inactive/Stakeholders (about 200). Individuals in 26 countries and territories:
Andorra, Argentina, Bolivia, Brazil, Canada, Chile, Colombia, Costa Rica, Cuba, Dominican Rep, Ecuador, El Salvador, France, Guatemala, Honduras, Mexico, Nicaragua, Panama, Paraguay, Peru, Portugal, Puerto Rico, Spain, Uruguay, USA, Venezuela.
IGO Relations Cooperates with numerous IGOs. **NGO Relations** Member of: *Aerospace Medical Association (ASMA).* [2020.03.04/XD6136/v/**D**]

♦ Asociación Iberoamericana de Medicina y Salud Escolar y Universitaria 02148

Pres Calle Amorós 3 – 1o A, 28028 Madrid, Spain. T. +34917250919. E-mail: saludescolar@telefonica.net.
URL: http://www.saludescolar.net/
History 2001. Founded with the support of *World Organization for Early Childhood Education (OMEP, #21689); Pan American Health Organization (PAHO, #18108)* and Asociación Española de Medicina Escolar. **Structure** President; 4 Vice-Presidents (Europe; North America; Central America and Caribbean; South America); Treasurer; Secretary. **Languages** English, French, Spanish. **Staff** Voluntary. **Finance** Voluntary contributions; foundations. **Activities** Organizes congresses. **Events** *Annual Doctors of Podiatric Medicine against SARS-COV-2 International Congress* Madrid (Spain) 2020, *International Congress of School Medicine* Cadiz (Spain) 2012, *International congress on school health* Evora (Portugal) 2009, *Encuentro internacional de expertos en cuidados de salud escolar* Oviedo (Spain) 2008. **Publications** Manuals; reviews. **NGO Relations** *Asociación Latinoamericana de Profesores de Medicina Familiar (ALPMF, #02258); International Union for Health Promotion and Education (IUHPE, #15778); Rädda Barnen – Save the Children Sweden.* [2020/XM8287/**D**]

♦ Asociación Iberoamericana de Medicina y Salud Escolar y Universitaria (#11017)
♦ Asociación Iberoamericana del Menor (inactive)

♦ Asociación Iberoamericana de Ministerios Públicos (AIAMP) 02149

Ibero-American Association of Public Prosecutors
Gen Sec c/o Fiscalía General, Calle de Fortuny, 4, 28010 Madrid, Spain.
URL: http://www.aiamp.info/
History 24 Nov 1954, Sao Paulo (Brazil). Former names and other names: *Asociación Interamericana del Ministerio Público* – former (1954 to 2002); *Inter-American Association of Public Prosecution* – former (1954 to 2002). **Aims** Strengthen ties and solidarity between public prosecution services of American countries; establish a common guidance in the light of fundamental problems concerning the institution. **Structure** General Assembly; Executive Committee; General Secretariat. **Events** *General Assembly* Madrid (Spain) 2020, *Congreso Interamericano del Ministerio Público* Cartagena de Indias (Colombia) 2002, *Congreso Interamericano del Ministerio Público* Antigua (Guatemala) 2000, *Extraordinary meeting* Buenos Aires (Argentina) 1999, *Congreso Interamericano del Ministerio Público* Brasilia (Brazil) 1998.
Members Prosecutors of 38 countries and territories:
Argentina, Aruba, Barbados, Belize, Bermuda, Bolivia, Brazil, Canada, Chile, Colombia, Costa Rica, Cuba, Dominica, Dominican Rep, Ecuador, El Salvador, Grenada, Guatemala, Guyana, Haiti, Honduras, Jamaica, Mexico, Montserrat, Neth Antilles, Nicaragua, Panama, Paraguay, Peru, Puerto Rico, St Lucia, St Vincent-Grenadines, Suriname, Trinidad-Tobago, Uruguay, USA, Venezuela, Virgin Is USA.
IGO Relations Listed in the Registro de Redes Iberoamericano, held by *Ibero-American General Secretariat (#11024).* **NGO Relations** Instrumental in setting up (1): *Red Iberoamericana de Cooperación Jurídica Internacional (IberRed, #18662).* [2020/XD7604/**D**]

♦ Asociación Iberoamericana de Motociclismo (unconfirmed)
♦ Asociación Iberoamericana de Odontologia Familiar (inactive)

♦ Asociación Iberoamericana de Organismos Gubernamentales de Defensa y Protección Civil 02150

Iberoamerican Association of Institutions on Civil Defence and Protection – Associação Iberoamericana das Organizações Governamentais da Defesa e Proteção Civil
Founder Dirección General de Protección Civil, Calle Quintiliano 21, 28002 Madrid, Spain. T. +34915373100. Fax +34915628926. E-mail: dgpce@procivil.mir.es.
Coodinator address not obtained.
URL: https://arce.dei.inf.uc3m.es/
History 7 Jul 1996. Statutes approved 1997. Former names and other names: *Asociación Iberoamericana de Defensa y Protección Civil* – alias. **Events** *Conference* Cartagena de Indias (Colombia) 2011, *Conference* Madrid (Spain) 2009, *Conference* Caracas (Venezuela) 2007, *Conference* Havana (Cuba) 2006, *Extraordinary conference* Caracas (Venezuela) 2005. [2020.09.10/XD8388/**D***]

♦ Asociación Iberoamericana de Ortodoncistas (AIO) 02151

Pres C/ Lleó11-13, 08911 Barcelona, Spain. T. +34933844705.
URL: http://www.iberortodoncia.com/
History 28 Sep 1978, Madrid (Spain). **Aims** Promote scientific advancement in the field; increase ties between orthodontists in Iberoamerican countries, thereby promoting scientific interchange; encourage training of members in orthodontics through continuing education and other means. **Structure** General Assembly (meets during Congress). General Scientific Committee, comprising President (Secretary General of AIO), Vice-President and 17 members. Executive Committee, comprising General Secretary, Treasurer, 2 Editors and 4 Vocals (Coordination with WFO; Continuing Education; Scientific Coordination; Coordination with President of National Committees). National Committees, each with its own President, Treasurer and Vocals. **Languages** English, Spanish. **Staff** 8.00 FTE, paid. **Finance** Members' dues. Other sources: meeting proceeds; sponsors; donations. **Activities** Groups together Organizes: congress; continuing education courses. **Events** *Congress* La Paz (Bolivia) 2019, *Congress* Madrid (Spain) 2016, *Congress* Lima (Peru) 2015, *Congress* Montevideo (Uruguay) 2013, *International Symposium* Madrid (Spain) 2012. **Publications** *Revista Iberoamericana de Ortodoncia* (3 a year). Monographs.
Members Categories Associate; Active; Founding; Honorary. National committees in 19 countries and territories:
Argentina, Bolivia, Brazil, Chile, Colombia, Cuba, Dominican Rep, Ecuador, El Salvador, Honduras, Mexico, Panama, Paraguay, Peru, Portugal, Puerto Rico, Spain, Uruguay, Venezuela.
NGO Relations Affiliated with: *World Federation of Orthodontists (#21469).* [2020/XJ0130/**D**]

♦ Asociación Iberoamericana de Periodismo Cientifico (#19140)

♦ Asociación Iberoamericana de Periodistas Especializados y Técnicos (AIPET Internacional) 02152

Pres C/Provenza 157 Bis 4o 1a, 08036 Barcelona, Spain. T. +34934516069. E-mail: secreaipet@hotmail.com – info@aipet.org.
URL: http://www.aipet.org/
History Founded 1981. **Aims** Represent interests of specialized journalists. **Structure** General Assembly; Board of Directors. **Languages** English, French, Spanish. **Staff** Voluntary. **Finance** Annual budget: euro 10,000. **Activities** Awards/prizes/competitions. **Events** *International Congress* Barcelona (Spain) 2011, *International congress* Barcelona (Spain) 2004, *International Congress* Bogota (Colombia) 2001, *International congress* Bogota (Colombia) 2001, *International congress* Barcelona (Spain) 1999. **Publications** *AIPET Bulletin* (4 a year).
Members Individuals in 15 countries:
Argentina, Bolivia, Chile, Colombia, Cuba, Dominican Rep, Mexico, Panama, Paraguay, Peru, Portugal, Spain, Uruguay, USA, Venezuela. [2016.12.28/XD1285/v/**D**]

♦ Asociación Iberoamericana de Profesionales para la Calidad y el Desarrollo (unconfirmed)
♦ Asociación Iberoamericana de Puertos y Costas (inactive)
♦ Asociación Iberoamericana de Rehabilitación Médica (inactive)
♦ Asociación Iberoamericana de Reproducción Animal (no recent information)
♦ Asociación Iberoamericana de Sociología de las Organizaciones / see Asociación Iberoamericana de Investigación en Sociología de las Organizaciones y Comunicación (#02145)
♦ Asociación Iberoamericanas para el Sindrome de Down (inactive)

♦ Asociación Iberoamericana de las Tecnologias del Agua y Riego (IBEROAQUA) 02153

Association ibéro-américaine des technologies de l'eau et de l'irrigation
Contact address not obtained. T. +34917819522. Fax +34915761866.
History Founded 19 Jun 2008, Saragossa (Spain). Registered in accordance with Spanish law. **Aims** Promote continuing innovation in the *sustainable management* of *water resources* through cooperation and transfer of technology between Latin American countries; represent, defend, promote and link the sector's common interests in the fields of water and irrigation. **Structure** General Assembly; Executive Committee; Permanent Commission. **Events** *Annual water and energy exchange summit* Cyprus 2010, *International Congress* Mexico 2010, *International irrigation congress* Mexico 2010, *Constituant assembly* Saragossa (Spain) 2008, *International irrigation congress / International Congress* Saragossa (Spain) 2008.
Members in 22 countries and territories:
Argentina, Bolivia, Brazil, Chile, Colombia, Costa Rica, Cuba, Dominican Rep, Ecuador, El Salvador, Guatemala, Honduras, Mexico, Nicaragua, Panama, Paraguay, Peru, Portugal, Puerto Rico, Spain, Uruguay, Venezuela. [2012/XJ0214/**D**]

♦ Asociación Iberoamericana de Tecnologias de Apoyo a la Discapacidad (AITADIS) 02154

Coordinator CSIC – Carretera Campo Real km 0, 200, La Poveda, Arganda del Rey, 28500 Madrid, Spain. T. +34918711900 ext 278. Fax +34918717050. E-mail: info@aitadis.org.
URL: http://www.aitadis.org/
History 22 Nov 2006, San Sebastian (Spain). Registered in accordance with Spanish law, 17 Jul 2007: 589 215. **Aims** Promote research and development, application, general distribution and use of assistive technologies, achievement of greater autonomy and social participation of people with disabilities and the elderly, and provision of a forum for integrating different actors involved in the field. **Structure** Board of Directors. **Languages** Portuguese, Spanish. **Staff** 7.00 FTE, voluntary. **Finance** Members' dues. Specials funds from external organizations. **Activities** Events/meetings. **Events** *IBERDISCAP : Congreso Iberoamericano de Tecnologias de Apoyo a la Discapacidad* Bogota (Colombia) 2017, *IBERDISCAP : Congreso Iberoamericano de Tecnologias de Apoyo a la Discapacidad* Punta Arenas (Chile) 2015, *IBERDISCAP : Congreso Iberoamericano de Tecnologias de Apoyo a la Discapacidad* Santo Domingo (Dominican Rep) 2013, *IBERDISCAP : Congreso Iberoamericano de Tecnologias de Apoyo a la Discapacidad* Palma (Spain) 2011, *IBERDISCAP : Congreso Iberoamericano de Tecnologias de Apoyo a la Discapacidad* Cartagena de Indias (Colombia) 2008. **Publications** Proceedings. [2019.04.26/XJ6922/**D**]

♦ Asociación Iberoamericana de Telesalud y Telemedicina (AITT) . . . 02155

Associação Iberoamericana de Telessaúde e Telemedicina (AITT)
Sec address not obtained.
Pres address not obtained. E-mail: marcial@cim.es.
URL: http://teleiberoamerica.com/
History Statutes adopted Feb 2011. **Structure** Board. **Events** *Congress* Seville (Spain) 2015, *Congress* Lima (Peru) 2014. **Publications** *Revista de la AITT.*
Members Branches in 23 countries and territories:
Argentina, Bolivia, Brazil, Chile, Colombia, Costa Rica, Cuba, Dominican Rep, Ecuador, El Salvador, Guatemala, Honduras, Mexico, Nicaragua, Panama, Paraguay, Peru, Portugal, Puerto Rico, Spain, Uruguay, USA, Venezuela.
NGO Relations *Latin American Clinical Pathology and Laboratory Medicine (ALAPAC/ML, #16299).* [2015/XJ9687/**D**]

♦ Asociación Iberoamericana de Terapeutas Florales (no recent information)
♦ Asociación Ibero-Americana Veterinaria Equina (no recent information)
♦ Asociación Ibero Latinoamericana de Asociaciones de Endodoncia / see Asociación Iberolatinoamericana de Endodoncia (#02157)

♦ Asociación Ibero Latinoamericana de Colombofilia (AILAC) 02156

Contact Bogota 13, 1405 Buenos Aires, Argentina. T. +541149823121. Fax +541179823121.
URL: http://www.fecoar.com.ar/ailac
History 1992. **Aims** Promote the hobby of breeding and racing *homing pigeons.* **Activities** Events/meetings. **Events** *Congress* Havana (Cuba) 2003.
Members National organizations in 13 countries:
Argentina, Brazil, Chile, Colombia, Costa Rica, Cuba, Mexico, Nicaragua, Peru, Portugal, Romania, Spain, Uruguay. [2019.06.05/XD9233/**D**]

♦ Asociación Iberolatinoamericana de Endodoncia (AILAE) 02157

Ibero-Latin American Endodontic Association
Sec address not obtained. E-mail: vdf@coem.org.es – webmaster@endodoncia.es.
URL: http://www.ailae.com/
History 1978. Also referred to as *Ibero-Latin American Association of Endodontists – Asociación Ibero-Latinoamericana de Endodontistas (AILAE)* and *Asociación Ibero Latinoamericana de Asociaciones de Endodoncia (AILAE).* **Events** *Congress* Madrid (Spain) 2013, *Congress* Asunción (Paraguay) 2003, *Congress* Viña del Mar (Chile) 1998.
Members Endodontic organizations in 12 countries:
Argentina, Bolivia, Brazil, Chile, Colombia, Ecuador, Mexico, Paraguay, Peru, Puerto Rico, Uruguay, Venezuela. [2013/XD1310/**D**]

♦ Asociación Ibero-Latinoamericana de Endodontistas / see Asociación Iberolatinoamericana de Endodoncia (#02157)
♦ Asociación IberoLatinoAmericana de Neurociencias y Psiquiatría (unconfirmed)
♦ Asociación de Iglesias Presbiterianas y Reformadas de América Latina / see Alliance of Presbyterian and Reformed Churches in Latin America (#00713)
♦ Asociación Indigena Mundial (#11166)
♦ Asociación de Industriales Latinoamericanos (#16341)

♦ Asociación de la Industrias de Alimentación Animal de América Latina y Caribe (FEEDLATINA) 02158

Associação das Indústrias de Alimentação Animal da América Latina e Caribe (FEEDLATINA)
Exec Dir Calle Andes, 1365 Of 310 Centro, Montevideo, Uruguay.
URL: http://www.feedlatina.org/
History 24 Jan 2008. Registered in accordance with Brazilian law. **Structure** Council; Board of Directors.
Members Full in 5 countries:
Argentina, Brazil, Cuba, Mexico, Uruguay.
IGO Relations *FAO (#09260).* **NGO Relations** Member of: *International Feed Industry Federation (IFIF, #13581).* [2015/XM4106/t/**D**]

♦ Asociación de Industrias Europeas del Yute (inactive)
♦ Asociación de Industrias de Fabricantes de Helados de la CEE / see EUROGLACES – European Ice Cream Association (#05688)
♦ Asociación de Industrias de Fabricantes de Helados de la UE / see EUROGLACES – European Ice Cream Association (#05688)
♦ Asociación de las Industrias de Margarina de los Paises de la CE / see European Margarine Association (#07736)
♦ Asociación de Inspectores Organicos Independientes / see International Organic Inspectors Association (#14421)

- ♦ Asociación de Inspectores Organicos Internationales (#14421)
- ♦ Asociación de Instituciones de Financiamiento Habitacional del Caribe (#03447)
- ♦ Asociación de Instituciones Financieras de Desarrollo del Asia y el Pacifico (#02472)
- ♦ Asociación de Instituciones Jesuitas de Enseñanza Superior de Europa y Lebanon (inactive)
- ♦ Asociación de Instituciones de Seguridad Social de Centroamérica y Panama (inactive)
- ♦ Asociación de Institutos de Estudios Europeos (inactive)
- ♦ Asociación Interamericana de Bibliotecarios, Documentalistas y Especialistas en Información Agricola (no recent information)
- ♦ Asociación Interamericana de Contabilidad (#11395)
- ♦ Asociación Interamericana para la Defensa del Ambiente (#11398)

♦ Asociación Interamericana de Defensorias Públicas (AIDEF) 02159

Iner-American Association of Public Defenders

Gen Coordinator Defensoria Penal Pública de Chile, Av Bernardo O'Higgins 1449, Pisos 5 y 8, 8340518 Santiago, Santiago Metropolitan, Chile. T. +56224396885 – +56224396831 – +56224790158. E-mail: conferenciasaidef@gmail.com.

Gen Sec Defensoria General, Callao 970 1 Piso, CP C1023AAP, Buenos Aires, Argentina. T. +541148148403. E-mail: internacional@mdp.gov.py.

URL: http://www.aidef.org/

History Founded 18 Oct 2003, Rio de Janeiro (Brazil), during 2nd Inter American Congress. Previously also referred to in English as *Iberoamerican Association of Public Defence Counsels*. **Aims** Defend the effectiveness of internationally recognized *Human Rights* and Guarantees; provide legal assistance and representation when required, with due regard for quality and excellence, allowing an effective access to justice; encourage that the existing legislation of the countries in the region and its reforms, respect the human rights of people in vulnerable situations; promote the independence and functional autonomy of the Public Defender's Offices, in order to ensure a wide access to high quality legal aid, not only in criminal matters; support institutional strengthening of the Public Defender's Offices, in balance with the Prosecutors' Offices. **Structure** Steering Committee (Comité Ejecutivo); Board (Consejo Directivo). **Languages** English, Portuguese, Spanish. **Activities** Conflict resolution; events/meetings. **Events** *Congress* Santo Domingo (Dominican Rep) 2014, *Congress* Fortaleza (Brazil) 2012, *Congress* Guatemala (Guatemala) 2010, *Congress* Buenos Aires (Argentina) 2008, *Congress* San Salvador (El Salvador) 2006. **Publications** *Regional Guide for the Public Defense and the Protection of Persons Deprived of Liberty* – with explanatory memorandum.

Members Public Defender's Offices and Associations in 20 countries and territories:

Antigua-Barbuda, Argentina, Bolivia, Brazil, Chile, Colombia, Costa Rica, Dominican Rep, Ecuador, El Salvador, Guatemala, Honduras, Mexico, Nicaragua, Panama, Paraguay, Peru, Puerto Rico, Uruguay, Venezuela.

IGO Relations Cooperates with: *Inter-American Commission on Human Rights (IACHR, #11411)*; *Corte Interamericana de Derechos Humanos (Corte IDH, #04851)*; *OAS (#17629)* – Secretariat for Legal Affairs. **NGO Relations** Cooperates with EUROsociAL Programme. [2020/XJ4179/**D**]

- ♦ Asociación Interamericana pro Democracia y Libertad (inactive)
- ♦ Asociación Interamericana de Directores de Coro (inactive)
- ♦ Asociación Interamericana de Educación (inactive)

♦ Asociación Interamericana de Empresas de Telecomunicaciones (ASIET) 02160

General Manager Rambla República de Mexico 6125, 11400 Montevideo, Uruguay. E-mail: contacto@tel.lat.

SG address not obtained.

Head Office C/ Príncipe de Vergara 109, 2º piso, 28002 Madrid, Spain. E-mail: fernando@tel.lat.

URL: https://asiet.lat/

History 1982, Madrid (Spain). Former names and other names: *Asociación Iberoamericana de Centros de Investigación y Empresas de Telecomunicaciones (AHCIET)* – former (1982); *Hispano-American Association of Research Centers and Telecommunications Enterprises* – former; *Association hispanoaméricaine des centres de recherches et des entreprises de télécommunication* – former. **Aims** Assist telecommunications development in all *Spanish-speaking* countries by bringing together study and research in the field; promote and cooperate in developing different aspects concerning technical and technological training and standards in telecommunications subjects. **Structure** General Assembly (annual); Board of Trustees; General Secretariat. Meetings closed. **Languages** Spanish. **Staff** 6.00 FTE, paid. **Finance** Sources: donations; grants; members' dues. Annual budget: 3,000,000 USD. **Activities** Awards/prizes/competitions; events/meetings; knowledge management/information dissemination; research and development; standards/guidelines; training/education. **Events** *Latin American Congress of Telecommunications* Córdoba (Argentina) 2019, *General Assembly* 2001, *Wireless communication meeting* 2001, *Iberoamerican week of telecommunications and society* Buenos Aires (Argentina) 2001, *Internet meeting* Santiago (Chile) 2001. **Publications** *Telecomunicaciones de América Latina* (6 a year); *Anuario de las Telecomunicaciones Hispanoamericanas* (annual). **Information Services** *Sistema de Información en Telecomunicaciones (SIT)* – creates and distributes cooperative databases.

Members Centres in 21 countries and territories:

Argentina, Bolivia, Brazil, Chile, Colombia, Costa Rica, Cuba, Dominican Rep, Ecuador, El Salvador, Guatemala, Honduras, Mexico, Nicaragua, Panama, Paraguay, Peru, Puerto Rico, Spain, Uruguay, Venezuela.

IGO Relations Cooperates with (1): *International Telecommunication Union (ITU, #15673)*. **NGO Relations** Partner of (1): *Centro de Estudios Avanzados en Banda Ancha para el Desarrollo (CEABAD, #03797)*. [2021.02.16/XD0707/**D**]

- ♦ Asociación Interamericana de Enseñanza Turistica y Hotelera (inactive)
- ♦ Asociación Interamericana de Gastroenterologia / see Organización Panamericana de Gastroenterologia (#17847)
- ♦ Asociación Interamericana de Hoteles (no recent information)
- ♦ Asociación Interamericana y Ibérica de Presupuesto Público / see Public Budget International Association (#18564)
- ♦ Asociación Interamericana de Ingenieria Sanitaria / see Inter-American Association of Sanitary and Environmental Engineering (#11400)
- ♦ Asociación Interamericana de Ingenieria Sanitaria y Ambiental (#11400)
- ♦ Asociación Interamericana de Jueces de Menores (inactive)
- ♦ Asociación Interamericana del Ministerio Público / see Asociación Iberoamericana de Ministerios Públicos (#02149)
- ♦ Asociación Interamericana de Otorrinolaringologia Pediátrica (#11399)
- ♦ Asociación Interamericana de Profesores de Derecho Internacional Privado (inactive)
- ♦ Asociación Interamericana de Profesores de Ingenieria Sanitaria y Ambiental (no recent information)
- ♦ Asociación Interamericana de la Propiedad Industrial / see Asociación Interamericana de la Propiedad Intelectual (#02161)

♦ Asociación Interamericana de la Propiedad Intelectual (ASIPI) 02161

Interamerican Association of Intellectual Property – Associação Interamericana da Propriedade Intelectual

Pres Vanrell Propiedad Intelectual – Abogados, Prof J C Sabat Pebet 1230/508, CP 11300 Montevideo, Uruguay. T. +59826286033.

Former Pres Triana/Uribe/Michelsen, Calle 93B No 12-48 P 4, Bogota, Bogota DC, Colombia. T. +5716019660 – +5716215810. Fax +5716114209.

URL: http://www.asipi.org/

History Founded 14 Apr 1963, Mexico City (Mexico), as *Inter-American Association of Industrial Property – Association interaméricaine de propriété industrielle – Asociación Interamericana de la Propiedad Industrial (ASIPI)*. Commenced activities in 1964. Constitution modified: Nov 1965, Buenos Aires (Argentina), during first Congress; 1968, Lima (Peru). Sometimes referred to by English initials *IAAIP*. **Aims** Promote, in the American countries, the development and harmonization of the laws, regulations and procedures related to industrial and intellectual property; advise governments and intergovernmental entities on the study of projects on legal dispositions related to intellectual property; encourage relationships with related entities, such as FICPI, WIP, AIPPI, INTA, AIPLA and IPO. **Structure** Congress (every 3 years); Board of Directors; Executive Committee (meets at least 3 times a year) of 9 members. Committees (23): Administration of Law Firms; Anti-Counterfeiting; Arbitration and Conciliation; Competition; Copyrights; Education; Enterprise; Entertainment; Events Coordination Program; Geographical Indications; Industrial Design Trade Dress; Madrid Protocol; New Creations; New Technologies; Non Traditional Trademarks; Notorious Trademarks; Regulations and Ethics; Regulatory; Social Actions, Sports Law, Trademarks; Trademarks; Country Guide; Traditional Knowledge. National Delegates (44). **Languages** English, French, Portuguese, Spanish. **Staff** Voluntary. **Finance** Members' dues. Other sources: contributions; funds from activities. **Activities** Events/meetings. **Events** *Triennial Congress* Punta Cana (Dominican Rep) 2021, *Triennial Congress* Rio de Janeiro (Brazil) 2018, *Triennial Congress* Cartagena de Indias (Colombia) 2015, *Unfair competition and intellectual property – contemporary problems that affect the industry* Antigua (Guatemala) 2012, *Triennial Congress* Punta del Este (Uruguay) 2012. **Publications** *Derechos Intelectuales* (annual); *ASIPInforma* (4-5 a year); *Derecho Farmacéutico y Propiedad Intelectual en América Latina*. *Geographical Indications*; *Tratados Internacionales en Materia de Propiedad Intelectual*. Congress and seminar reports.

Members Individuals (over 1,000) in 51 countries and territories:

Anguilla, Argentina, Aruba, Australia, Austria, Barbados, Belgium, Belize, Bolivia, Brazil, Canada, Chile, China, Colombia, Costa Rica, Cuba, Curaçao, Cyprus, Dominica, Dominican Rep, Ecuador, El Salvador, France, Germany, Guatemala, Haiti, Honduras, India, Ireland, Italy, Jamaica, Lebanon, Mexico, Neth Antilles, Nicaragua, Nigeria, Panama, Paraguay, Peru, Portugal, Puerto Rico, Russia, Spain, St Lucia, Suriname, Switzerland, Trinidad-Tobago, UK, Uruguay, USA, Venezuela.

Consultative Status Consultative status granted from: *World Intellectual Property Organization (WIPO, #21593)* (Permanent Observer Status). **NGO Relations** Member of: *MARQUES (#16588)*. [2015.09.04/XD1048/v/**D**]

- ♦ Asociación Interamericana de Radiodifusión / see International Association of Broadcasting (#11738)
- ♦ Asociación Interamericana de Servicios Legales Alternativos / see Inter-American Legal Services Association (#11439)
- ♦ Asociación Interamericana de Vivienda Rural (inactive)
- ♦ Asociación Interciencia (#11459)
- ♦ Asociación Internacional de Abogacia Preventiva (no recent information)
- ♦ Asociación Internacional de Actuarios (#11586)
- ♦ Asociación Internacional de Administración de Ciudades (#12579)
- ♦ Asociación Internacional de Aeropuertos Civiles (inactive)
- ♦ Asociación Internacional de Agencias de Turismo Receptivo (inactive)
- ♦ Asociación Internacional de Alergologia e Inmunologia Clinica / see World Allergy Organization – IAACI (#21077)
- ♦ Asociación Internacional de Anatomistas de la Madera (#12273)
- ♦ Asociación Internacional de Archivos Sonoros y Audiovisuales (#12172)
- ♦ Asociación Internacional de Armadores de Buques de Carga Seca (#11853)
- ♦ Asociación Internacional de Arqueologia del Caribe (#11756)
- ♦ Asociación Internacional de Arqueologia Clasica (#02988)
- ♦ Asociación Internacional de Artes Plasticas (#11710)
- ♦ Asociación Internacional Artes Renascentes (#02670)
- ♦ Asociación Internacional de Asistencia Legal (inactive)
- ♦ Asociación Internacional de Asmologia / see INTERASMA (#11457)
- ♦ Asociación Internacionala per l'Usança de la Lengas Regionalas a l'Escola (no recent information)
- ♦ Asociación Internacional de Auxologia Humana (no recent information)
- ♦ Asociación Internacional de Bancos Cooperativos (#12945)
- ♦ Asociación Internacional de Bibliófilos (#02673)
- ♦ Asociación Internacional de Bibliologia (inactive)
- ♦ Asociación Internacional de Bibliotecas y Centros de Información sobre Población y Planificación Familiar (internationally oriented national body)
- ♦ Asociación Internacional de Bibliotecas de las Universidades (#12247)
- ♦ Asociación Internacional de Bibliotecas de las Universidades Tecnológicas / see International Association of University Libraries (#12247)
- ♦ Asociación Internacional de Cabras (#13725)

♦ Asociación Internacional de Camineria (AIC) 02162

Contact c/José Abascal 49 – 6 D, 28003 Madrid, Spain. T. +34914411696. E-mail: cchs_camineria@cchs.csic.es.

URL: http://aicamineria.org/

History Founded 1996, Morelia (Mexico). **Aims** Promote the study of Hispanic *roads*. **Structure** General Assembly; Council. **Events** *International Congress of Hispanic Camineria / International Congress* Madrid (Spain) 2014, *International Congress* Madrid (Spain) 2012, *International congress of Hispanic camineria / International Congress* Madrid (Spain) 2010, *International Congress* Cadiz (Spain) 2008, *International congress of Hispanic camineria* Madrid (Spain) 2006. [2022/XM0137/**D**]

- ♦ Asociación Internacional por el Cannabis como Medicamento / see International Association for Cannabinoid Medicines (#11754)
- ♦ Asociación Internacional de Caridades (#02675)
- ♦ Asociación Internacional de Caridades de San Vincente de Paul / see Association Internationale des Charités (#02675)
- ♦ Asociación Internacional de Charters Aéreos / see Airlines International Representation in Europe (#00608)
- ♦ Asociación Internacional de Cibernética (inactive)
- ♦ Asociación Internacional de Ciencia y Diversidad Cultural (#12150)
- ♦ Asociación Internacional para las Ciencias Fisicas del Oceano (#12082)
- ♦ Asociación Internacional de Ciencias Juridicas (#11997)
- ♦ Asociación Internacional de Ciencias Politicas (#14615)
- ♦ Asociación Internacional para la Ciencia y la Tecnologia Cerealistas (#11048)
- ♦ Asociación Internacional para la Ciencia de la Vivienda (#11943)
- ♦ Asociación Internacional de Ciudadanos "Seniors" (inactive)
- ♦ Asociación Internacional de Ciudades contra la Droga (inactive)
- ♦ Asociación Internacional de Ciudades Educadoras (#11860)
- ♦ Asociación Internacional Ciudades y Puertos / see Association internationale villes et ports – réseau mondial des villes portuaires (#02751)
- ♦ Asociación Internacional de los Clubes de Leones / see Lions Clubs International (#16485)

♦ Asociación Internacional de la Comunicación Interactiva (AInCI) .. 02163

Coordinator Via Tabajani 1 – S 15 – CP 7, 24121 Bergamo BG, Italy. E-mail: info@ainci.com.

URL: http://www.ainci.com/

History 1997. **Aims** Research and promote the results achieved in the context of the high quality interactive communication. **Activities** Events/meetings. **Events** *International Conference on Multimedia, Scientific Information and Visualization for Information Systems and Metrics* Las Palmas de Gran Canaria (Spain) 2020, *International Symposium on Communicability, Computer Graphics and Innovative Design for Interactive Systems* Madrid (Spain) 2020, *International Conference on Software and Emerging Technologies for Education, Culture, Entertainment, and Commerce* Venice (Italy) 2020, *International Conference on Advances in New Technologies, Interactive Interfaces and Communicability* Córdoba (Argentina) 2019, *International Conference on Research and Development in Imaging, Nanotechnology, Industrial Design and Robotics* Las Palmas de Gran Canaria (Spain) 2019. **Publications** *International Scientific Journal of the AInCI and ALAIPO*.

Members Chapters in 28 countries and territories:

Argentina, Australia, Brazil, Canada, China, Costa Rica, Ecuador, Greece, India, Indonesia, Ireland, Italy, Jamaica, Japan, Korea Rep, Malta, Netherlands, Poland, Puerto Rico, Russia, Slovenia, Spain, Taiwan, Thailand, Türkiye, UK, USA, Venezuela.

NGO Relations *Asociación Latina Interacción Persona-Ordenador (ALAIPO, #02174)*. [2019/XM7670/**C**]

- ♦ Asociación Internacional de Constructores de Material Rodante (inactive)
- ♦ Asociación Internacional contra los Experimentos Dolorosos en Animales (#11694)
- ♦ Asociación Internacional contra la Fibrosis Quistica / Mucoviscidosis / (inactive)
- ♦ Asociación Internacional contra la Tortura (no recent information)
- ♦ Asociación Internacional de Coordinación del Transporte de Carga (inactive)

- ♦ Asociación Internacional de Correccionales y Prisiones para el Avance de Profesionales de las Correcciones (#12970)
- ♦ Asociación Internacional de Correccionales y Prisiones para el Avance de Profesionales de las Correcciones: Centro para el Intercambio de Mejores Practicas de las Correccionales / see International Corrections and Prisons Association for the Advancement of Professional Corrections (#12970)
- ♦ Asociación Internacional de Corredores de Fondo Veteranos (inactive)
- ♦ Asociación Internacional de Criadores de Aves Silvestres / see Aviornis International (#03048)
- ♦ Asociación Internacional de Criticos de Arte (#02680)
- ♦ Asociación Internacional de Criticos Literarios / see Association internationale de la critique littéraire (#02679)
- ♦ Asociación Internacional Datos para el Desarrollo (inactive)
- ♦ Asociación Internacional para la Defensa de las Lenguas y Culturas Amenazadas / see Association pour les Langues et Cultures Européennes Menacées (#02782)
- ♦ Asociación Internacional para la Defensa de la Libertad Religiosa (#02681)
- ♦ Asociación Internacional de Deportes para Ciegos / see International Blind Sports Federation (#12363)
- ♦ Asociación Internacional de Derecho de Aguas (#12263)
- ♦ Asociación Internacional de Derecho Deportivo (#12180)
- ♦ Asociación Internacional por el Derecho del Niño a Jugar (#14604)
- ♦ Asociación Internacional de Derecho Penal (#12074)
- ♦ Asociación Internacional de Derecho Procesal (#12102)
- ♦ Asociación Internacional de Derecho de Seguros (#02684)
- ♦ Asociación Internacional para el Desarrollo de los Intercambios Comerciales (inactive)
- ♦ Asociación Internacional para el Desarrollo Organizacional (#14444)
- ♦ Asociación Internacional de Desarrollo Rural (inactive)
- ♦ Asociación Internacional para el Desarrollo Urbano (#15832)
- ♦ Asociación Internacional de Documentalistas y Especialistas en Información (inactive)
- ♦ Asociación Internacional de Drama/Teatro y Educación (#13198)
- ♦ Asociación Internacional de Ecologia (#11856)
- ♦ Asociación Internacional de Economia (#13222)
- ♦ Asociación Internacional de Economia Alimentaria y Agroindustrial (inactive)
- ♦ Asociación Internacional para la Economía Feminista (#11889)
- ♦ Asociación Internacional de Economistas Agricolas (#11695)
- ♦ Asociación Internacional para Educación Cognoscitiva / see International Association for Cognitive Education and Psychology (#11782)
- ♦ Asociación Internacional de Educación de la Comunidad (inactive)
- ♦ Asociación Internacional de Educación Fisica y Deportes para la Joven y la Mujer (#12081)
- ♦ Asociación Internacional de Educación Infantil / see Childhood Education International
- ♦ Asociación Internacional de Educadores de Jóvenes Inadaptados / see International Association of Social Educators (#12167)
- ♦ Asociación Internacional de Educadores para la Paz (internationally oriented national body)
- ♦ Asociación Internacional de Educadores para la Paz Mundial (internationally oriented national body)
- ♦ Asociación Internacional de Educadores Sociales (#12167)
- ♦ Asociación Internacional de Empresarios de Electricidad / see EuropeOn (#09166)
- ♦ Asociación Internacional para la Energia del Hidrógeno (#11951)
- ♦ Asociación Internacional para la Enseñanza de Conducción y de Educación (inactive)
- ♦ Asociación Internacional de Epidemiologia (#13287)
- ♦ Asociación Internacional de Epigrafia Griega y Latina (#11924)
- ♦ Asociación Internacional de Ergonomia (#13294)
- ♦ Asociación Internacional de Escritores Policiacos (#11825)
- ♦ Asociación Internacional de Escuelas de Cine y Televisión / see International Association of Cinema, Audiovisual and Media Schools (#11771)
- ♦ Asociación Internacional de Escuelas Cristianas (#02430)
- ♦ Asociación Internacional de Escuelas e Institutos de Administración (#12147)
- ♦ Asociación Internacional de Escuelas de Negocios Jesuitas (#11974)
- ♦ Asociación Internacional de las Escuelas Superioras de Educación Fisica y Deporte (#02685)
- ♦ Asociación Internacional de Escuelas de Trabajo Social (#12149)
- ♦ Asociación Internacional de Escuelas de Vela (#14777)
- ♦ Asociación Internacional de Especialistas de Información Agricola (inactive)
- ♦ Asociación Internacional de Establecimientos Públicos de Crédito Pignoraticio (inactive)
- ♦ Asociación Internacional de Estructuras Laminares y Espaciales (#12162)
- ♦ Asociación Internacional de Estudiantes de Agricultura / see International Association of Students in Agricultural and Related Sciences (#12191)
- ♦ Asociación Internacional de Estudiantes de Lingüistica (#12002)
- ♦ Asociación Internacional para el Estudio Cientifico del Deficiencia Intelectual / see International Association for the Scientific Study of Intellectual and Developmental Disabilities (#12153)
- ♦ Asociación Internacional para el Estudio Cientifico de la Deficiencia Mental / see International Association for the Scientific Study of Intellectual and Developmental Disabilities (#12153)
- ♦ Asociación Internacional para el Estudio de la Economia del Seguro / see Geneva Association (#10119)
- ♦ Asociación Internacional para el Estudio del Higado (#12203)
- ♦ Asociación Internacional de Estudio Integral del Deporte (inactive)
- ♦ Asociación Internacional de Estudios del Discurso (#11850)
- ♦ Asociación Internacional de Estudios del Sur-Este Europeo (#02693)

♦ Asociación Internacional de Estudios Galegos (AIEG) 02164

International Association of Galician Studies

Main Office Consello da Cultura Galega, Pazo de Raxoi, 2o andar, 15705 Santiago de Compostela, La Coruña, Spain. T. +34986812342. Fax +34986812380. E-mail: estudosgalegos@gmail.com.
URL: http://www.estudosgalegos.org/

History 1985, Orono ME (USA). **Aims** Coordinate Galician studies on a worldwide basis. **Structure** Executive Committee, comprising President, Vice-President, Secretary, Institutional Relations Officer, Treasurer and 4 members. **Languages** English, Galician, Portuguese, Spanish. **Staff** 9.00 FTE, voluntary. **Finance** Members' dues. Public financing. **Activities** Multi- and inter-disciplinary coverage of fields. Organizes triennial conference. **Events** *Congress* Warsaw (Poland) 2022, *Triennial Congress* Madrid (Spain) 2018, *Triennial Congress* Buenos Aires (Argentina) 2015, *Triennial Congress* Cardiff (UK) 2012, *Triennial congress* Santiago de Compostela (Spain) / Vigo (Spain) 2009. **Publications** *Revista Internacional de Estudos Galegos* (annual) – journal. Congress proceedings.
Members Individuals and one organization in 17 countries:
Argentina, Australia, Austria, Brazil, Cuba, France, Germany, Italy, Mexico, Poland, Portugal, Romania, Russia, Spain, UK, USA, Venezuela. [2012/XD8916/**D**]

- ♦ Asociación Internacional de Estudios Latinoamericanos y del Caribe / see Federación Internacional de Estudios sobre América Latina y el Caribe (#09338)
- ♦ Asociación Internacional por los Estudios sobre la Mecanografia (inactive)
- ♦ Asociación Internacional de Estudios Médicos-Psicológicos y Religiosos (#12028)
- ♦ Asociación Internacional de Estudios de la Misión (#12032)
- ♦ Asociación Internacional de Estudios de Otto Gross (#12060)
- ♦ Asociación Internacional de Etica del Desarrollo (#13157)
- ♦ Asociación Internacional 'Europa 2000' (inactive)
- ♦ Asociación Internacional de Exorcistas (internationally oriented national body)
- ♦ Asociación Internacional de Expertos Cientificos del Turismo (#02697)
- ♦ Asociación Internacional de Expertos Filatélicos (#02696)
- ♦ Asociación Internacional de Fabricantes de Confiteria (inactive)
- ♦ Asociación Internacional de Fabricantes de Harina de Pescado / see The Marine Ingredients Organisation (#16579)
- ♦ Asociación Internacional de Fabricantes de Impermeables (inactive)
- ♦ Asociación Internacional de Ferias de América (#11886)
- ♦ Asociación Internacional Fibrodisplasia Osificante Progresiva (internationally oriented national body)
- ♦ Asociación Internacional de Fomento (#13155)
- ♦ Asociación Internacional de Geodesia (#11914)
- ♦ Asociación Internacional de Gerontologia / see International Association of Gerontology and Geriatrics (#11920)
- ♦ Asociación Internacional de Hidatidologia (#11949)
- ♦ Asociación Internacional de Higiene, Medicina Preventiva y Social (inactive)

♦ Asociación Internacional de Hispanistas (AIH) 02165

International Association of Hispanists – Association internationale des hispanistes

Pres Hebrew Univ, Dept of Spanish and Latin American Studies, Mt Scopus Campus, 9190501 Jerusalem, Israel. T. +97225883830.
SG Univ of Texas at Austin, Dept Spanish and Portuguese, 150 W 21st Street, Austin TX 78712-1155, USA.
URL: https://asociacioninternacionaldehispanistas.org/

History Sep 1962, Oxford (UK). Statutes adopted 1965; amended 1992, 1998, 2015. **Aims** Study Hispanic *literature*, *language*, linguistics, history and culture; promote Hispanic studies in all countries. **Structure** General Assembly (at Triennial Conference); Executive Committee; Honorary Presidents (9). **Languages** Spanish. **Staff** Voluntary. **Finance** Sources: grants; members' dues. Supported by: Fundación Duques de Soria (Madrid); *UNESCO (#20322)*. **Activities** Events/meetings. **Events** *Triennial Congress* Neuchâtel (Switzerland) 2023, *Triennial Congress* Jerusalem (Israel) 2019, *Triennial Congress* Münster (Germany) 2016, *Triennial Congress* Buenos Aires (Argentina) 2013, *Triennial Congress* Rome (Italy) 2010. **Publications** Conference proceedings. **Members** Individuals. Membership countries not specified. [2022.06.29/XC3857/v/**C**]

- ♦ Asociación Internacional de Historia y Civilización del Azúcar (internationally oriented national body)
- ♦ Asociación Internacional de Historia Oral (#14417)
- ♦ Asociación Internacional para la Historia de las Religiones (#11936)
- ♦ Asociación Internacional de Hosteleria / see International Hotel and Restaurant Association (#13813)
- ♦ Asociación Internacional de la Industria de los Fertilizantes / see International Fertilizer Association (#13589)
- ♦ Asociación Internacional de las Industrias de Preimpresión (inactive)
- ♦ Asociación Internacional de Información Escolar Universitaria y Profesional (inactive)
- ♦ Asociación Internacional de Informatica Médica para Latino América y Caribe (#14135)
- ♦ Asociación Internacional de la Inspección de Trabajo (#11983)
- ♦ Asociación Internacional para Instalaciones Deportivas y Recreativas (#13319)
- ♦ Asociación Internacional de Intercambio de Estudiantes para favorecer su Experiencia Técnica (#11885)
- ♦ Asociación Internacional de Intérpretes de Conferencias (#11807)
- ♦ Asociación Internacional de los Inversores en la Economia Social (#11971)
- ♦ Asociación Internacional de Investigación sobre la Comunicación Social (#12022)
- ♦ Asociación Internacional de Investigaciones Hidraulicas / see International Association for Hydro-Environment Engineering and Research (#11950)
- ♦ Asociación Internacional de Investigaciones Psicotrónicas (no recent information)
- ♦ Asociación Internacional de Investigaciones sobre Rentas y Riqueza (#12134)
- ♦ Asociación Internacional de Investigación de Literatura Infantil y Juvenil (#14742)
- ♦ Asociación Internacional de Investigación para la Paz (#14537)
- ♦ Asociación Internacional de Jefes de Policia (#11765)
- ♦ Asociación Internacional de Jóvenes Abogados (#12282)
- ♦ Asociación Internacional de Jóvenes Investigadores en Comunicación (internationally oriented national body)
- ♦ Asociación Internacional de Juristas Demócratas (#11837)
- ♦ Asociación Internacional Juventud Idente (internationally oriented national body)
- ♦ Asociación Internacional de Lectores de la Biblia (#12337)
- ♦ Asociación Internacional de Lectura / see International Literacy Association (#14057)
- ♦ Asociación Internacional de la Lepra (#14029)
- ♦ Asociación Internacional de Lesbianas y Gays / see ILGA World (#11120)

♦ Asociación Internacional de Lesbianas, Gays, Bisexuales, Trans e Intersex para América Latina y el Caribe (ILGALAC) 02166

Exec Dir Av Córdoba 4123, piso1, C1188AAH Buenos Aires, Argentina. T. +541148643716. E-mail: info@ilga-lac.org.
URL: https://www.ilga-lac.org/

History A regional structure of *ILGA World (International Lesbian, Gay, Bisexual, Trans and Intersex Association, #11120)*. **Structure** Regional Conference; Regional Council. **Languages** French, Portuguese, Spanish. **Staff** 8.00 FTE, paid; 2.00 FTE, voluntary. **Activities** Active in: Argentina, Bolivia, Brazil, Chile, Colombia, Costa Rica, Cuba, Dominican Rep, Ecuador, El Salvador, Guadeloupe, Guatemala, Guiana Fr, Haiti, Honduras, Martinique, Mexico, Nicaragua, Panama, Paraguay, Peru, Puerto Rico, Uruguay, Venezuela. **Events** *Regional Conference* La Paz (Bolivia) 2022, *Regional Conference* Bogota (Colombia) 2019, *Regional Conference* Guatemala (Guatemala) 2017, *Regional Conference* Havana (Cuba) / Varadero (Cuba) 2014, *Regional Conference* Curitiba (Brazil) 2010. **NGO Relations** Member of (2): Mira que te miro; *Red Iberoamericana de Organismos y Organizaciones contra la Discriminación (RIOOD, #18678)*. [2020.12.13/AA1247/**E**]

- ♦ **Asociación Internacional de Lesbianas, Gays, Bisexuales, Trans e Intersex** ILGA Mundo (#11120)
- ♦ Asociación Internacional para la Libertad de Religión (#12130)
- ♦ Asociación Internacional de Libre Pensamiento (#11906)
- ♦ Asociación Internacional de Limnologia Teórica y Aplicada / see International Society of Limnology (#15232)
- ♦ Asociación Internacional de Literatura y Cine Españoles Siglo XXI (internationally oriented national body)
- ♦ Asociación Internacional de Literature Comparada, la Sociedad y Cultura (#11796)
- ♦ Asociación Internacional de Logopedia y Foniatria / see International Association of Logopedics and Phoniatrics (#12005)
- ♦ Asociación Internacional de las Loterias de Estado (inactive)
- ♦ Asociación Internacional de Ludotecas (#15699)
- ♦ Asociación Internacional del Lupino / see International Lupin Association (#14068)
- ♦ Asociación Internacional de Magistrados de la Juventud y de la Familia (#12283)
- ♦ Asociación Internacional de Marketing de Periódicos (#14363)
- ♦ Asociación Internacional de Masaje Infantil (#11962)
- ♦ Asociación Internacional por los Medicamentos Cannabinoides (#11754)
- ♦ Asociación Internacional de Medicina de Accidentes y del Trafico / see International Traffic Medicine Association (#15713)
- ♦ Asociación Internacional de Medicina del Trafico (#15713)
- ♦ Asociación Internacional de Médicos Católicos / see International Federation of Catholic Medical Associations (#13378)
- ♦ Asociación Internacional de Médicos para la Prevención de la Guerra Nuclear (#14578)
- ♦ Asociación Internacional de Mercados Mayoristas dentro del Marco de Actividades de la IULA / see World Union of Wholesale Markets (#21889)
- ♦ Asociación Internacional de Mercadotecnia Social (inactive)
- ♦ Asociación Internacional Micológica (#14203)
- ♦ Asociación internacional de misionólogos católicos (#11760)
- ♦ Asociación Internacional de Mitocritica (internationally oriented national body)
- ♦ Asociación Internacional de los Movimientos Familiares de Formación Rural (#02719)
- ♦ Asociación Internacional Mujeres en las Artes (internationally oriented national body)
- ♦ Asociación Internacional de Mujeres Jueces (#12267)
- ♦ Asociación Internacional de Mujeres de Radio y Televisión (#12271)

- Asociación Internacional de Museos de Transportes y Comunicaciones (#12237)
- Asociación Internacional de Navateros, Almadieros y Gancheros (#15691)
- Asociación Internacional de Navegación / see PIANC (#18371)
- Asociación Internacional de Navieros (inactive)
- Asociación Internacional de Noticiarios Cinematograficos (no recent information)
- Asociación Internacional de Numismaticos Profesionales (#12104)
- Asociación Internacional de Organismos y Ciudades de Congresos de los Paises Interesados en el Mediterraneo (inactive)

♦ Asociación Internacional de Organismos de Supervisión de Fondos de Pensiones (AIOS) 02167

International Relations Officer Av Libertador Bernardo O'Higgins 1449 – Tower 2 – Flat 15, 8340518 Santiago, Santiago Metropolitan, Chile. T. +562227530157. E-mail: aios@aiosfp.org.
Pres Los Laureles 214, San Isidro, Lima, Peru.
URL: http://www.aiosfp.org/

History 1996. **Aims** Highlight the role of pension systems based on individual savings; strengthen communication between supervisors of pension funds; facilitate exchange of information (legislation, operating systems, control methods, procedures and practices of supervision and penalty system) as well as experiences in the field of pensions. **Structure** General Assembly; Board. **Languages** Spanish. **Staff** None. **Finance** Members' dues. **Activities** Knowledge management/information dissemination; networking/liaising; events/meetings. **Events** *General Assembly* Dominican Rep 2014, *General Assembly* Mexico City (Mexico) 2013, *General Assembly* San Salvador (El Salvador) 2012, *General Assembly* Mexico City (Mexico) 2011, *General Assembly* Lima (Peru) 2010.
Members (10) in 9 countries:
Chile, Colombia, Costa Rica, Dominican Rep, El Salvador, Mexico, Panama, Peru, Uruguay.
IGO Relations *Inter-American Development Bank (IDB, #11427).* **NGO Relations** Cooperates with: *Asociación de Supervisores de Seguros de América Latina (ASSAL, #02300); International Organisation of Pension Supervisors (IOPS, #14432).* [2020.03.03/XM1681/**D**]

- Asociación Internacional de Organizaciones Comerciales para un Mundo en Desarrollo (inactive)
- Asociación Internacional para la Orientación Educativa y Profesional (#11862)
- Asociación Internacional de Papirólogos (#02725)
- Asociación Internacional de Parlamentarios de Lengua Francesa / see Assemblée parlementaire de la Francophonie (#02312)
- Asociación Internacional de Parques Tecnológicos / see International Association of Science Parks and Areas of Innovation (#12151)
- Asociación Internacional de Pediatria (#14541)
- Asociación Internacional de la Pelicula Cientifica (inactive)
- Asociación Internacional de Periodistas Deportivos (#02729)
- Asociación Internacional Permanente de los Congresos de Carreteras / see World Road Association (#21754)
- Asociación Internacional Permanente de los Congresos de Navegación / see PIANC (#18371)
- Asociación Internacional de Pesca Deportiva (internationally oriented national body)
- Asociación Internacional de Policia (#14612)
- Asociación Internacional de Policia de Puertos y Aeropuertos / see InterPortPolice (#15963)
- Asociación Internacional de Politicas de Salud (#11930)
- Asociación Internacional de la Prensa Ajadrecistica (inactive)
- Asociación Internacional de la Prensa Médica (inactive)
- Asociación Internacional de Presupuesto Público (#18564)
- Asociación Internacional para la Prevención del Suicido / see International Association for Suicide Prevention and Crisis Intervention (#12213)

♦ Asociación Internacional de Prisiones y Correcciones Capitulo Latinoamericano (ICPALA) 02168

Address not obtained.
URL: http://www.icpala.com/

History 2011, Mexico City (Mexico). Set up as the Latin American chapter of *International Corrections and Prisons Association for the Advancement of Professional Corrections (ICPA, #12970).* **Aims** Develop the penitentiary function; reassess its contribution to public safety and the delivery of justice, with professional, ethical, efficient and effective prison systems, and respect for *human rights.* **Activities** Events/meetings. [2018/XM6536/**D**]

- Asociación Internacional de Productores Cinematograficos Independientes (no recent information)
- Asociación Internacional de Productores Horticolas (#11940)
- Asociación Internacional de Productores Independientes del Mediterraneo (#02731)
- Asociación Internacional de Profesionales Administrativos (internationally oriented national body)

♦ Asociación Internacional de Profesionales de Puertos y Costas (AIPPYC) 02169

Pres Av del Libertador 4510 PB, 1426 Buenos Aires, Argentina. T. +541147790369. E-mail: administracion@aippyc.org.
URL: http://www.aippyc.org/

Structure Consultative Council; Executive Commission; Techncial Commissions. **Events** *Conference on coasts, marine structures and breakwaters* Edinburgh (UK) 2009. **IGO Relations** *Inter-American Committee on Ports (#11415).* [2011/XJ3497/**D**]

- Asociación Internacional de Profesionales de la Traducción y la Interpretación (#12106)
- Asociación Internacional de Profesores y Conferenciantes Universitarios (#12250)
- Asociación Internacional de los Profesores de Inglés de la Universidades / see International Association of University Professors of English (#12249)
- Asociación Internacional de los Profesores de Italiano (#02989)
- Asociación Internacional de Profesores de Yoga Solar (internationally oriented national body)
- Asociación Internacional para el Progreso de la Enseñanza y de la Investigación de la Propiedad Intelectual (#11690)
- Asociación Internacional para el Progreso Social (inactive)
- Asociación Internacional para la Promoción de la Farmacologia Experimental y Clinica (inactive)
- Asociación Internacional de Promoción y Protección de Inversiones Privadas Extranjeras (inactive)
- Asociación Internacional de Propietarios Independientes de Buques Cisterna (#11959)
- Asociación Internacional para la Protección de la Propiedad Industrial / see International Association for the Protection of Intellectual Property (#12112)
- Asociación Internacional de Proveedores de Efectos Navales (#14850)
- Asociación Internacional de Psicoanalisis de Pareja y Familia (#11822)
- Asociación Internacional de Psicologia Analitica (#11700)
- Asociación Internacional de Psiquiatria Infantil y Profesiones Afines (#11766)
- Asociación Internacional de Publicidad (#11590)
- Asociación Internacional de los Puertos (#12096)
- Asociación Internacional de Quimica de los Cereales / see ICC – International Association for Cereal Science and Technology (#11048)
- Asociación Internacional de Radiodifusión (#11738)
- Asociación Internacional de Recursos Hidricos (#15871)
- Asociación Internacional de Registros del Cancer (#11753)
- Asociación Internacional Reina Elena (#02740)
- Asociación Internacional de Relaciones Públicas (#14671)
- Asociación Internacional de Relaciones de Trabajo / see International Labour and Employment Relations Association (#13997)
- Asociación Internacional Rural Católica (#12461)
- Asociación Internacional de la Seda (inactive)
- Asociación Internacional de Sedimentólogos (#12155)
- Asociación Internacional de la Seguridad Social (#14885)
- Asociación Internacional del Seguro de Defensa Juridica / see Legal Protection International (#16440)
- Asociación Internacional de Sémiotica (#12160)
- Asociación Internacional de Semiótica Visual (#12258)
- Asociación Internacional de Señalización Maritima (#12013)
- Asociación Internacional para la Sintesis del Conocimiento (no recent information)
- Asociación Internacional de Sistemas Agricolas (#13332)
- Asociación Internacional de Sociedades de Seguro Mutuo (inactive)
- Asociación Internacional de Sociologia (#15553)
- Asociación Internacional Soroptimista / see Soroptimist International (#19686)
- Asociación Internacional para la Supervisión Civil del Cumplimiento de la Ley (inactive)
- Asociación Internacional para la Taxonomia Vegetal (#12092)
- Asociación Internacional del Teatro de Arte (#11647)
- Asociación Internacional Teatro y Educación / see International Drama/Theatre and Education Association (#13198)
- Asociación Internacional de Teatro Universitario (#15831)
- Asociación Internacional de Técnicos, Expertos e Investigadores (#02745)
- Asociación Internacional de Técnicos de Laboratorios Médicos / see International Federation of Biomedical Laboratory Science (#13372)
- Asociación Internacional de los Trabajadores (#15906)
- Asociación Internacional para el Trabajo Social con Grupos (unconfirmed)
- Asociación Internacional de los Traductores de Conferencia (#02748)
- Asociación Internacional de Transporte Aéreo Latinoamericano / see Latin American and Caribbean Air Transport Association (#16263)
- Asociación Internacional Trapense (#15727)
- Asociación Internacional de Tubos (#15741)
- Asociación Internacional de Universidades (#12246)
- Asociación Internacional de Universidades La Salle (#12142)
- Asociación Internacional de las Universidades de la Tercera Edad (#02749)
- Asociación Internacional de Urbanistas (#15012)
- Asociación Internacional de Usuarios de Ramales Privados / see Cargo Rail Europe (#03431)
- Asociación Internacional Veterinaria de Producción Animal (inactive)
- Asociación Internacional para el Video en las Artes y la Cultura (inactive)
- Asociación Internacional de Webmasters (#15874)
- Asociación Internacional de Yogaterapia (no recent information)
- Asociación de Investigación y Especialización sobre Temas Iberoamericanos (internationally oriented national body)
- Asociación de Investigación por la Paz Gernika Gogoratuz / see Gernika Gogoratuz – Peace Research Center
- Asociación de Investigación Turistica (internationally oriented national body)
- Asociación Japonesa de Estudios Latinoamericanos (internationally oriented national body)

♦ Asociación de Jóvenes Doctores en Hispanismo (Asociación BETA) 02170

Contact Seminar B9, 122 Fac de Lletres, Univ Autònoma de Barcelona CAMPUS DE LA UAB, 08193 Bellaterra, Barcelona, Spain. E-mail: contacto@asociacionbeta.com.
URL: http://asociacionbeta.com/

History Dec 2009, Spain. **Aims** Promote Hispanic studies. **Structure** Board of Directors. **Activities** Awards/prizes/competitions; events/meetings; networking/liaising; training/education. **Events** *BETA International Congress* Barcelona (Spain) 2021, *BETA International Congress* La Laguna (Spain) 2020, *BETA International Congress* Barcelona (Spain) 2019, *BETA International Congress* Naples (Italy) 2018, *BETA International Congress* Santander (Spain) 2017. **Members** Individuals. Membership countries not specified. [2020/AA0635/v/**E**]

- Asociación de Jóvenes Funcionarios Europeos (#02772)
- Asociación de Jóvenes Investigadores de la Literatura Hispánica (internationally oriented national body)
- Asociación de Jóvenes Nucleares Latinoamericanos (unconfirmed)
- Asociación de los Juecez y Fiscales de la Union Europea (#07614)
- Asociación jurista esperantista (no recent information)
- Asociación de Laboratorios Marinos del Caribe (#02794)

♦ Asociación Latina para el Analisis de los Sistemas de Salud (ALASS) 02171

Association latine pour l'analyse des systèmes de santé – Associazione Latina per l'Analisi dei Sistemi Sanitari – Associação Latina para a Analise dos Sistemas de Saúde – Asocatia Latinâ pentru Analiza Sistemor de Sânàtate – Associació Llatina per a l'Anàlisi dels Sistemes de Salut
Sec Marc Aureli 5, Loc 3, 08006 Barcelona, Spain. T. +34932014461. Fax +34932023317. E-mail: alass@alass.org.
URL: http://www.alass.org/

History Founded 28 Jan 1989, Lugano (Switzerland). **Aims** Promote exchange and development of joint research and training of researchers in the field of health *systems analysis* in Latin countries. **Structure** Committee of 23 members. **Languages** Catalan, French, Italian, Portuguese, Romanian, Spanish. **Staff** 1.00 FTE, paid. **Finance** Members' dues. Annual budget: euro 35,000. **Activities** Events/meetings; training/education. **Events** *Cultures et transformation des systèmes de santé* Montréal, QC (Canada) 2019, *Congress* Lyon (France) 2018, *Congress* Liège (Belgium) 2017, *Congress* Brasilia (Brazil) 2016, *Congress* Ancona (Italy) 2015. **Publications** *PALASS* – scientific collection. Acts of Congress.
Members Individuals in 18 countries:
Belgium, Brazil, Canada, Chile, Colombia, France, Italy, Lebanon, Luxembourg, Mexico, Moldova, Morocco, Portugal, Romania, Spain, Switzerland, Tunisia, UK.
Collaborating national institutions in 10 countries and territories:
Belgium, Brazil, Canada, France, Italy, Luxembourg, Mexico, Moldova, Romania, Switzerland. [2020/XD6792/**D**]

♦ Asociación Latina de Filosofía del Deporte (ALFiD) 02172

Sec address not obtained. E-mail: alfid.info@gmail.com.
URL: https://asociacionlatinafild.wixsite.com/alfid-website

History Nov 2013. Registration: Spain. **Structure** General Assembly; Board of Directors. **Activities** Events/meetings. **Events** *Congress* Barcelona (Spain) 2020, *Congress* Porto (Portugal) 2016. [2022.03.04/AA1738/**D**]

♦ Asociación Latina e Ibérica Contra el Cancer (ALICC) 02173

Pres Liga Argentina de Lucha Contra el Cancer, Araoz 2380, 1425 Buenos Aires, Argentina. T. +541148341551. E-mail: info@lalcec.org.ar.
URL: http://www.alicc.org/

History 29 Mar 1993, Cartagena de Indias (Colombia), as *Asociación de Ligas Iberoamericanas de Lucha contra el Cancer.* Subsequently changed name to *Asociación de Ligas Iberoamericanas contra el Cancer.* Present name adopted 2016. **Aims** Address the problems of cancer in Spanish-speaking countries. **Structure** General Assembly. **Languages** English, Spanish.
Members National associations in 13 countries:
Argentina, Colombia, Cuba, Dominican Rep, Ecuador, El Salvador, Guatemala, Honduras, Mexico, Panama, Peru, Spain, Venezuela.
NGO Relations Cooperates with: COPES Programme of *Union for International Cancer Control (UICC, #20415).* [2017.06.01/XD9441/**D**]

♦ Asociación Latina Interacción Persona-Ordenador (ALAIPO) 02174

Main Office c/ Angel Baixeras 5, AP 1638, 08080 Barcelona, Spain. E-mail: info@alaipo.com.
URL: http://www.alaipo.com/

History 1997. **Aims** Research and promote results achieved in the HCI – Human-*Computer* Interaction – framework. **Activities** Events/meetings. **Events** *International Conference on Multimedia, Scientific Information and Visualization for Information Systems and Metrics* Las Palmas de Gran Canaria (Spain) 2020, *International Symposium on Communicability, Computer Graphics and Innovative Design for Interactive Systems* Madrid (Spain) 2020, *International Conference on Software and Emerging Technologies for Education, Culture, Entertainment, and Commerce* Venice (Italy) 2020, *International Conference on Advances in New Technologies, Interactive Interfaces and Communicability* Córdoba (Argentina) 2019, *International Conference on Research and Development in Imaging, Nanotechnology, Industrial Design and Robotics* Las Palmas de Gran Canaria (Spain) 2019. **Publications** *International Scientific Journal of the AInCI and ALAIPO.*
Members Chapters in 27 countries and territories:
Argentina, Belgium, Brazil, Canada, China, Costa Rica, Ecuador, India, Indonesia, Ireland, Italy, Jamaica, Japan, Korea Rep, Malta, Mexico, Netherlands, Puerto Rico, Russia, Slovenia, Spain, Taiwan, Türkiye, UK, Uruguay, USA, Venezuela.
NGO Relations *Asociación Internacional de la Comunicación Interactiva (AInCI, #02163).* [2022/XM7669/**C**]

♦ Asociación de Latinoamérica y del Caribe de Economia Agricola (no recent information)
♦ Asociación Latinoamericana de Abogados Laboralistas (unconfirmed)

♦ Asociación Latinoamericana de Academias Nacionales de Medicina (ALANAM) 02175

Association latinoaméricaine des académies nationales de médecine – Latin American Association of National Academies of Medicine

Exec Sec c/o UNAL, Carrera 45 No 26-85, Edif Uriel Gutiérrez, Bogota, Bogota DC, Colombia.
URL: http://redalanam.com/

History 1967, Bogota. **Aims** Promote mutual scientific and technical collaboration of national academies of medicine in Latin American countries and encourage their cooperation for the promotion of public health and social welfare; foster the exchange of publications and academic work; seek joint measures in benefit of medical education, scientific research and public health and well-being. **Structure** Board of Directors comprises presidents of member academies, among whom Chairmanship rotates. Honorary President, Permanent Secretary and Assistant Secretary. Secretariat in Bogota. **Languages** Portuguese, Spanish. **Staff** Voluntary. **Finance** Members' contributions. **Activities** Coordinates activities of medical academies which have legal status as consultative bodies for governments of Latin American countries; organizes preparatory meetings of experts present papers on specific problems of public health and medical and allied sciences, which are submitted to the Board of Directors who use them to produce final documents and recommendations for governments. **Events** *Congress / Reunión de las Academias Latinoamericanas Nacionales de Medicina* Quito (Ecuador) 2001, *Meeting* Quito (Ecuador) 2001, *Reunión de las Academias Latinoamericanas Nacionales de Medicina* Rio de Janeiro (Brazil) 1999, *Reunión de las Academias Latinoamericanas Nacionales de Medicina* Madrid (Spain) 1997, *Meeting of Executive Board* Quito (Ecuador) 1995. **Publications** *Boletin Informativo de ALANAM* (4 a year). Reports of meetings.
Members National academies of medicine in 11 countries:
Argentina, Bolivia, Brazil, Chile, Colombia, Ecuador, Mexico, Paraguay, Peru, Uruguay, Venezuela.
Honorary members national academies of medicine in 2 countries:
Portugal, Spain. [2018/XD4637/**D**]

♦ Asociación Latinoamericana del Acero (Alacero) 02176

Latin American Steel Association

Contact Al Santos 2300 conj 62, Cerqueira César, Sao Paulo SP, Brazil. T. +551131955802.
URL: http://www.alacero.org/

History Founded 3 Oct 1959, Santiago (Chile), as *Latin American Iron and Steel Institute – Institut Latinoaméricain du Fer et de l'Acier – Instituto Latinoamericano del Fierro y el Acero (ILAFA) – Instituto Latinoamericano de Ferro e Aço.* Registered under Chilean law. **Aims** Study the scientific, technical, industrial and economic problems connected with the production, marketing and use of steel products and by-products, steelmaking plants, raw materials and other inputs. **Structure** General Assembly (annual); Board of Directors; Executive Committee; General Secretariat, headed by Secretary General; Regional Secretariats (6). **Languages** English, Portuguese, Spanish. **Finance** Members' dues. **Activities** Knowledge management/ information dissemination; standards/guidelines; training/education; guidance/assistance/consulting. **Events** *Annual Latin American Iron and Steel Congress* Santiago (Chile) 2012, *Annual Latin American iron and steel congress* Rio de Janeiro (Brazil) 2011, *Annual Latin American iron and steel congress* Buenos Aires (Argentina) 2010, *Annual Latin American iron and steel congress* Quito (Ecuador) 2009, *Annual Latin American iron and steel congress* Cancún (Mexico) 2008. **Publications** *Acero Latinoamericano* (6 a year) in Spanish – magazine; *Monthly Newsletter and Statistical Bulletin.* Bulletins; Yearbooks; Directory. Technical books; electronic manuals.
Members Active Latin American companies producing steel, iron ore, raw materials or auxiliary equipment for the steelmaking and iron ore mining industry and national bodies within the area, grouping the steelmakers of their respective countries; Associate research institutions, universities and companies in the region or outside it, whose activities enable them to cooperate with the Institute objectives; Honorary. Members in 21 countries:
Argentina, Austria, Belgium, Brazil, Chile, Colombia, Costa Rica, Cuba, Dominican Rep, Ecuador, Germany, Italy, Korea Rep, Mexico, Paraguay, Peru, Russia, Switzerland, Uruguay, USA, Venezuela.
Consultative Status Consultative status granted from: *UNIDO (#20336); UNCTAD (#20285)* (General Category). **IGO Relations** Accredited by: *United Nations Office at Vienna (UNOV, #20604).* Participates in the work of: *United Nations Economic Commission for Europe (UNECE, #20555).* Associated with Department of Global Communications of the United Nations. [2020.03.04/XD2884/**D**]

♦ Asociación Latinoamericana de Acuicultura (ALA) 02177

Latin America Poultry Association

Contact c/o ABPA, Av Brigadeiro Faria Lima, 1912-20 Andar – cj 20L, Sao Paulo SP, 10452-001, Brazil. E-mail: abpa@abpa-br.org.

History Founded 1977. **Aims** Promote the scientific and technological research and the development and technological interchange in the poultry industry. **Structure** General Assembly (annual); Board of Directors of 6 officers and 2 members. **Languages** Spanish. **Staff** 4.00 FTE, paid. **Events** *Congress* El Salvador 2013, *Congress* Argentina 2011, *Congress* Havana (Cuba) 2009, *Congress* Porto Alegre (Brazil) 2007, *Congress* Panama (Panama) 2005. **Publications** *Boletin ALA Noticias CTC Informa; Boletin de Noticias ALA; ILH Newspaper; ILH Update.*
Members Full in 12 countries:
Argentina, Brazil, Chile, Colombia, Costa Rica, Cuba, Ecuador, Mexico, Peru, Uruguay, USA, Venezuela.
[2015.09.02/XD5489/**D**]

♦ Asociación Latinoamericana de Adiccionologia (unconfirmed)
♦ Asociación Latinoamericana de Administración Pública (inactive)

♦ Asociación Latinoamericana de Aféresis y Terapias celulares (ALAyTeC) 02178

Latin American Association for Apheresis and Cell Therapies

Pres Paraguay St 2302, Apt 5 FL 12, 1121 Buenos Aires, Argentina. T. +541149617344. Fax +541152391968.

History 1984, as *Latin American Hemapheresis Group – Grupo Latinoamericano de Hemaféresis (GLHEMA).* Present name adopted, 2009, during assembly held at WAA/ISFA congress in Buenos Aires (Argentina). **Aims** Promote *apheresis* procedures in *Latin America.* **Structure** Board, comprising President, Vice President, General Secretary, Treasurer. **Activities** Protocol Committee establishes practice guidelines. **Events** *Simposio latinoamericano de hemaféresis y medicina transfusional* Montevideo (Uruguay) 2001.
Members in 6 countries:
Argentina, Brazil, Paraguay, Peru, Uruguay, Venezuela.
NGO Relations Member of: *Grupo Cooperativo Iberoamericano de Medicina Transfusional (GCIAMT, #10801); World Apheresis Association (WAA, #21097).* [2011/XF3421/**F**]

♦ Asociación Latinoamericana de Agencias de Publicidad (#16235)
♦ Asociación Latinoamericana de Agrometeorologia (unconfirmed)

♦ Asociación Latinoamericana de Analisis y Modificación del Comportamiento (ALAMOC) 02179

Association latinoaméricaine de l'analyse et de la modification du comportement – Latin American Association of Analysis and Behavioural Modification

SG Depto de Psicologia Univ Andina, Urbanizacion Larapa Grande, San Jeronimo, Cusco, Peru. E-mail: alamoclatinoamerica@gmail.com.
URL: http://www.alamoc-web.org/

History 19 Feb 1975, Bogota (Colombia). **Aims** Promote, execute, diffuse, investigate, evaluate, accredit, analyse and reflect on the study of human behaviour. **Events** *Congreso Latinoamericano de Analisis, Modificación del Comportamiento y Terapia Cognitivo-Conductual (CLAMOC)* Panama (Panama) 2022, *Congreso Latinoamericano de Análisis, Modificación del Comportamiento y Terapia Cognitivo Conductual (CLAMOC)* Panama 2016, *Congreso Latinoamericano de Análisis, Modificación del Comportamiento y Terapia Cognitivo Conductual (CLAMOC)* Asunción (Paraguay) 2014, *World Congress of Behavioural and Cognitive Therapies* Lima (Peru) 2013, *Congreso Latinoamericano de Análisis, Modificación del Comportamiento y Terapia Cognitivo Conductual (CLAMOC)* Buenos Aires (Argentina) 2012. **Publications** Bulletin; review; books.
Members Full in 22 countries:
Argentina, Bolivia, Brazil, Chile, Colombia, Costa Rica, Cuba, Dominican Rep, Ecuador, El Salvador, Guatemala, Honduras, Mexico, Nicaragua, Panama, Paraguay, Peru, Puerto Rico, Spain, Uruguay, USA, Venezuela.
NGO Relations Member of (2): *Association for Behavior Analysis International (ABAI, #02395); World Confederation of Cognitive and Behavioural Therapies (WCCBT, #21292). European Association for Behavioural and Cognitive Therapies (EABCT, #05953).* [2021/XD1374/**D**]

♦ Asociación Latinoamericana de Analisis Transaccional (no recent information)
♦ Asociación Latinoamericana de Antropologia (#16234)

♦ Asociación Latinoamericana de Antropologia Biológica (ALAB) 02180

Latin American Association of Biological Anthropology

Pres Facultad de Filosofia – UBA, Puan 480, 1406 Buenos Aires, Argentina. E-mail: antbiol@filo.uba.ar.
Sec CIGEBA – UNLP, Casilla de Correo 296, La Plata, Argentina.

History 6 Nov 1989, Santiago (Chile). **Aims** Stimulate research and interchange in biological anthropology and other activities related to the progress of the science; defend professional interests of members; give impulses to education in biological anthropology; train professors and researchers. **Structure** Board of Directors, consisting of President, Vice-President, General Secretary, Treasurer and Past-President. **Languages** English, Portuguese, Spanish. **Staff** 6.00 FTE, paid. 6. **Finance** Members' dues. Other sources: sponsorships and collaborations of the host country of the congress. **Activities** Organizes biennial congress. **Events** *Biennial Congress* Havana (Cuba) 2014, *Biennial Congress / Congress* San José (Costa Rica) 2012, *Congress* Bogota (Colombia) 2010, *Biennial congress / Congress* La Plata (Argentina) 2008, *Biennial congress / Congress* Ouro Preto (Brazil) 2006. **Publications** *Magazine of Latin American Physical Anthropology.*
Members Full (325) in 16 countries:
Argentina, Australia, Brazil, Chile, Colombia, Costa Rica, Cuba, France, Italy, Mexico, Paraguay, Peru, Spain, Uruguay, USA, Venezuela.
NGO Relations Member of: *International Association of Human Biologists (IAHB, #11945).*
[2014/XD6993/**D**]

♦ Asociación Latinoamericana de Antropologia Forense (ALAF) 02181

Pres address not obtained. E-mail: omarbertoni@gmail.com.
Sec address not obtained. E-mail: nibya@yahoo.com.
URL: http://alafforense.org/

Structure Board of Directors, comprising President, Vice-President, Secretary, Treasurer, 2 members and Fiscal Editor. **Finance** Members' dues. **Events** *The challenge for Latin America* Caracas (Venezuela) 2013, *Congress* Antigua (Guatemala) 2012, *Congress* Ayacucho (Peru) 2011, *Congress* Manizales (Colombia) 2010, *Congress* Buenos Aires (Argentina) 2009.
Members Individuals in 8 countries:
Argentina, Colombia, Guatemala, Panama, Peru, Spain, Uruguay, Venezuela. [2016/XJ7218/**D**]

♦ Asociación Latinoamericana de Arbitraje (ALARB) 02182

Associação Latinoamericana de Arbitragem

Contact Calle 87 No 10-93, Oficina 302, Bogota 110231, Bogota DC, Colombia. T. +576017431005. E-mail: info@alarb.org – tesoreria@alarb.org.
URL: http://www.alarb.org/

History 2011, Bogota (Colombia). Registration: Colombia. **Structure** General Assembly; Board of Directors; Executive Committee. Working Committees. **Languages** English, Portuguese, Spanish. **Activities** Events/ meetings. Active in all member countries. **Publications** *Revista ALARB.* [2021.12.01/XM6483/**D**]

♦ Asociación Latinoamericana de Archivos (ALA) 02183

Latin American Association on Archives – Association latinoaméricaine des archives

Contact Archivo General de la Nación – México, Av Ing Eduardo Molina 113, Colonia Penitenciaria, Delegación Venustiano Carranza, 15280 Mexico City CDMX, Mexico. E-mail: informacion@alaarchivos.org.
URL: http://www.alaarchivos.org/

History 6 Apr 1973, Lima (Peru), as regional branch of *International Council on Archives (ICA, #12996).* Constitution modified: 1982; 1986; 1973; last revised 3 Mar 1995, Cartagena de Indias (Colombia). **Aims** Study, establish and maintain relations between institutions in the field of archives and public and private *professional* bodies in Spanish and Portuguese-speaking countries of Latin America, Spain and Portugal. **Structure** General Assembly (every 4 years). Steering Committee, comprising Chairman, 1st and 2nd Vice-Chairmen, Secretary-General, Treasurer and 2 members. **Finance** Members' dues. Other sources: contributions from national and international non-governmental and intergovernmental bodies; grants. **Activities** Recommendations and lobbying; studies and research; publishing activity. **Events** *Biennial international conference on preservation of archives in tropical climates* Curaçao 2003, *Conference* Rio de Janeiro (Brazil) 2002, *Conference* Santiago (Chile) 2002, *Conference* Mexico 2001, *Conference* Rio de Janeiro (Brazil) 2000. **Publications** *ALA* – magazine; *Circulares Informativas.* Translations; studies.
Members Class A general or national archives which officially represent the country in all the matters related to archives; Class B professional national associations in the field of archives; Class C historical and administrative archives; Class D training centres in the field of archives; Class E individual archivists. Members in 17 countries:
Argentina, Brazil, Chile, Colombia, Costa Rica, Cuba, Dominican Rep, Ecuador, Honduras, Mexico, Nicaragua, Panama, Paraguay, Peru, Puerto Rico, Uruguay, Venezuela.
IGO Relations *UNESCO (#20322).* [2018/XD6137/**E**]

♦ Asociación Latinoamericana de Armadores (#16369)
♦ Asociación Latinoamericana de Aseguradoras Agropecuarias / see Asociación Latinoamericana para el Desarrollo del Seguro Agropecuario (#02205)

♦ Asociación Latinoamericana de Autocuidado Responsable (ILAR) . . 02184

Latin American Association of Responsible Self-care

Contact 400 E Randolph St, Suite 3725, Chicago IL 60601, USA. T. +5511986666778. E-mail: info@infoilar.org.
URL: https://www.infoilar.org/

History 1996, as *Asociación Latinoamericana de Productores OTC (ALPO) – Latin American OTC Association.* Subsequently changed title to *Industria Latinoamericana de Automedicación Responsable (ILAR),* 2001. **Aims** Promote self-care in the use of medicines without prescription; optimize resources and social welfare systems; contribute to public health through responsible medication. **Events** *Latin American regional conference* Cartagena de Indias (Colombia) 2009, *Latin American regional conference* Sao Paulo (Brazil) 2005.
Members Companies in 6 countries:
Argentina, Brazil, Colombia, Dominican Rep, Mexico, Venezuela.
NGO Relations Member of: *Global Self-Care Federation (GSCF, #10588).* [2019/XD9064/**D**]

Asociación Latinoamericana Avicultura
02185

alphabetic sequence excludes
For the complete listing, see Yearbook Online at

♦ **Asociación Latinoamericana de Avicultura (ALA)** **02185**
Latin American Poultry Association
Exec Dir San Francisco Ave 5a Sur, Panama, Panamá, Panama PANAMá, Panama. T. +5072264656. E-mail: ala@avicolatina.com.
Pres address not obtained.
URL: http://www.avicolatina.com/
History 23 Apr 1970, Buenos Aires (Argentina). **Aims** Contribute to strengthening of efficient and responsible production, providing food security, representation in international forums and promoting businesses that generate employment and wealth in the region. **Structure** Associates Assebmly; Board of Directors; Executive Director; Committee; Institutes (2). **Languages** English, Portuguese, Spanish. **Staff** 4.00 FTE, paid. **Finance** Sources: meeting proceeds; members' dues. Support from cooperating partners. **Activities** Events/meetings. **Events** *Congress* San Pedro Sula (Honduras) 2022, *Congress* Lima (Peru) 2019, *Congress* Guadalajara (Mexico) 2017, *Congress* Guayaquil (Ecuador) 2015, *Congress* San Salvador (El Salvador) 2013. **Publications** *ALA News Bulletin*; *ALA Noticias CTC Informa*; *ILH Update*; *ILP Update*; *Newsletter ILH*; *Newsletter ILP*.
Members National members in 18 countries:
Argentina, Bolivia, Brazil, Chile, Costa Rica, Cuba, Dominican Rep, Ecuador, El Salvador, Guatemala, Honduras, Mexico, Nicaragua, Panama, Paraguay, Peru, Uruguay, Venezuela.
IGO Relations Observer status with (2): *Codex Alimentarius Commission (CAC, #04081)*; *OIE – World Organisation for Animal Health (#17703)*. **NGO Relations** Member of (1): *International Poultry Council (IPC, #14628)*. [2022/XD5294/y/**D**]

♦ **Asociación Latinoamericana de Bancos de Tejidos (ALABAT)** **02186**
Latin American Tissue Banking Association
Pres address not obtained.
URL: https://www.alabat.net/
History 1 Oct 2000, Sao Paulo (Brazil). **Aims** Promote and disseminate at the academic level the discipline and development of tissues, and *cell* preservation of biological origin for *therapeutic* purposes. **Structure** General Assembly; Board of Directors; Scientific Committee. **Languages** English, Portuguese, Spanish. **Staff** 13, part-time, paid and voluntary. **Finance** Sources: members' dues. Annual budget: 1,500 USD. **Activities** Events/meetings; projects/programmes; standards/guidelines. **Events** *Congress* Buenos Aires (Argentina) 2016, *World congress on tissue banking* Barcelona (Spain) 2011, *Congress* Bogota (Colombia) 2011, *Congress* Punta del Este (Uruguay) 2009, *Congress* Cancún (Mexico) 2007.
Members Physicians, nurses, technologists, biologists, biochemists and engineers contributing to development of tissue banking in the region. Members in 12 countries:
Argentina, Brazil, Chile, Colombia, Costa Rica, Cuba, Ecuador, El Salvador, Mexico, Peru, Uruguay, Venezuela.
NGO Relations Member of (1): *World Union of Tissue Banking Associations (WUTBA, #21888)*. [2020/XM0148/**D**]

♦ Asociación Latinoamericana de Biomatematica (inactive)
♦ Asociación Latinoamericana de Biotecnologia y Bioingenieria (unconfirmed)
♦ Asociación Latinoamericana de Botanica / see Asociación Latinoamericana de Botanica (#02187)

♦ **Asociación Latinoamericana de Botanica (ALB)** **02187**
Latin American Society for Botany
Exec Sec address not obtained. E-mail: alb@botanica-alb.org.
Exec Sec address not obtained.
URL: https://botanica-alb.org/
History 1986. A regional society of *Red Latinoamericana de Ciencias Biológicas (RELAB, #18706)*. Former names and other names: *Latin American Botanical Association* – alias; *Asociación Latinoamericana de Botanica* – alias. **Aims** Promote botany in Latin America; stimulate relations between botanists and between Latin American botanical institutions; represent the Latin American botanical community. **Structure** Executive Committee. **Languages** Portuguese, Spanish. **Events** *Congreso Latinoamericano de Botánica* Havana (Cuba) 2023, *Congreso Latinoamericano de Botánica* Havana (Cuba) 2022, *Congreso Latinoamericano de Botánica* Quito (Ecuador) 2018, *Congreso Latinoamericano de Botánica* Salvador (Brazil) 2014, *Congreso Latinoamericano de Botánica* La Serena (Chile) 2010. **Publications** *Boletin Botanico Latinoamericano* (periodical). **NGO Relations** *Latin American Plant Sciences Network (#16362)*. [2023/XD6281/**D**]

♦ Asociación Latinoamericana de Burós de Crédito / see Asociación Latinoamericana y del Caribe de Burós de Crédito (#02189)
♦ Asociación Latinoamericana para la Calidad (inactive)

♦ **Asociación Latinoamericana de Carcinologia (ALCARCINUS)** **02188**
Latin American Association of Carcinology
Pres ICML UNAM, Apdo Postal 811, 82040 Mazatlan SIN, Mexico. T. +6699852845 – +6699852846 – +6699852848. Fax +6699826133. E-mail: michel@ola.icmyl.unam.mx.
URL: http://www.alcarcinus.com/
History 1995, Mar del Plata (Argentina), at 6th Latin-American Congress in Marine Sciences. Previously also known under the acronym *ALCA*. Also referred to as *ALCARCINUS*. **Aims** Promote carcinology throughout Latin America; facilitate access to literature dealing with *crustaceans*; provide an electronic forum for inquiries related to crustaceans; maintain contact and seek collaboration with The Crustacean Society (TCS). **Structure** Board; Consulting Committee. **Languages** Spanish. **Staff** No full-time staff. **Finance** Voluntary fees. **Activities** Networking/liaising; events/meetings; awards/prizes/competitions. **Events** *Board Meeting* Frankfurt-Main (Germany) 2014, *Meeting* San José (Costa Rica) 2013, *Meeting* Coquimbo (Chile) 2007, *Meeting* Florianópolis (Brazil) 2007, *Meeting* Santos (Brazil) 1997.
Members in 19 countries:
Argentina, Brazil, Chile, Colombia, Costa Rica, Cuba, Ecuador, El Salvador, Germany, Mexico, Panama, Peru, Puerto Rico, Spain, UK, Uruguay, USA, Venezuela.
NGO Relations Brazilian Society of Carcinology; *The Crustacean Society (TCS, #04974)*. [2019.12.11/XJ3033/**D**]

♦ Asociación Latinoamericana y del Caribe de Agencias de Carga Aérea y Transporte / see Latin American and Caribbean Federation of National Associations of Cargo (#16276)

♦ **Asociación Latinoamericana y del Caribe de Burós de Crédito (ALACRED)** **02189**
Latin American and Caribbean Association of Credit Bureaus
Contact address not obtained. E-mail: alacred@burodecredito.com.mx.
URL: http://www.alacred.com/
History Founded 27 Aug 2004. Registered in accordance with Brazilian law. Former names and other names: *Latin American Association of Credit Bureaus* – former (2004 to 2015); *Asociación Latinoamericana de Burós de Crédito (ALACRED)* – former (2004 to 2015). **Events** *World Consumer Credit Reporting Conference* Barcelona (Spain) 2022, *World Consumer Credit Reporting Conference* Barcelona (Spain) 2021, *World Consumer Credit Reporting Conference* Barcelona (Spain) 2020.
Members Full in 10 countries:
Brazil, Chile, Colombia, Dominican Rep, Ecuador, Mexico, Panama, Paraguay, Peru, Venezuela.
NGO Relations Member of: *Latin American Banking Association (#16254)*. [2020/XJ1864/**D**]

♦ Asociación Latinoamericana y del Caribe de Derecho y Economia / see Latin American and Iberian Law and Economics Association (#16340)
♦ Asociación Latinoamericana y del Caribe de Economistas Ambientales y de Recursos Naturales (inactive)
♦ Asociación Latinoamericana y del Caribe de Educación en Salud Pública (inactive)
♦ Asociación Latinoamericana y del Caribe de Empresas de Agua Potable y Alcantarillado (no recent information)
♦ Asociación Latinoamericana y del Caribe de Estudiantes de Ingeniería Agrícola (unconfirmed)
♦ Asociación Latinoamericana y del Caribe sobre Estudios de la Mujer (inactive)

♦ **Asociación Latinoamericana y del Caribe de Ingeniería Agrícola (ALIA)** **02190**
Treas Av Villanueva 60, Depto 503 Nuñoa, Santiago, Santiago Metropolitan, Chile. T. +5629579413 – +56225033501.
Contact Universidad EARTH, Limón, Guácimo, 4442-10000, Costa Rica. T. +50689954101. E-mail: wrodrigu@earth.ac.cr – wedrocha@gmail.com.
URL: http://aliaweb.org/
History Nov 1994, Chillan (Chile). Current statutes adopted 2008. Former names and other names: *Latin American Association of Agricultural Engineering* – former. **Aims** Promote exchange of experience among agricultural engineers in different countries. **Structure** General Assembly; Board of Directors. **Languages** English, Portuguese, Spanish. **Staff** 1.00 FTE, paid. **Finance** Sources: members' dues. **Events** *Biennial Congress* San José (Costa Rica) 2020, *Congreso Latinoamericano y del Caribe de Ingeniería Agrícola (CLIA)* San José (Costa Rica) 2018, *Biennial Congress* Bogota (Colombia) 2016, *Biennial Congress / Congress* Cancún (Mexico) 2014, *Biennial Congress / Congress* Londrina (Brazil) 2012.
Members Full 23 in countries:
Argentina, Bolivia, Brazil, Canada, Chile, Colombia, Costa Rica, Cuba, Dominican Rep, Ecuador, El Salvador, Guatemala, Haiti, Honduras, Mexico, Nicaragua, Panama, Paraguay, Peru, Puerto Rico, Uruguay, USA, Venezuela.
NGO Relations Member of (1): *International Commission of Agricultural and Biosystems Engineering (#12661)*. [2022.10.25/XD4979/**D**]

♦ Asociación Latinoamericana y del Caribe de Mudanzas Internacionales (#16280)

♦ **Asociación Latinoamericana y Caribeña para el control de las Infecciones de Transmisión (ALAC-ITS)** **02191**
Pres FASPA, Univ Peruana Cayetano Heredia, Av Honorio Delgado 430, Urb Ingenieria, Lima, Peru. T. +5113190028ext2712.
URL: http://www.alacits.org/
History Founded 2003, Niterói (Brazil). **Aims** Bring together professionals in Latin America and the Caribbean from diverse specializations with a common interest in collaboration on services and applied research for control of *sexually transmitted* infections. **Structure** Board. **Events** *Meeting* Lima (Peru) 2008, *Meeting* Porto Alegre (Brazil) 2007. **Publications** *Revista oficial de ALACITS*. Bulletins.
Members Full in 19 countries:
Argentina, Bolivia, Brazil, Chile, Colombia, Costa Rica, Cuba, Dominican Rep, Ecuador, El Salvador, Guatemala, Honduras, Mexico, Nicaragua, Panama, Paraguay, Peru, Uruguay, Venezuela.
NGO Relations Cooperates with: *International Union against Sexually Transmitted Infections (IUSTI, #15751)*. [2014/XJ7525/**D**]

♦ Asociación Latinoamericana y Caribeña de Inmunología (#16265)
♦ Asociación Latinoamericana y del Caribe de Transporte Aéreo (#16263)

♦ **Asociación Latinoamericana de Carreras Universitarias de Relaciones Públicas (ALACAURP)** **02192**
Latin American Association of Universities of Public Relations Programmes – Association latinoaméricaine des études universitaires de relations publiques
Pres Fac Ciencias Comunicación-Turismo-Psicologia, Univ de San Martin de Porres, Av Tomas Marsano 242, Lima, Peru. T. +5115136300ext2010.
URL: http://www.alacaurp.org/
History 19 Aug 1999, Cusco (Peru). **Aims** Promote academic, cultural, research and promotion activities related to public relations in Latin America. **Structure** Officers: Honorary Life Chairman; President; Vice President; Directors (4). **Languages** Spanish. **Finance** Congress financed by host university. **Activities** Events/meetings. **Events** *Congress* Santa Cruz (Bolivia) 2018, *Extraordinary Congress* Guayaquil (Ecuador) 2016, *Congress* Medellin (Colombia) 2015, *Congress* Guayaquil (Ecuador) 2013, *Congress* Lima (Peru) 2011. **Publications** Scientific journal.
Members Universities (25) in 10 countries:
Argentina, Bolivia, Brazil, Chile, Colombia, Costa Rica, Ecuador, Mexico, Panama, Peru. [2019.02.18/XJ3464/**D**]

♦ Asociación Latinoamericana de Centros Binacionales (inactive)
♦ Asociación Latinoamericana de Centros de Educación Cooperativa (no recent information)
♦ Asociación Latinoamericana de Centros de Lucha contra las Intoxicaciones (inactive)

♦ **Asociación Latinoamericana de Ciencia Politica (ALACIP)** **02193**
Latin American Association of Political Science
SG Univ Estadual do Norte Fluminense (UENF) CCH, Av Alberto Lamego, n 2000 Campos dos Goytacazes, Rua Souza Franco num 448 casa 201, Rio de Janeiro RJ, 20551-120, Brazil. T. +5521980757888. E-mail: alacipinstitucional@gmail.com – contato@alacip.org.
URL: http://www.alacip.org/
Aims Promote development of Political Sciences studies about Latin America and the Caribbean. **Structure** General Assembly; Executive Committee. **Languages** Portuguese, Spanish. **Staff** 2.00 FTE, paid. **Activities** Awards/prizes/competitions; events/meetings; knowledge management/information dissemination; networking/liaising; politics/policy/regulatory; projects/programmes; publishing activities; research/documentation; training/education. **Events** *Congress* 2024, *Congress* Santiago (Chile) 2022, *Congress* Monterrey (Mexico) 2019, *Congress* Montevideo (Uruguay) 2017, *Congress* Lima (Peru) 2015. **Publications** *Boletin ALACIP*. [2021.07.02/XM2128/**D**]

♦ Asociación Latinoamericana de Ciencias Agricolas (inactive)
♦ Asociación Latinoamericana de Ciencias del Deporte Educación y Danza (unconfirmed)
♦ Asociación Latino-americana de Ciencias Fisiológicas (#16250)
♦ Asociación Latino Americana de Cirugia de Catarata y Segmento Anterior / see Asociación Latino Americana de Cirugia de Catarata, Segmento Anterior y Refractiva (#02194)

♦ **Asociación Latino Americana de Cirugia de Catarata, Segmento Anterior y Refractiva (ALACCSA-R)** **02194**
Latin American Association of Cataract, Anterior Segment and Refractive Surgery
Exec Sec 2446 W Whittier Blvd, Montebello CA 90640, USA. T. +13238878888. Fax +13232015093. E-mail: alaccsa@aol.com.
Chairman address not obtained.
URL: http://www.alaccsa.com/
History Founded 1991, as *Latin American Association of Cataract and Anterior Segment Surgery – Asociación Latino Americana de Cirugia de Catarata y Segmento Anterior (ALACCSA)*. Previously also referred to in English as *Latin American Society of Cataract and Refractive Surgeons (LASCRS)*. **Aims** Conduct scientific congresses and symposia. **Structure** Board of Executive Directors; Board of Directors; Committees. **Languages** Portuguese, Spanish. **Staff** 1.00 FTE, paid. **Activities** Events/meetings. **Events** *Congress of the Southern Cone* Bogota (Colombia) 2019, *Congress of the Southern Cone* Santiago (Chile) 2018, *Congress of the Northern Cone, Central America and Caribbean* Lima (Peru) 2016, *Congress of the Northern Cone, Central America and Caribbean / Congress* Cancún (Mexico) 2015, *Joint Meeting* San Diego, CA (USA) 2015. **Publications** *NOTICIERO ALACCSA-R* (12 a year) in Portuguese, Spanish – newsletter.
Members National organizations (26) in 20 countries:
Argentina, Bolivia, Brazil, Chile, Colombia, Costa Rica, Cuba, Dominican Rep, Ecuador, El Salvador, Guatemala, Mexico, Nicaragua, Panama, Paraguay, Peru, Spain, Uruguay, USA, Venezuela. [2018.09.10/XD6799/**D**]

♦ **Asociación Latinoamericana de Cirugía y Traumatología Bucomaxilofacial (ALACIBU)** **02195**
Latin American Association of Bucco-Maxillo-Facial Surgery
Pres Av República, CC Terras Plaza, Urb, Terrazas de Club Hípico, Venezuela. E-mail: secretaria@alacibu.net – marketingalacibu@gmail.com.
Contact Diagonal 74 nº 2571, La Plata (CP 1900), Buenos Aires, Argentina. T. +542214511859.
URL: https://alacibu.net/asociacion/

History 1962. **Structure** Executive Committee. **Events** *Congress* Cartagena de Indias (Colombia) 2022, *Congress* Cancún (Mexico) 2019, *Congress* Cancún (Mexico) 2017, *Congress* Lima (Peru) 2015, *Triennial Congress* Porlamar (Venezuela) 2013.
Members Full in 17 countries:
Argentina, Bolivia, Brazil, Chile, Colombia, Costa Rica, Cuba, Ecuador, El Salvador, Guatemala, Mexico, Nicaragua, Panama, Paraguay, Peru, Uruguay, Venezuela. [2021/XD2295/**D**]

♦ Asociación Latinoamericana de Cirugia Vascular y Angiologia (ALCVA) 02196

Pres address not obtained. E-mail: valente_angiologia@yahoo.com.mx – presidente@alcva.org.
URL: http://alcva.org/
History 25 Nov 2011, Cartagena de Indias (Colombia). Founded as a continuation of the now defunct *International Society for Vascular Specialists (ISVS, inactive)* Latin American chapter, set up 1951. **Structure** Board of Directors, comprising President, Vice-President, Secretary, Treasurer, Fiscal doctor and 11 members. **Events** *Congress* Cartagena de Indias (Colombia) 2014, *Congress* Santa Cruz (Bolivia) 2012, *Congress* Havana (Cuba) 2007, *Congress* Caracas (Venezuela) 2005, *Congress* Buenos Aires (Argentina) 2002. **Publications** *ALCVA Newsletter.*
Members Scientific societies in 20 countries:
Argentina, Bolivia, Brazil, Chile, Colombia, Costa Rica, Cuba, Dominican Rep, Ecuador, El Salvador, Guatemala, Honduras, Mexico, Nicaragua, Panama, Paraguay, Peru, Puerto Rico, Uruguay, Venezuela. [2014/XJ7229/**D**]

- ♦ Asociación Latinoamericana de Cirujanos Endoscópistas (#16239)
- ♦ Asociación Latinoamericana de Cirurgia Endoscópica / see Latin American Association of Endoscopic Surgeons (#16239)
- ♦ Asociación Latinoamericana de Coaching (unconfirmed)
- ♦ Asociación Latinoamericana de Colo-Proctologia (#16237)

♦ Asociación Latinoamericana de Conservatorios y Escuelas de Música (ALCEM) 02197

Pres 951 Ave Ponce de León, Pda 15 Miramar, San Juan PR 00907-3373, USA. T. +17877510160.
History Founded Feb 2006. **Aims** Serve as the official institutional body and represent all musical education institutions in Latin America. **Structure** Board of Directors.
Members Full in 9 countries and territories:
Argentina, Chile, Colombia, Costa Rica, Dominican Rep, Ecuador, Mexico, Peru, Puerto Rico.
NGO Relations Member of: *International Music Council (IMC, #14199).* [2015/XJ6300/**D**]

♦ Asociación Latinoamericana de Consultores Politicos (ALACOP) . . . 02198

Latin American Association for Political Consultants
Pres address not obtained. E-mail: alacop@alacoplatam.org.
URL: http://www.alacoplatam.org/
History Founded 1996. **Events** *Annual Meeting* Madrid (Spain) 2019, *Meeting* Mexico City (Mexico) 2005, *Meeting* Buenos Aires (Argentina) 2002, *Meeting* San José (Costa Rica) 2001, *Meeting* Miami, FL (USA) 2000. [2016/XD5980/**D**]

♦ Asociación Latinoamericana de Control de Calidad, Patologia y Recuperación de la Construcción (ALCONPAT) 02199

Latin American Association of Control of Quality, Pathology and Recovery of Construction
Contact IETcc-CSIC, C Serrano Galvache 4, 28033 Madrid, Spain. T. +34913020440. Fax +34913020700. E-mail: director.ietcc@csic.es.
URL: http://www.alconpat.org/
History 20 May 1993, Córdoba (Argentina). Also referred to as *ALCONPAT Internacional.* **Events** *Latin American Congress on Pathology of Construction* Lisbon (Portugal) 2015, *Latin American Congress on Control of Quality in Construction* Cartagena de Indias (Colombia) 2013, *Latin American Congress on Pathology of Construction / Congress* Cartagena de Indias (Colombia) 2013, *Congress* Guatemala (Guatemala) 2011, *Congress* Valparaíso (Chile) 2009. [2012/XM3075/**D**]

♦ Asociación Latinoamericana de Cooperación en Emergencia Médica y Desastres (ALACED) 02200

Latin American Association of Emergency Medicine and Disaster Cooperation
Contact Fundación emergencias, 1253, Av Melian 2752, C1430EYH Buenos Aires, Argentina. T. +5443230300. Fax +5443230300.
URL: http://www.alaced.org/
History Apr 2002, Havana (Cuba). **Structure** Executive Committee, comprising President, Vice-President, Treasurer and 4 further members. **Events** *Congress* Buenos Aires (Argentina) 2022, *Congress* Havana (Cuba) 2013, *Congress* Buenos Aires (Argentina) 2010, *Interamerican congress on emergency medicine* Buenos Aires (Argentina) 2010, *Interamerican congress on prehospital setting medicine* Buenos Aires (Argentina) 2010. [2022.05.10/XJ3369/**D**]

- ♦ Asociación Latinoamericana de Corporaciones Regionales de Desarrollo (inactive)

♦ Asociación Latinoamericana de Cuidados Paliativos (ALCP) 02201

Latin American Association of Palliative Care – Associação Latino-americana de Cuidados Paliativos
Main Office Diagonal 76 no 1-29, Bogota 110221, Bogota DC, Colombia. E-mail: contacto@alcp.lat.
URL: http://www.cuidadospaliativos.org/
History 23 Apr 2001, Buenos Aires (Argentina). Registration: Start date: 19 Feb 2019, Colombia; Argentina. **Aims** Promote development of palliative care in Latin America and the Caribbean through communication and integration of all those interested in improving the quality of life of patients with progressive, life limiting conditions and their families. **Structure** Board of Directors; Work Commissions; Administrative Director. **Languages** Portuguese, Spanish. **Staff** 2.00 FTE, paid; 6.00 FTE, voluntary. **Finance** Sources: contributions; donations; grants; meeting proceeds; members' dues; revenue from activities/projects; sponsorship. Annual budget: 31,000 USD. **Activities** Advocacy/lobbying/activism; events/meetings; guidance/assistance/consulting; knowledge management/information dissemination; networking/liaising; politics/policy/regulatory; projects/programmes; training/education. Active in: Argentina, Bolivia, Brazil, Chile, Colombia, Costa Rica, Ecuador, El Salvador, Guatemala, Mexico, Panama, Paraguay, Peru, Uruguay. **Events** *Congress* San José (Costa Rica) 2022, *Jornada Latinoamericana de Cuidados Paliativos* 2021, *Congress* San José (Costa Rica) 2020, *Congress* Santiago (Chile) 2018, *Congress* Mexico City (Mexico) 2016. **Publications** Monthly publication.
Members Full in 21 countries:
Argentina, Belize, Bolivia, Brazil, Canada, Chile, Colombia, Costa Rica, Cuba, Dominican Rep, Ecuador, El Salvador, Guatemala, Mexico, Nicaragua, Panama, Paraguay, Peru, Uruguay, USA, Venezuela.
NGO Relations Member of (1): *Worldwide Hospice Palliative Care Alliance (WHPCA, #21924).* [2022.05.11/XM8224/**D**]

♦ Asociación Latinoamericana de Derecho Aeronautico y Espacial (ALADA) 02202

Latin American Association for Aeronautical and Space Law
SG Arroyo 950, 6o piso A, 1007 Buenos Aires, Argentina. Fax +541143949430 – +541143270611. E-mail: aladasec@gmail.com.
URL: http://www.alada.org/
History Nov 1960, Buenos Aires (Argentina). **Aims** Unify Aeronautical Law; promote studies and development of Aeronautical and Space Law. **Structure** Assembly; Directive Board; Executive. **Languages** Spanish. **Finance** Members' dues. Income from courses. **Activities** Training/education; knowledge management/information dissemination; publishing activities; events/meetings. **Events** *Latin America/Polish Air and Space Law Conference* Warsaw (Poland) 2017, *Seminar* Madrid (Spain) 1989. **Publications** *Revista Latino Americana de Derecho Aeronautico.* Books. **Members** Membership countries not specified. **IGO Relations** Observer to: *International Civil Aviation Organization (ICAO, #12581); Latin American Civil Aviation Commission (LACAC, #16297).* **NGO Relations** *Latin American and Caribbean Federation of National Associations of Cargo (#16276);* universities. [2019/XD2424/**D***]

- ♦ Asociación Latinoamericana de Derecho Constitucional (no recent information)
- ♦ Asociación Latinoamericana de Derecho y Economia / see Latin American and Iberian Law and Economics Association (#16340)

♦ Asociación Latinoamericana de Derecho Médico (ASOLADEME) . . . 02203

Pres Fac de Medicina, Campus Univ de Espinardo, Univ de Murcia, Calle Campus Universitario, 30100 Murcia, Spain. T. +34868889362.
SG Apdo Postal 2331, 10 02 Paseo de los Estudiantes, San José, San José, San José, 02006, Costa Rica.
URL: http://asolademe.org/
History Nov 1996, San José (Costa Rica). **Aims** Know and debate aspects related to health and medical law in Latin America. **Structure** General Assembly; Board of Directors. **Languages** French, Italian, Portuguese, Spanish. **Activities** Healthcare; politics/policy/regulatory; projects/programmes; publishing activities; research/documentation; training/education. **Events** *Congress* Murcia (Spain) 2020, *Congress* San José (Costa Rica) 2016, *Congress* Lima (Peru) 2014, *Congress* Maceió (Brazil) 2012, *Congress* Santiago (Chile) 2010. **Publications** *Revista Latinoamericana de Derecho Médico y Medicina Legal.* [2020.06.22/XM0543/**D**]

- ♦ Asociación Latinoamericana de Derecho de la Navegación y del Mar (no recent information)
- ♦ Asociación Latinoamericana de Derecho Penal y Criminologia (unconfirmed)
- ♦ Asociación Latinoamericana para los Derechos Humanos (#16243)

♦ Asociación Latinoamericana de Desalación y Reúso del Agua (ALADYR) 02204

Latin American Association of Desalination and Water Reuse – Associação Latino-americana de Dessalinização e Reúso de Água
Contact address not obtained. E-mail: info@aladyr.net.
URL: http://www.aladyr.net/
History 30 Nov 2010, Antofagasta (Chile). Founded during the II International Desalination Seminar in Antofagasta City, Chile. **Aims** Be the benchmark in desalination, reuse and treatment of water and effluents in Latin America. **Structure** Board of Directors. **Languages** English, Portuguese, Spanish. **Finance** Sources: members' dues. **Activities** Awareness raising; events/meetings; guidance/assistance/consulting; knowledge management/information dissemination; publishing activities; research and development; research/documentation; training/education. Latin America. **Events** *Congress* Lima (Peru) 2022, *Water in Latin America* Miami, FL (USA) 2022, *International Congress* Santiago (Chile) 2022, *Seminar* Mexico City (Mexico) 2019, *Seminar* Santiago (Chile) 2019. [2022.05.10/XM7649/**D**]

- ♦ Asociación Latinoamericana para el Desarrollo y la Integración de la Mujer (inactive)
- ♦ Asociación Latinoamericana de Desarrollo Organizacional (no recent information)
- ♦ Asociación Latinoamericana para el Desarrollo del Seguro Agropecuario / see Asociación Latinoamericana para el Desarrollo del Seguro Agropecuario (#02205)

♦ Asociación Latinoamericana para el Desarrollo del Seguro Agropecuario (ALASA) 02205

Association latinoamèricaine pour le développement des assurances agricoles et du bétail – Latin American Association of Development of Crop and Livestock Insurance
Sec Ruta Nacional 34 – KM 257, Sunchales, Santa Fé, Argentina. T. +543493428500. E-mail: info@alasa-web.org.
URL: http://www.alasa-web.org/
History 21 Feb 1986, Santo Domingo (Dominican Rep). Also referred to as *Latin American Association for the Development of Agricultural and Livestock Insurance – Asociación Latinoamericana para el Desarrollo del Seguro Agropecuario; Latin American Association of Agriculture and Cattle Insurance Companies – Asociación Latinoamericana de Aseguradoras Agropecuarias.* **Aims** Secure cooperation and information between Caribbean and Latin American companies related to agricultural insurance. **Structure** General Assembly (annual). Board of Directors, comprising President, Vice-President, General Secretary, Chair of the Vigilance Committee and 3 members. **Languages** English, Spanish. **Staff** 6.00 FTE, voluntary. 6 voluntary. **Finance** Annual and extraordinary quotas; donations; payments for services; other incomes. **Activities** Organizes international symposia or congresses. **Events** *Congress* Punta del Este (Uruguay) 2016, *Congress* Puebla (Mexico) 2014, *Congress* Panama (Panama) 2008, *Congress* Viña del Mar (Chile) 2006, *Congress* Sao Paulo (Brazil) 2004.
Members Organizations in 14 countries:
Argentina, Brazil, Colombia, Costa Rica, Cuba, Ecuador, France, Germany, Mexico, Panama, Spain, Switzerland, USA, Venezuela.
Collaborating organizations (5) in 4 countries:
El Salvador, France, Peru, Spain.
IGO Relations *International Bank for Reconstruction and Development (IBRD, #12317).* **NGO Relations** *Association internationale des assureurs de la production agricole (AIAG, #02671); Asociación Latinoamericana de Instituciones Financieras para el Desarrollo (ALIDE, #02233).* [2022/XD1532/**D**]

- ♦ Asociación Latinoamericana de Diabetes (#16311)
- ♦ Asociación Latinoamericana de Diseño (#16238)
- ♦ Asociación Latinoamericana de Diseño Industrial / see Latin American Association of Design (#16238)
- ♦ Asociación Latinoamericana de Ecodesarrollo (inactive)

♦ Asociación Latinoamericana de Economia de la Energia (ALADEE) . 02206

Latin-American Association of Economy of the Energy
Sec address not obtained. E-mail: helder@ie.ufrj.br.
URL: http://aladee.org/
History Founded 17 Apr 2011, Buenos Aires (Argentina). **Structure** Executive. **Activities** Events/meetings. **Events** *Latin American Conference* Buenos Aires (Argentina) 2019, *Latin American Conference* Rio de Janeiro (Brazil) 2017, *Latin American Conference* Medellin (Colombia) 2015, *Latin American Conference* Montevideo (Uruguay) 2013, *Latin American Conference* Buenos Aires (Argentina) 2011. **NGO Relations** Member of: *International Association for Energy Economics (IAEE, #11869).* [2019/XM7665/**D**]

- ♦ Asociación Latinoamericana de Editores de Geociencias (inactive)
- ♦ Asociación Latinoamericana de Educación Agricola Superior (no recent information)

♦ Asociación Latinoamericana de Educación y Comunicación Popular (ALER) 02207

Association latinoaméricaine d'éducation et de communication populaire – Latin American Association of Popular Education and Communication
Gen Coordinator Calle Valladolid 511 y Madrid, Casilla 17 03 4639, Quito, Ecuador. T. +59322559012 – +59322524358 – +59322503996. Fax +59322559012 – +59322524358. E-mail: hugo@aler.org – aler@aler.org.
URL: http://www.aler.org/
History 7 Sep 1972, Colombia, as *Asociación Latinoamericana de Educación Radiofónica (ALER) – Association latinoaméricaine d'éducation radiophonique – Latin American Association of Radio Education.* **Aims** Strengthen the movement of popular radio and democratization of communications in Latin America and the Caribbean; contribute to construction of a democratic and participative society where the poor are protagonists of their own development. **Structure** General Assembly; Executive Council; General Coordination. **Languages** Spanish. **Staff** 14.00 FTE, paid; 25.00 FTE, voluntary. **Finance** European cooperation agencies. Annual budget: about US$ 300,000. **Activities** Organizes and produces: courses by radio; service activities on adult education; workshops. Lines of action: radio production; capacity building; research; technology; sustainability; relations. **Events** *International forum on communication and citizenship* San Salvador (El Salvador) 1998, *Meeting* Quito (Ecuador) 1994, *Meeting of Latin American popular and alternative media* Quito (Ecuador) 1992, *Meeting* Quito (Ecuador) 1991, *International seminar / Meeting* Quito (Ecuador) 1989. **Publications** *Boletin Informativo ALERta* (6 a year). *Experiencias* – series. Vocational training manuals; textbooks; booklets.
Members Educational broadcasting organizations (68) in 17 countries:
Argentina, Bolivia, Brazil, Chile, Colombia, Costa Rica, Dominican Rep, Ecuador, El Salvador, Guatemala, Honduras, Mexico, Nicaragua, Panama, Paraguay, Peru, Venezuela.

Consultative Status Consultative status granted from: *UNESCO (#20322)* (Consultative Status). **NGO Relations** Member of: *Redes de Comunicación de América Latina y el Caribe para el Desarrollo (G-8, no recent information)*; *Unda, International Catholic Association for Radio and Television (inactive)*. Honorary member of: *Federación Latinoamericana de Facultades de Comunicación Social (FELAFACS, #09353)*. Joint events with: *Agencia Latinoamericana de Información (ALAI, #00551)*; *Association mondiale des radiodiffuseurs communautaires (AMARC, #02810)*; *Association for Progressive Communications (APC, #02873)*.
[2019.06.24/XD5293/**D**]

- ♦ Asociación Latinoamericana de Educación Radiofónica / see Asociación Latinoamericana de Educación y Comunicación Popular (#02207)
- ♦ Asociación Latinoamericana de Educadoras del Hogar (inactive)
- ♦ Asociación Latinoamericana de Empresas Comercializadoras Internacionales (no recent information)

♦ Asociación Latinoamericana de Endocrinología Ginecológica (ALEG) 02208

Contact address not obtained. E-mail: aleg.latam@gmail.com.
URL: https://aleg-latam.com/
History 2008. Registration: Mexico. **Structure** General Assembly; Board of Directors. **Activities** Events/ meetings.
[2021/AA2148/**D**]

♦ Asociación Latinoamericana de Energia Eólica 02209

Latin American Wind Energy Association (LAWEA)
Office Av Terranova 1091-2, 44620 Guadalajara JAL, Mexico. T. +523353500176. Fax +523338178758.
URL: http://www.lawea.org/
History 2007. **Aims** Promote the use of wind energy as a clean electricity source to be supplied to Latin America countries. **Structure** Board of Directors. **Languages** English, Spanish. **Activities** Provides information on everything involved with installing wind turbines. Organizes workshops. **Events** *Conference* Mexico City (Mexico) 2011, *Conference* Mexico City (Mexico) 2010, *RETECH : international renewable energy technology conference* Las Vegas, NV (USA) 2009, *Conference* Panama (Panama) 2009, *Conference* Guadalajara (Mexico) 2008. **Publications** *LAWEA Yearbook*; *Windy News Bulletin*. **Members** Membership countries not specified. **NGO Relations** Member of: *World Wind Energy Association (WWEA, #21937)*.
[2011.06.01/XM3582/**D**]

- ♦ Asociación Latinoamericana de Energia Solar (inactive)

♦ Asociación Latinoamericana de Enseñanza e Investigación en Trabajo Social (ALAEITS) 02210

Latin American Association for Education and Research on Social Work – Associação Latinoamericana de Ensino e Pesquisa em Serviço Social
Sec address not obtained. E-mail: alaeits@gmail.com.
URL: http://www.ts.ucr.ac.cr/html/alaeits/alaeits-es.htm
History 30 Aug 2006, Santiago (Chile). Takes over activities of *Asociación Latinoamericana de Escuelas de Trabajo Social (ALAETS, inactive)*. **Events** *Seminar* Mexico 2008, *Assembly* Foz do Iguaçu (Brazil) 2007.
[2016/XM2629/**D**]

- ♦ Asociación Latinoamericana de Entidades de Tecnologia de la Información / see Federación de Asociaciones de América Latina, el Caribe, España y Portugal de Entidades de Tecnologias de Información y Comunicación (#09288)
- ♦ Asociación Latinoamericana de Entrenadores de Fútbol (unconfirmed)
- ♦ Asociación Latinoamericana de Escuelas de Biblioteconomia y Ciencias de la Información (inactive)

♦ Asociación Latinoamericana de Escuelas y Facultades de Enfermeria (ALADEFE) 02211

Latin American Association of Nursing Science Schools and Departments – Association latinoaméricaine d'écoles et de facultés de sciences infirmières
SG Campus de San Vicente del Raspeig, Ap 99, 03080 Alicante, Castellón, Spain. T. +34965903400 ext3920. Fax +34965909561. E-mail: jr.martinez@ua.es.
Pres Univ Nacional Autónoma de Mexico, Escuela Nac de Enfermeria y Obstrecia, Mexico City CDMX, Mexico. E-mail: eneolm@yahoo.com.
URL: http://www.aladefe.org/
History 1 Oct 1986, Havana (Cuba), as a consulting, cooperation and research body of *Association of Universities of Latin America and the Caribbean (#02970)*. **Aims** Promote and carry out the tasks connected with educational development, research and social impact in the field of *health* in general and of nursing in particular, in order to contribute to its improvement on national as well as on international level. **Structure** General Assembly; Executive Committee; Advisory Board. Includes: *Centro Latinoamericano de Desarrollo en Enfermeria (CLADE, no recent information)*. **Languages** English, Portuguese, Spanish. **Staff** None. **Finance** Members' dues. **Activities** Research and development. **Events** *Conference* Granada (Spain) 2021, *Conference* Panama (Panama) 2019, *Conference* Lima (Peru) 2017, *Conference / Ibero-American Conference* Rio de Janeiro (Brazil) 2015, *Conference / Ibero-American Conference* Montevideo (Uruguay) 2013. **Publications** *Boletin Informativo ALADEFE* (annual). Scientific journal. Conference proceedings.
Members Founding; Full; Associate. Nursing schools and departments in 18 countries:
Argentina, Bolivia, Brazil, Chile, Colombia, Costa Rica, Cuba, Dominican Rep, Ecuador, El Salvador, Honduras, Mexico, Panama, Peru, Portugal, Spain, Uruguay, Venezuela.
IGO Relations *Pan American Health Organization (PAHO, #18108)*.
[2022/XD1439/**D**]

- ♦ Asociación Latinoamericana de Escuelas de Trabajo Social (inactive)

♦ Asociación Latinoamericana de Escuelas de Urbanismo y Planeación (ALEUP) 02212

Association of Latin-American Schools of Urbanism and Planning
Pres address not obtained.
URL: https://aleup.org/
History 1999. **Events** *Congress* Buenos Aires (Argentina) 2021, *Congress* Buenos Aires (Argentina) 2020, *Congress* Santiago (Chile) 2018, *Congress* Mexico 2013. **Members** Membership countries not specified. **NGO Relations** Member of (1): *Global Planning Education Association Network (GPEAN, #10549)*.
[2021/XD9306/**D**]

- ♦ Asociación Latinoamericana de Especialistas en Pequeños Rumiantes y Camélidos Sudamericanos (unconfirmed)

♦ Asociación Latinoamericana de Estudiantes de Ciencias Forestales (ALECIF) 02213

Pres Fac de ciencias Forestales, Univ Nacional de Misiones, Carretera Nacional, Kilometro 145, NL 67700 Linares NL, Mexico. E-mail: v_vavc@hotmail.com.
URL: http://www.alecif.com/
History Founded 1995, Colombia, during the first Encuentro Hispanoamericano de Estudiantes de Ciencias Forestales. **Aims** Contribute to responsible formation of the forestry profession in Latin America through cultural exchange and enrichment. **Structure** General Assembly (annual). **Activities** Events/meetings. **Events** *Congress* Asunción (Paraguay) 2015, *Congress* San José (Costa Rica) 2014, *Congress* Mexico 2013, *Congress* Colombia 2012, *Congress* Peru 2011. **Members** Students in 12 countries. Membership countries not specified.
[2015/XD9004/**D**]

♦ Asociación Latinoamericana de Estudiantes de Ingenieria Industrial y Afines (ALEIIAF) 02214

Pres address not obtained. E-mail: presidencia@aleiiaf.net.
Exec Committee Dir address not obtained. E-mail: direccionce@aleiiaf.org.
URL: http://aleiiaf.org/
History Founded 1991, Lima (Peru). Restructured 1999. Registered in accordance with Chilean law, 2014. **Aims** Promote comprehensive development of students and professionals through activities that promote academic, cultural and social exchange, this leading to generation of knowledge and abilities of industrial engineering in Latin America. **Structure** CLEIN Congress (annual); Board of Directors. **Languages** English, Portuguese, Spanish. **Staff** 8.00 FTE, voluntary. **Finance** Congress fees. **Activities** Events/meetings. **Events** *Engineering well done* Antigua (Guatemala) 2019, *Congress* Cartagena de Indias (Colombia) 2018, *Desafia tus limites, revoluciona tu mundo* Santo Domingo (Dominican Rep) 2018, *Conference* Guayaquil (Ecuador) 2017, *Conference* Medellin (Colombia) 2016. **Publications** *ALEIIAF Newsletter* (12 a year); *Memorias del CLEIN (CLEIN Memoirs)* (annual).
Members Individuals in 20 countries:
Argentina, Bolivia, Brazil, Chile, Colombia, Costa Rica, Cuba, Dominican Rep, Ecuador, El Salvador, Guatemala, Honduras, Mexico, Nicaragua, Panama, Paraguay, Peru, Puerto Rico, Uruguay, Venezuela.
NGO Relations *AIESEC (#00593)*; national associations.
[2019/XJ6782/**D**]

♦ Asociación Latinoamericana de Estudiantes de Ingenieria Quimica (ALEIQ) 02215

Latin American Association of Chemical Engineering Students
Contact address not obtained. E-mail: presidencia@aleiq.org – secretaria@aleiq.org.
URL: http://www.aleiq.org/
History 1998, Mérida (Venezuela) during IV Congreso Latinoamericano de Estudiantes de Ingenieria Quimica. **Events** *Congress* Medellin (Colombia) 2016, *Congress* San José (Costa Rica) 2013, *Congress* Mexico City (Mexico) 2011, *Congress* San Salvador (El Salvador) 2009, *COLAEIQ annual congress / Congress* Rio de Janeiro (Brazil) 2008.
Members in 17 countries:
Argentina, Bolivia, Chile, Colombia, Costa Rica, Cuba, Dominican Rep, Ecuador, El Salvador, Guatemala, Honduras, Mexico, Paraguay, Peru, Puerto Rico, Uruguay, Venezuela.
NGO Relations Member of: *Inter-American Confederation of Chemical Engineering (IACChE, #11417)*.
[2015/XD7078/**D**]

- ♦ Asociación Latinoamericana para el Estudio del Higado (#16252)

♦ Asociación Latinoamericana para el Estudio de las Religiones (ALER) 02216

Pres EMK, Ap 21-456, 04000 Coyoacan CHIS, Mexico. E-mail: contacto@revistaacademica.com.
Coordinator Academic Program address not obtained. E-mail: coordinacionacademica.aler@gmail.com.
Journal: http://www.religioneslatinoamericanas.com.mx
History 1990, Mexico City (Mexico). Founded during III *Congreso Latinoamericano sobre Religión y Etnicidad* – 3rd Latin American Congress on Religion and Ethnicity. **Events** *Congreso Latinoamericano de Religión y Etnicidad* Mexico 2021, *Congreso Latinoamericano de Religión y Etnicidad* Toro (Spain) 2018, *Congreso Latinoamericano sobre Religión y Etnicidad* Heredia (Costa Rica) 2016, *Congreso Latinoamericano sobre Religión y Etnicidad* San Juan (Puerto Rico) 2014, *Congreso Latinoamericano sobre Religión y Etnicidad* San Salvador (El Salvador) 2012. **Publications** *Revista Religiones Latinoamericanas* – ISSN: 0188-4050. **NGO Relations** Member of: *International Association for the History of Religions (IAHR, #11936)*.
[2021/XD5509/**D**]

- ♦ Asociación Latinoamericana de Estudios de Asia y Africa (#16236)

♦ Asociación Latinoamericana de Estudios del Discurso (ALED) 02217

Associação Latino-Americana de Estudos do Discurso
Contact address not obtained. E-mail: revista.raled@gmail.com.
Main Website: http://comunidadaled.org/
History Feb 1995, Caracas (Venezuela). **Aims** Promote the scientific development of discourse studies in Latin America. **Structure** Assembly; Board of Directors. **Languages** Portuguese, Spanish. **Activities** Events/ meetings; publishing activities. **Events** *DiscourneNet Congress* Valencia (Spain) 2023, *DiscourneNet Congress* Budapest (Hungary) 2021, *Biennial Congress* Puebla (Mexico) 2021, *Biennial Congress* Santo Domingo (Dominican Rep) 2020, *DiscourneNet Congress* Paris (France) 2019. **Publications** *Revista ALED*.
Members Full in 11 countries:
Argentina, Brazil, Chile, Colombia, Costa Rica, Cuba, Dominican Rep, Mexico, Puerto Rico, Uruguay, Venezuela.
[2022.02.15/XM7640/**D**]

♦ Asociación Latinoamericana de Estudios de la Escritura en Educación Superior y Contextos Profesionales (ALES) 02218

Latin American Association of Writing Studies in Higher Education and Professional Contexts – Associação Latino-Americana de Estudos da Escrita na Educação Superior e em Contextos Profissionais
Contact address not obtained. E-mail: estudiosdelaescritura@gmail.com.
URL: http://www.estudiosdelaescritura.org/
History Founded 17 Oct 2016, Santiago (Chile). **Aims** Collaborate with inclusivity and quality in Higher Education and with the scientific and technological development of Latin America, mentoring initiatives linked with academic and professional writing, as well as promoting the conformation of a specific disciplinary space. **Languages** English, Portuguese, Spanish. **Activities** Advocacy/lobbying/activism; events/meetings. **Events** *Biennial Conference* João Pessoa (Brazil) 2021, *Biennial Conference* João Pessoa (Brazil) 2020, *Biennial Conference* Santiago (Chile) 2018, *Biennial Conference* Santiago (Chile) 2016. **Members** Full (856) in 31 countries. Membership countries not specified.
[2020.03.16/XM7638/t/**D**]

- ♦ Asociación Latinoamericana de Estudios del Trabajo / see Asociación Latinoamericana de Sociologia del Trabajo (#02268)
- ♦ Asociación Latinoamericana de Etica en los Negocios y Economia (#16262)
- ♦ Asociación Latinoamericana de Evaluadores de Proyectos (inactive)
- ♦ Asociación Latinoamericana de Exportadores de Carne (inactive)

♦ Asociación Latinoamericana de Exportadores de Servicios (ALES) 02219

Latin American Association of Services Exporters
Contact Rincón 518/528 (Oficinas de Uruguay XXI), CP 11000 Montevideo, Uruguay. E-mail: contacto@ales-lac.org – aleslatinoamerica@gmail.com.
URL: http://www.ales-lac.org/
History Registered in accordance with the law of Uruguay. **Aims** Promote Latin America as a knowledge exporter region and outsourcing destination. **Structure** General Assembly; Board of Directors; General Secretariat; Commissions.
Members Institutions (35) in 18 countries:
Argentina, Bolivia, Brazil, Chile, Colombia, Costa Rica, Curaçao, Dominican Rep, Ecuador, El Salvador, Guatemala, Honduras, Mexico, Nicaragua, Panama, Paraguay, Peru, Uruguay.
[2019/XM7636/**D**]

- ♦ Asociación Latinoamericana de Expositores (unconfirmed)
- ♦ Asociación Latinoamericana de Fabricantes de Alimentos Balanceados (no recent information)
- ♦ Asociación Latinoamericana de Fabricantes de Cerveza / see Cerveceros Latinoamericanos (#03836)
- ♦ Asociación Latinoamericana de Fabricantes de Materiales Refractarios (#16244)
- ♦ Asociación Latinoamericana de Fabricantes de Tableros y Fibras de Maderas y Similares (no recent information)
- ♦ Asociación Latino Americana de Fabricantes de Velas (unconfirmed)
- ♦ Asociación Latinoamericana de Facultades y Escuelas de Contaduria Administración (#02783)
- ♦ Asociación Latinoamericana de Facultades y Escuelas de Medicina (#16245)
- ♦ Asociación Latinoamericana de Facultades de Odontologia (inactive)

♦ Asociación Latinoamericana de Facultades de Optometria (ALDEFO) 02220

Latin American Association of Schools and Faculties of Optometry
Pres-Elect OD Urbanización El Caracol, Mz 624 V 11, Guayaquil, Ecuador. T. +59398404457.

History Feb 2003, Ecuador, by *Asociación Latinoamericana de Optometria y Optica (ALDOO, #02247).* **Aims** Represent schools and programmes of optometry; provide the opportunity for professional training in the field. **Structure** General Delegations Meetings; Governing Board. President. **Languages** Spanish. **Finance** Members' dues. Income from events. **Activities** Organizes Ibero American Congress of Optometry Teachers. **Events** *Congress* Guayaquil (Ecuador) 2009.
Members (19) in 7 countries and territories:
Argentina, Colombia, Ecuador, El Salvador, Mexico, Peru, Puerto Rico. [2009.06.01/XD9264/**D**]

♦ Asociación Latinoamericana de Farmacologia (#16249)
♦ Asociación Latinoamericana de Ferrocarriles (#16365)

♦ Asociación Latinoamericana de Filosofia Analitica (ALFAn) 02221

Latin American Association for Analytic Philosophy – Associação Latino-Americana de Filosofia Analitica
Pres Avenida de los Alpes 240, Lomas de Chapultepec I, Sección Miguel Hidalgo, DF 11000 Mexico City CDMX, Mexico. E-mail: info@alfa-n.org.
URL: http://alfa-n.org/
History Proposed Apr 2006, Mexico City (Mexico). **Aims** Promote, increase and disseminate studies and research in analytic philosophy as well as exchange between scholars, societies and higher education institutions with similar interests both at local and international levels. **Structure** Governing Board; Management Committee. **Languages** English, Portuguese, Spanish. **Staff** Part-time, voluntary. **Finance** Members' dues. **Activities** Events/meetings. **Events** *Congress* Santiago (Chile) 2020, *Congress* Villa de Leiva (Colombia) 2018, *Congress* San José (Costa Rica) 2016, *Congress* Fortaleza (Brazil) 2014, *Congress* Buenos Aires (Argentina) 2012. **Publications** *ALFAn Newsletter.*
Members Ordinary; Associate; Institutional. Institutional members in 12 countries:
Argentina, Brazil, Chile, Colombia, Costa Rica, Germany, Mexico, Panama, Peru, Portugal, Spain, Uruguay.
NGO Relations Member of: *International Federation of Philosophical Societies (FISP, #13507).* [2017.10.17/XM5333/**D**]

♦ Asociación Latinoamericana de Filosofia de la Educación (ALFE) .. 02222

Contact address not obtained. E-mail: wordpress@filosofiaeducacion.org.
URL: http://filosofiaeducacion.org/alfe/
History Founded Jul 2010, Bogota (Colombia). **Structure** Board of Directors. **Activities** Events/meetings. **Events** *Filosofia, educacion y ensenanza – dialogos de una relacion* Santiago (Chile) 2019, *Desafíos de la filosofía de la educación en América Latina* Buenos Aires (Argentina) 2017, *Congreso* Mexico City (Mexico) 2015, *Congreso* Montevideo (Uruguay) 2013, *Congreso* Sao Paulo (Brazil) 2011. **Publications** *Revista Latinoamericana de Filosofia de la Educación.* Proceedings. [2019/XM7634/**D**]

♦ Asociación Latinoamericana de Fisica Médica (#16246)

♦ Asociación Latinoamericana de Fitopatologia (ALF) 02223

Latin American Phytopathological Association
Sec-Treas CIP, Apartado 1558, La Molina, 12, Lima, Peru.
Pres address not obtained. E-mail: yanezmj@colpos.mx.
URL: http://www.alfitopatologia.org/
History 1964, Lima (Peru). **Aims** Promote research in *plant* pathology; organize plant pathology congresses. **Structure** Board of Directors, including President, Vice-President, Ex-President, Executive Secretary and Editor-in-chief. **Languages** English, French, Portuguese, Spanish. **Staff** 3.00 FTE, voluntary. **Finance** Members' dues. Sales of publication. **Events** *Biennial Congress* Mexico City (Mexico) 2015, *Biennial Congress* Lambayeque (Peru) 2013, *Biennial Congress* Bogota (Colombia) 2011, *Biennial Congress* Santiago (Chile) 2009, *Biennial Congress* Cancún (Mexico) 2007. **Publications** *Fitopatologia* (3 a year) – journal.
Members Full in 22 countries and territories:
Argentina, Bolivia, Brazil, Canada, Chile, Colombia, Costa Rica, Cuba, Dominican Rep, Ecuador, El Salvador, Guatemala, Honduras, Mexico, Nicaragua, Panama, Paraguay, Peru, Puerto Rico, Uruguay, USA, Venezuela.
Individuals in 9 countries:
Belgium, France, Germany, Italy, Japan, Netherlands, Portugal, Spain, UK.
NGO Relations Member of: *International Society for Plant Pathology (ISPP, #15371).* [2015/XD5635/**D**]

♦ Asociación Latinoamericana para la Formación y Enseñanza de la psicologia (ALFEPSI) 02224

Contact address not obtained. E-mail: contacto@alfepsi.org.
URL: http://www.alfepsi.org/
History Founded 20 May 2011, Cajamarca (Peru). **Aims** Contribute to the training and development of professionals in psychology. **Structure** General Assembly; Coordinating Board. **Activities** Events/meetings. **Events** *Discursos y practicas para una formación en psicologia latinoamericana culturalmente sensible* Medellin (Colombia) 2019, *Congreso* Rio de Janeiro (Brazil) 2018, *Congreso* Lima (Peru) 2017, *Congreso* San José (Costa Rica) 2016, *Congreso* Santa Marta (Colombia) 2015.
Members Individuals (246) in 16 countries:
Argentina, Bolivia, Brazil, Chile, Colombia, Costa Rica, Cuba, Ecuador, Mexico, Nicaragua, Panama, Paraguay, Peru, Uruguay, USA, Venezuela.
Institutional (59) in 12 countries:
Argentina, Brazil, Chile, Colombia, Costa Rica, Cuba, Ecuador, Mexico, Panama, Paraguay, Peru, Uruguay.
[2019/XM7633/**D**]

♦ Asociación Latinoamericana de Genética (ALAG) 02225

Latin American Association of Genetics – Association latinoaméricaine de génétique
Pres address not obtained. E-mail: alagsecretaria@gmail.com.
URL: https://www.alagenet.org/
History 3 Jul 1969, Porto Alegre (Brazil). First Congress was held in São Paulo (Brazil), 02-08 July 1972. Regional society of *Red Latinoamericana de Ciencias Biológicas (RELAB, #18706).* **Aims** Contribute to the progress of Genetics and Related Sciences, promoting conditions that allow advancement and improvement of knowledge in all its areas in Latin America. **Languages** English, Portuguese, Spanish. **Activities** Events/meetings. **Events** *Congress* Guadalajara (Mexico) 2024, *Congress* Mendoza (Argentina) 2019, *Congress* Montevideo (Uruguay) 2016, *Congress* Rosario (Argentina) 2012, *Congress* Viña del Mar (Chile) 2010. **NGO Relations** Member of (1): *Red de Redes Cientificas de América Latina y el Caribe (CCRCLA, no recent information).* [2023/XD8054/**D**]

♦ Asociación Latinoamericana de Geofisica Espacial / see Asociación Latinoamericana de Geofísica Espacial (#02226)

♦ Asociación Latinoamericana de Geofísica Espacial (ALAGE) 02226

Latin American Association of Space Geophysics
Information Sec address not obtained. E-mail: alage.information@gmail.com.
Intl Sec address not obtained.
URL: http://www.alage.org/
History Nov 1993, Havana (Cuba). Founded during the 3rd COLAGE congress. Former names and other names: *Asociación Latinoamericana de Geofisica Espacial* – former. **Aims** As a scientific autonomous society: motivate development of research in Space Geophysics, taking advantage of the human resources and cultural unity, as well as similar economic conditions of Latin America. **Structure** Officers. **Languages** English, Portuguese, Spanish. **Staff** Part-time, voluntary. **Finance** Sources: members' dues. **Activities** Events/meetings. Organizes *Congreso Latinoamericano de Geofísica Espacial* (COLAGE) / Latin American Conference on Space Geophysics. **Events** *Latin American Conference on Space Geophysics (COLAGE) / Congreso Latinoamericano de Geofísica Espacial* Chile 2021, *Latin American Conference on Space Geophysics (COLAGE) / Congreso Latinoamericano de Geofísica Espacial* Pucón (Chile) 2020, *Latin American Conference on Space Geophysics (COLAGE) / Congreso Latinoamericano de Geofísica Espacial* Buenos Aires (Argentina) 2018, *Latin American Conference on Space Geophysics (COLAGE) / Congreso Latinoamericano de Geofísica Espacial* Cusco (Peru) 2014, *Latin American Conference on Space Geophysics (COLAGE) / Congreso Latinoamericano de Geofísica Espacial* Puntarenas (Costa Rica) 2011. **Publications** *ALAGE Boletin.*
Members Members in 11 countries:
Argentina, Bolivia, Brazil, Chile, Colombia, Costa Rica, Cuba, Mexico, Peru, Uruguay, Venezuela.
NGO Relations *Scientific Committee on Solar-Terrestrial Physics (SCOSTEP, #19151).* [2021/XD5107/**D**]

♦ Asociación Latino Americana de Geoquimica Organica (#02331)

♦ Asociación Latinoamericana de Gerencia Deportiva (ALGEDE) 02227

Latin American Association for Sport Management
Sec Universidad Autónoma de Nuevo León, Ciudad Universitaria, Pedro de Alba s/n San Nicolás de los Garza, 66451 Monterrey NL, Mexico.
Pres Carrera 27 #10-02 Barrio Alamos, Edificio 7B – Oficina 108, Pereira 660003, Risaralda, Colombia.
URL: http://www.algede.org/homees.html
History 6 Mar 2009, Turmero (Venezuela). **Structure** Board of Directors. **Finance** Members' dues. **Events** *Biennial Congress* Colima (Mexico) 2019, *Biennial Congress* Buenos Aires (Argentina) 2017, *Biennial Congress* Sao Paulo (Brazil) 2015, *Biennial Congress* Pereira (Colombia) 2013, *Biennial Congress* Monterrey (Mexico) 2011. **Publications** *ALGeDe Bulletin*; *Journal de AlGeDe.* **NGO Relations** A regional organization of *World Association for Sport Management (WASM, #21194).* [2020/XJ9555/**D**]

♦ Asociación Latinoamericana de Gestión Tecnológica / see Asociación Latino-Iberoamericana de Gestión Tecnológica y de la Innovación (#02277)
♦ Asociación Latinoamericana de Hidrologia Subterranea para el Desarrollo (#16242)
♦ Asociación Latinoamericana e Ibérica de Derecho y Economia (#16340)
♦ Asociación Latinoamericana de la Industria del Cloro, Alcalis y Derivados (#16295)
♦ Asociación Latinoamericana de la Industria Curtidora (inactive)

♦ Asociación Latinoamericana de la Industria Eléctrica, Electrónica y de Gasodomésticos (ALAINEE) 02228

Associação Latino-Americana da Indústria Elétrica, Eletrônica e Gasodomésticos
Secretariat Calle Paraguay 1855, C1121ABA Buenos Aires, Argentina. T. +541148120232.
URL: http://www.alainee.org/
History A sectoral activity initiated and supported by the then *Latin American Free Trade Association (LAFTA, inactive)*, currently, since 12 Aug 1980, *Latin American Integration Association (LAIA, #16343).* **Aims** Defend sectorial issues of electrical and electronic companies in Latin America. **Structure** Regular Meeting (annual, always in Montevideo – Uruguay). **Languages** Portuguese, Spanish. **Staff** 3.00 FTE, voluntary. **Finance** No budget. **Events** *Meeting* Montevideo (Uruguay) 2008. **Members** Membership countries not specified. [2016/XD4704/t/**D**]

♦ Asociación Latinoamericana de Industriales y Camaras de la Alimentación (inactive)
♦ Asociación Latinoamericana de Industriales Molineros (no recent information)

♦ Asociación Latinoamericana de la Industria del Letrero (ALAIL) ... 02229

Main Office Agrelo 4049, 1224 Buenos Aires, Argentina. T. +541149583053.
History Mar 2008, Orlando FL (USA), during expo of *International Sign Association.* **Aims** Serve as a medium of cooperation and communication for the defence and strengthening of the sign-making market in Latin America. **Structure** Annual Assembly. Chairman and Secretary (renewable terms every 2 years). Management based in Buenos Aires (Argentina). **Languages** Spanish. **Staff** 20.00 FTE, voluntary. **Finance** by CAIL (Argentinian Sign Association). **Publications** Assembly proceedings.
Members in 10 countries:
Brazil, Chile, Colombia, Costa Rica, Ecuador, Guatemala, Mexico, Peru, Uruguay, Venezuela.
NGO Relations *Latin American Association of Design (ALADI, #16238)* is a founding member. Links with ISA. [2011.06.01/XM4034/t/**E**]

♦ Asociación Latinoamericana de la Industria Móvil (no recent information)

♦ Asociación Latinoamericana de la Industria Nacional de Agroquimicos (ALINA) 02230

Latin American Association of National Agrochemical Industries
Contact address not obtained. T. +50622712752. Fax +50622714184.
URL: http://www.alinainternacional.org/
Aims Unite and represent generic industrial and commercial distributors so as to increase agricultural production and competitiveness in the whole Latin American region. **Structure** Board of Directors, including President, Secretary, Assistant Secretary, Treasurer and Coordinator.
Members Companies and organizations (17) in 10 countries:
Argentina, Brazil, Colombia, Costa Rica, Ecuador, Guatemala, Mexico, Paraguay, Peru, Venezuela.
IGO Relations Participates as observer in the activities of: *Codex Alimentarius Commission (CAC, #04081).* [2011/XM4035/t/**D**]

♦ Asociación Latinoamericana de la Industria del Petróleo (ALIP) ... 02231

Latin America Petroleum Association – Associação Latino-americana da Indústria do Petróleo
Contact address not obtained. T. +5716411944.
URL: http://www.alip.org/
History 4 Dec 2009, Bogota (Colombia). **Aims** Promote petroleum-related activities in the region.
Members Active; Honorary Partners. National societies in 7 countries:
Argentina, Bolivia, Brazil, Colombia, Costa Rica, Ecuador, Venezuela. [2011/XM4033/t/**D**]

♦ Asociación Latinoamericana de Industrias de Bienes de Capital e Infraestructura (no recent information)

♦ Asociación Latinoamericana de Industrias Farmacéuticas (ALIFAR) 02232

Association latinoaméricaine des industries pharmaceutiques – Latin American Association of Pharmaceutical Industries
SG Av Del Libertador 602, Piso 6, Buenos Aires, Argentina. T. +541148199550. E-mail: secretariageneral@alifar.org.
URL: http://www.alifar.org/
History Nov 1980. **Aims** Promote cooperation between, and safeguard the interest of, national pharmaceutical industries of Latin America; encourage free competition in supply of raw materials and local production; support development of the industry and related research. **Structure** General Assembly; Board of Directors; Secretary-General. **Languages** Spanish. **Staff** 3.00 FTE, paid. **Finance** Contributions of affiliates. Budget (annual): US$ 40,000. **Events** *Annual Assembly* Santiago (Chile) 2015, *Annual Assembly* Bariloche (Argentina) 2014, *Annual Assembly* Cartagena de Indias (Colombia) 2013, *Annual Assembly* Mexico 2012, *Annual Assembly* Mexico City (Mexico) 2012.
Members Enterprises (400), representing 90 percent of the national enterprise market and acting together through national coordinating bodies, in 15 countries:
Argentina, Bolivia, Brazil, Chile, Colombia, Costa Rica, Dominican Rep, Ecuador, El Salvador, Guatemala, Mexico, Paraguay, Peru, Uruguay, Venezuela.
Consultative Status Consultative status granted from: *ECOSOC (#05331)* (Ros C); *UNCTAD (#20285)* (General Category); *World Intellectual Property Organization (WIPO, #21593)* (Permanent Observer Status); *UNIDO (#20336).* [2015/XD0362/t/**D**]

♦ Asociación Latinoamericana de Industrias Plasticas (no recent information)
♦ Asociación Latinoamericana de Informadores Comerciales (no recent information)
♦ Asociación Latino-americana de Ingenieros de Seguransa del Trabajo (#16314)
♦ Asociación Latinoamericana de Inmunología / see Latin American and Caribbean Association of Immunology (#16265)
♦ Asociación Latinoamericana de Instituciones de Educación Teológica (unconfirmed)

♦ Asociación Latinoamericana de Instituciones Financieras para el Desarrollo (ALIDE) 02233

Latin American Association of Development Financing Institutions – Association latinoaméricaine d'institutions pour le financement du développement – Associacão Latino-Americana de Instituições Financeiras para o Desenvolvimento
SG Av Paseo de la República 3211, 15047, Lima, Peru. T. +5114422400. Fax +5114428105. E-mail: secretariageneral@alide.org – bjcarbajal@alide.org.
Pres c/o COFIDE, Augusto Tamayo 160, 15072, Lima, Peru.
URL: http://www.alide.org.pe/

History 24 Jan 1968, Washington, DC (USA). Founded, at a meeting convened for that purpose by *Inter-American Development Bank (IDB, #11427)*. Updated By-laws approved by 2nd Special Meeting of the General Assembly, 17 May 1978, Buenos Aires (Argentina). Amendments approved at: 3rd Extraordinary General Assembly, 23 Oct 1979, Lima (Peru); 5th Extraordinary General Assembly, 26 May 1998, Lima. Recognized by the Peruvian Government and other Latin American countries (unspecified). **Aims** Highlight and strengthen the role that development finance institutions play in the more equitable growth of member countries; stimulate information exchange concerning products, services and better practices; contribute to the training and technical assistance of associates; promote collaboration to foster business and financial cooperation; encourage contribution to the social and economic development of the region; support financial viability and act as a spokesperson for development banking in Latin America and the Caribbean. **Structure** General Assembly (annual); Executive Committee; General Secretariat. Headquarters based in Lima (Peru). **Languages** English, Portuguese, Spanish. **Staff** 25.00 FTE, paid; 5.00 FTE, voluntary. **Finance** Sources: fees for services; meeting proceeds; members' dues. **Activities** Capacity building; events/meetings; financial and/or material support; publishing activities; research/documentation; training/education. **Events** *World Congress on Agricultural and Rural Finance* Morelia (Mexico) 2022, *General Assembly* Willemstad (Curaçao) 2022, *General Assembly* Lima (Peru) 2021, *General Assembly* Lima (Peru) 2020, *General Assembly* Willemstad (Curaçao) 2020. **Publications** *Banca and Desarrollo Review*. E-news bulletin.
Members Active; Associate; Collaborating. Active in 22 countries:
Argentina, Belize, Bolivia, Brazil, Chile, Colombia, Costa Rica, Cuba, Curaçao, Dominican Rep, Ecuador, El Salvador, Guatemala, Haiti, Honduras, Mexico, Nicaragua, Panama, Paraguay, Peru, Uruguay, Venezuela.
Associate in 8 countries:
Canada, China, France, Germany, India, Portugal, Russia, Spain.
Included in the above, 9 organizations listed in this Yearbook:
Agence française de développement (AFD); Banco Latinoamericano de Comercio Exterior (BLADEX, #03159); Central American Bank for Economic Integration (CABEI, #03658); Compañía Española de Financiación de Desarrollo (COFIDES); Development Bank of Latin America (CAF, #05055); European Investment Bank (EIB, #07599); Fondo Financiero para el Desarrollo de la Cuenca del Plata (FONPLATA, #09833); Inter-American Development Bank (IDB, #11427); Kreditanstalt für Wiederaufbau (KfW).
Collaborating members in 7 countries:
Argentina, Brazil, Costa Rica, Ecuador, Paraguay, Peru, Venezuela.
Consultative Status Consultative status granted from: *FAO (#09260)* (Liaison Status); *UNCTAD (#20285)* (General Category); *UNIDO (#20336)*; *OAS (#17629)* (Special Status). **IGO Relations** Observer status with (1): *Sistema Económico Latinoamericano (SELA, #19294)*. Associated with Department of Global Communications of the United Nations. **NGO Relations** Represents: *World Federation of Development Financing Institutions (WFDFI, #21428)*. [2021/XD2859/y/D]

♦ Asociación Latinoamericana de Integración (#16343)

♦ Asociación Latinoamericana de Internet (ALAI) 02234

Exec Dir Rambla República de México 6125, 11400 Montevideo, Uruguay. T. +59826042222. E-mail: info@alai.lat.
URL: https://alai.lat/ [2020/AA1304/D]

♦ Asociación Latinoamericana de Investigación y Desarrollo del Algodón (ALIDA) 02235

Latin American Association for Cotton Research and Development
Pres INTA, Centro Regional Chaco-Formosa, Av Wilde 5, 3500 Resistencia, Argentina. T. +543722426558 – +543722427471ext105.
URL: http://www.alida-algodon.org/
History Founded 1986. **Events** *Meeting* Cartagena de Indias (Colombia) 2013, *Meeting* Buenos Aires (Argentina) 2011, *Meeting* Resistencia (Argentina) 2010, *Meeting* Ibagué (Colombia) 2005, *Meeting* Goiânia (Brazil) 2003. [2013/XJ1126/D]

♦ Asociación Latino Americana de Investigaciones de Mercado y Opinión (no recent information)
♦ Asociación Latinoamericana de Investigaciones en Reproducción Humana / see Asociación Latinoamericana de Investigadores en Reproducción Humana (#02238)
♦ Asociación Latinoamericana de Investigación Institucional (inactive)

♦ Asociación Latinoamericana de Investigadores en Campañas Electorales (ALICE) 02236

Sec Avenida Ronda de Levante 10, 30008 Murcia, Spain. E-mail: info@alice-comunicacionpolitica.com.
URL: https://www.alice-comunicacionpolitica.com/
History 2012. **Aims** Promote, disseminate, study and analyse issues concerning electoral campaigns and political communication. **Structure** General Assembly; Board of Directors. **Activities** Events/meetings; networking/liaising; research/documentation. **Events** *International Congress* 2020, *International Congress* Murcia (Spain) 2018, *International Congress* Bogota (Colombia) 2017, *International Congress* Buenos Aires (Argentina) 2016, *International Congress* Belo Horizonte (Brazil) 2015. **Publications** *MARCO – Revista de Márketing y Comunicación Política* in Spanish; *Más Poder Local* in Spanish. [2021/AA1932/D]

♦ Asociación Latinoamericana de Investigadores de la Comunicación (ALAIC) 02237

Association latinoaméricaine de chercheurs sur la communication – Latin American Association of Communications Researchers
Pres Centro de Estudios de la Comunicación, Fac de Ciencias Politicas y Sociales, UNAM, Circuito Mario de la Cueva S/N, Cuidad Universitaria, Delegación Coyoacan, 04510 Mexico City CDMX, Mexico. E-mail: crovi@servidor.unam.mx.
Dir of International Relations address not obtained.
URL: http://www.alaic.net/
History Founded Nov 1978. **Aims** Group and assist the members of the Latin American scientific community specialized in research on communication and promote the development and improvement of these activities. **Structure** General Assembly; Executive Board. **Languages** Portuguese, Spanish. **Staff** 0.50 FTE, paid. **Finance** Contributions of members. Also support from the University of Guadalajara – Centre for the Study of Communication. **Events** *Congress* Lima (Peru) 2014, *Congress* Montevideo (Uruguay) 2012, *Congress* La Plata (Argentina) 2004, *Communication sciences and society – a dialogue for the digital era* Santa Cruz (Bolivia) 2002, *Latin American seminar on investigation in communications* La Plata (Argentina) 2001. **Publications** *Boletin ALAIC* (2 a year) in Portuguese, Spanish. **Information Services** *BILAC* – database – Latin American communication bibliography.
Members National associations in 9 countries:
Argentina, Brazil, Chile, Colombia, Mexico, Peru, Spain, Uruguay, Venezuela.
Individuals in 21 countries:
Argentina, Bolivia, Brazil, Canada, Chile, Colombia, Costa Rica, Cuba, Dominican Rep, Ecuador, El Salvador, Honduras, Mexico, Panama, Paraguay, Peru, Puerto Rico, Spain, Uruguay, USA, Venezuela.
Honorary members include one organization listed in this Yearbook:
Centro Internacional de Estudios Superiores de Comunicación para América Latina (CIESPAL, #03806).
NGO Relations Member of: *Confederación Iberoamericana de Asociaciones Científicas y Académicas de la Comunicación (CONFIBERCOM, #04448); Federación Latinoamericana de Facultades de Comunicación Social (FELAFACS, #09353); International Association for Media and Communication Research (IAMCR, #12022); World Journalism Education Council (WJEC, #21602).* [2015/XD8636/D]

♦ Asociación Latinoamericana de Investigadores en Reproducción Humana (ALIRH) 02238

Latin American Association for Human Reproduction Research – Association latinoaméricaine de recherches sur la reproduction humaine
Contact c/o CEMICAMP, Caixa Postal 6181, CEP 13084 – 971, Campinas SP, CEP 13084 – 971, Brazil. Fax +551932892440.
URL: http://www.alirh.org/
History Also referred to as *Asociación Latinoamericana de Investigaciones en Reproducción Humana (ALIRH)*. **Events** *Meeting* Sao Paulo (Brazil) 2009, *Meeting* Buenos Aires (Argentina) 2007, *Meeting* Cartagena de Indias (Colombia) 2005, *Meeting* Varadero (Cuba) 2003, *Meeting* Curitiba (Brazil) 2001. **Members** Membership countries not specified. [2017/XD0189/D]

♦ Asociación Latinoamericana de Jojoba (inactive)
♦ Asociación Latinoamericana de Libre Comercio (inactive)

♦ Asociación Latinoamericana de Logistica (ALALOG) 02239

Contact Rincón 500, CP 11000, Montevideo, Uruguay. T. +59825185037. E-mail: secretaria@alalog.org.
URL: http://www.alalog.org/
History Founded at the instigation of *Latin American Integration Association (LAIA, #16343)*. **Aims** Bring together chambers and associations of Latin American Operators, Entrepreneurs and Professionals involved in the management of the supply chain. **Structure** General Assembly; Executive Committee. **Events** *Summit* Mexico City (Mexico) 2019.
Members Full in 10 countries:
Argentina, Bolivia, Brazil, Colombia, Ecuador, Mexico, Paraguay, Peru, Uruguay, Venezuela. [2019/XM7631/D]

♦ Asociación Latinoamericana de Malezas / see Latin American Weed Society (#16394)
♦ Asociación Latinoamericana de Malherbologia (#16394)
♦ Asociación Latinoamericana de Managers Musicales (unconfirmed)
♦ Asociación Latinoamericana de Medicina de Aviación y del Espacio / see Asociación Iberoamericana de Medicina Aerospacial (#02147)
♦ Asociación Latinoamericana de Medicina del Estilo de Vida (#16347)
♦ Asociación Latinoamericana de Medicina Legal y Deontologia Médica (inactive)
♦ Asociación Latinoamericana de Medicina Legal y Deontologia Médica e Iberoamericana de Ciencias Forenses (no recent information)

♦ Asociación Latinoamericana de Medicina Reproductiva (ALMER) .. 02240

Sec address not obtained.
URL: http://www.almerweb.com/
History 3 Oct 2008, Quito (Ecuador), when replaced *Latin American Federation of Fertility and Sterility Societies (FLASEF, inactive)*. **Structure** Executive Committee. **Events** *Congress* Quito (Ecuador) 2016, *Congress* Lima (Peru) 2014, *Congress* Viña del Mar (Chile) 2012, *Congress* Bogota (Colombia) 2010. **NGO Relations** Associated with: *International Federation of Fertility Societies (IFFS, #13426)*. [2016/XJ8615/D]

♦ Asociación Latinoamericana de Medicina Social (ALAMES) 02241

Latin American Association of Social Medicine
Exec Sec 6o piso edif B, UNAM Fac de Medicina, Cd Universitaria, Mexico City CDMX, Mexico. E-mail: rgcs@unam.mx – rgcs@servidor.unam.mx.
Gen Coordinator address not obtained.
URL: http://www.alames.org/
History Nov 1984, Brazil. **Aims** Defend and promote the right to *health*. **Structure** General Coordination; Executive Secretary. **Languages** Portuguese, Spanish. **Staff** 4.00 FTE, paid. **Finance** Members' dues. **Events** *Congress* Santo Domingo (Dominican Rep) 2021, *Congress* La Paz (Bolivia) 2018, *Congress* Asunción (Paraguay) 2016, *Congress* San Salvador (El Salvador) 2014, *Congress* Montevideo (Uruguay) 2012.
Members in 20 countries:
Argentina, Bolivia, Brazil, Canada, Chile, Colombia, Costa Rica, Cuba, Dominican Rep, Ecuador, Guatemala, Haiti, Honduras, Mexico, Nicaragua, Paraguay, Peru, Uruguay, USA, Venezuela. [2016.10.18/XD8701/D]

♦ Asociación Latino Americana de Medio Ambiente y Desarrollo (no recent information)
♦ Asociación Latinoamericana de Mercadeo de Alimentos (no recent information)
♦ Asociación Latinoamericana de Mercadeo Social (unconfirmed)

♦ Asociación Latinoamericana de Metros y Subterraneos (ALAMYS) . 02242

Latin American Association of Metros and Subways
Secretariat Metro Madrid, Calle Cavanilles 58, 28007 Madrid, Spain. T. +34913798805. Fax +34913798995. E-mail: alamys@mail.metromadrid.es.
URL: http://www.alamys.org/
History 1986, Caracas (Venezuela), as *Latino-American Underground Committee (CLM)*. Current name adopted, 27 Nov 1987, at 1st official meeting. **Aims** Promote exchange of knowledge and experience among operators of urban and metropolitan *rail* and underground systems for mass *transport* of passengers in the countries of Latin America and the Iberian peninsula concerning relevant aspects of construction, operation, technology and management; contribute to increased productivity and optimization of resources. **Structure** General Assembly. Board, comprising President, 2 Vice-Chairmen, Secretary General and 3 members. Technical Committees (5): Management; New Undergrounds; Planning; Operation; Maintenance. **Languages** Portuguese, Spanish. **Finance** Members' dues. **Activities** Studies and evaluates technical and operational aspects of urban rail and underground public transport systems. **Events** *Meeting* Porto (Portugal) 2019, *Meeting* Madrid (Spain) 2018, *General Assembly* Quito (Ecuador) 2018, *General Assembly* Barcelona (Spain) 2017, *General Assembly* Buenos Aires (Argentina) 2013. **Publications** *ALAMYS Boletin* (4 a year).
Members Principal (31) organizations constructing and operating metropolitan rail systems transporting large numbers of passengers in 11 countries:
Argentina, Brazil, Chile, Colombia, Cuba, Mexico, Peru, Portugal, Puerto Rico, Spain, Venezuela.
Adhering (16) urban and suburban passenger transport organizations and companies providing equipment and services by metropolitan railways and developing their activity in a principal member country, in 8 countries:
Argentina, Belgium, Brazil, France, Mexico, Spain, Uruguay, Venezuela.
Included in the above, 2 organizations listed in this Yearbook:
International Association of Public Transport (#12118); Latin American Railways Association (#16365).
IGO Relations Collaboration agreement with: *United Nations Economic Commission for Latin America and the Caribbean (ECLAC, #20556).* [2013/XD3743/y/D]

♦ Asociación Latinoamericana de Micologia (#16248)
♦ Asociación Latinoamericana de Microbiologia (#16247)
♦ Asociación Latinoamericana de Micro, Pequeños y Medianos Empresarios (no recent information)
♦ Asociación Latinoamericana Multidisciplinaria de Planeación Estrategica del Medio Ambiente (inactive)
♦ Asociación Latinoamericana de Museos (inactive)
♦ Asociación Latinoamericana de Mutagenesis, Carcinogeneisi y Teratogenesis Ambiental (#16240)
♦ Asociación Latinoamericana de Nefrologia Pediatrica (#16379)
♦ Asociación Latinoamericana de Neumaticos y Llantas (#02332)
♦ Asociación Latinoamericana de neuropsicologia (unconfirmed)

♦ Asociación Latinoamericana de Obstetricia y Ginecologia Infantil y de la Adolescencia (ALOGIA) 02243

Pres address not obtained. E-mail: info@alogiaonline.org.
URL: http://www.alogiaonline.org/
History 20 Apr 1993, Santiago (Chile). **Structure** Executive Committee, comprising President, Secretary and Treasurer. **Events** *Congress* Asunción (Paraguay) 2019, *Congress* Montevideo (Uruguay) 2017, *Congress* San José (Costa Rica) 2015, *Congress* Lima (Peru) 2013, *Congress* Montevideo (Uruguay) 1997.
Members Full in 12 countries:
Argentina, Brazil, Chile, Colombia, Costa Rica, Cuba, Mexico, Panama, Paraguay, Peru, Uruguay, Venezuela.
NGO Relations *European Association of Paediatric and Adolescent Gynaecology (EURAPAG, #06140).* [2016/XJ6888/D]

♦ Asociación Latinoamericana de Odontologia Restauradora y Biomateriales (ALODYB) 02244

Latin American Operative Dentistry and Biomaterials Society
Main Office C/ Chacarilla 433, San Isidro, Lima, Peru. E-mail: alodybpy@gmail.com – alodybsecretaria@gmail.com.

URL: http://www.alodyb.com/
History 1996, Buenos Aires (Argentina). Former names and other names: *Asociación Latinoamericana de Operatoria Dental y Biomateriales* – former; *Associação Latinoamericana de Operação Dental e Biomateriais* – former. **Events** *Digital Congress* Paraguay 2021, *Congress* Asunción (Paraguay) 2019, *Congress* Bogota (Colombia) 2018, *Congress* Quito (Ecuador) 2017, *Congress* Concepción (Chile) 2015.
Members National organizations (13) in 11 countries:
Argentina, Brazil, Chile, Colombia, Dominican Rep, El Salvador, Guatemala, Paraguay, Peru, Uruguay, Venezuela.
[2021/XJ1048/**D**]

♦ Asociación Latinoamericana de Odontopediatría (ALOP) 02245

Acting Pres address not obtained. E-mail: alop.presidente@gmail.com.
URL: http://www.alopodontopediatria.org/
History 1993, Quito (Ecuador). Formalized 1993, following activities initiated 1971. **Aims** Promote improvement of *pediatric oral health* in Latin America. **Structure** Board of Directors. Officers: President, Honourary President, Vice-President, Secretary, Treasurer, Communications Officer. **Languages** English, Portuguese, Spanish. **Activities** Events/meetings; knowledge management/information dissemination; networking/liaising; training/education. **Events** *Congreso Latinoamericano de Odontopediatría* Monterrey (Mexico) 2022, *Congreso Latinoamericano de Odontopediatría* Antigua (Guatemala) 2021, *Congreso Latinoamericano de Odontopediatría* 2020, *Congreso Latinoamericano de Odontopediatría* Santa Marta (Colombia) 2016, *Congreso Latinoamericano de Odontopediatría* Sao Paulo (Brazil) 2014. **Publications** *Revista de Odontopediatria Latinoamericana.* Manuals; guides; brochures.
Members Full in 20 countries and territories:
Argentina, Bolivia, Brazil, Chile, Colombia, Costa Rica, Dominica, Ecuador, El Salvador, Guatemala, Honduras, Mexico, Nicaragua, Panama, Paraguay, Peru, Puerto Rico, Spain, Uruguay, Venezuela. [2023.02.15/XM7646/**D**]

♦ Asociación Latinoamericana de Operadores de Agua y Saneamiento (ALOAS) 02246

Address not obtained.
URL: http://www.aloas.org/
History Nov 2010. **Events** *Annual Meeting* Panama (Panama) 2017, *Annual Meeting* Buenos Aires (Argentina) 2015, *Annual Meeting* Buenos Aires (Argentina) 2014, *Annual Meeting* Buenos Aires (Argentina) 2013, *Annual Meeting* Buenos Aires (Argentina) 2012.
Members Full (107) in 15 countries:
Argentina, Bolivia, Brazil, Chile, Colombia, Costa Rica, Dominican Rep, Ecuador, El Salvador, Honduras, Mexico, Panama, Paraguay, Peru, Uruguay. [2017/XM5880/**D**]

- ♦ Asociación Latinoamericana de Operadores de Turismo (inactive)
- ♦ Asociación Latinoamericana de Operatoria Dental y Biomateriales / see Asociación Latinoamericana de Odontologia Restauradora y Biomateriales (#02244)

♦ Asociación Latinoamericana de Optometria y Optica (ALDOO) 02247

Admin PO Box 9192, Caguas PR 00726, USA. E-mail: secretaria@aldoo.info – administradora@aldoo.info.
URL: http://www.aldoo.info/
History 1969, Venezuela. **Aims** Represent optometry, the field of optics and the profession in all its aspects in Latin America. **Structure** General Delegations Meeting; Governing Board; President. Official office at the Interamerican University of Puerto Rico. **Languages** Spanish. **Staff** 6.00 FTE, paid. **Finance** Sources: meeting proceeds; members' dues. **Activities** Guidance/assistance/consulting; knowledge management/information dissemination. **Events** *Congress / Latin American Congress of Optometry and Optics* Lima (Peru) 2013, *Congress / Latin American Congress of Optometry and Optics* San Juan (Puerto Rico) 2008, *Congress / Latin American Congress of Optometry and Optics* Lima (Peru) 2006, *Meeting of the Latin American universities* Quito (Ecuador) 2003, *Central American congress / Latin American Congress of Optometry and Optics* San José (Costa Rica) 2003.
Members Associate; Affiliate; Honorary. Members in 9 countries and territories:
Argentina, Bolivia, Brazil, Chile, Colombia, Mexico, Panama, Puerto Rico, Uruguay.
Universities (4) in 3 countries and territories:
Bolivia, Colombia, Puerto Rico.
NGO Relations Regional member of: *World Council of Optometry (WCO, #21335).* Instrumental in setting up: *Asociación Latinoamericana de Facultades de Optometria (ALDEFO, #02220).* [2020.03.31/XD4077/**D**]

- ♦ Asociación Latinoamericana de Organismos de Seguros de Crédito a la Exportación (#16241)
- ♦ Asociación Latinoamericana de Organizaciones de Promoción (inactive)
- ♦ Asociación Latino Americana de Ostomizados (inactive)

♦ Asociación Latinoamericana Out of Home (ALOOH) 02248

Address not obtained.
URL: http://www.alooh.org/
Aims Promote and continue building on the prestige, prioritization, best creative and technical standards, and the unity and growth of the region's ooh advertising companies. **Structure** Board of Directors; Executive Committee.
Members Full in 20 countries:
Argentina, Bolivia, Brazil, Chile, Colombia, Costa Rica, Cuba, Dominican Rep, Ecuador, El Salvador, Guatemala, Haiti, Honduras, Mexico, Nicaragua, Panama, Paraguay, Peru, Uruguay, Venezuela.
NGO Relations *World Out of Home Organization (WOO, #21702).* [2018/XM7637/**D**]

♦ Asociación Latinoamericana de Paleobotanica y Palinologia (ALPP) 02249

Associação Latinoamericana de Paleobotânica e Palinologia – Latin American Association of Paleobotany and Palynology – Association latinoaméricaine de paléobotanique et palinologie
Pres CICyTTP-CONICET, Dr Matteri y España, E3105BWA Diamante, Argentina. E-mail: medipa@cicyttp.org.ar.
Main Website: http://www.ufrgs.br/alpp/
History Dec 1972, Mexico City (Mexico). Founded at *Congreso Latinoamericano de Botanica.* **Aims** Promote dissemination, knowledge and education of palaeobotany and palynology in Latin America and mutual exchange of data and information among members; encourage interchange with similar associations, either national or international. **Structure** Board; Executive Committee. **Languages** Portuguese, Spanish. **Staff** Part-time, voluntary. **Finance** Sources: members' dues. **Activities** Events/meetings; knowledge management/information dissemination. **Events** *Annual Meeting* Manizales (Colombia) 2022, *International Scientific Meeting* Salvador (Brazil) 2016, *Meeting of palaeobotany and palynology* Sao Paulo (Brazil) 1990. **Publications** *Boletin de la ALPP* (annual).
Members Individuals in 17 countries:
Argentina, Belgium, Bolivia, Brazil, Chile, Colombia, Cuba, Ecuador, Germany, India, Mexico, Panama, Peru, Portugal, Uruguay, USA, Venezuela.
NGO Relations Member of (1): *International Federation of Palynological Societies (IFPS, #13498).*
[2022.10.28/XD1224/v/**D**]

♦ Asociación Latinoamericana de la Papa (ALAP) 02250

Latin American Potato Association
Pres 14 de julio 2735, 7600 Mar del Plata, Argentina. E-mail: alapadm777@gmail.com.
URL: http://www.papaslatinas.org/
History 1977. Former names and other names: *Sociedad Latinoamericana de Investigadores de Papa (SLIP)* – former (1977 to 2002). **Aims** Contribute to connecting *potato* researchers, growers, merchants and processors; promote the exchange of technical and scientific staff and other associates, as well as genetic material, literature, etc. **Structure** General Assembly; Board; Editorial Board. **Languages** English, Portuguese, Spanish. **Staff** 16.00 FTE, voluntary. **Finance** Members' dues. Other sources: congress revenue; special projects. **Activities** Events/meetings; publishing activities. **Events** *Congress* Puerto Varas (Chile) 2022, *Congress* León (Mexico) 2020, *Congress* Cusco (Peru) 2018, *Congress* Panama (Panama) 2016, *Congress* Bogota (Colombia) 2014. **Publications** *Revista Latinoamericana de la Papa.*
Members Full in 16 countries:
Argentina, Brazil, Chile, Colombia, Costa Rica, Cuba, Dominican Rep, Ecuador, El Salvador, France, Guatemala, Mexico, Panama, Peru, Spain, USA.
Regional member:
International Potato Center (#14627).
IGO Relations Contacts with: *FAO (#09260)*; United Nations. **NGO Relations** Contacts with: *African Potato Association (APA, #00421)*; *European Association for Potato Research (EAPR, #06160)*; *International Potato Center (#14627)*; *World Potato Congress (WPC, #21734).* [2020/XJ6410/y/**D**]

- ♦ Asociación Latinoamericana de Parques Cementerios y Servicios Exequiales / see Asociación Latinoamericana de Parques Cementerios y Servicios Funderarios (#02251)

♦ Asociación Latinoamericana de Parques Cementerios y Servicios Funderarios (ALPAR) 02251

Exec Dir Calle 33 No 81A-51 Oficina 404, Medellin 050032, Antioquia, Colombia. T. +5744134411 – +5742508428.
URL: http://www.alpar.com.co/
History Founded 1988, Cartagena de Indias (Colombia), as *Asociación Latinoamericana de Parques Cementerios y Servicios Exequiales (ALPAR).* **Aims** Bring together individuals and entities linked to the funeral industry; encourage continuous learning. **Structure** Executive Board.
Members Full in 20 countries:
Argentina, Australia, Bolivia, Brazil, Chile, Colombia, Costa Rica, Dominican Rep, Ecuador, Guatemala, Honduras, Mexico, Nicaragua, Panama, Peru, San Marino, Spain, Uruguay, USA, Venezuela. [2016/XJ0443/**D**]

♦ Asociación Latinoamericana de Parques Zoológicos y Acuarios (ALPZA) 02252

Latin American Association of Zoos and Aquariums
Exec Dir Nuestra Sra del Rosario 165, Las Condes, Santiago, Santiago Metropolitan, Chile. E-mail: info@alpza.com – alpza@alpza.com.
Communications/Membership Manager address not obtained.
URL: http://www.alpza.com/
History 1990, as *Asociación Latinoamericana de Parques Zoológicos, Acuarios y Afines (ALPZA) – Latin American Association of Zoos, Aquariums and Similar Sites.* Previously also referred to in English as *Latin American Association of Zoological Gardens and Aquariums* and as *Latin American and Caribbean Association of Zoological Parks and Aquariums* and by initials *FUNPZA.* **Aims** Promote strategies for integral development of members; positively impact on Latin American *biodiversity conservation*; warranty the viability of populations of Latin American zoos and aquariums. **Languages** English, Portuguese, Spanish. **Staff** 2.00 FTE, paid. **Finance** Members' dues. Funding for projects and capacity building initiatives. **Events** *Annual Conference* Cali (Colombia) 2016, *Annual Conference / Congress* Córdoba (Argentina) 2015, *Annual Conference / Congress* Lima (Peru) 2014, *Annual Conference / Congress* Sao Paulo (Brazil) 2013, *Annual Conference / Congress* Puebla (Mexico) 2012. **Publications** *ALPZA Bulletin*; *ALPZA Conservation Newsletter.*
Members Institutional in 19 countries and territories:
Argentina, Bolivia, Brazil, Chile, Colombia, Cuba, Dominican Rep, Ecuador, France, Guadeloupe, Guatemala, Guiana Fr, Mexico, Panama, Peru, Portugal, Uruguay, USA, Venezuela.
IGO Relations *Secretariat of the Convention on International Trade in Endangered Species of Wild Fauna and Flora (CITES Secretariat, #19199).* **NGO Relations** Member of: *International Union for Conservation of Nature and Natural Resources (IUCN, #15766)*; *World Association of Zoos and Aquariums (WAZA, #21208).*
[2015.01.31/XD4240/**D**]

- ♦ Asociación Latinoamericana de Parques Zoológicos, Acuarios y Afines / see Asociación Latinoamericana de Parques Zoológicos y Acuarios (#02252)
- ♦ Asociación Latinoamericana de Patologia Clinica/Medicina de Laboratorio (#16299)
- ♦ Asociación Latinoamericana de Patologia Toxicologica (#16387)
- ♦ Asociación Latinoamericana de Pediatria (#16360)

♦ Asociación Latinoamericana de Perfusión (ALAP) 02253

Contact 25371 Patriot Terrace, Aldie VA 20105, USA. T. +19549017867. E-mail: operaciones@asociacionalap.com.
URL: https://www.asociacionalap.com/
History Current statutes adopted Mar 2016. **Aims** Promote continuous education, professional and union improvement of Latin American perfusionists, so as to achieve and maintain the highest standards of safety and quality in the care of our patients. **Structure** General Assembly; Board of Directors. **Publications** *EnBOMBA* – review. [2022/XM7664/**D**]

- ♦ Asociación Latinoamericana de Periodistas para el Desarrollo (inactive)

♦ Asociación Latinoamericana de Piso Pélvico (ALAPP) 02254

Secretariat address not obtained. T. +34913612600. E-mail: secretaria@alapp.org.
URL: http://www.alapp.org/
History Founded 2015. **Aims** Promote the training, dissemination and research of all aspects related to the area of voiding, *anorectal* and pelvic floor dysfunction. **Structure** Board of Directors; Scientific Committee; Secretariat. **Activities** Events/meetings. **Events** *Congreso* Santiago (Chile) 2019, *Congreso* Mexico City (Mexico) 2018, *Congreso* Sao Paulo (Brazil) 2017, *Congreso* Bogota (Colombia) 2016. [2019/XM7651/**D**]

- ♦ Asociación Latinoamericana de Planificadores Energéticos (inactive)

♦ Asociación Latinoamericana de Plantas de Rendimiento (ALAPRE) . 02255

Contact address not obtained. T. +50622324080. E-mail: info@alapre.org.
URL: http://www.alapre.org/
History Founded 2012. Registered in accordance with the law of Costa Rica. **Aims** Promote a sustainable industry and food biosecurity. **Structure** General Assembly; Board of Directors. **Activities** Events/meetings. **Events** *Congress* Cartagena de Indias (Colombia) 2019, *Congress* Cartagena de Indias (Colombia) 2018, *Congress* Cartagena de Indias (Colombia) 2017, *Congress* Cancún (Mexico) 2016, *Congress* Cancún (Mexico) 2015.
Members Full in 5 countries:
Brazil, Colombia, Costa Rica, Mexico, Venezuela. [2019/XM7635/**D**]

♦ Asociación Latinoamericana de Población (ALAP) 02256

Contact Rua André Cavalcanti 106, sala 502, Bairro de Fatima, Rio de Janeiro RJ, Brazil. T. +552122422077. E-mail: alap.secretaria@alapop.org.
Contact address not obtained.
URL: https://www.alapop.org/
History 19 Sep 2004, Caxambú (Brazil). **Structure** Board of Directors. **Events** *Congress* Valparaiso (Chile) 2022, *Congress* Rio de Janeiro (Brazil) 2020, *Congress* Puebla (Mexico) 2018, *Congress* Foz do Iguaçu (Brazil) 2016, *Congress* Lima (Peru) 2014. **Publications** *RELAP: Revista Latino Americana de Población* (2 a year).
[2022/XJ8964/**D**]

- ♦ Asociación Latinoamericana de Politica Cientifica y Tecnológica (inactive)
- ♦ Asociación Latinoamericana de Proctologia / see Latin American Association of Coloproctology (#16237)

♦ Asociación Latinoamericana para la Producción Animal (ALPA) ... 02257

Latin American Association for Animal Production – Association latinoaméricaine pour la production animale – Associação Latinoamericana da Produção Animal
Perm Sec 309-2528 Bowness Road NW, Calgary AB T2N 3L9, Canada. E-mail: secretariat@alpa.uy.
URL: http://www.alpa.uy/
History 1966. Statutes modified 1995; current statutes adopted 2021. **Aims** Carry out and promote studies, research and education which favor development of animal production; disseminate results of studies and research, especially those undertaken in various Latin American countries; promote and develop sustainable animal production and industry in Latin America, in harmony with the environment. **Structure** General Assembly (every 2 years); Executive Committee; Board of Directors; Consultative Council. **Languages** English,

Portuguese, Spanish. **Staff** 3.00 FTE, voluntary. Clerical staff partially paid from budget. **Finance** Sources: members' dues. Annual budget: 18,000 USD. **Activities** Knowledge management/information dissemination; research/documentation. **Events** *Biennial General Assembly* Guayaquil (Ecuador) 2018, *Biennial General Assembly* Pernambuco (Brazil) 2016, *Biennial General Assembly* Puerto Varas (Chile) 2015, *Biennial General Assembly* Havana (Cuba) 2013, *Biennial general assembly* Montevideo (Uruguay) 2011. **Publications** *ALPA en el Campo* (4 a year) in Spanish – Technical divulgation magazine; *Archivos Latinoamericanos de Producción Animal* (4 a year) in English, Portuguese, Spanish – journal. **Information Services** *Carta Electronica* in English, Portuguese, Spanish.
Members National organizations in 20 countries and territories:
Argentina, Bolivia, Brazil, Chile, Colombia, Costa Rica, Cuba, Dominican Rep, Ecuador, El Salvador, Guatemala, Honduras, Mexico, Nicaragua, Panama, Paraguay, Peru, Puerto Rico, Uruguay, Venezuela.
NGO Relations Member of (1): *World Association for Animal Production (WAAP, #21117)*. Also links with national associations. [2022.05.12/XD7335/D]

- ♦ Asociación Latinoamericana de Productores OTC / see Asociación Latinoamericana de Autocuidado Responsable (#02184)
- ♦ Asociación Latinoamericana de Productores de Vidrio (no recent information)

♦ Asociación Latinoamericana de Profesores de Medicina Familiar (ALPMF) 02258

Contact Avenida ävila Camacho 68 Centro, Xalapa, Veracruz CHIS, Mexico. E-mail: congreso.alpmf@gmail.com.
URL: http://www.alpmf.org/
History Founded 25 Feb 2001, Mexico City (Mexico), through an electronic communication system interconnecting Mexico City with Havana (Cuba), La Paz (Bolivia), San Juan (Puerto Rico), Santiago (Chile), Montevideo (Uruguay), and Monterrey, Xalapa and Queretaro (Mexico). **Aims** Promote, support, consolidate and spread knowledge of Family Medicine in undergraduate, postgraduate and continuing medical education, promote analysis of the principles and foundations of the specialty internationally. **Structure** Board of Directors (2 year terms), comprising President, Vice-President, Secretary, Treasurer-General, representatives of the 3 Commissions (Editorial and Diffusion, Membership, and Scientific). **Languages** Spanish. **Staff** 8.00 FTE, paid. **Finance** Proceeds from congresses, other events and journal sales. **Activities** Provides logistical support to professors of Family Medicine in order to publish research projects of undergraduate, postgraduate and continuing medical education students in scientific publications; promotes participation of members in local and international events; promotes and support formation of multinational groups for research on prevalent problems in Family Medicine in member countries; establishes strong relationships with associations and scientific organizations. Organizes annual virtual Congress (15 days in December). **Publications** *Revista Archivos en Medicina Familiar: An International Journal* – 13 vols published to date. Congress proceedings.
Members Full in 11 countries:
Argentina, Bolivia, Brazil, Colombia, Cuba, Ecuador, Mexico, Paraguay, Spain, Uruguay, Venezuela.
NGO Relations *Asociación Iberoamericana de Medicina y Salud Escolar y Universitaria (#02148)*; Colegio Mexicano de Medicina Familiar AC. [2012.09.14/XM8288/D]

- ♦ Asociación Latinoamericana para la Promoción del Habitat, del Urbanismo y de la Arquitectura (inactive)
- ♦ Asociación Latinoamericana de Promotores de Desarrollo Institucional (inactive)
- ♦ Asociación Latinoamericana para la Protección de los Cultivos / see CropLife Latin America (#04967)
- ♦ Asociación Latinoamericana de Psicologia Juridica y Forense (unconfirmed)

♦ Asociación Latinoamericana de Psicologia de la Salud (ALAPSA) . . 02259

Latin-American Society of Health Psychology
Pres Instituto de Investigaciones Psicologicas, Universidad Veracruzana, Xalapa VER, Mexico.
URL: http://www.alapsa.org/
Events *Congress* Colombia 2009, *Congress* Havana (Cuba) 2005, *Psicosalud : quadrennial international conference on health psychology* Havana (Cuba) 2004, *Congress* Cartagena de Indias (Colombia) 2003, *Congress* Veracruz, CHIS (Mexico) 2001. [2012/XJ4289/D]

- ♦ Asociación Latinoamericana de Psicologia Social (inactive)
- ♦ Asociación Latinoamericana de Psicólogos Sexólogos (inactive)
- ♦ Asociación Latinoamericana de Psicoterapias Cognitivas y Conductuales / see Federación Latinoamericana de Psicoterapias Cognitivas y Conductuales (#09363)

♦ Asociación Latinoamericana de Psicoterapias Integrativas (ALAPSI) 02260

Pres Zapata 552, Barrio de Belgrano, Buenos Aires, Argentina.
URL: http://www.alapsiweb.org/
History 25 Sep 2006, Quito (Ecuador). **Structure** Board, comprising President, Vice-President, Secretary, Treasurer and 3 members. **Events** *Encuentro Latinoamericano de Psicoterapias Integrativas* 2022, *Encuentro Latinoamericano de Psicoterapias Integrativas* Antigua (Guatemala) 2021, *Meeting* Montevideo (Uruguay) 2018, *Meeting* Buenos Aires (Argentina) 2016, *Meeting* Quito (Ecuador) 2014.
Members Full in 4 countries:
Argentina, Chile, Ecuador, Uruguay.
NGO Relations *Federación Latinoamericana de Psiconeuroinmunoendocrinologia (FLAPNIE, #09360).* [2021/XM4040/D]

- ♦ Asociación Latinoamericana de Psiquiatria / see Latin American Psychiatric Association (#16363)
- ♦ Asociación Latinoamericana de Pteridologia (inactive)
- ♦ Asociación Latinoamericana de Redactores de Revistas Biológicas (inactive)

♦ Asociación Latinoamericana de Relaciones Públicas (ALARP) 02261

Pres address not obtained. E-mail: presidencia@alarpargentina.com.ar.
URL: http://alarp-internacional.webnode.com.br/
History 1998, Brazil. **Events** *Congress* Mar del Plata (Argentina) 2012, *Congress* Bogota (Colombia) 2011, *Congress* Viña del Mar (Chile) 2010, *Congress* Asunción (Paraguay) 2009, *Congress* Montevideo (Uruguay) 2008.
Members Full in 6 countries:
Argentina, Brazil, Chile, Colombia, Paraguay, Uruguay. [2013/XJ6994/D]

♦ Asociación Latinoamericana de Rizobiologia (ALAR) 02262

Latin American Rhizobiology Association – Associação Latinoamericana de Rizobiologia
Exec Sec Ave Italia 3318, 11600 Montevideo, Uruguay. T. +59824871616ext146. Fax +59824875461. E-mail: secretaria.alar@gmail.com.
URL: http://www.alaronline.org/
History Founded 1964, Montevideo (Uruguay), during Reunion Latinoamericana de Rizobiologia (RELAR). Formalized 1980, Maracay (Venezuela), during 5th RELAR. **Aims** Promote activities of biological nitrogen fixation and use of microorganisms that promote plant growth in the countries of Latin America and the Caribbean. **Structure** General Assembly; Executive Committee; Consultative Council; Secretariat located in Montevideo (Uruguay). **Languages** English, Portuguese, Spanish. **Finance** Activities financed by BIAGRO. **Activities** Knowledge management/information dissemination; research and development; events/meetings. **Events** *Biennial Conference* Pucón (Chile) 2019, *Biennial Meeting* Lima (Peru) 2017, *Biennial Meeting* Londrina (Brazil) 2016, *Biennial Meeting* Seville (Spain) 2013, *Biennial Meeting* Maldonado (Uruguay) 2011. **Publications** *Boletim ALAR* in Spanish. **Members** Latin-American and Caribbean membership. Membership countries not specified. **IGO Relations** *FAO (#09260)*; *UNESCO (#20322)*. **NGO Relations** *International Centre for Tropical Agriculture (#12527)*; *UNESCO World Network of Microbiological Resources Centres MIRCEN (no recent information)*; national organizations. [2018.09.13/XD5142/D]

♦ Asociación Latinoamericana de Rorschach (ALAR) 02263

Latin American Rorschach Association
Exec Fac de Psicologia, Univ de Buenos Aires, Avda Independencia 3051, 1225 Buenos Aires, Argentina. E-mail: passalac@psi.uba.ar.
Contact Uriarte 2221, 1425 CABA Buenos Aires, Argentina. T. +541147774927 – +54110351.
History Also referred to as *Asociación Latinoamericana de Rorschach y Otras Técnicas Proyectivas.* **Events** *Congress* Santiago (Chile) 2015, *Latin America – Transformations in subjectivity* Montevideo (Uruguay) 2003, *Congress* Chile 1998. [2014/XE4469/E]

- ♦ Asociación Latinoamericana de Rorschach y Otras Técnicas Proyectivas / see Asociación Latinoamericana de Rorschach (#02263)

♦ Asociación Latinoamericana de Salud Ocupacional (ALSO) 02264

Latin American Association for Health at the Workplace
Pres INS-CENSOPAS, Cl Las Amapolas 350, Urb San Eugenio Lince, 14, Lima, Peru. E-mail: astetemed@gmail.com.
URL: http://congresosaludocupacional.org/
Events *Biennial Congress* Lima (Peru) 2015, *Biennial Congress* Buenos Aires (Argentina) 2013, *Biennial Congress* Puerto Vallarta (Mexico) 2000, *Biennial Latin American congress on occupational health* Bogota (Colombia) 1999, *Biennial Latin American congress on occupational health / Biennial Congress* Quito (Ecuador) 1997. [2017/XD6089/D]

- ♦ Asociación Latinoamericana de Seguridad (unconfirmed)

♦ Asociación Latinoamericana de Seguridad e Higiene en el Trabajo (ALASEHT) 02265

Latin American Association of Security and Hygiene at Work
Address not obtained.
URL: http://www.alaseht.com/
History Founded 25 Nov 1977, Buenos Aires (Argentina). Statutes adopted by General Assembly, Aug 1993, Santafé de Bogota (Colombia); modified Sep 2000, Buenos Aires. **Aims** Promote: prevention of risks of accident; security and hygiene at work; occupational safety; protection of the environment; quality of life in Latin American countries. **Structure** General Assembly (annual); Presidency. **Finance** Members' dues. **Activities** Events/meetings. **Events** *Latin American days on security and hygiene at work* Bogota (Colombia) 2003, *Annual General Assembly* Sao Paulo (Brazil) 2001, *Latin American days on security and hygiene at work* Buenos Aires (Argentina) 1999, *Annual General Assembly* Santiago (Chile) 1998, *General assembly / Annual General Assembly* Santiago (Chile) 1998.
Members Active; Adhering; Corresponding. Observers. National organizations in 11 countries:
Argentina, Brazil, Chile, Colombia, Costa Rica, Ecuador, Mexico, Panama, Paraguay, Spain, Uruguay. [2014/XD5937/D]

- ♦ Asociación Latinoamericana de Seguridad Ocupacional (no recent information)
- ♦ Asociación Latinoamericana de Seguridad Vial (internationally oriented national body)
- ♦ Asociación Latinoamericana de Sistemas Privados de Salud (unconfirmed)

♦ Asociación Latinoamericana de Sistémica (ALAS) 02266

Sec Explanada 705, 11000 Mexico City CDMX, Mexico. E-mail: ignaciopeon@gmail.com.
History 2007. **Aims** Connect Spanish speaking systemic organizations; develop systemic knowledge, methods and applications. **Structure** President; Secretary; Financial Department. **Languages** English, Spanish. **Finance** Self-financing. **Activities** Events/meetings. **Events** *Congress* Buenos Aires (Argentina) 2011, *Congress* Mexico City (Mexico) 2008, *Congress* Colombia 2007, *Congress* Argentina 2006. **NGO Relations** Affiliated with: *World Organisation of Systems and Cybernetics (WOSC, #21686).* [2016.10.18/XJ5274/D]

- ♦ Asociación Latinoamericana de Sociedades de Biologia y Medicina Nuclear (#16251)

♦ Asociación Latinoamericana de Sociologia (ALAS) 02267

Latin American Association of Sociology – Association latinoaméricaine de sociologie
Sec address not obtained. E-mail: carolgonzalez.alas@gmail.com – contactoalas2015@ucr.ac.cr.
URL: http://www.sociologia-alas.org/
History Set up, 1950, Zurich (Switzerland), at Congress of *International Sociological Association (ISA, #15553).* Previous attempts include: *Pan American Institute of Sociology*; *Inter-American Society of Sociology.* Also referred to as *Latin American Sociological Association.* **Aims** Create a space for reflection, from the point of view of the sociological sciences, on the current problems of the Latin American and Caribbean reality. **Structure** Executive Committee; Consultative Council. **Languages** Portuguese, Spanish. **Staff** Voluntary. **Activities** Events/meetings. **Events** *Congress* Lima (Peru) 2019, *Congress* Montevideo (Uruguay) 2017, *Congress* San José (Costa Rica) 2015, *Congress* Santiago (Chile) 2013, *Congress* Recife (Brazil) 2011. **Publications** *Boletin ALAS* (4 a year) – newsletter; *Controversias y Concurrencias Latinoamericanas* – electronic magazine.
Members Individuals in 22 countries:
Argentina, Bolivia, Brazil, Chile, Colombia, Costa Rica, Cuba, Dominican Rep, Ecuador, El Salvador, Guatemala, Haiti, Honduras, Mexico, Nicaragua, Panama, Paraguay, Peru, Puerto Rico, Uruguay, USA, Venezuela.
NGO Relations *Consejo Latinoamericano de Ciencias Sociales (CLACSO, #04718)*; *Coordinadora Regional de Investigaciones Económicas y Sociales (CRIES, #04812)*; *Programa de Estudios Conjuntos sobre las Relaciones Internacionales de América Latina (RIAL, no recent information)*; *Social Science Research Council (SSRC).* [2017.06.01/XD0194/v/D]

- ♦ Asociación Latinoamericana de Sociologia Rural (#16368)

♦ Asociación Latinoamericana de Sociologia del Trabajo (ALAST) . . . 02268

Latin American Association of Sociology of Work
Contact Martinez Trueba 1300, CP11200, Montevideo, Uruguay. E-mail: secretariaalast@gmail.com.
URL: http://alast.info/
History 1993, Mexico. Also referred to as *Asociación Latinoamericana de Estudios del Trabajo.* **Structure** Executive Committee, including President, Secretary and Treasurer. **Languages** Portuguese, Spanish. **Staff** Part-time, voluntary. **Finance** Members' dues. **Events** *Conference* Sao Paulo (Brazil) 2013, *Conference* Campinas (Brazil) 2012, *Conference* Mexico City (Mexico) 2010, *Conference* Mexico City (Mexico) 2009, *Conference* Montevideo (Uruguay) 2007. **Publications** *Revista Latinoamericana de Estudios del Trabajo.*
Members in 13 countries:
Argentina, Bolivia, Brazil, Chile, Colombia, Costa Rica, Cuba, Ecuador, Mexico, Peru, Puerto Rico, Uruguay, Venezuela.
IGO Relations *ILO (#11123).* [2017/XD9244/D]

♦ Asociación Latinoamericana de Supermercados (ALAS) 02269

Latin American Supermarket Association
Gen Dir Horacio 1855, piso 6, Col Chapultepec Morales, 11570 Mexico City CDMX, Mexico. T. +525555809900ext246.
URL: http://www.alasnet.org/
History 1986. **Aims** Support the supermarket sector in Latin America. **Structure** General Assembly; Board. **Languages** English, Portuguese, Spanish. **Staff** 1.00 FTE, paid. **Activities** Events/meetings. **Events** *Workshop* Cartagena de Indias (Colombia) 2015, *Workshop* Campinas (Brazil) 2014, *Workshop* Atibaia (Brazil) 2013, *Workshop* Atibaia (Brazil) 2012.
Members Active (15) in 13 countries:
Argentina, Bolivia, Brazil, Chile, Colombia, Dominican Rep, Mexico, Paraguay, Peru, Puerto Rico, Uruguay, USA, Venezuela.
Adhering (2) in 2 countries:
Colombia, USA. [2018/XD7534/D]

♦ Asociación Latinoamericana de Surfistas Profesionales (ALAS) 02270

Pres c/o PASA HQ, Av Larco 1239 – 3B, Miraflores, L-18, Lima, Peru. E-mail: central@alaslatintour.com.
URL: http://www.alaslatintour.com/
History 30 Apr 2001, Lima (Peru). **Aims** Develop and promote surfing throughout Latin America. **Activities** Sporting activities. **Publications** *ALAS Bulletin.* **NGO Relations** *Pan American Surf Association (PASA, #18135).* [2016/XM4715/D]

- Asociación Latinoamericana de Técnicos Radiólogos (unconfirmed)
- Asociación Latinoamericana de Tecnologias Alternativas (inactive)
- Asociación Latinoamericana de Teoria Económica / see Asociación Latino Americana de Teoria Económica (#02271)

♦ Asociación Latino Americana de Teoria Económica (ALTE) 02271

Latin-American Association of Economic Theory – Associação Latino-Americana de Teoria Económica

Pres Fac de Economia de la UASLP, Avda Pintores s/n, Colonia Burocratas del Estado, CP 78263 San Luis Potosí, Mexico.
URL: http://www.alte.uaslp.mx/

History Founded Oct 2008, San Luis (Argentina), with JOLATE meetings organized since 1999. Also referred to as *Asociación Latinoamericana de Teoria Económica*. **Aims** Promote awareness and research of economic theory in its more formal and modern aspects in Latin America; motivate students of economics, mathematics or other related areas to pursue postgraduate studies in mathematical economics or in general in modern economic theory; confirm work networks across the Latin American continent and link them with researchers from other regions. **Structure** General Assembly; Executive Committee. **Languages** English, Portuguese, Spanish. **Staff** 3.00 FTE, voluntary. **Finance** Support from sponsoring institutions of JOLATE. **Activities** Events/meetings. **Events** *Jornadas Latinoamericanas de Teoria Económica* Bahia Blanca (Argentina) 2019, *Jornadas Latinoamericanas de Teoria Económica* Madrid (Spain) 2018. **Publications** *Journal of Dynamics and Games. Trends in Mathematical Economics: Dialogues between Southern Europe and Latin America.* Proceedings. **Members** Individual; Institutional. Membership countries not specified. **NGO Relations** *Econometric Society (ES, #05310)* – Latin American region. *Game Theory Society (GTS, #10068).* [2019.12.13/XM7667/**D**]

♦ Asociación Latinoamericana de Terapia Radiante Oncológica (ALATRO) 02272

Latin American Society of Therapeutic Radiology and Oncology

Secretariat Calle Castello 128 CP, 28006 Madrid, Spain. T. +34917820030. Fax +34915615787. E-mail: secretaria@alatro.org.
Pres address not obtained.
URL: http://www.alatro.org/

History 31 Mar 2005, Lima (Peru), by merger of *Circulo de Radioterapeutas Ibero-Latinoamericanos (CRILA, inactive)* and *Grupo Latinoamericano de Curieterapia y Radioterapia Oncológica (GLAC-RO, inactive).* **Structure** Board of Directors. **Events** *Congress* Mexico City (Mexico) 2021, *Congress* Punta Cana (Dominican Rep) 2017, *World Congress of Brachytherapy* San Francisco, CA (USA) 2016, *Congress* Rosario (Argentina) 2015, *Congress* Cartagena de Indias (Colombia) 2013. [2017/XM1510/**D**]

- Asociación Latinoamericana de Tiempo Libre y Recreación (inactive)

♦ Asociación Latinoamericana del Tórax (ALAT) 02273

Associação Latino-americana do Tórax – Latin American Thoracic Association

Secretariat Mario Cassinoni 1689, CP 11200 Montevideo, Uruguay. E-mail: secretaria@alatorax.org.
URL: http://www.alatorax.org/

History Nov 1996, Caracas (Venezuela), as *Iberoamerican Society of Pneumonology*, during the 4th Latin-American Thoracic Conference. Previously also abbreviated as *ALATA*. Present name adopted 1998. **Aims** Promote the development of thoracic medicine in the region. **Structure** Assembly. Executive Committee, comprising President, Secretary, Treasurer and President Elect. Departments (11). Includes: *Unión Latinoamericana de Sociedades de Tisiologia y Enfermedades Respiratorias (ULASTER, no recent information).* **Languages** Portuguese, Spanish. **Finance** Members' dues. Donations. **Activities** Departments (11): Bronchial Asthma; Chronic Obstructive Pulmonary Diseases; Critical Care; Interstitial Diseases; Lung Surgery and Cancer; Paediatric Pneumology; Respiratory Endoscopy; Respiratory Pathophysiology; Smoking, Epidemiology, Occupational Diseases and Environment; Tropical Diseases; Tuberculosis. **Events** *Congress* Montevideo (Uruguay) 2012, *Congress* Lima (Peru) 2010, *Congress* Brasilia (Brazil) 2008, *Congress* Cancún (Mexico) 2006, *Congress* Buenos Aires (Argentina) 2004. **Publications** *Archivos de Bronconeumologia* (12 a year); *ALAT Newsletter* (4 a year).
Members Full in 27 countries:
Argentina, Belgium, Bolivia, Brazil, Canada, Chile, Colombia, Costa Rica, Cuba, Dominican Rep, Ecuador, El Salvador, France, Guatemala, Haiti, Honduras, Mexico, Nicaragua, Panama, Paraguay, Peru, Portugal, Puerto Rico, Spain, Uruguay, USA, Venezuela.
NGO Relations Member of: *Global Alliance Against Chronic Respiratory Diseases (GARD, #10182).* [2014/XD7503/**D**]

♦ Asociación Latinoamericana de Toxicologia (ALATOX) 02274

Latin American Association of Toxicology

Contact Ernesto Pinto Lagarrigue 281, Recoleta, Santiago, Santiago Metropolitan, Chile. T. +5627355863. Fax +5627350478. E-mail: pilarjulieta@gmail.com – asesorias.toxicologia@gmail.com.
URL: http://www.alatox.org/

History 13 Aug 1969, Bogota (Colombia). **Aims** Promote the creation of centres of toxicology, the teaching of this discipline, and the scientific exchange among all Latin American and Caribbean countries. **Structure** President, 1st Vice-President, 2nd Vice President, General Secretary, Assistant Secretary, Treasurer, Pro-Treasurer, and 5 Members. **Languages** Portuguese, Spanish. **Staff** 12.00 FTE, voluntary. **Finance** Members' dues. Voluntary contributions of institutions of the country where are located the headquarters and presidency of ALATOX. Budget (annual): US$ 20,000. **Activities** Organizes courses and congresses with the participation of scientists from Latin American and Caribbean countries. **Events** *Congress* Guayaquil (Ecuador) 2013, *Congress* Mérida (Mexico) 2009, *Congress* Santiago (Chile) 2006, *Congress* Campinas (Brazil) 2000, *Congress* Havana (Cuba) 1998. **Publications** Abstracts of meetings.
Members Full in 13 countries:
Argentina, Bolivia, Brazil, Chile, Colombia, Costa Rica, Cuba, Ecuador, Honduras, Mexico, Peru, Uruguay, Venezuela.
NGO Relations Member of: *International Union of Toxicology (IUTOX, #15824).* [2013/XD0871/**D**]

- Asociación Latinoamericana de Transportadores Aéreos de Carga (inactive)
- Asociación Latinoamericana de Transporte / see Latin American and Caribbean Air Transport Association (#16263)
- Asociación Latinoamericana del Transporte Automotor por Carreteras (inactive)
- Asociación Latino-Americana del Uro-oncologia (#16391)
- Asociación Latinoamericana de Veterinarios de Fauna Silvestre (unconfirmed)
- Asociación Latinoamericana de Volcanologia (unconfirmed)

♦ Asociación Latinoamericano de Administradores de Riesgos y Seguros (ALARYS) 02275

Latin American Association of Risk and Insurance Administrators

Contact Calle Guatemala, El Cangrejo, Plaza Dorchester – Planta Baja, Panama, Panamá, Panama PANAMá, Panama. T. +5072630000. Fax +5072152215. E-mail: info@alarys.org.
Pres c/o Pirelli Group, Maipu 757, Piso 6, 1006 Buenos Aires, Argentina. T. +5413227223. Fax +5413936578. E-mail: presidencia@alarys.org.
URL: http://www.alarys.org/

History 1993. **Aims** Support the growth of risk management in Latin America. **Events** *Biennial Congress* Hamilton (Bermuda) 2016, *Biennial Congress* Rio de Janeiro (Brazil) 2014, *Biennial Congress* Panama (Panama) 2012, *Biennial Congress* Bermuda 2010, *Biennial Congress* Buenos Aires (Argentina) 2008. **NGO Relations** Member of (1): *International Federation of Risk and Insurance Management Associations (IFRIMA, #13531).* [2021/XD6268/**D**]

♦ Asociación Latinoamericano y del Caribe de Ciencia y Tecnologia de los Alimentos (ALACCTA) 02276

Pres UNAM, Fac de Estudios Superiores Cuautitlan, Av 1o de Mayo s/n, Col Atlanta, 54440 Cuautitlan Izcalli MEX, Mexico. E-mail: sara@unam.mx.
Sec address not obtained. E-mail: maagio2@yahoo.com.mx.
URL: http://alaccta.org/

History 1988. **Aims** Help increase Food Science and Technology knowledge in Latin America and the Caribbean; promote scientific and technological exchange between members, students and professionals in the region. **Structure** General Assembly; Steering Committee; Fiscal Commission. **Languages** English, Portuguese, Spanish. **Finance** Members' dues. **Activities** Events/meetings; training/education; knowledge management/information dissemination; networking/liaising. **Events** *Latin American and Caribbean Congress of Food Science and Technology* Buenos Aires (Argentina) 2019, *Latin American Seminar of Food Science and Technology* Panama (Panama) 2018, *Latin American Seminar of Food Science and Technology* Montevideo (Uruguay) 2016, *Latin American Seminar of Food Science and Technology* San José (Costa Rica) 2014, *Food science and innovation conference* Guadalajara (Mexico) 2012. **Publications** *La Alimentación Latinoamericana* (5 a year) – magazine.
Members National Associations (12) in 10 countries:
Argentina, Brazil, Chile, Colombia, Costa Rica, Cuba, Mexico, Panama, Paraguay, Uruguay.
NGO Relations Member of: *International Union of Food Science and Technology (IUFoST, #15773).* [2022/XD7439/**D**]

- Asociación Latinoiberoamericana de Derecho a la Salud (no recent information)
- Asociación Latino-Iberoamericana de Gestión Tecnológica / see Asociación Latino-Iberoamericana de Gestión Tecnológica y de la Innovación (#02277)

♦ Asociación Latino-Iberoamericana de Gestión Tecnológica y de la Innovación (ALTEC) 02277

Latin Ibero-American Association of Technological Management and Innovation

Pres PUCP Fac de Gestión y Alta Dirección, Av Universitaria 1801, San Miguel, 15088, Lima, Peru. E-mail: altecasociacion@gmail.com. .
URL: http://www.asociacionaltec.org/

History 23 Oct 1984. Originated from Latin American Meeting on Technological Innovation Management promoted by OAS and the Government of Brazil, Oct 1983. Former names and other names: *Latin American Association of Technological Management* – former; *Asociación Latinoamericana de Gestión Tecnológica* – former; *Asociación Latino-Iberoamericana de Gestión Tecnológica (ALTEC)* – former; *Latin Ibero-American Association of Technological Management* – former; *Association latino-ibero-américaine de gestion technologique* – former. **Aims** Promote socio-economic development through continuous improvement of Technological Management in the region of Ibero-America, Latin America and the Caribbean. **Structure** Board of Directors consists of President, Past President and 5 Directors; Advisory Council; General Secretary. **Languages** English, Portuguese, Spanish. **Staff** 8.00 FTE, voluntary. **Finance** Sources: members' dues. **Activities** Events/meetings; guidance/assistance/consulting; knowledge management/information dissemination; management of treaties and agreements; monitoring/evaluation; publishing activities; research and development; research/documentation; training/education. **Events** *Congress* Paraná (Argentina) 2023, *Congress* Lima (Peru) 2021, *Biennial International Seminar* Buenos Aires (Argentina) 2007, *Biennial International Seminar* Salvador (Brazil) 2005, *Biennial Seminar* Salvador (Brazil) 2005. **Publications** *Repositorio institucional – Institutional repository* (2022) in English, Portuguese, Spanish – Seminar and conference proceedings since 1997..
Members Active in 19 countries:
Bolivia, Brazil, Chile, Colombia, Costa Rica, Cuba, Dominican Rep, Ecuador, El Salvador, Guatemala, Mexico, Panama, Paraguay, Peru, Portugal, Puerto Rico, Spain, Uruguay, Venezuela.
NGO Relations Formal contacts with: *Asociación Latinoamericana de Instituciones Financieras para el Desarrollo (ALIDE, #02233).* [2023.02.27/XD2126/**D**]

- Asociación Latino-Iberoamericana de Investigación Operativa (#16398)
- Asociación Latino-Ibero-Americana de Pesquisa Operacional (#16398)
- Asociación Lesbia y Gay Internacional / see ILGA World (#11120)
- Asociación de Ligas Iberoamericanas contra el Cancer / see Asociación Latina e Ibérica Contra el Cancer (#02173)
- Asociación de Ligas Iberoamericanas de Lucha contra el Cancer / see Asociación Latina e Ibérica Contra el Cancer (#02173)

♦ Asociación de Lingüistica y Filologia de la América Latina (ALFAL) 02278

Latin American Association of Linguistics and Philology – Associação de Lingüistica e Filologia da América Latina

SG address not obtained.
Pres address not obtained.
URL: http://www.mundoalfal.org/

History 1962, Cambridge, MA (USA). Founded at 9th *International Congress of Linguistics.* Statutes modified by General Assembly: 8 Aug 1990, Campinas (Brazil); 25 Jul 1996, Las Palmas de Gran Canaria (Spain). **Aims** Promote the study of applied and theoretical linguistics and philology in Latin America; establish close links between teachers and researchers; disseminate results of research. **Structure** General Assembly (every 3 years, at conference); Steering Committee; Regional Delegates (17); Working Committees. **Languages** Portuguese, Spanish. **Staff** 9.00 FTE, voluntary. **Finance** Sources: members' dues. **Activities** Events/meetings; knowledge management/information dissemination; networking/liaising. **Events** *Triennial International Congress* Concepción (Chile) 2024, *Triennial International Congress* Brasilia (Brazil) 2021, *Triennial International Congress* La Paz (Bolivia) 2020, *Triennial International Congress* Bogota (Colombia) 2017, *Triennial International Congress* João Pessoa (Brazil) 2014. **Publications** *Cuadernos de la ALFAL; Lingüistica* – official journal. Congress proceedings.
Members Honorary; Active. Individuals (over 1,000) in 36 countries:
Argentina, Austria, Belgium, Bolivia, Brazil, Canada, Chile, Colombia, Costa Rica, Cuba, Czechia, Dominican Rep, Ecuador, Finland, France, Germany, Guatemala, Honduras, Italy, Japan, Korea Rep, Mexico, Netherlands, Nicaragua, Norway, Panama, Peru, Portugal, Puerto Rico, Spain, Sweden, Switzerland, UK, Uruguay, USA, Venezuela.
NGO Relations Member of (1): *International Federation for Modern Languages and Literatures (#13480).* [2022/XD3859/v/**D**]

♦ Asociación de Lingüistica Sistémico Funcional de América Latina (ALSFAL) 02279

Latin American Systemic Functional Linguistics Association – Associação de Linguistica Sistemico-Funcional da América Latina

Editor Universidad Nacional de Cuyo, Centro Universitario – CP5500, Mendoza, Argentina. E-mail: lasfla@gmail.com.
Pres address not obtained.
Vice-Pres Fundacion Universidad del Norte, Km 5 Via Puerto Colombia, Barranquilla, Atlántico, Colombia. T. +5753509509.
URL: http://www4.pucsp.br/isfc/alsfal/

History 10 Apr 2004, Mendoza (Argentina). Previously also known under the English acronym *LASFLA*. **Aims** Promote and strengthen SFL in Latin America. **Structure** Executive Committee, comprising President, Vice-President, Secretary, 2 Newsletter Editors, 2 Website Coordinators and 2 Discussion Group Coordinators. **Languages** English, Portuguese, Spanish. **Staff** Voluntary. **Finance** None. **Events** *Conference* Puebla (Mexico) 2018, *Conference* Córdoba (Argentina) 2017, *Conference* Barranquilla (Colombia) 2016, *Conference* Santa Maria (Brazil) 2015, *Conference / Latin American Regional Conference* Mendoza (Argentina) 2014. **Publications** *ALSFAL Newsletter* (2 a year).
Members Full (140) in 11 countries:
Argentina, Australia, Brazil, Chile, Colombia, Mexico, UK, Uruguay, USA, Venezuela. [2012.06.01/XJ1153/**D**]

- Asociación Literaria y Artistica Internacional (#14058)
- Asociación Maritima Cristiana Internacional (#12561)
- Asociación Médica Aerospacial (internationally oriented national body)
- Asociación Médica del Caribe (internationally oriented national body)
- Asociación Médica Europea (#07761)
- Asociación Médica Internacional para el Estudio de las Condiciones de Vida y de Salud (inactive)

Asociación Médica Latinoamericana
02280
alphabetic sequence excludes
For the complete listing, see Yearbook Online at

♦ Asociación Médica Latinoamericana de Rehabilitación (AMLAR) .. 02280

Medical Latin American Association of Rehabilitation – Association médicale latinoaméricaine de réhabilitation

Contact address not obtained. E-mail: contacto@portalamlar.org.
URL: https://www.portalamlar.org/

History 1963, Mexico City (Mexico). **Aims** Enhance the scientific level of rehabilitation in Latin America. **Structure** Executive Committee. **Events** *Congress* Santa Cruz (Bolivia) 2021, *Congress* Santa Cruz (Bolivia) 2020, *Congress* Guayaquil (Ecuador) 2018, *Congress* San Pedro Sula (Honduras) 2016, *Congress* Viña del Mar (Chile) 2014. **Publications** *AMLAR Boletin.*

Members Societies in 24 countries:
Argentina, Bolivia, Brazil, Chile, Colombia, Costa Rica, Cuba, Dominican Rep, Ecuador, El Salvador, Guatemala, Guyana, Haiti, Honduras, Jamaica, Mexico, Nicaragua, Panama, Paraguay, Peru, Puerto Rico, Trinidad-Tobago, Uruguay, Venezuela.
[2020/XD5280/**D**]

♦ Asociación Médica Mundial (#21646)
♦ Asociación Médica Panamericana (no recent information)

♦ Asociación Medioambiental Internacional de Gestores del Olor (AMIGO) 02281

International Environmental Association of Odour Managers

Contact Uribitarte 6 – Ground floor, 48001 Bilbao, Biscay, Spain. T. +34946124671. E-mail: info@gestoresdelolor.org.
URL: http://gestoresdelolor.org/

History Set up following 3rd International Conference about Odour Management in the Environment, Nov 2015, Bilbao (Spain). Registered in accordance with Spanish law: AS / B / 21291/2017 NIF: G95891198. **Aims** Promote and disseminate the importance of a proper odour management. **Languages** Spanish. **Activities** Events/meetings; knowledge management/information dissemination; guidance/assistance/consulting. **Publications** *AMIGO Newsletter.*

Members Full in 4 countries:
Argentina, Chile, Colombia, Spain. [2019.02.20/XM7052/**D**]

♦ Asociación del Medio Oeste para Estudios latinoamericanos (internationally oriented national body)
♦ Asociación Mediterranea para la Avifauna Marina (#16661)
♦ Asociación Mediterranea de Biologia Marina y Oceanologia (inactive)
♦ Asociación Mediterranea de Psiquiatria (no recent information)
♦ Asociación Mensajeros de la Paz (internationally oriented national body)
♦ Asociación Mesoamericana y del Caribe de Zoológicos y Acuarios (#16730)
♦ Asociación Mesoamericana de Zoologia / see Meso-American and Caribbean Zoo and Aquarium Association (#16730)
♦ Asociación Mesoamericana de Zoológicos / see Meso-American and Caribbean Zoo and Aquarium Association (#16730)
♦ Asociación Mexicana para la Educación Internacional (internationally oriented national body)
♦ Asociación Mexicana de Estudios del Caribe (internationally oriented national body)
♦ Asociación Mexicana de Estudios Internacionales (internationally oriented national body)

♦ Asociación Miraismo Internacional (AMI) 02282

Miraism Assocation International – Association Miraisme International

Pres Rue des Charmilles 23, 1203 Geneva, Switzerland. E-mail: presidencia@miraismo.org – info@miraismo.org.
URL: http://miraismo.org/

History 10 May 2012. **Aims** Contribute to build harmonious societies, based on coexistence with respect, dignity and human security; spread, promote and defend human rights, peace and sustainable human development; empower women, migrants and young people for equal opportunities to enjoy their rights and fully develop their human potential. **Structure** Headquarters in Geneva (Switzerland); offices in 13 countries. **Languages** English, Spanish. **Staff** 4.00 FTE, voluntary. **Finance** Fundraising activities. **Activities** Awards/prizes/competitions; events/meetings.

Members Full in 4 countries:
Colombia, Spain, Switzerland, USA.

Consultative Status Consultative status granted from: *ECOSOC (#05331)* (Special). **IGO Relations** *European Union (EU, #08967); OAS (#17629); United Nations (UN, #20515).* [2017.03.09/XM5369/**E**]

♦ Asociación Monarquica Europea (no recent information)
♦ Asociación Mondial de Ciencias de la Educación (#02811)
♦ Asociación de Montañas Andinas (inactive)
♦ Asociación Montessori Internacional (#02812)
♦ Asociación para la Mujer y el Desarrollo / see Association for Women's Rights in Development (#02980)
♦ Asociación de Mujeres de América Latina para el Control del Tabaquismo (inactive)
♦ Asociación Mundial de Abogados Aeroportuarios (#21076)
♦ Asociación Mundial de Amigos de la Infancia (#02808)
♦ Asociación Mundial de Anatomistas Veterinarios (#21202)
♦ Asociación Mundial de Antiguas e Antiguos del Sagrado Corazón (#21116)
♦ Asociación Mundial de Antiguos Internistas y Becarios de la Organización de la Naciones Unidas (#21141)
♦ Asociación Mundial para el Avance de la Parasitologia Veterinaria (#21114)
♦ Asociación Mundial de Avicultura Cientifica (#21825)
♦ Asociación Mundial de Bandas y Ensambles (#21197)
♦ Asociación Mundial de Boxeo (#21241)
♦ Asociación Mundial de Buiatria (#21122)
♦ Asociación Mundial de Carreteras (#21754)
♦ Asociación Mundial del Cine Médico y de la Salud (#21163)
♦ Asociación Mundial para la Comunicación Cristiana (#21126)
♦ Asociación Mundial de Derecho Médico / see World Association for Medical Law (#21164)
♦ Asociación Mundial de Educación Especial (#21193)
♦ Asociación Mundial de Educadores Infantiles (#21136)
♦ Asociación Mundial del Ejecutivas de Empresa / see Femmes chefs d'entreprises mondiales (#09733)
♦ Asociación Mundial de Empresas Pequeñas y Medianas (#21189)
♦ Asociación Mundial por la Escuela Instrumento de Paz (#21184)
♦ Asociación Mundial para el Estudio de la Opinión Pública (#21180)
♦ Asociación Mundial para el Estudio y la Seguridad de los Animales de Transporte (internationally oriented national body)
♦ Asociación Mundial de Fisiólogos, Farmacólogos, Bioquimicos y Toxicólogos Veterinarios (no recent information)
♦ Asociación Mundial para la Formación Hotelera y Turistica (#21144)
♦ Asociación Mundial para la Formación Profesional Turistica / see World Association for Hospitality and Tourism Education and Training (#21144)
♦ Asociación Mundial de Fútbol de Salón / see World Futsal Association (#21532)
♦ Asociación Mundial de Futsal (#21532)
♦ Asociación Mundial Ganaderos de la Raza Parda (unconfirmed)
♦ Asociación Mundial de los GLP (#21629)
♦ Asociación Mundial de las Grandes Metrópolis (#21158)
♦ Asociación Mundial de las Guias Scouts (#21142)
♦ Asociación Mundial de Historia de la Medicina Veterinaria (#21143)
♦ Asociación Mundial de Ingenieros Agrónomos (#21115)
♦ Asociación Mundial de Juristas (#21604)
♦ Asociación Mundial de Loteria (#21628)
♦ Asociación Mundial de Lucha contra el Hambre (inactive)
♦ Asociación Mundial de Magistrados (#21150)
♦ Asociación Mundial de Mujeres Empresarias / see Femmes chefs d'entreprises mondiales (#09733)
♦ Asociación Mundial de Mujeres Periodistas y Escritoras (#21206)
♦ Asociación Mundial de Mujeres Rurales (#02338)
♦ Asociación Mundial de Organismos Electorales (#02984)
♦ Asociación Mundial de Patólogos Veterinarios (no recent information)
♦ Asociación Mundial Pedro Arrupe (#18287)
♦ Asociación Mundial de Periódicos (inactive)
♦ Asociación Mundial para la Producción Animal (#21117)
♦ Asociación Mundial de Productores de Caña y Remolacha Azucareras (#21120)
♦ Asociación Mundial de los Profesores Veterinarios (inactive)
♦ Asociación Mundial de Prospectiva Social (inactive)
♦ Asociación Mundial de Psicoanalisis (#21177)
♦ Asociación Mundial de Psicoterapia (#21337)
♦ Asociación Mundial de Psiquiatria (#21741)
♦ Asociación Mundial de Puentes Colgantes / see World Transporter Bridges Association (#21869)
♦ Asociación Mundial de Puentes Transbordadores (#21869)
♦ Asociación Mundial de Radios Comunitarias (#02810)
♦ Asociación Mundial para la Rehabilitación Psicosocial (#21178)
♦ Asociación Mundial para la Salud Mental Infantil / see World Association for Infant Mental Health (#21146)
♦ Asociación Mundial para la Salud Sexual (#21187)
♦ Asociación Mundial de Servicios Públicos de Empleo (#21179)
♦ Asociación Mundial de Sexologia / see World Association for Sexual Health (#21187)
♦ Asociación Mundial de Sexologia Médica (unconfirmed)
♦ Asociación Mundial de Sociedades de Cocineros (#21124)
♦ Asociación Mundial de las Sociedades de Patologia – Anatómica y Clinica / see World Association of Societies of Pathology and Laboratory Medicine (#21191)
♦ Asociación Mundial de Sociedades de Patologia y Medicina Laboratorial (#21191)
♦ Asociación Mundial de Tiempo Libre y Recreación / see World Leisure Organization (#21624)
♦ Asociación Mundial Veterinaria (#21901)
♦ Asociación Mundial Veterinaria de Avicultura (#21902)
♦ Asociación Mundial Veterinaria Equina (#21388)
♦ Asociación Mundial Veterinaria de Pequeños Animales (#21795)
♦ Asociación Mundial de Veterinarios Higienistas de los Alimentos (#21204)
♦ Asociación Mundial de los Veterinarios Microbiológios y Especialistas en Enfermedades Infecciosas (no recent information)
♦ Asociación Mundial de Vivienda Rural (inactive)
♦ Asociación de Museos del Caribe (#16909)
♦ Asociación de Museos Marítimos del Mediterráneo (#02801)
♦ Asociación de Naciones del Asia Sudoriental (#01141)
♦ Asociación de Neurocirujanos del Caribe (#03455)
♦ Asociación Nórdica para la Investigación sobre América Latina (inactive)
♦ Asociación Nórdica-Latinoamericana para la Educación Popular (no recent information)
♦ Asociación de Obtentores Horticolas Europeos (no recent information)
♦ Asociación Oceanica Europea (inactive)

♦ Asociación de Odontólogos Forenses de Sudamérica (AOFS) 02283

Contact address not obtained. E-mail: aofs.odontologiaforense@gmail.com.
URL: http://aofs-odontologiaforense.blogspot.be/

History 2010. **Events** *International Congress / Congress* Lima (Peru) 2014, *Meeting / Congress* Paraguay 2013.

Members Full in 4 countries:
Argentina, Brazil, Paraguay, Peru. [2014/XJ7965/**D**]

♦ Asociación de Ombudsman del Mediterraneo (#02802)
♦ Asociación de los ombudsmans mediterraneos / see Association of Mediterranean Ombudsmen (#02802)
♦ Asociación de Organismos Electorales de América del Sur (#02919)
♦ Asociación de Organismos Electorales del Caribe (#02405)
♦ Asociación de Organismos Electorales de Centroamérica y del Caribe (#02484)
♦ Asociación de Organizaciones Campesinas Centroamericanas para la Cooperación y el Desarrollo (inactive)
♦ Asociación de las Organizaciones Nacionales de Empresas de Pesca en la UE (#02841)
♦ Asociación de Paises Exportadores de Mineral de Hierro (inactive)
♦ Asociación de Palinólogos de Lengua Española (internationally oriented national body)
♦ Asociación Panamericana de Aerobiologia (#18078)
♦ Asociación Panamericana de Anatomia (#18079)

♦ Asociación Panamericana de Atletismo (APA) 02284

Association of Panamerican Athletics (APA)

Contact address not obtained. T. +17877233890. Fax +17872532982. E-mail: panamathletics@gmail.com.
Twitter: https://twitter.com/panamathletics

History Founded 1 Sep 1972, Munich (Germany FR), as *Panamerican Athletics Commission – Comisión Panamericana de Atletismo.* Previously also referred to in French as *Commission athlétique panaméricaine.* Restructured under current title 28 Oct 2011, Guadalajara (Mexico), when constitution was adopted. **Aims** Strive to bring together confederations and other bodies of the Americas which develop athletics in their respective areas; develop athletics exchanges within the Americas; unite concepts, methods and other formulae related to the *sport* of athletics; recognize Panamerican records and maintain statistics of both area and national records; promote competitions with other continents; promote activities to contribute to the strengthening of athletics and the greater spread of the sport throughout the hemisphere; indicate to fans that international *competitions* are a demonstration of agility and vigour of youth and of unity among peoples of the Americas. **Structure** Executive Council. **Languages** English, Spanish. **Staff** None. **Finance** Annual budget: 60,000 USD. **Activities** Sporting activities. **Events** *Meeting* Guadalajara (Mexico) 2011, *Meeting* Rio de Janeiro (Brazil) 2007, *Meeting* Santo Domingo (Dominican Rep) 2003, *Meeting* Winnipeg, MB (Canada) 1999, *Meeting* Mar del Plata (Argentina) 1995. **Publications** *The Americas and the World Cup in Athletics; The History of the Panamerican Junior Athletics Championships, 1980-2007.*

Members National organization in 44 countries and territories:
Anguilla, Antigua-Barbuda, Argentina, Aruba, Bahamas, Barbados, Belize, Bermuda, Bolivia, Brazil, Canada, Cayman Is, Chile, Colombia, Costa Rica, Cuba, Dominica, Dominican Rep, Ecuador, El Salvador, Grenada, Guatemala, Guyana, Haiti, Honduras, Jamaica, Mexico, Montserrat, Nicaragua, Panama, Paraguay, Peru, Puerto Rico, St Kitts-Nevis, St Lucia, St Vincent-Grenadines, Suriname, Trinidad-Tobago, Turks-Caicos, Uruguay, USA, Venezuela, Virgin Is UK, Virgin Is USA.

Regional organization affiliates (1), listed in this Yearbook:
Central American and Caribbean Athletic Confederation (CACAC, #03661).

NGO Relations Member of (1): *Asociación de Confederaciones Deportivas Panamericanas (ACODEPA, #02119).* Recognized by: *World Athletics (#21209); Panam Sports Organization (Panam Sports, #18138).*
[2022/XD1571/y/**D**]

♦ Asociación Panamericana para el Avance de la Mujer (inactive)

♦ Asociación Pan Americana de Bancos de Ojos (APABO) 02285

Pan American Association of Eye Banks – Associação Panamericana de Banco de Olhos

Pres Caixa Postal 210, CEP 37550-000, Pouso Alegre MG, Brazil. E-mail: lucienebarbosa@pobox.com – apabo@uninet.com.br – apabo@apabo.org.br.
URL: http://www.apaboeyebanks.org/

History Founded 1985, by eye bank executive directors from Argentina, Colombia, Ecuador, Panama, Paraguay, Peru and Puerto Rico. **Aims** Encourage establishment of eye banks throughout North, Central and South America and the states and regions of the Caribbean; set standards to be followed by member eye banks; train and certify qualified personnel as eye bank technicians; foster educational programmes concerning the importance of eye donation and the causes and prevention of blindness. **Structure** Executive Committee. **Languages** English, Portuguese, Spanish. **Staff** 2.00 FTE, paid. **Finance** Members' dues. Other sources: donations; course fees; registrations. **Activities** Standards/guidelines; training/education.
Members Active; Candidate; Associate; Affiliate. Nonprofit eye banks in 18 countries:
Argentina, Brazil, Chile, Colombia, Costa Rica, Cuba, Dominican Rep, Ecuador, El Salvador, Guatemala, Honduras, Mexico, Nicaragua, Panama, Paraguay, Peru, USA, Venezuela.
NGO Relations Member of: *Pan-American Association of Ophthalmology (PAAO, #18081)*. Founding partner of: *Global Alliance of Eye Bank Associations (GAEBA, #10197)*. [2017.06.01/XD8977/**F**]

- ♦ Asociación Panamericana de Bioética (no recent information)
- ♦ Asociación Panamericana de Bolsas de Productos (no recent information)

♦ Asociación Panamericana y Caribeña de Hipnosis Terapéutica (APCHT) 02286

Contact Dept de Psicologia Médica, Edif del Rectorado, Fac de Ciencias Médicas, No 1 Av de las Américas, Calle Eel, Reparto Fomento – Sueno, 90400 Santiago, Cuba. T. +532265301117ext114. E-mail: contacto@apcht.org.
URL: http://apcht.org/
History Founded 19 May 1999, Santiago (Cuba). Original title: *Interlighter – International Shipping Company*. **Aims** Demonstrate and disseminate knowledge of therapeutic hipnosis in a scientific and concrete manner; encourage the use of hypnotic techniques among public health and mental health professionals and other related professions; promote academic and scientific training of hypnotherapists in the region. **Structure** Board of Directors. Permanent Committees (2): Editorial and Publications; Education and Research. **Events** *Congress* Santiago de Cuba (Cuba) / Santiago (Cuba) 2015, *International meeting on natural and traditional medicine* Santiago de Cuba (Cuba) 2005, *International workshop of therapeutical hypnosis and related techniques* Santiago de Cuba (Cuba) 2005.
Members in 7 countries and territories:
Colombia, Costa Rica, Cuba, Dominican Rep, Guatemala, Panama, Puerto Rico. [2018/XM0150/**D**]

♦ Asociación Panamericana de Ciencias Veterinarias (PANVET) 02287

Association panaméricaine de sciences vétérinaires – Pan American Association of Veterinary Sciences
Secretariat Avenida Italia 1045, Providencia, Santiago, Santiago Metropolitan, Chile. E-mail: contacto@panvet.vet.
URL: http://www.panvet.vet/
History 7 Apr 1954, Sao Paulo (Brazil), as *Directing Council of Pan American Congresses of Veterinary Medicine*, replacing *Asociación Panamericana de Medicina Veterinaria*, set up 1951, Lima (Peru). Subsequently name changed to *Pan American Association of Veterinary Medicine and Zootechnics – Association panaméricaine de médecine vétérinaire et de zootechnie – Asociación Panamericana de Medicina Veterinaria y Zootecnia*. Present name adopted 1987. Current association formally set up 1992, when registered in accordance with the laws of Chile. **Aims** Serve the veterinary medical profession, promoting its rights and pointing out its obligations and quality standards; promote development of veterinary science in the areas of human and animal health, animal welfare, animal production and proyection; contribute to environmental protection and sustainability for the benefit of society. **Structure** Assembly of Delegates (every 2 years); Directing Council; Executive Secretariat. **Languages** English, Spanish. **Finance** Members' dues. Other sources: 10% of Congress registration fees. Administrative costs covered by country of Executive Secretariat.
Activities Events/meetings; networking/liaising; knowledge management/information dissemination. **Events** *Congress* Havana (Cuba) 2014, *Congress* Cartagena de Indias (Colombia) 2012, *Congress* Lima (Peru) 2010, *Congress* Guadalajara (Mexico) 2008, *Congress* Santiago (Chile) 2006. **Publications** *PANVET Magazine*.
Members National organizations (one per country) in 14 countries:
Argentina, Bolivia, Brazil, Canada, Chile, Colombia, Costa Rica, Cuba, Mexico, Paraguay, Peru, Uruguay, USA, Venezuela.
Included in the above, 1 organization listed in this Yearbook:
Association vétérinaire Euro-Arabe (AVEA, #02975).
NGO Relations Observer status with: *World Veterinary Association (WVA, #21901)*. Meetings held in conjunction with: *Asociación Iberoamericana de Academias de Ciencias Veterinarias (#02133)*. Together with: *Pan American Federation of University Faculties and Schools in Veterinary Sciences (#18105)*, set up: *Pan American Council on Education in Veterinary Science (#18091)*. Instrumental in setting up: *Ibero-American Animal Reproduction Association (IAARA, no recent information)*. [2021/XD3973/**D**]

- ♦ Asociación Panamericana de Cirugia Pediatrica / see Asociación Iberoamericana de Cirugia Pediatrica (#02134)
- ♦ Asociación Panamericana para la Conservación (internationally oriented national body)
- ♦ Asociación Panamericana de Fianzas (#18134)
- ♦ Asociación Panamericana de Implantes (inactive)
- ♦ Asociación Panamericana de Industria y Comercio Dentales (inactive)

♦ Asociación Panamericana de Infectologia (API) 02288

Panamerican Society for Infectious Diseases
Secretariat La Cresta, Ave José de Fabrega, Bella Vista, Panama, Panamá, Panama PANAMá, Panama. E-mail: juntadirectivaapi@gmail.com – juntadirectiva@apinfectologia.com.
URL: https://www.apiinfectologia.org/
History 1982, Guadalajara (Mexico), as *Pan American Infectious Diseases Association (PAIDA)*. Also referred to as *Pan American Infectious Diseases Society*. **Aims** Improve the care of patients with infectious diseases by promoting the exchange of information. **Structure** Board of Directors, consisting of 8 members. Regional and local (by countries) representatives. **Languages** English, Spanish. **Finance** Members' dues: US$ 30 per year. Other sources: mostly funding from pharmaceutical industry. **Events** *Pan American Congress of Infectology* Punta Cana (Dominican Rep) 2021, *Pan American Congress of Infectology* Luque (Paraguay) 2019, *Pan American Congress of Infectology* Quito (Ecuador) 2015, *Pan American Congress of Infectology* Santiago (Chile) 2013, *Pan American Congress of Infectology* Punta del Este (Uruguay) 2011. **Publications** *Revista Panamericana de Infectologia*.
Members Full in 19 countries:
Argentina, Bolivia, Brazil, Chile, Colombia, Costa Rica, Cuba, Ecuador, El Salvador, Guatemala, Honduras, Mexico, Nicaragua, Panama, Paraguay, Peru, Uruguay, USA, Venezuela.
NGO Relations Member of: *International Society of Antimicrobial Chemotherapy (ISAC, #14925)*. Instrumental in setting up: *Sociedad Iberoamericana de Infectologia (SIAI)*. [2018/XD2438/**D**]

♦ Asociación Panamericana de Ingenieros Agrónomos (APIA) 02289

Contact Pinto 215, 7000 Tandil, Argentina. T. +542494547404.
Facebook: https://www.facebook.com/asociacionpanamericanadeingenierosagronomos/
History 1994. **Structure** Assembly.
Members Full in 35 countries:
Antigua-Barbuda, Argentina, Barbados, Belize, Bolivia, Brazil, Canada, Chile, Colombia, Costa Rica, Cuba, Dominican Rep, Ecuador, El Salvador, Grenada, Guatemala, Guiana Fr, Guyana, Haiti, Honduras, Jamaica, Mexico, Nicaragua, Panama, Paraguay, Peru, Puerto Rico, St Kitts-Nevis, St Lucia, St Vincent-Grenadines, Suriname, Trinidad-Tobago, Uruguay, USA, Venezuela.
Cooperating in 1 country:
Spain.
IGO Relations *Inter-American Institute for Cooperation on Agriculture (IICA, #11434)*. **NGO Relations** Member of: *World Association of Agronomists (WAA, #21115)*. [2020/XM7738/**D**]

- ♦ Asociación Panamericana de Instituciones de Crédito Educativo (#18084)
- ♦ Asociación Panamericana de Medicina Veterinaria y Zootecnia / see Asociación Panamericana de Ciencias Veterinarias (#02287)
- ♦ Asociación Panamericana de Mercadeo Social (internationally oriented national body)

♦ Asociación Panamericana Nikkei (APN) 02290

Pan American Nikkei Association
Contact address not obtained. E-mail: asociacionpanamericananikkei@gmail.com.
URL: http://copani.org/
History 6 Dec 1981, Lima (Peru). **Structure** Executive Council, comprising President, Vice-President, Treasurer and Secretary. **Activities** Organizes 'Conventions of the Association of Pan American Nikkei (COPANI)'. **Events** *Convention* San Francisco, CA (USA) 2019, *Convention* Lima (Peru) 2017, *Convention* Santo Domingo (Dominican Rep) 2015, *Convention* Buenos Aires (Argentina) 2013, *Convention* Cancún (Mexico) 2011.
Members Full in 14 countries:
Argentina, Bolivia, Brazil, Canada, Chile, Colombia, Dominican Rep, Japan, Mexico, Paraguay, Peru, Uruguay, USA, Venezuela. [2018/XJ7364/**D**]

- ♦ Asociación Panamericana Oblatos Diocesanos (religious order)
- ♦ Asociación Panamericana de Oftalmologia (#18081)
- ♦ Asociación Panamericana de Otorrinolaringologia y Broncoesofagologia / see Pan American Association of Oto-Rhino-Laryngology – Head and Neck Surgery (#18082)
- ♦ Asociación Panamericana de Otorrinolaringologia – Cirugia de Cabeza y Cuello (#18082)
- ♦ Asociación Panamericana de Periodontologia / see Federación Iberopanamericana de Periodoncia (#09328)

♦ Asociación Panamericana de Profesionales de la Agrimensura y Topografia (APPAT) 02291

Contact address not obtained. T. +50621032440. E-mail: appat@colegiotopografoscr.com.
URL: http://www.colegiotopografoscr.com/appat/
History Founded 1999, but soon became inactive. Reactivated Sep 2010, Costa Rica. **Aims** Promote the role of the surveyor in the administration of natural and anthropic environments. **Structure** General Assembly; Board of Directors. **Publications** *APPAT Bulletin*.
Members Full in 13 countries:
Argentina, Colombia, Costa Rica, Cuba, Dominican Rep, Guatemala, Honduras, Mexico, Panama, Puerto Rico, Spain, Uruguay, USA.
NGO Relations *International Federation of Surveyors (FIG, #13561)*. [2018/XM7735/**D**]

- ♦ Asociación Panamericana de Rugby (#18127)
- ♦ Asociación Panamericana de Sociedades de Bioquimica / see Pan American Association for Biochemistry and Molecular Biology (#18080)
- ♦ Asociación Panamericana de Surf (#18135)

♦ Asociación Panamericana de Tecnólogos Médicos (APTM) 02292

Contact address not obtained. T. +51998781902. E-mail: pantecmed2@gmail.com – panamtecmed@gmail.com.
URL: https://www.panamtecmed.net/
History 18 Aug 1992, Arica (Chile). **Aims** Promote rationalization, development, protection, progress, prestige, competencies and prerogatives of the profession of medical technologist and equivalent professions. **Structure** Council. **Languages** Spanish. **Staff** 3.00 FTE, paid. **Finance** Self-financed. **Activities** Events/meetings. **Events** *Convention* Concepción (Chile) 2019. **Publications** *Boletin APTM*; *Informativo Iberoamericano*. [2021/XM7736/**D**]

♦ Asociación Panamericana de Trauma Ocular (APTO) 02293

Pan-American Association of Ocular Trauma
Pres address not obtained. E-mail: exilaserec@gmail.com.
History 26 Oct 1997, on the initiative of Dr José Dalma Weiszhausz. Also referred to as *Pan-American Society of Ocular Trauma – Sociedad Panamericana de Trauma Ocular*. **Events** *Latin American Congress* Santiago (Chile) 2019, *Meeting* Buenos Aires (Argentina) 2010. **NGO Relations** Affiliated member of: *Pan-American Association of Ophthalmology (PAAO, #18081)*. [2019/XM1749/**D**]

- ♦ Asociación Panibérica de Academias Olimpica (#18181)
- ♦ Asociación Pan Pakistana de Mujeres (internationally oriented national body)
- ♦ Asociación Parlementarios de Origen Italiano en el Mundo (#02992)
- ♦ Asociación por la Paz Continental (unconfirmed)
- ♦ Asociación Paz con Dignidad (internationally oriented national body)
- ♦ Asociación de Pequeñas y Medianas Empresas del Caribe (#03459)
- ♦ Asociación del Personal de la OMT / see UNWTO Staff Association, Madrid
- ♦ Asociación de Personal OPS/OMS (#18024)
- ♦ Asociación del Personal de la Organización de Aviación Civil Internacional (#19939)

♦ Asociación Petroquimica y Quimica Latinoamericana (APLA) 02294

Latin American Petrochemical Association – Association de pétrochimie latinoaméricaine
Contact Carlos Pellegrini 1069, Floor 7, Of A, C1009ABU Buenos Aires, Argentina. T. +541143251422. Fax +541143228202. E-mail: info@apla.com.ar.
URL: http://www.apla.com.ar/
History Founded Jun 1977, Buenos Aires (Argentina), as *Latin America Petrochemical Institute – Instituto Petroquimico Latinoamericano (IPLA)*, following decision of 1st Latin American Petrochemical Congress, Nov 1976, Bariloche (Argentina). Present name adopted at 3rd Congress, Nov 1980, Salvador (Brazil). **Aims** Promote the relationship and mutual cooperation between enterprises, institutes, research centres and other activities related to the petrochemical industry, to achieve its establishment and development in Latin America; prepare information and analytical studies on markets to assist greater sectoral development; promote and publicize research work so as to help avoid duplication of effort. **Structure** General Assembly; Board. **Languages** English, Portuguese, Spanish. **Staff** 8.00 FTE, paid. **Activities** Events/meetings; research/documentation; monitoring/evaluation. **Events** *Logistics Meeting* Buenos Aires (Argentina) 2021, *Latin American Petrochemical Annual Meeting* Sao Paulo (Brazil) 2021, *Logistics Meeting* Buenos Aires (Argentina) 2020, *Latin American Petrochemical Annual Meeting* Sao Paulo (Brazil) 2020, *Latin American Petrochemical Annual Meeting* Buenos Aires (Argentina) 2019. **Publications** *Latin American Petrochemical Yearbook*; *Petroquimica y Quimica al Dia* – electronic newsletter. *Latin American Chemical Industry Buyer's Guide*; *Latin American Logistics Guide*.
Members Active petrochemical companies with plants in Latin American countries. Associate scientific or technical institutes; businesses linked to petrochemicals. Members in 9 countries:
Argentina, Bolivia, Brazil, Chile, Colombia, Mexico, Peru, USA, Venezuela.
Also members in other countries (not specified). [2015.02.05/XD6444/**D**]

- ♦ Asociación de Pilotos Maritimos Internacionales (#14103)
- ♦ Asociación de Poblaciones de Montaña del Mundo (#21658)
- ♦ Asociación para la Prevención de la Tortura (#02869)
- ♦ Asociación para el Progreso de las Ciencias Agricolas en Africa (no recent information)
- ♦ Asociación para el Progreso de las Comunicaciones (#02873)
- ♦ Asociación para la Protección de la Propiedad Industrial en el Mundo Arabe (#02877)
- ♦ Asociación para la Proyección de las Lenguas Europeas / see Europe plurilingue
- ♦ Asociación Psicoanalitica Internacional (#14662)

♦ Asociación Psicológica Iberoamericana de Clinica y Salud (APICSA) 02295

Associação Psicológica Iberoamericana de Clinica e Saúde
Pres Aptdo de Correos 11060, 18080 Granada, Spain. E-mail: apicsa3@gmail.com.
URL: https://funveca.org/apicsa/
History 1998, Granada (Spain). **Aims** Promote communication among clinical and health psychologists from the Ibero-American countries. **Structure** Board of Directors. **Languages** English, Portuguese, Spanish. **Staff** 2.00 FTE, paid. Several voluntary. **Finance** Sources: meeting proceeds; members' dues. **Events** *Congress* Medellin (Colombia) 2019, *Congress* San Juan (Puerto Rico) 2016, *Congress* Córdoba (Argentina) 2012, *Congress* Santiago (Chile) 2009, *Congress* San José (Costa Rica) 2006. **Publications** *Behavioral Psychology – Psicologia Conductal* (3 a year) in English, Portuguese.

Members Full in 16 countries and territories:
Argentina, Brazil, Chile, Colombia, Costa Rica, Ecuador, El Salvador, Mexico, Paraguay, Peru, Portugal, Puerto Rico, Spain, Uruguay, USA, Venezuela. [2021.02.17/XD7892/**D**]

- Asociación Psiquiatria de América Latina (#16363)
- Asociación de Quimicos Analiticos Oficiales / see AOAC INTERNATIONAL (#00863)
- Asociación de Reaseguradores Latinoamericanos (no recent information)
- Asociación de la Red Iberoamericana de Hipercolesterolemia Familiar / see Red Iberoamericana de Hipercolesterolemia Familiar (#18668)
- Asociación de Refugiados de Latinoamérica y del Caribe (internationally oriented national body)
- Asociación Regional de Crédito Agricola para Asia y el Pacifico / see Asia Pacific Rural and Agricultural Credit Association (#02019)
- Asociación Regional de Educación Médica para el Sureste Asiatico (#19780)
- Asociación Regional de Empresas de Petroleo y Gas Natural en Latinoamérica y el Caribe / see Asociación Regional de Empresas del Sector Petróleo, Gas y Biocombustibles en Latinoamérica y el Caribe (#02296)

♦ Asociación Regional de Empresas del Sector Petróleo, Gas y Biocombustibles en Latinoamérica y el Caribe (ARPEL) 02296

Regional Association of Oil, Gas and Biofuels Sector Companies in Latin America and the Caribbean

Chairman Av Luis A de Herrera 1248, WTC Torre 2, Of 717, CP 11300 Montevideo, Uruguay. T. +59826236993. E-mail: presidencia@arpel.org.uy – info@arpel.org.uy.
URL: https://arpel.org/

History 2 Oct 1965, Rio de Janeiro (Brazil). Founded on signature of basic convention by eight governmental oil enterprises, at the 3rd *Conference of Latin American State Owned Oil Companies (CEPEL, no recent information).* Transformation process started, 1995. Former names and other names: *Mutual Assistance of the Latin American Government Oil Companies* – former (1965 to 1993); *Assistance mutuelle des entreprises pétrolières gouvernementales latinoaméricaines* – former (1965 to 1993); *Asistencia Reciproca Petrolera Estatal Latinoamericana* – former (1965 to 1993); *Mutual Assistance of the Latin American Oil Companies* – former (1993 to 1998); *Assistance mutuelle des entreprises pétrolières latinoaméricaines* – former (1993 to 1998); *Asistencia Reciproca Petrolera Empresarial Latinoamericana* – former (1993 to 1998); *Asociación Regional de Empresas de Petroleo y Gas Natural en Latinoamérica y el Caribe (ARPEL)* – former (1993 to 1998); *Regional Association of Oil and Natural Gas Companies in Latin America and the Caribbean* – former. **Aims** Promote the integration, growth, operational excellence and effective socio-environmental performance of the industry in the region. **Structure** Assembly (annual); Board of Directors; Executive Secretariat; Fiscal Committee. Technical Committees (7): Environment, Health and Safety; Social Responsibility; Human Talent and Knowledge Management; Exploration and Production; Pipelines and Terminals; Refining and Fuels; Gas and Energy. **Languages** English, Portuguese, Spanish. **Staff** 17.00 FTE, paid. **Finance** Members' dues. **Activities** Events/meetings; training/education. **Events** *Congress on natural gas in Latin America* 1992, *Annual Assembly* Costa Rica 1992, *Latin American hydrocarbon congress* Rio de Janeiro (Brazil) 1992, *Joint seminar* Angra dos Reis (Brazil) 1991, *Annual Assembly* Vancouver, BC (Canada) 1991. **Publications** Annual Report; annual Sustainability Report. Documents; guidelines; management reports; newsletters; technical reports.

Members Membership represents over 90% of the upstream and downstream activities in the region, and includes national, international and independent oil companies, providers of technology, goods and services to the industry value chain, and other national and international institutions in the industry. Active (29 companies and institutions) in 21 countries:
Argentina, Bolivia, Brazil, Chile, Colombia, Costa Rica, Ecuador, France, Germany, Jamaica, Mexico, Norway, Paraguay, Peru, Spain, Suriname, Trinidad-Tobago, UK, Uruguay, USA, Venezuela.

Consultative Status Consultative status granted from: *UNIDO (#20336).* **NGO Relations** Member of: *International Petroleum Industry Environmental Conservation Association (IPIECA, #14562).* [2022/XD2967/**D**]

- Asociación Regional Latinoamericana de Puertos de Pacifico (inactive)
- Asociación Regional para las Migraciones Forzadas (no recent information)
- Asociación de las Regiones de los Alpes Centrales (#01081)
- Asociación de las Regiones de los Alpes Orientales / see Alps-Adriatic-Alliance (#00747)
- Asociación de las Regiones Europeas de los Productos de Origen (#02890)
- Asociación de Regiones Fronterizas Europeas (#02499)
- Asociación para la Salud Integral y Ciudadania de América Latina y el Caribe (#02651)
- Asociación Las Segovias para la Cooperación con Centroamérica / see Asociación para la Cooperación con el Sur – Las Segovias
- Asociación Seminario Biblico Latinoamericano / see Universidad Biblica Latinoamericana
- Asociación de Seminarios e Instituciones Teológicas (#02912)
- Asociación de Seminarios e Instituciones Teológicas del Cono Sur / see Association of Seminaries and Theological Institutions (#02912)

♦ Asociación de Servicios de Geologia y Mineria Iberoamericanos (ASGMI) 02297

Iberoamerican Association of Geological and Mining Surveys

Main Office C/ Rios Rosas 23, 28003 Madrid, Spain. T. +34616516817. E-mail: asgmi@asgmi.org.
URL: http://www.asgmi.org/

History Founded May 1993, Cochabamba (Bolivia). **Aims** Foster institutional strengthening of associated members, socio-economic development of country members, preservation of the environment and inter-association cooperation. Promote projects designed to sensitize society towards: prevention and mitigation of natural hazards; sustainable management of mineral, water and energy resources; soil and underground water pollution; effects of climate change; production and diffusion of geological knowledge; economic resources and active processes as a supporting tool for land planning. **Structure** General Assembly (annual). **Languages** Portuguese, Spanish. **Staff** None. **Finance** Each survey pays for its own expenses. Annual meeting expenses supported by host survey. **Activities** Events/meetings. **Events** *General Assembly* Brasilia (Brazil) 2022, *General Assembly* 2021, *General Assembly* Tegucigalpa (Honduras) 2019, *Extraordinary General Assembly* Madrid (Spain) 2015, *General Assembly* Arequipa (Peru) 2014.

Members Full in 21 countries:
Argentina, Bolivia, Brazil, Chile, Colombia, Costa Rica, Cuba, Dominican Rep, Ecuador, El Salvador, Guatemala, Honduras, Mexico, Nicaragua, Panama, Paraguay, Peru, Portugal, Spain, Uruguay, Venezuela. [2015.02.11/XD9454/**D**]

- Asociación de Siderúrgicos Europeos Independientes (inactive)
- Asociación de Sociedades Centroamericanas de Neurocirugia (unconfirmed)
- Asociación de Sociedades Farmacéuticas del Mediterraneo Latino / see Société de pharmacie de la Méditerranée latine (#19508)

♦ Asociación de Sociedades Iberoamericanas de Andrologia (ANDRO) 02298

Pres address not obtained. E-mail: cortada@asesa.org.
URL: http://androiberoamericana.com/

History 2003, Santo Domingo (Dominican Rep). **Structure** General Assembly. Board of Directors, comprising President, President-Elect, Secretary, Treasurer and members. **Events** *Congress* Buenos Aires (Argentina) 2012, *Congress* Barcelona (Spain) 2009, *Congress* Havana (Cuba) 2006, *Congress* Santo Domingo (Dominican Rep) 2003, *Congress* Cartagena de Indias (Colombia) 2000. [2013/XJ6989/**D**]

- Asociación de Sociedades Nacionales Europeas y Mediterraneas de Gastro-Enterologia (inactive)

♦ Asociación Sudamericana de Atletas Máster (ASUDAMA) 02299

South American Association of Master Athletes

Pres Miguel B Sánchez 1050, C1429CABA Buenos Aires, Argentina. E-mail: asudama@asudama.org.
Sec address not obtained.
URL: https://asudama.org/

History 1979, Buenos Aires (Argentina). A regional body of *World Masters Athletics (WMA, #21640).* Former names and other names: *Association of South American Veteran Athletics* – former; *Asociación Sudamericana de Atletas Veteranos (ASUDAVE)* – former. **Aims** Organize master athletics championship competitions for athletes from the South American continent. **Structure** Governing Board. **Activities** Sporting activities.

Members Full in 10 countries:
Argentina, Bolivia, Brazil, Chile, Colombia, Ecuador, Paraguay, Peru, Uruguay, Venezuela. [2022/XD9102/**D**]

- Asociación Sudamericana de Atletas Veteranos / see Asociación Sudamericana de Atletas Máster (#02299)
- Asociación Sudamericana de Endoscopia Respiratoria (unconfirmed)
- Asociación Sudamericana de Estudios Geopoliticos e Internacionales, Montevideo (no recent information)
- Asociación Sudamericana del la Industria del Cloro-Soda y sus Derivados / see Latin American Chlor-Alkali and Derivatives Industry Association (#16295)
- Asociación Sudamericana de Ingenieria Estructural (#02336)
- Asociación Sudamericana de Jueces de Atletismo (inactive)
- Asociación Sudamericana de Museos (inactive)
- Asociación de Suicidologia de Latinoamérica y el Caribe (unconfirmed)
- Asociación Suiza para el Intercambio de Personas en la Cooperación Internacional (internationally oriented national body)
- Asociación de Supervisores Bancarios de América Latina y el Caribe / see Association of Supervisors of Banks of the Americas (#02944)
- Asociación de Supervisores Bancarios de las Américas (#02944)

♦ Asociación de Supervisores de Seguros de América Latina (ASSAL) 02300

Latin American Association of Insurance Supervisors

Pres Av Libertador Bernardo O'Higgins 1449, Torre I – Piso 9, 8340518 Santiago, Santiago Metropolitan, Chile. T. +56226174513. Fax +56226174001.
URL: http://www.assalweb.org/

History Founded 1979, but no concrete activities until 1991. **Aims** Promote exchange of information on legislation, regulatory control, market characteristics and operational systems in Latin America. **Structure** General Assembly; Executive Committee. **Events** *Annual Meeting* Santiago (Chile) 2021, *Annual Meeting* Lima (Peru) 2020, *Annual Meeting* Santa Cruz (Bolivia) 2019, *Annual Meeting* Santo Domingo (Dominican Rep) 2018, *Annual Meeting* Santiago (Chile) 2017.

Members Full in 19 countries:
Argentina, Bolivia, Brazil, Chile, Colombia, Costa Rica, Cuba, Dominican Rep, Ecuador, El Salvador, Guatemala, Honduras, Mexico, Nicaragua, Panama, Paraguay, Peru, Puerto Rico, Uruguay.
Associate in 2 countries:
Portugal, Spain.

NGO Relations Joint seminar and other activities with *International Association of Insurance Supervisors (IAIS, #11966).* [2019.07.18/XD9399/**D**]

- Asociación por un Tasa a las Transacciones financieras especulativas para Ayuda a los Ciudadanos (#02947)

♦ Asociación Técnica de Diarios Latinoamericanos (ATDL) 02301

Technical Association of Latin American Newspapers

Exec Dir address not obtained.
URL: http://www.atdl.org/

History Founded 1983. Registered in accordance with USA law. **Structure** Board. **Languages** Portuguese, Spanish. **Staff** 22.00 FTE, paid. **Events** *Meeting* Panama (Panama) 2014, *Meeting* Santiago (Chile) 2013, *Meeting* Madrid (Spain) 2012, *Meeting* Rio de Janeiro (Brazil) 2011, *Meeting* San Salvador (El Salvador) 2010. **Publications** *ATDL Newsletter* (weekly); *Intercambio Técnico* (6 a year) – technical magazine. [2020/XD7635/**D**]

- Asociación Técnica Internacional de las Maderas Tropicales (#15668)

♦ Asociación de Técnicos Andinos en Recubrimientos (STAR) 02302

Contact Carrera 43C No 4 Sur, 143 Of 147, Medellin, Antioquia, Colombia. T. +5742970658. E-mail: info@starandinapaint.com.
URL: http://starandinapaint.com/

History 1998. Also referred to as *STAR Andina Paint.* **Aims** Sponsor and increase the application of science, engineering and technology in the coatings industry, both among partners and at industrial level; promote research and education in fields that are of interest to members; promote social and professional exchange among members. **Structure** General Assembly; Administrative Council. **Events** *Congress* Bogota (Colombia) 2015, *Congress* Lima (Peru) 2014, *Congress* Bogota (Colombia) 2012, *Congress* Medellin (Colombia) 2010, *Congress* Bogota (Colombia) 2009.

Members Full in 5 countries:
Bolivia, Colombia, Ecuador, Peru, Venezuela.

NGO Relations Member of: *Coatings Societies International (CSI, #04075).* [2020.03.03/XJ9120/**D**]

- Asociación de Técnicos Municipales de América Latina (inactive)
- Asociación de Técnicos para la Solidaridad y Cooperación Internacional (internationally oriented national body)
- Asociación Tecnologia Iberoamericana de Pinturas, Adhesivos y Tintas (unconfirmed)

♦ Asociación de Televisión Educativa Iberoamericana (ATEI) 02303

Iberoamerican Educational Television Association – Associação das Televisoes Educativas e Culturais Ibero-americanas

Pres Calle Serpis 29, Taller de Audiovisuales 5a, 46022 Valencia, Spain. T. +34961625578 – +34659205823. E-mail: contacto@atei.mx.
URL: http://atei.mx/

History 1992. Previously referred to as *Televisión Educativa Iberoamericana (HISPASAT); Televisión Educativa Latinoamericana.* **Aims** Contribute, through cooperation, to the development of Iberoamerican education, culture and communication; explore the educational possibilities of the latest information and communication technologies and integrate them in the activities; promote means of communication and exchange of cultural, educational and scientific experiences. **Structure** General Assembly. Council, comprising 17 members (one for each national chapter). Committee, consisting of 5 members. **Staff** 13.00 FTE, paid. **Activities** Grants: Young Video Prize; ATEI Prize; Videoteca ATEI Prize; Educlip Prize. Runs an online radio program. **Events** *Assembly* Brazil 2013, *Assembly* Seville (Spain) 2010, *Virtual Educa : international conference on education, training and new technologies* São José dos Campos (Brazil) 2007, *European conference on multimedia applications* Madrid (Spain) 1999. **Publications** Press releases (weekly).

Members Institutions (200) in 24 countries:
Andorra, Argentina, Bolivia, Brazil, Chile, Colombia, Costa Rica, Cuba, Dominican Rep, Ecuador, El Salvador, Guatemala, Honduras, Mexico, Nicaragua, Panama, Paraguay, Peru, Portugal, Puerto Rico, Spain, Uruguay, USA, Venezuela.

NGO Relations Honorary member of: *Federación Latinoamericana de Facultades de Comunicación Social (FELAFACS, #09353).* [2021/XF3179/**F**]

♦ Asociación Transpersonal Iberoamericana (ATI) 02304

Ibero-American Transpersonal Association – Associação Ibero-Americana de Transpessoal

Pres Andres Mellado 65, 28015 Madrid, Spain. E-mail: contacto@ati-transpersonal.org.
URL: http://www.ati-transpersonal.org/

History 2015, Madrid (Spain). Founded after the foundation of the Journal of Transpersonal Research. Registration: Registro Nacional de Asociaciones del Ministerio del Interior, Start date: 25 Mar 2015, Spain. **Aims** Represent the transpersonal community from Iberoamerica. **Structure** Board of Directors; Departments. **Languages** English, Portuguese, Spanish. **Staff** 20.00 FTE, voluntary. **Finance** Sources: donations; members' dues; revenue from activities/projects. **Activities** Awareness raising; certification/accreditation; events/meetings; knowledge management/information dissemination; networking/liaising; publishing activities; research/documentation; training/education. **Publications** *ATI Magazine* (2 a year); *Journal of Transpersonal Research.*

Members Institutions and individuals in 11 countries:
Argentina, Brazil, Chile, Colombia, Costa Rica, Ecuador, Mexico, Peru, Portugal, Spain, Venezuela. [2023.02.20/AA1214/**C**]

♦ Asociación de Transporte Aéreo Internacional (#11614)
♦ Asociación de Turismo del Caribe Oriental (inactive)
♦ Asociación Turística de la Zona del Pacífico (#17932)
♦ Asociación UNESCO para la Promoción de la Etica en los Medios de Comunicación (internationally oriented national body)
♦ Asociación Universal del Esperanto (#20676)
♦ Asociación Universal de Federalistas Mundiales / see World Federalist Movement – Movement for a Just World Order through a Strengthened United Nations (#21404)
♦ Asociación de Universidades Africanas (#02361)
♦ Asociación de Universidades Amazónicas (#02366)

♦ Asociación de Universidades de América Latina y el Caribe para la Integración (AUALCPI) 02305

SG Exec Calle 222 No 55 – 37, Bogota, Bogota DC, Colombia. T. +5716684700 ext 220. E-mail: secretariageneral@aualcpi.org – info@aualcpi.org – aualcpi@udca.edu.co.
URL: https://www.aualcpi.org/

History 15 Apr 1993, Mendoza (Argentina). Registration: Colombia. **Aims** Promote inter-exchange between Latin American and Caribbean universities so as to develop activities leading to integration of the community of Latin American and Caribbean nations. **Structure** General Assembly; Directive Council; Officers. **Languages** Portuguese, Spanish. **Staff** 4.00 FTE, paid. **Finance** Sources: members' dues. Main funding from Universidad de Ciencias Aplicadas y Ambientales UDCA. **Activities** Events/meetings; knowledge management/information dissemination; training/education. **Publications** *Agora Latinoamericana.*
Members Higher education institutions (about 70) in 17 countries:
Argentina, Bolivia, Brazil, Chile, Colombia, Cuba, Ecuador, El Salvador, Haiti, Mexico, Nicaragua, Panama, Paraguay, Peru, Puerto Rico, USA, Venezuela.
NGO Relations Member of (2): *Association of Universities of Latin America and the Caribbean (#02970); Inter-American Organization for Higher Education (IOHE, #11442).* [2021.06.09/XJ9114/**D**]

♦ Asociación de Universidades del Commonwealth (#02440)
♦ Asociación de Universidades Confiadas a la Compañía de Jesús en América Latina (#02969)
♦ Asociación de Universidades Grupo Montevideo (#02971)
♦ Asociación de Universidades e Institutos de Investigación del Caribe / see Universities Caribbean (#20694)
♦ Asociación de Universidades Privadas de Centroamérica / see Asociación de Universidades Privadas de Centroamérica y Panama (#02306)

♦ Asociación de Universidades Privadas de Centroamérica y Panama (AUPRICA) 02306

Pres Rector UNIVO, 4a Calle Poniente No 705, San Miguel, El Salvador. T. +50326683700ext2706 – +50326683707. E-mail: parieta@univo.edu.sv – erodriguez@unibe.ac.cr.
Vice-Pres Univ Rural de Guatemala, 7 Calle 6-49, Zona 2, Guatemala, Guatemala. E-mail: rector@urural.edu.gt.
URL: http://www.auprica.org/

History Founded 14 Aug 1990, Tegucigalpa (Honduras), as *Federation of Private Universities of Central America and Panama – Fédération d'universités privés d'Amérique centrale et du Panama – Federación de Universidades Privadas de América Central y Panamá.* Derives from *Federation of Private Universities of Central America (FUPAC) – Asociación de Universidades Privadas de Centroamérica (PIECA),* set up 6 Aug 1966, Managua (Nicaragua). **Aims** Promote academic excellence as necessary and vital to development of quality *education* in member institutions; foster cooperation among member institutions; promote exchange of information, professors, students and inter-institutional research projects; contribute to student education, particularly those who have not had the opportunity to enter the higher education system; encourage preservation and restoration of the identity and cultures of Central America.
Members Universities in 6 countries:
Costa Rica, El Salvador, Guatemala, Honduras, Nicaragua, Panama.
Included in the above, 6 organizations listed in this Yearbook:
International Cooperative University (ICU, #12952); Pan American Agricultural School 'El Zamorano' (EAP); Universidad Adventista de Centro América (UNADECO, no recent information); Universidad de Iberoamérica; Universidad Latinoamericana de Ciencia y Tecnologia (ULACIT); Universidad Tecnológica Centroamericana (UNITEC). [2018/XE3495/y/**D**]

♦ Asociación de Universidades del Sureste de Asia (#02920)

♦ Asociación Universitaria Iberoamericana de Postgrado (AUIP) 02307

Iberoamerican Association of Postgraduate Universities

Managing Dir Hospedería Fonseca, C/ Fonseca 2, 37002 Salamanca, Spain. T. +34923210039. Fax +34923214949. E-mail: administracion@auip.org.
URL: http://www.auip.org/

History 1987. Founded on the initiative of OEI as a network of centres of postgraduate studies, for servicing especially the graduate students from Latin America, the Caribbean, Spain and Portugal. Former names and other names: *Ibero-American University for Graduate Studies* – former (1987 to 1994); *Université ibéroaméricaine d'études post-universitaires* – former (1987 to 1994); *Universidad Iberoamericana de Postgrado (UIP)* – former (1987 to 1994). Registration: Registro Nacional de Asociaciones del Ministerio de Interior de España, No/ID: 162841, Start date: 9 Oct 1997, Spain, SALAMANCA. **Aims** Advance *postgraduate* studies in the community of Ibero-American nations by: collecting information on them; making such information available to them and to others who may benefit from this network, such as graduate *students* and researchers; providing and facilitating program evaluation and accreditation processes; promoting international understanding, cooperation and academic integration. **Structure** General Assembly; Executive Commission; Managing Director. **Languages** Portuguese, Spanish. **Staff** 6.00 FTE, paid. **Finance** Sources: contributions; grants; members' dues. Supported by: Junta de Andalucia; Junta de Castilla y Leon. Annual budget: 3,000,000 EUR. **Activities** Financial and/or material support; guidance/assistance/consulting; networking/liaising; projects/programmes; training/education. **Events** *General Assembly* Salamanca (Spain) 2020, *General Assembly* Salamanca (Spain) 2019, *General Assembly* Santiago de los Caballeros (Dominican Rep) 2019, *General Assembly* Santa Cruz de Tenerife (Spain) 2018, *General Assembly* Lima (Peru) 2017. **Publications** *Boletin de Noticias de la AUIP; Boletin Informativo.* Guide.
Members Associated institutions (246) in 22 countries and territories:
Argentina, Bolivia, Brazil, Chile, Colombia, Costa Rica, Cuba, Dominican Rep, Ecuador, El Salvador, Guatemala, Honduras, Mexico, Nicaragua, Panama, Paraguay, Peru, Portugal, Puerto Rico, Spain, Uruguay, Venezuela.
Included in the above, 7 institutions listed in this Yearbook:
Confederación Universitaria Centroamericana (CSUCA, #04497); Instituto Andaluz del Deporte (inactive); Latin American Faculty of Social Sciences (#16316); Tropical Agriculture Research and Higher Education Center (#20246); Universidad Abierta Interamericana (UAI); Universidad Andina Simón Bolívar (UASB, #20687); Universidad Interamericana, Santo Domingo (no recent information).
IGO Relations Cooperates with (2): *International Development Research Centre (IDRC, #13162); United Nations University (UNU, #20642).* Consultative Status with: *UNESCO (#20322).* **NGO Relations** Cooperates with (3): *Association of Universities of Latin America and the Caribbean (#02970); Red Universitaria de Educación Continua de Latinoamérica y Europa (RECLA, #18734); United Nations Academic Impact (UNAI, #20516).* Supports (1): *Red Iberoamericana de Investigadores "Kant: Ética, Política y Sociedad (RIKEPS, #18671).* Also links with national organizations. [2021.02.17/XF2033/y/**F**]

♦ Asociación Universitaria Internacional del Vino y de los Productos de la Viña (unconfirmed)
♦ Asociación de Urologia del Mediterraneo Latino (inactive)
♦ Asociación de Usuarios del Transporte Maritimo, Terrestre y Aéreo del Istmo Centroamericano (no recent information)
♦ Asociación Veterinaria Euro-Arabe (#02975)
♦ Asociación de Zonas Francas de Latinoamérica y el Caribe (no recent information)
♦ Asociación de Zonas Mineras / see Association of Europe's Coalfield Regions (#02585)
♦ Asociatia Europeana pentru Educatie si Cultura (unconfirmed)
♦ Asociatia Internationalaa a gândirii libere (#11906)
♦ Asociatia Internationala a Plutasilor (#15691)
♦ Asociatiei Internationale a Fostilor Detinuti Politici si Victimelor Communismului (no recent information)
♦ Association of Institute for Euroregional Studies (IERS) "Jean Monnet" European Center of Excellence / see Institute for Euroregional Studies
♦ **ASOCIO** Asian-Oceanian Computing Industry Organisation (#01576)
♦ Asocio por Eúropa Konscio (internationally oriented national body)
♦ Asocio Internacia por la Defendo de la Minacataj Lingvoj kaj Kulturoj / see Association pour les Langues et Cultures Européennes Menacées (#02782)
♦ Asocio de Studado Internacia pri Spiritaj kaj Teologiaj Instruoj (inactive)
♦ Asocio de Verduloj Esperantistaj (#02494)
♦ ASOCODE – Asociación de Organizaciones Campesinas Centroamericanas para la Cooperación y el Desarrollo (inactive)
♦ **ASOG** African Society of Organization Gestosis (#00464)
♦ **ASOIF** Association of Summer Olympic International Federations (#02943)
♦ **ASOLADEME** Asociación Latinoamericana de Derecho Médico (#02203)
♦ ASOMPS – Asian Symposium on Medicinal Plants, Spices and Other Natural Products (meeting series)
♦ ASOPAZCO – Asociación por la Paz Continental (unconfirmed)
♦ **ASOP EU** Alliance for Safe Online Pharmacy – EU (#00720)
♦ ASOP Global – Alliance for Safe Online Pharmacies (internationally oriented national body)
♦ ASOR – Agreement on the International Carriage of Passengers by Road by Means of Occasional Coach and Bus Service (1982 treaty)
♦ ASOR – American Schools of Oriental Research (internationally oriented national body)
♦ **ASOSAI** Asian Organization of Supreme Audit Institutions (#01594)
♦ ASP / see Asian Studies Center, Pittsburgh
♦ ASPA / see Society for Human Resource Management
♦ ASPA / see Australasian Society for Physical Activity
♦ **ASPA** Asian Science Park Association (#01693)
♦ **ASPA** Asian Society of Paediatric Anaesthesiologists (#01732)
♦ ASPA – Asociación Andaluza por la Solidaridad y la Paz (internationally oriented national body)
♦ **ASPA** Association of South Pacific Airlines (#02926)
♦ ASPA – Australasian Society for Physical Activity (internationally oriented national body)
♦ ASPAB – Australasian Society of Phycology and Aquatic Botany (internationally oriented national body)
♦ ASPACAE – Asian Pacific Confederation for Arts Education (no recent information)
♦ ASPAC – Asian and Pacific Council (inactive)
♦ **ASPAC** Asia Pacific Grouping of Consulting Engineers (#01920)
♦ **ASPAC** Asia Pacific Network of Science and Technology Centres (#01974)
♦ ASPAC / see IWA Asia Pacific Region Grouping (#16083)
♦ **ASPAC** Kiwanis Asia-Pacific (#16194)
♦ ASPAC-NGO – Asia Pacific Non-Government Organization on Drug and Substance Abuse Prevention (inactive)
♦ ASPAC-TCIF – Asia-Pacific Textile and Clothing Industry Forum (meeting series)
♦ **ASP** Adriatic Society of Pathology (#00123)
♦ **ASPAE** African Society for Paediatric and Adolescent Endocrinology (#00465)
♦ ASPAFRIQUE-JICS-H2F / see ASPAFRIQUE-JICS-HFFUN
♦ ASPAFRIQUE-JICS-HFFUN (internationally oriented national body)
♦ ASPAL – Association de solidarité avec les peuples d'Amérique latine (internationally oriented national body)
♦ **ASPASP** Asian-South Pacific Association of Sport Psychology (#01755)
♦ ASP – Associazione Svizzera di politica estera (internationally oriented national body)
♦ **ASP** Astronomical Society of the Pacific (#02997)
♦ ASP – Australasian Society for Psychophysiology (internationally oriented national body)
♦ ASPBAE / see Asia South Pacific Association for Basic and Adult Education (#02098)
♦ **ASPBAE** Asia South Pacific Association for Basic and Adult Education (#02098)
♦ ASPB – Asian Student Press Bureau (inactive)
♦ ASPC – Asian Society of Protective Clothing (unconfirmed)
♦ **ASPC** Association of Sport Performance Centres (#02930)
♦ **ASPC** Association of Sport Performance Centres (#02929)
♦ **ASPCR** Asian Society for Pigment Cell Research (#01735)
♦ ASP-DAC – Asia and South Pacific Design Automation Conference (meeting series)
♦ **ASPE** Association of Standardized Patient Educators (#02932)
♦ ASPE – Association suisse de politique étrangère (internationally oriented national body)
♦ Aspect Foundation Student Exchange (internationally oriented national body)

♦ Aspect-Oriented Software Association (AOSA) 02308

Sec-Treas address not obtained.
URL: https://aosa-inc.org/

Aims Be the primary sponsor for the annual Conference on Aspect-Oriented Software Development. **Structure** Steering Committee, including Chair and Secretary/Treasurer. **Events** *International Conference on the Art, Science, and Engineering of Programming* Tokyo (Japan) 2023, *International Conference on the Art, Science, and Engineering of Programming* Porto (Portugal) 2022, *International Conference on the Art, Science, and Engineering of Programming* Cambridge (UK) 2021, *International Conference on the Art, Science, and Engineering of Programming* Porto (Portugal) 2020, *International Conference on the Art, Science, and Engineering of Programming* Genoa (Italy) 2019. [2021/XJ7001/**E**]

♦ **ASPED** Arab Society for Paediatric Endocrinology and Diabetes (#01048)
♦ ASPEI – Association of South Pacific Environmental Institutions (inactive)
♦ ASPEm – Associazione Solidarietà Paesi Emergenti (internationally oriented national body)
♦ **ASPEN** Asian Physics Education Network (#01664)
♦ **ASPEN** Asian Society for Precision Engineering and Nanotechnology (#01736)
♦ Aspen Global Change Institute (internationally oriented national body)

♦ Aspen Institute 02309

Institut Aspen – Instituto Aspen

Pres/CEO 2300 N Street NW, Ste 700, Washington DC 20037, USA. T. +12027365800. Fax +12024670790.
Aspen 1000 North Third St, Aspen CO 81611, USA. T. +19709257010. Fax +19709254188.
URL: http://www.aspeninst.org/

History 1950, Aspen CO (USA), at 1st Executive Seminar, as *Aspen Institute for Humanistic Studies.* Present name adopted 1988. **Aims** Enhance the ability of *leaders* in business, government, the nonprofit sector, academia and the media to understand and act upon the issues that challenge the national and international community; help leaders deepen their thinking and broaden their perspectives for *decision-making* by convening them in seminars and conferences that address topics of current interest, but place the debate and discussion of such issues within the context of the universal and enduring values and ideas that traditionally define civilization. Integrate humanistic values into the choices which must be made in selected areas of contemporary life; bring able people from all sectors of society together in a search for viable approaches to many of the most critical issues of our time. **Structure** Headed by Chairman/Chief Executive Officer. Board of Trustees, consisting of Chairman, 2 Vice Chairmen, Aspen Institute President, 56 Active Trustees, 4 ex-officio Trustees, 12 Honorary Trustees and 43 Emeritus Trustees. US offices in Washington DC (USA), Queenstown MD (USA), New York NY (USA), Aspen CO (USA) and Santa Barbara CA (USA). International offices in Berlin (Germany), Rome (Italy), Lyon (France) and Tokyo (Japan). **Finance** Members' dues. Other sources: foundation grants; corporate and individual contributions; fees; tuition. Budget (annual): about US$ 20 million. **Activities** Evens/meetings; training/education. Includes: *Aspen Network of Development Entrepreneurs (ANDE, #02310).* **Events** *Seminar* Aspen, CO (USA) 2012, *Round Table on Spectrum Policy* Queenstown, MD (USA) 2012,

Seminar Queenstown, MD (USA) 2012, *Global forum for responsible management education* New York, NY (USA) 2010, *Antarctic treaty summit* Washington, DC (USA) 2009. **Publications** *Aspen Peaks* – newsletter. Books, working papers, studies, reports in the following fields: arms control/national security, economics, education, energy an the environment, governance, international studies, media/communications, science and technology, sociology. Annual report; conference reports. **Members** Individuals. Membership countries not specified. **NGO Relations** Acts as secretariat for: *International Commission on the Balkans (no recent information)*. Partner of: *Global Knowledge Initiative*. Instrumental in setting up: *Applied Research and Development International (ARDI, inactive)*. [2019/XE4010/j/**E**]

♦ Aspen Institute for Humanistic Studies / see Aspen Institute (#02309)
♦ Aspen International Mountain Foundation (internationally oriented national body)

♦ Aspen Network of Development Entrepreneurs (ANDE) 02310

Exec Dir c/o Aspen Inst, 2300 N St. NW, Ste 700, Washington DC 20037-1122, USA. E-mail: ande.info@aspeninst.org.
URL: https://www.andeglobal.org/

History 2009, operating under *Aspen Institute (#02309)*. **Aims** Invest money and expertise to propel entrepreneurship in emerging markets. **Structure** Executive Committee, headed by Chair. **Activities** Programme areas (5): Knowledge Sharing and Networking: Training and Talent Development; Metrics and Evaluation; Capacity Building Fund; Advocacy and Education. **Events** *Annual Conference* Glen Cove, NY (USA) 2012, *Annual Conference* Ellicott City, MD (USA) 2011, *Annual Conference* Glen Cove, NY (USA) 2010.
Members Investment funds; non-governments organizations; research institutions; private philanthropic foundations. Members (136) include the following 26 organizations listed in this Yearbook:
- *ACCION International*;
- *Acumen*;
- *African Management Services Company (AMSCO, #00367)*;
- *Aga Khan Foundation (AKF, #00545)*;
- *Andes University (ULA)*;
- *Aspen Institute (#02309)*;
- *Bill and Melinda Gates Foundation (BMGF)*;
- *Energy 4 Impact (#05465)*;
- *Finance Alliance for Sustainable Trade (FAST, #09763)*;
- *Ford Foundation (#09858)*;
- *Forum on Business and Social Responsibility in the Americas (Forum EMPRESA)*;
- *Fundación para el Desarrollo Sostenible en América Latina (FUNDES, #10021)*;
- *Global Alliance for Improved Nutrition (GAIN, #10202)*;
- *Global Communities*;
- *ICCO – Interchurch Organization for Development Cooperation*;
- *International Finance Corporation (IFC, #13597)*;
- *Middlebury Institute of International Studies, Monterey (MIIS)*;
- *Oxfam International (#17922)*;
- *RTI International*;
- *Shell Foundation*;
- *Skoll Foundation*;
- *SNV Netherlands Development Organisation (SNV)*;
- *Special Emergency Assistance Fund for Drought and Famine in Africa (SEAF, #19908)*;
- *Swisscontact – Swiss Foundation for Technical Cooperation*;
- *The Rockefeller Foundation (#18966)*;
- *Youth Business International (YBI)*.

NGO Relations Member of: *Global Innovation Exchange (The Exchange, inactive)*; *InsideNGO (inactive)*. [2020/XJ3825/y/**E**]

♦ **ASPF** Arab Sea Ports Federation (#01040)
♦ **ASPHA** Association of Schools of Public Health in Africa (#02903)
♦ Asphalt Emulsion Manufacturers Association (internationally oriented national body)
♦ ASPH – Association of Schools of Public Health (internationally oriented national body)
♦ **ASPHER** Association of Schools of Public Health in the European Region (#02904)
♦ ASPI – Australasian Society of Paediatric Imaging (unconfirmed)
♦ **ASPID** Asian Society of Pediatric Infectious Diseases (#01733)
♦ ASPIP / see Arab Society for Intellectual Property (#01046)

♦ A.SPIRE 02311

Pres Rue Belliard 40, BP 21, 1040 Brussels, Belgium. T. +3226767308. E-mail: info@spire2030.eu.
URL: http://www.spire2030.eu/

History Signing ceremony, 18 Jul 2012, Brussels (Belgium). European Association committed to manage and implement the *Sustainable Process Industry through Resource and Energy Efficiency (SPIRE)* Public-Private Partnership (PPP), as part of the Horizon2020 framework programme. Registration: Banque-Carrefour des Entreprises, No/ID: 0848.414.953, Start date: 4 Sep 2012, Belgium; EU Transparency Register, No/ID: 568717115528-72, Start date: 12 Jan 2015. **Aims** Ensure development of enabling technologies and best practices along all stages of large scale existing value chain productions that will contribute to a resource efficient process industry. **Languages** English. **Staff** 4.00 FTE, paid. **Finance** Members' dues. **Events** *Public Private Partnerships Brokerage Meeting* Brussels (Belgium) 2015. **Publications** *SPIRE Roadmap*.
Members Members (over 140): Industries; Research; Associations; Associate. Research institutes include 5 organizations listed in this Yearbook:
European Nanoporous Materials Institute of Excellence (ENMIX, #07851); *European Research Institute of Catalysis (ERIC, #08369)*; *European Virtual Institute for Integrated Risk Management (EU-VRi, #09062)*; *SINTEF*.
Associations include 8 organizations listed in this Yearbook:
Association européenne des métaux (EUROMETAUX, #02578); *CEMBUREAU – The European Cement Association (CEMBUREAU, #03634)*; *Conseil européen de l'industrie chimique (CEFIC, #04687)*; *European Ceramic Industry Association (CERAME-UNIE, #06506)*; *European Engineering Industries Association (EUnited, #06991)*; *European Steel Association (EUROFER, #08835)*; *Industrial Minerals Association – Europe (IMA Europe, #11179)*.
Associate members include 2 organizations listed in this Yearbook:
European Federation of National Maintenance Societies (EFNMS, #07173); *Greenovate! Europe (#10726)*.
NGO Relations *Industry4Europe (#11181)*; *Knowledge4Innovation (K4I, #16198)*. [2021/XJ8754/y/**E**]

♦ **ASPIRE** Asia-Pacific Initiative on Reproduction (#01932)
♦ ASPL – Asian Symposium on Plant Lipids (meeting series)
♦ **ASPLF** Association des sociétés de philosophie de langue française (#02918)
♦ **AsPNA** Asian Pediatric Nephrology Association (#01659)
♦ **ASPnet** UNESCO Associated Schools Project Network (#20302)
♦ ASPNF – Arab Society for Plant Nutrition and Fertilization (inactive)
♦ **ASPOA** Asian and South Pacific Ostomy Association (#01756)
♦ **ASPO** Association for the Study of Peak Oil and Gas (#02940)
♦ **ASPP** Arab Society for Plant Protection (#01049)
♦ **ASPR** Asian Society for Pediatric Research (#01734)
♦ ASPR – Austrian Study Centre for Peace and Conflict Resolution (internationally oriented national body)
♦ ASPS – Association for the Study of Persianate Societies (internationally oriented national body)
♦ ASPT – American Society of Plant Taxonomists (internationally oriented national body)
♦ **ASPU** Asian Sports Press Union (#01759)
♦ ASP / see UNESCO Associated Schools Project Network (#20302)
♦ ASQ – American Society for Quality (internationally oriented national body)
♦ ASQC / see American Society for Quality
♦ **ASQH** African Society for Quality in Healthcare (#00467)
♦ **ASQua** Asian Society for Quality in Health Care (#01737)
♦ ASRA – Australasian Sound Recordings Association (internationally oriented national body)
♦ **ASR** African Society of Radiology (#00468)
♦ ASR – Asia Society of Researchers (unconfirmed)
♦ ASRC / see Kansas African Studies Center
♦ **ASRDLF** Association de science régionale de langue française (#02906)
♦ **ASREN** Arab States Research and Education Network (#01051)
♦ **AsRES** Asian Real Estate Society (#01680)
♦ ASRI / see Sinor Research Institute for Inner Asian Studies
♦ ASrIA – Association for Sustainable and Responsible Investment in Asia (inactive)
♦ **ASRIC** African Scientific Technical and Research Innovation Council (#00451)
♦ ASRO / see Academic Scientific Research Organization (#00023)
♦ **ASRO** Academic Scientific Research Organization (#00023)
♦ **ASRS** Asian Sleep Research Society (#01701)
♦ ASRY – Arab Shipbuilding and Repair Yard Company (see: #17854)
♦ ASSA – Anatomical Society of Southern Africa (internationally oriented national body)
♦ **ASSA** ASEAN Social Security Association (#01234)
♦ **ASSA** ASEAN Society for Sports Medicine and Arthroscopy (#01235)
♦ **ASSA** Association for the Study of Australasia in Asia (#02937)
♦ **ASSA-I** Aviation Security Services Association – International (#03046)
♦ ASSA International / see Aviation Security Services Association – International (#03046)
♦ **ASSAL** Asociación de Supervisores de Seguros de América Latina (#02300)
♦ **ASSB** Asian Society of Sport Biomechanics (#01740)
♦ ASSBI – Australasian Society for the Study of Brain Impairment (internationally oriented national body)
♦ **ASSC** Association for the Scientific Study of Consciousness (#02907)
♦ ASSE / see International Student Exchange Programs
♦ ASSEA / see Asian Surgical Association (#01763)
♦ **ASSECAA** Association of Senates, Shoora and Equivalent Councils in Africa and the Arab World (#02913)
♦ **ASSECAM** Association de l'education Catholique pour l'Afrique et Madagascar (#02415)
♦ **ASSEDIL** Association européenne des directeurs d'institutions lasalliennes (#02563)
♦ ASSE – International Student Exchange Programs (internationally oriented national body)
♦ Assemblea Generale dei Comitati Nazionali Olimpici / see Association of National Olympic Committees (#02819)
♦ Assemblea delle Regioni d'Europa (#02316)
♦ Assemblea delle Regioni Europee Viticole (#02317)
♦ Assemblée d'Accra (inactive)
♦ Assemblée de l'Atlantique Nord / see NATO Parliamentary Assembly (#16946)
♦ Assemblée balte (#03094)
♦ Assemblée des bibliothèques de l'Eurasie (#16458)
♦ Assemblée consultative balkanique (inactive)
♦ Assemblée des directeurs d'instituts de médecine tropicale d'Europe (inactive)
♦ Assemblée européenne des citoyens (#05922)
♦ Assemblée européenne des étudiants en architecture (meeting series)
♦ Assemblée générale des comités nationaux olympiques / see Association of National Olympic Committees (#02819)
♦ Assemblée générale des églises chrétiennes libres et unitaires (#10105)
♦ Assemblée hispano-luso-américano-philippine de tourisme (inactive)
♦ Assemblée internationale des fédérations des sports d'hiver / see Association of the International Olympic Winter Sports Federations (#02757)
♦ Assemblée internationale des ONG intéressées à l'environnement (inactive)
♦ Assemblée internationale des parlementaires de langue française / see Assemblée parlementaire de la Francophonie (#02312)
♦ Assemblée interparlementaire de la CEI / see Interparliamentary Assembly of Member Nations of the Commonwealth of Independent States (#15958)
♦ Assemblée législative de l'Afrique orientale (#05185)
♦ Assemblée mondiale des artisans de la radio communautaire / see Association mondiale des radiodiffuseurs communautaires (#02810)
♦ Assemblée mondiale des citoyens / see Association of World Citizens (#02982)
♦ Assemblée mondiale de la jeunesse (#21113)
♦ Assemblée mondiale des petites et moyennes entreprises / see World Association for Small and Medium Enterprises (#21189)
♦ Assemblée mondiale des radiodiffuseurs communautaires / see Association mondiale des radiodiffuseurs communautaires (#02810)
♦ Assemblée des Ordinaires Catholiques de Terre Sainte (religious order)
♦ Assemblée paritaire ACP-CE / see ACP-EU Joint Parliamentary Assembly (#00077)
♦ Assemblée paritaire ACP-UE / see ACP-EU Joint Parliamentary Assembly (#00077)
♦ Assemblée parlementaire de la Communauté des Etats indépendants / see Interparliamentary Assembly of Member Nations of the Commonwealth of Independent States (#15958)
♦ Assemblée parlementaire de la Conférence sur la sécurité et la coopération en Europe / see Parliamentary Assembly of the Organization for Security and Cooperation in Europe (#18214)
♦ Assemblée parlementaire du Conseil de l'Europe (#18211)
♦ Assemblée parlementaire euro-latino américaine (#05700)
♦ Assemblée parlementaire européenne / see European Parliament (#08146)

♦ Assemblée parlementaire de la Francophonie (APF) 02312

Parliamentary Assembly of the French-Speaking World – Asamblea Parlamentaria de la Francofonia

Mailing Address 126 rue de l'Université, 75355 Paris 07 SP, France.
SG 233 bd St-Germain, 75007 Paris, France. T. +33140639160. E-mail: info@apf-fr.org.
URL: http://apf.francophonie.org/

History 18 May 1967, Luxembourg, as *Association internationale des parlementaires de langue française (AIPLF) – International Association of French-Speaking Parliamentarians – Asociación Internacional de Parlamentarios de Lengua Francesa*, by Constituent Assembly. Following recognition of its vocation as the French-speaking interparliamentary organization by by *Conférence au sommet des chefs d'Etat et de gouvernement des pays ayant le français en partage (Sommet de la Francophonie, #04648)* May 1989, Dakar (Senegal), changed title to *Assemblée internationale des parlementaires de langue française (AIPLF) – International Assembly of French-Speaking Parliamentarians – Asamblea Internacional de Parlamentarios de Lengua Francesa* at General Assembly of Jul 1989, Paris (France). Subsequently recognized by 5th Summit, Oct 1993, Mauritius, as the consultative assembly of the French-speaking world. Following Summit of 1997, Hanoi (Vietnam), became an operating institution of the French-speaking world and modified statutes and modus operandi to comply with terms of *Organisation internationale de la Francophonie (OIF, #17809)* Charter and changed title to current title. Those changes were adopted Jul 1998, during Ordinary Assembly of Abidjan (Côte di'Ivoire). Registration: France. **Aims** Function as the democratic link between institutions and peoples of the French-speaking world; further the influence of the *French language*; contribute to the development and reciprocal understanding of cultures and civilizations of peoples habitually using the French language although not of French culture or civilization; promote cooperation and reinforce solidarity within the French-speaking community, respecting the right to development; promote democracy, the rule of law and individual rights, particularly within the French-speaking community; manage all issues of interest to the Parliamentary Assembly, particularly those related to current international politics, and transmit relevant information to authorities of the French-speaking world. **Structure** Plenary General Assembly (annual); Bureau; Executive Committee; Secretariat-General; Standing commissions (4); Regional Assemblies (4); National Sections. **Languages** French. **Staff** 15.00 FTE, paid. **Finance** Contributions from national sections; subventions. Annual budget: 2,239,185 EUR. **Activities** Events/meetings; knowledge management/information dissemination; training/education. Gives: opinions and recommendations at *Conférence ministérielle de la Francophonie (CMF, #04630)* and *Conseil permanent de la Francophonie (CPF, #04697)*. **Events** *European Regional Assembly* Barcelona (Spain) 2022, *General Assembly* Kigali (Rwanda) 2022, *African Regional Assembly* Rabat (Morocco) 2022, *General Assembly* 2021, *European Regional Assembly* Tirana (Albania) 2021. **Publications** *Lettre de la Francophonie Parlementaire*.

Members Membership Sections comprise parliaments or come within parliaments of states or communities whose official, administrative or common language is French. Associate Sections comprise parliaments or come within parliaments of other states which habitually use the French language, particularly in international meetings. Membership Sections in 54 countries, territories and provinces:
Armenia, Belgium (French Community/Wallonia-Brussels), Benin, Burkina Faso, Burundi, Cambodia, Cameroon, Canada, Cape Verde, Central African Rep, Chad, Comoros, Congo Brazzaville, Congo DR, Côte d'Ivoire, Djibouti, Egypt, Equatorial Guinea, France, Gabon, Greece, Guinea, Guinea-Bissau, Haiti, Jersey, Jura, Laos, Lebanon, Luxembourg, Madagascar, Mali, Manitoba, Mauritania, Mauritius, Monaco, Morocco, New Brunswick, New Caledonia, Niger, Nova Scotia, Ontario, Québec, Romania, Rwanda, Senegal, Seychelles, Switzerland, Syrian AR, Togo, Tunisia, Valle d'Aosta, Vanuatu, Vietnam.
Associate Sections in 14 countries, territories and provinces:
Albania, Andorra, British Columbia, Bulgaria, Geneva (Canton of), Hungary, Lithuania, Moldova, North Macedonia, Poland, Prince Edward Is, Saskatchewan, Valais (Canton of).
Observer members in 9 countries:
Bosnia, Catalunya (Spain), Croatia, Czechia, Georgia, Kosovo, Lithuania, Mexico, Serbia.
Observers also in the following 3 states in the USA: Louisiana, Maine, New Hampshire. Included in the above, 6 organizations listed in this Yearbook:
Included in the above, 6 organizations listed in this Yearbook:
Benelux Inter-Parliamentary Consultative Council (Benelux Parliament, #03201); *Communauté économique et monétaire d'Afrique centrale (CEMAC, #04374)* (Parliament); *Confederación Parlamentaria de las Américas (COPA, #04479)*; *Economic Community of West African States (ECOWAS, #05312)* (Parliament); *European Parliament (EP, #08146)*; *Union économique et monétaire Ouest africaine (UEMOA, #20377)*.
Consultative Status Consultative status granted from: *ILO (#11123)* (Special List). **IGO Relations** Consultative relationship with the Summit of la Francophonie and its related institutions. Accredited by: *United Nations Office at Vienna (UNOV, #20604)*. Informational and cooperative relations with: *WHO (#20950)*. Associated with Department of Global Communications of the United Nations. Other partnership agreements signed with: *UNESCO (#20322)* (2005); Association des Scretaires Gnraux de Parlements Francophones (ASGPF) (2009); *UNDP (#20292)* (2009); *Joint United Nations Programme on HIV/AIDS (UNAIDS, #16149)* (2010). **NGO Relations** Member of: *International Council on Archives (ICA, #12996)*. Library is member of: *International Federation of Library Associations and Institutions (IFLA, #13470)*. Cooperates with: *African Parliamentary Union (APU, #00412)*; *Agence universitaire de La Francophonie (AUF, #00548)*; *Commonwealth Parliamentary Association (CPA, #04355)*. [2021/XC4331/y/**C**]

- ♦ Assemblée parlementaire de la Méditerranée (#18212)
- ♦ Assemblée parlementaire des Nations Unies (unconfirmed)
- ♦ Assemblée parlementaire de l'Organisation pour la sécurité et la coopération en Europe (#18214)
- ♦ Assemblée parlementaire de la OSCE / see Parliamentary Assembly of the Organization for Security and Cooperation in Europe (#18214)
- ♦ Assemblée parlementaire de l'OTAN (#16946)
- ♦ Assemblée parlementaire paritaire de l'accord de partenariat entre les membres du groupe des états d'Afrique, des Caraïbes et du Pacifique et la Communauté Européenne et ses états membres / see ACP-EU Joint Parliamentary Assembly (#00077)
- ♦ Assemblée parlementaire paritaire ACP-UE (#00077)
- ♦ Assemblée parlementaire de l'UEO – Assemblée européenne de sécurité et de défense (inactive)
- ♦ Assemblée Parlementaire – Union pour la Méditerranée (#18216)
- ♦ Assemblée permanente des chambres de commerce et d'industrie de la Méditerranée / see Asociación de las Camaras de Comercio e Industria del Mediterraneo (#02112)
- ♦ Assemblée permanente pour les droits de l'homme (internationally oriented national body)

♦ Assemblée Régionale et Locale Euro-Méditerranéenne (ARLEM) . . . 02313

Euro-Mediterranean Regional and Local Assembly
Secretariat c/o CoR, Rue Belliard 101, 1040 Brussels, Belgium. T. +3222822444. E-mail: arlem-secretariat@cor.europa.eu.
URL: https://cor.europa.eu/en/our-work/Pages/ARLEM.aspx
History Set up 2010 by *European Committee of the Regions (CoR, #06665)*. **Aims** Give a territorial dimension to the Union for the Mediterranean; promote local democracy, multi-level governance and decentralized cooperation around the three shores of the Mediterranean; encourage North-South and South-South dialogue between local and regional authorities; promote the exchange of best practice, knowledge and technical experience in the areas for which local and regional authorities are responsible; promote regional integration and cohesion. **Structure** Composed of 80 members and 2 observers; Chaired by co-presidency representing equally the Mediterranean partners and *European Union (EU, #08967)*. Bureau.
Members Countries involved (15; indicates currently suspended):
Albania, Algeria, Bosnia-Herzegovina, Egypt, Israel, Jordan, Lebanon, Mauritania, Monaco, Montenegro, Morocco, Palestine, Syrian AR (*), Tunisia, Türkiye.
Observer country:
Libya.
IGO Relations Institutional relations with: *European Commission (EC, #06633)*; *European Economic and Social Committee (EESC, #06963)*; *European External Action Service (EEAS, #07018)*; *European Parliament (EP, #08146)*. Observer status with: Parliamentary Assembly of *Union for the Mediterranean (UfM, #20457)*. Observer status granted to: *Congress of Local and Regional Authorities of the Council of Europe (#04677)*. Cooperation agreement with: *European Training Foundation (ETF, #08934)*. **NGO Relations** Cooperation agreement with: *Euro-Mediterranean University (EMUNI, #05728)*. [2021/XM7077/**E***]

- ♦ Assemblée des régions d'Europe (#02316)

♦ Assemblée des Régions Européennes Fruitières, Légumières et Horticoles (AREFLH) 02314

Assembly of European Regions Producing Fruit, Vegetable and Plants
Main Office 110 Quai de Paludate, BP 26, 33000 Bordeaux, France. T. +33556488848. E-mail: contact@areflh.org – communication@areflh.org.
URL: http://www.areflh.org/
History 2000. Former names and other names: *Assembly of European Regions producing Fruit, Vegetable, Ornamental Plants and Olive Oil* – alias. Registration: EU Transparency Register, No/ID: 729014411618-96. **Aims** Defend economic and social interests of the fruit, vegetable and horticultural sectors with European authorities; promote exchange of experiences, partnerships and joint projects between regions and professional organizations; be proactive and come up with new solutions for the main issues which affect the future of fruit and vegetable production in Europe. **Structure** General Assembly; Administrative Board; Bureau; Administrative Office. Working Groups and Commissions. **Languages** English, French, Italian, Spanish. **Staff** 1.00 FTE, paid. **Finance** Sources: members' dues. **Activities** Knowledge management/information dissemination; networking/liaising; research and development; monitoring/evaluation; events/meetings. **Events** *International Pear Congress (INTERPERA)* Rotterdam (Netherlands) 2022, *International Pear Seminar* 2021, *International Pear Congress (INTERPERA)* Rotterdam (Netherlands) 2020, *International Pear Congress (INTERPERA)* Tours (France) 2019, *Assemblée générale* Brussels (Belgium) 2018.
Members Regions and associations of producers organizations in 7 countries:
Austria, Belgium, France, Greece, Italy, Portugal, Spain.
NGO Relations Member of (3): *Assembly of European Regions (AER, #02316)*; *EU Platform for Action on Diet, Physical Activity and Health (inactive)*; *Global Alliance to Promote Fruits and Vegetable Consumption "5 a day" (AIAM5, #10221)*. Instrumental in setting up (1): *European Chestnut Network (EUROCASTANEA)*. [2022/XF6747/**F**]

- ♦ Assemblée des régions européennes viticoles (#02317)

♦ Assembleia Parlamentar da Comunidade dos Países de Língua Portuguesa (AP-CPLP) 02315

Address not obtained.
URL: https://www.ap-cplp.org/
History Nov 2007, Lisbon (Portugal). Established by the XII Council of Ministers of *Comunidade dos Países de Língua Portuguesa (CPLP, #04430)*, following several meetings of *Fórum dos Parlamentos dos Países de Língua Portuguesa (FPLP, inactive)*. **Aims** Strengthen ties of cooperation, solidarity and exchange between member Parliaments, so as to contribute to the consolidation of peace, democracy and the rule of law in the respective countries. **Structure** Plenary; Conference of President of Parliament; President. **Activities** Events/meetings. **Events** *Meeting* Luanda (Angola) 2019, *Meeting* Praia (Cape Verde) 2019, *Meeting* Lisbon (Portugal) 2017, *Meeting* Brasilia (Brazil) 2016, *Meeting* Dili (Timor-Leste) 2014.
Members Parliaments of 9 countries:
Angola, Brazil, Cape Verde, Equatorial Guinea, Guinea-Bissau, Mozambique, Portugal, Sao Tomé-Principe, Timor-Leste. [2019/AA3040/**E***]

- ♦ Assembleia Parlamentar Euro-Latino-Americana (#05700)
- ♦ Assembleia das Regiões Européias Viticolas (#02317)
- ♦ Assemblies of God World Ministry (see: #10110)
- ♦ Assembly of Caribbean Community Parliamentarians (no recent information)

♦ Assembly of European Regions (AER) 02316

Assemblée des régions d'Europe (ARE) – Asamblea de las Regiones de Europa (ARE) – Versammlung der Regionen Europas (VRE) – Assemblea delle Regioni d'Europa (ARE)
SG 6 rue Oberlin, 67000 Strasbourg, France. T. +33388220707. Fax +33388756719. E-mail: info@aer.eu.
Brussels Office Rue d'Arlon 63, 1000 Brussels, Belgium. T. +3224001054.
URL: https://aer.eu/
History 15 Jun 1985, Louvain-la-Neuve (Belgium). Founded at constituent General Assembly, when statutes were adopted. Statutes revised by Extraordinary General Assemblies of: 21 Nov 1987; 28 Nov 1989; 5 Dec 1990; 5 Feb 1992; 3 Jul 1992; 2 Dec 1993; 4 Dec 1996; 7 Dec 2000; 26 Nov 2002. Foundation followed the setting up, 1971-1973, of the first European inter-regional associations – *Association of European Border Regions (AEBR, #02499)*, *Conference of Peripheral Maritime Regions of Europe (CPMR, #04638)* and the then *Committee for Cooperation of Alpine Regions (inactive)* – and the unanimous approval by 52 Regions, 4 Oct 1984, Trieste, of a proposal of a meeting of the 'Island Committee' made to CPMR, 27 Mar 1984, Azores. Continues the activities of *Liaison Office of the European Regional Organisations (inactive)*, created 1980, Strasbourg (France), which ceased to exist when CER – now AER – was set up. First General Assembly of European Regions held 24-26 Nov 1985, Strasbourg, in the hemicycle of the European Parliament. Former names and other names: *Council of European Regions (CER)* – former; *Conseil des régions d'Europe (CRE)* – former; *Consejo de las Regiones de Europa (CRE)* – former; *Rat der Regionen Europas (RRE)* – former; *Consiglio delle Regioni d'Europa (CRE)* – former. **Aims** Organize common dialogue, research and activities among regions belonging to member countries of the European Union and Council of Europe, with due regard to treaties and constitutions of the various states; strengthen representation of the regions within European institutions, and facilitate their participation in the construction of Europe and in Community life in all aspects concerning them; cooperate with European associations representing local authorities; support the action of the founder inter-regional organizations and of those which may later become members; promote regionalism and federalism in Europe. **Structure** General Assembly (annual); Political Bureau (executive arm); Executive Board; Praesidium; Youth Regional Network; Offices in Strasbourg (France) and Brussels (Belgium). **Languages** English, French, German, Italian, Spanish. **Staff** 8.00 FTE, paid. **Finance** Sources: members' dues. **Activities** Events/meetings; training/education; advocacy/lobbying/activism. **Events** *Forum on New Forms of Democratic Engagement* Brussels (Belgium) 2022, *General Assembly* Brussels (Belgium) 2022, *Regional Support for Ukraine* Brussels (Belgium) 2022, *Eurodyssey Forum* Brussels (Belgium) 2021, *General Assembly* Strasbourg (France) 2021.
Members Regions (270) in 27 countries:
Albania, Austria, Belgium, Bosnia-Herzegovina, Croatia, Cyprus, Denmark, Finland, France, Georgia, Hungary, Ireland, Italy, Montenegro, Netherlands, Norway, Portugal, Romania, Russia, Serbia, Slovenia, Spain, Sweden, Switzerland, Türkiye, UK (England – Scotland – Wales), Ukraine.
Geographical interregional organizations (12):
AEBR; *Alps-Adriatic-Alliance (#00747)*; *Arbeitsgemeinschaft Alpenländer (ARGE ALP, #01081)*; *Baltic Sea States Subregional Cooperation (BSSSC, #03150)*; Channel Arc Manche; Transjurasian Conference; Working Community Galicia – North Portugal; *Working Community of the Danube Regions (#21056)*; Working Community of the Low and Middle Adriatic; *Working Community of the Pyrenees (#21057)*; Working Community of the Western Alps (COTRAO); *World Mountain People Association (WMPA, #21658)*.
Sectorial Interregional Organizations (4):
Assemblée des Régions Européennes Fruitières, Légumières et Horticoles (AREFLH, #02314); *Assembly of European Wine Regions (AREV, #02317)*; *European Association for Local Democracy (ALDA, #06110)*; *Union of Local Authority Chief Executives of Europe (#20454)*.
Observers in 2 countries:
Poland, Russia.
Special guests in 2 countries:
Canada, South Africa.
IGO Relations Observer at: *European Committee of the Regions (CoR, #06665)*; *Congress of Local and Regional Authorities of the Council of Europe (#04677)*. Affiliated to: *Regions of Climate Action (R20, #18820)*.
NGO Relations Member of (1): *Citizens for Europe (CFEU, #03956)*. [2022/XE3500/y/**D**]

- ♦ Assembly of European Regions producing Fruit, Vegetable, Ornamental Plants and Olive Oil / see Assemblée des Régions Européennes Fruitières, Légumières et Horticoles (#02314)
- ♦ Assembly of European Regions Producing Fruit, Vegetable and Plants (#02314)
- ♦ Assembly of European Wine Producing European Regions / see Assembly of European Wine Regions (#02317)

♦ Assembly of European Wine Regions (AREV) 02317

Assemblée des régions européennes viticoles (AREV) – Asamblea de las Regiones Europeas Vitícolas (AREV) – Versammlung der Europäischen Weinbauregionen (AREV) – Assemblea delle Regioni Europee Viticole (AREV) – Assembleia das Regiões Européias Viticolas (AREV) – Sinelevsi Evropaikon Ampeloinikon Periohon (AREV)
Chairman Rond Point Robert Schuman 14 – 4ÈME ÉTAGE, 1049 Brussels, Belgium. E-mail: arev@arev.org.
Deputy Gen Sec address not obtained.
URL: http://www.arev.org/
History 1988. Statutes adopted 26 Oct 1994, Marsala (Italy). Current Statutes adopted 11 Jun 2005. Former names and other names: *European Conference of Wine Producing Regions* – former (1988 to 28 May 1994); *Conférence européenne des régions viticoles (CERV)* – former (1988 to 28 May 1994); *Conferencia Europea de las Regiones Viniculas* – former (1988 to 28 May 1994); *Europäische Konferenz der Weinbauregionen* – former (1988 to 28 May 1994); *Conferência Europeia das Regiões Vinicolas* – former (1988 to 28 May 1994); *Evropaïkí Diáskepsi ton Periferéión Oínou* – former (1988 to 28 May 1994); *Assembly of European Wine Producing European Regions (AWER)* – former (28 May 1994). Registration: Banque-Carrefour des Entreprises, No/ID: 0775.372.072, Start date: 24 Oct 1994, Belgium; EU Transparency Register, No/ID: 90526016248-05, Start date: 19 Jul 2011. **Aims** Promote common interests of wine-producing regions within the European and world economy; organize and develop dialogue, consultation, research and common action between wine-producing regions of Europe; reinforce representation of the AREV within European institutions. **Structure** General Assembly (annual); College of Regions; *Conseil européen professionnel du vin (CEPV)*; International Council; Bureau. **Languages** English, French, German, Italian, Portuguese, Spanish. **Finance** Sources: contributions; donations; gifts, legacies; grants; members' dues; revenue from activities/projects. **Activities** Advocacy/lobbying/activism; events/meetings. **Events** *General Assembly* Luxembourg (Luxembourg) 2014, *General Assembly* Stuttgart (Germany) 2013, *General Assembly* Turin (Italy) 2012, *General Assembly* Toledo (Spain) 2011, *General Assembly* Porec (Croatia) 2010. **Publications** *Etude sur les impacts socio-économiques et territoriaux de la libéralisation des droits de plantations viticoles – Tome 2.* (2013) by E Montaigne and A Coelho et al in French – UNITE MIXTE DE RECHERCHE MOISA- MONTPELLIER; *Etude sur les impacts socio-économiques et territoriaux de la libéralisation des droits de plantations viticoles – Tome 1.* (2012) by E Montaigne and A Coelho et al in French – UNITE MIXTE DE RECHERCHE MOISA- MONTPELLIER; *The Technical Guide to the Wine Routes* (1995); *The Wine and Health Guide* (1995). Brochures.

Members Members of the College of Regions; members of the Professional College; Observers (without voting right); Membres d'honneur (individuals); Qualified persons (called Counsellors – without voting right). Members in 14 countries:
Austria, Bosnia-Herzegovina, Croatia, Czechia, France, Germany, Greece, Hungary, Italy, Luxembourg, Portugal, Romania, Spain, Ukraine.
IGO Relations Observer status with (1): *International Organisation of Vine and Wine (OIV, #14435).* **NGO Relations** Member of (1): *Assembly of European Regions (AER, #02316).* [2022/XF2536/F]

♦ Assembly for the International Heat Transfer Conferences (AIHTC) . 02318

Pres c/o Tsinghua Univ, 30 Shuangqing Rd, Haidan Qu, Beijing, China.
URL: http://www.aihtc.org/

History Founded 1966, Chicago IL (USA) during 4th International Conference on Heat Transfer. Previous conferences were organized in London (UK) and Atlantic City NJ (USA) 1951, Boulder CO (USA) 1961 and London (UK) 1962. **Aims** Provide international cooperation in the planning and coordination of the International Conference on Heat Transfer; promote scientific understanding in the field of heat transfer. **Events** *International Heat Transfer Conference* Rio de Janeiro (Brazil) 2026, *International Heat Transfer Conference* Cape Town (South Africa) 2022, *International Heat Transfer Conference* Beijing (China) 2018, *International Heat Transfer Conference* Kyoto (Japan) 2014, *International Heat Transfer Conference* Washington, DC (USA) 2010.
Members in 18 countries:
Australia, Brazil, Canada, China, France, Germany, India, Israel, Italy, Japan, Korea Rep, Netherlands, Portugal, Russia, South Africa, Switzerland, UK, USA. [2018/XM2193/c/F]

- ♦ Assembly of Judges (meeting series)
- ♦ Assembly of the Mediterranean Chambers of Commerce and Industry / see Asociación de las Camaras de Comercio e Industria del Mediterraneo (#02112)
- ♦ Assembly of Organizations for Aid to the Eastern Churches (see: #04672)
- ♦ Asser International Sports Law Centre (unconfirmed)
- ♦ Assessment Capacities Project / see ACAPS (#00044)

♦ Assessment of SpondyloArthritis International Society (ASAS) 02319

Sec Korte Raarberg 46, 6231 KR Meerssen, Netherlands. E-mail: mail@asas-group.org.
URL: http://www.asas-group.org/

History Current bylaws approved 26 Jan 2008. **Aims** Support and promote the study of Axial and Peripheral Spondyloarthritis. **Structure** Executive Committee. Advisory Board. **Activities** Education; research; meeting activities. **Events** *Annual Workshop* Houston, TX (USA) 2020, *Annual Workshop* Amsterdam (Netherlands) 2019, *Annual Workshop* Lisbon (Portugal) 2018, *Workshop* Madrid (Spain) 2015, *Workshop* Madrid (Spain) 2013. **Publications** Handbooks; educational kits.
Members Full in 36 countries and territories:
Argentina, Australia, Austria, Belgium, Brazil, Canada, China, Colombia, Croatia, Denmark, Egypt, Finland, France, Germany, Hungary, Indonesia, Ireland, Italy, Korea Rep, Malta, Mexico, Netherlands, New Zealand, Norway, Portugal, Russia, Singapore, Spain, Sweden, Switzerland, Taiwan, Thailand, Türkiye, UK, Ukraine, USA. [2017/XJ7890/C]

- ♦ **ASSET** Association of Southern European Economic Theorists (#02925)

♦ Asset Recovery Interagency Network – Asia Pacific (ARIN-AP) 02320

Secretariat Office No 505, Intl Cooperation Ctr, Supreme Prosecutors' Office, 157 Banpo-daero, Seocho-gu, Seoul 06590, Korea Rep. T. +82234802338. Fax +8225353109. E-mail: arin-ap@spo.go.kr.
URL: http://www.arin-ap.org/

History Nov 2013. Officially launched as an informal network of contacts. **Aims** Increase the effectiveness of Members' efforts, on a multi-agency basis, in depriving *criminals* of their illicit profits. **Structure** Annual General Meeting; Steering Group; Presidency; Secretariat. **Languages** English. **Finance** Self-funded. **Activities** Training/education. **Events** *Annual General Meeting* Queenstown (New Zealand) 2022, *Annual General Meeting* Ulaanbaatar (Mongolia) 2019, *Annual General Meeting* Bali (Indonesia) 2018, *Annual General Meeting* Tokyo (Japan) 2017.
Members States and jurisdictions (25):
Australia, Brunei Darussalam, Cambodia, Cook Is, India, Indonesia, Japan, Kazakhstan, Korea Rep, Kyrgyzstan, Malaysia, Mongolia, Myanmar, Nepal, New Zealand, Pakistan, Palau, Papua New Guinea, Philippines, Singapore, Sri Lanka, Taiwan, Thailand, Timor-Leste, Tonga.
Observers (9), including 8 organizations listed in this Yearbook:
ARINSA (#01107); Asia/Pacific Group on Money Laundering (APG, #01921); Asset Recovery Inter-Agency Network for the Caribbean (ARIN-CARIB, #02321); Asset Recovery Inter-Agency Network in West and Central Asia (ARIN-WCA); International Bank for Reconstruction and Development (IBRD, #12317) (World Bank); *International Criminal Police Organization – INTERPOL (ICPO-INTERPOL, #13110); Pacific Transnational Crime Network (PTCN, #18010); United Nations Office on Drugs and Crime (UNODC, #20596).*
[2021.05.20/XJ9252/F]

♦ Asset Recovery Inter-Agency Network for the Caribbean (ARIN-CARIB) 02321

Dir c/o RSS Asset Recovery Unit (RSS ARU), Fusion Centre, Paragon Base, Christ Church BB17110, CHRIST CHURCH BB17110, Barbados. T. +12464281488. Fax +12464207316. E-mail: arin-carib@rss.org.bb.
URL: https://arin-carib.org/

History 2017. Founded as an informal network. **Aims** Increase the effectiveness of members' efforts, on a multi-agency basis, to deprive criminals of their illicit profits. **Structure** Annual General Meeting; Steering Group; Secretariat. **Languages** English. **Activities** Guidance/assistance/consulting; networking/liaising.
Members Law enforcement and judicial practitioners in 33 countries and territories:
Anguilla, Antigua-Barbuda, Aruba, Bahamas, Barbados, Belize, Bermuda, Bonaire Is, Cayman Is, Curaçao, Dominica, Dominican Rep, Grenada, Guadeloupe, Guiana Fr, Guyana, Haiti, Jamaica, Martinique, Montserrat, Saba, St Barthélemy, St Eustatius, St Kitts-Nevis, St Lucia, St Maarten, St Martin, St Vincent-Grenadines, Suriname, Trinidad-Tobago, Turks-Caicos, USA, Virgin Is UK.
IGO Relations Partner of (5): *Caribbean Community (CARICOM, #03476); Caribbean Financial Action Task Force (CFATF, #03505); CARICOM Implementation Agency for Crime and Security (IMPACS, #03573); Stolen Asset Recovery Initiative (StAR, #19996); United Nations Office on Drugs and Crime (UNODC, #20596).* **NGO Relations** Observer status with (1): *Asset Recovery Interagency Network – Asia Pacific (ARIN-AP, #02320).*
[2023.02.14/XM8742/F]

- ♦ Asset Recovery Inter-Agency Network for Southern Africa / see ARINSA (#01107)
- ♦ Asset Recovery Inter-Agency Network for West Africa (unconfirmed)
- ♦ Asset Recovery Inter-Agency Network in West and Central Asia (unconfirmed)
- ♦ ASSFCN / see Asian-Australasian Society for Stereotactic and Functional Neurosurgery (#01354)
- ♦ ASSH – Académie suisse des sciences humaines et sociales (internationally oriented national body)
- ♦ ASSHH – Association for the Social Sciences and Humanities in HIV (inactive)
- ♦ **ASSIAPS** Association Internationale des Acheteurs et Approvisionneurs Publics et Privés de la Santé (#02664)
- ♦ **ASSIBERCOM** Associação Ibero-Americana de Comunicação (#02328)
- ♦ ASSIDS / see International Association of Sports Law (#12180)
- ♦ **ASSIDS** Association internationale du droit des sports (#12180)
- ♦ ASSIFIC – Association de Solidarité Internationale pour la Formation, l'Instruction et la Coopération (internationally oriented national body)
- ♦ **ASSIFONTE** Association de l'industrie de la fonte de fromage de l'UE (#02642)
- ♦ ASSINSEL – Association internationale des sélectionneurs pour la protection des obtentions végétales (inactive)
- ♦ ASSIS – Association pour la sécurité des systèmes d'information de santé (unconfirmed)
- ♦ Assises européennes de la transition énergétique (meeting series)
- ♦ **ASSISi** Anti-Seismic Systems International Society (#00859)
- ♦ ASSISTANCE – Association for International Scientific and Technical Communication and Cooperation (inactive)

♦ Assistance Dogs Europe (ADEu) 02322

Address not obtained.
URL: http://assistancedogseurope.org/

History Set up 2000. Since 2007, a chapter of *Assistance Dogs International (ADI, #02323).* Current statutes adopted 2011. Registered in accordance with Dutch law. **Aims** Develop into the leading organization in Europe promoting the Assistance Dogs movement; promote contacts and coordination between European assistance dogs programmes so as to improve the movement and enlarge it. **Structure** Assembly (annual); Board. **Finance** Members' dues. Other sources: costs or charges; donations and gifts; subventions and subsidies; sponsorship; successions and legacies. **Events** *Conference* Prague (Czech Rep) 2016. **Publications** Manuals.
Members Full/Accredited (39); Candidate. Accredited in 15 countries:
Austria, Belgium, Croatia, Czechia, Denmark, Finland, Germany, Ireland, Netherlands, Norway, Portugal, Spain, Sweden, Switzerland, UK.
Candidate in 11 countries:
Belgium, Croatia, Czechia, France, Ireland, Netherlands, Slovakia, Slovenia, Spain, Sweden, UK.
NGO Relations Memorandum of Understanding with: *European Guide Dog Federation (EGDF, #07440).* Affiliate member of: *Animal Assisted Intervention International (AAII, #00834).* [2020/XM4718/D]

♦ Assistance Dogs International (ADI) 02323

Exec Dir PO Box 276, Maumee OH 43537-0276, USA. E-mail: info@assistancedogsinternational.org.
Sec 246 West Parade, Lincoln, LN1 1LY, UK. T. +447949921844. E-mail: steph@assistancedogsinternational.org.
URL: http://www.assistancedogsinternational.org/

History 1986. Set up originally as a North American organization. Developed into an international coalition, 2007. Registration: Start date: 1988, USA, State o f Oregon. **Aims** Establish and promote standards of excellence in all areas of assistance dog acquisition, training and partnership; facilitate communication and learning among member programmes; educate the public about the benefits of assistance dogs. **Structure** Board of Directors. Regional chapters (4): *Assistance Dogs Europe (ADEu, #02322)*; ADINA – North America; OCEANIA – Australia and New Zealand. **Languages** English. **Staff** 3.00 FTE, paid. **Finance** Sources: donations; grants; members' dues; sponsorship. **Activities** Events/meetings. **Events** *Conference* Concord, CA (USA) 2022, *The power of positivity* 2021, *Conference* Split (Croatia) 2020, *Conference* Noblesville, IN (USA) 2019, *Conference* Bloomington, MN (USA) 2018. **Members** Accredited members (142) and Candidate programmes (49) representing 23 countries. Membership countries not specified. **NGO Relations** *International Guide Dog Federation (IGDF, #13763).* Affiliate member of: *Animal Assisted Intervention International (AAII, #00834); Assistance Dogs Europe (ADEu, #02322).* [2022.06.15/XG2418/C]

- ♦ Assistance for Economic Restructuring in the Countries of Central and Eastern Europe (no recent information)
- ♦ Assistance mutuelle des entreprises pétrolières gouvernementales latinoaméricaines / see Asociación Regional de Empresas del Sector Petróleo, Gas y Biocombustibles en Latinoamérica y el Caribe (#02296)
- ♦ Assistance mutuelle des entreprises pétrolières latinoaméricaines / see Asociación Regional de Empresas del Sector Petróleo, Gas y Biocombustibles en Latinoamérica y el Caribe (#02296)
- ♦ Assistance Pays Bas aux réfugiés dans le monde / see ZOA
- ♦ Assistance pharmaceutique internationale / see Orbi-Pharma
- ♦ Assistance aux réfugiés et déplacés dans le monde / see ZOA
- ♦ Assistance to Support Humanity and Need for Aid Organization (internationally oriented national body)
- ♦ **ASSIST** Asia Society for Social Improvement and Sustainable Transformation (#02097)
- ♦ Assist International (internationally oriented national body)
- ♦ ASSITEB / see Association Internationale des Technologistes Biomédicaux (#02747)
- ♦ **ASSITEB-BIORIF** Association Internationale des Technologistes Biomédicaux (#02747)
- ♦ **ASSITEJ** Association internationale du théâtre pour l'enfance et la jeunesse (#12225)
- ♦ ASSLA – Associazione di Studi Sociali Latinoamericani (internationally oriented national body)
- ♦ ASSM – Accademia Svizzera di Science Morali e Sociali (internationally oriented national body)
- ♦ **ASSM** African Society for Sexual Medicine (#00470)
- ♦ ASSM – Asian Seafarers Summit Meeting (meeting series)
- ♦ **ASSM** Asian Society of Sleep Medicine (#01738)
- ♦ **ASSMO** Asian Society of Structural and Multidisciplinary Optimization (#01742)
- ♦ **ASSN** African Security Sector Network (#00453)
- ♦ ASS / see Nordic Acoustic Association (#17165)
- ♦ ASSO / see Australian and New Zealand Obesity Society
- ♦ Assoção dos Usuarios e Distribuidores de Agro-Quimicos Europa (no recent information)
- ♦ **Assocation Comenius** Réseau européen d'instituts de formation d'enseignants (#18875)
- ♦ Associação de Advogados Latinoamericanos pela Defesa dos Direitos Humanos (no recent information)
- ♦ Associação Africana de Bibliotecas e Instituições de Informação (#00363)
- ♦ Associação de Ambientalistas a Favor da Energia Nuclear (internationally oriented national body)
- ♦ Associação Americana de Juristas (#02110)
- ♦ Associação de Beisebol e Softbol da Africa (#00158)

♦ Associação de Brasilianistas na Europa (ABRE) 02324

Registered Address Emil Holms Kanal 6, 2300 Copenhagen, Denmark. E-mail: abre.associacao@gmail.com.
URL: http://abre.eu/

History 2017, Leiden (Netherlands). **Aims** Build, feed and maintain a network of teachers, researchers and students interested in Brazil linked to European teaching and research institutions. **Structure** General Assembly; Executive Committee. **Activities** Events/meetings. **Events** *Congress* Paris (France) 2019.
[2020/AA0901/E]

- ♦ Associação Canadense de Estudos Latino-americanos e do Caribe (internationally oriented national body)
- ♦ Associação das Cidades Para a Reciclagem / see Association of Cities and Regions for Sustainable Resource Management (#02433)
- ♦ Associação das Cidades e Regiões Para a Reciclagem / see Association of Cities and Regions for Sustainable Resource Management (#02433)
- ♦ Associação de Cientistas Sociais de Religião do MERCOSUR (#02118)
- ♦ Associação das Colectividades Têxteis Europeias (#02435)
- ♦ Associação Comite Ibero-Americano de Reumatologia / see Ibero-American College of Rheumatology (#11020)
- ♦ Associação do Congresso Panamericano de Estradas de Ferro (#18124)
- ♦ Associação para a Cooperação e Desenvolvimento (internationally oriented national body)
- ♦ Associação de Cooperativas e Mutuais de Seguros das Américas / see International Cooperative and Mutual Insurance Federation / Regional Association for The Americas (#12949)

♦ Associação de Crioulos de Base Lexical Portuguesa e Espanhola (ACBLPE) 02325

Asociación de Criollos de Base Lexical Portuguesa y Española – Association of Portuguese and Spanish-Lexified Creoles – Association des Créoles de Base Lexicale Portugaise et Espagnole
Sec address not obtained. E-mail: geral@acblpe.com.
URL: http://www.acblpe.com/

History 2001. **Aims** Promote the study of the Iberian-lexified creole languages and their communities. **Structure** General Assembly; Executive Committee. **Activities** Advocacy/lobbying/activism; events/meetings; research/documentation. **Events** *Annual Congress* Augsburg (Germany) 2022, *Annual Conference* Libolo (Angola) 2020, *Annual Conference* Lisbon (Portugal) 2019, *Annual Conference* Ziguinchor (Senegal) 2018, *Annual Conference* Stockholm (Sweden) 2017. **Publications** *Journal of Ibero-Romance Creoles (JIRC)* – until 2018 known as Revista de Crioulos de Base Lexical Portuguesa e Espanhola – RCBLPE. [2020/AA0343/C]

- ♦ Associação para o Desenvolvimento Coesivo da Amazônia (internationally oriented national body)
- ♦ Associação de Editoras para Deficientes Visuais de Ibero-América (inactive)

- ♦ Associação de Educação e Investigação em Ciência da Informação da Iberoamerica e Caribe (#02122)
- ♦ Associação Elevadores do Mercosul (unconfirmed)
- ♦ Associação das Escolas e Faculdades de Arquitetura Públicas da América do Sul (#02128)
- ♦ Associação Europa – Terceiro Mundo / see eu can aid (#05570)
- ♦ Associação Européia dos Assistentes Sociais Hospitalares e da Saúde (inactive)
- ♦ Associação Europeia de Caucionamento Mútuo / see European Association of Guarantee Institutions (#06061)
- ♦ Associação Europeia de Direção e Economia da Empresa / see European Academy of Management and Business Economics (#05801)
- ♦ Associação Européia para a Educação Pública pela Televisão (inactive)
- ♦ Associação Européia dos Eleitos de Montanha (#06021)
- ♦ Associação Européia de Energia Mini-Hidrica (#08495)
- ♦ Associação Européia de Medicamentos Genéricos / see Medicines for Europe (#16633)
- ♦ Associação Européia dos Médicos Hospitalares (#02577)
- ♦ Associação Européia dos Podólogos (inactive)
- ♦ Associação Européia da Siderurgia / see European Steel Association (#08835)

♦ Associação Evangélica de Educação Teológica na América Latina (AETAL) 02326

Evangelical Association of Theological Education in Latin America – Asociación Evangélica de Educación Teológica en América Latina

Pres Caixa Postal 7030, Campinas SP, 13076-970, Brazil. E-mail: atendimento@aetal.com – instituciones@aetal.com.
Gen Sec address not obtained.
URL: http://www.aetal.com/

History 1 Jul 1992, Sao Paulo (Brazil). Founded at Assembly of the former *'Evangelical Association for Theological Training, Brazil (AETTE)'*, which had existed since 1968. Constitution approved at founding meeting. In 1992 AETTE merged into AETAL. **Aims** Provide interchange between centres of theological education in Latin America; support development of member institutions and promote excellence in these programs of theological education in order to offer a holistic education which is committed to the church; recognize through a permanent commission of accreditation, biblical and theological institutions in Latin America that meet established requirements. **Structure** Assembly; Board of Directors; Fiscal Committee; Accrediting Committee. **Languages** Portuguese, Spanish. **Staff** 1.00 FTE, paid. Several voluntary. **Finance** Sources: members' dues. **Activities** Certification/accreditation; events/meetings; training/education. **Events** *Continental Conference* Quito (Ecuador) 2016, *Continental Conference* Campinas (Brazil) 2013, *Continental conference* Medellin (Colombia) 2010, *Continental conference* Sao Paulo (Brazil) 2007, *Continental conference* 2004. **Publications** *AETAL Newsletter* (2 a year) in Portuguese, Spanish.
Members Theological institutions (130) in 14 countries:
Argentina, Bolivia, Brazil, Colombia, Costa Rica, Ecuador, El Salvador, Guatemala, Honduras, Mexico, Paraguay, Peru, USA, Venezuela.
NGO Relations Member of (2): *International Council for Evangelical Theological Education (ICETE, #13020); World Evangelical Alliance (WEA, #21393).* [2022.05.23/XD3285/D]

- ♦ Associação dos Fabricantes de Gelatina da América do Sul (#19703)

♦ Associação de Farmacêuticos dos Paises de Lingua Portuguesa (AFPLP) 02327

Association of Pharmacists of the Portuguese-speaking Countries

Address not obtained.
URL: http://www.afplp.org/scid/farmempt/

History Founded Jun 1993, Lisbon (Portugal). **Aims** Promote pharmaceutical sciences, defend the interest of the pharmaceutical profession in all Portuguese-speaking countries. **Structure** General Assembly; Board; Fiscal Council. **Languages** Portuguese. **Finance** Donations, sponsorship. **Activities** Makes representation visits to official authorities in Portuguese-speaking countries; provides human resources training and support for associative sector organizations. **Events** *World congress* Luanda (Angola) 2013, *World congress* Praia (Cape Verde) 2008, *World Congress* Luanda (Angola) 2006, *World Congress* Funchal (Portugal) 2002, *World congress* Rio de Janeiro (Brazil) 2000. **Publications** *Noticias Farmacia em Português.* **NGO Relations** Observer Member of: *International Pharmaceutical Federation (#14566).* [2018/XD8160/D]

- ♦ Associação de Filosofia e História da Ciência do Cone Sul (#02130)
- ♦ Associação Geral dos Adventistas do Sétimo Dia (#10109)
- ♦ Associação de Historiadores Latinoamericanistas Europeus (#02517)

♦ Associação Ibero-Americana de Comunicação (ASSIBERCOM) 02328

Contact address not obtained. T. +351222002650. E-mail: ibercom@imultimedia.pt.
URL: http://www.imultimedia.pt/ibercom/

History Set up Nov 1998, Porto (Portugal), at 5th IBERCOM Meeting. Legally set up Apr 2000, Santiago (Chile). Registered in accordance with Portuguese law. **Structure** General Assembly. Board of Founders. Directorate, comprising President, 3 Vice-Presidents, Secretary-General and members. Fiscal Council. **Events** *Congress* Santiago de Compostela (Spain) 2013, *Congress* Santa Cruz (Bolivia) 2011, *Congress* Madeira (Portugal) 2009, *Congress* Guadalajara (Mexico) 2007, *Congress* Seville (Spain) 2006.
Members Full in 22 countries:
Andorra, Argentina, Bolivia, Brazil, Chile, Colombia, Costa Rica, Cuba, Dominican Rep, Ecuador, El Salvador, Guatemala, Honduras, Mexico, Nicaragua, Panama, Paraguay, Peru, Portugal, Spain, Uruguay, Venezuela.
NGO Relations Member of: *Confederación Iberoamericana de Asociaciones Científicas y Académicas de la Comunicación (CONFIBERCOM, #04448).* [2013/XJ7238/D]

- ♦ Associação Iberoamericana de Diagnóstico e Avaliação Psicológica (#02138)
- ♦ Associação Iberoamericana de Entidades Reguladoras da Energia (#02139)
- ♦ Associação Ibero-Americana de Estudos Ricoeurianos (unconfirmed)
- ♦ Associação Iberoamericana das Organizações Governamentais da Defesa e Proteção Civil (#02150)
- ♦ Associação Iberoamericana de Portas e Costas (inactive)
- ♦ Associação Iberoamericana de Telessaúde e Telemedicina (#02155)
- ♦ Associação Ibero-Americana de Transpessoal (#02304)
- ♦ Associação dos Industriais Latinoamericanos (#16341)
- ♦ Associação da Indústria de Margarinas dos Paises da CE / see European Margarine Association (#07736)
- ♦ Associação das Indústrias de Alimentação Animal da América Latina e Caribe (#02158)
- ♦ Associação Interamericana de Contabilidade (#11395)
- ♦ Associação Interamericana de Engenharia Sanitaria e Ambiental (#11400)
- ♦ Associação Interamericana de Gastroenterologia / see Organización Panamericana de Gastroenterología (#17847)
- ♦ Associação Interamericana da Propriedade Intelectual (#02161)
- ♦ Associação Interamericana de Radiodifusão / see International Association of Broadcasting (#11738)
- ♦ Associação Interciencia (#11459)
- ♦ Associação Internacional Artes Renascentes (#02670)
- ♦ Associação Internacional para Avaliação de Impactos Ambientais (#11956)
- ♦ Associação Internacional de Caprinos (#13725)

♦ Associação Internacional de Ciências Sociais e Humanas em Língua Portuguesa (AILPcsh) 02329

Secretariat Colégio de S. Jerónimo, Ap 3087, 3000-995 Coimbra, Portugal. E-mail: ailp.secretariado@ailpcsh.org.
URL: https://www.ailpcsh.org/

History Statutes approved 2 Mar 2012. Registration: Portugal. **Aims** Promote a space for cooperation between Portuguese-speaking social sciences and humanities scholars. **Structure** General Assembly; Executive; Scientific Policy Council; Advisory Board. **Activities** Events/meetings. **Events** *CONLAB – Luso-Afro-Brazilian Congress* 2021, *CONLAB – Luso-Afro-Brazilian Congress* Coimbra (Portugal) 2020, *CONLAB – Luso-Afro-Brazilian Congress* Sao Paulo (Brazil) 2018, *CONLAB – Luso-Afro-Brazilian Congress* Lisbon (Portugal) 2015, *CONLAB – Luso-Afro-Brazilian Congress* Salvador (Brazil) 2011. [2021/AA1944/D]

- ♦ Associação Internacional para a Defesa da Liberdade Religiosa (#02681)
- ♦ Associação Internacional de Desenvolvimento Rural (inactive)
- ♦ Associação Internacional de Educação Comunitaria (inactive)
- ♦ Associação Internacional de Educadores de Jovens Inadaptados / see International Association of Social Educators (#12167)
- ♦ Associação Internacional de Estudos do Discurso (#11850)
- ♦ Associação Internacional para Estudos Otto Gross (#12060)
- ♦ Associação Internacional de História e Civilização do Açúcar (internationally oriented national body)
- ♦ Associação Internacional dos Jovens Advogados (#12282)
- ♦ **Associação Internacional de Lésbicas, Gays, Bissexuais, Trans e Intersexo** ILGA World (#11120)

♦ Associação Internacional de Linguistica do Português (AILP) 02330

Contact R São Francisco Xavier 524, Maracanã, Rio de Janeiro RJ, 20550-013, Brazil. E-mail: ailplinguistica@gmail.com.
URL: https://ailp.wordpress.com/

History 2001. **Structure** General Assembly; Committee. **Events** *Congress* Macau 2014, *International Congress* Macau (Macau) 2014. [2020/XJ8690/D]

- ♦ Associação Internacional do Livre Pensamento (#11906)
- ♦ Associação Internacional de Lusitanistas (#12006)
- ♦ Associação Internacional de Massagem Infantil (#11962)
- ♦ Associação Internacional de Movimentes Familiares de Formação Rural (#02719)
- ♦ Associação Internacional de Orçamento Público (#18564)
- ♦ Associação Internacional de Pesquisa da Paz (#14537)
- ♦ Associação Internacional de Psiquiatria da Infância e Adolescência e Profissões Afins (#11766)
- ♦ Associação Internacional para o Uso Medicinal da Cannabis / see International Association for Cannabinoid Medicines (#11754)
- ♦ Associação Internacional Veterinaria de Produção Animale (inactive)
- ♦ Associação Japonesa de Estudos Latino-americanos (internationally oriented national body)
- ♦ Associação de Jornalistas Europeus (#02516)
- ♦ Associação Latina para a Analise dos Sistemas de Saúde (#02171)
- ♦ Associação Latino-Americana de Agências de Publicidade (#16235)
- ♦ Associação Latino Americana de Antropologia (#16234)
- ♦ Associação Latinoamericana de Arbitragem (#02182)
- ♦ Associação Latinoamericana de Armadores (#16369)
- ♦ Associação Latinoamericana de Boiatria (#19394)
- ♦ Associação Latino Americana e do Caribe de Direito e Economia / see Latin American and Iberian Law and Economics Association (#16340)
- ♦ Associação Latino-americana e do Caribe de Economia Agricola (no recent information)
- ♦ Associação Latino-Americana e do Caribe de Imunologia (#16265)
- ♦ Associação Latino-Americana de Ciências do Esporte, Educação Fisica e Dança (unconfirmed)
- ♦ Associação Latino-Americana de Ciências Fisiológicas (#16250)
- ♦ Associação Latino-Americana de Colo-Proctologia (#16237)
- ♦ Associação Latino-americana de Cuidados Paliativos (#02201)
- ♦ Associação Latino-americana de Dessalinização e Reúso de Água (#02204)
- ♦ Associação Latinoamericana de Direito Penal e Criminologia (unconfirmed)
- ♦ Associação Latinoamericana de Dragages (inactive)
- ♦ Associação Latino-Americana de Engenharia de Segurança do Trabalho (#16314)
- ♦ Associação Latinoamericana de Ensino e Pesquisa em Serviço Social (#02210)
- ♦ Associação Latinoamericana de Escolas de Biblioteconomia e Ciências da Informação (inactive)
- ♦ Associação Latinoamericana de Escolas de Serviço Social (inactive)
- ♦ Associação Latinoamericana de Estradas de Ferro (#16365)
- ♦ Associação Latinoamericana para o Estudo do Figado (#16252)
- ♦ Associação Latino-Americana de Estudos do Discurso (#02217)
- ♦ Associação Latino-Americana de Estudos da Escrita na Educação Superior e em Contextos Profissionais (#02218)
- ♦ Associação Latino-Americana de Filosofia Analitica (#02221)
- ♦ Associação Latinoamericana de Fisica Médica (#16246)

♦ Associação Latinoamericana de Geoquimica Orgânica (ALAGO) ... 02331

Asociación Latino Americana de Geoquimica Organica – Latin American Association of Organic Geochemistry

SG address not obtained. E-mail: debora@iq.ufrj.br – carlosbandeira@petrobras.com.br.
URL: http://www.alago.co/

History 29 Nov 1988, Rio de Janeiro (Brazil). Statutes adopted 6 Apr 1989, Porto Alegre (Brazil). **Aims** Promote and disseminate scientific and technological research in the field of organic geochemistry; unite professionals in the field and promote the integration of university/industry/research centres with emphasis in Latin America. **Structure** General Assembly (every 2 years, at Congress). Board of Directors, composed of 7-9 permanent members, including President, 1st and 2nd Treasurers and other officers as necessary. Permanent Committees (2): Elections and Statutes; Publications. Temporary Special Committees. Technical-Scientific Committees at the discretion of the Board of Directors. **Languages** English, Portuguese, Spanish. **Staff** All voluntary. **Finance** Members' dues. Sponsors. **Activities** Organizes: Latin American Congress on Organic Geochemistry (every 2 years); technical and scientific meetings; seminars, workshops and courses on specific subjects. **Events** *Biennial Congress* Niterói (Brazil) 2020, *Biennial Congress* Salvador (Brazil) 2018, *Biennial Congress* Armação de Búzios (Brazil) 2014, *Biennial Congress* Montevideo (Uruguay) 2010, *Biennial Congress* Porlamar (Venezuela) 2008. **Publications** *ALAGO Newsletter* (2 a year); *Revista Latinoamericana de Geoquimica Orgânica.*
Members Individuals (about 250) exercising technical or scientific activities in the field in 35 countries:
Argentina, Australia, Bolivia, Brazil, Canada, Chile, China, Colombia, Cuba, Ecuador, Egypt, France, Germany, India, Israel, Italy, Japan, Kenya, Mexico, Mozambique, Netherlands, Norway, Paraguay, Peru, Poland, Portugal, Russia, Spain, Switzerland, Trinidad-Tobago, Türkiye, UK, Uruguay, USA, Venezuela. [2021/XD6445/D]

- ♦ Associação Latino-Americana e Ibérica de Direito e Economia (#16340)
- ♦ Associação Latinoamericana de Imunologia / see Latin American and Caribbean Association of Immunology (#16265)
- ♦ Associação Latinoamericana da Indústria de Cloro, Alkalis e Derivados (#16295)
- ♦ Associação Latino-Americana da Indústria Elétrica, Eletrônica e Gasodomésticos (#02228)
- ♦ Associação Latinoamericana de Industriais e Camaras da Alimentação (inactive)
- ♦ Associação Latino-americana da Indústria do Petróleo (#02231)
- ♦ Associação Latino-Americana de Instituições Financeiras para o Desenvolvimento (#02233)
- ♦ Associação Latino-Americana de Integração (#16343)
- ♦ Associação Latino-Americana de Lazer e Recreação (inactive)
- ♦ Associação Latinoamericana de Livre Comércio (inactive)
- ♦ Associação Latinoamericana Multidisciplinar de Planeación Estr de Meio Ambiente (inactive)
- ♦ Associação Latino-Americana de Mutagênese, Carcinogênese e Teratogênese Ambiental (#16240)
- ♦ Associação Latinoamericana de Operação Dental e Biomateriais / see Asociación Latinoamericana de Odontologia Restauradora y Biomateriales (#02244)
- ♦ Associação Latinoamericana de Paleobotânica e Palinologia (#02249)
- ♦ Associação Latinoamericana de Patologia Toxicológica (#16387)
- ♦ Associação Latino-Americana de Pesquisa de Mercado e Opinião (no recent information)

Associação Latino Americana
02331
alphabetic sequence excludes
For the complete listing, see Yearbook Online at

♦ Associação Latino-Americana de Planejadores Energéticos (inactive)

♦ Associação Latino Americana de Pneus e Aros (ALAPA) 02332

Asociación Latinoamericana de Neumaticos y Llantas

Pres Rua Domingos Bertaglia 46 SV001, So Bernardo do Campo, Sao Paulo SP, 09891-110, Brazil. T. +551143316110. E-mail: contato@alapa.com.br.
URL: http://www.alapa.com.br/

History 2 Feb 1968, Sao Paulo (Brazil). **Aims** Study all technical problems referring to dimensions, condition of use and mounting of *tyres*, tubes, rims, valves and their components; establish standards and specifications, related to the above, trying to standardize them, as much as possible, with existing international standards and specifications related to the matter, and make sure that those standards are followed by its members; furnish the national automotive industry and all interested with standards and specifications issued by the Association; inform members of laws or regulation on national or regional levels. **Structure** Fiscal Council; President; Vice-President; Treasurer; Secretary. **Languages** Portuguese, Spanish. **Staff** 7.00 FTE, paid. **Finance** Members' dues. **Activities** Research/development; standards/guidelines; knowledge management/information dissemination. **Publications** Manuals; recommendations. **Members** Tyre; Rim and Wheel; Allied Part. Membership countries not specified. **NGO Relations** *European Tyre and Rim Technical Organisation (ETRTO, #08962)*; Tire and Rim Association (TRA). [2018.09.05/XD7988/**D**]

♦ Associação Latinoamericana da Produção Animal (#02257)
♦ Associação Latinoamericana dos Produtores de Vidro (no recent information)
♦ Associação Latino-americana de Registros de Câncer (no recent information)
♦ Associação Latino-Americana de Teoria Económica (#02271)
♦ Associação Latino-americana do Tórax (#02273)
♦ Associação Latinoamericana do Transporte Rodoviario (inactive)
♦ Associação Latino-Americana de Uro-oncologia (#16391)
♦ Associação Latinoamericana de Veterinarios de Fauna Silvestre (unconfirmed)
♦ Associação de Lingüistica e Filologia da América Latina (#02278)
♦ Associação de Linguistica Sistemico-Funcional da América Latina (#02279)
♦ Associação Lusófona de Energias Renovaveis (internationally oriented national body)
♦ Associação dos Magistrados da União Europeia (#07614)
♦ Associação Maritima Cristão Internacional (#12561)
♦ Associação Médica Europea (#07761)
♦ Associação de Medicina Chinesa e Acupuntura da América do Sul (no recent information)
♦ Associação de Mulheres da América Latina para o Controle do Tabagismo (inactive)
♦ Associação Mundial dos Amigos da Infância (#02808)
♦ Associação Mundial de Counselling e Psicoterapia Centrados-na-Pessoa (#21172)
♦ Associação Mundial de Ecologia / see AME World Ecology Foundation
♦ Associação Mundial de Educadores Infantis (#21136)
♦ Associação Mundial de Luta Contra a Fome (inactive)
♦ Associação Mundial de Psiquiatria (#21741)
♦ Associação dos Ombudsman e Mediadores (#02838)

♦ Associação dos Operadores de Correios e Telecomunicações dos Paises e Territórios de Lingua Oficial Portuguesa (AICEP) 02333

Association of Postal and Telecommunications Operators of the Portuguese Speaking Countries and Territories – Association des opérateurs des postes et des télécommunications des pays et territoires de langue officielle portugaise

SG Av Defensores de Chaves 15, 7A, 1000-109 Lisbon, Portugal. T. +351213129650. Fax +351213129668. E-mail: aicep@aicep.pt.
Pres address not obtained.
URL: http://www.aicep.pt/

History 26 Nov 1993. Recognized as a restricted union of *Universal Postal Union (UPU, #20682)*, 14 Dec 1998. Previously also referred to in English as *Association of Post Office and Telecommunications Operators of the Portuguese Speaking Countries and Territories*. **Aims** Contribute towards the development and modernization of the post and telecommunication services of portuguese speaking countries and territories. **Structure** General Assembly (annual). Board of Directors. Supervisory Board. **Languages** Portuguese. **Staff** 6.50 FTE, paid. **Finance** Members' dues. Subsidies from: Agência Portuguesa para o Apoio ao Desenvolvimento; *International Telecommunication Union (ITU, #15673)*; Universal Postal Union. **Activities** Organizes international conferences and seminars, training courses, workshops and case-studies. Provides information and documentation. Publishing activities. **Events** *Annual Forum* Macau 2006, *Annual Forum* Lisbon (Portugal) 2005, *Annual Forum* Sao Tomé-Principe 2002, *Annual Forum* Mozambique 2001, *Annual Forum* Brazil 2000. **Publications** *Convergir* (4 a year).
Members Postal operators in 9 signatory countries and territories:
Angola, Brazil, Cape Verde, Guinea-Bissau, Macau, Mozambique, Portugal, Sao Tomé-Principe, Timor-Leste.
IGO Relations Links with the other restricted unions: *African Postal Union (APU, no recent information)*; *Arab Permanent Postal Commission (APPC, #01025)*; *Asian-Pacific Postal Union (APPU, #01625)*; *Association of European Public Postal Operators (PostEurop, #02534)*; *Baltic Postal Union (BPU, #03137)*; *Caribbean Postal Union (CPU, #03541)*; *Conférence européenne des administrations des postes et des télécommunications (CEPT, #04602)*; *Conference of Posts and Telecommunications of Central Africa (#04642)*; *Nordic Postal Union (NPU, #17391)*; *Pan African Postal Union (PAPU, #18060)*; *Postal Union of the Americas, Spain and Portugal (PUASP, #18466)*. [2020/XD6891/**D***]

♦ Associação das Organizações Nacionais de Empresas de Pesca da UE (#02841)
♦ Associação Panamericana de Aerobiologia (#18078)
♦ Associação Panamericana de Anatomia (#18079)
♦ Associação Panamericana de Banco de Olhos (#02285)
♦ Associação Panamericana de Fianças e Garantias / see Panamerican Surety Association (#18134)
♦ Associação Panamericana de Gastroenterologia (#17847)
♦ Associação Panamericana de Implantes (inactive)
♦ Associação Panamericana de Medicina Social (inactive)
♦ Associação Panamericana de Oftalmologia (#18081)
♦ Associação Panamericana das Sociedades de Bioquimica / see Pan American Association for Biochemistry and Molecular Biology (#18080)
♦ Associação Parlamentares de Origem Italiana no Mundo (#02992)
♦ Associação de Pessoal OPAS/OMS (#18024)
♦ Associação Portuguesa para o Estudo das Relações Internacionais / see Instituto Português de Relações Internacionais e Segurança
♦ Associação Psicológica Iberoamericana de Clinica e Saúde (#02295)
♦ Associação das Regiões Fronteiriças Europaias (#02499)
♦ Associação de Reguladores de Agua e Saneamento das Américas (#02124)

♦ Associação de Secretários-Gerais dos Parlamentos de Língua Portuguesa (ASG-PLP) 02334

Presidency address not obtained.
URL: https://www.asg-plp.org/

History 30 Jan 1998, Lisbon (Portugal). **Aims** Promote the development of common technical-parliamentary cooperation; contribute to the modernization of parliamentary institutions; facilitate personal and institutional contacts between members. **Events** *Meeting* Praia (Cape Verde) 2022, *Meeting* Brazil 2020.
Members General Secretaries or equivalent positions of the Parliaments of 8 countries:
Angola, Brazil, Cape Verde, Guinea-Bissau, Mozambique, Portugal, Sao Tomé-Principe, Timor-Leste. [2022/AA3042/v/**D**]

♦ Associação Sons da Lusofonia 02335

Sounds of Lusofonia Association

Main Office Rua da Rosa 145, 1200-383 Lisbon, Portugal. T. +351213463244. Fax +351213463244. E-mail: geral@sonsdalusofonia.com.
URL: http://www.sonsdalusofonia.com/

History 1996, Portugal, when registered according to Portuguese law. **Aims** Contribute to *cultural cooperation* among *Portuguese-speaking* countries; promote development of a lusophone identity based on shared *traditions* but oriented towards the future; promote tolerance and raise awareness of the importance and benefits of *intercultural exchange*. **Finance** Sponsored by: President and Secretaries of State for Culture and Youth of the Portuguese Republic; Mayor of Lisbon (Portugal). **Activities** Research in: ethnomusicology; global education through music; technical and cultural cooperation; promotion of concerts, in particular through *Lusophone Orchestra (inactive)*. **Publications** Books; CDs; videos.
Members Individuals in 7 countries:
Angola, Brazil, Cape Verde, Guinea-Bissau, Mozambique, Portugal, Sao Tomé-Principe.
IGO Relations *Comunidade dos Paises de Lingua Portuguesa (CPLP, #04430)*. [2015/XF3533/**F**]

♦ Associação SOS Amazonia (internationally oriented national body)
♦ Associação Sudamericana de Juizes de Atletismo (inactive)
♦ Associação Suiça para o Intercâmbio de Pessoas na Cooperação Internacional (internationally oriented national body)
♦ Associação de Suicidologia da América Latina e do Caribe (unconfirmed)

♦ Associação Sul Americana de Engenharia Estrutural (ASAEE) 02336

South American Structural Engineering Association – Asociación Sudamericana de Ingenieria Estructural

Main Office Av Osvaldo Aranha, no 99 – térreo, Porto Alegre RS, 90035-140, Brazil. T. +555133083538. Fax +555133083333. E-mail: asaee.secretaria@gmail.com.
URL: http://www.asaee.org.br/

Publications *Revista Sul-Americana de Engenharia Estrutural* (3 a year). **Members** Individuals. Membership countries not specified. [2014/XJ8052/**D**]

♦ Associação Sul Americana da Indústria de Cloro-Soda e Derivados / see Latin American Chlor-Alkali and Derivatives Industry Association (#16295)
♦ Associação das Televisoes Educativas e Culturais Ibero-americanas (#02303)
♦ Associação de Universidades Amazónicas (#02366)

♦ Associação das Universidades de Lingua Portuguesa (AULP) 02337

SG Av Santos Dumont 67 – 2o, 1050-203 Lisbon, Portugal. T. +351217816360 – +351217816368. E-mail: aulp@aulp.org.
URL: http://www.aulp.org/

History 27 Nov 1986, Praia (Cape Verde). Founded at constitutive meeting, when statutes were adopted. Statutes revised at General Assembly, 19 Apr 1993, Macau. **Aims** Safeguard and develop the Portuguese language and the common culture of those speaking it; promote cooperation among *Portuguese-speaking* universities and institutes of higher education and research; increase exchange of faculty, researchers, students and technicians among them and the circulation of scientific, technical, educational and cultural information; stimulate bilateral agreements between institutes and the mutual recognition of literary, academic and scientific qualifications; promote reflection on the role of higher education; support the creation of new educational and research structures. **Structure** General Assembly. Administrative Council; Secretariat in Lisbon (Portugal). **Languages** Portuguese. **Staff** 2.50 FTE, voluntary. **Finance** Sources: donations; government support; members' dues. **Activities** Events/meetings; financial and/or material support; networking/liaising. **Events** *Annual conference* Lisbon (Portugal) 2019, *Annual Conference* Macau (Macau) 2010, *Conference* Brasilia (Brazil) 2008, *Conference* Praia (Cape Verde) 2007, *Conference* Macau (Macau) 2006. **Publications** *Carta Informativa*; *Revista Internacional da Lingua Portuguesa*. Meeting proceedings.
Members Universities in 8 countries and territories:
Angola, Brazil, Cape Verde, Guinea-Bissau, Macau, Mozambique, Portugal, Sao Tomé-Principe. [2021.02.17/XD2422/**D**]

♦ Associação Veterinaria Euro-Arabe (#02975)
♦ Associacija Evro-Atlanticeskogo Sotrudnicestva (no recent information)
♦ Associacija Mezdunarodnyh Issledovanij (#15615)
♦ Associacija Pisatelej Azii i Afriki (inactive)
♦ Associacija Skol Obscestvennogo Zdravoohranenija v Evropejskom Regione (#02904)
♦ Associaçio Cristo para Educaçio Teológica em Africa (#02431)
♦ Associació Internacional de Centres d'Alt Rendiment Esportiu / see Association of Sport Performance Centres (#02929)
♦ Associació Internacional de Centros de Alto Rendimiento Deportivo / see Association of Sport Performance Centres (#02929)
♦ Associació Internacional de Ciutats Educadores (#11860)
♦ Associació Internacional del Dret de l'Esport (#12180)
♦ Associació Internacional de Raiers (#15691)
♦ Associació Llatina per a l'Anàlisi dels Sistemes de Salut (#02171)
♦ Associació pel Voluntariat a Europa (#02978)
♦ Associated Boards for Christian Colleges in China / see United Board for Christian Higher Education in Asia
♦ Associated Countries and Territories / see Association of Overseas Countries and Territories of the European Union (#02843)

♦ Associated Country Women of the World (ACWW) 02338

Union mondiale des femmes rurales (UMFR) – Asociación Mundial de Mujeres Rurales – Weltlandfrauenverband

Main Office A04 Parkhall, 40 Martell Road, London, SE21 8EN, UK. T. +442077993875. E-mail: office@acww.org.uk.
URL: http://www.acww.org.uk/

History 1930, Vienna (Austria). Founded following recommendations 1927, Geneva (Switzerland), of *International Council of Women (ICW, #13093)*, and preliminary assembly 1929, London (UK). Constitution drawn up 1933, Stockholm (Sweden). Former names and other names: *Liaison Committee of Rural Women's and Homemakers' Organizations* – former (1930 to 1933). Registration: Charity Commission, No/ID: 1174798, England and Wales; No/ID: 290367. **Aims** Connect and support women and communities worldwide; raise *living standards* of *rural* women and families through education, training and community development projects; provide practical support to members, such as aid to women's groups to set up income-generating schemes; support educational opportunities for women and girls and eliminate *gender*-based *discrimination*; give rural women a voice at international level through links with UN agencies. **Structure** Conference (every 3 years); Executive Committee. Specified Committees (6): Agriculture; Finance; Projects; Promotion and Publications; Triennial Conference; United Nations. Meetings closed. **Languages** English. **Staff** 8.00 FTE, paid. **Finance** Sources: donations; members' dues.
Activities Does not fund other UK charities. Priorities: status of women; status of the girl child; health; education; communication. Speaks for rural women at UN meetings and keeps the UN informed about the work and concerns of members; keeps members informed about UN developments and helps them identify areas where they can become involved in supporting or actively participating in UN initiatives. Supports development programmes in rural communities through Projects and Trust Funds: leadership and skill training; nutrition/education projects; literacy and basic education programmes, including family planning and HIV/AIDS awareness; small business initiatives and small-scale agricultural, income-generating schemes.
Funds:
- *'Water for All'* – supports clean water and sanitation projects providing water tanks, bore wells and hand pumps;
- *'Women Feed the World'* – supports subsistence food production, cooperatives, training in appropriate agricultural techniques and credit savings schemes;
- *'Projects'* – supports projects worldwide to improve living conditions;
- *'Lady Aberdeen Scholarship'* – provides scholarships and courses in home economics, welfare and citizenship for leaders working in rural communities;
- *'Elsie Zimmern Memorial'* – supports advanced training in organization and leadership;
- *'Nutrition Education'* – promotes good nutrition, improved hygiene, food production and childcare.

Organizes: World Conference (every 3 years), Area Presidents organizing Area Conferences during each triennium; capacity-building workshops.

Events *Triennial World Conference* Kuala Lumpur (Malaysia) 2023, *Triennial Conference* Kuala Lumpur (Malaysia) 2022, *South East Asia and the Far East Area Conference* Kuching (Malaysia) 2022, *Special World Conference* 2021, *Triennial Conference* Melbourne, VIC (Australia) 2019. **Publications** *The Countrywoman* (4 a year) – magazine. Annual Report; conference reports; pamphlets.
Members Categories: I – associations of women with at least 500 members; II – associations of women with 100-500 members; III – umbrella or national organizations; IVa – groups; IVb – individuals. Organized bodies of countrywomen and homemakers or associations with a substantial number of women members in 66 countries:
Australia, Bangladesh, Belarus, Botswana, Brazil, Brunei Darussalam, Bulgaria, Cameroon, Canada, China, Colombia, Czechia, Denmark, Estonia, Eswatini, Fiji, Finland, Gambia, Germany, Ghana, Greece, Grenada, Guyana, Hungary, Iceland, India, Indonesia, Ireland, Jamaica, Kiribati, Korea Rep, Kyrgyzstan, Latvia, Lesotho, Malaysia, Mali, Mongolia, Namibia, Nepal, Netherlands, New Zealand, Niue, Norway, Pakistan, Papua New Guinea, Philippines, Poland, Romania, Russia, Sierra Leone, South Africa, Spain, Sri Lanka, St Lucia, St Vincent-Grenadines, Sweden, Switzerland, Tanzania UR, Timor-Leste, Tonga, Trinidad-Tobago, Uganda, UK, USA, Zambia, Zimbabwe.
Consultative Status Consultative status granted from: *ECOSOC (#05331)* (Special); *UNESCO (#20322)* (Consultative Status); *FAO (#09260)*; *UNICEF (#20332)*. **IGO Relations** Accredited by (1): *United Nations Office at Vienna (UNOV, #20604)*. Associated with Department of Global Communications of the United Nations. **NGO Relations** Member of (9): *Alliance for Health Promotion (A4HP, #00687)*; *Child Rights Connect (#03884)*; *Conference of Non-Governmental Organizations in Consultative Relationship with the United Nations (CONGO, #04635)*; NGO Committee on Human Rights; *NGO Committee on the Status of Women, Geneva (#17117)*; *NGO Committee on the Status of Women, New York NY (see: #04635)*; *NGO Committee on UNICEF (#17120)*; *NGO-UNESCO Liaison Committee (#17127)*; *Vienna NGO Committee on the Status of Women (#20775)*.
[2022.02.03/XB0098/**B**]

- ♦ Associated European Consultants (inactive)
- ♦ Associated European Divers (internationally oriented national body)
- ♦ Associated European Schools Network / see Accredited European Schools Network (#00064)
- ♦ Associated General Contractors of America (internationally oriented national body)

♦ Associated Humans 02339

Humains Associés
Contact 16 blvd Saint Germain, 75005 Paris, France.
URL: http://www.humains-associes.org/
History Founded 1984, Paris (France). **Aims** Bring together psychologists, journalists, scientists and artists with the aim of awakening individual awareness and promoting humanistic and ecological values through work and creative awareness. **Languages** English, French. **Publications** *Revue intemporelle* (annual); *Journal virtuel*. **Members** Individuals. Membership countries not specified. [2016.02.20/XF4253/v/**F**]

♦ Associated International Group of Nurseries (AIGN) 02340

Pres PO Box 3203, Union Gap WA 98903, USA. T. +15092484315. Fax +15092484421.
Exec Sec address not obtained.
URL: http://www.aign.org/
Aims Further enhance the worldwide availability of tree *fruit* varieties and related information. **Publications** *AIGN Newsletter*. **Information Services** *HERTHA* – database.
Members Full in 10 countries:
Argentina, Australia, Belgium, Chile, China, France, New Zealand, South Africa, Uruguay, USA. [2018/XJ3689/**C**]

- ♦ Associated research Centres for the Urban Underground Space (#02420)
- ♦ Associated Schools Project in Education for International Cooperation and Peace / see UNESCO Associated Schools Project Network (#20302)
- ♦ Associate Euro-Mediterranean Centre for Seismic Hazards Assessment and Prevention / see Euro-Mediterranean Centre on Evaluation and Prevention of Seismic Risk
- ♦ Associate European Centre on Flooding / see European Centre for Mitigation of Natural Risks
- ♦ Associate European Centre on Forest Fires / see European Centre on Forest Fires
- ♦ Associates of Clinical Pharmacology / see Association of Clinical Research Professionals (#02434)
- ♦ Associatie van Caraïbische Economen (no recent information)
- ♦ Associatie van Caribische Historici (#02407)
- ♦ Associatio pro Expansione Radiationis Internationalis Linguarum Europae Continentis (#02589)
- ♦ Association of Academic Health Centers International (internationally oriented national body)
- ♦ Association of Academies of Science for Asia (inactive)

♦ Association of Academies and Societies of Sciences in Asia (AASSA) 02341

Secretariat c/o KAST, KAST Bldg – 3rd Floor, 42 Dolma-Ro, Bundang-Gu, Seongnam GYEONGGI 463-808, Korea Rep. T. +82317104622. Fax +82317267909. E-mail: aassa@kast.or.kr.
URL: http://aassa.asia/
History 1 Jan 2012, on merger of *Federation of Asian Scientific Academies and Societies (FASAS, inactive)* and *Association of Academies of Science for Asia (AASA, inactive)*. **Aims** Achieve a society in Asia and Australasia in which science and technology play a major role in the development of the region. **Structure** Executive Board. Secretariat. **Events** *General Assembly* Seongnam (Korea Rep) 2021, *Seminar on Plastic Pollution* Seongnam (Korea Rep) 2021, *Regional Workshop on Crop Biotechnology for Sustainable Agriculture* Seoul (Korea Rep) 2019, *International Conference on Science and Technology for Sustainability* Tokyo (Japan) 2017, *Gender Summit Asia-Pacific* Seoul (Korea Rep) 2015.
Members Academies in 28 countries:
Afghanistan, Armenia, Australia, Azerbaijan, Bangladesh, China, Georgia, India, Indonesia, Iran Islamic Rep, Israel, Kazakhstan, Korea Rep, Kyrgyzstan, Malaysia, Mongolia, Nepal, New Zealand, Pakistan, Philippines, Russia, Singapore, Sri Lanka, Tajikistan, Thailand, Türkiye, Uzbekistan, Vietnam.
Associate academies in 2 countries:
Jordan, Saudi Arabia.
NGO Relations Regional network of: *InterAcademy Partnership (IAP, #11376)*. Affiliated member of: *International Science Council (ISC, #14796)*. [2014/XJ7954/**D**]

♦ Association Académique Internationale de Gouvernance (AAIG) ... 02342

Sec address not obtained. E-mail: contact@aaig.fr.
URL: https://www.aaig.fr/
History Jun 2009, Florence (Italy). **Structure** Board of Directors; Bureau. **Activities** Events/meetings. **Events** *Conférence Internationale de Gouvernance* Brussels (Belgium) 2019, *Conférence Internationale de Gouvernance* Nice (France) 2018, *Conférence Internationale de Gouvernance* Lausanne (Switzerland) 2017, *Conférence Internationale de Gouvernance* Montpellier (France) 2016, *Conférence Internationale de Gouvernance* Québec, QC (Canada) 2015.
Members Individuals in 4 countries:
Belgium, Canada, France, Switzerland. [2022/AA0077/v/**D**]

♦ Association of Accountancy Bodies in West Africa (ABWA) 02343

Main Office Akintola Williams House, Plot 2048 – Micheal Okpara Street, off Olusegun Obasanjo Way, PO Box 13109, Wuse District, Abuja, Federal Capital Territory, Nigeria. E-mail: magdeko@yahoo.com – abwa_secretariat@yahoo.com – abwa_abuja@yahoo.com.
URL: http://www.abwa-online.org/
History 1982. **Aims** Strengthen the accountancy profession in member countries; enhance technical competence and ethical standards of members for effective service delivery by adopting global best practices in the public interest; contribute to sustainable economic development of member countries; partner with other stakeholders in promoting, fostering and sustaining economic development in the African continent. **Languages** English, French. **Events** *Congress / Conference* Banjul (Gambia) 2004, *Congress* Accra (Ghana) 2001, *Congress / Conference* Nigeria 1999, *Conference* Freetown (Sierra Leone) 1994, *Conference* Accra (Ghana) 1988.
Members Professional institutes in 6 countries:
Gambia, Ghana, Liberia, Nigeria, Senegal, Sierra Leone.
NGO Relations Affiliated with: *International Federation of Accountants (IFAC, #13335)*.
[2011.08.01/XD9167/**D**]

♦ Association of Accountants and Auditors in Europe (AAAE) 02344

Association des Experts Comptables et Commissaires aux Comptes en Europe
Contact c/o McCabe Ford Williams, Bank Chambers, 1 Central Ave, Sittingbourne, ME10 4AE, UK. E-mail: webmaster@aaae-europe.eu.
URL: http://www.aaae-europe.eu/
History An organization of the type *European Economic Interest Grouping (EEIG, #06960)*. Registered in accordance with French law.
Members Full in 7 countries:
Belgium, Cyprus, France, Germany, Ireland, Netherlands, UK. [2016/XD5636/**D**]

- ♦ Association of Accredited Public Policy Advocates to the European Union (unconfirmed)
- ♦ Association des aciéries européennes indépendantes (inactive)

♦ Association of ACP National Chambers of Commerce, Industry and Other Economic Operators (ACP Chambers) 02345

Association des chambres nationales de commerce, d'industrie et des autres opérateurs économiques ACP
1st Vice-Pres 80 East Street, PO Box 1929, Kingston 8, Jamaica. T. +18769673845. Fax +18769673845.
Pres PO Box 5908, 269 Samora Machel Ave East, Harare, HARARE, Zimbabwe. T. +2634778603. Fax +2634778603.
Secretariat c/o APC Secretariat, Av George Henri 451, 1200 Brussels, Belgium.
URL: http://www.acpsec.org/
History 10 Jul 1981, Lomé (Togo), on recommendation of *ACP-EU Council of Ministers (#00076)*, meeting Jul 1980, Montego Bay (Jamaica). Present Constitution adopted 11 Oct 1996, Las Palmas de Gran Canaria (Spain). Registered in accordance with Spanish law. **Aims** Bearing in mind the new world trade environment, contribute to development and promotion of intra-ACP and ACP-EU trade; motivate and improve ACP and ACP-EU trade flows through more professional management, enhanced decentralized cooperation and regional integration; identify and analyse opportunities offered by the globalization process and liberalization of international trade; raise capacity building of ACP national chambers to the level required for dialogue amongst themselves and with EU chambers; upgrade level of, and foster contacts and flow of information among members; contribute to integration of the informal sector of ACP economies into the formal sector; assist in harmonizing commercial policies of ACP countries; serve as an instrument for promotion of economic activity, market research, human resource development, development of the private sector, of SMEs and of export-oriented investment in ACP countries and regions. **Structure** General Assembly (every 3 years). Bureau, comprising President, 2 Vice-Presidents, Rapporteur and 8 voting members, and including equal representation of 5 regions: Caribbean; Pacific; Southern Africa; Central Africa; East Africa; West Africa. Secretariat in Brussels (Belgium). Responsible for managing the affairs of the Association during the 3 year interval of General Assembly meetings. National Centres (national chambers of commerce, industry or appointed economic operators). **Languages** English, French. **Finance** Members' dues. Support from *European Development Fund (EDF, #06914)*. Funding for headquarters approved by meeting of *ACP-EU Joint Parliamentary Assembly (#00077)*, 17-20 Mar 1997, Brussels (Belgium). **Activities** Organizes meetings, in particular on business and investment promotion; assists members in establishing economic development programmes and in strengthening existing programmes; advises and makes recommendations to members on formulation of economic policy conducive to trade exchange and to increase intra-ACP trade and trade with other countries, investment and other cross-border initiatives. Current concerns: project of the ACP Council of Ministers to establish a *'Network of ACP National Chambers of Commerce'*; extending the BC-Net idea to ACP countries; collaborative training programmes; training to assist women in setting up their own businesses; joint meetings of ACP and EU chambers. **Events** *Conference on the role of the private sector in ACP-EU future relations* Las Palmas de Gran Canaria (Spain) 1999.
Members Open to economic operators in all countries signatory to the Lomé conventions. Full: national economic operators in ACP countries (one per country); Associate (non-voting): national/regional non-political organizations; Honorary. Members in 79 countries:
Angola, Antigua-Barbuda, Bahamas, Barbados, Belgium, Belize, Benin, Botswana, Burkina Faso, Burundi, Cameroon, Cape Verde, Central African Rep, Chad, Comoros, Congo Brazzaville, Congo DR, Côte d'Ivoire, Cuba, Djibouti, Dominica, Dominican Rep, Equatorial Guinea, Eritrea, Eswatini, Ethiopia, Fiji, Gabon, Gambia, Ghana, Grenada, Guinea, Guinea-Bissau, Guyana, Haiti, Jamaica, Kenya, Kiribati, Lesotho, Liberia, Madagascar, Malawi, Mali, Marshall Is, Mauritania, Micronesia FS, Mozambique, Namibia, Nauru, Niger, Nigeria, Niue, Palau, Papua New Guinea, Rwanda, Samoa, Sao Tomé-Principe, Senegal, Seychelles, Sierra Leone, Solomon Is, Somalia, South Africa, Spain, St Kitts-Nevis, St Lucia, St Vincent-Grenadines, Sudan, Suriname, Tanzania UR, Timor-Leste, Togo, Tonga, Trinidad-Tobago, Tuvalu, Uganda, Vanuatu, Zambia, Zimbabwe.
IGO Relations Operates closely with: *Organisation of African, Caribbean and Pacific States (OACPS, #17796)*; *European Commission (EC, #06633)*. **NGO Relations** Through Global Chamber Platform, links with: *Association des chambres de commerce et d'industrie européennes (EUROCHAMBRES, #02423)*. Representative bodies of the international business sector (not specified). [2011.06.01/XD6526/t/**D**]

- ♦ Association Actuarielle Européenne (#00105)
- ♦ Association actuarielle internationale (#11586)
- ♦ Association des administrations portuaires de l'Afrique du Nord / see North African Port Management Association (#17556)
- ♦ Association for the Advancement of Agricultural Sciences in Africa (no recent information)
- ♦ Association for the Advancement of Artificial Intelligence (internationally oriented national body)

♦ Association for the Advancement of Assistive Technology in Europe (AAATE) 02346

Contact c/o Institute Integriert Studieren, Altenberger Strasse 69, 4040 Linz, Austria. E-mail: office@aaate.net.
Pres address not obtained.
URL: http://www.aaate.net/
History Oct 1995. **Aims** Stimulate advancement of assistive technology in all its aspects for persons with disabilities and elderly people. **Structure** Board. **Languages** English. **Finance** Sources: members' dues. **Activities** Awareness raising; events/meetings; knowledge management/information dissemination; networking/liaising; projects/programmes; research and development. **Events** *Joint International Conference on Digital Inclusion, Assistive Technology & Accessibility* Lecco (Italy) 2022, *Biennial Conference* Paris (France) 2021, *Biennial Conference* Bologna (Italy) 2019, *Biennial Conference* Sheffield (UK) 2017, *Biennial Conference* Budapest (Hungary) 2015. **Publications** *Technology and Disability*. Reports; documents; conference proceedings.
Members Full in 33 countries and territories:
Australia, Austria, Belgium, Bulgaria, Canada, Croatia, Cyprus, Denmark, Egypt, Estonia, Faeroe Is, Finland, France, Germany, Greece, Hong Kong, Hungary, Iceland, Ireland, Israel, Italy, Japan, Korea Rep, Lithuania, Netherlands, Norway, Poland, Portugal, Serbia, Slovakia, Spain, Sweden, Switzerland, UK, USA.
NGO Relations Cooperates with (1): *International Conference on Computers Helping People with Special Needs (ICCHP)*. [2022/XD7733/**D**]

- ♦ Association for the Advancement of Automotive Medicine (internationally oriented national body)
- ♦ Association for Advancement of Behavioral Therapies / see Association for Behavioural and Cognitive Therapies
- ♦ Association for Advancement of Behavior Therapy / see Association for Behavioural and Cognitive Therapies
- ♦ Association for the Advancement of Computing in Education (internationally oriented national body)

♦ Association for the Advancement of Consumerism in the World (AACW) 02347

Contact Hollandstraat 13, 1060 Brussels, Belgium.
History 24 Jun 1976, as *Association des consommateurs Tiers-monde (ACTM) – Verbruikersunie Derde Wereld*. Present name adopted 2 Jan 1992. Previously registered in accordance with Belgian law. Since Oct 1999, registered in accordance with Dutch law. **Aims** Promote the setting up of consumer associations and of organizations whose main goal is the editing and dissemination of periodicals and other *publications* devoted to informing *consumers*. **Structure** Management Board, consisting of President, Vice-President, Secretary, Treasurer.

Members National organizations in 6 countries:
France, Italy, Luxembourg, Netherlands, Portugal, Spain. [2007/XF5521/**F**]

♦ Association for the Advancement of Cost Engineering / see AACE International (#00001)
♦ Association for the Advancement of Gestalt Therapy / see International Association for the Advancement of Gestalt Therapy
♦ Association for the Advancement of Gestalt Therapy – An International Community / see International Association for the Advancement of Gestalt Therapy
♦ Association for the Advancement of Industrial Crops (internationally oriented national body)
♦ Association for the Advancement of International Education (internationally oriented national body)
♦ Association for the Advancement of Policy, Research and Development in the Third World (inactive)
♦ Association for the Advancement of Scandinavian Studies in Canada (internationally oriented national body)
♦ Association for the Advancement of Women in Africa (no recent information)
♦ Association des aéroclubs nordiques (no recent information)
♦ Association des aéroports de l'Europe de l'Ouest (inactive)
♦ Association for Aerosol Research (#10140)
♦ Association Africa 21 (internationally oriented national body)
♦ Association Africa Culture Internationale / see Africa Culture Internationale Human Rights
♦ Association of AfricaFreeAid (internationally oriented national body)
♦ Association africaine des administrateurs africains des impôts (no recent information)
♦ Association africaine d'administration et de gestion publiques / see African Association for Public Administration and Management (#00215)
♦ Association africaine pour l'administration publique et le management (#00215)
♦ Association africaine des agroéconomistes (#00205)
♦ Association africaine pour l'alphabétisation et la formation des adultes (inactive)
♦ Association africaine des autorités électorales (#02355)
♦ Association africaine pour l'avancement des sciences et technique (no recent information)
♦ Association Africaine des Bibliothèques et des Institutions d'Information (#00363)
♦ Association africaine de boxe amateur / see African Boxing Confederation (#00228)

♦ Association africaine des centrales d'achats de médicaments essentiels (ACAME) 02348

African Association of Generic Essential Drugs Purchasing Centres

Permanent Sec BP 4877, Ouagadougou 01, Burkina Faso. T. +22625370267 – +22625379175. Fax +22625373757. E-mail: secretariat.acame@gmail.com – projet.acame@gmail.com.
URL: http://www.acame.net/

History Founded 19 Jul 1996, Ouagadougou (Burkina Faso). **Aims** Contribute to better performance of Generic Essential Drugs Purchasing Centres in African countries in order to assure regular procurement of essential generic drugs at accessible prices. **Structure** General Assembly (annual); Executive Committee; Permanent Secretariat. **Languages** English, French. **Staff** 5.00 FTE, paid. **Finance** Members' dues. Other sources: institutional donors; public and private partners. **Activities** Training/education; knowledge management/information dissemination; advocacy/lobbying/activism. **Events** *Forum pharmaceutique* Libreville (Gabon) 2008. **Publications** Annual Report.
Members Full in 22 countries:
Algeria, Benin, Burkina Faso, Burundi, Cameroon, Central African Rep, Chad, Comoros, Congo Brazzaville, Congo DR, Côte d'Ivoire, Djibouti, Gabon, Guinea, Guinea-Bissau, Madagascar, Mali, Mauritania, Niger, Senegal, Togo, Tunisia.
Consultative Status Consultative status granted from: *WHO (#20950)* (Official Relations). [2018.09.06/XM3796/**D**]

♦ Association Africaine des Centres d'Enseignement à Distance (#02354)
♦ Association africaine du commerce des semences (#00454)
♦ Association africaine de défense des droits de l'homme (internationally oriented national body)
♦ Association africaine de dermatologie (no recent information)
♦ Association africaine pour le développement (inactive)
♦ Association africaine pour le développement du palmier à huile (no recent information)
♦ Association africaine de droit international (#00208)
♦ Association Africaine de l'Eau (#00497)
♦ Association Africaine d'Economie et Politique de la Santé (#00335)
♦ Association africaine des educateurs et formateurs à l'assurance (inactive)
♦ Association africaine pour l'éducation des adultes (inactive)
♦ Association africaine d'éducation pour le développement (no recent information)
♦ Association africaine pour l'environnement et le développement communautaire (no recent information)
♦ Association africaine pour les établissements humains (inactive)
♦ Association africaine pour l'étude du foie (no recent information)
♦ Association Africaine d'Evaluation (#00304)
♦ Association africaine du fer et de l'acier (#00346)
♦ Association africaine pour la fixation de l'azote (#00206)
♦ Association africaine des formateurs et directeurs de personnel (inactive)
♦ Association africaine francophone de formation à distance (no recent information)

♦ Association africaine des laboratoires du bâtiment et des travaux publics (ALBTP) 02349

Address not obtained.

History Previously referred to as *Association des laboratoires africains des routes.* **Events** *JAG : Journées Africaines de la Géotechnique* Abidjan (Côte d'Ivoire) 2018, *JAG : Journées Africaines de la Géotechnique* Lomé (Togo) 2017, *JAG : Journées Africaines de la Géotechnique* Ouagadougou (Burkina Faso) 2015, *JAG : Journées Africaines de la Géotechnique* Ouagadougou (Burkina Faso) 2014, *JAG : Journées Africaines de la Géotechnique* Kribi (Cameroon) 2012. **Members** in 21 countries. Membership countries not specified. [2018/XD6848/**D**]

♦ Association africaine pour la liturgie, la musique et les arts (inactive)
♦ Association africaine des loteries d'état / see Association des Loteries d'Afrique (#02791)
♦ Association africaine pour les maladies rénales / see African Association of Nephrology (#00209)
♦ Association africaine pour le management (inactive)

♦ Association africaine de microbiologie et d'hygiène alimentaire (AAMHA) 02350

African Association of Microbiology and Food Hygiene

Pres Fac de Médecine Ibn El Jazzar, Lab de Biochimie, Ave Mohamed Karoui, 4002 Sousse, Tunisia. T. +21673219632. Fax +21673224899. E-mail: aamha@planet.tn.
URL: http://www.aamha.com/

History 29 Dec 1984, Sousse (Tunisia). **Aims** Promote, develop and diffuse knowledge and research in the fields of microbiology and food hygiene. **Structure** General Assembly; Executive Committee. **Languages** Arabic, English, French. **Staff** 12.00 FTE, voluntary. **Finance** Members' dues. National and international subsidies. **Activities** Organizes international courses, seminars and workshops on specific diseases, treatments and other topics. **Events** *Séminar sur l'HACCP* Sousse (Tunisia) 2011, *International Colloquium* Tunis (Tunisia) 2003, *Workshop on biochemistry and molecular biology at the post-doctoral level* Sousse (Tunisia) 1998, *International colloquium* Tunis (Tunisia) 1994, *Les techniques immunologiques appliquées au dosage des entérotoxines staphylococciques dans les aliments* Sousse (Tunisia) 1993. **Publications** *Microbiologie et hygiène alimentaire* (6 a year). Volumes of international courses. **Information Services** *Base de données pour une recherche bibliographique concernant les recherches en microbiologie et en hygiène alimentaire effectuées en Afrique francophone par les chercheurs autochtones ou non africains.*
Members Full in 12 countries:
Algeria, Benin, Burkina Faso, Côte d'Ivoire, Egypt, France, Gabon, Morocco, Niger, Senegal, Togo, Tunisia.
NGO Relations *Environnement et développement du Tiers-monde (enda, #05510); Fondation internationale pour la promotion de l'hygiène (Fondation HYGIE, inactive).* [2013/XD1156/**D**]

♦ Association africaine de néphrologie (#00209)
♦ Association africaine des professionnels de l'hygiène et de l'environnement (inactive)
♦ Association africaine de rédacteurs d'ouvrages scientifiques (no recent information)
♦ Association africaine de la science du sol (#00520)
♦ Association africaine de sciences politiques (unconfirmed)
♦ Association africaine de statistique (#00475)
♦ Association africaine de la télédétection et de l'environnement (#00216)
♦ Association africaine de tourisme (#00528)
♦ Association of African Airlines / see African Airlines Association (#00200)
♦ Association of African Amateur Basketball Federations / see FIBA Africa (#09744)

♦ Association of African Business Schools (AABS) 02351

Permanent Contact 26 Melville Road, Illovo Sandton, Johannesburg, 2196, South Africa. T. +270117714382. E-mail: info@aabschools.com.
URL: http://www.aabschools.com/

History Oct 2005, Lagos (Nigeria). Registration: Start date: Sep 2007, Nigeria. **Aims** Promote excellence in business and management education in Africa by supporting graduate business schools through capacity building, collaboration and quality improvement. **Structure** Governing Board; Secretariat.
Members Schools, universities and institutes in 9 countries:
Botswana, Egypt, Ghana, Kenya, Morocco, Nigeria, Senegal, South Africa, Tanzania UR.
NGO Relations Member of (1): *EFMD – The Management Development Network (#05387).* Partner of (1): *CEEMAN – International Association for Management Development in Dynamic Societies (CEEMAN, #03625).* [2021.07.16/XJ2429/**D**]

♦ Association of African Central Banks (AACB) 02352

Association des banques centrales africaines (ABCA)

Secretariat c/o BCXEAO, Ave Abdoulaye Fadiga, BP 3108, Dakar, Senegal. T. +2218390500. Fax +2218239335. E-mail: akangni@bceao.int.
URL: http://www.aacb.org/

History Established 13 Aug 1968, Accra (Ghana), on adoption by a Conference of Governors of African Central Banks of Articles of Association, which entered into force on 17 Dec 1968. **Aims** Promote cooperation in *monetary*, banking and *financial* sphere in the African region; assist in formulation of guidelines along which agreements among African countries in the monetary and financial fields shall proceed; help strengthen monetary and financial stability in the region; examine the effectiveness of international *economic* and financial institutions in which African countries have an interest and suggest ways of possible improvement. **Structure** Assembly of Governors (every 2 years, rotating among the 4 sub-regions) elects President and Vice-President for 2-year term. Executive Committee, consisting of President, Vice-President and the Chairmen of each of 4 sub-regional committees. Secretariat of West African Sub-Regional Committee provided by *West African Monetary Agency (WAMA, #20887)*; Secretariat of the North, Central, and East and Southern Committees, and of AACB itself, provided by *African Centre for Monetary Studies (ACMS, inactive).* **Languages** English, French. **Staff** 20.00 FTE, paid. **Finance** Members' dues. **Activities** Networking/liaising; knowledge management/information dissemination. **Events** *Annual Meeting* Balaclava (Mauritius) 2013, *Biennial ordinary meeting* Abuja (Nigeria) 1997, *Biennial ordinary meeting* Kinshasa (Zaire) 1995, *Biennial Ordinary Meeting* Khartoum (Sudan) 1993, *Biennial ordinary meeting* Harare (Zimbabwe) 1991.
Members African central banks and monetary authorities (34), in 46 countries in 4 regions:
Algeria, Benin, Botswana, Burkina Faso, Burundi, Cameroon, Cape Verde, Central African Rep, Chad, Congo Brazzaville, Congo DR, Côte d'Ivoire, Egypt, Equatorial Guinea, Eswatini, Ethiopia, Gabon, Gambia, Ghana, Guinea, Guinea-Bissau, Kenya, Lesotho, Liberia, Libya, Madagascar, Malawi, Mali, Mauritania, Mauritius, Morocco, Mozambique, Namibia, Niger, Nigeria, Rwanda, Senegal, Sierra Leone, Somalia, Sudan, Tanzania UR, Togo, Tunisia, Uganda, Zambia, Zimbabwe.
Regional banks (2):
Banque centrale des Etats de l'Afrique de l'Ouest (BCEAO, #03167); Banque des Etats de l'Afrique centrale (BEAC, #03169).
NGO Relations West African Regional Sub-Committee instrumental in setting up *West African Bankers' Association (WABA, no recent information).* [2016/XD4491/y/**D***]

♦ Association of African Church Planters (inactive)

♦ Association of African Development Finance Institutions (AADFI) . . 02353

Association des institutions africaines de financement du développement (AIAFD) – Asociación Africana de Instituciones Financieras de Desarrollo

Headquarters Immeuble AIAFD, Boulevard Latrille rue J61, Cocody-Deux Plateaux, 06 BP 321, Abidjan 06, Côte d'Ivoire. T. +22522527940. Fax +22522522584. E-mail: info@adfi-ci.org.
URL: http://www.adfi-ci.org/

History 6 Mar 1975, Abidjan (Côte d'Ivoire), on recommendation of leaders of African banking and financing institutions, under the auspices of *African Development Bank (ADB, #00283).* **Aims** Serve as a medium for technical exchange and cooperation in financing economic and social development of Africa. In particular: alleviate poverty and reduce social inequality in Africa; accelerate the process of economic integration in the region and ensure sustainable development; stimulate cooperation and solidarity among member institutions so as to ensure harmonization of financial policies. **Structure** General Assembly (annual); Executive Committee; Bureau; General Secretariat. **Languages** English, French. **Staff** 4 professionals; 4 general service staff. **Finance** Members' dues. Voluntary contributions. Other sources: donations, grants. **Activities** Networking/liaising; research and development; training/education; financial and/or material support; events/meetings. **Events** *Annual General Assembly* Malabo (Equatorial Guinea) 2019, *Annual General Assembly* Busan (Korea Rep) 2018, *Annual General Assembly* Ahmedabad (India) 2017, *Annual General Assembly* Lusaka (Zambia) 2016, *Annual General Assembly* Abidjan (Côte d'Ivoire) 2015. **Publications** *AADFI Information Bulletin* (4 a year) in English, French; *Finance and Development in Africa* (2 a year) in English, French; *Brief Note on AADFI* (every 2 years); *AADFI Directory.* Annual report; seminar reports; brochures. Information Services: Maintains databank.
Members Ordinary: African national and regional development banks and finance institutions (55) in 34 countries:
Algeria, Angola, Benin, Burundi, Chad, Comoros, Congo Brazzaville, Congo DR, Côte d'Ivoire, Djibouti, Egypt, Eswatini, Ethiopia, Ghana, Kenya, Liberia, Libya, Malawi, Mauritius, Morocco, Niger, Nigeria, Rwanda, Sao Tomé-Principe, Senegal, Seychelles, Sierra Leone, South Africa, Sudan, Tanzania UR, Togo, Tunisia, Uganda, Zambia.
Special (regional) members (11), including the following 9 listed in this Yearbook:
African Development Bank (ADB); *African Fund for Guarantee and Economic Cooperation (#00326); Arab Bank for Economic Development in Africa (#00904); Banque de développement des Etats de l'Afrique centrale (BDEAC, #03168); Banque ouest africaine de développement (BOAD, #03170); East African Development Bank (EADB, #05183); Fonds de solidarité africain (FSA, #09838); Mutual Aid and Loan Guaranty Fund of the Entente Council (EC-Fund, no recent information); Trade and Development Bank (TDB, #20181).*
Honorary members (7) in 5 non-African countries:
India, Italy, Portugal, Switzerland, USA.
Included in the above honorary members, 4 organizations listed in this Yearbook:
International Bank for Reconstruction and Development (IBRD, #12317); International Finance Corporation (IFC, #13597); SIFIDA Investment Company (inactive); World Association for Small and Medium Enterprises (WASME, #21189).
Consultative Status Consultative status granted from: *ECOSOC (#05331)* (Ros C); *UNIDO (#20336).* **IGO Relations** Cooperates with: *Africa Project Development Facility (APDF, inactive); African Development Bank Group (ADB Group, #00284); Association of African Central Banks (AACB, #02352); Association of Regional and Sub-regional Development Finance Institutions in West Africa (AIRFD, no recent information); ECOWAS Bank for Investment and Development (EBID, #05334); Institut africain d'informatique (IAI, #11235); UNCTAD (#20285); United Nations Economic Commission for Africa (ECA, #20554).* Partner of: *African Development Institute (ADI, #00286).* **NGO Relations** Member of: *World Federation of Development Financing Institutions (WFDFI, #21428).* Cooperates with: *Asociación Latinoamericana de Instituciones Financieras para el Desarrollo (ALIDE, #02233); Association of Development Financing Institutions in Asia and the Pacific (ADFIAP, #02472); Association of National Development Finance Institutions in Member Countries of the Islamic Development Bank (ADFIMI, #02817); Center for International Accounting Development; Centre international de formation de la profession bancaire (CIFPB, inactive); European Development Finance Institutions (EDFI, #06913); Institut Africain pour le Développement Economique et Social – Centre Africain de Formation (INADES-Formation, #11233).* [2018/XD4539/y/**D**]

♦ Association of African Distance Learning Centres (AADLC) 02354

Association Africaine des Centres d'Enseignement à Distance (AACED)

Contact TGDLC, Shaaban Robert Str, Block A – IFM, PO Box 2287, Dar es Salaam, Tanzania UR. T. +255222123705. Fax +255222123702. E-mail: info@aadlc.net.

Senegal Contact Centre d'Enseignement à Distance, BP 12997, BP 12997 Colobane, Dakar, Senegal. T. +22108250254. Fax +22108640305.

URL: http://www.aadlc.net/

History May 2003, Dar es Salaam (Tanzania UR), at 2nd Regional Meeting of African Distance Learning Centres, as part of *Global Development Learning Network (GDLN, #10317)*. **Aims** Fight poverty and promote development in Africa by developing skills and competencies for the public and private sectors, civil society, and academics for the delivery of best quality standards services through cost-effective distance learning using cutting-edge technology. **Events** *eLearning Africa : International Conference on ICT for Development, Education and Training* Cotonou (Benin) 2012.

Members Full in 10 countries:
Benin, Burkina Faso, Côte d'Ivoire, Ethiopia, Ghana, Kenya, Madagascar, Senegal, Tanzania UR, Uganda.

NGO Relations Associate member of: *International Council for Open and Distance Education (ICDE, #13056)*. [2015/XJ5101/**E**]

♦ Association of African Economists (inactive)

♦ Association of African Election Authorities (AAEA) 02355

Association africaine des autorités électorales

Contact c/o Instance Supérieure Indépendante pour les Elections, 5 rue de l'Ile de Sardaigne, Les Jardins du Lac, 1053 Tunis, Tunisia. T. +21670018555. Fax +21671289483. E-mail: contact@isie.tn.

History Jan 1997, Kampala (Uganda). Inaugural meeting 13-15 Aug 1998, Accra (Ghana). **Aims** Promote cooperation and mutual assistance among electoral organizations in the region in the pursuit of democracy by processes that ensure free, fair and peaceful elections. **Structure** General Assembly. Officers: Chairperson; Executive Secretary. Advisory Board. **Events** *Extraordinary General Assembly* Abidjan (Côte d'Ivoire) 2018, *Forum Annuel Continental des Organes de Gestion des Elections* Abidjan (Côte d'Ivoire) 2018, *Board Meeting* Kigali (Rwanda) 2006, *General Assembly* Accra (Ghana) 1998.

Members Full (15); Associate (6). Members in 17 countries:
Benin, Burkina Faso, Cameroon, Central African Rep, Gabon, Gambia, Ghana, Guinea, Kenya, Lesotho, Liberia, Mali, Senegal, Togo, Uganda, Zambia, Zimbabwe.

NGO Relations *International Foundation for Electoral Systems (IFES, #13669)*. [2018/XD6864/**D**]

♦ Association of African Entrepreneurs (AAE) 02356

Exec Officer Hse No PR-QK-008, Mandela Road, Prampram, Ghana. T. +233243785324. E-mail: info@aaeafrica.org.

URL: http://www.aaeafrica.org/

History May 2004. Proposed May 2003. **Aims** Establish a mutually beneficial sharing system where entrepreneurs and expert volunteers exchange experiences and participate in learning and service. **Structure** General Meeting (annual); Board; Committee; Sub-offices. **Languages** English. **Staff** 7.00 FTE, voluntary. **Finance** Sources: donations; grants; members' dues. **Activities** Advocacy/lobbying/activism; events/meetings; knowledge management/information dissemination; training/education.

Members Full (60) in 9 countries:
Gambia, Ghana, Guinea, Kenya, Nigeria, Philippines, South Africa, Uganda, USA. [2022.06.13/XJ6867/**D**]

♦ Association of African Exhibition Organisers (internationally oriented national body)
♦ Association of African Geological Surveys (inactive)

♦ Association of African Historians 02357

Association des historiens africains (AHA)

Exec Sec BP E 5484, Rue Mage, Porte 428, Bamako, Mali. T. +223238772. Fax +223238770. E-mail: doulaye@afribone.net.ml.

Pres address not obtained. E-mail: doulaye@afribone.net.ml.

URL: http://africanhistorians.org/

History Sep 1972, Dakar (Senegal), as an internal commission of *International Committee of Historical Sciences (ICHS, #12777)*. Current constitution adopted, 24 May 2007, Addis Ababa (Ethiopia). **Aims** Contribute to the development of historical research in Africa; spread knowledge of African history, especially in literature and the promotion of regional and continental history; provide a platform for researchers and history educators, in both primary and secondary education. **Structure** Congress (every 3 years). Executive Committee (meets annually), comprising President, Vice-President and 6 members representing Sub-Regions or tutelar Sector. Executive Secretariat, headed by Executive Secretary. Scientific Committee. Sub-Regions include: South Africa; Central Africa; East Africa; North Africa; West Africa; Overseas Chapter. **Languages** Arabic, English, French, Portuguese, Spanish. **Finance** Members' dues (annual): US$ 4.20. Other sources: private and governmental contributions; sale of products and publications; congress proceeds. **Events** *Congress* Abuja (Nigeria) 2013, *Congress* Addis Ababa (Ethiopia) 2007, *Congress* Bamako (Mali) 2001, *Congress* Yaoundé (Cameroon) 1975, *Congress* Dakar (Senegal) 1972. **Publications** *Afrika Zamani* (2 a year) in English, French, German, Italian, Spanish – journal.

Members includes all African countries. Representatives in 19 countries:
Representatives in 19 countries:
Algeria, Benin, Burkina Faso, Burundi, Cameroon, Central African Rep, Congo Brazzaville, Côte d'Ivoire, Gabon, Ghana, Liberia, Mali, Morocco, Nigeria, Rwanda, Senegal, Sierra Leone, Togo, Tunisia.

IGO Relations Observer to: *African Cultural Institute (ACI, inactive)*. **NGO Relations** Member of Permanent Council of: *International Congress of African Studies (ICAF, inactive)*. [2012/XD7784/v/**D**]

♦ Association of African Industrial Technology Organizations (inactive)

♦ Association of African Insurance Brokers (AAIB) 02358

Association des courtiers africains d'assurance (ACAA)

Chairman United African Insurance Brokers Ltd, 33B Bode Thomas Street, Surulere, PO Box 54334, Lagos, Nigeria. T. +23417738985 – +23417738987. Fax +23415850367.

History by *African Insurance Organization (AIO, #00343)*. Originally referred to as *Association of African Insurance Brokers and Consultants (AAIBC)*. Also referred to as *Association of African Insurance Brokers and Brokers Association (AAIBBA)*. **Aims** Promote competence, ethics and standards of African brokers. **Structure** Executive Committee, comprising Chairman, Vice-Chairman and Treasurer-Secretary. **Events** *EUROGLIA : European Meeting on Glial Cells in Health and Disease* Berlin (Germany) 2013. **NGO Relations** Member of: *World Federation of Insurance Intermediaries (WFII, #21443)*. [2008/XJ3656/**D**]

♦ Association of African Insurance Brokers and Brokers Association / see Association of African Insurance Brokers (#02358)
♦ Association of African Insurance Brokers and Consultants / see Association of African Insurance Brokers (#02358)
♦ Association of African Insurance Educators and Trainers (inactive)
♦ Association of African Insurance Supervisory Authorities (no recent information)
♦ Association of African Investment Promotion Agencies (no recent information)
♦ Association of African Managers and Partners of Roads (#02626)
♦ Association of African Maritime Training Institutes (no recent information)
♦ Association for African Medicinal Plants Standards (no recent information)
♦ Association of African Optometric Educators (no recent information)
♦ Association of African Palais de Congrès (inactive)

♦ Association of African Planning Schools (AAPS) 02359

Gen Sec African Centre for Cities, Univ of Cape Town, Rondebosch, 7700, South Africa.

URL: http://www.africanplanningschools.org.za/

History 2002. **Events** *Conference* Dar es Salaam (Tanzania UR) 2010, *Conference* Cape Town (South Africa) 2008.

Members Institutes and universities (54) in 8 countries:
Botswana, Ghana, Nigeria, South Africa, Tanzania UR, Uganda, Zambia, Zimbabwe.

NGO Relations Member of: *Global Planning Education Association Network (GPEAN, #10549)*; *Global Land Tool Network (GLTN, #10452)*. [2014/XD9305/**D**]

♦ Association of African Researchers for Economic and Social Development (inactive)
♦ Association of African Road Directors / see Association des Gestionnaires et Partenaires Africains de la Route (#02626)
♦ Association of African Schools and Faculties of Medicine / see Association of Medical Schools in Africa (#02798)

♦ Association of African Sports Confederations (AASC) 02360

Union des confédérations sportives africaines (UCSA) – Etihad Konfidiraliat al'Ifriqyah Lielriadha

SG PO Box 35205, Yaoundé, Cameroon. T. +237242218690. Fax +2372242218690.

URL: http://www.ucsa-aasc.org/

History 22 Jul 1983, Abidjan (Côte d'Ivoire), at Constitutive General Assembly. **Aims** Promote understanding, cooperation and mutual help among African sports confederations (ASCs); ensure affirmation of African sport at world level; encourage exchange of experience at the level of administrative and technical organization; combat racial discrimination in sports. **Structure** General Assembly (every 2 years); Bureau. President, Senior and Second Vice-Presidents are representatives of AASC within the Executive Committee of SCSA. The post of Secretary General/Treasurer is entrusted to the Secretary General of SCSA. **Languages** Arabic, English, French. **Staff** 10.00 FTE, paid. **Finance** Annual contributions of member confederations. Other sources: gifts; aids; grants; revenue from sport events. **Events** *General Assembly* Maputo (Mozambique) 2011, *General Assembly* Johannesburg (South Africa) 1998, *Joint meeting / General Assembly* Johannesburg (South Africa) 1998, *General Assembly* Algiers (Algeria) 1996, *General Assembly* Harare (Zimbabwe) 1994.

Members Sports Confederations in the 53 member States of the Organization of African Unity (OAU):
Algeria, Angola, Benin, Botswana, Burkina Faso, Burundi, Cameroon, Cape Verde, Central African Rep, Chad, Comoros, Congo Brazzaville, Congo DR, Côte d'Ivoire, Djibouti, Egypt, Equatorial Guinea, Eritrea, Eswatini, Ethiopia, Gabon, Gambia, Ghana, Guinea, Guinea-Bissau, Kenya, Lesotho, Liberia, Libya, Madagascar, Malawi, Mali, Mauritania, Mauritius, Morocco, Mozambique, Namibia, Niger, Nigeria, Rwanda, Sao Tomé-Principe, Senegal, Seychelles, Sierra Leone, Somalia, South Africa, Sudan, Tanzania UR, Togo, Tunisia, Uganda, Zambia, Zimbabwe.

International organizations (2):
Africa Baseball and Softball Association (ABSA, #00158); *African Sports Journalists Union (ASJU, inactive)*.

NGO Relations Affiliated with: *Confederation of Africa Deaf Sports (CADS, #04498)*. [2017/XD7304/y/**D**]

♦ Association of African Statisticians (inactive)
♦ Association of African Studies Programs (internationally oriented national body)
♦ Association of African Tax Administrators (no recent information)
♦ Association of African Trade Promotion Organizations (no recent information)
♦ Association of African Trading Enterprises (inactive)

♦ Association of African Universities (AAU) 02361

Association des Universités Africaines (AUA) – Asociación de Universidades Africanas

SG PO Box AN 5744, Accra, Ghana. T. +233302774495 – +233547728975. E-mail: secgen@aau.org – info@aau.org.

Street Address Trinity Avenue, Next to Ghana Tertiary Education Commission and NAPBTEX, East Legon, Accra, Ghana.

Main Website: http://www.aau.org/

History 12 Nov 1967, Rabat (Morocco). Founded when constitution was adopted and Officers and Executive Board elected. A preparatory committee had previously been set up, 16-19 Sep 1963, Khartoum (Sudan), at a Meeting of Heads of African Institutions of Higher Education, following recommendations of Conference on the Future of Higher Education in Africa, Sep 1962, Tananarive, under the auspices of UNESCO. Secretariat has been hosted in Ghana since 1970. **Aims** Promote interchange, contact and cooperation among Higher Education Institutions in Africa; collect, classify and disseminate information on higher education and research, particularly in Africa; promote cooperation among African institutions in curriculum development and in the determination of equivalence of degrees; encourage increased contact between members and the international academic world; study and make known the educational and related needs of African university institutions and, as far as practicable, coordinate the means whereby they may be met. **Structure** General Conference (every 4 years); *Conference of Vice-Chancellors, Presidents and Rectors of Institutions of Higher Learning in Africa (COREVIP)* (every 2 years); Governing Board; Secretariat, headed by Secretary-General. **Languages** Arabic, English, French, Portuguese. **Staff** 55.00 FTE, paid; 25.00 FTE, voluntary. **Finance** Sources: donations; grants; members' dues. Subventions, mainly from *African Union (AU, #00488)*. Donors include: *Association for the Development of Education in Africa (ADEA, #02471)*; AU; *Canadian International Development Agency (CIDA, inactive)*; *Carnegie Corporation of New York*; *Deutscher Akademischer Austauschdienst (DAAD)*; *Ford Foundation (#09858)*; Government of the Netherlands; *Norwegian Agency for Development Cooperation (Norad)*; *The Rockefeller Foundation (#18966)*; *Swedish International Development Cooperation Agency (Sida)*; UNESCO. **Activities** Financial and/or material support; knowledge management/information dissemination; projects/programmes; training/education. **Events** *General Conference* Accra (Ghana) 2021, *International Conference on Quality Assurance in Higher Education in Africa* Abuja (Nigeria) 2019, *Biennial Conference of Rectors, Vice Chancellors and Presidents of African Universities* Cairo (Egypt) 2019, *International Conference on Quality Assurance in Higher Education in Africa* Yaoundé (Cameroon) 2018, *International Conference on Quality Assurance in Higher Education in Africa* Accra (Ghana) 2017. **Publications** *AAU Newsletter* (12 a year); *Guide to Higher Education in Africa* (every 2 years). Annual Report; seminar and workshop reports and studies; press-releases. Information Services: Library and Documentation Centre, including need-based information service. **Information Services** *Database of African Theses and Dissertations (DATAD)*.

Members Universities and institutions of university rank (414) in 46 countries:
Algeria, Angola, Benin, Botswana, Burkina Faso, Burundi, Cameroon, Cape Verde, Central African Rep, Chad, Congo Brazzaville, Congo DR, Côte d'Ivoire, Egypt, Eritrea, Eswatini, Ethiopia, Gabon, Gambia, Ghana, Kenya, Lesotho, Liberia, Libya, Madagascar, Malawi, Mali, Mauritania, Mauritius, Morocco, Mozambique, Namibia, Niger, Nigeria, Rwanda, Senegal, Sierra Leone, Somalia, South Africa, Sudan, Tanzania UR, Togo, Tunisia, Uganda, Zambia, Zimbabwe.

Included in the above, 5 organizations listed in this Yearbook:
African Virtual University (AVU, #00496); *Euclid University (EUCLID, #05575)*; *Institut International d'Ingénierie de l'Eau et de l'Environnement (2iE, #11313)*; *Pan-Atlantic University (PAU)*; *Women's University in Africa (WUA)*.

Consultative Status Consultative status granted from: *ECOSOC (#05331)* (Ros C); *UNESCO (#20322)* (Associate Status). **IGO Relations** Cooperates with (6): *African and Malagasy Council for Higher Education (#00364)*; *African Union (AU, #00488)*; *Commonwealth of Learning (COL, #04346)*; *Commonwealth Secretariat (#04362)*; *United Nations Economic Commission for Africa (ECA, #20554)*; *United Nations University (UNU, #20642)*. **NGO Relations** Member of (2): *Global Sustainability Coalition for Open Science Services (SCOSS, #10616)*; *International Association of Universities (IAU, #12246)*. Instrumental in setting up (1): *African Quality Assurance Network (AfriQAN, #00427)*. [2022.05.11/XD0117/y/**D**]

♦ Association of African Women for Research and Development (AAWORD) 02362

Association des femmes africaines pour la recherche et le développement (AFARD)

Address not obtained.

URL: http://www.afard.org/

History 17 Dec 1977, Dakar (Senegal), following consultative meeting, Dec 1976, Lusaka (Zambia). **Aims** Promote multi-dimensional (political, economic, social, cultural and psychological) development of the African people; alert governments, public authorities and research centres to the need for decolonizing research; create and develop lines of communication between women researchers themselves and between them and others concerned with development problems in Africa; promote action oriented research; evaluate methodologies and research priorities. **Structure** General Assembly (every 4 years). Executive Committee, consisting of 9 elected members representing 9 regions (North Africa, Southern Africa, Central Africa, Eastern Africa, Anglophone West Africa, Francophone West Africa, Lusophone Africa, Europe, Americas), defined in the regulations and, ex-officio, Executive Secretary. Secretariat, headed by Executive Secretary. **Languages** English, French. **Staff** 5.00 FTE, paid. **Finance** Source: development research cooperation agencies. **Activities** Identifies resources for members. Encourages formation of National Research Working Groups; maintains contact with groups in other developing countries. Research Methodology Training Programme. Priority Programme Areas: Gender analysis and transformation of economic and social policy reforms in Africa; Natural resources management and reproductive health for sustainable human development; Governance,

democratization and women's political empowerment; Struggle for women's rights and against violence of women; Gender, equity and information technology. Organizes workshops and seminars on major topics of concern to women and sets up campaigns. **Events** *General Assembly* Dakar (Senegal) 2003, *General assembly and seminar / General Assembly* Dakar (Senegal) 1999, *Conference / General Assembly* Pretoria (South Africa) 1995, *Women and democratization in Africa* Johannesburg (South Africa) 1994, *WAAD : international conference on women in Africa and African diaspora* Nsukka (Nigeria) 1992. **Publications** *Echo* (4 a year) in English, French – newsletter. Books.
Members National chapters and organizations in 23 countries:
Cameroon, Cape Verde, Chad, Congo DR, Côte d'Ivoire, Egypt, Eswatini, Germany, Ghana, Guinea-Bissau, Kenya, Mauritania, Morocco, Niger, Nigeria, Senegal, South Africa, Tanzania UR, Togo, Tunisia, Uganda, USA, Zambia.
Individuals in 1 country:
USA.
Consultative Status Consultative status granted from: *ECOSOC (#05331)* (Special); *UNEP (#20299)*. **IGO Relations** Accredited by: *United Nations Office at Vienna (UNOV, #20604)*. **NGO Relations** Secretariat facilities provided by: *Council for the Development of Social Science Research in Africa (CODESRIA, #04879)*. Member of: *Council of Non-Governmental Organizations for Development Support (#04911)*; *EarthAction (EA, #05159)*. Associate member of: *Conference of Non-Governmental Organizations in Consultative Relationship with the United Nations (CONGO, #04635)*. Regional member of: *International Council for Adult Education (ICAE, #12983)*. AFARD Togo is member of: *Association for Women's Rights in Development (AWID, #02980)*.
[2017/XD7436/v/**D**]

- Association of African Women Specialized in Communication (no recent information)
- Association de l'Afrique de l'Est pour le commerce du thé (#05189)
- Association d'Afrique de l'Est pour la gestion portuaire / see Port Management Association of Eastern and Southern Africa (#18462)
- Association Afrique, Hambourg (internationally oriented national body)
- Association de l'Afrique orientale des contrôleurs du trafic aérien (inactive)
- Association des agences de la démocratie locale / see European Association for Local Democracy (#06110)

♦ Association des agents pensionnés des organisations coordonnées et de leurs ayants droit (AAPOCAD) 02363

Association of the Pensioned Staff of the Coordinated Organizations and of their Dependants
Secretariat 2 rue André Pascal, 75775 Paris CEDEX 16, France. T. +33145248587. E-mail: aapocad@oecd.org.
URL: http://www.aapocad.org/
Aims Ensure correct implementation of the pension scheme for *retired* staff of relevant organizations and defend their interests. **Structure** General Assembly; Board. **Finance** Sources: members' dues.
[2022.05.05/XE4155/**E**]

- Association des agriculteurs africains (inactive)
- Association of Agricultural Engineering of South Eastern Europe (inactive)

♦ Association of Agricultural Research Institutions in the Near East and North Africa (AARINENA) 02364

AARINENA-RAIS Secretariat Yemen Ave, Chamran Highway, Teheran, Iran Islamic Rep. T. +982122413931. Fax +982122413931.
Secretariat c/o WARP, PO Box 950764, Amman 11195, Jordan. T. +96265525750. Fax +96265525930.
URL: http://www.aarinena.org/
History 1985, Damascus (Syrian AR), as *Association of Agricultural Research Institutions in the Near East and North Africa Region*, at 1st General Meeting, when Officers were selected, following decision of meeting, 1983, Cyprus. Co-sponsored by *FAO (#09260)*, *International Center for Agricultural Research in the Dry Areas (ICARDA, #12466)* and *International Service for National Agricultural Research (ISNAR, inactive)*. Constitution currently being amended to allow membership from universities, institutions of higher agricultural education and civil society representatives. **Aims** Foster development of agricultural research; promote exchange of information and experience in the region; strengthen cooperative linkages in research and training in accordance with national and regional needs and priorities. **Structure** General Conference. Executive Committee, comprising President, Vice-President, 7 members and Executive Secretary. General Secretariat provided by ICARDA West Asia Regional Programme. **Languages** Arabic, English. **Staff** 3.00 FTE, voluntary. **Finance** Members' dues: US$ 3,000 for members and US$ 2,000 for associate members. **Activities** Seminars; workshops; exchange of germ plasm and genetic resources; exchange visits; exchange of information; studies. Proposed joint research projects: research priority setting, country profiles and biotechnology applications. Central register of holdings, personnel and specialist advice. **Events** *General Conference* Damascus (Syrian AR) 2008, *General Conference* Sanaa (Yemen) 2006, *General Conference* Muscat (Oman) 2004, *General Conference* Oman 2004, *Olive expert consultation meeting* Sfax (Tunisia) 2004. **Publications** *AARINENA Newsletter* (2 a year) in Arabic, English. Concept research papers. **Information Services** *Data Base on Human Resources and Expenditure*.
Members Governments of countries in the region (19):
Cyprus, Egypt, Iran Islamic Rep, Iraq, Jordan, Kuwait, Lebanon, Libya, Malta, Morocco, Oman, Pakistan, Palestine, Qatar, Sudan, Syrian AR, Tunisia, United Arab Emirates, Yemen.
International organizations (7):
Arab Centre for the Studies of Arid Zones and Dry Lands (ACSAD, #00918); *Arab Organization for Agricultural Development (AOAD, #01018)*; *Bioversity International (#03262)*; *FAO Regional Office for the Near East and North Africa (#09269)*; *International Centre for Biosaline Agriculture (ICBA, #12468)*; International Centre for Agricultural Research in the Dry Areas (ICARDA); *International Food Policy Research Institute (IFPRI, #13622)*.
NGO Relations Member of: *Global Forum on Agricultural Research (GFAR, #10370)*. Instrumental in setting up: *Inter-regional Network on Cotton in Asia and North Africa (INCANA, #15972)*. Works with: *Young Professionals for Agricultural Development (YPARD, #21996)*.
[2014/XD0785/y/**D***]

- Association of Agricultural Research Institutions in the Near East and North Africa Region / see Association of Agricultural Research Institutions in the Near East and North Africa (#02364)
- Association for AgriCulture and Ecology (internationally oriented national body)
- Association for Agro-Industrial Development of the Sahel (internationally oriented national body)
- Association Aide au Tiers-Monde (internationally oriented national body)
- Association to Aid Indochinese Refugees / see Association for Aid and Relief – Japan
- Association to Aid Refugees / see Association for Aid and Relief – Japan
- Association for Aid and Relief – Japan (internationally oriented national body)
- Association allemande de médecins pour la coopération humanitaire (internationally oriented national body)
- Association de l'alliance pour le commerce mondial (inactive)
- Association of Alpine Regions / see Association of Working Communities of the Alpine Regions (#02981)

♦ Association of Alumni of the College of Europe 02365

Association des anciens du collège d'Europe
Sec Breydelstraat 40, 1000 Brussels, Belgium. T. +32477841647. E-mail: anciens@coleurope.eu.
Coordinator address not obtained.
URL: http://www.coleurope-alumni.eu/
History Jun 1951, Bruges (Belgium). Founded as *Association of Former Students of the College of Europe – Association des anciens étudiants du Collège d'Europe*, after the first academic year of *College of Europe (#04105)*. Previously known as *College of Europe Alumni*. Registration: Banque-Carrefour des Entreprises, No/ID: 0408.296.160, Start date: 17 Mar 1956, Belgium. **Aims** Maintain and develop the links forged as students of the College of Europe; develop a network between the *alumni* and *private* and *public* sector *enterprises* and organizations; serve and promote the cause of European integration; enhance the College's reputation and position as one of the foremost centres for postgraduate studies in European affairs. **Structure** General Assembly (annual, in Bruges, Belgium). Administrative Council (elected for 3 years). Meetings closed. **Languages** English, French. **Finance** Members' dues. **Activities** Runs the Careers Office, which aims to promote the optimal use of each Alumnus' skills. Organizes conferences and meetings. Set up *Madariaga – College of Europe Foundation (inactive)*. **Publications** *College of Europe News* (2 a year). Information Services: Database – list of former students of the College of Europe, with addresses. **Members** Active; Associate; Honorary Membership. Regional Groups; Individuals (about 9,000). Membership countries not specified.
[2021/XF0133/**E**]

- Association des amateurs de musique de chambre (#00072)

♦ Association of Amazonian Universities (UNAMAZ) 02366

Association des universités de l'Amazonie – Asociación de Universidades Amazónicas – Associação de Universidades Amazônicas
Contact address not obtained. T. +559132105230.
URL: http://www.ufpa.br/unamaz/
History 18 Sep 1987, Belém (Brazil), during an international seminar. Current statutes adopted 1992. **Aims** Strengthen links among universities and other teaching, research and cultural institutions of countries in the Amazon region; discuss solutions to common regional problems through systematic cooperation, communication and information; raise the level of reciprocal knowledge among Amazonian universities so as to identify common needs, available resources and possibilities of institutional support; develop programmes and projects of common interest in science, technology and culture; define an integrated cultural policy for Amazonia, respecting different ethnic and social contexts, recovering the true cultural identity of the region and serving as as reference for regional scientific and technological policy; create/consolidate programmes to obtain qualified human resources; establish/strengthen links with national and international agencies, identify sources of finance and provide technical support in execution of programmes and events; promote development for the benefit of the population and ecology of Amazonian countries. **Structure** General Assembly (every 2 years). Central Commission, comprising: President, 8 Vice-Presidents (one for each member country) and Executive Secretary. Vice-President; Treasurer. **Languages** English, Portuguese, Spanish. **Staff** 9.00 FTE, paid. **Finance** Members' dues and their extraordinary contributions to *Association of Amazonian Universities Support Fund (FUNDUNAMAZ)*. National organizations in Amazonian countries. International agencies: *European Community (inactive)*; *Ford Foundation (#09858)*; *Inter-American Development Bank (IDB, #11427)*; *International Development Research Centre (IDRC, #13162)*; *OAS (#17629)*; UNESCO; UNICEF. Budget (annual): about US$ 200,000. **Activities** Training/education; events/meetings; knowledge management/information dissemination. **Events** *General Assembly* Iquitos (Peru) 2010, *Conference on environmentally sound socio-economic development in the humid tropics* Belém (Brazil) 1996, *General Assembly* Belém (Brazil) 1996, *Conference on environmentally sound socio-economic development in the humid tropics* Manaus (Brazil) 1992, *Joint conference / General Assembly* Manaus (Brazil) 1992. **Publications** *UNAMAZ Bulletin*; *UNAMAZ News* in English, Portuguese, Spanish. *Série Cooperação Amazônica* – series; *Série Informação Amazônica* – series; *Série Pobreza e Meio Ambiente na Amazônia* – series. Books.
Members Institutions (33) and other members (39) in the 8 Amazonian countries:
Bolivia, Brazil, Colombia, Ecuador, Guyana, Peru, Suriname, Venezuela.
Member in 1 non-Amazonian country:
Canada.
IGO Relations *UNESCO (#20322)*; *Programme on Man and the Biosphere (MAB, #18526)*; *UNDP (#20292)*; *UNICEF (#20332)*; *United Nations University (UNU, #20642)*. **NGO Relations** *Global University Network for Innovation (GUNI, #10641)*; *Centre for Amazonian Studies, Glasgow (no recent information)*; *Inter-American Distance Education Consortium (#11428)*; *International Centre for Tropical Agriculture (#12527)*; *Sistema de Informação da Amazônia (SIAMAZ, no recent information)*.
[2015/XD2421/**D**]

- Association of Ambulatory Vaginal and Incontinence Surgeons / see International Society for Pelviperineology (#15348)
- Association américaine des autorités portuaires (#00775)
- Association américaine des bibliothèques (internationally oriented national body)
- Association américaine de constructeurs de routes (internationally oriented national body)
- Association américaine pour les droits étrangers (internationally oriented national body)
- Association américaine de juristes (#02110)
- Association américaine de marketing cinématographique / see Independent Film and Television Alliance
- Association américaine de personnes à la retraite (internationally oriented national body)
- Association américaine pour le progrès de la science (internationally oriented national body)
- Association américaine des spécialistes en langues (#00774)
- Association of American Chambers of Commerce in Latin America (internationally oriented national body)
- Association of American Geographers (internationally oriented national body)
- Association of American International Colleges and Universities (internationally oriented national body)
- Association of American Schools of Central America (see: #02367)

♦ Association of American Schools of Central America, Colombia, Caribbean and Mexico (Tri-Association) 02367

Exec Dir 2637 Ascot Drive, Florence SC 29501, USA. T. +18437995754.
URL: http://www.tri-association.org/
History 1989. **Aims** Explore ways to achieve better understanding through international *education*; improve the quality of *teaching* and *learning* in member schools; promote communication and cooperation among member institutions; facilitate cooperation with national, state and local governmental and non-governmental agencies in the field of international education. **Structure** Board of Directors, comprising Executive Director and the Presidents of the 3 regional organizations: *Association of American Schools of Central America (AASCA, see: #02367)*; *Association of Colombian-Caribbean American Schools (ACCAS, see: #02367)*; *Association of American Schools in Mexico (ASOMEX)*. **Languages** English, Spanish. **Staff** 1.00 FTE, paid. **Finance** Sources: fees; grants. Budget (annual): US$ 500,000. **Activities** Knowledge management/information dissemination; guidance/assistance/consulting. **Events** *Annual Conference* Santo Domingo (Dominican Rep) 2018, *Annual Conference* San José (Costa Rica) 2014, *Annual Conference* San José (Costa Rica) 2008, *Annual Conference* Puerto Vallarta (Mexico) 2007, *Annual Conference* Bogota (Colombia) 2006. **Publications** *Tri-Association Newsletter* (3 a year).
Members Member schools of regional associations in 13 countries:
Colombia, Costa Rica, Dominican Rep, Ecuador, El Salvador, Guatemala, Haiti, Honduras, Jamaica, Mexico, Nicaragua, Panama, Venezuela.
Invitational members (9) in 6 countries and territories:
Aruba, Cayman Is, Colombia, Ecuador, Guatemala, Mexico.
Corporate members (15) in 3 countries:
Canada, UK, USA.
Sponsoring Members (10) in one country (not specified).
[2018/XE2003/**E**]

- Association for American Schools in South America / see American International Schools in the Americas
- Association of Americans Resident Overseas (internationally oriented national body)
- Association d'Amérique pour les langues modernes (internationally oriented national body)
- Association des amidonneries de céréales de l'UE / see Starch Europe (#19966)
- Association des amidonneries de maïs de la CEE / see Starch Europe (#19966)
- Association des amidonniers et féculiers / see Starch Europe (#19966)
- Association des amis des chasses traditionnelles / see Association européenne des chasses traditionnelles (#02557)
- Association des amis de Jean Monnet / see Jean Monnet Association

♦ Association des amis du parc archéologique européen de Bliesbruck-Reinheim 02368

Contact 1 rue Robert Schuman, 57200 Bliesbruck, France. T. +33387350220. E-mail: bliesbruck@moselle.fr.
URL: http://www.archeo57.com/

Aims Unite those wishing to support and promote the European Archaeological Park project of Bliesbruck-Reinheim. **Languages** French, German. **Finance** Members' dues. Donations. **Activities** Events/meetings.
Members Individuals (75) in 2 countries:
France, Germany. [2018.06.21/XM1583/**E**]

- ♦ Association des amis de Robert Schuman / see Association Robert Schuman (#02896)
- ♦ Association des amitiés internationales (inactive)
- ♦ Association pour l'amour et la fraternité universelles (#20678)
- ♦ Association anatonale mondiale (#16941)
- ♦ Association des anatomistes / see Association of Morphologists (#02814)
- ♦ Association of Anatomists / see Association of Morphologists (#02814)
- ♦ Association des anciens du collège d'Europe (#02365)
- ♦ Association des anciens députés au Parlement européen (#08151)
- ♦ Association des anciens élèves de l'Ecole interaméricaine de bibliothéconomie (#00759)
- ♦ Association des anciens ESCP-EAP / see Association of ESCP Europe Students and Graduates (#02493)
- ♦ Association des anciens étudiants du Collège d'Europe / see Association of Alumni of the College of Europe (#02365)
- ♦ Association des anciens fonctionnaires internationaux – Genève (#02599)
- ♦ Association des anciens fonctionnaires internationaux – New York (#02600)
- ♦ Association des anciens fonctionnaires de l'UNESCO (#02601)
- ♦ Association des anciens de l'OMS (#02604)
- ♦ Association des anciens résidents et amis de la Cité internationale universitaire de Paris / see Alliance Internationale – Association des anciens et amis de la Cité internationale universitaire de Paris (#00693)

♦ Association pour l'anthropologie du changement social et du développement (APAD) 02369

Association for the Anthropology of Social Change and Development

SG c/o Inst des régions chaudes, Montpellier SUPAGRO, 1101 av Agropolis, BP 5098, 34093 Montpellier CEDEX 5, France. E-mail: contact@apad-association.org.
Pres IRD, BP 64501, 34394 Montpellier CEDEX 5, France.
URL: http://apad-association.org/

History Founded 5 Mar 1991, Paris (France), as *Association euro-africaine pour l'anthropologie du changement social et du développement (APAD) – Euro-African Association for the Anthropology of Social Change and Development.* **Aims** Promote social change and development as an area of research in general anthropology; promote anthropological perspectives in development practice; encourage exchange of ideas and experience and the opening up of national scientific communities in a Euro-African and international partnership. **Structure** Bureau; National Correspondents. **Languages** English, French. **Staff** Voluntary. **Finance** Members' dues. Fundraising. Annual budget: euro 10,000. **Activities** Monitoring/evaluation; research/documentation; politics/policy/regulatory; networking/liaising; training/education; events/meetings. **Events** *International Conference on Fieldwork Relations in the Context of Development or Emergency Access, Risks, Knowledge, Restitutions / Meeting* Montpellier (France) 2013, *Conference on engaging anthropology in development and social change* Ouagadougou (Burkina Faso) 2010, *Development, liberalism and modernity – trajectories for an anthropology of social change* Tervuren (Belgium) / Louvain-la-Neuve (Belgium) 2007, *Meeting* Yaoundé (Cameroon) 2005, *Meeting* Leiden (Netherlands) 2002. **Publications** *Anthropologie et Développement* – journal; *Bulletin de l'APAD*; *OpenEdition*. Books.
Members Individuals in 27 countries:
Austria, Belgium, Benin, Burkina Faso, Cameroon, Canada, Congo Brazzaville, Congo DR, Côte d'Ivoire, Denmark, France, Gabon, Germany, Guinea, Italy, Madagascar, Mali, Mauritania, Netherlands, Niger, Senegal, Spain, Sweden, Switzerland, Togo, UK, USA. [2018.09.05/XD1237/v/**D**]

- ♦ Association d'anthropologie méditerranéenne (internationally oriented national body)
- ♦ Association d'anthropologie sociale en Océanie (internationally oriented national body)
- ♦ Association anthropologique internationale de langue française / see Groupement des anthropologistes de langue française (#10756)
- ♦ Association des anthropologistes de langue française / see Groupement des anthropologistes de langue française (#10756)
- ♦ Association for the Anthropology of Social Change and Development (#02369)
- ♦ Association for Anthropology in Southern Africa / see Anthropology Southern Africa (#00851)
- ♦ Association pour l'antiquité tardive (internationally oriented national body)

♦ Association of Anti Virus Asia Researchers (AVAR) 02370

Chair Flat C and D, 8/F Yally Industrial Bldg, 6 Yip Fat Street, Wong Chuk Hang, Hong Kong, Central and Western, Hong Kong. E-mail: secretary@aavar.org.
URL: http://www.aavar.org/

History Jun 1998. **Aims** Prevent the spread and damage caused by malicious *software*; develop a cooperative relationship among anti malicious software experts in Asia. **Structure** Board of Directors. **Events** *International Conference* Osaka (Japan) 2019, *International Conference* Goa (India) 2018, *International Conference* Beijing (China) 2017, *International Conference* Kuala Lumpur (Malaysia) 2016, *International Conference* Danang (Vietnam) 2015.
Members Corporations experts on computer virus in 11 countries and territories:
Australia, China, Hong Kong, India, Japan, Korea Rep, Philippines, Singapore, Taiwan, UK, USA. [2019.07.30/XJ1521/**D**]

- ♦ Association L'appel / see Appel aide aux enfants victimes de conflits
- ♦ Association pour l'Appel de Genève (internationally oriented national body)

♦ Association for Applied Animal Andrology (AAAA) 02371

Sec/Treas Univ of Calgary, 2500 University Dr NW, Calgary AB T2N 1N4, Canada. E-mail: animal-andr@gmail.com – animalandrology@gmail.com.
URL: https://animalandrology.wildapricot.org/

History Formally inaugurated Nov 1998, Herceghalom (Hungary). Registration: Canada. **Aims** Stimulate and disseminate information on applied animal andrology. **Structure** Board of Directors. **Languages** English. **Staff** 0.50 FTE, paid. **Finance** Sources: members' dues; sponsorship. Other sources: proceedings from meetings and CE programmes. **Activities** Events/meetings. **Events** *Conference* 2022, *Biennial Conference* Bologna (Italy) 2020, *Biennial Conference* New Orleans, LA (USA) 2018, *Biennial Conference* Tours (France) 2016, *Biennial Conference* Sydney, NSW (Australia) 2014. **Publications** Meeting proceedings. **Members** Individuals in 20-25 countries. Membership countries not specified. [2022/XJ4040/**C**]

- ♦ Association of Applied Biologists (internationally oriented national body)

♦ Association of Applied Geochemists (AAG) 02372

Business Manager c/o AEG Business Office, PO Box 26099, 72 Robertson Rd, Nepean ON K2H 9R0, Canada. T. +16138280199. Fax +16138289288. E-mail: office@sappliedgeochemists.org.
Sec US Geological Survey, PO Box 25046, MS 973, Denver Federal Centre, Denver CO 80225, USA. T. +13032361849. Fax +13032363200.
URL: http://www.appliedgeochemists.org/

History 1970. Former names and other names: *Association of Exploration Geochemists (AEG)* – former (1970). **Aims** Provide a forum for exchange of ideas and technical findings; advance the science of geochemistry as it relates to exploration and the environment; facilitate acquisition and distribution of scientific knowledge; promote exchange of information; encourage research and development; advance the status of the profession. **Structure** Executive Council; Councillors; Regional Councillors; Committees (13). **Languages** English. **Staff** 0.50 FTE, paid. **Finance** Members' dues. **Activities** Events/meetings; training/education; research and development; awards/prizes/competitions; knowledge management/information dissemination. **Events** *International Applied Geochemistry Symposium (IAGS)* Viña del Mar (Chile) 2022, *International Applied Geochemistry Symposium* Viña del Mar (Chile) 2021, *International Applied Geochemistry Symposium* Viña del Mar (Chile) 2020, *International Applied Geochemistry Symposium* Vancouver, BC (Canada) 2018, *International Applied Geochemistry Symposium* Tucson, AZ (USA) 2015. **Publications** *Explore* (4 a year); *Geochemistry: Exploration, Environment, Analysis* (4 a year). *Handbook of Exploration Geochemistry* – series. *Bibliography of Exploration Geochemistry.* **Members** Fellows (voting); Members (non-voting); Students individuals (500) in over 60 countries (not specified). **NGO Relations** Member of: *International Union of Geological Sciences (IUGS, #15777).* [2021/XD1493/v/**D**]

- ♦ Association for Applied Human Pharmacology (internationally oriented national body)
- ♦ Association for Applied Solar Energy / see International Solar Energy Society (#15564)
- ♦ Association Apprentissages Sans Frontières (internationally oriented national body)
- ♦ Association for Appropriate Technologies / see FAKT – Consult for Management, Training and Technologies
- ♦ Association arabe des journalistes sportifs (#00954)
- ♦ Association arabe de littérature comparée (inactive)
- ♦ Association arabe des pilotes de ligne (inactive)
- ♦ Association arabe des routes (inactive)
- ♦ Association arabe de science politique (inactive)
- ♦ Association arabe de sociologie (no recent information)

♦ Association of Arab and European Universities (AEUA) 02373

Secretariat PO Box 352, 2501 JC The Hague, Netherlands.
URL: http://www.aeua.net/

History 1998, Netherlands, by Lutfia Rabbani Foundation. Registered in accordance with Dutch law, 2000. **Aims** Facilitate and stimulate collaboration between universities in European and Arab countries at institutional, departmental and faculty levels; develop human resources and promote understanding between cultures and exchanges between the civil societies involved. **Structure** Board of 7, including Chairperson and representation from *Association of Arab Universities (AARU, #02374)* and *European University Association (EUA, #09027).* **Events** *Conference* Amman (Jordan) 2014, *Presidents Meeting* Groningen (Netherlands) 2011. **NGO Relations** Supports: *Programme for Palestinian-European-American Cooperation in Education (PEACE Programme, #18527).* [2014/XJ5020/**D**]

- ♦ Association of Arab Geologists / see Arab Geologists' Association (#00967)
- ♦ Association of Arab Institutes and Centres for Economic and Social Research (inactive)

♦ Association of Arab Universities (AARU) 02374

Association des universités arabes (AUA)

SG PO Box 121, Tabarbour, Amman 11947, Jordan. T. +96265062048. Fax +96265062051. E-mail: secgen@aaru.edu.jo.
URL: http://www.aaru.edu.jo/

History Dec 1964, Cairo (Egypt). Founded when representatives of Arab Universities drafted a Constitution which was approved by the Council of *League of Arab States (LAS, #16420)*, Sep 1964. Registration: Egypt. **Aims** Enhance cooperation among Arab universities and institutes of higher education and scientific research. **Structure** General Conference; Executive Council; General Secretariat. Affiliated institutions include: *Arab Council for Student Activities (no recent information).* **Languages** Arabic. **Staff** 23.00 FTE, paid. **Finance** Sources: fees for services; members' dues; sale of publications. **Activities** Certification/accreditation; events/meetings; financial and/or material support; knowledge management/information dissemination; projects/programmes; research and development; training/education. **Events** *International Arab Conference on Information Technology* Abu Dhabi (United Arab Emirates) 2022, *Arab-Euro Conference on Higher Education* Murcia (Spain) 2018, *Arab-Euro Conference on Higher Education* Rabat (Morocco) 2017, *Arab-Euro Conference on Higher Education* Barcelona (Spain) 2016, *Middle East and North Africa Higher Education Leadership Forum* Abu Dhabi (United Arab Emirates) 2015. **Publications** *Journal of the Association of Arab University* (4 a year). Specialized journals hosted by member universities and by societies of peer faculties; guides; directories; seminar reports.
Members Active; Associate. Arab universities and institutes (400) in 21 countries:
Algeria, Bahrain, Djibouti, Egypt, Iraq, Jordan, Kuwait, Lebanon, Libya, Mauritania, Morocco, Oman, Palestine, Qatar, Saudi Arabia, Somalia, Sudan, Syrian AR, Tunisia, United Arab Emirates, Yemen.
Included in the above, 6 institutions affiliated to Arab League, listed in this Yearbook:
Arab Academy for Science, Technology and Maritime Transport (AASTMT, #00891); Arab Academy of Banking and Financial Sciences (AABFS); Arab Open University (AOU); High Arab Institute for Translation (HAIT); Institute of Arab Research and Studies (no recent information); Naif Arab University for Security Sciences (NAUSS, #16929).
Consultative Status Consultative status granted from: *ECOSOC (#05331)* (Ros C); *UNESCO (#20322)* (Associate Status). **NGO Relations** Member of (1): *International Association of Universities (IAU, #12246).* Cooperates with (2): *Association of Arab and European Universities (AEUA, #02373); United Nations Academic Impact (UNAI, #20516).* [2021.06.21/XD3342/y/**D**]

- ♦ Association des architectes du Commonwealth (#04301)
- ♦ Association des archivistes ecclésiastiques (#05279)

♦ Association of Arctic Expedition Cruise Operators (AECO) 02375

Exec Dir Postboks 162, 9252 Tromsø, Norway. E-mail: aeco@aeco.no.
URL: http://www.aeco.no/

History 2003. **Aims** Manage responsible, environmentally friendly and safe tourism in the Arctic. **Structure** Executive Committee; Committees; Resource Groups. Secretariat. **Activities** Events/meetings. **Events** *Annual Meeting* Oslo (Norway) 2022, *Annual Meeting* Oslo (Norway) 2020, *Annual Meeting* Oslo (Norway) 2019, *Annual Meeting* Oslo (Norway) 2018.
Members Full in 11 countries:
Australia, Canada, Denmark, France, Germany, Netherlands, Norway, Sweden, Switzerland, UK, USA.
Provisional in 7 countries:
Germany, New Zealand, Norway, Portugal, Switzerland, UK, USA.
Associate in 5 countries:
France, Monaco, Poland, Sweden, USA.
Affiliate in 17 countries and territories:
Australia, Belgium, Canada, China, Croatia, Denmark, Finland, France, Germany, Greenland, Iceland, Netherlands, Norway, Russia, Switzerland, UK, USA. [2021/XM8035/**C**]

- ♦ Association arctique nordique (inactive)
- ♦ Association of Arid Lands Studies (internationally oriented national body)
- ♦ Association des armateurs d'Amérique centrale (no recent information)
- ♦ Association des armateurs des Caraïbes (#03554)
- ♦ Association des armateurs nordiques (#17501)
- ♦ Association of Arts Administration Educators (internationally oriented national body)
- ♦ Association des arts du Pacifique (#17928)
- ♦ Association d'asbeste du Pacifique Sud (inactive)

♦ Association of Asian Athletics Coaches (AAAC) 02376

Pres c/o Chinese Athletics Assn, no 4 Tiyuguan Road, 100763 Beijing, China. T. +861087183441. Fax +861067142515.

History 2002. **Structure** Council. Executive Committee, comprising President, Senior Vice-President and Secretary-Treasurer. **Events** *Congress* Wuxi (China) 2004.
Members in 45 countries and territories:
Afghanistan, Bahrain, Bangladesh, Bhutan, Brunei Darussalam, Cambodia, China, Hong Kong, India, Indonesia, Iran Islamic Rep, Iraq, Japan, Jordan, Kazakhstan, Korea DPR, Korea Rep, Kuwait, Kyrgyzstan, Laos, Lebanon, Macau, Malaysia, Maldives, Mongolia, Myanmar, Nepal, Oman, Pakistan, Palestine, Philippines, Qatar, Saudi Arabia, Singapore, Sri Lanka, Syrian AR, Taiwan, Tajikistan, Thailand, Timor-Leste, Turkmenistan, United Arab Emirates, Uzbekistan, Vietnam, Yemen.
NGO Relations *Asian Athletics Association (AAA, #01348); World Athletics (#21209).* [2008/XM0867/**D**]

♦ Association of Asian Confederation of Credit Unions (ACCU) 02377

Confédération des coopératives d'épargne et de crédit d'Asie

Chief Executive Office 5th Floor FSCT Bldg, No 199 Nakornin Rd (Rama V), Bangkruay District, Bangkok, 11130, Thailand. T. +6624961262 – +6624961264. Fax +6624961263. E-mail: ranjith@aaccu.coop – accumail@aaccu.coop.
URL: http://www.aaccu.coop/

History 28 Apr 1971. Incorporated into *World Council of Credit Unions (WOCCU, #21324)*, 19 May 1971. **Aims** Promote, strengthen and assist in organization and promoting credit unions and similar financial organizations so as to enable them to fulfil their potential as effective instruction instruments for socio-economic development of individuals in the market place. **Structure** General Meeting (annual); Board of Directors. Includes: *Asia Fund for Credit Union Development (AFCUD, see: #02377)*. **Languages** English. **Staff** 6.00 FTE, paid. 10 project staff. **Finance** Sources: members' dues. Funding from development assistance agencies, including: *Agriterra* Netherlands; *Catholic Organization for Relief and Development (Cordaid)* Netherlands; Canadian Cooperation Association (CCA). **Activities** Capacity building; events/meetings; research and development; training/education. **Events** *Annual General Meeting* Nonthaburi (Thailand) 2020, *Annual General Meeting* Kuala Lumpur (Malaysia) 2019, *Forum* Kuala Lumpur (Malaysia) 2019, *Annual General Meeting* Manila (Philippines) 2018, *Forum* Manila (Philippines) 2018. **Publications** *Monthly Management Report/ACCU Newsletter* (12 a year); *ACCU News* (4 a year). *ACCU Handbook*. Annual report; training reports and manuals.
Members Regular(16) in 13 countries and territories:
Bangladesh, Hong Kong, India, Indonesia, Japan, Korea Rep, Nepal, Papua New Guinea, Philippines, Sri Lanka, Taiwan, Thailand, Vietnam.
Affiliate (13) in 11 countries and territories:
Australia, Bangladesh, Cambodia, Germany, Malaysia, Mongolia, Myanmar, Pakistan, Philippines, Singapore, Timor-Leste.
Included in the above, 1 international organization listed in this Yearbook:
Internationale Raiffeisen Union e.V. (IRU, #13291).
Supporters (185 organizations) in 9 countries:
Australia, Bangladesh, India, Indonesia, Korea Rep, Malaysia, Nepal, New Zealand, Philippines.
Consultative Status Consultative status granted from: *ECOSOC (#05331)* (Special). **NGO Relations** Member partners: *International Co-operative Alliance (ICA, #12944)*; *Internationale Raiffeisen Union e.V. (IRU, #13291)*; *World Council of Credit Unions (WOCCU, #21324)*. Member of: *International Cooperative Banking Association (ICBA, #12945)*; *Social Performance Task Force (SPTF, #19343)*. Stakeholder in: *Child and Youth Finance International (CYFI, inactive)*. [2021.06.09/XD4279/**D**]

♦ Association of Asian Constitutional Courts / see Association of Asian Constitutional Courts and Equivalent Institutions (#02378)

♦ Association of Asian Constitutional Courts and Equivalent Institutions (ACC) 02378

Contact Mahkamah Konstitusi RI Jl, Medan Merdeka Barat No 6, Jakarta 10110, Indonesia. T. +62213529000. Fax +62213520177. E-mail: humas@mahkamahkonstitusi.go.id.
URL: https://aacc.mahkamahkonstitusi.go.id/

History Jul 2010, Jakarta (Indonesia), following conferences and preparatory committee activities. Original title: *Association of Asian Constitutional Courts (ACC)*. **Aims** Promote: protection of human rights; guarantee of democracy; implementation of the rule of law; independence of constitutional courts and equivalent institutions; cooperation and exchange of experience and information among members. **Structure** Congress; Board; Joint Permanent Secretariats in Indonesia and Korea Rep. **Languages** English, Russian. **Activities** Events/meetings; training/education; knowledge management/information dissemination; guidance/assistance/consulting; networking/liaising. **Events** *Secretariat for Research and Development International Symposium* Seoul (Korea Rep) 2021, *Secretariat for Research and Development International Symposium* Seoul (Korea Rep) 2019, *Conference of the AACC SRD Jurisdictions and Organization of AACC Members* Seoul (Korea Rep) 2018, *Meeting* Seoul (Korea Rep) 2017, *Congress* Bali (Indonesia) 2016.
Members Courts of 16 countries:
Afghanistan, Azerbaijan, Indonesia, Kazakhstan, Korea Rep, Kyrgyzstan, Malaysia, Mongolia, Myanmar, Pakistan, Philippines, Russia, Tajikistan, Thailand, Türkiye, Uzbekistan.
IGO Relations Participates in: *World Conference on Constitutional Justice (WCCJ, #21298)*. [2017/XJ8264/**D***]

♦ Association of Asian Election Authorities (AAEA) 02379

Association des autorités électorales en Asie

Election Commissioner c/o Election Commission of India, Nirvachan Sadan, Ashoka Road, New Delhi, Delhi 110001, New Delhi DELHI 110001, India.
URL: http://www.aaea-sec.org/

History 10 Feb 1998, Manila (Philippines). Founded by *International Foundation for Electoral Systems (IFES, #13669)*. **Aims** Promote and institutionalize open and transparent elections, independent election authorities, professional election administration, citizen participation in the electoral and civic process, information sharing; develop information resources. **Structure** General Assembly. Executive Board. **Languages** English. **Staff** 3.00 FTE, paid. **Finance** Sources: donations; members' dues. **Activities** Events/meetings; projects/programmes. Projects include: development of Asian-electoral information resources; election observation missions; exchange of election-related materials; arrangement of professional development opportunities. **Events** *General Assembly* Seoul (Korea Rep) 2011, *Executive Board Meeting* Seoul (Korea Rep) 2010, *International seminar on absentee voting* Taipei (Taiwan) 2010, *Executive Board Meeting* Taipei (Taiwan) 2009, *General Assembly* Taipei (Taiwan) 2008.
Members National Election Commissions of 17 countries and territories:
Afghanistan, Bangladesh, Bhutan, Cambodia, India, Indonesia, Kazakhstan, Korea Rep, Kyrgyzstan, Mongolia, Nepal, Pakistan, Papua New Guinea, Philippines, Sri Lanka, Taiwan, Tajikistan.
IGO Relations Cooperation agreement with: *International Institute for Democracy and Electoral Assistance (International IDEA, #13872)*. [2017/XD7003/**D**]

♦ Association of Asian Insurance Commissioners (no recent information)

♦ Association of Asian and Pacific Arts Festivals (AAPAF) 02380

Secretariat c/o China Shanghai Intl Arts Festival, No 211 Kangding Road – Room 2402, Yihai Bldg, 200041 Shanghai, China. T. +862167220440. Fax +862167220919. E-mail: secretariat@aapaf.org.
URL: http://www.aapaf.org/

History 19 Jun 2004, Singapore, as *Association of Asian Performing Arts Festivals (AAPAF)*. Current title adopted 2012. **Aims** Promote international cooperation between Asian festivals and similar organizations; support development and promotion of artists and festival organizations in Asia; facilitate and create opportunities for cooperation in artistic productions and operational fields; encourage exchange of experience and knowledge. **Structure** General Meeting (annual); Council, including Chair and Vice-Chair; Secretariat. **Finance** Members' dues. **Activities** Knowledge management/information dissemination; awards/prizes/competitions; training/education. **Events** *Annual Meeting* Shanghai (China) 2014, *Annual Meeting* Shanghai (China) 2013, *Annual Meeting* Shanghai (China) 2012, *Annual Meeting* Shanghai (China) 2010, *Annual general meeting / Annual Meeting* Seoul (Korea Rep) 2009.
Members Full; Associate. Members in 16 countries:
Australia, Belgium, Bosnia-Herzegovina, China, Hong Kong, Indonesia, Japan, Korea Rep, Macau, Mexico, New Zealand, Palestine, Russia, Singapore, Thailand, USA.
Included in the above, 1 organization listed in this Yearbook:
European Festivals Association (EFA, #07242). [2015.01.19/XM2442/**D**]

♦ Association of Asian-Pacific Operational Research Societies within IFORS (APORS) 02381

Gen Sec Suite 14 A Cyber One, 11, Eastwood Avenue, Eastwood City, Cyberpark, Bagumbayan, 1110 Quezon City, Philippines. T. +6324399496. E-mail: info@apors.org.
URL: http://apors.asia/

History 1985. Founded as a regional organization of national societies within *International Federation of Operational Research Societies (IFORS, #13493)*. **Aims** Advance operations research in the Asia-Pacific region. **Structure** Executive Committee; Organizing Committee. **Languages** English. **Finance** Sale of publications. **Events** *Triennial International Conference* Cebu City (Philippines) 2022, *Triennial Conference* Kathmandu (Nepal) 2018, *Triennial Conference* Kuching (Malaysia) 2015, *Triennial Conference* Xian (China) 2012, *Conference on Operations Research Pathways to Sustainable Development* Penang (Malaysia) 2010. **Publications** *Asia-Pacific Journal of Operational Research* (2 a year).
Members Societies (12), grouping 5,250 individuals, in 12 countries and territories:
Australia, China, Hong Kong, India, Iran Islamic Rep, Japan, Korea Rep, Malaysia, Nepal, New Zealand, Philippines, Singapore. [2022/XE3080/**E**]

♦ Association of Asian Parliaments for Peace / see Asian Parliamentary Assembly (#01653)
♦ Association of Asian Performing Arts Festivals / see Association of Asian and Pacific Arts Festivals (#02380)

♦ Association of Asian Social Science Research Councils (AASSREC) 02382

Association des conseils asiatiques pour la recherche en sciences sociales

SG c/o Academy of the Social Sciences in Australia, GPO Box 1956, Canberra ACT 2601, Australia. T. +61262491788.
URL: https://aassrec.org/

History 26 May 1973, Shimla (India). Founded within the framework of *Asia-Pacific Information Network in Social Sciences (APINESS, inactive)*, in accordance with the recommendation of Regional Conference of the National Commission for UNESCO. Statutes approved at 1st Conference, 1975, Teheran (Iran Islamic Rep); most recently amended at 14th Conference, Nov 2001, Hanoi (Vietnam). **Aims** Encourage development of social sciences in Asia and the Pacific, with due regard to their national and cultural traditions, and promote research, teaching, training and dissemination of knowledge in the field; identify major areas of national, regional and international development efforts in order to organize cross-national research. **Structure** General Conference (normally every 2 years); Executive Council. Secretariat, headed by Secretary-General. **Languages** English. **Finance** Sources: members' dues. **Activities** Events/meetings; knowledge management/information dissemination; projects/programmes; research and development. **Events** *Biennial General Conference* Hanoi (Vietnam) 2019, *Biennial General Conference* Beijing (China) 2017, *Biennial General Conference* Taipei (Taiwan) 2015, *Biennial General Conference* Cebu City (Philippines) 2013, *Biennial General Conference* Manado (Indonesia) 2011. **Publications** *Asian Social Scientists*. Conference reports and proceedings; brochures; research project publications.
Members Full: National Social Science Research Councils, Academies of Social Sciences or similar bodies in 14 countries:
Australia, Bangladesh, China, India, Indonesia, Iran Islamic Rep, Japan, Korea Rep, Malaysia, New Zealand, Philippines, Sri Lanka, Thailand, Vietnam.
Associate: national organizations with related functions; regional social sciences organizations; international funding agencies. Members in 2 countries and territories:
Philippines, Taiwan.
Consultative Status Consultative status granted from: *UNESCO (#20322)* (Consultative Status). **IGO Relations** *Management of Social Transformations (MOST, #16562)*; *UNESCO Asia and Pacific Regional Bureau for Education (#20301)*. [2020.06.23/XD6075/**D**]

♦ Association of Asian Societies for Bioinformatics (unconfirmed)

♦ Association for Asian Studies in Africa (A-ASIA) 02383

Secretariat Univ of Ghana, Legon, Ghana. T. +23330397462. E-mail: cas@ug.edu.gh.
URL: http://www.ukna.asia/

History Founded Nov 2012, Chisamba (Zambia), at Asian Studies in Africa Roundtable. Registered in accordance with the law of Ghana. **Aims** Increase capacity enhancement of institutions, programmes and scholars. **Structure** Steering Committee; Secretariat. **Activities** Events/meetings. **Events** *A-Asia Africa-Asia Conference* Dar es Salaam (Tanzania UR) 2018, *A-Asia Africa-Asia Conference* Accra (Ghana) 2015. **NGO Relations** *International Convention of Asia Scholars (ICAS)*; *International Institute for Asian Studies, Leiden (IIAS)*. [2020/XM7769/**E**]

♦ Association for Asian Studies, Ann Arbor (internationally oriented national body)

♦ Association of Asia Pacific Advertising Media (AAPAM) 02384

Contact 99 Building, Jl Mampang Prapatan Raya no 99, Jakarta 12760, Indonesia. T. +62217990005. Fax +62217990253.
URL: http://apmf.com/

History 2003. **Activities** *Asia Pacific Media Forum (APMF)*. **Events** *Forum* Bali (Indonesia) 2016, *Forum* Bali (Indonesia) 2008, *Forum* Bali (Indonesia) 2006, *Asia Pacific media forum* Bali (Indonesia) 2005. **NGO Relations** *Asian Federation of Advertising Associations (AFAA, #01452)*. [2018/XM0183/**D**]

♦ Association of Asia Pacific Airlines (AAPA) 02385

Main Office 36th Floor, Menara Maxis, Kuala Lumpur City Centre, 50088 Kuala Lumpur, Malaysia. E-mail: info@aapa.org.my – ap@aapa.org.my.
URL: http://www.aapairlines.org/

History 1966, Manila (Philippines). Former names and other names: *Orient Airlines Research Bureau* – former (1966 to 1970); *Orient Airlines Association (OAA)* – former (1970 to Apr 1997); *Asian Airline Association* – alias. Registration: EU Transparency Register, No/ID: 148659915430-51. **Aims** Serve as a forum for articulation of members' views on matters and problems of common interest; foster close cooperation and bring about an atmosphere conducive to stimulation of the travel and *tourism* industry; enhance role of national flag carriers as instruments for international cooperation in the economic, social and cultural fields. **Structure** Assembly of Presidents (annual); Secretariat; Executive Committee; Working Committees; Working Groups. Departments (3): Industry Affairs; Technical Affairs; Research and Statistics. **Languages** English. **Staff** 20.00 FTE, paid. **Finance** Members' dues. Annual assessments from members. **Activities** cover every aspect of civil aviation where airlines feel they can work together for mutual benefit. **Events** *Asia Pacific Aviation Safety Seminar* Ho Chi Minh City (Vietnam) 2021, *Asia Pacific Aviation Safety Seminar* Ho Chi Minh City (Vietnam) 2020, *Annual Assembly of Presidents* Kuala Lumpur (Malaysia) 2020, *Annual Assembly of Presidents* Kuala Lumpur (Malaysia) 2019, *Emergency Response Conference* Singapore (Singapore) 2019. **Publications** *AAPA Annual Statistical Report*. Annual Report.
Members Membership open to international airlines based within times zones GMTplus7 and GMTplus12. National airlines in 13 countries and territories:
Australia, Brunei Darussalam, China, Hong Kong, Indonesia, Japan, Malaysia, New Zealand, Philippines, Singapore, Taiwan, Thailand, Vietnam.
NGO Relations Member of: *Air Transport Action Group (ATAG, #00614)*; *Flight Safety Foundation (FSF, #09795)*. [2021/XD4470/**D**]

♦ Association of Asia-Pacific Business Schools (AAPBS) 02386

Manager KAIST Business School, 85 Hoegiro, Dongdaemoon-gu, Seoul 02455, Korea Rep. T. +8229583293. Fax +8229583290. E-mail: secretariat.aapbs@gmail.com.
URL: http://www.aapbs.org/

History 17 Oct 2004, Seoul (Korea Rep). **Aims** Advance and represent business and management education in the Asia-Pacific region. **Structure** Officers: President; Vice-President; Executive Members; Council Member; Executive Director. **Languages** English. **Finance** Sources: members' dues. **Activities** Events/meetings; training/education. **Events** *Academic Conference* Nagoya (Japan) 2022, *Annual Meeting* Chiang Mai (Thailand) 2021, *Academic Conference* Lanzhou (China) 2021, *Annual Meeting* Bangkok (Thailand) 2020, *Academic Conference* Lanzhou (China) 2020. **Publications** Annual Case Journal Compilation.
Members 139 in 32 countries and territories:
Abu Dhabi, Australia, Belgium, Brunei Darussalam, Chile, China, France, Germany, Hong Kong, India, Indonesia, Japan, Kazakhstan, Korea Rep, Kyrgyzstan, Lebanon, Malaysia, New Zealand, Pakistan, Papua New Guinea, Peru, Philippines, Poland, Russia, Singapore, Spain, Taiwan, Thailand, UK, United Arab Emirates, USA, Vietnam.
Included in the above, 1 organization listed in this Yearbook:
Asian Institute of Management (AIM, #01518).
NGO Relations Member of (1): *EFMD – The Management Development Network (#05387)*. [2022.02.16/XM2383/**D**]

♦ Association of Asia Pacific Performing Arts Centres (AAPPAC) 02387

SG 1 Esplanade Drive, Singapore 038981, Singapore. T. +6568288341. Fax +6563373633. E-mail: aappac@esplanade.com.
URL: https://www.aappac.com/en/home/

History 1996. **Aims** Establish the Asia Pacific region as a leader in the performing arts industry. **Structure** Executive Council; Secretariat. **Languages** English, Mandarin Chinese. **Activities** Awards/prizes/competitions; knowledge management/information dissemination; networking/liaising; research and development. **Events** *Annual Conference* Taipei (Taiwan) 2020, *Annual Conference* Manila (Philippines) 2019, *Annual Conference* Auckland (New Zealand) 2018, *Annual Conference* Tongyeong (Korea Rep) 2015, *Annual Conference* Singapore (Singapore) 2014. **Publications** *AAPPAC Newsletter* (4 a year).

Members Art centres and organizations (74) in over 20 countries. Full in 13 countries and territories:
Australia, China, Hong Kong, India, Japan, Korea Rep, Macau, Malaysia, New Zealand, Philippines, Singapore, Sri Lanka, Taiwan.
Peak Business Circles (3):
Global Cultural Districts Network; *International Artist Managers' Association (IAMA, #11673)*; *International Society for the Performing Arts Foundation (ISPA, #15350)*.
Business Circles in 12 countries and territories:
Australia, Canada, China, France, Hong Kong, Indonesia, Korea Rep, Russia, Singapore, Spain, UK, USA.
NGO Relations Member of (1): *International Artist Managers' Association (IAMA, #11673)*.
[2021/XM1719/y/**D**]

♦ Association of Asia Pacific Physical Societies (AAPPS) 02388

Association des sociétés de physique de l'Asie et du Pacifique

Headquarters Hogil Kim Memorial Bldg, 501 POSTECH, 67 Cheongam-ro, Nam-gu, Pohang-si, Gyeongsangbuk-do, Pohang NORTH GYEONGSANG 37673, Korea Rep. T. +82542798663. Fax +82542798679. E-mail: aapps@apctp.org.
URL: http://www.aapps.org/

History 15 Oct 1989, when formally constituted, following work of an ad hoc committee set up 1988, Hong Kong, at 3rd Asia Pacific Physics Conference. Regional network of *UNESCO Office, Jakarta – Regional Bureau for Sciences in Asia and the Pacific (#20313)*. **Aims** Advance knowledge of *physics* in the Asia Pacific region, including research, application and teaching, especially through international collaboration. **Structure** General Meeting. Council of 9 to 15 members. Conference Executive Committee. Officers: President; Vice-President; Secretary; Treasurer. Secretariat rotates. **Languages** English. **Finance** Members' dues: US$ 200. Other sources: voluntary donations. Annual budget: US$ 40,000. **Activities** Organizes: *Asia Pacific Physics Conference* (every 2 years); symposia; workshops. Grants AAPPS Physics Award. **Events** *Asia Pacific Physics Conference* Seoul (Korea Rep) 2022, *Asia Pacific Physics Conference* Kuching (Malaysia) 2019, *Council Meeting* Pohang (Korea Rep) 2018, *International Conference on Quantum Dots* Jeju (Korea Rep) 2016, *IUPAP Conference on Computational Physics* Guwahati (India) 2015. **Publications** *AAPPS Bulletin* (2 a year).
Members Full; associate, national organizations (17) in 15 countries and territories:
Australia, China, Hong Kong, India, Indonesia, Japan, Korea Rep, Malaysia, Nepal, New Zealand, Philippines, Singapore, Taiwan, Thailand, Vietnam.
Included in the above, 2 organizations listed in this Yearbook:
ASEAN Institute of Physics (ASEANIP, #01199); *South East Asia Theoretical Physics Association (SEATPA, #19799)*.
[2022/XD3054/**D**]

- ♦ Association asiatique d'aide aux hémophiles (inactive)
- ♦ Association asiatique des chirurgiens pédiatres (#01333)
- ♦ Association asiatique d'experts juridiques en brevets (#01655)
- ♦ Association asiatique de recherche sur la paix (#01991)
- ♦ Association asiatique de recyclage (inactive)
- ♦ Association asiatique de tourisme pour les étudiants (inactive)
- ♦ Association d'Asie et du Pacifique des institutions financières de développement (#02472)
- ♦ Association de l'Asie et du Pacifique des professeurs et éducateurs de physique (inactive)
- ♦ Association de l'Asie du Sud-Est (inactive)
- ♦ Association for Assessment and Accreditation of Laboratory Animal Care International / see AAALAC International
- ♦ Association pour l'assistance au développement / see AGIOMONDO
- ♦ Association des astronautes européens (inactive)
- ♦ Association d'athlétisme amateur d'Asie / see Asian Athletics Association (#01348)
- ♦ Association d'athlétisme amateur d'Océanie / see Oceania Athletics Association (#17651)
- ♦ Association d'athlétisme d'Amérique du Nord, d'Amérique centrale et des Caraïbes (#17563)
- ♦ Association d'athlétisme d'Océanie (#17651)
- ♦ Association of Australasian IB Schools / see IB Schools Australasia (#11039)
- ♦ Association of Australasian International Baccalaureate Schools / see IB Schools Australasia (#11039)
- ♦ Association of Authorized European Adoption Agencies / see Euradopt (#05596)
- ♦ Association des autorités électorales en Asie (#02379)
- ♦ Association des autorités locales européennes pour une politique énergétique locale durable / see Energy Cities (#05467)
- ♦ Association pour l'avancement en Afrique des sciences de l'agriculture (no recent information)
- ♦ Association pour l'avancement des études scandinaves au Canada (internationally oriented national body)
- ♦ Association pour l'avancement de la politique, de la recherche et du développement au Tiers-monde (inactive)

♦ Association of Avian Veterinarians (AAV) 02389

Exec Dir PO Box 9, Teaneck NJ 07666, USA. T. +17204584111. Fax +17203983496. E-mail: office@aav.org.
Pres address not obtained. E-mail: cgreenac@utk.edu.
International Committee address not obtained. E-mail: international-committee@aav.org.
URL: http://www.aav.org/

History 1980. **Aims** Advance and promote avian medicine, stewardship and conservation. **Structure** Includes *European Association of Avian Veterinarians (EAAV, #05949)*. **Activities** Research programs; scholarships. **Events** *AAV Annual Conference / Annual Conference* San Antonio, TX (USA) 2015, *Annual Conference* New Orleans, LA (USA) 2014, *Annual Conference* Jacksonville, FL (USA) 2013, *Annual Conference* Louisville, KY (USA) 2012, *Annual Conference* Seattle, WA (USA) 2011. **Publications** *Journal of Avian Medicine and Surgery (JAMS)* (4 a year).
Members Individuals Active; Associate; Technician; Student. Student Chapters. Members (mainly in USA) in 37 countries and territories:
Argentina, Australia, Austria, Belgium, Canada, China, Czechia, Denmark, Finland, France, Germany, Guam, Guatemala, Hong Kong, Israel, Italy, Japan, Luxembourg, Malaysia, Mexico, Netherlands, New Zealand, Norway, Poland, Portugal, Puerto Rico, Singapore, Slovenia, South Africa, Spain, Sweden, Switzerland, Thailand, UK, United Arab Emirates, USA.
NGO Relations Instrumental in setting up: *European College of Zoological Medicine (ECZM, #06631)*.
[2015/XF2268/**F**]

♦ Association de l'aviculture, de l'industrie et du commerce de volailles dans les pays de l'Union européenne (AVEC) 02390

Association of Poultry Processors and Poultry Trade in the EU Countries – Vereinigung der Geflügelschlächtereien des Geflügelimport- und Exporthandels der Europäischen Union

SG Rue du Luxembourg 47-51, 1050 Brussels, Belgium. T. +3222381082 – +3222381083. Fax +3222381084. E-mail: avec@avec-poultry.eu.
URL: https://avec-poultry.eu/

History 5 Oct 1966, Holten (Netherlands). Former names and other names: *Association of Poultry Processors and Poultry Import and Export Trade in the EC Countries* – former (1966); *Association des centres d'abattage de volailles et du commerce d'importation et d'exportation de volailles des pays de la CE* – former (1966); *Vereinigung der Geflügelschlächtereien des Geflügelimport- und Exporthandels der EG-Länder* – former (1966); *Association of Poultry Processors and Poultry Import and Export Trade in the EU Countries* – former (23 Nov 2004); *Association des centres d'abattage de volailles et du commerce d'importation et d'exportation de volailles des pays de l' Union européenne (AVEC)* – former (23 Nov 2004); *Vereinigung der Geflügelschlächtereien des Geflügelimport- und Exporthandels der Europäischen Union* – former (23 Nov 2004); *Association of Poultry Processors and Poultry Import and Export Trade in the EU Countries* – alias. Registration: EU Transparency Register, No/ID: 9803788883-16; Belgium. **Aims** Defend the interests of poultry processors and the poultry import and export trade in EU countries, as well as protect their rights and functions. **Structure** General Assembly (annual); Board; Presidency; Secretariat, headed by Secretary General and Director. **Languages** English, French. **Staff** 3.00 FTE, paid. **Finance** Members' dues. **Activities** Networking/liaising. **Events** *Annual General Assembly* Budapest (Hungary) 2019, *Annual General Assembly* Vienna (Austria) 2018, *Annual General Assembly* Helsinki (Finland) 2017, *Annual General Assembly* Lisbon (Portugal) 2016, *Annual General Assembly* Marseille (France) 2014.
Members Representative trade associations of poultry slaughterhouses and of poultry import and export trade (18) in 16 countries:
Austria, Belgium, Czechia, Denmark, Finland, France (2), Germany, Hungary, Italy, Netherlands, Poland, Portugal, Romania, Spain (2), Sweden, UK.
IGO Relations Recognized by: *European Commission (EC, #06633)*; *United Nations Economic Commission for Europe (UNECE, #20555)*. Regular contacts with: *Council of the European Union (#04895)*; *European Parliament (EP, #08146)*. **NGO Relations** Member of: *European Food Sustainable Consumption and Production Round Table (European Food SCP Roundtable, #07289)*; *Federation of European and International Associations Established in Belgium (FAIB, #09508)*; *International Poultry Council (IPC, #14628)*. Regular contacts with: *COPA – european farmers (COPA, #04829)*; *European Liaison Committee for Agricultural and Agri-Food Trades (#07687)*; *Fédération européenne des fabricants d'aliments composés pour animaux (FEFAC, #09566)*; *General Confederation of Agricultural Cooperatives in the European Union (#10107)*; *Liaison Centre for the Meat Processing Industry in the EU (#16452)*; *Union européenne du commerce du bétail et de la viande (UECBV, #20394)*.
[2021/XE0126/ty/**E**]

- ♦ Association des avocats latinoaméricains pour la défense des droits del'homme (no recent information)
- ♦ Association babel international / see Babel International

♦ Association for Baha'i Studies (ABS) 02391

Association d'études baha'ies

Office Manager 34 Copernicus Street, Ottawa ON K1N 7K4, Canada. T. +16132331903. Fax +16132333644. E-mail: abs-na@bahai-studies.ca.
URL: http://www.bahai-studies.ca/

History 1975, Toronto (Canada), as a Canadian association. Subsequently membership extended to North America and afterwards worldwide. **Aims** Stimulate, coordinate and present original research on the Baha'i *faith*. **Languages** English. **Staff** 2.00 FTE, paid. 1 contract. **Finance** Members' dues. Other sources: conference registrations; sale of publications. **Activities** Research/documentation; events/meetings. **Events** *Annual Conference* Garden Grove, CA (USA) 2015, *Annual Conference* Toronto, ON (Canada) 2014, *Annual Conference* Toronto, ON (Canada) 2014, *Annual Conference* Irvine, CA (USA) 2013, *Annual Conference* Montréal, QC (Canada) 2012. **Publications** *ABS Bulletin* (4 a year); *Journal of Baha'i Studies* (3 a year). *Baha'i Studies* – series.
Members Autonomous branches and affiliates 45 countries:
Albania, Argentina, Australia, Austria, Barbados, Belgium, Belize, Bolivia, Botswana, Brazil, Cameroon, Canada, Chile, China, Colombia, Cuba, Cyprus, Denmark, Finland, France, Germany, Greece, Haiti, Hong Kong, Iceland, India, Ireland, Israel, Italy, Japan, Kenya, Malta, Netherlands, New Zealand, Norway, Poland, South Africa, Spain, St Lucia, Sweden, Switzerland, Türkiye, UK, USA, Zambia.
[2015.08.26/XF3785/**F**]

♦ Association of the Balkan Chambers (ABC) 02392

No fixed address address not obtained. E-mail: ic@mchamber.mk – tmilunovic@pkcg.org – bcci@bcci.bg.
URL: https://www.bcci.bg/bulgarian/abc.htm

History Sep 1994, Mangalia (Romania). Sept 1994, Mangalia (Romania), at the initiative of the Bulgarian and Romanian Chambers of Commerce and Industry. **Aims** Ensure promotion and development of ABC business communities; facilitate communication and business cooperation by means of a modern and efficient network information system. **Structure** General Assembly. Office rotates annually among member countries. **Languages** English. **Finance** By the budget of each Chamber member. **Activities** Research and development; networking/liaising. **Events** *General Assembly* Macedonia 2015, *General Assembly* Athens (Greece) 2014, *General Assembly* Nicosia (Cyprus) 2012, *General Assembly* Sarajevo (Bosnia-Herzegovina) 2010, *General Assembly* Tirana (Albania) 2009. **Information Services** *ABC Network System*.
Members Chambers of Commerce in 10 countries:
Albania, Bosnia-Herzegovina, Bulgaria, Cyprus, Greece, Montenegro, North Macedonia, Romania, Serbia, Türkiye.
[2020.06.04/XD6449/**D**]

♦ Association of the Balkan News Agencies (ABNA) 02393

General Secretariat 154 Egnatias street, 546 36 Thessaloniki, Greece. T. +302310244101. Fax +302310244105.
Gen Sec Piata Presei Libere nr 1 – sector 1, Bucharest, Romania. T. +40212076110. Fax +40213170707.
Pres address not obtained. T. +35929881719.
URL: http://www.abnaorg.eu/

History 26 Jun 1995, Thessaloniki (Greece). **Aims** Increase cooperation between news agencies; promote peace and friendship in the region.
Members News agencies (11) in 9 countries:
Albania, Bosnia-Herzegovina, Bulgaria, Greece, North Macedonia, Romania, Serbia, Slovenia, Türkiye. [2017/XD9224/**D**]

- ♦ Association balte pour les enfants handicapés (no recent information)
- ♦ Association of Baltic National Parks (inactive)

♦ Association of Baltic Numismatists (ABN) 02394

Pres Estonian History Museum, Pikk 17, 10123 Tallinn, Estonia.

History Founded 28 Aug 2005, Riga (Latvia). **Aims** Maintain cooperation between numismatists in the Baltic countries. **Structure** Annual Meeting. **Languages** English, German, Russian. **Staff** None. **Finance** Members' dues. **Activities** Events/meetings; publishing activities. **Publications** *Numismatica Baltica* – series. *Between Klaipeda and Turku* (2016).
Members Individuals in 5 countries:
Belarus, Estonia, Finland, Latvia, Lithuania. [2017.09.18/XM1582/v/**D**]

- ♦ Association bancaire pour l'Euro (#05647)
- ♦ Association des banques centrales africaines (#02352)
- ♦ Association des banques populaires pour l'assistance aux pays en voie de développement / see Association des banques populaires pour la coopération et le développement
- ♦ Association des banques populaires pour la coopération et le développement (internationally oriented national body)
- ♦ Association des banquiers de l'Afrique de l'Ouest (no recent information)
- ♦ Association des banquiers arabes (#00905)
- ♦ Association des banquiers internationaux de Floride (internationally oriented national body)
- ♦ Association of Baptists for Evangelism in the Orient / see Association of Baptists for World Evangelism
- ♦ Association of Baptists for World Evangelism (internationally oriented national body)
- ♦ Association du Barreau Africain (#00220)
- ♦ Association du Barreau près la Cour Pénale Internationale (#13109)
- ♦ Association de la baryte (#03180)
- ♦ Association de baseball et softball de l'Afrique (#00158)
- ♦ Association of Basic Science Teachers in Dentistry (internationally oriented national body)
- ♦ Association de basketball des pays du Golfe arabe (inactive)
- ♦ Association BATIK International / see BATIK International
- ♦ Association Baytna pour le Soutien de la Société Civile (internationally oriented national body)
- ♦ Association for the Behavioral Treatment of Sexual Aggressives / see Association for the Treatment of Sexual Abusers

♦ Association for Behavior Analysis International (ABAI) 02395

CEO 550 W Centre Ave, Portage MI 49024, USA. T. +12694929310. Fax +12694929316.
URL: http://www.abainternational.org/

History 1974. Former names and other names: *ABA International* – alias. **Aims** Promote experimental, theoretical and applied analysis of behaviour. **Structure** Executive Council; Committees; Board. **Activities** Events/meetings. **Events** *International Conference* Dublin (Ireland) 2022, *International Conference* Dublin (Ireland) 2021, *Annual Convention* Portage, MI (USA) 2020, *International Conference* Stockholm (Sweden) 2019, *International Conference* Paris (France) 2017. **Publications** *Behavior Analysis in Practice* (4 a year); *Perspectives on Behavior Science* (4 a year); *The Psychological Record* (4 a year); *Inside Behavior Analysis* (3 a year); *Behavior and Social Issues* (2 a year); *The Analysis of Verbal Behavior* (2 a year).

Members Full in 48 countries:
Albania, Australia, Bahrain, Belgium, Bermuda, Brazil, Canada, Chile, China, Colombia, Cyprus, Denmark, Finland, France, Germany, Greece, Guatemala, Iceland, India, Indonesia, Ireland, Israel, Italy, Japan, Korea Rep, Kuwait, Mexico, Netherlands, New Zealand, Norway, Peru, Philippines, Poland, Portugal, Romania, Saudi Arabia, Singapore, Spain, Sweden, Switzerland, Taiwan, Thailand, Türkiye, UK, United Arab Emirates, USA, Venezuela, Vietnam.
Affiliated chapters (76) in 28 countries:
Albania, Australia, Brazil, Canada, China, Colombia, France, Iceland, India, Ireland, Israel, Italy, Japan, Jordan, Korea Rep, Mexico, New Zealand, Norway, Philippines, Poland, Saudi Arabia, Spain, Sweden, Switzerland, Taiwan, UK, USA, Venezuela.
International organizations (1):
Asociación Latinoamericana de Analisis y Modificación del Comportamiento (ALAMOC, #02179).
[2021/XF1572/F]

♦ Association for Behavioural and Cognitive Therapies (internationally oriented national body)

♦ Association of Behavioural Researchers on Asians (ABRA) 02396

Contact Ctr for Environment-Behaviour Studies, Fac of Architecture/Planning/Surveying, Univ Teknologi MARA, 40450 Shah Alam, Selangor, Malaysia. E-mail: amerabra@gmail.com – membership@amerabra.org.
URL: http://www.amerabra.org/

History Official formative meeting at Asia/Pacific International Conference on Environment-Behaviour Studies (AicE-Bs), 8 Dec 2010, Kuching (Malaysia). Registered in accordance with Malaysian law, Oct 2014. **Finance** Members' dues. **Events** *AicE-Bs Conference* Sydney, NSW (Australia) 2017, *AicE-Bs Conference* Edinburgh (UK) 2016, *AicE-Bs Conference* Barcelona (Spain) 2015, *Asia Pacific international conference on environment-behaviour studies* Cairo (Egypt) 2014, *Asia Pacific international conference on environment-behaviour studies* Taipei (Taiwan) 2014. [2016/XJ2658/D]

- ♦ Association belge des africanistes (internationally oriented national body)
- ♦ Association Belgique – Bolivie – Amérique latine (internationally oriented national body)
- ♦ Association Belgo-Hollandaise (inactive)
- ♦ Association Benelux des conseils en marques et modèles / see Benelux Association for Trademark and Design Law (#03199)
- ♦ Association Benelux pour le droit des marques et modèles (#03199)
- ♦ Association Benelux pour la science horticole (#03205)
- ♦ Association de béton armé de l'Amérique centrale et du Panama (inactive)
- ♦ Association for Better Land Husbandry (internationally oriented national body)
- ♦ Association for Better Living and Education (see: #03922)
- ♦ Association for Biblical Higher Education (internationally oriented national body)
- ♦ Association de bibliothécaires et documentalistes agricoles d'Afrique de l'Ouest (inactive)
- ♦ Association des bibliothèques d'Afrique orientale (inactive)
- ♦ Association des Bibliothèques Botaniques et Horticoles Européennes / see European Botanical and Horticultural Libraries Group (#06383)
- ♦ Association de bibliothèques internationales / see Association of International Librarians and Information Specialists (#02754)
- ♦ Association des bibliothèques de judaïca et hébraïca en Europe (inactive)
- ♦ Association des bibliothèques privées (#18505)
- ♦ Association des bibliothèques publiques d'Amérique latine et des Caraïbes (no recent information)
- ♦ Association des bibliothèques universitaires, de recherche et institutionnelles dans les Caraïbes (#02413)
- ♦ Association of Binational Centers in Latin America (inactive)
- ♦ Association of Binational Families and Partnerships (internationally oriented national body)
- ♦ Association for Biodiversity Information / see NatureServe
- ♦ Association biographique internationale (#12350)
- ♦ Association des biologistes des Communautés européennes / see European Countries Biologists Association (#06852)
- ♦ Association des biologistes des pays européens (#06852)
- ♦ Association biosophique universelle (inactive)
- ♦ Association of Bookseller and Publisher Training Organizations in Europe (inactive)

♦ Association for Borderlands Studies (ABS) 02397

Exec Sec Arizona State Univ, School of Transborder Studies, PO Box 876303, Tempe AZ 85287-6303, USA. E-mail: absborderlands@asu.edu.
URL: http://www.absborderlands.org/

History Founded 1976 with an emphasis on the United States-Mexico borderlands; currently global in scope. Current bylaws amended 1996; revised 2012. Registered in the State of New Mexico (USA). **Aims** Study and exchange ideas, information and analysis of international borders and the processes and communities engendered by such borders. **Structure** Annual Meeting; Board of Directors; Regional Chapters. **Languages** English, Spanish. **Staff** 3.00 FTE, paid. **Finance** Sources: members' dues. Royalties. **Events** *Annual Conference* Seattle, WA (USA) 2025, *Annual Conference* San Antonio, TX (USA) 2024, *Annual Conference* Tempe, AZ (USA) 2023, *Annual Conference* Denver, CO (USA) 2022, *Annual Conference* Albuquerque, NM (USA) 2021. **Publications** *Journal of Borderlands Studies* (4 a year); *La Frontera* (2 a year) – newsletter.
Members Full in 45 countries:
Argentina, Australia, Austria, Azerbaijan, Belgium, Brazil, Bulgaria, Canada, China, Colombia, Croatia, Czechia, Denmark, Finland, France, Georgia, Germany, Greece, Hungary, India, Indonesia, Israel, Italy, Japan, Korea Rep, Latvia, Luxembourg, Malaysia, Mexico, Nepal, Netherlands, New Zealand, Nigeria, Norway, Poland, Portugal, Romania, Russia, Slovenia, Spain, Sweden, Switzerland, Türkiye, UK, USA.
NGO Relations Academic institutions and associations. [2019.12.13/XJ7182/C]

- ♦ Association des botanistes de l'Afrique de l'ouest (no recent information)
- ♦ Association of Breeders and European Distributors of Flower Seed Varieties / see International Association of Breeders and Distributors of Ornamental Plant Varieties (#11735)

♦ Association of BRICS Business Schools (ABBS) 02398

Contact Xavier Inst of Management and Entrepreneurship, Electronics City, Phase II, Hosur Road, Bangalore, Karnataka 560100, Bangalore KARNATAKA 560100, India. T. +918028528477 – +918028528498. Fax +918028520809. E-mail: chairmanblr@xime.org.
URL: http://brics-abbs.com/

History 31 Jan 2009, Bangalore (India). 'BRICS' derives from: Brazil, Russia, India, China and South Africa. **Aims** Promote cooperation and exchanges among business schools of BRICS member countries. **Structure** Board; President and 4 Vice-Presidents (representing all countries). **Languages** English. **Staff** 5.00 FTE, voluntary. **Finance** Sources: members' dues. **Activities** Events/meetings. **Events** *Biennial Conference* Moscow (Russia) 2015, *International Conference on Revisiting the MBA in the Asia Pacific Context* Bangalore (India) 2014, *International Conference on Problems of Management in the Real Economy* Moscow (Russia) 2013, *Biennial Conference* Shanghai (China) 2013, *Students Meeting* Shanghai (China) 2013. **Publications** *ABBS E-Journal. Doing Business in BRIC Countries – Legal Aspects.*
Members Business schools, universities and institutes of business and management education in 5 countries:
Brazil, China, India, Russia, South Africa.
IGO Relations Memorandum of Cooperation with: *International Monetary Fund (IMF, #14180)* Network of Anti-Money Laundering and Counter Financing of Terrorism (AML/CFT). [2023.02.20/XJ8265/E]

- ♦ Association des bureaux de garantie européens / see International Association of Assay Offices (#11715)
- ♦ Association for Business Communication (internationally oriented national body)
- ♦ Association of Business and Industrial Marketing for Europe (no recent information)
- ♦ Association of Business Process Management Professionals International (internationally oriented national body)
- ♦ Association des Cabinets d'Avocats d'Affaires Africains (unconfirmed)
- ♦ Association du cadmium (inactive)
- ♦ Association cambiste interarabe (#11455)
- ♦ Association cambiste internationale / see Financial Markets Association (#09767)
- ♦ Association of Canadian Universities for Northern Studies (internationally oriented national body)
- ♦ Association canadienne des anciens fonctionnaires internationaux (internationally oriented national body)
- ♦ Association canadienne d'éducation et de recherche pour la paix (internationally oriented national body)
- ♦ Association canadienne des études africaines (internationally oriented national body)
- ♦ Association canadienne d'études du développement international (internationally oriented national body)
- ♦ Association canadienne des études latinoaméricaines et caraïbes (internationally oriented national body)
- ♦ Association canadienne-française pour l'avancement des sciences / see Acfas
- ♦ Association canadienne de normalisation (internationally oriented national body)
- ♦ Association canadienne pour la santé mondiale (internationally oriented national body)
- ♦ Association canadienne des slavistes (internationally oriented national body)

♦ Association for Cancer Immunotherapy (CIMT) 02399

Acting Managing Dir Hölderlinstr 8, 55131 Mainz, Germany. T. +4961315547400. E-mail: office@cimt.eu.
URL: https://www.cimt.eu/

History 2002. Registration: Rhineland-Palatinate District court, No/ID: VR 3783, Start date: 7 Feb 2003, Germany, Mainz. **Aims** Facilitate knowledge exchange between academic and industry scientists, physicians and regulatory authorities who research and develop cancer immunotherapies. **Structure** Executive Board; Management Board. **Finance** Sources: donations; grants; meeting proceeds; sponsorship. **Activities** Awards/prizes/competitions; events/meetings; training/education. **Events** *Annual Meeting* Mainz (Germany) 2021, *International Cancer Immunotherapy Conference* New York, NY (USA) 2018, *International Cancer Immunotherapy Conference* Mainz (Germany) 2017, *International Cancer Immunotherapy Conference* New York, NY (USA) 2016, *International Cancer Immunotherapy Conference* New York, NY (USA) 2015. **NGO Relations** Member of (1): *European Network for Cancer Immunotherapy (ENCI, #07872)* (Founding). [2021/AA1965/D]

- ♦ Association caraïbéenne pour la recherche et l'action féministe (#03445)
- ♦ Association caraïbe pour l'environnement (#03481)
- ♦ Association des Caraïbes sur l'arriération mentale et les autres retards du développement (inactive)
- ♦ Association des Caraïbes pour la réadaptation des handicapés (inactive)
- ♦ Association des Caraïbes des thérapeutes de réadaptation (inactive)

♦ Association of Career Firms International (ACF International) 02400

Pres Burg De Monchyplein 41, 2585 DD The Hague, Netherlands.
URL: http://www.acf-international.net/

History 1982, as *Association of Outplacement Consulting Firms International (AOCFI)*, as an international non-profit trade association. 1996, Merged with *European Association of Outplacement (inactive)*, 1996. Changed name to *Association of Career Management Consulting Firms International*, 1998. **Aims** Promote best practice in the areas of outplacement services, coaching, and related activities. **Structure** International Board. Chapters: North America; Europe. **Finance** Members' dues. Annual budget: about US$ 300,000. **Activities** Organizes biennial conferences and webinars. **Events** *Annual Conference* Washington, DC (USA) 1996. **Publications** *ACF Newsletter*. Surveys.
Members Firms in 13 countries:
Austria, Denmark, Finland, France, Germany, Greece, Ireland, Netherlands, Portugal, Spain, Switzerland, UK, USA.
NGO Relations Links with national organizations. [2013.11.25/XN6145/F]

- ♦ Association of Career Management Consulting Firms International / see Association of Career Firms International (#02400)

♦ Association of Caribbean Beekeepers Organisations (ACBO) 02401

Pres 11 Farm Road, Hope Village, Hope Village, Trinidad-Tobago. E-mail: associationofcaribbeanbeekeepers@yahoo.com.

History Founded 18 Sep 2002, Kingston (Jamaica), during 3rd Caribbean Beekeeping Congress. **Aims** Ensure the sustainability of the Caribbean beekeeping sector while developing its competitiveness. **Structure** General Assembly; Executive Committee; Advisory Board. **Languages** English. **Staff** Voluntary. **Activities** Events/meetings; training/education. **Events** *Congress* Crown Point (Trinidad-Tobago) 2016, *Congress* St Croix (Virgin Is USA) 2014, *Caribbean Beekeeping Congress* Virgin Is USA 2014, *Strengthening Caribbean beekeeping, enhancing growth, adding value, sweetening the future* St George's (Grenada) 2011, *Strengthening Caribbean beekeeping, enhancing growth, adding value, sweetening the future* St George's (Grenada) 2010. **Members** Full; Associate; Honorary. Membership countries not specified. **NGO Relations** Member of: *International Federation of Beekeepers' Associations (APIMONDIA, #13370).* [2015/XM4007/E]

♦ Association of Caribbean, Central and South American Corrugators (ACCCSA) 02402

Asociación de Corrugadores del Caribe, Centro y Sur América

Exec Dir PO Box 681-1260 Plaza Colonial, San José, San José, San José, 681-1260, Costa Rica. T. +50625882436. Fax +50625882438. E-mail: info@acccsa.org.
URL: http://www.acccsa.org/

History 1980. **Structure** General Assembly of Associates; Board of Directors. **Languages** English, Spanish. **Finance** Sources: conventions; seminars; courses; sales of publications. **Activities** Events/meetings. **Events** *Convention* San José (Costa Rica) 2010, *Convention* Medellin (Colombia) 2009, *Convention* Argentina 2008, *Convention* Buenos Aires (Argentina) 2008, *Convention* Santo Domingo (Dominican Rep) 2007.
Members Full in 24 countries and territories:
Argentina, Bolivia, Brazil, Chile, Colombia, Costa Rica, Cuba, Dominica, Dominican Rep, Ecuador, El Salvador, Guadeloupe, Guatemala, Guyana, Honduras, Jamaica, Mexico, Nicaragua, Panama, Paraguay, Peru, St Lucia, Uruguay, Venezuela.
NGO Relations Member of: *International Corrugated Case Association (ICCA, #12974).* [2022/XD8957/D]

♦ Association of Caribbean Commissioners of Police (ACCP) 02403

Secretariat Manager 1st Floor, Baobab Tower, Warrens, St Michael, ST MICHAEL, Barbados. T. +12462718684. Fax +12462718694. E-mail: admin@accpolice.org.
URL: http://www.accpolice.org/

History 20 Aug 1987, Castries (St Lucia), by a resolution passed by 13 members. Constitution amended 1993, St Kitts-Nevis. Constitution and bye laws revised and approved 20 May 2000, Cayman Is; amended: 25 May 2001, St Lucia; 2 May 2013, Bermuda. **Aims** Act as the principal regional organization for promoting and facilitating: collaboration and cooperation in development and implementation of policing strategies, systems and procedures; professional and technical skills development of police officers; proactive measures to prevent crime and improve police community relations. **Structure** General Meeting (annual); Executive Committee; Ad-hoc Committees; Permanent Secretariat. **Languages** English. **Staff** 2.00 FTE, paid. **Finance** Sources: members' dues. Annual budget: 192,000 USD. **Activities** Awards/prizes/competitions; financial and/or material support; projects/programmes. **Events** *Annual Conference* 2021, *Annual Conference* Grand Cayman Is (Cayman Is) 2019, *Annual Conference* Montego Bay (Jamaica) 2018, *Annual Conference* Oranjestad (Aruba) 2017, *Annual Conference* Paramaribo (Suriname) 2016. **Publications** *United Against Crime* (annual) – magazine. Conference reports.
Members Ordinary; Associate; Corporate; Life. Commissioners in 26 countries and territories:
Anguilla, Antigua-Barbuda, Aruba, Bahamas, Barbados, Belize, Bermuda, Cayman Is, Curaçao, Dominica, French Antilles, Grenada, Guyana, Haiti, Jamaica, Montserrat, St Kitts-Nevis, St Lucia, St Maarten, St Vincent-Grenadines, Suriname, Trinidad-Tobago, Turks-Caicos, United Arab Emirates, Virgin Is UK, Virgin Is USA.
IGO Relations Active partner of: *International Criminal Police Organization – INTERPOL (ICPO-INTERPOL, #13110).* Memorandum of Understanding with: *Caribbean Customs Law Enforcement Council (CCLEC, #03487).* [2022/XD6876/v/D]

- ♦ Association of Caribbean Community Foundations / see Caribbean Philanthropy Network (#03538)

♦ Association of Caribbean Copyright Societies (ACCS) 02404

Mailing Address 139-141 Abercromby Street, Port-of-Spain, Trinidad-Tobago. T. +18686236101 ext2239. Fax +18686234755.
URL: http://www.accscaribbean.com/

History 2000, as *Caribbean Copyright Link (CCL)*. Also referred to as *Caribbean Regional Centre for Collective Management of Copyright*. **Aims** Provide clients (by extension copyright and related rights holders) with *data* management services. **Structure** Board of Directors, comprising President, Vice-President and 2 Directors. **Languages** English, Spanish. **Staff** 3.00 FTE, paid. **Activities** Researches unidentified works and performances in cooperation with national societies; monitors and maintains data standards for all incoming data; researches, exports or otherwise make regional data available to all societies worldwide and to other international data centres; maintains the integrity and functionality of the regional data network; carries out royalty distribution processing operations.
Members Copyright societies in 4 countries:
Barbados, Jamaica, St Lucia, Trinidad-Tobago.
IGO Relations Organizations involved: *Caribbean Community (CARICOM, #03476)*; *World Intellectual Property Organization (WIPO, #21593)*. **NGO Relations** Associate member of: *Confédération internationale des sociétés d'auteurs et compositeurs (CISAC, #04563)*. [2012/XE3293/**E**]

♦ Association of Caribbean Economists (no recent information)

♦ Association of Caribbean Electoral Organizations (ACEO) 02405

Association des organismes électoraux de la Caraïbe – Asociación de Organismos Electorales del Caribe

Secretariat Electoral Office of Jamaica, 43 Duke Street, Kingston, Jamaica. T. +187692204259. Fax +18769224058. E-mail: eojinfo@eoj.com.jm.
URL: http://www.theaceo.com/

History 30 Mar 1998, Puerto Rico. 30 Mar – 1 Apr 1998, Puerto Rico, during Founding General Assembly, and following Caribbean Election Network Conference, Jan 1997, Kingston (Jamaica), hosted by *International Foundation for Electoral Systems (IFES, #13669)*. Charter drafted by working group, Apr 1997, San Juan (Puerto Rico); formally signed by 22 countries and dependent territories during the Founding General Assembly. **Aims** Promote cooperation and mutual assistance among electoral organizations in the region in the pursuit of *democracy* by processes that ensure free, fair and peaceful elections. **Structure** General Assembly (annual); Executive Board; Secretariat located in Electoral Office, Kingston (Jamaica). **Languages** English. **Staff** 1.50 FTE, voluntary. **Finance** Members' dues are main source. **Events** *General Assembly* Georgetown (Guyana) 2011, *Annual General Assembly / General Assembly* Port-of-Spain (Trinidad-Tobago) 2010, *Annual General Assembly / General Assembly* Bridgetown (Barbados) 2009, *General Assembly* Kingston (Jamaica) 2008, *General Assembly* Kingston (Jamaica) 2001. **Publications** General Assembly reports.
Members Full in 20 countries and territories:
Anguilla, Antigua-Barbuda, Bahamas, Barbados, Belize, Bermuda, Cayman Is, Grenada, Guyana, Haiti, Jamaica, Montserrat, St Kitts-Nevis, St Lucia, St Vincent-Grenadines, Suriname, Trinidad-Tobago, Turks-Caicos, Virgin Is UK, Virgin Is USA.
Associate in 3 countries and territories:
Dominican Rep, Neth Antilles, Puerto Rico. [2019.12.02/XD7002/v/**D**]

♦ Association of Caribbean Higher Education Administrators (ACHEA) 02406

Sec c/o Univ of the West Indies, Regional Head Quarters, Mona, Jamaica. T. +18769771710 – +18769704721. Fax +18769772885.
URL: http://acheacaribbean.org/

History 1 Jul 2001, Kingston (Jamaica), at *University of the West Indies (UWI, #20705)*. **Aims** Promote the highest professional and ethical standards and continuing development of management capacity among those who have administrative and managerial responsibilities in higher education in the Caribbean. **Structure** General Meeting (annual); Committees (5). **Languages** English. **Finance** Annual conference registration fees; sponsorship. **Activities** Training/education; capacity building; networking/liaising. **Events** *Annual Conference* St Augustine (Trinidad-Tobago) 2015, *Annual conference and general meeting* Scarborough (Trinidad-Tobago) 2005, *Annual conference and general meeting / Annual Conference* Montego Bay (Jamaica) 2004, *Annual conference and general meeting / Annual Conference* Barbados 2003, *Annual conference and general meeting / Annual Conference* Port-of-Spain (Trinidad-Tobago) 2002. **Publications** *Journal of Arts Science and Technology Special Issue – vol 12* (2019).
Members in 5 countries and territories:
Antigua-Barbuda, Barbados, Jamaica, Trinidad-Tobago, Turks-Caicos.
IGO Relations *Eastern Caribbean Institute of Agriculture and Forestry (ECIAF, #05234)* is member. [2019.11.04/XM0334/**D**]

♦ Association of Caribbean Historians (ACH) 02407

Association des historiens de la Caraïbe – Asociación de Historiadores del Caribe – Associatie van Caribische Historici

Sec-Treas c/o History Dept – Xavier Univ, 3800 Victory Pkwy, Cincinnati OH 45207, USA.
URL: https://associationofcaribbeanhistorians.org/

History 1974. Founded on the initiative of Jacques Adelaide-Merlande and others, founding followed conferences started in 1969. **Aims** Encourage and stimulate research, writing and dissemination of Caribbean history; keep other professionals in the field in touch with new areas of research. **Structure** General Meeting (annual, at Conference); Executive Committee; Secretariat. **Languages** English, French, Spanish. **Staff** No paid staff. **Finance** Members' dues. **Activities** Events/meetings; awards/prizes/competitions. **Events** *Annual Conference* San Juan (Puerto Rico) 2023, *Annual Conference* Kingston (Jamaica) 2022, *Annual Conference* Gosier (Guadeloupe) 2021, *Annual Conference* Gosier (Guadeloupe) 2020, *Annual Conference* Willemstad (Curaçao) 2019. **Publications** *ACHistorians Bulletin* (2 a year). *Directory of Caribbean Historians* (1995). Selected papers; conference proceedings.
Members Individuals (492) in 33 countries and territories:
Antigua-Barbuda, Aruba, Australia, Austria, Bahamas, Barbados, Canada, Colombia, Cuba, Curaçao, Denmark, Dominican Rep, England, France, Germany, Guatemala, Haiti, Jamaica, Japan, Martinique, Mexico, Netherlands, New Zealand, Puerto Rico, Scotland, Spain, St Kitts-Nevis, St Lucia, Suriname, Sweden, Trinidad-Tobago, USA, Venezuela. [2022/XD1269/v/**D**]

♦ Association of Caribbean Media Workers (ACM) 02408

Mailing address 55 Caiman Circle, Elizabeth Gardens, St Joseph, Trinidad-Tobago. E-mail: acmmail@gmail.com.
Acting Pres address not obtained.
URL: http://www.acmpress.org/

History 2001, Bridgetown (Barbados). Replaced *Caribbean Association of Media Workers (CAMWORK, inactive)*. Establishment facilitated by *Pan American Health Organization (PAHO, #18108)*. **Aims** Promote: free movement of *journalists* in the region; free press legislation; training; ethics; welfare of freelance journalists; improved international relations; freedom of expression. **Structure** Executive. **Languages** English. **Staff** 7.00 FTE, voluntary. **Finance** Sources: grants; members' dues; revenue from activities/projects. **Members** Covers all countries of Association of Caribbean States. **IGO Relations** Cooperates with: *Caribbean Community (CARICOM, #03476)*; *UNESCO (#20322)*; *University of the West Indies (UWI, #20705)*. **NGO Relations** Member of: *Global Forum for Media Development (GFMD, #10375)*; *IFEX (#11100)*. Cooperates with: *Caribbean School of Media and Communication (CARIMAC, #03552)*; *International News Safety Institute (INSI, #14364)*; *International Press Institute (IPI, #14636)*. [2020.07.21/XD8585/**D**]

♦ Association of Caribbean Occupational Therapists 02409

Contact c/o Occupational Therapy Dept, Psychiatric Hosp, Black Rock, St Michael, ST MICHAEL, Barbados. T. +12464257209. E-mail: caribbeanot@gmail.com – acotmembership@gmail.com.

History 1991. **Events** *Biennial conference* Trinidad-Tobago 2007. **Members** Membership countries not specified. **NGO Relations** Member of: *World Federation of Occupational Therapists (WFOT, #21468)*. [2019.10.28/XD5059/**D**]

♦ Association of Caribbean and Research Libraries / see Association of Caribbean University, Research and Institutional Libraries (#02413)

♦ Association of Caribbean Social Work Educators (ACSWE) 02410

Asociación de Educadores de Trabajo Social del Caribe

Pres c/o Social Work Unit, Univ of the West Indies – Mona Campus, Kingston, Jamaica. E-mail: acswe2014@gmail.com.
Sec address not obtained.
URL: http://www.iassw-aiets.org/

History 10 Jul 1997, Port-of-Spain (Trinidad-Tobago), within *North American and Caribbean Association of Schools of Social Work (NACASSW, #17562)*. **Aims** Seek ways of improving standards of social work education in the Caribbean, as well as address issues of relevance to Caribbean social work educators and practitioners involved in training residing outside of the region; provide a forum in which issues related to development of social work education in the region can be discussed, where policy proposals can be developed and where moral and practical support can be given to colleagues. **Structure** General Meeting (every 2 years); Executive Committee. **Languages** English. **Staff** None. **Finance** Members' dues. Other sources: conference fees; grants. **Activities** Knowledge management/information dissemination; events/meetings; certification/accreditation; research/documentation; networking/liaising. **Events** *Biennial Conference* Curaçao 2013, *Biennial Conference* Willemstad (Curaçao) 2013, *Biennial Conference* Martinique 2011, *Biennial Conference* Guyana 2009, *Biennial conference* Port-of-Spain (Trinidad-Tobago) 2007. **Publications** *Caribbean Journal of Social Work* – also occassional special issues. Newsletter.
Members Full – individuals teaching in social work programmes in accredited educational institutions in the Caribbean; Associate – accredited supervisors/instructors of social work students; social work educators, practicum supervisors or social work staff training officers; individuals engaged in social work education; Affiliate – organizations in the Caribbean engaged in provision of training or setting and maintenance of standards related to the profession. Membership in 13 countries and territories:
Bahamas, Barbados, Belize, Canada, Grenada, Guyana, Jamaica, St Lucia, Suriname, Trinidad-Tobago, UK, USA, Virgin Is USA. [2019.02.27/XE4496/**E**]

♦ Association of Caribbean States (ACS) 02411

Association des Etats de la Caraïbe (AEC) – Asociación de Estados del Caribe (AEC)

SG 5-7 Sweet Briar Road, St Clair, PO Box 660, Port-of-Spain, Trinidad-Tobago. T. +18686229575. Fax +18686221653. E-mail: communications@acs-aec.org – mail@acs-aec.org.
URL: http://www.acs-aec.org/

History 24 Jul 1994, Cartagena de Indias (Colombia). 24 Jul 1994, Cartagena da Indias (Colombia), on signature of a draft convention, having been proposed, May 1992, in the final report of *West Indian Commission (inactive)*; and Conference of Heads of Government of *Caribbean Community (CARICOM, #03476)* reaffirming their confidence in the proposed Association, 5-8 Jul 1993, Nassau (Bahamas). Designed to include all the countries of the Caribbean basin. Headquarters in Trinidad-Tobago. Convention establishing the ACS came into force in 2007. **Aims** Strengthen the regional cooperation and integration process, so as to create an enhanced economic space in the region; preserve the environmental integrity of the Caribbean Sea which is regarded as the common patrimony of the peoples of the region; promote the sustainable development of the Greater Caribbean. **Structure** Permanent organs: Ministerial Council (principal organ for policy-making and direction); Secretariat. Special Committees (5): Trade Development and External Economic Relations; Transport; Sustainable Tourism; Disaster Risk Reduction; Budget and Administration. Council of National Representatives of the Special Fund. **Languages** English, French, Spanish. **Staff** 31.00 FTE, paid. **Finance** Members' dues. Budget (annual): US$ 1.5 million. **Activities** Priority areas of the work programme are: Trade, Sustainable Tourism, Transport and Disaster Risk Reduction. **Events** *Forum of Airline and Tourism Executives* Martinique 2013, *Meeting* Panama (Panama) 2013, *Meeting* Port-of-Spain (Trinidad-Tobago) 2012, *Meeting* Port-of-Spain (Trinidad-Tobago) 2011, *Meeting* Cartagena de Indias (Colombia) 2010. **Publications** *ACS Yearbook*.
Members Governments of 25 countries:
Antigua-Barbuda, Bahamas, Barbados, Belize, Colombia, Costa Rica, Cuba, Dominica, Dominican Rep, El Salvador, Grenada, Guatemala, Guyana, Haiti, Honduras, Jamaica, Mexico, Nicaragua, Panama, St Kitts-Nevis, St Vincent-Grenadines, Suriname, Trinidad-Tobago, Venezuela.
Associate Members (11):
Aruba, Bonaire Is, Curaçao, Guadeloupe, Guiana Fr, Martinique, Saba, St Barthélemy, St Eustatius, St Maarten, St Martin.
Founding Observers (6):
Caribbean Community (CARICOM, #03476); *Caribbean Tourism Organization (CTO, #03561)*; *Central American Integration System (#03671)*; *Secretaria Permanente del Tratado General de Integración Económica Centroamericana (SIECA, #19195)*; *Sistema Económico Latinoamericano (SELA, #19294)*.
Observers in 18 countries:
Argentina, Brazil, Canada, Chile, Ecuador, Egypt, Finland, India, Italy, Korea Rep, Morocco, Netherlands, Peru, Russia, Spain, Türkiye, UK, Ukraine.
Observer:
IGO Relations Cooperation agreement with: *International Hydrographic Organization (IHO, #13825)*; *International Maritime Organization (IMO, #14102)*; *Organisation internationale de la Francophonie (OIF, #17809)*. Member of: *Intergovernmental Organizations Conference (IGO Conference, #11498)*. Observer member of: SELA. Observer to General Assembly of: *United Nations (UN, #20515)*. Permanent Observer to: *ECOSOC (#05331)*. Involved in development and participation of: *Caribbean Action Plan (CAR, #03432)*.
- *Caribbean Disaster Emergency Management Agency (CDEMA, #03493)*;
- *Forum of Caribbean States (CARIFORUM, #09904)*;
- *Institute for the Integration of Latin America and the Caribbean (#11271)*;
- *International Civil Aviation Organization (ICAO, #12581)*;
- *IOC Sub-Commission for the Caribbean and Adjacent Regions (IOCARIBE, #16003)*;
- *Latin American Civil Aviation Commission (LACAC, #16297)*;
- *PAHO/WHO Health Emergencies Department (PHE, #18023)*;
- *Preparatory Commission for the Comprehensive Nuclear-Test-Ban Treaty Organization (CTBTO, #18482)*;
- *UNEP (#20299)*;
- *UNESCO (#20322)*;
- *United Nations Office for Disaster Risk Reduction (UNDRR, #20595)*. [2017/XD4036/y/**D***]

♦ Association of Caribbean Studies (no recent information)

♦ Association of Caribbean Tertiary Institutions (ACTI) 02412

Secretariat Alister McIntyre Bldg, CARICOM Research Park, Univ of The West Indies, Cave Hill Campus, St Michael, ST MICHAEL, Barbados. T. +12464170203 – +12464174495. E-mail: acti.office@yahoo.com – acti@cavehill.uwi.edu.
URL: http://www.acticaribbean.org/

History Founded 9 Nov 1990, Kingston (Jamaica). **Aims** Facilitate cooperation and collaboration among member institutions in academic, administrative and other areas; liaise between member institutions and regional partners in the management of tertiary education; provide a forum for articulating issues, ideas and procedures in developing and enhancing tertiary education; mediate on issues involving alliances and cooperation strategies adopted by member institutions; coordinate efforts of member institutions and regional partners in the management of tertiary education; communicate to member institutions/territories information, advice and guidance in the delivery of tertiary education. **Structure** General Assembly (annual); Council; Executive Committee. **Languages** English. **Staff** 2.00 FTE, paid. **Finance** Members' dues. **Activities** Research/documentation; capacity building. **Events** *Annual General Assembly* Bermuda 2015, *Annual General Assembly* Grenada 2011, *Annual general assembly* St George's (Grenada) 2011, *Annual General Assembly* Tortola Is (Virgin Is UK) 2010, *Annual General Assembly* Virgin Is UK 2010. **Publications** *ACTI Newsletter* (annual). Directory; strategic plan.
Members Full (68); Associate (19); Honorary (12). Members in 21 countries and territories:
Anguilla, Antigua-Barbuda, Bahamas, Barbados, Belize, Bermuda, Cayman Is, Dominica, Grenada, Guyana, Jamaica, Montserrat, St Kitts-Nevis, St Lucia, St Martin, St Vincent-Grenadines, Suriname, Trinidad-Tobago, Turks-Caicos, Virgin Is UK, Virgin Is USA.
IGO Relations *Caribbean Community (CARICOM, #03476)* is an associate member. **NGO Relations** Member of: *World Federation of Colleges and Polytechnics (WFCP, #21421)*. *Caribbean Evangelical Theological Association (CETA, #03499)* is Associate member. [2018.06.19/XD3086/**D**]

♦ Association of Caribbean Universities and Research Institutes / see Universities Caribbean (#20694)
♦ Association of Caribbean University and Research Institute Libraries / see Association of Caribbean University, Research and Institutional Libraries (#02413)

♦ Association of Caribbean University, Research and Institutional Libraries (ACURIL) 02413

Association des bibliothèques universitaires, de recherche et institutionnelles dans les Caraïbes – Asociación de Bibliotecas Universitarias, de Investigación e Institucionales del Caribe

Exec Sec ACURILNET, Executive Secretariat, PO Box 21337, San Juan PR PR 00931, USA. T. +17876129343. E-mail: executivesecretariat@acuril.org.
URL: http://acuril.uprrp.edu/

History 1969, San Juan (Puerto Rico). Founded as *Association of Caribbean University and Research Institute Libraries*, at a conference under the auspices of *Universities Caribbean (#20694)*. Subsequently referred to as *Association of Caribbean and Research Libraries*. Present title adopted 1976. Most recent constitution adopted 1992. **Aims** Facilitate development and use of libraries, archives and information services, and identification, collection and preservation of information resources in support of all intellectual and educational endeavours in the Caribbean area; strengthen archival, library and information professions in the region. **Structure** Annual Meeting. Executive Council (meets twice a year), comprising President, Vice-President (who is President-Elect), Past-President and 10 members, plus Executive Director and Treasurer (non-voting). Permanent Committees (5): Constitution and Bylaws; Cyber Notes; Finance; Membership; Continued Education. Special Interest Groups. Official archives held at: *Caribbean and Latin American Studies Library*. **Languages** English, French, Spanish. **Staff** 2.00 FTE, voluntary. **Finance** Members' dues. **Activities** Organizes regional projects to improve access to information produced or published in the region, including: microfilming archives and newspapers; increasing availability of documents and publications through collection and circulation of books, journals, reports, etc, by various regional institutions; indexing regional social science journals; meetings for special interest groups to review and plan, and to identify common problems. Holds annual Conferences and mid-year Executive Council Meetings. **Events** *Annual Conference* San Juan (Puerto Rico) 2013, *Annual Conference* Pétion-Ville (Haiti) 2012, *Annual Conference* Tampa, FL (USA) 2011, *Annual Conference* Santo Domingo (Dominican Rep) 2010, *Annual Conference* Guadeloupe 2009. **Publications** *ACURIL Cypber Notes*. Directories; conference proceedings.

Members Institutional libraries, archives and schools; Organizational national library associations and regional and other special organizations and associations; Personal individual librarians, archivists and others; Associate any of these categories outside the geographic area. Members in 27 countries and territories:
Antigua-Barbuda, Argentina, Bahamas, Barbados, Belize, Brazil, Canada, Colombia, Costa Rica, Cuba, Dominica, Dominican Rep, France, Guyana, Haiti, Jamaica, Mexico, Netherlands, Puerto Rico, St Kitts-Nevis, St Lucia, St Vincent-Grenadines, Suriname, Trinidad-Tobago, USA, Venezuela.
International member (1), listed in this Yearbook:
Commonwealth Library Association (COMLA, no recent information).

IGO Relations *Association of Caribbean States (ACS, #02411)*; *Information Society Program for Latin America and the Caribbean (INFOLAC, inactive)*; *UNESCO (#20322)*. **NGO Relations** International association member of: *International Federation of Library Associations and Institutions (IFLA, #13470)*, being represented on IFLA/LAC Standing Committee for the regional Latin American and Caribbean Division. [2020/XD4171/y/**D**]

♦ Association Caritative et Humanitaire des Ordres de Chevalerie (unconfirmed)

♦ Association of the Carpathian Region Universities (ACRU) 02414

SG Univ Veterinary Medicine Pharmacy, Komenského 73, 041 81 Košice, Slovakia. T. +421908716521. Fax +421556325293.
Pres Univ Babes-Bolyai, M Kogalniceanu Str Nr 1, 400084 Cluj-Napoca, Romania. T. +40264405300. Fax +40264591906.
URL: http://acru.uvlf.sk/

History 1994, Lublin (Poland), by 16 universities and colleges from the Carpathian region. Registered in accordance with Slovakian law. **Aims** Advance academic, scientific and cultural cooperation, taking advantage of the particular dynamics of the long established historic and cultural links developed in the Carpathian Region. **Structure** Working groups. **Languages** English. **Staff** No full-time staff. **Finance** Members' dues (annual): euro 700. **Events** *Annual Conference* Yalta, Crimea (Ukraine) 2011, *Annual Conference* Chernivtsi, Vinnytsia (Ukraine) 2010, *Annual Conference* Alba Iulia (Romania) 2009, *Annual Conference* Trencin (Slovakia) 2007, *Annual Conference* Rzeszów (Poland) 2006.

Members Universities and colleges in 6 countries:
Hungary, Poland, Romania, Serbia, Slovakia, Ukraine. [2014.06.01/XM2575/**E**]

♦ Association of Car Rental Industry Systems Standards / see ACRISS EEIG (#00079)
♦ Association Cartographique Internationale (#12446)
♦ Association of Catering Excellence (unconfirmed)

♦ Association of Catholic Education for Africa and Madagascar 02415

Association de l'education Catholique pour l'Afrique et Madagascar (ASSECAM)

SG Km 11, Boulevard du Centenaire de la Commune de Dakar, BP 3164, Dakar, Senegal. T. +2218345685. Fax +2218345685. E-mail: snepc@orange.sn.

History 1962, as *Regional Secretariat of Catholic Education for Africa and Madagascar (SRAM)* under the Doctrinal and Pastoral Commission of *Symposium of Episcopal Conferences of Africa and Madagascar (SECAM, #20077)*. Current name adopted 1998. **Aims** Increase cooperation and communication between the national secretariats of Catholic education and represent them at the international organizations, particularly interafrican organizations. **Structure** General Assembly. Sub-regions (5): French-Speaking Western Africa; English-Speaking Western Africa; Central Africa; Eastern Africa; Southern Africa. **Finance** Members' dues (annual), calculated according to the country's GNP. Other sources: Catholic education institutions; fundraising. **Events** *General Assembly* Kinshasa (Congo DR) 2003, *General Assembly* Dar es Salaam (Tanzania UR) 2001, *General assembly* Nairobi (Kenya) 1996.

Members Governments of 8 countries:
Benin, Burkina Faso, Côte d'Ivoire, Guinea, Mali, Niger, Senegal, Togo.

NGO Relations Regional antenna of: *Catholic International Education Office (#03604)*. [2010/XE1213/**E**]

♦ Association of Catholic Institutes of Education / see International Catholic Association of Institutes of Educational Sciences (#12448)

♦ Association of Catholic Universities and Higher Institutes of Africa and Madagascar (ACUHIAM) 02416

Association des universités et instituts catholiques d'Afrique et de Madagascar (ASUNICAM)

Exec Sec PO Box 307, 33113 Mwanza, Tanzania UR. T. +255756058511. Fax +255282550167. E-mail: acuhiam.asunicam@saut.ac.tz.

History Oct 1989. Founded as a regional association of *International Federation of Catholic Universities (IFCU, #13381)*. Current statutes adopted 13 May 2000, Nairobi (Kenya). Former names and other names: *Association des universités catholiques d'Afrique et de Madagascar* – former. **Aims** Promote higher education and Catholic faith in Africa, and connect its higher education scene with other institutions of higher education in Europe, America and Asia. **Structure** General Assembly (every 2 years). Executive Committee, composed of President, Executive Secretary and members of the Scientific Committee. Scientific Committee. **Languages** English, French, Portuguese. **Staff** Paid. **Finance** Sources: members' dues; revenue from activities/projects; subsidies. **Events** *General Assembly* Kinshasa (Congo DR) 2012, *General Assembly* Mwanza (Tanzania UR) 2010, *General Assembly* Bukavu (Congo DR) 2008, *General Assembly* Abidjan (Côte d'Ivoire) 2006, *General Assembly* Yaoundé (Cameroon) 2004. **Publications** *ACUHIAM Journal* (2 a year).

Members Universities and colleges (20) in 15 countries:
Angola, Congo Brazzaville, Congo DR, Côte d'Ivoire, Egypt, Ghana, Kenya, Madagascar, Mozambique, Nigeria, Rwanda, South Africa, Tanzania UR, Uganda, Zambia.
Founding members include the following 2 organizations listed in this Yearbook:
Catholic University of Eastern Africa, The (CUEA, #03610); *Université catholique d'Afrique centrale (UCAC)*.

NGO Relations Member of: *International Federation of Catholic Universities (IFCU, #13381)*. [2022.05.04/XE3791/y/**E**]

♦ Association catholique d'aide à l'Orient (#03606)
♦ Association catholique de coopération internationale (inactive)
♦ Association catholique internationale d'études médico-psychologiques (inactive)
♦ Association catholique internationale des oeuvres de protection de la jeune fille / see Association Catholique Internationale de Services pour la Jeunesse Féminine (#02417)
♦ Association catholique internationale de protection de la jeune fille / see Association Catholique Internationale de Services pour la Jeunesse Féminine (#02417)
♦ Association catholique internationale des sciences de l'éducation (#12448)

♦ Association Catholique Internationale de Services pour la Jeunesse Féminine (ACISJF/In Via) 02417

International Catholic Society for Girls – Asociación Católica Internacional de Servicios para la Juventud Femenina

Vice-Pres Maison des Associations, Rue des Savoises 15, 1205 Geneva, Switzerland. T. +41228000835. E-mail: acisjf_invia@greenmail.ch – acsjf.paris@wanadoo.fr.
URL: https://www.acisjf-invia.org/

History 19 Aug 1897, Fribourg (Switzerland). In 1956, Mexico, activities extended from Europe to include Latin America and the Caribbean. Present constitution adopted 1968, Geneva (Switzerland); amended Sep-Oct 1980, Rome, when the Society set up Regional Commissions. Statutes revised, 26 Apr 2007. Former names and other names: *Association catholique internationale des oeuvres de protection de la jeune fille (ACIOPJF)* – former (1897 to Oct 1964); *Association catholique internationale de protection de la jeune fille* – former alias. Registration: Switzerland. **Aims** Promote interests of young *women* outside their family circle; coordinate the activities of organizations and institutions which, throughout the world, form a network of services contributing to the wellbeing and safety of feminine youth; seek to ensure all round advancement of girls outside their family context, providing assistance, education and training and helping them find employment and a place in society; promote the establishment of service networks at national and regional levels. **Structure** General Assembly (about every 4 years). Executive Bureau. Officers: President-General; Vice-President General; Secretary. Counsellors. International Council. Regional Commissions (4): Africa; Cono Sur; Europe; Northern Latin America. National committees or federal groups of regional and local committees. International secretariat. **Languages** English, French, German, Spanish. **Staff** 1.00 FTE, paid. Voluntary. **Finance** Sources: gifts, legacies; members' dues. **Activities** Members provide: hostels for students, young persons, persons in difficulty, those in transit, young unmarried mothers and others; self-service restaurants; centres of preparation for life; literacy, scholastic-level remedial courses, language courses; vocational and professional training, social, cultural and religious education; schools for nursing assistants and social workers; cultural and sports centres; employment centres – in Europe, placement of young women in families as "au pairs"; information and advice centres; welcome posts at railway stations, road transport terminals and airports. These services are carried out by professionals and by competent volunteers, for whom continuing training is provided in some countries. **Events** *International Council* Rome (Italy) 2012, *International Council* Paderborn (Germany) 2011, *International Council* Paris (France) 2010, *International Council* Geneva (Switzerland) 2009, *General Assembly* Tarija (Bolivia) 2009. **Publications** *Boletin Informativo* in Spanish; *Contactos* in Spanish; *Contacts* in French; *Information Letter* in English; *Informationsbrief* in German; *Kontakte* in German; *Lettre d'Information* in French.

Members National committees or federal groups in 26 countries:
Argentina, Belgium, Benin, Bolivia, Burkina Faso, Cameroon, Chad, Colombia, Congo Brazzaville, Congo DR, Dominican Rep, France, Germany, Greece, Haiti, Honduras, Italy, Lebanon, Mauritius, Mexico, Portugal, Senegal, Spain, Switzerland, Togo, Uruguay.

Consultative Status Consultative status granted from: *ECOSOC (#05331)* (Ros C); *UNESCO (#20322)* (Consultative Status); *Council of Europe (CE, #04881)* (Participatory Status). **NGO Relations** Represented with: *World Union of Catholic Women's Organisations (WUCWO, #21876)*. Member of: *Forum of Catholic Inspired NGOs (#09905)*; *International Catholic Centre of Geneva (ICCG, #12449)*. [2021/XC1455/**C**]

♦ Association catholique mondiale pour la communication (#21264)
♦ Association de la cause freudienne (internationally oriented national body)

♦ Association for Cemetery and Crematoria in the Nordic Countries . 02418

Nordiska Förbundet för Kyrkogårdar och Krematorier (NFKK)

Chair SKKFs kansil finns pa, Sveavagen 116 i Stockholm, Box 190 71, SE-104 32 Stockholm, Sweden.
URL: http://www.nfkk.eu/

History Founded Sep 1997, by merger of *Nordic Association for Churchyard Culture (inactive)* and *Nordisk Samarbejdsråd inden for Kirkegårds- og Krematoriespörsmål (NSKK, inactive)*. **Structure** Board of 5 members. **Events** *Congress* Tampere (Finland) 2022, *Congress* Tampere (Finland) 2021, *Seminar* Drammen (Norway) 2020, *Congress* Copenhagen (Denmark) 2017, *Congress* Oslo (Norway) 2013.

Members National organizations (10) in 5 countries:
Denmark, Finland, Iceland, Norway, Sweden. [2016.06.27/XD8282/**D**]

♦ Association of Central African Centres for the Handicapped 02419

Association des centres pour handicapés de l'Afrique centrale (ACHAC)

SG BP 51, Butare, Rwanda. E-mail: achac.rdc2013@gmail.com.

History 1974. Registered in accordance with the law of Rwanda. Currently inactive due to the political situation in Rwanda. **Aims** Defend the rights and improve the situation of handicapped people in society and achieve their maximum possible *rehabilitation*, by promoting effective collaboration among centres, in particular in the use of up-to-date techniques, and by acting as joint spokesman for the centres with governments and with national and international organizations. **Structure** General Assembly (every 2 years). Executive Committee, comprising Secretary-General, Permanent Secretary, Regional (national) Secretaries and Treasurer. Commissions (4): Blind; Physically Handicapped; Auditive Impaired and Mute; Mentally Handicapped and Mentally Ill. Advisers in these specialties. **Languages** English, French. **Staff** 1.00 FTE, paid; 8.00 FTE, voluntary. **Finance** Members' dues, donations. **Activities** Training of personnel in specific handicaps. **Events** *General assembly* Bujumbura (Burundi) 1993, *Meeting* Buhimba (Zaire) 1991, *General Assembly* Goma (Zaire) 1990, *General Assembly* Kinshasa (Zaire) 1987, *General Assembly* Bujumbura (Burundi) 1985. **Publications** *Homme comme toi* (4 a year) – bulletin. *Un état complet de bien-être.*

Members Centres for the handicapped (53) in 3 countries:
Burundi, Congo DR, Rwanda.
Honorary members in 1 country:
Belgium.

NGO Relations Member of: *World Federation for Mental Health (WFMH, #21455)*. [2015/XD6352/**D**]

♦ Association of Central African Episcopal Conferences (#02448)
♦ Association of the Central Alps (#01081)
♦ Association of Central American and Caribbean Electoral Organizations / see Association of Electoral Organizations of Central America and the Caribbean (#02484)
♦ Association of Central American Peasant Organizations for Cooperation and Development (inactive)
♦ Association of Central American Societies of Neurosurgeons (unconfirmed)
♦ Association of Central and Eastern European Election Officials / see Association of European Election Officials (#02508)
♦ Association for the Central Europe-Atlantic Road (#02899)
♦ Association centre-européenne de libre-échange (no recent information)
♦ Association des centres d'abattage de volailles et du commerce d'importation et d'exportation de volailles des pays de la CE / see Association de l'aviculture, de l'industrie et du commerce de volailles dans les pays de l'Union européenne (#02390)
♦ Association des centres d'abattage de volailles et du commerce d'importation et d'exportation de volailles des pays de l' Union européenne / see Association de l'aviculture, de l'industrie et du commerce de volailles dans les pays de l'Union européenne (#02390)
♦ Association des centres du commerce international (#21862)
♦ Association des Centres culturels de rencontre – Réseau européen (internationally oriented national body)
♦ Association des centres européens serveurs de banques de données (inactive)
♦ Association des centres d'evaluation en langues en Europe (#02779)
♦ Association des centres pour handicapés de l'Afrique centrale (#02419)

♦ Association de centres laïcs chrétiens en Afrique (#02429)

♦ Association des Centres de recherche sur l'Utilisation Urbaine du Sous-sol (ACUUS) 02420

Associated research Centres for the Urban Underground Space (ACUUS)

Gen Manager 34 Prom Seville, Dollard-des-Ormeaux QC H9B 2S5, Canada. T. +15148800808. E-mail: info@acuus.org.
Pres address not obtained.
URL: https://www.acuus.org/index.php

History 1983, Australia. Founded at first conference. Secretariat inaugurated, 1997, Montréal QC (Canada). Registration: Industry Canada, No/ID: 331552-5, Start date: 1996, Canada. **Aims** Promote partnerships among all actors in the field of planning, management, research and uses of urban underground space. **Structure** General Assembly; Board of Directors. **Languages** English, French. **Staff** 2.00 FTE, voluntary. **Finance** Sources: meeting proceeds; members' dues. **Activities** Awareness raising; events/meetings; publishing activities; research/documentation. **Events** *International Conference* Singapore (Singapore) 2023, *International Conference* Helsinki (Finland) 2021, *International Conference* Helsinki (Finland) 2020, *International Conference* Hong Kong (Hong Kong) 2018, *International Conference* St Petersburg (Russia) 2016. **Publications** *ACUUS E-Newsletter* (12 a year); *ScoopIt!* – https://www.scoop.it/topic/underground-space. Proceedings. **Information Services** *Database for Worldwide Underground Space Development.*

Members Institutes; associations; universities; firms and individuals. Members in 18 countries and territories:
Belgium, Canada, China, Finland, France, Greece, Hong Kong, Iran Islamic Rep, Israel, Italy, Japan, Korea Rep, Russia, Serbia, Singapore, Sweden, UK, USA.

NGO Relations Cooperates with (1): *World Urban Campaign (WUC, #21893).* [2022.05.04/XE4487/**E**]

♦ Association centroaméricaine des facultés de médecine (no recent information)
♦ Association centroaméricaine de familles de disparus (no recent information)
♦ Association of the Cereal Starch Industries of the EU / see Starch Europe (#19966)
♦ Association of Certified Accountants / see Association of Chartered Certified Accountants
♦ Association of Certified Anti-Money Laundering Specialists (internationally oriented national body)

♦ Association of Certified Fraud Examiners (ACFE) 02421

Main Office Gregor Building, 716 West Ave, Austin TX 78701, USA. T. +15124789000. Fax +15124789297. E-mail: memberservices@acfe.com – info@acfe.com.
European Office 78 York Street, London, W1H 1DP, UK. E-mail: ukinquiries@acfe.com.
URL: http://www.acfe.com/

History 1988. Founded on the initiative of Joseph T Wells. **Aims** Fight fraud and *white-collar crime.* **Events** *Global Fraud Conference* Washington, DC (USA) 2023, *Africa Conference & Exhibition* 2022, *Anti-Fraud Leadership Summit* New York, NY (USA) 2022, *Fraud Conference Asia-Pacific* Singapore (Singapore) 2022, *Asia-Pacific Fraud Conference* Singapore (Singapore) 2021.

Members Chapters in 12 countries:
Argentina, Australia, Canada, China, India, Netherlands, New Zealand, Puerto Rico, Saudi Arabia, South Africa, UK, USA. [2021/XF5897/**F**]

♦ Association of Certified International Investment Analysts (ACIIA) 02422

Chairman address not obtained. T. +496924005975. Fax +4969264848335. E-mail: info@aciia.org.
URL: http://www.aciia.org/

History Jun 2000, UK. **Aims** Provide a flexible global, internationally recognized qualification, which examines candidates at a high standard and in a practical fashion in the topic areas that are necessary to pursue a career in the investment profession. **Structure** Board. **Events** *Annual General Assembly* Madrid (Spain) 2012, *Annual General Assembly* Luxembourg (Luxembourg) 2006, *International seminar* Brussels (Belgium) 2005, *Annual General Assembly* Stockholm (Sweden) 2003.

Members Full in 33 countries and territories:
Argentina, Austria, Belgium, Brazil, China, Finland, France, Germany, Greece, Hong Kong, Hungary, India, Iran Islamic Rep, Italy, Japan, Kazakhstan, Kenya, Korea Rep, Lithuania, Luxembourg, Mexico, Morocco, Netherlands, Nigeria, Peru, Poland, Russia, Spain, Sweden, Switzerland, Taiwan, Tunisia, Ukraine.

NGO Relations *European Federation of Financial Analysts Societies (EFFAS, #07123)* is member. [2018/XD8445/**D**]

♦ Association of Chambers of Commerce and Industry of the Mediterranean Countries / see Asociación de las Camaras de Comercio e Industria del Mediterraneo (#02112)
♦ Association des chambres de commerce et d'industrie ACP / see Chamber of Commerce, Industry and Agriculture Belgium – Luxembourg – Africa-Caribbean-Pacific
♦ Association des chambres de commerce, industrie et autres opérateurs économiques des Iles du Pacifique (inactive)

♦ Association des chambres de commerce et d'industrie européennes (EUROCHAMBRES) 02423

Association of European Chambers of Commerce and Industry – Vereinigung der Europäischen Industrie und Handelskammern

CEO Av des Arts 19 A/D, 1000 Brussels, Belgium. T. +3222820850. Fax +3222300038. E-mail: eurochambres@eurochambres.eu.
Events Manager address not obtained.
URL: http://www.eurochambres.eu/

History 28 Feb 1958. Former names and other names: *Permanent Conference of Chambers of Commerce and Industry of the EEC* – former (1985); *Conférence permanente des chambres de commerce et de l'industrie de la CEE (CPCCI)* – former (1985); *Ständige Konferenz der Industrie- und Handelskammern der EWG* – former (1985). Registration: No/ID: 0417.324.583, Start date: 14 Jul 1977, Belgium; EU Transparency Register, No/ID: 0014082722-83, Start date: 4 Dec 2008. **Aims** Represent the needs, aspirations and opinions of members; promote European *integration*; provide information on *European Union* policies and programmes; promote *economic* and *trade* relations between the European Union and non-European countries; assist members in upgrading and adapting services they provide to their member enterprises in view of the rapid changes of the European Union. **Structure** General Assembly (twice a year); Board; Administration Department. **Languages** English, French. **Staff** 30.00 FTE, paid. **Finance** Members' dues. **Activities** Politics/policy/regulatory; projects/programmes; events/meetings; training/education; networking/liaising. **Events** *Corporate Sustainability Due Diligence Meeting* Brussels (Belgium) 2022, *Delivering the EU 2021 Industrial Strategy* Brussels (Belgium) 2022, *European Learning Experience Platform Kick-off Meting* Brussels (Belgium) 2022, *Meeting on Competitiveness Compass* Brussels (Belgium) 2022, *Migration of African Talents through Capacity building and Hiring (MATCH) Project Final Conference* Brussels (Belgium) 2022.

Members Full in 26 countries:
Austria, Belgium, Bulgaria, Croatia, Cyprus, Czechia, Estonia, Finland, France, Germany, Greece, Hungary, Ireland, Italy, Latvia, Lithuania, Luxembourg, Malta, Netherlands, Poland, Portugal, Romania, Slovakia, Slovenia, Spain, Sweden.

Affiliate in 15 countries:
Albania, Armenia, Azerbaijan, Belarus, Bosnia-Herzegovina, Georgia, Kosovo, Moldova, Montenegro, North Macedonia, Norway, Russia, Serbia, Türkiye, Ukraine.

Correspondent members (4):
Israel, Switzerland.
Forum of the Adriatic and Ionian Chambers of Commerce (AIC FORUM, #09891); Network of the Insular Chambers of Commerce and Industry of the European Union (INSULEUR, #17040).

Consultative Status Consultative status granted from: *UNCTAD (#20285)* (General Category). **IGO Relations** All institutions of the European Union, such as: *European Economic and Social Committee (EESC, #06963); European Parliament (EP, #08146).* Recognized by: *European Commission (EC, #06633).* Cooperation agreement with: *ASEAN (#01141).* **NGO Relations** Member of (1): *Citizens for Europe (CFEU, #03956).* Part of: *MedAlliance consortium (inactive).* Through Global Chamber Platform, cooperates with: *Asociación de las Camaras de Comercio e Industria del Mediterraneo (ASCAME, #02112); Association of ACP National Chambers of Commerce, Industry and Other Economic Operators (ACP Chambers, #02345); Caribbean Association of Industry and Commerce (CAIC, #03448); China Council for the Promotion of International Trade (CCPIT); Confederation of Asia-Pacific Chambers of Commerce and Industry (CACCI, #04512); Federation of GCC Chambers (FGCCC, #09590); Ibero-American Association of Chambers of Commerce (IACC, #11014); Junior Chamber International (JCI, #16168); Latin American Industrialists Association (#16341); SAARC Chamber of Commerce and Industry (SAARC CCI, #19015).* [2020/XE3287/ty/**E**]

♦ Association des chambres de commerce et d'industrie de la Méditerranée (#02112)
♦ Association des chambres nationales de commerce, d'industrie et des autres opérateurs économiques ACP (#02345)

♦ Association of Change Management Professionals (ACMP) 02424

Main Office 1809 East Broadway, Ste 173, Oviedo FL 32765, USA. T. +14073923373. E-mail: help@acmpglobal.org.
URL: http://www.acmpglobal.org/

History 2009. **Aims** Advance the discipline and profession of change management practices that support the success of individual and organizational change for the realization of intended business results. **Structure** Board of Directors. **Events** *Global Conference* New Orleans, LA (USA) 2017, *Global Conference* Dallas, TX (USA) 2016, *Middle East and North African Conference* Dubai (United Arab Emirates) 2016, *Regional Conference* Toronto, ON (Canada) 2016, *European Regional Conference* Brussels (Belgium) 2015. [2018/XJ7478/t/**D**]

♦ Association des chanteurs et musiciens nordiques (#17478)
♦ Association pour le charbon en Europe (inactive)

♦ Association of Charity Lotteries in Europe (ACLEU) 02425

Exec Dir PO Box 75025, 1070 AA Amsterdam, Netherlands. E-mail: info@acleu.eu.
Street address Beethovenstraat 200, 1077 JZ Amsterdam, Netherlands.
URL: http://www.acleu.eu/

History 2007. Registration: EU Transparency Register, No/ID: 54735291072-89. **Aims** Promote the charity lottery model; give a voice to charity lotteries and their beneficiaries in the European debate on games of chance and in all matters relating to fundraising through charity lotteries. **Structure** Board of Directors; Secretariat. **Languages** Dutch, English. **Staff** 0.20 FTE, paid. **Finance** Sources: members' dues. Annual budget: 15,000 EUR.

Members Full in 6 countries:
Germany, Ireland, Netherlands, Norway, Sweden, UK. [2022.10.18/XM5305/**D**]

♦ Association of Chartered Certified Accountants (internationally oriented national body)
♦ Association des chasseurs professionnels d'Afrique francophone (inactive)
♦ Association des chasseurs professionnels de l'Afrique orientale (inactive)
♦ Association de chefs d'entreprises latines (inactive)

♦ Association of Chemistry and the Environment (ACE) 02426

Address not obtained.
URL: http://www.europeanace.com/

History Oct 2000. Also known as *European Association of Chemistry and the Environment (ACE).* **Aims** Promote protection of the environment by collaboration between scientists. **Structure** Board. **Finance** Members' dues. **Events** *Meeting* Clermont-Ferrand (France) 2011, *Meeting* Portoroz (Slovenia) 2010, *Meeting* Limoges (France) 2009, *Meeting* Girona (Spain) 2008, *European meeting on environmental chemistry / Meeting* Inverness (UK) 2007. **Publications** *Environmental Chemistry Letter* – journal. [2012/XM0378/**D**]

♦ Association des chercheurs africains pour le développement économique et social (inactive)
♦ Association des chercheurs du maïs en Afrique (no recent information)
♦ Association of Chief Education Officers in the Caribbean (no recent information)
♦ Association of Chief Executives of Latin Countries (inactive)
♦ Association for Child and Adolescent Mental Health (internationally oriented national body)
♦ Association for Childhood Education / see Childhood Education International
♦ Association for Childhood Education International / see Childhood Education International
♦ Association for Child Psychology and Psychiatry / see Association for Child and Adolescent Mental Health
♦ Association des chimistes analytiques officiels / see AOAC INTERNATIONAL (#00863)
♦ Association des chimistes des peintures et vernis (#17707)
♦ Association of China and Mongolia International Schools (internationally oriented national body)
♦ Association chirurgicale d'Asie (#01763)
♦ Association de chirurgiens de l'Afrique de l'Est (inactive)
♦ Association des chirurgiens d'Afrique occidentale / see West African College of Surgeons (#20876)
♦ Association des chirurgiens pédiatres du Pacifique (#17933)
♦ Association of the Chocolate-, Biscuit- and Confectionery Industries of the EEC / see Association of the Chocolate, Biscuit and Confectionery Industries of the EU (#02427)

♦ Association of the Chocolate, Biscuit and Confectionery Industries of the EU (CAOBISCO) 02427

Association des industries de la chocolaterie, biscuiterie et confiserie de l'UE

SG Av des Nerviens 9-31, 1040 Brussels, Belgium. T. +3225081021. E-mail: caobisco@caobisco.eu.
URL: http://caobisco.eu/

History 12 May 1959, Rome (Italy). Former names and other names: *Association of the Chocolate-, Biscuit- and Confectionery Industries of the EEC* – former; *Association des industries de la chocolaterie, biscuiterie-biscotterie et confiserie de la CEE (CAOBISCO)* – former; *Verband der Schokolade-, Dauerbackwaren- und Zuckerwarenindustrien der EWG* – former; *Associazione delle Industrie del Cioccolato, della Biscotteria-Pasticceria e della Confetteria della CEE* – former; *Vereniging van de Chocolade-, Biscuit-, Beschuit- en Suikerwerkindustrieen in de EEG* – former; *Brancheforeningen for Chokolade-, Biscuit- og Konfekture Industrien i EØF* – former; *Sindesmos Viomihanion Sokolatopas, Biskotopas-, Friganopopas- ke Zaharodon Prionton tis EOK* – alias. Registration: Banque-Carrefour des Entreprises, Belgium; EU Transparency Register, No/ID: 496569221197-39. **Aims** Promote chocolate, biscuit and confectionery food categories to stakeholders through building confidence and trust; influence public policy at European and global levels via proactive networking; enhance value to members by addressing needs via a transparent, timely and efficient decision making process on non-competitive issues relevant to members' activities. **Structure** General Assembly; General Council; Executive Committee. Committees; Working Groups. **Languages** English. **Staff** 5.00 FTE, paid. **Finance** Sources: members' dues. **Activities** Networking/liaising; politics/policy/regulatory. **Events** *General Assembly* Oslo (Norway) 2015, *General Assembly* Amsterdam (Netherlands) 2014, *General Assembly* Brussels (Belgium) 2013, *General Assembly* Budapest (Hungary) 2011, *Conference* Brussels (Belgium) 2010. **Publications** Annual Report; statistical bulletin.

Members National Associations; Direct Member Companies; Observer; Affiliated. National Associations in 17 countries:
Austria, Belgium, Finland, France, Germany, Hungary, Ireland, Italy, Netherlands, Norway, Poland, Portugal, Slovenia, Spain, Sweden, Switzerland, UK.

Direct Member Companies in 3 countries:
Belgium, Italy, Switzerland.

Affiliated in 2 countries:
Greece, Malta.

Consultative Status Consultative status granted from: *UNCTAD (#20285)* (Special Category). **IGO Relations** Recognized by: *European Commission (EC, #06633).* **NGO Relations** Member of (4): *CIUS – European Sugar Users (#03961); Federation of European and International Associations Established in Belgium (FAIB, #09508); FoodDrinkEurope (#09841); International Confectionery Association (ICA, #12840).* Cooperates with (2): *European Cocoa Association (ECA, #06599); International Chewing Gum Association (ICGA, #12545).* Instrumental in setting up (1): *International Cocoa Initiative (ICI, #12626).* Liaison Organization of: *Comité européen de normalisation (CEN, #04162).* [2021.05.26/XE0168/t/**E**]

♦ Association chrétienne d'Asie (no recent information)
♦ Association chrétienne d'étudiants / see World Student Christian Federation (#21833)
♦ Association chrétienne internationale (#12556)
♦ Association chrétienne des jeunes gens / see World Student Christian Federation (#21833)
♦ Association of Christian Artists / see Christian Artists International Association (#03896)
♦ Association of Christian Democratic Latin Americans in Europe (inactive)

♦ Association of Christian Institutes for Social Concern in Asia (ACISCA) 02428

Contact c/o Ecumenical Christian Centre, Post Box 11, Whitefield, Bangalore, Karnataka 560066, Bangalore KARNATAKA 560066, India. T. +918028452270. Fax +918028452653. E-mail: director@eccbangalore.org.

History 25 Jul 1970, Kyoto (Japan), as *Association of Directors of Christian Institutes for Social Concern in Asia*, having formal links with the then *'East Asia Christian Conference (EACC)'*, currently, since 1973, *Christian Conference of Asia (CCA, #03898)*. Present name of the Association adopted 1972. **Aims** Stimulate links and cooperation among members; establish channels of communication by collecting information in relation to lay training, academic work and movements for social concern; share experiments and programmes; organize relations with churches, sister associations and other organizations with similar concerns; offer consultative or advisory service on the formation of new institutes; seek human development and social justice, liberation from poverty and restoration of basic human rights. **Structure** General Assembly (every 4 years); Executive Committee comprising Chairperson, Vice-Chairperson, Secretary, Treasurer and 4 Committee Members. **Languages** English. **Finance** Members' dues. Contributions from members and other funds. **Activities** Main topics: human rights; indigenous social action in Asia; role of co-workers in the struggle for peace and justice; links with people's movements; peace and disarmament; women and justice; indigenous culture. Organizes: training courses to help staff of various centres; Bible study courses; field trips; consultations; staff exchanges; ecumenical team visits. **Events** *Quadrennial General Assembly* Bangkok (Thailand) 2002, *Quadrennial general assembly* Bangkok (Thailand) 1998, *South Asian directors conference* Sri Lanka 1997, *Assembly* Seoul (Korea Rep) 1996, *Church and human rights on justice promoters and peace* 1995. **Publications** *ACISCA News Letter* (4 a year). Monographs; books.

Members Institutions (34) in 12 countries and territories:
Bangladesh, Hong Kong, India, Indonesia, Japan, Korea Rep, Malaysia, Pakistan, Philippines, Sri Lanka, Taiwan, Thailand.

NGO Relations A regional network of: *OIKOSNET (no recent information).* [2018/XD5926/**D**]

♦ Association of Christian Lay Centres in Africa (ACLCA) 02429

Association de centres laïcs chrétiens en Afrique

SG address not obtained.

History 1970, Kitwe (Zambia). Also referred to as *Association of Christian Lay Training Centres in Africa* and *OIKOSNET Africa*. **Aims** Promote contacts and development of a common purpose between lay training centres in Africa; encourage common planning and deepen the Church's responsibility in the world; strengthen programmes; encourage and coordinate research and study of common tasks; arrange joint training for staff and leaders so as to develop ecumenical leaders; stimulate production of materials and information related to lay training; offer advisory services in developing and establishing lay training activities in Africa; develop, where possible, an increasingly close relationship between lay training centres and work in close consultation with national christian councils; encourage dialogue between people of different faiths; strengthen links with similar associations in other continents. **Structure** General Assembly (normally every 3 years). Executive Committee of 9 to 12 members. Secretariat, headed by General Secretary. President; Treasurer. **Languages** English, French, Portuguese. **Staff** 10.00 FTE, paid. **Finance** Members' dues. Grants. **Activities** Programme priorities: CLLTs – Courses for Leadership in Lay Training focusing on leadership training, laity formation and ecumenical learning; Church Renewal, Justice, Peace and Creation; Youth and Women Concerns; Exchange Programme. Launched the *'Peace Building and Conflict Resolution Network'*, 1998. **Events** *General Assembly* Limuru (Kenya) 2004, *General assembly* Limuru (Kenya) 2003, *General Assembly* Abokobi (Ghana) 2000, *Peace building and conflict resolution network consultation* Johannesburg (South Africa) 2000, *Being the light of the world – challenges and hopes of the new millennium* Abetefi (Ghana) 1999. **Publications** *ACLCA News Update* (3 a year). *The Taproot of Environment and Development Crisis in Africa: The Challenge* (1992) by JJ Otim; *Debt Crisis: An African Perspective*; *Training for Transformation*. Resource materials; booklets; guides; manuals; videos; reports of workshops, etc.

Members Christian lay centres (60) and contact groups in 23 countries:
Angola, Benin, Burundi, Cameroon, Congo DR, Egypt, Ethiopia, Ghana, Kenya, Lesotho, Madagascar, Malawi, Mozambique, Nigeria, Rwanda, Senegal, Sierra Leone, South Africa, Sudan, Tanzania UR, Uganda, Zambia, Zimbabwe.
Associate in 1 country:
Kenya.

NGO Relations *World Council of Churches (WCC, #21320)*. Regional network of: *OIKOSNET (no recent information)*. Member of: *Conference of African Theological Institutions (CATI, #04580)*; *Fellowship of Councils of Churches in Southern Africa (FOCCISA, no recent information)*. Associate member of: *All Africa Conference of Churches (AACC, #00640)*. [2011/XD5878/**D**]

- ♦ Association of Christian Lay Training Centres in Africa / see Association of Christian Lay Centres in Africa (#02429)
- ♦ Association of Christian Resource Organisation Service Sudan / see ACROSS (#00080)
- ♦ Association of Christian Resource Organizations Serving Sudan / see ACROSS (#00080)

♦ Association of Christian Schools International (ACSI) 02430

Asociación Internacional de Escuelas Cristianas

Contact PO Box 62249, Colorado Springs CO 80962, USA. T. +18003675391. E-mail: communications@acsi.org.

URL: http://www.acsi.org/

History 1950. Present form assumed 1978, on merger of (USA) National Christian School Education Association (NCSEA), Ohio Association of Christian Schools (OACS) and the Western Association of Christian Schools. Registration: Section 501 (c)(3), USA. **Aims** Strengthen Christian schools and equip Christian educators worldwide as they prepare students academically and inspire them to become devoted followers of *Jesus Christ*. **Structure** Executive Board; Regional Offices (19); Headquarters in Colorado Springs CO (USA). **Languages** English, French, Hungarian, Indonesian, Korean, Portuguese, Spanish. **Staff** 150.00 FTE, paid. **Finance** Sources: fees for services; members' dues; sale of publications. Annual budget: 22,000,000 USD. **Activities** Certification/accreditation; events/meetings; knowledge management/information dissemination; networking/liaising. **Events** *International Christian Educators Conference Asia* Kuala Lumpur (Malaysia) 2018, *International Christian Educators Conference Asia* Hong Kong (Hong Kong) 2016, *International Christian Educator Conference Asia* Daejeon (Korea Rep) 2014. **Publications** *Legal Legislative Update* (3 a year). Textbooks. **Members** Schools (25,000) in 115 countries. Membership countries not specified. **NGO Relations** Member of (1): *World Evangelical Alliance (WEA, #21393)* (as Associate member of). [2022/XF6199/**F**]

- ♦ Association of Christians Ministering Among Internationals (internationally oriented national body)

♦ Association for Christian Theological Education in Africa (ACTEA) . 02431

Association pour l'Education Théologique Chrétienne en Afrique (COHETA) – Associaçio Cristo para Educaçio Teológica em Africa (ACETA)

Exec Dir AEA Plaza, 6th Floor,, PO Box 49332-00100, Nairobi, Nairobi, 00100, Kenya. T. +254721571549. E-mail: actea.africa@gmail.com.

Exec Admin Assistant address not obtained. T. +254725556644. E-mail: info@acteaweb.org – adm.ass.actea@gmail.com.

URL: http://www.acteaweb.org/

History 1976. Founded within the framework of *Association of Evangelicals in Africa (AEA, #02587)*. Former names and other names: *Accrediting Council for Theological Education in Africa (ACTEA)* – former; *Conseil pour l'homologation des établissements théologiques en Afrique (COHETA)* – former. **Aims** Strengthen member institutions in offering quality theological programmes for excellency and renewal. **Structure** Accreditation Council. **Languages** English, French, Portuguese. **Staff** 3.50 FTE, paid. **Finance** Sources: members' dues. Annual budget: 350,000 USD. **Activities** Capacity building; certification/accreditation; networking/liaising. **Events** *Conference* Addis Ababa (Ethiopia) 2015, *Conference* Jos (Nigeria) 2008, *Conference* Pietermaritzburg (South Africa) 2003, *Conference* Jos (Nigeria) 2001, *Conference* Nairobi (Kenya) 2000. **Publications** *ACTEA e-News*; *ACTEA Forum*; *ACTEA Librarian News*. *ACTEA Guide for Self-Evaluation*; *ACTEA Monographs*; *ACTEA Standards and Procedures*; *ACTEA Tools and Studies*.

Members Affiliate (30); Candidate for Accreditation (10); Accredited (30). Members in 28 countries:
Angola, Cameroon, Central African Rep, Chad, Côte d'Ivoire, Equatorial Guinea, Eswatini, Ethiopia, Gabon, Ghana, Kenya, Liberia, Madagascar, Malawi, Mauritius, Mozambique, Namibia, Niger, Nigeria, Rwanda, Sierra Leone, South Africa, Sudan, Tanzania UR, Togo, Uganda, Zambia, Zimbabwe.

NGO Relations Founding member of: *International Council for Evangelical Theological Education (ICETE, #13020)*. [2022.10.25/XF0485/**F**]

♦ Association of Christian Universities and Colleges in Asia (ACUCA) 02432

Association des universités et des collèges chrétiens d'Asie

Contact Payap Univ, Super-highway Chiang Mai – Lumpang Road, Amphur Muang, Chiang Mai, 50000, Thailand. T. +6653851478. E-mail: secretariat@acuca.net.

URL: http://www.acuca.net/

History Dec 1976, Taipei (Taiwan), when commenced operations, having been planned from Oct 1974. **Aims** Promote Christian higher education and provide cultural links among member institutions. **Structure** General Assembly (every 2 years); Executive Committee; Secretariat moves every 2 years. **Languages** English. **Staff** 2.00 FTE, paid. **Finance** Members' dues. Grants for special programmes, especially from *United Board for Christian Higher Education in Asia (UBCHEA)*. **Activities** *'ACUCA Student Mobility Scheme'* – students go on exchange studies at another member institution for a semester. *'ACUCA Student Camp'* (every 2 years) – students in member institutions gather and engage in various activities for a few days in the summer. Organizes: Conference and General Assembly (every 2 years); Management Conference (every 2 years). **Events** *Management Conference and General Assembly* Dumaguete City (Philippines) 2019, *Biennial General Assembly* Nakhon Pathom (Thailand) 2018, *Management Conference* Chiang Mai (Thailand) 2017, *Biennial General Assembly* Bali (Indonesia) 2016, *Biennial General Assembly* Tokyo (Japan) 2012. **Publications** *ACUCA Newsletter* (4 a year).

Members Member institutions (59) in 8 countries and territories:
Hong Kong, India, Indonesia, Japan, Korea Rep, Philippines, Taiwan, Thailand. [2017.03.21/XD4469/**D**]

- ♦ Association of Cider and Fruit Wine Industries of the EEC / see Association des Industries des Cidres et Vins de Fruits de l'UE (#02643)
- ♦ Association of the Cider and Fruit Wine Industry of the EEC / see Association des Industries des Cidres et Vins de Fruits de l'UE (#02643)
- ♦ Association of the Cider and Fruit Wine Industry of the EU / see Association des Industries des Cidres et Vins de Fruits de l'UE (#02643)
- ♦ Association des cimetières historique-monumentaux en Europe (#02915)
- ♦ Association des Cinémathèques Européennes (#02511)
- ♦ Association of Cities for Recycling / see Association of Cities and Regions for Sustainable Resource Management (#02433)
- ♦ Association of Cities and Regions Hosting an International Exhibition (no recent information)
- ♦ Association of Cities and Regions for Recycling and Sustainable Resource Management / see Association of Cities and Regions for Sustainable Resource Management (#02433)

♦ Association of Cities and Regions for Sustainable Resource Management (ACR+) 02433

SG Avenue d'Auderghem 63, 1040 Brussels, Belgium. T. +3222346500. Fax +3222346501. E-mail: fb@acrplus.org – info@acrplus.org.

Administrative Assistant address not obtained.

URL: http://www.acrplus.org/

History 28 May 1994, Pamplona (Spain). Founded at constitutive general meeting, following proclamation of a *'Charter of the Cities for Recycling'* at 2nd European Congress on Packaging and the Environment, 26 Oct 1993, Brussels (Belgium). Former names and other names: *Association of Cities for Recycling (ACR)* – former; *Association des villes pour le recyclage (AVR)* – former; *Asociación de Ciudades para el Reciclaje* – former; *Städteverband für Recycling* – former; *Associação das Cidades Para a Reciclagem* – former; *Associazione di Città per il Riciclaggio* – former; *Vereniging van Steden voor Recyclage* – former; *Network for the Exchange of Information between Cities and Urban Communities on Selective Waste Collection* – alias; *Association des villes et régions pour le recyclage* – former; *Asociación de Ciudades y Regiones para el Reciclaje* – former; *Associação das Cidades e Regiões Para a Reciclagem* – former; *Associazione di Città e Regioni per il Riciclaggio* – former; *Vereniging van Steden en Regio's voor Recyclage* – former; *Association of Cities and Regions for Recycling and Sustainable Resource Management (ACR+)* – former (2017). Registration: EU Transparency Register, No/ID: 302141215278-05. **Aims** Promote sustainable consumption of resources and management of *waste* in cities and urban communities through prevention at source, reuse and recycling, especially: technical data on waste management options; means of communication, education and sensitization; legal, economic or voluntary instruments. **Structure** General Meeting (annual); Board of Directors; Working Groups; Task Forces; Support Committee; Secretariat. **Languages** English, French, Spanish. **Staff** 13.00 FTE, paid. **Finance** Sources: members' dues. Other sources: *European Commission (EC, #06633)*; Brussels (Belgium) Institute for the Management of the Environment. **Activities** Advocacy/lobbying/activism; events/meetings; networking/liaising. **Events** *EPR principles as a bridge between waste and products policies* Brussels (Belgium) 2022, *General Assembly* Brussels (Belgium) 2022, *How Can EPR Promote Sustainable Consumption and Production?* Brussels (Belgium) 2022, *LCA from policy planning to implementation* Brussels (Belgium) 2022, *Waste Management Intelligent Systems and Policies Conference* Brussels (Belgium) 2022. **Publications** *ACR+ Update* (4 a year); *ACR+ Weekly Newsline*. Technical reports; conference, congress and seminar proceedings; surveys; papers; statistics. Information Services: Database on recycling in European cities.

Members Full and partner in 26 countries:
Austria, Belgium, Bulgaria, Croatia, Denmark, Egypt, France, Germany, Greece, Hungary, Ireland, Italy, Jordan, Luxembourg, Malta, Morocco, Netherlands, Palestine, Poland, Portugal, Romania, Slovenia, Spain, Tunisia, Türkiye, UK.
Included in the above, 3 organizations listed in this Yearbook:
European Association for Local Democracy (ALDA, #06110); *Reloop Platform (Reloop, #18835)*; *Zero Waste MENA (ZW MENA)*.

NGO Relations Member of (1): *Circular Plastics Alliance (#03936)*. [2022.10.19/XD3584/y/**D**]

- ♦ Association Civic Tech Europe (unconfirmed)
- ♦ Association for Clean and Sterile Products / see Association pour les Produits Propres et Parentéraux

♦ Association of Clinical Research Professionals (ACRP) 02434

Headquarters 99 Canal Center Plaza, Ste 150, Alexandria VA 22314, USA. T. +17032548100. E-mail: support@acrpnet.org.

URL: http://www.acrpnet.org/

History Founded 1976. Previously known as *Associates of Clinical Pharmacology (ACP)*. **Aims** Promote ethical and responsible conduct of clinical research. **Languages** English. **Activities** Provides support and service to members through delivery of professional development services and certification programmes. Organizes: Annual Global Conference (in April) in varying cities in the USA; certification exams (March and September); professional development live and e-learning courses. **Events** *Annual Global Conference* Orlando, FL (USA) 2022, *Annual Global Conference* Toronto, ON (Canada) 2021, *Annual Global Conference* Seattle, WA (USA) 2020, *Annual Global Conference* Nashville, TN (USA) 2019, *Annual Global Conference* Washington, DC (USA) 2018. **Publications** *The Monitor* (6 a year) – peer-reviewed journal. **Members** Chapters, comprising clinical research professionals, in 13 countries worldwide (not specified). [2019/XD8868/t/**D**]

- ♦ Association for Coal in Europe (inactive)
- ♦ Association of the Coal Producers of the European Community / see European Association for Coal and Lignite (#05978)
- ♦ Association coeur africain (internationally oriented national body)
- ♦ Association for the Cohesive Development of the Amazon (internationally oriented national body)
- ♦ Association des coiffeurs nordiques (#17307)

♦ Association des collectivités textiles européennes (ACTE) 02435

European Textile Collectivities Association – Asociación de Colectividades Textiles Europeas – Associação das Colectividades Têxteis Europeias – Associazione delle Comunità Tessili d'Europa

Pres Ajuntament de Terrassa, Edif Vapor Gran, C/Dels Telers 5-B 2a pl, Local 12, 08221 Terrassa, Barcelona, Spain. T. +34937397000. Fax +34937890354. E-mail: acte.presidency@terrassa.cat – acte.executivesecretariat@terrassa.cat.

URL: http://www.acte.net/

History 13 Apr 1991, Guimarães (Portugal), on signature of founding protocol by textile groupings, associations and groups of municipalities heavily dependent on the textile industry. Previously also referred to as *European Textile Association.* **Aims** Represent and defend interests of territorial collectivities and adherent organizations that represent territories with a presence of the textile, clothing, leather, footwear and fashion accessories sectors. **Structure** General Assembly; Executive Committee; Executive Secretariat. **Languages** English, French, Italian, Spanish. **Staff** 3.00 FTE, paid. **Activities** Advocacy/lobbying/activism; awareness raising; events/meetings. **Events** *General Assembly and Conference* Terrassa (Spain) 2014, *General Assembly and Conference / General Assembly* Biella (Italy) 2013, *General assembly and conference / General Assembly* Lódz (Poland) 2012, *General assembly and conference / General Assembly* Barcelona (Spain) 2011, *General assembly and conference / General Assembly* Guimarães (Portugal) 2010.
Members Effective – European local and regional authorities; Adherent (non-voting) – schools and universities, technology centres, business incubators, chambers of commerce, business and trade union organizations. Members in 9 countries:
Belgium, Croatia, France, Italy, North Macedonia, Poland, Portugal, Spain, Sweden. [2016/XD7009/**D**]

- ♦ Association of College Professors of Textiles and Clothing / see International Textile and Apparel Association
- ♦ Association of Collegiate Conference and Events Directors – International (internationally oriented national body)
- ♦ Association of Collegiate Schools of Business / see AACSB International – Association to Advance Collegiate Schools of Business
- ♦ Association of Colombian-Caribbean American Schools (see: #02367)
- ♦ Association des comités nationaux olympiques (#02819)
- ♦ Association des comités nationaux olympiques d'Afrique (#02820)
- ♦ Association des comités nationaux olympiques européens / see European Olympic Committees (#08083)
- ♦ Association des comités de simplification des procédures du commerce international au sein de l'Union européenne et de l'Association européenne de libre-échange / see European PRO Committee (#08280)
- ♦ Association du commerce de la banane dans la CE (inactive)
- ♦ Association du commerce international de bulbes à fleurs et de plantes (no recent information)
- ♦ Association du commerce du voyageur pour l'Europe centrale et orientale (#03699)

♦ Association of Commercial Television in Europe (ACT) 02436

Association des télévisions commerciales européennes
Dir Gen Rue des Deux Eglises 26, 1000 Brussels, Belgium. T. +3227360052. E-mail: gp@acte.be – info@acte.be.
URL: http://www.acte.be/
History 12 Jul 1989, Brussels (Belgium). Founded by 5 founder members. A grouping of the type *European Economic Interest Grouping (EEIG, #06960).* Registration: EU Transparency Register, No/ID: 18574111503-28, Start date: 9 Apr 2009. **Aims** Promote cooperation among members and with European enterprises active in the field of *communication*; defend interests of private *broadcasters* vis-à-vis the *European Union*; provide a forum for reflection leading to proposals in the regulatory field – advertising, intellectual property, public service, media ownership, new services, protection of minors, sports – and in the establishment of Community support initiatives with regard to production and distribution for both the internal market and for export. **Structure** College of Members; Executive Board. Working Groups (6): Legal Affairs; Advertising; Pay TV; New Services; Media Concentration; Competition. **Languages** English, French. **Staff** 4.00 FTE, paid. **Finance** Sources: members' dues. Annual budget: 800,000 EUR. **Activities** Guidance/assistance/consulting. **Events** *EU Media Policy Conference* Brussels (Belgium) 2019, *Annual Conference* Brussels (Belgium) 2008, *DTH world summit for satellite TV platforms and channels* Paris (France) 2004, *MIPCOM : international film and programme market for tv, video, cable and satellite conference* Cannes (France) 1996. **Publications** *TV News* (4 a year) in English, French. *Safeguarding the Future of the EU Audiovisual Market* (2004) – joint ACT/AER/EPC publication.
Members Private television channels (about 60) in 11 countries:
Belgium, Finland, France, Germany, Greece, Ireland, Italy, Luxembourg, Spain, Sweden, UK.
Consultative Status Consultative status granted from: *World Intellectual Property Organization (WIPO, #21593)* (Permanent Observer Status). **NGO Relations** Member of (8): *Centre for European Policy Studies (CEPS, #03741); Creative Media Business Alliance (CMBA, #04947); DVB Project (#05147); Ethical Journalism Network (EJN, #05554); European Advertising Standards Alliance (EASA, #05829); European Interactive Digital Advertising Alliance (EDAA, #07582); European Internet Forum (EIF, #07591); European Telecommunications Standards Institute (ETSI, #08897).* Instrumental in setting up (1): *European Cinema and Television Office (ECTO, inactive).* [2021/XD2450/**F**]

- ♦ Association of Committees of Simplified Procedures for International Trade within the European Community and the European Free Trade Association / see European PRO Committee (#08280)
- ♦ Association of Commodity Exchange Firms / see Futures Industry Association

♦ Association for Common European Nursing Diagnoses, Interventions and Outcomes (ACENDIO) 02437

Association pour des diagnostics, des interventions et des résultats infirmiers unifiés au niveau européen
Sec Saint Camillus International Univ of Health and Medical Sciences, Via di Sant'Alessandro 8, 00131 Rome RM, Italy. E-mail: secretary@acendio.net.
URL: http://www.acendio.net/
History 1995. **Aims** Promote a common European framework for development of nursing practice through employment of standardized nursing languages and information systems. **Structure** General Assembly (every 2 years, during conference); Board; Scientific Committee; Ad-hoc Committees. **Languages** English. **Staff** 8.00 FTE, paid. **Finance** Members' dues. **Activities** Events/meetings; training/education. **Events** *Biennial Conference* Falun (Sweden) 2019, *Biennial Conference* Bern (Switzerland) 2015, *Biennial Conference* Dublin (Ireland) 2013, *Biennial conference / Congress* Madeira (Portugal) 2011, *Biennial conference / Congress* Helsinki (Finland) 2009. **Publications** *ACENDIO Newsletter* (3 a year).
Members Full in 24 countries:
Andorra, Austria, Belgium, Brazil, Bulgaria, Estonia, Finland, Germany, Iceland, Ireland, Italy, Japan, Netherlands, New Zealand, Norway, Poland, Portugal, Romania, Slovenia, Spain, Sweden, Switzerland, UK, USA.
NGO Relations Member of: *European Specialist Nurses Organisation (ESNO, #08808).* [2020/XD6031/**D**]

- ♦ Association of Commonwealth Archivists and Records Managers (inactive)
- ♦ Association du Commonwealth britannique d'aide aux prisonniers (inactive)
- ♦ Association du Commonwealth pour l'éducation et la formation des adultes (inactive)
- ♦ Association du Commonwealth pour l'enseignement du droit (#04347)

♦ Association of Commonwealth Examination and Accreditation Bodies (ACEAB) 02438

Address not obtained.
History 1998. Also referred to as *Association for Commonwealth Examining and Accrediting Bodies.* **Aims** Promote quality and comparability of assessment, accreditation, certification and administration procedures in Commonwealth countries. **Structure** Executive Committee, including President, Vice-President, Secretary and Treasurer. **Events** *Biennial Conference* Johannesburg (South Africa) 2008, *Biennial Conference* Pretoria (South Africa) 2008, *Biennial Conference* Ocho Rios (Jamaica) 2006, *Biennial Conference* Fiji 2004, *Biennial conference* Nadi (Fiji) 2004.
Members Associate; individual; institutional. Members in 38 countries and territories:
Australia, Bahamas, Barbados, Belize, Bhutan, Botswana, Brunei Darussalam, Cook Is, Cyprus, Eswatini, Fiji, Guyana, Jamaica, Kiribati, Lesotho, Malawi, Maldives, Malta, Mauritius, Namibia, Nauru, New Zealand, Niue, Samoa, Seychelles, Singapore, Slovenia, Solomon Is, South Africa, St Lucia, Tanzania UR, Tokelau, Tonga, Trinidad-Tobago, Tuvalu, UK, Vanuatu, Zambia.
NGO Relations Member of: *Commonwealth Consortium for Education (CCfE, #04318) International Association for Educational Assessment (IAEA, #11861).* [2010/XD8888/**D**]

- ♦ Association for Commonwealth Examining and Accrediting Bodies / see Association of Commonwealth Examination and Accreditation Bodies (#02438)
- ♦ Association for Commonwealth Language and Literature Studies / see Association for Commonwealth Literature and Language Studies (#02439)

♦ Association for Commonwealth Literature and Language Studies (ACLALS) 02439

Association pour l'étude des littératures et langues du Commonwealth
Chair PO Box 30197, Nairobi, 00100, Kenya.
URL: http://www.aclals.net
History 16 Sep 1965, Leeds (UK). Articles amended 11 Mar 1966, Leeds (UK). Accredited to The Commonwealth in 2005. Former names and other names: *Association for Commonwealth Language and Literature Studies* – former; *Association pour l'étude des langues et littératures du Commonwealth* – former. **Aims** Encourage study and research on Commonwealth literature and languages and related fields of study. Publish and support publication of information relating to: study and teaching of Commonwealth languages and literatures; nature and location of source materials; comparative studies; relation between English and indigenous literatures and languages; mass media and new varieties of English. **Structure** General Meeting (every 3 years); Board; Branches (9) including: *European Association for Commonwealth Literature and Language Studies (EACLALS, #05981); South Pacific Association for Commonwealth Literature and Language Studies (SPACLALS, see: #02439); Southern African Association for Commonwealth Literature and Language Studies (SAACLALS, see: #02439) West Indian Association for Commonwealth Literature and Language Studies (WIACLALS, #20921).* **Languages** English. **Staff** Voluntary. **Finance** Sources: members' dues; sponsorship. Supported by: *Commonwealth Foundation (CF, #04330).* **Activities** Events/meetings. **Events** *Triennial Conference* Toronto, ON (Canada) 2022, *Triennial Conference* Auckland (New Zealand) 2019, *Triennial Conference* Stellenbosch (South Africa) 2016, *Triennial Conference* St Lucia 2013, *Triennial Conference* Nicosia (Cyprus) 2010. **Publications** *ACLALS Newsletter*, *Postcolonial Text* – peer-reviewed open access journal. Conference reports; occasional publications; regional and scholarly journals.
Members Ordinary individuals resident in Commonwealth countries; Associate individuals resident outside the Commonwealth; Corporate national associations. Individuals in 69 countries and territories:
Australia, Austria, Bahamas, Bangladesh, Barbados, Belarus, Belgium, Belize, Botswana, Cameroon, Canada, China, Cook Is, Cyprus, Czechia, Denmark, Dominica, Fiji, Finland, France, Germany, Ghana, Greece, Guyana, Hong Kong, Hungary, Iceland, India, Ireland, Italy, Jamaica, Kenya, Kiribati, Lesotho, Malawi, Malaysia, Malta, Mauritius, Montenegro, Netherlands, New Zealand, Nigeria, Norway, Pakistan, Papua New Guinea, Philippines, Poland, Romania, Russia, Samoa, Serbia, Sierra Leone, Singapore, Slovakia, Solomon Is, South Africa, Sri Lanka, St Kitts-Nevis, St Lucia, St Vincent-Grenadines, Sweden, Switzerland, Tanzania UR, Trinidad-Tobago, Uganda, UK, Ukraine, USA, Zimbabwe.
NGO Relations Member of (2): *Commonwealth Consortium for Education (CCfE, #04318); International Federation for Modern Languages and Literatures (#13480).* Instrumental in setting up (1): *Association for the Study of Australasia in Asia (ASSA, #02937).* [2022.06.14/XC0100/**C**]

- ♦ Association of Commonwealth Newspapers, News Agencies and Periodicals / see CPU Media Trust (#04941)
- ♦ Association of Commonwealth Studies (inactive)

♦ Association of Commonwealth Universities, The (ACU) 02440

L'Association des universités du Commonwealth – Asociación de Universidades del Commonwealth – Vereinigung der Commonwealth Universitäten
SG Woburn House, 20-24 Tavistock Square, London, WC1H 9HF, UK. T. +442073806700. Fax +442073872655. E-mail: communications@acu.ac.uk.
URL: http://www.acu.ac.uk/
History Founded 1913, London (UK), as *Universities Bureau of the British Empire.* Name changed to *Association of Universities of the British Commonwealth* in 1948; present name adopted in 1963. First incorporated in UK in 1919; Royal Charter 1963. Registered UK Charity: 314137. **Aims** Promote and support excellence in higher education for the benefit of individuals and societies throughout the Commonwealth and beyond. **Structure** Council; Professional Networks (6). **Languages** English. **Staff** 115.00 FTE, paid. **Finance** Sources: members' dues. Other sources: programme fees; scholarship schemes; conferences; benchmarking; member activity income. **Activities** Events/meetings; guidance/assistance/consulting; knowledge management/information dissemination; networking/liaising; research/documentation. **Events** *HR in HE Community Conference* Delhi (India) 2020, *Workshop on Developing the Next Generation of Researchers* Kumasi (Ghana) 2020, *Journeys to Belonging Conference* London (UK) 2019, *Conference* Waterloo, ON (Canada) 2018, *Developing innovative minds, how to foster independent thinking as student numbers rise* Singapore (Singapore) 2017. **Publications** *Bulletin* (4 a year); *Realising Research* (2 a year). Reports; papers.
Members Higher education institutions (500) in 37 Commonwealth countries and territories:
Australia, Bangladesh, Botswana, Brunei Darussalam, Cameroon, Canada, Cyprus, Eswatini, Fiji, Ghana, Guyana, Hong Kong, India, Jamaica, Kenya, Lesotho, Malawi, Malaysia, Malta, Mauritius, Mozambique, Namibia, New Zealand, Nigeria, Pakistan, Papua New Guinea, Rwanda, Sierra Leone, Singapore, South Africa, Sri Lanka, Tanzania UR, Trinidad-Tobago, Uganda, UK, Zambia, Zimbabwe.
Consultative Status Consultative status granted from: *ECOSOC (#05331)* (Ros C); *UNESCO (#20322)* (Associate Status). **IGO Relations** Cooperates with: *Australian Aid (inactive); Commonwealth Secretariat (#04362); Department for International Development (DFID, inactive); European Commission (EC, #06633);* Foreign and Commonwealth Office (FCO). **NGO Relations** Close contacts with national and regional inter-university organizations and agencies worldwide. Cooperates with: *British Council*; national departments and governmental offices. [2021/XC0122/y/**C**]

- ♦ Association communautaire du droit des marques / see ECTA (#05341)
- ♦ Association entre la Communauté économique européenne et les Etats partenaires de la Communauté de l'Afrique orientale (inactive)
- ♦ Association entre la Communauté européenne et les Etats africains et malgache associés (inactive)
- ♦ Association de communautés chrétiennes missionnaires indépendantes / see The Family International (#09253)
- ♦ Association des communautés de travail des régions alpines (#02981)
- ♦ Association des communications et échanges internationaux de Yokohama (internationally oriented national body)

♦ Association for Community Colleges (ACC) 02441

Contact Dobri Daskalov 1/1-24, 1000 Skopje, North Macedonia. T. +389076420010. E-mail: office@acc.eu.org.
URL: http://www.acc.eu.org/
History 11 Aug 1999. Up to 2012, an independent chapter of *Association for World Education (AWE, #02983).* **Aims** Work towards the formation of a European transnational public sphere so as to have a vivid European democracy. **Structure** General Assembly (annual); Board. **Languages** English. **Finance** Sources: subscriptions; gifts; grants. **Activities** Advocacy/lobbying/activism; networking/liaising; training/education. **Publications** *ACC Bulletin*; *ACCENT Magazine.*
Members in 38 countries:
Albania, Austria, Azerbaijan, Belarus, Belgium, Bosnia-Herzegovina, Bulgaria, Croatia, Cyprus, Czechia, Denmark, Estonia, Finland, France, Georgia, Germany, Greece, Hungary, Ireland, Italy, Latvia, Lithuania, Malta, Netherlands, North Macedonia, Poland, Portugal, Romania, Russia, Serbia, Slovakia, Slovenia, Spain, Sweden, Türkiye, UK, Ukraine, USA.
NGO Relations Supports (1): *European Alliance for the Statute of the European Association (EASEA, #05886).* [2021.02.26/XD8738/v/**D**]

- ♦ Association des compagnies aériennes africaines (#00200)
- ♦ Association des compagnies d'aviation des régions d'Europe (#08347)
- ♦ Association for Comparative Economic Studies (internationally oriented national body)

♦ Association of the Compendium of Cultural Policies and Trends (CCPT Association) 02442

Contact Herengracht 415, 1017 BP Amsterdam, Netherlands. T. +31206243739. E-mail: office@culturalpolicies.net.
URL: http://www.culturalpolicies.net/web/compendium.php

History Compendium run by *Council of Europe (CE, #04881)* as a joint venture with *European Institute for Comparative Cultural Research (ERICarts, #07547)* from 1998 to 2017. Association set up 2017, Netherlands, where it is registered. Seat at Boekman Foundation, Amsterdam (Netherlands). Since 1 Apr 2018, transitioned into a multi-stakeholder Association. **Aims** Manage and financially support the database, which monitors national cultural policies and related development; develop knowledge, interaction and exchange in the globalizing cultural policy community; support exchange of free information. **Structure** General Assembly; Board; Service Providing Team; Community of Experts. **Languages** English. **Staff** 1.60 FTE, paid. **Finance** Members' dues. **Activities** Knowledge management/information dissemination; research/documentation. **Events** *General Assembly* Paris (France) 2019, *General Assembly* Rijeka (Croatia) 2018. **Publications** *Compendium Association Newsletter*. Country profiles. **Information Services** *Compendium of Cultural Policies and Trends*.
Members Founding/Permanent members (2):
Council of Europe (CE, #04881); European Institute for Comparative Cultural Research (ERICarts, #07547).
Stakeholders in 14 countries:
Austria, Belgium, Croatia, Cyprus, Finland, France, Germany, Latvia, Lithuania, Malta, Netherlands, Romania, Sweden, Switzerland.
Included in the above, 2 organizations listed in this Yearbook:
Asia-Europe Foundation (ASEF, #01270); European Cultural Foundation (ECF, #06868).
Standing Member:
European Association of Cultural Researchers (ECURES, #06000).
IGO Relations Partners include: *Asia-Europe Foundation (ASEF, #01270); European Audiovisual Observatory (#06294); European Cultural Foundation (ECF, #06868); Statistical Office of the European Union (Eurostat, #19974).* **NGO Relations** Partners include: *International Association of the European Heritage Network (HEREIN Association, #11881); International Federation of Arts Councils and Culture Agencies (IFACCA, #13358).* [2019.12.11/XM7061/y/E]

♦ Association for Competition Economics (ACE) 02443

Pres address not obtained. E-mail: conference@competitioneconomics.org.
URL: https://www.competitioneconomics.org/
History 2003. **Aims** Bring together competition economists working in government, academia and the private sector; provide a forum for discussion and debate on policies and specific cases. **Structure** Steering Committee; Executive Committee. **Activities** Awards/prizes/competitions; events/meetings. **Events** *Annual ACE Conference* Barcelona (Spain) 2021, *ACE Conference* 2020, *ACE Conference* Copenhagen (Denmark) 2019, *ACE Conference* Bologna (Italy) 2018, *ACE Conference* Madrid (Spain) 2017. [2021/AA2551/D]

- ♦ Association for Compositional Data (unconfirmed)
- ♦ Association pour une compréhension européenne à travers les frontières linguistiques / see Europa Klubo

♦ Association Computability in Europe (CiE) 02444

SG Dipartimento di Filosofia, UNIMI, Festa del Perdono 7, 20122 Milan MI, Italy.
URL: http://www.computability.org.uk/
History 2008, Athens (Greece), with conference organized since 2005. Current constitution adopted 2016. **Aims** Promote development, particularly in Europe, of computability-related science, ranging over mathematics, computer science, and applications in various natural and engineering sciences such as physics and biology. **Structure** Executive Committee. **Activities** Events/meetings. **Events** *Conference* Salerno (Italy) 2020, *Sailing routes in the world of computation* Durham (UK) 2019, *Conference* Kiel (Germany) 2018, *Unveiling dynamics and complexity* Turku (Finland) 2017, *Conference* Paris (France) 2016. **Publications** *Computability* – journal. *Theory and Applications of Computability* – book series.
Members Individuals in 64 countries and territories:
Afghanistan, Algeria, Argentina, Armenia, Australia, Austria, Azerbaijan, Bangladesh, Belgium, Brazil, Bulgaria, Canada, China, Colombia, Czechia, Denmark, Egypt, Fiji, Finland, France, Georgia, Germany, Greece, Hungary, Iceland, India, Iran Islamic Rep, Ireland, Israel, Italy, Japan, Kazakhstan, Korea Rep, Latvia, Lithuania, Malaysia, Malta, Mexico, Netherlands, New Zealand, North Macedonia, Norway, Pakistan, Peru, Philippines, Poland, Portugal, Qatar, Romania, Russia, Singapore, Slovakia, Slovenia, South Africa, Spain, Sweden, Switzerland, Taiwan, Türkiye, UK, Ukraine, USA, Venezuela, Vietnam. [2018/XM5526/c/E]

- ♦ Association for Computational Learning (unconfirmed)

♦ Association for Computational Linguistics (ACL) 02445

Main Office 209 N Eighth St, Stroudsburg PA 18360, USA. T. +15704768006. Fax +15704760860. E-mail: acl@aclweb.org.
URL: http://www.aclweb.org/
History 1967, USA. **Aims** Provide a forum for the exchange of knowledge and ideas and for technical advancement in the field of computational linguistics. **Structure** Annual Meeting. Chapters: *European Chapter of the Association for Computational Linguistics (EACL, see: #02445)*; North American Chapter of the Association for Computational Linguistics (NAACL). Special Interest Groups (SIGs). **Languages** English. **Activities** Organizes: annual conferences; workshops and tutorials. Provides access to ACL and related research papers. Special Interest Groups (14): Linguistic Annotation; Linguistic Data and Corpus-Based Approaches to NLP; Dialogue Processing; Natural Language Generation; Chinese Language Processing; Lexicon; Multimedia Language Processing; Mathematics of Language; Natural Language Learning; Natural Language Parsing; Computational Phonology; Computational Semantics; Computational Approaches to Semitic Languages; Web as Corpus. **Events** *Conference* 2023, *Conference on Empirical Methods in Natural Language Processing* Abu Dhabi (United Arab Emirates) 2022, *International Joint Conference on Natural Language Processing* 2021, *Annual Meeting* Bangkok (Thailand) 2021, *International Joint Conference on Natural Language Processing* 2020. **Publications** *Computational Linguistics Journal* (4 a year); *ACL Anthology*. Conference proceedings.
Members Full in 57 countries and territories:
Australia, Austria, Bahrain, Belgium, Brazil, Bulgaria, Canada, China, Croatia, Cuba, Czechia, Denmark, Egypt, Estonia, Finland, France, Germany, Greece, Hong Kong, Hungary, Iceland, India, Indonesia, Ireland, Israel, Italy, Japan, Jordan, Korea Rep, Latvia, Lithuania, Malaysia, Malta, Mexico, Netherlands, New Zealand, Norway, Pakistan, Philippines, Poland, Portugal, Romania, Russia, Saudi Arabia, Singapore, Slovakia, Slovenia, South Africa, Spain, Sweden, Switzerland, Taiwan, Türkiye, UK, Ukraine, USA, Vietnam. [2021/XD3979/F]

- ♦ Association for Computer Aided Design in Architecture (internationally oriented national body)

♦ Association for Computers and the Humanities (ACH) 02446

Hon Sec Boston University Libraries, 771 Commonwealth Ave, Boston MA 02215, USA. T. +16173586370. E-mail: secretary@ach.org – webmaster@ach.org.
URL: http://www.ach.org/
History 1978. **Aims** Encourage appropriate uses of computers and related technologies in the study of the humanities. **Structure** Executive Council, including President, Immediate Past-President, Vice-President, Executive Secretary, Treasurer. **Languages** English. **Finance** Members' dues. **Events** *Annual Conference* Pittsburgh, PA (USA) 2019, *Digital Humanities Conference* Lausanne (Switzerland) 2014, *Digital Humanities Conference* Lincoln, NE (USA) 2013, *Digital humanities conference* Oulu (Finland) 2008, *Digital humanities conference* Urbana, IL (USA) 2007. **Publications** *Computers and the Humanities* (6 a year).
Members Individuals in 21 countries:
Austria, Belgium, Canada, France, Germany, Greece, Hungary, Ireland, Italy, Japan, Korea Rep, Lithuania, Mexico, Netherlands, Norway, Poland, Spain, Sweden, Türkiye, UK, USA.
NGO Relations Instrumental in setting up: *Alliance of Digital Humanities Organizations (ADHO, #00671).* [2020/XD6617/D]

♦ Association for Computing Machinery (ACM) 02447

Headquarters 2 Penn Plaza, Ste 701, New York NY 10121-0121, USA. T. +12128697440. Fax +12129441318. E-mail: acmhelp@acm.org.
URL: http://www.acm.org/
History 1947, New York, NY (USA). Founded as an international scientific and educational organization. 1949, constitution approved. Former names and other names: *Eastern Association for Computing Machinery* – former (1947 to 1948). **Aims** Deliver resources that advance computing as a science and a profession; provide the computing field's premier Digital Library; serve members and the computing profession with leading-edge publications, conferences and career resources. **Structure** Council; Executive Committee. Boards (3): Education; Practitioners; Publications. SGB Executive Committee. Regional Councils (3): Europe; India; China. Special Interest Groups (37). **Events** *Design, Automation and Test in Europe Conference (DATE)* Antwerp (Belgium) 2023, *Web Conference* Austin, TX (USA) 2023, *Annual Conference on Human-Robot Interaction* Stockholm (Sweden) 2023, *ACM Multimedia Asia Conference (MM Asia)* Tainan (Taiwan) 2023, *AINTEC: Asian Internet Engineering Conference* Hiroshima (Japan) 2022. **Publications** *ACM Communications* (12 a year); *Mobile Networks and Applications (MONET)* (4 a year) – jointly with Baltzer Publishers; *Journal of Experimental Algorithmics (JEA)* (periodical) – online publication through http, ftp, and ftpmail; *netWorker* (periodical); *StandardView* (periodical). **Members** Worldwide membership of 100,000. Membership countries not specified. **NGO Relations** Member of: *American Association for the Advancement of Science (AAAS); International Federation for Information Processing (IFIP, #13458); Internet Society (ISOC, #15952); ORCID (#17790).* European Council is member of: *European Forum for ICST (#07316).* Instrumental in setting up: *Environmental Design Research Association (EDRA).* Collaborates with: *European Society for Applied Mathematics (EUROSAM, #08521).* [2020/XN8383/F]

- ♦ Association of Concerned Africa Scholars (internationally oriented national body)
- ♦ Association de la Conférence mondiale sur la recherche dans les transports (#21301)

♦ Association des conférences épiscopales de l'Afrique centrale (ACEAC) 02448

Association of Central African Episcopal Conferences
SG rue Joseph Bolle 2, 6240 Farciennes, Belgium. E-mail: jpbadidi@yahoo.be.
Secretariat BP 20511, Gombe, Kinshasa, Congo DR. E-mail: aceac.secretariat@gmail.com.
History 3 Dec 1984, Kinshasa (Zaire). Registered in accordance with the law of Congo DR. One of the regions of *Symposium of Episcopal Conferences of Africa and Madagascar (SECAM, #20077).* **Aims** Study the means to promote dialogue, consultation, mutual aid and ecclesiastical cooperation between Episcopal conferences for the profound evangelization of the African man in his cultural, social and religious environment. **Structure** Plenary Assembly; Permanent Committee; Presidency; Bureau; Secretariat General; Commissions. **Languages** English, French. **Staff** 1.00 FTE, paid. **Finance** Members' dues. Budget (annual): euro 24,790. **Activities** Networking/liaising; events/meetings. **Events** *Young forum* Goma (Congo DR) 2009, *Extraordinary plenary assembly* Kinshasa (Congo DR) 2009, *Statutory meeting* Butare (Rwanda) 2008, *Congrès continental de justice et paix* Kinshasa (Congo DR) 2008, *Extraordinary plenary assembly / Plenary Assembly* Kinshasa (Congo DR) 2007. **Publications** *ACEAC Nouvelles* (3 a year) – bulletin.
Members Episcopal conferences of 3 countries:
Burundi, Congo DR, Rwanda. [2018/XD0779/D]

- ♦ Association des conférences épiscopales de l'Afrique de l'Ouest anglophone (inactive)
- ♦ Association des conférences épiscopales du Congo, Centrafrique et Tchad / Cameroun / see Association of the Episcopal Conferences of the Central African Region (#02491)
- ♦ Association des conférences épiscopales du Congo, de la République centrafricaine, du Tchad et du Cameroun / see Association of the Episcopal Conferences of the Central African Region (#02491)
- ♦ Association des conférences épiscopales membres de l'Afrique de l'Est (#02805)
- ♦ Association des conférences épiscopales de la région de l'Afrique centrale (#02491)
- ♦ Association for Conflict Resolution (internationally oriented national body)
- ♦ Association congrégationaliste internationale (#12889)
- ♦ Association du Congrès panaméricain des chemins de fer (#18124)
- ♦ Association du congrès de la propriété minière, du travail, de l'hygiène et de la sécurité dans les mines (inactive)
- ♦ Association of the Congress of Mining Property, of Work, Hygiene and Security in the Mines (inactive)
- ♦ Association des conjoints du service extérieur de la commission européenne (internationally oriented national body)
- ♦ Association Conoscere Eurasia (internationally oriented national body)
- ♦ Association of Consecrated Women in Eastern and Central Africa (unconfirmed)
- ♦ Association des conseillers européens (inactive)
- ♦ Association des conseils asiatiques pour la recherche en sciences sociales (#02382)
- ♦ Association des conseils chrétiens et eglises en afrique de l'ouest (#09724)
- ♦ Association for the Conservation of the Cultural Heritage for the Americas / see Association for Heritage Preservation of the Americas
- ♦ Association for the Conservation of the Cultural Patrimony of the Americas / see Association for Heritage Preservation of the Americas
- ♦ Association pour la conservation des ressources océaniques (inactive)
- ♦ Association des consommateurs des Caraïbes (inactive)
- ♦ Association des consommateurs Tiers-monde / see Association for the Advancement of Consumerism in the World (#02347)
- ♦ Association pour une constitution mondiale et un parlement mondial (#21313)

♦ Association for Constraint Programming (ACP) 02449

Past-Pres address not obtained.
Events Manager address not obtained.
URL: https://www.a4cp.org/
History 2005, France. Registration: Start date: 14 May 2005, France. **Aims** Promote constraint programming in every aspect of the scientific world, by encouraging its theoretical and practical developments, its teachning in the academic institutions, its adoption in the industrial world, and its use in the the application fields. **Structure** General Assembly; Executive Committee. **Languages** English, French. **Staff** 10.00 FTE, voluntary. **Activities** Events/meetings; research/documentation. **Events** *International Conference on Principles and Practice of Constraint Programming* Montpellier (France) 2021, *International Conference on Principles and Practice of Constraint Programming* Storrs, CT (USA) 2020, *International Conference on Principles and Practice of Constraint Programming* Stamford, CT (USA) 2019, *International Conference on Principles and Practice of Constraint Programming* Lille (France) 2018, *International Conference on Principles and Practice of Constraint Programming* Melbourne, VIC (Australia) 2017.
Members Individuals in 23 countries:
Algeria, Australia, Belgium, Cameroon, Canada, Czechia, Denmark, Finland, France, Germany, Greece, Italy, Morocco, Netherlands, Norway, Poland, Portugal, South Africa, Spain, Sweden, Switzerland, UK, USA. [2023.02.14/AA1475/v/C]

- ♦ Association des constructeurs européens d'automobiles (#06300)
- ♦ Association des constructeurs européens de machines électro-portatives / see European Power Tool Association (#08264)

♦ Association des constructeurs européens de motocycles (ACEM) . . 02450

Motorcycle Industry in Europe
SG ACEM GEIE/EEIG, Avenue de la Joyeuse Entrée 1, 1040 Brussels, Belgium. T. +3222309732. E-mail: acem@acem.eu.
URL: http://www.acem.eu/
History 12 Jan 1994. Founded on merger of a previous association 'ACEM', originally set up 1990, with *Comité de liaison des constructeurs de motocycles de la Communauté européenne (COLIMO, inactive)*, set up 1962. A grouping of the type *European Economic Interest Grouping (EEIG, #06960).* Former names and other names: *Association of European Motorcycle Manufacturers* – alias; *European Association of Motorcycle Manufacturers* – alias. Registration: No/ID: 0451.945.071, Start date: 12 Jan 1994, Belgium; EU Transparency Register, No/ID: 02480451230-88, Start date: 25 Feb 2009. **Aims** Develop and support the common interests of motorcycle manufacturers in European Union and other European countries; monitor, study, analyse and inform members and the general public on environmental, economic, safety, technical, transport, legal, fiscal and other issues of common interest; inform members about trends and developments; develop, coordinate and implement joint positions; support European Community authorities in dealing with matters of common interest; maintain contacts and present homogenous positions in dealing with other European and international bodies; support free and fair *competition*. **Structure** General Assembly; Executive Committee; Coordinating Committee; Secretariat in Brussels (Belgium). Committees (5) responding to Coordinating Committee: Legal; Safety; Environment; Market Transport Policy; E-Vehicles. **Languages** English, French. **Staff** 8.00 FTE, paid. **Finance** Budget (2015): euro 1,108,000. **Activities** Networking/liaising; knowledge management/information dissemiantion; advocacy/lobbying/activism; monitoring/evaluation; events/meetings. **Events** *General Assembly* Saint-Quentin (France) 2019, *Sustainable motorcycling in Europe* Brussels

(Belgium) 2018, *General Assembly* Berlin (Germany) 2017, *The safe ride to the future* Brussels (Belgium) 2016, *General Assembly* Salzburg (Austria) 2016. **Publications** Newsletters; Annual Report; position papers. **Members** Manufacturers (18) and national associations (17) in 15 countries:
Austria, Belgium, Czechia, France, Germany, Greece, Ireland, Italy, Netherlands, Poland, Romania, Spain, Sweden, Switzerland, UK.
NGO Relations Member of: *European Green Vehicles Initiative Association (EGVIA, #07410); Forum for Mobility and Society (FMS, #09924); Industry4Europe (#11181); International Motorcycle Manufacturers Association (IMMA, #14186); Mobility for Prosperity in Europe (MPE, #16839).* [2020/XD4097/t/F]

- ♦ Association des constructeurs européens de systèmes d'alarme, incendie et vol / see Association of European Manufacturers of Fire and Security Systems (#02520)
- ♦ Association des constructeurs et installateurs européens de systèmes de sécurité et d'incendie (#02520)
- ♦ Association de consultants internationaux en droits de l'homme (inactive)

♦ Association of Consumer Credit Information Suppliers (ACCIS) 02451

Dir-Gen Rue du Luxembourg 22-24, 1000 Brussels, Belgium. T. +3227616693. E-mail: secretariat@accis.eu.
URL: http://www.accis.eu/

History 1990, Dublin (Ireland). Registration: Banque-Carrefour des Entreprises, No/ID: 0884.372.853, Start date: 26 Jul 2006, Belgium; EU Transparency Register, No/ID: 21868711871-63, Start date: 22 Jun 2009. **Aims** Represent, promote, protect and preserve members' interests, and in particular with regard to international matters and questions arising in connection with the European Community. **Structure** General Assembly (at least annual); Management Board. **Activities** Events/meetings. **Events** *World Consumer Credit Reporting Conference* Barcelona (Spain) 2022, *World Consumer Credit Reporting Conference* Barcelona (Spain) 2021, *World Consumer Credit Reporting Conference* Barcelona (Spain) 2020, *World Consumer Credit Reporting Conference* New Delhi (India) 2018, *World Consumer Credit Reporting Conference* Toronto, ON (Canada) 2016.
Members Full in 30 countries:
Albania, Armenia, Austria, Belgium, Croatia, Cyprus, Czechia, Denmark, Estonia, Finland, Germany, Greece, Hungary, Iceland, Ireland, Italy, Kosovo, Lithuania, Netherlands, Norway, Poland, Romania, Russia, Slovakia, Slovenia, Spain, Sweden, Switzerland, Türkiye, UK.
Associate in 7 countries and territories:
China, Curaçao, Mexico, Suriname, Taiwan, Thailand, USA.
Affiliate in 2 countries:
Brazil, USA.
NGO Relations Member of (1): *SME Finance Forum (#19323).* [2020/XJ7981/D]

- ♦ Association of Container Reconditioners / see International Confederation of Container Reconditioners (#12854)

♦ Association for Contextual Behavioral Science (ACBS) 02452

Exec Dir 1880 Pinegrove Dr, Jenison MI 49428, USA. E-mail: acbs@contextualscience.org.
URL: http://contextualscience.org/

History Set up 2005; incorporated 2006. **Aims** Advance functional contextual cognitive and behavioral science and practice so as to alleviate human suffering and advance human well being. **Structure** Board of Directors; Committees. **Languages** English. **Staff** 3.00 FTE, paid. **Finance** Sources: meeting proceeds; members' dues. **Activities** Events/meetings; networking/liaising; training/education. **Events** *World Conference* San Francisco, CA (USA) 2022, *World Conference* Jenison, MI (USA) 2021, *World Conference* Jenison, MI (USA) 2020, *World Conference* Dublin (Ireland) 2019, *World Conference* Montréal, QC (Canada) 2018. **Publications** *ACBS Newsletter*; *Journal of Contextual Behavioral Science (JCBS).* **Members** Membership in over 50 countries. Membership countries not specified. [2015.06.01/XJ9540/C]

- ♦ Association of Contractors in the Amazon Region (inactive)
- ♦ Association pour la coopération académique (#00019)
- ♦ Association for Cooperation in Banana Research in the Caribbean and Tropical America (no recent information)
- ♦ Association de coopération et d'éducation aux développements (internationally oriented national body)
- ♦ Association pour la coopération des Eglises, l'environnement et le développement de l'Afrique centrale (no recent information)
- ♦ Association for the Cooperation of Employers (no recent information)
- ♦ Association pour la coopération des recherches bananières aux Antilles et en Amérique tropicale (no recent information)
- ♦ Association pour la coopération scientifique en Asie (no recent information)
- ♦ Association for Cooperation with the South – Las Segovias (internationally oriented national body)

♦ Association for Cooperation on Sustainable Development and Sustainable Construction in the Mediterranean (SD-MED Association) 02453

Pres 7 Pinotsi St, 117 41 Athens, Greece. T. +302109215981. Fax +302109215981. E-mail: sdmed.planning@gmail.com.
URL: http://sd-med.org/

History Sep 2004. **Aims** Promote sustainable development focusing on: terrestrial spatial planning and urban environment and construction; maritime spatial planning and ecosystem-based management; green infrastructure and ecosystem services based spatial planning, including in the urban context. **Structure** Administrative Council; International Forum; Scientific Council; National Team Coordinators (25); Corresponding Local Teams; Thematic Colleges (5). **Languages** English, French, Irish Gaelic. **Staff** 10.00 FTE, paid. **Finance** Members' dues. Other sources: grants; sponsorships. **Activities** Training/education; events/meetings. **Events** *ECHOPOLIS Conference* Athens (Greece) 2018, *ECHOPOLIS Conference* Athens (Greece) 2013, *Conference* Athens (Greece) 2012, *Conference* Athens (Greece) 2011, *Conference* Athens (Greece) 2010. **Publications** *SD-MED Guide to Sustainable Construction*; *SD-MED Process for Building*; *SD-MED Process for Neighborhoods.* Books; conference proceedings.
Members in 21 countries and territories:
Albania, Algeria, Argentina, Bulgaria, Canada, Egypt, France, Greece, Israel, Italy, Japan, Jordan, Morocco, Netherlands, Palestine, Romania, Serbia, Spain, Tunisia, UK, USA.
IGO Relations Partners: *OECD (#17693)*; *UNEP (#20299).* **NGO Relations** Partners: *Association Europa*; *International Council for Research and Innovation in Building and Construction (CIB, #13069)*; *Union internationale des architectes (UIA, #20419)*; *Union méditerranéenne des architectes (UMAR, #20459)*; national organizations; universities. [2018.04.04/XM0030/D]

♦ Association Coopérative des Automobilistes et des motocyclistes des Secrétariats et Bureaux des organisations Internationales et des institutions Accrédités (CASBIA) 02454

International Officials Motoring Association

Mailing address Bureau Salève 196, 150 route de Ferney, 1218 Le Grand-Saconnex GE, Switzerland. T. +41229200420. E-mail: info@casbia.ch.
URL: http://casbia.ch/

History 1926, as a cooperative membership organization for international civil servants. Registered in accordance with Swiss law. **Aims** Negotiate agreements with partners in the field of insurances, garages, car representative dealers, suppliers of tyres and gas, fitness centres, etc. **Publications** Information circular (1-2 a year).
Members Full in 2 countries:
France, Switzerland. [2016/XE5556/E]

- ♦ Association of Co-operative Banks of the EC / see European Association of Co-operative Banks (#05990)
- ♦ Association coopérative européenne des fonctionnaires internationaux / see Association coopérative financière des fonctionnaires internationaux (#02455)

♦ Association coopérative financière des fonctionnaires internationaux (AMFIE) 02455

Financial Cooperative Association of International Civil Servants (AMFIE)

Chairman Blvd Royal 25A, L-2449 Luxembourg, Luxembourg. T. +3524236611. Fax +352423660. E-mail: amfie@amfie.org.
Managing Dir address not obtained.
URL: http://www.amfie.org/

History Nov 1990, Luxembourg (Luxembourg). Founded by a group of 21 international officials. Statutes amended 5 Dec 1994; Jun 2001; Jun 2006; consolidated Jun 2007. Former names and other names: *Cooperative Society for Staff Members of Intergovernmental Organizations Having their Headquarters or Permanent Offices in Europe (AMFIE)* – former (Nov 1990); *Association coopérative européenne des fonctionnaires internationaux (AMFIE)* – former; *European Cooperative Association of International Civil Servants* – former. Registration: Registre de commerce et des sociétés RCS, No/ID: B35566, Start date: 24 Dec 1990, Luxembourg. **Aims** Serve intergovernmental civil servants and their families who work for (or have retired from) intergovernmental organizations; encourage mutual assistance among members, enabling them to *invest* their *savings*; offer a range of financial products, in particular the possibility of a savings account remunerated at advantageous rates. **Structure** General Meeting (annual); Board of Directors. **Languages** English, French. **Staff** 20.00 FTE, paid. **Finance** Sources: members' dues. Annual budget: 125,000 EUR. **Activities** Events/meetings; financial and/or material support. **Events** *Annual meeting* Luxembourg (Luxembourg) 2003, *Annual meeting* Luxembourg (Luxembourg) 2002, *Annual meeting* Luxembourg (Luxembourg) 2001, *Annual meeting* Luxembourg (Luxembourg) 2000, *Annual meeting* Luxembourg (Luxembourg) 1999. **Publications** Newsletters. Annual Report. **Members** Membership open to: intergovernmental organizations; serving, former and retired international civil servants employed by these organizations; representative bodies composed of serving or retired international civil servants, recognized by the intergovernmental organizations listed above; persons who have or have had regular and contractual links of a lasting or recurring nature with these organizations and meeting the requirements laid down by the Board of Directors; a member's spouse or partner within the meaning of the relevant laws, any person directly related to a member in the ascending or descending line (ie parents and children), a member's siblings and their children, together with any person receiving one or more shares by donation or legacy; employees in permanent posts with an international organization and consultants with a contract of six months or more. Over 8,000 members in 146 organizations. **NGO Relations** Member of (1): *Association for Human Resources Management in International Organizations (AHRMIO, #02634).* [2023.02.14/XD3151/F]

♦ Association for Cooperative Operations Research and Development (ACORD) 02456

Pres/CEO One Blue Hill Plaza, 15th Fl, PO Box 1529, Pearl River NY 10965-85290, USA. T. +18456201700. Fax +18456203600. E-mail: memberservices@acord.org.
London Office 8th Fl, 1 Minster Court, Mincing Lane, London, EC3R 7AA, UK. T. +442038086012.
URL: http://www.acord.org/

History 1970. **Aims** Serve the *insurance* and related industries. **Structure** Board of Directors. Standards Committee. **Activities** Events/meetings; knowledge management/information dissemination; standards/guidelines. **Events** *Conference* Boca Raton, FL (USA) 2016, *Forum Southern Africa* Johannesburg (South Africa) 2016, *Conference* Boca Raton, FL (USA) 2015. **NGO Relations** Liaison Organization of: *Comité européen de normalisation (CEN, #04162).* [2016/XM4796/C]

- ♦ Association of Co-operative Savings and Credit Institutions of the EEC / see European Association of Co-operative Banks (#05990)
- ♦ Association des coopératives d'épargne et de crédit d'Afrique (#00261)
- ♦ Association des coopératives et mutuelles d'assurances d'Amérique / see International Cooperative and Mutual Insurance Federation / Regional Association for The Americas (#12949)
- ♦ Association Coordinating Regulatory Matters for European National Aero Clubs and Associations of Member States of the European Civil Aviation Conference / see Europe Air Sports (#05776)
- ♦ Association of Corporate Treasurers (internationally oriented national body)
- ♦ Association cotonnière africaine (#00270)

♦ Association of Cotton Merchants in Europe (ACME) 02457

Association des marchands de coton en Europe

Secretariat International Cotton Association, 6th Floor – Walker House, Exchange Flags, Liverpool, L2 3YL, UK. T. +441512366041. Fax +441512550174. E-mail: info@ica-ltd.org.
Members Full in 53 countries and territories:
Argentina, Australia, Austria, Azerbaijan, Bangladesh, Belgium, Benin, Brazil, Chad, Chile, China, Denmark, Estonia, France, Germany, Greece, India, Israel, Italy, Japan, Kazakhstan, Kenya, Korea Rep, Latvia, Mexico, Pakistan, Panama, Paraguay, Poland, Portugal, Russia, Singapore, South Africa, Spain, Sudan, Switzerland, Syrian AR, Taiwan, Tajikistan, Tanzania UR, Thailand, Türkiye, Uganda, UK, Ukraine, United Arab Emirates, Uruguay, USA, Venezuela, Vietnam, Virgin Is UK, Zambia, Zimbabwe. [2017.03.08/XD2136/D]

♦ Association of the Councils of State and Supreme Administrative Jurisdictions of the European Union (ACA-Europe) 02458

Associations des conseils d'état et des juridictions administratives suprêmes de l'Union européenne

Contact Conseil d'état de Belgique, Rue de la Science 33, 1040 Brussels, Belgium. T. +3222349744. E-mail: info@aca-europe.eu.
URL: http://www.aca-europe.eu/

History Jun 1998, Stockholm (Sweden). Established after a series of colloquia. Statutes adopted May 2000, Vienna (Austria). Registration: Belgium. **Aims** Obtain a better understanding of EU law by the judges of the Supreme Administrative Courts across Europe and a better knowledge of the functioning of the other Supreme Administrative Courts in the implementation of EU law; improve mutual trust between judges of the Supreme Administrative Courts; foster an effectively and efficiently functioning of administrative justice in the EU; provide exchange of ideas on the rule of law in the administrative judicial systems; ensure access to the decisions of the Supreme Administrative Courts implementing EU law. **Structure** General Assembly (annual); Board; General Secretariat. **Languages** English, French. **Finance** Sources: contributions of member/participating states; subsidies. **Activities** Events/meetings; knowledge management/information dissemination; networking/liaising; research/documentation. **Events** *Biennal Colloquium* Leipzig (Germany) 2021, *Biennal Colloquium* The Hague (Netherlands) 2018, *Biennal Colloquium* Prague (Czechia) 2016, *Biennial Colloquium* Strasbourg (France) 2014, *Biennial Colloquium* Madrid (Spain) 2012. **Publications** *E-NEWS.*
Members Jurisdictions of 27 countries:
Austria, Belgium, Bulgaria, Croatia, Cyprus, Czechia, Denmark, Estonia, Finland, France, Germany, Greece, Hungary, Ireland, Italy, Latvia, Lithuania, Luxembourg, Malta, Netherlands, Poland, Portugal, Romania, Slovakia, Slovenia, Spain, Sweden.
Regional organization (1):
Court of Justice of the European Union (CJEU, #04938).
Observers (4):
Albania, Montenegro, Serbia, Türkiye.
Guests (3):
Norway, Switzerland, UK. [2022.11.30/XD2109/D*]

- ♦ Association de coureurs internationaux en multicoques océaniques (inactive)
- ♦ Association des cours constitutionnelles ayant en partage l'usage du français / see Association des cours constitutionnelles Francophone (#02459)

♦ Association des cours constitutionnelles Francophone (ACCF) 02459

SG 2 rue de Montpensier, 75001 Paris, France. T. +33140153050. Fax +33140153188. E-mail: relations-exterieures@conseil-constitutionnel.fr.
URL: https://accf-francophonie.org/

History 9 Apr 1997, Paris (France) as *Association des cours constitutionnelles ayant en partage l'usage du français (ACCPUF).* Present title adopted May 2019. Registered in accordance with French law. **Aims** Increase cooperation between *constitutional courts* of *French-speaking* countries. **Structure** General Assembly (every 3 years); Council; Permanent Secretariat in Paris (France). **Languages** French. **Staff** 5.00 FTE, paid. **Finance**

Association courtiers africains
02459

alphabetic sequence excludes
For the complete listing, see Yearbook Online at

Members' dues. **Activities** Monitoring/evaluation; events/meetings. **Events** *Congrès* Dakar (Senegal) 2022, *Congrès* Montréal, QC (Canada) 2019, *Congrès / Triennial Congress* Lausanne (Switzerland) 2015, *Congrès / Triennial Congress* Marrakech (Morocco) 2012, *Congrès / Triennial Congress* Cotonou (Benin) 2009. **Publications** *ACCF Bulletin* (annual). Congress proceedings.
Members Institutions in 45 countries:
Albania, Andorra, Angola, Belgium, Benin, Bulgaria, Burkina Faso, Burundi, Cambodia, Cameroon, Canada, Cape Verde, Central African Rep, Chad, Comoros, Congo Brazzaville, Congo DR, Côte d'Ivoire, Djibouti, Egypt, Equatorial Guinea, France, Gabon, Guinea, Guinea-Bissau, Haiti, Lebanon, Luxembourg, Madagascar, Mali, Mauritania, Mauritius, Moldova, Monaco, Morocco, Mozambique, Niger, Romania, Rwanda, Senegal, Serbia, Seychelles, Switzerland, Togo, Tunisia.
Observers in 3 countries:
Algeria, Bahrain, Hungary.
IGO Relations Participates in: *World Conference on Constitutional Justice (WCCJ, #21298)*. Agreement with: *Council of Europe (CE, #04881)*. [2019.07.11/XD7112/**D**]

♦ Association des courtiers africains d'assurance (#02358)
♦ Association des courtiers et intervenants frontaliers internationaux (internationally oriented national body)
♦ Association for the Creation of a Bureau of International Language (inactive)
♦ Association pour la création d'un bureau de la langue internationale (inactive)

♦ Association of Credit Rating Agencies in Asia (ACRAA) 02460

Chairman JCR-VIS Credit Rating Co Ltd, VIS House 128/C, 25th Lane Off Khayaban-e-Ittehad, Phase VII DHA, Karachi, Pakistan. T. +9221531186170.
SG address not obtained.
URL: http://acraa.com/
History 14 Sep 2001, Manila (Philippines), at headquarters of *Asian Development Bank (ADB, #01422)*. **Aims** Promote interaction and exchange of ideas, experiences, information, knowledge and skills among credit rating agencies in Asia; promote adoption of best practices and common standards than ensure high quality and comparability of credit ratings throughout the region; promote development of Asia's bond markets and cross-border investment. **Languages** English. **Activities** Events/meetings. **Events** *Workshop on Opportunities in Infrastructure Projects* Bangkok (Thailand) 2017.
Members Credit Rating Agencies (32) in 15 countries and territories:
Bahrain, Bangladesh, China, India, Indonesia, Japan, Kazakhstan, Korea Rep, Malaysia, Pakistan, Philippines, Sri Lanka, Taiwan, Thailand, Türkiye. [2015.11.06/XM0009/**D**]

♦ Association des Créoles de Base Lexicale Portugaise et Espagnole (#02325)

♦ Association of Critical Heritage Studies (ACHS) 02461

Pres address not obtained. E-mail: info@criticalheritagestudies.org.
URL: https://www.criticalheritagestudies.org/
History 2012, Gothenburg (Sweden). Registration: Canada. **Aims** Promote and develop heritage studies as a social, cultural, economic and political phenomenon and as an area of professional or governmental intervention from a perspective of sustainability and social and cultural equity. **Structure** General Meeting; Executive Committee. Chapters. **Events** *Conference* Auckland (New Zealand) 2026, *Conference* Galway (Ireland) 2024, *Conference* Santiago (Chile) 2022, *Conference* London (UK) 2020, *Conference* Hangzhou (China) 2018. [2020/AA0835/**C**]

♦ Association des cultivateurs de canne à sucre des Caraïbes (inactive)

♦ Association of Cultural Attachés from Latin American Countries, Spain and Portugal 02462

Asociación de Agregados Culturales de Latinoamérica, España y Portugal (ACALASP)
Contact c/o Embassy of Brasil in London, 14-16 Cockspur Street, London, SW1Y 5BL, UK. T. +442077474500. E-mail: viaartsprize@gmail.com.
URL: http://www.viaartsprize.org/
History Set up with the title: *Association of Cultural Attachés of Latin America, Spain and Portugal*. Also referred to as *Association of Ibero-American Cultural Attachés*. **Aims** Promote greater knowledge of Latin America and Iberia. **Activities** Events/meetings; awards/prizes/competitions. **IGO Relations** *OAS (#17629)*. **NGO Relations** *American Film Institute (AFI)*; *Cultural Foundation of the Americas (CFA)*. [2020/XJ7151/y/**D**]

♦ Association of Cultural Attachés of Latin America, Spain and Portugal / see Association of Cultural Attachés from Latin American Countries, Spain and Portugal (#02462)
♦ Association for Cultural Economics / see Association for Cultural Economics International (#02463)

♦ Association for Cultural Economics International (ACEI) 02463

Exec Sec-Treas c/o RMIT School of Economics, Finance & Marketing, Level 11, 445 Swanston Street, Melbourne VIC 3000, Australia.
URL: http://culturaleconomics.org/
History Oct 1992, Fort Worth, TX (USA). Founded at 7th international conference, conferences having been held since 1979 under the auspices of the then Association for Cultural Economics (ACE) which was founded by Prof William Hendon. **Aims** Promote scholarly investigation of issues involved in the economics of cultural activities; provide opportunities for sharing the results of this research among members of the academic community, the community of arts and heritage organizations, the community of arts practitioners, the community of the artists and other interested parties. **Structure** Executive Board consisting of President, President-Elect, Immediate Past President, Executive Secretary-Treasurer and 9 elected Board members. **Languages** English. **Staff** None. **Finance** Sources: members' dues. **Activities** Events/meetings; knowledge management/information dissemination; networking/liaising. **Events** *International Conference on Cultural Economics* Melbourne, VIC (Australia) / Copenhagen (Denmark) 2021, *International Conference on Cultural Economics'* Melbourne, VIC (Australia) 2018, *International Conference on Cultural Economics* Valladolid (Spain) 2016, *International Conference on Cultural Economics* Montréal, QC (Canada) 2014, *International Conference on Cultural Economics* Kyoto (Japan) 2012. **Publications** *Journal of Cultural Economics* (4 a year); *ACEI Newletter*.
Members Individuals (about 350) in 41 countries and territories:
Argentina, Australia, Austria, Belgium, Brazil, Canada, Chile, China, Cuba, Denmark, Finland, France, Germany, Greece, Hungary, India, Ireland, Italy, Japan, Korea Rep, Luxembourg, Mexico, Netherlands, Nigeria, Norway, Philippines, Poland, Portugal, Romania, Russia, Serbia, Singapore, South Africa, Spain, Sweden, Switzerland, Taiwan, UK, Uruguay, USA, Vietnam. [2022.02.23/XD4864/v/**D**]

♦ Association for Cultural Studies (ACS) 02464

Contact PO Box 35, Dept of Music, Art and Culture Studies, Univ of Jyväskylä, FI-40014 Jyväskylä, Finland. E-mail: info@cultstud.org.
URL: https://www.cultstud.org/
History 2002. Registration: No/ID: BID 1914311-6, Finland. **Aims** Form and promote an effective worldwide community of cultural studies. **Structure** Board; Executive Committee. Committees (4): Conference; Communications and Membership; Financial; ACS Development. **Finance** Sources: members' dues. **Activities** Awards/prizes/competitions; events/meetings. **Events** *International Conference on Crossroads in Cultural Studies* Lisbon (Portugal) 2022, *International Conference on Crossroads in Cultural Studies* Shanghai (China) 2018, *International Conference on Crossroads in Cultural Studies* Sydney, NSW (Australia) 2016, *International Conference on Crossroads in Cultural Studies* Tampere (Finland) 2014, *International Conference on Crossroads in Cultural Studies* Paris (France) 2012. [2023.02.17/AA0321/**B**]

♦ Association for Cultural, Technical and Educational Cooperation / see ACTEC – Association for Cultural, Technical and Educational Cooperation
♦ Association of Culture and Art Development in Balkans (internationally oriented national body)
♦ Association culturelle d'aide à la promotion éducative et sociale (internationally oriented national body)
♦ Association for Curative Education and Social Therapy in the Nordic countries (#17482)
♦ Association of Cyber Forensics and Threat Investigators (unconfirmed)
♦ Association des cyclistes de l'UE (#08984)
♦ Association des cytogénéticiens européens (#06880)

♦ Association des dames de la charité de Saint-Vincent-de-Paul, Oeuvre des pauvres malades / see Association Internationale des Charités (#02675)
♦ Association de Danemark pour la coopération internationale (internationally oriented national body)
♦ Association danoise pour la collaboration nordique (internationally oriented national body)

♦ Association Dealing with International Travel Facilities for Railway Staff 02465

Groupement pour les facilités de circulation internationale du personnel des chemins de fer (FIP) – Vereinigung für die internationalen Fahrvergünstigungen des Eisenbahnpersonals
Address not obtained.
URL: http://www.uic.org/spip.php?rubrique1817
History A special group of *International Union of Railways (#15813)*. [2010/XF5010/**F**]

♦ Association of Deans of Southeast Asian Graduate Schools of Management (no recent information)
♦ Association for the Defence of Human Rights and Democratic Liberties in the Arab World (no recent information)
♦ Association Defending Victims of Terrorism (internationally oriented national body)
♦ Association de défense des droits de l'homme et des libertés démocratiques dans le monde arabe (no recent information)
♦ Association des demeures historiques européennes (#07491)
♦ Association des démocrates chrétiens latinoaméricains en Europe (inactive)
♦ Association for Democratic Development and Cooperation (inactive)
♦ Association dentaire d'Afrique orientale (inactive)
♦ Association dentaire du Commonwealth (#04321)

♦ Association of Dental Dealers in Europe 02466

Association des dépôts dentaires européens (ADDE)
Pres Ten Houte 13, 8500 Kortrijk, Belgium. T. +32475831908. E-mail: info@adde.info.
URL: http://www.adde.info/
History 1964. Also referred to in English as *European Dental Dealers' Association*. Latest statutes adopted May 1996, Copenhagen (Denmark). Registration: Banque-Carrefour des Entreprises, No/ID: 0676.495.420, Start date: 23 Feb 2017, Belgium. **Aims** Bring together national dental dealers for exchange of information and experience on technical and legal matters; develop a spirit of fellowship among them; defend their interests vis-à-vis insurance and quality control authorities. **Structure** General Meeting (annual); Board. **Languages** English, French. **Finance** Members' dues. **Activities** Knowledge management/information dissemination; standards/guidelines; events/meetings. **Events** *Annual General Meeting* Brussels (Belgium) 2019, *Annual General Meeting* Madrid (Spain) 2018, *Annual General Meeting* Madrid (Spain) 2017, *Annual General Meeting* Amsterdam (Netherlands) 2015, *Annual General Meeting* Marseille (France) 2014. **Publications** *ADDE Newsletter* (4 a year) in English – summaries in other languages.
Members National associations, representing about 1,100 companies, in 15 countries:
Austria, Belgium, Bulgaria, Czechia, Denmark, France, Germany, Greece, Hungary, Ireland, Italy, Netherlands, Romania, Switzerland, UK.
Associate member in 1 country:
Finland.
NGO Relations Member of: *FDI – World Dental Federation (#09281)*; *Federation of European and International Associations Established in Belgium (FAIB, #09508)*. Cooperates with: *Fédération de l'industrie dentaire en Europe (FIDE, #09595)*. [2020/XD1803/**D**]

♦ Association for Dental Education in Europe (ADEE) 02467

Association européenne des enseignants dentaires (AEED)
Chief Admin Officer Dublin Dental Univ Hosp, Lincoln Place 2, Dublin, D02F859, CO. DUBLIN, D02 F859, Ireland. T. +35316127287. Fax +35316127294. E-mail: administrator@adee.org.
URL: http://www.adee.org/
History 9 Dec 1974, Strasbourg (France). Founded following Constitutive Committee having been set up in 1971. Current Bylaws and Constitution approved at General Assembly, 1986, London (UK). As of Oct 2007, takes over activities of European component of *DentEd*, a Thematic Network funded by *European Union (EU, #08967)* since 1997. Registration: Charities Regulator Ireland, No/ID: 20058111, Ireland. **Aims** Promote advancement and foster convergence towards high standards of dental education in Europe; contribute to co-ordinate peer review and quality assurance in dental educaton and training; promote the development of assessment and examination methods; encourage exchange of staff, students and programmes; provide a European link with other bodies concerned with education, particularly dental education. **Structure** General Assembly (annual); Executive Committee. **Languages** English, French. **Staff** 1.50 FTE, paid. **Finance** Sources: members' dues. **Activities** Awards/prizes/competitions; events/meetings; knowledge management/information dissemination; networking/liaising; projects/programmes; publishing activities. **Events** *ADEE Annual Meeting* Palma (Spain) 2022, *Annual General Assembly* Strasbourg (France) 2021, *Annual General Assembly* Dublin (Ireland) 2020, *Annual General Assembly* Berlin (Germany) 2019, *Joint International Meeting* Brescia (Italy) 2019. **Publications** *European Journal of Dental Education*.
Members Institutions and national associations in 30 countries:
Albania, Belgium, Croatia, Czechia, Denmark, Estonia, Finland, France, Germany, Greece, Hungary, Iceland, Ireland, Italy, Latvia, Lithuania, Malta, Netherlands, Norway, Poland, Portugal, Romania, Russia, Slovakia, Slovenia, Spain, Sweden, Switzerland, Türkiye, UK.
Affiliate members in 4 countries and territories:
China, Hong Kong, Japan, USA.
Members also in Middle East countries. Membership countries not specified.
NGO Relations Member of (2): *European Association for Quality Assurance in Higher Education (ENQA, #06183)*; *Platform for Better Oral Health in Europe (#18399)*. Also links with national dental associations. [2022.05.13/XD0008/**D**]

♦ Association déontologique européenne de graphologues (ADEG) .. 02468

European Deontological Association of Graphologists
SG Cabinet d'études graphologiques, Rue de la Vallée 67, 1000 Brussels, Belgium. T. +3226406276. Fax +3226402584.
Registered Office Rue Washington 40, 1050 Brussels, Belgium.
URL: http://adeg.secretaria-online.com/
History 16 Oct 1991, Paris (France). Registration: Banque-Carrefour des Entreprises, No/ID: 0457.771.902, Start date: 3 May 1996, Belgium. **Aims** Bring together groups and associations of *graphologists* respecting a common code; defend members' image and monitor their level of training and qualification. **Structure** General Assembly (annual) comprising presidents or equivalent of member associations. Executive Committee, composed of President, Vice-President, Secretary-General/Treasurer (these comprising the Bureau) and at least 3 directors. **Languages** French. **Finance** Members' dues. **Events** *Annual General Assembly* London (UK) 2013, *Annual General Assembly* Amsterdam (Netherlands) 2012, *Annual General Assembly* Rome (Italy) 2011, *Annual General Assembly* Rome (Italy) 2011, *Annual General Assembly* Brussels (Belgium) 2010.
Members Founder; full. National associations in 7 countries:
Belgium, France, Germany, Italy, Spain, Switzerland, UK.
NGO Relations Member of: *Federation of European and International Associations Established in Belgium (FAIB, #09508)*. [2016/XD5103/**D**]

♦ Association des dépôts dentaires européens (#02466)

♦ Association des dermatologistes francophones 02469

Association of French-Speaking Dermatologists
Contact address not obtained.
Pres address not obtained.
URL: https://www.dermatologie-francophone.com/
History 7 Jul 1923, Strasbourg (France), as *Association des dermatologistes et syphiligraphes de langue française – Association of French-Speaking Dermatologists and Syphiligraphers*. New statutes and present name adopted 10 Apr 1995. Registered in accordance with French law. **Aims** Develop clinical-medical, clinical-biological and fundamental research; promote public health activity aimed at prevention, epidemiology

and health education; develop and improve information, in particular through continuing education; evaluate treatment, in particular diagnostic and therapeutic innovation; promote any development or research activity in the dermatological field. **Structure** General Assembly. Executive Council (meets annually) comprising 15 to 21 members including the Bureau. Bureau, consisting of President, 4 Vice-Presidents, Secretary-General, Treasurer, Assistant Secretary-General and Assistant Treasurer. **Languages** French. **Staff** No permanent staff; Committee voluntary. **Finance** Members' dues (annual): euro 15. **Activities** Organizes scientific meetings, congresses, conferences, seminars, colloquia and training sessions, including *Congrès des dermatologistes et syphiligraphes de langue française*; awards prizes, fellowships and contributions for research projects. **Events** *Congress* Montréal, QC (Canada) 2024, *Congress* Hammamet (Tunisia) 2022, *Congress* Hammamet (Tunisia) 2020, *Congress* Brussels (Belgium) 2018, *Congress* Abidjan (Côte d'Ivoire) 2016. **Publications** *Annales de Dermatologie* – official journal. Congress papers. Information Services: Management, exhibition and provision of documents and medical and scientific materials.
Members Individuals in 27 countries:
Algeria, Argentina, Belgium, Benin, Brazil, Burkina Faso, Canada, Côte d'Ivoire, Czechia, France, Gabon, Guyana, Iran Islamic Rep, Italy, Lebanon, Luxembourg, Mexico, Montenegro, Morocco, Portugal, Romania, Senegal, Serbia, Spain, Switzerland, Togo, Tunisia.
NGO Relations Member of: *International League of Dermatological Societies (ILDS, #14018)*. [2020/XD0135/v/**C**]

♦ Association des dermatologistes et syphiligraphes de langue française / see Association des dermatologistes francophones (#02469)
♦ Association of Destination Management Executives / see Association of Destination Management Executives International
♦ Association of Destination Management Executives International (internationally oriented national body)

♦ Association for Development and Advancement for the Global Democracy Award 02470

Verein zur Entwicklung und Förderung des Global Democracy Award
Contact Servitengasse 19, 1090 Vienna, Austria. T. +43113195679. E-mail: office@democracyranking.org.
URL: http://www.democracyranking.org/
History Oct 2001. **Activities** Presents 'Global Democracy Award' to 2 states having made the most democratic progress politically. [2010/XM0309/**D**]

♦ Association for Development Aid / see AGIOMONDO
♦ Association for the Development of Commonwealth Cultural Knowledge (inactive)
♦ Association for Development Cooperation / see AGIOMONDO
♦ Association for the Development and Coordination of European Touristic Exchanges (inactive)

♦ Association for the Development of Education in Africa (ADEA) . . . 02471

Association pour le développement de l'éducation en Afrique
Main Office c/o – Immeuble CCIA Plateau, Av Jean Paul II, 01 BP 1387, Abidjan 01, Côte d'Ivoire. T. +22520265674. E-mail: adea@afdb.org.
URL: http://www.adeanet.org/
History 1988. Founded by *International Bank for Reconstruction and Development (IBRD, #12317)* and other funding agencies. Former names and other names: *Donors to African Education (DAE)* – former (1988 to 1995); *Bailleurs de fonds pour l'éducation en Afrique* – former (1988 to 1995). **Aims** Assist African countries to plan and implement their education reforms through policy dialogue. **Structure** Steering Committee; Bureau of Ministers; Executive Committee; Working Groups; Secretariat. **Languages** English, French. **Activities** Research/documentation; capacity building; advocacy/lobbying/activism; networking/liaising; events/meetings; publishing activities; awards/prizes/competitions. **Events** *Workshop on the Global Book Alliance* Abidjan (Côte d'Ivoire) 2018, *Triennial Plenary Meeting* Dakar (Senegal) 2017, *Forum Eurafric* Lyon (France) 2015, *Forum Eurafric* Lyon (France) 2014, *Triennial Plenary Meeting* Ouagadougou (Burkina Faso) 2012. **NGO Relations** Member of: *Next Einstein Forum (NEF, #17098)*. [2021/XE1750/y/**F**]

♦ Association for the Development of Environmental Information (inactive)
♦ Association for the Development of European Political Science (inactive)
♦ Association for the Development of Evaluation Methodologies in Education (#02474)

♦ Association of Development Financing Institutions in Asia and the Pacific (ADFIAP) 02472

Association d'Asie et du Pacifique des institutions financières de développement – Asociación de Instituciones Financieras de Desarrollo del Asia y el Pacifico
SG 2F Skyland Plaza, Sen Gil J Puyat Avenue, 1200 Makati, Philippines. T. +63288161672 – +63288430932. E-mail: inquiries@adfiap.org.
URL: http://www.adfiap.org/
History 1 Oct 1976, Manila (Philippines). Founded with the adoption of Constitution by 31 institutions attending 6th Regional Conference of Development Financing Institutions in Asia and the Pacific, held under the sponsorship of *Asian Development Bank (ADB, #01422)*. **Aims** Advance sustainable development by strengthening development finance function and institutions, enhancing member capacity and advocating development finance innovations. **Structure** General Assembly; Board of Directors; General Secretariat. **Languages** English. **Staff** 10.00 FTE, paid. **Finance** Sources: international organizations; members' dues; revenue from activities/projects; sponsorship. Supported by: *Asian Development Bank (ADB, #01422)*; *Center for International Private Enterprise (CIPE)*; *European Commission (EC, #06633)*; *International Finance Corporation (IFC, #13597)*; *International Trade Centre (ITC, #15703)*; *UNDP (#20292)*; *UNIDO (#20336)*. **Activities** Awards/prizes/competitions; certification/accreditation; events/meetings; guidance/assistance/consulting; standards/guidelines; training/education. **Events** *Annual Meeting* Manila (Philippines) 2022, *Annual Meeting* Manila (Philippines) 2021, *Annual Meeting* Manila (Philippines) 2020, *Annual Meeting* Muscat (Oman) 2019, *International CEO Forum* Kyrenia (Cyprus) 2018. **Publications** *ADVANCE Magazine*; *Touchpoint*. Reports; surveys; Sustainability Report. **Information Services** *ADFIAP E-Library*.
Members Development Financing Institutions (85) in 38 countries and territories:
Bangladesh, Belarus, Bhutan, Cambodia, Canada, China, Cook Is, Fiji, Germany, Guam, India, Indonesia, Iran Islamic Rep, Japan, Kiribati, Malaysia, Micronesia FS, Mongolia, Myanmar, Nepal, Northern Cyprus, Northern Mariana Is, Oman, Pakistan, Palau, Papua New Guinea, Philippines, Russia, Samoa, Saudi Arabia, Sri Lanka, Thailand, Tonga, Türkiye, Tuvalu, Uzbekistan, Vanuatu, Vietnam.
IGO Relations *ASEAN (#01141)*; *Asia-Pacific Economic Cooperation (APEC, #01887)*; *UNEP (#20299)*; *UNEP Finance Initiative (UNEP FI)*; *United Nations Economic and Social Commission for Asia and the Pacific (ESCAP, #20557)*; *United States Agency for International Development (USAID)*. **NGO Relations** *Asian Bankers Association (ABA, #01355)*; *Asociación Latinoamericana de Instituciones Financieras para el Desarrollo (ALIDE, #02233)*; *Association of African Development Finance Institutions (AADFI, #02353)*; *Association of Development Financing Institutions in the Pacific (ADFIP, #02473)*; *Association of National Development Finance Institutions in Member Countries of the Islamic Development Bank (ADFIMI, #02817)*; *European Development Finance Institutions (EDFI, #06913)*; *SME Finance Forum (#19323)*; *World Association for Small and Medium Enterprises (WASME, #21189)*; *World Federation of Development Financing Institutions (WFDFI, #21428)*; national institutions. [2021.09.05/XC7305/y/**C**]

♦ Association of Development Financing Institutions in the Pacific (ADFIP) 02473

Sec Level 1, FDB Centre, 360 Victoria Parade, Suva, Fiji. T. +6797753400. E-mail: adfipsecretariat@gmail.com – admin@adfip.net.
URL: http://adfip.net/
History 1986. **Aims** Promote interests of members; advance cooperation and establish machinery for systematic exchange of information; carry out studies; train staff to improve expertise and effectiveness of member DFIs. **Structure** General Assembly; Board of Directors; Secretariat in Suva (Fiji), headed by Executive Director. **Languages** English. **Staff** 1.00 FTE, paid. **Finance** Members' dues. Investments. **Activities** Training/education; knowledge management/information dissemination; advocacy/lobbying/activism. **Events** *Meeting* Nuku'alofa (Tonga) 2014, *Meeting* Rarotonga Is (Cook Is) 2013, *Meeting* Apia (Samoa) 2012, *Meeting* Funafuti (Tuvalu) 2011, *Meeting* Pohnpei (Micronesia FS) 2010. **Publications** Newsletter. Annual Report; press releases.
Members Development Banks in 13 countries and territories:
Cook Is, Fiji, Kiribati, Micronesia FS, Niue, Palau, Papua New Guinea, Samoa, Samoa USA, Solomon Is, Tonga, Tuvalu, Vanuatu.
Included in the above, 1 bank listed in this Yearbook:
Pacific Islands Development Bank (PIDB, #17966).
Special members (3):
European Investment Bank (EIB, #07599); *Société de crédit et de développement de l'Océanie (SOCREDO, no recent information)*; Societé Financière de Développement de la Polyneise. [2017/XD2289/y/**D**]

♦ Association of Development Innovations and Networks / see Development Innovations and Networks (#05057)
♦ Association for the Development of International Exchange of Food and Agricultural Products and Techniques / see Association for the Development of International Exchanges in Agricultural and Agrifood Products and Techniques
♦ Association for the Development of International Exchanges in Agricultural and Agrifood Products and Techniques (internationally oriented national body)
♦ Association of Development Research and Training Institutes of Asia and the Pacific (inactive)
♦ Association for the Development of the Study of Central American History (internationally oriented national body)
♦ Association for Development of Teaching, Education and Learning (internationally oriented national body)
♦ Association l'e-développement (internationally oriented national body)
♦ Association pour le développement agro-industriel du Sahel (internationally oriented national body)
♦ Association pour le développement et la coordination des échanges touristiques européens (inactive)
♦ Association pour le développement des échanges internationaux de produits et techniques agricoles et agro-alimentaires / see Association for the Development of International Exchanges in Agricultural and Agrifood Products and Techniques
♦ Association pour le développement des échanges internationaux de produits et techniques agro-alimentaires (internationally oriented national body)
♦ Association pour le développement de l'éducation en Afrique (#02471)
♦ Association du Développement de l'Elevage Caprin à l'International / see Elevages sans frontières
♦ Association pour le développement humain et l'approche (#10964)
♦ Association pour le développement de l'information environnementale (inactive)
♦ Association pour le développement international (inactive)
♦ Association pour le développement international en sciences de la terre (#02623)
♦ Association pour le développement du marché du zinc (inactive)

♦ Association pour le développement des méthodologies d'évaluation en éducation (ADMEE-Europe) 02474

Association for the Development of Evaluation Methodologies in Education
Pres c/o IRDP, Faubourg de l'Hôpital 43, CP 54, 2007 Neuchâtel, Switzerland. E-mail: info@admee-europe.org – info@admee.org.
URL: http://www.admee.org/
History 1986. **Aims** Meet the needs of people concerned with *evaluation* in *education*, by supporting their reciprocal communication and their efforts. **Structure** General Assembly; Board; Bureau; Thematic Networks. **Finance** Sources: members' dues. **Events** *Colloquium* Lausanne (Switzerland) 2019, *Colloquium* Esch-sur-Alzette (Luxembourg) 2018, *Colloquium* Dijon (France) 2017, *Colloquium* Lisbon (Portugal) 2016, *Colloquium* Liège (Belgium) 2015. **Publications** *Bulletin de l'ADMEE-Europe* (3 a year); *Mesure et évaluation en éducation* (3 a year) – magazine.
Members Full in 11 countries:
Belgium, Canada, France, Greece, Italy, Luxembourg, Morocco, Portugal, Romania, Spain, Switzerland. [2023/XF3656/**F**]

♦ Association pour le développement de la physique de l'atmosphère tropicale (no recent information)
♦ Association pour le développement de la recherche et de l'action intégrées / see Louvain Coopération
♦ Association pour le développement de la recherche agronomique intégrée / see Louvain Coopération
♦ Association pour le développement de la riziculture en Afrique de l'Ouest / see Africa Rice Center (#00518)
♦ Association pour le développement de la science politique européenne (inactive)
♦ Association pour le développement de la socio-économie / see Society for the Advancement of Socio-Economics (#19516)
♦ Association of Diaconal Organizations in Europe (inactive)
♦ Association pour des diagnostics, des interventions et des résultats infirmiers unifiés au niveau européen (#02437)
♦ Association pour le dialogue international islamo-chrétien / see International Union for Intercultural and Interfaith Dialogue and Peace Education (#15783)

♦ Association des diatomistes de langue française (ADLaF) 02475

Treas Villa Blanche La Feuillasse, 136 route d'Armoy, 74200 Thonon-les-Bains, France. T. +33450715563. Fax +33450265305. E-mail: lafeuillasse@wanadoo.fr.
URL: http://www.adlaf.fr/
History 1980. **Aims** Promote the study of diatoms; increase cooperation among francophone diatom specialists. **Structure** Council. Bureau, comprising President, Vice-President, Treasurer and Secretary-General. **Events** *Colloquium* Clermont-Ferrand (France) 2022, *Colloquium* Aix-en-Provence (France) 2021, *Colloquium* Clermont-Ferrand (France) 2014, *Colloquium* Thonon-les-Bains (France) 2013, *Colloquium* Le Mans (France) 2012. **Publications** *Diatomia* (annual).
Members in 4 countries:
Belgium, France, Luxembourg, Switzerland. [2022/XM3021/**D**]

♦ Association de didactique du français langue étrangère (internationally oriented national body)
♦ Association of Dietetic Foods Industries of the EEC / see Specialised Nutrition Europe (#19909)
♦ Association of Dietetic Foods Industries of the EU / see Specialised Nutrition Europe (#19909)
♦ Association des diététiciens de langue française (inactive)
♦ Association pour la diffusion internationale francophone de livres, ouvrages et revues (internationally oriented national body)
♦ Association DIOGENIS – Association DIOGENIS – Initiative for Drug Policy Dialogue in South East Europe (internationally oriented national body)
♦ Association DIOGENIS – Initiative for Drug Policy Dialogue in South East Europe (internationally oriented national body)
♦ Association des directeurs africains des routes / see Association des Gestionnaires et Partenaires Africains de la Route (#02626)
♦ Association des Directeurs des Institutions Lasalliennes / see Association européenne des directeurs d'institutions lasalliennes (#02563)
♦ Association of Directors of Christian Institutes for Social Concern in Asia / see Association of Christian Institutes for Social Concern in Asia (#02428)
♦ Association of Directors of Diplomatic Academies in Latin America and the Caribbean States (no recent information)
♦ Association of Directors of European Centres for Plastics (inactive)
♦ Association of Directors of the Lasallian Institutions (#02563)
♦ Association des distributeurs de l'alimentation européenne (inactive)
♦ Association des distributeurs alternatifs de l'Amérique latine et des Caraïbes (no recent information)
♦ Association of Diving Contractors International (internationally oriented national body)
♦ Association for the Documentation, Preservation and Enhancement of the Euro-Mediterranean Cultural Heritage (no recent information)
♦ Association des doyens des facultés et des établissements de lettres et sciences humaines / see Association des facultés ou établissements de lettres et sciences humaines des universités d'expression française (#02593)
♦ Association des doyens des facultés de médecine d'Europe / see Association of Medical Schools in Europe (#02799)

- ♦ Association de droit international (#14003)
- ♦ Association du droit juif (#16112)
- ♦ Association pour les droits de la femme et le développement (#02980)
- ♦ Association pour le droit et la société du Pacifique (inactive)

♦ Association for East Asian Environmental History (AEAEH) 02476

Contact address not obtained.
URL: http://www.aeaeh.org/

History Aug 2009. Founded during First World Congress of Environmental History, Copenhagen (Denmark) and Malmö (Sweden). Current bylaws adopted 26 Oct 2011. **Aims** Encourage, promote and foster the study of East Asian environmental history in general; foster communication among scholars interested in the field. **Structure** General Meeting; Council. **Activities** Events/meetings. **Events** *Conference of East Asian Environmental History* Kyoto (Japan) 2021, *Conference of East Asian Environmental History (EAEH 2019)* Tainan (Taiwan) 2019, *Conference of East Asia Environmental History* Takamatsu (Japan) 2015. **NGO Relations** Cooperates with (1): *International Consortium of Environmental History Organizations (ICEHO, #12912).* [2020/AA0233/**D**]

♦ Association of East Asian Research Universities (AEARU) 02477

Chair No1, Sec 4, Roosevelt Road, National Taiwan University, Taipei 10617, Taiwan. T. +886233662007 ext 220. E-mail: aearusec@ntu.edu.tw.
URL: http://www.aearu.com/

History Jan 1996, Hong Kong (Hong Kong). **Aims** Serve as a forum for leading research-oriented universities in the region; cooperate on academic and applied research projects; develop common curricula and transferable credits; exchange faculty and students; sponsor conferences and international events; identify and collaborate in areas of mutual interest; share facilities, information and materials. **Structure** The Board shall consist of the Chairperson, Vice-Chairperson, and five other Members for a total of seven, each being chief executives of their universities. **Languages** English. **Staff** 1 full-time; 19 part-time contact persons at each university. **Finance** Member Universities' support. **Activities** Organizes workshops, student leadership and friendship camps. **Events** *Annual General Meeting* Tokyo (Japan) 2020, *Annual General Meeting* Seoul (Korea Rep) 2019, *Forum* Seoul (Korea Rep) 2019, *Annual General Meeting* Taipei (Taiwan) 2018, *Advanced Materials Science Workshop* Suita (Japan) 2017. **Publications** Brochure.
Members Universities (19) in 5 countries and territories:
China, Hong Kong, Japan, Korea Rep, Taiwan. [2020.06.29/XD6118/**D**]

- ♦ Association of the Eastern Alps / see Alps-Adriatic-Alliance (#00747)
- ♦ Association of Eastern Caribbean Exporters (no recent information)
- ♦ Association of Eastern and Southern African Universities (inactive)
- ♦ Association pour l'échange électronique de données (inactive)
- ♦ Association d'échanges culturels en Méditerranée / see Echanges culturels en Méditerranée (#05281)
- ♦ Association pour les échanges culturels et scientifiques (no recent information)

♦ Association des Echanges Méditerranéens pour l'eau, la forêt, l'énergie, et le développement durable des territoires (AEM) 02478

Pres 19 av du Maine, 75732 Paris CEDEX 15, France.
URL: http://aem.portail-gref.org/

History Set up 20 Jun 2000. Registered in accordance with French law. **Structure** Presidents; Vice-Presidents; Secretary-General; Treasurer. **Events** *Rencontres Annuelles* Tangiers (Morocco) 2015, *Rencontres Annuelles* Béjaïa (Algeria) 2014, *SESAME : Séminaire International sur l'Eau et la Sécurité Alimentaire en Méditerranée* Montpellier (France) 2013, *Rencontres Annuelles* Khenchela (Algeria) 2011, *Rencontres Annuelles* Aix-en-Provence (France) 2010.
Members Individuals (over 350) in 6 countries:
Algeria, France, Lebanon, Morocco, Spain, Tunisia. [2018.03.22/XM4342/**D**]

- ♦ Association des écoles engagées dans des échanges internationaux (no recent information)
- ♦ Association des Ecoles d'études politiques du Conseil de l'Europe (#02902)
- ♦ Association des écoles et facultés de médecine d'Afrique / see Association of Medical Schools in Africa (#02798)
- ♦ Association des écoles internationales (#14789)
- ♦ Association des écoles de médecine d'Afrique (#02798)
- ♦ Association des écoles de médecine du Moyen-Orient / see Association for Medical Education in the Eastern Mediterranean Region (#02796)
- ♦ Association des écoles de santé publique pour l'Amérique du Nord / see Association of Schools of Public Health
- ♦ Association des écoles de santé publique de la région européenne (#02904)
- ♦ Association des Ecoles Supérieures des Polices Européennes (#02531)
- ♦ Association des écoles de théologie d'Asie du Nord-Est (no recent information)
- ♦ Association des écologistes pour le nucléaire (internationally oriented national body)

♦ Association of Economic Universities of South and Eastern Europe and the Black Sea Region (ASECU) 02479

Sec Univ of Macedonia, Egnatia st 156, PO BOX 1591, 540 06 Thessaloniki, Greece. T. +302310891793 – +302310891794. Fax +302310891748. E-mail: asecu@uom.gr.
Chairman address not obtained.
URL: http://www.asecu.gr/

History 1996, Thessaloniki (Greece). Former names and other names: *Association of South Eastern Europe Economic Universities (ASECU)* – former (1996 to 2007). **Aims** Promote the interests of economic universities which are public, recognized or financed by the state of origin. **Structure** General Assembly; Board. **Languages** English. **Staff** 1.00 FTE, paid. **Finance** Members' dues. **Activities** Events/meetings; training/education. **Events** *International Conference* Belgrade (Serbia) 2021, *International Conference* Sofia (Bulgaria) 2019, *International Conference* Nitra (Slovakia) 2018, *International Conference* Durrës (Albania) 2017, *International Conference* Eskisehir (Turkey) 2016. **Publications** *South Eastern Europe Journal of Economics (SEEJE)* (2 a year).
Members Universities (44) in 13 countries:
Albania, Armenia, Bosnia-Herzegovina, Bulgaria, Greece, Montenegro, North Macedonia, Poland, Romania, Russia, Serbia, Türkiye, Ukraine.
Associate (5) in 3 countries:
Egypt, Hungary, Lebanon. [2021/XD7709/**D**]

- ♦ Association pour l'économie familiale de la région d'Asie (#01682)
- ♦ Association économique de l'Afrique de l'Ouest (inactive)
- ♦ Association économique européenne du commerce extérieur (inactive)
- ♦ Association des économistes agricoles d'Afrique de l'Ouest (no recent information)
- ♦ Association d'économistes des caraïbes (no recent information)
- ♦ Association des économistes de langue française / see Association Internationale des Economistes de Langue Française (#02686)
- ♦ Association des économistes latinoaméricains et des Caraïbes (#02480)
- ♦ Association des économistes du Tiers-monde (inactive)

♦ Association of Economists of Latin America and the Caribbean (AELAC) 02480

Association des économistes latinoaméricains et des Caraïbes – Asociación de Economistas de América Latina y el Caribe (AEALC)

Permanent Secretariat c/o ANEC, 22 No 901 esq a 9na Miramar, Playa, 11300 Havana, Cuba. T. +5372049462. Fax +5372023456.

History 1980, Mexico. **Aims** Unite and collaborate with economists of the region; study and investigate economic problems; promote exchange of ideas and work experiences. **Structure** General Assembly and Congress; Executive Committee, headed by President. **Languages** Spanish. **Staff** 1.00 FTE, paid; 2.00 FTE, voluntary. **Finance** Sources: members' dues. **Activities** Events/meetings. **Events** *Congress* San Salvador (El Salvador) 2019, *Encuentro Internacional de Economistas* Panama (Panama) 2015, *Biennial Congress / Congress* Paris (France) 2012, *Congress* Havana (Cuba) 2010, *Congress* Bogota (Colombia) 2008. **Publications** *El Economista* (4 a year) – newspaper. *Globalization and Development Problems – Balance of a Decade* (2010).
Members Federations, associations and colleges in 18 countries:
Argentina, Bolivia, Brazil, Colombia, Costa Rica, Cuba, Dominican Rep, Ecuador, El Salvador, Guatemala, Honduras, Mexico, Panama, Paraguay, Peru, Puerto Rico, Spain, Uruguay.
Consultative Status Consultative status granted from: *UNCTAD (#20285)* (General Category).
[2019/XD4343/**D**]

- ♦ Association des écrivains afro-asiatiques (inactive)
- ♦ Association d'écrivains européens / see European Writers' Council (#09123)
- ♦ Association des écrivains européens, 1941 (inactive)
- ♦ Association des écrivains d'expression française de la mer et d'outre-mer / see Association des écrivains de langue française (#02481)

♦ Association des écrivains de langue française (ADELF) 02481

French-Language Writers' Association

Director of Publication c/o Maison des Associations, 22 rue Deparcieux, Bte 13, 75014 Paris, France. E-mail: adelf.paris@gmail.com.
URL: http://www.adelf.info/

History Jan 1926, Paris (France). Subsequently known as *Association nationale des écrivains de la mer et d'outre-mer*, *Association des écrivains d'expression française de la mer et d'outre-mer*, *Association internationale des écrivains de langue française*. Registered in accordance with French law. **Aims** Promote knowledge of *Francophone* writings and writers outside France, as well as of French writers; encourage *literary* extension of the French language; encourage and support French-language writers living inside and outside France. **Structure** Annual General Assembly, always in Paris (France). Board of Management, consisting of Honorary Presidents, President, 2 Vice-Presidents, Secretary General, Assistant Secretary General, Treasurer, Juridical Counsellor and 16 members. **Languages** French. **Finance** Sources: grants; members' dues. **Activities** Awards 10 literary prizes annually for French language writers from different areas of the world; organizes various meetings, colloquia and annual ceremony to award literary prizes; participates in various literary "salons". **Events** *General Assembly* Paris (France) 2005, *Les écrivains du Liban* Payrac (France) 1996, *Gaston Monnerville* Payrac (France) 1995. **Publications** *Liaison Bulletin* (4 a year); *Lettres et cultures de langue française* (2 a year). *La Francophonie en Afrique* (2000); *Regards croisés sur la Francophonie au Maroc* (1999); *Belgique-Wallonie-Bruxelles: une littérature francophone* (1998); *Les Chefs d'Etats écrivains en pays francophone* (1997); *La Francophonie au Liban* (1996); *Le Président Gaston Monnerville* (1995); *Les écrivains du Québec* (1994); *Les écrivains de la négritude et de la créolité* (1993); *Ismaïl Kadaré, gardien de mémoire* (1992); *Pierre Benoît, témoin de son temps* (1991).
Members Writers (about 1,000) in 50 countries:
Albania, Algeria, Angola, Belgium, Benin, Burkina Faso, Burundi, Cambodia, Cameroon, Canada, Central African Rep, Chad, Comoros, Congo Brazzaville, Congo DR, Côte d'Ivoire, Egypt, Ethiopia, Finland, France, Gabon, Germany, Greece, Haiti, Italy, Japan, Lebanon, Luxembourg, Madagascar, Mali, Mauritania, Mauritius, Mexico, Monaco, Morocco, Netherlands, Niger, Poland, Romania, Rwanda, Senegal, Seychelles, Spain, Sweden, Switzerland, Togo, Tunisia, UK, USA, Vietnam.
IGO Relations *Organisation internationale de la Francophonie (OIF, #17809).* **NGO Relations** Member of: *Association francophone d'amitié et de liaison (AFAL, #02605).* [2020/XC0146/v/**C**]

- ♦ Association des éditeurs de l'Asie du Sud-Est (inactive)
- ♦ Association of Editors of Andean Scientific Journals (no recent information)
- ♦ Association of Editors in the South-East Asia, Australasia and Oceania (inactive)
- ♦ Association des éducateurs à distance d'Afrique (no recent information)

♦ Association for Educational Assessment in Africa (AEAA) 02482

Contact Examinations Council of Eswatini, Next to Spintex Village, Ezulwini Valley, PO Box 1394, Mbabane, Eswatini. E-mail: registrar@examscouncil.org.sz.
URL: http://www.aeaafrica.org/

History 1982. **Aims** Promote cooperation between examining and assessment bodies in Africa. **Events** *Annual Conference* Mombasa (Kenya) 2021, *Annual Conference* Mombasa (Kenya) 2020, *Annual Conference* Abuja (Nigeria) 2019, *Annual Conference* Maseru (Lesotho) 2018, *Annual Conference* Kampala (Uganda) 2017. **IGO Relations** *West African Examinations Council (WAEC, #20879).* **NGO Relations** Member of: *International Association for Educational Assessment (IAEA, #11861).* [2014/XD8371/**D**]

♦ Association for Educational Assessment – Europe (AEA Europe) ... 02483

Exec Sec c/o AQA, 2nd Floor, Lynton House, 7-12 Tavistock Square, London, WC1H 9LT, UK. E-mail: admin@aea-europe.net.
URL: http://www.aea-europe.net/

History 2000. Registration: Handelsregister, No/ID: KVK 09112147, Netherlands. **Aims** Act as a European platform for discussion of developments in educational assessment; foster cooperation and facilitate liaison between organizations and individuals active in educational assessment throughout Europe. **Structure** General Assembly (annual); Council. **Languages** English. **Staff** 0.50 FTE, paid; 7.00 FTE, voluntary. **Finance** Sources: meeting proceeds; members' dues. **Events** *Annual Conference* 2021, *Annual Conference* Lisbon (Portugal) 2019, *Annual Conference* Arnhem (Netherlands) 2018, *Annual Conference* Prague (Czechia) 2017, *Annual Conference* Limassol (Cyprus) 2016.
Members Corporate; individual. Members in 36 countries and territories:
Armenia, Australia, Azerbaijan, Belarus, Belgium, Bosnia-Herzegovina, Bulgaria, Canada, Croatia, Cyprus, Czechia, Estonia, Finland, France, Georgia, Germany, Hong Kong, Ireland, Israel, Italy, Malta, Netherlands, Norway, Portugal, Russia, Saudi Arabia, Serbia, Slovakia, Slovenia, Spain, Sweden, Switzerland, Türkiye, UK, Ukraine, USA.
NGO Relations Member of (1): *International Association for Educational Assessment (IAEA, #11861).*
[2021/XD8900/**D**]

- ♦ Association de l'education Catholique pour l'Afrique et Madagascar (#02415)
- ♦ Association d'éducation comparée en Europe (#04410)
- ♦ Association for Education in International Business / see Academy of International Business (#00040)
- ♦ Association for Education Mladiinfo International / see Mladiinfo International (#16834)
- ♦ Association pour l'éducation mondiale (#02983)
- ♦ Association pour l'éducation publique européenne par télévision (inactive)
- ♦ Association of Education and Research in Information Science of Iberoamerica and the Caribbean (#02122)
- ♦ Association pour l'éducation technique dans le Sud et le centre asiatiques (inactive)
- ♦ Association d'éducation théologique en Asie du Sud-Est / see Association for Theological Education in South East Asia (#02952)
- ♦ Association pour l'Education Théologique Chrétienne en Afrique (#02431)
- ♦ Association for Education in World Government / see World Policy Institute
- ♦ Association of the EEC Manufacturers of Technical Ceramics for Electronic, Electrical, Mechanical and Other Applications / see European Technical Ceramics Federation (#08878)
- ♦ Association EFW – EUROFOODWATER (unconfirmed)
- ♦ Association d'églises de professants des pays francophones (inactive)

♦ Association of Electoral Organizations of Central America and the Caribbean (Tikal Protocol) 02484

Asociación de Organismos Electorales de Centroamérica y del Caribe

Contact c/o CAPEL, Av 8 calles 41 y 43, Casa 222, San José, San José, San José, Costa Rica. T. +50622340404. Fax +50622340955. E-mail: capel@iidh.ed.cr – actividades-capel@iidh.ed.cr.
URL: http://www.iidh.ed.cr/capel/

History Founded Sep 1985, Tikal (Guatemala), for the purpose of information, cooperation and consultations; decisions have the nature of recommendations. Also referred to as *Association of Central American and Caribbean Electoral Organizations.* Constitution changed, 16 Jul 1999. **Aims** Encourage international cooperation in order to promote representative *democracy*, and the free, universal and secret vote; promote effective political participation by means of efficient and clean electoral systems in their respective countries; encourage reciprocal consultations on any matters related to the electoral process, as well as exchange of information about the same and about the development of elections, within the framework of horizontal cooperation; foster electoral observation with the participation of member organizations, with the invitation of host country which will offer the necessary facilities; make recommendations of a technical nature about such matters; foster mutual support between the Electoral Organizations, independent of whether or not they are in an electoral period. **Structure** Conference; Coordination and Follow-Up Committee; Executive Secretariat. **Languages** English, Spanish. **Finance** Members' dues. Financed by: Electoral Organizations; *Centre for Electoral Promotion and Assistance (CAPEL, see: #11334).* **Events** *Conference* Panama 2013, *Conference* Honduras 2012.

Members Full (voting rights) Electoral Organizations of the Central American and Caribbean Region that have signed the Constitution of the Protocol, as well as those of other countries which have formally requested membership. Electoral Organizations (11) in 11 countries and territories:
Antigua-Barbuda, Costa Rica, Dominican Rep, El Salvador, Guatemala, Honduras, Jamaica, Nicaragua, Panama, Puerto Rico, St Lucia.

NGO Relations Located at: *Centre for Electoral Promotion and Assistance (CAPEL, see: #11334).* Together with *Association of South American Electoral Organizations (Quito Protocol, #02919),* constitutes: *Unión Interamericana de Organismos Electorales (UNIORE, #20413).* [2020.03.03/XM4590/**D**]

- ♦ Association of Electoral Organizations of South America / see Association of South American Electoral Organizations (#02919)

♦ Association of the Electricity Supply Industry of East Asia and the Western Pacific (AESIEAP) 02485

Association des industries électriques de l'Asie orientale et du Pacifique Ouest

Address not obtained.
URL: https://www.aesieap.com

History 1975, Hong Kong (Hong Kong). Founded following a first technical conference of representatives of the electrical supply industry in the region. Registration: Hong Kong. **Aims** Bring together and foster cooperation and exchange of expertise and technology between organizations which are responsible for one or more of the functions of generation, transmission and distribution of electricity for public use in the countries the region; study problems at the regional level, the solutions of which are likely to contribute to the development of electricity supply industry in the area. **Structure** Council, consisting of national/regional representatives of members. Executive Committee, comprising President, Immediate Past President, Vice-President, Secretary-General, Honorary Treasurer and 4 members approved by Council. **Finance** Members' dues: US$ 1,000; Associate (organizational) US$ 600; Associate (individual) US$ 100. **Activities** Organizes meetings, congresses and seminars, in particular regular regional CEO meetings/CEPSI. **Events** *CEPSI Conference* Xiamen (China) 2023, *CEO Conference* Haikou City (China) 2022, *CEPSI Biennial Conference* Manila (Philippines) 2020, *CEO Conference* Cebu City (Philippines) 2019, *CEPSI Biennial Conference* Kuala Lumpur (Malaysia) 2018. **Publications** *AESIEAP Newsletter. GOLDBOOK.*

Members Principal members (76) organizations responsible for providing or administering public electricity supply in 19 countries and territories:
Australia, Brunei Darussalam, China, Hong Kong, India, Indonesia, Japan, Korea Rep, Macau, Malaysia, New Zealand, Papua New Guinea, Philippines, Polynesia Fr, Singapore, Sri Lanka, Taiwan, Thailand, Vietnam.
Associate members (organizational) (44); Associate members (individual) (4). Membership countries not specified. [2022/XD1842/t/**D**]

- ♦ Association des électro-radiologistes de langue latine (inactive)
- ♦ Association of Embryo Technology in Europe / see Association européenne de transfert embryonnaire (#02582)
- ♦ Association for Emergency Aid and Solidarity Development Cooperation (internationally oriented national body)

♦ Association for Emissions Control by Catalyst (AECC) 02486

Exec Dir Blue Point, Bd Auguste Reyers 80, 1030 Brussels, Belgium. T. +3227068160. Fax +3227068169. E-mail: info@aecc.eu.
URL: http://www.aecc.eu/

History 1985. Registration: Banque-Carrefour des Entreprises, Belgium; EU Transparency Register, No/ID: 78711786419-61. **Aims** Assist development and implementation of advanced emissions control technology in the *European Union* by being a trusted source of information on catalytic solutions to limit emissions from *internal combustion* engines. **Structure** General Assembly; Executive Committee; Technical Steering Committee; Public Affairs Committee. **Languages** Dutch, English, French. **Staff** 3.00 FTE, paid. **Finance** Sources: members' dues. **Events** *Seminar on Euro 7 Emissions Standards* Brussels (Belgium) 2022. **Publications** *AECC Newsletter* (12 a year) in English.

Members European-based companies engaged in the development, production and testing of catalyst and filter based technologies for engine exhaust emissions control. Members in 4 countries:
Belgium, France, Germany, UK.

Consultative Status Consultative status granted from: *ECOSOC (#05331)* (Special). **IGO Relations** Member of the expert groups: *European Commission (EC, #06633)* (Motor Vehicles Emissions Group); *United Nations Economic Commission for Europe (UNECE, #20555)* (WP 29 – World Forum for Harmonization of Vehicle Regulations / GRPE – Working Party on Pollution and Energy). **NGO Relations** In liaison with technical committees of: *Comité européen de normalisation (CEN, #04162).* Member of: *Partnership for Clean Fuels and Vehicles (PCFV, #18231).* [2021.09.14/XE2851/**D**]

- ♦ Association pour encourager la lutte contre l'analphabétisme des adultes en Afrique (inactive)
- ♦ Association enfants et développement / see Planète Enfants & Développement
- ♦ Association for Engineering Education in South and Central Asia (no recent information)
- ♦ Association for Engineering Education in Southeast Asia / see Association for Engineering Education in Southeast Asia and the Pacific (#02487)

♦ Association for Engineering Education in Southeast Asia and the Pacific (AEESEAP) 02487

Association pour la formation des ingénieurs en Asie du Sud-Est et dans le Pacifique

Pres Tsinghua Univ, 100084 Beijing, China.
SG address not obtained.

History 1973. Founded with the support of *UNESCO (#20322).* Regional network of *UNESCO Office, Jakarta – Regional Bureau for Sciences in Asia and the Pacific (#20313).* Former names and other names: *Association for Engineering Education in Southeast Asia (AEESEA)* – former (1973 to May 1989). **Aims** Promote engineering education in Southeast Asia and the Pacific through regional cooperation; cover the entire spectrum of the education of technicians at all levels and professional engineers in both training and research. **Structure** Executive Committee. Since 1995 Secretariat located at Lae (Papua New Guinea). Voting Members (15). **Languages** English. **Staff** 0.50 FTE, paid. Voluntary. **Finance** Sources: members' dues. **Activities** Main activities include a regional survey of engineering education. **Events** *Workshop* Sendai (Japan) 2019, *Triennial Conference* Singapore (Singapore) 2014, *Workshop* Jeju (Korea Rep) 2013, *Workshop* Tokyo (Japan) 2012, *Mid-term conference* Seoul (Korea Rep) 2009. **Publications** *Links Newsletter* (4 a year); *AEESEAP Journal of Engineering Education* (2 a year). Directory of researchers; conference proceedings.

Members Voting; Ordinary; Individual; Corporate. Voting in 15 countries:
Australia, Brunei Darussalam, China, Fiji, Indonesia, Japan, Korea Rep, Laos, Malaysia, New Zealand, Papua New Guinea, Philippines, Singapore, Thailand, Vietnam.

NGO Relations Cooperates with (1): *Federation of Engineering Institutions of Asia and the Pacific (FEIAP, #09480).* Instrumental in setting up (1): *Cooperative Program in Technological Research and Higher Education in Southeast Asia and the Pacific (no recent information)* (and sponsor of). [2021/XD6501/**D**]

♦ Association of Engineering, Project, and Production Management (EPPM) 02488

Contact address not obtained. E-mail: eppm.association@gmail.com.
URL: http://www.ppml.url.tw/EPPM/association.htm

Aims Encourage the exchange of ideas, research, and other professional activities that are of an interdisciplinary nature relating to the engineering, project, and production management. **Structure** General Assembly; Board of Directors. **Activities** Advocacy/lobbying/activism; events/meetings; research/documentation. **Events** *International Conference on Engineering, Project, and Production Management (EPPM)* Krakow (Poland) 2021, *International Conference on Engineering, Project, and Production Management* 2020, *International Conference on Engineering, Project, and Production Management* Berlin (Germany) 2019, *International Conference on Engineering, Project, and Production Management* Cape Town (South Africa) 2018, *International Conference on Engineering, Project, and Production Management* Amman (Jordan) 2017. **Publications** *EPPM Journal.* [AA0745/**C**]

- ♦ Association des enseignants et chercheurs pour la coopération inter-universitaire en Europe (inactive)
- ♦ Association pour l'enseignement médical en Europe (#02797)
- ♦ Association pour l'enseignement social en Afrique (inactive)
- ♦ Association of Enterprise Architects (unconfirmed)
- ♦ Association entomologique internationale (inactive)
- ♦ Association des entrepreneurs de forage dirigé (#05133)
- ♦ Association des entrepreneurs de la région des Amazones (inactive)
- ♦ Association des entreprises africaines de commerce extérieur (inactive)
- ♦ Association des entreprises gouvernementales de télécommunications de l'Accord sous-régional andin / see Association of Telecommunication Enterprises of the Andean Community (#02951)
- ♦ Association des entreprises de télécommunications de l'Accord sous-régional andin / see Association of Telecommunication Enterprises of the Andean Community (#02951)
- ♦ Association des entreprises de télécommunications de la Communauté andine (#02951)
- ♦ Association for Environmental Archaeology (internationally oriented national body)
- ♦ Association for Environmental Education (no recent information)
- ♦ Association of Environmental Lawyers of Central and Eastern Europe and Newly Independent States (inactive)

♦ Association for Environmentally Friendly Carpets 02489

Gemeinschaft Umweltfreundlichen Teppichboden (GuT)

Secretariat Schönebergstrasse 2, 52068 Aachen, Germany. T. +4924196843411. E-mail: mail@gut-ev.de.
URL: http://www.gut-ev.de/

History Dec 1990, by European carpet manufacturers. **Aims** Ensure steady improvement of the textile floorcovering life cycle from the viewpoint of *consumer protection* and protection of the environment. **Structure** General Assembly. Managing Committee. **Activities** Research and development; research/docuemntation. **Events** *General Assembly* Vaals (Netherlands) 1995, *General Assembly* Vaals (Netherlands) 1994, *General Assembly* Bruges (Belgium) 1993, *General Assembly* Maastricht (Netherlands) 1992, *General Assembly* Münster (Germany) 1991.

Members European carpet manufacturers (87) in 9 countries:
Austria, Belgium, Denmark, France, Germany, Netherlands, Sweden, Switzerland, UK. [2014/XD3994/**D**]

- ♦ Association of Environmental and Resource Economists (internationally oriented national body)
- ♦ Association for the Epidemiological Study and Assessment of Disasters in Developing Countries / see Centre for Research on the Epidemiology of Disasters (#03781)
- ♦ Association pour l'épidémiologie des désastres / see Centre for Research on the Epidemiology of Disasters (#03781)

♦ Association des épidémiologistes de langue française (ADELF) . . . 02490

French Speaking Epidemiologist's Association

Main Office ISPED, Case 11, Univ de Bordeaux, CS 61292, 146 rue Léo Saignat, 33076 Bordeaux, France. T. +33557574527. Fax +33556991360. E-mail: adelf@u-bordeaux.fr.
URL: http://adelf.isped.u-bordeaux2.fr/

History 19 Feb 1976, France. **Aims** Facilitate exchanges between French-speaking epidemiologists; develop and diffuse epidemiological methods; promote study and research. **Structure** Administrative Council; Board. **Languages** French. **Staff** Part-time, voluntary. **Finance** Members' dues: euro 22 – euro 30. **Activities** Events/meetings; knowledge management/information dissemination; research/documentation. **Events** *Congrès International d'Epidémiologie* Québec, QC (Canada) 2022, *Congrès International d'Epidémiologie* Québec, QC (Canada) 2020, *Assemblée Générale* Lyon (France) 2018, *Congrès International d'Epidémiologie* Lyon (France) 2018, *Congrès International d'Epidémiologie* Rennes (France) 2016. **Publications** *Bulletin de l'ADELF* (2 a year).

Members Individuals (about 500) in 37 countries and territories:
Algeria, Austria, Belgium, Benin, Bolivia, Burkina Faso, Burundi, Cameroon, Canada, Central African Rep, Congo DR, Côte d'Ivoire, Croatia, Cuba, France, Gabon, Guinea, Haiti, Italy, Japan, Lebanon, Luxembourg, Mali, Mauritania, Morocco, Mozambique, Netherlands, Niger, Norway, Romania, Rwanda, Senegal, Switzerland, Tunisia, UK, Uruguay, USA. [2018/XD9210/v/**F**]

- ♦ Association for the Epidemiology of Disasters / see Centre for Research on the Epidemiology of Disasters (#03781)
- ♦ Association of Episcopal Conferences of Anglophone West Africa (inactive)

♦ Association of the Episcopal Conferences of the Central African Region 02491

Association des conférences épiscopales de la région de l'Afrique centrale (ACERAC)

Contact BP 200, Brazzaville, Congo Brazzaville. T. +242812770. Fax +242812770. E-mail: acerac_secreta@yahoo.fr.

History 6 May 1987, Yaoundé (Cameroon), as *Association des conférences épiscopales du Congo, Centrafrique et Tchad / Cameroun (ACECCT/CAMEROUN).* Also referred to as *Association des conférences épiscopales du Congo, de la République centrafricaine, du Tchad et du Cameroun (ACECCTC).* **Aims** Favour the ecclesial communion; deepen the practice of collegiality; promote a dynamic and interdependent pastoral. **Structure** Plenary Assembly; Presidency; Permanent Committee; Secretariat. Commissions. **Languages** English, French, Spanish. **Staff** 2.00 FTE, paid. **Finance** Members' dues. Grants. **Events** *Plenary Assembly* Malabo (Equatorial Guinea) 2002, *Plenary Assembly* Equatorial Guinea 1999, *Seminar / Plenary Assembly* Brazzaville (Congo Brazzaville) 1996, *Plenary Assembly* Congo Brazzaville 1995.

Members Episcopal Conferences in 6 countries:
Cameroon, Central African Rep, Chad, Congo Brazzaville, Equatorial Guinea, Gabon.

NGO Relations Member of: *Symposium of Episcopal Conferences of Africa and Madagascar (SECAM, #20077).* Set up: *Université catholique d'Afrique centrale (UCAC).* [2019/XD8903/**D**]

- ♦ Association of the Episcopal Conferences of West Africa / see Regional Episcopal Conference of West Africa (#18783)

♦ Association of ERC Grantees (AERG) 02492

Contact c/o ULB, Ave F D Roosevelt 50, CP 191, 1050 Brussels, Belgium. T. +3226503296. E-mail: contact@aerg.eu.
Sec address not obtained.
URL: https://aerg.eu/

History 24 Sep 2020. Registration: Banque-Carrefour des Entreprises, No/ID: 0758.965.414, Start date: 1 Dec 2020, Belgium. **Aims** Highlight, accelerate, and defend fundamental research in Europe. **Structure** General Assembly; Board. **NGO Relations** Signatory to agreement of *Coalition for Advancing Research Assessment (CoARA, #04045).* [2022/AA3084/**E**]

♦ Association of ESCP Europe Students and Graduates (ESCP Europe Alumni) 02493

Association des étudiants et diplômes ESCP Europe

Main Office 81 av de la République, 75543 Paris CEDEX 11, France. T. +33143572403 – +33148054627. Fax +33148052350. E-mail: info@escpeuropealumni.org.
URL: http://www.escpeuropealumni.org/

History 1872, as the alumni association of ESCP, then *ESCP Europe Business School (#05536)*. Original title: *ESCP-EAP Alumni Association – Association des anciens ESCP-EAP*. Registered in accordance with French law. **Aims** Bring together the worldwide community of graduates and students of ESCP Europe, promoting solidarity among them and providing them with a range of services and tools. **Structure** Board of 21 members. **Staff** 13.00 FTE, paid. **Activities** Network and career activities and services. Annual General Assembly; workshops; conferences; meetings. **Publications** *ESCP Europe Alumni Info* (12 a year); *ESCP Europe Alumni Career News* (12 a year); *ESCP Europe Alumni News* (12 a year); *ESCP Europe Alumni* – electronic newsletter. *ESCP Europe Directory*. **Members** Individuals (about 40,000) worldwide. Membership countries not specified. [2015/XM1426/**E**]

♦ Associationes Juventutis Salesianae / see Salesian Youth Movement (#19039)
♦ Association espérantiste des médecins (inactive)
♦ Association des espérantistes verts (#02494)
♦ Association espérantiste universelle / see Universal Esperanto Association (#20676)

♦ Association of Esperantist Greens (AEG) 02494

Association des espérantistes verts – Asocio de Verduloj Esperantistaj (AVE)

Sec Weissdornweg 68, 53177 Bonn, Germany. T. +4922890917149. E-mail: ave@verduloj.org.
URL: http://www.verduloj.org/

History 1984, Liège (Belgium). **Aims** Work towards the use of Esperanto as the 2nd language for all; promote Esperanto as the neutral language bridge for international communication; inform Green parties and ecological movements about the advantages of Esperanto; inform Esperanto users about Green and ecological issues. **Structure** Loose network of individuals. **Languages** Esperanto. **Staff** 0.40 FTE, voluntary. **Finance** Sources: donations; fundraising; members' dues. Other sources: funds from national ministries. **Activities** Financial and/or material support; knowledge management/information dissemination; projects/programmes; training/education. **Events** *Meeting* Turin (Italy) 2023, *Global Assembly* 2021, *Global Assembly* 2020, *Global Assembly* Lahti (Finland) 2019, *Global Assembly* Lisbon (Portugal) 2018. **Publications** *AVENO* (weekly).
Members Organizations and individuals (about 310) in 50 countries:
Albania, Argentina, Australia, Belgium, Benin, Brazil, Bulgaria, Canada, Chile, China, Congo DR, Cuba, Czechia, Denmark, Estonia, Finland, France, Germany, Hungary, India, Iran Islamic Rep, Ireland, Israel, Italy, Japan, Kazakhstan, Latvia, Lithuania, Madagascar, Netherlands, Niger, Norway, Pakistan, Poland, Portugal, Romania, Russia, Senegal, Serbia, Slovakia, Spain, Sri Lanka, Sweden, Taiwan, Tanzania UR, UK, Ukraine, Uruguay, USA, Uzbekistan.
NGO Relations Member of (1): *Universal Esperanto Association (UEA, #20676)*. [2021.09.01/XE3641/**E**]

♦ Association des établissements d'enseignement supérieur d'Asie du Sud-Est (#02920)
♦ Association des établissements jésuites d'enseignement supérieur d'Europe et du Liban (inactive)
♦ Association des Etats de la Caraïbe (#02411)

♦ Association des états généraux des étudiants de l'Europe (AEGEE-Europe) 02495

European Students' Forum

SG Rue du Noyer 55, 1000 Brussels, Belgium. T. +3222460320. Fax +3222460329. E-mail: headoffice@aegee.org.
Pres address not obtained. T. +3222460327. E-mail: president@aegee.org.
URL: http://www.aegee.org/

History 16 Apr 1985, Paris (France). Former names and other names: *General Assembly of European Students* – alias. Registration: Banque-Carrefour des Entreprises, No/ID: 0472.022.289, Start date: 22 Apr 2013, Belgium; EU Transparency Register, No/ID: 877041722506-79, Start date: 4 Jul 2016. **Aims** Promote the idea of a unified Europe, cross-border cooperation, communication and integration of young people and creation of an open and tolerant society by involving students and young graduates in valuable projects and discussions over topics of importance for the communities in which they live. **Structure** At European level: Agora – General Assembly (twice a year); European Planning Meeting (annual); Comité Directeur (CD) – European Board of Directors; Commissions (4); Committees (6); Working Groups (4); Liaison Officers. At local level: branches in academic cities across Europe (Antennae, Contact-Antennae and Contacts). **Languages** English. **Finance** Sources: donations; grants; members' dues; sponsorship. **Activities** Events/meetings; training/education. **Events** *Fall Agora* Istanbul (Turkey) 2018, *Spring Agora* Krakow (Poland) 2018, *Fall Agora* Catania (Italy) 2017, *Spring Agora* Enschede (Netherlands) 2017, *Conference* Brussels (Belgium) 2015. **Publications** *Key to Europe* (annual) – yearbook. *Summer University Book* – internal. Books; reports; flyers. Databases. **Information Services** *Young European Electronic Forum* – internal.
Members Local groups (160), one for each university city, where AEGEE is present, represent 13,000 members in 39 European countries:
Armenia, Austria, Azerbaijan, Belarus, Belgium, Bosnia-Herzegovina, Bulgaria, Croatia, Cyprus, Czechia, Denmark, Estonia, Finland, France, Georgia, Germany, Greece, Hungary, Italy, Kosovo, Latvia, Malta, Moldova, Montenegro, Netherlands, North Macedonia, Poland, Portugal, Romania, Russia, Serbia, Slovakia, Slovenia, Spain, Sweden, Switzerland, Türkiye, UK, Ukraine.
Consultative Status Consultative status granted from: *ECOSOC (#05331)* (Special); *UNESCO (#20322)* (Consultative Status); *Council of Europe (CE, #04881)* (Participatory Status); *UNEP (#20299)*. **IGO Relations** *European Commission (EC, #06633)*. **NGO Relations** Member of (9): *Citizens for Europe (CFEU, #03956)*; *Civil Society Europe*; *Eastern Partnership Civil Society Forum (EaP CSF, #05247)*; *European Civic Forum (ECF, #06563)*; *European Movement International (EMI, #07825)*; *European Youth Forum (#09140)*; *Generation Climate Europe (GCE, #10114)*; *Informal Forum of International Student Organizations (IFISO, #11193)*; *The Right to Research Coalition (no recent information)*. Supports: *European Alliance for the Statute of the European Association (EASEA, #05886)*. [2020/XF1801/**F**]

♦ Association for Ethnic and Regional Studies (internationally oriented national body)
♦ Association pour l'étude du développement économique, social et culturel (inactive)
♦ Association pour l'étude et l'évaluation épidémiologiques des désastres dans les pays en voie de développement / see Centre for Research on the Epidemiology of Disasters (#03781)
♦ Association d'étude des humanités modernes (#16843)
♦ Association pour l'étude de l'intégration européenne (inactive)
♦ Association pour l'étude des langues juives (no recent information)
♦ Association pour l'étude des langues et littératures du Commonwealth / see Association for Commonwealth Literature and Language Studies (#02439)
♦ Association pour l'étude des littératures et langues du Commonwealth (#02439)
♦ Association pour l'étude de la politique allemande / see International Association for the Study of German Politics (#12200)
♦ Association pour l'étude du problème mondial des réfugiés (#02942)
♦ Association pour l'étude des problèmes de l'Europe (inactive)
♦ Association d'études africaines dans les Antilles (inactive)
♦ Association d'études baha'ies (#02391)
♦ Association d'études baha'ies – Europe francophone / see Association francophone européenne d'études baha'ies (#02613)
♦ Association d'études canadiennes en Europe Centrale (#03704)
♦ Association d'études des Caraïbes (#03559)
♦ Association des études sur la Communauté européenne / see European Union Studies Association
♦ Association des études françaises en Afrique australe (internationally oriented national body)
♦ Association des études internationales (#15615)
♦ Association des études internationales (internationally oriented national body)
♦ Association d'études latinoaméricaines (#16388)
♦ Association d'études linguistiques interculturelles africaines (inactive)
♦ L'association des études du Maghreb (internationally oriented national body)
♦ Association du études Mande (#16564)
♦ Association des études du Proche-Orient ancien (internationally oriented national body)
♦ Association pour l'étude taxonomique de la flore d'Afrique tropicale (#02948)
♦ Association des étudiants d'Asie et de Pacifique (no recent information)
♦ Association des étudiants dentaires de l'Asie et du Pacifique (#01607)
♦ Association des étudiants et diplômes ESCP Europe (#02493)

♦ Association of Eurasian Central Securities Depositories (AECSD) .. 02496

Secretariat address not obtained. T. +74952344827. Fax +74959560938. E-mail: secretariat@aecsd.org – aecsd@aecsd.com.
URL: http://aecsd.org/en/

History 2001. **Aims** Develop and enhance depository operations; create a common depository "environment"; integrate the CSDs of the CIS countries into the global securities settlement system. **Structure** Board. **Events** *Conference* Almaty (Kazakhstan) 2015, *Conference* Baku (Azerbaijan) 2014, *Conference* Nizhniy Novgorod (Russia) 2013, *Conference* Kiev (Ukraine) 2012, *Conference* Yerevan (Armenia) 2011. **Publications** *AECDS Newsletter*.
Members Full in 10 countries:
Armenia, Azerbaijan, Belarus, Georgia, Kazakhstan, Kyrgyzstan, Moldova, Russia, Ukraine, Uzbekistan.
NGO Relations Member of: *World Forum of CSDs (WFC, #21514)*. Cooperates with: *European Central Securities Depositories Association (ECSDA, #06468)*. [2014/XJ8699/**D**]

♦ Association euro-africaine pour l'anthropologie du changement social et du développement / see Association pour l'anthropologie du changement social et du développement (#02369)
♦ Association for Euro-Atlantic Cooperation (no recent information)
♦ Association Euromed Capital Forum / see Euromed Capital (#05714)
♦ Association Europa (internationally oriented national body)
♦ Association of European Accumulator Manufacturers / see Association of European Automative and Industrial Battery Manufacturers (#02498)
♦ Association of the European Adhesive and Sealant Industry (#09572)
♦ Association of European Adhesives Manufacturers / see Fédération européenne des industries de colles et adhésifs (#09572)

♦ Association of European Administrative Judges (AEAJ) 02497

Fédération européenne des juges administratifs (FEJA) – Vereinigung Europäischer Verwaltungsrichter – Associazione Europea di Magistrati Amministrativi

Pres Verwaltungsgericht Wien, Muthgasse 64, 1190 Vienna, Austria. T. +431400038614. Fax +43140009938610. E-mail: info@aeaj.org.
Registered Office ERA, Metzer Allee 4, 54295 Trier, Germany. T. +49651937370. Fax +496519373790.
URL: http://www.aeaj.org/

History 25 Mar 2000, Trier (Germany). Founded at *Academy of European Law (#00035)*. Current statutes entered into force, 24 Mar 2000, Trier (Germany). Statutes amended: May 2008, Bari (Italy); May 2010, Freiburg (Germany); June 2012, Lisbon (Portugal). Former names and other names: *Union dei Magistrati Amministrativi Europea* – alias. Registration: Germany; EU Transparency Register, No/ID: 622038240860-29, Start date: 6 Jan 2021. **Aims** Further legal protection of individuals against public violence; further lawfulness of administrative actions; increase expansion of knowledge of European administrative judges in the European Union; strengthen the position of administrative judges in Europe. **Structure** General Assembly (annual); Board; Working Groups (4). **Languages** English. **Staff** 9.00 FTE, voluntary. **Finance** Sources: members' dues. Annual budget: 12,000 EUR. **Activities** Events/meetings. . **Events** *General Assembly* Heraklion (Greece) 2022, *General Assembly* Lyon (France) 2021, *General Assembly* Darmstadt (Germany) 2019, *General Assembly* Helsinki (Finland) 2014, *General Assembly* Utrecht (Netherlands) 2013.
Members Organizations in 19 countries:
Austria, Azerbaijan, Bulgaria, Estonia, Finland, France, Germany, Greece, Hungary, Italy, Latvia, Lithuania, Luxembourg, Portugal, Slovakia, Slovenia, Sweden, Türkiye, Ukraine.
Individual members in 15 countries:
Belgium, Croatia, Cyprus, Czechia, Georgia, Ireland, Malta, Montenegro, Netherlands, Poland, Romania, Serbia, Spain, Switzerland, UK.
IGO Relations Participant in Fundamental Rights Platform of: *European Union Agency for Fundamental Rights (FRA, #08969)*. [2022.02.18/XJ4110/**D**]

♦ Association of European Airlines (inactive)
♦ Association of European Assay Offices / see International Association of Assay Offices (#11715)
♦ Association for European Astronauts (inactive)

♦ Association of European Automative and Industrial Battery Manufacturers (EUROBAT) 02498

Association de fabricants européens d'accumulateurs – Vereinigung Europäischer Akkumulatoren-Hersteller

Exec Dir Av de Tervueren 188A – box 4, 1150 Brussels, Belgium. T. +3227611653. Fax +3227611699. E-mail: eurobat@eurobat.org.
General Manager address not obtained.
URL: https://www.eurobat.org/

History 1968. Former names and other names: *Association of European Battery Manufacturers* – former; *Association of European Accumulator Manufacturers* – former; *Association of European Storage Battery Manufacturers* – former. Registration: EU Transparency Register, No/ID: 39573492614-61. **Aims** Enhance relations between the industry and European institutions; develop collective solutions towards issues of common concern to the industry, regulators and consumers; coordinate exchange of information on European battery issues to European institutions, media and public; serve as an advisor on all information related to the starter and industrial battery domain. **Structure** General Meeting (annual); Board; Secretariat; Clusters; Task Forces. **Languages** English. **Staff** 5.00 FTE, paid. **Activities** Advocacy/lobbying/activism; capacity building; events/meetings; knowledge management/information dissemination; networking/liaising; politics/policy/regulatory; projects/programmes; research and development; research/documentation; standards/guidelines; training/education. **Events** *General Assembly and Forum* Madrid (Spain) 2023, *General Assembly and Forum* Brussels (Belgium) 2022, *Forum* Brussels (Belgium) 2021, *Forum* Brussels (Belgium) 2020, *Finnish European Union Presidency Conference on Supporting a Competitive and Sustainable Battery Value Chain in the EU* Brussels (Belgium) 2019. **Publications** EUROBAT Innovation Roadmap 2.0
Members Companies (49): Regular (manufacturers); Associate (suppliers). Members in 21 countries:
Austria, Belgium, Czechia, France, Germany, Greece, Italy, Luxembourg, Malta, Netherlands, Norway, Poland, Portugal, Slovenia, South Africa, Spain, Sweden, Switzerland, Türkiye, UK, United Arab Emirates.
IGO Relations Recognized by: *European Commission (EC, #06633)*. **NGO Relations** Member of (4): *Association européenne des métaux (EUROMETAUX, #02578)*; *Circular Plastics Alliance (#03936)*; *European Green Vehicles Initiative Association (EGVIA, #07410)*; *Industry4Europe (#11181)*. Cooperates with (1): *European Committee for Electrotechnical Standardization (CENELEC, #06647)*. [2022.11.14/XD3488/t/**D**]

♦ Association of European Automobile Manufacturers / see European Automobile Manufacturers' Association (#06300)
♦ Association of European Automotive Components and Parts Industry / see European Association of Automotive Suppliers (#05948)
♦ Association of European Battery Manufacturers / see Association of European Automative and Industrial Battery Manufacturers (#02498)
♦ Association of European Bedfeather and Bedding Industries / see European Down and Feather Association (#06941)

♦ Association of European Border Regions (AEBR) 02499

Association des Régions Frontalières Européennes (ARFE) – Asociación de Regiones Fronterizas Europeas (ARFE) – Arbeitsgemeinschaft Europäischer Grenzregionen (AGEG) – Associação das Regiões Fronteiriças Europaias (ARFE) – Comunità di Lavoro delle Regioni Europee di Confine – Europaeiske Graenseregioners Arbejdsfaellesskab – Werkgemeenschap van Europese Grensgebieden (WVEG) – Stowarzyseenie Europejskich Regionów Granicznych (SERG)

SG Enscheder Strasse 362, 48599 Gronau, Germany. T. +49256270219. Fax +49256270259. E-mail: info@aebr.eu.

Project Office c/o WeWork, Neue Schönhauserstrasse 3-5, 10178 Berlin, Germany.
URL: http://www.aebr.eu/

History Founded following a 'Regio Meeting', 1965, Basel (Switzerland), and the 'Anholt Talks', 1970-1971. Current statutes adopted 1981; revised 1987; 25 Nov 1994, Trieste (Italy). Former names and other names: *European Frontier Regions Joint Working Party* – former; *Associazione delle Regioni Frontaliere Europee* – former. Registration: EU Transparency Register, No/ID: 684213919233-18. **Aims** Act for the benefit of all European border and cross-border regions and therefore aim to: make their particular problems, opportunities, tasks and projects intelligible; represent their overall interests to national and international parliaments, organs, authorities and institutions; initiate, support and coordinate their co-operation throughout Europe (creation of a network); exchange know-how and information in order to formulate and coordinate common interests on the basis of various cross-border problems and opportunities, and to offer adequate solutions. **Structure** General Assembly (annual); Executive Committee; Advisory Committee for Cross-border Cooperation. **Languages** English, French, German. **Finance** Sources: grants; members' dues. **Activities** Advocacy/lobbying/activism; events/meetings. **Events** *General Assembly and Annual Conference* Eupen (Belgium) 2020, *General Assembly and Annual Conference* Dresden (Germany) 2019, *General Assembly* Oulu (Finland) 2018, *Joint Conference on the Future of Cross-Border Cooperation in Europe* Brussels (Belgium) 2015, *Annual Conference* Maastricht (Netherlands) / Liège (Belgium) 2013. **Publications** *AEBR Newsflash* (12 a year); *Cooperation Between European Border Regions – Review and Perspectives. European Charter, Practical Guide.* Brochure; information sheets; map.
Members Border and cross-border organizations (85). Full in 34 countries:
Austria, Belarus, Belgium, Bosnia-Herzegovina, Bulgaria, Croatia, Czechia, Denmark, Estonia, Finland, France, Germany, Greece, Hungary, Ireland, Italy, Latvia, Lithuania, Moldova, Netherlands, North Macedonia, Norway, Poland, Portugal, Romania, Russia, Serbia, Slovakia, Slovenia, Spain, Switzerland, Türkiye, UK, Ukraine.
Included in the above, 1 organization listed in this Yearbook:
EUREGIO.
Consultative Status Consultative status granted from: *Council of Europe (CE, #04881)* (Participatory Status).
[2021.07.07/XD6446/y/**D**]

♦ Association of European Building Surveyors / see Association of European Experts in Building and Construction (The) (#02510)

♦ Association of European Cancer Leagues (ECL) 02500

Association européenne des ligues nationales contre le cancer
Contact Chée de Louvain 479, 1030 Brussels, Belgium. T. +3222562000. E-mail: ecl@europeancancerleagues.org – info@europeancancerleagues.org.
URL: http://www.europeancancerleagues.org/

History Nov 1980, Rome (Italy). Statutes adopted 27 Oct 1981, Lausanne (Switzerland); most recently revised 21 Oct 2001, Lisbon (Portugal). Statutes adopted 2004, Brussels (Belgium). Registration: Belgium; EU Transparency Register, No/ID: 19265592757-25. **Aims** Influence and improve cancer control and cancer care in Europe through collaboration between members; influence EU and pan-European policies. **Structure** General Assembly; Executive Board; Secretariat in Brussels (Belgium). **Languages** English, French. **Staff** 4.00 FTE, paid. **Finance** Sources: donations; members' dues. Supported by: *European Union (EU, #08967).* **Activities** Events/meetings; knowledge management/information dissemination; politics/policy/regulatory. **Events** *European Conference on Tobacco or Health (ECToH)* Madrid (Spain) 2023, *ECToH : European Conference on Tobacco or Health* Berlin (Germany) 2020, *Annual General Assembly and Conference* Berlin (Germany) 2018, *Annual General Assembly and Conference* Copenhagen (Denmark) 2017, *ECToH : European Conference on Tobacco or Health* Porto (Portugal) 2017. **Publications** Annual Report; annual conference report; annual General Assembly report; meeting reports; European recommendations; European guidelines.
Members National and regional cancer leagues (29) in 24 countries, of which 21 EU Member States:
Belgium, Cyprus, Czechia, Denmark, Finland, France, Germany, Hungary, Iceland, Ireland, Israel, Italy, Luxembourg, Malta, Netherlands, Poland, Portugal, Romania, Slovakia, Slovenia, Spain, Switzerland, Türkiye, UK.
IGO Relations Cooperates with (4): *European Commission (EC, #06633); European Parliament (EP, #08146); International Agency for Research on Cancer (IARC, #11598); WHO Regional Office for Europe (#20945).* **NGO Relations** Member of (5): *European Cancer Organisation (ECO, #06432); European Cervical Cancer Association (ECCA, #06512); European Public Health Alliance (EPHA, #08297); Framework Convention Alliance (FCA, #09981); Health and Environment Alliance (HEAL, #10879).* Cooperates with (9): *European Alcohol Policy Alliance (Eurocare, #05856); European Cancer Patient Coalition (ECPC, #06433); European Network for Smoking and Tobacco Prevention (ENSP, #08002); European Oncology Nursing Society (EONS, #08086); European Society for Medical Oncology (ESMO, #08648); Organization of European Cancer Institutes (OECI, #17865); SIOP Europe (SIOPE, #19288); Smoke Free Partnership (SFP, #19329); Union for International Cancer Control (UICC, #20415).* Provides secretariat for: *MEPs against Cancer (MAC, #16717).*
[2020.06.23/XD8630/**D**]

♦ Association of European Candle Makers (inactive)

♦ Association for the European Cardiovascular Pathology (AECVP) . . 02501

Sec-Reas Univ Center of Legal Medicine – Lausanne, Rue du Bugnon 21, 1011 Lausanne VD, Switzerland. T. +41213147090.
URL: http://anpat.unipd.it/aecvp/

History Founded 2001, as a continuation of *European School for Cardiovascular Pathology (inactive).* **Aims** Bring together those in Europe actively involved in cardiovascular pathology; provide a platform to serve as a liaison between pathologists, cardiologists and surgeons, as well as basic researchers in the field of cardiovascular diseases. **Structure** Council; Executive Committee. Standing Committees (4): Education; Membership; Nominating; Cardiac Transplantation. **Languages** English. **Staff** None. **Finance** Members' dues. Industrial and institutional support for meetings. Budget (annual): euro 20,000. **Activities** Events/meetings; studies/documentation; training/education; awards/prizes/competitions. **Events** *Biennial Meeting* Cologne (Germany) 2016, *IALM Intersocietal Symposium* Venice (Italy) 2016, *Biennial Meeting* Amsterdam (Netherlands) 2014, *Biennial Meeting* Paris (France) 2014, *Biennial Meeting* Cadiz (Spain) 2012. **Publications** *AECVP Newsletter. Guidelines for Endomyocardial Biopsy.* Consensus documents (articles in journals).
Members Regular; Trainee; Honorary; Emeritus. Pathologists/trainees, cardiologists/cardiac surgeons and forensic pathologists with interest in cardiac morphology and researchs in the field of cardiovascular pathology. Membership countries not specified.
[2015/XJ1299/**D**]

♦ Association of European Cartonboard and Carton Manufacturers (PRO CARTON) 02502

Contact c/o AC- Fiduciaire, Todistrasse 42, PO Box 1507, 8027 Zurich ZH, Switzerland. T. +41767220244. E-mail: info@procarton.com.
Dir-Gen address not obtained.
URL: http://www.procarton.com/

History 1988, Zurich (Switzerland). A Participating Industry Sector of *Confederation of European Paper Industries (CEPI, #04529).* Former names and other names: *Europese Vereniging voor de Promotie van Vouwkartonnage* – former; *European Association of Carton and Cartonboard Manufacturers (Pro Carton)* – alias; *Association européenne des fabricants de cartonnages et de carton plat* – alias; *Europäischer Verband von Karton- und Faltschachtelherstellern* – alias; *Associazione Europea di Produttori di Cartone e Cartoncino* – alias. **Aims** Promote the functionalities and benefits of cartons and cartonboard as a renewable, recyclable and competitive packaging material to brand owners, retailers, designers, the media and EU policymakers. **Activities** Awards/prizes/competitions. **Events** *Congress* Sorrento (Italy) 2014, *Congress* Dubrovnik (Croatia) 2013, *Packaging in a digital world* Düsseldorf (Germany) 2012, *Congress* Düsseldorf (Germany) 2009, *General Assembly* Budapest (Hungary) 2004. **Members** Producers of cartonboard and folding cartons (16). Membership countries not specified. **NGO Relations** Grants annual Pro Carton/ECMA Award with: *European Carton Makers Association (ECMA, #06453).*
[2023.02.14/XD3016/**D**]

♦ Association of European Chambers of Commerce and Industry (#02423)
♦ Association of European Christian Fraternities / see European Federation of Christian Student Associations (#07076)
♦ Association of the European Cigarette Paper Converting Industry / see European Rolling Paper Association (#08399)
♦ Association of European Cities and Regions for Culture / see European Cities and Regions for Culture (#06554)
♦ Association of European Citizens (inactive)

♦ Association of European Civil Engineering Faculties (AECEF) 02503

Permanent SG DEC-FEUP R Dr Roberto Frias s/n, 4200-465 Porto, Portugal. T. +351225081856. Fax +351225081940. E-mail: aecef@fe.up.pt.
Main Website: http://www.aecef.net

History 14 Sep 1992. Registration: EU Transparency Register, No/ID: 913322240282-30, Start date: 11 Nov 2020. **Aims** Promote cooperation between civil engineering faculties in Europe; increase dissemination and application of research and teaching in the field. **Structure** General Assembly (every 2 years); Board of Directors; Secretariat. **Languages** English. **Staff** 0.50 FTE, paid. **Finance** Sources: members' dues. **Events** *Joint Conference* Pisa (Italy) 2023, *Joint Conference* Thessaloniki (Greece) 2021, *Biennial Symposium* Wroclaw (Poland) 2019, *Biennial Symposium* Prague (Czechia) 2017, *Biennial Symposium* Porto (Portugal) 2015. **Publications** *AECEF Newsletter* (6 a year).
Members Full in 21 countries:
Belarus, Croatia, Czechia, Denmark, Estonia, Finland, Greece, Hungary, Ireland, Italy, Latvia, Lithuania, Poland, Portugal, Romania, Russia, Slovakia, Slovenia, Türkiye, UK, Ukraine.
NGO Relations Participates in: *European Civil Engineering Education and Training (EUCEET Association, #06565).*
[2022.05.10/XJ3234/**D**]

♦ Association of European Coeliac Societies (AOECS) 02504

Association des sociétés coeliaques européennes
Contact Rue de la Presse 4, 1000 Brussels, Belgium.
URL: http://www.aoecs.org/

History 1988. Founded by national coeliac associations from France, Italy, Spain and UK. Current statutes adopted 2009. Registration: Belgium. **Aims** Represent people who are affected by coeliac disease or dermatitis herpetiformis (DH). **Structure** Annual General Assembly; Executive Board; Working Groups. **Languages** English. **Staff** None. **Finance** Members' dues. Fees resulting from Crossed Grain Trademark licensing. **Activities** Research and development; networking/liaising; awareness raising. **Events** *Annual Congress* Sintra (Portugal) 2021, *Annual Congress* Lisbon (Portugal) 2020, *Annual Congress* Milan (Italy) 2019, *Annual Congress* Amsterdam (Netherlands) 2013, *Better life for coeliacs* Helsinki (Finland) 2012. **Publications** *AOECS Newsletter* (4 a year).
Members National associations in 33 countries:
Andorra, Austria, Belgium, Bulgaria, Croatia, Cyprus, Czechia, Denmark, Estonia, Finland, France, Germany, Greece, Hungary, Ireland, Israel, Italy, Luxembourg, Malta, Netherlands, Norway, Poland, Portugal, Romania, Russia, Serbia, Slovenia, Spain, Sweden, Switzerland, UK, Ukraine, USA.
IGO Relations Participates as observer in the activities of: *Codex Alimentarius Commission (CAC, #04081).* **NGO Relations** Member of: *European Patients' Forum (EPF, #08172); European Society for Study of Coeliac Disease (ESSCD); International Alliance of Patients' Organizations (IAPO, #11633).*
[2020/XD5119/**D**]

♦ Association of European Colour Consultants/Colour Designers (#03357)
♦ Association of European Comparative Clinical Pathology (inactive)

♦ Association of European Competition Law Judges (AECLJ) 02505

SG c/o Comp Appeal Tribunal, Salisbury Square House, 8 Salisbury Square, London, EC4Y 8AP, UK.
URL: http://www.aeclj.com/

History 2001, Luxembourg. Registration: Companies House, England and Wales. **Aims** Provide a forum for discussing judicial issues in the competition law field. **Events** *Annual Conference* London (UK) 2021, *Annual Conference* Vilnius (Lithuania) 2020, *Annual Conference* Copenhagen (Denmark) 2019, *Annual Conference* Paris (France) 2018, *Annual Conference* Vienna (Austria) 2017. **Members** Membership restricted to judiciary of Member States of European Community.
[2021/XM3159/**D**]

♦ Association of European Conjuncture Institutes 02506

Association d'instituts européens de conjoncture économique (AIECE) – Vereinigung Europäischer Konjunktur-Institute – Associazione di Istituti Europei di Congiuntura Economica
Admin Sec c/o UCL-IRES, Place Montesquieu 3, 1348 Louvain-la-Neuve, Belgium. T. +3210474143. Fax +3210473945. E-mail: info@aiece.org.
Chairwoman OFCE, 10 Place de Catalogne, 75014 Paris, France. T. +33144185437.
URL: http://www.aiece.org/

History 25 Oct 1957, Liège (Belgium). Statutes modified Oct 1961, Rome (Italy); Oct 1973, Louvain (Belgium); May 1981, Hamburg (Germany FR); May 1987, Belgrade (Yugoslavia); May 1998, Zurich (Switzerland); Nov 2008, Brussels (Belgium); Nov 2018, Brussels (Belgium). **Aims** Stimulate exchanges between members with a view to improve their insight into international economic developments. **Structure** Plenary Assembly; Steering Committee; President; Permanent Secretary; Study Groups. **Languages** English, French. **Staff** 1.00 FTE, voluntary. **Finance** Sources: members' dues. **Activities** Knowledge management/information dissemination; networking/liaising; research and development. **Events** *Half-yearly Meeting* Kiel (Germany) 2022, *Half-yearly meeting* Brussels (Belgium) 2019, *Half-yearly meeting* The Hague (Netherlands) 2019, *Half-yearly meeting* Brussels (Belgium) 2018, *Half-yearly meeting* Warsaw (Poland) 2018. **Publications** Reports.
Members Institutes in 19 countries:
Austria, Belgium, Denmark, Finland, France, Germany, Greece, Hungary, Ireland, Italy, Netherlands, Norway, Poland, Slovakia, Slovenia, Spain, Sweden, Switzerland, UK.
[2022.05.11/XD0127/**D**]

♦ Association of European Consumers (no recent information)
♦ Association of European Correspondence Schools / see European Association for Distance Learning (#06015)
♦ Association of European Document Exchanges (no recent information)
♦ Association of European Dry Battery Manufacturers / see European Portable Battery Association (#08255)
♦ Association of the European Economic Community and the African and Malagasy States (inactive)
♦ Association between the European Economic Community and the Partner States of the East African Community (inactive)

♦ Association of European Economics Education (AEEE) 02507

Gen Sec address not obtained. E-mail: vecon@yourchance.nl.
Pres address not obtained.
URL: http://www.economicseducation.eu/

History 1990. Builds on the Working Committee of Secondary Economics Education in EEC Countries. Current constitution adopted 27 Aug 2009. **Aims** Bring together researchers and teachers to improve economics education. **Structure** Council; Executive. **Activities** Events/meetings; knowledge management/information dissemination; networking/liaising. **Events** *European Economics Education Conference* Leeuwarden (Netherlands) 2023, *European Economics Education Conference* Lyon (France) 2022, *European Economics Education Conference* Freiburg-Breisgau (Germany) 2021, *European Economics Education Conference* Freiburg-Breisgau (Germany) 2020, *International Conference* Copenhagen (Denmark) 2018. **Publications** *AEEE Newsletter.*
Members Full; Associate. Members in 13 countries:
Belgium, Denmark, France, Germany, Greece, Ireland, Italy, Luxembourg, Netherlands, Romania, Switzerland, UK, Ukraine.
[2023/XM7559/**D**]

♦ Association of European Election Officials (ACEEEO) 02508

SG Vas Street 6, Budapest 1088, Hungary. T. +3617868298. Fax +3617868298. E-mail: aceeeo@aceeeo.org.
URL: http://www.aceeeo.org/

History Nov 1991, Budapest (Hungary). Founded with the support of *International Foundation for Electoral Systems (IFES, #13669).* Formal agreement 27 Nov 1998, Vilnius (Lithuania). Former names and other names: *Association of Central and Eastern European Election Officials (ACEEEO)* – former (Nov 1991 to 2006). **Aims** Provide a non-partisan forum, independent of national governments, for information exchange among election officials and experts throughout the Central and Eastern European region to discuss and act upon ways to promote open and transparent elections with the objective of supporting good governance

and democracy. **Structure** General Assembly (annual); Executive Board; Secretariat. **Languages** English, Russian. **Staff** 1.50 FTE, paid; 10.00 FTE, voluntary. **Finance** Members' dues. Other sources: contributions and gifts. **Activities** Knowledge management/information dissemination; training/education; monitoring/evaluation. **Events** *Annual Conference* Bucharest (Romania) 2021, *Annual conference* Tbilisi (Georgia) 2020, *Annual conference* Ljubljana (Slovenia) 2019, *Annual conference* Vilnius (Lithuania) 2018, *Annual Conference* Sofia (Bulgaria) 2017. **Publications** *ACEEEO Newsletter* (4 a year). *ACEEEO Jubilee Book*; *Elections in Europe* – in 12 vols and 2 special issues. Conference, workshop and seminar proceedings; handbooks.
Members Institutional, Associate Institutional, Member-Supporters and Honorary Members. Institutional in 24 countries:
Albania, Armenia, Azerbaijan, Belarus, Bosnia-Herzegovina, Bulgaria, Croatia, Georgia, Hungary, Kazakhstan, Kosovo, Latvia, Lithuania, Moldova, Montenegro, North Macedonia, Poland, Romania, Russia, Serbia, Slovakia, Slovenia, Türkiye, Ukraine.
Associate Institutional Members in 3 countries:
Afghanistan, Azerbaijan, Kyrgyzstan.
Member-Supporter (1):
IFES.
Consultative Status Consultative status granted from: *Council of Europe (CE, #04881)* (Participatory Status). **IGO Relations** Formal contacts with: *International Institute for Democracy and Electoral Assistance (International IDEA, #13872)*; *Organization for Security and Cooperation in Europe (OSCE, #17887)*; *OSCE – Office for Democratic Institutions and Human Rights (OSCE/ODIHR, #17902)*. Associated with Department of Global Communications of the United Nations. [2021/XD7053/**D**]

♦ Association of European Electricity Meter Manufacturers (inactive)

♦ Association of European Energy Exchanges (EUROPEX) 02509

Gen Sec Rue Archimède 44, 1000 Brussels, Belgium. T. +3225123410. E-mail: secretariat@europex.org.
URL: http://www.europex.org/
History Former names and other names: *Association of European Power Exchanges (EuroPEX)* – former. Registration: Belgium; EU Transparency Register, No/ID: 50679663522-75. **Aims** Represent the interests of exchange based wholesale markets for electrical energy, gas and environmental markets with regard to development of the European regulatory framework for wholesale energy trading; provide a discussion platform on a European level. **Structure** General Assembly; Board; Secretariat. **Activities** Advocacy/lobbying/activism; knowledge management/information dissemination; networking/liaising. **Publications** Consultations; position papers; presenations; press releases; market data.
Members Exchanges (29) in 27 countries:
Austria, Belgium, Bulgaria, Czechia, Denmark, Finland, France, Georgia, Germany, Greece, Hungary, Ireland, Italy, Netherlands, North Macedonia, Norway, Poland, Portugal, Romania, Russia, Slovakia, Slovenia, Spain, Sweden, Türkiye, UK, Ukraine.
[2020.06.23/XJ8137/**D**]

♦ Association of European Engineering Periodicals (inactive)

♦ Association of European Experts in Building and Construction (The) (AEEBC) 02510

Association d'experts européens du bâtiment et de la construction (AEEBC)
General Manager RICS, 5 Willow Park, Haywards Heath, RH16 3UA, UK. T. +447461110365. E-mail: mrusselc@gmail.com – aeebcorg@gmail.com.
URL: http://www.aeebc.org/
History Founded 1990. Also referred to as *European Association of Building and Construction Experts*. **Aims** Facilitate exchange of experience and information between professionally qualified building surveyors, technical architects and building experts responsible for technological and management processes by which buildings are constructed, renewed and repaired; represent interests to the European Commission and other European institutions; facilitate training, qualification and mutual recognition; establish practice guidelines; support and develop construction industry services in line with European Community policy; promote the profession. **Structure** General Assembly (twice a year). Officers: President; Honorary Secretary; Vice-President; Treasurer; National Delegates and Observers. Executive Secretariat. **Languages** English, French. **Staff** 0.50 FTE, paid. **Finance** Members' dues. **Activities** Research/documentation. **Events** *Half-Yearly General Assembly* Riga (Latvia) 2015, *Half-Yearly General Assembly* Vienna (Austria) 2015, *Half-Yearly General Assembly* Prague (Czech Rep) 2014, *Half-Yearly General Assembly* Santander (Spain) 2013, *Half-Yearly General Assembly* Vilnius (Lithuania) 2013. **Publications** *Common Learning Outcomes for European Managers in Construction* – manuals. Books.
Members National organizations representing over 80,000 professionals in 11 countries:
Belgium, Denmark, Finland, Germany, Ireland, Italy, Netherlands, Poland, Spain, Sweden, UK.
NGO Relations Member of: *European Council for Construction Research, Development and Innovation (ECCREDI, #06813)*; *International Fire Safety Standards Coalition (IFSS Coalition, #13606)*.
[2015.10.20/XD3581/**D**]

♦ Association of European Express Carriers (inactive)
♦ Association of European Federations of Agro-Engineers (inactive)
♦ Association of European Fibre and Paper Research Organisations (inactive)

♦ Association of European Film Archives and Cinémathèques 02511

Association des Cinémathèques Européennes (ACE)
Chairperson c/o EYE Film Museum, IJpromenade 1, 1031 KT Amsterdam, Netherlands. E-mail: ace@eyefilm.nl.
Registered Office Cinémathèque Royale de Belgique, Hotel des Clèves, Rue Ravenstein 3, 1000 Brussels, Belgium. T. +3225511902. E-mail: secretariat@cinematek.be.
URL: http://www.ace-film.eu/
History Founded 1991, as *Association of Film Archives of the European Community (ACCE)*. Present name adopted 1996. Registered in accordance with Belgian law: 0475 110 354. EU Transparency Register: 45960464757-14. **Aims** Enhance awareness of the cultural and economic value of the European film heritage and raise sufficient funds to safeguard it; create economical and juridical conditions in which the European film archives can fulfil their archival mission; promote and facilitate collaboration among European film heritage institutions; promote digitization of and facilitate access to European film heritage. **Structure** General Assembly; Executive Committee. **Languages** English, French. **Staff** Part-time. **Finance** Members' dues. Additional resources link with European programmes. **Activities** Knowledge management/information dissemination; training/education; standards/guidelines; events/meetings. Database containing personal and professional information of all registered members. **Events** *Workshop on Film Literacy* Bologna (Italy) 2016. **Publications** *Challenges of the Digital Era for Europe's Film Heritage* – final report prepared for the European Commission, DG Information Society and Media; *FORWARD* – framework for EU-wide Audiovisual Orphan Works Registry (2013-2016). Information Services: Film archives online database; European Film Gateway.
Members Film archives (44) in 26 countries:
Austria, Belgium, Croatia, Czechia, Denmark, Finland, Germany, Greece, Holy See, Hungary, Ireland, Luxembourg, Montenegro, Netherlands, North Macedonia, Norway, Poland, Portugal, Romania, Russia, Serbia, Slovenia, Spain, Sweden, Switzerland, UK.
[2019.12.19/XD4695/**D**]

♦ Association of European Financial Centres (inactive)
♦ Association of European Foresters Practicing Management which Follows Natural Processes / see PRO SILVA (#18543)
♦ Association of European Fruit and Vegetable Processing Industries / see European Association of Fruit and Vegetable Processors (#06049)
♦ Association of European Gas Meter Manufacturers / see Association of European Manufacturers of Gas Meters, Gas Pressure Regulators, Safety Devices and Stations (#02521)

♦ Association of European Geographical Societies (EUGEO) 02512

Association des Sociétés Européennes de Géographie – Verband von Europäischen Geographischen Gesellschaften
Pres p/a MTA CSFK FTI, Budaorsi ut 45, Budapest 1112, Hungary. E-mail: info@eugeo.eu.
SG address not obtained.
URL: http://www.eugeo.eu/
History 1997, Brussels (Belgium). Founded with original titles: *European Society for Geography (EUGEO) – Société européenne pour la géographie – Sociedad Europea para la Geografia – Europäische Gesellschaft für Geographie – Sociedade Européia para a Geografia – Società Europea per la Geografia – Europese Associatie voor Geografie – Europaeiske Geografiske Selskab*. Registration: Banque-Carrefour des Entreprises, No/ID: 0462.145.414, Start date: 15 Mar 1997, Belgium. **Aims** Represent member Geographical Societies at European level; coordinate and initiate joint activities to advance research and education on, and promote discipline of, geography in Europe; communicate the relevance of geographical knowledge with the wider public. **Structure** General Assembly (annual); Executive Committee; Secretariat. **Languages** English, French. **Staff** Voluntary. **Finance** Members' dues. Contributions. **Activities** Events/meetings. **Events** *Congress* Barcelona (Spain) 2023, *Congress* Prague (Czechia) 2021, *Re-imagining Europe's future society and landscapes* Galway (Ireland) 2019, *Geography for Europe* Brussels (Belgium) 2017, *Convergences and divergences of geography in Europe* Budapest (Hungary) 2015.
Members National and regional geographical societies and associations of geographers throughout Europe. Members in 26 countries:
Austria, Belgium, Bulgaria, Croatia, Czechia, Denmark, Finland, France, Germany, Hungary, Ireland, Italy, Latvia, Lithuania, Netherlands, Norway, Poland, Portugal, Romania, Serbia, Slovakia, Slovenia, Spain, Sweden, Switzerland, UK.
[2022/XD6259/**D**]

♦ Association of European Geological Societies (AEGS) 02513

Association européenne des sociétés géologiques
Sec Univ of Torino, Dipto di Scienze della Terra, Via Valperga Caluso 35, 10125 Turin TO, Italy.
URL: http://www.aegs.de/
History Oct 1987, Dubrovnik (Yugoslavia), at 5th Meeting of European Geological Societies (MEGS), when statutes were adopted. Current statutes adopted Dec 1991. **Aims** Identify geological problems of Europe as a whole; promote investigation and research; assist in promoting a unified understanding of geology, geophysics and geochemistry of the solid earth of Europe; promote collaboration among workers of different countries, geological societies and branches of earth sciences; increase public understanding of geological knowledge and its application in solving future economic, technological and social problems. **Structure** Executive Committee, including President, Vice-President or their nominees, Secretary, representatives of societies due to hold future meetings and representatives of other societies. Organizing Committee. **Languages** English. **Staff** 1.00 FTE, voluntary. **Finance** Members' dues. Meetings financed through delegate registration fees. **Activities** Organizes periodic scientific meetings and colloquia. **Events** *Meeting* Belgrade (Serbia) 2011, *Geology for society – education and cultural heritage* Cluj-Napoca (Romania) 2009, *Georesources and public policy – research, management, environment* Tallinn (Estonia) 2007, *Natural hazard related to recent geological processes and regional evolution* Turin (Italy) 2005, *General Assembly* Hannover (Germany) 2003. **Publications** Proceedings of meetings.
Members Open to all NGOs, institutions and societies in Europe active in the field of geological or earth sciences. Members in 29 countries:
Albania, Austria, Belgium, Bulgaria, Croatia, Czechia, Denmark, Estonia, Finland, France, Germany, Greece, Hungary, Italy, Latvia, Lithuania, Netherlands, North Macedonia, Norway, Poland, Portugal, Romania, Russia, Serbia, Slovakia, Spain, Sweden, UK, Ukraine.
NGO Relations Affiliated member of: *International Union of Geological Sciences (IUGS, #15777)*.
[2011/XD2042/**D**]

♦ Association of European Gypsum Industries / see European Association of Plaster and Plaster Product Manufacturers (#06152)
♦ Association of the European Hat Industry (inactive)

♦ Association of the European Heating Industry (EHI) 02514

Association pour l'industrie européenne de chauffage
SG Avenue des Arts 40, 1040 Brussels, Belgium. T. +3228803070. E-mail: ehi@ehi.eu.
URL: http://www.ehi.eu/
History 11 Jun 2002. Founded on merger of *Association of European Manufacturers of Instantaneous Gas Water Heaters and Wall-Hung Boilers (AFECI, inactive)* and the previous EHI (2000-2002), which founded 30 Jun 2000, Cologne (Germany), as a merger of *European Heating Boilers Association (EBA, inactive)* and *European Committee of Burner Manufacturers (CEB, inactive)*. **Aims** Represent the joint technical and economic interests of the heating industry towards the European Commission, European Parliament and other EU institutions. **Structure** Executive Council, comprising Chairman, 2 Vice-Chairmen, Secretary General, 2 Advisors, Regulatory Affairs Director, 10 elected members and 2 ex-officio members. Commissions; Working Groups. **Languages** English. **Staff** 1.50 FTE, paid. **Activities** Commissions (2): *'Economic'*, comprising 3 Working Groups: Market Research, Renewable Energies, WEEE; *'Technical'*, comprising 4 Departments: Burners, Floor-standing boilers, Component integration, Gas fired wall-hung boilers and water heaters; and 2 Working Groups: Energy saving, Energy labelling. **Events** *General Assembly and Conference* Cologne (Germany) 2022, *Conference on the Future of Heating for Buildings in Europe* Brussels (Belgium) 2018, *General Assembly* Brussels (Belgium) 2018, *General Assembly* Vienna (Austria) 2017.
Members Direct members and associations. Members in 12 countries:
Austria, Belgium, Denmark, France, Germany, Italy, Liechtenstein, Netherlands, Slovakia, Spain, Sweden, UK.
NGO Relations Member of: *European Association for the Streamlining of Energy Exchange-gas (EASEE-gas, #06224)*. In liaison with technical committees of: *Comité européen de normalisation (CEN, #04162)*.
[2021/XD7839/t/**D**]

♦ Association of European Home Warranty Organisations (see: #13816)
♦ Association of European Horticultural Breeders (no recent information)
♦ Association of the European Host Operators Groups (inactive)
♦ Association for European Inland Navigation and Waterways (internationally oriented national body)
♦ Association of European Inventors (inactive)

♦ Association of European Jewish Museums (AEJM) 02515

Administrator PO Box 16737, 1001 RE Amsterdam, Netherlands. E-mail: aejm@aejm.org.
URL: http://www.aejm.org/
History Registered in accordance with Dutch law. **Aims** Promote cooperation and communication between Jewish Museums in Europe; assist members in meeting the challenges facing Jewish Museums today. **Structure** General Meeting (annual). Board, comprising President, Treasurer, Secretary and 3 members. **Activities** Offers: annual Curatorial Education Programmes (CEP); (ETP) educational workshops (at annual conference). **Events** *Annual Conference* Copenhagen (Denmark) 2016, *Annual Conference* Munich (Germany) 2013, *Annual Conference* Vienna (Austria) 2012. **Publications** *AEJM Newsletter*.
Members Full; Associate; Honorary. Full in 22 countries:
Austria, Belgium, Czechia, Denmark, France, Germany, Greece, Hungary, Ireland, Italy, Lithuania, Netherlands, Norway, Poland, Russia, Slovakia, Spain, Sweden, Switzerland, Türkiye, UK, Ukraine.
Associate in 7 countries:
France, Germany, Israel, Russia, Spain, Türkiye, UK.
Honorary in 3 countries:
Austria, Germany, UK. [2013/XJ6625/**D**]

♦ Association of European Journalists (AEJ) 02516

Association des journalistes européens (AJE) – Vereinigung Europäischer Journalisten – Associação de Jornalistas Europeus – Associazione dei Giornalisti Europei – Vereniging van Europese Journalisten – Sammenslutningen af Europaeiske Journalister – Cumann Scriobhnoiri Eorpach
SG Emile Maxlaan 51, 1030 Brussels, Belgium.
URL: http://www.aej.org/
History 11 Oct 1963, Brussels (Belgium). Founded following conferences: Jun 1961, Ostend (Belgium), organized by *Centre international de formation européenne (CIFE, #03755)*; May 1962, San Remo (Italy); Oct 1962, Cologne (Germany FR). Statutes most recently modified: 2005. Registration: Banque-Carrefour des Entreprises, No/ID: 0458.856.619, Start date: 23 Feb 1996, Belgium; EU Transparency Register, No/ID: 018214429231-64, Start date: 7 Dec 2017. **Aims** Participate actively in development of a European consciousness; promote deeper knowledge of European problems; facilitate members' access to sources of European information; promote professional journalism in member countries of the Council of Europe; promote freedom of the press in Europe. **Structure** General Assembly; Executive Committee; Committees

(2). **Languages** English, French. **Staff** Voluntary. **Finance** Sources: contributions; members' dues. **Activities** Events/meetings. **Events** *Congress and General Assembly* Athens (Greece) 2021, *Congress* 2020, *Conference on Freedom of the Press in Europe* Paris (France) 2019, *Congress* Messolonghi (Greece) 2018, *Congress* Vilnius (Lithuania) 2017. **Publications** *AEJ Newsletter*. Articles.
Members National sections in 31 countries:
Albania, Armenia, Austria, Belarus, Belgium, Bosnia-Herzegovina, Bulgaria, Croatia, Cyprus, Czechia, Estonia, France, Georgia, Greece, Hungary, Ireland, Italy, Luxembourg, Malta, Moldova, Netherlands, North Macedonia, Poland, Portugal, Romania, Serbia, Slovakia, Spain, Türkiye, UK, Ukraine.
Consultative Status Consultative status granted from: *UNESCO (#20322)* (Consultative Status); *Council of Europe (CE, #04881)* (Participatory Status); *Organization for Security and Cooperation in Europe (OSCE, #17887)*. **IGO Relations** Recognized by: *European Committee of the Regions (CoR, #06665)*; *European Commission (EC, #06633)*; *European Economic and Social Committee (EESC, #06963)*; *European Parliament (EP, #08146)*. **NGO Relations** Member of (1): *Citizens for Europe (CFEU, #03956)*. [2021.02.16/XD0128/**D**]

♦ Association of European Jute Industries (inactive)
♦ Association of European Landscape and Sports Ground Contractors / see European Landscape Contractors Association (#07642)

♦ Association of European Latin Americanist Historians 02517

Association des historiens latinoaméricanistes européens – Asociación de Historiadores Latinoamericanistas Europeos (AHILA) – Associação de Historiadores Latinoamericanistas Europeus

Pres Dipto di Studi Umanistici, Univ degli Studi Roma 3, Via Ostiense 234, 00146 Rome RM, Italy. E-mail: luigi.guarnieri@uniroma3.it.
Gen Sec School of European Language and Culture, Univ of Kent, Canterbury, CT2 7NF, UK. E-mail: n.sobrevilla@kent.ac.uk.
URL: http://www.ahila.eu/

History Formally set up, 1978, Torun (Poland), following earlier meetings held 1970, 1972 and 1975. **Aims** Promote research and education relating to Latin America in Europe; act as a liaison body with other organizations of Latin Americanist historians; participate in programmes of international cooperation in the field of historical sciences; organize meetings and promote specialized symposia. **Structure** Executive Committee. **Languages** Portuguese, Spanish. **Staff** 3.50 FTE, voluntary. **Finance** Members' dues. **Activities** Events/meetings; research/documentation; financial and/or material support; awards/prizes/competitions. **Events** *Congress* Naples (Italy) 2024, *Triennial Congress* Paris (France) 2021, *Triennial Congress* Paris (France) 2020, *Triennial Congress* Valencia (Spain) 2017, *Triennial Congress* Berlin (Germany) 2014. **Publications** *Estudios AHILA*.
Members Honorary; Regular. Individuals in 26 countries:
Argentina, Austria, Brazil, Canada, Chile, Colombia, Costa Rica, Denmark, Ecuador, France, Germany, Hungary, Italy, Mexico, Netherlands, Peru, Poland, Portugal, Puerto Rico, Russia, Spain, Switzerland, UK, Uruguay, USA, Venezuela.
NGO Relations Instrumental in setting up: *Commission internationale d'études historiques latinoaméricaines et des Caraïbes (CIHL, inactive)*. [2020.03.03/XD1716/**D**]

♦ Association of European-level Research Infrastructure Facilities (ERF-AISBL) 02518

Registered Office c/o Leibniz Assn, Rue du Trône 98, 1050 Brussels, Belgium. E-mail: info@erf-aisbl.eu.
URL: https://erf-aisbl.eu/

History Registration: Banque-Carrefour des Entreprises, No/ID: 0534.481.777, Start date: 15 May 2013, Belgium. **Aims** Promote cooperation and projects between European-level research infrastructures which are open, at international level, to external researchers. **Structure** General Assembly; Executive Board; Chair. **Languages** English. **Finance** Sources: members' dues. **Activities** Events/meetings.
Members Full in 8 countries:
France, Germany, Hungary, Italy, Spain, Sweden, Switzerland, UK.
Members also include 5 organizations listed in this Yearbook:
Central European Research Infrastructure Consortium (CERIC, #03716); *EGI Foundation (EGI.eu, #05395)*; *Extreme Light Infrastructure ERIC (ELI ERIC, #09230)*; *Laserlab-Europe AISBL (#16233)*; *Partnership for Advanced Computing Europe (PRACE, #18229)*. [2020/XM6075/y/**D**]

♦ Association for European Life Science Universities (ICA) 02519

Secretariat Intl Relations Office, Czech Univ of Life Sciences Prague, Kamycka 129, 165 00 Prague 6, Czechia. T. +420224384080. Fax +420234381817. E-mail: icasecretariat@ica-europe.org.
Registered Office Marcus Van Vaernewijckstraat 21, 9030 Mariakerke, Belgium.
URL: http://www.ica-europe.info/

History Jun 1997, Vienna (Austria). Founded taking over the activities of *Interfaculty Committee Agraria (ICA, inactive)*, set up 1988. Current title adopted to reflect activities relating to agriculture, forestry, food, natural resources, rural development and the environment. Former names and other names: *Interuniversity Conference for Agricultural and Related Sciences in Europe (ICA)* – former (Jun 1997 to 1999); *Conférence interuniversitaire pour les sciences agronomiques et les disciplines connexes en Europe* – former (Jun 1997 to 1999); *Interuniversity Consortium for Agricultural and Related Sciences in Europe (ICA)* – former (1999 to 2006). Registration: No/ID: 0461 925 876, Belgium. **Aims** Enhance members' success in the international market place, in Europe and globally, by providing a supportive environment to share experience, cooperate in new ventures and benefit from the resulting synergy. **Structure** General Assembly (annual); Council; Board. Standing Committees (8): *AGRINATURA (#00578)*; *'Education and Research in Biosystems Engineering in Europe Thematic Network (ERABEE)'*; *European Forest Science Academic Network (Silva Network, #07300)*; *European Network of International Relations Officers at Higher Education Institutions for Agricultural and Related Sciences (IROICA, #07935)*; *'ICA Network for Innovation in Higher Education in the Life Sciences (ICA-Edu)' 'ICA Regional Network for Central and South Eastern Europe (CASEE)'*; *International Network for the MBA in Agribusiness and Commerce (AGRIMBA, #14295)*; *ISEKI-Food Association (#16027)*. **Languages** English. **Staff** 1.00 FTE, paid; 4.00 FTE, voluntary. **Finance** Members' dues. **Activities** Disciplines: Agriculture; Food; Forestry; Natural Resources; Rural Development; Environment. Organizes conferences and seminars; leads Commission-funded projects. **Events** *The role of life science universities in redirecting land use from threat to guardian of ecosystem* Sarajevo (Bosnia-Herzegovina) 2019, *Research based education at life science universities in the Danube region towards a sustainable future* Bucharest (Romania) 2018, *Rectors and Deans Forum* Wageningen (Netherlands) 2018, *Rectors and Deans Forum* Louvain-la-Neuve (Belgium) 2017, *Conference* Vienna (Austria) 2017. **Publications** Studies; monographs; case studies.
Members Institutions (61) in 31 countries:
Albania, Austria, Belgium, Bulgaria, Croatia, Cyprus, Czechia, Denmark, Estonia, Finland, France, Germany, Greece, Hungary, Iceland, Ireland, Italy, Latvia, Lithuania, Netherlands, Poland, Portugal, Romania, Russia, Slovakia, Slovenia, Spain, Sweden, Türkiye, UK, Ukraine.
IGO Relations *FAO (#09260)*; *UNESCO (#20322)*. [2019/XE2905/**E**]

♦ Association of European Local Authorities Promoting Local Sustainable Energy Policies / see Energy Cities (#05467)
♦ Association of European Machine Tool Merchants / see European Association of Machine Tool Merchants (#06114)
♦ Association of European Manufacturers of Automobile Spare Parts (inactive)
♦ Association of European Manufacturers of Carbonless Paper (no recent information)
♦ Association of the European Manufacturers of Feed Mineral Materials / see European Manufacturers of Feed Minerals Association (#07733)
♦ Association of European Manufacturers of Fire and Intruder Alarm Systems / see Association of European Manufacturers of Fire and Security Systems (#02520)

♦ Association of European Manufacturers of Fire and Security Systems (EURALARM) 02520

Association des constructeurs et installateurs européens de systèmes de sécurité et d'incendie – Vereinigung Europäischer Hersteller und Errichter von Sicherheitsanlagen

SG Gubelstrasse 22, 6300 Zug, Switzerland. E-mail: secretariat@euralarm.org.
URL: http://www.euralarm.org/

History 1970, as *Association of European Manufacturers of Fire and Intruder Alarm Systems – Association des constructeurs européens de systèmes d'alarme, incendie et vol – Vereinigung Europäischer Hersteller von Alarmanlagen für Brand, Einbruch und Überfall*. EU Transparency Register: 94201247949-87. **Aims** Represent on an international level the interests of European manufacturers and service providers of fire safety and security systems, in cooperation with economic and technical organizations; assist in preparation of standards, rules and recommendations; endeavour to eliminate trade barriers; support research and testing organizations; promote technological development for improvement of systems reliability. **Structure** General Assembly; Board; Sections (3); General Secretariat. **Languages** English. **Staff** Voluntary. **Finance** Members' dues. **Activities** Standards/guidelines; research and development; certification/accreditation. **Events** *General Assembly* Brussels (Belgium) 2020, *General Assembly* Madrid (Spain) 2019, *General Assembly* Bucharest (Romania) 2018, *Annual General Assembly* London (UK) 2017, *Annual General Assembly* Lisbon (Portugal) 2016.
Members Associations and companies in 17 countries:
Austria, Belgium, Bulgaria, Czechia, Denmark, Finland, France, Germany, Italy, Netherlands, Norway, Romania, Spain, Sweden, Switzerland, UK, Ukraine.
NGO Relations In liaison with technical committees of: *Comité européen de normalisation (CEN, #04162)*; *European Committee for Electrotechnical Standardization (CENELEC, #06647)*; *International Organization for Standardization (ISO, #14473)*. [2021/XD2158/**D**]

♦ Association of European Manufacturers of Gas Meters, Gas Pressure Regulators, Safety Devices and Stations (FARECOGAZ) 02521

SG Marienburgerstrasse 15, 50968 Cologne, Germany. T. +492213766857. Fax +492213766861.
URL: http://www.farecogaz.org/

History Founded 1968. Original title: *Union of European Manufacturers of Gas Meters – Union des fabricants européens de compteurs de gaz – Vereinigung der Europäischen Gaszähler-Hersteller*. Has also been referred to: in French as *Chambre syndicale des fabricants de compteurs de gaz*; in English and French as *Association of European Gas Meter Manufacturers – Association des fabricants européens de compteurs de gaz (FACOGAZ)*. New name adopted 2011, upon merger with *European Association of the Manufacturers of Gas Pressure Regulators and Safety Devices (inactive)*. **Aims** Act as a forum for exchange of views cooperating towards a regulatory framework; promote safety, quality, reliability, cost effectiveness, sustainability and environmental aspects of gas metering equipment, gas pressure regulators and associated safety devices and stations; actively promote and monitor standardization activities; monitor and take action on technical legislation at EU level. **Structure** Executive Committee. Technical Committees (2). **Languages** English. **Staff** 1.00 FTE, voluntary. **Finance** Members' dues, depending on annual turnover. **Activities** Knowledge management/information dissemination; guidance/assistance/consulting; advocacy/lobbying/activism; events/meetings. **Publications** Guidelines. **Members** European manufacturers of gas meters (17). Membership countries not specified. [2017/XD2810/**D**]

♦ Association of European Manufacturers of Heatmeters and Meters applied within the District Cooling Industry (inactive)
♦ Association of European Manufacturers of Industrial Gas Turbines (inactive)
♦ Association of European Manufacturers of Instantaneous Gas Water Heaters and Wall-Hung Boilers (inactive)
♦ Association of European Manufacturers of Internal Combustion Engines / see European Association of Internal Combustion Engine Manufacturers (#06090)

♦ Association of European Manufacturers of Sporting Ammunition . . 02522

Association des fabricants européens de munitions de sport (AFEMS)

Secretariat Viale dell'Astronomia 30, 00144 Rome RM, Italy. T. +39065903510. Fax +390654282691. E-mail: secretariat@afems.org.
Registered Office Rue Th De Cuyper 1000, 1200 Brussels, Belgium.
URL: http://www.afems.org/

History 1975. Former names and other names: *European Association of Sporting Ammunition Manufacturers* – alias. Registration: Banque-Carrefour des Entreprises, No/ID: 0420.679.201, Start date: 3 Sep 1980, Belgium; EU Transparency Register, No/ID: 131992710104-83, Start date: 12 Nov 2012. **Aims** Establish dialogue with decision-making bodies; provide a forum for members to work together to tackle the technical, scientific and legislative challenges of a competitive business environment. **Structure** General Assembly; Board of Directors; Secretary-General. Committees (3): Strategic; Technical; Legislative. **Languages** English. **Finance** Sources: members' dues. **Events** *Congress* Cascais (Portugal) 2022, *Congress* Helsinki (Finland) 2019, *Congress* Palma (Spain) 2016, *Congress* Belgrade (Serbia) 2015, *Congress* Spain 2011.
Members Manufacturers in 19 countries:
Austria, Belgium, Cyprus, Czechia, Denmark, Finland, France, Germany, Greece, Hungary, Italy, Norway, Serbia, Slovenia, Spain, Sweden, Switzerland, Türkiye, UK.
Consultative Status Consultative status granted from: *ECOSOC (#05331)* (Special). **NGO Relations** Member of (3): *Conseil européen de l'industrie chimique (CEFIC, #04687)* (Affiliated); *SAFEX International (#19030)* (Associate); *World Forum on Shooting Activities (WFSA, #21523)*. Partner of (1): *Association of European Manufacturers of Sporting Firearms (ESFAM, #02523)*. [2021/XD7485/**D**]

♦ Association of European Manufacturers of Sporting Firearms (ESFAM) 02523

SG Rue Th de Cuyper 100, 1200 Brussels, Belgium.
URL: https://www.esfam.eu/

History 2009. Registration: Banque-Carrefour des Entreprises, No/ID: 0812.363.320, Start date: 18 Jun 2009, Belgium; EU Transparency Register, No/ID: 572813043948-74, Start date: 30 Aug 2021. **Aims** Represent members towards the European and international authorities.
Members Companies in 4 countries:
Austria, Belgium, Germany, Italy.
NGO Relations Member of (1): *Institut Européen des Armes de Chasse et de Sport (IEACS, #11299)* (Associate). Partner of (7): *Association of European Manufacturers of Sporting Ammunition (#02522)*; *European Association of the Civil Commerce of Weapons (#05975)*; *European Shooting Confederation (ESC, #08481)*; *Federation of Associations for Hunting and Conservation of the EU (#09459)*; *Foundation for European Societies of Arms Collectors (FESAC, #09955)*; US National Rifle Association; *World Forum on Shooting Activities (WFSA, #21523)*. [2021/AA2088/**D**]

♦ Association of the European Manufacturers of Storage Gas-Waterheaters (inactive)
♦ Association of the European Manufacturers of Technical Ceramics for Electronic, Electrical, Mechanical and Other Applications / see European Technical Ceramics Federation (#08878)
♦ Association of the European Manufacturers of Vitreous Enamelled Hollow Ware (inactive)
♦ Association of European Market Research Institutes / see Alliance of International Market Research Institutes (#00695)
♦ Association of European Metal Sink Manufacturers (inactive)

♦ Association of European Migration Institutions (AEMI) 02524

Sec c/o LWL Industriemuseum, Zeche Hannover, Am Rübenkamp 8, 44793 Bochum, Germany. T. +4923428253911. Fax +4923428253919.
URL: http://www.aemi.eu/

History 1989, Aalborg (Denmark). Enlarged 1991, Bremerhaven (Germany) to a European organization, when current title was adopted. Statutes amended 1995, Liverpool (UK). Current statutes carried out 28 Sep 1996, Krakow-Przegorzaly (Poland). Former names and other names: *Association of Scandinavian Migration Institutions* – former. **Aims** Provide members with an international forum through which they may advance the knowledge of European migration, including, but not limited to initiation and pursuit of common research projects, arrangement of meetings, international symposia and multinational events and dissemination of knowledge supplied by members acting individually or in concern through all appropriate media. **Structure** General Assembly (annual); Executive Board. **Languages** English. **Finance** Sources: meeting proceeds; members' dues. **Events** *Annual Meeting* Fafe (Portugal) 2022, *Annual Meeting* San Sebastian (Spain) 2021, *Annual Meeting* Omagh (UK) 2020, *Annual Meeting* Antwerp (Belgium) 2019, *Annual Meeting* Riga (Latvia) 2014. **Publications** *Aemi Journal* (annual).

Members Individuals; institutions and organizations (34) in 23 countries and territories:
Åland, Canada, Croatia, Czechia, Denmark (2), England, Finland, France, Germany (4), Greece, Iceland, Ireland, Italy (2), Luxembourg, Northern Ireland, Norway (4), Poland, Portugal, San Marino, Scotland, Slovenia (2), Sweden (2), USA.
[2022/XD5925/**D**]

- ♦ Association of European Military Parachutists / see European Paratroopers Association (#08141)
- ♦ Association of European Motorcycle Manufacturers / see Association des constructeurs européens de motocycles (#02450)
- ♦ Association of European Municipalities Towards Urban Energy Efficiency / see Energy Cities (#05467)

♦ Association for European NanoElectronics ActivitieS (AENEAS) 02525

Dir-Gen 44 rue Cambronne, 75015 Paris, France. T. +33140644580. E-mail: contact@aeneas-office.org.
Office Manager address not obtained.
URL: https://aeneas-office.org/

History 30 Nov 2006. *European Commission (EC, #06633)*, Member States and associated countries and AENEAS together created *ENIAC Joint Undertaking*, set up 2008, which ended prior to 2015. AENEAS currently part of Private Members Board of a new public private partnership called *ECSEL Joint Undertaking*. Former names and other names: *European Nanoelectronics Initiative Advisory Council (ENIAC)* – former; *European Technology Platform for Nanoelectronics (ENIAC)* – former (2004 to 2006). **Aims** Enhance competitiveness of the European micro and nanoelectronics components and systems industry. **Structure** General Assembly; Steering Board; Support Group; Scientific Committee; Working Groups. **Languages** English. **Finance** Sources: members' dues. **Activities** Research and development. **Events** *Electronic Components and Systems Brokerage Event* Brussels (Belgium) 2022, *Electronic Components and Systems Brokerage Event* Eindhoven (Netherlands) 2021, *European Forum for Electronic Components and Systems (EFECS)* Netherlands 2021, *Electronic Components and Systems Brokerage Event* Brussels (Belgium) 2020, *European Forum for Electronic Components and Systems* Helsinki (Finland) 2019. **Members** Organizations (401). Membership countries not specified. **NGO Relations** Member of (1): *European Partnership for Key Digital Technologies (KDT, #08158)*.
[2022/XM2975/**E**]

- ♦ Association of the European National Olympic Committees / see European Olympic Committees (#08083)

♦ Association of European Ocularists (AEO) 02526

Contact address not obtained. E-mail: info@aeo2021.com.

Events *Congress* Palermo (Italy) 2023, *Congress* Palermo (Italy) 2022, *Congress* Palermo (Italy) 2021, *Congress* Athens (Greece) 2019, *Congress* Moscow (Russia) 2017. [2020/XJ5235/**D**]

♦ Association of European Open Air Museums (AEOM) 02527

Association des musées de plein air européens – Verband Europäischer Freilichtmuseen

Pres c/o Jamtli Foundation, Museiplan, SE-731 31 Östersund, Sweden.
URL: http://www.aeom.org/

History 26 Apr 1966, Bokrijk (Belgium), when a first meeting of 12 open air professionals was held. The initial working group was transformed into an association at the constituent assembly, 1972, Helsinki (Finland). **Aims** Exchange scientific, technical, practical and organizational experience relative to open air museums; promote the activities of open air museums in general, such museums being defined as scientific collections in the open air of various types of structures, which, as constructional and functional entities, illustrate settlement patterns, dwellings, economy, and technology. **Structure** Assembly (every 2 years). Board, consisting of President, Vice-President and 5 additional members (all from different countries). **Languages** English, French, German. **Staff** 5.00 FTE, voluntary. **Events** *Biennial Conference* Stockholm (Sweden) 2022, *Biennial Conference* Oslo (Norway) / Lillehammer (Norway) 2015, *Biennial Conference* Germany 2013, *Biennial Conference* Bardejov (Slovakia) / Roznov pod Radhostem (Czech Rep) 2011, *Biennial Conference* Aarhus (Denmark) 2009. **Publications** Conference reports.
Members Personal directors or leading persons of scientific staff of open air museums. Institutional open air museums. Members in 24 countries:
Austria, Belgium, Bulgaria, Czechia, Denmark, Estonia, Finland, France, Germany, Greece, Hungary, Ireland, Latvia, Lithuania, Netherlands, Norway, Poland, Romania, Russia, Slovakia, Slovenia, Sweden, Switzerland, UK.
IGO Relations *UNESCO (#20322)*. **NGO Relations** Affiliated member of: *International Council of Museums (ICOM, #13051)*. [2017/XD4393/v/**D**]

♦ Association of European Operational Research Societies (EURO) .. 02528

Manager PO Box 513, Meanwood, Leeds, LS6 9DT, UK. E-mail: office@euro-online.org – manager@euro-online.org.
Registered Office c/o Univ de Fribourg, Dépt d'Informatique, Bd de Pérolles 90, 1700 Fribourg, Switzerland.
Main Website: http://www.euro-online.org/

History 27 Jan 1975, Brussels (Belgium). Founded as a regional grouping within *International Federation of Operational Research Societies (IFORS, #13493)*, on signature of the first association agreement by 9 societies, following discussion at IFORS conferences and meetings, 1972, 1973 and 1974. Formally constituted 5 Mar 1976. Statutes amended: 18 Jun 1976; 1989; 1990; 2003; 2019. Registration: Swiss Civil Code, No/ID: CH-217 3 541 128-3, Switzerland. **Aims** Promote Operational Research throughout Europe. **Structure** Council; Executive Committee; Working Groups. **Languages** English. **Finance** Sources: meeting proceeds; members' dues; sale of publications. **Activities** Awards/prizes/competitions; events/meetings; research/documentation; training/education. **Events** *European Conference on Operational Research (EURO-k Conference)* Copenhagen (Denmark) 2024, *European Conference on Operational Research (EURO-k Conference)* Espoo (Finland) 2022, *PATAT: International Conference on the Practice and Theory of Automated Timetabling* Leuven (Belgium) 2022, *PATAT: International Conference on the Practice and Theory of Automated Timetabling* Bruges (Belgium) 2021, *Conference on Sustainable Supply Chains* Lisbon (Portugal) 2021. **Publications** *EURO Electronic Newsletter* (12 a year); *EURO Journal on Computational Optimization (EJCO)*; *EURO Journal on Decision Processes (EJDP)*; *EURO Journal on Transportation and Logistics (EJTL)*; *European Journal of Operational Research (EJOR)*. *EURO Advanced Tutorials in Operational Research*.
Members National organizations (normally full members of IFORS) in 32 countries:
Austria, Belarus, Belgium, Croatia, Czechia, Denmark, Estonia, Finland, France, Germany, Greece, Hungary, Iceland, Ireland, Israel, Italy, Lithuania, Netherlands, Norway, Poland, Portugal, Russia, Serbia, Slovakia, Slovenia, South Africa, Spain, Sweden, Switzerland, Tunisia, Türkiye, UK. [2022.06.12/XD5785/**E**]

- ♦ Association of European Paediatric Cardiology / see Association for European Paediatric and Congenital Cardiology (#02529)

♦ Association for European Paediatric and Congenital Cardiology (AEPC) 02529

Permanent Secretariat c/o Kenes Associations, Rue François Versonnex 7, 1207 Geneva, Switzerland. T. +41229080483. E-mail: office@aepc.org.
Registered Address Herestraat 49, 3000 Leuven, Belgium.
URL: http://www.aepc.org/

History 30 Jun 1963, Lyon (France). Statutes amended 20 May 1995, Bologna (Italy); May 2013. Statutes fully revised 2020. Former names and other names: *Association des pédiatres cardiologues européens* – former; *Association of European Paediatric Cardiology (AEPC)* – former (2011); *Association européenne pour la cardiologie pédiatrique* – former (2011); *Association européene de cardiologie pédiatrique et congénitale* – former (2011 to 2020). **Aims** Defend the interests of all European patients, doctors and care providers in the field of paediatric and congenital cardiology; promote knowledge of the normal and abnormal heart and the cardiovascular physiology during growth and development from foetus until adulthood; assure a high level of professional practice in the field of paediatric congenital heart disease. **Structure** Business Meeting (General Assembly); Council; Board of National Delegates; Scientific Advisory Committee (SAC); Educational Committee; Working Groups. **Languages** English. **Staff** Voluntary. **Finance** Sources: meeting proceeds; subscriptions. **Activities** Awards/prizes/competitions; events/meetings; training/education. **Events** *Annual Meeting* Hamburg (Germany) 2025, *Annual Meeting* Porto (Portugal) 2024, *Annual Meeting* Dublin (Ireland) 2023, *Annual Meeting* Geneva (Switzerland) 2022, *Annual Meeting* Gothenburg (Sweden) 2021. **Publications** *Cardiology in the Young* (10 a year). *AEPC Recommendations* in English.
Members About 1,100 members in 53 countries:
Afghanistan, Argentina, Australia, Austria, Belgium, Bosnia-Herzegovina, Bulgaria, Croatia, Cyprus, Czechia, Denmark, Estonia, Finland, France, Germany, Greece, Holy See, Hungary, Iceland, India, Indonesia, Iran Islamic Rep, Iraq, Ireland, Israel, Italy, Japan, Latvia, Lithuania, Luxembourg, Monaco, Morocco, Namibia, Netherlands, North Macedonia, Norway, Poland, Portugal, Romania, Russia, Serbia, Slovakia, Slovenia, South Africa, Spain, Sweden, Switzerland, Tunisia, Turkey, Türkiye, UK, Ukraine, USA.
NGO Relations Member of (1): *World Federation of Pediatric Intensive and Critical Care Societies (WFPICCS, #21473)*. [2022.11.07/XD0130/v/**D**]

♦ Association of European Performers' Organisations (AEPO-ARTIS) . 02530

Association des organisations européennes d'artistes interprètes

Secretariat Avenue de Cortenbergh 116, 1000 Brussels, Belgium. T. +3222801934. Fax +3222303507. E-mail: aepo-artis@aepo-artis.org.
URL: http://www.aepo-artis.org/

History 20 May 1994, Brussels (Belgium). Founded under the acronym *AEPO*. Current title adopted on merger with *ARTES EEIG (ARTIS, inactive)*, Nov 2004. Registration: France; EU Transparency Register, No/ID: 69221462428-97. **Aims** Develop, strengthen and protect performers' rights; highlight the contribution they make to Europe's cultural sector. **Structure** General Assembly; Administrative Council. Standing Committees. **Languages** English. **Activities** Advocacy/lobbying/activism. **Events** *Seminar* Brussels (Belgium) 2019, *Conference on collective management of copyright and related rights in Europe* Brussels (Belgium) 2008.
Members Federations, national performer's societies, performers' sections, representatives in 26 countries:
Austria, Belgium, Croatia, Czechia, Denmark, Finland, France, Germany, Greece, Hungary, Ireland, Italy, Latvia, Lithuania, Netherlands, Norway, Poland, Portugal, Romania, Serbia, Slovakia, Slovenia, Spain, Sweden, Switzerland, UK.
International organization representing European member unions:
International Federation of Musicians (#13486).
Consultative Status Consultative status granted from: *World Intellectual Property Organization (WIPO, #21593)* (Permanent Observer Status). **IGO Relations** *Council of Europe (CE, #04881)*; *Intergovernmental Committee of the International Convention of Rome for the Protection of Performers, Producers of Phonograms and Broadcasting Organizations (#11474)*. **NGO Relations** Member of: *Culture First Coalition (inactive)*.
[2021/XD6946/**D**]

- ♦ Association of European Pharmaceutical Inspectors (no recent information)

♦ Association of European Police Colleges (AEPC) 02531

Association des Ecoles Supérieures des Polices Européennes – Vereinigung Europäischer Polizeiakademien

SG BMI-SIAK, Herrengasse 7, 1010 Vienna, Austria. E-mail: aepc-secretariat@bmi.gv.at – info@aepc.net.
URL: http://www.aepc.net/

History 10 Jan 1996. **Aims** Improve cooperation and coordination on police training between member colleges. **Structure** Governing Board; Executive Committee; Secretariat. **Languages** English. **Finance** No budget of its own. External financing for execution of activities. **Activities** Events/meetings. **Events** *Conference & Governing Board Meeting* Czechia 2023, *Annual Conference* Baku (Azerbaijan) 2015, *Annual Conference* Riga (Latvia) 2014, *Conference* Belgrade (Serbia) 2011, *Annual European police congress* Berlin (Germany) 2011. **Publications** *Ten Candidate Member States on Their Way to the EU* (2002); *Police and Justice Systems in the European Union* (2000). Reports.
Members Police colleges in 43 countries:
Albania, Armenia, Austria, Azerbaijan, Belgium, Bosnia-Herzegovina, Bulgaria, Croatia, Cyprus, Czechia, Denmark, Estonia, Finland, France, Georgia, Germany, Greece, Hungary, Ireland, Italy, Kosovo, Latvia, Lithuania, Luxembourg, Malta, Moldova, Montenegro, Netherlands, North Macedonia, Norway, Poland, Portugal, Romania, Russia, Serbia, Slovakia, Slovenia, Spain, Sweden, Switzerland, Türkiye, UK, Ukraine.
IGO Relations Participant in Fundamental Rights Platform of: *European Union Agency for Fundamental Rights (FRA, #08969)*. [2023/XD7279/**D**]

- ♦ Association of European Power Exchanges / see Association of European Energy Exchanges (#02509)

♦ Association of European Printing Museums (AEPM) 02532

Contact Rue de la Mutualité 58, 1180 Brussels, Belgium. E-mail: info@aepm.eu.
URL: http://www.aepm.eu/

History Registered in accordance with Belgian law. **Aims** Encourage the sharing of knowledge, experience, initiatives, and resources in all fields of the graphic arts as practised from the time of Gutenberg until the present day. **Structure** General Assembly; Managing Board. **Finance** Members' dues. **Activities** Events/meetings. **Events** *Annual Conference* Turnhout (Belgium) 2019, *Annual Conference* Madrid (Spain) 2018. **Publications** Papers; proceedings.
Members Full in 31 countries:
Armenia, Australia, Austria, Belgium, Brazil, Canada, Cyprus, Czechia, Denmark, Estonia, Finland, France, Germany, Greece, Ireland, Italy, Korea Rep, Latvia, Luxembourg, Netherlands, Norway, Poland, Portugal, Romania, Serbia, South Africa, Spain, Sweden, Switzerland, UK, USA. [2020.03.03/XM7690/**D**]

♦ Association of European Producers of Laminate Flooring (EPLF) ... 02533

Fédération européenne des fabricants de revêtements de sol stratifiés – Verband der Europäischen Laminatfussbodenhersteller

Communications Officer Rue Defacqz 52, 1050 Brussels, Belgium. E-mail: info@eplf.com.
Registered Office Mittelstr 50, 33602 Bielefeld, Germany.
URL: http://www.eplf.com/

History 1994, Bonn (Germany). **Aims** Promote research, development and standards of laminate flooring; increase cooperation in the field.
Members Companies (21) in 9 countries:
Austria, Belgium, France, Germany, Italy, Spain, Sweden, Switzerland, Türkiye.
NGO Relations Member of: *European Floor Coverings Association (EUFCA, #07271)*. [2022/XD8684/**D**]

- ♦ Association of European Psychiatrists / see European Psychiatric Association (#08290)
- ♦ Association of European Publication Paper Producers / see European Association of Graphic Paper Producers (#06060)
- ♦ Association for European Public Information by Television (inactive)

♦ Association of European Public Postal Operators (PostEurop) 02534

Association des opérateurs postaux publics européens

SG Bvd Brand Whitlock 114, 1200 Brussels, Belgium. T. +3227731190 – +3227619650. Fax +3227714858. E-mail: info@posteurop.org.
URL: http://www.posteurop.org/

History Sep 1992, Athens (Greece). Set up at conference of *Conférence européenne des administrations des postes et des télécommunications (CEPT, #04602)*. First statutes adopted by 26 founding members, 12 Jan 1993, London (UK). Most recent statutes adopted 1 Aug 2019. A Restricted Union of *Universal Postal Union (UPU, #20682)*. Registration: Banque-Carrefour des Entreprises, No/ID: 0450.024.174, Start date: 29 Apr 1993, Belgium. **Aims** Promote postal services, including diverse mail and parcel services, which constitute key elements of members' activities; support members in finding new and innovative ways of developing their activities in response to ever-changing market conditions and demanding customer needs. **Structure** Plenary Assembly (annual); Management Board; Committees/Circles/Transversals/Working Groups; Headquarters managed by Secretary General. **Languages** English, French. **Staff** 12.00 FTE, paid. **Finance** Members' dues. **Activities** Advocacy/lobbying/activism; training/education; politics/policy/regulatory; events/meetings. **Events** *Plenary Assembly* Dublin (Ireland) 2020, *Plenary Assembly* Jersey (UK) 2019, *Plenary Assembly* Tbilisi (Georgia) 2018, *Annual SAFEPOST Working Group Meeting* Brussels (Belgium) 2017, *Security Working Group Meeting* Brussels (Belgium) 2017. **Publications** *PostEurop News* (2 a year). Position papers; thematic brochures.
Members Membership is restricted to European Postal Operators of countries falling within the definition of the European Territory (CEPT decision of Dresden 1993) and have designation as postal operators to UPU. Members in 52 countries and territories:
Åland, Albania, Armenia, Austria, Belarus, Belgium, Bosnia-Herzegovina, Bulgaria, Croatia, Cyprus, Czechia, Denmark, Estonia, Finland, France, Georgia, Germany, Greece, Guernsey, Holy See, Hungary, Iceland, Ireland, Isle of Man, Italy, Jersey, Kazakhstan, Latvia, Liechtenstein, Lithuania, Luxembourg, Malta, Moldova, Monaco, Montenegro, Netherlands, North Macedonia, Norway, Poland, Portugal, Romania, Russia, San Marino, Serbia, Slovakia, Slovenia, Spain, Sweden, Switzerland, Türkiye, UK, Ukraine.

IGO Relations Special links with: *European Commission (EC, #06633)*; *European Committee for Postal Regulation (CERP, see: #04602)*. Links with the other UPU Restricted Unions:.
- *African Postal Union (APU, no recent information)*;
- *Arab Permanent Postal Commission (APPC, #01025)*;
- *Asian-Pacific Postal Union (APPU, #01625)*;
- *Associação dos Operadores de Correios e Telecomunicações dos Paises e Territórios de Lingua Oficial Portuguesa (AICEP, #02333)*;
- *Baltic Postal Union (BPU, #03137)*;
- *Caribbean Postal Union (CPU, #03541)*;
- *Conference of Posts and Telecommunications of Central Africa (#04642)*;
- European Conference of Postal and Telecommunications Administrations (CEPT);
- *Nordic Postal Union (NPU, #17391)*;
- *Pan African Postal Union (PAPU, #18060)*;
- *Postal Union of the Americas, Spain and Portugal (PUASP, #18466)*;
- *Southern Africa Postal Operators Association (SAPOA, #19866)*.

NGO Relations In liaison with technical committees of: *Comité européen de normalisation (CEN, #04162)*. Member of: *European Services Forum (ESF, #08469)*; *Federation of European and International Associations Established in Belgium (FAIB, #09508)*. [2021/XD3688/**D***]

♦ Association of European Radios (AER) 02535

Association européenne des radios (AER)

Contact Rue des Deux Eglises 26, 1000 Brussels, Belgium. T. +3227369131. Fax +3227328990.
URL: http://www.aereurope.org/

History 1992. **Aims** Develop and improve the most suitable framework for private commercial radio activity; promote the diffusion and use of new technologies in radio transmission. **Structure** Executive Board. **Languages** English, French. **Staff** 1.00 FTE, paid; 2.00 FTE, voluntary. **Finance** Sources: members' dues. **Events** *EU Media Policy Conference* Brussels (Belgium) 2019.
Members National organizations in 14 countries:
Belgium, Bulgaria, Finland, France, Germany, Greece, Hungary, Italy, Netherlands, Romania, Slovakia, Spain, Switzerland, UK.
Consultative Status Consultative status granted from: *World Intellectual Property Organization (WIPO, #21593)* (Permanent Observer Status). **NGO Relations** Member of (4): *European Advertising Standards Alliance (EASA, #05829)*; *European Interactive Digital Advertising Alliance (EDAA, #07582)*; *European Internet Forum (EIF, #07591)* (Associate); *WorldDAB (#21351)*. [2019/XD4419/**D**]

♦ Association of the European Rail Supply Industry (UNIFE) 02536

Union des industries ferroviaires européennes (UNIFE) – Verband der Europäischen Eisenbahn-Industrien

Dir Gen Avenue Louise 221, Bte 11, 1050 Brussels, Belgium. T. +3226261260. Fax +3226261261. E-mail: general@unife.org.
Office Manager address not obtained.
URL: http://www.unife.org

History 31 Oct 1975, Paris (France). On 8 Nov 1991, took over activities of *European Association of Railway Equipment Manufacturers (AFEDEF, inactive)*, *European Builders of Diesel Engine and Electric Locomotives (CELTE, inactive)* and *Association internationale des constructeurs de matériel roulant (AICMR, inactive)*, their members becoming direct members of UNIFE. Registration: Start date: 31 Jan 1992, End date: 26 May 1995, France; Banque-Carrefour des Entreprises, No/ID: 0453.405.417, Start date: 8 Sep 1994, Belgium; EU Transparency Register, No/ID: 9624415524-28, Start date: 17 Oct 2008. **Aims** Promote rail transport through dialogue with EU institutions and all important stakeholders; lobby for rail issues by leading initiatives with national rail supply industry associations; deliver railway interoperability and standardization for improved LCC and RAMS; ensure European rail supply industry leadership through joint research and innovation; convince the public that rail transport is the favourable solution for the 21st century challenges of increased mobility, economic growth and environmental protection by other transport modes on innovative materials and production methods. **Structure** General Assembly (annual); Presiding Board; Secretariat, headed by Director-General. **Languages** English. **Staff** 24.00 FTE, paid. **Finance** Sources: members' dues. **Activities** Advocacy/lobbying/activism; events/meetings; research/documentation. Active in all member countries. **Events** *General Assembly* Paris (France) 2022, *General Assembly* Lisbon (Portugal) 2021, *General Assembly* Berlin (Germany) 2020, *General Assembly* Dublin (Ireland) 2019, *Meeting on the MEAT Principle* Brussels (Belgium) 2018. **Publications** *UNIFE Newsletter* (4 a year). *UNIFE World Rail Market Study*. Annual Report. Information Services: Databank on: EU regulations and activities; national policies; Market developments; company news.
Members Full (companies); Associate (national associations). Companies (118) and national associations (12) in 25 countries:
Austria, Belgium, Bulgaria, Croatia, Czechia, Estonia, Finland, France, Germany, Israel, Italy, Latvia, Lithuania, Luxembourg, Netherlands, Norway, Poland, Portugal, Romania, Slovakia, Slovenia, Spain, Sweden, Switzerland, UK.
Associate includes 1 organization listed in this Yearbook:
European Federation of Railway Trackworks Contractors (EFRTC, #07205).
IGO Relations Recognized by: *European Commission (EC, #06633)*. **NGO Relations** Member of (3): *Federation of European and International Associations Established in Belgium (FAIB, #09508)*; *Industry4Europe (#11181)*; *Rail Forum Europe (RFE, #18607)* (Associate). Partner of (1): *Partnership on Sustainable, Low Carbon Transport Foundation (SLoCaT Foundation, #18244)*. Cooperates with (1): *International Union of Railways (#15813)*. Instrumental in setting up (1): *European Rail Research Advisory Council (ERRAC, #08325)*. In liaison with technical committees of: *Comité européen de normalisation (CEN, #04162)*; *European Committee for Electrotechnical Standardization (CENELEC, #06647)*. Associate Expert Group of: *Business and Industry Advisory Committee to the OECD (BIAC, #03385)*. [2023.02.16/XD5224/t/**D**]

♦ Association of European Railway Staff (#02558)

♦ Association of European Refrigeration Component Manufacturers (ASERCOM) 02537

Registered Office Rue du Congrès 35, 1000 Brussels, Belgium. E-mail: office@asercom.org.
URL: http://www.asercom.org/

History Statutes adopted 25 Jun 1992; amended 9 Oct 1996; 2002; 2005; 2010; 2016. Former names and other names: *Association of European Refrigeration Compressor and Controls Manufacturers (ASERCOM)* – former. Registration: Banque-Carrefour des Entreprises, Belgium. **Aims** Be the platform for dealing with scientific and technical topics and their challenges, promoting standards for performance rating, methods of testing and product safety, focusing on improved environmental protection, serving the refrigeration and air conditioning industry and its customers. **Structure** General Assembly (annual); Administrative Board; Executive Committee. **Languages** English. **Staff** 3.00 FTE, paid. **Finance** Sources: members' dues. **Activities** Certification/accreditation; events/meetings; knowledge management/information dissemination; research/documentation; standards/guidelines. **Events** *Annual symposium* Essen (Germany) 1999, *Annual symposium* Nürburg (Germany) 1998, *Annual Symposium* Essen (Germany) 1997, *Annual symposium* Essen (Germany) / Nürburg (Germany) 1996.
Members Individuals (20) in 7 countries:
Czechia, Denmark, France, Germany, Italy, Netherlands, UK.
NGO Relations Also links with national associations. [2022.05.10/XD3297/v/**D**]

♦ Association of European Refrigeration Compressor and Controls Manufacturers / see Association of European Refrigeration Component Manufacturers (#02537)
♦ Association of European Regions for Products of Origin (#02890)

♦ Association of European Registered Experts 02538

Association des experts européens agréés (AEXEA) – Arbeitsgemeinschaft der Europäischen Anerkannten Sachverständigen

Pres 3 rue du Colonel Moll, 75017 Paris, France. T. +33467643710. E-mail: aexea.contact@gmail.com.
Registered Office Rue des Champs 2, L-8218 Mamer, Luxembourg.
URL: http://www.aexea.org/

History 29 Sep 1989, Luxembourg. Registered in accordance with Luxembourg law. **Structure** General Assembly. Board of Directors. Administrative Committee, comprising President, 3 Vice-Presidents, Secretary-General and Treasurer. **Members** Individuals (approx 170) in 14 countries. Membership countries not specified. **NGO Relations** Member of: *World Union of Professions (WUP, #21882)*. [2016/XG2822/**D**]

♦ Association of European Research Establishments in Aeronautics (EREA) 02539

Exec Secretariat c/o ONERA, International Affairs Directorate, Chemin de la Hunière – BP 80100, 91123 Palaiseau CEDEX, France. T. +33180386748.
URL: http://www.erea.org/

History 11 Oct 1994, Brussels (Belgium). Founded on signature of an agreement by 7 research centres in the European Union. Former names and other names: *AEREA* – alias. Registration: Start date: 3 May 1999, Netherlands. **Aims** Promote and represent interests of members; intensify cooperation between members to further integrate their activities in civil, military and space related *aeronautics*; improve cooperation with third parties; facilitate integrated management of joint activities, thereby contributing to Europe's role as a global player in *aeronautics*. **Structure** Board; Executive Secretariat; Aviation Research Group (ARG); Security Research Group (SRG). **Languages** English. **Activities** Research and development; events/meetings. **Events** *Annual Event* Brussels (Belgium) 2022, *EREA Welcome Back Event* Brussels (Belgium) 2021, *Annual Event* Brussels (Belgium) 2020, *Meeting* Brussels (Belgium) 2018, *Meeting* Brussels (Belgium) 2017. **Publications** *EREA Newsletter*. Studies.
Members Full; Affiliate; Strategic Partners. Full in 12 countries:
Austria, Czechia, France, Germany, Italy, Netherlands, Poland, Portugal, Romania, Spain, Sweden, Switzerland.
Affiliate in 1 country:
Poland.
Strategic partners in 2 countries:
Belgium, Russia. [2021/XD5657/**D**]

♦ Association of European Research Libraries 02540

Ligue des Bibliothèques Européennes de Recherche (LIBER)

Exec Dir c/o Koninklijke Bibliotheek, PO Box 90407, 2509 LK The Hague, Netherlands. T. +31703140767. E-mail: liber@libereurope.eu.
SG address not obtained.
URL: https://libereurope.eu/

History 18 Mar 1971, Strasbourg (France). Founded under the auspices of the *Council of Europe (CE, #04881)*, constituent Assembly, when statutes were adopted. New statutes adopted, 7 Jul 1994, Göttingen (Germany). The former Association was dissolved at the Annual General Assembly, Jul 2009. Statutes and Rules and Regulations adopted 1 Jan 2009. Former names and other names: *League of European Research Libraries* – former. Registration: KVK, No/ID: 78491096, Start date: 1 Jan 2009, Netherlands; EU Transparency Register, No/ID: 24973952940-04, Start date: 5 Jan 2010. **Aims** Represent the interests of research libraries of Europe, their universities and researchers. Promote in particular: efficient information services; access to research information, in any form whatsoever; innovation in end-user services provided by research libraries in support of teaching, learning and research; preservation of cultural heritage; efficient and effective management in research libraries. **Structure** Meeting of Participants (annual); Executive Board; Steering Committees (3): Scholarly Communication and Research Infrastructures; Reshaping the Research Library; Advocacy and Communications. Office based in The Hague (Netherlands). **Languages** English. **Staff** 4.00 FTE, paid. Plus project staff, paid. **Finance** Sources: grants; members' dues; revenue from activities/projects; sponsorship. Supported by: *European Union (EU, #08967)*. **Activities** Events/meetings; networking/liaising. **Events** *Annual Conference* Budapest (Hungary) 2023, *Annual Conference* Odense (Denmark) 2022, *Annual General Conference* The Hague (Netherlands) 2021, *Annual General Conference* The Hague (Netherlands) 2020, *Annual General Conference* Dublin (Ireland) 2019. **Publications** *LIBER Quarterly* (4 a year).
Members Institutional – major research libraries, including national, university, libraries of institutions conducting teaching and research at postgraduate level, libraries with major research collections and national archives; Organizational – library organizations that are members of the Council of Europe; Associate – companies or consortia supplying services to research libraries and/or library organizations in countries that are not members of the Council of Europe; Individual – professional librarians who work/have worked in research libraries; Honorary. Members (about 450) in 38 countries and territories:
Albania, Armenia, Austria, Belgium, Bosnia-Herzegovina, Bulgaria, Canada, Croatia, Cyprus, Czechia, Denmark, Estonia, Finland, France, Germany, Greece, Hungary, Ireland, Italy, Latvia, Lithuania, Luxembourg, Malta, Netherlands, North Macedonia, Norway, Poland, Portugal, Romania, Saudi Arabia, Serbia, Slovakia, Slovenia, Spain, Sweden, Switzerland, Türkiye, UK.
NGO Relations Memorandum of Understanding with (9): *Common Language Resources and Technology Infrastructure (CLARIN, #04295)*; *Confederation of Open Access Repositories (COAR, #04573)*; *Conference of European National Librarians (CENL, #04597)*; *Consortium of European Research Libraries (CERL, #04742)*; *Digital Research Infrastructure for the Arts and Humanities (DARIAH-EU, #05083)*; *EUDAT Collaborative Data Infrastructure (EUDAT CDI, #05580)*; *European Bureau of Library, Information and Documentation Associations (EBLIDA, #06413)*; *International Federation of Library Associations and Institutions (IFLA, #13470)*; *SPARC Europe (#19902)*. Member of (4): *Copyright for Creativity (C4C, #04832)*; *European Alliance for Research Excellence (EARE)*; *Global Sustainability Coalition for Open Science Services (SCOSS, #10616)*; *International Alliance of Research Library Associations (IARLA, #11636)*. [2022/XD3805/**D**]

♦ Association for European Rural Universities (APURE) 02541

Permanent Secretariat Rua de Santana 277, 6030-230 Vila Velha de Ródão, Portugal. T. +351272540200. Fax +351272540209. E-mail: apure@adraces.pt.
Headquarters Université de Provence, Institut de Géografie, 9 Av Robert Schuman, 13621 Aix-en-Provence CEDEX 1, France.
URL: http://www.ure-apure.org/

History 1989, France, as *European Rural University (ERU)* – *Université rurale européenne (URE)*. **Aims** Support rural areas, with a focus on the people who work in rural development. **Members** Membership countries not specified. **NGO Relations** Cooperates with: *Rurality – Environment – Development (RED, #19003)*. [2008/XF7097/**F**]

♦ Association of European Scaffolding Companies / see Union Europäischer Gerüstbaubetriebe (#20382)

♦ Association of European Schools of Planning (AESOP) 02542

Association européenne de facultés et autres établissements d'enseignement supérieur formant des spécialistes de l'aménagement du territoire – Europäische Vereinigung der Raumplanerfakultetgplan

SG University of Reading, Henley Business School, Whiteknights, Reading, RG6 6UD, UK. E-mail: secretariat@aesop-planning.eu.
URL: http://www.aesop-planning.eu/

History 24 Jan 1987, Schloss Cappenberg (Germany FR). Founded at meeting of planning schools of European institutions of higher education. Initiative for the Association came from Klaus R Kunzmann and Patsy Healey who attended and were inspired by the Annual Congress of the American Association of Planning Schools (ACSP), 1985, Atlanta GA (USA). Charter signed by Foundation Members. Replaces *International Association for Urban and Regional Research and Education (IAURRE, inactive)*. Registration: No/ID: 0448.474.352, Start date: 8 Oct 1992, Belgium. **Aims** Represent interests of planning schools in Europe, at national and international level, and before both public and private institutions. **Structure** Council of Representatives; Executive Committee; National Representatives; Working Groups; Young Academics Network; Thematic Groups (14). **Languages** English. **Staff** None. Staff connected to projects. **Finance** Members' dues. Other sources: projects; grants. Annual budget: euro 115,000. **Activities** Events/meetings; research/documentation; training/education; politics/policy/regulatory; guidance/assistance/consulting; awards/prizes/competitions. **Events** *Annual Congress* Tartu (Estonia) 2022, *Conference* Gdansk (Poland) 2021, *Head of Schools Meeting* Vienna (Austria) 2021, *Head of Schools Meeting* Vienna (Austria) 2021, *Annual Congress* Bristol (UK) 2020. **Publications** *AESOP Yearbook* (every 4 years); *Planning Education* – journal. *City in Water* (2017) by G Warsawa and I Mironowicz; *Sustainability of Protected Areas* (2015) by L Verdelli et al; *Heritage Conservation and Urban Sustainable Development* (2014) by L Verdelli; *Strategies for Post-Speculative City* (2014) by J Arana and T Franchini; *Arhitecture and Planning in Times of Scarcity: Reclaiming the Possibility of Making* (2013) by D Iossifova; *Urban Change: The prospect of Transformation* (2011) by I Mironowicz and J Ryser.
Members Full (112) European universities and their schools, departments, faculties, running autonomous programmes in planning and conferring degrees in urban/rural/regional/environmental planning. Associate (29) European universities and their schools, departments, faculties, running courses in planning. Corresponding (8) universities located out of Europe and their schools, departments, faculties, running courses

in planning. Affiliate (18) private and public companies, institutions, organizations, agencies or other entity focused on planning. Honorary (5) persons who made a significant contribution to AESOP and/or discipling of planning. Members in 42 countries and territories:
Albania, Australia, Austria, Belgium, Bulgaria, Canada, China, Croatia, Czechia, Denmark, Estonia, Finland, France, Germany, Greece, India, Ireland, Israel, Italy, Japan, Kenya, Kosovo, Latvia, Malaysia, Malta, Netherlands, Norway, Poland, Portugal, Romania, Russia, Saudi Arabia, Serbia, Slovakia, Slovenia, Spain, Sweden, Switzerland, Syrian AR, Türkiye, UK, USA.
NGO Relations Member of: *Global Planning Education Association Network (GPEAN, #10549)*. Cooperates with: *Association pour la promotion de l'enseignement et de la recherche en aménagement et urbanisme (APERAU, #02875)*; *European Council of Spatial Planners (ECTP-CEU, #06843)*; *European Regional Science Association (ERSA, #08346)*; *European Urban Research Association (EURA, #09040)*; *International Academic Association on Planning, Law and Property Rights (PLPR, #11531)*; *International Federation for Housing and Planning (IFHP, #13450)*; *International Planning History Society (#14590)*; *International Society of City and Regional Planners (ISOCARP, #15012)*. [2022/XD0974/D]

- ♦ Association of European Science and Technology Transfer Professionals (inactive)
- ♦ Association of European Scientists 'Pro Vita' (inactive)
- ♦ Association for the European Self-Adhesive Labelling and Adjacent Narrow Web Converting Industries / see FINAT (#09773)

♦ Association of the European Self-Care Industry 02543
Association européenne des spécialités pharmaceutiques grand public (AESGP) – Europäischer Fachverband der Arzneimittel-Hersteller

Dir Gen Av de Tervueren 7, 1040 Brussels, Belgium. T. +3227355130. Fax +3227355222. E-mail: info@aesgp.eu.
URL: http://www.aesgp.eu/

History 1964, Paris (France). Present statutes adopted 3 Jun 1991, Cannes (France). Former names and other names: *Association européenne des spécialités grand public* – former; *European Proprietary Medicines Manufacturers' Association* – former; *Association of the European Self-Medication Industry* – former. Registration: Banque Carrefour des Entreprises, No/ID: 0850.689.703, Start date: 1 Oct 1989, Belgium; EU Transparency Register, No/ID: 99565011637-64, Start date: 4 May 2009. **Aims** Advance responsible self-care enabling citizens to take better care of their *health* needs; contribute to sustainability of European health care systems. **Structure** General Assembly (annual); Board of Directors; Expert Commissions. **Languages** English. **Staff** 9.00 FTE, paid. **Finance** Sources: members' dues. **Activities** Advocacy/lobbying/activism; events/meetings. **Events** *Annual Meeting* Milan (Italy) 2022, *Annual Meeting* Brussels (Belgium) 2021, *Regulatory Conference* Brussels (Belgium) 2021, *Annual Meeting* Milan (Italy) 2020, *Conference on a Renewed Agenda for Self-Care Products* Brussels (Belgium) 2019. **Publications** *50 Years AESGP* (2014); *Economic and Legal Framework for Non-Prescription Medicines* (18th ed 2013); *Legal and Regulatory Framework for Herbal Medicines* (2012); *Regulatory Framework for Food Supplements in Europe* (2012); *Economic and Public Health Value of Self-Medication* (2004); *AESGP Self-Care Agenda 2020*. Annual Report; annual meeting proceedings.
Members National proprietary medicine associations in 22 countries:
Austria, Belgium, Croatia, Czechia, Denmark, Finland, France, Germany, Greece, Hungary, Ireland, Italy, Netherlands, Norway, Poland, Portugal, Romania, Slovenia, Spain, Sweden, Switzerland, UK.
Consultative Status Consultative status granted from: *Council of Europe (CE, #04881)* (Participatory Status).
IGO Relations Recognized by: *European Commission (EC, #06633)*. Participates as observer in the activities of: *Codex Alimentarius Commission (CAC, #04081)*; *World Intellectual Property Organization (WIPO, #21593)*.
NGO Relations Member of (2): *EU Health Coalition*; *Global Self-Care Federation (GSCF, #10588)*. Stakeholder in: *European Network for Health Technology Assessment (EUnetHTA, #07921)*. Associate Expert Group of *Business and Industry Advisory Committee to the OECD (BIAC, #03385)*. [2022/XD3970/t/D]

- ♦ Association of the European Self-Medication Industry / see Association of the European Self-Care Industry (#02543)
- ♦ Association of European Senates (#02914)
- ♦ Association of European Shipbuilders and Shiprepairers (inactive)
- ♦ Association of European Slate Producers (inactive)

♦ Association of European Space Industry (EUROSPACE) 02544
SG 22 rue du Quatre Septembre, 75002 Paris, France. T. +33144420070. Fax +33144420079. E-mail: letterbox@eurospace.org.
Office Management address not obtained.
Brussels Office c/o EUROSPACE/ASD, Rue Montoyer 10, 1000 Brussels, Belgium. T. +3227758120. Fax +3227758139.
URL: http://www.eurospace.org/

History 21 Sep 1961, Paris (France). Previously also referred to as *European Industrial Space Study Group – Groupement industriel européen d'études spatiales – Grupo Industrial Europeo de Estudio Espacial – Europäische Industriegruppe für Raumfahrtstudien*. Registered in accordance with French law. Along with *European Association of Aerospace Industries (AECMA, inactive)* and *European Defence Industries Group (EDIG, inactive)*, merged into *Aerospace and Defence Industries Association of Europe (ASD, #00146)* to become the Space subsidiary on 22 Apr 2004. Registered in accordance with French law. EU Transparency Register: 959028733673-17. **Aims** Foster development of space activities in Europe, with the main focus being on space policy and strategy; promote better understanding of space industry related issues and problems. **Structure** General Assembly; Council (Board of Directors); Executive; Policy Committee; Financial Committee; Temporary Committees or Working Groups. **Languages** English, French, Italian. **Staff** 7.00 FTE, paid. **Finance** Members' dues. Other sources: study contracts; sale of publications; conferences. Annual budget: about euro 1,800,000. **Activities** Networking/liaising; knowledge management/information dissemination; guidance/assistance/consulting; standards/guidelines; events/meetings. **Events** *Annual DASIA Conference* Warsaw (Poland) 2014, *Annual DASIA Conference* Porto (Portugal) 2013, *European Space Industry R and T Priorities Conference* Belgirate (Italy) 2012, *DASIA : Annual Symposium on Data Systems in Aerospace / Annual DASIA Conference* Dubrovnik (Croatia) 2012, *DASIA : Annual Symposium on Data Systems in Aerospace* San Anton (Malta) 2011. **Publications** *Eurospace Facts and Figures* (annual); *Space Trends* (annual). *European Space Industry R and T Priorities* (3rd ed 2014); *European Space Industry – Building the Future* (2002); *European Strategic Dependence* (1999) in English, French; *European Top 10 Research Priorities and Development Priorities* (1999). Studies; reports. **Information Services** *Launch events Database* – 1983-2013.
Members Main European space systems manufacturers and launch service providers (44) in 14 countries:
Austria, Belgium, Denmark, Finland, France, Germany, Italy, Netherlands, Norway, Portugal, Spain, Sweden, Switzerland, UK.
IGO Relations Recognized by: *European Commission (EC, #06633)*. Recognized by, and since 2001, Memorandum of Understanding with: *European Space Agency (ESA, #08798)*. **NGO Relations** Recognized by: *European Cooperation for Space Standardization (ECSS, #06785)*. [2021/XD0784/t/D]

♦ Association of European Space Research Establishments (ESRE) .. 02545
Sec Rue du Trône 98, 1050 Brussels, Belgium. T. +31885113621. E-mail: info@esre-space.org.
URL: http://esre-space.org/

History Formally set up 10 Mar 2016. Registered in accordance with Belgian law. **Aims** Intensify cooperation between members, so as to further coordination and integration of their space related research activities; improve and intensify cooperation with 3rd parties in the space domain; contribute to the global competitiveness of the European space sector; offer harmonized views to European industry, governments and institutions in the field of space and innovative research.
Members Space research centres of 5 countries:
France, Germany, Italy, Netherlands, Spain. [2017/XM6065/D]

- ♦ Association of European Stock Exchanges (inactive)
- ♦ Association of European Storage Battery Manufacturers / see Association of European Automative and Industrial Battery Manufacturers (#02498)
- ♦ Association of European Studies, Moscow (internationally oriented national body)
- ♦ Association for European Surface Treatment on Aluminium / see European association for Surface Treatment on Aluminium (#06242)
- ♦ Association of European Tax Law Professors / see European Association of Tax Law Professors (#06247)

♦ Association of European Team Sports (ETS) 02546
Contact Rue Marie-Thérèse 21, 1000 Brussels, Belgium. T. +3226260469. Fax +3226260464.
URL: http://www.europeanteamsports.com/

History Dec 2009. Registered in accordance with Swiss Civil Code. **Aims** Promote, develop and represent the interests of European team sport.
Members European team sports (6):
European Handball Federation (EHF, #07446); *European Volleyball Confederation (#09078)*; *FIBA-Europe (#09747)*; *International Ice Hockey Federation (IIHF, #13831)*; *Rugby Europe (#18998)*; *Union of European Football Associations (UEFA, #20386)*. [2019/XJ8518/y/D]

♦ Association of European Threat Assessment Professionals (AETAP) 02547
Association européenne des professionnel/-les de l'évaluation des menaces

Mailing Address Postfach 11 01 05, 64216 Darmstadt, Germany. E-mail: info@aetap.eu.
Registered Address PO Box 475, 4012 Basel BS, Switzerland. T. +41613316113.
URL: http://www.aetap.eu/

History Current statutes adopted 2 Mar 2008, Lucerne (Switzerland). Registration: Swiss Civile Code, Switzerland. **Aims** Promote research on threat assessment and management; implement tools and structures in relation to the topic; offer teaching and training to professionals in threat assessment and management. **Structure** Board of Directors. **Finance** Sources: members' dues. **Activities** Events/meetings. **Events** *Conference* Darmstadt (Germany) 2022, *Conference* Budapest (Hungary) 2021, *Conference* 2020, *Annual Conference* Amsterdam (Netherlands) 2019, *Annual Conference* Helsinki (Finland) 2018. **NGO Relations** Associated with (2): *African Association of Threat Assessment Professionals (AfATAP)*; *Asia Pacific Association of Threat Assessment Professionals (APATAP)*. [2023.02.14/XJ2661/t/D]

- ♦ Association of European Tomato Processing Industries / see European Organisation of Tomato Industries (#08104)
- ♦ Association of European Toxicologists and Societies of Toxicology / see EUROTOX (#09191)
- ♦ Association of European Trade Mark Proprietors / see MARQUES (#16588)

♦ Association for European Transport (AET) 02548
Secretariat Forrester House, Doctors Lane, Henley-in-Arden, Newbury, B95 5AW, UK. T. +441564793552. E-mail: info@aetransport.org.
URL: http://www.aetransport.org/

History Feb 1998. Statutes modified: 2009. Registration: Handelsregister, No/ID: 27170096, Netherlands, Haaglanden. **Aims** Promote understanding, cooperation, discussion, research and development with regard to all aspects of transport. **Structure** General Meeting; Council. Board, including Chairman, Secretary, Treasurer; Advisory Group. **Languages** English. **Staff** 1.00 FTE, paid. **Finance** Sources: members' dues. **Events** *European Transport Conference (ETC)* Milan (Italy) 2022, *European Transport Conference (ETC)* 2021, *Annual Conference* Brussels (Belgium) 2020, *Annual Conference* Dublin (Ireland) 2019, *Annual Conference* Dublin (Ireland) 2018.
Members Associations and individuals. Members in 43 countries and territories:
Albania, Australia, Austria, Barbados, Belgium, Bulgaria, Chile, China, Croatia, Cyprus, Czechia, Denmark, Egypt, Finland, France, Germany, Greece, Hungary, India, Ireland, Israel, Italy, Japan, Korea Rep, Kosovo, Kuwait, Luxembourg, Malta, Netherlands, New Zealand, Norway, Poland, Portugal, Romania, Russia, Serbia, Spain, Sweden, Switzerland, Trinidad-Tobago, Türkiye, UK, USA. [2022.05.10/XD6854/D]

- ♦ Association of the European Two-Wheeler Parts' and Accessories' Industry (inactive)
- ♦ Association of European Union Premier Professional Football Leagues / see European Leagues (#07672)
- ♦ Association of European Union Sport Shooting Federations (inactive)
- ♦ Association of European Universities (inactive)
- ♦ Association of European University Graduates (inactive)

♦ Association of European University Public Relations and Information Officers (EUPRIO) 02549
Pres c/o CPE Lyon, 43 bd du 11 novembre 1918, 69100 Villeurbanne, France. T. +33472431703. Fax +33472431668.
URL: http://www.euprio.eu/

History 12 May 1986, Brussels (Belgium), with support from European Community officials. Re-set up, 27 Jun 2009, Leuven (Belgium), when registered in accordance with Belgian law. **Aims** Serve as a professional association for colleagues in higher education institutions in Europe; promote exchange of public relations ideas, techniques and information; promote members' professional excellence; facilitate intra-European awareness of study programmes and scientific developments of relevance to industry and economic advance across national borders, including those sponsored by the European Union; promote dissemination of information on, and reputation of, European higher education, science, research and development. **Structure** Steering Committee; Executive Board; National Representatives; Deputy National Representatives; President acts as National Representative for countries with less than 5 members. *EUPRIO Network*. **Languages** English. **Staff** Voluntary. **Finance** Members' dues. **Activities** Events/meetings. **Events** *Annual Conference* Innsbruck (Austria) 2014, *Annual Conference* Canterbury (UK) 2013, *Annual Conference* Gothenburg (Sweden) 2012, *Annual Conference* Prague (Czech Rep) 2011, *Annual Conference* Stresa (Italy) 2010.
Members Individuals and institutions (751) in 23 countries:
Austria, Belgium, Croatia, Czechia, Denmark, Finland, France, Germany, Iceland, Ireland, Italy, Lebanon, Lithuania, Luxembourg, Montenegro, Netherlands, Norway, Poland, Portugal, Spain, Sweden, Switzerland, UK.
NGO Relations Memorandum of Understanding with: *European Citizen Science Association (ECSA, #06557)*. [2016.10.25/XD2061/D]

- ♦ Association of European Vegetable Processing Industries (inactive)

♦ Association of European Vehicle and Driver Registration Authorities (EReg) 02550
Secretariat Rue Froissart 95, 1040 Brussels, Belgium. T. +31793458352 – +31793458161. E-mail: info@ereg-association.eu – secretariat@ereg-association.eu.
Chairman address not obtained.
URL: http://www.ereg-association.eu/

History May 2006, Cyprus. Registration: No/ID: 0847.563.828, Start date: 20 Jul 2012, Belgium; EU Transparency Register, No/ID: 745331538710-86, Start date: 24 Jun 2020. **Aims** Bring together European vehicle and driver registration authorities. **Structure** General Meeting; Advisory Board; Chairman; Secretariat. Topic Groups. **Languages** English. **Staff** 1.00 FTE, paid. **Finance** Sources: members' dues. Annual budget: 105,000 EUR. **Activities** Advocacy/lobbying/activism; events/meetings; knowledge management/information dissemination. **Events** *Annual Conference* The Hague (Netherlands) 2021, *General Meeting and Annual Conference* The Hague (Netherlands) 2020, *General Meeting* The Hague (Netherlands) 2020, *General Meeting and Annual Conference* Lisbon (Portugal) 2019, *General Meeting and Annual Conference* Berlin (Germany) 2018. **Publications** *EReg Vehicle Chain* (every 3 years); *EReg Newsletter*.
Members Full in 25 countries and territories:
Belgium, Cyprus, Denmark, Estonia, Finland, France, Germany, Gibraltar, Hungary, Iceland, Ireland, Isle of Man, Jersey, Latvia, Lithuania, Luxembourg, Malta, Netherlands, Norway, Poland, Romania, Slovakia, Spain, Sweden, Switzerland, UK. [2021/XJ9299/D]

♦ Association of European Vehicle Logistics (ECG) 02551
Exec Dir BluePoint Brussels, Bd Auguste Reyers 80, 1030 Brussels, Belgium. T. +3227068280. E-mail: info@ecgassociation.eu.
URL: http://www.ecgassociation.eu/

History May 1997. Former names and other names: *European Car-Transport Group of Interest* – legal name. Registration: Banque Carrefour des Entreprises, No/ID: 0464.984.346, Start date: 21 Jan 1999, Belgium; EU Transparency Register, No/ID: 2297093238-71, Start date: 27 Jul 2008. **Aims** Represent the interests of the European finished vehicle logistics sector towards EU institutions and other European associations active in the field of the automotive sector; represent the interests of the European automobile logistics trade towards automotive manufacturers and importers. **Structure** General Assembly (annual); Board; Working Groups; Secretariat. **Languages** English. **Staff** 5.50 FTE, paid. **Finance** Sources: members' dues. **Activities** Events/

meetings; training/education. **Events** *25th Anniversary Meeting* Brussels (Belgium) 2022, *General Assembly and Spring Congress* Malaga (Spain) 2022, *Conference* Vienna (Austria) 2022, *Conference* Brussels (Belgium) 2021, *General Assembly* Brussels (Belgium) 2021. **Publications** *ECG Survey on Vehicle Logistics* (every 2 years). *ECG Operations Quality Manual.* Annual Activities Report; position papers; reports.
Members Companies in 26 countries:
Austria, Belgium, Bulgaria, Denmark, Finland, France, Germany, Greece, Hungary, Ireland, Italy, Latvia, Lithuania, Netherlands, Norway, Poland, Russia, Serbia, Slovakia, Slovenia, Spain, Sweden, Switzerland, Türkiye, UK, Ukraine.
NGO Relations Member of (4): *European Logistics Platform (ELP, #07711); European Technology Platform ALICE (ALICE, #08888); International Road Transport Union (IRU, #14761); Mobility for Prosperity in Europe (MPE, #16839).* [2022.02.17/XD6906/**D**]

♦ Association of European Wheel Manufacturers (EUWA) 02552
Association des fabricants européens de roues – Verband der Europäischen Hersteller von Fahrzeugrädern – Associazione dei Costruttori Europei di Ruote
Vice Pres c/o ALCAR Ruote SA, Via Violino 4, 5928 Lugano TI, Switzerland. E-mail: euwa@euwa.org.
URL: http://www.euwa.org/
History 17 Jan 1989. Non-profit. Registered in accordance with Swiss law. EU Transparency Register: 168439722478-68. **Aims** Protect and promote the interests of member manufacturers of wheels for road vehicles – cars, trucks, buses – and for agricultural tractors and earthmoving machines, within the framework of free and fair competition; ensure exchange of technical opinions and experience; address technical and basic problems in the field; study requirements of the European Single Market; represent members with national and international authorities. **Structure** General Assembly (annual); Executive Council; Technical Commission; Logistic Commission. **Languages** English. **Staff** 0.50 FTE, paid; 1.50 FTE, voluntary. **Finance** Members' dues, according to company size. **Activities** Standards/guidelines; knowledge management/information dissemination. **Events** *General Assembly* Valencia (Spain) 2019, *Annual General Assembly* 2003, *Annual General Assembly* 2002, *Annual General Assembly* 2001. **Publications** *EUWA Yearbook* – CD-Rom. Technical dictionary in English/French/German/Italian; Safety Recommendations in English/French/German/Italian.
Members Full in 10 countries:
Czechia, France, Germany, Hungary, Italy, Switzerland, Türkiye, UK, Ukraine.
Associate in 2 countries:
Germany, Italy.
NGO Relations In liaison with technical committees of: *International Organization for Standardization (ISO, #14473).* Member of: *AEGIS Europe; European Association of Automotive Suppliers (CLEPA, #05948).* [2018/XD5011/**D**]

♦ Association européen art éducation – nouvelles technologies (ARENOTECH) 02553
Art Education – New Technologies in Europe – Arte Educación – Nuevas Tecnologias en Europa – Kunst Bildung – Neue Technologien in Europa – Arte Educazione – Nuove Technologie in Europa
Contact 22 avenue de Laumière, 75019 Paris, France. T. +33143584573. Fax +33146368320.
URL: http://www.arenotech.org/
History 24 Apr 1996, Venice (Italy), by *European Network of Digital Cities (#07893).* **Structure** Council. President; Honorary President; Scientific Director; Secretary General; Deputy Secretary General. **Languages** English, French, German, Spanish. **Finance** Funding depends on projects. **Activities** Organizes seminars and symposia. Organizes European and international innovation projects. **Events** *Meeting* Fontevraud-l'Abbaye (France) 2005. **Publications** *ARENOTECH Newsletter* – electronic newsletter. **NGO Relations** *European Network of Digital Cities (#07893); Observatoire européen des éspaces multimédia.* [2018/XM0652/**F**]

- ♦ Association européene de cardiologie pédiatrique et congénitale / see Association for European Paediatric and Congenital Cardiology (#02529)
- ♦ Association européen des marchands de machines-outils (#06114)
- ♦ Association européenne des académiques turcs (inactive)
- ♦ Association européenne des administrateurs locaux démocrates-chrétiens (no recent information)
- ♦ Association européenne pour l'administration de la recherche industrielle (#07531)
- ♦ Association européenne des agences de développement / see European Association of Regional Development Agencies (#06187)
- ♦ Association européenne des agences de développement régionales (#06187)
- ♦ Association européenne des agences de publicité / see European Association of Communications Agencies (#05983)

♦ Association Européenne des Agents Artistiques (AEAA) 02554
European Association of Artist Managers – Europäischer Verband der Künstleragenturen
Exec Sec c/o Mark Stephan Buhl Artists Management, Geylinggasse 1, 1130 Vienna, Austria.
Gen Sec address not obtained.
URL: http://www.aeaa.info/
History 1947, Paris (France), as *European Association of Concert Managers – Association européenne des directeurs de bureaux de concerts et spectacles (AEDBCS).* **Aims** Facilitate relations of members with promoters of concerts, lectures and shows in all foreign countries; arbitrate in disputes between members; establish professional rules of conduct. **Structure** General Assembly; Board; Executive Secretary. **Languages** English, French, German. **Finance** Members' dues. **Activities** Events/meetings. **Events** *Annual General Assembly* Moscow (Russia) 2019, *Annual General Assembly* Cologne (Germany) 2018, *Annual General Assembly* Paris (France) 2017, *Annual General Assembly* Rotterdam (Netherlands) 2016, *Annual General Assembly* Krakow (Poland) 2015. **Publications** *Classical Music Artists – Who Represents Whom* – jointly with IAMA.
Members Directors of concert and theatrical agencies (over 70) in 17 countries:
Austria, Belgium, Czechia, Denmark, France, Germany, Hungary, Italy, Japan, Netherlands, Poland, Romania, Russia, Spain, Sweden, Switzerland, UK. [2018.09.11/XD9757/v/**D**]

- ♦ Association européenne d'agriculture biologique et de santé (inactive)
- ♦ Association européenne de l'aluminium (#05893)
- ♦ Association européenne de l'aluminium atomisé (inactive)
- ♦ Association européenne pour l'amélioration des plantes / see EUCARPIA (#05571)
- ♦ Association européenne d'analyse transactionnelle (#06257)
- ♦ Association Européenne pour l'Analyse Transculturelle de Groupe (#06258)
- ♦ Association européenne des anatomistes vétérinaires (#06268)
- ♦ Association Européenne des Anciens Parlementaires (#06047)
- ♦ Association européenne des anciens parlementaires des pays membres du Conseil de l'Europe / see European Association of Former Parliamentarians (#06047)
- ♦ Association européenne des animateurs / see european playwork association (#08236)
- ♦ Association européenne des anodiseurs (inactive)
- ♦ Association européenne d'anthropologie (#05904)
- ♦ Association Européenne des Anthropologues Sociaux (#06209)
- ♦ Association européenne des apiculteurs professionnels (#08284)
- ♦ Association européenne d'apithérapie (inactive)
- ♦ Association européenne d'archéologie (#05940)
- ♦ Association européenne des archéologues d'Asie du Sud / see European Association for South Asian Archaeology and Art (#06214)
- ♦ Association européenne de l'asphalte / see International Mastic Asphalt Association (#14119)
- ♦ Association européenne des assistants sociaux hospitaliers et de la santé (inactive)

♦ Association européenne des associations du commerce de gros de bière et boissons des pays de l'Europe (CEGROBB) 02555
European Federation of Associations of Beer and Beverages Wholesalers in European countries – Europäische Gemeinschaft der Bier-Grosshandels-Verbände der EG-Länder – Comunità Europea delle Associazioni del Commercio all'Ingrosso di Birra dei Paesi Membri della CEE – Europese Gemeenschap van Verenigingen voor de Groothandel in Bier van de Lid-Staten van de EEG – Europaeiske Faellesskab for EØF- Landenes Organisationer for Engroshandelen med OEl
Gen Sec c/o FEBED, Edmond Machtenslaan 83, Bte 1, 1080 Brussels, Belgium. T. +3224103347. Fax +3224103545. E-mail: info@cegrobb.org.
URL: http://www.cegrobb.org/
History 20 Mar 1959. Former names and other names: *European Community of Wholesale Beer Trade Associations of Member Countries of the EEC* – former (20 Mar 1959); *Communauté européenne des associations du commerce gros de bière des pays membres de la CEE* – former (20 Mar 1959). Registration: EU Transparency Register, No/ID: 522936628455-80. **Aims** Offer European beverage wholesalers a platform for information exchange and the preparation of reactions on European developments. **Structure** General Assembly; Secretariat. **Languages** English, French. **Finance** Contributions. Annual budget: euro 15,000. **Activities** Events/meetings. **Events** *General Assembly* Italy 2015, *General Assembly* Belgium 2014, *General Assembly* Poperinge (Belgium) 2014, *General Assembly* Netherlands 2013, *Re-Use Conference* Brussels (Belgium) 2012.
Members National organizations in 8 countries:
Belgium, France, Germany, Italy, Luxembourg, Netherlands, Portugal, Switzerland.
NGO Relations Member of: *Reloop Platform (Reloop, #18835).* [2022/XE0676/**E**]

- ♦ Association européenne des associations nationales de l'industrie de l'ascenseur (#07695)
- ♦ Association européenne des assurés de l'industrie / see Federation of European Risk Management Associations (#09539)
- ♦ Association Européenne d'Athlétisme / see European Athletics (#06291)
- ♦ Association Européenne des Audioprothésistes (#06066)
- ♦ Association européenne des auteurs "DIE KOGGE" (#05749)
- ♦ Association européenne des autorités locales qui inventent leur futur énergétique / see Energy Cities (#05467)
- ♦ Association européenne des autorités régionales et locales pour l'apprentissage tout au long de la vie (#06188)
- ♦ Association européenne des avocats / see AEA – International Lawyers Network (#00142)
- ♦ Association européenne des avocats (#07661)
- ♦ Association européenne d'avocats spécialisés dans le contentieux des brevets d'invention (#08165)
- ♦ Association européenne baha'ie de management / see ebbf – ethical business building the future (#05269)
- ♦ Association européenne du bambou (#06309)
- ♦ Association européenne de banques et organismes financiers interpellés par les questions d'écologie, de culture, de gestion démocratique de l'économie sociale / see International Association of Investors in the Social Economy (#11971)
- ♦ Association européenne de banques publiques (#06178)
- ♦ Association européenne de banques publiques et d'institutions communales de financement / see European Association of Public Banks (#06178)
- ♦ Association européenne des barreaux des cours suprêmes (inactive)
- ♦ Association européenne des bateliers (#08491)
- ♦ Association européenne du béton prêt à l'emploi (#08330)
- ♦ Association européenne de biologie comparée de la peau (inactive)
- ♦ Association européenne pour la biomasse / see Bioenergy Europe (#03247)
- ♦ Association européenne de biomécanique / see European Society of Biomechanics (#08531)
- ♦ Association européenne du bitume (#06348)
- ♦ Association européenne des bourses de valeurs (inactive)
- ♦ Association européenne de boxe amateur / see European Boxing Confederation (#06387)
- ♦ Association Européenne pour le Buis et l'Art Topiaire (#06389)

♦ Association Européenne des Cadres de l'Assurance (AECA) 02556
European Association of Insurance Company Managers
Pres AECA Secretariat, c/o CFE-CGC Assurance/SNCAPA, 43 rue de Provence, 75009 Paris, France. T. +33155078760. Fax +33155319675. E-mail: asso.euro.cadres@cgc-assurance.com.
URL: http://www.cec-managers.org/
History Founded 29 Nov 1980, Düsseldorf (Germany FR). Previous title in English: *European Federation of Executives and Managerial Staff of the Insurance Sector.* EU Transparency Register: 56852692897-76. **Aims** In accordance with the aims of CEC: bring together, analyse and distribute economic and social information related to the European insurance context; contribute to European social dialogue by passing on opinions to the CEC in regards to positions adopted by the European Commission; study and defend common professional interest; improve, by all appropriate measures, the working, economic and living conditions of members, and safeguard their general interests; develop, wherever possible, professional training and good managerial practices in a spirit of European collaboration; represent interests of member associations and their members in all European organizations in the geographical area where AECA members exist and where the insurance sector is concerned; ensure best relations with European organizations of insurance employers and share common views about economic and social key points. **Structure** Steering Committee; Head Office in Paris (France); Office in Brussels (Belgium). **Languages** English, French. **Events** *General Meeting* Paris (France) 2009, *Meeting* Cologne (Germany FR) 1988.
Members National organizations in 7 countries:
Belgium, France, Germany, Italy, Luxembourg, Netherlands, UK.
IGO Relations *ECOSOC (#05331); European Economic and Social Committee (EESC, #06963).* **NGO Relations** Professional federation member of: *CEC European Managers (#03623).* [2015.01.07/XD3281/**D**]

- ♦ Association européenne des cadres de banque / see European Federation of Managers in the Banking Sector (#07161)
- ♦ Association européenne Camac (no recent information)
- ♦ Association européenne de capital investissement / see Invest Europe – The Voice of Private Capital (#15997)
- ♦ Association européenne de capital investissement et capital risque / see Invest Europe – The Voice of Private Capital (#15997)
- ♦ Association européenne de capital à risque / see Invest Europe – The Voice of Private Capital (#15997)
- ♦ Association européenne de capsules de surbouchage (no recent information)
- ♦ Association européenne pour la cardiologie pédiatrique / see Association for European Paediatric and Congenital Cardiology (#02529)
- ♦ Association européenne des Cartes jeunes (#09137)
- ♦ Association européenne de catalyse (no recent information)
- ♦ Association européenne de Cautionnement (#06061)
- ♦ Association européenne du cautionnement mutuel / see European Association of Guarantee Institutions (#06061)
- ♦ Association européenne des centres anti-poisons / see European Association of Poisons Centres and Clinical Toxicologists (#06155)
- ♦ Association européenne des centres d'audiophonologie (inactive)
- ♦ Association européenne des centres communautaires juifs (#06097)
- ♦ Association européenne des centres d'éthique médicale (#05968)
- ♦ Association européenne des centres de formation professionnelle (#06085)
- ♦ Association européenne des centres de formation au travail socio-éducatif / see Formation d'éducateurs sociaux européens (#09873)
- ♦ Association européenne des centres de manifestations / see European Association of Event Centers (#06032)
- ♦ Association européenne des centres nationaux de productivité (#06130)
- ♦ Association européenne des centres de perfectionnement dans la direction des entreprises (inactive)
- ♦ Association européenne des centres de rééducation fonctionnelle et de formation professionnelle d'orthopédie de précision et de haute botterie pour jeunes handicapés physiques (inactive)
- ♦ Association européenne de céramique (inactive)
- ♦ Association européenne du charbon et du lignite / see European Association for Coal and Lignite (#05978)

♦ Association européenne des chasses traditionnelles 02557

SG Conseil régional de la chasse de la région PACA, Le Mercure B, 80 rue Charles Duchesne, Pole d'activités d'Ais-les-Milles, 13851 Aix-en-Provence CEDEX 3, France.

History Previously referred to as *Association des amis des chasses traditionnelles (AACT)*. Registered in accordance with Belgian law. **Structure** General Assembly (annual). Administrative Council, consisting of 5 delegates for each country represented in the membership and including the President of *Federation of Associations for Hunting and Conservation of the EU (#09459)* (ex officio) and the Bureau, comprising President, 2 Vice-Presidents, Secretary and Treasurer. **Finance** Members' dues.
Members Founder members in 4 countries:
Belgium, France, Italy, Spain. [2015/XD5816/**D**]

- ♦ Association européenne de la chaux (#07699)
- ♦ Association européenne des chefs d'établissements (#08431)
- ♦ Association européenne des chefs d'établissements du secondaire / see European School Heads Association (#08431)

♦ Association européenne des cheminots (AEC) 02558

Association of European Railway Staff – Asociación Europea de Ferroviaros – Europäische Vereinigung der Eisenbahner – Associazione Europea dei Ferrovieri – Europese Vereniging van Spoorwegpersoneel – Europa Asocio de la Fervojistoj

Contact Quartier de Cairol, 30120 Avèze, France. T. +33467811414.
Pres Eppens Allee 16, 21423 Winsen, Germany.
Registered Office Square dd Meeûs 25, 1000 Brussels, Belgium.
Germany: https://www.a-e-c.net/

History 23 Jul 1961, Turin (Italy), on the initiative of *Commission fédéraliste européenne des Alpes (no recent information)*. Registered in accordance with Belgian law, 4 Feb 1985. **Aims** Promote amicable, cultural and scientific activities designed to generate a European attitude of mind among present and former members of *railway* staff, in conjunction with like-minded persons and bodies. **Structure** General Assembly (every 3 years). European Bureau, comprising President, Vice-President, Secretary-General, Assistant Secretary-General, Treasurer and Assistant Treasurer. Executive Committee, consisting of European Bureau and the presidents, secretaries-general and treasurers of all sections. Commissions (6): Administrative; Finance; Cultural; Press; Transport; Training. **Languages** English, French, German, Italian. **Staff** Voluntary. **Finance** European budget (annual): about euro 7,745. Training budget: euro 10,000. **Activities** Organizes congresses, symposia and exhibitions. **Events** *Congress* Salzburg (Austria) 2013, *Congress* Roubaix (France) / Lille (France) 2012, *Congress* Castelnuovo del Garda (Italy) 2011, *Congress* Sibiu (Romania) 2011, *Congress* Santiago de Compostela (Spain) 2010. **Publications** *Die Dreh Schiebe* (4 a year) – in Austria; *Europa Ferroviaria* (4 a year) – in Italy and Spain; *European Friendship* (4 a year) – in UK; *Fereurop* (4 a year) – in Belgium; *Schiene Europas* (4 a year) – in Germany; *Fer-Europ* (annual) – in France.
Members Full; Honorary; Associate. Individuals in 17 countries:
Albania, Austria, Belgium, Bulgaria, Czechia, France, Germany, Greece, Hungary, Italy, Latvia, Lithuania, Poland, Romania, Slovakia, Spain, UK.
Consultative Status Consultative status granted from: *Council of Europe (CE, #04881)* (Participatory Status).
NGO Relations Member of: *Permanent Forum of European Civil Society (#18322)*. [2011.11.28/XD5955/v/**D**]

- ♦ Association européenne de chimie (no recent information)
- ♦ Association européenne des chiropraticiens (#06538)
- ♦ Association européenne de chirurgie de l'arthrose rhumatoïde / see European Rheumatism and Arthritis Surgical Society (#08387)
- ♦ Association européenne de chirurgie buccale (#07040)
- ♦ Association européenne pour la chirurgie cardio-thoracique (#05964)
- ♦ Association européenne des chirurgiens plasticiens (#06154)
- ♦ Association européenne de chirurgie viscérale (no recent information)
- ♦ Association Européenne du Cinéma pour l'Enfance et la Jeunesse (#06530)
- ♦ Association européenne des classes moyennes (inactive)
- ♦ Association européenne des clubs de figurinistes (inactive)
- ♦ Association européenne de coléoptérologie (#02125)
- ♦ Association européenne du commerce / see EuroCommerce (#05665)
- ♦ Association Européenne de Commerce d'Armes Civiles (#05975)
- ♦ Association européenne du commerce de détail en jouets (inactive)
- ♦ Association européenne pour un commerce équitable (#07026)
- ♦ Association européenne du commerce en gros des viandes (inactive)
- ♦ Association européenne de commerce international / see European International Business Academy (#07585)
- ♦ Association européenne du commerce des oeufs, de la volaille et du gibier (#08258)
- ♦ Association européenne du commerce des pommes de terre (#08257)
- ♦ Association européenne pour le commerce des produits de jute (#06256)
- ♦ Association européenne du commerce des produits laitiers et dérivés (#06003)
- ♦ Association Européenne pour la Communication Parlée (#15578)
- ♦ Association européenne des companies pétrolières pour l'environnement, la santé et la sécurité dans le raffinage et la distribution (#17708)
- ♦ Association européenne pour la compétitivité par les ressources humaines (inactive)
- ♦ Association européenne de comptabilité (#05820)

♦ Association Européenne des Concessionnaires d'Autoroutes et d'Ouvrages à Péage (ASECAP) 02559

European Association of Operators of Toll Road Infrastructures – Asociación Europea de Concesionarias de Autopistas, Túneles, Puentes y Vias de Peaje – Europäischer Verband der Konzessionäre von Gebührenpflichtigen Autobahnen und Bauwerken

SG Rue Guimard 15, 3rd Floor, 1040 Brussels, Belgium. T. +3222892620. Fax +3225146628. E-mail: secretariat@asecap.com.
Head Office 152 avenue de Malakoff, 75116 Paris, France.
URL: https://www.asecap.com/

History 1973. Legally set up and statutes adopted, 1993 Former names and other names: *Secrétariat européen des concessionnaires d'autoroutes à péage (SECAP)* – former; *European Secretary for Toll Motorway Concessionaires* – former; *Secretariato Europeo delle Concessionarie de Autostrade a Pedaggio* – former; *European Association of Tolled Motorway, Bridge and Tunnel Concessionaires* – former. **Aims** Defend and develop the system of motorways and road infrastructures in Europe, applying tolls as a means to ensure financing of their construction, maintenance and operation. **Structure** General Assembly; Steering Committee; Executive Committee; Permanent Committees (4). **Languages** English, French. **Staff** 5.00 FTE, paid. **Finance** Sources: members' dues; sponsorship. Other sources: EU project funding; exhibitors' fees. **Activities** Advocacy/lobbying/activism; events/meetings; projects/programmes; publishing activities. **Events** *Road Safety Conference* Salzburg (Austria) 2023, *ASECAP Study and Information Days* Brussels (Belgium) 2022, *Road Safety Conference* Trento (Italy) 2022, *ASECAP Study and Information Days* Brussels (Belgium) 2021, *ASECAP Study and Information Days* Brussels (Belgium) 2020. **Publications** *ASECAP Key Figures* (annual); *ASECAP Statistical Bulletin* (annual). Press releases; position papers; policy papers; statements; manifestos.
Members Full; Associate. Full in 17 countries:
Austria, Croatia, Denmark, France, Greece, Hungary, Ireland, Italy, Netherlands, Poland, Portugal, Serbia, Slovenia, Spain, Türkiye, UK.
Associate in 5 countries:
Germany, Morocco, Russia, Slovakia.
Supporting Partner((1):
Ukraine.
IGO Relations Memorandum of Understanding with: *United Nations Economic Commission for Europe (UNECE, #20555)*. **NGO Relations** Memorandum of Understanding with (1): *International Bridge, Tunnel and Turnpike Association (IBTTA, #12400)*. Member of (2): *European Road Transport Research Advisory Council (ERTRAC, #08396)*; *Mobility for Prosperity in Europe (MPE, #16839)*. Partner of (1): *International Road Federation (IRF, #14758)*. [2023/XF2356/**F**]

- ♦ Association européenne pour la conservation du sol (#08739)

♦ Association Européenne des Conservatoires, Académies de Musique et Musikhochschulen (AEC) 02560

European Association of Conservatories (AEC)

Chief Exec AEC Office, Av des Celtes 20, 1040 Brussels, Belgium. T. +3227371670. E-mail: info@aec-music.eu – events@aec-music.eu.
Events Manager address not obtained.
URL: http://www.aec-music.eu/

History 3 Jul 1953, Salzburg (Austria). Statutes adopted 10 Oct 1963, Copenhagen (Denmark). Statutes revised: 12 Nov 1982, Stockholm (Sweden); 26 Nov 1993, Tel Aviv; 21 Nov 1997, Brussels (Belgium); 19 Nov 2001, Groningen (Netherlands). Former names and other names: *European Association of Music Conservatories, Academies and High Schools* – alias. **Aims** Encourage and develop contacts and exchanges in the field of professional *music* training. **Structure** General Assembly (annual); Council; Executive Committee; Working Groups and Platforms. **Languages** English, French, German. **Staff** 6.00 FTE, paid. **Finance** Sources: grants; members' dues. Supported by: *European Union (EU, #08967)*. **Activities** Events/meetings; training/education. **Events** *European Platform for Artistic Research in Music Conference* London (UK) 2022, *Annual Congress and General Assembly* Lyon (France) 2022, *Pop and Jazz Platform Meeting* Lódz (Poland) 2022, *Annual Congress and General Assembly* Antwerp (Belgium) 2021, *European Platform for Artistic Research in Music Conference* Brussels (Belgium) 2021. **Publications** *AEC Newsletter* (11 a year). *AEC Connect*; *AEC Promuse Leonardo*; *AEC Socrates*. *AEC Declaration to the Bologna Declaration* (1999) in English; *History of the AEC 1953-1988* (1996) in English, French. *Handbook on the Effects of the Bologna Declaration on Professional Music Training*. Information brochure; congress proceedings; project publications; studies; reports.
Members Active; Associate: institutions (298) in 58 countries and territories:
Albania, Australia, Austria, Azerbaijan, Belarus, Belgium, Bosnia-Herzegovina, Bulgaria, Canada, China, Croatia, Cyprus, Czechia, Denmark, Estonia, Finland, France, Georgia, Germany, Greece, Hong Kong, Hungary, Iceland, Ireland, Israel, Italy, Japan, Jordan, Kazakhstan, Korea Rep, Kosovo, Latvia, Lebanon, Lithuania, Luxembourg, Malta, Mexico, Montenegro, Netherlands, New Zealand, North Macedonia, Norway, Poland, Portugal, Puerto Rico, Romania, Russia, Serbia, Singapore, Slovakia, Slovenia, Spain, Sweden, Switzerland, Türkiye, UK, Ukraine, USA.
NGO Relations Member of (4): *Culture Action Europe (CAE, #04981)*; *European Alliance for Culture and the Arts (#05866)*; *European Music Council (EMC, #07837)*; *International Music Council (IMC, #14199)* (as Associate Member). Founding member of: *European Alliance of Subject-Specific and Professional Accreditation and Quality Assurance (EASPA, #05887)*. Also links with national organizations. [2022.02.15/XD0571/**D**]

- ♦ Association européenne des consommateurs (no recent information)
- ♦ Association européenne des constructeurs de corps de chauffe (inactive)
- ♦ Association européenne de constructeurs d'ordinateurs / see Ecma International (#05288)
- ♦ Association européenne des constructeurs de pompes (#06182)
- ♦ Association européenne de constructeurs d'usines métallurgiques (inactive)
- ♦ Association européenne pour la construction en profiles minces en acier (no recent information)
- ♦ Association européenne des consultants en innovation (#06084)
- ♦ Association européenne contre les leucodystrophies (#07684)
- ♦ Association européenne contre les violences faites aux femmes au travail (#05931)
- ♦ Association européenne des contribuables (#20102)
- ♦ Association européenne pour le contrôle des eaux usées (inactive)
- ♦ Association européenne de contrôle de la pollution des eaux / see European Water Association (#09080)
- ♦ Association européenne pour la coopération (inactive)
- ♦ Association européenne pour la coopération interrégionale (no recent information)

♦ Association européenne pour la coordination de la représentation des consommateurs pour la normalisation (ANEC) 02561

European Association for the Coordination of Consumer Representation in Standardization (ANEC)

SG Rue d'Arlon 80, 1040 Brussels, Belgium. T. +3227432470. E-mail: anec@anec.eu.
Communications Officer address not obtained.
URL: http://www.anec.eu/

History Feb 1995. Founded by *Conseil consultatif des consommateurs de la Commission des communautés européennes (CCC/CCE, inactive)* and *EFTA Consultative Committee (CC)*. Registration: Banque-Carrefour des Entreprises, No/ID: 0457.696.181, Start date: 4 Apr 1996, Belgium; EU Transparency Register, No/ID: 507800799-30, Start date: 30 Jun 2008. **Aims** Represent the collective voice of European consumers in development of European (CEN-CENELEC-ETSI) standards and selected international (ISO-IEC) standards; influence related EU legislation in order to achieve optimal levels of consumer protection, welfare and sustainability. **Structure** General Assembly (annual); Steering Committee (Executive Board). **Languages** English. **Staff** 8.30 FTE, paid. **Finance** Sources: contributions. Supported by: *EFTA (#05391)*; *European Commission (EC, #06633)*. Annual budget: 1,870,000 EUR. **Activities** Advocacy/lobbying/activism; guidance/assistance/consulting; standards/guidelines. **Events** *General Assembly* Dublin (Ireland) 2021, *General Assembly* 2020, *General Assembly* Brussels (Belgium) 2019, *General Assembly* Brussels (Belgium) 2018, *General Assembly* Brussels (Belgium) 2003. **Publications** *ANEC Annual Review* (annual); *ANEC e-Newsletter* (9 a year). Technical reports; position papers; press releases; background flyers.
Members Full in 34 countries:
Austria, Belgium, Bulgaria, Croatia, Cyprus, Czechia, Denmark, Estonia, Finland, France, Germany, Greece, Hungary, Iceland, Ireland, Italy, Latvia, Lithuania, Luxembourg, Malta, Netherlands, North Macedonia, Norway, Poland, Portugal, Romania, Serbia, Slovakia, Slovenia, Spain, Sweden, Switzerland, Türkiye, UK.
Included in above, 2 organizations listed in this Yearbook:
EFTA (#05391); *European Union (EU, #08967)*.
NGO Relations Member of (5): *European Accreditation Advisory Board (EAAB, see: #06782)*; *European Policy Centre (EPC, #08240)*; *European Telecommunications Standards Institute (ETSI, #08897)*; *Federation of European and International Associations Established in Belgium (FAIB, #09508)*; *Transatlantic Consumer Dialogue (TACD, #20203)*. Partner of (2): *Comité européen de normalisation (CEN, #04162)*; *European Committee for Electrotechnical Standardization (CENELEC, #06647)*. [2022/XD4993/y/**D**]

- ♦ Association européenne de counselling (#05993)
- ♦ Association européenne pour la créativité des personnes handicapées (#11713)
- ♦ Association européenne pour la culture juive (no recent information)
- ♦ Association européenne de cyclosport (internationally oriented national body)
- ♦ Association européenne des décaféineurs (inactive)
- ♦ Association européenne pour le décompte des coûts énergétiques sur la base de la consommation (#05989)
- ♦ Association Européenne pour la défense des Droits de l'Homme (no recent information)
- ♦ Association européenne pour la démocratie locale (#06110)
- ♦ Association européenne de démolition (#06902)
- ♦ Association européenne pour le développement des banques de données sur la formation et l'éducation (inactive)
- ♦ Association européenne pour le développement de l'enseignement supérieur et de la recherche sur Internet / see Interdisciplines
- ♦ Association européenne pour le développement des exportations de programmes de television (no recent information)
- ♦ Association européenne pour le développement de l'information et la connaissance de l'environnement (inactive)

♦ Association européenne pour le développement et la santé (AEDES) 02562

European Agency for the Development and Health

Dir Gen Rue Joseph II 34, 1000 Brussels, Belgium. T. +3222190306. Fax +3222190938. E-mail: jpdaltilia@aedes.be – aedes@aedes.be.
URL: http://www.aedes.be/

History Founded 13 Nov 1984, by members of *Bureau international des Médecins sans frontières (MSF International, #03366)*. Also referred to as *European Association for Health Development*. Registered in accordance with Belgian law. **Structure** General Assembly; Board of Directors. Set up *Fondation AEDES*. **Staff** Brussels (Belgium) office: 13. Experts in the field: 25. **Events** *NGO conference on the reduction of drug consumption* Brussels (Belgium) 1992. **Members** Membership countries not specified. [2016/XD6080/**D**]

- ♦ Association européenne pour le développement du transport ferroviaire (#06011)
- ♦ Association européenne du diagnostic de la gastrocamera / see European Association for Gastroenterology, Endoscopy and Nutrition (#06051)
- ♦ Association européenne de dialyse et de transplantation – Association européenne de maladies rénales / see European Renal Association – European Dialysis and Transplant Association (#08353)
- ♦ Association européenne de didactique de la biologie (inactive)
- ♦ Association européenne des directeurs d'abattoirs publics / see Union européenne des vétérinaires hygiénistes (#20404)
- ♦ Association européenne des directeurs de bureaux de concerts et spectacles / see Association Européenne des Agents Artistiques (#02554)
- ♦ Association européenne des directeurs des centres plastiques (inactive)
- ♦ Association européenne des directeurs d'écoles hôtelières / see International Association of Hotel School Directors (#11942)
- ♦ Association européenne des directeurs d'hôpitaux (#06073)
- ♦ Association européenne des directeurs d'hôtels (#07502)

♦ Association européenne des directeurs d'institutions lasalliennes (ASSEDIL) 02563

Association of Directors of the Lasallian Institutions – Asociación de directores de las Instituciones Lasalianas

Registered Address 30 rue du Général Leclerc, 92136 Issy-les-Moulineaux, France. E-mail: assedil.info@lasalle.org.
URL: https://lasalle-assedil.org/

History Former names and other names: *Association des Directeurs des Institutions Lasalliennes* – alias. Registration: France. **Aims** Promote various types of training and education, in line with national directives, in the establishments conducted by the Brothers of the *Christian Schools* or under their trusteeship in European countries; foster exchanges of pupils and teachers in the interests of language learning, teaching of technologies and developing an awareness of European culture; represent members' interests in relation to the relevant offices of the *European Union*. **Structure** General Assembly. Administration Council. Bureau, comprising President, one or more Vice-Presidents, Secretary and Treasurer, plus possible General Delegate. **Finance** Members' dues. **Events** *Congress* Gdansk (Poland) 2021, *Congress* 2020, *Congress* Thessaloniki (Greece) 2018, *Congress* Santa Cruz de Tenerife (Spain) 2017, *Congress* Paris (France) 2016.
Members Full in 7 countries:
Belgium, Egypt, France, Italy, Jordan, Lebanon, Türkiye. [2021/XJ6616/**E**]

- ♦ Association européenne des directeurs du son (no recent information)
- ♦ Association Européenne des Directeurs de Structures d'Accueil et de Services aux Personnes Agées (inactive)
- ♦ Association européenne de direction et économie de l'entreprise / see European Academy of Management and Business Economics (#05801)
- ♦ Association européenne pour la direction du personnel / see European Association for People Management (#06146)
- ♦ Association européenne de la distribution automatique / see European Vending and Coffee Service Association (#09049)
- ♦ Association européenne de dragage (#06946)
- ♦ Association européenne pour le droit des affaires entre l'Est et l'Ouest (inactive)
- ♦ Association Européenne pour le Droit de l'Alimentation (#07286)

♦ Association européenne pour le droit bancaire et financier (AEDBF) 02564

Europese Vereniging voor Bank- en Financieel Recht (EVBFR)

Administrative Seat Avenue de Tervueren 268A, 1150 Brussels, Belgium. T. +3227802448. E-mail: info@aedbf.be.
URL: http://www.aedbf.be/

History 1988, Paris (France). Registered in accordance with French law. Belgian section founded, 1991, Brussels (Belgium) and registered in accordance with Belgian law. **Aims** Promote knowledge of national and EC legislation in the field of banking and finance; promote the legal profession in the context of the establishment of the European financial area. **Structure** General Assembly; Board of Directors. **Languages** Dutch, English, French. **Finance** Members' dues. Colloquia. **Activities** Knowledge management/information dissemination; events/meetings. **Events** *Study Day* Brussels (Belgium) 2012, *Capital and decision-making in commercial companies* Luxembourg (Luxembourg) 1993.
Members National committees in 5 countries:
Belgium, France, Italy, Luxembourg, Netherlands.
Correspondents in 6 countries:
Denmark, Greece, Ireland, Spain, Switzerland, UK. [2018/XD2683/**D**]

- ♦ Association européenne de droit de l'environnement (inactive)
- ♦ Association européenne pour l'échange de la littérature technique dans le domaine de la sidérurgie (inactive)
- ♦ Association européenne des éco-conseillers/ères (inactive)
- ♦ Association européenne des écoles d'architecture / see European Association for Architectural Education (#05941)
- ♦ Association européenne des écoles d'hôtellerie et de tourisme (#06075)
- ♦ Association européenne des écoles primaires (inactive)
- ♦ Association Européenne des Ecoles de Travailleurs Sociaux (#06200)
- ♦ Association européenne d'écologie humaine (inactive)
- ♦ Association européenne d'économie (#06958)
- ♦ Association européenne des économistes du travail (#06102)
- ♦ Association européenne des éditeurs de journaux (#08048)
- ♦ Association européenne des éditeurs juridiques et économiques (inactive)
- ♦ Association européenne des éditeurs de la presse périodique d'information féminine ou familiale (inactive)
- ♦ Association européenne des éditeurs de publications pour la jeunesse (inactive)
- ♦ Association européenne pour l'éducation des adultes (#06018)
- ♦ Association européenne pour l'éducation aux médias audiovisuels (#05946)
- ♦ Association européenne pour l'éducation en milieu pénitentiaire (#08276)
- ♦ Association européenne pour l'éducation spéciale (no recent information)
- ♦ Association européenne pour l'éducation technologique (#08757)
- ♦ Association européenne EEST / see European Interuniversity Association on Society, Science and Technology (#07597)
- ♦ Association européenne en électronique de puissance et entraînements électriques (#08261)
- ♦ Association Européenne pour l'Elevage de Volailles, de Pigeons, d'Oiseaux, de Lapins et de Cobayes (#05492)
- ♦ Association européenne des élus de montagne (#06021)
- ♦ Association européenne d'emballages alimentaires à usage unique / see Pack2Go Europe (#18014)
- ♦ Association européenne de l'énergie / see European Energy Forum (#06986)
- ♦ Association européenne de l'énergie éolienne / see WindEurope (#20965)
- ♦ Association européenne pour les enfants à l'hôpital (#05970)

♦ Association européenne des enseignants (AEDE) 02565

European Association of Teachers – Asociación Europea de Enseñantes – Europäischer Erzieherbund – Associazione Europea degli Insegnanti – Europese Vereniging van het Onderwijzend Personeel – Europaeiske Laerersammenslutning – Cumann Eorpach na Muinteoiri – Ghaqda Ewropea Tal-Ghalliema

Pres MEI, Place due Luxembourg 2, 1050 Brussels, Belgium. E-mail: aedeeuropea@gmail.com.
Contact Via Lalia,72, 72013 Ceglie Messapica BR, Italy. E-mail: aede.italia@gmail.com.
URL: http://www.aede.eu/

History 18 Jul 1956, Paris (France). Former names and other names: *EAT* – alias. Registration: Belgium. **Aims** Unite teachers willing to cooperate in the creation of the European Union; widen teachers' knowledge of European problems; make known the common basic features of European civilization and assure its defence; pass on this knowledge to pupils and all circles where teachers can exercise an influence. **Structure** Congress of delegates of national sections; European Committe;. Executive Board, consisting of President, 4 Vice-Presidents, Secretary-General, 2 Assistant Secretaries-General and Treasurer. **Languages** English, French, Italian. **Staff** 5.00 FTE, voluntary. **Finance** Sources: grants; members' dues. **Activities** Events/meetings; networking/liaising; publishing activities; training/education. **Events** *European Cultural Heritage Summit* Paris (France) 2019, *Triennial Congress* Strasbourg (France) 2014, *Triennial Congress* Bucharest (Romania) / Constantza (Romania) 2011, *Congress* Ostuni (Italy) 2008, *Congress* Ceské Budejovice (Czech Rep) 2004. **Publications** *Documents pour l'enseignement* (periodical); *AEDE News*; *Context: European Education Magazine* in English, French. *AEDE Manual for European Educational Exchanges*.
Members National sections (21), regional groups and contacts representing over 25,000 teachers, heads and inspectors (" also individual members) in 22 countries:
Austria, Belgium, Bulgaria, Canaries, Cyprus (*; Portugal), Czechia, Denmark, Finland, France, Germany, Greece, Italy, Luxembourg, Malta, Netherlands, Poland, Romania, Slovakia, Spain, Sweden, Switzerland, UK.
Consultative Status Consultative status granted from: *Council of Europe (CE, #04881)* (Participatory Status).
NGO Relations Member of (4): *European Civic Forum (ECF, #06562)*; *European Movement International (EMI, #07825)*; *Federation of European and International Associations Established in Belgium (FAIB, #09508)*; *Permanent Forum of European Civil Society (#18322)*. [2021.06.08/XD0583/**D**]

- ♦ Association européenne des enseignants dentaires (#02467)
- ♦ Association européenne pour l'enseignement de l'architecture (#05941)
- ♦ Association Européenne pour l'enseignement de la pédiatrie (#02847)
- ♦ Association européenne pour l'enseignement de la théorie du droit (#06250)
- ♦ Association européenne des entreprises d'équipement électrique / see EuropeOn (#09166)
- ♦ Association européenne des entreprises de l'installation électrique / see EuropeOn (#09166)
- ♦ Association européenne des entreprises du patrimoine architectural / see European Association Architectural Heritage Restoration Firms (#05942)
- ♦ Association Européenne des Entreprises de Restauration du Patrimoine Architectural (#05942)
- ♦ Association européenne des entreprises de services en télécommunications (inactive)
- ♦ Association européenne d'ergonomie cognitive (#05980)
- ♦ Association européenne pour les essais comparatifs (inactive)
- ♦ Association européenne d'essais de semences / see International Seed Testing Association (#14829)
- ♦ Association Européenne des Etablissements d'Enseignement Vétérinaire (#06031)
- ♦ Association européenne de l'étanchéité (#08452)
- ♦ Association européenne de l'étanchéité au moyen de matières synthétiques / see European Single Ply Waterproofing Association (#08488)
- ♦ Association européenne de l'ethnie française (inactive)

♦ Association Européenne pour l'Etude de l'Alimentation et du Développement de l'Enfant (ADE) 02566

Pres Hôpital Trousseau, 26 avenue Dr Arnold Netter, 75012 Paris, France. T. +33144736739. Fax +33144736739. E-mail: ade.france@wanadoo.fr.
Head Office 4 Place de Breteuil, 75015 Paris, France.
URL: http://www.ade-ong.com/

History Founded 1 Dec 1976, Paris (France). **Aims** Promote research on the influence of nutrition on intellectual and psychomotor development of children and disseminate results of this research; use these results in aiding *developing countries*. **Languages** Arabic, English, French, German, Polish, Russian. **Staff** 1.00 FTE, paid; 10.00 FTE, voluntary. **Finance** Members' dues. Other sources: donations; grants; proceeds from exhibitions. Annual budget: less than euro 500,000. **Activities** Research/documentation; training/education; events/meetings. Active in: South Sudan, Sudan. **Events** *Meeting* Gdansk (Poland) 2014, *Meeting* Juba (South Sudan) 2013, *Meeting* Paris (France) 2013, *Meeting* Beijing (China) 2012, *Meeting* Juba (South Sudan) 2012. **Publications** *ADE Bulletin* (periodical). Books; food tables; conference proceedings.
Members Principal scientists, medical and non-medical (100) organizations. Members mainly in France, but in a total of 13 countries:
Albania, China, France, Georgia, Germany, Kenya, Philippines, Poland, Russia, South Sudan, Sudan, Uganda, Ukraine.
NGO Relations Member of: *NGO/UNICEF Regional Network for Children in CEE, CIS and Baltic States (RNC, inactive)*. [2019/XD6511/**F**]

- ♦ Association européenne pour l'étude du diabète (#06228)
- ♦ Association européenne pour l'étude du droit chinois (#05971)
- ♦ Association européenne pour l'étude du foie / see European Association for the Study of the Liver (#06233)
- ♦ Association européenne pour l'étude des jeux de hasard (#06231)
- ♦ Association européenne pour l'étude du marché pharmaceutique (#08196)
- ♦ Association européenne pour l'étude de la population (#06158)
- ♦ Association européenne pour l'étude des problèmes de sécurité dans la fabrication et l'emploi des poudres propulsives (inactive)
- ♦ Association européenne pour l'étude et la recherche en matière d'enseignement supérieur (inactive)
- ♦ Association européenne d'étude et de réflexion sur les problèmes de consommation (inactive)
- ♦ Association européenne pour l'étude du rêve (#06230)
- ♦ Association européenne d'études chinoises (#05973)
- ♦ Association européenne pour l'étude de la science et de la technologie (#06236)
- ♦ Association européenne des études juives / see European Association for Jewish Studies (#06098)
- ♦ Association européenne d'études juridiques et fiscales (no recent information)
- ♦ Association européenne d'études de motivation économique, commerciale et industrielle (inactive)
- ♦ Association européenne pour les études d'opinion et de marketing / see World Association of Research Professionals (#21182)
- ♦ Association européenne d'étude des traumatisés crâniens et de leur réinsertion (#06394)
- ♦ Association européenne des étudiants de la défense (inactive)
- ♦ Association européenne des étudiants en médecine (#07764)
- ♦ Association européenne d'experts comptables / see European Accounting Association (#05820)
- ♦ Association européenne des exploitations frigorifiques (inactive)
- ♦ Association européenne des expositions scientifiques, techniques et industrielles / see European Network of Science Centres and Museums (#07998)
- ♦ Association européenne de fabricants d'aiguilles (inactive)
- ♦ Association européenne de fabricants d'amortisseurs (inactive)
- ♦ Association européenne des fabricants d'articles de papeterie scolaire et de bureau (inactive)
- ♦ Association européenne des fabricants d'articles à usage unique / see Pack2Go Europe (#18014)
- ♦ Association européenne des fabricants de beton cellulaire (#06297)
- ♦ Association européenne des fabricants de blocs de mousse souple de polyuréthane (#06042)
- ♦ Association européenne des fabricants de boîtes en aluminium pour aérosol / see International Organization of Aluminium Aerosol Container Manufacturers (#14437)
- ♦ Association européenne des fabricants de caramel (#08877)
- ♦ Association européenne des fabricants de cartonnages et de carton plat / see Association of European Cartonboard and Carton Manufacturers (#02502)
- ♦ Association européenne des fabricants de cartonnages pliants (#06453)

♦ Association européenne des fabricants de composants électroniques (#06974)
♦ Association européenne de fabricants de compteurs d'eau / see Association européenne de fabricants de compteurs d'eau et d'énergie thermique (#02567)

♦ Association européenne de fabricants de compteurs d'eau et d'énergie thermique (AQUA) 02567

European Association of Water and Heat Meter Manufacturers – Europäische Vereinigung der Hersteller von Wasserzählern und Wärmezählern

Secretariat c/o Syndicat de la Mesure, 39-41 rue Louis Blanc, Courbevoie, 92038 Paris La Défense CEDEX, France.
SG 22 rue Saint Fiacre, 94210 Varenne-Saint-Hilaire, France. T. +33767331105.
URL: http://www.aqua-metering.org/

History 1960. Former names and other names: *European Association of Water Meters Manufacturers* – former (1960); *Association européenne de fabricants de compteurs d'eau (AQUA)* – former (1960); *Europäische Vereinigung der Hersteller von Wasserzählern* – former (1960). Registration: EU Transparency Register, No/ID: 66027272133-77. **Aims** Promote evaluation and resolution among members of problems of common interests of scientific, technical or legal nature relating to manufacturing of water and/or heat meters and application of technical standards and regulation. **Structure** General Assembly; Executive Committee; Working Groups (4). **Languages** English. **Staff** 0.50 FTE, voluntary. **Finance** Sources: members' dues. **Events** *Executive Committee Meeting* Vienna (Austria) 2021, *Executive Committee Meeting* Vienna (Austria) 2021, *General Assembly* Vienna (Austria) 2021, *General Assembly* Vienna (Austria) 2021, *Executive Committee Meeting* Lyon (France) 2020. **Members** in 14 EU member countries. Membership countries not specified. **NGO Relations** Cooperates with (6): *Comité européen de normalisation (CEN, #04162)*; *ESMIG (#05539)*; *European Committee for Electrotechnical Standardization (CENELEC, #06647)*; *NoBoMet (#17145)*; *Orgalim – Europe's Technology Industries (#17794)*; *WELMEC – European Cooperation in Legal Metrology (#20857)*.
[2022/XD2714/**D**]

♦ Association Européenne des Fabricants de demi-produits corroyés en aluminium (inactive)
♦ Association européenne des fabricants d'emballages plastiques (inactive)
♦ Association européenne des fabricants d'équipement électronique grand public (inactive)
♦ Association européenne des fabricants d'équipements pour la boulangerie (inactive)
♦ Association européenne des fabricants de ferments à usage agro-alimentaire (#07282)
♦ Association européenne des fabricants de feuilles, membranes et revêtements en matière plastique (inactive)
♦ Association européenne des fabricants de feuillets de téréphtalate (inactive)
♦ Association européenne des fabricants de filets (inactive)
♦ Association européenne de fabricants de gélatine / see Gelatin Manufacturers Association of Europe (#10090)
♦ Association européenne des fabricants de jauges, d'outils de mesure de précision, d'appareils et de machines pour la technique de longueur (no recent information)
♦ Association européenne des fabricants de matériaux isolants (#07577)

♦ Association européenne des fabricants de médicaments utilisés en thérapeutique anthroposophique (AEFMUTA) 02568

European Anthroposophic Manufacturers Association – Europäischer Verband der Arzneimittelhersteller der Anthroposophischen Therapierichtung

Contact 9 rue Eugène Jung, 68330 Huningue, France.

History Founded Apr 1989. **Members** Companies (18) in 12 countries. Membership countries not specified.
[2015/XM3377/**D**]

♦ Association européenne des fabricants de panneaux radiants lumineux à gaz (#05758)
♦ Association européenne des fabricants de pièces moulées de polyuréthane destinées à l'industrie automobile (#06116)
♦ Association européenne des fabricants de quadricycles / see European Quadricycle League (#08309)
♦ Association européenne des fabricants de raccords (inactive)
♦ Association Européenne des Fabricants de Réactifs Vétérinaires / see Diagnostics For Animals (#05062)
♦ Association européenne de fabricants et de revendeurs de matériel didactique / see Worlddidac Association (#21361)
♦ Association européenne des fabricants de snacks (#08498)
♦ Association européenne des fabricants de tubes souples / see european tube manufacturers association (#08953)
♦ Association européenne de fabricants de tuyaux métalliques flexibles et de compensateurs de dilatation de qualité (inactive)
♦ Association européenne de facultés et autres établissements d'enseignement supérieur formant des spécialistes de l'aménagement du territoire (#02542)

♦ Association Européenne des Facultés Libres (AEFLib) 02569

Exec Pres 70 av Denfert Rochereau, 75014 Paris, France. E-mail: contact@aeflib.eu.
URL: http://www.aeflib.eu/

History Nov 2008, Paris (France). Founded by institutions in Austria, France, Czech Rep and Spain, including *International Theological Institute (ITI)*. Registration: France; EU Transparency Register, No/ID: 739094715664-45. **Aims** Act as forum for reflection, discussion and proposals leading to concrete projects and offering opportunities to develop and promote education in the context of *Christian humanism*; develop a proposal for each of *European Union* state and for the European Union concerning policies for free *higher education*. **Languages** English, French. **Staff** 2.00 FTE, voluntary. **Finance** Sources: members' dues. Annual budget: 9,300 EUR. **Activities** Events/meetings; networking/liaising; research and development.
Members Full in 5 countries:
Austria, Czechia, France, Italy, Spain.
[2022.05.17/XM6244/**D**]

♦ Association européenne des facultés de pharmacie (#06036)
♦ Association européenne des femmes chefs d'entreprise / see Femmes chefs d'entreprises mondiales (#09733)
♦ Association européenne des femmes juristes (#09098)
♦ Association européenne des femmes pour la recherche théologique (#08789)
♦ Association européenne des festivals / see European Festivals Association (#07242)
♦ Association européenne des festivals de musique / see European Festivals Association (#07242)
♦ Association européenne de finance / see European Finance Association (#07248)

♦ Association européenne pour le fleurissement et le paysage (AEFP) 02570

European Association for Flowers and Landscaping – Europäische Vereinigung für Grün und Blumen – Europese Vereniging voor Bloemen en Groenvoorziening

SG address not obtained. T. +353871007633. E-mail: info@entente-florale.eu.
Pres Kappaertstraat E/1, 8550 Zwevegem, Belgium.
URL: http://www.entente-florale.eu/

History 1996. Statutes published in Belgian Monitor, 8 Sep 1998. Amended articles, by law of 2 May 2002, published in Belgian Monitor, 28 Apr 2006, and again 23 Mar 2008. Registration: Banque-Carrefour des Entreprises, No/ID: 0462.242.315, Start date: 8 Jan 1998, Belgium. **Aims** Promote landscaping, greening and flowering of towns and villages in Europe; promote development of *horticulture*, tourism and environment; increase the quality of life of inhabitants and visitors. **Structure** General Assembly (annual). Council of Members. Board of Directors (meets twice a year), including President, 2 Vice-Presidents, Secretary General, Secretary, Project Manager VR and Chairperson International Jury EFL. Working groups. **Languages** English, French. **Staff** 0.50 FTE, paid; 1.00 FTE, voluntary. **Finance** Members' dues. Other sources: subsidies from state sources such as ministries of tourism and environment, horticultural organizations and official institutions. **Activities** Events/meetings; awards/prizes/competitions. **Events** *Conference* Nieuwpoort (Belgium) 2013, *Conference* Düsseldorf (Germany) 2012, *Conference* Sentjernej (Slovenia) 2011, *Conference* Cervia (Italy) 2010, *Conference / Conference and Entente Florale Europe* Vienna (Austria) 2010.
Members Active, representatives officially mandated by national ministries or other official tourism, horticulture or related organizations. Members in 12 countries:
Austria, Belgium, Croatia, Czechia, France, Germany, Hungary, Ireland, Italy, Netherlands, Slovenia, UK. [2021/XD4881/**D**]

♦ Association européenne de football de table (inactive)

♦ Association européenne des formateurs du transport (EuroTra) . . . 02571

European Transport Training Association

Secretariat Rue Archimède 5, 1000 Brussels, Belgium. T. +3222343010. Fax +3222307534. E-mail: eurotra@eurotra.eu.
URL: http://www.eurotra.eu/

History Founded 16 Dec 1990. Registered in accordance with Belgian law. **Aims** Develop links among European organizations concerned with training in the field of transport; harmonize training programmes and standards; become recognized as representative of transport training organizations with national, international and European Community authorities; cooperate in exchange of training programmes, educational supports and practical training courses; obtain recognition for a European level qualification or diploma. **Structure** General Assembly (annual); Board of Directors; Registered office in Brussels (Belgium). **Languages** English. **Staff** 0.50 FTE, paid. **Finance** Members' dues.
Members Transport training centres in 12 countries:
Belgium, Czechia, Denmark, Finland, France, Germany, Hungary, Netherlands, Romania, Spain, Sweden, Ukraine.
[2014.12.05/XD3296/**D**]

♦ Association européenne pour la formation en gestion de l'environnement (inactive)
♦ Association européenne de formation au journalisme (#07613)
♦ Association européenne de formation paysanne et rurale (inactive)
♦ Association européenne pour la formation professionnelle (#09075)
♦ Association Européenne des Fournisseurs Automobiles (#05948)
♦ Association européenne de fournisseurs d'information (inactive)
♦ Association européenne de fournisseurs de services Internet (#07592)
♦ Association Européenne des Foyers (internationally oriented national body)
♦ Association européenne francophone pour les études baha'ies / see Association francophone européenne d'études baha'ies (#02613)
♦ Association Européenne des Gaz Industriels (#07525)
♦ Association européenne des gaz de pétrole liquéfiés / see Liquid Gas Europe (#16488)
♦ Association européenne de génie sismique (#06017)
♦ Association européenne des géophysiciens d'exploration (inactive)
♦ Association européenne de gestion des systèmes de santé (#07458)
♦ Association européenne de golf (#07399)
♦ Association européenne pour les graphiques sur l'ordinateur (#05986)

♦ Association européenne des graveurs et des flexographes (AEGRAFLEX) 02572

European Association of Engravers and Flexographers – Europäische Vereinigung der Graveure und Flexografen

Pres c/o Marburger STS, Alte Kasseler Str 22, 35039 Marburg, Germany. T. +492352260296. Fax +492352331087. E-mail: aegraflex_gf@t-online.de.
URL: http://www.aegraflex.org/

History 11 Jun 1966, Amsterdam (Netherlands). Registration: Commercial Register, Start date: 1975, Netherlands, Amsterdam. **Aims** Promote engraving techniques and flexography – manufacture of stamps, form preparation for flexographic printing; act as group representatives of the profession. **Structure** Assembly; Board. **Languages** English, French, German, Norwegian. **Staff** 2.00 FTE, paid. **Finance** Members' dues. **Activities** Training/education; knowledge management/information dissemination; publishing activities; guidance/assistance/consulting; events/meetings. **Events** *GraFlex Conference* Netherlands 2021, *GraFlex Conference* Netherlands 2020, *GraFlex Conference* Feldkirch (Austria) 2018, *GraFlex Conference* Strasbourg (France) 2016, *GraFlex Conference* Dresden (Germany) 2014. **Publications** *Graflex Bulletin Professionnel* (3 a year) in English, French, German, Norwegian.
Members Associations (8) in 7 countries. Firms in 12 countries:
Austria, Belgium, Denmark, Finland, France, Germany, Netherlands, Norway, Portugal, Spain, Sweden, Switzerland.
IGO Relations Recognized by: *European Commission (EC, #06633)*. **NGO Relations** *SMEunited (#19327)*.
[2020/XD8570/**D**]

♦ Association européenne des grossistes en produits du tabac (#08919)
♦ Association européenne de gynécologie et d'obstétrique (inactive)
♦ Association européenne des hélicoptères (#07472)
♦ Association européenne d'hématopathologie (#06062)
♦ Association européenne d'histoire contemporaine / see Association internationale d'histoire contemporaine de l'Europe (#02705)
♦ Association européenne pour l'histoire de la médecine et de la santé (#06070)
♦ Association européenne pour l'histoire de la photographie (#08622)
♦ Association européenne d'histoire de la psychiatrie (inactive)
♦ Association Européenne d'Histoire Urbaine (#06262)
♦ Association Européenne des Historiens and Collectionneurs de Golf (#06059)
♦ Association européenne des historiens de la danse (#06004)

♦ Association Européenne des Illustrateurs Médicaux et Scientifiques (AEIMS) 02573

Pres 18 Bd Auguste Blanqui, 75013 Paris, France. E-mail: info@aeims.eu.
Treas 26 rue des Dragons, 67700 Ernolsheim-lès-Saverne, France. E-mail: treasurer.aeims@gmail.com.
URL: https://www.aeims.eu/

History 1986. Former names and other names: *European Associaton of Medical and Scientific Illustrators (AEIMS)* – full title (1986). **Aims** Bring together medical and scientific artists of Europe for the purpose of education and social contact; share work experience and contribute to innovation within the profession; establish recognition for the skilled work carried out by its members; encourage further establishment of centres for the training of students; attract professional sponsorship for the assistance of students; promote the profession where possible through exhibition and publicity. **Structure** Administrative Council. **Languages** English. **Staff** 10.00 FTE, voluntary. **Finance** Sources: members' dues. **Activities** Events/meetings. **Events** *Annual Congress* Riga (Latvia) 2021, *Annual Congress* Riga (Latvia) 2020, *Annual Congress* Antwerp (Belgium) 2018, *Annual Congress* Maastricht (Netherlands) 2017, *Annual Congress* Bristol (UK) 2015.
Members Professional (Active); Associate; Student. Individuals in 9 countries:
Belgium, France, Germany, Italy, Netherlands, Portugal, Switzerland, UK, USA.
NGO Relations Member of (1): *European Federation of the Scientific Image (EFSI, no recent information)*.
[2022.10.19/XD8543/**D**]

♦ Association européenne de l'ILSMH / see Inclusion Europe – European Association of Societies of Persons with Intellectual Disability and their Families (#11144)
♦ Association européenne d'importateurs de produits finis (inactive)
♦ Association européenne de l'industrie de la bureautique et de l'informatique (inactive)
♦ Association européenne de l'industrie photographique (inactive)
♦ Association européenne de l'industrie du plâtre / see European Association of Plaster and Plaster Product Manufacturers (#06152)
♦ Association européenne des industries aérospatiales (inactive)
♦ Association européenne des industries du bois lamellé-collé (no recent information)
♦ Association européenne des industries de cartonnage (inactive)
♦ Association européenne des industries et commerces de boyauderie (#07854)
♦ Association européenne des industries de la galvanisation d'articles divers (#07383)
♦ Association européenne des industries de l'informatique et des télécommunications / see DIGITAL-EUROPE (#05073)
♦ Association européenne de l'industrie solaire / see Solar Heat Europe (#19674)
♦ Association européenne de l'industrie solaire thermique / see Solar Heat Europe (#19674)
♦ Association européenne des industries de plumes et articles de literie / see European Down and Feather Association (#06941)

- ♦ Association européenne des industries de produits de marque / see European Brands Association (#06397)
- ♦ Association européenne de l'industrie de transformation du papier à cigarettes / see European Rolling Paper Association (#08399)

♦ Association européenne Inédits (AEI) 02574

European Association 'Inédits'

Contact Centre national de l'audiovisuel, Rue de Centenaire 1b, L-3475 Dudelange, Luxembourg. E-mail: inedits.europe@gmail.com.
URL: http://inedits-europe.org/

History Jun 1991, Paris (France), following the issue of a *European Amateur Film Charter – Charte européenne des Inédits*, Mar 1989, Spa (Belgium). Registered in accordance with Belgian law. **Aims** Promote and coordinate research, restoration, archiving, conservation, safeguarding, improvement and diffusion of moving pictures on any aspect of social life and not destined for the professional audio-visual circuits; encourage creation and development of centres responsible for such activity in all European regions; initiate and develop cooperation in international registry, in technical, legal and methodological cooperation, and in exchange and co-production of amateur, unpublished film; encourage cooperation to save the unique cultural heritage such films represent. **Structure** General Assembly (annual); Governing Board. **Languages** English, French. **Staff** 0.50 FTE, paid. **Finance** None. **Activities** Projects/programmes; events/meetings; knowledge management/ information dissemination; training/education. **Events** *Annual meeting* Luxembourg (Luxembourg) 2009, *Annual meeting* Reus (Spain) 2008, *Annual meeting* Annecy (France) 2007, *Annual meeting* Brest (France) 2006, *Annual meeting* Nancy (France) 2005. **Publications** *AEI Newsletter* (12 a year); *Inédits Mémo. Jubilee Book* – series of essays on different aspects of inedits films; *Une guerre inconnue* – TV series. *Restor Inédits* – restoration of amateur films.

Members Active in 17 countries:
Belgium, Czechia, Denmark, Finland, France, Germany, Greece, Hungary, Italy, Luxembourg, Monaco, Netherlands, New Zealand, Portugal, Spain, Switzerland, UK. [2017.12.04/XD3277/**D**]

- ♦ Association européenne d'infirmières et infirmiers de dialyse et de transplantation – Association européenne pour les soins des reins (#06918)
- ♦ Association européenne pour l'information et les bibliothèques de santé / see European Association for Health Information and Libraries (#06064)
- ♦ Association européenne pour l'information et le conseil des jeunes / see European Youth Information and Counselling Agency (#09142)
- ♦ Association européenne pour l'information sur le développement local (#00143)
- ♦ Association européenne pour l'informatique de la navigation maritime (inactive)
- ♦ Association européenne pour l'informatique portuaire (inactive)
- ♦ Association européenne d'informatique théorique (#06253)
- ♦ Association européenne pour l'ingénierie et la médecine / see Educating Students in Engineering and Medicine (#05364)
- ♦ Association européenne des ingénieurs électriciens et électroniciens (inactive)
- ♦ Association Européenne des Ingrédient Spécifiques pour la nutrition animale et leur mélanges (#09720)
- ♦ Association européenne des institutions d'aménagement rural (#06198)
- ♦ Association Européenne des Institutions d'Enseignement Supérieur (#06086)
- ♦ Association européenne des institutions de loisirs des enfants et des jeunes (#06087)
- ♦ Association européenne des institutions paritaires / see Association Européenne des Institutions Paritaires de la Protection Sociale (#02575)

♦ Association Européenne des Institutions Paritaires de la Protection Sociale (AEIP) 02575

European Association of Paritarian Institutions of Social Protection

Main Office Rue Montoyer 24, 1000 Brussels, Belgium. T. +3222335421. Fax +3222335429. E-mail: general@aeip.net.
Exec Dir address not obtained.
URL: http://www.aeip.net/

History Sep 1996. Statutes adopted 18 Feb 1997, Brussels (Belgium); modified 24 Nov 2007, Brussels, and 6 Mar 2012, Brussels. Former names and other names: *Association européenne des institutions paritaires (AEIP)* – former; *European Association of Paritarian Institutions* – former. Registration: Banque-Carrefour des Entreprises, No/ID: 0461.338.532, Start date: 11 Sep 1997, Belgium; EU Transparency Register, No/ID: 69133399372-91, Start date: 21 Aug 2012. **Aims** Promote development of representative *management* as a means of social protection; offer to institutions of social protection and social partners the possibility of exchanges on negotiation and management of social funds set up by collective agreements beyond national reference systems; promote equal partnership as of employers' and employees' representatives as a way of optimizing the social coverage of workers who are increasingly concerned with mobility. **Structure** General Assembly (annual); Management Board. **Languages** English, French. **Staff** 4.00 FTE, paid. **Finance** Sources: members' dues. Annual budget: 500,000 EUR. **Activities** Advocacy/lobbying/activism; events/meetings. **Events** *Annual Conference* Brussels (Belgium) 2022, *Meeting on the Care Strategy* Brussels (Belgium) 2022, *World Pension Alliance and Transatlantic Conference* Melbourne, VIC (Australia) 2022, *Annual Transatlantic Conference* Brussels (Belgium) 2021, *Annual Transatlantic Conference* Brussels (Belgium) 2020. **Publications** Annual Activity Report.

Members Partner; Associate; Observer; Correspondant. Organizations in 12 countries:
Austria, Belgium, Finland, France, Germany, Greece, Ireland, Italy, Luxembourg, Netherlands, Spain, Switzerland.

NGO Relations Member of (2): *European Alliance for Mental Health – Employment & Work (EUMH Alliance, #05875)*; *World Pension Alliance (WPA, #21719)*. Partner of (1): *Education and Solidarity Network (#05374)*. [2022/XD6194/**D**]

- ♦ Association Européenne des institutions de retraite du secteur public (#06180)
- ♦ Association européenne des instituts de recherche et de formation en matière de développement (#06012)
- ♦ Association européenne d'instituts de transport (inactive)
- ♦ Association européenne pour une interaction entre les organismes universitaires (inactive)
- ♦ Association européenne pour l'interopérabilité ferroviaire (inactive)
- ♦ Association Européenne des Inventeurs (inactive)
- ♦ Association européenne des investisseurs individuels (inactive)
- ♦ Association européenne de l'irrigation (#07603)
- ♦ Association européenne de la jeune Croix-Bleue (inactive)
- ♦ Association européenne des jeunes demandeurs d'emploi européens (inactive)

♦ Association Européenne des Jeunes Entrepreneurs (AEJE) 02576

Pres 9c rue des Balayeurs, 67000 Strasbourg, France. T. +33618606560. E-mail: aeje@jeunes-entrepreneurs.eu.
URL: http://www.jeunes-entrepreneurs.eu/

History Jul 2010. EU Transparency Register: 901016036362-23. **Aims** Work in favour of young entrepreneurs through assistance and support, and through examining how to improve their status at European level, in cooperation with the institutions. **Activities** Events/meetings. **Members** Full (around 600) in 17 countries. Membership countries not specified. [2019.02.21/XM5234/**D**]

- ♦ Association européenne des jeunes historiens (inactive)
- ♦ Association européenne des jeunes médiateurs (no recent information)
- ♦ Association européenne des jeux et sports traditionnels (#08931)
- ♦ Association européenne des juristes pour la démocratie et les droits de l'homme dans le monde (#06105)
- ♦ Association européenne des juristes d'entreprises (#06686)
- ♦ Association européenne des kinésithérapeutes photographes et cinéastes (inactive)
- ♦ Association européenne de laboratoires de télédétection (#06191)
- ♦ Association Européenne de l'Eau (#09080)
- ♦ Association européenne de lexicographie (#06107)
- ♦ Association européenne de libre-échange (#05391)
- ♦ Association européenne de la Ligue internationale des associations pour les personnes handicapées mentales / see Inclusion Europe – European Association of Societies of Persons with Intellectual Disability and their Families (#11144)
- ♦ Association européenne des ligues nationales contre le cancer (#02500)
- ♦ Association européenne des linguistes et des professeurs de langues (no recent information)
- ♦ Association européenne du loisir (inactive)
- ♦ Association européenne des loteries d'Etat / see European State Lotteries and Toto Association (#08833)
- ♦ Association Européenne des Loteries et Totos d'Etat (#08833)
- ♦ Association européenne des loueurs de voitures et de camions (inactive)
- ♦ Association européenne des magistrats (#06100)
- ♦ Association européenne des maîtres luthiers et archetiers (#06273)
- ♦ Association européenne pour la maîtrise de l'eau / see European Water Association (#09080)
- ♦ Association européenne pour la maladie de Parkinson (#08145)
- ♦ Association européenne des maladies rares / see EURORDIS – Rare Diseases Europe (#09175)
- ♦ Association européenne de maladies rénales – Association européenne de dialyse et de transplantation (#08353)
- ♦ Association européenne pour les mammifères marins (#05938)
- ♦ Association européenne de management et de marketing financiers / see Efma (#05386)
- ♦ Association européenne pour un marché audiovisuel indépendant (inactive)
- ♦ Association européenne des marchés aux bestiaux (#06109)
- ♦ Association européenne du marketing direct (inactive)
- ♦ Association européenne de marketing financier / see Efma (#05386)
- ♦ Association européenne de matériel didactique / see Worlddidac Association (#21361)
- ♦ Association européenne de Mayanistes (#02126)
- ♦ Association européenne de médecine interne / see European Federation of Internal Medicine (#07147)
- ♦ Association européenne de médecine interne d'ensemble / see European Federation of Internal Medicine (#07147)
- ♦ Association européenne de médecine nucléaire (#06136)
- ♦ Association européenne de médecine périnatale (#06148)
- ♦ Association Européenne de Médecine Prédictive et Personnalisée (#06163)
- ♦ Association européenne de médecine thermale et bioclimatologie (inactive)
- ♦ Association européenne des médecins des équipes de football (inactive)

♦ Association européenne des médecins des hôpitaux (AEMH) 02577

European Association of Senior Hospital Physicians – Asociación Europea de Médicos de Hospitales – Europäische Vereinigung der Leitenden Krankenhausärzte – Associação Européia dos Médicos Hospitalares – Associazione Europea dei Medici Ospedalieri – Europese Vereniging van Stafartsen – Europaeiske Overlaegeforening

Secretariat Rue Guimard 15, 1040 Brussels, Belgium. T. +3227366066. Fax +3227329972. E-mail: secretariat@aemh.org.
Pres address not obtained.
URL: http://www.aemh.org/

History 1963. Current statutes adopted 2002. Registration: EU Transparency Register, No/ID: 29179039021-46. **Aims** Promote public health care at the European level, in particular in the hospital sector; for this purpose, study conditions for practice of the medical profession in hospitals, forms of hospital health care in the various countries, modalities for cooperation with other members of the hospital community and possibilities for improving care and treatment of patients in hospital. **Structure** Plenary Assembly (annual); Board; Executive Committee; Working Groups. **Languages** English, French. **Staff** 0.50 FTE, paid. **Finance** Members' dues. **Activities** Training/education; monitoring/evaluation; networking/liaising; events/meetings; certification/accreditation. **Events** *Annual Plenary Assembly* Oslo (Norway) 2019, *Annual Plenary Assembly* Lisbon (Portugal) 2018, *Annual Plenary Assembly* Vienna (Austria) 2015, *Annual Plenary Assembly* Stockholm (Sweden) 2014, *Patient safety – antimicrobial resistant* Stockholm (Sweden) 2014.

Members National organizations of senior hospital doctors (one per country) in 15 countries:
Austria, Belgium, Croatia, France, Germany, Greece, Italy, Luxembourg, Norway, Portugal, Romania, Slovakia, Spain, Sweden, Switzerland.

NGO Relations Observer status with: *European Federation of Salaried Doctors (#07209)*; *European Forum of Medical Associations and WHO (EFMA, #07320)*; *European Union of Medical Specialists (UEMS, #09001)*; *Standing Committee of European Doctors (#19955)*. Associated organizations: *European Medical Students' Association (EMSA, #07764)*; *European Junior Doctors Association (EJD, #07620)*. [2020.03.03/XD0580/**D**]

- ♦ Association européenne des média numériques / see DOT Europe (#05125)
- ♦ Association européenne du médicament générique / see Medicines for Europe (#16633)
- ♦ Association européenne et méditerranéenne de coloproctologie / see Mediterranean Society of Coloproctology (#16676)
- ♦ Association européenne de membres de Corps et Organismes Publics de Sécurité et de Défense (internationally oriented national body)
- ♦ Association européenne de la mesure industrielle (inactive)
- ♦ Association européenne de mesures par ordinateur (inactive)
- ♦ Association européenne de la métallurgie des poudres (#08260)

♦ Association européenne des métaux (EUROMETAUX) 02578

European Association of Metals

SG Av de Tervueren 168, Box 13, 1150 Brussels, Belgium. T. +3227756311. Fax +3227790523. E-mail: eurometaux@eurometaux.be.
Office Manager address not obtained.
URL: http://www.eurometaux.eu/

History 1957, Paris (France). Statutes modified: 22 Jun 1988; 22 May 1997. Current statutes adopted: 20 Jan 2000; since modified (date not specified). Former names and other names: *Comité de liaison des industries de métaux non-ferreux de la Communauté européenne (CDL)* – former (1957). Registration: Banque-Carrefour des Entreprises, No/ID: 0421.833.204, Start date: 19 Aug 1981, Belgium; EU Transparency Register, No/ID: 61650796093-48. **Aims** Promote sustainable production, use and recycling of non-ferrous metals in europe. **Structure** General Assembly (annual); Executive Committee; Management Board; Committees (5); Secretariat. **Languages** English. **Staff** 14.00 FTE, paid. **Activities** Events/meetings; knowledge management/information dissemination; networking/liaising. **Events** *General Assembly* Brussels (Belgium) 2022, *General Assembly* Brussels (Belgium) 2017, *Annual environment health and safety seminar* Brussels (Belgium) 2008, *Annual environment health and safety seminar* Brussels (Belgium) 2005, *Annual environment, health and safety seminar* Brussels (Belgium) 2004. **Publications** *Flash Infos*. Annual Report; activity reports; position papers; meeting proceedings; brochures; press releases.

Members Company (20); International (7); National (15); Associate (14); EU Commodities (6). National associations in 13 countries:
Austria, Belgium, Bulgaria, Finland, France, Germany, Italy, Netherlands, Norway, Spain, Sweden, Switzerland, UK.
International members (6):
European Aluminium (#05893); *European Copper Institute (ECI, #06796)*; *European Precious Metals Federation (EPMF, #08267)*; *International Lead Association (ILA, #14009)*; *International Zinc Association (IZA, #15942) (Europe)*; *Nickel Institute (#17133)*.
Associate members include 8 organizations listed in this Yearbook:
Association of European Automotive and Industrial Battery Manufacturers (EUROBAT, #02498); *Cobalt Institute (CI, #04076)*; *Euroalliages (#05629)*; *European Powder Metallurgy Association (EPMA, #08260)*; *International Antimony Association (i2a, #11657)*; *International Molybdenum Association (IMOA, #14178)*; *RECHARGE (#18627)*; *Vanadium International Technical Committee (VANITEC, #20746)*.

IGO Relations Recognized by: *European Commission (EC, #06633)*. Permanent observer to: *International Copper Study Group (ICSG, #12963)*; *International Lead and Zinc Study Group (ILZSG, #14012)*. Observer to: *International Commission of the Schelde River (#12727)*. **NGO Relations** Member of (6): *AEGIS Europe*; *Alliance for a Competitive European Industry (ACEI, #00670)*; *European Policy Centre (EPC, #08240)*; *Industry4Europe (#11181)*; *International Council on Mining and Metals (ICMM, #13048)*; *METALS FOR BUILDINGS (#16737)*. Associate expert of: *Business and Industry Advisory Committee to the OECD (BIAC, #03385)*.
[2023/XE0508/ty/**D**]

♦ Association européenne de méthodes médicales nouvelles 02579

Contact address not obtained. T. +352250226.

History Founded 25 Feb 1987, Luxembourg, when statutes were adopted. **Aims** Promote research, develop exchanges and gather evidence for the *efficacity* of new *medical methods*; act as a catalyst in creative innovation but also moderate hasty conclusions. **Structure** General Assembly (annual); Administrative Council. Sections (4): Acupuncture; Laser; Magnetotherapy; Phytotherapy. **Languages** English, French, German. **Staff** Voluntary. **Finance** Members' dues. Budget (annual): US$ 5,000. **Activities** Events/meetings. **Events** *Congress* Pétange (Luxembourg) 2011, *Congrès / Congress* Pétange (Luxembourg) 2010, *Congrès* Luxembourg (Luxembourg) 2009, *Congress* Luxembourg 2008, *Congrès* Luxembourg (Luxembourg) 2008. **Publications** *La santé par l'électrothérapie* by Chou Quang Pham and Robert Vansinay. Reprints; bibliographies; other documents.

Members Active; Sympathizer; Honorary. Active members 10 countries:
Belgium, Côte d'Ivoire, France, Germany, Luxembourg, Morocco, Spain, Tunisia, UK, USA. [2011.10.20/XD1458/v/**D**]

- ♦ Association européenne des meuniers exportateurs (inactive)
- ♦ Association européenne de micro-ondes (#07796)
- ♦ Association européenne des minéraux pour l'alimentation animale (#07733)
- ♦ Association européenne des moniteurs d'auto-école / see Fédération européenne des auto-écoles (#09560)
- ♦ Association européenne des moniteurs de plongée professionnels (#06663)
- ♦ Association européenne du moulinage (inactive)
- ♦ Association européenne des musées de l'histoire des sciences médicales (#06125)
- ♦ Association européenne pour la musique à l'école (#06127)
- ♦ Association européenne de navigation de plaisance (#06376)
- ♦ Association européenne de négociants en timbre-poste (inactive)
- ♦ Association européenne des négociateurs en valeurs mobilières (inactive)
- ♦ Association européenne de neuroendocrinologie (#08040)
- ♦ Association européenne /NOE tourisme/ (inactive)
- ♦ Association européenne de numérotation des articles / see GS1 (#10809)
- ♦ Association européenne océanique (inactive)
- ♦ Association européenne des officiers de l'Etat civil (#05760)
- ♦ Association européenne des officiers professionnels sapeurs-pompiers (no recent information)
- ♦ Association Européenne des Sous-Officiers de Réserve / see Confédération Interalliée des Sous-Officiers de Réserve (#04556)
- ♦ Association européenne des opérateurs de satellites / see Global Satellite Operators' Association (#10586)
- ♦ Association européenne des orchestres d'amateurs (inactive)
- ♦ Association européenne d'organisations d'aides et de soins à domicile (inactive)
- ♦ Association européenne des organisations non-gouvernementales sur la question de la Palestine / see European Association for Non-Governmental Organizations Working on Palestine (#06135)
- ♦ Association européenne des organisations non-gouvernementales travaillant sur la Palestine (#06135)
- ♦ Association Européenne des Organisations de Practiciens de l'Insolvabilité / see European Insolvency Practitioners Association (#07543)
- ♦ Association Européenne des Organisations de Producteurs dans le secteur de la pêche (#06041)
- ♦ Association européenne des organisations de recherche sous contrat (inactive)
- ♦ Association européenne pour l'orientation, la guidance et l'information scolaires et professionnelles (inactive)
- ♦ Association européenne pour l'osséointégration (#06139)
- ♦ Association européenne de l'outillage électrique (#08264)
- ♦ Association européenne d'outils de coupe (#06873)
- ♦ Association européenne de paléontologues des vertébrés (#06266)
- ♦ Association européenne des parents d'élèves / see European Parents' Association (#08142)
- ♦ Association européenne de la parfumerie, des produits cosmétiques et de toilette / see Cosmetics Europe – The Personal Care Association (#04852)
- ♦ Association européenne de pathologie clinique (inactive)
- ♦ Association Européenne de la Pensée Libre (#06048)
- ♦ Association européenne de périodiques scolaires (inactive)
- ♦ Association Européenne des Personnes Chargées de Veiller au Respect de la Réglementation Relative aux Dispositifs Médicaux (unconfirmed)
- ♦ Association européenne pour la petite hydraulique (#08495)
- ♦ Association Européenne de la Pétrochimie / see European Petrochemical Association, The (#08192)
- ♦ Association européenne de pharma biotechnologie (#06150)
- ♦ Association européenne des pharmaciens des hôpitaux (#06074)
- ♦ Association européenne des e-pharmacies / see European Association of E-Pharmacies (#06029)
- ♦ Association européenne de photochimie (#08204)
- ♦ Association européenne des photographes professionnels (inactive)
- ♦ Association européenne des podologues (inactive)
- ♦ Association européenne des porteurs d'un implant cochléaire (#05979)
- ♦ Association européenne des ports de pêche et criées (inactive)
- ♦ Association européenne des praticiens des procédures collectives / see INSOL Europe (#11231)

♦ Association européenne de pratiques multidisciplinaires en santé mentale de l'enfant, l'adolescent et de la famille (AESMEAF) 02580

Contact address not obtained. T. +33467541245. Fax +33467541245.

History Founded 22 Mar 1992, Paris (France). **Aims** Create a network of information exchanges. **Structure** General Assembly; Board of Directors; Bureau. **Languages** English, French, German, Italian, Spanish. **Staff** 8.00 FTE, voluntary. **Finance** Self-financing. **Activities** Events/meetings.

Members Individuals and organizations in 9 countries:
Belgium, France, Germany, Greece, Italy, Norway, Portugal, Spain, Switzerland. [2012.09.12/XD5644/**D**]

- ♦ Association européenne pour la presse d'information sur l'antiquité, la brocante et la collection (inactive)
- ♦ Association Européenne de la presse militaire (#07803)
- ♦ Association européenne de la presse musicale / see Presse musicale internationale (#18488)
- ♦ Association européenne de prévision technologique (inactive)
- ♦ Association européenne principale des fabricants des panneaux infrarouges lumineux à gaz / see Europäischer Leit-Verband der Hersteller von Gas-Infrarot- Hellstrahlern (#05758)
- ♦ Association européenne principale des fabricants de panneaux radiants lumineux à gaz / see Europäischer Leit-Verband der Hersteller von Gas-Infrarot- Hellstrahlern (#05758)
- ♦ Association européenne des producteurs d'acides gras / see European Oleochemicals and Allied Products Group (#08081)
- ♦ Association européenne de producteurs et de distributeurs de médicaments naturels (no recent information)
- ♦ Association européenne des producteurs d'enrobés bitumineux (#05920)
- ♦ Association européenne des producteurs de matériel de chauffage en fonte (inactive)
- ♦ Association européenne de producteurs de mollusques (#07818)
- ♦ Association européenne des producteurs de mozzarella (inactive)
- ♦ Association européenne des producteurs de papier décoratif (no recent information)
- ♦ Association européenne des producteurs de protéines unicellulaires (inactive)
- ♦ Association européenne des producteurs et revendeurs de feuilles plastiques décoratives et de papeterie (inactive)
- ♦ Association européenne des producteurs de solvants oxygénés (#17923)
- ♦ Association Européenne des Produits d'Investissement Structurés (#08845)
- ♦ Association européenne des produits de lactosérum (#09093)
- ♦ Association européenne des produits de lactosérum (inactive)
- ♦ Association européenne des professeurs d'espagnol (#02127)
- ♦ Association européenne de professeurs d'instruments à cordes (#08842)
- ♦ Association européenne de professeurs de langues anciennes de l'enseignement supérieur (#06260)
- ♦ Association européenne des professionnel/-les de l'évaluation des menaces (#02547)
- ♦ Association européenne des Professions immobilières (#06186)
- ♦ Association européenne des professions supérieures d'ingénieurs et de la technique (#07484)
- ♦ Association européenne pour le progrès social et culturel (inactive)
- ♦ Association Européenne de la Projection Thermique (#08908)
- ♦ Association européenne des promoteurs de centres commerciaux (inactive)
- ♦ Association Européenne de promotion des droits et de soutien des Personnes en Situation de Fragilité (unconfirmed)
- ♦ Association européenne pour la promotion des études du comportement dynamique des matériaux et applications / see DYMAT Association (#05148)
- ♦ Association européenne pour la promotion de l'hygiène des mains (inactive)
- ♦ Association européenne de promotion de la pêche durable et responsable / see Blue Fish Europe (#03284)
- ♦ Association européenne pour la promotion de la poésie (inactive)
- ♦ Association européenne de promotion des quadricycles (#08309)
- ♦ Association européenne pour la promotion de la santé / see European network for health promotion and economic development (#07920)
- ♦ Association européenne pour la promotion de la science et de la technologie (#05927)
- ♦ Association européenne de propriétaires de remorqueurs (#08956)
- ♦ Association européenne pour la protection des oeuvres et services cryptés / see Audiovisual Anti-Piracy Alliance (#03015)
- ♦ Association européenne pour la protection passive contre l'incendie (#06143)
- ♦ Association européenne des protéines végétales (#09047)
- ♦ Association européenne de psychiatrie (#08290)
- ♦ Association européenne de psychiatrie gériatrique (#06057)
- ♦ Association européenne de psycholinguistique (inactive)
- ♦ Association Européenne pour la Psychologie Aéronautique (#05950)
- ♦ Association européenne pour la psychologie humaniste (inactive)
- ♦ Association Européenne de Psychologie Transpersonnelle (#08938)

♦ Association européenne de psychopathologie de l'enfant et de l'adolescent (AEPEA) 02581

Pres c/o Hôpital Necker Enfants, 149 rue de Sèvres, 75015 Paris, France.
URL: http://www.aepea.org/

History 1996. **Aims** Group specialists interested in psychopathology of children and adolescents; promote, within Europe, meetings and exchanges between specialists and speakers of the various European countries in the field of the psychopathology of the child and the adolescent; create a European network of research in this field; sensitize the public authorities of the European States to these questions. **Structure** General Assembly (annual). Council, comprising President, Vice-President, Secretary, Treasurer and 8 members. Scientific Council of 32 members. **Languages** French. **Staff** Voluntary. **Finance** Members' dues. **Activities** Coordinates research at European level; organizes colloquia and international and national meetings; disseminates information. In the area of research, proposes to: set up an European research network in psychopathology; put protocols in place for common research concerning developmental psychopathology; offer expertise on research projects carried out by members of the association. **Events** *Congrès* Paris (France) 2023, *Congrès* Paris (France) 2021, *Congrès* Bilbao (Spain) 2018, *Congress* Brussels (Belgium) 2014, *Evaluer pour bien soigner – l'évaluation, un défi pour la psychopathologie* Paris (France) 2004. **Publications** *Lettre d'Information*.

Members Individuals in 21 countries:
Argentina, Belgium, Brazil, Colombia, Denmark, France, Greece, Iceland, Israel, Italy, Lebanon, Luxembourg, Monaco, Norway, Palestine, Portugal, Spain, Switzerland, Syrian AR, Tunisia, UK. [2021/XD7675/v/**D**]

- ♦ Association européenne de psychothérapie (#06176)
- ♦ Association Européenne de Psychothérapie Corporelle (#05958)
- ♦ Association européenne pour la psycho-thérapie neuro-linguistique (#06131)
- ♦ Association européenne de pyrotechnie (inactive)
- ♦ Association européenne de radiologie (inactive)
- ♦ Association européenne des radios (#02535)
- ♦ Association européenne pour la rationalisation des échanges d'énergie-gaz (#06224)
- ♦ Association européenne de réassurance et d'assurances mutuelles (inactive)
- ♦ Association européenne de recherche en activité adaptée / see European Federation of Adapted Physical Activity (#07038)
- ♦ Association européenne pour la recherche en adolescence (#06192)
- ♦ Association européenne de recherche sur le cancer (#05962)
- ♦ Association européenne de la recherche en économie industrielle (#06193)
- ♦ Association européenne de recherche en education (#06967)
- ♦ Association européenne pour la recherche sur la pomme de terre (#06160)
- ♦ Association européenne de recherche sur les protéagineux (inactive)
- ♦ Association européenne de recherches biologiques (no recent information)
- ♦ Association européenne de recherches sur la glande thyroïde / see European Thyroid Association (#08913)
- ♦ Association européenne des recycleurs de plastiques / see Plastics Recyclers Europe (#18394)
- ♦ Association européenne de rédacteurs-en-chef de publications relatives aux sciences de la terre (inactive)
- ♦ Association européenne de rédacteurs d'ouvrages scientifiques (#06201)
- ♦ Association européenne des rédacteurs de périodiques de chimie et de physique (inactive)
- ♦ Association européenne pour la réduction de la pollution due aux fibres (inactive)
- ♦ Association européenne de réflexion sur les religions du monde dans l'éducation (#06279)
- ♦ Association européenne des régies de quartier (internationally oriented national body)
- ♦ Association européenne pour la réhabilitation sociale du mourir (inactive)
- ♦ Association européenne de représentants territoriaux de l'état (#06220)
- ♦ Association européenne des réserves naturelles libres (inactive)
- ♦ Association européenne pour les ressources linguistiques (#07650)
- ♦ Association européenne de la restauration moderne / see Serving Europe (#19248)
- ♦ Association européenne de rhinologie (#08388)
- ♦ Association européenne du rhum (no recent information)
- ♦ Association Européenne du Rorschach pour le Système Intégré / see Comprehensive System International Rorschach Association (#04421)
- ♦ Association européenne de rotogravure (#08404)
- ♦ Association européenne rubans, tresses, tissus élastiques (inactive)
- ♦ Association européenne de science régionale (#08346)
- ♦ Association européenne pour les sciences chimiques et moléculaires / see European Chemical Society (#06524)
- ♦ Association européenne pour les sciences cognitives de la musique (#08555)
- ♦ Association européenne des sciences et techniques de la mer (no recent information)

♦ Association européenne de la sécurité sur les campus (inactive)
♦ Association européenne pour la sécurité des consommateurs (inactive)
♦ Association européenne de seniors golfeurs (#08464)
♦ Association européenne des services d'information (no recent information)
♦ Association européenne des services informatiques (inactive)
♦ Association européenne des services d'investissement (inactive)
♦ Association Européenne SIBIU2020 pour L'Éducation et la Culture (unconfirmed)
♦ Association européenne de la sidérurgie (#08835)
♦ Association européenne de sinologie / see European Association for Chinese Studies (#05973)
♦ Association européenne des sociétés géologiques (#02513)
♦ Association européenne de sociétés de neurochirurgie (#06134)
♦ Association européenne des sociétés de télédétection (#06190)
♦ Association européenne de soins et aides à domicile (inactive)
♦ Association européenne pour les soins palliatifs (#06141)
♦ Association Européenne pour les Soins de Soutien au Développement (#06009)
♦ Association européenne des spécialités grand public / see Association of the European Self-Care Industry (#02543)
♦ Association européenne des spécialités pharmaceutiques grand public (#02543)
♦ Association européenne des stations nucléaires à haute température (inactive)
♦ Association européenne pour la sûreté, la fiabilité et les données (#08420)
♦ Association européenne pour le syndrome de Down (#06942)
♦ Association européenne du tapis / see European Carpet and Rug Association (#06452)
♦ Association européenne de technologie en pultrusion (#08307)
♦ Association Européenne des Technologies de l'Embryon / see Association européenne de transfert embryonnaire (#02582)
♦ Association européenne des télévisions régionales (#06189)
♦ Association européenne de terminologie (#06252)
♦ Association européenne des textiles polyoléfines (inactive)
♦ Association européenne de thanatologie (inactive)
♦ Association européenne de théologie catholique (#08540)
♦ Association européenne de théologiens évangéliques (#09727)
♦ Association Européenne de Thérapie Familiale (#07031)
♦ Association européenne du thermalisme et du climatisme (#08805)
♦ Association européenne de thermographie (inactive)
♦ Association européenne de thermologie (#06254)
♦ Association européenne thyroïde / see European Thyroid Association (#08913)
♦ Association européenne de tisseurs de verre (no recent information)
♦ Association européenne de tourisme pédestre / see European Ramblers' Association (#08328)
♦ Association européenne du traitement de surface sur aluminium (#06242)

♦ Association européenne de transfert embryonnaire (AETE) 02582

European Embryo Transfer Association

Main Office c/o ALLICE, 149 Rue de Bercy, 75595 Paris CEDEX 12, France. E-mail: info@aete.eu.
URL: http://www.aete.eu/

History Former names and other names: *Association européenne de transferts embryonnaires vétérinaires* – former; *Association of Embryo Technology in Europe* – alias; *Association Européenne des Technologies de l'Embryon* – alias. Registration: France. **Aims** Facilitate the diffusion and application of knowledge relative to embryo transfer in mammals. **Structure** Board. **Languages** English. **Finance** Members' dues. **Events** *AETE Meeting* Greece 2023, *AETE Meeting* Utrecht (Netherlands) 2022, *AETE Meeting* 2021, *AETE Meeting* 2020, *AETE Meeting* Murcia (Spain) 2019. **Publications** *AETE Newsletter*. [2021/XD7515/**D**]

♦ Association européenne de transferts embryonnaires vétérinaires / see Association européenne de transfert embryonnaire (#02582)
♦ Association européenne pour le transfert des technologies, de l'innovation et de l'information industrielle (#06259)
♦ Association européenne de transplantation des tissus de l'appareil locomoteur (inactive)
♦ Association européenne du transport et convoyage de valeurs (#08458)
♦ Association européenne pour les transports exceptionnels et les grues automobiles / see European Association of Abnormal Road Transport and Mobile Cranes (#05923)

♦ Association Européenne des Trésors et Musées d'Eglises (Europae Thesauri) 02583

European Association of Treasures and Churchesmuseums

Address not obtained.
URL: http://www.europaethesauri.eu/

History 2004. **Aims** Preserve and enhance European *religious heritage*.
Members Individuals in 10 countries:
Austria, Belgium, France, Germany, Italy, Luxembourg, Netherlands, Portugal, Spain, UK. [2019/XM8579/**D**]

♦ Association européenne du tube d'acier (#08837)
♦ Association européenne des tubes carton (#06797)
♦ Association européenne de l'université (#09027)
♦ Association européenne des universités et écoles d'optométrie (inactive)
♦ Association européenne des véhicules électriques – batteries, hybrides et piles à combustible / see European Association for Electromobility (#06024)
♦ Association européenne des véhicules électriques routiers / see European Association for Electromobility (#06024)
♦ Association européenne pour la vente à distance (no recent information)
♦ Association européenne des viandes (inactive)
♦ Association européenne des villes intéressées par l'utilisation de véhicules électriques (#05974)
♦ Association européenne des villes et régions historiques (#06068)

♦ Association européenne des villes de la toison d'or 02584

Contact Fondation Toison d'Or, Rue de la Procession 4, 1331 Rosières, Belgium. T. +3226535324. Fax +3226541908.

History Founded 1970, Bruges (Belgium), by *Fondation Toison d'Or – Académie Européenne d'Histoire (#09830)*. **Aims** Promote collaboration between cities associated with the Order of the Golden Fleece or the Maison de Bourgogne.
Members Cities in 11 countries:
Austria, Belgium, Czechia, France, Germany, Hungary, Italy, Netherlands, Portugal, Slovakia, Spain. [2011.09.06/XM2418/**D**]

♦ Association Européenne des voies vertes (#07412)
♦ Association Européenne des Volailles Rurales (#08416)
♦ Association européenne des voyages d'affaires (inactive)
♦ Association européenne pour les zones de montagne / see Euromontana (#05737)
♦ Association Europe-Finances-Régulations (internationally oriented national body)
♦ Association Europe des kinésithérapeutes pour la maladie de Parkinson (#02860)
♦ Association de l'Europe occidentale pour la psychologie aéronautique / see European Association for Aviation Psychology (#05950)

♦ Association of Europe's Coalfield Regions (EURACOM) 02585

Pres Hôtel de Ville, BP 49, 62801 Lievin CEDEX, France. T. +33321448625. Fax +33321448622. E-mail: euracom@nordnet.fr.
Gen Sec Ctr administratif – Les Grands Bureaux, 45 rue Edouard Vaillant, BP 49, 62801 Lievin, France. T. +33321448625. Fax +33321448622. E-mail: acom.france@nordnet.fr.
URL: https://www.facebook.com/Euracom-633730626637933

History 1989. Also referred to as *Partnership of Mining Areas – Association des zones minières – Asociación de Zonas Mineras – Partnerschaft der Bergbauregionen* and *Action for Mining Communities – Action pour les régions minières – Acción para las Comarcas Mineras – Aktion für Bergbauregionen*. Previously also referred to as *European Association of Local Authorities of Coal Mining Areas (EUR-ACOM)*. **Aims** Represent the interests of local authorities situated in the current or former coal mining regions of the European Union at European level. **Structure** Executive Committee. **Languages** English, French, German, Polish, Spanish. **Staff** 1.00 FTE, paid. **Finance** Members' dues. **Activities** Advocacy/lobbying/activism; events/meetings; projects/programmes. **Events** *Conference* Houthalen-Helchteren (Belgium) 2012. **Publications** *Promoting Entrepreneurship and New SMEs in the Mining Regions*.
Members National associations of coal mining municipalities (over 800) in 9 countries:
Czechia, France, Germany, Poland, Russia, Slovenia, Spain, UK, Ukraine. [2017.01.11/XD5482/**D**]

♦ Association Europe and Society 02586

Europe et Société – Europa y Sociedad – Europa und Gesellschaft – Europa e Società

Contact address not obtained. T. +33155651919. Fax +33147630883. E-mail: europeetsociete@wanadoo.fr.

History 15 Nov 1985, Paris (France). Founded by Jacques Moreau. Former names and other names: *Foundation Europe and Society* – former; *Fondation Europe et société* – former; *Stiftung Europa und Gesellschaft* – former. Registration: France. **Aims** Allow *economic* and *social* actors to think together; suggest initiatives which could help master unavoidable evolutions of the European social and economic system. **Structure** Board, consisting of Chairman, Vice-Chairman, Treasurer and General Delegate. **Staff** 8.00 FTE, paid. **Activities** Organizes European conferences, colloquia, symposia, study days, auditions and working parties. **Events** *Conference* Paris (France) 2011, *Conference* Paris (France) 2010, *Conference* Paris (France) 2009, *Colloque* Paris (France) 2008, *Conference* Paris (France) 2008. **Publications** *Les cahiers de la Fondation* (2 a year) in English, French; *La lettre de la Fondation* in English, French. **Members** Firms, professional and trade union organizations, institutions (45). Membership countries not specified. [2012/XF0719/**F**]

♦ Association Europe – Tiers-monde / see eu can aid (#05570)
♦ Association of Evangelical Missions (internationally oriented national body)
♦ Association of Evangelical Relief and Development Organizations / see Accord Network

♦ Association of Evangelicals in Africa (AEA) 02587

Association des évangéliques d'Afrique

Gen Sec PO Box 49332, Nairobi, 00100, Kenya. E-mail: info@aeafrica.org.
Communications Manager address not obtained.
URL: http://www.aeafrica.org/

History 26 Feb 1966, Limuru (Kenya). Founded at a meeting of 192 evangelical Christian leaders from 23 African nations and missionaries from other continents, following setting up of *'African Evangelical Office'*, 1961, Nairobi (Kenya). **Aims** Function as a centre for evangelical witness throughout Africa and Madagascar; strive for the furtherance of the Gospel; provide a working fellowship for all evangelical Churches and para-Church organizations. **Structure** General Assembly (every 4 years). General Council (meets every 2 years), consisting of President and Vice-President, Regional Associate Presidents, Chief Executives of National Fellowships, Executive Directors of Associate Members or their representatives, Heads of Special Member Churches, General Secretary and Associate General Secretary, Executive Secretaries of AEA Commissions (non-voting members) and AEA Treasurer. Executive Committee (meets annually), composed of President and Vice-President, Regional Associate Presidents, 3 members-at-large (representing Youth, Women and the Laity), General Secretary and Associate General Secretary, Treasurer, Executive Secretaries of AEA Commissions (non-voting members), any co-opted members (up to 3). General Secretariat. Regional Offices (8): Northern (Arabic); Western (Anglophone); Western (Francophone); Central (Francophone); Eastern (Anglophone); Southern (Anglophone); Oceanic (Francophone); Lusophone. Commissions (9): Evangelism and Missions (EMC); *Pan African Christian Women Alliance (PACWA, #18043)*; Ethics, Peace and Justice (EPJC); Prayer and Church Renewal (PCRC); Relief and Development (RDC); Theological and Christian Education (TCEC); Communications (CC); Evangelical Focus on Children (EFOC); Stewardship and Accountability (SAAC). Registered Trustees. **Languages** English, French. **Staff** 38.00 FTE, paid. **Finance** Sources: grants. **Activities** Maintains faculties of African Protestant Theology -*Bangui Evangelical Graduate School of Theology (BEST, no recent information)* (for French speakers) and *Nairobi Evangelical Graduate School of Theology (NEGST, no recent information)* (for English speakers). *'Department on Discipleship and Leadership Training'* organizes leadership training seminars for African Christian leaders and pastors in 29 countries, complemented by Church Growth workshops. *'Theological Education by Extension'* sponsors graduate schools, provides materials and services to Churches and schools for education by extension and offers courses in English, French and a number of local languages. *'Department on Development and Social Transformation'* serves the evangelical constituency and wider society with programmes aimed at empowering the poor, enhancing available resources and transforming society, enabling evangelical Churches to develop a positive attitude and involvement in relief, development and social transformation. *'Commission on Evangelism and Missions'* encourages and assists emerging indigenous mission organizations by providing a platform for fellowship and exchange of ideas and strategies. *'Pan African Christian Women Alliance'* encourages women to rise to their full potential. *'Communications Department'* organizes training programmes to equip pastors and Christian workers with skills to communicate and publishes materials from seminars and institutes. Communications Commission project: *Proclamation de l'évangile par les médias en Afrique (PEMA, see: #02587)*. *'Peace and Justice Department'* provides short courses on ethics and morality. *Christian Learning Materials Centre, Nairobi (CLMC, #03904)* produces Sunday School materials and Bible Study books for Christian colleges. *'Sports Outreach Ministry'* assists Churches in creating opportunities for expression of body-life, evangelism and discipleship. *Association for Christian Theological Education in Africa (ACTEA, #02431)* serves as a medium for contact and cooperation among evangelical theological colleges. *Win Africa for Jesus* declaration adopted 9 Nov 1993, Lagos (Nigeria). **Events** *General Assembly* Nairobi (Kenya) 2021, *General Assembly* Harare (Zimbabwe) 2015, *Quadrennial General Assembly* Accra (Ghana) 2014, *General Assembly* Freetown (Sierra Leone) 2014, *General Assembly* Botswana 2001. **Publications** *Afroscope* (4 a year) in English, French; *Prayer Bulletin* (4 a year) in English, French. Seminar and conference proceedings; news from members and Churches.
Members Full (28); Associate (34); Special (14). Membership groups over 60 million people in Africa. Full members in 28 countries:
Angola, Benin, Botswana, Burkina Faso, Central African Rep, Chad, Côte d'Ivoire, Egypt, Eswatini, Ethiopia, Gambia, Ghana, Guinea, Guinea-Bissau, Kenya, Liberia, Malawi, Mali, Mozambique, Namibia, Nigeria, Rwanda, Senegal, Sierra Leone, South Africa, Sudan, Zambia, Zimbabwe.
Associate members in 11 countries:
Burkina Faso, Côte d'Ivoire, Eswatini, Ghana, Kenya, Netherlands, New Zealand, South Africa, Tanzania UR, UK, Zimbabwe.
Of the above-mentioned Church groups, 22 organizations listed in this Yearbook:
- *Africa Cooperative Action Trust – International (ACAT International, #00165)*;
- *Africa Inland Mission International (AIM International, #00182)*;
- *Africa Ministry Resources (AMR)* (Kenya);
- *Biblica*;
- *Campus Crusade for Christ International (CCCI)*;
- *Compassion International (CI, #04413)* (Kenya);
- *Every Home for Christ International (EHCI, #09214)*;
- *Fellowship of Christian Communicators in Africa and Madagascar (FOCCAM, no recent information)*;
- *Leprosy Mission International (TLMI, #16446)*;
- *MAP International (#16569)*;
- *METDEV International (no recent information)*;
- *Navigators Africa Region (no recent information)*;
- *Open Door International: for the Economic Emancipation of the Woman Worker (ODI, no recent information)*;
- *Prison Fellowship International (PFI, #18503)* (Zimbabwe);
- *SIM International*;
- *Trans World Radio (TWR)*;
- *World Concern International (#21290)*;
- *World Mission Associates (no recent information)*;
- *World Relief*;
- *World Renew*;
- *World Vision International (WVI, #21904)*;
- *Youth for Christ International (YFCI, #22009)*.

Special members in 8 countries:
Burundi, Cameroon, Congo DR, Kenya, Madagascar, Rwanda, Tanzania UR, Togo.
Of the above-mentioned Church groups, 3 organizations listed in this Yearbook:
Communauté évangélique du centre de l'Afrique (CECA, no recent information); Communauté évangélique du Christ au coeur de l'Afrique (CECCA, no recent information); WEC International (WEC, #20850).
NGO Relations Member of (2): *Micah Global (#16741); World Evangelical Alliance (WEA, #21393).*
[2021/XD6561/y/**D**]

- ♦ Association of Evangelicals in Africa and Madagascar / see Association of Evangelicals in Africa (#02587)
- ♦ Association évangélique des Caraïbes (#09210)
- ♦ Association évangélique européenne d'accréditation / see European Council for Theological Education (#06846)
- ♦ Association des évangéliques d'Afrique (#02587)
- ♦ Association des évangéliques d'Afrique et de Madagascar / see Association of Evangelicals in Africa (#02587)
- ♦ Association for Evolutionary Economics (internationally oriented national body)
- ♦ Association for the Exchange of Culture and Science between East and West (no recent information)
- ♦ Association of Executive Recruiting Consultants / see Association of Executive Search and Leadership Consultants (#02588)
- ♦ Association of Executive Search Consultants / see Association of Executive Search and Leadership Consultants (#02588)

♦ Association of Executive Search and Leadership Consultants (AESC) 02588

Pres/CEO AESC Headquarters, Fifth Ave, 4th Floor, New York NY 10016, USA. T. +12123989556.
URL: http://www.aesc.org/

History 1959. Former names and other names: *Association of Executive Recruiting Consultants (AERC)* – former (1959 to 1982); *Association of Executive Search Consultants (AESC)* – former (1982 to 2014). **Aims** Promote the highest professional standards in retained executive search consulting; broaden public understanding of the executive search process, serve as an advocate for the interests of member firms. **Structure** Board of Directors; Regional councils (3); Regional office in Brussels (Belgium). **Languages** English. **Staff** 20.00 FTE, paid. **Finance** Members' dues. Career Management Service Revenue. **Activities** Training/education; certification/accreditation. **Events** *Global Conference* London (UK) 2022, *Global Conference* New York, NY (USA) 2020, *Global Conference* New York, NY (USA) 2019, *Asia Pacific conference* Singapore (Singapore) 2018, *Annual European Conference* Brussels (Belgium) 2017. **Publications** *Search Wire* (twice a month) – electronic newsletter. **Members** Firms (over 250) in 74 countries and territories (not specified).
[2022/XJ4532/**D**]

♦ Association for the Expansion of International Roles of the Languages of Continental Europe 02589

Association pour l'expansion du rôle international des langues d'Europe continentale (PERIL-Europe) – Association pro le Expansion del Rol International del Linguas de Europa Continental – Associatio pro Expansione Radiationis Internationalis Linguarum Europae Continentis
Pres 4 rue de la Monnaie, 30400 Villeneuve-lès-Avignon, France. T. +33413665228. Fax +33413665228. E-mail: escriveme.unpoc@yahoo.fr.
URL: http://www.interland.eu/

History Founded 1987. Sometimes also referred to as *Péril-Europe.* **Aims** Break the current hegemony of one national language – English – in all international relations; promote development of solutions enabling more justice and convenience in international communication for everyone, in Europe and in the world; promote Interlingua, or modern Latin, and *Esperanto.* **Structure** General Meeting (annual); national groups; cultural and humanitarian commissions. **Languages** Esperanto, French, Interlingua. **Staff** 1.50 FTE, voluntary. **Finance** Members' dues. Annual budget: euro 1,600. **Events** *English-speaking Europe or European-speaking Europe – which one would be the better for people ?* Avignon (France) 1990. **Publications** *Europe en péril?* (4 a year).
Members Full in 6 countries:
Australia, Belgium, France, Italy, Netherlands, UK. [2019.06.28/XD1971/**D**]

- ♦ Association pour l'expansion du rôle international des langues d'Europe continentale (#02589)
- ♦ Association pro le Expansion del Rol International del Linguas de Europa Continental (#02589)
- ♦ Association des expéditeurs des pays du Nord / see Nordiskt Speditörförbund (#17543)

♦ Association for Experiential Education (AEE) 02590

Exec Dir 2315 18th St S, St Petersburg FL 33712, USA. T. +13034408844. E-mail: membership@aee.org – anna@aee.org.
Main Website: http://www.aee.org/

History 1972, USA. Registration: Nonprofit 501(c)(3), No/ID: 84-0737619, Start date: 1977, USA. **Aims** Support the community and provide resources that help expand and elevate the capacity of Experiential Education around the world. **Structure** Board of Directors; Executive Director. **Languages** English. Some Standards translated into Mandarin Chinese. **Staff** 2.50 FTE, paid. **Finance** Sources: contributions; members' dues; revenue from activities/projects; sale of publications; sponsorship; subscriptions. Annual budget: 462,000 USD (2022). **Activities** Certification/accreditation; events/meetings; knowledge management/information dissemination; monitoring/evaluation; networking/liaising; publishing activities; research and development; research/documentation; standards/guidelines; training/education. **Events** *Annual International Conference* Madison, WI (USA) 2023, *Annual International Conference* Black Mountain, NC (USA) 2022, *Annual International Conference* St Petersburg, FL (USA) 2021, *Annual International Conference* St Petersburg, FL (USA) 2020, *Annual International Conference* Spokane, WA (USA) 2019. **Publications** *Journal of Experiential Education* (4 a year). Manuals; proceedings. **Members** Accredited; Organizational; Individual. Membership countries not specified. [2023.02.27/XM6316/**C**]

- ♦ Association des Experts Comptables et Commissaires aux Comptes en Europe (#02344)
- ♦ Association des experts-comptables internationaux (#02654)
- ♦ Association of Experts Dealing with the Protection and Enhancement of the Marine and Coastal Environment (inactive)
- ♦ Association des experts européens agréés (#02538)
- ♦ Association d'experts européens du bâtiment et de la construction (#02510)
- ♦ Association of Exploration Geochemists / see Association of Applied Geochemists (#02372)
- ♦ Association des exportateurs de sucre du Commonwealth (inactive)
- ♦ Association of Export Credit Insurers and of Export Promotion Organizations (inactive)
- ♦ Association expression européenne / see European Expression

♦ Association of Eye Banks of Asia (AEBA) 02591

Contact c/o Asia Cornea Soc, One Orchard Boulevard 13-03, Camden Medical Centre, Singapore 248649, Singapore.
URL: http://www.eyebankingasia.org/

History Jan 2009. Founded under the auspices of *Asia Cornea Society (ACS, #01262).* **Aims** Formulate Asian standards and guidelines in eye banking, accreditation and certification of member eye banks; set up eye banking and cornea transplantation research programmes. **Structure** Board. **NGO Relations** Member of: *Global Alliance of Eye Bank Associations (GAEBA, #10197).* [2015/XM4080/**E**]

- ♦ Association for Eye Research (inactive)
- ♦ Association de fabricants de claie de l'Afrique orientale (inactive)
- ♦ Association des fabricants européens d'accumulateurs (#02498)
- ♦ Association des fabricants européens d'appareils de contrôle / see Association des fabricants européens d'appareils de contrôle et de régulation (#02592)
- ♦ Association des fabricants européens d'appareils de contrôle pour le gaz / see Association des fabricants européens d'appareils de contrôle et de régulation (#02592)

♦ Association des fabricants européens d'appareils de contrôle et de régulation (AFECOR) 02592

European Control Manufacturers Association – Europäischer Verband der Regelgerätehersteller
Pres c/o Siemens AG, Berliner Ring 23, 76437 Rastatt, Germany. T. +497222598270. Fax +4972225989270.
URL: http://www.afecor.org/

History 1963, Brussels (Belgium). Title changed in 1968 when manufacturers of safety and control devices for installations and appliances using oil and energy sources other than gas were also admitted. Present name adopted to reflect the fact that members also provide controls and systems for building energy management (BEMS). Former names and other names: *European Gas Control Manufacturers' Association (EGCMA)* – former (1963 to 1968); *Association des fabricants européens d'appareils de contrôle pour le gaz* – former (1963 to 1968); *Verband Europäischer Gaskontrollgerätehersteller* – former (1963 to 1968); *European Control Manufacturers' Association* – former (1968 to 1989); *Association des fabricants européens d'appareils de contrôle (AFECOGAZ)* – former (1968 to 1989); *Verband Europäischer Kontrollgerätehersteller* – former (1968 to 1989). Registration: EU Transparency Register, No/ID: 18638678159-24. **Aims** Provide technical assistance in establishing national standards and harmonization of international standards. **Structure** General Assembly (annual) in Belgium; Council of Administration. **Languages** English, French, German. **Staff** 0.50 FTE, paid. **Finance** Members' dues. **Activities** Guidance/assistance/consulting. **Events** *Seminar* Berlin (Germany) 2013, *Joint conference* Berlin (Germany) 2010, *Seminar* Berlin (Germany) 2007. **Publications** Information Circulars; Circular letters.
Members Companies in 6 countries:
Belgium, Germany, Italy, Netherlands, Switzerland, UK.
IGO Relations Recognized by: *European Commission (EC, #06633).* **NGO Relations** Cooperates with: *Comité européen de normalisation (CEN, #04162); International Organization for Standardization (ISO, #14473).*
[2021/XD0770/**D**]

- ♦ Association des fabricants européens de chauffe-bains et chauffe-eau instantanés et de chaudières murales au gaz (inactive)
- ♦ Association des fabricants européens de chauffe-eau à accumulation au gaz (inactive)
- ♦ Association des fabricants européens de compteurs d'électricité (inactive)
- ♦ Association des fabricants européens de compteurs de gaz / see Association of European Manufacturers of Gas Meters, Gas Pressure Regulators, Safety Devices and Stations (#02521)
- ♦ Association des fabricants européens d'émulsifiants alimentaires (#07281)
- ♦ Association des fabricants européens d'équipements ferroviaires (inactive)
- ♦ Association des fabricants européens de munitions de sport (#02522)
- ♦ Association des fabricants européens de pièces automobiles (inactive)
- ♦ Association des fabricants européens de piles électriques / see European Portable Battery Association (#08255)
- ♦ Association des fabricants européens de roues (#02552)
- ♦ Association des fabricants européens de rubans auto-adhésifs / see European Adhesive Tape Association (#05826)
- ♦ Association des fabricants européens pour la sérigraphie / see European Specialist Printing Manufacturers Associations (#08809)
- ♦ Association de fabricants et d'importateurs de tronçonneuses opérant en Europe (inactive)
- ♦ Association des facultés agronomiques d'Afrique (inactive)
- ♦ Association des facultés dentaires de l'Amérique latine (inactive)
- ♦ Association des facultés de droit en Europe (#07656)
- ♦ Association des facultés, écoles et instituts d'économie d'Amérique latine (#02784)
- ♦ Association des facultés et des écoles latinoaméricaines de comptabilité publique (#02783)
- ♦ Association des Facultés et Établissements de Lettres et Sciences Humaines / see Association des facultés ou établissements de lettres et sciences humaines des universités d'expression française (#02593)

♦ Association des facultés ou établissements de lettres et sciences humaines des universités d'expression française (AFELSH) 02593

Pres Univ de Hanoi, 144 Xuan Thuy, Hanoi, Vietnam.
URL: http://afelsh.org/

History 9 Jan 1988, Dakar (Senegal). Founded following an international colloquium, as an institutional network of *Université des réseaux d'expression française (UREF, inactive)* within the framework of *Agence universitaire de La Francophonie (AUF, #00548).* Former names and other names: *Association des doyens des facultés et des établissements de lettres et sciences humaines* – former; *Association des Facultés et Établissements de Lettres et Sciences Humaines* – alias. **Aims** Exchange information, in particular regarding transformation of *teaching methods* and new directions of research; promote comparative studies on *professional* acceptance of students of the *humanities* and improve public opinion of training institutions in the field. **Structure** General Assembly (at least every 3 years); Executive Committee. **Languages** French. **Finance** Members' dues. AUF subvention. **Activities** Events/meetings; projects/programmes; publishing activities; training/education. **Events** *Colloque sur le devenir et l'insertion professionnelle des diplômés en lettres, langues, arts, sciences humaines et sociales / Colloquium* Libreville (Gabon) 2008, *Colloque / Colloquium* Sofia (Bulgaria) 2006, *Colloquium* Saint Louis (Senegal) 2004, *L'harmonisation des études* Saint Louis (Senegal) 2004, *Colloque / Colloquium* Beirut (Lebanon) 1998. **Publications** Colloquium proceedings.
Members Universities, faculties and other higher institutes of learning in 17 countries:
Algeria, Bulgaria, Burundi, Cameroon, Canada, Central African Rep, Congo DR, France, Gabon, Georgia, Lebanon, Madagascar, Moldova, Morocco, Romania, Tunisia, Vietnam. [2019.12.13/XD2386/**C**]

- ♦ Association des facultés de médecine d'Europe (#02799)
- ♦ Association des facultés des sciences des universités africaines (inactive)
- ♦ Association of Faculties of Agriculture in Africa (inactive)
- ♦ Association of Faculties of Science in African Universities (inactive)
- ♦ Association for Farming Systems Research and Extension / see International Farming Systems Association (#13332)
- ♦ Association of Fashion Advertising and Editorial Photographers / see Association of Photographers
- ♦ Association fédérale internationale des promoteurs et organisateurs de courses océaniques (inactive)
- ♦ Association fédéraliste africaine (inactive)
- ♦ Association des fédérations africaines de basketball / see FIBA Africa (#09744)
- ♦ Association of Federations and Associations of Business Women in the Mediterranean / see Association of Organisations of Mediterranean Businesswomen (#02840)
- ♦ Association des fédérations internationales olympiques d'été (#02943)
- ♦ Association des fédérations internationales olympiques des sports d'hiver (#02757)
- ♦ Association des fédérations internationales des sports d'hiver / see Association of the International Olympic Winter Sports Federations (#02757)
- ♦ Association des fédérations nordiques de natation (#17442)
- ♦ Association des fédérations de tir sportif de la CE (inactive)
- ♦ Association féminine nordique pour la tempérance intégrale (inactive)
- ♦ Association féminine pluridisciplinaire d'études et de recherches en Afrique (inactive)
- ♦ Association des femmes africaines pour la recherche et le développement (#02362)
- ♦ Association des femmes de l'Afrique de l'Ouest (#20900)
- ♦ Association pour les femmes et le développement / see Association for Women's Rights in Development (#02980)
- ♦ Association Femmes et développement (internationally oriented national body)
- ♦ Association femmes d'Europe (internationally oriented national body)

♦ Association des femmes de l'Europe méridionale (AFEM) 02594

Pres Maison de l'Europe, 29 avenue de Villiers, 75017 Paris, France. T. +33144545058.
URL: http://www.afem-europa.org/

History 1996, Paris (France). **Aims** Work for the effective realization of equal rights and opportunities for women and men in all fields; contribute to the setting up of a coordinated strategy to improve women's participation in decision-making; contribute to the defence of various cultures, of multilinguism and of concepts which permit their safeguard; develop common projects within the European Union and in partnership with associations in other countries, especially in the framework of Euro-Mediterranean policy. **Structure** Management Board; Bureau. **Languages** French, Italian, Portuguese, Spanish. **Staff** 2.00 FTE, paid. Volunteers. **Finance** Members' dues. Other sources: *European Commission (EC, #06633)*; French government; Italian and Spanish local authorities. **Activities** Organizes: conferences and colloquia; awareness campaigns focused on political authorities; project "Stratégies d'accès des femmes". Participates in feminist and human rights networks. **Events** *Conférence / Conference* Paris (France) 2000, *Conference* Strasbourg (France) 2000, *Conference* Strasbourg (France) 2000, *Conference* Naples (Italy) 1999, *Colloque international sur la parité de l'accès des femmes et des hommes à la vie publique* Reims (France) 1999. **Publications** *La Gazette* (6 a year) – newsletter. Books. Videos.
Members Organizations in 7 countries:
Andorra, France, Greece, Italy, Portugal, Spain, Sweden.
Individuals in 13 countries:
Belgium, Cape Verde, Cyprus, Finland, France, Greece, Italy, Japan, Morocco, Poland, Portugal, Spain, Tunisia.
Consultative Status Consultative status granted from: *Council of Europe (CE, #04881)* (Participatory Status). **IGO Relations** Participant in Fundamental Rights Platform of: *European Union Agency for Fundamental Rights (FRA, #08969)*. **NGO Relations** Member of: *Conference of INGOs of the Council of Europe (#04607)*; *EuroMed Non-Governmental Platform (#05730)*; *Permanent Forum of European Civil Society (#18322)*; *Social Platform (#19344)*. Affiliated with: *International Alliance of Women (IAW, #11639)*. Partners include: *Comité international de liaison des associations féminines (CILAF)*; *European Movement International (EMI, #07825)* (Women's Commission); *Nordic Women's Network (NWN, no recent information)*. Supports: *European Alliance for the Statute of the European Association (EASEA, #05886)*. [2018/XD6320/**D**]

♦ Association des femmes au foyer des pays nordiques (no recent information)
♦ Association des femmes et des jeunes de la diaspora africaine pour le développement socio-éducatif et agricole de l'afrique (internationally oriented national body)
♦ Association femmes et jeunesse dans l'environnement maghrébin (no recent information)
♦ Association femmes méditerranée rencontres (inactive)
♦ Association des femmes du Pacifique et d'Asie du Sud-Est (#18186)
♦ Association des femmes pakistanaises (internationally oriented national body)
♦ Association of Film Archives of the European Community / see Association of European Film Archives and Cinémathèques (#02511)

♦ Association of Film Commissioners International (AFCI) 02595

Address not obtained.
URL: http://www.afci.org/
History 1975. **Structure** Board of Directors; Executive Committee; Advisory Board. **Finance** Members' dues. Budget (annual): US$ 1 million. **Activities** *'Locations Trade Show'* annual tradeshow of film and television production. *'Cineposium'* annual educational meeting. **Events** *Annual Cineposium* St Petersburg (Russia) 2019, *Annual Cineposium* Los Angeles, CA (USA) 2018, *Annual Cineposium* Los Angeles, CA (USA) 2017, *Annual Cineposium* Atlanta, GA (USA) 2016, *Global Cineposium* Barcelona (Spain) 2015. **Publications** *AFCI News-Notes* (12 a year); *Locations Magazine* (annual).
Members Primarily North American membership, but membership covers 44 countries:
Argentina, Australia, Austria, Bahamas, Barbados, Belgium, Brazil, Canada, Chile, Denmark, Fiji, Finland, France, Germany, Guatemala, Hong Kong, Hungary, Iceland, Indonesia, Ireland, Italy, Jamaica, Japan, Jordan, Korea Rep, Malaysia, Mexico, Namibia, Netherlands, New Zealand, Norway, Peru, Poland, Portugal, Romania, South Africa, Spain, Sweden, Switzerland, Thailand, Trinidad-Tobago, UK, USA, Venezuela. [2019/XD2360/**F**]

♦ Association for Financial Markets in Europe (AFME) 02596

Main Office 39th floor, 25 Canada Square, London, E14 5LQ, UK. T. +442038282700. E-mail: londonreception@afme.eu.
Brussels Office Rue de la Loi 82, 1040 Brussels, Belgium. T. +3227883971.
URL: http://www.afme.eu/
History Nov 2009. Founded by merger of London Investment Banking Association (LIBA) and the European arm of the *Securities Industries and Financial Markets Association (SIFMA)*. Also integrated with the merger: *European Covered Bond Dealers Association (ECBDA)*; *European High yield Association (EHYA)*; *European Primary Dealers Association (EPDA)*; *European Primary Markets Division (EPMD)*; *European Securitisation Forum (ESF)*; *European Securities Services Forum (ESSF)*. Registration: EU Transparency Register, No/ID: 65110063986-76; Companies House, No/ID: 06996678, England and Wales. **Aims** Offer a single voice for Europe's capital market participants and advocate their views at national, EU and global levels; represent leading global and European banks and other significant capital market players, focusing on a wide range of market, business and prudential issues; offer a pan-European perspective, bringing to bear policy and technical expertise and constructive influence with European and global policymakers to help achieve a balanced and stable regulatory environment; advocate stable, competitive, sustainable European financial markets that support economic growth and benefit society; build constructive dialogue with regulators and policymakers; promote contribution of the financial sector to society. **Structure** Board of Directors; Senior Management Team; Divisions. **Activities** Advocacy/lobbying/activism; politics/policy/regulatory; networking/liaising; events/liaising. **Events** *Annual European Government Bond Conference* Brussels (Belgium) 2022, *Annual Capital Markets Technology and Innovation Conference* Paris (France) 2019, *Annual Spanish Funding Conference* Madrid (Spain) 2017, *Annual European Government Bond Conference* Brussels (Belgium) 2016, *Conference on the Future of the CMU* Brussels (Belgium) 2016. **Members** Open to all participants in wholesale financial markets. Full banks; corporate finance advisors; brokers. Associate service providers; professional advisors. Membership countries not specified. **NGO Relations** Member of: *Asia Securities Industry and Financial Markets Association (ASIFMA, #02094)*; *Global Financial Markets Association (GFMA, #10359)*; *International Council of Securities Associations (ICSA, #13071)*. [2021/XJ2825/**D**]

♦ Association for Financial Professionals (internationally oriented national body)
♦ Association of Financial Supervisors of Pacific Countries (inactive)
♦ Association of Finno-Ugric Literatures (unconfirmed)

♦ Association for Fire Ecology (AFE) 02597

Admin Dir PO Box 50412, Eugene OR 97405, USA. T. +15418527903. E-mail: office@fireecology.net.
URL: https://fireecology.org/
History Jul 2000, USA. Founded by members of the California Association for Fire Ecology (CAFE). **Aims** Improve knowledge and use of fire in land management through science and education. **Structure** Board of Directors. Committees. **Activities** Awards/prizes/competitions; events/meetings. **Events** *International Fire Ecology and Management Congress* Miramar Beach, FL (USA) 2021, *International Fire Ecology and Management Congress* Tucson, AZ (USA) 2019, *International Fire Ecology and Management Congress* Orlando, FL (USA) 2017, *International Fire Ecology and Management Congress* San Antonio, TX (USA) 2015, *Conference on Large Wildland Fires* Missoula, MT (USA) 2014. **Publications** *Fire Ecology* – online. [2021/AA1954/**D**]

♦ Association of Fire Testing Laboratories of European Industries (inactive)
♦ Association fiscale internationale (#13608)
♦ Association des foires internationales d'Amérique (#11886)
♦ Association fonds d'aide internationale au développement (internationally oriented national body)
♦ Association des fonds d'assurance de la santé (#13442)
♦ Association des fonds d'entretien routier africains (#00443)
♦ Association of Food and Agricultural Marketing Agencies in Asia and the Pacific / see Agricultural and Food Marketing Association for Asia and the Pacific (#00569)
♦ Association of the Food Industries for Particular Nutritional Uses of the European Union / see Specialised Nutrition Europe (#19909)
♦ Association of Food Marketing Agencies in Asia and the Pacific / see Agricultural and Food Marketing Association for Asia and the Pacific (#00569)
♦ Association of Food Marketing Enterprises in Eastern and Southern Africa (inactive)
♦ Association of Forensic Radiographers / see International Association of Forensic Radiographers

♦ Association for Forest Spatial Analysis Technologies (ForestSAT) .. 02598

Chair address not obtained. E-mail: forestsat@forestsat.com – forestsat@gmail.com.
URL: https://www.forestsat.com/
History Informal group organizing the ForestSAT conference in existence since 2002, but formally organized since Dec 2015, when constitution was adopted. Since 2014, conference organized alternatingly with *SilviLaser*. **Aims** Promote and advance the application of spatial analysis technologies in forestry. **Structure** Board of Directors; Committees. **Activities** Awards/prizes/competitions; events/meetings. **Events** *ForestSAT Conference* Berlin (Germany) 2022, *ForestSAT Conference* Krakow (Poland) 2020, *ForestSAT Conference* College Park, MD (USA) 2018, *ForestSAT Conference* Santiago (Chile) 2016, *ForestSAT Conference* Riva del Garda (Italy) 2014. [2022.05.04/AA2495/c/**E**]

♦ Association Forêt Méditerranéenne (internationally oriented national body)
♦ Association pour la formation des enseignants en Europe (#02949)
♦ Association pour la formation des ingénieurs en Asie du Sud-Est et dans le Pacifique (#02487)
♦ Association pour la formation de maîtres en Afrique (no recent information)
♦ Association of Former FAO Officials / see Former FAO and Other United Nations Staff Association
♦ Association of Former FAO and WFP Staff Members / see Former FAO and Other United Nations Staff Association
♦ Association of Former ILO Turin International Centre Officials / see Former Officials Association Turin
♦ Association of Former International Civil Servants for Development (internationally oriented national body)

♦ Association of Former International Civil Servants – Geneva (AAFI-AFICS Geneva) 02599

Association des anciens fonctionnaires internationaux – Genève – Asociación des los Ex Funcionarios Internacionales – Geneva
Pres AAFI-AFICS Geneva, c/o Palais des Nations, Room A-265, 1211 Geneva 10, Switzerland. T. +41229173330. Fax +41229170075. E-mail: aafi-afics@unog.ch.
URL: http://www.unog.ch/afics/afics.htm
History 1955, Geneva (Switzerland), succeeding *'Amicale des anciens du BIT'*, set up 1940, Geneva. Present title adopted 1955. Current Statutes adopted 30 May 1989, Geneva. Statutes revised 27 May 1997; 23 May 2000. **Aims** Promote the work of the UN system; foster friendly relations among members; promote and defend pension and health insurance rights of former international civil servants in international and national bodies. **Structure** Annual General Assembly; Committee. **Finance** Members' dues. Gifts. **Activities** Organizes information meetings; advises members on pensions, health insurance, taxation and problems they may encounter as pensioners; organizes several lunch meetings and group travel of cultural interest. **Events** *Annual General Assembly* Geneva (Switzerland) 2002, *Annual General Assembly* Geneva (Switzerland) 1989. **Publications** *Bulletin AAFI-AFICS* (5 a year). Special brochures.
Members Persons (3,700) belonging or having belonged to the staff of the United Nations or the Specialized Agencies and their surviving dependants in 86 countries:
Algeria, Andorra, Argentina, Australia, Austria, Bangladesh, Barbados, Belarus, Belgium, Benin, Brazil, Burundi, Canada, Chile, China, Colombia, Congo DR, Côte d'Ivoire, Croatia, Cyprus, Czechia, Denmark, Ecuador, Egypt, Ethiopia, Finland, France, Gabon, Gambia, Germany, Ghana, Greece, Hungary, India, Iran Islamic Rep, Ireland, Israel, Italy, Japan, Jordan, Kenya, Lebanon, Luxembourg, Madagascar, Mali, Malta, Mauritius, Mexico, Monaco, Montenegro, Morocco, Nepal, Netherlands, New Zealand, Norway, Pakistan, Panama, Paraguay, Peru, Philippines, Poland, Portugal, Romania, Russia, Rwanda, Saudi Arabia, Senegal, Serbia, Singapore, Slovakia, Slovenia, Somalia, South Africa, Spain, Sri Lanka, Sweden, Switzerland, Syrian AR, Tanzania UR, Thailand, Tunisia, Türkiye, UK, Uruguay, USA, Venezuela.
NGO Relations Member of: *Federation of Associations of Former International Civil Servants (FAFICS, #09457)*; *NGO-UNESCO Liaison Committee (#17127)*. [2013.07.22/XE0194/v/**E**]

♦ Association of Former International Civil Servants – New York (AFICS New York) 02600

Association des anciens fonctionnaires internationaux – New York (AAFI New York) – Asociación de ex Funcionarios Públicos Internacionales – New York (AFICS New York)
Contact Room DC1-580, United Nations Plaza, New York NY 10017, USA. T. +12129632943. Fax +12129635702. E-mail: afics@un.org.
URL: http://www.un.org/other/afics/
History 1970, New York, NY (USA). Founded at *United Nations (UN, #20515)* Headquarters, with support of the then Secretary-General. Building in New York, as distinct from the body of the same name based at Geneva (Switzerland) offices of the United Nations. **Aims** Support and promote the purposes, principles and programmes of the UN system; advise and assist former international civil servants and those about to separate from service; represent the interests of members within the system; foster social and personal relationships among members, promote their well-being and encourage mutual support of individual members. **Structure** Assembly (annual); Governing Board; Standing Committees (6). **Finance** Sources: members' dues. **Activities** Events/meetings; guidance/assistance/consulting. **Events** *Annual Assembly* New York, NY (USA) 2022, *Annual meeting* New York, NY (USA) 1992. **Publications** *AFICS Quarterly Bulletin*.
Members Former staff members of the United Nations and specialized agencies, or their surviving spouses in 96 countries and territories:
Andorra, Anguilla, Antigua-Barbuda, Argentina, Australia, Austria, Bangladesh, Barbados, Belgium, Benin, Bermuda, Bolivia, Brazil, Bulgaria, Cameroon, Canada, Central African Rep, Chile, China, Colombia, Congo DR, Costa Rica, Croatia, Cuba, Cyprus, Czechia, Denmark, Dominica, Dominican Rep, Ecuador, Egypt, Ethiopia, Finland, France, Germany, Ghana, Greece, Guatemala, Guinea, Guyana, Haiti, Honduras, Iceland, India, Indonesia, Iran Islamic Rep, Ireland, Israel, Italy, Jamaica, Japan, Jordan, Kenya, Lebanon, Madagascar, Malaysia, Mali, Malta, Mexico, Morocco, Myanmar, Nepal, Netherlands, New Zealand, Niger, Nigeria, Norway, Pakistan, Panama, Paraguay, Peru, Philippines, Poland, Portugal, Russia, Senegal, Serbia, Sierra Leone, Slovenia, Spain, Sri Lanka, Sudan, Sweden, Switzerland, Taiwan, Tanzania UR, Thailand, Togo, Trinidad-Tobago, Türkiye, UK, Uruguay, USA, Venezuela, Vietnam, Zimbabwe.
IGO Relations *ECOSOC (#05331)*. Associated with Department of Global Communications of the United Nations. **NGO Relations** Founding member of: *Federation of Associations of Former International Civil Servants (FAFICS, #09457)*. [2022.10.19/XE4591/v/**E**]

♦ Association of Former Staff of the European Union / see Association internationale des anciens de l'Union Européenne (#02667)
♦ Association of Former Students of the College of Europe / see Association of Alumni of the College of Europe (#02365)

♦ Association of Former UNESCO Staff Members (AFUS Paris) 02601

Association des anciens fonctionnaires de l'UNESCO (AAFU Paris)
Contact Bldg VI Office 121, 1 rue Miollis, 75732 Paris CEDEX 15, France. T. +33145684655. E-mail: afus@afus.unesco.org.
Pres address not obtained.
URL: http://www.afus-unesco.org/
History 1972, Paris (France), as *Committee of Former UNESCO Staff Members – Comité des anciens fonctionnaires de l'UNESCO (CAF-UNESCO Paris)*, to represent former staff members of *UNESCO (#20322)*, Paris. Present title adopted 1991, when, through an amendment to its statutes, became independent of *UNESCO Staff Union (STU, #20321)*. **Aims** Represent, protect and inform former international *civil servants*; support UNESCO and United Nations. **Structure** General Assembly (annual); Executive Committees (12); Commissions (8). **Languages** English, French. **Staff** 0.80 FTE, paid; 15.00 FTE, voluntary. **Finance** Members' dues. UNESCO subsidy (2018): US$ 13,000. **Activities** Networking/liaising; guidance/assistance/consulting; financial and/or material support; events/meetings. **Events** *General Assembly* Paris (France) 1999. **Publications** *Lien/Link Periodical* (4 a year). *Cahiers d'Histoire/History Papers*. Books.
Members Individuals in 67 countries:
Algeria, Andorra, Argentina, Australia, Austria, Belgium, Brazil, Burkina Faso, Cameroon, Canada, Chile, Colombia, Congo DR, Costa Rica, Côte d'Ivoire, Croatia, Cyprus, Denmark, Egypt, Eritrea, Ethiopia, Finland, France, Germany, Ghana, Greece, Hungary, Iceland, India, Ireland, Italy, Jamaica, Japan, Jordan, Kenya, Lebanon, Liberia, Luxembourg, Mali, Malta, Mauritania, Mexico, Monaco, Morocco, New Zealand, Nigeria, Norway, Pakistan, Paraguay, Peru, Poland, Portugal, Romania, Senegal, Spain, Sweden, Switzerland, Syrian AR, Tanzania UR, Thailand, Tunisia, Türkiye, UK, Uruguay, USA, Venezuela, Zimbabwe.
NGO Relations Member of: *Federation of Associations of Former International Civil Servants (FAFICS, #09457)*. [2019.10.04/XE4431/v/**E**]

♦ Association of Former United Nations Industry and Development Experts (AFIDE) 02602

Contact address not obtained. T. +43126026ext5204. Fax +43196104088.
History Registered in accordance with Austrian law. **Aims** Serve as a forum for economic and industrial development to developing countries and economies in transition to improve their socio-economic conditions. **Structure** General Assembly; Board. **Consultative Status** Consultative status granted from: *UNIDO (#20336)*. [2010/XE4311/E]

♦ Association of Former United Nations Personnel in and of India (AFUNPI) 02603

Contact PO Box 5569, Bangalore, Karnataka 560 055, Bangalore KARNATAKA 560 055, India. T. +918023317747. E-mail: afunpi@hotmail.com.
URL: http://www.un.org/other/afics/
History Founded 3 May 1975, Bangalore (India). Statutes revised Jan 2002. Also referred to as *Association of United Nations Pensioners in India*. **Aims** Provide counsel, information and assistance to members; study, promote and take all possible measures to safeguard the welfare, rights and interests of former UN personnel and their spouses in and of India. **Structure** General Body. Executive Committee, consisting of Chairman, Secretary, Treasurer and 7 additional members from General Body, elected for 2 year terms. Members inscribed upon request. **Staff** Voluntary. **Finance** Members' contributions (no dues). **Events** *General Body Meeting* Chennai (India) 2012, *General Body Meeting* Bangalore (India) 2010. **Publications** *AFUNPI Circular* (2-3 a year) – on UN pension matters. **NGO Relations** Member of: *Federation of Associations of Former International Civil Servants (FAFICS, #09457)*. [2012.06.01/XE1530/v/E]

♦ Association of Former WHO Staff Members (AFSM) 02604

Association des anciens de l'OMS (AOMS)
Pres Office 4141, 1211 Geneva 27, Switzerland. T. +41227913103. Fax +41227913111. E-mail: aoms@who.int.
URL: http://www.who.int/formerstaff/
History Set up to represent former staff members of *WHO (#20950)* worldwide. **Aims** Defend the interests of persons formerly employed by WHO, as well as their surviving spouses, and, in cooperation with the Staff Committee, maintain and strengthen their links both with WHO as an institution and with serving staff; develop effective solidarity between WHO staff and their former colleagues; place at the service of former WHO staff members and their families such information and mutual aid services as they may need. **Structure** General Assembly (every 2 years); Executive Committee. **Languages** English, French. **Staff** 12.00 FTE, voluntary. **Finance** Sources: members' dues. **Activities** Guidance/assistance/consulting. **Publications** *Quarterly News* in English, French. Members' Directory (every 2 years).
Members Full in 81 countries:
Algeria, Argentina, Australia, Austria, Bangladesh, Belgium, Brazil, Burkina Faso, Burundi, Canada, Chad, Chile, China, Colombia, Comoros, Côte d'Ivoire, Croatia, Czechia, Denmark, Egypt, Finland, France, Gambia, Germany, Ghana, Greece, Guinea, Hungary, India, Indonesia, Iraq, Ireland, Israel, Italy, Japan, Jordan, Kenya, Laos, Lebanon, Lesotho, Libya, Luxembourg, Malaysia, Mali, Mauritania, Mauritius, Mexico, Morocco, Nepal, Netherlands, New Caledonia, New Zealand, Niger, Nigeria, Pakistan, Paraguay, Peru, Philippines, Poland, Portugal, Russia, Serbia, Singapore, South Africa, Spain, St Lucia, Sweden, Switzerland, Syrian AR, Tanzania UR, Thailand, Togo, Trinidad-Tobago, Tunisia, Türkiye, Uganda, UK, USA, Vietnam, Zambia, Zimbabwe. [2021.05.28/XE1625/v/E]

- ♦ Association pour le forum mondial de la société civile / see World Civil Society Forum (#21278)
- ♦ Association for the Foundations of Science, Language and Cognition (no recent information)
- ♦ Association des foyers internationaux (internationally oriented national body)
- ♦ Association des foyers de marins scandinaves dans les ports étrangers (inactive)
- ♦ Association française d'amitié et de solidarité avec les peuples d'Afrique (internationally oriented national body)
- ♦ Association française de chirurgie endocrinienne / see Association francophone de chirurgie endocrinienne (#02607)
- ♦ Association française de comptabilité / see Association francophone de comptabilité (#02609)
- ♦ Association française pour le développement des échanges internationaux de produits et techniques agricoles et agro-alimentaires / see Association for the Development of International Exchanges in Agricultural and Agrifood Products and Techniques
- ♦ Association française d'études américaines (internationally oriented national body)
- ♦ Association Française d'Études Européennes (internationally oriented national body)
- ♦ Association française des experts de la coopération technique internationale / see Association francophone des experts et des consultants de la coopération technique internationale
- ♦ Association française de science politique (internationally oriented national body)
- ♦ Association française des volontaires du progrès / see France Volontaires
- ♦ Association franco-européenne de Waterloo (internationally oriented national body)
- ♦ Association François-Xavier Bagnoud (internationally oriented national body)
- ♦ Association francophone d'accueil et de liaison / see Association francophone d'amitié et de liaison (#02605)
- ♦ Association francophone des aéroports / see Les Aéroports Francophones (#00145)

♦ Association francophone d'amitié et de liaison (AFAL) 02605

Contact 60 rue de la Belle-Feuille, 92100 Boulogne-Billancourt, France. E-mail: afalassociation@gmail.com.
URL: http://www.afalassociation.com/
History 1974, France. 1974. Subsequently ceased to exist, but revived in 1983 as *Association francophone d'accueil et de liaison*. Previous statutes adopted 25 Nov 1997, Paris (France). Most recent statutes adopted, 3 Sep 2005, Paris (France). Registered in accordance with French law. **Aims** Contribute to the defence and expansion of the *French language* worldwide; unite francophone associations, assure dialogue among them and promote their activities, in particular through joint information; participate in international francophone institutions. **Structure** General Assembly (annual). Administrative Council of 25 members. Bureau, consisting of President, Honorary President, 6 Vice-Presidents, Honorary Vice-President, Secretary General, Honorary Secretary General, Treasurer, General Delegate and Honorary Member. Committee of Honour of 17 members. Secretariat in Paris (France). **Languages** French. **Staff** 1.00 FTE, paid; 6.00 FTE, voluntary. **Finance** Members' dues. Subventions from: French government; other sources. **Activities** Maintains regular relations with official authorities. Organizes: *'Festi'phonie'*; international contests; writing contests. Organizes, co-sponsors or participates in international, regional and national meetings; provides a "post box" for members without their own permanent office. **Events** *Conférence Festi'phonie* Paris (France) 2007, *Francophonie, associations, échanges dans les relations avec l'Europe centrale et orientale* Paris (France) 1991, *Espace éditorial et audiovisuel francophone* Paris (France) 1988. **Publications** *Liaisons – Revue des associations ayant le français en partage* (4 a year); *AFAL Directory* (annual).
Members Associations (123) in 18 countries:
Albania, Algeria, Belgium, Bulgaria, Cameroon, Canada, Djibouti, Estonia, France, Georgia, Italy, Moldova, Poland, Romania, Russia, Tunisia, Ukraine, Vietnam.
Of the above-mentioned bodies, 44 organizations listed in this Yearbook:
- *Académie internationale des arts et des lettres, Paris (AIAL)*;
- *Agence universitaire de La Francophonie (AUF, #00548)*;
- *Alliance francophone (#00681)*;
- *Alliance israélite universelle (AIU, #00698)*;
- *Amitiés acadiennes*;
- *Amitiés catholiques françaises dans le mondes (ACFM)*;
- *Association des écrivains de langue française (ADELF, #02481)*;
- *Association des informaticiens de langue française (AILF, #02644)*;
- *Association du notariat francophone (ANF, #02836)*;
- *Association franco-européenne de Waterloo*;
- *Association francophone des experts et des consultants de la coopération technique internationale (AFECTI)*;
- *Association francophone du tourisme d'affaires (AFTA)*;
- *Association générale des intervenants retraités (AGIRabcd)*;
- *Association internationale de la presse francophone (AIPF)*;
- *Association internationale des établissements francophones de formation à l'assurance (AIEFFA, #02687)*;
- *Association Internationale des Maires et responsables des capitales et métropoles partiellement ou entièrement Francophones (AIMF, #02715)*;
- *Association of International Studies (AEI)*;
- *Association pour la diffusion internationale francophone de livres, ouvrages et revues (ADIFLOR)*;
- *Association pour la recherche didactique du français langue étrangère (ARDIFLE)*;
- *Avenir de la langue française (ALF)*;
- *Biblionef International*;
- *Biennale de la langue française (BLF, #03231)*;
- *Centre d'étude et de rencontres francophones (CERF)*;
- *Centre international de documentation et d'échanges de la Francophonie – L'Agora francophone internationale (CIDEF-AFI)*;
- *Cercle Richelieu Senghor*;
- *Coésio – Destinations Francophone de Congrès (#04082)*;
- *Comité international de liaison des associations féminines (CILAF)*;
- *Comité Orthodoxe des amitiés françaises dans le monde*;
- *Comité protestant des amitiés françaises à l'étranger (COPAFE)*;
- *Comité universitaire francophone pour le développement des échanges scientifiques (CUFDES)*;
- *Echanges internationaux*;
- *Fédération Internationale des Accueils Français et francophones d'Expatriés (FIAFE, #09606)*;
- *Fédération internationale des experts-comptables francophones (FIDEF, #09630)*;
- *Fédération internationale des professeurs de français (FIPF, #09652)*;
- *Forum francophone des affaires (FFA, #09916)*;
- *Foyer d'échanges et de rencontres administratifs mondiaux (FERAM, no recent information)*;
- *Groupe d'échanges scientifiques et technologiques éducation-environnement (GESTE)*;
- *Groupement des associations dentaires francophones (GADEF, #10757)*;
- *Institut international de droit d'expression et d'inspiration françaises (IDEF, #11310)*;
- *Jeune francophonie*;
- *Oeuvre d'Orient*;
- *School and Cultural Help and Equipment (AESCO)*;
- *Sud-ouest sans frontières (LSJF)*;
- *Union culturelle et technique de langue française (UCTF, #20374)*.

Consultative Status Consultative status granted from: *UNESCO (#20322)* (Consultative Status); *Organisation internationale de la Francophonie (OIF, #17809)*. **IGO Relations** *Conférence au sommet des chefs d'Etat et de gouvernement des pays ayant le français en partage (Sommet de la Francophonie, #04648)*. Associated with Department of Global Communications of the United Nations. **NGO Relations** Member of: *Comité pour les Partenariats avec l'Europe Continentale (Comité PECO)*. [2017/XD1006/y/F]

♦ Association francophone des autorités de protection des données personnelles (AFAPDP) 02606

French-Speaking Association of Personal Data Protection Authorities
Pres 3 Place de Fontenoy, TSA 80715, 75334 Paris CEDEX 07, France.
URL: http://www.afapdp.org/
History 24 Sep 2007, Montréal QC (Canada). **Aims** Promote personal data protection principles and rules in French-speaking countries; enhance French expertise on personal data protection; develop good practices. **Structure** General Assembly; Board. **Languages** French. **Staff** 1.00 FTE, paid. **Finance** Members' dues. Other sources: subventions; donations. **Activities** Events/meetings. **Events** *Conference* Ouagadougou (Burkina Faso) 2014, *Conference* Marrakech (Morocco) 2013, *Conference* Monte Carlo (Monaco) 2012, *Conference* Dakar (Senegal) 2011, *Conference* Mexico City (Mexico) 2011.
Members Data protection authorities in 20 OIF member states:
Albania, Andorra, Belgium, Benin, Burkina Faso, Canada, Cape Verde, Côte d'Ivoire, France, Gabon, Greece, Luxembourg, Mali, Mauritius, Monaco, Morocco, Québec, Senegal, Switzerland, Tunisia.
IGO Relations *Council of Europe (CE, #04881)* (Data protection division); *Organisation internationale de la Francophonie (OIF, #17809)*. [2018.06.14/XJ0819/E]

- ♦ Association francophone pour l'avancement des technologies en transformation des aliments (no recent information)

♦ Association francophone de chirurgie endocrinienne (AFCE) 02607

Sec Clinique Chirurgicale A, Hotel Dieu CHU, Place Alexis Ricordeau, 44035 Nantes CEDEX, France.
URL: https://afce-chirurgie-endocrinienne.com/
History 1988, Paris (France). Sometimes referred to as *Association française de chirurgie endocrinienne*. **Aims** Promote progress in surgical endocrinology. **Structure** Executive Board. Officers: President; Vice-President; Secretary General; Deputy Secretary General; Treasurer; Coordinator to Scientific Council. Scientific Council. **Languages** French. **Staff** 6.00 FTE, voluntary. **Finance** Members' dues. Budget (annual): about euro 15,245. **Activities** Organizes biennial congresses and annual scientific meetings. Offers post-graduate courses in surgical endocrinology. Undertakes national and international scientific work. **Events** *Congrès* Cassis (France) 2023, *Congrès* Lille (France) 2019, *Congrès* Nantes (France) 2017, *Congrès* Geneva (Switzerland) 2015, *Congrès* Lyon (France) 2013. **Publications** *Journal of Viscerol Surgery* – periodical.
Members Individuals in 21 countries:
Algeria, Argentina, Australia, Belgium, Cambodia, Czechia, France, Germany, Greece, Guatemala, Italy, Lebanon, Mali, Mexico, Portugal, Romania, Spain, Sweden, Switzerland, UK, USA. [2020/XD4996/v/D]

♦ Association francophone des commissions nationales des droits de l'Homme (AFCNDH) 02608

SG 20 avenue de Ségur, TSA 40720-75334, 75007 Paris CEDEX 07, France. T. +33142757191 – +33142755166. E-mail: afcndh@afcndh.org.
URL: http://afcndh.org/
History May 2002. Created with the support of *Organisation internationale de la Francophonie (OIF, #17809)*. **Aims** Enhance and strengthen the role of national human rights commissions in the promotion and protection of human rights. **Structure** General Assemlby; Board of Directors; Bureau.
Members National Institutes for Human Rights in 36 countries:
Algeria (Observer), Belgium, Benin, Burkina Faso, Burundi, Cameroon, Canada, Cape Verde, Central African Rep, Chad, Comoros, Congo Brazzaville, Congo DR, Côte d'Ivoire, Djibouti, Egypt, France, Gabon, Ghana, Greece, Guinea, Guinea-Bissau, Haiti, Luxembourg, Madagascar, Mali, Mauritania, Mauritius, Morocco, Niger, Romania, Rwanda, Senegal, Switzerland, Togo, Tunisia.
IGO Relations Partner of (1): *Organisation internationale de la Francophonie (OIF, #17809)*. [2021/AA2317/E]

♦ Association francophone de comptabilité (AFC) 02609

SG CSOEC – attn: l'AFC, 200-216 rue Raymond Losserand, 75014 Paris, France. E-mail: associationafc1980@gmail.com.
Contact IAE Nancy, 13 rue Michel Ney, 54000 Nancy, France.
URL: http://www.afc-cca.com/
History 1979. Former names and other names: *Association française de comptabilité* – former (1979 to 2002). **Aims** Contribute to the development and dissemination of knowledge in the field of accounting, control and audit; develop exchange networks between professionals, teachers and researchers. **Structure** General Assembly; Administrative Board; Bureau. **Languages** French. **Activities** Awards/prizes/competitions; events/meetings; financial and/or material support; knowledge management/information dissemination; networking/liaising. **Events** *Congrès Annuel* Montpellier (France) 2020, *Congrès Annuel* Paris (France) 2019, *Congrès Annuel* Nantes (France) 2018, *Congrès Annuel* Poitiers (France) 2017, *Congrès Annuel* Clermont-Ferrand (France) 2016. **Publications** *Comptabilité Contrôle Audit CCA* (3 a year) in English, French – journal; *Audit Comptabilité Contrôle: Recherches Appliquées ACCRA* (3 a year) – online journal; *AFC Informe* – online newsletter. Congress proceedings. **Members** Full (400). Membership countries not specified. [2021.09.11/XM3709/D]

- ♦ Association Francophone contre la Polychondrite Chronique Atrophiante (internationally oriented national body)
- ♦ Association francophone pour le développement de l'éducation médicale (inactive)
- ♦ Association francophone des droits de l'homme âgé (internationally oriented national body)

♦ Association francophone d'éducation comparée (AFEC) 02610

French-Speaking Comparative Education Association (FCES)

Pres LACES, Université de Bordeaux Segalen, Site de la Victoire, 33076 Bordeaux CEDEX, France. E-mail: afecbureau2012@gmail.com.
URL: http://web.mediateam.fr/afec/

History 19 Jan 1973, Sèvres (France). **Aims** Bring together individuals who understand French and are concerned with problems of comparative education: promote the pooling of their experience and research; provide administrators, researchers and teachers with material likely to encourage educational renewal and innovation in their respective countries; develop exchanges with all other national, European and world-wide associations concerned with problems of comparative education. **Structure** General Assembly (annual); Board of Directors. **Languages** English, French. **Staff** Part-time, voluntary. **Finance** Sources: members' dues. **Activities** Organizes symposia, seminars, colloquia and study sessions; regular information exchange. **Events** *Annual International Colloquium General Assembly* Montréal, QC (Canada) 2012, *Annual International Colloquium General Assembly* Dijon (France) 2009, *Annual International Colloquium General Assembly* Alexandria (Egypt) 2007, *International conference on education and training* Ho Chi Minh City (Vietnam) 2006, *International conference on education and training / Annual International Colloquium General Assembly* Villeneuve d'Ascq (France) 2006. **Publications** *Education Comparée* (2 a year) – revue; *Bulletin d'information et de liaison* (2 a year) in French; *Annuaire de l'éducation comparée* (annual) in French.
Members Individuals and students in 51 countries and territories:
Algeria, Argentina, Belgium, Benin, Brazil, Bulgaria, Burkina Faso, Cameroon, Canada, Central African Rep, Chad, Chile, China, Congo Brazzaville, Congo DR, Côte d'Ivoire, Denmark, France, Gabon, Germany, Greece, Haiti, Hong Kong, Hungary, India, Israel, Italy, Korea Rep, Madagascar, Mali, Netherlands, New Zealand, Nicaragua, Niger, Norway, Paraguay, Poland, Portugal, Romania, Russia, Rwanda, South Africa, Spain, Switzerland, Togo, Tunisia, Türkiye, UK, USA, Vanuatu, Vietnam.
NGO Relations Member of (1): *World Council of Comparative Education Societies (WCCES, #21322).*
[2019/XD4430/v/**C**]

♦ Association Francophone pour l'Etude et la Recherche sur les Urgences Psychiatriques (AFERUP) 02611

SG Unité d'Accueil des Urgences Psychiatriques, Hôp Central, 29 Avenue du Maréchal de Lattre de Tassigny, 54035 Nancy CEDEX, France. T. +33383852088. Fax +33383521031.
URL: http://www.aferup.fr/

History Founded in 1986, as a francophone scholarly society. **Structure** Council. Bureau, comprising President, 2 Vice-Presidents, Secretary-General, Deputy Secretary-General, Treasurer and Deputy Treasurer. **Events** *Annual Congrès* La Rochelle (France) 2015, *Congress* Toulouse (France) 2014, *Congrès Annuel* Toulouse (France) 2013, *Congress* Turin (Italy) 2013, *Congrès annuel / Congress* Brussels (Belgium) 2011.
[2017/XJ5535/**D**]

♦ Association Francophone Européenne des Diagnostics Infirmiers / see Association Francophone Européenne des Diagnostics Interventions Résultats Infirmiers (#02612)

♦ Association Francophone Européenne des Diagnostics Interventions Résultats Infirmiers (AFEDI) 02612

Contact Rue Royale 336, 1030 Brussels, Belgium. E-mail: af.gadisseux@skynet.be.
URL: http://www.afedi.com/

History Jan 1991, Paris (France), as *Association Francophone Européenne des Diagnostics Infirmiers.* Registered in accordance with Belgian law, 8 Aug 1991. **Aims** Develop *nursing diagnostics* as a contribution to promoting quality, recognition and management of nursing *care*; participate in international research in the field, including international *taxonomy* of nursing diagnostics; develop exchange networks and guarantee the scientific base of French-speaking diagnostic nursing. **Structure** General Assembly (every 2 years). Council, consisting of 18 members plus 18 alternate members. Bureau, consisting of President, Vice-Presidents, Secretaries, Treasurer and Advisers. Committees. Divisions. **Languages** French. **Staff** 3.00 FTE, voluntary. **Finance** Members' dues. **Activities** Programme: action on quality and management of nursing care; integration of diagnostic nurses in the hospital environment; exchanges with nurses in different sectors and European countries; development of nursing knowledge through practice; identification of new nursing diagnostics; validation of those already existing. **Events** *Study Days* Paris (France) 2012, *General Assembly* Brussels (Belgium) 1993, *Study days / General Assembly* Brussels (Belgium) 1993.
Members Full qualified nurses; Adhering students of nursing science. Individuals in 6 countries:
Belgium, France, Italy, Luxembourg, Spain, Switzerland. [2013.10.08/XD3265/**D**]

♦ Association francophone européenne d'études baha'ies (AFEEB) .. 02613

Contact c/o Centre baha'i, 45 rue Pergolèse, 75116 Paris, France. E-mail: afeeb@afeeb.org.
URL: http://www.afeeb.org/

History 1983, Geneva (Switzerland), as *Association européenne francophone pour les études baha'ies.* Name subsequently changed to: *Association d'études baha'ies – Europe francophone.* **Aims** Contribute to progress and development of *knowledge* in the light of Baha'i *teachings*; encourage and sustain *young* people in this research; promote and carry out research in scientific, artistic, philosophical and religious fields; contribute to contemporary essential debates, especially on transition towards a *global society*; favour dialogue between thinkers of various horizons and all those interested in the *ethical* dimension of things and in *interdisciplinary* approaches to problems. **Structure** Committee, consisting of representatives of the 4 member countries. Secretariat lies with the Executive Committee. **Languages** French. **Staff** None. **Finance** Members' dues. Baha'i institutions. **Activities** Organizes: study groups and conferences on regional and national level; meetings on European level. **Events** *Meeting* Luxembourg (Luxembourg) 2009, *Meeting* Paris (France) 2008, *Conference* Paris (France) 2007, *Conference / Meeting* Luxembourg (Luxembourg) 2006, *Conference / Meeting* Brussels (Belgium) 2005. **Publications** *Histoire du salut et changement de paradigme* by U Schaefer; *Justice ou miséricorde ?* by Udo Schaefer; *Une preuve scientifique de l'existence de Dieu* by William S Hatcher. Proceedings.
Members Organizations and individuals in 5 countries:
Belgium, Canada, France, Luxembourg, Switzerland.
NGO Relations Affiliated to: *Association for Baha'i Studies (ABS, #02391).* Collaborates with: *Baha'i International Community (#03062).* [2009.07.29/XE1469/v/**E**]

♦ Association francophone des experts et des consultants de la coopération technique internationale (internationally oriented national body)
♦ Association Francophone de Formation et Recherche en Thérapie Comportementale et Cognitive (unconfirmed)
♦ Association Francophone des Glycogénoses (internationally oriented national body)
♦ Association francophone des humanités numériques/digitales / see Humanistica (#10971)
♦ Association francophone internationale du diabète (inactive)
♦ Association francophone internationale des directeurs d'établissements scolaires (inactive)

♦ Association francophone internationale des groupes d'animation de la paraplégie (AFIGAP) 02614

Contact address not obtained. E-mail: contact@afigap.com.
URL: https://afigap.com/

History 1979, Paris (France). Founder and initial Permanent Secretary was Marc Maury. Registration: France. **Aims** Study and develop ways of increasing knowledge and treatment of paraplegics. **Structure** Executive Council of 24, includes representatives of all professional groupings included among the members. Bureau, consisting of President, 4 Vice-Presidents, Secretary-General, Secretary, Treasurer, Deputy Treasurer and up to 6 other members. **Languages** French. **Staff** 0.50 FTE, paid. **Finance** Members' dues. **Activities** Organizes annual congress, regional meetings, meetings on specific subjects. **Events** *Congress* Lyon (France) 2009, *Congress* Namur (Belgium) 2009, *Congress* Bordeaux (France) / Mulhouse (France) 2008, *Congress* France 2007, *Congress* Rouen (France) 2006. **Publications** Congress proceedings – separately or in 'Annales de réadaptation et de médecine physique'.
Members Individuals – medical and paramedical personnel – in 17 countries:
Algeria, Belgium, France, Gabon, Germany, Greece, Italy, Morocco, Portugal, Romania, Senegal, Slovenia, Spain, Sweden, Switzerland, Togo, Tunisia.
NGO Relations Affiliated with: *International Spinal Cord Society (ISCoS, #15581).* [2021/XD1030/v/**D**]

♦ Association francophone internationale de recherche scientifique en éducation (AFIRSE) 02615

Pres 7 Le Feuil, 35580 Saint-Senoux, France.
URL: http://www.afirse.com/

History 1952, as *Association internationale de pédagogie expérimentale de langue française (AIPELF).* Constitution adopted 1958, Paris (France); amended 1963. Present name adopted 1990, when restructured into current form. Registered in accordance with French law. **Aims** Encourage development of scientific educational research in a critical perspective, and its use in the advancement of education; promote cooperation and exchange between those engaged in relevant research; improve techniques and materials for more thorough and accurate research; promote international teams of searches; disseminate research results to education authorities. **Structure** General Assembly; Board. **Languages** French. **Finance** Members' dues. Grants; sale of publications. **Activities** Knowledge management/information dissemination; events/ meetings. **Events** *Rhétoriques, résistances, reprises d'initiatives dans les nouvelles approches pluriculturelles en éducation* Beirut (Lebanon) 2019, *Colloque* Lisbon (Portugal) 2017, *Colloque* Lisbon (Portugal) 2016, *Congress* Lecce (Italy) 2015, *Diversité et complexité de l'évaluation en éducation et formation – contributions de la recherche* Lisbon (Portugal) 2015. **Publications** *L'année internationale de la recherche et sciences de l'éducation* (annual) – review; *Recherches et éducation* – electronic review. Proceedings.
Members Full (those directly involved in relevant research in higher educational or nationally approved establishments); Associate (those having an interest in experimental pedagogics, but outside the above definition). Full in 19 countries:
Algeria, Belgium, Brazil, Burundi, Cameroon, Canada, Cape Verde, Congo Brazzaville, Congo DR, France, Gabon, Greece, Guinea, Italy, Mexico, Niger, Portugal, Spain, Switzerland.
National sections in 6 countries:
Belgium, Brazil, Canada, France, Mexico, Portugal.
Regional section in Africa.
NGO Relations Located at: *International Centre for Educational Research, Sèvres (CIEP).*
[2019.12.13/XD0978/v/**D**]

♦ Association francophone internationale des spécialistes du traitement des abuseurs sexuels (no recent information)
♦ Association Francophone de MAnagement du Tourisme (internationally oriented national body)

♦ Association francophone oecuménique de missiologie (AFOM) 02616

Pres Centre d'études Istina, 45 rue de la Glacière, 75013 Paris, France.
Administration 102 bd Arago, 75014 Paris, France. E-mail: info@afom.org.
URL: http://www.afom.org/

History 23 Apr 1994. **Aims** Promote: specific contribution of the Francophone world to Christian missiology in an ecumenical approach; theological research on the mission in connection with the experience; missiological training at university and Church level, pastoral and lay; communication and spreading of the work done in this direction. **Structure** General Assembly (annual), always in Paris (France); Committee. **Languages** French. **Staff** No paid staff. **Finance** Members' dues. **Events** *Assemblée Générale* Paris (France) 2021, *Assemblée Générale* Paris (France) 2019, *Assemblée Générale* Paris (France) 2018, *Assemblée Générale* Paris (France) 2017, *Assemblée Générale* Paris (France) 2016. **Publications** Books; anthologies.
Members in 7 countries:
Belgium, Benin, Finland, France, Germany, Luxembourg, Switzerland.
NGO Relations Member of: *International Association for Mission Studies (IAMS, #12032).*
[2017.10.30/XM0180/**D**]

♦ Association francophone pour la prévention-réadaptation cardiovasculaire (AFPRC) 02617

Francophone Association for Cardiovascular Prevention and Rehabilitation

Scientific Sec CRC Leopold Bellan, 38 rue de Choisy, 60170 Tracy le Mont, France.
Tech Secretariat OVERCOME, 3-5 bd Paul-Emile Victor, 92523 Neuilly-sur-Seine CEDEX, France. T. +33141920120. Fax +33146410521. E-mail: afprc@overcome.fr.

Structure General Assembly (annual). Committee, comprising President, Secretary, Treasurer and 3 further members. **Events** *Congress* Tunis (Tunisia) 2010, *Congress* Lausanne (Switzerland) 2009, *Congrès* Paris (France) 2006, *Congress* Paris (France) 2005, *Congress* Crans-Montana (Switzerland) 2004.
Members in 5 countries:
Belgium, Canada, France, Luxembourg, Switzerland. [2014/XM2703/**D**]

♦ Association francophone des professionnels de l'aéronautique (internationally oriented national body)

♦ Association francophone des professionnels de l'expérience utilisateur (Flupa) 02618

Contact 30 Ter Bd Val Claret, Bat A, 03300 Antibes, France. E-mail: info@flupa.eu.
URL: http://flupa.eu/

History Founded 2008, as a chapter of *User Experience Professionals Association (UXPA, #20735).* **Aims** Act as a network where professionals can exchange experience; promote the practice of experience professionals. **Structure** Council; Committee. **Events** *Ux Days* Paris (France) 2021, *Ux Days* Paris (France) 2020, *Ux Days* Paris (France) 2019, *Ux Days* Paris (France) 2018.
Members Full in 4 countries:
Belgium, France, Luxembourg, Switzerland. [2018/XM6640/t/**E**]

♦ Association francophone pour la recherche en activités physiques et sportives (AFRAPS) 02619

Pres 230 chemin des Térébinthes, 34830 Clapiers, France.
URL: https://afraps.org/

History Registered in accordance with French law. **Structure** General Assembly (annual). Board of Directors of 14 members, including President, Secretary and Treasurer. **Finance** Members' dues. **Publications** *AFRAPS Bulletin*; *STAPS* – newsletter. Books. **Members** Membership countries not specified. [2020/XD9366/**D**]

♦ Association Francophone du Rotomoulage (internationally oriented national body)
♦ Association francophone pour le savoir / see Acfas
♦ Association Francophone pour les Soins Oncologiques de Support (internationally oriented national body)
♦ Association francophone de spectrométrie de masses des solides (no recent information)
♦ Association francophone du tourisme d'affaires (internationally oriented national body)
♦ Association Francophone des Types Psychologiques (internationally oriented national body)

♦ Association francophone des utilisateurs de Linux et des logiciels libres (AFUL) 02620

French Speaking Linux and Free Software Users' Association

Contact AFUL, Boîte Associative 14, 23 rue Grenetta, 75002 Paris, France. E-mail: secretaire@aful.org.
URL: https://aful.org/

History Registered in accordance with French law. **NGO Relations** *Association des informaticiens de langue française (AILF, #02644)*; *EuroLinux Alliance for a Free Information Infrastructure (#05707)*; *Organization of Internet Users (no recent information).* [2017.03.09/XE4292/**E**]

♦ Association fraternelle internationale (#11465)
♦ Association of Free Trade Zones of Latin America and the Caribbean (no recent information)
♦ Association of French-Language Countries Nationless Esperantist Workers (#20488)
♦ Association of French Language Jurists / see Association Henri Capitant des amis de la culture juridique française (#02631)
♦ Association of French-Language Leprologists (#02787)
♦ Association of French-Speaking African Employers' Organizations (no recent information)
♦ Association of French-Speaking Airports / see Les Aéroports Francophones (#00145)
♦ Association of French-Speaking Computer Professionals and Users (#02644)

- ♦ Association of French-Speaking Dermatologists (#02469)
- ♦ Association of French-Speaking Dermatologists and Syphiligraphers / see Association des dermatologistes francophones (#02469)
- ♦ Association of French-Speaking Dieticians (inactive)
- ♦ Association of French-Speaking and European University Administrations in Medicine and Odontology (#00115)
- ♦ Association of French-Speaking Microbiologists (inactive)
- ♦ Association of French-Speaking Palynologists (#02849)
- ♦ Association of French-Speaking Pediatricians (#02855)
- ♦ Association of French Speaking Planetaria (internationally oriented national body)
- ♦ Association of French-Speaking Psychologists of the Working Environment / see Association internationale de psychologie du travail de langue française (#02734)
- ♦ Association of French-Speaking Societies of Philosophy (#02918)
- ♦ Association of French Speaking Veterinarians (no recent information)
- ♦ Association for French Studies in Southern Africa (internationally oriented national body)
- ♦ Association of French Teachers in Africa (no recent information)
- ♦ Association of Fundraising Professionals (internationally oriented national body)
- ♦ Association FUTURALLIA (#10045)

♦ Association of Futures Markets (AFM) 02621

SG Racz Aladar út 26, Budapest 1121, Hungary. T. +36303435370. Fax +36302490057.
URL: http://www.afmorg.net/

History 1998, Buenos Aires (Argentina). Registered in accordance with Hungarian law. **Aims** Promote and encourage the establishment of new derivative and related markets. **Structure** General Assembly. Executive Board, including Chairman and Secretary. Secretariat. **Finance** Sources: members' dues. **Events** *Conference* London (UK) 2022, *Conference* Budapest (Hungary) 2020, *Conference* Chicago, IL (USA) 2019, *Conference* Bangkok (Thailand) 2018, *Conference* Buenos Aires (Argentina) / Rosario (Argentina) 2017. **Members** Full; Associate. Membership countries not specified. **NGO Relations** Memorandum of Understanding with: *South Asian Federation of Exchanges (SAFE, #19729).* [2014/XJ4828/**C**]

- ♦ Association de gastroentérologie de l'Asie et du Pacifique / see Asian Pan-Pacific Society for Paediatric Gastroenterology, Hepatology, and Nutrition (#01651)
- ♦ Association gay internationale / see ILGA World (#11120)
- ♦ Association of Gay and Lesbian Choruses in Europe / see LEGATO (#16441)
- ♦ Association générale de l'automobile / see Fédération Internationale de l'Automobile (#09613)
- ♦ Association générale des entrepreneurs d'Amérique (internationally oriented national body)
- ♦ Association générale des intervenants retraités (internationally oriented national body)
- ♦ Association générale des intervenants retraités – actions de bénévoles pour la coopération et le développement / see Association générale des intervenants retraités
- ♦ Association de Genève (#10119)
- ♦ Association genevoise pour l'alimentation infantile (internationally oriented national body)
- ♦ Association genevoise internationale des employés d'hôtel et restaurant (inactive)
- ♦ Association de géodésie et d'économie foncière du Commonwealth (#04313)
- ♦ Association géodésique internationale / see International Association of Geodesy (#11914)
- ♦ Association des géographes africains (no recent information)

♦ Association of Geographic Information Laboratories for Europe (AGILE) 02622

Sec address not obtained.
URL: http://www.agile-online.org/

History Apr 1998, Enschede (Netherlands). **Aims** Promote academic teaching and research on geographic information laboratories at the European level; promote cooperation in the field. **Structure** Council, Chairman, Secretary/Treasurer and 6 members. **Languages** English. **Finance** Members' dues. **Events** *Conference* Crete (Greece) 2021, *Conference* Chania (Greece) 2020, *Conference* Lund (Sweden) 2018, *Conference* Wageningen (Netherlands) 2017, *Conference* Helsinki (Finland) 2016. **Publications** *AGILE Newsletter* – online.
Members Full (91) in 24 countries:
Austria, Belgium, Bosnia-Herzegovina, Czechia, Denmark, Finland, France, Germany, Greece, Hungary, Ireland, Israel, Italy, Netherlands, Norway, Poland, Portugal, Serbia, Slovenia, Spain, Sweden, Switzerland, Türkiye, UK.
NGO Relations Memorandum of Understanding with: *Geographical Information Systems International Group (GISIG, #10133).* Member of: *European Geographic Information Network (EGIN, #07387); International Society for Photogrammetry and Remote Sensing (ISPRS, #15362).* [2021/XD7277/**D**]

- ♦ Association de géologie carpato-balkanique (#03586)
- ♦ Association de géologues arabes (#00967)
- ♦ Association des géophysiciens en exploration et recherches en Afrique de l'Ouest (inactive)

♦ Association of Geoscientists for International Development (AGID) . 02623

Association pour le développement international en sciences de la terre – Asociación de Geocientificos para el Desarrollo Internacional

Pres Geological Survey of Bangladesh, Segunbagicha, 153 Pioneer Rd, Dhaka 1000, Bangladesh. T. +88028322855 – +88029337559.
Vice-Pres address not obtained.
URL: http://www.agid-international.org/

History 19 May 1974, Canada. 19 May 1974, St Johns (Canada). Also referred to in French as *Association pour le développement international en sciences de la terre.* **Aims** Encourage communication among individuals, societies, agencies and corporations interested in applying geosciences to international development; promote geoscientific activities related to needs of *developing countries*; promote and encourage among earth scientists an awareness of their responsibility in the management of *natural resources*; emphasize the fundamental role of the geosciences in social and economic development. **Structure** General Assembly (every 4 years during International Geological Congress). Executive Committee, consisting of President, Secretary/Treasurer and Past President. Other officers: 5 Vice-Presidents (Africa; Asia; Europe; Latin America; North America). **Languages** English. **Staff** part-time, voluntary. **Finance** Sources: grants; members' dues. Supported by: *International Union of Geological Sciences (IUGS, #15777).* **Activities** Events/meetings; financial and/or material support. **Events** *Quadrennial General Assembly* Brisbane, QLD (Australia) 2012, *International conference on geoscience for global development* Dhaka (Bangladesh) 2009, *Quadrennial General Assembly* Oslo (Norway) 2008, *Quadrennial General Assembly* Florence (Italy) 2004, *International symposium on land subsidence* Ravenna (Italy) 2000. **Publications** *Geoscience Newsletter* (4 a year); *Geoscience and Development* (annual). *AGID Report Series.* Directories of organizations and individuals interested in international development. **Members** Individual Life and Ordinary Members (about 500). Membership countries not specified. **Consultative Status** Consultative status granted from: *ECOSOC (#05331)* (Ros A). **NGO Relations** *Geological Society of Africa (GSAf, #10135).* [2020.04.01/XB0042/**C**]

♦ Association for Geospatial Information in South-East Europe (AGISEE) 02624

Exec Sec Mladost 1, bl 98 B, Entr B – apt 49, 1797 Sofia, Bulgaria. T. +35928702878. E-mail: rsp@tu-sofia.bg.

Aims Promote access to, sharing and use of geospatial information (GI); work towards development of a spatial data infrastructure (SDI) allowing users and providers globally and regionally to distribute and access GI independent of scale, formats and standards. **Structure** General Assembly; Managing Board. **Activities** Events/meetings.
Members Full in 11 countries:
Albania, Bosnia-Herzegovina, Bulgaria, Croatia, Germany, Italy, Kosovo, North Macedonia, Romania, Serbia, Türkiye.
NGO Relations *South-East European Research Institute on Geo Sciences (Geo-SEE Institute).* [2021/XJ9086/**D**]

♦ Association of Geotechnical Societies in Southeast Asia (AGSSEA) . 02625

Secretariat c/o AIT, Km 42 Paholyothin Highway, Klong Luang, Pathumthani, Bangkok, 12120, Thailand. T. +6625245864. Fax +6625245865. E-mail: seags@ait.ac.th.
URL: http://www.seags.ait.ac.th/

History Originated 2007, Kuala Lumpur (Malaysia), at 16th Southeast Asian Geotechnical Conference. Inaugurated 5 Dec 2007, Malaysia. Statutes revised May 2010. An enlarged society of *Southeast Asian Geotechnical Society (SEAGS, #19769).* **Aims** Promote cooperation among geotechnical societies in Southeast Asia for the advancement of knowledge in geotechnical engineering. **Structure** Council; General Committee; Secretariat. **Finance** Members' dues. **Activities** Events/meetings; training/education.
Members Societies in 7 countries:
Hong Kong, Indonesia, Malaysia, Singapore, Taiwan, Thailand, Vietnam. [2019/XM7501/**D**]

- ♦ Association of German Development and Humanitarian Aid NGOs (internationally oriented national body)
- ♦ Association of German Development Non-Governmental Organizations / see Verband Entwicklungspolitik und Humanitäre Hilfe e.V.
- ♦ Association de gestion internationale collective des oeuvres audiovisuelles (#02658)

♦ Association des Gestionnaires et Partenaires Africains de la Route (AGEPAR) 02626

Association of African Managers and Partners of Roads

SG DGIR, BP 351, Cotonou, Benin. T. +22670200506 – +22995283672 – +22997764042. Fax +22921316774. E-mail: berestani876@gmail.com – fidzit2017@gmail.com.
AGEPAR: https://www.a-gepar.org

History 27 Oct 1995, Yamoussoukro (Côte d'Ivoire). Former names and other names: *Association of African Road Directors (ADAR)* – former; *Association des directeurs africains des routes* – former. Registration: Préfecture de l'Atlantique et du Littoral, No/ID: 2006/0220 DEP-ATL, Start date: 27 Oct 1995, Benin. **Aims** Promote development of the road sector; encourage research, professional training and the dissemination of road related information; promote harmonization of *construction*, maintenance and operation standards between the members. **Structure** Located in Cotonou. **Staff** 8.00 FTE, voluntary. **Finance** Sources: meeting proceeds; members' dues. Annual budget: 60,980 EUR (2021). **Events** *Assises* Yamoussoukro (Côte d'Ivoire) 2016, *Assises* Yaoundé (Cameroon) 2013, *Assises* Libreville (Gabon) 2011, *Assises* Dakar (Senegal) 2009, *Seminar* Ouagadougou (Burkina Faso) 2007.
Members National committees in 15 countries:
Benin, Burkina Faso, Cameroon, Chad, Congo Brazzaville, Congo DR, Côte d'Ivoire, Gabon, Guinea, Madagascar, Mali, Mauritania, Niger, Senegal, Togo. [2022.02.15/XD5052/**D**]

- ♦ Association de Gestionnaires des Réseaux de Transport de l'électricité Méditerranéens (#02803)
- ♦ Association de gestion du PDM / see Municipal Development Partnership for West and Central Africa (#16902)
- ♦ Association de gestion des ports de l'Afrique de l'Est et australe (#18462)
- ♦ Association de gestion des ports de l'Afrique de l'Ouest et du Centre (#18463)
- ♦ Association of Global Automakers (internationally oriented national body)

♦ Association of Global Custodians (AGC) 02627

Counsel c/o Baker and McKenzie LLP, 815 Connecticut Ave NW, Washington DC 20006-4078, USA. T. +12024527000. Fax +12024527074. E-mail: john.conroy@bakermckenzie.com – info@theagc.com.
URL: http://www.theagc.com/

History 1996. **Aims** Provide securities safekeeping services and asset-servicing functions to primarily institutional cross-border investors worldwide; represent common interests of *financial* member institutions on *regulatory* and *market* structure matters. **Structure** Committees (8). **Languages** English. **Activities** Advocacy/lobbying/activism; knowledge management/information dissemination; politics/policy/regulatory. **Members** Financial institutions (12). Membership countries not specified. [2019.12.16/XJ8819/**C**]

- ♦ Association for Global Strategic Information (inactive)

♦ Association for Gnotobiotics 02628

Main Office address not obtained. E-mail: gnoto.association@gmail.com.
URL: http://gnotobiotics.wildapricot.org/

History 1961, by several organizations including *Association for Gnotobiotics.* Reorganized, 2017, following years of inactivity. Registered in accordance with USA law. **Aims** Stimulate research in the field of gnotobiotics. **Structure** General Assembly. Board, comprising 12 members, elects officers: President, President-Elect, Secretary-Treasurer. **Languages** English. **Staff** Voluntary; occasional contractual. **Finance** Members' dues: individual, corporate. Annual budget: US$ 3,000. **Events** *Annual meeting* St Louis, MO (USA) 2006, *Annual meeting* Raleigh, NC (USA) 2002, *Annual meeting* Belo Horizonte (Brazil) 2001, *Annual Meeting* Raleigh, NC (USA) 2000.
Members Individuals in 20 countries:
Australia, Belgium, Brazil, Canada, China, Denmark, France, Germany, Hungary, Israel, Italy, Japan, Mexico, Netherlands, Romania, South Africa, Sweden, Switzerland, UK, USA.
NGO Relations Affiliated with: *International Association for Gnotobiology (IAG, #11921).* [2018/XD6555/**D**]

- ♦ Association of Gospel Rescue Missions (internationally oriented national body)
- ♦ Association des grands parcs d'expositions européens (#07726)
- ♦ Association des Guides et Scouts d'Europe / see Union Internationale des Guides et Scouts d'Europe – Fédération du Scoutisme Européen (#20426)
- ♦ Association de gymnastique des pays nordiques (inactive)
- ♦ Association haltérophile nordique (#17465)

♦ Association des hautes juridictions de cassation des pays ayant en partage l'usage du Français (AHJUCAF) 02629

SG Cour de Cassation de France, 5 quai de l'Horloge, 75001 Paris, France. T. +33146346740. Fax +33144346740. E-mail: sgahjucaf@ahjucaf.org – mehdi.ben-mimoun@justice.fr.
General: http://www.ahjucaf.org/

History 17 May 2001, Paris (France). Founded by *Agence intergouvernementale de La Francophonie (inactive)*, now *Organisation internationale de la Francophonie (OIF, #17809).* Registration: Start date: 1 Jun 2001, France. **Aims** Promote understanding, solidarity, cooperation and exchange of information between members. **Structure** General Assembly (every 3 years). Bureau, including President, Past-President, 5 Vice-Presidents, Secretary-General, Treasurer and 1 observer of the Organisation internationale de la Francophonie. **Languages** French. **Staff** 1.00 FTE, paid. **Finance** Members' dues. **Activities** Organizes thematic congresses; publishing activity. **Events** *Congrès / Congress* Beirut (Lebanon) 2013, *Congress* Ottawa, ON (Canada) 2010, *Congrès* Ottawa, ON (Canada) 2010, *Congrès / Congress* Dakar (Senegal) 2007, *Congrès / Congress* Marrakech (Morocco) 2004. **Publications** *Le juge de cassation à l'aube du 21ème ciècle* (2006). **Information Services** *JURICAF* – database.
Members Supreme Courts (48) in 45 countries:
Albania, Belgium, Benin, Bulgaria, Burkina Faso, Burundi, Cambodia, Cameroon, Canada, Cape Verde, Central African Rep, Chad, Comoros, Congo Brazzaville, Congo DR, Côte d'Ivoire, Czechia, Dominican Rep, Egypt, Equatorial Guinea, France, Gabon, Guinea, Guinea-Bissau, Haiti, Hungary, Lebanon, Madagascar, Mali, Mauritania, Mauritius, Moldova, Monaco, Morocco, Niger, North Macedonia, Poland, Romania, Rwanda, Sao Tomé-Principe, Senegal, Slovakia, Switzerland, Togo, Tunisia, Vanuatu, Vietnam.
Regional organizations (3), listed in this Yearbook:
Communauté économique et monétaire d'Afrique centrale (CEMAC, #04374); Organisation pour l'Harmonisation en Afrique du Droit des Affaires (OHADA, #17806); Union économique et monétaire Ouest africaine (UEMOA, #20377). [2020/XD9295/y/**D**]

♦ Association for Health Information and Libraries in Africa (AHILA) . 02630

Association pour l'information et les bibliothèques de santé en Afrique (AIBSA)

Pres c/o ITOCA, 276 West Avenue, Centurion, South Africa. E-mail: president@ahila.org – executive@ahila.org.

URL: http://www.ahila.org/
History 1980, Belgrade (Yugoslavia), as *African Medical Library Association (AMLA)*. Inaugurated and constitution adopted, 23 Aug 1984, Nairobi (Kenya). **Aims** Improve the provision of information to health and *medical* workers in Africa; encourage *professional* development of members; promote resource-sharing and exchange of experience and information among African health and *biomedical* libraries and documentation centres; promote the development and standardization of national databases of medical and health literature produced in African countries and eventually an African Index Medicus. **Structure** General Assembly (every 2 years, at Congress); Executive Council. **Languages** English, French, Portuguese. **Finance** Members' dues. Other sources: donations; grants. Most regular sponsor: *WHO Regional Office for Africa (AFRO, #20943)*. **Activities** Events/meetings; publishing activities. **Events** *Congress* Pretoria (South Africa) 2022, *Congress* Pretoria (South Africa) 2021, *Biennial Congress and General Assembly* Ibadan (Nigeria) 2019, *Biennial Congress and General Assembly* Kampala (Uganda) 2016, *Biennial Congress and General Assembly* Dar es Salaam (Tanzania UR) 2014. **Publications** *AHILA Information Bulletin*. *Directory of Health Sciences Libraries and Information Centres in Africa* (1996); *AHILA Directory* (1996); *African Index Medicus*.
Members Individual librarians, documentalists and others involved in the field in the African Region of WHO; Associate (non-voting) nationals of countries outside the region; Institutional medical and health services libraries and documentation centres in the region; Associate (non-voting) institutional similar outside the region; Fellows; Honorary Members. Members in 41 countries:
Algeria, Benin, Botswana, Burkina Faso, Burundi, Cameroon, Cape Verde, Central African Rep, Chad, Comoros, Congo Brazzaville, Congo DR, Côte d'Ivoire, Eritrea, Gambia, Ghana, Guinea, Guinea-Bissau, Kenya, Lesotho, Liberia, Malawi, Mali, Mauritania, Mozambique, Namibia, Niger, Rwanda, Senegal, Seychelles, Sierra Leone, South Africa, Sweden, Switzerland, Tanzania UR, Togo, Uganda, UK, USA, Zambia, Zimbabwe.
IGO Relations *UNESCO (#20322)*. [2019.12.12/XD0907/**D**]

♦ Association Henri Capitant des amis de la culture juridique française 02631

Henri Capitant Association for the French Legal System
SG 12 place du Panthéon, 75005 Paris, France. T. +33143544317. Fax +33140518652.
URL: http://www.henricapitant.org/
History 1935, Paris (France), as *Association of French Language Jurists – Association des juristes de langue française*. Statutes last modified 3 Mar 1977. **Aims** Promote the spread of French legal methods by means of regular international congresses. **Structure** General Assembly (once a year). Council, consisting of not less than 16 and not more than 24 members. Board, consisting of President, 2 Vice-Presidents, Secretary General, Assistant Secretary General and Treasurer. **Languages** French. **Finance** Members' dues. **Events** *Congrès Annuel* Paris (France) 2019, *Congrès Annuel* Montréal, QC (Canada) / Ottawa, ON (Canada) 2018, *Congrès Annuel* Münster (Germany) / Berlin (Germany) 2016, *Congrès Annuel* Panama (Panama) 2015, *Congrès Annuel* Madrid (Spain) / Barcelona (Spain) 2014. **Publications** Congress proceedings.
Members National groups and individuals in 54 countries:
Albania, Algeria, Argentina, Austria, Belgium, Benin, Brazil, Bulgaria, Cambodia, Cameroon, Canada, Chad, Chile, Colombia, Costa Rica, Côte d'Ivoire, Dominican Rep, Egypt, Finland, France, Germany, Greece, Guatemala, Haiti, Iran Islamic Rep, Italy, Japan, Kuwait, Lebanon, Luxembourg, Mali, Mexico, Morocco, Netherlands, Panama, Peru, Poland, Portugal, Puerto Rico, Senegal, Serbia, Seychelles, Spain, Sweden, Switzerland, Syrian AR, Togo, Tunisia, Türkiye, UK, Uruguay, USA, Venezuela, Vietnam. [2014/XE8272/**E**]

- ♦ Association d'hépato-gastro-entérologie de l'Afrique noire francophone (no recent information)
- ♦ Association for Heritage Preservation of the Americas (internationally oriented national body)
- ♦ Association of Higher Education Facilities Officers / see APPA-Leadership in Educational Facilities
- ♦ Association hispanoaméricaine des centres de recherches et des entreprises de télécommunication / see Asociación Interamericana de Empresas de Telecomunicaciones (#02160)

♦ Association of Historians of Latin America and the Caribbean 02632

Association des historiens latinoaméricains et des Caraïbes – Asociación de Historiadores Latinoamericanos y del Caribe (ADHILAC)
Exec Sec address not obtained.
URL: http://www.adhilac.com.ar/
History 1974, Mexico. Former names and other names: *ADHILAC Internacional* – alias. **Aims** Promote better understanding among historians of Latin America and the Caribbean. **Structure** International Executive Committee. **Languages** English, Portuguese, Spanish. **Staff** Voluntary. **Finance** Members' dues. Donations. **Activities** Events/meetings. **Events** *Congress* Vienna (Austria) 2014, *Conference* Santa Marta (Colombia) 2010, *Conference* Cadiz (Spain) 2009, *Conference* Caracas (Venezuela) 2007, *Congress* Havana (Cuba) 2003. **Publications** Occasional publications. **Members** National Sections. Membership countries not specified. **NGO Relations** Instrumental in setting up: *Commission internationale d'études historiques latinoaméricaines et des Caraïbes (CIHL, inactive)*. [2022/XD9332/**D**]

- ♦ Association des historiens africains (#02357)
- ♦ Association des historiens de la Caraïbe (#02407)
- ♦ Association des historiens latinoaméricains et des Caraïbes (#02632)
- ♦ Association des historiens latinoaméricanistes européens (#02517)
- ♦ Association for the History of the Northern Seas (no recent information)
- ♦ Association of Holocaust Organizations (internationally oriented national body)
- ♦ Association hôtelière des Caraïbes / see Caribbean Hotel and Tourism Association (#03516)
- ♦ Association des hôtels et restaurants de l'Asie et de l'Australasie (inactive)

♦ Association for Humanistic Psychology (AHP) 02633

Association pour la psychologie humaniste
Exec Dir 2007 Bert Ave, Austin TX 78704, USA. T. +15124418988. Fax +15124412688. E-mail: memberservices@ahpweb.org.
Pres address not obtained.
URL: https://ahpweb.org/
History 1962, San Francisco, CA (USA). Registration: Nonprofit 501(c)(3), USA. **Aims** Explore and further the evolution of the human spirit. **Structure** Board of Directors. **Languages** English. **Finance** Sources: donations; members' dues. Annual budget: 20,000 USD (2020). **Activities** Events/meetings; publishing activities; training/education. **Events** *Annual international conference on conflict resolution* St Petersburg (Russia) 2006, *Annual international youth conference on the ecology of war and peace* St Petersburg (Russia) 2006, *Quest for global healing conference* Ubud (Indonesia) 2006, *Annual international conference on conflict resolution* St Petersburg (Russia) 2005, *Annual international youth conference on the ecology of war and peace* St Petersburg (Russia) 2004. **Publications** *Journal of Humanistic Psychology* (6 a year); *AHP Perspective*. *Directory of Humanistic Professionals*.
Members Individuals in 32 countries and territories:
Argentina, Australia, Bolivia, Bosnia-Herzegovina, Canada, Chile, China, Czechia, Denmark, France, Germany, Hong Kong, Hungary, India, Iran Islamic Rep, Israel, Italy, Japan, Korea Rep, Latvia, Lithuania, Mexico, Netherlands, New Zealand, Norway, Philippines, Russia, Singapore, Switzerland, Taiwan, UK, USA.
Nationals in 6 countries:
Iran Islamic Rep, Italy, Japan, Mexico, UK, USA.
NGO Relations Instrumental in setting up (1): *Common Bond Institute (CBI)*. [2022/XF4985/**F**]

♦ Association for Human Resources Management in International Organizations (AHRMIO) 02634

Chair c/o EFMD Global Network, Grand-Montfleury 48, 1290 Versoix GE, Switzerland. T. +41227554410. Fax +41225948130. E-mail: info@ahrmio.org.
URL: http://www.ahrmio.org/
History 2000. Registered in accordance with French law. **Aims** Promote study and dissemination of information in the field of human resources management in not-for-profit international organizations. **Structure** General Assembly (annual). Board, including President and Treasurer. Advisory Council. Committees (2): Credentials; Finance. **Events** *Annual Conference* Versoix (Switzerland) 2021, *Annual Conference* Brussels (Belgium) 2020, *Annual Conference* Boston, MA (USA) 2019, *Annual Conference* Braga (Portugal) 2018, *Annual Conference* Milan (Italy) 2017.
Members International organizations (44):
- *African Development Bank (ADB, #00283)*;
- *Asian Development Bank (ADB, #01422)*;
- *Association coopérative financière des fonctionnaires internationaux (AMFIE, #02455)*;
- *Bank for International Settlements (BIS, #03165)*;
- *Caribbean Development Bank (CDB, #03492)*;
- *CGIAR System Organization (CGIAR, #03843)*;
- *European Central Bank (ECB, #06466)*;
- *European Court of Auditors (#06854)*;
- *European Organization for Nuclear Research (CERN, #08108)*;
- *European Space Agency (ESA, #08798)*;
- *FAO (#09260)*;
- *ILO (#11123)*;
- *International Atomic Energy Agency (IAEA, #12294)*;
- *International Bank for Reconstruction and Development (IBRD, #12317)*;
- *International Civil Aviation Organization (ICAO, #12581)*;
- *International Criminal Court (ICC, #13108)*;
- *International Criminal Police Organization – INTERPOL (ICPO-INTERPOL, #13110)*;
- *International Federation of Red Cross and Red Crescent Societies (#13526)*;
- *International Maritime Organization (IMO, #14102)*;
- *International Monetary Fund (IMF, #14180)*;
- *International Organization for Migration (IOM, #14454)*;
- *International Telecommunication Union (ITU, #15673)*;
- *Joint United Nations Programme on HIV/AIDS (UNAIDS, #16149)*;
- *NATO (#16945)*;
- *OECD (#17693)*;
- *OPEC Fund for International Development (OFID, #17745)*;
- *Organisation for the Prohibition of Chemical Weapons (OPCW, #17823)*;
- *Organization for Security and Cooperation in Europe (OSCE, #17887)*;
- *Pan American Health Organization (PAHO, #18108)*;
- *UNCTAD (#20285)*;
- *UNDP (#20292)*;
- *UNESCO (#20322)*;
- *UNHCR (#20327)*;
- *UNICEF (#20332)*;
- *UNIDO (#20336)*;
- *United Nations Field Staff Union (UNFSU, #20561)*;
- *United Nations Office for Project Services (UNOPS, #20602)*;
- *United Nations Population Fund (UNFPA, #20612)*;
- *United Nations Relief and Works Agency for Palestine Refugees in the Near East (UNRWA, #20622)*;
- *United Nations (UN, #20515)*;
- *WHO (#20950)*;
- *World Food Programme (WFP, #21510)*;
- *World Intellectual Property Organization (WIPO, #21593)*;
- *World Trade Organization (WTO, #21864)*.

NGO Relations Partners: *Escuela Superior de Administración y Dirección de Empresas (ESADE)*; national organizations and companies. [2017/XM0413/y/**D**]

- ♦ Association for Human Rights and Democracy in Africa (internationally oriented national body)

♦ Association of Human Rights Institutes (AHRI) 02635

Exec Sec c/o Global Justice Academy, Law School, University of Edinburgh, Old College, B18, Edinburgh, EH8 9YL, UK. E-mail: administration@ahri-network.org.
URL: https://new.ahri-network.org/
History Sep 2000, Reykjavik (Iceland). **Events** *Annual Conference* Bilbao (Spain) 2023, *Annual Conference* Pretoria (South Africa) 2022, *Annual Conference* Edinburgh (UK) 2020, *Annual Conference* Potsdam (Germany) 2019, *Annual Conference* Edinburgh (UK) 2018.
Members Associations and institutes (49) in 22 countries:
Austria, Belgium, Denmark, Finland, Germany, Hungary, Iceland, Ireland, Italy, Latvia, Luxembourg, Netherlands, Norway, Poland, Serbia, South Africa, Spain, Sweden, Switzerland, UK.
NGO Relations *Icelandic Human Rights Centre* is a member. [2022/XD9217/**D**]

- ♦ Association of Hydro-Meteorological Equipment Industry / see Association of Hydro-Meteorological Industry (#02636)

♦ Association of Hydro-Meteorological Industry (HMEI) 02636

Exec Sec WMO Bldg, 7 bis Ave de la Paix, 1211 Geneva 2, Switzerland. T. +41227308334. E-mail: hmei@wmo.int.
Administrator address not obtained.
URL: http://www.hmei.org/
History 26 Sep 2001, Budapest (Hungary). Founded during conference of *European Meteorological Society (EMS, #07786)*. Foundation followed the WMO Technical Conference on Instruments and Methods of Observation (CIMO), Oct 2000, Beijing (China). Former names and other names: *Association of Hydro-Meteorological Equipment Industry* – former. **Aims** Promote the views of the providers of products and services in the meteorological, *hydrological*, environmental and related fields in collaboration with WMO. **Structure** General Assembly; Council; Office in Geneva (Switzerland); Secretariat. **Languages** English. **Staff** 1.00 FTE, paid. **Finance** Sources: members' dues. **Activities** Events/meetings; knowledge management/information dissemination; networking/liaising; standards/guidelines. **Events** *General Assembly* Paris (France) 2022, *Global Weather Enterprise Forum* Singapore (Singapore) 2018, *General Assembly* Amsterdam (Netherlands) 2017, *General Assembly* Madrid (Spain) 2016. **Publications** *Member Products Catalogue*.
Members Companies (150) in 30 countries:
Australia, Austria, Brazil, Canada, China, Czechia, Egypt, Finland, France, Germany, Greece, India, Iran Islamic Rep, Italy, Japan, Korea Rep, Netherlands, Norway, Philippines, Poland, Portugal, Russia, Slovakia, South Africa, Spain, Switzerland, Türkiye, UK, United Arab Emirates, USA.
Consultative Status Consultative status granted from: *World Meteorological Organization (WMO, #21649)*.
NGO Relations Liaison status with: *International Organization for Standardization (ISO, #14473)*. [2023.02.16/XJ4034/t/**D**]

♦ Association of Iberian and Latin American Studies of Australasia (AILASA) 02637

Sec c/o JCU-LCRC, PO Box 6811, Cairns QLD 4870, Australia.
URL: http://www.ailasa.org/
History 1993. Statutes most recently amended in Jul 1999. **Aims** Promote: research and teaching of Iberian and Latin American studies in Australasia; professional development of members; public interest in the Iberian Peninsula and Latin America; interchange between Australasia and the Iberian Peninsula and Latin America. **Structure** General Meeting (every 2 years). Coordinating Committee, comprising Executive Committee (President, Secretary and Treasurer) and representatives of 7 states or regions. **Languages** English, Portuguese, Spanish. **Staff** 10.00 FTE, voluntary. **Finance** Members' dues. **Events** *Biennial Conference* Cairns, QLD (Australia) 2020, *Biennial Conference* Melbourne, VIC (Australia) 2018, *Biennial Conference* Auckland (New Zealand) 2016, *Biennial Conference* Sydney, NSW (Australia) 2014, *Biennial Conference* Wellington (New Zealand) 2012. **Publications** *Journal of Iberian and Latin American Studies (JILAS)* (periodical).
Members Individuals in 13 countries:
Argentina, Australia, Brazil, China, Colombia, Ireland, Japan, Korea Rep, New Zealand, Peru, UK, USA, Venezuela. [2018/XD5501/v/**D**]

- ♦ Association ibéroaméricaine des académies olympiques / see Pan-Iberican Association of Olympic Academies (#18181)
- ♦ Association ibéroaméricaine d'athlétisme (inactive)
- ♦ Association ibéroaméricaine des chambres de commerce (#11014)
- ♦ Association ibéroaméricaine d'éditeurs pour handicapés visuels (inactive)
- ♦ Association ibéroaméricaine de l'enseignement supérieur à distance (#11015)
- ♦ Association ibéroaméricaine d'étude des problèmes de l'alcool et de la drogue (no recent information)
- ♦ Association ibéroaméricaine d'information et promotion professionnelle d'assurances (no recent information)
- ♦ Association ibéroaméricaine pour les jeunes mineurs (inactive)

- ♦ Association Ibéroaméricaine de Médecine Aérospatiale / see Asociación Iberoamericana de Medicina Aerospacial (#02147)
- ♦ Association ibéroaméricaine pour la réadaptation des handicapés (inactive)
- ♦ Association ibéro-américaine des technologies de l'eau et de l'irrigation (#02153)
- ♦ Association of Ibero-American Cultural Attachés / see Association of Cultural Attachés from Latin American Countries, Spain and Portugal (#02462)

♦ Association of Ibero-American States for the Development of National Libraries (ABINIA) 02638

Asociación de Estados Iberoamericanos para el Desarrollo de las Bibliotecas Nacionales de Iberoamérica (ABINIA)

Exec Sec Final Av Panteón, Sede Administrativa de la Biblioteca Nacional de Venezuela, Nivel AP4 Foro Libertador, Altagracia, Caracas 1010 DF, Venezuela. T. +582125643189.

History 14 Dec 1989, Mexico City (Mexico). Initially founded as a nongovernmental meeting of library directors to organize an exhibition in 1992 of ancient rare books, manuscripts, engravings and maps. Current title adopted when became an intergovernmental organization, on signature of an agreement by ambassadors of 13 Latin American countries, Oct 1999, Lima (Peru). Former names and other names: *Ibero-American National Library Association* – former (1989 to Oct 1999); *Asociación de Bibliotecas Nacionales de Iberoamérica (ABINIA)* – former (1989 to Oct 1999). **Aims** Encourage exchange of knowledge, information and experience and growth and development of each library, through common policy, technical standards, cooperation programmes and mutual assistance; solve common problems through mutual cooperation; help national libraries in the region respond to challenges of the information society. **Structure** General Assembly of Directors of Member National Libraries. Board of Directors; Technical Committees. Executive Secretariat; Technical Secretariat. **Languages** Portuguese, Spanish. **Staff** 3.00 FTE, paid. **Finance** Annual contribution from Venezuelan government; national libraries membership. Budget (annual): US$ 150,000. **Activities** Designs and carries out projects for recovery, organization and diffusion of regional memory, including participation in UNESCO's *Memory of the World Programme (Memoria Mundi, see: #20322)* and Memory of Iberoamerica. **Events** *General Assembly* Lima (Peru) 2019, *General Assembly* Panama (Panama) 2013, *General Assembly* Madrid (Spain) 2012, *General Assembly* Mexico 2011, *General Assembly* Buenos Aires (Argentina) 2010. **Publications** *ABINIA Newsletter* (4 a year). Members' list; Website Directory. **Information Services** *ABINIA Database.*

Members National libraries in 22 countries:
Argentina, Bolivia, Brazil, Chile, Colombia, Costa Rica, Cuba, Dominican Rep, Ecuador, El Salvador, Guatemala, Honduras, Mexico, Nicaragua, Panama, Paraguay, Peru, Portugal, Puerto Rico, Spain, Uruguay, Venezuela.
Associate libraries (3) in 2 countries:
Colombia, Spain (2).

IGO Relations *Agencia Española de Cooperación Internacional para el Desarrollo (AECID); Information Society Program for Latin America and the Caribbean (INFOLAC, inactive); UNESCO (#20322).* **NGO Relations** International association member of: *International Federation of Library Associations and Institutions (IFLA, #13470).* [2019/XD4338/D*]

♦ Association of IBM Computer Users (COMMON Europe) 02639

Vice Pres address not obtained.
URL: http://www.comeur.org/

History 1962, Switzerland. **Aims** Encourage members to exchange experience and information related to the use of IT; offer members advanced education and training; influence strategy for product development and service levels; encourage ongoing dialogue between members; influence setting of international standards. **Structure** General Assembly; Board of Directors; Executive Committee. **Languages** English. **Staff** 1.00 FTE, paid. **Finance** Members' dues. **Activities** Events/meetings. **Events** *Common Europe Annual Conference* Alicante (Spain) 2022, *Common Europe Annual Conference* Copenhagen (Denmark) 2021, *Common Europe Annual Conference* 2020, *Common Europe Annual Conference* Berlin (Germany) 2019, *Common Europe Annual Conference* Warsaw (Poland) 2018.

Members Country offices in 16 countries:
Austria, Belgium, Czechia, Denmark, France, Germany, Italy, Luxembourg, Netherlands, Norway, Poland, Russia, Slovakia, Sweden, Switzerland, UK. [2020.03.10/XD8605/D]

- ♦ Association of the Ice Cream Industries of the EEC / see EUROGLACES – European Ice Cream Association (#05688)
- ♦ Association of the Ice Cream Industries of the EU / see EUROGLACES – European Ice Cream Association (#05688)
- ♦ Association of Imaging Producers and Equipment Suppliers / see Nuclear Medicine Europe (#17619)
- ♦ Association for Improvement of Safety (no recent information)
- ♦ Association of Independent Discographers – Regional Association of Independent Discographers Balkans / see RUNDA (#18999)
- ♦ Association of Independent Electronic Mass Media Organization of Central Asia (no recent information)

♦ Association of Independent European Lawyers (AIEL) 02640

Sec 2nd Floor, Burwood House, 14-16 Caxton Street, London, SW1H 0QY, UK. T. +442078731000. E-mail: contact@aiel.com.
URL: http://www.aiel.com/

History Founded 1991. **Aims** Offer a cost effective, yet experienced, alternative to large international law firms. **Members** Small to medium sized law firms. Membership countries not specified. [2016/XD6460/D]

- ♦ Association of Independent Mediterranean Producers / see Association internationale des producteurs indépendants de la méditerranée (#02731)
- ♦ Association of the Indigenous Minorities of the North, Siberia and the Far East of the Russian Federation / see Russian Association of Indigenous Peoples of the North

♦ Association of Industrial Ceiling Manufacturers (TAIM) 02641

Verband Industrieller Metalldeckenhersteller

Contact Leostr 22, 40545 Düsseldorf, Germany. T. +492119559327. Fax +49211556466. E-mail: mail@taim.info.
URL: http://www.taim.info/

History 1988, emerging from *Technical Association of Industrial Metal Ceilings (TAIM).* **Aims** Promote quality and positive aspects of metal ceiling systems above and beyond the minimum requirements of standards. **Activities** Certification/accreditation.

Members Full in 6 countries:
Belgium, Denmark, Germany, Switzerland, Türkiye, UK. [2018/XJ4992/t/D]

- ♦ Association of Industrial Metallizers, Coaters and Laminators / see Association of International Metallizers, Coaters and Laminators
- ♦ Association de l'industrie chimique pour la compréhension scientifique (inactive)
- ♦ Association pour l'industrie européenne de chauffage (#02514)
- ♦ Association de l'industrie européenne du coco (inactive)
- ♦ Association de l'industrie européenne des mortiers (#07822)
- ♦ Association de l'industrie de la fonte de fromage de la CEE / see Association de l'industrie de la fonte de fromage de l'UE (#02642)

♦ Association de l'industrie de la fonte de fromage de l'UE (ASSIFONTE) 02642

Association of the Processed Cheese Industry in the EU – Vereinigung der Schmelzkäse-Industrie in der EU

Contact c/o Euromilk, Avenue d'Auderghem 22-28, 1040 Brussels, Belgium. T. +3225495041. E-mail: aanton@euromilk.org.
URL: http://www.assifonte.eu/

History 21 Jan 1964, Brussels (Belgium), as *EEC Association of the Processed Cheese Industry – Association de l'industrie de la fonte de fromage de la CEE – Vereinigung der Schmelzkäse-Industrie in der EWG.* Present name adopted 1994. **Aims** Coordinate and defend the interests of the *processed cheese industry.* **Structure** General Assembly; Comité Directeur; General Secretariat. **Finance** Members' dues. **Events** *Joint Annual Congress* Vienna (Austria) 2019, *Joint Annual Congress* Dublin (Ireland) 2018, *Joint Annual Congress* Stockholm (Sweden) 2017, *Joint Annual Congress* Nice (France) 2016, *Joint Annual Congress* Edinburgh (UK) 2015.

Members Member delegations in 13 countries:
Austria, Czechia, Denmark, Finland, France, Germany, Ireland, Italy, Netherlands, Poland, Spain, Sweden, UK.

IGO Relations Recognized by: *European Commission (EC, #06633).* [2018/XE0485/t/E]

- ♦ Association de l'industrie des jus et nectars de fruits et de légumes de la Communauté économique européenne / see European Fruit Juice Association (#07362)
- ♦ Association de l'industrie des jus et nectars de fruits et de légumes de l'Union européenne / see European Fruit Juice Association (#07362)
- ♦ Association de l'industrie latinoaméricaine de la tannerie (inactive)
- ♦ Association des industriels de l'Amérique latine (#16341)
- ♦ Association de l'industrie pétrolière européenne / see FuelsEurope (#10014)
- ♦ Association des industries des aliments diététiques de la CEE / see Specialised Nutrition Europe (#19909)
- ♦ Association des industries des aliments diététiques de l'Union européenne / see Specialised Nutrition Europe (#19909)
- ♦ Association des industries de la chocolaterie, biscuiterie-biscotterie et confiserie de la CEE / see Association of the Chocolate, Biscuit and Confectionery Industries of the EU (#02427)
- ♦ Association des industries de la chocolaterie, biscuiterie et confiserie de l'UE (#02427)
- ♦ Association des industries des cidres et vins de fruits de la CEE / see Association des Industries des Cidres et Vins de Fruits de l'UE (#02643)

♦ Association des Industries des Cidres et Vins de Fruits de l'UE (AICV) 02643

European Cider and Fruit Wine Association

SG Rue de la Loi 221 – Boîte 5, 1040 Brussels, Belgium. T. +3222350620. Fax +3222829420. E-mail: aicv@aicv.org.
Office Manager address not obtained.
URL: http://www.aicv.org/

History 1961. Former names and other names: *Committee of the Cider and Fruit Wine Industry of the EEC* – former (1961 to 19 Sep 1969); *Association of the Cider and Fruit Wine Industry of the EEC* – former (19 Sep 1969); *Association des industries des cidres et vins de fruits de la CEE* – former (19 Sep 1969); *Vereinigung der Obst- und Fruchtweinindustrie der EWG* – former (19 Sep 1969); *Vereniging van de Cider- en Vruchtenwijnindustrie van de EEG* – former (19 Sep 1969); *Association of Cider and Fruit Wine Industries of the EEC* – former; *Association of the Cider and Fruit Wine Industry of the EU* – former. Registration: EU Transparency Register, No/ID: 27459429876-64. **Aims** Represent member interests among EU authorities and institutions; develop initiatives so as to promote its industries; constitute a forum for development of greater cooperation and solidarity. **Structure** General Assembly; Executive Committee; Secretariat. **Languages** English, French. **Finance** Annual budget: 105,000 EUR (2021). **Activities** Events/meetings. **Events** *Global Cider Forum* Frankfurt-Main (Germany) 2020, *Global Cider Forum* Frankfurt-Main (Germany) 2019, *Global Cider Forum* Frankfurt-Main (Germany) 2018, *Global Cider Forum* Frankfurt-Main (Germany) 2017. **Publications** *European Cider Trends.*

Members National organizations in 11 countries:
Belgium, Denmark, Finland, France, Germany, Ireland, Luxembourg, Poland, Spain, Sweden, UK.
Observer members in 4 countries:
Russia, South Africa, Switzerland, UK.

IGO Relations Affiliated with (1): *European Commission (EC, #06633).* [2022.05.04/XE0487/t/E]

- ♦ Association des industries du Commonwealth (inactive)
- ♦ Association des industries électriques de l'Asie orientale et du Pacifique Ouest (#02485)
- ♦ Association des industries européennes de chapellerie (inactive)
- ♦ Association des industries européennes du plâtre / see European Association of Plaster and Plaster Product Manufacturers (#06152)
- ♦ Association des industries des glaces alimentaires de la CEE / see EUROGLACES – European Ice Cream Association (#05688)
- ♦ Association des industries des glaces alimentaires et crèmes glacées de la CEE / see EUROGLACES – European Ice Cream Association (#05688)
- ♦ Association des industries des glaces alimentaires de l'UE / see EUROGLACES – European Ice Cream Association (#05688)
- ♦ Association des industries du jute européennes (inactive)
- ♦ Association des industries margarinières des pays de la CE / see European Margarine Association (#07736)
- ♦ Association des industries de marques (#06397)
- ♦ Association des industries du papier (#18191)
- ♦ Association des industries du poisson de la CEE / see European Union Fish Processors Association (#08989)
- ♦ Association des industries du poisson de l'Union Européenne (#08989)
- ♦ Association of the Industry of Juices and Nectars from Fruits and Vegetables of the European Economic Community / see European Fruit Juice Association (#07362)
- ♦ Association of the Industry of Juices and Nectars from Fruits and Vegetables of the European Union / see European Fruit Juice Association (#07362)
- ♦ Association des infirmières des pays du Nord (#17371)

♦ Association des informaticiens de langue française (AILF) 02644

Association of French-Speaking Computer Professionals and Users

Contact c/o AFAL, Carré Belle-Feuille, 60 rue de la Belle-Feuille, 92100 Boulogne-Billancourt, France.

History Founded 24 Dec 1981. Registered in accordance with French law, 1982. **Aims** Further the use, development and promotion of the *French language* in the framework of *computing* technology, while respecting other languages and cultures. **Languages** French. **Staff** 6.00 FTE, voluntary. **Finance** Members' dues. Biennial colloquium sponsored by *Délégation générale à la langue française et aux langues de France (DGLFLF).* **Activities** Events/meetings. **Events** *LexiPraxi* Paris (France) 2002, *LexiPraxi* Paris (France) 2000, *LexiPraxi colloquium / LexiPraxi* Paris (France) 1998, *Inforoutes, édition électronique, radio et télévision numériques* Paris (France) 1994, *LexiPraxi* Québec, QC (Canada) 1994. **Publications** *AILF Info* (12 a year); *Bulletin de l'AILF* (periodical).

Members Full in 6 countries:
Belgium, Canada, France, Germany, Italy, Senegal.

NGO Relations Member of: *Association francophone d'amitié et de liaison (AFAL, #02605).* [2018/XD1570/D]

- ♦ Association pour l'information et les bibliothèques de santé en Afrique (#02630)
- ♦ Association for Information and Image Management International / see Association for Intelligent Information Management (#02652)
- ♦ Association of Information Managers Professionals / see ARMA International
- ♦ Association pour une information médicale éthique et le développement (inactive)
- ♦ Association for Information Science and Technology (internationally oriented national body)

♦ Association for Information Systems (AIS) 02645

COO PO Box 2712, Atlanta GA 30301-2712, USA. T. +14046510348. Fax +14046514938. E-mail: office@aisnet.org – membership@aisnet.org.
URL: http://www.aisnet.org/

History 1994. *International Academy for Information Management (IAIM, inactive)* became part of AIS, Jan 2003. Former names and other names: *International Conference on Information Systems* – former (1994). **Aims** Serve society through advancement of knowledge and promotion of excellence in the practice and study of information systems. **Structure** Council; Executive Committee; Standing Committees; Ad Hoc Committees; Regions (3): Americas; Europe and Africa; Asia and the Pacific – *Urban Environmental Accords (UEA, #20732)*. **Languages** English. **Staff** 6.00 FTE, paid. **Finance** Members' dues. Other sources: conference registration fees; corporate sponsorships; donations. **Activities** Awards/prizes/competitions; awareness raising; financial and/or material support; knowledge management/information dissemination; networking/liaising; publishing activities; research and development; research/documentation; training/education. **Events** *AMCIS : Annual Americas Conference on Information Systems* Salt Lake City, UT (USA) 2024, *ICIS : Annual International Conference on Information Systems* Hyderabad (India) 2023, *AMCIS : Annual Americas Conference on Information Systems* Panama (Panama) 2023, *ICIS : Annual International Conference on Information Systems* Copenhagen (Denmark) 2022, *AMCIS : Annual Americas Conference on Information Systems* Minneapolis, MN (USA) 2022. **Publications** *AIS Insider Member Newsletter*; *AIS Transactions on Human-Computer Interaction (THCI)*; *AIS Transactions on Replication Research (TRR)*; *Communications of the Association for Information Systems (CAIS)*; *Journal of Information Technology Theory and Application (JITTA)*; *Journal of the Association for Information Systems (JAIS)*; *Journal of the Midwest Association for Information Systems (JMWAIS)*; *Pacific Asia Journal of the Association for Information Systems (PAJAIS)*; *Revista Latinoamericana Y Del Caribe De La Associacion De Sistemas De Informacion (RELCASI)*; *Scandinavian Journal of Information Systems (SJIS)*. Conference proceedings. **Members** Membership countries not specified. **NGO Relations** Sponsors: *European Conference on Information Systems (ECIS, #06733)*; *Pacific Asia Conference on Information Systems (PACIS)*. [2022/XD9267/**D**]

- ♦ Association of Information Systems Professionals (inactive)
- ♦ Association d'ingénierie routière d'Asie et d'Australasie (#18955)
- ♦ Association des ingénieurs de la route d'Asie et d'Australasie / see Road Engineering Association of Asia and Australasia (#18955)

♦ Association of Inhalation Toxicologists (AIT) 02646

Contact LabCorp, Woolley Road, Alconbury, Huntingdon, PE28 4HS, UK. T. +441480892015. E-mail: aitoxicology@gmail.com.
URL: http://www.aitoxicology.org/

History 1981. **Aims** Promote open discussion, exchange of ideas and the presentation of high quality scientific research in the field of inhalation toxicology. **Structure** Officers: Chairman; Vice-Chairman; Committee Secretary; Membership Secretary; Treasurer. **Languages** English. **Staff** 0.50 FTE, paid; 15.00 FTE, voluntary. **Finance** Sources: meeting proceeds. **Activities** Events/meetings. **Events** *Annual Meeting* Huntingdon (UK) 2021, *Annual Meeting* Huntingdon (UK) 2020, *Annual Meeting* Brighton (UK) 2019, *Annual Meeting* Research Triangle Park, NC (USA) 2018, *Annual Meeting* Copenhagen (Denmark) 2017.
Members Full in 12 countries:
Canada, Denmark, France, Germany, India, Italy, Japan, Korea Rep, Spain, Sweden, UK, USA. [2023.02.14/XJ6956/**D**]

- ♦ Association of Inner Wheel Clubs / see International Inner Wheel (#13855)
- ♦ Association for Innovative Cooperation in Europe / see Network of European Foundations (#17019)
- ♦ Association des inspecteurs automobiles nordiques (inactive)
- ♦ Association des inspecteurs organiques indépendants / see International Organic Inspectors Association (#14421)
- ♦ Association des inspecteurs organiques internationals (#14421)
- ♦ Association of Institutes of European Studies (inactive)
- ♦ Association of Institutes for Research and Development in the Indian Ocean (inactive)
- ♦ Association for Institutional Research (internationally oriented national body)
- ♦ Association des institutions africaines de financement du développement (#02353)
- ♦ Association des Institutions d'Enseignement Theologique en Afrique Occidentale (#02953)
- ♦ Association of Institutions for Feminist Education and Research in Europe (inactive)
- ♦ Association des institutions de formation et de perfectionnement au management d'Afrique francophone (no recent information)
- ♦ Association des institutions nationales de financement du développement des pays membres de la Banque islamique de développement (#02817)
- ♦ Association des institutions de recherche et développement de l'océan Indien (inactive)
- ♦ Association des institutions régionales et sous-régionales de financement du développement en Afrique de l'Ouest (no recent information)
- ♦ Association des institutions responsables de l'enseignement avancé de santé publique et des écoles de santé publique en Europe / see Association of Schools of Public Health in the European Region (#02904)
- ♦ Association of Institutions responsible for Advanced Teaching in Public Health and of Schools of Public Health in Europe / see Association of Schools of Public Health in the European Region (#02904)
- ♦ Association des institutions de sécurité sociale d'Amérique centrale et de Panama (inactive)

♦ Association des institutions supérieures de contrôle ayant en commun l'usage du français (AISCCUF) 02647

SG Cour des comptes, 13 rue Cambon, 75100 Paris CEDEX 01, France. T. +33142989500. Fax +33142989602.
URL: http://www.aisccuf.org/

History 15 Mar 1995. Statutes revised, 28 Jan 2008, Marrakech (Morocco). **Aims** At a time when increasingly democratic government in *French-speaking* countries has renewed interest in monitoring public finances; contribute to consolidating the rule of law; promote strategic development of *auditing* procedures and reinforce independence of the auditor; promote French-speaking juridical and accounting traditions; use its privileged position to encourage technical exchanges North-South and South-South in order to link the experience of legal institutions to the latest auditing techniques. **Structure** General Assembly; Board. **Publications** *Bulletin de l'AISCCUF* (2 a year).
Members Full: Institutions in 35 countries:
Andorra, Belgium, Benin, Burkina Faso, Burundi, Cameroon, Canada, Cape Verde, Central African Rep, Chad, Comoros, Congo Brazzaville, Congo DR, Côte d'Ivoire, Djibouti, France, Gabon, Guinea, Guinea-Bissau, Haiti, Lebanon, Luxembourg, Madagascar, Mali, Mauritania, Moldova, Monaco, Morocco, Niger, Romania, Senegal, Switzerland, Togo, Tunisia, Vietnam.
Communauté économique et monétaire d'Afrique centrale (CEMAC, #04374); *Cour des comptes de l'UEMOA (see: #20377)*.
Permanent observers in 5 countries and territories:
Algeria, Mozambique, Québec, Switzerland (Valais Canton), Vietnam.
IGO Relations Partner of (1): *Organisation internationale de la Francophonie (OIF, #17809)*. **NGO Relations** Partner of (2): *Association des ombudsmans et médiateurs de la Francophonie (AOMF, #02839)*; *International Organization of Supreme Audit Institutions (INTOSAI, #14478)*. [2020/XD5849/**D**]

♦ Association of Institutions of Tropical Veterinary Medicine (AITVM) 02648

Gen Sec Fac of Veterinary Medicine, Office for Intl Cooperation, PO Box 80163, 3508 TD Utrecht, Netherlands. T. +31302532116. Fax +31302531815.

History Registered in accordance with Dutch law. **Aims** Improve human health and quality of life by means of increased and safe food production in tropical regions through enhancement of research, training and education in veterinary medicine and lifestock production, within the framework of sustainable development. **Structure** General Assembly; Standing Committee; Executive Committee. **Finance** Members' dues. Budget (annual): euro 100. **Events** *Joint Conference on Tropical Animal Diseases and Veterinary Public Health* Buenos Aires (Argentina) 2018, *Joint Conference on Tropical Animal Diseases and Veterinary Public Health* Berlin (Germany) 2016, *Triennial Conference* Pretoria (South Africa) 2013, *Triennial Conference* Bangkok (Thailand) 2010, *Triennial international conference* Montpellier (France) 2007.
Members Institutions of Tropical Veterinary Medicine (26) in 19 countries:
Belgium, Denmark, France, Germany, Indonesia, Iran Islamic Rep, Italy, Malaysia, Mozambique, Netherlands, Nigeria, Portugal, Senegal, South Africa, St Kitts-Nevis, Sweden, Thailand, UK, Zimbabwe.
Included in the above, 5 organizations listed in this Yearbook:
Centre de coopération internationale en recherche agronomique pour le développement (CIRAD, #03733); *Centre for Tropical Veterinary Medicine, Edinburgh (CTVM)*; *Institute of Tropical Medicine Antwerp (IMT)*; *Inter-State School of Veterinary Sciences and Medicine (#15982)*; *Tropical Science Research Institute (IICT)*. [2016.02.23/XD3663/y/**D**]

- ♦ Association des instituts africains de formation maritime (no recent information)
- ♦ Association des instituts et centres arabes de recherche pour le développement économique et social (inactive)
- ♦ Association des instituts d'études européennes (inactive)
- ♦ Association d'instituts européens de conjoncture économique (#02506)
- ♦ Association des instituts polytechniques africains du Commonwealth (#04308)
- ♦ Association des instituts de recherche et de formation en matière de développement de l'Asie et du Pacifique (inactive)
- ♦ Association des instituts de théologie du Moyen-Orient / see Association of Theological Seminaries and Institutes in the Middle East (#02954)
- ♦ Association des instituts et universités agronomiques d'Asie (#01312)

♦ Association of Insurance Supervisory Authorities of Developing Countries (AISADC) 02649

SG IIAP, 26th floor BPI-Philam Life Makati, 6811 Ayala Avenue, Makati, Philippines. T. +6328877446. Fax +6328877443. E-mail: airdc@iiap.com.ph – airdc2013@gmail.com.
Facebook: https://www.facebook.com/airdc.aisadc/

History Formally set up 28 Jan 1983. **Aims** Develop and expand interregional collaboration and cooperation in the field of insurance supervision or regulation; extend assistance to any developing country upon its request, in the establishment or strengthening of insurance supervision in such country. **Structure** Council. **Languages** English. **Staff** 1.50 FTE, paid; 1.00 FTE, voluntary. **Finance** Members' dues. **Activities** Programmes: Education and Training Surveys; Profile of Insurance Companies doing Business in the Third World. Provides practical training for staff of supervisory authorities in developing countries. **Events** *Conference* Ghana 2021, *Conference* Ghana 2020, *Conference* Kathmandu (Nepal) 2018, *Conference* Manama (Bahrain) 2016, *Special Meeting* Colombo (Sri Lanka) 2013. **Publications** *Insurance Research and Studies* (2 a year). Reports.
Members Insurance supervisory authorities in 14 countries:
Cuba, Curaçao, Ecuador, Egypt, Ghana, India, Nepal, Nigeria, Papua New Guinea, Philippines, Sri Lanka, Tanzania UR, Thailand, Zimbabwe.
IGO Relations *UNDP (#20292)*. **NGO Relations** Secretariat provided by: *Insurance Institute for Asia and the Pacific (IIAP)*. [2020/XD0260/**D**]

♦ Association of Insurers and Reinsurers of Developing Countries (AIRDC) 02650

SG IIAP, 26th floor BPI-Philam Life Makati, 6811 Ayala Avenue, Makati, Philippines. T. +6328877446. Fax +6328877443. E-mail: airdc@iiap.com.ph – airdc2013@gmail.com.
URL: https://www.airdevc.org/

History Takes over activities of *Third World Insurance Congress (TWIC, inactive)*. **Aims** Develop and expand international collaboration in the fields of insurance and reinsurance of every type. **Structure** Executive Board. **Languages** English. **Staff** 1.50 FTE, paid; 1.00 FTE, voluntary. **Finance** Members' dues. **Activities** Events/meetings; training/education. **Events** *Conference* Ghana 2021, *Conference* Ghana 2020, *Congress / Conference* Victoria Falls (Zimbabwe) 2014, *Congress / Conference* Colombo (Sri Lanka) 2013, *Achieving financial stability through collaboration and understanding* Makati (Philippines) 2009. **Publications** *Insurance Research and Studies* (2 a year) – newsletter. *Insurance Research and Studies of the Developing Countries*.
Members Full in 32 countries and territories:
Bahrain, Bangladesh, Belgium, Belize, Bhutan, Ghana, Hong Kong, India, Jordan, Kenya, Korea DPR, Malawi, Malaysia, Maldives, Mauritius, Mozambique, Nepal, Netherlands, Nigeria, Pakistan, Philippines, Qatar, Russia, Seychelles, Sri Lanka, Tanzania UR, Thailand, United Arab Emirates, USA, Vietnam, Zambia, Zimbabwe.
Supporting in 2 countries:
Fiji, UK.
NGO Relations *Insurance Institute for Asia and the Pacific (IIAP)*. [2020/XG0296/**D**]

♦ Association for an Integral Health and Citizenship of Latin America and the Caribbean 02651

Asociación para la Salud Integral y Ciudadania de América Latina y el Caribe (ASICAL)
Contact Baquerizo Moreno E7-86 y Diego de Almagro, 3 piso, Quito, Ecuador. T. +59322253548 – +59322544337. Fax +59322253548.
URL: http://www.asical.org/

NGO Relations Partner of: *Horizontal Technical Cooperation Group of Latin America and the Caribbean on HIV/AIDS (HTGC, #10945)*. [2009/XM3590/**D**]

♦ Association for Intelligent Information Management (AIIM) 02652

Pres-CEO 8403 Colesville Rd, Ste 1100, Silver Spring MD 20910, USA. T. +13015878202. Fax +13015872711. E-mail: aiim@aiim.org.
Chief Operating Officer address not obtained.
URL: http://www.aiim.org/

History 1945, USA. Took over activities of *International Information Management Congress (IMC, inactive)*, Apr 1999. Former names and other names: *Association for Information and Image Management International (AIIM)* – former; *National Microfilm Association* – former (1945); *National Micrographics Association* – former. **Activities** Annual conference and exhibition. **Events** *Conference* Dallas, TX (USA) 2020, *Conference* San Diego, CA (USA) 2019, *Conference* San Diego, CA (USA) 2015, *Information opportunity vs information chaos* Orlando, FL (USA) 2014, *Conference* San Francisco, CA (USA) 2012. **Publications** *inform* (10 a year).
Members Associate; Sustaining; Affiliate (individual membership), in 32 countries and territories:
Argentina, Australia, Austria, Brazil, Canada, Chile, Colombia, Denmark, Egypt, Finland, France, Germany, India, Israel, Italy, Japan, Korea Rep, Malaysia, Mexico, Morocco, Netherlands, New Zealand, Norway, Poland, Singapore, Spain, Sweden, Switzerland, Taiwan, UK, USA, Venezuela.
NGO Relations Member of: *Workflow Management Coalition (WfMC, #21053)*. In liaison with technical committees of: *International Organization for Standardization (ISO, #14473)*. [2020/XC0107/**C**]

- ♦ Association interaméricaine de bibliographie et des bibliothèques (inactive)
- ♦ Association interaméricaine des bibliothécaires, documentalistes et spécialistes en information agricoles (no recent information)
- ♦ Association interaméricaine de comptabilité (#11395)
- ♦ Association interaméricaine pour la démocratie et la liberté (inactive)
- ♦ Association interaméricaine des directeurs de choeurs (inactive)
- ♦ Association interaméricaine d'éducation (inactive)
- ♦ Association interaméricaine de formation pour le tourisme et l'hôtellerie (inactive)
- ♦ Association interaméricaine de génie sanitaire et des sciences de l'environnement (#11400)
- ♦ Association interaméricaine d'habitat rural (inactive)
- ♦ Association interaméricaine des hôpitaux (inactive)
- ♦ Association interaméricaine de l'hôtellerie (no recent information)
- ♦ Association interaméricaine des magistrats de la jeunesse (inactive)
- ♦ Association interaméricaine des philosophes catholiques (inactive)
- ♦ Association interaméricaine de la presse (#11444)
- ♦ Association interaméricaine de propriété industrielle / see Asociación Interamericana de la Propiedad Intelectual (#02161)
- ♦ Association interaméricaine de radiodiffusion / see International Association of Broadcasting (#11738)

♦ Association of Interbalkan Women's Cooperation Societies, Thessaloniki (AIWCS) 02653

Pres 30 Ploutonos – G Papandreou Str, 546 55 Thessaloniki, Greece. T. +302310422270 – +302310423152. Fax +302310422271. E-mail: unescenter@the.forthnet.gr.

URL: http://www.unescocenter.gr/
History Nov 1992, Thessaloniki (Greece), at 1st Congress. **Aims** Establish links of friendship and cooperation with women, targeted at ensuring peace and stability in the Balkan region; promote the enforcement of human rights and eliminate all forms of discrimination against women; advocate for women's advancement; support creation of a culture of peace by disseminating its values; promote intercultural dialogue and respect for cultural diversity. **Structure** General Assembly (every 2 years); Executive Board; Secretariat. **Languages** English. **Staff** 1.00 FTE, paid. **Finance** Private donations and grants from UNESCO, CE, etc, for specific projects. **Activities** Together with *UNESCO Centre for Women and Peace in the Balkan Countries (#20303)*, undertakes (short and medium-term) projects, organizes seminars, workshops, international conferences, training programmes and cultural festivals. **Events** *Congress* Burgas (Bulgaria) 2009, *Congress* Athens (Greece) 2003, *Congress* Tirana (Albania) 1999, *Congress* Nicosia (Cyprus) 1998, *Congress* Thessaloniki (Greece) 1997. **Publications** Newsletters; Annual Report; leaflets, pamphlets and information booklets.
Members Society members (national associations) (8):
Albania, Bulgaria, Cyprus, Greece, Montenegro, Romania, Serbia, Türkiye.
Participants to AIWCS programmes in 30 countries. Membership countries not specified.
Consultative Status Consultative status granted from: *UNESCO (#20322)* (Consultative Status); *FAO (#09260)* (Liaison Status). **IGO Relations** Cooperates with: *UNESCO Centre for Women and Peace in the Balkan Countries (#20303)*. Permanent relations with: *Anna Lindh Euro-Mediterranean Foundation for the Dialogue between Cultures (Anna Lindh Foundation, #00847)*. [2016/XD6715/**D**]

♦ Association Interciencia (#11459)
♦ Association for Intercultural Research (#02888)
♦ Association interculturelle / see Inter-Cultural Association (#11465)
♦ Association interculturelle pour le Développement Artistique (unconfirmed)
♦ Association of Intergovernmental Organizations of West Africa (inactive)

♦ Association of International Accountants (AIA) 02654

Association des experts-comptables internationaux
Chief Exec Staithes 3, The Watermark, Metro Riverside, Newcastle upon Tyne, NE11 9SN, UK. T. +441914930277. Fax +441914930278. E-mail: aia@aiaworldwide.com.
URL: http://www.aiaworldwide.com/
History 1928, UK. Incorporated as Company Limited by Guarantee, Apr 1932, London (UK). Merged with *Institute of Company Accountants (IComA, inactive)* in 2003. **Aims** Promote the concept of 'international accounting'. **Structure** Council of Management; Secretariat, headed by Chief Executive; Branches in Europe, Asia and Africa, controlled by local committees. **Languages** English. **Staff** 20.00 FTE, paid. **Activities** Certification/accreditation; events/meetings; politics/policy/regulatory. **Publications** *Accountancy E-news* (weekly); *International Accountant* (6 a year) – magazine.
Members Individuals in 96 countries and territories:
Antigua-Barbuda, Australia, Austria, Bahamas, Bahrain, Barbados, Belarus, Belgium, Belize, Bolivia, Botswana, Brunei Darussalam, Cambodia, Cameroon, Canada, China, Côte d'Ivoire, Cyprus, Czechia, Dominica, Eritrea, Eswatini, Ethiopia, France, Gambia, Germany, Ghana, Greece, Grenada, Guernsey, Guyana, Hong Kong, India, Indonesia, Iran Islamic Rep, Ireland, Isle of Man, Italy, Jamaica, Japan, Jersey, Jordan, Kazakhstan, Kenya, Lebanon, Libya, Luxembourg, Macau, Malawi, Malaysia, Maldives, Malta, Mauritius, Mongolia, Montserrat, Netherlands, New Zealand, Nigeria, Northern Ireland, Norway, Oman, Pakistan, Papua New Guinea, Philippines, Poland, Portugal, Qatar, Saudi Arabia, Seychelles, Sierra Leone, Singapore, South Africa, Spain, Sri Lanka, St Kitts-Nevis, St Lucia, St Vincent-Grenadines, Sudan, Sweden, Switzerland, Taiwan, Tanzania UR, Thailand, Trinidad-Tobago, Tunisia, Türkiye, Uganda, UK, Ukraine, United Arab Emirates, USA, Venezuela, Vietnam, Zambia, Zimbabwe. [2022.05.13/XD4384/v/**D**]

♦ Association for International Affairs, Prague (internationally oriented national body)
♦ Association for International Agriculture and Rural Development (internationally oriented national body)
♦ Association international des approvisionneurs de navires / see International Ship Suppliers and Services Association (#14850)
♦ Association international d'approvisionneurs de navires (#14850)

♦ Association for International Arbitration (AIA) 02655

Pres Avenue Louise 146, 1050 Brussels, Belgium. T. +3226433307. Fax +3226432431. E-mail: administration@arbitration-adr.org.
URL: http://arbitration-adr.org/
History Founded 2001. **Aims** Bring together the global community in the field of Alternative *Dispute* Resolution (ADR) through promotion, education and scholarship. **Structure** Executive Board. **Languages** English. **Staff** 2.00 FTE, voluntary. **Finance** Sources: members' dues. Other sources: Fees from seminars and trainings. **Activities** Events/meetings; knowledge management/information dissemination; training/education. **Publications** Newsletters; books.
Members Individuals in 50 countries and territories:
Argentina, Australia, Austria, Bahrain, Barbados, Belgium, Brunei Darussalam, Canada, Costa Rica, Cyprus, Czechia, Denmark, Ecuador, Finland, France, Germany, Greece, Hong Kong, India, Iran Islamic Rep, Israel, Italy, Korea Rep, Kosovo, Kuwait, Kyrgyzstan, Lebanon, Luxembourg, Mauritius, Netherlands, Nigeria, Philippines, Portugal, Romania, Russia, Saudi Arabia, Serbia, Singapore, Spain, Sweden, Switzerland, Tunisia, Türkiye, Uganda, UK, Ukraine, United Arab Emirates, USA, Virgin Is UK, Zambia.
NGO Relations *Diplomatic Council (DC).* [2017.12.14/XM6097/v/**C**]

♦ Association of International Automobile Manufacturers / see Association of Global Automakers
♦ Association of International Bond Dealers / see International Capital Market Association (#12438)

♦ Association for International Broadcasting (AIB) 02656

CEO PO Box 112, Downham Market, PE38 8DX, UK. T. +442079932557. E-mail: contactaib@aib.org.uk.
URL: http://www.aib.org.uk/
History 1993. **Aims** Bring together the international television, radio and digital *media* industry. **Structure** Executive Committee. **Languages** English. **Staff** 8.00 FTE, paid. **Finance** Sources: members' dues; sponsorship. Other sources: advertising. **Activities** Advocacy/lobbying/activism; awards/prizes/competitions; events/meetings; knowledge management/information dissemination; networking/liaising. **Events** *BroadcastAsia : international digital multimedia and entertainment technology conference* Singapore (Singapore) 2010, *Global media business conference* Prague (Czech Rep) 2004, *Global media business conference* London (UK) 2003.
Members Corporate; Individual. Members in 26 countries and territories:
Australia, Canada, Czechia, France, Germany, Hong Kong, India, Japan, Kazakhstan, Korea Rep, Luxembourg, Malaysia, Montenegro, Netherlands, New Zealand, Nigeria, Norway, Poland, Romania, Saudi Arabia, Singapore, Sweden, Taiwan, UK, United Arab Emirates, USA.
NGO Relations Institutional Member of: *Asia-Pacific Broadcasting Union (ABU, #01863).* [2023.02.14/XD9262/**D**]

♦ Association of International Cardio Sports / see International Federation of Cardio HIIT BodyWeight Exercise
♦ Association of International Certified Professional Accountants (internationally oriented national body)
♦ The Association of International Churches (Ecumenical – English Speaking – Europe and the Middle East) / see Association of International Churches in Europe and the Middle East (#02657)

♦ Association of International Churches in Europe and the Middle East (AICEME) 02657

Contact Ester De Boer-Van Rijklaan 20, 2597 TJ The Hague, Netherlands. E-mail: secretary@aiceme.net.
URL: http://www.aiceme.net/
History 1960. Former names and other names: *Annual Conference of Pastors and Wives Serving English Speaking Churches in Europe and the Middle East* – former (1960 to 1974); *The Association of International Churches (Ecumenical – English Speaking – Europe and the Middle East)* – former (1974 to 1981). Registration: Start date: 2018, Netherlands. **Aims** Enable mutual encouragement and support among pastors and spouses of English speaking Christian congregations in Europe and the Middle East; provide resources for pastoral ministry. **Structure** Executive Team. **Languages** English. **Staff** None. **Finance** Sources: members' dues. **Events** *Pastors and Spouses Conference* Cairo (Egypt) 2019, *Pastors and Spouses Conference* Greece 2018, *Pastors and Spouses Conference* Bratislava (Slovakia) / Vienna (Austria) 2017, *Pastors and Spouses Conference* Geneva (Switzerland) / Interlaken (Switzerland) 2016, *Pastors and Spouses Conference* Geneva (Switzerland) / Interlaken (Switzerland) / Nyon (Switzerland) 2016.
Members Churches (over 30) in 20 countries:
Austria, Belgium, Denmark, Egypt, Finland, France, Germany, Lebanon, Lithuania, Luxembourg, Netherlands, Norway, Palestine, Russia, Slovakia, Spain, Sweden, Switzerland, Türkiye, UK. [2020.06.29/XD5933/**D**]

♦ Association for the International Collective Management of Audiovisual Works (AGICOA) 02658

Association de gestion internationale collective des oeuvres audiovisuelles – Asociación para la Gestión Colectiva Internacional de Obras Audiovisuales
Managing Dir Rue Pestalozzi 1, 1202 Geneva, Switzerland. T. +41225448300. Fax +41223403432. E-mail: info@agicoa.org.
Corporate Communication Manager address not obtained.
URL: https://www.agicoa.org/
History Dec 1981, Geneva (Switzerland). Former names and other names: *AGICOA Alliance* – alias. Registration: Swiss Civil Code, No/ID: CH-660-0184984-7, Switzerland. **Aims** Manage *copyright* and related rights of producers of audiovisual works, their successors in title and entities representing them. **Structure** General Assembly; Administrative Board. **Languages** English, French. **Staff** 30.00 FTE, paid. **Finance** Cost of perceiving and collecting royalties deducted from royalties collected. **Activities** Certification/accreditation. **Publications** Annual Report; Transparency Report.
Members Worldwide producers associations, representing about 20,000 rightsholders in 36 countries:
Australia, Austria, Belgium, Bosnia-Herzegovina, Bulgaria, Canada, Croatia, Denmark, Estonia, Finland, France, Germany, Hungary, Iceland, Ireland, Israel, Kosovo, Latvia, Lithuania, Luxembourg, Moldova, Montenegro, Netherlands, North Macedonia, Norway, Poland, Portugal, Romania, Serbia, Slovakia, Slovenia, South Africa, Spain, Sweden, Switzerland, UK.
Consultative Status Consultative status granted from: *World Intellectual Property Organization (WIPO, #21593)* (Permanent Observer Status). **IGO Relations** Observer to: *Union for the International Registration of Audiovisual Works (#20444).* **NGO Relations** In liaison with technical committees of: *International Organization for Standardization (ISO, #14473)*. Together with: *Confédération internationale des sociétés d'auteurs et compositeurs (CISAC, #04563)* and *International Federation of Film Producers' Associations (#13429)*, set up: *ISAN International Agency (ISAN-IA, #16023).* [2020.06.23/XD2081/**D**]

♦ Association of International Colleges and Universities / see Association of American International Colleges and Universities
♦ Association of International Communication for Building and Housing / see Institute of International Harmonization for Building and Housing
♦ Association of International Competitors on Oceanic Multihulls (inactive)
♦ Association for International Conciliation (inactive)
♦ Association of International Consultants on Human Rights (inactive)
♦ Association for International Cooperation in Agriculture and Forestry / see Japan Association for International Collaboration of Agriculture and Forestry

♦ Association for International Cooperation and Research in Steel-Concrete Composite Structures (ASCCS) 02659

Pres Engineering – Univ of Bradford, Chesham Bldg, Richmond Road, Bradford, BD7 1DP, UK.
Aims Advance the use of steel-concrete composite construction. **Structure** Officers: President; Past-President; Vice-President; Secretary/Treasurer. **Languages** English. **Activities** Events/meetings. **Events** *International Conference on Advances in Steel Concrete Composite and Hybrid Structures* Valencia (Spain) 2018, *International Conference on Advances in Steel Concrete Composite and Hybrid Structures* Beijing (China) 2015, *International Conference on Advances in Steel Concrete Composite and Hybrid Structures* Singapore (Singapore) 2012, *Triennial international conference on composite construction / Triennal International Conference* Leeds (UK) 2009, *Triennial international conference on composite construction* Harbin (China) 2006. **Publications** Conference proceedings.
Members Individuals (226) in 34 countries and territories:
Australia, Bahrain, Belarus, Belgium, Canada, China, Egypt, Finland, France, Germany, Greece, Hong Kong, Hungary, India, Italy, Japan, Jordan, Korea Rep, Lithuania, Netherlands, Norway, Poland, Portugal, Romania, Saudi Arabia, Singapore, Slovakia, South Africa, Spain, Sweden, Switzerland, UK, Ukraine, USA. [2016.02.18/XD7641/**D**]

♦ Association of International Credit and Trade Finance Professionals (ICTF) 02660

Pres 1820 Lancaster St, Ste 210, Baltimore MD 21231, USA. E-mail: info@ictfworld.org.
URL: http://www.ictfworld.org/
History 2010. **Aims** Advance the profession of international credit management by providing expertise, leadership, powerful connections, leading-edge educational programs and resources, and a forum for the exchange of information and best practices. **Structure** Board of Directors. Advisory Council. **Finance** Members' dues. Contributions. **Activities** Courses; meeting activities in USA and Europe. **Events** *Global Credit Professionals Symposium* Chicago, IL (USA) 2022, *Global Credit Symposium* Fort Lauderdale, FL (USA) 2022, *International Credit Professionals Symposium* Lisbon (Portugal) 2022, *Symposium* Cap d'Ail (France) 2017, *Annual Global Trade Symposium* Fort Lauderdale, FL (USA) 2017. **Publications** *ICTF Newsletter.* [2022/XJ7910/t/**D**]

♦ Association of International Customs and Border Agencies (internationally oriented national body)

♦ Association of International Dental Manufacturers (IDM) 02661

Pres Weissbadstr. 1, 9050 Appenzell AI, Switzerland. E-mail: info@idm-vox.org.
URL: http://www.idm-vox.org/
History 1988, Washington, DC (USA). Founded at annual congress of FDI. Former names and other names: *International Dental Manufacturers (IDM)* – former. **Aims** Represent as an association the common interests of member associations and through them support the interests of the global dental industry as a whole. **Structure** Membership Meeting (2 a year); Board of Directors; Board of Officers. **Languages** English. **Staff** 1.00 FTE, voluntary. **Finance** Sources: members' dues. Annual budget: 40,000 USD. **Events** *General Assembly* Cologne (Germany) 2021. **Publications** *IDM Global Dental Event Planner.* Membership Directory.
Members National dental industry associations in 8 countries:
Argentina, Australia, Brazil, Germany, Japan, Korea Rep, Mexico, USA.
Regional organizations (2) listed in this Yearbook:
Fédération de l'industrie dentaire en Europe (FIDE, #09595); Latin American Dental Industry and Trade Association (LADIA, no recent information). [2021.06.10/XD2528/y/**D**]

♦ Association for International Development (inactive)

♦ Association for International Development of Natural Gums (AIDGUM) 02662

Association internationale pour le développement des gommes naturelles
Permanent Headquarters 129 Chemin de Croisset, CS 94151, 76723 Rouen CEDEX, France. T. +33232831818. Fax +33232831919.
URL: http://www.aidgum.com/
History Founded Jun 1974, as *Association internationale pour le développement des hydrocolloides (AIDHRO)*. Current name adopted 1985. Also referred to in English as *International Association for the Development of Natural Gums*. Registered in accordance with French law. **Aims** Ensure scientific and technological services to forest and agriculture departments of gum-producing countries; undertake and promote measures leading to development and improvement of natural plant gums from land and aquatic sources; provide a location for those concerned with collection, distribution and technical or scientific research into plant hydrocolloids and their modifications to meet for exchange of views and information; promote and cooperate in training of specialists from gum-producing countries; collect scientific, technical and statistical information from whatever source; present recommendations and resolutions to governments and national and international agencies. **Structure** General Assembly (annual); Administrative Council; Bureau. **Finance** Members' dues. **Activities** Events/meetings; guidance/assistance/consulting; research and development.
Members Companies in 3 producing countries (" indicates also NGO member):
Chad, Mali (*), Senegal (*).
Expert members (9) in 4 countries:
France, Mali, Senegal, Sudan.

Final users and importers (5) in 5 countries:
Brazil, France, Mexico, UK, USA.
IGO Relations Observer status with: *Codex Alimentarius Commission (CAC, #04081).*
[2014.10.29/XF1795/F]

♦ Association for International Dialogue on the Transition to a Global Society (no recent information)
♦ Association of International Diving Schools / see International Diving Schools Association (#13183)
♦ Association International DNAI (#16961)

♦ Association of International Dressage Event Organizers (AIDEO) . . . 02663

Contact c/o Macrostr 4, 49692 Cappeln, Germany.
NGO Relations Member of: *International Equestrian Organisers' Alliance (IEOA, #13289).* [2017/XD8383/D]

♦ Association internationale des abattoirs d'animaux de basse-cour (inactive)
♦ Association internationale des abstinents du personnel du chemin de fer (inactive)
♦ Association internationale des académies (inactive)
♦ Association internationale des accordéonistes / see International Confederation of Accordionists (#12841)

♦ Association Internationale des Acheteurs et Approvisionneurs Publics et Privés de la Santé (ASSIAPS) 02664

Contact 858 Terasse Turcotte, Trois Rivières QC G9A 5C5, Canada. T. +14187808111ext315. Fax +14187808118. E-mail: contact@assiaps-belgique.be.
Belgian Member: http://www.assiaps-belgique.be/
History Founded Sep 2008, Trois Rivières QC (Canada). **Aims** Assemble at international level those responsible for group purchase and procurement for public and private organizations in the healthcare and social services industry; facilitate information exchange between professionals. **Structure** General Assembly. Board of Directors. Committees (2): Executive; Ethics. **Languages** English, French, Italian. **Staff** 14.00 FTE, paid. **Finance** Members' dues. Other sources: proceeds from conferences, trainings, symposia. **Events** *Biennial Symposium* Québec, QC (Canada) 2016, *Symposium* Québec, QC (Canada) 2016, *Biennial Symposium / Symposium* Milan (Italy) 2014, *Biennial Symposium / Symposium* Brussels (Belgium) 2012, *Biennial symposium / Symposium* Paris (France) 2010.
Members Full in 4 countries:
Belgium, Canada, France. [2015/XJ2333/D]

♦ Association internationale des actuaires consultants (#11813)
♦ Association internationale de l'administration des villes (#12579)
♦ Association internationale des adultes avec la mucoviscidose (inactive)
♦ Association internationale d'aérobiologie (#11691)
♦ Association internationale des aéroports civils (inactive)
♦ Association internationale des aérosols (inactive)
♦ Association internationale des affaires correctionnelles et des pénitenciers pour l'avancement des services correctionnels professionnels (#12970)
♦ Association internationale des affaires correctionnelles et des pénitenciers pour l'avancement des services correctionnels professionnels: Centre pour l'échange des meilleures pratiques correctionnelles / see International Corrections and Prisons Association for the Advancement of Professional Corrections (#12970)
♦ Association internationale africaine (inactive)
♦ Association internationale des agents des compagnies de navigation aérienne / see Airline Sports and Cultural Association (#00609)
♦ Association internationale des agents et courtiers aériens (inactive)
♦ Association internationale des agents d'éditeurs de publicité (inactive)
♦ Association internationale des agriculteurs (inactive)
♦ Association internationale d'aide spirituelle aux personnes souffrant de troubles auditifs (#13500)
♦ Association internationale d'alimentation animale (#13581)
♦ Association internationale des allergistes / see World Allergy Organization – IAACI (#21077)
♦ Association internationale d'allergologie / see World Allergy Organization – IAACI (#21077)
♦ Association internationale d'allergologie et d'immunologie clinique / see World Allergy Organization – IAACI (#21077)
♦ Association internationale de l'amiante / see International Chrysotile Association (#12570)
♦ Association internationale des amis de plume / see International Pen Friends (#14554)
♦ Association internationale Les amis de la reliure d'art / see ARA International (#01080)
♦ Association internationale d'analyse transactionnelle (#15719)
♦ Association internationale des anatomistes du bois (#12273)
♦ Association internationale des anatomistes vétérinaires / see World Association of Veterinary Anatomists (#21202)

♦ Association internationale des anciens agents, retraités de l'OTAN et de leurs ayants-droits (ARO) 02665

International Association of Retired NATO Civilian Staff and their Dependents (ARNS)
Main Office c/o Centre du personnel, NATO HQ, 1110 Brussels, Belgium. T. +3227072688. Fax +3227072689. E-mail: aro-arns@cnrcsa.nato.int.
URL: http://www.aro-arns.org/
History 24 Jan 1987, Brussels (Belgium), to represent ex and retired staff and their dependents of *NATO (#16945).* Registered in accordance with Belgian law, 2 Sep 1987. **Aims** Study all measures meant to protect the interests of retired NATO civilian staff and their dependents. **Structure** General Assembly (annual); Executive Committee; Board, consisting of President, Vice-President and Secretary; National Delegations; Experts/Advisers. **Languages** English, French. **Finance** Members' dues. **Activities** Participates in various activities organized by NATO. **Events** *General Assembly* Brussels (Belgium) 1997, *General Assembly* Brussels (Belgium) 1996, *General Assembly* Brussels (Belgium) 1995, *General Assembly* Brussels (Belgium) 1994, *General Assembly* Brussels (Belgium) 1993.
Members Civilian staff and their dependents in 18 countries (not NATO member countries):
Andorra (*), Belgium, Canada, Denmark, France, Germany, Greece, Iceland, Italy, Luxembourg, Netherlands, Norway, Portugal, Spain, Switzerland (*), Türkiye, UK, USA. [2013/XE6057/v/E]

♦ Association internationale des anciens des Communautés européennes / see Association internationale des anciens de l'Union Européenne (#02667)

♦ Association internationale des anciens d'EUROCONTROL (AIAE) . . . 02666

International Association of Former Officials of EUROCONTROL
Sec c/o EUROCONTROL, Rue de la Fusée 96, 1130 Brussels, Belgium. T. +3227293341. Fax +3227299080. E-mail: info@exeurocontrol.eu.
URL: http://www.exeurocontrol.eu/
History 1984, Brussels (Belgium). Former names and other names: *Internationale Vereinigung des Ehemaligen Beamten und Bediensteten von EUROCONTROL* – former; *Internationale Vereniging van Oud-Personeelsleden van EUROCONTROL* – former. Registration: Banque-Carrefour des Entreprises, No/ID: 0425.751.014, Start date: 30 May 1984, Belgium. **Aims** Maintain and develop bonds of friendship among former officials of EUROCONTROL; provide a real and effective link between them and EUROCONTROL; liaise with EUROCONTROL Agency and its serving staff; protect members' individual and collective rights. In liaison with the Director General of the EUROCONTROL Agency: contribute to the study of problems relating to *safety* of international *air traffic*; stimulate *European* cooperation in the field of air navigation; draw attention of business and social circles to the importance of this cooperation. **Structure** General Assembly (annual); Board of Governors; Executive Bureau. **Languages** English, French. **Staff** None. **Finance** Sources: members' dues. **Activities** Events/meetings. **Events** *Annual General Assembly* Brussels (Belgium) 2006, *Annual General Assembly* Brussels (Belgium) 2005, *Annual General Assembly* Brussels (Belgium) 2004, *Annual General Assembly* Brussels (Belgium) 2004, *Annual General Assembly* Brussels (Belgium) 2003. **Publications** *Directory/Annuaire* (annual).
Members Individuals in 15 countries:
Austria, Belgium, France, Germany, Ireland, Italy, Luxembourg, Mexico, Netherlands, Portugal, Spain, Sweden, Switzerland, UK, USA.
NGO Relations Cooperates with (1): *AIPE-International Association of EUROCONTROL Staff (#00597).*
[2022/XE2970/v/E]

♦ Association internationale des anciens de l'OECE et de l'OCDE (#11904)

♦ Association internationale des anciens de l'Union Européenne (AIACE) 02667

International Association of Former Officials of the European Union – Internationale Vereinigung der Ehemaligen Bediensteten Europäischen Union – Associazione Internazionale degli Anziani delle Comunità Europee – International Forening af Forhenvaerende EU-Medarbejdere
Secretariat 105 Ave des Nerviens, N 105 00/036, 1049 Brussels, Belgium. E-mail: aiace-int@ec.europa.eu.
URL: http://www.aiace-europa.eu/
History 1969, Brussels (Belgium). Founded by 35 former officials of various nationalities. Former names and other names: *Association internationale des anciens des Communautés européennes (AIACE)* – former; *International Association of Former Officials of the European Communities* – former; *Internationale Vereinigung der Ehemaligen Angehörigen der Europäischen Gemeinschaften* – former; *Associazione Internazionale dagli Ex-Comunitari Europei* – former; *Internationale Vereniging van Oudpersoneelsleden van de Europese Gemeenschappen* – former; *Internationale Forening af Forhenvaerende EF-Medarbejdere* – former; *Association of Former Staff of the European Union* – former. Registration: Belgium. **Aims** Improve the well-being of all pensioners; nurture, in a spirit of friendship and good humour, the links among pensioners and with the administrative services of the institutions. **Structure** General Assembly (annual, during Congress); Conseil d'Administration (Governing Board); Board; Sections. **Languages** English, French. **Staff** 1.50 FTE, paid; 8.00 FTE, voluntary. **Finance** Members' dues. EC/EU contributions. **Events** *Annual Congress* Lisbon (Portugal) 2019, *Annual Congress* Valencia (Spain) 2018, *Annual Congress* Maastricht (Netherlands) 2017, *Annual Congress* Trieste (Italy) 2016, *Annual Congress* Bratislava (Slovakia) 2015. **Publications** *VOX* (3 a year).
Members Individuals (10,000) in 15 countries:
Austria, Belgium, Denmark, Finland, France, Germany, Greece, Ireland, Italy, Luxembourg, Netherlands, Portugal, Spain, Sweden, UK.
NGO Relations Member of: *European Movement International (EMI, #07825).* [2021/XE3897/v/E]

♦ Association internationale des anesthésistes-réanimateurs d'expression française (inactive)
♦ Association internationale des anthropobiologistes (#11945)
♦ Association internationale d'anthropologie du sudest européen (#12173)
♦ Association internationale antimilitariste (inactive)
♦ Association Internationale Aphasia / see Association internationale aphasie (#02668)

♦ Association internationale aphasie (AIA) 02668

Gen Sec c/o Stroke Association House, 240 City Road, London, EC1V 2PR, UK.
Pres address not obtained.
URL: http://www.aphasia-international.com/
History 27 May 1989, Brussels (Belgium). Founded at 1st Congress. Statutes adopted 31 May 1991; amended 24 Nov 2001. Former names and other names: *Association Internationale Aphasia* – alias; *Aphasia International* – alias. Registration: Belgium. **Aims** Promote the rehabilitation and in particular the restitution of the communication capacity of the *aphasic* person; preserve his or her human dignity; defend his or her interest and those of their close proximity in the fields of therapy and familiar, social and professional reintegration. **Structure** Administrative Board. National associations represented each by AIA Vice-President. **Languages** English, French, German. **Staff** Voluntary. **Finance** Sources: donations; members' dues. **Activities** Events/meetings. **Events** *General Assembly* London (UK) 2020, *Annual General Assembly* Toulouse (France) 2012, *Annual General Assembly* Nice (France) 2006, *Annual General Assembly* Örebro (Sweden) 2005, *Annual General Assembly* Luxembourg (Luxembourg) 2004. **Publications** *International Guide for Aphasics.* Brochures; bibliographies; directories; film and video.
Members National organizations in 18 countries:
Argentina, Austria, Belgium, Estonia, Finland, France, Germany, Greece, Italy, Japan, Luxembourg, Netherlands, Portugal, Spain, Sweden, Switzerland, UK, USA.
NGO Relations Member of (1): *European Disability Forum (EDF, #06929).* [2022/XD3387/D]

♦ Association internationale des arbitres de water polo (inactive)
♦ Association internationale d'archéologie de la Caraïbe (#11756)
♦ Association internationale d'archéologie classique (#02988)
♦ Association internationale des architectes de la CEI (inactive)

♦ Association internationale des archives francophones (AIAF) 02669

Sec-Treas Pav Louis-Jacques-Casault, 1055 ave du Séminaire, local 3212, Québec QC G1V 5C8, Canada. T. +14186444800. Fax +14186460868. E-mail: aiaf.gestion@gmail.com.
URL: https://www.piaf-archives.org/AIAF/association-internationale-des-archives-francophones
History Oct 1989. Current statutes revised, 21 Jul 2008, Kuala Lumpur (Malaysia). Registration: Canada. **Aims** Support and develop cooperation among member associations by: training of specialists; professional exchanges; disseminating specialized literature; organizing and modernizing archive services; disseminating archive contents; supporting *professional* archive associations. **Structure** General Assembly (annual); Council. **Languages** French. **Finance** Members' dues. Other sources: voluntary contributions; subsidies; income from services. **Activities** Events/meetings. **Events** *International colloquium on management of current and intermediary records* Dakar (Senegal) 1998, *Symposium on archival legislation for francophone developing countries* Tunis (Tunisia) 1994, *Assemblée générale* Montréal, QC (Canada) 1992. **Information Services** *Portail international archivistique francophone.*
Members Associations in 43 countries:
Belgium, Benin, Bulgaria, Burkina Faso, Burundi, Cambodia, Cameroon, Canada, Cape Verde, Central African Rep, Chad, Comoros, Congo Brazzaville, Congo DR, Côte d'Ivoire, Djibouti, Dominica, Egypt, Equatorial Guinea, France, Gabon, Guinea, Guinea-Bissau, Haiti, Laos, Lebanon, Luxembourg, Madagascar, Mali, Mauritania, Mauritius, Morocco, Niger, Romania, Rwanda, Senegal, Seychelles, St Lucia, Switzerland, Togo, Tunisia, Vanuatu, Vietnam.
NGO Relations Institutional member of: *International Council on Archives (ICA, #12996).* [2022/XD2595/F]

♦ Association internationale d'archives sonores / see International Association of Sound and Audiovisual Archives (#12172)
♦ Association internationale d'archives sonores et audiovisuelles (#12172)
♦ Association internationale des armateurs (inactive)
♦ Association internationale des armateurs et commanditaires de compétitions (no recent information)
♦ Association internationale des armateurs indépendants de pétroliers (#11959)
♦ Association Internationale d'Art Dramatique/ Théâtre et Education (#13198)

♦ Association Internationale Artes Renascentes (ARTES RENASCENTES) 02670

International Association Artes Renascentes – Asociación Internacional Artes Renascentes – Associação Internacional Artes Renascentes – Associazione Internazionale Artes Renascentes
Registered Office Ctr natl de la Recherche scientifique, Ctr Jean Pépin, 7 rue Guy Môquet, 94801 Villejuif, France.
URL: http://www.artesrenascentes.eu/
History Registered in accordance with French law. **Aims** Study and disseminate the history, literature, thought, science and arts of the tradition of Greco-*Roman* antiquity, of *Humanism* and of the *Renaissance*, in their broadest sense. **Structure** Annual General Meeting; Executive Council; Board of Directors; Editorial Board. **Finance** Sources: members' dues. **Activities** Events/meetings; knowledge management/information dissemination. **Publications** *HVMANISTICA – An international journal of early Renaissance studies. Series Gallica; Series Germanica; Series Italia.*
Members Individual founding; Honorary; Supporting; Active; Assistant Institutional. Members in 8 countries:
Austria, Brazil, France, Holy See, Italy, Spain, Switzerland, USA. [2018/XM7054/C]

♦ Association internationale des artistes chrétiens (#03896)

- ♦ Association internationale pour l'art et les moyens audio-visuels (inactive)
- ♦ Association internationale des arts plastiques (#11710)
- ♦ Association internationale – Art-thérapie (no recent information)
- ♦ Association internationale de l'asphalte (#14119)
- ♦ Association internationale de l'asphalte appliqué à la construction (inactive)
- ♦ Association internationale d'assistance juridique (inactive)
- ♦ Association internationale pour l'assistance médicale aux voyageurs (internationally oriented national body)
- ♦ Association internationale de l'assurance de protection juridique / see Legal Protection International (#16440)
- ♦ Association internationale d'assurance technique (#11874)
- ♦ Association internationale des assureurs contre la grêle / see Association internationale des assureurs de la production agricole (#02671)
- ♦ Association internationale des assureurs-crédit / see International Credit Insurance & Surety Association (#13103)

♦ Association internationale des assureurs de la production agricole (AIAG) 02671

International Association of Agricultural Production Insurers – Internationale Vereinigung der Versicherer der Landwirtschaftlichen Produktion – Associazione Internazionale degli Assicuratori della Produzione Agricola

Secretariat Seilergraben 61, 8001 Zurich ZH, Switzerland. T. +41442572211. Fax +41442572212. E-mail: info@aiag-iahi.org.
URL: http://www.aiag-iahi.org/

History 22 Oct 1951, Paris (France). Former names and other names: *International Association of Hail Insurance Companies* – former (Oct 1951); *Association internationale des compagnies d'assurance contre la grêle* – former (Oct 1951); *International Association of Hail Insurers* – former (2007); *Association internationale des assureurs contre la grêle (AIAG)* – former (2007); *Internationale Vereinigung der Hagelversicherer* – former (2007); *Associazione Internazionale degli Assicuratori contro la Grandine* – former (2007). **Aims** Unite agricultural production insurers as well as reinsurers and brokers. **Languages** English, French, German, Italian. **Staff** 2.00 FTE, paid. **Finance** Sources: members' dues. **Activities** Events/meetings. **Events** *Congress* Geneva (Switzerland) 2023, *Congress* Istanbul (Türkiye) 2022, *Biennial Congress* Bordeaux (France) 2019, *Biennial Congress* Warsaw (Poland) 2017, *Biennial Congress* Kansas City, MO (USA) 2015.
Members Full direct hail insurers (52) in 20 countries:
Austria, Brazil, China, Czechia, Denmark, France, Germany, Israel, Italy, Netherlands, Poland, Romania, Russia, Slovakia, Slovenia, South Africa, Spain, Sweden, Switzerland, USA.
Subscribing members reinsurance companies and professional organizations (45), in 21 countries and territories:
Argentina, Australia, Austria, Belgium, Cyprus, France, Germany, Greece, Hong Kong, Italy, Korea Rep, Poland, Portugal, Russia, South Africa, Spain, Switzerland, Türkiye, UK, Ukraine, USA. [2022/XC1294/**C**]

- ♦ Association internationale d'astacologie (#11717)
- ♦ Association internationale d'asthmologie / see INTERASMA (#11457)
- ♦ Association internationale d'aumôniers de l'aviation civile (#11774)
- ♦ Association internationale des auteurs de l'audiovisuel (no recent information)
- ♦ Association internationale des auteurs de comics et de cartoons (inactive)
- ♦ Association internationale d'auteurs, compositeurs et écrivains (inactive)
- ♦ Association internationale des auteurs de romans policiers (#11825)
- ♦ Association internationale Autisme – Europe / see Autism-Europe (#03040)
- ♦ Association internationale pour l'automation de la chimie analytique (inactive)
- ♦ Association internationale des automobile-clubs reconnus / see Fédération Internationale de l'Automobile (#09613)
- ♦ Association internationale d'auxologie humaine (no recent information)
- ♦ Association internationale pour l'avancement de la recherche et de la technologie aux hautes pressions (#11686)
- ♦ Association internationale des avocats (inactive)
- ♦ Association internationale des avocats de la défense (inactive)

♦ Association Internationale des Avocats du Football (AIAF) 02672

International Association for Football Lawyers

Contact 197 boulevard Saint Germain, 75007 Paris, France. E-mail: contact@aiaf-law.com.
URL: https://www.aiaf-law.com/

History Registered in accordance with French law. **Aims** Value and assert the activity and image of football lawyers. **Structure** General Meeting; Executive Committee. **Activities** Advocacy/lobbying/activism; events/meetings; knowledge management/information dissemination. **Events** *Congress* Rio de Janeiro (Brazil) 2022, *Congress* Seville (Spain) 2021, *Congress* Cairo (Egypt) 2019, *Congress* Lausanne (Switzerland) 2018, *Congress* Kiev (Ukraine) 2017. **Publications** *AIAF Newsletter*. **Members** Lawyers. Membership countries not specified. **NGO Relations** Member of: *Sport Integrity Global Alliance (SIGA, #19925)*. [2020/XM8979/v/**C**]

- ♦ Association internationale des avocats et juristes juifs (#11977)
- ♦ Association internationale des avocats, juristes et spécialistes du droit aéronautique (inactive)
- ♦ Association internationale des avocats du monde et des industries du spectacle (#11875)
- ♦ Association internationale des avocats-pilotes (inactive)
- ♦ Association internationale des banques coopératives (#12945)
- ♦ Association internationale des banques islamiques (no recent information)
- ♦ Association internationale de banquiers (no recent information)
- ♦ Association internationale des banquiers espérantistes (inactive)
- ♦ Association internationale du barreau (#12320)
- ♦ Association internationale de la bauxite (inactive)
- ♦ Association internationale Bible et informatique (inactive)
- ♦ Association internationale de bibliologie (inactive)

♦ Association internationale de bibliophilie (AIB) 02673

International Association of Bibliophiles – Asociación Internacional de Bibliófilos

SG AIB Registered Office, Bibliothèque Nat de France, Réserve des livres rares, Quai François Mauriac, 75706 Paris CEDEX 13, France. T. +33153795452.
Sec address not obtained. T. +33153795481.

History 10 Oct 1963, Barcelona (Spain), at 3rd International Bibliophilic Congress. **Aims** Encourage love of books; stimulate an appreciation for rare *books* and the diffusion of knowledge about them. **Structure** Congress (every 2 years); Council. **Languages** English, French. **Staff** Voluntary. **Finance** Sources: members' dues. **Activities** Events/meetings. **Events** *Colloquium* Milan (Italy) / Genoa (Italy) 2016, *Congress / Biennial Congress* Madrid (Spain) 2015, *Colloquium* France 2014, *Biennial Congress* Munich (Germany) 2013, *Colloquium* Brazil 2012. **Publications** *Bulletin du bibliophile* (2 a year).
Members Societies; Libraries; Individuals. Members in 26 countries:
Australia, Austria, Belgium, Brazil, Canada, Czechia, Denmark, Egypt, Finland, France, Germany, Greece, Italy, Japan, Netherlands, New Zealand, Norway, Poland, Portugal, Russia, South Africa, Spain, Sweden, Switzerland, UK, USA. [2019.07.08/XC2530/**C**]

- ♦ Association internationale de bibliothécaires orientalistes (inactive)
- ♦ Association internationale des bibliothécaires scolaires (#12146)
- ♦ Association internationale de bibliothéconomie scolaire / see International Association of School Librarianship (#12146)
- ♦ Association internationale des bibliothèques, archives et centres de documentation musicaux (#12042)
- ♦ Association internationale pour les bibliothèques et centres d'information spécialisés dans les questions de population et de planification de la famille (internationally oriented national body)
- ♦ Association internationale des bibliothèques juridiques (#11992)
- ♦ Association internationale des bibliothèques musicales / see International Association of Music Libraries, Archives and Documentation Centres (#12042)
- ♦ Association internationale des bibliothèques théologiques (inactive)
- ♦ Association internationale des bibliothèques d'universités (#12247)
- ♦ Association internationale des bibliothèques d'universités polytechniques / see International Association of University Libraries (#12247)
- ♦ Association internationale de biblistes et orientalistes (inactive)
- ♦ Association internationale de bienfaisance (inactive)
- ♦ Association internationale pour la Biennale des jeunes créateurs de l'Europe et de la Méditerranée (#11724)
- ♦ Association internationale de bioéthique (#11725)
- ♦ Association internationale Blaise Cendrars (#03279)
- ♦ Association internationale des botanistes (inactive)

♦ Association internationale de la boulangerie industrielle (AIBI) 02674

International Association of Plant Bakers – Internationaler Verband der Brotindustrie – Associazione Internazionale della Panificazione Industriale – Internationale Vereniging van de Industriële Bakkerijen – Industribageriernes Internationale Forening

SG Grand Place 10, 1000 Brussels, Belgium. T. +3223611900. Fax +3223811800. E-mail: info@aibi.eu.
URL: http://www.aibi.eu/

History 20 Dec 1956, Paris (France). Former names and other names: *International Association of the Bread Industry* – alias. Registration: Banque-Carrefour des Entreprises, No/ID: 0844 968 285, Start date: 3 Apr 2012, Belgium; EU Transparency Register, No/ID: 55835028654-55, Start date: 24 Apr 2012. **Aims** Represent, promote and protect the interests of plant bakers in Europe and beyond. **Structure** General Assembly (annual); Board of Directors. **Languages** English. **Staff** 1.00 FTE, paid. **Finance** Members' dues. **Activities** Research/documentation. **Events** *Biennial Congress* Bled (Slovenia) 2021, *Biennial Congress* Manchester (UK) 2019, *Biennial Congress* Paris (France) 2017, *Biennial Congress* Athens (Greece) 2015, *Biennial Congress* Amsterdam (Netherlands) 2013. **Publications** *AIBI Bread Report* (annual); *Presentation of Market Data* (annual). **Information Services** *FLOURplus Project*.
Members National organizations in 15 countries:
Austria, Belgium, Bulgaria, Denmark, Finland, France, Germany, Italy, Netherlands, Portugal, Russia, Slovenia, Spain, UK, Ukraine.
Associate member in 2 countries:
Greece, Netherlands.
IGO Relations Liaises with: *European Community (inactive)*. Recognized by: *European Commission (EC, #06633)*. **NGO Relations** Member of: *Federation of European and International Associations Established in Belgium (FAIB, #09508)*. [2020/XD1358/t/**D**]

- ♦ Association internationale de boxe (#12385)
- ♦ Association internationale de boxe amateur / see International Boxing Association (#12385)
- ♦ Association internationale de broncho-pneumologie (inactive)
- ♦ Association internationale du budget public (#18564)
- ♦ Association internationale des bureaux de congrès et de tourisme / see Destinations International (#05046)
- ♦ Association internationale de cadres de marketing-communications (#16586)
- ♦ Association internationale des cadres médicaux olympiques (inactive)
- ♦ Association internationale pour le calcul analogique / see International Association for Mathematics and Computers in Simulation (#12019)
- ♦ Association internationale pour le calendrier mondial / see The World Calendar Association – International (#21255)
- ♦ Association Internationale pour les Cannabinoïdes en Médecine (#11754)
- ♦ Association internationale pour le cannabis médicale / see International Association for Cannabinoid Medicines (#11754)
- ♦ Association internationale des capitaines au long cours 'cap-horniers' (#11755)
- ♦ Association internationale caprine (#13725)
- ♦ Association internationale cardijn (internationally oriented national body)
- ♦ Association internationale pour la carte à mémoire (inactive)
- ♦ Association internationale des catholiques pour le progrès de la science (inactive)
- ♦ Association internationale des centres d'études du mouvement ouvrier (inactive)
- ♦ Association internationale des cercles Richard Wagner (#12261)

♦ Association Internationale des Charités (AIC) 02675

International Association of Charities – Asociación Internacional de Caridades

Gen Manager Rampe des Ardennais 23, 1348 Louvain-la-Neuve, Belgium. T. +3210456353. E-mail: info@aic-international.org.
Project Officer address not obtained. E-mail: service.projet@aic-international.org.
URL: http://www.aic-international.org/

History 23 Aug 1617. Founded by Saint Vincent de Paul. Currently an international organization composed of feminine associations or federations founded by Saint Vincent de Paul or following his tradition. AIC is an International Catholic Nongovernmental Organization (ICNO), recognized as such by the Holy See. International statutes adopted 1971, Rome (Italy), when organization was set up under current title. New statutes adopted 2015. Former names and other names: *Confraternity of Ladies of Charity* – former; *Association of the Ladies of Charity of Saint-Vincent-de-Paul, Mission for the Sick Poor* – former; *Association des dames de la charité de Saint-Vincent-de-Paul, Oeuvre des pauvres malades* – former; *International Association of Charities of St Vincent de Paul* – former; *Association internationale des charités de Saint Vincent de Paul* – former; *Asociación Internacional de Caridades de San Vincente de Paul* – former. Registration: Banque-Carrefour des Entreprises, No/ID: 0428.602.418, Start date: 12 Mar 1986, Belgium. **Aims** Fight against *poverty* and exclusion; accompany *women* in their search for empowerment and autonomy; speak out against injustice, and put pressure on structures and decision makers to fight against the causes of poverty. **Structure** Assembly of Delegates; Board (meets annually); Permanent Committee; Working Commissions; International Secretariat, headed by General Manager. **Languages** English, French, Spanish. **Staff** 4.00 FTE, paid; 100000.00 FTE, voluntary. Staff and volunteers generally work part-time. **Finance** Sources: donations; members' dues. **Activities** Events/meetings; networking/liaising; training/education. **Events** *General Assembly* Bogota (Colombia) 2020, *Delegates Assembly* Châtillon-sur-Chalaronne (France) 2017, *Delegates Assembly* Guatemala (Guatemala) 2015, *Delegates Assembly* Bangkok (Thailand) 2013, *Meeting* Aparecida (Brazil) 2012. **Publications** *AIC Newsletter* in English, French, Spanish. Activity Report; training booklets; meeting reports.
Members Associations in 55 countries and territories:
Argentina, Belgium, Bolivia, Brazil, Burundi, Cambodia, Cameroon, Central African Rep, Chad, Chile, Colombia, Congo DR, Costa Rica, Cuba, Curaçao, Dominican Rep, Ecuador, Egypt, El Salvador, Ethiopia, France, Germany, Guatemala, Guyana, Haiti, Honduras, Indonesia, Ireland, Italy, Japan, Laos, Lebanon, Madagascar, Mexico, Mozambique, Nicaragua, Nigeria, Panama, Paraguay, Peru, Philippines, Poland, Portugal, Puerto Rico, Slovakia, Spain, Switzerland, Syrian AR, Taiwan, Thailand, UK, Ukraine, USA, Venezuela, Vietnam.
Consultative Status Consultative status granted from: *UNESCO (#20322)* (Consultative Status); *Council of Europe (CE, #04881)* (Participatory Status). **NGO Relations** Member of (5): *Crescendo Worldwide Network (#04950)*; *Federation of European and International Associations Established in Belgium (FAIB, #09508)*; *Forum of Catholic Inspired NGOs (#09905)*; *International Catholic Centre of Geneva (ICCG, #12449)*; *Vienna NGO Committee on the Family (#20774)*. Cooperates with (5): *Company of the Daughters of Charity of St Vincent de Paul (DC)*; *Consejo Episcopal Latinoamericano (CELAM, #04709)*; *Council of European Bishops' Conferences (#04884)*; *Daughters of Charity of the Sacred Heart of Jesus (DCSHJ)*; *International Catholic Cooperation Centre for UNESCO (CCIC, #12454)*. Links with religious orders created by: *Pères et Frères Religieux de Saint Vincent-de-Paul (RSV)*. [2021.06.01/XF0589/v/**F**]

- ♦ Association internationale des charités de Saint Vincent de Paul / see Association Internationale des Charités (#02675)
- ♦ Association internationale de charter aérien / see Airlines International Representation in Europe (#00608)

- ♦ Association internationale de chasseurs professionnels (#14647)
- ♦ Association internationale pour le chauffage urbain, le refroidissement à distance et la cogénération / see Euroheat and Power (#05694)
- ♦ Association internationale des chauves (no recent information)
- ♦ Association internationale de la chaux (#14049)
- ♦ Association internationale des chefs de police (#11765)
- ♦ Association internationale des chefs pompiers d'Asie (#13605)
- ♦ Association internationale de chimie cérçalière / see ICC – International Association for Cereal Science and Technology (#11048)
- ♦ Association internationale de la chimie environnementale analytique (#11876)
- ♦ Association internationale des chimistes de l'industrie du cuir (inactive)
- ♦ Association internationale de chiropraxie (internationally oriented national body)
- ♦ Association internationale pour la chirurgie ambulatoire (#11698)
- ♦ Association internationale de chirurgie buccale et maxillo-faciale (#12057)
- ♦ Association Internationale de Chirurgie Endocrine (#11868)
- ♦ Association internationale de chirurgie maxillo-faciale / see International College for Maxillo-Facial Surgery (#12645)
- ♦ Association internationale chrétienne de police (inactive)
- ♦ Association internationale chrétienne de la radio et de la télévision (inactive)
- ♦ Association internationale pour le christianisme libéral et la liberté religieuse / see International Association for Religious Freedom (#12130)
- ♦ Association internationale de chronométrie (inactive)
- ♦ Association internationale du chrysotile (#12570)
- ♦ Association internationale: le cinéma contre la guerre (inactive)
- ♦ Association internationale du cinéma scientifique (inactive)
- ♦ Association internationale des circuits permanents (#03934)
- ♦ Association internationale des cités-jardins linéaires (inactive)
- ♦ Association internationale des citoyens "senior" (inactive)
- ♦ Association internationale de la classe 470 (see: #21760)

♦ Association internationale de climatologie (AIC) 02676

Sec Université Grenoble Alpes, Institut d'urbanisme et de Géographie Alpine, 14bis av Marie Reynoard, 38100 Grenoble, France.
Treas Laboratoire LETG-Rennes, UMR6554, Université Rennes2, place du Recteur H. Le Moal, 35043 Rennes, France.
URL: http://www.climato.be/aic/

History Jun 1988. **Aims** Further development of relations and contacts between climatologists through climatological studies and scientific activities. **Structure** Council, including 3 officers. **Languages** English, French. **Staff** 100.00 FTE, paid. **Finance** Sources: meeting proceeds; members' dues. **Activities** Events/ meetings. **Events** *Colloque Annuel* Toulouse (France) 2022, *Colloque Annuel* Mohammedia (Morocco) 2021, *Colloque Annuel* Rennes (France) 2020, *Colloque Annuel* Thessaloniki (Greece) 2019, *Colloque Annuel* Nice (France) 2018. **Publications** *Climatologie* (annual) – magazine; *Publications de l'Association Internationale de Climatologie* (annual).
Members Individuals in 24 countries:
Albania, Algeria, Argentina, Belgium, Brazil, Cameroon, Canada, Congo Brazzaville, France, Gabon, Germany, Greece, Israel, Italy, Mali, Morocco, Poland, Portugal, Romania, Senegal, Spain, Switzerland, Togo, Tunisia. [2022.03.08/XD6101/v/**D**]

- ♦ Association internationale de clubs des fumeurs de pipes (#12089)
- ♦ Association internationale des cokes (inactive)

♦ Association Internationale des Collectionneurs Olympiques (AICO) . 02677

International Olympic Collectors Association (IOCA)
Président Maison du Sport Français, 1 av Pierre de Coubertin, 75013 Paris, France. E-mail: president@aicolympic.org.
URL: http://www.aicolympic.org/

History 22 May 2014, Lausanne (Switzerland). Set up prior to opening of 20th World Olympic Collectors Fair. Replaced *International Olympic Philately Federation (inactive)*. **Aims** Promote the quality of Olympic *philately*, *numismatic* and *memorabilia* collections linked to historical and cultural aspects of the Olympic Movement. **Structure** General Assembly; Board. **Languages** English, French. **Finance** Sources: members' dues. Olympic Foundation. **Events** *General Assembly* Lausanne (Switzerland) 2014.
Members Full in 17 Countries:
Belgium, Canada, China, Croatia, Czechia, Ecuador, France, Germany, Hungary, Italy, Norway, Poland, Slovakia, Slovenia, Spain, UK, USA.
NGO Relations Association Française des Collectionneurs Olympiques et Sportifs (AFCOS); *International Olympic Committee (IOC, #14408)* – Olympic Philately, Numismatic and Memorabilia Commission; *Olympic Movement (#17719)*; *Sports Philatelists International (SPI, #19928)*. [2022.02.01/XJ8721/**E**]

- ♦ Association internationale des collèges privés d'enseignement professionnel (unconfirmed)
- ♦ Association internationale de combustible et énergie (#13688)
- ♦ Association internationale des commandants des sapeurs-pompiers (internationally oriented national body)
- ♦ Association internationale de commerce et de gestion (inactive)
- ♦ Association internationale pour la communication interculturelle (inactive)
- ♦ Association internationale des compagnies d'assurance contre la grêle / see Association internationale des assureurs de la production agricole (#02671)
- ♦ Association internationale des compagnies de dragage (#11852)
- ♦ Association internationale des compagnons-bâtisseurs (#11745)
- ♦ Association internationale sur les comportements de déplacements / see International Association for Travel Behaviour Research (#12240)
- ♦ Association internationale de comptabilité (inactive)
- ♦ Association internationale des conducteurs anti-alcooliques (inactive)
- ♦ Association internationale de conducteurs courriers professionnels (inactive)
- ♦ Association internationale des conférences de psychotechnique (inactive)
- ♦ Association Internationale des Conférenciers Professionnels de la Francophonie (internationally oriented national body)
- ♦ Association internationale du Congo (inactive)
- ♦ Association internationale du congrès des chemins de fer (inactive)
- ♦ Association internationale pour la conscience de Krishna (religious order)
- ♦ Association internationale sur le conseil de la lactation (internationally oriented national body)
- ♦ Association internationale conseils en campagnes politiques / see International Association of Political Consultants (#12094)
- ♦ Association internationale des conseils économiques et sociaux et institutions similaires (#11858)
- ♦ Association internationale de conseils politiques (#12094)
- ♦ Association internationale pour la conservation des livres, du papier et du matériel d'archives / see International Association of Book and Paper Conservators (#11729)
- ♦ Association internationale des constructeurs de matériel roulant (inactive)
- ♦ Association internationale des constructeurs de motocycles (#14186)
- ♦ Association internationale des constructeurs de transporteurs aériens (#12139)
- ♦ Association internationale de la construction de carrosseries et de remorques (#11727)
- ♦ Association internationale de la construction, de l'urbanisme et de l'environnement (#11812)
- ♦ Association internationale des consultants en établissements d'enseignement supérieur (inactive)
- ♦ Association internationale contre l'emploi de l'opium (inactive)
- ♦ Association internationale contre les expériences douloureuses sur les animaux (#11694)
- ♦ Association internationale contre l'exploitation des foetus humains (inactive)
- ♦ Association internationale contre la lèpre (#14029)
- ♦ Association internationale contre la torture (no recent information)
- ♦ Association internationale contre la tuberculose / see International Union Against Tuberculosis and Lung Disease (#15752)
- ♦ Association internationale contre l'utilisation de la psychiatrie à des fins politiques / see Human Rights in Mental Health (#10988)
- ♦ Association internationale pour le contrôle et la promotion de la santé (#13781)
- ♦ Association internationale des contrôleurs des assurances (#11966)
- ♦ Association internationale de coopération et d'animation régionales (inactive)
- ♦ Association internationale pour la coopération et le développement en Afrique australe (no recent information)
- ♦ Association internationale de coopération pour les pays en voie de développement (inactive)
- ♦ Association internationale coopérative bancaire / see International Cooperative Banking Association (#12945)
- ♦ Association internationale pour la coordination de la manutention des marchandises (inactive)
- ♦ Association Internationale de la Couleur (#12655)
- ♦ Association internationale de courses de grand fond (#12244)

♦ Association internationale des criminologues de langue française (AICLF) 02678

International Association of French-Speaking Criminologists
SG ESC, Univ de Lausanne, Quartier UNIL-Sorge, Bâtiment Batochime, 1015 Lausanne VD, Switzerland. E-mail: secretariat@aiclf.net.
URL: http://www.aiclf.net/

History Founded 1987, Geneva. **Aims** Foster relationships between academics, practitioners and researchers studying or working in criminology. **Languages** French. **Events** *Colloquium* Paris (France) 2016, *Colloquium* Liège (Belgium) 2014, *Colloquium* Montréal, QC (Canada) 2012, *Colloquium* Fribourg (Switzerland) 2010, *Colloquium* Rabat (Morocco) 2008. **Publications** *Revue Internationale de Criminologie et de Police Technique et Scientifique* (4 a year). **Members** Membership countries not specified. **NGO Relations** Member of: *Association des universités partiellement ou entièrement de langue française (AUPELF, inactive)*. *International Centre for Comparative Criminology (ICCC, #12482)* is a member. [2017.12.05/XD1436/**D**]

♦ Association internationale de la critique littéraire (AICL) 02679

Pres Hôtel de Massa, 38 rue du Faubourg-Saint-Jacques, 75014 Paris, France. E-mail: aicl@aicl-fr.com.
UNESCO Representative 19 rue Saint-Saëns, 75015 Paris, France.
URL: http://aicl-fr.com/

History 17 May 1969, Parma (Italy). Former names and other names: *International Association of Literary Critics (IALC)* – former; *Association internationale des critiques littéraires (AICL)* – former; *Asociación Internacional de Criticos Literarios* – former; *Associazione Internazione del Critici Letterari* – former. Registration: Start date: 6 Nov 2004, France. **Aims** Strengthen links among cultures, in particular in the area of writing and literary criticism; promote cultural development in the contemporary world; increase exchange among literatures by means of *translation*; study common problems that concern the function of critic; promote the *book* as the essential element of culture and as the irreplaceable medium of its diffusion. **Structure** Executive Committee (meets annually), comprising one representative of each national centre. International Bureau: President; 3 Vice-Presidents; Treasurer. **Languages** English, French. **Staff** 2.00 FTE, voluntary. **Finance** Sources: members' dues. Other sources. **Activities** Congresses; round tables; colloquia. **Events** *International Colloquium* La Riche (France) 2020, *General Assembly* 2019, *International Colloquium* 2019, *International Conference* Lecce (Italy) 2013, *Congress* Piatra-Neamt (Romania) 2008. **Publications** *Revue internationale des critiques littéraires* (2 a year). *L'écrivain et la ville*. Congress proceedings; books.
Members National centres in 28 countries:
Belgium, Benin, Brazil, Canada, Colombia, Costa Rica, Cuba, Cyprus, Czechia, Denmark, Finland, France, Germany, Greece, India, Iraq, Italy, Japan, Norway, Poland, Portugal, Romania, Russia, Spain, Switzerland, Tunisia, UK, USA.
Consultative Status Consultative status granted from: *ECOSOC (#05331)* (Ros C). **IGO Relations** Informal relations with: *UNESCO (#20322)*. [2020/XC4199/**C**]

♦ Association internationale des critiques d'art (AICA) 02680

International Association of Art Critics – Asociación Internacional de Criticos de Arte
Contact 32 rue Yves Toudic, 75010 Paris, France. T. +33147701742. E-mail: aica.office@gmail.com.
URL: http://www.aicainternational.news/

History 21 Jun 1948, Paris (France). 21-26 Jun 1948, Paris (France), at first congress, as *International Congress of Art Critics – Congrès international des critiques d'art*. **Aims** Develop international cooperation in the visual, graphic and applied arts and architecture, and their creation, diffusion and culture, by safeguarding the prestige and professional interests of art critics; encourage international exchange in the field of plastic art. **Structure** General Assembly (annual); Board of Directors; Directing Committee. Congresses open; Assemblies closed. **Languages** English, French, Spanish. **Staff** 1.00 FTE, paid. **Finance** Sources: members' dues. **Activities** Events/meetings. **Events** *Annual Congress* Valparaiso (Chile) 2022, *Annual Congress* Istanbul (Turkey) 2021, *Annual Congress* Cologne (Germany) / Berlin (Germany) 2019, *Annual Congress* Taipei (Taiwan) 2018, *Annual Congress* Paris (France) 2017. **Publications** *AICA in the Age of Globalisation* (2010). Congress reports; minutes of assemblies; directory (1996); articles in specialist journals. Information Services: International Art Information Office.
Members National sections representing over 4,200 members in 63 countries and territories:
Argentina, Armenia, Australia, Austria, Barbados, Belgium, Bosnia-Herzegovina, Brazil, Bulgaria, Canada, Catalunya, Chile, Colombia, Congo Brazzaville, Congo DR, Côte d'Ivoire, Croatia, Czechia, Denmark, Dominican Rep, Egypt, Finland, France, Germany, Greece, Haiti, Hong Kong, Hungary, Ireland, Israel, Italy, Japan, Kazakhstan, Korea Rep, Lebanon, Lithuania, Luxembourg, Mexico, Netherlands, Nigeria, North Macedonia, Norway, Pakistan, Paraguay, Poland, Portugal, Puerto Rico, Romania, Russia, Senegal, Serbia, Slovakia, Slovenia, Spain, Sweden, Switzerland, Taiwan, Türkiye, UK, Ukraine, Uruguay, USA, Venezuela.
Open sections representing 63 members in 29 countries. Membership countries not specified.
Consultative Status Consultative status granted from: *UNESCO (#20322)* (Consultative Status). **IGO Relations** *Intergovernmental Committee for Promoting the Return of Cultural Property to its Countries of Origin or its Restitution in case of Illicit Appropriation (#11476)*. **NGO Relations** Member of: *Union des organisations internationales non-gouvernementales établies en France (UOIF, inactive)*. [2019.03.05/XC1255/**B**]

- ♦ Association internationale des critiques littéraires / see Association internationale de la critique littéraire (#02679)
- ♦ Association internationale des critiques de théâtre (#12226)
- ♦ Association internationale pour le cuivre (#12962)
- ♦ Association internationale pour la culture des tissus des plantes / see International Association of Plant Biotechnology (#12090)
- ♦ Association internationale de cybernétique (inactive)
- ♦ Association internationale des cyclistes espérantophones (#11878)
- ♦ Association internationale des cyclistes professionnels (inactive)
- ♦ Association internationale de dart / see International DART 18 Association (#13135)
- ♦ Association internationale de défense des artistes (inactive)
- ♦ Association internationale pour la défense des langues et cultures menacées / see Association pour les Langues et Cultures Européennes Menacées (#02782)

♦ Association internationale pour la défense de la liberté religieuse (AIDLR) 02681

International Association for the Defence of Religious Liberty – Asociación Internacional para la Defensa de la Libertad Religiosa – Vereinigung für die Verteidigung der Religionsfreiheit – Associação Internacional para a Defesa da Liberdade Religiosa – Associazione Internazionale per la Difesa della Libertà Religiosa
SG Schlosshaldenstr 17, 3006 Bern, Switzerland. T. +41313591527 – +41313591535. Fax +41313591566. E-mail: info@aidlr.org.
URL: http://www.aidlr.org/

History 1946, France. Sister organization of *International Religious Liberty Association (IRLA)*. Registration: Switzerland. **Aims** Protect, in all legitimate ways, the right of every man to worship as he chooses or to practice no religion at all. **Structure** Committee of Honour – International Committee. **Languages** English, French, German, Italian, Portuguese, Spanish. **Finance** Sources: members' dues. **Activities** Events/meetings. **Events** *Global Summit on Religion , Peace and Security* Geneva (Switzerland) 2019, *Global Summit on Religion , Peace and Security* Geneva (Switzerland) 2016, *International Conference on Religion, Peace and Security* Madrid (Spain) 2016, *Joint Congress* Dominican Rep 2012, *Joint Congress* Cape Town (South Africa) 2007. **Publications** *Conscience et liberté* (annual) in English, French, German, Italian, Portuguese, Spanish.
Members National associations in 16 countries and territories:
Angola, Austria, Belgium, Bulgaria, Canada, Czechia, France, French Antilles, Germany, Italy, Mozambique, Portugal, Romania, Slovakia, Spain, Switzerland.
Individuals in 39 countries and territories:
Albania, Algeria, Argentina, Australia, Burundi, Cameroon, Chile, Côte d'Ivoire, Croatia, Czechia, Gabon, Ghana, Greece, Guyana, Hungary, India, Israel, Lebanon, Luxembourg, Madagascar, Malta, Mauritania, Mauritius, Morocco, Netherlands, New Caledonia, Nigeria, Pakistan, Poland, Polynesia Fr, Réunion, Russia, Rwanda, Senegal, Seychelles, Togo, Tunisia, UK, USA.
Consultative Status Consultative status granted from: *ECOSOC (#05331)* (Special); *Council of Europe (CE, #04881)* (Participatory Status). **IGO Relations** *UNESCO (#20322)*. Consultative Status with: *European Parliament (EP, #08146)*; *Organization for Security and Cooperation in Europe (OSCE, #17887)*. Cooperates with: *United Nations Human Rights Council (HRC, #20571)*. Accredited by: *United Nations Office at Vienna (UNOV, #20604)*. **NGO Relations** Member of (3): *Committee of NGOs on Human Rights, Geneva (#04275)*; *Conference of Non-Governmental Organizations in Consultative Relationship with the United Nations (CONGO, #04635)*; *NGO Committee on Freedom of Religion or Belief, New York NY (#17109)*. Cooperates with (1): *G20 Interfaith Forum Association (IF20, #10055)*. [2020.03.03/XD1215/**C**]

- ♦ Association internationale de défense des producteurs de lait, des agriculteurs et des industries de transformation connexes (inactive)
- ♦ Association internationale de défense du saumon atlantique (internationally oriented national body)
- ♦ Association internationale pour la démocratie en Afrique (#11836)

♦ Association internationale des démographes de langue française (AIDELF) 02682

International Association of French-speaking Demographers
Sec 9 Cours des Humanités, CS 50004, 93322 Aubervilliers CEDEX, France. T. +33156062237. E-mail: aidelf@ined.fr.
URL: http://www.aidelf.org/
History Founded 1978. **Aims** Study population problems; promote *demography* and its applications; disseminate knowledge on population matters; widen the public for demography and assist in preventing mono-lingualism and encouraging scientific diversity in ways of thinking by promoting use of the *French language* in publications and international meetings. **Languages** French. **Staff** 1.50 FTE, voluntary. **Finance** Sources: members' dues. **Activities** Events/meetings. **Events** *Démographie et Crises* Athens (Greece) 2022, *Démographie et Crises* Athens (Greece) 2020, *Comment vieillissons-nous?* Louvain-la-Neuve (Belgium) 2018, *Colloque* Strasbourg (France) 2016, *Colloque* Bari (Italy) 2014. **Publications** *AIDELF-Actualités*. Colloquium and seminar proceedings.
Members Individuals (over 500) in 55 countries:
Albania, Algeria, Angola, Argentina, Belgium, Belize, Benin, Bosnia-Herzegovina, Brazil, Burkina Faso, Burundi, Cameroon, Canada, Chad, Congo Brazzaville, Congo DR, Côte d'Ivoire, Croatia, Czechia, Estonia, France, Germany, Greece, Guinea, Hungary, Ireland, Israel, Italy, Japan, Lebanon, Luxembourg, Madagascar, Mali, Mauritania, Montenegro, Morocco, Netherlands, New Zealand, Niger, Poland, Portugal, Romania, Russia, Senegal, Serbia, Slovenia, South Africa, Spain, Suriname, Switzerland, Togo, Tunisia, UK, USA, Venezuela. [2020/XD0062/v/**C**]

- ♦ Association internationale des denrées congelées (#13686)
- ♦ Association internationale de dentisterie pour les handicapés / see International Association for Disability and Oral Health (#11848)
- ♦ Association internationale de dentisterie pédiatrique / see International Association of Paediatric Dentistry (#12064)
- ♦ Association internationale des dentistes contre la guerre (inactive)
- ♦ Association internationale Pro Deo (inactive)
- ♦ Association internationale pour la destruction des rats (inactive)
- ♦ Association internationale de développement (#13155)
- ♦ Association internationale de développement et d'action communautaires / see International Association for Community Development (#11793)
- ♦ Association internationale pour le développement et la communication / see Eurometrika-Euroskopia (#05734)
- ♦ Association internationale pour le développement de la documentation, des bibliothèques et des archives en Afrique (inactive)
- ♦ Association internationale pour le développement des échanges commerciaux (inactive)
- ♦ Association internationale pour le développement économique et l'aide technique / see Conseil français des investisseurs en Afrique
- ♦ Association internationale pour le développement et la gestion des villes anciennes et nouvelles / see International Urban Development Association (#15832)
- ♦ Association internationale pour le développement des gommes naturelles (#02662)
- ♦ Association internationale pour le développement des hydrocolloides / see Association for International Development of Natural Gums (#02662)
- ♦ Association internationale pour le développement de logements coopératifs (inactive)
- ♦ Association internationale pour le développement de l'odonto-stomatologie tropicale (no recent information)
- ♦ Association internationale pour le développement organisationnel (#14444)
- ♦ Association Internationale pour le Développement de la Propriété Intellectuelle (#15056)
- ♦ Association internationale pour le développement de la recherche en didactique du français langue maternelle / see Association internationale pour la recherche en didactique du français (#02736)
- ♦ Association internationale pour le développement des ressources humaines (inactive)
- ♦ Association internationale de développement rural (inactive)
- ♦ Association internationale de développement de tontines (internationally oriented national body)
- ♦ Association internationale pour le développement des universités internationales et mondiales (no recent information)
- ♦ Association internationale du développement urbain (#15832)

♦ Association internationale de dialectologie arabe (AIDA) 02683

International Association of Arabic Dialectology
Gen Sec Fac der Geesteswetenschappen, Semitische talen en culturen, Univ Amsterdam, Spuistr 134, 1012 VB Amsterdam, Netherlands. T. +31205244680.
URL: https://independent.academia.edu/AIDAAssociationInternationaledeDialectologieArabe
History 1993, Paris (France). **Aims** Encourage and promote the study of Arabic dialects. **Structure** General Assembly; Executive Board. **Activities** Events/meetings. **Events** *Biennial Congress* Granada (Spain) 2022, *Biennial Congress* Kutaisi (Georgia) 2019, *Biennial Congress* Marseille (France) 2017, *Biennial Congress* Bucharest (Romania) 2015, *Biennial Congress* Doha (Qatar) 2013. **Publications** Conference proceedings. [2016.03.10/XM2753/**D**]

- ♦ Association internationale des diffuseurs d'oeuvres d'art originales / see Federation of European Art Galleries Associations (#09492)
- ♦ Association internationale pour la diffusion des cultures et des langues (inactive)
- ♦ Association internationale des diplômés des institutions éducatives soviétiques / see International Coordination Council of Educational Institutions Alumni (#12959)
- ♦ Association internationale des diplômés de la restauration et de l'hôtellerie (no recent information)
- ♦ Association internationale des directeurs d'écoles hôtelières (#11942)
- ♦ Association internationale des directeurs d'opéra (inactive)
- ♦ Association internationale de dispacheurs européens / see Association mondiale de dispacheurs (#02809)
- ♦ Association internationale de la distribution (#11851)
- ♦ Association internationale de la distribution des produits alimentaires et des produits de grande consommation / see International Association for the Distributive Trade (#11851)
- ♦ Association internationale de la distribution des produits alimentaires pour le progrès des techniques et des services / see International Association for the Distributive Trade (#11851)
- ♦ Association internationale des docteurs en économie du tourisme (inactive)
- ♦ Association internationale des documentalistes et techniciens de l'information (inactive)
- ♦ Association internationale des documentaristes (inactive)
- ♦ Association internationale Données pour le développement (inactive)
- ♦ Association internationale de la droguerie (inactive)
- ♦ Association internationale de droit africain (inactive)

♦ Association Internationale de Droit des Assurances (AIDA) 02684

International Insurance Law Association – Asociación Internacional de Derecho de Seguros – Internationale Vereinigung für Versicherungsrecht – Associazione Internazionale di Diritto delle Assicurazioni
Secretariat address not obtained. E-mail: secretariat@aidainsurance.org.
SG Limburgo 1447, 11400 Montevideo, Uruguay. T. +59894459239. E-mail: asignorino@netgate.com.uy – andreasignorino@gmail.com.
URL: https://aidainsurance.org/
History 28 Apr 1960, Luxembourg. Registration: Switzerland. **Aims** Further and develop international collaboration in the field of insurance law. **Structure** General Assembly (at least every 4 years, at World Congress); Presidential Council; Executive Committee; Finance Committee; Scientific Council; Working Parties; General Secretariat. Regional groups: *AIDA Europe*; *Ibero-Latin American Committee (CILA)*. **Languages** English, French, German, Italian, Spanish. **Staff** Voluntary. **Finance** Sources: members' dues. **Activities** Awards/prizes/competitions; events/meetings; knowledge management/information dissemination. **Events** *World Congress* Melbourne, VIC (Australia) 2023, *Europe Conference* Zurich (Switzerland) 2022, *Europe Conference* Zurich (Switzerland) 2020, *Europe Conference* Lisbon (Portugal) 2019, *Quadrennial World Congress* Rio de Janeiro (Brazil) 2018. **Publications** Reports; proceedings.
Members National sections, associations in 54 countries and territories:
Argentina, Australia, Austria, Belgium, Brazil, Bulgaria, Chile, China, Colombia, Costa Rica, Croatia, Cuba, Denmark, El Salvador, Estonia, Finland, France, Germany, Greece, Guatemala, Honduras, Hong Kong, Hungary, Iceland, Indonesia, Israel, Italy, Japan, Korea DPR, Korea Rep, Lebanon, Mexico, Morocco, Netherlands, New Zealand, Norway, Paraguay, Peru, Poland, Romania, Russia, Serbia, Singapore, Slovenia, South Africa, Spain, Sweden, Switzerland, Tunisia, Türkiye, UK, Uruguay, USA, Venezuela.
NGO Relations Cooperates with: *International Credit Insurance & Surety Association (ICISA, #13103)*; *International Insurance Library, Leuven*. [2019/XC3896/**C**]

- ♦ Association internationale de droit de la communication, Paris (unconfirmed)
- ♦ Association internationale de droit de la consommation (#11814)
- ♦ Association internationale de droit constitutionnel (#11811)
- ♦ Association internationale du droit des eaux (#12263)
- ♦ Association internationale de droit économique (inactive)
- ♦ Association internationale de droit de la famille (#15114)
- ♦ Association internationale pour le droit financier et fiscal / see International Fiscal Association (#13608)
- ♦ Association internationale pour le droit au jeu de l'enfant (#14604)
- ♦ Association internationale de droit judiciaire / see International Association for Procedural Law (#12102)
- ♦ Association internationale du droit nucléaire (#14379)
- ♦ Association internationale de droit pénal (#12074)
- ♦ Association internationale de droit processuel (#12102)
- ♦ Association Internationale des Droits de l'enfant en difficulté et dans la souffrance (internationally oriented national body)
- ♦ Association Internationale des Droits de l'Homme (internationally oriented national body)
- ♦ Association internationale du droit des sports (#12180)
- ♦ Association of International Education Administrators (internationally oriented national body)
- ♦ Association internationale pour l'échange de droits d'émission (#13262)
- ♦ Association internationale pour l'échange d'étudiants en vue de l'acquisition d'une expérience technique (#11885)
- ♦ Association internationale des échecs en Braille (#12388)
- ♦ Association Internationale des Écoles de Cinéma et de Télévision / see International Association of Cinema, Audiovisual and Media Schools (#11771)
- ♦ Association internationale des écoles et instituts d'administration (#12147)
- ♦ Association internationale des écoles ou instituts supérieurs d'éducation physique et sportive / see Association internationale des écoles supérieures d'éducation physique (#02685)
- ♦ Association internationale des écoles partiellement ou entièrement de langue française (inactive)
- ♦ Association internationale des écoles de publicité (inactive)

♦ Association internationale des écoles supérieures d'éducation physique (AIESEP) 02685

International Association for Physical Education in Higher Education – Asociación Internacional de las Escuelas Superioras de Educación Fisica y Deporte
Gen Sec Sport Studies and Physical Education, Univ College Cork, Gaol Walk, T12 YN60, Cork, CO. CORK, Ireland. T. +353214902107.
Pres Dept of Sport Sciences, Univ de Liège, Allée des Sports 4 – Bât B-21, 4000 Liège, Belgium. T. +3243663880.
URL: http://www.aiesep.org/
History Aug 1962, Lisbon (Portugal). Former names and other names: *International Association of Schools or Higher Institutes of Physical Education* – former (Aug 1962); *Association internationale des écoles ou instituts supérieurs d'éducation physique et sportive* – former (Aug 1962); *International Association of Colleges of Physical Education* – former alias. **Aims** Promote high quality research in the areas of physical education, physical activity and sport pedagogy across the lifespan. **Structure** General Assembly (every 4 years); Board of Directors; Committees; Special Interest Groups (2). **Languages** English. **Staff** Voluntary. **Finance** Sources: members' dues. **Activities** Awards/prizes/competitions; events/meetings; guidance/assistance/consulting; knowledge management/information dissemination; networking/liaising; politics/policy/regulatory; research/documentation. **Events** *International Conference* 2025, *International Conference* Santiago (Chile) 2023, *Scientific Meeting* Gold Coast, QLD (Australia) 2022, *Scientific Meeting* Banff, AB (Canada) 2021, *Scientific Meeting* Hong Kong (Hong Kong) 2020. **Publications** *AIESEP Flash Newsletter*. *The Cagigal Lecture Series*. Position statements; conference proceedings.
Members Schools and higher institutes of education; individuals. Members in 51 countries and territories:
Algeria, Argentina, Australia, Austria, Belgium, Brazil, Bulgaria, Canada, Chile, China, Cuba, Czechia, Denmark, Finland, France, Germany, Greece, Hong Kong, Hungary, India, Ireland, Israel, Italy, Japan, Mauritius, Mexico, Morocco, Netherlands, New Zealand, Norway, Paraguay, Poland, Portugal, Romania, Russia, Saudi Arabia, Senegal, Singapore, Slovakia, South Africa, Spain, Sweden, Switzerland, Taiwan, Thailand, Tunisia, UK, United Arab Emirates, Uruguay, USA, Venezuela.
NGO Relations Member of: *European Physical Education Association (EUPEA, #08206)*; *International Council of Sport Science and Physical Education (ICSSPE, #13077)*. [2020.03.07/XC1338/**C**]

- ♦ Association internationale des écoles supérieures d'hôtellerie (inactive)
- ♦ Association internationale des écoles de travail social (#12149)
- ♦ Association internationale des écoles de voiles (#14777)
- ♦ Association internationale d'écologie (#11856)
- ♦ Association internationale d'économie alimentaire et agro-industrielle (inactive)
- ♦ Association internationale d'économie de la participation (#11859)
- ♦ Association internationale des économistes agronomiques (#11695)
- ♦ Association internationale des économistes de l'énergie / see International Association for Energy Economics (#11869)

♦ Association Internationale des Economistes de Langue Française (AIELF) 02686

Pres 12 place du Panthéon, 75231 Paris, France. E-mail: info@aielf.org.
SG Université de Dschang, Rectorat de l'UDs BP 96, Dschang, Cameroon. T. +237233451381. E-mail: courrier.rectorat@univ-dschang.org – udsrectorat@univ-dschang.org.
Scientific Dir Dept of Mathematics, Faculty of Informatics and Electronic Economy, Poznan University of Economics and Business, al Niepodleglosci 10, 61-875 Poznań, Poland. T. +48618543743.
URL: http://aielf.org/

History Replaces *Congrès International des Economistes de Langue Française*, set up 27 Apr 1970. Also referred to as *Association des économistes de langue française.* Current statutes adopted 20 May 2015. Registration: RNA, No/ID: W751023711, Start date: 2 Jun 2015, France. **Aims** Bring together academics, researchers and men of culture who think, cooperate and disseminate economic thought riveted to the passion of the language of Molière. **Structure** General Assembly; Board; Scientific Council. **Languages** French. **Staff** 4.00 FTE, paid. **Finance** Sources: members' dues. **Activities** Events/meetings. **Events** *International Congress* Beirut (Lebanon) 2021, *International Congress* Santiago (Chile) 2019, *International Congress* Poznań (Poland) 2017, *International Congress* Paris (France) 2015, *Congress* Warsaw (Poland) 2007. **Publications** *Revue Internationale des Economistes de Lange Française (RIELF).* Congress proceedings. **Members** Individuals (over 160) in about 40 countries. Membership countries not specified. [2020/XD4573/**C**]

- ♦ Association internationale des économistes du sport (#12177)
- ♦ Association internationale des écrivains de langue française / see Association des écrivains de langue française (#02481)
- ♦ Association internationale des écrivains de langue française (inactive)
- ♦ Association internationale des écrivains scientifiques (#14800)
- ♦ Association internationale des éditeurs africains francophones (no recent information)
- ♦ Association internationale des éditeurs de catalogues de timbres-poste / see ASCAT – International Association of Stamp Catalogue, Stamp Album and Philatelic Magazine Publishers (#01130)
- ♦ Association internationale d'éditeurs de linguistique appliquée (inactive)
- ♦ Association internationale des éditeurs d'ouvrages savants (inactive)
- ♦ Association internationale d'éditeurs scientifiques, techniques et médicaux (#12154)
- ♦ Association internationale d'éducateurs de communauté (inactive)
- ♦ Association internationale des éducateurs de jeunes inadaptés / see International Association of Social Educators (#12167)
- ♦ Association internationale des éducateurs à la paix (internationally oriented national body)
- ♦ Association internationale des éducateurs pour la paix du monde (internationally oriented national body)
- ♦ Association internationale des éducateurs sociaux (#12167)
- ♦ Association internationale pour l'éducation cognitive / see International Association for Cognitive Education and Psychology (#11782)
- ♦ Association internationale pour l'éducation de l'enfance / see Childhood Education International
- ♦ Association internationale pour l'éducation intégrative (inactive)
- ♦ Association internationale pour l'éducation interculturelle (#11969)
- ♦ Association internationale d'éducation physique et sportive féminine (#12081)
- ♦ Association internationale pour l'éducation des sourds-aveugles / see Deafblind International (#05014)
- ♦ Association internationale pour l'éducation des sourds-muets / see Deafblind International (#05014)
- ♦ Association Internationale pour les Edulcorants (#15639)
- ♦ Association internationale pour l'égalité des femmes (unconfirmed)
- ♦ Association internationale des égyptologues (#11865)
- ♦ Association internationale Pro Electron (inactive)
- ♦ Association internationale d'éleveurs de bétail Pinzgauer (#14585)
- ♦ Association internationale des employés de chemin de fer espérantistes (inactive)
- ♦ Association internationale d'endoscopie / see World Endoscopy Organization (#21380)
- ♦ Association internationale pour l'énergie hydrogène (#11951)
- ♦ Association internationale des enquêteurs de la sécurité aérienne (#14914)
- ♦ Association internationale des enseignants et chercheurs des droits de l'homme (inactive)
- ♦ Association internationale pour l'enseignement de la conduite et de l'éducation routière (inactive)
- ♦ Association internationale pour l'enseignement du droit comparé (inactive)
- ♦ Association internationale pour l'enseignement des langues vivantes par les méthodes modernes (inactive)
- ♦ Association internationale pour l'enseignement programmé (inactive)
- ♦ Association internationale pour l'enseignement statistique (#12184)
- ♦ Association internationale des entraîneurs d'athlétisme (#15702)
- ♦ Association internationale des entrepreneurs en pipe lines onshore et offshore (#14586)
- ♦ Association internationale des entreprises d'équipement électrique / see EuropeOn (#09166)
- ♦ Association Internationale d'Entreprises Familiales and Bicentenaires (#11723)
- ♦ Association Internationale d'épidémiologie (#13287)
- ♦ Association internationale d'épigraphie Grecque et Latine (#11924)
- ♦ Association internationale d'épigraphie latine / see International Association for Greek and Latin Epigraphy (#11924)
- ♦ Association internationale équipements de sport et de loisirs (#13319)
- ♦ Association internationale d'ergonomie (#13294)
- ♦ Association internationale espérantiste d'employés de la police (inactive)
- ♦ Association internationale espérantiste des juristes (inactive)
- ♦ Association internationale pour l'essai des matériaux (inactive)
- ♦ Association internationale d'essais de semences / see International Seed Testing Association (#14829)
- ♦ Association internationale d'esthétique (#11692)
- ♦ Association internationale d'esthétique expérimentale (#11867)

♦ Association internationale des établissements francophones de formation à l'assurance (AIEFFA) 02687

SG 14 rue Gay-Lussac, 75005 Paris, France. T. +33613097881.
SG address not obtained. T. +33147765811.
URL: http://aieffa.org/

History Founded 20 Nov 1995, Paris (France). Registered in accordance with French law. **Aims** Encourage establishment of insurance training institutions in French-speaking countries; promote exchange of information, and of teachers and trainees. **Languages** French. **Staff** Voluntary. **Finance** Members' dues. **Activities** Events/meetings; awards/prizes/competitions. **Events** *General Assembly* Casablanca (Morocco) 2015, *General Assembly* Paris (France) 2013, *General Assembly* Paris (France) 2011, *General Assembly* Paris (France) 2009, *General Assembly* Paris (France) 2008. **Publications** Onlin information.
Members Full in 20 countries:
Algeria, Burkina Faso, Benin, Burkina Faso, Cameroon, Central African Rep, Chad, Comoros, Congo Brazzaville, Côte d'Ivoire, Equatorial Guinea, France, Gabon, Lebanon, Mali, Morocco, Niger, Senegal, Togo, Tunisia.
IGO Relations Cooperates with: *Institut international des assurances, Yaoundé (IIA, #11309).* **NGO Relations** Member of: *Association francophone d'amitié et de liaison (AFAL, #02605).* [2018/XD6696/**D**]

- ♦ Association internationale des établissements publics de crédit sur gages (inactive)
- ♦ Association internationale de l'étanchéité / see European Waterproofing Association (#09084)
- ♦ Association internationale d'ethnopsychiatrie et d'ethnopsychanalyse (inactive)

♦ Association internationale pour l'étude des argiles (AIPEA) 02688

International Association for the Study of Clays – Internationale Vereinigung zum Studium der Tone – Mezdunarodnaja Associacija po Izuceniju Glin

Pres address not obtained.
Past Pres Microminerals/Health/Environment Research Group, Inst Methodologies for Environmental Analysis, Natl Research Council Italy, c/o Dept of Earth/Geoenvironmental Sciences, c/o Dept of Earth/Geoenvironmental Sciences, Via Orabona 4, 70125 Bari BA, Italy. T. +39805442618. Fax +39805442591. E-mail: president@aipea.org.
URL: http://www.aipea.org/

History 1948, London (UK). Founded at International Geological Congress. Statutes adopted 24 Jun 1966, Jerusalem (Israel). Former names and other names: *International Committee for the Study of Clays* – former (1948 to Jun 1966); *Comité international pour l'études des argiles* – former (1948 to Jun 1966). **Aims** Promote international cooperation in clay research and technology; cooperate with other organizations having an interest in these fields. **Structure** General Assembly (at International Clay Conference); Council; Committees. **Languages** English, French, German, Russian, Spanish. **Staff** Voluntary. **Finance** Sources: contributions; members' dues. **Activities** Advocacy/lobbying/activism; awards/prizes/competitions; events/meetings. **Events** *International Clay Conference* Istanbul (Türkiye) 2022, *EUROCLAY : International Conference on Clay Science and Technology* Paris (France) 2019, *International Clay Conference* Rio de Janeiro (Brazil) 2013, *International Conference on Clays, Clay Minerals and Layered Materials* St Petersburg (Russia) 2013, *International clay conference* Taranto (Italy) 2009. **Publications** *AIPEA Newsletter. AIPEA Education Series.* Conference proceedings.
Members Individuals (clay scientists); Institutions; Companies; Sustaining members; Patrons. Affiliated societies in 24 countries:
Algeria, Australia, Austria, China, Croatia, Czechia, France, Germany, Hungary, India, Israel, Italy, Japan, Korea Rep, Poland, Portugal, Russia, Slovakia, Spain, Switzerland, Tunisia, Türkiye, UK, Ukraine.
European affiliated society:
NGO Relations Affiliated member of: *International Union of Geological Sciences (IUGS, #15777).* [2021/XC1238/**C**]

- ♦ Association internationale pour l'étude du cancer (inactive)
- ♦ Association internationale pour l'étude du cancer du poumon (#12204)
- ♦ Association internationale pour l'étude des céramiques médiévales méditerranéennes / see Association Internationale pour l'Étude des Céramiques Médiévales et Modernes en Méditerranée (#02711)
- ♦ Association internationale d'étude des civilisations méditerranéennes (inactive)
- ♦ Association internationale pour l'étude du comportement des conducteurs (inactive)
- ♦ Association internationale d'étude de la concurrence / see Ligue internationale du droit de la concurrence (#16478)
- ♦ Association internationale pour l'étude de la douleur (#12206)
- ♦ Association internationale pour l'étude du droit canon (#12193)
- ♦ Association internationale d'étude sur les eaux dans des mines (#14168)
- ♦ Association internationale pour l'étude de l'économie de l'assurance / see Geneva Association (#10119)
- ♦ Association internationale pour l'étude empirique de la littérature (#15085)
- ♦ Association internationale d'étude des enseignements spirituels et théologiques (inactive)
- ♦ Association internationale pour l'étude des états proches de la mort (#12047)
- ♦ Association internationale pour l'étude du foie (#12203)
- ♦ Association internationale de l'étude intégrale du sport (inactive)
- ♦ Association Internationale pour l'Etude du Langage Enfantin (#12194)
- ♦ Association internationale pour l'étude de la langue et la littérature italienne (#12202)
- ♦ Association internationale d'étude des micro-Etats (inactive)
- ♦ Association internationale d'étude de la mission (#12032)

♦ Association internationale pour l'étude de la mosaïque antique (AIEMA) 02689

International Association for the Study of Ancient Mosaics

Contact Ecole Normale Supérieure, rue d'Ulm, 75230 Paris CEDEX 05, France. E-mail: aiema75rs@gmail.com.
URL: https://aiema75rs.wixsite.com/aiema/

History Founded 3 Sep 1963, Paris (France). Registered in accordance with French law. **Aims** Promote and coordinate scientific research on ancient and *mediaeval* mosaics; establish cultural links among researchers and organizations in the field; improve dissemination of research results through specialized indexes and libraries. **Structure** General Assembly (every 3-4 years, on the eve of International Congress); Administrative Council; Bureau. **Languages** English, French, German, Italian, Spanish. **Staff** 40.00 FTE, voluntary. **Finance** Sources: members' dues. **Activities** Events/meetings; knowledge management/information dissemination; networking/liaising; research/documentation. **Events** *International Colloquium* Lyon (France) / Saint-Romain-en-Gal (France) 2022, *International Colloquium* Nicosia (Cyprus) 2018, *International Colloquium* Madrid (Spain) 2015, *International colloquium* Venice (Italy) 2012, *International colloquium* Bursa (Turkey) 2009. **Publications** *Bulletin de l'AIEMA* (every 2 years) – including international bibliography. Proceedings of international colloquia.
Members Institutions in 16 countries (not specified). Individuals in 34 countries:
Algeria, Australia, Austria, Azerbaijan, Belgium, Bulgaria, Canada, Croatia, Cyprus, Czechia, Denmark, France, Germany, Greece, Israel, Italy, Japan, Morocco, Netherlands, New Zealand, Poland, Portugal, Romania, Serbia, Slovenia, Spain, Sweden, Switzerland, Syrian AR, Tunisia, Türkiye, UK, Ukraine, USA.
NGO Relations Affiliated to: *Fédération internationale des associations d'études classiques (FIEC, #09607).* [2019/XC1235/y/**C**]

- ♦ Association internationale pour l'étude de la musique populaire (#12207)
- ♦ Association internationale pour l'étude d'Otto Gross (#12060)
- ♦ Association internationale pour l'étude de la paléontologie humaine (no recent information)
- ♦ Association internationale pour l'étude du quaternaire / see International Union for Quaternary Research (#15811)
- ♦ Association internationale pour l'étude du quaternaire européen / see International Union for Quaternary Research (#15811)
- ♦ Association internationale pour l'étude des questions relatives à l'enseignement technique supérieur (inactive)
- ♦ Association internationale pour l'étude des rapports entre texte et image (#12276)
- ♦ Association internationale pour l'étude des relations homme-environnement (#12075)
- ♦ Association internationale des études arméniennes (#11709)
- ♦ Association internationale des études de l'Asie du Sud-Est (inactive)
- ♦ Association internationale d'études bouddhiques (#11743)
- ♦ Association internationale des études byzantines (#11751)
- ♦ Association internationale pour l'étude scientifique de l'arriération mentale / see International Association for the Scientific Study of Intellectual and Developmental Disabilities (#12153)
- ♦ Association internationale pour l'étude scientifique de la déficience intellectuelle / see International Association for the Scientific Study of Intellectual and Developmental Disabilities (#12153)
- ♦ Association internationale des études coptes (#11820)
- ♦ Association internationale des Études du discours (#11850)

♦ Association internationale des études françaises (AIEF) 02690

International Association of French Studies

Treas Bureau 20, Pavillon Saint-Jacques, 11 pl Marcelin Berthelot, 75005 Paris, France.
URL: http://www.aief.fr/

History 21 Sep 1949, Paris (France). **Aims** Promote *French language* and culture. **Structure** Board of Directors of 24 members. Bureau, comprising President, Vice-President, Secretary General, Treasurer and Editor. **Languages** French. **Staff** 1.50 FTE, voluntary. **Finance** Sources: grants; members' dues; sale of publications. **Activities** Organizes annual congress (always in Paris). **Events** *Congrès* Paris (France) 2021, *Congrès* Paris (France) 2016, *Congrès* Paris (France) 2012, *Congrès* Paris (France) 2011, *Congrès* Paris (France) 2010. **Publications** *Cahiers de l'Association internationale des études françaises (CAIEF)* (annual). Congress proceedings.
Members Individuals in 53 countries and territories:
Algeria, Andorra, Argentina, Australia, Austria, Belgium, Bosnia-Herzegovina, Brazil, Bulgaria, Burkina Faso, Cambodia, Canada, Chad, China, Congo Brazzaville, Côte d'Ivoire, Croatia, Denmark, Finland, France, Germany, Greece, Hungary, India, Ireland, Israel, Italy, Japan, Korea Rep, Liechtenstein, Luxembourg, Madagascar, Mexico, Monaco, Netherlands, New Zealand, Norway, Poland, Portugal, Romania, Russia, Senegal, Serbia, South Africa, Spain, Sweden, Switzerland, Taiwan, Türkiye, UK, Ukraine, USA, Vietnam. [2018/XD1289/v/**C**]

- ♦ Association internationale d'études de la genèse des minerais (#11910)
- ♦ Association internationale des études hongroises (#11948)
- ♦ Association internationale des études sur la mécanographie (inactive)
- ♦ Association internationale d'études médicales psychologiques et religieuses / see International Association for Medico-Psychological and Religious Studies (#12028)
- ♦ Association Internationale d'études medico-psychologiques et religieuses (#12028)
- ♦ Association internationale d'études missionnaires / see International Association for Mission Studies (#12032)
- ♦ Association internationale des études mongoles (#12035)
- ♦ Association Internationale d'Études néo-latines (#12048)

♦ Association internationale d'études occitanes (AIEO) 02691

International Association of Occitan Studies

Pres Dept de Filologia Clasica y Romanica, Univ de Oviedo, C/ Teniente Alfonso Martinez s/n, 33011 Oviedo, Asturias, Spain. T. +34985104605. E-mail: president@aieo.org.
Sec Dept de Langues/Littéatures/Arts/Cultures des Suds, Univ Paul-Valéry, Route de Mende, 34103 Montpellier, France. E-mail: secretaire@aieo.org.
URL: http://www.aieo.org/

History 1981. Registered in accordance with French law. Registration: RNA, No/ID: W343028686, Start date: 5 Feb 2021, France, Montpellier. **Aims** Contribute to research on the Occitan domain and humanities and social societies. **Structure** General Assembly (every 3 years); Council (meets annually); working groups. **Languages** Occitan. **Staff** Voluntary. **Finance** Members' dues. **Activities** Events/meetings; knowledge management/information dissemination; publishing activity. **Events** *International Congress* Munich (Germany) 2023, *International Congress* Oviedo (Spain) 2021, *International Congress* Albi (France) 2017, *Triennial International Congress* Lleida (Spain) 2014, *Triennial congress / Triennial International Congress* Béziers (France) 2011. **Publications** *Bulletin de l'AIEO* – closed.
Members Individuals in 26 countries:
Australia, Austria, Belgium, Brazil, Bulgaria, Canada, Denmark, Finland, France, Germany, Hungary, Ireland, Italy, Japan, Luxembourg, Netherlands, New Zealand, Norway, Portugal, Romania, Russia, Spain, Sweden, Switzerland, UK, USA.
[2022/XD1891/v/D]

♦ Association internationale d'études patristiques (AIEP) 02692

International Association of Patristic Studies (IAPS)

Pres Univ Nac de San Juan – Univ Católica de Cuyo, Esteban Echeverria, 5400 San Juan, Argentina.
Sec Dipto de Scienze religiose, Univ Cattolica del Sacro Cuore, Largo Gemelli 1, 20123 Milan MI, Italy.
Registered Office Bibliothèque d'Histoire des Religions, Univ Paris IV Sorbonne, 28 rue Serpente, 75006 Paris, France.
URL: http://www.aiep-iaps.org/

History 26 Jun 1965, Paris (France). Statutes adopted 1965; modified: 1979; 1987; 2003; 2012. Registration: Start date: 28 Jun 1967, France. **Aims** Promote study of *Christian antiquity*, especially the Church Fathers; establish by all appropriate means links and exchanges of information among qualified researchers in the field, particular educators, directors of research and those responsible for publications and museum collections. **Structure** General Assembly (at quadrennial conference); Council; Executive Committee. **Languages** English, French, German, Italian, Spanish. **Staff** 5.00 FTE, voluntary. **Finance** Sources: members' dues. **Activities** Events/meetings. **Events** *Quadrennial International Conference on Patristic Studies* Oxford (UK) 2019, *Quadrennial International Conference on Patristic Studies* Oxford (UK) 2015, *Quadrennial International Conference on Patristic Studies* Oxford (UK) 2011, *Quadrennial International Conference on Patristic Studies* Oxford (UK) 2007, *Quadrennial International Conference on Patristic Studies* Oxford (UK) 2003. **Publications** *Bulletin d'information et de liaison* (annual).
Members Individuals qualified in relevant fields and as agreed by the Executive Council (responding research centres and libraries may receive documentation as corresponding members). Members in 53 countries:
Angola, Argentina, Armenia, Australia, Austria, Belgium, Bosnia-Herzegovina, Brazil, Bulgaria, Canada, Chile, China, Colombia, Congo DR, Croatia, Czechia, Denmark, Egypt, Finland, France, Georgia, Germany, Greece, Hungary, India, Ireland, Israel, Italy, Japan, Korea Rep, Lebanon, Lithuania, Malta, Mexico, Montenegro, Netherlands, Norway, Poland, Portugal, Puerto Rico, Romania, Russia, Serbia, Singapore, Slovakia, Slovenia, South Africa, Spain, Sweden, Switzerland, UK, Ukraine, USA.
NGO Relations *Fédération internationale des associations d'études classiques (FIEC, #09607); International Council for Philosophy and Human Sciences (CIPSH, #13061).* [2022/XC3030/v/C]

- ♦ Association internationale des études québécoises (internationally oriented national body)
- ♦ Association internationale des études et recherches sur l'information (#12022)
- ♦ Association internationale pour les études sanskrites (#12143)
- ♦ Association internationale d'études scandinaves (#12145)

♦ Association internationale d'études du Sud-Est européen (AIESEE) 02693

International Association of South-East European Studies – Asociación Internacional de Estudios del Sur-Este Europeo – Internationale Vereinigung für Südosteuropäische Studien – Mezdunarodnaja Associacija po Izuceniju Jugo-Vostocnoj Evropy

Contact Daniel Constantin Str 17, 010631 Bucharest, Romania.
URL: http://www.aiesee.org/

History 23 Apr 1963, Bucharest (Romania). Also referred to as *International Association for the History of South-East Europe – Association internationale pour l'histoire de l'Europe du Sud-Est.* **Aims** Promote *Balkan* and South-East European studies generally in all fields of humanistic sciences, from the earliest times up to the present day; develop knowledge of the South-East European civilizations and their role in cultural exchanges between East and West. **Structure** International Committee (meeting every 4 years), composed of delegates of affiliated national committees or institutions. Bureau, consisting of President, 7 Vice-Presidents, Secretary-General and Treasurer. **Languages** English, French, Russian, Spanish. **Staff** 2.00 FTE, paid. **Finance** Members' dues: Committees or Institutions $200. Other sources: grants from *International Council for Philosophy and Human Sciences (CIPSH, #13061)*, UNESCO and the Romanian Academy (also provides for Secretariat expenses). **Activities** Organization of study groups on different problems of Balkan civilizations; facilitation of international scientific and cultural exchanges. Scientific meetings. **Events** *Quinquennial Congress* Sofia (Bulgaria) 2015, *Quinquennial congress / Annual Meeting* Paris (France) 2009, *Quinquennial Congress* Tirana (Albania) 2004, *Colloquium / Annual Meeting* Italy 2003, *Quinquennial congress / Annual Meeting* Bucharest (Romania) 1999. **Publications** *Bulletin de l'AIESEE* (annual) in English, French. Studies; documents; proceedings.
Members National Committees (25); other institutions. Members in 25 countries:
Albania, Austria, Bosnia-Herzegovina, Bulgaria, Cyprus, Czechia, France, Germany, Greece, Hungary, Italy, Japan, Lebanon, Moldova, Netherlands, North Macedonia, Poland, Romania, Russia, Serbia, Slovakia, Spain, Türkiye, UK, USA.
IGO Relations *UNESCO (#20322).* **NGO Relations** Affiliated to: *International Committee of Historical Sciences (ICHS, #12777).* [2016/XD1346/D]

- ♦ Association internationale des études tamil (no recent information)
- ♦ Association internationale d'étude des substances de croissance de plantes (#14591)
- ♦ Association Internationale des Etudiants en Agriculture / see International Association of Students in Agricultural and Related Sciences (#12191)
- ♦ Association internationale d'étudiants en agronomie des Amériques (inactive)
- ♦ Association internationale des étudiants aveugles (inactive)

♦ Association internationale des étudiants cavaliers (AIEC) 02694

International University Equestrian Federation

Contact address not obtained. E-mail: board@aiecworld.com.
URL: http://www.aiecworld.com/

History 8 Dec 1984. Registered in accordance with German law. Also referred to as *World University Equestrian Federation.* Since 2001, registered in the Netherlands. **Structure** General Assembly; Executive Committee. **Activities** Sporting activities. **Events** *General Assembly* Netherlands 2001, *General Assembly* Luxembourg (Luxembourg) 2000, *General Assembly* Belgium 1999, *General Assembly* Luxembourg (Luxembourg) 1998, *General Assembly* Germany 1997.
Members Individuals in 24 countries:
Algeria, Austria, Belgium, Bermuda, Canada, Estonia, Finland, France, Germany, Hungary, Ireland, Italy, Luxembourg, Monaco, Netherlands, Norway, Poland, Slovenia, Spain, Sweden, Switzerland, UK, USA, Zimbabwe. [2020.03.03/XD6088/v/D]

- ♦ Association internationale des étudiants linguistiques (#12002)
- ♦ Association internationale 'Europe 2000' (inactive)

♦ Association internationale Europe's 500 (Growth Plus) 02695

Exec Dir c/o White and Case, Rue de la Loi 62, 1040 Brussels, Belgium. T. +3222098231. Fax +3222191626.
Pres Zugspitzstrasse 15, Pullach, 82049 Munich, Germany.
URL: http://www.europes500.eu/

History 1996. Registration: No/ID: 0464.218.937, Belgium. **Aims** Promote *entrepreneurship* throughout Europe; advise policy makers to improve the environment for growth companies. **Structure** General Assembly. Board of Directors, comprising President, Vice-President, Honorary President, Founding President, Institutional Representative, Corporate Representative, Executive Director and 6 Chapter Representatives (Austria, Belgium, France, Germany, Netherlands and Spain). Registered office in Brussels (Belgium). **Finance** Members' dues. Income from sponsors, projects. **Activities** Set up 'Europe's 500 – Entrepreneurs for Growth' in 1995. **Events** *Meeting* Brussels (Belgium) 2001, *Meeting* Cannes (France) 2000, *Meeting* Edinburgh (UK) 1999.
Members Individuals in 21 countries:
Austria, Belgium, Bulgaria, Czechia, Denmark, Finland, France, Germany, Greece, Hungary, Iceland, Ireland, Italy, Liechtenstein, Luxembourg, Netherlands, Norway, Spain, Sweden, Switzerland, UK. [2013/XD7732/v/D]

- ♦ Association internationale pour l'évaluation éducative (#11861)
- ♦ Association internationale pour l'évaluation d'impacts (#11956)
- ♦ Association internationale pour l'évaluation du rendement scolaire (#11882)
- ♦ Association internationale d'expertise chimique (inactive)

♦ Association internationale des experts en philatélie (AIEP) 02696

International Association of Philatelic Experts – Asociación Internacional de Expertos Filatélicos – Internationaler Verband der Philatelistischen Experten

Pres Herzog-Friedrich-Strasse 19, 6020 Innsbruck, Austria.
URL: http://www.aiep-experts.net/

History 10 Oct 1954, Merano (Italy). **Aims** Unite leading philatelic experts of all nations and promote and encourage personal contact and cooperation between them; facilitate and promote exchanges of views and opinions; uphold common interests; inform its members of new technologies in the production and/or detection of forgeries; cooperate in detection of forgeries of all kinds and support national and international organizations which are similarly engaged; impress on *collectors* and dealers the role of expert opinions for the benefit and protection of philately; issue and/or support studies and publications dealing with "expertizing" and/or forgeries. **Structure** General Meeting (annual). Board, consisting of President, Vice-President/Treasurer, Vice-President, Secretary and 3 Directors. **Languages** English. **Finance** Members' dues. **Activities** Annually awards the Hunziker Medal for a significant literary contribution or research work concerned with forgeries or philatelic expert activities. Organizes seminars. **Events** *General Meeting* Athens (Greece) 2015, *General Meeting* Venice (Italy) 2014, *General Meeting* Verona (Italy) 2013, *General Meeting* Paris (France) 2012, *General Meeting* Sindelfingen (Germany) 2011. **Publications** *Fakes, Forgeries, Experts* (annual) – jointly with FIP. Yearbook.
Members Individuals; Expert Committees. Full (122) in 37 countries and territories:
Argentina, Australia, Austria, Belgium, Brazil, Canada, Colombia, Cyprus, Czechia, Denmark, Finland, France, Germany, Greece, Hong Kong, Hungary, India, Ireland, Israel, Italy, Luxembourg, Monaco, Netherlands, New Zealand, Norway, Peru, Romania, Russia, Serbia, Singapore, Spain, Sweden, Switzerland, Thailand, Türkiye, UK, USA.
Affiliate organizations (13) in 10 countries:
Australia, Austria, Czechia, Finland, Japan, New Zealand, Spain, Switzerland, UK, USA. [2015.01.02/XD5807/D]

♦ Association internationale d'experts scientifiques du tourisme (AIEST) 02697

International Association of Scientific Experts in Tourism – Asociación Internacional de Expertos Científicos del Turismo – Internationale Vereinigung Wissenschaftlicher Fremdenverkehrsexperten – Associazione internationale degli esperti scientifici del turismo

SG Dufourstrasse 40a, 9000 St Gallen, Switzerland. T. +41712242530. Fax +41712242536. E-mail: info@aiest.org.
URL: http://www.aiest.org/

History 31 May 1951, Rome (Italy). Founded at meeting of founder members, following a meeting of experts held 1949, Lugano (Switzerland), on the initiative of Walter Hunziker and Kurt Krapf. Statutes amended: 23 Jun 1954, Palermo (Italy); 24 Sep 1960, Stresa (Italy); 5 Sep 1975, Belgrade (Yugoslavia) and 21 Sep 1978, Alexandria (Egypt). New statutes adopted 2 Sep 1986, Montreux (Switzerland); amended 29 Aug 2005, Brainerd MN (USA), 20 Aug 2007, Macau and 29 Aug 2011, Barcelona (Spain). **Aims** Act a an international catalyst to promote scientific activity in the field of tourism; promote members' scientific activity, in particular by developing personal contacts, providing documentation and facilitating exchange of views and experience; support activity of scientific institutes of tourism and other centres of research and education in the field. **Structure** General Meeting (annual). Committee, consisting of President, Vice-President and 8 members. Secretariat General, headed by Secretary-General. Auditors. Membership by election. **Languages** English, German. **Staff** 0.50 FTE, paid; 0.50 FTE, voluntary. **Finance** Members' dues: euro 100 – euro 675. Other sources: donations. Budget (annual): about Swiss Fr 100,000. **Activities** Events/meetings. **Events** *Conference* Cologne (Germany) 2022, *Annual Congress* Lucerne (Switzerland) 2021, *Annual Congress* Cologne (Germany) 2020, *Annual Congress* Varna (Bulgaria) 2019, *Annual Congress* Treviso (Italy) 2018. **Publications** *Tourism Review* (4 a year) in English.
Members Individual; Junior; Senior; Honorary; Associate. Individuals and organizations in 47 countries:
Argentina, Australia, Austria, Belgium, Brazil, Canada, China, Croatia, Cyprus, Czechia, Egypt, Ethiopia, Finland, France, Germany, Greece, Hungary, Indonesia, Ireland, Israel, Italy, Kenya, Korea Rep, Mexico, Morocco, Netherlands, New Zealand, Nigeria, North Macedonia, Norway, Poland, Russia, Serbia, Slovakia, Slovenia, South Africa, Spain, Sweden, Switzerland, Thailand, Tunisia, Türkiye, UK, Ukraine, United Arab Emirates, USA, Yemen. [2021/XC1339/v/C]

- ♦ Association internationale pour l'exploration de l'Asie centrale et de l'Extrême-Orient (inactive)
- ♦ Association internationale des fabricants d'aliments pour l'enfance (#11961)
- ♦ Association internationale des fabricants de caisses en carton ondulé (#12974)
- ♦ Association internationale des fabricants de confiserie (inactive)
- ♦ Association internationale des fabricants de diamants (#13171)
- ♦ Association internationale de fabricants d'équipements de sauvetage (#14039)
- ♦ Association internationale de fabricants de farine de poisson / see The Marine Ingredients Organisation (#16579)
- ♦ Association internationale des fabricants d'oxygène (#14493)
- ♦ Association internationale des fabricants de produits biodégradables (inactive)
- ♦ Association internationale des fabricants de prothèses médicales (inactive)
- ♦ Association internationale des facultés de lettres des pays d'expression française (inactive)
- ♦ Association internationale des facultés de médecine catholiques (#11759)
- ♦ Association internationale de la fauconnerie et de la conservation des oiseaux de proie (#11888)
- ♦ Association Internationale de la Femme Marocaine à l'Étranger (internationally oriented national body)
- ♦ Association internationale des femmes écrivains (inactive)
- ♦ Association internationale des femmes francophones (no recent information)
- ♦ Association internationale des femmes juges (#12267)
- ♦ Association Internationale Pour les Femmes du Karité (unconfirmed)
- ♦ Association internationale des femmes médecins (#16630)
- ♦ Association internationale de femmes philosophes (#12269)
- ♦ Association internationale de femmes à la radio et à la télévision (#12271)
- ♦ Association internationale de fertilité / see International Federation of Fertility Societies (#13426)
- ♦ Association internationale du fil de fer (internationally oriented national body)

♦ Association internationale du film d'animation (ASIFA) 02698

International Animated Film Association – Internationale Vereniging van de Animatiefilm – Mezdunarodnaja Associacija Multiplikacionnogo Kino

Vice-Pres Communications AG Animationsfilm eV, Funkenburgstr 16 04105 Leipzig, 04105 Leipzig, Germany. E-mail: gf@ag-animationsfilm.de.
Pres address not obtained.
URL: http://asifa.net/

History 1960. **Aims** Establish worldwide communication among members and thereby help solve their problems; inform government organizations and the public in order to develop appreciation of animation art. **Structure** General Assembly (every 3 years). Board of Directors, consisting of Representatives of all National Chapters. Executive Board, consisting of President, up to 4 Vice-Presidents, General Secretary, Executive Director and Treasurer. **Languages** English, French. **Finance** Members' dues. **Activities** Triennial General Assembly, meetings, conferences, seminars, exhibitions, children's workshops and international exchange of films made by children; maintains film archives; sponsors competitions. Field of activity: promotion of the art of animation; exchange of films and artists; sale of art work; education and workshops; film archives; publications; research. **Events** *Festival* Hiroshima (Japan) 2006, *Festival* Ottawa, ON (Canada) 2006, *Festival* Zagreb (Croatia) 2006, *Festival* Seoul (Korea Rep) 2005, *Festival* Zagreb (Croatia) 2004. **Publications** *Cartoons* (2 a year) – magazine. Studies; reports; reviews; interviews. National and regional groups produce their own newsletters and brochures.

Members Individuals in 61 countries and territories:
Argentina, Australia, Austria, Belarus, Belgium, Bosnia-Herzegovina, Brazil, Bulgaria, Canada, China, Côte d'Ivoire, Croatia, Cuba, Cyprus, Czechia, Denmark, Egypt, Estonia, Finland, France, Germany, Ghana, Greece, Hungary, India, Iran Islamic Rep, Ireland, Israel, Italy, Japan, Kazakhstan, Korea Rep, Latvia, Lebanon, Lithuania, Luxembourg, Malaysia, Mexico, Mongolia, Netherlands, New Zealand, North Macedonia, Norway, Poland, Portugal, Romania, Russia, Serbia, Singapore, Slovakia, Slovenia, South Africa, Spain, Sweden, Switzerland, Taiwan, Türkiye, UK, Ukraine, USA, Uzbekistan.

NGO Relations Member of: *International Council for Film, Television and Audiovisual Communication (IFTC, #13022).* [2022/XD3953/v/**D**]

- ♦ Association internationale du fil métallique et des machines (#15893)
- ♦ Association internationale des flotteurs et radeliers (#15691)
- ♦ Association internationale Foi et lumière (#09246)
- ♦ Association internationale des fonctionnaires de musée (inactive)
- ♦ Association internationale de la fonction publique (no recent information)
- ♦ Association internationale des fondations Raoul Follereau / see Raoul Follereau International Union (#18618)
- ♦ Association internationale des fonds d'investissement (#13952)

♦ Association internationale forêts méditerranéennes (AIFM) 02699

International Association for Mediterranean Forests (IAFM)

Coordinator 14 rue Louis Astouin, 13002 Marseille, France. T. +33491907670. E-mail: contact@aifm.org.
URL: http://www.aifm.org/

History 11 Oct 1996, Nice (France), following a preparatory meeting, 7 Jun 1996, Arles (France), on the initiative of *Association Forêt Méditerranéenne*. Registered in accordance with French law. EU Transparency Register: 13362983294-04. **Aims** Identify and solve the different issues for sustainable management of Mediterranean forest areas. **Structure** General Assembly (annual); Board of Directors; Secretariat. **Languages** Arabic, English, French, Italian, Spanish. **Staff** 2.00 FTE, paid. **Finance** Members' dues. Subsidies from: French government; *European Commission (EC, #06633); FAO (#09260).* **Activities** Events/meetings. **Events** *Mediterranean Forest Week* Broummana (Lebanon) 2019, *Mediterranean Forest Week* Agadir (Morocco) 2017, *Annual General Assembly* Rome (Italy) 2014, *Annual General Assembly* Rome (Italy) 2014, *Annual General Assembly* Marseille (France) 2013. **Publications** *IAMF Newsletter* (6 a year) in English, French.

Members Categories Active; Active Benefactor; Honorary; Associate – organizations, legal entities and individuals. Organizations in 7 countries:
Croatia, Cyprus, France, Italy, Portugal, Slovenia, Spain.
Individuals in 11 countries:
Algeria, Croatia, France, Greece, Israel, Italy, Morocco, Portugal, Spain, Tunisia, Türkiye.

IGO Relations Accredited by: *United Nations Framework Convention on Climate Change – Secretariat (UNFCCC, #20564).* Accredited to the Conference of the Parties of: *Secretariat of the United Nations Convention to Combat Desertification (Secretariat of the UNCCD, #19208).* **NGO Relations** Partner of: *1% for the Planet.* Member of: *European Forest Institute Mediterranean Facility (EFIMED, #07298).* [2020.03.03/XD5527/**D**]

- ♦ Association internationale pour la formation des cadres (inactive)
- ♦ Association internationale pour la formation pédagogique des ingénieurs (#15089)
- ♦ Association internationale pour la formation professionnelle en aménagement urbain et régional (inactive)

♦ Association internationale de formation et de recherche en éducation familiale (AIFREF) 02700

International Association of Training and Research in Family Education

Pres UMONS, ASBL Education et Famille, Rue des Dominicans 24, 7000 Mons, Belgium. T. +3265373106.
URL: http://www.aifref.org/

History 1987. Registration: Canada, Québec QC. **Aims** Develop research and training in family education; enable researchers and practitioners worldwide to share their work, their research orientations and their respective practices; promote dissemination of research and intervention models in family education; strengthen cooperation between universities and between fields of intervention; with a view to the development of teaching, research and action in family education. **Languages** English, French, Spanish. **Staff** Voluntary. **Finance** Members' dues. **Activities** Events/meetings. **Events** *Congress* Mestre (Italy) 2022, *Congress* Fort de France (Martinique) 2019, *Congress* Bilbao (Spain) 2015, *Congress* Patras (Greece) 2013, *Congress* Florence (Italy) 2011. **Publications** *Nouvelles de l'AIFREF* (2 a year); *Revue internationale de l'éducation familiale* (2 a year). [2022/XD9008/**D**]

♦ Association Internationale pour la Formation, la Recherche et l'Intervention Sociale (AIFRIS) 02701

Pres 1 rue Alfred Vigny, 25000 Besançon, France. E-mail: contact@afris-france.org – secretariat@aifris.eu.
URL: http://aifris.eu/

History 28 Jun 2008, Paris (France). Registration: Start date: 18 Nov 2016, France; End date: 18 Nov 2016, Belgium. **Aims** Promote scientific, educational, professional and international influence of social intervention. **Structure** General Assembly; Board of Directors. **Languages** French. **Staff** 11.00 FTE, paid. **Activities** Events/meetings; knowledge management/information dissemination. **Events** *International Congress* Paris (France) 2023, *Congress* Brussels (Belgium) 2022, *Congress* Beirut (Lebanon) 2019, *Solidarités en questions et en actes – quelles recompositions?* Montréal, QC (Canada) 2017, *Multiplication des précarités – quelles interventions sociales?* Porto (Portugal) 2015. **Publications** *La Lettre* (4 a year) – newsletter; *Ecrire le social – Le revue de l'AIFRIS* (periodical) – journal. Communications.

Members Full in 15 countries:
Algeria, Belgium, Canada, Congo DR, Côte d'Ivoire, France, Italy, Lebanon, Luxembourg, Mali, Morocco, Portugal, Romania, Switzerland, Tunisia.

NGO Relations Member of (1): *International Council on Social Welfare (ICSW, #13076).* [2023/XJ4630/**C**]

♦ Association internationale francophone des aînés (AIFA) 02702

SG 25 Ave du Couvent, Québec QC G1E 6R9, Canada. T. +14186678161. Fax +14186617011. E-mail: aifa.quebec@yahoo.ca.
URL: http://www.aifa.ca/

History Jul 1981. **Aims** Bring together the Francophone elder citizens of the world; develop their autonomy; promote French language and culture. **Finance** Annual budget: 149,000 CAD. **Events** *Conférence Internationale* Ouagadougou (Burkina Faso) 2010, *Conférence internationale* Québec, QC (Canada) 2008, *Conférence internationale* Paris (France) 2006, *Conférence internationale* Québec, QC (Canada) 2004, *Ralliement* Québec, QC (Canada) 1995. **Publications** *Maturité* (4 a year).

Members Individuals in 12 countries and territories:
Belgium, Benin, Burkina Faso, Canada, Côte d'Ivoire, France, Guadeloupe, Guyana, Luxembourg, Martinique, Senegal, USA. [2014/XD1284/v/**D**]

♦ Association internationale francophone des bibliothécaires et documentalistes (AIFBD) 02703

Pres address not obtained. E-mail: aifbd@aifbd.org.
Sec address not obtained.
URL: http://aifbd.org/

History 2001, Boston MA (USA), at annual congress of *International Federation of Library Associations and Institutions (IFLA, #13470),* as a working group. Decision to formalize organization at annual congress, Aug 2004, Buenos Aires (Argentina). Statutes adopted, Feb 2008. Registered in accordance with French law. **Structure** General Assembly; Board of Directors. **Languages** French. **Events** *Congress* Limoges (France) 2014, *Congress* Martinique 2011, *Congress* Montréal, QC (Canada) 2008, *Congrès mondial* Montréal, QC (Canada) 2008. [2017.06.01/XM3053/**E**]

♦ Association internationale francophone des intervenants auprès des familles séparées (AIFI) 02704

Sec 445 boulevard Saint-Laurent, bureau 500, Montréal QC H2Y 3T8, Canada. E-mail: secretariat@aifi.info.
URL: http://www.aifi.info/

Aims Promote constructive ways of resolving family conflicts; provide a forum for exchange and ideas for social and legal actors working with separated families; provide an opportunity for these stakeholders to develop concerted action with separated families; create an international network between these various stakeholders to promote the transfer of knowledge and expertise. **Structure** Board of Directors; Secretariat. **Languages** French. **Activities** Events/meetings; training/education. **Events** *Colloque International* Montréal, QC (Canada) 2019, *Colloque International* Brussels (Belgium) 2017. **Publications** *Liaison AIFI* (5 a year); *AIFI Bulletin.*

Members Individuals in 5 countries:
Belgium, Canada, France, Luxembourg, Switzerland. [2018/XM6662/v/**C**]

- ♦ Association internationale francophone de recherche odontologique (no recent information)
- ♦ Association internationale du froid (inactive)
- ♦ Association internationale futuribles / see Futuribles International (#10052)
- ♦ Association internationale des gays et des lesbiennes / see ILGA World (#11120)
- ♦ Association internationale des gays et lesbiennes espérantistes / see Ligo de Samseksamaj Geesperantistoj (#16475)
- ♦ Association internationale des gédéons (#10149)
- ♦ Association internationale de génétique pédiatrique (inactive)
- ♦ Association internationale de génie séismique (#11855)
- ♦ Association internationale de géochimie et de cosmochimie / see International Association of GeoChemistry (#11913)
- ♦ Association internationale de géodésie (#11914)
- ♦ Association internationale de géographie /espérantiste/ (inactive)
- ♦ Association internationale de géologie de l'ingénieur / see International Association of Engineering Geology and the Environment (#11872)
- ♦ Association internationale pour la géologie mathématique / see International Association for Mathematical Geosciences (#12017)
- ♦ Association internationale de géomagnetisme et d'aéronomie (#11916)
- ♦ Association internationale des germanistes (#13317)
- ♦ Association internationale de gérodontologie (#11919)
- ♦ Association Internationale de Gérontologie / see International Association of Gerontology and Geriatrics (#11920)
- ♦ Association internationale de gérontologie psychanalytique (inactive)
- ♦ Association internationale de gestion agricole (#13333)
- ♦ Association for International Egg Donation Research and Information (no recent information)
- ♦ Association internationale du goudron (#15655)
- ♦ Association Internationale de Gouvernance du Cachet Electronique Visible (internationally oriented national body)
- ♦ Association internationale de grands magasins (#11842)
- ♦ Association internationale des grottes aménagées (#14856)
- ♦ Association internationale des groupements d'achat et de marketing (inactive)
- ♦ Association internationale de l'habitation (inactive)
- ♦ Association internationale de l'habitat rural (inactive)
- ♦ Association internationale des hautes juridictions administratives (#12215)
- ♦ Association internationale des hispanistes (#02165)
- ♦ Association Internationale pour l'Histoire des Alpes (#02990)
- ♦ Association internationale d'histoire de l'art dentaire (no recent information)

♦ Association internationale d'histoire contemporaine de l'Europe (AICHE) 02705

International Association of Contemporary History of Europe

Pres Dept Politics and International Studies, Univ of Cambridge, Room 321 Alison Richard Bldg, 7 West Road, Cambridge, CB3 9DT, UK.
SG IEP – UStrasb, 47 ave Forêt-Noire, 67082 Strasbourg CEDEX, France.
URL: http://iache.hypotheses.org/

History 30 Nov 1968, Strasbourg (France), as *European Association for Contemporary History – Association européenne d'histoire contemporaine.* Present name adopted 1980. Registered in accordance with French law. **Aims** Facilitate and develop exchanges between teachers of and researchers in contemporary history of Europe; promote and develop teaching and research in the field; collaborate with national and international organizations to this end. **Structure** General Assembly (every 5 years); Governing Council. **Languages** English, French. **Staff** Voluntary. **Finance** Members' dues. **Activities** Events/meetings. **Events** *International Conference on East Central Europe in the First Half of the 20th Century* Leipzig (Germany) 2016, *General Assembly* Cambridge (UK) 2015, *Colloquium* Amsterdam (Netherlands) 2010, *Colloquium* Geneva (Switzerland) 2009, *Colloquium* Florence (Italy) 2008. **Publications** *Bulletin de liaison et d'information.* Conference proceedings. **Members** Individuals professors, lecturers, teachers and research workers in universities, academies and equivalent institutions, concerned with history of Europe post-1815; Collective organizations or committees concerned with the same period. Membership countries not specified. **NGO Relations** Affiliate member of: *International Committee of Historical Sciences (ICHS, #12777).* [2019/XD0549/**D**]

- ♦ Association internationale d'histoire du droit et des institutions (inactive)
- ♦ Association internationale d'histoire économique (#13224)
- ♦ Association internationale d'histoire de l'éducation physique et du sport (inactive)
- ♦ Association internationale pour l'histoire de l'État et de l'administration (unconfirmed)
- ♦ Association internationale pour l'histoire de l'Europe du Sud-Est / see Association internationale d'études du Sud-Est européen (#02693)
- ♦ Association internationale pour l'histoire de la justice et de la criminalité (#11934)
- ♦ Association internationale d'histoire des mers nordiques de l'Europe (no recent information)
- ♦ Association internationale d'histoire de la psychanalyse / see International Association Interactions of Psychoanalysis (#11968)
- ♦ Association internationale pour l'histoire des religions (#11936)
- ♦ Association internationale d'histoire des télécommunications et de l'informatique (inactive)

♦ Association internationale pour l'histoire du verre (AIHV) 02706

International Association for the History of Glass – Internationale Vereinigung für die Geschichte des Glases – Associazione Internazionale per la Storia del Vetro

Pres Kalavryton 14, 5133 Kalamaria, Greece. E-mail: andonar@physics.auth.gr.
SG Via Andrea Alciato 2, 27100 Pavia PV, Italy.
URL: http://www.aihv.org/

History Founded 23 Aug 1958, Liège (Belgium), as *Journées internationales du verre*. Statutes and present title adopted May 1967, Ravenna (Italy), during 4th 'Journées internationales'. **Aims** Advance knowledge of glass from antiquity to present times; promote study of glass from historical, archaeological, artistic and museum stand-points and technological and conservational problems but not with respect to industrial production. **Structure** General Assembly (at Congress); Executive Committee; Bureau. **Languages** English, French. **Staff** Voluntary. **Finance** Sources: members' dues. **Activities** Knowledge management/information dissemination. **Events** *Congress* Lisbon (Portugal) 2021, *Congress* Istanbul (Turkey) 2018, *Congress* Fribourg (Switzerland) / Romont (Switzerland) 2015, *Congress* Piran (Slovenia) 2012, *Congress* Thessaloniki (Greece) 2009. **Publications** *AIHV Annales* – congress reports.
Members Individuals in 39 countries:
Australia, Austria, Belarus, Belgium, Canada, Congo Brazzaville, Croatia, Czechia, Denmark, Egypt, Finland, France, Germany, Greece, Hungary, Ireland, Israel, Italy, Japan, Jordan, Korea Rep, Liechtenstein, Luxembourg, Montenegro, Morocco, Netherlands, Norway, Poland, Portugal, Qatar, Romania, Serbia, Slovenia, Spain, Sweden, Switzerland, Türkiye, UK, USA.
[2020/XD1220/v/**C**]

- ♦ Association internationale des historiens de l'Asie (#11932)
- ♦ Association internationale des historiens du papier (#12066)
- ♦ Association internationale des hommes d'affaires chrétiens (#13316)
- ♦ Association internationale des hôpitaux (inactive)
- ♦ Association internationale de l'hôtellerie / see International Hotel and Restaurant Association (#13813)
- ♦ Association internationale de l'hôtellerie et de la restauration (#13813)
- ♦ Association internationale Hubbard des scientologistes / see Church of Scientology International (#03922)
- ♦ Association internationale des humoristes (inactive)
- ♦ Association internationale d'hydatidologie (#11949)
- ♦ Association internationale des hydrogéologues (#11953)
- ♦ Association internationale de l'hydrologie scientifique / see International Association of Hydrological Sciences (#11954)
- ♦ Association internationale de l'icône et des objects de culte (no recent information)
- ♦ Association internationale de l'image corporelle (inactive)
- ♦ Association internationale de l'industrie des bouillons et potages (inactive)
- ♦ Association internationale de l'industrie des engrais / see International Fertilizer Association (#13589)
- ♦ Association internationale de l'industrie des fertilisants / see International Fertilizer Association (#13589)
- ♦ Association internationale des industries margarinières des pays d'Europe / see European Margarine Association (#07736)
- ♦ Association internationale des industries de prépress (inactive)
- ♦ Association internationale des informateurs scientifiques / see International Science Writers' Association (#14800)
- ♦ Association internationale d'information et de documentation en administration publique (inactive)
- ♦ Association internationale d'information scolaire universitaire et professionnelle (inactive)
- ♦ Association internationale d'informatique médicale (#14134)
- ♦ Association internationale d'informatique médicale pour l'Amérique latine et les Caraïbes (#14135)
- ♦ Association internationale pour l'informatique statistique (#12183)
- ♦ Association internationale d'ingénierie éolienne (#12266)
- ♦ Association internationale d'ingénierie et de recherches hydrauliques / see International Association for Hydro-Environment Engineering and Research (#11950)
- ♦ Association internationale d'ingénierie et de recherches hydrauliques et environmentales (#11950)
- ♦ Association internationale des ingenieurs agronomes francophones (inactive)
- ♦ Association internationale des ingénieurs et techniciens du sondage (inactive)
- ♦ Association internationale des inspecteurs de fabriques (inactive)
- ♦ Association internationale de l'inspection du travail (#11983)
- ♦ Association internationale des institutions d'évaluation et de prospective technologique (inactive)
- ♦ Association internationale d'institutions d'histoire ouvrière (#11982)
- ♦ Association internationale des institutions sanitaires catholiques (no recent information)
- ♦ Association internationale de l'Institut Marey (inactive)
- ♦ Association internationale des instituts de navigation (#11965)
- ♦ Association internationale des instituts de recherche sur l'emballage (#12063)
- ♦ Association internationale des instituts de recherches des industries graphiques / see International Association of Research Organizations for the Information, Media and Graphic Arts Industries (#12136)
- ♦ Association internationale d'instructeurs et instructrices en massage pour bébé / see International Association of Infant Massage (#11962)
- ♦ Association internationale 'Interaction' – Partenariats Est-Ouest pour un monde meilleur (inactive)
- ♦ Association internationale interactions de la psychanalyse (#11968)

♦ Association internationale et interdisciplinaire sur la chaîne des médicaments (AIICM) 02707

International and Interdisciplinary Association on the Pharmaceutical Life Cycle (IIAPC)

SG c/o CRDP, Fac de droit, Univ de Montréal, CP 6128 succ Centre-ville, Montréal QC H3C 3J7, Canada. E-mail: aicm.iapc@gmail.com.
Street Address Pavillon Maximilien-Caron – 8e étage, Univ de Montréal, 3101 chemin de la Tour, Montréal QC H3T 1J7, Canada.
URL: http://www.aiicm-iiapc.com/

Aims Promote interdisciplinary scientific research on drugs, specifically on natural and *homeopathic* health products, by assembling researchers of various disciplines and from different countries, and health professionals and professionals from various associations. **Structure** Board of Directors. **Events** *Congress* Montréal, QC (Canada) 2015, *International Conference* Montréal, QC (Canada) 2015, *Congress* Amsterdam (Netherlands) 2013, *Congress* Paris (France) 2011, *Congress* Milan (Italy) 2009. **Publications** *Revue internatinale sur le médicament (RIM)*. Reports. [2015/XM4676/**D**]

- ♦ Association internationale des intérêts radio-maritimes (inactive)
- ♦ Association internationale des interprètes de conférence (#11807)
- ♦ Association internationale des interprètes et traducteurs de conférences (inactive)
- ♦ Association internationale des investisseurs dans l'économie sociale (#11971)
- ♦ Association internationale d'irradiation industrielle (inactive)
- ♦ Association Internationale Jacques Ellul (internationally oriented national body)
- ♦ Association internationale des jardins botaniques (#11731)
- ♦ Association Internationale des jeunes Africains (unconfirmed)
- ♦ Association internationale des jeunes avocats (#12282)
- ♦ Association internationale des jeunes francophones (no recent information)
- ♦ Association internationale des journalistes accrédités auprès de la Société des Nations (inactive)

♦ Association Internationale des Journalistes de Cyclisme (AIJC) ... 02708

International Association of Cycling Journalists

Pres Reuters, 101 Quai Gallieni, 94500 Champigny-sur-Marne, France. E-mail: info@aijc.org.
URL: https://www.aijc.org/

Structure Officers include: President; 3 Vice-Presidents; Treasurer. **Members** Journalists (around 300) in 19 countries. Membership countries not specified. [2021/XJ6274/**D**]

- ♦ Association internationale des journalistes ferroviaires (no recent information)

♦ Association internationale des journalistes philatéliques (AIJP) ... 02709

International Association of Philatelic Journalists

SG Tucholskyweg 5, 55127 Mainz, Germany. E-mail: info@aijp.org.
Pres address not obtained.
URL: http://www.aijp.org/

History 19 Aug 1962, Prague (Czech Rep). Registered in accordance with Dutch law, 22 May 1981. **Aims** Develop international cooperation among philatelic journalists and *authors* contributing regularly or periodically to philatelic publications throughout the world; defend the integrity of philately against forgeries, speculations, harmful issues and all things which could damage it; support cooperation between organs of the philatelic press for exchange, translation and distribution of articles; promote the authorship of manuscripts; improve the position of philatelic exhibitions. **Structure** General Assembly (every 2 years); Council; Board. **Languages** English, French, German. **Staff** Honorary. **Finance** Sources: members' dues. **Activities** Knowledge management/information dissemination. **Events** *Congress* Essen (Germany) 2013, *Congress* Chur (Switzerland) 2011, *Congress* Lisbon (Portugal) 2010, *Congress* Essen (Germany) 2009, *Congress* Leipzig (Germany) 2007. **Publications** *AIJP Bulletin* (3 a year). Yearbook.
Members Journalists and authors (totalling 450) in 52 countries:
Algeria, Argentina, Armenia, Australia, Austria, Bangladesh, Belgium, Brazil, Bulgaria, Canada, Costa Rica, Croatia, Cyprus, Czechia, Denmark, Estonia, Finland, France, Germany, Greece, Guatemala, Hungary, Iceland, India, Iraq, Ireland, Israel, Italy, Japan, Liechtenstein, Luxembourg, Malaysia, Netherlands, New Zealand, North Macedonia, Norway, Pakistan, Poland, Portugal, Romania, Russia, Serbia, Slovakia, Slovenia, South Africa, Spain, Sri Lanka, Sweden, Switzerland, Tunisia, UK, USA.
NGO Relations Member of: *World Association for the Development of Philately (WADP, #21132)*.
[2020/XC1325/**C**]

♦ Association internationale des journalistes du ski (AIJS) 02710

International Association of Ski Journalists – Internationale Vereinigung der Ski-Journalisten – Associazione Internationale dei Giornalisti dello Sci

Vice Pres address not obtained. T. +41793562321. E-mail: skinews@hotmail.com.

History 1961, Mürren (Switzerland). Also referred to as *International Association of Ski Writers*. **Structure** Annual Convention; Board; President; Secretary-General. **Languages** English, French, German, Italian. **Staff** 0.50 FTE, paid. Other voluntary. **Finance** Members' dues. **Activities** Elects skier of the year. **Members** Individuals (200) from 13 countries. Primarily European membership. Membership countries not specified.
[2013/XD3470/**D**]

- ♦ Association internationale des juges des enfants / see International Association of Youth and Family Judges and Magistrates (#12283)
- ♦ Association internationale des juges en matière de droit des réfugiés / see International Association of Refugee and Migration Judges (#12126)
- ♦ Association internationale des juristes africains (inactive)
- ♦ Association internationale des juristes démocrates (#11837)
- ♦ Association internationale des juristes du droit de la vigne et du vin (#15891)
- ♦ Association internationale des juristes espérantistes (inactive)
- ♦ Association internationale des juristes portuaires (no recent information)
- ♦ Association internationale de kinésiologistes spécialisés (#12175)
- ♦ Association internationale Kosmopolit (inactive)
- ♦ Association internationale de laboratoires textiles lainiers (#12275)
- ♦ Association internationale laïcs volontaires (internationally oriented national body)
- ♦ Association internationale langue et économie (#11987)
- ♦ Association internationale des langues et littératures germaniques / see Internationale Vereinigung für Germanistik (#13317)
- ♦ Association internationale des langues et littératures slaves (inactive)
- ♦ Association internationale pour la lecture / see International Literacy Association (#14057)
- ♦ Association internationale pour la lecture de la Bible (#12337)
- ♦ Association internationale de législation et d'économie politique comparée (inactive)
- ♦ **Association internationale des lesbiennes, gays, bisexuels, trans et intersexes** ILGA World (#11120)

♦ Association Internationale pour l'Étude des Céramiques Médiévales et Modernes en Méditerranée (AIECM3) 02711

International Association for the Study of Medieval and Modern Period Mediterranean Ceramics

Dir c/o MMSH, 5 Rue Château de l'Horloge, 13090 Aix-en-Provence, France.
URL: http://aiecm3.com/

History 1992. Former names and other names: *Association internationale pour l'étude des céramiques médiévales méditerranéennes (AIECM2)* – former (1992 to 2012). Registration: France. **Aims** Promote and increase research in Mediterranean ceramics in the Middle Ages and post-Middle Ages. **Structure** General Assembly. Committee, comprising President, 2 Vice-Presidents, Secretary, Vice-Secretary, Treasurer and Vice-Treasurer. **Activities** Organizes congresses and colloquies. **Events** *Congress on Medieval and Modern Period Mediterranean Ceramics (CICM3)* Granada (Spain) 2021, *International Congress on Medieval and Modern Period Mediterranean Ceramics* Athens (Greece) 2018, *Congrès International Thématique* Faenza (Italy) 2015, *Congrès International Thématique* Montpellier (France) 2014, *Congress* Silves (Portugal) 2012.
Members Individuals and organizations in 9 countries:
Croatia, France, Greece, Italy, Lebanon, Morocco, Netherlands, Spain, Switzerland. [2020/XD8964/**D**]

- ♦ Association internationale pour la liberté de la culture (inactive)
- ♦ Association internationale pour la liberté religieuse (#12130)

♦ Association internationale des libraires francophones (AILF) 02712

Coordinator BP 49, 11 rue Caillaux, 75013 Paris, France. T. +33140511145. E-mail: contact@librairesfrancophones.org.
URL: http://www.librairesfrancophones.org/

History 27 Mar 2002, Beirut (Lebanon). Founded during the *Conférence au sommet des chefs d'Etat et de gouvernement des pays ayant le français en partage (Sommet de la Francophonie, #04648)*. Registration: France. **Aims** Develop the French language and francophone cultures through a network of francophone bookshops around the world. **Structure** General Assembly; Board of Directors; Secretariat in Paris (France). **Languages** French. **Staff** 2.00 FTE, paid. **Finance** Members' contributions. Supported by, amongst others: French Government; *Organisation internationale de la Francophonie (OIF, #17809)*; Centre National du Livre (France); Wallonie-Bruxelles International (Belgium); national associations; individuals. Annual budget: about euro 150,000. **Activities** Training/education; networking/liaising; events/meetings. **Events** *Maghreb regional seminar* 2007. **Publications** *AILF Newsletter* (4 a year). Leaflets.
Members Booksellers (79) in 40 countries and territories:
Algeria, Argentina, Australia, Belgium, Benin, Burkina Faso, Burundi, Cameroon, Canada, Chad, Chile, Comoros, Congo DR, Côte d'Ivoire, Cyprus, Djibouti, Egypt, France, Germany, Greece, Guinea, Haiti, Lebanon, Madagascar, Mauritania, Mauritius, Morocco, Niger, Romania, Rwanda, Senegal, Spain, Switzerland, Syrian AR, Taiwan, Togo, Tunisia, UK, United Arab Emirates, Vietnam. [2020/XM0519/**D**]

- ♦ Association Internationale de Libre Pensée (#11906)
- ♦ Association internationale du libre service (no recent information)
- ♦ Association internationale de limnologie théorique et appliquée / see International Society of Limnology (#15232)

♦ Association internationale de linguistique appliquée (AILA) 02713

International Association of Applied Linguistics

SG Indiana Univ, Dept of Spanish & Portuguese, 355 North Jordan Ave, Bloomington IN 47405, USA. T. +18128556392. E-mail: secretariat@aila.info.
Registered Address c/o School of Applied Linguistics, Zurich Univ of Applied Sciences, Theaterstrasse 15c, 8401 Winterthur ZH, Switzerland.
URL: http://www.aila.info/

History 31 Oct 1964, Nancy (France). Founded at international colloquium, following 2 years preparatory work and discussion. New statutes adopted at Congress, Jul 2005, Madison WI (USA). Registration: Swiss Civil Code, Switzerland. **Aims** Encourage research within the field of applied linguistics; support dissemination of findings; promote implementation of practical implications emerging from such findings. **Structure** International Committee; Executive Board. **Languages** English, French. **Staff** 1.00 FTE, paid. **Finance** Sources: members' dues. **Activities** Events/meetings; financial and/or material support. **Events** *World Congress* Vancouver, BC (Canada) 2027, *60th Anniversary World Congress* Kuala Lumpur (Malaysia) 2024, *World Congress* Lyon (France) 2023, *World Congress* Groningen (Netherlands) 2021, *World Congress* Groningen (Netherlands) 2020. **Publications** *AILA Review* (annual) in English; *AILA Newsletter* in English. *AILA Applied Linguistics Series*.

Members Associations, institutes or societies. Membership classes (6): Regular Affiliate; Temporary Affiliate; Associate; Individual Associate; Benefactor; Honorary. Affiliate in 33 countries:
Australia, Austria, Belgium, Brazil, Cameroon, Canada, China, Estonia, Finland, France, Germany, Greece, Ireland, Israel, Italy, Japan, Korea Rep, Malaysia, Mexico, Netherlands, New Zealand, Norway, Philippines, Russia, Serbia, Singapore, Slovenia, South Africa, Spain, Sweden, Switzerland, UK, USA.
Associate in 2 countries:
Gambia, Türkiye.
International Associate (1):
International Pragmatics Association (IPrA, #14634).
Consultative Status Consultative status granted from: *ECOSOC (#05331)* (Ros C). **IGO Relations** Accredited by (2): *Council of Europe (CE, #04881); European Centre for Modern Languages (ECML, #06491).* **NGO Relations** Cooperates with (1): *International Organization for Standardization (ISO, #14473).* Instrumental in setting up (1): *International Society of Applied Psycholinguistics (ISAPL, #14933).* [2022.02.02/XC1252/y/**C**]

- ♦ Association internationale des Lions clubs / see Lions Clubs International (#16485)
- ♦ Association internationale de littérature comparée (#12829)
- ♦ Association internationale de littérature comparée, société et culture (#11796)
- ♦ Association internationale de logopédie et phoniatrie / see International Association of Logopedics and Phoniatrics (#12005)
- ♦ Association internationale des loteries d'Etat (inactive)
- ♦ Association internationale des Ludothèques (#15699)
- ♦ Association internationale pour la lutte contre le chômage (inactive)

♦ Association internationale de lutte contre la cybercriminalité (AILCC) . . . 02714

International Association of Cybercrime Prevention

Contact Maison des associations du 20ème arrondissement, 1-3 rue Fréderick Lemaître, Boîte No 5, 75020 Paris, France. T. +33140333361. E-mail: info@cybercrime-fr.org.
URL: http://www.cybercrime-fr.org/

History Feb 2006. Registered in accordance with French law. **Aims** Fight cybercrime by encouraging scholars, experts and professionals of *cyberlaw* to engage more fully with the IT industry, policymakers and members of the general public. **Structure** General Assembly. Board of Directors, comprising President, Vice-President, Secretary General, Treasurer and 2 members. **Languages** English, French. **Events** *Regional Conference* Sydney, NSW (Australia) 2011.
Members Chapters in 8 countries:
Argentina, Australia, Belgium, Brazil, Mauritius, Oman, South Africa, Tunisia.
IGO Relations Memorandum of Understanding with: *United Nations African Institute for the Prevention of Crime and the Treatment of Offenders (UNAFRI, #20519).* [2012/XJ0958/**C**]

- ♦ Association internationale de lutte contre la mucoviscidose (inactive)
- ♦ Association internationale des Lyceum Clubs (#12007)
- ♦ Association internationale des magistrats de la jeunesse / see International Association of Youth and Family Judges and Magistrates (#12283)
- ♦ Association internationale des magistrats de la jeunesse et de la famille (#12283)
- ♦ Association internationale de magnétisme et électricité terrestre / see International Association of Geomagnetism and Aeronomy (#11916)
- ♦ Association internationale des maires francophones / see Association Internationale des Maires et responsables des capitales et métropoles partiellement ou entièrement Francophones (#02715)

♦ Association Internationale des Maires et responsables des capitales et métropoles partiellement ou entièrement Francophones (AIMF) 02715

Permanent Sec 9 rue des Halles, 75001 Paris, France. T. +33144882288. Fax +33140390662.
URL: http://www.aimf.asso.fr/

History 1 May 1979, Québec (Canada). Statutes ratified Apr 1979. Since formalization of *Organisation internationale de la Francophonie (OIF, #17809)*, 2-4 Dec 1995, Cotonou (Benin), an operating institution of 'La Francophonie'. Also referred to as *Association internationale des maires francophones.* Statutes adopted 1 May 1979; modified Apr 1982, Sep 1983, Jul 1988, Jul 1996, Nov 2004, Sep 2006, Oct 2007, Oct 2009, Oct 2010 and Nov 2014. **Aims** Through use of the *French language*, promote solidarity between *municipalities* by a greater exchange of information and experience and collaboration in municipal activities. **Structure** General Assembly; Board (meets twice a year); Bureau; Permanent Secretariat. Commissions (6): Decentralization and Local Democracy; Urban and Sustainable Development; Modernization of the Services and Municipal Staff Training; Animation of the Cities Network and Multicultural Exchanges; Local Health and Policy; Humanitarian Aid. **Languages** French. **Staff** 13.00 FTE, paid. **Finance** Sources: international organizations; subsidies. Other sources: emergency fund. Supported by: *European Commission (EC, #06633).* Annual budget: 6,870,000 EUR. **Activities** Politics/policy/regulatory; projects/programmes; training/education. **Events** *Assemblée Générale Annuelle* Abidjan (Côte d'Ivoire) 2022, *Assemblée Générale Annuelle* Kigali (Rwanda) 2021, *Somme International du Numérique* Namur (Belgium) 2021, *Assemblée Générale Annuelle* Tunis (Tunisia) 2020, *Assemblée Générale Annuelle* Phnom Penh (Cambodia) 2019. **Publications** Meeting reports; microfinance guide.
Members Cities (176) and associations of local governments (15) in 46 countries:
Albania, Armenia, Belgium, Benin, Bulgaria, Burkina Faso, Burundi, Cambodia, Cameroon, Canada, Cape Verde, Central African Rep, Chad, Comoros, Congo Brazzaville, Congo DR, Côte d'Ivoire, Djibouti, Egypt, France, Gabon, Georgia, Guinea, Haiti, Italy, Laos, Lebanon, Luxembourg, Madagascar, Mali, Mauritania, Mauritius, Moldova, Monaco, Morocco, Niger, North Macedonia, Romania, Rwanda, Senegal, Seychelles, Switzerland, Togo, Tunisia, Vanuatu, Vietnam.
Included in the above, 1 organization listed in this Yearbook:
Association pour la diffusion internationale francophone de livres, ouvrages et revues (ADIFLOR).
IGO Relations Implements relevant decisions of: *Conférence au sommet des chefs d'Etat et de gouvernement des pays ayant le français en partage (Sommet de la Francophonie, #04648).* Associated with: *Conseil permanent de la Francophonie (CPF, #04697).* Cooperates with: *United Nations Institute for Training and Research (UNITAR, #20576).* **NGO Relations** Observer to: *Association francophone d'amitié et de liaison (AFAL, #02605).* Framework Partnership Agreement with: *PLATFORMA (#18397).* Member of: *Global Taskforce of Local and Regional Governments (Global Taskforce, #10622).* [2020/XC7332/**C**]

- ♦ Association internationale des maisons familiales rurales / see Association internationale des mouvements familiaux de formation rurale (#02719)
- ♦ Association Internationale des Maîtres Coiffeurs de Dames / see Internationale des coiffeurs de dames (#13218)
- ♦ Association internationale de Maître Suprême Ching Hai (internationally oriented national body)

♦ Association internationale de management de l'art et de la culture (AIMAC) 02716

International Association of Arts and Cultural Management

Chair HEC Montréal, 3000 chemin de la Côte-Sainte-Catherine, Montréal QC H3T 2A7, Canada. T. +15143405629. E-mail: ijam@hec.ca – gestiondesarts@hec.ca.
URL: https://gestiondesarts.hec.ca/en/activities/aimac/?noredirect=en_US

History 1991, Montréal, QC (Canada). Former names and other names: *Management, Arts and Culture International Association* – former. **Aims** Provide a forum for exchange of insights and perspectives in the discipline of arts management. **Structure** Scientific Committee. **Languages** English, French. **Activities** Events/meetings. **Events** *Biennial Conference* Mexico City (Mexico) 2022, *Biennial Conference* Venice (Italy) 2019, *Biennial Conference* Beijing (China) 2017, *Biennial Conference* Aix-en-Provence (France) / Marseille (France) 2015, *Biennial Conference* Bogota (Colombia) 2013. **Publications** *International Journal of Arts Management.* Conference proceedings.
Members Full in 48 countries and territories:
Argentina, Australia, Austria, Belgium, Bosnia-Herzegovina, Brazil, Cameroon, Canada, Chile, China, Colombia, Czechia, Denmark, Estonia, Finland, France, Germany, Greece, Iceland, India, Indonesia, Iran Islamic Rep, Ireland, Italy, Japan, Korea Rep, Latvia, Lithuania, Malaysia, Malta, Mexico, Netherlands, New Zealand, Norway, Portugal, Romania, Russia, Singapore, Slovenia, South Africa, Spain, Sweden, Switzerland, Taiwan, Trinidad-Tobago, Tunisia, UK, USA. [2021.09.23/XF4968/**F**]

- ♦ Association internationale pour le management du sport (inactive)

♦ Association internationale du management stratégique (AIMS) . . . 02717

International Strategic Management Association

Secretariat UP Sud – Fac J Monnet, Bureau D202, 54 bd Desgranges, 92331 Sceaux CEDEX, France. E-mail: secretariat@strategie-aims.com.
URL: http://www.strategie-aims.com/

History 1991. **Aims** Promote and diffuse research in management. **Structure** Executive Board; Scientific Committee. **Languages** English, French. **Finance** Members' dues. Annual conference. Annual budget: euro 25,000. **Activities** Events/meetings. **Events** *Annual Conference* Strasbourg (France) 2023, *Annual Conference* Annecy (France) 2022, *Annual Conference* 2021, *Annual Conference* 2020, *Annual Conference* Dakar (Senegal) 2019. **Publications** *Management* (4-5 a year).
Members Full in 5 countries:
Belgium, Canada, France, Luxembourg, Switzerland.
Members also in North and West Africa. Membership countries not specified. [2022/XD9432/**D**]

- ♦ Association internationale des marchés de gros au sein de la IULA / see World Union of Wholesale Markets (#21889)
- ♦ Association internationale de la marine (inactive)
- ♦ Association internationale de marketing de journaux (#14363)
- ♦ Association internationale de marketing social (inactive)
- ♦ Association Internationale en Massage pour Bébé (#11962)
- ♦ Association internationale de matériel de terrassement (#15505)
- ♦ Association internationale pour les mathématiques et calculateurs en simulation (#12019)
- ♦ Association internationale des matières premières pour la parfumerie / see International Fragrance Association (#13680)
- ♦ Association internationale pour la mécanisation de la culture de la vigne, du fruit et du légume (inactive)
- ♦ Association internationale de mécanisation des essais en plein champ (#12021)
- ♦ Association internationale des mécanothérapeutes (inactive)
- ♦ Association internationale de médecine des accidents et du trafic / see International Traffic Medicine Association (#15713)
- ♦ Association internationale de médecine agricole et de santé rurale / see International Association of Rural Health and Medicine (#12140)
- ♦ Association internationale de médecine et de biologie de l'environnement (inactive)
- ♦ Association internationale de médecine maritime (#14099)
- ♦ Association internationale de médecine physique et de physiothérapie (inactive)
- ♦ Association internationale de médecine du trafic (#15713)
- ♦ Association internationale des médecins audiologistes (#12084)
- ♦ Association internationale des médecins-experts de compagnies d'assurance / see International Committee for Insurance Medicine (#12780)
- ♦ Association internationale des médecins inspecteurs des écoles (inactive)
- ♦ Association internationale des médecins pour la prévention de la guerre nucléaire (#14578)

♦ Association Internationale des Médecins pour la promotion de l'Education et de la Santé en Afrique (AIMES -AFRIQUE) 02718

Registered Office Immeuble AIMES-AFRIQUE, Lomé, Togo. T. +22870183939 – +22898397896. E-mail: info@aimes-afrique.org.
Founder/Pres address not obtained.
URL: http://www.aimes-afrique.org/

History 19 Jan 2005, Lomé (Togo). **Aims** Cultivate a sense of social responsibility and volunteering so as to promote health and education in Africa. **Structure** Congress; Board of Directors; Executive Board; Scientific and Pedagogic Council. **Languages** English, French. **Staff** 40.00 FTE, paid; 350.00 FTE, voluntary. **Finance** Supported by: AKTIONPIT TOGOHILFE (BMZ). Annual budget: 15,000,000 EUR (2020). **Activities** Healthcare; research and development; training/education. Active in all member countries. **Publications** Activities reports; press release.
Members Full in 15 countries:
Benin, Burkina Faso, Cameroon, Côte d'Ivoire, France, Germany, Guinea, Japan, Kenya, Mali, Morocco, Senegal, Switzerland, Togo, USA.
Consultative Status Consultative status granted from: *ECOSOC (#05331)* (Special). **NGO Relations** Cooperates with (1): *Hanns Seidel Foundation.* [2023.02.27/XJ9763/**D**]

- ♦ Association internationale des médecins scolaires (inactive)
- ♦ Association internationale de médecins socialistes (inactive)
- ♦ Association internationale pour les media dans la science (#12024)
- ♦ Association internationale de méditation du Maître Suprême Ching Hai / see Supreme Master Ching Hai International Association
- ♦ Association internationale de météorologie / see International Association of Meteorology and Atmospheric Sciences (#12031)
- ♦ Association internationale de météorologie et de physique de l'atmosphère / see International Association of Meteorology and Atmospheric Sciences (#12031)
- ♦ Association internationale de météorologie et de sciences de l'atmosphère (#12031)
- ♦ Association internationale pour la méthode Margaret Morris (#12012)
- ♦ Association internationale de méthodologie juridique (#11996)
- ♦ Association internationale des métiers et enseignements d'art (inactive)
- ♦ Association internationale de la meunerie (inactive)
- ♦ Association internationale de micro-chirurgie (inactive)
- ♦ Association internationale de microscopie (inactive)
- ♦ Association Internationale des Ministères de Guérison (unconfirmed)
- ♦ Association internationale des missiologues catholiques (#11760)
- ♦ Association internationale missionnaire (internationally oriented national body)
- ♦ Association internationale du mohair (inactive)
- ♦ Association internationale du molybdène (#14178)
- ♦ Association internationale des moniteurs de ski (#14870)
- ♦ Association internationale des mosaïstes contemporains (#11816)

♦ Association internationale des mouvements familiaux de formation rurale (AIMFR) 02719

International Association of Family Movements for Rural Training – Asociación Internacional de los Movimientos Familiares de Formación Rural – Associação Internacional de Movimentes Familiares de Formação Rural – Associazione Internazionale dei Movimenti Familiari di Formazione Rurale

SG Carrer de Barcelona 126-128, 08820 Barcelona, Spain. T. +33144918686. Fax +34693215128. E-mail: secretariageneral@aimfr.org.
Registered Address c/o Union Nationale des MFR d'Education et d'Orientation, 58 rue Notre-Dame de Lorette, 75009 Paris, France. E-mail: info@aimfr.org.
URL: http://www.aimfr.org/

History 16 May 1975, Dakar (Senegal). Founded by *Union nationale des maisons familiales rurales d'éducation et d'orientation (UNMFREO)*, as *Association internationale des maisons familiales rurales*, at Constituent General Assembly, the first 'Maisons familiales rurales' having been set up in France in 1935, and others subsequently established in Italy, Spain, Portugal, Africa, Central and South America, Asia and North America. **Aims** Encourage and promote the development of rural training centres in all parts of the world, to serve as educational centres and provide general training for young people in rural areas. **Structure** General Assembly (every 4 years). Bureau (meets once a year). **Languages** French, Spanish. **Staff** 0.50 FTE, voluntary. **Finance** Sources: members' dues. **Activities** Organizes meetings, regional seminars and congresses. Instrumental in setting up *Solidarité internationale des maisons familiales rurales (SIMFR, see:*

Association internationale musées
02720

alphabetic sequence excludes
For the complete listing, see Yearbook Online at

#02719). **Events** *International Colloquium* Sherbrooke, QC (Canada) 2019, *Congress* Rouen (France) 2013, *Congress* Brazil 2005, *Congress* Guatemala (Guatemala) 2004, *Congress* France 2003. **Publications** *La Lettre de l'AIMFR – Bulletin d'information de l'Association internationale des mouvements familiaux de formation rurale.*
Members Centres (approx 1,000) in 39 countries and territories:
Argentina, Benin, Brazil, Burkina Faso, Cameroon, Canada, Central African Rep, Chad, Chile, Colombia, Congo Brazzaville, Congo DR, Dominican Rep, Ecuador, El Salvador, France, Guatemala, Honduras, Italy, Madagascar, Mali, Mauritius, Mexico, Morocco, Mozambique, Nicaragua, Panama, Paraguay, Peru, Philippines, Polynesia Fr, Portugal, Rwanda, Senegal, Spain, Togo, Uruguay, Venezuela, Vietnam.
Consultative Status Consultative status granted from: *FAO (#09260)* (Liaison Status). **IGO Relations** Contacts with: *UNESCO (#20322)*. **NGO Relations** Cooperates with: *Rurality – Environment – Development (RED, #19003)*. [2022/XC4532/**C**]

♦ Association internationale des musées d'agriculture (AIMA) 02720
International Association of Agricultural Museums – Internationale Vereinigung der Agrarrmuseen
Pres address not obtained. E-mail: agriculturemuseums.president@gmail.com.
Sec address not obtained. E-mail: agriculturemuseums.secretary@gmail.com.
URL: https://www.agriculturalmuseums.org/
History 1968, following proposals made at an International Conference of Agricultural Museums, 1966, Liblice (Czechoslovakia). Part of *European System of Cooperative Research Networks in Agriculture (ESCORENA, #08871)*. **Events** *Triennial Congress* Reading (UK) 2021, *Triennial Congress* Reading (UK) 2020, *Triennial Congress* Tartu (Estonia) 2017, *Triennial Congress* Marseille (France) 2014, *Triennial Congress* Slobozia (Romania) 2011.
Members Agricultural museums in 15 countries:
Austria, Belgium, Denmark, France, Germany, Greece, Hungary, Israel, Italy, Japan, Mexico, Norway, Sweden, UK, USA.
IGO Relations *UNESCO (#20322)*. **NGO Relations** Affiliated member of: *International Council of Museums (ICOM, #13051)*. [2018/XD4872/**E**]

- ♦ Association internationale des musées d'armes et d'histoire militaire / see International Committee of Museums and Collections of Arms and Military History (#12790)
- ♦ Association internationale pour les musées et les collections d'instruments de musique (inactive)
- ♦ Association internationale des musées des douanes (#11831)
- ♦ Association internationale des musées d'histoire (#12040)
- ♦ Association internationale des musées médicaux / see International Academy of Pathology (#11567)
- ♦ Association internationale des musées de transports et de communications (#12237)
- ♦ Association internationale de musicologie (inactive)
- ♦ Association internationale des musiques traditionnelles (no recent information)

♦ Association internationale de la mutualité (AIM) 02721
International Association of Mutual Benefit Societies
Exec Dir Rue d'Arlon 50, 1000 Brussels, Belgium. T. +3222345700. Fax +3222345708. E-mail: aim.secretariat@aim-mutual.org.
Registered Office 50, rue d'Arlon, 1000 Brussels, Belgium. T. +3222345700. Fax +3222345708. E-mail: aim.secretariat@aim-mutual.org.
URL: http://www.aim-mutual.org/
History 1947, Geneva (Switzerland). Former names and other names: *Centre international d'information de la mutualité (CIIM)* – former; *International Centre for Information on Mutuality* – former. Registration: Moniteur belge, No/ID: 0809673153, Start date: 19 Feb 2009, Belgium; EU Transparency Register, No/ID: 595328413083-91, Start date: 28 Feb 2014. **Aims** Develop and defend universal access to high-quality, affordable healthcare along with social protection based on solidarity and democracy. **Structure** General Assembly (annual); Board of Directors; Praesidium. **Languages** English, French, German, Spanish. **Staff** 6.00 FTE, paid. **Finance** Sources: members' dues. **Activities** Events/meetings; networking/liaising; training/education. **Events** *Meeting on the Care Strategy* Brussels (Belgium) 2022, *Meeting* Brussels (Belgium) 2019, *General Assembly* Luxembourg (Luxembourg) 2019, *Meeting* Brussels (Belgium) 2018, *General Assembly* Brussels (Belgium) 2013. **Publications** *AIM Flash Newsletter* (12 a year) in English, French, German, Spanish; *AIM Weekly*. Monographs; activity reports; working programme.
Members Mutual benefit societies in 28 countries:
Argentina, Austria, Belgium, Burkina Faso, Burundi, Colombia, Congo DR, Côte d'Ivoire, Cyprus, Czechia, Estonia, France, Germany, Greece, Hungary, Italy, Lebanon, Lithuania, Luxembourg, Mali, Morocco, Netherlands, Poland, Portugal, Slovenia, Spain, Switzerland, Uruguay.
Consultative Status Consultative status granted from: *ILO (#11123)* (Special List). **NGO Relations** Member of (7): *Education and Solidarity Network (#05374)* (Founding); *European Alliance for Cardiovascular Health (EACH, #05863)*; *European Alliance for Mental Health – Employment & Work (EUMH Alliance, #05875)*; *European Alliance for Personalised Medicine (EAPM, #05878)*; *European Migration Centre (EMZ)*; *European Nutrition for Health Alliance, The (ENHA, #08069)*; *Social Economy Europe (SEE, #19335)* (Founding). Close relationship with: *International Federation of Health Plans (iFHP, #13442)*, each organization being represented at the other's meetings. Stakeholder in: *European Network for Health Technology Assessment (EUnetHTA, #07921)*. [2022/XD1200/**D**]

- ♦ Association internationale de mycologie (#14203)
- ♦ Association internationale de natalité et de conception (inactive)
- ♦ Association internationale des navigants de langue française (inactive)
- ♦ Association internationale de navigation / see PIANC (#18371)
- ♦ Association internationale du négoce du papier peint (inactive)
- ♦ Association internationale de néphrologie infantile (#14543)

♦ Association of International Energy Negotiators (AIEN) 02722
Exec Dir 11111 Katy Freeway, Ste 615, Houston TX 77079, USA. T. +12815587715. Fax +12815587073. E-mail: aien@aien.org.
Events Manager address not obtained.
URL: https://www.aien.org/
History 1981, USA. Former names and other names: *Association of International Petroleum Negotiators (AIPN)* – former. **Structure** Board of Directors. Regional Chapters: Africa; Asia; Australia-Pacific; Canada; CIS-FSU; Europe; Latin America & Caribbean; MENA; US. **Staff** 5.00 FTE, paid; 45.00 FTE, voluntary. **Activities** Events/meetings; standards/guidelines; training/education. **Events** *International Energy Summit* Miami, FL (USA) 2023, *International Energy Summit* London (UK) 2022, *International Petroleum Summit* Bangkok (Thailand) 2021, *Model Contracts Workshop* Rio de Janeiro (Brazil) 2021, *International Petroleum Summit* Bangkok (Thailand) 2020. **Publications** *Advisor* – newsletter. Membership Directory; model contracts.
Members Individuals in 71 countries and territories:
Angola, Argentina, Australia, Austria, Azerbaijan, Belgium, Bolivia, Brazil, Cameroon, Canada, Chile, China, Colombia, Congo Brazzaville, Côte d'Ivoire, Denmark, Ecuador, Egypt, France, Georgia, Germany, Greece, Hong Kong, Hungary, India, Indonesia, Ireland, Israel, Italy, Japan, Kazakhstan, Korea Rep, Kuwait, Malaysia, Mexico, Morocco, Namibia, Netherlands, New Zealand, Nigeria, Norway, Oman, Pakistan, Palau, Papua New Guinea, Peru, Poland, Portugal, Qatar, Russia, Saudi Arabia, Singapore, South Africa, Spain, Sudan, Suriname, Switzerland, Taiwan, Tanzania UR, Thailand, Timor-Leste, Trinidad-Tobago, Tunisia, Türkiye, UK, United Arab Emirates, Uruguay, USA, Venezuela, Vietnam, Yemen. [2022.10.11/XN8596/v/**B**]

- ♦ Association internationale du nettoiement public / see International Solid Waste Association (#15567)
- ♦ Association internationale des nettoyeurs (#13207)
- ♦ Association internationale de neurologie infantile (#12550)
- ♦ Association internationale NORCOFEL /normalisation et commercialisation des fruits et légumes/ (inactive)
- ♦ Association internationale de numérotation des articles / see GS1 (#10809)
- ♦ Association internationale des numismates professionnels (#12104)
- ♦ Association internationale d'océanographie biologique (#11726)
- ♦ Association internationale d'océanographie médicale (inactive)
- ♦ Association internationale d'océanographie physique / see International Association for the Physical Sciences of the Oceans (#12082)
- ♦ Association internationale d'odonto-stomatologie infantile / see International Association of Paediatric Dentistry (#12064)
- ♦ Association internationale d'odonto-stomatologie pédiatrique / see International Association of Paediatric Dentistry (#12064)

♦ Association internationale pour l'oeuvre du docteur Albert Schweitzer de Lambaréné (AISL) 02723
International Association for the Work of Doctor Albert Schweitzer of Lambaréné
Sec Maison Albert Schweitzer, Route de Munster 8, 68140 Gunsbach, France. T. +33389773142. E-mail: gunsbach@schweitzer.org.
Pres Weissenaustr 17, 3800 Unterseen BE, Switzerland. T. +41338266464. Fax +41338266453.
URL: http://www.schweitzer.org/
History 1930. **Aims** Disseminate information about the life and thought of *Albert Schweitzer* in Lambaréné and maintain his legacy. **Structure** Board of Directors; Bureau. Includes *Fondation internationale de l'Hôpital du docteur Albert Schweitzer à Lambaréné*. **Languages** English, French, German. **Staff** Voluntary. **Finance** Sources: government support; private foundations. . Annual budget: 300,000 CHF. **Activities** Events/meetings. **Events** *Annual General Meeting* Gunsbach (France) 2018, *Annual General Meeting* Gunsbach (France) 2017, *Annual General Meeting* Gunsbach (France) 2016, *Annual General Meeting* Konigsfeld im Schwarzwald (Germany) 2014, *Colloque International* Libreville (Gabon) 2013. **Publications** Annual Report; books.
Members Individuals in 10 countries:
France, Germany, Hungary, Italy, Netherlands, Poland, Russia, Switzerland, UK, USA. [2022/XE0193/**E**]

- ♦ Association internationale des officiers contre le stupéfiants et le terrorisme (internationally oriented national body)
- ♦ Association internationale des officiers de la marine marchande (inactive)
- ♦ Association internationale d'onirothérapie / see Société internationale des techniques d'imagerie mentale onirique (#19498)
- ♦ Association internationale des opticiens (#14415)
- ♦ Association internationale pour l'optimisation de la nutrition des plantes (inactive)
- ♦ Association internationale des organisateurs de courses cyclistes (inactive)
- ♦ Association internationale des organisateurs d'excursions et de visites de villes (inactive)
- ♦ Association internationale des organisateurs professionnels de congrès (#12103)
- ♦ Association internationale de l'organisation du théâtre public (inactive)
- ♦ Association internationale des organismes de commerce pour un monde en développement (inactive)
- ♦ Association internationale des organismes et des villes de congrès des pays intéressés à la Méditerranée (inactive)
- ♦ Association internationale d'orientation scolaire et professionelle / see International Association for Educational and Vocational Guidance (#11862)
- ♦ Association internationale d'orientation scolaire et professionnelle (#11862)
- ♦ Association internationale d'orthodontie (#12058)

♦ Association Internationale des Orthodontistes Francophones (AIOF) 02724
Pres Avenue Brugmann 326, 1180 Brussels, Belgium. T. +3223449484. Fax +3223440932. E-mail: info@aiof.org.
URL: http://www.aiof.org/
History 6 Nov 2011, Paris (France). Registered in accordance with Belgian law. **Aims** Encourage, promote and realize all means to further development of orthodontics in francophone countries. **Structure** General Assembly; Board of Directors. **Finance** Members' dues. **Activities** Events/meetings. **Events** *Congrès* Iasi (Romania) 2019, *Congrès International* Montréal, QC (Canada) 2017, *Congrès* Ostend (Belgium) 2015, *Congrès* Paris (France) 2013, *Congrès* Bucharest (Romania) 2011. **Members** Individuals. Membership countries not specified. [2018/XM6261/**D**]

- ♦ Association internationale des orthoptistes (#14489)
- ♦ Association internationale pour l'ostéosynthèse dynamique / see Osteosynthesis and Trauma Care Foundation (#17911)
- ♦ Association internationale de l'ozone (#14494)
- ♦ Association internationale 'Paix par la culture' (#12070)
- ♦ Association internationale des palais de congrès / see International Association of Convention Centres (#11818)
- ♦ Association internationale de pancréatologie (#12065)

♦ Association internationale de papyrologues (AIP) 02725
International Association of Papyrologists – Asociación Internacional de Papirólogos – Internationale Vereinigung Papyrologen
Sec Assn Egyptologique Reine Elisabeth, Musées Royaux d'Art et d'Histoire, Parc du Cinquantenaire 10, 1000 Brussels, Belgium. T. +3227417364.
URL: https://aip.ulb.be/
History 30 Aug 1947, Brussels (Belgium). Took over activities of the previous *International Committee of Papyrology (inactive)*, founded 1930. **Aims** Encourage international cooperation in the field of papyrology; contribute to progress of the science. **Structure** General Assembly (every 3 years); International Committee. **Languages** English, French, German, Italian. **Finance** Sources: members' dues. **Activities** Events/meetings. **Events** *Triennial Congress* Paris (France) 2022, *Triennial Congress* Salento (Italy) 2019, *Triennial Congress* Barcelona (Spain) 2016, *Triennial Congress* Warsaw (Poland) 2013, *Triennial Congress* Geneva (Switzerland) 2010. **Publications** Reference books; congress proceedings.
Members Individuals; universities. Members in 22 countries:
Australia, Austria, Belgium, Canada, Denmark, Egypt, Finland, France, Germany, Greece, Ireland, Israel, Italy, Japan, Mexico, Netherlands, Norway, Poland, Spain, Switzerland, UK, USA.
NGO Relations Member of (1): *Fédération internationale des associations d'études classiques (FIEC, #09607)*. [2022.06.14/XC1323/**C**]

- ♦ Association internationale des parcs d'amusement et de distraction (#11699)
- ♦ Association internationale des parlementaires de langue française / see Assemblée parlementaire de la Francophonie (#02312)
- ♦ Association internationale pour la participation financière (#11891)
- ♦ Association internationale pour le patrimoine souterrain (no recent information)

♦ Association internationale des pays du pourtour de la Méditerranée et de l'Union européenne (STRADEMED) 02726
Seat Université de Mons, 20 Place du Parc, 7000 Mons, Belgium.
Secretariat STRATEMED Safar H, Ave Maistriau 8, 7000 Mons, Belgium. E-mail: cerm.umh@gmail.com.
URL: http://strademed.cermumons.be/
History 1995, Marseille (France). Founded during international colloquium of *Fondation méditerranéenne d'études stratégiques (FMES)*. Former names and other names: *Association internationale STRADEMED* – alias; *Stratégies et Développement en Méditerranée* – alias. Registration: Banque-Carrefour des Entreprises, Start date: 1 Apr 1996. **Aims** Organize a *higher education* programme to equip executives and other decision makers in Mediterranean countries with the tools necessary to integrate the idea of inter-Mediterranean *cooperation* in their *professional* activities; develop a Mediterranean centre to analyse cooperation, development and security strategy. **Structure** General Meeting; Board of Directors; FMES provides Permanent Secretariat. **Languages** English, French. **Staff** 21.00 FTE, paid. **Finance** Sources: members' dues; subsidies. **Activities** Events/meetings; networking/liaising; training/education. **IGO Relations** EU institutions. [2022.10.18/XD5735/**D**]

- ♦ Association internationale de la pêche (inactive)
- ♦ Association internationale pour la pêche sportive à la ligne (internationally oriented national body)
- ♦ Association internationale de pédagogie expérimentale de langue française / see Association francophone internationale de recherche scientifique en éducation (#02615)

♦ Association Internationale de Pédagogie Universitaire (AIPU) 02727

Pres 2500 bd de l'Université, Sherbrooke QC J1K 2R1, Canada. T. +18198218000ext65685.
SG HEP Vaud, Av de Cour 33, 1014 Lausanne VD, Switzerland. T. +41213160789.
URL: http://www.aipu-international.org/

History Jan 1981, Canada. Statutes adopted 11 Aug 1995, Hull (UK); amended 4 Nov 1996, Hammamet (Tunisia) and May 2008, Montpellier (France). Registered under Belgian law. **Aims** Develop a new system of education in the context of solidarity among nations and preservation of cultural heritage; promote research and development in and about *higher education*; encourage educational exchange between developed and developing countries. **Structure** General Assembly (biannual); Board; Secretariat located in Lausanne (Switzerland). Offices in Africa, Americas and Europe. **Languages** French. **Finance** Sources: members' dues; sale of publications. **Activities** Events/meetings; publishing activities; research/documentation. **Events** *Congress* Québec, QC (Canada) 2020, *Congress* Cotonou (Benin) 2018, *Congress* Lausanne (Switzerland) 2016, *Congress / International Meeting* Mons (Belgium) 2014, *Congress* Trois Rivières, QC (Canada) 2012. **Publications** *Pédagogiques* (periodical); *Revue Internationale de Pédagogie de l'Enseignement Supérieur (RIPES)* – electronic review. Congress proceedings. **Information Services** *Qui fait quoi?* – database.
Members Sections (12) in 13 countries:
Algeria, Belgium, Benin, Burundi, Canada, Congo DR, France, Lebanon, Madagascar, Morocco, Niger, Switzerland, Tunisia.
Individuals in 24 countries:
Benin, Bolivia, Brazil, Burkina Faso, Burundi, Cameroon, Central African Rep, Chad, Chile, Colombia, Comoros, Congo Brazzaville, Congo DR, Côte d'Ivoire, Gabon, Greece, Guinea, Madagascar, Mali, Mauritius, Mexico, Romania, Rwanda, Senegal.
NGO Relations Formal contacts with: *Agence universitaire de La Francophonie (AUF, #00548)*; Alliance Citoyenne pour l'Education (ACE-Tunisia); *Association pour le développement des méthodologies d'évaluation en éducation (ADMEE-Europe, #02474)*. [2018.09.29/XD9968/**C**]

- ♦ Association internationale de pédiatrie (#14541)
- ♦ Association internationale de pédiatrie préventive (inactive)
- ♦ Association internationale du pergélisol (#14558)
- ♦ Association internationale permanente des congrès de navigation / see PIANC (#18371)
- ♦ Association internationale permanente des congrès de la route / see World Road Association (#21754)
- ♦ Association internationale du personnel d'EUROCONTROL (#00597)
- ♦ Association internationale du personnel de l'Organisation européenne pour la sécurité de la navigation aérienne / see AIPE-International Association of EUROCONTROL Staff (#00597)
- ♦ Association internationale du personnel de la sécurité de l'emploi / see International Association of Workforce Professionals (#12278)
- ♦ Association internationale du personnel de l'UNESCO (#15597)
- ♦ Association internationale des pharmaciens espérantistes (inactive)
- ♦ Association internationale des philatélistes (inactive)
- ♦ Association internationale de philosophie du droit et de philosophie sociale (#13318)
- ♦ Association internationale de photobiologie / see International Union of Photobiology (#15798)
- ♦ Association internationale des photographes (inactive)
- ♦ Association internationale pour la physiologie des plantes (inactive)
- ♦ Association internationale de physique mathématique (#12018)
- ♦ Association internationale de phytothérapie et aromathérapie (inactive)
- ♦ Association internationale des pilotes maritimes (#14103)
- ♦ Association internationale des podo-orthésists (#12059)
- ♦ Association internationale de poésie (inactive)
- ♦ Association internationale de police (#14612)
- ♦ Association Internationale de la Police (internationally oriented national body)
- ♦ Association internationale de la police des ports et des aéroports / see InterPortPolice (#15963)
- ♦ Association internationale des pompiers / see CTIF International Association of Fire and Rescue Services (#04979)
- ♦ Association internationale des pompiers (internationally oriented national body)
- ♦ Association internationale des ponts et charpentes (#11737)
- ♦ Association internationale du pont, du tunnel et de l'autoroute à péage (#12400)
- ♦ Association internationale des ports (#12096)
- ♦ Association internationale des ports et rades / see International Association of Ports and Harbors (#12096)
- ♦ Association internationale de la poupée (inactive)
- ♦ Association internationale de pragmatique (#14634)

♦ Association internationale des Praticiens de la méthode GDS (APGDS) 02728

Registered Seat 6 rue de la Cavée, 62690 Camblain-l'Abbé, France. T. +33321585769. E-mail: apgdsfrance@gmail.com.
URL: http://www.apgds.com/

History Registration: Start date: 27 Nov 1995, France. **Events** *Congress* Brussels (Belgium) 2010.
Members Full in 12 countries:
Belgium, Brazil, France, Germany, Italy, Lebanon, Mexico, Netherlands, Norway, Poland, Spain, UK. [2020/XJ2441/**D**]

- ♦ Association internationale pour la préservation et ses techniques (internationally oriented national body)
- ♦ Association Internationale des Press Clubs (#12099)
- ♦ Association internationale de presse pour le développement de l'habitat (inactive)
- ♦ Association internationale de la presse échiquéenne (inactive)
- ♦ Association internationale de presse pour l'étude des problèmes d'outre-mer (inactive)
- ♦ Association internationale de la presse filmée (no recent information)
- ♦ Association internationale de la presse francophone (internationally oriented national body)
- ♦ Association internationale de la presse médicale (inactive)

♦ Association internationale de la presse sportive (AIPS) 02729

International Sports Press Association – Asociación Internacional de Periodistas Deportivos – Internationaler Sportpresse-Verband – Associazione Internazionale della Stampa Sportiva

Headquarters Avenue de la Gare 12, 1003 Lausanne VD, Switzerland. T. +39381690636. E-mail: info@aipsmedia.com.
Pres Via Marazzani 7, 27029 Vigevano PV, Italy. T. +39381690636. Fax +39381690638.
URL: http://www.aipsmedia.com/

History Founded 1924, Paris (France). Statutes modified and approved by the Extraordinary Congress, 26 Mar 1996, Kuala Lumpur (Malaysia). Most recent Statutes adopted, Apr 2006, Doha (Qatar). **Aims** Enhance cooperation between member associations in defending sport and professional interest of members; strengthen friendship, solidarity and common interests between sports *journalists* of all nations; assure the best possible working conditions for members. **Structure** Congress (annual); Executive Committee (serving 4-year terms). Continental sections: *African Sports Journalists Union (ASJU, inactive)*; *Asian Sports Press Union (ASPU, #01759)*; *European Sports Press Union (AIPS Europe, #08822)*; *AIPS America (#00599)*. Bureau; Specialist Commissions (27); Sub-Commissions of the Executive Committee (2); Secretariat located in Lausanne (Switzerland). **Languages** English, French, Spanish. **Staff** 5.00 FTE, paid. **Finance** Sources: contributions; members' dues. Other sources: supporters, advertisers. **Activities** Awards/prizes/competitions; events/meetings; projects/programmes. **Events** *Congress* Rome (Italy) 2022, *Congress* Budapest (Hungary) 2020, *Congress* Lausanne (Switzerland) 2019, *Congress* Brussels (Belgium) 2018, *Congress* Seoul (Korea Rep) 2017. **Publications** *AIPS Magazine* (4 a year). *AIPS Historical Book (1924-2014)*.
Members National Sports Journalists Associations (NSJAs); Individual; Honorary; Associate. National associations in 148 countries and territories:
Albania, Algeria, Angola, Argentina, Armenia, Australia, Austria, Azerbaijan, Bahrain, Bangladesh, Barbados, Belarus, Belgium, Benin, Bolivia, Bosnia-Herzegovina, Brazil, Bulgaria, Burkina Faso, Burundi, Cameroon, Canada, Central African Rep, Chile, China, Colombia, Congo Brazzaville, Congo DR, Costa Rica, Côte d'Ivoire, Croatia, Cuba, Cyprus, Czechia, Denmark, Dominican Rep, Ecuador, Egypt, El Salvador, Equatorial Guinea, Estonia, Eswatini, Ethiopia, Fiji, Finland, France, Gabon, Georgia, Germany, Ghana, Greece, Grenada, Guam, Guatemala, Guinea, Haiti, Honduras, Hong Kong, Hungary, Iceland, India, Indonesia, Iran Islamic Rep, Iraq, Ireland, Israel, Italy, Jamaica, Japan, Jordan, Kazakhstan, Kenya, Korea DPR, Korea Rep, Kuwait, Kyrgyzstan, Latvia, Lebanon, Liberia, Libya, Liechtenstein, Lithuania, Luxembourg, Macau, Madagascar, Malaysia, Mali, Malta, Mauritania, Mauritius, Mexico, Moldova, Monaco, Mongolia, Morocco, Nepal, Netherlands, New Zealand, Nicaragua, Niger, Nigeria, North Macedonia, Norway, Pakistan, Palestine, Panama, Paraguay, Peru, Poland, Portugal, Puerto Rico, Qatar, Romania, Russia, Rwanda, San Marino, Saudi Arabia, Senegal, Serbia, Sierra Leone, Slovakia, Slovenia, Somalia, South Africa, Spain, Sri Lanka, Sudan, Suriname, Sweden, Switzerland, Syrian AR, Tanzania UR, Thailand, Togo, Trinidad-Tobago, Tunisia, Türkiye, Turkmenistan, Uganda, UK, Ukraine, United Arab Emirates, Uruguay, USA, Uzbekistan, Venezuela, Yemen, Zimbabwe.
NGO Relations Member of (1): *Olympic Movement (#17719)*. Cooperates with (1): *Fédération internationale de SAMBO (FIAS, #09655)*. [2022.10.11/XB2583/**B**]

- ♦ Association internationale des presses universitaires de langue française (inactive)
- ♦ Association internationale pour la prévention du suicide / see International Association for Suicide Prevention and Crisis Intervention (#12213)
- ♦ Association internationale pour la prévention du suicide et l'intervention en cas de suicide (#12213)

♦ Association internationale des procureurs et poursuivants francophones (AIPPF) 02730

Contact Complexe Jules Dallaire, 2828 boulevard Laurier, Tour 1, Bur 500, Québec QC G1V 0B9, Canada. E-mail: gabrielle.mercier@dpcp.gouv.qc.ca.
Contact 13 place Vendôme, 75042 Paris CEDEX 01, France.
URL: http://aippf.org/

History 25 Feb 2009, Yaoundé (Cameroon). **Aims** Develop solidarity, cooperation exchange of ideas, knowledge and experience between Francophone prosecutors on all issues relating to the actions of prosecutors worldwide. **Structure** General Assembly; Board of Directors; Bureau. **Events** *General Assembly* 2021. **IGO Relations** Partner of (1): *Organisation internationale de la Francophonie (OIF, #17809)*. [2021/AA2319/**C**]

- ♦ Association internationale des producteurs et consommateurs de méthanol (#14153)
- ♦ Association internationale des producteurs de coton (inactive)
- ♦ Association internationale des producteurs de l'horticulture (#11940)

♦ Association internationale des producteurs indépendants de la méditerranée (APIMED) 02731

International Association of Independent Producers of the Mediterranean – Asociación Internacional de Productores Independientes del Mediterraneo

Gen Manager Calle Girona 20-22, 5a planta, 08010 Barcelona, Spain. T. +34935560991. Fax +34932470165. E-mail: info@apimed.org.
Pres address not obtained.
URL: http://www.apimed.org/

History Jan 1997, Marseille (France). Also referred to as *Association of Independent Mediterranean Producers – Association des producteurs indépendants de la méditerranée.* **Aims** Contribute to preserve all cultures in the Mediterranean area; promote their diversity in the *audiovisual* industry. **Structure** Board of Directors of 16 members. Presidency, comprising President, 4 Vice-Presidents and General Secretary. Central Office in Barcelona (Spain). **Languages** Catalan, English, French, Spanish. **Staff** 1.00 FTE, paid. **Activities** Organizes: *'Euro-Mediterranean Documentary Market (MEDIMED)'*, annually in Sitges (Spain); seminars. **Publications** *Viability of TV Co-production between Europe and the Mediterranean* (2003).
Members Independent producers; main producers' associations. Members (over 400) in 16 countries:
Algeria, Austria, Belgium, Egypt, France, Germany, Greece, Ireland, Italy, Libya, Malta, Morocco, Spain, Tunisia, Türkiye, UK. [2013.11.19/XD8051/**D**]

- ♦ Association internationale des producteurs de pectine (#14539)
- ♦ Association internationale des producteurs de rails de chemin de fer (inactive)
- ♦ Association internationale pour la production d'équipement technologique pour l'industrie textile (inactive)
- ♦ Association internationale des professeurs d'allemand (#13228)
- ♦ Association internationale des professeurs d'anglais comme langue étrangère (#12222)
- ♦ Association internationale des professeurs d'anglais des universités / see International Association of University Professors of English (#12249)
- ♦ Association internationale des professeurs de danse (#13133)
- ♦ Association internationale des professeurs d'italien (#02989)
- ♦ Association internationale des professeurs de langue et littérature russes (#16739)
- ♦ Association internationale des professeurs et maîtres de conférences des universités (#12250)

♦ Association internationale des professeurs de philosophie (AIPPh) 02732

Pres Torhoutsesteenweg 296, 8400 Ostend, Belgium.
URL: http://www.aipph.eu/

History Founded 1 Nov 1964, Sèvres (France), as *International Committee on the Teaching of Philosophy – Comité international de l'enseignement philosophique*, at 3rd International Congress on the Teaching of Philosophy in European Secondary Schools. New Statutes and present name adopted at 5th International Congress, Nov 1971, Brussels (Belgium). Registered in accordance with Belgian law, Jun 1974. **Aims** Promote the teaching of philosophy in schools and universities of member countries; provide information on philosophy teaching in Europe; ensure that philosophy teaching is based on the fundamental condition of freedom of thought and expression; ensure that working conditions for philosophy teaching guarantee its free and effective development; promote cooperation of national associations concerned with philosophy teaching with regard to the formation and implementation of the Association's aims. **Structure** General Assembly; Executive Board. **Languages** English, French, German. **Staff** 9.00 FTE, voluntary. **Finance** Members' dues. **Activities** Organizes: triennial congress; and annual regional congresses; symposia. Documentation centre and archives on all aspects of philosophy teaching. **Events** *Regional Congress* Wesseling (Germany) 2012, *Regional Congress* Münster (Germany) 2011, *Regional Congress* Leusden (Netherlands) 2009, *Regional Congress* Bonn (Germany) 2006, *Triennial international congress / Triennial Congress / Regional Congress* Bonn (Germany) 2003. **Publications** *Bulletin d'information AIPPh*; *Documentation Europa Forum Philosophie. Das Wechselspiel von Mythos und Logos* (1998).
Members Individuals in 30 countries:
Austria, Belarus, Belgium, Bulgaria, Croatia, Czechia, Denmark, Estonia, Finland, France, Germany, Greece, Hungary, Ireland, Italy, Latvia, Lithuania, Luxembourg, Netherlands, Norway, Poland, Portugal, Romania, Russia, Slovakia, Slovenia, Spain, Sweden, Switzerland, UK.
IGO Relations *UNESCO (#20322)*. **NGO Relations** *International Federation of Philosophical Societies (FISP, #13507)*. [2013.08.21/XD1640/v/**D**]

- ♦ Association internationale professionnelle des médecins (inactive)
- ♦ Association internationale des professionnels administratifs (internationally oriented national body)
- ♦ Association internationale des professionnels de la bioénergie / see Bioenergy Institute
- ♦ Association internationale des professionnels de la recherche et du marketing en matière de voyages / see Travel and Tourism Research Association
- ♦ Association Internationale de Professionnels de Tourisme / see Association Internationale des Skål Clubs (#02743)
- ♦ Association internationale des professions de la santé (inactive)
- ♦ Association internationale pour le progrès social (inactive)
- ♦ Association Internationale pour la Promotion et a la Diffusion de la Recherche sur la Résilience (#12108)
- ♦ Association internationale pour la promotion de l'enseignement et de la recherche en propriété intellectuelle (#11690)
- ♦ Association internationale pour la promotion des études hégéliennes / see International Hegel Society (#13788)
- ♦ Association internationale pour la promotion des études hégéliennes (#13247)
- ♦ Association internationale pour la promotion de femmes d'Europe (#12109)
- ♦ Association internationale pour la promotion des fluids supercritiques (#14904)

Association Internationale promotion
02733

alphabetic sequence excludes
For the complete listing, see Yearbook Online at

♦ Association Internationale pour la promotion de Formations Spécialisées en Médecine et en Sciences Biologiques (AFISM) 02733

Treas c/o Publi Créations SAM, 74 boulevard d'Italie, 98000 Monaco, Monaco. T. +37797973555. E-mail: info@afism.org.
URL: http://www.afism.org/

History 2017, Monaco. **Aims** Promote and enhance the continuing professional development and post-degree education in medical, scientific and technical professions. **Structure** Scientific Committee. **Languages** English. **Staff** 3.00 FTE, voluntary. **Activities** Advocacy/lobbying/activism; awards/prizes/competitions; awareness raising; events/meetings; knowledge management/information dissemination; networking/liaising; publishing activities; training/education. **Events** *Monaco Age Oncologie* Monaco (Monaco) 2023, *International Workshop on Lung Health* The Hague (Netherlands) 2022. **NGO Relations** Cooperates with (1): *International Forum on Mood and Anxiety Disorders (IFMAD, #13646).* [2022/AA0942/**D**]

- ♦ Association internationale pour la promotion de la pharmacologie expérimentale et clinique (inactive)
- ♦ Association internationale pour la promotion et la protection des investissements privés en territoires étrangers (inactive)
- ♦ Association internationale pour la promotion de la recherche clinique en médecine (inactive)
- ♦ Association internationale pour la promotion du thé (inactive)
- ♦ Association internationale pour promouvoir l'étude des quaternions et des systèmes connexes (inactive)
- ♦ Association internationale de prophylaxie de la cécité (inactive)
- ♦ Association internationale pour les propriétés de l'eau et de la vapeur (#12110)
- ♦ Association internationale pour les propriétés de la vapeur / see International Association for the Properties of Water and Steam (#12110)
- ♦ Association internationale pour la protection contre les radiations (#14686)
- ♦ Association internationale pour la protection des droits de l'homme à Chypre (internationally oriented national body)
- ♦ Association internationale pour la protection des droits privés (inactive)
- ♦ Association internationale pour la protection de l'enfance (inactive)
- ♦ Association internationale pour la protection de l'environnement en Afrique (no recent information)
- ♦ Association internationale pour la protection des espèces en péril / see Aviornis International (#03048)
- ♦ Association internationale pour la protection légale des travailleurs, 1889 (inactive)
- ♦ Association internationale pour la protection légale des travailleurs, 1901 (inactive)
- ♦ Association internationale pour la protection de la mère et pour la réforme de la vie sexuelle (inactive)
- ♦ Association internationale pour la protection des populations civiles, des monuments historiques et oeuvres d'art en temps de guerre / see International Civil Defence Organization (#12582)
- ♦ Association internationale pour la protection de la propriété industrielle / see International Association for the Protection of Intellectual Property (#12112)
- ♦ Association internationale pour la protection de la propriété intellectuelle (#12112)
- ♦ Association Internationale de Psychanalyse de Couple et de Famille (#11822)
- ♦ Association internationale de psychanalyse éclectique (inactive)
- ♦ Association Internationale de Psychiatrie de l'Enfant, de l'Adolescent, et des Professions Associees (#11766)
- ♦ Association internationale de psychiatrie spirituelle (inactive)
- ♦ Association Internationale de la Psychologie Adlérienne (#11960)
- ♦ Association internationale de psychologie analytique (#11700)
- ♦ Association internationale de psychologie appliquée (#11705)
- ♦ Association internationale de psychologie scolaire (#14788)

♦ Association internationale de psychologie du travail de langue française (AIPTLF) 02734

International Association of Work Psychology in French Language

Pres Univ Paris Ouest Nanterre La Défense, 200 av de la République, 92001 Nanterre CEDEX, France. E-mail: contactaiptlf@gmail.com.
SG Psytc, Faculté des Sciences psychologiques et de l'éducation, Université Libre de Bruxelles, Av Depage 30, 1050 Brussels, Belgium.
URL: https://www.aiptlf.net/

History Nov 1980, as *Association of French-Speaking Psychologists of the Working Environment – Association de psychologie du travail de langue française (APTLF).* **Aims** Develop exchanges among French-speaking psychologists practising in the working environment; contribute to their training and information. **Structure** Bureau; Congress Organization Council. **Languages** French. **Staff** Voluntary. **Finance** Sources: members' dues. Annual budget: 76,225 EUR. **Events** *Congrès International de Psychologie du Travail* Paris (France) 2021, *Congrès International de Psychologie du Travail* 2020, *Biennial Congress* Brussels (Belgium) 2016, *Biennial Congress* Florence (Italy) 2014, *Biennial Congress* Lyon (France) 2012. **Publications** *Psychologie du travail et des organisations* – review. Congress proceedings.
Members Psychologists in 37 countries and territories:
Algeria, Angola, Argentina, Austria, Belgium, Brazil, Bulgaria, Burkina Faso, Cameroon, Canada, Colombia, Congo DR, Côte d'Ivoire, Cyprus, Equatorial Guinea, France, Germany, Greece, Hungary, Israel, Italy, Japan, Luxembourg, Mexico, Morocco, Netherlands, New Caledonia, Poland, Portugal, Romania, Senegal, Spain, Switzerland, Tunisia, Türkiye, UK, USA. [2020/XD0351/v/**C**]

♦ Association Internationale de Psychomécanique du Langage (AIPL) 02735

Address not obtained.
URL: http://www.fondsgustaveguillaume.ulaval.ca/aipl/

Structure Bureau, comprising President, 2 Vice-Presidents (Europe; North America); 2 Secretaries (Europe; North America) and Treasurer. **Events** *Congress* Brussels (Belgium) 2010. [2010/XJ1390/**F**]

- ♦ Association internationale de psychotechnique / see International Association of Applied Psychology (#11705)
- ♦ Association internationale de publicité (#11590)
- ♦ Association internationale de publicité cinématographique (inactive)
- ♦ Association internationale pour la qualité de l'eau (inactive)
- ♦ Association internationale de radiodiffusion (#11738)
- ♦ Association internationale de radiologie dento-maxillo-faciale (#11841)
- ♦ Association internationale de radiologie vétérinaire (#15850)
- ♦ Association internationale de radioprotection / see International Radiation Protection Association (#14686)
- ♦ Association internationale de réadaptation médicale (inactive)
- ♦ Association internationale de réassurance mutuelle (inactive)
- ♦ Association internationale des receveurs de la poste (inactive)
- ♦ Association internationale pour la recherche et l'aménagement des métropoles (inactive)
- ♦ Association internationale de recherche apicole (#12330)
- ♦ Association internationale de la recherche et de l'avancement de la musique à vent (#13237)
- ♦ Association internationale de recherche sur le bois (inactive)
- ♦ Association internationale pour la recherche comparée dans les leucémies et les maladies voisines (#11799)
- ♦ Association internationale pour la recherche en criminologie juvénile (no recent information)

♦ Association internationale pour la recherche en didactique du français (AIRDF) 02736

Pres Univ de Lille, BP 149, 59653 Villeneuve d'Ascq, France. E-mail: airdf@ouvaton.org.
Permanent Contact address not obtained.
URL: http://airdf.ouvaton.org

History 1986. Former names and other names: *Association internationale pour le développement de la recherche en didactique du français langue maternelle (DFLM)* – former. **Aims** Work for recognition of the *didactics* of *French language* as a full-fledged field of research and as a training branch of instruction. **Structure** Bureau; Council; Working Groups. **Languages** French. **Activities** Events/meetings; publishing activities. **Events** *International Colloquium* Lyon (France) 2019, *International Colloquium* Montréal, QC (Canada) 2016, *International Colloquium* Lausanne (Switzerland) 2013, *International Colloquium* Liège (Belgium) 2010, *International Colloquium* Lille (France) 2007. **Publications** *La lettre de la DFLM* (2 a year). *Recherches en didactique du français.*
Members Individuals; institutions. Members in 4 countries:
Belgium, Canada, France, Switzerland. [2020.08.27/XF3795/**F**]

- ♦ Association internationale de recherche en didactique de l'histoire et des sciences sociales (#14718)

♦ Association internationale de recherche en entrepreneuriat et PME (AIREPME) 02737

Chairman PeeL, Univ de Lorraine, Site Artem, 2 allée André Guinier, 54000 Nancy, France.
URL: https://www.airepme.org/

History 1996. **Aims** Contribute to the international influence of French-speaking work in entrepreneurship and SMEs. **Structure** General Assembly; Council; Board. **Languages** French. **Staff** 2.00 FTE, voluntary. **Finance** Sources: members' dues. **Activities** Events/meetings; research/documentation; training/education. **Events** *Congrès International Francophone en Entrepreneuriat et PME* Lyon (France) 2022, *Congrès International Francophone en Entrepreneuriat et PME* 2021, *Congrès International Francophone en Entrepreneuriat et PME* Nice (France) 2020, *Congrès International Francophone en Entrepreneuriat et PME* Toulouse (France) 2018, *Congrès International Francophone en Entrepreneuriat et PME* Trois Rivières, QC (Canada) 2016. **Publications** *RIPME – Revue International PME.*
Members Individuals in 19 countries:
Algeria, Belgium, Benin, Brazil, Cameroon, Canada, Colombia, Congo Brazzaville, France, Gabon, Italy, Lebanon, Mexico, Morocco, Romania, Rwanda, Switzerland, Tunisia, Vietnam. [2022/XD8968/**D**]

- ♦ Association internationale de recherche et de formation soutenue par l'UNESCO / see Centre de culture européenne, Bruxelles
- ♦ Association internationale pour la recherche en hygiène hospitalière (no recent information)
- ♦ Association internationale de recherche en informatique toxicologique (inactive)
- ♦ Association internationale pour la recherche sur le jouet (#15700)
- ♦ Association Internationale de Recherche en Management Public (internationally oriented national body)
- ♦ Association internationale pour la recherche médicale et les échanges culturels (no recent information)
- ♦ Association internationale de recherche sur la paix (#14537)
- ♦ Association internationale de recherche en psychologie économique (#12132)
- ♦ Association internationale de recherche psychotronique (no recent information)
- ♦ Association internationale de recherche sur les radiations (#12119)
- ♦ Association internationale de recherches sur la banane plantain et la banane (inactive)

♦ Association internationale de recherche scientifique en faveur des personnes handicapées mentales (AIRHM) 02738

International Association for Research in Favour of Persons with Mental Handicap

SG 28 rue Georges Clémenceau, 91400 Orsay, France.
URL: http://www.airhm.org/

History 1988, Lausanne (Switzerland), at first Congress. Registered in accordance with French law. **Aims** Promote *francophone* study and research on mental deficiency; encourage cooperation between researchers and practitioners; exchange information with local or international organizations in similar fields. **Structure** Council; Regional delegations (8). **Languages** French. **Finance** Members' dues. **Activities** Events/meetings; training/education. **Events** *Congress* Mons (Belgium) 2022, *Congress* Mons (Belgium) 2020, *La convention de l'ONU relative aux droits des personnes handicapées – une utopie?* Geneva (Switzerland) 2017, *Créativité des pratiques sur le terrain – voies nouvelles pour la recherche* Beaune (France) 2014, *Recherche, droits et gouvernance en faveur de la personne et de ses proches* Mont-Tremblant, QC (Canada) 2012. **Publications** *Nouvelles de l'AIRHM* (2 a year) in French – bulletin; *Revue francophone de la déficience intellectuelle* (2 a year) in French. Proceedings of congresses and study days.
Members Individuals (over 120). Researchers, educators and practitioners in relevant disciplines in 13 countries:
Albania, Belgium, Brazil, Bulgaria, Canada, France, Germany, Italy, Lebanon, Mauritania, Morocco, Romania, Switzerland. [2016.06.20/XD6373/v/**D**]

- ♦ Association internationale de recherches dentaires (#11838)
- ♦ Association internationale de recherches hydrauliques / see International Association for Hydro-Environment Engineering and Research (#11950)
- ♦ Association internationale de recherches sur la qualité des plantes alimentaires (inactive)
- ♦ Association internationale de recherches sur le revenu et la fortune / see International Association for Research in Income and Wealth (#12134)
- ♦ Association internationale de recherches sur le revenu et la richesse (#12134)
- ♦ Association internationale de recherches pour travaux hydrauliques / see International Association for Hydro-Environment Engineering and Research (#11950)
- ♦ Association internationale de recherches sur les voyages interplanétaires (inactive)
- ♦ Association internationale pour la reconnaissance des formes (#12069)
- ♦ Association internationale des recteurs d'universités (#12248)
- ♦ Association Internationale RED / see Rurality – Environment – Development (#19003)
- ♦ Association internationale des rédacteurs de télévision (inactive)
- ♦ Association internationale pour les réformes douanières (inactive)
- ♦ Association internationale des régies et commissions des accidents du travail (internationally oriented national body)

♦ Association internationale des régions francophones (AIRF) 02739

Dir 8 rue Paul Montrochet, 69002 Lyon, France. T. +33426734650. Fax +33426735757. E-mail: contact@regions-francophones.org.
URL: http://www.regions-francophones.org/

History 4 Oct 2002, Lyon (France). **Aims** Establish between *French-speaking* collectivities, territories and communities cooperation, exchange of information and expertise in their fields of activity. **Languages** French. **Staff** 3.00 FTE, paid; 1.00 FTE, voluntary. **Finance** Members' dues. Subsidies. Budget (annual): euro 360,000. **Events** *Assemblée Générale* Dakar (Senegal) 2012, *Etats généraux de la francophonie décentralisée / Rencontres Internationales des Régions francophones* Dakar (Senegal) 2012, *Rencontres Internationales des Régions francophones* Ouagadougou (Burkina Faso) 2011, *Assemblée générale* Yerevan (Armenia) 2011, *Assemblée générale* Lyon (France) 2010. **Publications** *L'écho des Régions Francophones* – newsletter.
Members Collectivities (149) in 28 countries and territories:
Albania, Armenia, Belgium, Benin, Bulgaria, Burkina Faso, Cambodia, Cameroon, Cape Verde, Comoros, Congo Brazzaville, Congo DR, Côte d'Ivoire, Djibouti, France, Gabon, Italy, Lebanon, Madagascar, Mali, Mauritania, Morocco, Niger, Québec, Romania, Senegal, Tunisia, Vietnam.
Consultative Status Consultative status granted from: *Organisation internationale de la Francophonie (OIF, #17809).* **IGO Relations** *UNDP (#20292); United Nations (UN, #20515); United Nations Institute for Training and Research (UNITAR, #20576).* **NGO Relations** Member of: *FMDV (#09804).* [2021/XM3503/**D**]

- ♦ Association internationale du registre des bateaux du Rhin / see International Association for the Representation of the Mutual Interests of the Inland Shipping and the Insurance and for Keeping the Register of Inland Vessels in Europe (#12131)
- ♦ Association internationale des registres du cancer (#11753)

♦ Association internationale Reine Hélène (AIRH) 02740

Queen Helen's International Association – Asociación Internacional Reina Elena – Associazione Internazionale Regina Elena

Contact via Gherarda 9, 41121 Modena MO, Italy. E-mail: airh.onlus@gmail.com.
URL: http://www.reginaelenaonlus.eu

History 18 Mar 1990, deriving from *'Committee for the Raising at Montpellier of a Bust of H M Queen Helen of Italy – Comité pour l'érection à Montpellier d'un buste de S M la Reine Hélène d'Italie'*, set up 28 Feb 1989. **Aims** Make known and recognize the life and example of *Helen of Savoy*; make contributions in the *spiritual*, *social*, *charitable* and *cultural* fields. **Structure** International Management Board; Board of Directors; Central Council. **Finance** Members' dues. Other sources: subsidies; grants. **Activities** Presents annually the 'Prix de la Charité Reine Hélène d'Italie' and 'Prix International de la Paix Mafalde de Savoie'. Organizes about 4 conferences a year. **Events** *Colloquium and assembly* Montpellier (France) 1995, *Colloquium and assembly* Rome (Italy) 1995. **Publications** *Caritas Augusta* (6 a year); *La Croix du Midi* (2 a year).
Members National Delegations in 15 countries. Individuals in 61 countries and territories:
Afghanistan, Albania, Andorra, Angola, Argentina, Australia, Austria, Belgium, Brazil, Bulgaria, Cambodia, Canada, Cape Verde, Chile, Côte d'Ivoire, Croatia, Cuba, Czechia, Denmark, Egypt, Estonia, France, Germany, Greece, Guinea, Haiti, Holy See, Hungary, India, Israel, Italy, Lebanon, Liechtenstein, Lithuania, Luxembourg, Malta, Mexico, Moldova, Monaco, Netherlands, Nigeria, Peru, Poland, Portugal, Romania, Russia, Senegal, Serbia, Slovakia, Slovenia, Spain, Sweden, Switzerland, Syrian AR, Tunisia, Türkiye, Uganda, UK, USA, Venezuela.
NGO Relations Member of: *Union des organisations internationales non-gouvernementales établies en France (UOIF, inactive).* [2022/XE3194/**E**]

- ♦ Association internationale Relais Dessert (internationally oriented national body)
- ♦ Association internationale de relations professionnelles / see International Labour and Employment Relations Association (#13997)
- ♦ Association internationale de relations publiques (#14671)

♦ Association Internationale des Réparateurs en Carosserie (AIRC) .. 02741

International Association of Bodywork Repairers

SG c/o ZKF, Grüner WEg 12, 61169 Friedberg, Germany. T. +496031794790. Fax +4960317947910. E-mail: airc@zkf.de.
URL: http://www.airc-int.com/

History 1969, Sassenheim (Netherlands). Registered in accordance with Dutch law. **Aims** Join forces in order to ensure the future of the *vehicle* repair industry; promote vehicle repairs and the vehicle repair industry; engage in international economic and political lobbying; promote international exchange of knowledge and information. **Structure** General Meeting; Council; Board; Regional Chapters (3); Secretariat in Friedberg (Germany). **Languages** English, French, German, Spanish. **Staff** 7.00 FTE, voluntary. **Finance** Members' dues. Annual budget: about euro 50,000. **Activities** Events/meetings; advocacy/lobbying/activism; certification/accreditation; training/education. **Events** *World congress* Amsterdam (Netherlands) 2004, *World congress* Brussels (Belgium) 2000, *World congress* Dallas, TX (USA) 1993, *World congress* Amsterdam (Netherlands) 1991, *World congress* Adelaide, SA (Australia) 1989. **Publications** *AIRC News*.
Members National trade organizations representing over 40,000 vehicle repair companies in 15 countries and territories:
Austria, Belgium, Croatia, Denmark, England, Germany, Iceland, Ireland, Japan, Luxembourg, Netherlands, Sweden, Switzerland, Trentino-South Tyrol, USA.
NGO Relations Member of: *Alliance for the Freedom of Car Repair in the EU (AFCAR, #00682).*
[2019.12.12/XD1498/**D**]

- ♦ Association internationale des représentants fiscaux (#15841)
- ♦ Association internationale pour la repression de la traite des blanches (inactive)
- ♦ Association internationale de la reproduction humaine / see International Academy of Human Reproduction (#11551)
- ♦ Association internationale du réseau européen du patrimoine (#11881)
- ♦ Association internationale pour les résidus solides (#15567)
- ♦ Association internationale pour les résidus solides et du nettoiement des villes / see International Solid Waste Association (#15567)
- ♦ Association internationale pour le respect des droits des peuples autochtones (inactive)
- ♦ Association internationale des responsables des libérations conditionnelles (internationally oriented national body)
- ♦ Association internationale des ressources en eau (#15871)
- ♦ Association internationale des retraités (inactive)
- ♦ Association internationale pour la revitalization des quartiers en crise / see Local Urban Development European Network (#16508)
- ♦ Association internationale du roman policier / see International Association of Crime Writers (#11825)
- ♦ Association internationale rurale catholique (#12461)
- ♦ Association internationale salésienne du sport (internationally oriented national body)
- ♦ Association internationale de santé bucco-dentaire (inactive)
- ♦ Association internationale pour la santé de la mère et du nouveau-né (inactive)
- ♦ Association internationale pour la santé des touristes (no recent information)
- ♦ Association internationale pour la sauvegarde des intérêts communs de la navigation intérieure européenne et de l'assurance et pour la tenue d'un registre des bateaux intérieurs en Europe (#12131)
- ♦ Association Internationale pour la Sauvegarde de Tyr (#12144)
- ♦ Association internationale de la savonnerie et de la détergence (inactive)
- ♦ Association internationale de la savonnerie, de la détergence et des produits d'entretien (#12166)
- ♦ Association internationale pour la science et l'information sur le café / see Association for the Science and Information on Coffee (#02905)
- ♦ Association internationale pour la science du logement (#11943)
- ♦ Association internationale de la science de la marchandise et de la technologie de base (#11790)
- ♦ Association internationale de science politique (#14615)
- ♦ Association internationale pour les sciences auxiliaires de l'histoire (inactive)
- ♦ Association internationale des sciences de la circulation et de la sécurité routières (#12235)
- ♦ Association internationale des sciences économiques (#13222)
- ♦ Association internationale des sciences de l'éducation / see Association mondiale des sciences de l'éducation (#02811)
- ♦ Association internationale de sciences expérimentales ou d'érudition, pures et appliquées, pour un humanisme objectif (inactive)
- ♦ Association internationale des sciences hydrologiques (#11954)
- ♦ Association internationale des sciences juridiques (#11997)
- ♦ Association internationale des sciences et de la médecine légale (#11900)
- ♦ Association internationale de la science du sol / see International Union of Soil Sciences (#15817)
- ♦ Association internationale des sciences physiques de l'océan (#12082)
- ♦ Association internationale des sciences et technologies céréalières (#11048)
- ♦ Association internationale pour la science du tabac (inactive)
- ♦ Association internationale des secrétaires de sociétés ophtalmologiques et otolaryngologiques (inactive)
- ♦ Association internationale pour la sécurité aérienne (inactive)
- ♦ Association internationale de sécurité professionnelle (#14649)
- ♦ Association Internationale de Sécurité Routière (#16874)
- ♦ Association internationale de la sécurité sociale (#14885)

♦ Association internationale pour la sécurité du transport des jeunes (AIST) 02742

International Association for Youth Transportation Safety

AIST Europe 8 rue Edouard Lockroy, 75011 Paris, France. T. +33143574286. Fax +33143570394. E-mail: aist@anateep.fr.

AIST America 5300 boulevard des Galeries, Bureau 300, Québec QC G2K 2A2, Canada. T. +14186226544. Fax +14186226595.
URL: http://www.aist-europe.org/

History 1994. **Languages** English, French, Spanish. **Publications** *Bulletin de l'AIST*.
Members Founder members (national organizations) in 5 countries:
Belgium, Canada, France, Spain, USA. [2010/XD9489/**D**]

- ♦ Association internationale de sédimentologie / see International Association of Sedimentologists (#12155)
- ♦ Association internationale de sédimentologistes (#12155)
- ♦ Association Internationale de Séismologie / see International Association of Seismology and Physics of the Earth's Interior (#12157)
- ♦ Association internationale de séismologie et de physique de l'intérieur de la Terre (#12157)
- ♦ Association internationale des sélectionneurs pour la protection des obtentions végétales (inactive)
- ♦ Association internationale de sémiologie de l'image / see International Association for Visual Semiotics (#12258)
- ♦ Association internationale de sémiotique (#12160)
- ♦ Association internationale de sémiotique de l'espace / see International Association for the Semiotics of Space and Time (#12159)
- ♦ Association internationale de sémiotique juridique (inactive)
- ♦ Association Internationale de Sémiotique de l'Espace et du Temps (#12159)
- ♦ Association internationale de sémiotique visuelle (#12258)
- ♦ Association Internationale des Seniors pour la Santé (#19228)
- ♦ Association internationale des services d'eau (inactive)
- ♦ Association internationale des services d'incendie et de secours CTIF (#04979)
- ♦ Association internationale des services secrets (inactive)
- ♦ Association internationale pour les services et techniques d'information en sciences sociales (#12169)
- ♦ Association internationale des settlements (inactive)
- ♦ Association internationale de signalisation maritime (#12013)
- ♦ Association internationale de la simulation dans la construction (#12409)
- ♦ Association internationale de simulation et de jeux d'entreprises (#14861)

♦ Association Internationale des Skål Clubs (AISC) 02743

Skål International

CEO Avda Palma de Mallorca, No 15 – 1 Edificio España, 29620 Torremolinos, Málaga, Spain. T. +34952389111. Fax +34952370013. E-mail: skal@skal.org.
Pres address not obtained.
URL: http://www.skal.travel/

History Apr 1934, Paris (France). First club set up 1932, Paris (France). Constitution modified: 1951; 1957; 1964; 1966; 1969; 1972; 1976; 1998; 2004; 2008. Former names and other names: *Association Internationale de Professionnels de Tourisme* – alias; *International Association of Professionals in Tourism* – alias. **Aims** Maximize networking opportunities and develop a responsible *tourism* industry; promote global tourism and friendship. **Structure** General Assembly (annual during World Congress); International Council; Executive Committee; General Secretariat based in Torremolinos (Spain). **Languages** English, French, Spanish. **Staff** 6.00 FTE, paid. **Finance** Sources: members' dues; sponsorship. **Activities** Awards/prizes/competitions; networking/liaising. **Events** *World Congress* Miami, FL (USA) 2019, *North American Congress* Isla Mujeres (Mexico) 2018, *Asian Assembly* Macau (Macau) 2018, *World Congress* Mombasa (Kenya) 2018, *Latin American Congress* Panama (Panama) 2018. **Publications** Electronic newsletters; magazine; press releases; position papers; directory. **Members** Active membership limited to individuals holding managerial positions in the travel and tourism industry, working full-time and directly involved in sales, marketing or promotion. Skål Young membership limited to tourism students and young professionals in the travel and tourism industry. Individuals (about 18,000) in Clubs (450) in 85 countries and territories. Membership countries not specified. **IGO Relations** Affiliate member of: *World Tourism Organization (UNWTO, #21861)* Business Council. Member of: UNWTO Task Force on the Prevention of Exploitation of Children in Tourism. Supports UNWTO ST-EP. **NGO Relations** Member of (1): *World Tourism Network (WTN, #21860).* Founder and coalition partner of: *International Institute for Peace through Tourism (IIPT).* [2021/XB1345/**B**]

- ♦ Association internationale du ski sur herbe (inactive)
- ♦ Association internationale sociale chrétienne (inactive)
- ♦ Association internationale des sociétés d'assurance mutuelle (inactive)
- ♦ Association internationale des sociétés de botanique et de mycologie (#11730)
- ♦ Association internationale des sociétés chimiques (inactive)
- ♦ Association internationale des sociétés de classification (#11778)
- ♦ Association internationale des sociétés de microbiologie / see International Union of Microbiological Societies (#15794)
- ♦ Association internationale des sociétés de la mutagenèse de l'environnement (#11877)
- ♦ Association internationale de sociologie (#15553)
- ♦ Association internationale de sociologie de la famille (no recent information)
- ♦ Association internationale de sociologie rurale (#14774)

♦ Association internationale des sociologues de langue française (AISLF) 02744

International Association of French-Speaking Sociologists

Pres Univ Toulouse Jean Jaurès, Maison de la Recherche, 5 allée Antonio Machado, 31058 Toulouse CEDEX 9, France. E-mail: aislf@aislf.org.
URL: http://www.aislf.org/

History 1958, Brussels (Belgium). Founded on initiative of Georges Gurvitch and Henri Janne, following colloquium, May 1956, Royaumont (France). Statutes adopted 20 Mar 1959, Paris (France). Registration: SIRET, No/ID: 37938015700022, France. **Aims** Encourage exchange between French-speaking sociologists of their theories and work relating to the evolution of societies in the contemporary world. **Structure** General Assembly (every 4 years, with congress); Bureau. **Languages** French. **Staff** 1.00 FTE, paid. **Finance** Sources: donations; grants; members' dues. **Activities** Awards/prizes/competitions; events/meetings; research/documentation. **Events** *Quadrennial Plenary Congress* Ottawa, ON (Canada) 2024, *Quadrennial Plenary Congress* Tunis (Tunisia) 2021, *Quadrennial Plenary Congress* Tunis (Tunisia) 2020, *Critiques du monde contemporain – quelles formes pour la contestation?* Paris (France) 2017, *Des identités collectives – approches comparatives* Tunis (Tunisia) 2016. **Publications** *Lettre de l'Aislf* (2 a year); *SociologieS* (3-4 a year) – online magazine; *Annuaire de l'AISLF*. Proceedings of colloquia, symposia and roundtables; research committee, working group and ad hoc group reports.
Members Honorary; Regular: individual sociologists and other social science specialists whose work has some bearing on sociology, all using French to a notable extent in their professional activities. Members (over 2,000) in 61 countries:
Algeria, Argentina, Austria, Belgium, Benin, Bosnia-Herzegovina, Brazil, Bulgaria, Burkina Faso, Burundi, Cameroon, Canada, China, Colombia, Congo Brazzaville, Congo DR, Costa Rica, Côte d'Ivoire, Czechia, Egypt, Finland, France, Gabon, Georgia, Germany, Greece, Haiti, Iran Islamic Rep, Israel, Italy, Japan, Lebanon, Luxembourg, Madagascar, Mali, Mauritania, Mexico, Monaco, Morocco, Mozambique, Netherlands, North Macedonia, Norway, Palestine, Poland, Portugal, Romania, Russia, Senegal, Serbia, Slovakia, Spain, Sweden, Switzerland, Togo, Tunisia, Türkiye, UK, Uruguay, USA, Venezuela.
NGO Relations Cooperates with: *Agence universitaire de La Francophonie (AUF, #00548).*
[2022/XC1286/v/**C**]

- ♦ Association internationale de la soie (inactive)
- ♦ Association internationale des soldats de la paix (#19678)
- ♦ Association internationale de solidarité francophone (inactive)
- ♦ Association internationale de somatothérapie (no recent information)
- ♦ Association Internationale Soufie Alâwiyya (unconfirmed)
- ♦ Association internationale de spécialistes en énergie (no recent information)
- ♦ Association internationale des spécialistes de l'information agricole (inactive)

Association internationale sport
02744

- Association internationale pour le sport des aveugles / see International Blind Sports Federation (#12363)
- Association internationale pour un sport sans violence (no recent information)
- Association internationale de standardization biologique / see International Alliance for Biological Standardization (#11622)
- Association internationale des statisticiens d'enquêtes (#12218)
- Association internationale de statisticiens municipaux / see International Association for Official Statistics (#12052)
- Association internationale pour la statistique régionale et urbaine (inactive)
- Association internationale pour la statistique dans les sciences physiques / see Bernoulli Society for Mathematical Statistics and Probability (#03212)
- Association internationale pour les statistiques officielles (#12052)
- Association internationale des stomisés (#14491)
- Association internationale de strabisme (#15609)
- Association internationale STRADEMED / see Association internationale des pays du pourtour de la Méditerranée et de l'Union européenne (#02726)
- Association internationale des sylviculteurs et des utilisateurs de produits de la forêt et du bois (inactive)
- Association internationale des syndicats d'initiative et groupements similaires (inactive)
- Association internationale pour la synthèse de la connaissance (no recent information)
- Association internationale sur les systèmes de production (#13332)
- Association internationale Tai Chi Chuan (#15653)
- Association internationale des tarifeurs / see International Association of Tariff-Specialists – Organization of Tariff and Transport Experts (#12219)
- Association internationale des tarifeurs – Organisation des experts des tarifs et des transports (#12219)
- Association internationale pour la taxonomie végétale (#12092)
- Association Internationale des Techniciens Biologistes / see Association Internationale des Technologistes Biomédicaux (#02747)
- Association internationale des techniciens biologistes de langue française / see Association Internationale des Technologistes Biomédicaux (#02747)
- Association internationale des techniciens de chaussures orthopédiques / see International Association of Orthopaedic Footwear (#12059)

♦ Association internationale de techniciens, experts et chercheurs (AITEC)   02745

International Association of Technicians, Experts and Researchers – Asociación Internacional de Técnicos, Expertos e Investigadores
Pres 21ter rue Voltaire, 75011 Paris, France. T. +33143712222. Fax +33144647455. E-mail: contact.aitec@reseau-ipam.org.
Co-Pres address not obtained.
URL: http://aitec.reseau-ipam.org/
History 1983. Registration: Start date: 24 May 1983, France. **Aims** Bring together specialists, association activists and experts in developed and developing countries working on free trade agreements, environment, urban policy and habitat. **Activities** Networking/liaising; guidance/assistance/consulting; events/meetings. **Events** Seminar on public services regulation in Europe Paris (France) 2005, Séminaire sur la régularisation des établissements irréguliers dans le Tiers-monde Mexico City (Mexico) 1993, Study day Paris (France) 1993. **Publications** Les carnets de l'AITEC (4 a year) – common publication with AEC, CEDETIM and CEDIDELP. Housing in Europe: Time to evict the crisis; Lobby Planet Paris; Stop à l'accaparement des ressources du sud par l'Union européenne. **Members** Individual jurists, architects, urban developers, geographers, engineers, economists, sociologists, managers (300). Membership countries not specified. **NGO Relations** Member of (1): Citizens for Europe (CFEU, #03956). Alternative Trade Mandate Alliance (ATM); Bellanet Alliance of Social Entrepreneurs (BASE, #03196); Centre de documentation internationale pour le développement, les libertés et la paix (CEDIDELP); Centre d'études et initiatives de solidarité internationale (CEDETIM); Centre de recherche et d'information pour le développement, Paris (CRID); Climate Justice Now ! (CJN!, inactive); European Anti-Poverty Network (EAPN, #05908); European Assembly of Citizens (EAC, #05922); European Network for the Respect of the Right to Housing (no recent information); Habitat International Coalition (HIC, #10845); Initiatives Pour un Autre Monde (IPAM).   [2020/XD3844/v/**D**]

- Association internationale des techniciens de laboratoire médical / see International Federation of Biomedical Laboratory Science (#13372)
- Association internationale des techniciens de théâtre (inactive)
- Association internationale pour la technologie aéroportuaire mondiale (inactive)
- Association internationale de technologie des conférences (inactive)
- Association internationale pour la technologie pharmaceutique (#01082)

♦ Association internationale pour les technologies objets (AITO)   02746

Sec DIBRIS Via Dodecaneso 35, 16146 Genoa GE, Italy. T. +39103536636. Fax +39103536699.
URL: http://www.aito.org/
History Registered in accordance with German law. **Aims** Promote advancement of research in object-related technology in Europe. **Structure** General Assembly (annual); Executive Board. **Languages** English. **Activities** Events/meetings; awards/prizes/competitions. **Events** European Conference on Object Oriented Programming Aarhus (Denmark) 2021, European Conference on Object Oriented Programming Genoa (Italy) 2020, European Conference on Object Oriented Programming London (UK) 2019, European Conference on Object Oriented Programming Amsterdam (Netherlands) 2018, European Conference on Object Oriented Programming Barcelona (Spain) 2017. **Publications** The Journal of Object Technology (JOT). **Members** 51 members in 16 countries. Membership countries not specified.   [2016.10.26/XM3062/**D**]

♦ Association Internationale des Technologistes Biomédicaux (ASSITEB-BIORIF)   02747

International Association of Biologists Technicians
Secretariat 33 rue de Metz, 94170 Le Perreux-sur-Marne, France. T. +33148729274 – +33148729275. Fax +33148729051. E-mail: assisteb@wanadoo.fr – assiteb-biorif@orange.fr.
Registered Seat 3 rue Pierre Brossolette, 94130 Nogent-sur-Marne, France.
URL: http://www.assiteb-biorif.org/
History 1981. Former names and other names: Association Internationale des Techniciens Biologistes (ASSITEB) – former; Association internationale des techniciens biologistes de langue française – former; International Association of Technologists in Biology – former. Registration: RNA, No/ID: W942001720, France. **Activities** Events/meetings; training/education. **Events** Rencontre Africaine Yaoundé (Cameroon) 2015, Rencontre africaine Brazzaville (Congo Brazzaville) 2013, Rencontre africaine Lomé (Togo) 2011, Rencontre africaine Ouagadougou (Burkina Faso) 2009, Rencontre Africaine Tours (France) 2008. **Publications** Biotechnologiste International (6 a year).
Members Associations (27); individuals – biologist technicians, bio-technologists and biology teachers; governmental organs – ministers, research centres, universities, other teaching establishments. Members in 54 countries and territories:
Algeria, Andorra, Argentina, Austria, Belgium, Benin, Bolivia, Brazil, Burkina Faso, Burundi, Cambodia, Cameroon, Canada, Central African Rep, Chad, Chile, Comoros, Congo Brazzaville, Congo DR, Côte d'Ivoire, Cyprus, Djibouti, Equatorial Guinea, Eritrea, Ethiopia, France, Gabon, Germany, Greece, Guinea, Guinea-Bissau, Haiti, Israel, Italy, Lebanon, Madagascar, Mali, Mauritania, Mauritius, Morocco, Niger, Nigeria, Portugal, Romania, Rwanda, Sao Tomé-Principe, Saudi Arabia, Senegal, Spain, Switzerland, Togo, Tunisia, UK, Vietnam.
Consultative Status Consultative status granted from: WHO (#20950) (Official Relations). **IGO Relations** Accredited by (1): Organisation internationale de la Francophonie (OIF, #17809). **NGO Relations** PMNCH (#18410); Union internationale des ingénieurs et des scientifiques utilisant la langue française (UISF, #18410).   [2021/XJ1563/**C**]

- Association internationale des technologistes de laboratoire médical / see International Federation of Biomedical Laboratory Science (#13372)

- Association internationale de la teinture et de l'impression textiles (inactive)
- Association internationale de la teinture textile (inactive)
- Association internationale des télévisions d'éducation et de découverte (no recent information)
- Association internationale de terminologie (inactive)
- Association internationale des terrains de jeux / see International Play Association (#14604)
- Association internationale de thalassothérapie (no recent information)
- Association internationale du théâtre amateur (#11647)
- Association internationale théâtre et éducation / see International Drama/Theatre and Education Association (#13198)
- Association internationale du théâtre pour l'enfance et la jeunesse (#12225)
- Association internationale du théâtre lyrique (no recent information)
- Association internationale du théâtre à l'université (#15831)
- Association internationale de tourisme des espérantistes (inactive)
- Association internationale pour le tourisme social (no recent information)
- Association internationale de tour managers (#12231)
- Association internationale du tournesol (#15625)
- Association internationale de toxicologie légale (#11902)
- Association internationale de la traction à la corde (#20259)

♦ Association internationale des traducteurs de conférence (AITC)   02748

International Association of Conference Translators – Asociación Internacional de los Traductores de Conferencia – Internationaler Verband der Konferenz Übersetzer
Exec Sec AITC Secretariat, Route des Morillons 15, Grand-Saconnex, 1218 Geneva, Switzerland. T. +41227910666. E-mail: secretariat@aitc.ch.
Pres address not obtained.
URL: http://www.aitc.ch/
History 3 Jun 1962, Geneva (Switzerland). Constitution adopted 26 May 1963, and amended: 30 May 1965, 8 May 1966, 7 May 1967, 20 Jun 1971, 25 Jun 1972, 19 May 1974, 8 May 1977, 8 May 1978, 21 Jun 1980, Jun 1981, Jul 1983, Jul 1989, 30 Jun 1990, 27 Jun 1998, 23 Jun 2007 and 19 Jun 2010. Registration: Swiss Civil Code, Switzerland. **Aims** Study problems connected with exercising the professions of translators, revisers, précis-writers, editors and terminologists working for international conferences and organizations; help to ensure high professional standards; defend these occupations. **Structure** Assembly (annual); Executive Committee; Specialized Committees. **Languages** Arabic, Bosnian, Bulgarian, Catalan, Chinese, Croatian, Czech, Danish, Dutch, English, French, German, Greek, Hebrew, Irish Gaelic, Italian, Latvian, Lithuanian, Polish, Portuguese, Romanian, Russian, Serbian, Spanish, Swahili, Swedish, Turkish, Ukrainian. **Staff** 1.00 FTE, paid. **Finance** Sources: members' dues. **Activities** Guidance/assistance/consulting; monitoring/evaluation. **Events** Meeting Paris (France) 2000, Annual General Assembly Geneva (Switzerland) 1986. **Publications** AITC Annuaire/Directory (annual). Guidelines on External Translation. Presentation brochure in English, French, Spanish.
Members Active (249); Associate (156); Candidate (15). Members in 38 countries and territories:
Argentina, Australia, Austria, Belgium, Bulgaria, Cameroon, Canada, China, Congo Brazzaville, Côte d'Ivoire, Denmark, Egypt, Ethiopia, France, Germany, Ghana, Italy, Kenya, Lebanon, Luxembourg, Malaysia, Martinique, Morocco, Namibia, Netherlands, New Caledonia, New Zealand, Puerto Rico, Romania, Saudi Arabia, Spain, Sweden, Switzerland, Thailand, Togo, UK, USA, Zambia.
Consultative Status Consultative status granted from: ECOSOC (#05331) (Ros A).
IGO Relations Representatives to:
- European Organization for Nuclear Research (CERN, #08108);
- FAO (#09260);
- ILO (#11123);
- International Atomic Energy Agency (IAEA, #12294);
- International Maritime Organization (IMO, #14102);
- International Oil Pollution Compensation Funds (IOPC Funds, #14402);
- International Organization for Migration (IOM, #14454);
- International Telecommunication Union (ITU, #15673);
- Organisation for the Prohibition of Chemical Weapons (OPCW, #17823);
- Pacific Community (SPC, #17942);
- UNESCO (#20322);
- United Nations (UN, #20515) (New York Office);
- United Nations Office at Geneva (UNOG, #20597);
- United Nations Office at Vienna (UNOV, #20604);
- WHO (#20950);
- World Intellectual Property Organization (WIPO, #21593);
- World Meteorological Organization (WMO, #21649);
- World Trade Organization (WTO, #21864).
NGO Relations Representatives to: Inter-Parliamentary Union (IPU, #15961). Consultative status with: Federation of International Civil Servants' Associations (FICSA, #09603).   [2022.02.18/XC1267/v/**C**]

- Association internationale des traducteurs et des linguistes arabes (#21118)
- Association internationale de traitement thermique et de l'ingénierie des surfaces (#13443)
- Association internationale de traitement thermique des matériaux / see International Federation for Heat Treatment and Surface Engineering (#13443)
- Association internationale des transformateurs de graines oléagineuses (inactive)
- Association internationale des transporteurs de marchandises solides (#11853)
- Association internationale trappist (#15727)
- Association internationale de traumatologie dentaire (#11840)
- Association internationale des travailleurs, 1864 (inactive)
- Association internationale des travailleurs, 1923 (inactive)
- Association internationale pour le travail social avec les groupes (unconfirmed)
- Association Internationale des Travaux en Souterrain / see International Tunnelling and Underground Space Association (#15744)
- Association internationale du tube (#15741)
- Association internationale des tunnels et de l'espace souterrain (#15744)
- Association internationale pour l'union des démocraties (inactive)
- Association internationale des universitaires, écrivains et artistes de langue française (inactive)
- Association internationale des Universités (#12246)

♦ Association internationale des universités du troisième âge (AIUTA)   02749

International Association of Universities of the Third Age – Asociación Internacional de las Universidades de la Tercera Edad – Internationale Vereinigung der Senioren Universitäten – Associazione Internazionale delle Università della Terza Età
Secretariat Univ Toulouse 1-Capitole, 2 rue du Doyen G Marty, 31042 Toulouse CEDEX 9, France. T. +33561633637. Fax +33561633640. E-mail: secretariat.aiuta@gmail.com.
URL: https://aiu3a.org/
History 1973. Former names and other names: Réseau européen des universités du troisième âge – former (1973 to 1976). **Aims** Establish cooperation among Third-Age Universities (UTAs) – universities for the elderly – and similar higher education institutions in all countries and also among institutions whose activities relate to higher education and to living conditions of elderly people. **Structure** General Assembly (annual); Board of Governors; Management Committee. **Languages** English, French. **Staff** 0.50 FTE, paid. 0.5 FTE. **Finance** Members' dues. **Activities** Events/meetings. **Events** International Conference Lebanon 2019, International Conference Osaka (Japan) 2016, International Conference Melbourne, VIC (Australia) 2013, Biennial Congress Lisbon (Portugal) 2012, Conference Singapore (Singapore) 2011. **Publications** AIUTA Infos (4 a year); Les Cahiers de l'AIUTA (annual) in English, French. Information Services: Computerized documentation service. Congress proceedings. Books.
Members Voting; Associate; Honorary. UTAs in 20 countries:
Argentina, Austria, Belgium, Brazil, Canada, Chile, China, Finland, France, Germany, Italy, Netherlands, Poland, Senegal, Slovakia, Spain, Sweden, Switzerland, UK, USA.

Consultative Status Consultative status granted from: *ECOSOC (#05331)* (Ros C); *ILO (#11123)* (Special List). **IGO Relations** Accredited by: *United Nations Office at Vienna (UNOV, #20604)*. Associated with Department of Global Communications of the United Nations. **NGO Relations** Instrumental in setting up: *Réseau mondial francophone pour la promotion de l'apprentissage continu des aînés (RESEAU FRANCOPHONE, no recent information)*. [2021/XD7103/**D**]

- ♦ Association internationale urbanisme et commerce (#12232)
- ♦ Association internationale des urbanistes (#15012)
- ♦ Association internationale d'urologie / see Société Internationale d'Urologie (#19499)
- ♦ Association internationale des usagers d'embranchements particuliers / see Cargo Rail Europe (#03431)
- ♦ Association internationale des utilisateurs de filés de fibres artificielles et synthétiques / see Association internationale des utilisateurs de fils de filaments artificiels et synthétiques et de soie naturelle (#02750)
- ♦ Association internationale des utilisateurs de filés de fibres artificielles et synthétiques et de soie naturelle / see Association internationale des utilisateurs de fils de filaments artificiels et synthétiques et de soie naturelle (#02750)

♦ Association internationale des utilisateurs de fils de filaments artificiels et synthétiques et de soie naturelle (AIUFFASS) 02750

International Association of Users of Artificial and Synthetic Filament Yarns and of Natural Silk – Internationaler Verband der Verarbeiter von Chemiefaser Filament- und Naturseidengaren

SG Villa Creatis, 2 rue des Mûriers, 69009 Lyon, France.
Dir Gen Via Raimondi 1, 22100 Como CO, Italy. T. +3931234280.
URL: https://www.aiuffass.eu/en/

History 1954, Geneva (Switzerland). Assimilated *European Silk Weavers (inactive)* as a second section., 1991. *European Throwsters' Association (inactive)* became the third section on 1 Jan 1992. Former names and other names: *International Association of Users of Yarn of Man-Made Fibres* – former (1954); *Association internationale des utilisateurs de filés de fibres artificielles et synthétiques (AIUFFASS)* – former (1954); *International Association of Users of Yarn of Man-Made Fibres and of Natural Silk* – former; *Association internationale des utilisateurs de filés de fibres artificielles et synthétiques et de soie naturelle* – former; *International Association of Users of Man-Made Fibres Filament Yarns and of Natural Silk* – former. Registration: Switzerland. **Aims** Promote the use of artificial and synthetic fibres; undertake research on problems facing industries using such fibres. **Structure** General Assembly (annual). Executive Bureau, consisting of one representative per member country. Technical Committee; Commercial Committee. **Languages** English. **Staff** 2.00 FTE, paid. **Finance** Sources: members' dues. **Events** *Congress* Vilnius (Lithuania) 2020, *Congress* Schaffhausen (Switzerland) 2019, *Congress* Leuven (Belgium) 2014, *Congress* Moltrasio (Italy) 2013, *Congress* Lyon (France) 2012.
Members National organizations in 5 countries:
Belgium, France, Italy, Switzerland, Türkiye.
Individuals in 3 countries:
Germany, Lithuania, UK.
NGO Relations Cooperates with: *International Organization for Standardization (ISO, #14473)*. Member of: *EURATEX – The European Apparel and Textile Confederation (EURATEX, #05616)*. [2020/XD1368/**D**]

- ♦ Association internationale pour l'utilisation des langues régionales à l'école (no recent information)
- ♦ Association internationale pour les véhicules à traction humaine (#13822)
- ♦ Association internationale vétérinaire de production animale (inactive)
- ♦ Association internationale pour la vidéo dans les arts et la culture (inactive)
- ♦ Association internationale des ville éducatrices (#11860)
- ♦ Association internationale des villes (inactive)
- ♦ Association internationale des villes d'avenir (inactive)
- ♦ Association internationale de villes contre la drogue (inactive)
- ♦ Association internationale des villes francophones de congrès / see Coésio – Destinations Francophone de Congrès (#04082)
- ♦ Association internationale des villes messagères de la paix (#12073)
- ♦ Association internationale des villes nouvelles / see International Urban Development Association (#15832)
- ♦ Association internationale villes et ports / see Association internationale villes et ports – réseau mondial des villes portuaires (#02751)

♦ Association internationale villes et ports – réseau mondial des villes portuaires (AIVP) 02751

Worldwide Network of Port Cities – Red Mundial de las Ciudades Portuarias

Dir Gen 5 Quai de la Saône, 76600 Le Havre, France. T. +33235427884. Fax +33235422194. E-mail: aivp@aivp.org.
Pres address not obtained.
URL: http://www.aivp.org/

History Jul 1988. Former names and other names: *International Association Cities and Ports (IACP)* – former; *Association internationale villes et ports (AIVP)* – former; *Asociación Internacional Ciudades y Puertos (AICP)* – former; *International Town and Port Association* – former. Registration: RNA, No/ID: W762000561, Start date: 31 Aug 2009, France, Normandie. **Aims** Bring together all public and private development stakeholders in port cities. **Structure** General Assembly; Board of Directors; Bureau; Network of Experts; General Director; Heads of Mission (4); Secretariats (2). **Languages** English, French, Spanish. **Staff** 10.00 FTE, paid. **Finance** Sources: meeting proceeds; members' dues; revenue from activities/projects; subsidies. Annual budget: 1,000,000 EUR. **Activities** Events/meetings; research/documentation. **Events** *World Conference Cities and Ports* Tangiers (Morocco) 2022, *Congress* Tangiers (Morocco) 2020, *Congress* Québec, QC (Canada) 2018, *Days* Le Havre (France) 2017, *Congress* Rotterdam (Netherlands) 2016. **Publications** *Dock infos Bulletin* (5 a year); *AIVP E-Newsletter* (2 a week). Reference books; congress and seminar proceedings; studies; good practice guides. Information Services: Computerized database; searches on request.
Members Cities; territorial organizations; autonomous and other ports; organizations, companies, universities, research institutes, self-employed. Organizations (180), mainly in France but in a total of 44 countries:
Albania, Argentina, Australia, Belgium, Benin, Brazil, Cameroon, Canada, Chile, China, Colombia, Congo Brazzaville, Côte d'Ivoire, Croatia, Ecuador, Estonia, Finland, France, Gabon, Ghana, Guinea, Ireland, Israel, Italy, Kenya, Latvia, Madagascar, Mauritania, Mauritius, Morocco, Mozambique, Netherlands, Norway, Papua New Guinea, Portugal, Saudi Arabia, Senegal, South Africa, Spain, Suriname, Sweden, Togo, Tunisia, USA.
Consultative Status Consultative status granted from: *UNCTAD (#20285)* (Special Category). **IGO Relations** *International Bank for Reconstruction and Development (IBRD, #12317)* (World Bank); *OECD (#17693)*; *Port Management Association of Eastern and Southern Africa (PMAESA, #18462)*; *Port Management Association of West and Central Africa (PMAWCA, #18463)*; *UNCTAD (#20285)*. **NGO Relations** Associate partner of: *World Urban Campaign (WUC, #21893)*. [2023.02.14/XD2184/**D**]

- ♦ Association internationale pour les voiles minces et les voiles spatiaux (#12162)
- ♦ Association internationale de volcanologie / see International Association of Volcanology and Chemistry of the Earth's Interior (#12259)
- ♦ Association internationale de volcanologie et de chimie de l'intérieur de la Terre (#12259)
- ♦ Association internationale Walras (#15862)
- ♦ Association internationale des Walser (#12262)
- ♦ Association internationale des webmasters (#15874)
- ♦ Association internationale du yoga intégré (no recent information)
- ♦ Association of International Friendships (inactive)
- ♦ Association of International Glaucoma Societies / see World Glaucoma Association (#21540)
- ♦ Association of International Industrial Irradiation (inactive)
- ♦ Association international de l'industrie du tungstène (#15743)

♦ Association des internationalistes 02752

Registered Office c/o Centre Panthéon, 12 place du Panthéon, 75005 Paris, France. E-mail: asso.inter@gmail.com.
URL: http://www.association-des-internationalistes.org/

History 9 Oct 2009, France, on the initiative of Bernard Kouchner. **Aims** Promote a 'French School' of *international relations* theory and practice. **Events** *General Assembly* Paris (France) 2010. **Members** Membership countries not specified. [2009/XJ8233/**D**]

♦ Association of International Law Firm Networks (AILFN) 02753

Pres 3730 Kirby Dr, Ste 1200, Houston TX 77098, USA. T. +18327889260.
URL: https://www.ailfn.com/

History Founded by *Global Governance Institute (GGI, #10391)* and *MSI Global Alliance (MSI, #16878)*. **Aims** Demonstrate and promote the value of legal networks to general counsel and the wider legal community, and networks' reach, attorney numbers, and cost effectiveness value. **Structure** Board of Directors. **Publications** *Independent Business Law Firm Newsletter (IBLF Newsletter)* (12 a year); *Law Firm Network Alert*.
Members Organizations (15), including:
Cicero League of International Lawyers (CICERO, #03924); *EuroCollectNet (ECN, #05664)*; *GGI Global Alliance*; *IAPA (#11005)*; *Interlex Group (#11518)*; *Legal Network International (LNI, #16439)*; *LEX Africa (#16449)*; *MSI Global Alliance (MSI, #16878)*. [2020/XM8485/y/**C**]

♦ Association of International Librarians and Information Specialists (AILIS) 02754

Pres route de Meyrin 385, 1217 Meyrin GE, Switzerland. E-mail: ailis.committee@gmail.com.
URL: https://sites.google.com/site/ailisgeneva/

History Founded Sep 1963, Sofia (Bulgaria), as *Association of International Libraries (AIL) – Association de bibliothèques internationales – Asociación de Bibliotecas Internacionales*, at a meeting of the Council of *International Federation of Library Associations and Institutions (IFLA, #13470)*. **Aims** Foster better communication and closer cooperation amongst international librarians and information specialists in the Geneva – Lausanne area; provide opportunities to learn about current trends in the profession. **Structure** General Assembly elects Executive Committee for 3-year term. **Languages** English, French. **Finance** Members' dues. **Activities** Co-sponsors the programme Library Science Talks, consisting of 5-6 lectures per year given by internationally recognized specialists in the field. Organizes: conferences; seminars; training courses; regular visits to international libraries and information centres. Provides a meeting point for members. **Events** *Seminar* 1990.
Members Librarians and information specialists of international organizations; non-profit institutions dealing with international issues. Membership open to librarians and information specialists outside international organizations, as well as to LIS students. Membership countries not specified. [2019/XC0147/**E**]

- ♦ Association of International Libraries / see Association of International Librarians and Information Specialists (#02754)

♦ Association of International Life Offices (AILO) 02755

Admin Dir 1st Floor College Park House, South Frederick Street, Dublin 2, Dublin, CO. DUBLIN, D02 VY46, Ireland. T. +447891201870. E-mail: secretariat@ailo.org.
Registered Office 1st Floor, Tudor House, Le Bordage, St Peter Port, GY1 1DB, UK.
URL: http://www.ailo.org/

History 1987. Registration: EU Transparency Register, No/ID: 952334430978-51. **Aims** Represent members' interests to governments, regulators, insurance and other trade bodies; influence and monitor the development of policy measures in relevant jurisdictions; encourage integrity and professionalism of members and promote these standards to governments, media and other channels; provide a forum of discussion and knowledge sharing among members. **Structure** General Committee; Executive Committee; Management Committee; Committees (6). **Languages** English, French, German. **Staff** 1.75 FTE, paid; 2.00 FTE, voluntary. **Finance** Sources: members' dues. **Activities** Advocacy/lobbying/activism; knowledge management/information dissemination; monitoring/evaluation; networking/liaising.
Members Companies (45) in 8 countries and territories:
Bermuda, Cayman Is, Guernsey, Ireland, Isle of Man, Liechtenstein, Luxembourg, UK. [2021.06.11/XD8251/**D**]

- ♦ Association of International Marathons / see Association of International Marathons and Distance Races (#02756)

♦ Association of International Marathons and Distance Races (AIMS) 02756

Sec 19 Kelly Street, London, NW1 8PG, UK. T. +442072093193. E-mail: aimssec@aol.com.
Pres address not obtained.
URL: http://www.aimsworldrunning.org/

History 7 May 1982, London (UK), as *Association of International Marathons*. Subsequently changed title to *Association of International Marathons and Road Races – Association des marathons internationaux*. Present title adopted 2007. **Aims** Foster and promote distance *running* throughout the world; exchange expertise and information among members; cooperate with IAAF in furthering these objectives. **Structure** Board; Sub-Committees (4). **Languages** English, French, German, Japanese, Spanish. **Staff** 1.50 FTE, paid. **Finance** Sources: members' dues; sponsorship. Annual budget: 500,000 USD. **Activities** Awards/prizes/competitions; events/meetings. **Events** *World Congress* Osaka (Japan) 2023, *World Congress* Batumi (Georgia) 2021, *World Congress* Batumi (Georgia) 2020, *Congress* Tallinn (Estonia) 2018, *Congress* Quito (Ecuador) 2015. **Publications** *AIMS Newsletter* (10 a year); *Distance Running* (4 a year) – magazine. **Members** 360 in 102 countries and territories. Membership countries not specified. [2022/XD1754/**C**]

- ♦ Association of International Marathons and Road Races / see Association of International Marathons and Distance Races (#02756)
- ♦ Association for International Meetings People and Religions (#11148)
- ♦ Association of International Metallizers, Coaters and Laminators (internationally oriented national body)
- ♦ Association of International Mission Services / see Accelerating International Mission Strategies

♦ Association of the International Olympic Winter Sports Federations (AIOWF) 02757

Association des fédérations internationales olympiques des sports d'hiver

Contact Blochstr 2, 3653 Oberhofen-Thunersee BE, Switzerland. T. +41332446161.
URL: https://olympics.com/ioc/international-federations/aiowf

History 1976, Innsbruck (Austria). Former names and other names: *International Assembly of Winter Sports Federations* – former; *Assemblée internationale des fédérations des sports d'hiver* – former; *Association of the International Winter Sports Federations (AIWF)* – former; *Association des fédérations internationales des sports d'hiver* – former. Registration: Swiss Civil Code, Switzerland. **Aims** Encourage cooperation between members; deal with specific questions connected with winter sports in general, and with the Olympic Games in particular; choose the joint delegation and/or appointments of winter sports representatives on the commissions of the International Olympic Committee (IOC) and other international organizations. **Structure** General Assembly. Council. **Languages** English. **Staff** 2.00 FTE, paid. **Finance** IOC contribution from Olympic revenues. Annual budget: 350,000 CHF. **Activities** Sporting activities. **Events** *IF Sports Forum* Lausanne (Switzerland) 2012, *IF sports forum* Lausanne (Switzerland) 2008, *IF sports forum* Lausanne (Switzerland) 2007.
Members International Federations governing a sport which appears on the programme of the Olympic Winter Games (7), included in this Yearbook:
Fédération Internationale de Ski (FIS, #09659); *International Biathlon Union (IBU, #12336)*; *International Bobsleigh and Skeleton Federation (IBSF, #12375)*; *International Ice Hockey Federation (IIHF, #13831)*; *International Luge Federation (FIL, #14066)*; *International Skating Union (ISU, #14865)*; *World Curling Federation (WCF, #21348)*.
NGO Relations Member of (1): *Olympic Movement (#17719)*. Recognized Organization by: *International Olympic Committee (IOC, #14408)*. Stakeholder in: *SportAccord (#19923)*. [2021/XF0630/y/**E**]

- ♦ Association of International Organizations for Workers' Culture (inactive)
- ♦ Association of International Petroleum Negotiators / see Association of International Energy Negotiators (#02722)

♦ Association of International Private Committees for the Safeguarding of Venice 02758

Comitati Privati Internazionali per la Salvaguardia di Venezia

Main Office c/o Fondazione di Venezia, Dorsoduro 3488/u, 30123 Venice VE, Italy. E-mail: info@comprive.org.
URL: http://www.comprive.org/

History Former names and other names: *Private Committees, Associations and Organizations for the Safeguarding of Venice* – former alias; *Comités, associations et organisations privés pour la sauvegarde de Venise* – former alias; *Association of Private Committees for the Safeguarding of Venice* – former alias. **Aims** Preserve the historic, cultural and artistic heritage of Venice. **Structure** Annual General Meeting; Executive Committee. **Languages** English, French, Italian. **Staff** 1.00 FTE, paid. **Activities** Events/meetings; research and development; training/education. **Events** *Annual General Meeting* Venice (Italy) 2017.
Members Full (26) in 10 countries:
Austria, Denmark, France, Germany, Italy, Netherlands, Sweden, Switzerland, UK, USA.
Consultative Status Consultative status granted from: *UNESCO (#20322)* (Consultative Status).
[2023.02.14/XE3392/**E**]

♦ Association for International Promotion of Gums (AIPG) 02759

Secretariat WGA Group, Sonninstrasse 28, 4th Floor, 20097 Hamburg, Germany. T. +494023601634. Fax +494023601610. E-mail: aipg@wga-hh.de.
URL: http://www.treegums.org/

History Registered in accordance with UK law. Nov 2000, absorbed *International Natural Gums Association for Research (INGAR, inactive)*. **Aims** Safeguard the position of gum Acacia – *gum arabic* – as a recognized safe *food additive* and ingredient; maintain and extend use of gum Acacia in food, pharmaceutical and other industries so as to regain traditional areas which have been lost; identify and promote new applications and boost consumption of gum Acacia. **Structure** General Meeting (annual); Board of Directors; Scientific Advisors; Secretariat. **Languages** English, French. **Finance** Members' dues. **Events** *Annual General Meeting* London (UK) 1997, *Regional conference for Africa on conservation, management and utilisation of plant gums, resins and oils* Nairobi (Kenya) 1996, *Annual General Meeting* Paris (France) 1996, *Annual General Meeting* Frankfurt-Main (Germany) 1995. **Members** Full (41) in 14 countries. Membership countries not specified. **IGO Relations** *European Pharmacopoeia Commission (#08198)*. Participates as observer in the activities of: *Codex Alimentarius Commission (CAC, #04081)*. [2019.10.14/XD4879/**D**]

♦ Association of International Property Professionals (internationally oriented national body)
♦ Association of International Relations / see Institute of International Relations, Taipei
♦ Association for International Research / see Association for Institutional Research

♦ Association of International Research and Development Centers for Agriculture (AIRCA) 02760

Chair AVRDC Headuarters, PO Box 42 Shanhua, Tainan 74199, Taiwan. T. +88665837801ext100.
Exec Sec icipe Duduville, Kasarani, PO Box 30772, Nairobi, 00100, Kenya. T. +254715497193.
URL: http://www.airca.org/

History 2012, Punta del Este (Uruguay). **Aims** Increase global food security by supporting smallholder agriculture within healthy, sustainable and climate-smart landscapes.
Members Centres (9):
AVRDC – The World Vegetable Center (#03051); *CABI (#03393)*; *Crops For the Future (CFF, #04968)*; *International Center for Biosaline Agriculture (ICBA, #12468)*; *International Centre for Integrated Mountain Development (ICIMOD, #12500)*; *International Centre of Insect Physiology and Ecology (ICIPE, #12499)*; *International Fertilizer Development Center (IFDC, #13590)*; *International Network for Bamboo and Rattan (INBAR, #14234)*; *Tropical Agriculture Research and Higher Education Center (#20246)*.
NGO Relations Cooperates with: *Global Forum on Agricultural Research (GFAR, #10370)*.
[2015.08.31/XJ7329/y/**E**]

♦ Association of the International Rubber Trade / see Rubber Trade Association of Europe (#18995)

♦ Association of International Schools in Africa (AISA) 02761

Exec Dir Peponi Road, PO Box 14103-00800, Nairobi, Kenya. T. +254202697442 – +2548076067. E-mail: director@aisa.or.ke – info@aisa.or.ke.
Chair American Intl School of Cape Town, 42 Soetvlei Ave, Sweet Valley, Cape Town, 7806, South Africa.
URL: http://www.aisa.or.ke/

History 1969, to represent international schools in sub-Saharan Africa offering international education to an international study body in Africa. **Aims** Transform student learning by leading and supporting strategic thinking, professional growth and school effectiveness. **Structure** Board of Directors. **Languages** English. **Staff** 5.00 FTE, paid. **Finance** Members' dues. **Activities** Events/meetings; guidance/assistance/consulting; networking/liaising; knowledge management/information dissemination; projects/programmes. **Events** *Annual Leadership Conference* Cape Town (South Africa) 2019, *Invitational Conference* Lagos (Nigeria) 2019, *Annual Leadership Conference* Nairobi (Kenya) 2018, *Annual Leadership Conference* Johannesburg (South Africa) 2017, *Annual Educators Conference* Nairobi (Kenya) 2017. **Publications** *Connexions* (2 a year). Annual prospectus; biannual salary and benefits survey; regular member e-updates.
Members Schools (76) in 35 countries:
Angola, Botswana, Burkina Faso, Cameroon, Congo Brazzaville, Congo DR, Côte d'Ivoire, Eritrea, Ethiopia, Gabon, Gambia, Ghana, Guinea, Kenya, Lesotho, Liberia, Madagascar, Malawi, Mali, Mauritania, Mauritius, Mozambique, Namibia, Niger, Nigeria, Rwanda, Senegal, Sierra Leone, South Africa, Sudan, Tanzania UR, Togo, Uganda, Zambia, Zimbabwe.
Associate members (71) in 13 countries:
Australia, Canada, Egypt, Ireland, Kenya, Netherlands, South Africa, Spain, Switzerland, Thailand, UK, USA, Zimbabwe.
[2019.12.19/XD0704/**D**]

♦ Association for International Scientific and Technical Communication and Cooperation (inactive)

♦ Association of International Seafood Professionals (AISP) 02762

Contact level 11, 65 York St, Sydney NSW 2000, Australia. E-mail: admin@seafoodprofessionals.org.
URL: http://seafoodprofessionals.org/

Aims Bring the global seafood community together to define a comprehensive agenda created by the seafood industry community. **Activities** Events/meetings; networking/liaising. [2022/XM4765/t/**C**]

♦ Association internationale des sélectionneurs (inactive)

♦ The Association for International Sport for All (TAFISA) 02763

SG c/o Commerzbank / Filiale Höchst, Hostatostr 2, 65929 Frankfurt-Main, Germany. T. +49699739359990. Fax +4969973935995. E-mail: info@tafisa.org.
URL: http://www.tafisa.org/

History 9 Mar 1990, Stuttgart (Germany). Biennial *'Trim and Fitness'* congresses having been held since 1969, Oslo (Norway). Office set up, 2005, Frankfurt-Main (Germany). As of end 2009, *International Assembly of National Organizations of Sport (IANOS, inactive)* merged into the organization. Former names and other names: *Trim and Fitness International Sport for All Association* – former. Registration: Hesse District Court, No/ID: VR 9727, Start date: 5 Mar 1991, Germany, Frankfurt-Main; EU Transparency Register, No/ID: 362405025078-34, Start date: 21 Dec 2016. **Aims** Globally promote and facilitate access for every person to sport for all and physical activity; lobby internationally; provide and coordinate programmes and events; provide networking and experience transfer platforms. **Structure** General Assembly; Board of Directors. Regional bodies (3): *TAFISA Europe (#20087)*; *Asiania Sport For All Association (ASFAA, #01510)*; TAFISA Africa; Pan-American Federation of Sport for All (PASFAF). **Languages** English. **Staff** 2.00 FTE, paid. **Finance** Sources: donations; fees for services; members' dues; sponsorship. Annual budget: 300,000 EUR. **Activities** Awards/prizes/competitions; events/meetings; sporting activities; training/education. **Events** *World Sport for All Congress* Düsseldorf (Germany) 2023, *World Congress* Portoroz (Slovenia) 2022, *World Congress* Portoroz (Slovenia) 2021, *World Congress* Tokyo (Japan) 2019, *Biennial Congress* Seoul (Korea Rep) 2017. **Publications** *TAFISA Newsletter* in English. Magazines.
Members National organizations in 153 countries and territories:
Albania, Angola, Anguilla, Antigua-Barbuda, Argentina, Aruba, Australia, Austria, Azerbaijan, Bahamas, Bahrain, Bangladesh, Barbados, Belarus, Belgium, Belize, Benin, Bermuda, Bolivia, Bosnia-Herzegovina, Botswana, Brazil, Brunei Darussalam, Bulgaria, Burundi, Cameroon, Canada, Cape Verde, Cayman Is, Chile, China, Colombia, Congo Brazzaville, Costa Rica, Côte d'Ivoire, Croatia, Cuba, Cyprus, Denmark, Djibouti, Dominica, Dominican Rep, Ecuador, Egypt, El Salvador, England, Estonia, Ethiopia, Faeroe Is, Fiji, Finland, France, Gabon, Georgia, Germany, Ghana, Greece, Grenada, Guadeloupe, Guam, Guatemala, Guyana, Haiti, Hong Kong, Hungary, Iceland, India, Indonesia, Iran Islamic Rep, Iraq, Israel, Italy, Jamaica, Japan, Jordan, Kazakhstan, Kenya, Korea Rep, Kosovo, Kuwait, Latvia, Lebanon, Liechtenstein, Lithuania, Macau, Malaysia, Maldives, Martinique, Mauritius, Mexico, Micronesia FS, Mongolia, Montserrat, Mozambique, Nepal, Netherlands, New Zealand, Nigeria, North Macedonia, Norway, Oman, Pakistan, Palau, Palestine, Papua New Guinea, Philippines, Poland, Portugal, Puerto Rico, Qatar, Romania, Russia, Samoa USA, Sao Tomé-Principe, Saudi Arabia, Senegal, Serbia, Sierra Leone, Singapore, Slovakia, Slovenia, Solomon Is, South Africa, Spain, St Kitts-Nevis, St Lucia, St Vincent-Grenadines, Suriname, Sweden, Switzerland, Syrian AR, Taiwan, Tanzania UR, Thailand, Togo, Trinidad-Tobago, Tunisia, Türkiye, Turks-Caicos, Uganda, Ukraine, United Arab Emirates, Uruguay, USA, Uzbekistan, Vanuatu, Venezuela, Vietnam, Virgin Is UK, Virgin Is USA, Yemen, Zambia, Zimbabwe.
International members (58):
- *Badminton World Federation (BWF, #03060)*;
- *IML Walking Association (IML, #11130)*;
- *International Cheer Union (ICU, #12539)*;
- *International Dance Organization (IDO, #13131)*;
- *International Dance Sport Association (IDSA, #13132)*;
- *International Draughts Federation (IDF, #13199)*;
- *International Esports Federation (IESF, #13303)*;
- *International Federation of Cardio HIIT BodyWeight Exercise (IFCH)*;
- *International Federation of Cheerleading (IFC, #13386)*;
- *International Federation of Kitesports Organizations (IFKO, #13464)*;
- *International Federation of Muaythai Associations (IFMA, #13482)*;
- *International Federation of Popular Sports (#13515)*;
- *International Federation of Wrestling on Belts "Alysh"*;
- *International Field Archery Association (IFAA, #13595)*;
- *International Fistball Association (IFA, #13609)*;
- *International Functional Fitness Federation (iF3, #13691)*;
- *International Jukskei Federation (IJF)*;
- *International Jump Rope Union (IJRU, #13978)*;
- *International Mind Sports Association (IMSA, #14164)*;
- *International NaB Golf Association (INGA)*;
- *International Nordic Walking Federation (INWA, #14375)*;
- *International Pole Sports Federation (IPSF, #14611)*;
- *International Qwan Ki Do Federation (IQKDF, #14682)*;
- *International Sport Lawyers Association (ISLA, #15591)*;
- *International Sports Chanbara Association (ISCA)*;
- *International Table Tennis Federation Foundation (ITTF Foundation, #15651)*;
- *International Taekwon-Do Federation (ITF, #15652)*;
- *International Tchoukball Federation (FITB, #15661)*;
- *International Traditional Taekwon-Do Federation (ITTAF, #15712)*;
- *International Union of Kettlebell Lifting (IUKL, #15786)*;
- *International Zurkhaneh Sports Federation (IZSF, #15946)*;
- *Spoqcs International Federation (SIF, #19922)*;
- *Sport Jiu-Jitsu International Federation (SJJIF, #19926)*;
- *United World Wrestling (UWW, #20665)*;
- *World Baton Twirling Federation (WBTF, #21225)*;
- *World Bodybuilding and Physique Sports Federation (WBPF, #21237)*;
- *World Budo Martial Arts Federation*;
- *World Council of Ju-Jitsu Organisations (WCJJO, #21333)*;
- *World Dance Council (WDC, #21353)*;
- *World Flying Disc Federation (WFDF, #21509)*;
- World Hangung Association;
- *World Hapkido Confederation (WHC)*;
- *World Hapkido Federation (WHF)*;
- *World Jiu Jitsu Confederation (WJJC)*;
- *World Judo Federation (WJF, #21603)*;
- *World Karate Confederation (WKC, #21607)*;
- *World Kettlebell Sport Federation (WKSF)*;
- *World Kickboxing League (WKL)*;
- World Kungfu Dragon and Lion Dance Federation;
- *World Martial Arts Committee (WMAC, #21636)*;
- *World Martial Arts Games Committee (WMAGC, #21637)*;
- *World Minigolf Sport Federation (WMF, #21653)*;
- World Mixed Jitsu Union;
- *World Muay Federation (WMF, #21662)*;
- *World O-Sport Federation (WOF, #21700)*;
- *World Silambam Federation (WSF)*;
- *World Ssireum Federation (WSF, #21827)*;
- *World Traditional Kickboxing Association (WTKA, no recent information)*.

Supporter members in 50 countries and territories:
Argentina, Australia, Austria, Bahrain, Bolivia, Brazil, Brunei Darussalam, Canada, Denmark, Ecuador, Germany, Ghana, Greece, Hungary, India, Indonesia, Iran Islamic Rep, Italy, Japan, Kazakhstan, Kenya, Korea Rep, Kosovo, Kuwait, Latvia, Lebanon, Malaysia, Mexico, Mozambique, Nepal, Netherlands, Oman, Pakistan, Philippines, Poland, Portugal, Sierra Leone, Slovenia, South Africa, Spain, Switzerland, Taiwan, Tanzania UR, Togo, Trinidad-Tobago, Türkiye, Uganda, UK, United Arab Emirates, USA.
International Health and Fitness Association (IHFA); *World Ninja Federation (WNF)*; *World Pahuyuth Federation (WPF, #21706)*.
Consultative Status Consultative status granted from: *UNESCO (#20322)* (Consultative Status). **IGO Relations** Recognized by: *UNESCO (#20322)*; United Nations Office on Sport for Development and Peace; *WHO (#20950)*. **NGO Relations** Recognized by: *International Olympic Committee (IOC, #14408)*. Member of: *International Council of Sport Science and Physical Education (ICSSPE, #13077)*. Memorandum of Understanding with: *World Ethnosport Society (#21392)*. [2021/XD2173/y/**B**]

♦ Association of International Studies (internationally oriented national body)
♦ Association international du textile naturel (#14217)
♦ Association of International Trade Fairs of America / see International Association of Exhibitions in Latin America (#11886)
♦ Association of the International Trade in Flowerbulbs and Plants (no recent information)
♦ Association of International Travel Agents / see Association of International Travel Agents Network (#02764)

♦ Association of International Travel Agents Network (AITAN) 02764

Contact 703 Waterford Way, Ste 600, Miami FL 33126, USA.
URL: http://www.iatan.org/Pages/default.aspx

History Original title: *Association of International Travel Agents (AITA)*.
Members Travel agents and agencies in 13 countries:
Australia, Belgium, Czechia, Germany, Italy, Netherlands, Pakistan, Philippines, Russia, Sweden, Switzerland, Thailand, USA.
[2015/XD7132/**D**]

♦ Association of International Vascular Surgeons (AIVS) 02765

Chairperson Freeman Hospital, Freeman Road, Newcastle upon Tyne, NE7 7DN, UK.
URL: http://aivsconf.com/

History 26 Mar 1982, Zürs (Austria). 26 Mar 1982, Zurs (Austria), at 3rd International Vascular Winter Workshop, on the initiative of Roger Greenhalgh. Previously also referred to as *International Society of Vascular Surgeons*. Memorandum of Association signed, Davos (Switzerland), 2006. **Aims** Promote good fellowship and exchange of scientifique ideas in an informal setting. **Events** *Annual Meeting* Gosau (Austria) 2023, *Annual Meeting* Sölden (Austria) 2022, *Annual Meeting* Sölden (Austria) 2021, *Annual Meeting* Whistler, BC (Canada) 2020, *Annual Meeting* Jasna (Slovakia) 2019.
Members Individuals in 14 countries:
Australia, Austria, Belgium, Denmark, Finland, France, Germany, Italy, Netherlands, Norway, Poland, Sweden, UK, USA.
[2021/XD1588/v/**F**]

♦ Association for International Water and Forest Studies / see Foreningen for Internasjonale Vannstudier
♦ Association for International Water Studies (internationally oriented national body)

♦ Association of International Wealth Management (AIWM) 02766

Contact Feldstr 80, 8180 Bülach ZH, Switzerland. T. +41448723551. Fax +41448723532. E-mail: info@aiwm.org.
URL: http://www.aiwm.org/

History 2007. Articles of Association amended 21 Feb 2011 and 8 Feb 2013. Registered in accordance with Swiss Civil Code. **Aims** Encourage, promote and strengthen global education in the private banking industry; set a globally recognized standard for the qualification of private banking professionals. **Structure** General Assembly; Board of Directors; Secretariat. **Finance** Sources: members' dues. **Activities** Awards/prizes/ competitions; events/meetings; training/education. **Publications** *AIWM Newsletter* (2 a year) – electronic. **Members** Regular; Affiliate. Membership countries not specified. [2016/XJ9874/**C**]

- ♦ Association of the International Winter Sports Federations / see Association of the International Olympic Winter Sports Federations (#02757)
- ♦ Association for International Youth Exchange and Tourism / see INEX – Association of Voluntary Activities
- ♦ Association of Interprofessional Employers / Businessmen of European Capital Cities / see Business European Capital Cities (#03382)
- ♦ Association of Interprofessional Employers/Businessmen Organisations of European Capital Cities / see Business European Capital Cities (#03382)
- ♦ Association interuniversitaire européenne Société, science et technologie (#07597)
- ♦ Association for Investment Management and Research / see CFA Institute

♦ Association of the IOC Recognized International Sports Federations (ARISF) 02767

SG Maison du Sport Intl, Av de Rhodanie 54, 1007 Lausanne VD, Switzerland. T. +41216147568. E-mail: arisf@arisf.sport.
URL: https://www.arisf.sport/

History 1985, Seoul (Korea Rep). Current statutes adopted Apr 2015. **Aims** Unite, promote and support the IOC Recognized International Sport Federations; coordinate their common interests and goals while preserving their autonomy and promoting their values. **Structure** General Assembly; Council; Secretariat. **Languages** English. **Staff** 1.00 FTE, paid. **Finance** Sources: members' dues. **Events** *Meeting* Dubai (United Arab Emirates) 2010.

Members International Federations (42), listed in this Yearbook:
- *Federación Internacional de Pelota Vasca (FIPV, #09340);*
- *Fédération aéronautique internationale (FAI, #09397);*
- *Fédération Internationale de l'Automobile (FIA, #09613);*
- *Fédération Internationale de Motocyclisme (FIM, #09643);*
- *Fédération internationale de SAMBO (FIAS, #09655);*
- *Fédération internationale des échecs (FIDE, #09627);*
- *Federation of International Bandy (FIB, #09601);*
- *Federation of International Polo (FIP, #09675);*
- *International Bowling Federation (IBF, #12384);*
- *International Cheer Union (ICU, #12539);*
- *International Cricket Council (ICC, #13105);*
- *International Federation Icestocksport (IFI, #13455);*
- *International Federation of American Football (IFAF, #13354);*
- *International Federation of Muaythai Associations (IFMA, #13482);*
- *International Federation of Sport Climbing (IFSC, #13553);*
- *International Floorball Federation (IFF, #13615);*
- *International Korfball Federation (IKF, #13992);*
- *International Life Saving Federation (ILS, #14040);*
- *International Orienteering Federation (IOF, #14485);*
- *International Racquetball Federation (IRF, #14683);*
- *International Ski Mountaineering Federation (ISMF, #14871);*
- *International Sumo Federation (IFS, #15624);*
- *International Surfing Association (ISA, #15630);*
- *International University Sports Federation (FISU, #15830);*
- *International Waterski and Wakeboard Federation (IWWF, #15872);*
- *International Wushu Federation (IWUF, #15918);*
- *Tug of War International Federation (TWIF, #20259);*
- *Union internationale des associations d'alpinisme (UIAA, #20420);*
- *Union internationale Motonautique (UIM, #20431);*
- *World Association of Kickboxing Organizations (WAKO, #21151);*
- *World Baseball Softball Confederation (WBSC, #21222);*
- *World Bridge Federation (WBF, #21246);*
- *World Confederation of Billiards Sports (WCBS, #21291);*
- *World DanceSport Federation (WDSF, #21354);*
- *World Flying Disc Federation (WFDF, #21509);*
- *World Karate Federation (WKF, #21608);*
- *World Lacrosse (#21616);*
- *World Netball (WN, #21668);*
- *World Pétanque and Bowls Federation (WPBF, #21721);*
- *World Skate (#21786);*
- *World Squash Federation (WSF, #21826);*
- *World Underwater Federation (#21873).*

NGO Relations Member of (1): *Olympic Movement (#17719).* Recognized Organization by: *International Olympic Committee (IOC, #14408).* Stakeholder in: *SportAccord (#19923).* [2022/XE3330/y/**E**]

- ♦ Association for Iranian Studies (internationally oriented national body)
- ♦ Association iranienne des relations internationales (internationally oriented national body)
- ♦ Association IRENE – Initiatives, Researches, Experiences for a New Europe (internationally oriented national body)
- ♦ Association of Iron Ore Exporting Countries (inactive)
- ♦ Association islamique des armateurs / see Organization of the Islamic Shipowners' Association (#17876)
- ♦ Association of Island Laboratories of the Caribbean / see Association of Marine Laboratories of the Caribbean (#02794)
- ♦ Association of Island Marine Laboratories / see Association of Marine Laboratories of the Caribbean (#02794)
- ♦ Association of Island Marine Laboratories of the Caribbean / see Association of Marine Laboratories of the Caribbean (#02794)

♦ Association of Issuing Bodies (AIB) 02768

SG Visverkopersstraat 13, 1000 Brussels, Belgium. T. +32486558301. E-mail: info@aib-net.org.
URL: http://www.aib-net.org/

History May 2002. Former names and other names: *Association of Issuing Bodies of The Renewable Energy Certification System* – former. Registration: Banque-Carrefour des Entreprises, No/ID: 0864.645.330, Start date: 19 Mar 2004, Belgium. **Aims** Develop, use and promote the *European Energy Certificate System* (EECS), thereby guaranteeing the origin of European energy. **Structure** General Meeting (twice a year); Board; Units; Scheme Groups; Task Forces; Secretariat. **Languages** English. **Staff** 4.00 FTE, paid. **Finance** Sources: members' dues. Annual budget: 1,880,520 EUR (2023). **Activities** Certification/accreditation. European Union, EFTA countries, Contracting Parties to the Energy Community. **Events** *Meeting* Madrid (Spain) 2018, *Meeting* Vienna (Austria) 2017. **Publications** *AIB Newsletter* (2 a year). Annual Report.

Members Electricity regulators; energy agencies; transmission system operators; electricity market operators; others. Members (38) in 30 countries:
Austria, Belgium, Bosnia-Herzegovina, Bulgaria, Croatia, Cyprus, Czechia, Denmark, Estonia, Finland, France, Germany, Greece, Hungary, Iceland, Ireland, Italy, Latvia, Lithuania, Luxembourg, Montenegro, Netherlands, Norway, Portugal, Serbia, Slovakia, Slovenia, Spain, Sweden, Switzerland.

NGO Relations Member of (2): *European Society of Association Executives (ESAE, #08526); Federation of European and International Associations Established in Belgium (FAIB, #09508).* Partner of (1): *RECS International (#18631).* In liaison with technical committees of: *Comité européen de normalisation (CEN, #04162).* [2023.01.06/XJ4951/**F**]

- ♦ Association of Issuing Bodies of The Renewable Energy Certification System / see Association of Issuing Bodies (#02768)
- ♦ Association italienne des femmes pour le développement ONLUS (internationally oriented national body)

♦ Association of Japanese Language Teachers in Europe (AJE) 02769

Chair Univ Ca'Foscari Venezia, Dorsoduro 3246, 30123 Venice VE, Italy.
Office Homberger Str 16, 47441 Moers, Germany.
URL: http://www.eaje.eu/en.html

History 1995. Since 2009 registered in accordance with German law. **Aims** Enhance and promote teaching and learning Japanese language and culture in the European countries. **Structure** Executive Committee. **Finance** Members' dues. **Activities** Events/meetings; knowledge management/information dissemination. **Events** *Symposium* Ljubljana (Slovenia) 2014, *Symposium* Madrid (Spain) 2013, *Symposium* Tallinn (Estonia) 2011, *Symposium* Bucharest (Romania) 2010, *Symposium* Berlin (Germany) 2009. **Publications** *Japanese Language Education in Europe* (annual). **Members** Full (over 300) in about 30 countries. Membership countries not specified. **NGO Relations** Member of: *Global Network of Japanese Language Education (GN, #10492).* [2017/XJ1363/**E**]

- ♦ Association japonaise de droit international (internationally oriented national body)
- ♦ Association Jean Monnet (internationally oriented national body)

♦ Association of Jesuit Colleges and Universities in Asia Pacific (AJCU-AP) 02770

Chairman Sanata Dharma Univ, Affandi Street, Tromol Pos 29 Mrican, Sleman, Yogyakarta 55281, Indonesia. T. +62274513301 – +62274515352. Fax +62274562383. E-mail: eko@usd.ac.id – ajcuap@gmail.com.
URL: http://www.ajcu-ap.org/

History 2002, as *Association of Jesuit Colleges and Universities in East Asia and Oceania (AJCU-EAO).* Constitution and bylaws approved 2002, Perth (Australia); revised 2006, Seoul (Korea Rep). Current title adopted, 2010, Chiang Mai (Thailand). **Aims** Support and promote Jesuit higher education in the Asia Pacific region. **Structure** General Assembly; Board. **Languages** English. **Staff** 4-5 FTE, voluntary. **Finance** Tuition fees; donations. Annual budget: up to US$ 45,000. **Activities** Training/education; research/documentation; events/meetings; networking/liaising.

Members Full: universities or institutions (22) in 11 countries and territories:
Australia, China, Indonesia, Japan, Korea Rep, Myanmar, Philippines, Taiwan, Thailand, Timor-Leste, Vietnam.

NGO Relations *International Association of Jesuit Universities (IAJU, #11975); Jesuit Conference of Asia Pacific (JCAP, #16099); Society of Jesus (SJ).* [2019.12.27/XM5359/**E**]

- ♦ Association of Jesuit Colleges and Universities in East Asia and Oceania / see Association of Jesuit Colleges and Universities in Asia Pacific (#02770)
- ♦ Association of Jesuit Higher Education Institutions in Europe and Lebanon (inactive)

♦ Association des Jeunes Chercheurs Européens en études québécoise (AJCEEQ) 02771

Contact address not obtained. E-mail: ajceeq@gmail.com.

History Feb 1995, Besançon (France), as *Association des jeunes chercheurs européens en littérature québécoise (AJCELQ).* Current title adopted 2013. Registered in accordance with French law. **Finance** Members' dues. Subsidies for colloquia. **Events** *Le Québec recto-verso* Berlin (Germany) 2013, *Colloquium* Venice (Italy) 2006, *Colloque* Innsbruck (Austria) 2002, *Colloque* Montréal, QC (Canada) 2000, *Colloque / Colloquium* Genoa (Italy) 1999.

Members Individuals (about 66) in 14 countries:
Austria, Canada, France, Germany, Hungary, India, Italy, Luxembourg, Netherlands, New Zealand, Norway, Poland, Spain, UK. [2015/XE2582/v/**E**]

- ♦ Association des jeunes chercheurs européens en littérature québécoise / see Association des Jeunes Chercheurs Européens en études québécoise (#02771)

♦ Association des jeunes fonctionnaires européens (AJFE) 02772

Association of Young European Administrators – Asociación de Jóvenes Funcionarios Europeos – Vereinigung Junger Europäischer Beamter (VJEB)

Address not obtained.

History 1968. The Commission section, set up in 1974, is registered in accordance with Belgian law. Also referred to as *Association Of Young European Civil Servants (AYECS).* New statutes adopted 2005. **Aims** Create links between young *officials*; study problems relating to the creation of a *united Europe.* **Structure** General Assembly (annual). Board of Management, consisting of President, Vice-President, Secretary-General and Treasurer. **Events** *Annual Congress* Cologne (Germany) 2004, *Annual Congress* Graz (Austria) 2003, *Annual Congress* Lincoln (UK) 2001, *Annual Congress* Liverpool (UK) 1997, *Annual Congress* Meissen (Germany) 1996.

Members Sections (4). National sections (3) in 5 countries:
Belgium, Finland, France, Germany, UK.
A fourth section, the Commission section, is at:
European Commission (EC, #06633).
Individuals in 12 countries:
Belgium, Denmark, France, Germany, Greece, Ireland, Italy, Luxembourg, Monaco, Netherlands, Spain, UK. [2010/XE4079/**E**]

- ♦ Association des jeunes juristes africains / see African Jurists' Association (#00351)
- ♦ Association jeunes du traité atlantique (#22006)
- ♦ Association des Jeunes Volontaires au Service du Monde Environnemental (internationally oriented national body)
- ♦ Association of Jewish Genealogical Societies / see International Association of Jewish Genealogical Societies (#11976)
- ♦ Association of Jewish Religious Professionals from the Soviet Union and Eastern Europe / see Israel Association of Jewish Professionals from the Former Soviet Union
- ♦ Association des joueurs de tennis professionnels / see ATP World Tour (#03011)
- ♦ Association de joueurs de tournois continentaux (inactive)

♦ Association des journalistes accrédités auprès du Vatican 02773

Associazione Internazionale dei Giornalisti Accreditati in Vaticano (AIGAV) – Association of Journalists Accredited to the Vatican

Pres CNS Rome, Via dei Branchi Vecchi 58, Int 7, 00186 Rome RM, Italy. T. +39668300498. Fax +39668300511 – +39668823209. E-mail: cns@catholicnews.com.

History 6 Jun 1978, Rome (Italy), as *Association de la presse internationale auprès de la salle de la presse du Saint-Siège (ASISS)*; name changed 1982. **Aims** In the spirit of the Helsinki (Finland) Agreement, contribute to the dissemination of information on the activities of the Holy See and of Catholic institutions; assure a continuing dialogue between journalists and the organization of the Holy See. **Events** *General Assembly* Vatican City (Vatican) 1983, *General Assembly* Vatican City (Vatican) 1982, *General Assembly* Vatican City (Vatican) 1981, *General Assembly* Vatican City (Vatican) 1980, *General Assembly* Vatican City (Vatican) 1979.

Members Representatives of national newspapers and radio-TV stations in 22 countries:
Argentina, Australia, Austria, Belgium, Brazil, Canada, France, Germany, Hungary, Ireland, Italy, Japan, Mexico, Netherlands, Poland, Portugal, Russia, Spain, Switzerland, UK, USA, Venezuela. [2015/XE5209/**E**]

- ♦ Association des journalistes d'Afrique occidentale / see West African Journalists' Union (#20885)
- ♦ Association des journalistes du Commonwealth (#04344)
- ♦ Association des journalistes européens (#02516)
- ♦ Association des journalistes latinoaméricains pour le développement (inactive)
- ♦ Association des journalistes du Pacifique (inactive)
- ♦ Association des journalistes de la presse francophone (no recent information)
- ♦ Association of Journalists Accredited to the Vatican (#02773)
- ♦ Association des journaux techniques européens (inactive)

- ♦ Association juive pour la protection des jeunes filles, des femmes et des enfants (inactive)
- ♦ Association juridique de l'Asie et du Pacifique (#16406)
- ♦ Association des juristes africains (#00351)
- ♦ Association des juristes canadiens pour le respect des droits humains dans le monde / see Canadian Lawyers for International Human Rights
- ♦ Association des juristes de langue française / see Association Henri Capitant des amis de la culture juridique française (#02631)

♦ Association Justice and Environment, z.s. (J&E) 02774

Coordinator Udolni 33, 602 00 Brno, Czechia. T. +3613228462. Fax +3617901381. E-mail: secretariat@justiceandenvironment.org.
URL: http://www.justiceandenvironment.org/

History 2003, Czech Rep. Former names and other names: *Environmental Legal Organizations' Network Central and Eastern Europe (ELONETCE)* – former; *Justice and Environment (J&E)* – former. Registration: Ministry of Interior, No/ID: CZ 75141892, Start date: 2008, Czechia; EU Transparency Register, No/ID: 81849786507-65, Start date: 30 Aug 2011; Start date: 2004, End date: 2008, Netherlands. **Aims** Improve EU environmental laws and their implementation for the benefit of the environment and people across Europe. **Structure** General Meeting; Executive Committee; Advisory Board; Chairman; Treasurer; Coordinator; Financial Manager; Communications Consultant. **Languages** Bulgarian, Croatian, Czech, English, Estonian, German, Greek, Hungarian, Macedonian, Romanian, Slovakian, Slovene, Spanish. **Staff** 20.00 FTE, paid. **Finance** Supported by: *Central European Initiative (CEI, #03708)*; *European Commission (EC, #06633)*. **Activities** Advocacy/lobbying/activism; awareness raising; capacity building; events/meetings; guidance/assistance/consulting; knowledge management/information dissemination; monitoring/evaluation; networking/liaising; projects/programmes; publishing activities; training/education. Legal service/legal advice/litigation. **Publications** http://www.justiceandenvironment.org/publications/.
Members Organizations in 14 countries:
Austria, Belgium, Bulgaria, Croatia, Czechia, Estonia, Germany, Greece, Hungary, North Macedonia, Romania, Slovakia, Slovenia, Spain.
Included in the above, 2 organizations listed in this Yearbook:
Frank Bold Society; *Instituto Internacional de Derecho y Medio Ambiente (IIDMA)*. [2023.02.14/XM5642/y/F]

♦ Association Kangourou sans Frontières (AKSF) 02775

Sec 7 rue de Castellane, 75008 Paris, France. E-mail: info@aksf.org.
URL: http://aksf.org/

History Jun 1994, Strasbourg (France). Current by-laws adopted 1996; revised 2004, 2008, 2011, 2017, 2018 and 2021. Former names and other names: *Kangourou sans Frontières* – alias. Registration: RNA, No/ID: W751120290, Start date: 1995, France. **Aims** Promote basic mathematical culture by every possible means. **Structure** General Assembly; Board of Directors. **Activities** Awards/prizes/competitions; events/meetings. **Events** *Annual Meeting* Istanbul (Türkiye) 2025, *Annual Meeting* Salvador (Brazil) 2024, *Annual Meeting* Ohrid (North Macedonia) 2023, *Annual Meeting* Cervia (Italy) 2022, *Annual Meeting* Antwerp (Belgium) 2021.
Members Active in 71 countries and territories:
Albania, Argentina, Armenia, Australia, Austria, Azerbaijan, Belarus, Belgium, Bolivia, Bosnia-Herzegovina, Brazil, Bulgaria, Canada, Chile, Colombia, Costa Rica, Croatia, Cyprus, Czechia, Denmark, Dominican Rep, Ecuador, Estonia, Finland, France, Germany, Greece, Hungary, India, Iran Islamic Rep, Israel, Italy, Kazakhstan, Kosovo, Latvia, Lithuania, Malaysia, Mexico, Moldova, Mongolia, Myanmar, Netherlands, Nigeria, North Macedonia, Norway, Pakistan, Panama, Paraguay, Philippines, Poland, Portugal, Puerto Rico, Romania, Russia, Saudi Arabia, Serbia, Singapore, Slovakia, Slovenia, Spain, Sweden, Switzerland, Tajikistan, Tunisia, Türkiye, UK, Ukraine, Uruguay, USA, Uzbekistan, Venezuela. [2022/AA2584/C]

♦ Association for Korean Studies in Europe (AKSE) 02776

Sec Inst of Oriental Studies, Fac of Philosophy and Letters, Univ of Rome Sapienza, Via Principe Amedeo 182b, 00185 Rome RM, Italy.
URL: http://koreanstudies.eu/

History 1977. **Aims** Stimulate and coordinate academic Korean studies in all countries of Europe; contribute to the spread of knowledge of Korea among a wider public. **Structure** Council. **Languages** English, French, German, Korean. **Staff** No permanent staff. **Finance** Members' dues. Contributions from sponsoring associations in Korea Rep. **Activities** Events/meetings. **Events** *Biennial Conference* Copenhagen (Denmark) 2023, *Biennial Conference* La Rochelle (France) 2021, *Biennial Conference* Rome (Italy) 2019, *Biennial Conference* Prague (Czechia) 2017, *Biennial Conference* Bochum (Germany) 2015. **Publications** *AKSE Newsletter* (annual).
Members Full: Ordinary (230); Honorary (19). Associate: Individual; Corporate. Individuals in 26 countries:
Austria, Belgium, Bulgaria, Canada, Croatia, Czechia, Denmark, Finland, France, Germany, Hungary, Ireland, Italy, Japan, Kazakhstan, Korea Rep, Netherlands, Poland, Romania, Russia, Slovakia, Spain, Sweden, Switzerland, UK, USA. [2018.06.14/XD5728/D]

- ♦ Association des laboratoires africains des routes / see Association africaine des laboratoires du bâtiment et des travaux publics (#02349)
- ♦ Association des laboratoires marins des Caraïbes (#02794)

♦ Association for Laboratory Phonology (labphon) 02777

Contact address not obtained. E-mail: admin@labphon.org.
URL: http://labphon.org/

History Current bylaws adopted Jan 2011. A US non-profit of the type 501(c)(3) . Registered in the District of Columbia (USA). **Aims** Promote the scientific study of the phonologies of diverse languages through the use of quantitative and laboratory methods. **Structure** Executive Council. Standing Committees. **Finance** Sources: members' dues. **Activities** Advocacy/lobbying/activism; events/meetings. **Events** *Conference on Laboratory Phonology* Seoul (Korea Rep) 2024, *Conference on Laboratory Phonology* 2022, *Conference on Laboratory Phonology* 2020, *Conference on Laboratory Phonology* Lisbon (Portugal) 2018. **Publications** *Laboratory Phonology* – journal. [2019/XM7956/C]

- ♦ Association of Labor and Management Administrators and Consultants on Alcoholism / see International Employee Assistance Professionals Association (#13264)
- ♦ Association of Lactose Manufacturers (inactive)
- ♦ Association of the Ladies of Charity of Saint-Vincent-de-Paul, Mission for the Sick Poor / see Association Internationale des Charités (#02675)
- ♦ Association laitière européenne (#06883)

♦ Association for Language Awareness (ALA) 02778

Pres School of Modern Languages and Literatures, Dept of English, Univ of Kassel, Kurt-Wolters-Strasse 5, 34109 Kassel, Germany. E-mail: languageaware@gmail.com.
URL: https://www.languageawareness.org/

History 12 Apr 1994. Registration: Charity Commission, No/ID: 1038988, England and Wales. **Aims** Support and promote activities across the whole breadth of language awareness. **Structure** Committee. **Finance** Sources: members' dues. **Activities** Advocacy/lobbying/activism; events/meetings; knowledge management/information dissemination. **Events** *International Conference* Bauru (Brazil) 2022, *International Conference* Geelong, VIC (Australia) 2020, *International Conference* Amsterdam (Netherlands) 2018, *International Conference* Vienna (Austria) 2016, *International Conference* Hamar (Norway) 2014. **Publications** *Language Awareness* (4 a year). [2022/AA1955/C]

♦ Association of Language Testers in Europe (ALTE) 02779

Association des centres d'evaluation en langues en Europe – Asociación Europea de Examinadores de Lenguas

Secretariat The Triangle Bldg, Shaftesbury Road, Cambridge, CB2 8EA, UK. T. +441223552828. Fax +441223553083. E-mail: secretariat@alte.org.
URL: http://www.alte.org/

History 1990. Registration: Charity Commission, No/ID: 1184799, England and Wales. **Aims** Promote multilingualism across Europe and beyond by supporting institutions which produce examinations and certification for language learners. **Structure** Meeting (biannual); Sub-groups (7); Secretariat. **Languages** English. **Staff** Paid; voluntary. **Finance** Sources: members' dues. **Activities** Events/meetings; standards/guidelines; training/education. **Events** *Conference* Paris (France) 2022, *International Digital Symposium* Madrid (Spain) 2021, *Meeting* Perugia (Italy) 2021, *Meeting* Istanbul (Turkey) 2020, *International Conference* Madrid (Spain) 2020. **Publications** *Guidelines for the Development of Language for Specific Purposes Tests* (2018); *Language Tests for Access, Integration and Citizenship: An Outline for Policy Makers* (2016); *Manual for Language Test Development and Examining* (2011).
Members Universities, ministries or charitable organizations (33 institutions in total) involved in language test development and production, representing 25 European languages, in 22 countries:
Austria, Belgium, Bulgaria, Czechia, Denmark, Estonia, Finland, France, Germany, Hungary, Ireland, Italy, Lithuania, Luxembourg, Norway, Poland, Portugal, Romania, Slovenia, Spain, Sweden, UK.
Consultative Status Consultative status granted from: *Council of Europe (CE, #04881)* (Participatory Status).
NGO Relations Member of (2): *European Civil Society Platform for Multilingualism (ECSPM, #06569)*; *European Institute for E-Learning (EIfEL, #07552)*. [2022.02.15/XD6458/D]

♦ Association of Language Travel Organizations (ALTO) 02780

Manager 259 Greenwich High Road, London, SE10 8NB, UK. T. +442032396551. E-mail: mailbox@altonet.org.
URL: http://www.altonet.org/

History 28 Sep 1998, Miami FL (USA), by *Federation of International Youth Travel Organizations (FIYTO, inactive)*. **Aims** Provide a global platform for leaders and decision makers within the language travel industry to further develop and let the industry grow through networking, professional development, idea and information exchange. **Structure** General Meeting (annual). Board, comprising Chairman, Treasurer and 4 members. Manager. **Languages** English. **Staff** 1.00 FTE, paid. **Finance** Members' dues. **Activities** Organizes conferences and seminars. **Events** *Conference* Lisbon (Portugal) 2019, *Conference* New York, NY (USA) 2015, *Annual general meeting / Conference* Rhodes Is (Greece) 2002, *Annual general meeting / Conference* Cancún (Mexico) 2001, *Conference* Düsseldorf (Germany) 2000.
Members Full in 31 countries and territories:
Albania, Argentina, Australia, Austria, Belgium, Brazil, Canada, Chile, Czechia, France, Germany, Hungary, Ireland, Italy, Japan, Korea Rep, Lebanon, Malta, Mexico, Monaco, Netherlands, Philippines, Russia, Saudi Arabia, South Africa, Spain, Sweden, Switzerland, Türkiye, UK, USA. [2016/XD6773/D]

- ♦ Association de langue française pour l'étude du diabète et des maladies métaboliques / see Société Francophone du Diabète (#19468)
- ♦ Association de la langue française pour l'étude du stress et du trauma / see Association de la langue française de l'étude du stress et du traumatisme (#02781)

♦ Association de la langue française de l'étude du stress et du traumatisme (ALFEST) 02781

SG PAV/ALFEST, 12 rue Charles Fourier, 75013 Paris, France. T. +33145884100.
URL: http://www.alfest-trauma.com/

History Founded 1990. Previously also referred to as *Association de la langue française pour l'étude du stress et du trauma*. **Aims** Unite academics and experts specialized in the field of trauma so as to learn more about hospitalization and let psychotherapeutic practices evolve. **Structure** Bureau. **Languages** French. **Staff** Voluntary. **Finance** Members' dues. **Activities** Organizes: 2 or more scientific days annually; international colloquium. **Publications** *Traumas: la revue de l'alfest* (6 a year).
Members in 8 countries:
Algeria, Argentina, Belgium, Canada, France, Luxembourg, Morocco, Switzerland.
NGO Relations *Australasian Society for Traumatic Stress Studies (ASTSS, #03029)*; *European Society for Traumatic Stress Studies (ESTSS, #08769)*; *International Society for Traumatic Stress Studies (ISTSS, #15518)*. [2016/XD6492/D]

♦ Association pour les Langues et Cultures Européennes Menacées (ALCEM) 02782

SG 84 rue des 3 Frères Carasso, 13004 Marseille, France. T. +33491490974.
Pres address not obtained.
URL: https://www.alcem.net/

History 1 May 1962, Lund (Sweden). Statutes adopted 31 Jul 1967, Issime (Italy). Statutes amended: 25 Jul 1972, Celovec (Austria); 23 Jul 1982, Montpellier (France); 1984. Original title: *Association internationale pour la défense des langues et cultures menacées (AIDLCM) – International Association for the Defence of Menaced Languages and Cultures – Asociación Internacional para la Defensa de las Lenguas y Culturas Amenazadas – Internationaler Verband zum Schutz Bedrohter Sprachen und Kulturen – Associazione Internazionale per la Difesa delle Lingue e Culture Minacciate – Asocio Internacia por la Defendo de la Minacataj Lingvoj kaj Kulturoj*. Current title adopted 2011. Registered first in accordance with Swiss law. Registered in accordance with French law in 1999, Morlaix (France). Currently registered in accordance with Belgian law; headquarters in Liège (Belgium). **Aims** Create and maintain in all countries an opinion in favour of, and defend and promote, languages and cultures threatened with extinction either as a whole or in a certain part of their traditional territory, through decadence, corruption or suppression as a result of discrimination in education or public life. **Structure** General Assembly (at least every 2 years); Federal Council, consisting of a permanent member and deputy of each member association and including the Officers – President, 4 Vice-Presidents, Secretary-General, 1 or more Deputy Secretaries-General, Treasurer and Territorial Secretaries – who comprise the Federal Bureau. **Languages** Accepts all languages spoken by members or under threat of extinction. **Staff** Voluntary. **Finance** Members' dues: Individuals euro 15; Associations euro 30. **Activities** Events/meetings; knowledge management/information dissemination; research/documentation. **Events** *Congrès* Klagenfurt am Wörthersee (Austria) 2022, *Congrès* Klagenfurt am Wörthersee (Austria) / Celovec (Austria) 2021, *Congrès* Klagenfurt am Wörthersee (Austria) 2020, *Congrès* Nice (France) 2018, *Congrès* Huesca (Spain) 2015. **Publications** Articles.
Members Associations; individuals. Members in 7 countries:
Austria, Belgium, France, Italy, Portugal, Slovenia, Spain. [2021/XC4588/C]

- ♦ Association des langues et littératures des universités d'Australasie (#03033)
- ♦ Association des langues vivantes pour l'Afrique occidentale (inactive)
- ♦ Association Latina-américaine de Droit pénal et Criminologie (unconfirmed)
- ♦ Association of Latin American and Caribbean Refugees (internationally oriented national body)
- ♦ Association of Latin American Composers of Art Music (#04092)
- ♦ Association of Latin American Faculties, Schools and Institutes of Law (#02129)

♦ Association of Latin American Faculties and Schools of Public Accountancy 02783

Association des facultés et des écoles latinoaméricaines de comptabilité publique – Asociación Latinoamericana de Facultades y Escuelas de Contaduria Administración (ALAFEC)

Exec Sec Univ Nacional Autónoma de México, Ciudad Universitaria, Fac de Contaduria y Admón, Circuito Ext s/n, 04570 Mexico City CDMX, Mexico. E-mail: trosales@fca.unam.mx.
SG Univ Popular Autónoma del Estado de Puebla, Escuela de Administración 21 Sur, 1103 CP, 72160 Puebla, Mexico. T. +52222299495.
URL: http://www.alafec.unam.mx/

History 17 Jun 1982, under the auspices of *Association of Universities of Latin America and the Caribbean (#02970)*. Previously also referred to as *Asociación de Facultades y Escuelas de Contaduria Pública de América Latina*. **Structure** General Assembly; Executive Committee. **Events** *Biennial general assembly / General Assembly* Lima (Peru) 2010, *Biennial general assembly / General Assembly* Guayaquil (Ecuador) 2009, *Biennial General Assembly* Santo Domingo (Dominican Rep) 2007, *Biennial General Assembly* Havana (Cuba) 2005, *Biennial general assembly / General Assembly* Mérida (Mexico) 2003. **Publications** *Revista Alafec* – online.
Members Membership countries not specified. [2019/XD7323/D]

- ♦ Association of Latin American Faculties of Systems Engineering (inactive)
- ♦ Association of Latin American Lawyers for the Defense of Human Rights (no recent information)
- ♦ Association of Latin American Marine Scientists (inactive)
- ♦ Association of Latin American Reinsurers (no recent information)

♦ Association of Latin American Schools and Institutes of Economy . 02784

Association des facultés, écoles et instituts d'économie d'Amérique latine – Asociación de Facultades, Escuelas e Institutos de Economia de América Latina (AFEIEAL)

Pres UNAM – Fac Economia, Circuito Interior s/n, Ciudad Univ, Coyoacan, 04510, 24107 Mexico City CDMX, Mexico.
SG address not obtained. E-mail: iph@servidor.unam.mx.
URL: http://www.economia.unam.mx/afeieal/

History 4 Dec 1953, Santiago (Chile), with the assistance of *Association of Universities of Latin America and the Caribbean (#02970)*. **Structure** Executive Council, comprising President, Secretary-General, 8 Vice-Presidents. **Events** *Conference* Mexico City (Mexico) 2011, *Conference* Maracaibo (Venezuela) 2010, *Conference* Mexico 2009, *Conference* Mexico City (Mexico) 2008, *Conference* Puebla (Mexico) 2006. **Members** Membership countries not specified. [2012/XD9362/**D**]

- ♦ Association of Latin-American Schools of Urbanism and Planning (#02212)
- ♦ Association latine pour l'analyse des systèmes de santé (#02171)
- ♦ Association latinoaméricaine des académies nationales de médecine (#02175)
- ♦ Association latinoaméricaine d'administration publique (inactive)
- ♦ Association latinoaméricaine d'agriculture scientifique (inactive)
- ♦ Association latinoaméricaine de l'analyse et de la modification du comportement (#02179)
- ♦ Association latinoaméricaine d'analyse transactionnelle (no recent information)
- ♦ Association latinoaméricaine des archives (#02183)
- ♦ Association latinoaméricaine des armateurs (#16369)
- ♦ Association latinoaméricaine de biotechnologie et de biotechnique (unconfirmed)
- ♦ Association latinoaméricaine et des Caraïbes des entreprises d'eau potable et d'assainissement (no recent information)
- ♦ Association latinoaméricaine et des Caraïbes d'études sur les femmes (inactive)
- ♦ Association latinoaméricaine des centres anti-poisons (inactive)
- ♦ Association latinoaméricaine des centres d'éducation coopérative (no recent information)
- ♦ Association latinoaméricaine des chemins de fer (#16365)
- ♦ Association latinoaméricaine de chercheurs sur la communication (#02237)
- ♦ Association latinoaméricaine de communicateurs démographiques (inactive)
- ♦ Association latinoaméricaine des corporations régionales de développement (inactive)
- ♦ Association latinoaméricaine de dessin industriel / see Latin American Association of Design (#16238)
- ♦ Association latinoaméricaine pour le développement des assurances agricoles et du bétail (#02205)
- ♦ Association latinoaméricaine por le développement et l'intégration des femmes (inactive)
- ♦ Association latinoaméricaine de dragage (inactive)
- ♦ Association latinoaméricaine pour le droit constitutionnel (no recent information)
- ♦ Association latinoaméricaine pour les droits de l'homme (#16243)
- ♦ Association latinoaméricaine pour l'écodéveloppement (inactive)
- ♦ Association latinoaméricaine des écoles de bibliothéconomie et des sciences de l'information (inactive)
- ♦ Association latinoaméricaine d'écoles et de facultés de sciences infirmières (#02211)
- ♦ Association latinoaméricaine des écoles de service social (inactive)
- ♦ Association latinoaméricaine d'éducation agricole supérieure (no recent information)
- ♦ Association latinoaméricaine d'éducation et de communication populaire (#02207)
- ♦ Association latinoaméricaine d'éducation ménagère (inactive)
- ♦ Association latinoaméricaine d'éducation radiophonique / see Asociación Latinoamericana de Educación y Comunicación Popular (#02207)
- ♦ Association latinoaméricaine d'énergie solaire (inactive)
- ♦ Association latinoaméricaine pour l'étude du foie (#16252)
- ♦ Association latinoaméricaine d'étude des mutagènes, carcinogènes et tératogènes présents dans l'environnement (#16240)
- ♦ Association latino-américaine d'études afro-asiatiques (#16236)
- ♦ Association latinoaméricaine des études universitaires de relations publiques (#02192)
- ♦ Association latinoaméricaine des évaluateurs de projets (inactive)
- ♦ Association latinoaméricaine des exportateurs de viande (inactive)
- ♦ Association latinoaméricaine des facultés et écoles de médecine (#16245)
- ♦ Association latinoaméricaine de génétique (#02225)
- ♦ Association latinoaméricaine des industriels et des chambres de l'industrie de l'alimentation (inactive)
- ♦ Association latinoaméricaine des industries pharmaceutiques (#02232)
- ♦ Association latinoaméricaine des industries plastiques (no recent information)
- ♦ Association latinoaméricaine d'institutions pour le financement du développement (#02233)
- ♦ Association latinoaméricaine d'intégration (#16343)
- ♦ Association latinoaméricaine de libre échange (inactive)
- ♦ Association latinoaméricaine des matières réfractaires (#16244)
- ♦ Association latinoaméricaine de microbiologie (#16247)
- ♦ Association latinoaméricaine de muséologie (inactive)
- ♦ Association latinoaméricaine des opérateurs de tourisme (inactive)
- ♦ Association latinoaméricaine de paléobotanique et palinologie (#02249)
- ♦ Association latinoaméricaine de pédiatrie (#16360)
- ♦ Association latinoaméricaine de pharmacologie (#16249)
- ♦ Association latinoaméricaine de physique médicale (#16246)
- ♦ Association latinoaméricaine des producteurs de verre (no recent information)
- ♦ Association latinoaméricaine pour la production animale (#02257)
- ♦ Association latinoaméricaine pour la promotion de l'habitat, de l'architecture et de l'urbanisme (inactive)
- ♦ Association latinoaméricaine de psychiatrie (#16363)
- ♦ Association latinoaméricaine de psychologie sociale (inactive)
- ♦ Association latinoaméricaine pour la qualité (inactive)
- ♦ Association latinoaméricaine de recherches institutionnelles (inactive)
- ♦ Association latinoaméricaine de recherches sur la reproduction humaine (#02238)
- ♦ Association latinoaméricaine de récréation et de loisirs (inactive)
- ♦ Association latinoaméricaine des rédacteurs de périodiques de biologie (inactive)
- ♦ Association latinoaméricaine de rédacteurs de publications spécialisées dans les sciences de la terre (inactive)
- ♦ Association latinoaméricaine des sciences physiologiques (#16250)
- ♦ Association latinoaméricaine des sociétés de biologie et médecine nucléaires (#16251)
- ♦ Association latinoaméricaine des sociétés commerciales internationales (no recent information)
- ♦ Association latinoaméricaine de sociologie (#02267)
- ♦ Association latinoaméricaine de sociologie rurale (#16368)
- ♦ Association latinoaméricaine pour les technologies alternatives (inactive)
- ♦ Association latinoaméricaine de transport autoroutier (inactive)
- ♦ Association latino-ibero-américaine de gestion technologique / see Asociación Latino-Iberoamericana de Gestión Tecnológica y de la Innovación (#02277)
- ♦ Association of Latin-Speaking Electro-Radiologists (inactive)

♦ Association for Law, Property and Society (ALPS) 02785

Treas address not obtained.
URL: http://www.alps-law.org/

Aims Encourage dialogue across and among people in many disciplines who are interested in property law, policy, and theory. **Structure** Board of Directors. Committees (3): Outreach; Program; Mentoring. **Activities** Awards/prizes/competitions; events/meetings. **Events** *Annual Conference* Syracuse, NY (USA) 2019, *Annual Conference* Maastricht (Netherlands) 2018, *Annual Conference* Ann Arbor, MI (USA) 2017, *Annual Conference* Belfast (UK) 2016, *Annual Conference* Athens, GA (USA) 2015. **Publications** *ALPS Law Journal*. [2019/XM7815/**C**]

♦ Association of Learned and Professional Society Publishers (ALPSP) 02786

Chief Exec Egale 1, 80 St Albans Road, Watford, WD17 1DL, UK. E-mail: admin@alpsp.org.
Conference and Events Manager address not obtained.
URL: http://www.alpsp.org/

History 1972. Revised version of the Constitution adopted Nov 1994. Registration: Companies House, No/ID: 04081634, Start date: 2 Oct 2000, England and Wales; EU Transparency Register, No/ID: 11119336625-36, Start date: 9 Sep 2011. **Aims** Connect, inform, develop and represent the international scholarly and professional publishing community. **Structure** General Assembly (annual); Council; Committees (5); Working Groups. **Languages** English. **Staff** 8.00 FTE, paid. **Finance** Sources: fees for services; meeting proceeds; members' dues; sale of publications; sponsorship. Annual budget: 900,000 GBP. **Activities** Awards/prizes/competitions; events/meetings; training/education. **Events** *Conference* UK 2022, *Conference* 2021, *Conference* Manchester (UK) 2020, *Conference* Windsor (UK) 2019, *Conference* Windsor (UK) 2018. **Publications** *ALPSP Alert* (12 a year); *Learned Publishing* (4 a year); *Policy Bulletin* (4 a year).
Members Full; Associate; Honorary. Members in 32 countries and territories:
Australia, Austria, Brazil, Canada, China, Croatia, Denmark, Finland, France, Germany, Greece, Hong Kong, Hungary, India, Ireland, Italy, Jamaica, Korea Rep, Lithuania, Netherlands, New Zealand, Norway, Pakistan, Qatar, Slovenia, Spain, Sweden, Switzerland, UK, Ukraine, United Arab Emirates, USA.
NGO Relations Member of (1): *International Council for Scientific and Technical Information (ICSTI, #13070)*. [2022.02.14/XD1212/ty/**D**]

- ♦ Association Learning and Assisting Overseas (internationally oriented national body)
- ♦ Association for Learning Environments (internationally oriented national body)

♦ Association des léprologues de langue française (ALLF) 02787

Association of French-Language Leprologists

SG 4 Rue Jean Jacques Bel, 33000 Bordeaux, France. T. +33556523214. Fax +33556523214. E-mail: maheant@yahoo.fr.
Registered Office Centre René Labusquière, Université Victor Ségalen Bordeaux 2, 146 rue Léo-Saignat, 33076 Bordeaux CEDEX, France.
URL: https://allf.medicalistes.fr/

History 1959, Hammamet (Tunisia). **Aims** Ensure cooperation among French language countries in leprosy research and control; promote technical, scientific and administrative collaboration and facilitate exchanges in all branches of the field. **Structure** General Assembly (meeting as required) elects Bureau, which includes an Executive Committee consisting of President, Secretary General and Treasurer. **Languages** French. **Staff** 1.50 FTE, voluntary. **Finance** Sources: gifts, legacies; members' dues; subsidies. **Activities** Projects depending on financial resources. **Events** *Congress* Yaoundé (Cameroon) 1996, *La lèpre – clinique thérapeutique, immunologie, épidémiologie* Bamako (Mali) 1992. **Publications** *Le Bulletin de l'ALLF* (2 a year) in French.
Members Collective; Individual Honorary; Corresponding; Technical Advisors. Individuals in 38 countries:
Algeria, Argentina, Australia, Belgium, Benin, Brazil, Burkina Faso, Cameroon, Canada, Central African Rep, Chad, Congo Brazzaville, Congo DR, Côte d'Ivoire, Ethiopia, France, Gabon, Germany, Guinea, Haiti, India, Italy, Lebanon, Madagascar, Mali, Mauritania, Morocco, Netherlands, Niger, Senegal, Spain, Switzerland, Togo, Tunisia, UK, USA, Vietnam, Zimbabwe.
IGO Relations *WHO (#20950)*. **NGO Relations** *Raoul Follereau International Union (#18618)* (French association). [2022/XD4272/v/**C**]

- ♦ Association of Lesbian and Gay Writers Living in Europe (inactive)
- ♦ Association of Libraries of Judaica and Hebraica in Europe (inactive)
- ♦ Association de libre-échange des Caraïbes (inactive)
- ♦ Association pro un Lingua Auxiliari International (inactive)

♦ Association for Linguistic Typology (ALT) 02788

Sec-Treas address not obtained. E-mail: honohiiri@yandex.ru.
URL: http://linguistic-typology.org/

History Mar 1994. Inaugural meeting Sep 1995, Vitoria-Gasteiz (Spain). **Aims** Advance scientific study of typology. **Structure** Executive Committee, including President, Secretary-Treasurer. **Finance** Members' dues. **Activities** Organizes meetings and workshops. **Events** *Biennial Conference / Biennial Meeting* Albuquerque, NM (USA) 2015, *Biennial Conference / Biennial Meeting* Leipzig (Germany) 2013, *Biennial Conference / Biennial Meeting* Hong Kong (Hong Kong) 2011, *Biennial Conference / Biennial Meeting* Berkeley, CA (USA) 2009, *Biennial conference / Biennial Meeting* Paris (France) 2007. **Publications** *Linguistic Typology* (3 a year); *ALT News*; *World Atlas of Language Structures*.
Members Individuals (391) in 43 countries and territories:
Australia, Austria, Belgium, Canada, Croatia, Czechia, Denmark, Egypt, Finland, France, Germany, Hong Kong, Hungary, India, Ireland, Israel, Italy, Jamaica, Japan, Malaysia, Mali, Malta, Mexico, Morocco, Netherlands, New Zealand, Norway, Peru, Philippines, Poland, Russia, Serbia, Singapore, Slovenia, South Africa, Spain, Sweden, Switzerland, Taiwan, Thailand, UK, Ukraine, USA. [2018/XD6626/**D**]

- ♦ Association linguistique du Canada et des Etats Unis (internationally oriented national body)
- ♦ Association linguistique interméditerranéenne (inactive)
- ♦ Association for Literary and Linguistic Computing / see European Association for Digital Humanities (#06014)
- ♦ Association for Literary Urban Studies (internationally oriented national body)
- ♦ Association littéraire et artistique internationale (#14058)
- ♦ Association of the Local Democracy Agencies / see European Association for Local Democracy (#06110)
- ♦ Association of Local and Regional Authorities of Europe / see Council of European Municipalities and Regions (#04891)

♦ Association of Logic, Language and Information (FoLLI) 02789

Sec address not obtained. E-mail: secretary@folli.info.
URL: http://www.folli.info/

History 1991. Former names and other names: *European Association of Logic, Language and Information* – former. Registration: Netherlands. **Aims** Advance the practice of research and education at the interfaces between logic, linguistics, computer science and cognitive science and related disciplines; represent members views at local, national and international levels. **Structure** General Meeting (annual); Management Board. **Languages** English. **Finance** Members' dues. **Activities** Training/education; publishing activities; events/meetings; awards/prizes/competitions; research/documentation. **Publications** *Journal of Logic, Language and Information (JoLLI)*. *Studies in Logic, Language and Information (SiLLI)* – book series.
Members Individuals (219) in 30 countries and territories:
Australia, Belgium, Brazil, Bulgaria, Canada, Chile, Cuba, Czechia, Denmark, France, Germany, Hungary, Ireland, Israel, Italy, Japan, Netherlands, Norway, Oman, Poland, Portugal, Russia, South Africa, Spain, Sweden, Taiwan, Türkiye, UK, Ukraine, USA.
NGO Relations Member of (2): *International Federation for Computational Logic (IFCoLog, #13397)*; *International Union of History and Philosophy of Science and Technology (IUHPST, #15779)* (Division of Logic, Methodology and Philosophy of Science and Technology (DLMPST)). Cooperates with (2): *European Science Foundation (ESF, #08441)*; *Expert Advisory Group on Language Engineering Standards (EAGLES, inactive)*. Sponsors: *Workshop on Logic, Language, Information and Computation (WoLLIC)*. [2020/XD4669/v/**D**]

♦ Association of Logic Programming (ALP) 02790

Sec and Dir Dept of Computer Science, State University of New York at Stony Brook, Stony Brook NY 11794-4400, USA. T. +15166328454. Fax +15166328334.
URL: http://www.logicprogramming.org/

History 1986, London (UK). **Aims** Contribute to the development of Logic Programming; relate it to other formal and also to humanistic sciences; promote its uses in academia and industry all over the world. **Structure** Elected Executive Committee, including President, Past President, Secretary, Treasurer. **Events** *International Conference on Logic Programming / Conference* Vienna (Austria) 2014, *International Conference on Logic Programming / Conference* Budapest (Hungary) 2012, *International Conference on Logic Programming / Conference* Lexington, KY (USA) 2011, *Conference* Edinburgh (UK) 2010, *Conference* Pasadena, CA (USA) 2009. **Publications** *Theory and Practice of Logic Programming*. Conference proceedings.
Members Affiliated societies (4) in 4 countries:
France, Germany, Italy, UK.

Association Loteries Afrique
02791

alphabetic sequence excludes
For the complete listing, see Yearbook Online at

Individuals in 58 countries and territories:
Australia, Bulgaria, Canada, China, Croatia, Cyprus, Czechia, Denmark, Dominican Rep, Egypt, Estonia, Finland, France, Georgia, Germany, Greece, Hong Kong, Hungary, Iceland, India, Indonesia, Iraq, Ireland, Israel, Italy, Japan, Korea Rep, Latvia, Liechtenstein, Lithuania, Luxembourg, Malta, Mexico, Netherlands, New Zealand, Norway, Philippines, Poland, Portugal, Puerto Rico, Romania, Russia, Saudi Arabia, Serbia, Singapore, Slovakia, Slovenia, Spain, Sri Lanka, Sweden, Switzerland, Thailand, Türkiye, UK, Ukraine, USA, Venezuela, Vietnam.
NGO Relations Member of: *International Federation for Computational Logic (IFCoLog, #13397).* [2014/XD6618/**D**]

♦ Association des Loteries d'Afrique (ALA) 02791

African Lotteries Association
Main Office 33 Boulevard Rachidi, 20070 Casablanca, Morocco. E-mail: sg_ala@africanlotteries.com.
URL: https://www.africanlotteries.com/

History 1981, Dakar (Senegal). Former names and other names: *Association des PMU et des loteries d'Afrique* – former (1981); *African Association of States Lotteries* – former alias; *Association africaine des loteries d'état (AALE)* – former alias; *Association des pari mutuel urbain et des loteries d'Afrique* – former alias. **Aims** Unite African lotteries. **Structure** General Assembly (annual); Executive Committee. **Events** *Legal and Tax Seminar* Abidjan (Côte d'Ivoire) 2019, *Congress* Casablanca (Morocco) 2019, *Lottery organisations and corporate social responsibility* Dakar (Senegal) 2014, *Congress* Johannesburg (South Africa) 2003.
Members African State lotteries in 9 countries:
Benin, Burkina Faso, Congo Brazzaville, Congo DR, Côte d'Ivoire, Mali, Niger, Senegal, Togo.
NGO Relations Regional association of: *World Lottery Association (WLA, #21628).* [2021/XD1296/**D**]

- ♦ Association de Louvain pour la coopération au développement / see Louvain Coopération
- ♦ Association for Low Flow Anaesthesia (no recent information)
- ♦ Association luthérienne de l'Asie du Sud-Est pour l'enseignement supérieur (inactive)
- ♦ Association de lutte contre le sida (internationally oriented national body)
- ♦ Association for Machine Translation in the Americas (internationally oriented national body)
- ♦ Association maçonnique internationale (inactive)
- ♦ Association des magistrats et juges du Commonwealth (#04349)
- ♦ Association des Magistrats de l'Union Européenne (#07614)
- ♦ Association de magnétisme et électricité terrestres de l'UISG / see International Association of Geomagnetism and Aeronomy (#11916)
- ♦ Association Maison Chance (#16550)
- ♦ Association des maisons internationales (inactive)
- ♦ Association of Maize Researchers in Africa (no recent information)
- ♦ Association of the Maize Starch Industries of the EEC / see Starch Europe (#19966)
- ♦ Association of Management Development Institutions in French-Speaking Africa (no recent information)

♦ Association of Management Development Institutions in South Asia (AMDISA) 02792

Exec Dir Univ of Hyderabad Campus, Central Univ Post Office, Hyderabad, Telangana 500046, Hyderabad TELANGANA 500046, India. T. +914023013346. Fax +914023013346. E-mail: amdisa.org@gmail.com – amdisa@amdisa.org.
Pres Sukkur IBA University, Air Port Road, Sukkur 65200, Pakistan.
URL: https://www.amdisa.org/

History 1989, Kathmandu (Nepal). Founded with the initial support of *Commonwealth Secretariat (#04362), International Management Development Network (INTERMAN, no recent information), Canadian International Development Agency (CIDA, inactive)* and the Canadian Federation of Deans of Management and Business Schools. **Aims** Promote management education and management development activities in South Asia, taking into account the economic, social and cultural context of the Region, with firm dedication to worldwide exchange of experience and ideas in the fields concerned. **Structure** General Assembly (every 2 years); Executive Board; Committees (8). **Languages** English. **Staff** 18.00 FTE, paid. **Finance** Sources: members' dues. Other sources: accreditation fees; journal subscriptions; project support from organizations. **Activities** Certification/accreditation; events/meetings; networking/liaising; research/documentation. **Events** *Biennial South Asian Management Forum and Academic Conference* Dhaka (Bangladesh) 2021, *Biennial South Asian Management Forum and Academic Conference* Sukkur (Pakistan) 2019, *Biennial South Asian Management Forum and Academic Conference* Malé (Maldives) 2017, *Biennial South Asian Management Forum and Academic Conference* Colombo (Sri Lanka) 2015, *International Conference on Accreditation for Institutional Learning and Growth* Hyderabad (India) 2015. **Publications** *South Asian Journal of Management* (4 a year); *AMDISA Newsletter* (3 a year). Studies; books; reports; recommendations.
Members Affiliate (7); Institutional (280); Corporate (1); Reciprocal (15). Institutional and Corporate Members in 9 countries:
Afghanistan, Bangladesh, Bhutan, India, Maldives, Nepal, Pakistan, Sri Lanka, United Arab Emirates.
Reciprocal members in 12 countries:
Belgium, Canada, India, Kazakhstan, Kenya, Nigeria, Philippines, Romania, Russia, UK, USA, Venezuela.
IGO Relations *South Asian Association for Regional Cooperation (SAARC, #19721).* **NGO Relations** *AACSB International – Association to Advance Collegiate Schools of Business; CEEMAN – International Association for Management Development in Dynamic Societies (CEEMAN, #03625); Commonwealth Association for Public Administration and Management (CAPAM, #04310); EFMD – The Management Development Network (#05387).* [2022.02.25/XD2454/**D**]

- ♦ Association for Management Education and Development (internationally oriented national body)
- ♦ Association of Management Training Institutions of Eastern and Southern Africa (no recent information)
- ♦ Association of Manufacturers of Animal-Derived Food Enzymes (no recent information)
- ♦ Association of Manufacturers of Fermentation Enzyme Products / see Association of Manufacturers and Formulators of Enzyme Products (#02793)

♦ Association of Manufacturers and Formulators of Enzyme Products (AMFEP) 02793

Gen Sec c/o Kellen, Av de Tervueren 188A, Box 4, 1150 Brussels, Belgium. T. +3227611677. Fax +3227611699. E-mail: amfep@kellencompany.com.
URL: http://www.amfep.org/

History 1 Aug 1977, Brussels (Belgium). Statutes amended by General Assembly, Oct 2015. Former names and other names: *Association of Microbial Food Enzyme Producers within the EEC* – former (1977); *Association des producteurs d'enzymes dans la CEE* – former (1977); *Association of Microbial Food Enzyme Producers in Western Europe* – former; *Association of Manufacturers of Fermentation Enzyme Products* – former (1995). **Aims** Represent, promote and defend the interests, safe use and regulatory framework of manufacturers and formulators of enzyme products. **Structure** General Assembly (annual); Executive Committee; Food Enzymes Committee; Feed Enzymes Committee; Technical Enzymes Committee; Expert Groups. **Languages** English. **Staff** 2.00 FTE, paid. **Finance** Sources: members' dues. **Events** *Annual General Assembly* Røskilde (Denmark) 2012, *Annual General Assembly* Barcelona (Spain) 2006, *Annual General Assembly* Odense (Denmark) 2005, *Annual General Assembly* Bruges (Belgium) 2004, *Annual General Assembly* Paris (France) 2003. **Publications** *Microbial Enzymes and Their Uses*; *Regulatory Aspects of Microbial Food Enzymes*; *Safety Aspects of Enzymes Produced by Genetically Modified Micro-Organismes*; *The Classification and Labelling of Microbial Enzyme Preparations*; *The Safe Handling of Microbial Enzyme Preparations*. **Members** Companies (31). Membership countries not specified. **IGO Relations** Liaises with: *European Community (inactive).* Recognized by: *European Commission (EC, #06633).* Participates as observer in the activities of: *Codex Alimentarius Commission (CAC, #04081).* **NGO Relations** Member of: *EU Specialty Food Ingredients (#09200); International Association for Soaps, Detergents and Maintenance Products (#12166).* [2021.09.01/XE1636/**D**]

- ♦ Association of Manufacturers and Importers of Chain Saws in Europe (inactive)
- ♦ Association of Manufacturers of Polyester Film (inactive)
- ♦ Association des marathons internationaux / see Association of International Marathons and Distance Races (#02756)
- ♦ Association Marcel Hicter (internationally oriented national body)
- ♦ Association Marcel Hicter pour la démocratie culturelle / see Association Marcel Hicter
- ♦ Association des marchands de coton en Europe (#02457)
- ♦ Association of the Margarine Industry of the EC Countries / see European Margarine Association (#07736)
- ♦ Association marinecultures.org / see marinecultures.org

♦ Association of Marine Laboratories of the Caribbean (AMLC) 02794

Association des laboratoires marins des Caraïbes – Asociación de Laboratorios Marinos del Caribe
Exec Dir 800 17th St NW, Washington DC 20006, USA. E-mail: ron.oleynik@hklaw.com – mdenni12@utk.edu.
Pres address not obtained.
URL: http://www.amlc-carib.org/

History 1957. Former names and other names: *Association of Island Marine Laboratories* – former (1957 to 1964); *Association of Island Marine Laboratories of the Caribbean (AIMLC)* – former (1964); *Association of Island Laboratories of the Caribbean* – former (1988). **Aims** Advance common interest in marine sciences by arranging meetings, fostering personal and official relations among members and assisting or initiating cooperative research programmes. **Structure** Board of Directors. **Languages** English, Spanish. **Staff** 10.00 FTE, voluntary. **Finance** Sources: donations; members' dues. **Activities** Events/meetings. **Events** *Biennial Scientific Meeting* Punta Cana (Dominican Rep) 2019, *Annual Meeting* Calabash Caye (Belize) 2018, *Biennial Scientific Meeting* Mérida (Mexico) 2017, *Annual Meeting* Willemstad (Curaçao) 2015, *Biennial Scientific Meeting* Willemstad (Curaçao) 2015. **Publications** Conference proceedings.
Members Institutional: laboratories (37) of the subtropical Atlantic and Caribbean; Individual: staff members (350) of such laboratories and scientists. Members in 40 countries and territories:
Alabama, Australia, Austria, Bahamas, Barbados, Belize, Bermuda, Bonaire Is, Brazil, Canada, Cayman Is, Colombia, Costa Rica, Cuba, Curaçao, Dominica, Dominican Rep, Florida, Georgia, Germany, Grenada, Jamaica, Japan, Louisiana, Mexico, Mississippi, Netherlands, Panama, Puerto Rico, St Lucia, St Vincent-Grenadines, Texas, Trinidad-Tobago, Turks-Caicos, UK, USA, Venezuela, Virgin Is UK, Virgin Is USA.
Included in the above, 3 organizations listed in this Yearbook:
Caribbean Research and Management of Biodiversity (CARMABI); Central Caribbean Marine Institute (CCMI); Coral Restoration Foundation (CRF).
NGO Relations Member of (1): *World Association of Marine Stations (WAMS, #21161).* [2022/XD4682/**D**]

- ♦ Association maritime chrétienne internationale (#12561)
- ♦ Association of Maritime Education and Training Institutions in Asia Pacific / see Global Maritime Education and Training Association (#10464)
- ♦ Association of Maritime, Road and Air Transport Users in the Central American Isthmus (no recent information)
- ♦ Association de marketing pour les hôtels / see Hospitality Sales and Marketing Association International (#10948)
- ♦ Association des marques des Etats-Unis / see International Trademark Association (#15706)
- ♦ Association for Mass Media and Communication Culture on the Balkans / see Balkanmedia Association (#03077)
- ♦ Association for Mass Spectrometry & Advances in the Clinical Lab (unconfirmed)
- ♦ Association mastologie Nord et Sud Méditerranée / see Mobile Mediterranean University of Mastology (#16836)

♦ Association of MBAs (AMBA) 02795

CEO 25 Hosier Lane, London, EC1A 9LQ, UK. T. +442072462686. Fax +442072462687.
URL: https://www.associationofmbas.com/

History Jun 1967. Former names and other names: *Business Graduates Association (BGA)* – former (Jun 1967 to 1987). **Aims** Achieve international recognition as the authoritative voice in *postgraduate management education*. **Structure** International Management Board. **Languages** English. **Activities** Serves as accreditation body for Master in Business Administration programmes worldwide. Also accredits Doctor of Business Administration and Masters in Management degrees. Organizes: events for business school staff; fairs for potential students; networking events; annual Gala Dinner. **Events** *AMBA & BGA Latin America Conference for Deans and Directors* Cartagena de Indias (Colombia) 2022, *Global Deans and Directors Conference* Stockholm (Sweden) 2022, *Global Deans and Directors Conference* Istanbul (Turkey) 2019, *Business School Professionals Conference* Vienna (Austria) 2019, *Global Deans and Directors Conference* Stockholm (Sweden) 2018. **Publications** *Ambition* (4 a year) – magazine; *Business Leadership Review* (4 a year); *MBAworld* (24 a year) – electronic newsletter. *Official Guide to Choosing an MBA*. **Members** MBA students and graduates (9,000) in 88 countries. Corporate members (Business Schools). Membership countries not specified. **NGO Relations** Co-convenor of: *Principles for Responsible Management Education (PRME, #18500).* Member of: *EFMD – The Management Development Network (#05387).* [2021/XJ2427/**F**]

- ♦ Association de médecine aéronautique et spatiale (internationally oriented national body)
- ♦ Association de médecine endocrinienne d'Amérique centrale et des Caraïbes (inactive)
- ♦ Association des médecins de langue française de l'hémisphère américain (unconfirmed)
- ♦ Association des médias électroniques indépendants d'Asie centrale (no recent information)
- ♦ Association for Medical Deans in Europe / see Association of Medical Schools in Europe (#02799)
- ♦ Association of Medical Doctors of Asia (internationally oriented national body)
- ♦ Association médicale arménienne mondiale (unconfirmed)
- ♦ Association médicale du Commonwealth (#04351)

♦ Association for Medical Education in the Eastern Mediterranean Region (AMEEMR) 02796

Pres PO Box 22490, Mail Code 3133, Riyadh 11426, Saudi Arabia. T. +966114299999ext95209. E-mail: ame-emr@ksau-hs.edu.sa.
URL: http://ame-emr.org/ameemr/

History Set as *Association of Medical Schools in the Middle East (AMSME) – Association des écoles de médecine du Moyen-Orient.* Previously also referred to as *Association for Medical Education in the Middle East.* One of 6 regional organizations of *World Federation for Medical Education (WFME, #21454).* **Aims** Advance high scientific and ethical standards in medical education and innovative management of medical education focusing in the Eastern Mediterranean region at all levels. **Structure** Executive Committee. **Events** *Conference* Sharm el Sheikh (Egypt) 2015, *Conference* Tunis (Tunisia) 2011. **Publications** *AMEEMR Newsletter.* Handbook.
Members Schools of medicine in 8 countries:
Egypt, Iran Islamic Rep, Iraq, Lebanon, Libya, Pakistan, Sudan, Türkiye. [2015/XD5948/**D**]

♦ Association for Medical Education in Europe (AMEE) 02797

Association pour l'enseignement médical en Europe (AEME) – Asociación para la Educación Médica en Europa
COO 12 Airlie Place, Dundee, DD1 4HJ, UK. T. +441382381953. Fax +441382381987. E-mail: services@amee.org.
URL: http://www.amee.org/

History 1972, Copenhagen (Denmark). Registration: Scottish Charity Regulator, No/ID: SC031618, Start date: 28 Aug 2000, Scotland. **Aims** Bring together medical educators in Europe; promote national associations; support national bodies, organizations and teachers in medical and other health care professions through services designed to share and facilitate developments in undergraduate, postgraduate and continuing medical education in the European context; facilitate high quality research and disseminate findings. **Structure** General Assembly; Executive Committee. **Languages** English. **Staff** 7.00 FTE, paid. **Finance** Sources: members' dues. **Activities** Awards/prizes/competitions; events/meetings; guidance/assistance/consulting; knowledge management/information dissemination. **Events** *Annual Conference* Glasgow (UK) 2023, *Annual Conference* Lyon (France) 2022, *Biennial Ottawa Conference on the Assessment of Competence in Medicine and the Healthcare Professions* Lyon (France) 2022, *Redefining Health Professions Together* 2021, *Annual Conference* Glasgow (UK) 2020. **Publications** *AMEE Occasional Papers.* Guides; books; other publications. Information Services: Information on opportunities and programmes funded by international agencies. Education Resource Index. Data base of members' special interests. **Information Services** *System for Education Article Retrieval from Categorized Headings (SEARCH)* – provides access to medical literature. **Members** Teachers in medicine or health care professions and organizations or national bodies committed to high standards in medical education. Membership Corporate or Associate Corporate; Institutional; Individual; Student. Members in 80 countries. Membership countries not specified. **IGO Relations** *WHO (#20950)* (European Office); *WHO Regional Office for Europe (#20945)*. **NGO Relations** Member of (3): *International Federation of Medical Students' Associations (IFMSA, #13478)*; *Nordic Federation for Medical Education (NFME, no recent information)*; *World Federation for Medical Education (WFME, #21454)*. Instrumental in setting up (2): *Association of Medical Schools in Europe (AMSE, #02799)*; *Veterinary Education Worldwide (ViEW, #20761)*. [2021/XD3245/**D**]

- ♦ Association for Medical Education in the Middle East / see Association for Medical Education in the Eastern Mediterranean Region (#02796)
- ♦ Association for Medical Education in South-East Asia / see South-East Asian Regional Association for Medical Education (#19780)
- ♦ Association for Medical Education in the Western Pacific Region / see Western Pacific Association for Medical Education (#20917)
- ♦ Association médicale espérantiste universelle (#20672)
- ♦ Association médicale européenne (#07761)
- ♦ Association médicale européenne tabac ou santé (#07762)
- ♦ Association médicale internationale contre la guerre (inactive)
- ♦ Association médicale internationale pour l'étude des conditions de vie et de santé (inactive)
- ♦ Association médicale islamique (internationally oriented national body)
- ♦ Association médicale latine (inactive)
- ♦ Association médicale latinoaméricaine de réhabilitation (#02280)
- ♦ Association médicale mondiale (#21646)
- ♦ Association médicale mondiale de tennis (#21647)
- ♦ Association médicale panaméricaine (no recent information)

♦ Association of Medical Schools in Africa (AMSA) 02798

Association des écoles de médecine d'Afrique

Chair AMSA Secretariat, c/o Principal's Office, Makarere College of Health Sciences, Kampala, Uganda.
URL: http://www.amsafrica.org/

History Inaugurated Dec 1963, Kampala (Uganda), having first been proposed at conference of medical schools in 1961, Ibadan (Nigeria). Also referred to as *Association of African Schools and Faculties of Medicine – Association des écoles et facultés de médecine d'Afrique*. **Aims** Improve standards, value and relevance of medical schools on the African continent through education, research, service and collaboration. **Languages** English, French, Portuguese. **Staff** Voluntary. **Finance** Members' dues. Assistance from schools and WHO. **Activities** Events/meetings. **Events** *Annual meeting* Khartoum (Sudan) 1988, *Annual Meeting* Arusha (Tanzania UR) 1986, *Annual Meeting* Algiers (Algeria) 1984. **Publications** *AMSA Newsletter*.
Members Schools of medicine; Individuals, members in 17 countries:
Algeria, Angola, Benin, Congo DR, Morocco, Mozambique, Niger, Nigeria, Rwanda, Senegal, Sierra Leone, Sudan, Tanzania UR, Tunisia, Uganda, Zambia, Zimbabwe.
IGO Relations *WHO (#20950)*. **NGO Relations** Member of: *World Federation for Medical Education (WFME, #21454)*. [2014/XD6114/**D**]

♦ Association of Medical Schools in Europe (AMSE) 02799

Association des facultés de médecine d'Europe

Pres Alt-Moabit 96, 10559 Berlin, Germany. T. +49306449855944. E-mail: office@amse-med.eu.
Gen Sec Fac of Medicine, Univ of Ljubljana, Vrazov trg 2, 1104 Ljubljana, Slovenia. T. +38615437700. Fax +38615437701.
URL: http://www.amse-med.eu/

History 1979, Athens (Greece). Former names and other names: *Association for Medical Deans in Europe (AMDE)* – former; *Association des doyens des facultés de médecine d'Europe* – former. Registration: Berlin District Court, No/ID: VR 34019, Start date: 20 Apr 2015, Germany, Charlottenburg; Companies House, No/ID: 6559004, End date: 2 Nov 2010, England and Wales. **Aims** Create a forum for European medical faculties to share experiences in the fields of education, research and management; stimulate cooperation between medical schools in Europe and initiate and sustain relations with other professional, governmental and non-governmental organizations in education, research and health care. **Structure** General Assembly (annual); Executive Committee. **Languages** English. **Staff** 0.50 FTE, paid. **Finance** Sources: members' dues. **Activities** Events/meetings; networking/liaising. **Events** *Annual Conference* Vilnius (Lithuania) 2021, *Annual Conference* Belgrade (Serbia) 2020, *Annual General Meeting* Lódz (Poland) 2019, *European Conference on Assessment in Medical Education* Lódz (Poland) 2019, *Annual General Meeting* Berlin (Germany) 2014.
Members Deans or representatives of schools in 29 countries:
Austria, Belarus, Bosnia-Herzegovina, Czechia, Denmark, Finland, France, Georgia, Germany, Hungary, Ireland, Italy, Kazakhstan, Kyrgyzstan, Lithuania, Malta, Moldova, Netherlands, Poland, Portugal, Romania, Russia, Serbia, Slovakia, Slovenia, Spain, Sweden, Switzerland, UK. [2021/XD9169/**D**]

- ♦ Association of Medical Schools in the Middle East / see Association for Medical Education in the Eastern Mediterranean Region (#02796)
- ♦ Association for Medical Technologists / see Caribbean Association of Medical Technologists (#03453)
- ♦ Association médico-sociale protestante de langue française (no recent information)
- ♦ Association of the Mediterranean Chambers of Commerce and Industry (#02112)
- ♦ The Association of Mediterranean Cruise Ports / see MedCruise (#16611)

♦ Association of Mediterranean Energy Regulators (MEDREG) 02800

Deputy SG Via Fieno 3, 20123 Milan MI, Italy. T. +393402938023. E-mail: info@medreg-regulators.org.
URL: http://www.medreg-regulators.org/

History May 2006. Founded as a Working Group. Became a non-profit association, supported by *European Commission (EC, #06633)*. Former names and other names: *Mediterranean Energy Regulators (MedReg)* – alias; *Association of the Mediterranean Regulators for Electricity and Gas (MEDREG)* – former. Registration: Start date: Nov 2007, Italy; EU Transparency Register, No/ID: 350106937818-26, Start date: 20 Apr 2020. **Aims** Establish a fair, functioning and integrated Euro-Mediterranean energy market through regulatory cooperation and support. **Structure** General Assembly; Presidency; Steering Committee; Communication Officers Network; Working Groups (5); Secretariat. **Languages** Arabic, English, French. **Staff** 9.00 FTE, paid. **Finance** Sources: members' dues. Supported by: *European Commission (EC, #06633)* (DG NEAR). **Activities** Capacity building; events/meetings; guidance/assistance/consulting; politics/policy/regulatory; publishing activities; training/education. **Events** *Energy Forum* Brussels (Belgium) 2019, *Trilateral Workshop on Consumer Involvement and Retail Market Opening* Brussels (Belgium) 2019, *Presidents Meeting* Rome (Italy) 2019, *General Assembly* St Julian's (Malta) 2016, *General Assembly* Tirana (Albania) 2015. **Publications** *MedReg Newsletter*. Annual Report; news alerts; technical reports; pedagogical leaflets; case studies; booklets; handbooks.
Members Energy regulators (27) from 22 countries and territories:
Albania, Algeria, Bosnia-Herzegovina, Croatia, Cyprus, Egypt, France, Greece, Israel, Italy, Jordan, Lebanon, Libya, Malta, Montenegro, Morocco, Palestine, Portugal, Slovenia, Spain, Tunisia, Türkiye.
NGO Relations Member of (1): *International Confederation of Energy Regulators (ICER, #12859)*. [2021.05.26/XJ4587/**E**]

- ♦ Association of Mediterranean Forest Owners / see ARCMED

♦ Association of Mediterranean Maritime Museums (AMMM) 02801

Asociación de Museos Marítimos del Mediterráneo (AMMM)

Address not obtained.
URL: https://www.ammm-info.net/

History 14 Oct 1998, Dubrovnik (Croatia). Founded during 8th Triennial Conference of the International Congress of Maritime Museums (ICMM). **Aims** Promote the diffusion, safeguard and awareness of the maritime heritage of the Mediterranean basin. **Structure** General Assembly; Executive Committee. **Activities** Events/meetings; projects/programmes. **Events** *Forum* Barcelona (Spain) 2021, *Forum* Barcelona (Spain) 2020, *Forum* Betina (Croatia) 2019, *Forum* Naples (Italy) 2018, *Forum* Cesenatico (Italy) 2017.
Members Full in countries:
Algeria, Croatia, France, Greece, Italy, Malta, Monaco, Montenegro, Portugal, Slovenia, Spain, Türkiye.
European Maritime Heritage (EMH, #07741).
Affiliate in 3 countries:
France, Italy, Spain. [2021/AA0958/**D**]

♦ Association of Mediterranean Ombudsmen 02802

Association des Ombudsmans de la Méditerranée (AOM) – Asociación de Ombudsman del Mediterraneo

Headquarters TSA 907167, 75334 Paris CEDEX 07, France.
URL: http://www.ombudsman-med.org/

History 19 Dec 2008, Marseille (France), at 2nd meeting of the Mediterranean network of Ombudsmen, according to Declaration of Rabat. Previous names include: *Mediterranean Ombudsmen Network*; *Association des ombudsmans de la méditerranée*; *Asociación de los ombudsmans mediterraneos*. Registered in accordance with Moroccan law. **Aims** Promote the creation of new institutions of mediators, ombudsmen, Diwan Al Madhalim or people's defenders; consolidate existing institutions and promote and defend their independence; promote and defend democracy, human rights and social peace around the Mediterranean region. **Structure** General Assembly (at least every 2 years). Governing Board of 10, including Executive Committee, comprising President, 1st and 2nd Vice-Presidents, Secretary-General and Treasurer. **Languages** Arabic, English, French, Spanish. **Finance** Members' dues. **Activities** Organizes: encounters among members and institutions for promotion of human rights in the region; training sessions; conferences and awareness programmes. **Events** *General assembly and conference* Madrid (Spain) 2010, *General assembly and conference* Athens (Greece) 2009, *General assembly and conference* Marseille (France) 2008, *General assembly and conference* Rabat (Morocco) 2007. **Publications** *AOM Newsletter*.
Members Full in 25 countries and territories:
Albania, Algeria, Andorra, Bosnia-Herzegovina, Croatia, Cyprus, Egypt, France, Greece, Israel, Italy, Jordan, Lebanon, Malta, Mauritania, Montenegro, Morocco, North Macedonia, Palestine, Portugal, Serbia, Slovenia, Spain, Tunisia, Türkiye.
IGO Relations Observers: *Council of Europe (CE, #04881)* – Human Rights Commissioner; *League of Arab States (LAS, #16420)* – Human Rights Department; *European Ombudsman (#08084)*; *Office of the United Nations High Commissioner for Human Rights (OHCHR, #17697)*; *Organisation internationale de la Francophonie (OIF, #17809)*. [2018/XJ1839/**D**]

- ♦ Association of the Mediterranean Regulators for Electricity and Gas / see Association of Mediterranean Energy Regulators (#02800)

♦ Association of the Mediterranean Transmission System Operators (Med-TSO) 02803

Association de Gestionnaires des Réseaux de Transport de l'électricité Méditerranéens

Contact Via della Marcigliana 911, 00138 Rome RM, Italy. E-mail: info@med-tso.com.
Registered Address Viale Egidio Galbani 70, 00156 Rome RM, Italy.
URL: http://www.med-tso.com/

History Established 19 Apr 2012, Rome (Italy), as a technical platform. **Aims** Support institutional initiatives aimed at facilitating creation of a Mediterranean energy market by fostering development of an integrated, secure and sustainable regional *electricity* transmission grid. **Structure** General Assembly; Executive Board; Secretariat. **Languages** English, French, Italian.
Members TSOs (21) in 19 countries:
Albania, Algeria, Croatia, Cyprus, Egypt, France, Greece, Israel, Italy, Jordan, Libya, Mongolia, Morocco, Palestine, Portugal, Slovenia, Spain, Tunisia, Türkiye. [2018.06.18/XM6431/**D**]

- ♦ Association méditerranéenne d'andrologie (inactive)
- ♦ Association méditerranéenne pour l'avifaune marine (#16661)
- ♦ Association méditerranéenne de biologie marine et d'océanologie (inactive)
- ♦ Association méditerranéenne de dermato-vénéréologie (inactive)
- ♦ Association méditerranéenne pour l'éducation des adultes (inactive)
- ♦ Association méditerranéenne internationale de la tomate transformée (#16659)
- ♦ Association méditerranéenne de motocyclisme (no recent information)

♦ Association Méditerranéenne et Moyen-orientale de Chirurgie Endoscopique 02804

Mediterranean and Middle Eastern Endoscopic Surgery Association (MMESA)

SG address not obtained.
URL: http://www.mmesa.org/

History Founded 20 Nov 2000, Beirut (Lebanon). Registered in accordance with Lebanese law. **Aims** Develop endoscopic surgery and interventional techniques in the Mediterranean, Middle Eastern and surrounding countries; coordinate and train these techniques; develop common standards; promote scientific studies so as to develop and identity for endoscopic surgery. **Structure** General Assembly (annual); Administrative Board; Executive Board; Executive Office. No formal headquarters. **Languages** English, French. **Staff** None. **Finance** Members' dues. Contributions. **Activities** Events/meetings; education/training. Annual Congress, Annual Winter Meeting and Spring Meeting, always using – as much as possible – alternate places (North, South, East and West of the Mediterranean Basin). **Events** *Congress* United Arab Emirates 2016, *Congress* 2015, *Congress* Tbilisi (Georgia) 2014, *Congress* Amman (Jordan) 2012, *Congress* Catania (Italy) 2011. **Publications** *Journal of Minimally Invasive Surgical Sciences* (4 a year); *MMESA Newsletter*.
Members Founding; Active; International; Honorary. Members in 32 countries and territories:
Algeria, Armenia, Bahrain, Croatia, Egypt, France, Georgia, Iran Islamic Rep, Iraq, Italy, Jordan, Kuwait, Lebanon, Libya, Malta, Morocco, Oman, Palestine, Portugal, Qatar, Romania, Saudi Arabia, Serbia, Slovenia, Spain, Sudan, Switzerland, Syrian AR, Tunisia, Türkiye, United Arab Emirates, Yemen.
NGO Relations National scientific associations. [2020/XJ8974/**D**]

- ♦ Association méditerranéenne pour la physiologie des plantes (inactive)
- ♦ Association méditerranéenne de psychiatrie (no recent information)
- ♦ Association méditerranéennes des sciences de l'environnement et de l'espace (inactive)
- ♦ Association Med-Vet-Net de Recherche sur les Zoonoses / see Med-Vet-Net Association (#16693)
- ♦ Association of Meiobenthologists / see International Association of Meiobenthologists (#12029)

♦ Association of Member Episcopal Conferences in Eastern Africa (AMECEA) 02805

Association des conférences épiscopales membres de l'Afrique de l'Est

SG PO Box 21191, Nairobi, 00505, Kenya. T. +254783189081. E-mail: secgeneral@amecea.org – amecea@amecea.org.
URL: http://www.amecea.org/

History Founded 26 Jul 1961, Dar es Salaam (Tanganyika), as *Inter-Territorial Episcopal Board of Eastern Africa (ITEBEA)*, at 1st Inter-Territorial Episcopal Meeting. Full time Secretariat from 1964. **Aims** Inspire and empower God's family in AMECEA to a credible and prophetic witness to Christ by promoting unity, justice, peace and solidarity. **Structure** Plenary Assembly (every 4 years); Executive Board; Secretariat in Nairobi (Kenya). Coordinates activities of: (1) *AMECEA Pastoral Institute (API/Gaba, #00771)*, set up 1967, Eldoret (Kenya). (2) AMECEA Social Communications Department, set up 1968, whose activities include: training workshops, seminars and lectures; publications; communication surveys and research; representing AMECEA with other bodies. (3) AMECEA Documentation Service (ADS), now a desk under AMECEA Social Communications Department, set up 1973 to share pastoral initiatives and experience among the dioceses and publicize AMECEA activities. (4) Apostolate to Nomads. (5) *Catholic University of Eastern Africa, The (CUEA, #03610)*, set up 3 Nov 1992, to train clergy, religious and lay people, having previously functioned as *Catholic Higher Institute of Eastern Africa (CHIEA)*. (6) AMECEA Pastoral Department, set up 1994. (7) Blessed Bakanja AMECEA College, set up 1998; a regional theological seminary/house of formation. **Languages** English. **Staff**

15.00 FTE, paid. **Finance** Contributions from Bishops. Annual budget: Kenyan Shillings 9,000,000. **Activities** Networking/liaising; religious activities; research/documentation. **Events** *Triennial plenary meeting* Zambia 2008, *Triennial plenary meeting* Kampala (Uganda) 2005, *Triennial plenary meeting* Dar es Salaam (Tanzania UR) 2002, *Annual social communications meeting* Addis Ababa (Ethiopia) 2000, *Triennial plenary meeting* Nairobi (Kenya) 1999. **Publications** *African Ecclesiastical Review* (6 a year); *Spearhead* (6 a year); *African Christian Studies* (4 a year) – produced by CUEA; *AMECEA News*.
Members National Conferences of Bishops, totalling 124 dioceses. Full in 9 countries:
Eritrea, Ethiopia, Kenya, Malawi, South Sudan, Sudan, Tanzania UR, Uganda, Zambia.
Affiliate in 2 countries:
Djibouti, Somalia.
NGO Relations Member of: *Freshwater Action Network (FAN, inactive)*; *Laudato Si' Movement (#16403)*. Cooperates with: *Anglophone West Africa Catechetical Commission (AWACC, inactive)*; *Symposium of Episcopal Conferences of Africa and Madagascar (SECAM, #20077)*. Works with many overseas mission-partners in the pastoral, educational and socio-economic fields. [2019.12.06/XD4339/**D**]

♦ Association des messageries européennes (inactive)
♦ Association of Microbial Food Enzyme Producers within the EEC / see Association of Manufacturers and Formulators of Enzyme Products (#02793)
♦ Association of Microbial Food Enzyme Producers in Western Europe / see Association of Manufacturers and Formulators of Enzyme Products (#02793)
♦ Association des microbiologistes de langue française (inactive)
♦ Association of Microbiologists for Latin America / see Latin American Association of Microbiology (#16247)

♦ Association for Microwave Power in Europe for Research and Education (AMPERE Europe) 02806

General Secretariat UPCT Dpto Tec Comunicaciones, Plaza del Hospital 1, 30202 Cartagena, Murcia, Spain. E-mail: contact@ampereeurope.org.
URL: http://www.ampereeurope.org/
History Sep 1993, Gothenburg (Sweden), at International Conference on Microwave and High Frequency Heating. To be recognized throughout the EU and beyond, registered as a non-profit company, 22 Jan 2003, UK. Registered in accordance with French law, 10 Dec 2008. **Aims** Promote microwave and radio frequency heating techniques for research and industrial applications. **Structure** General Assembly (every 2 years). Management Committee, including President, General Secretary and Treasurer. **Events** *International Conference on Microwave and High Frequency Applications* Gothenburg (Sweden) 2021, *International Conference on Microwave and High Frequency Heating* Valencia (Spain) 2019, *International Conference on Microwave and High Frequency Heating* Delft (Netherlands) 2017, *International Conference on Microwave and High Frequency Heating* Krakow (Poland) 2015, *International Conference on Microwave and High Frequency Heating* Nottingham (UK) 2013. **Publications** *AMPERE Newsletter* (4 a year). **NGO Relations** Founding member of: *International Federation of Associations in the Field of Microwave and RF Power Engineering (MAJIC, #13362)*. [2014/XJ0065/**E**]

♦ Association for Middle Eastern Public Policy and Administration (AMEPPA) 02807

Main Office c/o AUC, PO Box 74, New Cairo CAIRO, Egypt. E-mail: merppa@aucegypt.edu.
URL: https://ameppa.org/
History 2012. **Aims** Promote peace and prosperity in the Middle East through sound governance. **Structure** Executive Council; Executive Board; Advisory Board. **Languages** Arabic, English, Kurdish, Persian. **Staff** 25.00 FTE, voluntary. **Finance** Sources: donations. **Activities** Events/meetings. **Events** *Conference* Cairo (Egypt) 2022, *Conference* Doha (Qatar) 2021, *Global Conference On Public Policy and Administration in the Middle East* Qatar 2020, *Conference* Cairo (Egypt) 2019, *Conference* Cairo (Egypt) 2018. **Publications** *Middle Eastern Review of Public Administration* (4 a year). Books.
Members Full (approx 600) in 49 countries:
Afghanistan, Algeria, Azerbaijan, Bahrain, Bangladesh, Belgium, Canada, China, Denmark, Egypt, France, Germany, Greece, India, Indonesia, Iran Islamic Rep, Iraq, Ireland, Israel, Italy, Jordan, Kazakhstan, Kenya, Kuwait, Lebanon, Morocco, Netherlands, Nigeria, Pakistan, Philippines, Poland, Qatar, Russia, Saudi Arabia, Singapore, Somalia, Spain, Sri Lanka, Sudan, Sweden, Switzerland, Tunisia, Türkiye, UK, United Arab Emirates, USA, Uzbekistan, Yemen, Zimbabwe.
IGO Relations *ECOSOC (#05331)*. **NGO Relations** *African Association for Public Administration and Management (AAPAM, #00215)*; *Global Science and Technology Forum (GSTF)*; *International Comparative Policy Analysis Forum (ICPA-Forum, #12830)*; *International Institute of Administrative Sciences (IIAS, #13859)*; *International Political Science Association (IPSA, #14615)*. [2022/XJ5951/**C**]

♦ Association de la migration africaine (internationally oriented national body)
♦ Association of Military Christian Fellowships (internationally oriented national body)
♦ Association Miraisme International (#02282)
♦ Association for Modelling and Forecasting Economies in Transition (unconfirmed)
♦ Association monarchiste européenne (no recent information)
♦ Association du monde indigène (#11166)
♦ Association Monde juste (internationally oriented national body)
♦ Association mondiale d'acoustique (inactive)
♦ Association mondiale des airlines clubs (#21075)

♦ Association Mondiale des Amis de l'Enfance (AMADE) 02808

World Association of Children's Friends – Asociación Mundial de Amigos de la Infancia – Weltverband der Kinderfreunde – Associação Mundial dos Amigos da Infância – Associazione Mondiale degli Amici dell' Infanzia – Wereldvereniging der Kindervrienden
SG 4 rue des Iris, 98000 Monte Carlo, Monaco. T. +37797705260. Fax +37797705272.
URL: http://www.amade-mondiale.org/
History 1963, Monaco. Founded by Princess Grace of Monaco, Grace Patricia Kelly (1929-1982). Most recent statutes adopted 27 May 2010. Former names and other names: *AMADE MONDIALE* – alias. Registration: Monaco. **Aims** Without distinction of gender, race, religion, language, culture, social background or political opinion: contribute to bring access to education and healthcare for every child worldwide; promote the defence of the children's essential rights; raise public awareness of the place of the child in society. **Structure** General Assembly (annual, always in Monaco); Board of Directors; Secretariat. Branches (12): Belgium; Burundi, Cambodia; Chad; Chile; Congo DR; Cyprus; Guinea; Italy; Lithuania; Monaco; Niger. **Languages** English, French, Spanish. **Staff** 3.00 FTE, paid. **Finance** Sources: donations; government support; members' dues. **Activities** Awards/prizes/competitions; projects/programmes. **Events** *Annual meeting* Monte Carlo (Monaco) 2006, *Annual meeting* Monte Carlo (Monaco) 2005, *Annual meeting* Monte Carlo (Monaco) 2004, *Annual meeting* Monte Carlo (Monaco) 2003, *General Assembly* Monte Carlo (Monaco) 1996. **Publications** Annual Report; leaflets; brochures; project summaries; mission reports.
Members National associations in 12 countries:
Belgium, Burundi, Cambodia, Chad, Chile, Congo DR, Cyprus, Guinea, Italy, Lithuania, Monaco, Niger.
Consultative Status Consultative status granted from: *UNESCO (#20322)* (Foundations); *UNICEF (#20332)*; *Council of Europe (CE, #04881)* (Participatory Status). **NGO Relations** Member of: *NGO Committee on UNICEF (#17120)*. *'UNESCO NGO Working Group on the Protection of Children during National and International Armed Conflicts'*. [2022/XD3478/**C**]

♦ Association mondiale des anatomistes vétérinaires (#21202)
♦ Association mondiale des anciennes et anciens du Sacré Coeur (#21116)
♦ Association mondiale des anciens stagiaires et boursiers de l'Organisation des Nations Unies (#21141)
♦ Association mondiale pour l'appel islamique (inactive)
♦ Association mondiale d'archéologie (#21104)
♦ Association mondiale pour l'avancement de parasitologie vétérinaire (#21114)
♦ Association mondiale chrétienne anti-communiste (no recent information)
♦ Association mondiale du cinéma médical et de la santé (#21163)
♦ Association mondiale pour la communication chrétienne (#21126)
♦ Association mondiale pour la conservation du sol et de l'eau (#21192)
♦ Association mondiale pour la construction par éléments et la préfabrication (inactive)
♦ Association mondiale pour le counseling et la psychothérapie centrés-sur-la-personne (#21172)
♦ Association mondiale de courses en montagne (#21659)
♦ Association mondiale de cybernétique d'informatique et de la théorie des systèmes (inactive)
♦ Association mondiale des détectives (#21131)
♦ Association mondiale pour le développement de la philatélie (#21132)

♦ Association mondiale de dispacheurs (AMD) 02809

International Association of Average Adjusters
SG c/o Seven Seas and Co, Av Royale 16, 1330 Rixensart, Belgium. E-mail: mdk@7seas.bg.
URL: http://www.amdadjusters.org/
History 1961, as *International Association of European General Average Adjusters*. Later known as *International Association of Average Adjusters – Association internationale de dispacheurs européens (AIDE)*. Present name adopted, 2007. **Aims** Promote and study general average and marine insurance claims handling; maintain good practice of all members and inform about Rules of practice and legal or insurance news. **Structure** General Assembly; President. **Languages** English, French. **Publications** Annual Report; studies.
Members Membership in 22 countries:
Angola, Argentina, Brazil, Canada, China, Croatia, Cyprus, Denmark, Finland, Greece, India, Japan, Morocco, New Zealand, Norway, Poland, Singapore, Spain, Sweden, UK, Ukraine, USA.
Consultative Status Consultative status granted from: *UNCTAD (#20285)* (Special Category). **NGO Relations** Consultative member of: *International Salvage Union (ISU, #14779)*. [2019.06.29/XD3261/**D**]

♦ Association mondiale de droit médical / see World Association for Medical Law (#21164)
♦ Association mondiale pour l'école instrument de paix (#21184)
♦ Association mondiale des éditeurs, fabricants et revendeurs de matériels didactiques / see Worlddidac Association (#21361)
♦ Association mondiale des éleveurs de la race brune (unconfirmed)
♦ Association mondiale des enseignants espérantistes (inactive)
♦ Association mondiale des enseignants vétérinaires (inactive)
♦ Association mondiale des entraîneurs de plongée (inactive)
♦ Association mondiale des esperantophones professionnels du bâtiment et des travaux publics (#20266)
♦ Association mondiale pour l'étude et la sécurité des animaux de transport (internationally oriented national body)
♦ Association mondiale des fabricants de matériel vidéo (inactive)
♦ Association mondiale des fédéralistes mondiaux / see World Federalist Movement – Movement for a Just World Order through a Strengthened United Nations (#21404)
♦ Association mondiale des femmes chefs d'entreprises / see Femmes chefs d'entreprises mondiales (#09733)
♦ Association mondiale des formateurs de développement (no recent information)
♦ Association mondiale pour la formation hôtelière et touristique (#21144)
♦ Association mondiale pour la formation professionnelle touristique / see World Association for Hospitality and Tourism Education and Training (#21144)
♦ Association mondiale de la gastronomie / see Chaîne des Rôtisseurs – Association Mondiale de la Gastronomie (#03845)
♦ Association mondiale des GPL (#21629)
♦ Association mondiale des grandes métropoles (#21158)
♦ Association mondiale des guides et des éclaireuses (#21142)
♦ Association mondiale de l'histoire de la médecine vétérinaire (#21143)
♦ Association mondiale des industries de traitement des algues marines (#21185)
♦ Association mondiale d'informatique médicale (inactive)
♦ Association mondiale des inventeurs et chercheurs scientifiques (inactive)
♦ Association mondiale pour l'investissement immobilier et la construction (inactive)
♦ Association mondiale des jeunes bouddhistes (#21502)
♦ Association mondiale des journalistes espérantistes (#21138)
♦ Association mondiale des journaux (inactive)
♦ Association mondiale de juges (#21150)
♦ Association mondiale de juristes (#21604)
♦ Association mondiale pour les loisirs et la récréation / see World Leisure Organization (#21624)
♦ Association mondiale de loterie (#21628)
♦ Association mondiale de lutte contre la faim (inactive)
♦ Association mondiale des MBA en aéronautique (internationally oriented national body)
♦ Association mondiale pour la médecine de catastrophe et d'urgence (#21133)
♦ Association mondiale de médecine naturelle (inactive)
♦ Association mondiale pour la médecine d'urgence et de catastrophe / see World Association for Disaster and Emergency Medicine (#21133)
♦ Association mondiale des médecins francophones (no recent information)
♦ Association mondiale des moyens de communication (#21644)
♦ Association mondiale de navigation (inactive)
♦ Association mondiale des olympiens (#21682)
♦ Association mondiale d'organismes de gestion des élections (#02984)
♦ Association mondiale des pathologistes vétérinaires (no recent information)
♦ Association mondiale de patinage artistique sur patins en ligne (#21584)
♦ Association mondiale Pedro Arrupe (#18287)
♦ Association mondiale des petites et moyennes entreprises (#21189)
♦ Association mondiale de physiologistes, pharmacologistes, biochimistes et toxicologistes vétérinaires (no recent information)
♦ Association mondiale de phytothérapie (inactive)
♦ Association mondiale des planteurs de betteraves et de canne à sucre (#21120)
♦ Association mondiale de la presse fédéraliste (inactive)
♦ Association mondiale de prévention du cancer gynécologique (inactive)
♦ Association mondiale des producteurs de betteraves et de canne à sucre / see World Association of Beet and Cane Growers (#21120)
♦ Association mondiale des producteurs d'extraits d'algues / see World Association of Seaweed Processors (#21185)
♦ Association mondiale des professeurs d'université / see International Association of University Professors and Lecturers (#12250)
♦ Association mondiale pour la promotion culturelle (inactive)
♦ Association mondiale de prospective sociale (inactive)
♦ Association mondiale de psychanalyse (#21177)
♦ Association Mondiale de Psychanalyse du Champ freudien / see World Association for Psychoanalysis (#21177)
♦ Association mondiale de psychiatrie (#21741)
♦ Association mondiale de psychiatrie dynamique (#21135)
♦ Association mondiale de psychiatrie et psychologie légale (no recent information)
♦ Association mondiale de psychiatrie sociale (#21190)
♦ Association mondiale de la publicité cinématographique (#19158)
♦ Association mondiale des radiodiffuseurs communautaires / see Association mondiale des radiodiffuseurs communautaires (#02810)

♦ Association mondiale des radiodiffuseurs communautaires (AMARC) 02810

World Association of Community Radio Broadcasters – Asociación Mundial de Radios Comunitarias

SG 2 Sainte-Catherine Est, Ste 202, Montréal QC H2X 1K4, Canada. T. +15149820351. Fax +15148497129. E-mail: secretariat@si.amarc.org.
AMARC Europe Rue de la Linière 11, B-1060 Brussels, Belgium. T. +3226094440.
URL: https://amarc.radio/

History 1983, Montréal, QC (Canada). Former names and other names: *World Association of Community Radios* – alias; *Association mondiale des radios communautaires* – alias; *World Association of Community Broadcasters* – alias; *Association mondiale des radiodiffuseurs communautaires* – alias; *Assemblée mondiale des artisans de la radio communautaire* – alias; *Assemblée mondiale des radiodiffuseurs communautaires* – alias; *AMARC International* – alias. **Aims** Support and contribute to the development of participatory radio along the principles of solidarity and international cooperation; develop and further a general understanding of the concept and role of community radio; promote use of community radio as a viable alternative model for communication; promote use of community radio as a tool for development, peace, justice and solidarity; promote and facilitate cooperation and information exchange between community radio broadcasters; defend community radio broadcasters who are threatened by political developments; contribute to the democratization of communication that meets the needs and demands of communities, in the pursuit of a new world information balance. **Structure** General Assembly (at least every 4 years); Board of Directors (meets annually); Executive Committee; General Secretariat. Regional Sections (4): ALC; African; Asia-Pacific; *AMARC Europe (#00764)*. Action Committees. Includes: Women's International Network. **Languages** English, French, Portuguese, Spanish.
Finance Sources: contributions; grants; members' dues. Programmes and projects funded by organizations and foundations, including:
- *British Council*;
- *Catholic Agency for Overseas Development (CAFOD)*;
- *Catholic Organization for Relief and Development (Cordaid)*;
- *DANIDA*;
- *Department for International Development (DFID, inactive)*;
- *Development and Peace (CCODP)*;
- *European Commission (EC, #06633)*;
- *Friedrich-Ebert-Stiftung (FES)*;
- *German Catholic Bishops' Organisation for Development Cooperation (MISEREOR)*;
- *Global Ministries of The United Methodist Church (GM-UMC)*;
- *International Development Research Centre (IDRC, #13162)*;
- *Oxfam GB*;
- *Broederlijk Delen*;
- *Swedish International Development Cooperation Agency (Sida)*;
- *Three Kings Action (DKA Austria)*;
- *UNESCO (#20322)*;
- *UNICEF (#20332)*;
- *United Nations Development Fund for Women (UNIFEM, inactive)*;
- *World Association for Christian Communication (WACC, #21126)*.

Activities Events/meetings. **Events** *World Conference* Accra (Ghana) 2015, *Asia Pacific Assembly and Conference* Seoul (Korea Rep) 2013, *Asia Pacific assembly and conference* Bangalore (India) 2010, *General assembly and conference / World Conference* La Plata (Argentina) 2010, *Joint workshop on codes of practice for community media* La Plata (Argentina) 2010. **Publications** *AMARC-Link* (4 a year) in English, French, Spanish – bulletin; *InteRadio* (annual) in English, French, Spanish – magazine. *Radio Forum* – series. Studies; conference reports.
Members Regular (voting): community radio stations, production groups, federations and associations of community radio stations; Associate (non-voting): individuals, groups and organizations who are in agreement with AMARC objectives. Members (almost 4000) in 120 countries and territories:
Albania, Angola, Argentina, Austria, Bahrain, Bangladesh, Belarus, Belgium, Benin, Bolivia, Bosnia-Herzegovina, Botswana, Brazil, Burkina Faso, Burundi, Cambodia, Cameroon, Canada, Cape Verde, Chad, Chile, Colombia, Comoros, Congo Brazzaville, Congo DR, Costa Rica, Côte d'Ivoire, Croatia, Cuba, Czechia, Denmark, Dominican Rep, Ecuador, El Salvador, Estonia, Eswatini, Ethiopia, Finland, France, Gambia, Georgia, Germany, Ghana, Guatemala, Guiana Fr, Guinea, Guinea-Bissau, Guyana, Haiti, Honduras, Hungary, India, Ireland, Israel, Italy, Japan, Jordan, Kazakhstan, Kenya, Korea Rep, Kyrgyzstan, Latvia, Lesotho, Liberia, Luxembourg, Madagascar, Malawi, Malaysia, Mali, Martinique, Mauritania, Mexico, Moldova, Morocco, Mozambique, Namibia, Nepal, Netherlands, Nicaragua, Niger, Nigeria, North Macedonia, Norway, Pakistan, Panama, Paraguay, Peru, Philippines, Poland, Portugal, Puerto Rico, Réunion, Romania, Russia, Rwanda, Senegal, Serbia, Sierra Leone, Slovenia, Somalia, South Africa, Spain, Sri Lanka, Sweden, Switzerland, Tanzania UR, Thailand, Timor-Leste, Togo, Trinidad-Tobago, Tunisia, Uganda, UK, Ukraine, Uruguay, USA, Venezuela, Yemen, Zambia, Zimbabwe.
Consultative Status Consultative status granted from: *UNESCO (#20322)* (Associate Status). **IGO Relations** Observer status with: *International Telecommunication Union (ITU, #15673)*. **NGO Relations** Member of: *Global Forum for Media Development (GFMD, #10375)*; *Redes de Comunicación de América Latina y el Caribe para el Desarrollo (G-8, no recent information)*; *World Social Forum (WSF, #21797)*. Member of: *Community Media Forum Europe (CMFE, #04402)*, through Europe office; *Federación Latinoamericana de Facultades de Comunicación Social (FELAFACS, #09353)*. Cooperates with: *African Network for Popular and Participatory Radio Producers (no recent information)*; *International Council for Adult Education (ICAE, #12983)*. Instrumental in setting up: *Voices Without Frontiers (VWF, #20805)* via AMARC-Europe.
[2018/XF0332/**F**]

♦ Association mondiale pour la radiodiffusion chrétienne (inactive)
♦ Association mondiale des radios communautaires / see Association mondiale des radiodiffuseurs communautaires (#02810)
♦ Association mondiale pour la réadaptation psychosociale (#21178)
♦ Association mondiale de recherches sur l'opinion publique (#21180)
♦ Association mondiale de la route (#21754)
♦ Association mondiale de santé mentale du nourrisson / see World Association for Infant Mental Health (#21146)
♦ Association mondiale pour la santé sexuelle (#21187)

♦ Association mondiale des sciences de l'éducation (AMSE) 02811

World Association for Educational Research (WAER) – Asociación Mondial de Ciencias de la Educación (AMCE)
SG Inspé de l'académie de Reims, 23 rue Clément Ader, 51680 Reims, France. T. +332691821.
URL: http://www.amse-amce-waer.org/

History 12 Sep 1953, Ghent (Belgium). Founded at 1st International Congress for the University Study of Education, on the initiative of Prof Dr R L Plancke and Prof Dr R Verbist.. Former names and other names: *International Secretariat for Teaching Educational Sciences in Universities* – former (12 Sep 1953 to 9 Aug 1961); *Secrétariat international de l'enseignement universitaire des sciences pédagogiques* – former (12 Sep 1953 to 9 Aug 1961); *International Association for the Advancement of Educational Research (IAAER)* – former (9 Aug 1961 to 29 Jul 1977); *Association internationale des sciences de l'éducation* – former (9 Aug 1961 to 29 Jul 1977). Registration: Start date: 9 Jul 1979, Belgium. **Aims** At an international level, foster development of research in the field of education. **Structure** General Assembly (every 4 years on occasion of Congress) elects Executive Committee, comprising President, Vice-President and Secretary General for 4-year term. Advisory Council, consisting of Vice-President and country representatives appointed by regional members. Membership limited to individuals of university standing and for non-profit organizations in education. **Languages** English, French, Spanish. **Staff** 7.00 FTE, voluntary. **Finance** Sources: members' dues; revenue from activities/projects; subsidies. **Activities** Events/meetings; knowledge management/information dissemination; networking/liaising. **Events** *Biennial International Congress* Buenos Aires (Argentina) 2021, *Biennial International Congress* Buenos Aires (Argentina) 2020, *Biennial International Congress* Suceava (Romania) 2018, *Biennial International Congress* Eskisehir (Turkey) 2016, *International Congress* Reims (France) 2012. **Publications** *Short Letter of the AMSE-AMCE-WAER* (2 a year) – electronic. Congress reports; books.
Members Individuals in 35 countries:
Argentina, Australia, Belgium, Brazil, Cameroon, Canada, Chile, Colombia, Costa Rica, Cuba, Czechia, France, Germany, Greece, Israel, Italy, Lebanon, Luxembourg, Mexico, Morocco, Peru, Portugal, Romania, Saudi Arabia, Senegal, Slovakia, Slovenia, South Africa, Spain, Switzerland, Tunisia, Türkiye, Uruguay, USA, Venezuela.
Consultative Status Consultative status granted from: *ECOSOC (#05331)* (Ros C). **IGO Relations** Accredited by (1): *United Nations Office at Vienna (UNOV, #20604)*. [2021/XB1212/v/**B**]

♦ Association mondiale des services d'emploi publics (#21179)
♦ Association mondiale des sociétés d'histoire du travail (inactive)
♦ Association mondiale des sociétés de pathologie – anatomie pathologique et biologie médicale / see World Association of Societies of Pathology and Laboratory Medicine (#21191)
♦ Association mondiale des sociétés de pathologie anatomique et clinique / see World Association of Societies of Pathology and Laboratory Medicine (#21191)
♦ Association mondiale des sociétés de pathologie et biologie médicale (#21191)
♦ Association mondiale de spécialistes dans l'expertise de documents (inactive)
♦ Association mondiale pour l'union du troisième âge (inactive)
♦ Association mondiale des végétariens espérantistes (#21389)
♦ Association mondiale vétérinaire (#21901)
♦ Association mondiale vétérinaire d'aviculture (#21902)
♦ Association mondiale vétérinaire de petits animaux (#21795)
♦ Association mondiale des vétérinaires équins (#21388)
♦ Association mondiale des vétérinaires microbiologistes, immunologistes et spécialistes des maladies infectieuses (no recent information)
♦ Association mondiale des zones franches industrielles / see World Economic Processing Zones Association (#21368)
♦ Association mondiale des zones industrielles d'exportation / see World Economic Processing Zones Association (#21368)
♦ Association mondiale des zones industrielles libres / see World Economic Processing Zones Association (#21368)
♦ Association mondiale de zootechnie (#21117)
♦ Association pour les montagnes africaines (inactive)

♦ Association Montessori Internationale (AMI) 02812

International Montessori Association – Asociación Montessori Internacional – Internationale Montessori Vereinigung – Associazione Montessori Internazionale
Exec Dir Koninginneweg 161, 1075 CN Amsterdam, Netherlands. T. +31206798932. E-mail: publications@montessori-ami.org – info@montessori-ami.org.
Pres address not obtained.
URL: http://www.montessori-ami.org/

History Aug 1929, Helsingør (Denmark). Statutes modified in 1953 to comply with Dutch legislation. Articles of Association changed in 1983. Registration: Dutch Royal Decree, No/ID: 40, Start date: 24 Jan 1954. **Aims** Maintain, propagate and further the ideas and principles of Dr Maria Montessori for the full development of the human being. **Structure** Annual General Meeting; Board; AMI Secretariat; Training Centres; Affiliated Societies; Assemblies of Educators without Borders. **Languages** Dutch, English, French, German, Italian, Spanish. **Finance** Sources: gifts, legacies; members' dues; sponsorship. Other sources: percentage of students' fees. **Activities** Awareness raising; events/meetings; networking/liaising; training/education. **Events** *Education for a New World* Bangkok (Thailand) 2023, *Annual General Meeting* Amsterdam (Netherlands) 2022, *Congress* Bangkok (Thailand) 2021, *Annual General Meeting* Amsterdam (Netherlands) 2019, *Annual Meeting* Amsterdam (Netherlands) 2018. **Publications** *Newsletter* (weekly) – Free newsletter for non-members; *AMI Journal* (annual); *AMI Digital Newsletter* (8 a year). Annual Report to membership – digital.
Members Individuals in 106 countries and territories:
Albania, Argentina, Aruba, Australia, Austria, Bahamas, Bahrain, Bangladesh, Belgium, Bermuda, Bolivia, Bosnia-Herzegovina, Brazil, Bulgaria, Cambodia, Canada, Cayman Is, Chile, China, Colombia, Costa Rica, Croatia, Curaçao, Cyprus, Czechia, Denmark, Dominican Rep, Ecuador, Egypt, El Salvador, Estonia, Finland, France, Germany, Ghana, Greece, Guatemala, Haiti, Hong Kong, Hungary, Iceland, India, Indonesia, Iran Islamic Rep, Ireland, Israel, Italy, Japan, Jordan, Kazakhstan, Kenya, Korea Rep, Kosovo, Kuwait, Latvia, Lithuania, Luxembourg, Madagascar, Malaysia, Mexico, Mongolia, Morocco, Nepal, Netherlands, New Zealand, Nigeria, North Macedonia, Norway, Oman, Pakistan, Paraguay, Peru, Philippines, Poland, Portugal, Puerto Rico, Romania, Russia, Saudi Arabia, Serbia, Singapore, Slovakia, Slovenia, South Africa, Spain, Sri Lanka, St Lucia, Sweden, Switzerland, Taiwan, Tanzania UR, Thailand, Trinidad-Tobago, Tunisia, Türkiye, Uganda, UK, Ukraine, United Arab Emirates, Uruguay, USA, Uzbekistan, Vietnam, Virgin Is UK, Yemen, Zimbabwe.
Consultative Status Consultative status granted from: *UNESCO (#20322)* (Consultative Status). **IGO Relations** Associated with Department of Global Communications of the United Nations. **NGO Relations** Member of (1): *International Network for a Culture of Nonviolence and Peace (#14247)*. [2022/XE2267/v/**E**]

♦ Association for Moral Education (AME) 02813

Sec Dept of Psychology, Gordon College, 255 Grapevine Rd, Wenham MA 01984, USA.
URL: http://www.amenetwork.org/

History 1976. **Aims** Provide an interdisciplinary forum for professionals interested in the moral dimensions of educational theory and practice. **Structure** Executive Board. **Languages** English. **Events** *Conference* Manchester (UK) 2022, *Conference* Wenham, MA (USA) 2021, *Conference* Wenham, MA (USA) 2020, *Annual Conference* Barcelona (Spain) 2018, *Annual Conference* Montréal, QC (Canada) 2013. **Publications** *AME Forum* (2 a year).
Members Individuals in 30 countries and territories:
Australia, Brazil, Canada, China, Colombia, Costa Rica, Denmark, England, Finland, Germany, Greece, Iceland, Ireland, Israel, Japan, Korea Rep, Mexico, Netherlands, Nigeria, Norway, Peru, Russia, Scotland, Slovakia, Slovenia, Switzerland, Taiwan, Türkiye, UK, USA. [2012.06.19/XD8016/v/**D**]

♦ Association des morphologistes (#02814)

♦ Association of Morphologists 02814

Association des morphologistes
Contact 9 av de la Forêt de Haye – bte 184, 54500 Vandoeuvre-les-Nancy, France.

History Founded 1899, France, as *Association of Anatomists – Association des anatomistes*. **Aims** Encourage presentation, discussion and publication of original papers on anatomy, histology and embryology. **Structure** General Assembly (annual); Council (meets twice a year); Executive Committee; Committee on Lectures; Secretariat. **Languages** French. **Finance** Members' dues. Donations. **Activities** Events/meetings. **Events** *Annual Congress* Toulouse (France) 2016, *Annual Congress* Montpellier (France) 2010, *Annual Congress* Leuven (Belgium) 2009, *Annual Congress* Bordeaux (France) 2008, *Annual Congress* Nantes (France) 2006. **Publications** *Bulletin de l'Association des anatomistes* (4 a year) in French – summaries in English. **Members** Individuals worldwide. Membership countries not specified. **NGO Relations** Member of: *International Federation of Associations of Anatomists (IFAA, #13361)*. [2018/XD7055/**D**]

♦ Association of Moving Image Archivists (internationally oriented national body)
♦ Association MPs of Italian Origin in the World (#02992)
♦ Association of Multiethnic Cities of Southeast Europe (no recent information)
♦ Association Mundial de Antiguas del Sagrado Corazón / see World Association of Alumnae of the Sacred Heart (#21116)
♦ Association de municipalités européennes pour la maîtrise de l'énergie en milieu urbain / see Energy Cities (#05467)
♦ Association of Municipal Technicians of Latin America (inactive)
♦ Association des Musées de la Caraïbe (#16909)
♦ Association des musées du Commonwealth (#04305)
♦ Association des musées des îles du Pacifique (#17959)
♦ Association des musées de l'océan Indien (inactive)
♦ Association des musées de plein air européens (#02527)

♦ Association of Museums and Castles around the Baltic Sea 02815

Itämeren alueen museoiden ja linnojen yhdistyksessä
Chairperson c/o Pilskalns, Bauska LV-3901, Latvia.
Sec Häggeby Kyrkväg 36, SE-746 94 Häggeby, Sweden. E-mail: c.n@bredband2.com.
URL: http://www.visitcastles.eu/

History Jul 1991. **Aims** Promote cultural cooperation between countries around the Baltic Sea; increase knowledge of the region's history and arts; promote tourism in the region. **Structure** General Assembly; Board; Executive Committee; Working Group. **Languages** English, Finnish. **Staff** Voluntary. **Finance** Sources: donations; members' dues; sale of publications. **Activities** Awareness raising; events/meetings; networking/

liaising; publishing activities. **Events** *Annual General Assembly* 2021, *Annual General Assembly and History Conference* Kalmar (Sweden) 2020, *Annual General Assembly and History Conference* Haapsalu (Estonia) 2019, *Annual General Assembly and History Conference* Elblag (Poland) 2018, *Annual General Assembly and History Conference* Turku (Finland) 2017. **Publications** *Castles Around the Baltic Sea* (3rd ed 2019) in English.
Members Museums and historic sites in countries around the Baltic Sea. Members in 9 countries:
Denmark, Estonia, Finland, Germany, Latvia, Lithuania, Poland, Russia, Sweden. [2021.06.14/XD5674/**D**]

♦ Association of Museums of the Indian Ocean (inactive)
♦ Association for Muslim-Christian Dialogue / see International Union for Intercultural and Interfaith Dialogue and Peace Education (#15783)
♦ Association of Muslim Schools in Europe (see: #09682)
♦ Association of Muslim Social Scientists, UK (internationally oriented national body)

♦ Association of Mutual Insurers and Insurance Cooperatives in Europe (AMICE) 02816

Permanent SG Rue du Trône 98/14, 1050 Brussels, Belgium. T. +3225033878. Fax +3225033055. E-mail: secretariat@amice-eu.org.
URL: http://www.amice-eu.org/
History 2007. Founded by *International Association of Mutual Insurance Companies (AISAM, inactive)* and *Association of European Cooperative and Mutual Insurers (inactive)*, whose activities it took over early 2008. Registration: Banque-Carrefour des Entreprises, No/ID: 0893.970.608, Start date: 6 Dec 2007, Belgium; EU Transparency Register, No/ID: 62503501759-81, Start date: 26 May 2009. **Aims** Promote the mutual and cooperative insurance business model; create opportunities and address challenges for mutual and cooperative insurers; advocate for appropriate and fair treatment of all mutual and cooperative insurers in the European Union; enable members, and in particular small and medium-sized insurance undertakings, to be successful. **Structure** General Meeting; Board; Executive Committee. **Languages** English. **Staff** 5.00 FTE, paid. **Finance** Sources: members' dues. Annual budget: 1,200,000 EUR. **Activities** Advocacy/lobbying/activism; events/meetings; knowledge management/information dissemination; networking/liaising; politics/policy/regulatory. **Events** *Biennial Congress* Bilbao (Spain) 2024, *Biennial Congress* Mainz (Germany) / Wiesbaden (Germany) 2022, *Biennial Congress* 2021, *Biennial Congress* Bilbao (Spain) 2020, *Biennial Congress* Stockholm (Sweden) 2018. **Publications** *AMICE Newsletter* (4 a year) in English, French, German, Spanish. *European Mutual Market Share 2022* (2022) – In association with ICMIF; *Facts & Figures: Mutual and cooperatives insurance in Europe* (2 2018) – In association with ICMIF; *Good Practices* (2017); *From Past to Present: A Valuable Model* (2016); *Facts and Figures – Mutual and Cooperative Insurance in Europe*; *MarketInsights 2016* – In association with ICMIF; *MarketInsights Europe 2015* in English, French – with ICMIF; *United in Diversity – European Mutual Insurance Manifesto 2014*. Annual Report.
Members Full members in 19 countries:
Austria, Belgium, Denmark, Finland, France, Germany, Greece, Hungary, Ireland, Italy, Luxembourg, Netherlands, Norway, Poland, Portugal, Slovenia, Spain, Sweden, Switzerland.
Supporting members in 3 countries:
Belgium, France, Lebanon.
Associate member:
France.
NGO Relations Member of (3): *Federation of European and International Associations Established in Belgium (FAIB, #09508)*; *Global Federation of Insurance Associations (GFIA, #10356)*; *Social Economy Europe (SEE, #19335)*. [2023.03.01/XM3677/**D**]

♦ Association mutuelle des fonctionnaires internationaux (#12585)
♦ Association of National Charity Monitoring Agencies / see International Committee on Fundraising Organizations (#12773)
♦ Association of National Committees of the Blue Shield / see Blue Shield International (#03286)
♦ Association of National Committees of the Blue Shield (inactive)

♦ Association of National Development Finance Institutions in Member Countries of the Islamic Development Bank (ADFIMI) 02817

Association des institutions nationales de financement du développement des pays membres de la Banque islamique de développement
SG Saka Mehmet Sokak No 33-39 – Kat 2, Sultanhamam, Eminonu, 34116 Istanbul/Istanbul, Türkiye. T. +902125265126-5265127. Fax +902125265128. E-mail: info@adfimi.org.
URL: http://www.adfimi.org/
History 1986, Jeddah (Saudi Arabia), as a Regional Association of Development Finance Institutions (DFIs) in the Member Countries of *Islamic Development Bank (IsDB, #16044)*. Headquarters transferred to Istanbul (Turkey), 1987, in accordance with a resolution adopted at 2nd General Assembly Meeting, 30 Mar 1987. Registered in accordance with Turkish law. **Aims** Disseminate experience gained from multilateral agencies and regional associations. **Structure** General Assembly (annual); Management Committee; General Secretariat. **Languages** Arabic, English, French. **Finance** Members' dues. Other sources: voluntary donations and co-sponsorship of members. **Activities** Events/meetings; training/education; knowledge management/information dissemination; research/documentation. **Events** *General Assembly* Maputo (Mozambique) 2015, *General Assembly* Jeddah (Saudi Arabia) 2014, *International Development Forum* Kuala Lumpur (Malaysia) 2014, *General Assembly* Dushanbe (Tajikistan) 2013, *General Assembly* Khartoum (Sudan) 2012. **Publications** *ADFIMI Newsletter*.
Members Ordinary; Associate; Honorary. National development finance institutions (43) in 14 Islamic Development Bank member countries:
Bangladesh, Cameroon, Iran Islamic Rep, Jordan, Kazakhstan, Malaysia, Northern Cyprus, Oman, Pakistan, Qatar, Sudan, Türkiye, Uganda, Yemen.
NGO Relations Member of: *World Federation of Development Financing Institutions (WFDFI, #21428)*. Memorandum of Understanding with: *Association of Development Financing Institutions in Asia and the Pacific (ADFIAP, #02472)*; *Asociación Latinoamericana de Instituciones Financieras para el Desarrollo (ALIDE, #02233)*. [2019/XE5921/**E**]

♦ Association nationale cultures du monde (internationally oriented national body)
♦ Association Nationale Cultures and Traditions / see Association nationale cultures du monde
♦ Association nationale pour le développement culturel du monde du travail / see Culture et Liberté
♦ Association nationale pour le développement culturel et solidaire / see Culture et Liberté
♦ Association nationale des directeurs et responsables des relations internationales et de la coopération décentralisée des collectivités territoriales (internationally oriented national body)
♦ Association nationale des écrivains de la mer et d'outre-mer / see Association des écrivains de langue française (#02481)
♦ Association nationale renaissance des cités de France / see Renaissance des cités d'Europe
♦ Association of National European and Mediterranean Societies of Gastroenterology (inactive)

♦ Association of National Numbering Agencies (ANNA) 02818

Exec Dir c/o WM Datenservice, Düsseldorfer Str 16, 60329 Frankfurt-Main, Germany. T. +49692732226. E-mail: secretariat@anna-web.org.
Registered Office Av Marnix 17, 1000 Brussels, Belgium.
URL: http://www.anna-web.org/
History Most recent Articles of Incorporation adopted 30 Sep 2010. Registration: No/ID: 0446.525.840, Start date: 29 Jan 1992, Belgium. **Aims** Adopt a common standard for identifying securities to make the financial world a more efficient, safer and more stable environment for investors and the financial institutions that serve them. **Structure** General Meeting (annual); Board of Directors; Committees; Task Forces (2); Working Groups (2). **Languages** English, French. **Finance** Shares. **Activities** Events/meetings; guidance/assistance/consulting; standards/guidelines. **Events** *Extraordinary General Meeting* Antigua (Guatemala) 2021, *Ordinary General Meeting* Brussels (Belgium) 2021, *Extraordinary General Meeting* Seoul (Korea Rep) 2020, *Ordinary General Meeting* Split (Croatia) 2020, *Extraordinary General Meeting* Montevideo (Uruguay) 2019. **Publications** *Standards Report* (annual). *CFI Guidelines*; *ISIN Guidelines*.
Members National numbering agencies in 65 countries and territories:
Argentina, Australia, Austria, Belgium, Brazil, Bulgaria, Canada, Chile, Costa Rica, Croatia, Cyprus, Czechia, Denmark, Egypt, Estonia, Finland, France, Germany, Greece, Hong Kong, Hungary, Iceland, India, Indonesia, Iran Islamic Rep, Ireland, Israel, Italy, Japan, Jordan, Korea Rep, Kuwait, Latvia, Lebanon, Luxembourg, Malaysia, Mexico, Morocco, Netherlands, Norway, Pakistan, Panama, Peru, Philippines, Poland, Portugal, Romania, Russia, Serbia, Singapore, Slovakia, Slovenia, South Africa, Spain, Sri Lanka, Sweden, Switzerland, Taiwan, Thailand, Tunisia, Türkiye, UK, Ukraine, USA, Venezuela.
Substitute agencies representing 237 countries and territories:
Afghanistan, Albania, Algeria, Andorra, Angola, Anguilla, Antigua-Barbuda, Argentina, Armenia, Aruba, Australia, Austria, Azerbaijan, Bahamas, Bahrain, Bangladesh, Barbados, Belarus, Belgium, Belize, Benin, Bermuda, Bhutan, Bolivia, Bosnia-Herzegovina, Botswana, Brazil, British Antarctic Terr, British Indian Ocean Terr, Brunei Darussalam, Bulgaria, Burkina Faso, Burundi, Cambodia, Cameroon, Canada, Canaries, Cape Verde, Cayman Is, Central African Rep, Chad, Chile, China, Christmas Is, Cocos-Keeling Is, Colombia, Comoros, Congo DR, Cook Is, Costa Rica, Côte d'Ivoire, Croatia, Cuba, Cyprus, Czechia, Denmark, Djibouti, Dominica, Dominican Rep, Ecuador, Egypt, El Salvador, Equatorial Guinea, Eritrea, Estonia, Eswatini, Ethiopia, Faeroe Is, Falklands/Malvinas, Fiji, Finland, France, French Southern and Antarctic Terr, Gabon, Gambia, Georgia, Germany, Ghana, Gibraltar, Greece, Greenland, Grenada, Guadeloupe, Guam, Guatemala, Guernsey, Guiana Fr, Guinea, Guinea-Bissau, Guyana, Haiti, Heard Is, Holy See, Honduras, Hong Kong, Hungary, Iceland, India, Indonesia, Iran Islamic Rep, Iraq, Ireland, Israel, Italy, Jamaica, Japan, Jersey, Jordan, Kazakhstan, Kenya, Kiribati, Korea DPR, Korea Rep, Kuwait, Kyrgyzstan, Laos, Latvia, Lebanon, Lesotho, Liberia, Libya, Liechtenstein, Lithuania, Luxembourg, Macau, Madagascar, Malawi, Malaysia, Maldives, Mali, Malta, Marshall Is, Martinique, Mauritania, Mauritius, McDonald Is, Mexico, Micronesia FS, Moldova, Monaco, Mongolia, Montserrat, Morocco, Mozambique, Myanmar, Namibia, Nauru, Nepal, Netherlands, New Caledonia, New Zealand, Nicaragua, Niger, Nigeria, Niue, Norfolk Is, North Macedonia, Northern Mariana Is, Norway, Oman, Pakistan, Palau, Panama, Papua New Guinea, Paraguay, Peru, Philippines, Pitcairn, Poland, Polynesia Fr, Portugal, Puerto Rico, Qatar, Réunion, Romania, Russia, Rwanda, Sahara West, Samoa, Samoa USA, San Marino, Sao Tomé-Principe, Saudi Arabia, Senegal, Serbia, Seychelles, Sierra Leone, Singapore, Slovakia, Slovenia, Solomon Is, Somalia, South Africa, Spain, Sri Lanka, St Helena, St Kitts-Nevis, St Lucia, St Pierre-Miquelon, St Vincent-Grenadines, Sudan, Suriname, Sweden, Switzerland, Syrian AR, Taiwan, Tajikistan, Tanzania UR, Thailand, Timor-Leste, Togo, Tokelau, Tonga, Trinidad-Tobago, Tunisia, Türkiye, Turkmenistan, Turks-Caicos, Tuvalu, Uganda, UK, Ukraine, United Arab Emirates, Uruguay, USA, Uzbekistan, Vanuatu, Venezuela, Vietnam, Virgin Is UK, Virgin Is USA, Wallis-Futuna, Yemen, Zambia, Zimbabwe.
Also substitute agencies representing Bouvet Is, Canton and Enderbury Is, Neutral Zone, Ceuta Melilla, Svålbard and Jan Mayen Is, USA Minor Outlying Terr. Agreements signed by the following 14 countries (countries allocating ISINs, "):
Agreements signed by the following 14 countries (countries allocating ISINs, "):
Bangladesh (*), Botswana (*), Eswatini, Ghana (*), Honduras, Jordan (*), Kenya (*), Lithuania, Mauritius (*), Nicaragua, Tanzania UR, Uganda (*), Zambia, Zimbabwe (*).
Included in the above, one organization listed in this Yearbook:
Union économique et monétaire Ouest africaine (UEMOA, #20377).
NGO Relations In liaison with technical committees of: *International Organization for Standardization (ISO, #14473)*. [2020/XE2221/**C**]

♦ Association of National Olympic Committees (ANOC) 02819

Association des comités nationaux olympiques (ACNO) – Asociación de Comités Olimpicos Nacionales
SG Chemin des Charmettes 4, 1003 Lausanne VD, Switzerland. T. +41213215260. Fax +41213215261. E-mail: info@anocolympic.org.
URL: https://www.anocolympic.org/
History 26 Jun 1979, San Juan (Puerto Rico). Founded at 1st ANOC General Assembly, a Permanent General Assembly of National Olympic Committees (PGA-NOC) having been set up at 3rd General Assembly of National Olympic Committees (NOCs), 1 Oct 1968, Mexico City (Mexico), held at 19th Olympic Games. Present Constitution in force from 9 Apr 2008. **Aims** Serve the International Olympic Movement in the framework of the philosophical, spiritual and *sporting* principles defined by the International Olympic Committee; promote close collaboration and exchange of information and experience among NOCs and strengthen their role at national level; educate young people through *sport* for a peaceful world; present IOC with suggestions and projects aimed at developing or improving the International Olympic Movement. **Structure** General Assembly; Executive Council. Commissions (8): Communications; Marketing; Sports Venues; Juridical; Medical; Merit Award; Technical; Coordination of the National Olympic Academies' Activities. **Languages** English, French, Spanish. **Staff** 3.00 FTE, paid. **Events** *Annual General Assembly* Crete (Greece) 2021, *Annual General Assembly* Seoul (Korea Rep) 2020, *Annual General Assembly* Doha (Qatar) 2019, *Annual General Assembly* Tokyo (Japan) 2018, *Meeting* Tokyo (Japan) 2018. **Publications** *Annuaire ACNO/ANOC Yearbook*.
Members National Olympic Committees recognized by IOC in 205 countries and territories:
Afghanistan, Albania, Algeria, Andorra, Angola, Antigua-Barbuda, Argentina, Armenia, Aruba, Australia, Austria, Azerbaijan, Bahamas, Bahrain, Bangladesh, Barbados, Belarus, Belgium, Belize, Benin, Bermuda, Bhutan, Bolivia, Bosnia-Herzegovina, Botswana, Brazil, Brunei Darussalam, Bulgaria, Burkina Faso, Burundi, Cambodia, Cameroon, Canada, Cape Verde, Cayman Is, Central African Rep, Chad, Chile, China, Colombia, Comoros, Congo Brazzaville, Congo DR, Cook Is, Costa Rica, Côte d'Ivoire, Croatia, Cuba, Cyprus, Czechia, Denmark, Djibouti, Dominica, Dominican Rep, Ecuador, Egypt, El Salvador, Equatorial Guinea, Eritrea, Estonia, Eswatini, Ethiopia, Fiji, Finland, France, Gabon, Gambia, Georgia, Germany, Ghana, Great Britain, Greece, Grenada, Guam, Guatemala, Guinea, Guinea-Bissau, Guyana, Haiti, Honduras, Hong Kong, Hungary, Iceland, India, Indonesia, Iran Islamic Rep, Iraq, Ireland, Israel, Italy, Jamaica, Japan, Jordan, Kazakhstan, Kenya, Kiribati, Korea DPR, Korea Rep, Kuwait, Kyrgyzstan, Laos, Latvia, Lebanon, Lesotho, Liberia, Libya, Liechtenstein, Lithuania, Luxembourg, Madagascar, Malawi, Malaysia, Maldives, Mali, Malta, Marshall Is, Mauritania, Mauritius, Mexico, Micronesia FS, Moldova, Monaco, Mongolia, Montenegro, Morocco, Mozambique, Myanmar, Namibia, Nauru, Nepal, Netherlands, New Zealand, Nicaragua, Niger, Nigeria, North Macedonia, Norway, Oman, Pakistan, Palau, Palestine, Panama, Papua New Guinea, Paraguay, Peru, Philippines, Poland, Portugal, Puerto Rico, Qatar, Romania, Russia, Rwanda, Samoa, Samoa USA, San Marino, Sao Tomé-Principe, Saudi Arabia, Senegal, Serbia, Seychelles, Sierra Leone, Singapore, Slovakia, Slovenia, Solomon Is, Somalia, South Africa, Spain, Sri Lanka, St Kitts-Nevis, St Lucia, St Vincent-Grenadines, Sudan, Suriname, Sweden, Switzerland, Syrian AR, Taiwan, Tajikistan, Tanzania UR, Thailand, Timor-Leste, Togo, Tonga, Trinidad-Tobago, Tunisia, Türkiye, Turkmenistan, Tuvalu, Uganda, Ukraine, United Arab Emirates, Uruguay, USA, Uzbekistan, Vanuatu, Venezuela, Vietnam, Virgin Is UK, Virgin Is USA, Yemen, Zambia, Zimbabwe.
Continental Associations (5):
Association of National Olympic Committees of Africa (ANOCA, #02820); *European Olympic Committees (EOC, #08083)*; *Oceania National Olympic Committees (ONOC, #17667)*; *Olympic Council of Asia (OCA, #17718)*; *Panam Sports Organization (Panam Sports, #18138)*.
Consultative Status Consultative status granted from: *UNESCO (#20322)* (Consultative Status). **NGO Relations** Instrumental in setting up (1): *Asociación de Confederaciones Deportivas Panamericanas (ACODEPA, #02119)*. Recognized Organization by: *International Olympic Committee (IOC, #14408)*. Grants from IOC through the intermediary of: *Olympic Solidarity (OS, #17721)*. [2020/XB3109/y/**B**]

♦ Association of National Olympic Committees of Africa (ANOCA) . . . 02820

Association des comités nationaux olympiques d'Afrique (ACNOA) – Asociación de Comités Olimpicos Nacionales de Africa
Headquarters PMB 645, Maitama, Abuja, Federal Capital Territory, Nigeria. T. +2348175627455. E-mail: infos@africaolympic.org.
History 27 Jun 1981, Lomé (Togo). 27-28 Jun 1981, Lomé (Togo), at first Constitutive General Assembly. **Aims** Promote understanding, cooperation and mutual help among the National Olympic Committees (NOCs) of Africa; help African NOCs to spread, develop and protect the Olympic ethic throughout the African continent; plan and coordinate the action of African NOCs; organize and coordinate the preparation and participation of Africa in Olympic Games; celebrate in close collaboration with the NOCs concerned, African Sports Confederations and SCSA, the African Games and such in accordance with the Olympic Charter; collaborate closely with SCSA and in a general manner with government and non-governmental sports bodies in order to facilitate the working out and the implementation in Africa of a coherent strategy of sports development which translates in terms of operational programmes the right for all to the practice of sports and physical activities. **Structure** General Assembly. Executive Committee (meets at least annually), consisting of President, 4 Vice-Presidents, 7 Zone Representatives, Secretary-General, Treasurer General, 4 Honorary Presidents and Honorary Secretary-General. Autonomous Secretariat, headed by Secretary General. 8 Standing Committees. **Languages** Arabic, English, French. **Staff** 2.50 FTE, paid; 2.00 FTE, voluntary. **Finance** Members' dues. Other sources: donations; subventions. **Activities** Standing Committees (8): Games; Development; Communication; Finance; Marketing and New Sources of Financing; Sport for All; Medical; National Olympic Academies. Organizes 4-year programmes include symposia, seminars and training courses. **Events** *General Assembly* Lomé (Togo) 2011, *General Assembly* Cairo (Egypt) 2010, *General assembly / African Games* Algiers (Algeria) 2007, *General Assembly* Accra (Ghana) 2005, *General assembly / African Games* Mombasa (Kenya) 2001. **Publications** *ANOCA Update* (12 a year) – electroni newsletter; *ACNOA Magazine*.
Members National Olympic Committees in 53 of the member States of the Organization of African Unity (OAU):

Algeria, Angola, Benin, Botswana, Burkina Faso, Burundi, Cameroon, Cape Verde, Central African Rep, Chad, Comoros, Congo Brazzaville, Congo DR, Côte d'Ivoire, Djibouti, Egypt, Equatorial Guinea, Eswatini, Ethiopia, Gabon, Gambia, Ghana, Guinea, Guinea-Bissau, Kenya, Lesotho, Liberia, Libya, Madagascar, Malawi, Mali, Mauritania, Mauritius, Morocco, Mozambique, Namibia, Niger, Nigeria, Rwanda, Sao Tomé-Principe, Senegal, Seychelles, Sierra Leone, Somalia, South Africa, Sudan, Tanzania UR, Togo, Tunisia, Uganda, Zambia, Zimbabwe.
Individuals in 13 countries:
Cameroon, Côte d'Ivoire, Egypt, Guinea, Kenya, Mauritius, Morocco, Nigeria, Senegal, South Africa, Tunisia, Uganda, Zimbabwe.
NGO Relations Continental Association of: *Association of National Olympic Committees (ANOC, #02819).* Recognized Organization of: *International Olympic Committee (IOC, #14408).* Formal contacts with: *African Sports Journalists Union (ASJU, inactive).* Grants from IOC through the intermediary of: *Olympic Solidarity (OS, #17721).* Affiliated with: *Confederation of Africa Deaf Sports (CADS, #04498).* [2017/XD1525/**D**]

♦ Association of National Organisations for Supervision in Europe (ANSE) 02821

Sec ANSE Office, Heinrichsgasse 4/8, 1010 Vienna, Austria. E-mail: i.stankusvisa@anse.eu – office@anse.eu.
Pres address not obtained.
URL: http://www.anse.eu/
History Set up 21 Nov 1997, by national organizations of Austria, Germany, Hungary, Netherlands and Switzerland. Registered in accordance with Austrian law. **Aims** Meet the need for European cooperation and Europe-wide exchange of views among professionals in the field of supervision, coaching and the professional guidance of learning and work processes; promote learning about cultural diversity and support cross border cooperation. **Structure** General Assembly; Board. **Languages** English. **Staff** Voluntary. **Finance** Members' dues. Annual budget: about euro 27,500. **Activities** Training/education; events/meetings; knowledge management/information dissemination; projects/programmes. **Events** *Conference* Budapest (Hungary) 2015, *Conference* Berlin (Germany) 2014, *General Assembly* Vienna (Austria) 2014, *General Assembly* Berlin (Germany) 2012, *General Assembly* Vienna (Austria) 2010.
Members Full in 15 countries:
Austria, Bosnia-Herzegovina, Croatia, Estonia, Germany, Hungary, Ireland, Italy, Latvia, Lithuania, Netherlands, Norway, Slovenia, Spain, Switzerland.
Associate in 2 countries:
Slovenia, Ukraine.
Members of ANSE Network in 8 countries:
Czechia, Finland, Greece, Iceland, Poland, Romania, Sweden, UK.
NGO Relations Agreement with: *EUROCADRES – Council of European Professional and Managerial Staff (#05651).* Partner of: *European Association for Supervision and Coaching (EASC, #06240); EMCC Global (EMCC, #05434).* [2016.10.27/XJ9089/**D**]

- ♦ Association of National Organizations of Fishing Enterprises of the EEC / see Association des organisations nationales d'entreprises de pêche de l'UE (#02841)
- ♦ Association of National Organizations of Fishing Enterprises in the EU (#02841)
- ♦ Association of Nationless Esperantist Workers / see Nationless Worldwide Association (#16941)
- ♦ Association des nations de l'Asie du Sud-Est (#01141)
- ♦ Association of Natural Medicine in Europe (internationally oriented national body)

♦ Association of Natural Rubber Producing Countries (ANRPC) 02822

Association des pays producteurs de caoutchouc naturel
SG 7th Floor, Bangunan Getah Asli, 148 Jalan Ampang, 50450 Kuala Lumpur, Malaysia. T. +60321611900. Fax +60321613014. E-mail: secretariat@anrpc.org.
URL: http://www.anrpc.org/
History Constitution came into force 8 Apr 1970. First Session of the Assembly, 14-16 Oct 1970, Kuala Lumpur (Malaysia). *International Natural Rubber Agreement on Price Stabilisation (1976)* was signed, Nov 1976, by five member countries. Re-constituted May 1982. Statutes registered in *'UNTS 1/15731'.* **Aims** Improve productivity of rubber holdings, reduce cost, increase value addition in downstream rubber sector, explore sources of ancillary income, capitalize on eco-friendly credentials of natural rubber and thereby improve the well-being of rubber farmers. **Structure** Assembly; Executive Committee; Committees (2); Working Groups (2). **Languages** English. **Staff** 6.00 FTE, paid. **Finance** Members' dues. **Activities** Makes studies of the world rubber position and examines the short and long term problems facing the natural rubber industry; promotes research and development in production, marketing and processing of natural rubber; sets up institutional arrangements as required; cooperates with appropriate organizations. Organizes Annual Conference, seminars, workshops and meetings connected with: (a) progress and development of rubber smallholders; (b) natural rubber statistics; (c) production and marketing of natural rubber; (d) demand-supply of natural rubber. **Events** *Annual Rubber Conference* Yogyakarta (Indonesia) 2019, *Annual Rubber Conference* Chiang Rai (Thailand) 2018, *Annual Rubber Conference* Ho Chi Minh City (Vietnam) 2017, *Annual Rubber Conference* Krabi (Thailand) 2016, *Annual Rubber Conference* Colombo (Sri Lanka) 2013. **Publications** *ANRPC Monthly Bulletin on Rubber Statistics* (12 a year); *Quarterly Natural Rubber Market Review* (4 a year); *Industry Updatte* (28 a year); *Market Update* (28 a year); *Statistical Profile of Smallholdings* (occasional); *Annual Bulletin on Rubber Statistics. ANRPC Directory of Natural Rubber Organizations* (2008); *ANRPC Directory of Rubber Suppliers* (2008).
Members Governments of 13 countries:
Bangladesh, Cambodia, China, India, Indonesia, Malaysia, Myanmar, Papua New Guinea, Philippines, Singapore, Sri Lanka, Thailand, Vietnam.
IGO Relations Participates in the activities of: *UNCTAD (#20285).* Relationship agreement with: *United Nations Framework Convention on Climate Change (UNFCCC, 1992); UNIDO (#20336).* Liaison with: *FAO Regional Office for Asia and the Pacific (RAP, #09266).* [2019.04.25/XD5434/**D***]

- ♦ Association pour la navigation fluviale et les voies navigables européennes (internationally oriented national body)
- ♦ Association néerlandaise des africanists (internationally oriented national body)
- ♦ Association des négociateurs-conseils en propriété industrielle (inactive)

♦ Association of the Network for International Research on Desertification (DesertNet International) 02823

Reseau pour la recherche internationale sur la desertification – Red de Investigación Internacional sobre la Desertificación
SG c/o NRD, Univ of Sassari, Viale Italia 39, 07100 Sassari SS, Italy. T. +39079229267. Fax +39079229394. E-mail: nrd@uniss.it.
Chair 16 rue Juliette Savar, 94000 Créteil, France.
URL: http://www.desertnet-international.org/
History Oct 2007, Bonn (Germany). Current title adopted to reflect international membership. Former names and other names: *European Network for Global Desertification Research (European DesertNet)* – former; *DNI* – alias. **Aims** Generate and enhance knowledge and understanding of the biophysical and socio-economic processes of desertification. **Structure** Steering Committee; Advisory Board; Secretariat. **Languages** English. **Staff** Voluntary. **Finance** Sponsored by universities, research institutes and ministries. **Activities** Capacity building; politics/policy/regulatory; projects/programmes; research and development.
Members Full (328) in 51 countries:
Algeria, Argentina, Australia, Belgium, Brazil, Bulgaria, Burkina Faso, Canada, Chile, China, Cuba, Egypt, Ethiopia, Finland, France, Georgia, Germany, Greece, Hungary, India, Indonesia, Iran Islamic Rep, Israel, Italy, Jordan, Kazakhstan, Kenya, Lebanon, Mali, Morocco, Myanmar, Namibia, Netherlands, Norway, Pakistan, Portugal, Romania, Russia, Slovakia, South Africa, Spain, Sudan, Sweden, Switzerland, Thailand, Togo, Tunisia, UK, United Arab Emirates, USA, Vietnam.
IGO Relations Accredited to the Conference of the Parties of: *Secretariat of the United Nations Convention to Combat Desertification (Secretariat of the UNCCD, #19208).* **NGO Relations** Member of (1): *Sustainable Development Solutions Network (SDSN, #20054).* Also links with other NGOs (not specified). [2023.02.14/XM2985/**D**]

♦ Association de neuro-anesthésie-réanimation de langue française (ANARLF) 02824

Pres c/o CHU de Bicêtre, Dept d'anesthésie Réanimation, 78 rue du Général Leclerc, 94270 Le Kremlin-Bicêtre, France.
Main Office c/o CHU Pellegrin, 33076 Bordeaux, France.
URL: http://www.anarlf.eu/
History 1982, Bordeaux (France). Registration: RNA, No/ID: W943004798, Start date: 19 Jul 2017, France. **Aims** Promote postgraduate proficiency; encourage scientific and clinical research in the field of neuro-anaesthesia-intensive care; further exchanges. **Structure** General Assembly (annual). Administrative Council of 12 to 21 members, comprising Bureau – President, Immediate Past President, 3 Vice-Presidents, Secretary-General, 2 Assistant Secretaries-General and Treasurer – and 20 members. **Languages** French. **Staff** 1.00 FTE, paid; 20.00 FTE, voluntary. **Finance** Members' dues: euro 30. Donations. Budget (annual): euro 2,000. **Activities** Participates in experts conferences; organizes congress (annual), conferences and symposia. **Events** *Annual Congress* Grenoble (France) 2022, *Annual Congress* Le Kremlin-Bicêtre (France) 2021, *Annual Congress* Le Kremlin-Bicêtre (France) 2020, *Annual Congress* Paris (France) 2018, *Annual Congress* Nice (France) 2017.
Members Regular; Associate; Founder individuals in 8 countries:
Belgium, Canada, France, Italy, Liechtenstein, Switzerland, UK, USA. [2022/XD3263/v/**D**]

- ♦ Association de neurologie d'Asie et d'Océanie (#01352)
- ♦ Association de la noblesse russe / see Russian Nobility Union (#19009)
- ♦ Association of Non-Governmental Organizations in SEE / see Association of Non-Governmental Organizations of Southeast Europe (#02825)

♦ Association of Non-Governmental Organizations of Southeast Europe (CIVIS) 02825

Project Manager Dobracina 15/VII, Belgrade, PAK 11000, Serbia. T. +381112621723. Fax +381112626332.
URL: http://www.civis-see.org/
History 4 Jun 2007. Also referred to as *Association of Non-Governmental Organizations in SEE.* **Aims** Promote and improve the rights of all citizens in the area of Southeast Europe; fulfill the highest standards of civil society; support civic dialogue; improve education, cooperation and exchange information between members and between European institutions committed to the same objective; provide assistance to all those having European integration as objective, as well as to NGOs in the region and their activities and relations with European institutions and organizations. **Structure** General Assembly; Executive Board. **Languages** Bosnian, Croatian, English, French, Serbian. **Staff** 3.00 FTE, paid; 6.00 FTE, voluntary. **Finance** Members' dues. Funding from: *Peace and Crises Management Foundation.* **Activities** Organizes: conference; round tables; workshops; TV serial. Promotes COE documents. Advocacy; publishing activity. Participates in: World Energy Efficiency Day (5 March); International Human Rights Day (10 December). **Publications** *Everlasting Value and Permanent Actuality of the Edict of Milan-On the Way to the Great Jubilee in 2013* (2013); *Neo-Ottomanism: A Doctrine and Foreign Policy Practice* (2013); *Neoclassicism in the Balkans and Other Essays* (2012); *New Economic Diplomacy – Opportunities and Challenges* (2012); *Everyone Should Believe as His Heart Wishes* (2011); *The Role of Churches and Religious Communities in Sustainable Peace-Building in Southeast Europe* (2008). Newsletter.
Members Full in 12 countries:
Albania, Bosnia-Herzegovina, Bulgaria, Croatia, France, Greece, Kosovo, Montenegro, Romania, Serbia, Slovenia, Switzerland.
Included in the above, 3 organizations listed in this Yearbook:
Association of Multiethnic Cities of Southeast Europe (PHILIA, no recent information); Centrul Euroregional pentru Democratie (CED); Robert Schuman Institute for Europe (IRSE, #18959).
Consultative Status Consultative status granted from: *Council of Europe (CE, #04881)* (Participatory Status). [2016/XJ0973/y/**D**]

- ♦ Association Nord-Américaine des Etudes Jean-Jacques Rousseau / see Rousseau Association
- ♦ Association of Nordic Aeroclubs (no recent information)
- ♦ Association of Nordic Automobile Inspectors (inactive)

♦ Association of Nordic Cancer Registries (ANCR) 02826

Contact Icelandic Cancer Society, Icelandic Cancer Registry, Skógarhlid 8, PO Box 5420, 125 Reykjavik, Iceland. T. +3548995333. E-mail: helgi.birgisson@krabb.is.
URL: http://www.ancr.nu/
History Founded 1984. **Aims** Provide a continuing, organized framework for Nordic cancer registries so as to: facilitate exchange of scientific and technical information; contribute to uniformity of definitions use by registries; facilitate organization of inter-Nordic and international studies. **Structure** Board of Directors. Presidency rotates annually. **Languages** Danish, English, Faroese, Icelandic, Norwegian, Swedish. **Staff** None. **Finance** No budget. Running costs paid by member registries. **Activities** Research/documentation; knowledge management/information dissemination; events/meetings. **Events** *Annual Scientific Meeting* Denmark 2021, *Annual Scientific Meeting* Copenhagen (Denmark) 2020, *Annual Scientific Meeting* Stockholm (Sweden) 2019, *Annual Scientific Meeting* Hella (Iceland) 2018, *Annual Scientific Meeting* Stavanger (Norway) 2017. **Publications** Reports; monographs.
Members Cancer registries in 6 countries and territories:
Denmark, Faeroe Is, Finland, Iceland, Norway, Sweden.
IGO Relations Links with *Nordic Council (NC, #17256).* [2019.01.18/XD2811/**D**]

♦ Association for Nordic Dialysis and Transplant Personnel 02827

Association du personnel nordique en dialyse et transplantation – Foreningen for Nordisk Dialyse og Transplantation Personale (NORDIATRANS)
Pres Dialysis units, Helsinki Univ Hosp, Haartmaninkatu 4, FI-00029 Helsinki, Finland.
URL: https://www.nordiatrans.org/
History 1972. **Aims** Increase knowledge of care of patients with *renal disease*; exchange experience in the field; increase cooperation among persons working with dialysis and transplantation in the Nordic countries. **Structure** President; Secretary. **Languages** Danish, English, Norwegian, Swedish. **Staff** 6.00 FTE, voluntary. **Finance** Sources: meeting proceeds; members' dues. **Activities** Events/meetings. **Events** *Congress* Visby (Sweden) 2017, *Congress* Copenhagen (Denmark) 2015, *Congress* Oslo (Norway) 2013, *Congress / Annual Nordiatrans Congress* Lund (Sweden) 2012, *Congress / Annual Nordiatrans Congress* Helsinki (Finland) 2011.
Members Personnel in the transplant and dialysis fields in the 5 Nordic countries:
Denmark, Finland, Iceland, Norway, Sweden. [2021/XD0782/v/**D**]

♦ Association of Nordic Engineers (ANE) 02828

Gen Sec Kalvebod Brygge 31-33, 1780 Copenhagen, Denmark. T. +4529743960. E-mail: nordic-engineers@ida.dk.
URL: http://nordicengineers.org/
History May 2007. **Aims** Serve as a platform for affiliates to generate ideas and share know-how; focus on securing sustainable working life for engineers, and on demonstrating the role of engineers impacting the sustainable transition of our societies and in achieving the UN's Sustainable Development Goals. **Structure** Advisory Board; Students Network; Secretariat. **Languages** English. **Staff** 2.50 FTE, paid. **Finance** Sources: members' dues. **Activities** Advocacy/lobbying/activism; awareness raising; events/meetings; knowledge management/information dissemination; networking/liaising; projects/programmes. **Publications** Policy recommendations; guidelines; reports.
Members Full in 5 countries:
Denmark, Finland, Iceland, Norway, Sweden. [2023.02.15/XM7798/**D**]

♦ Association for the Nordic Game Industry (ANGI) 02829

Secretariat Kommunikation2, Hoveporten 2, 2650 Hvidovre, Denmark. T. +4536890890. E-mail: mm@k-2.dk.
URL: http://angi-nordic.com/
History 2012. **Aims** Support and maintain the Nordics as an ideal environment to publish and distribute video games and interactive entertainment. **Structure** Board; Secretariat.
Members Full in 4 countries:
Denmark, Finland, Norway, Sweden.
NGO Relations Member of (1): *Interactive Software Federation of Europe (ISFE, #11380).* [2020/AA1886/**D**]

♦ **Association of Nordic Music Academies (ANMA)** **02830**
Conseil nordique des académies de musique – Nordisk Konservatorieråd
SG Royal Academy of Music Aarhus/Aalborg, Skovgaardsgade 2C, 8000 Aarhus, Denmark. T. +4572267400.
URL: http://www.nordplusmusic.net/index.php?id=6
History 1964. Founded by Nordic music conservatoires and academies. Former names and other names: *Nordic Council for Music Conservatories* – former. **Aims** Strengthen higher education in music in the Nordic countries through Nordic cooperation; provide a forum for consideration of common issues concerning higher education in music; provide a coordinating body for cooperation in Nordic projects; safeguard the Nordic perspective on international cooperation. **Structure** General Assembly (annual); Executive Committee; Secretariat. **Languages** Danish, English, Norwegian, Swedish. **Staff** None. **Finance** Sources: members' dues. **Activities** Awards/prizes/competitions; events/meetings. **Events** *General Assembly* 2021, *General Assembly* Reykjavik (Iceland) 2019, *Nordtrad Network Conference* Voss (Norway) 2018, *Annual Meeting* Oslo (Norway) 2011, *Festival* Riga (Latvia) 2011. **Publications** Conference proceedings; reports.
Members Institutions in 11 countries and territories:
Denmark, Estonia, Finland, Georgia, Iceland, Latvia, Lithuania, Norway, Poland, Scotland, Sweden. [2021/XD1894/**D**]

♦ Association of Nordic Organizations (inactive)

♦ **Association of Nordic Paper Historians** **02831**
Association nordique des historiens du papier – Verein Nordischer Papierhistoriker – Föreningen Nordiska Pappershistoriker
Chairman Adolf Lemons väg 56, SE-187 76 Täby, Sweden. T. +46851010169.
URL: http://www.nph.nu/
History Founded 1968. Also referred to in English as *Scandinavian Paper History Association.* **Aims** Encourage cooperation and study of paper history, handmade paper and watermarks as well as the history of industry based paper production, processes, products, converting and related subjects. **Structure** Annual meeting; Board. **Languages** Danish, Norwegian, Swedish. **Staff** Voluntary. **Finance** Members' dues. Annual budget: Swedish Kr 60,000. **Events** *Annual Meeting* Sønderborg (Denmark) 2014, *Annual Meeting* Lappeenranta (Finland) 2013, *Annual Meeting* Östanå (Sweden) 2012, *Annual Meeting* Oslo (Norway) 2011, *Annual Meeting* Mänttä-Vilppula (Finland) 2010. **Publications** *Nordisk Pappershistorisk Tidskrift* (4 a year).
Members Individuals and corporations in 4 countries:
Denmark, Finland, Norway, Sweden. [2020/XD1407/**D**]

♦ Association of Nordic and Pol-Balt Lesbian, Gay, Bisexual, Transgender and Queer Student Organizations / see Association of Nordic and Pol-Balt LGBTQ Student Organizations (#02832)

♦ **Association of Nordic and Pol-Balt LGBTQ Student Organizations (ANSO)** **02832**
Contact c/o KPH, ul Solec 30 A, 00-403 Warsaw, Poland.
URL: http://ansoblog.wordpress.com/
History Full title: *Association of Nordic and Pol-Balt Lesbian, Gay, Bisexual, Transgender and Queer Student Organizations.* **Aims** Combat *discrimination* based on *homophobia* and transphobia in *universities*; increase the quality of higher education by combating heteronormativity. **Structure** Board, comprising President, Vice President, Treasurer, Secretary and 5 members.
Members Full in 8 countries:
Denmark, Estonia, Finland, Iceland, Lithuania, Norway, Poland, Sweden.
NGO Relations Member of: *ILGA-Europe (#11118); International Lesbian, Gay, Bisexual, Transgender, Queer and Intersex Youth and Student Organization (IGLYO, #14032).* [2013/XJ6336/**D**]

♦ Association of Nordic Reserve Officers (inactive)

♦ **Association for Nordic Theatre Scholars (ANTS)** **02833**
Föreningen Nordiska Teaterforskare
Pres Iceland Academy of the Arts, Sölvhólsgata 13, 101 Reykjavik, Iceland. E-mail: magnusthor@lhi.is – magnusthor@simnet.is.
URL: https://blogs.uta.fi/nordictheatrestudies/the-association/
Aims Encourage cooperation between Nordic theatre scholars and students. **Structure** General Assembly; Board. **Activities** Events/meetings; knowledge management/information dissemination. **Events** *Conference* Helsinki (Finland) 2019, *Conference* Aarhus (Denmark) 2017, *Conference* Reykjavik (Iceland) 2016, *Conference* Helsinki (Finland) 2015. **Publications** *Nordic Theatre Studies* – journal.
Members Full in 7 countries:
Denmark, Estonia, Finland, Iceland, Lithuania, Norway, Sweden. [2019/XM7797/**D**]

♦ Association of Nordic University Rectors' Conferences / see Nordic University Association (#17458)

♦ **Association of Nordic War and UN Military Veterans (ANWUNMV)** . . **02834**
Nordiska Krigs-och FN-Veteranförbundet
Address not obtained.
History 1974. **Aims** Maintain and strengthen *friendship* and unity between members; commemorate and strengthen friendship between those who: for the Nordic countries took part in *World War II*, took part in the *Korean War* under UN Command, have participates in the UN Peace Keeping Force; look after the interests of the individuals within member organizations; cooperate with other veterans' organizations to promote peace, liberty, human rights and self-determination of all peoples. **Structure** Annual Meeting; Board. **Languages** English, Swedish. **Staff** 7.00 FTE, voluntary. **Finance** Sources: members' dues. **Activities** Events/meetings; financial and/or material support.
Members Regional veterans' organizations, other veterans' organizations, and individuals in 10 countries and territories:
Denmark, Estonia, Finland, Iceland, Korea Rep, Norway, Philippines, Sweden, Taiwan, Thailand.
NGO Relations Member of (1): *World League for Freedom and Democracy (WLFD, #21621)* (as International Organization Member Unit). [2021/XE6113/**E**]

♦ Association nordique des administrateurs d'université (#17206)
♦ Association nordique des agences de publicité (no recent information)
♦ Association nordique pour l'aménagement du marché (inactive)
♦ Association nordique des apprentis du textile (no recent information)
♦ Association nordique d'aviculture scientifique (inactive)
♦ Association nordique de bibliothécaires (inactive)
♦ Association nordique de bowling (inactive)
♦ Association nordique de canoë (inactive)
♦ Association nordique des chanteurs (#17532)
♦ Association nordique des chimistes du cuir (inactive)
♦ Association nordique des coiffeurs pour dames et pour messieurs / see Nordic Hairdressers' Association (#17307)
♦ Association nordique des confiseurs (inactive)
♦ Association nordique de conseillers en orientation (inactive)
♦ Association nordique pour l'économie domestique (#17160)
♦ Association nordique d'éducation comparée et internationale (#17249)
♦ Association nordique d'éthologie (inactive)
♦ Association nordique des études canadiennes (#17181)
♦ Association nordique pour les études sur la condition féminine et la recherche sur l'égalité des sexes (#17208)
♦ Association nordique des experts comptables enregistrés (inactive)
♦ Association nordique des fabricants de postes électroniques (inactive)
♦ Association nordique des fabricants de violons (inactive)
♦ Association nordique de gastroentérologie (inactive)
♦ Association nordique de géophysique appliquée (no recent information)
♦ Association nordique de gymnastique féminine (inactive)
♦ Association nordique des gynécologues et obstétriciens (#17286)
♦ Association nordique des handicapés (#17308)
♦ Association nordique des historiens du papier (#02831)
♦ Association nordique de l'horlogerie (no recent information)
♦ Association nordique des hôtels et restaurants / see Nordic Union Hotels, Restaurants, Catering and Tourism (#17454)
♦ Association nordique des industries de plomberie (inactive)
♦ Association nordique des ingénieurs (inactive)
♦ Association nordique des lotissements (#17177)
♦ Association nordique de lutte amateur (no recent information)
♦ Association nordique de médecine interne (inactive)
♦ Association nordique de médecine manuelle (inactive)
♦ Association Nordique des Médecins Catholiques (#17506)
♦ Association nordique des mycologistes de terrain (inactive)
♦ Association nordique de neurologie (inactive)
♦ Association nordique d'odontologie (#19070)
♦ Association nordique d'orientation scolaire et professionnelle (#17191)
♦ Association nordique pour la paix (inactive)
♦ Association nordique de pathologie et microbiologie (inactive)
♦ Association nordique de pathologie pédiatrique (inactive)
♦ Association nordique de pédicures (inactive)
♦ Association nordique de pédodontie (inactive)
♦ Association nordique de plombiers et étameurs (inactive)
♦ Association nordique de podologie (inactive)
♦ Association nordique de protection contre les radiations (#17428)
♦ Association nordique de récupération (inactive)
♦ Association nordique de la route / see Nordic Road Association (#17402)
♦ Association nordique des sapeurs pompiers (inactive)
♦ Association nordique de science politique (#17389)
♦ Association nordique des sciences administratives (#17477)
♦ Association nordique des télécommunications (inactive)
♦ Association nordique de transitaires (#17543)
♦ Association nordique des travailleurs de la bijouterie (inactive)
♦ Association of North American Operations Research Societies within IFORS (internationally oriented national body)

♦ **Association of North East Asia Regional Governments (NEAR)** **02835**
Secretariat 3F Pohang Technopark, 601 Jigok-dong, Nam-gu, Pohang NORTH GYEONGSANG 37668, Korea Rep. T. +82542232318. Fax +82542232309. E-mail: neargov@gmail.com.
URL: http://www.neargov.org/
History 12 Sep 1996, Gyeongju (Korea Rep). 12 Sep 1996, Kyung-ju City (Korea Rep), after an initial meeting Oct 1993, Japan. **Aims** Promote all local authorities within Northeast Asia to form a network for interaction and cooperation, based on the philosophy of equality and mutual benefit. **Structure** General Assembly (every 2 years); Working Committee; Sub-Committees. **Languages** Chinese, English, Japanese, Korean, Mongolian, Russian. **Staff** 12.00 FTE, paid. 4 seconded from member regions. **Finance** Financed by host member region of Secretariat. **Activities** Advocacy/lobbying/activism. **Events** *General Assembly* Pohang (Korea Rep) 2021, *International Forum on Cruise Tourism* Pohang (Korea Rep) 2019, *Economic Cooperation Forum of CEO in Northeast Asia* Pohang (Korea Rep) 2018, *Northeast Asia Young Leaders Forum* Pohang (Korea Rep) 2018, *General Assembly* Zhangjiajie (China) 2018. **Publications** *NEAR News* (6 a year).
Members Regional governments in 6 countries:
China (6), Japan (10), Korea DPR (2), Korea Rep (16), Mongolia (22), Russia (15).
IGO Relations Affiliated to: *Regions of Climate Action (R20, #18820).* [2020/XD6588/**D**]

♦ Association North Mediterranean Mastology / see Mobile Mediterranean University of Mastology (#16836)

♦ **Association du notariat francophone (ANF)** **02836**
Pres 60 blvd de La Tour Maubourg, 75007 Paris, France. T. +33144404040. Fax +33144903030.
URL: http://www.notariat-francophone.org/
History 17 Mar 1992. Founded on initiative of French notaries with support from the Ministère français de la Francophonie (French Ministry of French-speaking People). **Aims** Develop links among *French-speaking* notaries; promote humane and legal values that underlie Latin right; facilitate the sharing and exchange of materials, persons and experience. **Structure** General Assembly; Board of Directors; Bureau. **Languages** French. **Finance** Sources: members' dues. **Activities** Events/meetings; training/education. **Events** *Annual General Assembly* Montpellier (France) 2012, *Annual General Assembly* Bordeaux (France) 2010, *Annual General Assembly* Lille (France) 2009, *Triennial Extraordinary General Assembly* Nice (France) 2008, *Colloque sur le notaire, acteur de la sécurité juridique et régulateur dans une économie de marché* Paris (France) 2007. **Publications** *Lettre d'information* (2 a year).
Members Organizations and individuals in 28 countries:
Belgium, Benin, Bulgaria, Burkina Faso, Cameroon, Central African Rep, Chad, Congo Brazzaville, Congo DR, Côte d'Ivoire, France, Gabon, Guinea, Lebanon, Luxembourg, Madagascar, Mali, Mauritius, Morocco, Niger, North Macedonia, Poland, Québec, Romania, Senegal, Switzerland, Togo, Tunisia.
NGO Relations Member of: *Association francophone d'amitié et de liaison (AFAL, #02605); Forum francophone des affaires (FFA, #09916); Institut international de droit d'expression et d'inspiration françaises (IDEF, #11310).* [2022/XD9485/**C**]

♦ Association de Notre-Dame de la Bonne-Mort (religious order)
♦ Association du Numéro d'Urgence Européen (#06978)
♦ Association des obtenteurs horticoles européens (no recent information)
♦ Association occidentale de dragage (#20913)
♦ Association oecuménique des centres de recherche et de rencontre en Europe (#17706)
♦ Association oecuménique des femmes européennes en recherche théologique / see European Society of Women in Theological Research (#08789)
♦ Association oecuménique des théologiens africains (no recent information)
♦ Association oecuménique des théologiens du Tiers-monde (#05344)
♦ Association des offices de commercialisation des produits alimentaires au Proche-Orient et en Afrique du Nord (no recent information)
♦ Association of Official Agricultural Chemists / see AOAC INTERNATIONAL (#00863)
♦ Association of Official Analytical Chemists / see AOAC INTERNATIONAL (#00863)
♦ Association of Official Analytical Collaboration / see AOAC INTERNATIONAL (#00863)
♦ Association of Official Racing Chemists (unconfirmed)

♦ **Association of Official Seed Certifying Agencies (AOSCA)** **02837**
CEO 3105 Research Rd, Champaign IL 61822, USA.
URL: http://www.aosca.org/
History 1919. Former names and other names: *International Crop Improvement Association* – former (1919 to 1968). **Aims** Promote and facilitate the movement of seed or plant products in local, national, and international markets through the coordinated efforts of official seed certification agencies acting to evaluate, document, and verify that a seed or plant product meets certain accepted standards. **Structure** Board of Directors. **Events** *Annual Meeting* Bloomington, MN (USA) 2023, *Annual Meeting* Dearborn, MI (USA) 2013, *Annual meeting* Sun Valley, ID (USA) 2012, *Annual meeting* St Louis, MO (USA) 2011, *Annual meeting* Niagara Falls, NY (USA) 2010. **Publications** Annual Report. Newsletters; handbook.
Members Agencies in 6 countries:
Argentina, Australia, Canada, Chile, New Zealand, USA.
IGO Relations *OECD (#17693).* [2022/XD8141/t/**D**]

♦ Association d'officiers de réserve nordiques (inactive)
♦ Association of Old Crows (internationally oriented national body)
♦ Association Ollier Maffuci Europe (internationally oriented national body)

♦ Association olympique internationale (inactive)
♦ Association olympique internationale pour la recherche médico-sportive (no recent information)

♦ Association des ombudsmans et médiateurs africains (AOMA) 02838

African Ombudsman and Mediators Association – Associação dos Ombudsman e Mediadores

SG PO Box 201414, Nairobi, 00200, Kenya. T. +25472768261. Fax +254202302666. E-mail: aoma.kenya@ombudsman.go.ke.

URL: http://aoma.ukzn.ac.za/Home.aspx

History 2001, as *Centre africain de l'Ombudsman*. Present name and structure adopted, 2003. Current constitution adopted 2014, Addis Ababa (Ethiopia). **Aims** Advance the development of the Ombudsman institution for the furtherance of good governance, the rule of law, and human rights in Africa. **Structure** General Assembly; Executive Committee; Secretariat. **Activities** Events/meetings; training/education. **Events** *General Assembly* Kigali (Rwanda) 2018, *Congress* Tripoli (Libyan AJ) 2008.

Members Full in 40 countries:

Angola, Benin, Botswana, Burkina Faso, Burundi, Cape Verde, Central African Rep, Chad, Congo Brazzaville, Côte d'Ivoire, Djibouti, Ethiopia, Gabon, Gambia, Ghana, Guinea, Kenya, Lesotho, Libya, Madagascar, Malawi, Mali, Mauritania, Mauritius, Mozambique, Namibia, Niger, Nigeria, Rwanda, Senegal, Seychelles, Sierra Leone, South Africa, Sudan, Tanzania UR, Togo, Tunisia, Uganda, Zambia, Zimbabwe.

NGO Relations Member of: *International Partnership on Religion and Sustainable Development (PaRD, #14524).* [2019/XM3909/**D**]

♦ Association des ombudsmans et médiateurs de la Francophonie (AOMF) 02839

Association of Ombudsmen and Mediators of the French-speaking World

Permanent Secretariat TSA 90716, 75334 Paris CEDEX 07, France. E-mail: secretariat.aomf@defenseurdesdroits.fr.

Pres address not obtained.

URL: http://www.aomf-ombudsmans-francophonie.org/

History 20 May 1998, Nouakchott (Mauritania). Founded with the support of *Organisation internationale de la Francophonie (OIF, #17809).* **Aims** Encourage dispute resolution and *conflict prevention*; support democracy and human rights; promote the institutions of ombudsmen and mediators in French speaking countries. **Languages** French. **Staff** 0.50 FTE, paid. **Finance** Sources: grants; members' dues. Supported by: *Organisation internationale de la Francophonie (OIF, #17809).* **Activities** Events/meetings; training/education. **Events** *Conférence* Monaco (Monaco) 2021, *Joint Conference* Rabat (Morocco) 2019, *Congrès* Brussels (Belgium) 2018, *Congrès* Québec, QC (Canada) 2015, *Congrès* Dakar (Senegal) 2013. **Publications** *AOMF Newsletter.* Guides.

Members Full in 36 countries:

Albania, Andorra, Armenia, Belgium, Benin, Bulgaria, Burkina Faso, Burundi, Canada, Central African Rep, Congo Brazzaville, Côte d'Ivoire, Djibouti, Egypt, France, Gabon, Guinea, Haiti, Italy, Kosovo, Luxembourg, Madagascar, Mali, Mauritius, Moldova, Monaco, Morocco, Niger, Romania, Senegal, Seychelles, Spain, Switzerland, Togo, Tunisia, Vanuatu. [2022/XJ8248/**D**]

♦ Association des Ombudsmans de la Méditerranée (#02802)
♦ Association of Ombudsmen and Mediators of the French-speaking World (#02839)
♦ Association des ONGs des Iles du Pacifique (#17961)
♦ Association des opérateurs postaux publics européens (#02534)
♦ Association des opérateurs des postes et des télécommunications des pays et territoires de langue officielle portugaise (#02333)
♦ Association of Operative Millers / see International Association of Operative Millers
♦ Association des organisations africaines de promotion commerciale (no recent information)
♦ Association des organisations africaines de technologie industrielle (inactive)
♦ Association des organisations européennes d'artistes interprètes (#02530)
♦ Association des organisations de gestion d'Asie (#01329)
♦ Association des organisations intergouvernementales d'Afrique de l'Ouest (inactive)
♦ Association des organisations internationales de culture ouvrière (inactive)
♦ Association des Organisations interProfessionnelles d'entrepreneurs des Capitales Européennes / see Business European Capital Cities (#03382)

♦ Association of Organisations of Mediterranean Businesswomen ... 02840

Asociación de Federaciones y Asociaciones de Empresarias del Mediterraneo (AFAEMME)

Pres C/ Provença 301 bajos, 08037 Barcelona, Spain. E-mail: afaemme@afaemme.org.

URL: http://www.afaemme.org/

History Jul 2002, Barcelona (Spain). Former names and other names: *Association of Federations and Associations of Business Women in the Mediterranean (AFAEMME)* – alias. Registration: Spain. **Aims** Promote equality at work and improve women's *professional* development by eliminating discrimination; promote development of relations between Mediterranean *business women* and women entrepreneurs; promote international cooperation in the field of the promotion of equal opportunities for men and women; contribute to the cultural development of business women and women entrepreneurs in the Mediterranean. **Structure** General Assembly (annual); Board of Directors. **Languages** English. **Staff** 4.00 FTE, paid; 6.00 FTE, voluntary. **Activities** Research/documentation; networking/liaising; advocacy/lobbying/activism. **Events** *Mediterranean Women Entrepreneurs Forum* Alexandria (Egypt) 2022, *Mediterranean Women Entrepreneurs Forum* Barcelona (Spain) 2021, *Mediterranean Women Entrepreneurs Forum* Barcelona (Spain) 2020, *Forum* Barcelona (Spain) 2019, *Forum* Barcelona (Spain) 2017. **Publications** *afaemme Bulletin* (4 a year) – electronic bulletin. Reports.

Members National organizations (60) in 23 countries and territories:

Albania, Algeria, Bosnia-Herzegovina, Croatia, Cyprus, Egypt, France, Greece, Italy, Jordan, Lebanon, Libya, Malta, Monaco, Montenegro, Morocco, Palestine, Slovenia, Spain, Syrian AR, Tunisia, Türkiye, UK.

Arab International Women's Forum (AIWF, #00994).

Consultative Status Consultative status granted from: *ECOSOC (#05331)* (Special). **IGO Relations** Collaborate with: *ECOSOC (#05331); European Commission (EC, #06633); European Parliament (EP, #08146); Union for the Mediterranean (UfM, #20457).* Member of: *Anna Lindh Euro-Mediterranean Foundation for the Dialogue between Cultures (Anna Lindh Foundation, #00847).* **NGO Relations** Member of (3): *ANIMA Investment Network (#00833); Asociación de las Camaras de Comercio e Industria del Mediterraneo (ASCAME, #02112); Euro-Mediterranean Women's Foundation (#05729).* Member of: *Institut de Prospective économique du Monde Méditerranéen (IPEMED, #11352).* Collaborates with: *European Union Women Inventors and Innovators Network (EUWIIN, #09023); International Alliance for Learning (IAL, no recent information).* Partnership agreement with: *GlobeWomen.* [2022/XM0610/y/**D**]

♦ Association des organisations nationales de la boulangerie et de la pâtisserie de la CEE / see European Confederation of National Bakery and Confectionery Organizations (#06714)
♦ Association des organisations nationales de la boulangerie, de la pâtisserie, de la confiserie, de la chocolaterie artisanales de la CEE / see European Confederation of National Bakery and Confectionery Organizations (#06714)
♦ Association des organisations nationales d'entreprises de pêche de la CEE Asociación de las Organizaciones Nacionales de Empresas de Pesca en la CEE / see Association des organisations nationales d'entreprises de pêche de l'UE (#02841)

♦ Association des organisations nationales d'entreprises de pêche de l'UE (EUROPECHE) 02841

Association of National Organizations of Fishing Enterprises in the EU – Asociación de las Organizaciones Nacionales de Empresas de Pesca en la UE – Vereinigung der Nationalen Verbände von Fischereiunternehmen in der EU – Associação das Organizações Nacionais de Empresas de Pesca da UE – Associazione delle Organizzazioni Nazionali delle Imprese di Pesca della UE – Vereniging der Nationale Organisaties van Visserijondernemingen in de EU

Dir Rue Montoyer 24, 1000 Brussels, Belgium. T. +3222304848. Fax +3222302680. E-mail: europeche@europeche.org.

URL: http://www.europeche.org/

History Founded 4 May 1962, Brussels (Belgium), as *Association of National Organizations of Fishing Enterprises of the EEC – Association des organisations nationales d'entreprises de pêche de la CEE Asociación de las Organizaciones Nacionales de Empresas de Pesca en la CEE – Vereinigung der Nationalen Verbände von Fischereiunternehmen in der EWG – Associazione delle Organizzazioni Nazionali delle Imprese di Pesca della CEE – Vereniging der Nationale Organisaties van Visserijondernemingen in de EEG.* Current Statutes adopted by General Assembly, 14 Dec 1987. EU Transparency Register: 2312395253-25. **Aims** Represent the common interests of member organizations in dealings with various European Union authorities and with other groups and organizations; promote relations between all the national organizations of fishing enterprises in EU and defend their general and specific interests; look for the points of agreement on all fishery-related questions which are of interest at EU level. **Structure** General Assembly (at least annual). **Languages** English, French, Spanish. **Staff** 2.50 FTE, paid. **Finance** Members' dues. **Activities** Politics/policy/regulatory; advocacy/lobbying/activism; events/meetings. **Events** *European seminar* Concarneau (France) 2000, *Forum for partnership in the fisheries industry between the European Union and the Islamic Republic of Mauritania* Nouakchott (Mauritania) 2000, *European seminar* Puerto de Santa Maria (Spain) 1997, *Ordinary meeting* Brussels (Belgium) 1992. **Publications** *The Fisheries Sector in the Islamic Republic of Mauritania* (1999); *Handbook for the Prevention of Accidents at Sea and the Safety of Fishermen*; *The Creation of the European Network for Vocational Training and Employment in the Fisheries Sector in the EU*; *The Mutual Recognition of Certificates in the Fisheries Sector.*

Members National organizations in 10 countries:

Belgium, Denmark, France, Germany, Italy, Malta, Netherlands, Poland, Spain, UK.

IGO Relations *European Economic and Social Committee (EESC, #06963); OSPAR Commission for the Protection of the Marine Environment of the North-East Atlantic (OSPAR Commission, #17905).* **NGO Relations** *International Coalition of Fisheries Associations (ICFA, #12614); Market Advisory Council (MAC, #16584); Waste Free Oceans (WFO, #20820).* [2022/XE0154/**E**]

♦ Association des organisations nordiques (inactive)
♦ Association des organisations patronales interprofessionnelles des capitales européennes / see Business European Capital Cities (#03382)
♦ Association des organisations professionnelles du commerce des sucres pour les pays de la CEE / see European Association of Sugar Traders (#06239)
♦ Association des organisations professionnelles du commerce des sucres pour les pays de l'UE / see European Association of Sugar Traders (#06239)
♦ Association des organismes d'assurance-crédit à l'exportation et de promotion du commerce extérieur (inactive)
♦ Association des organismes électoraux de la Caraïbe (#02405)
♦ Association des organismes d'habitat social pour le développement d'un réseau international de coopération / see Réseau habitat et francophonie (#18888)
♦ Association orientale de dragage (#05238)
♦ Association for Oriental Studies (internationally oriented national body)
♦ Association ornithologique internationale (inactive)
♦ Association des ornithologistes espérantistes (no recent information)

♦ Association des orthopédistes de langue française (AOLF) 02842

French-Language Association for Orthopaedics

SG address not obtained.

URL: http://www.aolf.ch/

History 1986. **Aims** Promote cooperation among orthopaedic surgeons through cultural and technical exchanges. **Structure** Congress (every 2 years). Bureau, consisting of President, Vice-President, Immediate Past President, President of forthcoming Congress, Secretary-General/Treasurer, Deputy Secretary. Council. **Finance** Members' dues. **Events** *Congrès* Oran (Algeria) 2016, *Congrès / Congress* St Petersburg (Russia) 2014, *Congrès* Dakar (Senegal) 2012, *Congrès / Congress* Geneva (Switzerland) 2010, *Congrès / Congress* Marrakech (Morocco) 2008. **Publications** *AOLF Newsletter.*

Members National associations of French-speaking orthopaedic surgeons and individuals. Members in 33 countries:

Algeria, Argentina, Austria, Belgium, Brazil, Bulgaria, Burkina Faso, Canada, Congo Brazzaville, Côte d'Ivoire, El Salvador, France, Germany, Greece, Guinea, Iran Islamic Rep, Italy, Lebanon, Luxembourg, Mali, Mexico, Morocco, North Macedonia, Portugal, Romania, Senegal, Serbia, South Africa, Spain, Switzerland, Togo, Tunisia, Vietnam. [2017/XF2050/**F**]

♦ Association ouest africaine d'archéologie (#20866)
♦ Association ouest africaine des chirurgiens plasticiens (no recent information)
♦ Association ouest africaine pour le développement de la pêche artisanale (#20867)
♦ Association ouest africaine pour l'évaluation environnementale (#20868)
♦ Association ouest et centre africaine de la science du sol (no recent information)
♦ Association of Outplacement Consulting Firms International / see Association of Career Firms International (#02400)
♦ Association of Overseas Countries and Territories / see Association of Overseas Countries and Territories of the European Union (#02843).

♦ Association of Overseas Countries and Territories of the European Union (OCTA) 02843

Association des pays et territoires d'outre-mer de l'Union européenne

Contact Schumanplein 6, 1040 Brussels, Belgium. T. +3227917578.

Contact address not obtained.

Main Website: https://www.overseas-association.eu/

History Established as an association under Part Four of *Treaty Establishing the European Econonomci Community (Treaty of Rome).* In Jun 2000, OCTs representatives in Brussels (Belgium) started meeting together in order to coordinate their views with respect to a common position to be taken on the draft for a new OCT decision, which was at the time being prepared by the *European Commission (EC, #06633)* for adoption by European Union Ministers meeting in the General Council. The first meeting took place, 16-17 Nov 2000, Brussels, where governments of the OCTs decided to re-establish the Association. Agreement reached on the Articles of the Association, 18 Sep 2002, at the second OCT Ministerial Conference in Bonaire. Re-established 5 Mar 2003, Brussels.

The OCTs are associated with the European Union through a regime based on the provisions of Part IV of the *Treaty on the Functioning of the European Union (TFEU, 1957).* Article 355 of the Treaty provides the possibility for the OCTs to become outermost regions, and inversely. Twelve OCTs are constitutionally linked to the UK, 6 to the French Republic, 6 to the Kingdom of Netherlands and 1 to the Kingdom of Denmark. Following an extensive consultation process, a new OAD governs EU-OCT relations as of 1 Jan 2014. Former names and other names: *Association of Overseas Countries and Territories (OCTA)* – former; *Other Countries and Territories (OCTs)* – former; *Associated Countries and Territories (AOCT)* – former; *Overseas Countries and Territories (OCT)* – former; *Overseas Countries and Territories of the European Union Association* – former. Registration: Crossroads Bank for Enterprises, No/ID: 0872.157.880, Start date: 28 Feb 2005, Belgium, Brussels.

Aims Serve as a platform through which Overseas Countries and Territories realize their common goals by working collectively through cooperation, policy dialogue, promotion of common positions and partnerships for sustainable development of OCTs. **Structure** Ministerial Conference (General Assembly); Rotating Chairmanship; Executive Committee (Administrative Board); Permanent Secretariat. /Members/ Territory under the Danish Crown: Greenland. Overseas countries and territories of France: French Polynesia; French Southern and Antarctic Lands; New Caledonia and dependencies; Saint Barthelemy; St Pierre-Miquelon; Wallis and Futuna Islands. Overseas countries of the Netherlands: Aruba; Bonaire; Curaçao; Saba; Sint Eustatius; Sint Maarten. **Languages** English, French. **Staff** 2.00 FTE, paid; 10.00 FTE, voluntary. **Finance** Sources: members' dues. Supported by: *European Commission (EC, #06633); European Development Fund (EDF, #06914).* **Activities** Advocacy/lobbying/activism; events/meetings; networking/liaising; politics/policy/regulatory. **Events** *Cultural mobility in European Outermost Regions and Overseas Countries and Territories* Brussels (Belgium) 2022, *OCTA Youth Days* Brussels (Belgium) 2022, *Presenting LIFE programme to the OCTs* Brussels (Belgium) 2022, *Annual OCT-EU Forum* Nouméa (New Caledonia) 2022, *Conference on Oceans* Brussels (Belgium) 2019. **Publications** *OCTA Newsletter.* [2023.02.14/XF3413/**F***]

♦ Association for Overseas Technical Cooperation and Sustainable Partnerships (internationally oriented national body)
♦ Association for Overseas Technical Scholarship / see Association for Overseas Technical Cooperation and Sustainable Partnerships
♦ Association of Pacific and Far East Ports / see Association of Pacific Ports (#02845)

♦ Association of Pacific Island Legislatures (APIL) 02844

Mailing Address PO Box V, Hagatna GU 96932, USA.
URL: http://www.apilpacific.com/

History 1981. **Aims** Organize a permanent association of mutual assistance by representatives of the people of the Pacific Islands. **Structure** General Assembly; Board of Directors. **Languages** English. **Staff** 1.00 FTE, paid. **Finance** Annual budget: US$ 120,000. **Events** *General Assembly* Honolulu, HI (USA) 2020, *General Assembly* Pohnpei (Micronesia FS) 2018, *General Assembly* Kiribati 2017, *General Assembly* Guam 2016, *East Asia and Southeast Asia Regional conference on Ethical Recruitment and Policy Harmonization in Fishing Industry* Seoul (Korea Rep) 2016. **Publications** Assembly proceedings.
Members Legislative representatives from 12 governments:
Chuuk, Guam, Hawaii, Kiribati, Kosrae, Marshall Is, Nauru, Northern Mariana Is, Palau, Pohnpei, Samoa USA, Yap.
[2022/XD0786/**D**]

♦ Association of Pacific Islands Maritime Training Institutions and Maritime Authorities / see Pacific Islands Maritime Association (#17974)
♦ Association of Pacific Ports / see Pacific Maritime Transport Alliance (#17982)

♦ Association of Pacific Ports (APP) 02845

Address not obtained.
URL: http://www.pacificports.org/

History 1913, as *Association of Pacific and Far East Ports*. Present name adopted 1934. **Aims** Promote efficiency and effectiveness of the ports of the Pacific. **Structure** Executive Committee, comprising President, 3 Vice-Presidents, Immediate Past-President, 5 Regional Representatives, Executive Staff Representative. **Events** *Winter Conference* Hawaii (USA) 2024, *Annual Conference* Kaohsiung (Taiwan) 2024, *Winter Conference* Honolulu, HI (USA) 2023, *Annual Conference* Long Beach, CA (USA) 2023, *Annual Conference* Saipan (Northern Mariana Is) 2022. **Publications** *Pacific Current* – newsletter.
Members Ports (28) in 7 countries and territories:
Guam, Mexico, Micronesia FS, Northern Mariana Is, Samoa USA, Taiwan, USA. [2021/XM1793/**D**]

♦ Association of Pacific Rim Universities (APRU) 02846

Communications Dir Unit 902, Cyberport 2, 100 Cyberport Road, Kowloon, Hong Kong. E-mail: info@apru.org.
URL: http://www.apru.org/

History 3 Jun 1997, Los Angeles, CA (USA). Founded as a not-for-profit research institute. **Aims** Serve as an advisory body to international organizations, governments and business on development of science and innovation as well as the broader development of higher education in the region. **Structure** Steering Committee. **Languages** English. **Staff** 7.00 FTE, paid. **Finance** Sources: members' dues. **Activities** Events/meetings. **Events** *Annual Presidents Meeting* Hong Kong (Hong Kong) 2022, *Annual Presidents Meeting* Kowloon (Hong Kong) 2021, *Global Health Conference* Pokfulam (Hong Kong) 2021, *Sustainable Cities and Landscapes Conference* Kowloon (Hong Kong) 2020, *Global Health Conference* Shanghai (China) 2020. **Publications** *APRU Impact Report 2016*.
Members Universities (45) in 17 countries and territories:
Australia, Canada, Chile, China, Hong Kong, Indonesia, Japan, Korea Rep, Malaysia, Mexico, New Zealand, Philippines, Russia, Singapore, Taiwan, Thailand, USA.
Consultative Status Consultative status granted from: *ECOSOC (#05331)* (Special). **NGO Relations** Member of (1): *International Association of Universities (IAU, #12246)*. [2023.02.20/XD7584/**D**]

♦ Association of Pacific Systematists (no recent information)
♦ Association pacifiste internationale (inactive)

♦ Association for Paediatric Education in Europe (APEE) 02847

Association Européenne pour l'enseignement de la pédiatrie (AEPE)
SG 49 rue d'Alzon, 33000 Bordeaux, France. T. +33688237374.
URL: http://www.aeep.asso.fr/

History 1970. Previously referred to in Spanish as *Asociación Europea de Educación Pediatrica*. Also known as *European Association for Paediatric Education (EAPE)*. **Aims** Promote research and advances in paediatric education. **Structure** Executive Committee, comprising President, Vice-President, Secretary, Treasurer and 3 members. Specific working groups/committees. **Languages** English, French. **Staff** Voluntary. **Finance** Members' dues. **Activities** Projects carried out through Standing Committees (3): Inventory of the Curricula of Undergraduate Teaching of Paediatrics in the Different Countries of Europe; Handbook on Teaching Paediatrics; Computers in Paediatric Education. Task force for programme on teaching paediatrics for the general practitioner in Europe. **Events** *World Pediatrics Conference* Singapore (Singapore) 2019, *Teaching pediatrics to school teachers* Budapest (Hungary) 2015, *Annual meeting* Bordeaux (France) 2003, *Annual meeting* Aix-en-Provence (France) 2001, *Annual meeting* London (UK) 2000. **Publications** *The Journal of APEE* (annual) in English, French.
Members Individual mainly university teachers and paediatricians actively interested in medical education; Institutional groups, associations, institutions. Members (about 80) in 21 countries:
Austria, Croatia, Czechia, Denmark, Estonia, Finland, France, Germany, Greece, Hungary, Ireland, Italy, Luxembourg, Netherlands, Poland, Portugal, Spain, Sweden, Switzerland, Türkiye, UK.
IGO Relations *WHO (#20950)*. **NGO Relations** Cooperates with: *Association for Medical Education in Europe (AMEE, #02797)*; *European Academy of Paediatrics (EAP, #05811)*; *European Society for Paediatric Research (ESPR, #08687)*; *International Society for Social Pediatrics and Child Health (ISSOP, #15448)*; *European Paediatric Association (EPA/UNEPSA, #08124)*. [2015/XD3644/**D**]

♦ Association des palais de congrès africains (inactive)

♦ Association paléographique internationale – culture, écriture, société (APICES) 02848

SG CNRS-IRHT, Campus Condorcet, bât recherche nord, 14 cours des Humanités, 93322 Aubervilliers CEDEX, France. T. +33188120017. E-mail: secretariat.apices@cnrs-orleans.fr.
Registered Office Ecole nationale des chartes, 19 rue de la Sorbonne, 75005 Paris, France.
URL: http://www.palaeographia.org/apices/apices.htm

History 24 Oct 1993, Erice (Italy). Founded by *Comité international de paléographie latine (CIPL, #04180)*. Registration: France. **Aims** Bring together people interested in scholarly study of ancient and *medieval scripts*. **Structure** General Assembly; Council (Moderamen); Officers: President, Secretary General, Treasurer. **Languages** English, French, Italian. **Staff** Voluntary. **Finance** Sources: members' dues. **Activities** Events/meetings; knowledge management/information dissemination; research and development. **Events** *General Assembly* Florence (Italy) 2020, *General assembly* New Haven, CT (USA) 2017, *General Assembly* Berlin (Germany) 2015, *General Assembly* St Gallen (Switzerland) 2013, *General Assembly* Ljubljana (Slovenia) 2010. **Publications** *Gazette du Livre médiéval* – partnership publication.
Members Corporate; Adhering. Members in 22 countries:
Austria, Belgium, Canada, Finland, France, Germany, Iceland, Ireland, Israel, Italy, Japan, Luxembourg, Netherlands, Norway, Poland, Portugal, Romania, Spain, Sweden, Switzerland, UK, USA.
NGO Relations Statutory partner of: *Comité international de paléographie latine (CIPL, #04180)*.
[2022.02.01/XD2950/**E**]

♦ Association paléontologique internationale (#14501)

♦ Association des palynologues de langue française (APLF) 02849

Association of French-Speaking Palynologists
Secretariat c/o Maison de la Géologie, 77 rue Claude Bernard, 75005 Paris, France. E-mail: didier.galop@univ-tlse2.fr.
URL: http://w3.laplf.univ-tlse2.fr/

History 1967. Registered in accordance with French law. **Aims** Assist the progress, illustration, representation and defence of palynology (pollens – spores – microplankton – dinoflagellates – acritarchs) – principally palynostratigraphy, paleoecology, paleoclimatology, morphology, melissopalynology, systematic, phylogeny, aeropalynology, archeology. **Structure** General Assembly (at least every 2 years). Bureau of at least 4 persons (meeting at least annually). Working Groups. **Languages** English, French. **Staff** None. **Finance** Members' dues. **Activities** Organizes conferences and meetings, including geological and botanical trips. Works on international pollen and dinocyst databases. **Events** *International Symposium* Pontarlier (France) 2015, *International Congress* Madrid (Spain) 2013, *International Symposium* Madrid (Spain) 2013, *Symposium* Meudon (France) 2011, *International Symposium* Lille (France) 2009. **Publications** *Palynosciences* – review. Reports (annual).
Members Individuals in 36 countries and territories:
Algeria, Belgium, Brazil, Burkina Faso, Cameroon, Canada, Chile, China, Congo Brazzaville, Congo DR, Côte d'Ivoire, France, Gabon, Germany, Greece, Hungary, India, Israel, Italy, Madagascar, Mexico, Morocco, Netherlands, Niger, Nigeria, Norway, Poland, Portugal, Romania, Saudi Arabia, Spain, Sweden, Switzerland, Uganda, UK, USA.
NGO Relations Member of: *International Federation of Palynological Societies (IFPS, #13498)*.
[2013/XD4710/v/**D**]

♦ Association pan-africaine d'anthropologie (#18036)
♦ Association panafricaine d'archéologie (#18035)
♦ Association pan-africaine de coopération portuaire (#18038)
♦ Association panafricaine pour le développement communautaire (no recent information)
♦ Association panafricaine des écrivains (#18075)
♦ Association panafricaine de l'éducation et de la formation des adultes (no recent information)
♦ Association panafricaine des étudiants en droit (no recent information)
♦ Association panafricaine des exégètes catholiques (inactive)
♦ Association panafricaine des femmes professionnelles des télécommunications et des Technologies de l'information (no recent information)
♦ Association panafricaine des historiens (inactive)
♦ Association panafricaine de musique d'Eglise (inactive)
♦ Association panafricaine pour la préhistoire et les sciences auxilliaires / see Pan-African Archaeological Association (#18035)
♦ Association panafricaine des sciences neurologiques (#18037)
♦ Association pan-américaine d'aérobiologie (#18078)
♦ Association panaméricaine d'anatomie (#18079)
♦ Association panaméricaine de cautionnement / see Panamerican Surety Association (#18134)
♦ Association panaméricaine de chirurgie pédiatrique / see Asociación Iberoamericana de Cirugia Pediatrica (#02134)
♦ Association panaméricaine des femmes (inactive)
♦ Association panaméricaine des implants (inactive)
♦ Association Panaméricaine des Institutions de Crédit Éducatif (#18084)
♦ Association panaméricaine de médecine légale (inactive)
♦ Association panaméricaine de médecine sociale (inactive)
♦ Association panaméricaine de médecine vétérinaire et de zootechnie / see Asociación Panamericana de Ciencias Veterinarias (#02287)
♦ Association panaméricaine d'odontologie (inactive)
♦ Association panaméricaine d'ophtalmologie (#18081)
♦ Association panaméricaine d'oto-rhino-laryngologie et de broncho-oesophagologie / see Pan American Association of Oto-Rhino-Laryngology – Head and Neck Surgery (#18082)
♦ Association panaméricaine d'oto-rhino-laryngologie – chirurgie de la tête et du cou (#18082)
♦ Association panaméricaine de sciences vétérinaires (#02287)
♦ Association of Panamerican Athletics (#02284)
♦ Association of Pan American Sport Confederations (#02119)
♦ Association pan arabe des sociétés de radiologie (#18141)
♦ Association Panibérique des Académies Olympiques (#18181)
♦ Association pan Pacifique de chirurgie (#18187)

♦ Association of Paralympic Sports Organisations (APSO) 02850

Honorary Secretary General address not obtained.
URL: http://apso.sport/

History Constituent General Meeting and first General Assembly took place on 4 Sep 2017, Abu Dhabi (United Arab Emirates). Registration: Switzerland, Vaud. **Aims** Protect and promote the interests of member sport organisations and athletes within the Paralympic movement. **Structure** General Assembly; Executive Board. **Languages** English. **Staff** 0.00 FTE, paid.
Members Organizations (17):
Badminton World Federation (BWF, #03060); *Fédération Équestre Internationale (FEI, #09484)*; *International Blind Sports Federation (IBSA, #12363)*; *International Canoe Federation (ICF, #12437)*; *International Table Tennis Federation (ITTF, #15650)*; *International Tennis Federation (ITF, #15676)*; *International Wheelchair and Amputee Sports Federation (IWAS, #15881)*; *International Wheelchair Basketball Federation (IWBF, #15882)*; *International Wheelchair Rugby Federation (IWRF, #15883)*; *Union Cycliste Internationale (UCI, #20375)*; *World Archery (#21105)*; *World Boccia (#21236)*; *World Curling Federation (WCF, #21348)*; *World ParaVolley (#21710)*; *World Rowing (#21756)*; *World Taekwondo (#21844)*; *World Triathlon (#21872)*.
NGO Relations Member of (1): *Olympic Movement (#17719)*. [2022.10.11/AA1356/y/**B**]

♦ Association des pari mutuel urbain et des loteries d'Afrique / see Association des Loteries d'Afrique (#02791)
♦ Association of Parkinsonism and Related Disorders / see International Association of Parkinsonism and Related Disorders (#12068)
♦ Association parlementaire du Commonwealth (#04355)
♦ Association parlementaire pour la coopération euro-arabe (#18217)
♦ Association parlementaire européenne (internationally oriented national body)
♦ Association parlementaire mondiale pour les droits de l'animal (inactive)
♦ Association Parlementaires d'Origine Italienne dans le Monde (#02992)
♦ Association pour un parlement mondial (inactive)

♦ Association of Parliamentary Librarians of Asia and the Pacific (APLAP) 02851

Acting Sec address not obtained.
URL: https://www.asiapacificparllibs.org/

History 1990. **Aims** Encourage cooperation and knowledge sharing between bodies that provide library and research services to Parliaments in Asia and the Pacific. **Structure** Executive Committee. **Activities** Events/meetings; training/education; capacity building. **Events** *Conference* Tokyo (Japan) 2018, *Moving towards a big data era – the roles of parliamentary libraries and research services* Seoul (Korea Rep) 2017, *Conference* Canberra, ACT (Australia) 2015, *Conference* Wellington (New Zealand) 2006, *Conference* Delhi (India) 2005.
Members Full in 39 countries and territories:
Afghanistan, Australia, Bangladesh, Bhutan, Cambodia, China, Cook Is, Fiji, Hong Kong, India, Indonesia, Iran Islamic Rep, Japan, Kiribati, Korea Rep, Malaysia, Marshall Is, Micronesia FS, Mongolia, Myanmar, Nepal, New Zealand, Niue, Oman, Pakistan, Papua New Guinea, Philippines, Samoa, Singapore, Solomon Is, Sri Lanka, Taiwan, Thailand, Timor-Leste, Tonga, Türkiye, Tuvalu, Vanuatu, Vietnam.
NGO Relations International Association member of: *International Federation of Library Associations and Institutions (IFLA, #13470)*. [2022/XJ9485/**D**]

♦ Association of Parliamentary Libraries of Australasia (internationally oriented national body)

♦ Association of Parliamentary Libraries of Eastern and Southern Africa (APLESA) 02852

Chairperson/Pres Parliament of Uganda, PO Box 7178, Kampala, Uganda. T. +256414377242.
URL: http://www.aplesa.org/

History 1994. **Aims** Serve as a forum for professional networking and resource sharing among parliamentary libraries in the sub-region. **Languages** English, French, Portuguese. **Staff** 2.00 FTE, paid. **Finance** Members' dues. Other sources: conference fees; funding from donors. **Activities** Knowledge management/information dissemination; events/meetings; networking/liaising; capacity building. **Events** *Conference* Kampala (Uganda) 2019, *Conference* Nairobi (Kenya) 2015, *Conference* Lobamba (Swaziland) 2013, *Conference* Swakopmund (Namibia) 2012, *Conference* Blantyre (Malawi) 2010.
Members Parliamentary libraries in 13 countries:
Angola, Botswana, Eswatini, Kenya, Lesotho, Malawi, Namibia, Rwanda, South Africa, Tanzania UR, Uganda, Zambia, Zimbabwe. [2019.07.11/XD9354/D]

♦ Association of Paroling Authorities International (internationally oriented national body)
♦ Association for Partnership and Citizens Activity Support / see Balkan Assist

♦ Association of Pathologists of East, Central and Southern Africa (APECSA) — 02853
Pres address not obtained. E-mail: slylukas@gmail.com.
URL: http://www.apecsa.org/
History Founded Sep 1991, Dar es Salaam (Tanzania UR). **Aims** Oversee and improve training in the field, thus increasing the number of qualified pathologists. **Activities** Standards/guidelines; guidance/assistance/consulting. **Events** *Annual Meeting* Kigali (Rwanda) 2016, *Annual Meeting* Arusha (Tanzania UR) 2014, *Annual Meeting* Cape Town (South Africa) 2012, *Annual Meeting* Kampala (Uganda) 2010, *Biennial congress / Annual Meeting / Biennial Congress* Mombasa (Kenya) 2008.
Members Full in 12 countries:
Botswana, Eswatini, Kenya, Lesotho, Malawi, Mauritius, Namibia, Seychelles, Tanzania UR, Uganda, Zambia, Zimbabwe.
NGO Relations *College of Pathologists of East Central and Southern Africa (COPECSA, #04109).*
[2016/XD3315/D]

♦ Association des pays exportateurs de minerai de fer (inactive)
♦ Association des pays producteurs de caoutchouc naturel (#02822)
♦ Association des pays producteurs d'étain (inactive)
♦ Association des pays et territoires d'outre-mer de l'Union européenne (#02843)
♦ Association of Peace Messengers (internationally oriented national body)
♦ Association for Peace, Rome (internationally oriented national body)
♦ Association for Peace and Understanding in the Middle East (internationally oriented national body)

♦ Association des pédiatres d'Afrique noire francophone (APANF) — 02854
Contact BP 523, Cotonou, Benin.
History Founded Dec 1981, Dakar (Senegal). Also referred to in English as as *Pediatric Association of Black-French-Speaking Africa*. **Aims** Group all physicians in French-speaking Black Africa who work in the field of child health; collect, exchange and disseminate information concerning the practice and teaching of paediatrics; promote development of paediatrics in member countries. **Structure** Congress (every 2 years); Bureau. **Languages** French. **Finance** Members' dues. Other sources: subsidies; grants; donations. Budget (annual): CFA Fr 15 million. **Events** *Survie de l'enfant africain – où en sommes-nous au 3ème millénaire?* Kinshasa (Congo DR) 2015, *Congress* Yamoussoukro (Côte d'Ivoire) 2012, *OMD 4 – réduire la mortalité* Brazzaville (Congo Brazzaville) 2009, *Congress* Dakar (Senegal) 2007, *Annual general assembly / Medical Days* Bangui (Central African Rep) 1990.
Members Individuals Full; Honorary; Associate; Corresponding. Members in 16 countries:
Benin, Burkina Faso, Burundi, Cameroon, Central African Rep, Chad, Congo Brazzaville, Congo DR, Côte d'Ivoire, Gabon, Guinea, Madagascar, Mali, Niger, Senegal, Togo. [2015/XD9559/D]

♦ Association des pédiatres cardiologues européens / see Association for European Paediatric and Congenital Cardiology (#02529)

♦ Association des pédiatres de langue française (APLF) — 02855
Association of French-Speaking Pediatricians
Secretariat Hôpital Necker Enfants Malades, 149 rue de Sèvres, 75743 Paris CEDEX, France. T. +33144494882. E-mail: hello@aplf2022.ma.
History Founded 1978, a French national organization having existed since 1910. In French also referred to as *Société de pédiatrie de langue française*. **Aims** Bring together doctors specializing in diseases of children and whose primary language is French. **Structure** Executive Council; Board. **Languages** French. **Staff** Voluntary. **Finance** Sources: grants; subsidies. **Activities** Instrumental in setting up *European Academy of Paediatrics (EAP, #05811)*. **Events** *Congrès National de Pédiatrie* Marrakech (Morocco) 2022, *Triennial Congress* Paris (France) 2019, *Triennial Congress* Tours (France) 2015, *Triennial Congress* Hammamet (Tunisia) 2011, *Triennial Congress* Paris (France) 2005. **Publications** Congress proceedings.
Members Individuals; National organizations (marked "). Members (over 4,000) in 27 countries:
Algeria (*), Austria, Belgium, Benin (*), Cameroon, Canada, Central African Rep, Congo Brazzaville, Congo DR, Côte d'Ivoire (*), Equatorial Guinea, France (*), Gabon, Guinea, Haiti, Italy, Lebanon, Luxembourg (*), Madagascar, Monaco, Morocco (*), Poland, Portugal, Senegal, Spain, Switzerland, Tunisia (*). [2022/XD0141/C]

♦ Association of Pediatric Societies of the Southeast Asian Region / see Asia Pacific Pediatric Association (#01992)
♦ Association pénitentiaire africaine (no recent information)
♦ Association of the Pensioned Staff of the Coordinated Organizations and of their Dependants (#02363)

♦ Association of Pension and Social Funds of the CIS (APSF) — 02856
Head Office 23 Skolkovskoye shosse, Moscow MOSKVA, Russia, 121353. E-mail: apsf@apsf.ru.
URL: http://www.apsf.ru/
History 1992. Also referred to as *International Association of Pension and Social Funds (IAPSF)*. **Aims** Coordinate activities of pension and social funds of CIS member countries for implementation of their commitments ensuing from international agreements on provision of pensions and social insurance of citizens of these countries and for representation of the interests of the association members on their behalf in relations with interstate and international organizations. **Structure** General Meeting. **Finance** Members' dues. **Activities** Generalizes and popularizes information on related questions; prepares and publishes collections of normative material; arranges international meetings and refresher courses; studies problems of mutual interest. **Events** *Annual Conference* Tbilisi (Georgia) 2002, *Annual Conference* Dushanbe (Tajikistan) 2001. **Publications** *Social Newsletter for Pension Social funds of CIS Baltia* (4 a year) – magazine.
Members Full in 11 countries:
Armenia, Azerbaijan, Belarus, Georgia, Kazakhstan, Kyrgyzstan, Moldova, Russia, Tajikistan, Ukraine, Uzbekistan.
NGO Relations *International Social Security Association (ISSA, #14885)*. [2018/XE3701/E]

♦ Association permanente des producteurs de l'horticulture (inactive)
♦ Association permanente de la sellerie (inactive)
♦ Association du personnel du CERN (#03834)
♦ Association du personnel nordique en dialyse et transplantation (#02827)
♦ Association du personnel de l'OCDE (#19940)
♦ **Association du personnel de L'OMPI** Association du personnel de l'Organisation mondiale de la propriété intellectuelle (#19942)
♦ Association du personnel de l'OMT / see UNWTO Staff Association, Madrid
♦ Association du personnel OPS/OMS (#18024)
♦ Association du personnel de l'Organisation de l'aviation civile internationale (#19939)
♦ Association du personnel de l'Organisation mondiale de la propriété intellectuelle (#19942)
♦ Association du personnel de la Région européenne de l'Organisation mondiale de la santé / see Staff Association of the WHO Regional Office for Europe (#19941)
♦ Association du personnel de siège l'OMS, Genève (#20938)
♦ Association du personnel de l'UNESCO / see UNESCO Staff Union (#20321)
♦ Association of Persons of the Legal Communities of the SAARC Countries / see South Asian Association for Regional Cooperation in Law (#19723)
♦ Association of Petrochemicals Producers in Europe / see Petrochemicals Europe (#18342)

♦ Association de pétrochimie latinoaméricaine (#02294)
♦ Association pour les peuples menacés international (#19654)
♦ Association pharmaceutique française pour l'hydrologie / see Association scientifique européenne pour l'eau et la santé (#02908)
♦ Association des pharmaciens inspecteurs européens (no recent information)
♦ Association of Pharmacists of the Portuguese-speaking Countries (#02327)
♦ Association for Pharmacoeconomics and Outcomes Research / see International Society for Pharmacoeconomics and Outcomes Research (#15354)

♦ Association of Philosophers from South-Eastern Europe — 02857
Gen Sec 14 Lerin St, 1612 Sofia, Bulgaria. T. +35929583262. Fax +35929583262.
Pres Eng Ivan Ivanov Blvd 88, 1303 Sofia, Bulgaria. T. +35929315780. Fax +35929315780.
Structure Officers include: President; Vice-President; General Secretary. **NGO Relations** Member of: *International Federation of Philosophical Societies (FISP, #13507)*. [2017.11.26/XM2989/D]

♦ Association of Philosophical Journals Editors / see Association of Philosophy Journal Editors (#02858)

♦ Association of Philosophy Journal Editors (APJE) — 02858
Chair Philosophy Program CUNY Graduate Ctr, 365 Fifth Ave, New York NY 10016, USA.
History Founded 1971, as *Association of Philosophical Journals Editors*. Present name adopted 1980. Revived, 2009, after a dormant period. **Aims** Provide a forum for discussion between philosophy journal editors and issues in the profession. **Languages** English. **Staff** None. **Activities** Meets annually with American Philosophical Association and once every 5 years with World Congress of Philosophy. **Members** Editors of philosophy journals (90). Membership countries not specified. [2013.11.22/XD0513/D]

♦ Association for Philosophy and Liberation (internationally oriented national body)

♦ Association for the Philosophy of Mathematical Practice (APMP) — 02859
Contact address not obtained.
URL: http://institucional.us.es/apmp/index.htm
History 2009. Current statutes adopted 30 Dec 2013. **Aims** Become a common forum that will stimulate research in philosophy of mathematics related to mathematical activity, past and present, and foster joint actions. **Structure** Directive Committee. **Activities** Events/meetings. **Events** *International Meeting* Zurich (Switzerland) 2020, *International Meeting* Salvador (Brazil) 2017, *International Meeting* Paris (France) 2015, *International Meeting* Urbana, IL (USA) 2013, *International Meeting* Brussels (Belgium) 2010. **Members** Individuals. Membership countries not specified. [2019/XM4733/v/C]

♦ Association phonétique internationale (#14573)
♦ Association phonétique des professeurs de langues vivantes / see International Phonetic Association (#14573)
♦ Association of Photographers (internationally oriented national body)
♦ Association des photographes nordiques (no recent information)
♦ Association des physiologistes / see Société de Physiologie (#19509)
♦ Association des physiologistes de langue française / see Société de Physiologie (#19509)

♦ Association of Physiotherapists in Parkinson's Disease Europe (APPDE) — 02860
Association Europe des kinésithérapeutes pour la maladie de Parkinson (AEKMP)
Pres Résidence Lara, 16 rue Boltgen, L-4037 Esch-sur-Alzette, Luxembourg.
URL: http://www.appde.eu/
History 2000, Brussels (Belgium). Registered in accordance with Belgian law. **Aims** Facilitate networking to promote best practice within the context of individual health care systems; enable educational initiatives to be developed and supported; provide a forum for discussion of potential research programmes in additional to facilitating and supporting collaborative networks in their pursuit of appropriate research funding; raise the profile of the contribution of physiotherapy to multidisciplinary team management of PD. **Structure** General Assembly (annual). Board, comprising President, Vice-President, Events and Professional Development Secretary, Treasurer/Membership Secretary and 2 members. **Events** *Annual General Meeting* Vienna (Austria) 2002. **NGO Relations** Member of: *European Parkinson's Disease Association (EPDA, #08145)*.
[2011/XN1292/D]

♦ Association de physique théorique de l'Asie du Sud-Est (#19799)
♦ Association de pilotage des conférences B (#12328)
♦ Association pisciculture et développement rural en Afrique tropicale humide (internationally oriented national body)
♦ Association des planétariums de langue française (internationally oriented national body)

♦ Association for Plant Breeding for the Benefit of Society (APBREBES) — 02861
Coordinator c/o Public Eye, Av Charles-Dickens 4, 1006 Lausanne VD, Switzerland. E-mail: contact@apbrebes.org.
URL: http://www.apbrebes.org/
History 2009, by 7 civil society organizations. Registered in accordance with Swiss Civil Code. **Aims** Promote plant breeding for the benefit of society, fully implementing farmers' rights to plant genetic resources and promoting biodiversity. **Structure** Assembly. Board. **Staff** 1.00 FTE, paid. **Publications** *APBREBES Updates on Plant Variety Protection* – newsletter.
Members Organizations (7) in 7 countries:
Malaysia, Nepal, Norway, Philippines, Switzerland, USA, Zimbabwe.
Included in the above, 4 organizations listed in this Yearbook:
Center for International Environmental Law (CIEL); *Public Eye*; *Southeast Asia Regional Initiatives for Community Empowerment (SEARICE, #19795)*; *Third World Network (TWN, #20151)*.
IGO Relations Observer status with: *International Treaty on Plant Genetic Resources for Food and Agriculture (2001)*; *Union internationale pour la protection des obtentions végétales (UPOV, #20436)*.
[2019.04.16/XJ7928/y/C]

♦ Association des planteurs d'hévéas / see Tropical Growers' Association (#20250)
♦ Association of Plant Physiologists of SAARC Countries (no recent information)
♦ Association of Plant Resources in South East Asia / see Plant Resources of South-East Asia (#18391)
♦ Association of Plastic and Reconstructive Surgeons of Southern Africa (internationally oriented national body)
♦ Association of Plastics Manufacturers in Europe / see Association of Plastics Manufacturers in Europe (#02862)

♦ Association of Plastics Manufacturers in Europe (Plastics Europe) — 02862
Managing Dir Rue Belliard 40, 1040 Brussels, Belgium. T. +3227923000. Fax +3227923009. E-mail: info@plasticseurope.org.
URL: http://www.plasticseurope.org/
History 15 Jan 1976, Munich (Germany). Present name adopted upon merging of APME and national plastics industry bodies into one single networked organization. By-Laws modified: 19 Jun 1979; Jun 1988; May 1993; Nov 1994; Nov 1995; 24 May 2018. Most recently modified 13 Jun 2019. Former names and other names: *Association of Plastics Manufacturers in Europe (APME)* – former (15 Jun 1976); *Association des producteurs de matières plastiques en Europe* – former (15 Jun 1976). Registration: Banque-Carrefour des Entreprises, No/ID: 0416.155.338, Start date: 11 Jun 1976, Belgium; EU Transparency Register, No/ID: 454264611835-56, Start date: 24 Sep 2013. **Aims** Serve as the catalyst for the industry with a responsibility to openly engage with stakeholders and deliver solutions which are safe, circular and sustainable; implement long-lasting positive change. **Structure** General Assembly (annual); Steering Board; Strategic Councils (Climate and Production – Sustainability – End-of-life and Circularity); Communications Committee; Advocacy Committee; Leadership Team; Product Groups; Working Groups. Regional Offices (5): Frankfurt; London; Madrid; Milan; Paris. Headquarters, located in Brussels (Belgium). **Languages** English. **Staff** 21.00 FTE, paid. **Finance** Sources: members' dues. **Activities** Events/meetings; knowledge management/information dissemination;

research/documentation. **Events** *Biennial Identiplast Conference* London (UK) 2019, *Packaging Waste and Sustainability Forum* Brussels (Belgium) 2017, *Biennial Identiplast Conference* Vienna (Austria) 2017, *Biennial Identiplast Conference* Rome (Italy) 2015, *Biennial Identiplast Conference* Paris (France) 2013. **Publications** Facts & figures; plastics & circular economy report, plastics eco-profiles programme; position papers. **Information Services** *European Plastics Industry market data.*
Members Companies (over 100) producing over 90% of all polymers, in 31 countries:
Austria, Belgium, Bulgaria, Croatia, Cyprus, Czechia, Denmark, Estonia, Finland, France, Germany, Greece, Hungary, Ireland, Italy, Latvia, Lithuania, Luxembourg, Malta, Netherlands, Norway, Poland, Portugal, Romania, Slovakia, Slovenia, Spain, Sweden, Switzerland, Türkiye, UK.
NGO Relations Member of (9): *Circular Plastics Alliance (#03936)*; *Construction Products Europe AISBL (#04761)*; *European Association of Automotive Suppliers (CLEPA, #05948)* (Associate); *Federation of European and International Associations Established in Belgium (FAIB, #09508)*; *Flame Retardants Europe (FRE, #09791)* (Guest); *Industry4Europe (#11181)*; *Modern Building Alliance (#16842)*; *Network of Reference Laboratories for Monitoring of Emerging Environmental Pollutants (NORMAN Network, #17053)*; *World Plastics Council (WPC, #21730)* (Associate). Affiliated with (1): *Conseil européen de l'industrie chimique (CEFIC, #04687)*. Supports (1): *Life Cycle Initiative (LCI, #16464)*. Instrumental in setting up (1): *European Council of Vinyl Manufacturers (ECVM, #06849)*. In liaison with technical committees of: *Comité européen de normalisation (CEN, #04162)*. Associate Expert Group of *Business and Industry Advisory Committee to the OECD (BIAC, #03385)*. Links with various stakeholders, trade associations and organizations. [2022.04.21/XD0052/**D**]

♦ Association of Plastic Surgery of Central America and the Caribbean (no recent information)
♦ Association pluridisciplinaire pour la recherche et l'action en matière de développement (internationally oriented national body)
♦ Association des PMU et des loteries d'Afrique / see Association des Loteries d'Afrique (#02791)

♦ Association Points-Coeur 02863
Heart's Home
Contact Rue de Lausanne 67, 1202 Geneva, Switzerland. T. +41223463972. E-mail: contact.onu@pointscoeur.org.
Main Website: https://pointscoeur.org/
History 1990. **Aims** Welcome and visit neighbors and suffering individuals, in order to assist and form personal bonds with troubled, disadvantaged and socially isolated people in the world's most desperate areas. **Structure** Council. **Languages** English, French. **Activities** Awareness raising; certification/accreditation; humanitarian/emergency aid; religious activities. Active in: Argentina, Austria, Brazil, Chile, Costa Rica, Cuba, Ecuador, El Salvador, France, Germany, Greece, Honduras, India, Italy, Japan, Lebanon, Peru, Philippines, Poland, Romania, Senegal, Switzerland, Thailand, Ukraine, Uruguay, USA. **Consultative Status** Consultative status granted from: *ECOSOC (#05331)* (Special). **NGO Relations** Member of (2): *Forum of Catholic Inspired NGOs (#09905)*; *International Catholic Centre of Geneva (ICCG, #12449)*. [2022.11.15/XM8824/**C**]

♦ Association of Polar Early Career Scientists (APECS) 02864
Exec Dir c/o UiT, Huginbakken 14, 9019 Tromsø, Norway. E-mail: info@apecs.is.
Main Website: http://www.apecs.is/
History 2006. Founded growing out of ICARP II (2005) and the 4th International Polar Year (2007-2008), which emphasized the need to nurture the next generation of scientists in order to foster a continuum of engagement and capacity in the leadership of international research initiatives. **Aims** Stimulate interdisciplinary and international research collaborations; develop effective future leaders in polar research, education and outreach; facilitate international and interdisciplinary networking to share ideas and experiences and to develop new research directions and collaborations; provide opportunities for professional career development; promote education and outreach as an integral component of polar research and stimulate future generations of polar researchers. **Structure** Council; Executive Committee; Advisory Committee; International Directorate; National Committee Representatives; Project Groups. **Languages** English. **Staff** 1.50 FTE, paid. Several voluntary. **Finance** Sources: international organizations; revenue from activities/projects. Office staff and operational expenses funded by Alfred Wegener Institute (AWI). Project officer positions funded through EU Horizon 2020 projects ARICE and INTERACT III. **Activities** Capacity building; events/meetings; networking/liaising; training/education. **Events** *International Online Conference* 2022, *Polar Symposium* 2022, *Annual Arctic Science Summit* Arkhangelsk (Russia) 2019, *Annual Arctic Science Summit* Davos (Switzerland) 2018, *Annual Arctic Science Summit* Prague (Czechia) 2017.
Members National Committees in 29 countries:
Argentina, Australia, Belgium, Brazil, Bulgaria, Canada, Chile, China, Colombia, Denmark, France, Germany, Iceland, India, Italy, Luxembourg, Malaysia, Netherlands, New Zealand, Norway, Portugal, Russia, South Africa, Spain, Sweden, Switzerland, Türkiye, UK, USA. [2022/XJ1201/**E**]

♦ Association des polices nordiques (#17489)

♦ Association for Politics and the Life Sciences (APLS) 02865
Contact School of Public Policy, Univ of Maryland, College Park MD 20742, USA.
URL: http://www.aplsnet.org/
History 1980. **Aims** Advance knowledge of politics; promote better *policymaking* through multidisciplinary analysis that draws on life sciences. **Structure** Council, comprising 11 members. **Languages** English. **Finance** Members' dues. Indexing royalties. **Activities** Holds annual meetings (in conjunction with the annual convention of the American Political Science Association). **Events** *Annual meeting* Washington, DC (USA) 2005, *Annual meeting* 1989. **Publications** *Politics and the Life Sciences* (2 a year).
Members Individual; Library; Institutional. Members (mostly in USA) in 19 countries:
Australia, Belgium, Brazil, Canada, China, Colombia, Finland, Germany, Italy, Japan, Netherlands, Portugal, South Africa, Sweden, Switzerland, Türkiye, UK, United Arab Emirates, USA. [2012.07.30/XF2585/**F**]

♦ Association for Population / Family Planning Libraries and Information Centers – International (internationally oriented national body)
♦ Association des populations des montagnes du monde (#21658)
♦ Association of Portuguese and Spanish-Lexified Creoles (#02325)
♦ Association of Postal and Telecommunications Operators of the Portuguese Speaking Countries and Territories (#02333)
♦ Association of Post Office and Telecommunications Operators of the Portuguese Speaking Countries and Territories / see Associação dos Operadores de Correios e Telecomunicações dos Paises e Territórios de Lingua Oficial Portuguesa (#02333)
♦ Association of Poultry Processors and Poultry Import and Export Trade in the EC Countries / see Association de l'aviculture, de l'industrie et du commerce de volailles dans les pays de l'Union européenne (#02390)
♦ Association of Poultry Processors and Poultry Import and Export Trade in the EU Countries / see Association de l'aviculture, de l'industrie et du commerce de volailles dans les pays de l'Union européenne (#02390)
♦ Association of Poultry Processors and Poultry Trade in the EU Countries (#02390)

♦ Association of Power Exchanges (APEx) 02866
Main Office 2750 Monroe Blvd, Audubon PA 19403, USA. E-mail: michelle.harhai@pjm.com.
URL: http://www.theapex.org/
History 1996. **Aims** Facilitate development and communication of ideas and practices in the operation of global competitive *electricity* markets. **Structure** Board. **Languages** English. **Staff** No FTE. **Finance** Members' dues. **Events** *Annual Conference* Toronto, ON (Canada) 2019, *Annual Conference* Brussels (Belgium) 2017, *Annual Conference* Krakow (Poland) 2014, *Annual Conference* New York, NY (USA) 2013, *Annual Conference* Delhi (India) 2012.
Members Full companies in 31 countries:
Argentina, Australia, Austria, Canada, Colombia, El Salvador, France, Georgia, Germany, Guatemala, India, Ireland, Japan, Kazakhstan, Korea Rep, Netherlands, New Zealand, Norway, Panama, Philippines, Poland, Portugal, Romania, Russia, Saudi Arabia, Singapore, Slovenia, Spain, UK, USA, Vietnam.
Associate companies in 3 countries:
Brazil, Italy, Malaysia. [2017/XM3138/**D**]

♦ Association of Power Utilities in Africa (APUA) 02867
Association des Sociétés d'Electricité d'Afrique (ASEA)
SG 01 BP 1345, Abidjan 01, Côte d'Ivoire. T. +22520206053 – +22520312660. Fax +22520331210. E-mail: secgen@apua-asea.org.
URL: http://www.apua-asea.org/
History May 1970, Abidjan (Côte d'Ivoire), as *Union of Producers, Transporters and Distributors of Electric Power in Africa (UPDEA) – Union des producteurs, transporteurs et distributeurs d'énergie électrique d'Afrique.* Also previously known in English as *Union of Producers, Conveyors and Distributors of Electric Power in Africa.* Current title adopted 2013. **Aims** Be the primary catalyst in the realization of access to electricity for all the people of Africa; in this framework, support and facilitate development and integration of the African power sector. **Structure** Congress (every 3 years); General Assembly (annual), comprising all Active and Affiliate members. Executive Committee (meets twice a year), composed of 16 members representing the various sub-regions of the continent (North, West, Central, South and East) and includes President, 5 Vice-Presidents and General Comptroller. Scientific Committee is the technical organ. Study Committees (6): Operation, Maintenance and Development of Electric Systems in Africa; Rural Electrification; Customer Management; Energy Efficiency and Development of Renewable Energies; Restructuring and Financing of the Electric Sector in Africa; Competitiveness of Human Resources of Member Companies of the Union. General Secretariat, led by Secretary General. **Languages** English, French. **Staff** 17.00 FTE, paid. **Finance** Members' dues. Grants. Budget (annual): US$ 1 million. **Activities** Research/documentation; knowledge management/information dissemination; events/meetings; training/education; standards/guidelines. **Events** *Triennial Congress* Dakar (Senegal) 2021, *Triennial Congress* Dakar (Senegal) 2020, *Workshop on Power Sector Leadership on Governance and Loss Reduction* Abidjan (Côte d'Ivoire) 2017, *Triennial Congress* Livingstone (Zambia) 2017, *Triennial Congress* Luanda (Angola) 2014. **Publications** *APUA Information* (4 a year). Official directory; technical papers. Information Services: Databank of African power sector.
Members Active (53) companies or utilities. Active in 42 countries:
Algeria, Angola, Benin, Botswana, Burkina Faso, Burundi, Cameroon, Central African Rep, Chad, Congo Brazzaville, Congo DR, Côte d'Ivoire, Djibouti, Egypt, Ethiopia, Gabon, Gambia, Ghana, Guinea, Guinea-Bissau, Kenya, Lesotho, Liberia, Libya, Madagascar, Malawi, Mali, Mauritania, Morocco, Mozambiqûe, Namibia, Niger, Nigeria, Rwanda, Senegal, South Africa, Sudan, Togo, Tunisia, Uganda, Zambia, Zimbabwe.
Included in the above, 2 multilateral authorities:
Benin Electricity Community (CEB) (for Benin and Togo); Manantali Management Company (SOGEM) for Mali, Mauritania and Senegal.
Affiliated (14) companies and organizations. Membership countries not specified.
Consultative Status Consultative status granted from: *ECOSOC (#05331)* (Ros C); *UNIDO (#20336)*. **IGO Relations** Formal relations with: *African Development Bank (ADB, #00283)*; *Common Market for Eastern and Southern Africa (COMESA, #04296)*; *Economic Community of Central African States (ECCAS, #05311)*; *Economic Community of West African States (ECOWAS, #05312)*; *Southern African Development Community (SADC, #19843)*. Permanent Member of the Executive Council of: *African Energy Commission (AFREC, #00298)*. Permanent Member of the Management Committee of: *African Electrotechnical Standardization Commission (AFSEC)*. Observer member of and specialized consulting body of: *African Union (AU, #00488)*. Partner of: *New Partnership for Africa's Development (NEPAD, #17091)*. Associate Member and Supporting Partner of: COMELEC *Eastern Africa Power Pool (EAPP, #05226)*; *Southern African Power Pool (SAPP, #19858)*. **NGO Relations** Member of: *MEDELEC (#16614)*. Associate Member and Supporting Partner of: *Central African Power Pool (CAPP, #03655)*; *West African Power Pool (WAPP, #20894)*. Consultative status with: *World Energy Council (WEC, #21381)*. Represented in: *African Electrotechnical Standardization Commission (AFSEC, #00295)*. [2016/XD6104/y/**D**]

♦ Association des praticiens des Communautés européennes dans le domaine des marques / see ECTA (#05341)
♦ Association des Praticiens du Droit des Marques et des Modèles (internationally oriented national body)
♦ Association de préhistoire de la région Indo-Pacifique (#11171)
♦ Association for Pre- and Perinatal Psychology and Health (internationally oriented national body)
♦ Association of Presbyterian and Reformed Churches in Latin America / see Alliance of Presbyterian and Reformed Churches in Latin America (#00713)
♦ Association for Preservation Technology / see Association for Preservation Technology International
♦ Association for Preservation Technology International (internationally oriented national body)
♦ Association de la presse francophone / see Association internationale de la presse francophone
♦ Association de la presse gaie internationale (inactive)

♦ Association de la presse internationale (API) 02868
International Press Association (IPA)
Admin Sec Intl Press Center Residence Palace, Bloc C, Office 2 223 – 2nd Floor, Rue de la Loi 155, 1040 Brussels, Belgium. T. +3222352224. Fax +3222309718. E-mail: info@api-ipa.org.
Pres address not obtained.
URL: http://www.api-ipa.org/
History 27 Jun 1975, Belgium. Founded to replace the *Union of Foreign Press in Belgium.* Registration: Belgium. **Aims** Represent foreign journalists based in Brussels covering European institutions, NATO and Belgium. **Structure** Council; Bureau. **Languages** English, French. **Staff** 1.00 FTE, paid. **Finance** Sources: members' dues. **Activities** Events/meetings; financial and/or material support; knowledge management/information dissemination; training/education. [2022.10.18/XN8457/**E**]

♦ Association de la presse internationale auprès de la salle de la presse du Saint-Siège / see Association des journalistes accrédités auprès du Vatican (#02773)
♦ Association de la presse militaire de l'Europe / see European Military Press Association (#07803)
♦ Association de la presse philatélique francophone (inactive)
♦ Association des Prêtres du Prado (religious order)
♦ Association pour la prévention de la torture (#02869)

♦ Association for the Prevention of Torture (APT) 02869
Association pour la prévention de la torture – Asociación para la Prevención de la Tortura – Vereinigung für die Verhütung der Folter
Head Office Centre J-J Gautier, 10 route de Ferney, 1202 Geneva, Switzerland. T. +41229192170. Fax +41229192180. E-mail: apt@apt.ch.
URL: http://www.apt.ch/
History 1977. Founded by Jean-Jacques Gautier. Present name adopted on revision of CSCT statutes, when the organization became international. Statutes further amended by General Assembly, 12 Feb 1994. Former names and other names: *Comité suisse contre la torture (CSCT)* – former (1977 to 29 Jun 1992); *Swiss Committee Against Torture (SCAT)* – former (1977 to 29 Jun 1992). Registration: Swiss Civil Code, Switzerland. **Aims** Promote transparency and accountability of places of deprivation of liberty as the most effective way to prevent torture and abuses from happening. **Structure** General Assembly (annual); Board; Secretariat in Geneva (Switzerland). **Languages** English, French, Portuguese, Spanish. **Staff** 9.00 FTE, paid. **Finance** Annual budget: 1,919,500 CHF (2021). **Activities** Advocacy/lobbying/activism; capacity building; guidance/assistance/consulting; knowledge management/information dissemination; management of treaties and agreements; monitoring/evaluation. Manages the following treaties/agreements: *Optional Protocol to the UN Convention Against Torture and other Cruel, Inhuman or Degrading Treatment or Punishment (OPCAT, 2002)*. **Events** *High Level Conference on the occasion of the 30th anniversary of the European Committee for the Prevention of Torture* Strasbourg (France) 2019, *Meeting on Torture Prevention, for National Preventive Mechanisms and Civil Society Organisations* Milan (Italy) 2018, *Symposium on Procedural Safeguards in the first hours of police detention* Geneva (Switzerland) 2017, *National Preventive Mechanisms Symposium on Monitoring Psychiatric Institutions* Geneva (Switzerland) 2016, *Annual Meeting of National Preventive Mechanisms for the OSCE Region* Vienna (Austria) 2016. **Publications** *APT Reporter* (6 a year). *Does prevention of Torture works* (2016) by Prof Richard Carver and Prof Lisa Handley – Liverpool University Press. Annual Report; guides; manuals; general documents; position papers; fact sheets; thematic studies; reports. **Information Services** *Knowledge Hub* – videos, Podcast, Detention focus Database, OPCAT Database Toolkit, Prevention Learning Village.
Members Individuals (133) in 28 countries:

Argentina, Australia, Austria, Brazil, Bulgaria, Burundi, Cameroon, Canada, Chile, Colombia, Congo DR, Denmark, France, Gambia, Germany, Maldives, Netherlands, Peru, Philippines, Senegal, Sierra Leone, Spain, Switzerland, Togo, Tunisia, UK, Uruguay, USA.
Consultative Status Consultative status granted from: *African Commission on Human and Peoples' Rights (ACHPR, #00255)* (Observer); *ECOSOC (#05331)* (Special); *Council of Europe (CE, #04881)* (Participatory Status); *Organisation internationale de la Francophonie (OIF, #17809)*. **IGO Relations** Observer status with (1): *OAS (#17629)* (Permanent observer status). **NGO Relations** Member of (4): *End Corporal Punishment (#05457)*; *Human Rights and Democracy Network (HRDN, #10980)*; *NGO Committee on the Status of Women, Geneva (#17117)*; *World Organisation Against Torture (OMCT, #21685)*. Cooperates with (8): *Amnesty International (AI, #00801)*; *DIGNITY – Danish Institute Against Torture*; *Human Rights Watch (HRW, #10990)*; *International Commission of Jurists (ICJ, #12695)*; *International Committee of the Red Cross (ICRC, #12799)*; *International Federation of ACATs – Action by Christians for the Abolition of Torture (#13334)*; *Penal Reform International (PRI, #18290)*; *REDRESS*. [2021.06.21/XE2863/v/**D**]

♦ Association of the Primary Food Processors of the EU / see Primary Food Processors (#18496)

♦ Association of Principals of Jewish Schools of Australasia (APJSA) 02870

Pres Moriah College, PO Box 986, Bondi Junction NSW 1355, Australia. T. +61293751600.
Structure President, elected every 2 years. **Events** *Biennial Asia Pacific regional conference on education* Melbourne, VIC (Australia) 1998. [2015.01.07/XD8415/**D**]

♦ Association for Private Capital Investment in Latin America (LAVCA) 02871

Pres/Exec Dir 589 Eighth Avenue, 18th Floor, New York NY 10018, USA. T. +16463156735. Fax +16463491047. E-mail: contact@lavca.org – policy@lavca.org.
URL: http://lavca.org/
History 2002. Founded with the support of *Multilateral Investment Fund (MIF, #16887)* of *Inter-American Development Bank (IDB, #11427)* the National Venture Capital Association (NVCA), and Development Capital Networks (DCN). **Aims** Support growth of the private equity and venture capital industry in Latin America. **Structure** Board of Directors; Executive Director. **Staff** 12.00 FTE, paid. **Activities** Advocacy/lobbying/activism; awards/prizes/competitions; events/meetings; knowledge management/information dissemination; networking/liaising; politics/policy/regulatory; research/documentation; training/education. **Events** *Annual Summit* New York, NY (USA) 2019, *Annual Summit* New York, NY (USA) 2014, *Annual Summit* New York, NY (USA) 2012, *Annual Summit* New York, NY (USA) 2011. **Publications** *Annual LAVCA Industry Data and Analysis*; *The Latin American Private Equity Deal Book and ESG Cases*. Reports; updates; directories. **Members** Full; Associate. Membership countries not identified. **IGO Relations** Partner of (7): *DEG – Deutsche Investitions- und Entwicklungsgesellschaft*; *Development Bank of Latin America (CAF, #05055)*; *European Investment Bank (EIB, #07599)*; *Inter-American Investment Corporation (IIC, #11438)*; *International Finance Corporation (IFC, #13597)*; *Multilateral Investment Fund (MIF, #16887)*; *Swiss Investment Fund for Emerging Markets (SIFEM)*. **NGO Relations** Partner of (4): *Aspen Network of Development Entrepreneurs (ANDE, #02310)*; *Global Private Capital Association (GPCA, #10556)*; *Invest Europe – The Voice of Private Capital (Invest Europe, #15997)*; *Nederlandse Financierings-Maatschappij voor Ontwikkelingslanden (FMO)*. [2021.06.08/XJ5329/**D**]

♦ Association of Private Committees for the Safeguarding of Venice / see Association of International Private Committees for the Safeguarding of Venice (#02758)
♦ Association of Private Development Agencies / see Association of Private Organizations for Development Service
♦ Association of Private European Cable Operators (inactive)
♦ Association of Private Organizations for Development Service (internationally oriented national body)
♦ Association of the Processed Cheese Industry in the EU (#02642)
♦ Association of Producers of Cinema and Television / see EUROCINEMA (#05661)
♦ Association de Producteurs de Cinéma et de Télévision / see EUROCINEMA (#05661)
♦ Association des producteurs et coucheurs de papiers thermo-réactifs (inactive)
♦ Association des producteurs d'enzymes dans la CEE / see Association of Manufacturers and Formulators of Enzyme Products (#02793)
♦ Association des producteurs européens d'azote (inactive)

♦ Association des producteurs européens de potasse (APEP) 02872

European Potash Producers Association – Verband der Europäischen Kaliproduzenten
Main Office Avenue Louise 489, 1050 Brussels, Belgium. T. +3222376151.
URL: http://www.apep.eu/
History 3 May 1982, Brussels (Belgium). Registered in accordance with Belgian law. **Structure** General Assembly. Council, including President, Vice-President and Secretary. [2017/XD8069/**D**]

♦ Association des producteurs de fibres de verre européens / see GlassFibreEurope (#10158)
♦ Association des producteurs de film de polypropylène orienté (inactive)
♦ Association des producteurs indépendants de la méditerranée / see Association internationale des producteurs indépendants de la méditerranée (#02731)
♦ Association des producteurs de matières plastiques en Europe / see Association of Plastics Manufacturers in Europe (#02862)
♦ Association des producteurs de pétrole africains / see African Petroleum Producers's Organization (#00414)
♦ Association des producteurs de produits pétrochimiques en Europe / see Petrochemicals Europe (#18342)
♦ Association des producteurs de tungstène (inactive)
♦ Association for Products Propres and Parentals (internationally oriented national body)
♦ Association pour les Produits Propres et Parentéraux (internationally oriented national body)
♦ Association pour les produits propres et stériles / see Association pour les Produits Propres et Parentéraux
♦ Association des professeurs catholiques des Caraïbes (#03444)
♦ Association des professeurs de français en Afrique (no recent information)
♦ Association des professeurs de phonétique / see International Phonetic Association (#14573)
♦ Association des professeurs scandinaves pour la paix (inactive)
♦ Association of Professional Organizations of the Sugar Trade for EEC Countries / see European Association of Sugar Traders (#06239)
♦ Association of Professional Organizations of the Sugar Trade for EU Countries / see European Association of Sugar Traders (#06239)
♦ Association of Professional Schools of International Affairs (internationally oriented national body)
♦ Association professionnelle du caoutchouc naturel en Afrique (no recent information)
♦ Association professionnelle des producteurs européens d'aciers pour emballage (#06167)
♦ Association professionnelle internationale des médecins ophtalmologistes (inactive)
♦ Association professionnelle des producteurs européens d'aciers pour emballage / see European Association of Producers of Steel for Packaging (#06167)
♦ Association des professionnelles africaines de la communication (no recent information)

♦ Association for Progressive Communications (APC) 02873

Asociación para el Progreso de las Comunicaciones
Exec Dir PO Box 29755, Melville, 2109, South Africa. T. +27117261692. Fax +27117261692. E-mail: adolfo@apc.org – info@apc.org.
Secretariat c/o IGC, PO Box 29047, San Francisco CA 94129-0047, USA.
URL: http://www.apc.org/
History May 1990, by 7 networks in Sweden, Canada, Brazil, Nicarague, Australia, UK and USA, including *GreenNet (#10725)* and *Institute for Global Communications (IGC, inactive)*. **Aims** Empower and support organizations, social movements and individuals in and through the use of information and communication technologies (ICTs) to build strategic communities and initiatives for the purpose of making meaningful contributions to equitable human development, social justice, participatory political processes and environmental sustainability. **Structure** Council; Board of Directors. **Finance** Members' dues. **Activities** Knowledge management/information dissemination. **Events** *International forum on communication and citizenship* San Salvador (El Salvador) 1998.
Members Independent networks (whose users total over 45,000 in 133 countries – not specified), based in 30 countries:
Argentina, Australia, Bangladesh, Brazil, Bulgaria, Cambodia, Cameroon, Canada, Chile, Colombia, Congo Brazzaville, Costa Rica, Egypt, India, Japan, Kenya, Korea Rep, Nigeria, North Macedonia, Pakistan, Paraguay, Philippines, Romania, South Africa, Spain, Thailand, Uganda, UK, USA, Venezuela.
Included in the above, 7 organizations listed in this Yearbook:
Alternatives – Action and Communication Network for International Development; *Collaboration on International ICT Policy-Making for East and Southern Africa (CIPESA)*; *Computer Aid International*; *GreenNet (#10725)*; *Latin American Networks School (ESLARED)*; *Oneworld – Platform for South East Europe (OWPSEE, inactive)*; *Southern African Non-Governmental Development Organization Network (SANGONeT, #19854)*.
Consultative Status Consultative status granted from: *ECOSOC (#05331)* (General). **IGO Relations** *UNDP (#20292)*. Assisted in *Global Electronic Network* of: *United Nations Conference on Environment and Development (UNCED)*. **NGO Relations** Member of: *Alliance for Affordable Internet (A4AI, #00651)*; *Asian Women's Resource Exchange (AWORC, no recent information)*; *Conference of Non-Governmental Organizations in Consultative Relationship with the United Nations (CONGO, #04635)*; *World Social Forum (WSF, #21797)*. *Instituto del Tercer Mundo, Montevideo (ITEM)*, is a member. Coordinates: *WomenAction 2000 (no recent information)*. [2015/XF1003/y/**F**]

♦ Association for Promoting European Soya Production – Danube Soya / see Donau Soja (#05116)

♦ Association for the Promotion of African Community Initiatives 02874

Association pour la promotion des initiatives communautaires africaines (APICA)
Contact address not obtained. T. +237370405. Fax +237370402.
Pres address not obtained.
History May 1980, Douala (Cameroon). Commenced activities 1981. **Aims** Study and improve traditional technologies in order to assist, encourage and support local *development* initiatives. **Structure** Group of General Members; Assembly of Delegates from the Group of General Members; Executive Bureau; Secretary General; Administrative and Financial Service. Central Services (Communication Service; Documentation Service; Service for Assistance to Programs); East Central African Office (Service for Development Assistance and Training; Service for Technical Assistance); West African Office (Service for Development Assistance and Training; Service for Technical Assistance). **Staff** 7.00 FTE, paid. **Finance** Operations supported by: *Entreprise Works / VITA*; Protestant Central Agency for Development Aid (EZE); Coopération technique suisse (CTS). **Activities** APICA generally intervenes in 3 areas: assistance for development; assistance in technology; information-communication. In these three areas the following activities are carried out: (1) Training activities; (2) Assistance in the form of advice; (3) Study and research; (4) Technological activities; (5) Extension Teaching; (6) Information and Communication. **Events** *Séminaire sur la méthodologie d'appui aux organisations paysannes et aux ONG congolaises d'appui* Brazzaville (Congo Brazzaville) 1993. **Publications** *Communautés africaines* (4 a year).
Members Individuals in 10 countries:
Belgium, Benin, Chad, Congo DR, France, Gabon, Mali, Niger, Rwanda, Sweden.
NGO Relations Partner of: *Development Innovations and Networks (#05057)*. [2009/XF0201/**F**]

♦ Association pour la promotion de la coopération internationale (internationally oriented national body)
♦ Association pour la promotion de la diffusion internationale de la presse (#02876)
♦ Association pour la promotion des droits de l'homme en Afrique centrale (internationally oriented national body)
♦ Association pour la promotion de l'éducation et de la formation à l'étranger (internationally oriented national body)
♦ Association for the Promotion of Education and Training Abroad (internationally oriented national body)
♦ Association pour la Promotion de l'Enseignement et de la Recherche en Aménagement et Urbanisme / see Association pour la promotion de l'enseignement et de la recherche en aménagement et urbanisme (#02875)

♦ Association pour la promotion de l'enseignement et de la recherche en aménagement et urbanisme (APERAU) 02875

Sec address not obtained.
Contact 8 rue Jean Sébastien Bach, 75013 Paris, France.
URL: http://www.aperau.org/
History 1984. Registered in accordance with French law. An institutional network member of *Agence universitaire de La Francophonie (AUF, #00548)* and its *Université des réseaux d'expression française (UREF, inactive)*. Former names and other names: *Association pour la Promotion de l'Enseignement et de la Recherche en Aménagement et Urbanisme (APERAU-Internationale)* – alias. **Aims** Identify new and old curricula of *urban* planning, town and country planning. **Structure** Board, comprising President, 4 Vice-Presidents, Secretary and Treasurer. **Languages** French. **Activities** Set up a charter aiming to create a framework for its programmes; manages a process of programme evaluation. Programmes organized with credits, corresponding to a way of teaching and practices: lessons, applied works; seminaries; workshops; internship; field trips; individual and collective theses. Organizes international days. **Events** *Rencontres Internationales en Urbanisme* 2021, *Rencontres Internationales en Urbanisme* Rabat (Morocco) 2020, *Seminar* Montréal, QC (Canada) 2014, *Journées internationales* Tours (France) 2009, *Journées internationales* Québec, QC (Canada) 2008.
Members Schools and universities in 10 countries:
Algeria, Belgium, Brazil, Canada, France, Lebanon, Morocco, Switzerland, Togo, Tunisia.
NGO Relations Member of (1): *Global Planning Education Association Network (GPEAN, #10549)*. Cooperates with (1): *Association of European Schools of Planning (AESOP, #02542)*. [2020/XD9439/**D**]

♦ Association for the Promotion of European Chamber Music / see European Chamber Music Academy (#06515)
♦ Association for the Promotion of Human Rights in Central Africa (internationally oriented national body)
♦ Association pour la promotion et l'information des techniques et des applications spatiales en Europe (inactive)
♦ Association pour la promotion des initiatives communautaires africaines (#02874)
♦ Association for the Promotion of the International Circulation of the Press / see Association for the Promotion of the International Circulation of the Press (#02876)

♦ Association for the Promotion of the International Circulation of the Press (DISTRIPRESS) 02876

Association pour la promotion de la diffusion internationale de la presse – Vereinigung zur Förderung des Internationalen Pressevertriebes
Managing Dir Riesbachstrasse 57, Postfach, 8034 Zurich ZH, Switzerland. E-mail: welcome@distripress.org.
Community Manager address not obtained.
URL: http://www.distripress.org/
History Sep 1955, Bad Kissingen (Germany). Officially constituted Sep 1957. Most recent statutes adopted 13 Sep 2004, Vancouver BC (Canada). Former names and other names: *Association for the Promotion of the International Circulation of the Press (DISTRIPRESS – Bringing the world of press distribution together)* – full title. Registration: Swiss Civil Code, Switzerland. **Aims** Assist in promoting *freedom* of the press worldwide; support and aid all national and international action promoting free flow of ideas by word or image, and intervention against all measures which hinder or aim to prevent such a free flow; further the interests of the press circulation trade. **Structure** General Assembly (every 3 years); Executive Committee; Secretariat. Participates in educational activities in cooperation with 'Distripress Training Foundation'. **Languages** English, French, German. **Staff** 2.00 FTE, paid. **Finance** Sources: members' dues.
Activities Advocacy/lobbying/activism; events/meetings; research/documentation; training/education. Intervenes directly or through national or international authorities when free international circulation of the press is held up or hindered. Engages in improvement of overall environment for member companies and press distribution in general in the following areas:

– *'Freedom of the Press'* – engages worldwide for free flow of information by word and image, in accordance with the UN *Universal Declaration of Human Rights (UDHR, 1948)* and with UNESCO Constitution;
– *'Taxation'* – based on the 1950 Agreement of UNESCO, Florence (Italy), intervenes against duties on press products and against taxation on reading materials;
– *'Marketing'* – promotes exchange of information and experience on sales promotion, profitability of press products in retail trade, retail classification, sales analysis, data quality and sales information;
– *'Transportation'* – maintains contact with forwarders to secure speedy and efficient transportation by land or air, to facilitate customs clearance and to obtain adequate freight rates;
– *'New Technologies'* – fosters exchange of information and experience on new methods of bundling, packing, processing unsold items, bar-coding etc;
– *'European Union'* – maintains contact with EU institutions to safeguard efficient press distribution systems guaranteeing a wide variety of publications and a sufficient density of sales points throughout the European Union.

Events *Annual Congress* Estoril (Portugal) 2021, *Annual Congress* Berlin (Germany) 2019, *Annual Congress* Rome (Italy) 2018, *Annual Congress* Lisbon (Portugal) 2017, *Annual Congress* Dubai (United Arab Emirates) 2016. **Publications** *Distripress Flash* (bi-weekly); *Distripress News* (4 a year); *Distripress Gazette* (annual); *Who's Who in Distripress* (annual).
Members Regular – press distributors, international publishers, ancillary services; Affiliate; Honorary. Enterprises engaged in international publishing and marketing of newspapers, magazines, periodicals and paperbacks (308), in 71 countries and territories:
Albania, Australia, Austria, Bahrain, Belgium, Brazil, Canada, Chile, China, Congo Brazzaville, Cyprus, Czechia, Denmark, Egypt, Estonia, Finland, France, Germany, Ghana, Gibraltar, Greece, Hungary, Iceland, India, Indonesia, Iran Islamic Rep, Ireland, Israel, Italy, Jamaica, Japan, Jordan, Kenya, Korea Rep, Latvia, Lebanon, Lithuania, Luxembourg, Malta, Mauritius, Mexico, Morocco, Nepal, Netherlands, Nigeria, Norway, Oman, Pakistan, Panama, Philippines, Poland, Polynesia Fr, Portugal, Qatar, Romania, Russia, Saudi Arabia, Singapore, Slovakia, Slovenia, South Africa, Spain, Sweden, Switzerland, Taiwan, Thailand, Türkiye, UK, UK Overseas Territories, United Arab Emirates, USA.
Ancillary services (30) in 10 countries:
Canada, Finland, France, Germany, Italy, Netherlands, Norway, Switzerland, UK, USA.
Consultative Status Consultative status granted from: *ECOSOC (#05331)* (Ros C); *UNESCO (#20322)* (Consultative Status). **NGO Relations** Member of (3): *European Magazine Media Association (EMMA, #07723); European Newspaper Publishers' Association (ENPA, #08048); World Association of Newspapers and News Publishers (WAN-IFRA, #21166).* [2023.02.16/XB0111/**B**]

♦ Association for Promotion of International Cooperation (internationally oriented national body)
♦ Association of Promotion Marketing Agencies Worldwide / see Marketing Agencies Association Worldwide (#16585)
♦ Association de Promotion de l'Organisation Mondiale de l'Environnement (unconfirmed)
♦ Association de promotion des produits marins de l'Atlantique Nord (inactive)
♦ Association pour la promotion de la propriété intellectuelle en Afrique / see African Intellectual Property Organization (#00344)
♦ Association pour la promotion des publications scientifiques en langue française (inactive)
♦ Association for the Promotion of Space Activities in Europe (inactive)
♦ Association for the Promotion of Traditional Medicine International / see PROMETRA International (#18539)
♦ Association des propriétaires européens de marques de commerce / see MARQUES (#16588)

♦ Association for the Protection of Industrial Property in the Arab World 02877

Association pour la protection de la propriété industrielle dans le monde arabe (APPIMAF) – Asociación para la Protección de la Propiedad Industrial en el Mundo Arabe
Contact AIPPI, Tödistrasse 16, PO Box, 8027 Zurich ZH, Switzerland. T. +41442805880. Fax +41442805885. E-mail: mail@aippi.org.
Pres PO Box 116-2039, Beirut, Lebanon. T. +9611481681. Fax +9611490826.
URL: http://www.appimaf.org/
History Founded 1973, Beirut (Lebanon), as *Association for the Protection of Industrial Property in the Middle East and North Africa – Association pour la protection de la propriété industrielle au Moyen-Orient et en Afrique du Nord.* Regional group of: *International Association for the Protection of Intellectual Property (#12112).* **Aims** Promote awareness of industrial and *intellectual property* rights and the concept of their protection in the Arab World. **Structure** General Assembly; Executive Committee; Bureau. **Languages** Arabic, English, French. **Staff** 5.00 FTE, voluntary. **Finance** Self-financed. **Activities** Events/meetings. **Events** *General Assembly* Beirut (Lebanon) 2013, *General Assembly* Cairo (Egypt) 2009, *Conference* Casablanca (Morocco) 1994, *Conference and annual meeting* Dubai (United Arab Emirates) 1990. **Publications** *APPIMAF Newsletter* (4 a year).
Members Individuals and organizations in 16 countries:
Algeria, Bahrain, Djibouti, Iraq, Kuwait, Lebanon, Libya, Morocco, Oman, Qatar, Saudi Arabia, Sudan, Syrian AR, Tunisia, United Arab Emirates, Yemen.
Consultative Status Consultative status granted from: *World Intellectual Property Organization (WIPO, #21593)* (Permanent Observer Status). **IGO Relations** Associated with Department of Global Communications of the United Nations. [2016.10.20/XE1445/t/**E**]

♦ Association for the Protection of Industrial Property in the Middle East and North Africa / see Association for the Protection of Industrial Property in the Arab World (#02877)
♦ Association pour la protection de la propriété industrielle dans le monde arabe (#02877)
♦ Association pour la protección de la propriété industrielle au Moyen-Orient et en Afrique du Nord / see Association for the Protection of Industrial Property in the Arab World (#02877)
♦ Association of Protestant Churches and Missions in Germany (internationally oriented national body)
♦ Association of Protestant Development Organizations in Europe / see ACT Alliance EU (#00082)
♦ Association protestante pour la formation des adultes en Europe (inactive)
♦ Association protestante internationale de prêt (inactive)
♦ Association psychanalytique internationale (#14662)
♦ Association des psychiatres en Afrique (inactive)
♦ Association de psychiatrie des Caraïbes (no recent information)
♦ Association of Psychiatrists in Africa (inactive)

♦ Association of Psychological and Educational Counsellors of Asia (ABAECA) 02878

Pres c/o PGCA, PSS Center, Commonwealth Avenue Diliman, Quezon City, Philippines.
Facebook: https://www.facebook.com/APECA-1431334430440549/
History 1976, Manila (Philippines). Former names and other names: *Association of Psychological and Educational Counsellors of Asia Pacific (APECA)* – alias. **Events** *Biennial Conference* Singapore (Singapore) 2014, *Biennial Conference* Chiba (Japan) 2012, *Biennial conference* Penang (Malaysia) 2010, *Biennial Conference* Cebu City (Philippines) 2006, *Biennial Conference* Johor Bahru (Malaysia) 2004. **Publications** *Asian Journal of Counselling* (6 a year). [2016/XD8061/**D**]

♦ Association of Psychological and Educational Counsellors of Asia Pacific / see Association of Psychological and Educational Counsellors of Asia (#02878)

♦ Association for Psychological Science (APS) 02879

Exec Dir 1800 Massachusetts Ave NW, Suite 402, Washington DC 20036, USA. T. +12022939300. Fax +12022939350.
URL: https://www.psychologicalscience.org/
History 1988. Former names and other names: *American Psychological Society* – former (1988 to 31 Dec 2005). **Aims** Promote, protect, and advance the interests of scientifically oriented psychology in research, application, teaching, and the improvement of human welfare. **Structure** Board of Directors; Student Caucus Executive Board. **Activities** Awards/prizes/competitions; events/meetings; research/documentation. **Events** *International Convention of Psychological Science (ICPS)* Kyoto (Japan) 2025, *Annual Convention* Washington, DC (USA) 2024, *International Convention of Psychological Science* Brussels (Belgium) 2023, *Annual Convention* Washington, DC (USA) 2023, *Annual Convention* Chicago, IL (USA) 2022. **Publications** *Advances in Methods and Practices in Psychological Science; Current Directions in Psychological Science; Psychological Science; Psychological Science in the Public Interest (PSPI).* [2020/AA0910/**D**]

♦ Association for Psychological Type International (APTi) 02880

Mailing Address PO Box 4538, Itasca IL 60143, USA. E-mail: apti.contactus@gmail.com.
URL: http://www.aptinternational.org/
History 1979. **Aims** Promote practical application and ethical use of psychological type. **Structure** Board of Directors. Regional Chapters (7). International Chapters (9). **Events** *Biennial Conference* Chicago, IL (USA) 2021, *Biennial Conference / Conference* Miami, FL (USA) 2015, *Biennial Conference / Conference* Miami, FL (USA) 2013, *Biennial conference / Conference* San Francisco, CA (USA) 2011, *Biennial Conference / Conference* Dallas, TX (USA) 2009. **Publications** *APTi Bulleting.*
Members Chapters in 10 countries:
Australia, Canada, France, Japan, Korea Rep, New Zealand, Peru, South Africa, UK, USA. [2021/XM2591/**D**]

♦ Association pour la psychologie humaniste (#02633)
♦ Association de psychologie scientifique de langue française (no recent information)
♦ Association de psychologie transpersonnelle (#02960)
♦ Association de psychologie du travail de langue française / see Association internationale de psychologie du travail de langue française (#02734)

♦ Association for Public Economic Theory (APET) 02881

Contact Head of School of Economics, North Terrace, Nexus 10 Tower, Floor 3, Room 3 54, Adelaide SA 5005, Australia. T. +61883134768. Fax +61882231460.
URL: http://www.apet-jpet.org/
History 1999. **Aims** Promote theoretical research in all areas of public finance; facilitate communication amongst economists working in these areas. **Finance** Voluntary contributions; partner organizations host conferences and workshops. **Events** *Conference* Paris (France) 2017, *Conference* Lisbon (Portugal) 2013, *Conference* Taipei (Taiwan) 2012, *Conference* Bloomington, IN (USA) 2011, *Conference* Istanbul (Turkey) 2010. **Publications** *Journal of Public Economic Theory.* **Members** Individuals worldwide. Membership countries not specified. **NGO Relations** Cooperates with: *Coalition Theory Network (CTN, #04069).* [2018/XJ2624/**E**]

♦ Association of Publishers of European Legal and Economic Works (inactive)

♦ Association of Quality Assurance Agencies of the Islamic World (QA-Islamic) 02882

Exec Sec Natl Authority Qualifications/Quality Assurance/Education/Training, PO Box 30347, Manama, Bahrain. T. +93717562313. Fax +93717562306.
URL: http://www.mqa.gov.my/aqaaiw/
History Nov 2009. Constitution adopted 4 May 2011, Astana (Kazakhstan). Previously known under the acronym *AQAAIW.* **Aims** Enhance the capacity of quality assurance agencies in countries of the Islamic world; facilitate collaboration and exchanges of best practices, experiences and expertise among quality assurance agencies of countries of the Islamic world; encourage cooperation with regional and international quality assurance organizations. **Structure** Roundtable (at least every 2 years). Executive Board, comprising President, Vice-President, Executive Secretary and up to 7 members. Secretariat, headed by Executive Secretary. **Languages** English. **Finance** Members' dues. Event expenses covered by host. **Events** *Seminar and Round Table / Roundtable* Bahrain 2013, *Seminar and Round Table* Cairo (Egypt) 2012, *Roundtable* Egypt 2012, *Roundtable* Astana (Kazakhstan) 2011.
Members Full national external quality assurance agencies or authorities. Associate other organizations with an interest and involvement in the subject. Full in 17 countries and territories:
Algeria, Azerbaijan, Bahrain, Bosnia-Herzegovina, Brunei Darussalam, Egypt, Gambia, Indonesia, Iran Islamic Rep, Kazakhstan, Malaysia, Northern Cyprus, Pakistan, Saudi Arabia, Sudan, Türkiye, Uganda.
Associate in 6 countries and territories:
Egypt, Iraq, Lebanon, Pakistan, Palestine, Saudi Arabia.
NGO Relations Cooperation agreement with: *International Network of Quality Assurance Agencies in Higher Education (INQAAHE, #14312).* [2014.03.20/XJ4642/**D***]

♦ Association of Quality Control in the Lacquering, Painting and Coating Industry / see QUALICOAT (#18590)
♦ Association québécoise des organismes de coopération internationale (internationally oriented national body)
♦ Association of Racing Commissioners International / see Racing Commissioners International
♦ Association des radiobiologistes des pays de l'Euratom / see European Radiation Research Society (#08319)
♦ Association of Radiobiologists of Euratom Countries / see European Radiation Research Society (#08319)

♦ Association Radiodays Europe (RDE) 02883

General Manager Danish Broadcasting Corporation, Emil Holms kanal 20 (3,5), 0999 Copenhagen, Denmark.
URL: http://www.radiodayseurope.com/
History First Radiodays Europe organized 2010, Copenhagen (Denmark). Registration: Denmark. **Aims** Organize annual radio and conferences. **Structure** Executive Committee; Board. **Activities** Events/meetings. **Events** *Conference* Malmö (Sweden) 2022, *Conference* Lisbon (Portugal) 2021, *Conference* Lisbon (Portugal) 2020, *Conference* Lausanne (Switzerland) 2019, *Conference* Vienna (Austria) 2018. [2021/XM7986/c/**E**]

♦ Association de radiodiffusion du Commonwealth / see Public Media Alliance (#18568)
♦ Association de radiologie d'Afrique francophone (no recent information)

♦ Association of Radiologists of West Africa (ARAWA) 02884

Contact Radiology Dept, University Teaching Hospital, Ituku-Ozalla, Enugu, Nigeria. E-mail: editor_wajr@yahoo.com.
Contact address not obtained. E-mail: ybmensah@yahoo.com.
History 1963. **Events** *Annual Conference* Ibadan (Nigeria) 2012, *Annual Conference* Ibadan (Nigeria) 2011, *Annual Conference* Kano (Nigeria) 2011, *Annual Conference* Accra (Ghana) 2010, *Annual Conference* Enugu (Nigeria) 2004. **Publications** *West African Journal of Radiology.* **NGO Relations** *International Skeletal Society (ISS, #14867).* [2011/XD7399/**D**]

♦ Association of Radiopharmaceutical Producers and Equipment Suppliers / see Nuclear Medicine Europe (#17619)
♦ Association of Radiopharmaceutical producers Europe / see Nuclear Medicine Europe (#17619)
♦ Association des Raffineurs Africains (#00429)

♦ Association for the Rational Treatment of Fractures (ARTOF) 02885

Contact c/o Valentine Accountants, Lynton House, 7-12 Tavistock Sq, London, WC1H 9BQ, UK.
URL: http://artof-online.org/
History Founded 1997, Amsterdam (Netherlands). UK Registered Charity: 1094981. **Aims** Provide a logical approach to the management of fractures by choosing from all available methods. **Structure** Board of Directors; Executive Committee. **Languages** English. **Staff** None. **Finance** Donations. Budget (annual): pounds9,000. **Activities** Events/meetings; training/education.
Members in 11 countries:
Austria, Canada, Czechia, Finland, Germany, Hungary, Philippines, Poland, Russia, UK, USA.
NGO Relations *European Federation of National Associations of Orthopaedics and Traumatology (EFORT, #07169); International Society of Orthopaedic Surgery and Traumatology (#15335).* [2016/XM0853/**D**]

♦ Association pour le rayonnement de l'art pariétal européen (ARAPE) 02886

Contact 11 rue du Fourcat, 09000 Foix, France.
URL: http://www.inoraonline.org/
History 1991. Registered in accordance with French law. **Aims** Promote study and conservation, and increase knowledge of *rock art.* **Languages** English, French. **Staff** 0.50 FTE, paid; 3.00 FTE, voluntary. **Finance** Members' dues. Supported by the French Government, Ministry of Culture and the 'Ariège Département'. **Publications** *Lettre internationale d'information* (3 a year) in English, French.
Members Covers 72 countries:

Albania, Algeria, Andorra, Argentina, Armenia, Australia, Austria, Azerbaijan, Belgium, Bolivia, Brazil, Bulgaria, Canada, Chile, China, Colombia, Croatia, Cuba, Czechia, Denmark, Dominican Rep, Estonia, Ethiopia, Finland, France, Georgia, Germany, Greece, Guatemala, Hungary, India, Indonesia, Ireland, Israel, Italy, Japan, Korea Rep, Lebanon, Luxembourg, Malawi, Malaysia, Malta, Mexico, Monaco, Namibia, Netherlands, New Zealand, Nicaragua, Niger, Norway, Paraguay, Peru, Philippines, Poland, Portugal, Romania, Russia, Saudi Arabia, Serbia, Slovakia, South Africa, Spain, Sri Lanka, Sweden, Switzerland, Türkiye, UK, Ukraine, Uruguay, USA, Venezuela, Zimbabwe.
NGO Relations Member of: *International Federation of Rock Art Organizations (IFRAO, #13533).*
[2018.09.06/XD6103/**D**]

- ♦ Association pour le rayonnement des langues européennes / see Europe plurilingue
- ♦ Association des réalisateurs de journaux ruraux africains (inactive)
- ♦ Association Réalités et Relations Internationales (internationally oriented national body)
- ♦ Association for Real Property and Infrastructure (internationally oriented national body)
- ♦ Association des réassureurs latinoaméricains (no recent information)
- ♦ Association pour la recherche des aérosols (#10140)
- ♦ Association de recherche pour l'aménagement de l'habitat dans le Tiers-monde (internationally oriented national body)
- ♦ Association pour la recherche didactique du français langue étrangère (internationally oriented national body)

♦ Association de recherche et de formation sur l'insertion en Europe (ARFIE) 02887

Association for Research and Training on Integration in Europe
Contact Square Ambiorix 32 – Bte 47, 1000 Brussels, Belgium. T. +3222304761. E-mail: arfie@arfie.info.
URL: https://arfie.info/
History 1992, Paris (France). Registration: Registre des Personnes Morales – Bruxelles, No/ID: 0833.571.181, Start date: 8 Feb 2011, Belgium. **Aims** As a network of social service providers and professionals: improve support, social inclusion and availability of services for people with disabilities, people with important dependency needs and with associated mental health needs; promote and develop innovative and inclusive approaches in the field of service provision for people with disabilities; promote quality staff training for social service providers; support and contribute to the implementation of the UN Convention on the Rights of Persons with Disabilities. **Structure** Working Groups. **Languages** English, French. **Finance** Sources: members' dues. Supported by: *European Union (EU, #08967)* (EU funded projects). **Activities** Events/meetings; knowledge management/information dissemination; politics/policy/regulatory; training/education. **Events** *General Assembly* Brussels (Belgium) 2020, *General Assembly* Barcelona (Spain) 2019, *Handicaps et travail – Regards croisés européens* Brest (France) 2018. **Publications** *ARFIE Newsletter* (3 a year) in English, French; *ARFIE Reports* – journal. **Members** Corporate; Individual. Full (80) in 14 European countries. Membership countries not specified. **NGO Relations** Member of (1): *European Disability Forum (EDF, #06929).*
[2020.06.23/XD6968/**D**]

- ♦ Association de recherche sur les innovations monétaires et les systèmes de monnaies complémentaires (#18851)

♦ Association pour la recherche interculturelle (ARIC) 02888

Association for Intercultural Research
Sec c/o Univ de Fribourg, Dpt des Sciences de L'éducation, Rue P. – A. de Faucigny 2, 1700 Fribourg, Switzerland. E-mail: info@aric-interculturel.com.
Gen Sec address not obtained.
URL: https://www.aric-interculturel.com/
History 1984, Geneva (Switzerland). **Aims** Encourage intercultural research; facilitate exchange of information; promote interdisciplinary collaboration and collaboration between researchers and practitioners. **Structure** General Assembly (at Colloquium); Council. **Languages** French. **Staff** Voluntary. **Finance** Sources: members' dues. **Activities** Events/meetings. **Events** *Congrès* Nice (France) 2021, *Congrès* Nice (France) 2021, *Congrès* Geneva (Switzerland) 2019, *Congrès* Antananarivo (Madagascar) 2017, *Congrès* Strasbourg (France) 2015. **Publications** *Espaces interculturels* – collection; *Répertoire des membres.* Colloquium proceedings.
Members Individual; Collective members in 25 countries:
Algeria, Belgium, Bolivia, Brazil, Burkina Faso, Cameroon, Canada, Côte d'Ivoire, France, Germany, Haiti, Italy, Lebanon, Mali, Morocco, Netherlands, Portugal, Romania, Senegal, Spain, Sweden, Switzerland, Togo, Tunisia, USA.
NGO Relations Cooperates with: *International Association for Intercultural Education (IAIE, #11969).*
[2020/XD0356/**C**]

- ♦ Association pour la Recherche de l'Unité, la Solidarité et l'Identité Africaine (unconfirmed)
- ♦ Association pour la recherche médicale en Afrique de l'Ouest (inactive)
- ♦ Association pour la recherche en neuroéducation (internationally oriented national body)
- ♦ Association de recherche ouest africaine (internationally oriented national body)
- ♦ Association pour la Recherche et la Promotion de l'Energie Durable en Afrique Centrale (unconfirmed)
- ♦ Association Recherche et régulation (internationally oriented national body)
- ♦ Association de recherches islamiques (inactive)
- ♦ Association pour les recherches sur les parodontopathies (inactive)
- ♦ Association pour la reconstruction rurale de l'Asie du Sud (#19748)
- ♦ Association of Records Managers and Administrators / see ARMA International
- ♦ Association de rédacteurs de publications de l'Asie du Sud-Est, de l'Australasie et de l'Océanie (inactive)
- ♦ Association for the Reform and Codification of the Law of Nations / see International Law Association (#14003)
- ♦ Association pour la réforme et la codification du droit des nations / see International Law Association (#14003)
- ♦ Association of Reformers in Psychiatry (no recent information)
- ♦ Association des réfugiés latino-américains et de caraïbes (internationally oriented national body)
- ♦ Association for the Regeneration of Neighbourhoods in Crisis / see Local Urban Development European Network (#16508)
- ♦ Association régionale du crédit agricole pour l'Afrique (#00446)
- ♦ Association régionale du crédit agricole pour l'Asie et le Pacifique / see Asia Pacific Rural and Agricultural Credit Association (#02019)
- ♦ Association régionale pour le développement de la coopération industrielle internationale (internationally oriented national body)
- ♦ Association régionale européenne sur la société de l'information (no recent information)

♦ Association Régionale pour l'Irrigation et le Drainage en Afrique de l'Ouest et du Centre (ARID) 02889

Pres Dept Génie Rural/Eaux/Forêts, Fac Agronomie, Univ Abdou Moumouni, BP 10960, Niamey, Niger. E-mail: info@arid-afrique.org.
URL: http://arid-afrique.org/
History 1996. **Aims** Contribute to food security through promotion of sustainable enhancement of soil and water. **Structure** General Assembly; Bureau. **Finance** Members' dues.
Members Full in 23 countries:
Benin, Burkina Faso, Cameroon, Cape Verde, Central African Rep, Chad, Congo Brazzaville, Côte d'Ivoire, Equatorial Guinea, Gabon, Gambia, Ghana, Guinea, Guinea-Bissau, Liberia, Mali, Mauritania, Niger, Nigeria, Sao Tomé-Principe, Senegal, Sierra Leone, Togo.
IGO Relations *Institut International d'Ingénierie de l'Eau et de l'Environnement (2iE, #11313).*
[2020.03.11/XM4214/**D**]

- ♦ Association régionale latinoaméricaine des ports du Pacifique (inactive)
- ♦ Association of Regional and Sub-regional Development Finance Institutions in West Africa (no recent information)
- ♦ Association des Régions des Alpes centrales (#01081)
- ♦ Association des régions des Alpes orientales / see Alps-Adriatic-Alliance (#00747)
- ♦ Association des régions alpines / see Association of Working Communities of the Alpine Regions (#02981)

♦ Association des Régions Européennes des Produits d'Origine (AREPO) 02890

Association of European Regions for Products of Origin – Asociación de las Regiones Europeas de los Productos de Origen – Associazione delle Regioni Europee per i Prodotti di Origine
SG Hôtel de Région, 14 rue François de Sourdis, 33077 Bordeaux CEDEX, France. T. +33610131189. E-mail: secgen@arepoquality.eu – info@arepoquality.eu.
Brussels' Office Emilia-Romagna Office, Rue Montoyer 21, 1000 Brussels, Belgium.
URL: http://www.arepoquality.eu/
History May 2004, Bordeaux (France), by 16 regions from 6 European countries. **Aims** Promote and defend the interests of producers and consumers of European Regions involved in the valorization of quality food products. **Structure** Board of Directors; Board of Regions; Board of Producer Representatives; Committees (2); Representation Office in Brussels (Belgium). **Languages** English, French, Italian, Spanish. **Activities** Advocacy/lobbying/activism.
Members Full in 7 countries:
France, Germany, Greece, Italy, Poland, Portugal, Spain.
Observer in 1 country:
Croatia.
[2020.03.04/XJ8994/**D**]

- ♦ Association des Régions Frontalières Européennes (#02499)
- ♦ Association des régions industrielles européennes (inactive)
- ♦ Association du registre des bateaux du Rhin (inactive)
- ♦ Association of Regulators of Information and Communications for Eastern and Southern Africa (no recent information)
- ♦ Association of Regulators of Water and Sanitation of the Americas (#02124)
- ♦ Association for Relations between Soviet and Foreign Cities / see Twin Cities International Association (#20271)
- ♦ Association Relative à la Télévision Européenne (internationally oriented national body)
- ♦ Association Rencontre CEFIR (internationally oriented national body)
- ♦ Association Rencontre – Centre d'Education et de Formation Interculturel Rencontre / see Association Rencontre CEFIR
- ♦ Association pour les Rencontres internationales Hommes et religions (#11148)
- ♦ Association pour le renforcement de la recherche agricole en Afrique orientale et centrale (#02933)
- ♦ Association des Représentants de Groupes d'Intérêts Accrédités auprès de l'Union Européenne (unconfirmed)

♦ Association for Research into Arterial Structure and Physiology (ARTERY) 02891

Secretariat c/o Conference Collective, 8 Waldegrave Road, Teddington, TW11 8HT, UK. T. +442089777997. E-mail: artery@conferencecollective.co.uk.
URL: http://www.arterysociety.org/
History Constitution adopted 14 Sep 2007; amended 15 Oct 2011. **Aims** Promote advancement of knowledge and dissemination of information concerning pathophysiology, pharmacology, epidemiology, detection, investigation and treatment of arterial structure and function. **Structure** Council; Executive Committee. **Finance** Members' dues. **Events** *Conference* Nancy (France) 2022, *Conference* Paris (France) 2021, *Conference* Teddington (UK) 2020, *Conference* Budapest (Hungary) 2019, *Annual Meeting* Copenhagen (Denmark) 2016. **Publications** *Artery Research* – journal.
[2022/XJ7577/**D**]

- ♦ Association for Research on Civil Society in Africa (internationally oriented national body)

♦ Association for Research in Digital Interactive Narratives (ARDIN) . 02892

Contact address not obtained. E-mail: info@ardin.online.
URL: https://ardin.online/
History 2018. Founded at 11th *International Conference on Interactive Digital Storytelling (ICIDS)*, which organization it then took over. Registration: No/ID: KVK 73017892, Netherlands, Amsterdam. **Aims** Support the study of and practice of Interactive Digital Narratives. **Structure** General Assembly; Board; Executive Board. **Activities** Events/meetings; research/documentation. **Events** *International Conference on Interactive Digital Storytelling* Santa Cruz, CA (USA) 2022, *International Conference on Interactive Digital Storytelling* Tallinn (Estonia) 2021, *International Conference on Interactive Digital Storytelling* Bournemouth (UK) 2020, *International Conference on Interactive Digital Storytelling* Salt Lake City, UT (USA) 2019. **Publications** *ARDIN Newsletter* (12 a year).
[2022/AA2481/**C**]

♦ Association for Research and Enlightenment (Edgar Cayce's ARE) . 02893

Exec Dir and CEO 215 67th St, Virginia Beach VA 23451, USA.
International Contact address not obtained.
URL: http://www.edgarcayce.org/
History 1931, Virginia Beach VA (USA). Primarily a US organization with many international study groups. **Aims** Disseminate the *Edgar Cayce* information dealing with the purposefulness of life and healing of body, mind and spirit; promote study and the power of the human mind. **Structure** Board; Headquarters in Virginia Beach VA (USA), managed by Executive Director/CEO. **Languages** English. **Staff** 85.00 FTE, paid. **Finance** Members' dues. Other sources: book sales; programme fees; school tuition; contributions. Annual budget: about US$ 8,500,000. **Activities** Events/meetings; training/education. **Events** *Conference to create a bridge for true understanding, cooperation and healing* Virginia Beach, VA (USA) 1998, *Annual Congress* Virginia Beach, VA (USA) 1987, *Year-round conference* Virginia Beach, VA (USA) 1986. **Publications** *ARE Newsletter* (4 a year); *Venture Inward* (4 a year) – magazine. Books; videos; online materials. **Members** Individuals in over 65 countries. Membership countries not specified.
[2019.02.12/XF5494/v/**F**]

- ♦ Association – Research Group in Government, Administration and Public Policies (internationally oriented national body)
- ♦ Association for Research in Neuroeducation (internationally oriented national body)
- ♦ Association for Research on Nonprofit Organizations and Voluntary Action (internationally oriented national body)
- ♦ Association for Research in Ophthalmology / see Association for Research in Vision and Ophthalmology (#02894)
- ♦ Association for Research on Periodontal Diseases (inactive)
- ♦ Association for Research and Study of Iberoamerican Issues (internationally oriented national body)
- ♦ Association for Research and Training on Integration in Europe (#02887)

♦ Association for Research in Vision and Ophthalmology (ARVO) 02894

Main Office 5515 Security Ln, Ste 500, Rockville MD 20852, USA. E-mail: arvo@arvo.org.
URL: http://www.arvo.org/
History 1928, Washington, DC (USA). Former names and other names: *Association for Research in Ophthalmology (ARO)* – former (1928 to 1970). **Structure** Board of Trustees. **Languages** English. **Staff** 32.00 FTE, paid. **Finance** Members' dues. Other sources: proceeds of meeting; sales of publications. Budget (annual) US$ 68 million. **Activities** Events/meetings. **Events** *Annual Meeting* Austin, TX (USA) 2025, *Annual Meeting* Seattle, WA (USA) 2024, *Annual Meeting* New Orleans, LA (USA) 2023, *Annual Meeting* Denver, CO (USA) 2022, *Annual Meeting* Rockville, MD (USA) 2021. **Publications** *Investigative Ophthalmology and Visual Science – Journal of Vision.*
Members Individuals (about 12,600) in 75 countries and territories:
Angola, Argentina, Armenia, Australia, Austria, Belgium, Benin, Bosnia-Herzegovina, Brazil, Bulgaria, Chile, China, Colombia, Costa Rica, Croatia, Cuba, Czechia, Denmark, Dominica, Dominican Rep, Egypt, Finland, France, Germany, Greece, Grenada, Hong Kong, Hungary, Iceland, India, Indonesia, Iraq, Ireland, Israel, Italy, Jamaica, Japan, Korea Rep, Kuwait, Latvia, Lebanon, Lithuania, Luxembourg, Malaysia, Mexico, Moldova, Nepal, Netherlands, New Zealand, Nigeria, Norway, Oman, Palestine, Peru, Philippines, Poland, Portugal, Romania, Russia, Saudi Arabia, Singapore, Slovenia, South Africa, Spain, Sweden, Switzerland, Taiwan, Tanzania UR, Thailand, Trinidad-Tobago, Tunisia, Türkiye, UK, United Arab Emirates, Uruguay.
NGO Relations Full member of: *International Agency for the Prevention of Blindness (IAPB, #11597).*
[2022/XM8236/**D**]

Association Réseau Européen
02894

alphabetic sequence excludes
For the complete listing, see Yearbook Online at

♦ Association du Réseau Européen des Registres Testamentaires (#07984)
♦ Association des responsables des bibliothèques et centres de documentation universitaires et de recherche d'expression française (inactive)
♦ Association of Retailer-Owned Wholesalers of Europe / see Independent Retail Europe (#11154)
♦ Association of Retailer-Owned Wholesalers in Foodstuff / see Independent Retail Europe (#11154)
♦ Association of Retired International Civil Servants, Austria (internationally oriented national body)
♦ Association of Retired Persons International (inactive)
♦ Association for Rhetoric and Communication in Southern Africa (internationally oriented national body)
♦ Association of Rhine and Meuse Water Supply Companies / see Association of River Water Companies (#02895)
♦ Association for the Rhine Ships Register (inactive)
♦ Association of Rhine Waterworks / see Internationale Arbeitsgemeinschaft der Wasserwerke im Rheineinzugsgebiet (#13215)
♦ **Association RICHIE** Réseau international de jeunes chercheurs en histoire de l'intégration européenne (#14739)

♦ Association of River Water Companies (RIWA) 02895

Association des sociétés d'eau de rivière – Verein der Flusswasserwerke – Vereniging van Rivierwaterbedrijven

Address not obtained.
URL: http://www.riwa.org/

History 15 Jun 1950, as *Association of Rhine and Meuse Water Supply Companies – Association des services d'eau du Rhin et de la Meuse – Arbeitsgemeinschaft der Rhein- und Maaswasserwerke – Samenwerkende Rijn- en Maaswaterleidingbedrijven.* EU Transparency Register: 20739609188-97. **Aims** Promote measures taken for prevention and reduction of the *pollution* of Rhine, Meuse, Ijsselmeer and Haringvliet. **Structure** Sections: RIWA-Rhine; RIWA-Meuse; RIWA-Scheldt. **Languages** Dutch, French. **Activities** Operates an international sampling network with a total of 11 sampling points. For the Rhine basin these are situated in the Netherlands (Lobith, Hagestein, Andijk, Stellendam), for the Meuse basin in France (Remilly, Taillefer), Belgium (Namêche, Liège) and the Netherlands (Eijsden, Belfeld, Keizersveer). Instrumental in setting up: *Internationale Arbeitsgemeinschaft der Wasserwerke im Rheineinzugsgebiet (IAWR, #13215).* **Publications** Annual Report.

Members Water companies (11) in 2 countries:
Belgium, Netherlands.

NGO Relations Member of: *Internationale Arbeitsgemeinschaft der Wasserwerke im Rheineinzugsgebiet (IAWR, #13215).* [2012/XN8450/**F**]

♦ Association Robert Schuman 02896

Association Robert Schuman – Verein Robert Schuman – Vereniging Robert Schuman

Pres BP 40037, 57160 Scy-Chazelles, France. T. +33387604397. Fax +33387601471.
URL: http://www.association-robert-schuman.eu/

History 1968. amended statutes, 13 Dec 1997. Former names and other names: *Association of Robert Schuman's Friends* – former (1968); *Association des amis de Robert Schuman* – former (1968); *Verein der Freunde Robert Schumans* – former (1968); *Vereniging der Vrienden van Robert Schuman* – former (1968). **Aims** Group individuals supporting the idea of a *supranational* Europe, as advocated by Robert Schuman. **Languages** French, German. **Finance** Annual budget: 100,000 EUR. **Events** *Seminar on the revision of the common European agricultural policy* Karpenisi (Greece) 1999, *Conference on young employees in Europe* Otzenhausen (Germany) 1999, *Meeting on Switzerland and Europe* Otzenhausen (Germany) 1999, *Conference on the evolution of the EU beyond the borders of the Central European countries* Ustron (Poland) 1999, *Seminar on employment of young people, women and disadvantaged groups* Walbrzych (Poland) 1999.

Members Individuals in 6 countries:
Belgium, France, Germany, Greece, Luxembourg, Switzerland.

NGO Relations Member of (2): *Permanent Forum of European Civil Society (#18322); Robert Schuman Institute for Europe (IRSE, #18959).* [2020.11.17/XE4316/v/**E**]

♦ Association of Robert Schuman's Friends / see Association Robert Schuman (#02896)
♦ Association Roger Riou (internationally oriented national body)
♦ Association of Roman Ceramic Archaeologists (#18827)
♦ Association Rorschach Internationale pour le Système Intégré (#04421)
♦ Association of Rosin and Hydrocarbon Resins Producers / see Hydrocarbon and Rosin Resins Producers Association (#10996)
♦ Association des Rotary clubs belges pour la coopération au développement (internationally oriented national body)

♦ Association of Rotational Molders International (ARM International) 02897

Exec Dir 3400 W Stonegate Road, Suite 2315, Arlington Heights IL 60005, USA. T. +16309426589. Fax +16309426589. E-mail: info@rotomolding.org.
URL: http://www.rotomolding.org/

Aims Support research and development of rotational molding. **Structure** Board of Directors, comprising President; Vice-President; Immediate Past President; Secretary-Treasurer and 10 Directors. Committees (14). **Finance** Members' dues. **Events** *Annual Fall Meeting* Rosemont, IL (USA) 2020, *Annual Fall Meeting* Montréal, QC (Canada) 2018, *Annual Fall Meeting* Cleveland, OH (USA) 2013, *Annual Fall Meeting* Minneapolis, MN (USA) 2012, *Annual fall meeting* Montréal, QC (Canada) 2010. **Members** Companies in 58 countries. Membership countries not specified. **NGO Relations** *Society of Asian Rotomoulders (StAR).* [2021/XJ3299/**D**]

♦ Association of Rotational Moulders Australasia (internationally oriented national body)
♦ Association of Rotational Moulders of Southern Africa (internationally oriented national body)
♦ Association of Rotational Moulding – Central Europe (internationally oriented national body)
♦ Association of Round Tables in the Arabian Gulf / see Round Table Arabian Gulf (#18979)

♦ Association of Round Tables in Eastern Africa (ARTEA) 02898

Pres Kahama Group, PO Box 33003, Nairobi, 00600, Kenya. T. +254203749042. Fax +254203747099.

History Founded 1954, within the framework of *Round Table International (RTI, #18982).* **Events** *Annual General Meeting* Kisumu (Kenya) 2006.

Members Round Tables in 3 countries:
Ethiopia, Kenya, Tanzania UR.

NGO Relations Member of: *World Council of Service Clubs (WOCO, no recent information).* [2016/XE2312/**E**]

♦ Association of Round Tables in Southern Africa / see Round Table Southern Africa (#18984)
♦ Association Rousseau (internationally oriented national body)

♦ Association pour la route Centre Europe-Atlantique (ARCEA) 02899

Association for the Central Europe-Atlantic Road

SG Hôtel de Ville, 322 quai Lamartine, 71018 Mâcon CEDEX, France. T. +33685935532.

History 25 Nov 1967. Statutes modified: 10 Oct 1982; 25 Jun 1983; 16 Dec 1987; 29 Oct 1993; 19 Jun 1996. Statutes adopted: 19 Jun 1996, Paris (France). **Aims** Promote, at national and international level, any economic, touristic and cultural action leading to the improvement and promotion of *roads.* **Structure** General Assembly; Presidency Council; Bureau, composed of President, 5 Presidents-Delegate, Administrative Adviser, Secretary-General, General Director, General Treasurer, Assistant Treasurer and 4 members. **Finance** Members' dues. Other sources: subsidies, gifts, contributions, exceptional incomes. Budget: euro 67,816. **Activities** Studies. **Events** *Assemblée générale* Paris (France) 2012, *Assemblée Générale* Paris (France) 2008, *Assemblée Générale / General Assembly* Paris (France) 2007, *Assemblée générale / General Assembly* Paris (France) 2006, *Assemblée générale / General Assembly* Paris (France) 2005. **Publications** *ARCEAinfos* – newsletter. [2008.07.14/XF0370/**E**]

♦ Association routière maghrébine (no recent information)
♦ Association routière des pays baltes (#03138)
♦ Association for Rural Cooperation in Africa and Latin America (internationally oriented national body)

♦ Association of SAARC Speakers and Parliamentarians 02900

Contact c/o SAARC, PO Box 4222, Tridevi Marg, Kathmandu, Nepal. T. +97714221785 – +97714226350 – +9771423134. Fax +97714227033 – +97714223991. E-mail: saarc@saarc-sec.org.

History 15 Nov 1992, Kathmandu (Nepal), within *South Asian Association for Regional Cooperation (SAARC, #19721),* when Charter of the Association adopted by speakers of SAARC parliaments. **Aims** Promote contact, coordinate and exchange experience among parliaments and parliamentarians of the SAARC countries. **Events** *Opportunities and challenges for women political participation in South Africa* Bandos Is (Maldives) 2013, *Conference* Islamabad (Pakistan) 2012, *Conference* Dhaka (Bangladesh) 1999, *Meeting* Bangladesh 1998, *Conference* Islamabad (Pakistan) 1997. [2010/XE2293/**E***]

♦ Association of SADC Chambers of Commerce and Industry (ASCCI) 02901

Headquarters PO Box 432, Gaborone, Botswana. T. +2673953459. Fax +2673973142.
URL: http://www.ascci.info/

History 1992. Formally founded, 21 Oct 1999, Mauritius, by National Chambers of Commerce and Industry and/or equivalent bodies of the *Southern African Development Community (SADC, #19843).* **Aims** Create a forum for dialogue with regional governments through the SADC Secretariat; promote a free market economy system in SADC; promote interests of the private sector in the region and cross border trade and investment activities. **Structure** General Meeting (annual). Executive Council, composed of President, Vice-President, Chief Executive Officer, Treasurer and one Executive Officer. Rotating Presidency; Permanent Secretariat. **Languages** English. **Staff** 4.00 FTE, paid. **Finance** Members' dues. Sponsorship. **Activities** Organizes and participates in conferences, fora and meetings. **Events** *Annual General Meeting* Johannesburg (South Africa) 2005, *Asia-Africa conference* Kuala Lumpur (Malaysia) 2000. **Publications** *ASCCI Newsletter.*

Members Full in 15 countries:
Angola, Botswana, Congo DR, Eswatini, Lesotho, Madagascar, Malawi, Mauritius, Mozambique, Namibia, Seychelles, South Africa, Tanzania UR, Zambia, Zimbabwe.

IGO Relations Memorandum of Understanding with: SADC. [2014/XD7286/t/**D**]

♦ Association for Safe International Road Travel (internationally oriented national body)
♦ Association for Safer Drug Policies (internationally oriented national body)
♦ Association Saint François de Sales (religious order)
♦ Associations d'armateurs des Communautés européennes (#06683)
♦ Association de sauvetage des pays nordiques (inactive)
♦ Association des savants chrétiens pour la paix (inactive)
♦ Association of Savings Banks of CIS (no recent information)
♦ Association scandinave de campanologie et carillon (#17533)
♦ Association scandinave de chirurgie cardiothoracique (#19079)
♦ Association scandinave des chirurgiens de la bouche (#19074)
♦ Association scandinave de chirurgie plastique (#19075)
♦ Association scandinave des dentistes (inactive)
♦ Association scandinave de l'emballage (#19095)
♦ Association scandinave d'endodontie (#19085)
♦ Association scandinave d'enseignantes (inactive)
♦ Association scandinave d'étude de la fertilité (inactive)
♦ Association scandinave des généticiens (no recent information)
♦ Association scandinave d'immunologie (#19110)
♦ Association scandinave de médecine sociale (inactive)
♦ Association scandinave des navigateurs aériens (inactive)
♦ Association scandinave de parodontologie (#19114)
♦ Association scandinave du plomb et du zinc (inactive)
♦ Association scandinave de recherches agricoles (#17486)
♦ Association scandinave de réforme pénale (inactive)
♦ Association scandinave pour la sociologie du droit (inactive)
♦ Association scandinave de yachting (inactive)
♦ Association of Scandinavian Migration Institutions / see Association of European Migration Institutions (#02524)

♦ Association of Schools of Political Studies of the Council of Europe 02902

Association des Ecoles d'études politiques du Conseil de l'Europe

Main Office Palais de l'Europe, 67075 Strasbourg CEDEX, France. T. +33388412994. E-mail: aspscoe@gmail.com.
URL: https://www.schoolsofpoliticalstudies.eu/

History Jul 2008. Founded after 3rd Summer University for Democracy was set up. Present statutes adopted Jun 2008. Former names and other names: *European Association of Schools of Political Studies of the Council of Europe (EASPS)* – alias. Registration: France. **Aims** Promote democracy, human rights and the rule of law; strengthen ties and promote exchanges between the schools of political studies of the Council of Europe. **Structure** General Assembly; Board of Administration; Bureau. **Finance** Sources: members' dues. **Publications** *Schools of Political Studies Newsletter* (4 a year).

Members Schools of Political Studies; Associate; Individual; Benefactor. Schools in 21 countries:
Albania, Armenia, Azerbaijan, Belarus, Bosnia-Herzegovina, Bulgaria, Croatia, Georgia, Greece, Kosovo, Moldova, Montenegro, Morocco, North Macedonia, Poland, Romania, Russia, Serbia, Tunisia, Türkiye, Ukraine. [2023.03.03/XM8882/**E**]

♦ Association of Schools of Public Health (internationally oriented national body)

♦ Association of Schools of Public Health in Africa (ASPHA) 02903

Secretariat address not obtained. E-mail: info@asphaafrica.net.
URL: https://asphaafrica.net/

History 23 Oct 2010. Registration: Ghana. **Aims** Serve the collective needs of member institutions in the education and training of public health professionals by building their capacity to maximize and excel in academic training and advocacy, and in the process serve to provide a strong unified voice for promoting public health in Africa. **Structure** General Meeting (annual); Board; Executive Committee; Secretariat. Committees (3): Advocacy and Fund Raising; Technical; Collaboration/Partnership. **Events** *Annual General Meeting* Kampala (Uganda) 2019, *Annual General Meeting* Cape Town (South Africa) 2014, *Annual General Meeting* Accra (Ghana) 2012, *Annual General Meeting* Nairobi (Kenya) 2011.

Members Schools in 9 countries:
Botswana, Egypt, Ethiopia, Ghana, Kenya, Malawi, Nigeria, South Africa, Tunisia.

NGO Relations Member of (1): *World Federation of Public Health Associations (WFPHA, #21476).* [2020/XJ8771/**D**]

♦ Association of Schools of Public Health in Afro-Asian Regions (inactive)

♦ Association of Schools of Public Health in the European Region (ASPHER) 02904

Association des écoles de santé publique de la région européenne (AESPRE) – Vereinigung von Schulen für den Öffentlichen Gesundheitswesen in der Europäische Region – Associacija Skol Obscestvennogo Zdravoohranenija v Evropejskom Regione

Dir UM Brussels Campus, Avenue de Tervueren 153, 1150 Brussels, Belgium. T. +3227350890. E-mail: office@aspher.org.
Registered Address 9-11 rue Benoît Malon, 92150 Suresnes, France.
URL: http://www.aspher.org/

History 1966, Ankara (Türkiye). Constitution revised 1977, Düsseldorf (Germany FR), to incorporate a class of individual membership; 1996, Utrecht (Netherlands), to take in account the appointment of a full-time executive director. Former names and other names: *Association of Institutions responsible for Advanced Teaching in Public Health and of Schools of Public Health in Europe* – former; *Association des institutions responsables de l'enseignement avancé de santé publique et des écoles de santé publique en Europe* –

former. Registration: EU Transparency Register, No/ID: 124269043440-45, Start date: 7 Jul 2021. **Aims** Strengthen the role of public health by improving training of public health professionals for both practice and research within the European region, as defined by WHO; serve collective needs of directors and deans, faculty and staff, as they educate and train professional public health personnel; assist schools and university departments of public health to achieve their missions of professional and graduate education, research and service; build coalitions with other programs and public health organizations to increase public awareness, appreciation and support of public health; secure the recognition of ASPHER's position as a leader in public health. **Structure** General Assembly (annual); Executive Board. **Languages** English. **Staff** 2.00 FTE, paid. **Finance** Sources: grants; members' dues; sponsorship. **Activities** Awards/prizes/competitions; events/meetings; training/education. **Events** *World Congress on Public Health* Rome (Italy) 2023, *European Public Health Conference* Milan (Italy) 2015, *European Public Health Conference* Glasgow (UK) 2014, *European Public Health Conference* Brussels (Belgium) 2013, *European Public Health Conference* Valletta (Malta) 2012. **Publications** *Collaboration in European Public Health Training* (1994); *The Athens Memorandum: Training and Research in Public Health* (1994); *Health Care Management Workbook* (1988); *Motivation Workbook* (1987); *ASPHER Newsletter*; *Training Manpower for Health Managers* – report on Joint Working Group with WHO Regional Office for Europe.

Members Full – 107 schools; Associate – 9 institutions. Full in 42 countries and territories:
Albania, Armenia, Austria, Belgium, Bulgaria, Croatia, Cyprus, Czechia, Denmark, Estonia, Finland, France, Georgia, Germany, Greece, Hungary, Iceland, Ireland, Israel, Italy, Kazakhstan, Kosovo, Latvia, Lithuania, Moldova, Netherlands, North Macedonia, Norway, Palestine, Poland, Portugal, Romania, Russia, Serbia, Slovakia, Slovenia, Spain, Sweden, Switzerland, Türkiye, UK, Ukraine.
Associate in 9 countries:
Australia, Canada, Japan, Lebanon, Malta, Mexico, Morocco, Syrian AR, Ukraine.

NGO Relations Member of (2): *European Public Health Alliance (EPHA, #08297)*; *World Federation of Public Health Associations (WFPHA, #21476)*. Participating organization of: *European Alliance for Personalised Medicine (EAPM, #05878)*. Instrumental in setting up: *Agency for Public Health Education Accreditation (APHEA, #00555)*; *European Academic Global Health Alliance (EAGHA, inactive)*. [2021/XD4509/**D**]

- ♦ Association of Schools of Public Health for North America / see Association of Schools of Public Health
- ♦ Association of Schools of Social Work in Africa (inactive)
- ♦ Association for Science Cooperation in Asia (no recent information)
- ♦ Association pour la science et l'information sur le café (#02905)

♦ Association for the Science and Information on Coffee 02905

Association pour la science et l'information sur le café (ASIC)

Pres Dorfstrasse 11, Allenwinden, 6319 Baar ZG, Switzerland. T. +41218013609. Fax +41217010041. E-mail: coffee-science@asic-cafe.org.
Sec c/o CIRAD, TA80/IRD, 34398 Montpellier CEDEX 5, France.
URL: http://www.asic-cafe.org/

History 7 May 1965, Paris (France). Founded following International Colloquia on the Chemistry of Coffee, 1963 and 1965, Paris, organized by the Institut français du café et du cacao (IFCC). Statutes adopted 1966. Up to 1981, membership was limited to individuals. Since 2 Apr 1981, interested groups may also join the association. Former names and other names: *International Scientific Association of Coffee* – former (7 May 1965); *Association scientifique internationale du café (ASIC)* – former (7 May 1965); *International Association for the Science and Information on Coffee* – former; *Association internationale pour la science et l'information sur le café* – former. Registration: France. **Aims** Compile an inventory of scientific, technical and applied knowledge likely to lead to better use of coffee and its derivatives and improve its quality, in the joint interests of producers, dealers, industrialists and consumers. **Structure** General Assembly (every 2 years); Governing Council. **Languages** English, French. **Staff** 0.50 FTE, paid. **Finance** Sources: grants; members' dues. **Activities** Events/meetings; knowledge management/information dissemination. **Events** *Biennial Colloquium* Montpellier (France) 2021, *Biennial Colloquium* Montpellier (France) 2020, *Biennial Colloquium* Portland, OR (USA) 2018, *Biennial Colloquium* Kunming (China) 2016, *Biennial Colloquium* Armenia (Colombia) 2014. **Publications** Conference proceedings; online science alerts.

Members Individuals and corporate in 25 countries:
Australia, Brazil, Canada, China, Colombia, Costa Rica, Finland, France, Germany, Guatemala, Italy, Jamaica, Japan, Kenya, Mexico, Netherlands, New Zealand, Portugal, Saudi Arabia, Spain, Switzerland, Tanzania UR, UK, USA, Zambia.

IGO Relations Cooperates with (1): *International Coffee Organization (ICO, #12630)*. **NGO Relations** In liaison with technical committees of: *International Organization for Standardization (ISO, #14473)*. [2022/XC2432/**C**]

♦ Association de science régionale de langue française (ASRDLF) . . . 02906

Pres Université Lyon 3, UMR 5600 EVS, 1C Av des Frères Lumières, CS 78242, 69372 Lyon CEDEX 08, France. T. +33481652655.
URL: http://www.asrdlf.org/

History 1961. **Structure** Officers: President; Vice-President, Treasurer and Secretary-General. **Finance** Sources: members' dues. **Activities** Awards/prizes/competitions; events/meetings; research and development. **Events** *Annual Congress* Avignon (France) 2021, *Annual Congress* Avignon (France) 2020, *Annual Congress* Gatineau, QC (Canada) 2016, *Annual Congress* Montpellier (France) 2015, *Annual Congress* Marne-la-Vallée (France) 2014. **Publications** *Revue d'économie régionale et urbaine (RERU)*.

Members Individuals in 15 countries:
Algeria, Belgium, Brazil, Canada, France, Italy, Lebanon, Mexico, Morocco, Portugal, Spain, Switzerland, Tunisia, Türkiye, USA.

NGO Relations Member of (2): *European Regional Science Association (ERSA, #08346)*; *Regional Science Association International (RSAI, #18813)*. [2021.05.20/XF5548/v/**F**]

- ♦ Association for the Sciences of Limnology and Oceanography (internationally oriented national body)
- ♦ Association des sciences de la mer d'océan Indien occidental (#20916)
- ♦ Association de science sociale de l'Asie du Sud-Est (inactive)
- ♦ Association for Sciences and Politics (internationally oriented national body)
- ♦ Association pour les sciences sociales du Pacifique Sud (inactive)
- ♦ Association of Science-Technology Centers (internationally oriented national body)
- ♦ Association of Scientific Centres in a Changing Europe (inactive)

♦ Association for the Scientific Study of Consciousness (ASSC) 02907

Exec Dir c/o Wellcome Neuroimaging, 12 Queen Square, London, WC1N 3BG, UK. E-mail: assc1997.director@gmail.com – assc1997.secretary@gmail.com.
URL: http://www.theassc.org/

History 1994. Founded on the initiative of Patrick Wilken. **Aims** Encourage research on consciousness in *cognitive* science, *neuroscience*, within the framework of philosophy and other relevant disciplines in the sciences and humanities, directed toward understanding the nature, function and underlying mechanisms of consciousness. **Structure** Board of Directors, comprising President, Past-President, President-Elect and 6 Members-at-Large. Advisory Board. **Events** *Meeting* Amsterdam (Netherlands) 2022, *Meeting* Tel Aviv (Israel) 2021, *Meeting* London, ON (Canada) 2019, *Meeting* Krakow (Poland) 2018, *Meeting* Beijing (China) 2017. **Publications** *Neuroscience of Consciouslness*. [2021/XN9288/**C**]

- ♦ Association for the Scientific Study of Near-Death Phenomena / see International Association for Near-Death Studies (#12047)
- ♦ Association scientifique pour l'étude du quaternaire africain (inactive)

♦ Association scientifique européenne pour l'eau et la santé (ASEES) 02908

Pres Facu de Pharmacie, case 57, 4 ave de l'Observatoire, 75006 Paris, France.
General: http://www.asees.eu/

History Founded 1969, by Prof A Morette, as *'Association pharmaceutique française pour l'hydrologie'*. Current title adopted 1993, when expanded activities beyond France. **Aims** Publish research work in hydrology related to human health. **Languages** English, French. **Staff** Voluntary. **Finance** Members' dues. Colloquia registration. **Activities** Events/meetings. **Events** *Colloquium* Lyon (France) 2014, *Colloquium* Paris (France) 2014, *Colloquium* Paris (France) 2013, *Colloquium* Limoges (France) 2012, *Colloquium* Paris (France) 2012. **Publications** *European Journal of Water Quality – Eur j water qual* (2 a year) – print and online; *Cahiers* (annual).

Members Full in 26 countries:
Algeria, Andorra, Argentina, Austria, Belgium, Bulgaria, Chad, Côte d'Ivoire, France, Germany, Hungary, Italy, Japan, Lebanon, Morocco, Netherlands, Poland, Portugal, Romania, Spain, Sweden, Switzerland, Syrian AR, Tunisia, UK, USA. [2018/XD3513/**D**]

- ♦ Association scientifique européenne d'économie appliquée (no recent information)
- ♦ Association scientifique de l'industrie européenne du talc (#19146)
- ♦ Association scientifique internationale d'agriculture des pays chauds (inactive)
- ♦ Association scientifique internationale d'auriculothérapie (inactive)
- ♦ Association scientifique internationale du café / see Association for the Science and Information on Coffee (#02905)
- ♦ Association scientifique internationale des espérantistes (#13301)
- ♦ Association scientifique mondiale de cuniculture (#21744)
- ♦ Association scientifique de l'Ouest africain (no recent information)
- ♦ Association scientifique du Pacifique (#18003)
- ♦ Association scientifique des pays de l'Océan Indien (inactive)
- ♦ Association des scientifiques européens 'Pro Vita' (inactive)
- ♦ Associations Collaborating on Hepatitis to Immunise and Eliminate the Viruses in Europe / see ACHIEVE (#00068)

♦ Associations and Conference Forum (AC Forum) 02909

Admin Dir Templeorum, Piltown, CO. KILKENNY, E32 H729, Ireland. T. +35351644020. E-mail: secretariat@acforum.net.
Registered Address c/o Herbst Kinsky Rechtsanwälte, Dr Karl Lueger-Platz 5, 1010 Vienna, Austria.
URL: http://www.acforum.net/

History 24 May 2000, Vienna (Austria). Founded by *European Association for the Study of Diabetes (EASD, #06228)*, *European Association of Urology (EAU, #06264)*, *European College of Neuropsychopharmacology (ECNP, #06612)*, *European Society of Radiology (ESR, #08720)*, *European Society for Medical Oncology (ESMO, #08648)*, *European Society of Cardiology (ESC, #08536)*, *European Cancer Organisation (ECO, #06432)*, *International Bureau for Epilepsy (IBE, #12414)*, *FDI – World Dental Federation (#09281)* and *International Pharmaceutical Federation (#14566)*. Registration: Austria. **Aims** Provide members with a variety of opportunities to network and exchange experiences in environments that are confidential, trusting and free from commercial influence; use expertise from among our members and from external experts to deliver quality, cost-effective, needs-led educational offerings that support association leadership, management and innovation; serve as a platform for communication and networking amongst association executives in relation to association and conference management and related activities; contribute and work towards better organized associations and conferences; increase the level of professionalism, in-house knowledge and expertise available within associations and association executives in association and conference management. **Structure** General Assembly (annual); Board. **Languages** English. **Activities** Events/meetings. Active in all member countries. **Events** *Annual Meeting and General Assembly* Hamburg (Germany) 2024, *Annual Meeting and General Assembly* Rotterdam (Netherlands) 2023, *General Assembly* 2022, *General Assembly* 2021, *Annual Meeting* Helsinki (Finland) 2020.

Members Full members
- *Cardiovascular and Interventional Radiological Society of Europe (CIRSE, #03427)*;
- *European Academy of Allergy and Clinical Immunology (EAACI, #05779)*;
- *European Academy of Dermatology and Venereology (EADV, #05788)*;
- *European Academy of Neurology (EAN, #05803)*;
- *European Alliance of Associations for Rheumatology (EULAR, #05862)*;
- *European Association for Cardio-Thoracic Surgery (EACTS, #05964)*;
- *European Association for International Education (EAIE, #06092)*;
- *European Association for Osseointegration (EAO, #06139)*;
- *European Association for the Study of the Liver (EASL, #06233)*;
- *European Association of Nuclear Medicine (EANM, #06136)*;
- *European Association of Urology (EAU, #06264)*;
- *European College of Neuropsychopharmacology (ECNP, #06612)*;
- *European Crohn's and Colitis Organisation (ECCO, #06864)*;
- *European Federation of National Associations of Orthopaedics and Traumatology (EFORT, #07169)*;
- *European Organisation for Research and Treatment of Cancer (EORTC, #08101)*;
- *European Renal Association (ERA, inactive)*;
- *European Respiratory Society (ERS, #08383)*;
- *European Society for Blood and Marrow Transplantation (EBMT, #08533)*;
- *European Society for Medical Oncology (ESMO, #08648)*;
- *European Society for Organ Transplantation (ESOT, #08676)*;
- *European SocieTy for Radiotherapy and Oncology (ESTRO, #08721)*;
- *European Society of Anaesthesiology and Intensive Care (ESAIC, #08518)*;
- *European Society of Cardiology (ESC, #08536)*;
- *European Society of Human Reproduction and Embryology (ESHRE, #08625)*;
- *European Society of Sports Traumatology, Knee Surgery and Arthroscopy (ESSKA, #08741)*;
- *International AIDS Society (IAS, #11601)*;
- *International Association for the Study of Pain (IASP, #12206)*;
- *International Council of Nurses (ICN, #13054)*;
- *International Diabetes Federation (IDF, #13164)*;
- *International League Against Epilepsy (ILAE, #14013)*;
- *International Pharmaceutical Federation (#14566)*;
- *International Society for Microbial Ecology (ISME, #15266)*;
- *International Society of Nephrology (ISN, #15294)*;
- *International Society of Ultrasound in Obstetrics and Gynaecology (ISUOG, #15527)*;
- *International Society on Thrombosis and Haemostasis (ISTH, #15511)*;
- *International Union Against Tuberculosis and Lung Disease (The Union, #15752)*;
- *United European Gastroenterology (UEG, #20506)*;
- *WindEurope (#20965)*;
- *World Confederation for Physical Therapy (WCPT, #21293)*.

Provisional members
European Society for Emergency Medicine (EuSEM, #08590); *Federation of European Microbiological Societies (FEMS, #09516)*. [2022.10.19/XF7024/y/**F**]

- ♦ Associations des conseils d'état et des juridictions administratives suprêmes de l'Union européenne (#02458)
- ♦ Association des secrétaires généraux des facultés de médecine et d'odontologie francophones / see Administration universitaire francophone et européenne en médecine et odontologie (#00115)
- ♦ Association des secrétaires généraux des parlements (#02911)

♦ Association of Secretaries and Administrative Professionals in Asia Pacific (ASA) 02910

Secretariat c/o PAS, Unit 2418 – 24th Floor Cityland 10, Tower 2, 154 H V dela Costa corner Valero Street, Makati, Philippines. T. +6328136468. Fax +6328185136.
URL: http://www.asapap.org/

History 1974, Manila (Philippines), as *Association of Secretaries in Asia*. Present name adopted, 1998. **Events** *Biennial Congress / Congress* Karachi (Pakistan) 2014, *Biennial Congress / Congress* Dhaka (Bangladesh) 2012, *Congress* Taipei (Taiwan) 2010, *Congress* Kuala Lumpur (Malaysia) 2008, *Congress* Jakarta (Indonesia) 2007.

Members National associations in 15 countries and territories:
Bangladesh, Brunei Darussalam, Hong Kong, India, Indonesia, Japan, Korea Rep, Malaysia, Pakistan, Papua New Guinea, Philippines, Singapore, Sri Lanka, Taiwan, Thailand.

NGO Relations Affiliate of: *International Association of Administrative Professionals (IAAP)*. [2014/XD5510/t/**D**]

- ♦ Association of Secretaries in Asia / see Association of Secretaries and Administrative Professionals in Asia Pacific (#02910)
- ♦ Association of Secretaries General of French-Speaking Faculties of Medicine and Odontology / see Administration universitaire francophone et européenne en médecine et odontologie (#00115)

♦ Association of Secretaries General of Parliaments (ASGP) 02911
Association des secrétaires généraux des parlements

Contact Committee Office, House of Commons, London, SW1A 0AA, UK. T. +442072193292. E-mail: asgp@parliament.uk.
URL: http://www.asgp.co/

History 23 Aug 1938, The Hague (Netherlands), as Autonomous Section of Secretaries General of Parliaments of the *Inter-Parliamentary Union (IPU, #15961)*. Present title adopted 12 Sep 1957, London (UK). **Aims** Facilitate personal contacts between holders of the office of Secretary General in any Parliamentary Assembly, whether such Assembly is a member of the Inter-Parliamentary Union or not, for the purpose of studying the *law*, procedure, practice and working methods of different Parliaments and of proposing measures for improving those methods and securing cooperation between the services of different Parliaments. **Structure** Plenary Meeting (2 a year); Executive Committee; Secretaries. Members are officers (normally the Secretary-General and his/her Deputy) of parliamentary assemblies. Meetings closed. **Languages** English, French. **Staff** 2.50 FTE, paid. **Finance** Expenses borne by Inter-Parliamentary Union or by national Parliaments. **Events** *Plenary Meeting* Geneva (Switzerland) 2020, *Plenary Meeting* Belgrade (Serbia) 2019, *Plenary Meeting* Doha (Qatar) 2019, *Plenary Meeting* Geneva (Switzerland) 2018, *Plenary Meeting* Dhaka (Bangladesh) 2017. **Publications** *Constitutional and Parliamentary Information* (2 a year) in English, French.
Members Officers of Parliamentary Assemblies in 135 countries:
Afghanistan, Algeria, Andorra, Angola, Argentina, Armenia, Australia, Austria, Bahrain, Bangladesh, Belarus, Belgium, Belize, Benin, Bosnia-Herzegovina, Botswana, Brazil, Bulgaria, Burkina Faso, Burundi, Cambodia, Cameroon, Canada, Cape Verde, Chad, Chile, China, Colombia, Congo Brazzaville, Congo DR, Côte d'Ivoire, Croatia, Cyprus, Czechia, Denmark, Dominican Rep, Egypt, El Salvador, Estonia, Ethiopia, Fiji, Finland, France, Gabon, Georgia, Germany, Ghana, Greece, Grenada, Guinea, Guyana, Haiti, Hungary, Iceland, India, Indonesia, Iran Islamic Rep, Iraq, Ireland, Israel, Italy, Japan, Jordan, Kenya, Korea DPR, Korea Rep, Kuwait, Latvia, Lebanon, Lesotho, Liberia, Lithuania, Luxembourg, Malawi, Malaysia, Maldives, Mali, Malta, Mauritania, Mauritius, Monaco, Mongolia, Montenegro, Morocco, Mozambique, Namibia, Nepal, Netherlands, New Zealand, Niger, Nigeria, North Macedonia, Norway, Oman, Pakistan, Panama, Papua New Guinea, Philippines, Poland, Portugal, Romania, Russia, Rwanda, Samoa, Sao Tomé-Principe, Saudi Arabia, Senegal, Seychelles, Singapore, Slovakia, Slovenia, Somalia, South Africa, South Sudan, Spain, Sri Lanka, Sudan, Suriname, Sweden, Switzerland, Tanzania UR, Thailand, Timor-Leste, Togo, Türkiye, Uganda, UK, Ukraine, United Arab Emirates, Uruguay, USA, Vietnam, Yemen, Zambia, Zimbabwe.
Also includes 7 organizations with individual members:
Consultative Council of the Arab Maghreb Union (#04765); *Council of Europe (CE, #04881)*; *East African Legislative Assembly (EALA, #05185)*; *Economic Community of West African States (ECOWAS, #05312)*; *SADC Parliamentary Forum (SADC PF, #19023)*; *Union économique et monétaire Ouest africaine (UEMOA, #20377)* (Inter-parliamentary Committee); Union of Belarus and the Russian Federation. [2021/XB0160/vy/**E**]

♦ Association pour la sécurité des systèmes d'information de santé (unconfirmed)
♦ Association for Security in HealthCare Information Systems (unconfirmed)

♦ Association of Seminaries and Theological Institutions 02912
Asociación de Seminarios e Instituciones Teológicas (ASIT)

Pres Miraflores 590, piso 6 oficina 11, Santiago, Santiago Metropolitan, Chile.
Sec address not obtained. E-mail: info@asit.edu.ar.
URL: https://asit.edu.ar/

History 20 Nov 1963. Former names and other names: *South American Association of Theological Institutions* – former; *Asociación de Seminarios e Instituciones Teológicas del Cono Sur* – alias. **Aims** Promote fraternity among theological evangelical education institutions. **Structure** Board of Directors; Area Managers; National Secretaries. **Languages** Spanish. **Activities** Events/meetings; networking/liaising; training/education. **Events** *Assembly* Buenos Aires (Argentina) 2018, *Assembly* Santiago (Chile) 2016, *Assembly* Buenos Aires (Argentina) 2012.
Members Seminaries and theological institutions (21) in 5 countries:
Argentina, Bolivia, Chile, Paraguay, Uruguay.
NGO Relations Member of (1): *World Conference of Associations of Theological Institutions (WOCATI, #21296)*. Instrumental in setting up (2): Evangelisches Missionswerk (EMW); *Foro de Educación Teológica Ecuménica de América Latina y el Caribe (FETELAC)*. [2021/XD9113/**D**]

♦ Association of Senates and Second Chambers of Africa and the Arab World / see Association of Senates, Shoora and Equivalent Councils in Africa and the Arab World (#02913)

♦ Association of Senates, Shoora and Equivalent Councils in Africa and the Arab World (ASSECAA) 02913
Association des sénats, shoora et conseils équivalents d'Afrique et du Monde Arabe

Headquarters PO Box 8899, Haddah, Sanaa, Yemen. T. +9671433925 – +9671433926 – +9671433928. Fax +9671433927. E-mail: assecaa@gmail.com.
Street Address Villa 31, Medina Sofan, Al-Hasaba, Sanaa, Yemen.
URL: http://www.assecaa.org/

History Apr 2004, Sanaa (Yemen). Founded following a proposal 7 Jun 2002, Rabat (Morocco). Former names and other names: *Association of Senates and Second Chambers of Africa and the Arab World* – alias; *Association des sénats et secondes chambres d'Afrique et du monde arabe* – alias. **Aims** Encourage, support and strengthen *parliamentary* bicameral systems in the African and Arab regions; reinforce economic, political, cultural cooperation and security in the regions. **Structure** Officers: President; Immediate Past President; Secretary-General; 2 Assistant Secretaries-General. **Languages** Arabic, English, French. **Staff** 20.00 FTE, paid. **Finance** Budget (2010): US$ 807,460. **Activities** Participates in international fora (IPU, Arab League, etc); works on parliamentary diplomacy initiatives. Parliamentary study visit exchange programme. Organizes: Women Parliamentary Meetings; Meeting of Chambers of Commerce and Industry in Africa and the Arab World; peace and conflict resolution meetings; student exchange programmes. **Events** *Meeting of women parliamentarians in Africa and the Arab world* Khartoum (Sudan) 2010, *Meeting of chambers of commerce and industries* Manama (Bahrain) 2010, *Meeting of women parliamentarians in Africa and Arab world* Abuja (Nigeria) 2009, *Conference* Rabat (Morocco) 2009, *Meeting of chambers of commerce and industries* Cape Town (South Africa) 2008. **Publications** Reports of meetings and conferences.
Members in 22 countries:
Algeria, Bahrain, Botswana, Burundi, Congo Brazzaville, Egypt, Eswatini, Ethiopia, Gabon, Jordan, Lesotho, Madagascar, Mauritania, Morocco, Namibia, Nigeria, Oman, Qatar, Saudi Arabia, South Africa, Sudan, Yemen.
NGO Relations Observer status with: *Inter-Parliamentary Union (IPU, #15961)*. [2019/XJ4672/**D**]

♦ Association des Sénats d'Europe (SENATEUROPE) 02914
Association of European Senates

Address not obtained.
URL: http://www.senateurope.org/

History 8 Nov 2000, Paris (France). **Aims** Develop relationships between members; promote bicameralism within the framework of parliamentary democracy; strengthen European identity and awareness. **Activities** Events/meetings. **Events** *Annual Meeting* Paris (France) 2019, *Annual Meeting* Bucharest (Romania) 2018, *Annual Meeting* Ljubljana (Slovenia) 2017, *Annual Meeting* Bern (Switzerland) 2016, *Annual Meeting* The Hague (Netherlands) 2015.
Members Federal Councils; Senates; (National) Councils. Members in 16 countries:
Austria, Belgium, Bosnia-Herzegovina, Czechia, France, Germany, Ireland, Italy, Netherlands, Poland, Romania, Russia, Slovenia, Spain, Switzerland, UK.
Observer in 1 country:
Luxembourg. [2019/AA1844/**D**]

♦ Association des sénats et secondes chambres d'Afrique et du monde arabe / see Association of Senates, Shoora and Equivalent Councils in Africa and the Arab World (#02913)
♦ Association des sénats, shoora et conseils équivalents d'Afrique et du Monde Arabe (#02913)
♦ Association of Senior European Counsellors / see Confederation of European Senior Expert Services (#04533)
♦ Association of Seniors of the European Community / see Confederation of European Senior Expert Services (#04533)
♦ Association de seniors de l'Europe communautaire / see Confederation of European Senior Expert Services (#04533)
♦ Association de seniors européens conseillers / see Confederation of European Senior Expert Services (#04533)
♦ The Association of Service Civil International / see Service Civil International (#19238)
♦ Association of Service and Computer Dealers International / see AscdiNatd (#01131)
♦ Association des services d'eau du Rhin et de la Meuse / see Association of River Water Companies (#02895)
♦ Association des services géologiques africains (inactive)
♦ Association for the Shopping Center Industry in Scandinavia / see Nordic Council of Shopping Centres (#17261)
♦ Association of Shortwave-Listeners and DX Organizations in Europe / see European DX Council (#06950)
♦ Association de la sidérurgie nordique (inactive)

♦ Association of Significant Cemeteries in Europe (ASCE) 02915
Association des cimetières historique-monumentaux en Europe – Vereinigung Bedeutender Friedhöfe in Europa – Asociación de los Cementerios Históricos-Monumentales en Europa – Associazione dei Cimiteri Storico-Monumentali in Europa – Zdruzenje Kulturno Pomembnih Evropskih Pokopalisc

Pres Pogrebno podjetje Maribor dd, Cesta XIV divizije 39a, 2000 Maribor, Slovenia. T. +38624800900. Fax +38624800908. E-mail: president@significantcemeteries.org.
Vice-Pres Comune di Bologna, Istituzione Bologna Musei, Via Don Giovanni Minzoni 14, 40121 Bologna BO, Italy. E-mail: secretariat@significantcemeteries.org.
URL: http://www.significantcemeteries.org/

History 2001, Bologna (Italy). **Aims** Promote European cemeteries as *cultural heritage* sites; increase cooperation in order to protect, restore and maintain cemeteries; raise awareness of the importance of significant cemeteries. **Structure** General Meeting (annual); Steering Committee. **Languages** English. **Staff** 1.00 FTE, voluntary. **Finance** Members' dues. **Activities** Events/meetings. **Events** *Annual General Meeting* Ghent (Belgium) 2019, *Annual general meeting* Innsbruck (Austria) 2018, *Annual general meeting* Athens (Greece) 2017, *Annual general meeting* Granada (Spain) 2009, *General Meeting* Liverpool (UK) 2008.
Members Cities (98) in 22 countries:
Austria, Belgium, Bosnia-Herzegovina, Croatia, Denmark, Estonia, France, Germany, Greece, Ireland, Italy, Lithuania, Netherlands, Norway, Poland, Portugal, Romania, Serbia, Slovenia, Spain, Sweden, UK. [2019/XM3237/**D**]

♦ Association for Slavic, East European, and Eurasian Studies (internationally oriented national body)
♦ Association for Small Animal Endoscopy and Endosurgery (unconfirmed)

♦ Association for Smart Learning Ecosystem and Regional Development (ASLERD) 02916

Sec Uni Rostock, Inst für Informatik, Praktische Informatik, Räum 253 – Konrad-Zuse-Haus, Albert-Einstein-Str 22, 18051 Rostock, Germany. T. +493814987640. Fax +493814987642. E-mail: aslerd.org@gmail.com.
URL: http://www.aslerd.org/

Aims Support schools and other learning ecosystems to improve their smartness so as to achieve the well-being of all players involved in the learning process. **Structure** Executive Committee. **Finance** Members' dues. **Activities** Events/meetings; research/documentation; training/education. **Events** *International Conference on Smart Learning Ecosystems and Regional Development* Tallinn (Estonia) 2023, *International Conference on Smart Learning Ecosystems and Regional Development* Bucharest (Romania) 2022, *International Conference on Smart Learning Ecosystems and Regional Development* Rostock (Germany) 2021, *International Conference on Smart Learning Ecosystems and Regional Development* Rostock (Germany) 2020, *International Conference on Smart Learning Ecosystems and Regional Development* Rome (Italy) 2019. [2017/XM5557/**D**]

♦ Association of Social Anthropologists of the Commonwealth / see Association of Social Anthropologists of the UK (#02917)

♦ Association of Social Anthropologists of the UK (ASA) 02917

Chair c/o The Royal Anthropological Inst, 50 Fitzroy St, London, W1I 5BT, UK. E-mail: secretary@theasa.org.
URL: http://www.theasa.org/

History 1946, London (UK). Former names and other names: *Association of Social Anthropologists of the Commonwealth* – former; *Association of Social Anthropologists of the UK and Commonwealth* – former. **Aims** Promote the study and teaching of social anthropology; present its interests; maintain its *professional* status. **Structure** General Meeting (annual); Committee. **Languages** English. **Staff** 0.50 FTE, paid. **Finance** Sources: meeting proceeds; members' dues; sale of publications. **Activities** Events/meetings; publishing activities. **Events** *Conference* St Andrews (UK) 2021, *Annual Conference* London (UK) 2020, *Annual Conference* Norwich (UK) 2019, *Annual Conference* Oxford (UK) 2018, *Annual Conference* Adelaide, SA (Australia) 2017. **Publications** *ASA Online*. *ASA Monograph Series*; *ASA Research Methods Series*. Directory of members.
Members Individuals in 46 countries and territories:
Australia, Bangladesh, Bolivia, Brazil, Canada, Colombia, Cyprus, Denmark, Ethiopia, France, Germany, Ghana, Greece, Guyana, Hong Kong, India, Ireland, Israel, Italy, Jamaica, Japan, Jordan, Kenya, Malawi, Malaysia, Nepal, Netherlands, New Zealand, Nigeria, Norway, Pakistan, Papua New Guinea, Portugal, Senegal, South Africa, Spain, Sri Lanka, Switzerland, Tanzania UR, Tonga, Türkiye, Uganda, UK, USA, Zambia, Zimbabwe.
NGO Relations Member of (1): *World Council of Anthropological Associations (WCAA, #21317)*. [2020.11.16/XE0731/v/**E**]

♦ Association of Social Anthropologists of the UK and Commowealth / see Association of Social Anthropologists of the UK (#02917)
♦ Association for Social Anthropology in Eastern Oceania / see Association for Social Anthropology in Oceania
♦ Association for Social Anthropology in Oceania (internationally oriented national body)
♦ Association for Social and Medical Action and Education (internationally oriented national body)
♦ Association for the Social Sciences and Humanities in HIV (inactive)
♦ Association of Social Security Institutions of Central America and Panama (inactive)
♦ Association for Social Work Education in Africa (inactive)
♦ Association des sociétés coeliaques européennes (#02504)
♦ Association des sociétés d'eau de rivière (#02895)
♦ Association des Sociétés d'Electricité d'Afrique (#02867)
♦ Association des Sociétés Européennes de Géographie (#02512)
♦ Association des sociétés nationales européennes et méditerranéennes de gastro-entérologie (inactive)
♦ Association des sociétés de pharmacie de la Méditerranée latine / see Société de pharmacie de la Méditerranée latine (#19508)

♦ Association des sociétés de philosophie de langue française (ASPLF) 02918
Association of French-Speaking Societies of Philosophy

SG Università degli Studi di Padova, Dipartimento FISPPA, Piazza Capitaniato, 3, 35139 Padua PD, Italy.
Pres Université Libre de Bruxelles – FNRS, CIERL, avenue Franklin Roosevelt 17, 1050 Brussels, Belgium.
URL: http://www.asplf.org/

History 1937. Statutes adopted 2 Sep 1990, Hammamet (Tunisia). Registration: France, Start date: 21 Oct 1990. **Aims** Communicate information on philosophical activity in the French language; establish friendly relations among members and liaise among them. **Structure** General Assembly (annual). Bureau of at least 5 members, including President, Secretary-General and Vice-Presidents. **Languages** French. **Staff** Voluntary. **Finance** Sources: members' dues. **Activities** Events/meetings. **Events** *Congrès* Rio de Janeiro (Brazil) 2018, *Congrès* Iasi (Romania) 2016, *Congrès* Rabat (Morocco) 2014, *Congrès Biennal / Biennial Congress* Louvain-la-Neuve (Belgium) 2012, *Congrès biennal / Biennial Congress* Venice (Italy) 2010. **Publications** *Bulletin de l'Association des sociétés de philosophie de langue française*.
Members French-speaking societies of philosophy in 24 countries:
Albania, Belgium, Benin, Bulgaria, Cameroon, Canada, Central African Rep, Congo Brazzaville, Congo DR, Côte d'Ivoire, France, Germany, Greece, Hungary, Italy, Japan, Luxembourg, Poland, Romania, Senegal, Switzerland, Togo, Tunisia, USA.
NGO Relations Member of (1): *International Federation of Philosophical Societies (FISP, #13507)*. Instrumental in setting up (1): *Société d'études kantiennes de langue française (SEKLF)*. [2022/XD6254/**D**]

- ♦ Association des sociétés de physique de l'Asie et du Pacifique (#02388)
- ♦ Association des sociétés scientifiques agricoles du Commonwealth (no recent information)
- ♦ Association des sociologues du Tiers-Monde (inactive)
- ♦ Association of solidarists-corporatists NTS / see Alliance of Russian Solidarists
- ♦ Association pour la solidarité entre les femmes arabes (inactive)
- ♦ Association de Solidarité Internationale pour la Formation, l'Instruction et la Coopération (internationally oriented national body)
- ♦ Association de solidarité avec les paysans d'Amérique latine / see Association de solidarité avec les peuples d'Amérique latine
- ♦ Association de solidarité avec les peuples d'Amérique latine (internationally oriented national body)
- ♦ Association de solidarité avec Timor oriental (internationally oriented national body)
- ♦ Association for Solidarity with Developing Countries (internationally oriented national body)
- ♦ Association de la sommellerie internationale (internationally oriented national body)
- ♦ Association soroptimiste internationale / see Soroptimist International (#19686)
- ♦ Association SOS-Sahel International / see SOS SAHEL (#19695)

♦ Association of South American Electoral Organizations (Quito Protocol) 02919

Asociación de Organismos Electorales de América del Sur

Dir Av 8, calles 41 y 43, Casa 222, San José, San José, San José, Costa Rica. T. +50622340404. Fax +50622340955. E-mail: capel@iidh.ed.cr – actividades-capel@iidh.ed.cr.
URL: http://www.iidh.ed.cr/capel/

History Founded 21 Sep 1989, Quito (Ecuador). Previously also referred to as *Association of Electoral Organizations of South America*. **Aims** Increase cooperation between all member organizations by highlighting the need for permanent democratic government in South America through universal suffrage and free and secret ballots and by suggesting adoption of policies and procedures which contribute to the enhancement of electoral processes, thereby guaranteeing their absolute fairness and unconditional respect for their outcome. **Structure** Conference of Electoral Organizations (meets periodically in different member countries on a rotating basis). **Languages** Spanish. **Finance** Support from: *Centre for Electoral Promotion and Assistance (CAPEL, see: #11334)*. **Events** *Conference* Paraguay 2011.
Members Electoral organizations in 10 countries:
Argentina, Bolivia, Brazil, Chile, Colombia, Ecuador, Paraguay, Peru, Uruguay, Venezuela.
NGO Relations *Association of Electoral Organizations of Central America and the Caribbean (Tikal Protocol, #02484)*; *Centre for Electoral Promotion and Assistance (CAPEL, see: #11334)*; *Unión Interamericana de Organismos Electorales (UNIORE, #20413)*. [2020.03.03/XD6193/**D**]

- ♦ Association of South American Sporting Confederations (no recent information)
- ♦ Association of South American Veteran Athletics / see Asociación Sudamericana de Atletas Máster (#02299)
- ♦ Association of South Asian Archaeologists in Western Europe / see European Association for South Asian Archaeology and Art (#06214)
- ♦ Association of South-East Asia (inactive)
- ♦ Association of Southeast Asian Cinemas (unconfirmed)

♦ Association of Southeast Asian Institutions of Higher Learning (ASAIHL) 02920

Association des établissements d'enseignement supérieur d'Asie du Sud-Est – Asociación de Universidades del Sureste de Asia

SG 16th Floor, Chaloem Rajakumari 60 Bldg, Chulalongkorn Univ, Bangkok, 10330, Thailand. Fax +6622537909. E-mail: asaihl1956@gmail.com.
URL: http://asaihl.stou.ac.th/

History 1956, Bangkok (Thailand). **Aims** Assist member institutions to strengthen themselves through mutual self-help and thus to achieve international distinction in teaching, research and public service, thereby contributing strength to their respective nations and to the entire region. **Structure** General Conference (every 2 years); Administrative Board. **Languages** English. **Staff** 6.50 FTE, paid. **Finance** Members' dues. Other sources: foundations' support; governmental contributions. **Activities** Knowledge management/information dissemination; networking/liaising; guidance/assistance/consulting; events/meetings. **Events** *ASAIHL Conference* Indonesia 2024, *ASAIHL Conference* Iran Islamic Rep 2024, *ASAIHL Conference* Japan 2023, *ASAIHL Conference* Sukhothai (Thailand) 2022, *ASAIHL Conference* Warsaw (Poland) 2022. **Publications** *ASAIHL Handbook* (annual); *ASAIHL Newsletter*. Seminar reports.
Members Institutions (180) in 11 countries and territories:
Brunei Darussalam, Cambodia, Hong Kong, Indonesia, Malaysia, Myanmar, Philippines, Singapore, Thailand, Timor-Leste, Vietnam.
Associate members in 15 countries and territories:
Australia, Belgium, Canada, China, France, India, Iran Islamic Rep, Japan, New Zealand, Poland, Sri Lanka, Sweden, Taiwan, UK, USA.
Consultative Status Consultative status granted from: *UNESCO (#20322)* (Consultative Status). **IGO Relations** Formal contacts with: *Southeast Asian Ministers of Education Organization (SEAMEO, #19774)*. **NGO Relations** Member of: *Global University Network for Innovation (GUNI, #10641)*. Supports: *Programme for Palestinian-European-American Cooperation in Education (PEACE Programme, #18527)*. [2021/XD0164/**D**]

- ♦ Association of Southeast Asian Marine Scientists (no recent information)
- ♦ Association of South-East Asian Nation Countries' Union of Polymer Science (inactive)
- ♦ Association of South East Asian Nations (#01141)
- ♦ Association of South-East Asian Nations Regional Forum / see ASEAN Regional Forum (#01228)

♦ Association of Southeast Asian Networks of Food Data Systems (ASEANFOODS) 02921

Regional Coordinator Institute of Nutrition, Mahidol Univ, Salaya Phuttamonthon 4, Nakhon Pathom, 73170, Thailand. T. +6628002380ext324.
URL: http://www.inmu.mahidol.ac.th/aseanfoods/

History 1986, by ASEAN Subcommittee on Protein. ASEAN arm of *International Network of Food Data Systems (INFOODS, #14271)* since 1991. **Aims** Strengthen the development of national and regional food composition data with high quality, adequate quantity and accessibility to the users in ASEAN and other regions. **Languages** English. **Activities** Training/education; events/meetings; research/documentation; knowledge management/information dissemination. **Information Services** *ASEAN Food Composition Tables*.
Members Full in 10 countries:
Brunei Darussalam, Cambodia, Indonesia, Laos, Malaysia, Myanmar, Philippines, Singapore, Thailand, Vietnam.
[2017.10.10/XJ4991/**E**]

♦ Association of South-East Asian Pain Societies (ASEAPS) 02922

Contact Anesthesiology Dept – Fac of Medicine, Hasanuddin Univ, Dr Wahidin Sudirohusodo Hosp Jl Perintis, Kemerdekaan KM 11 Tamalanrea, Makassar 90245, Indonesia. T. +62411582583. Fax +62411590290.
URL: http://www.aseaps2013.org/

History Sep 2004, Singapore (Singapore). **Aims** Promote pain management in the region. **Structure** Executive Council. **Events** *Congress* Bangkok (Thailand) 2023, *Congress* Kuching (Malaysia) 2019, *Congress* Yangon (Myanmar) 2017, *Congress* Manila (Philippines) 2015, *Congress* Singapore (Singapore) 2013.
Members Full in 5 countries:
Indonesia, Malaysia, Philippines, Singapore, Thailand. [2014/XM2919/**D**]

- ♦ Association of South East Asian Publishers (inactive)
- ♦ Association of Southeast Asian Studies (UK) (internationally oriented national body)

♦ Association of Southeast and East Asian Catholic Colleges and Universities (ASEACCU) 02923

Exec Sec Office of the Rector, Univ Santo Tomas, 2nd Fl Main Bldg, España, 1015 Manila, Philippines. T. +6327313123. Fax +6327327486. E-mail: aseaccu@ust.edu.ph.
URL: http://aseaccu.org/

History Founded Aug 1991, as *Asian Desk of the International Federation of Catholic Universities*. Subsequently referred to as *Association of Southeast and East Asian Catholic Universities (ASEACU)*. Present name adopted 1997. Regional association of *International Federation of Catholic Universities (IFCU, #13381)*. **Aims** Promote *Christian* higher *education* and provide cultural links among member institutions. **Structure** General Assembly; Advisory Committee. **Languages** English. **Staff** Voluntary. **Finance** Members' dues. Expenses for Annual Conference and Students' Forum paid by participating institutions. **Activities** Events/meetings. **Events** *Annual Conference* Phnom Penh (Cambodia) 2020, *Annual Conference* Seoul (Korea Rep) 2019, *Annual Conference* Hiroshima (Japan) 2018, *Annual Conference* Bangkok (Thailand) 2017, *Annual Conference* Semarang (Indonesia) 2015.
Members Universities and colleges in 8 countries and territories:
Australia, Cambodia, Indonesia, Japan, Korea Rep, Philippines, Taiwan, Thailand. [2020/XD4699/**D**]

- ♦ Association of Southeast and East Asian Catholic Universities / see Association of Southeast and East Asian Catholic Colleges and Universities (#02923)
- ♦ Association of South Eastern Europe Economic Universities / see Association of Economic Universities of South and Eastern Europe and the Black Sea Region (#02479)

♦ Association of Southern African National Road Agencies (ASANRA) 02924

Secretariat PO Box 754, Lilongwe, Malawi. T. +2651775088. Fax +2651775088. E-mail: asanrasec@asanra.com.
Street Address Pacific Villas, Area 14/25, Flat No 4, Lilongwe, Malawi.
URL: http://www.asanra.int.mw/

Aims Support and develop an integrated *transportation* system that meets national and regional goals and objectives through adoption of initiatives. **Structure** Board of Directors; Executive Committee. Standing Committees (6): Network Management and Financing; Construction and Maintenance; Materials and Design Standards; Road Safety; Research and Development; Technology Transfer and Capacity Building. **Languages** English. **Staff** 3.00 FTE, paid. **Finance** Members' dues. **Events** *Africa Regional Seminar and Workshop on Performance-Based Contracts for Roads* Arusha (Tanzania UR) 2016. **Publications** *ASANRA Quarterly Newsletter*.
Members Full in 10 countries:
Angola, Botswana, Congo DR, Lesotho, Malawi, Mozambique, Namibia, South Africa, Zambia, Zimbabwe.
IGO Relations *African Development Bank (ADB, #00283)*; *Africa Transport Policy Program (SSATP, #00527)*; *Southern African Development Community (SADC, #19843)*; *United Nations Economic Commission for Africa (ECA, #20554)*. **NGO Relations** *African Road Maintenance Funds Association (ARMFA, #00443)*; *International Road Federation (IRF Global, #14759)*; *World Road Association (PIARC, #21754)*. [2017.03.10/XM5244/**D**]

- ♦ Association of Southern African States (inactive)
- ♦ Association of Southern African Travel Agents (now national)

♦ Association of Southern European Economic Theorists (ASSET) ... 02925

SG Univ of Basque Country – Economics, Avda Lehendakari Agirre 83, 48015 Bilbao, Biscay, Spain.
URL: http://www.econ.boun.edu.tr/asset/

History Founded 1979. **Aims** Encourage among participating research institutions the development of economic problems that meet international standards of quality in quantitative economics and econometrics; promote exchanges of researches and of ideas among institutions based in Southern Europe and the Mediterranean. **Structure** Executive Committee of 4 officers. **Languages** English. **Staff** 1.00 FTE, voluntary. **Events** *Annual Meeting* Crete (Greece) 2020, *Annual Meeting* Athens (Greece) 2019, *Annual Conference* Granada (Spain) 2015, *Annual Conference* Aix-en-Provence (France) 2014, *Annual Conference* Bilbao (Spain) 2013.
Members Departments and centres (20) in 10 countries:
Algeria, Cyprus, France, Greece, Israel, Italy, Portugal, Spain, Tunisia, Türkiye. [2021/XD8238/**D**]

♦ Association of South Pacific Airlines (ASPA) 02926

SG PO Box 9817, Nadi Airport, Nadi, Fiji. T. +6796723526. Fax +6796720196.
URL: http://www.aspa.aero/

History 30 Mar 1979, Suva (Fiji). Founded at inaugural meeting convened by *Pacific Islands Forum Secretariat (#17970)*, when Articles were adopted. Articles subsequently amended: 22 Apr 1982, Suva; 5 Aug 1986, Brisbane (Australia). **Aims** Develop regular, safe and economical commercial *aviation* within, to and from the South Pacific. **Structure** General Meeting (annual); Executive Committee; Technical and Commercial Committees. **Languages** English. **Staff** 2.00 FTE, paid. **Finance** Members' dues. Development projects funded by donor agencies. **Activities** Standards/guidelines; training/education. **Events** *General Session* Christchurch (New Zealand) 2019, *General Session* Brisbane, QLD (Australia) 2018, *General Session* Nuku'alofa (Tonga) 2018, *General Session* Auckland (New Zealand) 2017, *General Session* Papeete (Polynesia Fr) 2017. **Publications** *Pacific Skies* (3 a year) – magazine.
Members Regional airlines (13) and industry service providers (46) in 15 countries and territories:
Australia, Cook Is, Fiji, Kiribati, Marshall Is, Nauru, New Caledonia, New Zealand, Papua New Guinea, Polynesia Fr, Samoa, Samoa USA, Solomon Is, Tonga, Vanuatu.
IGO Relations *International Civil Aviation Organization (ICAO, #12581)*; *Pacific Community (SPC, #17942)*. **NGO Relations** *African Airlines Association (AFRAA, #00200)*; *Arab Air Carriers Organization (AACO, #00896)*; *International Air Transport Association (IATA, #11614)*. [2020.03.05/XF6327/**D**]

- ♦ Association of South Pacific Environmental Institutions (inactive)
- ♦ Association de soutien de la mission évangélique Afrique-France / see Association de soutien des missions des assemblées de France
- ♦ Association de soutien des missions des assemblées de France (internationally oriented national body)

♦ Association of Space Explorers (ASE) 02927

ASE-USA Office – Exec Dir 141 Bay Area Blvd, Webster TX 77598, USA. T. +12812808172. E-mail: astronauts@space-explorers.org.
URL: http://www.space-explorers.org/

History 2 Oct 1985, Cernay (France). 2-6 Oct 1985, Cernay (France), stemming from initiatives commencing 1981. **Aims** Provide a forum for professional dialogue among individuals who have flown in space; support space science and exploration for the benefit of all; promote education in science and engineering; foster greater environmental awareness; encourage international cooperation in the human exploration of space. **Structure** Congress (annual); Executive Committee; ASE-USA Board of Directors; ASE-Russia Board of Directors; Standing Committees (4). **Languages** English, Russian. **Staff** 2.00 FTE, paid. **Finance** Sources: contributions; members' dues. Other sources: corporate memberships; retail. **Activities** Advocacy/lobbying/activism; awards/prizes/competitions; events/meetings; networking/liaising; projects/programmes; publishing activities. **Events** *Annual Plenary Congress* 2025, *Annual Plenary Congress* Netherlands 2024, *Annual Plenary Congress* Bursa (Türkiye) 2023, *Annual Plenary Congress* 2022, *Annual Planetary Congress* Budapest (Hungary) 2021. **Publications** *Space Explorer* – USA newsletter; *The Greatest Adventure*; *The Home Planet*. Annual Report.
Members Individuals who have travelled in space (over 400) in 38 countries:
Afghanistan, Austria, Belgium, Brazil, Bulgaria, Canada, China, Costa Rica, Cuba, Czechia, Denmark, France, Germany, Hungary, India, Israel, Italy, Japan, Kazakhstan, Korea Rep, Malaysia, Mexico, Mongolia, Netherlands, Poland, Romania, Russia, Saudi Arabia, Slovakia, South Africa, Spain, Sweden, Switzerland, Syrian AR, UK, Ukraine, USA, Vietnam.
IGO Relations Observer status with (1): *Committee on the Peaceful Uses of Outer Space (COPUOS, #04277)*. **NGO Relations** Associated member of: *Bull Foundation (no recent information)*. [2023.02.14/XD0908/v/**C**]

- ♦ Association of Spanish Speaking Palynologists (internationally oriented national body)
- ♦ Association spatiale européenne (inactive)
- ♦ Associations for Peace in the Continents (unconfirmed)

♦ Association of Special Fares Agents (ASFA) 02928

Contact Sofronii Vrachanski 1, 3rd Floor, 1303 Sofia, Bulgaria. T. +35929879911 – +35929873598. E-mail: asfaagent@gmail.com.

History 1986, by international airline ticket brokers, consolidators and independent travel agents. Former names and other names: *International Travel Association (ITA)* – former (1986 to 1987). **Events** *Conference* Jakarta (Indonesia) 1997.
Members in 42 countries:
Albania, Australia, Austria, Belgium, Brazil, Canada, China, Czechia, Denmark, Egypt, France, Germany, Greece, India, Indonesia, Israel, Jordan, Kazakhstan, Kyrgyzstan, Latvia, Libya, Lithuania, Moldova, Mongolia, Nigeria, Norway, Philippines, Portugal, Russia, Serbia, Singapore, South Africa, Spain, Sri Lanka, Sweden, Switzerland, Thailand, Türkiye, UK, Ukraine, USA, Uzbekistan.
NGO Relations *Association of International Travel Agents Network (AITAN, #02764).* [2017/XD5838/**D**]

- ♦ Association des spécialistes latinoaméricains en sciences de la mer (inactive)
- ♦ Association of Spiritual Academies International (internationally oriented national body)
- ♦ Association of Sport Climbers International (inactive)
- ♦ Association sportive académique des pays nordiques (inactive)
- ♦ Association sportive et culturelle des agents des compagnies de navigation aérienne (#00609)
- ♦ Association sportive mondiale des avocats (inactive)
- ♦ Association sportive nordique de la police (inactive)

♦ Association of Sport Performance Centres (ASPC) 02930

SG Centre d'Alt Rendiment, Av Alcalde Barnils 3-5, 08174 Sant Cugat del Vallés, Barcelona, Spain. E-mail: secretariat@sportperformancecentres.org.
URL: https://sportperformancecentres.org/
History Sep 1999, Sydney, NSW (Australia). By-laws amended 30 Nov 2021; 9 Nov 2022. Former names and other names: *International Association of High Performance Sport Training Centres* – former (2011). Registration: No/ID: 586667, Spain. **Aims** Provide opportunities that enhance training for high performance sport worldwide. **Structure** General Assembly; Board of Directors; Secretariat. **Languages** English. **Staff** 14.00 FTE, voluntary. **Finance** Sources: members' dues. **Events** *International Forum On Elite Sport* Barcelona (Spain) 2019.
Members Sport Performance Centres in 40 countries and territories:
Australia, Austria, Barbados, Botswana, Brazil, Canada, China, Finland, France, Germany, Greece, Guadeloupe, Guatemala, India, Ireland, Israel, Italy, Japan, Luxembourg, Malawi, Malaysia, Mauritius, Mexico, Namibia, Netherlands, New Zealand, Norway, Papua New Guinea, Portugal, Puerto Rico, Réunion, Serbia, Singapore, Slovakia, South Africa, Spain, Switzerland, UK, USA, Zambia. [2023.02.15/AA0650/**C**]

♦ Association of Sport Performance Centres (ASPC) 02929

Main Office Centre d'Alt Rendiment, Av Alcalde Barnils 3-5, 08174 Sant Cugat del Vallés, Barcelona, Spain. T. +34935891572. Fax +34936754106. E-mail: secretariat@sportperformancecentres.org.
URL: https://sportperformancecentres.org/
History 2005, Montréal, QC (Canada). Founded during IV International Forum on Elite Sport. Former names and other names: *International Association of High Performance Sports Training Centers (IAHPSTC)* – former (2005 to 2011); *Associació Internacional de Centros de Alto Rendimiento Deportivo* – former (2005 to 2011); *Associació Internacional de Centres d'Alt Rendiment Esportiu* – former (2005 to 2011). Registration: Spain. **Aims** Respect the autonomy of each of the high performance sports centres; foster collaboration; maintain an ethical approach; enhance staff development; share information and knowledge; identify best practices. **Structure** General Assembly; Board of Directors; Secretariat. **Languages** English. **Staff** 0.00 FTE, paid; 13.00 FTE, voluntary. **Finance** Sources: donations; gifts, legacies; grants; members' dues. **Activities** Events/meetings. **Events** *International Forum on Elite Sport* Sha Tin (Hong Kong) 2022, *International Forum on Elite Sport* 2021, *International Forum on Elite Sport* Barcelona (Spain) 2019, *International Forum on Elite Sport* Durban (South Africa) 2017, *Forum on Elite Sport* San Juan (Puerto Rico) 2015. **Publications** Online publications for members only.
Members Centres (101) in 40 countries and territories:
Australia, Austria, Barbados, Brazil, Canada, Colombia, Ecuador, England, Finland, France, Germany, Greece, Guadeloupe, Hong Kong, India, Israel, Italy, Japan, Lesotho, Luxembourg, Malawi, Malaysia, Mexico, Namibia, Netherlands, New Zealand, Norway, Papua New Guinea, Portugal, Puerto Rico, Réunion, Singapore, Slovakia, Slovenia, South Africa, Spain, Switzerland, UK, USA, Zambia. [2022.06.14/XJ8069/**C**]

♦ Association of Sports Institutes in Asia (ASIA) 02931

Sec address not obtained.
URL: http://www.sportasia.org/
History Mar 2015. **Aims** Make connections with Asian countries on the foundation of high performance development to support the sporting ambitions of members. **Structure** Annual General Meeting; Steering Committee. **Activities** Events/meetings. **Events** *Annual Congress* 2021, *Congress* Doha (Qatar) 2019, *Congress* Singapore (Singapore) 2018.
Members Sport organizations in 11 countries and territories:
Bangladesh, Cambodia, China, Hong Kong, Japan, Malaysia, Nepal, Philippines, Qatar, Singapore, Thailand. [2021/AA1850/**D**]

♦ Association of Standardized Patient Educators (ASPE) 02932

Contact 222 S Westmonte Dr Ste 101, Altamonte Springs FL 32714, USA. T. +14077747880. Fax +14077746440. E-mail: admin@aspeducators.org.
URL: http://www.aspeducators.org/
History 2001. **Aims** Promote best practices in the application of Standardized Patient (SP) methodology for education, assessment and research; foster dissemination of research and scholarship in the field of SP methodology; advance professional knowledge and skills. **Structure** Board of Directors; Committees; Special Interest Groups (SIGs). **Activities** Awards/prizes/competitions; events/meetings; training/education; research/documentation. **Events** *Annual Conference* Tampa, FL (USA) 2016, *Annual Conference* Denver, CO (USA) 2015, *Annual Conference* Indianapolis, IN (USA) 2014, *Annual Conference* Atlanta, GA (USA) 2013, *Annual Conference* San Diego, CA (USA) 2012. **NGO Relations** Affiliated with: *International Nursing Association for Clinical Simulation and Learning (INACSL)*; *Society in Europe for Simulation Applied to Medicine (SESAM, #19555)*; national associations. [2015/XJ9972/**D**]

- ♦ Association of State Telecommunication Undertakings of the Andean Subregional Agreement / see Association of Telecommunication Enterprises of the Andean Community (#02951)
- ♦ Association des statisticiens africains (inactive)
- ♦ Association des statisticiens de l'athlétisme (#02957)
- ♦ Association stomatologique internationale (inactive)
- ♦ Association STOP à la destruction du monde (#19997)
- ♦ Association strabismologique européenne (#08840)

♦ Association for Strengthening Agricultural Research in Eastern and Central Africa (ASARECA) 02933

Association pour le renforcement de la recherche agricole en Afrique orientale et centrale
Exec Dir Plot 5 Mpigi Road, PO Box 765, Entebbe, Uganda. T. +256414320556 – +256414320212. Fax +256414321126. E-mail: secretariat@asareca.org.
URL: http://www.asareca.org/
History 8 Sep 1994. Founded on signature of a Memorandum of Agreement by directors of member institutes, following their decision of Jun 1994. Constitution and by-laws formally adopted and headquarters agreement with the host country (Uganda) signed, Mar 1995, Kampala (Uganda). Former names and other names: *Association for Strengthening Agriculture Research in East and Central Africa* – former. **Aims** Strengthen and increase the efficiency of agricultural research in the Eastern and Central Africa region; facilitate the achievement of economic growth, food security and export competitiveness through productive and sustainable agriculture; promote regional cooperation in agricultural research so as to exploit economies of scale and scope. **Structure** General Assembly; Board of Directors; Secretariat. **Languages** English, French. **Staff** 11.00 FTE, paid. **Finance** Sources: *DANIDA*; *European Union (EU, #08967)*; *International Bank for Reconstruction and Development (IBRD, #12317)*; *Swedish International Development Cooperation Agency (Sida)*; *Swiss Agency for Development and Cooperation (SDC)*; *Centre technique de coopération agricole et rurale (CTA, inactive)*; *UNDP (#20292)*; *United States Agency for International Development (USAID)*; national agricultural research institutes (NARIs). Budget (annual): US$ 7.3 million. **Activities** Research and development. **Events** *General Assembly* Entebbe (Uganda) 2011, *Seminar on assessing the opportunities for developing and diversifying markets for bananas and banana-based products in Sub-Saharan Africa* Kampala (Uganda) 2004, *Joint ministers of agriculture meeting* Nairobi (Kenya) 2004, *Meeting* Nairobi (Kenya) 2004, *Meeting* Nairobi (Kenya) 2002. **Publications** *AgriForum* (4 a year) – newsletter.
Members National agricultural research institutes (NARIs) in 10 countries:
Burundi, Congo DR, Eritrea, Ethiopia, Kenya, Madagascar, Rwanda, Sudan, Tanzania UR, Uganda.
NGO Relations Member of (1): *Global Forum on Agricultural Research (GFAR, #10370)*. Instrumental in setting up (1): *Forum for Agricultural Research in Africa (FARA, #09897).* [2021/XD5643/**D**]

- ♦ Association for Strengthening Agriculture Research in East and Central Africa / see Association for Strengthening Agricultural Research in Eastern and Central Africa (#02933)
- ♦ Association of Student International Law Societies / see International Law Students Association

♦ Association for Studies in International Education (ASIE) 02934

Chair Nuffic, Kortenaerkade 11, 2518 ZX The Hague, Netherlands. T. +31704260231. Fax +31704260399.
Editor Fac of Economics and Management, Amsterdam Univ of Applied Sciences, Entrepotdok 206, 1018 AD Amsterdam, Netherlands. T. +31654744089.
Editor Univ of Southern Australia, GPO Box 2471, Adelaide SA 5001, Australia.
URL: http://www.asie.org/
History 2000. **Aims** Encourage international education and serious research and publications dealing with this topic. **Structure** Secretary. **Languages** English. **Staff** 1.00 FTE, paid. **Finance** Members' dues. Other sources: royalties; donations. **Publications** *Journal of Studies in International Education (JSIE)* (5 a year).
Members International organizations (13):
Asia-Pacific Association for International Education (APAIE, #01844); *Association of International Education Administrators (AIEA)*; *British Council*; *Canadian Bureau for International Education (CBIE)*; *Council on International Educational Exchange (CIEE, #04901)*; *European Association for International Education (EAIE, #06092)*; *International Education Association of Australia (IEAA)*; *International Education Association of South Africa (IEASA)*; *Japan Network for International Education (JAFSA)*; *Mexican Association for International Education (AMPEI)*; *NAFSA – Association of International Educators*; *Netherlands Organization for International Cooperation in Higher Education (NUFFIC)*; *World Education Services (WES).* [2011.11.28/XD7808/y/**D**]

- ♦ Association for the Study of African American Life and History (internationally oriented national body)
- ♦ Association for the Study of Afro-American Life and History / see Association for the Study of African American Life and History
- ♦ Association for the Study of Alternative Futures / see World Future Society (#21534)

♦ Association for the Study of Animal Behaviour (ASAB) 02935

Sec Mammalian Behaviour and Evolution Group, Univ of Liverpool, Leahurst Campus, Chester High Rd, Neston, CH64 7TE, UK. T. +441517946103.
Membership Sec Univ of Lincoln, Brayford Way, Brayford Pool, Lincoln, LN6 7TS, UK.
URL: http://www.asab.org/
History Founded 1936. **Aims** Promote the study of animal behaviour; encourage teaching of animal behaviour in schools. **Structure** General Meeting (annual); Council; Committees (5). **Languages** English. **Staff** None. **Finance** Sources: members' dues. **Activities** Events/meetings; financial and/or material support. **Events** *Summer Conference* Konstanz (Germany) 2019, *Easter Meeting* York (UK) 2019, *European Conference on Behavioural Biology* Liverpool (UK) 2018, *Winter Meeting* London (UK) 2018, *Easter Meeting* Plymouth (UK) 2018. **Publications** *Animal Behaviour* (12 a year) – scientific journal, jointly with the Animal Behaviour Society; *ASAB Newsletter* (3 a year). Books; videos.
Members Professionals and students (about 1,900) in 56 countries and territories:
Argentina, Australia, Austria, Bangladesh, Belgium, Botswana, Brazil, Canada, Chile, China, Costa Rica, Côte d'Ivoire, Czechia, Denmark, Ecuador, Finland, France, Germany, Hong Kong, Hungary, Iceland, India, Ireland, Israel, Italy, Japan, Kenya, Korea Rep, Malaysia, Malta, Mexico, Monaco, Namibia, Nepal, Netherlands, New Zealand, Norway, Panama, Peru, Poland, Portugal, Romania, Russia, Saudi Arabia, South Africa, Spain, Sweden, Switzerland, Taiwan, Türkiye, Uganda, United Arab Emirates, USA, Venezuela, Zambia, Zimbabwe. [2019.07.04/XF2592/v/**C**]

♦ Association for the Study of the Art of Record Production (ASARP) . 02936

Contact Univ of West London, London College of Music, St Mary's Road, Ealing, W5 5RF, UK.
URL: http://artofrecordproduction.com/
History 2005. **Aims** Promote the study of the production of recorded *music*. **Structure** Executive Committee. **Languages** English. **Staff** Part-time, voluntary. **Finance** Sources: members' dues. **Events** *International Conference* Boston, MA (USA) 2019, *International Conference* Stockholm (Sweden) 2017, *International Conference* Aalborg (Denmark) 2016, *International Conference* Philadelphia, PA (USA) 2015, *International Conference* Philadelphia, PA (USA) 2015. **Publications** *Journal on the Art of Record Production (JARP).*
Members Full in 24 countries:
Australia, Austria, Belgium, Brazil, Canada, Colombia, Cyprus, Denmark, Finland, France, Germany, Greece, Israel, Italy, Jamaica, Japan, New Zealand, Nigeria, Norway, Portugal, Spain, Sweden, UK, USA. [2015.06.01/XJ9502/**C**]

♦ Association for the Study of Australasia in Asia (ASSA) 02937

Pres Australia Fac of Art and Humanities, Univ of Western Australia, 35 Stirling Hwy, Crawley WA 6009, Australia.
Pres Asia Dept of Humanities, Indian Inst of Technology, Kharagpur, West Bengal, Kharagpur WEST BENGAL, India. E-mail: agera_99@yahoo.com.
URL: http://www.asaa.net.au/
History Aug 1995, Colombo (Sri Lanka), as *Asian Association for the Study of Australia (AASA)*, during 10th conference of *Association for Commonwealth Literature and Language Studies (ACLALS, #02439)*. Oct 1998, Mysore (India), name changed to *Asian-Australian Association for the Study of Australasia (A-AASA)*. Present name adopted 1999. **Aims** Bring together individuals, institutions and associations concerned with the study and teaching of Australasian studies in Asia; foster interest; promote research and projects in all aspects of Australasian life. **Structure** Executive Committee. **Languages** English. **Staff** Voluntary. **Finance** Members' dues (biennial): Australian $ – 20 / Indian Rs 1,000. Other sources: subsidies from Australian government. **Events** *Conference* 2015, *Conference* Hyderabad (India) 2012, *Conference* Hyderabad (India) 2011, *Conference* Kandy (Sri Lanka) 2008, *Conference* Thiruvananthapuram (India) 2004. **Publications** *A-AASA Newsletter* (2 a year). *Globalisation: Austral-Asian Scenarios* (2013); *Change: Conflict and Convergence* (2009); *Diaspora: The Australian Experience* (2005); *Asian-Australian Encounters* (2002); *New Directions in Australian Studies* (1999).
Members Full in 15 countries:
Australia, Bangladesh, Canada, China, Fiji, India, Korea DPR, Korea Rep, Malaysia, New Zealand, Pakistan, Singapore, South Africa, Spain, Sri Lanka.
IGO Relations Australia India Council. **NGO Relations** Asia Society AustralAsia Centre. [2020/XE3827/**E**]

- ♦ Association for the Study of Classical African Civilizations (internationally oriented national body)
- ♦ Association for the Study of Economic, Social and Cultural Development (inactive)
- ♦ Association for the Study of Ethnicity and Nationalism (internationally oriented national body)
- ♦ Association for the Study of European Problems (inactive)
- ♦ Association for the Study of German Politics / see International Association for the Study of German Politics (#12200)
- ♦ Association for the Study of Internal Fixation / see AO Foundation (#00866)
- ♦ Association for the Study of Jewish Languages (no recent information)

♦ Association for the Study of Language In Prehistory (ASLIP) 02938

Sec-Treas 20 Duane Ave, West Newton MA 02465, USA. T. +16179640978.
Information Officer address not obtained. T. +551131512667.
Editor – Mother Tongue Journal 5108 Credit River Dr, Savage MN 55378, USA. T. +16128393649. E-mail: palaeojdb@hotmail.com.
URL: http://www.aslip.org/
History Founded 1986. Incorporated in the State of Massachusetts (USA). **Aims** Encourage international, interdisciplinary information sharing, discussion and debate among bio-geneticists, paleo-anthropologists, archaeologists and historical linguists on questions relating to the emerging synthesis on language origins and ancestral human spoken languages. **Structure** Annual Meeting; Board of Directors; Council of Fellows. **Languages** English, French, German. **Staff** Voluntary. **Finance** Members' dues. **Activities** Knowledge

management/information dissemination. **Events** *Annual Meeting* Cambridge, MA (USA) 2016, *Annual Meeting* Cambridge, MA (USA) 2015, *Harvard round table on the ethnogenesis of South and Central Asia* Cambridge, MA (USA) 2008, *Round table on South and Central Asia* Cambridge, MA (USA) 2008, *Harvard round table on the ethnogenesis of South and Central Asia* Edinburgh (UK) 2007. **Publications** *Mother Tongue* (annual) – journal; *The Long Ranger* – newsletter. **Members** in North and South America, Europe, Asia, Australia and Africa. Membership countries not specified. [2016.06.01/XD6628/**D**]

♦ Association for the Study of Man Environment Relations (inactive)

♦ Association for the Study of Marble and Other Stones in Antiquity (ASMOSIA) 02939

Sec-Treas Earth Sciences Dept, Petrology and Geochemistry, Zaragoza University, 50009 Saragossa, Spain. T. +34976762125. E-mail: plapuent@unizar.es.
Pres Lab of Archaeometry, Inst of Materials Sciences, NCSR "Demokritos", Aghia Paraskevi, 153 10 Attiki, Greece. T. +3016524821. Fax +3016519430.
URL: http://www.asmosia.org/

History 13 May 1988, Il Ciocco (Italy). **Aims** Promote the exchange of knowledge related to the study of marble and other stones of art historical or archaeological interest. **Structure** Executive Committee, comprising President, Honorary President, Immediate Past-President, Vice-President, Secretary-Treasurer and several councillors. **Languages** English. **Staff** Voluntary. **Finance** Members' dues. **Events** *Biennial Meeting* Tarragona (Spain) 2009, *Conference / Biennial Meeting* Aix-en-Provence (France) 2006, *Conference* Greece 2003, *Conference / Biennial Meeting* Venice (Italy) 2000, *Biennial Meeting* Boston, MA (USA) 1998. **Publications** *ASMOSIA Newsletter* (2 a year). Conference proceedings.
Members Individuals in 27 countries:
Albania, Australia, Austria, Belgium, Croatia, Cyprus, Czechia, Denmark, Egypt, France, Germany, Greece, Ireland, Israel, Italy, Japan, Malta, Norway, Poland, Portugal, Romania, Slovenia, Spain, Switzerland, Türkiye, UK, USA. [2010.06.01/XD8793/v/**D**]

♦ Association for the Study of Negro Life and History / see Association for the Study of African American Life and History
♦ Association for the Study of Neurons and Diseases (internationally oriented national body)

♦ Association for the Study of Peak Oil and Gas (ASPO) 02940

Sec c/o Uppsala Univ, Dept of Earth Sciences – Natural Resources and Sustainable Development, Villavägen 16, SE-752 36 Uppsala, Sweden.
URL: http://www.peakoil.net/

Aims Evaluate the world's endowment and definition of oil and gas; study depletion, taking due account of economics, demand, technology and politics; raise awareness of the serious consequences for mankind. **Structure** Board, including President, Honorary Chairman and Secretary. **Events** *Conference* Vienna (Austria) 2012, *Conference* Brussels (Belgium) 2011, *Conference* Denver, CO (USA) 2009, *Conference* Barcelona (Spain) 2008, *Conference* Cork (Ireland) 2007. **Publications** *ASPO Newsletter*.
Members Scientists in 14 countries:
Austria, Denmark, Finland, France, Germany, Ireland, Italy, Netherlands, Norway, Portugal, Spain, Sweden, Switzerland, UK. [2018/XD9358/**D**]

♦ Association for the Study of Persianate Societies (internationally oriented national body)
♦ Association for the Study of Snow and Ice / see International Glaciological Society (#13718)

♦ Association for the Study of Sport and the European Union (Sport&EU) 02941

Exec Dir address not obtained.
URL: https://www.sportandeu.com/

History 2005. **Aims** Provide a home for scholars and practitioners interested in the relationship between sport and the EU. **Structure** Board. **Activities** Events/meetings. **Events** *Conference* Lausanne (Switzerland) 2022, *Annual Conference* Rijeka (Croatia) 2021, *Annual Conference* Rijeka (Croatia) 2020, *Annual Conference* Valletta (Malta) 2019, *Annual Conference* Ormskirk (UK) 2018. [2021/AA1960/**D**]

♦ Association for the Study of the World Refugee Problem (AWR) 02942

Association pour l'étude du problème mondial des réfugiés – Forschungsgesellschaft für das Weltflüchtlingsproblem – Associazione per lo Studio del Problema Mondiale dei Rifugiati
Contact Leiterin des operativen Bereichs, Postfach 1241, 97201 Höchberg, Germany.
URL: http://www.awr-int.de/

History Sep 1954, Istanbul (Turkey). 15 Oct 1961, Athens (Greece), merged with *European Association for the Study of Refugee Problems – Association européenne pour l'étude du problème des réfugiés AER* – which had been set up Sep 1950, Rome (Italy), and first met 1951, Hannover (Germany FR) – to form a new association but retaining the same name. Registered in Liechtenstein. **Aims** Promote, intensify and coordinate scholarly research in the refugee problem, by mutual comparison and exchange of results, by establishing general working principles, by publications and dissemination of results achieved in any other appropriate form; contribute, through scientific findings, to the search for theoretical and practical solutions to the problem. **Structure** General Assembly (annual). Board of Trustees, composed of presidents and secretaries of each national section. Executive Committee. Officers: President; Vice-President; Secretary-General. International Committees of Experts (CIE). **Languages** English, French, German, Italian. **Staff** 9.00 FTE, voluntary. **Finance** Members' contributions and donations. Budget (annual): Swiss Fr 45,000. **Activities** International Committees (10) on special problems such as rights of asylum and social integration. Results of studies and analyses are placed at the disposal of competent governments and international organizations. Promotes annual meetings, seminars, roundtables. **Events** *Congress* Freising (Germany) 2012, *Congress* Ljubljana (Slovenia) 2005, *Congress* Lucerne (Switzerland) 2004, *The enlargement of the European Union – implications for migration and sylum* Vienna (Austria) 2003, *Congress* Würzburg (Germany) 2002. **Publications** *AWR Bulletin* (4 a year) in English, French, German, Italian. *L'Ingresso degu Stranieri Extra-Communitari ed il Tratamento delle Domande d'Asilo nelle Legislazioni dei Paesi della CEE* (1993); *Menschenrechte und Souveränitätslehre* (1976); *25 Jahre Flüchtlingsfrage* (1975); *Die Palästinafrage und die Vereinten Nationen* (1974); *Les refugiés en Afrique* (1974); *Rechtspositivismus*.
Members Full Honorary; Sponsors; Branches; correspondents. Universities, organizations, scholars, social assistants, teachers, in 21 countries:
Australia, Austria, Belgium, Croatia, Denmark, Finland, France, Germany, Hungary, Italy, Liechtenstein, Luxembourg, Malta, Netherlands, Poland, San Marino, Slovakia, Slovenia, Spain, Switzerland, Türkiye.
IGO Relations *UNHCR (#20327)*. Accredited by: *United Nations Office at Vienna (UNOV, #20604)*. [2012/XD0113/**D**]

♦ Association of Subscription Agents and Intermediaries (inactive)
♦ Association sud-américaine des arbitres athlétiques (inactive)
♦ Association sud-américaine des musées (inactive)
♦ Association sud-asiatique de coopération régionale (#19721)
♦ Association sud-asiatique pour la coopération régionale des architectes (#19722)
♦ Association suisse pour un développement solidaire / see Public Eye
♦ Association Suisse pour l'échange de personnes dans la coopération internationale (internationally oriented national body)
♦ Association suisse de politique étrangère (internationally oriented national body)

♦ Association of Summer Olympic International Federations (ASOIF) 02943

Association des fédérations internationales olympiques d'été
Exec Dir Maison du Sport Intl, Bldg A – 2nd floor, Av de Rhodanie 54, 1007 Lausanne VD, Switzerland. T. +41216014888. Fax +41216014889. E-mail: info@asoif.com.
URL: https://www.asoif.com/

History 30 May 1983. Current constitution adopted, 18 Oct 1989, Budapest (Hungary); modified: 9 Nov 1992, Acapulco (Mexico); 19 Apr 2000, Lausanne (Switzerland); 17 May 2001, Lausanne (Switzerland); 17 May 2004; 24 Apr 2007, Beijing (China); 28 Apr 2010, Dubai (United Arab Emirates); 4 Apr 2011, London (UK); 22 May 2012 Québec QC (Canada); 28 May 2013, St Petersburg (Russia); 8 Apr 2014, Belek (Turkey); 22 Apr 2015, Sochi (Russia); 19 Apr 2016, Lausanne (Switzerland); 17 Apr 2018, Bangkok (Thailand). Registration: Swiss Civil Code, Switzerland. **Aims** Unite, promote and support the International Summer *Olympic* Federations; preserve their autonomy, while coordinating their common interests and goals. **Structure** General Assembly (annual); Council; Secretariat. Consultative and Advisory Groups. **Languages** English, French. **Staff** 7.00 FTE, paid. **Finance** Olympic Summer Games revenue share. **Events** *General Assembly* Lausanne (Switzerland) 2022, *Annual General Assembly* Lausanne (Switzerland) 2021, *Annual General Assembly* Lausanne (Switzerland) 2020, *Annual General Assembly* Gold Coast, QLD (Australia) 2019, *Annual General Assembly* Bangkok (Thailand) 2018.
Members Federations – Full (28):
- *Badminton World Federation (BWF, #03060)*;
- *Fédération Équestre Internationale (FEI, #09484)*;
- *Fédération internationale de basketball (FIBA, #09614)*;
- *Fédération internationale de gymnastique (FIG, #09636)*;
- *Fédération internationale d'escrime (FIE, #09629)*;
- *Fédération internationale de volleyball (FIVB, #09670)*;
- *International Boxing Association (IBA, #12385)*;
- *International Canoe Federation (ICF, #12437)*;
- *International Federation of Association Football (#13360)*;
- *International Golf Federation (IGF, #13727)*;
- *International Handball Federation (IHF, #13771)*;
- *International Hockey Federation (#13802)*;
- *International Judo Federation (IJF, #13975)*;
- *International Shooting Sport Federation (ISSF, #14852)*;
- *International Table Tennis Federation (ITTF, #15650)*;
- *International Tennis Federation (ITF, #15676)*;
- *International Weightlifting Federation (IWF, #15876)*;
- *Union Cycliste Internationale (UCI, #20375)*;
- *United World Wrestling (UWW, #20665)*;
- *World Aquatics (#21100)*;
- *World Archery (#21105)*;
- *World Athletics (#21209)*;
- *World Penthathlon (UIPM, #21720)*;
- *World Rowing (#21756)*;
- *World Rugby (#21757)*;
- *World Sailing (#21760)*;
- *World Taekwondo (#21844)*;
- *World Triathlon (#21872)*.

Associate (4):
International Federation of Sport Climbing (IFSC, #13553); *International Surfing Association (ISA, #15630)*; *World DanceSport Federation (WDSF, #21354)*; *World Skate (#21786)*.
NGO Relations Member of (1): *Olympic Movement (#17719)*. Stakeholder in: *SportAccord (#19923)*. [2022/XD8400/y/**E**]

♦ Association of Supervisors of Banks of the Americas (ASBA) 02944

Asociación de Supervisores Bancarios de las Américas
Address not obtained.
URL: http://asbaweb.org/

History 29 Jul 1981, Mexico, at 1st Assembly, as *Commission of Latin American and Caribbean Banking Supervisory and Inspection Organizations – Comisión de Organismos de Supervisión y Fiscalización Bancaria de América Latina y el Caribe*. Statutes approved at 2nd Assembly, 1982, Lima (Peru), and amended at: 4th Assembly, 1984, Rome (Italy); 8th Assembly, 1991, Cartagena de Indias (Colombia). Statutes modifications approved by the Commission for change of name to *Association of Supervisors of Banks of Latin America and the Caribbean – Asociación de Supervisores Bancarios de América Latina y el Caribe (ASBALC)* at: 9th Assembly, 1992, Santa Cruz de la Sierra (Bolivia); 14th Assembly, 1997, Santiago (Chile). Present name adopted 14 May 1999. **Structure** Assembly (annual); Governing Board; Technicians Meeting (twice a year each, on banking supervision, legal advisors and on automated information systems); Working Groups to define minimum regulatory and supervisory standards. **Languages** English, Spanish. **Staff** 3.00 FTE, paid. **Finance** Members' dues. Assessment established for annual working program. **Activities** Defines and improves supervisory systems through training, research, working groups and providing a high level forum for the discussion and exchange of ideas and experiences. **Events** *International Standards for Financial Reporting and Accounting Seminar* Bogota (Colombia) 2015, *Annual Assembly* Porto Alegre (Brazil) 1998, *Annual Assembly* Santiago (Chile) 1997, *Annual Assembly* Santo Domingo (Dominican Rep) 1996, *Annual Assembly* Buenos Aires (Argentina) 1995. **Publications** *Bank Supervision and Inspection Bulletin* (3 a year). Meetings, seminars and resarch papers.
Members Bank supervision authorities in 35 countries and territories of South America, Central America and the Caribbean:
Antigua-Barbuda, Argentina, Bahamas, Barbados, Belize, Bolivia, Brazil, Chile, Colombia, Costa Rica, Cuba, Dominica, Dominican Rep, Ecuador, El Salvador, Grenada, Guatemala, Guyana, Haiti, Honduras, Jamaica, Mexico, Neth Antilles, Nicaragua, Panama, Paraguay, Peru, Puerto Rico, St Kitts-Nevis, St Lucia, St Vincent-Grenadines, Suriname, Trinidad-Tobago, Uruguay, Venezuela.
NGO Relations Member of: *Latin American Banking Association (#16254)*. [2018/XD7423/**D**]

♦ Association of Supervisors of Banks of Latin America and the Caribbean / see Association of Supervisors of Banks of the Americas (#02944)
♦ Association of Surgeons of East Africa (inactive)
♦ Association of Surgeons of South East Asia / see Asian Surgical Association (#01763)
♦ Association of Surgeons of West Africa / see West African College of Surgeons (#20876)
♦ Association for Sustainable and Responsible Investment in Asia (inactive)
♦ Association for the Sustainable Use and Recovery of Resources in Europe (inactive)

♦ Association for Symbolic Logic (ASL) 02945

Business Office Dept of Mathematics, Univ of Connecticut, 341 Mansfiel Rd U-1009, Storrs CT 06269-10009, USA. T. +18604863989. Fax +18604864238. E-mail: asl@uconn.edu.
Pres Research Group Logic, Dept of Mathematics – Technische Uni Darmstadt, Schlossgartenstrasse 7, 64289 Darmstadt, Germany. T. +4961511622862.
URL: http://www.aslonline.org/

History 1936. **Aims** Support research and critical studies in logic; provide an effective forum for the presentation, publication and discussion of scholarly work in the field; promote awareness and appreciation of advances in logic among all who may benefit; present current research in logic to all logicians in such a way as to preserve the essential integrity of the entire subject and to promote interactions of all aspects of logic with each other. **Activities** Awards/prizes/competitions; events/meetings. **Events** *European Summer Meeting / Logic Colloquium* Poznań (Poland) 2021, *European Summer Meeting / Logic Colloquium* Poznań (Poland) 2020, *Winter Meeting* San Francisco, CA (USA) 2020, *European Summer Meeting* Prague (Czechia) 2019, *European Summer Meeting* Udine (Italy) 2018. **Publications** *ASL Newsletter* (4 a year); *Journal of Symbolic Logic* (4 a year); *Bulletin of Symbolic Logic*; *The Review of Symbolic Logic*. *Lecture Notes in Logic*; *Perspectives in Logic*. Books. **Members** Individual; Student; Institutional; Corporate; Corporate Associate. Membership countries not specified. **NGO Relations** Member of (1): *International Union of History and Philosophy of Science and Technology (IUHPST, #15779)* (Division of Logic, Methodology and Philosophy of Science and Technology (DLMPST)). Sponsors: *Workshop on Logic, Language, Information and Computation (WoLLIC)*. [2021/XN8104/**C**]

♦ Association of Synthetic Amorphous Silica Producers (ASASP) 02946

Manager c/o CEFIC, Rue Belliard 40, Boîte 15, 1040 Brussels, Belgium. T. +3224369300. E-mail: bpi@cefic.be.
URL: http://www.asasp.eu/

History 1992, as a sector group of *Conseil européen de l'industrie chimique (CEFIC, #04687)*. **Aims** Be concerned with related health, safety and environmental issues. **Structure** General Assembly. Working Group. **Members** Producers (9) in 5 countries:
Finland, France, Germany, Netherlands, UK. [2016/XE3103/**E**]

♦ Association of Systematics Collections / see Natural Science Collections Alliance

♦ Association for the Taxation of Financial Transactions for the Aid of Citizens 02947

Association pour une taxation des transactions financières pour l'aide aux citoyens (ATTAC) – Asociación por un Tasa a las Transacciones financieras especulativas para Ayuda a los Ciudadanos – Foreininga for ei regulering og demokratisering av finansverda til beste for menneska

ATTAC France 21 ter rue Voltaire, 75011 Paris, France. T. +33156064360.
URL: http://www.attac.org/

History 3 Jun 1998, France. Not a formal organization, but a network. Former names and other names: *Association for a Tobin Tax in Aid of Citizens* – alias. **Events** *Conference on another UNO for another world* Geneva (Switzerland) 2010, *Conference on the environment in the trap of globalisation* Berlin (Germany) 2003, *Conference* Paris (France) 1999. **Publications** *ATTAC News* (weekly).

Members in 6 countries:
Belgium, Brazil, Canada, France, Senegal, Switzerland.

NGO Relations Member of (2): *Tax Justice Network (TJN, #20100)*; *World Social Forum (WSF, #21797)*. Cooperates with (1): *Economy for the Common Good (ECG, #05323)*. Signatory to the 'Publish What You Pay' appeal of: *Publish What You Pay Coalition (PWYP, #18573)*. Signatory to Founding Statement of: *Alliance for Lobbying Transparency and Ethics Regulation (ALTER-EU, #00705)*. Supports: *Global Call for Action Against Poverty (GCAP, #10263)*; *International Campaign Against Mass Surveillance (ICAMS, no recent information)*. Endorses: *Ban Terminator Campaign (#03172)*. [2016/XD8616/**D**]

♦ Association pour une taxation des transactions financières pour l'aide aux citoyens (#02947)

♦ Association for the Taxonomic Study of the Flora of Tropical Africa 02948

Association pour l'étude taxonomique de la flore d'Afrique tropicale (AETFAT) – Asociación para el Estudio Taxonómico de la Flora del Africa Tropical – Verband für die Taxonomische Untersuchung der Flora des Tropischen Afrikas

Contact address not obtained. T. +260975166497. E-mail: info@aetfat.com – leeanne@es.events.
URL: http://www.aetfat.org/

History Founded 15 Sep 1950, Kew (UK). Also referred to as *Association for the Taxonomic Study of Tropical African Flora*. **Aims** Facilitate cooperation and liaison between *botanists* engaged in the study of the flora of tropical Africa. **Structure** General Assembly (every 3 years); Secretariat rotates every 3 years. Meetings closed. **Languages** English, French. **Staff** Voluntary. **Finance** Grants from official or private sources. **Activities** Knowledge management/information dissemination. **Events** *Congress* Livingstone (Zambia) 2022, *Triennial General Assembly and Congress* Livingstone (Zambia) 2020, *Triennial General Assembly and Congress* Nairobi (Kenya) 2017, *Triennial General Assembly and Congress / General Assembly* Stellenbosch (South Africa) 2014, *Triennial general assembly and congress / General Assembly* Antananarivo (Madagascar) 2010. **Publications** Congress proceedings (every 3 years).

Members Individuals in 60 countries:
Angola, Australia, Austria, Belgium, Benin, Botswana, Burkina Faso, Burundi, Cameroon, Canada, Chad, Congo Brazzaville, Congo DR, Côte d'Ivoire, Czechia, Denmark, Egypt, Eswatini, Ethiopia, Finland, France, Gabon, Germany, Ghana, Hungary, India, Indonesia, Italy, Japan, Kenya, Madagascar, Malawi, Malaysia, Mali, Mauritius, Mexico, Morocco, Mozambique, Namibia, Netherlands, Niger, Nigeria, Norway, Poland, Portugal, Russia, Rwanda, Senegal, Sierra Leone, South Africa, Sudan, Sweden, Switzerland, Tanzania UR, Togo, Uganda, UK, USA, Zambia, Zimbabwe.

NGO Relations Set up: *African Ethnobotany Network (AEN, no recent information)*. [2023/XD0114/v/**D**]

♦ Association for the Taxonomic Study of Tropical African Flora / see Association for the Taxonomic Study of the Flora of Tropical Africa (#02948)
♦ Association for Teacher Education in Africa (no recent information)

♦ Association for Teacher Education in Europe (ATEE) 02949

Association pour la formation des enseignants en Europe

Head of Office Rue de la Presse 4, 1000 Brussels, Belgium. T. +32479604119. E-mail: secretariat@atee.education.
URL: https://atee.education/

History 1976, Brussels (Belgium). Founded with support from *European Cultural Foundation (ECF, #06868)*. Current statutes updated May 2016. Registration: Banque-Carrefour des Entreprises, No/ID: 0416.419.911, Start date: 11 Oct 1976, Belgium; EU Transparency Register, No/ID: 474040833982-65, Start date: 17 Feb 2019. **Aims** Enhance the quality of teacher education in Europe; support professional development of teachers and teacher educators at all levels. **Structure** General Assembly (at Annual Conference); Administrative Council; Secretariat. **Languages** English, French. **Staff** 1.00 FTE, paid; 1.00 FTE, voluntary. **Finance** Sources: fees for services; members' dues; revenue from activities/projects. **Activities** Events/meetings; guidance/assistance/consulting; knowledge management/information dissemination; networking/liaising; research and development; training/education. **Events** *Spring Conference* Dublin (Ireland) 2022, *ATEE Annual Conference* Riga (Latvia) 2022, *Winter Conference* Sestri Levante (Italy) 2022, *Spring Conference* Florence (Italy) 2021, *ATEE Annual Conference* Warsaw (Poland) 2021. **Publications** *European Journal of Teacher Education* (5 a year); *ATEE News* (periodical). *Life and Work of Teacher Educators*. ATEE book series; guides; conference proceedings.

Members Institutional in 44 countries and territories:
Albania, Austria, Belarus, Belgium, Bulgaria, Canada, Central Serbia, Croatia, Czechia, Denmark, England, Estonia, Finland, France, Germany, Greece, Hungary, Iceland, Ireland, Israel, Italy, Kosovo, Latvia, Lithuania, Malaysia, Malta, Montenegro, Netherlands, Norway, Poland, Portugal, Romania, Russia, Serbia, Slovakia, Slovenia, Spain, Sweden, Switzerland, Türkiye, UK, Ukraine, Vojvodina, Wales.

Individuals and universities in 40 countries and territories:
Albania, Australia, Austria, Belgium, Canada, Czechia, Denmark, Estonia, Faeroe Is, Finland, France, Germany, Greece, Hungary, Iceland, India, Ireland, Israel, Italy, Japan, Latvia, Lithuania, Malta, Moldova, Namibia, Netherlands, Norway, Poland, Portugal, Romania, Slovakia, Slovenia, South Africa, Spain, Sweden, Switzerland, Taiwan, UK, Ukraine, USA.

NGO Relations Member of (3): *European Policy Network on School Leadership (EPNoSL, #08245)*; *Federation of European and International Associations Established in Belgium (FAIB, #09508)*; *Lifelong Learning Platform – European Civil Society for Education (LLLP, #16466)*. Instrumental in setting up (1): *Permanent Liaison Committee of European Associations in Education (PLEASE, inactive)*. [2022.05.11/XD8705/**D**]

♦ Association of Teachers of Latin American Studies (internationally oriented national body)
♦ Association of Teachers of Management / see Association for Management Education and Development
♦ Association for Technical Education in South and South East Asia (inactive)
♦ Association of Technical Universities of Baltic States (no recent information)
♦ Association of Technicians for International Cooperation and Solidarity (internationally oriented national body)
♦ Association de techniciens municipaux d'Amérique latine (inactive)
♦ Association technique africaine (inactive)
♦ Association technique européenne des revêtements de protection (inactive)

♦ Association technique de l'industrie européenne des lubrifiants (ATIEL) 02950

Technical Association of the European Lubricant Industry

Secretariat Rue de la Science 14b, 1040 Brussels, Belgium. T. +3225669137. Fax +3225669136. E-mail: info@atiel.eu.
URL: http://www.atiel.org/

History 1976, Brussels (Belgium). A grouping of the type *European Economic Interest Grouping (EEIG, #06960)* since 1995. Registration: Banque Carrefour des Entreprises, No/ID: 0750.488.604, Start date: 10 Jul 2020, Belgium; EU Transparency Register, No/ID: 673525317243-17, Start date: 6 May 2015. **Aims** Promote the dialogue on technical concerns and issues reflected in regulations, specifications and relevant self-imposed codes, between its members and the *automotive* manufacturing industries and their professional bodies, and relevant administrative bodies; monitor technical issues concerning product performance needs and environmental legislation; develop, coordinate and adopt common positions of its members; inform relevant bodies. **Structure** General Meeting; Executive Committee; Technical Council; Technical Committees. **Languages** English. **Staff** 0.50 FTE, paid; 2.00 FTE, voluntary. **Finance** Sources: members' dues. **Publications** *ATIEL Code of Practice*.

Members European oil companies developing and marketing lubricants (24) in 12 countries:
Austria, Belgium, Finland, France, Germany, Italy, Netherlands, Norway, Portugal, Spain, Sweden, UK.

European professional bodies (1):
Union Européenne de l'Industrie des Lubrifiants (UEIL, #20398).

NGO Relations Member of: *Coordinating European Council for the Development of Performance Tests for Transportation Fuels, Lubricants and Other Fluids (CEC, #04822)*; *Industry4Europe (#11181)*. Associate member of: *European Energy Forum (EEF, #06986)*. [2020/XD8670/t/**D**]

♦ Association technique internationale des bois tropicaux (#15668)
♦ Association technique et scientifique pour la conservation et la restauration des bâtiments et des monuments (#12152)
♦ Association for Technology Implementation in Europe / see Taftie – The European Network of leading national innovation agencies (#20088)

♦ Association of Telecommunication Enterprises of the Andean Community 02951

Association des entreprises de télécommunications de la Communauté andine – Asociación de Empresas de Telecomunicaciones de la Comunidad Andina (ASETA)

Secretariat Av La Coruña N 27-36 y Francisco de Orellana, 170523 Quito, Ecuador. T. +59322556094 – +59322231393. E-mail: aseta@aseta.org.
URL: http://www.aseta.org/

History 24 Jul 1974, Lima (Peru). Established 24-26 Jul 1974, Lima (Peru), as *Association of State Telecommunication Undertakings of the Andean Subregional Agreement – Association des entreprises gouvernementales de télécommunications de l'Accord sous-régional andin – Asociación de Empresas Estatales de Telecomunicaciones del Acuerdo Subregional Andino*, when first statutes were adopted. Registered in accordance with law of Ecuador, 11 Jun 1975. New statutes entered into force 1 Jan 1994, when title changed to *Association of Telecommunication Enterprises of the Andean Subregional Agreement – Association des entreprises de télécommunications de l'Accord sous-régional andin – Asociación de Empresas de Telecomunicaciones del Acuerdo Subregional Andino*. An Andean integration organ of *Andean Subregional Integration Agreement (Cartagena Agreement, 1969)*, coming within the framework of *Andean Community (#00817)*. **Aims** Contribute to the achievement of business objectives of members, and integral development of the telecommunication and ICT sectors into a converged environment; strengthen regional integration. **Structure** Board of Directors (meets annually), consisting of the General Managers or Chief Executive Officers of each member enterprise. General Secretariat, headed by Secretary-General, includes 2 Departments (each coordinating 3 Standing Committees): Studies and Projects Department – Planning and Standardization, Operations, Training; International Relations Department – Tariffs, Sales and Marketing, Regulatory Issues. Secretariat located in Quito (Ecuador). **Languages** Spanish. **Staff** Staff at Secretariat; consultants and experts. **Finance** Members' contributions (periodical); revenue from studies and projects. **Activities** Promotes harmonious development of telecommunications in the Andean Community countries; works to achieve goals agreed upon by member companies, involving a series of studies, projects and events at the subregional and international level; provides support to *'General Secretariat of Andean Community – Comunidad Andina de Naciones (CAN)'* and to *'Comité Andino de Autoridades de Telecomunicaciones (CAATEL)'* in specific telecommunications and information topics and areas; joins efforts in discussion of standardization, services, regulation, rates and other issues with international agencies; promotes seminars, courses, internships and events to disseminate new technologies and exchange experience; supports telecommunications authorities of Andean Community countries and other operators and network and service providers; organizes seminars, studies, curses, other international events and local training and development programmes. **Publications** *Boletin Andino de Noticias* (weekly) – newsletter; *Boletin Sectorial Andino* (4 a year); *Enlace Andino* (2 a year) – magazine.

Members Telecommunications companies (12) in 5 countries:
Bolivia, Colombia, Ecuador, Peru, Venezuela.

IGO Relations Working relations with: *International Telecommunication Union (ITU, #15673)*. Formal agreement with: *International Telecommunications Satellite Organization (ITSO, #15670)*. *Comisión Técnica Regional de Telecomunicaciones (COMTELCA, #04144)*. [2018/XD5906/**D***]

♦ Association of Telecommunication Enterprises of the Andean Subregional Agreement / see Association of Telecommunication Enterprises of the Andean Community (#02951)
♦ Association des télévisions commerciales européennes (#02436)
♦ Association Ten-Chi international (inactive)
♦ Association of Tennis Professionals / see ATP World Tour (#03011)
♦ Association pour la terminologie et le transfert des connaissances (#10145)
♦ Association for Terminology and Knowledge Transfer (#10145)
♦ Association of Terrestrial Magnetism and Electricity of the IUGG / see International Association of Geomagnetism and Aeronomy (#11916)
♦ Association of Test Publishers (unconfirmed)
♦ Association for Theological Education in the Near East / see Association of Theological Seminaries and Institutes in the Middle East (#02954)

♦ Association for Theological Education in South East Asia (ATESEA) 02952

Main Office c/o 2F Henry Luce Library – CPU, Jaro, 5000 Iloilo ILI, Philippines. T. +63333274556. Fax +63333291971. E-mail: atesea.info@gmail.com.
URL: http://atesea.net/

History 1957, Singapore (Singapore). New constitution and name adopted July 1981, Philippines. New structure adopted 2009. Former names and other names: *Association of Theological Schools in South East Asia* – former; *Association d'éducation théologique en Asie du Sud-Est* – former. **Aims** Promote creative relationships among institutions and agencies engaged in theological education and the Churches in the region; facilitate regional efforts in theological education; set guidelines and standards and provide accreditation services to member-institutions and to others requesting it; work for the improvement and renewal of theological education in the region. **Structure** Board of Trustees; Accreditation Commission; Executive, Policy and Finance Committees. **Languages** Burmese, English, Indonesian, Mandarin Chinese, Thai. **Staff** 2.00 FTE, paid. **Finance** Sources: grants. Annual budget: 160,000 USD. **Activities** Events/meetings; training/education. **Events** *Quadrennial General Assembly* Malang (Indonesia) 2009, *Quadrennial General Assembly* Hong Kong (Hong Kong) 1997, *Quadrennial General Assembly* Hong Kong (Hong Kong) 1997, *Annual General Meeting* Bali (Indonesia) 1996, *Annual General Meeting* Myanmar 1995. **Publications** *Asia Journal of Theology* (2 a year).

Members Regular (institutions regularly engaged in training for Christian ministry in South East Asia) and Affiliate (institutions involved in theological education in South East Asia), totalling 94, in 13 countries and territories:
Australia, Cambodia, China, Hong Kong, Indonesia, Malaysia, Myanmar, Philippines, Singapore, Sri Lanka, Taiwan, Thailand, Vietnam.

NGO Relations Instrumental in setting up (1): *World Conference of Associations of Theological Institutions (WOCATI, #21296)*. [2023.02.15/XD6703/**D**]

♦ Association of Theological Institutes in the Middle East / see Association of Theological Seminaries and Institutes in the Middle East (#02954)

♦ Association of Theological Institutions of Eastern Africa (ATIEA) . . 02953

Association des Institutions d'Enseignement Theologique en Afrique Occidentale (AIETAO)

Gen Sec PO Box 15055-00509, Lang'ata, Kenya. E-mail: glad4phil@yahoo.com.
Facebook: https://www.facebook.com/Association-of-Theological-Institutions-in-Eastern-Africa-1641662296089238/

Events *World conference of associations of theological institutions* Nairobi (Kenya) 1996, *Annual general meeting* Nairobi (Kenya) 1995, *Annual general meeting* Dar es Salaam (Tanzania UR) 1993. **NGO Relations** Member of: *World Conference of Associations of Theological Institutions (WOCATI, #21296)*. [2009/XE1685/**E**]

♦ Association of Theological Schools in South East Asia / see Association for Theological Education in South East Asia (#02952)

♦ Association of Theological Seminaries and Institutes in the Middle East (ATIME) 02954

Contact c/o MECC, PO Box 11-5376, Beirut, Lebanon. E-mail: info@mecc.org.
URL: https://www.mecc.org/atime

History 1967. Founded as *Association for Theological Education in the Near East (ATENE)*. Became *Association of Theological Institutes in the Middle East – Association des instituts de théologie du Moyen-Orient* in 1980, at General Assembly, when new statutes were adopted. Present name adopted, 3 Jun 1992. Since 1975, affiliated with *Middle East Council of Churches (MECC, #16756)*. Activities suspended from 1999 to 2019, then reactivated. **Aims** Academic: help theological instruction be more in keeping with growing needs of the region; practical: pool material and human resources to cope better with academic needs; ecclesiastical: prepare future *clergy* and *lay* people to assume responsibility in the *Churches* of the region; general: promote fraternal relationships among institutes, instructors and student bodies, helping institutes to share information, raising standards of theological *education*, encouraging relationship between theological studies and the life of the Churches and increasing theological cooperation with other institutes in and outside the region. **Structure** Deans of theological academies (meeting annually), elect Chairman (1-year term) and Executive Secretary (3-year term). **Activities** Programmes (4): Consultations; Publications; Students; Information-Documentation. **Events** *Meeting* Cairo (Egypt) 2019.
Members Church-affiliated (11) institutes in 3 countries:
Egypt, Lebanon, Syrian AR.
Internationally orientated member (1):
Near East School of Theology (NEST).
NGO Relations Member of: *Middle East Association of Training and Retreat Centres (MEATRC, no recent information)*; *World Conference of Associations of Theological Institutions (WOCATI, #21296)*.
[2022/XD2523/**D**]

♦ Association of Third World Economists (inactive)

♦ Association of Thoracic and Cardiovascular Surgeons of Asia (ATCSA) 02955

SG c/o Cardio Thoracic Surgical Centre, Mnt Elizabeth Medical Cenre, 3 Mnt Elizabeth 17 – 18, Singapore 228510, Singapore. T. +6567346393. Fax +6567330728.
URL: http://www.atcsa.org/

History 1971. Previously also known under the acronym *ATCVSA*. **Events** *Annual Congress* Bangkok (Thailand) 2021, *Annual Congress* Phuket (Thailand) 2020, *Annual Congress* Taipei (Taiwan) 2019, *Annual Congress* Yogyakarta (Indonesia) 2018, *Annual Congress* Melbourne, VIC (Australia) 2017. **Publications** *Annals of Thoracic and Cardiovascular Surgery* (periodical). **NGO Relations** Associate member of: *World Heart Federation (WHF, #21562)*. [2021/XD8381/**D**]

♦ Association of Tin Producing Countries (inactive)
♦ Association for a Tobin Tax in Aid of Citizens / see Association for the Taxation of Financial Transactions for the Aid of Citizens (#02947)
♦ Association pour le tourisme dans les Caraïbes de l'Est (inactive)
♦ Association de tourisme du Pacifique-Asie (#17932)
♦ Association for Tourism and Leisure Education / see Association for Tourism and Leisure Education and Research (#02956)

♦ Association for Tourism and Leisure Education and Research (ATLAS) 02956

Administration Travit – PO Box 109, 6800 AC Arnhem, Netherlands. T. +31208932166. E-mail: admin@atlas-euro.org.
Chair/Coordinator Wageningen Univ, Cultural Geography Group, PO Box 47, 6700 AA Wageningen, Netherlands. T. +31317485395.
URL: http://www.atlas-euro.org/

History 1991, as *European Association for Tourism and Leisure Education*. Subsequently changed title to *Association for Tourism and Leisure Education (ATLAS)*, 2000. Current title adopted 2012. **Aims** Develop transnational initiatives in tourism and leisure. **Structure** Executive; Regional Associations (4); Special Interest Groups (7). **Languages** English. **Staff** 2.00 FTE, paid. **Finance** Members' dues. **Activities** Projects/programmes; training/education; events/meetings; publishing activities. **Events** *Annual Conference* Girona (Spain) 2019, *Business Tourism Conference* Porvoo (Finland) 2019, *Annual Conference* Copenhagen (Denmark) 2018, *Africa Conference* Eldoret (Kenya) 2017, *Annual Conference* Viana do Castelo (Portugal) 2017. **Publications** *ATLAS Tourism and Leisure Review* (periodical). Books; reports; working papers.
Members Full and Associate in 63 countries and territories:
Argentina, Australia, Austria, Belgium, Bolivia, Botswana, Brazil, Bulgaria, Cameroon, Canada, China, Costa Rica, Croatia, Cyprus, Czechia, Denmark, Estonia, Fiji, Finland, France, Georgia, Germany, Greece, Hungary, India, Indonesia, Ireland, Italy, Kazakhstan, Kenya, Latvia, Malaysia, Malta, Mexico, Mongolia, Mozambique, Nepal, Netherlands, New Zealand, Nigeria, North Macedonia, Norway, Poland, Portugal, Romania, Russia, Rwanda, Sao Tomé-Principe, Serbia, Singapore, Slovakia, Slovenia, South Africa, Spain, Sweden, Switzerland, Tanzania UR, Thailand, Türkiye, Uganda, UK, United Arab Emirates, USA.
IGO Relations *European Commission (EC, #06633)*. [2017.11.02/XD6296/**D**]

♦ Association touristique pour les Caraïbes (inactive)

♦ Association of Track and Field Statisticians (ATFS) 02957

Association des statisticiens de l'athlétisme

Sec PO Box 1001, Huntley IL 60142-1001, USA. E-mail: secretary@atfs.org.
URL: http://www.atfs.org/

History Founded 26 Aug 1950, Brussels (Belgium). Constitution revised: 5 Sep 1974, Rome (Italy); 12 Sep 1982, Athens (Greece); 31 Aug 1986, Stuttgart (Germany FR); 27 Sep 1988, Seoul (Korea Rep). **Aims** Promote development and rationalization of track and field statistics internationally, by publishing and coordinating complete data on track field *athletics*, performance and history. **Structure** General Session (every 4 years, at Olympic Games); Executive Committee. **Languages** English. **Staff** 7.00 FTE, voluntary. **Finance** Sources: members' dues; sale of publications. **Activities** Publishing activities. **Events** *Biennial general meeting* Barcelona (Spain) 2010, *Biennial Convention* Berlin (Germany) 2009, *Biennial convention / Biennial General Meeting* Osaka (Japan) 2007, *Biennial convention / Biennial General Session* Helsinki (Finland) 2005, *Biennial Convention* Athens (Greece) 2004. **Publications** *ATFS Bulletin* (3 a year); *ATFS International Athletics Annual*. *ATFS National Statistics*. *FIDAL/ATFS World Almanac 1981*; *Track and Field Performances through the Years 1929-49*. Statistics handbooks; up-to-date statistics (since 1950); in progress – pre-1950 track and field statistics.
Members Track and field statisticians and patron organizations in 40 countries and territories:
Argentina, Australia, Austria, Belgium, Brazil, Canada, Croatia, Cuba, Czechia, Denmark, Estonia, Finland, France, Germany, Greece, Hungary, India, Ireland, Israel, Italy, Japan, Malaysia, Netherlands, New Zealand, Norway, Philippines, Poland, Portugal, Russia, Serbia, Slovakia, South Africa, Spain, Sweden, Switzerland, Trinidad-Tobago, Türkiye, UK, USA, Virgin Is UK.
[2018.12.09/XB0174/**B**]

♦ Association of Trade and Forfaiting in the Americas (internationally oriented national body)
♦ Association du Traité Atlantique (#03010)
♦ Association transeuropéenne d'études politiques / see Trans European Policy Studies Association (#20209)

♦ Association transfrontalière du pôle européen de développement (PED) 02958

Contact 2 rue de Lexy, CS 11432 Réhon, 54414 Longwy, France. T. +33382260320. Fax +33382260321.
Contact Secrétariats permanents d'Interreg Wallonie-Lorraine-Luxembourg et e-Bird, IDELUX, Drève de l'Arc-en-Ciel 98, 6700 Arlon, Belgium. T. +3263231843. Fax +3263231895.

History 19 Jul 1985, Kirchberg (Luxembourg). Also referred to as: *Pôle européen de développement Athus-Longwy-Rodange*; *Pôle européen des trois frontières*; *Europese Ontwikkelingspool*. Registered in accordance with Belgian law. **Aims** Assist the *steel industry* in French Lorraine, Belgian Luxembourg (Luxembourg) Province and the Grand Duchy of Luxembourg through a trans-frontier initiative which permits a test case for 'Europe without Frontiers' to be enforced throughout the European Union; allow the region to profit from customs advantages and direct investment. **Structure** Permanent Commission. Proposed projects include: *Collège européen de technologie (CET, no recent information)*. Instrumental in setting up *Centre européen de ressources sur les reconversions et les mutations (CERRM, no recent information)*.
Members Governments of 3 countries:
Belgium, France, Luxembourg. [2009/XF1137/**F***]

♦ Association transnationale de service civique (ATSC) 02959

Transnational Civic Service Trust

Pres CIC Case Postale 20, 1211 Geneva 20, Switzerland. T. +41227336717.

History 1980, Geneva (Switzerland). **Languages** English, French. **Staff** 1.00 FTE, paid. **Finance** Donations.
Members Bodies in 12 countries:
Australia, Canada, Denmark, Egypt, France, Israel, Kenya, Netherlands, Poland, Switzerland, UK, USA.
NGO Relations Member of: *Environment Liaison Centre International (ELCI, no recent information)*.
[2017.09.16/XF1917/**F**]

♦ Association for Transpersonal Psychology (ATP) 02960

Association de psychologie transpersonnelle

Co-Pres PO Box 50187, Palo Alto CA 94303, USA. T. +16504248764. Fax +16506181851. E-mail: info@atpweb.org.
URL: http://atpweb.org/

History 1972. **Aims** Encourage individual and group learning, cooperation among disciplines, research in theory and application, and the dissemination of information about the field. **Structure** Board of Directors, consisting of 2 Co-Presidents, Vice-President, Secretary, Treasurer, Editor and 8 members. Conference Committee, comprising 5 members. **Staff** 3.00 FTE, paid. **Finance** Members' dues. **Events** *Annual conference* Berkeley, CA (USA) 2005, *International conference* London (UK) 2004, *International conference* Vancouver, BC (Canada) 2000, *Global cyberconference* 1999, *Annual Conference* California (USA) 1999. **Publications** *ATP Newsletter* (4 a year); *Journal of Transpersonal Psychology* (2 a year). Listings.
Members Membership Professional; Student; Organizational; Supporting; Joint. Members (mostly in USA) in 47 countries and territories:
Argentina, Australia, Austria, Belgium, Belize, Brazil, Canada, Chile, Colombia, Costa Rica, Czechia, Denmark, Egypt, Estonia, Fiji, Finland, France, Germany, Greece, Hong Kong, Hungary, India, Indonesia, Ireland, Israel, Italy, Japan, Kenya, Korea Rep, Lithuania, Mexico, Netherlands, New Zealand, Norway, Philippines, Poland, Romania, Russia, Slovakia, South Africa, Spain, Sweden, Switzerland, Taiwan, Türkiye, UK, USA. [2010/XF5493/**F**]

♦ Association du transport aérien international (#11614)
♦ Association du transport aérien latinoaméricain / see Latin American and Caribbean Air Transport Association (#16263)
♦ Association des transporteurs aériens francophones / see ATAF – Association internationale de transporteurs aériens (#03000)
♦ Association des transporteurs aériens francophones – de l'Afrique, du Maghreb et de la France / see ATAF – Association internationale de transporteurs aériens (#03000)
♦ Association des transporteurs aériens de la Zone franc / see ATAF – Association internationale de transporteurs aériens (#03000)

♦ Association of Traumatic Stress Specialists (ATSS) 02961

Office Administrator 5000 Old Buncombe Rd, Ste 27-11, Greenville SC 29617, USA. T. +18642944337. E-mail: admin@atss.info.
URL: http://www.atss.info/

History 1987, as *International Association of Trauma Counseling (IATC)*. **Aims** Assist those affected by trauma; provide professional education and certification to those actively involved in crisis intervention, trauma response, management, treatment and the recovery of those affected by traumatic stress. **Structure** Board of Directors, consisting of President, Immediate Past President, Vice President, Secretary, Treasurer, 2 Certification Chairs, 7 Directors and ATSS Executive Director. Administrative Staff. **Languages** English. **Staff** 2.00 FTE, paid. **Finance** Members' dues. Other sources: certification fees; grants; donations. **Activities** Offers 3 distinct international specialized trauma certifications for qualified individuals: CTS – Certified Trauma Specialist, for counsellors, clinicians and treatment specialists who provide therapy, counselling and/or intervention; CTR – Certified Trauma Responder, for those who provide immediate trauma intervention through critical incident stress debriefing/management, peer-counselling and trauma response; CTSS-Certified Trauma Services Specialist, for those who provide immediate trauma intervention, crisis support, advocacy, or victim assistance. Recognizes educational standards in the field of trauma counselling and services. **Events** *Annual Conference* Toronto, ON (Canada) 2012, *Annual conference* Portland, ME (USA) 2008, *Annual conference* Palm Beach, FL (USA) 2006, *Annual Conference* West Palm Beach, FL (USA) 2006, *Annual conference* Dallas, TX (USA) 2005. **Publications** *Trauma Lines* (4 a year).
Members Individuals (mostly in USA) and associations. Members in 21 countries and territories:
Australia, Barbados, Belize, Canada, China, Croatia, Italy, Japan, Mexico, Norway, Poland, Puerto Rico, Russia, Samoa, South Africa, Sri Lanka, Switzerland, Trinidad-Tobago, UK, United Arab Emirates, USA. [2016/XF4575/v/**F**]

♦ Association for the Treatment of Sexual Abusers (internationally oriented national body)

♦ Association for Tree-Ring Research (ATR) 02962

Pres PO Box 47, 6700 AA Wageningen, Netherlands.
URL: http://www.tree-ring.org/

History 2002. **Aims** Provide information and facilitate networking on the field of dendrochronology. **Structure** Board; Scientific Advisory Board. **Finance** Members' dues. **Activities** Events/meetings; knowledge management/information dissemination; networking/liaising; financial and/or material support. **Events** *TRACE Meeting* Lund (Sweden) 2021, *TRACE Meeting* Greifswald (Germany) 2018, *TRACE Meeting* Svetlogorsk, Krasnoyarsk Krai (Russia) 2017, *TRACE Meeting* Poland 2016, *International Symposium on Wood Structure in Plant Biology and Ecology* Naples (Italy) 2013. **Publications** *ATR Newsletter*. Conference volumes. **Members** Individuals (400). Membership countries not specified. [2017.11.27/XJ6253/**D**]

♦ Association des trois mondes (internationally oriented national body)
♦ Association for Tropical Biology / see Association for Tropical Biology and Conservation (#02963)

♦ Association for Tropical Biology and Conservation (ATBC) 02963

Exec Dir Univ de Sao Paulo, Inst de Biociências, Depto de Botânica, Rua do Matão, 277, Sao Paulo SP, 05508-090, Brazil. T. +5511999117440. E-mail: director@tropicalbio.org.
Secretary Univ of Hawaii at Manoa, Dept of Botany, 3190 Maile Way, Honolulu HI 96822, USA.
URL: http://www.tropicalbio.org/

History 1963. Former names and other names: *Association for Tropical Biology (ATB)* – former (1963 to 2003). **Aims** Foster scientific understanding and conservation of tropical ecosystems by supporting research, collaboration, capacity building and communication among tropical biologists and conservationists. **Structure** Council; Executive Board; Regional Chapters. **Languages** English. **Staff** 1.00 FTE, paid. **Finance** Sources: members' dues. **Activities** Awards/prizes/competitions; capacity building; events/meetings; networking/liaising; publishing activities; training/education. **Events** *ATBC Annual Meeting* Cartagena de Indias (Colombia) 2022, *Virtual ATBC Annual Meeting* 2021, *ATBC Annual Meeting* Cartagena de Indias (Colombia) 2020, *ATBC Annual Meeting* Antananarivo (Madagascar) 2019, *ATBC Asia Pacific Chapter Meeting* Thulhiriya (Sri Lanka) 2019. **Publications** *ATBC Newsletter*, *BIOTROPICA* – journal. **Members** Full (over 1,000) in over 70 countries. Membership countries not specified. **NGO Relations** Member of (2): *Dryad (#05139)*; *International Union for Conservation of Nature and Natural Resources (IUCN, #15766)*. Cooperates with (1): *Organization for Tropical Studies (OTS)*. [2022.10.13/XN7001/**C**]

♦ Association for Tropical Lepidoptera (ATL) 02964

Exec Dir PO Box 141210, Gainesville FL 32614-1210, USA. E-mail: jdtatl@gmail.com.
SG address not obtained. E-mail: pjeatl@gmail.com.
URL: http://www.troplep.org/

History Founded 1989. **Aims** Promote the study and conservation of lepidoptera worldwide. **Structure** Board of Directors of 10 members. Advisory Council. **Languages** English, German, Spanish. **Staff** 2.00 FTE, voluntary. **Finance** Members' dues. Donations; contributions. Budget (annual): US$ 120,000. **Activities** Organizes annual meeting. Offers field expeditions to members. Runs conservation and research projects. **Events** *Annual International Meeting* Gainesville, FL (USA) 2016, *Annual International Meeting* Gainesville, FL (USA) 2015, *Annual International Meeting* Gainesville, FL (USA) 2014, *Annual International Meeting* Gainesville, FL (USA) 2013, *Annual international meeting* Gainesville, FL (USA) 2002. **Publications** *Lepidoptera News* (4 a year); *Holarctic Lepidoptera* (2 a year) – journal; *Tropical Lepidoptera* (2 a year) – journal; *Altas of North American Lepidoptera*; *Atlas of Palearctic Lepidoptera*; *Lepidoptera of Taiwan*; *Lepidoptera Species Data Sheets (LSDS)*; *Lepidopterum Catalogus*. *Atlas of Neotropical Lepidoptera*.
Members in 112 countries and territories:
Albania, Antigua-Barbuda, Argentina, Armenia, Australia, Austria, Azerbaijan, Bahamas, Barbados, Belarus, Belgium, Belize, Bolivia, Bosnia-Herzegovina, Botswana, Brazil, Bulgaria, Cambodia, Canada, Chile, China, Colombia, Costa Rica, Côte d'Ivoire, Croatia, Cuba, Cyprus, Czechia, Denmark, Dominican Rep, Ecuador, Egypt, El Salvador, Fiji, Finland, France, Georgia, Germany, Ghana, Greece, Guatemala, Guyana, Honduras, Hong Kong, Hungary, Iceland, India, Indonesia, Iran Islamic Rep, Ireland, Israel, Italy, Jamaica, Japan, Jordan, Kenya, Korea Rep, Kuwait, Laos, Lithuania, Luxembourg, Madagascar, Malaysia, Maldives, Malta, Mexico, Monaco, Nepal, Netherlands, New Zealand, Nicaragua, North Macedonia (former Yugoslav Rep of), Norway, Pakistan, Palestine, Panama, Papua New Guinea, Paraguay, Peru, Philippines, Poland, Portugal, Puerto Rico, Romania, Russia, Saudi Arabia, Serbia, Seychelles, Singapore, Slovakia, Solomon Is, South Africa, Spain, Sri Lanka, Suriname, Sweden, Switzerland, Taiwan, Tanzania UR, Thailand, Trinidad-Tobago, Türkiye, Uganda, UK, Ukraine, Uruguay, USA, Venezuela, Vietnam, Yemen, Zimbabwe. [2016/XD6467/**D**]

♦ Association typographique internationale (ATypI) 02965

Exec Dir/Secretariat address not obtained. E-mail: secretariat@atypi.org.
Registered Address 1011 Camino Del Rio S, Ste 150, San Diego CA 92108, USA.
URL: http://www.atypi.org/

History 11 Jun 1957, Lausanne (Switzerland). Founded at constituting General Assembly, when Statutes were accepted and went into effect, an Interim Committee having been set up in Jun 1956, Paris (France). Statutes amended and approved by General Assembly, 27 Sep 1993, Antwerp (Belgium); 2018. Registration: USA, California. **Aims** Provide the structure for communication, information and action relating to all matters typographic for the international type community; preserve the culture, tradition and history of type and typography; promote contemporary digital *fonts*; encourage outstanding typography and typographic *design*. **Structure** General Assembly (annual, at Conference). Board, consisting of President and 5 to 20 members. Steering Committee of 3 to 5 members. Officers: President, 2 Vice-Presidents, Honorary Presidents, Treasurer. Committees (6): Arbitration; Business and Legal; Designers and Typographers; Marketing; Research and Education; Technology. Country delegations. Full-time secretariat. **Languages** English. **Staff** 2.00 FTE, paid. Voluntary. **Finance** Members' dues: pounds62 – 50. Other sources: contributions from sponsors and public institutions; donations and settlements of all kinds; voluntary special contributions; income from ATypI activities. **Activities** Members form special interest sub-groups and committees and contribute to publication, conference programmes and other international initiatives. Awards Charles Peignot Prize. Organizes design competition. Campaigns for the protection of typeface designs. **Events** *Annual Conference* Stockholm (Sweden) 2024, *Annual Conference* Paris (France) 2023, *Annual Conference* 2021, *Annual Conference* 2020, *Annual Conference* Tokyo (Japan) 2019. **Publications** *Type* – journal. ATypI official annual papers; reports; meeting and seminar proceedings; lectures; members' address book; country delegates report.
Members Corporate (manufacturers); Professional Bodies (institutions etc); Individuals (typeface designers, educators). Members in 41 countries and territories:
Argentina, Armenia, Australia, Austria, Belgium, Brazil, Canada, Chile, Croatia, Cyprus, Czechia, Denmark, Finland, France, Germany, Greece, Hong Kong, Hungary, Iceland, India, Ireland, Israel, Italy, Japan, Lebanon, Malaysia, Mexico, Netherlands, New Zealand, Norway, Poland, Portugal, Russia, Singapore, Slovenia, Spain, Sweden, Switzerland, UK, United Arab Emirates, USA.
IGO Relations *UNESCO (#20322)*. **NGO Relations** Affiliate member of: *International Council of Design (ICoD, #13013)*. [2021/XC2647/**C**]

♦ Association typologique Benelux (#20272)

♦ Association for Uncertainty in Artificial Intelligence (AUAI) 02966

Sec Dept of Management Science and Engineering, Stanford Univ, Huang Engineering Ctr, 475 Via Ortega, Room 337, Stanford CA 94305-4121, USA.
Chair Dept of Computer Science, Univ of British Columbia, 2366 Main Mall, Vancouver BC V6T 1Z4, Canada.
URL: http://www.auai.org/

Aims Promote research in pursuit of advances in knowledge representation, learning and reasoning under uncertainty. **Structure** Board of Directors. **Activities** Events/meetings. **Events** *International Conference* Sydney, NSW (Australia) 2017, *International Conference* New York, NY (USA) 2016, *International Conference* Amsterdam (Netherlands) 2015, *International Conference* Québec, QC (Canada) 2014, *International Conference* Bellevue, WA (USA) 2013. [2017/XW0036/c/**E**]

♦ Association unie de l'Afrique centrale (inactive)
♦ Association pour l'Unification du Christianisme Mondial (religious order)
♦ Association des unions des architectes baltes (#03093)
♦ Association des unions de journalistes nordiques / see Nordiska Journalistförbundet (#17487)
♦ Association for Unitarian Universalist Music Ministries (internationally oriented national body)
♦ Association of United Nations Correspondents / see United Nations Correspondents Association
♦ Association of United Nations Pensioners in India / see Association of Former United Nations Personnel in and of India (#02603)
♦ Association universelle pour l'amélioration de la race nègre et Société des collectivités africaines / see Universal Negro Improvement Association and African Communities League of the World
♦ Association universelle pour l'amélioration de la race nègre et Société des collectivités africaines du monde (internationally oriented national body)
♦ Association universelle d'aviculture scientifique (#21825)
♦ Association universelle des bons templiers espérantistes (inactive)
♦ Association universelle du calendrier (inactive)
♦ Association universelle pour l'éducation des adultes (inactive)
♦ Association universelle de l'espéranto (#20676)
♦ Association universitaire canadienne d'études nordiques (internationally oriented national body)
♦ Association Universitaire Internationale du Vin et des Produits de la Vigne (unconfirmed)
♦ Association des universitaires d'Europe (inactive)
♦ Association des Universités Africaines (#02361)
♦ Association des universités de l'Afrique de l'Est et du Sud (inactive)
♦ Association des universités de l'Amazonie (#02366)
♦ Association des universités arabes (#02374)
♦ Association des universités d'Asie et du Pacifique (#02968)
♦ Association des universités catholiques d'Afrique et de Madagascar / see Association of Catholic Universities and Higher Institutes of Africa and Madagascar (#02416)
♦ Association des Universités et Centres de Recherche de la Caraïbe / see Universities Caribbean (#20694)
♦ Association des universités et des collèges chrétiens d'Asie (#02432)
♦ L'Association des universités du Commonwealth (#02440)
♦ Association des universités européennes (inactive)
♦ Association des universités du Groupe de Montevideo (#02971)
♦ Association des universités et instituts catholiques d'Afrique et de Madagascar (#02416)
♦ Association des universités partiellement ou entièrement de langue française / see Agence universitaire de La Francophonie (#00548)

♦ Association pour les universités rurales européennes (APURE) 02967

Contact c/o ADRACES, Rua de Santana 277, 6030-230 Vila Velha de Ródão, Portugal. T. +351272540200. Fax +351272540209. E-mail: apure@adraces.pt – adraces@adraces.pt.
URL: http://www.ure-apure.org/

History May 1988. Registered in accordance with French law. **Events** *Conference* Valle Soana (Italy) 1998, *Conference* Vejle (Denmark) 1996, *Conference* Evora (Portugal) 1993, *Conference* Schull (Ireland) 1991, *Conference* Viuz-en-Sallaz (France) 1989. **Members** Membership countries not specified. **NGO Relations** *Association for European Rural Universities (APURE, #02541)*. [2014/XD9321/**D**]

♦ Association of Universities of Asia and the Pacific (AUAP) 02968

Association des universités d'Asie et du Pacifique

SG Suranaree Univ Technology, Academic Bldg 2, Room C2-228, 111 University Ave Suranaree Sub-District Muang District, Nakhon Ratchasima, 30000, Thailand. T. +6644224141 – +6644224142 – +6644224146. Fax +6644224140. E-mail: auapheadquarter@gmail.com – auapheadquarter1995@gmail.com.
Pres Rector, Univ of Macau, Fac of Science and Technology, Room T301, Av Padre Tomas Pereira SJ, Taipa, Macau. T. +8533974301. Fax +85328831694.
Facebook: https://www.facebook.com/AssociationofUniversitiesofAsiaandthePacific/

History 28 Jul 1995, Nakhon Ratchasima (Thailand), at Suranaree University of Technology during founding conference. **Aims** Provide means for universities of the Asian and Pacific region to work together so as to: discharge more effectively their responsibility to provide higher education and training, extend the frontiers of knowledge and contribute actively to the well-being of the community, develop human resources, preserve and enhance cultural heritage and thus serve the cause of socio-economic development and peace; promote wider understanding of the value and importance of these basic goals; implement programmes which will assist in development of member institutions. **Structure** General Conference (every 2 years). Board, consisting of President, Immediate Past President, 1st and 2nd Vice-Presidents and 5 to 7 members. Advisory Council, comprising representatives of associate members. Secretariat, headed by Secretary-General. **Languages** English, Thai. **Staff** 3.00 FTE, paid. **Finance** Members' dues (annual): Regular, US$ 500; Associate, US$ 250. **Activities** Cooperates with university bodies at international, regional, sub-regional and national levels and with intergovernmental, governmental and private bodies concerned with higher education; implements programmes to assist development of member institutions; organizes conferences, seminars and workshops. **Events** *General Conference* Dhaka (Bangladesh) 2022, *Allied Health Science International Symposium* Daegu (Korea Rep) 2021, *General Conference* Manila (Philippines) 2020, *AUAP Learning and Sharing Forum* Dapitan (Philippines) 2019, *Joint Conference* Xinzheng (China) 2019. **Publications** *AUAP Gazette* (4 a year).
Members Founding, in 17 countries and territories:
Australia, Bangladesh, Cambodia, China, Fiji, Hong Kong, India, Indonesia, Japan, Korea Rep, Macau, Malaysia, New Zealand, Pakistan, Philippines, Thailand, Vietnam.
Universities and other degree-conferring institutions; national associations. Members in 21 countries and territories:
Australia, Bangladesh, Cambodia, China, Hong Kong, India, Indonesia, Iran Islamic Rep, Japan, Kazakhstan, Korea Rep, Macau, Malaysia, New Zealand, Pakistan, Philippines, Taiwan, Thailand, UK, USA, Vietnam.
Included in the above, 3 institutions listed in this Yearbook:
Asian Institute of Technology (AIT, #01519); *Euclid University (EUCLID, #05575)*; *International Islamic University Malaysia (IIUM, #13961)*.
IGO Relations Cooperates with: *UNESCO Office, Jakarta – Regional Bureau for Sciences in Asia and the Pacific (#20313)*. [2019/XD4630/y/**D**]

♦ Association of Universities of the British Commonwealth / see Association of Commonwealth Universities, The (#02440)

♦ Association of Universities Entrusted to the Society of Jesus in Latin-America 02969

Asociación de Universidades Confiadas a la Compañia de Jesús en América Latina (AUSJAL)

Main Office Prol Paseo de Reforma 880, Col Lomas de Santa Fe, 01219 Mexico City CDMX, Mexico. E-mail: contacto@ausjal.org.
URL: http://www.ausjal.org/

History 10 Nov 1985, Rome (Italy). Founded by decision of university rectors. Decision ratified and Statutes approved at 4th General Assembly, 31 Oct 1987, Rio de Janeiro (Brazil). Statutes modified at: 4th General Assembly, 1987, Rio de Janeiro; 9th General Assembly, 1997, Guatemala (Guatemala). **Aims** Favour reflection on *Jesuit educational* ideals and their implementation in each university; further integration of Latin American universities in their aim of transforming social structures in favour of the *poor*, give priority to integrated training of students through educational *curricula* and educational processes in which teaching of *Christian*-inspired *values* and religious and social choice are encouraged and applied in contrast to current poverty and dehumanizing secularism; ensure continuing education of teachers, researchers and administrators and their participation in University ideals, including pedagogy and Ignatian spirituality; provide a university environment allowing growth of religious experience and an adequate synthesis of faith and science, Christian experience and social and professional practice; improve *living standards* through increasing scientific and technological capacity encouraged through plural responsibility and organization of *civil society*. **Structure** General Assembly; Executive Council of 4 officers. **Languages** English, Portuguese, Spanish. **Staff** 5.00 FTE, paid. **Activities** Events/meetings; networking/liaising; training/education. **Events** *General Assembly* Cali (Colombia) 2021, *General Assembly* Guadalajara (Mexico) 2019, *General Assembly* Pernambuco (Brazil) 2017, *Assembly* Cali (Colombia) 2007, *Meeting* Cali (Colombia) 2005. **Publications** *AUSJAL Al Dia* (10 a year) – newsletter; *Carta de AUSJAL* (2 a year); *Directorio de AUSJAL* (every 2 years). Proceedings.
Members Universities (30) of 14 countries:
Argentina, Brazil, Chile, Colombia, Dominican Rep, Ecuador, El Salvador, Guatemala, Mexico, Nicaragua, Paraguay, Peru, Uruguay, Venezuela.
Included in the above, 5 regional bodies listed in this Yearbook:
Centro de Investigación de la Universidad del Pacifico (CIUP); *Instituto Latinoamericano de Doctrinas y Estudios Sociales (ILADES, #11345)*; *Universidad Centroamericana José Simeón Cañas (UCA)*; *Universidad Centroamericana, Managua (UCA)*; *Universidad Iberoamericana, México (UIA)*. [2021/XD1630/y/**E**]

♦ Association of Universities of Latin America and the Caribbean . . . 02970

Union des universités de l'Amérique latine et les Caraïbes – Unión de Universidades de América Latina y el Caribe (UDUAL) – União das Universidades de América Latina e das Caraïbes

SG Ricardo Flores Magón 1, Piso 9, Col Nonoalco-Tlatelolco, Delegación Cuauhtémoc, CP 06995, 70232 Mexico City CDMX, Mexico. T. +525551172818 ext 49762. E-mail: roberto.escalante@udual.org – admin1@udual.org – enlace@udual.org.
URL: http://www.udual.org/

History 22 Sep 1949, Guatemala (Guatemala). Founded at 1st Congress. Current statutes approved by General Assembly, 22 Sep 2014, Guatemala (Guatemala). Former names and other names: *Union of Latin American Universities (ULAU)* – former; *Union des universités de l'Amérique latine* – former; *Unión de Universidades de América Latina* – former. **Aims** Support academic exchange, mobility, recognition and transfer of credits; strengthen the evaluation process and assurance of the quality of higher education. **Structure** General Assembly (at least every 3 years); Executive Committee; Committees (2); General Secretariat, headed by Secretary-General. **Languages** Portuguese, Spanish. **Staff** 30.00 FTE, paid. **Finance** Sources: members' dues. **Activities** Training/education; events/meetings; research/documentation; financial and/or material support. **Events** *Foro Latinoamericano de Universidades Tecnologicas y Politecnicas* Córdoba (Argentina) 2015, *Reunion Latinoamericana y del Caribe de Dependencias Academicas de las Artes* Tuxtla Gutiérrez (Mexico) 2015, *Extraordinary General Assembly / General Assembly* Guatemala (Guatemala) 2014, *General Assembly* Tunja (Colombia) 2012, *General Assembly* Lima (Peru) 2010. **Publications** *Boletin UDUAL* (12 a year); *Revista Universidades* (6 a year); *Gaceta UDUAL* (4 a year); *Sistema de Información SIESALC* (every 2 years). *Colección UDUAL* – series. Studies on: university legislation; statistics. Assembly and Conference Reports. **Information Services** *Centro de Información y Documentación (CIDU)*; *Sistema de Información de Educación Superior de América Latina y el Caribe (SIESALC)*.
Members Universities (230) and university networks (10) in 21 countries:
Argentina, Bolivia, Brazil, Chile, Colombia, Costa Rica, Cuba, Dominican Rep, Ecuador, El Salvador, Guatemala, Haiti, Honduras, Mexico, Nicaragua, Panama, Paraguay, Peru, Puerto Rico, Uruguay, Venezuela.
Included in the above, organizations listed in this Yearbook (1):
Technical University of Latin America, San Salvador (UTLA).
Consultative Status Consultative status granted from: *UNESCO (#20322)* (Associate Status). **NGO Relations** Member of: *Consejo Universitario Iberoamericano (CUIB, #04727)*; *Global University Network for Innovation (GUNI, #10641)*; *International Association of Universities (IAU, #12246)*. Cooperates with: *United Nations Academic Impact (UNAI, #20516)*. Instrumental in setting up: *Asociación Latinoamericana de Escuelas y Facultades de Enfermeria (ALADEFE, #02211)*; *Association of Latin American Faculties and Schools of Public Accountancy (#02783)*; *Association of Latin American Schools and Institutes of Economy (#02784)*;

Institutional Development Programme between European and Latin American Universities (COLUMBUS Association, #11316); Latin American Association of Medical Faculties and Schools (#16245); Organización de Facultades, Escuelas y Departamentos de Odontología de la Unión de Universidades de América Latina (OFEDO/UDUAL, #17837). [2020/XD3357/y/**D**]

♦ Association of Universities of the Montevideo Group (AUGM) 02971

Association des universités du Groupe de Montevideo – Asociación de Universidades Grupo Montevideo

Exec Sec Edif del Notariado, Torre Guayabo, Guayabo 1729, Apto 502, 11 200 Montevideo, Uruguay. T. +59824005401. Fax +59824005411. E-mail: grmont@seciu.edu.uy.

URL: http://www.grupomontevideo.edu.uy/

History Founded Aug 1991, Montevideo (Uruguay). Located at: *UNESCO Office, Montevideo – Regional Bureau for Sciences in Latin America and the Caribbean (#20314).* **Aims** Promote the process of integration through creation of a 'wider common academic area' based on scientific, technological, educational and cultural cooperation among members; strengthen and consolidate a critical mass of high-level human resources to profit from the comparative advantages offered by the capacities installed in the region; strengthen and consolidate scientific and technological research, including the process of innovation, adaptation and transfer of technology in strategic areas. **Structure** Discipline Groups (12); Academic Committees (6). **Languages** Portuguese, Spanish. **Finance** Members' dues. Agreements with other institutions. **Activities** Training/education; capacity building; events/meetings. **Events** *Europe-Latin America Bi-Regional University Association And Leadership Conference* Sao Paulo (Brazil) 2012, *Conference on the university and regional development* Mar del Plata (Argentina) 1997.

Members Higher education centres in 6 countries:
Argentina, Bolivia, Brazil, Chile, Paraguay, Uruguay. [2015.02.06/XD6202/**D**]

♦ Association of Universities for Textiles (AUTEX) 02972

Sec Dept of Materials/Textiles/Chemical Engineering, Ghent Univ, Technologiepark 907, 9052 Zwijnaarde, Belgium. T. +3292645735. Fax +3292645846.

Pres Lodz Univ of Technology, ul Zeromskiego 116, 90-924 Lódz, Poland.

URL: http://www.autex.org/

History Jul 1994, Manchester (UK). **Aims** Facilitate European cooperation in high level textile education and research. **Languages** English. **Finance** Members' dues. **Events** *Conference* Lódz (Poland) 2022, *Conference* Lisbon (Portugal) 2021, *Conference* Guimarães (Portugal) 2020, *Conference* Ghent (Belgium) 2019, *Conference* Istanbul (Turkey) 2018. **Publications** *AUTEX Research Journal.*

Members Full and Associate (39) in 31 countries and territories:
Albania, Australia, Belgium, Croatia, Czechia, Finland, France, Germany, Greece, Hong Kong, Iran Islamic Rep, Italy, Japan, Latvia, Lithuania, Morocco, Netherlands, Pakistan, Poland, Portugal, Romania, Russia, Serbia, Slovenia, Spain, Sweden, Tunisia, Türkiye, UK, USA, Uzbekistan. [2018.09.18/XD7888/**D**]

- ♦ Association of University Chief Security Officers (internationally oriented national body)
- ♦ Association of University English Teachers of Southern Africa (internationally oriented national body)
- ♦ Association of University Leaders for a Sustainable Future (internationally oriented national body)
- ♦ Association of University Programs in Health Administration (internationally oriented national body)
- ♦ Association of University Related Research Parks / see Association of University Research Parks (#02973)

♦ Association of University Research Parks (AURP) 02973

CEO 6262 N Swan Rd, Ste 125, Tucson AZ 85718, USA. T. +15205292524 – +15205292521. Fax +15205292499. E-mail: info@aurp.net.

URL: http://www.aurp.net/

History Founded 1986, Tempe AZ (USA), at first international conference, as *Association of University Related Research Parks (AURRP).* Current title adopted 2001. **Aims** Promote university research parks, *technology* incubators and associated programmes; facilitate development, transfer and commercialization of technology. **Structure** Board of Directors; Executive Committee. **Staff** 3.00 FTE, paid. **Finance** Members' dues. Other sources: conference fees; income from publications. **Activities** Events/meetings; training/education; guidance/assistance/consulting. **Events** *Annual Conference* Atlanta, GA (USA) 2019, *Annual Conference* College Park, MD (USA) 2018, *Annual Conference* Huntsville, AL (USA) 2017, *Annual Conference* Oklahoma City, OK (USA) 2016, *Annual Conference* Buffalo, NY (USA) 2015. **Publications** *Research Park Forum* (6 a year) – newsletter; *AURP Newsletter. AURP Consultants Directory; AURP Membership Directory; Statistics on Research Parks; Technology Incubator Directory; Worldwide Research Park Directory.* Information Services: Access to: AURRP Listserv; library; database.

Members Individuals, companies and institutions (300) in 33 countries and territories:
Argentina, Australia, Austria, Belgium, Brazil, Canada, China, Czechia, Dominican Rep, Finland, France, Greece, India, Iran Islamic Rep, Ireland, Italy, Japan, Korea Rep, Malaysia, Mexico, Poland, Portugal, Russia, Singapore, Slovakia, South Africa, Spain, Sweden, Taiwan, Thailand, Türkiye, UK, USA.

NGO Relations Member of: *World Alliance for Innovation (WAINOVA, #21082).* [2018/XC0053/**F**]

- ♦ Association of University Staff to Promote Inter-University Cooperation in Europe (inactive)

♦ Association of University Surgeons of Asia 02974

Contact address not obtained. Fax +6567795678.

URL: http://www.e-asianjournalsurgery.com/

History Previously known as *University Surgeons of South-East Asia.* **Events** *Scientific congress* Singapore (Singapore) 2000, *Scientific congress / Congress* Singapore (Singapore) 1998, *Scientific congress / Congress* Singapore (Singapore) 1996, *Scientific congress / Congress* Singapore (Singapore) 1994. **Publications** *Asian Journal of Surgery* (4 a year). [2015/XD3811/**F**]

- ♦ Association of University Technology Managers (internationally oriented national body)
- ♦ Association des urbanistes du Commonwealth (#04307)
- ♦ Association des usagers du canal de Suez (inactive)
- ♦ Association of Users and Distributors of AgroChemicals in Europe (no recent information)
- ♦ Association of US University Directors of International Agricultural Programs / see Association for International Agriculture and Rural Development
- ♦ Association des utilisateurs et distributeurs de l'agrochimie européenne (no recent information)
- ♦ Association des utilisateurs du transport maritime, routier et aérien dans l'isthme centroaméricain (no recent information)
- ♦ Association pour l'utilisation du coke en Scandinavie (inactive)
- ♦ Association for UU Music Ministries / see Association for Unitarian Universalist Music Ministries
- ♦ Association for Vertical Farming (unconfirmed)
- ♦ Association Vétérinaire Africaine (#00495)
- ♦ Association vétérinaire du Commonwealth (#04366)

♦ Association vétérinaire Euro-Arabe (AVEA) 02975

Euro-Arab Veterinary Association (EAVA) – Asociación Veterinaria Euro-Arabe – Associação Veterinaria Euro-Arabe

Pres PO Box 267, Cité Mahrajène, 1082 Tunis, Tunisia. T. +21698317601. Fax +21671237339. E-mail: vetatvac@yahoo.com.

URL: http://www.euroarabeveterinaryassociation.org/

History Preparatory Meeting, May 1996, Córdoba (Spain); Constitutive General Assembly, 22 Nov 1997, Tunis (Tunisia). **Aims** Promote the interest of health and Welfare of animals and people in respect of One Health Initiative as well as the interest of its veterinary statutory bodies, professional organizations and their members. **Structure** General Assembly; Executive Board; Technical Commissions (8). **Languages** Arabic, English, French. **Staff** 3.00 FTE, paid. **Finance** Sources: members' dues; sponsorship. Other sources: partnership. **Activities** Events/meetings; healthcare; research/documentation; training/education. **Events** *Symposium International Vétérinaire* 2022, *World Rabies Day Celebration* Djerba (Tunisia) 2022, *African and Euro-Arab Veterinary Congress* Tunis (Tunisia) 2022, *World Veterinary Day Celebration* Tunis (Tunisia) 2022.

Members Full in 39 countries and territories:
Albania, Algeria, Austria, Bahrain, Belgium, Bulgaria, Cyprus, Czechia, Djibouti, Egypt, France, Germany, Greece, Hungary, Iraq, Italy, Jordan, Kuwait, Lebanon, Libya, Malta, Mauritania, Morocco, Netherlands, Oman, Palestine, Portugal, Qatar, Romania, Saudi Arabia, Serbia, Somalia, Spain, Sudan, Switzerland, Syrian AR, Tunisia, Türkiye, Yemen.

Observers in 5 countries:
Azerbaijan, Georgia, Kazakhstan, Turkmenistan, Ukraine.

Also Observer member, one organization listed in this Yearbook:
World Union of Professions (WUP, #21882).

NGO Relations Member of (4): *Asociación Panamericana de Ciencias Veterinarias (PANVET, #02287); Federation of Asian Veterinary Associations (FAVA, #09451); World Association for Buiatrics (WAB, #21122); World Veterinary Association (WVA, #21901).* [2022.03.04/XJ2259/**D**]

- ♦ Association vétérinaire européenne pour la reproduction des petits animaux (#09059)
- ♦ Association vétérinaire mondiale d'hygiène alimentaire (#21204)
- ♦ Association vétérinaire nordique pour la recherche et la prévention de la mastite (inactive)
- ♦ Association des vétérinaires francophones (no recent information)

♦ Association of Veterinary Anaesthetists (AVA) 02976

Pres address not obtained. E-mail: secretary@ava.eu.com.

URL: http://www.ava.eu.com/

History 1964, as *'Association of Veterinary Anaesthetists of Great Britain and Ireland'.* Current title adopted, 1991, when became international society. **Aims** Teach the subject of veterinary anaesthesia and *analgesia* and promote its advancement. **Structure** Officers: President; Senior Vice-President; Junior Vice-President; Treasurer; Secretary; Editor. **Languages** English. **Staff** None. **Finance** Members' dues. Meeting fees and sponsorships. **Activities** Two main meetings annually, one in UK one elsewhere in Europe. Local meetings (often continuing education courses). **Events** *Autumn Meeting* Bern (Switzerland) 2022, *Spring Meeting* Nafplion (Greece) 2022, *Autumn Meeting* 2021, *Autumn Meeting* Nafplion (Greece) 2021, *Autumn Meeting* 2020. **Publications** *Veterinary Anaesthesia and Analgesia* – journal.

Members Full veterinary surgeons resident in Europe; corresponding; veterinary surgeons from elsewhere; associate interested non-veterinarians; technical animal nurses and technicians. Individuals (about 500) in 33 countries:
Australia, Austria, Belgium, Brazil, Canada, Croatia, Czechia, Denmark, Estonia, Finland, France, Germany, Greece, Hungary, Iran Islamic Rep, Ireland, Israel, Italy, Japan, Mexico, Netherlands, New Zealand, Nigeria, Norway, Poland, Portugal, Slovenia, South Africa, Spain, Sweden, Switzerland, UK, USA.

Also members in South America and West Indies. Membership countries not specified.

NGO Relations Instrumental in setting up: *European College of Veterinary Anaesthesia and Analgesia (ECVAA, #06619).* [2018/XD4063/v/**D**]

- ♦ Association of Veterinary Anaesthetists of Great Britain and Ireland / see Association of Veterinary Anaesthetists (#02976)
- ♦ Association of Vietnamese Scientists and Experts (internationally oriented national body)
- ♦ Association Ville des Alpes de l'Année (#20753)
- ♦ Association des Villes Numériques / see European Network of Digital Cities (#07893)
- ♦ Association des villes pour le recyclage / see Association of Cities and Regions for Sustainable Resource Management (#02433)
- ♦ Association des villes et régions de la grande Europe pour la culture / see European Cities and Regions for Culture (#06554)
- ♦ Association des Villes et Régions Hôtes d'Expositions Internationales (no recent information)
- ♦ Association des villes et régions pour le recyclage / see Association of Cities and Regions for Sustainable Resource Management (#02433)
- ♦ Association villes et territoires méditerranéens (no recent information)

♦ Association for Visual Pedagogies (AVP) 02977

Contact address not obtained.

Sec University of Canterbury, Fac of Education, Rehua Level 5, Private Bag 4800, Christchurch 8140, New Zealand.

URL: https://visualpedagogies.com/

History 2015. **Aims** Promote and advance diverse ways of working with the image and its impact in contemporary and future worlds for learners. **Structure** Executive Committee. **Activities** Events/meetings. **Events** *International AVP Conference* Christchurch (New Zealand) 2023, *Its Autotune But Not as we Know it : Provocations for Time-Based Media in Education* Christchurch (New Zealand) 2022, *Symposium on New Materialist Visual Methodologies* Christchurch (New Zealand) 2022, *Visual Ethics Summit* Christchurch (New Zealand) 2022, *Immersive Possibilities of Education in VR* Auckland (New Zealand) 2021. **Publications** *AVP Newsletter, Video Journal of Education and Pedagogy.* [2022/AA2580/**C**]

- ♦ Association volcanologique européenne (#09077)
- ♦ Association pour le volontariat à l'acte gratuit en Europe / see Association pour le volontariat en Europe (#02978)

♦ Association pour le volontariat en Europe (AVE) 02978

Association for Voluntary Action in Europe – Associació pel Voluntariat a Europa

General Secretariat BP 2541, 69218 Lyon CEDEX 02, France. T. +33620592710. E-mail: info@ave-europe.org.

URL: http://www.ave-europe.org/

History 12 Sep 1972, Lyon (France). Founded following decisions of 2nd Congress for voluntary action (LIVE 72). Former names and other names: *Association pour le volontariat à l'acte gratuit en Europe* – alias. Registration: Start date: 22 Sep 1972, France. **Aims** Promote the spirit of volunteerism; enhance the volunteer efforts of European citizens helping to build a society based on solidarity. **Structure** Administrative Council; General Secretariat. **Languages** English, French, Italian, Spanish. **Staff** Voluntary. **Finance** Institutional support; donations. **Activities** Organizes and participates in national and international conferences which enable exchanges among the various volunteer networks in Europe. Established *Université européenne du volontariat (UEV, see: #02978),* an itinerant university which organizes sessions for professors, students and volunteers to study current affairs in the area of volunteerism. The theme of the following UEV is based on new information technologies and communication, aiming to benefit development of digital networks in order to increase the exchange of debates between European volunteers. **Events** *General Assembly* Italy 2007, *General Assembly* Lucerne (Switzerland) 2005, *General Assembly* Freiburg-Breisgau (Germany) 2001, *Volunteering – culture of peace* Lyon (France) 2000, *Joint conference* Lyon (France) 1999. **Publications** *AVE Connexion* (periodical). University acts.

Members Affiliate associations in 13 countries:
Belgium, Cyprus, France, Germany, Greece, Hungary, Italy, Luxembourg, Poland, Portugal, Spain, Switzerland, UK.

Consultative Status Consultative status granted from: *Council of Europe (CE, #04881)* (Participatory Status). **IGO Relations** Contacts with: *European Commission (EC, #06633)* (DG V and DG XXII). **NGO Relations** Member of: *International Association for Volunteer Effort (IAVE, #12260).* [2019/XD4021/**D**]

- ♦ Association for Voluntary Action in Europe (#02978)
- ♦ Association of Voluntary Action Scholars / see Association for Research on Nonprofit Organizations and Voluntary Action
- ♦ Association of Voluntary Agencies for Rural Development (internationally oriented national body)
- ♦ Association for Voluntary Surgical Contraception / see EngenderHealth
- ♦ Association of Volunteers for Programs of Economic and Social Development (internationally oriented national body)
- ♦ Association Voûte Nubienne (#17614)
- ♦ Association of Waterworks Lake Constance-Rhine / see Internationale Arbeitsgemeinschaft der Wasserwerke im Rheineinzugsgebiet (#13215)
- ♦ Association of West African Exploration and Research Geophysicists (inactive)
- ♦ Association of West Indian Gastroenterologists (internationally oriented national body)
- ♦ Association for Women in Development / see Association for Women's Rights in Development (#02980)

♦ Association of Women Managers in the Maritime Sector in Eastern and Southern Africa (WOMESA) 02979

Secretariat PO Box 95076 – 80104, Mombasa, Kenya. T. +254412318398 – +254412318399. Fax +254412318397. E-mail: info@womesa.org.

URL: http://womesa.org/
History Initiated by *International Maritime Organization (IMO, #14102)* and launched Dec 2007, Mombasa (Kenya), under IMO's programme on the Integration of Women in the Maritime Sector (IWMS). **Aims** Advocate gender equity; improve women's access to maritime training and technology; promote their advancement to key decision making levels in the maritime sector in Eastern and Southern Africa. **Structure** Governing Council (regional level); National Chapters (local level). **Languages** English. **Staff** 2.00 FTE, voluntary. **Finance** Sources: contributions of member/participating states; sponsorship. **Activities** Events/meetings; training/education. Other activities: beach cleaning, mentorship. Active in: Comoros, Madagascar, Malawi, Mauritius, Mozambique, South Africa, South Sudan. **Events** *Annual Conference* Antananarivo (Madagascar) 2017, *Annual Conference* Bishoftu (Ethiopia) 2016. **Publications** *WOMESA Regional Newsletter*.
Members Individual; Corporate; Associate; Honorary. Members in 23 countries:
Angola, Botswana, Burundi, Comoros, Congo DR, Djibouti, Eritrea, Eswatini, Ethiopia, Kenya, Madagascar, Malawi, Mauritius, Mozambique, Namibia, Rwanda, Seychelles, South Africa, Sudan, Tanzania UR, Uganda, Zambia, Zimbabwe.
[2022.04.07/XM5070/**D**]

♦ Association of Women of the Mediterranean Region (no recent information)
♦ Association of Women's Health, Obstetric and Neonatal Nurses (internationally oriented national body)

♦ Association for Women's Rights in Development (AWID) 02980

Association pour les droits de la femme et le développement – Asociación para los Derechos de la Mujer y el Desarrollo
Co-Exec Dir 215 Spadina Avenue, Ste 225, Toronto ON M5T 2C7, Canada. T. +14165943773.
Co-Exec Dir address not obtained.
URL: http://www.awid.org/
History 1982, Racine, WI (USA). Office in Washington DC (USA) with permanent staff opened in 1995. Secretariat moved to Toronto (Canada), 2000. Took over activities of: *Women Human Rights Net (WHRnet, inactive)*. Evolved into a virtual office. Former names and other names: *Association for Women in Development* – former; *Association pour les femmes et le développement* – former; *Asociación para la Mujer y el Desarrollo* – former. **Aims** Act as an international, feminist, creative and multi-generational membership organization for women's rights and *gender* justice; strengthen the voice, impact and influence of women's rights advocates, organizations and movements internationally to effectively advance rights and justice. **Structure** Board of Directors. **Languages** English, French, Spanish. **Activities** Networking/liaising; research/documentation; knowledge management/information dissemination; advocacy/lobbying/activism; events/meetings; capacity building. **Events** *International Forum* Taipei (Taiwan) 2021, *International Forum* Costa do Sauipe (Brazil) 2016, *International forum* Istanbul (Turkey) 2012, *International forum / Triennial Forum* Cape Town (South Africa) 2008, *International forum / Triennial Forum* Bangkok (Thailand) 2005. **Publications** *Primers*. Forum Papers; occasional papers; special collaborative publications; books; booklets; guides; reports; policy briefs; videos.
Members Individual (about 5,200) and institutional (nearly 320) membership. Members in 179 countries and territories:
Afghanistan, Albania, Algeria, Angola, Antigua-Barbuda, Argentina, Armenia, Aruba, Australia, Austria, Azerbaijan, Bahamas, Bahrain, Bangladesh, Barbados, Belarus, Belgium, Benin, Bhutan, Bolivia, Bosnia-Herzegovina, Botswana, Brazil, Bulgaria, Burkina Faso, Burundi, Cambodia, Cameroon, Canada, Central African Rep, Chad, Chile, China, Colombia, Congo DR, Cook Is, Costa Rica, Côte d'Ivoire, Croatia, Cuba, Cyprus, Czechia, Denmark, Djibouti, Dominican Rep, Ecuador, Egypt, El Salvador, Eritrea, Estonia, Eswatini, Ethiopia, Fiji, Finland, France, Gabon, Gambia, Georgia, Germany, Ghana, Greece, Grenada, Guadeloupe, Guatemala, Guinea, Guinea-Bissau, Guyana, Haiti, Honduras, Hong Kong, Hungary, Iceland, India, Indonesia, Iran Islamic Rep, Iraq, Ireland, Isle of Man, Israel, Italy, Jamaica, Japan, Jordan, Kazakhstan, Kenya, Korea Rep, Kosovo, Kuwait, Kyrgyzstan, Laos, Latvia, Lebanon, Lesotho, Liberia, Libya, Lithuania, Luxembourg, Madagascar, Malawi, Malaysia, Maldives, Mali, Malta, Martinique, Mauritania, Mauritius, Mexico, Moldova, Mongolia, Montenegro, Morocco, Mozambique, Myanmar, Namibia, Nepal, Netherlands, New Zealand, Nicaragua, Niger, Nigeria, North Macedonia, Norway, Oman, Pakistan, Palestine, Panama, Papua New Guinea, Paraguay, Peru, Philippines, Poland, Portugal, Puerto Rico, Qatar, Romania, Russia, Rwanda, Saudi Arabia, Senegal, Serbia, Seychelles, Sierra Leone, Singapore, Slovakia, Slovenia, Solomon Is, Somalia, South Africa, South Sudan, Spain, Sri Lanka, St Lucia, St Vincent-Grenadines, Sudan, Sweden, Switzerland, Syrian AR, Taiwan, Tajikistan, Tanzania UR, Thailand, Timor-Leste, Togo, Trinidad-Tobago, Tunisia, Türkiye, Turkmenistan, Uganda, UK, Ukraine, Uruguay, USA, Uzbekistan, Vanuatu, Venezuela, Vietnam, Yemen, Zambia, Zimbabwe.
Included in the above, 62 organizations listed in this Yearbook:
- *ActionAid (#00087)*;
- *Action Without Borders (AWB)*;
- *African Women's Development and Communication Network (FEMNET, #00503)*;
- *African Women's Development Fund (AWDF, #00504)*;
- *American Council for Voluntary International Action (InterAction)*;
- *American Jewish World Service (AJWS)*;
- *Amnesty International (AI, #00801)*;
- *Asia Foundation*;
- *Asia Japan Women's Resource Centre (AJWRC)*;
- *Asia Pacific Forum on Women, Law and Development (APWLD, #01912)*;
- *Association of African Women for Research and Development (AAWORD, #02362)*;
- *Canadian International Development Agency (CIDA, inactive)*;
- *CARE International (CI, #03429)*;
- *Central American Solar Energy Project (CASEP)*;
- *Coady International Institute (CII)*;
- *Comisión Interamericana de Mujeres (CIM, #04137)*;
- *Creating Hope International (CHI)*;
- *Freedom House*;
- *Future Group International, The (TFGI)*;
- *Gender Concerns International (GCI)*;
- *Global Alliance Against Traffic in Women (GAATW, #10184)*;
- *Global Communities*;
- *Global Fund for Women (GFW, #10384)*;
- *Global Grassroots*;
- *Global Ministries of The United Methodist Church (GM-UMC)*;
- *Global Rights*;
- *Global Sisters of Moral Fibre*;
- *Global Urban Development (GUD, #10643)*;
- *Heifer International*;
- *HomeWorkers Worldwide (HWW)*;
- *Humanistisch Instituut voor Ontwikkelingssamenwerking (Hivos)*;
- *Hunger Project (#10994)*;
- *Institute of Development Studies, Brighton (IDS)*;
- *International Development Research Centre (IDRC, #13162)*;
- *International Fund for Agricultural Development (IFAD, #13692)*;
- *International Women's Development Agency (IWDA)*;
- *International Women's Health Coalition (IWHC)*;
- *Inter Pares*;
- *Japan Centre for International Exchange (JCIE)*;
- *Japan International Cooperation Agency (JICA)*;
- *Josef Korbel School of International Studies*;
- *Latin American and Caribbean Women's Health Network (LACWHN, #16288)*;
- *MADRE*;
- *Mama Cash (#16560)*;
- *Mediterranean Institute of Gender Studies (MIGS)*;
- *Monde solidarité Afrique*;
- *New Field Foundation*;
- *Nippon Foundation*;
- *OutRight Action International*;
- *Oxfam GB*;
- *Pro-Hope International (PHIN)*;
- *Prospera – International Network of Women's Funds (INWF, #18545)*;
- *Rural Integrated Development Program of Africa (RIDPA)*;
- *Swedish NGO Centre for Development Cooperation (Forum Syd)*;
- *The Eastern African Sub-Regional Support Initiative for the Advancement of Women (EASSI, #05225)*;
- *UNICEF (#20332)*;
- *Urgent Action Fund for Women's Human Rights (UAF)*;
- *WIDE+ (#20951)*;
- *Womankind Worldwide (#20982)*;
- *Women on Waves*;
- *Women's Environment and Development Organization (WEDO, #21016)*;
- *Women's Link Worldwide*.

Consultative Status Consultative status granted from: *ECOSOC (#05331)* (General).
NGO Relations Member of: *International Network for Economic, Social and Cultural Rights (ESCR-Net, #14255)*; *Society for International Development (SID, #19581)*; *Women's Working Group on Financing for Development (WWG on FfD, #21036)*. Supports: *Global Call for Action Against Poverty (GCAP, #10263)*. Instrumental in setting up: *Women in Migration Network (WIMN, #21008)*. Cooperates with:
- *ActionAid (#00087)*;
- *African Women's Development and Communication Network (FEMNET, #00503)*;
- *Asian Women's Human Rights Council (AWHRC, #01783)*;
- *Center for Women's Global Leadership (CWGL)*;
- *Development Alternatives with Women for a New Era (DAWN, #05054)*;
- *International Alliance of Women (IAW, #11639)*;
- *Global Women's Strike (GWS, #10660)*;
- *International Women's Tribune Centre (IWTC, inactive)*;
- *Sisterhood Is Global Institute (SIGI, #19298)*;
- *Women in Law and Development in Africa-Afrique de l'Ouest (WiLDAF-AO, #21005)*;
- *Women, Law and Development International (WLDI, inactive)*;
- *Women Living under Muslim Laws (WLUML, #21007)*.

[2021/XF4222/y/**F**]

♦ Association of Working Communities of the Alpine Regions (AWCAR) 02981

Association des communautés de travail des régions alpines
Contact ARGE ALP, Amt der Tiroler Landesregierung, Eduard-Wallnöfer-Platz 3, 6020 Innsbruck, Austria. T. +435125082340. Fax +43512508742345. E-mail: info@argealp.org.
URL: https://www.argealp.org/de
History 1989. Former names and other names: *Association des régions alpines* – alias; *Association of Alpine Regions* – alias. **Consultative Status** Consultative status granted from: *Council of Europe (CE, #04881)* (Participatory Status). **IGO Relations** Observer at: *European Committee of the Regions (CoR, #06665)*; *Congress of Local and Regional Authorities of the Council of Europe (#04677)*. [2022/XE1901/**E**]

♦ ASSOCIATIONWORLD (unconfirmed)

♦ Association of World Citizens (AWC) 02982

Vice-Pres PO Box 1206, Novato CA 94948, USA.
Head Office Le Passe, 07140 Gravières, France.
URL: https://www.associationofworldcitizens.com/
History 25 Jul 1975, San Francisco CA (USA), as *World Citizens Assembly (WCA) – Assemblée mondiale des citoyens (AMC)*. Absorbed activities of the International Steering Committee for *Peoples' World Convention – Assemblée constituante des peuples*, which had been instrumental in setting up *World Council for the Peoples World Convention (CMACP, inactive)*. Name changed, 1988, to *World Citizens*. Current name adopted 1990. **Aims** Convene Assemblies for people, groups and organizations concerned about the state of the Earth and committed to the ongoing effort of building a global village of economic/social justice, lasting peace, and a sustainable environment for the 21st Century. **Structure** Advisory Committee; Commissions; Secretariat. Includes *World Citizen Diplomats (no recent information)*. **Languages** English, French, Japanese, Spanish. **Staff** 10.00 FTE, voluntary. **Finance** Contributions, pledges by members. Financial support from *World Citizens Foundation*, a tax exempt membership organization. **Activities** Events/meetings; advocacy/lobbying/activism; awards/prizes/competitions. **Events** *World Summit of Love and Peace* Gyeongju (Korea Rep) 2016, *World citizens assembly* Taipei (Taiwan) 2001, *Planning assembly* San Francisco, CA (USA) 1998, *Conference on global governance* San Francisco, CA (USA) 1995, *World citizens assembly* San Francisco, CA (USA) 1995. **Publications** *World Citizen* (2 or 3 a year). *Action Handbook of the World Citizens Assembly*. Proceedings of World Assemblies.
Members World citizen centers and individual world citizens in 59 countries and territories:
Argentina, Australia, Austria, Bangladesh, Belgium, Botswana, Bulgaria, Burundi, Canada, China, Congo DR, Costa Rica, Côte d'Ivoire, Cuba, Denmark, Egypt, Ethiopia, Finland, France, Gambia, Germany, Ghana, Greece, Guatemala, Hungary, India, Israel, Italy, Jamaica, Japan, Kenya, Libya, Madagascar, Mexico, Netherlands, New Zealand, Nigeria, Pakistan, Philippines, Portugal, Puerto Rico, Romania, Russia, Senegal, Sierra Leone, South Africa, Spain, Sri Lanka, Sudan, Sweden, Switzerland, Taiwan, Thailand, Togo, Uganda, UK, Ukraine, USA, Vietnam.
Consultative Status Consultative status granted from: *ECOSOC (#05331)* (Ros A). **IGO Relations** Associated with Department of Global Communications of the United Nations. [2019.06.30/XF8714/**F**]

♦ Association for the World Civil Society Forum / see World Civil Society Forum (#21278)
♦ Association of World Colleges and Universities / see Association for World Education (#02983)
♦ Association of World Council of Churches Related Development Organizations in Europe / see ACT Alliance EU (#00082)
♦ Association of World Economic Studies (unconfirmed)

♦ Association for World Education (AWE) 02983

Association pour l'éducation mondiale – Asociación para la Educación Mundial
Chairman PO Box 424, Portland ME 04112-0424, USA. T. +12076719131.
Secretariat Landevejen 6, 5683 Haarby, Denmark.
URL: http://www.world-education.org/
History Nov 1970, Westbury, NY (USA). Charter having been granted by the State of New York (USA), 20 Jan 1971. Former names and other names: *Association of World Colleges and Universities* – former. **Aims** Maintain and grow a dynamic and supportive network of educators, lifelong learners and organizations from around the globe doing work that draws inspiration from the Nordic Folk High School Movement to influence and improve social and ecological conditions at local, national, regional and global levels. **Structure** Global Presidency; International Council (meets every 3 years); Committees (4); Secretariat. **Languages** Arabic, Bengali, Danish, Dutch, English, Filipino, French, Hawaiian, Hindi, Japanese, Ladakhi, Malayalam, Portuguese, Russian, Sinhala, Spanish, Swahili, Tamil, Telugu. **Staff** Voluntary. **Finance** Sources: contributions; members' dues; sponsorship. **Activities** Capacity building; events/meetings; networking/liaising; projects/programmes; publishing activities; research/documentation; training/education. **Events** *International Council Meeting* Denmark 2022, *International Council Meeting* Denmark 2019, *Meeting* Cairo (Egypt) 2017, *Meeting* Copenhagen (Denmark) 2017, *International Conference* Moscow (Russia) 2006. **Publications** *Journal for World Education* (2 a year). Regional newsletters; conference reports; Global Action Report.
Members Individuals in 21 countries:
Argentina, Bangladesh, Belgium, Brazil, Denmark, Egypt, France, India, Japan, Kenya, North Macedonia, Philippines, Russia, Sri Lanka, Tajikistan, Uganda, Ukraine, USA, Venezuela, Zambia, Zimbabwe.
Institutional members include:
The Global Institute (#10427).
Consultative Status Consultative status granted from: *ECOSOC (#05331)* (Roster); *UNICEF (#20332)*. **IGO Relations** Associated with Department of Global Communications of the United Nations.
[2021.03.18/XC4001/**C**]

♦ Association of World Election Bodies (A-WEB) 02984

Association mondiale d'organismes de gestion des élections – Asociación Mundial de Organismos Electorales
Secretariat 19th Floor, 12 Gaetbeol-ro, Yeonsu-gu, Incheon 21999, Korea Rep. T. +82324557200. Fax +82324557299. E-mail: aweb201310@gmail.com.
URL: http://aweb.org/
History Oct 2013, Incheon (Korea Rep). Adoption of Resolution to Establish A-WEB Oct, 2011. Secretariat launched Apr, 2014. **Aims** Contribute to the development of democracy by supporting a conduct of a free, fair, transparent, and participatory elections around the world. **Structure** General Assembly; Executive Board; Committees (2); Secretariat, located in Songdo Incheon (Korea Rep). **Languages** English. **Staff** 30.00 FTE, paid. **Activities** Awareness raising; capacity building; events/meetings; guidance/assistance/consulting; research/documentation; training/education. **Events** *Executive Board Meeting* Incheon (Korea Rep) 2021, *Biennial General Assembly* Bangalore (India) 2019, *Executive Board Meeting* Sofia (Bulgaria) 2019, *Executive Board Meeting* Nadi (Fiji) 2018, *Biennial General Assembly* Bucharest (Romania) 2017. **Publications** *A-WEB Newsletter* (12 a year). Annual Report.
Members Full (115) in 106 countries and territories:

Afghanistan, Albania, Angola, Argentina, Australia, Bahamas, Bangladesh, Barbados, Belarus, Benin, Bhutan, Bolivia, Bosnia-Herzegovina, Brazil, Bulgaria, Burkina Faso, Burundi, Cambodia, Cameroon, Canada, Colombia, Congo DR, Costa Rica, Côte d'Ivoire, Croatia, Djibouti, Dominica, Dominican Rep, Ecuador, Egypt, El Salvador, Ethiopia, Fiji, France, Gabon, Gambia, Georgia, Ghana, Guatemala, Guinea, Guyana, Haiti, India, Indonesia, Iraq, Jamaica, Kazakhstan, Kenya, Korea Rep, Kosovo, Kyrgyzstan, Latvia, Lebanon, Libya, Madagascar, Malawi, Maldives, Mali, Mauritius, Mexico, Moldova, Mongolia, Mozambique, Myanmar, Nicaragua, Nigeria, Pakistan, Palestine, Panama, Paraguay, Peru, Philippines, Poland, Portugal, Puerto Rico, Romania, Russia, Rwanda, Samoa, Sao Tomé-Principe, Senegal, Serbia, Sierra Leone, Slovenia, Somalia, South Africa, South Sudan, Sri Lanka, St Lucia, Suriname, Taiwan, Tanzania UR, Thailand, Timor-Leste, Togo, Tonga, Trinidad-Tobago, Tunisia, Türkiye, Uganda, Ukraine, Uzbekistan, Vanuatu, Venezuela, Yemen, Zambia. [2022/XM5308/**B**]

♦ Association of World Reindeer Herders (WRH) 02985

Admin Sec c/o ICRH, PO Box 109, 9520 Kautokeino, Norway. T. +4778607670. Fax +4778607671. E-mail: office@reindeerworld.org.
SG address not obtained.
URL: http://reindeerherding.org/wrh/

History Mar 1997, Nadym (Russia). **Aims** Provide a forum for contacts between the reindeer peoples; facilitate the exchange of information on the tame reindeer industry. **Events** *Quadrennial Congress* Genhe (China) 2013, *Quadrennial Congress* Kautokeino (Norway) 2009, *Quadrennial Congress* Yakutsk (Russia) 2005, *Quadrennial Congress* Inari (Finland) 2001, *Quadrennial Congress* Nadym (Russia) 1997. **Publications** *The Reindeer Herder* in English, Finnish, Norwegian, Russian.
Members Individuals in 5 countries:
China, Finland, Norway, Russia, Sweden.
Consultative Status Consultative status granted from: *ECOSOC (#05331)* (Special). **IGO Relations** Observer to: *Arctic Council (#01097)*; *Conservation of Arctic Flora and Fauna (CAFF, #04728)*. Member of: *Arctic Monitoring and Assessment Programme (AMAP, #01100)*. [2016/XD8286/**D**]

- ♦ Association pour le XIème Congrès international d'archéologie chrétienne / see Association pour l'antiquité tardive

♦ Association of Yacht Support Services (AYSS) 02986

Contact address not obtained. E-mail: info@ayss.org – admin@ayss.org.
URL: http://ayss.org/

History 1991. Also referred to as *AYSS Superyacht Global Network*. **Aims** Bring together local suppliers and yacht captains; assist the smooth passage of superyachts across the region. **Structure** Annual General Meeting; Council. **Finance** Sources: members' dues. **NGO Relations** Member of: *Professional Yachting Association (PYA, #18519)*. [2017/XM5839/**C**]

- ♦ Association of Young European Administrators (#02772)
- ♦ Association Of Young European Civil Servants / see Association des jeunes fonctionnaires européens (#02772)

♦ Association of Young Legal Historians (AYLH) 02987

Vereinigung Junger RechtshistorikerInnen (VJR)
Contact address not obtained. E-mail: info@aylh.org.
URL: http://www.aylh.org/

History 2007, Seville (Spain). Founded at annual European Forum of Young Legal Historians, which was first organized 1992. Registration: Swiss Civil Code, Switzerland. **Aims** Organize the annual conference European Forum of Young Legal Historians; promote academic legal history in Europe and beyond. **Structure** General Assembly; Executive Board. **Languages** English. **Finance** Sources: members' dues. **Events** *Annual Forum of Young Legal Historians* Istanbul (Türkiye) 2022, *Annual Forum of Young Legal Historians* Brussels (Belgium) 2019, *Annual Forum of Young Legal Historians* Warsaw (Poland) 2018, *Annual Forum of Young Legal Historians* Naples (Italy) 2017, *Annual Forum of Young Legal Historians* Belgrade (Serbia) 2016. **Publications** *Yearbook of Young Legal Historians*. [2020/AA0065/c/**E**]

- ♦ Association Zen d'Europe / see International Zen Association (#15940)
- ♦ Association Zen internationale (#15940)
- ♦ Association des zones minières / see Association of Europe's Coalfield Regions (#02585)
- ♦ Associazione Accademia Internazionale per la Riproduzione Umana (#11551)
- ♦ Associazione delle Acciaierie Europee Indipendenti (inactive)
- ♦ Associazione Ambientalisti per il Nucleare (internationally oriented national body)
- ♦ Associazione Amici dei Bambini (internationally oriented national body)
- ♦ Associazione Archivistica Ecclesiastica (#05279)
- ♦ Associazione Azione per un Mondo Unito (internationally oriented national body)
- ♦ Associazione Bertoni Cooperazione Sviluppo Terzo Mondo (internationally oriented national body)
- ♦ Association dei Biologi delle Comunità Europee / see European Countries Biologists Association (#06852)
- ♦ Associazione Biosofica Universale (inactive)
- ♦ Associazione Botteghe del Mondo (internationally oriented national body)
- ♦ Associazione Cattolica Internazionale di Studi Medico-Psicologici (inactive)
- ♦ Associazione Centro Aiuti Volontari Cooperazione Sviluppo Terzo Mondo (internationally oriented national body)
- ♦ Associazione dei Cimiteri Storico-Monumentali in Europa (#02915)
- ♦ Associazione Città alpina dell'anno (#20753)
- ♦ Associazione di Città e Regioni per il Riciclaggio / see Association of Cities and Regions for Sustainable Resource Management (#02433)
- ♦ Associazione di Città per il Riciclaggio / see Association of Cities and Regions for Sustainable Resource Management (#02433)
- ♦ Associazione Commercio Internazionale di Bulbi da Fiore e di Pianti (no recent information)
- ♦ Associazione Comunità Papa Giovanni (internationally oriented national body)
- ♦ Associazione Comunità Papa Giovanni XXIII / see Associazione Comunità Papa Giovanni
- ♦ Associazione delle Comunità Tessili d'Europa (#02435)
- ♦ Associazione Conoscere Eurasia (internationally oriented national body)
- ♦ Associazione Controllo Strutture (no recent information)
- ♦ Associazione di Cooperazione Cristiana Internazionale (internationally oriented national body)
- ♦ Associazione per la Cooperazione Internazionale e l'Aiuto Umanitario (internationally oriented national body)
- ♦ Associazione per la Cooperazione Internazionale allo Sviluppo (internationally oriented national body)
- ♦ Associazione di Cooperazione Rurale in Africa e America Latina (internationally oriented national body)
- ♦ Associazione dei Costruttori Europei di Ruote (#02552)
- ♦ Associazione Cultura Assistenza Popolare / see Comunità di Sant'Egidio – ACAP
- ♦ Associazione per la Diffusione delle Lingue Europee / see Europe plurilingue
- ♦ Associazione Economica Europea del Commercio Estero (inactive)
- ♦ Associazione Europa – Terzo Mondo / see eu can aid (#05570)
- ♦ Associazione Europea degli Assistenti Sociali Ospedalieri e della Sanitari (inactive)
- ♦ Associazione Europea Audio-Protesisti / see European Association of Hearing Aid Professionals (#06066)
- ♦ Associazione Europea di Avvocati / see AEA – International Lawyers Network (#00142)
- ♦ Associazione Europea della Carne (inactive)
- ♦ Associazione Europea di Centri che Offrono Servizi per Persone Handicappate (#06204)
- ♦ Associazione Europea Ceto Medio (inactive)
- ♦ Associazione Europea del Commercio all'Ingrosso delle Carni Macellate (inactive)
- ♦ Associazione Europea del Commercio al Dettaglio in Giocattoli (inactive)
- ♦ Associazione Europea per la Cooperazione (inactive)
- ♦ Associazione Europea Costruttori Macchine per Ufficio e Tecnologie dell'Informazione (inactive)
- ♦ Associazione Europea per le Cure Palliative (#06141)
- ♦ Associazione Europea Decaffeinizzatori (inactive)
- ♦ Associazione Europea delle Donne Poliziotto (#07970)
- ♦ Associazione Europea per l'Educazione Cattolica degli Adulti (#05966)
- ♦ Associazione Europea per l'Educazione die Fanciulli Precoci e dei Giovani con Alto Potenziale (#06664)
- ♦ Associazione Europea degli Eletti della Montagna (#06021)
- ♦ Associazione Europea dei Ferrovieri (#02558)
- ♦ Associazione Europea fra le Industrie di Prodotti di Marca / see European Brands Association (#06397)
- ♦ Associazione Europea di Garanzia Mutua / see European Association of Guarantee Institutions (#06061)
- ♦ Associazione Europea delle Giuriste e dei Giuristi per la Democrazia e i Diritti dell'Uomo nel Mondo (#06105)
- ♦ Associazione Europea dell'Industria Fotografica (inactive)
- ♦ Associazione Europea per l'Informatica nella Navigazione (inactive)
- ♦ Associazione Europea per la Informatica Portuaria (inactive)
- ♦ Associazione Europea di Informazione Pubblica Televisiva (inactive)
- ♦ Associazione Europea di Ingegneria di Precisione (#08710)
- ♦ Associazione Europea degli Insegnanti (#02565)
- ♦ Associazione Europea Installatori Impianti Elettrici / see EuropeOn (#09166)
- ♦ Associazione Europea Maestri Liutai e Archettai (#06273)
- ♦ Associazione Europea dei Magistrati (#06100)
- ♦ Associazione Europea di Magistrati Amministrativi (#02497)
- ♦ Associazione Europea di Medicina Interna / see European Federation of Internal Medicine (#07147)
- ♦ Associazione Europea dei Medici Ospedalieri (#02577)
- ♦ Associazione Europea Nastri, Treccia, Tessuti Elastici (inactive)
- ♦ Associazione Europea degli Organismi di Garanzia (#06061)
- ♦ Associazione Europea delle Organizzazioni Operanti nel Settore delle Strutture e delle Trasformazioni Fondiario-Agrarie (#06198)
- ♦ Associazione Europea dei Paleontologi dei vertebrati (#06266)
- ♦ Associazione Europea del Pensiero Libero (#06048)
- ♦ Associazione Europea per il Piccolo Idroelettrico (#08495)
- ♦ Associazione Europea dei Podologi (inactive)
- ♦ Associazione Europea di Produttori di Cartone e Cartoncino / see Association of European Cartonboard and Carton Manufacturers (#02502)
- ♦ Associazione Europea di Produttori di Molluschi (#07818)
- ♦ Associazione Europea dei Produttori di Pompe (#06182)
- ♦ Associazione Europea di Produttori di Proteine Unicellulari (inactive)
- ♦ Associazione Europea per il Progresso Sociale e Culturale (inactive)
- ♦ Associazione Europea Proteine Vegetali (#09047)
- ♦ Associazione Europea dei Quotidiani in Lingua Minoritaria e Regionale (#06002)
- ♦ Associazione Europea per la ricerca dell' educazione degli adulti (#08725)
- ♦ Associazione Europea per le Ricerche sul Cancro (#05962)
- ♦ Associazione Europea della Siderurgia (#08835)
- ♦ Associazione Europea della Stampa Militare (#07803)
- ♦ Associazione Europea per lo Studio del Giudaismo / see European Association for Jewish Studies (#06098)
- ♦ Associazione Europea per lo Studio del Mercato Farmaceutico (#08196)
- ♦ Associazione Europea per lo Sviluppo delle Banche Dati sulla Formazione Iniziale e Continua (inactive)
- ♦ Associazione Europea per lo Sviluppo del Transporto Ferroviario (#06011)
- ♦ Associazione Europea del Termalismo e Climatismo (#08805)
- ♦ Associazione Europea per la Terminologia (#06252)
- ♦ Associazione Europea della Torcitura (inactive)
- ♦ Associazione Europea delle Ufficialesse e degli Ufficiali dello Stato Civile (#05760)
- ♦ Associazione Europea degli Ufficiali Professionisti dei Vigili del Fuoco (no recent information)
- ♦ Associazione Europea di Volatili Rurali (#08416)
- ♦ Associazione Europea di Zincatura Generale (#07383)
- ♦ Associazione dei Fabbricanti Europei di Emulsionanti Alimentari (#07281)
- ♦ Associazione dei Fabbricanti Europei di Scaldacqua ad Accumulazione Funzionanti a Gas (inactive)
- ♦ Associazione fra le Industrie Alimentari del Gelato della CEE / see EUROGLACES – European Ice Cream Association (#05688)
- ♦ Associazione fra le Industrie Alimentari del Gelato della UE / see EUROGLACES – European Ice Cream Association (#05688)
- ♦ Associazione Genitori d'Europa / see European Parents' Association (#08142)
- ♦ Associazione dei Giornalisti Europei (#02516)
- ♦ Associazione ICS (internationally oriented national body)
- ♦ Associazione della Industria Margariniera dei Paesi della CE / see European Margarine Association (#07736)
- ♦ Associazione delle Industrie del Cioccolato, della Biscotteria-Pasticceria e della Confetteria della CEE / see Association of the Chocolate, Biscuit and Confectionery Industries of the EU (#02427)
- ♦ Associazione delle Industrie Conserviere Ittiche della CEE / see European Union Fish Processors Association (#08989)
- ♦ Associazione delle Industrie Conserviere Ittiche della Commissione Europea (#08989)
- ♦ Associazione internationale degli esperti scientifici del turismo (#02697)
- ♦ Associazione Internationale dei Giornalisti dello Sci (#02710)
- ♦ Associazione Internationale Installatori Impianti Elettrici / see EuropeOn (#09166)
- ♦ Associazione Internationale dei Maestri di sci professionisti (#14870)
- ♦ Associazione Internationale di Medicina Ortomolecolare / see International Society for Orthomolecular Medicine (#15334)
- ♦ Associazione Internationale della Sandplay Therapy (#15432)
- ♦ Associazione internationale per i Walser (#12262)
- ♦ Associazione Internazionale degli Anziani delle Comunità Europee (#02667)

♦ Associazione Internazionale di Archeologia Classica (AIAC) 02988

Association internationale d'archéologie classique – Asociación Internacional de Arqueologia Clasica – Internationaler Verband für Klassiche Archeologie – International Association for Classical Archaeology
SG Via di S Apollinare 8, c/o Palazzo Altemps, 00186 Rome RM, Italy. T. +3966798798. Fax +3966798798. E-mail: segreteria@aiac.org – info@aiac.org.
URL: http://www.aiac.org/

History Mar 1945, Rome (Italy). Registered in accordance with Italian law, 4 Oct 1957. **Aims** Promote: study and knowledge of classical archaeology; international collaboration among classical archaeologists. **Structure** Council, composed of Directors of national institutes of archaeology and of individual scholars of archaeology established in Rome (Italy). **Languages** English, Italian. **Staff** 1.00 FTE, paid. **Finance** Annual budget: 126,000 EUR. **Events** *Congress* Cologne (Germany) / Bonn (Germany) 2018, *Quinquennial Congress* Mérida (Spain) 2013, *Quinquennial Congress* Rome (Italy) 2008, *Quinquennial Congress* Rome (Italy) 2008, *Quinquennial Congress* Boston, MA (USA) 2003. **Publications** *AIACNews*; *FOLD and R*.
Members Institutes and scientists (500) in 30 countries:
Albania, Australia, Austria, Belgium, Bulgaria, Canada, Croatia, Cyprus, Denmark, Finland, France, Germany, Greece, Holy See, Hungary, Israel, Italy, Japan, Netherlands, New Zealand, Norway, Poland, Portugal, Romania, Slovenia, Spain, Sweden, Switzerland, Türkiye, USA.
NGO Relations Member of: *Association internationale pour l'étude de la mosaïque antique (AIEMA, #02689)*; *Fédération internationale des associations d'études classiques (FIEC, #09607)*; *International Union of Institutes of Archaeology, History and Art History in Rome (#15782)*. [2020/XC1182/v/**C**]

- ♦ Associazione Internazionale di Archeologia Computazionale (no recent information)
- ♦ Associazione Internazionale Artes Renascentes (#02670)
- ♦ Associazione Internazionale degli Assicuratori contro la Grandine / see Association internationale des assureurs de la production agricole (#02671)

- ♦ Associazione Internazionale degli Assicuratori della Produzione Agricola (#02671)
- ♦ Associazione Internazionale dell'Assicurazione di Difesa Legale / see Legal Protection International (#16440)
- ♦ Associazione Internazionale dei Calvi (no recent information)
- ♦ Associazione Internazionale per la Cannabis come Medicina / see International Association for Cannabinoid Medicines (#11754)
- ♦ Associazione Internazionale della Capra (#13725)
- ♦ Associazione Internazionale per la Comunicazione Ambientale (internationally oriented national body)
- ♦ Associazione Internazionale contra la Tortura (no recent information)
- ♦ Associazione Internazionale dagli Ex-Comunitari Europei / see Association internationale des anciens de l'Union Européenne (#02667)
- ♦ Associazione Internazionale per la Difesa della Libertà Religiosa (#02681)
- ♦ Associazione Internazionale per la Difesa delle Lingue e Culture Minacciate / see Association pour les Langues et Cultures Européennes Menacées (#02782)
- ♦ Associazione Internazionale dei Direttori d'Opera (inactive)
- ♦ Associazione Internazionale di Diritto delle Assicurazioni (#02684)
- ♦ Associazione Internazionale di Diritto Processuale (#12102)
- ♦ Associazione Internazionale Disarmo e Sviluppo (internationally oriented national body)
- ♦ Associazione Internazionale delle Donne per la Comunicazione – Mediterranea Media (internationally oriented national body)
- ♦ Associazione Internazionale degli Educatori dei Giovani Disadattati / see International Association of Social Educators (#12167)
- ♦ Associazione Internazionale degli Educatori della Gioventù in Difficoltà / see International Association of Social Educators (#12167)
- ♦ Associazione Internazionale di Epigrafia Greca e Latina (#11924)
- ♦ Associazione Internazionale di Estetica Empirica (#11867)
- ♦ Associazione Internazionale del Filo Metallico e Macchinario (#15893)
- ♦ Associazione Internazionale delle Fondazioni Raoul Follereau / see Raoul Follereau International Union (#18618)
- ♦ Associazione Internazionale di Ginecologia Endocrinologica (#15150)
- ♦ Associazione Internazionale dei Giornalisti Accreditati in Vaticano (#02773)
- ♦ Associazione Internazionale dei Giovani Avvocati (#12282)
- ♦ Associazione Internazionale di Igiene, Medicina Preventiva e Sociale (inactive)
- ♦ Associazione Internazionale delle Industrie di Prestampa (inactive)
- ♦ Associazione Internazionale delle Istituzioni Sanitarie Cattoliche (no recent information)
- ♦ Associazione Internazionale IUS Primi Viri (internationally oriented national body)
- ♦ Associazione Internazionale di Libero Pensiero (#11906)
- ♦ Associazione Internazionale di Massagio Infantile (#11962)
- ♦ Associazione Internazionale di Medicina degli Infortuni e del Traffico / see International Traffic Medicine Association (#15713)
- ♦ Associazione Internazionale di Medicina del Traffico (#15713)
- ♦ Associazione internazionale dei missiologi cattolici (#11760)
- ♦ Associazione Internazionale Mosaicisti Contemporanei (#11816)
- ♦ Associazione Internazionale dei Movimenti Familiari di Formazione Rurale (#02719)
- ♦ Associazione Internazionale di Ontopsicologia (internationally oriented national body)
- ♦ Associazione Internazionale della Panificazione Industriale (#02674)
- ♦ Associazione Internazionale dei Platonisti (#14603)
- ♦ Associazione Internazionale di Polizia / see International Police Association (#14612)
- ♦ Associazione Internazionale di Polizia (internationally oriented national body)

♦ Associazione Internazionale dei Professori d'Italiano (AIPI) 02989

Association internationale des professeurs d'italien – Asociación Internacional de los Profesores de Italiano – Internationaler Verband der Italienischen Lehrer – International Association of Professors of Italian

Contact KU Leuven, Fac of Arts, Blijde Inkomststraat 21 – box 3311, 3000 Leuven, Belgium.
URL: http://www.infoaipi.org/

History 21 Sep 1975, Vicenza (Italy). Registered in accordance with Belgian law, 30 Oct 1982, Brussels (Belgium). **Aims** Promote contact and collaboration between individuals and associations interested in teaching Italian *language* and culture at all educational levels; facilitate exchanges of educational, linguistic and cultural nature; offer discussion in the latest didactic findings and fundamental research in Italian studies. **Structure** General Assembly (every 2 years at Conference); Executive Committee. **Languages** Italian. **Staff** Voluntary. **Finance** Sources: members' dues. **Activities** Events/meetings; publishing activities; training/education. **Events** *Biennial Congress and General Assembly / Biennial Congress* Bari (Italy) 2014, *Biennial Congress and General Assembly / Biennial Congress* Salzburg (Austria) 2012, *Biennial Congress and General Assembly / Biennial Congress* Cagliari (Italy) 2010, *Biennial Congress and General Assembly / Biennial Congress* Oviedo (Spain) 2008, *Biennial Congress and General Assembly / Biennial Congress* Ascoli Piceno (Italy) 2006. **Publications** *Notiziario dell'AIPI* (2 a year); *Civiltà Italiana* (annual). Peer-reviewed publications; conference proceedings. **Members** Associations and individuals in 37 countries. Membership countries not specified. [2019/XD4576/**C**]

- ♦ Associazione Internazionale per il Progresso Sociale (inactive)
- ♦ Associazione Internazionale per la Promozione della Geoetica (#12107)
- ♦ Associazione Internazionale per la Promozione dello Studio della Filosofia di Hegel (#13247)
- ♦ Associazione Internazionale per il Provimento della Farmacologia Sperimentale e Clinica (inactive)
- ♦ Associazione Internazionale di Psicanalisi Eclettica (inactive)
- ♦ Associazione Internazionale di Psicologia Analitica (#11700)
- ♦ Associazione Internazionale dei Pubblici Istituti di Credito su Pegno (inactive)
- ♦ Associazione Internazionale Regina Elena (#02740)
- ♦ Associazione Internazionale Rurale Cattolica (#12461)
- ♦ Associazione Internazionale per la Sintesi della Conoscenza (no recent information)
- ♦ Associazione Internazionale della Stampa Medica (inactive)
- ♦ Associazione Internazionale della Stampa Sportiva (#02729)

♦ Associazione Internazionale per la Storia delle Alpi (AISA) 02990

Association Internationale pour l'Histoire des Alpes – Internationale Gesellschaft für historische Alpenforschung (IGHA)

SG Lab di Storia delle Alpi, Accademia di architettura, Largo Bernasconi 2, 6850 Mendrisio TI, Switzerland. T. +41586665819. Fax +41586665868. E-mail: labisalp.arc@usi.ch.
URL: http://www.labisalp.arc.usi.ch/it/aisa/

History 7 Oct 1995, Lucerne (Switzerland). **Aims** Conduct historical research concerning the whole *alpine* area. **Structure** General Assembly; Board of Directors; Executive Committee. **Languages** French, German, Italian. **Staff** 1.50 FTE, paid. **Finance** Members' dues. **Activities** Research/documentation. Active in: Austria, France, Germany, Italy, Slovenia, Switzerland. **Publications** *Histoire des Alpes – Storia delli Alpi – Geschichte der Alpen* (annual) – review.
Members Full in 6 countries:
Austria, France, Italy, Liechtenstein, Slovenia, Switzerland.
IGO Relations None. **NGO Relations** *International Scientific Committee on Research in the Alps (ISCAR, #14804).* [2015.06.01/XJ9534/**E**]

- ♦ Associazione Internazionale per la Storia del Vetro (#02706)

♦ Associazione Internazionale Studi di Canto Gregoriano (AISCGre) .. 02991

International Society for the Study of Gregorian Chants – Internationale Gesellschaft für Studien des Gregorianischen Chorals

Pres Johann-Mutter-Str 22, 86899 Landsberg am Lech, Germany. T. +447990570401.
URL: http://www.aiscgre.org/

History Founded 1975, Rome (Italy). Registered in accordance with Italian law, Cremona (Italy). **Aims** Promote and further develop the *semiological* orientation of *Gregorian Chant*, basing interpretation on historical evidence based theory, bringing together theory and practice. **Structure** Sections (5): German; Italian; Japanese; Polish; Spanish. **Finance** Members' dues. **Activities** Training/education; research/documentation; events/meetings. **Events** *International Congress* Lugano (Switzerland) 2015, *Congress / International Congress* Poznań (Poland) 2011, *Congress / International Congress* Florence (Italy) 2007, *Congress / International Congress* Hildesheim (Germany) 2003, *Congress / International Congress* Verona (Italy) 1999. **Publications** *Studi Gregoriani* (2 a year); *Beiträge zur Gregorianik*; *Estudius Gregorianos*.
Members In 25 countries:
Austria, Belgium, Colombia, Croatia, Czechia, Finland, France, Germany, Hungary, Israel, Italy, Japan, Korea Rep, Latvia, Mexico, Netherlands, Norway, Poland, Romania, Slovakia, Spain, Sweden, Switzerland, USA, Venezuela. [2016.03.03/XE3823/**E**]

- ♦ Associazione Internazionale degli Studi Latini Umanistici e Moderni (#12048)
- ♦ Associazione Internazionale per gli Studi di Lingua e Letteratura Italiana (#12202)
- ♦ Associazione Internazionale di Studi sulla Meccanografia ed Informatica (inactive)
- ♦ Associazione Internazionale di Studi Medico-Psicologici e Religiosi (#12028)
- ♦ Associazione Internazionale per lo Studio e la Promozione della Musica per Fiatti (#13237)
- ♦ Associazione Internazionale di Studi su Otto Gross (#12060)
- ♦ Associazione Internazionale di Studi sul Discorso (#11850)
- ♦ Associazione Internazionale di Studi sul Mediterraneo e l'Oriente (internationally oriented national body)
- ♦ Associazione Internazionale per lo Sviluppo degli Scambi Commerciali (inactive)
- ♦ Associazione Internazionale per lo Sviluppo Urbano (#15832)
- ♦ Associazione Internazionale dei Teatri Lirici (no recent information)
- ♦ Associazione Internazionale del Tessile Naturale (#14217)
- ♦ Associazione Internazionale Trappista (#15727)
- ♦ Associazione Internazionale del Trasporto Multimodale (inactive)
- ♦ Associazione Internazionale dei Tubi Metallici (#15741)
- ♦ Associazione Internazionale delle Università della Terza Età (#02749)
- ♦ Associazione Internazionale per il Video nelle Arti e nella Cultura (inactive)
- ♦ Associazione Internazionale Volontari Laici (internationally oriented national body)
- ♦ Associazione Internazionale degli Zattieri (#15691)
- ♦ Associazione Internazione del Critici Letterari / see Association internationale de la critique littéraire (#02679)
- ♦ Associazione IRENE – Iniziative, Ricerche, Esperienze per una Nuova Europa (internationally oriented national body)
- ♦ Associazione di Istituti Europei di Congiuntura Economica (#02506)
- ♦ Associazione Italiana Amici di Raoul Follereau (internationally oriented national body)
- ♦ Associazione Italiana Donne per lo Sviluppo ONLUS (internationally oriented national body)
- ♦ Associazione Italiana degli Slavisti (internationally oriented national body)
- ♦ Associazione Laicale Missionaria (internationally oriented national body)
- ♦ Associazione Latina per l'Analisi dei Sistemi Sanitari (#02171)
- ♦ Associazione Medica Europea (#07761)
- ♦ Associazione Mediterranea per l'Avifauna Marina (#16661)
- ♦ Associazione Mediterranea di Educazione degli Adulti (inactive)
- ♦ Associazione Mediterranea di Psichiatria (no recent information)
- ♦ Associazione Mondiale Allevatori Bovini della Razza Bruna (unconfirmed)
- ♦ Associazione Mondiale degli Amici dell' Infanzia (#02808)
- ♦ Associazione Mondiale Barbe e Baffi (#21226)
- ♦ Associazione Mondiale per la Protezione del Patrimonio Culturale, Tangibile ed Intangibile in Tempo di Conflitti Armati (#21176)
- ♦ Associazione Mondiale di Psicoanalisi (#21177)
- ♦ Associazione Mondiale di Psicoterapia (#21337)
- ♦ Associazione Mondiale per la Scuola Strumento di Pace (#21184)
- ♦ Associazione Mondo Giusto (internationally oriented national body)
- ♦ Associazione Montessori Internazionale (#02812)
- ♦ Associazione delle ONG Italiane / see Associazione delle organizzazioni italiane di cooperazione e solidarietà internazionale
- ♦ Associazione delle organizzazioni italiane di cooperazione e solidarietà internazionale (internationally oriented national body)
- ♦ Associazione delle Organizzazioni Nazionali delle Imprese di Pesca della CEE / see Association des organisations nationales d'entreprises de pêche de l'UE (#02841)
- ♦ Associazione delle Organizzazioni Nazionali delle Imprese di Pesca della UE (#02841)
- ♦ Associazione delle Organizzazioni Professionali del Commercio degli Zuccheri per i Paesi Membri della UE / see European Association of Sugar Traders (#06239)
- ♦ Associazione per la Pace, Roma (internationally oriented national body)

♦ Associazione Parlamentari di Origine Italiana nel Mondo 02992

Association MPs of Italian Origin in the World – Association Parlementaires d'Origine Italienne dans le Monde – Asociación Parlementarios de Origen Italiano en el Mundo – Associação Parlamentares de Origem Italiana no Mundo

Address not obtained.
URL: http://www.italorigin.it/

History 20 Nov 2000, Rome (Italy).
Members Members of Parliament from 43 countries:
Albania, Argentina, Australia, Austria, Belgium, Bolivia, Brazil, Cameroon, Canada, Cape Verde, Chile, Colombia, Costa Rica, Croatia, Cuba, Cyprus, Dominican Rep, Ecuador, France, Germany, Guatemala, Honduras, India, Ireland, Luxembourg, Malta, Mexico, Monaco, New Zealand, Panama, Paraguay, Peru, Poland, Romania, San Marino, Slovenia, South Africa, Sweden, Switzerland, UK, Uruguay, USA, Venezuela. [2020/AA2282/v/**E**]

- ♦ Associazione Patologie Autoimmuni Internazionale (internationally oriented national body)
- ♦ Associazione delle Popolazioni delle Montagne del Mondo (#21658)
- ♦ Associazione per i Popoli Minacciati Internazionale (#19654)
- ♦ Associazione dei Produttori Europei di Scaldacqua e Scaldabagni Instantanei a Gas e di Caldaie Murali a Gas (inactive)
- ♦ Associazione delle Regioni delle Alpi Orientali / see Alps-Adriatic-Alliance (#00747)
- ♦ Associazione delle Regioni Europee per i Prodotti di Origine (#02890)
- ♦ Associazione delle Regioni Frontaliere Europee / see Association of European Border Regions (#02499)
- ♦ Associazione Ricerca e Cooperazione / see Ricerca e Cooperazione
- ♦ Associazione Sanitaria Internazionale (internationally oriented national body)
- ♦ Associazione per gli Scambi Culturali e Scientifici Est-Ovest (no recent information)
- ♦ Associazione delle Società Farmaceutiche del Mediterraneo Latino / see Société de pharmacie de la Méditerranée latine (#19508)
- ♦ Associazione per la Solidarietà Internazionale in Asia (internationally oriented national body)
- ♦ Associazione Solidarietà Paesi Emergenti (internationally oriented national body)
- ♦ Associazione per lo Studio del Problema Mondiale dei Rifugiati (#02942)
- ♦ Associazione di Studi Sociali Latinoamericani (internationally oriented national body)
- ♦ Associazione A Sud – Ecologia e Cooperazione ONLUS (internationally oriented national body)
- ♦ Associazione per lo Sviluppo e la Coordinazione di Scambi Turistici Europei (inactive)
- ♦ Associazione Svizzera di politica estera (internationally oriented national body)
- ♦ Associazione Svizzera per lo Scambio di Persone nella Cooperazione Internazionale (internationally oriented national body)
- ♦ Associazione di tecnici per la solidarietà e cooperazione internazionale (internationally oriented national body)
- ♦ Associazione della Teoria della Gestalt e delle sue Applicazioni (internationally oriented national body)

- ♦ Associazione Pro Terra Sancta (internationally oriented national body)
- ♦ Associazione Universitaria Internazionale del Vino (unconfirmed)
- ♦ Associazione Volontari Iniziative di Sviluppo Economico e Sociale (internationally oriented national body)
- ♦ Associazione Volontari per il Servizio Internazionale / see AVSI Foundation
- ♦ Assomptionnistes – Augustins de l'Assomption (religious order)
- ♦ Assoziation Europa für Sozialen und Kulturellen Fortschritt (inactive)
- ♦ **ASSR** Asian Society of Stoma Rehabilitation (#01741)
- ♦ **ASSS** Africa Soil Science Society (#00520)
- ♦ **ASSSI** Asian Society for Solid State Ionics (#01739)
- ♦ ASST / see ASM International
- ♦ ASST – Arab School of Science and Technology (internationally oriented national body)
- ♦ ASSTC / see Naif Arab University for Security Sciences (#16929)
- ♦ **ASSUC** European Association of Sugar Traders (#06239)
- ♦ Assumptionists – Augustinians of the Assumption (religious order)
- ♦ Assunzionisti – Agostiniani dell'Assunzione (religious order)

♦ Assurance Services International (ASI) 02993

Managing Dir Friedrich-Ebert-Allee 69, 53113 Bonn, Germany. T. +492282272370. Fax +4922822723730. E-mail: asi-info@asi-assurance.org.
Asia-Pacific Menara MBMR (Floor 11 – Unit 5), Jalan Syed PUtra, Mid Valley City, 58000 Kuala Lumpur, Malaysia.
URL: http://www.asi-assurance.org/

History Founded 2006. Registered in accordance with German law. **Aims** Bring sustainability intentions to life through partnerships with leading sustainability standards and initiatives. **Structure** Supervisory Board of Directors; Accreditation Committee; Senior Management Team; Managing Director. **Activities** Certification/accreditation; training/education; research/documentation. **NGO Relations** Full member of: *ISEAL (#16026).* [2020/XM8971/**F**]

- ♦ ASSURRE – Association for the Sustainable Use and Recovery of Resources in Europe (inactive)
- ♦ ASSWA – Association of Schools of Social Work in Africa (inactive)
- ♦ Assyrian Universal Alliance (internationally oriented national body)
- ♦ ASTA / see American Society of Travel Advisors
- ♦ ASTA / see Arab Academy for Science, Technology and Maritime Transport (#00891)
- ♦ ASTA – Asian Society of Tumor Ablation (unconfirmed)
- ♦ **ASTA** Asian Software Testing Alliance (#01753)
- ♦ ASTA – Australasian Sleep Technologists Association (internationally oriented national body)
- ♦ **ASTA** Australasian Sports Technology Alliance (#03032)
- ♦ ASTAF – Asian Sepak Takraw Federation (inactive)
- ♦ ast Asia Conference on Developing Clinical Pharmacy Practice and Clinical Pharmacy Education / see Asian Conference on Clinical Pharmacy (#01399)
- ♦ **AST** Asian Society of Transplantation (#01745)
- ♦ **AST** Atlantic Salmon Trust (#03009)
- ♦ **ASTC** Asian Triathlon Confederation (#01769)
- ♦ ASTC – Association of Science-Technology Centers (internationally oriented national body)
- ♦ ASTE / see SME
- ♦ ASTERIA – Asociación Internacional de Mitocritica (internationally oriented national body)
- ♦ **ASTF** Africa Solidarity Trust Fund (#00522)
- ♦ **ASTF** Arab Science and Technology Foundation (#01039)
- ♦ **ASTF** Asian Soft Tennis Federation (#01752)
- ♦ ASTH – Australasian Society of Thrombosis and Haemostasis (internationally oriented national body)
- ♦ ASTINFO – Regional Network for the Exchange of Information and Experience in Science and Technology in Asia and the Pacific (inactive)
- ♦ ASTM – Action solidarité Tiers-monde (internationally oriented national body)
- ♦ ASTM / see Asia Pacific Travel Health Society (#02070)
- ♦ ASTM / see ASTM International (#02994)
- ♦ ASTMH – American Society of Tropical Medicine and Hygiene (internationally oriented national body)

♦ ASTM International 02994

Pres 100 Barr Harbor Dr, PO Box C700, Conshohocken PA 19428-2959, USA. T. +16108329721. E-mail: service@astm.org.
Contact Rue de la Loi 67, 1040 Brussels, Belgium.
URL: http://www.astm.org/

History 16 Jun 1898. Founded as the American Section of *International Association for Materials Testing (AIEM, inactive)*. Former names and other names: *American Society for Testing and Materials (ASTM)* – former (1902 to 2001). **Structure** Board of Directors; Committees. Offices in: Belgium; Canada; China; Mexico; USA (2). **Activities** Events/meetings. **Events** *International Conference on Additive Manufacturing (ICAM)* Orlando, FL (USA) 2022, *International Conference for Sustainable Construction Materials* Dubai (United Arab Emirates) 2019, *International Conference for Sustainable Construction Materials* Dubai (United Arab Emirates) 2018, *Gulf Building Code Conference* Dubai (United Arab Emirates) 2017, *International Conference for Sustainable Construction Materials* Dubai (United Arab Emirates) 2017. **Members** Individuals (30,000) in 150 countries and territories. Membership countries not specified. **NGO Relations** Member of (2): *International Property Measurement Standards Coalition (IPMSC, #14656)*; *ORCID (#17790).* [2022.05.17/XG3990/**D**]

- ♦ ASTMP – ASEAN Society of Tropical Medicine and Parasitology (unconfirmed)
- ♦ ASTO – Association de solidarité avec Timor oriental (internationally oriented national body)

♦ ASTP 02995

Chief Exec Stationsweg 28A, 2312 AV Leiden, Netherlands. T. +31717113511. E-mail: hq@astp4kt.eu.
Communications Manager address not obtained.
URL: http://www.astp4KT.eu/

History May 2013. Founded on merger of *Public Research Organizations Transfer Offices Network – Europe (ProTon Europe, inactive)* and *Association of European Science and Technology Transfer Professionals (ASTP, inactive)*. Known only by acronym since 2018. Former names and other names: *ASTP-Proton – Knowledge Transfer Europe* – former. Registration: No/ID: KVK 27185978, Netherlands. **Aims** Promote and professionalize *knowledge transfer* practice so as to enhance the impact of *public research* on society and the economy. **Structure** Board; Committees. **Languages** English. **Staff** 5.50 FTE, paid. **Activities** Events/meetings; training/education; networking/liaising; knowledge management/information dissemination. **Events** *Annual Conference* Lisbon (Portugal) 2022, *Annual Conference* Lisbon (Portugal) 2021, *Annual Conference* Dublin (Ireland) 2019, *Annual Conference* Liège (Belgium) 2018, *Annual Conference* Budapest (Hungary) 2017. **Publications** Annual Survey. **Members** Individuals (over 1,000) from over 50 countries, primarily in Europe. Membership countries not specified. [2021/XJ8689/**F**]

- ♦ ASTP – Association of European Science and Technology Transfer Professionals (inactive)
- ♦ ASTP-Proton – Knowledge Transfer Europe / see ASTP (#02995)

♦ ASTRA – Central and Eastern European Women's Network for Sexual and Reproductive Health and Rights (ASTRA Network) 02996

Contact Nowolipie 13/15, 01-150 Warsaw, Poland. T. +48226359395. Fax +48228878140. E-mail: federa@astra.org.pl – info@astra.org.pl.
URL: http://www.astra.org.pl/

History Dec 1999. **Aims** Promote women's sexual and reproductive health and rights in the region. **Activities** Events/meetings. **Publications** *ASTRA Bulletin* (12 a year) – online. Reports; guides.
Members Organizations (39) in 21 countries:
Albania, Armenia, Azerbaijan, Belarus, Bosnia-Herzegovina, Bulgaria, Croatia, Georgia, Hungary, Kazakhstan, Latvia, Lithuania, Moldova, North Macedonia, Poland, Romania, Russia, Slovakia, Tajikistan, Ukraine, Uzbekistan.
NGO Relations Member of: *International AIDS Women's Caucus (IAWC, #11603).* [2019.04.24/XF6778/**F**]

- ♦ Astraea International Fund For Sexual Minorities (internationally oriented national body)
- ♦ **ASTRA Network** ASTRA – Central and Eastern European Women's Network for Sexual and Reproductive Health and Rights (#02996)
- ♦ **ASTR** Asian Society of Thoracic Radiology (#01743)
- ♦ ASTRO – International Association of Trading Organizations for a Developing World (inactive)
- ♦ Astrological Federation of Southern Europe (no recent information)
- ♦ Astronomers Without Borders (internationally oriented national body)
- ♦ Astronomical Data Analysis Software & Systems (meeting series)

♦ Astronomical Society of the Pacific (ASP) 02997

Exec Dir 390 Ashton Ave, San Francisco CA 94112, USA. T. +14153371100. Fax +14153375205. E-mail: director@astrosociety.org.
URL: http://www.astrosociety.org/

History 7 Feb 1889, San Francisco CA (USA). **Aims** Improve public understanding of astronomy; encourage astronomical research; advance science education. **Structure** Annual Membership Meeting; Board of Directors; Executive Committee. **Languages** English. **Staff** 21.00 FTE, paid; 5.00 FTE, voluntary. **Finance** Members' dues. Other sources: grants; sales of publications; catalogue of Educational Products. **Activities** Events/meetings; awards/prizes/competitions. **Events** *Annual Meeting / Annual Scientific Meeting* Oakland, CA (USA) 2015, *Annual Meeting / Annual Scientific Meeting* Burlingame, CA (USA) 2014, *Annual Meeting / Annual Scientific Meeting* San Jose, CA (USA) 2013, *Annual Meeting / Annual Scientific Meeting* Tucson, AZ (USA) 2012, *Annual Meeting / Annual Scientific Meeting* Baltimore, MD (USA) 2011. **Publications** *Publications of the ASP* (12 a year); *Mercury* (6 a year); *The Universe in the Classroom* (4 a year) – online. Educational materials; information packets; conference proceedings; journals; newlsetter for teachers; mail order catalogue of educational materials. **Members** Regular; Technical; Institutional. Members (6,000) in over 75 countries. Membership countries not specified. [2015/XF0890/**F**]

- ♦ Astronomy Society of Spain and America (no recent information)
- ♦ ASTRONUM – International Conference on Numerical Modeling of Space Plasma Flows (meeting series)

♦ Astroparticle Physics European Consortium (APPEC) 02998

Gen Sec address not obtained. E-mail: appec@desy.de.
URL: http://www.appec.org/

History 2012, emanating from the *Astroparticle Physics European Coordination (APPEC)* committee, set up 2001. **Aims** Coordinate and fund national research efforts in Astroparticle Physics. **Structure** General Assembly; Joint Secretariat; Scientific Advisory Committee. **Languages** English. **Staff** 2.00 FTE, paid. **Finance** In-kind contributions. Annual budget: about euro 60,000. **Events** *International Meeting for Large Neutrino Infrastructures* Tsukuba (Japan) 2016.
Members Funding agencies; governmental institutions and institutes. Members in 16 countries:
Belgium, Czechia, Finland, France, Germany, Greece, Ireland, Italy, Netherlands, Portugal, Romania, Russia, Spain, Sweden, Switzerland, UK.
Included in the above, 1 organization listed in this Yearbook:
Joint Institute for Nuclear Research (JINR, #16134).
Observers (5) include the following 3 organizations listed in this Yearbook:
European Committee for Future Accelerators (ECFA, #06650); *European Organization for Astronomical Research in the Southern hemisphere (ESO, #08106)*; *European Organization for Nuclear Research (CERN, #08108).*
NGO Relations Instrumental in setting up (1): *European Centre for AstroParticle Theory (EuCAPT, #06470).* [2018.09.19/XM4931/**D**]

- ♦ **ASTSA** Asia Semiconductor Trading Support Association (#02095)
- ♦ **ASTSS** Australasian Society for Traumatic Stress Studies (#03029)
- ♦ ASTT – Australasian Society for Trenchless Technology (internationally oriented national body)
- ♦ ASUA / see PanAm Aquatics (#18077)
- ♦ ASU – Asian School of Urology (see: #20733)
- ♦ **ASUDAMA** Asociación Sudamericana de Atletas Máster (#02299)
- ♦ A Sud – Associazione A Sud – Ecologia e Cooperazione ONLUS (internationally oriented national body)
- ♦ ASUDAVE / see Asociación Sudamericana de Atletas Máster (#02299)
- ♦ ASUDEC (internationally oriented national body)
- ♦ ASULAC – Asociación de Suicidologia de Latinoamérica y el Caribe (unconfirmed)
- ♦ **ASUM** Australasian Society for Ultrasound in Medicine (#03030)
- ♦ **ASUNICAM** Association des universités et instituts catholiques d'Afrique et de Madagascar (#02416)
- ♦ Asuntoviranomaisten Kokous (meeting series)
- ♦ ASUPA – Asian Union of Pankration Athlima (inactive)
- ♦ ASUS – Asian Surgical Ultrasound Society (unconfirmed)
- ♦ ASV – Australasian Society of Victimology (internationally oriented national body)
- ♦ **ASVB** Asian Society for Vascular Biology (#01747)
- ♦ ASVSA / see Infectious Diseases Society of Southern Africa
- ♦ **ASVS** Asian Society for Vascular Surgery (#01748)
- ♦ **ASWA** African Sex Workers Alliance (#00455)
- ♦ ASW – Aktionsgemeinschaft Solidarische Welt (internationally oriented national body)
- ♦ ASWEA – Association for Social Work Education in Africa (inactive)
- ♦ Asylum Access (internationally oriented national body)

♦ Asymmetric Threats Contingency Alliance (ATCA) 02999

Contact c/o mi2g, The Philanthropia, 29th Floor, One Canada Square, London, E14 5DY, UK. T. +442077121782. Fax +442077121501. E-mail: intelligence.unit@mi2g.com.
URL: http://www.mi2g.com/

History 2001, as an elite global think tank. **Aims** Promote discussion and awareness of *warfare* threats facing today's society among decision makers; facilitate better understanding and cooperation between government and business in both mitigating and responding to all forms of *terrorist* attacks. **Members** Individuals (over 5,000) in over 120 countries. Membership countries not specified. [2015/XM3214/**F**]

- ♦ **ASZK** Australasian Society of Zoo Keeping (#03031)
- ♦ ASZWM / see Asian Society of Conservation Medicine (#01714)
- ♦ ATA / see Airlines for America
- ♦ ATA – African Technical Association (inactive)
- ♦ **ATA** Africa Travel Association (#00528)
- ♦ **ATA** Animal Transportation Association (#00844)
- ♦ ATA – Appropriate Technology Asia (internationally oriented national body)
- ♦ ATA / see Asia Theological Association (#02101)
- ♦ **ATA** Asia Theological Association (#02101)
- ♦ ATA – Association technique africaine (inactive)
- ♦ **ATA** Atlantic Treaty Association (#03010)
- ♦ ATA Convention – Customs Convention on the ATA Carnet for the Temporary Admission of Goods (1961 treaty)
- ♦ **ATAF** African Tax Administration Forum (#00479)

♦ ATAF – Association internationale de transporteurs aériens 03000

SG Tour Altaïs – CS90012, 76 rue du Capitaine Dreyfus, CEDEX, 93102 Montreuil, France. T. +33142891861. Fax +33142891857.
URL: http://www.ataf.fr/

History 9 Jan 1950, Paris (France). Former names and other names: *Association des transporteurs aériens de la Zone franc* – former; *Association des transporteurs aériens francophones – de l'Afrique, du Maghreb et de la France* – former; *Association des transporteurs aériens francophones (ATAF)* – former. **Aims** Study common problems related to air transport; ensure well-balanced development of member companies; establish a North-South dialogue, in particular with respect to Africa and the outer islands; promote cooperation between companies involved in long-haul flights and those providing internal connections. **Structure** General Assembly

(annual); Executive Committee; Permanent Committees (3); Special Committees (2); Secretariat in Paris (France). **Languages** French. **Staff** 6.00 FTE, paid. **Finance** Sources: members' dues. **Activities** Networking/liaising; training/education. **Events** *General Assembly* Trou-aux-Biches (Mauritius) 2022, *General Assembly* Nice (France) 2021, *General Assembly* Algiers (Algeria) 2019, *General Assembly* Porticcio (France) 2018, *General Assembly* Abidjan (Côte d'Ivoire) 2017.
Members Companies (21) covering 37 countries and territories:
Algeria, Burkina Faso, Corsica, France, Lebanon, Madagascar, Mali, Mauritius, Morocco, Seychelles, Tunisia.
Countries and territories entering into ATAF's competence zone (37):
Algeria, Andorra, Benin, Burkina Faso, Cameroon, Cape Verde, Central African Rep, Chad, Comoros, Congo Brazzaville, Côte d'Ivoire, Djibouti, France, Gabon, Guadeloupe, Guinea, Guinea-Bissau, Guyana, Lebanon, Madagascar, Mali, Martinique, Mauritania, Mayotte, Monaco, Morocco, New Caledonia, Niger, Polynesia Fr, Réunion, Senegal, Seychelles, St Pierre-Miquelon, Togo, Tunisia, Vanuatu, Wallis-Futuna. [2022.10.21/XD6353/**D**]

- ♦ ATAF / see ATAF – Association internationale de transporteurs aériens (#03000)
- ♦ **ATAF** Forum sur l'Administration Fiscale Africaine (#00479)
- ♦ **ATAF** Fórum Africano das Administrações Tributárias (#00479)
- ♦ **ATAG** Air Transport Action Group (#00614)
- ♦ ATA – Inter-American Association of Translators (inactive)
- ♦ **AT** Americas Triathlon (#00795)
- ♦ **AT** Antarctic Treaty (#00850)
- ♦ ATASP – Arbeitsstelle Transnationale Beziehungen, Aussen- und Sicherheitspolitik (internationally oriented national body)
- ♦ ATB / see Association for Tropical Biology and Conservation (#02963)
- ♦ **ATBC** Association for Tropical Biology and Conservation (#02963)
- ♦ ATBF / see Biotherapeutics Association of Australasia
- ♦ ATBF / see Asia Pacific Tchoukball Federation (#02063)
- ♦ **ATCA** African Tobacco Control Alliance (#00484)
- ♦ **ATCA** Asymmetric Threats Contingency Alliance (#02999)
- ♦ ATCA – Australasian Therapeutic Communities Association (internationally oriented national body)
- ♦ ATC – African Trade Center (internationally oriented national body)
- ♦ **ATC** Alpine Tourist Commission (#00745)
- ♦ **ATC** Aquarian Tabernacle Church (#00888)
- ♦ ATC – Arab Taekwondo Confederation (inactive)
- ♦ ATC – Asian Trade Centre (unconfirmed)
- ♦ **ATC** Asian Tribology Council (#01770)
- ♦ **ATCF** Adventure Travel Conservation Fund (#00134)
- ♦ **ATCPDE** ASEAN Training Center for Preventive Drug Education (#01241)
- ♦ ATC/PHC / see ASEAN Institute for Health Development (#01197)
- ♦ **ATCRI** Africa Tobacco Control Regional Initiative (#00524)
- ♦ **ATCSA** Association of Thoracic and Cardiovascular Surgeons of Asia (#02955)
- ♦ **ATC** Technical Committee of Petroleum Additive Manufacturers in Europe (#20115)
- ♦ ATCVSA / see Association of Thoracic and Cardiovascular Surgeons of Asia (#02955)
- ♦ ATDC – Asian TV Drama Conference (meeting series)
- ♦ **ATDF** Arab Towns Development Fund (#01058)
- ♦ **ATDL** Asociación Técnica de Diarios Latinoamericanos (#02301)
- ♦ ATEA – Association for Teacher Education in Africa (no recent information)
- ♦ **ATEE** Association for Teacher Education in Europe (#02949)
- ♦ **ATEI** Asociación de Televisión Educativa Iberoamericana (#02303)

♦ Ateista Tutmonda Esperanto-Organizo (ATEO) 03001

Sec 22 St Pancras Court, High Road, London, N2 9AE, UK. T. +442084442018 – +447943137891. E-mail: ateismo.bulteno@gmail.com.
Pres address not obtained.
URL: http://ateisto.org/

History 29 Jul 1987, Warsaw (Poland). Founded during the 72nd World Esperanto Congress. Entered into official working relations with the World Esperanto Association, 1990. Inactive during the 1990s and revived at 85th World Esperanto Congress, Tel Aviv (Israël), 2000. **Aims** Promote rational thinking within the Esperanto movement, and Esperanto among atheists. **Structure** Executive Body consisting of President, Vice-President, Secretary, Editor and Treasurer. **Languages** Esperanto. **Finance** Sources: members' dues. **Activities** Events/meetings. **Events** *Annual ATEO Assembly* 2021, *Associations Forum* 2021, *Meeting* 2021, *Annual ATEO Assembly* 2020, *Meeting* Lisbon (Portugal) 2018. **Publications** *Ateismo* (2 a year).
Members Individuals (mainly) and organizations in 28 countries:
Argentina, Australia, Austria, Belgium, Bosnia-Herzegovina, Canada, China, Costa Rica, Czechia, Denmark, France, Germany, Hungary, India, Israel, Italy, Luxembourg, Mexico, Netherlands, Poland, Portugal, Russia, Spain, Sweden, Switzerland, Uganda, UK, USA.
NGO Relations Member of (1): *Universal Esperanto Association (UEA, #20676).* [2022.03.04/XE1095/**E**]

- ♦ Atelier de développement autrichien (internationally oriented national body)
- ♦ Ateliers du cinéma européen / see ACE Producers (#00067)
- ♦ Ateliers sans frontières (internationally oriented national body)
- ♦ ATENE / see Association of Theological Seminaries and Institutes in the Middle East (#02954)
- ♦ **ATEO** Ateista Tutmonda Esperanto-Organizo (#03001)
- ♦ **ATESEA** Association for Theological Education in South East Asia (#02952)

♦ ATESEA Theological Union (ATU) 03002

Exec Dir Henry Luce III Library, Central Philippine Univ, Jaro, 5000 Iloilo ILI, Philippines. T. +63333213714.
URL: http://atesea.net/

History Founded 1966, as *South East Asia Graduate School of Theology (SEAGST)*, under the auspices of *Association for Theological Education in South East Asia (ATESEA, #02952).* Present name adopted, 2009. **Aims** Assist in the intellectual and spiritual development of *Asian* theologians; contribute to the emergence of a contextual and Asia oriented theology; further the building-up of competent seminary *teachers*; provide opportunities for exchange of graduate students and seminary teachers. **Structure** Structured on a cluster system with 6 Areas: Burma-Malaysia-Singapore-Thailand; Hong Kong; Indonesia; Korea Rep; Philippines; Taiwan (China). **Languages** Burmese, English, Indonesian, Mandarin Chinese, Thai. **Staff** Members of participating schools, all full time. **Finance** The participating schools contribute 60 % of the annual budget, with SEAGST providing the remaining funds. Budget (annual): US$ 100,000. **Activities** Training/education; events/meetings. **Events** *Annual Senate Meeting* Hong Kong (Hong Kong) 1997, *Annual senate meeting* Hong Kong (Hong Kong) 1997, *Annual senate meeting* 1996, *Annual Senate Meeting* Bali (Indonesia) 1996, *Annual senate meeting* Myanmar 1995. **Publications** *The Asia Journal of Theology* (2 a year). ATESEA occasional papers (usually 2 a year).
Members Participating schools (17) in 13 countries and territories:
Australia, Hong Kong, Indonesia, Malaysia, Myanmar, New Zealand, Pakistan, Philippines, Singapore, Sri Lanka, Taiwan, Thailand, Vietnam.
NGO Relations Cooperates with: *Programme for Theology and Cultures in Asia (PTCA, inactive)*; *World Conference of Associations of Theological Institutions (WOCATI, #21296)*; *World Council of Churches (WCC, #21320).* [2016/XF0020/**F**]

- ♦ ATFA – Association of Trade and Forfaiting in the Americas (internationally oriented national body)
- ♦ ATF – African Technology Foundation (internationally oriented national body)
- ♦ **ATF** African Theological Fellowship (#00483)
- ♦ **ATF** Arab Thought Forum (#01055)
- ♦ **ATF** Arab Thought Foundation (#01056)
- ♦ **ATF** Asian Tennis Federation (#01767)
- ♦ ATF / see Asia-Pacific Tax Forum (#02061)
- ♦ **ATF** Asia Taekwondo Federation (#02100)
- ♦ ATFCA – Asian Track and Field Coaches Association (inactive)
- ♦ ATF-CLTH – Asian Trade Federation of Clothing, Leather, Textile and Handloom Workers (inactive)
- ♦ ATF-MIG – Asian Trade Federation for the Mixed Industries Group (no recent information)
- ♦ **ATFP** Arab Trade Financing Programme (#01060)
- ♦ **ATFS** Association of Track and Field Statisticians (#02957)
- ♦ ATF-TW – Asian Trade Federation of Transport Workers, Dhaka (inactive)
- ♦ **ATGENDER** The European Association for Gender Research, Education and Documentation (#06052)
- ♦ Atheist Alliance / see Atheist Alliance International (#03003)

♦ Atheist Alliance International (AAI) 03003

Pres 216 Mt Hermon Rd, Ste 178, Scotts Valley CA 95066, USA. E-mail: info@atheistalliance.org.
URL: http://www.atheistalliance.org/

History 1991, USA. Restructured, 2011, when US-focused operations, known as Atheist Alliance of America, ceded from the international entity. **Aims** Confront and challenge *religious* discrimination and privilege; support atheist individuals and establish and expand atheist organizations worldwide. **Structure** Board of Directors, comprising President, Vice-President, Treasurer, Secretary, Membership Director and members-at-large. **Languages** English, Spanish. **Staff** 1.00 FTE, paid. Voluntary. **Finance** Members' dues. Other sources: donations; merchandise sales; proceeds from conventions. **Activities** Training/education; advocacy/lobbying/activism; events/meetings; networking/liaising. **Events** *Global Convention* Boston, MA (USA) 2013, *European Convention* Cologne (Germany) 2012, *Convention* Melbourne, VIC (Australia) 2012, *European convention / Global Convention* Dublin (Ireland) 2011, *Annual Convention* Montréal, QC (Canada) 2010. **Publications** *Secular World* (4 a year) – magazine. **Members** Affiliate; Associate; Individual. Members in about 40 countries. Membership countries not specified. **Consultative Status** Consultative status granted from: *ECOSOC (#05331)* (Special); *Council of Europe (CE, #04881)* (Participatory Status). **IGO Relations** *African Union (AU, #00488)*; *European Commission (EC, #06633).* **NGO Relations** Working relationships with: *Humanists International (#10972)*; *International League of Non-Religious and Atheists (ILNA, #14020).* [2022/XM1919/**F**]

- ♦ ATHENA – Advancing gender equity and human rights in the global HIV response / see ATHENA Network (#03004)
- ♦ **ATHENA** ATHENA Network (#03004)
- ♦ 'Athenaeum' International Cultural Center (internationally oriented national body)
- ♦ Athena Intelligence (internationally oriented national body)

♦ ATHENA Network (ATHENA) 03004

Contact address not obtained. E-mail: comms.athena@gmail.com.
Main Website: https://networkathena.org/

History 2006. Former names and other names: *ATHENA – Advancing gender equity and human rights in the global HIV response* – full title. **Aims** Work at the intersection of SRHR, HIV, gender equity and human rights, and to bring feminist and youth power into that work. **Structure** Board of Directors. **Languages** English. **Staff** 8.00 FTE, paid. **Activities** Advocacy/lobbying/activism. Eastern and Southern Africa. **Publications** Reports; toolkits; articles.
Members Founding members in 8 countries:
Argentina, Bolivia, Canada, Netherlands, South Africa, Spain, Thailand, USA.
Included in the above, 4 organizations listed in this Yearbook:
Center for Health and Gender Equity (CHANGE); *Human Rights Watch (HRW, #10990)*; *International AIDS Women's Caucus (IAWC, #11603)*; *International Community of Women Living with HIV/AIDS (ICW, #12826).* [2022.03.09/XM4925/y/**F**]

- ♦ Athens Convention Relating to the Carriage of Passengers and Their Luggage by Sea (1974 treaty)
- ♦ ATHG / see Alcohol and Drugs History Society (#00623)
- ♦ ATHGO International – Alliance Toward Harnessing Global Opportunities Corporation (internationally oriented national body)

♦ Athletes in Action International (AIA) 03005

Pres 651 Taylor Dr, Xenia OH 45385, USA. T. +19373521000. E-mail: becky.arnett@athletesinaction.org – info@athletesinaction.org.
International Dir address not obtained.
URL: http://www.athletesinaction.org/

History Founded 1966, USA, by Dave Hannah, within *Campus Crusade for Christ International (CCCI).* **Aims** Assist athletes in their relationship with *Christ*; encourage them to use their influence to share their *faith* with others. **Structure** Board of Trustees. Headquarters in Xenia OH (USA). Part of CCCI; international staff report to CCCI country directors. **Languages** English, German, Spanish. **Finance** Contributions from churches, businesses and individuals. **Activities** Sporting activities; events/meetings; religious activities. **Members** Membership covers 66 countries. Membership countries not specified. [2018.09.19/XF5033/**F**]

- ♦ Athletes United for Peace (internationally oriented national body)

♦ Athletic Association of the Small States of Europe (AASSE) 03006

Pres/Treas Gibraltar Amateur Athletic Assn, 6E Riesling, Vineyards, PO Box 483, Gibraltar, GX11 1AA, Gibraltar. T. +35054955000.
Hon Sec Féd Monégasque d'Athlétisme, Stade Louis II – 4ème étage, 7 av des Castelans, 98000 Monte Carlo, Monaco. T. +33607933328.

History 1994. Following activities begun in 1989. **Aims** Promote athletics among the small federations in Europe. **Structure** Committee (meets annually); Council. **Languages** English, French. **Staff** None. **Finance** Members' dues.
Members National federations in 10 countries:
Andorra, Cyprus, Gibraltar, Iceland, Liechtenstein, Luxembourg, Malta, Monaco, Montenegro, San Marino. [2022/XD7804/**D**]

- ♦ Athletic Confederation of the Central American Isthmus (#04441)
- ♦ ATHS / see World Association for Triple Helix and Future Strategy Studies
- ♦ ATHS – Australasian TeleHealth Society (internationally oriented national body)
- ♦ ATIA / see African Trade Insurance Agency (#00485)
- ♦ **ATI** African Trade Insurance Agency (#00485)
- ♦ **ATI** Alexander Technique International (#00625)
- ♦ ATI – Arab Theatre Institute (internationally oriented national body)
- ♦ **ATI** Asociación Transpersonal Iberoamericana (#02304)
- ♦ **ATIBT** Association technique internationale des bois tropicaux (#15668)
- ♦ **ATIC** Adventure Therapy International Committee (#00133)
- ♦ **ATIEA** Association of Theological Institutions of Eastern Africa (#02953)
- ♦ ATIE – Asian Telecom and Information Exchange Forum (unconfirmed)
- ♦ **ATIEL** Association technique de l'industrie européenne des lubrifiants (#02950)
- ♦ ATIGA – ASEAN Trade in Goods Agreement (2009 treaty)
- ♦ **ATIME** Association of Theological Seminaries and Institutes in the Middle East (#02954)
- ♦ ATIPAT – Asociación Tecnologia Iberoamericana de Pinturas, Adhesivos y Tintas (unconfirmed)
- ♦ **ATLAFCO** Ministerial Conference on Fisheries Cooperation Among African States Bordering the Atlantic Ocean (#16816)

♦ Atlantic Arc Commission 03007

Commission de l'Arc Atlantique – Comisión Arco Atlantico – Atlantikbogen-Kommission – Comissão Arco Atlântico – Commissione dell'Arco Atlantico – Epitropi tu Atlantiku Tosu
Exec Sec Rond-point Schuman 14, 1040 Brussels, Belgium. T. +3226121705.
Rennes Office 6 rue Saint-Martin, 35700 Rennes, France. T. +33299354050. Fax +33299350919. E-mail: catherine.petiau@crpm.org.
URL: http://cpmr-atlantic.org/

History 13 Oct 1989, Faro (Portugal), within the framework of *Conference of Peripheral Maritime Regions of Europe (CPMR, #04638).* First meeting: Apr 1990. **Aims** Define a balanced and sustainable development strategy to reduce the effects of peripherality and develop their assets and complementarities, through inter-regional cooperation, especially with regard to the maritime domain and, more generally, all aspects of regional development. **Structure** Bureau; Executive Secretariat; National Coordinators. Working Groups.

Staff 3.00 FTE, paid. **Finance** Sources include: contribution from the regions; grant from *Conference of Peripheral Maritime Regions of Europe (CPMR, #04638)*; payment for running costs for EU programmes. **Activities** Politics/policy/regulatory; projects/programmes; advocacy/lobbying/activism. **Events** *General Assembly* Pamplona (Spain) 2016, *General Assembly* Bilbao (Spain) 2015, *General Assembly* Bordeaux (France) 2014, *Annual General Assembly* Porto (Portugal) 2013, *Annual General Assembly* Spain 2009.
Members Regions (17) in 5 countries:
France, Ireland, Portugal, Spain, UK. [2018/XK0374/**E**]

♦ Atlantic Centre for Atomistic Modelling (internationally oriented national body)
♦ Atlantic Charter (1941 treaty)

♦ Atlantic Cities 03008
Villes Atlantiques – Ciudades Atlanticas – Cidades Atlânticas
SG 12 rue du Nivernais, 35000 Rennes, France. T. +33223252089. E-mail: info@atlanticcities.eu – headquarters@atlanticcities.eu.
URL: http://www.atlanticcities.eu/
History 7 Jul 2000, Rennes (France). Former names and other names: *Conference of the Atlantic Arc Cities (CAAC)* – former (7 Jul 2000); *Conférence des Villes de l'Arc Atlantique (CVAA)* – former (7 Jul 2000); *Conferencia de las Ciudades del Arco Atlantico (CCAA)* – former (7 Jul 2000); *Conferência das Cidades do Arco Atlântico (CCAA)* – former (7 Jul 2000). Registration: France. **Aims** Promote the role of cities in Europe and highlight the specificity of the Atlantic Arc; represent interests of European Atlantic Arc cities before European institutions; coordinate members at political level; create technical projects between these cities. **Structure** General Assembly (annual); Executive Bureau; Commissions (3); General Secretariat headed by Secretary General. **Languages** English, French, Portuguese, Spanish. **Staff** 3.00 FTE, paid. **Finance** Members' dues. EU project funding. **Activities** Awareness raising; events/meetings; networking/liaising; training/education; knowledge management/information dissemination. **Events** *General Assembly* Dublin (Ireland) 2015, *General Assembly* Brest (France) 2012, *General Assembly* Niort (France) 2011. **Publications** *Atlantic Cities Newsletter* (6 a year). Articles; policy positions; strategy documents.
Members Full (cities with at least 50,000 inhabitants, situated in Atlantic Arc); Associate (cities with less than 50,000 inhabitants, situated in Atlantic Arc); Observer (institutions located in Atlantic cities). Cities, local organizations and city networks in 5 countries:
France, Ireland, Portugal, Spain, UK.
NGO Relations Member of: *Conference of European Cross-border and Interregional Cities Network (CECICN, #04595)*. [2022/XD9417/**D**]

♦ Atlantic Community Development Group for Latin America (inactive)
♦ Atlantic Council (internationally oriented national body)
♦ Atlantic Council for International Cooperation (internationally oriented national body)
♦ Atlantic Council of the United States / see Atlantic Council
♦ Atlantic Economic Society / see International Atlantic Economic Society (#12291)
♦ Atlantic Euro Mediterranean Academy of Medical Science (internationally oriented national body)
♦ Atlantic Federation of African Press Agencies (#09462)
♦ Atlantic Gas Research Exchange (inactive)
♦ Atlantic Initiative (internationally oriented national body)
♦ Atlantic Institute (internationally oriented national body)
♦ Atlantic Philanthropies (internationally oriented national body)
♦ Atlantic Salmon Federation (internationally oriented national body)
♦ Atlantic Salmon Research Trust / see Atlantic Salmon Trust (#03009)

♦ Atlantic Salmon Trust (AST) 03009
Contact Battleby House, Redgorton, Perth, PH1 3EW, UK. T. +441738827200. E-mail: administrator@atlanticsalmontrust.org.
URL: http://www.atlanticsalmontrust.org/
History 1967. Former names and other names: *Atlantic Salmon Research Trust* – former. Registration: Charity Commission, No/ID: 252742, England and Wales; Scottish Charity Regulator, No/ID: SC037902, Start date: 6 Mar 2007, Scotland. **Aims** Work for *conservation* and *restoration* of wild salmon and sea trout stocks to a level which allows sustainable exploitation; promote enlightened fishery management at local, national and international level; act as focal point for research into, and collection and dissemination of, new knowledge about Atlantic salmon and *sea trout*. **Structure** Board of Directors; Honorary Scientific Advisory Panel. **Languages** English. **Staff** 2.50 FTE, paid. **Finance** Sources: contributions. Other sources: annual online auction; endowment funds. **Activities** Events/meetings; financial and/or material support; guidance/assistance/consulting; networking/liaising. **Events** *Conference on Salmon Stocking / Symposium* Glasgow (UK) 2013, *Ocean silver conference* London (UK) 2011, *Symposium* UK 2011, *Symposium* Southampton (UK) 2007, *Salmon at the edge* Edinburgh (UK) 2002. **Publications** *Blue Books* – reports covering AST's scientific work, national overviews and examinations of particular aspects and problems. **Members** Elected (58) and supporters worldwide. Membership countries not specified. **IGO Relations** Observer status with (1): *International Council for the Exploration of the Sea (ICES, #13021)*. [2022/XF3786/v/**F**]

♦ Atlantic States Legal Foundation (internationally oriented national body)

♦ Atlantic Treaty Association (ATA) 03010
Association du Traité Atlantique
Secretariat Rue des Petits Carmes 20, 1000 Brussels, Belgium. T. +3225023160. E-mail: program.assistant@atahq.org.
URL: http://www.atahq.org/
History Founded 18 Jun 1954, The Hague (Netherlands), replacing *International Atlantic Committee (inactive)*, set up 1952, Oxford (UK). Registered office in Brussels (Belgium). Serves as the umbrella organization for the 36 Atlantic Councils of the NATO Alliance, both Allied and Partner countries. Registered in accordance with Belgian law, 2006. **Aims** Educate and inform the public regarding NATO's missions and responsibilities; engage the successor generation in promoting the importance of the Transatlantic security relationship, while simultaneously helping to shape its future; develop and maintain a strong network of responsible future political leaders; promote solidarity of the populations of the North Atlantic area, and of those whose governments have signed NATO PfP or Mediterranean Dialogue Agreements, and/or those who are directly concerned with the affairs of Euro-Atlantic security; support development of civil society in the Black Sea area, the Transcaucasus, and Central Asia; conduct research into the role of NATO and its expansion to the countries of Central Europe and the former Soviet Union; pursue dialogues with countries bordering the Mediterranean and in the Middle East which work in cooperation with the Alliance; deepen cooperation between the ATA, its Member Associations, the governments of its Member Associations, NATO, the NATO Parliamentary Assembly and the European Union. **Structure** General Assembly (annual, in Fall); Council (meets annually, in Spring); Bureau; Committee of Patrons; Chapters (36). **Languages** English, French. **Staff** 8.00 FTE, paid. **Finance** Members' contributions; grants; donations. **Activities** Events/meetings; politics/policy/regulatory; training/education. **Events** *Annual General Assembly* Madrid (Spain) 2022, *Annual General Assembly* Brussels (Belgium) 2019, *Annual General Assembly* Bucharest (Romania) 2018, *Annual General Assembly* Brussels (Belgium) 2017, *Meeting on Cooperation on Cyber-Security* Brussels (Belgium) 2017. **Publications** *Atlantic Voices* (12 a year). Bilateral briefs; commentaries; newsletters; policy briefs.
Members Full; Associate; Observer: national organizations in 24 countries:
Belgium, Bulgaria, Canada, Czechia, Denmark, Estonia, Germany, Greece, Hungary, Iceland, Italy, Latvia, Lithuania, Luxembourg, Netherlands, Norway, Portugal, Romania, Slovakia, Slovenia, Spain, Türkiye, UK, USA.
Associate members in 12 countries:
Albania, Armenia, Austria, Azerbaijan, Croatia, Finland, Georgia, Montenegro, North Macedonia, Russia, Serbia, Ukraine.
Also member: one organization listed in this Yearbook:
Youth Atlantic Treaty Association (YATA, #22006). [2020/XC0179/**F**]

♦ Atlantikbogen-Kommission (#03007)
♦ Atlantische Commissie (internationally oriented national body)
♦ Atlantische Initiative (internationally oriented national body)
♦ Atlantische Initiative (internationally oriented national body)
♦ Atlantsammenslutningen (internationally oriented national body)
♦ Atlantshafssattmalinn (1949 treaty)
♦ ATLAS – African Transformative Leapfrogging Advisory Services (unconfirmed)
♦ ATLAS – Agrupación de Trabajadores Latinoamericanos Sindicalistas (inactive)
♦ Atlas Alliance (internationally oriented national body)
♦ Atlas-alliansen (internationally oriented national body)
♦ ATLAS – Association of Teachers of Latin American Studies (internationally oriented national body)
♦ ATLAS / see Association for Tourism and Leisure Education and Research (#02956)
♦ **ATLAS** Association for Tourism and Leisure Education and Research (#02956)
♦ Atlas Corps / see Atlas Service Corps
♦ Atlas Economic Research Foundation (internationally oriented national body)
♦ Atlas Florae Europaeae (#04268)
♦ Atlas Network – Atlas Economic Research Foundation (internationally oriented national body)
♦ Atlas Service Corps (internationally oriented national body)
♦ **ATL** Association for Tropical Lepidoptera (#02964)
♦ ATLCOM – Atlantische Commissie (internationally oriented national body)
♦ ATM / see Association for Management Education and Development
♦ ATM – Alternative Trade Mandate Alliance (unconfirmed)
♦ **ATM** Amici Thomae Mori (#00799)
♦ ATM – Association Aide au Tiers-Monde (internationally oriented national body)
♦ ATM – Association des trois mondes (internationally oriented national body)
♦ ATMCS – Algebraic Topology: Methods, Computation, and Science (meeting series)
♦ **ATMF** Arab Transfusion Medicine Forum (#01061)
♦ ATMIA – ATM Industry Association (internationally oriented national body)
♦ ATM Industry Association (internationally oriented national body)
♦ AtmoDust – International Network of AtmoDust Scientists (unconfirmed)
♦ ATMOS – Symposium on Algorithmic Approaches for Transportation Modeling, Optimization, and Systems (meeting series)
♦ ATM Owners Association / see ATM Industry Association
♦ ATM Parrainages / see Association Aide au Tiers-Monde
♦ **ATN** Africa Trade Network (#00526)
♦ **ATN-APTS** Arab Translators Network – Arab Professional Translators Society (#01062)
♦ **ATN** Asia Trails Network (#02102)
♦ **ATNESA** Animal Traction Network for Eastern and Southern Africa (#00843)
♦ ATNUTO – Administration transitoire des Nations Unies au Timor oriental (inactive)
♦ ATO – African Timber Organization (no recent information)
♦ **ATO** Arab Tourism Organization (#01057)
♦ **ATO** Arab Towns Organization (#01059)
♦ ATOI – Alliance touristique de l'Océan Indien (inactive)
♦ Atomes et Molécules Par Études Radio-Électriques / see Groupement AMPERE (#10755)
♦ ATP / see Gesellschaft für Tropenpädiatrie und Internationale Kindergesundheit
♦ ATP1A3 In Disease – Annual Symposium on ATP1A3 in Disease (meeting series)
♦ ATP – Accord relatif aux transports internationaux de denrées périssables et aux engins spéciaux à utiliser pour ces transports (1970 treaty)
♦ ATP – Agreement on the International Carriage of Perishable Foodstuffs and on the Special Equipment to be Used for Such Carriage (1970 treaty)
♦ ATP – Association of Test Publishers (unconfirmed)
♦ **ATP** Association for Transpersonal Psychology (#02960)
♦ ATP / see ATP World Tour (#03011)
♦ ATPC – Asian Thermophysical Properties Conference (meeting series)
♦ ATPC – Association of Tin Producing Countries (inactive)
♦ ATPF – Asian Trade Promotion Forum (meeting series)
♦ **ATPS** African Technology Policy Studies Network (#00481)
♦ ATP Tour / see ATP World Tour (#03011)

♦ ATP World Tour 03011
Chairman ATP London, Palliser House, Palliser Road, London, W14 9EB, UK. T. +442073817890. Fax +442073817895.
European Office Monte Carlo Sun, 74 bd d'Italie, 98000 Monte Carlo, Monaco. T. +37797970404. Fax +37797970400.
International Office Suite 208, 46a Macleay Street, Potts Point, Sydney NSW 2011, Australia. T. +61293367000. Fax +61283541945.
URL: http://www.atpworldtour.com/
History 1990, as *Association of Tennis Professionals (ATP)* – *Association des joueurs de tennis professionnels*. Previously also referred to as *International Professional Tennis Players Association* and *ATP Tour*. **Aims** As the governing body for *men's professional tennis*: manage and promote the game on a global scale; help the partnership of *players* and *tournaments* maximize its growth potential. **Structure** Board of Directors, presided over by Chief Executive Officer and including 3 representatives from the Player Council (which consists of 10 members elected by the Tour players) and 3 from the Tournament Council (which consists of 12 members elected by the tournament directors). **Finance** Main sources: television; marketing; sponsorship. Total revenues 2004: US$ 40.2 million, of which expenses accounted for 35 percent, the rest being distributed to players, tournaments and charities. **Activities** Conducts sponsored tournaments in many countries and world championships; grants and revokes tournament memberships; approves sale and transfer of tournaments; negotiates television, sponsorship and licensing contracts; calculates official standard rankings; enforces code of conduct; hires and trains supervisors and chair umpires; supports players on-site with Tour managers and trainers; services the media; administers charities. *'ATP Tour University'* prepares young players for life on the circuit. **Publications** *ATP Players' Weekly*; *DEUCE Magazine* – online. *ATP Insider*, *Barclays ATP World Tour Finals Media Guide*; *Official ATP World Tour Media Guide*. Press releases; promotions brochures. **Members** Players and tournaments. Membership countries not specified. **NGO Relations** Member of: *Sports Rights Owners Coalition (SROC, #19929)*. Cooperates with: *European Tennis Federation (#08898)*. [2018/XD6580/**F**]

♦ **ATRA** Adventure Tourism Research Association (internationally oriented national body)
♦ **ATRA** ASEAN Tourism Research Association (#01239)
♦ **ATR** Association for Tree-Ring Research (#02962)
♦ Atria – Institute for Gender Equality and Women's History (internationally oriented national body)
♦ **ATRIP** International Association for the Advancement of Teaching and Research in Intellectual Property (#11690)
♦ Atrium Society (internationally oriented national body)
♦ **ATRN** African Tax Research Network (#00480)
♦ **ATRS** Air Transport Research Society (#00615)
♦ ATSA – Association for the Treatment of Sexual Abusers (internationally oriented national body)
♦ **ATSAF** – Arbeitsgemeinschaft Tropische und Subtropische Agrarforschung (internationally oriented national body)
♦ ATS – American Thoracic Society (internationally oriented national body)
♦ ATS – ASEAN Thalassaemia Society (no recent information)
♦ ATS – Asian Theological Seminary, Metro Manila (internationally oriented national body)
♦ ATS – Associazione Pro Terra Sancta (internationally oriented national body)
♦ ATS – Australasian Trauma Society (internationally oriented national body)
♦ ATS – Australasian Tunnelling Society (internationally oriented national body)
♦ ATSC – Asian Thoracic Surgical Club (unconfirmed)
♦ **ATSC** Association transnationale de service civique (#02959)
♦ ATSE Crawford Fund / see Crawford Fund for International Agricultural Research
♦ ATSGA – Asian Traditional Sports and Games Association (unconfirmed)
♦ **ATSS** Asian Thermal Spray Society (#01768)
♦ **ATSS** Association of Traumatic Stress Specialists (#02961)

- ♦ ATSS – Australasian Tuberous Sclerosis Society (internationally oriented national body)
- ♦ **ATTA** Adventure Travel Trade Association (#00135)
- ♦ ATTA / see Asia Pacific Histocompatibility and Immunogenetics Association (#01927)
- ♦ **ATTAC** Association pour une taxation des transactions financières pour l'aide aux citoyens (#02947)
- ♦ Attack Avoidable Maternal Mortality/Morbidity (internationally oriented national body)
- ♦ ATT – Arms Trade Treaty (2013 treaty)
- ♦ ATTD – International Conference on Advanced Technologies and Treatments for Diabetes (meeting series)
- ♦ ATTEN – ASEAN Tourism Training and Education Network (no recent information)
- ♦ ATTF – Arab Table Tennis Federation (inactive)
- ♦ ATTO – Asia-Pacific Tropical Timber Organization (inactive)

♦ ATTP 03012

Contact address not obtained. E-mail: office@attp.info.
URL: http://www.attp.info/

History Founded 2010, as *Alliance of Technology Transfer Professionals (ATTP)*. Registered in accordance with Scottish law. **Aims** Unify and educate technology transfer professionals around the world to successfully move technology from research to the marketplace. **Structure** Board of Directors. **Finance** Sources: members' dues. **Activities** Training/education.
Members Organizations (14). National organizations in 12 countries:
Australia, China, Germany, India, Italy, Japan, Malaysia, Spain, Sweden, Türkiye, UK, USA.
Included in the above, 3 organizations listed in this Yearbook:
Association of University Technology Managers (AUTM); *International Strategic Technology Alliance (ISTA)*; *Knowledge Commercialisation Australasia (KCA)*.
Regional organizations (2):
ASTP (#02995); *Southern African Research and Innovation Management Association (SARIMA)*.
[2020.01.24/XJ6835/y/**C**]

- ♦ **ATTU** Asian Table Tennis Union (#01765)
- ♦ **ATU** African Telecommunications Union (#00482)
- ♦ **ATU** African Triathlon Union (#00487)
- ♦ ATU – Arab Telecommunication Union (inactive)
- ♦ ATU / see Arab Tourism Organization (#01057)
- ♦ **ATU** Asian Taekwondo Union (#01766)
- ♦ **ATU** ATESEA Theological Union (#03002)
- ♦ ATUBS – Association of Technical Universities of Baltic States (no recent information)
- ♦ ATUC – African Trade Union Confederation (inactive)
- ♦ **ATUC** ASEAN Trade Union Council (#01240)
- ♦ **ATVEA** All Terrain Vehicle Industry European Association (#00739)
- ♦ **'at'WAS** International Organization for Information Integration and Web-Based Applications and Services (#14449)
- ♦ ATWE – Association of Third World Economists (inactive)
- ♦ **ATypI** Association typographique internationale (#02965)
- ♦ AU / see Africa Unite
- ♦ **AUA** Africa Union of Architects (#00529)
- ♦ **AUA** Association des Universités Africaines (#02361)
- ♦ **AUA** Association des universités arabes (#02374)
- ♦ AUA – Assyrian Universal Alliance (internationally oriented national body)
- ♦ **AU** African Union (#00488)
- ♦ AU – Africa Unite (internationally oriented national body)
- ♦ **AUAI** Association for Uncertainty in Artificial Intelligence (#02966)
- ♦ AUAIR – Alliance universelle pour l'amitié universelle par la religion (inactive)
- ♦ **AUALCPI** Asociación de Universidades de América Latina y el Caribe para la Integración (#02305)
- ♦ **AU** Alliance universelle (#20671)
- ♦ AU – Americans for UNESCO (internationally oriented national body)
- ♦ **AUAP** Association of Universities of Asia and the Pacific (#02968)
- ♦ **AUASS** Arab Union for Astronomy and Space Sciences (#01063)
- ♦ **AUB** African Union of Broadcasting (#00490)
- ♦ AUBE – International Conference on Automatic Fire Detection (meeting series)
- ♦ Aubert League – International Entente Against the Third International (inactive)
- ♦ **AUCBM** Arab Union for Cement and Building Materials (#01065)
- ♦ **AUCD** African University for Cooperative Development (#00494)
- ♦ AUCEN – Association universitaire canadienne d'études nordiques (internationally oriented national body)
- ♦ **AU/CIEFFA** African Union International Centre for Girls' and Women's Education in Africa (#03752)
- ♦ AUCM – Association pour l'Unification du Christianisme Mondial (religious order)
- ♦ AU Commission on Refugees (inactive)
- ♦ AUCOS – Association pour l'utilisation du coke en Scandinavie (inactive)
- ♦ AUCSO – Association of University Chief Security Officers (internationally oriented national body)
- ♦ AUDACE – Association of Users and Distributors of AgroChemicals in Europe (no recent information)
- ♦ **AUDEM** Alliance of Universities for Democracy (#00725)
- ♦ **AUDI** Arab Urban Development Institute (#01071)

♦ Audiences Europe Network (AEN) 03013

Address not obtained.
URL: http://www.audienceseurope.net/

History Apr 2004. **Structure** Board.
Members Cultural professionals in 9 countries:
Belgium, Czechia, France, Germany, Ireland, Italy, Netherlands, Spain, UK.
NGO Relations Cooperates with *International Festivals and Events Association Europe (IFEA-E, #13591)*. *European Festivals Association (EFA, #07242)* is a member. [2014/XJ4449/**F**]

♦ Audio Engineering Society (AES) 03014

Headquarters 551 Fifth Ave, Ste 1225, New York NY 10176, USA. T. +12126618528. Fax +12126820477. E-mail: hq@aes.org.
URL: http://www.aes.org/

History 1948, New York NY (USA). Commenced operating internationally, 1970. **Structure** National/local sections grouped in 8 Regions: USA/Canada (3 – Eastern, Central and Western); Europe (3 – Northern, Central, Southern); Latin America; 'International' (other continents). Based in New York NY (USA). **Activities** Organizes: annual conference; biannual conventions, alternately in North America and Europe; technical meetings, exhibitions of professional equipment. **Events** *Convention* Vienna (Austria) 2020, *Convention* New York, NY (USA) 2019, *International Conference on Audio Forensics* Porto (Portugal) 2019, *International Conference on Headphone Technology* San Francisco, CA (USA) 2019, *International Conference on Immersive and Interactive Audio* York (UK) 2019. **Publications** *Journal of the Audio Engineering Society*.
Members Engineers, scientists, executives, educators and students. Basically a North American organization, but with sections (73) and student sections (41) in a total of in 44 countries and territories:
Argentina, Australia, Austria, Belarus, Belgium, Brazil, Bulgaria, Canada, Chile, Colombia, Croatia, Czechia, Denmark, Finland, France, Germany, Greece, Hong Kong, Hungary, India, Israel, Italy, Japan, Korea Rep, Lithuania, Mexico, Netherlands, Norway, Philippines, Poland, Romania, Russia, Serbia, Singapore, Slovakia, Slovenia, Spain, Sweden, Switzerland, UK, Ukraine, Uruguay, USA, Venezuela.
Included in the above, one university listed in this Yearbook:
Baltic D F Ustinov Technical University (no recent information).
NGO Relations Affiliate Member of: *International Commission for Acoustics (ICA, #12658)*.
[2020/XF4621/**F**]

- ♦ Audio Scripture Ministries (internationally oriented national body)

♦ Audiovisual Anti-Piracy Alliance (AAPA) 03015

Exec Vice Pres c/o Mark Garrett Tax and Accountancy Ltd, Box House, Bath Road, Corsham, SN13 8AA, UK. E-mail: contact@aapa.eu.
URL: http://www.aapa.eu/

History Set up with the original title *Association européenne pour la protection des oeuvres et services cryptés (AEPOC) – European Association for the Protection of Encrypted Works and Services*. Reorganized under current title 2012. Registered in accordance with UK law. **Aims** Enable the fight against piracy where this involves development, promotion, distribution, application or use of technologies resulting in unauthorized use of protected audiovisual content, by coordinating intelligence and action supported by effective legislation and its implementation. **Structure** General Meeting (annual); Council; Working Groups. **Languages** English. **Staff** 0.50 FTE, paid. **Finance** Members' dues. **Activities** Active in: Europe and Middle East. **Members** Leading European digital television and telecommunication companies (TV channels, conditional access providers, providers of transmission infrastructures and manufacturers of related hardware). Membership countries not specified. **IGO Relations** Ad Hoc Observer Status with: *World Intellectual Property Organization (WIPO, #21593)*. Member of: *European Police Office (Europol, #08239)* – IPC3 Advisory Group; *European Union Intellectual Property Office (EUIPO, #08996)* – Observatory. [2022/XN8375/**D**]

- ♦ Audiovisual and Integrated Experience Association (internationally oriented national body)

♦ Auditeurs consultants experts européens (ACEE) 03016

Gen Sec Sarl Arraou and Associés, 66 chemin Mirassou, 64140 Lons, France. T. +33559802804. Fax +33559843716.
Registered Office c/o Arraou and Associés SARL, 133 bis rue de l'Université, 75007 Paris, France.

History 1989. A grouping of the type *European Economic Interest Grouping (EEIG, #06960)*. **Aims** Offer an international service in order to lead and aid businesses to develop in Europe. **Structure** Bureau. **Languages** English, French. **Staff** 0.50 FTE, paid. **Finance** Members' dues. **Activities** Guidance/assistance/consulting. **Events** *Meeting* Milan (Italy) 2015, *Meeting* Strasbourg (France) 2015, *Meeting* Milan (Italy) 2014, *Meeting* Luxembourg (Luxembourg) 2013, *Meeting* Paris (France) 2012.
Members Individuals in 6 countries:
Belgium, France, Germany, Italy, Luxembourg, Spain. [2016.10.24/XD5623/v/**F**]

- ♦ Auditorium Managers Association / see International Association of Venue Managers
- ♦ Audubon International (internationally oriented national body)
- ♦ Audubon Society of New York State / see Audubon International
- ♦ **AUE** Arab Union of Electricity (#01066)
- ♦ AUE – Association des universitaires d'Europe (inactive)
- ♦ **AUEDM** Asian University Network of Environment and Disaster Risk Management (#01774)
- ♦ AUETSA – Association of University English Teachers of Southern Africa (internationally oriented national body)
- ♦ **AUF** Agence universitaire de La Francophonie (#00548)
- ♦ **AUF** Asian Underwater Federation (#01771)
- ♦ **AUFEMO** Administration universitaire francophone et européenne en médecine et odontologie (#00115)
- ♦ AUFM / see World Federalist Movement – Movement for a Just World Order through a Strengthened United Nations (#21404)
- ♦ AUFP – Arab Union of Forensic Physicians (unconfirmed)
- ♦ **AUGM** Association of Universities of the Montevideo Group (#02971)

♦ Augmented Cognition International Society 03017

Contact c/o CTNSP, Natl Defense Univ, 260 5th Ave, Fort Lesley J McNair, Lincoln Hall Building 64, Ste 3600, Washington DC 20319, USA.

History Set up founded on the initiative of Dylan Schmorrow. **Events** *Conference* Orlando, FL (USA) 2010, *Conference* San Diego, CA (USA) 2009, *Conference* Baltimore, MD (USA) 2007, *International conference / Conference* Beijing (China) 2007, *International conference / Conference* San Francisco, CA (USA) 2006. **Publications** *Journal of Cognitive Engineering and Decision Making*. [2015/XM2099/**D**]

- ♦ Augmented Reality for Enterprise Alliance (internationally oriented national body)
- ♦ Augustine Canons – Confederation of the Canons Regular of Saint Augustine (religious order)
- ♦ Augustines Déchaussées (religious order)
- ♦ Augustines de Meaux – Soeurs Augustines (religious order)
- ♦ Augustines de Notre-Dame de Paris (religious order)
- ♦ Augustinian Nuns (religious order)
- ♦ Augustinians of the Assumption (religious order)
- ♦ Augustinians International – Order of St Augustine (religious order)
- ♦ Augustins de l'Assomption (religious order)
- ♦ Augustins – Ordre de Saint Augustin (religious order)
- ♦ Augustins Récollects (religious order)
- ♦ Augustins séculiers (religious order)
- ♦ **AUHF** African Union for Housing Finance (#00491)
- ♦ **AUIA** Arab Union of International Arbitration (#01068)
- ♦ **AUI** Action d'urgence internationale (#13258)
- ♦ **AU-IAPSC** Inter-African Phytosanitary Council (#11386)
- ♦ **AU-IBAR** Interafrican Bureau for Animal Resources (#11382)
- ♦ AUICK – Asian Urban Information Center of Kobe (internationally oriented national body)
- ♦ AUIEC – Arab Union for International Exhibitions and Conferences, Cairo (no recent information)
- ♦ **AUIP** Asociación Universitaria Iberoamericana de Postgrado (#02307)
- ♦ AUIV – Association Universitaire Internationale du Vin et des Produits de la Vigne (unconfirmed)
- ♦ Aujourd'hui l'Afrique / see Association française d'amitié et de solidarité avec les peuples d'Afrique
- ♦ AUJS – Australasian Union of Jewish Students (internationally oriented national body)
- ♦ **AULLA** Australasian Universities Language and Literature Association (#03033)
- ♦ **AULP** Associação das Universidades de Lingua Portuguesa (#02337)
- ♦ **AULT** Arab Union of Land Transport (#01069)
- ♦ Aum / see Aum Supreme Truth (#03018)
- ♦ AUM – Asian Union for Microcirculation (no recent information)
- ♦ Aumôniers du Travail (religious order)
- ♦ **AUMS** Asian Union of Magnetics Societies (#01772)
- ♦ Aum Shinri Kyo (#03018)

♦ Aum Supreme Truth 03018

Aum Shinri Kyo

Address not obtained.

History 1987, Japan, by Shoko Asahara. Also referred to simply as *Aum*. Registered, 1989, as a religious entity in accordance with Japanese law. As such, disbanded in Oct 1995, but still exists de facto. In 1998 reportedly earned 30 million pounds from discount computer stores. 2000, name changed to *Aleph*. **Aims** Take over Japan and subsequently the world, in part at least through *terrorism*. **Structure** Functions like a nation state: ministries; pope secretariat. **Activities** Notably the release of poisonous gas in the underground railway complex, 20 Mar 1995, Tokyo (Japan), killing 12 and injuring over 5,000.
Members As of 2004, membership estimated at 1,500 to 2,000 individuals. Members mainly in Japan, but in a total of 9 countries and territories:
Australia, Germany, Japan, Russia, Serbia-Montenegro, Sri Lanka, Taiwan, Ukraine, USA. [2008/XF4249/s/**F**]

- ♦ **AUN** ASEAN University Network (#01243)
- ♦ AUOD – Alliance universelle des ouvriers diamantaires (inactive)
- ♦ AUOLT / see Arab Union of Land Transport (#01069)
- ♦ AUP – African Union of Physics (inactive)
- ♦ **AUPAM** Arab Union of Manufacturers of Pharmaceuticals and Medical Appliances (#01070)
- ♦ **AU-PANVAC** Pan African Veterinary Vaccine Center of the African Union (#18073)
- ♦ AUPELF / see Agence universitaire de La Francophonie (#00548)

♦ AUPELF-UREF / see Agence universitaire de La Francophonie (#00548)
♦ AUPEMEC – Asociación UNESCO para la Promoción de la Etica en los Medios de Comunicación (internationally oriented national body)
♦ AUPHA – Association of University Programs in Health Administration (internationally oriented national body)
♦ **AUPRICA** Asociación de Universidades Privadas de Centroamérica y Panama (#02306)
♦ AuPSA – Austrian Political Science Association (internationally oriented national body)
♦ AUPTDE / see Arab Union of Electricity (#01066)
♦ **AURA** Asian Urban Research Association (#01776)
♦ Aura Freedom International (internationally oriented national body)
♦ AUR – Arab Union of Railways (inactive)
♦ AURE – Academic University Radiologists in Europe (inactive)
♦ **AURG** Asian Urban Research Group (#01777)

♦ Auroville Foundation 03019

Secretariat Bhavan – Administrative Area, Auroville 605 101, Rajapalayam, Tamil Nadu, Rajapalayam TAMIL NADU, India. T. +914132622222 – +914132623496 – +914132622414. Fax +914132623496. E-mail: avfoundation@auroville.org.in – info@auroville.org.in.
URL: http://www.auroville.org/

History Inaugurated 28 Feb 1968, Auroville (India). Recognized by an Act of Parliament of India, viz, Auroville Foundation Act, 1988 and 4 Resolutions of UNESCO. Previously also referred to as *Auroville International Township, Auroville Universal City* or *City of Dawn*. Registered as a foundation under Indian law. **Aims** Develop Auroville as a universal *township* for an actual human unity, inspired by the vision of Sri Aurobindo and Mirra Alfassa (also known as the Mother) for a conscious transformation of mankind through unending education and future oriented material, *spiritual*, environmental and inter-cultural research. **Structure** Residents' Assembly; Governing Board; International Advisory Council; Working Committees. *Auroville International (AVI, see: #03019)*, with 30 centres worldwide, was set up to support the Auroville experiment. **Languages** English, French, Sanskrit, Tamil. **Staff** All residents (about 2,500) are "honorary voluntary workers". **Finance** Grants from Government of India; support from: *UNESCO (#20322)*; income generated by small industries, handicraft units, Internet services and various consultancies; donations from international organizations and individuals. **Activities** Networking/liaising; training/education. **Events** *International seminar* Auroville (India) 1994, *Anniversary meeting* Paris (France) 1993. **Publications** *News and Notes* (weekly) – internal news bulletin; *Auroville Today* (12 a year) in English – journal; *Land Fund Newsletter*; *La Revue d'Auroville*; *Periodical Savitri Bhavan Newsletter*; *Ritam – SAIIER.*
Members Individuals (over 2,500) in 52 countries and territories:
Algeria, Argentina, Australia, Austria, Belarus, Belgium, Brazil, Bulgaria, Burkina Faso, Canada, China, Colombia, Czechia, Denmark, Egypt, Ethiopia, France, Germany, Greece, Hungary, Iceland, India, Ireland, Israel, Italy, Japan, Kazakhstan, Korea Rep, Latvia, Lithuania, Luxembourg, Moldova, Nepal, Netherlands, New Zealand, Nigeria, North Macedonia, Poland, Portugal, Russia, Slovenia, South Africa, Spain, Sri Lanka, Sweden, Switzerland, Taiwan, Thailand, Tibet, Türkiye, UK, Ukraine, USA.
NGO Relations Affiliate: *Sri Aurobindo International Institute of Educational Research (SAIIER).*
[2016.12.30/XF6458/fv/**F**]

♦ Auroville International (see: #03019)
♦ Auroville International Township / see Auroville Foundation (#03019)
♦ Auroville Universal City / see Auroville Foundation (#03019)
♦ **AURP** Association of University Research Parks (#02973)
♦ AURRP / see Association of University Research Parks (#02973)
♦ **AUSACE** Arab-US Association for Communication Educators (#01072)
♦ AusACPDM – Australasian Academy of Cerebral Palsy and Developmental Medicine (internationally oriented national body)
♦ AuSAE – Australasian Society of Association Executives (internationally oriented national body)
♦ **AU SAFGRAD** Semi-Arid Food Grain Research and Development (#19226)
♦ AUS / see Arab Federation of Surveyors (#00955)
♦ AUSBC / see US-ASEAN Business Council
♦ AUSC – African Union Sports Council (unconfirmed)
♦ **AUSC** ASEAN University Sports Council (#01244)
♦ Auschwitz Institute for Peace and Reconciliation / see Auschwitz Institute for the Prevention of Genocide and Mass Atrocities
♦ Auschwitz Institute for the Prevention of Genocide and Mass Atrocities (internationally oriented national body)
♦ AUSE – Arab Union for Small Enterprises (inactive)
♦ **AUSF** Asian University Sports Federation (#01775)
♦ AUSIC – Arab Union of Sport Information Centers (no recent information)
♦ Ausiliatrici del Purgatorio (religious order)
♦ AusIMM – Australasian Institute of Mining and Metallurgy (internationally oriented national body)
♦ **AUSJAL** Asociación de Universidades Confiadas a la Compañia de Jesús en América Latina (#02969)
♦ Auslandsgesellschaft Nordrhein-Westfalen (internationally oriented national body)
♦ AuSPEN – Australasian Society for Parenteral and Enteral Nutrition (unconfirmed)
♦ AUSPICE – Association of University Staff to Promote Inter-University Cooperation in Europe (inactive)
♦ Aussätzigenhilfe Emmaus / see FAIRMED
♦ Ausschuss der Bäckerhefersteller in der EWG / see Confédération des Fabricants de Levure de l'Union Européenne (#04551)
♦ Ausschuss für Bankenbestimmungen und Überwachung / see Basel Committee on Banking Supervision (#03183)
♦ Ausschuss der Berufsständischen Landwirtschaftlichen Organisationen der EG / see COPA – european farmers (#04829)
♦ Ausschuss der Berufsständischen Landwirtschaftlichen Organisationen der Europäischen Union / see COPA – european farmers (#04829)
♦ Ausschuss der EWG-Reederverbände / see European Community Shipowners' Associations (#06683)
♦ Ausschuss für Gesellschaft, Entwicklung und Frieden des Oekumenischen Rates der Kirchen und der Päpstlichen Kommission für Gerechtigkeit und Frieden (inactive)
♦ Ausschuss für Holzverwertung (inactive)
♦ Ausschuss der Kirchen für Ausländerfragen in Europa / see Churches' Commission for Migrants in Europe (#03912)
♦ Ausschuss der Kirchen für Fragen der Ausländischen Arbeitnehmer in Westeuropa / see Churches' Commission for Migrants in Europe (#03912)
♦ Ausschuss der Kirchen für Fragen Ausländischer Arbeitnehmer in Europa / see Churches' Commission for Migrants in Europe (#03912)
♦ Ausschuss der Krankenhäuser der Europäischen Gemeinschaft / see European Hospital and Healthcare Federation (#07501)
♦ Ausschuss der Präsidenten der Zentralbanken der Mitgliedstaaten der Europäischen Wirtschaftsgemeinschaft (inactive)
♦ Aussie Rules International (internationally oriented national body)
♦ AustLII – Australasian Legal Information Institute (internationally oriented national body)
♦ Australasian Academy of Cerebral Palsy and Developmental Medicine (internationally oriented national body)
♦ Australasian Academy of Facial Plastic Surgery (internationally oriented national body)
♦ Australasian Academy of Paediatric Dentistry (internationally oriented national body)
♦ Australasian Airline Ground Safety Council / see Australasian Aviation Ground Safety Council (#03021)
♦ Australasian Association for Clinical Biochemistry and Laboratory Medicine (internationally oriented national body)
♦ Australasian Association of Clinical Biochemists / see Australasian Association for Clinical Biochemistry and Laboratory Medicine
♦ Australasian Association of Clinical Geneticists (internationally oriented national body)
♦ Australasian Association of College and University Housing Officers / see Asia-Pacific Student Accommodation Association (#02058)
♦ Australasian Association for Communist and Post-Communist Studies (internationally oriented national body)
♦ Australasian Association for Digital Humanities (internationally oriented national body)
♦ Australasian Association for Engineering Education (internationally oriented national body)
♦ Australasian Association of Genealogists and Record Agents (internationally oriented national body)
♦ Australasian Association for Information Systems (internationally oriented national body)
♦ Australasian Association for Institutional Research (internationally oriented national body)
♦ Australasian Association for Lexicography (internationally oriented national body)
♦ Australasian Association for Logic (internationally oriented national body)
♦ Australasian Association of Nematologists
♦ Australasian Association of Paediatric Teaching Hospitals / see Children's Healthcare Australasia
♦ Australasian Association of Philosophy (internationally oriented national body)

♦ Australasian Association of Schools of Dentistry (AASD) 03020

Address not obtained.
Pres Dental School, Univ of Adelaide, Adelaide SA 2005, Australia.

History 1987. As of 2008, inactive. **Aims** Foster and advance *dental* education, research and training for all recognized education programmes for dental *health care* workers. **Structure** General Meeting (annual). Executive, composed of President, Vice-President, Secretary-Treasurer and one member-at-large. **Languages** English. **Finance** Biannual subscriptions from member institutions. **Events** *Annual General Meeting* Dunedin (New Zealand) 2005, *Annual General Meeting* Queenstown (New Zealand) 2005, *Annual General Meeting* Fiji 2004, *Annual General Meeting* Melbourne, VIC (Australia) 2003, *Annual General Meeting* Sydney, NSW (Australia) 2002.
Members in 3 countries:
Australia, Fiji, New Zealand.
NGO Relations Member of: *International Federation of Dental Educators and Associations (IFDEA, #13404).*
[2011.06.01/XE4235/*d*/**E**]

♦ Australasian Association for the Study of Socialist Countries / see Australasian Association for Communist and Post-Communist Studies
♦ Australasian Association for Theatre, Drama and Performance Studies (internationally oriented national body)
♦ Australasian Association of Veterinary Diagnostic Imaging (internationally oriented national body)

♦ Australasian Aviation Ground Safety Council (AAGSC) 03021

Executive address not obtained.
Executive address not obtained.
URL: http://www.aagsc.org/

History 1982, Sydney (Australia), as *Australasian Airline Ground Safety Council*, under the patronage of Australasian Airline Flight Safety Council (AFFSC). Charter revised 1 Jan 2011. **Aims** Provide a forum for the open exchange of ground safety related information so as to maintain highest overall safety standards of members; further the cause of safety education within the industry; recommend, formulate and pursue ground safety policies and practices relating to operational standards within the industry. **Structure** General Meeting; Council; Executive. **Languages** English. **Staff** Voluntary. **Finance** Members' dues: Corporate – Australian $ 300; Individual – Australian $ 80. **Activities** Standards/guidelines; awards/prizes/competitions; events/meetings; knowledge management/information dissemination. **Events** *Conference* Perth, WA (Australia) 2000, *Seminar* Sydney, NSW (Australia) 1996. **Publications** *Safety Watch* (12 a year) – newsletter. Series of ramp safety training videos; industry practice documents; safety audit checklists.
Members Full; Associate. Organizations (59) in 5 countries and territories:
Australia, Greece, New Zealand, United Arab Emirates, Vanuatu.
IGO Relations Formal contacts with: *International Civil Aviation Organization (ICAO, #12581).* **NGO Relations** Formal contacts with: *International Air Transport Association (IATA, #11614)*; national aviation authorities of Australia and New Zealand.
[2016.02.26/XD4815/**D**]

♦ Australasian Bone Marrow Transplant Recipient Registry (internationally oriented national body)
♦ Australasian Chapter of Sexual Health Medicine (internationally oriented national body)
♦ Australasian Cognitive Neuroscience Society (internationally oriented national body)
♦ Australasian College of Advancement in Medicine (internationally oriented national body)
♦ Australasian College of Aesthetic Medicine (internationally oriented national body)
♦ Australasian College of Behavioural Optometrists (internationally oriented national body)
♦ Australasian College of Cosmetic Surgery (internationally oriented national body)
♦ Australasian College of Dermatologists (internationally oriented national body)
♦ Australasian College for Emergency Medicine (internationally oriented national body)
♦ Australasian College of Phlebology (internationally oriented national body)
♦ Australasian College of Physical Scientists and Engineers in Medicine (internationally oriented national body)
♦ Australasian College of Physical Scientists in Medicine / see Australasian College of Physical Scientists and Engineers in Medicine
♦ Australasian College of Podiatric Surgeons (internationally oriented national body)
♦ Australasian College of Sexual Health Physicians / see Australasian Chapter of Sexual Health Medicine

♦ Australasian College of Tropical Medicine (ACTM) 03022

Main Office PO Box 123, Red Hill QLD 4059, Australia. T. +61738722246. Fax +61738564727. E-mail: actm@tropmed.org.
URL: http://www.tropmed.org/

History 29 May 1991, Townsville (Australia). **Aims** Encourage continuing education and exchange of knowledge in tropical medicine; promote research in the field. **Structure** Executive Council, comprising President, Vice-President, Honorary Secretary, Honorary Treasurer and 8 members. Committees. **Finance** Members' dues. Other sources: donations; sponsors. **Activities** Publishing activity. Annual and regional scientific meetings. Scholarships, awards and honours. Accreditation and support of teaching and research. Committees (9): Membership (Board of Censors); Scientific Programme; Membership Promotion; Incorporation (Constitutional); Editorial (Editorial Board); Editorial Advisory; Electronic Networking; Scholarships, Awards and Honours; Research and Development Finance. **Events** *Annual Scientific Meeting* Melbourne, VIC (Australia) 2008, *Annual scientific meeting* Cairns, QLD (Australia) 2004, *Asia Pacific forum on tropical health innovation* Cairns, QLD (Australia) 2004, *Annual scientific meeting* Melbourne, VIC (Australia) 2003, *Annual scientific meeting* Cairns, QLD (Australia) 2002. **Publications** *ACTM Bulletin* (4 a year). *ACTM Tropical Medicine Books* – series; *ACTM Tropical Medicine Papers* – series. Abstracts and proceedings of Scientific Meetings.
Members Fellow; Member; Associate; Affiliate/Student; Retired; Life. Members (over 500) in 7 countries and territories:
Australia, Hong Kong, Malaysia, Myanmar, New Zealand, Papua New Guinea, Thailand.
NGO Relations Affiliated with: *International Consortium for Jellyfish Stings* (and joint publication); *International Federation for Tropical Medicine (IFTM, #13575)*; *International Society of Travel Medicine (ISTM, #15519)*; *International Society of Tropical Pediatrics (ISTP, #15523).*
[2012/XD5896/v/**D**]

♦ Australasian College of Venereologists / see Australasian Chapter of Sexual Health Medicine
♦ Australasian Conference on Chemical Engineering (meeting series)
♦ Australasian Conference on Information Security and Privacy (meeting series)
♦ Australasian Container Reconditioners Association (internationally oriented national body)

♦ The Australasian Corrosion Association (ACA) 03023

Communications Manager 30A Jessie Street, Preston VIC 3072, Australia. T. +610386087900. Fax +61398907866. E-mail: aca@corrosion.com.au.
Street address Suite 1, 458 Middleborough Road, Blackburn VIC 3130, Australia.
URL: https://membership.corrosion.com.au/

History Founded 1955. **Aims** Reduce the cost of corrosion to the community and *industry*; disseminate corrosion information, research data and related technological material; promote and provide *education* in corrosion control at all levels. **Structure** Board; Council; Branches. **Languages** English. **Staff** 7.00 FTE, paid. **Finance** Sources: fees for services; meeting proceeds; members' dues. **Activities** Events/meetings; guidance/assistance/consulting; training/education. **Events** *Annual Conference* Newcastle, NSW (Australia) 2022, *Annual Conference* 2020, *Annual Conference* Melbourne, VIC (Australia) 2019, *Annual Conference* Adelaide, SA (Australia) 2018, *Annual Conference* Sydney, NSW (Australia) 2017. **Publications** *Corrosion and Materials*; *Corrosion Matters*. **Members** Individuals; industrial organizations; government departments. Branches in all Australian states and New Zealand. Membership countries not specified. **NGO Relations** Member of: *World Corrosion Organization (WCO, #21316)*. [2023.02.14/XE0854/**E**]

- ♦ Australasian Council of Auditors-General (internationally oriented national body)
- ♦ Australasian Council on Open, Distance and E-Learning (internationally oriented national body)
- ♦ Australasian Council of Women and Policing (internationally oriented national body)
- ♦ Australasian Cytometry Society (internationally oriented national body)
- ♦ Australasian Democratic Education Community (internationally oriented national body)
- ♦ Australasian Diabetes in Pregnancy Society (internationally oriented national body)
- ♦ Australasian Drama Studies Association / see Australasian Association for Theatre, Drama and Performance Studies
- ♦ Australasian Environmental Law Enforcement and Regulators Network (internationally oriented national body)
- ♦ Australasian Epidemiological Association (internationally oriented national body)
- ♦ Australasian Ethics Network (internationally oriented national body)
- ♦ Australasian Exploration Geoscience Conference (meeting series)
- ♦ Australasian Facilitators' Network (internationally oriented national body)
- ♦ Australasian Federation of Family History Organizations (internationally oriented national body)
- ♦ Australasian Federation for Medical and Veterinary Mycology (internationally oriented national body)
- ♦ Australasian Fire Authorities Council (internationally oriented national body)
- ♦ Australasian Flow Cytometry Group / see Australasian Cytometry Society
- ♦ Australasian Fluids and Thermal Engineering Society (internationally oriented national body)

♦ Australasian Forum for International Arbitration (AFIA) 03024

Sec and Public Officer c/o Norton Rose Fulbright, Level 18, Grosvenor Place/225 George Street, Sydney NSW 2000, Australia. T. +61293308000. E-mail: mail@afia.asia.
URL: http://www.afia.net.au/

History 2004. **Aims** Provide young practitioners with a forum to discuss issues and developments in international arbitration, with particular focus on the Asia-Pacific region. **Structure** Annual General Meeting. Executive Committee, comprising Co-Chairs, Secretary/Public Officer, Deputy Secretary, 10 regional representatives and ACICA Liaison. General Committee. **Activities** Organizes AFIA Symposium on International Arbitration. **Events** *FIAA International Arbitration Advocacy Workshop* Singapore (Singapore) 2013, *Symposium* Sydney, NSW (Australia) 2012, *Symposium* Sydney, NSW (Australia) 2011, *Symposium* Shanghai (China) 2010, *Symposium* Sydney, NSW (Australia) 2010. **Publications** *AFIA News* (irregular).
Members (350) in 20 countries and territories:
Australia, Bahrain, China, France, Germany, Hong Kong, India, Indonesia, Ireland, Italy, Japan, Malaysia, Netherlands, New Zealand, Singapore, Sri Lanka, Thailand, UK, United Arab Emirates, USA. [2013/XJ0308/**D**]

- ♦ Australasian Genomic Technologies Association (internationally oriented national body)
- ♦ Australasian Gynaecological Endoscopy and Surgery (internationally oriented national body)
- ♦ Australasian Hair and Wool Research Society (internationally oriented national body)
- ♦ Australasian Hernia Society (internationally oriented national body)
- ♦ Australasian Human Development Association (internationally oriented national body)
- ♦ Australasian Hydrographic Society (internationally oriented national body)
- ♦ Australasian Injury Prevention Network (internationally oriented national body)
- ♦ Australasian Institute of Banking and Finance / see Financial Services Institute of Australasia
- ♦ Australasian Institute of Chartered Loss Adjusters (internationally oriented national body)
- ♦ Australasian Institute for Ethnomethodology and Conversation Analysis (internationally oriented national body)
- ♦ Australasian Institute of Judicial Administration (internationally oriented national body)
- ♦ Australasian Institute of Metals / see Institute of Materials Engineering, Australasia
- ♦ Australasian Institute of Mining and Metallurgy (internationally oriented national body)
- ♦ Australasian Interprofessional Practice and Education Network (internationally oriented national body)

♦ Australasian Law Academics Association (ALAA) 03025

Secretariat ANU College of Law, 5 Fellows Rd, Acton ACT 2601, Australia. T. +612554178. E-mail: admin@alta.edu.au.
SG Fac of Law, Univ of Technology Sydney, Eton Road, Lindfield NSW 2070, Australia.
URL: https://www.alaa.asn.au/

History 5 Jun 1946, Sydney, NSW (Australia). Former names and other names: *Australian Universities Law Schools Association* – former (5 Jun 1946); *Australasian Universities Law Schools Association* – former; *Australasian Law Teachers Association (ALTA)* – former (1988 to 1 Jul 2019). **Aims** Further legal education in Australia, New Zealand and Papua New Guinea and the Pacific Islands, and the work and interests of law teachers in these countries; encourage and organize legal research and the publication of contributions to legal knowledge; promote active co-operation of the law teachers of this region and elsewhere; co-operate with professional legal associations, law reform agencies and other bodies in the work of law reform. **Languages** English. **Staff** 0.50 FTE, paid; 12.00 FTE, voluntary. **Finance** Sources: members' dues. **Activities** Awards/prizes/competitions; events/meetings; research/documentation. **Events** *Annual Conference* Sydney, NSW (Australia) 2021, *Annual Conference* Sydney, NSW (Australia) 2020, *Annual Conference* Gold Coast, QLD (Australia) 2019, *Annual Conference* Perth, WA (Australia) 2018, *Annual Conference* Adelaide, SA (Australia) 2017. **Publications** *ALTA Newsletter* (2 a year); *Journal of the Australasian Law Teachers Association*; *Legal Education Digest*; *Legal Education Review*. *ALTA Law Research Series*.
Members Law teachers in 5 countries:
Australia, Fiji, New Zealand, Papua New Guinea, Vanuatu. [2021/XD5702/v/**D**]

- ♦ Australasian Law Students' Association (internationally oriented national body)
- ♦ Australasian Law Teachers Association / see Australasian Law Academics Association (#03025)
- ♦ Australasian Legal Information Institute (internationally oriented national body)
- ♦ Australasian Lymphology Association (internationally oriented national body)

♦ Australasian Menopause Society (AMS) 03026

Exec Dir PO Box 280, Healesville VIC 3777, Australia. T. +61359626241. Fax +61399236569. E-mail: ams@menopause.org.au.
URL: http://www.menopause.org.au/

History 1988. **Aims** Improve the quality of life of women during and after the menopause; promote discussion, study and understanding of midlife women's health; encourage and support research into all aspects of midlife women's health; disseminate quality information to health professionals and the public; encourage the application of that information and knowledge as clinical best practice. **Structure** Council, including Executive, comprising President, President-elect, Honorary Treasurer, Honorary Secretary, Chair Education and Research and Immediate Past-President. **Languages** English. **Staff** 1.00 FTE, paid. **Finance** Sources: members' dues. **Activities** Events/meetings. **Events** *World Congress* Melbourne, VIC (Australia) 2024, *Annual Congress* Adelaide, SA (Australia) 2021, *Annual Congress* Hobart, TAS (Australia) 2019, *Annual Congress* Brisbane, QLD (Australia) 2018, *Annual Congress* Sydney, NSW (Australia) 2017. **Publications** *AMS Newsletter* (4 a year).
Members Full in 6 countries:
Australia, China, Malaysia, New Zealand, Singapore, United Arab Emirates. [2021/XD6788/**D**]

- ♦ Australasian Microarray and Associated Technologies Association / see Australasian Genomic Technologies Association
- ♦ Australasian Musculoskeletal Imaging Group (internationally oriented national body)
- ♦ Australasian Mycological Society (internationally oriented national body)
- ♦ Australasian Neurogastroenterology and Motility Association (internationally oriented national body)
- ♦ Australasian Neuromuscular Network (internationally oriented national body)
- ♦ Australasian Neuroscience Nurses' Association (internationally oriented national body)
- ♦ Australasian and New Zealand Association for Medical Education / see Australian and New Zealand Association for Health Professional Educators
- ♦ Australasian Paediatric Endocrine Group (internationally oriented national body)
- ♦ Australasian Particle Technology Society (internationally oriented national body)
- ♦ Australasian Performing Right Association (internationally oriented national body)
- ♦ Australasian Personal Construct Group (internationally oriented national body)
- ♦ Australasian Pharmaceutical Science Association (internationally oriented national body)
- ♦ Australasian Philosophy of Religion Association (internationally oriented national body)
- ♦ Australasian Piano Tuners and Technicians Association (internationally oriented national body)
- ♦ Australasian Planetarium Society (internationally oriented national body)
- ♦ Australasian Plant Breeding Conference (meeting series)
- ♦ Australasian Plant Pathology Society (internationally oriented national body)
- ♦ Australasian Podiatry Council (internationally oriented national body)
- ♦ Australasian Political Studies Association (internationally oriented national body)
- ♦ Australasian Pool Association (no recent information)
- ♦ Australasian Postharvest Conference (meeting series)
- ♦ Australasian Primate Society (internationally oriented national body)
- ♦ Australasian Professional Society on Alcohol and Other Drugs (internationally oriented national body)
- ♦ Australasian Radiation Protection Society (internationally oriented national body)
- ♦ Australasian Regional Association of Zoological Parks and Aquaria / see Zoo and Aquarium Association Australasia (#22039)
- ♦ Australasian Remote Sensing and Photogrammetry Conference (meeting series)

♦ Australasian Research Management Society (ARMS) 03027

Pres c/o Flinders Univ, GPO Box 2100, Adelaide SA 5001, Australia. T. +61882015592. E-mail: arms.adminofficer@flinders.edu.au.
URL: http://researchmanagement.org.au/

History 1991. Constitution revised 21 Sep 2007, Adelaide (Australia); 4 Mar 2011, Sydney (Australia); 13 Sep 2016, Australia. Registration: Associations Incorporation Act, No/ID: ARBN 6090514431, Australia, State of Victoria. **Aims** Create an internationally connected community of research management professionals who operate at the highest standards to influence, support and enhance the global delivery of research excellence. **Structure** Annual General Meeting; Board; Committees (5); Chapters (10); Special Interest Groups (9); Accreditation Council. **Languages** English. **Staff** 4.00 FTE, paid. **Finance** Sources: fees for services; meeting proceeds; members' dues; revenue from activities/projects; sponsorship. **Activities** Advocacy/lobbying/activism; awards/prizes/competitions; certification/accreditation; events/meetings; knowledge management/information dissemination; training/education. **Events** *Annual Conference* 2021, *Annual Conference* Perth, WA (Australia) 2020, *Annual Conference* Adelaide, SA (Australia) 2019, *Annual Conference* Hobart, TAS (Australia) 2018, *Annual Conference* Wellington (New Zealand) 2017. **Publications** *Up in ARMS* (about 12 a year) – newsletter. Yearbook.
Members Individual; Corporate. Members (about 3,000) in 5 countries:
Australia, New Zealand, Singapore, Thailand, Vietnam.
IGO Relations Government agencies in Australia, Singapore and New Zealand. **NGO Relations** Member of: *International Network of Research Management Societies (INORMS, #14317)*. Strategic alliance with: *Australasian Ethics Network (AEN)*; Australasian Research Training Network (ARTN). [2021.06.07/XJ0179/**D**]

- ♦ Australasian Road Rescue Organisation (internationally oriented national body)
- ♦ Australasian Science Education Research Association (internationally oriented national body)
- ♦ Australasian Seabird Group (internationally oriented national body)
- ♦ Australasian Sexual Health Alliance (internationally oriented national body)
- ♦ Australasian Sexual Health and HIV Nurses Association (internationally oriented national body)
- ♦ Australasian Sexual Health Nurses Association / see Australasian Sexual Health and HIV Nurses Association
- ♦ Australasian Sleep Association (internationally oriented national body)
- ♦ Australasian Sleep Technologists Association (internationally oriented national body)
- ♦ Australasian Society of Aerospace Medicine (internationally oriented national body)
- ♦ Australasian Society of Aesthetic Plastic Surgeons (internationally oriented national body)
- ♦ Australasian Society of Aesthetic Plastic Surgery / see Australasian Society of Aesthetic Plastic Surgeons
- ♦ Australasian Society for Asian and Comparative Philosophy (no recent information)
- ♦ Australasian Society of Association Executives (internationally oriented national body)
- ♦ Australasian Society for Biomaterials / see Australasian Society for for Biomaterials and Tissue Engineering
- ♦ Australasian Society for for Biomaterials and Tissue Engineering (internationally oriented national body)
- ♦ Australasian Society for Bipolar and Depressive Disorders (internationally oriented national body)
- ♦ Australasian Society for Bipolar Disorders / see Australasian Society for Bipolar and Depressive Disorders
- ♦ Australasian Society for Breast Disease (internationally oriented national body)
- ♦ Australasian Society of Cardiac and Thoracic Surgeons (internationally oriented national body)
- ♦ Australasian Society of Chefs and Cooks (inactive)
- ♦ Australasian Society for Classical Studies (internationally oriented national body)
- ♦ Australasian Society of Clinical and Experimental Pharmacologists / see Australasian Society of Clinical and Experimental Pharmacology and Toxicology
- ♦ Australasian Society of Clinical and Experimental Pharmacology and Toxicology (internationally oriented national body)
- ♦ Australasian Society of Clinical Immunology and Allergy (internationally oriented national body)
- ♦ Australasian Society for Computers in Learning in Tertiary Education (internationally oriented national body)
- ♦ Australasian Society of Cytogeneticists / see Australasian Society of Diagnostic Genomics
- ♦ Australasian Society for Dermatology Research (internationally oriented national body)
- ♦ Australasian Society of Diagnostic Genomics (internationally oriented national body)
- ♦ Australasian Society for Emergency Medicine (internationally oriented national body)

♦ Australasian Society for General Relativity and Gravitation (ASGRG) 03028

Sec Mathematical and Computing Sciences, Univ Brunei Darussalam, Jalan Tungku Link, Negaru, Negaru, Brunei Darussalam. T. +6732463001ext1304. E-mail: asgrg@hotmail.com.
URL: http://www.asgrg.org/

History Sep 1994, Canberra (Australia). **Aims** Support and encourage research in general relativity and related areas in Australasia. **Structure** Committee, comprising President, Vice-President, Treasurer, Secretary, 2 Ordinary Members and co-opted members when necessary. **Languages** English. **Staff** Voluntary. **Finance** Members' dues. **Activities** Events/meetings. **Events** *Australasian Conference on General Relativity and Gravitation* Hobart, TAS (Australia) 2022, *Australasian Conference on General Relativity and Gravitation* Wellington (New Zealand) 2019, *Australasian Conference on General Relativity and Gravitation* Gingin, WA (Australia) 2017, *Australasian Conference on General Relativity and Gravitation* Melbourne, VIC (Australia) 2015, *Australasian Conference on General Relativity and Gravitation* Hamilton Is, QLD (Australia) 2013. **Publications** *ASGRG Newsletter* in Danish, English, Finnish, Norwegian, Swedish.
Members Individuals in 7 countries:
Australia, Brunei Darussalam, France, New Zealand, South Africa, UK, USA. [2021/XD6572/**D**]

- ♦ Australasian Society of Genetic Counsellors (internationally oriented national body)
- ♦ Australasian Society for HIV Medicine / see Australasian Society for HIV, Viral Hepatitis and Sexual Health Medicine

♦ Australasian Society for HIV, Viral Hepatitis and Sexual Health Medicine (internationally oriented national body)
♦ Australasian Society for Immunology (internationally oriented national body)
♦ Australasian Society for Inborn Errors of Metabolism (internationally oriented national body)
♦ Australasian Society for Infectious Diseases (internationally oriented national body)
♦ Australasian Society for Intellectual Disability (internationally oriented national body)
♦ Australasian Society of Lifestyle Medicine (internationally oriented national body)
♦ Australasian Society of Paediatric Imaging (unconfirmed)
♦ Australasian Society for Parenteral and Enteral Nutrition (unconfirmed)
♦ Australasian Society of Phycology and Aquatic Botany (internationally oriented national body)
♦ Australasian Society for Physical Activity (internationally oriented national body)
♦ Australasian Society for Psychophysiology (internationally oriented national body)
♦ Australasian Society for the Study of Brain Impairment (internationally oriented national body)
♦ Australasian Society for the Study of Obesity / see Australian and New Zealand Obesity Society
♦ Australasian Society of Thrombosis and Haemostasis (internationally oriented national body)

♦ Australasian Society for Traumatic Stress Studies (ASTSS) 03029

Main Office C/-QUT Psychology and Counselling, Level 5 – B Wing – O Block, Victoria Park Rd, Kelvin Grove QLD 4059, Australia. E-mail: tjlsdesign@googlemail.com.
URL: http://www.astss.org.au/

History Dec 1990, Melbourne (Australia), following initiatives among groups in Australia since the 1980s. **Aims** Serve as a forum to extend prevention and treatment of major stress and trauma within the Australasian region; promote the advancement of knowledge on nature, consequences, prevention and treatment of highly stressful experiences; foster development of policy and programmes and service initiatives which prevent the unwanted consequences of such experiences; contribute to informed discussion on ethical issues and standards of practice and to development of professionalism in the field; support research and the dissemination of information; heighten awareness of the subject within the wider professional community and the general public. **Structure** General Assembly (annual). Individual regional chapters. **Languages** English. **Staff** 1.50 FTE, paid. **Finance** Members' dues: Australian $ 65. **Activities** Organizes regular scientific meetings and speaker tours. **Events** *Australasian Conference on Traumatic Stress* Kelvin Grove, QLD (Australia) 2021, *Australasian Conference on Traumatic Stress* Sydney, NSW (Australia) 2019, *Australasian Conference on Traumatic Stress* Gold Coast, QLD (Australia) 2016, *Annual conference* Melbourne, VIC (Australia) 2014, *Annual Conference* Perth, WA (Australia) 2012. **Publications** *Australasian Traumatic Stress Points* (3 a year) – newsletter.
Members Organizations (indicated) and individuals in 4 countries:
Australia, New Zealand, Singapore, USA (*). [2018/XD4992/**D**]

♦ Australasian Society for Trenchless Technology (internationally oriented national body)

♦ Australasian Society for Ultrasound in Medicine (ASUM) 03030

CEO 9 Help Street, Suite 3.01, Chatswood NSW 2067, Australia. T. +61294382078. Fax +61294383686. E-mail: ceo@asum.com.au – asum@asum.com.au.
URL: http://www.asum.com.au/

History 1970. The Australian society merged with New Zealand and altered the society name to include Australasian. Former names and other names: *Australian Society for Ultrasound in Medicine and Biology* – former (1970 to 5 Aug 1992). **Aims** Create healthier lives for all by driving excellence in ultrasound. **Structure** General Meeting; Council. A company limited by guarantee. **Languages** English. **Staff** 10.00 FTE, paid. **Finance** Sources: members' dues. **Activities** Certification/accreditation; events/meetings; healthcare; networking/liaising; publishing activities; research/documentation; standards/guidelines; training/education. **Events** *Annual Scientific Meeting* Adelaide, SA (Australia) 2022, *Annual Scientific Meeting* 2021, *Annual Scientific Meeting* Sydney, NSW (Australia) 2020, *Annual Scientific Meeting* Melbourne, VIC (Australia) 2019, *Annual Scientific Meeting* Auckland (New Zealand) 2018. **Publications** *Australasian Journal of Ultrasound in Medicine (AJUM)*.
Members Medical; Sonographer; Scientific; Allied Health; Student; Associate; Corresponding; Corporate. Members in 2 countries:
Australia, New Zealand. [2022.05.12/XD3415/**D**]

♦ Australasian Society of Victimology (internationally oriented national body)

♦ Australasian Society of Zoo Keeping (ASZK) 03031

Contact address not obtained. E-mail: eo@aszk.org.au.
URL: http://www.aszk.org.au/

History 1976, Adelaide, SA (Australia). Incorporated in 1991. **Aims** Support and encourage professional development of *animal husbandry* within the zoo industry; increase liaison among zoo personnel, particularly in the Australasian region. **Structure** Management Committee; Committees (9); Branches (7). **Languages** English. **Staff** 12.00 FTE, voluntary. **Finance** Sources: fundraising; members' dues. **Activities** Advocacy/lobbying/activism; awards/prizes/competitions; events/meetings; training/education. **Events** *Annual Conference* Sydney, NSW (Australia) 2021, *Annual Conference* Healesville, VIC (Australia) 2014, *Annual Conference* Auckland (New Zealand) 2013, *International Congress on Zoo Keeping* Singapore (Singapore) 2012, *Annual Conference* Gold Coast, QLD (Australia) 2011. **Publications** *Thylacinus* (4 a year); *Cybercinus* (occassional) – electronic newsletter. Pamphlets.
Members Categories Full (178); Associate (40); Overseas (5); Corporate (3); Overseas Corporate (17); Life (7). Individuals in 14 countries:
Canada, France, Germany, Japan, Nepal, Netherlands, New Zealand, Philippines, Singapore, South Africa, Spain, Switzerland, UK, USA.
NGO Relations Member of (1): *International Congress of Zookeepers (ICZ, #12902)*. [2021/XD4999/**D**]

♦ Australasian Sound Recordings Association (internationally oriented national body)
♦ Australasian and Southeast Asian Tissue Typing Association / see Asia Pacific Histocompatibility and Immunogenetics Association (#01927)

♦ Australasian Sports Technology Alliance (ASTA) 03032

Contact RMIT Engineering Dept, PO Box 71, Bundoora VIC 3083, Australia.

Activities Asia-Pacific Congress on Sports Technology (APCST). **Events** *Biennial Congress / Conference* Barcelona (Spain) 2015, *Conference* Hong Kong (Hong Kong) 2013, *Biennial congress / Conference* Melbourne, VIC (Australia) 2011, *Biennial congress / Conference* Honolulu, HI (USA) 2009, *Biennial Congress* Singapore (Singapore) 2007. **Members** Membership countries not specified. [2014/XJ8095/**D**]

♦ Australasian TeleHealth Society (internationally oriented national body)
♦ Australasian Tertiary Education Facilities Management Association / see Tertiary Education Facilities Management Association
♦ Australasian Therapeutic Communities Association (internationally oriented national body)
♦ Australasian Tissue and Biotherapeutics Forum / see Biotherapeutics Association of Australasia
♦ Australasian Tissue Typing Association / see Asia Pacific Histocompatibility and Immunogenetics Association (#01927)
♦ Australasian Transplant Coordinators Association (internationally oriented national body)
♦ Australasian Trauma Society (internationally oriented national body)
♦ Australasian Tuberous Sclerosis Society (internationally oriented national body)
♦ Australasian Tunnelling Society (internationally oriented national body)
♦ Australasian Union of Jewish Students (internationally oriented national body)

♦ Australasian Universities Language and Literature Association (AULLA) 03033

Association des langues et littératures des universités d'Australasie

Pres College of the Arts, Victoria Univ, Melbourne VIC 8001, Australia.
URL: http://aulla.com.au/

History Founded 1950, as *Australasian Universities Modern Languages Association*. Present title adopted 1957. **Aims** Advance study and research in all fields of language and literature, including linguistics, films studies and cultural studies, in the universities and tertiary institutions of Australia, New Zealand and the Asia-Pacific; promote cross-disciplinary connections and synergies; encourage innovative research directions in language, literature and cultural studies. **Structure** General Meeting; Standing Committee. **Languages** English, French, German. **Staff** None. **Finance** Members' dues. **Activities** Awards/prizes/competitions. **Events** *Triennial Conference* Darwin, NT (Australia) 2022, *Triennial Conference* Wollongong, NSW (Australia) 2019, *Triennial Conference* Melbourne, VIC (Australia) 2016, *Biennial Congress* Brisbane, QLD (Australia) 2013, *Biennial congress* Auckland (New Zealand) 2011. **Publications** *The Journal of Literature, Language and Culture (JLLC)* (3 a year).
Members Individuals in 22 countries and territories:
Australia, Brazil, Canada, China, France, Germany, Greece, Hong Kong, Iceland, India, Indonesia, Italy, Japan, Korea Rep, Monaco, New Zealand, Papua New Guinea, Russia, South Africa, Switzerland, Tonga, UK, USA.
NGO Relations *International Federation for Modern Languages and Literatures (#13480)*.
[2017.03.21/XD3856/v/**D**]

♦ Australasian Universities Law Schools Association / see Australasian Law Academics Association (#03025)
♦ Australasian Universities Modern Languages Association / see Australasian Universities Language and Literature Association (#03033)
♦ Australasian Veterinary Poultry Association (internationally oriented national body)

♦ Australasian Victorian Studies Association (AVSA) 03034

Pres School of Humnaities, Univ of Adelaide, Adelaide SA 5005, Australia.
URL: http://www.avsa.unimelb.edu.au/

Aims Promote the activities and research of scholars in Victorian studies in Australia, New Zealand and East Asia. **Structure** Annual General Meeting (usually in conjunction with Annual Conference); Executive Committee; Regional Representatives. **Finance** Members' dues. **Events** *Annual Conference* Melbourne, VIC (Australia) 2020, *Annual Conference* Dunedin (New Zealand) 2019, *Annual Conference* Melbourne, VIC (Australia) 2017, *Annual Conference* Ballarat, VIC (Australia) 2016, *Annual Conference* Auckland (New Zealand) 2015. **Publications** *Australasian Journal of Victorian Studies* (2 a year).
Members Organizations and individuals in 9 countries and territories:
Australia, Canada, Hong Kong, Japan, New Zealand, Singapore, Sweden, UK, USA. [2018.06.25/XE2793/**E**]

♦ Australasian Wader Studies Group (internationally oriented national body)
♦ Australasian Wind Engineering Society (internationally oriented national body)
♦ Australasian Wound and Tissue Repair Society (internationally oriented national body)

♦ Australasia Pacific Extension Network (APEN) 03035

Secretariat PO Box 1239, Wodonga VIC 3689, Australia. T. +61260245349. E-mail: info@apen.org.au.
URL: http://www.apen.org.au/

History Oct 1993, Gold Coast, QLD (Australia). Founded at *International Extension Conference*. Original network formalized under current title in 1994. First Annual General Meeting, 1995. **Aims** Enable change in primary industries, natural resource management and communities so as to support *professional* development and networking for workers in extension and related fields in Australia, New Zealand and the Asia-Pacific region. **Structure** Management Committee; Cluster Coordinators; Regional Coordinators (7). Regions: Australian States and Northern Territory; New Zealand/Overseas. **Languages** English. **Staff** 1.00 FTE, paid. **Finance** Members' dues. Other sources: sponsors; corporate members; surplus from events. **Activities** Events/meetings; advocacy/lobbying/activism; politics/policy/regulatory. **Events** *Conference* Parkville, VIC (Australia) 2022, *Extending horizons – extension's role in climate, rural industries, and community challenges* Darwin, NT (Australia) 2019, *Conference* Townsville, QLD (Australia) 2017, *Conference* Adelaide, SA (Australia) 2015, *Transformative change – chosen or unchosen, pathways to innovation, resilience and prosperity* Christchurch (New Zealand) 2013. **Publications** *APEN eBulletin* (12 a year); *ExtensionNet* (4 a year); *Rural Extension and innovation Systems Journal. Shaping Change: Natural Resource Management, Agriculture and the Role of Extension* (2011). Conference proceedings.
Members Professional practitioners in 19 countries:
Australia, Canada, India, Indonesia, Iran Islamic Rep, Kenya, Malaysia, Netherlands, New Zealand, Pakistan, Papua New Guinea, Philippines, Solomon Is, South Africa, Sweden, Tonga, UK, USA, Vietnam. [2021/XF4520/**F**]

♦ AUSTRALEX – Australasian Association for Lexicography (internationally oriented national body)
♦ Australia, Asian and New Zealand Union for Progressive Judaism / see Union for Progressive Judaism

♦ Australia Group (AG) 03036

Groupe d'Australie – Grupo de Australia – Australische Gruppe

Address not obtained.
URL: http://www.australiagroup.net/

History 1984. **Aims** Use licensing measures to ensure that exports of certain *chemicals*, biological agents, and dual-use chemical and biological manufacturing facilities and equipment, do not contribute to the spread of chemical and biological *weapons*. **Structure** An informal forum of countries.
Members Governments of 42 countries:
Argentina, Australia, Austria, Belgium, Bulgaria, Canada, Croatia, Cyprus, Czechia, Denmark, Estonia, Finland, France, Germany, Greece, Hungary, Iceland, India, Ireland, Italy, Japan, Korea Rep, Latvia, Lithuania, Luxembourg, Malta, Mexico, Netherlands, New Zealand, Norway, Poland, Portugal, Romania, Slovakia, Slovenia, Spain, Sweden, Switzerland, Türkiye, UK, Ukraine, USA.
Regional organization (1):
European Union (EU, #08967).
Adherent government (1):
Kazakhstan.
IGO Relations *Nuclear Suppliers Group (NSG, #17621)*. [2018/XE3131/c/**E***]

♦ Australian APEC Study Centre (internationally oriented national body)
♦ Australian Association for the Advancement of Pacific Studies / see Australian Association for Pacific Studies
♦ Australian Association for Pacific Studies (internationally oriented national body)
♦ Australian Baptist Foreign Mission / see Global Interaction
♦ Australian Baptist Mission / see Global Interaction
♦ Australian Baptist Missionary Society / see Global Interaction
♦ Australian Baptist World Aid / see Baptist World Aid Australia
♦ Australian Baptist World Aid and Relief Committee / see Baptist World Aid Australia
♦ Australian Business Volunteers (internationally oriented national body)
♦ Australian Catholic Migrant and Refugee Office (internationally oriented national body)
♦ Australian Catholic Relief / see Caritas Australia
♦ Australian Centre for International Agricultural Research (internationally oriented national body)
♦ Australian Centre for International Commercial Arbitration (internationally oriented national body)
♦ Australian Council for International Development (internationally oriented national body)
♦ Australian Council for Overseas Aid / see Australian Council for International Development
♦ Australian Doctors for Africa (internationally oriented national body)
♦ Australian Doctors International (internationally oriented national body)
♦ Australia and New Zealand Pulp and Paper Industry Technical Association / see Appita – Australia and New Zealand Pulp and Paper Industry Technical Association
♦ Australia and New Zealand Union for Progressive Judaism / see Union for Progressive Judaism
♦ Australian Executive Service Overseas Program / see Australian Business Volunteers
♦ Australian Expert Service Overseas Program / see Australian Business Volunteers
♦ Australian Foundation for Asia and the Pacific / see Action on Poverty
♦ Australian Foundation for International Credit Union Development / see Credit Union Foundation Australia
♦ Australian Foundation for the Peoples of the South Pacific / see Action on Poverty
♦ Australian Injury Prevention Network / see Australasian Injury Prevention Network
♦ Australian Institute of Evangelism / see Ambassadors for Christ International (#00768)

Australian Institute International
03036

alphabetic sequence excludes
For the complete listing, see Yearbook Online at

- ♦ Australian Institute of International Affairs (internationally oriented national body)
- ♦ Australian Medical and Professional Society on Alcohol and Other Drugs / see Australasian Professional Society on Alcohol and Other Drugs
- ♦ Australian Medical Society on Alcohol and other Drug Problems / see Australasian Professional Society on Alcohol and Other Drugs
- ♦ Australian Mercy / see Australian Relief and Mercy Services
- ♦ Australian and New Zealand Architectural Science Association / see Architectural Science Association
- ♦ Australian and New Zealand Association for Health Professional Educators (internationally oriented national body)
- ♦ Australian and New Zealand Comparative and International Education Society / see Oceania Comparative and International Education Society
- ♦ Australian and New Zealand Council for the Care of Animals in Research and Teaching (internationally oriented national body)
- ♦ Australian and New Zealand Obesity Society (internationally oriented national body)
- ♦ Australian and New Zealand Society of International Law (internationally oriented national body)
- ♦ Australian People for Health, Education and Development Abroad / see Union Aid Abroad-APHEDA
- ♦ Australian Professional Society on Alcohol and other Drugs / see Australasian Professional Society on Alcohol and Other Drugs
- ♦ Australian Relief and Mercy Services (internationally oriented national body)
- ♦ Australian Science Education Research Association / see Australasian Science Education Research Association
- ♦ Australian Society for Biomaterials / see Australasian Society for for Biomaterials and Tissue Engineering
- ♦ Australian Society for Ultrasound in Medicine and Biology / see Australasian Society for Ultrasound in Medicine (#03030)
- ♦ Australian Universities Law Schools Association / see Australasian Law Academics Association (#03025)
- ♦ Australian Volunteers International / see AVI
- ♦ Australia South Asia Research Centre (internationally oriented national body)
- ♦ Australische Gruppe (#03036)
- ♦ **AU STRC** African Union Scientific Technical Research Commission (#00493)
- ♦ Austrian Agency for International Cooperation in Education and Research (internationally oriented national body)
- ♦ Austrian Association for Development and Cooperation / see Hilfswerk International
- ♦ Austrian Association for Foreign Policy and International Relations / see Österreichische Gesellschaft für Aussenpolitik und die Vereinten Nationen
- ♦ Austrian Development Agency (internationally oriented national body)

♦ Austrian Economics Meeting Europe Foundation (AEME Foundation) 03037

Sec address not obtained.
URL: http://www.aem-europe.com/

History 2014. Founded by European alumni of Mises University. Registration: Stichting, No/ID: 72994665, Netherlands. **Activities** Events/meetings. **Events** *Meeting* Madrid (Spain) 2019, *Meeting* Budapest (Hungary) 2018, *Meeting* Krakow (Poland) 2017, *Meeting* Prague (Czech Rep) 2016, *Meeting* Vienna (Austria) 2015. **Publications** *AEME Newsletter*. [2020/AA0558/f/F]

- ♦ Austrian Exchange Service / see Österreichische Austauschdienst
- ♦ Austrian Exchange Service – Agency for International Cooperation in Education and Research / see Österreichische Austauschdienst
- ♦ Austrian Foundation for Development Research / see Austrian Research Foundation for Development Cooperation
- ♦ Austrian Institute for European Law and Policy (internationally oriented national body)
- ♦ Austrian Institute for International Affairs (internationally oriented national body)
- ♦ Austrian Institute for Peace Research / see Austrian Study Centre for Peace and Conflict Resolution
- ♦ Austrian Institute for Peace Research and Peace Education / see Austrian Study Centre for Peace and Conflict Resolution
- ♦ Austrian Latin America Institute (internationally oriented national body)
- ♦ Austrian North-South Institute for Development Cooperation (internationally oriented national body)
- ♦ Austrian Organisation for Development Co-operation / see HORIZONT 3000
- ♦ Austrian Peace Council (internationally oriented national body)
- ♦ Austrian Political Science Association (internationally oriented national body)
- ♦ Austrian Research Foundation for Development Cooperation (internationally oriented national body)
- ♦ Austrian Senior Experts Pool (internationally oriented national body)
- ♦ Austrian Service for Development Education / see SÜDWIND – Verein für Entwicklungspolitische Bildungs- und Öffentlichkeitsarbeit
- ♦ Austrian Society for Environment and Technology (internationally oriented national body)
- ♦ Austrian South-East Asian University Partnership Network / see ASEAN-European Academic University Network (#01170)
- ♦ Austrian Study Centre for Peace and Conflict Resolution (internationally oriented national body)

♦ Austronesian Formal Linguistics Association (AFLA) 03038

Contact UWO Linguistics Prog, Univ College Room 138, London ON ONT N6A 3K7, Canada.
URL: https://www.uwo.ca/linguistics/research/afla/index.html

History Founded 1994, Toronto (Canada). **Aims** Promote the study of Austronesian languages from a formal perspective. **Events** *AFLA Meeting* Singapore (Singapore) 2021, *Conference* Taipei (Taiwan) 2012, *Conference* Cambridge, MA (USA) 2011, *Conference* Stony Brook, NY (USA) 2010, *Annual meeting / Conference* Santa Cruz, CA (USA) 2009. [2020/XJ0100/F]

♦ Austronesian and Papuan Languages and Linguistics research group (APLL) 03039

Address not obtained.
URL: https://sites.google.com/view/apllconference/

History Successor to UK Austronesian Research Group (of UKARG), set up 2005. **Aims** Encourage research in Austronesian and Papuan languages. **Structure** Steering Committee; Programme Committee. **Activities** Events/meetings. **Events** *APLL – International Austronesian and Papuan Languages and Linguistics Conference* Edinburgh (UK) 2021, *APLL – International Austronesian and Papuan Languages and Linguistics Conference* Oslo (Norway) 2020, *APLL – International Austronesian and Papuan Languages and Linguistics Conference* Leiden (Netherlands) 2019, *APLL – International Austronesian and Papuan Languages and Linguistics Conference* Guildford (UK) 2018, *APLL – International Austronesian and Papuan Languages and Linguistics Conference* Paris (France) 2017. [2021/AA1831/c/E]

- ♦ AUSUDIAP / see Association for International Agriculture and Rural Development
- ♦ **AUTEX** Association of Universities for Textiles (#02972)
- ♦ Autisme-Europe (#03040)

♦ Autism-Europe (AE) 03040

Autisme-Europe (AE)

Main Office Rue Montoyer 39, Box 11, 1000 Brussels, Belgium. T. +3226757505. Fax +3226757270. E-mail: secretariat@autismeurope.org.
URL: http://www.autismeurope.org/

History 12 Jun 1983. Current Statutes adopted by Extraordinary General Assemblies of Oct 2009. Former names and other names: *International Association Autism – Europe (IAAE)* – former (12 Jun 1983); *Association internationale Autisme – Europe (AIAE)* – former (12 Jun 1983). Registration: Banque Carrefour des Entreprises, No/ID: 0424.600.969, Start date: 2 Sep 1983, Belgium; EU Transparency Register, No/ID: 396580546242-82, Start date: 26 Apr 2022. **Aims** Advance the rights of persons with autism and their families; help them improve their quality of life. **Structure** General Assembly (annually); Council; Executive Committee. President must be parent of an autistic person. Committees; working parties. Secretariat in Brussels (Belgium). **Languages** English, French. **Staff** 4.20 FTE, paid. **Finance** Sources: donations; members' dues. Other sources: European funding. **Activities** Advocacy/lobbying/activism; events/meetings. *Charter of Rights*, drawn up May 1992, adopted as a Written Declaration by the European Parliament, May 1996. Set up *World Autism Organisation (WAO, #21211)*, 21 Nov 1998, Luxembourg (Luxembourg). Cooperates with *WHO (#20950)*, founder of 'Coalition for independent living'. **Events** *International Congress* Dublin (Ireland) 2025, *International Congress* Krakow (Poland) 2022, *Early Childhood Mental Health International Conference (EMentH)* 2021, *Triennial Congress* Nice (France) 2019, *Final Conference* Madrid (Spain) 2018. **Publications** *AE Newsletter* (5 a year); *LINK* (2 a year) in English, French – magazine. *Access to Health and Rehabilitation* (2010); *Autistic Spectrum Disorders: Identification, Understanding, Intervention* (2009); *Toolkits for Self-advocates on Education* (2009); *Case Law on Education* (2006); *Code of Good Practice* (1998). Position Papers.
Members Associations and individuals in 34 countries:
Austria, Belgium, Bosnia-Herzegovina, Bulgaria, Croatia, Cyprus, Czechia, Denmark, Estonia, Finland, France, Germany, Greece, Hungary, Iceland, Ireland, Italy, Lithuania, Luxembourg, Morocco, Netherlands, North Macedonia, Norway, Poland, Portugal, Romania, Slovakia, Slovenia, Spain, Sweden, Switzerland, Türkiye, UK, Ukraine.
Consultative Status Consultative status granted from: *Council of Europe (CE, #04881)* (Participatory Status). **IGO Relations** Participant in Fundamental Rights Platform of: *European Union Agency for Fundamental Rights (FRA, #08969)*. **NGO Relations** Member of (3): *European Disability Forum (EDF, #06929)*; *Social Platform (#19344)*; *World Autism Organisation (WAO, #21211)* (as Funding member). [2022/XD9564/D]

♦ Autism Network International (ANI) 03041

Address not obtained.
Facebook: https://www.facebook.com/autismnetworkinternational/

History 1992. **Aims** Promote self- and peer-advocacy for autistic people; educate parents and professionals about autism from an advocacy and cultural perspective. **Activities** Events/meetings. **Events** *Conference* Brantingham, NY (USA) 2002, *Celebrating autistic culture* Canandaigua, NY (USA) 1998, *MAAPing the future* Indianapolis, IN (USA) 1995. **Publications** Reference library of educational materials on autism, self-advocacy and civil rights. **Information Services** *ANI-L* – internet discussion list; *Reference library of educational materials on autism, self-advocacy and civil rights*.
Members Individuals, mostly in USA but in a total of 11 countries and territories:
Australia, Canada, Denmark, Germany, Hong Kong, Israel, Japan, Namibia, Puerto Rico, UK, USA. [2021/XF3105/v/F]

♦ Autismo Latinoamérica Federación (ALaFe) 03042

Contact address not obtained. E-mail: info@apadea.org.ar.
Facebook: https://www.facebook.com/alafeAutismo/

History 21 Sep 2019.
Members Organizations in 10 countries:
Argentina, Bolivia, Brazil, Costa Rica, Ecuador, Guatemala, Honduras, Paraguay, Peru, Uruguay. [2021/AA1333/D]

- ♦ Autistic Minority International (unconfirmed)
- ♦ AUTM – Association of University Technology Managers (internationally oriented national body)
- ♦ Automated Teller Machine Industry Association / see ATM Industry Association
- ♦ Automated Valuation Models / see European AVM Alliance (#06305)
- ♦ Automatic Car Wash Association International / see International Carwash Association
- ♦ Automatic Identification Manufacturers Association / see AIM
- ♦ Automobile License Plate Collectors Association (internationally oriented national body)
- ♦ Automotive Parts Rebuilders Association / see Automotive Parts Remanufacturers Association
- ♦ Automotive Parts Remanufacturers Association (internationally oriented national body)

♦ Autonome Lokomotivführer-Gewerkschaften Europas (ALE) 03043

Autonomous Traindrivers' Union in Europe (LE)

Sec Paseo de las Delicias 20, Planta 3a, 28045 Madrid, Spain. T. +34917749400. E-mail: semaf@semaf.org – sec_general@semaf.org.
URL: http://ale-org.eu/

History 1989, Rome (Italy). Current statutes adopted 27 Oct 2006, Brno (Czech Rep). **Aims** Advocate a harmonized development of rail in Europe; require the establishment of clear rules to ensure the future viability of the railways, the employment of its workers and the conditions in which it develops its activity and safe rail transport. **Structure** Congress (every 4 years); Board of Management. **Languages** English, German, Spanish. **Staff** 26.00 FTE, paid. **Finance** Sources: members' dues. **Activities** Knowledge management/information dissemination; management of treaties and agreements; networking/liaising; standards/guidelines. Active in all member countries.
Members Train drivers' unions in 13 countries:
Belgium, Bulgaria, Croatia, Czechia, Greece, Hungary, Italy, Poland, Portugal, Romania, Serbia, Slovakia, Spain. [2020.04.29/XF3928/F]

- ♦ Autonomous Traindrivers' Union in Europe (#03043)
- ♦ Autoridad Internacional de los Fondos Marinos (#14813)
- ♦ Autoridad de Servicio Mundial (see: #21543)
- ♦ Autorità Europa di Sicurezza Alimentare (#07287)
- ♦ Autorité alimentaire européenne / see European Food Safety Authority (#07287)
- ♦ Autorité arabe pour les investissements et le développement agricoles (#00902)
- ♦ Autorité du bassin du Niger (#17134)
- ♦ Autorité du Bassin de la Volta (#20808)
- ♦ Autorité de contrôle allié de l'Allemagne (inactive)
- ♦ Autorité de coordination de transit et de transport du Corridor Nord (#17582)
- ♦ Autorité de coordination du transport de transit du Corridor Nord / see Northern Corridor Transit and Transport Coordination Authority (#17582)
- ♦ Autorité du développement intégré de Liptako-Gourma (no recent information)
- ♦ Autorité écossaise des réfugiés (internationally oriented national body)
- ♦ Autorité européenne de sécurité des aliments (#07287)
- ♦ Autorité intergouvernementale pour le développement (#11472)
- ♦ Autorité intergouvernementale sur la sécheresse et le développement (inactive)
- ♦ Autorité internationale des fonds marins (#14813)
- ♦ Autorité internationale de la Ruhr (inactive)
- ♦ Autorité de la route transafricaine Mombasa-Lagos (inactive)
- ♦ Autorité de la Route trans-est-africaine Le Caire-Gaborone (inactive)
- ♦ Autorité de surveillance AELE (#05392)
- ♦ Autoroute transeuropéenne Nord-Sud (#20208)
- ♦ AUTOSAR – AUTOSAR Partnership (unconfirmed)
- ♦ AUTOSAR Partnership (unconfirmed)

♦ Autre Terre 03044

Dir Parc Industriel des Hauts-Sarts, 4ème Avenue 45, 4040 Herstal, Belgium. T. +3242406848. Fax +3242406842. E-mail: info@autreterre.org.
URL: http://www.autreterre.org/

History 1982. Former names and other names: *Terre Tiers-monde et information (TTMI)* – former (2002); *Terre* – former. Registration: Banque-Carrefour des Entreprises, No/ID: 0423.588.904, Start date: 23 Sep 1982, Belgium; EU Transparency Register, No/ID: 03188475271-44, Start date: 9 Feb 2011. **Aims** Remain active in the North with education in World and solidarity Citizenship, and in the South with projects in agroecology and urban sanitation (collection, sorting and recovery of household waste). **Structure** General Assembly; Board of Directors; Executive Director; internal services. **Languages** English, French, Spanish. **Staff** Belgium: 14; Peru: 1; Africa 3; 100 voluntary. **Finance** Sources: donations; fundraising; gifts, legacies; government support; grants; private foundations; revenue from activities/projects; subsidies. Annual budget: 1,728,696 EUR (2021). **Activities** Awareness raising; capacity building; events/meetings; financial and/or material support; guidance/assistance/consulting; networking/liaising; projects/programmes; training/education. Active in: Belgium, Benin, Burkina Faso, Mali, Peru, Senegal. **Publications** *Autre Terre* (4 a year) in French. Annual activity report.

NGO Relations Member of (5): *Action pour le développement – SOS Faim (SOS Faim)*; *CNCD Opération 11 11 11*; *Fédération des employeurs ONG (FEONG)*; *Fédération francophone et germanophone des associations de coopération au développement (ACODEV, #09587)*; *RIPESS Europe – Economy Solidarity Europe (RIPESS Europe, #18952)*.

[2023.02.14/XF2974/F]

♦ **AUTSE** Asian Union of Thermal Science and Engineering (#01773)
♦ **AUU** / see Americans for UNESCO
♦ **AUUMM** – Association for Unitarian Universalist Music Ministries (internationally oriented national body)
♦ **AUW** – Action for a United World (internationally oriented national body)
♦ **AUW** – Asian University for Women (unconfirmed)
♦ **Auxiliadoras del Purgatorio** (religious order)
♦ **Auxiliaires féminines internationales** / see Inter-Cultural Association (#11465)
♦ **Auxiliaires Laïques des Mission** / see Inter-Cultural Association (#11465)
♦ **Auxiliatrices de la Charité** (religious order)
♦ **Auxiliatrices du Purgatoire** (religious order)
♦ **Auxilio Mundial** (internationally oriented national body)
♦ **AVAA** / see African Masters Athletics (#00368)
♦ **AVAA** / see Asia Masters Athletics (#01291)
♦ **AVA** African Veterinary Association (#00495)
♦ **AVA** ASEAN Valuers Association (#01245)
♦ **AVA** Association of Veterinary Anaesthetists (#02976)

♦ **Avaaz Foundation** **03045**
Dir 857 Broadway, New York NY 10003, USA. E-mail: media@avaaz.org – partnerships@avaaz.org.
URL: http://www.avaaz.org
History Feb 2007. Founded as a community of global citizens. Name derives from the words for "voice" in several languages. Registration: USA, State of Delaware. **Aims** Unite *citizens* worldwide and ensure their views and *values* shape global *decisions*; close the gap between the world as it is and the world as it should be on human rights, environmental protection, poverty, global justice, etc. **Structure** Managed by a small team of campaigners in 4 continents. **Finance** Sources: donations. Small online donations only (maximum euro5000); none accepted from corporations, governments or foundations. Individual donations up to August 2008: over euro 2.5 million. **Activities** Launches internet campaigns, collecting signatures on matters of global importance and presents the results to the authorities concerned. Funds (over US $8 million to Apr 2014) humanitarian causes and partner organizations doing work unlikely to be funded by corporations and foundations. **Members** As of Feb 2022, membership comprises over 69 million individuals in over 190 countries. Membership countries not specified. **NGO Relations** Member of (1): *Global Call for Climate Action (GCCA, inactive)*.

[2022.02.23/XM2609/fv/F]

♦ **AVAC** / see Global Advocacy for HIV Prevention (#10172)
♦ **AVAC** Global Advocacy for HIV Prevention (#10172)
♦ **Avannaamioqatigiit Arnanur Suiaassusersiornermulu Ilisimatusarfiat** / see Nordic Information for Gender Knowledge (#17317)
♦ **Avant Ministries** (internationally oriented national body)
♦ **AVAR** Association of Anti Virus Asia Researchers (#02370)
♦ **AVARD** – Association of Voluntary Agencies for Rural Development (internationally oriented national body)
♦ **AVAS** / see Association for Research on Nonprofit Organizations and Voluntary Action
♦ **AVCA** African Private Equity and Venture Capital Association (#00425)
♦ **AVC** Asian Volleyball Confederation (#01779)
♦ **Avdelningen för Utvecklingssamarbete** (internationally oriented national body)
♦ **AVEA** Association vétérinaire Euro-Arabe (#02975)
♦ **AVE** Asocio de Verduloj Esperantistaj (#02494)
♦ **AVE** – Association des Villes et Régions Hôtes d'Expositions Internationales (no recent information)
♦ **AVE** Association pour le volontariat en Europe (#02978)
♦ **AVEC** / see Alliance de Villes Euro-méditerranéennes de Culture (#00726)
♦ **AVEC** Alliance de Villes Euro-méditerranéennes de Culture (#00726)
♦ **AVEC** / see Association de l'aviculture, de l'industrie et du commerce de volailles dans les pays de l'Union européenne (#02390)
♦ **AVEC** Association de l'aviculture, de l'industrie et du commerce de volailles dans les pays de l'Union européenne (#02390)
♦ **Avenir pour l'Enfant des Rizières** (internationally oriented national body)
♦ **Avenir de la langue française** (internationally oriented national body)
♦ **AVERE** / see European Association for Electromobility (#06024)
♦ **AVERE** European Association for Electromobility (#06024)
♦ **AVF** / see Asian Volleyball Confederation (#01779)
♦ **AVF** – Association for Vertical Farming (unconfirmed)
♦ **AVF** – Association des vétérinaires francophones (no recent information)
♦ **AVFT** Association européenne contre les violences faites aux femmes au travail (#05931)
♦ **AvH** – Alexander von Humboldt Foundation (internationally oriented national body)
♦ **AvH** – Alexander von Humboldt-Stiftung (internationally oriented national body)
♦ **AVI** (internationally oriented national body)
♦ **AVIA** Asia Video Industry Association (#02103)
♦ **Avian Immunology Research Group** (meeting series)
♦ **AVI** Association universelle d'aviculture scientifique (#21825)
♦ **Aviation Without Borders** (internationally oriented national body)
♦ **Aviation Without Borders** – Wings for the World / see Aviation Without Borders
♦ **Aviation Sans Frontières** (unconfirmed)
♦ **Aviation sans frontières, Belgique** (internationally oriented national body)
♦ **Aviation sans frontières, France** (internationally oriented national body)

♦ **Aviation Security Services Association – International (ASSA-I)** ... **03046**
Dir Gen Jan Bogemansstraat 249, 1780 Wemmel, Belgium. T. +3224620776. Fax +3224601431.
URL: http://www.assa-i.org/
History Founded Jun 2002, as *European Aviation Security Association*. Also known as *ASSA International*. Registered in accordance with Belgian law. **Aims** Be the single voice of private security providers and, as such, promote high quality standards and professionalism in aviation security. **Structure** General Assembly (annual); Board of Directors; General Secretariat. **Languages** English. **Staff** 1.00 FTE, paid. **Finance** Members' dues. **Activities** Politics/policy/regulatory; knowledge management/information dissemination; standards/guidelines. **Publications** Reports; studies; position papers.
Members Companies (7) with headquarters in 6 countries:
Belgium, Germany, Netherlands, Spain, Switzerland, UK.
NGO Relations Corresponding member of: *Confederation of European Security Services (CoESS, #04532)*.

[2019.12.12/XJ4563/D]

♦ **AVI** – Auroville International (see: #03019)

♦ **Avicenna Alliance** **03047**
SG RPP Group SPRL, Rue Guimard 10, 1040 Brussels, Belgium. E-mail: secgen@avicenna-alliance.com.
URL: https://avicenna-alliance.com/
History Founded 2016, as an initiative of *Avicenna* and *Virtual Physiological Human Institute for Integrative Biomedical Research (VPH Institute, #20790)*. Full title: *Avicenna Alliance – Association for Predictive Medicine*. **Aims** Significantly accelerate medical innovation and its practical implementation, to ensure safe, affordable and cost effective *health care* through the large scale adoption of in silico medicine – *Computer Modelling* and *Simulation*, CM and S. **Structure** Board. Working Groups (3): Research; Policy Development; International Affairs. **Languages** English. **Activities** Events/meetings; knowledge management/information dissemination. **Publications** *Avicenna Alliance Newsletter*. **Members** Representation of healthcare industry (50%); Virtual Physiological Human Institute for Integrative Biomedical Research (50%). Membership countries not specified.

[2020.03.12/XM8641/E]

♦ **Avicenna Alliance** – Association for Predictive Medicine / see Avicenna Alliance (#03047)
♦ **AVICOM** – ICOM International Committee for Audiovisual and New Technologies of Image and Sound (see: #13051)
♦ **Avions sans frontières** / see Terre sans frontières
♦ **Aviornis** / see Aviornis International (#03048)

♦ **Aviornis International** **03048**
Registered Office Wuytsbergen 118, 2200 Herentals, Belgium.
History 1973, Tienen (Belgium) as *Aviornis*. In French also referred to as *Association internationale pour la protection des espèces en péril (AVIORNIS)*. In Spanish also known as *Asociación Internacional de Criadores de Aves Silvestres*. Current title adopted 1975. Registered in accordance with Belgian law. **NGO Relations** Supports: *World Pheasant Association (WPA, #21724)*.

[2019/XN2960/F]

♦ **AViTeM** – Agence des Villes et Territoires Méditerranéens Durables (internationally oriented national body)
♦ **AVIXA** – Audiovisual and Integrated Experience Association (internationally oriented national body)
♦ **AVL** Alliance Vietnam liberté (#09990)
♦ **AVN** Asiavision (#02104)
♦ **AVN** Association Voûte Nubienne (#17614)
♦ **Avocats/Conseils pour l'Afrique** / see LEX Africa (#16449)

♦ **Avocats européens démocrates (AED)** **03049**
European Democratic Lawyers – Abogados Europeos Democraticos (AED) – Europäische Demokratische Anwälte (EDA)
Contact 2 rue Louis Pergaud, 94706 Maisons-Alfort, France. T. +33149804367. Fax +33143396502.
Pres c/ Provença 332 – 3r, 08037 Barcelona, Spain. T. +34934578358.
URL: https://www.aeud.org/
History Oct 1987. Registration: Start date: 4 Jul 1990, France. **Aims** Introduce a debate between lawyers of various countries in order to promote a democratic Europe, in particular concerning recourse to the debate towards litigation solutions, the respect of rights of defence and the harmonization of the statutes and practices of professional lawyers; guarantee independence of Bars and their members in any capacity, and in particular, the capacity of the State; defend and extend rights and prerogatives of defence, and in particular, of the physical integrity and the political, economic, social and individual freedom of lawyers at the international level; promote on behalf of citizens, notably the weakest or victims of infringements of human rights, the access to rights and to modern and humaine democratic justice; carry out action for respect of the essential rights and fundamental public and individual freedoms, in particular against any abuse of the Public Power and in any capacity; develop European, democratic juridic culture, notably by regular exchange of information, continuous study of subject of common interest and organization of joint working meetings. **Structure** General Assembly; Directors Committee; Bureau; Commissions. **Languages** English, French. **Staff** 1.00 FTE, paid. **Finance** Members' dues. **Activities** Organizes seminars, colloquia and international conferences. As an association, AED is a civil party together with other human rights associations in diverse trials. Members participate in international solidarity missions with lawyers from around the world. **Events** *Conférence internationale sur les frontières de l'Europe – zone de non-droit* Barcelona (Spain) 2006, *Conférence internationale sur les droits sociaux en Europe* Berlin (Germany) 2006, *L'enfermement des étrangers aux frontières européennes* Malaga (Spain) 2005, *Dérives pénales européennes* Bordeaux (France) 2004, *L'Europe – espace de liberté, de sécurité et de droit* Berlin (Germany) 2003. **Publications** All available online.
Members National organizations of lawyers (10) in 6 countries:
Belgium, France, Germany, Italy, Netherlands, Spain.

[2021/XD8608/D]

♦ **Avocats Sans Frontières (ASF)** **03050**
Abogados Sin Fronteras – Anwälte Ohne Grenzen – Advocaten Zonder Grenzen
Dir Gen Av de la Chasse 140, 1040 Brussels, Belgium. T. +3222233654. E-mail: communication@asf.be.
URL: http://www.asf.be/
History 1992, Brussels (Belgium). Registered in accordance with Belgian law. **Aims** Promote and protect *human rights*, and particularly the right of defence; seek to ensure organization of proper defence and fair process of *law*; protect the rights of more vulnerable persons and groups and ensure that they can exercise their rights; prevent conflict and promote respect for persons and peoples and for their social, cultural, economic and political development. **Structure** General Assembly; Administrative Council. **Languages** Dutch, English, French. **Staff** 65.00 FTE, paid; 2.00 FTE, voluntary. **Finance** Members' dues. Donations; support from institutional donors from Belgium, Congo DR, France, UK, Switzerland, Netherlands, USA. Including supports from: *European Union (EU, #08967)*; Heinrich Böll Foundation; Institut für Auslandsbeziehungen, Stuttgart (ifa); *Natural Resource Governance Institute (NRGI, #16957)*; *Open Society Foundations (OSF, #17763)*; *UNDP (#20292)*. **Activities** Guidance/assistance/consulting; capacity building; knowledge management/information dissemination; monitoring/evaluation; advocacy/lobbying/activism. Active in: Belgium, Burundi, Central African Rep, Chad, Congo DR, Indonesia, Morocco, Tunisia, Uganda. **Events** *Conférence sur l'Accès à la Justice en République Centrafricaine* Brussels (Belgium) 2018, *Conference on the establishment of an international criminal bar* Montréal, QC (Canada) 2002. **Publications** *ASF Newsletter* (8 a year) – by e-mail. Annual Report. **Consultative Status** Consultative status granted from: *ECOSOC (#05331)* (Special); *Organisation internationale de la Francophonie (OIF, #17809)*; *African Commission on Human and Peoples' Rights (ACHPR, #00255)* (Observer). **IGO Relations** Cooperates with: *UNHCR (#20327)*. Associated with Department of Global Communications of the United Nations. **NGO Relations** Member of: *Coalition for an Effective African Court on Human and Peoples' Rights (African Court Coalition, #04055)*; *ETO Consortium (ETOs, #05560)*; *International Criminal Bar (ICB, #13107)*; *Transparency, Accountability and Participation Network (TAP Network, #20222)*. Instrumental in setting up: *Arusha School on International Criminal Law and Human Rights* (no recent information).

[2019.06.17/XF5401/v/F]

♦ **Avocats pour la Santé dans le Monde** / see Global Health Advocates (#10400)
♦ **Avoided Deforestation Partners** (internationally oriented national body)
♦ **AVPA** – African Venture Philanthropy Alliance (unconfirmed)
♦ **AVPA** – Australasian Veterinary Poultry Association (internationally oriented national body)
♦ **AVP** Association for Visual Pedagogies (#02977)
♦ **AVP International** Alternatives to Violence Project International (#00755)
♦ **AVPN** Asian Venture Philanthropy Network (#01778)
♦ **AVR** / see Association of Cities and Regions for Sustainable Resource Management (#02433)
♦ **Avrasya Üniversiteler Birligi** (#05615)
♦ **AVRDC** / see AVRDC – The World Vegetable Center (#03051)

♦ **AVRDC – The World Vegetable Center** **03051**
Dir Gen PO Box 42, Shanhua, Tainan 74199, Taiwan. T. +88665837801. Fax +88665830009.
URL: http://avrdc.org/
History Established 22 May 1971, Tainan (Taiwan), on acceptance of Charter and Memorandum of Understanding by representatives of 7 governments. Original mandate covered humid and semihumid tropics of Asia; from 1991, activities expanded to Africa, Latin America and the Caribbean. Original title: *Asian Vegetable Research and Development Center (AVRDC) – Centre asiatique de recherche et de développement dans le domaine des végétaux*. Has been referred to in French as *Centre de recherche et de développement sur les légumes en Asie*. **Aims** Enhance *nutritional well-being* and raise incomes of *poor people* in rural and urban areas of *developing countries* through improved varieties and methods of vegetable production, marketing, distribution and consumption, taking into account preservation of the quality of the environment. **Structure** Board of Directors; Director-General; Regional Offices (4); Research Units (12). Set up and administers 5 international regional research networks: *ASEAN-AVRDC Regional Network on Vegetable Research and Development (AARNET, #01143)*. **Languages** English. **Staff** 350.00 FTE, paid. **Finance** Grants from: *African Development Bank (ADB, #00283)*; *Australian Centre for International Agricultural Research (ACIAR)*; EuropeAID; *Global Crop Diversity Trust (Crop Trust, #10313)*; *United States Agency for International Development (USAID)*; member governments. Donations for special project funds. Annual budget: about US$ 20,000,000. **Activities** Research and development; training/education; guidance/assistance/consulting;

knowledge management/information dissemination; events/meetings. Comprises the major global depository of vegetable germplasm (62,000 accessions). Annually supplies about 6,000 to 10,000 seed samples to university researchers, private companies, NGOs and others. Main research and development groups: biotechnology/molecular breeding; entomology; genetic resources and genebank management; nutrition; plant breeding; plant pathology; postharvest; socioeconomics; technology dissemination. **Events** *International Conference* Manila (Philippines) 2015, *Regional Symposium on Sustaining Small Scale Vegetable Poduction and Marketing Systems for Food and Nutrition Security / International Symposium* Bangkok (Thailand) 2014, *International Symposium on Indigenous Vegetables / International Symposium* Brisbane, QLD (Australia) 2014, *International Conference* Hyderabad (India) 2014, *International Plant Virus Epidemiology Symposium* Arusha (Tanzania UR) 2013. **Publications** *Fresh* (12 a year) – newsletter. Annual Report; progress reports; technical bulletins; cooperators' guides; proceedings; bibliographies; directories of crop researchers; catalogues; field guides; syllabuses; training materials.
Members Governments of 9 countries and territories:
Australia, Germany, Japan, Korea Rep, Philippines, Taiwan, Thailand, UK, USA.
IGO Relations Member of: *Asia-Pacific Association of Agricultural Research Institutions (APAARI, #01830).* Cooperates with: *International Center for Agricultural Research in the Dry Areas (ICARDA, #12466); International Crops Research Institute for the Semi-Arid Tropics (ICRISAT, #13116).* **NGO Relations** Member of: *Association of International Research and Development Centers for Agriculture (AIRCA, #02760); Global Alliance to Promote Fruits and Vegetable Consumption "5 a day" (AIAM5, #10221); Global Open Data for Agriculture and Nutrition (GODAN, #10514); Inland Valley Consortium (IVC, no recent information); International Society for Horticultural Science (ISHS, #15180).* Cooperates with: *Global Forum on Agricultural Research (GFAR, #10370); Global Horticulture Initiative (GlobalHort, #10412); International Potato Center (#14627); WorldFish (#21507).* [2016.10.18/XD4635/**E***]

- ♦ AVRD Symposium – International Symposium on Avian Viral Respiratory Diseases (meeting series)
- ♦ Avrupa Dogal Afetler Egitim Merkezi (internationally oriented national body)
- ♦ Avrupa Icin Liberaller ve Demokratlar Ittifaki Partisi (#00703)
- ♦ Avrupa Liberal, Demokrat ve Reform Partisi / see Alliance of Liberals and Democrats for Europe Party (#00703)
- ♦ AVSA – Anatomiese Vereniging van Suider Afrika (internationally oriented national body)
- ♦ **AVSA** Australasian Victorian Studies Association (#03034)
- ♦ AVSC / see EngenderHealth
- ♦ AVSC International / see EngenderHealth
- ♦ AVSE Global – Association of Vietnamese Scientists and Experts (internationally oriented national body)
- ♦ AVSF – Agronomes et vétérinaires sans frontières (internationally oriented national body)
- ♦ AVSI / see AVSI Foundation
- ♦ AVSI Foundation (internationally oriented national body)
- ♦ Avtale om gjennomføring av visse bestemmelser om statsborgerrett (2002 treaty)
- ♦ Avtale om kulturelt samarbeid (1971 treaty)
- ♦ Avtale mellom Danmark, Island, Norge og Sverige om samarbeid i konkurransesaker (2001 treaty)
- ♦ Avtal om kulturellt samarbete (1971 treaty)
- ♦ Avtal mellan Danmark, Finland, Island, Norge och Sverige om genomförande av vissa bestämmelser om medborgarskap (2002 treaty)
- ♦ Avtal mellan Danmark, Island, Norge och Sverige om samarbete i konkurrensfrågor (2001 treaty)
- ♦ **AVU** African Virtual University (#00496)
- ♦ **AVUS** Adriatic Vascular Ultrasound Society (#00124)
- ♦ **AWO** Arab Women Organization (#01078)
- ♦ **AW2I** Arab World Internet Institute (#01079)
- ♦ AWAFC – American West African Freight Conference (meeting series)
- ♦ **AWANICh** African Women's Active Nonviolence Initiatives for Social Change (#00502)
- ♦ AWARE International (internationally oriented national body)
- ♦ **Awarenet** Arab Water Network for Capacity Building (#01076)
- ♦ AW – ASSOCIATIONWORLD (unconfirmed)
- ♦ AWB – Academics Without Borders (internationally oriented national body)
- ♦ AWB – Action Without Borders (internationally oriented national body)
- ♦ **AWB** Acupuncture Without Borders (#00106)
- ♦ AWB – Advertisers without Borders (unconfirmed)
- ♦ AWBAF – Asian Wrestling on Belts Alysh Federation (unconfirmed)
- ♦ AWB – Astronomers Without Borders (internationally oriented national body)
- ♦ AWB – Aviation Without Borders (internationally oriented national body)
- ♦ **AwB International** Archivists without Borders International (#01091)
- ♦ AWBR / see Internationale Arbeitsgemeinschaft der Wasserwerke im Rheineinzugsgebiet (#13215)
- ♦ AWCA – Asian Wound Care Association (unconfirmed)
- ♦ AWC – African Woman and Child Features Service (internationally oriented national body)
- ♦ AWC – Amazigh World Congress (internationally oriented national body)
- ♦ **AWC** Arab Watch Coalition (#01074)
- ♦ **AWC** Arab Water Council (#01075)
- ♦ **AWCAR** Association of Working Communities of the Alpine Regions (#02981)
- ♦ **AWC** Asia Water Council (#02105)
- ♦ **AWC** Association of World Citizens (#02982)
- ♦ **AWCE** Alan Walker College of Evangelism (#00619)
- ♦ AWCF – Apostolic World Christian Fellowship (internationally oriented national body)
- ♦ AWCFS / see African Woman and Child Features Service
- ♦ AWCTR / see Center of Arab Women for Training and Research, Tunis (#03637)
- ♦ **AWDF** African Women's Development Fund (#00504)
- ♦ AWDSA – Asia Working Dog Support Association (internationally oriented national body)
- ♦ **AWE** Association for World Education (#02983)
- ♦ **A-WEB** Association of World Election Bodies (#02984)
- ♦ AWEG – African Women Empowerment Guild (internationally oriented national body)
- ♦ AWEMA – Arab World Evangelical Ministers Association (internationally oriented national body)
- ♦ AWEPON – African Women's Economic Policy Network (inactive)
- ♦ AWER / see Assembly of European Wine Regions (#02317)
- ♦ AWES – Association of European Shipbuilders and Shiprepairers (inactive)
- ♦ AWES – Association of World Economic Studies (unconfirmed)
- ♦ AWES – Australasian Wind Engineering Society (internationally oriented national body)
- ♦ AWF – Afghanistan World Foundation (internationally oriented national body)
- ♦ **AWF** African Water Facility (#09233)
- ♦ **AWF** African Wildlife Foundation (#00498)
- ♦ **AWF** Alliance World Fellowship (#00728)
- ♦ AWF – Arab Weightlifting Federation (inactive)
- ♦ AWF – Arab West Foundation (internationally oriented national body)
- ♦ **AWF** Asian Weightlifting Federation (#01781)
- ♦ **AWF** Asian Welding Federation (#01782)
- ♦ AWF-International – Animals without Frontiers – International (internationally oriented national body)
- ♦ **AWG SF** ASEAN Working Group on Social Forestry (#01247)
- ♦ **AWHF** African World Heritage Fund (#00505)
- ♦ AWHONN – Association of Women's Health, Obstetric and Neonatal Nurses (internationally oriented national body)
- ♦ **AWHRC** Asian Women's Human Rights Council (#01783)
- ♦ **AWID** Association for Women's Rights in Development (#02980)
- ♦ **AWIEF** Africa Women Innovation and Entrepreneurship Forum (#00531)
- ♦ AWIG – Association of West Indian Gastroenterologists (internationally oriented national body)
- ♦ AWiMA – Arab Women in Maritime Association (unconfirmed)
- ♦ AWIMA – Asia Women in Motorsport Association (unconfirmed)
- ♦ A WISH – World Institute for a Sustainable Humanity (internationally oriented national body)
- ♦ **AWIU** Arab Women Investors Union (#01077)
- ♦ AWJN – Africa Water Journalist Network (internationally oriented national body)
- ♦ AWLAE – African Women Leaders in Agriculture and the Environment (internationally oriented national body)
- ♦ AWLCO – Arab Well Logging Company (see: #17854)
- ♦ **AWLO** African Women in Leadership Organisation (#00501)
- ♦ A and WMA – Air and Waste Management Association (internationally oriented national body)
- ♦ AWM International – Arab World Ministries (internationally oriented national body)
- ♦ AWMM – Arbeitsgemeinschaft für Werbung, Markt- und Meinungsforschung (inactive)
- ♦ AWMR – Association of Women of the Mediterranean Region (no recent information)
- ♦ **AWNA** Asian Women's Neurosurgical Association (#01784)
- ♦ AWO International – Arbeiterwohlfahrt International (internationally oriented national body)
- ♦ AWP – Arbeitsgemeinschaft für Wissenschaft und Politik (internationally oriented national body)
- ♦ **AWR** Association for the Study of the World Refugee Problem (#02942)
- ♦ **AWRC** Asian Women's Resource Centre for Culture and Theology (#01785)
- ♦ AWRN – Arab World Regional EC Network (unconfirmed)
- ♦ AWSA – Arab Women's Solidarity Association (inactive)
- ♦ **AWS** Alliance for Water Stewardship (#00727)
- ♦ AWS – American Welding Society (internationally oriented national body)
- ♦ AWSE – African Women in Science and Engineering (internationally oriented national body)
- ♦ AWSG – Australasian Wader Studies Group (internationally oriented national body)
- ♦ AWTRS – Australasian Wound and Tissue Repair Society (internationally oriented national body)
- ♦ **AWWA** American Water Works Association (#00791)
- ♦ **AXF** Asian Xiangqi Federation (#01786)

♦ Axial Spondyloarthritis International Federation (ASIF) 03052

Assistant Administrator 27 Old Gloucester Street, London, WC1N 3AX, UK. E-mail: office@asif.info.
Pres address not obtained.
URL: http://www.asif.info/

History 1988, Bath (UK). Founded when statutes were adopted with original title *Ankylosing Spondylitis International Federation (ASIF).* Current constitution adopted Oct 2016, Moscow (Russia); amended Jun 2017, Madrid (Spain). Registration: Charity Commission, No/ID: 1173902, Start date: 21 Jul 2017, England and Wales. **Aims** Increase public awareness of Ankylosing Spondylitis; disseminate knowledge of the *disease* worldwide. Encourage and support research into ankylosing spondylitis and its associated diseases; act as a central body for national self-help organizations. **Structure** General Council; Executive Committee. **Languages** English. **Finance** Members' dues. **Activities** Research and development; research/documentation; events/meetings. **Events** *Meeting* Copenhagen (Denmark) 2022, *Meeting* Guangzhou (China) 2018, *Meeting* Sofia (Bulgaria) 2014, *Meeting / Council Meeting* Izmir (Turkey) 2011, *Meeting / Council Meeting* Bad Gastein (Austria) 2009. **Publications** *ASIF News* (2 a year) – electronically.
Members National organizations in 36 countries and territories:
Australia, Austria, Belgium, Bulgaria, Canada, Chile, China, Colombia, Croatia, Cyprus, Czechia, Denmark, France, Germany, Hungary, India, Ireland, Italy, Japan, Korea Rep, Lithuania, Moldova, Netherlands, Norway, Portugal, Russia, Singapore, Slovenia, South Africa, Spain, Sweden, Switzerland, Taiwan, Türkiye, UK, USA. [2022/XD7215/**D**]

- ♦ The Axis – Triple Alliance (inactive)
- ♦ AY+ – African Young Positives Network (unconfirmed)
- ♦ Aya Worldwide (internationally oriented national body)
- ♦ AYA / see World Youth Alliance – Africa (#21950)
- ♦ AYC – Africa Youth Trust (internationally oriented national body)
- ♦ **AYC** Asian Youth Centre (#01787)
- ♦ **AYC** Asian Youth Council (#01788)
- ♦ AYECS / see Association des jeunes fonctionnaires européens (#02772)
- ♦ AYF – African Youth Foundation (internationally oriented national body)
- ♦ AYF – Africa Yoga Federation (internationally oriented national body)
- ♦ **AYF** Aikido Yoshinkai Foundation (#00595)
- ♦ AYF – Asian Yachting Federation (no recent information)
- ♦ **AYF** Asian Youth Forum (#01789)
- ♦ AYF International / see Asian Youth Forum (#01789)
- ♦ AYFT / see Youth for Transparency International
- ♦ AYGF – African Youth Growth Foundation (internationally oriented national body)
- ♦ AYICRIP – African Youths Initiative on Crime Prevention (internationally oriented national body)
- ♦ **AYLH** Association of Young Legal Historians (#02987)
- ♦ **AYM** African Youth Movement (#00506)
- ♦ AYM – Arab Youth Movement (see: #13327)
- ♦ AYNLA – Alliance of Young Nurse Leaders and Advocates International (internationally oriented national body)
- ♦ **AYO** Asian Youth Orchestra (#01790)
- ♦ **AYOSA** African Youth Safe Abortion Alliance (#00508)
- ♦ AYPAD – Africa Youth for Peace and Development (internationally oriented national body)
- ♦ **AYPN** African Youth in Philanthropy Network (#00507)
- ♦ AYPVC – ASEAN Young Professionals Volunteers Corps (unconfirmed)
- ♦ AYRCOB – Asian Young Researchers Conference on Computational and Omics Biology (meeting series)
- ♦ Ayrshires-International / see World Federation of Ayrshire Breed Societies (#21414)
- ♦ **AYSS** Association of Yacht Support Services (#02986)
- ♦ AYSS Superyacht Global Network / see Association of Yacht Support Services (#02986)
- ♦ AYU – Arab Youth Union (no recent information)
- ♦ Ayuda en Acción (#00087)
- ♦ AYUDA – American Youth Understanding Diabetes Abroad (internationally oriented national body)
- ♦ Ayuda a la Iglesia Necesitada (#00587)
- ♦ Ayuda de la Iglesia Noruega (internationally oriented national body)
- ♦ Ayuda de las Iglesias Evangelicas de Suiza (internationally oriented national body)
- ♦ Ayuda Obrera Internacional / see SOLIDAR (#19680)
- ♦ Ayuda Popular Noruega (internationally oriented national body)
- ♦ AYUSA – Ayusa International (internationally oriented national body)
- ♦ Ayusa International (internationally oriented national body)
- ♦ AZA / see B'nai B'rith Youth Organization (#03291)
- ♦ **AZE** Alliance for Zero Extinction (#00730)
- ♦ AZEC – Asian Zoo Educators Conference (meeting series)
- ♦ Az Egyesitett Atomkutató Intézet / see Joint Institute for Nuclear Research (#16134)
- ♦ Azerbaijan International Development Agency (internationally oriented national body)
- ♦ Azerbaycan Insan Hüquqlarini Mudafie Merkezi (internationally oriented national body)
- ♦ Az eurócsoport (#05689)
- ♦ Az Európai Parlament Szocialista Képviselöcsoportja / see Group of the Progressive Alliance of Socialists and Democrats in the European Parliament (#10786)
- ♦ Az Európai Unió Kiadóhivatala (#18562)
- ♦ Az Európai Unió Tanacsa (#04895)
- ♦ **AZI** Association Zen internationale (#15940)
- ♦ AZI-LIA' / see International Lead Zinc Research Organization (#14011)
- ♦ Azione Aiuto (#00087)
- ♦ Azione contro la Fame (#00086)
- ♦ Azione Globale dei Popoli contra il comercio 'libre' (#18304)
- ♦ AZOLCA – Asociación de Zonas Francas de Latinoamérica y el Caribe (no recent information)

♦ AZV – Artsen Zonder Vakantie (internationally oriented national body)
♦ Azzurra della Nostra Signora di Fatima (religious order)
♦ B1G1 (unconfirmed)
♦ B20 Coalition / see Global Business Coalition (#10257)
♦ B4H – Bicycles for Humanity (internationally oriented national body)
♦ **B4IG** Business for Inclusive Growth (#03384)
♦ **B7** Islands of the Baltic Sea (#16060)
♦ **BAAC** Baltic Audiovisual Archival Council (#03103)
♦ BAA / see Jesuit Conference of Asia Pacific (#16099)
♦ **BA** Baltic Assembly (#03094)
♦ Babel International (internationally oriented national body)
♦ BABFD – Baltic Association of Burns and Fire Disasters (no recent information)
♦ **BA** Borderless Alliance (#03303)
♦ BABS – Benelux Association of Bariatric Surgeons (no recent information)
♦ BaBSEVA – Balkan and Black Sea Veterinary Association (no recent information)

♦ Baby Friendly Hospital Initiative (BFHI) 03053

Address not obtained.
URL: http://www.unicef.org/programme/breastfeeding/baby.htm

History Jun 1991, as a worldwide effort to protect, promote and support breastfeeding. **Aims** Promote a worldwide return to breastfeeding, particularly exclusive breastfeeding for the first 4 to 6 months of a baby's life by encouraging women to breastfeed, instituting hospital procedures that enable them to breastfeed and ending the supply of free or low-cost infant formula to maternity institutions. **Structure** Not an organization but a project carried out by UNICEF. **Activities** Carries out advocacy and awareness-raising actions at all levels, provides information and supports the training necessary to help hospitals and maternity institutions everywhere to achieve baby-friendly status by implementing the "Ten Steps to Successful Breastfeeding" as elaborated by WHO and UNICEF. As of Jan 1998, 13,127 hospitals and maternity institutions in 117 countries had become "baby-friendly". **Events** *Euro workshop on BFHI and lactation management* Nymburk (Czech Rep) 1994. **Publications** *BFHI News* (12 a year) in English – newsletter. **IGO Relations** Supported by: *UNICEF (#20332)*; *WHO (#20950)*. [2016/XF5269/**F**]

♦ Babylon / see Centre for the Study of Superdiversity
♦ Babylon – Centre for the Study of Superdiversity (internationally oriented national body)
♦ BAC / see Badminton Asia (#03056)
♦ BAC – Benelux Afro Center (internationally oriented national body)
♦ **BAC** Business Advisory Council (#03376)
♦ Baccalauréat International (#12306)
♦ **BACEE** Banking Association for Central and Eastern Europe (#03163)

♦ Bachelier Finance Society (BFS) 03054

Exec Sec ETH Zürich, Dept of Mathematics, Rämistrasse 101, 8092 Zurich ZH, Switzerland. T. +41446322755. Fax +41446321474.
URL: http://www.bachelierfinance.org/

History 1996. **Aims** Promote the discipline of finance by applying the theory of *stochastic* processes as well as *statistical* and *mathematical* theory. **Structure** General Assembly. Council of 10. Executive Committee, comprising President, Vice-President, Executive Secretary, Past-President and Treasurer. **Events** *World Congress* Brussels (Belgium) 2014, *World Congress* Sydney, NSW (Australia) 2012, *World congress* Sydney, NSW (Australia) 2012, *World Congress* Paris (France) 2010, *World Congress* Toronto, ON (Canada) 2010. **Members** Individual; Institutional; Sponsoring. Membership countries not specified. [2013/XJ6481/**E**]

♦ Bachillerato Internacional (#12306)
♦ BAC / see International Center for Biosaline Agriculture (#12468)
♦ BAC – International Union of Bricklayers and Allied Craftworkers (internationally oriented national body)
♦ **BACSA** Black, Caspian Seas and Central Asia Silk Association (#03269)
♦ **BACS** Balkan Academy of Cosmetic Surgery (#03064)
♦ Badawiya Ahmadiya (religious order)
♦ **BAD** Banque africaine de développement (#00283)
♦ **BAD** Banque asiatique de développement (#01422)
♦ **BADEA** Banque arabe pour le développement économique en Afrique (#00904)

♦ Baden-Powell World Fellowship 03055

Fraternité mondiale Baden-Powell

Dir c/o World Scout Foundation, Box 2116, 1211 Geneva 1, Switzerland. T. +41227051090. Fax +41227051099. E-mail: info@worldscoutfoundation.org.
URL: http://www.scout.org/

History 22 Feb 1982, as a special programme of the *World Scout Foundation (WSF, #21772)*. **Aims** Generate and duly recognize support for the promotion of *scouting* around the globe through the World Organization of the Scout Movement. **Structure** Chapters (8): Athens (Greece); Cayman Is; Ireland; Japan; London (UK); Thailand; Denmark, Australia. **Languages** English. **Staff** 1.00 FTE, paid. **Finance** Members' dues: US$ 10,000. **Activities** Organizes periodic Fellowhip Meeting. **Events** *Meeting* Seoul (Korea Rep) 2008. **Publications** Annual Report; Membership list.
Members Individuals (over 1,838) in 72 countries and territories:
Argentina, Armenia, Australia, Austria, Bahamas, Bangladesh, Belgium, Bermuda, Brazil, Brunei Darussalam, Cameroon, Canada, Cayman Is, Chile, China, Colombia, Costa Rica, Côte d'Ivoire, Czechia, Denmark, Egypt, Ethiopia, Finland, France, Germany, Greece, Guatemala, Hong Kong, Hungary, India, Indonesia, Ireland, Italy, Jamaica, Japan, Kenya, Korea Rep, Kuwait, Lebanon, Liechtenstein, Luxembourg, Malaysia, Mexico, Monaco, Netherlands, New Zealand, Nigeria, Norway, Oman, Panama, Philippines, Portugal, Romania, Russia, Saudi Arabia, Senegal, Singapore, Slovakia, South Africa, Spain, Sweden, Switzerland, Syrian AR, Taiwan, Thailand, Uganda, UK, Ukraine, United Arab Emirates, USA, Venezuela, Zimbabwe.
NGO Relations Close relations with: *World Organization of the Scout Movement (WOSM, #21693)*. [2013/XF7422/v/**F**]

♦ BADLE – Bureau africain pour la défense des libertés de l'écrivain (no recent information)

♦ Badminton Asia 03056

COO Unit 1016 – 10th Floor, Block A – Damansara Intan, Jalan SS20/27, 47400 Petaling Jaya, Selangor, Malaysia. T. +60377338962 – +60377338964. Fax +60377328958. E-mail: admin@badmintonasia.org.
URL: http://www.badmintonasia.org/

History 30 Jul 1959, Kuala Lumpur (Malaysia). Constitution approved 31 Mar 1994; amended 13 Nov 1972, Jakarta (Indonesia). Former names and other names: *Asian Badminton Confederation (ABC)* – former; *Confédération asiatique de badminton* – former; *Badminton Asia Confederation (BAC)* – former; *Gabungan Badminton Asia* – former. **Aims** Promote and upgrade the interests of badminton in Asia; organize badminton *championship* tournaments in Asia. **Structure** General Meeting (annual); Executive Committee. Subcommittees (8): Umpires Board; Business; Finance; Coaching and Training; Tournament; Publicity; Awards; Rules and Laws. **Languages** English. **Staff** 1.00 FTE, paid. **Finance** Sources: members' dues; sponsorship. Tournament levies to IBF. **Activities** Sporting activities; training/education. **Events** *Championships and General Meeting* Jakarta (Indonesia) 2003, *Championships and General Meeting* Bangkok (Thailand) 2002, *Championships and General Meeting* Manila (Philippines) 2001, *Championships and General Meeting* Jakarta (Indonesia) 2000, *Championships and General Meeting* Kuala Lumpur (Malaysia) 1999. **Publications** *Asian Badminton Bulletin* (4 a year).
Members National associations in 43 countries and territories:
Afghanistan, Bahrain, Bangladesh, Bhutan, Brunei Darussalam, Cambodia, China, Hong Kong, India, Indonesia, Iran Islamic Rep, Iraq, Japan, Jordan, Kazakhstan, Korea DPR, Korea Rep, Kuwait, Kyrgyzstan, Laos, Lebanon, Macau, Malaysia, Maldives, Mongolia, Myanmar, Nepal, Pakistan, Palestine, Philippines, Qatar, Saudi Arabia, Singapore, Sri Lanka, Syrian AR, Taiwan, Tajikistan, Thailand, Timor-Leste, Turkmenistan, United Arab Emirates, Uzbekistan, Vietnam.
NGO Relations Member of (1): *Badminton World Federation (BWF, #03060)*. [2021/XD0073/**D**]

♦ Badminton Asia Confederation / see Badminton Asia (#03056)

♦ Badminton Confederation of Africa (BCA) 03057

Contact Shop No 2 Centurion Galleries, c/o Jean and South Avenue 279 Jean Avenue, Doringkloof, Centurion, South Africa. T. +27120350093.
URL: http://badmintonafrica.org/

History Founded 1974, as *African Badminton Federation (ABF)*. **Aims** Promote and develop the sport of Badminton in Africa. **Structure** General Meeting; Executive Board; Council. **Languages** English, French. **Staff** 4.50 FTE, paid; 14.00 FTE, voluntary. **Finance** Contributions from members; subsidy from BWF; sponsors. Budget (annual): US$ 600,000. **Activities** Organizes: continental and regional championships and technical courses; national courses.
Members National associations in 37 countries:
Algeria, Benin, Botswana, Burundi, Cameroon, Central African Rep, Congo Brazzaville, Congo DR, Côte d'Ivoire, Egypt, Equatorial Guinea, Eritrea, Eswatini, Ethiopia, Ghana, Kenya, Lesotho, Madagascar, Malawi, Mauritania, Mauritius, Morocco, Mozambique, Namibia, Nigeria, Seychelles, Sierra Leone, Somalia, South Africa, St Helena, Sudan, Tanzania UR, Togo, Tunisia, Uganda, Zambia, Zimbabwe.
NGO Relations Member of: *Badminton World Federation (BWF, #03060)*. [2018/XD9631/**D**]

♦ Badminton Europe (BEC) 03058

Gen Sec Brøndbytoften 14, 2605 Brøndby, Denmark. E-mail: info@badmintoneurope.com.
Acting Pres address not obtained.
URL: http://www.badmintoneurope.com/

History 24 Sep 1967, Frankfurt-Main (Germany). Former names and other names: *European Badminton Union (EBU)* – former (24 Sep 1967); *Union européenne de badminton (UEB)* – former (24 Sep 1967); *Badminton Europe Confederation (BEC)* – former. **Aims** Develop the *game* of badminton in Europe. **Structure** Annual Delegates' Meeting; Board of Directors; Commissions; Committees. **Languages** English. **Staff** 15.00 FTE, paid. 15 FTE. **Finance** Sources: fees for services; grants. Supported by: *Badminton World Federation (BWF, #03060)*. **Activities** Awards/prizes/competitions; events/meetings; sporting activities; training/education. **Events** *Annual Delegates Meeting* Bucharest (Romania) 2020, *Annual Delegates Meeting* Kiev (Ukraine) 2019, *Annual Delegates Meeting* Dubrovnik (Croatia) 2018, *Annual Delegates Meeting* Paris (France) 2015, *Annual Delegates Meeting* Dublin (Ireland) 2014. **Publications** *Badminton Europe* (4 a year) – online magazine.
Members National badminton associations in 53 countries and territories:
Albania, Armenia, Austria, Azerbaijan, Belarus, Belgium, Bosnia-Herzegovina, Bulgaria, Croatia, Cyprus, Czechia, Denmark, England, Estonia, Faeroe Is, Finland, France, Georgia, Germany, Gibraltar, Greece, Greenland, Hungary, Iceland, Ireland, Israel, Italy, Kosovo, Latvia, Liechtenstein, Lithuania, Luxembourg, Malta, Moldova, Monaco, Montenegro, Netherlands, North Macedonia, Norway, Poland, Portugal, Romania, Russia, Scotland, Serbia, Slovakia, Slovenia, Spain, Sweden, Switzerland, Türkiye, Ukraine, Wales.
Associate member in 1 territory:
Isle of Man.
NGO Relations Member of (1): *Badminton World Federation (BWF, #03060)*. [2022/XD9626/**D**]

♦ Badminton Europe Confederation / see Badminton Europe (#03058)

♦ Badminton Oceania (BOC) 03059

SG/CEO PO Box 11-216, Ellerslie, Auckland 1542, New Zealand. T. +6421760327. E-mail: office@badmintonoceania.org.
Pres address not obtained.
URL: http://badmintonoceania.org/

History 21 May 1987. Former names and other names: *Oceania Badminton Confederation* – alias. **Aims** Promote and develop badminton throughout Oceania. **Structure** General Meeting (annual); Executive Board. **Languages** English. **Staff** 5.00 FTE, paid. **Finance** Sources: sponsorship; subscriptions. Supported by: *Badminton World Federation (BWF, #03060)*; *Oceania National Olympic Committees (ONOC, #17667)*. **Activities** Events/meetings; research and development; sporting activities; training/education. **Events** *Annual General Meeting* Auckland (New Zealand) 2021, *Annual General Meeting* Ballarat, VIC (Australia) 2020, *Annual General Meeting* Nanning (China) 2019, *Annual General Meeting* Bangkok (Thailand) 2018, *Annual General Meeting* Gold Coast, QLD (Australia) 2017. **Publications** *BOC Newsletter*.
Members National Badminton Federations in 17 countries and territories:
Australia, Cook Is, Fiji, Guam, Kiribati, Nauru, New Caledonia, New Zealand, Norfolk Is, Northern Mariana Is, Papua New Guinea, Samoa, Solomon Is, Tahiti Is, Tonga, Tuvalu, Wallis-Futuna.
NGO Relations Member of (3): *Badminton World Federation (BWF, #03060)*; *Oceania National Olympic Committees (ONOC, #17667)*; *Organisation of Sports Federations of Oceania (OSFO, #17828)*. [2022.05.11/XD1903/**D**]

♦ Badminton Pan American Confederation (#04467)

♦ Badminton World Federation (BWF) 03060

SG Unit 1 Level 29, Naza Tower, Platinium Park, No 10 Persiaran KLCC, 50088 Kuala Lumpur, Malaysia. T. +60326319188. Fax +60326319688. E-mail: bwf@bwfbadminton.org.
URL: http://www.bwfbadminton.org/

History 5 Jul 1934, London (UK). Incorporated *Parabadminton World Federation (PBWF, inactive)*, 2009. Current constitution adopted 30 January 2021. Former names and other names: *International Badminton Federation (IBF)* – former. **Aims** Develop the *sport* of badminton world-wide; establish uniform rules; encourage creation of new national organizations. **Structure** Annual General Meeting; Council; Executive Board; Management Team. Committees (8): Administration; Finance; Marketing; Communications and Media; Events; Para-Badminton; Development and Sport for All; IOC and International Relations. Commissions (11): Governance and Ethics; Gender Equity; HR; Awards; Para-Badminton; Athletes', Para-Badminton Athletes' TUE. **Languages** English. **Staff** 44.00 FTE, paid. **Finance** Sources: members' dues. Other sources: sanction fees from open tournaments; IBF-run events; sale of TV rights. **Activities** Sporting activities. **Events** *Annual General Meeting* Bangkok (Thailand) 2022, *Annual General Meeting* Kuala Lumpur (Malaysia) 2021, *Annual General Meeting* Copenhagen (Denmark) 2020, *Annual General Meeting* Nanning (China) 2019, *World Congress of Racket Sport Science* Bangkok (Thailand) 2018. **Publications** *Statute Book* (annual). Technical leaflets.
Members Full: affiliated national associations in 187 countries and territories:
Afghanistan, Albania, Algeria, Argentina, Armenia, Aruba, Australia, Austria, Azerbaijan, Bahrain, Bangladesh, Barbados, Belarus, Belgium, Benin, Bermuda, Bhutan, Bolivia, Bosnia-Herzegovina, Botswana, Brazil, Brunei Darussalam, Bulgaria, Burkina Faso, Burundi, Cambodia, Cameroon, Canada, Cayman Is, Central African Rep, Chile, China, Colombia, Congo Brazzaville, Congo DR, Cook Is, Costa Rica, Côte d'Ivoire, Croatia, Cuba, Curaçao, Cyprus, Czechia, Denmark, Djibouti, Dominican Rep, Ecuador, Egypt, El Salvador, England, Equatorial Guinea, Eritrea, Estonia, Eswatini, Ethiopia, Faeroe Is, Falklands/Malvinas, Fiji, Finland, France, Gambia, Georgia, Germany, Ghana, Gibraltar, Greece, Greenland, Grenada, Guam, Guatemala, Guinea, Guyana, Haiti, Honduras, Hong Kong, Hungary, Iceland, India, Indonesia, Iran Islamic Rep, Iraq, Ireland, Israel, Italy, Jamaica, Japan, Jordan, Kazakhstan, Kenya, Kiribati, Korea DPR, Korea Rep, Kosovo, Kuwait, Kyrgyzstan, Laos, Latvia, Lebanon, Lesotho, Libya, Liechtenstein, Lithuania, Luxembourg, Macau, Madagascar, Malawi, Malaysia, Maldives, Malta, Mauritania, Mauritius, Mexico, Moldova, Monaco, Mongolia, Montenegro, Morocco, Mozambique, Myanmar, Namibia, Nauru, Nepal, Netherlands, New Zealand, Niger, Nigeria, Norfolk Is, North Macedonia, Norway, Pakistan, Palestine, Panama, Papua New Guinea, Paraguay, Peru, Philippines, Poland, Polynesia Fr, Portugal, Puerto Rico, Qatar, Romania, Russia, Samoa, Saudi Arabia, Scotland, Serbia, Seychelles, Sierra Leone, Singapore, Slovakia, Slovenia, Solomon Is, Somalia, South Africa, Spain, Sri Lanka, St Helena, St Lucia, Sudan, Suriname, Sweden, Switzerland, Syrian AR, Taiwan, Tajikistan, Tanzania UR, Thailand, Timor-Leste, Togo, Tonga, Trinidad-Tobago, Tunisia, Türkiye, Turkmenistan, Tuvalu, Uganda, Ukraine, United Arab Emirates, Uruguay, USA, Uzbekistan, Venezuela, Vietnam, Wales, Zambia, Zimbabwe.
Associate in 10 countries and territories:
Guadeloupe, Guiana Fr, Isle of Man, Martinique, New Caledonia, Northern Mariana Is, Oman, Réunion, Senegal, Wallis-Futuna.
Continental Confederations (5):
Badminton Asia (#03056); *Badminton Confederation of Africa (BCA, #03057)*; *Badminton Europe (BEC, #03058)*; *Badminton Oceania (BOC, #03059)*; *Confederación Panamericana de Badminton (PABC, #04467)*.
NGO Relations Member of (7): *Association of Paralympic Sports Organisations (APSO, #02850)*; *Association of Summer Olympic International Federations (ASOIF, #02943)*; *International Council for Coaching Excellence (ICCE, #13008)*; *International Masters Games Association (IMGA, #14117)*; *International Paralympic Committee (IPC, #14512)*; *Olympic Movement (#17719)*; *The Association for International Sport for All (TAFISA, #02763)*. Cooperates with (1): *International Testing Agency (ITA, #15678)*. Olympic Summer Sport, from 1992, at: *International Olympic Committee (IOC, #14408)*. [2021.10.26/XB0135/y/**B**]

♦ BADV / see Baltic Association of Dermatovenereologists (#03095)
♦ **BADV** Baltic Association of Dermatovenereologists (#03095)

- ♦ **BAE** Bibliotechnoj Assamblei Evrazii (#16458)
- ♦ **BAEE** Benelux Association for Energy Economics (#03198)
- ♦ BAFTA – Baltic Free Trade Agreement (1993 treaty)
- ♦ **BAFT** Bankers Association for Finance and Trade (#03162)
- ♦ BAFT-IFSA / see Bankers Association for Finance and Trade (#03162)
- ♦ BAFUNCS – British Association of Former United Nations Civil Servants (internationally oriented national body)
- ♦ BAFWAC – Business Alliance for Water and Climate (unconfirmed)
- ♦ BAGECO – Symposium on Bacterial Genetics and Ecology (meeting series)

♦ Bahaa Esperanto-Ligo (BEL) 03061

Ligue espérantiste baha'ie – Baha'i Esperanto League

Sec Eppsteiner Str 89, 65719 Hofheim-Langenhain, Germany. Fax +496192992999. E-mail: bel@bahai.de.

URL: http://www.bel.bahai.de/

History Founded 18 Mar 1973, Fortaleza (Brazil), with approval of the Baha'i *'Universal House of Justice'*, Haifa (Israel). **Aims** Link Esperanto-speaking people of the Baha'i Faith; represent the International Baha'i Community in the Esperanto movement. **Structure** Meeting (annual); Governing Board; ad hoc temporary internal commissions. **Languages** English, Esperanto. **Staff** Voluntary. **Finance** Voluntary contributions from members only. **Activities** Events/meetings. Congress. **Events** *Annual meeting* Hanoi (Vietnam) 2012, *Annual meeting* Copenhagen (Denmark) 2011, *Annual meeting* Havana (Cuba) 2010, *Annual meeting* Bialystok (Poland) 2009, *Annual meeting* Rotterdam (Netherlands) 2008. **Publications** *La BEL-Monda Letero* (2 a year). Baha'i literature in Esperanto. Information service on the Baha'i faith in Esperanto; information of the Baha'i Community on the Esperanto movement. **Members** Individuals (about 200) in 50 countries (not specified). **NGO Relations** Member of: *Universal Esperanto Association (UEA, #20676).* [2014.10.23/XD8278/**E**]

- ♦ **BAHA** Balkan Alliance of Hotel Associations (#03065)
- ♦ Baha'i Esperanto League (#03061)

♦ Baha'i International Community 03062

Communauté Internationale Baha'ie – Comunidad Internacional Baha'i

Contact Route des Morillons, 15, 1218 Le Grand-Saconnex GE, Switzerland. T. +41227985400. Fax +12128032566. E-mail: geneva@bic.org.

Geneva Office – Representative to the UN address not obtained.

URL: http://www.bic.org/

History Persia, by Mirza Husayn-'Ali (1817-1892), known as Baha'u'llah, the Glory of God. Comprises members of the Baha'i Faith, an independent world religion, The Baha'i Faith is intimately linked with the Babi Faith, founded in 1844 by Mirza 'Ali-Muhammad (1819-1850), known as the Bab, who proclaimed the imminent approach of the prophet (Messenger of God) foretold by all world religions: in 1863, Baha'u'llah declared that he was this prophet. After successive banishments, he arrived in the Holy Land, where he passed away. He appointed his eldest son, 'Abdu'l-Baha (1844-1921), to succeed him in leading the Baha'i Community and in interpreting the Baha'i Writings. 'Abdu'l-Baha in turn appointed his eldest grandson, Shoghi Effendi (1896-1957), as his successor, Guardian of the Cause, and authorized interpreter of the Baha'i teachings. Registration: EU Transparency Register, No/ID: 30317703883-03. **Aims** Promote and apply principles derived from the teaching of the Baha-i Faith which contribute to the resolution of current day challenges facing humanity and to the development of a united, peaceful, just and sustainable civilization, with the core principles including: oneness of humanity; equality of men and women; universal standard of human rights; equitable and just socio-economic development; universal education; environmental stewardship. **Structure** Offices at: UN New York NY (USA), Geneva (Switzerland) and Brussels (Belgium). Representations to *European Commission (EC, #06633).* UN Regional Commissions based in: Addis Ababa (Ethiopia); Bangkok (Thailand); Nairobi (Kenya); Rome (Italy); Santiago (Chile); Vienna (Austria). Office of Public Information. **Languages** English, French. **Staff** New York NY (USA) Office: 12; Geneva (Switzerland) Office: 5. **Finance** Voluntary contributions from registered members only. **Activities** Monitoring/evaluation; networking/liaising. Representatives actively engage in numerous committees, consultation and conferences at UN as well as other international conferences. Facilitates participation of civil society representatives in UN consultations and regularly contributes to debates regarding the strengthening of gender equality and human rights mechanisms at the UN. Monitors sessions of UN General Assembly and ECOSOC. **Events** *Nordic Baha'i Youth Conference* Drammen (Norway) 2020, *Nordic Baha'i Youth Conference* Drammen (Norway) 2019, *Nordic Baha'i youth conference* Lillehammer (Norway) 2011, *Conference on social and economic development* Sydney, NSW (Australia) 2009, *Nordic Baha'i youth conference* Oulu (Finland) 2008. **Publications** *ONE COUNTRY* (4 a year) in Chinese, English, French, German, Russian, Spanish – newsletter. Writings; books.

Members comprise over 5 million people in 181 countries. Affiliates in 164 countries and territories:

Afghanistan, Albania, Angola, Antigua-Barbuda, Argentina, Armenia, Australia, Austria, Azerbaijan, Bahamas, Bahrain, Bangladesh, Barbados, Belarus, Belgium, Belize, Benin, Bolivia, Botswana, Brazil, Bulgaria, Burkina Faso, Cambodia, Cameroon, Canada, Cape Verde, Central African Rep, Chad, Chile, Colombia, Comoros, Congo Brazzaville, Congo DR, Costa Rica, Côte d'Ivoire, Cuba, Cyprus, Czechia, Denmark, Dominica, Dominican Rep, Ecuador, El Salvador, Equatorial Guinea, Eritrea, Estonia, Eswatini, Ethiopia, Fiji, Finland, France, Gabon, Gambia, Georgia, Germany, Ghana, Greece, Grenada, Guatemala, Guinea, Guinea-Bissau, Guyana, Haiti, Honduras, Hungary, Iceland, India, Indonesia, Iraq, Ireland, Italy, Jamaica, Japan, Jordan, Kazakhstan, Kenya, Kiribati, Korea Rep, Kuwait, Kyrgyzstan, Laos, Latvia, Lebanon, Lesotho, Liberia, Lithuania, Luxembourg, Madagascar, Malawi, Malaysia, Mali, Marshall Is, Mauritius, Mexico, Micronesia FS, Moldova, Mongolia, Morocco, Mozambique, Myanmar, Namibia, Nepal, Netherlands, New Zealand, Nicaragua, Niger, Nigeria, Norway, Oman, Pakistan, Palau, Panama, Papua New Guinea, Paraguay, Peru, Poland, Portugal, Qatar, Romania, Russia, Rwanda, Samoa, Sao Tomé-Principe, Saudi Arabia, Senegal, Seychelles, Sierra Leone, Singapore, Slovakia, Solomon Is, South Africa, Spain, Sri Lanka, St Kitts-Nevis, St Lucia, St Vincent-Grenadines, Sudan, Suriname, Sweden, Switzerland, Taiwan, Tajikistan, Tanzania UR, Thailand, Togo, Tonga, Trinidad-Tobago, Tunisia, Türkiye, Turkmenistan, Tuvalu, Uganda, UK, Ukraine, United Arab Emirates, Uruguay, USA, Uzbekistan, Vanuatu, Venezuela, Vietnam, Yemen, Zambia, Zimbabwe.

Consultative Status Consultative status granted from: *ECOSOC (#05331)* (Special); *UNICEF (#20332); UNEP (#20299).* **IGO Relations** Working relations with: *WHO (#20950).* Cooperative relations with: *Office of the United Nations High Commissioner for Human Rights (OHCHR, #17697); UNDP (#20292); UNESCO (#20322); United Nations Economic Commission for Africa (ECA, #20554); United Nations Economic Commission for Latin America and the Caribbean (ECLAC, #20556); United Nations Economic and Social Commission for Asia and the Pacific (ESCAP, #20557).* Associated with Department of Global Communications of the United Nations. **NGO Relations** Member of: *Conference of Non-Governmental Organizations in Consultative Relationship with the United Nations (CONGO, #04635); CONGO Committee on Human Rights (#04663); Faith and Ethics Network for the International Criminal Court; Global Gender and Climate Alliance (GGCA, no recent information); Joint Learning Initiative on Faith and Local Communities (JLI, #16139); NGO Committee on Ageing, New York (#17103); NGO Committee on Financing for Development, New York (#17108); NGO Committee on Migration, New York (#17112); NGO Committee on Social Development (#17115); NGO Committee on the Status of Women, Geneva (#17117); NGO Committee on Sustainable Development, New York (#17118); NGO Working Group on the Security Council (#17128); Committee of NGOs on Human Rights, Geneva (#04275)* and its *NGO Committee on Freedom of Religion or Belief, New York NY (#17109); NGO Committee on UNICEF (#17120).* [2021.08.31/XF0180/**F**]

- ♦ **BAHPS** Baltic Association of the History and Philosophy of Science (#03096)
- ♦ BAICE – British Association for International and Comparative Education (internationally oriented national body)
- ♦ Bailleurs de fonds pour l'éducation en Afrique / see Association for the Development of Education in Africa (#02471)
- ♦ Baitulmaal (internationally oriented national body)
- ♦ Baitulmaal AHED / see Baitulmaal
- ♦ Baker Institute for Peace and Conflict Studies (internationally oriented national body)
- ♦ Bakery Equipment Manufacturers Association / see BEMA – The Baking Industry Suppliers Association
- ♦ Bakery Yeast Manufacturers Committee of the European Union / see Confédération des Fabricants de Levure de l'Union Européenne (#04551)
- ♦ Baku Training-Information Centre / see European Centre on Training and Formation of Local and Regional Authorities and Population in the Field of Natural and Technological Disasters
- ♦ **BALAS** Business Association of Latin American Studies (#03378)
- ♦ Balaton Group / see International Network of Resource Information Centers (#14320)
- ♦ Bali Democracy Forum (meeting series)
- ♦ **Bali Process** Bali Process on People Smuggling, Trafficking in Persons and Related Transnational Crime (#03063)

♦ Bali Process on People Smuggling, Trafficking in Persons and Related Transnational Crime (Bali Process) 03063

Regional Support Office Level 27 – Rajanakarn Bldg, 183 South Sathorn Road, Sathorn, Bangkok, 10120, Thailand. T. +6623439477.

Co-Chair R G Casey Bldg, John McEwan Crescent, Barton ACT 0221, Australia. T. +61262611111.

Co-Chair Jalan Pejambon 6 Jakarta DKI, Jakarta, Indonesia. T. +62213849350.

URL: http://www.baliprocess.net/

History 2002. **Aims** Raise regional awareness of the consequences of people smuggling, trafficking in persons and related transnational crime. **Structure** Ministerial Conference; Senior Official Meeting. Co-Chairs: governments of Australia and Indonesia. Bali Process Strategy for Cooperation; Ad Hoc Group; Regional Support Office. **Events** *Annual Meeting* Bali (Indonesia) 2017, *Regional Ministerial Conference* Bali (Indonesia) 2016, *Annual Meeting* Bangkok (Thailand) 2016, *Regional Ministerial Conference* Bali (Indonesia) 2013, *Regional Ministerial Conference* Bali (Indonesia) 2011.

Members Governments (45):

Afghanistan, Australia, Bangladesh, Bhutan, Brunei Darussalam, Cambodia, China, Fiji, Hong Kong, India, Indonesia, Iran Islamic Rep, Iraq, Japan, Jordan, Kiribati, Korea DPR, Korea Rep, Laos, Macau, Malaysia, Maldives, Mongolia, Myanmar, Nauru, Nepal, New Caledonia, New Zealand, Pakistan, Palau, Papua New Guinea, Philippines, Samoa, Singapore, Sri Lanka, Syrian AR, Thailand, Timor-Leste, United Arab Emirates, USA, Vietnam.

Regional membership of the following (3) organizations listed in this Yearbook:

International Organization for Migration (IOM, #14454); UNHCR (#20327); United Nations Office on Drugs and Crime (UNODC, #20596).

IGO Relations Cooperates with: *Budapest Process (#03344).* [2017/XM5882/**E***]

♦ Balkan Academy of Cosmetic Surgery (BACS) 03064

Chairman Medical Centre – Aesthetic Surgery, Aesthetic Medicine, 11 20th April Street, 1606 Sofia, Bulgaria. T. +35929524652. Fax +35929515668.

Pres Halaskargazi, Cad Cifcurt Apt no 368/4, Sisli, Istanbul/Istanbul, Türkiye. T. +902122965333. Fax +902122304567.

Structure Board of 5 members. **Events** *Annual meeting / World Congress* Varna (Bulgaria) 2007, *International congress on cosmetics surgery and medicine* Buenos Aires (Argentina) 2003, *International symposium on applied esthetics* Buenos Aires (Argentina) 2003, *Annual meeting / World Congress* Varna (Bulgaria) 2003, *International congress of aesthetic-cosmetic surgery and medicine* Istanbul (Turkey) 2001.

Members Societies in 5 countries:

Bulgaria, Cyprus, Romania, Serbia, Türkiye.

NGO Relations Division of: *International Academy of Cosmetic Surgery (IACS, #11543).* [2010/XD8119/**D**]

- ♦ Balkanactie van de Gemeenten (internationally oriented national body)
- ♦ Balkan Alliance (inactive)

♦ Balkan Alliance of Hotel Associations (BAHA) 03065

Contact Dobrinska 11, Belgrade, Serbia. T. +38163200097. E-mail: baha@bahah.org.

URL: http://www.bahah.org/

Members Associations in 7 countries:

Albania, Bosnia-Herzegovina, Bulgaria, Montenegro, North Macedonia, Romania, Serbia.

IGO Relations Affiliate member of: *World Tourism Organization (UNWTO, #21861).* [2016.08.19/XJ5012/**D**]

- ♦ Balkan Assist (internationally oriented national body)

♦ Balkan Association for Workers' Sport (BAWS) 03066

Contact Macedonia Sq 1, Sofia, Bulgaria. T. +35924010461. Fax +35929874142. E-mail: kparzulov@abv.bg. [2010/XJ2154/**D**]

♦ Balkan Badminton Association 03067

Contact c/o Bulgarian Badminton Fed, 75 Vasil Levski Blvd, 1040 Sofia, Bulgaria. T. +35929300550 – +35929867781. Fax +35929867781 – +35929815728.

URL: https://www.facebook.com/balkanbadminton/

History Founded 1992, Bucharest (Romania), as *Balkan Badminton Committee.* Present name adopted, 1997. **NGO Relations** Member of: *Badminton World Federation (BWF, #03060).* [2015/XD6745/**D**]

- ♦ Balkan Badminton Committee / see Balkan Badminton Association (#03067)
- ♦ Balkan Berligi Cemiyeti (inactive)
- ♦ Balkan Black Sea Baltic ICT Clusters Network (unconfirmed)
- ♦ Balkan and Black Sea Petroleum Association (unconfirmed)

♦ Balkan and Black Sea Regional Commission (BBSC) 03068

Exec Sec Rond Point Schuman 14, 1040 Brussels, Belgium. T. +3226121700. Fax +3222802765.

Contact 6 Rue Saint-Martin, 35700 Rennes, France. E-mail: lejla.becirovic@crpm.org.

URL: https://cpmr-balkan-blacksea.org/

History 2004, within the framework of *Conference of Peripheral Maritime Regions of Europe (CPMR, #04638),* by merger of *Balkan Commission (inactive)* and *CPMR Association of the Black Sea Area Regions (ABSAR, inactive).* Full title: *CPMR – Balkan and Black Sea Regional Commission.* **Aims** Encourage dialogue and cooperation between sub-state spheres of *government*; constitute a lasting institutional framework to support the integration in the EU in the context of enlargement and beyond; contribute to efficient and peaceful neighbourhood relationships. **Structure** General Assembly (annual). President; 2 Vice-Presidents. Secretariat in Kavala (Greece). **Languages** English, French, Irish Gaelic. **Finance** Members' dues. **Activities** Events/meetings. **Events** *General Assembly* Istanbul (Turkey) 2016, *General Assembly* Edirne (Turkey) 2014, *General Assembly* Odessa (Ukraine) 2013, *General Assembly* Rhodes Is (Greece) 2008, *General Assembly* Canakkale (Turkey) 2007.

Members Regions (22) in 7 countries:

Albania, Bulgaria, Greece, Moldova, Romania, Türkiye, Ukraine. [2022/XM0883/**E**]

- ♦ Balkan and Black Sea Veterinary Association (no recent information)
- ♦ Balkan Blockchain Association (unconfirmed)
- ♦ Balkan Centre for Peace and Culture (internationally oriented national body)
- ♦ Balkan Centre for Regional Development (internationally oriented national body)
- ♦ Balkan Centre of Study and Research in Ecology and Environmental Protection / see Balkan Science and Education Centre of Ecology and Environment

♦ Balkan Cities Association of Nephrology, Dialysis, Transplantation and Artificial Organs (BANTAO) 03069

Pres address not obtained.

URL: http://www.bantao.org/

History Sep 1995. Sept 1995. **Aims** Encourage, promote and realize relations, collaboration and friendship across political boundaries between scientists and health professionals of Balkan countries in the fields of: Basic and Clinical Nephrology; Paediatric Nephrology; Hemodialysis; Peritoneal Dialysis; Kidney Transplantation; Artificial Organs; Hypertension; Urinary Tract Infections; Autoimmune Diseases; Renal Pathology. **Structure** General Assembly. Board, comprising President, Past President, President Elect, Secretary/Treasurer, Journal Editor-in-Chief (all ex-officio) and 4 ordinary members. **Languages** English. **Staff** No secretariat staff. **Finance** Members' dues (biannual). Other sources: congress proceeds; gifts; donations; legacies. **Activities** Organizes rotating biennial congress. **Events** *Congress* Skopje (North Macedonia) 2019, *Congress* Budva (Montenegro) 2018, *Congress* Opatija (Croatia) 2015, *Congress* Timisoara (Romania) 2013, *Congress* Chalkidiki (Greece) 2010. **Publications** *BANTAO Journal* (4 a year) in English.

Members Individuals (over 400) in 10 countries:

Albania, Bosnia-Herzegovina, Bulgaria, Croatia, Cyprus, Greece, Montenegro, North Macedonia, Romania, Serbia, Slovenia, Türkiye. [2015/XD7586/v/**D**]

♦ Balkan Civil Society Development Network (BCSDN) 03070

Exec Dir Macedonia Street 43-1/9, 1000 Skopje, North Macedonia. T. +38926144211. Fax +38926144211. E-mail: executiveoffice@balkancsd.net.
URL: https://www.balkancsd.net/

History Dec 2003. Founded as an informal network. Founding Assembly held 6 Jul 2009, Skopje (Macedonia). Registration: Start date: 30 Sep 2009, North Macedonia; EU Transparency Register, No/ID: 63794152825-82, Start date: 17 Dec 2009. **Aims** Empower civil society and influence European and national policies towards more enabling environment for civil society development in order to ensure sustainable and functioning democracies in the Balkans. **Structure** Council; Board; Executive Office. **Languages** Albanian, English, Macedonian, Serbian, Turkish. **Staff** 5.00 FTE, paid. **Activities** Advocacy/lobbying/activism; capacity building; monitoring/evaluation; networking/liaising; politics/policy/regulatory. **Publications** *BCSDN Newsletter* (4 a year); *BCSDN News* (26 a year) – email alerts; *Balkan Civic Practices* (irregular). Reports; analyses; briefs.
Members Civil society organizations (15) in 10 countries:
Albania, Bosnia-Herzegovina, Croatia, Kosovo, Montenegro, North Macedonia, Romania, Serbia, Slovenia, Türkiye.
Included in the above, 1 organization listed in this Yearbook:
Macedonian Centre for International Cooperation (MCIC).
Consultative Status Consultative status granted from: *Council of Europe (CE, #04881)* (Participatory Status).
NGO Relations Cooperates with: *ACT Alliance EU (#00082); Central and Eastern European Citizens Network (CEE CN, #03689); CIVICUS: World Alliance for Citizen Participation (#03962); Confédération européenne des ong d'urgence et de développement (CONCORD, #04547); Conference of INGOs of the Council of Europe (#04607); European Association for Local Democracy (ALDA, #06110); European Center for Not-for-Profit Law (ECNL, #06463); European Citizen Action Service (ECAS, #06555); European Network of National Civil Society Associations (ENNA, inactive)*; Third Sector Impact; *Thomson Reuters Foundation (TRF).* [2023/XJ9305/F]

♦ Balkan Clinical Laboratory Federation (BCLF) 03071

Admin Ilica 94b, I sprat stan 7, Belgrade, PAK 11050, Serbia. T. +381113475183. Fax +381113615631. E-mail: dmbj@eunet.rs.
Sec address not obtained.
URL: http://www.bclf.info/

History 15 May 1993, Sofia (Bulgaria). Former names and other names: *Balkan Federation of Clinical Chemistry* – former (15 May 1993). **Aims** Encourage collaboration among member countries; improve quality assurance, management and accreditation programs; encourage education and training; enhance clinical laboratory practice by implementing new medical discoveries and new technologies; promote partnerships among countries of the Federation and with nearby countries; establish laboratories for specialized investigation in Balkan countries; investigate specific pathology of the Balkan region. **Structure** Executive Board. **Languages** English. **Finance** No separate budget; each national federation supports its own activities. Supported by: *European Commission (EC, #06633).* **Activities** Events/meetings; healthcare; training/education. **Events** *Annual Scientific Meeting* Sofia (Bulgaria) 2020, *Annual Scientific Meeting* Antalya (Turkey) 2019, *Annual Scientific Meeting* Skopje (Macedonia) 2018, *Annual Scientific Meeting* Athens (Greece) 2017, *Annual Scientific Meeting* Tirana (Albania) 2016. **Publications** Meeting reports.
Members Full; Affiliate; Corporate; Honorary Individual. Full in 9 countries:
Albania, Bosnia-Herzegovina, Bulgaria, Greece, Montenegro, North Macedonia, Romania, Serbia, Türkiye.
[2022/XD4936/D]

- ♦ Balkan Communist Federation (inactive)
- ♦ Balkan Consultative Assembly (inactive)
- ♦ Balkan Entente (inactive)

♦ Balkan Environmental Association (BENA) 03072

Exec Dir Alexander Tech Ed Inst, PO Box 141 Sindos, Thessaloniki, 574 00 Thessaloniki, Greece. T. +302310791420. Fax +302310-791300. E-mail: bena@gen.teithe.gr.
Journal: http://www.jepe-journal.info/bena

History 19 Nov 1998, Thessaloniki (Greece). Founded at 1st Balkan Conference. **Aims** Promote cooperation among all Balkan countries on environmental research projects and on formulating common environmental *policies* for the region; organize cooperation on current environmental protection problems in the region; integrate common efforts of scientists, specialists, educators and industrial enterprises for the environment and its *sustainable development* between the Balkan countries and the European Union and other countries; make suggestions and recommendations concerning environmental quality and *safety* to regulatory bodies in Balkan countries; develop programmes to reduce *transboundary pollution* and to protect Balkan rivers, lakes, seawater and soil from pollution by chemicals and other agents. **Structure** General Assembly (annual); Executive Committee. **Languages** English. **Staff** One paid; voluntary. **Finance** Members' dues. Other sources: projects. **Activities** Events/meetings; research/documentation; training/education. Operates *Balkan Institute for Environmental Research, Greece (BIER, no recent information).* **Events** *International symposium on marine and inland pollution control and prevention in the Black sea and Mediterranean sea* Istanbul (Turkey) 2003, *Meeting on coastal erosion* Mangalia (Romania) 2003, *Conference* Belgrade (Yugoslavia) 2002, *Conference* Edirne (Turkey) 2001, *Conference* Bucharest (Romania) 2000. **Publications** *Journal of Environmental Protection and Ecology (JEPE)* – official journal.
Members Full in 28 countries:
Albania, Belgium, Bosnia-Herzegovina, Bulgaria, Cyprus, Egypt, Georgia, Germany, Greece, Israel, Italy, Moldova, Montenegro, Netherlands, North Macedonia, Portugal, Romania, Russia, Serbia, Slovakia, Slovenia, Spain, Sweden, Switzerland, Syrian AR, Türkiye, UK, Ukraine. [2019/XD8050/D]

♦ Balkan Federation of Apicultural Associations 03073

Federatia Balcanică a Asociatiilor Apicole

Main Office Bd Ficusului nr 40, 013975 Bucharest, Romania. E-mail: balkan.apifederation@abv.bg.
URL: http://www.apibalcanica.org/

History Also referred to as *Balkan Federation of Beekeeping Associations.* **Events** *Congress* Istanbul (Turkey) 2007.
Members Organizations in 8 countries:
Albania, Bulgaria, Greece, Montenegro, North Macedonia, Romania, Serbia, Türkiye.
Included in the above, one organization listed in this Yearbook:
Fundatia Institutul International de Tehnologie si Economie Apicola (FIITEA).
NGO Relations Member of: *International Federation of Beekeepers' Associations (APIMONDIA, #13370).*
[2015.01.12/XM1303/y/D]

- ♦ Balkan Federation of Beekeeping Associations / see Balkan Federation of Apicultural Associations (#03073)
- ♦ Balkan Federation of Clinical Chemistry / see Balkan Clinical Laboratory Federation (#03071)
- ♦ Balkan Foundation for Sustainable Development (internationally oriented national body)

♦ Balkan Geophysical Society (BGS) 03074

Contact Technical University of Crete, Applied Geophysics Lab, Polytechnioupolis, 731 00 Chania, Greece. T. +302821037643. Fax +302821069554.
URL: http://www.balkangeophysoc.gr/

History 1993. **Structure** Executive Committee, comprising President, 2 Vice-Presidents, Scientific Secretary, Secretary-Treasurer and 2 further members. **Events** *Congress* Bucharest (Romania) 2021, *Congress* Albena (Bulgaria) 2019, *Congress* Antalya (Turkey) 2017, *Congress* Chania (Greece) 2015, *Congress* Tirana (Albania) 2013. **Publications** *Journal of the Balkan Geophysical Society.*
Members National organizations (7) in 7 countries:
Albania, Bulgaria, Greece, Hungary, Romania, Serbia, Türkiye.
NGO Relations Affiliated with (1): *International Union of Geological Sciences (IUGS, #15777).* Associate of: *European Association of Geoscientists and Engineers (EAGE, #06055).* [2021/XJ3075/D]

- ♦ Balkan Göçmenleri ve Mülteci Dernekleri Federasyonu / see Balkan Türkleri Göçmenleri ve Mülteci Dernekleri Federasyonu (#03089)

♦ Balkan Investigative Reporting Network (BIRN) 03075

Regional Hub Branilaca Sarajeva 14, 71000 Sarajevo, Bosnia-Herzegovina. T. +38733266615. Fax +38733266616. E-mail: office@birn.eu.com.
URL: http://www.birn.eu.com/

History 2005. Emerged from Balkans Programme of *Institute for War and Peace Reporting (IWPR, #11302).* **Aims** Secure its position as the premier Balkan investigative and analytical journalism organization, addressing the need for objective, quality, sustainable reporting on the region's political, economic and European Union integration challenges. **Languages** Albanian, Bulgarian, English, Macedonian, Romanian. **Staff** 30.00 FTE, paid. **Activities** Reports; offers training; organizes debates and round tables.
Members Journalists in 6 countries:
Bosnia-Herzegovina, Bulgaria, Montenegro, North Macedonia, Romania, Serbia.
NGO Relations Member of: *Global Forum for Media Development (GFMD, #10375).* Cooperates with: *ERSTE Foundation.* [2021/XM3154/F]

♦ BALKANI Wildlife Society 03076

Chairman 93 Evlogi i Hristo Georgievi Blvd, 1st Floor, 1142 Sofia, Bulgaria. T. +35929631470. Fax +35929631470. E-mail: office@balkani.org.
URL: http://www.balkani.org/

History Founded 1989, as *Green Balkans Movement.* Registered in accordance with Bulgarian law, 1992. **Aims** Promote: conservation, research and restoration of *biodiversity* in Bulgaria and the Balkans; improvement and public control on the implementation of the *nature protection* legislation; public awareness about *ecological* problems and environmental education. **Structure** General Assembly; Board. **Languages** Bulgarian, English. **Finance** Members' dues. Other sources: donations; grants; sponsorship. **Activities** Advocacy/lobbying/activism; awareness raising; events/meetings. **Publications** *Management Plan for Brown Bear.* In Bulgarian: leaflets; posters; brochures. **Members** (54). Membership countries not specified. **NGO Relations** Member of: *CEEweb for Biodiversity (#03626).* [2014.11.17/XF3200/E]

- ♦ Balkan League (inactive)
- ♦ Balkan Mathematical Union (inactive)
- ♦ Balkan Media Association (no recent information)

♦ Balkanmedia Association 03077

Pres 24 Bor Str, 1434 Sofia, Bulgaria. T. +35929611688. Fax +35929611688.
Head Office 96 Lubotren Str, 1407 Sofia, Bulgaria. T. +35928622497.
URL: https://monoskop.org/Balkanmedia_Association

History 28 Dec 1990, Sofia (Bulgaria). Former names and other names: *Association for Mass Media and Communication Culture on the Balkans* – alias; *BALKANMEDIA Organization* – former. Registration: Bulgaria. **Aims** Contribute to incorporating *media* development of the *Balkan* countries into the all-European integration process in the field of *mass communications* and culture; promote collaboration with mass media institutions worldwide; through research and promotion activities, protect *copyright* and full freedom of *creativity* of the mass media; contribute to economic, political and cultural integration of the Balkan countries, their cooperation in the areas of science, publishing, television, broadcasting and arts, and to establishment of closer and long-term contacts among researchers, journalists and creators. **Structure** General Assembly; Management Board, headed by Chairman; Consulting Committee; Auditing Committee; Secretariat. **Finance** Sources: contributions; donations; gifts, legacies; subsidies. **Activities** Awards/prizes/competitions; events/meetings; training/education. **Publications** *Balkanmedia Magazine* (4 a year). *Scriptura mundi* – series, in preparation as of 2011. *Bugarian Media Studies; European Media and Communication History; Gotite – The Goths.* Analyses; reports.
Members Full; Associate. Organizations and individuals in 13 countries:
Albania, Bosnia-Herzegovina, Bulgaria, Croatia, Cyprus, Greece, Moldova, Montenegro, North Macedonia, Romania, Serbia, Slovenia, Türkiye.
Associates in 6 countries:
Austria, France, Germany, Switzerland, UK, USA.
IGO Relations Cooperation on scientific and research projects with international and national institutions, including: *Council of Europe (CE, #04881); European Audiovisual Observatory (#06294); European Commission (EC, #06633); UNESCO (#20322).* **NGO Relations** Member of (1): *European Communication Research and Education Association (ECREA, #06675).* Cooperates on scientific and research projects with international and national institutions, including: *European Cultural Foundation (ECF, #06868); European Institute for the Media (EIM, no recent information); World Public Forum – Dialogue of Civilizations (WPF-DoC, inactive).*
[2020/XD4538/D]

- ♦ BALKANMEDIA Organization / see Balkanmedia Association (#03077)

♦ Balkan Medical Union 03078

Union médicale balkanique (UMB)

Contact str T Ciorba no 1, MD-2004 Chisinau, Moldova. T. +3722205306. Fax +3722235309. E-mail: codolg@gmail.com – umb@urgenta.md.
URL: http://www.umbalk.org/

History 24 Oct 1932, Bucharest (Romania). Statutes modified: 12 May 1962, Bucharest; 10 June, 1964, Sofia (Bulgaria); 3 Apr 1977, Heraklion (Crete); 11-14 Sep 1977, Belgrade (Yugoslavia); 10-15 Sep 1978, Athens (Greece); Nov 1989, Bucharest; Jun 1990, Varna (Bulgaria); 5 Dec 1992, Edirne (Turkey). **Aims** Study *morbidity* problems and *prophylactic* and *curative* methods with special reference to the Balkan region; promote reciprocal understanding, develop contacts and strengthen links of friendship among *doctors.* **Structure** General Council, consisting of delegates of each national section and sub-sections. Standing Committee; Secretariat-General. **Languages** English, French. **Staff** 1.00 FTE, paid; 2.00 FTE, voluntary. **Finance** Members' dues. Grants from official bodies. **Events** *Biennial Balkan Medical Week* Chisinau (Moldova) 2013, *Biennial Balkan medical week* Athens (Greece) 2010, *Biennial Balkan medical week* Chisinau (Moldova) 2008, *Biennial Balkan medical week* Chisinau (Moldova) 2002, *Biennial Balkan medical days session* Borovets (Bulgaria) 2001. **Publications** *Archives de l'Union médicale balkanique* (4 a year) – 1963- ; *UMB – Annuaire des membres* (every 2 years); *Bulletin de l'Union médicale balkanique* – supplement to 'Archives'.
Members National sections and individuals. Members in 11 countries:
Albania, Bosnia-Herzegovina, Bulgaria, Cyprus, France, Greece, Italy, Moldova, North Macedonia, Romania, Serbia, Türkiye.
[2013/XD0182/D]

♦ Balkan Mountaineering Union (BMU) 03079

SG address not obtained.
Pres address not obtained.
URL: http://www.bmumagazine.com/

History 16 Oct 2009, Bosnia-Herzegovina. **Structure** Executive Board; Supervisory Board. **Publications** *BMU Magazine.*
Members Associations in 11 countries:
Albania, Bosnia-Herzegovina, Bulgaria, Croatia, Czechia, Greece, Montenegro, North Macedonia, Serbia, Slovenia, Türkiye.
NGO Relations Cooperates with (1): *European Union of Mountaineering Associations (EUMA, #09002).*
[2021/AA1437/D]

♦ Balkan Museum Network (BM Network) 03080

Balkanska mreza muzeja – Rjeti i Muzeve të Ballkanit

Contact Radiceva 17/V, 71000 Sarajevo, Bosnia-Herzegovina. E-mail: info@bmuseums.net.
URL: http://www.bmuseums.net/

History Founded Apr 2006, Uppsala (Sweden), originally facilitated by *Cultural Heritage without Borders (CHwB).* Also known under the acronym *BMN.* Registered in accordance with the law of Bosnia-Herzegovina. **Aims** Improve support and development for museums and galleries; improve the work of museums and cultural institutions that work to preservan and promote cultural *heritage.* **Structure** Assembly; Steering Board. **Finance** Members' dues. **Activities** Events/meetings; networking/liaising; awards/prizes/competitions.
Members Museums and institutes in 9 countries:
Albania, Bosnia-Herzegovina, Croatia, Greece, Kosovo, Montenegro, North Macedonia, Romania, Serbia.
NGO Relations *Cultural Heritage without Borders (CHwB).* [2020/XM8578/F]

♦ Balkan and Near East Railway Rates Union (inactive)
♦ Balkan Network on Obesity / see Balkan Network for the Study of Obesity (#03081)

♦ Balkan Network for the Study of Obesity (BALNESO) 03081

Exec Dir 46 Kifissias Ave, 115 26 Athens, Greece. T. +302106985987. Fax +302106985986.
URL: http://www.balneso.com/

History 20 Apr 2002, Athens (Greece), as *Balkan Network on Obesity.* **Aims** Promote collaboration in the field of obesity in the region; increase awareness of the growing problem of obesity as a disease. **Activities** *Balkan Congress on Obesity* series. **Events** *Biennial congress / Congress* Thessaloniki (Greece) 2008, *Biennial congress / Congress* Albena (Bulgaria) 2006, *Biennial Congress* Athens (Greece) 2003, *Congress* Greece 2003.
Members in 6 countries:
Bulgaria, Greece, Israel, Romania, Serbia, Türkiye. [2008/XF6835/F]

♦ Balkan Physical Union (BPU) 03082

Pres Fac of Sciences and Mathematics, Univ of Nis, Visegradska 33, Nis, PAK 18000, Serbia.
URL: http://www.balkanphysicalunion.info/

History Founded 1985. **Aims** Promote: research in *physics* and related sciences in the Balkans; *teaching* of physics at primary, secondary and high school levels and in universities; application of physics *research* in industry, economy and environment; collaboration and mutual assistance in research and education among physicists in Balkans; peace and friendship among Balkan people. **Structure** Council (meeting every 3 years); Executive Committee. **Languages** English. **Staff** None. **Finance** Members' dues. Other sources: official grants, donations. **Activities** Events/meetings; training/education; networking/liaising; knowledge management/information dissemination. **Events** *Conference* Sofia (Bulgaria) 2018, *Conference* Istanbul (Turkey) 2015, *Conference* Constantza (Romania) 2012, *Conference* Alexandroupoli (Greece) 2009, *Conference* Istanbul (Turkey) 2006. **Publications** *Balkan Physics Letters* (periodical).
Members National Physical Societies in 10 countries:
Albania, Bulgaria, Cyprus, Greece, Moldova, Montenegro, North Macedonia, Romania, Serbia, Türkiye.
[2019.02.26/XF2371/F]

♦ Balkan Point (internationally oriented national body)
♦ Balkan Postal Union (inactive)

♦ Balkan Rowing Association (BRA) 03083

SG str Vasile Conta nr 16, sector 2, Bucharest, Romania. T. +4021317200. Fax +4021317201.
URL: http://www.balkanrowing.com/

History 14 Apr 1973, Athens (Greece), as *Balkan Rowing Championships (BRC).* Present name adopted 9 Sep 2000, Kastoria (Greece). **Aims** Develop and promote all forms of rowing sport; improve the relationships among the member federations and the Balkan countries. **Structure** Congress; President and Secretary-General. Headquarters with office of Secretary-General. **Languages** English. **Finance** Members' dues. **Activities** Organizes championships. **Events** *Congress* Belgrade (Serbia) 2013, *Congress* Plovdiv (Bulgaria) 2012, *Congress* Istanbul (Turkey) 2011, *Congress* Kastoria (Greece) 2010, *Congress* Romania 2009.
Members National organizations (8) in 8 countries:
Albania, Bosnia-Herzegovina, Bulgaria, Greece, North Macedonia, Romania, Serbia, Türkiye.
NGO Relations *World Rowing (#21756).* [2017.11.27/XJ4090/D]

♦ Balkan Rowing Championships / see Balkan Rowing Association (#03083)
♦ Balkan Science and Education Centre of Ecology and Environment (internationally oriented national body)
♦ Balkanska Asocijaciaja za Transakcionu Analizu (unconfirmed)
♦ Balkanska mreza muzeja (#03080)

♦ Balkan Society of Geometers (BSG) 03084

Pres Univ Politehnica of Bucharest, Fac of Applied Sciences, Dept of Mathematics-Informatics, Splaiul Independentei 313, 060042 Bucharest, Romania. T. +40214029150. Fax +40214029622.
Vice-president address not obtained.
URL: http://www.mathem.pub.ro/dept/bsg.htm

History 20 Aug 1994, Athens (Greece). **Aims** Provide a framework within which geometers and other specialists from Balkan countries and worldwide; exchange information, study and debate up-to-date problems concerning the evolution of geometry and its applications. **Structure** Director Committee; Executive Board; Censor Committee. **Languages** English, French. **Staff** Part-time, voluntary. **Finance** Sources: donations; meeting proceeds; members' dues; sale of publications; sponsorship; subscriptions. **Activities** Events/meetings. **Events** *International Conference on Differential Geometry and Dynamical Systems* Bucharest (Romania) 2020, *International Conference on Differential Geometry and Dynamical Systems* Bucharest (Romania) 2019, *International Conference on Differential Geometry and Dynamical Systems* Mangalia (Romania) 2018, *International Conference on Differential Geometry and Dynamical Systems* Bucharest (Romania) 2017, *International Conference on Differential Geometry and Dynamical Systems* Bucharest (Romania) 2015. **Publications** *Applied Sciences (APPS)*; *Balkan Journal of Geometry and Its Applications (BJGA)*; *BSG Proceedings (BSGP)*; *Differential Geometry and Dynamical Systems (DGDS).* Books; studies; monographs.
Members Individuals (204) in 29 countries:
Belgium, Brazil, Bulgaria, Canada, China, Czechia, Egypt, Estonia, France, Germany, Greece, Hungary, India, Iran Islamic Rep, Israel, Italy, Japan, Korea Rep, Malaysia, North Macedonia, Oman, Poland, Romania, Saudi Arabia, Serbia, Spain, Türkiye, UK, USA. [2020.06.24/XJ1836/v/D]

♦ Balkan Society of Haematology (no recent information)

♦ Balkan Society of Oto-Rhino-Laryngology, Head and Neck Surgery (BSOHNS) 03085

Pres address not obtained.

History 23 Jun 2001, Athens (Greece), during 2nd World Congress of Otorhinolaryngologic Allergy, Endoscopy and Laser Surgery. **Aims** Promote advancement of otorhinolaryngology head and neck surgery in the Balkan countries; encourage close relationships between otorhinolaryngologists and allied professionals in the Balkan countries. **Structure** General Assembly. Board of Directors, including President, Vice-President and General Secretary. **Languages** English. **Events** *Congress* Targu-Mures (Romania) 2012, *Congress* Nis (Serbia) 2010, *Congress* Thessaloniki (Greece) 2008, *Congress* Edirne (Turkey) 2006, *Congress* Sunny Beach (Bulgaria) 2004.
Members National societies in 8 countries:
Albania, Bosnia-Herzegovina, Bulgaria, Greece, North Macedonia, Romania, Serbia, Türkiye. [2012/XM3218/D]

♦ Balkan Society of Radiology (BSR) 03086

Office address not obtained. T. +905373937447.

History Current bylaws adopted 4 Nov 2012. **Structure** Executive Board. Committees (4): Programme Planning; Membership; Bylaws; Nomination's. Council of National Representatives. **Activities** Training/education; events/meetings. **Events** *Balkan Congress of Radiology* Plovdiv (Bulgaria) 2020, *Balkan Congress of Radiology* Budapest (Hungary) 2017, *Balkan Congress of Radiology* Thessaloniki (Greece) 2016, *Balkan Congress of Radiology* Sarajevo (Bosnia-Herzegovina) 2015, *Balkan Congress of Radiology* Istanbul (Turkey) 2014. [2020/XJ9056/D]

♦ Balkan Speleological Union (BSU) 03087

Gen Sec Bulgarian Federation of Speleology, 75 Vasil Levsky Blvd, 1040 Sofia, Bulgaria. T. +35929300650. Fax +35929878812. E-mail: balkanspeleo@yahoo.com.
URL: http://www.balkan-speleo.org/

History Sep 2002, Vratsa (Bulgaria). Registered in accordance with Greek law. **Structure** General Assembly. Bureau, comprising President, Vice-President, General Secretary and 2 members.
Members National associations in 10 countries:
Albania, Bosnia-Herzegovina, Bulgaria, Croatia, Greece, Montenegro, North Macedonia, Romania, Serbia, Slovenia.
[2011/XJ2210/D]

♦ Balkan Stomatological Society (BaSS) 03088

SG PO Box 1531, Aristotle Univ Campus, 541 24 Thessaloniki, Greece. T. +302310999546. Fax +302310999621. E-mail: pissioti@dent.auth.gr.
URL: http://www.e-bass.org/

Structure Council. Executive Committee, comprising President, Past President, President-Elect, Vice President, Secretary General, Honorary Treasurer and Editor-in-Chief. **Events** *Congress* Skopje (Macedonia) 2013. **Publications** *Balkan Journal of Stomatology.*
Members Full in 10 countries:
Albania, Bosnia-Herzegovina, Bulgaria, Cyprus, Greece, Montenegro, North Macedonia, Romania, Serbia, Türkiye.
NGO Relations Supporting member of: *FDI – World Dental Federation (#09281).* [2013/XJ6484/D]

♦ Balkan Trust Network, Greece (internationally oriented national body)

♦ Balkan Türkleri Göçmenleri ve Mülteci Dernekleri Federasyonu (BGF) 03089

Federation of Balkan Turk Migrants and Refugee Associations (BTF)
Gen Pres Ankara cad, DSI Karsisi, Okumus ap 292/3, Yildirim, Bursa/Bursa, Türkiye. T. +902243603685 – +902243610062. Fax +902243617448. E-mail: balgocmerkez@gmail.com.
Gen Sec address not obtained.
URL: http://www.bgf.org.tr/

History Founded 16 Dec 1987, as *Balkan Göçmenleri ve Mülteci Dernekleri Federasyonu – Federation of Balkan Turks Migrants and Refugees Associations.* Also referred to as *Federation of Balkan Turks and Associations for Emigrés* and as *Federation of Balkanite Turks Immigrants and Refugee Associations.* **Aims** Facilitate adaptation to life in places of refuge of migrants from Balkan countries to Turkey or other countries in order to increase solidarity and find solutions to problems of work, shelter, citizenship and refugee status. **Structure** General Assembly (every 3 years); Executive Board; Headquarters in Bursa (Turkey). **Languages** Turkish. **Staff** 3.00 FTE, paid; 1.50 FTE, voluntary. **Finance** Members' dues. Donations. Annual budget: about US$ 200,000. **Activities** Networking/liaising; projects/programmes; events/meetings. **Publications** *Balkanlarda Türk Kültürü* (4 a year) – journal. Studies.
Members Individuals (about 100,000) belonging to Balkan Migrant Associations (5) in 1 country:
Türkiye. [2018.09.19/XJ3976/D]

♦ Balkan Union of Oncology (inactive)

♦ Balkan Volleyball Association (BVA) 03090

SG TVF 50 Yil Spor Salonu, Burhan Felek por Sitesi, Nuh Kuyusu Cad Seyit Ahmet Deresi Sok NO-5, Zeynep Kamil, Uskudar, 81150 Istanbul/Istanbul, Türkiye. T. +903122214040. Fax +903122214010. E-mail: bva@tvf.org.tr.
URL: http://www.balkanvolleyball.org/

History 1998, Orestiada (Greece), but briefly afterwards activities were suspended. Revived 2000, Athens (Greece). **Aims** Further develop Volleyball and Beach Volleyball in the Balkan Region. **Structure** Presidency rotates annually. Commissions; Sub-commissions; Secretariat situated in Istanbul (Turkey). **Languages** English. **Staff** 2.00 FTE, voluntary. **Finance** Members' dues. Support from: *European Volleyball Confederation (#09078)*; *Fédération internationale de volleyball (FIVB, #09670).* **Activities** Sporting activities; events/meetings. **Events** *General Assembly* Istanbul (Turkey) 2011, *General Assembly* Podgorica (Montenegro) 2010, *General Assembly* Sarajevo (Bosnia-Herzegovina) 2009, *General Assembly* Orestiada (Greece) 2008, *General Assembly* Sofia (Bulgaria) 2007. **Publications** Activity books (annual).
Members Federation in 10 countries:
Albania, Bosnia-Herzegovina, Bulgaria, Greece, Moldova, Montenegro, North Macedonia, Romania, Serbia, Türkiye.
NGO Relations Affiliated with: *European Volleyball Confederation (#09078)*; *Fédération internationale de volleyball (FIVB, #09670).* [2016.06.01/XJ8512/D]

♦ Ballroom Dancers' Federation International 03091

Coordinating Dir Tumbelturn, Copped Hall Drive, Camberley, GU15 1NP, UK. T. +441276500213. E-mail: sec@bdfi.org.
URL: http://www.bdfi.org/

History 1997. **Aims** Promote the spirit of good fellowship and sportsmanship in the competitive dance world; protect and advance the interests of all those interested in the competitive dance world. To promote the spirit of good fellowship and sportsmanship and to protect and advance the interests of all those, who have an interest in the competitive dance world. **Structure** Council, comprising Honorary President, Chairman, Vice-Chairman, Honorary Secretary, Membership Director, Public Relations Director, Financial Director, Coordinating Director, 7 International Directors. **Events** *UK congress* Bournemouth (UK) 2005, *Biennial Meeting* Blackpool (UK) 2004, *Biennial general meeting* Blackpool (UK) 2004, *UK congress* Bournemouth (UK) 2004, *International congress* Rome (Italy) 2004.
Members in 21 countries and territories:
Australia, Austria, Belgium, Canada, Greece, Israel, Italy, Japan, Korea Rep, Lebanon, Malta, Netherlands, Portugal, Russia, Singapore, South Africa, Taiwan, Thailand, UK, Ukraine, USA. [2012/XJ4083/D]

♦ **BALNESO** Balkan Network for the Study of Obesity (#03081)
♦ BalS – Baltic Society for Immunology (inactive)
♦ BALTBAT – Baltic Battalion (inactive)
♦ BaltCF – Baltic Sea Conservation Foundation (internationally oriented national body)
♦ Baltchambers / see Baltic Sea Chambers of Commerce Association (#03140)
♦ **BALTDEFCOL** Baltic Defence College (#03110)
♦ **BALTGRAF** International Association for Engineering Graphics (#11873)
♦ Balti Assamblee (#03094)
♦ Baltic 21 (inactive)
♦ Baltic Academy of Tourism and Entrepreneurship (internationally oriented national body)
♦ Pro Baltica Forum / see Baltic Sea Forum (#03142)

♦ Baltic Air Surveillance Network (BALTNET) 03092

Contact CRC Karmelava, Paslapiu g7, Karmelava, LT-54458 Kaunas, Lithuania. T. +3707307511. Fax +3707307523.

History 1996, within *Baltic Security Assistance Forum (BALTSEA, inactive).* **Aims** Survey and control air space in Baltic countries compatible with similar Western and NATO air defence entities in provision of airspace sovereignty. **Languages** English. **Finance** Annual budget costs shared between Baltic states.
Members Governments of 3 countries:
Estonia, Latvia, Lithuania.
IGO Relations *NATO (#16945).* [2016.07.07/XM0807/F*]

♦ **Baltic Antiviral Network** Baltic Network against Life-Threatening Viral Infections (#03130)

♦ Baltic Architects Unions Association (BAUA) 03093

Association des unions des architectes baltes
Address not obtained.

Languages English, Estonian, Russian. **Staff** 1.00 FTE, paid.
Members in 3 countries:
Estonia, Latvia, Lithuania.
NGO Relations Member of: *Union internationale des architectes (UIA, #20419).* [2018/XD4155/D]

♦ Baltic Assembly (BA) 03094

Assemblée balte – Balti Assamblee – Baltijas Asambleja – Baltijos Asambleja
SG Citadeles St 2-616, Riga LV-1010, Latvia. Fax +37167225178.
Contact address not obtained.
URL: http://www.baltasam.org/

History 8 Nov 1991, Tallinn (Estonia). Founded based on Joint Decision adopted by members of Supreme Councils of Estonia, Latvia and Lithuania, Vilnius (Lithuania), 1 Dec 1990. Agreement on Parliamentary and Intergovernmental Cooperation of the Baltic States signed in Tallinn (Estonia), 13 June 1994, specifying responsibilities of the Baltic Assembly and those of the *Baltic Council of Ministers (BCM, #03109)*, as well as the cooperation format between the BA and *Baltic Council (#03108)*. Statutes most recently adopted 10 Nov 2017, Riga (Latvia). **Aims** Coordinate cooperation between the national parliaments of the Baltic states; discuss issues and various projects which are of mutual interest to the members of the national delegations and the member states; adopt decisions in compliance with the principles of equality, mutual benefit and unanimity; and develop cooperation with other regional, international, and inter-parliamentary organisations. **Structure** Sessions (annual). Baltic Assembly, composed of 12 to 16 parliamentarians appointed by parliament of each of the Baltic States. Presidium, composed of Chairperson of each national delegation and a deputy appointed by the parliament of the respective state. Committees of the Baltic Assembly (6): Economics, Energy and Innovation; Education, Science and Culture; Health, Welfare and Family; Natural Resources and Environment; Security and Defence; Budget and Audit. Secretariat. **Languages** Estonian, Latvian, Lithuanian. **Staff** 6, including 3 secretaries of national delegations to the Baltic Assembly. **Finance** Sources: members' dues. **Activities** Events/meetings. Priorities (2022): *'Baltic Assembly'*: (I) Rapid recovery and sustainable growth of the Baltic States. (II) Socially protected people living in a safe and resilient Baltic region. (III) Interconnected and innovative Baltic States. *'Baltic Assembly and Baltic Council of Ministers'*: (I) Regional security and defence, countering hybrid threats and disinformation. (II) Modernizing economy by advancing green and digital transition, connectivity and development of regional infrastructure projects. (III) Strengthening strategic and ambitious Eastern Partnership and support to civil society in Belarus. **Events** *Session* Riga (Latvia) 2022, *Session* Vilnius (Lithuania) 2021, *Session* 2020, *Session* Riga (Latvia) 2019, *Session* Vilnius (Lithuania) 2018. **Publications** *Fifteen Years of the Baltic Assembly*; *Ten Years of the Baltic Assembly*; *Twenty Years of the Baltic Cooperation*. Brochures.
Members Comprises 12-20 parliamentarians from each Parliament of the Baltic States:
Estonia, Latvia, Lithuania.
IGO Relations Member of (1): *Baltic Sea Parliamentary Conference (BSPC, #03146)* (since 1992). Cooperates with (1): *Baltic Council of Ministers (BCM, #03109)* (since 1994). Agreements on parliamentary cooperation signed with: *Nordic Council (NC, #17256)* (1992); *Benelux Inter-Parliamentary Consultative Council (Benelux Parliament, #03201)* (1994). Declaration on cooperation between BA and GUAM Parliamentary Assembly, signed 19 Jun 2009, Vilnius (Lithuania). Trilateral cooperation among the BA, Nordic Council and Benelux Parliament. [2022.10.17/XF3174/F*]

♦ Baltic Association of Burns and Fire Disasters (no recent information)

♦ Baltic Association of Dermatovenereologists (BADV) 03095

Pres 14-3 Perses Str, Riga LV-1011, Latvia. T. +37129481725. Fax +37167361615. E-mail: info.badv@gmail.com.
URL: http://www.badv.lv/
History Former names and other names: *Baltic Association of Dermatovenerology (BADV)* – former. **Aims** Support and promote clinical and scientific Dermatovenereology in the Baltic States. **Activities** Training/education; events/meetings; publishing activities. **Events** *Congress* Riga (Latvia) 2022, *Congress* Kaunas (Lithuania) 2021, *Congress* Riga (Latvia) 2020, *Congress* Riga (Latvia) 2018, *Congress* Vilnius (Lithuania) 2017. [2022/XM0139/D]

♦ Baltic Association of Dermatovenerology / see Baltic Association of Dermatovenereologists (#03095)

♦ Baltic Association of the History and Philosophy of Science (BAHPS) 03096

Chairperson address not obtained.
URL: https://www.bahps.org/
History 1990, Riga (Latvia). Founded following series of conferences initiated in 1958. **Events** *Baltic Conference on the History and Philosophy of Science* Tartu (Estonia) 2024, *Baltic Conference on the History and Philosophy of Science* Oulu (Finland) 2022, *Baltic Conference on the History of Science* Vilnius (Lithuania) 2019, *Conference* Tartu (Estonia) 2017, *Conference* Riga (Latvia) / Jelgava (Latvia) 2015. **Publications** *Acta Baltica Historiae et Philosophiae Scientiarum*. [2022/AA3070/D]

♦ Baltic Association for Maxillofacial and Plastic Surgery (BAMPS) . . 03097

Pres Tartu Univ Hospital, Surgery Dept, 1a L Puusepa St, Tartu, Estonia.
History 1990. **Events** *Congress* Kaunas (Lithuania) 2013, *Triennial congress / Congress* Tallinn (Estonia) 2008, *Triennial congress / Congress* Kaunas (Lithuania) 2005, *Triennial congress / Congress* Riga (Latvia) 2002, *Triennial congress / Congress* Tartu (Estonia) 1999. [2013/XD8704/D]

♦ Baltic Association for Media Research (BAMR) 03098

Contact Tartu Univ, Inst of Social Studies, Lossi 36, 51003 Tartu, Estonia. T. +3727375188. Fax +3727375356.
History 23 May 1993, Tartu (Estonia). **Aims** Develop contacts among Baltic countries and between them and other countries in the field of media research, publication of results and training of journalists; represent Baltic media researchers with enterprises, organizations and private persons of other countries; develop *publishing* and other pertinent activities. **Structure** Board. **Languages** English. **Staff** None. **Finance** Members' dues. Research and development projects. Annnual budget (2016): US$ 1,000. **Activities** Projects/programmes; research and development. **Publications** *Baltic Media in Transition* (2002); *Towards a Civic Society: Baltic Media's Long Road to Freedom* (1993).
Members Individuals in 4 countries:
Estonia, Finland, Latvia, Lithuania.
NGO Relations Associate member of: *International Association for Media and Communication Research (IAMCR, #12022)*; *International Communication Association (ICA, #12814)*. [2017.11.07/XD5051/D]

♦ Baltic Association for Medical Libraries (inactive)

♦ Baltic Association of Neuropathologists (BAN) 03099

Pres Dept of Pathology, LUHS Hosp Kauno Klinikos, Eiveniu 2, LT-50009 Kaunas, Lithuania.
URL: https://www.euro-cns.org/national-societies/
History 31 May 2003, Riga (Latvia). Previously referred to as *Baltic Society of Neuropathologists*. **Aims** Promote the science and medical practice of neuropathology so as to facilitate the diagnostics, study and prevention of diseases of the *nervous* system and the musculature as well as neuroscience in a broader sense in the Baltic states. **Structure** Officers: President; 2 Vice-Presidents. **Languages** English, Russian. **Activities** Organizes workshops, scientific meetings and teaching events. **Events** *Meeting* Riga (Latvia) 2018, *Workshop* Kaunas (Lithuania) 2011, *Workshop* Kaunas (Lithuania) 2009, *Workshop* Riga (Latvia) 2007, *Meeting* Tartu (Estonia) 2005.
Members in 6 countries:
Estonia, Finland, Germany, Latvia, Lithuania, USA.
NGO Relations Member of: *European Confederation of Neuropathological Societies (Euro-CNS, #06715)*. [2018/XM1497/D]

♦ Baltic Association of Paediatric Surgeons (BAOPS) 03100

Contact Dept of Paediatric Surgery, Univ Children's Hosp, Vieibas Gatve 45, Riga LV-1004, Latvia. T. +37128769660. Fax +37167064473.
History 1992. **Activities** Events/meetings. **Events** *Conference* Riga (Latvia) 2018, *Conference* Tartu (Estonia) 2016, *Conference* Vilnius (Lithuania) 2014, *Conference* Riga (Latvia) 2012, *Conference* Tallinn (Estonia) 2010.
Members Full in 3 countries:
Estonia, Latvia, Lithuania. [2018/XM6978/D]

♦ Baltic Association for Rehabilitation (no recent information)

♦ Baltic Association of Science/Technology Parks and Innovation Centres (BASTIC) 03101

Dir Kaunaus Univ of Technology, Regional Business Incubator (KTC), K Petrausko G 26, Kaunas, Lithuania. T. +37037300818. Fax +37037451599.
URL: http://www.innovation.lv/bastic/
Aims Bring and keep together the corresponding institutions in the three Baltic States. **Activities** Organizes: 'BALTIC DYNAMICS' – annual conference rotating between Estonia, Lithuania and Latvia. **Events** *Baltic Dynamics Annual International Conference* Stockholm (Sweden) 2017, *Annual Conference* Riga (Latvia) 2013.
NGO Relations Member of: *World Alliance for Innovation (WAINOVA, #21082)*. [2013/XJ2638/D]

♦ Baltic Association of Surgeons (BAS) 03102

Pres FACS, North Estonian Medical Centre Foundation, Sütiste 19, 13419 Tallinn, Estonia. T. +3725079764. Fax +3726171244.
Structure Board. **Events** *Triennial Congress / Congress* Tallinn (Estonia) 2015, *Triennial Congress / Congress* Riga (Latvia) 2012, *Triennial congress / Congress* Pärnu (Estonia) 2006, *Triennial congress / Congress* Liepaja (Latvia) 2004, *Triennial congress / Congress* Vilnius (Lithuania) 2001. **NGO Relations** *International Federation of Surgical Colleges (IFSC, #13560)*. [2014.01.15/XD8447/D]

♦ Baltic Audiovisual Archival Council (BAAC) 03103

Contact Pirita tee 56, 10012 Tallinn, Estonia. E-mail: maria@baacouncil.org.
URL: http://www.baacouncil.org/
History Founded 16 Oct 2005. **Aims** Foster cooperation between public and private archives, broadcasting and TV archives, libraries and museums that possess collections of audiovisual materials about the Baltic States, Scandinavian countries and the worldwide Baltic diaspora. **Structure** Board. **Languages** English, Estonian. **Staff** No paid staff. **Finance** Members' dues. **Activities** Networking/liaising; awareness raising; training/education; events/meetings. **Events** *Annual Conference* Riga (Latvia) 2019, *Annual Conference* Tallinn (Estonia) 2018, *Annual Conference* Warsaw (Poland) 2017, *Annual Conference* Vilnius (Lithuania) 2016, *Annual Conference* Tallinn (Estonia) 2015.
Members Institutional (13) in 6 countries:
Estonia, Finland, Latvia, Norway, Poland, Sweden.
Individuals and Honorary (32) in 10 countries:
Canada, Czechia, Estonia, Finland, Latvia, Lithuania, Netherlands, Norway, Sweden, USA. [2017.10.12/XM0634/y/E]

♦ Baltic Badminton Association (inactive)
♦ Baltic Bast Crops Growers' and Producers' Association (internationally oriented national body)
♦ Baltic Battalion (inactive)
♦ **BALTICCARE** Baltic Network for Infection Control and Containment of Antibiotic Resistance (#03131)

♦ Baltic Centre for Media Excellence (BCME) 03104

Exec Dir Palasta street 5/1, Riga LV-1050, Latvia. E-mail: info@baltic.media.
URL: https://www.bcme.eu/
History Registration: EU Transparency Register, No/ID: 641737539199-17, Start date: 12 Aug 2020. **Aims** Promote professional growth, media intelligence and critical thinking; strive for positive change in journalism and communities it serves. **Structure** Board. **Activities** Events/meetings; networking/liaising; research/documentation; training/education. [2021/AA1018/D]

♦ Baltic Centre for Strategic Studies (internationally oriented national body)

♦ Baltic Centre for Writers and Translators (BCWT) 03105

Östersjöns Författar- och Översättarcentrum
Dir Uddens gränd 3, SE-621 56 Visby, Sweden. T. +46498218764 – +46498218385. Fax +46498218798. E-mail: baltic.centre@gotlandica.se – bcwt@gotlandica.se.
URL: http://www.bcwt.org/
History May 1993. Founded as a result of the writers' cruise, 1992, "Baltic Waves", following activities arranged by *ARS BALTICA (#01114)* and the setting up of *Baltic Writers' Council (BWC, #03156)*, 1992. **Aims** Serve as a working and meeting place for *professional* writers and translators from the Baltic sea region and other parts of Europe. **Finance** Funded by: Swedish Government, Municipality and County Administration of Gotland (Sweden). Budget (annual): about Swedish Kr 2 millions. **Activities** Organizes seminars, meetings, conferences and poetry festivals. Maintains a library. **Events** *Meeting on the creation of a worldwide network of international literary centres* Rhodes Is (Greece) 2000, *Conference on combatting stereotypes and prejudice in history textbooks of South-East Europe / Conference* Visby (Sweden) 1999. **Publications** Newsletter. Proceedings.
Members Writers' Unions in 11 countries:
Denmark, Estonia, Finland, Germany, Iceland, Latvia, Lithuania, Norway, Poland, Russia (St Petersburg), Sweden.
IGO Relations *UNESCO (#20322)*. **NGO Relations** Member of: *Réseau européen des centres internationaux de traducteurs littéraires (RECIT, #18873)*. [2021/XE2635/E]

♦ Baltic Chambers of Commerce Association / see Baltic Sea Chambers of Commerce Association (#03140)

♦ Baltic Child Neurology Association (BCNA) 03106

Pres Dept of Pediatrics, Univ of Tartu, Lunini Str 6, 51014 Tartu, Estonia. T. +3727319500.
History 7 Sep 1990, Tartu (USSR). **Aims** Unite Baltic child neurologists to ensure better possibilities for learning and training; create patient and family oriented medical care for children; develop friendship between paediatric neurologists of the Baltic States. **Structure** Officers: President, 2 Vice-Presidents, Secretary. **Languages** English, Russian. **Staff** Part-time, voluntary. **Finance** Members' dues. Sponsoring. **Activities** Networking/liaising; training/education. **Events** *International Conference* Pärnu (Estonia) 2022, *International Conference* Narva (Estonia) 2021, *Conference* Kaunas (Lithuania) 2019, *Conference* Riga (Latvia) 2017, *Conference* Tartu (Estonia) 2015.
Members Child neurologists and other specialists in near connection with child neurologists in 9 countries:
Estonia, Finland, Germany, Latvia, Lithuania, Russia, Sweden, UK, USA.
NGO Relations Cooperates with: *Nordic Neuropediatric Society (#17367)*. [2022/XD3486/v/D]

♦ Baltic Cities Healthy Cities Association (internationally oriented national body)
♦ Baltic Club / see Union of the Baltic Cities (#20366)
♦ Baltic Coalition for People Living with HIV / see Baltic Coalition for PLWHIV (#03107)

♦ Baltic Coalition for PLWHIV (NGO BaCo) 03107

Contact address not obtained. T. +37120207737. E-mail: baco5@inbox.lv.
History Founded 16 Feb 2018. Full title: *Baltic Coalition for People Living with HIV*. **Aims** Create life improvements and recognition of the rights of those affected by HIV/AIDS; inform and educate society, patients and those around them on the HIV infection, its risks and prevention tools; increase adherence to HIV diagnostics, therapy and disease management. **Structure** Board.
Members Full in 5 countries:
Estonia, Germany, Latvia, Lithuania, Poland. [2019/XM8821/D]

♦ Baltic Council 03108

Conseil baltique
Address not obtained.
URL: http://www.baltasam.org/
History 12 May 1990, USSR. 12 May 1990, Tallinn (USSR), developing from the reconstituted *Baltic Entente (inactive)*. Since 13 Jun 1994, following signature of the Agreement on Baltic Parliamentary and Governmental Cooperation between the Republic of Estonia, the Republic of Latvia and the Republic of Lithuania, functions as the main forum of *Baltic Assembly (BA, #03094)* and *Baltic Council of Ministers (BCM, #03109)*. Also referred to as *Conseil de la Baltique*; *Conseil des Etats baltes*. **Aims** Monitor cooperation of the Baltic States both on the legislative and executive level; ensure follow-up of the adopted decisions. **Structure** Not a formal organization, but a joint annual session held between the Baltic Council of Ministers and the Baltic Assembly, as stipulated in Article 3 of the 'Protocol Amending the Agreement on Baltic Parliamentary and Governmental Cooperation between the Republic of Estonia, the Republic of Latvia and the Republic of Lithuania', signed

by the Prime Ministers of the respective countries, 28 Nov 2003. Prime Ministers do not participate, only the Foreign Minister of the chairing country in his/her capacity as a Cooperation Minister. No formal secretariat. **Languages** English. **Staff** None. **Finance** Budget covered on a rotation basis. **Activities** Events/meetings; politics/policy/regulatory.
Members Governments and parliaments of 3 countries:
Estonia, Latvia, Lithuania. [2016/XF2714/**F***]

♦ Baltic Council of Ministers (BCM) 03109
Conseil des ministres baltes – Balti Ministrite Nõukogu
Contact Ministry of Foreign Affairs of the Republic of Estonia, Islandi Väljak 1, 15049 Tallinn, Estonia. T. +3726377000. E-mail: vminfo@vm.ee.
Contact Ministry of Foreign Affairs of the Republic of Latvia, K Valdmara iela 3, Riga LV-1395, Latvia. T. +37167016201. E-mail: minsek@mfa.gov.lv.
Contact Ministry of Foreign Affairs of the Republic of Lithuania, J Tumo-Vaizganto Str 2, LT-01511 Vilnius, Lithuania. T. +37052362444. E-mail: urm@urm.lt.
History 13 Jun 1994, Tallinn (Estonia), as a means of regional cooperation among Estonian, Latvian and Lithuanian Governments. Through *Baltic Council (#03108)*, coöperates with *Baltic Assembly (BA, #03094)*. **Aims** Ensure continuity of cooperation at the executive level of the States. **Structure** Not a formal organization. Prime Ministers' Council (meets at least annually). Cooperation Council, consisting of Ministers of Foreign Affairs. Committees of Senior Officials, comprising one senior official from each country and a number of experts, acting in a certain area of cooperation. No permanent secretariat. Rotating Presidency. **Languages** English. **Finance** Each party covers its own expenses through its national budget. **Activities** Networking/liaising; events/meetings. **Events** *International conference on information technologies and telecommunications in the Baltic States* Riga (Latvia) 2000.
Members 3 Member States:
Estonia, Latvia, Lithuania.
IGO Relations *Nordic Council (NC, #17256)*; *Nordic Council of Ministers (NCM, #17260)*. [2023/XD5517/**D***]

♦ Baltic Defence College (BALTDEFCOL) 03110
Commandant Riia 12, 51013 Tartu, Estonia. T. +3727176000. Fax +3727176050. E-mail: eve.vahtra@baltdefcol.org – info@baltdefcol.org.
URL: http://www.baltdefcol.org/
History 1998, within *Baltic Security Assistance Forum (BALTSEA, inactive)*. Officially opened, 25 Feb 1999. Registered in accordance with Estonian law: 98000012. **Aims** Educate and further the personal and professional development of the military staff of the Baltic states; participate in enhancement of academic studies in selected, relevant fields in close cooperation with the military national defence academies. **Structure** Ministerial Committee, consisting of Ministers of Defence; Military Committee, comprising Chiefs of Defence. Baltic Management Group. Coordination Group. Commandant. Departments (2): Political Studies and Officership; Operations. **Staff** 52.00 FTE, paid. From 14 countries. **Finance** Funded by governments of member states. **Activities** Main functions: Joint Staff College (Joint Command and General Staff Course); Level 4 course (Higher Command Studies Course); Education of Civil Servants in Security and Defence (Civil Servants Course). Research. Annual Baltic Conference on Defence. **Publications** *Baltic Security and Defence Review* (annual).
Members Governments of 3 countries:
Estonia, Latvia, Lithuania.
NGO Relations Participant in: *PfP Consortium of Defence Academies and Security Studies Institutes (#18345)*. Member of: *International Society of Military Sciences (ISMS, #15271)*. [2017/XM0808/**D***]

♦ Baltic Development Forum 03111
Dir Nytorv 3, 1st Floor, 1450 Copenhagen K, Denmark. T. +4570209394. Fax +4570209395. E-mail: bdf@bdforum.org.
URL: http://www.bdforum.org/
History 1998. **Aims** Promote the Baltic Sea Region as an integrated, prosperous and internationally competitive growth region. **Structure** Board; Advisory Board; Secretariat. **Finance** Members' dues. Other sources: sponsorship; conference fees. **Activities** Networking/liaising; projects/programmes; events/meetings. **Events** *Annual Summit* Tallinn (Estonia) 2018, *Annual Summit* Berlin (Germany) 2017, *Annual Summit* Stockholm (Sweden) 2016, *Annual Summit* Copenhagen (Denmark) 2015, *Annual Summit* Turku (Finland) 2014. **Publications** Annual State of the Region Report; Annual Summit Report; thematic reports.
Members Full members from large companies, major cities, institutional investors and business associations in the Baltic Sea region. Members in 12 countries:
Denmark, Estonia, Finland, Germany, Latvia, Lithuania, Netherlands, Norway, Poland, Russia, Sweden, UK.
IGO Relations Cooperating Partner: *Council of the Baltic Sea States (CBSS, #04870)*; *Nordic Council (NC, #17256)*; *Nordic Council of Ministers (NCM, #17260)*. Regular relations with: *Interparliamentary Assembly of Member Nations of the Commonwealth of Independent States (IPA CIS, #15958)*. **NGO Relations** Cooperating Partners: *Baltic Sea Chambers of Commerce Association (BCCA, #03140)*; *Business Advisory Council (BAC, #03376)*; *Konrad Adenauer Foundation (KAF)*; *ScanBalt (#19065)*; *World Economic Forum (WEF, #21367)*. Member of: *Nordic Center for Sustainable Healthcare (NCSH, #17229)*. [2018/XF5898/**F**]

♦ Baltic Earth 03112
Secretariat Helmholtz-Zentrum Geesthacht, Max-Planck-Str 1, 21502 Geesthacht, Germany. T. +494152871693. E-mail: bearth@hzg.de – balticearth@hereon.de – silke.koeppen@hereon.de.
URL: https://baltic.earth/
History Successor to *Baltic Sea Experiment (BALTEX)* (1993-2013), a Regional Hydroclimate Project (RHP) within the Global Energy and Water Exchanges Project (GEWEX) of *World Climate Research Programme (WCRP, #21279)* – *World Meteorological Organization (WMO, #21649)*. **Aims** Foster and improve multidisciplinary scientific collaboration, outreach and education in the Baltic Sea region; achieve an improved Earth system understanding of the region. **Structure** Baltic Earth Science Steering Group (BESSG); Baltic Earth Senior Advisory Board (BESAB); Baltic Earth Working Groups; International Baltic Earth Secretariat. **Languages** English. **Staff** 3.00 FTE, paid. **Finance** International Baltic Earth Secretariat funded by Helmholtz-Zentrum Geesthacht. Scientific and educational events co-sponsored by participating institutions. **Activities** Events/meetings; monitoring/evaluation; networking/liaising; publishing activities; research and development; training/education. **Events** *Assessing the Baltic Sea Earth System* Jastarnia (Poland) 2022, *Earth system changes and Baltic Sea coasts* Jastarnia (Poland) 2020, *The Baltic Sea Region in Transition* Helsingør (Denmark) 2018, *Multiple drivers for earth system changes in the Baltic sea region* Nida (Lithuania) 2016. **Publications** *Baltic Earth Newsletter* (2-4 a year). Scientific and assessment reports; workshop and conference proceedings. Information Services: Online Publication Library database. **IGO Relations** Close collaboration with: *Baltic Marine Environment Protection Commission – Helsinki Commission (HELCOM, #03126)*. [2022.05.04/XJ9229/**E**]

♦ Baltic and East European Graduate School (internationally oriented national body)

♦ Baltic Economic Association (BEA) 03113
Sec address not obtained.
URL: http://balticecon.org
History Jun 2018, Vilnius (Lithuania). Statutes approved 12 June 2018, Vilnius (Lithuania). **Aims** Foster the development and application of economics as as science in the Baltic States; promote and reinforce cooperation among economists from the region. **Structure** General Meeting; Board. **Activities** Events/meetings; training/education. **Publications** *Baltic Journal of Economics.*
Members Individual; Institutional. Members in 3 countries:
Estonia, Latvia, Lithuania. [2019/AA0029/**D**]

♦ Baltic Ecovillage Network (BEN) 03114
Chair address not obtained.
URL: http://balticecovillages.net/
Aims Promote *environmental* protection and restoration of *nature*; carry out outreach for societal transition and support socio-cultural, economical and ecological sustainability. **Structure** Board. **Publications** *BEN Newsletter.*
Members Full in 9 countries:
Denmark, Estonia, Finland, Germany, Latvia, Lithuania, Norway, Poland, Russia.
NGO Relations *Global Ecovillage Network (GEN, #10331)*; *Global Ecovillage Network – Europe (GEN Europe, #10332)*. Member of: *European Network for Community-Led Initiatives on Climate Change and Sustainability (ECOLISE, #07882)*. [2016/XM5116/**F**]

♦ Baltic Educational Travel and Work Association (no recent information)

♦ Baltic Energy Innovation Centre (BEIC) 03115
Exec Dir Skarpskyttev 10D, SE-226 42 Lund, Sweden. T. +46725199425. E-mail: info@beic.nu.
URL: http://www.beic.nu/
History Current statutes adopted Jun 2017. Registration: No/ID: 769635-0185, Sweden; EU Transparency Register, No/ID: 183063439272-89, Start date: 21 Aug 2020. **Aims** Provide a long lasting platform for collaboration associated with the challenges the Baltic Sea region and neighbouring areas are facing. **Structure** General Assembly; Board of Directors. **Activities** Events/meetings; guidance/assistance/consulting.
Members Full in 4 countries:
Germany, Lithuania, Poland, Sweden. [2020/AA1039/**D**]

♦ Baltic Entente (inactive)

♦ Baltic Environmental Forum (BEF) 03116
Chair Antonijas 3-8, Riga LV-1010, Latvia. T. +37167357555. E-mail: bef@bef.lv.
Latvia: http://www.bef.lv/
History Jun 1995. Founded on adoption of initial working programme to 1997, as the technical assistance project to the Baltic ministers of the Environment, based on environmental cooperation agreement between the 3 Baltic states, signed 21 Jul 1995. Subtitle: *Baltic States Regional Environmental Development*. New legal entity since 2003, when became an NGO. **Aims** Promote the significance of environmental protection, by developing cooperation and dialogue between various institutions and stakeholders, and by increasing their capacities in implementation of environmental management. **Structure** General Assembly (annual); Board. **Languages** English, Estonian, German, Latvian, Lithuanian, Russian. **Activities** Advocacy/lobbying/activism; events/meetings; training/education; research/documentation. **Events** *International workshop for stakeholders of the printing industry supply chain within the Baltic Sea region* Jurmala (Latvia) 2006, *Meeting of Baltic environmental NGO coalitions and committees* Jurmala (Latvia) 2006, *Workshop on concept development for management plans of marine protected areas in the Baltic states* Jurmala (Latvia) 2006, *Workshop on REACH* Sigulda (Latvia) 2006, *Conference about the society participation in the household waste management* Valmiera (Latvia) 2006.
Members NGOs in 5 countries:
Estonia, Germany, Latvia, Lithuania, Russia.
NGO Relations Member of: *EDC Free Europe (#05355)*. [2019/XF4084/**F**]

♦ Baltic Euregional Network (inactive)

♦ Baltic Farmers Forum on Environment (BFFE) 03117
Chairman c/o LRF, Franzingatan 6, SE-105 33 Stockholm, Sweden.
History 2 Apr 1998, Visby (Sweden), on the initiative of *Central Council of the Nordic Farmers' Associations (NBC, no recent information)*. **Aims** Involve farmers from the Baltic Sea region and their organizations in the process of environmental improvement. **Events** *Conference on Agricultural Water Protection and Sustainable Food Production* Espoo (Finland) 2015, *Conference* Finland 2004.
Members Organizations in 11 countries:
Denmark, Estonia, Finland, Germany, Iceland, Latvia, Lithuania, Norway, Poland, Russia, Sweden.
IGO Relations Observer to: *Baltic Marine Environment Protection Commission – Helsinki Commission (HELCOM, #03126)*. [2013/XF6117/**F**]

♦ BalticFem (internationally oriented national body)

♦ Baltic Fishermen's Association (BFA) 03118
Secretariat Nordensvej 3, Taulov, 7000 Fredericia, Denmark. T. +4570104040. Fax +4575451928. E-mail: mail@dkfisk.dk.
URL: http://www.fiskeriforening.dk/
Aims Increase cooperation between the national fishery associations in the Baltic area. **Structure** General Meeting (annual). Board elects Chairman. **Finance** Members' dues. **Events** *Meeting* Hamburg (Germany) 1999.
Members National fishery associations (7) in 7 countries:
Denmark, Estonia, Finland, Germany, Iceland, Lithuania, Sweden. [2011/XD8759/**D**]

♦ Baltic Fishing Fleet State Academy (internationally oriented national body)

♦ Baltic Forestry, Veterinary and Agricultural University Network (BOVA UN) 03119
Secretary Latvia University of Life Sciences and Technologies, Liela iela 2, Jelgava LV-3001, Latvia. T. +371630005684.
Rector address not obtained.
URL: http://www.bova-university.org/
History 1996. Established when agreement between founding universities was signed. Permanent secretariat functioning since 2002. Former names and other names: *Nordic Forestry, Veterinary and Agricultural University, NOVA – Baltic University Cooperation (NOVABA)* – former. **Aims** Initiate, administer and promote active educational cooperation among Baltic forestry, veterinary and agricultural universities in education, teaching and research; share competence among Baltic universities in the field; serve as a forum for discussion of teaching and education matters among members. **Structure** Rector Board, headed by Rector and coordinated by Coordination Committee and Rotating Secretariat (every 3 years). **Languages** English. **Staff** 3.00 FTE, paid. **Finance** Sources: grants; members' dues. Annual budget: 100,000 EUR. **Activities** Events/meetings; research/documentation; training/education.
Members Universities (4) in 3 Baltic countries:
Estonia, Latvia, Lithuania.
NGO Relations Close links with: *Nordic Forestry, Veterinary and Agricultural University Network (NOVA University Network, #17297)*. [2020.10.13/XF4086/**F**]

♦ Baltic Free Trade Agreement (1993 treaty)
♦ Baltic Free Trade Area (no recent information)
♦ Baltic Fund for Nature (internationally oriented national body)
♦ Baltic Head and Neck Oncology Association / see Baltic States Head and Neck Oncology Association

♦ Baltic HIV Association 03120
Contact address not obtained. T. +37129630960 – +37128441324. E-mail: balthiv@balthiv.com.
URL: https://balthiv.com/
History Founded 2010, by healthcare professionals. **Aims** Limit the spread of HIV and related infections by implementing health promotion and prevention activities and participating in the integration of this area into state and municipal policy planning documents and activities in the Baltic States. **Structure** Board. **Languages** English, Latvian, Russian. **Finance** Project financing; funding from Latvian government. **Activities** Advocacy/lobbying/activism; guidance/assistance/consulting; research/documentation. [2020.03.16/XM8820/**D**]

♦ Baltic Institute of Corporate Governance (BICG) 03121
Pres Jogailos st 4, LT-01116 Vilnius, Lithuania. T. +37061113344.
URL: http://www.corporategovernance.lt/
History Founded 2009. **Aims** Deliver value to stakeholders by promoting global competitiveness of Baltic companies through adoption of leading corporate governance practices. **Structure** Board. **Finance** Members' dues. **Activities** Training/education. **Members** Corporate; Individual. Membership countries not specified. [2015.01.05/XJ2238/j/**D**]

♦ Baltic Institute of Social Science (BISS) 03122

Baltijas sociâlo zinâtòu institûts (BSZI)

Office Terbatas Str 53 – 6 (4th floor), Riga LV-1011, Latvia. T. +37167217554. Fax +37167217560. E-mail: biss@biss.soc.lv.

Legal Address Pikola Str 31 -4, Riga LV-1006, Latvia.

URL: http://www.biss.soc.lv/

History Jan 2000. **Aims** Provide policy analysis and sociological research. **Structure** Board of 3 members. **Staff** 6.00 FTE, paid. **Activities** Research/documentation; knowledge management/information dissemination. **Events** *International conference on corruption and party finance* Riga (Latvia) 2000. **Publications** Books; articles. [2015/XE4082/j/**E**]

♦ Baltic International Airlines / see Air Baltic Corporation (#00600)
♦ Baltic International Centre for Economic Policy Studies (internationally oriented national body)
♦ Baltic International Institute of Tourism, St Petersburg / see Baltic Academy of Tourism and Entrepreneurship
♦ Baltic and International Maritime Conference / see BIMCO (#03236)
♦ Baltic and International Maritime Council / see BIMCO (#03236)
♦ Baltic Laboratory Animal Science Association (internationally oriented national body)

♦ Baltic Management Development Association (BMDA) 03123

Baltijos Vadybos Pletros Asociacija (BMDA)

Pres Gedimino str 50, LT-44239 Kaunas, Lithuania. T. +37037302206. Fax +37037205676. E-mail: info@bmda.net.

Project Manager address not obtained. E-mail: projects@bmda.net.

URL: http://www.bmda.net/

History 2002. Founded on the initiative of universities, business schools, individuals professors and business professionals from the Baltic and other countries. **Aims** Induce the quality of management development in the Baltic region and beyond. **Structure** Board. **Languages** English, Lithuanian. **Staff** 3.00 FTE, paid. **Finance** Sources: meeting proceeds; members' dues. **Activities** Events/meetings; research/documentation; training/education. **Events** *Annual Conference* Tallinn (Estonia) 2021, *Annual Conference* 2020, *Annual Conference* Casablanca (Morocco) 2019, *Annual Conference* Porto (Portugal) 2018, *Annual Conference* Podgorica (Montenegro) 2017. **Publications** *Baltic Journal of Management*; *BMDA Newsletter*. Proceedings.

Members Full (70) in 25 countries:
Austria, Belarus, Belgium, Croatia, Denmark, Estonia, Finland, France, Georgia, Germany, Italy, Kazakhstan, Latvia, Lithuania, Montenegro, Netherlands, Norway, Poland, Portugal, Russia, Slovenia, Sweden, UK, Ukraine, USA.
Included in the above, 4 organizations listed in this Yearbook:
BMI Executive Institute (BMI, #03288); *EFMD – The Management Development Network (#05387)*; *Moscow International Higher Business School (MIRBIS)*; *Riga International School of Economics and Business Administration (RISEBA)*.

NGO Relations Member of: *EFMD – The Management Development Network (#05387)*. [2020/XM0431/y/**D**]

♦ Baltic Management Foundation (BMF) 03124

Contact Vytautas Magnus Univ, Fac of Economics and Management, K Donelacio g 58, LT-44246 Kaunas, Lithuania. T. +37037327857. Fax +37037327857.

History Founded 1992. Registered in accordance with Lithuanian law. **Aims** Assist in development of *free enterprise*, a culture of professional management and formation of national schools of management in Baltic countries. **Activities** Projects/programmes; training/education. **Events** *International conference / Conference* Kaunas (Lithuania) 2007, *International conference / Annual Assembly / Conference* Kaunas (Lithuania) 2005.

Members Founder members in 5 countries:
Estonia, Latvia, Lithuania, Poland, USA.

NGO Relations Member of: *European Management Association (EMA, #07729)*. [2017.07.05/XF6542/f/**F**]

♦ Baltic Management Institute / see BMI Executive Institute (#03288)

♦ Baltic Marine Biologists (BMB) 03125

Spécialistes baltes de biologie marine

Contact address not obtained. T. +3726204302. Fax +3726204301. E-mail: georg.martin@ut.ee.

URL: http://www.vaxtbio.uu.se/

History 20 Sep 1968, Rostock (German DR). Revised statutes adopted 4 Nov 1988, Kämpinge (Sweden). **Aims** Facilitate contacts between Baltic marine biologists. **Structure** Steering Committee (meets once or twice a year). **Languages** English. **Staff** 5.00 FTE, voluntary. **Finance** Voluntary contributions. **Activities** Organizes working groups and courses; elaborates standardized methods for research; promotes joint investigations and cruises; arranges scientific meetings and symposia. Active partner in guidelines for and execution of HELCOM's *'Baltic Monitoring Programme'*. Organizes *Baltic Sea Science Congress* with CBO and BSG. **Events** *Baltic sea science congress / Conference* Helsinki (Finland) 2003, *Biennial symposium / Conference* Stockholm (Sweden) 2001, *Biennial symposium* Klaipeda (Lithuania) 1999, *Conference* Lithuania 1999, *Conference* Hel (Poland) 1998. **Publications** *BMB Publications* (irregular). Proceedings.

Members Individual professionals (about 500) in 9 Baltic Sea countries:
Denmark, Estonia, Finland, Germany, Latvia, Lithuania, Poland, Russia, Sweden.

IGO Relations Observer status with (1): *International Council for the Exploration of the Sea (ICES, #13021)*.
NGO Relations *Baltic Sea Geologists (BSG, #03143)*. [2013/XD3566/v/**D**]

♦ Baltic Marine Environment Protection Commission – Helsinki Commission (HELCOM) 03126

Commission pour la protection de l'environnement marin de la Mer Baltique

Exec Sec Katajanokanlaituri 6 B, 3rd floor, FI-00160 Helsinki, Finland. T. +358207412649. E-mail: secretariat@helcom.fi – info@helcom.fi.

URL: http://www.helcom.fi/

History *Convention on the Protection of the Marine Environment of the Baltic Sea Area (Helsinki Convention, 1974, 1974)* signed 22 Mar 1974, Helsinki (Finland). A new treaty, *Convention on the Protection of the Marine Environment of the Baltic Sea Area, 1992 (Helsinki Convention, 1992, 1992)*, signed 9 Apr 1992, Helsinki, entered into force 17 Jan 2000. *HELCOM Baltic Sea Action Plan*, adopted 2007; updated 2021. Ministerial Declarations: Moscow 2010; Copenhagen 2013; Brussels 2018; Lübeck 2021 (Ministerial Statement). Former names and other names: *Interim Baltic Marine Environment Protection Commission* – former. **Aims** Protect the marine environment of the Baltic Sea area from all sources of *pollution* through inter-governmental cooperation. **Structure** Meeting (annually in Helsinki, Finland); Ministerial level meeting (occasionally). All 9 Baltic Sea States and *European Union (EU, #08967)* are Contracting Parties to the 1992 Convention on an equal basis. Rotating Chairmanship. Working structure: meetings of the Helsinki Commission; meetings of the Heads of Delegation; Main Working Groups (8). Also cooperation platforms, expert groups/networks and projects as necessary. Secretariat located in Helsinki (Finland). **Languages** English. **Staff** 26.50 FTE, paid. **Finance** Administrative costs and any supplementary expenses are shared by the Contracting Parties in equal parts (11%), unless unanimously decided otherwise by the Commission, except for the EU, which contributes 3% of the costs. Finland as the host country for the Commission headquarters provides additional contribution. Annual budget: 2,000,000 EUR (2022). **Activities** Advocacy/lobbying/activism; events/meetings; politics/policy/regulatory. **Events** *Meeting of the Cooperation Platform on Port Reception Facilities* Helsinki (Finland) 2022, *Meeting of the HELCOM Group on Ecosystem-Based Sustainable Fisheries* Helsinki (Finland) 2022, *Targeted Assessment Methodology Workshop for HOLAS 3 on Economic and Social Analyses* Helsinki (Finland) 2022, *Targeted Assessment Methodology Workshop for HOLAS 3* Helsinki (Finland) 2022, *International Environmental Forum* St Petersburg (Russia) 2022. **Publications** *Baltic Sea Environment Proceedings (BSEP)* – series. Reports; brochures; press releases; news.

Members Contracting Parties to the Helsinki Convention – governments of 9 countries:
Denmark, Estonia, Finland, Germany, Latvia, Lithuania, Poland, Russia, Sweden.
Regional economic integration organization (1):
European Union (EU, #08967).
Observer Governments (2):
Belarus, Ukraine.

IGO Relations Observer status with:
- *Agreement for cooperation in dealing with pollution of the North Sea by oil and other harmful substances (Bonn Agreement, #00564)*;
- *Baltic Sea Parliamentary Conference (BSPC, #03146)*;
- *Commission on the Protection of the Black Sea Against Pollution (Black Sea Commission, #04237)*;
- *Council of the Baltic Sea States (CBSS, #04870)*;
- *ECOSOC (#05331)*;
- *European Environment Agency (EEA, #06995)*;
- *Great Lakes Commission (GLC)*;
- *Intergovernmental Oceanographic Commission (IOC, #11496)*;
- *International Council for the Exploration of the Sea (ICES, #13021)*;
- *International Maritime Organization (IMO, #14102)*;
- *International Oil Pollution Compensation Funds (IOPC Funds, #14402)*;
- *OSPAR Commission for the Protection of the Marine Environment of the North-East Atlantic (OSPAR Commission, #17905)*;
- *Permanent Secretariat to the Agreement on the Conservation of African-Eurasian Migratory Waterbirds (#18330)*;
- *UNEP (#20299)*;
- *United Nations Framework Convention on Climate Change – Secretariat (UNFCCC, #20564)*;
- *World Meteorological Organization (WMO, #21649)*.

The following intergovernmental organizations have observer status: *African-Eurasian Migratory /Water Bird/ Agreement (AEWA, 1995)*; *Agreement on the Conservation of Small Cetaceans of the Baltic, North East Atlantic, Irish and North Seas (ASCOBANS, 1992)*; *Baltic Pilotage Authorities Commission (BPAC, #03135)*; *Baltic Sea States Subregional Cooperation (BSSSC, #03150)*; *Council of the Baltic Sea States (CBSS, #04870)* Expert Group on Sustainable Development (Baltic 2030); *Baltic Sea Parliamentary Conference (BSPC, #03146)*; *International Atomic Energy Agency (IAEA, #12294)*; *United Nations Economic Commission for Europe (UNECE, #20555)*; *WHO Regional Office for Europe (#20945)*. Links with (among others): *Convention on Biological Diversity (Biodiversity convention, 1992)*; *Cooperative Programme for Monitoring and Evaluation of the Long-range Transmission of Air Pollutants in Europe (EMEP, #04800)*; *Global Programme of Action for the Protection of the Marine Environment from Land-Based Activities (GPA, see: #20299)*; *International Bank for Reconstruction and Dévelopment (IBRD, #12317)*; *Vision and Strategies around the Baltic Sea (VASAB, #20798)*.

NGO Relations Nongovernmental observer organizations:
- *Association of Plastics Manufacturers in Europe (Plastics Europe, #02862)*;
- *Baltic Farmers Forum on Environment (BFFE, #03117)*;
- *Baltic Marine Environment Protection Commission – Helsinki Commission (HELCOM, #03126)*;
- *Baltic Operational Oceanographic System (BOOS, #03133)*;
- *Baltic Organisations' Network for Funding Science EEIG (BONUS EEIG, inactive)*;
- *Baltic Ports Organization (BPO, #03136)*;
- *Baltic Sea Forum (#03142)*;
- *BirdLife International (#03266)*;
- *CLIA Europe (#03995)*;
- *Coalition Clean Baltic (CCB, #04053)*;
- *Coastal and Marine Union – EUCC (#04072)*;
- *Conference of Peripheral Maritime Regions of Europe (CPMR, #04638)* – Baltic Sea Commission;
- *Conseil européen de l'industrie chimique (CEFIC, #04687)*;
- *Cruise Lines International Association (CLIA, #04973)*;
- *Euro Chlor (#05659)*;
- *European Anglers Alliance (EAA, #05900)*;
- *European Boating Association (EBA, #06376)*;
- *European Community Shipowners' Associations (ECSA, #06683)*;
- *European Dredging Association (EuDA, #06946)*;
- *European Federation of National Associations of Water and Waste Water Services (#07170)*;
- *European Network of Freshwater Research Organisations (EurAqua, #07911)*;
- *European Sea Ports Organisation (ESPO, #08453)*;
- *Federation of European Aquaculture Producers (FEAP, #09491)*;
- *Federation of European Private Port Companies and Terminals (FEPORT, #09531)*;
- *Fertilizers Europe (#09738)*;
- *Global Water Partnership (GWP, #10653)* – Central and Eastern Europe;
- *INTERFERRY (#11470)*;
- *International Association of Oil and Gas Producers (IOGP, #12053)*;
- *International Chamber of Shipping (ICS, #12535)*;
- *International Dialogue on Underwater Munitions (IDUM, #13169)*;
- *KIMO International (#16192)*;
- *Low Impact Fishers of Europe (LIFE, #16517)*;
- *Marine Stewardship Council (MSC, #16580)*;
- *Nordic Hunters' Alliance (NHA, #17313)*;
- *Oceana*;
- *Sea Alarm Foundation (#19164)*;
- *Union of the Baltic Cities (UBC, #20366)*;
- *World Wide Fund for Nature (WWF, #21922)*. [2023.02.16/XD0107/y/**E***]

♦ Baltic Maritime Coordinating Meeting (meeting series)

♦ Baltic Medico-Legal Association (BMLA) 03127

Conference Pres c/o Eesti Kohtuekspertiisi Instituut, Tervise 30, 13419 Tallinn, Estonia. T. +3726636600. E-mail: registration@ekei.ee – info@ekei.ee.

URL: http://www.ekei.ee/en/international-cooperation/bmla-baltic-medico- legal-association/

History 1990. **Structure** Officers: President; 4 Vice-Presidents; Secretary General. **Events** *International congress* Helsinki (Finland) 2010, *International congress / Congress* Vilnius (Lithuania) 2007, *Congress* St Petersburg (Russia) 2004, *Congress* Tartu (Estonia) 2001, *Congress* Riga (Latvia) 1998. [2016/XJ1713/**E**]

♦ Baltic Naval Squadron (BALTRON) 03128

Contact Tallinn Miinisadam, Box 1549, 54 Tööstuse St, 10402 Tallinn, Estonia. T. +3727177150. Fax +3727177158. E-mail: baltron@mil.ee.

History 1997, within *Baltic Security Assistance Forum (BALTSEA, inactive)*. **Aims** Minimize mine hazards, improve safety of peacetime navigation and help to remediate environmental damage in the territorial waters and economic zone of Estonia, Latvia and Lithuania. **Structure** Comprises International Staff of the Baltic States and ships of the navies of Estonia, Latvia and Lithuania. Every state allocates 1-2 Mine Countermeasures ships to BALTRON. The authorities of the Baltic States annually agree on the allocation of ships, appointment of staff members and specific exercises – the annual plan of BALTRON's activity is prepared accordingly. The ships allocated to BALTRON remain parts of the Baltic navies and therefore the joint squadron is based on the support of the three navies. One ship performs the tasks of a command and support ship, as well as base platform for staff and Commanding Officer. **Languages** English. **Staff** BALTRON staff is formed of representatives from the Estonian, Latvian and Lithuanian navies. The staff positions are rotated between the officers of the 3 states. This helps to ensure an equal participation of the navies involved in the project; participants also gain an equal share of experience to be able to act in accordance with the internationally established terms of cooperation. **Finance** Based on Memorandum of Understanding between 3 Baltic States, the budget is agreed and split by participant nations. **Activities** International cooperation in the framework of BALTRON and the foreign aid accompanying the project help to speed up the development of the Baltic navies, thereby enhancing the defence capabilities of each state. Improves mutual understanding between the navies of the Baltic States and their interoperability and helps to integrate them with the other NATO units. Plans conferences for the annual NATO and PfP exercises; BALTRON squadron participates annually in International Maritime Exercises and Mine Countermeasures Historical Ordnance Operations in Baltic and North Sea.

Members Governments of 3 countries:
Estonia, Latvia, Lithuania.

IGO Relations *NATO (#16945)*. [2014.01.20/XM0803/**F***]

♦ Baltic Nest Institute (BNI) 03129

Dir Sweden Stockholm Resilience Ctr, Stockholm Univ, SE-106 91 Stockholm, Sweden. T. +4686747668.

Denmark Dept of Ecoscience, Aarhus Univ, Frederiksborgsvej 399, 4000 Roskilde, Denmark. T. +4526701387. E-mail: jac@ecos.au.dk.

Finland Finnish Environment Inst, PO Box 140, FI-00251 Helsinki, Finland. T. +35820610123.

URL: http://www.balticnest.org/

History 2007. Developed from *'MArine Research on Eutrophication (MARE)'* programme (1999-2006), which developed the 'Baltic Nest'. **Aims** Host the Baltic Nest decision support system to facilitate adaptive *management* of *environmental* concern in the *Baltic Sea*. **Structure** Executive Board; Management Group; Advisory Group.
Members Centres in 3 countries:
Denmark, Finland, Sweden. [2022.02.01/XJ4796/j/**E**]

♦ Baltic Network against Life-Threatening Viral Infections (Baltic Antiviral Network) 03130

Coordinator Dept of Microbiology/Tumor/Cell Biology, Karolinska Inst, SE-171 77 Stockholm, Sweden. T. +46852485993.
Co-coordinator Dept of Clinical Virology, Lund Univ, Box 117, SE-221 00 Lund, Sweden. T. +46462221489.
URL: http://mtcexternal.ki.se.preview.binero.se/Baltic-Antiviral-Network/
History 1 Jul 2013, transforming from New Visby Hepatitis C Network. **Aims** Protect the population of the Baltic region from viral hepatitis, HIV-1 and pandemic influenza. **Finance** Networking grants of Swedish Institute of Ministry of Foreign Affairs (2003-2016). **Activities** Events/meetings. **Events** *Conference* Moscow (Russia) 2017, *Virus as moving targets* Vilnius (Lithuania) 2016, *Viral infections of regional significance* Moscow (Russia) 2015, *Conference* Vilnius (Lithuania) 2014, *Conference* Riga (Latvia) 2013. **NGO Relations** *European Society for translational Antiviral Research (ESAR, #08764).* [2016/XM4936/**F**]

♦ Baltic Network for Infection Control and Containment of Antibiotic Resistance (BALTICCARE) 03131

Contact address not obtained.
URL: http://www.balticcare.org/
History Mar 2004, Riga (Latvia). **Aims** Increase patient safety by: reducing health care associated infections; promoting prudent use of antibiotics. **Structure** Steering Group; Advisory Board. **Activities** Working Groups (5): Susceptibility testing; Surveillance; Isolation precautions; Education; Website.
Members Specialists in 4 countries:
Estonia, Latvia, Lithuania, Russia.
NGO Relations *International Federation of Infection Control (IFIC, #13457).* [2009/XM3005/v/**F**]

♦ Baltic Neurosurgical Association (no recent information)

♦ Baltic and North Sea Forum of Physical and Rehabilitation Medicine (BNF-PRM) 03132

Pres Hannover Medical School, Carl-Neuberg-Str 1, 30625 Hannover, Germany. T. +495115324140. Fax +495115328124.
History 7 Sep 2008, Riga (Latvia). **Aims** Promote communication, education and science in the field of physical and rehabilitation medicine (PRM) and related fields in the countries with borders to the Baltic Sea and the North Sea. **Structure** Executive Committee. **Finance** Members' dues. **Events** *Conference* Hannover (Germany) 2013, *Conference* Vilnius (Lithuania) 2011. [2014/XJ8561/**F**]

♦ Baltic Operational Oceanographic System (BOOS) 03133

Chair MSI Ehitajate tee 5, 19086 Tallinn, Estonia.
URL: http://www.boos.org/
Aims Provide integrated marine services to the marine users and policy makers. **Structure** Plenary Meeting. Steering Group, comprising Chair and 5 members.
Members Full institutions which signed the Memorandum of Understanding. Full in 9 countries:
Denmark, Estonia, Finland, Germany, Latvia, Lithuania, Poland, Russia, Sweden.
Associate institutions which have not yet signed the MoU. Associate in 3 countries:
Germany, Lithuania, Russia.
IGO Relations Observer to: *Baltic Marine Environment Protection Commission – Helsinki Commission (HELCOM, #03126).* [2013/XJ6844/**F**]

♦ Baltic Organization of Democrat Youth (inactive)

♦ Baltic Orthodontic Association (BOA) 03134

Pres Institute of Stomatology, Riga Stradins Univ, Dzirciema Street 20, Riga LV-1007, Latvia. T. +37167455586. Fax +37167815323. E-mail: eestiortodontideselts@gmail.com.
Contact address not obtained.
History 1999. **Events** *Congress* Estonia 2020, *Biennial Congress* Vilnius (Lithuania) 2018, *Biennial Congress* Riga (Latvia) 2016, *Congress* Tallinn (Estonia) 2013, *Biennial congress / Congress* Riga (Latvia) 2008. [2020/XD8703/**D**]

♦ Baltic Pilotage Authorities Commission (BPAC) 03135

SG c/o DMA, Caspar Brands Plads 9, 4220 Korsør, Denmark. T. +4572196177. E-mail: fgo@dma.dk – bil@dma.dk.
Pres c/o TRAFICOM, Kumpulantie 9, FI-00520 Helsinki, Finland. T. +358295346466.
History 1981, Rostock (Germany). **Aims** Improve *maritime* and *shipping* safety and protect the environment in the Baltic Sea region; promote the exchange of deep-sea pilotage experience between national authorities and pilotage providers in the region; forward recommendations and influence decision making related to pilotage in the region in cooperation with other interested parties. **Structure** Executive Committee. **Languages** English. **Staff** 3.00 FTE, voluntary. **Finance** No budget. **Activities** Events/meetings. **Events** *Conference* Liepaja (Latvia) 2022, *Conference* Copenhagen (Denmark) 2019, *Conference* St Petersburg (Russia) 2018, *Conference* Bergen (Norway) 2017, *Conference* Stockholm (Sweden) 2016. **Publications** Conferences presentations and summaries.
Members Member States (10):
Denmark, Estonia, Finland, Germany, Latvia, Lithuania, Norway, Poland, Russia, Sweden.
IGO Relations Observer status with (1): *Baltic Marine Environment Protection Commission – Helsinki Commission (HELCOM, #03126).* [2021.08.31/XJ6843/**D***]

♦ Baltic Plastic Pipes Association (no recent information)

♦ Baltic Ports Organization (BPO) 03136

SG c/o Actia Forum Ltd, ul Pulaskiego 8, 81-368 Gdynia, Poland. T. +48586272467. Fax +48586272427. E-mail: bpo.sg@actiaforum.pl – bpo.office@actiaforum.pl.
Registered Address Port of Tallinn, Sadama 25, 15051 Tallinn, Estonia.
URL: http://www.bpoports.com/
History 10 Oct 1991, Copenhagen (Denmark). Statutes adopted 26-27 Mar 1992, Tallinn (Estonia), at 1st General Assembly; most recently revised 1 Jun 2006, Stockholm (Sweden). Former names and other names: *Organization of the Baltic Ports* – alias. Registration: Estonia; EU Transparency Register, No/ID: 891210440298-53, Start date: 12 Nov 2020. **Aims** Increase transfer of cargo and passengers between ports of the Baltic Sea; improve competitiveness of maritime transport in the Baltic region; promote policies and viewpoints of ports in the region with relevant international bodies; study problems relating to the port industry in the context of international treaties so as to keep members informed and to seek common positions; cooperate on subjects concerning preservation of the environment. **Structure** General Assembly (annually); Board; Secretariat. **Languages** English. **Staff** 1.00 FTE, paid. **Finance** Sources: members' dues. Annual budget: 100,000 EUR. **Activities** Events/meetings; training/education. **Events** *General Assembly* Stockholm (Sweden) 2019, *General Assembly* Helsinki (Finland) 2016, *General Assembly* Riga (Latvia) 2015, *General Assembly* Klaipeda (Lithuania) 2013, *General Assembly* Turku (Finland) 2012. **Publications** *BPO e-Newsletter* (6 a year); *BPO Newsletter* (6 a year).
Members Harbour and port authorities (50) and their national organizations, in 8 countries:
Denmark, Estonia, Finland, Germany, Latvia, Lithuania, Poland, Sweden.
IGO Relations Observer to: *Baltic Marine Environment Protection Commission – Helsinki Commission (HELCOM, #03126).* [2020/XD3697/**D**]

♦ Baltic Postal Union (BPU) 03137

Union postale balte (UPB)
Contact Lithuania Post, J Jasinskio g 16, LT-03500 Vilnius, Lithuania. T. +370570055400.
History 1 Feb 1994, legally based on UPU Charter 49/1994. A Restricted Union of *Universal Postal Union (UPU, #20682).* **Aims** Improve and develop cooperation among postal administrations of Baltic countries; develop and introduce integrated services within the territory of the 3 countries; coordinate and represent them in international developments and attend to their common interests; participate in promotion of international postal development issues and postal business operations. **Structure** No permanent administrative body. Chairmanship rotates annually among member countries. **Languages** English, Russian. **Staff** None. Participants are responsible for their own administrative work. **Finance** Expenses for task forces covered by member countries; some organizational expenses covered by country hosting annual meeting. **Activities** Information dissemination; meeting activities; 3-country stamps. **Events** *Annual Meeting* Tallinn (Estonia) 2011, *Annual meeting* Vilnius (Lithuania) 2004, *Annual meeting* Riga (Latvia) 2003, *Annual Meeting* Pärnu (Estonia) 2002, *Annual meeting* Vilnius (Lithuania) 2001.
Members Postal administrations of 3 countries:
Estonia, Latvia, Lithuania.
IGO Relations Links with the other Restricted Unions: *Association of European Public Postal Operators (PostEurop, #02534); Nordic Postal Union (NPU, #17391).* [2013.11.19/XD4870/**D***]

♦ Baltic Road Association (BRA) 03138

Association routière des pays baltes – Balti Maanteeliit (BML) – Baltijas Celinieku Asociacija (BCA) – Baltijos Saliu Kelininku Asociacija (BKA)
Contact 4 Valge Road, 11413 Tallinn, Estonia.
URL: http://www.balticroads.org/
History 20 Apr 1989. Established following conferences dating back to 1932. Former names and other names: *Baltic Road Council (BRC)* – former; *Baltijos Kelininku Asociacija (BKA)* – former. Registration: Estonia. **Aims** Coordinate activities of road sector organizations in the Baltic States in order to prepare and implement a uniform road maintenance strategy in the region. **Structure** Council (meets twice a year); Technical Committees. Each Baltic country is responsible for managing the Association for 4 years. **Languages** English. **Staff** None. **Finance** Sources: members' dues. **Activities** Events/meetings. **Events** *Baltic Road Conference* 2021, *Triennial Conference* Tallinn (Estonia) 2017, *Triennial Conference* Vilnius (Lithuania) 2013, *Triennial conference* Riga (Latvia) 2009, *NordBalt seminar on steel pipe bridges* Stockholm (Sweden) 2007. **Publications** *Baltic Journal of Road and Bridge Engineering.* Conference proceedings.
Members Organizations, institutions and companies. Full in 3 countries:
Estonia, Latvia, Lithuania. [2023.02.14/XD4325/**D**]

♦ Baltic Road Council / see Baltic Road Association (#03138)
♦ Baltic Sail (unconfirmed)
♦ BalticSea2020 (internationally oriented national body)
♦ Baltic Sea 7 Islands / see Islands of the Baltic Sea (#16060)
♦ Baltic Sea Action Group / see Foundation for a Living Baltic Sea

♦ Baltic Sea Advisory Council (BSAC) 03139

Exec Sec HC Andersens Boulevard 37, Third Floor, 1553 Copenhagen V, Denmark. T. +4533935000. Fax +4532176461.
URL: http://www.bsac.dk/
History Mar 2006. Founded following *European Commission (EC, #06633)* – Council Decision 2004/585/EC to create Regional Advisory Councils in the fisheries sector. Common Fisheries Policy reform finalized Dec 2013. Former names and other names: *Baltic Sea Regional Advisory Council (BS RAC)* – former. **Aims** Advise the European Commission and Member States on matters relating to management of the *fisheries* in the Baltic Sea. **Structure** General Assembly; Executive Committee. Working Groups. **Finance** Funded by: *European Union (EU, #08967)*; Member States around the Baltic Sea; members. **Events** *General Assembly* Helsinki (Finland) 2015, *General Assembly* Gdynia (Poland) 2014, *General Assembly* Copenhagen (Denmark) 2013, *General Assembly* Tallinn (Estonia) 2012, *General Assembly* Riga (Latvia) 2011.
Members Stakeholders in 8 countries:
Denmark, Estonia, Finland, Germany, Latvia, Lithuania, Poland, Sweden.
Included in the above, 11 organizations listed in this Yearbook:
BalticSea2020; Coalition Clean Baltic (CCB, #04053); Comité des organisations nationales des importateurs et exportateurs de poisson de l'UE (CEP, #04194); Environmental Defense Fund (EDF); European Anglers Alliance (EAA, #05900); European Fismeal and Fish Oil Producers (European Fishmeal, #07268); European Transport Workers' Federation (ETF, #08941); European Union Fish Processors Association (#08989); International Sea Sportfishing Federation (FIPS-M, see: #04562); Oceana; World Wide Fund for Nature (WWF, #21922).
NGO Relations *Long Distance Advisory Council (LDAC, #16511); Mediterranean Advisory Council (MEDAC, #16639); North Sea Advisory Council (NSAC, #17603); North Western Waters Advisory Council (NWWAC, #17607); Pelagic Advisory Council (Pelagic AC, #18289); South West Waters Advisory Council (SWWAC, #19896).* [2022/XJ9732/y/**E**]

♦ Baltic Sea Alliance (inactive)
♦ Baltic Sea Business Advisory Council / see Business Advisory Council (#03376)

♦ Baltic Sea Chambers of Commerce Association (BCCA) 03140

SG c/o Sydsvenska Handelskammaren, Skeppsbron 2, SE-211 20 Malmö, Sweden. T. +46406902400. Fax +46406902409. E-mail: info@bcca.eu.
Pres address not obtained.
URL: http://www.bcca.ws/
History 4th Jun 1992, Rostock (Germany)/Warnemünde (Germany), *Conferences of the Baltic Chambers of Commerce* having taken place since 1972. Also referred to as *Baltic Chambers of Commerce Association.* Also abbreviated as *Baltchambers.* **Aims** Foster and strengthen economic development and the integration process in the region, especially through creation of company contacts; represent and give one voice to private business and companies in regional dialogue; establish a network among companies in the region to promote trade and other forms of economic cooperation and development; identify and combat barriers to trade; protect and uphold the interests of private entrepreneurship. **Structure** General Conference of Members (annual). Praesidium, comprising President and 4 Vice-Presidents. Ad hoc working groups. Secretariat. **Languages** English. **Staff** 1.50 FTE, paid. **Finance** Members' dues. **Activities** Events/meetings; advocacy/loybbing/activism. **Events** *Annual General Conference* Riga (Latvia) 2014, *Annual General Conference / General Conference* Stockholm (Sweden) 2013, *Annual General Conference / General Conference* Helsinki (Finland) 2012, *Annual general conference* Kiel (Germany) 2005, *Annual general conference* Turku (Finland) 2004. **Publications** *Baltchambers News. Arbitration in the Baltic Sea Region; Cross-Cultural Management Guide.* Annual Report. Information Services: Collects and publishes information on trade barriers; drafts investors' guidelines. Integrated databanks: member list; news; calendar of events.
Members Full (43); corresponding (8) Chambers of industry and commerce representing 430,000 businesses in 10 countries:
Denmark, Estonia, Finland, Germany, Latvia, Lithuania, Norway, Poland, Russia, Sweden. [2014/XD4424/**D**]

♦ Baltic Sea Commission (BSC) 03141

Commission de la Mer baltique
Exec Sec c/o North Sweden EU Office, Av Palmerston 26, 1000 Brussels, Belgium.
URL: http://cpmr-baltic.org/
History 1996, Kotka (Finland), within the framework of *Conference of Peripheral Maritime Regions of Europe (CPMR, #04638).* **Aims** Support the main goals, and work for stronger involvement of regional stakeholders in the governance and implementation of the EU Strategy of the Baltic Sea Region. **Structure** General Assembly (annual); Executive Committee; Presidency; Executive Secretary; Working Groups. **Languages** English. **Finance** Members' dues. Other sources: hosting regions of the secretariat; project funds. **Activities** Politics/policy/regulatory; events/meetings; projects/programmes. **Events** *Annual Forum on the EU Strategy for the Baltic Sea Region* Gdansk (Poland) 2019, *General Assembly* Gdansk (Poland) 2019, *Future of Europe Conference* Lahti (Finland) 2019, *International Seminar on Circular Economy* Lahti (Finland) 2019, *Annual Forum on the EU Strategy for the Baltic Sea Region* Tallinn (Estonia) 2018.

Members Regions (19) in 6 countries:
Estonia, Finland, Germany, Norway, Poland, Sweden.
IGO Relations Special participant status with: *Council of the Baltic Sea States (CBSS, #04870)*. Member of: EGSD-Baltic 2030. Observer to: *Baltic Marine Environment Protection Commission – Helsinki Commission (HELCOM, #03126)*. [2017.06.01/XK1437/E]

♦ Baltic Sea Conference of Ministers of Transport (meeting series)
♦ Baltic Sea Conservation Foundation (internationally oriented national body)
♦ Baltic Sea Culture Centre, Gdansk (internationally oriented national body)

♦ Baltic Sea Forum 03142

Contact Am Kaiserkai 69, 20457 Hamburg, Germany. T. +4940239369810. Fax +4940239369820. E-mail: info@baltic-sea-forum.org.
URL: http://www.baltic-sea-forum.org/

History 1992, as *Pro Baltica Forum*. Current name adopted 20 Mar 2003. **Aims** Improve cooperation between the sectors of *economics, politics* and *cultural* activities in the Baltic Sea Region. **Structure** Advisory Board, comprising 2 Chairmen and 15 members. Board, consisting of Chairman, 2 Vice-Chairmen and 8 members. Board office with Managing Director. **Languages** English, German. **Staff** 1.50 FTE, paid. 1-2 interns. **Finance** Members' dues. Donations. **Activities** Arranges conferences, meetings and events; provides information; provides support and contact for development of projects and publications. **Events** *International congress on cognitive design* Lübeck (Germany) 2004, *Eastern Europe conference on transport* Berlin (Germany) 2003, *South-North Europe Economic forum* Brioni (Croatia) 2003, *Conference on public private partnership in the Baltic sea region* Kiel (Germany) 2003, *Environmental forum* Rovaniemi (Finland) 2003. **Publications** *Baltic Sea Magazine*. Calendar.
Members Individuals, companies and institutions in 12 countries:
Austria, Denmark, Estonia, Finland, Germany, Latvia, Lithuania, Norway, Poland, Russia, Sweden, Switzerland.
Business members include 1 organization listed in this Yearbook:
Wiener Institut für Internationale Wirtschaftsvergleiche (WIIW).
Consultative Status Consultative status granted from: *ECOSOC (#05331)* (Special). **IGO Relations** Observer to: *Baltic Marine Environment Protection Commission – Helsinki Commission (HELCOM, #03126)*. **NGO Relations** Member of: *European Association of Service Providers for Persons with Disabilities (EASPD, #06204)*. Partner organizations include: *Baltic Development Forum (#03111)*; *EastWest Institute (EWI, #05264)*; *Union of the Baltic Cities (UBC, #20366)*. [2019/XF5760/y/F]

♦ Baltic Sea Geologists (BSG) 03143

Chairman Inst of Geology, Univ of Tartu, Vanemuise 46, 51014 Tartu, Estonia. T. +3727375879.
URL: http://www.pgi.gda.pl/

History 2001, Stockholm (Sweden), during *Baltic Sea Science Congress*. **Aims** Promote geological studies of the Baltic Sea and adjacent areas. **Structure** Chairman elected for 2 years during Baltic Sea Science Congress. **Events** *Conference* Jurmala (Latvia) 2006.
Members Individuals (31) in 9 countries:
Belarus, Denmark, Estonia, Finland, Germany, Lithuania, Poland, Russia, Sweden.
NGO Relations *Baltic Sea Research Institute (IOW)*. [2007.08.27/XM0259/F]

♦ Baltic Sea Hydrographic Commission (see: #13825)
♦ Baltic Sea Institute / see European-Latvian Institute
♦ Baltic Sea Joint Comprehensive Environmental Action Programme (inactive)

♦ Baltic Sea Network on Occupational Health and Safety (BSN) 03144

Secretariat Finnish Inst of Occupational Health, Arinatie 3A, PO Box 18, FI-00391 Helsinki, Finland.
URL: http://www.balticseaosh.net/

History Founded 7 Nov 1995, Copenhagen (Denmark), during the Consultation on Strengthening of Occupational Health Services in Baltic Countries, organized by *WHO Regional Office for Europe (#20945)*. **Aims** Provide direction and a platform for strengthening peer-to-peer networking and collaboration on occupational health and safety between and within countries around the Baltic Sea. **Structure** National focal points; Secretariat, based in Helsinki (Finland). **Languages** English. **Staff** No permanent staff. Member-country participating institutes cooperate voluntarily. Secretariat supported by Finnish Institute of Occupational Health. **Finance** No funding. Joint surveys financed by different organizations. **Activities** Research/documentation. **Events** *Annual Meeting* Tallinn (Estonia) 2015, *Annual Meeting* Vilnius (Lithuania) 2014, *Annual Meeting* Espoo (Finland) 2013, *Annual Meeting* St Petersburg (Russia) 2012, *Annual Meeting* Riga (Latvia) 2011. **Publications** *Barents Newsletter on Occupational Health and Safety* (3 a year). Proceedings-books.
Members Participants in 10 countries:
Denmark, Estonia, Finland, Germany, Latvia, Lithuania, Norway, Poland, Russia, Sweden. [2015.09.04/XF4661/F]

♦ Baltic Sea NGO Network (BS NGO Network) 03145

Contact Kastrupvej 78 – 3 th, 2300 Copenhagen S, Denmark. E-mail: mail@bs-ngo.dk.
URL: http://www.bsngoforum.net/

Structure Coordination Committee. **Activities** Events/meetings. **Events** *Annual Forum* Tallinn (Estonia) 2015, *Annual Forum* Turku (Finland) 2014, *Annual Forum* St Petersburg (Russia) 2013, *Annual Forum* Berlin (Germany) 2012, *Annual Forum* Vilnius (Lithuania) 2010.
Members Full in 11 countries:
Denmark, Estonia, Finland, Germany, Iceland, Latvia, Lithuania, Norway, Poland, Russia, Sweden.
IGO Relations *Council of the Baltic Sea States (CBSS, #04870)*. [2019/XJ9024/F]

♦ Baltic Sea Parliamentary Conference (BSPC) 03146

SG Schlossgartenallee 15, 19061 Schwerin, Germany. T. +491715512557.
URL: http://www.bspc.net/

History 1991, Helsinki (Finland). Founded with the administrative support of *Nordic Council (NC, #17256)*. New rules adopted 8 Sep 1999, Mariehamn (Finland). Former names and other names: *Parliamentary Conference on Cooperation in the Baltic Sea Region* – former (1999). Registration: EU Transparency Register, No/ID: 480302138737-71, Start date: 24 Jun 2020. **Aims** Strengthen the common identity of the Baltic Sea Region by means of close cooperation between national and regional parliaments on the basis of equality; initiate and guide political activities in the region, endowing them with additional democratic legitimacy and parliamentary authority; further cooperation in the region, especially towards the CBSS and other governmental as well as non-governmental organizations; act as a forum for debate and exchange of information between parliaments and other bodies and organizations. **Structure** Conference (annual); Standing Committee; Secretary Level meeting; Secretariat. Working Group on Innovation in Social and Health Care. Secretariat at the Nordic Council. **Languages** Danish, English, Faroese, German, Icelandic, Norwegian, Russian, Swedish. **Staff** 2.50 FTE, paid. **Finance** All costs of the conference covered by Host Parliament. **Activities** Events/meetings; politics/policy/regulatory. **Events** *Baltic Sea Parliamentary Conference* Stockholm (Sweden) 2022, *Baltic Sea Parliamentary Conference* Schwerin (Germany) 2020, *Annual Conference* Oslo (Norway) 2019, *Annual Conference* Mariehamn (Finland) 2018, *Annual Conference* Hamburg (Germany) 2017.
Members Parliamentarians of 11 countries:
Denmark, Estonia, Finland, Germany, Iceland, Latvia, Lithuania, Norway, Poland, Russia, Sweden.
Member Parliaments (4):
Baltic Assembly (BA, #03094); *European Parliament (EP, #08146)*; *Nordic Council (NC, #17256)*; *Parliamentary Assembly of the Council of Europe (PACE, #18211)*.
IGO Relations Mutual observer status with: *Baltic Marine Environment Protection Commission – Helsinki Commission (HELCOM, #03126)*. Invited observers: *Baltic Sea States Subregional Cooperation (BSSSC, #03150)*; *Conférence des Organes Parlementaires Spécialisés dans les Affaires de l'Union des Parlements de l'Union Européenne (COSAC, #04637)*; *Council of the Baltic Sea States (CBSS, #04870)*; *European Commission (EC, #06633)*; *Standing Committee of Parliamentarians of the Arctic Region (SCPAR, #19958)*. **NGO Relations** Invited observers: *Baltic Sea Chambers of Commerce Association (BCCA, #03140)*; *Baltic Sea Commission (BSC, #03141)*; *Conference of Peripheral Maritime Regions of Europe (CPMR, #04638)*; *Inter-Parliamentary Union (IPU, #15961)*; *Union of the Baltic Cities (UBC, #20366)*. [2022/XF5712/F*]

♦ Baltic Sea Project (BSP) 03147

Gen Coordinator address not obtained. T. +8123142336.
URL: http://www.b-s-p.org/

History 1989, by *UNESCO Associated Schools Project Network (ASPnet, #20302)* and *International Network for Information in Science and Technology Education (INISTE, inactive)*. **Aims** Increase among students an awareness of *environmental* problems in the Baltic Sea area; give them an understanding of the scientific, social and cultural aspects of the *interdependence* of man and *nature*; develop their ability to study *changes* in the environment; encourage them to participate in developing a *sustainable future*. Educational approach of BSP schools is to: achieve a balance between holistic view and individual subject studies; change student's role from passive recipient to active constructor; change teacher's role from supervisor to guide in the learning process; use networks to provide participants with opportunities to learn and pass on new ideas; use international cooperation as an inherent element of school work. **Structure** National Coordinators (meet annually); Programme Coordinators; Coordinators from Sister Projects. General Coordinator, appointed by host country. **Languages** English. **Staff** 0.50 FTE, paid. Voluntary. **Finance** Annual budget the responsibility of host country: 2001-2003 – hosted by German Commission for UNESCO; 2003-2006 – hosted by Polish Commission for UNESCO and Polish Ministry for Education; 2006 – hosted by Lithuania. Budget (annual): about Danish Kr 1 million. **Activities** Building up networks of schools, teachers and educational institutions in the Baltic drainage area – basic characteristics of BSP schools are: active participation in seeking solutions to environmental problems of the Baltic Sea area; networking; pilot function in promoting environmental education in the spirit of the Rio Declaration, Agenda 21 and Baltic 21 (an Agenda 21 for the Baltic region). Creates and develops educational approaches and joint programmes for environmental and international education. *'Programmes'*: Water Quality of the Baltic Sea; Air Quality of the Baltic Sea Area; Rivers; BSP Coast Watch; Phenological Studies; Bird Ecology; Environmental History. Organizes joint activities and events. Sponsors: thematic Baltic Weeks in schools; seminars; lectures and fieldwork for teachers and students; summer camps and courses; Agenda 21; Baltic 21. **Events** *Annual Coordinators Meeting* St Petersburg (Russia) 2016, *Conference* Tallinn (Estonia) 2016, *Science of changes* Tallinn (Estonia) 2015, *Conference* Katowice (Poland) 2006, *Conference* Travemünde (Germany) 2005. **Publications** *Baltic Sea Project Newsletter* (2 a year). *Learner's Guide* – series. Catalogue.
Members Associated schools (350) and national coordinators in school authorities of the 9 countries surrounding the Baltic Sea:
Denmark, Estonia, Finland, Germany, Latvia, Lithuania, Poland, Russia, Sweden.
IGO Relations Promotes: *Global Action Plan for Environment and Development in the 21st Century (Agenda 21, inactive)*. [2016/XK0478/E]

♦ Baltic Sea Regional Advisory Council / see Baltic Sea Advisory Council (#03139)

♦ Baltic Sea Region Energy Cooperation (BASREC) 03148

Address not obtained.

History Oct 1999. Established by *European Commission (EC, #06633)* and the Energy Ministers of the 11 Baltic Sea Region countries. Working body of *Council of the Baltic Sea States (CBSS, #04870)*. Revised format since Mar 2015, since when no activities have been planned. **Aims** Serve as a cooperation forum between energy authorities of Baltic Sea Region countries and the European Commission for development of framework conditions towards effective, economically and environmentally sound and more integrated energy systems. **Structure** Group of Senior Energy Officials (GSEO) steers the cooperation. Ad-hoc working groups are appointed in a flexible manner when the need arises (currently 2 working bodies active). **Languages** English. **Activities** Mandate to cover virtually all aspects of energy policy. Organizes conferences in the fields of renewable energy sources, energy efficiency and energy related climate change. **Events** *Energy Efficiency Seminar* Helsinki (Finland) 2014, *Energy Efficiency Seminar* Helsinki (Finland) 2014, *Ministerial Conference* Copenhagen (Denmark) 2008, *Seminar* Lahti (Finland) 2006, *Ministerial conference* Reykjavik (Iceland) 2005.
Members Governments of 11 countries:
Denmark, Estonia, Finland, Germany, Iceland, Latvia, Lithuania, Norway, Poland, Russia, Sweden.
Includes 1 organization, listed in this Yearbook;:
European Commission (EC, #06633) (represented by DG TREN).
Observers governments of 6 countries:
France, Italy, Netherlands, Slovakia, Ukraine, USA.
IGO Relations Observer members: *Energy Charter Conference (#05466)*; *International Energy Agency (IEA, #13270)*. [2009/XF6259/d/F*]

♦ Baltic Sea Region University Network (BSRUN) 03149

President Univ of Latvia, Aspazijas Bulvaris 5, Room 120, Riga LV-1505, Latvia. T. +37167034600. E-mail: bsrun@lu.lv – president@bsrun.org.
Secretariat St Petersburg State Univ of Economics, Sadovaya Street 21, St Petersburg SANKT-PETERBURG, Russia, 191023. T. +78123101963. E-mail: bsrun@unecon.ru.
URL: http://www.bsrun.org/

History 28 Feb 2000, Turku (Finland). New rules and regulations approved 25 Feb 2010, Turku (Finland) and in force from 1 Jul 2010; revised and approved Mar 2013; came into force 1 Jan 2014; amended 25 Oct 2016. **Aims** Serve as a network for university governance, management and administration, and as a platform for new ideas, contacts and projects; facilitate and enhance cooperation between members. **Structure** Steering Committee; Secretarial Offices (2). **Languages** English. **Finance** Sources: members' dues. **Activities** Events/meetings. **Events** *Embedding Sustainable Development Goals into the Universities DNA* 2022, *Re-inventing Students Housing* Riga (Latvia) 2021, *University Governance Reforms – Expectations and Experiences* Riga (Latvia) 2021, *University Governance Reforms in Poland – Expectations and Experiences* Riga (Latvia) 2021, *UN Sustainable Development Goals in Universities* St Petersburg (Russia) 2021.
Members Institutions (24) in 7 countries:
Belarus, Estonia, Finland, Germany, Latvia, Poland, Russia.
IGO Relations Partner of (1): *Council of the Baltic Sea States (CBSS, #04870)*. **NGO Relations** Partner of (4): *EAIR, The European Higher Education Society (#05153)*; *European Association for International Education (EAIE, #06092)*; *Nordic Association of University Administrators (NAUA, #17206)*; *United Nations Academic Impact (UNAI, #20516)*. Links with regional organizations. [2022.05.04/XM3171/F]

♦ Baltic Sea Research Institute (internationally oriented national body)
♦ Baltic Sea Science Congress (meeting series)
♦ Baltic Sea Secretariat for Youth Affairs (inactive)

♦ Baltic Sea States Subregional Cooperation (BSSSC) 03150

Chairmanship – 2013-2015 c/o Uusimaa Regional Council, Esterinportti 2B, FI-00240 Helsinki, Finland. E-mail: bsssc@bsssc.com.
URL: http://www.bsssc.com/

History Established Oct 1993, Stavanger (Norway), based on the Stavanger declaration, and as a result of the establishment of the Council of Baltic Sea States (CBSS) in 1992. EU Transparency Register: 9016880835-58. **Aims** Act as a political network organization open to all subregions (regional authorities) around the Baltic Sea area, bringing added value to regional cooperation on every side of the Baltic Sea, so as to strengthen regional cooperation, using the BSSSC image as a *political* network and a regional partner to CBSS; promote and advocate the interests of the regions of the Baltic Sea area to decision makers, such as national governments, the EU and globally; provide expertise, best practice examples and implementation capacity. **Structure** Board, comprising 2 representatives from each of the Baltic Sea region countries, 2 youth representatives and one representative each of *Union of the Baltic Cities (UBC, #20366)*, *Baltic Sea Commission (BSC, #03141)* – CPMR and *Islands of the Baltic Sea (B7, #16060)*, and one observer representative of *Council of the Baltic Sea States (CBSS, #04870)*. Secretariat; Ad-hoc Working Groups. **Languages** English. **Staff** 2.00 FTE, paid. **Finance** No membership fees. **Activities** Politics/policy/regulatory; networking/liaising; capacity building; advocacy/lobbying/activism; guidance/assistance/consulting. **Events** *Annual Conference* Visby (Sweden) 2015, *Annual Conference* Jurmala (Latvia) 2014, *Annual Conference* Helsinki (Finland) 2013, *Annual Conference* Oslo (Norway) / Lillestrøm (Norway) 2012, *Annual Conference* Ringsted (Denmark) 2009. **Publications** *BSSSC Newsletter* (3-4 a year). *Administrative Structures* (2001); *Administrative Structures 2001*; *Baltic Sea Cooperation Beyond 2000 – Visions and Strategies on the Local and Regional Level*; *Quality of Life – A Subregional Contribution to the Implementation of the Northern Dimension*; *Youth Policies in the Baltic Sea Region*. Calendar of Baltic events; position papers; forum reports; surveys.

Members Regional governments of 10 countries:
Denmark, Estonia, Finland, Germany, Latvia, Lithuania, Norway, Poland, Russia, Sweden.
IGO Relations Observer status with: *European Committee of the Regions (CoR, #06665)*. Member of: *Northern Dimension Partnership in Public Health and Social Well-being (NDPHS, #17587)*. [2014.11.17/XD5919/**D***]

♦ Baltic Sea Trade Union Network (BASTUN) 03151

Policy Officer c/o NFS/TCO, Linnégatan 14, SE-114 47 Stockholm, Sweden. T. +46722373723. E-mail: jenny@nfs.net.
URL: http://www.bastun.nu/
History Jul 1999. Founded in connection with Congress of *European Trade Union Confederation (ETUC, #08927)*.
Members Organizations in 10 countries:
Denmark, Estonia, Finland, Germany, Latvia, Lithuania, Norway, Poland, Russia, Sweden.
NGO Relations Secretariat at: *Nordens Fackliga Samorganisation (NFS, #17158)*. [2020.04.29/XF6066/t/**F**]

♦ Baltic Society of Andrology 03152

Contact Fertility Clinic Nordic, Pärnu mnt 67a, 7th Floor, 10134 Tallinn, Estonia. E-mail: info@ivfnordic.com.
Events *Conference* Kaunas (Lithuania) 2004. [2009/XJ3491/**D**]

- ♦ Baltic Society for Immunology (inactive)
- ♦ Baltic Society of Neuropathologists / see Baltic Association of Neuropathologists (#03099)

♦ Baltic Society of Phlebology (BSP) 03153

Pres Keguma iela 13-2, Riga LV-1006, Latvia. T. +37129230123.
URL: http://baltic-phlebology.org/
History May 2009. Registered in accordance with Latvian law: 40008152001. **Aims** Contribute to the qualification of doctors; encourage the development of science and praxis of phlebology. **Structure** Board. **Finance** Members' dues. **Activities** Events/meetings; training/education.
Members Full in 4 countries:
Belarus, Estonia, Latvia, Lithuania. [2015/XJ9323/**D**]

- ♦ Baltic Society of Thoracic and Cardiovascular Surgery (inactive)

♦ Baltic Sport Science Society (BSSS) 03154

Sec Latvian Academy of Sport Education, Brivibas Str 333, Riga LV-1006, Latvia. T. +37167543410.
URL: http://www.balticsportsciencesociety.com/
History Apr 2009, Vilnius (Lithuania). **Aims** Promote the study and development of sport sciences in the Baltic States; enhance the quality of doctoral studies. **Structure** Council. **Languages** English. **Activities** Events/meetings; training/education. **Events** *Conference* Kaunas (Lithuania) 2016, *Conference* Vilnius (Lithuania) 2015, *Conference* Tartu (Estonia) 2014, *Conference* Riga (Latvia) 2013, *Conference* Kaunas (Lithuania) 2012.
Members Full in 3 countries:
Estonia, Latvia, Lithuania. [2016/XM4456/**D**]

- ♦ Baltic States Freedom Council (inactive)
- ♦ Baltic States Genetical Societies Federation (inactive)
- ♦ Baltic States Head and Neck Oncology Association (internationally oriented national body)
- ♦ Baltic States Regional Environmental Development / see Baltic Environmental Forum (#03116)
- ♦ Baltic Studies Programme / see Institute of Baltic Studies
- ♦ Baltic United Special Printing Association (inactive)
- ♦ Baltic University / see The Baltic University Programme (#03155)

♦ The Baltic University Programme (BUP) 03155

Secretariat Villavägen 16, SE-752 36 Uppsala, Sweden. E-mail: info@balticuniv.uu.se.
URL: http://www.balticuniv.uu.se/
History Founded following planning conference, 1991, Uppsala (Sweden). Since 2016, an organization of participating universities in the Baltic Sea Region. Former names and other names: *Baltic University* – alias. **Aims** Promote and support universities and corresponding institutions in development of the Baltic Sea region towards peaceful cooperation, democracy and economic, social and ecological sustainable development. **Structure** International Board; Coordinating Secretariat at Uppsala University (Sweden). Associated Secretariats: Åbo Akademi University; Hamburg University of Applied Sciences; Lodz University of Technology. **Languages** English. **Staff** 5.00 FTE, paid. **Finance** Sources: members' dues. **Activities** Capacity building; events/meetings; projects/programmes; training/education. . **Events** *International conference on integrative approaches towards sustainability* Jurmala (Latvia) 2005, *Baltic meeting point conference on sustainable community development* Uppsala (Sweden) 2001. **Publications** *City 2000 Video Series*; *Environmental Management* – book series, 4 vols to date. *Cultures, Politics, Societies*; *Environmental Science*; *SUPERBS Case Studies* – in 4 vols; *The Baltic Sea Region*. Annual Report; books.
Members Participating Universities (nearly 90) in 10 countries:
Czechia, Estonia, Finland, Germany, Latvia, Lithuania, Poland, Slovakia, Sweden, Ukraine.
NGO Relations Member of (1): *International Climate Change Information Programme (ICCIP, #12597)* (Founding). [2022.10.19/XF3599/**F**]

- ♦ BalticWaters2030 (internationally oriented national body)
- ♦ Baltic and White Sea Conference / see BIMCO (#03236)

♦ Baltic Writers' Council (BWC) 03156

Contact Uddens gränd 3, SE-621 56 Visby, Sweden. T. +46498218385. Fax +46498218798.
URL: http://www.balticwriterscouncil.info/
History 1992. Founded following the *Baltic Waves' Cruise*. Former names and other names: *Baltic Writers and Translators' Council (BWTC)* – alias. **Events** *General Assembly* Visby (Sweden) 2013, *General Assembly* Visby (Sweden) 2012, *General Assembly* Visby (Sweden) 2011, *General Assembly* Visby (Sweden) 2010, *General Assembly* Visby (Sweden) 2009.
Members Writers ' unions in 11 countries:
Denmark, Estonia, Finland, Germany, Iceland, Latvia, Lithuania, Norway, Poland, Russia, Sweden.
NGO Relations Instrumental in setting up: *Baltic Centre for Writers and Translators (BCWT, #03105)*. [2020/XD6976/**D**]

- ♦ Baltic Writers and Translators' Council / see Baltic Writers' Council (#03156)

♦ Baltic Youth Philharmonic (BYP) 03157

Contact c/o Baltic Sea Music Education Foundation, Strasse der Pariser Kommune 38, 10243 Berlin, Germany. T. +493029770290. Fax +493029770292. E-mail: contact@bmef.eu.
URL: http://www.baltic-youth-philharmonic.org/
History Founded 2008, as a joint initiative of the Usedom Music Festival and the consortium Nord Stream AG – which is still the orchestra's main sponsor. **Aims** Bring together highly talented young *musicians* from the countries of the Baltic Sea region. **Staff** 4.00 FTE, paid. **Activities** Events/meetings. **NGO Relations** Member of: *European Federation of National Youth Orchestras (EFNYO, #07176)*. [2015.03.19/XJ2901/**F**]

- ♦ Baltijas Asambleja (#03094)
- ♦ Baltijas Celinieku Asociacija (#03138)
- ♦ Baltijas Rehabilitologu Asociacijas (no recent information)
- ♦ Baltijas sociâlo zinâtòu institûts (#03122)
- ♦ Baltijos Asambleja (#03094)
- ♦ Baltijos Kelininku Asociacija / see Baltic Road Association (#03138)
- ♦ Baltijos Saliu Kelininku Asociacija (#03138)
- ♦ Baltijos Vadybos Pletros Asociacija (#03123)
- ♦ Baltijskij Meždunarodnyj Institut Turizma / see Baltic Academy of Tourism and Entrepreneurship
- ♦ Balti Maanteeliit (#03138)
- ♦ Balti Ministrite Nõukogu (#03109)
- ♦ Balti Rahvusparkide Assotsiatsioon (inactive)
- ♦ Balt-LASA – Baltic Laboratory Animal Science Association (internationally oriented national body)
- ♦ **BALTNET** Baltic Air Surveillance Network (#03092)
- ♦ **BALTRON** Baltic Naval Squadron (#03128)
- ♦ BALTSO – Organization of Estonian, Latvian and Lithuanian Transmission System Operators (inactive)
- ♦ Bamako Convention – Convention on the Ban of the Import of Hazardous Wastes into Africa and on the Control of Their Transboundary Movements within Africa (1991 treaty)
- ♦ Bamboo of the Americas (internationally oriented national body)
- ♦ Bamboo Foundation (internationally oriented national body)
- ♦ **BAM** Brothers to All Men (#03339)
- ♦ Bambúes de las Américas (internationally oriented national body)
- ♦ BAM – IUMS Division of Bacteriology and Applied Microbiology (see: #15794)
- ♦ BAML – Baltic Association for Medical Libraries (inactive)
- ♦ **BAMPS** Baltic Association for Maxillofacial and Plastic Surgery (#03097)
- ♦ **BAMR** Baltic Association for Media Research (#03098)
- ♦ BAMREL – Bureau africain et mauricien de recherches et d'études législatives (inactive)
- ♦ Banach Centre / see Stefan Banach International Mathematical Center at the Institute of Mathematics of the Polish Academy of Sciences (#19981)
- ♦ Banafair (internationally oriented national body)
- ♦ Ban All Nukes generation / see European Youth Network for Nuclear Disarmament (#09143)
- ♦ Banana Link (internationally oriented national body)

♦ Banana Research Network for Eastern and Southern Africa (BARNESA) 03158

Secretariat PO Box 24384, Plot 106, Katalima road, Nagura, Kampala, Uganda. T. +256414286213 – +256414286948. Fax +256414286949.
URL: http://banana-networks.org/barnesa/
History 1994. Coordinated by *International Network for the Improvement of Banana and Plantain (INIBAP, inactive)* from 1997 to 1998. From 1998 until 2007, coordinated by *Association for Strengthening Agricultural Research in Eastern and Central Africa (ASARECA, #02933)*. Since 2007, coordinated by *Bioversity International (#03262)*. Located in Kampala (Uganda). **Aims** Ensure enhanced sustainable productivity, value added and competitiveness of bananas and *plantain* in Eastern and Southern Africa. **Structure** Regional Steering Committee. **Finance** Government of Belgium. Budget (annual): US$ 120,000. **Activities** Research and development; projects/programmes; capacity building.
Members Full in 12 countries:
Burundi, Congo DR, Ethiopia, Kenya, Madagascar, Malawi, Mozambique, Rwanda, South Africa, Sudan, Tanzania UR, Uganda. [2017/XK1491/**F**]

- ♦ Banana Research Network for West and Central Africa (unconfirmed)
- ♦ **BAN** Baltic Association of Neuropathologists (#03099)
- ♦ **BAN** Basel Action Network (#03182)
- ♦ Banca Europea per gli Investimenti (#07599)
- ♦ Bancaja International Centre for Peace and Development (internationally oriented national body)
- ♦ Banca dei Regolamenti Internazionali (#03165)
- ♦ Banco del Sur (unconfirmed)
- ♦ Banco Africano de Desarrollo (#00283)
- ♦ Banco Africano de Investimento (unconfirmed)
- ♦ Banco Arabe para el Desarrollo de Africa (#00904)
- ♦ Banco Asiatico de Desarrollo (#01422)
- ♦ Banco Centroamericano de Integración Económica (#03658)
- ♦ Banco de Desarrollo de América Latina (#05055)
- ♦ Banco de Desarrollo del Caribe (#03492)
- ♦ Banco de Desarrollo Económico y Social de Venezuela (internationally oriented national body)
- ♦ Banco de Desenvolvimento de América Latina (#05055)
- ♦ Banco Europeo de Inversiones (#07599)
- ♦ Banco Europeu de Investimento (#07599)
- ♦ Banco Interamericano de Desarrollo (#11427)
- ♦ Banco Interamericano de Desenvolvimento (#11427)
- ♦ Banco Internacional de Reconstrucción y Fomento (#12317)
- ♦ Banco de Investimento e de Desenvolvimento da CEDEAO (#05334)

♦ Banco Latinoamericano de Comercio Exterior (BLADEX) 03159

Foreign Trade Bank of Latin America

Head Office Torre V, Business Park, Ave La Rotonda, Urb Costa del Este, PO Box 0819-08730, Panama, Panamá, Panama PANAMá, Panama. T. +5072108500. Fax +5072696333.
URL: http://www.bladex.com/
History Sep 1977, pursuant to proposal of 20th Assembly of Governors of Latin American Central Banks, May 1975; commenced operations Jan 1979, Panama. Original title: *Banco Latinoamericano de Exportaciones (BLADEX) – Latin American Export Bank*. Current title effective since 17 Jun 2009. Incorporated under the laws of Panama. **Aims** Promote trade of goods and services of Latin American origin, through trade credit system comprising the granting of loans, including import, pre-export and post-export financing and the advise and confirmation of letters of credit. **Structure** General Assembly of Shareholders: Board of Directors; Executive Committee; Executive Vice President (CEO). **Finance** Loan and investment activity funded with interbank dollar deposits, short-term credit facilities, floating and fixed rate placements, and medium and long-term obligations issued in regional and international markets. Funds are supplied by central banks, state-owned and private Latin American banks, and government and international finance institutions. Resources include agreement with *Inter-American Development Bank (IDB, #11427)*, which assists in promoting a market for Latin American bankers' acceptances created for BLADEX. **Activities** Financial and/or material support. **Events** *Latin american meeting on the extension of international trade* Buenos Aires (Argentina) 1988.
Members Shareholders are 280 banks and financial institutions represented by central banks or designated government institutions in 22 countries of the Region; Latin American commercial banks (242); international commercial banks (23); in addition, approximately 6,000 institutional and retail investors (the latter is the result of an initial public offering of common shares completed on 1 Oct 1992). Members in 33 countries:
Argentina, Bahrain, Barbados, Bolivia, Brazil, Canada, Chile, Colombia, Costa Rica, Dominican Rep, Ecuador, El Salvador, Germany, Guatemala, Haiti, Honduras, India, Jamaica, Japan, Korea Rep, Mexico, Netherlands, Nicaragua, Panama, Paraguay, Peru, Spain, Switzerland, Trinidad-Tobago, UK, Uruguay, USA, Venezuela.
IGO Relations Observer member of: *Sistema Económico Latinoamericano (SELA, #19294)*. **NGO Relations** Associate member of: *Asociación Latinoamericana de Instituciones Financieras para el Desarrollo (ALIDE, #02233)*; *Latin American Banking Association (#16254)*. [2019/XF5451/et/**F**]

- ♦ Banco Latinoamericano de Exportaciones / see Banco Latinoamericano de Comercio Exterior (#03159)
- ♦ Banco Mundial / see International Bank for Reconstruction and Development (#12317)
- ♦ Banco Mundial de la Mujer (#21037)
- ♦ Bancroft Global Development (internationally oriented national body)

♦ Bancs d'essai internationaux (BEI) 03160

Dance Roads

Contact c/o Theaterwerkplaats, Rijnstraat 42, 6811 EX Arnhem, Netherlands.
URL: http://danceroads.eu/
History 1990. **Aims** Promote young *choreographers* and international *artistic* exchange; create long term support systems for the *'Bancs d'essai'* companies; develop training and work experience schemes for young choreographic authors. **Finance** Sponsored by: *European Commission (EC, #06633)*; *British Council*; the Governments of Austria, Canada, France, Germany, Switzerland; national foundations and organizations. **Activities** Serves as small-scale programmer's network in the field of contemporary dance. European and North American members are committed to practical support of young choreographers from member countries in "Dance Roads" touring project.
Members Partners in 6 countries:
Austria, Canada, France, Spain, Switzerland, UK. [2016/XF4336/**F**]

- ♦ Band Aid Charitable Trust (internationally oriented national body)

♦ Bandaranaike Centre for International Studies (internationally oriented national body)
♦ BANDES – Banco de Desarrollo Económico y Social de Venezuela (internationally oriented national body)
♦ **Bandidos MC** Bandidos Motorcycle Club Worldwide (#03161)

♦ Bandidos Motorcycle Club Worldwide (Bandidos MC) 03161

Address not obtained.
URL: http://www.bandidosmc.com/
History 1966, Houston, TX (USA). 1966, North Houston TX (USA).
Members Chapters in 9 countries:
Australia, Denmark, Finland, France, Germany, Luxembourg, Norway, Spain, USA. [2010/XF5948/s/**F**]

♦ **BANg** European Youth Network for Nuclear Disarmament (#09143)
♦ Bangkok agreement – Agreement on Trade Negotiations among Developing Member Countries (1975 treaty)
♦ Bangkok Treaty – Treaty on the Southeast Asia Nuclear Weapon-free Zone (1995 treaty)
♦ Bangladesh Asiatic Society (internationally oriented national body)
♦ Bangladesh, India, Myanmar, Sri Lanka, Thailand Economic Cooperation / see Bay of Bengal Initiative for Multi-Sectoral Technical and Economic Cooperation (#03188)
♦ Bangladesh, India, Sri Lanka, Thailand Economic Cooperation / see Bay of Bengal Initiative for Multi-Sectoral Technical and Economic Cooperation (#03188)
♦ Bangladesh Institute of Development Studies (internationally oriented national body)
♦ Bangladesh Institute of International and Strategic Studies (internationally oriented national body)
♦ Bangladesh Maritime Academy (internationally oriented national body)
♦ Bangladesh Rehabilitation Assistance Committee / see BRAC (#03310)
♦ Bangladesh Rural Advancement Committee / see BRAC (#03310)
♦ Bangladesh Unnayan Gobeshona Protishtan (internationally oriented national body)
♦ Banjul Protocol – African Charter of Human and Peoples' Rights (1981 treaty)
♦ Banjul Protocol on Marks (1993 treaty)
♦ Bank of the Central African States (#03169)
♦ Bank for Economic Cooperation and Development in the Middle East and North Africa (no recent information)

♦ Bankers Association for Finance and Trade (BAFT) 03162

Pres/CEO 1120 Connecticut Ave NW, Washington DC 20036, USA. T. +12026635252 – +12026637575. Fax +12026635538. E-mail: info@baft.org.
URL: http://www.baft.org/
History 19 Jan 2010. Founded on merger of *International Financial Services Association (IFSA, inactive)* and *Bankers' Association for Finance and Trade (BAFT, inactive)*. Former names and other names: *BAFT-IFSA* – former (2010 to 2013). **Aims** Bring the *financial* community and its suppliers together to collaborate on shaping *market* practices; influence *regulation* and legislation through global advocacy; develop and adapt new and existing instruments that facilitate settlement of products and service offerings for clients; provide education and training; contribute to the safety and soundness of the global financial system. **Structure** Board of Directors; Councils (7); Committees; Working Groups. **Languages** English. **Staff** 10.00 FTE, paid. **Finance** Sources: members' dues. **Activities** Advocacy/lobbying/activism; guidance/assistance/consulting; networking/liaising; politics/policy/regulatory; training/education. **Events** *MENA Bank to Bank Forum* Dubai (United Arab Emirates) 2020, *Europe Bank to Bank Forum* London (UK) 2019, *Europe Annual Conference* Madrid (Spain) 2017, *Europe Bank to Bank Forum* Madrid (Spain) 2017, *North America Conference* Miami, FL (USA) 2017. **Publications** *BAFT Newsletter* (12 a year). Best practices; policy comment letters.
Members Financial Institutions; Suppliers; Government Agencies. Membership countries not specified but including 1 organization listed in this Yearbook:
Japan Bank for International Cooperation (JBIC).
IGO Relations Over 115 government agencies and regulators. **NGO Relations** Over 25 multi-lateral NGOs and 115 industry associations. [2019.12.23/XJ7155/t/**C**]

♦ Bank Information Center (internationally oriented national body)
♦ Bank Information Center Europe / see Recourse (#18630)

♦ Banking Association for Central and Eastern Europe (BACEE) 03163

SG Feszty Arpad u 2, 3rd floor, Budapest 1013, Hungary. T. +3613568581 – +3612126210. Fax +3612120313. E-mail: bacee@bacee.hu.
URL: http://www.bacee.hu/
History 1996, following the activities of the 'Clearing Bank Association (CBA)' founded in 1993. **Events** *Banking Conference* Budapest (Hungary) 2013, *Country and Bank Conference* Budapest (Hungary) 2013, *Country and Bank Conference* Budapest (Hungary) 2013, *Country and bank conference* Budapest (Hungary) 2011, *Fraud and operational risk summit* Budapest (Hungary) 2011.
Members Banks – countries not specified but including 1 organization listed in this Yearbook:
International Bank for Economic Co-operation (IBEC, #12310). [2018/XD8547/**D**]

♦ Banking Federation of the European Community / see European Banking Federation (#06312)

♦ Banking With the Poor Network (BWTP Network) 03164

Contact PO Box 990, Kenmore QLD 4069, Australia. E-mail: info@bwtp.org.
URL: http://www.bwtp.org/
Aims Promote the growth of *self-help* groups of the poor; increase access of the poor to financial services. **Publications** *Banking With the Poor Newsletter.*
Members Banks and organizations in 10 countries:
Australia, Bangladesh, India, Indonesia, Malaysia, Nepal, Pakistan, Philippines, Sri Lanka, Thailand. [2020/XF5663/**F**]

♦ Bank für Internationalen Zahlungsausgleich (#03165)

♦ Bank for International Settlements (BIS) 03165

Banque des règlements internationaux (BRI) – Bank für Internationalen Zahlungsausgleich (BIZ) – Banca dei Regolamenti Internazionali (BRI)
Press-Publications Officer Centralbahnplatz 2, 4002 Basel BS, Switzerland. T. +41612808188 – +41612808900. Fax +41612809100 – +41612808100. E-mail: press@bis.org – email@bis.org.
Main: http://www.bis.org/
History 27 Feb 1930, pursuant to signature of intergovernmental convention – *The Hague Agreements*, 20 Jan 1930, and benefiting from statutes and a special charter granted by the Swiss Confederation; commenced operations 17 May 1930. Statutes adopted 20 Jan 1930; and amended: 3 May 1937; 12 Jun 1950; 9 Oct 1961; 9 Jun 1969; 10 Jun 1974; 8 Jul 1975; 14 Jun 1993; 13 Sep 1994; 8 Nov 1999; Jun 2005. Protocol regarding the immunities of the Bank signed 30 Jul 1936, Brussels (Belgium). Headquarters Agreement concluded with Swiss authorities 10 Feb 1987. Also referred to as *Central Banks' Bank*. Statutes registered in *'LNTS 1/2398'*. **Aims** Promote discussion and facilitate decision-making processes among central banks and within the international *financial* community; act as a prime counterpart for central banks in their financial transactions; conduct *economic* and *monetary* research; act as an agent or trustee in connection with international financial operations. **Structure** General Meeting (annual) at which member central banks have representation and voting rights in proportion to the number of shares subscribed by their respective countries. Executive Committee, including General Manager and Deputy General Manager. Board of Directors of 19 members, including Chair and Vice-Chair; its 6 ex-officio directors are the central bank Governors of Belgium, France, Germany, Italy and the UK and the Chairman of the Board of Governors of the US Federal Reserve System; each may appoint another member of the same nationality. Statutes also provide for election to the Board of a maximum of 9 Governors of other member central banks; currently elected members are the central bank Governors of Canada, China, Japan, Mexico, Netherlands, Sweden, Switzerland and the President of *European Central Bank (ECB, #06466)*. General Manager; Deputy General Manager. General Secretariat. Monetary and Economic Department; Banking Department. General Counsel. **Languages** English, French, German, Italian, Spanish. **Staff** 650.00 FTE, paid. Staff from over 50 countries. **Finance** Balance-sheet data as at 31 Mar 2014: total assets – SDR 222,510 million (1 Special Drawing Right, SDR, is equivalent to US$ 1.54 as at 31 Mar 2013); authorized capital – SDR 3,000 million as 600,000 shares (of SDR 5,000); issued capital – SDR 698.9 million as 559,125 shares paid up to the extent of 25%, all of which is held by central banks (except for 1,000 shares that are held in treasury); equity – SDR 17,728 million; deposits – SDR 191,770 million. **Activities** Acts as regular meeting place for governors of central banks. AGM approves the annual report and accounts, makes appropriations to reserve and special funds and considers declaration of dividend. The Bank: carries out wide range of banking operations with central banks and assists them in managing and investing some of their foreign exchange reserves; as banker to central banks, accepts deposits from central banks and places the funds received in international markets; makes liquid resources available to central banks in the form of credits or stand-by facilities; buys and sells gold on its own account or for central banks; holds gold on its own account and accepts custody of gold for the account of central banks; functions as trustee for certain international government loans; carries out financial and economic research, including collection of statistical data on financing of external surpluses and deficits, acting as data bank for central banks; organizes meetings of groups of experts on gold market, foreign exchange markets, Euro-currency market, payment systems, monetary and economic data bank questions.
Permanent Committees hosted by BIS:
– *Basel Committee on Banking Supervision (BCBS, #03183)* – addresses supervision at the level of individual institutions and its relation to macroprudential supervision;
– *Committee on the Global Financial System (CGFS, #04258)* – monitors and analyses macrofinancial stability issues;
– Committee on Payments and Market Infrastructures;
– Markets Committee – examines the functioning of financial markets;
– Central Bank Governance Group – examines issues related to the design and operation of central banks;
– *Irving Fisher Committee on Central Bank Statistics (IFC, #16020)* – addresses statistical issues of concern to central banks, including those relating to economic, monetary and financial stability.
Hosts secretariat for:
– *Financial Stability Board (FSB, #09770)*;
– *Financial Stability Institute (FSI, #09771)* – promotes international financial stability by coordinating the work of national financial authorities and international standard-setting bodies in developing strong regulatory, supervisory and other financial sector policies;
– *International Association of Deposit Insurers (IADI, #11843)* – contributes to the stability of financial systems by promoting international cooperation and encouraging wide international contact among deposit insurers and other interested parties;
– *International Association of Insurance Supervisors (IAIS, #11966)* – serves as the international standard-setting body for prudential supervision of the insurance industry.
Events *International Conference on Statistics for Sustainable Finance* Paris (France) 2021, *Annual General Meeting* Basel (Switzerland) 2019, *Meeting* Busan (Korea Rep) 2018, *Global Public Investor Symposium* Singapore (Singapore) 2018, *Regional Seminar on Problem Bank Identification, Supervision and Early Intervention* Singapore (Singapore) 2016. **Publications** *BIS Quarterly Review*; *International Journal of Central Banking (IJCB)* – in collaboration with ECB and G-10. Annual Report in English, French, German, Italian, Spanish.
Members Central banks (60) of 58 countries and territories:
Algeria, Argentina, Australia, Austria, Belgium, Bosnia-Herzegovina, Brazil, Bulgaria, Canada, Chile, China, Colombia, Croatia, Czechia, Denmark, Estonia, Finland, France, Germany, Greece, Hong Kong, Hungary, Iceland, India, Indonesia, Ireland, Israel, Italy, Japan, Korea Rep, Latvia, Lithuania, Luxembourg, Malaysia, Mexico, Netherlands, New Zealand, North Macedonia, Norway, Peru, Philippines, Poland, Portugal, Romania, Russia, Saudi Arabia, Serbia, Singapore, Slovakia, Slovenia, South Africa, Spain, Sweden, Switzerland, Thailand, Türkiye, UK, USA.
Regional Central Bank (1), listed in this Yearbook:
European Central Bank (ECB, #06466).
IGO Relations Observer to: *International Monetary and Financial Committee (IMFC, #14179)* (previously 'Interim Committee') of *International Monetary Fund (IMF, #14180)*. **NGO Relations** In liaison with technical committees of: *International Organization for Standardization (ISO, #14473)*. Member of: *Association for Human Resources Management in International Organizations (AHRMIO, #02634)*; *European Association for Banking and Financial History (#05951).* [2020/XF0184/**F***]

♦ Bank of Medical Equipment for Humanitarian Aid (internationally oriented national body)
♦ Bank of the South (unconfirmed)

♦ BankTrack 03166

Dir Vismarkt 15, 6511 VJ Nijmegen, Netherlands. T. +31243249220. E-mail: contact@banktrack.org.
URL: https://www.banktrack.org/
History 31 Oct 2003, Netherlands. Former names and other names: *BankTrack Foundation* – former; *Stichting BankTrack* – former. Registration: Handelsregister, No/ID: 30198568, Start date: 13 Sep 2004, Netherlands. **Aims** Stop banks from financing harmful business activities; promote a banking sector that contributes to just societies and a healthy planet. **Structure** Board of Directors; Office based in Nijmegen (Netherlands). **Languages** English. **Staff** 12.00 FTE, paid. **Activities** Advocacy/lobbying/activism; guidance/assistance/consulting; knowledge management/information dissemination; monitoring/evaluation; publishing activities; training/education. Worldwide. **Events** *Meeting* Hassocks (UK) 2006. **Members** Not a membership organization. **NGO Relations** Working relations with numerous civil society organizations, not specified. [2023.02.14/XM0876/fy/**F**]

♦ BankTrack Foundation / see BankTrack (#03166)
♦ Banque africaine de développement (#00283)
♦ Banque africaine d'import-export (#00305)
♦ Banque africaine d'investissement (unconfirmed)
♦ Banque de l'Afrique occidentale (inactive)
♦ Banque arabe pour le développement économique en Afrique (#00904)
♦ Banque arabe et internationale (#00992)
♦ Banque asiatique de développement (#01422)
♦ Banque canadienne de grains (internationally oriented national body)
♦ Banque canadienne de ressources pour la démocratie et les droits de la personne (internationally oriented national body)
♦ Banque centrale des Caraïbes orientales (#05231)
♦ Banque centrale des Etats de l'Afrique équatoriale et du Cameroun (inactive)

♦ Banque centrale des Etats de l'Afrique de l'Ouest (BCEAO) 03167

Central Bank of the West African States
SG Avenue Abdoulaye Fadiga, BP 3108, Dakar, Senegal. T. +2218390500. Fax +2218239335 – +2218226109. E-mail: akangni@bceao.int.
Paris Office 29 rue du Colisée, 75008 Paris, France. T. +33142257160. Fax +33142560037.
URL: http://www.bceao.int/
History 1 Nov 1962, on coming into force of a Convention signed 12 May 1962, replacing the *Institut d'émission de l'AOF et du Togo*, set up 1955, Paris (France). Currently governed by Treaty signed 14 Nov 1973, Paris, and entered into force 11 Oct 1974, setting up *Union monétaire Ouest africaine (UMOA, inactive)* – now subsumed in *Union économique et monétaire Ouest africaine (UEMOA, #20377)* – to which BCEAO statutes are annexed. The Treaty also formed agreement with government of France. Since the establishment of UEMOA, 1 Aug 1994, the Bank is common Issuing Institute of all UEMOA member states. Comes within the framework of *Communauté financière africaine (CFA, #04377)*, all member countries being part of *Pays africains de la Zone franc (PAZF, #18270)* and having the common currency *'CFA Franc'*. The Bank is unofficially referred to by English initials *CBWAS*. **Aims** Act as issuing institute for member states of WAMU, managing their common unit of currency, the CFA franc, and the monetary, banking and financial system; organize and monitor distribution of credit; provide professional training in banking and finance. **Structure** Management: Governor; 2 Deputy Governors; Secretary General; 2 Special Advisors to the Governor, 2 Advisors to the Governor and Assistant to the Governor. General Control Office. Departments (5): General Administration and Training; Issuance, Accounting and Finance; Economic Studies and Money; Projects and Missions; Security and Legal Affairs. Secretariat General. BCEAO representation to European cooperation institutions. BCEAO representation to WAEMU Commission. National Directorates (8). **Languages** French. **Activities** Has the exclusive privilege of issuing monetary devices that are legal currency and tender in member states. Although monetary reserves of CFA countries are normally held in French francs in the French treasury, BCEAO may hold up to 35 percent of its foreign exchange in other currencies. *WAMU Banking Commission* functions as supervision and control organ to guarantee protection of depositors and stability of the financial system, according to an agreement in force from 1 Oct 1990. The Commission: conducts on-site and off-site inspections of banks and financial establishments; comments on requests for authorization by banks and financial institutions; makes warnings, injunctions or disciplinary procedures if applicable provisions are not respected; takes disciplinary sanctions in relation to the infraction committed. **Events** *Seminar for journalists* Dakar (Senegal) 1993. **Publications** *Notes d'information et statistiques* (12 a year); *Annuaire des banques UMOA* (annual); *Bilan des banques UMOA* (annual); *Rapport d'activités* (annual).

Members Governments of 8 countries:
Benin, Burkina Faso, Côte d'Ivoire, Guinea-Bissau, Mali, Niger, Senegal, Togo.
Regional member (1):
Banque ouest africaine de développement (BOAD, #03170).
IGO Relations Member of: *West African Monetary Agency (WAMA, #20887).* Participates in the activities of: *UNCTAD (#20285).* Represented in: *Commission de l'UEMOA (see: #20377).* Partner of: *Inter-African Conference on Insurance Markets (#11385); Organisation pour l'Harmonisation en Afrique du Droit des Affaires (OHADA, #17806).* Cooperates with: *United Nations Institute for Training and Research (UNITAR, #20576).* Contact with: *Société Ouest Africaine de Gestion d'Actifs (SOAGA, see: #03170).* As one of the regions within the *Zone franc (#22037)*, links with: *Conférence des ministres des finances des pays de la Zone franc (#04633).* **NGO Relations** Administers: *West African Centre for Banking Education and Research (no recent information).* Member of: *Association for Soft Commodities, European Union / Africa-Caribbean-Pacific (no recent information); Islamic Financial Services Board (IFSB, #16045).* [2009/XF4541/y/**F***]

- ♦ Banque centrale européenne (#06466)
- ♦ Banque centroaméricaine d'intégration économique (#03658)
- ♦ Banque de commerce et de développement pour l'Afrique de l'Est et du Sud / see Trade and Development Bank (#20181)
- ♦ Banque pour le développement en Afrique australe (internationally oriented national body)
- ♦ Banque de développement de l'Afrique de l'Est (#05183)
- ♦ Banque de développement des Caraïbes (#03492)
- ♦ Banque de développement du Conseil de l'Europe (#04897)

♦ Banque de développement des Etats de l'Afrique centrale (BDEAC) 03168

Central African States' Development Bank (CASDB)

Registered Office Place du Gouvernement, BP 1177, Brazzaville, Congo Brazzaville. T. +2422811885. Fax +2422811880. E-mail: bdeac@bdeac.org.
URL: http://www.bdeac.org/

History 3 Dec 1975, within the framework of *Union douanière et économique de l'Afrique centrale (UDEAC, inactive)*, on signature of Agreement by representatives of the Governments of Cameroon, Central African Republic, Congo and Gabon; Chad and Equatorial Guinea subsequently adhered to the Agreement. Statutes approved 30 Apr 1976, Brazzaville (Congo Brazzaville), by Constituent General Assembly; amended 1978, 2002 and 2009. Commencement of activities: 2 Jan 1977. **Aims** Promote economic and social development of member states, especially through the financing of national and multinational investments and of projects of economic *integration*; support states, sub-regional organizations, financial institutions and economic operators in their efforts to mobilize financial resources and project financing and in the financing of feasibility studies in respect of programmes and projects. **Structure** General Assembly; Board of Directors. **Languages** English, French. **Staff** 55.00 FTE, paid. **Finance** Registered Capital: authorized, CFA Fr 1,200,000 million; subscribed, CFA Fr 1,036,595 million; called up and paid, CFA Fr 92,646 million; callable, CFA Fr 929,439 million. Equity capital: CFA Fr 134,774 million. Total balance: CFA Fr 163,405 million. **Activities** Advocacy/lobbying/activism; financial and/or material support.
Members Governments of 8 States:
Cameroon, Central African Rep, Chad, Congo Brazzaville, Equatorial Guinea, France, Gabon, Kuwait.
International organizational members (2):
African Development Bank (ADB, #00283); Banque des Etats de l'Afrique centrale (BEAC, #03169).
IGO Relations Relationship agreement signed with: *UNIDO (#20336).* Cooperation Agreement with: *FAO Investment Centre (#09264).* **NGO Relations** Special member of: *Association of African Development Finance Institutions (AADFI, #02353).* Member of: *Global Network of Export-Import Banks and Development Finance Institutions (G-NEXID, #10489).* [2019.12.17/XF4179/y/**F***]

- ♦ Banque de développement des Etats des Grands Lacs (inactive)
- ♦ Banque de développement du Moyen-Orient et d'Afrique du nord (no recent information)

♦ Banque des Etats de l'Afrique centrale (BEAC) 03169

Bank of the Central African States

Contact Siège Social et Services Centraux, Boîte Postal 1917, Yaoundé, Cameroon. T. +23722334030 – +2372222340060. Fax +237222233329 – +237222233350. E-mail: beacyde@beac.int.
URL: http://www.beac.int/

History 22 Nov 1972, Brazzaville (Congo Brazzaville). 22-23 Nov 1972, Brazzaville (Congo Brazzaville), on the setting up of *Union monétaire de l'Afrique centrale (UMAC, #20463)* and the signature of Conventions between the initial 5 African founding partners and between them and France. Continues the activities of *Banque centrale des Etats de l'Afrique équatoriale et du Cameroun (BCEAC, inactive)*, formed 4 Apr 1959, and itself a continuation of *Issuing Institute of Equatorial Africa and Cameroon – Institut d'émission de l'Afrique équatoriale et du Cameroun*, set up 15 Jul 1955, Paris (France). Commenced operations 2 Apr 1973, Brazzaville, on signature of Convention for Monetary Cooperation by the Governments of France and Cameroon, Central African Republic, Chad, Congo, Gabon. Central Services and General Direction transferred, 1 Jan 1977, from Paris to Yaoundé (Cameroon). Equatorial Guinea adhered to BEAC, 1 Jan 1985. Currently a principal organ of *Communauté économique et monétaire d'Afrique centrale (CEMAC, #04374)*, set up 16 Mar 1994. **Aims** Act as exclusive issuing house for notes and coins for circulation within member states, devise monetary policy, supervise its execution, monitor compliance by the banks with the banking and credit regulations and assist the banks and financial establishments of member states and their governments; contribute to financing of infrastructure and communal facilities. **Structure** Comité Ministériel; Administrative Council; Governing Body; College of Censors; Committee of 5 members (one for Cameroon, 2 for France, 2 for Gabon). Central Directions (9); National Directions (7); National Monitoring Committee in each member state. Serves as secretariat for *Union économique de l'Afrique centrale (UEAC, #20376).* **Languages** Arabic, English, French, Spanish. **Staff** 2400.00 FTE, paid. **Finance** Common currency throughout the area, the CFA franc, within *Communauté financière africaine (CFA, #04377).* Although, within the framework of the *Zone franc (#22037)*, monetary reserves of CFA countries are normally held in French francs in the French treasury, BOAD may hold up to 35% of its foreign exchange in other currencies. **Events** *Seminar for journalists* Dakar (Senegal) 1993. **Publications** *Etudes et statistiques* (12 a year) – bulletin. Annual report.
Members Governments of 6 states:
Cameroon, Central African Rep, Chad, Congo Brazzaville, Equatorial Guinea, Gabon.
Non-member participating in management and supervision:
France.
IGO Relations As one of the regions within the Zone franc, links with: *Conférence des ministres des finances des pays de la Zone franc (#04633).* Serves as secretariat for: *Commission bancaire de l'Afrique centrale (COBAC, #04204).* Partner of: *Inter-African Conference on Insurance Markets (#11385); Organisation pour l'Harmonisation en Afrique du Droit des Affaires (OHADA, #17806).* Cooperates with: *United Nations Institute for Training and Research (UNITAR, #20576).*
- *African Development Bank (ADB, #00283);*
- *African Development Fund (ADF, #00285);*
- *Agency for the Safety of Aerial Navigation in Africa and Madagascar (#00556);*
- *Association of African Central Banks (AACB, #02352);*
- *Bank for International Settlements (BIS, #03165);*
- *Banque centrale des Etats de l'Afrique de l'Ouest (BCEAO, #03167);*
- *Banque de développement des Etats de l'Afrique centrale (BDEAC, #03168);*
- *Central African Clearing House (CAfCH, no recent information);*
- *Comité monétaire de la Zone franc (#04193);*
- *Commission régionale de contrôle des assurances dans les Etats africains (CRCA, see: #11385);*
- *Conference of Ministers of Agriculture of West and Central Africa (CMA/WCA, #04631);*
- *Economic Community of Central African States (ECCAS, #05311);*
- *Institut sous-régional multisectoriel de technologie appliquée, de planification et d'évaluation de projets (ISTA, no recent information);*
- *International Bank for Reconstruction and Development (IBRD, #12317);*
- *International Development Association (IDA, #13155);*
- *International Monetary Fund (IMF, #14180).*

NGO Relations Member of: *African Centre for Monetary Studies (ACMS, inactive).* [2023/XF4535/**F***]

- ♦ Banque européenne d'investissement (#07599)
- ♦ Banque européenne pour la reconstruction et le développement (#06315)
- ♦ Banque européenne de sang congelé de groupes rares / see Sanquin Bank of Frozen Blood (#19052)
- ♦ Banque de l'Indochine (inactive)
- ♦ Banque interaméricaine (inactive)
- ♦ Banque interaméricaine de développement (#11427)
- ♦ Banque inter-Etats (#15978)
- ♦ Banque internationale pour l'Afrique de l'Ouest (inactive)
- ♦ Banque internationale pour la coopération économique (#12310)
- ♦ Banque internationale d'investissements (#13951)
- ♦ Banque internationale pour la reconstruction et le développement (#12317)
- ♦ Banque d'Investissement et de Développement de la CEDEAO (#05334)
- ♦ Banque islamique de développement (#16044)
- ♦ Banque de matériel médical pour l'aide humanitaire (internationally oriented national body)
- ♦ Banque mondiale / see International Bank for Reconstruction and Development (#12317)
- ♦ Banque Mondiale des Femmes (#21037)
- ♦ Banque nord-américaine de vaccin de la fièvre aphteus – Banco de Vacuna de Fiebre Aftosa de América del Norte (#17564)
- ♦ Banque nordique de génétique / see Nordic Genetic Resource Centre (#17303)
- ♦ Banque nordique de génétique agricole et horticole / see Nordic Genetic Resource Centre (#17303)

♦ Banque ouest africaine de développement (BOAD) 03170

West African Development Bank (WADB)

Acting Pres BOAD Head Office, 68 av de la Libération – BP 1172, Lomé, Togo. T. +2282215906 – +2282214244 – +2282210113. Fax +2282215267 – +2282217269. E-mail: boadsiege@boad.org.
URL: http://www.boad.org/

History 14 Nov 1973, Paris (France), and 4 Dec 1973, Dakar (Senegal), on signature of Treaty by the then 6 member states of *Union monétaire Ouest africaine (UMOA, inactive).* Treaty came into force in Oct 1974; BOAD became operational in 1976. Statutes adopted 1974; amended at meetings of the Council of Ministers of UMOA: 20 Dec 1977; 10 Apr 1979; 10 Apr 1980; 22 Dec 1981; 1 Jul 1982; 29 Dec 1982; 12 Sep 1984; 19 Sep 1987; 16 Sep 1988; 10 Apr 1991; 28 Mar 1996; 2 Jul 1998. Mali joined UMOA and BOAD as from 1 Jun 1984 and Guinea-Bissau joined UEMOA and BOAD from 2 May 1997. Since 1 Aug 1994, BOAD is a financial institution of *Union économique et monétaire Ouest africaine (UEMOA, #20377).* **Aims** As a joint *financing* institution of UEMOA member states, promote their balanced development and achieve *economic* integration of West Africa; assist in pooling available internal resources; mobilize external *capital*, both loans and grants; finance by means of loans, guarantees, shareholdings, etc, projects designed to build up the infrastructure needed for development; establish new activities; improve conditions and means of production, transferring ownership of means of production and of distribution of goods and services to public or private legal entities in UEMOA countries or to individual citizens of those countries; prepare and evaluate development projects. **Structure** Headed by President, appointed by UEMOA Council of Ministers. President is assisted by Vice-President and the Governing Board, consisting of: President of the Bank; a representative and a substitute appointed by each member state of the Union; Governor of the Central Bank West African States or his representative; representatives of Class B shareholders. Head Office in Lomé (Togo) includes: Office of the President; 4 departments – General affairs, Operation evaluation and internal audit, Finance and accounting, Funding and studies; Risk management unit. Representation Offices (6) attached to the Vice-Presidency. **Languages** French. **Staff** 205.00 FTE, paid. **Finance** Monetary unit is the franc of *Communauté financière africaine (CFA, #04377)* (CFA franc), which is linked to the French franc within the *Zone franc (#22037)* and is legal tender throughout the territory of the Union. Authorized capital (31 Dec 2006): CFA Fr 654,900 million; subscribed capital: CFA Fr 336,800 million; called-up capital: CFA Fr 66,526 million; paid-up capital: CFA Fr 103,506 million; callable capital: CFA Fr 484,867 million. Resources comprise internal available funds of UMOA and by external aid (loans and non-refundable grants). Distribution of subscribed capital: BCEAO – 47.8%; member countries – 47.8% in equal parts; external partners (Belgium, France, Germany, European Investment Bank, African Development Bank) – 4.4 %. Special funds (5) via endowments of founder member states: interest rate subsidy; backing operation guarantee; redemption guarantee; study financing; exchange risk cover. The Bank participates in the mobilization of financial resources and is empowered to float loans on the internal market of the Union or on foreign financial markets and to obtain loans from international or foreign organizations. **Activities** Member countries are divided into 3 groups so as to grant priority to the least developed: (1) Burkina Faso, Mali and Niger; (2) Benin and Togo; (3) Côte d'Ivoire and Senegal. Services include: provision of medium and long-term loans; equity participation in capital stock; backing of guarantees; easing of loan terms and conditions through interest subsidies; financing feasibility studies. Beneficiaries include governments, communities, public institutions, organizations, firms and private individuals. Sectors of operation: industry and agroindustry; rural development (in particular, village water supplies); basic and modern infrastructures; small and medium-scale enterprises producing goods and services; transfer of ownership of means of production and distribution of goods and services to nationals of the Union. Together with a number of commercial partners, set up *West African Investment Fund (FOAI, see: #03170)*, 27 Aug 2001, Lomé (Togo), with assets managed by *Société Ouest Africaine de Gestion d'Actifs (SOAGA, see: #03170).* Also set up: *CAURIS Investissement SA* – risk capital company set up 1995, in cooperation with EIB, FAGACE, PROPARCO and others; *Fonds de garantie des investissements privés en Afrique de l'Ouest (Fonds GARI, see: #03170)* – 1995, with AFD; *Project d'utilisation du fonds suisse (PUFS)* – set up in agreement with Swiss Bank and Government, 20 Dec 1993, became operational Jan 1994. **Events** *Ordinary meeting* Abidjan (Côte d'Ivoire) 1998, *Ordinary meeting* Bamako (Mali) 1998, *Rural technologies in youth development* Lomé (Togo) 1988, *Meeting* Ouagadougou (Burkina Faso) 1987, *Meeting* Lomé (Togo) 1986. **Publications** *BOAD Info* (4 a year). Annual Report in English/French. Sectoral and other studies.
Members Category A: members of the UMOA and BCEAO; Category B: States not members of the Union but wishing to cooperate in its economic development and approved by the Council of Ministers of the Union and international or regional intergovernmental bodies. Class A – Shareholders: Governments of 8 countries:
Class A – Shareholders: Governments of 8 countries:
Benin, Burkina Faso, Côte d'Ivoire, Guinea-Bissau, Mali, Niger, Senegal, Togo.
Common issuing institute for member states:
Banque centrale des Etats de l'Afrique de l'Ouest (BCEAO, #03167).
Class B – Shareholders: Governments of 5 countries:
Belgium, China (through Popular Bank of China), France, Germany (through DEG), India (through Exim Bank).
Class B shareholder listed in this Yearbook:
African Development Bank (ADB, #00283).
IGO Relations Invited as observer to meetings of: *Joint Ministerial Committee of the Boards of Governors of the Bank and the Fund on the Transfer of Real Resources to Developing Countries (Development Committee, #16141).* Accredited by: *United Nations Framework Convention on Climate Change – Secretariat (UNFCCC, #20564).* Member of: *Association of Regional and Sub-regional Development Finance Institutions in West Africa (AIRFD, no recent information); African Legal Support Facility (ALSF, #00361).* Bilateral cooperation with governments of several industrialized countries. Partner of: *Organisation pour l'Harmonisation en Afrique du Droit des Affaires (OHADA, #17806).* Implementing agency of: *Global Environment Facility (GEF, #10346).*
Regional cooperation with:
- ADB;
- *African Fund for Guarantee and Economic Cooperation (#00326);*
- *Banque de développement des Etats de l'Afrique centrale (BDEAC, #03168);*
- *ECOWAS Bank for Investment and Development (EBID, #05334).*

International cooperation with:
- *Arab Bank for Economic Development in Africa (#00904);*
- *Canadian International Development Agency (CIDA, inactive);*
- EIB;
- *International Bank for Reconstruction and Development (IBRD, #12317);*
- *International Finance Corporation (IFC, #13597);*
- *International Fund for Agricultural Development (IFAD, #13692);*
- *International Monetary Fund (IMF, #14180);*
- *Islamic Development Bank (IsDB, #16044);*
- *OPEC Fund for International Development (OFID, #17745);*

– *UNDP (#20292).*

Cooperation agreements with:
– *African Regional Centre for Engineering Design and Manufacturing (ARCEDEM, no recent information);*
– *Comité permanent inter-Etats de lutte contre la sécheresse dans le Sahel (CILSS, #04195);*
– *International Telecommunication Union (ITU, #15673);*
– *UNIDO (#20336);*
– *Union of African Railways (UAR, #20347);*
– *United Nations Economic Commission for Africa (ECA, #20554);*
– *United States Agency for International Development (USAID).*

NGO Relations Special member of: *Association of African Development Finance Institutions (AADFI, #02353).* Member of: *International Development Finance Club (IDFC, #13159).* Cooperation agreements with: *Agency for Technological Development and Design with Developing Countries (no recent information). International Agency for Rural Industrialization (INARI, no recent information); SIFIDA Investment Company (inactive); Universal Engineering and Finance Corporation (UNEFICO, no recent information).* International cooperation with: *Kreditanstalt für Wiederaufbau (KfW); Skandinaviska Enskilda Banken (SEB).* [2008/XF4540/y/**F***]

♦ Banque des règlements internationaux (#03165)
♦ Banques coopératives / see European Association of Co-operative Banks (#05990)
♦ Banque du sud (unconfirmed)
♦ Banque de la Zep / see Trade and Development Bank (#20181)
♦ BANSEA – Business Angel Network Southeast Asia (internationally oriented national body)

♦ Bantani Education 03171

Dir Steenputten 21, 3080 Tervuren, Belgium.
Dir address not obtained.
URL: https://bantani.com/

History 2017, Brussels (Belgium). Bantani means "Away We Go" in Welsh. Registration: Banque-Carrefour des Entreprises, No/ID: 0672.526.734, Start date: 8 Mar 2017, Belgium. **Aims** Drive entrepreneurial and creative learning; bring together extensive policy and practical experience working with public, community and private sector partners, with the experience to research, co-create, test and embed high quality entrepreneurial learning practice and policy. **Languages** English, French, Spanish. **Staff** 5.00 FTE, paid; 1.00 FTE, voluntary. **Activities** Advocacy/lobbying/activism; guidance/assistance/consulting; networking/liaising; politics/policy/regulatory; research/documentation. Active in all member countries. **Publications** *EntreComp at Work* (1st ed 2020) by Elin McCallum and Lisa McMullan et al in English; *EntreComp into Action: get ideas, make it happen* (1st ed 2018) by Elin McCallum and Rebecca Weicht et al in English. [2021.02.08/AA1262/**F**]

♦ **BANTAO** Balkan Cities Association of Nephrology, Dialysis, Transplantation and Artificial Organs (#03069)

♦ Ban Terminator Campaign 03172

La campagne Interdire terminator – Campaña Terminar Terminator

Contact 431 Gilmour Street, Second Fl, Ottawa ON K2P 0R5, Canada. T. +16132412267. Fax +16132412506. E-mail: contact@banterminator.org.
URL: http://www.banterminator.org/

Aims Promote government bans on terminator technology – *genetically engineered* plants to produce sterile *seeds* – at national and international levels; support the efforts of civil society, farmers, indigenous peoples and social movements to campaign against it. **Structure** Steering Committee.
NGO Relations Endorsers: national and international organizations, including the following bodies listed in this Yearbook:
– *Action Group on Erosion, Technology and Concentration (ETC Group, #00091);*
– *Action for Solidarity, Equality, Environment and Diversity (A SEED, #00098);*
– *ActionAid France – Peuples Solidaires;*
– *African Centre for Biodiversity (ACB);*
– *Afrika-Europa Netwerk (AEN);*
– *Amazon Cooperation Network (no recent information);*
– *Asian Network for Culture and Development (ANCAD);*
– *Association for the Taxation of Financial Transactions for the Aid of Citizens (#02947);*
– *Bread for All;*
– *Brot für die Welt;*
– *Centro de Estudios Rurales y de Agricultura Internacional (CERAI);*
– *Earth Rights Institute (ERI);*
– *Earthlife Africa (ELA);*
– *Earthsave International;*
– *Equal Access International AIDS Network, Canada (no recent information);*
– *Equiterre;*
– *Gaia Foundation;*
– *Grassroots International (GI);*
– *Greenpeace International (#10727);*
– *Inter Pares;*
– *International Center for Technology Assessment (ICTA);*
– *International Code Documentation Centre (ICDC, see: #12305);*
– *International People's Health Council (IPHC);*
– *International Union of Food, Agricultural, Hotel, Restaurant, Catering, Tobacco and Allied Workers Associations (IUF, #15772);*
– *Irish Missionary Union (IMU);*
– *La Via Campesina (#20765);*
– *Local Futures (#16506);*
– *Missionary Sisters of St Columban (SSC);*
– *Missionary Society of St Columban (SSCME);*
– *Pesticide Action Network (PAN, #18336);*
– *Practical Action (#18475);*
– *Progressio (inactive);*
– *Public Eye;*
– *Red por una América Latina Libre de Transgénicos (RALLT, #18733);*
– *St Patrick's Society for the Foreign Missions (Kiltegan Fathers);*
– *Society of the Sacred Heart of Jesus (St Madeleine-Sophie Barat);*
– *Union of Concerned Scientists (UCS);*
– *UPA International Development (UPA DI);*
– *Women for a Better World (WBW);*
– *Women Working Worldwide (WWW);*
– *Women's International League for Peace and Freedom (WILPF, #21024);*
– *World Community Development Education Society (WCDES).* [2013/XM1330/**F**]

♦ **BAOPS** Baltic Association of Paediatric Surgeons (#03100)
♦ BAPS Swaminarayan Sanstha / see Bochasanwasi Shri Akshar Purushottam Swaminarayan Sanstha
♦ Baptisternas Skandinaviska Samarbetskommitté (inactive)
♦ Baptistines – Congrégation des Soeurs de Saint Jean-Baptiste (religious order)
♦ Baptistischer Weltbund (#03176)
♦ Baptist Missionary Society, UK / see BMS World Mission
♦ Baptist Peace Fellowship of North America (internationally oriented national body)

♦ Baptist Women of the Pacific (BWP) 03173

Pres c/o BRBC, 47 Norris Rd, Bracken Ridge QLD 4017, Australia.
URL: https://bwpacific.org/

History within *Baptist World Alliance (BWA, #03176).* Former names and other names: *Baptist Women's Union of the South West Pacific (BWUSWP)* – former. **Aims** Support and implement the objectives and ideals of the BWA among Baptist women of the world and in particular the South West Pacific; promote fellowship, deeper sympathy and fuller understanding among Baptist women; encourage and promote development of women's leadership at all levels of Baptist world fellowship; facilitate information exchange concerning activities and methods of work in women's organizations; promote the worldwide Baptist Women's World Day of Prayer. **Structure** General Assembly. Executive, comprising President, Vice-President, Secretary, Treasurer and representative members. Nominating Committee. **Languages** English, Fijian, Tok Pisin. **Staff** 1.50 FTE, voluntary. **Finance** Day of Prayer offerings; individual donations; gifts. **Activities** Organizes: Annual Day of Prayer; development projects within the region; quinquennial regional conference; quinquennial international leadership conference with sister members of the BWA Women's Department. **Events** *Quinquennial conference* Nadi (Fiji) 2004.

Members Women's organizations in 5 countries:
Australia, Fiji, Indonesia, New Zealand, Papua New Guinea. [2020/XD8140/**E**]

♦ Baptist Women's Union of Africa (BWUA) 03174

Union des femmes baptistes d'Afrique

Exec Dir BWA Women, 405 N Washington St, Falls Church VA 22046, USA. T. +17037908980. Fax +17038935160.
Pres address not obtained.
URL: https://www.bwawd.org/

History within *Baptist World Alliance (BWA, #03176).* **Events** *Annual Conference* Kinshasa (Congo DR) 2012, *Annual Conference* Legon (Ghana) 2002. **NGO Relations** *All Africa Baptist Fellowship (AABF, #00639).* [2022/XD1464/**D**]

♦ Baptist Women's Union of the South West Pacific / see Baptist Women of the Pacific (#03173)

♦ Baptist World Aid (BWAid) 03175

Contact 405 N Washington St, Falls Church VA 22046, USA. T. +17037908980. Fax +17038935160. E-mail: bwaid@bwanet.org.
URL: http://www.bwanet.org/

History Founded 1920, as the relief and development arm of *Baptist World Alliance (BWA, #03176).* **Aims** Provide *disaster relief* and *sustainable* community *development* aid and training to the member bodies of the BWA; act as a broker between those who develop projects and those who offer funding; coordinate disaster emergency response around the world. **Languages** English. **Staff** 2.00 FTE, paid. **Finance** Donations made through *Baptist World Alliance (BWA, #03176).* **Publications** *BWA Connect* (12 a year); *Baptist World Magazine* (4 a year). **Members** National Baptist conventions and unions (220), with 44,000 baptized members in 120 countries and territories (not specified). [2016/XF1378/**F**]

♦ Baptist World Aid Australia (internationally oriented national body)

♦ Baptist World Alliance (BWA) 03176

Alliance baptiste mondiale – Alianza Bautista Mundial – Baptistischer Weltbund

SG 405 North Washington St, Falls Church VA 22046, USA. T. +17037908980. Fax +17038935160. E-mail: info@baptistworld.org.
Main Website: http://www.baptistworld.org

History Jul 1905, London (UK). Founded at 1st Baptist World Congress. **Aims** As a global movement of Baptists, support, encourage and strengthen one another while proclaiming and living the Gospel of Jesus Christ in the power of the Holy Spirit before a lost and hurting world.
Structure General Council (annual); Executive Committee (usually meeting twice a year). Departments (3): Women's; Men's; Youth. Divisions (5): Worship, Fellowship & Unity; Mission & Evangelism; Aid, Relief & Community Development; Religious Freedom, Human Rights & Justice; and Theological Reflection & Transformational Leadership.
Regional Fellowships (6):
– *All Africa Baptist Fellowship (AABF, #00639);*
– *Asia Pacific Baptist Federation (APBF, #01857);*
– *Caribbean Baptist Fellowship (#03464);*
– *European Baptist Federation (EBF, #06316);*
– *North American Baptist Fellowship (NABF);*
– *Union of Baptists in Latin America (UBLA, #20368).*

Continental unions within the Women's Department (7):
– *Asian Baptist Women's Union (ABWU, #01356);*
– *Baptist Women's Union of Africa (BWUA, #03174);*
– *Baptist Women of the Pacific (BWP, #03173);*
– *Caribbean Baptist Women's Union (see: #03176);*
– *European Baptist Women United (EBWU, #06317);*
– *Latin American Baptist Women's Union (#16255);*
– *North American Baptist Women's Union (NABWU, no recent information).*

Relief and development arm (1):
– *Baptist World Aid (BWAid, #03175).*

Languages English, French, Portuguese, Spanish. **Staff** None. **Finance** Sources: contributions. **Activities** Events/meetings; training/education. **Events** *World Congress* Brisbane, QLD (Australia) 2025, *Annual Gathering* Stavanger (Norway) 2023, *Annual Gathering* Birmingham, AL (USA) 2022, *Quinquennial Congress* 2021, *Quinquennial Congress* Rio de Janeiro (Brazil) 2020. **Publications** *Baptist World* (4 a year); *Annual Gathering Agenda Book*; *BWA Yearbook.* Congress report book and resolutions; divisional and regional newsletters; papers and studies. **Information Services** *BWA Communications.*
Members Baptist conventions and unions (246), comprising over 49 million baptized believers and a community of 110 million, in 128 countries and territories:
Angola, Antigua-Barbuda, Argentina, Armenia, Australia, Austria, Azerbaijan, Bahamas, Bangladesh, Barbados, Belarus, Belgium, Belize, Benin, Bermuda, Bolivia, Bosnia-Herzegovina, Botswana, Brazil, Bulgaria, Burkina Faso, Burundi, Cambodia, Cameroon, Canada, Central African Rep, Chad, Chile, Colombia, Congo DR, Costa Rica, Côte d'Ivoire, Croatia, Cuba, Czechia, Denmark, Dominican Rep, Ecuador, Egypt, El Salvador, Equatorial Guinea, Estonia, Ethiopia, Fiji, Finland, France, Gambia, Georgia, Germany, Ghana, Grenada, Guadeloupe, Guatemala, Guyana, Haiti, Honduras, Hong Kong, Hungary, India, Indonesia, Israel, Italy, Jamaica, Japan, Jordan, Kenya, Korea Rep, Latvia, Lebanon, Liberia, Lithuania, Macau, Madagascar, Malawi, Malaysia, Mexico, Moldova, Mozambique, Myanmar, Namibia, Nepal, Netherlands, New Zealand, Nicaragua, Nigeria, Norway, Panama, Papua New Guinea, Paraguay, Peru, Philippines, Poland, Portugal, Romania, Russia, Rwanda, Serbia, Sierra Leone, Singapore, Slovakia, Slovenia, South Africa, South Sudan, Spain, Sri Lanka, St Kitts-Nevis, St Vincent-Grenadines, Sudan, Sweden, Switzerland, Syrian AR, Taiwan, Tanzania UR, Thailand, Togo, Trinidad-Tobago, Turkey, Turks-Caicos, Uganda, UK, Ukraine, Uruguay, USA, Uzbekistan, Venezuela, Vietnam, Zambia, Zimbabwe.
Consultative Status Consultative status granted from: *ECOSOC (#05331)* (Special); *UNICEF (#20332).* **IGO Relations** Associated with Department of Global Communications of the United Nations. **NGO Relations** Member of (3): *Conference of Non-Governmental Organizations in Consultative Relationship with the United Nations (CONGO, #04635); International Council of Voluntary Agencies (ICVA, #13092); NGO Committee on UNICEF (#17120).* [2022.12.16/XB0186/**B**]

♦ **Barany Society** International Academy of Equilibrium Researchers (#11547)
♦ Bar Association of International Governmental Organizations (unconfirmed)
♦ BAR – Baltic Association for Rehabilitation (no recent information)
♦ Barcelona Centre for International Affairs / see Centre for International Information and Documentation, Barcelona
♦ Barcelona Convention – Convention for the Protection of the Marine Environment and the Coastal Region of the Mediterranean (1976 treaty)
♦ Barcelona Institute for Global Health (internationally oriented national body)
♦ Barcelona Institute for International Studies Foundation (internationally oriented national body)
♦ The Barcelona Process: Union for the Mediterranean / see Union for the Mediterranean (#20457)
♦ Barcelona protocol – Protocol Concerning Specially Protected Areas and Biological Diversity in the Mediterranean (1995 treaty)
♦ BarefootLawyers International (internationally oriented national body)
♦ Barents Euro-Arctic Council / see Barents Euro-Arctic Council (#03177)

♦ Barents Euro-Arctic Council (BEAC) 03177

Head of Secretariat Wiulls gate 3, 9900 Kirkenes, Norway. T. +4790149277. E-mail: ibs@barents-council.org.
URL: https://www.barents-council.org

History 11 Jan 1993, Kirkenes (Norway). Founded as *Barents Euro-Arctic Council (BEAC),* on signature of an agreement, the *'Kirkenes Declaration',* by foreign ministers of the Nordic countries, Russia and a representative of the European Commission. At the same time, representatives of the Barents Region county governors and their equivalents, together with a representative of the indigenous peoples, signed a cooperation protocol that established the Barents Regional Council, with similar objectives as the BEAC. *International Barents Secretariat (IBS)* set up by Agreement on the Establishment of an International Barents Secretariat (IBS), 15 Nov 2007, Rovaniemi (Finland). **Aims** Support and promote intergovernmental and regional cooperation in various fields, including: economic, social and environmental issues, education, culture, transport, logistics and rescue services. **Structure** Cooperation covers 2 levels: intergovernmental – Barents

Euro-Arctic Council; interregional – *Barents Regional Council (BRC, see: #03177)*, comprised of 13 counties or similar subregional entities in Finland, Norway, Russia and Sweden. BEAC Chairmanship rotates every 2 years between Finland, Norway, Russia and Sweden. Committee of Senior Officials. Meetings at Foreign Minister level (every second year). Working Groups; Sub-groups; Task Forces. **Languages** English, Finnish, Norwegian, Russian, Swedish. **Staff** 3.00 FTE, paid. **Finance** Sources: contributions of member/participating states. Annual budget: 420,000 EUR (2017). **Activities** Cooperation is both intergovernmental among all countries of the region (BEAC), and cross-border among regional administrations of Northwest Russia, Northern Finland, Northern Norway and Northern Sweden (BRC). Projects: Barents Industrial Partnership – promotes economic development and business contacts in the Barents region; Environment and Climate Change – aims to implement environmental Hot Spots projects and develop cooperation on climate change; Health and Social Well-Being – aims to continue implementation of the Barents HIV/AIDS programme and support new initiatives; Emergency and Rescue Services; Logistics, Transport and Border Crossings – aims to improve accessibility across borders; project on development of cross-border entrepreneurship of indigenous youth; Steering Committee for the *'Barents Euro-Arctic Pan-European Transport Area (BEATA)'*. Organizes conferences on economic cooperation, transport, environment, raw materials and indigenous issues. **Events** *Barents Press International Annual Media Conference* Joensuu (Finland) 2022, *Conference* Kirkenes (Norway) 2016, *Barents Industrial Partnership Meeting* Oulu (Finland) 2015, *Foreign Ministers Session* Oulu (Finland) 2015, *Meeting* Oulu (Finland) 2015.
Members Governments of 6 countries:
Denmark, Finland, Iceland, Norway, Russia, Sweden.
Regional EU integration body (1), listed in this Yearbook:
European Commission (EC, #06633).
Observers governments of 10 countries:
Canada, Finland (North Karelia), France, Germany, Italy, Japan, Netherlands, Poland, UK, USA. [2022.10.11/XE1716/y/**E***]

♦ Barents Euro Arctic Region / see Barents Euro-Arctic Council (#03177)

♦ Barents Press International 03178

Chairman address not obtained.
URL: http://www.barentspress.org/
History 1994. **Aims** Support and develop journalistic cooperation in the region. **Structure** Rotating Presidency. **Events** *Annual Meeting* Tromsø (Norway) 2019.
Members Journalists of 4 countries:
Finland, Norway, Russia, Sweden. [2019/AA0723/v/**E**]

♦ Barents Regional Council (see: #03177)
♦ Bar European Group (internationally oriented national body)
♦ Barilla Center for Food and Nutrition Foundation (internationally oriented national body)
♦ Bariloche Foundation (internationally oriented national body)
♦ **Bari MAI** Mediterranean Agronomic Institute of Bari (#16641)
♦ Baring Foundation (internationally oriented national body)
♦ BARKA Foundation for Mutual Help (internationally oriented national body)
♦ Barmherzige Brüder von Maria Hilfe (religious order)
♦ Barmherzige Brüder von Montabaur (religious order)
♦ Barmherzige Schwestern vom Heiligen Karl Barromäus (religious order)
♦ Barmherzige Schwestern vom Heiligen Kreuz (religious order)
♦ Barnabas International (internationally oriented national body)
♦ Barnabas Outreach Trust (internationally oriented national body)
♦ Barnabites – Clercs Réguliers de Saint-Paul (religious order)
♦ Barnabites – Clerics Regular of St Paul (religious order)
♦ Barnabiti – Chierici Regolari di San Paolo (religious order)
♦ Barndrømmen (unconfirmed)

♦ Barnekulturforskning i Norden (BIN-Norden) 03179

Contact address not obtained.
URL: https://bin-norden.org/
History Former names and other names: *Barnekulturforskning i Norden – et nordisk tverrfaglig forskningsnettverk* – full title. **Aims** Act as a Nordic research network based on humanistic, social science, cultural-historical and aesthetical studies. **Activities** Events/meetings. [2023/AA2554/**F**]

♦ Barnekulturforskning i Norden – et nordisk tverrfaglig forskningsnettverk / see Barnekulturforskning i Norden (#03179)
♦ **BARNESA** Banana Research Network for Eastern and Southern Africa (#03158)
♦ Barreau des organisations internationales (unconfirmed)
♦ Barreau Pénal International (#13107)
♦ Barrow Cadbury Trust (internationally oriented national body)
♦ Barrow and Geraldine S Cadbury Trust / see Barrow Cadbury Trust

♦ Barytes Association, The 03180

Association de la baryte
Contact Av de Tervuren 168, box 15, 1150 Brussels, Belgium. T. +3222050840. E-mail: barytes@barytes.org.
URL: http://www.barytes.org/
History Oct 2000. Registered in accordance with Belgian law. **Aims** Provide a forum for the international barytes industry in all its activities including technical, legislative and environmental matters. **Structure** General Assembly (annual); Executive Committee. **Languages** English. **Finance** Members' dues.
Members Companies (29) in 14 countries:
Brazil, Bulgaria, China, France, Germany, India, Mexico, Morocco, Netherlands, Spain, Türkiye, UK, United Arab Emirates, USA.
NGO Relations Secretariat provided by: *European Association of Mining Industries, Metal Ores and Industrial Minerals (EUROMINES, #06122)*. Member of: *Critical Raw Materials Alliance (CRM Alliance, #04959)*. [2020.03.10/XD8997/**D**]

♦ BASAS – British Association for South Asian Studies (internationally oriented national body)
♦ **BAS** Baltic Association of Surgeons (#03102)
♦ The Base / see Al-Qa'ida (#00748)
♦ Baseball Confederation of Oceania (inactive)

♦ Baseball Federation of Asia (BFA) 03181

Exec Dir F -3 – No 288, Sec 6 Civic Blvd, Xinyi Dist, New Taipei City 110, Taiwan. T. +8862473368. Fax +886227470068. E-mail: bfa@baseballasia.org.
URL: http://www.baseballasia.org/
History Also referred to as *Asian Baseball Federation*. **Structure** Congress. **Activities** Sporting activities. **Publications** *Asian Baseball Cheers*.
Members National baseball associations in 24 countries and territories:
Afghanistan, Brunei Darussalam, Cambodia, China, Hong Kong, India, Indonesia, Iran Islamic Rep, Iraq, Japan, Kazakhstan, Korea DPR, Korea Rep, Malaysia, Mongolia, Myanmar, Nepal, Pakistan, Philippines, Singapore, Sri Lanka, Taiwan, Thailand, Uzbekistan.
NGO Relations Continental confederation of: *World Baseball Softball Confederation (WBSC, #21222)*. [2016/XD2110/**D**]

♦ BASE – Basel Agency for Sustainable Energy (internationally oriented national body)
♦ **BASE** Bellanet Alliance of Social Entrepreneurs (#03196)
♦ BASE – Bureau africain des sciences de l'éducation (no recent information)
♦ Base de Datos de Recursos Mundiale (#10578)
♦ Base de données mondiale d'information sur les ressources (#10578)
♦ BASEES – British Association for Slavonic and East European Studies (internationally oriented national body)

♦ Basel Action Network (BAN) 03182

Exec Dir 80 Yesler Way, Suite 300, Seattle WA 98104, USA. T. +12066525555. E-mail: inform@ban.org.
URL: http://www.ban.org/
History 1997. Founded by *Earth Economics*. Registration: Charity, USA; EU Transparency Register, No/ID: 979092139046-24, Start date: 22 Jul 2020. **Aims** Work in opposition to toxic trade in *toxic wastes*, toxic products and toxic technologies that are exported from rich to poorer countries; ensure national self-sufficiency in *waste management* through clean production and toxics use reductions and in support of the principle of global *environmental* justice. **Structure** Board. **Languages** English. **Staff** 6.00 FTE, paid. **Finance** Sources: grants. Annual budget: 1,000,000 USD. **Activities** Events/meetings; knowledge management/information dissemination; management of treaties and agreements; research/documentation; training/education. *Basel Convention on the Control of Transboundary Movements of Hazardous Wastes and Their Disposal (UNCRTD, 1989)*. **Members** Organizations around the world. Membership countries not specified.
IGO Relations Cooperates with (1): *Secretariat of the Basel Convention (SBC, #19196)*. **NGO Relations** Member of (4): Break Free from Plastics; *GoodElectronics (#10679)*; *International Pollutants Elimination Network (IPEN, #14616)*; *NGO Shipbreaking Platform (#17126)*. [2021.08.31/XF4662/**F**]

♦ Basel Agency for Sustainable Energy (internationally oriented national body)
♦ Basel Ban Amendment – Amendment to the Basel Convention on the Control of Transboundary Movements of Hazardous Wastes and their Disposal (1995 treaty)
♦ Basel Capital Accord (1988 treaty)

♦ Basel Committee on Banking Supervision (BCBS) 03183

Comité de Bâle sur le contrôle bancaire – Basler Ausschuss für Bankenaufsicht – Comitato di Basilea per la Vigilanza Bancaria
SG c/o BIS, Centralbahnplatz 2, 4002 Basel BS, Switzerland. T. +41612808080. Fax +41612809100 – +41612808100. E-mail: baselcommittee@bis.org.
URL: http://www.bis.org/bcbs/index.htm
History Dec 1974, Basel (Switzerland), by Governors of Central Banks of countries of the *Group of Ten (G-10, inactive)*, as *Committee on Banking Regulations and Supervisory Practices – Comité des règles et pratiques de contrôle bancaire – Ausschuss für Bankenbestimmungen und Überwachung – Comitato per la Regolamentazione Bancaria e le Procedure di Vigilanza*. **Aims** Provide a regular forum for closer *international cooperation* on banking supervisory matters; work towards improving the cohesion of arrangements for supervising activities of banks operating in international *markets*; improve the effectiveness of techniques for supervising international banking business. **Structure** Group of Central Bank Governors and heads of Supervision. Meetings usually at *Bank for International Settlements (BIS, #03165)*, where permanent Secretariat is located. **Activities** Guidance; information exchange; standard setting; training; meeting activities. Has concluded work on reform of the *Basel Capital Accord (1988)* so as to improve the way regulatory capital requirements reflect underlying risks and to better address recent financial innovations. Together with BIS, set up *Financial Stability Institute (FSI, #09771)*, 1999. **Events** *Asia-Pacific High Level Meeting on Banking Supervision* Sydney, NSW (Australia) 2019, *Asia-Pacific High Level Meeting on Banking Supervision* Singapore (Singapore) 2018, *Meeting* Seoul (Korea Rep) 2013, *Conference* Istanbul (Turkey) 2012, *Joint forum* Tokyo (Japan) 2010.
Members Senior representatives of bank supervisory authorities and central banks fromm 27 countries and territories:
Argentina, Australia, Belgium, Brazil, Canada, China, France, Germany, Hong Kong, India, Indonesia, Italy, Japan, Korea Rep, Luxembourg, Mexico, Netherlands, Russia, Saudi Arabia, Singapore, South Africa, Spain, Sweden, Switzerland, Türkiye, UK, USA.
IGO Relations Observer with: *Financial Action Task Force (FATF, #09765)*; *OECD (#17693)* Corporate Governance Committee. **NGO Relations** Instrumental in setting up, and occasionally holds meetings with: *Group of International Finance Centre Supervisors (GIFCS, #10782)*. Observer to: *International Forum of Independent Audit Regulators (IFIAR, #13639)*. Instrumental in setting up: *Joint Forum (#16130)*. [2020/XE0385/**E**]

♦ Basel Concordat – Principles for the Supervision of Banks' Foreign Establishments (1983 treaty)
♦ Basel Convention / see Secretariat of the Basel Convention (#19196)
♦ Basel Convention on the Control of Transboundary Movements of Hazardous Wastes and Their Disposal (1989 treaty)
♦ Basel Declaration Society / see Animal Research Tomorrow (#00840)
♦ Basel Institute on Governance (internationally oriented national body)
♦ Basel Peace Office (internationally oriented national body)
♦ Basel Protocol on Liability and Compensation for Damage Resulting from Transboundary Movements of Hazardous Wastes and Their Disposal (1999 treaty)
♦ BASIC – British-American Security Information Council (internationally oriented national body)

♦ Basic Education Coalition (BEC) 03184

General Enquiries 1400 16th St NW, Ste 210, Washington DC 20036, USA. T. +12027296712.
URL: http://www.basiced.org/
History 2001, by members. Registration: USA. **Aims** Maximize resources in broadening the reach of members' efforts; share experience and lessons learnt, so as to enhance investment in basic education; raise public and private support for quality basic education as a key element in economic development and human well-being – *'Education For All'*. **Structure** Board of Directors. **Publications** *International Basic Education Update* (24 a year) – newsletter. *Teach a Child, Transform a Nation*. Fact sheets.
Members Development organizations (18), working in more than 100 countries, including the following 13 organizations listed in this Yearbook:
CARE International (CI, #03429); *Catholic Relief Services (CRS, #03608)*; *ChildFund International (#03869)*; *International Research and Exchanges Board (IREX)*; *International Youth Foundation (IYF)*; *Plan International (#18386)*; *RTI International*; *Save the Children Federation (SCF)*; *SIL LEAD*; *Women Thrive Alliance*; *World Education (WE)*; *World Learning*; *World Vision International (WVI, #21904)*.
NGO Relations Member of: *American Council for Voluntary International Action (InterAction)*. [2020/XM0044/y/**F**]

♦ Basic Education Resource Centre (BERC) 03185

Contact Faculty of Education, Kenyatta University, PO Box 43844-00100, Nairobi, Kenya. T. +25420810901 – +25420811622 – +25420812722. Fax +25420811575.
URL: http://www.ku.ac.ke/
History 1975, as a joint venture, by *UNESCO (#20322)*, *UNICEF (#20332)* and Kenyatta University (Kenya). Full title: *Basic Education Resource Centre – Eastern and Southern Africa*. **Aims** Collect and disseminate information on basic education; establish areas of priority for research into the problems associated with basic education and identify persons and organizations willing to participate in coordinated basic research projects. **Finance** Financed by: Kenyatta University (Nairobi); Kenya Government; UNICEF. **Activities** Major sections (5): (i) Early childhood education; (ii) Adult out of school education; (iii) Primary education; (iv) Special education; (v) Community studies. Administrative BERC is sub-divided into the following sections: (i) Administrative and finance; (ii) research projects, post-graduate studies and examinations; (iii) Documentation/Library, BERC links; (iv) Seminars, workshops, social welfare, research associates; (v) Publications, academic/staff meetings. **Publications** *Basic Education Forum* – journal.
Members Covers 19 countries:
Botswana, Burundi, Comoros, Djibouti, Eswatini, Ethiopia, Kenya, Lesotho, Madagascar, Malawi, Mauritius, Mozambique, Rwanda, Seychelles, Somalia, Tanzania UR, Uganda, Zambia, Zimbabwe.
IGO Relations *International Development Research Centre (IDRC, #13162)*. Associated regional institution of: *Network of Educational Innovation for Development in Africa (NEIDA, no recent information)*. **NGO Relations** *African Society for Environmental Studies Programme (ASESP, no recent information)*. [2008/XF1569/**F**]

♦ Basic Education Resource Centre – Eastern and Southern Africa / see Basic Education Resource Centre (#03185)
♦ Basic Health International (internationally oriented national body)

♦ Basic Income Earth Network (BIEN) ... 03186
Sec 286 Ivydale Road, London, SE15 3DF, UK. T. +4476357916. E-mail: bien@basicincome.org.
URL: http://www.basicincome.org/
History Sep 1986, Louvain-la-Neuve (Belgium). Founded at 1st international conference on basic income. Original Statutes adopted 24 Sep 1988, Antwerp (Belgium), during General Assembly and finalized 5 Dec 1988, Brussels (Belgium), by Executive Committee. Current Statutes adopted 20 Sep 2004, Barcelona (Spain), during General Assembly, and finalized 4 Dec 2006, Cape Town (South Africa), during General Assembly. Former names and other names: *Basic Income European Network (BIEN)* – former (1988 to 2004). **Aims** Serve as a link between individuals and groups committed to, or interested in, basic income, ie an income unconditionally granted to all on an individual basis, without means test or work requirement; stimulate and disseminate research; foster informed public discussion on this topic throughout the world. **Structure** Annual General Assembly (at Congress); Executive Committee. **Languages** English. **Staff** Voluntary. **Finance** Sources: members' dues. **Activities** Events/meetings; knowledge management/information dissemination; networking/liaising; research/documentation. **Events** *Congress* Brisbane, QLD (Australia) 2022, *Congress* Glasgow (UK) 2021, *Congress* Hyderabad (India) 2019, *Congress* Tampere (Finland) 2018, *Congress* Lisbon (Portugal) 2017. **Publications** *BIEN Newsletter* (12 a year); *BIEN News Flash* (6 a year) – electronic bulletin. **Members** Individuals (about 400). Membership countries not specified. [2022.11.04/XF1107/**F**]

- ♦ Basic Income European Network / see Basic Income Earth Network (#03186)
- ♦ BasicNeeds (internationally oriented national body)
- ♦ Basilian Fathers – Congregation of St Basil (religious order)
- ♦ Basiliani (religious order)
- ♦ Basilians – Order of St Basil the Great (religious order)
- ♦ **BASIN** Building Advisory Service and Information Network (#03351)
- ♦ BASIS – Benelux Association for Stable Isotope Scientists (internationally oriented national body)
- ♦ Basler Ausschuss für Bankenaufsicht (#03183)
- ♦ **BASPA** Black and Azov Seas Ports Association (#03268)
- ♦ Basque Country University / see International Centre for Research on Delinquency, Marginality and Social Relationships (#12510)
- ♦ **BASREC** Baltic Sea Region Energy Cooperation (#03148)
- ♦ **BaSS** Balkan Stomatological Society (#03088)
- ♦ **BASSEUROPE** European Society of Bassists (#08528)
- ♦ **BASTIC** Baltic Association of Science/Technology Parks and Innovation Centres (#03101)
- ♦ **BASTUN** Baltic Sea Trade Union Network (#03151)
- ♦ Båtbranchens Nordiska Samarbetskommitté (inactive)
- ♦ Bat Conservation International (internationally oriented national body)
- ♦ Batey Relief Alliance (internationally oriented national body)
- ♦ Bathurst Meeting – International Meeting of Carbonate Sedimentologists (meeting series)
- ♦ BATIK International (internationally oriented national body)
- ♦ Bâtisseurs pour le développement en Afrique (internationally oriented national body)

♦ Battelle Memorial Institute (BMI) ... 03187
Institut Battelle
Headquarters 505 King Avenue, Columbus OH 43201-2693, USA. T. +16144246424. E-mail: solutions@battelle.org.
Pres/CEO address not obtained.
URL: http://www.battelle.org/
History 1925, USA, under the terms of the will of Gordon Battelle, as a nonprofit, public purpose organization. **Aims** Serve industry and government in the development, commercialization and management of *technology*. **Structure** Board of Directors. Centres (6). **Staff** 9000.00 FTE, paid. **Finance** Total revenue: US$ 1,157 million. **Activities** Provides technology development and commercialization services. Markets include: aerospace; environment; energy; health and human service; transportation; material security; homeland defense. **Events** *International symposium on in situ and on-site bioremediation* Baltimore, MD (USA) 2009, *International symposium on in situ and on-site bioremediation* Baltimore, MD (USA) 2007, *International conference on remediation of contaminated sediments* Savannah, GA (USA) 2007, *International China biopharmaceutical symposium* Beijing (China) 2006, *International conference on the remediation of contaminated sediments* New Orleans, LA (USA) 2005. **Publications** *Solutions Update*. Technical books and papers. **Members** Not a membership organization. **Consultative Status** Consultative status granted from: *ECOSOC (#05331)* (Ros A). **IGO Relations** Accredited by: *United Nations Framework Convention on Climate Change – Secretariat (UNFCCC, #20564)*; *United Nations Office at Vienna (UNOV, #20604)*. Associated with Department of Global Communications of the United Nations. **NGO Relations** Member of: *Global Research Alliance (GRA, no recent information)*; *World Association of Industrial and Technological Research Organizations (WAITRO, #21145)*. [2018/XF0187/j/**E**]

- ♦ Battery Council International (internationally oriented national body)
- ♦ BATU – Brotherhood of Asian Trade Unionists (inactive)
- ♦ **BAUA** Baltic Architects Unions Association (#03093)
- ♦ BAU – Beirut Arab University (internationally oriented national body)
- ♦ Bau- und Holzarbeiter Internationale (#03355)
- ♦ Bautistas de Norte América Unidos por la Paz (internationally oriented national body)
- ♦ **BAWS** Balkan Association for Workers' Sport (#03066)

♦ Bay of Bengal Initiative for Multi-Sectoral Technical and Economic Cooperation (BIMSTEC) ... 03188
Permanent Secretariat c/o Ministry of Foreign Affairs, Gov of People's Rep of Bangladesh, Shegun Bagicha, Dhaka 1000, Bangladesh. T. +880295560209. Fax +88029572259. E-mail: asbimstec@mofa.gov.bd – dirbimstec@mofa.gov.bd.
URL: http://www.bimstec.org/
History 6 Jun 1997, Bangkok (Thailand), with adoption of Bangkok Declaration, as *Bangladesh, India, Sri Lanka, Thailand Economic Cooperation (BIST-EC)*. Following inclusion of Myanmar, 22 Dec 1997, during special Ministerial Meeting, Bangkok, changed name to *Bangladesh, India, Myanmar, Sri Lanka, Thailand Economic Cooperation (BIMST-EC)*. At 6th Ministerial Meeting, Feb 2004, Phuket (Thailand), Bhutan and Nepal became members, and present name was adopted. *Framework Agreement on BIMSTEC Free Trade Area (2004)* was signed 8 Feb 2004, Phuket. Permanent Secretariat established in Dhaka (Bangladesh) at 13th Ministerial Meeting, 22 Jan 2011, Nay Pyi Taw (Myanmar). **Aims** Create an enabling environment for rapid economic *development*; accelerate social progress in the sub-region; promote active collaboration and mutual assistance on matters of common interest; provide assistance to each other in the form of training and research facilities; cooperate more effectively in joint efforts that are supportive of, and complementary to, national development plans of member states; promote socio-economic development; create an enabling environment for cooperation in various fields between member countries in order to enhance the livelihoods of the peoples of the region. **Structure** Policy making bodies: Summit; Annual Ministerial Meeting, comprising Foreign Ministerial Meeting and Trade and Economic Ministerial Meeting. Operational bodies: Senior Officials' Meeting (SOM) meetings on regular basis as and when required; BIMSTEC Working Group (coordinating body). Chairmanship rotates by alphabetical order of member country name. Specialized Task Forces and other mechanisms as may be deemed necessary by Senior Officials, coordinated by Member States as appropriate. **Finance** Contributions from member states. **Activities** Encourages active collaboration and mutual assistance on matters of common interest that are supportive of, and complementary to, national development plans of member states, including: training; research facilities; joint efforts. Maintains close and beneficial cooperation with existing international and regional organizations; cooperates in projects that can be dealt with most productively on a sub-regional basis and which make best use of available synergies. Lead Countries of the 14 priority sectors of cooperation host Expert Group Meetings of their responsible sectors regularly, and report the result to the BIMSTEC Working Group. Outcome is then reported to the SOM, Economic Forum and Business Forum Meetings. Areas of cooperation in 14 Priority Sectors: Trade and Investment; Transport and Communication; Energy; Tourism; Technology; Fisheries; Agriculture; Public Health; Poverty Alleviation; Counter-Terrorism and Transnational Crime; Environment and Natural Disaster Management; Culture; People to People Contact; Climate Change. **Events** *Meeting of the Joint Working Group on Counter-Terrorism and Transnational Crime* Bangkok (Thailand) 2015, *Meeting* Bangkok (Thailand) 2015, *Meeting* Khon Kaen (Thailand) 2015, *Ministerial Meeting* Nay Pyi Taw (Myanmar) 2011, *Ministerial Meeting* Nay Pyi Taw (Myanmar) 2011. **Publications** *BIMSTEC News Letter* (12 a year).
Members Governments of 7 countries:
Bangladesh, Bhutan, India, Myanmar, Nepal, Sri Lanka, Thailand.
IGO Relations Cooperates with: *Asian Development Bank (ADB, #01422)*; *Research and Information System for Developing Countries, India (RIS, India)*. [2012.01.09/XM0273/**F***]

♦ Bay of Bengal Programme Inter-Governmental Organization (BOBP-IGO) ... 03189
Dir PO Box 1054, 91 St Mary's Road, Abhiramapuram, Chennai, Tamil Nadu 600 018, Chennai TAMIL NADU 600 018, India. T. +914442040024. Fax +914424936102. E-mail: info@bobpigo.org.
URL: http://www.bobpigo.org/
History 26 Apr 2003, Chennai (India). Founded on signature of an Agreement between the Governments of Bangladesh, India and Sri Lanka. Agreement with the Government of Maldives was signed 21 May 2003. Evolved from Bay of Bengal Programme of *FAO (#09260)*. **Aims** Promote and establish responsible *fisheries* in a time bound manner to ensure socio-economic security of the coastal small-scale fishers and ecological security of fisheries resources in the Bay of Bengal while catalyzing growth of the sector to substantiate economic development of member countries. **Structure** Governing Council; Technical Advisory Committee; Secretariat, located in Chennai (India). **Languages** Bengali, Dhivehi, English, Oriya, Sinhala, Tamil, Telugu. **Staff** 20.00 FTE, paid. **Finance** Financed by Governments of Bangladesh, India, Maldives and Sri Lanka. **Activities** Politics/policy/regulatory; awareness raising; knowledge management/information dissemination; guidance/assistance/consulting; training/education; events/meetings. **Events** *Governing Council Meeting* Chennai (India) 2022, *International Conference on the Promotion of Seaweed Value Chain in India* Chennai (India) 2022, *Regional Workshop on Best Practices for Instruments and Methods of Ocean Observation* Chennai (India) 2012, *Governing Council Meeting* Malé (Maldives) 2011, *Regional Consultation on Preparation of Management Plant for Hilsa Fisheries* Chittagong (Bangladesh) 2010.
Members Governments of 4 countries:
Bangladesh, India, Maldives, Sri Lanka.
IGO Relations Cooperates with: *Asia-Pacific Fishery Commission (APFIC, #01907)*. [2022/XM3389/**E***]

- ♦ Bayozefiti – Fratelli Figli Giuseppini del Rwanda (religious order)
- ♦ Baytna – Association Baytna pour le Soutien de la Société Civile (internationally oriented national body)
- ♦ **BBA** – Balkan Blockchain Association (unconfirmed)
- ♦ **BB** Boys' Brigade, The (#03308)
- ♦ **BBBSI** – Big Brothers Big Sisters International (internationally oriented national body)
- ♦ **BBCGPA** – Baltic Bast Crops Growers' and Producers' Association (internationally oriented national body)
- ♦ **BBC** Media Action (internationally oriented national body)
- ♦ BBC World Service Trust / see BBC Media Action
- ♦ BBC WST / see BBC Media Action
- ♦ **BBE** B'nai B'rith Europe (#03289)
- ♦ **BBI** – Best Buddies International (internationally oriented national body)
- ♦ **BBI** B'nai B'rith International (#03290)
- ♦ **BBI** – Bridge Builders International (internationally oriented national body)
- ♦ **BBIE** Benelux-Bureau voor de Intellectuele Eigendom (#03202)
- ♦ **BBI JU** Bio-based Industries Joint Undertaking (#03239)
- ♦ **BBMRI-ERIC** Biobanking and BioMolecular resources Research Infrastructure (#03237)
- ♦ **BBSC** Balkan and Black Sea Regional Commission (#03068)
- ♦ **BBS** Europe (internationally oriented national body)
- ♦ BBS Europe – European Citizenship Education / see BBS Europe
- ♦ **BBSPA** – Balkan and Black Sea Petroleum Association (unconfirmed)
- ♦ BBW / see Jewish Women International (#16114)
- ♦ **BBYO** B'nai B'rith Youth Organization (#03291)
- ♦ **BCA** Badminton Confederation of Africa (#03057)
- ♦ **BCA** Baltijas Celinieku Asociacija (#03138)
- ♦ BCA – Billiard Congress of America (internationally oriented national body)
- ♦ BCA – Biocosmological Association (unconfirmed)
- ♦ **BCA** Bureau de coordination de l'arabisation (#00999)
- ♦ **BCAH** Bureau de la coordination des affaires humanitaires (#20593)
- ♦ **BCARE** International (internationally oriented national body)
- ♦ BCAS – Brussels Centre of African Studies (internationally oriented national body)
- ♦ BC – Brighton Collaboration (inactive)
- ♦ **BCBS** Basel Committee on Banking Supervision (#03183)
- ♦ **BCB** Union of Black Sea and Caspian Business (#20369)
- ♦ **BCCA** Baltic Sea Chambers of Commerce Association (#03140)
- ♦ BCC / see African Network for Strategic Communication in Health and Development (#00396)
- ♦ **BCCIC** – BC Council for International Cooperation (internationally oriented national body)
- ♦ BCC / see ICC Financial Investigation Bureau (#11046)
- ♦ BCCM – Bureau central de compensation maghrébin (no recent information)
- ♦ BC Council for International Cooperation (internationally oriented national body)
- ♦ BCDA – Bureau de développement de coopérative d'assurance (inactive)
- ♦ **BCEAC** – Banque centrale des Etats de l'Afrique équatoriale et du Cameroun (inactive)
- ♦ **BCEAM** / see European Business Council for Africa (#06416)
- ♦ **BCEAO** Banque centrale des Etats de l'Afrique de l'Ouest (#03167)
- ♦ **BCE** Banque centrale européenne (#06466)
- ♦ **BCE** Butterfly Conservation Europe (#03388)
- ♦ BCEI – Bureau canadien de l'éducation internationale (internationally oriented national body)
- ♦ **BCEL** / see Royal Commonwealth Ex-Services League (#18989)
- ♦ BCEPS / see Pacific Islands Forum Secretariat (#17970)
- ♦ **BCF** Blind Children's Fund (#03280)
- ♦ **BCFN** Foundation – Barilla Center for Food and Nutrition Foundation (internationally oriented national body)
- ♦ BCG Society / see European Society for Noninvasive and Preventive Cardiology (#08668)
- ♦ **BCHV** – Belgisch Comité voor Hulp aan Vluchtelingen (internationally oriented national body)
- ♦ BCI – Bat Conservation International (internationally oriented national body)
- ♦ BCI – Battery Council International (internationally oriented national body)
- ♦ **BCI** Better Cotton Initiative (#03218)
- ♦ BCI – Bonobo Conservation Initiative (internationally oriented national body)
- ♦ **BCI** Bonsai Clubs International (#03301)
- ♦ BCID – Bradford Centre for International Development (internationally oriented national body)
- ♦ **BCIE** Banco Centroamericano de Integración Económica (#03658)
- ♦ BCIRG / see Translational Research In Oncology
- ♦ BCIS – Bandaranaike Centre for International Studies (internationally oriented national body)
- ♦ BCIS – Bureau central international de séismologie (inactive)
- ♦ **BCI Society** Brain-Computer Interface Society (#03313)
- ♦ BCIU – Business Council for International Understanding (internationally oriented national body)
- ♦ **BCLF** Balkan Clinical Laboratory Federation (#03071)
- ♦ **BCMA** – Branded Content Marketing Association (unconfirmed)
- ♦ **BCM** Baltic Council of Ministers (#03109)
- ♦ **BCME** Baltic Centre for Media Excellence (#03104)
- ♦ BCMS / see Crosslinks
- ♦ BCMSB / see Catholic Bishops' Conference of Malaysia-Singapore-Brunei (#03601)
- ♦ BCMS Crosslinks / see Crosslinks

- ♦ **BCNA** Baltic Child Neurology Association (#03106)
- ♦ **BCN** Breast Centres Network (#03317)
- ♦ BCO – Baseball Confederation of Oceania (inactive)
- ♦ BCRD – Balkan Centre for Regional Development (internationally oriented national body)
- ♦ BCRRA – International Conference on the Bearing Capacity of Roads, Railways and Airfields (meeting series)
- ♦ BCS – BCS – The Chartered Institute for IT (unconfirmed)
- ♦ BCS – The Chartered Institute for IT (unconfirmed)
- ♦ BCSD – Business Council for Sustainable Development (inactive)
- ♦ **BCSDN** Balkan Civil Society Development Network (#03070)
- ♦ BCSIA – Belfer Center for Science and International Affairs (internationally oriented national body)
- ♦ BCUN – Business Council for the United Nations (internationally oriented national body)
- ♦ BCWG / see European Breast Cancer Council (#06400)
- ♦ BCWLF / see Commonwealth Weightlifting Federation (#04368)
- ♦ **BCWT** Baltic Centre for Writers and Translators (#03105)
- ♦ BD / see Public Eye
- ♦ BDAASA – Biodynamic Agricultural Association of Southern Africa (internationally oriented national body)
- ♦ BDA – Blu-ray Disc Association (unconfirmed)
- ♦ BDA / see Cancer Drug Development Forum (#03413)
- ♦ BDA – Conférence sur la Gestion de Données – Principes, Technologies et Applications (meeting series)
- ♦ BDC / see CODE
- ♦ **BDC** Banco de Desarrollo del Caribe (#03492)
- ♦ **BDC** Bentley Drivers Club (#03209)
- ♦ **BDCD** Brussels Dialogue on Climate Diplomacy (#03341)
- ♦ BDCM Workshop – International Workshop on Business Data Collection Methodology (meeting series)
- ♦ BDCP – Bioresources Development and Conservation Programme (internationally oriented national body)
- ♦ **BDEAC** Banque de développement des Etats de l'Afrique centrale (#03168)
- ♦ BDEGL – Banque de développement des Etats des Grands Lacs (inactive)
- ♦ BDFA – Benelux Duty Free Association (no recent information)
- ♦ BDF – Bali Democracy Forum (meeting series)
- ♦ bdi – business disability international (internationally oriented national body)
- ♦ B and D – International Workshop on Bubble and Drop Interfaces (meeting series)
- ♦ BDLN Overeenkomst (1986 treaty)
- ♦ BDS – International Conference on Broadband Dielectric Spectroscopy and its Applications (meeting series)
- ♦ **BDT** Bureau de développement des télécommunications (#03358)
- ♦ **BDVA** Big Data Value Association (#03232)
- ♦ **BEA** Baltic Economic Association (#03113)
- ♦ **BEAC** Banque des Etats de l'Afrique centrale (#03169)
- ♦ BEAC / see Barents Euro-Arctic Council (#03177)
- ♦ **BEAC** Barents Euro-Arctic Council (#03177)

♦ Beach Ultimate Lovers Association (BULA) 03190

Contact Rua Joao Luis Ricardo 65-4b, 2775-211 Parede, Portugal. T. +351918412363. E-mail: info@beachultimate.org.
URL: http://beachultimate.org/

History Dec 2000, having existed as an informal organization since 1999. **Aims** Assist, educate and promote the spirit and the game of beach ultimate worldwide. **Structure** Board. Officers: President; Europe President; Coordinator; Contributor. **NGO Relations** Member of: *World Flying Disc Federation (WFDF, #21509).*
[2013/XJ7686/**F**]

- ♦ BEAR Council / see Barents Euro-Arctic Council (#03177)
- ♦ Bear Information Centre (internationally oriented national body)
- ♦ Bears in Mind (internationally oriented national body)
- ♦ Bears in Mind – Fund for bears / see Bears in Mind
- ♦ Bears in Mind – Stichting voor beren / see Bears in Mind
- ♦ **BEBPA** BioPharmaceutical Emerging Best Practices Association (#03254)
- ♦ **BE** The Butterfly Effect (#03389)
- ♦ **BecA** Biosciences Eastern and Central Africa (#03259)
- ♦ Be-cause Health / see Belgian Platform for International Health
- ♦ Be-cause health – Belgian Platform for International Health (internationally oriented national body)
- ♦ BEC / see Badminton Europe (#03058)
- ♦ **BEC** Badminton Europe (#03058)
- ♦ **BEC** Basic Education Coalition (#03184)
- ♦ **BEC** Bureau d'enquêtes de la CCI sur la contrefaçon (#11043)
- ♦ BEC – Bureau européen de café (inactive)
- ♦ BEC – Bureau européen de coordination des organisations internationales de jeunesse (inactive)
- ♦ **BECC** Business European Capital Cities (#03382)
- ♦ Be The Change Earth Alliance (internationally oriented national body)
- ♦ BECSA – Bulgarian European Community Studies Association (internationally oriented national body)
- ♦ **BEDA** Bureau of European Design Associations (#03359)
- ♦ Bedömningskommittén för Nordiska Rådets Litteraturpris (#00114)
- ♦ BEDSE – Bureau d'étude et de documentation sur la santé des étudiants (inactive)
- ♦ BEE / see European Environmental Bureau (#06996)
- ♦ BEEGS – Baltic and East European Graduate School (internationally oriented national body)

♦ Beekeeping Network North-South (BNNS) 03191

Pres Rue Ste-Walburge 207, 4000 Liège, Belgium. T. +3243800618.

History Memorandum signed, Oct 2010, Brussels (Belgium). Registered in accordance with Belgian law. Registration: AISBL/IVZW, No/ID: 0847.349.735, Belgium. **Aims** Promote beekeeping as a development tool. **Structure** General Assembly (annually). Advisory Committee; Steering Committee. **Activities** Events/meetings. **Members** Effective; Supporting; Honorary. Membership countries not specified.
[2015.02.24/XJ8470/**F**]

- ♦ BEEP / see European Association for the Education of Adults (#06018)
- ♦ Bee Research Association / see International Bee Research Association (#12330)
- ♦ **Beeronomics Society** International Association for the Economics of Beer and Brewing (#11857)
- ♦ Bees for Development Trust (internationally oriented national body)
- ♦ **BEF** Baltic Environmental Forum (#03116)
- ♦ **BEF** Bund Europäischer Farbberater/Farbdesigner (#03357)
- ♦ The Befrienders / see Samaritans
- ♦ Befrienders International (inactive)

♦ Befrienders Worldwide 03192

Treas 7 Woodberry Avenue, Harrow, HA2 6AU, UK. E-mail: treasurer@befrienders.org – info@befrienders.org.
URL: http://www.befrienders.org/

History 1974. Originally founded within *Samaritans*. Launched as an independent organization, 2012. Registration: Charity Commission, No/ID: 1146717, England and Wales; Companies House, No/ID: 07964782, Start date: 24 Feb 2012, England. **Aims** Provide emotional support to prevent *suicide* worldwide. **Structure** Trustees. **Publications** *Befrienders Worldwide Newsletter.*

Members Centres in 34 countries and territories:
Argentina, Australia, Brazil, China, Cyprus, Denmark, France, Hong Kong, Hungary, India, Italy, Japan, Kenya, Lithuania, Malaysia, Mauritius, Moldova, Morocco, New Zealand, Norway, Poland, Portugal, Serbia, Singapore, South Africa, Spain, Sri Lanka, St Vincent-Grenadines, Sweden, Thailand, UK, Uruguay, USA, Zimbabwe.
[2020/XJ6864/**F**]

- ♦ BEG – Bar European Group (internationally oriented national body)
- ♦ Begin-Sadat Centre for Strategic Studies (internationally oriented national body)
- ♦ BEGS / see Pelargonium and Geranium Society

♦ Behavioral Optometry Academy Foundation (BOAF) 03193

Pres Bankstrasse 17, 8610 Uster ZH, Switzerland. T. +41798833700. E-mail: office@boaf-eu.org.
URL: https://www.boaf-eu.org/

History 2012. Registration: KVK, No/ID: 54479126, Netherlands. **Structure** Officers; Secretariat. **Languages** English, German, Italian. **Activities** Events/meetings. **Events** *Congress of Behavioural Optometry* Sydney, NSW (Australia) 2018, *Annual Conference on Behavioural Optometry* Berlin (Germany) 2015.

Members Individuals in 7 countries:
Austria, Belgium, Germany, Italy, Netherlands, Switzerland, USA.
[2022/XJ8477/f/**F**]

♦ Behavior Genetics Association (BGA) 03194

Information Officer address not obtained.
Sec address not obtained.
URL: http://www.bga.org/

History Bylaws adopted Apr 1973; revised Jun 1974, Mar 1975, Oct 1981, Jun 1990, Jul 1992, Jul 1997, Jul 2002, Jul 2003, Jul 2005, Sep 2009, Jul 2013, Apr 2015, Aug 2015, Jun 2018 and Nov 2018. Registered in the State of Illinois (USA). Registration: USA. **Aims** Promote the scientific study of the interrelationship of genetic mechanisms and human and animal behavior. **Structure** Annual Meeting; Executive Committee. **Finance** Sources: members' dues. **Activities** Events/meetings; knowledge management/information dissemination; training/education. **Events** *Annual International Meeting* Stockholm (Sweden) 2019, *Annual International Meeting* Oslo (Norway) 2017, *Annual international meeting* Seoul (Korea Rep) 2010, *Annual international meeting* Stockholm (Sweden) 1998, *Annual international meeting* Nijmegen (Netherlands) 1988. **Publications** *Behavior Genetics.*
[2020/XW1347/**C**]

- ♦ Behavioural Exchange – International Behavioural Insights Conference Behavioural Exchange (meeting series)
- ♦ Beiaard Wereld Federatie (#21260)
- ♦ **BEI** Banca Europea per gli Investimenti (#07599)
- ♦ **BEI** Banco Europeo de Inversiones (#07599)
- ♦ **BEI** Banco Europeu de Investimento (#07599)
- ♦ **BEI** Bancs d'essai internationaux (#03160)
- ♦ **BEI** Banque européenne d'investissement (#07599)
- ♦ **BEI** Bridge Engineering Institute (#03327)
- ♦ **BEIC** Baltic Energy Innovation Centre (#03115)
- ♦ BEIC – Bureau européen d'informations charbonnières (inactive)
- ♦ Beijer Institute – International Institute of Ecological Economics (internationally oriented national body)
- ♦ Beijer Institute – International Institute for Energy, Resources and the Human Environment / see Beijer Institute – International Institute of Ecological Economics
- ♦ Beijerinstitutet (internationally oriented national body)
- ♦ Beijer International Institute of Ecological Economics / see Beijer Institute – International Institute of Ecological Economics
- ♦ Beijing amendment – Amendment to the Montreal Protocol on Substances That Deplete the Ozone Layer, 1999 (1999 treaty)
- ♦ Beijing Convention – Convention on the Suppression of Unlawful Acts Relating to International Civil Aviation (2010 treaty)
- ♦ Beijing Declaration / see International Civil Defence Organization (#12582)
- ♦ Beijing Institute of Foreign Trade / see University of International Business and Economics
- ♦ Beijing Institute for International Strategic Studies / see China Institute for International Strategic Studies
- ♦ Beijing Protocol – Protocol Supplementary to the Convention for the Suppression of Unlawful Seizure of Aircraft (2010 treaty)
- ♦ Beijing Treaty on Audiovisual Performances (2012 treaty)
- ♦ Beira-Lobito Trans Southern African Highway Coordinating Committee (inactive)
- ♦ Beirut Agreement – Agreement for Facilitating the International Circulation of Visual and Auditory Materials of an Educational, Scientific and Cultural Character (1948 treaty)
- ♦ Beirut Arab University (internationally oriented national body)
- ♦ BEJE – Bureau européen de la jeunesse et de l'enfance (inactive)
- ♦ **BEL** Bahaa Esperanto-Ligo (#03061)
- ♦ BelBol / see CATAPA
- ♦ Belfer Center for Science and International Affairs (internationally oriented national body)
- ♦ Belgian Administration for Development Cooperation / see Directorate-General for Development Cooperation
- ♦ Belgian African Chamber of Commerce / see Chamber of Commerce, Industry and Agriculture Belgium – Luxembourg – Africa-Caribbean-Pacific
- ♦ Belgian Association of Africanists (internationally oriented national body)
- ♦ Belgian Centre of Slav Studies (internationally oriented national body)
- ♦ Belgian Committee for Refugee Aid (internationally oriented national body)
- ♦ Belgian Corporation for International Investment (internationally oriented national body)
- ♦ Belgian Development Agency / see Enabel
- ♦ Belgian Fund for Food Security (internationally oriented national body)

♦ Belgian-Luxembourg Economic Union (BLEU) 03195

Union économique belgo-luxembourgeoise (UEBL) – Belgisch-Luxemburgs Economische Unie (BLEU)

Contact Ministère des Affaires Etrangères et de l'Immigration, Direction des relations économiques internationales, 6 rue de l'Ancien Athénée, L-2911 Luxembourg, Luxembourg. T. +35247824782478. Fax +352478222048.
Contact Secrétariat, Cmsn admin belgo-luxembourgeoise, Rue des Petits Carmes 15, 1000 Brussels, Belgium.

History 1921, when the Convention on Belgo-Luxembourg Economic Union was signed. Initially intended to remain in force for 50 years, the Convention was renewed by tacit agreement for further periods of 10 years in 1982 and 1992. Dec 2002, a new Convention was signed between the 2 countries and 3 regions of Belgium. **Activities** In the context of the times BLEU, was very much like a common market; other arrangements subsequently drafted on to the original 1921 Treaty adapted to a constantly changing international situation. Especially important was the monetary association of Belgium and the Grand Duchy of Luxembourg (Luxembourg), being a forerunner of *European Economic and Monetary Union (EMU, #06961).*

Members Governments of 2 countries:
Belgium, Luxembourg.
[2010.11.15/XF0924/b/**F***]

- ♦ Belgian Platform for Education and Development (internationally oriented national body)
- ♦ Belgian Platform for International Health (internationally oriented national body)
- ♦ Belgian Society of Tropical Medicine (internationally oriented national body)
- ♦ Belgian Survival Fund / see Belgian Fund for Food Security
- ♦ Belgian Survival Fund for the Third World / see Belgian Fund for Food Security
- ♦ Belgian Technical Cooperation / see Enabel
- ♦ Belgisch Afrikaanse Kamer van Koophandel / see Chamber of Commerce, Industry and Agriculture Belgium – Luxembourg – Africa-Caribbean-Pacific
- ♦ Belgisch Agentschap voor Ontwikkelingssamenwerking / see Enabel
- ♦ Belgisch Centrum voor Slavische Studies (internationally oriented national body)
- ♦ Belgisch Comité voor Hulp aan Vluchtelingen (internationally oriented national body)
- ♦ Belgische Maatschappij voor Internationale Investering (internationally oriented national body)
- ♦ Belgische Technische Coöperatie / see Enabel
- ♦ Belgische Vereniging van Afrikanisten (internationally oriented national body)
- ♦ Belgische Vereniging voor Tropische Geneeskunde (internationally oriented national body)
- ♦ Belgisch-Luxemburgs-Duitse Kamer van Koophandel (internationally oriented national body)

♦ Belgisch-Luxemburgs Economische Unie (#03195)
♦ Belgisch-Nederlands-Luxemburgse Unie (inactive)
♦ Bellagio Group / see International Working Group on Education (#15909)
♦ Bellanet / see Bellanet Alliance of Social Entrepreneurs (#03196)

♦ Bellanet Alliance of Social Entrepreneurs (BASE) 03196

Africa Contact Aitec Uganda, Plot 22 Bukoto Street, PO Box 26970, Kampala, Uganda. E-mail: abasajjabaka@bellanet.org – contact@bellanet.org.
North America Contact 19 Carnochan Chelsea, Québec QC J9B 2L6, Canada. E-mail: mroberts@bellanet.org.
URL: http://www.bellanet.org/

History Jan 1995, Ottawa (Canada), by *International Development Research Centre (IDRC, #13162)*, for a 4-year experimental phase. Originally referred to as *Donornet*. Subsequently changed title to *Bellanet*. Evolved into an independent alliance, under current title. **Aims** Broaden collaboration, increase participation and transparency of action and diffuse lessons learned. **Languages** English, French, Nepali, Spanish. **Staff** 15.00 FTE, paid. **Finance** Current phase funded by: IDRC; *Swiss Agency for Development and Cooperation (SDC)*. **Activities** Supports collaboration in the development community by sharing expertise in information and communication technologies, as well as skills in facilitating organizational learning and the sharing of knowledge. Delivers work through 3 main programme lines: Online Communities; Knowledge Sharing; Open Development. Working areas: Gender Equality; Capacity Development; Monitoring and Evaluation; Learning. **Publications** *Bellanews* (3 a year); *KM4Dev Journal* (3 a year). Annual Report. **IGO Relations** Relations and cooperation with: *CGIAR System Organization (CGIAR, #03843)*; *Department for International Development (DFID, inactive)*; *Deutsche Gesellschaft für Technische Zusammenarbeit (GTZ, inactive)*; *Institute for Connectivity in the Americas (ICA, #11249)*; *International Bank for Reconstruction and Development (IBRD, #12317)* (World Bank); *Bioversity International (#03262)*. **NGO Relations** Partnerships, including with: *Acceso*; *Association internationale de techniciens, experts et chercheurs (AITEC, #02745)*; *South Asia Partnership International (SAP International, inactive)*. Cooperates with: *Association for the Development of Education in Africa (ADEA, #02471)*. Relations and cooperation with: *European Centre for Development Policy Management (ECDPM, #06473)*; *Humanistisch Instituut voor Ontwikkelingssamenwerking (Hivos)*; *International Centre for Tropical Agriculture (#12527)*; *International Water Management Institute (IWMI, #15867)*; *OneWorld International Foundation (OWIF, #17738)*. Links with various organizations, including: *Global Knowledge Partnership Foundation (GKPF, #10443)*. [2012/XK1503/**E**]

♦ Bell International (internationally oriented national body)
♦ Bell International NGO / see Bell International
♦ Bellona Europa (internationally oriented national body)
♦ Bellona Europe / see Bellona Europa
♦ Bellona Foundation / see Bellona Europa
♦ Bellona International / see Bellona Europa

♦ Belmont Forum 03197

Admin Office c/o IAI, Avenida Italia 6201, Edif Los Tilos 102, 11500 Montevideo, Uruguay. E-mail: info@belmontforum.org.
URL: http://www.belmontforum.org/

History Set up following a conference, Jun 2009, Elkridge MD (USA). Became Council of Principals for *International Group of Funding Agencies for Global Change Research (IGFA, inactive)*. As of Oct 2014, IGFA and Belmont Forum merged under current title. **Aims** Deliver knowledge needed for action to avoid and adapt to detrimental *environmental* change including extreme hazardous events. **Structure** Steering Committee; Secretariat. **Staff** 9.00 FTE, paid. **Activities** Research/documentation; events/meetings. **Events** *Sustainability Research and Innovation Congress* Pretoria (South Africa) 2022, *Sustainability Research and Innovation Congress* Brisbane, QLD (Australia) 2021.
Members Organizations that are legally allowed to mobilize resources from national or international research funds. Full in 17 countries:
Australia, Austria, Brazil, China, France, Germany, India, Italy, Japan, Netherlands, Norway, Qatar, South Africa, Sweden, Taiwan, UK, USA.
Included in the above, 1 organization listed in this Yearbook:
Commonwealth Scientific and Industrial Research Organization (CSIRO); *Inter-American Institute for Global Change Research (IAI, #11437)*.
Regional entity:
European Commission (EC, #06633).
IGO Relations Partner of: *Group on Earth Observations (GEO, #10735)*. **NGO Relations** Member of: *Science and Technology Alliance for Global Sustainability (Alliance, #19143)* and its *Future Earth (#10048)*. [2020/XM5334/**F**]

♦ BELRA / see LEPRA Health in Action
♦ BEMA – The Baking Industry Suppliers Association (internationally oriented national body)
♦ **BEMI** Biciklista Esperantista Movado Internacia (#11878)
♦ **BEMS** The Bioelectromagnetics Society (#03245)
♦ **BENA** Balkan Environmental Association (#03072)
♦ **BEN-Africa** Business Ethics Network of Africa (#03380)
♦ **BEN** Baltic Ecovillage Network (#03114)
♦ BEN – Baltic Euregional Network (inactive)
♦ Bendrijos Augalu Veisliu Tarnyba (#04404)
♦ Benedettine della Federazione di Santa Gertrude (religious order)
♦ Benedettine Missionarie (religious order)
♦ Benedictine Confederation (religious order)
♦ Benedictine Nuns (religious order)
♦ Bénédictine Adoratrices de Bellemagny (religious order)
♦ Benedictine Sisters of the Federation of Saint Benedict (religious order)
♦ Benedictine Sisters of the Federation of Saint Gertrude (religious order)
♦ Benedictine Sisters of the Federation of Saint Scholastica (religious order)
♦ Bénédictines de Jésus Crucifié (religious order)
♦ Bénédictines de Sainte Bathilde (religious order)
♦ Bénédictines de Sainte-Lioba (religious order)
♦ Benelux Afro Center (internationally oriented national body)
♦ Benelux Association of Bariatric Surgeons (no recent information)

♦ Benelux Association for Energy Economics (BAEE) 03198

Sec Van Ostadestraat 151-II, 1073 TK Amsterdam, Netherlands. T. +31619150224.
Registered Office Slijkstraat 52, 3212 Pellenberg, Belgium.
URL: http://www.baee.eu/

History 23 Feb 1984, as a branch of *International Association for Energy Economics (IAEE, #11869)*. Registered in accordance with Belgian law, 21 Dec 1984. **Aims** Further understanding of all aspects of energy economics, both within the Benelux (Belgium, Netherlands, Luxembourg) and internationally. **Structure** General Assembly; Board. **Languages** Dutch, English, French. **Finance** Members' dues. Sponsors. **Activities** Events/meetings. **Events** *Meeting* Luxembourg (Luxembourg) 1988, *Meeting* Brussels (Belgium) 1987. **Publications** Annual Report.
Members Individuals in 3 countries:
Belgium, Luxembourg, Netherlands. [2018/XE1480/v/**E**]

♦ Benelux Association for Stable Isotope Scientists (internationally oriented national body)

♦ Benelux Association for Trademark and Design Law 03199

Association Benelux pour le droit des marques et modèles – Benelux Vereniging voor Merken- en Modellenrecht (BMM)
Mailing Address p/a Postbus 78, 2640 AB Pijnacker, Netherlands. E-mail: secretariaat@bmm.nl.
URL: https://bmm.eu/

History 6 Sep 1974, Brussels (Belgium). Former names and other names: *Benelux Association for Trademark and Design Law* – alias; *Association Benelux des conseils en marques et modèles* – former alias. **Structure** Administrative Council, comprising President, Vice-President, Secretary, Treasurer and 6 members. Statutory commissions (3): Surveillance; Appeals; Education and Examination. Non-statutory commissions (9): Editorial; Programmes; Legislation; Offices; Professional Recognition; Benelux concertation; PR and Communication. **Languages** Dutch, English, French. **Staff** All voluntary. **Events** *Meeting* Utrecht (Netherlands) 2022, *Meeting* Ghent (Belgium) 2019, *Meeting* Arnhem (Netherlands) 1994. **Publications** *Bulletin BMM* (4 a year).
Members Mandatory; Ordinary (603). Individuals in 3 countries:
Belgium, Luxembourg, Netherlands.
Foreign members in 17 countries and territories:
Channel Is, Cyprus, France, Germany, Greece, India, Ireland, Japan, Nigeria, Pakistan, Portugal, South Africa, Spain, Sweden, Switzerland, UK, USA.
Consultative Status Consultative status granted from: *World Intellectual Property Organization (WIPO, #21593)* (Permanent Observer Status). **IGO Relations** Cooperates with: *European Union Intellectual Property Office (EUIPO, #08996)*. [2022/XD5210/t/**D**]

♦ Benelux-Bureau voor de Intellectuele Eigendom (#03202)
♦ Benelux conventie inzake grensoverschrijdende samenwerking tussen territoriale samenwerkingsverbanden of autoriteiten (1986 treaty)
♦ Benelux Convention on Co-decedents (1972 treaty)
♦ Benelux Convention on Designs or Models (1966 treaty)
♦ Benelux Convention on the Hunting and Protection of Birds (1970 treaty)
♦ Benelux Convention on Mandatory Civil Liability Insurance for Motor Vehicles (1966 treaty)
♦ Benelux Convention on Nature Conservation and Landscape Protection (1982 treaty)
♦ Benelux Convention on Trade Marks (1962 treaty)
♦ Benelux Convention on a Uniform Law Concerning Progressive Penalties for Non-compliance (1973 treaty)

♦ Benelux Court of Justice 03200

Cour de justice Benelux – Benelux-Gerechtshof
Registrar Rue de la Régence 39, 1000 Brussels, Belgium. T. +3225193861. Fax +3225134206. E-mail: info@courbeneluxhof.int.
URL: http://www.courbeneluxhof.be/

History 1 Jan 1974. Established on entry into force of a treaty signed 31 Mar 1965. Commenced operations 11 May 1974, Brussels (Belgium). Closely related to, although not formally an institution of, *Benelux Union (#03207)*, and based at the Union's Secretariat General. Treaty modified by the Protocols of 10 Jun 1981 and 23 Nov 1984. Statutes registered in *'UNTS/1 13176'*. **Aims** Ensure uniformity in applying and interpreting specifically designed *juridical* rules common to countries of the Benelux Economic Union; settle disputes in administration of Benelux affairs. **Structure** General Assembly (every 3 years). Members of the Court are nominated by Benelux Committee of Ministers and include: 9 judges, 3 from each country, and including a President and First and Second Vice-Presidents; 10 substitute judges (normally 2 from each country but with the option of up to 5); 3 Solicitors General, one from each country, of whom one is the Chief Prosecutor and each of whom may have a substitute; 3 Recorders, of whom one is Clerk of the Court. Chambers (2): Procedural Chamber; Chamber of Litigation. Judges of the Court also hold the highest judicial offices in their respective countries. **Languages** Dutch, French. **Staff** 2.50 FTE, paid. **Finance** Government contributions. Logistic support from *Benelux Union (#03207)*. Varying budget. **Activities** Functions: (i) *'Direct jurisdiction'* – if, in trying a case, a national court is unable to rule on an aspect of Benelux law, that court has the option, or in some cases the obligation, to refer the matter to the Benelux Court of Justice, whose ruling is binding on the national court. (ii) *'Consultative function'* – each of the three governments may consult the Court on the interpretation of a common legal provision. (iii) *'Jurisdiction on disputes involving officials'* of the Benelux Economic Union (Brussels) and of *Benelux Trademarks Office (BBM, inactive)* (The Hague) – if a Benelux official feels that he or she has been unfairly treated by his or her employer, the official in question may appeal to the Benelux Court, once an advisory committee of national civil servants and Benelux officials has delivered its opinion. **Events** *General Assembly* Niederanven (Luxembourg) 1998. **Publications** *Jurisprudentie – Jurisprudence* (annual).
Members Senior judges in 3 countries:
Belgium, Luxembourg, Netherlands. [2022/XF9017/**F***]

♦ Benelux Customs Union (inactive)
♦ Benelux Deployable Air Task Force (1996 treaty)
♦ Benelux Duty Free Association (no recent information)
♦ Benelux Economic Union / see Benelux Union (#03207)
♦ Benelux Economische Unie / see Benelux Union (#03207)
♦ Benelux EPR Discussie Groep (internationally oriented national body)
♦ Benelux EPR Discussion Group (internationally oriented national body)
♦ Benelux EPR Group / see Benelux EPR Discussion Group
♦ Benelux EPR Society / see Benelux EPR Discussion Group
♦ Benelux-Gerechtshof (#03200)

♦ Benelux Inter-Parliamentary Consultative Council (Benelux Parliament) 03201

Conseil interparlementaire consultatif de Benelux (Parlement Benelux) – Raadgevende Interparlementaire Beneluxraad (Benelux-Parlement)
SG Palais de la Nation, Place de la Nation 2, 1008 Brussels, Belgium. T. +3225498552. Fax +3225498520. E-mail: secr@beneluxparl.eu.
URL: https://www.beneluxparl.eu/

History 5 Nov 1955, Brussels (Belgium). Established by a Convention which entered into force 9 Sep 1956, as a consultative council of *Benelux Union (#03207)*. First session 1957. Former names and other names: *CICB* – former; *Inter-Parliamentary Consultative Council of Benelux* – alias. **Aims** Serve as a consultative body concerning all problems connected with the Economic Union; contribute to rapprochement and cooperation among member countries in the *cultural* field, in *foreign policy*, in unification of the *law* and in all issues of common interest. **Structure** Council of 49 members (21 from Belgium, 21 from Netherlands, 7 from Luxembourg), meeting in plenary session at least 3 times a year. Bureau; Permanent Committee. General Committees (7), each comprising 12 members. National Delegations (3), each comprising Head and Members of the country concerned. Secretariat, located in Brussels (Belgium). Secretary-General (appointed by the Council). **Languages** Dutch, French. **Finance** National contributions to the budget of the Benelux Parliament. **Activities** Politics/policy/regulatory. Protocols, conventions and agreements of the Union have to be presented to the Council for advice before being ratified by member parliaments. Since 1987, President of the Parliament has functioned as ombudsman for the Union, dealing with complaints about errors made in implementing legislation or contradicting the Benelux ideal. **Events** *Interparliamentary Conference* The Hague (Netherlands) 2012, *Interparliamentary Conference* Luxembourg (Luxembourg) 2011, *Interparliamentary Conference* Brussels (Belgium) 2010, *Interparliamentary Conference* Brussels (Belgium) 2009, *Interparliamentary Conference* Tallinn (Estonia) 2008. **Publications** Annual Report; conference reports; committee reports; reports of plenary sessions; resolutions; recommendations.
Members Members of parliament (49) nominated by their respective parliaments in the 3 Benelux countries:
Belgium, Luxembourg, Netherlands.
IGO Relations Cooperation agreements with: *Baltic Assembly (BA, #03094)*; *Council of Europe (CE, #04881)*; *Parliamentary Assembly of the Council of Europe (PACE, #18211)*. **NGO Relations** Observer of: *Assemblée parlementaire de la Francophonie (APF, #02312)*. [2021/XD2831/**E***]

♦ Benelux Interuniversitaire Groepering van Vervoerseconomen (#15985)
♦ Benelux Mathematical Society (no recent information)

♦ Benelux Office for Intellectual Property (BOIP) 03202

Office Benelux de la propriété intellectuelle (OBPI) – Benelux-Bureau voor de Intellectuele Eigendom (BBIE)
Contact Bordewijklaan 15, 2591 XR The Hague, Netherlands. T. +31703491111. Fax +31703475708. E-mail: info@boip.int.

URL: http://www.boip.int/
History Established 1 Sep 2006, on merger of *Benelux Designs Office (inactive)* and *Benelux Trademarks Office (BBM, inactive)*, within *Benelux Organization for Intellectual Property (BOIP, #03203)*. **Aims** Give effect to the Benelux Convention concerning Intellectual Property; ensure that all trademarks, designs and ideas in the Benelux region are registered and that business know where, why and how to protect their intellectual property. **Languages** Dutch, English, French. **Staff** 81.50 FTE, paid. **Finance** Self-supporting. **Activities** Monitoring/evaluation; events/meetings. Management of treaties and agreements: *Convention Benelux en Matière de Propriété Intellectuelle (2005)*. **Publications** Annual Report – in Dutch/French.
Members Covers the 3 Benelux countries:
Belgium, Luxembourg, Netherlands.
IGO Relations Member of: *Intergovernmental Organizations Conference (IGO Conference, #11498)*.
[2018.07.24/XM2322/**E***]

- ♦ Benelux Orgaan Inzake Verkeersveiligheid (no recent information)
- ♦ Benelux Organisatie voor de Intellectuele Eigendom (#03203)
- ♦ Benelux Organism on Road Safety (no recent information)

♦ Benelux Organization for Intellectual Property (BOIP) 03203

Organisation Benelux de la propriété intellectuelle – Benelux Organisatie voor de Intellectuele Eigendom

Postal address PO Box 90404, 2509 LK The Hague, Netherlands. T. +31703491111. E-mail: info@ boip.int.
Street address Bordewijklaan 15, 2591 XR The Hague, Netherlands.
URL: http://www.boip.int/
History Established 2006, when *Convention Benelux en Matière de Propriété Intellectuelle (2005)* came into force. **Structure** Committee of Ministers; Administrative Board; *Benelux Office for Intellectual Property (BOIP, #03202)*. **Languages** Dutch, English, French.
Members Covers the 3 Benelux countries:
Belgium, Luxembourg, Netherlands.
Consultative Status Consultative status granted from: *World Intellectual Property Organization (WIPO, #21593)* (Observer Status). **IGO Relations** Contracting party to: *Singapore Treaty on the Law of Trademarks (Singapore Treaty, 2006)*. [2020.09.04/XM0249/**D***]

- ♦ Benelux overeenkomst betreffende de verplichte aansprakelijkheidsverzekering inzake motorrijtuigen (1966 treaty)
- ♦ Benelux overeenkomst op het gebied van de jacht en vogelbescherming (1970 treaty)
- ♦ Benelux overeenkomst op het gebied van natuurbehoud en landschapsbescherming (1982 treaty)
- ♦ Benelux overeenkomst houdende eenvormige wet betreffende de dwangsom (1973 treaty)
- ♦ Benelux overeenkomst inzake commoriëntes (1972 treaty)
- ♦ **Benelux-Parlement** Raadgevende Interparlementaire Beneluxraad (#03201)
- ♦ **Benelux Parliament** Benelux Inter-Parliamentary Consultative Council (#03201)

♦ Benelux Phlebology Society (BPS) 03204

Société béneluxienne de phlébologie – Benelux Vereniging voor Flebologie

Chair Winston Churchilllaan 11 box 30, 1180 Brussels, Belgium. E-mail: secretariaat@bvf-sbp.org.
Registered Office Avenue Winston Churchill 11 box 30, 1180 Brussels, Belgium.
URL: http://www.phlebologybenelux.org/
History 16 Nov 1957, Eindhoven (Netherlands). Registration: Banque-Carrefour des Entreprises, No/ID: 0408.616.656, Start date: 9 Mar 1961. **Aims** Promote phlebology and lymphology in the BENELUX countries; keep members informed about latest developments in the field. **Languages** Dutch, English, French. **Staff** 7.00 FTE, voluntary. **Activities** Events/meetings; financial and/or material support. **Events** *Annual meeting* Rotterdam (Netherlands) 2023, *Annual Meeting* Leuven (Belgium) 2022, *Annual Meeting* Leuven (Belgium) 2021, *Annual Meeting* Ghent (Belgium) 2016, *Annual Meeting* The Hague (Netherlands) 2015.
Members Full in 3 countries:
Belgium, Luxembourg, Netherlands. [2022.11.07/XD4379/**D**]

- ♦ Benelux Rapprochement Committee (inactive)

♦ Benelux Society for Horticultural Science 03205

Association Benelux pour la science horticole – Benelux Vereniging voor Tuinbouwwetenschap

Chair ASTA, BP 1904, L-1019 Luxembourg, Luxembourg.
Contact Federal Public Office for Economy, Rue du Progrès 50, City Atrium C-5-B20, 1210 Brussels, Belgium.
URL: http://www.beneluxshs.eu/
History 4 Sep 1996, Brussels (Belgium). Originally founded to host the 1998 XXV International Horticultural Congress. Revived in 2002. Registration: Belgium. **Aims** Promote national and international cooperation on scientific and technical topics of interest for members; stimulate cooperative research on any theme related to horticultural science. **Structure** General Assembly (annual); Council. **Languages** English. **Staff** None. **Finance** Members' dues. Sponsorship. **Events** *Annual Symposium* Ghent (Belgium) 2016, *Annual Symposium* Wageningen (Netherlands) 2015, *Annual Symposium* Delft (Netherlands) 2014, *Annual Symposium* Ghent (Belgium) 2013, *Annual Symposium* Angers (France) 2012.
Members Full in 3 countries:
Belgium, Luxembourg, Netherlands. [2015.01.08/XD6184/**D**]

- ♦ Benelux Society for Microcirculation (inactive)

♦ BeNeLux Travel Retail Association (BTRA) 03206

Chairman PO Box 3065, 2130 KB Hoofddorp, Netherlands. T. +31204058402. Fax +31206534355.
Street Address Hoeksteen 57, 2132 MT Hoofddorp, Netherlands.
URL: http://www.btra.nl/
Aims Protect and promote branch interests of producers, suppliers, sales and marketing organizations of consumer products and transporters who are involved in cross-border traffic and travel retail sales in the widest sense of the word. **NGO Relations** Member of: *European Travel Retail Confederation (ETRC, #08945)*.
[2017/XM6040/**D**]

- ♦ Benelux Treaty on the Execution of Legal Decisions in Penal Matters (1968 treaty)
- ♦ Benelux Treaty on Extradition and Mutual Assistance in Penal Matters (1962 treaty)
- ♦ Benelux Unie (#03207)

♦ Benelux Union 03207

Union Benelux – Benelux Unie

SG Rue de la Régence 39, 1000 Brussels, Belgium. T. +3225193811. Fax +3225134206. E-mail: info@benelux.int.
PR and Communication address not obtained. T. +3225193830.
URL: http://www.benelux.int/
History 3 Feb 1958, The Hague (Netherlands). Established on signature of the Treaty of Union by representatives of Belgium, Luxembourg (Luxembourg), Netherlands; Treaty came into force 1 Nov 1960. Belgium and the Grand Duchy of Luxembourg had been linked, since 1921, by the *Belgian-Luxembourg Economic Union (BLEU, #03195)*, which still exists within the Benelux Union. The political initiative to bring together the economies of the Netherlands, Belgium and Luxembourg, taken during World War II, and which eventually led to the economic integration of these countries, had been started with the adoption of a Monetary Agreement, 21 Oct 1943, London (UK), a Customs Union Treaty, 5 Sep 1944, London, and the setting up of *Benelux Customs Union (inactive)*, 1 Jan 1948. Belgium (in all its component parts), Netherlands and Luxembourg signed new Benelux Treaty, 17 Jun 2008, The Hague (Netherlands). Statutes registered in *'UNTS 1/11096'*. Former names and other names: *Benelux Economic Union* – former; *Union économique Benelux* – former; *Benelux-Wirtschaftsunion* – former; *Benelux Economische Unie* – former. **Aims** Deepen and expand cooperation between Belgium, the Netherlands and Luxembourg so that it can continue its role as precursor within the European Union and strengthen and improve cross-border cooperation at every level.
Structure Institutions:
Committee of Ministers is the supreme organ of the Benelux and meets several times a year. It comprises at least one representative at Ministerial level of the 3 countries. Composition varies according to the agenda. Rotating chairmanship.
Benelux Council consists of high civil servants of the appropriate ministries and composition varies according the the agenda. Its main taks is to prepare files for the Ministers.
Benelux Inter-Parliamentary Consultative Council (Benelux Parliament, #03201), with permanent secretariat in Brussels (Belgium), comprises delegates of the 3 national parliaments: 21 from Belgium, 21 from Netherlands and 7 from Luxembourg, drawn from the whole political spectrum of their countries of origin. The Council is a consultative body which sends opinions to the Committee of Ministers, who often amend a draft Convention on the basis of the Council's opinion. Despite its essentially advisory role, the Council may also debate and send own-initiative questions, opinions and recommendations to the 3 governments.
Benelux Court of Justice (#03200), whose membership follows the same pattern as all the Benelux institutions, has 3 functions: direct jurisdiction (the Court's ruling is binding on the national court); consultative (each of the 3 governments may consult the Court on the interpretation of a common legal provision); jurisdiction on disputes involving officials of the Union. Judges of the Court hold also high judicial offices in their respective countries.
'General Secretariat' headed by a 'college' consisting of a Dutch Secretary-General and 2 Deputy Secretaries-General, one from Belgium and one from Luxembourg, who are appointed for renewable 5-year terms. In 1975 the Committee of Ministers granted the college of Secretaries-General the right to initiate directives aimed at encouraging cooperation between the Benelux partners.
Also includes: *Benelux Organization for Intellectual Property (BOIP, #03203)* and its *Benelux Office for Intellectual Property (BOIP, #03202)*.
Languages Dutch, French. **Staff** 49.00 FTE, paid. **Finance** Expenses borne by member governments: Netherlands 53%; Belgium 41%; Luxembourg 6%.
Activities Projects/programmes. Management of treaties and agreements:
- *Parc des trois pays – Espace ouvert sans frontières (#18195)*;
- *Convention Benelux Concernant la Coopération Transfrontalière entre Collectivités ou Autorités Territoriales (1986)*;
- *Benelux Convention on Nature Conservation and Landscape Protection (1982)*;
- *Accord de Senningen (1996)*;
- *Labour Treaty (1956)*, in force 1 Nov 1960, covering free movement of employed workers;
- *Convention on the Transfer of Control of Persons to the External Frontiers of Benelux Territory (1960)*, signed 11 Apr 1960, covering free movement of persons within the Benelux countries;
- *Benelux Treaty on Extradition and Mutual Assistance in Penal Matters (1962)*, in force 11 Dec 1967;
- *Protocol on the Abolition of Controls and Formalities at Internal Benelux Frontiers, and the Abolition of Barriers to Free Movement*, in force 1971;
- *Benelux Convention on Co-decedents (1972)*, signed 29 Dec 1972;
- *Benelux Treaty on the Execution of Legal Decisions in Penal Matters (1968)*, signed 26 Sep 1968;
- *Benelux Convention on Mandatory Civil Liability Insurance for Motor Vehicles (1966)*, in force 1 Jun 1976;
- *Convention on the Unification of the Benelux Customs Area (1969)*, in force 1971, covering abolition of customs formalities relating to trade goods at internal Benelux frontiers;
- *Benelux Convention on Trade Marks (1962)*, signed 19 Mar 1962, Brussels (Belgium) and *Benelux Convention on Designs or Models (1966)*, concluded 25 Oct 1966, Brussels, providing for single registration of a trademark or design to be effective in all 3 Benelux countries;
- *Benelux Convention on the Hunting and Protection of Birds (1970)*;
- *Benelux Convention on a Uniform Law Concerning Progressive Penalties for Non-compliance (1973)*;
- *Schengen Agreement (1985)*, setting up *Group of Schengen (inactive)*;
- *Accord sur les Transports Routiers entre le Benelux et les Etats Baltes (1992)*;
- *Protocol amending the Benelux Convention on the Hunting and Protection of Birds, 2016 (2016)*, signed 17 Feb 2016.

Events *Working conference* Hoeven (Netherlands) 1998, *Meeting* Antwerp (Belgium) 1992, *Congress* Brussels (Belgium) 1988, *Doing business with Pakistan* Brussels (Belgium) 1988, *Benelux Congress* The Hague (Netherlands) 1988. **Publications** *Bulletin Benelux* (irregular). Annual Report; reports; brochures.
Members Governments of 3 countries:
Belgium, Luxembourg, Netherlands.
IGO Relations Instrumental in setting up: *Parc des trois pays – Espace ouvert sans frontières (#18195)*.
[2020.03.03/XD0190/**D***]

- ♦ Benelux vedrag inzake de tenuitvoerlegging van rechterlijke beslissingen in strafzaken (1968 treaty)
- ♦ Benelux verdrag aangaande de uitlevering en de rechtshulp in strafzaken (1962 treaty)
- ♦ Benelux verdrag inzake de intellectuele eigendom (2005 treaty)
- ♦ Benelux verdrag inzake tekeningen of modellen (1966 treaty)
- ♦ Benelux Vereniging voor Flebologie (#03204)
- ♦ BeNeLux Vereniging voor Kunstmatige Intelligentie (#03292)
- ♦ Benelux Vereniging voor Merken- en Modellenrecht (#03199)
- ♦ Benelux Vereniging voor Microcirculatie (inactive)
- ♦ Benelux Vereniging voor Tuinbouwwetenschap (#03205)
- ♦ Benelux-Wirtschaftsunion / see Benelux Union (#03207)
- ♦ Benin Electricity Community (internationally oriented national body)
- ♦ Benjamin Franklin Institute of Global Education (internationally oriented national body)

♦ Benthological Society of Asia (BSA) 03208

SG No 425 Life Science West Bldg, Korea Univ, Anam-ro 145, Seongbuk-gu, Seoul 02841, Korea Rep. T. +82232903963. Fax +82232903623. E-mail: benthosaisa@gmail.com.
ManagingSec address not obtained.
URL: http://benthosasia.org/
History Sep 1998, Matsumoto (Japan). Former names and other names: *Aquatic Entomological Societies in East Asia (AESEA)* – former (1998 to 2009). **Aims** Lead development of benthological sciences academically and contribute to conservation and sustainable management of aquatic ecosystems in Asian countries; promote information exchange. **Structure** Executive Board. **Events** *International Symposium* Chiang Mai (Thailand) 2022, *International Symposium* Chiang Mai (Thailand) 2020, *International Symposium* Nanjing (China) 2018, *International Symposium* Vladivostok (Russia) 2016, *International Symposium* Busan (Korea Rep) 2014.
Members Individuals in 12 countries:
Australia, Cambodia, China, India, Japan, Korea Rep, Laos, Mongolia, Russia, Singapore, Thailand, Vietnam.
[2021/AA1993/v/**D**]

- ♦ Bentley Community / see BE User Group (#03221)

♦ Bentley Drivers Club (BDC) 03209

General Manager c/o W O Bentley Memorial Bldg, Ironstone Lane, Wroxton, Banbury, OX15 6ED, UK. T. +441295738886. Fax +441295738887. E-mail: info@bdcl.org.
URL: http://www.bdcl.org/
History Apr 1936. **Aims** Promote the sport and pastime of *motoring* in Bentley cars; keep alive the spirit of *sportsmanship* and comradeship created by Bentley teams of the past. **Structure** A federation of Bentley Clubs. Committee. **Finance** Members' dues. Entrance fees. **Publications** *Club Notes* (12 a year); *BDC Advertiser* (6 a year); *BDC Review* (4 a year).
Members Owner; Associate; Family; Junior. Club regions in 11 countries and territories:
Australia, Canada, Germany, Hong Kong, Japan, Netherlands, New Zealand, South Africa, Switzerland, UK, USA.
[2018/XE1475/**F**]

- ♦ Ben-Zvi Institute for the Study of Jewish Communities in the East (internationally oriented national body)
- ♦ Ben-Zvi Institute for the Study of Jewish Communities in the Middle East / see Ben-Zvi Institute for the Study of Jewish Communities in the East
- ♦ **BEOC** Bureau européen de l'objection de conscience (#06411)
- ♦ BEO – European Office of Processors and Distributors of Organic Products (no recent information)
- ♦ BEPA / see European Political Strategy Centre (#08248)
- ♦ BEPIC – Built Environment Professions in the Commonwealth (internationally oriented national body)

♦ BERAS International Foundation 03210

Contact Skillebyholm 4, SE-153 91 Järna, Sweden. T. +46735627738. E-mail: info@ berasinternational.se – hans@berasinternational.se.
URL: https://www.berasinternational.se/?lang=en

History Set up 2015. BERAS stands for: *Building Ecological Recycling Agriculture and Societies* and previously for *Baltic Ecological Recycling Agriculture and Society.* **Aims** Stimulate research, conceptual development, implementation of good examples, communication and education for the whole food chain from farmer to consumer. **Structure** Secretariat.
Members Partners in 10 countries:
Denmark, Estonia, Finland, Germany, Latvia, Lithuania, Norway, Poland, Russia, Sweden.
NGO Relations Member of: *TP Organics – European Technology Platform (TP Organics, #20180).*
[2022/XM6455/f/**F**]

- ♦ Beratendes Weltkomitee der Freunde (#10004)
- ♦ Beratungsbüro für Internationale Kongresszentren (inactive)
- ♦ **BERC** Basic Education Resource Centre (#03185)
- ♦ **BERD** Banque européenne pour la reconstruction et le développement (#06315)

♦ Bereavement Network Europe (BNE) 03211

Coordinator Danish National Center for Grief, Kejsergade 2, 1 og 2 sal, 1155 Copenhagen, Denmark. E-mail: info@bereavement.eu.
Chair address not obtained.
URL: https://bereavement.eu/
History Sep 2014, Leuven (Belgium). Proposed Feb 2013, Dublin (Ireland). Former names and other names: *Family Bereavement Network* – former. **Aims** Improve support and understanding for bereaved people. **Structure** Steering Group. **Events** *European Grief Conference* Copenhagen (Denmark) 2022.
[2020/AA2518/**F**]

- ♦ **BEREC** Body of European Regulators for Electronic Communications (#03299)
- ♦ Berggorilla und Regenwald Direkthilfe (internationally oriented national body)
- ♦ Berghof Foundation (internationally oriented national body)
- ♦ Berghof Foundation for Conflict Studies / see Berghof Foundation
- ♦ Berghof Stiftung für Konfliktforschung / see Berghof Foundation
- ♦ Berhan Children's Home / see African Development Aid Association
- ♦ Berkeley Stanford Joint Center for African Studies (internationally oriented national body)
- ♦ Berlin Civil Society Center / see International Civil Society Centre (#12589)
- ♦ Berlin College for Comparative European History (internationally oriented national body)
- ♦ Berliner Informationszentrum für Transatlantische Sicherheit (internationally oriented national body)
- ♦ Berliner Kolleg für Vergleichende Geschichte Europas (internationally oriented national body)
- ♦ Berlin Forum / see Fossil Fuels Forum (#09938)
- ♦ Berlin Forum on Fossil Fuels / see Fossil Fuels Forum (#09938)
- ♦ Berlin Information Centre for Transatlantic Security (internationally oriented national body)
- ♦ Bermuda Institute of Ocean Sciences (internationally oriented national body)
- ♦ Bernardines d'Esquermes (religious order)
- ♦ Bernard van Leer Foundation (internationally oriented national body)
- ♦ Bern convention – Convention on the Conservation of European Wildlife and Natural Habitats (1979 treaty)
- ♦ Bern Convention for the Protection of Literary and Artistic Works, 1886 (1886 treaty)
- ♦ Bern Declaration / see Public Eye
- ♦ Bern Declaration Group / see Public Eye
- ♦ **Berner Union** Internationale Union der Kreditversicherer (#15767)
- ♦ Bernhard Nocht Institute for Tropical Medicine (internationally oriented national body)
- ♦ Bernhard Nocht Institut für Tropenmedizin (internationally oriented national body)
- ♦ Bern International (inactive)
- ♦ Bernoulli Society / see Bernoulli Society for Mathematical Statistics and Probability (#03212)

♦ Bernoulli Society for Mathematical Statistics and Probability (BSMSP) 03212

Société Bernoulli pour la statistique mathématique et la probabilité (SBSMP)
Exec Sec Henri Faasdreef 312, PO Box 24070, 2490 AB The Hague, Netherlands. T. +31703375737. Fax +31703860025.
URL: https://bernoullisociety.org/
History 1961. Adopted current title when it became a section of *International Statistical Institute (ISI, #15603).* Former names and other names: *International Association for Statistics in Physical Sciences (IASPS)* – former (1961 to 1975); *Association internationale pour la statistique dans les sciences physiques* – former (1961 to 1975); *Bernoulli Society (BernSoc)* – alias. **Aims** Promote advancement of the sciences of probability (including stochastic processes) and mathematical statistics of their application to all those aspects of human endeavour, which are directed towards the increase of natural knowledge and the welfare of mankind. **Structure** General Assembly; Council; Executive Committee. Standing Committees (7): Conferences on Stochastic Processes; Probability and Statistics in the Physical Sciences; Publications; European Regional; East-Asian and Pacific Regional; Latin American Regional; Schramm/Doob Lecture Selection. **Finance** Members' dues. Sales of publications. **Activities** Events/meetings; awards/prizes/competitions; training/education; research/documentation; guidance/assistance/consulting; financial and/or material support. **Events** *International Conference on Stochastic Processes and their Applications* Lisbon (Portugal) 2023, *European Meeting of Statisticians* Moscow (Russia) 2022, *International Conference on Stochastic Processes and their Applications* Wuhan (China) 2022, *Quadrennial World Congress* Seoul (Korea Rep) 2021, *Quadrennial World Congress* Seoul (Korea Rep) 2020. **Publications** *Bernoulli Journal* (4 a year); *Bernoulli News* (2 a year). *Stochastic Processes and their Applications.*
Members Individuals (1,004) in 84 countries and territories:
Algeria, Argentina, Armenia, Australia, Austria, Azerbaijan, Bangladesh, Belarus, Belgium, Brazil, Bulgaria, Canada, Chile, China, Colombia, Croatia, Cyprus, Czechia, Denmark, Ecuador, Egypt, Estonia, Ethiopia, Finland, France, Georgia, Germany, Ghana, Greece, Hong Kong, Hungary, Iceland, India, Indonesia, Iran Islamic Rep, Iraq, Ireland, Israel, Italy, Japan, Kenya, Korea Rep, Kuwait, Latvia, Lithuania, Luxembourg, Malawi, Malaysia, Mauritius, Mexico, Moldova, Mongolia, Montenegro, Morocco, Netherlands, New Zealand, Nigeria, Norway, Pakistan, Peru, Philippines, Poland, Portugal, Romania, Russia, Saudi Arabia, Senegal, Serbia, Singapore, Slovakia, Slovenia, South Africa, Spain, Sweden, Switzerland, Thailand, Türkiye, UK, Ukraine, Uruguay, USA, Uzbekistan, Venezuela, Vietnam.
[2020/XE1209/v/**E**]

- ♦ BernSoc / see Bernoulli Society for Mathematical Statistics and Probability (#03212)
- ♦ **Bern Union** International Union of Credit and Investment Insurers (#15767)
- ♦ **Bern Union** International Union for the Protection of Literary and Artistic Works (#15806)
- ♦ Bertelsmann Foundation (internationally oriented national body)
- ♦ Bertelsmann Stiftung (internationally oriented national body)

♦ Bertrand Russell Peace Foundation (BRPF) 03213

Fondation Bertrand Russell pour la paix
Contact 5 Churchill Park, Nottingham, NG4 2HF, UK. T. +441159708318.
Main: http://www.russfound.org/
History Sep 1963. Registered in accordance with UK law, 1966, London (UK). **Aims** Carry forward Bertrand Russell's work for nuclear disarmament, international peace, human rights, and social justice; identify and counter the causes of violence and the obstacles to worldwide community; promote research into disarmament, wars and threats of war, and publish the results. **Structure** General Assembly (annual); Board of Directors. **Languages** English. **Staff** 3.00 FTE, paid. **Activities** Events/meetings; research/documentation. **Events** *Consultation to prepare the European conference for peace and human rights* Brussels (Belgium) 2000, *Symposium on oppressed people* Amsterdam (Netherlands) 1992, *CAMDUN : conference on a more democratic United Nations* New York, NY (USA) 1990, *END convention* Vitoria-Gasteiz (Spain) 1989, *END convention / Convention* Lund (Sweden) 1988. **Publications** *The Spokesman* (3 a year) – journal; *ENDinfo Newsletter.* Books; pamphlets. **NGO Relations** Member of: *International Coalition to Ban Uranium Weapons (ICBUW, #12609).*
[2019.08.01/XF0106/f/**F**]

- ♦ Berufsschule für Kaufleute der Grundstücks- und Wohnungswirtschaft / see Europäisches Bildungszentrum der Wohnungs- und Immobilienwirtschaft

♦ Beryllium Science and Technology Association (BeST) 03214

Contact Avenue Marnix 30, 1000 Brussels, Belgium. T. +3222137420. E-mail: info@beryllium.eu.
URL: http://beryllium.eu/
History EU Transparency Register: 40023137761-50. **Aims** Provide the best available scientific information related to Beryllium; ensure that its benefits to society in critical applications are realized and embraced and maintained by industry, governmental authorities and the general public. **Structure** Board. **NGO Relations** Member of: *Critical Raw Materials Alliance (CRM Alliance, #04959).*
[2018/XM5762/**D**]

- ♦ BESA – Begin-Sadat Centre for Strategic Studies (internationally oriented national body)
- ♦ **BES** Bioelectrochemical Society (#03244)

♦ Beshara Trust 03215

Treas address not obtained. E-mail: trust@beshara.org.
URL: http://www.beshara.org/
History 1971, UK. **Aims** Promote *spiritual* orientation to life without the bounds of dogma or religion; advance *education* in the consideration of the basic *unity* of all *religions*, in particular by provision of courses on understanding the relationship of man to the universe, the earth, the environment and the society he lives in, to reality and to *God.* **Structure** Board of Trustees. **Staff** 8.00 FTE, voluntary. **Activities** Events/meetings; training/education. **Publications** *Addresses 1* by Bulent Rauf; *Addresses 2* by Bulent Rauf; *Commentaries on Meister Eckhart Sermons* by Dom Sylvester Houedard; *Intimations* by John Bennett; *Kernel of the Kernel* by Ibn Arabi – translated by Bulent Rauf; *Mystical Astrology According to Ibn Arabi* by Titus Burckhardt – translated Bulent Rauf; *Sufis of Andalusia* by Ibn Arabi – translated by R W J Austin; *The Twenty-Nine Pages*; *The Wisdom of the Prophets* by Ibn Arabi – translated by A Culme-Seymour; *Treatise on Being* by Ibn Arabi – translated by T H Weir. *A Garden Amidst the Flames* – CD of Ibn Arabi extracts.
Members Centres and individuals, in 17 countries:
Australia, Brazil, Canada, Denmark, Finland, France, Germany, Indonesia, Israel, Netherlands, Norway, South Africa, Spain, Türkiye, UK, USA, Venezuela.
[2021.05.20/XF1966/**F**]

- ♦ **B and ESI** Business and Economics Society International (#03379)
- ♦ **BES-Net** Biodiversity and Ecosystem Services Network (#03241)
- ♦ BESQD – Bureau européen des qualifications et spécialisations en médecine dentaire (inactive)
- ♦ **BeST** Beryllium Science and Technology Association (#03214)
- ♦ **BEST** Board of European Students of Technology (#03294)
- ♦ Best Buddies International (internationally oriented national body)

♦ BestCities Global Alliance 03216

Head Office 08-01A Far East Finanace Bldg, 14 Robinson Road, Singapore 048545, Singapore. T. +6584532641. E-mail: info@bestcities.net.
Managing Dir address not obtained.
URL: http://www.bestcities.net/
History Feb 2000. **Aims** Harness the power of collaboration and community to create positive impact through business events. **Structure** Board of Directors; Strategic Business Development Committee; Strategic Thinkers Group; Management Office. **Languages** English. **Staff** 5.00 FTE, paid. **Finance** Sources: members' dues. **Activities** Events/meetings. **Events** *Global Forum* Vancouver, BC (Canada) 2022, *Global Forum* Madrid (Spain) 2021, *Global Forum* 2020, *Global Forum* Copenhagen (Denmark) 2019, *Global Forum* Bogota (Colombia) 2018. **Publications** Monthly Round-Up.
Members Convention bureaux in 12 cities and countries:
Australia (Melbourne), Canada (Vancouver BC), Denmark (Copenhagen), Germany (Berlin), Ireland (Dublin), Japan (Tokyo), México (Guadalajara), Singapore (Singapore), South Africa (Cape Town), Spain (Madrid), United Arab Emirates (Dubai), USA (Houston TX).
NGO Relations Meetings Industry contact with various trade and professional organizations including: *International Congress and Convention Association (ICCA, #12892)*; *Professional Convention Management Association (PCMA).*
[2022.11.10/XM3058/**F**]

- ♦ di Betania – Ordine dell'Imitazione di Cristo (religious order)

♦ Betar 03217

World Headquarters Bet Meridor, Emek Hamasleva, 64 Niut St, Jerusalem, Israel. T. +97226792954. Fax +97226791713. E-mail: myriam@betar.org.il.
URL: http://www.betar.org.il/
History 1923. **Aims** Function as a *zionist youth* movement. **Activities** Instrumental in setting up: *Tagar Zionist Student Activist Movement (see: #03217).*
Members Branches (15) in 14 countries:
Argentina, Australia, Brazil, Canada, Chile, France, Israel, Lithuania, Russia, South Africa, Türkiye, UK, Uruguay, USA.
[2011/XE2983/**E**]

- ♦ Bethany – Order of the Imitation of Christ (religious order)
- ♦ **BETH** Bibliothèques européennes de théologie (#08906)
- ♦ Bethlehem Mission Society (religious order)
- ♦ Betlemitas – Orden de los Hermanos de Belén (religious order)
- ♦ Betlemiti – Ordine dei Fratelli di Betlemme (religious order)
- ♦ Betonvereniging van Suidelike Afrika (internationally oriented national body)

♦ Better Cotton Initiative (BCI) 03218

CEO Ch de Balexert 7-9, 1219 Châtelaine, Switzerland. T. +41229391250.
London Office Unit 4, 27 Corsham Street, Hoxton, London, N1 6DR, UK.
URL: https://bettercotton.org/
History 2009. Registration: Switzerland. **Aims** Make global cotton production better for the people who produce it, better for the environment it grows in and better for the sector's future. **Structure** General Assembly; Council. **Activities** Events/meetings; standards/guidelines; training/education. **Events** *Better Cotton Conference* Amsterdam (Netherlands) 2023.
Members Members (over 2500). Associate; Civil Society; Producer Organisation; Retailer and Brand; Supplier and Manufacturer. Membership countries not specified.
Civil society members include 8 organizations listed in this Yearbook:
African Institute of Corporate Citizenship (AICC); *Alliance for Water Stewardship (AWS, #00727)*; *HCV Network Ltd (HCV Network, #10865)*; *Laudes Foundation*; *SOLIDARIDAD Network (#19681)*; *Terre des hommes Foundation (Tdh Foundation, #20132)*; *The Sustainable Trade Initiative (IDH, #20070)*; *World Wide Fund for Nature (WWF, #21922).*
Associate members include 1 organization:
International Finance Corporation (IFC, #13597).
NGO Relations Member of (2): *Cool Farm Alliance (CFA)*; *ISEAL (#16026)* (Full).
[2023/XM8972/y/**F**]

♦ BETTER FINANCE (BF) 03219

Acting Managing Dir Rue d'Arenberg 44, 1000 Brussels, Belgium. T. +3225143777. E-mail: info@betterfinance.eu.
URL: http://www.betterfinance.eu/
History 2009. Founded by *Euroshareholders (inactive)* and French Association for Independent Pension Savers (FAIDER). *EuroInvestors* completely merged into the then *EuroFinUse*, 2012. Former names and other names: *European Federation of Investors (EuroInvestors)* – former (2009 to 2012); *European Federation of Financial Services Users (EuroFinUse)* – former (2012); *European shareholders associations (Euroshareholders)* – former; *The European Federation of Investors and Financial Services Users (BETTER FINANCE (BF))* – full title (2013); *Fédération Européenne des Épargnants et Usagers des Services Financiers (BETTER FINANCE)* – full title (2013). Registration: Banque-Carrefour des Entreprises, No/ID: 0818.951.402, Start date: 22 Sep 2009, Belgium; EU Transparency Register, No/ID: 24633926420-79, Start date: 11 Aug 2011. **Aims** Advocate and defend the interests of European citizens as financial services users at the European level to lawmakers and the public. **Structure** Board; Scientific Council. **Staff** 9.00 FTE, paid; 1.00 FTE, voluntary. **Finance** Sources: donations; grants; members' dues. Supported by: *European Commission (EC, #06633).* **Activities** Advocacy/lobbying/activism; knowledge management/information dissemination; research/documentation; training/education. **Events** *European Retirement Week | Pension Adequacy and Value for Money in the Time of Financial Repression* Brussels (Belgium) 2022, *High Level Expert Forum for Sustainable Finance (HLEF)*

Brussels (Belgium) 2022, *BETTER FINANCE and DSW International Investors Conference* Frankfurt-Main (Germany) 2022, *Post-Brexit Capital Markets Union – How to make it work for people?* Brussels (Belgium) 2021, *Joint DSW and BETTER FINANCE International Conference on European Capital Markets' Union & the new Green Deal* Frankfurt-Main (Germany) 2020.
Members Shareholders' associations. Full (26) in 23 countries:
Austria, Belgium, Bulgaria, Denmark, Finland, France, Germany, Greece, Iceland, Italy, Lithuania, Luxembourg, Malta, Netherlands, Norway, Poland, Portugal, Romania, Slovenia, Spain, Sweden, Türkiye, UK.
Associate (6) in 6 countries:
Belgium, Cameroon, Cyprus, Lebanon, Russia, Spain.
NGO Relations Member of (1): *European Responsible Investment Network (ERIN).* [2022.10.28/XJ9423/**D**]

- ♦ BETTER FINANCE / see BETTER FINANCE (#03219)
- ♦ BETTER FINANCE (BF) / see BETTER FINANCE (#03219)
- ♦ Better Sugarcane Initiative / see Bonsucro (#03302)

♦ Better Than Cash Alliance 03220

Communications Dir Two UN Plaza, 26th Floor, New York NY 10017, USA. T. +12129065443. E-mail: info@betterthancash.org.
URL: http://www.betterthancash.org/
Aims Accelerate the transition from cash to digital payments globally through excellence in advocacy, knowledge and services. **Structure** Executive Committee; Secretariat, provided by *United Nations Capital Development Fund (UNCDF, #20524).* Committees (2): Member Services; Editorial and Publications. **Finance** Funded by: *Bill and Melinda Gates Foundation (BMGF);* Citi Foundation; *Ford Foundation (#09858);* MasterCard; Omidyar Network; *United States Agency for International Development (USAID);* Visa. **Activities** Advocacy/lobbying/activism; research/documentation.
Members Governments; International Organizations; Companies; Resource Partners. Governments (23):
Afghanistan, Bangladesh, Benin, Colombia, Dominican Rep, Ethiopia, Ghana, India, Kenya, Liberia, Malawi, Mexico, Moldova, Nepal, Pakistan, Papua New Guinea, Peru, Philippines, Rwanda, Senegal, Sierra Leone, Uruguay, Vietnam.
International Organizations, include 20 organizations listed in this Yearbook:
ACDI/VOCA; CARE International (CI, #03429); Catholic Relief Services (CRS, #03608); Concern Worldwide; European Bank for Reconstruction and Development (EBRD, #06315); Grameen Foundation (GF, #10694); Inter-American Development Bank (IDB, #11427); International Fund for Agricultural Development (IFAD, #13692); International Rescue Committee (IRC, #14717); Mennonite Economic Development Associates (MEDA); Mercy Corps International (MCI); Save the Children International (#19058); UNDP (#20292); United Nations Population Fund (UNFPA, #20612); United Nations (UN, #20515); Universal Postal Union (UPU, #20682); William J Clinton Foundation (Clinton Development Initiative); *Women's World Banking (WWB, #21037); World Food Programme (WFP, #21510); World Savings Banks Institute (WSBI, #21764).*
Resource partners include:
Bill and Melinda Gates Foundation (BMGF); United Nations Capital Development Fund (UNCDF, #20524); United States Agency for International Development (USAID).
NGO Relations Partner of: *Responsible Finance Forum (RFF).* [2021/XM5384/y/**E**]

- ♦ Better Tourism Africa (internationally oriented national body)
- ♦ Better World Fund (internationally oriented national body)
- ♦ Better World International (unconfirmed)
- ♦ BETWA – Baltic Educational Travel and Work Association (no recent information)
- ♦ **BEUC** Bureau Européen des Unions de Consommateurs (#03360)

♦ BE User Group 03221

Contact 685 Stockton Drive, Exton PA 19341, USA. T. +16104585000. E-mail: beusergroup@bentley.com.
URL: http://www.be.org/
History as *Bentley Community.* **Aims** Share ideas and exchange knowledge between groups using Bentley *technology.*
Members Groups in 19 countries:
Australia, Belgium, Canada, Czechia, Denmark, Finland, France, Germany, Iceland, India, Ireland, Luxembourg, Netherlands, Norway, Russia, Slovakia, Sweden, UK, USA. [2009/XM0518/**E**]

- ♦ Bevrijdende Internationale Actie / see International Action for Liberation
- ♦ Bevrijde Wereld / see Solidagro
- ♦ **BEWC** Black European Women's Council (#03270)

♦ Beyond the Horizon International Strategic Studies Group (Beyond the Horizon ISSG) 03222

Contact Davincilaan 1, 1930 Zaventem, Belgium. T. +3228011357 – +3228011358. E-mail: info@behorizon.org.
URL: https://behorizon.org/
History 7 Feb 2018, Zaventem (Belgium). Former names and other names: *BtH* – alias. Registration: Banque-Carrefour des Entreprises, No/ID: 0688.914.586, Start date: 26 Jan 2018, Belgium; EU Transparency Register, No/ID: 146054127966-91, Start date: 8 Aug 2017. **Aims** Promote local and global peace and security. **Languages** Dutch, English, French. **Finance** Sources: government support; grants; international organizations; members' dues. Supported by: *European Commission (EC, #06633); European Parliament (EP, #08146); European Social Fund (ESF, #08501).* **Activities** Events/meetings; knowledge management/information dissemination; networking/liaising; projects/programmes; research/documentation; training/education. **Events** *Emerging High-Tech Cyber and Hybrid Threats – Building Europe at Peace and Harmony* Brussels (Belgium) 2021, *New Horizons Summit* Brussels (Belgium) 2019. **Publications** *Horizon Weekly* (weekly); *Horizon Insights* (4 a year). **NGO Relations** Also links with national partners. [2022.05.05/AA0062/**F**]

- ♦ **Beyond the Horizon ISSG** Beyond the Horizon International Strategic Studies Group (#03222)
- ♦ Beyond Nickel-Based Superalloys (meeting series)

♦ Beyond Sciences Initiative (BSI) 03223

Contact address not obtained. E-mail: beyondsciencesinitiative@gmail.com.
URL: http://www.beyondsciences.org/
History 2013, Toronto ON (Canada), in partnership with the Department of Immunology and Trinity College, University of Toronto, Canada. **Aims** Develop strong *student* leaders and sustainable partnerships across the world with a mandate to engage scholars to promote scientific advancement and social justice. **Structure** Trainee-led organization. Co-supervision provided by faculty at Depart of Immunology, University of Toronto. **Languages** English. **Staff** 10-20 voluntary. **Finance** Largely financed through scholarships and sponsors. **Activities** Projects/programmes; events/meetings; financial and/or material support. **Events** *Conference* 2016, *International Remote Conference* 2016. **Publications** None.
Members Full in 21 countries:
Brazil, Canada, Egypt, Ethiopia, Germany, India, Iran Islamic Rep, Japan, Kenya, New Zealand, Poland, Portugal, Russia, South Africa, Sudan, Sweden, Switzerland, Türkiye, Uganda, Ukraine, USA.
IGO Relations None. **NGO Relations** None. [2016.02.24/XM4463/**F**]

- ♦ Beyond War Movement / see Foundation for Global Community – Global Initiatives Team for the CSCE
- ♦ BFAAME / see Bridge Federation of Asia & the Middle East (#03328)
- ♦ **BFA** Baltic Fishermen's Association (#03118)
- ♦ **BFA** Baseball Federation of Asia (#03181)
- ♦ BFA – Biodiversity Foundation for Africa (internationally oriented national body)
- ♦ **BFA** Boao Forum for Asia (#03293)
- ♦ BFA – Books For Africa (internationally oriented national body)
- ♦ BFA – International Workshop on Boolean Functions and their Applications (meeting series)
- ♦ **BFAME** Bridge Federation of Asia & the Middle East (#03328)
- ♦ **BF** BETTER FINANCE (#03219)
- ♦ BfdW / see Brot für die Welt
- ♦ **BFE** Biofeedback Foundation of Europe (#03249)
- ♦ **BFFE** Baltic Farmers Forum on Environment (#03117)
- ♦ BFFS – Belgian Fund for Food Security (internationally oriented national body)
- ♦ BFG – Bund Freier Gewerkschaften (no recent information)
- ♦ **BFHI** Baby Friendly Hospital Initiative (#03053)
- ♦ BFI – Bright Future International (internationally oriented national body)
- ♦ BFIC – Busan Foundation for International Cooperation (internationally oriented national body)
- ♦ BFM / see Tallinna Ülikool – Balti filmi, meedia, kunstide ja kommunikatsiooni instituut (#20092)
- ♦ BFN – Baltic Fund for Nature (internationally oriented national body)
- ♦ BFR – International Workshop on Brominated Flame Retardants (meeting series)
- ♦ **BFS** Bachelier Finance Society (#03054)
- ♦ BFSD – Balkan Foundation for Sustainable Development (internationally oriented national body)

♦ BFS International Operators Association (BFS IOA) 03224

Contact c/o Melitek, Hartvig Jensensvej 1, 4840 Nørre Alslev, Denmark. T. +4570250255. Fax +4570250277. E-mail: bfs@melitek.com.
URL: http://www.bfsioa.org/
History Founded 1988, as an interest group of pharmaceutical and associated actively involved with BFS processing. **Aims** Provide information on blow-fill-seal (BFS) *technology;* increase quality and common understanding between the user industry and the authorities. **Structure** General Meeting (annual) in European, Asia/Pacific and American regions; Board. **Finance** Subscriptions. **Activities** Events/meetings. **Events** *European Meeting* Stockholm (Sweden) 2019, *American Meeting* Columbia, SC (USA) 2014, *European Meeting* Lyon (France) 2014, *American Meeting* Boston, MA (USA) 2013, *Asia-Pacific Meeting* Sydney, NSW (Australia) 2013. **Publications** *BSF Newsletter.*
Members Pharmaceutical and associated companies (over 60) in 27 countries and territories:
Australia, Bangladesh, Belgium, Canada, China, Czechia, Denmark, Finland, France, Germany, Greece, India, Ireland, Italy, Japan, Kenya, Kuwait, Malaysia, Norway, Puerto Rico, Saudi Arabia, South Africa, Sweden, Switzerland, UK, United Arab Emirates, USA. [2015.06.01/XJ3116/**E**]

- ♦ **BFS IOA** BFS International Operators Association (#03224)
- ♦ **BFS IOA** Pharmaceutical BFS International Operators Association (#18347)
- ♦ BFTA – Baltic Free Trade Area (no recent information)
- ♦ BFW – Bread for the World, USA (internationally oriented national body)
- ♦ BFWI / see Bread for the World Institute
- ♦ BFW Institute – Bread for the World Institute (internationally oriented national body)
- ♦ BGA / see Association of MBAs (#02795)
- ♦ **BGA** Behavior Genetics Association (#03194)
- ♦ **BGCI** Botanic Gardens Conservation International (#03306)
- ♦ **BGF** Balkan Türkleri Göçmenleri ve Mülteci Dernekleri Federasyonu (#03089)
- ♦ BGF – Borngreat Foundation (internationally oriented national body)
- ♦ **BGI** Bureau gravimétrique international (#03361)
- ♦ BGR – Buddhist Global Relief (internationally oriented national body)
- ♦ **BGRI** Borlaug Global Rust Initiative (#03305)
- ♦ **BGS** Balkan Geophysical Society (#03074)
- ♦ BGS / see International Glaciological Society (#13718)
- ♦ **BGS** International Society for Board Game Studies (#14980)
- ♦ BGS – Parvi Fratres Boni Pastoris (religious order)
- ♦ Bhaktivédanta Archives Europe / see Bhaktivedanta Library Services asbl
- ♦ Bhaktivedanta College / see Bhaktivedanta Library Services asbl
- ♦ Bhaktivedanta Library Services asbl (internationally oriented national body)
- ♦ **BHF** Business Humanitarian Forum (#03383)
- ♦ **BHGI** Breast Health Global Initiative (#03318)
- ♦ BHI – Basic Health International (internationally oriented national body)
- ♦ **BHI** Bau- und Holzarbeiter Internationale (#03355)
- ♦ BHNO Association – Baltic States Head and Neck Oncology Association (internationally oriented national body)
- ♦ BHVI – Brien Holden Vision Institute (internationally oriented national body)
- ♦ BIA / see International Action for Liberation
- ♦ BIA – Bureau international antimilitariste contre la guerre et la réaction (inactive)
- ♦ **BIAC** Business and Industry Advisory Committee to the OECD (#03385)
- ♦ BIAD – Bureau international d'anthropologie différentielle (inactive)
- ♦ BIAMS – International Conference on Beam Injection Assessment of Microstructures in Semiconductors (meeting series)
- ♦ BIAO – Banque internationale pour l'Afrique de l'Ouest (inactive)
- ♦ **BIAP** Bureau international d'audiophonologie (#03362)
- ♦ **BIAU** Bienal Iberoamericana de Arquitectura y Urbanismo (#03230)
- ♦ **BI** Baccalauréat International (#12306)
- ♦ **BIBC** Brussels International Banking Club (#03342)
- ♦ BI – Befrienders International (inactive)
- ♦ **BI** Bildungsinternationale (#05371)
- ♦ BI – Bioline International (internationally oriented national body)
- ♦ **BI** BioNET INTERNATIONAL – Global Network for Taxonomy (#03253)
- ♦ Bible Churchmen's Missionary Society / see Crosslinks
- ♦ BibleLands / see Embrace the Middle East
- ♦ Bible Lands Society / see Embrace the Middle East
- ♦ Bible League / see Bible League International (#03225)

♦ Bible League International 03225

Headquarters 1 Bible League Plaza, Crete IL 60417, USA. T. +18668254636. Fax +17083678600. E-mail: info@bibleleague.org.
URL: http://www.bibleleague.org/
History 1938, USA. 1938, as *World Home Bible League.* Subsequently referred to as *International Association of Bible Leagues.* From 1989 referred to as *Bible League.* **Aims** Provide scriptures worldwide; ensure that the scriptures are used for *evangelism, discipleship* and *church* growth. **Structure** Board of Directors; Executive Team; President. **Activities** Networking/liaising; training/education; guidance/assistance/consulting.
Members Bible leagues in 9 countries:
Australia, Canada, Germany, Netherlands, New Zealand, Singapore, Switzerland, UK, USA.
Bible League offices in 27 countries ("*" indicates head office):
Australia, Belarus, Bulgaria, Cambodia, Canada, Colombia, Dominican Rep, Egypt, Ethiopia, Germany, Kenya, Mexico, Moldova, Mozambique, Netherlands, New Zealand, Philippines, Romania, Russia, South Africa, Taiwan, Thailand, Uganda, UK, Ukraine, USA (*), Zimbabwe.
NGO Relations Member of: *Forum of Bible Agencies International (#09903).* [2020/XG1192/**D**]

- ♦ Bible Medical and Missionary Fellowship / see Interserve (#15974)
- ♦ Bible Society (internationally oriented national body)
- ♦ BI – Blessings International (internationally oriented national body)
- ♦ Biblica (internationally oriented national body)

♦ Bibliographical Society 03226

Hon Sec c/o Inst of English Studies, Senate House, Malet Street, London, WC1E 7H4, UK. T. +442078628680.
URL: http://www.bibsoc.org.uk/
History 1892. **Aims** Promote and encourage study and research in the fields of: historical, analytical, descriptive and textual bibliography; the history of printing, publishing, bookselling, bookbinding and collecting. **Languages** English. **Finance** Members' dues. **Activities** Holds meetings; publishes work concerned with bibliography; maintains bibliographical library; awards a medal for services to bibliography; awards grants and bursaries. **Publications** *The Library* (4 a year).
Members Individuals in 26 countries and territories:
Argentina, Australia, Belgium, Canada, China, Denmark, Finland, France, Germany, Greece, Ireland, Italy, Japan, Korea Rep, Luxembourg, Netherlands, New Zealand, Poland, Russia, South Africa, Spain, Sweden, Switzerland, Taiwan, UK, USA. [2018.01.24/XF4694/v/**F**]

- ♦ Biblionef International (internationally oriented national body)
- ♦ Biblioteca Interamericana Simón Bolivar (#19283)
- ♦ Biblioteca Internacional de la Juventud (#15936)
- ♦ Biblioteca Regional de Caribe / see Caribbean and Latin American Studies Library
- ♦ Biblioteca Regional del Caribe y de Estudios Latinoamericanos (internationally oriented national body)
- ♦ Biblioteca Regional de Medicina / see Latin American and Caribbean Centre on Health Sciences Information (#16267)
- ♦ Bibliotechnoj Assamblei Evrazii (#16458)

♦ Bibliotheca Alexandrina Council of Patrons 03227

Contact Bibliotheca Alexandrina, PO Box 138, El Shatby, Alexandria, 21526, Egypt. T. +2034839999. Fax +2034820450. E-mail: secretariat@bibalex.org.
URL: http://www.bibalex.org/

History Apr 2002, on inauguration of the Library, replacing *International Commission for the Revival of the Ancient Library of Alexandria (inactive)*. **Aims** Provide high-level patronage and moral support to the project for the revival of the Ancient Library of Alexandria (Bibliotheca Alexandrina). **Structure** Council of up to 24 members, meets every 3 years. Board of Trustees. **Members** High-ranking persons (24) in the field of politics, sciences, literature and arts. Membership countries not specified. **IGO Relations** *European Commission (EC, #06633)*; *UNESCO (#20322)*. Houses: *Anna Lindh Euro-Mediterranean Foundation for the Dialogue between Cultures (Anna Lindh Foundation, #00847)*. **NGO Relations** Houses: *Arab Network for Women in Science and Technology (ANWST, #01015)*; *Arab Society for Ethics in Science and Technology (ASEST)*; *Middle East and North Africa Network for Environmental Economics (MENANEE, no recent information)*. Affiliate of: *International Association of Universities (IAU, #12246)*. [2015/XE4332/E*]

♦ Bibliotheca Baltica 03228

Sec c/o Herder-Inst – Forschungsbibliothek, Gisonenweg 5-7, 35037 Marburg, Germany. T. +496421184150. Fax +496421184139.
Pres c/o Gaia Leadership, M.aster Samuelsgatan 42, SE-111 57 Stockholm, Sweden.
URL: http://baltica.lnb.lv/

History 1992, during the first symposium in Lübeck (Germany), in the framework of *ARS BALTICA (#01114)*. Full title: *Bibliotheca Baltica – Working Group for the Cooperation between Libraries of the Baltic Sea Area*. **Aims** Promote cooperation between libraries in the Baltic Sea area; promote the awareness of the cultural, historical and artistic heritage of the Baltic Sea region by fostering information exchange between *libraries* as keepers of this heritage. **Structure** Board, comprising Director, Treasurer, Secretary and 3 members. **Languages** English. **Staff** None. **Finance** Members' dues. Support from bilateral and national organizations. **Activities** Organizes symposia (every 2 years). Maintains electronic discussion list. **Events** *Symposium* Lübeck (Germany) 2022, *Symposium* Rostock (Germany) 2018, *Symposium* Riga (Latvia) 2016, *Symposium* Stockholm (Sweden) 2014, *Symposium* Tallinn (Estonia) 2012. **Publications** *Bibliotheca Baltica Newsletter* (2 a year). Proceedings.
Members Libraries, librarians' organizations and individuals. Members in 10 countries:
Denmark, Estonia, Finland, Germany, Latvia, Lithuania, Norway, Poland, Russia, Sweden. [2012.07.03/XE2299/D]

- ♦ Bibliotheca Baltica – Working Group for the Cooperation between Libraries of the Baltic Sea Area / see Bibliotheca Baltica (#03228)
- ♦ Bibliotheksassemblee Eurasiens (#16458)
- ♦ Bibliothèque interaméricaine Simón Bolivar (#19283)
- ♦ Bibliothèque internationale sur l'architecture de terre (internationally oriented national body)
- ♦ Bibliothèque internationale des assurances de Louvain (internationally oriented national body)
- ♦ Bibliothèque internationale de la jeunesse (#15936)
- ♦ Bibliothèques européennes de théologie (#08906)

♦ Bibliothèques Sans Frontières (BSF) 03229

Libraries Without Borders (LWB)

Paris Office 8-10 rue de Valmy, 93100 Montreuil, France. T. +33184161903.
Washington DC Office 1342 Florida Avenue NW, Washington DC 20009, USA.
URL: http://www.bibliosansfrontieres.org/

History 2007, France. US Branch set up 2008. Canadian branch functions under title *Fondation pour une bibliothèque globale (FBG) BSF*. **Aims** Address the structural causes of economic and human underdevelopment through promotion of better and innovative educative practices, providing access to lifelong learning and training, helping disseminate information and knowledge, reducing the digital divide and promoting cultural heritage. **Structure** Branches in 5 countries: France; USA; Canada; Belgium; Switzerland. **Activities** Capacity building; knowledge management/information dissemination; training/education. [2022/XN6903/F]

- ♦ BIBM / see Bureau international du béton manufacturé (#03363)
- ♦ **BIBM** Bureau international du béton manufacturé (#03363)
- ♦ BIBOA / see CIBJO – The World Jewellery Confederation (#03923)
- ♦ BIBOAH / see CIBJO – The World Jewellery Confederation (#03923)
- ♦ BI – Bridge Initiative International (internationally oriented national body)
- ♦ BI – Brookings Institution (internationally oriented national body)
- ♦ BICA – Biologically Inspired Cognitive Architectures Society (internationally oriented national body)
- ♦ **BICAM** Catholic Biblical Centre for Africa and Madagascar (#03599)
- ♦ BICA Society / see Biologically Inspired Cognitive Architectures Society
- ♦ BIC – Bank Information Center (internationally oriented national body)
- ♦ BIC – Bear Information Centre (internationally oriented national body)
- ♦ **BIC** Bio-based Industries Consortium (#03238)
- ♦ BIC – Bureau international de la chaussure et de cuir (inactive)
- ♦ BIC – Bureau international du cinéma (inactive)
- ♦ BIC / see Bureau international des containers et du transport intermodal (#03364)
- ♦ **BIC** Bureau international des containers et du transport intermodal (#03364)
- ♦ **BICC** Bonn International Center for Conversion (#03300)
- ♦ BICC / see World Chambers Federation (#21269)
- ♦ **BICE** Bureau international catholique de l'enfance (#12450)
- ♦ BICEPS – Baltic International Centre for Economic Policy Studies (internationally oriented national body)
- ♦ **BICG** Baltic Institute of Corporate Governance (#03121)
- ♦ BICG – BioNET INTERNATIONAL Consultative Group (inactive)
- ♦ Biciklista Esperantista Movado Internacia (#11878)
- ♦ BICO – Bureau international d'information et de coopération des éditeurs de musique (inactive)
- ♦ **BICSI** Building Industry Consulting Service International (#03352)
- ♦ BICWM – Brethren in Christ World Missions (internationally oriented national body)
- ♦ Bicycles for Africa / see velafrica
- ♦ Bicycles for Humanity (internationally oriented national body)
- ♦ **BID** Banco Interamericano de Desarrollo (#11427)
- ♦ **BID** Banco Interamericano de Desenvolvimento (#11427)
- ♦ **BID** Banque interaméricaine de développement (#11427)
- ♦ **BID** Banque islamique de développement (#16044)
- ♦ BID – Bund Internationaler Detektive (internationally oriented national body)
- ♦ **BIDC** Banque d'Investissement et de Développement de la CEDEAO (#05334)
- ♦ BIDC – Bureau interafricain de développement et de coopération (inactive)
- ♦ BIDE – Bureau international de documentation éducative (inactive)
- ♦ BiD Network – Business in Development Network (internationally oriented national body)
- ♦ BIDR – Jacob Blaustein Institute for Desert Research (internationally oriented national body)
- ♦ BIDS – Bangladesh Institute of Development Studies (internationally oriented national body)
- ♦ BIE / see Institute for Housing and Urban Development Studies
- ♦ BIEA – British Institute in Eastern Africa (internationally oriented national body)
- ♦ **BIE** Bureau international d'éducation (#12413)
- ♦ BIE – Bureau international de l'environnement (inactive)
- ♦ **BIE** Bureau International des Expositions (#03365)
- ♦ BIEF – Bureau international de l'édition française (internationally oriented national body)
- ♦ BIE / see International Union for Electricity Applications (#15770)
- ♦ **BIEM** Bureau international des sociétés gérant les droits d'enregistrement et de reproduction mécanique (#12416)

♦ Bienal Iberoamericana de Arquitectura y Urbanismo (BIAU) 03230

Permanent Secretariat CSCAE, Paseo de la Castellana 12, 28046 Madrid, Spain. T. +34914352200. Fax +34915753839. E-mail: biau@cscae.com.
URL: http://www.bienalesdearquitectura.es/

History Spain, by the government of Spain. **Structure** Executive Committee; Management Committee; Permanent Secretariat. **Staff** 2.00 FTE, paid. **Events** *Meeting* Rosario (Argentina) 2014, *Meeting* Cadiz (Spain) 2012, *Meeting* Medellin (Colombia) 2010, *Meeting* Lisbon (Portugal) 2008, *Meeting* Montevideo (Uruguay) 2006. [2018/XJ6975/c/E]

- ♦ BIEN / see Basic Income Earth Network (#03186)
- ♦ **BIEN** Basic Income Earth Network (#03186)

♦ Biennale de la langue française (BLF) 03231

SG 146 rue de Paris, 94220 Charenton-le-Pont, France. E-mail: info@biennale-lf.org.
Registered Office 23 rue Greneta, 75002 Paris, France.
URL: http://www.biennale-lf.org/

History 14 May 1963. Founded as *Société des amis du français universel*. Took over activities of *Fédération du français universel (inactive)*, 1991. Registration: Start date: 11 Apr 2000, France. **Aims** Assist and support individuals, notably professors of the *French language*, and organizations who work to protect the specific qualities and unity of the French language in its diversity and also in the diversity of cultures that it conveys. **Structure** General Assembly (annual); Administrative Council; Bureau; Honorary Committee. **Languages** French. **Staff** 7.00 FTE, paid. **Finance** Members' dues. Grants. **Activities** Events/meetings. **Events** *Biennale de la Langue Française* Berlin (Germany) 2022, *Biennale de la Langue Française* Chicago, IL (USA) 2019, *Biennale de la Langue Française* Paris (France) 2017, *Biennale de la Langue Française* Cluj-Napoca (Romania) 2015, *Biennale de la Langue Française* Bordeaux (France) 2013. **Publications** *Florilège des vingt premières biennales de la langue française* by Jeanne Ogée. Actes des biennales; bulletin; books.
Members Honorary; Benefactor; Active/Adhering. Organizations in 6 countries:
Canada, Congo DR, France, Senegal, Switzerland, USA.
Individuals in 20 countries:
Algeria, Belgium, Benin, Burkina Faso, Canada, Dominican Rep, France, Italy, Mali, Mauritius, Morocco, Nigeria, Norway, Romania, Senegal, Slovakia, Switzerland, Tunisia, UK, USA.
Consultative Status Consultative status granted from: *Organisation internationale de la Francophonie (OIF, #17809)*. **NGO Relations** Member of: *Association francophone d'amitié et de liaison (AFAL, #02605)*. [2022/XF6233/v/F]

- ♦ Biennial of the Americas (internationally oriented national body)
- ♦ Biennial Symposium on Measuring Techniques in Turbomachinery (meeting series)
- ♦ **BIF-EC** Brain Injured and Families European Confederation (#03314)
- ♦ BIF European Confederation / see Brain Injured and Families European Confederation (#03314)
- ♦ BIFMA / see BIFMA International
- ♦ BIFMA International (internationally oriented national body)
- ♦ BIG against breast cancer / see Breast International Group (#03319)
- ♦ **BIG** Breast International Group (#03319)
- ♦ Big Brothers Big Sisters International (internationally oriented national body)

♦ Big Data Value Association (BDVA) 03232

Secretariat c/o INDRA, Rue Froissart 95, 1040 Brussels, Belgium. E-mail: info@core.bdva.eu – secretariat1@core.bdva.eu.
URL: http://www.bdva.eu/

History Founded as the private counterpart to the *European Commission (EC, #06633)* to implement the Bid Data Value PPP programme, which was launched 2014. **Aims** Develop the Innovation Ecosystem that will enable the data and AI-driven digital transformation in Europe delivering maximum economic and societal benefit, and, achieving and sustaining Europe's leadership on Big Data Value creation and Artificial Intelligence. **Structure** General Assembly; Board of Directors; Partnership Board; Secretariat. Task Forces. **Events** *European Big Data Community Forum* Brussels (Belgium) 2019, *European Big Data Community Forum* Brussels (Belgium) 2019, *European Big Data Value Forum* Helsinki (Finland) 2019, *European Big Data Value Forum* Paris (France) 2017, *Summit* Madrid (Spain) 2015.
Members Full; Associate. Members in 27 countries:
Austria, Belgium, Bulgaria, Croatia, Cyprus, Czechia, Denmark, Finland, France, Germany, Greece, Ireland, Israel, Italy, Latvia, Luxembourg, Netherlands, Norway, Poland, Portugal, Romania, Serbia, Slovakia, Spain, Sweden, Türkiye, UK.
NGO Relations Member of (1): *European High Performance Computing Joint Undertaking (EuroHPC JU, #07485)*. [2020/XM8842/E]

- ♦ BIGGA – British and International Golf Greenkeepers Association (internationally oriented national body)
- ♦ **Big Life** Big Life Foundation (#03233)

♦ Big Life Foundation (Big Life) 03233

Outreach Associate 1715 North Heron Drive, Ridgefield WA 98642, USA. T. +19713223326. E-mail: donations@biglife.org.
UK c/o Chapel and York Ltd, Unit 12 Ladycross Business Park, Hollow Lane, Dormansland, RH7 6PB, UK. E-mail: uk@biglife.org.
URL: http://biglife.org/

History Sep 2010. Registration: 501(c)(3) organization, Start date: 2011, USA, WA; List of Charities, No/ID: 82252 3288 RR0001, Canada; Charity Commission, No/ID: 1158772, Start date: 3 Oct 2014, England and Wales. **Aims** Collaborate with local communities, partner NGOs, national parks and government agencies to protect and sustain East Africa's *wildlife* and wild lands, including one of the greatest populations of *elephants* left in East Africa. **Structure** Board of Directors. Branches in: Kenya; USA; Canada; UK. **Activities** Awareness raising; networking/liaising; projects/programmes. Active in: Canada, Kenya, Tanzania UR, UK, USA. **NGO Relations** Partners include: *African Wildlife Foundation (AWF, #00498)*; *Elephant Protection Initiative Foundation (EPI Foundation, #05429)*; *Empowers Africa*; *Ivory For Elephants (IFE)*; *Perfect World Foundation*; *Save the Elephants (STE)*; *Save the Rhino International (SRI, #19061)*; *Sheldrick Wildlife Trust (SWT)*; *Space for Giants*; *Thin Green Line Foundation*; *TUSK*; *WildAid*. [2022.05.03/XM5137/f/F]

- ♦ BI – Global Network for Biosystematics of Invertebrates and Microorganisms / see BioNET INTERNATIONAL – Global Network for Taxonomy (#03253)
- ♦ BIH – Bureau international de l'heure (inactive)
- ♦ BIHR – British Institute of Human Rights (internationally oriented national body)
- ♦ **BIIA** Business Information Industry Association (#03386)
- ♦ BIICL – British Institute of International and Comparative Law (internationally oriented national body)
- ♦ BIISS – Bangladesh Institute of International and Strategic Studies (internationally oriented national body)
- ♦ **BIJ** Biblioteca Internacional de la Juventud (#15936)
- ♦ BIJ – Bureau international jeunesse de la Communauté française de Belgique (internationally oriented national body)
- ♦ Bike for Peace (internationally oriented national body)
- ♦ BIL – Bureau international du loisir (inactive)
- ♦ Bilderbergers / see Bilderberg Meetings (#03234)
- ♦ Bilderberg Group / see Bilderberg Meetings (#03234)

♦ Bilderberg Meetings 03234

Réunions Bilderberg

Chair c/o AXA, 25 Avenue Matignon, 75008 Paris, France.
URL: http://www.bilderbergmeetings.org

History May 1954, Oosterbeek (Netherlands), at the Hotel de Bilderberg, as a series of annual conferences. Also referred to as *Bilderberg Group – Groupe Bilderberg*; *Bilderbergers*. **Aims** Provide an informal atmosphere for off-the-record discussions on *political, economic* and *military problems* of mutual concern, between politicians, scholars, businessmen and labour leaders from the *North Atlantic* countries. **Structure** No formal organization; no membership, charter or elected group of officers. Invitations to Bilderberg conferences are made by Chairman, following consultation and recommendations by Steering Committee membership, Advisory Group and Honorary Secretaries General. Attendance is by invitation of the Chairman. **Finance** Expenses of meetings covered wholly by private subscription. Hospitality costs of the annual meeting are the responsibility of Steering Committee member(s) of the host country. **Activities** Principal activity is the Conference programme. **Events** *Conference* Copenhagen (Denmark) 2014, *Conference* Watford (UK) 2013, *Conference* Chantilly, VA (USA) 2012, *Conference* St Moritz (Switzerland) 2011, *Conference* Sitges (Spain) 2010.

Members Steering Committee and Advisory Group members from 19 countries:
Austria, Belgium, Canada, Denmark, Finland, France, Germany, Greece, Iceland, Italy, Netherlands, Norway, Portugal, Spain, Sweden, Switzerland, Türkiye, UK, USA. [2013/XF4365/c/F]

- ♦ Bildner Center for Western Hemisphere Studies, New York (internationally oriented national body)
- ♦ Bildungs- und Begegnungsstätte für gewaltfreie Aktion / see KURVE Wustrow
- ♦ Bildungsinternationale (#05371)

♦ Bilingual World 03235

Monde bilingue

Pres 9 rue de la Famille, 25000 Besançon, France. T. +33381884779. Fax +33381506874.

History Founded 27 Aug 1951, Paris (France), by a group of former members of the Resistance Movement, to bring about peace by direct people-to-people cooperation, through bilingual education and town-twinning. Registered in accordance with French law. **Aims** With a view to improving communications among peoples, introduce a new education in the field of living languages based on education conducted right from childhood in two *languages*; remove the linguistic factor from racism so that peoples no longer see each other as foreign; construct a multilingual Europe. **Structure** Set up the international programme *Pax Linguis*, Aosta (Italy). **Staff** Voluntary. **Finance** Voluntary contributions; subsidies. **Events** *International Conference* Tlemcen (Algeria) 2002, *Babylon international conference / International Conference* Baghdad (Iraq) 2001, *International Conference* Luxembourg (Luxembourg) 1996, *International Conference* Luxembourg (Luxembourg) 1994, *International conference on multilingualism in Europe / International Conference* Barcelona (Spain) 1991. **Publications** *La paix par les langues* in English, French, German; *Trilogie d'une politique linguistique pluraliste* in English, French, German.

Members Full in 63 countries:
Albania, Angola, Austria, Bahrain, Bangladesh, Belgium, Brazil, Bulgaria, Burundi, Canada, Cape Verde, Chad, Chile, China, Colombia, Côte d'Ivoire, Croatia, Cuba, Czechia, Ecuador, Egypt, Finland, France, Gabon, Germany, Greece, Guyana, Haiti, Holy See, Hungary, India, Indonesia, Ireland, Italy, Jamaica, Japan, Kuwait, Lebanon, Libya, Luxembourg, Madagascar, Mali, Morocco, Nicaragua, Niger, Nigeria, Palestine, Peru, Poland, Portugal, Romania, Russia, Rwanda, Senegal, Spain, Switzerland, Syrian AR, Togo, Tunisia, UK, Ukraine, USA, Vietnam.

NGO Relations Instrumental in setting up and close relations with: *European Language Council (ELC, #07646)*; *World Federation of United Cities (UTO, inactive)*. [2014/XF2479/F]

- ♦ Billiard Congress of America (internationally oriented national body)
- ♦ Billion Minds Foundation – Global Foundation for the Sustainability of Billion Minds (internationally oriented national body)
- ♦ Bill and Melinda Gates Foundation (internationally oriented national body)
- ♦ BILYAY – Insanligi Birlestiren Bilgiyi Yayma Vakfi (internationally oriented national body)
- ♦ BIM / see American Baptist International Ministries

♦ BIMCO 03236

SG/CEO Bagsvaerdvej 161, 2880 Bagsvaerd, Denmark. T. +4544366800. E-mail: mailbox@bimco.org.
Brussels Office Sq de Meeûs 35, 1000 Brussels, Belgium. E-mail: gja@bimco.org.
URL: http://www.bimco.org/

History 1905, Copenhagen (Denmark). Former names and other names: *Baltic and White Sea Conference* – former (1905 to 1927); *Baltic and International Maritime Conference* – former (1927 to 1985); *Conférence maritime baltique et internationale* – former (1927 to 1985); *Baltic and International Maritime Council* – full title (1985); *Conseil maritime baltique et international* – full title (1985). Registration: EU Transparency Register, No/ID: 31226213614-86. **Aims** Unite *shipowners* and other companies and individuals connected with the shipping industry; be a spokesman for and give advice on matters affecting the industry; gather and communicate to members useful information and also instances of unfair charges and claims, freight speculation, objectionable charter-parties and other practices; prepare and improve charter-parties and other shipping documents. **Structure** General Meeting (every 2 years); Board of Directors; Executive Committee; Documentary Committee. Meetings closed. **Languages** English. **Staff** 45.00 FTE, paid. **Finance** Sources: members' dues. **Activities** Advocacy/lobbying/activism; guidance/assistance/consulting; standards/guidelines; training/education. **Events** *Asia Pacific Maritime Conference* Singapore (Singapore) 2020, *Bunker Fuel and Ballast Water Compliance Conference* Singapore (Singapore) 2019, *Piracy and Sea Robbery Conference* Singapore (Singapore) 2019, *Road to Recovery Seminar* Singapore (Singapore) 2018, *Supplytime Seminar* Singapore (Singapore) 2018. **Publications** *BIMCO Bulletin* (4 a year); *BIMCO Holiday Calendar* (annual); *BIMCO Reflections* (annual); *Freight Taxes* (annual); *Check before Fixing* (every 2 years); *Forms of Approved Documents*. *BIMCO/ISF Manpower Update* (2005). Bulletins; handbooks, Shipmasters security manual.

Members Owner-members, broker-members, club-members, associate members (508 million deadweight tons of shipping entered). Individuals in 117 countries and territories:
Algeria, Angola, Argentina, Australia, Austria, Azerbaijan, Azores, Bahamas, Bahrain, Bangladesh, Belgium, Bermuda, Brazil, Bulgaria, Canada, Canaries, Cape Verde, Cayman Is, Chile, China, Colombia, Costa Rica, Côte d'Ivoire, Croatia, Cuba, Cyprus, Czechia, Denmark, Dominican Rep, Ecuador, Egypt, Equatorial Guinea, Estonia, Ethiopia, Faeroe Is, Finland, France, Gambia, Georgia, Germany, Ghana, Gibraltar, Greece, Haiti, Honduras, Hong Kong, Hungary, Iceland, India, Indonesia, Iran Islamic Rep, Ireland, Israel, Italy, Japan, Jordan, Kenya, Korea DPR, Korea Rep, Kuwait, Latvia, Lebanon, Liberia, Libya, Lithuania, Malaysia, Malta, Mauritius, Mexico, Monaco, Morocco, Mozambique, Netherlands, New Zealand, Nigeria, Norway, Oman, Pakistan, Panama, Papua New Guinea, Peru, Philippines, Poland, Portugal, Qatar, Romania, Russia, Saudi Arabia, Senegal, Serbia, Sierra Leone, Singapore, Slovakia, Slovenia, South Africa, Spain, Sri Lanka, Sudan, Sweden, Switzerland, Syrian AR, Taiwan, Tanzania UR, Thailand, Trinidad-Tobago, Tunisia, Türkiye, UK, Ukraine, United Arab Emirates, Uruguay, USA, Venezuela, Vietnam, Virgin Is UK, Yemen.

Consultative Status Consultative status granted from: *ECOSOC (#05331)* (Ros C); *UNCTAD (#20285)* (Special Category); *International Maritime Organization (IMO, #14102)*. **IGO Relations** Memorandum of Understanding with: *Regional Cooperation Agreement on Combating Piracy and Armed Robbery against Ships in Asia – Information Sharing Centre (ReCAAP ISC, #18771)*; *World Customs Organization (WCO, #21350)*. Observer status with: *International Oil Pollution Compensation Funds (IOPC Funds, #14402)*. **NGO Relations** Member of: *International Maritime Statistics Forum (IMSF, #14105)*; *International Salvage Union (ISU, #14779)*; *Maritime Piracy Humanitarian Response Programme (MPHRP, #16583)*. Instrumental in setting up: *Maritime Industry Foundation*. [2023/XD0183/v/C]

- ♦ **BIMP-EAGA** Brunei Darussalam-Indonesia-Malaysia-Philippine – East ASEAN Growth Area (#03340)
- ♦ **BIMST-EC** / see Bay of Bengal Initiative for Multi-Sectoral Technical and Economic Cooperation (#03188)
- ♦ **BIMSTEC** Bay of Bengal Initiative for Multi-Sectoral Technical and Economic Cooperation (#03188)
- ♦ **BIMT** Bureau international de mécanique des terrains (#12417)
- ♦ BINA – Bureau international de normalisation de l'automobile (inactive)
- ♦ BING / see Federation of European Rigid Polyurethane Foam Associations (#09538)
- ♦ **BIN-Norden** Barnekulturforskning i Norden (#03179)
- ♦ **BINSA** International Black Sea Region Association of Shipowners (#12359)
- ♦ BINUB – United Nations Integrated Office in Burundi (inactive)
- ♦ BINUC – Bureau intégré des Nations Unies pour le Cambodge (no recent information)
- ♦ BIO / see Biotechnology Innovation Organization

♦ Biobanking and BioMolecular resources Research Infrastructure (BBMRI-ERIC) 03237

Dir Gen Neue Stiftingtalstr 2/B/6, 8010 Graz, Austria. T. +433163499170. Fax +4331634991799. E-mail: contact@bbmri-eric.eu.
URL: https://www.bbmri-eric.eu/

History 3 Dec 2013, Graz (Austria). Set up initially as a project under *European Research Infrastructure Preparatory Phase*, 2008. Awarded the status of *European Research Infrastructure Consortium (ERIC)*, 3 Dec 2013. **Aims** Establish, operate and develop a pan-European distributed research infrastructure of biobanks and biomolecular resources so as to facilitate access to resources as well as facilities and support high quality biomolecular and medical research. **Structure** Assembly; Steering Committee; Finance Committee; Scientific and Ethical Advisory Board; Stakeholder Forum; Management Committee. **Staff** 20.00 FTE, paid. **Finance** Sources: members' dues. **Activities** Events/meetings; projects/programmes. **Events** *Europe Biobank Week Meeting* Aix-en-Provence (France) 2020, *Europe Biobank Week Meeting* Lübeck (Germany) 2019, *Biobank Conference* Oslo (Norway) 2018. **Publications** *BBMRI-ERIC Newsletter* (12 a year). *Handbook of Biomarkers and Precision Medicine* (2019) by Claudio Carini et al; *Biobanking of Human Biospecimens – Principles and Practice* (2017) by Markus Pasterk et al. Articles; reports; papers. **Information Services** *BBMRI-ERIC Directory* – biobank catalogue.

Members Members States (16):
Austria, Belgium, Bulgaria, Czechia, Estonia, Finland, Germany, Greece, Italy, Latvia, Malta, Netherlands, Norway, Poland, Sweden, UK.

Observer countries (4):
Cyprus, Lithuania, Switzerland, Türkiye.

Observer organization (1):
International Agency for Research on Cancer (IARC, #11598).

IGO Relations *European Commission (EC, #06633)*. **NGO Relations** Member of (1): *EU Health Coalition*. [2020.09.02/XM5204/E*]

♦ Bio-based Industries Consortium (BIC) 03238

Exec Dir c/o European Forestry House, Rue du Luxembourg 66, 1000 Brussels, Belgium. E-mail: info@biconsortium.eu.
URL: http://biconsortium.eu/

History 2013, Brussels (Belgium). Represents the private sector in a Public-Private Partnership (PPP) with *European Commission (EC, #06633)*, also known as *Bio-based Industries Joint Undertaking (BBI JU, #03239)*. Registration: Banque-Carrefour des Entreprises, No/ID: 0521.857.822, Start date: 8 Mar 2013, Belgium. **Aims** Accelerate the innovation and market uptake of bio-based products; position Europe as a world-leading, competitive bio-based economy where the basic building blocks for chemicals, materials and advanced *biofuels* are derived from *renewable* biological *resources*. **Structure** General Assembly; Board; Executive Committee; Office. Working Groups. **Events** *General Assembly* Brussels (Belgium) 2020, *General Assembly* Brussels (Belgium) 2019, *Stakeholder Forum on Bio-based Industries Joint Undertaking Programme* Brussels (Belgium) 2019, *Bioeconomy Conference* Brussels (Belgium) 2018, *Meeting* Brussels (Belgium) 2018. **Members** Full; Associate. Membership countries not specified. **IGO Relations** *European Union (EU, #08967)*. **NGO Relations** Member of (2): *European Bioeconomy Alliance (EUBA, #06334)* (Founding); *Industry4Europe (#11181)*. [2021/XM5748/t/D]

♦ Bio-based Industries Joint Undertaking (BBI JU) 03239

Exec Dir address not obtained.
URL: https://www.bbi.europa.eu/

History Established under *Council of the European Union (#04895)* Regulation No 560/2014, 6 May 2014. An independent legal entity managing the Public-Private Partnership (PPP) between *European Commission (EC, #06633)* and *Bio-based Industries Consortium (BIC, #03238)*. **Aims** Strengthen and structure the bio-based industries sector in Europe. **Structure** Governing Board; States Representative Group; Scientific Committee; Executive Director. **Finance** Budget: euro 3,700,000,000. **Events** *Stakeholder Forum on Bio-based Industries Joint Undertaking Programme* Brussels (Belgium) 2019. **NGO Relations** Member of (1): *EU Agencies Network (EUAN, #05564)*. [2020/AA1422/E]

- ♦ Bio Base Europe (internationally oriented national body)
- ♦ BIO – Biopolitics International Organisation (internationally oriented national body)
- ♦ BIO – Biotechnology Innovation Organization (internationally oriented national body)
- ♦ BIO – Brit Ivrit Olamit (no recent information)
- ♦ Biochemical Society (internationally oriented national body)
- ♦ BioCode / see International Committee on Bionomenclature (#12748)
- ♦ Biocosmological Association (unconfirmed)
- ♦ The Biodeterioration Society / see The International Biodeterioration and Biodegradation Society (#12344)
- ♦ Biodiversity Conservancy International (internationally oriented national body)
- ♦ Biodiversity convention – Convention on Biological Diversity (1992 treaty)

♦ Biodiversity and Economics for Conservation (BIOECON) 03240

Communications Officer c/o iDiv, Puschst 4, 04103 Leipzig, Germany.
URL: http://www.bioecon-network.org/

History Founded 2000, by *European Commission (EC, #06633)*, *DIVERSITAS – International Programme of Biodiversity Science (inactive)*, *International Food Policy Research Institute (IFPRI, #13622)*, *International Union for Conservation of Nature and Natural Resources (IUCN, #15766)*, *OECD (#17693)*, *UN Environment Programme World Conservation Monitoring Centre (UNEP-WCMC, #20295)*, Genetic Resources Institute and UK-DEFRA. **Aims** Investigate economic and policy driven forces responsible for decline of biodiversity; develop and implement tools accordingly. **Structure** Moderator. **Languages** English. **Staff** Part-time. **Finance** Founding partners provide contribution to organize the BIOECON Annual Conference: about US$ 70,000. **Activities** Research/documentation; events/meetings. **Events** *Annual BIOECON Conference* Jackson, WY (USA) 2021, *BIOECON Conference* Wageningen (Netherlands) 2019, *International BIOECON Conference* Cambridge (UK) 2018, *BIOECON Conference* Tilburg (Netherlands) 2017, *International BIOECON Conference* Cambridge (UK) 2016. **Publications** Special issues.

Members Partners (29) in 17 countries:
Australia, Belgium, Denmark, France, Germany, Israel, Italy, Japan, Kenya, Monaco, Netherlands, Norway, South Africa, Spain, Switzerland, UK, USA.

Included in the above, 1 organization listed in this Yearbook:
Commonwealth Scientific and Industrial Research Organization (CSIRO). [2020/XJ3671/y/F]

♦ Biodiversity and Ecosystem Services Network (BES-Net) 03241

Project Manager GC-RED, Gigiri, Block M, Middle Level, PO Box 30218-00100, Nairobi, 30218, Kenya. T. +254207624640 – +254207624642. E-mail: info@besnet.world.
URL: http://www.besnet.world/

History 2016, Kenya. **Aims** Build capacity and commitment for biodiversity action across the world by translating the latest IPBES products into action for biodiversity and conservation on the ground. **Structure** Jointly implemented by UNDP, UNEP-WCMC (hosting the National Ecosystem Assessment Initiative) and UNESCO (providing technical support on indigenous and local knowledge since 2020). **Finance** Funded by the Government of Germany (through the International Climate Initiative) and SwedBio. **Activities** Awareness raising; capacity building; events/meetings; knowledge management/information dissemination; monitoring/evaluation; networking/liaising; projects/programmes; publishing activities. First phase (2016–2022) has successfully strengthened institutional coordination between science, policy and practice communities in more than 20 countries. Second phase kicked off in 2020, continuing to support countries with National Ecosystem Assessments and Trialogues to foster collaboration, prioritizing greater inclusion of indigenous peoples and local voices in decision-making, as well as channelling catalytic investments for biodiversity solutions that are locally led. Active in: Azerbaijan, Bosnia-Herzegovina, Botswana, Cambodia, Cameroon, Colombia, Dominican Rep, Ethiopia, Grenada, Kazakhstan, Kenya, Malawi, Nigeria, Thailand, Trinidad-Tobago, Vietnam. [2023.02.23/XM6841/F]

♦ Biodiversity Foundation for Africa (internationally oriented national body)

♦ Biodiversity Indicators Partnership (BIP) 03242

Secretariat UNEP World Conservation Monitoring Ctr, 219 Huntingdon Rd, Cambridge, CB3 0DL, UK. T. +441223814664. E-mail: info@bipindicators.net.
URL: http://www.bipindicators.net/

History 2004, as *2010 Biodiversity Indicators Partnership (2010 BIP)*, when Conference of Parties (COP 7) of *Convention on Biological Diversity (Biodiversity convention, 1992)* adopted a framework recommending the use of indicators (Decision VII/30) and requested its scientific advisory body to work further on these with a specially created expert group, called Ad Hoc Technical Expert Group (AHTEG). COP 8 further elaborated this framework in 2006 and acknowledged establishment of the Partnership listed under current title, 2007. Since 2007, has been mandated by several COP Decisions to support the identification and development of indicators for current Strategic Plan for Biodiversity 2011-2020. **Aims** Further develop and promote indicators for the consistent monitoring and assessment of biodiversity. **Structure** Steering Committee, including indicator users, providers and supporters: *Convention on Biological Diversity (Biodiversity convention, 1992)*; *Convention on Wetlands of International Importance Especially as Waterfowl Habitat (Convention on Wetlands, 1971)*; *European Commission (EC, #06633)*; *European Environment Agency (EEA, #06995)*; *FAO (#09260)*; *Forest Peoples Programme (FPP, #09865)*; *Global Footprint Network (#10367)*; *Group on Earth Observations (GEO, #10735)*; *Intergovernmental Science-Policy Platform on Biodiversity and Ecosystem Services (IPBES, #11500)*; *International Union for Conservation of Nature and Natural Resources (IUCN, #15766)*; *NatureServe*; *PEFC Council (#18288)*; *United Nations Convention to Combat Desertification (UNCCD, 1994)*; *UNEP (#20299)*; UN Statistics Division (UNSD); government representatives from China, Switzerland and Grenada. **Languages** Arabic, Chinese, English, French, Russian, Spanish.

Members International Indicator Partners (44):
- *Alliance for Zero Extinction (AZE, #00730)*;
- *ASEAN Centre for Biodiversity (ACB, #01149)*;
- *Bioversity International (#03262)*;
- *BirdLife International (#03266)*;
- *Circumpolar Biodiversity Monitoring Program (CBMP, #03941)*;
- *Commonwealth Scientific and Industrial Research Organization (CSIRO)*;
- *Conservation International (CI)*;
- *Convention on Biological Diversity (Biodiversity convention, 1992)*;
- *Convention on International Trade in Endangered Species of Wild Fauna and Flora (CITES, 1973)*;
- *Convention on Wetlands of International Importance Especially as Waterfowl Habitat (Convention on Wetlands, 1971)*;
- *European Bird Census Council (EBCC, #06347)*;
- *Forest Stewardship Council (FSC, #09869)*;
- *GEMS/Water (see: #20299)*;
- *Global Biodiversity Information Facility (GBIF, #10250)*;
- *Global Coral Reef Monitoring Network (GCRMN, #10306)*;
- *Global Crop Diversity Trust (Crop Trust, #10313)*;
- *Global Ocean Observing System (GOOS, #10511)*;
- *Global Reporting Initiative (GRI, #10567)*;
- *International Centre for Integrated Mountain Development (ICIMOD, #12500)*;
- *International Centre for Tropical Agriculture (#12527)*;
- *International Indigenous Forum on Biodiversity (IIFB, #13837)*;
- *International Nitrogen Initiative (INI, #14372)*;
- *International Treaty on Plant Genetic Resources for Food and Agriculture (2001)*;
- *Island Conservation (CI)*;
- IUCN Red List Partnership;
- IUCN Species Survival Commission (SSC);
- IUCN World Commission on Protected Areas (WCPA / CMAP);
- *Joint Research Centre (JRC, #16147)*;
- KBA Partnership;
- *Marine Stewardship Council (MSC, #16580)*;
- Nitrogen Footprint;
- *OECD (#17693)*;
- Reef Life Survey;
- Sea Around Us;
- *Terralingua – Unity in Biocultural Diversity (Terralingua, #20129)*;
- *TRAFFIC International (#20196)*;
- *UN Environment Programme World Conservation Monitoring Centre (UNEP-WCMC, #20295)*;
- *UNESCO (#20322)*;
- *Union for Ethical BioTrade (UEBT, #20381)*;
- *United Nations University – Institute for Water, Environment and Health (UNU-INWEH, see: #20642)*;
- *WHO (#20950)*;
- *Wildlife Conservation Society (WCS)*;
- Wildlife Insights;
- *World Association of Zoos and Aquariums (WAZA, #21208)*;
- *World Wide Fund for Nature (WWF, #21922)*. [2019.10.19/XJ2094/y/**E**]

♦ Biodiversity Information Standards (TDWG) 03243

Sec 57 rue Cuvier CP39, 75005 Paris, France. E-mail: secretary@tdwg.org.
Contact 1342 34th Ave, San Francisco CA 94122, USA. T. +14154203724.
URL: http://www.tdwg.org/

History 1985. Constituted as an association. Former names and other names: *International Working Group on Taxonomic Databases for Plant Sciences* – former (1985); *International Working Group on Taxonomic Databases* – former; *IUBS Commission on Taxonomic Databases* – alias. Registration: USA, State of California. **Aims** Develop standards for exchange of biological/biodiversity data. **Structure** General Assembly (annual); Executive Committee; Regional Secretaries (5); Functional Committees; Interest Groups; Task Groups. **Languages** English. **Staff** 0.50 FTE, paid. Several voluntary. **Finance** Sources: grants; members' dues; sponsorship. **Activities** Events/meetings; knowledge management/information dissemination; standards/guidelines. **Events** *Annual conference* Sofia (Bulgaria) 2022, *Annual Conference* Gainesville, FL (USA) 2021, *Annual Meeting* Meise (Belgium) 2020, *Conference* Meise (Belgium) 2020, *Annual Meeting* Leiden (Netherlands) 2019. **Publications** *Biodiversity Information Science and Standards (BISS)*. **Information Services** *Biodiversity Information Networks Database*.

Members Institutions and individuals in 15 countries:
Australia, Belgium, Brazil, Canada, Denmark, Germany, Japan, Netherlands, New Zealand, Norway, Spain, Sweden, Switzerland, UK, USA.

IGO Relations Cooperates with (1): *Global Biodiversity Information Facility (GBIF, #10250)*. **NGO Relations** Cooperates with (1): *Committee on Data for Science and Technology (CODATA, #04247)*. Scientific member of: *International Union of Biological Sciences (IUBS, #15760)*. [2022.12.13/XD2824/**D**]

♦ Biodynamic Agricultural Association of Southern Africa (internationally oriented national body)
♦ **BIOECON** Biodiversity and Economics for Conservation (#03240)

♦ Bioelectrochemical Society (BES) 03244

Société de bioélectrochimie

Pres Analytical Chemistry/Biochemistry, Lund Univ, SE-221 00 Lund, Sweden.
URL: http://www.bioelectrochemical-soc.org/

History 1979. **Aims** Promote understanding and cooperation among scientists interested in application of electrochemical concepts or techniques to the fundamental or applied study of living systems. **Structure** General Assembly; Council. **Languages** English, French. **Staff** Voluntary. **Finance** Members' dues. **Activities** Events/meetings; publishing activities; knowledge management/information dissemination; awards/prizes/competitions. **Events** *Biennial Symposium* Malmö (Sweden) 2015, *Biennial Symposium* Bochum (Germany) 2013, *Biennial Symposium* Krakow (Poland) 2011, *Biennial Symposium* Sibiu (Romania) 2009, *Biennial Symposium* Toulouse (France) 2007. **Publications** *Bioelectrochemistry* – journal.

Members Individuals in 37 countries:
Algeria, Argentina, Austria, Belgium, Bulgaria, Canada, Czechia, Denmark, Egypt, Finland, France, Germany, Greece, Hungary, India, Ireland, Israel, Italy, Japan, Lithuania, Morocco, Netherlands, New Zealand, Norway, Poland, Portugal, Romania, Russia, Saudi Arabia, Slovakia, Slovenia, South Africa, Spain, Sweden, Switzerland, UK, USA.

NGO Relations *European BioElectromagnetics Association (EBEA, #06335)*; *International Society of Electrochemistry (ISE, #15079)*. [2017/XD4649/v/**D**]

♦ The Bioelectromagnetics Society (BEMS) 03245

Contact c/o Hildebrand Limparis, 7101 Guilford Dr, Ste 200, Frederick MD 21704, USA. E-mail: office@bems.org – secretary@bems.org.
URL: http://www.bems.org/

History 1978, Washington, DC (USA). **Aims** Promote research on understanding of biological interactions of electromagnetic energy. **Structure** Board Officers: President; Treasurer; Secretary; Editor-in-Chief. **Languages** English. **Staff** Voluntary. **Events** *BioEM Annual Meeting* Nagoya (Japan) 2022, *BioEM Annual Meeting* Ghent (Belgium) 2021, *BioEM Annual Meeting* Oxford (UK) 2020, *BioEM Annual Meeting* Montpellier (France) 2019, *Annual Meeting* Portoroz (Slovenia) 2018. **Publications** *BEMS Journal* (8 a year). Conference proceedings.

Members Full in 41 countries and territories:
Argentina, Australia, Austria, Belgium, Brazil, Canada, Chile, China, Czechia, Denmark, Finland, France, Germany, Greece, Hungary, India, Ireland, Israel, Italy, Japan, Korea Rep, Latvia, Luxembourg, Mexico, Netherlands, New Zealand, Norway, Peru, Poland, Romania, Russia, Singapore, Slovenia, South Africa, Spain, Sweden, Switzerland, Taiwan, UK, Ukraine, USA. [2022/XF3047/**F**]

♦ Bioencapsulation Research Group (BRG) 03246

Pres 114 Allée Paul Signac, 44240 Sucé sur Erdre, France.
URL: http://bioencapsulation.net/

History 1990, Canada. Registration: Start date: 23 May 1994, France. **Aims** Promote exchange, collaboration and collaborative projects in microencapsulation. **Structure** Informal Steering Committee. President; Secretary; Treasurer. **Languages** English. **Staff** None paid. **Finance** Mainly through event participation fees. **Activities** Events/meetings; training/education. **Events** *International Conference on Bioencapsulation* Strasbourg (France) 2019, *International Conference on Bioencapsulation* La Chapelle-sur-Erdre (France) 2017, *International Conference on Bioencapsulation* Lisbon (Portugal) 2016, *International Conference on Bioencapsulation* Delft (Netherlands) 2015, *Latin America Symposium on Encapsulation* João Pessoa (Brazil) 2014. **Publications** *Bioencapsulation Innovations* (4 a year) – newsletter. **Members** Members (around 7000) in over 80 countries. Membership countries not specified. [2021/XJ8675/**F**]

♦ Bioenergy Europe 03247

SG Place du Champs de Mars 2, 1050 Brussels, Belgium. T. +3223184100. E-mail: info@bioenergyeurope.org.
URL: https://bioenergyeurope.org/

History 1990, Brussels (Belgium). Former names and other names: *European Biomass Association* – former; *Association européenne pour la biomasse (AEBIOM)* – former. Registration: Banque Carrefour des Entreprises, No/ID: 0871.481.553, Start date: 15 Jan 2005, Belgium; EU Transparency Register, No/ID: 97810874431-67, Start date: 28 Oct 2010. **Aims** Promote biomass production and applications, especially in the countries of the European Union and Eastern Europe; develop and publicize global solutions to boost biomass production; encourage sharing of experience; provide direct or indirect assistance in setting up national associations; promote transfer of appropriate technology. **Structure** General Assembly; Board of Directors; Core Group. Networks: *International Biomass Torrefaction Council (IBTC, #12352)*; *European Pellet Council (EPC, #08179)*. Working Groups (6). **Languages** English, French. **Staff** 10.00 FTE, paid. **Finance** Sources: members' dues. Supported by: *European Commission (EC, #06633)*. **Activities** Advocacy/lobbying/activism; awareness raising; events/meetings; knowledge management/information dissemination. **Events** *Agrobiomass: A Rural Solution in the Green Transformation* Brussels (Belgium) 2022, *European Bioenergy Future Conference* Brussels (Belgium) 2022, *International Biomass Congress* Brussels (Belgium) 2022, *Joint Session* Brussels (Belgium) 2022, *Seeing the Wood for the Trees Conference* Brussels (Belgium) 2022. **Publications** *Biomass News* (4 a year). *AEBIOM Statistical Report – European Bionergy Overview*. Annual Report.

Members Full: biomass associations in 22 countries:
Austria, Bosnia-Herzegovina, Croatia, Czechia, Denmark, Estonia, Finland, France, Germany, Greece, Ireland, Italy, Latvia, Lithuania, Norway, Poland, Portugal, Romania, Russia, Spain, Sweden, Ukraine.
Included in the above, 1 regional organization:
European Bioeconomy Alliance (EUBA, #06334).
Associate: companies; associations. Associate in 15 countries:
Austria, Belgium, Finland, France, Germany, Hungary, Italy, Latvia, Netherlands, Portugal, Romania, Sweden, Switzerland, UK, USA.

NGO Relations Supporting member of: *European Forum for Renewable Energy Sources (EUFORES, #07329)*. Stakeholder member of: *PEFC Council (#18288)*. Member of: *Industry4Europe (#11181)*. Instrumental in setting up: *European Bioenergy Business Forum (EBBF)*; *European Technology Platform on Renewable Heating and Cooling (RHC-Platform, #08891)*. [2021/XD4307/y/**D**]

♦ Bioenergy Institute (internationally oriented national body)

♦ Bioethics Network on Women's Issues in the Arab Region 03248

Contact UNESCO Cairo Office, Regional Bureau for Science in Arab States, 8 Abdel Rahman Fahmy Str, Garden City, Cairo, 11541, Egypt. E-mail: o.ikebe@unesco.org – arab.bioethics@unesco.org.
URL: http://bioethicsnetwork.wordpress.com/

History Initiated by *UNESCO (#20322)* Cairo Office, Egypt. **Aims** Open a dialogue on ethical issues surrounding women's health and welfare in the Arab region; establish a network among experts and institutions working on these issues in the region and outside the region. **Structure** Advisory Board. **IGO Relations** *UNESCO (#20322)*. [2013/XJ7479/**E**]

♦ Biofeedback Foundation of Europe (BFE) 03249

Main Office 10 John St, London, WC1N 2EB, UK. T. +442032898033. E-mail: mail@bfe.org – info@bfe.org.
URL: http://www.bfe.org/

History Mar 1997. **Aims** Promote greater awareness of biofeedback among European *health professionals*. **Structure** Board of Directors. **Finance** Member's dues. **Activities** Research and development. **Events** *European Conference on Neurotherapies* Madrid (Spain) 2016, *Annual Meeting* Rome (Italy) 2015, *Annual Meeting* Venice (Italy) 2014, *Annual Meeting* Rzeszów (Poland) 2012, *Annual Meeting* Munich (Germany) 2011. **Members** Not a membership organization. [2016.02.17/XF4377/fv/**F**]

♦ Bioheterocycles – International Conference on Heterocycles in Bioorganic Chemistry (meeting series)
♦ Bioline International (internationally oriented national body)
♦ Biological Control Center for Africa (see: #13933)
♦ Biologically Inspired Cognitive Architectures Society (internationally oriented national body)
♦ Biological Science Graduate Congress (meeting series)
♦ Biologie Sans Frontières (internationally oriented national body)

♦ BIOMAT Consortium 03250

Contact Caixa Postal 68511, Rio de Janeiro RJ, CEP 21941-972 RJ, Brazil. T. +552125628689. E-mail: contato@biomat.org – biomatconsortium2015@gmail.com – biomatconsortium2014@gmail.com.
URL: http://www.biomat.org/

History BIOMAT stands for: Mathematical and Computational Biology. Full title: *BIOMAT Consortium – International Institute for Interdisciplinary Sciences*. **Aims** Serve as a reference institution on *biomathematics* and *bioinformatics*. **Structure** Board. **Activities** Events/meetings. **Events** *International Symposium on Mathematical and Computational Biology* 2021, *International Symposium on Mathematical and Computational Biology* 2020, *International Symposium on Mathematical and Computational Biology* Szeged (Hungary) 2019, *International Symposium on Mathematical and Computational Biology* Mohammedia (Morocco) 2018, *International Symposium on Mathematical and Computational Biology* Moscow (Russia) 2017. **Publications** *World Scientific* – book series. [2015/XM2356/**F**]

♦ BIOMAT Consortium – International Institute for Interdisciplinary Sciences / see BIOMAT Consortium (#03250)
♦ Biomed Alliance / see Biomedical Alliance in Europe (#03251)

♦ **Biomedical Alliance in Europe** **03251**
Exec Dir 29 Square de Meeûs, 1050 Brussels, Belgium. T. +3222741073. E-mail: info@biomedeurope.org.
URL: http://www.biomedeurope.org/
History 2011. Founded by *European Cancer Organisation (ECO, #06432)*, *European Respiratory Society (ERS, #08383)*, *European Society of Cardiology (ESC, #08536)* and *European Association for the Study of Diabetes (EASD, #06228)*. Former names and other names: *Alliance for Biomedical Research in Europe (Biomed Alliance)* – former (2010 to 2018). Registration: Banque-Carrfour des Entreprises, No/ID: 0831.609.704, Start date: 3 Dec 2010, Belgium; EU Transparency Register, No/ID: 876034021209-88, Start date: 30 Mar 2016. **Aims** Promote the best interests and values of researchers and *healthcare* professionals organized in not-for-profit scientific medical associations and organizations, across all medical disciplines in Europe, in those general areas where common interest is identified. **Structure** General Assembly (annual); Spring Meeting (annual); Board of Directors; Executive Committee. **Languages** English. **Staff** 3.50 FTE, paid. **Finance** Sources: members' dues. **Activities** Events/meetings; politics/policy/regulatory. **Events** *General Assembly* Brussels (Belgium) 2022, *Joint Workshop on the European Health Data Space Proposal* Brussels (Belgium) 2022, *General Assembly* Brussels (Belgium) 2021, *Spring Meeting* Brussels (Belgium) 2021, *General Assembly* Brussels (Belgium) 2020.
Members Organizations (36):
- *European Academy of Allergy and Clinical Immunology (EAACI, #05779)*;
- *European Academy of Neurology (EAN, #05803)*;
- *European Alliance of Associations for Rheumatology (EULAR, #05862)*;
- *European Association for Cardio-Thoracic Surgery (EACTS, #05964)*;
- *European Association for the Study of Diabetes (EASD, #06228)*;
- *European Association for the Study of Obesity (EASO, #06234)*;
- *European Association for the Study of the Liver (EASL, #06233)*;
- *European Association of Nuclear Medicine (EANM, #06136)*;
- *European Association of Urology (EAU, #06264)*;
- *European Atherosclerosis Society (EAS, #06289)*;
- *European Brain Council (EBC, #06391)*;
- *European Calcified Tissue Society (ECTS, #06429)*;
- *European Cancer Organisation (ECO, #06432)*;
- *European College of Neuropsychopharmacology (ECNP, #06612)*;
- *European Federation of Clinical Chemistry and Laboratory Medicine (EFLM, #07080)*;
- *European Federation of Immunological Societies (EFIS, #07142)*;
- *European Federation of National Associations of Orthopaedics and Traumatology (EFORT, #07169)*;
- *European Forum for Research and Education in Allergy and Airway Diseases (EUFOREA, #07330)*;
- *European Hematology Association (EHA, #07473)*;
- *European Organisation for Research and Treatment of Cancer (EORTC, #08101)*;
- *European Renal Association – European Dialysis and Transplant Association (ERA-EDTA, #08353)*;
- *European Respiratory Society (ERS, #08383)*;
- *European Society for Molecular Imaging (ESMI, #08655)*;
- *European Society for Paediatric Gastroenterology, Hepatology and Nutrition (ESPGHAN, #08680)*;
- *European Society for Paediatric Research (ESPR, #08687)*;
- *European Society of Anaesthesiology and Intensive Care (ESAIC, #08518)*;
- *European Society of Cardiology (ESC, #08536)*;
- *European Society of Clinical Microbiology and Infectious Diseases (ESCMID, #08548)*;
- *European Society of Endocrinology (ESE, #08594)*;
- *European Society of Human Genetics (ESHG, #08624)*;
- *European Society of Human Reproduction and Embryology (ESHRE, #08625)*;
- *European Society of Intensive Care Medicine (ESICM, #08632)*;
- *European Society of Pathology (ESP, #08689)*;
- *European Society of Radiology (ESR, #08720)*;
- *Federation of European Biochemical Societies (FEBS, #09494)*;
- *United European Gastroenterology (UEG, #20506)*.

NGO Relations Accredited by (3): *EIT Health (#05406)*; *EU Health Coalition*; *Federation of European and International Associations Established in Belgium (FAIB, #09508)*. [2021.05.27/XJ5560/y/**E**]

♦ **Biometrics Institute** **03252**
Chief Exec 4th Fl – Imperial House, 15 Kingsway, London, WC2B 6UN, UK. T. +442075814827. E-mail: manager@biometricsinstitute.org.
Australia PO Box 576, Crows Nest NSW 1585, Australia. T. +61294318688. Fax +61294318677.
URL: http://www.biometricsinstitute.org/
History Jul 2001, Australia, as a company limited by guarantee with not-for-profit status. **Aims** Promote responsible use of biometrics as an independent and impartial international forum for biometric users and other interested parties. **Structure** Board of Directors; Management Team; Committees. **Languages** English. **Staff** 4.00 FTE, paid. **Finance** Sources: meeting proceeds; members' dues. **Activities** Awareness raising; events/meetings; guidance/assistance/consulting; knowledge management/information dissemination; monitoring/evaluation; networking/liaising; publishing activities; research/documentation; standards/guidelines; training/education. Active in: Europe; USA; Australia; New Zealand; Singapore. **Events** *Congress* London (UK) 2020, *Congress* London (UK) 2019, *Annual Asia-Pacific Conference* Sydney, NSW (Australia) 2018, *Annual American Conference* Washington, DC (USA) 2018, *Congress* London (UK) 2017. **Publications** *Biometrics Institute eNewsletter* (every 8 weeks); *Annual Industry Survey*.
Members Full in 25 countries and territories:
Australia, Belgium, Brazil, Chile, China, Denmark, Estonia, Finland, France, Germany, Ghana, Hong Kong, Ireland, Luxembourg, Mexico, Netherlands, New Zealand, Norway, Portugal, Singapore, South Africa, Spain, Sweden, UK, USA.
[2021/XM4854/**C**]

♦ BioNET INTERNATIONAL Consultative Group (inactive)
♦ BioNET INTERNATIONAL – Global Network for Biosystematics / see BioNET INTERNATIONAL – Global Network for Taxonomy (#03253)

♦ **BioNET INTERNATIONAL – Global Network for Taxonomy (BI)** **03253**
Dir BI Technical Secretariat, Bakeham Lane, Egham, TW20 9TY, UK. T. +441491829036 – +441491829037 – +441491829038. Fax +441491829082.
URL: http://www.bionet-intl.org/
History following recommendations of *CABI (#03393)*, 1991. Concept endorsed, Jul 1993, at a meeting of representatives of various sub-regions of the developing world, major expert centres of developed countries, international organizations and UN agencies and some donors, who set up *BioNET INTERNATIONAL Consultative Group (BICG)* – (BIOCON) to promote and foster the Network. Original full title *Global Network for Biosystematics of Arthropods, Nematodes and Microorganisms*; subsequent full title: *BioNET INTERNATIONAL – Global Network for Biosystematics (BI) – Global Network for Biosystematics of Invertebrates and Microorganisms*. **Aims** Promote the science and use of taxonomy, especially in the economically poorer countries of the world.
Structure Locally Owned and Operated Partnerships (LOOPs), delimited by UN subregions, each comprising: LOOP Coordinating Committee (LCC); Regional Coordinating Institute; National Coordinating Institutions; Network Institutions. Secretariat. Host Organization: *CABI (#03393)*. BioNET Fund managed by BioNET Board. Current LOOPs (12):
- *ANDINONET*, set up 2004;
- *ASEANET – ASEAN Network on Taxonomy*, set up 1998 and endorsed by *ASEAN (#01141)*;
- *CARINET – Biosystematics Network of the Caribbean*, set up 1993 and endorsed by *Caribbean Community (CARICOM, #03476)*;
- *EAFRINET*, set up 1998;
- *EASIANET*, set up 2002;
- *NAFRINET*, set up 2004;
- *PACINET – Pacific Island Network for Taxonomy*, set up 2000 and endorsed by *Council of Regional Organisations of the Pacific (CROP, #04914)*;
- *SACNET*, set up 2006;
- *SAFRINET*, set up 1996 and endorsed by *Southern African Development Community (SADC, #19843)*;
- *WAFRINET*, set up 1998 and endorsed *West and Central African Council for Agricultural Research and Development (WECARD, #20907)*;
- *LATINET*, planned;
- *MESOAMERINET*, developed 2003 and awaiting endorsement.

Finance Technical Secretariat funded by *BioNET FUND*. LOOP establishment and activities financed from a wide variety of sources, including: Government support; donor contributions; UN agencies. **Activities** Knowledge management/information dissemination; training/education; research and development. **Events** *Global workshop* Pretoria (South Africa) 2002, *Global workshop* Cardiff (UK) 1999, *Global workshop* Cardiff (UK) 1995. **Publications** *BioNet Bulletin*; *BioNet-International News*.
Members Membership open to all countries and relevant institutions wishing to participate in and assist implementation of BioNET and in actioning its aims, currently in 97 countries and territories:
Angola, Bahamas, Barbados, Belgium, Belize, Benin, Botswana, Brunei Darussalam, Bulgaria, Burkina Faso, Cambodia, Cameroon, Cape Verde, Chad, Cook Is, Costa Rica, Côte d'Ivoire, Croatia, Denmark, Eritrea, Eswatini, Ethiopia, Fiji, Finland, France, Gambia, Germany, Ghana, Guam, Guinea, Guinea-Bissau, Guyana, Honduras, Hungary, Indonesia, Ireland, Italy, Jamaica, Kenya, Kiribati, Laos, Leeward Is, Lesotho, Liberia, Lithuania, Malawi, Malaysia, Mali, Marshall Is, Mauritania, Mauritius, Micronesia FS, Mozambique, Namibia, Nauru, Netherlands, New Caledonia, Niger, Nigeria, Niue, Norway, Palau, Papua New Guinea, Philippines, Pitcairn, Poland, Polynesia Fr, Portugal, Samoa, Samoa USA, Senegal, Sierra Leone, Singapore, Slovenia, Solomon Is, South Africa, Spain, Suriname, Sweden, Switzerland, Tanzania UR, Thailand, Togo, Tokelau, Tonga, Trinidad-Tobago, Tuvalu, Uganda, UK, Vanuatu, Venezuela, Vietnam, Wallis-Futuna, Windward Is, Zambia, Zimbabwe.
IGO Relations Member of: *Global Biodiversity Information Facility (GBIF, #10250)*. **NGO Relations** Member of: *Consortium for the Barcode of Life (CBOL, #04737)*. [2010/XF3332/**F***]

♦ **BioPharmaceutical Emerging Best Practices Association (BEBPA)** . **03254**
Office PO Box 5825, Bremerton WA 98312, USA. T. +12066514542. E-mail: contactus@bebpa.org.
URL: http://www.bebpa.org/
Aims Foster publication of white papers clarifying problems faced by biopharmaceutical community. **Structure** Board; Scientific Committee. **Activities** Events/meetings. **Events** *European Biological Assays Conference* Bremerton, WA (USA) 2020, *European Biological Assays Conference* Prague (Czechia) 2019, *European Biological Assays Conference* Budapest (Hungary) 2018, *Biological Assays Conference* St Julian's (Malta) 2017, *Biological Assays Conference* Dubrovnik (Croatia) 2016. [2020/XJ7467/**C**]

♦ **Biophysical Society (BPS)** **03255**
Main Office 5515 Security Ln, Suite 1110, Rockville MD 20852, USA. T. +12402905600. Fax +12402905555. E-mail: society@biophysics.org.
URL: http://www.biophysics.org/
History Apr 1956, Atlanta, GA (USA). Constitution adopted Feb 1958, Cambridge MA (USA); amended Sep 1991, Aug 1999, Aug 2002, Aug 2006, Apr 2012 and Feb 2020. **Aims** Eencourage the development and dissemination of knowledge in biophysics. **Structure** Council; Committees. **Activities** Advocacy/lobbying/activism; awards/prizes/competitions; events/meetings; training/education. **Events** *Annual Meeting* Los Angeles, CA (USA) 2025, *Annual Meeting* Philadelphia, PA (USA) 2024, *Annual Meeting* San Diego, CA (USA) 2023, *Physical and Quantitative Approaches to Overcome Antibiotic Resistance* Stockholm (Sweden) 2022, *Physical and Quantitative Approaches to Overcome Antibiotic Resistance* Stockholm (Sweden) 2021. **Publications** *BPS Bulletin* (12 a year); *Biophyiscal Journal*. [2022/XW0367/**C**]

♦ Biopolitics International Organisation (internationally oriented national body)

♦ **Biopolymer International** **03256**
SG Av de Tervueren 13A, Bte 7, 1040 Brussels, Belgium. T. +3227365354. Fax +3227323427. E-mail: biopolymer@ecco-eu.com.
URL: http://www.biopolymer-international.com/
History 1989, Paris (France). Full title: *World Association of Food Grade Biopolymer Producers (BIOPOLYMER International)*. **Aims** Promote a better understanding of the safety and use of xanthan gum and gellan gum among consumers, health professionals, legislators and customers; provide regulatory bodies with data necessary to demonstrate the safety and technological justification of biopolymers. **Structure** General Assembly (annual); Standing Committees. **Languages** English. **Finance** Members' dues. **Events** *General assembly* London (UK) 1994, *General Assembly* Paris (France) 1993, *General Assembly* Paris (France) 1992.
Members Producers (6) in 6 countries:
China, Denmark, France, Netherlands, Switzerland, USA.
NGO Relations Member of: *EU Specialty Food Ingredients (#09200)*. [2019.10.14/XD2525/**D**]

♦ **BioProtection Global (BPG)** **03257**
Address not obtained.
URL: https://www.bioprotectionglobal.org/
Aims Represent the bioprotection industry for key topics on a global scale so as to promote bioprotection and harmonize proportionate regulations.
Members Associations in 7 countries:
Argentina, Brazil, Colombia, India, Japan, South Africa, USA.
International Biocontrol Manufacturers Association (IBMA, #12343).
IGO Relations Partner of (1): *CABI (#03393)*. **NGO Relations** Partner of (1): *Food and Land Use Coalition (FOLU)*. [2020/AA2000/y/**F**]

♦ **BiOptic Driving Network** **03258**
Contact address not obtained. Fax +448723527874.
Contact 5520 Ridgeton Hill Court, Fairfax VA 22032, USA.
URL: http://www.biopticdriving.org/
History 2001. **Aims** Develop and advance the use of BiOptics for driving. **Events** *International BiOptic Driving Conference* London (UK) 2004.
Members National networks in 5 countries:
Australia, Canada, Netherlands, UK, USA. [2012/XF7020/**F**]

♦ Bioresonanz-Ärztegesellschaft / see International Society of Medical Doctors for Biophysical Information Therapy (#15253)
♦ Bioresources Development and Conservation Programme (internationally oriented national body)
♦ Biosaline Agriculture Centre / see International Center for Biosaline Agriculture (#12468)
♦ BIOS – Bermuda Institute of Ocean Sciences (internationally oriented national body)

♦ **Biosciences Eastern and Central Africa (BecA)** **03259**
Dir PO Box 30709, Nairobi, 00100, Kenya. T. +254204223805. E-mail: beca-hub@cgiar.org.
URL: http://hub.africabiosciences.org/
History on the initiative of *New Partnership for Africa's Development (NEPAD, #17091)*. **Structure** Steering Committee of 8. **NGO Relations** Agreement with: *International Foundation for Science (IFS, #13677)*. Supports: *International Institute of Tropical Agriculture (IITA, #13933)*. [2008/XM3469/**E**]

♦ Biosciences Research Support Foundation (internationally oriented national body)
♦ Biospeological Society / see International Society of Biospeleology (#14975)

♦ **Biosphere Expeditions** **03260**
Exec Dir 69 Main Street, Blackrock, CO. DUBLIN, A94 N6D0, Ireland. T. +35314428750. E-mail: info@biosphere-expeditions.org – ireland@biosphere-expeditions.org.
URL: https://www.biosphere-expeditions.org/
History 1999, UK. First expedition ran, 2001. Headquarters moved from UK to Ireland, 2018. Registration: No/ID: 601133, Ireland; Companies House, No/ID: 3906154, England and Wales; 501(c)(3), No/ID: EIN 72-1614948, USA; No/ID: VR 200383, Germany; No/ID: 05/3750, France; No/ID: A004912Y, Australia, Victoria. **Aims** Unite citizen science, ethical volunteering and hands-on wildlife conservation through expedition holidays. **Structure** Offices in Australia, France, Germany, UK and USA. **Languages** English. **Activities** Awareness raising; capacity building; research/documentation; training/education. **Publications** *Biosphere Expeditions Magazine* (annual). **Information Services** *Lab* – scientific reports and publications. **Consultative Status** Consultative status granted from: *UNEP (#20299)*. **IGO Relations** Accredited by (1): *UNEP (#20299)*. **NGO Relations** Partner of (4): *European Citizen Science Association (ECSA, #06557)*; *International Union for Conservation of Nature and Natural Resources (IUCN, #15766)*; NABU; Reef Check. [2022.05.04/XJ9015/**F**]

♦ Biosphere Foundation (internationally oriented national body)
♦ **BioSyst EU** Federation of European Biological Systematic Societies (#09495)
♦ Biotechnology Industry Organization / see Biotechnology Innovation Organization
♦ Biotechnology Innovation Organization (internationally oriented national body)

♦ Biotherapeutics Association of Australasia (internationally oriented national body)
♦ Biotherapy Development Association / see Cancer Drug Development Forum (#03413)

♦ BioTrade Initiative 03261

Chief UNCTAD Biodiversity and Climate Change Section, Palais des Nations, Building E, 1211 Geneva, Switzerland. T. +41229175731. Fax +41229170247. E-mail: biotrade@unctad.org.
URL: http://www.biotrade.org/

History 1996, by *UNCTAD (#20285)*, during 3rd Conference of Parties of *Convention on Biological Diversity (Biodiversity convention, 1992)*. **Aims** Stimulate trade and investment in *biological resources* to further sustainable development in line with the CBD objectives. **Activities** Since 2003, hosts *BioTrade Facilitation Programme (BTFP)*. [2016/XJ2096/t/**E**]

♦ BIOTROP / see Southeast Asian Regional Centre for Tropical Biology (#19782)
♦ BIO Ventures for Global Health (internationally oriented national body)

♦ Bioversity International 03262

Dir Gen Via dei Tre Denari 472/a, 00054 Maccarese RM, Italy. T. +39661181. Fax +3966118402. E-mail: bioversity@cgiar.org.
URL: https://www.bioversityinternational.org/

History 1974. Founded by *CGIAR System Organization (CGIAR, #03843)*. 1991, became an autonomous international scientific organization of CGIAR. Following a decision of CGIAR in 1994, *International Network for the Improvement of Banana and Plantain (INIBAP, inactive)*, based in Montpellier (France), became one of IPGRI's programmes. 2006, INIBAP completed integration process into IPGRI and both organizations adopted the same new name. In 2020, Bioversity International and the International Center for Tropical Agriculture (CIAT) established an Alliance, with one Director General, one Board of Trustees and one strategy. Former names and other names: *International Board for Plant Genetic Resources (IBPGR)* – former (1974 to 1991); *Conseil international des ressources phytogénétiques* – former (1974 to 1991); *Consejo Internacional de Recursos Fitogenéticos* – former (1974 to 1991); *International Plant Genetic Resources Institute (IPGRI)* – former (1991 to 2006); *Instituto Internacional de Recursos Fitogenéticos* – former (1991 to 2006). Registration: Section 501 (c)(3), USA; Charity Commission, No/ID: 1131854, England and Wales. **Aims** Deliver research-based solutions that harness agricultural biodiversity and sustainably transform food systems to improve people's lives in a climate crisis. **Structure** Board of Trustees; Director General Office; Leadership Team. Headquarters: Rome (Italy). Offices: Belgium; France; Costa Rica; Peru; India; Uzbekistan; China; Malaysia; Benin; Cameroon; Burundi; Ethiopia; Kenya; Uganda. **Languages** English. **Staff** 290.00 FTE, paid. **Finance** Unrestricted and restricted funding from several partners. Annual budget: 31,000,000 USD (2019). **Activities** Events/meetings; knowledge management/information dissemination; networking/liaising; research and development. Coordinates several networks including: *Plantain and Banana Research and Development Network for Latin America and the Caribbean (#18389)*; *Banana Research Network for West and Central Africa (Innovate Plantain)*; *Banana Research Network for Eastern and Southern Africa (BARNESA, #03158)*; *Banana Asia-Pacific Network (BAPNET, no recent information)*; *MusaNet (#16904)*; *Global Network for Cacao Genetic Resources (CacaoNet, #10484)*; *Coconut Genetic Resources Network (COGENT, #04080)*; *European Cooperative Programme for Plant Genetic Resources (ECPGR, #06787)*. **Events** *International Agrobiodiversity Congress* Delhi (India) 2016, *International Conference on Forests for Food Security and Nutrition* Rome (Italy) 2013, *Meeting* Montpellier (France) 2010, *International scientific symposium on biodiversity and sustainable diets* Rome (Italy) 2010, *Meeting* Rome (Italy) 2010. **Publications** Peer-reviewed papers; journal articles; books; conference proceedings; newsletters; surveys; training material; reports; databases. **Members** Not a membership organization. **IGO Relations** Extensive IGO relations with selected organizations, including: *Commission on Genetic Resources for Food and Agriculture (CGRFA, #04215)*; *European Commission (EC, #06633)*; *FAO (#09260)*; *Global Crop Diversity Trust (Crop Trust, #10313)*; *Intergovernmental Science-Policy Platform on Biodiversity and Ecosystem Services (IPBES, #11500)*; *International Cocoa Organization (ICCO, #12627)*; *International Fund for Agricultural Development (IFAD, #13692)*; *International Treaty on Plant Genetic Resources for Food and Agriculture (2001)*; national governments; *Secretariat of the Convention on Biological Diversity (SCBD, #19197)*; *Secretariat of the United Nations Convention to Combat Desertification (Secretariat of the UNCCD, #19208)*; *UNEP (#20299)*; *World Food Programme (WFP, #21510)*.
NGO Relations Extensive NGO relationships, including with:
- *Association for Strengthening Agricultural Research in Eastern and Central Africa (ASARECA, #02933)*;
- *Bill and Melinda Gates Foundation (BMGF)*;
- *Catholic Relief Services (CRS, #03608)*;
- *Christensen Fund (TCF)*;
- *Fairtrade International (FLO, #09240)*;
- *Humanistisch Instituut voor Ontwikkelingssamenwerking (Hivos)*;
- *International Union for Conservation of Nature and Natural Resources (IUCN, #15766)*;
- *Lutheran World Relief (LWR)*;
- *McKnight Foundation*;
- *Natural Capital Coalition (NCC, #16952)*;
- *The Nature Conservancy (TNC)*;
- *SNV Netherlands Development Organisation (SNV)*;
- *Oxfam Novib*;
- *Save the Children International (#19058)*;
- *Trocaire – Catholic Agency for World Development*;
- *World Cocoa Foundation (WCF)*;
- *World Resources Institute (WRI, #21753)*. [2022/XE3150/**E***]

♦ Biovision Africa Trust (unconfirmed)
♦ Biovision – Fondation pour un développement écologique (internationally oriented national body)
♦ Biovision – Foundation for Ecological Development (internationally oriented national body)
♦ Biovision – Stiftung für Ökologische Entwicklung (internationally oriented national body)
♦ BioVision – World Life Sciences Forum (unconfirmed)
♦ BIPAR / see BIPAR – European Federation of Insurance Intermediaries (#03263)

♦ BIPAR – European Federation of Insurance Intermediaries 03263

BIPAR – Fédération européenne des intermédiaires d'assurances

Permanent Secretariat Av Albert Elisabeth 40, 1200 Brussels, Belgium. T. +3227356048. E-mail: bipar@bipar.eu.
URL: https://www.bipar.eu/

History 1937, Paris (France). Founded at international congress. Statutes modified: 29 Jun 1953; 26 Jan 1954; 29 Jan 1957; 30 Oct 1964; 19 Apr 1967; 26 June 1968; 9 June 1969; 4 June 1974; 26 June 1976; 21 June 1979; 17 June 1982; 21 Sep 1984; 30 May 1990; 24 May 2000; 20 Aug 2009. Former names and other names: *International Association of Insurance and Reinsurance Intermediaries* – former; *Bureau international des producteurs d'assurances et de réassurances (BIPAR)* – former; *Internacional de Productores de Seguros y Reaseguros* – former. Registration: Start date: 2 Dec 1938, France; Banque-Carrefour des Entreprises, No/ID: 0562.817.754, Start date: 19 Sep 2014, Belgium. **Aims** Link professional associations or groups interested in insurance or reinsurance mediation; study problems of direct or indirect interest to the profession; encourage action concerned with improving the standing of the profession in relations with international and governmental bodies. **Structure** General Assembly (annual); Steering Committee; Governing Board; Management Committee; Standing Committees; Permanent Secretariat. **Languages** English, French. **Staff** 6.00 FTE, paid; 6.00 FTE, voluntary. **Finance** Sources: members' dues. **Activities** Advocacy/lobbying/activism; knowledge management/information dissemination. **Events** *Annual General Assembly* Brussels (Belgium) 2015, *Annual General Assembly* Rome (Italy) 2014, *Annual General Assembly* Brussels (Belgium) 2013, *Annual General Assembly* Brussels (Belgium) 2012, *Annual General Assembly* Brussels (Belgium) 2011. **Publications** *BIPAR Press* (6 a year).
Members National professional associations (48) in 30 countries:
Austria, Belgium, Bulgaria, Cyprus, Czechia, Denmark, Estonia, Finland, France, Germany, Greece, Hungary, Ireland, Israel, Italy, Lebanon, Lithuania, Luxembourg, Malta, Netherlands, Norway, Poland, Portugal, Romania, Slovakia, Spain, Sweden, Switzerland, Türkiye, UK.
Consultative Status Consultative status granted from: *UNCTAD (#20285)* (Special Category). **NGO Relations** Member of (5): *European Services Forum (ESF, #08469)*; *Federation of European and International Associations Established in Belgium (FAIB, #09508)*; *SMEunited (#19327)*; *World Federation of Insurance Intermediaries (WFII, #21443)*; *World Union of Professions (WUP, #21882)*. Instrumental in setting up (1): *Partners of Intermediaries (POI, #18246)*. Liaison Organization of: *Comité européen de normalisation (CEN, #04162)*. [2023/XC1431/**D**]

♦ BIPAR – Fédération européenne des intermédiaires d'assurances (#03263)
♦ BIPAVER / see BIPAVER – European Retread Manufacturers Association (#03264)

♦ BIPAVER – European Retread Manufacturers Association 03264

Contact Archimedesweg 31, PO Box 33, 2300 AA Leiden, Netherlands. T. +31715686970. E-mail: info@bipaver.org.
URL: http://bipaver.org/

History Founded 1 Oct 1954, Bern (Switzerland), as *International Federation of National Associations of Tyre Specialists and Retreaders – Bureau international permanent des associations de vendeurs et rechapeurs de pneumatiques (BIPAVER) – Internationale Federation der Nationalen Verbände der Reifenspezialisten und Runderneuerer – Federación Internacional de Asociaciones Nacionales de Especialistas de Neumatico y Recauchutadores*. Current name adopted 2003. Restructured 2011. **Aims** Represent the *tyre* retreading industry. **Structure** General Assembly; Executive Board; Technical Committee. **Languages** English. **Staff** 1.00 FTE, paid. **Finance** Members' dues. **Activities** Events/meetings; knowledge management/information dissemination. **Events** *General Assembly* Leiden (Netherlands) 2022, *General Assembly* Leiden (Netherlands) 2020, *General Assembly* Cologne (Germany) 2018, *Congress* Essen (Germany) 2016, *Congress* Bologna (Italy) 2015.
Members Ordinary: national associations in 11 countries:
Austria, Denmark, Finland, Germany, Italy, Netherlands, Portugal, Spain, Sweden, UK, USA.
Extraordinary: individual tyre retreaders in 2 countries:
Poland, Türkiye.
Supplier: suppliers or manufacturers of equipment (11) in 7 countries:
Belgium, Brazil, Germany, Italy, Netherlands, Portugal, UK. [2019.02.14/XD3117/**D**]

♦ **BIP** Biodiversity Indicators Partnership (#03242)
♦ BIPCA – Bureau international permanent de chimie analytique pour les matières destinées à l'alimentation de l'homme et des animaux (inactive)
♦ BIPF – BRICS Intellectual Property Forum (meeting series)
♦ **BIPM** Bureau international des poids et mesures (#03367)
♦ BIPP / see International Peace Bureau (#14535)
♦ BIRA / see Interafrican Bureau for Animal Resources (#11382)
♦ BIRBE – Bureau international de recherches balnéo-économiques (inactive)
♦ **BIR** Bureau of International Recycling (#03368)
♦ Bircham International University (internationally oriented national body)
♦ **BIRD** Banque internationale pour la reconstruction et le développement (#12317)

♦ BirdLife Europe 03265

Dir c/o Hive5, Cours Saint-Michel 30 B, 1040 Brussels, Belgium. T. +3222800830. Fax +3222303802. E-mail: europe@birdlife.org.
Registered Address Boulevard 12, 3707 AM Zeist, Netherlands.
URL: https://www.birdlife.org/europe-and-central-asia

History Founded as the European and Central Asian Division of *BirdLife International (#03266)*. Former names and other names: *BirdLife Europe and Central Asia* – former. Registration: Handelsregister, No/ID: KVK 09101082, Netherlands; EU Transparency Register, No/ID: 1083162721-43, Start date: 4 Dec 2008. **Aims** Prevent extinction of birds living in the wild; maintain and when possible improve the protection and conservation of all birds; protect and conserve the arcas and biotopes/habitats that are important to birds and other bio-diversity; support the vital ecological system that sustain people's livelihood and improve the quality of life. **Structure** Board of Directors. **Consultative Status** Consultative status granted from: *Council of Europe (CE, #04881)* (Participatory Status). **NGO Relations** Member of (1): *Conference of INGOs of the Council of Europe (#04607)*. [2022/AA2429/**E**]

♦ BirdLife Europe and Central Asia / see BirdLife Europe (#03265)

♦ BirdLife International 03266

CEO David Attenborough Building, 1st Floor, Pembroke Street, Cambridge, CB2 3QZ, UK. T. +441223277318. Fax +441223281441. E-mail: communications@birdlife.org – birdlife@birdlife.org.
URL: http://www.birdlife.org/

History 20 Jun 1922, London (UK). By-Laws modified: 1959; 1962; 1970; 1978; 1982; 1987; 1993. Reorganized under present name, Mar 1993. Former names and other names: *International Committee for Bird Protection* – former (1922); *Comité international pour la protection des oiseaux* – former (1922); *International Council for Bird Preservation (ICBP)* – former; *Conseil international pour la préservation des oiseaux (CIPO)* – former; *Consejo Internacional para la Preservación de las Aves* – former; *Internationale Rat für Vogelschutz (IRV)* – former. Registration: Charity Commission, No/ID: 1042125, England and Wales. **Aims** Conserve wild birds, their habitats and global *biodiversity*; prevent extinction in the wild; maintain and, where possible, improve the *conservation* status of all bird species; sustain vital ecological systems that underpin human livelihoods; enrich the quality of people's lives; empower people, contribute to the alleviation of poverty and, by people working together, strive to ensure sustainability in the use of natural resources. **Structure** Global Partnership Meeting (every 4-5 years). International Council (meets twice a year); Board; International Advisory Group; Executive Team; Regional Directors. Regional Offices: Accra (Ghana); Amman (Jordan); *BirdLife Europe (#03265)* – Belgium; Cambridge (UK); Nairobi (Kenya); Singapore; Suva (Fiji); Tokyo (Japan); Quito (Ecuador). **Languages** English, French, German, Spanish. **Staff** 6519.00 FTE, paid; 217599.00 FTE, voluntary. **Finance** Sources: grants; in-kind support; members' dues. *Rare Bird Club* members provides unrestricted funding. **Activities** Advocacy/lobbying/activism; events/meetings; guidance/assistance/consulting; projects/programmes. **Events** *Extinction or Regeneration Conference* London (UK) 2023, *Quadrennial World Conference* London (UK) 2022, *Workshop on Implementing Collaborative Waterbird Conservation in the Republic of Korea and the East Asian-Australasian Flyway* Incheon (Korea Rep) 2018, *African Great Lakes Conference* Entebbe (Uganda) 2017, *Quadrennial World Conference* Singapore (Singapore) 2017. **Publications** *Bird Conservation International* (4 a year) – journal; *World Birdwatch Magazine* (4 a year). *BirdLife Conservation Series*. *Birds in Europe: Population Estimates, Trends and Conservation Status* (2004); *Birds in the European Union: A Status Assessment* (2004); *Important Bird Areas of Asia: Key Sites for Conservation* (2004); *State of the World's Birds: Indicators for our Changing World* (2004). Annual Report. BirdLife International Study Reports; CD-Roms; technical publications series; monograph series.
Members Partner national conservation organizations with a focus on birds and working together on shared priorities, policies and programmes of conservation exchanging skills, achievements and information, in 112 countries and territories:
Andorra, Argentina, Austria, Azerbaijan, Bahamas, Bahrain, Belarus, Belgium, Belize, Bolivia, Botswana, Brazil, Bulgaria, Burkina Faso, Burundi, Cambodia, Cameroon, Canada, Chile, Cook Is, Croatia, Cuba, Cyprus, Czechia, Denmark, Ecuador, Egypt, El Salvador, Estonia, Ethiopia, Faeroe Is, Falklands/Malvinas, Fiji, Finland, France, Georgia, Germany, Ghana, Gibraltar, Greece, Hong Kong, Hungary, Iceland, India, Indonesia, Iran Islamic Rep, Ireland, Israel, Italy, Japan, Jordan, Kenya, Kuwait, Laos, Latvia, Lebanon, Liberia, Liechtenstein, Lithuania, Luxembourg, Madagascar, Malawi, Malaysia, Malta, Mexico, Myanmar, Nepal, Netherlands, New Caledonia, New Zealand, Nigeria, Norway, Pakistan, Palau, Palestine, Panama, Paraguay, Philippines, Poland, Polynesia Fr, Portugal, Puerto Rico, Romania, Russia, Rwanda, Samoa, Saudi Arabia, Seychelles, Sierra Leone, Singapore, Slovakia, Slovenia, South Africa, Spain, Sri Lanka, Suriname, Sweden, Switzerland, Taiwan, Thailand, Tunisia, Türkiye, Uganda, UK, Ukraine, Uruguay, USA, Venezuela, Vietnam, Yemen, Zambia, Zimbabwe.
Consultative Status Consultative status granted from: *ECOSOC (#05331)* (Ros A); *UNEP (#20299)*. **IGO Relations** Accredited by (2): *Green Climate Fund (GCF, #10714)*; *United Nations Framework Convention on Climate Change – Secretariat (UNFCCC, #20564)*. Observer status with (4): *Baltic Marine Environment Protection Commission – Helsinki Commission (HELCOM, #03126)*; *Intergovernmental Negotiating Committee for a Legally Binding Agreement on Forests in Europe (INC-Forests, inactive)*; *OSPAR Commission for the Protection of the Marine Environment of the North-East Atlantic (OSPAR Commission, #17905)*; *Standing Committee to the Bern Convention on the Conservation of European Wildlife and Natural Habitats (#19949)*. Member of (1): *Secretariat of the Convention of Wetlands (#19200)*. Participates in the work of: *United Nations Economic Commission for Europe (UNECE, #20555)*. Involved in development and participation of: *Caribbean Action Plan (CAR, #03432)*. **NGO Relations** Member of (10): *Antarctic and Southern Ocean Coalition (ASOC, #00849)*; *Biodiversity Indicators Partnership (BIP, #03242)*; *European Federation for Transport and Environment (T and E, #07230)*; *European Habitats Forum (EHF, #07443)*; *Freshwater Action Network (FAN, inactive)*; *GEF CSO Network (GCN, #10087)*; *High Seas Alliance (HSA, #10918)*; *International Union for Conservation of Nature and Natural Resources (IUCN, #15766)*; *Philanthropy Impact*; *The Green 10 (#10711)*.

Instrumental in setting up (4): *African Bird Club (ABC, #00224)*; *Global Forest Policy Project (GFPP)*; *World Pheasant Association (WPA, #21724)*; *World Working Group on Birds of Prey and Owls (WWGBP, #21945)*. [2022/XB1722/**B**]

♦ BirdsCaribbean 03267

Exec Dir address not obtained. E-mail: lsoren@bu.edu.
Pres address not obtained. E-mail: howien@hotmail.com.
URL: http://www.scscb.org/

History 1988, as *Society of Caribbean Ornithology (SCO)*. Subsequently changed title to *Society for the Conservation and Study of Caribbean Birds (SCSCB) – Société pur la conservation et l'etude des oiseaux de la Caraïbe – Sociedad para la Conservación n y Estudio de las Aves Caribeñas*. Also referred to as *Caribbean Birds*. **Aims** Promote the scientific study and conservation of *Caribbean birds* and their habitats; provide a link among *ornithologists* with those elsewhere; provide a written forum for researchers in the region; provide data and technical assistance to governments and conservation groups in the Caribbean. **Structure** Board. **Finance** Members' dues. **Events** *Meeting* Bahamas 2011, *Meeting* Veracruz, CHIS (Mexico) 2008, *Meeting* Veracruz, CHIS (Mexico) 2007, *Meeting* Guadeloupe 2006, *Meeting* Trinidad-Tobago 2003. **Publications** *The Journal of Caribbean Ornithology*. **Members** Full (about 300). Membership countries not specified. **NGO Relations** Member of: *Alliance for Zero Extinction (AZE, #00730)*; *World Seabird Union (WSU, #21774)*. [2014/XD7461/**D**]

- ♦ **BIREME** Latin American and Caribbean Centre on Health Sciences Information (#16267)
- ♦ BIRFA – Brigade multinationale d'intervention rapide des forces en attente des Nations Unies (inactive)
- ♦ **BIRF** Banco Internacional de Reconstrucción y Fomento (#12317)
- ♦ BIR – International Conference on Perspectives in Business Informatics Research (meeting series)
- ♦ Birlesmis Kentler Ve Yerel Yönetimler Orta Dogu Ve Bati Asya Bölge Teskilati (#20502)
- ♦ **BIRN** Balkan Investigative Reporting Network (#03075)
- ♦ BIROE – Bureau international de recherches sur les oiseaux d'eau et les zones humides (inactive)
- ♦ BIRSH – Bureau of Information and Research on Student Health (inactive)
- ♦ Birthright, Inc / see EngenderHealth
- ♦ BISA – British International Spa Association (inactive)
- ♦ BISA – British International Studies Association (internationally oriented national body)
- ♦ **BIS** Bank for International Settlements (#03165)
- ♦ Bischöfliche Aktion ADVENIAT (internationally oriented national body)
- ♦ Bischöfliches Hilfswerk Misereor, Aktion gegen Hunger und Krankheit in der Welt (internationally oriented national body)
- ♦ Biserica Lui Dumnezeu Ministerul Lui Isus Hristos (religious order)
- ♦ **BISFA** Bureau international pour la standardisation de la rayonne et des fibres synthétiques (#03369)
- ♦ BISFed / see World Boccia (#21236)
- ♦ **BISS** Baltic Institute of Social Science (#03122)
- ♦ BIST-EC / see Bay of Bengal Initiative for Multi-Sectoral Technical and Economic Cooperation (#03188)
- ♦ BITAC / see International Road Transport Union (#14761)
- ♦ BITC / see Euro Chlor (#05659)
- ♦ **BITD** Bureau international des tarifs douaniers (#13124)
- ♦ BITEJ – Bureau international pour le tourisme et les échanges de la jeunesse (inactive)
- ♦ **BITH** Bureau international des textiles et de l'habillement (#15680)
- ♦ **BIT** International Society of Medical Doctors for Biophysical Information Therapy (#15253)
- ♦ BITOM – Bureau international d'information pour les toiles métalliques (internationally oriented national body)
- ♦ BITS – Berliner Informationszentrum für Transatlantische Sicherheit (internationally oriented national body)
- ♦ BITS/EU / see OITS/ European Commission for Social Tourism (#17713)
- ♦ BITS – Europe / see OITS/ European Commission for Social Tourism (#17713)
- ♦ BITS/European Union / see OITS/ European Commission for Social Tourism (#17713)
- ♦ BITS / see International Social Tourism Organisation (#14889)
- ♦ Bitumen Waterproofing Association / see European Waterproofing Association (#09084)
- ♦ BIU – Bircham International University (internationally oriented national body)
- ♦ BIUDP – Bureau international pour l'unification du droit pénal (inactive)
- ♦ **BIVEC** Benelux Interuniversitaire Groepering van Vervoerseconomen (#15985)
- ♦ **BIWF** British Israel World Federation (#03331)
- ♦ Bixby Center for Global Reproductive Health (internationally oriented national body)
- ♦ **BIZ** Bank für Internationalen Zahlungsausgleich (#03165)
- ♦ **BJCEM** Association internationale pour la Biennale des jeunes créateurs de l'Europe et de la Méditerranée (#11724)
- ♦ BJD / see Global Alliance for Musculoskeletal Health (#10213)
- ♦ Björn Carlsons Östersjöstiftelse / see BalticSea2020
- ♦ Bjuro Koordinacii Frahtovanija Sudov (inactive)
- ♦ BKA / see Baltic Road Association (#03138)
- ♦ **BKA** Baltijos Saliu Kelininku Asociacija (#03138)
- ♦ **BK** Blue Knights' International Law Enforcement Motorcycle Club (#03285)
- ♦ BKFS – Bjuro Koordinacii Frahtovanija Sudov (inactive)
- ♦ BKR International (internationally oriented national body)
- ♦ BKVGE – Berliner Kolleg für Vergleichende Geschichte Europas (internationally oriented national body)
- ♦ **BKWSU** Brahma Kumaris World Spiritual University (#03311)

♦ Black and Azov Seas Ports Association (BASPA) 03268

Exec Dir 6 Truda str, Illichivsk, Odessa, 68001, Ukraine. T. +380486891494. Fax +380486891494.
URL: http://www.bsec-organization.org/partners

History 24 Mar 1999, Georgia. Set up 24 Mar 1999, Poti (Georgia), by Conference of the General Directors of the ports of Black and Azov Seas, on the initiative of *Organization of Black Sea Economic Cooperation (BSEC, #17857)*, with which it has status of sectoral dialogue partnership. Creation approved by General Directorate for Energy and Transport of *European Commission (EC, #06633)*. **Aims** Participate in: formation of effective and comprehensible transport policy in the EU, world community and BSEC countries; development of Trans-Black Sea transport network with priority to international maritime transport lines, development of ports and key reference points of the network; development of shipping lines with access to the Mediterranean Sea and ocean transport routes; promotion of exchange of information in areas of mutual interest; development of cooperation between ports in the region and international bodies. **Structure** Council; Directorate, headed by Executive Director. **Languages** English, Russian. **Staff** 3.00 FTE, paid. **Finance** Members' dues. **Activities** Events/meetings. **Events** *Port Expansion Summit* Istanbul (Turkey) 2012.
Members Ports and organizations in 6 countries:
Bulgaria, Georgia, Romania, Russia, Türkiye, Ukraine.
IGO Relations Member of: *Organization of Black Sea Economic Cooperation (BSEC, #17857)*. Close cooperation with: *European Bank for Reconstruction and Development (EBRD, #06315)*; *European Commission (EC, #06633)* – General Directorate for Transport; *United Nations Economic Commission for Europe (UNECE, #20555)* Transport Division; ministries of foreign relations and of Transport. **NGO Relations** Close cooperation with: *European Sea Ports Organisation (ESPO, #08453)*. [2014.06.24/XJ1861/**E**]

♦ Black, Caspian Seas and Central Asia Silk Association (BACSA) . . . 03269

Pres 5-A Stamboliiski Str, 3000 Vratsa, Bulgaria. T. +359888479438. Fax +35992642028.
Vice-Pres Europe NAGREF Ag Research Station, Merarhias serron 18, 691 00 Komotini, Greece. T. +302531022731. Fax +30531033556. E-mail: nagrefk@otenet.gr.
Vice-Pres Central Asia/Caucasus Sericulture Research Inst, 1 Ipakchi Str, Tashkent, Uzbekistan. T. +998712490766. Fax +998712490061.
URL: http://www.bacsa-silk.org/

History Apr 2005, Tashkent (Uzbekistan). Founded following 'International Workshop on Revival and Promotion of Sericulture Industries and Small Enterprise Development in the Black, Caspian Seas and Central Asia Region' sponsored by *FAO (#09260)*. **Aims** Promote *sericulture* production in the region countries. **Structure** Executive Committee; National Coordinators. **Languages** English, Russian. **Staff** 5.00 FTE, voluntary. **Finance** Sponsorship. Budget (annual): euro 20,000. **Activities** Research/documentation; events/meetings. Active in: Azerbaijan, Bulgaria, Georgia, Greece, Italy, Romania, Türkiye, Uzbekistan. **Events** *Conference* Batumi (Georgia) 2019, *Conference* Sheki (Azerbaijan) 2017, *Conference* Sinaia (Romania) 2015, *Conference* Padua (Italy) 2013, *Conference* Romania 2011.
Members Full in 19 countries:
Albania, Armenia, Azerbaijan, Bulgaria, Georgia, Germany, Greece, Iran Islamic Rep, Italy, Kazakhstan, Poland, Romania, Russia, Spain, Switzerland, Tajikistan, Türkiye, Ukraine, Uzbekistan. [2022/XJ8152/**D**]

- ♦ Black Cross / see Anarchist Black Cross Network (#00812)

♦ Black European Women's Council (BEWC) 03270

Pres address not obtained. E-mail: contact@blackwomenineurope.com.

History Sep 2007, Vienna (Austria). Officially launched Sep 2008, Brussels (Belgium). **Structure** Board, comprising President, Vice-President, Treasurer and 5 members. **Events** *General Assembly* Netherlands 2009. [2015/XJ6068/**D**]

- ♦ Black Parliament of the Americas (unconfirmed)

♦ Black Sea Advisory Council (BISAC) 03271

Pres Ohrid Street 24-26 – fl 1, Odessos District, 9000 Varna, Bulgaria. T. +35952632092. E-mail: office@blsaceu.eu – elena.peneva@blsaceu.eu.
SG address not obtained.
URL: http://www.blsaceu.eu/

History 20 Jul 2015. Registration: Bulgaria. **Aims** Promote a balanced representation of all *fisheries* and aquaculture stakeholders; contribute to the achievement of the objectives of the Common Fisheries Policy. **Structure** General Assembly; Executive Committee; Secretariat. **Languages** Bulgarian, English, Romanian. **Staff** 5.00 FTE, paid. **Finance** Sources: members' dues; subsidies. **Members** Associations, non-governmental organizations and societies whose activities cover all major areas of fisheries in Bulgaria and Romania; environmental NGOs and other stakeholders having activities related to the sea. Membership countries not specified. [2022.10.19/XM7030/**E**]

- ♦ Black Sea Area Research Group (internationally oriented national body)

♦ Black Sea Broadcasting Regulatory Authorities Forum (BRAF) 03272

SG RTUK, Universiteler Mah 1597 Cad No 13, Bilkent, 06800 Ankara/Ankara, Türkiye. T. +903122975034. Fax +903122975459. E-mail: braf@rtuk.gov.tr.
URL: http://www.braf.info/

History Proposal to set up BRAF accepted Dec 2007, Kiev (Ukraine). Joint Declaration concerning Establishment released 30 Jun 2008, Istanbul (Turkey). **Aims** Establish and promote regular coordination, communication and cooperation; provide a forum for exchange of information, opinion and experiences about common issues of broadcasting. **Structure** Annual Conference; Executive Board; Committee of Experts; Permanent Secretariat. **Languages** English. **Staff** 3.00 FTE, paid. **Finance** No stipulated budget. Operation of Permanent Secretariat covered by Turkish Supreme Council of Radio and Television; meetings expenses covered by host country. **Activities** Events/meetings.
Members National authorities in 12 countries:
Albania, Armenia, Azerbaijan, Bulgaria, Georgia, Greece, Moldova, Romania, Russia, Serbia, Türkiye, Ukraine.
IGO Relations Observer Status in: Steering Committee on Media and Information Society of *Council of Europe (CE, #04881)*. Sectoral Dialogue Partnership in: *Organization of Black Sea Economic Cooperation (BSEC, #17857)*. [2022.02.08/XM5712/**F**]

- ♦ Black Sea – Caspian Sea International Fund / see International Foundation for Sustainable Peace and Development (#13678)
- ♦ Black Sea Coastal Association (internationally oriented national body)
- ♦ **Black Sea Commission** Commission on the Protection of the Black Sea Against Pollution (#04237)
- ♦ Black Sea Convention on Combating Organized Crime and Terrorism (1998 treaty)
- ♦ Black Sea Economic Cooperation / see Organization of Black Sea Economic Cooperation (#17857)

♦ Black Sea Economic Cooperation Centre for the Exchange of Statistical Data and Economic Information (BSECCESDEI) 03273

Permanent Intl Secretariat Sakip Sabanci Caddesi, Müsir Fuad Pasa Yalisi, Eski Tersane, 34460 Istanbul/Istanbul, Türkiye. T. +902122296330. Fax +902122296336. E-mail: info@bsec-organization.org.
URL: http://www.bsec-organization.org/

History 9 Dec 1993, pursuant to approval of Ministers of Foreign Affairs of the countries of *Organization of Black Sea Economic Cooperation (BSEC, #17857)*. Located at the State Institute of Statistics, Ankara (Turkey). **Aims** Compile relevant data from participating countries; establish a system of exchange of statistical data and economic information; realize common projects; represent the regional identity in the international arena; enhance cooperation and achieve comparable statistical data among BSEC countries. **Finance** Supported by the State Institute of Statistics of Turkey. **Activities** Knowledge management/information dissemination; projects/programmes; training/education. **Events** *Workshop* Ankara (Turkey) 1998. **Publications** *Turkey's Foreign Trade with the Black Sea Economic Cooperation Countries* (4 a year); *Social and Economic Indicators of the Black Sea Economic Cooperation Countries* (annual). Surveys; reports.
Members Participating States (12):
Albania, Armenia, Azerbaijan, Bulgaria, Georgia, Greece, Moldova, Romania, Russia, Serbia, Türkiye, Ukraine.
IGO Relations Collaborates with: *OECD (#17693)*; *Statistical Office of the European Union (Eurostat, #19974)*; *United Nations (UN, #20515)*. [2016.01.21/XE2651/**E***]

- ♦ Black Sea Economic Cooperation Free Trade Area (unconfirmed)
- ♦ Black Sea Economic Cooperation Pact (1993 treaty)

♦ Black Sea Energy Research Centre (BSERC) 03274

Manager 7 Viktor Grigorovich Str, 1606 Sofia, Bulgaria. T. +35929806854. E-mail: office@bsrec.bg.
URL: http://www.bserc.eu/

History 2007. Took over activities of *Black Sea Regional Energy Centre (BSREC, inactive)*. Registration: Bulgaria. **Aims** Foster cooperation between the Black Sea Region countries and the European Union in the field of energy and *climate change* mitigation with emphasis on research. **Structure** General Assembly. **Languages** Bulgarian, English, French, Russian. **Staff** 6.00 FTE, paid. **Finance** Funded on project basis. **Activities** Politics/policy/regulatory; research/documentation; knowledge management/information dissemination; networking/liaising; training/education; research and development. **Publications** Newsletters; country reports; brochures; articles. [2022/XM4454/**D**]

- ♦ Black Sea Environmental Programme (inactive)

♦ Black Sea Euroregion (BSER) 03275

Gen Dir General Directorate for Projects, Constanta County Council, Bd Tomis Nr 51, 900725 Constantza, Romania. T. +40241488009 – +40241488442. Fax +40241488489. E-mail: bser@cjc.ro.
URL: http://www.bser.eu/

History Founded 26 Sep 2008, Varna (Bulgaria). Registered in accordance with Romanian law. **Aims** Develop cooperation among members; represent and support common interests; cooperate with existing Black Sea international organizations. **Structure** General Assembly; Board of Directors, including President; Standing Committees; Board of Auditors. **Languages** English. **Staff** from Constanta County Council. **Finance** Members' dues. Other sources: endowments, donations and other voluntary contributions; sponsorship; participation fees for events; interests or dividends; other legal sources. **Activities** Has developed four projects submitted twice under the Joint Operational Program Black Sea Basin 2007-2013 (both rejected). **Events** *General Assembly* Constantza (Romania) 2008.
Members Regions, cities and counties (14) in 5 countries:

Armenia, Bulgaria, Georgia, Moldova, Romania.
Observers:
Black Sea Bulgarian Local Authorities; National Union of Counties in Romania.
IGO Relations *Congress of Local and Regional Authorities of the Council of Europe (#04677)* is Honorary Member. [2012.09.03/XM2968/**D**]

♦ Black Sea MOU – Memorandum of Understanding on Port State Control in the Black Sea (2000 treaty)

♦ Black Sea NGO Network (BSNN) 03276

Exec Dir Sheinovo 12, PO Box 91, 9000 Varna, Bulgaria. T. +35952615856. Fax +35952602047. E-mail: bsnn@bsnn.org.
URL: http://www.bsnn.org/

History 5 Sep 1998, Varna (Bulgaria), with the initial support of *Oxfam Novib*. Took over activities of *Black Sea NGO Forum (BS NGO Forum, inactive)*. Also referred to as *International Black Sea NGO Network*. Registered in accordance with Bulgarian law. **Aims** Contribute to the *protection* and rehabilitation of the Black Sea, including the Azov Sea and to the *sustainable development* of the Black Sea countries. **Structure** General Assembly (every 2 years). Board of 6 members, one from each of the Black Sea countries. National assemblies. Regional office in Bulgaria; national offices (5) in the other member countries. **Languages** Bulgarian, English. **Staff** 8.00 FTE, paid; 8.00 FTE, voluntary. **Finance** Members' dues. Projects. **Activities** Informs the public; organizes seminars, workshops, public hearings and conferences; promotes campaigns, environmental education, environmental survey activities and lobbying and advocacy at national, regional and international levels; develops and implements projects on priority issues; maintains active contacts with similar organizations. **Events** *Black Sea youth leaders conference* Varna (Bulgaria) 2006. **Publications** *Black Sea Shared* (annual) – newsletter.
Members NGOs (64) in 6 countries:
Bulgaria, Georgia, Romania, Russia, Türkiye, Ukraine.
IGO Relations Permanent Observer of: *Commission on the Protection of the Black Sea Against Pollution (Black Sea Commission, #04237)*. **NGO Relations** Member of: *International Federation for Sustainable Development and Fight to Poverty in the Mediterranean-Black Sea (FISPMED, #13562)*. Instrumental in setting up: *European Seas Environmental Cooperation (ESEC, inactive)*. [2011.06.01/XF6273/**F**]

♦ Black Sea Regional Energy Centre (inactive)

♦ Black Sea Region Association of Shipbuilders and Ship Repairers (BRASS) 03277

Address not obtained.

History 8 Oct 1993, Varna (Bulgaria), when statutes were adopted. Association created in conformity with *Black Sea Economic Cooperation Pact (1993)*. Registered in accordance with Bulgarian law, Feb 1994. **Aims** Promote economic, scientific, technical and commercial cooperation among member shipbuilders and ship repairers, while recognizing and respecting historically established political, social and cultural systems and the need for a unified ecological policy in the region. **Structure** General Assembly (annual). Managing Council, comprising Chairman, 3 Deputies and Executive Director. Executive Body of 3 members, managed by Executive Director. Control Commission. Head Office in Varna (Bulgaria). **Languages** English, Russian. **Staff** 2.00 FTE, paid. **Finance** Members' dues. Grants. **Activities** Defends members' interests and extends mutual help in solution of production issues; organizes meetings and conferences. exchanges technological, economic, financial, commercial and pricing information. **Events** *Meeting / General Assembly* St Petersburg (Russia) 2005, *Joint conference* Varna (Bulgaria) 2001, *Conference* Varna (Bulgaria) 2000, *Conference* Odessa (Ukraine) 1999, *Joint conference / Conference* Varna (Bulgaria) 1997. **Publications** *Information List* (4 a year); *Infopont Bulletin* (2 a year) in English, Russian.
Members Companies (16) in 3 countries:
Bulgaria, Russia, Ukraine.
IGO Relations Official contacts with: *OECD (#17693)*. Sectoral dialogue partnership status (status renewed for 1 Nov 2004 to 1 Nov 2006) with: *Organization of Black Sea Economic Cooperation (BSEC, #17857)*. **NGO Relations** Official contacts with: *Organization of the Black Sea Economic Cooperation Business Council (BSEC BC, no recent information)*; *International Black Sea Club (IBSC, #12358)*; *International Black Sea Region Association of Shipowners (BINSA, #12359)*; national shipbuilder associations. [2010/XD5601/**D**]

♦ Black Sea Society of Clinical Microbiology and Infectious Diseases (unconfirmed)

♦ Black Sea Trade and Development Bank (BSTDB) 03278

SG 1 Komninon Street, 546 24 Thessaloniki, Greece. T. +302310290400. Fax +302310221796. E-mail: info@bstdb.org.
Pres address not obtained.
URL: http://www.bstdb.org/

History 1998, Thessaloniki (Greece). Established as an international financial institution by an international treaty called the Agreement Establishing the Black Sea Trade and Development Bank, signed 30 Jun 1994, Tbilisi (Georgia) and entered into force 24 Jan 1997 (UN registration number 36909), pursuant to Art 102 of the UN Charter. Became fully operational 1 Jun 1999. Financial pillar of *Organization of Black Sea Economic Cooperation (BSEC, #17857)*. Registration: No/ID: 36909, Start date: 23 Oct 2000. **Aims** Accelerate economic development; promote cooperation among shareholder countries; promote regional trade and project/corporate finance; facilitate the efforts of member states to create stronger links among their economies. **Structure** Board of Governors; Board of Directors; Headquarters located in Thessaloniki (Greece). **Languages** English. **Staff** 113.00 FTE, paid. **Finance** Annual budget: 25,000,000 EUR (2023). **Activities** Events/meetings; financial and/or material support. As the financial pillar of the BSEC, supports economic development and regional cooperation in the Black Sea Region through trade and project finance lending, guarantees, and equity participation in private enterprises and public entities in member countries. Rated A-/A-2 by Standard and Poor's, and A2/P1 by Moody's. Active in all member countries. **Events** *Annual Meeting and Business Forum* Baku (Azerbaijan) 2022, *Annual Meeting and Business Forum* Istanbul (Turkey) 2019, *Annual Meeting and Business Forum* Sochi (Russia) 2018, *Annual Meeting and Business Forum* Chisinau (Moldova) 2017, *Annual Meeting and Business Forum* Chania (Greece) 2016. **Publications** Annual Report.
Members Participating States/Shareholders (11):
Albania, Armenia, Azerbaijan, Bulgaria, Georgia, Greece, Moldova, Romania, Russia, Türkiye, Ukraine.
Observer institutions (12), including 9 organizations listed in this Yearbook:
Asian Development Bank (ADB, #01422); *European Bank for Reconstruction and Development (EBRD, #06315)*; *European Development Finance Institutions (EDFI, #06913)*; *European Investment Bank (EIB, #07599)*; *International Finance Corporation (IFC, #13597)*; *International Investment Bank (IIB, #13951)*; *Islamic Corporation for the Development of the Private Sector (ICD, see: #16044)*; *Nordic Investment Bank (NIB, #17327)*; *Société de promotion et de participations pour la coopération économique, Paris (PROPARCO)*.
IGO Relations Accredited by (1): *United Nations Framework Convention on Climate Change (UNFCCC, 1992)*. Observer status with (1): *The World Bank Group (#21218)*. Member of (1): *Global Partnership for Effective Development Co-operation (GPEDC, #10532)*. **NGO Relations** Member of (4): *European Development Finance Institutions (EDFI, #06913)*; Evaluation Cooperation Group (ECG); *International Council on Archives (ICA, #12996)*; *International Development Finance Club (IDFC, #13159)*. [2023.02.16/XF5680/t/**F***]

♦ Black Sea University Foundation
♦ Black Sea University Network (internationally oriented national body)
♦ Black Sea University for Women (meeting series)
♦ Blacksmith Institute / see Pure Earth (#18578)
♦ Black Women in Europe Social Media Group (internationally oriented national body)
♦ BLADEX / see Banco Latinoamericano de Comercio Exterior (#03159)
♦ **BLADEX** Banco Latinoamericano de Comercio Exterior (#03159)
♦ BLA / see European Flavour Association (#07269)

♦ Blaise Cendrars International Society 03279

Association internationale Blaise Cendrars (AIBC)
Contact 16 rue du Rempart Châtelet, 28000 Chartres, France.
URL: http://www.cebc-cendrars.ch/

History 1978, USA, on the initiative of Monique Chefdor and Jean-François Marie Thibault. **Aims** Promote study and appreciation of the works of Swiss *author* Frédéric Sauser aka Blaise Cendrars (1887-1961). **Publications** *Feuille de routes* (periodical). [2016.03.04/XN1881/**E**]

♦ Blaue Weltkette (#21235)
♦ Blauwe Wereldketen: voor de Bescherming van de Dieren en de Natuur (#21235)
♦ **BLE** Budhana Ligo Esperantista (#03348)
♦ Blessed Sacrament Sisters (religious order)
♦ Blessed Trinity Missionary Institute (religious order)
♦ Blessing of Africa Empowerment Foundation (internationally oriented national body)
♦ Blessings International (internationally oriented national body)
♦ **BLEU** Belgian-Luxembourg Economic Union (#03195)
♦ **BLEU** Belgisch-Luxemburgs Economische Unie (#03195)
♦ **BLF** Biennale de la langue française (#03231)
♦ **BLIA** Buddha's Light International Association (#03346)
♦ BLIC / see European Tyre and Rubber Manufacturers' Association (#08963)
♦ **BLIET** Bureau de liaison internationale des écoles de théâtre (#03370)

♦ Blind Children's Fund (BCF) 03280

Exec Dir PO Box 187, Grand Ledge MI 48837, USA. T. +15174884887.
Facebook: https://www.facebook.com/Blind-Childrens-Fund-121361740748/

History 1978, Lansing, MI (USA). Former names and other names: *International Institute for Visually Impaired* – former (1978). **Aims** Improve the quality of life for infant and young blind or visually impaired pre-school children world-wide; promote, foster, encourage and develop activities and programmes pertaining to their growth, development, education and welfare; increase awareness among the world community regarding the need for early services for pre-school blind or visually impaired children and their parents; engage in activities to meet that need. **Structure** Board (meets 4 to 8 times a year); Advisory Board; local Parent Groups. **Languages** English, Spanish. **Staff** 1.00 FTE, paid; 50.00 FTE, voluntary. **Finance** Members' dues. Other sources: fund raising; donations from service clubs, churches and individuals; sale of material. **Activities** Organizes: in-service teacher education; information clearing house; pre-school programmes; annual seminar meetings; international symposia; workshops. **Events** *Conference* Albuquerque, NM (USA) 1992, *International Symposium* Edinburgh (UK) 1988, *International symposium* Edinburgh (UK) 1987, *International Symposium* Aruba 1983, *International Symposium* Tel Aviv (Israel) 1981. **Publications** *VIP Newsletter* (4 a year) – also in Braille. Books; symposium proceedings.
Members Principally in North-America Contributing; Agency; Support; Sponsoring; Patron; Benefactor. Members in 43 countries and territories:
Antigua-Barbuda, Argentina, Australia, Austria, Bangladesh, Belgium, Canada, China, Colombia, Costa Rica, Denmark, Dominican Rep, Finland, Germany, Greece, Guatemala, India, Indonesia, Israel, Italy, Jamaica, Kenya, Mexico, Neth Antilles, New Zealand, Nigeria, Norway, Panama, Peru, Philippines, Puerto Rico, South Africa, Spain, St Lucia, Sweden, Switzerland, Taiwan, Trinidad-Tobago, UK, Uruguay, USA, Virgin Is USA, Zimbabwe. [2015/XF5810/f/**F**]

♦ Blinken European Institute, Columbia University, New York (internationally oriented national body)

♦ Blockchain for Europe 03281

SG Rue Montoyer 47, 1000 Brussels, Belgium. E-mail: secretariat@blockchain4europe.eu.
URL: http://www.blockchain4europe.eu/

History EU Transparency Register: 910251734425-24. Registration: EU Transparency Register, No/ID: 910251734425-24. **Aims** Create a coherent voice of the Distributed Ledger Technologies (DLT) and blockchain industry; share expertise and engage with European decision-makers about the true nature and potential of Blockchain and DLT; ensure that upcoming regulation promotes and protects innovation in the ecosystem. **Structure** Board; Secretariat. **Languages** English. **Finance** Sources: members' dues. **Activities** Awareness raising; events/meetings; knowledge management/information dissemination; politics/policy/regulatory; training/education. **Events** *Blockchain for Europe Summit* Brussels (Belgium) 2021, *Blockchain for Europe Summit* Brussels (Belgium) 2019, *Blockchain for Europe Summit* Brussels (Belgium) 2018.
Members Full in 9 countries:
Belgium, China, Costa Rica, Estonia, Germany, Poland, Singapore, UK, USA. [2021.06.23/XM8503/**D**]

♦ Blood and Honour (Blood and Honour) 03282

Address not obtained.
URL: http://www.bloodandhonour.org/

History 1987. A militant neo-Nazi network. **Activities** Organizes concerts; distributes records by Rock Against Communism bands. **Publications** *B and Honour Magazine*.
Members Divisions in 20 countries:
Australia, Belgium, Canada, Croatia, Cyprus, Czechia, Finland, France, Germany, Greece, Hungary, Italy, Netherlands, New Zealand, Portugal, Slovenia, Spain, UK, Ukraine, USA. [2006/XM1394/s/**F**]

♦ Bloomberg Philanthropies (internationally oriented national body)
♦ **BISAC** Black Sea Advisory Council (#03271)
♦ Blue Army – World Apostolate of Fatima (religious order)
♦ BLUE – Blue Marine Foundation (internationally oriented national body)

♦ Blue Finance 03283

CEO address not obtained. E-mail: info@blue-finance.org.
URL: http://blue-finance.org/

Aims Improve the management of at least 20 *Marine* Protected Areas (MPAs) by 2030. **Structure** Works under the institutional umbrella of *United Nations (UN, #20515)*. **Activities** Advocacy/lobbying/activism. **IGO Relations** Partners include: *European Investment Bank (EIB, #07599)*; *Partnerships in Environmental Management for the Seas of East Asia (PEMSEA, #18242)*; *UNDP (#20292)*; *University of the West Indies (UWI, #20705)*. **NGO Relations** Partners include: *AIDA*; *Caribbean Biodiversity Fund (CBF)*; *Conservation Finance Alliance (CFA)*; *Conservation International (CI)*; *Fauna & Flora International (FFI, #09277)*; *International Coral Reef Initiative (ICRI, #12965)*; *International Institute for Environment and Development (IIED, #13877)*; *The Nature Conservancy (TNC)*; *WildAid*. Member of: *High Level Panel for a Sustainable Ocean Economy (Panel, #10917)* Advisory Network. [2020/XM8930/**F**]

♦ Blue Fish / see Blue Fish Europe (#03284)

♦ Blue Fish Europe 03284

Pres 1 rue Fulvy, 56100 Lorient CEDEX, France. T. +33297891325. E-mail: contact@bluefish.fr – president@bluefish.fr.
Registered Address Rue Montoyer 47, 1000 Brussels, Belgium.
URL: https://bluefisheurope.org/en/

History Former names and other names: *European Association for the Promotion of Sustainable and Responsible Fisheries (Blue Fish)* – former; *Association européenne de promotion de la pêche durable et responsable* – former. Registration: Crossroads Bank for Enterprises, No/ID: 0561.720.961, Start date: 5 Sep 2014, Belgium. **Aims** Promote excellence in the European fishing sector; safeguard marine resources while supporting the socio-economic dynamism of European coastal communities. **Structure** Board of Directors.
Members Full in 1 country:
France.
NGO Relations Member of (1): *North Western Waters Advisory Council (NWWAC, #17607)*. [2023.02.14/XJ9739/**D**]

♦ Blue Knights' International Law Enforcement Motorcycle Club (BK) 03285

Main Office 38 Alden St, Bangor ME 04401, USA. T. +12079474600. Fax +12079415814. E-mail: hq@blueknights.org – international@blueknights.org.
URL: http://www.blueknights.org/

History 1974, as Blue Knights. Constitution and current name adopted 22 May 1983. Constitution amended: 21 Jul 1986; 20 Jul 1987; 18 Jul 1988; 17 Jul 1990. By-laws approved 24 May 1983; amended: 20 Jul 1987; 18 Jul 1988; 31 Dec 1990. **Aims** Promote and advance the *sport* of motorcycling; serve the interests of motorcycle owners and users. **Structure** International Board of Directors, composed of President, Immediate Past President, Vice-President, Secretary, Treasurer, Chairman of the Board of Governors and one representative from each of the sanctioned Conferences. Executive Committee, comprising President, Vice President, Secretary and Treasurer. **Finance** Members' dues. Budget (annual): US$ 300,000. **Publications** *Blue Knights News* (4 a year).

Members Chapters in 16 countries:
Australia, Austria, Belgium, Canada, Croatia, Finland, France, Germany, Ireland, Italy, Netherlands, Norway, Sweden, Switzerland, UK, USA. [2018/XN3542/v/**F**]

- ♦ Blue Marine Foundation (internationally oriented national body)
- ♦ Blue Moon Fund (internationally oriented national body)
- ♦ Blue Ocean Institute / see Safina Center
- ♦ Blue Planet Foundation (internationally oriented national body)
- ♦ Blue Planet Project (internationally oriented national body)
- ♦ Blue Plan – Regional Activity Centre for the Mediterranean / see Plan Bleu pour l'environnement et le développement en Méditerranée (#18379)

♦ Blue Shield International (BSI) 03286

Contact School of Arts and Cultures – Armstrong Bldg, Newcastle Univ, Newcastle upon Tyne, NE1 7RU, UK. E-mail: blueshield.international@theblueshield.org.
URL: https://theblueshield.org/

History Founded on merger of *International Committee of the Blue Shield (ICBS, inactive)* and *Association of National Committees of the Blue Shield (ANCBS, inactive)*. Statutes adopted 6 Apr 2016, Amsterdam (Netherlands). Registration: Netherlands. **Aims** Protect cultural property and cultural heritage in crisis, conflicts, natural, and human-made disasters around the world. **Structure** General Assembly; International Board; Secretariat. Represented on the Board: *International Council on Archives (ICA, #12996)*; *International Council of Museums (ICOM, #13051)*; *International Council on Monuments and Sites (ICOMOS, #13049)*; *International Federation of Library Associations and Institutions (IFLA, #13470)*. **Languages** English. **Staff** 2.50 FTE, paid. Voluntary. **Activities** Advocacy/lobbying/activism; awareness raising; capacity building; events/meetings; guidance/assistance/consulting; humanitarian/emergency aid; knowledge management/information dissemination; networking/liaising; projects/programmes; research/documentation; standards/guidelines; training/education.
Members National Committees in 30 countries and territories:
Argentina, Australia, Austria, Belgium, Cameroon, Curaçao, Czechia, Denmark, Fiji, France, Georgia, Germany, Greece, Guatemala, Iceland, Ireland, Korea Rep, Lebanon, Mali, Netherlands, Niger, North Macedonia, Norway, Peru, Poland, Senegal, Slovakia, Türkiye, UK, USA.
IGO Relations Official advisory body to the Committee for the Protection of Cultural Property in the Event of Armed Conflict, established under the Article 27 (3) of *Second Protocol to The Hague Convention for the Protection of Cultural Property in the Event of Armed Conflict (1999)*. **NGO Relations** Memorandum of Understanding with (1): *International Committee of the Red Cross (ICRC, #12799)*. Member of (1): *European Heritage Alliance 3.3 (#07477)*. [2022.05.04/XM8899/**F**]

♦ Bluetooth SIG 03287

CEO 5209 Lake Washington Blvd NE, Suite 350, Kirkland WA 98033, USA. T. +14256913535. Fax +14254846366.
URL: https://www.bluetooth.com/

History Incorporated in the State of Delaware (USA). Registration: Start date: 13 Nov 2000, USA. **Aims** Expand Bluetooth technology by fostering member collaboration to create new and improved specifications; drive global Bluetooth interoperability; grow the Bluetooth brand by increasing the awareness, understanding, and adoption of Bluetooth technology. **Structure** Board of Directors; Executive Team. **Activities** Networking/liaising; standards/guidelines. **Events** *Meeting* Vienna (Austria) 2019. **Members** Companies (over 34000). Membership countries not specified. [2020/AA0592/**F**]

- ♦ Blue Ventures (internationally oriented national body)
- ♦ Blue Ventures Conservation / see Blue Ventures
- ♦ Blue World Institute of Marine Research and Conservation (internationally oriented national body)
- ♦ Blumont International (internationally oriented national body)
- ♦ Blu-ray Disc Association (unconfirmed)
- ♦ BLV – International Workshop on Baryon and Lepton Number Violation (meeting series)
- ♦ BMA – Bangladesh Maritime Academy (internationally oriented national body)
- ♦ **BMB** Baltic Marine Biologists (#03125)
- ♦ **BMDA** Baltic Management Development Association (#03123)
- ♦ **BMDA** Baltijos Vadybos Pletros Asociacija (#03123)
- ♦ BMF / see Global Foundation for the Sustainability of Billion Minds
- ♦ **BMF** Baltic Management Foundation (#03124)
- ♦ BMGF – Bill and Melinda Gates Foundation (internationally oriented national body)
- ♦ BMG – International Conference on Bulk Metallic Glasses (with High Entropy Alloys) (meeting series)
- ♦ **BMI** Battelle Memorial Institute (#03187)
- ♦ BMI – Belgische Maatschappij voor Internationale Investering (internationally oriented national body)
- ♦ BMI / see BMI Executive Institute (#03288)
- ♦ **BMI** BMI Executive Institute (#03288)
- ♦ **BMI** Bureau maritime international (#14097)

♦ BMI Executive Institute (BMI) 03288

Dir-Gen Konstitucijos ave 7, LT-09308 Vilnius, Lithuania. T. +37060177438. E-mail: info@bmiinstitute.com.
BMI Brussels Av Louise 65, 1050 Brussels, Belgium. Fax +3225357980. E-mail: info@bmibrussels.com.
URL: http://www.bmiinstitute.com

History Jan 1999, Vilnius (Lithuania). Train high-level executives with quality content from top European business schools, taught by top management educators. Former names and other names: *Baltic Management Institute (BMI)* – former. **Aims** Enhance management skills of executives and business people in the wider Baltic-Nordic region so as to ensure its continuing economic success and its integration in the global economy. **Structure** Governing Board; International Academic Council. **Languages** English. **Activities** Training/education.
Members Universities and educational institutions in 6 countries:
Belgium, China, Denmark, France, Lithuania, Norway.
NGO Relations Member of (4): *Baltic Management Development Association (BMDA, #03123)*; *CEEMAN – International Association for Management Development in Dynamic Societies (CEEMAN, #03625)*; *EFMD – The Management Development Network (#05387)*; *United Nations Global Compact (#20567)*. [2021.08.31/XM0533/j/**D**]

- ♦ BMJD – World Congress on Controversies, Debates and Consensus in Bone, Muscle and Joint Diseases (meeting series)
- ♦ **BMLA** Baltic Medico-Legal Association (#03127)
- ♦ **BML** Balti Maanteeliit (#03138)
- ♦ **BMM** Benelux Vereniging voor Merken- en Modellenrecht (#03199)
- ♦ BMMF / see Interserve (#15974)
- ♦ BMN / see Balkan Museum Network (#03080)
- ♦ **BM Network** Balkan Museum Network (#03080)
- ♦ BMR – Bureau of Middle East Recycling (internationally oriented national body)
- ♦ BMS / see International Masonry Society (#14114)
- ♦ BMS – International Symposium on Biomechanics and Medicine in Swimming (meeting series)
- ♦ BMS World Mission (internationally oriented national body)
- ♦ **BMU** Balkan Mountaineering Union (#03079)
- ♦ BMW Center for German and European Studies (internationally oriented national body)
- ♦ BN / see Digni
- ♦ BNA – Baltic Neurosurgical Association (no recent information)

♦ B'nai B'rith Europe (BBE) 03289

Dir Rue Dautzenberg 36, 1050 Brussels, Belgium. T. +3226469298. E-mail: direction@bnaibritheurope.org.
SG address not obtained.
URL: https://www.bnaibritheurope.org/

History 1999. Founded when District 19 Continental Europe (all European countries and B'nai B'rith France) merged with District 15 United Kingdom. Part if *B'nai B'rith International (BBI, #03290)*. Registration: Banque-Carrrefour des Entreprises, No/ID: 0733.537.655, Start date: 30 Aug 2019, Belgium; EU Transparency Register, No/ID: 794476524670-73, Start date: 23 Nov 2016. **Aims** Combat anti-Semitism as well as promote tolerance and intergroup understanding around the globe according to its motto "Benevolence, Brotherly & Sisterly Love and Harmony". **Structure** Executive Committee. **Activities** Advocacy/lobbying/activism; events/meetings; projects/programmes.
Members Lodges in 23 countries:
Austria, Belgium, Bulgaria, Croatia, Czechia, Denmark, France, Germany, Greece, Hungary, Italy, Netherlands, Norway, Poland, Romania, Russia, Serbia, Slovakia, Spain, Sweden, Switzerland, UK, Ukraine. [2021/AA2384/**D**]

♦ B'nai B'rith International (BBI) 03290

Pres 1120 20th St NW, Ste 300 North, Washington DC 20036, USA. T. +12028576500. E-mail: info@bnaibrith.org – president@bnaibrith.org.
Main: http://www.bnaibrith.org/

History 13 Oct 1843, New York, NY (USA). Founded as a (US national) Jewish service organization. Internationalized 28 May 1959, Jerusalem (Israel), on setting up of the now defunct *International Council of B'nai B'rith (ICBB) – Conseil international B'nai B'rith*. Registration: EU Transparency Register, No/ID: 162711719247-82, Start date: 20 Oct 2015. **Aims** Advance human rights; advocate for Israel and on issues concerning seniors and their families; ensure access to safe and affordable housing for low-income seniors; improve communities and help communities in crisis. **Structure** Policy Forum (annual); Board of Governors; Executive Board of Directors; Units; Lodges; Chapters. Includes: *B'nai B'rith Europe (BBE, #03289)*. **Languages** Danish, Dutch, English, French, German, Hebrew, Italian, Norwegian, Portuguese, Russian, Spanish, Swedish. **Staff** Paid. **Activities** Advocacy/lobbying/activism; events/meetings; humanitarian/emergency aid; knowledge management/information dissemination; networking/liaising; politics/policy/regulatory; projects/programmes. **Events** *International Conference* Budapest (Hungary) 2020, *International Leadership Forum* Washington, DC (USA) 2019, *Policy Conference* Washington, DC (USA) 2015, *Policy Conference* Panama (Panama) 2014, *Policy Conference* Washington, DC (USA) 2013. **Publications** *B'nai B'rith Magazine* (4 a year); *IMPACT* (4 a year); *International Center for Human Rights and Public Policy This Week*; *Real News from Israel*; *Seniority Review*.
Members Individuals (500,000) in 51 countries and territories:
Argentina, Australia, Austria, Belgium, Bolivia, Brazil, Bulgaria, Canada, Chile, Colombia, Costa Rica, Croatia, Cuba, Curaçao, Czechia, Denmark, Ecuador, El Salvador, France, Germany, Greece, Guatemala, Hungary, Israel, Italy, Jamaica, Luxembourg, Mexico, Netherlands, New Zealand, Nicaragua, Norway, Panama, Paraguay, Peru, Poland, Portugal, Romania, Russia, Serbia, Singapore, Slovakia, South Africa, Spain, Sweden, Switzerland, UK, Ukraine, Uruguay, USA, Venezuela.
Consultative Status Consultative status granted from: *ECOSOC (#05331)* (Ros C); *UNESCO (#20322)* (Consultative Status); *Council of Europe (CE, #04881)* (Participatory Status). **IGO Relations** Cooperates with (1): *OAS (#17629)*. Associated with Department of Global Communications of the United Nations. **NGO Relations** Member of (3): *American Council for Voluntary International Action (InterAction)*; *Committee of Religious NGOs at the United Nations (CRNGOs, #04282)*; *World Jewish Restitution Organization (WJRO, #21601)*. Instrumental in setting up (1): *Hillel International (see: #03290)*. Former constituent organizations, now separate: *Anti-Defamation League of B'nai B'rith (ADL)*; *B'nai B'rith Youth Organization (BBYO, #03291)*; *Jewish Women International (JWI, #16114)*; *Jewish Prisoner Services International (JPSI)*. *'B'nai B'rith Center for Jewish Identity (CJI)'* – includes the work of the former *B'nai B'rith International Commission on Continuing Jewish Education (inactive)*. [2021.03.10/XC0193/v/**C**]

- ♦ B'nai B'rith Women / see Jewish Women International (#16114)

♦ B'nai B'rith Youth Organization (BBYO) 03291

Noar Le'noar

Main Office 800 Eighth St NW, Washington DC 20001, USA. T. +12028576633. Fax +12028576568.
URL: http://www.bbyo.org/

History 1924, Omaha, NE (USA). Formerly the youth branch of *B'nai B'rith International (BBI, #03290)*; now operates separately. Encompasses *Aleph Zadik Aleph (AZA)* and *B'nai B'rith Girls (BBG)*. **Aims** Assist *young Jewish* people to achieve personal growth according to their individual capacities, leading to personally satisfying and socially useful lives in the Jewish community and the larger communities of which they are a part. **Structure** Chapters (700) in 60 countries. **Activities** Components: B'nai B'rith Girls (BBG) for young women and Aleph Zadik Aleph (AZA) for young men; Teen Connection; B'nai B'rith Beber Camp and B'nai B'rith Perlman Camp; Summer Leadership Programs: International Kallah, International Leadership Training Conference (ILTC), Chapter Leadership Training Conference (CLTC), Israel Summer Institute (ISI), annual BBYO International Convention (always in Starlight PA – USA). **Events** *International Convention* Dallas, TX (USA) 2023, *International convention* Starlight, PA (USA) 1995. **Publications** *The Shofar* (4 a year).
Members Young people (30,000) in 12 countries:
Australia, Belgium, Canada, France, Germany, Ireland, Israel, Netherlands, Russia, Switzerland, UK, USA. [2022/XE3944/**E**]

- ♦ **BNE** Bereavement Network Europe (#03211)
- ♦ **BNE** Broadcast Network Europe (#03335)
- ♦ **BNF-PRM** Baltic and North Sea Forum of Physical and Rehabilitation Medicine (#03132)
- ♦ **BNI** Baltic Nest Institute (#03129)
- ♦ BNITM – Bernhard Nocht Institut für Tropenmedizin (internationally oriented national body)
- ♦ **BNNS** Beekeeping Network North-South (#03191)

♦ BNVKI-AIABN: Benelux Association for Artificial Intelligence (BNVKI-AIABN) 03292

BeNeLux Vereniging voor Kunstmatige Intelligentie (BNVKI)

Sec Eindhoven Univ of Technology, Dept of Industrial Engineering, De lismortel 2, Room Pav D20, 5600 MB Eindhoven, Netherlands. T. +31402472872. E-mail: board@bnvki.org.
Chair VU Amsterdam, Dept of Computer Science, De Boelelaan 1081a, Room T3-02c, 1081 HV Amsterdam, Netherlands. T. +31205987750.
URL: http://bnvki.org/

History 1981, Netherlands, as BNVKI. Merged with Belgian AI Associations to become BNVKI-AIABN. Current title adopted when merged with Luxembourg organization, 2008. **Aims** Stimulate research on, and the application and education of Artificial Intelligence (AI), as well as dissemination of knowledge about AI. **Structure** Board. **Finance** Members' dues. **Activities** Events/meetings. **Events** *Annual Conference* Amsterdam (Netherlands) 2016, *Annual Conference* Hasselt (Belgium) 2015, *Annual Conference* Nijmegen (Netherlands) 2014, *Annual Conference* Delft (Netherlands) 2013, *Annual Conference* Maastricht (Netherlands) 2012. **Publications** *Benelux AI Newsletter*.
Members Full in 3 countries:
Belgium, Luxembourg, Netherlands.
NGO Relations *European Association for Artificial Intelligence (EurAI, #05943)*. [2019/XJ9451/**D**]

- ♦ **BNVKI-AIABN** BNVKI-AIABN: Benelux Association for Artificial Intelligence (#03292)
- ♦ **BNVKI** BeNeLux Vereniging voor Kunstmatige Intelligentie (#03292)
- ♦ **BOA** Baltic Orthodontic Association (#03134)
- ♦ BOA – Blessing of Africa Empowerment Foundation (internationally oriented national body)
- ♦ **BOAD** Banque ouest africaine de développement (#03170)
- ♦ **BOAF** Behavioral Optometry Academy Foundation (#03193)
- ♦ BOAG – British Overseas Aid Group (internationally oriented national body)

♦ Boao Forum for Asia (BFA) 03293

Secretariat Room 2210 – China World Tower, No 1 Jianguomenwai Ave, 100004 Beijing, China. T. +861065057377. Fax +861065051833. E-mail: bfa@boaoforum.org.
URL: http://www.boaoforum.org/

History 27 Feb 2001, Boao (China). **Aims** Promote regional *economic integration* throughout Asia. **Structure** General Meeting (annual). Board of Directors; Council of Advisors; Secretariat. **Finance** Membership fees. **Activities** Annual conference in Boao (China). **Events** *Annual conference* Boao (China) 2019, *Seoul Conference* Seoul (Korea Rep) 2018, *Financial Cooperation Conference* Bangkok (Thailand) 2017, *Financial Cooperation Conference* Sydney, NSW (Australia) 2015, *Financial Cooperation Conference* Dubai (United Arab Emirates) 2014. **IGO Relations** *Research and Information System for Developing Countries, India (RIS, India)*. [2014/XM2382/**E**]

♦ Board of European Students of Technology (BEST) 03294

Bureau des étudiants européens en technologie

Pres Rond Point Schuman 6, 5th floor, 1040 Brussels, Belgium. E-mail: info@best.eu.org – president@best-eu.org.
URL: http://www.best.eu.org/

History Apr 1988, Grenoble (France). Meeting: Nov 1988, Eindhoven (Netherlands); 1st General Assembly and registration: Apr 1989, Berlin West (Germany FR). Registration: AISBL/IVZW, Belgium; EU Transparency Register, No/ID: 83163169410-75. **Aims** Help European students to achieve an international mindset and to develop the capacity to work in culturally diverse environments; create opportunities for personal development of students and support them in reaching their full potential. **Structure** General Assembly (2 a year); International Board; Departments; Projects. **Languages** English. **Staff** 7.00 FTE, voluntary. **Finance** Support from: *European Commission (EC, #06633)*; universities; foundations; private companies. Annual budget: 120,000 EUR (2021). **Activities** Awards/prizes/competitions; training/education. **Events** *BEST Virtual Summit* Brussels (Belgium) 2021, *Career Day Meeting* Brussels (Belgium) 2017, *Madrid Forum* Madrid (Spain) 2016, *World Engineering Education Forum* Florence (Italy) 2015, *Annual General Assembly* Paris (France) 2012. **Publications** Public conferences and scientific papers.

Members Local BEST groups (92) in 33 countries:
Austria, Belgium, Bosnia-Herzegovina, Bulgaria, Croatia, Czechia, Denmark, Estonia, Finland, France, Germany, Greece, Hungary, Iceland, Italy, Latvia, Lithuania, Moldova, Montenegro, Netherlands, North Macedonia, Norway, Poland, Portugal, Romania, Russia, Serbia, Slovakia, Slovenia, Spain, Sweden, Türkiye, Ukraine.

NGO Relations Member of (3): *European Youth Forum (#09140)*; *Informal Forum of International Student Organizations (IFISO, #11193)*; *International Federation of Engineering Education Societies (IFEES, #13412)*. Partner of (3): *Association des états généraux des étudiants de l'Europe (AEGEE-Europe, #02495)*; *Electrical Engineering STudents' European assoCiation (EESTEC, #05416)*; *European Students of Industrial Engineering and Management (ESTIEM, #08846)*. Cooperates with (2): *Fédération Européenne d'Associations Nationales d'Ingénieurs (FEANI, #09558)*; *Société européenne pour la formation des ingénieurs (SEFI, #19462)*.
[2021.06.11/XF2321/**F**]

- ♦ Board européen de pédiatrie (#06368)
- ♦ Board of Governors of Arab Central Banks and Monetary Agencies / see Council of Arab Central Banks and Monetary Agencies' Governors (#04858)
- ♦ Board of Governors of Central Banks and Heads of Arab Monetary Agencies / see Council of Arab Central Banks and Monetary Agencies' Governors (#04858)

♦ Board of Governors of the European Schools 03295

Conseil supérieur des Ecoles européennes – Oberster Rat der Europäischen Schulen – Consiglio Superiore delle Scuole Europee – Raad van Bestuur van de Europese Scholen

SG Office of Sec Gen for European Schools, Rue de la Science 23, 1040 Brussels, Belgium. T. +3228952611. Fax +3222302085. E-mail: osg-secretary-general@eursc.eu.
URL: http://www.eursc.eu/

History 12 Apr 1957, Luxembourg. Established on signature of an agreement by member governments of the *European Coal and Steel Community (ECSC, inactive)*, recognizing the operation in Luxembourg since 1953 of a school by the *Association des intérêts éducatifs et familiaux des fonctionnaires de la Communauté européenne du charbon et de l'acier*. A protocol to the agreement was signed, 13 Apr 1962, Luxembourg, providing for the creation of further European schools for the education and instruction of children of the staff of the European Communities, on the same model and according to a curriculum specified by the regulations of the European Baccalaureate, signed in 15 Jul 1957 in Luxembourg. The protocol further specified that the powers originally given to the Board of Governors of the Luxembourg school and to its Boards of Inspectors, should be extended to cover all such schools. On 15 Dec 1975, Luxembourg, a supplementary protocol to the protocol on the establishment of the European Schools was signed, providing for the creation of a European School in Munich (Germany), for the education and instruction of children of the staff of the European Patent Office. Statutes registered in *'UNTS 1/6362'*. **Aims** Ensure that *children* and *young people* from *European Union* member countries are educated together in a European spirit from minimum school age to university entrance level. **Structure** Board of Governors, composed of Ministers of Education of each of the Union countries, normally represented by senior civil servants from Ministries of Education or Foreign Affairs, together with representative of *European Commission (EC, #06633)* and representative of *European Patent Office (EPO, #08166)*. Office of the Secretary-General, including 7 Units (Administrative; Human Resources; Accounts; Pedagogical Development; European Baccalaureate; ICT and Statistics; Financial Control) and Complaints Board. Preparatory Committees (Joint Teaching; Budgetary); Boards of Inspectors; Administrative Boards; Directors (Headteachers) and the teachers; Staff Committee; Parents' Association; Pupils' Committee; Financial Controller. **Languages** English, French, German. **Finance** Schools budget – sources: national contributions for teachers' salaries (30%); *European Commission (EC, #06633)* (65%); other contributions including private pupil school fees (20%). **Activities** Training/education.

Members EU governments (27):
Austria, Belgium, Bulgaria, Croatia, Cyprus, Czechia, Denmark, Estonia, Finland, France, Germany, Greece, Hungary, Ireland, Italy, Latvia, Lithuania, Luxembourg, Malta, Netherlands, Poland, Portugal, Romania, Slovakia, Slovenia, Spain, Sweden.
Schools (13) in 6 countries:
Belgium (5), Germany (3), Italy, Luxembourg (2), Netherlands, Spain. [2021.11.04/XF1016/**F***]

- ♦ Board of International Ministries / see American Baptist International Ministries
- ♦ Board of the Ministers of Information of the Arab Gulf States (meeting series)
- ♦ Board of Nordic Development Projects (inactive)
- ♦ Board of Quality Standards (internationally oriented national body)

♦ BOBCATSSS Association 03296

Chair University of Library Studies and Information Technologies, 119 Tzarigradsko shosse, 1784 Sofia, Bulgaria.
URL: https://bobcatsss.info/

History Previously organized by *European Association for Library and Information Education and Research (EUCLID, inactive)*. Currently independent non-governmental and non-profit association. Acronym describes the university network and the letters stand for the first letters of the cities of the universities that initiated the BOBCATSSS symposium in 1993: Budapest, Oslo, Barcelona, Copenhagen, Amsterdam, Tampere, Stuttgart, Szombathely and Sheffield. Former names and other names: *European Association for Library and Information Education & Research (EUCLID)* – former (1991 to 2019). **Aims** Unite *library* and *information science* schools in a number of *European* cities. **Structure** Board; rotating Secretariat. **Languages** English. **Staff** 8.00 FTE, paid. **Activities** Events/meetings. **Events** *BOBCATSSS International Symposium* Coimbra (Portugal) 2024, *BOBCATSSS International Symposium* Oslo (Norway) 2023, *BOBCATSSS International Symposium* Debrecen (Hungary) 2022, *Conference* The Hague (Netherlands) 2022, *BOBCATSSS International Symposium* Oslo (Norway) 2021. **Publications** *BOBCATSSS Association Newsletter*. *Information Management, Fake News and Disinformation* (2021) by Assoc Prof Joumana Boustany and Prof Tania Todorova in English – Information Management, Fake News and Disinformation : Proceedings Book. BOBCATSSS Conference 2020, Paris, France, January 22-24, 2020. Eds. by Joumana Boustany & Tania Todorova. – Paris : InLitAs, 2020, 268 p. ISBN: 978-2-9561952-2-1; *Digital Transformation: Book of Abstracts at BOBCATSSS 2021 Virtual Conference* (20) by Dr Ana Lúcia Terra and Dr Milena Carvalho et al in English – Digital Transformation: Book of Abstracts at BOBCATSSS 2021 Virtual Conference, 21st-22nd January 2021, Porto / Ed. by Ana Lúcia Terra, Milena Carvalho, Tania Todorova, María Carmen Rodríguez López. Porto : Instituto Superior de Contabilidade e Administração, 2021, 73 p. ISBN: 978-972-98646-2-9. Conference proceedings. **Members** No membership in its current form. [2022.06.25/XF3682/c/**F**]

- ♦ **BOBP-IGO** Bay of Bengal Programme Inter-Governmental Organization (#03189)
- ♦ **BOC** Badminton Oceania (#03059)
- ♦ Boccia International Sports Federation / see World Boccia (#21236)
- ♦ Boccone del Povero – Missionari Servi dei Poveri (religious order)
- ♦ Bochasanwasi Shri Akshar Purushottam Swaminarayan Sanstha (internationally oriented national body)
- ♦ BOD – Brotherhood of Dragons (internationally oriented national body)

♦ Bodensee Stiftung 03297

Lake Constance Foundation

Exec Dir Fritz-Reichle-Ring 4, 78315 Radolfzell, Germany. T. +49773232999545 – +49773232999540. Fax +49773232999549.
URL: http://www.bodensee-stiftung.org/

History Originates from a projected conducted 1994. **Aims** Works towards sustainable economy in the international Lake Constance region and beyond. **Structure** Executive Committee; Advisory Board. **Languages** English, French, German, Spanish. **Staff** 14.00 FTE, paid. **Finance** Mainly project funding. Other sources: *European Commission (EC, #06633)*; national and regional ministries; private foundations; companies.

Members Full in 3 countries:
Austria, Germany, Switzerland.

IGO Relations *European Union (EU, #08967)* Business@Biodiversity Platform; *Internationale Bodenseekonferenz (IBK, #13217)*; *Secretariat of the Convention of Wetlands (#19200)*. **NGO Relations** Project partners include: *Global Nature Fund (GNF, #10479)*; *Research Institute of Organic Agriculture (#18857)*; environmental NGOs; research institutes; local authorities; companies. Founding member of: International Living Lakes Network. [2018.09.06/XM4900/f/**F**]

♦ Bodhimitra – International Lay Buddhist Forum 03298

Address not obtained.
URL: https://bodhimitra.com/

History Set up 2007, Seoul (Korea Rep) as a lay Buddhist movement. Formally constituted 2011. Former names and other names: *International Lay Buddhist Forum (ILBF)* – former. **Aims** Represent and further the interests and roles of lay Buddhists in the development of local and global Buddhisms in the world today. **Structure** International Steering Committee. **Activities** Events/meetings. **Events** *Forum* Seoul (Korea Rep) / Gyeongju (Korea Rep) 2021, *Forum* Seoul (Korea Rep) / Gyeongju (Korea Rep) 2020, *Forum* Nakhon Pathom (Thailand) 2018, *Forum* Padang (Indonesia) 2016, *Forum* Tokyo (Japan) 2014. [2018/XM6712/**F**]

- ♦ BODY – Baltic Organization of Democrat Youth (inactive)

♦ Body of European Regulators for Electronic Communications (BEREC) 03299

Head Office Zigfrida Annas Meierovica bd 14, Riga LV-1050, Latvia. T. +37129578999. E-mail: berecoffice@berec.europa.eu – berec@berec.europa.eu.
Main Website: http://berec.europa.eu/

History 29 Jul 2002, by *European Commission (EC, #06633)* decision 2002/627/EC, as *European Regulators Group (ERG)*. Restructured under current title by Regulation (EC) No 1211/2009, 25 Nov 2009. Commenced activities Jan 2010. A decentralized agency of *European Union (EU, #08967)*. The legal basis for the Body of European Regulators for Electronic Communications (BEREC) is set out in Regulation (EU) 2018/1971 of the European Parliament and of the Council of 11 December 2018. The new Regulation replaces the previous one, Regulation (EC) No 1211/2009, which was part of the Telecoms Reform package. **Aims** Foster the independent, consistent and high-quality regulation of digital markets for the benefit of Europe and its citizens. **Structure** Board of Regulators. **Languages** English. **Activities** Events/meetings; guidance/assistance/consulting; knowledge management/information dissemination; networking/liaising. **Events** *Stakeholder Forum* Brussels (Belgium) 2022, *Workshop on Experience Sharing on the Implementation of Article 22 EECC Geographical Surverys of Network Deployments* Brussels (Belgium) 2022, *Ordinary Meeting* Riga (Latvia) 2021, *Stakeholder Forum* Riga (Latvia) 2021, *Workshop on DMA* Riga (Latvia) 2021. **IGO Relations** Audited by: *European Court of Auditors (#06854)*. **NGO Relations** Member of (1): *EU Agencies Network (EUAN, #05564)*. [2021.09.01/XM2741/**E***]

- ♦ Boilermakers Union / see International Brotherhood of Boilermakers, Iron Shipbuilders, Blacksmiths, Forgers and Helpers
- ♦ **BOIP** Benelux Office for Intellectual Property (#03202)
- ♦ **BOIP** Benelux Organization for Intellectual Property (#03203)
- ♦ Bókun um ad leysa rikisborgara Islands Danmerkur, Finnlands, Noregs og Svipjódar undan skyldu til ad hafa i höndum vegabréf og dvalarleyfi við dvöl i ödru norraenu landi en heimalandinu (1954 treaty)
- ♦ BOLCEN – Asociación de Bolsas de Comercio de Centroamérica, Panama y República Dominicana (inactive)
- ♦ Bolivarian Alliance for the Americas (#00627)
- ♦ Bolivarian Alternative for Latin America and the Caribbean / see Alianza Bolivariana de los Pueblos de Nuestra América (#00627)
- ♦ Bolivia Inti – Sud Soleil / see INTI – Energies Solidaires
- ♦ Bolivian Association for Research and Conservation of Amazonian Andean Ecosystem (internationally oriented national body)
- ♦ Bolivian High Altitude Biology Institute (internationally oriented national body)
- ♦ Bolsa de Comercio Europea (#06674)
- ♦ Bolsa Europea de Productos Basicos / see European Commodities Exchange (#06674)
- ♦ BOMA – Building Owners and Managers Association International (internationally oriented national body)
- ♦ BOMA International / see Building Owners and Managers Association International
- ♦ Bomberos Unidos sin Fronteras (#09779)
- ♦ BOMS / see International Health Exchange
- ♦ BOND – British Overseas NGO's for Development (internationally oriented national body)
- ♦ Bond van Europese Ambtenaren / see European Public Service Union (#08303)
- ♦ Bond van Europese Ambtenaren (#06567)
- ♦ Bond van Internationale en Europese Ambtenaren / see European Public Service Union (#08303)
- ♦ Bone and Joint Decade / see Global Alliance for Musculoskeletal Health (#10213)
- ♦ BoneUS – International Bone Ultrasound Society (unconfirmed)
- ♦ **Bonn Agreement** Agreement for cooperation in dealing with pollution of the North Sea by oil and other harmful substances (#00564)
- ♦ Bonn Convention – Convention on the Conservation of Migratory Species of Wild Animals (1979 treaty)

♦ Bonn International Center for Conversion (BICC) 03300

Internationales Konversionszentrum Bonn

Dir Research Pfarrer-Byns-Str 1, 53121 Bonn, Germany. T. +492289119630. Fax +492289119622. E-mail: bicc@bicc.de.
Dir Admin address not obtained.
URL: http://www.bicc.de/

History Founded Apr 1994, Bonn (Germany), with support from the State Government of North Rhine Westphalia. Registered in accordance with German law. **Aims** Conduct critical, problem-oriented, policy relevant research in response to the problems posed by organized *violence*. **Structure** Supervisory Board; Board of Trustees; International Board; Director for Research; Director for Administration. **Languages** English, German. **Staff** 50.00 FTE, paid. **Finance** Sources: public funds raised by founders; funding from government agencies, German State, NGOs, international and multilateral organizations. **Activities** Research and development; policy/politics/regulatory; capacity building; knowledge management/information dissemination; events/meetings. **Events** *Regional Conference on Middle East and North African Sustainable Electricity Pathways* Amman (Jordan) 2019, *International Conference on Networks of Organized Violence / International Academic Conference* Bonn (Germany) 2015, *International Conference on Facing Organized Violence / International Academic Conference* Bonn (Germany) 2014, *International Academic Conference* Berlin (Germany) 2013, *DW Global Media forum* Bonn (Germany) 2009. **Publications** *Global Militarisation Index (GMI)* (annual). *Knowledge Notes* – series; *Policy Brief* – series; *Workking Paper* – series. Annual Report. [2019.03.11/XE2177/**E**]

- ♦ Bonobo Conservation Initiative (internationally oriented national body)

Bonsai Clubs International
03301

alphabetic sequence excludes
For the complete listing, see Yearbook Online at

♦ **Bonsai Clubs International (BCI)** **03301**
Pres PO Box 40463, Bay Village OH 44140-9998, USA. T. +14408714797. Fax +14408714797. E-mail: office@bonsai-bci.com.
URL: http://www.bonsai-bci.com/
History 1958, as Bonsai Club Association. Present title adopted 1966. Primarily North American membership. **Aims** Assists clubs and individual bonsai enthusiasts. **Structure** Officers; Directors. **Languages** Chinese, English, French, German, Italian, Spanish. **Staff** Voluntary. **Finance** Members' dues. Other sources: donations; proceeds from Annual Conventions. **Events** *Asia-Pacific Bonsai and Suiseki Convention* Ho Chi Minh City (Vietnam) 2019, *Asia-Pacific Bonsai and Suiseki Convention* Changhua (Taiwan) 2017, *Convention* Gold Coast, QLD (Australia) 2014, *Convention* Yangzhou (China) 2013, *Annual Convention* Tianjin (China) 2010. **Publications** *Bonsai and Stone Appreciation Magazine* (4 a year).
Members Clubs (245); individuals (over 2000). Members in 50 countries and territories:
Argentina, Australia, Austria, Bangladesh, Barbados, Belgium, Brazil, Canada, Chile, China, Colombia, Costa Rica, Czechia, Denmark, France, Georgia, Germany, Greece, Hong Kong, Hungary, India, Indonesia, Italy, Japan, Korea Rep, Lithuania, Malaysia, Mexico, Netherlands, New Zealand, Panama, Peru, Philippines, Poland, Portugal, San Marino, Singapore, Slovakia, South Africa, Spain, St Lucia, Switzerland, Taiwan, Thailand, Trinidad-Tobago, UK, USA, Venezuela, Vietnam.
NGO Relations *Latin American and Caribbean Bonsai Federation (FELAB, #16266)* is member.
[2018/XF1875/**F**]

♦ Bonsai Latin American Federation / see Latin American and Caribbean Bonsai Federation (#16266)

♦ **Bonsucro** **03302**
Secretariat Wenlock Centre, 50-52 Wharf Road, London, N1 7EU, UK. T. +442037358515. E-mail: info@bonsucro.com – laura@bonsucro.com.
URL: http://www.bonsucro.com/
History 2008. Former names and other names: *Better Sugarcane Initiative* – former (2008 to 2016). **Aims** Collectively accelerate sustainable production and uses of sugarcane. **Structure** Board of Directors; Members Council; Technical Advisory Board; Secretariat. **Languages** English, Portuguese, Spanish. **Staff** 18.00 FTE, paid. **Finance** Sources: fees for services; members' dues; revenue from activities/projects. Annual budget: 2,000,000 GBP. **Activities** Events/meetings; guidance/assistance/consulting; knowledge management/information dissemination; monitoring/evaluation; networking/liaising; projects/programmes; standards/guidelines; training/education. **Events** *Bonsucro Global Week* Guadalajara (Mexico) 2021, *Bonsucro Global Week* Guadalajara (Mexico) 2020, *Bonsucro Global Week* Sao Paulo (Brazil) 2015. **Publications** *Outcome Report* (annual). Impact assessment reports; research studies.
Members Full in 52 countries and territories:
Algeria, Argentina, Australia, Austria, Barbados, Bolivia, Brazil, Canada, China, Colombia, Costa Rica, Denmark, Dominican Rep, Ecuador, Egypt, El Salvador, Eswatini, France, Germany, Guatemala, Haiti, Honduras, Hungary, India, Indonesia, Japan, Kenya, Luxembourg, Malawi, Mauritius, Mexico, Netherlands, Nicaragua, Pakistan, Panama, Paraguay, Peru, Philippines, Poland, Portugal, Russia, Singapore, South Africa, Spain, Sweden, Switzerland, Taiwan, Thailand, Türkiye, UK, United Arab Emirates, USA.
NGO Relations Member of (2): *ISEAL (#16026)*; *United Nations Global Compact (#20567)*.
[2021.06.29/XJ8449/**C**]

♦ bon't worry (internationally oriented national body)
♦ Book Aid (internationally oriented national body)
♦ Book Aid International (internationally oriented national body)
♦ Book of Hope International / see OneHope
♦ Book Publishers Group of EEC / see Federation of European Publishers (#09536)
♦ Books2Africa (internationally oriented national body)
♦ Books Abroad (internationally oriented national body)
♦ Books For Africa (internationally oriented national body)
♦ Books for Developing Countries / see CODE
♦ **BOOS** Baltic Operational Oceanographic System (#03133)
♦ BORDA – Bremen Overseas Research and Development Association (internationally oriented national body)

♦ **Borderless Alliance (BA)** **03303**
Exec Sec 4th Str, Kuku Hill, Jubilee House, Osu, Accra, Ghana. T. +233302762696 – +233302762935. E-mail: info@borderlesswa.com.
URL: https://borderlesswa.com/
History May 2012. Officially launched with support from *United States Agency for International Development (USAID)* West Africa Trade Hub and its partners. Former names and other names: *Borderless Alliance – Removing trade barriers in West Africa* – full title. **Aims** Increase *trade* across the region, by working towards the elimination of all non-tariff barriers to trade. **Structure** Executive Council; Secretariat. **Events** *Annual Conference* Abidjan (Côte d'Ivoire) 2022, *Conference* Accra (Ghana) 2019, *Conference* Bamako (Mali) 2018. **Publications** *In-Transit* – newsletter. **IGO Relations** Partners: *African Development Bank (ADB, #00283)*; *Economic Community of West African States (ECOWAS, #05312)*; *Deutsche Gesellschaft für Internationale Zusammenarbeit (GIZ)*; *United States Agency for International Development (USAID)* *Union économique et monétaire Ouest africaine (UEMOA, #20377)*. [2022/XM7520/**D**]

♦ Borderless Alliance – Removing trade barriers in West Africa / see Borderless Alliance (#03303)
♦ borderline-europe (internationally oriented national body)
♦ borderline-europe – Menschenrechte ohne Grenzen / see borderline-europe

♦ **BORDERPOL** **03304**
Exec Dir 81 Crescent Street, Box 1071, Grand Bend ON N0M 1T0, Canada. T. +15092781660. Fax +15092781660. E-mail: member.services@borderpol.org – borderpol@borderpol.org.
URL: http://www.borderpol.org/
History Mar 2003. Founded by border security, migration management and human rights professionals. Restructured 2022. Former names and other names: *World Border Organization (BORDERPOL)* – former. Registration: Corporations Act, No/ID: 415442-9, Canada. **Aims** Work for a safer and more prosperous world through smart borders and transparent/lawful border management practices and *policies*; bridge policy and programme gaps in international border management; bring together diverse lawmakers, border and law enforcement managers, stakeholders with interests in border security, traveller and migration management and industry security experts. **Structure** Executive Committee; Membership Committee. **Languages** English, French, Spanish. **Staff** 5.00 FTE, voluntary. Stipend paid. **Finance** Sources: grants; members' dues. Cost recovery systems. Annual budget: 2,500 USD (2022). **Activities** Awards/prizes/competitions; events/meetings; guidance/assistance/consulting; training/education. **Events** *Annual Forum* Gandhinagar (India) 2020, *Annual World Congress* Madrid (Spain) 2019, *Annual World Congress* Prague (Czechia) 2018, *Annual World Congress* Budapest (Hungary) 2016, *World Congress* The Hague (Netherlands) 2015. **Publications** *BORDERPOL Journal*. **Members** Associate; Agency; Corporate. Membership countries not specified. **NGO Relations** Consultative status with: BORDERPOL Services UK. [2022.06.15/XJ8886/**C**]

♦ **Borlaug Global Rust Initiative (BGRI)** **03305**
Main Office Cornell Univ, Global Dev Dept, B75 Mann Library, Ithaca NY 14853, USA. E-mail: bgri@cornell.edu.
URL: https://bgri.cornell.edu/
History May 2005. Founded by Dr Norman E Borlaug. Set up under its current form by Indian Council of Agricultural Research (ICAR), *International Maize and Wheat Improvement Center (#14077)*, *FAO (#09260)* and Cornell University (USA). Former names and other names: *Global Rust Initiative (GRI)* – former (May 2005). **Aims** Systematically reduce the world's vulnerability to stem, yellow, and *leaf rusts* of *wheat*; advocate and facilitate the evolution of a sustainable international system to contain the threat of wheat rusts and continue the enhancements in productivity required to withstand future global threats to wheat. **Structure** Executive Committee, representing national and organizational stakeholders. **Activities** Knowledge management/information dissemination; events/meetings; awards/prizes/competitions. **Events** *Technical Workshop* Marrakech (Morocco) 2018, *Technical Workshop* Sydney, NSW (Australia) 2015, *Technical Workshop* Beijing (China) 2012, *Technical Workshop* St Paul, MN (USA) 2011, *International wheat conference* St Petersburg (Russia) 2010. **Publications** *BGRI Newsletter*.
Members Scientists (over 1,000) in 46 countries:
Afghanistan, Argentina, Australia, Azerbaijan, Bangladesh, Bhutan, Canada, Chile, China, Denmark, Egypt, Ethiopia, France, Georgia, Hungary, India, Iran Islamic Rep, Iraq, Israel, Italy, Japan, Jordan, Kazakhstan, Kenya, Lebanon, Mexico, Morocco, Nepal, New Zealand, Pakistan, Russia, South Africa, Sudan, Sweden, Syrian AR, Tajikistan, Tanzania UR, Tunisia, Türkiye, Uganda, UK, Uruguay, USA, Uzbekistan, Yemen, Zimbabwe.
IGO Relations Partners include: *CGIAR System Organization (CGIAR, #03843)*; *Common Market for Eastern and Southern Africa (COMESA, #04296)*; *FAO (#09260)*; *International Center for Agricultural Research in the Dry Areas (ICARDA, #12466)*; *International Rice Research Institute (IRRI, #14754)*. **NGO Relations** Partners include: *Bill and Melinda Gates Foundation (BMGF)*; *Canadian International Development Agency (CIDA, inactive)*; *Commonwealth Scientific and Industrial Research Organization (CSIRO)*. [2022/XJ1566/**E**]

♦ Borneo Orangutan Survival International / see Save the Orangutan (#19060)
♦ Born Free Foundation (internationally oriented national body)
♦ Borngreat Foundation (internationally oriented national body)
♦ Borsa Europea del Commercio (#06674)
♦ Borsa Merci Europea / see European Commodities Exchange (#06674)
♦ BOS / see Vereniging Tropische Bossen
♦ **BoSF** Bomberos Unidos sin Fronteras (#09779)
♦ BOS International / see Save the Orangutan (#19060)
♦ Bosques del Mundo (internationally oriented national body)
♦ Bostadsadministrativa Mötet (meeting series)
♦ Boston Church of Christ / see International Churches of Christ
♦ Boston College Center for International Higher Education (internationally oriented national body)
♦ Boston Movement / see International Churches of Christ
♦ BOTA – Bamboo of the Americas (internationally oriented national body)
♦ **BOTA** Builders of the Adytum (#03349)

♦ **Botanic Gardens Conservation International (BGCI)** **03306**
SG Descanso House, 199 Kew Road, Richmond, TW9 3BW, UK. T. +442083325940. Fax +442083325956. E-mail: info@bgci.org.
Admin and Membership Officer address not obtained.
URL: http://www.bgci.org/
History 1987. Founded under the auspices of *International Union for Conservation of Nature and Natural Resources (IUCN, #15766)* and *World Wide Fund for Nature (WWF, #21922)*. Registration: Charity Commission, No/ID: 1098834, England and Wales; USA. **Aims** Mobilize botanic gardens and engage partners in securing plant diversity for the well-being of people and the planet. **Structure** Headquarters located in the UK. Country offices: China; Kenya; Russia; Taiwan; USA. **Languages** English, French, Mandarin Chinese, Spanish. **Staff** 25.00 FTE, paid. **Finance** Members' dues. Other sources: sponsors; foundation grants; research contracts; donations. **Activities** Training/education; politics/policy/regulatory; events/meetings; knowledge management/information dissemination. **Events** *EUROGARD : European Botanic Gardens Congress* Budapest (Hungary) 2022, *International Congress on Education in Botanic Gardens* Buenos Aires (Argentina) 2022, *Global Botanic Gardens Congress* Melbourne, VIC (Australia) 2022, *Global Botanic Gardens Congress* Melbourne, VIC (Australia) 2021, *International Congress on Education in Botanic Gardens* Warsaw (Poland) 2018. **Publications** *Cultivate* (6 a year) – electronic newsletter; *BG Journal* (periodical); *Roots* (periodical). Handbooks; technical guidelines; newsletters, posters; slide packs; videos. **Information Services** *GardenSearch*; *GlobalTreeSearch*; *PlantSearch*; *ThreatSearch*.
Members Botanic gardens (over 700) in 124 countries and territories:
Albania, Argentina, Armenia, Australia, Austria, Azerbaijan, Bahamas, Bangladesh, Barbados, Belarus, Belgium, Belize, Bermuda, Bhutan, Bolivia, Bosnia-Herzegovina, Botswana, Brazil, Bulgaria, Burkina Faso, Cameroon, Canada, Cape Verde, Cayman Is, Chile, China, Colombia, Congo DR, Costa Rica, Croatia, Cuba, Czechia, Denmark, Dominica, Dominican Rep, Ecuador, Egypt, El Salvador, Estonia, Finland, France, Georgia, Germany, Ghana, Greece, Guatemala, Haiti, Honduras, Hong Kong, Hungary, Iceland, India, Indonesia, Ireland, Israel, Italy, Jamaica, Japan, Kazakhstan, Kenya, Korea Rep, Kuwait, Kyrgyzstan, Laos, Latvia, Lesotho, Lithuania, Luxembourg, Madagascar, Malawi, Malaysia, Malta, Mauritius, Mexico, Moldova, Monaco, Morocco, Myanmar, Namibia, Nepal, Netherlands, New Zealand, Nigeria, Norway, Oman, Pakistan, Papua New Guinea, Peru, Philippines, Poland, Portugal, Réunion, Romania, Russia, Saudi Arabia, Seychelles, Singapore, Slovakia, Slovenia, Solomon Is, South Africa, Spain, Sri Lanka, St Kitts-Nevis, St Vincent-Grenadines, Sweden, Switzerland, Taiwan, Tajikistan, Tanzania UR, Thailand, Trinidad-Tobago, Tunisia, Türkiye, Uganda, UK, Ukraine, United Arab Emirates, USA, Uzbekistan, Venezuela, Vietnam, Zambia, Zimbabwe.
IGO Relations Memorandum of Understanding with: *Programme on Man and the Biosphere (MAB, #18526)*. Member of: *Global Biodiversity Information Facility (GBIF, #10250)*. **NGO Relations** Partner with: *Fauna & Flora International (FFI, #09277)* (Global Trees Campaign). [2021/XF3621/**F**]

♦ Bóthar (internationally oriented national body)

♦ **Both ENDS** **03307**
Mailing Address Nobelstraat 4, 3512 EN Utrecht, Netherlands. E-mail: info@bothends.org.
URL: http://www.bothends.org/
History Dec 1986, Amsterdam (Netherlands). As of Jan 2003, incorporates activities of *INZET – Association for North South Campaigns (inactive)*. Former names and other names: *Environment and Development Service for Third World Citizens' Groups (ENDS)* – former; *Environment and Development Service for NGOs (Both ENDS)* – former. **Aims** Identify and strengthen civil society organizations (CSOs), mostly in developing countries, that come up with sustainable solutions for *environmental* and poverty-related issues. **Structure** Board; Director; Departments. **Languages** Dutch, English, Spanish. **Staff** 36.00 FTE, paid. **Finance** Support from: *European Union (EU, #08967)*; Dutch Ministry of Foreign Affairs; Dutch, European and US donor agencies; project funding; gifts; payments. Annual budget (2016): euro 6,018,189. **Activities** Networking/liaising. **Events** *Coordination of activities of international networks on women, environment and development* Amsterdam (Netherlands) 1992. **Publications** Working papers; policy notes; briefing papers. **Consultative Status** Consultative status granted from: *ECOSOC (#05331)* (Special). **IGO Relations** Accredited to the Conference of the Parties of: *Secretariat of the United Nations Convention to Combat Desertification (Secretariat of the UNCCD, #19208)*. Accredited by: *Green Climate Fund (GCF, #10714)*; *United Nations Framework Convention on Climate Change – Secretariat (UNFCCC, #20564)*.
NGO Relations Founding member of: *GEF CSO Network (GCN, #10087)*; *Global Water Solidarity (GWS, #10655)*. Member of:
- *Alternative Trade Mandate Alliance (ATM)*;
- *Climate Action Network Europe (CAN Europe, #04001)*;
- *Drynet (#05140)*;
- *ECA Watch*;
- *Environmental Paper Network (EPN, #05507)*;
- *European Network on Debt and Development (EURODAD, #07891)*;
- *International Union for Conservation of Nature and Natural Resources (IUCN, #15766)*;
- *NGO Forum on ADB (#17123)*;
- *OECD Watch (#17694)*;
- *Tax Justice Network (TJN, #20100)*.

Partner in: *Africa-EU Innovation Alliance for Water and Climate (AfriAlliance, #00169)*; *Wetlands International (#20928)*. Signatory to Founding Statement of: *Alliance for Lobbying Transparency and Ethics Regulation (ALTER-EU, #00705)*. Cooperates with: *International Analog Forestry Network (IAFN, #11650)*; *Transnational Institute (TNI, #20219)*; Operates closely with: *Environment Liaison Centre International (ELCI, no recent information)*. [2021/XF2019/**F**]

♦ Bountifield International (internationally oriented national body)
♦ Bourse de Commerce Européenne (#06674)
♦ Bouwcentrum / see Institute for Housing and Urban Development Studies
♦ Bouwcentrum International Education / see Institute for Housing and Urban Development Studies
♦ **BOVA UN** Baltic Forestry, Veterinary and Agricultural University Network (#03119)

♦ **Boys' Brigade, The (BB)** **03308**
Contact Felden Lodge, Hemel Hempstead, HP3 0BL, UK. E-mail: enquiries@boys-brigade.org.uk.
URL: http://boys-brigade.org.uk/

History Founded 1883, Glasgow (UK), by Sir William Alexander Smith. **Aims** Advance *Christ's* Kingdom among boys; promote habits of obedience, reverence, discipline, self-respect, and all that tends towards a true *Christian* manliness. **Structure** *Global Fellowship of Christian Youth (Global Fellowship, #10357)* (international coordinating body); Executive. Regional offices (5): England; Ireland; Northern Ireland; Scotland; Wales. **Languages** English. **Staff** 6.00 FTE, voluntary. **Finance** Members' dues. Other sources: donations; grants. **Activities** Training/education. **Events** *Annual Meeting* Glasgow (UK) 2014, *Annual Meeting* Belfast (UK) 2013, *Annual Meeting* London (UK) 2012, *Annual meeting* Birmingham (UK) 2002, *Annual Meeting* Northampton (UK) 2001. **Publications** *The Gazette* (4 a year) – magazine.
Members Membership covers 16 countries:
Australia, Canada, Denmark, Finland, Ghana, Guyana, Haiti, Jamaica, New Zealand, Nigeria, Singapore, St Kitts-Nevis, Sweden, Uganda, UK, Zambia.
IGO Relations *Commonwealth Secretariat (#04362).* **NGO Relations** *Commonwealth Youth Exchange Council (CYEC); European Fellowship of Christian Youth (EF, #07238).* [2018/XF5003/**F**]

- ♦ **BPAC** Badminton Pan American Confederation (#04467)
- ♦ **BPAC** Baltic Pilotage Authorities Commission (#03135)
- ♦ BP Amoco Foundation / see BP Foundation
- ♦ BP – BP Translation Conference (meeting series)
- ♦ BPF – Buddhist Peace Fellowship (internationally oriented national body)
- ♦ BPFNA – Baptist Peace Fellowship of North America (internationally oriented national body)
- ♦ BP Foundation (internationally oriented national body)
- ♦ **BPG** BioProtection Global (#03257)
- ♦ **BPI** Barreau Pénal International (#13107)
- ♦ BPICA / see International Organization of Motor Vehicle Manufacturers (#14455)
- ♦ BPICM / see International Motorcycle Manufacturers Association (#14186)
- ♦ **BPIE** Buildings Performance Institute Europe (#03354)
- ♦ BPM – International Conference on Business Process Management (meeting series)
- ♦ **BPO** Baltic Ports Organization (#03136)
- ♦ B-PO – Tariff Union of Balkan and Near East Countries (no recent information)
- ♦ BPO – Union tarifaire Balkans-Proche-Orient (inactive)
- ♦ BPPA – Baltic Plastic Pipes Association (no recent information)
- ♦ BPP – Blue Planet Project (internationally oriented national body)
- ♦ BP/RAC / see Plan Bleu pour l'environnement et le développement en Méditerranée (#18379)
- ♦ **BPS** Benelux Phlebology Society (#03204)
- ♦ **BPS** Biophysical Society (#03255)
- ♦ BP Translation Conference (meeting series)
- ♦ **BPU** Balkan Physical Union (#03082)
- ♦ **BPU** Baltic Postal Union (#03137)
- ♦ BPW European Coordination / see BPW Europe – European Region of BPW International (#03309)

♦ BPW Europe – European Region of BPW International 03309

Contact Avenue Paul Deschanel 252, 1030 Brussels, Belgium. E-mail: giuseppa.bombaci@bpw-europe.org.
URL: http://www.bpw-europe.org/

History Founded Oct 1985, as *European Federation of Business and Professional Women (EFBPW).* A region of *International Federation of Business and Professional Women (BPW International, #13376).* Registered in accordance with Belgian law, as *BPW European Coordination.* **Aims** Attain equal opportunities and status for *business* and *professional women* in economic, civil and political life. **Structure** European Coordinating Committee; Board of BPW European Coordination. **Languages** English, French, Italian, Spanish. **Staff** 5.00 FTE, voluntary. **Activities** Advocacy/lobbying/activism; events/meetings; training/education. **Events** *European Conference* Reykjavik (Iceland) 2022, *European Congress* Galway (Ireland) 2019, *European Presidents Meeting* Vienna (Austria) 2018, *Young BPW Symposium* Rome (Italy) 2017, *European Congress* Zurich (Switzerland) 2016.
Members Affiliate Federations in 16 countries:
Austria, Belgium, Cyprus, Estonia, Finland, France, Germany, Ireland, Italy, Netherlands, Poland, Spain, Sweden, Switzerland, Türkiye, UK.
Affiliate Clubs, totalling about 20,000 individuals, in 16 countries:
Bulgaria, Croatia, Czechia, Greece, Hungary, Iceland, Israel, Latvia, Malta, Moldova, Norway, Romania, Russia, Serbia, Slovakia, Ukraine.
IGO Relations Consultative status with: *ECOSOC (#05331).* **NGO Relations** Member of: *European Institute of Women's Health (EIWH, #07574); European Women's Lobby (EWL, #09102).* [2018/XD0498/**D**]

- ♦ BPWI / see International Federation of Business and Professional Women (#13376)
- ♦ **BPW International** International Federation of Business and Professional Women (#13376)
- ♦ BQS – Board of Quality Standards (internationally oriented national body)
- ♦ **BRA** Balkan Rowing Association (#03083)
- ♦ **BRA** Baltic Road Association (#03138)
- ♦ BRA – Batey Relief Alliance (internationally oriented national body)

♦ BRAC 03310

Exec Dir 75 Mohakhali, Dhaka 1212, Bangladesh. T. +88029881265 – +880288241807. Fax +88028823542. E-mail: info@brac.net – webmaster@brac.net.
URL: http://www.brac.net/

History Founded 1972, Bangladesh, by Fazle Hasan Abed, as as small relief and rehabilitation project under the title *Bangladesh Rehabilitation Assistance Committee (BRAC).* Changed title to *Bangladesh Rural Advancement Committee,* 1973. BRAC UK and BRAC USA set up 2006. Registered in Pakistan, 2007, in Sierra Leone and Liberia, 2008 and in Netherlands, 2009. **Aims** Empower people and communities in situations of poverty, illiteracy, disease and *social injustice*; achieve large scale, positive changes through economic and social programmes that enable men and women to realize their potential. **Languages** Bengali, English. **Staff** 115634.00 FTE, paid. **Finance** Budget (2014): US$ 845 million. **Activities** Advocacy/lobbying/activism. **Publications** Annual Report; BRAC at a Glance. **IGO Relations** Accredited organization of: *Green Climate Fund (GCF, #10714).* **NGO Relations** Member of: *CHS Alliance (#03911); Global Coalition to End Child Poverty (#10292); InsideNGO (inactive); PMNCH (#18410); Partnership for Responsible Financial Inclusion (PRFI, #18241).* Partner of: *UN Climate Resilience Initiative (A2R, #20284).* Supports: *Global Call for Action Against Poverty (GCAP, #10263).* [2018/XJ1141/**F**]

- ♦ BRA – Clusterize – Business Roaming Agreement (unconfirmed)
- ♦ Bradford Centre for International Development (internationally oriented national body)
- ♦ Bradshaw Foundation (internationally oriented national body)
- ♦ **BRAF** Black Sea Broadcasting Regulatory Authorities Forum (#03272)
- ♦ Brahma Kumaris Universidad Espiritual Mundial (#03311)

♦ Brahma Kumaris World Spiritual University (BKWSU) 03311

Université spirituelle internationale des Brahma Kumaris – Brahma Kumaris Universidad Espiritual Mundial – Prajapita Brahma Kumaris Ishwariya Vishwa Vidyalaya

Address not obtained.
Headquarters Pandav Bhavan, Post Box No 2, Rajasthan, Mount Abu, Rajasthan 307501, Mount Abu RAJASTHAN 307501, India. T. +912974238261 – +912974238262 – +912974238268. E-mail: abu@bkivv.org.
URL: http://www.brahmakumaris.org/

History 1936. Founded in Sind (India, currently Pakistan). Headquarters moved to Mount Abu (India), 1950. **Aims** Promote peace and freedom as the right of every human being; encourage cooperation among leaders of different communities, religions and nations; provide individuals with the necessary support and assistance to develop their spiritual and humanitarian awareness, leading to practical and positive changes within relationships throughout the workplace and community; encourage individuals to develop cooperation, creativity and communication and to use those skills in working towards a better world. **Structure** Management Committee (meets twice a year); Advisory Boards; Zonal Management Committees. **Languages** English, French, Hindi, Portuguese, Spanish. **Staff** Voluntary teachers (4,250) in 120 countries. **Finance** Sources: contributions; sponsorship. **Activities** Events/meetings; training/education. **Events** *International forum* Mount Abu (India) 1999, *International forum* Mount Abu (India) 1998, *International forum* Mount Abu (India) 1997, *Abu dialogue* Mount Abu (India) 1996, *International forum* Mount Abu (India) 1996. **Publications** *Purity* (12 a year); *World Renewal* (12 a year). Books; CDs; DVDs; audio tapes; newsletters and other publications in language of country concerned. **Members** Individuals (900,000) in 120 countries and territories. Membership countries not specified. **Consultative Status** Consultative status granted from: *ECOSOC (#05331)* (General); *UNICEF (#20332); UNEP (#20299).* **IGO Relations** Accredited by (1): *United Nations Office at Vienna (UNOV, #20604).* Associated with Department of Global Communications of the United Nations. **NGO Relations** Member of (7): *Committee of NGOs on Human Rights, Geneva (#04275); Committee of Religious NGOs at the United Nations (CRNGOs, #04282); Conference of Non-Governmental Organizations in Consultative Relationship with the United Nations (CONGO, #04635); NGO Alliance on Global Concerns and Values (NGO Alliance, #17102); NGO Committee on the Status of Women, Geneva (#17117); NGO Committee on UNICEF (#17120); Vienna NGO Committee on the Family (#20774).* [2022.10.20/XF8409/v/**F**]

♦ Braille Without Borders (BWB) 03312

Braille ohne Grenzen

Contact Im Auel 34, 53913 Swisttal, Germany. T. +492226913403. Fax +492226913404.
URL: http://www.braillewithoutborders.org/

History 1998. **Aims** Empower *blind* people from developing countries of Africa, Asia, Latin America and the Pacific Regions so they themselves can set up projects and schools for other blind people. [2017/XJ6337/**F**]

- ♦ Braille ohne Grenzen (#03312)

♦ Brain-Computer Interface Society (BCI Society) 03313

Contact Podium Conference Specialists, 2661 Queenswood Drive, Victoria BC V8N 1X6, Canada. T. +12504727644.
URL: https://bcisociety.org/

History 13 Mar 2015. Proposed at 5th International Brain-Computer Interface Meeting, with first meeting held, 1999. Registration: Handelsregister, No/ID: KVK 62866974, Start date: 2015, Netherlands. **Aims** Foster research leading to technologies that enable people to interact with the world through brain signals. **Structure** Board of Directors; Secretariat. Committees. **Activities** Events/meetings; networking/liaising; research/documentation. **Events** *International BCI Meeting* Victoria, BC (Canada) 2021, *International BCI Meeting* Pacific Grove, CA (USA) 2018, *International BCI Meeting* Pacific Grove, CA (USA) 2016, *International BCI Meeting* Pacific Grove, CA (USA) 2013, *International BCI Meeting* Pacific Grove, CA (USA) 2010. **Members** Members (over 300) in about 25 countries worldwide. Membership countries not specified. [2021/AA1463/**C**]

♦ Brain Injured and Families European Confederation (BIF-EC) 03314

Confédération européenne des associations de familles de traumatisés crâniens

SG ÖGSHT, Lascygasse 20/18, 1170 Vienna, Austria. T. +436644205214. Fax +43125330333204.
Registered Office Allée de Clerlande 6, 1340 Ottignies, Belgium. T. +3210430236. Fax +3210430440.
Pres HEADWAY-Nelson Hosp, Kingston Road, London, SW20 8DB, UK. T. +442085459640. Fax +442085459649. E-mail: e.velyn129@yahoo.co.uk.
URL: http://www.bif-ec.eu/

History 11 Apr 1999, Brussels (Belgium), by the General Assembly of the 7 founder organizations. Registered in accordance with Belgian law, 2 Mar 2000. Also known as *BIF European Confederation.* **Aims** Raise awareness of brain injury by creating a common European platform through coordination and cooperation between national associations of people with brain injury and their families. **Structure** General Assembly (annual). Board of Directors elects Executive Committee, comprising President, Vice-President, Treasurer and Secretary General. **Languages** English, French. **Staff** Voluntary. **Finance** Members' dues. **Activities** cover the following goals: brain injury to be recognized as a separate disability; establishment of a good model for rehabilitation; guidelines for good practice; all European countries working together; personal injury insurance for everyone; delivery of prevention message; lobbying national and European parliaments and governments; recognition of long-term consequences of brain injury, including physical and sensory impairment, cognitive difficulties, behavioural and emotional problems and social exclusion. Organizes biennial TBI-Challenge Conference. **Events** *Tbi Challenge Europe Congress* Vienna (Austria) 2021, *Tbi Challenge Europe Congress* Vienna (Austria) 2020, *Biennial Conference* Vienna (Austria) 2015, *Biennial Conference / TBI Challenge Conference* Vienna (Austria) 2013, *Biennial Conference / TBI Challenge Conference* Vienna (Austria) 2011.
Members Full; Associate. National organizations (" indicates founding members) in 18 countries:
Austria, Belgium (*), Czechia, Denmark (*), Finland, France (*), Germany, Iceland, Ireland, Italy (*), Netherlands, Poland, Portugal, Slovenia, Spain (*), Sweden, Switzerland (*), UK (*).
NGO Relations Full member of: *European Disability Forum (EDF, #06929).* [2020/XD7271/**D**]

♦ Brains for Brain 03315

Contact Dept of Paediatrics – Univ of Padova, Via N Giustiniania 3, 35128 Padua PD, Italy. T. +39498213505. Fax +39498213502.
Contact Kings College London, Blood-Brain Barrier Group, Wolfson Ctr for Age-Related Diseases, Hodgking Bldg, London, SE1 1UL, UK. T. +442078486262. Fax +442078586250.
URL: http://www.brains4brain.eu/

History Full title: *Brains for Brain Foundation – Onlus.* Serves as a *European Task Force on Brain and Neurodegenerative Lysosomal Storage Diseases.* Registered in accordance with Italian law. **Aims** Develop innovative therapeutic strategies to overcome the blood-brain barrier, the network of capillaries which, while protecting the brain from harmful substances, is opposing to all the treatments available today.
Members Full in 11 countries:
Australia, France, Germany, Greece, Israel, Italy, Netherlands, Russia, Spain, Sweden, UK.
NGO Relations Member of: *European Brain Council (EBC, #06391).* Cooperates with: *European Study Group on Lysosomal Diseases (ESGLD, #08850).* [2013/XJ6522/f/**F**]

- ♦ Brains for Brain Foundation – Onlus / see Brains for Brain (#03315)
- ♦ BRA / see International Bee Research Association (#12330)

♦ Brain Tumor Epidemiology Consortium (BTEC) 03316

Sec address not obtained. E-mail: ckcbtrus@aol.com.
Treas address not obtained.
URL: https://sites.usc.edu/braintumorcause/

History 2003. Registration: Non-profit 503(c)(3), No/ID: 46-1737519, Start date: 2013, USA, Illinois. **Aims** Support collaborative research; educate the public on new findings in brain *cancer* research. **Structure** Board of Directors. **Activities** Events/meetings. **Events** *Annual Meeting* Lyon (France) 2021, *Annual Meeting* Lyon (France) 2020, *Annual Meeting* Hawthorne, CA (USA) 2019, *Annual Meeting* Copenhagen (Denmark) 2018, *Annual Meeting* Banff, AB (Canada) 2017. [2020/XM7543/**C**]

- ♦ Brancheforeningen for Chokolade-, Biscuit- og Konfekture Industrien i EØF / see Association of the Chocolate, Biscuit and Confectionery Industries of the EU (#02427)
- ♦ Brancheforeningen for Oliefabrikker i EF / see FEDIOL – The EU Vegetable Oil and Proteinmeal Industry (#09718)
- ♦ Branche régionale antillaise du Conseil international des archives (see: #12996)
- ♦ Branche régionale arabe du Conseil international des archives (see: #12996)
- ♦ Branche régionale du Conseil international des archives pour l'Afrique centrale (see: #12996)
- ♦ Branche régionale du Conseil international des archives pour l'Afrique de l'Ouest (see: #12996)
- ♦ Branche régionale du Conseil international des archives pour l'Asie de l'Est (see: #12996)
- ♦ Branche régionale du Conseil international des archives pour l'Asie du Sud-Est (see: #12996)
- ♦ Branche régionale du Conseil international des archives pour l'Asie du Sud et de l'Ouest (see: #12996)
- ♦ Branche régionale du Conseil international des archives pour le Pacifique (see: #12996)
- ♦ Branche régionale européenne – Conseil international des archives (see: #12996)
- ♦ Branchforeningen for Olje-och Fett-Industrin i EG / see FEDIOL – The EU Vegetable Oil and Proteinmeal Industry (#09718)
- ♦ Branded Content Marketing Association (unconfirmed)
- ♦ Brand Registry Group (unconfirmed)
- ♦ **BRASS** Black Sea Region Association of Shipbuilders and Ship Repairers (#03277)
- ♦ Les brasseurs européens / see The Brewers of Europe (#03324)

♦ Braun Holocaust Institute / see ADL Braun Holocaust Institute
♦ Brazilian Association for Nature Protection / see AME World Ecology Foundation
♦ Brazilian Institute of International Relations (internationally oriented national body)
♦ Brazzaville Group – African and Malagasy Union (inactive)
♦ BRC / see Balkan Rowing Association (#03083)
♦ BRC / see Baltic Road Association (#03138)
♦ BRC – Barents Regional Council (see: #03177)
♦ BRD – Berggorilla und Regenwald Direkthilfe (internationally oriented national body)
♦ Bread for All (internationally oriented national body)
♦ Bread for Brethren / see Bread for All
♦ **BREAD** Bureau for Research and Economic Analysis of Development (#03373)
♦ Breadline (internationally oriented national body)
♦ Bread for the World (internationally oriented national body)
♦ Bread for the World Educational Fund / see Bread for the World Institute
♦ Bread for the World Institute (internationally oriented national body)
♦ Bread for the World, Stuttgart / see Brot für die Welt
♦ Bread for the World, USA (internationally oriented national body)
♦ Break Free Run / see 3Strands Global Foundation
♦ BrEAST – Breast European Adjuvant Study Team (internationally oriented national body)
♦ Breast Cancer International Research Group / see Translational Research In Oncology
♦ Breast Cancer Working Group / see European Breast Cancer Council (#06400)

♦ Breast Centres Network (BCN) 03317

Project Manager Senologic Intl Soc, 17 rue Albert Calmette, 67200 Strasbourg, France. E-mail: bcn@bcnbreast.org.
URL: https://www.breastcentresnetwork.org/

History Created by *European School of Oncology (ESO, #08434)*. Since 2020, administered by *Senologic International Society (SIS, #19230)*. **Aims** Promote and improve breast cancer care in Europe and throughout the world.
Members Breast units (nearly 250) in 55 countries:
Argentina, Armenia, Australia, Austria, Azerbaijan, Belgium, Bosnia-Herzegovina, Brazil, Bulgaria, Chile, China, Colombia, Croatia, Cyprus, Czechia, Ecuador, Egypt, Estonia, France, Germany, Greece, Hungary, India, Iraq, Ireland, Israel, Italy, Japan, Jordan, Latvia, Lebanon, Lithuania, Malta, Mexico, Netherlands, Pakistan, Peru, Poland, Portugal, Romania, Serbia, Slovakia, Slovenia, South Africa, Spain, Sudan, Sweden, Switzerland, Tanzania UR, Tunisia, Türkiye, UK, Ukraine, Uruguay, USA.
[2021/AA2294/**F**]

♦ Breast European Adjuvant Study Team (internationally oriented national body)

♦ Breast Health Global Initiative (BHGI) 03318

Administrator c/o FHCRC, PO Box 19024, Seattle WA 98109, USA. T. +12066673538. E-mail: bhgi@fredhutch.org.
URL: http://portal.bhgi.org/

History 2002, by Fred Hutchinson Cancer Research Center and Susan G Komen for the Cure. **Aims** Improve breast health outcomes and access to breast cancer screening, detection and treatment for women in low- and middle-income countries. **Structure** Steering Committee; Executive Committee. **Finance** Supported by founded founding organizations. **Activities** Events/meetings; guidance/assistance/consulting. **Events** *Global Summit on International Breast Health / Global Summit* Vienna (Austria) 2012, *Global Summit* Chicago, IL (USA) 2010, *Global Summit* Budapest (Hungary) 2007, *Global Summit* Bethesda, MD (USA) 2005, *Global Summit* Seattle, WA (USA) 2002.
Members Participants (6):
International Association for Hospice and Palliative Care (IAHPC, #11941); International Society for Nurses in Cancer Care (ISNCC, #15312); Latin-American and Caribbean Society of Medical Oncology (#16286); Multinational Association of Supportive Care in Cancer (MASCC, #16895); Union for International Cancer Control (UICC, #20415); WHO (#20950).
IGO Relations Scientific partners include: *Pan American Health Organization (PAHO, #18108).* **NGO Relations** Collaborates with: *European Society for Medical Oncology (ESMO, #08648); European School of Oncology (ESO, #08434).*
[2017/XJ6593/y/**C**]

♦ Breast International Group (BIG) 03319

Chair Bd de Waterloo 76, 1000 Brussels, Belgium. T. +3224861600. E-mail: gia.questiaux@bigagainstbc.org – info@bigagainstbc.org.
URL: http://www.BIGagainstbreastcancer.org/

History 1996. Public face of BIG is called *BIG against breast cancer*. Registration: Banque-Carrefour des Entreprises, No/ID: 0468.176.240, Start date: 23 Dec 1999, Belgium. **Aims** Facilitate and accelerate breast cancer research at international level by stimulating cooperation between members and other academic networks, and collaborating with, but working independently from, the pharmaceutical industry. **Structure** General Assembly (annual); Executive Board; Headquarters in Brussels (Belgium). **Languages** English, French. **Staff** 40.00 FTE, paid. **Finance** Members'dues. Other sources: private donations; fundraising activities; awards; fees from pharmaceutical and biotechnology industry partners for management services provided in connection with clinical trials; research and educational grants from private foundations and charities. **Activities** Research/documentation; projects/programmes; events/meetings. **Events** *IMPAKT Breast Cancer Conference* Brussels (Belgium) 2017, *IMPAKT Breast Cancer Conference* Brussels (Belgium) 2016, *IMPAKT Breast Cancer Conference* Brussels (Belgium) 2015, *IMPAKT Breast Cancer Conference* Brussels (Belgium) 2014, *IMPAKT Breast Cancer Conference* Brussels (Belgium) 2013. **Publications** *BIG Research in Focus* (2 a year). Annual Reports; Articles. Information Services: Database listing peer-reviewed articles related to clinic trials.
Members Organizations in 63 countries and territories:
Argentina, Australia, Austria, Belgium, Bolivia, Brazil, Bulgaria, Canada, Chile, China, Colombia, Cuba, Cyprus, Czechia, Denmark, Ecuador, Egypt, El Salvador, Finland, France, Germany, Greece, Guatemala, Hong Kong, Hungary, Iceland, India, Iran Islamic Rep, Ireland, Israel, Italy, Japan, Korea Rep, Luxembourg, Malta, Mexico, Montenegro, Netherlands, New Zealand, Nicaragua, Nigeria, North Macedonia, Norway, Pakistan, Panama, Peru, Poland, Portugal, Romania, Russia, Serbia, Singapore, Slovakia, Slovenia, South Africa, Spain, Sweden, Switzerland, Taiwan, Türkiye, UK, Uruguay, Venezuela.
Included in the above, 5 organizations listed in this Yearbook:
Breast European Adjuvant Study Team (BrEAST); Central and East European Oncology Group (CEEOG, #03701); European Organisation for Research and Treatment of Cancer (EORTC, #08101); International Breast Cancer Study Group (IBCSG, #12394); International Collaborative Cancer Group (ICCG, no recent information).
IGO Relations *European Commission (EC, #06633).* **NGO Relations** Member of: *Federation of European and International Associations Established in Belgium (FAIB, #09508).*
[2020.03.04/XF5609/y/**F**]

♦ Breast Surgery International (BSI) 03320

Admin Office c/o ISS-SIC, Seefeldstrasse 88, 8008 Zurich ZH, Switzerland. E-mail: surgery@iss-sic.com.
URL: http://www.bsisurgery.org/

History 1999, Vienna (Austria). **Aims** Maintain high standards in the practice and art of breast surgery; provide a forum for exchanging information and developing new knowledge in the field; support advancement of the science and art of breast surgery through clinical experience or laboratory investigation. **Structure** Assembly (every 2 years); Council. Officers: President; Secretary; Council Coordinator; Treasurer. Standing Committees (2): Membership/Nomination; Publications/Program. **Finance** Sources: members' dues. **Activities** Events/meetings; healthcare; training/education. **Events** *Meeting* Krakow (Poland) 2019, *Meeting* Basel (Switzerland) 2017, *Meeting* Bangkok (Thailand) 2015, *Meeting* Helsinki (Finland) 2013, *Meeting* Yokohama (Japan) 2011.
Members Active; Senior; Honorary. Surgeons in 39 countries and territories:
Australia, Austria, Belgium, China, Croatia, Czechia, Denmark, Egypt, France, Germany, Greece, Guatemala, Hong Kong, India, Israel, Italy, Japan, Korea Rep, Malaysia, Mexico, Nepal, Netherlands, New Zealand, Nigeria, Norway, Poland, Portugal, Saudi Arabia, Singapore, South Africa, Spain, Sri Lanka, Sweden, Switzerland, Taiwan, Thailand, Türkiye, UK, USA.
NGO Relations An integrated society of: *International Society of Surgery (ISS, #15496).*
[2021.02.09/XD7980/**D**]

♦ BREDA – Bureau régional de l'Unesco pour l'éducation en Afrique (inactive)

♦ **BREF** Bridging Europe (#03329)
♦ Breiz Europe (unconfirmed)
♦ Bremen Overseas Research and Development Association (internationally oriented national body)
♦ Bremer Arbeitsgemeinschaft für Überseeforschung und Entwicklung (internationally oriented national body)
♦ **BRESCE** UNESCO Office in Venice – UNESCO Regional Bureau for Science and Culture in Europe (#20316)
♦ Brethren in Christ World Missions (internationally oriented national body)
♦ Brethren Church – International Ministries (internationally oriented national body)
♦ Brethren Church Missionary Board / see Brethren Church – International Ministries

♦ Brethren Volunteer Service (BVS) 03321

Orientation Coordinator 1451 Dundee Ave, Elgin IL 60120, USA. T. +18474294396. Fax +18474294393. E-mail: bvs@brethren.org.
URL: http://www.brethrenvolunteerservice.org/

History Founded 1948, following a proposal by younger members of the Church of the Brethren to found a volunteer service programme which was presented before gathered Brethren delegates, 1948, at Colorado Springs Annual Conference. Work formally began Sep 1948. **Aims** Seek persons willing to act on their commitment and values; challenge individuals to offer themselves, their time, and their talents for work that is both demanding and rewarding, and to work for peace, advocate justice, serve human needs and care for creation. **Structure** A ministry of the *Church of the Brethren*. **Staff** 3.00 FTE, paid; 1.00 FTE, voluntary. **Finance** through Church of Brethren. **Activities** Humanitarian/emergency aid; projects/programmes. **Publications** *Volunteer* (2 a year) – newsletter. Project book; brochure.
Members Volunteers (mostly from USA) active in 12 countries:
Brazil, China, El Salvador, Guatemala, Haiti, Honduras, Ireland, Japan, Nigeria, Northern Ireland, South Sudan, USA.
NGO Relations *Church and Peace (#03916); Trees for Life International; World Council of Churches (WCC, #21320); World Friendship Center (WFC).*
[2019.02.12/XF5039/**F**]

♦ Bretton Woods Committee (internationally oriented national body)

♦ Bretton Woods Institutions (BWIs) 03322

Address not obtained.
URL: http://www.brettonwoods.org/

History Used as a description of the institutions set up or instigated in Jul 1944, Bretton Woods NH (USA), by representatives of 45 countries at the *Bretton Woods Conference*. These are *International Monetary Fund (IMF, #14180)* and *International Bank for Reconstruction and Development (IBRD, #12317)* (World Bank), the latter having subsequently been expanded so that, besides the IBRD, the *The World Bank Group (#21218)* includes *International Development Association (IDA, #13155)* (established 1960), *International Finance Corporation (IFC, #13597)* (set up 1956) and *Multilateral Investment Guarantee Agency (MIGA, #16888)* (set up 1988), together with *International Centre for Settlement of Investment Disputes (ICSID, #12515)*, which was added to the Group in 1966 to provide conciliation and arbitration services. Other entities sometimes included under the BWI heading: *World Trade Organization (WTO, #21864); General Agreement on Tariffs and Trade (GATT, inactive); International Fund for Agricultural Development (IFAD, #13692).* **Aims** Spur *economic* growth and *development* worldwide. **Structure** Not an organization as such. **Events** *Spring meeting* Washington, DC (USA) 2011, *Special high-level meeting* New York, NY (USA) 2010, *Special high-level meeting* New York, NY (USA) 2009, *Special high-level meeting* New York, NY (USA) 1999. **IGO Relations** Comes within: *United Nations System (#20635).* **NGO Relations** *Bretton Woods Committee.*
[2012/XE4376/**E***]

♦ Bretton Woods Project (internationally oriented national body)

♦ Brevets Randonneurs Mondiaux (BRM) 03323

Treas 76 rue de la République, 78920 Ecquevilly, France. T. +33134759857.
Pres address not obtained.
URL: http://www.lesrandonneursmondiaux.org/

History Founded 1983, as *Randonneurs mondiaux (RM)*, *Randonneurs européens* having been formed in 1976, Randonneurs français in 1921, and Audax club parisien – founder of Randonneurs Français – in 1904. **Aims** Promote worldwide the knowledge and practice of *cycling* 'grande randonnÃƒÂ©e'. **Structure** General Assembly; Officers: President, Vice-President, Treasurer. **Languages** English, French. **Staff** Voluntary. **Finance** Members' dues. **Activities** Events/meetings. **Events** *Meeting* Guyancourt (France) 2007, *General Assembly* Paris (France) 2007, *Meeting* Guyancourt (France) 2003. **Publications** *La lettre du président Randonneurs mondiaux* (about 4 a year).
Members Clubs; federations; individuals. Members in 60 countries and territories:
Argentina, Australia, Austria, Belarus, Belgium, Bosnia-Herzegovina, Brazil, Bulgaria, Canada, Chile, China, Colombia, Croatia, Czechia, Denmark, Estonia, Finland, France, Germany, Greece, Hungary, Iceland, India, Indonesia, Ireland, Israel, Italy, Japan, Kazakhstan, Korea Rep, Kyrgyzstan, Luxembourg, Macau, Malaysia, Mexico, Moldova, Mongolia, Netherlands, New Zealand, Norway, Philippines, Poland, Portugal, Romania, Russia, Serbia, Singapore, Slovakia, Slovenia, South Africa, Spain, Sri Lanka, Sweden, Switzerland, Taiwan, Thailand, UK, Ukraine, USA, Uzbekistan.
[2018.09.04/XF5487/**F**]

♦ The Brewers of Europe 03324

Office Manager Rue Caroly 23-25, 1050 Brussels, Belgium. T. +3225511810. E-mail: info@brewersofeurope.eu.
Gen Sec address not obtained.
URL: https://brewersofeurope.org/

History 19 Sep 1958, Amsterdam (Netherlands). Former names and other names: *Working Committee of Common Market Brewers* – former (19 Sep 1958 to 1990); *Communauté de travail des brasseurs du Marché commun* – former (19 Sep 1958 to 1990); *Confederation of Common Market Breweries* – former (1990 to 1999); *Confédération des brasseurs du Marché commun (CBMC)* – former (1990 to 1999); *Zusammenschluss der Brauereien des Gemeinsamen Marktes* – former (1990 to 1999); *Les brasseurs européens* – former; *Die Europäischen Brauer* – former. Registration: Banque-Carrefour des Entreprises, No/ID: 0428.031.108, Start date: 14 Nov 1985, Belgium; EU Transparency Register, No/ID: 81610896372-23, Start date: 4 Aug 2011. **Aims** Promote the positive role played by *beer* and the brewing sector in Europe; advocate creation of the right conditions to allow brewers to freely, cost-effectively and responsibly brew and market beer. **Structure** Includes: *European Brewery Convention (EBC, #06401).* **Languages** English. **Staff** 6.00 FTE, paid. **Finance** Sources: members' dues. **Activities** Advocacy/lobbying/activism; politics/policy/regulatory. **Events** *Forum* Brussels (Belgium) 2021, *Forum* Brussels (Belgium) 2020, *Forum* Antwerp (Belgium) 2019, *Beer and beyond* Brussels (Belgium) 2018, *Meeting* Vienna (Austria) 2014.
Members Associations of brewers in 26 countries:
Austria, Belgium, Bulgaria, Croatia, Cyprus, Czechia, Denmark, Finland, France, Germany, Greece, Hungary, Ireland, Italy, Lithuania, Luxembourg, Malta, Netherlands, Poland, Portugal, Romania, Slovakia, Slovenia, Spain, Sweden, UK.
Associate in 3 countries:
Norway, Switzerland, Türkiye.
IGO Relations Accredited by (1): *European Commission (EC, #06633).* **NGO Relations** Member of (3): *European Policy Centre (EPC, #08240); Federation of European and International Associations Established in Belgium (FAIB, #09508); Worldwide Brewing Alliance (WBA, #21917).* Affiliated with (2): *Business and Industry Advisory Committee to the OECD (BIAC, #03385)* (as Affiliated member of); *FoodDrinkEurope (#09841)* (as Affiliated member of).
[2022.05.04/XE3446/**E**]

♦ Brewers' Guild / see International Brewers' Guild
♦ Brewers' Guild Publications Ltd / see International Brewers' Guild
♦ **BRG** Bioencapsulation Research Group (#03246)
♦ BRG – Brand Registry Group (unconfirmed)
♦ **BRI** Banca dei Regolamenti Internazionali (#03165)
♦ **BRI** Banque des règlements internationaux (#03165)
♦ BRIC / see BRICS (#03325)
♦ Bricklayers, Masons and Plasterers International Union of America / see International Union of Bricklayers and Allied Craftworkers

♦ **BRICS** **03325**

Address not obtained.

URL: http://brics.itamaraty.gov.br/

History Originated in meeting held Sep 2006, New York NY (USA), as *BRIC* – the states of Brazil, Russia, India and China. Diplomatic meeting and 1st summit held Jun 2009, Yekaterinburg (Russia). South Africa joined 2010, follwoing which current title was adopted. BRICS stands for: Brazil, Russia, India, China and South Africa. **Aims** Promote dialogue and cooperation among the BRIC countries. **Activities** Politics/policy/regulatory; events/meetings. **Events** *BRICS Summit* India 2021, *BRICS Summit* St Petersburg (Russia) 2020, *Summit* Xiamen (China) 2017, *Summit* Benaulim (India) 2016, *Summit* Ufa (Russia) 2015.

Members Governments (5):
Brazil, China, India, Russia, South Africa. [2021/XM5886/**E***]

♦ **BRICS Forum** **03326**

Contact 24 Firoz Shah Road, Delhi 110001, DELHI 110001, India. T. +919911970905.

URL: http://www.bricsforum.in/

History Founded 2011, as an independent international organization. **Aims** Work for a structured social, economic and environmentally *sustainable* BRICS block – Brazil, Russia, India, China, South Africa. [2017/XJ5850/**F**]

♦ BRICS Intellectual Property Forum (meeting series)
♦ Bridderlech Deelen / see Fondation Partage Luxembourg
♦ The Bridge / see IFLAC – International Forum for the Literature and Culture of Peace (#11102)
♦ Bridge to Asia / see Bridge to Asia Foundation
♦ Bridge to Asia Foundation (internationally oriented national body)
♦ Bridge Builders International (internationally oriented national body)

♦ **Bridge Engineering Institute (BEI)** **03327**

Sec address not obtained. E-mail: bei_institute@outlook.com.

URL: https://www.beibridge.org/

Aims Advance the knowledge of bridge engineering and related fields; foster young professionals who will lead tomorrow's technology; provide a forum for international cooperation. **Structure** Executive Committee; International Advisory Committee. **Activities** Awards/prizes/competitions; events/meetings. **Events** *Bridge Engineering Conference* 2025, *Bridge Engineering Conference* Singapore (Singapore) 2024, *Bridge Engineering Conference* Rome (Italy) 2023, *Bridge Engineering Conference* Singapore (Singapore) 2021, *Bridge Engineering Conference* Honolulu, HI (USA) 2019. [2022/AA2789/**D**]

♦ Bridge EU (unconfirmed)
♦ Bridge Federation of Africa, Asia & the Middle East / see Bridge Federation of Asia & the Middle East (#03328)
♦ Bridge Federation of Asia & the Middle East / see Bridge Federation of Asia & the Middle East (#03328)

♦ **Bridge Federation of Asia & the Middle East (BFAME)** **03328**

Sec 14 – 18th Street, DHA Phase 5, Karachi 75500, Pakistan.

Pres Jordan Bridge Federation, PO Box 142637, Al Rawnaq, Amman 11184, Jordan.

URL: https://www.bridgewebs.com/bfame/

History 1979. A zone of *World Bridge Federation (WBF, #21246). African Bridge Federation (ABF, #00230)* split from BFAME, 2000. Former names and other names: *Bridge Federation of Asia & the Middle East* – former (1979 to 1993); *Bridge Federation of Africa, Asia & the Middle East (BFAAME)* – former (1993 to 2000). **Structure** Executive Council. **Activities** Events/meetings.

Members Full in 10 countries:
Bangladesh, India, Jordan, Kuwait, Pakistan, Palestine, Saudi Arabia, Sri Lanka, Syrian AR, United Arab Emirates. [2019/AA0985/**D**]

♦ The Bridge – Forum Dialogue (internationally oriented national body)
♦ Bridge Fund Europe (internationally oriented national body)
♦ Bridge Initiative International (internationally oriented national body)
♦ The Bridge: Jewish and Arab Women for Peace / see IFLAC – International Forum for the Literature and Culture of Peace (#11102)
♦ The Bridge: Jewish and Arab Women for Peace in the Middle East (see: #11102)
♦ Bridges/dot/Org (internationally oriented national body)
♦ Bridges International (internationally oriented national body)
♦ Bridges for Peace (internationally oriented national body)
♦ Bridgettine Order – Order of the Most Holy Saviour of Saint Bridget (religious order)
♦ Bridgettines – Ordo Sanctissimi Salvatoris (religious order)

♦ **Bridging Europe (BREF)** **03329**

Dir 28 Karaiskaki Street, 105 54 Athens, Greece. T. +302107255174. E-mail: connect@bridging-europe.org.

URL: https://www.bridging-europe.org/

History Jan 2014, Athens (Greece). **Aims** Conduct research on EU and regional topics, opinion polling, consulting services and forecasting; execute social media campaigns. **Structure** Core Team; Project Associates. **Languages** Chinese, English, French, Irish Gaelic, Italian, Portuguese, Spanish, Turkish. **Finance** Sources: donations; members' dues; revenue from activities/projects. **Activities** Events/meetings; publishing activities; research/documentation; training/education. **Publications** *BREF Newsletter. BREF Commentary.* Reports; policy briefs; books; studies; opinion surveys. **Members** Full – individuals; Institutional – companies, intergovernmental bodies, trade unions, universities, embassies, think-tanks, NGOs. Membership countries not specified. **NGO Relations** Member of (1): *Citizens for Europe (CFEU, #03956).* [2020/XJ8547/**D**]

♦ Bridging the Gap Foundation (internationally oriented national body)
♦ Bridging Nations (internationally oriented national body)
♦ BRIE – Bulgarisch-Rumänisches Interuniversitäres Europazentrum (internationally oriented national body)
♦ Brien Holden Vision Institute (internationally oriented national body)
♦ Brigadas Internacionales de Paz (#18277)
♦ Brigade mondiale de la paix /pour l'action non-violente/ (inactive)
♦ Brigade multinationale d'intervention rapide des forces en attente des Nations Unies (inactive)
♦ Brigades internationales (inactive)
♦ Brigades de paix internationales (#18277)
♦ Brighter Green (internationally oriented national body)
♦ Bright Future International (internationally oriented national body)
♦ Bright Hope International (internationally oriented national body)
♦ Brighton Collaboration (inactive)
♦ **Bright Star Foundation** Bright Star Foundation for Maternal and Child Health (#03330)

♦ **Bright Star Foundation for Maternal and Child Health (Bright Star Foundation)** **03330**

Head Office Avenue de Louis-Casaï 18, 1209 Geneva, Switzerland. T. +41225182776. E-mail: info@brightstartfoundation.org.

URL: https://brightstartfoundation.org/

Aims Optimize children's physical, cognitive, social, and emotional development in all settings where young children spend their time; work towards improving early childhood care and education across the world. **Structure** Board; Advisory Councils. **Activities** Advocacy/lobbying/activism; events/meetings; projects/programmes; training/education. **Events** *Annual Bright Start International Conference* 2022, *Middle East and North Africa Regional Conference* Abu Dhabi (United Arab Emirates) 2019. **Publications** *1st Voices of Children International Project_REPORT* (2022) in English – Honouring the Voices of Children; *2022 Bright Start Conference Resources* (2022) in English – Resources & Guides for early childhood educators; *The 1st Early Years Playbook* (1st 2022) in English – Child-Led Play Through Children's Eyes. [2023.02.14/AA0457/**f**/**F**]

♦ Brigidine – Suore di Santa Brigida (religious order)
♦ Brigittine Monks (religious order)
♦ La Brique (internationally oriented national body)
♦ BRISMES – British Society for Middle Eastern Studies (internationally oriented national body)
♦ British-American Security Information Council (internationally oriented national body)
♦ British Association of Concert Agents / see International Artist Managers' Association (#11673)
♦ British Association of Former United Nations Civil Servants (internationally oriented national body)
♦ British Association for International and Comparative Education (internationally oriented national body)
♦ British Association for Slavonic and East European Studies (internationally oriented national body)
♦ British Association for South Asian Studies (internationally oriented national body)
♦ British Association for Soviet, Slavonic and Eastern European Studies / see British Association for Slavonic and East European Studies
♦ British Boxing Board of Control (internationally oriented national body)
♦ British Caribbean Association (internationally oriented national body)
♦ British Commonwealth Association of Prisoners' Aid Society (inactive)
♦ British Commonwealth Ex-Services League / see Royal Commonwealth Ex-Services League (#18989)
♦ British Commonwealth Fencing Federation / see Commonwealth Fencing Federation (#04328)
♦ British Commonwealth Games Federation / see Commonwealth Games Federation (#04332)
♦ British Commonwealth League / see Commonwealth Countries League (#04320)
♦ British Commonwealth Merchant Shipping (1931 treaty)
♦ British Commonwealth Scientific Committee / see Commonwealth Science Council (#04361)
♦ British Commonwealth Weightlifting Federation / see Commonwealth Weightlifting Federation (#04368)
♦ British Council (internationally oriented national body)
♦ British Empire and Commonwealth Games Federation / see Commonwealth Games Federation (#04332)
♦ British Empire and Commonwealth Weightlifting Council / see Commonwealth Weightlifting Federation (#04368)
♦ British Empire Games Federation / see Commonwealth Games Federation (#04332)
♦ British Empire Leprosy Relief Association / see LEPRA Health in Action
♦ British Empire Service League / see Royal Commonwealth Ex-Services League (#18989)
♦ British Empire Society for the Blind / see Sightsavers International (#19270)
♦ British and European Geranium Society / see Pelargonium and Geranium Society
♦ British and Foreign Anti-Slavery Society / see Anti-Slavery International (#00860)
♦ British and Foreign Bible Society / see Bible Society
♦ British Glaciological Society / see International Glaciological Society (#13718)
♦ British Guild of Typographers / see International Society of Typographic Designers
♦ British Institute in Eastern Africa (internationally oriented national body)
♦ British Institute of History and Archaeology in East Africa / see British Institute in Eastern Africa
♦ British Institute of Human Rights (internationally oriented national body)
♦ British Institute of International and Comparative Law (internationally oriented national body)
♦ British and International Golf Greenkeepers Association (internationally oriented national body)
♦ British International Spa Association (inactive)
♦ British International Studies Association (internationally oriented national body)
♦ British Israelism / see Christian Identity

♦ **British Israel World Federation (BIWF)** **03331**

Fédération mondiale des israélites britanniques

Main Office 121 Low Etherley, Bishop Auckland, Durham, DL14 0HA, UK. T. +441388834395. Fax +441388835957. E-mail: admin@britishisrael.co.uk.

URL: http://www.britishisrael.co.uk/

History 1919. British Israelism movement itself was founded in about 1840, UK, by John Wilson. It is sometimes referred to as *Anglo-Israelism.* A Christian sectarian movement that holds distinctive beliefs in addition to those basic to Christianity. UK Registered Charity: 208079. **Aims** Further the belief that Great Britain is the geographical home of the Lost Ten tribes of the Northern House of Israel, whose descendants are to be found in the Anglo-Saxon-Celtic and kindred peoples of today; promote the belief that the covenants made between God and Abraham, Isaac and Jacob (Israel) are everlasting and the British nation plays an important part of God's Plan. **Events** *Annual Congress* Gilsland (UK) 2015, *Annual Congress* Newbury (UK) 2006. **Publications** *BIWF Quarterly.* Books; pamphlets.

Members Full in 15 countries:
Australia, Canada, France, Iceland, Ireland, Kenya, Netherlands, New Zealand, Norway, Solomon Is, South Africa, Switzerland, UK, USA, Zimbabwe.

NGO Relations *Christian Identity.* [2014/XF6522/**F**]

♦ British Leprosy Relief Association / see LEPRA Health in Action
♦ British Masonry Society / see International Masonry Society (#14114)
♦ British Micropalaeontological Group / see Micropalaeontology Society, The (#16749)
♦ British Micropalaeontological Society / see Micropalaeontology Society, The (#16749)
♦ British Overseas Aid Group (internationally oriented national body)
♦ British Overseas NGO's for Development (internationally oriented national body)
♦ British Pestalozzi Children's Village Association / see Pestalozzi International Foundation
♦ British Record Producers Guild / see Music Producers Guild (#16914)
♦ British Refugee Council / see Refugee Council (#18739)
♦ British Relief Association / see LEPRA Health in Action

♦ **British Schools of the Middle East (BSME)** **03332**

Contact 12-14 Carlton Place, Southampton, S015 2EA, UK. E-mail: business@bsme.org.uk – administrator@bsme.org.uk.

URL: http://www.bsme.org.uk/

History 1982. **Aims** Keep members abreast of current developments in UK education; enable head teachers to update their knowledge and understanding of matters that impact upon learning and teaching; discuss school leadership and management issues; explore possible futures for BSME. **Structure** Executive Committee; Country Representatives; BSME Team. **Languages** English. **Staff** 7.00 FTE, paid. **Finance** Sources: members' dues; sale of publications. **Activities** Awards/prizes/competitions; events/meetings; training/education. **Events** *Conference* Abu Dhabi (United Arab Emirates) 2019, *Conference* Abu Dhabi (United Arab Emirates) 2018, *Annual Conference* Abu Dhabi (United Arab Emirates) 2011, *Annual Conference* Manama (Bahrain) 2010, *Annual Conference* Cyprus 2009. **Publications** *BSME Newsletter.* **Members** Schools (over 130); Partners (over 100). Membership countries not specified. [2020.07.09/XM0258/**D**]

♦ British Society for Middle Eastern Studies (internationally oriented national body)
♦ British Union / see Cruelty Free International
♦ British Union for the Abolition of Vivisection / see Cruelty Free International
♦ British Veterinary Radiology Association / see European Association of Veterinary Diagnostic Imaging (#06269)
♦ British West Indies Federation (inactive)
♦ British West Indies Sugar Association / see Sugar Association of the Caribbean (#20033)
♦ Brit Ivrit Olamit (no recent information)
♦ **BRM** Brevets Randonneurs Mondiaux (#03323)

♦ **Broadband Commission for Sustainable Development** **03333**

Exec Dir c/o ITU, Place des Nations, 1211 Geneva 20, Switzerland. T. +41227305111. Fax +41227337256. E-mail: bbcommission@itu.int.

URL: http://www.broadbandcommission.org/

History May 2010. Set up may 2010, by *International Telecommunication Union (ITU, #15673)* and *UNESCO (#20322)*. **Aims** Boost the importance of broadband on the international policy agenda; expand broadband access in every country as key to accelerating progress towards national and international development targets. **Structure** Commissioners. **Activities** Advocacy/lobbying/activism; monitoring/evaluation. **Events** *Annual Spring Meeting* Menlo Park, CA (USA) 2019, *Annual Meeting* New York, NY (USA) 2019, *Special Session* Port Vila (Vanuatu) 2019, *Annual Spring Meeting* Kigali (Rwanda) 2018, *Annual Meeting* New York, NY (USA) 2018. **IGO Relations** *European Telecommunications Satellite Organization (EUTELSAT IGO, #08896)*.
[2021/XM6465/**E***]

♦ Broadband Forum 03334

CEO 5177 Brandin Court, Fremont CA 94538, USA. T. +15104924020. Fax +15104924001. E-mail: info@broadband-forum.org.
URL: http://www.broadband-forum.org/

History 1991, as *Frame Relay Forum (FRF)*. Merged 2003 with *MPLS Forum* and was renamed *MPLS and Frame Relay Alliance*. Merged with *ATM Forum* and became *MFA Forum*, 2005. Subsequently changed title to *IP/MPLS Forum*. *ADSL Forum*, set up 1994, changed title to *DSL Forum*, 1999, and to *Broadband Forum (inactive)*, 2008. IP/MPLS Forum merged with Broadband Forum, 2009 and adopted its title. **Aims** Drive global adoption of IP-MPLS based technology, networks, services and solutions; advance the deployment of multi-vendor, multi-service packet-based networks, associated applications and interworking solutions. **Structure** Board of Directors; Executive Advisory Council. Board Committees; Special Committees; Working Committees. **Languages** English. **Staff** 7.00 FTE, paid. **Events** *MultiProtocol Label Switching Forum* Paris (France) 2019, *Q2 Meeting* Seoul (Korea Rep) 2019, *Q3 Meeting* Berlin (Germany) 2016.
Members Companies in 18 countries:
Australia, Austria, Canada, Denmark, Finland, France, Germany, India, Israel, Italy, Japan, Russia, Spain, Sweden, Thailand, Türkiye, UK, USA.
[2017/XF5616/**F**]

♦ Broadcast Network Europe (BNE) 03335

Association Manager Rue du Luxembourg 22-24, 1000 Brussels, Belgium. T. +3222131384. Fax +3222131363. E-mail: info@broadcast-networks.eu.
URL: http://www.broadcast-networks.eu/

History Registered in accordance with Belgian law. **Aims** Maintain an efficient and fair regulatory and operational environment for terrestrial broadcast network operators so as to ensure European citizens continue to have universal access to a broad range of *TV* and *radio* programmes and content as well as other over-the-air services. **Structure** General Assembly (annual); Board of Directors; Working Groups (3). **Languages** English.
Members Full; Associate.* Full in 18 countries:
Austria, Croatia, Czechia, Finland, France, Germany, Greece, Hungary, Ireland, Italy, Norway, Poland, Romania, Serbia, Spain, Sweden, Switzerland, UK.
Associate in 1 country:
Serbia.
NGO Relations Member of: *Digital Television Action Group (DigiTAG, #05084)*.
[2019/XJ4540/**F**]

- ♦ Brock Chisholm Trust / see International Association for Humanitarian Medicine Chisholm-Gunn (#11946)
- ♦ Broederlijk Delen (internationally oriented national body)
- ♦ Broeders van de Heilige Aloysius Gonzaga (religious order)
- ♦ Broeders van Huijbergen – Broeders van de Onbevlekte Ontvangenis van de Allerheiligste Maagd en Moeder Gods Maria (religious order)
- ♦ Broeders van Liefde (religious order)
- ♦ Broeders van de Onbevlekte Ontvangenis van de Allerheiligste Maagd en Moeder Gods Maria (religious order)
- ♦ Broeders van Onze Lieve Vrouw van Lourdes (religious order)
- ♦ The Broker (internationally oriented national body)

♦ Bromeliad Society International (BSI) 03336

Sec 7540 SW 158th Terrace, Miami FL 33157-2450, USA. E-mail: secretary@bsi.org – membership@bsi.org.
URL: http://bsi.org/

History 1950, Los Angeles CA (USA). Incorporated in the State of California. **Aims** Promote and maintain interest in research, development, preservation and distribution of bromeliads. **Structure** Board of Directors. **Finance** Members' dues; donations. **Events** *Biennial Meeting* Houston, TX (USA) 2016, *Biennial Meeting* Honolulu, HI (USA) 2014, *Biennial Meeting* Orlando, FL (USA) 2012, *Biennial Meeting* New Orleans, LA (USA) 2010, *Biennial Meeting* Cairns, QLD (Australia) 2008. **Publications** *Journal of the Bromeliad Society* (4 a year).
Members National organizations in 11 countries:
Australia, Brazil, France, Germany, Japan, Netherlands, New Zealand, Philippines, UK, USA, Venezuela.
Individuals in 56 countries and territories:
Argentina, Aruba, Australia, Austria, Bahamas, Belgium, Belize, Bermuda, Brazil, Canada, Cayman Is, China, Colombia, Costa Rica, Czechia, Dominican Rep, Ecuador, France, Germany, Grenada, Guatemala, Guiana Fr, Hong Kong, India, Indonesia, Ireland, Israel, Italy, Japan, Kenya, Luxembourg, Malaysia, Mauritius, Mexico, Netherlands, New Zealand, Panama, Philippines, Puerto Rico, Saudi Arabia, Singapore, South Africa, Spain, Sri Lanka, Sweden, Switzerland, Tahiti Is, Taiwan, Thailand, Trinidad-Tobago, UK, Ukraine, Uruguay, USA, Venezuela, Virgin Is UK.
[2019/XE3416/**E**]

♦ Bromine Science and Environmental Forum (BSEF) 03337

SG Rue Belliard 40, Box 17, 1000 Brussels, Belgium. T. +3224369602. E-mail: info@bsef.org.
URL: http://www.bsef.com/

History 1997. Also referred to as *International Bromine Council*. Registration: EU Transparency Register, No/ID: 464193921314-91, Start date: 10 Apr 2016; Banque-Carrefour des Entreprises, No/ID: 0650.805.662, Start date: 25 Mar 2016, Belgium. **Aims** Commission science on brominated flame retardant (BFRs) and bromine; inform decision-makers and other stakeholders on science results and represent the bromine industry on issues of environment and human health. **Languages** English. **Activities** Knowledge management/information dissemination; advocacy/lobbying/activism. **Publications** Reports; factsheets. **Members** Bromine producers (3). Membership countries not specified. **NGO Relations** Member of: *Industry4Europe (#11181)*.
[2020/XF6953/**F**]

♦ The Brooke 03338

Chief Exec 5th Floor Friars Bridge Court, 41-45 Blackfriars Road, London, SE1 8NZ, UK. T. +442030123456. Fax +442030120156. E-mail: info@thebrooke.org.
URL: http://www.thebrooke.org/

History UK Registered Charity: 1085760. **Aims** Improve the lives of working *horses*, *donkeys* and mules in the poorest parts of the world. **Structure** Board of Trustees; Chief Executive. International Office based in UK. Networks in: Egypt, India, Pakistan, Ethiopia, Jordan, Netherlands, USA. **Consultative Status** Consultative status granted from: *ECOSOC (#05331)* (Special). **NGO Relations** Member of: *CHS Alliance (#03911)*.
[2016/XM4453/**F**]

- ♦ Brookings Institution (internationally oriented national body)
- ♦ Brot für Alle (internationally oriented national body)
- ♦ Brot für Brüder / see Bread for All
- ♦ Brot für die Welt (internationally oriented national body)
- ♦ Brot für die Welt – EED / see Brot für die Welt
- ♦ Brot für die Welt – Evangelischer Entwicklungsdienst / see Brot für die Welt
- ♦ BROTHERHOOD / see Asian Brotherhood of Clerical Workers (#01366)
- ♦ Brotherhood of Asian Trade Unionists (inactive)
- ♦ Brotherhood of Dragons (internationally oriented national body)
- ♦ Brotherhood of Locomotive Engineers, International (internationally oriented national body)

♦ Brothers to All Men (BAM) 03339

Frères des hommes (FDH) – Fratelli dell'Uomo

Secretariat Frères des hommes, Rue Renkin 2, 1030 Brussels, Belgium. T. +3225129794. Fax +3225114761. E-mail: fdhbel@skynet.be.
URL: http://www.freresdeshommes.org/

History 17 Sep 1964, Paris (France), when registered in accordance with French law; registered in accordance with UK law, 27 Jun 1968. Also referred to as: *Frères des hommes – Europe*. Previously known in Spanish as *Hermanos de los Hombres* and in Dutch as *Mensenbroeders*. **Aims** Promote fair and sustainable self-development of rural and urban populations in the *Third World*; make people in Europe aware of Third World problems. **Structure** General Assembly; Coordinating Committee; Local Teams (25); Secretariat in Paris (France) at headquarters of French national branch. **Languages** English, French, Italian, Spanish. **Staff** 50.00 FTE, paid. **Finance** Subsidies; donations; subscriptions. **Activities** Advocacy/lobbying/activism; knowledge management/information dissemination. **Events** *General Assembly* Brussels (Belgium) 1996, *General Assembly* Brussels (Belgium) 1996, *General Assembly* Brussels (Belgium) 1995, *General Assembly* Brussels (Belgium) 1994, *General Assembly* Brussels (Belgium) 1986. **Publications** *Peuples en March* (12 a year) – magazine; *Info Terra* (12 a year); *Témoignages et Dossiers* (4 a year); *Actualités* (2 a year) – newsletter. National bulletins.
Members Teams/branches in 4 countries:
Belgium, France, Italy, Luxembourg.
IGO Relations Member of: *Global Information and Early Warning System on Food and Agriculture (GIEWS, #10416)*. **NGO Relations** Member of: *Afrique verte*; *Centre de recherche et d'information pour le développement, Paris (CRID)*; *Confédération européenne des ong d'urgence et de développement (CONCORD, #04547)*; *Coordination SUD*; *Fédération des employeurs ONG (FEONG)*; *Fédération francophone et germanophone des associations de coopération au développement (ACODEV, #09587)*. Supports: *Global Call for Action Against Poverty (GCAP, #10263)*. Instrumental in setting up: *Maison des citoyens du monde (MCM)*.
[2019/XD0201/**F**]

- ♦ Brother's Brother Foundation (internationally oriented national body)
- ♦ Brothers of Charity (religious order)
- ♦ Brothers of the Christian Doctrine (religious order)
- ♦ Brothers of Christian Instruction of Ploërmel (religious order)
- ♦ Brothers of Christian Instruction of St Gabriel (religious order)
- ♦ Brothers of the Christian Schools (religious order)
- ♦ Brothers of the Immaculate Conception of the Blessed Virgin Mary, Mother of God (religious order)
- ♦ Brothers of Mercy of Montabaur (religious order)
- ♦ Brothers of Our Lady of Lourdes (religious order)
- ♦ Brothers of Our Lady, Mother of Mercy (religious order)
- ♦ Brothers of the Poor of St Francis (religious order)
- ♦ Brothers of Saint Patrick (religious order)
- ♦ Brothers of St Francis Xavier (religious order)
- ♦ Brown Cattle Breeders' World Association (unconfirmed)
- ♦ **BRPF** Bertrand Russell Peace Foundation (#03213)
- ♦ BRSF – Biosciences Research Support Foundation (internationally oriented national body)
- ♦ Brücke-CECOTRET / see Brücke-Le pont
- ♦ Brücke-Le pont (internationally oriented national body)
- ♦ Brücke zum Süden / see Brücke-Le pont
- ♦ Bruderan Karitas (religious order)
- ♦ Bruder-Bruder Budi Mulia (religious order)
- ♦ Bruderhof Communities (religious order)
- ♦ Bruderschaft der Drachen (internationally oriented national body)
- ♦ Bruderschaft Unser Lieber Frau vom Berge Karmel (religious order)
- ♦ Bruegel (internationally oriented national body)

♦ Brunei Darussalam-Indonesia-Malaysia-Philippine – East ASEAN Growth Area (BIMP-EAGA) 03340

Liaison Officer 25th Floor, Block A, State Admin Centre, Jalan Sulaman, Teluk Likas, 88400 Kota Kinabalu, Sabah, Malaysia. E-mail: info@bimp-eaga.asia.
URL: https://bimp-eaga.asia/

History 26 Mar 1994, Davao (Philippines). Former names and other names: *East ASEAN Growth Area* – alias. **Aims** Promote *trade*, transport, *tourism* and communication in the area. **Activities** Working Groups (13): Agro-Industry; Air Linkages; Capital Formation/Financial Services; Construction/Construction Materials; Energy; Environment; Fisheries; Forestry; Human Resource Development; People Mobility; Sea Linkages; Telecommunications; Tourism. **Events** *Summit / Meeting* Phnom Penh (Cambodia) 2012, *Senior officials meeting / Meeting* Kota Kinabalu (Malaysia) 2005, *Biennial industry conference* Manila (Philippines) 2004, *Orchid congress* Kota Kinabalu (Malaysia) 2003, *Tourism conference* Kuching (Malaysia) 2003. **Publications** *EAGA Review*.
Members Participating countries (4):
Brunei Darussalam, Indonesia, Malaysia, Philippines.
IGO Relations Instrumental in setting up: *Coral Triangle Initiative on Coral Reefs, Fisheries and Food Security (CTI-CFF, #04833)*.
[2021/XF6448/**F***]

- ♦ Bruno Kreisky Forum for International Dialogue (internationally oriented national body)
- ♦ Bruno Kreisky Forum für Internationalen Dialog (internationally oriented national body)
- ♦ Bruno Kreisky Foundation for Outstanding Achievements in the Area of Human Rights (internationally oriented national body)
- ♦ Bruno-Kreisky-Stiftung für Verdienste um die Menschenrechte (internationally oriented national body)
- ♦ Brussels Centre of African Studies (internationally oriented national body)
- ♦ Brussels Convention – Convention Relating to the Distribution of Programme-carrying Signals Transmitted by Satellite (1974 treaty)
- ♦ Brussels Democratic Association (inactive)

♦ Brussels Dialogue on Climate Diplomacy (BDCD) 03341

Coordinator address not obtained. E-mail: info@brusselsdialogue.net.
URL: https://www.brusselsdialogue.net/

History 2016, Brussels (Belgium). An informal network. **Aims** Promote information exchange and cooperation among European institutions, international organizations, NGOs and think-tanks active in the nexus between climate change and international, national, human and environmental security. **Structure** Coordinated by *Environment and Development Resource Centre (EDRC)*. **Activities** Events/meetings; knowledge management/information dissemination; networking/liaising; publishing activities; research/documentation.
Members Participating organizations, including 31 organizations listed in this Yearbook:
- *Centre for Research on the Epidemiology of Disasters (CRED, #03781)*;
- *E3G – Third Generation Environmentalism*;
- *Environment and Development Resource Centre (EDRC)*;
- *European Commission (EC, #06633)*;
- *European Defence Agency (EDA, #06895)*;
- *European Economic and Social Committee (EESC, #06963)* (Sustainable Development Observatory);
- *European Environmental Bureau (EEB, #06996)*;
- *European External Action Service (EEAS, #07018)*;
- *European Institute of Peace (EIP, #07567)*;
- *European Organisation of Military Associations and Trade Unions (EUROMIL, #08099)*;
- *Foundation for European Progressive Studies (FEPS, #09954)*;
- *Foundation for Global Governance and Sustainability (FOGGS, #09958)*;
- *German Marshall Fund of the United States (GMF)*;
- *Global Military Advisory Council On Climate Change (GMACCC, #10474)*;
- *GLOBE – European Union (GLOBE EU, #10667)*;
- *Heinrich Böll Foundation* (European Union);
- *Institute for Environmental Security (IES)*;
- *Institute for European Environmental Policy (IEEP, #11261)*;
- *International Organization for Migration (IOM, #14454)* (Regional Office Brussels);
- *International Union for Conservation of Nature and Natural Resources (IUCN, #15766)* (European Regional Office);
- *NATO (#16945)* (Emerging Security Challenges Division);
- *NATO Parliamentary Assembly (NATO PA, #16946)*;
- *Netherlands Institute of International Relations – Clingendael*;

- *Organisation of African, Caribbean and Pacific States (OACPS, #17796)*;
- *Organization for Security and Cooperation in Europe (OSCE, #17887)*;
- *Planetary Security Initiative (PSI)*;
- *Quaker Council for European Affairs (QCEA, #18587)*;
- *Supreme Headquarters Allied Powers Europe (SHAPE, #20039)* (Civil Military Cooperation Liaision Branch + Infrastructure & Engineering Division);
- *UNEP (#20299)* (Regional Office for Europe);
- *United Nations Liaison Office for Peace and Security (UNLOPS, #20583)*;
- *World Resources Institute (WRI, #21753)* (Europe). [2022.01.26/AA2419/y/**F**]

♦ Brussels International Banking Club (BIBC) 03342

Secretariat Rue England 94 – Bte 4, 1180 Brussels, Belgium. T. +3223743653. Fax +3223743282.

History Nov 1996, Brussels (Belgium), by *Information Fund of the Commonwealth of Independent States (no recent information)*. Registered in accordance with Belgian law, 6 Jul 1997. **Aims** Promote cooperation between financial institutions of the Commonwealth of Independent States and the European Union; facilitate the preparation of CIS banks for European Monetary Union and introduction of the Single European Currency; act as a forum for discussion. **Structure** General Assembly (annual). Board of Directors, comprising 14 members. Secretariat in Brussels (Belgium). **Languages** English, French, Russian. **Finance** Members' dues. Other sources: contributions; grants. **Activities** Dissemination of information; conferences, round tables, workshops and seminars; studies and research; special training sessions. **Events** *International Conference* Milan (Italy) / Rome (Italy) 2006, *International Conference* Brussels (Belgium) 2004, *International Conference* Luxembourg 2003, *International Forum* Brussels (Belgium) 2002, *Conference / International Forum* Brussels (Belgium) 1999.

Members Corporate (Permanent or Associate) and individual membership. Banks, banking associations and investment companies (about 30) in 11 countries:
Azerbaijan, Belarus, Belgium, Germany, Italy, Kyrgyzstan, Moldova, Netherlands, Russia, Tajikistan, Ukraine.
[2012.07.03/XF4495/**F**]

♦ Brussels International of Freethinkers (inactive)
♦ Brussels supplementary convention – Convention Supplementary to the Paris Convention on Third Party Liability in the Field of Nuclear Energy (1963 treaty)
♦ Brussels Treaty – Treaty for Collaboration in Economic, Social and Cultural Matters and for Collective Self-defence (1948 treaty)
♦ **BSA** Benthological Society of Asia (#03208)
♦ **BSA** Business Software Alliance (#03387)
♦ **BSAC** Baltic Sea Advisory Council (#03139)
♦ BSAG / see Foundation for a Living Baltic Sea
♦ BSARG – Black Sea Area Research Group (internationally oriented national body)
♦ BS – Biochemical Society (internationally oriented national body)
♦ BSC / see Commission on the Protection of the Black Sea Against Pollution (#04237)
♦ BSCA – Black Sea Coastal Association (internationally oriented national body)
♦ BSCAI – Building Service Contractors Association International (internationally oriented national body)
♦ **BSC** Baltic Sea Commission (#03141)
♦ BSCMID – Black Sea Society of Clinical Microbiology and Infectious Diseases (unconfirmed)
♦ BSCSIF / see International Foundation for Sustainable Peace and Development (#13678)
♦ BSEC BC – Organization of the Black Sea Economic Cooperation Business Council (no recent information)
♦ **BSECCESDEI** Black Sea Economic Cooperation Centre for the Exchange of Statistical Data and Economic Information (#03273)
♦ BSECEE – Balkan Science and Education Centre of Ecology and Environment (internationally oriented national body)
♦ BSEC Free Trade Area – Black Sea Economic Cooperation Free Trade Area (unconfirmed)
♦ **BSEC** Organization of Black Sea Economic Cooperation (#17857)
♦ **BSEC-URTA** Union of Road Transport Associations in the Black Sea Economic Cooperation Region (#20477)
♦ **BSEF** Bromine Science and Environmental Forum (#03337)
♦ BSEP – Black Sea Environmental Programme (inactive)
♦ **BSER** Black Sea Euroregion (#03275)
♦ **BSERC** Black Sea Energy Research Centre (#03274)
♦ BSF / see Belgian Fund for Food Security
♦ **BSF** Bibliothèques Sans Frontières (#03229)
♦ BSF – Biologie Sans Frontières (internationally oriented national body)
♦ **BSG** Balkan Society of Geometers (#03084)
♦ **BSG** Baltic Sea Geologists (#03143)
♦ BSGC – Biological Science Graduate Congress (meeting series)
♦ BSHC – Baltic Sea Hydrographic Commission (see: #13825)
♦ BSHF / see World Habitat
♦ **BSI** Beyond Sciences Initiative (#03223)
♦ **BSI** Blue Shield International (#03286)
♦ **BSI** Breast Surgery International (#03320)
♦ **BSI** Bromeliad Society International (#03336)
♦ **bSI** buildingSMART International (#03353)
♦ BSIEU / see Service Employees International Union
♦ BSK / see Berghof Foundation
♦ **BSME** British Schools of the Middle East (#03332)
♦ **BSMSP** Bernoulli Society for Mathematical Statistics and Probability (#03212)
♦ **BSN** Baltic Sea Network on Occupational Health and Safety (#03144)
♦ **BS NGO Network** Baltic Sea NGO Network (#03145)
♦ **BSNN** Black Sea NGO Network (#03276)
♦ **BSOHNS** Balkan Society of Oto-Rhino-Laryngology, Head and Neck Surgery (#03085)
♦ **BSP** Baltic Sea Project (#03147)
♦ **BSP** Baltic Society of Phlebology (#03153)
♦ **BSPC** Baltic Sea Parliamentary Conference (#03146)
♦ BS RAC / see Baltic Sea Advisory Council (#03139)
♦ **BSR-AO** CEA bureau sous-régional pour l'Afrique de l'Ouest (#05277)
♦ **BSR** Balkan Society of Radiology (#03086)
♦ BSR – Business for Social Responsibility (internationally oriented national body)
♦ BSREC – Black Sea Regional Energy Centre (inactive)
♦ **BSRUN** Baltic Sea Region University Network (#03149)
♦ **BSSS** Baltic Sport Science Society (#03154)
♦ **BSSSC** Baltic Sea States Subregional Cooperation (#03150)
♦ **BSTDB** Black Sea Trade and Development Bank (#03278)
♦ **BSU** Balkan Speleological Union (#03087)
♦ BSUF – Black Sea University Foundation
♦ BSUN – Black Sea University Network (internationally oriented national body)
♦ **BSZI** Baltijas sociālo zinātņu institūts (#03122)
♦ BTA – Bridge to Asia Foundation (internationally oriented national body)
♦ BTC / see Enabel
♦ BTCEA – Be The Change Earth Alliance (internationally oriented national body)

♦ The B Team 03343

Contact address not obtained. E-mail: info@bteam.org – media@bteam.org.
URL: http://bteam.org/

History 2013. **Aims** Catalyze a movement of business leaders driving a better way of doing business for the wellbeing of people and *planet*. **Structure** Leaders; Executive. **Finance** Support from various sources, including: *Ford Foundation (#09858)*; *The Rockefeller Foundation (#18966)*. **Members** Business leaders. Membership countries not specified. **NGO Relations** Member of: *We Mean Business*. [2017/XM5932/v/**F**]

♦ **BTEC** Brain Tumor Epidemiology Consortium (#03316)
♦ **BTF** Federation of Balkan Turk Migrants and Refugee Associations (#03089)
♦ BTG – Bridging the Gap Foundation (internationally oriented national body)
♦ BtH / see Beyond the Horizon International Strategic Studies Group (#03222)
♦ **BTI** Byggnads- ocht Träarbetar-Internationalen (#03355)
♦ BTK / see International Study Group for Systems Biology (#15619)
♦ **BTK** World Congress of Tatars (#21310)
♦ BTMI – Blessed Trinity Missionary Institute (religious order)
♦ **BTRA** BeNeLux Travel Retail Association (#03206)
♦ BUAV / see Cruelty Free International
♦ BUAV Charitable Trust / see Cruelty Free International
♦ BuBgA / see KURVE Wustrow
♦ Bucharest convention – Convention on the Protection of the Black Sea Against Pollution (1992 treaty)
♦ Budapest Centre for the International Prevention of Genocide and Mass Atrocities (unconfirmed)
♦ Budapest Convention – Convention on Cybercrime (2001 treaty)
♦ Budapesti Obszervatórium – Kelet-Közép-Európai Kulturalis Obszervatórium Alapitvany (internationally oriented national body)
♦ The Budapest Observatory – Regional Observatory on Financing Culture in East-Central Europe (internationally oriented national body)

♦ Budapest Process 03344

Head of Secretariat c/o ICMPD, Gonzagagasse 1, 5th floor, 1010 Vienna, Austria. T. +4366488451451. E-mail: budapestprocess@icmpd.org.
URL: http://www.budapestprocess.org/

History Feb 1993, Budapest (Hungary). Established as an interregional dialogue on migration stretching from Europe to the Silk Routes region, including over 40 countries. In 2013, the Istanbul Ministerial Declaration led to the establishment of "A Silk Routes Partnership for Migration" offering a framework for cooperation. "Istanbul Commitments on the Silk Routes Partnership for Migration and its Call for Action – a five year plan" was adopted, Feb 2019 **Aims** Master the balance and interplay between political dialogue and operational action; improve the capacities of administrations to better manage all aspects related to the movement of people, including awareness of how migration could be more beneficial for the development of each country; promote a common understanding of migration concepts and policies, as well as a common language on migration issues through dialogue, information and experience exchange between states and other stakeholders. **Structure** Senior Officials meet annually or bi-annually; Chairmanship held by Turkey, with Hungary as Co-Chair; Regional Working Groups (3): Black Sea Region; Silk Routes Region; South East European Region. **Languages** Arabic, English, Persian, Russian. **Staff** Part-time. **Finance** Sources: contributions. Bilateral funding from participating countries including Turkey, Hungary, Switzerland, Sweden, Poland, Norway and Finland. EU-funding through regional projects from 2014-2022. **Activities** Capacity building; events/meetings; monitoring/evaluation; politics/policy/regulatory; projects/programmes; research and development. Main focus on the Silk Routes Region. Projects currently active in Bangladesh, Iraq and Pakistan. **Events** *Meeting on Return and Reintegration* Istanbul (Türkiye) 2022, *Joint Meeting of the South East Europe and the Silk Routes Regional Working Groups of the Budapest Process* Skopje (North Macedonia) 2022, *Meeting on Return and Reintegration* Budapest (Hungary) 2020, *Meeting on Labour Migration in the Current Covid-19 Pandemic* Vienna (Austria) 2020, *Senior Officials Meeting* Istanbul (Turkey) 2019.

Members Budapest Process involves migration related ministries and agencies of 51 participating States:
Albania, Armenia, Austria, Azerbaijan, Belarus, Belgium, Bosnia-Herzegovina, Bulgaria, Croatia, Cyprus, Czechia, Denmark, Estonia, Finland, France, Georgia, Germany, Greece, Hungary, Iraq, Ireland, Italy, Kazakhstan, Kyrgyzstan, Latvia, Liechtenstein, Lithuania, Luxembourg, Malta, Moldova, Montenegro, Netherlands, North Macedonia, Norway, Pakistan, Poland, Portugal, Romania, Russia, Serbia, Slovakia, Slovenia, Spain, Sweden, Switzerland, Tajikistan, Türkiye, Turkmenistan, UK, Ukraine, Uzbekistan.
Cooperation with Afghanistan came to a halt in 2021.
Observers in 7 countries:
Australia, Bangladesh, Canada, China, India, Iran Islamic Rep, USA.
Intergovernmental organizations cooperating in the Process (17):
Bali Process on People Smuggling, Trafficking in Persons and Related Transnational Crime (Bali Process, #03063); *Council of Europe (CE, #04881)*; *Economic Cooperation Organization (ECO, #05313)*; *European Commission (EC, #06633)*; *European Police Office (Europol, #08239)*; *European Union (EU, #08967)* (European Asylum Support Office EASO); *Frontex, the European Border and Coast Guard Agency (#10005)*; *ILO (#11123)*; International Centre for Migration Policy Development, Vienna (ICMPD); *International Criminal Police Organization – INTERPOL (ICPO-INTERPOL, #13110)*; *International Organization for Migration (IOM, #14454)*; *Migration, Asylum, Refugees Regional Initiative (MARRI, #16800)*; *Organization for Security and Cooperation in Europe (OSCE, #17887)*; *Organization of Black Sea Economic Cooperation (BSEC, #17857)*; *UNDP (#20292)*; *UNHCR (#20327)*; *United Nations Office on Drugs and Crime (UNODC, #20596)*.
NGO Relations NGOs are invited to expert working group meetings on an ad-hoc basis.
[2022.10.19/XF4929/y/**E***]

♦ Budapest Treaty of 1977 – Budapest Treaty on the International Recognition of the Deposit of Microorganisms for the Purposes of Patent Procedure (1977 treaty)
♦ Budapest Treaty on the International Recognition of the Deposit of Microorganisms for the Purposes of Patent Procedure (1977 treaty)

♦ Budapest Union for the International Recognition of the Deposit of Microorganisms for the Purposes of Patent Procedure 03345

Union de Budapest pour la reconnaissance internationale du dépôt des microorganismes aux fins de la procédure en matière de brevets

Address not obtained.
URL: http://www.wipo.org/

History 28 Apr 1977, Budapest (Hungary), by *Budapest Treaty on the International Recognition of the Deposit of Microorganisms for the Purposes of Patent Procedure (Budapest Treaty of 1977, 1977)*. A union administered by *World Intellectual Property Organization (WIPO, #21593)*. **Aims** Facilitate the obtention of patents in respect of *inventions* involving microorganisms. **Activities** The Treaty allows for one deposit with an international depositary authority to suffice before national patent offices of all contracting States and before any regional patent office recognizing the effects of the Treaty – currently EPO.

Members Open to States party to the Budapest Treaty. States party to the Treaty, as of Jan 2012 (75):
Albania, Armenia, Australia, Austria, Azerbaijan, Belarus, Belgium, Bosnia-Herzegovina, Bulgaria, Canada, Chile, China, Costa Rica, Croatia, Cuba, Czechia, Denmark, Dominican Rep, El Salvador, Estonia, Finland, France, Georgia, Germany, Greece, Guatemala, Honduras, Hungary, Iceland, India, Ireland, Israel, Italy, Japan, Jordan, Kazakhstan, Korea DPR, Korea Rep, Kyrgyzstan, Latvia, Liechtenstein, Lithuania, Luxembourg, Mexico, Moldova, Monaco, Montenegro, Morocco, Netherlands, Nicaragua, North Macedonia, Norway, Oman, Peru, Philippines, Poland, Portugal, Romania, Russia, Serbia, Singapore, Slovakia, Slovenia, South Africa, Spain, Sweden, Switzerland, Tajikistan, Trinidad-Tobago, Tunisia, Türkiye, UK, Ukraine, USA, Uzbekistan.
Declarations of acceptance by intergovernmental organizations (2):
African Regional Intellectual Property Organization (ARIPO, #00434); *European Patent Office (EPO, #08166)*.
International depositary authorities (37), including the following body listed in this Yearbook:
European Collection of Authenticated Cell Cultures (ECACC, #06604). [2015/XF4181/y/**F***]

♦ Buddhalainen Yhteiso Triratna (#20243)

♦ Buddha's Light International Association (BLIA) 03346

Founder-Pres Hsi Lai Temple, 3456 South Glenmark Drive, Hacienda Heights CA 91745, USA. T. +16169235128. Fax +16169376544. E-mail: bliaeuro@blia.org.
Main Temple Fo Guang Shan, Ta Shu, Kaohsiung 84010, Taiwan. T. +88676561921.
URL: http://www.bliahq.org/

History 3 Feb 1991, Taiwan, on formal inauguration, following work of Taiwan chapter/organizing committee set up 1990. Comes within the framework of *International Buddhist Progress Society (IBPS, no recent information)*. **Aims** Follow and propagate the Buddha's teaching; venerate the triple gems, abide by Buddhist precepts, harmonize the five vehicles, practice the three teachings and perfect human character; promote living, dynamic Buddhism; work for the welfare and awakening of the world; facilitate communications and activities among Buddhist lay people worldwide; provide them with an opportunity to sponsor spiritual

activities, purify the human mind, fulfil individual human potential and establish Buddha's 'Light Pure Land' on earth; answer human need and actualize the humanistic Buddhist approach of benevolence and compassion to all by bringing Buddhism to the masses across national boundaries. **Structure** Board of Directors comprising 17 members, including President and 6 Vice-Presidents. Committees. World headquarters in Los Angeles CA (USA), inaugurated 17-22 May 1992. Regional/national headquarters; regional chapters (over 100); local chapters. **Activities** Celebrates 16 May as International Buddha's Light Day. **Events** *Meeting* Hong Kong (Hong Kong) 2013, *Asia Forum* Jenjarom (Malaysia) 2012, *Conference* Sydney, NSW (Australia) 2011, *Meeting of the fourth board of directors of Buddha's* Singapore (Singapore) 2009, *Annual members meeting* Hong Kong (Hong Kong) 1997.
Members Individuals and groups. Chapters in 15 countries:
Australia, Belgium, Brazil, Canada, France, Hong Kong, Indonesia, Japan, Malaysia, New Zealand, Paraguay, Philippines, South Africa, Taiwan, USA.
Consultative Status Consultative status granted from: *ECOSOC (#05331)* (Special). **IGO Relations** Associated with Department of Global Communications of the United Nations. **NGO Relations** Founding member of: *NGO Forum on Environment (FOE, #17125)*. Member of: *Conference of Non-Governmental Organizations in Consultative Relationship with the United Nations (CONGO, #04635)*. [2012/XF4320/**F**]

♦ Buddhist Global Relief (internationally oriented national body)
♦ Buddhistische Gemeinschaft Triratna (#20243)
♦ Buddhistiska Gemenskapen Triratna (#20243)
♦ Buddhist Peace Fellowship (internationally oriented national body)

♦ Buddhist Tzu Chi Foundation 03347

USA Headquarters 1100 S Valley Center Ave, San Dimas CA 91773, USA. T. +19094477799. Fax +19094477948. E-mail: info@us.tzuchi.org.
URL: http://www.tzuchi.org/
History May 1966, Hualien (Taiwan), as *Tzu Chi Merits Society* by Venerable Dharma Master Cheng Yen, as a humanitarian organization which started with 30 supporters, housewives who saved 2 cents from their grocery money each day to help the poor. Subsequently changed name to *Tzu Chi Foundation*. Tzu Chi means "compassion and relief". **Aims** Help the poor and educate the rich; give material aid to the needy and inspire love and humanity in both givers and receivers; relieve suffering for all living beings, regardless of nationality, religion, ethnicity or socio-economic status. As volunteers of the organizations, apply the Buddhist principle of "kindness, compassion, joy and selfless giving' when helping others, cultivate the virtues of "sincerity, integrity, trust and honesty", and treat everyone with gratitude, respect and love. **Activities** Major missions: charity; medicine; education; humanistic culture. Engages in international disaster relief, bone marrow donation, community volunteerism and environmental protection; builds schools, housing and medical clinics around the world; provides medical care, food, clothing, blanket and comfort to the poor, elderly, sick and underprivileged. Has assisted individuals and communities in 72 countries, including people suffering from disasters such as the Southeast Asia tsunami, Myanmar cyclone, floods in Pakistan, Australia and United States, and earthquakes in Turkey, Pakistan, Sichuan China, Haiti, Chile and Japan.
Members Offices (432) in 50 countries and territories:
Argentina, Australia, Austria, Belgium, Bolivia, Brazil, Brunei Darussalam, Canada, Chile, China, Costa Rica, Denmark, Dominican Rep, El Salvador, Eswatini, France, Germany, Guatemala, Haiti, Honduras, Hong Kong, Indonesia, Italy, Japan, Jordan, Korea Rep, Lesotho, Malaysia, Marshall Is, Mexico, Mozambique, Myanmar, Netherlands, New Zealand, Paraguay, Philippines, Singapore, South Africa, Spain, Sri Lanka, St Martin, Sweden, Switzerland, Taiwan, Thailand, Türkiye, UK, USA, Vietnam, Zimbabwe.
Consultative Status Consultative status granted from: *ECOSOC (#05331)* (Special); *UNEP (#20299)*. **NGO Relations** Member of: *American Council for Voluntary International Action (InterAction)*; *International Council of Voluntary Agencies (ICVA, #13092)*. [2020/XF7112/f/**F**]

♦ Buddhist Union of Europe / see European Buddhist Union (#06407)

♦ Budhana Ligo Esperantista (BLE) 03348

Ligue bouddhiste espérantiste – League of Buddhist Esperantists
Contact Tutihara 3-205, Tenpaku-ku, Nagoya-si, Ait-ken, 468-0026 Japan. E-mail: gan@starling.us.
URL: http://budhana.org/
History Jul 1928, UK. **Aims** Propagate the Buddha's basic teaching – without prejudicing any school or direction – by using the international language Esperanto. **Structure** Free Brotherhood, keeping contact mainly by correspondence and occasional meetings on the occasion of annual International Esperanto-Congresses. **Staff** 7.00 FTE, voluntary. **Finance** Voluntary grants. **Activities** Correspondence courses in Buddhism; translation and treatment of canonical Buddhist texts and doctrines. **Publications** *La Budhana Kuriero* (periodical) in Esperanto.
Members Individuals in 45 countries and territories:
Argentina, Australia, Austria, Belgium, Brazil, Bulgaria, Canada, Chile, China, Czechoslovakia, Denmark, Finland, France, Germany, Greece, Hungary, India, Indonesia, Iran Islamic Rep, Ireland, Israel, Italy, Japan, Korea Rep, Malaysia, Mexico, Myanmar, Nepal, Netherlands, New Caledonia, Norway, Poland, Portugal, Romania, Russia, Serbia, Spain, Sri Lanka, Sweden, Switzerland, Thailand, Tunisia, UK, USA, Vietnam.
NGO Relations Associated with: *Universal Esperanto Association (UEA, #20676)*. [2014/XC0202/v/**F**]

♦ BUE / see European Buddhist Union (#06407)
♦ **Buffalo Network** Inter-Regional Cooperative Research Network on Buffalo (#15967)
♦ Build Africa (internationally oriented national body)
♦ BUILD – Building Understanding through International Links for Development (internationally oriented national body)

♦ Builders of the Adytum (BOTA) 03349

Headquarters 5101 North Figueroa St, Los Angeles CA 90042, USA. T. +13232557141. Fax +13232554166. E-mail: inquiries@bota.org.
URL: http://www.bota.org/
History USA, by Paul Foster Case. A spiritual organization whose teachings are based on the Holy *Qabalah* and the Sacred *Tarot*. **Finance** Sources: members' dues. **Publications** *BOTA Online Newsletter* (4 a year).
Members Groups in 10 countries:
Australia, Colombia, France, Germany, Mexico, New Zealand, Spain, UK, USA, Venezuela. [2023.02.13/XF6735/**F**]

♦ Build Europe 03350

Acting Managing Dir Rue de la Violette 43, 1000 Brussels, Belgium. T. +3228939726. E-mail: info@buildeurope.net.
URL: https://buildeurope.net/
History 17 Nov 1958, Paris (France). Former names and other names: *Union européenne des constructeurs de logements /Secteur privé/ (UECL)* – former; *European Union of Independent Home-Builders* – former; *Europäische Union der Freien und Privaten Wohnungsunternehmen* – former; *Union européenne des promoteurs-constructeurs (UEPC)* – former (1991); *European Union of Developers and House Builders* – former (1991); *Europäische Union der Freien Wohnungsunternehmen* – former (1991). Registration: Banque-Carrefour des Entreprises, No/ID: 0410.819.942, Start date: 11 Apr 1960, Belgium; EU Transparency Register, No/ID: 80003592094-64, Start date: 30 Jul 2009. **Aims** Bring together and exchange experience among members in the scientific, social, technical, financial and legal fields of house building and developing; study the European market and the factors which influence it; encourage constant improvement in *construction* techniques; suggest and apply relevant legislative and administrative measures. **Structure** General Assembly (biannual); Board of Directors; Joint Committee; Secretariat. **Languages** English, French. **Finance** Members' dues. Subsidies. **Activities** Events/meetings; guidance/assistance/consulting; networking/liaising; research/documentation. **Events** *General Assembly* Malta 2015, *General Assembly* St Julian's (Malta) 2015, *General Assembly* Madrid (Spain) 2014, *General Assembly* Wroclaw (Poland) 2014, *General Assembly* Brussels (Belgium) 2013.
Members Full in 12 countries:
Belgium, Bulgaria, France, Germany, Ireland, Luxembourg, Malta, Norway, Poland, Romania, Spain, UK.
Consultative Status Consultative status granted from: *ECOSOC (#05331)* (Ros). **IGO Relations** Member of: FOCOPE of *European Parliament (EP, #08146)*. **NGO Relations** Observer status with (1): *European Organisation for Technical Assessment (EOTA, #08103)*. Member of (3): *European Construction Forum (ECF, #06765)*; *European Housing Forum (EHF, #07504)*; *International Housing Association (IHA, #13815)*. [2022/XD0892/**D**]

♦ Building Advisory and Information Network / see Building Advisory Service and Information Network (#03351)

♦ Building Advisory Service and Information Network (BASIN) 03351

Réseau de services consultatifs et d'information pour le secteur de la construction – Red de Servicios e Información en el Sector de la Construcción
Coordinator c/o CRATerre-EAG, BP 53, Maison Levrat, Parc Fallavier, 38092 Villefontaine CEDEX, France. T. +33474954391. Fax +33474956421.
Contact c/o SKAT, Vadianstrasse 42, 9000 St Gallen, Switzerland. T. +41712285454. Fax +41712285455. E-mail: info@skat.ch.
History 1988, by: SKAT, Switzerland; Practical Action (formerly ITDG), UK; GTZ-GATE, Germany. Statutes adopted and registered in accordance with French law, 31 Mar 1992. Reconstituted, 1997, allowing 2 categories of membership: Managing Partners; Network Partners. Also referred to as *Building Advisory and Information Network – Réseau d'information, documentation et conseil en bâtiment*. **Aims** Provide information and advice on appropriate building *technology*; create links between information resources and those requiring it worldwide – government officials, financiers, builders and developers, architects, planners, producers of building materials – covering up-to-date information and advice on manufacture, performance and availability of appropriate outputs and technology from all regions and on effective management of local resources; maximize returns from local resources and skills and collect and provide customer-oriented information on appropriate technology for cost-effective building and *low-cost housing*; stimulate popular initiative and profitable investment in provision of low-cost housing; strengthen local capacities for promoting a vibrant building industry. **Structure** General Assembly (annual). Management Team of 4 partners. Joint activities coordinated by a non-executive Chair. No permanent secretariat. **Languages** English. **Staff** 52.00 FTE, paid. **Finance** Sources: subsidies; contracts; donations; remuneration for services rendered. **Activities** Assesses local resources, skills and opportunities; develops enabling and people-focused policy approaches; reviews standards and regulations; appraises investment for profitable local production; carries out training programmes for technology awareness and construction; disseminates information; carries out research and development programmes; manages projects. Offers professional competence in a wide range of project activities including: post-disaster reconstruction and resettlement schemes for displaced people and refugees; upgrading of urban slum areas; provision of rural housing; settlement planning; enterprise promotion programmes; educational and health facility programmes; formulation of appropriate standards and regulations. **Events** *Sustainable building technology seminar* India 1999, *Awareness seminar* Cairo (Egypt) 1996. **Publications** *BASIN news* (2 a year) – newsletter. Books; videos; films; technical briefs; information leafleats; bibliographies.
Members Network Partners (9) in 9 countries:
Argentina, France, Germany, India, Kenya, Nicaragua, Philippines, Switzerland, UK.
Included in the above, 6 organizations listed in this Yearbook:
German Appropriate Technology Exchange (GATE, inactive); *International Centre for Earth Construction (#12485)*; *Network for an Economical and Ecological Habitat (EcoSouth Network, #17007)*; *Practical Action (#18475)*; *SKAT Foundation*; *Society for Development Alternatives*. [2008.06.01/XF3502/y/**F**]

♦ Building Industry Consulting Service International (BICSI) 03352

Secretariat 8610 Hidden River Pkwy, Tampa FL 33637-1000, USA. T. +18139791991. Fax +18139714311. E-mail: bicsi@bicsi.org.
BICSI South Pacific PO Box 318, South, Melbourne VIC 3205, Australia. E-mail: info@bicsi.com.au.
BICSI Japan Sagami Bldg 2nd fl, 7-13-6 Ginza, Chuo-ku, Tokyo, 104-0061 Japan. E-mail: bicsi-japan@bicsi.jp.
URL: http://www.bicsi.org/
History 1977. Registration: 501(c)6, USA. **Aims** Advance the economical technical efficiency, performance and safety of telecommunications services, networks and pathways for commercial and residential buildings and campus properties. **Structure** Board of Directors, comprising President, President Elect, Secretary, Treasurer, Executive Director. Committees (8). **Finance** Members' dues. Fees for services. Budget (annual): US$ 15 million. **Activities** Conducts registration (certification) programmes for designers and installers of telecommunications cabling systems. Organizes conferences. **Events** *Fall Conference* Las Vegas, NV (USA) 2022, *Annual Southeast Asia conference* Singapore (Singapore) 2021, *Winter Conference* Tampa, FL (USA) 2020, *Europe, Middle East and Africa ACE Summit* Dubai (United Arab Emirates) 2019, *Annual Southeast Asia conference* Manila (Philippines) 2019. **Publications** Manuals. **Members** Individuals (about 22,000) in 85 countries. Membership countries not specified. [2020/XN4469/t/**D**]

♦ Building Owners and Managers Association International (internationally oriented national body)
♦ Building Service Contractors Association International (internationally oriented national body)
♦ Building Service Employees' International Union / see Service Employees International Union

♦ buildingSMART International (bSI) 03353

Communications Dir Kings House, Station Road, Kings Langley, WD4 8LZ, UK. T. +441923277953. E-mail: contact@buildingsmart.org.
URL: http://www.buildingsmart.org/
History 1994, USA. Founded as (US) Industry Alliance for Interoperability. Former names and other names: *International Alliance for Interoperability (IAI)* – former (1996 to 2008). **Aims** Create and develop open digital ways of working for built asset environment. **Structure** International Council; Strategic Advisory Council; Board; Management Executive. **Events** *International Standards Summit* Montréal, QC (Canada) 2022, *International Standards Summit* 2021, *International Standards Summit* 2020, *International Standards Summit* Lillestrøm (Norway) 2020, *International Standards Summit* Beijing (China) 2019.
Members Organizations and companies (about 600). Chapters (9) in 27 countries and territories:
Australia, Austria, Canada, China, Denmark, Finland, France, Germany, Hong Kong, Ireland, Italy, Japan, Korea Rep, Netherlands, New Zealand, Norway, Poland, Russia, Singapore, Slovenia, Spain, Sweden, Switzerland, Türkiye, UK, United Arab Emirates, USA.
NGO Relations Liaison Organization of: *Comité européen de normalisation (CEN, #04162)*. [2022.05.04/XF5622/**F**]

♦ Building and Social Housing Foundation / see World Habitat

♦ Buildings Performance Institute Europe (BPIE) 03354

Exec Dir Rue de la Science 23, 1040 Brussels, Belgium. T. +3227893000. E-mail: info@bpie.eu.
Main Website: http://www.bpie.eu/
History 2010. Founded with support of *ClimateWorks Foundation (#04024)* and *European Climate Foundation (ECF, #06574)*. *European Council for an Energy Efficient Economy (ECEEE, #06818)* also provided support during its creation. Registration: Belgium. **Aims** Make a sustainable and low carbon built environment a reality in Europe. **Structure** Board of Directors; Strategy Advisory Group; Regional Office; Headquarters in Brussels (Belgium). **Languages** Croatian, Dutch, English, French, German, Hungarian, Italian, Polish, Portuguese, Romanian, Russian, Serbian, Slovakian, Spanish, Swedish. **Staff** 21.85 FTE, paid. **Finance** Sources: donations; grants; private foundations. **Activities** Advocacy/lobbying/activism; capacity building; events/meetings; knowledge management/information dissemination; politics/policy/regulatory; research/documentation. **Publications** Studies; reports.
Members National initiatives in 4 countries:
Bulgaria, Germany, Poland, Romania.
NGO Relations Member of (7): *Active House Alliance (#00100)*; Build Up; *Coalition for Energy Savings (#04056)*; Construction 21; *European Council for an Energy Efficient Economy (ECEEE, #06818)*; *Global Alliance for Buildings and Construction (GlobalABC, #10187)*; *Global Buildings Performance Network (GBPN, #10256)*. [2022.05.13/XJ2712/j/**D**]

♦ Building Understanding through International Links for Development (internationally oriented national body)

♦ Building and Wood Workers' International (BWI) 03355

Internationale des travailleurs du bâtiment et du bois (IBB) – Internacional de Trabajadores de la Construcción y la Madera (ICM) – Bau- und Holzarbeiter Internationale (BHI) – Byggnads- ocht Träarbetar-Internationalen (BTI)
Gen Sec Route des Acacias 54, 1227 Carouge GE, Switzerland. T. +41228273773. E-mail: info@bwint.org.

URL: http://www.bwint.org/
History 9 Dec 2005, Buenos Aires (Argentina). Founded on merger of *International Federation of Building and Wood Workers (IFBWW, inactive)* and *World Federation of Building and Woodworkers Unions (WFBWU, inactive)*. **Aims** Promote development of *trade unions* in the building, woodworking and *forestry* industries worldwide; promote and enforce workers *rights* in the context of *sustainable development*. **Structure** Congress (every 4 years). Council (meets every year), comprising representatives of 26 groups of countries, General Secretary and Women's Committee. Board (meets twice a year), including President and 5 Vice-Presidents. Regional office (3): BWI South African and Middle East Regional Office; *BWI Regional Office for Asia and the Pacific*; *BWI Latin American and Caribbean Regional Office*. Committees: Auditors; International Women; Regional Women. **Languages** English, French, German, Spanish, Swedish. **Staff** 14.00 FTE, paid. **Finance** Affiliation fees. Donations. **Events** *Quadrennial World Congress* Brazil 2021, *Asia Pacific Regional Strategy Meeting on Trade Justice* Singapore (Singapore) 2018, *Quadrennial world congress* Durban (South Africa) 2017, *Africa and Middle East, Europe, Latin America and Caribbean, Asia and Pacific regional committees meeting* Lille (France) 2009, *Quadrennial world congress* Lille (France) 2009.
Members Affiliated unions (324), grouping over 12 million individual members in 121 countries and territories:
Albania, Angola, Argentina, Austria, Azerbaijan, Bangladesh, Barbados, Belgium, Bermuda, Bosnia-Herzegovina, Botswana, Brazil, Bulgaria, Burkina Faso, Cambodia, Cameroon, Canada, Chad, Chile, Colombia, Congo DR, Costa Rica, Côte d'Ivoire, Croatia, Curaçao, Cyprus, Czechia, Denmark, Djibouti, Dominican Rep, Egypt, El Salvador, Estonia, Eswatini, Ethiopia, Faeroe Is, Fiji, Finland, France, Georgia, Germany, Ghana, Greece, Guatemala, Guinea, Guyana, Hong Kong, Hungary, Iceland, India, Indonesia, Ireland, Israel, Italy, Japan, Jordan, Kazakhstan, Kenya, Korea Rep, Kyrgyzstan, Latvia, Lesotho, Liberia, Lithuania, Luxembourg, Malawi, Malaysia, Mali, Malta, Mauritania, Mauritius, Moldova, Mongolia, Montenegro, Morocco, Mozambique, Nepal, Netherlands, New Zealand, Nicaragua, Nigeria, North Macedonia, Norway, Pakistan, Palestine, Panama, Papua New Guinea, Peru, Philippines, Poland, Portugal, Romania, Russia, Senegal, Serbia, Seychelles, Sierra Leone, Singapore, Slovakia, Slovenia, Solomon Is, South Africa, Spain, Sri Lanka, Sweden, Switzerland, Taiwan, Tanzania UR, Thailand, Togo, Tunisia, Türkiye, Uganda, UK, Ukraine, USA, Uzbekistan, Venezuela, Yemen, Zambia, Zimbabwe.
Consultative Status Consultative status granted from: *ECOSOC (#05331)* (Special). **IGO Relations** Observer Status with: *Intergovernmental Negotiating Committee for a Legally Binding Agreement on Forests in Europe (INC-Forests, inactive)*. Participates in: *United Nations Forum on Forests (UNFF, #20562)*. Accredited by: *United Nations Framework Convention on Climate Change – Secretariat (UNFCCC, #20564)*. Through ITUC links with: *FAO (#09260)*; *United Nations Economic Commission for Europe (UNECE, #20555)*; *UNIDO (#20336)*; *United Nations Human Settlements Programme (UN-Habitat, #20572)*. **NGO Relations** Member of (5): *Conference of Non-Governmental Organizations in Consultative Relationship with the United Nations (CONGO, #04635)*; *Fédération des Institutions Internationales établies à Genève (FIIG, #09599)*; *Global Labour University (GLU, #10448)*; *Global Union Federations (GUF, #10638)*; *Women in Migration Network (WIMN, #21008)*. Stakeholder in: *PEFC Council (#18288)*. Partner of: *World Urban Campaign (WUC, #21893)*. Close cooperation with: *Confederation of International Contractors Associations (CICA, #04558)*; *Education International (EI, #05371)*; *European Federation of Building and Woodworkers (EFBWW, #07065)*; *International Federation of Chemical, Energy, Mine and General Workers' Unions (ICEM, inactive)*; *International Federation of Journalists (IFJ, #13462)*; *International Trade Union Confederation (ITUC, #15708)*; *International Transport Workers' Federation (ITF, #15726)*; *Nordic Federation of Building and Wood Workers (NFBWW, #17283)*; *Public Services International (PSI, #18572)*; *Trade Union Advisory Committee to the OECD (TUAC, #20186)*; *UNI Global Union (#20338)*. [2021/XM1784/**B**]

- ♦ Building Workers International (inactive)
- ♦ Built Environment Professions in the Commonwealth (internationally oriented national body)

♦ Bukido World Federation (BWF) 03356

Exec Officer 273 Last Morh, Sarwal, Jammu, Jammu and Kashmir 180005, Jammu JAMMU AND KASHMIR 180005, India. E-mail: bukidofederation@gmail.com.
URL: http://www.bukidoworld.com/
History 2018, India. **Aims** Promote the game of bukido. **Structure** Executive Committee.
Members Full in 17 countries:
Afghanistan, Azerbaijan, Bangladesh, Brazil, Burkina Faso, Congo DR, Denmark, India, Iran Islamic Rep, Italy, Korea Rep, Malaysia, Maldives, Sierra Leone, Sri Lanka, Tanzania UR, Türkiye.
NGO Relations Member of (2): *General Association of Asia Pacific Sports Federations (GAAPSF, #10106)*; *International Sport Network Organization (ISNO, #15592)*. [2021/AA1082/**C**]

- ♦ BUKO – Bundeskoordination Internationalismus (internationally oriented national body)
- ♦ **BULA** Beach Ultimate Lovers Association (#03190)
- ♦ Bulgarian European Community Studies Association (internationally oriented national body)
- ♦ Bulgarian-Romanian Inter-University European Centre / see Bulgarian-Romanian Inter-University Europe Center
- ♦ Bulgarian-Romanian Inter-University Europe Center (internationally oriented national body)
- ♦ Bulgarisch-Rumänisches Interuniversitäres Europazentrum (internationally oriented national body)
- ♦ The BulLion Foundation (internationally oriented national body)
- ♦ Bund der Älteren Generation Europas (#05597)
- ♦ Bundeskoordination Internationalismus (internationally oriented national body)

♦ Bund Europäischer Farbberater/Farbdesigner (BEF) 03357

Association of European Colour Consultants/Colour Designers
Contact Putlitzst 13, 76137 Karlsruhe, Germany. T. +491709076640.
URL: https://bef-farbdesign.com/
Aims Promote and supports members in their work as colour consultants and colour designers; strengthen their reputation. **Structure** Board. **Languages** English, German. **Staff** Voluntary. **Finance** Members' dues. **Activities** Training/education.
Members Full in 4 countries:
Austria, Germany, Italy, Switzerland.
NGO Relations Official representative of *International Association of Colour Consultants/Designers (IACC)*. [2020.01.16/XM8395/**D**]

- ♦ Bund Europäischer Jugend / see Young European Federalists (#21984)
- ♦ Bund Europäischer Pfadfinder (#04531)
- ♦ Bund Europäischer Philatelistenverbände (inactive)
- ♦ Bund der Familienorganisationen der Europäischen Union / see COFACE Families Europe (#04084)
- ♦ Bund Freier Gewerkschaften (no recent information)
- ♦ Bund der Internationalen Christlichen Arbeitnehmerverbände / see International Federation of ACLI (#13336)
- ♦ Bund Internationaler Detektive (internationally oriented national body)
- ♦ Bündnis Entwicklung Hilft (internationally oriented national body)
- ♦ Bündnis Entwicklung Hilft – Gemeinsam für Menschen in Not / see Bündnis Entwicklung Hilft
- ♦ Bund der Personalverbände der Internationalen Beamten (#09603)
- ♦ Bund Russlicher Solidaristen (internationally oriented national body)
- ♦ Bund der Sozialdemokratischen Parteien der Europäischen Gemeinschaft / see Party of European Socialists (#18249)
- ♦ Bund der Vereinigungen der im Ausland Lebenden Bürger der Europäischen Gemeinschaft / see Europeans throughout the World (#08839)
- ♦ BUNKERS – International Convention on Civil Liability for Bunker Oil Pollution Damage (2001 treaty)
- ♦ BUON – Balkan Union of Oncology (inactive)
- ♦ **BUP** The Baltic University Programme (#03155)
- ♦ Bureau des affaires de désarmement des Nations Unies (#20594)
- ♦ Bureau africain pour la défense des libertés de l'écrivain (no recent information)
- ♦ Bureau africain et mauricien de recherches et d'études législatives (inactive)
- ♦ Bureau africain des sciences de l'éducation (no recent information)
- ♦ Bureau d'amélioration et de génétique végétales du CABI (inactive)
- ♦ Bureau arabe de l'éducation pour les Etats du Golfe (#00910)
- ♦ Bureau of Arab Sports Ministers for the Arab League / see Council of Arab Ministers for Youth and Sports (#04866)
- ♦ Bureau of Asian Affairs / see Jesuit Conference of Asia Pacific (#16099)
- ♦ Bureau de l'Asie et du Pacifique Sud de l'éducation des adultes (#02098)
- ♦ Bureau des associations de designers européens / see Bureau of European Design Associations (#03359)
- ♦ Bureau des associations européennes de design (#03359)
- ♦ Bureau du CABI d'horticulture et des cultures de plantation (inactive)
- ♦ Bureau canadien de l'éducation internationale (internationally oriented national body)
- ♦ Bureau de la CEA pour l'Afrique du Nord (#05273)
- ♦ Bureau central de compensation maghrébin (no recent information)
- ♦ Bureau central des congrès internationaux de pédologie (inactive)
- ♦ Bureau central international de séismologie (inactive)
- ♦ Bureau central météorique (inactive)
- ♦ Bureau central panaméricain d'eugénisme (inactive)
- ♦ Bureau central pour la prévention de la tuberculose (inactive)
- ♦ Bureau de la CESAP pour le Pacifique (see: #20557)
- ♦ Bureau commun nordique des éditeurs de journaux (no recent information)
- ♦ Bureau du Conseiller spécial pour l'Afrique (see: #20515)
- ♦ Bureau de coopération des associations nordiques de clergés (inactive)
- ♦ Bureau de coopération économique du Pacifique Sud / see Pacific Islands Forum Secretariat (#17970)
- ♦ Bureau de coordination de l'action des quinze pays de la CE en matière de sécurité publique (inactive)
- ♦ Bureau de la coordination des affaires humanitaires (#20593)
- ♦ Bureau de coordination de l'arabisation (#00999)
- ♦ Bureau of Coordination of Arabization / see Arabization Coordination Bureau (#00999)
- ♦ Bureau de coordination de la Conférence épiscopale autrichienne pour le développement international et la mission (internationally oriented national body)
- ♦ Bureau de coordination de frêt maritime (inactive)
- ♦ Bureau de coordination industrielle (inactive)
- ♦ Bureau de coordination des pays non alignés (#04815)
- ♦ Bureau de coordination des secours en cas d'urgence / see PAHO/WHO Health Emergencies Department (#18023)
- ♦ Bureau du Coordonnateur des Nations Unies pour les secours en cas de catastrophe (inactive)
- ♦ Bureau du Coordonnateur spécial pour l'Afrique et les pays les moins avancés (inactive)
- ♦ Bureau du Coordonnateur spécial des Nations Unies pour le processus de paix au Moyen-Orient (#17698)
- ♦ Bureau Croix-Rouge auprès de l'UE (#18643)
- ♦ Bureau de développement de coopérative d'assurance (inactive)

♦ Bureau de développement des télécommunications (BDT) 03358

Telecommunication Development Bureau – Oficina de Desarrollo de las Telecomunicaciones
Dir ITU-D, Place des Nations, 1211 Geneva 20, Switzerland. T. +41227306085. Fax +41227305484. E-mail: bdtdirector@itu.int – bdtmail@itu.int.
URL: http://www.itu.int/ITU-D/index.asp
History 1989, Nice (France), by the Plenipotentiary Conference of *International Telecommunication Union (ITU, #15673)*, having from 1959 been the department of ITU General Secretariat responsible for technical cooperation. Became operational 1 Jan 1990. Legal status: Article 21 of the Geneva Convention. Functions of *Centre for Telecommunications Development (CTD, inactive)*, set up Jul 1985, Geneva, by Resolution No 929 of ITU Administrative Council, and which ceased to exist 31 Dec 1991, have been integrated into the structure of the Bureau. **Aims** Foster international cooperation and solidarity in delivery of technical assistance and in creation, development and improvement of telecommunication and ICT equipment and networks in developing countries. **Structure** Functions as the executive arm of the Sector, headed by Director and assisted by *'Telecommunications Development Advisory Group (TDAG)'*. Headquarters in Geneva (Switzerland); field offices (11) in Africa, the Americas, the Arab States and Asia. **Languages** Arabic, Chinese, English, French, Russian, Spanish. **Finance** Contributions of ITU member states; voluntary contributions from a number of sources, including the following organizations listed in this Yearbook: *Abdus Salam International Centre for Theoretical Physics (ICTP, #00005)*; *Canadian International Development Agency (CIDA, inactive)*; *European Space Agency (ESA, #08798)*; *European Telecommunications Satellite Organization (EUTELSAT IGO, #08896)*; *Department for International Development Cooperation*; *International Far-Eastern Numismatics (IFEN, no recent information)*; *International Maritime Organization (IMO, #14102)*; *Pacific Islands Forum Secretariat (#17970)*; *Swedish International Development Cooperation Agency (Sida)*. Annual budget at least Swiss Fr 62 million, actual figure depending on voluntary contributions. **Activities** The Bureau's duties, as listed in Article 14 of the Nice Constitution, consist in principle of discharging, in the field of assistance to developing countries, the ITU's dual responsibility as a United Nations agency specialized in telecommunications and as an executing agency for implementing projects financed by UNDP and other sources. It offers, organizes and coordinates technical cooperation and assistance activities to facilitate and enhance telecommunications development and organizes regional and global development conferences plus numerous seminars/workshops/meetings in all areas of telecommunications. Functions include programme supervision and technical advice. Expert service recruits specialists from public and private sectors to provide missions with high-level expertise in a variety of telecommunication specialties. Computer-based assistance programmes. **Events** *General Affairs Meeting* Brussels (Belgium) 2014, *WTIS : World Telecommunication/ICT Indicators Symposium* Tbilisi (Georgia) 2014, *WTIS : World Telecommunication/ICT Indicators Symposium* Mexico City (Mexico) 2013, *Annual global symposium for regulators* Geneva (Switzerland) 2000, *World conference on telecommunications development / Quadrennial World Telecommunication Development Conference* Valletta (Malta) 1998. **Publications** Reports; handbooks; guidelines; toolkits. Information Services: Computer-based assistance programmes.
Members Member states of ITU. Sector Members, Academia and Associates in 188 countries and territories:
Afghanistan, Albania, Algeria, Andorra, Angola, Antigua-Barbuda, Argentina, Aruba, Australia, Austria, Bahamas, Bahrain, Bangladesh, Barbados, Belgium, Belize, Benin, Bermuda, Bhutan, Bolivia, Bosnia-Herzegovina, Botswana, Brazil, Brunei Darussalam, Bulgaria, Burkina Faso, Burundi, Cambodia, Cameroon, Canada, Cape Verde, Central African Rep, Chad, Chile, China, Colombia, Comoros, Congo Brazzaville, Congo DR, Costa Rica, Côte d'Ivoire, Croatia, Cuba, Curaçao, Cyprus, Czechia, Denmark, Djibouti, Dominica, Dominican Rep, Ecuador, Egypt, El Salvador, Equatorial Guinea, Eritrea, Estonia, Eswatini, Ethiopia, Fiji, Finland, France, Gabon, Gambia, Germany, Ghana, Greece, Grenada, Guatemala, Guinea, Guinea-Bissau, Guyana, Haiti, Holy See, Honduras, Hong Kong, Hungary, Iceland, India, Indonesia, Iran Islamic Rep, Iraq, Ireland, Israel, Italy, Jamaica, Japan, Jordan, Kenya, Kiribati, Korea DPR, Korea Rep, Kuwait, Laos, Latvia, Lebanon, Lesotho, Libya, Liechtenstein, Lithuania, Luxembourg, Madagascar, Malawi, Malaysia, Maldives, Mali, Malta, Marshall Is, Mauritania, Mauritius, Mexico, Micronesia FS, Monaco, Mongolia, Montserrat, Morocco, Mozambique, Myanmar, Namibia, Nauru, Nepal, Netherlands, New Zealand, Nicaragua, Niger, Nigeria, North Macedonia, Norway, Oman, Pakistan, Palestine, Panama, Papua New Guinea, Paraguay, Peru, Philippines, Poland, Portugal, Qatar, Romania, Rwanda, Samoa, San Marino, Sao Tomé-Principe, Saudi Arabia, Senegal, Serbia, Seychelles, Sierra Leone, Singapore, Slovakia, Slovenia, Solomon Is, Somalia, South Africa, South Sudan, Spain, Sri Lanka, St Kitts-Nevis, St Lucia, St Vincent-Grenadines, Sudan, Suriname, Sweden, Switzerland, Syrian AR, Tanzania UR, Thailand, Timor-Leste, Togo, Tonga, Trinidad-Tobago, Tunisia, Türkiye, Turks-Caicos, Tuvalu, Uganda, UK, United Arab Emirates, Uruguay, USA, Vanuatu, Venezuela, Vietnam, Virgin Is UK, Yemen, Zambia, Zimbabwe.
Included in the above-mentioned members, 10 bodies listed in this Yearbook:
Asia-Pacific Broadcasting Union (ABU, #01863); *Asia-Pacific Telecommunity (APT, #02064)*; *Caribbean Telecommunications Union (CTU, #03560)*; *European Broadcasting Union (EBU, #06404)*; *European Commission (EC, #06633)*; *International Amateur Radio Union (IARU, #11646)*; *International Mobile Satellite Organization (IMSO, #14174)*; *International Telecommunications Users Group (INTUG, #15672)*; *Pacific Telecommunications Council (PTC, #18007)*; *Regional Commonwealth in the Field of Communications (RCC, #18767)*.
IGO Relations *UNDP (#20292)*. Instrumental in setting up: *Global Telecommunication University (GTU, no recent information)*. **NGO Relations** Multinational telecommunications operators and manufacturers. [2019/XE3058/y/**E***]

- ♦ Bureau de l'économie rurale du CABI (inactive)
- ♦ Bureau pour les élections libres / see OSCE – Office for Democratic Institutions and Human Rights (#17902)
- ♦ Bureau d'enquêtes de la CCI sur la contrefaçon (#11043)
- ♦ Bureau d'étude et de documentation sur la santé des étudiants (inactive)
- ♦ Bureau des étudiants européens en technologie (#03294)

Bureau European Design
03359

alphabetic sequence excludes
For the complete listing, see Yearbook Online at

♦ Bureau of European Design Associations (BEDA) 03359

Bureau des associations européennes de design – Comité de Asociaciones Europeas de Diseño – Büro des Europäischen Design Verbandes – Comitato delle associazioni europee di design – Bureau van Europese Design Associations

Pres AWEX – C/O WBDM, Place Sainctelette 2, 1080 Brussels, Belgium. T. +33615680483. E-mail: office@beda.org.
URL: http://www.beda.org/

History 1969. Former names and other names: *Bureau of European Designers Associations* – former; *Bureau des associations de designers européens* – former; *Büro des Europäischen Designer Verbandes* – former; *Comitato delle Associazioni di Designers Europei* – former; *Bureau van Europese Designers Verenigingen* – former. Registration: Banque-Carrefour des Entreprises, No/ID: 0844.127.553, Start date: 2 Mar 2012, Belgium; EU Transparency Register, No/ID: 71028143474-84, Start date: 20 Apr 2010. **Aims** Ensure permanent liaison between professional societies of designers within EC/EU countries; act as a liaison committee between them and the EC/EU authorities. **Structure** General Assembly (annual); Board; Rotating Chairmanship (every 2 years). **Languages** English. **Staff** 0.50 FTE, paid. **Finance** Sources: members' dues. Annual budget: 90,000 EUR. **Activities** Events/meetings; networking/liaising; research/documentation. **Events** *BEDA Design Forum* Copenhagen (Denmark) 2023, *General Assembly* Copenhagen (Denmark) 2023, *BEDA Design Forum* Kaunas (Lithuania) 2022, *BEDA Design Forum* Saint-Étienne (France) 2022, *General Assembly* Saint-Étienne (France) 2022. **Publications** *BEDA Dossier*, *BEDA Register of European Designers*. Guides; reports.
Members Associations in 28 countries:
Austria, Belgium, Czechia, Denmark, Estonia, Finland, France, Germany, Greece, Hungary, Iceland, Ireland, Italy, Latvia, Lithuania, Luxembourg, Malta, Netherlands, Poland, Portugal, Serbia, Slovakia, Slovenia, Spain, Sweden, Switzerland, Türkiye, UK.
IGO Relations Cooperates with (1): *European Union Intellectual Property Office (EUIPO, #08996)*. Recognized by: *European Commission (EC, #06633)*. **NGO Relations** Together with: *International Federation of Interior Architects / Designers (IFI, #13460)*, took over activities of *Comité européen d'architectes d'intérieurs (inactive)*. [2022.10.18/XD3749/**D**]

- ♦ Bureau of European Designers Associations / see Bureau of European Design Associations (#03359)
- ♦ Bureau of European Policy Advisers / see European Political Strategy Centre (#08248)
- ♦ Bureau européen de café (inactive)
- ♦ Bureau européen certification des produits en laine minérale (#06510)
- ♦ Bureau européen des communications (#06676)
- ♦ Bureau européen pour la conservation et le développement (#06412)
- ♦ Bureau européen de coordination des organisations internationales de jeunesse (inactive)
- ♦ Bureau européen de l'éducation populaire / see European Association for the Education of Adults (#06018)
- ♦ Bureau européen de l'environnement / see European Environmental Bureau (#06996)
- ♦ Bureau européen d'information pour le développement de la santé animale / see Centre européen d'études pour la santé animale (#03745)
- ♦ Bureau européen d'informations charbonnières (inactive)
- ♦ Bureau européen d'investissement pour la santé et le développement (see: #20945)
- ♦ Bureau européen de la jeunesse et de l'enfance (inactive)
- ♦ Bureau européen de médecine physique et de réadaptation (#06371)
- ♦ Bureau européen du mouvement scout / see World Scout Bureau – European Regional Office (#21771)
- ♦ Bureau européen de la musique (no recent information)
- ♦ Bureau européen de l'objection de conscience (#06411)
- ♦ Bureau européen des préparateurs et distributeurs de produits de l'agriculture biologique (no recent information)
- ♦ Bureau européen des qualifications et spécialisations en médecine dentaire (inactive)
- ♦ Bureau européen des radiocommunications / see European Communications Office (#06676)

♦ Bureau Européen des Unions de Consommateurs (BEUC) 03360

European Consumers' Organisation – Europäischer Verbraucherschutzverband

Dir Rue d'Arlon 80 – Bte 1, 1040 Brussels, Belgium. T. +3227431591.
URL: http://www.beuc.eu/

History 6 Feb 1962, Brussels (Belgium). Founded following establishment of a provisional bureau, 20 Sep 1961. Former names and other names: *European Bureau of Consumers' Unions* – former; *European Office of Consumer Unions* – former; *ECO* – former; *Europäisches Büro der Verbraucherverbände* – former. Registration: Banque-Carrefour des Entreprises, No/ID: 0422.071.051, Start date: 5 Nov 1981, Belgium; EU Transparency Register, No/ID: 9505781573-45, Start date: 29 Oct 2008. **Aims** Unite consumers' unions of European Union, accession and European Economic Area countries to promote representation and support for European consumer interests; promote relevant initiatives by member organizations. **Structure** General Assembly (annual); Executive; Departments (2). Secretariat, located in Brussels (Belgium). **Languages** English, French, German. **Staff** 38.00 FTE, paid. **Finance** Sources: members' dues. Supported by: *European Union (EU, #08967)*. **Activities** Knowledge management/information dissemination; standards/guidelines. **Events** *To empower, not to weaken: Rethinking consumer protection in the digital world* Brussels (Belgium) 2022, *Conference on Protecting Consumers Freedom in the Digital Era* Brussels (Belgium) 2019, *Workshop on Bundled Products : Dispute Resolution and Consumer Rights Enforcement* Brussels (Belgium) 2019, *Joint Conference on the Financial Crisis Ten Years Later* Brussels (Belgium) 2018, *General Assembly* Brussels (Belgium) 2014. **Publications** Annual Report.
Members Full: organizations (41) in countries of the European Union or European Economic Area, in 30 countries:
Austria, Belgium, Bulgaria, Cyprus, Czechia, Denmark, Estonia, Finland, France, Germany, Greece, Hungary, Iceland, Ireland, Italy, Latvia, Luxembourg, Malta, Netherlands, North Macedonia, Norway, Poland, Portugal, Romania, Slovakia, Slovenia, Spain, Sweden, Switzerland, UK.
Consultative Status Consultative status granted from: *World Intellectual Property Organization (WIPO, #21593)* (Permanent Observer Status). **IGO Relations** Member of (1): *European Consumer Consultative Group (ECCG, #06771)*. **NGO Relations** Member of (5): *Copyright for Creativity (C4C, #04832)*; *European Alliance for Responsible R and D and Affordable Medicines (#05879)*; *Federation of European and International Associations Established in Belgium (FAIB, #09508)*; *Finance Watch (#09764)*; *Transatlantic Consumer Dialogue (TACD, #20203)*. Instrumental in setting up (1): *Peter Goldman Fund (inactive)*. Stakeholder in: *European Network for Health Technology Assessment (EUnetHTA, #07921)*. [2019.10.01/XD0602/**D**]

- ♦ Bureau van Europese Design Associations (#03359)
- ♦ Bureau van Europese Designers Verenigingen / see Bureau of European Design Associations (#03359)
- ♦ Bureau van de Europese Unie voor de Grondrechten (#08969)
- ♦ Bureau d'Experts de la Rage du continent Africain (unconfirmed)
- ♦ Bureau des fédérations européennes de gymnastique / see Fédération internationale de gymnastique (#09636)
- ♦ Bureau forestier du CABI (inactive)
- ♦ Bureau des géographes du Commonwealth (#04333)

♦ Bureau gravimétrique international (BGI) 03361

International Gravimetric Bureau

Dir 14 ave Edouard Belin, 31400 Toulouse CEDEX 4, France. T. +33561332651. Fax +33561332560.
URL: http://bgi.omp.obs-mip.fr/

History 1951, as one of the offices of *Federation of Astronomical and Geophysical Data Analysis Services (FAGS, inactive)*. **Aims** Collect, on a worldwide basis, all gravimetry *measurements* and pertinent information about the gravity field of the *Earth*; compile and store them in a computerized data base in order to redistribute them on request to a large variety of users for *scientific* purposes. **Structure** One of the constituent associations of *International Union of Geodesy and Geophysics (IUGG, #15776)*. Internal service of *International Association of Geodesy (IAG, #11914)*. International working groups (4). **Finance** Funded especially by France, through 7 host bodies. Subsidy from FAGS. **Activities** Services: data retrieval; data coverage plots; data screening; gridding; contour maps; computation of mean gravity anomalies; gravity anomaly maps. Digitalization of world bathymetry (1985-1989). Gravimetry station. Database of absolute gravity measurements. **Events** *Meeting* Sapporo (Japan) 2003, *Quadrennial international gravity commission meeting / International Gravity Commission Meeting* Thessaloniki (Greece) 2002, *Meeting* Budapest (Hungary) 2001, *Meeting* Banff, AB (Canada) 2000, *Meeting* Birmingham (UK) 1999. **Publications** *Newton's Bulletin* (annual). CD-Roms on land and marine points gravity measurements.
Members Institutions; Individuals. Members in 139 countries and territories:
Afghanistan, Albania, Algeria, Argentina, Australia, Austria, Bahrain, Bangladesh, Belgium, Belize, Benin, Bermuda, Bolivia, Botswana, Brazil, Bulgaria, Burkina Faso, Burundi, Cambodia, Cameroon, Canada, Central African Rep, Chad, Chile, China, Colombia, Congo Brazzaville, Congo DR, Costa Rica, Côte d'Ivoire, Cuba, Cyprus, Czechia, Denmark, Djibouti, Dominican Rep, Ecuador, Egypt, El Salvador, Equatorial Guinea, Eswatini, Ethiopia, Fiji, Finland, France, Gabon, Gambia, Germany, Ghana, Greece, Guatemala, Guinea-Bissau, Guyana, Haiti, Holy See, Honduras, Hong Kong, Hungary, Iceland, India, Indonesia, Iran Islamic Rep, Iraq, Ireland, Israel, Italy, Japan, Jordan, Kenya, Korea DPR, Korea Rep, Kuwait, Laos, Lebanon, Liberia, Libya, Luxembourg, Madagascar, Malawi, Malaysia, Mali, Mauritania, Mexico, Monaco, Morocco, Mozambique, Myanmar, Namibia, Nepal, Netherlands, New Zealand, Nicaragua, Niger, Nigeria, Norway, Oman, Pakistan, Panama, Papua New Guinea, Paraguay, Peru, Poland, Portugal, Puerto Rico, Qatar, Romania, Russia, Rwanda, Saudi Arabia, Senegal, Serbia, Sierra Leone, Singapore, Slovakia, Somalia, South Africa, Spain, Sri Lanka, Sudan, Suriname, Sweden, Switzerland, Syrian AR, Taiwan, Tanzania UR, Thailand, Togo, Tonga, Tunisia, Türkiye, Uganda, UK, United Arab Emirates, Uruguay, USA, Venezuela, Vietnam, Zambia, Zimbabwe.
NGO Relations Member of: *Global Geodetic Observing System (GGOS, see: #11914)*; *International Centre for Earth Simulation (ICES Foundation)*. [2012/XF4066/**F**]

- ♦ Bureau du Haut Représentant des Nations Unies pour les pays les moins avancés, les pays en développement sans littoral et les petits États insulaires en développement (#20599)
- ♦ Bureau hydrographique international / see International Hydrographic Organization (#13825)
- ♦ Bureau d'information des étudiants européens / see European Students' Union (#08848)
- ♦ Bureau d'information des étudiants ouest-européens / see European Students' Union (#08848)
- ♦ Bureau d'information des partis communistes et ouvriers (inactive)
- ♦ Bureau of Information and Research on Student Health (inactive)
- ♦ Bureau d'informations Amérique latine (internationally oriented national body)
- ♦ Bureau Intégré des Nations Unies au Burundi (inactive)
- ♦ Bureau intégré des Nations Unies pour le Cambodge (no recent information)
- ♦ Bureau voor Intellectuele Eigendom van de Europese Unie (#08996)
- ♦ Bureau interafricain de développement et de coopération (inactive)
- ♦ Bureau interafricain des épizooties (inactive)
- ♦ Bureau interafricain des ressources animales (#11382)
- ♦ Bureau interaméricain des marques de fabrique (inactive)
- ♦ Bureau intergouvernemental pour l'informatique (inactive)
- ♦ Bureau international agraire (inactive)
- ♦ Bureau international d'anthropologie différentielle (inactive)
- ♦ Bureau international antimilitariste contre la guerre et la réaction (inactive)
- ♦ Bureau international de l'Association des lignes de la jeunesse socialiste (inactive)
- ♦ Bureau international des associations de fabricants, grossistes et détaillants de bijouterie et argenterie / see CIBJO – The World Jewellery Confederation (#03923)

♦ Bureau international d'audiophonologie (BIAP) 03362

International Office for Audiophonology – Internationales Büro für Audiophonologie

Gen Sec ENT Dpt, CHU Liège, Bd de l'Hopital, 4000 Liège, Belgium. T. +3243667525. Fax +3243667525.
Registered Address Boucle des Chevreuils (BAR), 3500 Beaumont, Belgium.
URL: http://www.biap.org/

History 1967, Brussels (Belgium). Statutes approved by Belgian Royal Decree, 24 Mar 1967; modified by Extraordinary General Assembly, 3 May 1976, modifications approved by Belgian Royal Decree, 11 Oct 1976. New statutes registered 4 Apr 1996. Former names and other names: *International Bureau for Audiophonology* – alias; *IOAP* – alias. Registration: Banque-Carrefour des Entreprises, No/ID: 0408.297.645, Start date: 24 Mar 1967, Belgium. **Aims** Create a framework for interdisciplinary study; foster contact among scientific and professional workers in the field; create a scientific and professional documentation centre. **Structure** General Assembly (annual); Administrative Council; Executive Committee; Technical Commissions (6). **Languages** English, French, German, Spanish. **Staff** Voluntary. **Finance** Sources: grants; members' dues. **Activities** Monitoring/evaluation; networking/liaising; research/documentation; training/education. **Events** *Annual Convention* Palma (Spain) 2023, *Annual Convention* Palma (Spain) 2022, *Annual Mini-Convention* Belgium 2021, *Annual Convention* Bucharest (Romania) 2021, *Annual Mini-Convention* Paris (France) 2020. **Publications** *BIAP Information Bulletin*. Recommendations.
Members Individuals Founder; Honorary; Full; Associate. Members in 21 countries:
Austria, Belgium, Brazil, Canada, Denmark, Finland, France, Germany, Greece, Hungary, Italy, Lebanon, Luxembourg, Mexico, Netherlands, Poland, Portugal, Spain, Switzerland, UK, USA.
NGO Relations In liaison with technical committees of: *International Organization for Standardization (ISO, #14473)*. [2021/XD2287/**D**]

♦ Bureau international du béton manufacturé (BIBM) 03363

Federation of the European Precast Concrete Industry – Internationales Büro der Beton- und Fertigteil-Industrie – Internationaal Bureau van de Betonwarenindustrie

SG Rue d'Arlon 55, 1040 Brussels, Belgium. T. +3223401828. E-mail: info@bibm.eu.
URL: http://www.bibm.eu/

History Founded 15 Oct 1954, Brussels (Belgium), at 1st International Congress for Precast Concrete. New statutes 1993. Original name in English: *European Federation for Precast Concrete (BIBM)*. Previously also known in English as *International Bureau for Precast Concrete*. Registered 9 Feb 1965, under Belgian law of 25 Oct 1919 (modified 6 Dec 1954). **Aims** Encourage circulation of information, experience and know-how at a supra-national level to find global solutions to issues affecting precast concrete and its image; cooperate closely on technical and environmental issues. **Structure** General Assembly (annual); Board; Committee of the Chief Executives of Member Federations; Vertical Commissions (4); Horizontal Commissions (4). **Languages** English, French, German. **Staff** 2.00 FTE, paid. **Finance** Members' dues. **Events** *Congress* Amsterdam (Netherlands) 2023, *Triennial Congress* Copenhagen (Denmark) 2021, *Triennial Congress* Copenhagen (Denmark) 2020, *Triennial Congress* Madrid (Spain) 2017, *Triennial Congress* Istanbul (Turkey) 2014. **Publications** *BIBM Newsletter* (4 a year).
Members National federations in 16 countries:
Austria, Belgium, Denmark, Finland, France, Germany, Greece, Ireland, Italy, Netherlands, Norway, Poland, Portugal, Spain, Sweden, UK.
NGO Relations Member of: *Construction Products Europe AISBL (#04761)*; *Concrete Europe (#04433)*; *European Network on Silica (NEPSI, #08001)*. Cooperates with: *Comité européen de normalisation (CEN, #04162)*; *Industry4Europe (#11181)*; *International Organization for Standardization (ISO, #14473)*. *European Federation of Concrete Admixtures Associations (EFCA, #07085)*. [2022/XC1416/t/**D**]

- ♦ Bureau international catholique de l'enfance (#12450)
- ♦ Bureau international central américain (inactive)
- ♦ Bureau international de la chaussure et de cuir (inactive)
- ♦ Bureau international du cinéma (inactive)
- ♦ Bureau international et comité d'action pour la protection civile en temps de guerre (inactive)
- ♦ Bureau international des containers / see Bureau international des containers et du transport intermodal (#03364)

♦ Bureau international des containers et du transport intermodal (BIC) 03364

Chair 41 rue Réaumur, 75003 Paris, France. T. +33147660390. Fax +33147660891. E-mail: dow@bic-code.org – bic@bic-code.org.
URL: http://www.bic-code.org/

History 22 Feb 1933, Paris (France), as *Bureau international des containers (BIC)*, under the auspices of International Chamber of Commerce (ICC), being devoted to rail and road transportation. Ceased activities in summer 1939. Became intermodal and resumed activities 1 Jul 1948. Registered by French Ministerial Decree, 31 Oct 1949. **Aims** Contribute to expansion of safe, secure and sustainable *containerization* and *intermodal transport*; facilitate professional discussions on all subjects connected with containers and intermodal transport; obtain specialized documentation for the benefit of members. **Structure** Ordinary General Meeting (at least once a year); Board of Directors; Secretariat, headed by Secretary General. **Languages** English, French. **Staff** 4.00 FTE, paid. **Finance** Members' dues. Other sources: income derived from the sales of publications; remuneration for services rendered; remuneration for special studies requested by third parties. **Activities** Events/meetings; guidance/assistance/consulting. **Events** *Seminar* Verona (Italy) 1993, *Symposium sur les problèmes confrontant l'industrie des transports de fret* Hamburg (Germany FR) 1988, *Forum* Budapest (Hungary) 1987, *Seminar on intermodal transport issues in the enlarged European community / World Conference* Barcelona (Spain) 1986, *Transport forum* Munich (Germany FR) 1986. **Publications** *Containers Review* (4 a year) in English; *Containers Bic-Code Register: The Official Register of Internationally Protected ISO Alpha Codes for Identification of Container Owners* (annual) in English. Maintains documentation centre. **Members** Active (about 2,300): individual and corporate bodies interested in containerization and modal transport; forwarders, manufacturers, leasing agents, repair and transit companies, transport agents (land, sea, air); Honorary; Ordinary. Members in 127 countries and territories. Membership countries not specified. **Consultative Status** Consultative status granted from: *UNCTAD (#20285)* (Special Category); *International Maritime Organization (IMO, #14102)*. **IGO Relations** Accredited by: *United Nations Office at Vienna (UNOV, #20604)*. Observer at: *International Maritime Organization (IMO, #14102)*; *United Nations Economic Commission for Europe (UNECE, #20555)*; *World Customs Organization (WCO, #21350)*. **NGO Relations** Observer at: *International Organization for Standardization (ISO, #14473)*. Partner member of: *Container Owners Association (COA, #04777)*. [2019.02.20/XE1703/E]

- ♦ Bureau international contre l'alcoolisme / see International Council on Alcohol and Addictions (#12989)
- ♦ Bureau international de correspondance et de résistance néo-malthusienne (inactive)
- ♦ Bureau international des déclarations de décès (inactive)
- ♦ Bureau international pour le développement professionnel (inactive)
- ♦ Bureau international de documentation éducative (inactive)
- ♦ Bureau international de documentation fiscale / see International Bureau of Fiscal Documentation (#12415)
- ♦ Bureau international des droits des enfants (#12412)
- ♦ Bureau international des duvets et des plumes (#13195)
- ♦ Bureau international des écoles nouvelles (inactive)
- ♦ Bureau international de l'édition française (internationally oriented national body)
- ♦ Bureau international d'éducation (#12413)
- ♦ Bureau international pour l'éducation juive (inactive)
- ♦ Bureau international d'électrothermie / see International Union for Electricity Applications (#15770)
- ♦ Bureau international de l'enseignement technique (inactive)
- ♦ Bureau international de l'environnement (inactive)
- ♦ Bureau international pour l'épilepsie (#12414)
- ♦ Bureau international des étalons physico-chimiques (inactive)
- ♦ Bureau international d'ethnographie (inactive)
- ♦ Bureau international des étudiants (inactive)

♦ Bureau International des Expositions (BIE) 03365

SG 34 av d'Iéna, 75116 Paris, France. T. +33145003863. Fax +33145009615. E-mail: info@bie-paris.org.
URL: http://www.bie-paris.org/

History Established 1931, Paris (France), by *Convention Regarding International Exhibitions (1928)*, signed 22 Nov 1928, Paris. Updated by protocol signed 10 May 1948, 16 Nov 1966, 30 Nov 1972 and amended 24 Jun 1982, 31 May 1988. Former names and other names: *International Exhibitions Bureau* – former. **Aims** Lead, promote and foster international exhibitions for the benefit of the citizens of the international community. **Structure** General Assembly (twice a year); Committees (4); Secretariat. **Languages** English, French. **Staff** 18.00 FTE, paid. **Finance** Sources: members' dues. **Activities** Capacity building; events/meetings; guidance/assistance/consulting; networking/liaising. **Events** *General Assembly* Paris (France) 2022, *General assembly* Paris (France) 2022, *International Conference on Hosting the 2030 World Exposition* Busan (Korea Rep) 2014, *Theme Symposium* Dubai (United Arab Emirates) 2013, *Planning Meeting* Seoul (Korea Rep) 2012. **Publications** *BIE Bulletin*.
Members Any government may at any time accede to the 1928 Convention and to the Protocol of 1972. Governments of 170 countries:
Afghanistan, Albania, Algeria, Andorra, Angola, Antigua-Barbuda, Argentina, Armenia, Austria, Azerbaijan, Bahamas, Bahrain, Bangladesh, Barbados, Belarus, Belgium, Belize, Benin, Bosnia-Herzegovina, Brazil, Bulgaria, Burkina Faso, Burundi, Cambodia, Cameroon, Central African Rep, Chad, Chile, China, Colombia, Comoros, Congo Brazzaville, Congo DR, Costa Rica, Côte d'Ivoire, Croatia, Cuba, Cyprus, Czechia, Denmark, Djibouti, Dominica, Dominican Rep, Ecuador, Egypt, El Salvador, Equatorial Guinea, Eritrea, Estonia, Eswatini, Fiji, Finland, France, Gabon, Gambia, Georgia, Germany, Ghana, Greece, Grenada, Guatemala, Guinea, Guinea-Bissau, Guyana, Haiti, Honduras, Hungary, Iceland, Indonesia, Iran Islamic Rep, Israel, Italy, Japan, Jordan, Kazakhstan, Kenya, Kiribati, Korea DPR, Korea Rep, Kuwait, Kyrgyzstan, Laos, Lebanon, Lesotho, Liberia, Libya, Lithuania, Madagascar, Malawi, Malaysia, Maldives, Mali, Malta, Marshall Is, Mauritania, Mauritius, Mexico, Monaco, Mongolia, Montenegro, Morocco, Mozambique, Namibia, Nauru, Nepal, Netherlands, New Zealand, Nicaragua, Niger, Nigeria, Norway, Oman, Pakistan, Palau, Panama, Paraguay, Peru, Philippines, Poland, Portugal, Qatar, Romania, Russia, Rwanda, Samoa, San Marino, Saudi Arabia, Senegal, Serbia, Seychelles, Sierra Leone, Slovakia, Slovenia, Solomon Is, Somalia, South Africa, South Sudan, Spain, Sri Lanka, St Kitts-Nevis, St Lucia, St Vincent-Grenadines, Sudan, Suriname, Sweden, Switzerland, Syrian AR, Tajikistan, Tanzania UR, Thailand, Timor-Leste, Togo, Tonga, Tunisia, Türkiye, Turkmenistan, Tuvalu, Uganda, UK, Ukraine, United Arab Emirates, Uruguay, USA, Uzbekistan, Vanuatu, Venezuela, Vietnam, Yemen, Zambia. [2022.10.11/XB1819/B*]

- ♦ Bureau international des fédérations d'instituteurs (inactive)
- ♦ Bureau international des fédérations et sociétés protectrices des animaux et d'antivivisection (inactive)
- ♦ Bureau international de filmologie (inactive)
- ♦ Bureau international des gélatines / see Gelatin Manufacturers Association of Europe (#10090)
- ♦ Bureau international de l'heure (inactive)
- ♦ Bureau international humanitaire zoophile (inactive)
- ♦ Bureau international d'information /contre la littérature immorale/ (inactive)
- ♦ Bureau international d'information et de coopération des éditeurs de musique (inactive)
- ♦ Bureau international d'information et d'études sur l'assistance aux étrangers (inactive)
- ♦ Bureau international d'information pour les toiles métalliques (internationally oriented national body)
- ♦ Bureau international d'information des travailleurs du commerce (inactive)
- ♦ Bureau international jeunesse de la Communauté française de Belgique (internationally oriented national body)
- ♦ Bureau international de la jeunesse estudiantine abstinente (inactive)
- ♦ Bureau international du loisir (inactive)
- ♦ Bureau international des maisons du peuple (inactive)
- ♦ Bureau international de mécanique des roches / see International Bureau of Strata Mechanics (#12417)
- ♦ Bureau international de mécanique des terrains (#12417)

♦ Bureau international des Médecins sans frontières (MSF International) 03366

Doctors Without Borders – Artsen Zonder Grenzen

Secretariat Rue de Lausanne 78, Case Postale 1016, 1211 Geneva 21, Switzerland. T. +41228498916.
URL: http://www.msf.org/

History 20 Dec 1971, Paris (France). Founded as the first national organization with the title *Médecins sans frontières (MSF)*, first steps having been taken in 1968 during the Biafra crisis and during solidarity appeal following floods in East Pakistan, 1970. International bureau set up, 1991, Brussels (Belgium), to link national MSF sections. Currently registered mainly of doctors and health sector workers and is also open to all other. Registration: Swiss Civil Code, Switzerland. **Aims** Deliver emergency aid to people affected by armed conflict, epidemics, natural disasters and exclusion from healthcare. **Structure** International Board (IB); Full Executive Committee; Core Executive Committee; RIOD; Medical Director Platform. **Staff** Headquarters: 2,493; field positions: 32,234. **Finance** Sources: donations. Private donations: 90.8%. **Activities** Awareness raising; humanitarian/emergency aid. **Events** *Humanitarian Congress Tokyo* Tokyo (Japan) 2022, *Paediatric Days* Stockholm (Sweden) 2019, *Conference on Multinational Cooperation Program in the Asia-Pacific* Tokyo (Japan) 2012, *Conference on exploring the future of medical humanity / General Assembly* Amsterdam (Netherlands) 2010, *General Assembly* Copenhagen (Denmark) 2009. **Publications** *Speaking Out* – series. *Practical Guide to Humanitarian Law* (4th ed 2013); *Humanitarian Negotiations Revealed* (2011). Annual International Activity Report.
Members Operational Centres in 5 countries:
Belgium, France, Netherlands, Spain, Switzerland.
Sections and institutional association members in 19 countries and territories:
Australia, Austria, Belgium, Canada, Denmark, France, Germany, Greece, Hong Kong, Italy, Japan, Luxembourg, Netherlands, Norway, Spain, Sweden, Switzerland, UK, USA.
Present, via missions, in 65 countries and territories:
Afghanistan, Armenia, Bangladesh, Burkina Faso, Burundi, Cambodia, Cameroon, Central African Rep, Chad, China, Colombia, Congo Brazzaville, Congo DR, Côte d'Ivoire, Egypt, Eswatini, Ethiopia, Georgia, Greece, Guinea, Haiti, Honduras, India, Iran Islamic Rep, Iraq, Italy, Jordan, Kenya, Korea DPR, Kyrgyzstan, Laos, Lebanon, Lesotho, Liberia, Libya, Madagascar, Malawi, Mali, Mauritania, Mexico, Morocco, Mozambique, Myanmar, Niger, Nigeria, Pakistan, Palestine, Papua New Guinea, Paraguay, Philippines, Russia, Sierra Leone, Somalia, South Africa, South Sudan, Sudan, Syrian AR, Tajikistan, Türkiye, Uganda, Ukraine, Uzbekistan, Yemen, Zambia, Zimbabwe.
Consultative Status Consultative status granted from: *ECOSOC (#05331)* (General); *World Intellectual Property Organization (WIPO, #21593)* (Permanent Observer Status); *WHO (#20950)* (Official). **IGO Relations** Accredited by (2): *United Nations Office at Geneva (UNOG, #20597)*; *United Nations Office at Vienna (UNOV, #20604)*. Observer status with (1): *Codex Alimentarius Commission (CAC, #04081)*. Links with major humanitarian actors, including UN agencies. **NGO Relations** Permanent observer to: *International Council of Voluntary Agencies (ICVA, #13092)*. Links with major humanitarian actors, including international and national NGOs, donors, academics, research institutes, think tanks, etc. [2021/XF8357/F]

- ♦ Bureau international des musiciens (inactive)
- ♦ Bureau international de normalisation de l'automobile (inactive)
- ♦ Bureau international de la paix (#14535)
- ♦ Bureau international permanent des associations de vendeurs et rechapeurs de pneumatiques / see BIPAVER – European Retread Manufacturers Association (#03264)
- ♦ Bureau international permanent de chimie analytique pour les matières destinées à l'alimentation de l'homme et des animaux (inactive)
- ♦ Bureau international permanent d'études et de statistiques mutualistes et Fédération internationale de la mutualité libre (inactive)
- ♦ Bureau international permanent de la paix / see International Peace Bureau (#14535)
- ♦ Bureau international permanent pour le perfectionnement du chronométrage sportif (inactive)
- ♦ Bureau international permanent de la viande / see International Meat Secretariat (#14125)

♦ Bureau international des poids et mesures (BIPM) 03367

Dir Pavillon de Breteuil, 92312 Sèvres CEDEX, France.
URL: http://www.bipm.org/

History 20 May 1875, Paris (France). Established by *Metre Convention (1875)*, signed by 17 States. Modified 6 Oct 1921, Sèvres (France). Agreement signed with French Government, 25 Apr 1969; amended 23 Jul 2007. Statutes Registered in *'LNTS 427'*. Former names and other names: *International Bureau of Weights and Measures* – alias. **Aims** Work with NMIs of Member States, RMOs and strategic partners, using international and impartial status to promote and advance the global comparability of measurements. **Structure** Conférence générale des poids et mesures (CGPM) (General Conference on Weights and Measures); Comité international des poids et mesures (CIPM) International Committee for Weights and Measures; Consultative Committees (10); Joint Committees (4). **Languages** English, French. **Staff** 70.00 FTE, paid. *Administrative Tribunal of the International Labour Organization (ILO Tribunal, #00118)* is competent to settle disputes. **Finance** Contributions by member states; subscriptions from associate states and economies. **Events** *International Conference of Weighing* Berlin (Germany) 2023, *General Conference* Versailles (France) 2018, *General Conference* Paris (France) 2014, *Workshop on Challenges in Metrology for Dynamic Measurement* Sèvres (France) 2012, *Quadrennial General Conference* Paris (France) 2011. **Publications** *Circular T on Time* (12 a year); *Metrologia* – journal. *The International System of Units* (8th ed 2006); *Comptes rendus des séances de la Conférence générale des poids et mesures*; *Procès-verbaux des séances du Comité international des poids et mesures*. Reports on sessions of Consultative Committees. **Information Services** *Key Comparison Database (KCDB)*; *Time Section Data Service* – online (24 hours a day).
Members Governments of 62 countries:
Argentina, Australia, Austria, Belarus, Belgium, Brazil, Bulgaria, Canada, Chile, China, Colombia, Croatia, Czechia, Denmark, Ecuador, Egypt, Finland, France, Germany, Greece, Hungary, India, Indonesia, Iran Islamic Rep, Iraq, Ireland, Israel, Italy, Japan, Kazakhstan, Kenya, Korea Rep, Lithuania, Malaysia, Mexico, Montenegro, Morocco, Netherlands, New Zealand, Norway, Pakistan, Poland, Portugal, Romania, Russia, Saudi Arabia, Serbia, Singapore, Slovakia, Slovenia, South Africa, Spain, Sweden, Switzerland, Thailand, Tunisia, Türkiye, UK, Ukraine, United Arab Emirates, Uruguay, USA.
Associates of the CGPM (40):
Albania, Azerbaijan, Bangladesh, Bolivia, Bosnia-Herzegovina, Botswana, Costa Rica, Cuba, Estonia, Ethiopia, Georgia, Ghana, Hong Kong, Jamaica, Kuwait, Latvia, Luxembourg, Malta, Mauritius, Moldova, Mongolia, Namibia, North Macedonia, Oman, Panama, Paraguay, Peru, Philippines, Qatar, Seychelles, Sri Lanka, Sudan, Syrian AR, Taiwan, Tanzania UR, Uzbekistan, Vietnam, Zambia, Zimbabwe.
Caribbean Community (CARICOM, #03476).
IGO Relations Agreements with: *International Atomic Energy Agency (IAEA, #12294)* (1961 and 1967); *International Organization of Legal Metrology (#14451)* (1970); *OECD (#17693)*. Participates as observer in the activities of: *Codex Alimentarius Commission (CAC, #04081)*. Working relations with: *International Telecommunication Union (ITU, #15673)*, especially its Radiocommunication Sector. **NGO Relations** In liaison with technical committees of: *International Organization for Standardization (ISO, #14473)*. Responsible for time scale activities, including *International Atomic Time Scale*, previously administered by: *Bureau international de l'heure (BIH, inactive)* which ceased to exist, 31 Dec 1987. The BIH earth rotation activities are carried out by: *International Earth Rotation and Reference Systems Service (IERS, #13216)*. Instrumental in setting up: *Joint Committee for Traceability in Laboratory Medicine (JCTLM, #16127)*.
[2019.12.12/XC1440/y/C*]

- ♦ Bureau international pour la presse pacifiste (inactive)
- ♦ Bureau international pour les problèmes d'échecs (inactive)
- ♦ Bureau international des producteurs d'assurances et de réassurances / see BIPAR – European Federation of Insurance Intermediaries (#03263)
- ♦ Bureau international de recherches balnéo-économiques (inactive)
- ♦ Bureau international de recherches sur les oiseaux d'eau et les zones humides (inactive)
- ♦ Bureau international de la récupération / see Bureau of International Recycling (#03368)
- ♦ Bureau international de la récupération et du recyclage / see Bureau of International Recycling (#03368)
- ♦ Bureau International du Recyclage (#03368)

♦ Bureau of International Recycling (BIR) 03368

Bureau International du Recyclage

Dir Gen Av Franklin Roosevelt 24, 1050 Brussels, Belgium. T. +3226275770. E-mail: bir@bir.org.
Communications Dir address not obtained.
URL: http://www.bir.org/

History 29 Jun 1948, Brussels (Belgium). New statutes: 18 Dec 1973; 28 Sep 1995. Former names and other names: *Bureau international de la récupération* – former; *International Recovery Bureau* – former; *International Recycling Organization* – former; *International Recovering/Recycling Bureau* – former; *International Reclamation Bureau* – former; *Bureau international de la récupération et du recyclage* – former. Registration: Banque-Carrefour des Entreprises, No/ID: 0408.270.228, Start date: 3 May 1971, Belgium. **Aims** Promote recycling and recyclability, thereby conserving *natural resources*, protecting the environment and facilitating free trade; study and undertake research work on technical, scientific and environmental problems relative to the various sectors of recycling; act as the unified voice of international recycling industries associated on a worldwide level; develop public awareness of the economic and environmental contributions of membership; promote free trade in, and increased usage of, recyclable and recycled materials and encourage manufacturers to design products with increased understanding of recycling; act as a forum for members to exchange commercial, technical, economic, legal and environmental information. **Structure** General Assembly (annual); Advisory Council (meets twice a year); Executive Committee. Special Committees (12): Ambassadors; Arbitration; Articles of Association and Internal rules; Communications; Convention; Finance; International Trade Council; Membership; Nominating; International Environment Council; Young Traders Group. Working Committees. General Secretariat. **Languages** English, French, German. **Staff** Paid. **Finance** Sources: members' dues. **Activities** Events/meetings; knowledge management/information dissemination. **Events** *World Recycling Convention* Barcelona (Spain) 2022, *Autumn Round Table Session* Dubai (United Arab Emirates) 2022, *World Recycling Convention* 2021, *Global e-Forum* 2020, *World Recycling Convention* 2020. **Publications** *BIR Newsletter* (2 a year). Annual Report; Market 'Mirrors'; Membership Directory; Membership Toolkit. Proceedings of divisional meetings; press releases; technical, commercial and legislative information.
Members Effective (supporting or associate), including professional organizations involved in collecting, trading and/or processing of secondary raw materials, whose activities are principally in the recycling sector. Partner (non-voting): others interested/involved in recycling. Members in 69 countries and territories:
Albania, Algeria, Argentina, Australia, Austria, Bahrain, Bangladesh, Belgium, Brazil, Bulgaria, Canada, China, Cuba, Curaçao, Cyprus, Czechia, Denmark, Egypt, Estonia, Finland, France, Germany, Greece, Haiti, Honduras, Hungary, Iceland, India, Iran Islamic Rep, Ireland, Israel, Italy, Japan, Jordan, Korea DPR, Kuwait, Lebanon, Luxembourg, Malaysia, Mexico, Monaco, Morocco, Netherlands, New Zealand, North Macedonia, Norway, Pakistan, Poland, Portugal, Romania, Russia, Saudi Arabia, Serbia, Singapore, Slovakia, Slovenia, South Africa, Spain, Sweden, Switzerland, Taiwan, Thailand, Tunisia, Türkiye, UK, United Arab Emirates, Uruguay, USA, Yemen.
Bureau of Middle East Recycling (BMR); *European Recycling Industries' Confederation (EuRIC, #08335)*.
Consultative Status Consultative status granted from: *ECOSOC (#05331)* (Roster); *UNCTAD (#20285)* (Special Category). **IGO Relations** Recognized by: *European Commission (EC, #06633)*. Close contacts with: *OECD (#17693)*; *UNEP (#20299)*; *United Nations Economic Commission for Europe (UNECE, #20555)*; *World Customs Organization (WCO, #21350)*; *World Trade Organization (WTO, #21864)*. **NGO Relations** Member of (1): *Federation of European and International Associations Established in Belgium (FAIB, #09508)*. Close contacts with: *International Chamber of Commerce (ICC, #12534)*. Associate expert of: *Business and Industry Advisory Committee to the OECD (BIAC, #03385)*. [2022/XC2403/**C**]

- ♦ Bureau international des relations maçonniques (inactive)
- ♦ Bureau international de renseignements à l'usage des professeurs de langues vivantes (inactive)
- ♦ Bureau international pour la répression de la traite des êtres humains (inactive)
- ♦ Bureau international des sociétés gérant les droits d'enregistrement et de reproduction mécanique (#12416)
- ♦ Bureau international pour la standardisation des fibres artificielles / see Bureau international pour la standardisation de la rayonne et des fibres synthétiques (#03369)

♦ Bureau international pour la standardisation de la rayonne et des fibres synthétiques (BISFA) 03369

International Bureau for the Standardization of Man-Made Fibres – Oficina Internacional para la Estandardización de las Fibras Quimicas – Internationale Vereinigung für Chemiefasernormen – Ente Internazionale per la Standardizzazione delle Fibre Man-made

Secretariat 40 rue Belliard, 1040 Brussels, Belgium. T. +3224369635. Fax +3224369638. E-mail: secretariat@cirfs.org.
URL: http://www.bisfa.org/

History 25 Sep 1928, Paris (France). Most recent statutes: 24 May 1989. Former names and other names: *Bureau international pour la standardisation des fibres artificielles* – former (25 Sep 1928); *Organismo Internacional para la Normalización del Rayón y las Fibras Sintéticas* – alias; *Ufficio Internazionale per la Standardizzazione del Raion e delle Fibre Artificiali e Sintetiche* – alias. Registration: France. **Aims** Establish internationally agreed methods for testing different categories of man-made fibre, and relevant testing procedures; establish terminology for the categorization, designation and standardization of man-made fibres; provide an international voice for the man-made fibre industry in these matters, and promote the adoption of its methods and terminology by official standardization organizations. **Structure** General Assembly (annual) of delegates (one per member); voting depends on members' financial contributions. Policy Committee, meeting at least once a year (in liaison with CIRFS). Operational Committee; Technical Coordination Committee; General Secretariat. **Languages** English, French, German, Italian. **Staff** 2.00 FTE, paid. **Finance** Members' admission fees and subscriptions. **Activities** Regular meetings of Operational Committee and Technical Coordination Committee. **Events** *Annual General Assembly* Brussels (Belgium) 2013, *Annual General Assembly* Brussels (Belgium) 2012, *Annual General Assembly* Brussels (Belgium) 2011, *Annual General Assembly* Brussels (Belgium) 2010, *Annual General Assembly* Brussels (Belgium) 2009. **Publications** *Internationally agreed Methods for Testing Man-Made Fibres*.
Members Individual producers in 14 countries:
Austria, Brazil, Czechia, France, Germany, Ireland, Italy, Luxembourg, Netherlands, Portugal, Spain, Switzerland, Türkiye, UK.
NGO Relations *ASTM International (#02994)*; *CIRFS – European Man-made Fibres Association (#03944)*; *International Organization for Standardization (ISO, #14473)*. [2017/XD1419/**C**]

- ♦ Bureau international de statistique commerciale (inactive)
- ♦ Bureau international de statistique universitaire (inactive)
- ♦ Bureau international pour la suppression des contrefaçons de monnaies / see International Bureau for the Suppression of Counterfeit Coins
- ♦ Bureau international pour la suppression de monnaies fausses (internationally oriented national body)
- ♦ Bureau international des tarifs douaniers (#13124)
- ♦ Bureau international technique du chlore / see Euro Chlor (#05659)
- ♦ Bureau international technique des gélatines / see Gelatin Manufacturers Association of Europe (#10090)
- ♦ Bureau international des textiles et de l'habillement (#15680)
- ♦ Bureau international pour le tourisme et les échanges de la jeunesse (inactive)
- ♦ Bureau international du tourisme social / see International Social Tourism Organisation (#14889)
- ♦ Bureau international de traductions juridiques (inactive)
- ♦ Bureau international de transport par autocar et camion / see International Road Transport Union (#14761)
- ♦ Bureau international pour l'unification du droit pénal (inactive)
- ♦ Bureau de Législation Dramatique / see Société des auteurs et compositeurs dramatiques
- ♦ Bureau de liaison des associations de fabricants de peintures et d'encres d'imprimerie des pays du Marché commun / see Conseil européen de l'industrie des peintures, des encres d'imprimerie et des couleurs d'art (#04688)
- ♦ Bureau de liaison Croix-Rouge / UE / see Red Cross EU Office (#18643)
- ♦ Bureau de liaison des industries du caoutchouc de la Communauté économique européenne / see European Tyre and Rubber Manufacturers' Association (#08963)
- ♦ Bureau de liaison des industries du caoutchouc du Marché commun européen / see European Tyre and Rubber Manufacturers' Association (#08963)
- ♦ Bureau de liaison des industries du caoutchouc de l'Union européenne / see European Tyre and Rubber Manufacturers' Association (#08963)
- ♦ Bureau de liaison des industries céramiques européennes / see European Ceramic Industry Association (#06506)
- ♦ Bureau de liaison des industries céramiques du Marché commun / see European Ceramic Industry Association (#06506)

♦ Bureau de liaison internationale des écoles de théâtre (BLIET) 03370

International Coordination Bureau of Theatre Schools

Contact c/o Fondation René Hainaux, Chaussée de Nivelle 6A/01, 4300 Waremme, Belgium.
History Founded 1975, Berlin West (Germany FR), during 17th Congress of *International Theatre Institute (ITI, #15683)*, as an office of the Theatre Training Committee of ITI. **Aims** Coordinates international dissemination of information and *pedagogical* material among institutions specialized in dramatic *art*; fosters contacts and exchanges between schools. **Finance** Self-financed. **Activities** Collects documents and publications concerning theatre education; provides services to theatre schools. **Publications** *BLIET Bulletin* in English, French. Books.
Members Individuals in 46 countries and territories:
Argentina, Australia, Austria, Belgium, Brazil, Bulgaria, Burkina Faso, Canada, Chile, China, Congo DR, Costa Rica, Cuba, Czechia, Denmark, Egypt, Finland, France, Germany, Greece, Hong Kong, Hungary, Iceland, India, Indonesia, Israel, Italy, Jordan, Korea Rep, Mexico, Netherlands, Norway, Peru, Poland, Portugal, Romania, Russia, Senegal, Serbia, Slovakia, Spain, Sweden, Switzerland, Syrian AR, USA, Venezuela. [2013.09.10/XE5395/v/**E**]

- ♦ Bureau de liaison des ONG intéressées à l'environnement (inactive)
- ♦ Bureau de liaison des secrétariats professionnels internationaux (inactive)
- ♦ Bureau de liaison des syndicats européens – CEE / des produits aromatiques / see European Flavour Association (#07269)
- ♦ Bureau maritime international (#14097)
- ♦ Bureau maritime international de Zanzibar contre la traite des esclaves (inactive)
- ♦ Bureau méditerranéen d'information sur l'environnement, la culture et le développement durable (#16657)
- ♦ Bureau of Middle East Recycling (internationally oriented national body)
- ♦ Bureau mixte des femmes nordiques de droite (inactive)
- ♦ Bureau mondial des éleveurs de bétail Jersey (#21598)
- ♦ Bureau mondial du scoutisme (see: #21693)
- ♦ Bureau mondial du scoutisme – Bureau régional européen (#21771)
- ♦ Bureau des Nations Unies pour les affaires spatiales (#20601)
- ♦ Bureau des Nations Unies pour les services d'appui aux projets (#20602)

♦ Bureau of Nordic Family Forestry 03371

Contact European Forestry House, Rue du Luxembourg 66, 1000 Brussels, Belgium. T. +3222392313 – +322(32471139628. Fax +3222192191.
URL: http://www.nordicforestry.org/

History 1996, Brussels (Belgium). **Aims** Inform *European Union* institutions on the interests of small-scale forest owners. **Structure** Joint lobbying office at EU-level of the 4 Nordic forest owner's national organizations; based in Brussels (Belgium). **Languages** English. **Staff** 1.00 FTE, paid. **Finance** Through non-governmental organizations.
Members Private forest owners' federations (4) in 4 countries:
Denmark, Finland, Norway, Sweden. [2015/XG0410/**E**]

- ♦ Bureau nordique des droits d'auteur (#17500)
- ♦ Bureau nordique des musiciens amateurs (#19048)
- ♦ Bureau for Overseas Medical Service / see International Health Exchange
- ♦ Bureau panaméricain du café (inactive)
- ♦ Bureau permanent pour l'arabisation / see Arabization Coordination Bureau (#00999)

♦ Bureau permanent des congrès internationaux des sciences généalogique et héraldique 03372

Permanent Bureau of the International Congress of Genealogical and Heraldic Sciences

Sec c/o Stiftung Heraldic Intern, Hauffstrasse 35, 72622 Nürtingen, Germany. E-mail: c-drs@web.de.
History 1958, Brussels (Belgium), the first Congress having been held in 1929, Barcelona (Spain). Statutes revised 1982, Madrid (Spain). **Structure** Permanent Bureau consists of President and Secretary General of past Congresses and future Congress plus President of *International Academy of Heraldry (#11549)* and President of International Academy of Genealogy. **Activities** Surveys and advises on the biennial Congress run by the member organization in whose locality it takes place. **Events** *International Congress of Genealogical and Heraldic Sciences* Boston, MA (USA) 2024, *International Congress of Genealogical and Heraldic Sciences* Cambridge (UK) 2022, *Biennial Congress* Madrid (Spain) 2021, *Biennial Congress* Arras (France) 2018, *Biennial Congress* Maastricht (Netherlands) 2012.
Members Individuals in 13 countries:
Austria, Belgium, Canada, Denmark, Finland, Germany, Hungary, Luxembourg, Netherlands, Portugal, Spain, Sweden, UK.
NGO Relations *Confédération internationale de généalogie et d'héraldique (CIGH, #04561)*.
[2010.10.15/XD9924/v/**E**]

- ♦ Bureau permanent de coordination de l'arabisation dans le monde arabe / see Arabization Coordination Bureau (#00999)
- ♦ Bureau permanent des fédérations internationales sportives (inactive)
- ♦ Bureau permanent international des constructeurs d'automobiles / see International Organization of Motor Vehicle Manufacturers (#14455)
- ♦ Bureau permanent international des constructeurs de motocycles / see International Motorcycle Manufacturers Association (#14186)
- ♦ Bureau permanent international des secrétaires communaux (inactive)
- ♦ Bureau permanent international du spiritisme (inactive)
- ♦ Bureau de presse estudiantine asiatique (inactive)
- ♦ Bureau des projets de développement nordiques (inactive)
- ♦ Bureau voor publicaties van de Europese Unie (#18562)
- ♦ Bureau Quaker auprès des Nations Unies (#18588)
- ♦ Bureau de recherches sur l'économie islamique (internationally oriented national body)
- ♦ Bureau sous-régional de la CEA pour l'Afrique du Nord / see ECA Office for North Africa (#05273)
- ♦ Bureau régional de la FAO pour l'Amérique Latine et les Caraïbes (#09268)
- ♦ Bureau régional de l'OMS pour l'Afrique (#20943)
- ♦ Bureau régional de l'OMS pour les Amériques / see Pan American Sanitary Bureau (#18129)
- ♦ Bureau régional de l'OMS pour l'Europe (#20945)
- ♦ Bureau régional de l'OMS pour la Méditerranée orientale (#20944)
- ♦ Bureau régional du Pacifique occidental de l'OMS (#20947)
- ♦ Bureau régional principal de l'UNESCO en Asie et dans le Pacifique / see UNESCO Asia and Pacific Regional Bureau for Education (#20301)
- ♦ Bureau régional de science et de technologie de l'UNESCO pour l'Amérique latine et les Caraïbes / see UNESCO Office, Montevideo – Regional Bureau for Sciences in Latin America and the Caribbean (#20314)
- ♦ Bureau régional de science et de technologie pour de l'UNESCO pour l'Europe / see UNESCO Office in Venice – UNESCO Regional Bureau for Science and Culture in Europe (#20316)
- ♦ Bureau régional de science de l'UNESCO pour l'Amérique latine et les Caraïbes (#20314)
- ♦ Bureau régional de l'UNESCO pour la culture en Amérique latine et dans les Caraïbes (#20317)
- ♦ Bureau régional de l'Unesco pour l'éducation en Afrique (inactive)
- ♦ Bureau régional de l'UNESCO d'éducation pour l'Amérique latine et la région des Caraïbes (#20318)
- ♦ Bureau régional de l'UNESCO pour l'éducation en Asie et dans le Pacifique / see UNESCO Asia and Pacific Regional Bureau for Education (#20301)
- ♦ Bureau régional de 'Unesco de l'éducation pour les Etats arabes (#20320)
- ♦ Bureau régional de l'UNESCO de Jakarta de science et de technologie pour l'Asie du Sud-Est / see UNESCO Office, Jakarta – Regional Bureau for Sciences in Asia and the Pacific (#20313)
- ♦ Bureau régional de l'UNESCO de science pour les Etats arabes / see UNESCO Office, Cairo – Regional Bureau for Sciences in the Arab States (#20312)

♦ Bureau régional de l'UNESCO pour la science et la technologie en Afrique (inactive)
♦ Bureau régional de l'UNESCO de science et technologie pour l'Asie du Sud et l'Asie centrale / see UNESCO Asia-Pacific Regional Bureau for Communication and Information (#20300)
♦ Bureau régional de l'UNESCO de science et de technologie pour l'Asie du Sud-Est / see UNESCO Office, Jakarta – Regional Bureau for Sciences in Asia and the Pacific (#20313)
♦ Bureau régional de l'UNESCO de science et de technologie pour les Etats arabes (#20312)
♦ Bureau pour la répression de la traite (inactive)
♦ Bureau de reproduction et de génétique animale du CABI (inactive)

♦ Bureau for Research and Economic Analysis of Development (BREAD) 03373

Pres Economics Dept, 270 Bay State Rd, Boston MA 02215, USA. T. +16173534392. Fax +16173534143. E-mail: dilipm@bu.edu – bread@duke.edu.
Sec-Treas 64 Waterman St, Providence RI 02912, USA.
URL: http://ipl.econ.duke.edu/bread/

History 2002. **Aims** Encourage research and scholarship in development economics. **Structure** Board of Directors. Executive Committee, comprising President, Secretary/Treasurer and 4 members. **Activities** Organizes: conferences; summer school. **Events** *Development Economics Conference* Paris (France) 2011. **Publications** Working papers; policy paper series. **NGO Relations** Partner of: *Global Development Network (GDN, #10318).* [2013.03.07/XJ6588/v/F]

♦ Bureau des résumés analytiques du Conseil international des unions scientifiques / see International Council for Scientific and Technical Information (#13070)
♦ Bureau sanitaire international / see Pan American Sanitary Bureau (#18129)
♦ Bureau sanitaire panaméricain (#18129)
♦ Bureau des services médicaux outre-mer / see International Health Exchange
♦ Bureau socialiste international (inactive)
♦ Bureau voor de Statistiek van de Europese Gemeenschappen / see Statistical Office of the European Union (#19974)
♦ Bureau voor de Statistiek van de Europese Unie (#19974)
♦ Bureau for the Suppression of Slave-Trading (inactive)

♦ Bureau du Tibet – Bureau de représentation de sa Sainteté le Dalaï Lama 03374

Sec 84 bd Adolphe Pinard, 75014 Paris, France. T. +33146565453. Fax +33141170014. E-mail: tibetoffice@orange.fr – francebureau@tibet.net.
Brussels Office Av des Arts 24, 1000 Brussels, Belgium. T. +3222804922. Fax +3222802944. E-mail: rep.be@tibet.net.
URL: http://www.tibet.net/

History 1992. Registration: France. **Aims** Promote a better comprehension of the situation in Tibet. **Structure** General Assembly (annual); Executive Committee, comprising Representative of the Dalaï-Lama, Treasurer, Secretary and Assistant; Bureaus of Representation (14). **Finance** Financed by the Tibetan Government in Exile. Annual budget: 195,000 USD. **Activities** Events/meetings. **Publications** *Actualités Tibétaines* (4 a year). **NGO Relations** Cooperates with (1): *Unrepresented Nations and Peoples Organization (UNPO, #20714).* [2023.02.14/XD4217/E]

♦ Bureau de l'UNESCO à Apia / see UNESCO Office for the Pacific States (#20315)
♦ Bureau de l'UNESCO à Beirut / see UNESCO Regional Office for Education in the Arab States (#20320)
♦ Bureau de l'UNESCO au Caire / see UNESCO Office, Cairo – Regional Bureau for Sciences in the Arab States (#20312)
♦ Bureau de l'UNESCO à Delhi / see UNESCO Asia-Pacific Regional Bureau for Communication and Information (#20300)
♦ Bureau de l'UNESCO de l'éducation pour les Etats arabes / see UNESCO Regional Office for Education in the Arab States (#20320)
♦ Bureau de l'UNESCO pour les Etats du Pacifique (#20315)
♦ Bureau de l'UNESCO à la Havane / see UNESCO Regional Bureau for Culture for Latin America and the Caribbean (#20317)
♦ Bureau de l'UNESCO à Jakarta / see UNESCO Office, Jakarta – Regional Bureau for Sciences in Asia and the Pacific (#20313)
♦ Bureau de l'UNESCO à Montevideo / see UNESCO Office, Montevideo – Regional Bureau for Sciences in Latin America and the Caribbean (#20314)
♦ Bureau de l'UNESCO à Santiago / see UNESCO Regional Bureau for Education in Latin America and the Caribbean (#20318)
♦ Burkle Center for International Relations (internationally oriented national body)
♦ Burners Without Borders (internationally oriented national body)
♦ Büro des Europäischen Designer Verbandes / see Bureau of European Design Associations (#03359)
♦ Büro des Europäischen Design Verbandes (#03359)
♦ Buró Internacional para el Estudio de Aves Acuaticas y de Humedales (inactive)
♦ Buró Internazionale del Turismo Sociale / see International Social Tourism Organisation (#14889)
♦ Busan Foundation for International Cooperation (internationally oriented national body)
♦ Busan Partnership for Effective Development Co-operation / see Global Partnership for Effective Development Co-operation (#10532)
♦ Busan University of Foreign Studies (internationally oriented national body)
♦ BUSF / see Firemen without Borders (#09779)

♦ Business Action for Africa 03375

Action commerciale pour l'Afrique

Dir c/o Inspiris, Amadeus House, Floral Street, Covent Garden, London, WC2E 9DP, UK.
URL: http://www.businessactionforafrica.org/

Aims Create a platform for a clear African and international business voice; highlight business success stories and promote balanced reporting; facilitate new partnerships. [2008/XM1363/F]

♦ Business Advisory Council (BAC) 03376

Contact c/o CBSS, Strömsburg, PO Box 2010, SE-103 11 Stockholm, Sweden. T. +4684401920. Fax +4684401944. E-mail: cbss@cbss.org.
URL: http://www.cbss.org/Economic-Development/business-advisory-council/

History 1996, by *Council of the Baltic Sea States (CBSS, #04870).* Previously also referred to as *Baltic Sea Business Advisory Council.* **Aims** Identify *economic development* bottlenecks and suggest possible solutions. **Structure** Council of 11 delegates nominated by state-designated organizations (1 per country), headed by Chairman. **Languages** English. **Finance** Organizations of national delegates, including the Chairman, pay for all BAC expenses. **Activities** Carries out surveys on trade procedures, investments and business opportunities in the region; presents recommendations to various bodies within CBSS. **Events** *Meeting* Riga (Latvia) 2001, *Meeting* Stockholm (Sweden) 2000.
Members Delegates of the 11 CBSS countries:
Denmark, Estonia, Finland, Germany, Iceland, Latvia, Lithuania, Norway, Poland, Russia, Sweden.
NGO Relations Close cooperation with: *Baltic Sea Chambers of Commerce Association (BCCA, #03140).* [2010.07.01/XD6733/E]

♦ Business Africa (BUSINESSAFRICA) 03377

SG Waajiri House, Off Argwings Kodhek Road, Milimani, PO Box 48311-00100, Nairobi, Kenya. T. +254202721929 – +254202721948. Fax +254202720295 – +254202721990. E-mail: info@businessafrica-emp.org.
Pres address not obtained.
URL: http://www.businessafrica-emp.org/

History 12 Oct 1986, as *Pan-African Employers' Confederation (PEC) – Confédération panafricaine des employeurs (CPE) – Confederación Panafricana de Empleadores.* Statutes most recently revised: Jun 1993. 7 Jun 2012, present name adopted. **Aims** Contribute to economic and social development of Africa through the promotion of the enterprise, investment and employment. **Structure** General Assembly (annual). Executive Council, consisting of President, 1st and 2nd Vice-Presidents, Secretary-General, Deputy-Secretary-General, Treasurer, Deputy Treasurer and 5 members. Secretariat. **Languages** Arabic, English, French. **Staff** 5.00 FTE, voluntary. **Finance** Members' due (annual): Swiss Fr 1000. **Activities** Strategies: Networking; Information and Research; Marketing and Communication; Operational. Conducts studies; organizes meetings. **Events** *Biennial Conference* Dakar (Senegal) 1999, *Biennial Conference* Dakar (Senegal) 1999, *Biennial conference* Johannesburg (South Africa) 1997. **Publications** *PEC Newsletter* (4 a year). Annual Report. Brochure; books; case studies; tools.
Members Employers' organizations in 39 countries:
Algeria, Angola, Benin, Botswana, Burkina Faso, Cameroon, Chad, Comoros, Congo Brazzaville, Congo DR, Côte d'Ivoire, Egypt, Eritrea, Eswatini, Ethiopia, Gabon, Ghana, Guinea, Kenya, Lesotho, Madagascar, Mali, Mauritania, Mauritius, Morocco, Mozambique, Namibia, Niger, Nigeria, Rwanda, Senegal, South Africa, Sudan, Tanzania UR, Togo, Tunisia, Uganda, Zambia, Zimbabwe.
Consultative Status Consultative status granted from: *ILO (#11123)* (General). **IGO Relations** Consultative Status with: *African Union (AU, #00488).* **NGO Relations** Cooperates with: *International Organisation of Employers (IOE, #14428).* Signed a declaration together with: *BUSINESSEUROPE (#03381).* [2017/XD1071/D]

♦ **BUSINESSAFRICA** Business Africa (#03377)
♦ Business Alliance for Water and Climate (unconfirmed)
♦ Business Angel Network Southeast Asia (internationally oriented national body)

♦ Business Association of Latin American Studies (BALAS) 03378

Exec Dir address not obtained. E-mail: balas@balas.org.
URL: http://www.balas.org/

Aims Bring together scholars, professional managers and decision-makers to facilitate exchange of information and ideas and to provide leadership in the areas of Latin American business and economic research and practice. **Structure** Officers: President; Executive Secretary; Vice President – Membership; Immediate Past President; Treasurer; Programme Chair; 7 Regional Representatives. **Languages** English. **Staff** Voluntary. **Finance** Members' dues (annual): Institutional US$ 500; Individual US$ 45. **Activities** Provides a leadership role in sponsoring forums for exchange of ideas, information dissemination, research collaboration and educational activities; organizes annual conference. **Events** *Annual Conference* Mexico City (Mexico) 2023, *Annual Conference* Lima (Peru) 2019, *Annual Conference* San Diego, CA (USA) 2018, *Annual Conference* Santiago (Chile) 2017, *Annual Conference* Guayaquil (Ecuador) 2016. **Publications** *Latin American Business Review* (4 a year); *BALAS Newsletter* (2 a year); *BALAS Membership Directory* (annual). Newsletter for members only. **Members** Researchers, professors, business people, graduate students (500), in 30 countries. Membership countries not specified. **NGO Relations** *EFMD – The Management Development Network (#05387); Latin American Council of Business Schools (#16308);* national associations. [2018/XF0174/v/F]

♦ Business Council Europe – Africa – Mediterranean / see European Business Council for Africa (#06416)
♦ Business Council Europe – Afrique – Méditerranée / see European Business Council for Africa (#06416)
♦ Business Council for International Understanding (internationally oriented national body)
♦ Business Council for Sustainable Development (inactive)
♦ Business Council for the United Nations (internationally oriented national body)
♦ Business in Development Network (internationally oriented national body)
♦ business disability international (internationally oriented national body)

♦ Business and Economics Society International (B and ESI) 03379

Main Office 64 Holden St, Worcester MA 01605, USA. T. +15088523937. Fax +15085950089. E-mail: hkan@besiweb.com.
URL: http://www.besiweb.com/

History 1996, USA. **Aims** Bring together economics and business academicians and practitioners worldwide to exchange research findings. **Structure** Trustees. **Languages** English. **Activities** Events/meetings; networking/liaising; publishing activities; research and development; research/documentation; training/education. **Events** *Conference* Buenos Aires (Argentina) 2019, *Conference* Vienna (Austria) 2019, *Conference* Cusco (Peru) 2018, *Conference* Lugano (Switzerland) 2018, *Conference* Chania (Greece) 2017. **Publications** *International Journal of Behavioral and Healthcare Research* (4 a year); *Global Business and Economics Review* (4 a year); *Global Business and Economics Anthology (GBEA)* (2 a year); *International Journal of Economics and Business Research* (8 a year). **Members** Individuals (135) from 30 countries. Membership countries not specified. [2019.12.23/XN2524/D]

♦ Business Ethics Network of Africa (BEN-Africa) 03380

Contact PO Box 12700, Die Boord, Stellenbosch, 7613, South Africa. E-mail: info@benafrica.org.
URL: http://www.benafrica.org/

History 1999. **Aims** Strengthen the commitment and competence of Africans to do business with moral integrity by facilitating interaction between academics and practitioners who share an interest in business ethics. **Structure** Executive Committee. **Languages** English. **Staff** Voluntary. **Activities** Events/meetings; knowledge management/information dissemination; projects/programmes; research/documentation. **Events** *Conference* Mombasa (Kenya) 2019, *Conference* Maputo (Mozambique) 2018, *Annual Conference* Johannesburg (South Africa) 2015, *Annual Conference* Lagos (Nigeria) 2013, *Annual Conference* Entebbe (Uganda) 2012. **Publications** *African Journal of Business Ethics*; *BEN-Africa Newsletter*. *BEN-Africa Book Series.*
Members Full in 34 countries:
Angola, Australia, Belgium, Benin, Botswana, Brazil, Burkina Faso, Cameroon, Congo DR, Egypt, Eswatini, Ethiopia, Germany, Ghana, Kenya, Malawi, Mauritius, Mozambique, Namibia, Niger, Nigeria, Norway, Russia, Rwanda, South Africa, Spain, Sudan, Tanzania UR, Togo, Uganda, UK, USA, Zambia, Zimbabwe.
NGO Relations Partner of (1): *Globethics.net Foundation (#10669).* [2021.05.20/XF6746/F]

♦ BUSINESSEUROPE 03381

Dir Gen Av de Cortenbergh 168, 1000 Brussels, Belgium. T. +3222376511. Fax +3222311445. E-mail: main@businesseurope.eu.
Main Website: http://www.businesseurope.eu/

History Mar 1958. Former member of *Council of the Industrial Federations of EFTA (CIFEFTA, inactive)*; became associate member, 22 June 1987. Current statutes adopted, Dec 2007. Former names and other names: *Union of Industries of the European Community* – former (1958 to 1987); *Union des industries de la Communauté européenne* – former (1958 to 1987); *Union of Industrial and Employers' Confederations of Europe* – former (22 Jun 1987 to 2007); *Union des confédérations de l'industrie et des employeurs d'Europe (UNICE)* – former (22 Jun 1987 to 2007); *BUSINESSEUROPE – The Confederation of European Business* – full title (23 Jan 2007). Registration: EU Transparency Register, No/ID: 3978240953-79. **Aims** Influence EU policies to create a business-friendly environment; represent and promote actively *business* interests in *Europe*, advocate a conducive and competitive business environment to foster sustainable economic growth. **Structure** Council of Presidents (meets at least twice a year); Executive Committee; Executive Bureau; Committee of Permanent Delegates; Policy Committees; Working Groups; Secretariat, headed by Director General. Meetings closed. **Languages** English. **Staff** 50.00 FTE, paid. **Finance** Sources: members' dues. **Activities** Advocacy/lobbying/activism; awareness raising; events/meetings. **Events** *European Business Summit* Brussels (Belgium) 2022, *European Business Summit* Brussels (Belgium) 2021, *Business Europe Day* Brussels (Belgium) 2020, *European Business Summit* Brussels (Belgium) 2020, *Conference on a Trade Strategy Fit for the 21st Century* Brussels (Belgium) 2019. **Publications** *BUSINESSEUROPE Headlines* (45 a year) in English – electronic bulletin.
Members National industrial and employers' confederations in 35 countries:
Austria, Belgium, Bulgaria, Croatia, Cyprus, Czechia, Denmark (2), Estonia, Finland, France, Germany (2), Greece, Hungary, Iceland (2), Ireland, Italy, Latvia, Lithuania, Luxembourg, Malta, Montenegro, Netherlands, Norway, Poland, Portugal, Romania, San Marino, Serbia, Slovakia, Slovenia, Spain, Sweden, Switzerland (2), Türkiye (2), UK.

Consultative Status Consultative status granted from: *ECOSOC (#05331)* (Ros C); *ILO (#11123)*; *UNCTAD (#20285)* (General Category); *UNIDO (#20336)*; *World Intellectual Property Organization (WIPO, #21593)* (Permanent Observer Status). **IGO Relations** Observer to: *Union internationale pour la protection des obtentions végétales (UPOV, #20436)*. Social Partner of: *European Quality Assurance in Vocational Education and Training (EQAVET, #08312)*. Consultative member of: *European Higher Education Area (EHEA, #07483)*. Cooperates with: *EFTA (#05391)*; *European Commission (EC, #06633)*; *European Union Intellectual Property Office (EUIPO, #08996)*. Accredited by: *United Nations Framework Convention on Climate Change – Secretariat (UNFCCC, #20564)*; *United Nations Office at Vienna (UNOV, #20604)*. Observer to: *OSPAR Commission for the Protection of the Marine Environment of the North-East Atlantic (OSPAR Commission, #17905)*. Contact with: *United Nations Commission on International Trade Law (UNCITRAL, #20531)*. **NGO Relations** Member of: *Global Business Coalition (GBC, #10257)*; *European Accreditation Advisory Board (EAAB, see: #06782)*; *European Financial Reporting Advisory Group (EFRAG, #07254)*; *European Organisation for Conformity Assessment (EOTC, inactive)*; *European Policy Centre (EPC, #08240)*; *European Quality Assurance Register for Higher Education (EQAR, #08311)*. Associate member of: *European Registry of Internet Domain Names (EURid, #08351)*. Partner of: *World Business Council for Sustainable Development (WBCSD, #21254)*. Joint discussions with: *European Trade Union Confederation (ETUC, #08927)*. Cooperation agreement with: *European Committee for Electrotechnical Standardization (CENELEC, #06647)*. Instrumental in setting up: *Alliance for a Competitive European Industry (ACEI, #00670)*; *European Centre for Industrial Relations (ECIR, inactive)*; *Integrated Waste Management Network (IWMN, no recent information)*. [2022.02.16/XE3351/**D**]

♦ Business European Capital Cities (BECC) 03382

SG c/o MEDEF, 55 Ave Bosquet, 75007 Paris, France. T. +33153591996. Fax +33145512044.

History 1989, France. Founded on the initiative of the *Union Patronale de Paris*, following a meeting of entrepreneurs' associations in Paris. Former names and other names: *Organisation interProfessionnelle des Capitales Européennes (OPCE)* – former; *Association des organisations patronales interprofessionnelles des capitales européennes* – former; *Association of Interprofessional Employers/Businessmen Organisations of European Capital Cities* – former; *Organisation Patronale des Capitales Europeennes (OPCE)* – former; *Association des Organisations interProfessionnelles d'entrepreneurs des Capitales Européennes (OPCE)* – former; *Association of Interprofessional Employers / Businessmen of European Capital Cities* – former. Registration: Start date: 8 Jun 1990, France, Paris. **Aims** Provide a connection between businessmen organisations of the European capital cities. **Activities** Networking/liaising; advocacy/lobbying/activism; events/meetings. **Events** *Congress* Rome (Italy) 2015, *Congress* Paris (France) 2014, *Congress* Rome (Italy) 2011, *Congress* Rome (Italy) 2006, *Congress* Moscow (Russia) 2005.
Members National or local unions in 14 countries:
Austria, Belgium, France, Germany, Greece, Hungary, Italy, Malta, Norway, Poland, Portugal, Spain, Sweden, UK.
[2018/XD7549/t/**D**]

♦ BUSINESSEUROPE – The Confederation of European Business / see BUSINESSEUROPE (#03381)
♦ Business Graduates Association / see Association of MBAs (#02795)

♦ Business Humanitarian Forum (BHF) 03383

Pres Rue du Conseil-General 6, 1205 Geneva, Switzerland.
Dir address not obtained.

History Founded Jan 1999, Geneva (Switzerland), by business corporations and humanitarian organizations. Registered in accordance with Swiss Civil Code. **Aims** Encourage private sector support and public-private sector cooperation for economic and human development in post-conflict areas and poor countries where investment is needed. **Structure** Association Council; Board of Advisors. **Languages** English, French. **Staff** 3.00 FTE, paid. **Finance** Support from foundations, corporations and individuals. **Activities** Guidance/assistance/consulting; capacity building; humanitarian/emergency aid. **Publications** Articles; speeches; press releases. **Consultative Status** Consultative status granted from: *ECOSOC (#05331)* (Ros A). **IGO Relations** Cooperates with: *DEG – Deutsche Investitions- und Entwicklungsgesellschaft*; Governments of Afghanistan, Germany and Switzerland; *International Bank for Reconstruction and Development (IBRD, #12317)* (World Bank); *International Finance Corporation (IFC, #13597)*; *New Partnership for Africa's Development (NEPAD, #17091)*; *OECD (#17693)*; *OSCE – Office for Democratic Institutions and Human Rights (OSCE/ODIHR, #17902)*; *UNDP (#20292)*; *UNEP (#20299)*; *UNHCR (#20327)*; *United Nations Economic Commission for Europe (UNECE, #20555)*; *United Nations Institute for Training and Research (UNITAR, #20576)*; *United States Agency for International Development (USAID)*; *WHO (#20950)*. **NGO Relations** Cooperates with: *The Conference Board in Europe (#04583)*; *Geneva Centre for Security Policy (GCSP)*; *International Chamber of Commerce (ICC, #12534)*; *International Committee of the Red Cross (ICRC, #12799)*; *International Rescue Committee (IRC, #14717)*; *Transparency International (TI, #20223)*; *United States Institute of Peace (USIP)*.
[2018.09.05/XF6064/**F**]

♦ Business and Human Rights Resource Centre (internationally oriented national body)

♦ Business for Inclusive Growth (B4IG) 03384

CEO 17 boulevard Haussmann, 75009 Paris, France. E-mail: contact@b4ig.org.
URL: https://www.b4ig.org/

History Founded as a partnership between *OECD (#17693)* and major corporations worldwide. Registration: SIREN, No/ID: 884.182.320, France; RNA, No/ID: W751256594, Start date: 12 May 2020, France. **Aims** Pool and strengthen efforts by private companies to reduce inequalities linked to opportunity, gender and territory; build greater synergies with government-led efforts. **Structure** Co-Chairs (2); Board. Hosted by *OECD (#17693)*. **Members** Corporations. Membership countries not specified. **IGO Relations** Partner of (3): *Group of Seven (G-7, #10788)*; *ILO (#11123)*; *UN Women (#20724)*. **NGO Relations** Partner of (5): *Bill and Melinda Gates Foundation (BMGF)*; *Business and Industry Advisory Committee to the OECD (BIAC, #03385)*; *International Trade Union Confederation (ITUC, #15708)*; *The Rockefeller Foundation (#18966)*; *Trade Union Advisory Committee to the OECD (TUAC, #20186)*. [2021/AA2150/**E**]

♦ Business and Industry Advisory Committee to the OECD (BIAC) ... 03385

Comité consultatif économique et industriel auprès de l'OCDE

Exec Dir 13-15 chée de la Muette, 75016 Paris, France. T. +33142300960. Fax +33142887838. E-mail: contact@biac.org.
URL: https://www.businessatoecd.org/

History 9 Mar 1962, Paris (France). Founded as an independent organization. Officially recognized representative of OECD business community. **Aims** Provide expertise to national businesses and employers' federations via participation with the OECD and governments promoting competitive economies and better business. **Structure** General Assembly (annual); Executive Board; Policy Groups; Committees; Expert Groups; Secretariat, headed by Secretary-General. Meetings closed. **Languages** English, French. **Staff** 12.00 FTE, paid. **Finance** Sources: members' dues. **Activities** Events/meetings; guidance/assistance/consulting. **Events** *Conference on International Taxation* Tokyo (Japan) 2021, *General Assembly* Paris (France) 2013, *General Assembly* Budapest (Hungary) 2011, *General Assembly* Mexico City (Mexico) 2007, *General Assembly* Istanbul (Turkey) 2005. **Publications** *Economic Review*. Annual Report; policy group publications.
Members Full: major business organizations in 37 OECD countries:
Australia, Austria, Belgium, Canada, Chile, Colombia, Costa Rica, Czechia, Denmark, Estonia, Finland, France, Germany, Greece, Hungary, Iceland, Ireland, Israel, Italy, Japan, Korea Rep, Latvia, Lithuania, Luxembourg, Mexico, Netherlands, New Zealand, Norway, Portugal, Slovakia, Slovenia, Spain, Sweden, Switzerland, Türkiye, UK, USA.
Observer: organizations representing business in 12 non-OECD countries:
Argentina, Brazil, Bulgaria, Croatia, Egypt, India, Indonesia, Peru, Romania, Singapore, South Africa, Ukraine.
Associate experts groups (58):
- *Asociación Interamericana de Empresas de Telecomunicaciones (ASIET, #02160)*;
- *Association européenne des métaux (EUROMETAUX, #02578)*;
- *Association of Chartered Certified Accountants (ACCA)*;
- *Association of Plastics Manufacturers in Europe (Plastics Europe, #02862)*;
- *Association of the European Rail Supply Industry (UNIFE, #02536)*;
- *Association of the European Self-Care Industry (#02543)*;
- *Bureau of International Recycling (BIR, #03368)*;
- *Computer and Communications Industry Association (CCIA)*;
- *Confederation of European Waste-to-Energy Plants (CEWEP, #04535)*;
- *Conseil européen de l'industrie chimique (CEFIC, #04687)*;
- *Cosmetics Europe – The Personal Care Association (#04852)*;
- *Council of European Employers of the Metal, Engineering and Technology-Based Industries (CEEMET, #04887)*;
- *CropLife International (#04966)*;
- *DIGITALEUROPE (#05073)*;
- *European Aluminium (#05893)*;
- *European Association of Bioindustries (EuropaBio, #05956)*;
- *European Association of Mining Industries, Metal Ores and Industrial Minerals (EUROMINES, #06122)*;
- *European Association of the Machine tool Industries and related Manufacturing Technologies (CECIMO, #06113)*;
- *European Banking Federation (EBF, #06312)*;
- *European Carbon and Graphite Association (ECGA, #06447)*;
- *European Construction Industry Federation (#06766)*;
- *European Coordination Committee of the Radiological, Electromedical Healthcare IT Industry (COCIR, #06792)*;
- *European Federation of Pharmaceutical Industries and Associations (EFPIA, #07191)*;
- *European Industrial Research Management Association (EIRMA, #07531)*;
- *European Insulation Manufacturers Association (EURIMA, #07577)*;
- *European Recycling Industries' Confederation (EuRIC, #08335)*;
- *European Savings and Retail Banking Group (ESBG, #08426)*;
- *European Telecommunications Network Operators' Association (ETNO, #08895)*;
- *FoodDrinkEurope (#09841)*;
- *Global Self-Care Federation (GSCF, #10588)*;
- *GS1 (#10809)*;
- *GSM Association (GSMA, #10813)*;
- *Insurance Europe (#11362)*;
- *International Aluminium Institute (IAI, #11643)*;
- *International Chamber of Shipping (ICS, #12535)*;
- *International Council on Mining and Metals (ICMM, #13048)*;
- *International Federation of Accountants (IFAC, #13335)*;
- *International Federation of Pharmaceutical Manufacturers and Associations (IFPMA, #13505)*;
- *International Federation of Private Water Operators (AquaFed, #13517)*;
- *International Federation of the Phonographic Industry (IFPI, #13508)*;
- *International Fertilizer Association (IFA, #13589)*;
- *International Fragrance Association (IFRA, #13680)*;
- *International Health, Racquet and Sportsclub Association (IHRSA, #13783)*;
- *International Seed Federation (ISF, #14828)*;
- *International Textile Manufacturers Federation (ITMF, #15679)*;
- Investment Company Institute;
- *MedTech Europe (#16692)*;
- *spiritsEUROPE (#19921)*;
- *The Brewers of Europe (#03324)*;
- *Transnational Alliance to Combat Illicit Trade (TRACIT)*;
- *UNESDA Soft Drinks Europe (UNESDA, #20323)*;
- *Union européenne de l'hospitalisation privée (UEHP, #20397)*;
- *World Employment Confederation (WEC, #21376)*;
- *World Federation of Advertisers (WFA, #21407)*;
- *World Pharmacy Council (WPV, #21723)*;
- *World Savings Banks Institute (WSBI, #21764)*;
- *World Steel Association (worldsteel, #21829)*;
- *Worldwide Brewing Alliance (WBA, #21917)*.

Consultative Status Consultative status granted from: *OECD (#17693)*. **IGO Relations** Accredited by: *United Nations Framework Convention on Climate Change – Secretariat (UNFCCC, #20564)*. Represented in Steering Group of: *Anti-Corruption Network for Eastern Europe and Central Asia (ACN, #00853)*. Coordination with: *ILO (#11123)*. Adheres to: *Global Partnership for Effective Development Co-operation (GPEDC, #10532)*.
[2023/XE0204/ty/**E**]

♦ Business Information Industry Association (BIIA) 03386

Managing Dir Ste 4114, Hong Kong Plaza, 188 Connaught Road West, Hong Kong, Central and Western, Hong Kong. T. +85225256120. Fax +85225256171. E-mail: biiainfoasia@gmail.com.
Registered Office Unit B – 8th Floor, Jonsim Place, 228 Queen's Road East, Hong Kong, Central and Western, Hong Kong.
URL: http://www.biia.com/

History 2005, Hong Kong. Registered in accordance with the law of Hong Kong: 979425. Registration: Corporation, No/ID: 979425, Hong Kong. **Aims** Provide a platform to network and work on common issues facing the business information industry globally. **Structure** Board of Directors. **Languages** English. **Finance** Sources: members' dues. **Events** *World Consumer Credit Reporting Conference* Barcelona (Spain) 2022, *World Consumer Credit Reporting Conference* Barcelona (Spain) 2021, *World Consumer Credit Reporting Conference* Barcelona (Spain) 2020, *Biennial Conference* Bangkok (Thailand) 2019, *Biennial Conference* Bangkok (Thailand) 2017. **Publications** *BIIA Newsletter*. **Members** Individuals (75). Membership countries not specified. **NGO Relations** Cooperates with: *International Credit Insurance & Surety Association (ICISA, #13103)*. Member of: *SME Finance Forum (#19323)*. [2020/XJ5908/t/**C**]

♦ Business and Institutional Furniture Manufacturer's Association / see BIFMA International
♦ **BUSINESSMED** Union of Mediterranean Confederations of Enterprises (#20458)
♦ Business for Peace Foundation (internationally oriented national body)
♦ Business and Professional Women International / see International Federation of Business and Professional Women (#13376)
♦ Business for Social Responsibility (internationally oriented national body)

♦ Business Software Alliance (BSA) 03387

Pres and CEO 20 F St NW, Ste 800, Washington DC 20001, USA. T. +12028725500. Fax +12028725501. E-mail: info@bsa.org.
BSA Asia 300 Beach Road, 25-08 The Concourse, Singapore 199555, Singapore.
BSA EMEA Office 44 Avenue des Arts, 1040 Brussels, Belgium.
URL: http://www.bsa.org/

History 1988. **Aims** Promote conditions in which the *information technology* (IT) industry can thrive and contribute to the prosperity, security and quality of life of all people. **Structure** Executive, comprising President/CEO and 4 Vice-Presidents. **Activities** Educates computer users about software copyrights; advocates public policy; fights software piracy; operates "hotlines"; organizes fora. **Events** *Annual European Data Protection and Privacy Conference* Brussels (Belgium) 2015. **Publications** *Global Software Piracy Study* (annual); *Guide to Software Management*; *Piracy Impact Study: The Economic Benefits of Reducing Software Piracy*; *Software Review*. Studies. **Members** Leading publishers of PC software worldwide. Regional membership program has participants throughout Europe, Asia, North and Latin America. Membership countries not specified. **Consultative Status** Consultative status granted from: *World Intellectual Property Organization (WIPO, #21593)* (Permanent Observer Status). **IGO Relations** Memorandum of Understanding signed with: *World Customs Organization (WCO, #21350)*. **NGO Relations** Instrumental in setting up: *Software Action Group for Europe (SAGE, no recent information)*. Associate Member of: *European Internet Forum (EIF, #07591)*. Member of: *International Intellectual Property Alliance (IIPA)*. [2020/XF3369/**F**]

♦ **BUSINET** Global Business Education Network (#10258)
♦ BUSPA – Baltic United Special Printing Association (inactive)

♦ Butterfly Conservation Europe (BCE) 03388

Contact PO Box 506, 6700 AM Wageningen, Netherlands. E-mail: info@bc-europe.eu.
URL: http://www.bc-europe.eu/

History 2004. Registered in accordance with Dutch law. EU Transparency Register: 94537798584-35. **Aims** Halt and reverse the decline of butterflies, moths and their habitats throughout Europe. **Structure** Board; Secretariat. **Activities** Advocacy/lobbying/activism.
Members Partners in 35 countries:
Andorra, Armenia, Austria, Belarus, Belgium, Bulgaria, Croatia, Cyprus, Czechia, Denmark, Estonia, Finland, France, Germany, Hungary, Ireland, Isle of Man, Italy, Lithuania, Luxembourg, Netherlands, North Macedonia, Norway, Poland, Portugal, Romania, Russia, Serbia, Slovakia, Slovenia, Spain, Sweden, Switzerland, Türkiye, UK.
NGO Relations Member of: *European Habitats Forum (EHF, #07443)*. [2017/XM5978/**F**]

♦ The Butterfly Effect (BE) 03389

L'Effet Papillon – El Efecto Mariposa

Secretariat SIE/ISW/SIA, 9623 Lajeunesse, Montréal QC H3L 2C7, Canada. T. +15148494262. E-mail: butterflyeffectcoalition@gmail.com.
URL: http://www.effetpapillon.org/
History 17 Dec 2010, Paris (France). **Aims** Ensure that the NGOs/CSOs voice, from all world regions is strong and heard in the international agenda when it comes to advocating water's essential role in a sustainable and equitable development. **Structure** General Assembly; Steering Committee; Secretariat. Working Groups. **Activities** Advocacy/lobbying/activism. **Publications** *The Butterfly Effect Newsletter.*
Members Organizations (over 90), including the following 14 listed in this Yearbook:
Action Against Hunger (#00086); African Civil Society Network on Water and Sanitation (ANEW, #00250); Asociación Regional Centroamericana para el Agua el Ambiente (ARCA, no recent information); Comité Catholique contre la Faim et pour le Développement-Terre Solidaire (CCFD-Terre Solidaire); Freshwater Action Network South Asia (FANSA, #09996); Hydraulique sans frontières (HSF); International Secretariat for Water (ISW, #14822); Progressio (inactive); Red Centroamericana de Acción del Agua (#18638); Secours catholique – Caritas France; Women Engage for a Common Future (WECF, #20992); Women for Water Partnership (WfWP, #21041); Women's Voice International (inactive); World Wide Fund for Nature (WWF, #21922).
NGO Relations *World Water Council (WWC, #21908).* [2014/XJ5854/y/F]

♦ Buy Nothing Project 03390

Contact address not obtained. E-mail: thebuynothingproject@gmail.com – info@buynothinggeteverything.com.
URL: https://buynothingproject.org/
History Jul 2013, Bainbridge Island, WA (USA). Began when Rebecca Rockefeller and Liesl Clark created an experimental hyper-local gift economy. Evolved into a worldwide social movement. **Aims** Offer people a way to give and receive, share, lend, and express gratitude through a worldwide network of hyper-local gift economies in which the true wealth is the web of connections formed between people who are real-life neighbors. **Publications** *The Buy Nothing, Get Everything Plan* (1st ed 2020) by Liesl Clark and Rebecca Rockefeller. **Members** Participants (over 1500000 individuals) in local groups in over 25 countries. [2020/AA1308/v/F]

- ♦ **BVA** Balkan Volleyball Association (#03090)
- ♦ BVA – Belgische Vereniging van Afrikanisten (internationally oriented national body)
- ♦ BvAT – Biovision Africa Trust (unconfirmed)
- ♦ BVGH – BIO Ventures for Global Health (internationally oriented national body)
- ♦ BvLF – Bernard van Leer Foundation (internationally oriented national body)
- ♦ BVMs – Sisters of Charity of the Blessed Virgin Mary (religious order)
- ♦ BVRA' / see European Association of Veterinary Diagnostic Imaging (#06269)
- ♦ **BVS** Brethren Volunteer Service (#03321)
- ♦ BW2030 – BalticWaters2030 (internationally oriented national body)
- ♦ **BWA** Baptist World Alliance (#03176)
- ♦ BWA / see European Waterproofing Association (#09084)
- ♦ **BWAid** Baptist World Aid (#03175)
- ♦ **BWB** Braille Without Borders (#03312)
- ♦ BWB – Burners Without Borders (internationally oriented national body)
- ♦ **BWC** Baltic Writers' Council (#03156)
- ♦ **BWF** Badminton World Federation (#03060)
- ♦ **BWF** Beiaard Wereld Federatie (#21260)
- ♦ **BWF** Beratendes Weltkomitee der Freunde (#10004)
- ♦ **BWF** Bukido World Federation (#03356)
- ♦ **BWI** Building and Wood Workers' International (#03355)
- ♦ BWIESMG – Black Women in Europe Social Media Group (internationally oriented national body)
- ♦ BWI Latin American and Caribbean Regional Office
- ♦ BWI Regional Office for Asia and the Pacific
- ♦ **BWIs** Bretton Woods Institutions (#03322)
- ♦ BWM 2004 – International Convention for the Control and Management of Ships' Ballast Water and Sediments (2004 treaty)
- ♦ **BWP** Baptist Women of the Pacific (#03173)
- ♦ BWR – International Conference on Biological Waste as Resource (meeting series)
- ♦ BWTC / see Baltic Writers' Council (#03156)
- ♦ **BWTP Network** Banking With the Poor Network (#03164)
- ♦ **BWUA** Baptist Women's Union of Africa (#03174)
- ♦ BWUSWP / see Baptist Women of the Pacific (#03173)
- ♦ Byggnads- ocht Träarbetar-Internationalen (#03355)
- ♦ **BYP** Baltic Youth Philharmonic (#03157)
- ♦ C189 – Domestic Workers Convention, 2011 (2011 treaty)
- ♦ C2 / see Campbell Collaboration (#03408)
- ♦ C20 / see C40 (#03391)
- ♦ **C200** Committee of 200 (#04240)
- ♦ **C-24** Comité Especial de Descolonización (#19906)
- ♦ **C-24** Special Committee on Decolonization (#19906)

♦ C40 03391

Exec Dir 3 Queen Victoria St, London, EC4N 4TQ, UK. E-mail: contact@c40.org.
USA Office 120 Park Ave, 23rd Floor, New York NY 10017, USA.
URL: http://www.c40.org/
History Oct 2005, London (UK). Founded during World Cities Leadership Climate Change Summit. Previously referred to as *C20*. Previous full title: *C40 Large Cities – Climate Leadership Group.* Current title adopted, Aug 2006, on partnership with 'Clinton Climate Initiative', with full title: *C40 – Climate Leadership Group.* Also referred to as *C40 Cities.* Former names and other names: *Large Cities Climate Leadership Group (LCCLG)* – former (2005); *C20* – former; *C40 Large Cities – Climate Leadership Group* – former; *C40 – Climate Leadership Group* – former; *C40 Cities* – former. Registration: Charity Commission, No/ID: 1173124, England and Wales; South Africa; USA. **Aims** Reduce *greenhouse gas emissions* in participating *cities*; provide leadership on *climate change* issues. **Structure** Board of Directors; Steering Committee. **Activities** Guidance/assistance/consulting; research/documentation; events/meetings. **Events** *C40 World Mayors Summit* Buenos Aires (Argentina) 2022, *Mayors Summit* Copenhagen (Denmark) 2019, *Annual Women4Climate Conference* Paris (France) 2019, *Urban 20 Mayors Summit* Tokyo (Japan) 2019, *Conference on Tackling Climate Change through Technological Innovation* Singapore (Singapore) 2018.
Members Cities (96) in 47 countries and territories:
Argentina, Australia, Bangladesh, Brazil, Canada, Chile, China, Colombia, Côte d'Ivoire, Denmark, Ecuador, Ethiopia, France, Germany, Ghana, Greece, Hong Kong, India, Indonesia, Israel, Italy, Japan, Jordan, Korea Rep, Malaysia, Mexico, Netherlands, New Zealand, Nigeria, Norway, Pakistan, Peru, Philippines, Poland, Russia, Senegal, Singapore, South Africa, Spain, Switzerland, Tanzania UR, Thailand, Türkiye, UK, United Arab Emirates, USA, Vietnam.
NGO Relations Partnership agreement with: Climate Initiative of *William J Clinton Foundation.* Also partner of: *Local Governments for Sustainability (ICLEI, #16507).* Member of: *Cities Climate Finance Leadership Alliance (CCFLA, #03952); Climate and Clean Air Coalition (CCAC, #04010); Global Taskforce of Local and Regional Governments (Global Taskforce, #10622).* [2020/XM2097/F]

- ♦ C40 Cities / see C40 (#03391)
- ♦ C40 – Climate Leadership Group / see C40 (#03391)
- ♦ C40 Large Cities – Climate Leadership Group / see C40 (#03391)
- ♦ **C4C** Copyright for Creativity (#04832)
- ♦ CA4TA – Canada – Central America Four Free Trade Agreement (unconfirmed)
- ♦ CAAA / see Confederation of African Athletics (#04504)
- ♦ CAABU – Council for the Advancement of Arab-British Understanding (internationally oriented national body)
- ♦ **CAA** Caribbean Actuarial Association (#03433)
- ♦ CAA – Caribbean Aquaculture Association (inactive)
- ♦ CAAC / see Atlantic Cities (#03008)
- ♦ CAACE / see European Community Shipowners' Associations (#06683)
- ♦ **CAA** Circumpolar Agricultural Association (#03940)
- ♦ **CAA** Climate Action Accelerator (#03998)
- ♦ **CAA** Club Arc Alpin (#04030)
- ♦ **CAA** Cocoa Association of Asia (#04079)
- ♦ CAA – Commission for American Affairs (see: #15795)
- ♦ **CAA** Commonwealth Association of Architects (#04301)
- ♦ CAA – Computer Applications and Quantitative Methods in Archaeology (unconfirmed)
- ♦ **CAA** Confédération africaine d'athlétisme (#04504)
- ♦ **CAA** Confederation of African Athletics (#04504)
- ♦ **CAA** Conseil africain de l'arachide (#00332)

♦ CAADFutures Foundation 03392

Secretariat TUE – Built Environment, VRT 9-08, PO Box 513, 5600 MB Eindhoven, Netherlands.
URL: http://www.caadfutures.org/
History 1985. Registration: Netherlands. **Aims** Promote research interaction and collaboration among researchers and provide a platform for communication among researchers in the field of *Computer* Aided *Architectural Design*; play an active role in disseminating such progress to the scientific architectural community and architectural practice. **Structure** Board, comprising Chairman, Vice-Chairman/Secretary and Treasurer. **Events** *Conference* Los Angeles, CA (USA) 2021, *Conference* Daejeon (Korea Rep) 2019, *International CAAD Futures Conference* Istanbul (Turkey) 2017, *Global design and local materialization* Sao Paulo (Brazil) 2015, *Conference* Shanghai (China) 2013. **Publications** Conference proceedings. **NGO Relations** Related organizations: *Arab Society for Computer Aided Architectural Design (ASCAAD, #01044); Association for Computer Aided Design in Architecture (ACADIA); Computer Aided Architectural Design Research in Asia (CAADRIA, #04425); Education and research in Computer Aided Architectural Design in Europe (eCAADe, #05373); Sociedad Iberoamericana de Grafica Digital (SIGraDI, #19370).* [2021/XJ6188/f/F]

- ♦ **CAADRIA** Computer Aided Architectural Design Research in Asia (#04425)
- ♦ CAAf – Commission pour les affaires africaines (see: #15795)
- ♦ CAAF – Compassion Africa Aged Foundation (internationally oriented national body)
- ♦ CAAFL – Commonwealth Association of Armed Forces Lawyers (no recent information)
- ♦ **CAAPAS** Confederation of American Associations for the Production of Sustainable Agriculture (#04508)
- ♦ CAAP – Centro Andino de Acción Popular (internationally oriented national body)
- ♦ CAARC – Commonwealth Advisory Aeronautical Research Council (internationally oriented national body)
- ♦ CAAR – Collegium for African American Research (internationally oriented national body)
- ♦ **CAASA** Commercial Aviation Association of Southern Africa (#04201)
- ♦ CAAS – Canadian Association of African Studies (internationally oriented national body)
- ♦ CAAS – Centre for African Area Studies, Kyoto University (internationally oriented national body)
- ♦ **CAAS** Consortium for Asian and African Studies (#04736)
- ♦ C and A – Association for the Promotion of Space Activities in Europe (inactive)
- ♦ **CAATA** Comité Andino de Autoridades de Transporte Acuatico (#04147)
- ♦ CAAT – Campaign Against Arms Trade (internationally oriented national body)
- ♦ CAAWO – Coalition of African Animal Welfare Organisations (internationally oriented national body)
- ♦ CAAYE – Commonwealth Asia Alliance of Young Entrepreneurs (unconfirmed)
- ♦ **CABA** Caribbean AgriBusiness Association (#03434)
- ♦ CABA – Continental Automated Building Association (internationally oriented national body)
- ♦ CaBC / see Caribbean Broadcasting Corporation
- ♦ **CAB** Caribbean Association of Banks (#03443)
- ♦ CABC / see Caribbean Evangelical Theological Association (#03499)
- ♦ CAB – Commonwealth Agricultural Bureaux (inactive)
- ♦ **CAB** Confédération africain de boxe (#00228)
- ♦ CAB – Confédération asiatique de billard (inactive)
- ♦ **CABEI** Central American Bank for Economic Integration (#03658)
- ♦ CABEI / see Comité Intergubernamental Coordinador de los Paises de la Cuenca del Plata (#04172)

♦ CABI 03393

CEO Nosworthy Way, Wallingford, OX10 8DE, UK. T. +441491829215 – +441491832111. Fax +441491833508. E-mail: corporate@cabi.org – enquiries@cabi.org.
URL: http://www.cabi.org/
History 1985. Founded on adoption of *'Agreement on CAB INTERNATIONAL'.* Derives from formation in 1910, London (UK), of the *'Entomological Research Committee (Tropical Africa)'*, with entomologists posted in East Africa and West Africa to collect and study insects injurious to humans, crops and animals. Subsequently other organisms and disciplines were covered and services brought together under the auspices of the Imperial Agricultural Bureaux (IAB), which was formally constituted in 1929. IAB became *Commonwealth Agricultural Bureaux (CAB, inactive)* in 1930. Under the constitution of CAB INTERNATIONAL, the scope changed from being exclusively Commonwealth to fully international, with membership open to any country. Former names and other names: *CAB INTERNATIONAL – Offices agricoes du CAB INTERNATIONAL (CABI)* – former (1986); *Centre for Agricultural Biosciences International* – full title (2008). Registration: EU Transparency Register, No/ID: 02182818502-38, Start date: 4 Apr 2012. **Aims** Improve people's lives worldwide by providing information and applying scientific expertise to solve problems in *agriculture* and the *environment.* **Structure** Review Conference (convened periodically) reviews work programmes and determines broad policies and strategies. Executive Council comprises representatives of each member country; it monitors CABI's affairs and implements Review Conference resolutions. Board is an advisory board which oversees programmes and guides management on operational and strategic issues. Management team is headed by CEO, who is directly accountable to the Chair of Council. Head office: Wallingford (UK). Offices in: Europe (Egham, UK; Delémont, Switzerland); Asia (Rawalpindi, Pakistan; Delhi, India; Serdang, Malaysia; Beijing, China); Africa (Nairobi, Kenya); Americas (Curepe, Trinidad-Tobago; Cambridge MA, USA). Each member designates a National Implementing Agency (NIA) and nominates a Liaison Officer from this NIA who maintains close contact with CABI headquarters and appropriate regional centres. **Languages** English. **Staff** 400.00 FTE, paid.
Finance Member states' contributions (about 2.5% of annual budget); sale of publications; charges for scientific and information services including training courses; contracted or sponsored research; miscellaneous sources. Annual budget: about pounds20 million. Funders include the following:
- *Asia-Pacific Economic Cooperation (APEC, #01887);*
- *Australian Aid (inactive);*
- *Australian Centre for International Agricultural Research (ACIAR);*
- *Centre technique de coopération agricole et rurale (CTA, inactive);*
- *Common Fund for Commodities (CFC, #04293);*
- *Commonwealth Scientific and Industrial Research Organization (CSIRO);*
- *DANIDA;*
- Department for Environment Food and Rural Affairs (DEFRA) – UK;
- *Department for International Development (DFID, inactive);*
- Environment Agency (UK);
- *European Commission (EC, #06633);*
- *Global Environment Facility (GEF, #10346);*
- *Inter-American Institute for Cooperation on Agriculture (IICA, #11434);*
- *International Coffee Organization (ICO, #12630);*
- *International Fund for Agricultural Development (IFAD, #13692);*
- *International Union for Conservation of Nature and Natural Resources (IUCN, #15766);*
- *Swiss Agency for Development and Cooperation (SDC);*
- *UNDP (#20292);*
- *UNESCO (#20322);*
- *United States Agency for International Development (USAID);*
- United States Department of Agriculture (USDA).

Activities Events/meetings; projects/programmes; research/documentation; standards/guidelines. Manages one of the world's largest genetic resource collections of fungus cultures. **Events** *Triennial Review Conference* Egham (UK) 2019, *AFSC : Annual Africa Food Security Conference* Nairobi (Kenya) 2017, *Triennial Review Conference* Egham (UK) 2016, *Triennial Review Conference* Oxford (UK) 2013, *Triennial Review Conference* London (UK) 2011. **Publications** Books; compendia; abstract journals. Information Services: Multimedia compendia; books; e-books; interactive electronic resources. Expertise includes: Agriculture and International Development; Animal Sciences and Veterinary; Environmental Sciences; Human Health and Nutrition; Leisure Tourism; Plant Sciences. **Information Services** *CAB Abstracts* – database covering agriculture and environment.

Members Membership is by invitation from existing members and by application authorized at level of Head of State or Foreign Ministry or by a delegated authority. Governments of 48 countries and territories:
Anguilla, Australia, Bahamas, Bangladesh, Barbados, Bermuda, Botswana, Brunei Darussalam, Burundi, Canada, Chile, China, Colombia, Côte d'Ivoire, Cyprus, Gambia, Ghana, Grenada, Guyana, India, Jamaica, Kenya, Korea DPR, Malawi, Malaysia, Mauritius, Montserrat, Myanmar, Netherlands, Nigeria, Pakistan, Papua New Guinea, Philippines, Rwanda, Sierra Leone, Solomon Is, South Africa, Sri Lanka, St Helena, Switzerland, Tanzania UR, Trinidad-Tobago, Uganda, UK, Vietnam, Virgin Is UK, Zambia, Zimbabwe.

IGO Relations Accredited by (1): *United Nations Framework Convention on Climate Change – Secretariat (UNFCCC, #20564)*. Member of (2): *Asia-Pacific Association of Agricultural Research Institutions (APAARI, #01830)*; *Global Biodiversity Information Facility (GBIF, #10250)*. Instrumental in setting up (1): *BioNET INTERNATIONAL – Global Network for Taxonomy (BI, #03253)*. Special agreement with: *UNESCO (#20322)*. Relationship agreement with: *FAO (#09260)*. Observer Status with: ADB; FAO. *CGIAR System Organization (CGIAR, #03843)*. Accredited to the Conference of the Parties of: *Secretariat of the United Nations Convention to Combat Desertification (Secretariat of the UNCCD, #19208)*. Close links with: *Commonwealth Secretariat (#04362)*. **NGO Relations** Member of (8): *African Smallholder Farmers Group (ASFG, inactive)*; *Asia-Pacific Association of Forestry Research Institutions (APAFRI, #01841)*; *Association of International Research and Development Centers for Agriculture (AIRCA, #02760)*; *Association of Learned and Professional Society Publishers (ALPSP, #02786)*; *CHS Alliance (#03911)*; *International Society for Horticultural Science (ISHS, #15180)*; *International Union of Forest Research Organizations (IUFRO, #15774)*; *ORCID (#17790)*. Cooperates with (2): *Global Forum on Agricultural Research (GFAR, #10370)*; *International Fertilizer Development Center (IFDC, #13590)*. Instrumental in setting up (2): *International Committee on Bionomenclature (ICB, #12748)*; *Tree Pest Management Network for Central, Eastern and Southern Africa (no recent information)*. Member of and hosts: *Global Open Data for Agriculture and Nutrition (GODAN, #10514)*. [2017.06.01/XC0359/**C***]

- ♦ CABI Bureau of Agricultural Economics (inactive)
- ♦ CABI Bureau of Animal Breeding and Genetics (inactive)
- ♦ CABI Bureau of Animal Health (inactive)
- ♦ CABI Bureau of Crop Protection (inactive)
- ♦ CABI Bureau of Dairy Sciences and Technology (inactive)
- ♦ CABI Bureau of Horticulture and Plantation Crops (inactive)
- ♦ CABI Bureau of Plant Breeding and Genetics (inactive)
- ♦ CABI Forestry Bureau (inactive)
- ♦ CAB International Bureau of Nutrition (inactive)
- ♦ CAB International Bureau of Pastures and Field Crops (inactive)
- ♦ CAB International Bureau of Soils (inactive)
- ♦ CAB INTERNATIONAL – Offices agricoes du CAB INTERNATIONAL / see CABI (#03393)
- ♦ Cable Damage Committee / see International Cable Protection Committee (#12423)
- ♦ Cable Europe / see GIGAEurope AISBL (#10151)

♦ CableLabs 03394

Contact 858 Coal Creek Cir, Louisville CO 80027, USA. T. +13036619100. E-mail: info@cablelabs.com.
URL: https://www.cablelabs.com/

History Set up as a non-profit research and development consortium. **Aims** Invent new ways to keep people connected by making *broadband* stronger and cementing the cable network as the platform of choice. **Structure** Board of Directors. **Languages** English. **Staff** 20.00 FTE, paid. **Finance** Funded by cable operators. Annual budget: US$ 70,000,000.

Members Companies in 18 countries:
Austria, Canada, China, Cyprus, Denmark, France, Germany, Indonesia, Japan, Mexico, Netherlands, Norway, Portugal, Singapore, Spain, Sweden, UK, USA.
Also members in South America. Membership countries not specified.

NGO Relations *European Telecommunications Standards Institute (ETSI, #08897)*; *Institute of Electrical and Electronics Engineers (IEEE, #11259)*; *Small Cell Forum (#19312)*; *Wireless Broadband Alliance (WBA, #20969)*; national organizations. [2019.06.03/XJ8747/**D**]

- ♦ Cable and Satellite Broadcasting Association of Asia / see Asia Video Industry Association (#02103)
- ♦ Cable and Telecommunications Association for Marketing / see CTAM Europe (#04978)
- ♦ **CABO** Central American Black Organization (#03659)
- ♦ **CABRI** Collaborative Africa Budget Reform Initiative (#04097)
- ♦ **CABRI** Common Access to Biological Resources and Information (#04291)
- ♦ CABSA – Christian AIDS Bureau for Southern Africa (internationally oriented national body)
- ♦ CABS – Committee Against Bird Slaughter (internationally oriented national body)
- ♦ CABSHFI / see Caribbean Association of Housing Finance Institutions (#03447)
- ♦ CAC / see International Clinical Cytometry Society
- ♦ **CACAARI** Central Asia and the Caucasus Association of Agricultural Research Institutions (#03678)
- ♦ **CACAC** Central American and Caribbean Athletic Confederation (#03661)
- ♦ CA – Cadmium Association (inactive)
- ♦ **CacaoNet** Global Network for Cacao Genetic Resources (#10484)
- ♦ CACBF / see Central American & Caribbean Bridge Federation (#03662)
- ♦ **CAC** Central American & Caribbean Bridge Federation (#03662)
- ♦ **CACCI** Confederation of Asia-Pacific Chambers of Commerce and Industry (#04512)
- ♦ CAC – Coaches Across Continents (internationally oriented national body)
- ♦ **CAC** Codex Alimentarius Commission (#04081)
- ♦ **CAC** Confédération africaine de cyclisme (#04499)
- ♦ **CAC** Confédération africaine des échecs (#00244)
- ♦ **CAC** Confederation of African Canoeing (#04505)
- ♦ CAC – Conseil africain de la comptabilité (no recent information)
- ♦ **CAC** Consejo Agropecuario Centroamericano (#03657)
- ♦ CACESCO – Central American and Caribbean Confederation of Esports (unconfirmed)
- ♦ CACEU – Central African Customs and Economic Union (inactive)
- ♦ **CACF** Central Asian Cellular Forum (#03680)
- ♦ **CACFish** Central Asian and Caucasus Regional Fisheries and Aquaculture Commission (#03679)
- ♦ CACG – Commonwealth Association for Corporate Governance (inactive)
- ♦ CACGP / see International Commission on Atmospheric Chemistry and Global Pollution (#12664)
- ♦ **CACHE** Caribbean Council of Higher Education in Agriculture (#03484)
- ♦ CACI – Conferencia de Autoridades Cinematograficas de Iberoamérica (no recent information)
- ♦ CACI – Conseil atlantique pour la coopération internationale (internationally oriented national body)
- ♦ CACI-SRSP – Central Asia-Caucasus Institute and Silk Road Studies Program (internationally oriented national body)
- ♦ CACLALS / see West Indian Association for Commonwealth Literature and Language Studies (#20921)
- ♦ CACM – Center for Applied Conflict Management (internationally oriented national body)
- ♦ **CACM** Central American Common Market (#03666)
- ♦ CACMF – Central American Common Market Fund (inactive)
- ♦ CACMI – Comité africain pour la coordination des moyens d'information (inactive)
- ♦ CACOFD / see Latin American and Caribbean Conference on Theoretical and Applied Mechanics (#16269)
- ♦ **CA** COPERNICUS Alliance – European Network on Higher Education for Sustainable Development (#04830)
- ♦ CACRA – Caribbean Agricultural Association (inactive)
- ♦ CACR – Caribbean Association for Communication Research (no recent information)
- ♦ **CACSO** Central American and Caribbean Sports Organization (#03665)
- ♦ **CACT** Caribbean Association of Catholic Teachers (#03444)
- ♦ CACTM – Comité d'aide aux calaminois du Tiers-Monde (internationally oriented national body)
- ♦ CACTUSNET FAO / see FAO-ICARDA International Technical Cooperation Network on Cactus (#09262)
- ♦ **CACTUSNET** FAO-ICARDA International Technical Cooperation Network on Cactus (#09262)
- ♦ **CACU** African Confederation of UNESCO Clubs, Centres and Associations (#00264)
- ♦ CAC / see United Nations System Chief Executives Board for Coordination (#20636)
- ♦ CADA – Centre for Africa Democratic Affairs (internationally oriented national body)
- ♦ CADAL – Centro para la Apertura y el Desarrollo de América Latina (internationally oriented national body)
- ♦ CADAP – Centre d'administration du développement pour l'Asie et le Pacifique (inactive)
- ♦ CAD – Comité d'aide au développement de l'OCDE (see: #17693)
- ♦ CAD – Commonwealth Association for Development (no recent information)
- ♦ CADEB – Confederación Americana de Empleados Bancarios (inactive)
- ♦ **CADE** Centre africain pour le développement des engrais (#00241)
- ♦ **CADE** Coordination pour l'Afrique de demain (#04828)
- ♦ **CADEDH** Centre africain pour la démocratie et les études des droits de l'homme (#00239)
- ♦ Cadena de Asadores / see Chaîne des Rôtisseurs – Association Mondiale de la Gastronomie (#03845)
- ♦ Cadena Azul Mundial (#21235)
- ♦ **CADHP** Commission africaine des droits de l'homme et des peuples (#00255)
- ♦ **CADICA** Confederación Atlética del Istmo Centroamericano (#04441)
- ♦ CAD – International CAD Conference (meeting series)
- ♦ Cadmium Association (inactive)
- ♦ CADS / see Confederation of Africa Deaf Sports (#04498)
- ♦ **CADS** Confederation of Africa Deaf Sports (#04498)
- ♦ **CADTM** Comité pour l'annulation de la dette du Tiers-monde (#04148)
- ♦ CAE / see Allied Command Operations (#00731)
- ♦ **CAEC** Conseil africain d'enseignement de la communication (#00273)
- ♦ CAEC – Council for Asia Europe Cooperation (no recent information)
- ♦ CAE – Commission pour les affaires européennes (see: #15795)
- ♦ **CAE** Conseil des Architectes d'Europe (#01086)
- ♦ **CAE/CPLP** Centro de Análise Estratégica da Comunidade dos Países de Língua Portuguesa (#03793)
- ♦ **CAE** Culture Action Europe (#04981)
- ♦ CAEDEL / see Mouvement Europe et laïcité
- ♦ CAEDHU – Centre africain pour l'éducation aux droits humains (internationally oriented national body)
- ♦ **CAEF** European Foundry Association, The (#07352)
- ♦ **CAEI** Congrès des Amériques sur l'éducation internationale (#04581)
- ♦ **CAEI** Congreso de las Américas sobre la Educación Internacional (#04581)
- ♦ **CAEI** Congresso das Américas sobre Educação Internacional (#04581)
- ♦ CAEJAC – Commonwealth Association for Education in Journalism and Communication (no recent information)
- ♦ **CAEMC** Central Africa Economic and Monetary Community (#04374)
- ♦ CAEMC – Comité d'associations européennes de médecins catholiques (inactive)
- ♦ CAEM – Conseil d'assistance économique mutuelle (inactive)
- ♦ CAERD – Centre for African Entrepreneurship Research and Development (internationally oriented national body)
- ♦ **CAERT** Centre Africain d'Etudes et de Recherches sur le Terrorisme (#00236)
- ♦ **CAES** Caribbean Agro-Economic Society (#03437)
- ♦ CAETA – Commonwealth Association for the Education and Training of Adults (inactive)
- ♦ **CAETS** International Council of Academies of Engineering and Technological Sciences (#12982)
- ♦ **CAEU** Council of Arab Economic Unity (#04859)
- ♦ **CAFAC** Commission africaine de l'aviation civile (#00248)
- ♦ **CAFA** Central Asian Football Association (#03681)
- ♦ CAFA – Committee for Academic Freedom in Africa (internationally oriented national body)
- ♦ CAF America – Charities Aid Foundation of America (internationally oriented national body)
- ♦ **CaFAN** Caribbean Farmers Network (#03503)
- ♦ CAF – Canadian Arab Federation (internationally oriented national body)
- ♦ CAF – Charities Aid Foundation (internationally oriented national body)
- ♦ CAfCH – Central African Clearing House (no recent information)
- ♦ CAFCO – Confédération africaine de football corporatif (unconfirmed)
- ♦ **CAF** Common Action Forum (#04292)
- ♦ **CAF** Confédération africaine de football (#04500)
- ♦ CAF / see Development Bank of Latin America (#05055)
- ♦ **CAF** Development Bank of Latin America (#05055)
- ♦ **CAFE** Centre for Access to Football in Europe (#03722)
- ♦ CAFED – Centre africain de formation à l'édition et à la diffusion (internationally oriented national body)
- ♦ CAFEDD / see Centre africain de formation à l'édition et à la diffusion
- ♦ Café Mundial (inactive)
- ♦ Cafés Suaves Centrales (inactive)
- ♦ **CAFF** Conservation of Arctic Flora and Fauna (#04728)
- ♦ CAFICS – Canadian Association of Former International Civil Servants (internationally oriented national body)
- ♦ CAFIM / see Confederation of European Music Industries (#04527)
- ♦ **CAFIM** Confederation of European Music Industries (#04527)
- ♦ CAFIU – Chinese Association for International Understanding (internationally oriented national body)
- ♦ **CAFMET** Comité Africain de Métrologie (#00258)
- ♦ CAFMICRO – Centre africain de formation à la maintenance des équipements de la micro-informatique (internationally oriented national body)
- ♦ CAFMS – Central American Federation of Medical Students (inactive)
- ♦ CAFO – Conference of Asian Foundations and Organizations (unconfirmed)
- ♦ CAFOD / see Catholic Agency for Overseas Development
- ♦ CAFOD – Catholic Agency for Overseas Development (internationally oriented national body)
- ♦ **CAFRA** Caribbean Association for Feminist Research and Action (#03445)
- ♦ **CAFRAD** African Training and Research Centre in Administration for Development (#00486)
- ♦ **CAFRAD** Centre Africain de Formation et de Recherche Administratives pour le Développement (#00486)
- ♦ **CAFRADES** Centre africain de recherche appliquée et de formation en matière de développement social (#00237)
- ♦ CAFS – Caribbean Association of Forensic Scientists (no recent information)
- ♦ **CAFS** Centre for African Family Studies (#03726)
- ♦ **CAFS** Confederation of Asian Futsal (#04510)
- ♦ CAF Southern Africa – Charities Aid Foundation Southern Africa (unconfirmed)
- ♦ CAFTA – Conférence africaine des tarifs aériens (no recent information)
- ♦ CAFTA – US-Central American Free Trade Agreement (2004 treaty)
- ♦ CAF-UNESCO Paris / see Association of Former UNESCO Staff Members (#02601)
- ♦ CAF – UNWTO Commission for Africa (see: #21861)
- ♦ CAFUSA – Confédération Africaine de Futsal (unconfirmed)
- ♦ **CAG** Centre on Asia and Globalisation (#03730)
- ♦ **CAG** Confédération africaine de golf (#00329)
- ♦ CAGE – Centre for Arctic Gas Hydrate, Environment and Climate (internationally oriented national body)

- ♦ CAGH – Canadian Association Global Health (internationally oriented national body)
- ♦ **CAGRIS** Caribbean Information System for the Agricultural Sciences (#03518)
- ♦ **CAGS** Centre for Arab Genomic Studies (#03729)
- ♦ **CAHB** Confédération Africaine de Handball (#04501)
- ♦ CAH – Conference on Asian History (internationally oriented national body)
- ♦ **CAHDI** Committee of Legal Advisers on Public International Law (#04267)
- ♦ **CAHE** Caribbean Association of Home Economists (#03446)
- ♦ **CAHF** Centre for Affordable Housing Finance in Africa (#03723)
- ♦ **CAHFSA** Caribbean Agricultural Health and Food Safety Agency (#03435)
- ♦ CAHI – Caribbean Association for the Hearing Impaired (inactive)
- ♦ CAHIPE – Committee of the Associations of Honey Imports and Packers of Europe (inactive)
- ♦ CAI / see Conserve Africa Foundation
- ♦ CAIA Association – Chartered Alternative Investment Analyst Association (internationally oriented national body)
- ♦ CAIAG – Central-Asian Institute for Applied Geosciences (internationally oriented national body)
- ♦ CAI-Asia / see Clean Air Asia (#03983)
- ♦ CAIB / see Caribbean Association of Banks (#03443)
- ♦ CAIB – Council of Insurance Agents & Brokers (internationally oriented national body)
- ♦ **CAIBI** Conferencia de Autoridades Iberoamericanas de Informatica (#04606)
- ♦ **CAIC** Caribbean Association of Industry and Commerce (#03448)
- ♦ **CAI** Citizens Advice International (#03954)
- ♦ **CAI** Clean Air Initiative for Cities Around the World (#03984)
- ♦ **CAI** Clean Air Institute (#03985)
- ♦ CAI / see Communitas International (#04388)
- ♦ CAI – Consejo Andino de Ingenieria (inactive)
- ♦ CAIDS / see Canadian Association for the Study of International Development
- ♦ **CAIE** Conference of the Americas on International Education (#04581)
- ♦ CAIFC – China Association for International Friendly Contact (internationally oriented national body)
- ♦ CAIL / see Institute for Transnational Arbitration
- ♦ Caillou Blanc (religious order)
- ♦ CAIMED – Centro per l'Innovazione Amministrativa nelle Regione Euro-mediterranea (internationally oriented national body)
- ♦ **CAIPA** Caribbean Association of Investment Promotion Agencies (#03449)
- ♦ CAIP – Commonwealth Association of Indigenous Peoples (internationally oriented national body)
- ♦ Cairdeas – Cairdeas International Palliative Care Trust (internationally oriented national body)
- ♦ Cairdeas International Palliative Care Trust (internationally oriented national body)

♦ Cairns Group 03395

Address not obtained.
URL: http://www.cairnsgroup.org/

History Aug 1986, Cairns (Australia). **Aims** Function as an informal group of *agricultural exporting* countries. **Structure** Includes 'Cairns Group of Farm Leaders'. **Events** *Ministerial Meeting* Bali (Indonesia) 2013, *Ministerial Meeting* Geneva (Switzerland) 2011, *Ministerial Meeting* Saskatoon, SK (Canada) 2011, *Ministerial Meeting* Saskatoon, SK (Canada) 2011, *Ministerial Meeting* Punta del Este (Uruguay) 2010.
Members Governments of 17 countries:
Argentina, Australia, Bolivia, Brazil, Canada, Chile, Colombia, Costa Rica, Guatemala, Indonesia, Malaysia, New Zealand, Paraguay, Philippines, South Africa, Thailand, Uruguay. [2008/XF1159/**F***]

♦ Cairo Demographic Centre (CDC) 03396

Dir 78 St No 4, El-Hadaba Elolya, Mokattam, Cairo, 11571, Egypt. T. +20225080735 – +20225080745. Fax +20225082797. E-mail: info@cdc.edu.eg.
Facebook: https://www.facebook.com/people/Cairo-Demographic-Center/100064758428756/

History 1963, Cairo (Egypt). Founded under an agreement on joint sponsorship between *United Nations (UN, #20515)* and the Government of Egypt. Became an independent establishment of the Egyptian Government, Jan 1992, following termination of this agreement, Dec 1991. **Aims** Provide demographic training to persons working in the field of *population*; undertake research and provide advisory services in population and related fields to interested governments and other organizations. **Structure** Governing Council; Advisory Committee, consisting of representatives of countries served by CDC, scientific bodies and former graduates. **Languages** English. **Staff** 1.00 FTE, paid. **Finance** Funded by the Government of Egypt. Annual budget: 1,000,000 EGP. **Activities** Events/meetings; research/documentation; training/education. Training at 4 levels leads to: (1) General Diploma in Demography; (2) Special Diploma in Population and Development; (3) Master of Philosophy in Demography; (4) Doctor of Philosophy with specialization in Demography. *International Programme of Training in Population and Development (IPTPD)*, also referred to as *International Training Programme in Population and Development*, forms part of UNFPA, previously sponsored by *Global Programme in Population and Sustainable Development (inactive)*. **Events** *Arab regional population conference* Cairo (Egypt) 1996, *Annual seminar* Cairo (Egypt) 1995, *Annual seminar* Cairo (Egypt) 1993, *Annual seminar* Cairo (Egypt) 1992, *Annual seminar* Cairo (Egypt) 1991. **Publications** *CDC Acquisitions List* (4 a year); *CDC Newsletter* (2 a year). *Occasional Paper Series*; *Research Monograph Series*; *Working Paper Series*. Surveys. Manuals. Information Services: Library; computer.
Members Covers 7 countries:
Algeria, Egypt, Senegal, Somalia, Sudan, Tanzania UR, Uganda.
IGO Relations Supports (1): *Bioversity International (#03262)*. Assistance provided by: *United Nations Population Fund (UNFPA, #20612)*. **NGO Relations** Member of (1): *Population Information Network for Africa (POPIN-Africa, no recent information)*. [2022.10.16/XE8585/**E***]

- ♦ Cairo-Gaborone Trans East African Highway Authority (inactive)

♦ Cairo Institute for Human Rights Studies (CIHRS) 03397

Institut du Caire pour les études des droits de l'Homme

Contact 21 rue El Hijaz, Belvédère, 1002 Tunis, Tunisia. E-mail: info@cihrs.org.
URL: http://www.cihrs.org/

History 1993. Officially commenced operations in 1994. **Aims** Focus on analyzing the difficulties facing the application of international human rights law, disseminating a culture of respect for human rights in the region, and engaging in dialogue between cultures regarding various international human rights treaties and declarations. **Structure** General Assembly; Board of Directors; Management Committee. **Languages** Arabic, English, French. **Staff** 38.00 FTE, paid. **Finance** Sources: grants; international organizations; private foundations. Annual budget: 1,500,000 USD (2022). **Activities** Advocacy/lobbying/activism; capacity building; events/meetings; networking/liaising; politics/policy/regulatory; projects/programmes; research/documentation; training/education. Active in: Algeria, Egypt, Libya, Palestine, Syrian AR, Yemen. **Events** *Regional Forum for the Human Rights Movement* Brussels (Belgium) 2022, *Regional Forum for the Human Rights Movement* 2021, *Regional Forum for the Human Rights Movement* 2021, *Regional Forum for the Human Rights Movement* 2020, *Regional Forum for the Human Rights Movement* Brussels (Belgium) 2019. **Publications** *Rowaq Arabi* (periodical) in Arabic, English. *Prospects for Reform in the Arab Region in Post COVID-19 Realities* (2021) in Arabic, English – The freely accessible ebook is a compilation of contributions by ten authors, who explore the question of reform in the Arab world amidst the COVID-19 pandemic and its political and socio-economic ramifications.; *Violations against civilians, including journalists, human rights defenders and academics in Yemen* (2021) in Arabic, English; *Libya 2011: A Democratic Transition Derailed* (2020) in Arabic – In four chapters, seven Libyan researchers, academics and politicians analyse the obstacles to the democratic transition in Libya.; *Tunisia: The Difficult Democratic Transition* (2018) in Arabic – On the 7th anniversary of the Tunisian Revolution, Tunisian researchers and advocates examine crucial aspects of the ongoing transition, including social movements and economic development, the role of women, transitional justice, civil society, Islamic ideologies and movements, the Tunisian constitution, and media freedom.; *Arab Authoritarianism: the Incubators of Terror* (2017) in Arabic, English – This book, to which ten authors as well as CIHRS Director Bahey el-Din Hassan have contributed, analyses the link between the authoritarian policies and practices of most Arab governments on the one hand and the proliferation of terrorism across the region on the other.. *CIHRS Tenth Annual Report: New aspects of human rights crises during the Covid-19 pandemic* (2021) in Arabic, English – The tenth annual report gives a cursory overview of major human rights trends across the Arab world in 2020.; *CIHRS Ninth Annual Report: Evocations of the Arab Spring Amid Newly Drawn Armed Conflicts* (2020) in Arabic, English – The ninth annual report gives a cursory overview of major human rights trends across the Arab world in 2019. Annual Report on Human Rights; statements; open letters; investigative reports; toolkits; ebooks.
Members Board of Directors is composed of 7 leading rights defenders from 5 countries across the Arab region:
Egypt, Morocco, Palestine, Tunisia, Yemen.
Consultative Status Consultative status granted from: *African Commission on Human and Peoples' Rights (ACHPR, #00255)* (Observer); *ECOSOC (#05331)* (Special). **IGO Relations** Observer status with (1): *UNESCO (#20322)*. Associated with Department of Global Communications of the United Nations. **NGO Relations** Member of (2): *EuroMed Rights (#05733)*; *IFEX (#11100)*. Sub-regional member of: *Pan-African Human Rights Defenders Network (AfricanDefenders, #18052)*. [2023.02.23/XE3488/j/**E**]

♦ Cairo Regional Centre for International Commercial Arbitration (CRCICA) 03398

Dir 1 Al Saleh Ayoub Street, Zamalek 11211, Cairo, 11211, Egypt. T. +20227351333 – +20227351335 – +20227351337. Fax +20227351336. E-mail: info@crcica.org – conferences@crcica.org.
Chairman Board of Trustees address not obtained.
URL: http://www.crcica.org/

History 28 Jan 1978. Founded in accordance with decision of 19th Session of *Asian-African Legal Consultative Organization (AALCO, #01303)*, 23 Jan 1978, Doha (Qatar), as part of AALCC's integrated disputes settlement scheme in the economic and commercial field. Accorded privileges diplomatic immunities accorded to international organizations under Headquarters Agreement between AALCC and the Arab Republic of Egypt, Dec 1987. **Aims** Provide a system for settlement of international commercial *disputes* for parties engaged in *trade*, *commerce* and *investments* with and within the *Arabo-African* region; promote international commercial arbitration in the region; provide training so as to procure international arbitrators; coordinate and assist activities of existing arbitration institutions, particularly those in the region; assist countries of the region to harmonize with recent international investment and trade trends and techniques. **Structure** Board of Directors. Branches and institutes: *Alexandria Centre for International Maritime Arbitration (ACIMA)*; *Arab-African Arbitrators Association (no recent information)*; Investment and Arbitration Institute; Cairo (Egypt) Branch of the Chartered Institute of Arbitrators (CIArb); General Secretariat of the *Arab Union of International Arbitration (AUIA, #01068)*; Institute of Investment and Arbitration, set up Jul 1989 as an independent department within the Centre. **Languages** Arabic, English, French. **Finance** Self-allocated financial sources generated from administrative costs of cases. **Activities** Events/meetings; guidance/assistance/consulting. **Events** *Sharm El Sheikh Conference* Sharm el Sheikh (Egypt) 2016, *International conference on banking risk management and dispute settlement* Cairo (Egypt) 2005, *Arab engineering arbitration meeting* Cairo (Egypt) 2004, *International conference on international energy law and practice* Cairo (Egypt) 2004, *International procurement conference* Cairo (Egypt) 2004. **Publications** *Arab Arbitration Journal*; *CIArb Cairo Branch Newsletter*; *CRCICA Newsletter*; *Journal of Arab Arbitration*. *Arbitral Awards of the Cairo Regional Centre for International Commercial Arbitration – Part II* (2002) in Arabic, English. *CRCICA Handbook*. **Information Services** *Electronic data bank on legal information in the fields of international business law, investment and arbitration* in Arabic, English, French. **Members** Countries in the Asian-African Region (not specified). **Consultative Status** Consultative status granted from: *ECOSOC (#05331)* (Ros C); *UNIDO (#20336)*. **NGO Relations** Cooperation agreements (43) with arbitration institutions (not specified). [2020.05.06/XE0624/**E**]

- ♦ CAIS – Centre for Arab and Islamic Studies, Middle East and Central Asia (internationally oriented national body)
- ♦ CAIS / see European Union of Arabists and Islamicists (#08976)
- ♦ Caisse centrale de coopération économique / see Agence française de développement
- ♦ Caisse centrale de la France libre / see Agence française de développement
- ♦ Caisse commune des pensions du personnel des Nations Unies (#20581)
- ♦ Caisse française de développement / see Agence française de développement
- ♦ CAISTC – China Association for International Science and Technology Cooperation (internationally oriented national body)
- ♦ CAJ / see Coalition for Justice and Peace in Africa
- ♦ Caja Común de Pensiones del Personal de las Naciones Unidas (#20581)
- ♦ **CAJ** Comisión Andina de Juristas (#00816)
- ♦ **CAJ** Confederation of ASEAN Journalists (#04509)
- ♦ CALACS – Canadian Association for Latin American and Caribbean Studies (internationally oriented national body)
- ♦ CALA / see Global Council for Anthropological Linguistics (#10310)
- ♦ CALAI / see Conference of Iberoamerican Authorities on Informatics (#04606)
- ♦ Calala – CALALA – Fondo de Mujeres (internationally oriented national body)
- ♦ CALALA – Fondo de Mujeres (internationally oriented national body)
- ♦ Calasantini – Congregazione degli Operai Cristiani di San Giuseppe Calasanzio (religious order)
- ♦ Calasantins – Congrégation des Ouvriers Chrétiens de Saint Joseph Calasanz (religious order)
- ♦ CALB – Confédération africano-levantine de billard (inactive)
- ♦ **CALC** Commonwealth Association of Legislative Counsel (#04304)
- ♦ Calced Carmelites – Carmelite Nuns of the Ancient Observance (religious order)
- ♦ Calcio contro il Razzismo in Europa (#09853)

♦ Calcium Carbonate Association – Europe (CCA-Europe) 03399

SG c/o IMA-Europe, Rue des Deux Eglises 26, 1000 Brussels, Belgium. T. +3222104410. E-mail: secretariat@ima-europe.eu.
URL: http://www.ima-europe.eu/about-ima-europe/associations/cca-europe/

History 11 May 1995, when statutes were adopted. Registered in accordance with Belgian law. **Aims** Provide representation at EU level for the industry; study questions relevant industry, in particular those linked to public health, the environment, improved and standardized working conditions and hygiene, definition of standards and specifications and information on members, users and Community and national regulatory authorities; promote the common interests of member producers; collect, exchange and circulate economic, social and scientific data. **Structure** General Assembly (annual); Administrative Council; Secretariat. **Languages** English. **Staff** 9.00 FTE, paid. **Finance** Members' dues.
Members Companies in 13 countries:
Austria, Belgium, Finland, France, Germany, Italy, Netherlands, Poland, Spain, Sweden, Switzerland, UK, USA.
IGO Relations Cooperates on a regular basis with Directorates-General of: *European Commission (EC, #06633)*. **NGO Relations** Member of: *Industrial Minerals Association – Europe (IMA Europe, #11179)*. Shares office staff with: *European Association of Feldspar Producers (EUROFEL, #06037)*; *European Association of Industrial Silica Producers (EUROSIL, #06082)*; *European Bentonite Producers Association (EUBA, #06328)*; *European Borates Association (EBA, #06382)*; *European Kaolin and Plastic Clays Association (KPC Europe, #07623)*; *European Lime Association (EuLA, #07699)*; *European Speciality Minerals Association (ESMA, #08811)*; *International Diatomite Producers Association (IDPA, #13172)*; *Scientific Association of European Talc Industry (Eurotalc, #19146)*; IMA Europe. Close contact with: *Conseil européen de l'industrie chimique (CEFIC, #04687)*; *Cosmetics Europe – The Personal Care Association (#04852)*; *BUSINESSEUROPE (#03381)*. [2018.09.06/XD4803/**D**]

- ♦ **CAL** Coalition of African Lesbians (#04046)
- ♦ CALCO – International Conference on Algebra and Coalgebra in Computer Science (meeting series)
- ♦ CAL – Confederación Anti-Comunista Latinoamericana (inactive)
- ♦ **CALD** Council of Asian Liberals and Democrats (#04867)
- ♦ Caleb Project / see Initiative 360
- ♦ **CALED** Instituto Latinoamericano y del Caribe de Calidad en Educación Superior a Distancia (#11342)
- ♦ **CALGA** Caribbean Association of Local Government Authorities (#03451)
- ♦ California Institute of Asian Studies / see California Institute of Integral Studies

- ♦ California Institute of Integral Studies (internationally oriented national body)
- ♦ California Institute of International Studies / see World Association of International Studies
- ♦ California Institute of Pan African Studies (internationally oriented national body)
- ♦ California Institution of International Studies / see World Association of International Studies
- ♦ CALM Africa – Children's Rights Advocacy and Lobby Mission – Africa (internationally oriented national body)
- ♦ CALMEADOW / see Calmeadow Charitable Foundation
- ♦ Calmeadow Charitable Foundation (internationally oriented national body)
- ♦ CALM Uganda / see Children's Rights Advocacy and Lobby Mission – Africa
- ♦ Calorie Control Council (internationally oriented national body)
- ♦ Calouste Gulbenkian Foundation (internationally oriented national body)
- ♦ **CALPHAD** Computer Coupling of Phase Diagrams and Thermochemistry (#04426)
- ♦ **CALRAs** Commonwealth Association of Law Reform Agencies (#04303)
- ♦ **CALRE** Conférence des assemblées législatives régionales d'Europe (#04582)
- ♦ CALS – Centre for Asian Legal Studies, Vancouver (internationally oriented national body)
- ♦ CAM / see CAM International
- ♦ **CAMA** Civil Aviation Medical Association (#03964)
- ♦ CAMA' / see Communauté économique et monétaire d'Afrique centrale (#04374)
- ♦ Camaldolese Hermits of the Congregation of Monte Corona (religious order)
- ♦ **CAMAN** Central Asian Foundation for Management Development (#03682)
- ♦ Camara de Comercio de las Américas (inactive)
- ♦ Cámara de Comercio del Caribe para Europa (#03471)
- ♦ Camara de Comercio de los Estados Unidos (internationally oriented national body)
- ♦ Camara de Comercio Internacional (#12534)

♦ Cámara Interamericana de Asociaciones Nacionales de Agentes Marítimos (C.I.A.N.A.M.) 03400

Inter-American Chamber of Shipping Agent National Associations

Sec address not obtained. E-mail: secretaria@cianam.org.
URL: http://www.cianam.org/

Aims Promote, in harmony with the highest Inter-American interests, the rights and interests of the Shipping Agents. **Structure** General Assembly; Board of Directors; Tax Committee. **Activities** Events/meetings. **Publications** *Newsletter.*
Members Organizations in 12 countries:
Argentina, Brazil, Chile, Costa Rica, Ecuador, Guatemala, Mexico, Panama, Paraguay, Peru, Uruguay, USA.
[2020/AA1038/**D**]

- ♦ Câmara Interamericana de Transporte / see International Chamber of the Transport Industry (#12536)
- ♦ Camara Interamericana de Transportes / see International Chamber of the Transport Industry (#12536)
- ♦ Cámara Internacional de la Industria de Transportes (#12536)
- ♦ Câmara Internacional da Indústria de Transportes (#12536)
- ♦ Camara Júnior Internacional (#16168)
- ♦ CAMAS – Confederation of African Medical Associations and Societies (no recent information)
- ♦ CAMAS / see South Atlantic Maritime Area (#19750)
- ♦ CAMA / see Union monétaire de l'Afrique centrale (#20463)
- ♦ Cambia (internationally oriented national body)
- ♦ CAMBIA – Centre for the Application of Molecular Biology to International Agriculture (internationally oriented national body)
- ♦ Cambodia Action (internationally oriented national body)
- ♦ Cambodian Institute for Cooperation and Peace (internationally oriented national body)
- ♦ Cambrai League Treaty (1508 treaty)
- ♦ Cambridge Centre for Christianity Worldwide (internationally oriented national body)

♦ Cambridge Conference for National Mapping Organizations 03401

Conférence de Cambridge des géomètres et des fonctionnaires des instituts géographiques nationaux du monde

Communications Manager c/o Ordnance Survey, Explorer House, Adanac Drive, Southampton, SO16 0AS, UK. T. +443456050505. E-mail: cconf@os.uk.
URL: http://www.cambridgeconference.com/

History 1928, Cambridge (UK), as *Conference of Commonwealth Surveyors – Conférence des géomètres et des fonctionnaires du cadastre du Commonwealth*, known also as *Commonwealth Survey Officers' Conference.* Present title adopted 1994, when it was decided to open the Conference to the most senior staff of all national survey and mapping agencies worldwide. **Aims** Facilitate strategic duscussion between leaders of national mapping and *geospatial* information organizations. **Structure** Not a permanent organization; conferences every 4 years. **Events** *Conference* London (UK) 2020, *Quadrennial conference* Cambridge (UK) 2017, *Quadrennial Conference* Cambridge (UK) 2013, *Quadrennial Conference* Southampton (UK) 2009, *Quadrennial Conference* Cambridge (UK) 2007. **Publications** Conference proceedings (every 4 years). **Members** Attendance varies from Conference to Conference. Invited guests only. Currently covers all countries of the world. [2016.07.08/XF3473/c/**F***]

- ♦ Cambridge Female Education Trust / see CamFed International
- ♦ Cambridge Italian Dialect Syntax-Morphology Meeting (meeting series)
- ♦ CAMCA – Commercial Arbitration and Mediation Center for the Americas (inactive)
- ♦ CAM – CAM International (internationally oriented national body)
- ♦ **CAMC** Caribbean Association of Medical Councils (#03452)
- ♦ CAM – Central African Missions (internationally oriented national body)
- ♦ CAM – Combat Antisemitism Movement (internationally oriented national body)
- ♦ **CAM** Commonwealth Association of Museums (#04305)
- ♦ CaMDA – Caribbean Management Development Association (inactive)

♦ CAMDOC Alliance 03402

Secretariat Rue du Trône 194, 1050 Brussels, Belgium. T. +3226440020.
URL: http://www.camdoc.eu/

History CAM stands for *Complementary and Alternative Medicine.* **Aims** Develop and facilitate integration of well established and respectable CAM-methods into *European* Health Policies so as to provide European citizens with the added value to medicine that CAM provides.
Members International organizations (4):
European Committee for Homeopathy (ECH, #06651); European Council of Doctors for Plurality in Medicine (ECPM, #06816); International Council of Medical Acupuncture and Related Techniques (ICMART, #13046); Internationale Vereinigung Anthroposophischer Ärztegesellschaften (IVAA, #13314). [2015/XJ0712/y/**E**]

- ♦ CAMECO / see Catholic Media Council (#03605)
- ♦ **CAMECO** Catholic Media Council (#03605)
- ♦ CAME – Consejo de Ayuda Mutua Económica (inactive)
- ♦ Camera Europea degli Arbitri Stragiudiziali e degli Esperti d'Europa (internationally oriented national body)
- ♦ Camera Europea degli Arbitri Stragiudiziali e dei Periti Esperti-Consulenti Tecnici / see European Chamber of Extrajudicial Adjudicators and Experts of Europe
- ♦ Camera Europea Esperti / see European Chamber of Extrajudicial Adjudicators and Experts of Europe
- ♦ Camera Internazionale del Film (inactive)
- ♦ CAMES – Chinese Association for Middle East Studies (internationally oriented national body)
- ♦ **CAMES** Conseil africain et malgache pour l'enseignement supérieur (#00364)
- ♦ CamFed / see CamFed International
- ♦ CamFed International (internationally oriented national body)
- ♦ CAMHADD / see Commonwealth Association for Health and Disability (#04302)
- ♦ **CAMHR** Council of Arab Ministers for Housing and Reconstruction (#04862)
- ♦ CAMI / see Arab Interior Ministers' Council (#00990)
- ♦ CAM-I / see Consortium for Advanced Management – International (#04734)
- ♦ **CAM-I** Consortium for Advanced Management – International (#04734)
- ♦ Camilliani – Ordine dei Chierici Regolari Ministri degli Infermi (religious order)
- ♦ Camillians – Order of the Servants of the Sick (religious order)
- ♦ **CAMILLIANUM** Istituto Internazionale di Teologia Pastorale Sanitaria (#13906)
- ♦ Camilliens – Ordre de Saint-Camille de Lellis (religious order)
- ♦ Camilliens – Ordre des Serviteurs des Malades (religious order)
- ♦ Caminos de Arte Rupestre Prehistórico (#18478)
- ♦ El Camino de la Vida (#19901)
- ♦ CAM International (internationally oriented national body)
- ♦ CAMLOG Foundation / see Oral Reconstruction Foundation (#17781)
- ♦ CAMMINA – Alianza para las Migraciones en Centroamérica y México (unconfirmed)
- ♦ **CAMOC** ICOM International Committee for the Collections and Activities of Museums of Cities (#11056)
- ♦ Campagne pour une Assemblée parlementaire de l'ONU (#03406)
- ♦ La campagne Interdire terminator (#03172)
- ♦ Campagne internationale pour la contraception, l'avortement et la stérilisation / see Women's Global Network for Reproductive Rights (#21019)

♦ Campagne Internationale de l'Ordre de Malte contre la lèpre (Fondation CIOMAL) 03403

Main Office Chemin du Petit Saconnex 28-A, 1209 Geneva, Switzerland. T. +41227332252. Fax +41227340060. E-mail: info@ciomal.org.
URL: https://ciomal.org/

History 22 Oct 1958, Geneva (Switzerland). Founded following the Conférence internationale pour la Défense et la Réhabilitation sociale des Lépreux. Comes within the framework of *Sovereign Military Hospitaller Order of St John of Jerusalem, of Rhodes and of Malta (SMOM).* Statutes revised 22 Apr 1999. Former names and other names: *International Committee of the Order of Malta for Leprosy Relief* – former (22 Oct 1958 to 1999); *Comité exécutif international de l'Ordre de Malte pour l'assistance aux lépreux (CIOMAL)* – former (22 Oct 1958 to 1999); *International Committee of the Order of Malta* – former (1999); *Comité international de l'Ordre de Malte (CIOMAL)* – former (1999). Registration: Switzerland. **Aims** Provide *medical* and social assistance for leprosy sufferers and aid their *rehabilitation.* **Structure** Executive Committee, comprising President and 12 members. Council. Technical Adviser. Secretary-General. **Finance** Sources: subsidies from some national member associations of SMOM; grants and fund-raising activity in Switzerland. Budget (annual): Swiss Fr 700,000. **Activities** Assists in national anti-leprosy programmes; provides medicine, bandages, vehicles and building maintenance for treatment centres and dispensaries; provides training for medical and paramedical staff; assists research institutes. **Consultative Status** Consultative status granted from: *ECOSOC (#05331)* (Special). [2022/XE0809/**E**]

- ♦ Campagne internationale pour mettre fin aux génocides / see Alliance Against Genocide (#00655)
- ♦ Campagne mondiale pour l'éducation (#10264)
- ♦ Campagne mondiale en faveur de la ratification de la Convention sur les droits des migrants / see Global Campaign for Ratification of the Convention on the Rights of Migrant Workers (#10267)
- ♦ Campagne mondiale en faveur de la ratification de la Convention sur les droits des travailleurs migrants (#10267)
- ♦ Campagne du sommet du microcrédit (#16743)
- ♦ Campagne vêtements propres: les droits de l'homme dans le travail (#03986)
- ♦ Campagne des villes européennes durables (#08863)
- ♦ Campaign Against Arms Trade (internationally oriented national body)
- ♦ Campaign for Development and Solidarity (internationally oriented national body)
- ♦ Campaign for Female Education / see CamFed International
- ♦ Campaign to Free Mordechai Vanunu and for a Nuclear-Free Middle East / see Campaign for a Nuclear-Free Middle East
- ♦ Campaign for Innocent Victims in Conflict / see Center for Civilians in Conflict
- ♦ Campaign for an Interamerican Convention on Sexual and Reproductive Rights (internationally oriented national body)
- ♦ Campaign for International Cooperation and Disarmament (internationally oriented national body)
- ♦ Campaign for Nuclear Disarmament (internationally oriented national body)
- ♦ Campaign for a Nuclear-Free Middle East (internationally oriented national body)

♦ Campaign For Safer Alternatives (CASA) 03404

Contact PO Box 43109, Nairobi, 00100, Kenya. E-mail: info@safer-alternatives.org.
URL: https://safer-alternatives.org/

Aims Achieve 100% smoke free environments in Africa. **Activities** Advocacy/lobbying/activism; awareness raising; capacity building; research/documentation.
Members Organizations in 8 countries:
Burkina Faso, Congo Brazzaville, Congo DR, Kenya, Liberia, Malawi, Nigeria, Uganda.
NGO Relations Member of (1): *International Network of Nicotine Consumer Organisations (INNCO, #14298).* Partner of (1): *World Vapers' Alliance (WVA, #21899).* [2020/AA1325/**F**]

♦ Campaign to Stop Killer Robots 03405

Global Coordinator Human Rights Watch, 350 Fifth Ave, 34th floor, New York NY 10118-3299, USA. T. +12126124360.
URL: http://www.stopkillerrobots.org/

History Apr 2013. **Aims** Ban fully autonomous *weapons.* **Structure** Steering Committee.
Members International, regional and national NGOs in 23 countries:
Afghanistan, Austria, Cameroon, Canada, Egypt, Finland, Georgia, Germany, India, Ireland, Italy, Japan, Libya, Netherlands, New Zealand, Nigeria, Norway, Pakistan, South Africa, Spain, Sweden, UK, USA.
Included in the above, 19 organizations listed in this Yearbook:
Amnesty International (AI, #00801); Article 36; Campaign Against Arms Trade (CAAT); Foundation for Peace, Humanity and Inclusion (HI, #10975); Human Rights Watch (HRW, #10990); International Committee for Robot Arms Control (ICRAC, #12803); International Peace Bureau (IPB, #14535); Nobel Women's Initiative (#17144); Norwegian Peace Association (NPA); PAX; Peace Union of Finland; Pugwash Conferences on Science and World Affairs (#18574); Seguridad Humana en América Latina y el Caribe (SEHLAC, #19218); Swedish Peace and Arbitration Society (SPAS); War on Want; Washington Office on Latin America (WOLA); Women's International League for Peace and Freedom (WILPF, #21024). [2014/XJ8318/y/**F**]

- ♦ Campaign for Tobacco-Free Kids (internationally oriented national body)

♦ Campaign for a UN Parliamentary Assembly (UNPA Campaign) 03406

Campagne pour une Assemblée parlementaire de l'ONU – Campaña para una Asamblea Parlamentaria en la ONU – Kampagne für ein Parlament bei der UNO

Global Coordinator c/o Democracy Without Borders, Pariser Platz 6, 10117 Berlin, Germany. T. +493013881634. E-mail: contact@unpacampaign.org.
URL: https://www.unpacampaign.org/

History Based on the international appeal for the establishment of a parliamentary assembly at the UN, published 2007. **Aims** Mobilize governmental, parliamentary, civil society and public support for the establishment of a UNPA. **Structure** Secretariat, hosted by: *Democracy Without Borders (DWB).* **Activities** Advocacy/lobbying/activism; events/meetings. [2023.02.14/XM6143/y/**E**]

- ♦ Campaign for UN Reform / see Citizens for Global Solutions
- ♦ Campaign Whale (internationally oriented national body)
- ♦ CaMPAM – Caribbean Marine Protected Areas Management Network (internationally oriented national body)
- ♦ Campaña de la Cumbre de Microcrédito (#16743)
- ♦ Campaña Internacional sobre la Contracepción, el Aborto y la Esterilización / see Women's Global Network for Reproductive Rights (#21019)

♦ Campaña Internacional para Eliminar el Genocidio / see Alliance Against Genocide (#00655)

♦ Campaña Latinoamericana por el Derecho a la Educación (CLADE) . 03407

Latin-American Campaign for the Right to Education

Gen Coordinator Av Professor Alfonso Bovero 430, Perdizes, Sao Paulo SP, 01254-000, Brazil. T. +551138537900. E-mail: clade@redclade.org.
URL: https://redclade.org/

History 2002. Acquired legal status, 2010. **Aims** Act in defence of the right to transformative, secular and free public quality education for all throughout life as a State responsibility; contribute to the debate and implementation of the Education 2030 Agenda in LAC, as well as carry out advocacy strategies targeting educational policies of Latin-American countries and of the region as a whole. **Structure** General Assembly; Board; Executive Coordination; Working Groups. **Languages** English, Portuguese, Spanish. **Staff** 8.00 FTE, paid. **Finance** Financed by international agencies and NGOs, including: *ActionAid (#00087); EDUCO; Global Partnership for Education (GPE, #10531); Institut für Internationale Zusammenarbeit des Deutschen Volkshochschul-Verbandes (DVV-International); Studentenes og Akademikernes Internasjonale Hjelpefond (SAIH); UNESCO Regional Bureau for Education in Latin America and the Caribbean (#20318); UNICEF (#20332)* – Latin America and Caribbean Office. **Activities** Advocacy/lobbying/activism; research/documentation; awareness raising; events/meetings.

Members National forums, regional networks and organizations including the following 2 listed in this Yearbook:
ActionAid (#00087); Consejo de Educación de Adultos de América Latina (CEAAL, #04707).

Consultative Status Consultative status granted from: *UNESCO (#20322)* (Consultative Status). **IGO Relations** Member of the Board of: *Global Partnership for Education (GPE, #10531).* Cooperation agreement with: *Coordinación Educativa y Cultural Centroamericana (CECC, #04803).* **NGO Relations** Member of: *Global Campaign for Education (GCE, #10264); International Council for Adult Education (ICAE, #12983).*
[2020.01.07/XJ0242/y/**F**]

♦ Campaña del Milenio (#20709)
♦ Campaña Mundial por la Educación (#10264)
♦ Campaña mundial por la ratificación de la Convención sobre los derechos de los trabajadores migratorios (#10267)
♦ Campaña Ropa Limpia (#03986)
♦ Campaña Terminar Terminator (#03172)
♦ Campaña para una Asamblea Parlamentaria en la ONU (#03406)
♦ Campaña por una Convención Interamericana de los Derechos Sexuales y los Derechos Reproductivos (internationally oriented national body)
♦ Campanha Internacional para Eliminar o Genocidio / see Alliance Against Genocide (#00655)

♦ Campbell Collaboration 03408

CEO PO Box 4404 Nydalen, 0403 Oslo, Norway. E-mail: info@campbellcollaboration.org.
Pres Ottawa Hosp Research Inst, 1053 Carling Ave, Ottawa ON K1Y 4E9, Canada.
URL: http://campbellcollaboration.org/

History 2000, in honour of Dr Donald T Campbell (1916-1996), following a meeting 1999, London (UK). Previously known with acronym *C2*. **Aims** Promote positive social and economic change through production and use of systematic reviews and other evidence syntheses for evidence-based policy and practice. **Structure** Board; Coordinating Groups (9); International Secretariat. **Languages** English. **Finance** Local financing, with central activities supported by Norwegian government agencies. **Activities** Research/documentation; knowledge management/information dissemination; events/meetings; training/education. **Events** *Annual Colloquium* Belfast (UK) 2014, *Annual Colloquium* Chicago, IL (USA) 2013, *Annual Colloquium* Copenhagen (Denmark) 2012, *Annual Colloquium* Washington, DC (USA) 2011, *Annual Colloquium* Keystone, CO (USA) 2010. **Publications** *Campbell Newsletter*, *Campbell Systematic Reviews*. Goordinating Group newsletters Methods series. Policies; guidelines. **Information Services** *Campbell Library*.

Members Full in 11 countries:
Australia, Canada, Denmark, Germany, India, Ireland, Netherlands, Norway, UK, USA, Venezuela.

NGO Relations Partner of (1): *International Initiative for Impact Evaluation (3ie, #13851).*
[2017.10.13/XJ1075/**F**]

♦ **CAMP** Cybersecurity Alliance for Mutual Progress (#04987)

♦ Camphill Movement 03409

Dir 17-21 East Mayfield, Edinburgh, EH9 1SE, UK. E-mail: info@camphillscotland.org.uk.
URL: http://www.camphillscotland.org.uk/

History 1939, Aberdeen (UK), by Austrian refugees. Former names and other names: *Camphill Worldwide* – former. Registration: OSCR, No/ID: SC024428, Scotland. **Aims** Create *communities* in which children and adults, many with *learning disabilities*, can live, learn and work together based on mutual care and respect. **Structure** Each Camphill community is independently registered. **Finance** Sources: donations; fees for services; gifts, legacies; government support; in-kind support; members' dues; private foundations; revenue from activities/projects; sale of products. **Activities** Guidance/assistance/consulting; training/education. **Publications** Annual Review.

Members Camphill communities (107) in 24 countries:
Austria, Botswana, Canada, Czechia, Estonia, Finland, France, Germany, Hungary, India, Ireland, Italy, Latvia, Lithuania, Netherlands, Norway, Poland, Russia, South Africa, Sweden, Switzerland, UK, USA, Vietnam.

NGO Relations *International Communal Studies Association (ICSA, #12813).* [2020.10.15/XF4634/**F**]

♦ Camphill Worldwide / see Camphill Movement (#03409)
♦ CAMPSF – Comité d'aide médicale et de parrainage sans frontières (internationally oriented national body)
♦ Campus Crusade for Christ International (internationally oriented national body)
♦ Campus européens de l'environnement
♦ CAMRDC – Central African Mineral Resources Development Centre (no recent information)
♦ **CAMRE** Council of Arab Ministers Responsible for the Environment (#04863)
♦ CAMRODD – Caribbean Association on Mental Retardation and Other Developmental Disabilities (inactive)
♦ **CAMSE** Caribbean Association of Small and Medium Enterprises (#03459)
♦ CAMTRI / see Americas Triathlon (#00795)
♦ **CAMU** Central African Monetary Union (#20463)
♦ Camunian Center for Prehistoric Studies (internationally oriented national body)
♦ CAM – UNWTO Commission for the Americas (see: #21861)
♦ CAMWORK – Caribbean Association of Media Workers (inactive)
♦ **CANA** Caribbean News Agency (#03530)
♦ **CANACOM** Caribbean and North American Council for Mission (#03531)
♦ **CANA** Confédération africaine de natation amateur (#04502)
♦ Canada Africa Partnership on AIDS / see Canada Africa Partnership Network
♦ Canada Africa Partnership Network (internationally oriented national body)
♦ Canada – Central America Four Free Trade Agreement (unconfirmed)

♦ Canada-Europe Roundtable for Business (CERT) 03410

Forum sur le commerce Canada-Europe (FORCCE)

Secretariat 4000 – 199 Bay Str, Commerce Court West, Toronto ON M5L 1A9, Canada. T. +14163627143. Fax +14168635270. E-mail: info@canada-europe.org.
Europe Avenue de Messidor 208 – box 1, 1180 Brussels, Belgium. T. +3223445949. Fax +3223445343.
URL: http://canada-europe.org/

History 16 Jun 1999. EU Transparency Register: 468830015802-86. **Aims** Create business opportunities between Canada and the European Union. **Structure** Steering Committee. [2017/XM5443/**E**]

♦ Canada World Youth (internationally oriented national body)
♦ CANADEM – Canadian Resource Bank for Democracy and Human Rights (internationally oriented national body)
♦ Canadian Arab Federation (internationally oriented national body)
♦ Canadian Association of African Studies (internationally oriented national body)
♦ Canadian Association of Former International Civil Servants (internationally oriented national body)
♦ Canadian Association Global Health (internationally oriented national body)
♦ Canadian Association for Global Health Research / see Canadian Association Global Health
♦ Canadian Association of International Development Studies / see Canadian Association for the Study of International Development
♦ Canadian Association for Latin American and Caribbean Studies (internationally oriented national body)
♦ Canadian Association of Slavists (internationally oriented national body)
♦ Canadian Association for the Study of International Development (internationally oriented national body)
♦ Canadian Baptist International Ministries / see Canadian Baptist Ministries
♦ Canadian Baptist Ministries (internationally oriented national body)
♦ Canadian Baptist Overseas Mission Board / see Canadian Baptist Ministries
♦ Canadian Bureau for International Education (internationally oriented national body)
♦ Canadian Catholic Organization for Development and Peace / see Development and Peace
♦ Canadian Centre for International Studies and Cooperation (internationally oriented national body)
♦ Canadian Civilian Standby Support for UN Operations / see Canadian Resource Bank for Democracy and Human Rights
♦ Canadian Council for International Co-operation / see Cooperation Canada
♦ Canadian Council on International Law (internationally oriented national body)
♦ Canadian Council for Refugees (internationally oriented national body)
♦ Canadian Council for Southeast Asian Studies (internationally oriented national body)
♦ Canadian Crossroads International (internationally oriented national body)
♦ Canadian Disarmament Information Service (internationally oriented national body)
♦ Canadian Ecumenical Justice Initiatives (internationally oriented national body)
♦ Canadian Executive Service Organization (internationally oriented national body)
♦ Canadian Feminist Alliance for International Action (internationally oriented national body)
♦ Canadian Foodgrains Bank (internationally oriented national body)
♦ Canadian Friends Service Committee (internationally oriented national body)
♦ Canadian Human Rights Foundation / see Equitas – International Centre for Human Rights Education
♦ Canadian Information Centre for International Credentials (internationally oriented national body)
♦ Canadian Initiative for Nordic Studies / see Canadian Institute for Nordic Studies
♦ Canadian Institute of International Affairs (internationally oriented national body)
♦ Canadian Institute for International Order (internationally oriented national body)
♦ Canadian Institute for Nordic Studies (internationally oriented national body)
♦ Canadian Institute of Strategic Studies (internationally oriented national body)
♦ Canadian International Demining Centre / see Canadian International Demining Corps
♦ Canadian International Demining Corps (internationally oriented national body)
♦ Canadian and International Education Society of Canada / see Comparative and International Education Society of Canada
♦ Canadian International Institute of Applied Negotiation (internationally oriented national body)
♦ Canadian Lawyers Association for International Human Rights / see Canadian Lawyers for International Human Rights
♦ Canadian Lawyers for International Human Rights (internationally oriented national body)
♦ Canadian Lutheran World Relief (internationally oriented national body)
♦ Canadian Network for International Surgery (internationally oriented national body)
♦ Canadian Organization for Development through Education / see CODE
♦ Canadian Peace Alliance (internationally oriented national body)
♦ Canadian Peacebuilding Coordinating Committee (internationally oriented national body)
♦ Canadian Peace Research and Education Association (internationally oriented national body)
♦ Canadian Physicians for Aid and Relief (internationally oriented national body)
♦ Canadian Physicians for the Prevention of Nuclear War / see Physicians for Global Survival, Canada
♦ Canadian Resource Bank for Democracy and Human Rights (internationally oriented national body)
♦ Canadian Society for International Health / see Canadian Association Global Health
♦ Canadian Society for Tropical Medicine and International Health / see Canadian Association Global Health
♦ Canadian Standards Association (internationally oriented national body)
♦ Canadian University Service Overseas / see Cuso International
♦ Canadian Voice of Women for Peace (internationally oriented national body)
♦ Canarian Institute for International Law Studies (internationally oriented national body)
♦ **CANARI** Caribbean Natural Resources Institute (#03525)
♦ CANASO – Central African Network of AIDS Service Organizations (see: #00272)

♦ CAN in Automation (CiA) 03411

Contact Kontumazgarten 3, 90429 Nürburg, Germany. T. +499119288190. Fax +4991192881979. E-mail: headquarters@can-cia.org.
URL: http://www.can-cia.org/

History 1992. Former names and other names: *CAN in Automation – international users' and manufacturers group* – full title. Registration: Germany. **Aims** Provide technical, product and marketing information; promote the image of Controller Area Network (CAN) and provide a path for future developments of the CAN protocol. **Structure** General Assembly; Board of Directors; Technical Committee with Interest Groups; Business Committee with Marketing Groups. **Languages** English. **Staff** 16.00 FTE, paid. **Finance** Sources: members' dues. Annual budget: 1,000,000 EUR. **Activities** Events/meetings; standards/guidelines; training/education. **Events** *International CAN Conference* Vienna (Austria) 2015, *International CAN Conference / CAN Conference* Paris (France) 2013, *International CAN Conference* Neustadt-Weinstrasse (Germany) 2012, *CAN Conference* Barcelona (Spain) 2008, *CAN Conference* Stockholm (Sweden) 2006. **Publications** *CAN Newsletter*. Product guides. **Members** Companies (about 640). Membership countries not specified. [2020.11.18/XJ6670/**F**]

♦ CAN in Automation – international users' and manufacturers group / see CAN in Automation (#03411)
♦ **CAN** CBR Africa Network (#03616)
♦ CANCEE / see Climate Action Network Eastern Europe, Caucasus and Central Asia (#04000)

♦ Cancer Core Europe (CCE) 03412

Contact address not obtained. E-mail: info@cancercoreeurope.eu.
URL: https://cancercoreeurope.eu/

History 2014. **Aims** Connect and unite innovative centers of excellence so as to more rapidly translate cancer discovery to the clinic for the benefit of patients. **Structure** Board of Directors; Operational Board. **Activities** Research and development. **Events** *Annual Meeting* Stockholm (Sweden) 2021.

Members Research institutes (7) in countries:
France, Germany, Italy, Netherlands, Spain, Sweden, UK. [AA2449/**F**]

♦ Cancer Drug Development Forum (CDDF) 03413

Exec Dir c/o BLSI, Clos Chapelle-aux-Champs 30, 1200 Sint-Lambrechts-Woluwe, Belgium. T. +3228806270. E-mail: info@cddf.org.
URL: http://cddf.org/

History 2001. Former names and other names: *Biotherapy Development Association (BDA)* – former. Registration: Banque-Carrefour des Entreprises, No/ID: 0738.523.752, Start date: 28 Nov 2019, Belgium; Austria. **Aims** Facilitate collaboration between stakeholders, increase efficiency in cancer drug development and accelerate delivery of effective oncology treatment to patients. **Structure** Board of Directors; Administrative Office located in Brussels (Belgium). **Languages** English. **Staff** 2.00 FTE, paid. **Finance** Sources: donations; grants; meeting proceeds; members' dues. **Activities** Events/meetings. **Events** *Immunotherapy of Cancer Conference* Munich (Germany) 2021, *Spring Conference* Noordwijk (Netherlands) 2021, *Immunotherapy of Cancer Conference* Munich (Germany) 2020, *Spring Conference* Noordwijk-aan-Zee (Netherlands) 2020, *Immunotherapy of Cancer Conference* Vienna (Austria) 2019. **Publications** Articles; meeting reports; press releases. **NGO Relations** Cooperates with (4): *European Cancer Patient Coalition (ECPC, #06433); European*

Federation of Pharmaceutical Industries and Associations (EFPIA, #07191); European Organisation for Research and Treatment of Cancer (EORTC, #08101); Workgroup of European Cancer Patient Advocacy Networks (WECAN, #21054). Instrumental in setting up (1): *ACCELERATE (#00046).* [2023/XM5172/**F**]

♦ Cancer International Research Group / see Translational Research In Oncology

♦ Cancer and the Kidney International Network (C-KIN) 03414

Headquarters c/o UZ Leuven, Herestraat 49, 3000 Leuven, Belgium. T. +3216344580. Fax +3216344599.
Exec Sec address not obtained.
Events – Conference Coordinator address not obtained.
URL: http://www.c-kin.org/

History Mar 2014. **Aims** Improve patient care through better knowledge, education and awareness on cancer and the kidney related issues and research. **Structure** General Assembly. Governing Board, comprising Executive Committee and Council. Working Groups. **Languages** English. **Staff** 4.00 FTE, paid. **Finance** Sources: members' dues. **Activities** Events/meetings. **Events** *Annual Conference* Brussels (Belgium) 2016, *Annual Conference* Brussels (Belgium) 2015.
Members Full in 5 countries:
Belgium, Brazil, France, Poland, USA. [2017/XJ8377/**C**]

♦ Cancer and Primary Care Research International Network (Ca-PRI) . 03415

Contact Usher Inst – Univ of Edinburgh – NINE, 9 Little France Road, Edinburgh BioQuarter, Edinburgh, EH16 4UX, UK.
URL: http://www.ca-pri.org/

History Founded 2008. **Aims** Promote greater international collaboration in primary care and cancer research. **Structure** Executive Committee. **Activities** Events/meetings. **Events** *Annual Meeting* Toronto, ON (Canada) 2019, *Annual Meeting* Groningen (Netherlands) 2018, *Annual Meeting* Edinburgh (UK) 2017, *Annual Meeting* Boston, MA (USA) 2016, *Annual Meeting* Aarhus (Denmark) 2015. **NGO Relations** Associated member of: *European Forum for Primary Care (EFPC, #07326).* [2019/XM7518/**F**]

♦ **CAN** Climate Action Network (#03999)
♦ CAN – Community Action in Europe Network (inactive)
♦ **CANDI** Caribbean Association of Nutritionists and Dietitians (#03456)
♦ Candid (internationally oriented national body)
♦ Candid Foundation (internationally oriented national body)
♦ Candidus et Canonicus Ordo Praemonstratensis (religious order)
♦ CANDIS – Canadian Disarmament Information Service (internationally oriented national body)
♦ CANEEE / see Climate Action Network Eastern Europe, Caucasus and Central Asia (#04000)
♦ **CANENA** Consejo de Armonización de Normas Electrotécnicas de las Naciones en las Américas (#04700)
♦ **CANENA** Council for Harmonization of Electrotechnical Standards of the Nations in the Americas (#04700)
♦ **CAN Europe** Climate Action Network Europe (#04001)
♦ Canine Science Forum (meeting series)
♦ **CANLA** Climate Action Network Latin America (#04002)
♦ **CANOC** Caribbean Association of National Olympic Committees (#03454)
♦ Canolfan y Dechnoleg Amgen (internationally oriented national body)
♦ Canolfan Diwylliannau Traddodiadol a Rhanbarthol Ewrop / see European Centre for Training and Regional Cooperation (#06503)
♦ Canolfan Efrydiau Datblygu, Abertawe (internationally oriented national body)
♦ Canolfan Hyfforddiant a Diwylliannau Rhanbarthol Ewrop (#06503)
♦ Canolfan Materion Rhyngwladol Cymru (internationally oriented national body)
♦ Canon Collins Educational and Legal Assistance Trust (internationally oriented national body)
♦ Canon Collins Educational Trust for Southern Africa / see Canon Collins Educational and Legal Assistance Trust
♦ Canon Collins Trust Education for Southern Africa / see Canon Collins Educational and Legal Assistance Trust
♦ Canonichesse Regolari Ospedaliere della Misericordia di Gesù dell'Ordine di San Agostino (religious order)
♦ Canonici Regolari Premostratensi (religious order)
♦ Canonici Regolari di San Agostino Confederati (religious order)
♦ Canonici Regolari della Santa Croce (religious order)
♦ Canons Regular of the Immaculate Conception (religious order)
♦ Canons Regular of the Order of the Holy Cross (religious order)
♦ Canons of St Victor (inactive)
♦ Canopy (internationally oriented national body)
♦ Canopy Planet / see Canopy
♦ Canossian Daughters of Charity (religious order)
♦ Canossiani – Figli della Carità – Canossiani (religious order)
♦ Canossian International Voluntary Service / see Fondazione Canossiana Voica
♦ Canossian International Volunteers / see Fondazione Canossiana Voica
♦ Canossians – Sons of Charity – Canossians (religious order)
♦ Canossiens – Fils de la Charité – Canossiens (religious order)
♦ **CANPA** Caribbean Alliance of National Psychological Associations (#03438)
♦ **CANQATE** Caribbean Area Network for Quality Assurance in Tertiary Education (#03441)
♦ **CANSA** Climate Action Network South Asia (#04003)
♦ **CANS** Caribbean Association of Neurological Surgeons (#03455)
♦ **CANSEA** Climate Action Network South East Asia (#04004)
♦ **CANSO** Civil Air Navigation Services Organisation (#03963)

♦ CANTO 03416

SG 67 Picton Street, Newton, Port-of-Spain, Trinidad-Tobago. T. +18686223770 – +18686227448 – +18686220929. Fax +18686223751. E-mail: canto@canto.org.
URL: http://www.canto.org/

History Apr 1985, Port-of-Spain (Trinidad-Tobago), at inaugural conference. Formerly known as *Caribbean Association of National Telecommunications Organizations.* Now known only by acronym. **Aims** Influence innovation and development of *ICT* solutions. **Structure** General Assembly; Board of Directors; Finance Advisory Committee; Ad-hoc Working Committees; Secretariat, headed by Secretary General. **Languages** English, French, Papiamento, Spanish. **Staff** 9.00 FTE, paid. **Finance** Members' dues. Other sources: advertising revenue; corporate sponsorships; sales of publications; proceeds of annual trade exhibition. Annual budget: about US$ 400,000. **Activities** Networking/liaising; advocacy/lobbying/activism; events/meetings; knowledge management/information dissemination. **Events** *Annual General Meeting* Georgetown (Guyana) 2019, *Annual General Meeting* Port-of-Spain (Trinidad-Tobago) 2018, *Annual Conference* Punta Cana (Dominican Rep) 2017, *Annual General Meeting* Willemstad (Curaçao) 2017, *Annual Conference* Punta Cana (Dominican Rep) 2006. **Publications** *Cancion* (4 a year) – newsletter; *CANTO Connect Newsletter* (irregular); *CANTO Annual Directory.* Press releases. Information Services: CANTO database. **Information Services** *CANTO* – database.
Members Full; Associate; Honorary. Members in 35 countries and territories:
Anguilla, Antigua-Barbuda, Aruba, Bahamas, Barbados, Belgium, Belize, Bermuda, Bonaire Is, Canada, Cayman Is, Costa Rica, Cuba, Curaçao, Dominica, Grenada, Guiana Fr, Guyana, Haiti, Ireland, Jamaica, Jersey, Puerto Rico, St Kitts-Nevis, St Lucia, St Maarten, St Vincent-Grenadines, Suriname, Tortola Is, Trinidad-Tobago, Turks-Caicos, Uruguay, USA, Venezuela, Virgin Is UK.
IGO Relations Cooperates with: *International Telecommunication Union (ITU, #15673).* Formal contacts with: *Sistema Económico Latinoamericano (SELA, #19294).* Support from: *Commonwealth Telecommunications Organisation (CTO, #04365).* **NGO Relations** Affiliate of: *Internet Society (ISOC, #15952).* [2017.10.12/XD0874/**D**]

♦ CANVAS – Center for Applied Nonviolent Action and Strategies (internationally oriented national body)
♦ Canvas Products Association International / see Industrial Fabrics Association International (#11174)
♦ CANWFZ – Treaty on a Nuclear-Weapon-Free Zone in Central Asia (2006 treaty)

♦ CANZUK International 03417

Chief Exec address not obtained. E-mail: admin@canzukinternational.com.
URL: https://www.canzukinternational.com/

History Jan 2015. Former names and other names: *Commonwealth Freedom of Movement Organisation* – former. Registration: Canada. **Aims** Promote reciprocal migration, free trade and foreign policy coordination between Canada, Australia, New Zealand and the United Kingdom (the "CANZUK" countries). **Structure** Executive Board of Directors; Advisory Board. **Languages** English, French. **Activities** Advocacy/lobbying/activism.
Members Full in 4 countries:
Australia, Canada, New Zealand, UK. [2021.12.03/AA1924/**E**]

♦ CAOBISCO / see Association of the Chocolate, Biscuit and Confectionery Industries of the EU (#02427)
♦ **CAOBISCO** Association of the Chocolate, Biscuit and Confectionery Industries of the EU (#02427)
♦ **CAO** Caribbean Association of Otolaryngologists (#03457)
♦ **CAO** Centre Afrika Obota (#03728)
♦ CAO – Commonwealth Arts Organization (inactive)
♦ CAO – Communauté de l'Afrique orientale – 1967 (inactive)
♦ **CAOI** Coordinadora Andina de Organizaciones Indígenas (#04804)
♦ CAOM / see Archives nationales d'Outre mer
♦ CAORC – Council of American Overseas Research Centers (internationally oriented national body)
♦ **CAOS Asia** Asian Society for Computer Assisted Surgery (#01713)
♦ **CAOS-International** International Society for Computer Assisted Orthopaedic Surgery (#15029)
♦ CAPAC – Commonwealth Association of Public Accounts Committees (unconfirmed)
♦ Capacetes Brancos (#20933)
♦ CAPA – CILECT Asia-Pacific Association (see: #11771)

♦ Capacity Development Network in Nutrition in Central and Eastern Europe (CAPNUTRA) 03418

Coordinator Trnska 3, Belgrade, PAK 11000, Serbia. E-mail: office@capnutra.org.
Coordinator Tadeusa Koscuska 1, Belgrade, PAK 11000, Serbia.
URL: http://www.agrowebcee.net/ncdn/

History Founded 2005, Budapest (Hungary) by United Nations System Standing Committee on Nutrition (SCN) and *United Nations University (UNU, #20642),* as *UNU/SCN Network for Capacity Development in Nutrition in Central and Eastern Europe (NCDN-CEE).* Current name adopted, 2013, as a follow-up of NCDN-CEE. **Aims** Initiate and support establishment of networks for capacity development in Central and Eastern Europe and West Balkan countries. **Structure** Scientific Board. **Languages** Bosnian, Croatian, English, Hungarian, Macedonian, Russian, Serbian, Slovene, Ukrainian. **Staff** 4.00 FTE, voluntary. **Finance** Members' dues. Other sources: European Commission funded projects; support from non-profit associations and SMEs. **Activities** Capacity building; knowledge management/information dissemination; events/meetings; research and development; training/education; standards/guidelines; networking/liaising. **Events** *Balkan food platform – regional food composition data base development* Belgrade (Serbia) 2013. **Publications** Reports; scientific publications.
Members Full in 19 countries:
Albania, Bosnia-Herzegovina, Bulgaria, Croatia, Czechia, Estonia, Hungary, Moldova, Montenegro, Netherlands, North Macedonia, Norway, Poland, Russia, Serbia, Slovakia, Slovenia, UK, Ukraine.
IGO Relations Cooperates with: *European System of Cooperative Research Networks in Agriculture (ESCORENA, #08871); FAO Regional Office for Europe and Central Asia (FAO/REU, #09267); United Nations (UN, #20515)* and its Standing Committee on Nutrition; *WHO Regional Office for Europe (#20945).* **NGO Relations** Cooperates with: *European Food Information Council (EUFIC, #07284); European Food Information Resource (EuroFIR, #07285);* national organizations. [2017/XJ5086/**E**]

♦ CAPA – Comisión Americana Permanente de Aviación (inactive)
♦ **CAPA** Commonwealth Association of Polytechnics in Africa (#04308)
♦ **CAPA** Confederation of Asian and Pacific Accountants (#04511)
♦ **CAPA** Council of Anglican Provinces of Africa (#04857)
♦ CAP AIDS / see Canada Africa Partnership Network
♦ **CAPAJ** Comisión Jurídica para el Autodesarrollo de los Pueblos Originarios Andinos (#04139)
♦ **CAPAM** Commonwealth Association for Public Administration and Management (#04310)
♦ Cap Anamur – Cap Anamur – Deutsche Not-Ärzte (internationally oriented national body)
♦ Cap Anamur – Deutsche Not-Ärzte (internationally oriented national body)
♦ Cap Anamur – German Emergency Doctor (internationally oriented national body)
♦ CAPAS – Centre for Asia-Pacific Area Studies (internationally oriented national body)
♦ CAPAS – Coordinated African Programme of Assistance on Services (no recent information)

♦ Cap Business Océan Indien 03419

Exec Dir Bureau 4, 2nd Floor, 51A rue du Savoir, Ebene 72201, Mauritius. T. +2304631537. E-mail: direction@capbusiness.io.
URL: http://www.capbusiness.io

History 2005. Created by the chambers of commerce and industry of the six territories of the South-West of the Indian Ocean. Change of name in 2019 in order to broaden its membership base to professional organisations. Roadmap of projects and activities, 2021-2026. Former names and other names: *Cap Business OI* – alias; *Union des chambres de commerce et de l'industrie de l'Océan Indien (UCCIOI)* – former (2005 to 2019); *Fédération des chambres de commerce de l'industrie de l'Océan Indien (FCCI-OI)* – former (1989 to 2005). Registration: Registry of Associations, No/ID: 13074, Start date: 2005, Mauritius. **Aims** Facilitate dialogue among all relevant stakeholders on a number of issues; participate in the identification of solutions; support projects and companies through financial and/or technical support. **Structure** General Assembly; Steering Committee (two year tenure, meets every 2 or 3 months); General Secretariat. **Languages** English, French. **Staff** 10.00 FTE, paid. **Finance** Sources: members' dues. Supported by: *Agence française de développement (AFD); INTERREG V (#15966).* **Activities** Awareness raising; capacity building; events/meetings; guidance/assistance/consulting; networking/liaising; projects/programmes; research/documentation. **Events** *Forum économique des îles de l'océan Indien* Madagascar 2011, *Forum économique des îles de l'océan Indien* Seychelles 2010, *Forum économique des îles de l'océan Indien* Mayotte 2009, *Forum économique des îles de l'océan Indien* Moroni (Comoros) 2008, *Forum économique des iles de l'océan indien / Forum* Mauritius 2007.
Members Chambers of commerce in 6 countries and territories:
Comoros, Madagascar, Mauritius, Mayotte, Réunion, Seychelles.
NGO Relations Links with NGOs in all six territories of the South-West of the Indian Ocean. [2022.03.09/XD2197/**t**/**D**]

♦ Cap Business OI / see Cap Business Océan Indien (#03419)
♦ **CAP** Caribbean Association of Pharmacists (#03458)
♦ **CAPC** Commonwealth Association of Professional Centres (#04309)
♦ CAP – Centro de Amigos para la Paz (internationally oriented national body)
♦ CAP – Centrum für angewandte Politikforschung (internationally oriented national body)
♦ **CAP** Commonwealth Association of Planners (#04307)
♦ CAPEC – Conference of Asia Pacific Express Carriers (internationally oriented national body)
♦ **CAPE** Coalition pour des accords de pêche équitables (#04060)
♦ **CAPE** Confederation of Asia-Pacific Employers (#04513)
♦ CAPEL – Centro de Asesoria y Promoción Electoral (see: #11334)
♦ Cape Town convention – UNIDROIT Convention on International Interests in Mobile Equipment (2001 treaty)
♦ Cape Town Talent Exchange / see Community Exchange System (#04399)
♦ CAP Europe / see European Coordination of Associations and Individuals for Freedom of Conscience
♦ **CaPFA** Caribbean Public Finance Association (#03543)
♦ CAPFD – Centre de l'Asie et du Pacifique pour la femme et le développement (inactive)

- ♦ CAP Freedom of Conscience / see European Coordination of Associations and Individuals for Freedom of Conscience
- ♦ **CAPGAN** Commonwealth Association of Paediatric Gastroenterology and Nutrition (#04306)
- ♦ **CAPHRA** Coalition of Asia Pacific Tobacco Harm Reduction Advocates (#04052)
- ♦ **CAPI** – Centre for Asia-Pacific Initiatives (internationally oriented national body)
- ♦ **CAPI** Colegio de Abogados Penal Internacional (#13107)
- ♦ **CAPI** Comisión de Administración Pública Internacional (#12587)
- ♦ **CAPI** – Council of Asian Press Institutes (no recent information)
- ♦ **CAPIEL** / see European Coordinating Committee of Manufacturers of Electrical Switchgear and Controlgear (#06790)
- ♦ **CAPIEL** European Coordinating Committee of Manufacturers of Electrical Switchgear and Controlgear (#06790)
- ♦ CAPIS – Centre for Asia-Pacific Island Studies (internationally oriented national body)
- ♦ CapitalPlus Exchange (internationally oriented national body)
- ♦ Capital Policing Europe (meeting series)

♦ Capitals Coalition 03420
CEO Bezuidenhoutseweg 2, 2594 AV The Hague, Netherlands. E-mail: info@capitalscoalition.org.
URL: https://capitalscoalition.org/
History 23 Jan 2020, Davos (Switzerland). Founded on union of *Natural Capital Coalition (NCC, #16952)* and *Social & Human Capital Coalition (inactive)*. Registration: RSIN, No/ID: 860780375, Netherlands; KVK, No/ID: 76727149, Netherlands; EU Transparency Register, No/ID: 658097538474-53, Start date: 10 Jun 2020. **Aims** Transform the way decisions are made by including the value provided by nature, people and society. **Structure** Management Board; Advisory Panel; Team.
Members Organizations (over 370) affiliated with the Coalition through Natural Capital Coalition and Social and Human Capitals Coalition. Organizations include:
Global Green Growth Institute (GGGI, #10392); *Green Economy Coalition (GEC, #10717)*; *International Union for Conservation of Nature and Natural Resources (IUCN, #15766)*; *UN Environment Programme World Conservation Monitoring Centre (UNEP-WCMC, #20295)*; *Wellbeing Economy Alliance (WEAll, #20856)*; *World Business Council for Sustainable Development (WBCSD, #21254)*; *World Wide Fund for Nature (WWF, #21922)*.
[2020/AA1160/y/**F**]

- ♦ CAPJC – Centre africain de perfectionnement des journalistes et communicateurs (internationally oriented national body)
- ♦ CAP LC / see European Coordination of Associations and Individuals for Freedom of Conscience
- ♦ CAPLC – Coordination des Associations and Particuliers pour la Liberté de Conscience (internationally oriented national body)
- ♦ **CAPNET** Caribbean Publishers Network (#03546)
- ♦ **CAP-Net** Network for Capacity Building in Integrated Water Resources Management (#17000)
- ♦ **CAP Network** – Canada Africa Partnership Network (internationally oriented national body)
- ♦ **CAPNUTRA** Capacity Development Network in Nutrition in Central and Eastern Europe (#03418)
- ♦ **CAPoC** – International Congress on Catalysis and Automotive Pollution Control (meeting series)
- ♦ **CAPP** Centesimus Annus Pro Pontifice Foundation (#03654)
- ♦ **CAPP** Central African Power Pool (#03655)
- ♦ **CAPP** Commission arabe permanente des postes (#01025)
- ♦ **CAPP** Council of Africa Political Parties (#04856)
- ♦ CapPlus – CapitalPlus Exchange (internationally oriented national body)
- ♦ **CAPP** – RAND Center for Asia Pacific Policy (internationally oriented national body)
- ♦ CAPRC – Centre Africain de Prévention et Résolution des Conflits (internationally oriented national body)
- ♦ CAPREC – Centre Africain pour la Prévention et la Résolution des Conflits (internationally oriented national body)
- ♦ **Ca-PRI** Cancer and Primary Care Research International Network (#03415)
- ♦ CAPRI – Center d'analyse politique des relations internationales (internationally oriented national body)
- ♦ Capri Institute for International Social Philosophy (internationally oriented national body)
- ♦ CAPS / see School of Pacific and Asian Studies
- ♦ CAPSA-ESCAP – Centre for Alleviation of Poverty through Sustainable Agriculture (inactive)
- ♦ CAPS – Center for Asian and Pacific Studies, Eugene OR (internationally oriented national body)
- ♦ CAPS – Center of Asian and Pacific Studies, Iowa City (internationally oriented national body)
- ♦ CAPS – Centre for Asian Pacific Studies, Hong Kong (internationally oriented national body)
- ♦ CAPSDH – Commission africaine des promoteurs de la santé et des droits de l'homme (internationally oriented national body)
- ♦ CAPSEM / see Committee of Asia/Pacific Societies for Microscopy (#04244)
- ♦ CAPSICUM – Caribbean Association for Plant Science, Industry, Commerce and Use in Medicine (internationally oriented national body)
- ♦ **CAPSM** Committee of Asia/Pacific Societies for Microscopy (#04244)
- ♦ CAPTAC / see Conference of Posts and Telecommunications of Central Africa (#04642)
- ♦ Captain Planet Foundation (internationally oriented national body)
- ♦ **CAPTEAO** Conférence des administrations des postes et télécommunications des Etats de l'Afrique de l'Ouest (#04641)
- ♦ CAP – UNWTO Commission for East Asia and the Pacific (see: #21861)
- ♦ **CAPWIP** Centre for Asia-Pacific Women in Politics (#03731)
- ♦ **CAR 2 CAR** CAR 2 CAR Communication Consortium (#03421)

♦ CAR 2 CAR Communication Consortium (CAR 2 CAR) 03421
Administrator c/o ITS mobility GmbH, Hermann-Blenk-Str 18, 38108 Braunschweig, Germany. T. +4953123172127. Fax +4953123172119. E-mail: contact@car-2-car.org.
URL: http://www.car-2-car.org/
History 2002. **Aims** Assist towards accident free traffic (vision zero); support the highest safety level at improved *traffic* efficiency. **Structure** Annual Meeting; Steering Committee; Technical Organisation. **Languages** English. **Finance** Sources: members' dues. **Activities** Events/meetings. **Publications** *CAR 2 CAR Journal* (2 a year). **Members** Partner (11): vehicle manufacturers; Associate (31): suppliers, service providers, SMEs; Development (29): universities and research organizations. Membership countries not specified. **NGO Relations** Cooperates with (1): *European Telecommunications Standards Institute (ETSI, #08897)*.
[2021.06.08/XJ2133/**D**]

- ♦ Caracciolini – Chierici Regolari Minori (religious order)
- ♦ Caracciolins – Clercs Réguliers Mineurs (religious order)
- ♦ **CARA** Central American Water Resource Management Network (#03676)
- ♦ CARA – CILECT Africa Regional Association (see: #11771)
- ♦ CARA – Committee of African Road Associations (inactive)
- ♦ CARADOL – Caribbean Association for Distance and Open Learning (no recent information)
- ♦ CARAH – International Conference on Artificial Reefs and Related Aquatic Habitats (meeting series)
- ♦ Caraïbische Gezinsplanning Affiliatie (#03502)
- ♦ CARAIO – Caribbean Regional Accident and Incident Investigation Organization (unconfirmed)
- ♦ **CARALL** Caribbean Association of Law Libraries (#03450)
- ♦ **CARAM Asia** – Coordination of Action Research on AIDS and Mobility – Asia (internationally oriented national body)
- ♦ CARAPA – Caribbean Association of Researchers and Herbal Practitioners Association (no recent information)
- ♦ CARA / see Rugby Africa (#18996)
- ♦ **CAR/ASP** Centre d'Activités Régionales pour les Aires Spécialement Protégées (#18746)
- ♦ CARASRA / see Caribbean Area Squash Association (#03442)
- ♦ CARATE – Caribbean Association for the Teaching of English (inactive)
- ♦ Caravane des dix mots (internationally oriented national body)
- ♦ CARAVAN – European Youth Circus and Education Network / see CARAVAN – International Youth and Social Circus Network (#03422)

♦ CARAVAN – International Youth and Social Circus Network 03422
Coordinator c/o Ecole de Cirque de Bruxelles, Rue Picard 11, 1000 Brussels, Belgium. E-mail: info@caravancircusnetwork.eu.
URL: http://www.caravancircusnetwork.eu/
History 2008. Founded by 6 European circus schools. Former names and other names: *CARAVAN – European Youth Circus and Education Network* – former. **Aims** Use circus arts to create positive personal, community and social change. **Structure** General Assembly; Board; Development Manager. **Languages** English, French. **Staff** 1.00 FTE, paid. **Finance** Supported by: *European Commission (EC, #06633)* Erasmus+. **Activities** Events/meetings; projects/programmes; training/education.
Members Circus schools in 23 countries and territories:
Afghanistan, Belgium, Cambodia, Czechia, Ethiopia, Finland, France, Guadeloupe, Iceland, Ireland, Korea Rep, Lebanon, Luxembourg, Netherlands, Palestine, Romania, Russia, Slovenia, South Africa, Spain, Sweden, Türkiye, UK.
NGO Relations Partner: *Network of International Circus Exchange (NICE)*.
[2020.06.24/XJ5264/**D**]

- ♦ **CARBAP** Centre Africain de Recherches sur Bananiers et Plantains (#03725)
- ♦ **CARBICA** – Caribbean Regional Branch of the International Council on Archives (see: #12996)
- ♦ CarbonBC / see Climate Ledger Initiative (#04017)
- ♦ Carbon Capture and Storage Association (unconfirmed)
- ♦ Carbon Disclosure Project / see CDP (#03621)

♦ Carbon Market Watch 03423
Dir Avenue Marnix 17, 1000 Brussels, Belgium. T. +3226694319. E-mail: info@carbonmarketwatch.org.
URL: http://www.carbonmarketwatch.org/
History 2012. Launched to expand the work of watchdog organization *CDM Watch*, which was set up 2009. CDM stands for *Clean Development Mechanism*. Registration: Start date: 2019, Belgium. **Aims** Ensure carbon pricing and other climate policies cut pollution and drive a just transition towards zero-carbon societies. **Structure** General Assembly (annual); Board. **Languages** English. **Staff** 14.00 FTE, paid. **Finance** Supported by: *Brot für die Welt*; *ClimateWorks Foundation (#04024)*; *European Climate Foundation (ECF, #06574)*; *European Union (EU, #08967)* (Life Programme); *German Catholic Bishops' Organisation for Development Cooperation (MISEREOR)*; Quadrature. **Activities** Advocacy/lobbying/activism; events/meetings; monitoring/evaluation; standards/guidelines. **Publications** Annual Report; briefings; policy submissions; investigative research; articles; letters. **Members** Individual (20); Organizational. Membership countries not specified.
NGO Relations Member of: *European Environmental Bureau (EEB, #06996)*; *Climate Action Network (CAN, #03999)*; *International Coalition for Sustainable Aviation (ICSA, #12623)*; the Clean Shipping Coalition.
[2022.03.04/XJ2960/**F**]

- ♦ Carbon Neutral Action and Cooperation Organization (unconfirmed)

♦ Carbon Neutral Cities Alliance (CNCA) 03424
Communications Dir address not obtained. E-mail: contact@carbonneutralcities.org.
URL: https://carbonneutralcities.org/
History A project of Urban Sustainability Directors Network. **Aims** Enable leading cities worldwide that are working aggressively toward a zero-carbon future to advance their own transformational efforts, collaborate with each other and key partners to overcome barriers, foster innovative approaches, and share lessons with other cities ready to pursue similar goals. **Structure** Steering Committee; Innovation Committee; Game Changer Committee. **Finance** Sources: contributions; donations. Supported by: *McKnight Foundation*; *Rockefeller Brothers Fund (RBF)*. **Activities** Advocacy/lobbying/activism; financial and/or material support; networking/liaising; standards/guidelines. **Events** Meeting Helsinki (Finland) 2019.
Members Cities in 12 countries:
Australia (Adelaide; Melbourne; Sydney), Brazil (Rio de Janeiro), Canada (Toronto; Vancouver), Denmark (Copenhagen), Finland (Helsinki), Germany (Hamburg), Japan (Yokohama), Netherlands (Amsterdam), Norway (Oslo), Sweden (Stockholm), UK (Glasgow; London), USA (Boulder TX; Minneapolis MN; New York NY; Portland OR; San Francisco CA; Seattle WA; Washington DC).
[2020/AA0503/**C**]

- ♦ Carbon Offsets To Alleviate Poverty (internationally oriented national body)

♦ Carbon Sequestration Leadership Forum (CSLF) 03425
Secretariat c/o US Dept of Energy, FE-27, Germantown Bldg, 1000 Independence Ave SW, Washington DC 20585, USA. E-mail: cslfsecretariat@hq.doe.gov.
URL: http://www.cslforum.org/
History Established 23 Jun 2003, Tysons Corner VA (USA). Charter signed 25 Jun 2003, Washington DC (USA); charter revised 2011. **Aims** Facilitate development of improved cost-effective *technologies* for separation and capture of *carbon dioxide* for its *transport*, utilization and long-term safe *storage*; make these technologies broadly available internationally; identify and address wider issues relating to carbon capture, utilization and storage. **Structure** Policy Group; Technical Group; Secretariat; Task Forces; sub-groups. **Languages** English. **Staff** Varies based on requirements. **Finance** No fixed budget. **Activities** Capacity building; research/documentation; standards/guidelines; guidance/assistance/consulting; networking/liaising. **Events** *Annual Meeting* Melbourne, VIC (Australia) 2018, *Meeting* Venice (Italy) 2018, *Ministerial Meeting* Abu Dhabi (United Arab Emirates) 2017, *Annual Meeting* Tokyo (Japan) 2016, *Ministerial Meeting* Riyadh (Saudi Arabia) 2015.
Members Signatories to the charter governments of 22 countries:
Australia, Brazil, Canada, China, France, Germany, Greece, India, Italy, Japan, Korea Rep, Mexico, Netherlands, New Zealand, Norway, Poland, Russia, Saudi Arabia, South Africa, UK, United Arab Emirates, USA.
Regional organization (1), listed in this Yearbook:
European Commission (EC, #06633).
[2014.12.10/XJ0367/**F***]

- ♦ Carbon War Room (internationally oriented national body)
- ♦ **CARCAE** – Caribbean Regional Council for Adult Education (inactive)
- ♦ **CAR** Caribbean Action Plan (#03432)
- ♦ **CARC** – Conflict Analysis Research Centre (internationally oriented national body)
- ♦ **CAR** Comité international pour l'art rupestre de l'ICOMOS (#11066)
- ♦ **CAR** – Commission for Art Recovery (internationally oriented national body)
- ♦ **CARD** – Caribbean Association for the Rehabilitation of the Disabled (inactive)

♦ Cardiac Bioassist Association (CBAA) 03426
Pres European Hosp Georges Pompidou, Dept Cardiovascular Surgery, 56 rue Leblanc, 75015 Paris, France. T. +33613144398. Fax +33156095903.
URL: http://www.cb2a.org/
History Registered in accordance with French law, 7 Jul 2004. **Aims** Increase cooperation between those interested in the science and practice of cardiac bioassist technologies, focused on new emerging therapies for refractory heart failure, including biological approaches to cardiac assist as gene therapy, as well as cellular, vascular, muscular and tissue engineering methods to improve cardiac function; encourage and stimulate investigation and study to increase knowledge of cardiac physiology, pathology and therapy, as well as nanotechnologies for creation of bioartificial myocardium, bioprostheses for cardiac support and regeneration and bioartificial heart. **Structure** General Meeting; Council (Board of Directors). **Languages** English. **Staff** Voluntary. **Finance** Members' dues. **Activities** Events/meetings. **Events** *International Congress* Milan (Italy) 2015, *International congress* Santander (Spain) 2013, *International congress* Lima (Peru) 2012, *International congress* Montréal, QC (Canada) 2011, *International congress* Madrid (Spain) 2010.
Members Active; Honorary. Individuals in 64 countries and territories:
Algeria, Argentina, Australia, Austria, Belgium, Brazil, Canada, Chile, China, Colombia, Costa Rica, Cuba, Czechia, Denmark, Dominican Rep, Egypt, Finland, France, Germany, Greece, Hong Kong, Hungary, India, Indonesia, Ireland, Israel, Italy, Japan, Jordan, Korea Rep, Lebanon, Malaysia, Mexico, Monaco, Morocco, Netherlands, New Zealand, Norway, Pakistan, Panama, Paraguay, Peru, Philippines, Poland, Portugal, Puerto Rico, Romania, Russia, Saudi Arabia, Singapore, South Africa, Spain, Sweden, Switzerland, Taiwan, Thailand, Tunisia, Türkiye, UK, United Arab Emirates, Uruguay, USA, Venezuela, Vietnam.
NGO Relations Association Cardio-Monde, France.
[2017.01.29/XJ4369/**D**]

- ♦ Cardiac Physiome Society (unconfirmed)
- ♦ **CARDI** Caribbean Agricultural Research and Development Institute (#03436)

♦ Cardinal Mindszenty Foundation (internationally oriented national body)

♦ Cardiovascular and Interventional Radiological Society of Europe (CIRSE) 03427

Central Office Neutorgasse 9/6, 1010 Vienna, Austria. T. +4319042003. Fax +431904200330. E-mail: info@cirse.org.
URL: http://www.cirse.org/

History 24 Apr 1985, Vienna (Austria), on merger of *European Society of Cardio-Vascular Radiology and Interventional Radiology (inactive)*, which had been set up on 21 Jul 1975, Lyon (France), with *European College of Angiography (inactive)*. **Aims** Improve patient care through the support of teaching, science, research and clinical practice in the field of cardiovascular and interventional radiology. **Structure** General Assembly (annual); Executive Committee; Standing Committees; Subcommittees; Task Forces. **Languages** English. **Staff** 50.00 FTE, paid. **Finance** Members' dues. Congress registration fees. **Events** *Annual Congress* Barcelona (Spain) 2022, *European Conference on Embolotherapy* Nice (France) 2022, *European Conference on Interventional Oncology* Vienna (Austria) 2022, *Annual Congress* Lisbon (Portugal) 2021, *European Conference on Embolotherapy* Nice (France) 2021. **Publications** *CVIR – Cardiovascular and Interventional Radiology* (6 a year) – peer-reviewed journal; *IR News* (3 a year); *CVIR Endovascular* – peer-reviewed open access journal.
Members Groups: European and international IR societies in 34 countries and territories:
Austria, Belgium, Brazil, Bulgaria, Canada, Croatia, Czechia, Denmark, Finland, France, Georgia, Germany, Greece, Hong Kong, Hungary, India, Israel, Italy, Japan, Korea Rep, Latvia, Netherlands, Norway, Poland, Portugal, Russia, Serbia, Singapore, Slovakia, Spain, Sweden, Switzerland, Türkiye, UK.
Included in the above, 2 organizations listed in this Yearbook:
Interventional Radiology Society of Australasia (IRSA); Sociedad Iberoamericana de Intervencionismo (SIDI, #19373).
NGO Relations Member of: *Associations and Conference Forum (AC Forum, #02909); European Cancer Organisation (ECO, #06432); European ALARA Network (EAN, #05855)*. Shareholder in: *European Institute for Biomedical Imaging Research (EIBIR, #07546).* [2020/XD4503/**D**]

♦ Cardiovascular System Dynamics Society (CSDS) 03428

Sec-Treas 304 Hamilton Hall, 1645 Neil Avenue, Columbus OH 43210-1218, USA. T. +16142477838. Fax +16142924888. E-mail: secretary@csds.org.
URL: http://www.csds.org/

History 5 Oct 1976, Philadelphia PA (USA). **Aims** Bring together investigators – biophysicists, bio-engineers, cardiovascular physiologists or clinicians – with interests from the subcellular level to the entire cardiovascular system. **Structure** Executive Committee, comprising President, President-Elect, Secretary/Treasurer and 4 officers-at-large. **Languages** English. **Staff** None. **Activities** Witzig Memorial Lecture; Isaac Starr Lecture. Kiichi Sagawa Young Investigator's Award; Nico Westerhof Trainee's Award. International Conferences (every 2 years). **Events** *Biennial International Conference* Rhodes Is (Greece) 2012, *Biennial International Conference* Fukuoka (Japan) 2010, *Biennial international conference* St Louis, MO (USA) 2008, *Biennial international conference* Vaals (Netherlands) 2006, *Biennial international conference* Banff, AB (Canada) 2004. **Publications** *Journal of Cardiovascular Diagnosis and Preceedings* (1994); *Cardiac Mechanics and Function in the Normal and Diseased Heart* (1989); *Cardiovascular Dynamics* (1982); *Cardiac Dynamics* (1980); *Cardiovascular System Dynamics* (1978). Conference proceedings; abstracts.
Members Individuals in 17 countries:
Australia, Austria, Belgium, Canada, Germany, Greece, Israel, Italy, Japan, Korea Rep, Netherlands, Norway, Russia, Slovenia, Switzerland, UK, USA. [2012/XD2025/v/**F**]

♦ **CARDNE** Centre régional de la réforme agraire et de développement rural au Proche-Orient (#18755)
♦ **Care4BrittleBones** Foundation Care4BrittleBones (#09943)
♦ **Care4BrittleBones** Stichting Care4BrittleBones (#09943)
♦ CAREBACO / see Caribbean Badminton Confederation (#03463)
♦ CARE / see CARE International (#03429)
♦ CAREC – Caribbean Epidemiology Centre (inactive)
♦ **CAREC** Central Asia Regional Economic Cooperation (#03684)
♦ CARECE / see Europeans throughout the World (#08839)
♦ CAREC – Regional Environmental Centre for Central Asia (internationally oriented national body)
♦ Y Care International (internationally oriented national body)

♦ CARE International (CI) 03429

SG Rue du Trone 12, 1000 Brussels, Belgium. T. +3225024333. E-mail: cisecretariat@careinternational.org.
Geneva Chemin de Balexert 7-9, 1219 Châtelaine, Switzerland. T. +41227951020. Fax +41227951029.
URL: http://www.care-international.org/

History 27 Nov 1945, Washington, DC (USA). Previously registered in France and Switzerland. Former names and other names: *Cooperative for American Remittances to Europe (CARE)* – former; *Cooperative for American Relief Everywhere* – former (1985); *Cooperative for Assistance and Relief Everywhere* – former (1994). Registration: Banque-Carrefour des Entreprises, No/ID: 0447.380.925, Start date: 30 Jan 1992, Belgium; EU Transparency Register, No/ID: 90237823189-97, Start date: 8 Feb 2010. **Aims** Work around the globe to save lives, defeat poverty and achieve social justice. **Structure** Supervisory Board; Council; National Directors Committee (NDC); CI Secretariat; Strategic Leadership Teams. **Languages** English. **Staff** Secretariat: over 50; Overseas-based: 9,000.
Finance Donations from the private sector; contributions-in-kind; agricultural commodities donated by governments; governments grants of national offices; multilateral contracts; corporate and private donations. Current donors include:
- *Agence française de développement (AFD);*
- *Australian Aid (inactive);*
- *Canadian International Development Agency (CIDA, inactive);*
- *DANIDA;*
- *Department for International Development (DFID, inactive);*
- ECHO;
- European Commission;
- *Global Fund to Fight AIDS, Tuberculosis and Malaria (Global Fund, #10383);*
- IFAD;
- *International Bank for Reconstruction and Development (IBRD, #12317);*
- *Norwegian Agency for Development Cooperation (Norad);*
- *UNDP (#20292);*
- UNHCR;
- UNICEF;
- *United Nations Development Fund for Women (UNIFEM, inactive);*
- *United Nations Human Settlements Programme (UN-Habitat, #20572);*
- *United Nations Population Fund (UNFPA, #20612);*
- *United States Agency for International Development (USAID);*
- *WHO (#20950);*
- *World Food Programme (WFP, #21510).*

Activities Humanitarian/emergency aid; training/education; advocacy/lobbying/activism; events/meetings; capacity building. **Events** *International Conference on Language and Education* Bangkok (Thailand) 2016, *Meeting* Atlanta, GA (USA) 2001, *Meeting* Melbourne, VIC (Australia) 2001, *Meeting* Delhi (India) 2000, *Meeting* Cambodia 1999. **Publications** Annual Report; thematic publications.
Members CARE International members in 16 countries:
Australia, Austria, Canada, Denmark, Egypt, France, Germany, India, Japan, Luxembourg, Netherlands, Norway, Peru, Thailand, UK, USA.
Consultative Status Consultative status granted from: *ECOSOC (#05331)* (General); *UNICEF (#20332)*. **IGO Relations** Consultative Status with: *United Nations Framework Convention on Climate Change – Secretariat (UNFCCC, #20564)*. Contacts with: *FAO (#09260); European Commission (EC, #06633)*. Accredited by: *United Nations Office at Vienna (UNOV, #20604)*. Observer to: *International Organization for Migration (IOM, #14454)*. Associated with Department of Global Communications of the United Nations.
NGO Relations Member of:
- *Accountable Now (#00060);*
- *Active Learning Network for Accountability and Performance in Humanitarian Action (ALNAP, #00101);*
- *Association for African Medicinal Plants Standards (AAMPS, no recent information);*
- *Better Than Cash Alliance (#03220);*
- *Confédération européenne des ong d'urgence et de développement (CONCORD, #04547);*
- *End Water Poverty (EWP, #05464);*
- *Girls not Brides (#10154);*
- *Global Call for Climate Action (GCCA, inactive);*
- *Global Gender and Climate Alliance (GGCA, no recent information);*
- *Global Health Council (GHC, #10402);*
- *Global Partnership for Sustainable Development Data (Data4SDGS, #10542);*
- *Global WASH Cluster (GWC, #10651);*
- *International Council of Voluntary Agencies (ICVA, #13092);*
- *NetHope (#16979);*
- *NGO Committee on Sustainable Development, Vienna (#17119);*
- *NGO Working Group on the Security Council (#17128);*
- *Regional Inter-Agency Task Team on Children and AIDS in Eastern and Southern Africa (RIATT-ESA, #18791);*
- *The Sphere Project (#19918);*
- *Steering Committee for Humanitarian Response (SCHR, #19978).*

Partner of: *Global Health Cluster (GHC, #10401); Global Shelter Cluster (GSC, #10594)*. Supports: *Global Call for Action Against Poverty (GCAP, #10263).* [2022/XF1846/f/**F**]

♦ Carelift International (internationally oriented national body)
♦ Care and Relief for the Young (internationally oriented national body)
♦ Carers Worldwide (internationally oriented national body)
♦ **CAREST** Caribbean Network of Researchers on Sickle Cell Disease and Thalassemia (#03529)

♦ Caretakers of the Environment International (CEI) 03430

Netherlands Branch address not obtained.
URL: http://www.caretakers4all.org/

History 1986, as an international network of high school students and teachers. **Aims** Provide *students* with an understanding of their role as caretakers of the *earth's resources*. **Structure** Board of Directors. **Finance** Members' dues. Annual budget: US$ 2,500. **Activities** Promote environmental projects in and out of the classroom. Organizes international conferences on environmental-related themes. **Events** *International Conference* Ardlui (UK) 2013, *International Conference* Maastricht (Netherlands) 2012, *International environmental education conference* Aberdeen (UK) 2009, *International Environmental Education Conference* Aalborg (Denmark) 2008, *International Environmental Education Conference* Hong Kong (Hong Kong) 2007. **Publications** *Global Forum* (2 a year).
Members Organizations () and individuals in 81 countries:
Algeria, Angola, Argentina, Australia, Austria, Bangladesh, Belgium, Botswana, Brazil, Burundi, Cameroon (*), Canada (*), Congo DR, Costa Rica (*), Croatia, Cuba, Czechia, Denmark, Dominican Rep, Ecuador, Egypt, Equatorial Guinea, Eswatini, Ethiopia, Finland, France, Germany, Ghana, Greece, Guatemala, Guyana, Honduras, Hungary, Iceland, India (*), Indonesia (*), Ireland (*), Israel (*), Italy, Japan, Jordan, Kenya (*), Korea DPR, Kuwait, Malaysia, Malta, Mauritius, Mexico, Mozambique, Netherlands (*), New Zealand, Nicaragua, Niger, Nigeria, Norway, Pakistan (*), Panama, Peru, Philippines, Poland, Portugal (*), Puerto Rico, Russia, Serbia, South Africa, Spain, Sri Lanka, Sweden (*), Switzerland, Taiwan, Tanzania UR, Thailand, Türkiye, UK (*), Ukraine, USA (*), Venezuela, Vietnam, Zambia, Zimbabwe. [2020/XF1791/**F**]

♦ Careth Foundation (internationally oriented national body)
♦ CARFAD – Centre Africain de Recherches Forestières Appliquées et de Développement (internationally oriented national body)

♦ Cargo Rail Europe 03431

SG Ringlikerstr 70, 8142 Zurich ZH, Switzerland. T. +41444911595. Fax +41444912880.
URL: http://www.cargoraileurope.com/

History Founded 26 Oct 1954, Essen (Germany FR), as *International Association of Users of Private Sidings – Association internationale des usagers d'embranchements particuliers (AIEP) – Asociación Internacional de Usuarios de Ramales Privados – Internationale Vereinigung der Anschlussgeleise-Benützer (IVA)*. Registered in accordance with Swiss Civil Code. **Aims** Defend the common interests of users of private sidings; enter into relations with international *railway* authorities. **Structure** General Assembly (every 2 years); Executive Committee; Management. Membership and meetings closed. **Languages** French, German. **Staff** 1.00 FTE, paid; 1.00 FTE, voluntary. **Finance** Members' dues.
Members National nongovernmental organizations (13) in 8 countries:
Austria, Belgium, France, Germany (5), Liechtenstein, Luxembourg, Netherlands, Switzerland (2).
IGO Relations *European Commission (EC, #06633); Organisation intergouvernementale pour les transports internationaux ferroviaires (OTIF, #17807); United Nations Economic Commission for Europe (UNECE, #20555)*. **NGO Relations** *Comité international des transports ferroviaires (CIT, #04188): European Rail Freight Association (ERFA, #08323); European Rail Infrastructure Managers (EIM, #08324); European Shippers' Council (ESC, #08477); International Union of Wagon Keepers (#15827); International Union of Railways (#15813).* [2015/XD1367/**D**]

♦ **CARIAD** Caribbean Institute on Alcoholism and Other Drug Problems (#03519)
♦ CARI – Argentine Council for International Relations (internationally oriented national body)
♦ Caribank / see Caribbean Development Bank (#03492)
♦ Caribbean Academy of Sciences (internationally oriented national body)

♦ Caribbean Action Plan (CAR) 03432

Contact c/o UNEP-CAR/RCU, 14-20 Port Royal Street, Kingston, Jamaica. T. +18769229267. Fax +18769229292. E-mail: unep-cartagenaconvention@un.org.
URL: https://www.unep.org/cep/who-we-are

History 6 Apr 1981, Montego Bay (Jamaica). 6-8 Apr 1981, Montego Bay (Jamaica), by an intergovernmental meeting, when *Action Plan for the Caribbean Environment Programme* was adopted. Also referred to as: *Regional Seas Action Plan for the Wider Caribbean (CEPPOL); UNEP Caribbean Environment Programme.* Legal framework is *Convention for the Protection and Development of the Marine Environment of the Wider Caribbean Region (Cartagena Convention, 1983)*, signed in 1983, entered into force in 1986. An Action Plan of *UNEP (#20299)* within *Regional Seas Programme (#18814)*. Originally coordinated by *UNEP Water Branch (inactive)* but currently operated by *Caribbean Environment Programme (CEP, #03497)* through a Regional Coordinating Unit, *CAR/RCU*, opened, 11 May 1987, Kingston (Jamaica), as an organizational unit of UNEP. **Aims** Assist governments of the region to prevent and control environmental degradation by: promoting environmental management policies for each nation, based on the sustainable development of the region's resources; promoting cooperation among Caribbean governments in environment-related issues; providing technical assistance to countries of the region, especially smaller island countries; fostering technical cooperation and common efforts to resolve transnational and international problems; fostering improvement of environmental impact assessment capability; strengthening national and subregional institutions, including capabilities for improving environmental health services; assisting implementation of watershed management guidelines; preventing or minimizing effects of natural or man-made disasters, including a regional oil spill contingency plan; increasing public interest in, and awareness of, the environment-development relationship. **Structure** Meeting of Intergovernmental and Contracting Parties comprises ministers/plenipotentiaries of participating states and territories. Monitoring Committee (meets annually), consisting of 9 member countries. Regional Coordinating Unit (RCU) in Kingston (Jamaica). National Focal Points. Scientific and Academic Institutions. Subregional and Regional Institutions. **Languages** English, French, Spanish. **Finance** Since Apr 1981, funded through *Regional Trust Fund for the Implementation of the Action Plan for the Caribbean Environment Programme (see: #20299). Caribbean Trust Fund (CTF)* active from 1983. Other sources: national, bilateral and multilateral contributions; financial support from universities, corporations, private foundations and nongovernmental organizations with interests in the Caribbean Region. **Activities** Integrated and implemented through sub-programmes of the Caribbean Environment Programme, addressing priority areas of the Cartagena Convention and its protocols -*Protocol Concerning Cooperation in Combating Oil Spills in the Wider Caribbean Region (1983), Protocol Concerning Specially Protected Areas and Wildlife to the Convention for the Protection and Development of the Marine Environment of the Wider Caribbean Region (1990), Protocol Concerning Pollution from Land-based Sources and Activities (1999)* – and other related global and regional initiatives. Programmes also include development of: *Global Action Plan for Environment and Development in the 21st Century (Agenda 21, inactive)*; conservation of coastal ecosystems and its relation to private and public tourism sectors. Executes studies and surveys on environmental resources

and problems. Supports pilot projects that demonstrate sound environmental management practices. **Events** *Intergovernmental meeting* Montego Bay (Jamaica) 2006, *Intergovernmental meeting* Montego Bay (Jamaica) 2004, *Intergovernmental meeting* Montego Bay (Jamaica) 2002, *Meeting of contracting parties / Intergovernmental Meeting* Montego Bay (Jamaica) 2002, *Intergovernmental meeting* Kingston (Jamaica) 2000. **Publications** *CEPNews* (4 a year). Information Services: Operates a clearinghouse for regional environmental data. Databases accessible via Website include: Geographic Information System (GIS); Marine Protected Areas (MPA); Caribbean Capacity Building for Environmental Management (CCBEM).
Members Participating states (38):
Anguilla, Antigua-Barbuda, Aruba, Bahamas, Barbados, Belize, Bonaire Is, Cayman Is, Colombia, Costa Rica, Cuba, Curaçao, Dominica, Dominican Rep, France, Grenada, Guadeloupe, Guatemala, Guiana Fr, Guyana, Haiti, Honduras, Jamaica, Martinique, Mexico, Montserrat, Netherlands, Nicaragua, Panama, St Kitts-Nevis, St Lucia, St Vincent-Grenadines, Suriname, Trinidad-Tobago, UK, USA, Venezuela, Virgin Is UK.
IGO Relations Instrumental in setting up: *Regional Marine Pollution Emergency Information and Training Centre – Wider Caribbean (REMPEITC-Carib, #18794).* International organizations participating in the development and implementation of the Plan:
- *Association of Caribbean States (ACS, #02411);*
- *Caribbean Community (CARICOM, #03476);*
- *Caribbean Tourism Organization (CTO, #03561);*
- *Comisión Permanente del Pacífico Sur (CPPS, #04141);*
- *FAO (#09260);*
- *FAO Regional Office for Latin America and the Caribbean (FAO/RLC, #09268);*
- *Global Environment Facility (GEF, #10346);*
- *Inter-American Development Bank (IDB, #11427);*
- *Intergovernmental Oceanographic Commission (IOC, #11496);*
- *International Bank for Reconstruction and Development (IBRD, #12317)* (World Bank);
- *International Coral Reef Action Network (ICRAN, #12964);*
- *International Maritime Organization (IMO, #14102);*
- *OAS (#17629);*
- *Pan American Health Organization (PAHO, #18108);*
- *Swedish International Development Cooperation Agency (Sida);*
- *Tropical Agriculture Research and Higher Education Center (#20246);*
- *UNDP (#20292);*
- *UNESCO (#20322);*
- *United Nations Economic Commission for Latin America and the Caribbean (ECLAC, #20556);*
- *University of the West Indies (UWI, #20705);*
- *World Meteorological Organization (WMO, #21649).*

NGO Relations International organizations participating in the development and implementation of the Plan: *BirdLife International (#03266); Caribbean Conservation Association (CCA, #03481); International Union for Conservation of Nature and Natural Resources (IUCN, #15766); The Nature Conservancy (TNC); United Nations Foundation (UNF, #20563). Whale and Dolphin Conservation (WDC); World Resources Institute (WRI, #21753).* [2014/XF1971/**F***]

♦ Caribbean Action for Sustainable Tourism / see Caribbean Alliance for Sustainable Tourism (#03439)

♦ Caribbean Actuarial Association (CAA) 03433

Sec address not obtained. E-mail: caa.secretariat@gmail.com.
URL: http://www.caa.com.bb/

History Dec 1991, Jamaica. **Aims** Encourage and support the development of actuarial science in the Caribbean; maintain the high standard and image of the actuarial profession. **Structure** Executive Council, comprising President, 1st and 2nd Vice-Presidents, Secretary/Treasurer, Students' Representative and 3 members. **Events** *Annual Conference* Bridgetown (Barbados) 2014, *Joint Conference* Montego Bay (Jamaica) 2012, *Annual Conference* Port-of-Spain (Trinidad-Tobago) 2008, *Annual Conference* Paradise Is (Bahamas) 2007, *Annual Conference* Paramaribo (Suriname) 2006. [2016/XD7519/**D**]

♦ Caribbean Agri-business Association / see Caribbean AgriBusiness Association (#03434)

♦ Caribbean AgriBusiness Association (CABA) 03434

Main Office 2 Uquire Road Extension, Freeport, Bahamas. E-mail: cabasecretariat@gmail.com.
URL: http://www.cabacaribbean.com/

History 7 May 1998, Santo Domingo (Dominican Rep). Also referred to as *Caribbean Agri-business Association.* **Aims** Promote the interests of the agro-business industry in the region. **Structure** General Assembly (annual). Board of Directors of 15 members (meets twice a year). **Languages** English, French, Spanish. **Staff** 0.50 FTE, paid. **Finance** Members' dues. Supported by: *Inter-American Institute for Cooperation on Agriculture (IICA, #11434).* **Activities** Organizes annual *Caribbean Week of Agriculture*, which includes an exhibition of fruit and fruit value-added niche products and an Agri-Development Conference. Develops CD-ROM courses. **Events** *General Assembly* Punta Cana (Dominican Rep) 2001, *Caribbean week of agriculture* Jamaica 2000, *Annual General Assembly* Kingstown (St Vincent-Grenadines) 2000, *Annual General Assembly* Trinidad-Tobago 1999, *Caribbean week of agriculture* Trinidad-Tobago 1999.
Members in 15 countries:
Antigua-Barbuda, Argentina, Bahamas, Barbados, Dominica, Dominican Rep, Grenada, Guyana, Haiti, Jamaica, St Kitts-Nevis, St Lucia, St Vincent-Grenadines, Suriname, Trinidad-Tobago.
NGO Relations Member of: *Inter-American Network of Organizations of Agrifood Exporters (AGRIEXPORTAMERICAS, no recent information).* Collaborates with: *Caribbean Association of Industry and Commerce (CAIC, #03448).* [2016/XD7202/**D**]

♦ Caribbean Agricultural Association (inactive)

♦ Caribbean Agricultural Health and Food Safety Agency (CAHFSA) . . 03435

Contact Letitia Vriesdelaan No 10, Paramaribo, Suriname. T. +597422546. E-mail: info@cahfsa.org.
URL: http://www.cahfsa.org/

History 12 Mar 2010, Roseau (Dominica). Created following signing Agreement among Member States of, and as an institution of, *Caribbean Community (CARICOM, #03476),*. Officially launched 18 Mar 2010. Agreement establishing CAHFSA replaced by Revised CAHFSA Agreement, 25 Feb 2011, St George's (Grenada). Became operational Oct 2014. **Aims** Enhance regional development in agricultural health and food safety through the application of SPS measures that meet the expectation of all stakeholders and contribute to the welfare of citizens. **Structure** Board of Directors. **Events** *IPPC Regional Workshop for Caribbean* Rome (Italy) 2020, *IPPC Regional Workshop for Caribbean* Port-of-Spain (Trinidad-Tobago) 2018, *IPPC Regional Workshop for Caribbean* Bridgetown (Barbados) 2017.
Members States (15):
Antigua-Barbuda, Bahamas, Barbados, Belize, Dominica, Grenada, Guyana, Haiti, Jamaica, Montenegro, St Kitts-Nevis, St Lucia, St Vincent-Grenadines, Suriname, Trinidad-Tobago.
IGO Relations Partner of (5): *Caribbean Agricultural Research and Development Institute (CARDI, #03436); Caribbean Community (CARICOM, #03476); Caribbean Regional Fisheries Mechanism (CRFM, #03547); CARICOM Regional Organization for Standards and Quality (CROSQ, #03574); Inter-American Institute for Cooperation on Agriculture (IICA, #11434).* Serves as one of 10 Regional Plant Protection Organizations of *International Plant Protection Convention, 1951 (IPPC, 1951).* **NGO Relations** Member of (1): *Caribbean Plant Health Directors Forum (CPHD Forum, #03539).* Partner of (1): *Caribbean Animal Health Network (CaribVET, #03440).* [2020/XM6099/**D***]

♦ Caribbean Agricultural Research and Development Institute (CARDI) 03436

Institut de recherche et de développement agricoles des Caraïbes
Exec Dir PO Bag 212, Frederic Hardy Bldg, Univ of the West Indies, St. Augustine Campus, St Augustine, Trinidad-Tobago. T. +18686451205 – +18686451206 – +18686451207. Fax +18686451208. E-mail: infocentre@cardi.org – executive@cardi.org.
URL: http://www.cardi.org/

History Established 1975, as an autonomous institution of the *Caribbean Community (CARICOM, #03476).* Only regional agricultural institution listed in CARICOM's Revised *Treaty of Chaguaramas (1973)*, 1975. **Aims** Contribute to sustainable development of the Caribbean by co-generation, diffusion and application of knowledge through agricultural research for development. **Structure** Board of Governors, consisting of Ministers for Agriculture of member countries. Board of Directors, comprising Ministers' representatives, plus representatives of *Caribbean Community (CARICOM, #03476)* Secretariat, *Caribbean Development Bank (CDB, #03492),* University of Guyana and *University of the West Indies (UWI, #20705),* with *FAO (#09260)* and *Inter-American Institute for Cooperation on Agriculture (IICA, #11434)* as observers. Management Committee; Country Units in each member country. **Languages** English. **Staff** 96.00 FTE, paid. **Finance** Main sources: CARICOM member governments. Other sources – support for projects from donors which include: *Caribbean Development Bank (CDB, #03492); Inter-American Institute for Cooperation on Agriculture (IICA, #11434).* **Activities** Knowledge management/information dissemination; research and development. **Events** *Workshop on technical writing* Belize 1994, *Workshop on technical writing* Jamaica 1994, *Small farmer in agricultural development* Belize 1991, *Post-harvest management of tropical fruit and ornamentals in the Caribbean region* Trinidad-Tobago 1991, *Caribbean livestock nutrition and health* Antigua-Barbuda 1990. **Publications** *CARDI Ministers' Brief* (12 a year) in English; *CARDI Review.* Annual Report; Factsheets; Technical Manuals and other technical materials.
Members Governments of 14 countries and territories:
Antigua-Barbuda, Bahamas, Barbados, Belize, Cayman Is, Dominica, Grenada, Guyana, Jamaica, Montserrat, St Kitts-Nevis, St Lucia, St Vincent-Grenadines, Trinidad-Tobago.
IGO Relations Member of (1): *Caribbean Community (CARICOM, #03476)* (Agriculture Cluster). **NGO Relations** Also links with national organizations and universities. [2022.12.16/XE3268/j/**E***]

♦ Caribbean Agricultural Science and Technology Networking System (no recent information)

♦ Caribbean Agro-Economic Society (CAES) 03437

Contact Faculty of Agriculture, Univ of the West Indies, St Augustine, Trinidad-Tobago. T. +18686622002ext3275. Fax +18686638355. E-mail: info@caestt.com.
URL: http://www.caestt.com/

History 8 Apr 1974, Jamaica, at 9th West Indies Agricultural Economics Conference. **Aims** Provide a forum for examination of *agricultural* institutions, policies, systems and practices in the region; focus attention on economic problems of agricultural production and marketing with a view to improving economic efficiency; disseminate agricultural information throughout the region; establish a closer working relationship between the public and private sectors in agricultural production and marketing. **Structure** Executive Committee. Local representation in Caribbean States, USA and Canada. **Languages** English. **Finance** Conference attracts the support of: *Caribbean Community (CARICOM, #03476); Ford Foundation (#09858); Inter-American Institute for Cooperation on Agriculture (IICA, #11434); International Development Research Centre (IDRC, #13162); Department for International Development (DFID, inactive);* government ministries and other public sector agencies and private sector organizations throughout the region. **Activities** Since 1975, organizes West Indies Agricultural Economics Conferences. Uses membership as a resource pool of expertise for specific studies for which grants have been obtained. **Events** *West Indies Agricultural Economics Conference* St Vincent-Grenadines 2011, *West Indies Agricultural Economics Conference* St Augustine (Trinidad-Tobago) 2009, *West Indies Agricultural Economics Conference* Belize 2007, *West Indies Agricultural Economics Conference* Puerto Rico 2006, *West Indies Agricultural Economics Conference* Paramaribo (Suriname) 2004. **Publications** *Farm and Business* (2 a year); *Caribbean Agro-Economic Society Newsletter* (2 a year); *Caribbean Agro-Economic Society Journal.* Conference proceedings. **Members** Membership countries not specified. **IGO Relations** *Caribbean Development Bank (CDB, #03492).* [2012/XD2331/**D**]

♦ Caribbean Aid for Trade and Regional Integration Trust Fund (inactive)
♦ Caribbean Air Line Pilots Association (no recent information)

♦ Caribbean Alliance of National Psychological Associations (CANPA) 03438

Secretariat PO Box CB-13015, Nassau, Bahamas. E-mail: secretariat@canpanet.org.
URL: http://canpanet.org/

History 2013. **Aims** Advance psychological knowledge, research, skills and practice in the service of Caribbean well-being and development, while addressing the professional interests of psychological practitioners, academics and researchers. **Structure** General Assembly; Executive Council; Presidents and Elders Council; International Advisory Committee. Committees. **Events** *CRCP Conference* St Croix (Virgin Is USA) 2021, *CRCP Conference* St Croix (Virgin Is USA) 2020.
Members National associations in 13 countries and territories:
Bahamas, Barbados, Cuba, Dominica, Dominican Rep, Grenada, Haiti, Jamaica, Martinique, Puerto Rico, Suriname, Trinidad-Tobago, Virgin Is USA. [2020/AA0358/**D**]

♦ Caribbean Alliance for Sustainable Tourism (CAST) 03439

Contact CHTA, 2655 Le Jeune Rd, Ste 910, Coral Gables FL 33134, USA. T. +13054433040ext104.
URL: http://www.caribbeanhotelandtourism.com/cast/

History Founded 1997, as the environmental subsidiary of *Caribbean Hotel and Tourism Association (CHTA, #03516).* Also referred to as *Caribbean Action for Sustainable Tourism.* **Aims** Enhance the practices of the region's hotel and tourism operators by providing high quality *education* and training related to sustainable tourism; promote the industry's efforts and successes to the travelling public and other stakeholders; serve as a vital link to all stakeholders with sustainable tourism interests in the Caribbean region. **Structure** Governing Council (meets annually). Director; Programme Manager. **Finance** Members' dues. Other sources: 'Friends of Cast' programme; grant funding; donations; training courses; sale of publications. **Activities** *'Strategic focus':* Sustainable tourism certification and standards development, including promotion of standards for environmental leadership and performance in the hotel sector; development of best practice tools; advocacy; fund raising. *'Programmes and Services':* Sustainability – Hotel Environmental Leadership and Performance (HELP) programme; Training; Advocacy; Fund Raising; Environmental Best Practice Tools. **Publications** *BroadCAST* (4 a year) – newsletter. *Environmental Management Systems for Hotels and Resorts – A Users Manual; Environmental Toolkit for Caribbean Hoteliers; Waste Audit Manual for Caribbean Hotels and Resorts.* Video; case studies.
Members Full in 17 countries:
Antigua-Barbuda, Bahamas, Barbados, Belize, Cuba, Dominica, Dominican Rep, Grenada, Haiti, Jamaica, Mexico, Neth Antilles, Puerto Rico, St Kitts-Nevis, St Lucia, St Vincent-Grenadines, Trinidad-Tobago.
IGO Relations Represented in Governing Council: *Caribbean Tourism Organization (CTO, #03561); Pan American Health Organization (PAHO, #18108).* **NGO Relations** Member of: *Global Islands Network (GIN, #10437); Sustainable Tourism Certification Network of the Americas (STCNA, #20069).* [2016/XE3541/**E**]

♦ Caribbean ALPA – Caribbean Air Line Pilots Association (no recent information)

♦ Caribbean Animal Health Network (CaribVET) 03440

Réseau caraïbéen de santé animale – Red del Caribe de Sanidad Animal
Sec address not obtained.
URL: http://www.caribvet.net/

History 1998. **Aims** Improve animal health and the quality and safety of animal products throughout the Caribbean. **Structure** Steering Committee, including Chair and Co-Chair. Coordination Unit. Working Groups. **Languages** English, French, Spanish. **Finance** Supported by: *European Regional Development Fund (ERDF, #08342).* **Events** *General Assembly* Aruba 2021, *Annual meeting* Port-of-Spain (Trinidad-Tobago) 2006, *Joint meeting on animal disease surveillance and preparedness* Port-of-Spain (Trinidad-Tobago) 2006. [2021.11.22/XM2379/**F**]

♦ Caribbean Aquaculture Association (inactive)

♦ Caribbean Area Network for Quality Assurance in Tertiary Education (CANQATE) 03441

Pres c/o Accreditation Council Trinidad-Tobago, Level 1, Maritime Centre, 29 Tenth Avenue, Barataria, Port-of-Spain 500000, Trinidad-Tobago. T. +18682859177. E-mail: canqateinfo@gmail.com.
URL: http://www.canqate.org/

History 2002, Montego Bay (Jamaica). Founded as a sub-network of *International Network of Quality Assurance Agencies in Higher Education (INQAAHE, #14312).* **Aims** Share information and best practice in the field of tertiary education quality assurance; strengthen and harmonize tertiary education quality assurance policies and standards in the region. **Structure** General Assembly; Board of Management. **Languages** English. **Staff** 0.50 FTE, paid; 10.00 FTE, voluntary. **Finance** Sources: members' dues. **Activities** Advocacy/lobbying/activism; events/meetings; knowledge management/information dissemination. **Events** *Annual Conference* Willemstad (Curaçao) 2022, *Annual Conference* 2021, *Annual Conference* St Vincent-Grenadines 2020, *Annual Conference* Grand Anse (Grenada) 2019, *Annual Conference* Tobago (Trinidad-Tobago) 2018. **Publications** *CANQATE Newsletter.*

Members Categories: Full; Associate; Individual. National accreditation bodies; tertiary institutions; Ministries of Education; professional bodies and agencies; individuals. Members in 12 countries and territories:
Bahamas, Barbados, Belize, Bermuda, Dominica, Guyana, Jamaica, St Lucia, St Vincent-Grenadines, Suriname, Trinidad-Tobago, Turks-Caicos.
Included in the above, 3 organizations listed in this Yearbook:
Caribbean College of Family Physicians (CCFP, #03474); Caribbean Evangelical Theological Association (CETA, #03499); Eastern Caribbean Institute of Agriculture and Forestry (ECIAF, #05234). [2022.05.09/XM3488/y/**E**]

♦ Caribbean Area Squash Association (CASA) 03442

Sec c/o Barbados Squash Association BOA, Olympic Centre, Garfield Sobers Sports Complex, Wildey, St Michael BB 15094, ST MICHAEL BB 15094, Barbados.
Pres address not obtained.
URL: http://www.caribbeansquash.org/

History Founded 1977, as *Caribbean Area Squash Rackets Association (CARASRA).* **Aims** Promote the game of squash in the Caribbean sub-region. **Languages** English. **Staff** Voluntary. **Finance** Members' dues. **Activities** Events/meetings; sporting activities. **Events** *General Meeting* Trinidad-Tobago 2012, *General Meeting* Cayman Is 2011, *General Meeting* St Vincent-Grenadines 2010, *General Meeting* Cayman Is 2009, *General Meeting* Trinidad-Tobago 2005.
Members Associations in 8 countries:
Bahamas, Barbados, Bermuda, Cayman Is, Guyana, Jamaica, Trinidad-Tobago, Venezuela.
Included in the above, 1 organization listed in this Yearbook:
Organisation of Eastern Caribbean States (OECS, #17804). [2017.02.07/XE5877/**E**]

- ♦ Caribbean Area Squash Rackets Association / see Caribbean Area Squash Association (#03442)
- ♦ Caribbean ASEAN Council – Caribbean ASEAN Voluntary Council for Sustainable Development Goals (unconfirmed)
- ♦ Caribbean ASEAN Voluntary Council for Sustainable Development Goals (unconfirmed)

♦ Caribbean Association of Banks (CAB) 03443

CEO Chakiro Court, Vide Bouteille, PO Box CP 5404, Castries, St Lucia. T. +17584522877. Fax +17584522878. E-mail: cab@candw.lc.
Communications/Member Relations Officer address not obtained.
URL: http://www.cab-inc.com/

History Founded 1974, as *Caribbean Association of Indigenous Banks (CAIB).* **Aims** Foster a spirit of goodwill and camaraderie among indigenous banks of the region with a view to solving their common problems through understanding and cooperation. **Structure** Executive Committee (Directors); Chief Executive Officer; Office Manager; Project Officer; Administrative Officer. **Languages** English. **Staff** 4.00 FTE, paid. **Finance** Members' dues. **Activities** Knowledge management/information dissemination; awareness raising; capacity building; standards/guidelines; advocacy/lobbying/activism; publishing activities. **Events** *Annual General Meeting and Conference* 2020, *Annual General Meeting and Conference* St Maarten 2019, *Annual General Meeting and Conference* Nassau (Bahamas) 2018, *Annual General Meeting and Conference* Santo Domingo (Dominican Rep) 2017, *Annual General Meeting and Conference* Willemstad (Curaçao) 2016. **Publications** *CAB Newsletter* (6 a year); *Caribbean Account Magazine* (annual).
Members Full in 17 countries and territories:
Anguilla, Antigua-Barbuda, Barbados, Belize, Cayman Is, Dominica, Grenada, Guyana, Haiti, Jamaica, Montserrat, St Kitts-Nevis, St Lucia, St Vincent-Grenadines, Suriname, Trinidad-Tobago, Virgin Is UK.
NGO Relations *Caribbean Confederation of Credit Unions (CCCU, #03478)* is member. [2021/XD3899/**D**]

- ♦ Caribbean Association of, Bible Colleges / see Caribbean Evangelical Theological Association (#03499)
- ♦ Caribbean Association of Building Societies and Housing Finance Institutions / see Caribbean Association of Housing Finance Institutions (#03447)

♦ Caribbean Association of Catholic Teachers (CACT) 03444

Association des professeurs catholiques des Caraïbes

SG 48 Potter Street, Pottersville, Roseau, Dominica. T. +17674482837.
Secretariat PO Box 836, St John's, St John, Antigua-Barbuda.

History Founded 1967, Castries (St Lucia), originally as an annual meeting of Caribbean member associations of *UMEC-WUCT (#20280).* Current statutes adopted 18 Aug 1988; amended 4 Aug 1990. **Aims** Assist Catholic teachers' associations to increase the effectiveness of Catholic schools and teachers' organizations; make available documentation and assist in the pastoral care of Catholic teachers in their personal lives and professional development. **Structure** General Assembly (every 2 years); Council (meets annually), comprising 5 officers; Secretariat in Antigua-Barbuda. **Activities** Events/meetings. **Events** *Biennial conference* Grenada 2008, *Biennial conference* Kingston (Jamaica) 2000, *Biennial Conference* 1998, *Biennial Conference* 1996.
Members Catholic teachers' associations in 14 countries and territories:
Antigua-Barbuda, Bahamas, Barbados, Dominica, Grenada, Guadeloupe, Jamaica, Montserrat, Neth Antilles, St Kitts-Nevis, St Lucia, St Vincent-Grenadines, Trinidad-Tobago, Virgin Is UK. [2014/XD6990/**D**]

- ♦ Caribbean Association for Commonwealth Literature and Language Studies / see West Indian Association for Commonwealth Literature and Language Studies (#20921)
- ♦ Caribbean Association for Communication Research (no recent information)
- ♦ Caribbean Association for Distance and Open Learning (no recent information)
- ♦ Caribbean Association of Endo-laparoscopic Surgeons (unconfirmed)
- ♦ Caribbean Association of Environmental Educators (inactive)

♦ Caribbean Association for Feminist Research and Action (CAFRA) . 03445

Association caraïbéenne pour la recherche et l'action féministe – Asociación Caribeña para la Investigación y Acción Feministas

Coordinator PO Box 1599, Castries, St Lucia. T. +17584531608.

History 2 Apr 1985, Barbados. Registration: Start date: 16 Jul 1990, Trinidad-Tobago. **Aims** Celebrate and promote the collective power of women for individual and societal transformation, thus creating a climate in which social justice is realized; understand the relationship between the oppression of women and other forms of oppression in society and work actively for change; serve as facilitator of the regional women's movement. **Structure** General Meeting (every 3 years); Regional Committee (meets annually); Management Committee; Secretariat. **Languages** English, Spanish. **Staff** 5.50 FTE, paid. **Finance** Members' dues. Funding partners include: the Dutch government; Heinrich Boell Foundation (HBF); *Humanistisch Instituut voor Ontwikkelingssamenwerking (Hivos)*; Oxfam Canada; *WIDE+ (#20951).* **Activities** Awareness raising; events/meetings; knowledge management/information dissemination; projects/programmes; research/documentation. **Events** *Regional Committee Meeting* Macoya (Trinidad-Tobago) 2000, *Annual meeting / Regional Committee Meeting* Belize City (Belize) 1999, *Conference on sex tourism, sex work and Caribbean development paradigms* Kingston (Jamaica) 1998, *Regional Committee Meeting* Puerto Rico 1998, *Annual meeting* Suriname 1998. **Publications** *CAFRA News* (2 a year) in English; *Novedades CAFRA* (2 a year) in Spanish. *Publishing Handbook for Caribbean Women Writers* (1992); *Creation Fire: A CAFRA Anthology of Caribbean Women's Poetry* (1990); *Domestic Violence and the Law.* Annual Report. Project-specific reports. Information Services: Documentation centre; reference service.
Members Feminists, individual researchers, activists and women's organizations. Individuals in 20 countries:
Antigua-Barbuda, Bahamas, Barbados, Belize, Canada, Cuba, Dominica, Dominican Rep, Grenada, Guyana, Haiti, Jamaica, Neth Antilles, St Kitts-Nevis, St Lucia, St Vincent-Grenadines, Suriname, Trinidad-Tobago, UK, USA.
Consultative Status Consultative status granted from: *ECOSOC (#05331)* (Special). **NGO Relations** Regional network of: *Caribbean Policy Development Centre (CPDC, #03540).* Member of: *EarthAction (EA, #05159); Latin American and Caribbean Feminist Network Against Domestic and Sexual Violence (#16277).* Close cooperation with: *Caribbean Network for Integrated Rural Development (CNIRD, #03528); Caribbean Peoples Development Agency (CARIPEDA, no recent information); Development Alternatives with Women for a New Era (DAWN, #05054); International Gender and Trade Network (IGTN, #13707); Latin American and Caribbean Women's Health Network (LACWHN, #16288);* WIDE. [2018/XD3789/**D**]

- ♦ Caribbean Association of Forensic Scientists (no recent information)
- ♦ Caribbean Association for the Hearing Impaired (inactive)

♦ Caribbean Association of Home Economists (CAHE) 03446

Sec address not obtained.
Pres address not obtained.
URL: http://www.caribbeanhomeeconomist.org/

History 1972, Castries (St Lucia). **Aims** Promote awareness of social, economic and political issues and participate in activities affecting families; promote high professional standards among regional home economists through continuing education and professional development programmes; improve and strengthen education in Home Economics and incorporate it in school curricula at all levels of the education system; encourage research in home economics and related fields and assist in the dissemination and application of findings; strengthen the profession regionally and internationally by means of communication and linkages with organizations and institutions of like disciplines and/or similar interests. **Structure** Executive Team. **Languages** English. **Staff** Voluntary. **Finance** Members' dues. Fundraising. **Activities** Certification/accreditation; events/meetings; training/education. **Events** *Conference* 2021, *Conference* St John's (Antigua-Barbuda) 2019, *Biennial Conference* Georgetown (Guyana) 2015, *Biennial Conference* Nassau (Bahamas) 2007, *Biennial Conference* Antigua-Barbuda 2003. **Publications** *Caribbean Association of Home Economists Quarterly* (4 a year); *Caribbean Journal of Home Economics. History of Home Economics in the Caribbean* (1997); *Caribbean Home Economics in Action Books* – in 3 vols. Guides.
Members National and other organizations in 12 countries and territories:
Antigua-Barbuda, Bahamas, Barbados, Belize, Dominica, Grenada, Guyana, Jamaica, St Lucia, St Vincent-Grenadines, Trinidad-Tobago, Turks-Caicos.
Individuals in 7 countries and territories:
Anguilla, Canada, Montserrat, Puerto Rico, St Croix Is, St Kitts-Nevis, USA.
IGO Relations Cooperates with (1): *Caribbean Public Health Agency (CARPHA, #03544). Caribbean Community (CARICOM, #03476).* **NGO Relations** Member of (1): *International Federation for Home Economics (IFHE, #13447). Caribbean Association of Nutritionists and Dietitians (CANDI, #03456).* [2021/XD3781/**D**]

♦ Caribbean Association of Housing Finance Institutions (CASHFI) . . 03447

Asociación de Instituciones de Financiamiento Habitacional del Caribe

SG 1 Holborn Road, Kingston, Jamaica. T. +18767545268. Fax +18767549633. E-mail: cashfi@cwjamaica.com.
URL: http://www.cashfi.com/

History Founded 1984, Washington DC (USA), as *Caribbean Association of Building Societies and Housing Finance Institutions (CABSHFI).* **Aims** Promote the principles of savings and home ownership; assist in establishment and development of housing finance institutions in the Caribbean area, including Bermuda and the Bahamas. **Structure** Council; Executive Board; Sub-Committees (3). **Languages** English. **Staff** 2.00 FTE, paid. **Finance** Members' dues. Revenue from conferences and seminars. **Activities** Events/meetings; projects/programmes. **Events** *Regional Housing Conference* Kingston (Jamaica) 2014, *Regional housing conference* Antigua-Barbuda 2008, *International Shelter Conference* Montego Bay (Jamaica) 2006, *Joint conference* Montego Bay (Jamaica) 1994. **Publications** Newsletter (2 a year).
Members National associations of building societies and housing finance institutions in 13 countries and territories:
Bahamas, Barbados, Dominican Rep, Haiti, Jamaica, Montserrat, St Kitts-Nevis, St Lucia, St Vincent-Grenadines, Suriname, Trinidad-Tobago, UK, USA. [2017.10.26/XD1626/**D**]

- ♦ Caribbean Association of Indigenous Banks / see Caribbean Association of Banks (#03443)

♦ Caribbean Association of Industry and Commerce (CAIC) 03448

Secretariat PO Box 6541, Lady Young Road, TT Post, Maraval, Trinidad-Tobago. T. +18686234478. Fax +18686228936.
Facebook: https://www.facebook.com/theCAIC/

History Founded Apr 1955, an *Incorporated Commonwealth Chambers of Commerce and Industry of the Caribbean* having been set up in 1917. Articles of Association amended 1970. Re-organized 28 Apr 1981, Sam Lord's Castle (Barbados). **Aims** Stimulate the private sector to play greater role in national and regional development; increase employment, income, productivity and economic growth in Caribbean countries; assist in developing privately-owned productive enterprises, increasing the ability of local entrepreneurs to establish, expand or increase the efficiency of their enterprises; act as private sector spokesman on political advocacy, trade and regional integration. **Structure** General Meeting (annual); Board of Directors; Secretariat, headed by Executive Director. **Languages** English. **Staff** 6.00 FTE, paid. **Finance** Members' dues. **Activities** Advocacy/lobbying/activism; training/education; research/documentation. **Events** *Annual General Meeting* Port-of-Spain (Trinidad-Tobago) 2005, *Annual private sector conference* Port-of-Spain (Trinidad-Tobago) 2005, *Annual private sector conference* Port-of-Spain (Trinidad-Tobago) 2003, *Annual General Meeting* St George's (Grenada) 2000, *Annual private sector conference* St George's (Grenada) 2000. **Publications** *CAIC Speaks* (12 a year); *Business Wave* (6 a year); *CAIC Times* (4 a year); *CAIC News* (24 a year). **Information Services** *Caribbean Trade Information System (CARTIS).*
Members Organizational national chambers of commerce and manufacturers' associations; Corporate individual companies belonging to the national body most relevant to the nature of their business; Associate corporations with majority private sector equity, consulting firms, insurance companies, finance companies and brokers, banks, accounting firms. Members in 20 countries and territories:
Antigua-Barbuda, Barbados, Belize, Cuba, Dominica, Dominican Rep, Grenada, Guadeloupe, Guyana, Haiti, Jamaica, Martinique, Montserrat, Neth Antilles, Puerto Rico, St Kitts-Nevis, St Lucia, St Vincent-Grenadines, Trinidad-Tobago, Virgin Is UK.
IGO Relations Regular relations with: *UNDP (#20292); UNIDO (#20336); Caribbean Community (CARICOM, #03476); Caribbean Development Bank (CDB, #03492); Caribbean Forum for Development (CFD, no recent information); European Development Fund (EDF, #06914); Inter-American Development Bank (IDB, #11427); International Finance Corporation (IFC, #13597); OAS (#17629).* Through SEAP, interfaces with: *Organisation of Eastern Caribbean States (OECS, #17804)* and *United States Agency for International Development (USAID).* Under Lomé Conventions, links with: *European Commission (EC, #06633).* **NGO Relations** Member of: *Commonwealth Business Organizations International Network (no recent information).* Close links with: *Canadian Association for Latin American and Caribbean Studies (CALACS); Caribbean – Central American Action (CCAA, inactive); West Indies Rum and Spirits Producers' Association Inc (WIRSPA, #20923).* Represented on Board of Directors of: *Caribbean Hotel and Tourism Association (CHTA, #03516).* Through SEAP, interfaces with: *Association of Eastern Caribbean Exporters (AECE, no recent information).* Through Global Chamber Platform, links with: *Association des chambres de commerce et d'industrie européennes (EUROCHAMBRES, #02423).* [2020/XD5332/t/**D**]

♦ Caribbean Association of Investment Promotion Agencies (CAIPA) . 03449

Secretariat c/o Caribbean Export Development Agency, Baobab Tower, PO Box 34B, Warrens, St Michael BB1400 , ST MICHAEL BB1400 , Barbados. T. +12464360578. Fax +12464369999. E-mail: info@carib-export.com.
URL: http://www.caipainvest.org

History Launched 20 Nov 2007, Kingstown (Jamaica), following several meetings held Jun 2004, Port-of-Spain (Trinidad-Tobago). **Aims** Enable collaboration among the CARIFORUM Investment Promotion Agencies (IPAs). **Structure** Board. **Finance** Funding provided by *European Union (EU, #08967).* **Events** *Caribbean Sub-Regional Meeting on Attracting Foreign Direct Investment in the Caribbean* Miami, FL (USA) 2016.
Members Investment Promotion Agencies of 19 countries and territories:
Antigua-Barbuda, Bahamas, Barbados, Belize, Cayman Is, Curaçao, Dominica, Dominican Rep, Grenada, Guyana, Haiti, Jamaica, Montserrat, St Kitts-Nevis, St Lucia, St Vincent-Grenadines, Suriname, Trinidad-Tobago, Turks-Caicos.
IGO Relations *Forum of Caribbean States (CARIFORUM, #09904).* [2019/XM4992/**D**]

♦ Caribbean Association of Law Libraries (CARALL) 03450

Sec c/o June Renie Law Library, Hugh Wooding Law School, P.O. Bag 323, Tunapuna, 100-114 Gordon Street , St. Augustine, Tunapuna 331314, Trinidad-Tobago. T. +118682254288 ext 1111. E-mail: caribbeanassociationll@gmail.com.
Pres Mona Campus, UWI, Kingston, Jamaica.
URL: https://carallonline.weebly.com/

History May 1984. Inaugurated during a two-day meeting at the Hugh Wooding Law School, Trinidad-Tobago, attended by 19 representatives from 5 countries. **Aims** Promote better administration of law libraries; foster a spirit of cooperation among members of the profession through, inter alia, holding conferences and discussions; promote improvement of the status and qualifications of law librarians; encourage bibliographical study and research, and creation and organization of legal information through appropriate technology; publish information of service or interest to members; support and cooperate with, or become affiliated to, other organizations or activities which tend to enhance the control and dissemination of legal information generally. **Structure** Executive Committee of 5 officers. **Languages** English. **Staff** None. **Finance** Sources: members' dues. **Activities** Events/meetings. **Events** *Annual Conference* Port-of-Spain (Trinidad-Tobago) 2021, *Annual Conference* Guyana 2020, *Annual Conference* Antigua-Barbuda 2019, *Annual Conference* Port-of-Spain (Trinidad-Tobago) 2018, *Annual Conference* Nassau (Bahamas) 2017. **Publications** *CARALL Communications* (annual) – newsletter. **Members** Personal; Institutional; Associate; Student. Membership countries not specified. [2022.11.01/XD7731/**D**]

♦ Caribbean Association of Local Government Authorities (CALGA) . . 03451

Pres c/o Chaguanas Borough Corporation, Cumberbatch Street, Chaguanas, Trinidad-Tobago. T. +18682225608. E-mail: calgaoffice@gmail.com.
URL: http://www.calga.org/

History 1992, Belize City (Belize). Founded 1992, Belize (Belize). **Aims** Foster and maintain a high standard of *administration* within the local government system; assist member states of *CARICOM* to establish a system of local government where such system does not exist. **Structure** General Assembly (annual). Executive Committee, comprising President, Vice-President, Secretary, Treasurer, Public Relations Officer. Secretariat in Port-of-Spain. **Finance** Members' dues. Supported by the Government of Trinidad-Tobago. Donations. **Activities** Induction training for local government practitioners, following local government elections in Trinidad-Tobago and the Bahamas, 1996. Holds regional events in the form of an annual general meeting which combines with a training workshop for delegates and other local government practitioners from particular host country. **Events** *Regional symposium for women in local government within Commonwealth Caribbean* St Lucia 1997. **Publications** *Caribbean Local Government* (4 a year) – newsletter.
Members Local government authorities in 13 countries and territories:
Antigua-Barbuda, Bahamas, Barbados, Belize, Dominica, Grenada, Guyana, Jamaica, Montserrat, St Kitts-Nevis, St Lucia, St Vincent-Grenadines, Trinidad-Tobago. [2019/XD5695/**D**]

♦ Caribbean Association of Media Workers (inactive)

♦ Caribbean Association of Medical Councils (CAMC) 03452

Chairman 37 Windsor Ave, Unit 5, Kingston, Jamaica. T. +18769782159. Fax +18769782118. E-mail: medcojam@cwjamaica.com – contact@camcouncils.org.
Registrar address not obtained.
URL: http://camcouncils.org/

History Nov 1998. **Languages** English. **IGO Relations** *Caribbean Community (CARICOM, #03476).* **NGO Relations** Affiliated with: *Caribbean College of Family Physicians (CCFP, #03474).* [2016.07.07/XM2804/**D**]

♦ Caribbean Association of Medical Technologists (CASMET) 03453

Contact PO Box SS19793, 6 Terrace Centerville, Nassau, Bahamas. T. +12424624037. E-mail: casmet@ymail.com.
URL: http://www.casmet.org/

History 28 Sep 1954, as *Society of Medical Technologists, West Indies* following meeting in May 1953, Jamaica, held by senior technologists from government laboratories and from the Department of Pathology, University of the West Indies, Mona, to establish *Association for Medical Technologists* in Jamaica. Current name adopted Oct 1979, Bahamas. **Aims** Promote development and interchange of technical knowledge in the field of medical technology; make representation on behalf of members with reference to matters of professional interest, employment status and recognition; encourage formation of new Branches; encourage high standards of professional conduct; consider, promote, support or oppose proposed and/or existing legislation or other measures affecting the welfare of members; establish and improve dialogue with other teaching institutions, funding agencies and governments in all matters related to the field. **Structure** Regional Council, comprising President, Vice-President, President Elect, Immediate Past President, Secretary, Assistant Secretary, Treasurer, Assistant Treasurer, Public Relations Officer, 4 members, Chairperson of a Branch or his/her nominee and one nominee from each non-represented member country. At Branch level, Council consists of Chairperson, Vice Chairperson, Secretary, Assistant Secretary, Treasurer, Public Relations Officer and 4 Council members. **Languages** English. **Staff** None. **Finance** Members' dues. **Activities** Reviews periodically the role of CASMET as an examining body in member countries; offers advisory and collaboratory services to educational institutions in member countries in the development of technical aspects of medical technology training programmes; exercises professional supervision over members; organizes meetings, conferences, lectures, short courses; undertakes, if requested, settlement of disputes between members; offers services to relevant Ministries of Health in member countries in coordinating and monitoring standards of internship of medical technology programmes; publishing activity. **Events** *Biennial Meeting and Symposium* Bahamas 2013, *Biennial Meeting and Symposium* Miami, FL (USA) 2011, *Biennial Meeting and Symposium* Trinidad-Tobago 2009, *Meeting / Biennial Meeting and Symposium* Castries (St Lucia) 2007, *Biennial general meeting and scientific symposium* Vieux-Fort (St Lucia) 2007. **Publications** *CASMET Newsletter* (2 a year); *CASMET E-News.*
Members Full in 18 countries:
Antigua-Barbuda, Bahamas, Barbados, Belize, Costa Rica, Dominica, Dominican Rep, Grenada, Guyana, Haiti, Jamaica, Neth Antilles, St Kitts-Nevis, St Lucia, St Vincent-Grenadines, Suriname, Trinidad-Tobago, USA.
NGO Relations Links with national organizations. [2017/XD1878/v/**D**]

♦ Caribbean Association on Mental Retardation and Other Developmental Disabilities (inactive)

♦ Caribbean Association of National Olympic Committees (CANOC) . . 03454

Contact Villa Point, Box 1644, Indian Bay Road, Kingstown, St Vincent-Grenadines. T. +17844572970. E-mail: admin@canoc.net.
URL: https://canoc.net/

History Founded 31 Jul 2003. **Aims** Celebrate and conduct the Caribbean Games; promote develop and protect Sport as well as the Olympic Movement in the Caribbean. **Structure** Assembly; Executive.
Members National committees of 29 countries and territories:
Anguilla, Antigua-Barbuda, Aruba, Bahamas, Barbados, Belize, Bermuda, Cayman Is, Cuba, Curaçao, Dominica, Dominican Rep, Grenada, Guadeloupe, Guiana Fr, Guyana, Haiti, Jamaica, Martinique, Montserrat, Puerto Rico, St Kitts-Nevis, St Lucia, St Vincent-Grenadines, Suriname, Trinidad-Tobago, Turks-Caicos, Virgin Is UK, Virgin Is USA.
NGO Relations Founding member of: *Sport Integrity Global Alliance (SIGA, #19925).* [2020/XM8977/**D**]

♦ Caribbean Association of National Telecommunications Organizations / see CANTO (#03416)

♦ Caribbean Association of Neurological Surgeons (CANS) 03455

Asociación de Neurocirujanos del Caribe

Pres Edif Médico Santa Cruz, 73 Calle Santa Cruz, Ste 316, Bayamón PR, USA.
URL: http://www.caribbeanneurosurgery.com/

History 27 Apr 1973, Dominican Rep. Also referred to as *Caribbean Association of Neurological Surgery.* **Languages** English, French, Spanish. **Events** *Conference* San Juan (Puerto Rico) 2014, *Conference* Mexico 2013, *Conference* Cartagena de Indias (Colombia) 2012, *Conference* Panama (Panama) 2011, *Conference* Dominican Rep 2010. [2016/XD8203/**D**]

♦ Caribbean Association of Neurological Surgery / see Caribbean Association of Neurological Surgeons (#03455)

♦ Caribbean Association of Nutritionists and Dietitians (CANDI) 03456

Contact Good Health Medical Ctr, 7 Fitzblackman Dr, Woodbrook, Trinidad-Tobago. E-mail: flemtt@yahoo.com.
Contact address not obtained. E-mail: dbcpeace2009@gmail.com.

History 29 Jun 1972, Port-of-Spain (Trinidad-Tobago). **Aims** Collaborate with other disciplines in the improvement of the nutritional status of the peoples of the region; encourage standards of excellence in the practice of nutrition and dietetics in the region; promote and encourage continuing education in nutrition and other allied fields; promote, encourage and improve the status of nutritionists and dieticians in the region; establish standards of nutritionists, dieticians and auxiliary personnel. **Structure** General Meeting (every 2 years, previously annual). Board of Directors. Executive Committee, consisting of President, Vice President, President Elect, Secretary, Immediate Past President and Treasurer. Standing Committees (7): Nominating; Admissions; Finance; Nutrition; Education; Public Relations; Career Guidance. Country Representatives. **Languages** English. **Staff** None. **Finance** Subscriptions; pledges. **Activities** Provides nutrition education and health promotion through National Nutrition Week, lectures, discussions and seminars; collaborates with other organizations to provide training and workshops and develop management tools for nutritionists and dieticians. **Events** *Biennial general meeting and conference* Montego Bay (Jamaica) 2007, *Biennial General Meeting* Jamaica 2005, *Biennial general meeting and conference* Kingston (Jamaica) 2005, *Biennial general meeting and conference / Biennial General Meeting* Trinidad-Tobago 2003, *Biennial general meeting and conference / Biennial General Meeting* Barbados 2001. **Publications** *CANDi Line* (4 a year) – online newsletter.
Members Active; Graduate; Retired; Honorary; National Groups. Members in 14 countries and territories:
Antigua-Barbuda, Bahamas, Barbados, Canada, Dominica, Grenada, Guadeloupe, Guyana, Jamaica, Neth Antilles, St Lucia, Trinidad-Tobago, USA, Virgin Is USA.
IGO Relations Observer status with: *Caribbean Community (CARICOM, #03476).* **NGO Relations** Member of: *International Confederation of Dietetic Associations (ICDA, #12856).* [2013/XD5030/**D**]

♦ Caribbean Association of Otolaryngologists (CAO) 03457

Pres 54 Market Street, Montego Bay, Jamaica. T. +8769521332. Fax +8769524099. E-mail: grandi@cwjamaica.com.
URL: http://www.caoent.com/

History 1994. Former names and other names: *Caribbean Association of Otolaryngology* – alias. **Aims** Increase cooperation between otolaryngologists in the Caribbean. **Structure** Officers: 2 Presidents; Vice-President. **Events** *Annual Conference* Nassau (Bahamas) 2015, *Annual Conference* St Vincent-Grenadines 2011. **NGO Relations** Member of: *International Federation of Oto-Rhino-Laryngological Societies (IFOS, #13496).* [2015/XD7769/**D**]

♦ Caribbean Association of Otolaryngology / see Caribbean Association of Otolaryngologists (#03457)

♦ Caribbean Association of Pharmacists (CAP) 03458

Pres 91 Dumbarton Ave, Kingston, Jamaica. T. +18768180962. E-mail: thecapoffice@gmail.com.
URL: http://ww2.cap-pharmacists.com/

History Sep 1976, Kingston (Jamaica). **Aims** Advance development and empowerment of the people of the Caribbean through excellence in provision of all aspects of pharmacy practice. **Structure** Executive Council (meets 3 times a year). **Languages** Dutch, English, French, Spanish. **Staff** 11.00 FTE, voluntary. **Finance** Members' dues. Registration fees for sessions and meetings; project support. **Activities** Events/meetings. **Events** *Annual Convention* Orlando, FL (USA) 2019, *Annual Convention* Grand Cayman Is (Cayman Is) 2018, *Annual Convention* Belize City (Belize) 2017, *Annual Convention* Montego Bay (Jamaica) 2016, *Annual Convention* Georgetown (Guyana) 2015. **Publications** *CAP Journal and Review.*
Members Full (2,500) in 24 countries and territories:
Anguilla, Antigua-Barbuda, Aruba, Bahamas, Barbados, Belize, Bermuda, Canada, Cayman Is, Curaçao, Dominica, Grenada, Guyana, Jamaica, Montserrat, St Kitts-Nevis, St Lucia, St Vincent-Grenadines, Suriname, Trinidad-Tobago, Turks-Caicos, UK, USA, Virgin Is UK.
IGO Relations *Caribbean Community (CARICOM, #03476).* **NGO Relations** Member of: *Pharmaceutical Forum of the Americas (#18351).* [2018.11.04/XD9254/**D**]

♦ Caribbean Association for Plant Science, Industry, Commerce and Use in Medicine (internationally oriented national body)
♦ Caribbean Association for the Rehabilitation of the Disabled (inactive)
♦ Caribbean Association for Rehabilitation Therapists (inactive)
♦ Caribbean Association for Reproductive and Sexual Health (no recent information)
♦ Caribbean Association of Researchers and Herbal Practitioners Association (no recent information)

♦ Caribbean Association of Small and Medium Enterprises (CAMSE) . 03459

Asociación de Pequeñas y Medianas Empresas del Caribe

Pres 10 Waterloo Avenue, Kingston, Jamaica. T. +8767547444. Fax +8767545513. E-mail: chinmook@gmail.com.

History Founded 2005. Also referred to as *Caribbean Association of Small and Medium Size Enterprises.* **Aims** Promote and advance small and medium sized enterprises in the Caribbean. [2017.06.01/XM2197/**D**]

♦ Caribbean Association of Small and Medium Size Enterprises / see Caribbean Association of Small and Medium Enterprises (#03459)
♦ Caribbean Association for the Teaching of English (inactive)
♦ Caribbean Association for Technical and Vocational Education and Training (internationally oriented national body)

♦ Caribbean Association of Technologists, Technicians and Craftsmen (CATTAC) 03460

Chairman 1-3 St Mary's Junction, Freeport, Trinidad-Tobago. T. +8687629109. E-mail: cattaccaribbean@yahoo.com.

History 1998. **Aims** Influence members and individuals on, and cooperate with other agencies and affiliates in, prevention of accidents, fire and occupational diseases; organize, establish and conduct programmes to educate members in methods and procedures and initiate, advise, recommend and comment on matters relating to technical training and education; collect and analyse data on technical issues; assist in determining engineering requirements for safe design, construction and use of plants and machines; assist in formulating safety regulations; act as a clearing-house for information on scholarships, fellowships, grants, bursaries, courses and programmes. **Structure** Executive; Divisional Representatives. **Languages** English. **Staff** 1.50 FTE, paid. Voluntary. **Finance** Budget (annual): US$ 50,000. Members' dues. Corporate sponsorship, donations, fund raising activities. **Activities** Training/education. **Events** *Conference* Castries (St Lucia) 2000, *Conference* Bridgetown (Barbados) 1999, *Annual Conference* Port-of-Spain (Trinidad-Tobago) 1999, *Annual technical conference / Annual Conference* Port-of-Spain (Trinidad-Tobago) 1999, *Annual technical symposium* St George's (Grenada) 1999. **Publications** *CATTAC Newsletter* (4 a year). Bulletins; annual review.
Members General (corporate and non-corporate); Honorary. Members in 12 countries:
Antigua-Barbuda, Barbados, Belize, Cuba, Dominica, Grenada, Guyana, Martinique, St Kitts-Nevis, St Lucia, St Vincent-Grenadines, Trinidad-Tobago. [2014.09.23/XD6317/**D**]

♦ Caribbean Association of Theological Schools (CATS) 03461

Chairman United Theological College of the West Indies, PO Box 136, Kingston, Jamaica. T. +18769272868.
Contact Codrington College, BB20027, St John BB20027, ST JOHN BB20027, Barbados. T. +12464231140. Fax +12464231592.

History 1986, the four member schools being associated since 1970. **Aims** Coordinate theological programmes presently undertaken by member colleges; review existing programmes and develop new ones as the need arises; promote *continuing education* in theology. **Structure** Meeting (annual). Officers: Chairperson; Secretary-Treasurer. **Languages** English. **Staff** None. **Finance** Members' dues: US$ 100. Other source: occasional support from agencies. **Events** *Conference* Jamaica 2011, *Paul yesterday and today* Jamaica 2001, *Conference* Barbados 1995, *Conference* Jamaica 1993. **Publications** *Biblical Resistance Hermeneutics within a Caribbean Context* (2010) by Oral Thomas; *Conflicts and Contradictions* (1998) by Noel Titus; *Caribbean Theology* (1994) by Lewin Williams; *The Development of Methodism in Barbados, 1823-1883* (1994) by Noel Titus.
Members Theological colleges (4) in 3 countries:
Barbados, Jamaica (2), Trinidad-Tobago.
NGO Relations Member of: *World Conference of Associations of Theological Institutions (WOCATI, #21296).* [2011.09.12/XD3145/**D**]

♦ Caribbean Association of Women Police (inactive)

♦ Caribbean Aviation Safety and Security Oversight System (CASSOS) 03462

Secretariat 4 Winchester Road, Kingston, Jamaica. T. +18769604364. Fax +18769294532. E-mail: info@cassos.org.
URL: http://cassos.org/

History Agreement establishing CASSOS entered into force 3 Jul 2008. Formally launched Feb 2009, Guyana, at Headquarters of *Caribbean Community (CARICOM, #03476)* Secretariat. Successor to *Interim Regional Aviation Safety Oversight System (RASOS) Office*, which was operating arm of *Association of Civil Aviation Authorities of the Caribbean (ACAAC)*, set up 2001. An Institution of CARICOM. **Aims** Grow a safe, secure, vibrant and orderly civil aviation system, making a key contribution to the development of the Region through partnership. **Structure** Board of Directors. **Finance** Equal contributions from each Member State. Other sources: technical and financial assistance from donors.
Members Governments (6):
Barbados, Guyana, Haiti, Jamaica, Suriname, Trinidad-Tobago.
Regional organization:
Member governments participating through OECS (9):
Anguilla, Antigua-Barbuda, Dominica, Grenada, Montserrat, St Kitts-Nevis, St Lucia, St Vincent-Grenadines, Virgin Is UK.
[2017/XM6100/**F***]

♦ Caribbean Badminton Confederation 03463

Contact Barbados Badminton Association, PO BOX 659, Bridgetown, St Michael, Bridgetown ST MICHAEL, Barbados. E-mail: bba.association@gmail.com.
History 1972, as *Caribbean Regional Badminton Confederation (CAREBACO)*. **Aims** Promote the sport of badminton in the region. **Structure** Board, comprising one representative of each Member Country. President; Vice-President; Secretary/Treasurer. **Languages** English. **Finance** Members' dues. Budget (annual) US$ 500. **Activities** Annual meeting in host country of yearly CAREBACO Championships. **Events** *Annual meeting* Port-of-Spain (Trinidad-Tobago) 1991, *Annual Meeting* Bridgetown (Barbados) 1988. **Publications** *CAREBACO Newsletter* (12 a year).
Members Badminton national associations in 9 countries and territories (" indicates associate member):
Aruba, Barbados, Bermuda, Curaçao, Guatemala (*), Guyana, Jamaica, Suriname, Trinidad-Tobago.
NGO Relations Member of: *Badminton World Federation (BWF, #03060)*. [2011/XD9628/**D**]

♦ Caribbean Baptist Fellowship 03464

Executive Secretary/Treasurer 6-8 Pembroke Street, Port of Spain 100506, Trinidad-Tobago. T. +17377551. E-mail: caribbaptistfell@gmail.com.
URL: http://caribbeanbaptistfellowship.com/
History 14 Apr 1970. Established as a regional office of *Baptist World Alliance (BWA, #03176)*. **Aims** Disseminate and share information and resources; cooperate in planning and implementation of programmes; contribute to the strengthening, foundation and growth of (indigenous) *Churches*; provide special ministry to men, women and youth. **Structure** General Assembly (every 4 years); Executive (meets annually); Officers. **Staff** 1.00 FTE, paid. **Finance** Financed by regional and international support. Annual budget: 80,000 USD. **Activities** Events/meetings; projects/programmes; publishing activities; training/education. **Events** *Quinquennial General Assembly* Santo Domingo (Dominican Rep) 2003, *Quinquennial General Assembly* Lake Yale, FL (USA) 1993.
Members Full in 23 countries and territories:
Antigua-Barbuda, Bahamas, Barbados, Belize, Bermuda, Cayman Is, Dominica, Dominican Rep, Grenada, Guadeloupe, Guiana Fr, Guyana, Haiti, Jamaica, Martinique, St Kitts-Nevis, St Lucia, St Vincent-Grenadines, Suriname, Trinidad-Tobago, Turks-Caicos, Virgin Is UK, Virgin Is USA. [2022.02.02/XE8170/**E**]

- ♦ Caribbean Baptist Women's Union (see: #03176)
- ♦ Caribbean Baseball Confederation (inactive)
- ♦ Caribbean Basin Corrections Association (inactive)
- ♦ Caribbean Basin Investment Fund (inactive)
- ♦ Caribbean Basin Management Project / see Caribbean Water and Sewerage Association (#03567)
- ♦ Caribbean Basin Water Management Programme / see Caribbean Water and Sewerage Association (#03567)
- ♦ Caribbean Biodiversity Fund (unconfirmed)
- ♦ Caribbean Birds / see BirdsCaribbean (#03267)
- ♦ Caribbean Brain Research Organization (inactive)
- ♦ Caribbean Broadcasting Corporation (internationally oriented national body)

♦ Caribbean Broadcasting Union (CBU) 03465

Union des radiodiffusions des Caraïbes
SG Suite 1B Bldg 6A, Harbour Industrial Estate, Harbour Road, St Michael BB11145, ST MICHAEL BB11145, Barbados. T. +12464301017. Fax +12462289524. E-mail: cbusg@caribsurf.com – cbuadmin@caribsurf.com.
URL: http://www.caribroadcastunion.org/
History 1970, Barbados. From 1999, business operations undertaken by *Caribbean Media Corporation (CMC)*. **Aims** Stimulate the flow of broadcast material between radio and television systems in the region, and, through the exchange of programming, assist the strengthening of the process of Caribbean integration. **Structure** General Assembly (annual); Board of Directors; Permanent Secretariat in Barbados. **Languages** English. **Staff** 3.00 FTE, paid. **Finance** Members' dues. **Activities** Training/education; advocacy/lobbying/activism; events/meetings. **Events** *General Assembly* 2021, *General Assembly* 2020, *General Assembly* San Andrés (Colombia) 2019, *General Assembly* Kingston (Jamaica) 2018, *General Assembly* Nassau (Bahamas) 2017.
Members Full in 22 countries and territories:
Anguilla, Antigua-Barbuda, Bahamas, Barbados, Belize, Bermuda, Cayman Is, Colombia, Cuba, Curaçao, Grenada, Guyana, Jamaica, Montserrat, St Croix Is, St Kitts Is, St Lucia, St Maarten, St Vincent-Grenadines, Suriname, Trinidad-Tobago, Turks-Caicos.
Associate members in 16 countries and territories:
Anguilla, Antigua-Barbuda, Barbados, Canada, Dominica, France, Guyana, Jamaica, Netherlands, St Lucia, Suriname, Tortola Is, Trinidad-Tobago, UK, USA, Virgin Is USA.
Included in the above-mentioned associate members, 2 organizations listed in this Yearbook:
Caribbean School of Media and Communication (CARIMAC, #03552); *International Communications Network (no recent information)*.
Consultative Status Consultative status granted from: *World Intellectual Property Organization (WIPO, #21593)* (Permanent Observer Status). **NGO Relations** Member of: *Public Media Alliance (PMA, #18568)*; *World Broadcasting Unions (WBU, #21247)*. [2021/XD8615/y/**D**]

♦ Caribbean Business and Investment Support Network (CARIBIS-NET) 03466

Contact Caribbean Export, PO Box 34B, Bridgetown, St Michael, Bridgetown ST MICHAEL, Barbados. T. +12464360578. Fax +12464369999. E-mail: info@carib-export.com.
URL: http://www.carib-export.com/
History 21 Jul 2006, Barbados. **Aims** Enhance collaboration, information sharing and the development of common services among Caribbean business support organizations.
Members in 8 countries:
Bahamas, Barbados, Dominica, Dominican Rep, Guyana, Haiti, St Kitts-Nevis, Trinidad-Tobago.
IGO Relations *Caribbean Export Development Agency (Caribbean Export, #03501)*. [2008/XM2217/**F**]

- ♦ Caribbean-Canada Trade Agreement (treaty)
- ♦ Caribbean Cane Farmers' Association (inactive)

♦ Caribbean Cardiac Society (CCS) 03467

Main Office Ste 20 Seymour Park, 2 Seymour Ave, Kingston 10, Jamaica. T. +8769782276. Fax +8769274199. E-mail: ccs@cwjamaica.com.
URL: http://www.caribbeancardiac.org/
History 12 Apr 1988, Kingston (Jamaica), during 3rd Caribbean Cardiology Conference. **Aims** Advance knowledge of disease of the heart and circulation among medical and paramedical professions in the Caribbean. **Structure** Council, including President, Vice-President, Secretary, Assistant-Secretary and Treasurer. Committees (6). **Events** *Annual Conference* Fort de France (Martinique) 2007, *Annual Conference* Montego Bay (Jamaica) 2006, *Annual Conference* Miami, FL (USA) 2005, *Annual Conference* St Lucia 2004, *Annual Conference* Barbados 2001. **Publications** *Caribbean Cardiac Society Bulletin*.
Members in 28 countries and territories:
Antigua, Argentina, Aruba, Bahamas, Barbados, Belize, Canada, Cuba, Curaçao, Dominica, Dominican Rep, France, Grenada, Guadeloupe, Guyana, Haiti, Jamaica, Martinique, St Kitts-Nevis, St Lucia, St Vincent-Grenadines, Suriname, Trinidad-Tobago, Turks-Caicos, UK, USA, Venezuela, Virgin Is UK.
IGO Relations Located at: *University of the West Indies (UWI, #20705)*. **NGO Relations** Member of: *Healthy Caribbean Coalition (HCC, #10893)*; *InterAmerican Heart Foundation (IAHF, #11432)*. Affiliate of: *European Society of Cardiology (ESC, #08536)*. [2013.10.03/XM2482/**D**]

- ♦ Caribbean and Central American Conference on Physical Education and Sports for the Handicapped (meeting series)

♦ Caribbean Centre for Development Administration (CARICAD) 03468

Centre des Caraïbes pour l'administration du développement
Exec Dir 1st Floor Weymouth Corporate Centre, Roebuck Street, St Michael 11080, ST MICHAEL 11080, Barbados. T. +12464278535 – +12464278536. Fax +12464361709. E-mail: jastaphan@caricad.net – caricad@caricad.net.
URL: http://www.caricad.net/
History by decision of *Caribbean Community (CARICOM, #03476)* Heads of Government in 1975. Became operational in 1980. **Aims** Facilitate and enhance development and sustainability of a strong leadership and governance framework within the public sector of the Caribbean Community, effectively encouraging social partnerships in the process. **Structure** Small core secretariat includes Executive Director. **Languages** English. **Staff** 24.00 FTE, paid. **Finance** Financed by annual contributions from member governments. **Activities** Research and development; projects/programmes; networking/liaising. **Events** *Conference* St Lucia 2000, *Workshop* Trinidad-Tobago 2000, *Caribbean policy forum conference* Virgin Is UK 2000, *Annual General Meeting* Bridgetown (Barbados) 1999, *Joint international conference* Bridgetown (Barbados) 1999. **Publications** *Caricad Chronicle* (6 a year) – e-newsletter.
Members Membership open to CARICOM States and Overseas Territories within the Caribbean Region. Members at present 16 countries and territories:
Antigua-Barbuda, Bahamas, Barbados, Belize, Dominica, Grenada, Guyana, Jamaica, Montserrat, St Kitts-Nevis, St Lucia, St Vincent-Grenadines, Suriname, Trinidad-Tobago, Turks-Caicos, Virgin Is UK.
IGO Relations Works closely with various regional and international developmental partners including: *Canadian International Development Agency (CIDA, inactive)*; *Caribbean Community (CARICOM, #03476)* Secretariat; *Caribbean Development Bank (CDB, #03492)*; *Caribbean Regional Technical Assistance Centre (CARTAC, #03550)*; *CARICOM Implementation Agency for Crime and Security (IMPACS, #03573)*; *CARICOM Single Market and Economy (CSME, #03575)*; *Commonwealth Secretariat (#04362)*; *Department for International Development (DFID, inactive)*; *ILO (#11123)*; *International Bank for Reconstruction and Development (IBRD, #12317)* (World Bank); *Organisation of Eastern Caribbean States (OECS, #17804)*; United Nations Department of Economic and Social Affairs (UNDESA); *United Nations Public Administration Network (UNPAN, #20615)*. **NGO Relations** Works closely with various regional and international developmental partners including: *Commonwealth Association for Public Administration and Management (CAPAM, #04310)*.
[2016.06.30/XE4838/**E***]

- ♦ Caribbean Centre for Monetary Studies / see Caribbean Centre for Money and Finance (#03469)

♦ Caribbean Centre for Money and Finance 03469

OIC Univ of the West Indies, St Augustine, Trinidad-Tobago. T. +18686451172 – +18686621701. Fax +18686456017.
URL: http://www.ccmf-uwi.org/
History May 1995, under the auspices of the central banks of *Caribbean Community (CARICOM, #03476)* and *University of the West Indies (UWI, #20705)*. Became fully operational 1 Aug 1995. Evolved out of the *Regional Programme of Monetary Studies (RPMS)*, established 1968, whose first conference was held in 1969, Port-of-Spain (Trinidad-Tobago). Original title: *Caribbean Centre for Monetary Studies (CCMS)*. **Aims** Assist *policy* formulation through research on monetary and financial matters; provide a forum for officials of *central banks* to exchange views and discuss research findings; increase efficiency and flexibility of response to emerging needs and rapidly changing environment of the region; enhance efforts in the area of central bank training and creation of an adequate and specialist regional repository of information. **Structure** Board, comprising Central Bank Governors, Vice-Chancellor of the University of the West Indies or his designate and a representative of the University of the West Indies. **Languages** English. **Staff** 4.00 FTE, paid. **Finance** Sponsored by 10 regional (Central) Banks of: Bahamas; Barbados; Belize; Curaçao; *Eastern Caribbean Central Bank (ECCB, #05231)*; Guyana; Haiti; Jamaica; Suriname; Trinidad-Tobago. **Activities** Events/meetings; training/education; research/documentation; publishing activities. **Events** *Annual Conference* Nassau (Bahamas) 2016, *Annual conference* Georgetown (Guyana) 2015, *Annual conference* Port-of-Spain (Trinidad-Tobago) 2014, *Annual conference* Kingston (Jamaica) 2013, *Annual conference* Paramaribo (Suriname) 2012. **Publications** *Caribbean Centre for Money and Finance Newsletter* (12 a year); *Journal of Business Finance and Economics in Emerging Economies* (2 a year); *Aldith Brown Memorial Lectures* (annual). Annual report; conference papers; financial statistics papers; monographs; technical papers; working papers.
Members Central banks (12) in 12 countries:
Antigua-Barbuda, Bahamas, Barbados, Belize, Guyana, Haiti, Jamaica, St Kitts-Nevis, St Lucia, St Vincent-Grenadines, Suriname, Trinidad-Tobago.
IGO Relations *Caribbean Development Bank (CDB, #03492)*; *Inter-American Development Bank (IDB, #11427)*; *International Bank for Reconstruction and Development (IBRD, #12317)*; *International Monetary Fund (IMF, #14180)*. Member of: *Latin American and Caribbean Research Network (#16284)*.
[2016.09.28/XE3792/**E**]

♦ Caribbean Centre for Renewable Energy and Energy Efficiency (CCREEE) 03470

Exec Dir Trinity Office Ctr, Country Road, St Michael, ST MICHAEL, Barbados. E-mail: info@ccreee.org.
URL: http://www.ccreee.org/
History Memorandum of Understanding signed 17 Mar 2014, between *Small Island Developing States – Island Energy for Island Life (SIDS DOCK, #19314)*, *UNIDO (#20336)* and Government of Austria, to assist Small Island Developing States (SIDS) in creation of a network. Technical and institutional design validated, Jul 2014, Roseau (Dominica). Establishment endorsed by *Caribbean Community (CARICOM, #03476)*, Jul 2015, Bridgetown (Barbados). Officially inaugurated 28 Oct 2015, Bridgetown (Barbados). Legal Agreement adopted 6 Jul 2017, Grenada, at Meeting of the Conference of Heads of Government of CARICOM. A CARICOM Institution. **Aims** Improve access to modern, affordable and reliable energy services, energy security and mitigation of negative externalities of the energy system by promoting renewable energy and energy efficiency investments, markets and industries in the Caribbean. **Structure** Council; Executive Board; Technical Advisory Committee; Secretariat. National Focal Institutions; Thematic Hubs.
Members States (10):
Barbados, Belize, Dominica, Grenada, Guyana, Jamaica, St Kitts-Nevis, St Lucia, St Vincent-Grenadines, Suriname.
Additional Partner States (5):
Antigua-Barbuda, Bahamas, Haiti, Montserrat, Trinidad-Tobago.
IGO Relations Core Partners: *Austrian Development Agency (ADA)*; Energy Unit of *Caribbean Community (CARICOM, #03476)*; *Small Island Developing States – Island Energy for Island Life (SIDS DOCK, #19314)*; *UNIDO (#20336)*. Cooperates with: *ECOWAS Centre for Renewable Energy and Energy Efficiency (ECREEE, #05335)*; *Pacific Centre for Renewable Energy and Energy Efficiency (PCREEE, #17941)*. [2017/XM6103/**D***]

♦ Caribbean Chamber of Commerce in Europe (CCCE) 03471

Chambre de Commerce et d'Industrie des Caraïbes en Europe (CCCE) – Cámara de Comercio del Caribe para Europa (CCCE)
SG c/o BECI, Avenue Louise 500, 1050 Brussels, Belgium. T. +3226810393. Fax +3226409328. E-mail: admin@caribbeanchamber.eu – info@caribbeanchamber.eu.
URL: http://www.caribbeanchamber.eu/

History 5 Nov 2019, Brussels (Belgium). Registration: Banque-Carrefour des Entreprises, No/ID: 0737.425.078, Start date: 5 Nov 2019, Belgium, Brussels. **Aims** Promote trade and commerce between the greater Caribbean and the UK/Europe; attract European investment to strengthen the Caribbean economy. **Structure** Advisory Board; Board of Directors; Investment Board. Executive Director. **Languages** Dutch, English, French, Spanish. **Staff** 1.00 FTE, paid; 10.00 FTE, voluntary. **Finance** Sources: donations; members' dues; subsidies. **Activities** Awareness raising; capacity building; events/meetings; financial and/or material support; guidance/assistance/consulting; humanitarian/emergency aid; knowledge management/information dissemination; monitoring/evaluation; networking/liaising; publishing activities; research/documentation; standards/guidelines; training/education. Active in: Andorra, Anguilla, Antigua-Barbuda, Aruba, Austria, Bahamas, Barbados, Belgium, Belize, Bermuda, Bonaire Is, Bulgaria, Canaries, Cayman Is, Croatia, Cuba, Curaçao, Cyprus, Czechia, Denmark, Dominica, Dominican Rep, Dutch Caribbean, England, Estonia, Faeroe Is, Finland, France, Germany, Gibraltar, Greece, Grenada, Guadeloupe, Guiana Fr, Guyana, Haiti, Holy See, Hungary, Iceland, Ireland, Isle of Man, Isle of Wight, Italy, Jamaica, Latvia, Liechtenstein, Lithuania, Luxembourg, Malta, Martinique, Moldova, Monaco, Montserrat, Netherlands, Norway, Portugal, Puerto Rico, Romania, Russia, San Marino, Scotland, Slovakia, Slovenia, Spain, St Barthélemy, St Kitts-Nevis, St Lucia, St Maarten, St Martin, St Vincent-Grenadines, Suriname, Sweden, Switzerland, Türkiye, Turks-Caicos, UK, Virgin Is UK, Virgin Is USA, Wales. [2022/XM8908/t/E]

♦ Caribbean Child Development Centre (internationally oriented national body)
♦ Caribbean Citrus Growers Association (no recent information)

♦ Caribbean Coalition for Development and Reduction of Armed Violence (CDRAV) 03472

Secretariat c/o Women's Inst for Alternative Development (WINAD), 11 Meyler Street, Belmont, Port-of-Spain, Trinidad-Tobago. T. +18686212495. Fax +18686212495.
URL: http://www.cdrav.org/

Aims Advocate for policy reform on armed violence. **Publications** *CDRAV Bulletin* (12 a year).
Members Full in 14 countries and territories:
Antigua-Barbuda, Barbados, Belize, Dominica, Dominican Rep, Grenada, Guyana, Haiti, Jamaica, St Kitts-Nevis, St Lucia, St Vincent-Grenadines, Trinidad-Tobago, Turks-Caicos.
NGO Relations Member of: *Control Arms (#04782).* [2013/XJ7672/D]

♦ Caribbean Coalition of National AIDS Programme Coordinator (CCNAPC) 03473

Secretariat 4 O'Connor Street, Woodbrook, Port-of-Spain, Trinidad-Tobago. T. +18686241526 – +18686235527. Fax +18686247396.
URL: http://www.ccnapc.org/

Aims Advocate for an expanded and sustainable response to the *HIV*/AIDS epidemic by providing high level technical and managerial leadership in member countries and supporting alliances to reduce the spread and mitigate the impact of HIV/AIDS in the region. [2009.07.15/XM2028/F]

♦ Caribbean College of Family Physicians (CCFP) 03474

Pres 19A Windsor Avenue, Kingston 5, Jamaica. T. +18769460954. Fax +18769460954. E-mail: ccfp@cwjamaica.com – worldfamilydoctorday@gmail.com.
Exec Dir address not obtained.
URL: http://www.caribgp.org/

History 1987, Jamaica. Officially deemed a Liaison Organization within *Caribbean Community (CARICOM, #03476)* in 1992. At the 10th Meeting of COHSOD-Ministers of Health and Social Services within *Caribbean Community (CARICOM, #03476)* 2004, officially accorded "Observer Status" within that grouping. **Aims** Improve the health status of Caribbean people by providing the highest standard of family practice patient care through continuing medical education (CME) and advocacy. **Structure** Board of Directors; Regional Secretariat. **Languages** Creoles and pidgins, Dutch, English. **Staff** 1.00 FTE, paid. **Finance** Sources: meeting proceeds; members' dues. **Activities** Advocacy/lobbying/activism; awards/prizes/competitions; events/meetings. **Events** *Pan Caribbean Conference* Jamaica 2014, *Pan Caribbean Conference* Jamaica 2013, *Pan Caribbean Conference* Trinidad-Tobago 2012, *Pan Caribbean Conference* Jamaica 2011, *Pan-Caribbean conference / Pan Caribbean Conference* Barbados 2009.
Members Chapters in 4 countries:
Bahamas, Jamaica, St Lucia, Trinidad-Tobago.
Individuals in 16 countries and territories:
Antigua-Barbuda, Barbados, Belize, Bermuda, Cayman Is, Curaçao, Dominica, Grenada, Guyana, St Kitts-Nevis, St Lucia, St Maarten, St Vincent-Grenadines, Suriname, Turks-Caicos, Virgin Is UK.
IGO Relations Liaison organization within: *Caribbean Community (CARICOM, #03476).* Through WONCA, recognized by: *Pan American Health Organization (PAHO, #18108); WHO (#20950).* **NGO Relations** Member of (4): *Caribbean Area Network for Quality Assurance in Tertiary Education (CANQATE, #03441); Healthy Caribbean Coalition (HCC, #10893); Planetary Health Alliance (PHA, #18383); World Organization of Family Doctors (WONCA, #21690).* [2021/XD4479/D]

♦ Caribbean College of Surgeons (CCOS) 03475

Contact 34 Sandy Lane Estate, St James, ST JAMES, Barbados. T. +12464327508. Fax +12464321830. E-mail: collsurg@caribsurf.com.
URL: http://www.caribbeancollegeofsurgeons.com/

History 2001. **Aims** Improve quality of care for the surgical patient by setting high standards for surgical education and practice. **Structure** General Assembly (annual). Executive Committee, including President, President-Elect, Secretary and Treasurer. **Events** *Annual Conference* Bridgetown (Barbados) 2015, *Annual Conference* Willemstad (Curaçao) 2014, *Annual Conference* Tortola Is (Virgin Is UK) 2013, *Annual Conference* Grenada 2011, *Annual Conference* Georgetown (Guyana) 2010. [2014/XM3236/D]

♦ Caribbean Commission (inactive)

♦ Caribbean Community (CARICOM) 03476

Communauté des Caraïbes – Comunidad del Caribe

SG Turkeyen, Greater Georgetown, Georgetown, Guyana. T. +5922220001 – +592222002 – +5922220075. Fax +5922220171. E-mail: communications@caricom.org – registry@caricom.org.
URL: http://www.caricom.org/

History Established 4 Jul 1973, Chaguaramas (Trinidad-Tobago), on signature of *Treaty of Chaguaramas (1973)* by Prime Ministers of Barbados, Guyana, Jamaica and Tobago. Belize, Dominica, Grenada, Montserrat, St Lucia and St Vincent became members in May 1974; and Antigua and St Kitts-Nevis-Anguilla in Jul 1974. Bahamas became member of the Community, but not the Common Market, in Jul 1983. Suriname became Full member, 4-7 Jul 1995. Haiti became the 15th Full member on deposit of an instrument of accession, 3 Jul 2002. Associate membership granted to: Virgin Is UK, Jul 1991; Turks-Caicos, Jul 1991; Anguilla, Jul 1988; Cayman Is, 16 May 2002; Bermuda, 2 Jul 2003. Neth Antilles is currently seeking an interest in closer cooperation with CARICOM through observer status in the *Council for Human and Social Development (COHSOD)* and the *Council for Trade and Economic Development (COTED).*
CARICOM replaces and extends the work of previous attempts at regional integration, namely of *British West Indies Federation (inactive)* (1958-1962) and of *Caribbean Free Trade Association (CARIFTA, inactive).* The independent *West Indian Commission (inactive)* recommended considerable changes, proposed enhancement of activities of the Council of Ministers and advised development of *Association of Caribbean States (ACS, #02411),* to include all countries of the Caribbean Basin. In the context of a revised Treaty of Chaguaramas, CARICOM member governments would subscribe to a *'CARICOM Charter of Civil Society'* covering wider issues than economic circumstances. A multi-disciplinary intergovernmental task force was set up to oversee revision of the Treaty in order to make *CARICOM Single Market and Economy (CSME, #03575)* a reality. Heads of Government reaffirmed the benefit to the entire region of the ACS, 5-8 Jul 1993, Nassau (Bahamas). *Treaty of Chaguaramas – Revised (2001),* signed Jul 2001, Georgetown (Guyana), paved the way for implementation of the new Treaty provisions and the subsequent establishment of the CSME. The 13th Inter-Sessional Meeting of CARICOM leaders, 2001, Belize, approved programmes for the removal of restrictions on the right of establishment, the provision of services and the movement of capital as required by member states in fulfillment of obligations under Protocol II; these came into effect on 1 Mar 2002. Member states have committed to remove all other restrictions by 2005, thus completing the Single Market for goods, services, capital and significant movement of persons.
Aims Improve standards of living and work; work towards full employment of labour and other factors of production; accelerate, coordinate and sustain economic development and convergence; expand trade and economic relations with third states; enhance levels of international competitiveness; organize increased production and productivity; achieve a greater measure of economic leverage and effectiveness of Member States in dealing with third states, groups of states and entities of any description; enhance coordination of Member States' foreign and economic policies and enhance functional cooperation, including more efficient cooperation of common services and activities for the benefit of its people, accelerated promotion of greater understanding among its people and the advancement of their social, cultural and technological development, and intensified activities in areas such as health, education, transportation and telecommunications.
Structure Governance set out in establishing 1793 and revised 2002 Treaties.
Decision-making/Principal Bodies: *Conference of Heads of Government (The Conference)* as supreme organ, with *Bureau of the Conference of Heads of Government* as Sub-Committee; *Community Council of Ministers (The Council).* Assisted by: Organs (5); Bodies (4). Organs (5): *Council for Finance and Planning (COFAP); Council for Foreign and Community Relations (COFCOR); Council for Human and Social Development (COHSOD); Council for National Security and Law Enforcement (CONSLE); Council for Trade and Economic Development (COTED).* Bodies (4): Budget Committee; Committee of Central Bank Governors; Legal Affairs Committee; CARICOM Committee of Ambassadors. Quasi Cabinet, comprising Heads of Government.
CARICOM Secretariat (CCS), as principal Administrative Organ. Includes Offices; Directorates; Other Unites and Special Projects. Offices (4): Secretary-General; Deputy Secretary-General; General Counsel; Trade Negotiations. Directorates (3): Foreign and Community Relations; Human and Social Development, including responsibility for *Caribbean Festival of Creative Arts (CARIFESTA, #03504);* Trade and Economic Integration. Other Unit: PANCAP Coordinating Unit – coordinating arm of *Pan Caribbean Partnership against HIV and AIDS (PANCAP, #18171).*
/Institutions/ Entities established by or under the auspices of the Community and recognized as Institutions of the Community:
- *Caribbean Agricultural Research and Development Institute (CARDI, #03436);*
- *Caribbean Agricultural Health and Food Safety Agency (CAHFSA, #03435);*
- *Caribbean Aviation Safety and Security Oversight System (CASSOS, #03462);*
- *Caribbean Centre for Renewable Energy and Energy Efficiency (CCREEE, #03470);*
- *Caribbean Centre for Development Administration (CARICAD, #03468);*
- *Caribbean Community Climate Change Centre (CCCCC, #03477);*
- *Caribbean Court of Justice (CCJ, #03486);*
- *Caribbean Disaster Emergency Management Agency (CDEMA, #03493);*
- *Caribbean Examinations Council (CXC, #03500);*
- *Caribbean Institute for Meteorology and Hydrology (CIMH, #03520);*
- *Caribbean Meteorological Organization (CMO, #03524);*
- *Caribbean Public Health Agency (CARPHA, #03544);*
- *Caribbean Regional Fisheries Mechanism (CRFM, #03547);*
- *Caribbean Telecommunications Union (CTU, #03560);*
- *CARICOM Competition Commission (CCC, #03571);*
- *CARICOM Development Fund (CDF, #03572);*
- *CARICOM Implementation Agency for Crime and Security (IMPACS, #03573);*
- *CARICOM Regional Organization for Standards and Quality (CROSQ, #03574).*

/Associate Institutions/ – specialized operating bodies, each of which has its independent charter or legal instrument dictating its structure, mode of operation and lines of authority:
- *Caribbean Development Bank (CDB, #03492);*
- *Caribbean Law Institute (CLI, #03523)* and Caribbean Law Institute Centre (CLIC);
- University of Guyana;
- *University of the West Indies (UWI, #20705).*

/Functional Cooperation Institutions/:
- *Caribbean Export Development Agency (Caribbean Export, #03501);*
- *Caribbean Regional Information and Translation Institute (CRITI, #03548);*
- *Caribbean Tourism Organization (CTO, #03561);*
- *Council of Legal Education (CLE, #04908).*
- *Forum of Caribbean States (CARIFORUM, #09904).*

Languages English. **Staff** 238.00 FTE, paid. **Finance** Government contributions. **Activities** Politics/policy/regulator. Areas of Work: Agriculture; *CARICOM Single Market and Economy (CSME, #03575);* Crime and Security; Culture; Education; Energy; Environment and Sustainable Development; Foreign Policy and Community Relations; Gender; Health Sector Development Human Development; ICT for Development; Services; Sports Development; Statistics; Tourism; Trade Negotiations; Transportation; Youth Development. Management of treaties and agreements: *Agreement on the Harmonisation of Fiscal Incentives to Industry (1973); Agreement for the Avoidance of Double Taxation and the Prevention of Fiscal Evasion with Respect to Taxes on Income and for the Encouragement of International Trade and Investment (1973); Caribbean-Canada Trade Agreement (CARIBCAN).* **Events** *Caribbean renewable energy forum* Bridgetown (Barbados) 2011, *Caricom – European Union senior officials meeting on political dialogue* Kingston (Jamaica) 2010, *Japan-CARICOM ministerial level conference* Tokyo (Japan) 2010, *Annual Meeting of the Conference of Heads of Government* Georgetown (Guyana) 2009, *Summit of heads of state and government of the European Union, Latin America and the Caribbean* Lima (Peru) 2008. **Publications** *CARICOM Perspective* (annual); *CARICOM View* (irregular) – newsletter. *A CARICOM Handbook for Schools* (Rev ed 2008); *Common External Tariff of the Caribbean Community: Based on the Harmonised Commodity Description and Coding System* (2007); *Directory of Caribbean Publishers* (7th ed 2007); *International Standard Book Number (ISBN) Users' Manual – Caribbean* (6th ed 2006); *List of CARICOM Meetings Arranged Alphabetically by Acronym/Abbreviation, 1973-2005* (2006); *Caribbean Trade and Investment Report* (2005); *CARICOM: Our Caribbean Community* (2005); *Women and Men in CARICOM Member States – Power and Decision-making: 1980-2002* (2003); *Revised Treaty of Chaguaramas Establishing the Caribbean Community, including the CARICOM Single Market and Economy* (2001). Information Services: *Caribbean Information Action Group (CARINFO, inactive),* chaired by CDB.
Members Governments of 15 countries and territories:
Antigua-Barbuda, Bahamas, Barbados, Belize, Dominica, Grenada, Guyana, Haiti, Jamaica, Montserrat, St Kitts-Nevis, St Lucia, St Vincent-Grenadines, Suriname, Trinidad-Tobago.
Associate members (5):
Anguilla, Bermuda, Cayman Is, Turks-Caicos, Virgin Is UK.
Associate institutions listed in this Yearbook (5):
Caribbean Conference of Churches (CCC, #03479); Caribbean Development Bank (CDB, #03492); Caribbean Examinations Council (CXC, #03500); Caribbean Law Institute (CLI, #03523) (and the Caribbean Law Institute Centre CLIC); *Organisation of Eastern Caribbean States/Competitive Business Unit (OECS/CBU, #17805).*
IGO Relations Formal agreement with: *UNESCO (#20322); UNIDO (#20336); World Trade Organization (WTO, #21864)* (Observer Status). Relationship agreement with: *FAO (#09260).* Permanent observer status with: *World Intellectual Property Organization (WIPO, #21593).* Accredited by: *United Nations Framework Convention on Climate Change – Secretariat (UNFCCC, #20564).* Invited to sessions of Intergovernmental Council of: *International Programme for the Development of Communication (IPDC, #14651).* Relevant Treaty: *CARICOM Multilateral Air Services Agreement (1996).* [2017/XD4579/y/D*]

♦ Caribbean Community Climate Change Centre (CCCCC) 03477

Main Office Lawrence Nicholas Bldg, 2nd Fl, Ring Road, PO Box 563, Belmopan, Belmopan, Belize. T. +5018221094 – +5018221104. E-mail: pr@caribbeanclimate.bz – info@caribbeanclimate.bz.
URL: http://caribbeanclimate.bz/

History 2001, within *Caribbean Community (CARICOM, #03476).* Became fully operational Feb 2004. Also referred to as *5Cs.* A CARICOM Institution. **Aims** Serve as a clearing house for information on climate change issues and on the region's response to managing and adapting to climate change. **Structure** Board of Directors. **Languages** English. **Staff** 30.00 FTE, paid. **Activities** Regional Framework for Achieving Development Resilient to Climate Change and Implementation Plan. **IGO Relations** Accredited by: *United Nations Framework Convention on Climate Change – Secretariat (UNFCCC, #20564).* Recognized by: *UNEP (#20299); United Nations Institute for Training and Research (UNITAR, #20576).* **NGO Relations** Member of: *Climate Knowledge Brokers (CKB, #04016).* Participates in: *Global Center on Adaptation (GCA).* Partner of: *Many Strong Voices (MSV, #16568).* [2020/XM3130/E*]

Caribbean Confederation Credit
03478

♦ Caribbean Confederation of Credit Unions (CCCU) 03478
Confédération des coopératives d'épargne et de crédit des Caraïbes – Confederación Caribeña de Cooperativas de Ahorro y Crédito

Sec PO Box 1213, Corner Wilkin Street and St Johnston Ave, Fortlands, Basseterre, ST KITTS, St Kitts-Nevis. T. +18694669453. Fax +18694666957. E-mail: admin@caribccu.coop.
Events – Convention Coordinator address not obtained.
URL: http://www.caribccu.coop/

History 17 Aug 1972, Roseau (Dominica), as *Eastern Caribbean Council of Credit Unions*, as the successor of the *'West Indies Conferences of Credit Societies'*. **Aims** Serve as the apex trade and development organization for financial and non-financial cooperatives in the Caribbean. **Structure** Board of Directors of 7 members, elected from Member Delegates. Executive Officers: President; Vice-President; Treasurer; Secretary; CEO. **Languages** English. **Staff** 7.00 FTE, paid. **Finance** Members' dues. Other sources: grants; fees for services. **Activities** Defends and represents interests of the cooperative sector; provides technical and managerial assistance to strengthen and expand the sector; promotes and facilitates technology transfers and expertise; conducts promotional and educational campaigns to showcase cooperative sector achievements and benefits; organizes educational conventions and other fora to strengthen leadership, governance and management; provides directors and employees opportunities for skills training with regional and international certification; mobilizes financial and technical resources for expanding the sector. Programmes: Training and Development; Technical Assistance; Fund Mobilization; Participatory Strategic Planning. **Events** *Annual International Convention* St Maarten 2010, *Annual Convention* Grenada 2008, *Annual general meeting / Annual International Convention* Grenada 2008, *Annual Convention* Barbados 2007, *Annual general meeting / Annual International Convention* Barbados 2007. **Publications** *Revised Credit Union Examination and Supervision Manual* (2005); *Teachers Manual for Caribbean School Cooperative Societies* (1998).
Members Affiliate national and single-island credit union associations (19) in 18 countries and territories: Antigua-Barbuda, Bahamas, Barbados, Belize, Bermuda, Cayman Is, Dominica, Grenada, Guyana, Jamaica, Montserrat, Neth Antilles, St Kitts-Nevis, St Lucia, St Vincent-Grenadines, Suriname, Tortola Is, Trinidad-Tobago.
NGO Relations Member of: *Caribbean Association of Banks (CAB, #03443)*; *International Co-operative Alliance (ICA, #12944)*; *World Council of Credit Unions (WOCCU, #21324)*. [2019/XD2853/D]

♦ Caribbean Conference of Churches (CCC) 03479
Conférence des Eglises de la Caraïbe – Conferencia de Iglesias del Caribe – Conferentie van Caraïbische Kerken

Gen Sec CCC Head Office and Trinidad Programme Centre, PO Box 876, Port-of-Spain, Trinidad-Tobago. T. +18686623064. Fax +18686621303. E-mail: cccgensec@gmail.com – trinidadheadoffice@ccc-caribe.org.
Street address No 3B Warren Street, St Augustine, Trinidad-Tobago.
Jamaica Programme Centre 14 South Ave, PO Box 527, Kingston, Jamaica. T. +18769267114. Fax +18769236990. E-mail: jamaica-sro@ccc-caribe.org.
URL: http://www.ccc-caribe.org/

History 13 Nov 1973, Kingston (Jamaica). Founded following initiatives started in 1970, the first ecumenical agency, *Caribbean Committee on Joint Christian Action (CCJCA)*, having been set up in 1955, and followed up, 1971, Chaguaramas (Trinidad). **Aims** Promote ecumenism and social change in obedience to Jesus Christ and in solidarity with the poor. **Structure** General Assembly (every 5 years). Continuation Committee (Management Board), meets twice a year, between Assemblies and consists of 15 voting members, headed by a Praesidium (appointed by Assembly), comprising 3 Presidents, at least one of whom must be a woman. Finance Committee is special sub-committee of the Continuation Committee. Regional Office, located in Trinidad, including Regional Programme Coordinators who are responsible for management and coordination of programmatic initiatives. Sub-Regional Offices (2), headed by Senior Programme Officers, supported by Programme Staff. Programme Centres (2): Antigua; Jamaica; Trinidad. Secretariat, comprising Staff Executive Group (SEG), including General Secretary (Head), supported by 2 Associate General Secretaries (responsible for portfolios of Ecumenical Relations and Theological Affairs and of Organizations Development, Planning and Administration) and a Regional Financial Officer. Programme Executive for International Relations, Public and Cultural Affairs, also at Secretariat. Legally incorporated entity: *Christian Action for Development in the Caribbean (CADEC, no recent information)*. **Languages** Dutch, English, French, Spanish. **Staff** Paid; voluntary; intern. **Finance** Sources: grants; members' dues. **Activities** Advocacy/lobbying/activism; projects/programmes. **Events** *Quinquennial General Assembly* Panama 2005, *Quinquennial General Assembly* Cuba 1996, *Quinquennial General Assembly* Trinidad-Tobago 1991, *Caribbean workshop on theological reflection on tourism* 1987, *Quinquennial General Assembly* Barbados 1986. **Publications** *Ecuscope Caribbean* (4 a year). **Information Services** *CCC Documentation Centre* – located at Secretariat.
Members Churches (33) in 11 countries and territories: Cuba, Curaçao, Dominica, Grenada, Guyana, Haiti, Jamaica, Neth Antilles, Puerto Rico, Suriname, Trinidad-Tobago.
Included in the above, 7 regional and international members and groupings, including 4 listed in this Yearbook: *Antilles Episcopal Conference (AEC, #00856)*; *Church in the Province of the West Indies (CPWI, #03921)*; Ethiopian Orthodox Church; *Evangelical Lutheran Church in America (ELCA)* (Caribbean Synod); Methodist Church in the Caribbean and the Americas; Moravian Church – East West Indies Province; Salvation Army (#19041).
Work covers 32 countries and territories:
Anguilla, Antigua-Barbuda, Aruba, Bahamas, Barbados, Belize, Bermuda, Bonaire Is, Cayman Is, Costa Rica, Cuba, Curaçao, Dominica, Dominican Rep, Grenada, Guadeloupe, Guyana, Haiti, Honduras, Jamaica, Martinique, Montserrat, Panama, Puerto Rico, St Kitts-Nevis, St Lucia, St Maarten, St Vincent-Grenadines, Suriname, Trinidad-Tobago, Virgin Is UK, Virgin Is USA.
IGO Relations Member of (1): *Pan Caribbean Partnership against HIV and AIDS (PANCAP, #18171)*. Collaborates with: *Canadian International Development Agency (CIDA, inactive)*; *Caribbean Community (CARICOM, #03476)*; *Department for International Development (DFID, inactive)*; *Joint United Nations Programme on HIV/AIDS (UNAIDS, #16149)*; *UNHCR (#20327)*; *UNICEF (#20332)*; *United Nations Office on Drugs and Crime (UNODC, #20596)*; other UN agencies; regional governmental and state bodies. **NGO Relations** Close links with community-based organizations, NGOs and other regional and international organizations committed to working in development programmes such as the Priority Regional Initiatives (PRIs). Regional network of: *Caribbean Policy Development Centre (CPDC, #03540)*. [2011.06.01/XD4341/y/D]

♦ Caribbean Congress of Fluid Dynamics / see Latin American and Caribbean Conference on Theoretical and Applied Mechanics (#16269)

♦ Caribbean Congress of Labour (CCL) 03480
Congrès du travail des Caraïbes – Congreso de Trabajadores del Caribe

Pres c/o UTEB, PO Box EE1187, Nassau, Bahamas.
Secretariat Claphan Close, Wildey, PO Box 90-B, St Michael, ST MICHAEL, Barbados. T. +12464275067. Fax +12464272496. E-mail: cclres@caribsurf.com.
URL: http://www.caribbeancongressoflabour.com/

History 15 Sep 1960, St George's (Grenada). **Aims** Work for: achievement of the economic, social, educational, cultural and other aspirations of workers of the Caribbean region; recognition of the trade union movement as the legitimate instrument of working people to achieve their rights. Support the accepted principles of free and democratic trade unionism as subscribed to by ICFTU and ORIT; seek to represent the free trade union movement in all regional agencies which perform functions affecting the social/economic interests of working people; encourage the formation of national groupings and/or centres of trade unions. **Structure** Congress of delegates of affiliated organizations (every 3 years). General Council; Administrative Committee. Officers: President; Secretary-General; 1st, 2nd and 3rd Vice-Presidents. **Languages** English. **Staff** 7.00 FTE, paid. **Finance** Affiliation fees pro rata to member organizations' membership. **Activities** Events/meetings: training/education; knowledge management/information dissemination. Functions as a regional clearing house for information and research on trade union organizations, wages and working conditions, labour legislation, collective bargaining, etc. **Events** *Tripartite Caribbean conference on the global financial crisis and its social and labour dimensions* Kingston (Jamaica) 2009, *Meeting* Barbados 1997, *Subregional women conference* Barbados 1997, *Congress* Bahamas 1995, *Congress* Antigua (Antigua-Barbuda) 1992. **Publications** *Labour Viewpoint*; *On Behalf of Women*.
Members Organizations (28) in 17 countries and territories:
Antigua-Barbuda, Bahamas, Barbados, Belize, Bermuda, Curaçao, Dominica, Grenada, Guyana, Jamaica, Montserrat, St Kitts-Nevis, St Lucia, St Maarten, St Vincent-Grenadines, Suriname, Trinidad-Tobago.
Consultative Status Consultative status granted from: *ILO (#11123)* (Regional). **IGO Relations** Affiliate member of: *Caribbean Tourism Organization (CTO, #03561)*. [2018/XD0208/F]

♦ Caribbean Conservation Association (CCA) 03481
Association caraïbe pour l'environnement (ACE) – Asociación para la Conservación del Caribe (ACC)

Contact address not obtained. E-mail: admin@caribbeanconservation.org.
URL: http://www.caribbeanconservation.org/

History Founded 1967, St Thomas (Virgin Is USA). Headquarters moved to Barbados in 1975. Registered in accordance with the law of Barbados; original By-Laws adopted, Jun 1995; last amended Aug 1995. **Aims** Create a greater awareness of priority issues and of the value of the Caribbean's natural resources; enhance the quality of life for present and future generations by facilitating development and implementation of policies, programmes and practices to contribute to the sustainable use of Caribbean natural resources; improve ability to manage these resources and ascertain on a continuing basis the needs of the region in relation to them; enhance access to and information exchange; identify and implement priority projects; promote integration of conservation into socio-economic development; improve links within the region and outside to develop a broad base for supporting activities for the conservation and management of natural resources. **Structure** General Meeting (annual). Board of Directors, comprising 6 nongovernmental members, 4 governmental members and 2 individual members, Executive, comprising President, Vice-President, Secretary/Treasurer and Executive Director. Secretariat, headed by Executive Director, assisted by Administrative Support Staff and Technical Working Groups. **Languages** English, French, Spanish. **Staff** 3 full-time professionals; 2 administrative support staff; project consultants. **Finance** Members' dues: Organizational US$ 100; Individual US$ 25; Student US$ 15; Sponsoring US$ 1,000. Main source: member governments and external funding agencies. **Activities** Main categories (4): environmental education; information management; project development; project implementation. Acts as a clearing house for information on environmental projects; supports and assists in identifying, development and promotion of natural sites of potential global significance in the Caribbean to the World Heritage Committee; carries out regional inventories, surveys and assessments; participates in formulating and implementing regional plans and strategies; participates in and conducts regional education and communication activities; monitors and reviews existing environmental multi-lateral agreements and environmental legislation in the region, encouraging appropriate harmonization of legislation and programme activities; encourages governments to accept, ratify or accede to appropriate conventions, protocols, agreements, especially *Convention Concerning the Protection of the World Cultural and Natural Heritage (World Heritage Convention, 1972)*; supports training programmes, including part of the UWI Programme in Marine Sciences and Environmental Management; provides assistance in project development and management. Field projects and activities, including the 3-year *'Darwin Initiative Coral Reef Education Project'* to promote Biodiversity in the Caribbean programme activities, compatible with the programme approved by the Caribbean Environment Programme (UNEP's Caribbean Action Plan). Received *'Global 500 (UNEP) Award'* in 1997 for outstanding action and achievement in the field in the Wider Caribbean Region. Instrumental in setting up: *Caribbean Environmental Reporters' Network (CERN, no recent information)*; *Caribbean Heritage Programme (no recent information)*; *Caribbean Marine Parks and Protected Areas Management Network (no recent information)* (with CIDA); *Marine Resources Programme for the Eastern Caribbean (no recent information)*; *Museums Association of the Caribbean (MAC, #16909)*. **Events** *Annual General Meeting* Christ Church (Barbados) 2003, *Annual general meeting* Trinidad-Tobago 2002, *Annual General Meeting* Bridgetown (Barbados) 2001, *Annual General Meeting* Barbados 2000, *Annual General Meeting* Barbados 1999. **Publications** *CCA Journal* (4 a year); *Artificial Reefs: A Handbook for the Eastern Caribbean*. *Caribbean Environment Environmental Studies* – series. *Birds of Our Islands*; *Corals and Coral Reefs* – environmental education manual; *Environmental Guidelines for Caribbean Planners*; *Guide to Seamoss Cultivation in the West Indies*. Books: monographs; education and training manuals; occasional publications; country environmental profiles; booklets; fact sheets. Information Services: Environmental conservation and management databases. Library facilities, including monographs and other documentary material, slide sets, audio tapes, videotapes, film strips and CD-ROMs, including CABI's E-CD on the world's environmental literature. **Information Services** *Caribbean Contacts Database*; *Caribbean Contacts Database*.
Members Governmental members (18), NGO (310) and individuals in 35 countries and territories: Anguilla, Antigua-Barbuda, Aruba, Bahamas, Barbados, Belize, Bermuda, Brazil, Canada, Cayman Is, Dominica, Dominican Rep, France, Grenada, Guadeloupe, Guiana Fr, Guyana, Haiti, Jamaica, Martinique, Mexico, Montserrat, Netherlands, Puerto Rico, St Kitts-Nevis, St Lucia, St Vincent-Grenadines, Tanzania UR, Trinidad-Tobago, UK, USA, Venezuela, Virgin Is UK, Virgin Is USA.
Consultative Status Consultative status granted from: *ECOSOC (#05331)* (Ros A).
IGO Relations Accredited by: *International Whaling Commission (IWC, #15879)*. Cooperates with:
– *Canadian International Development Agency (CIDA, inactive)*;
– *Caribbean Action Plan (CAR, #03432)*;
– *Caribbean Community (CARICOM, #03476)*;
– *Caribbean Forum for Development (CFD, no recent information)*;
– *Caribbean Institute for Meteorology and Hydrology (CIMH, #03520)*;
– *Commonwealth Secretariat (#04362)*;
– *Global Environment Facility (GEF, #10346)*;
– *International Bank for Reconstruction and Development (IBRD, #12317)*;
– *OAS (#17629)*;
– *Organisation of Eastern Caribbean States (OECS, #17804)*;
– *UNEP (#20299)*;
– *UNDP (#20292)*;
– *UNESCO (#20322)*;
– *United States Agency for International Development (USAID)*;
– *University of the West Indies (UWI, #20705)*.
Associated with Department of Global Communications of the United Nations.
NGO Relations Member of: *Environment Liaison Centre International (ELCI, no recent information)*; *GEF CSO Network (GCN, #10087)*; *International Union for Conservation of Nature and Natural Resources (IUCN, #15766)*. [2020/XD4292/D]

♦ Caribbean Conservation Corporation / see Sea Turtle Conservancy
♦ Caribbean Consumers' Association (inactive)
♦ Caribbean Copyright Link / see Association of Caribbean Copyright Societies (#02404)

♦ The Caribbean Council (CC) 03482
Conseil des Caraïbes – Consejo del Caribe – Parat der Karibik

Managing Dir Temple Chambers, 3-7 Temple Avenue, London, EC4Y 0HP, UK. T. +442075838739. Fax +442075839657.
Contact address not obtained.
URL: http://www.caribbean-council.org/

History May 1992. Founded by *Caribbean Association of Industry and Commerce (CAIC, #03448)*, *West India Committee (WIC, #20920)* and *'Private Sector Organization of Jamaica'*, following regional conferences held by these organizations: 1988, London (UK); 1989, Barbados; 1990, Jamaica; 1991, Brussels (Belgium); 1992, Curaçao; 1993, Santo Domingo (Dominican Rep). Registered company, owned by a UK registered Charity, *Caribbean Foundation*, until 2010, when Charity ceased to operate. Former names and other names: *Caribbean Council for Europe (CCE)* – former; *Conseil des Caraïbes pour l'Europe* – former; *Consejo del Caribe para Europea* – former; *Europarat der Karibik* – former; *Caribbean Foundation* – former. **Aims** Support development of Caribbean and of Caribbean economic interests; provide specialist consultancy services to private companies, trade associations, governments, public sector organizations and regional and multilateral organizations in: international trade negotiations and regulatory affairs; export development and investment promotion; event and conference organization. **Structure** Board of Directors. Parent organization of: Caribbean-Britain Business Council; Cuba Initiative; Central American Business Council. **Languages** English, French, Spanish. **Staff** 4.00 FTE, paid. **Finance** Sources: contributions; fees for services; meeting proceeds; sale of publications. **Activities** Events/meetings: guidance/assistance/consulting; research/documentation. **Events** *Annual Europe-Caribbean Conference* Paris (France) 1999, *Conference* Brussels (Belgium) 1998, *Conference / Annual Europe-Caribbean Conference* Havana (Cuba) 1997, *Conference* Havana (Cuba) 1996, *Conference / Annual Europe-Caribbean Conference* Port-of-Spain (Trinidad-Tobago) 1995. **Publications** *The View from Europe* (weekly); *Caribbean Insight* (23 a year); *Central America Briefing* (23 a year); *Cuba Briefing* (45 a year); *The Business of Tourism* (26 a year).
Members Full in 18 countries and territories:
Antigua-Barbuda, Bahamas, Barbados, Belize, Cuba, Dominica, Dominican Rep, France, Grenada, Guyana, Jamaica, Netherlands, St Kitts-Nevis, St Lucia, St Vincent-Grenadines, Suriname, Trinidad-Tobago, UK.
NGO Relations Cooperates with (2): *Caribbean Association of Industry and Commerce (CAIC, #03448)*; *Caribbean Hotel and Tourism Association (CHTA, #03516)*. [2021.09.01/XD3206/D]

♦ Caribbean Council for the Blind (CCB) 03483

Exec Dir Lower All Saints Road, PO Box 1517, St John's, St John, Antigua-Barbuda. T. +12684624111. Fax +12684626371.

URL: http://www.eyecarecaribbean.com/

History Founded 1967, Trinidad-Tobago. **Aims** Give sight while creating opportunities for people whose sight cannot be restored. **Structure** Executive Committee; President; Secretary/Executive Director. **Languages** Dutch, English, French. **Staff** 12.50 FTE, paid. **Finance** Funding from international NGOs. Budget (annual): about US$ 900,000. **Activities** Major projects, programmes and plans include: Blindness Prevention and Sight Restoration; Education Services for the Blind and Visually Impaired Children; Adjustment to Blindness Services; Resource Mobilization; Capacity Building. *VISION 2020 – The Right to Sight (inactive)* Working Group for the Caribbean; Biennial Conference; participation in regional meetings; regular training workshops and symposia; Education services for children with blindness and visual impairments. **Publications** *Quarterly Performance Indicator.* Annual Report.

Members Societies (30) in 19 countries and territories:

Anguilla, Antigua-Barbuda, Bahamas, Barbados, Belize, Cayman Is, Dominica, Grenada, Guadeloupe, Guyana, Haiti, Jamaica, Martinique, Montserrat, St Kitts-Nevis, St Lucia, St Vincent-Grenadines, Trinidad-Tobago, Turks-Caicos.

IGO Relations *WHO (#20950).* [2014/XD5020/**D**]

♦ Caribbean Council of Engineering Organizations / see Council of Caribbean Engineering Organizations (#04874)

♦ Caribbean Council for Europe / see The Caribbean Council (#03482)

♦ Caribbean Council of Forensic Laboratory Heads (inactive)

♦ Caribbean Council of Higher Education in Agriculture (CACHE) 03484

Conseil caraïbe d'éducation supérieure en agriculture – Consejo Caribeño de Educación Superior en Agricultura

Secretariat Fac of Food and Agriculture, Univ of the West Indies, St Augustine, Trinidad-Tobago. T. +18686623719 – +18686622002ext83322. E-mail: ffadd.outreach@sta.uwi.edu.

Exec Sec Univ ISA, Av Pres Antonio Guzman km 5 1/2, La Herradura, Santiago, Dominican Rep. T. +18092472000 ext213.

URL: http://cache-caribbean.org/

History Nov 1997, Dominican Rep, under the auspices of *Inter-American Institute for Cooperation on Agriculture (IICA, #11434).* **Aims** Foster *human resource* development for sustainable transformation of agriculture in the Caribbean. **Structure** General Assembly (annual); Board of Directors. **Languages** Dutch, English, French, Spanish. **Finance** Members' dues. **Activities** Training/education; networking/liaising. **Events** *General Assembly* Guadeloupe 2016, *Meeting* Homestead, FL (USA) 2016, *Meeting* Barbados 2015, *General Assembly / Annual General Assembly* Suriname 2015, *General Assembly* Punta Cana (Dominican Rep) 2001. **Publications** *CACHE News.* **Members** Higher education institutions (30) in 11 countries and territories of the Caribbean. Membership countries not specified. **IGO Relations** *Eastern Caribbean Institute of Agriculture and Forestry (ECIAF, #05234);* Ministries of Agriculture of CACHE country members. [2015.09.09/XE4134/**E**]

♦ Caribbean Council of Legal Education / see Council of Legal Education (#04908)

♦ Caribbean Council for Science and Technology (CCST) 03485

Conseil des Caraïbes pour la science et la technologie – Consejo de Ciencia y Tecnologia para el Caribe

Secretary c/o NIHERST, 43-45 Woodford Street, PO Box 113, Newtown, Trinidad-Tobago. T. +18686227880 – +18686288523. Fax +18686221589. E-mail: ccst@niherst.gov.tt.

URL: http://www.ccst-caribbean.org/

History Apr 1980, Kingston, where statutes were adopted and signed, by *Caribbean Development and Cooperation Committee (CDCC, inactive)*, a permanent subsidiary body of *United Nations Economic Commission for Latin America and the Caribbean (ECLAC, #20556)*, the decision to establish CCST having been taken by CDCC at its 2nd session, Mar 1977, Santo Domingo (Dominican Rep). 1st session: 1981, Bridgetown. **Aims** Promote cooperation in the field of science and technology aimed at furthering the social and economic development of member nations, including the implementation of provisions of the Constituent Declaration of CDCC to promote efforts to cooperate in the mutual transfer of science and technology in order to facilitate the adaptation of imported technology and the development of domestic technologies and increase the bargaining power of the Caribbean countries in their relations with countries outside the area. **Structure** Regular Plenary Session (once a year). Executive Committee, consisting of Chairman, Vice-Chairman, Honorary Treasurer and two other members. Executive Secretariat, headed by Executive Secretary. **Finance** Sources: contributions from Member Governments, with additional support from organizations within the United Nations system and other institutions; funds for projects sponsored or launched by the Council. **Activities** Projects: National Consultations on science and technology; Technology Extension Service of the OECS countries and Belize (Belize); Renewable Energy; Science education and science popularization. Organizes or sponsors workshops. Collaborates on regional science and technology activities with other organizations/institutions. Provides advice on formulation of national science and technology policies and on environmentally friendly technologies. **Events** *Seminar on integrated water resource management in the Caribbean islands* Port-of-Spain (Trinidad-Tobago) 1997, *Plenary Session* Granada (Spain) 1996, *Plenary Session* Grenada 1996, *Plenary Session* Cuba 1995, *Plenary Session* Guyana 1994. **Publications** *CCST Newsletter* (4 a year). Reports; papers.

Members Governments of 15 countries and territories:

Antigua-Barbuda, Barbados, Belize, Cuba, Dominica, Grenada, Guyana, Haiti, Jamaica, St Kitts-Nevis, St Lucia, St Vincent-Grenadines, Suriname, Trinidad-Tobago, Virgin Is USA.

IGO Relations Cooperation agreements signed with: *Latin American Energy Organization (#16313).* Close working relations with: *Sistema Económico Latinoamericano (SELA, #19294); SSC WIDE (no recent information); UNESCO (#20322); University of the West Indies (UWI, #20705).* **NGO Relations** Close working relations with: *UWI Centre for Environment and Development, Mona (UWICED, see: #20705).* [2014/XE8871/**E***]

♦ Caribbean Court of Justice (CCJ) 03486

Contact 134 Henry Street, PO Box 1768, Port-of-Spain, Trinidad-Tobago. T. +18686232225. E-mail: info@ccj.org.

President of the Court address not obtained.

URL: http://ccj.org/

History 14 Feb 2001, Barbados, on signature of Agreement Establishing the Caribbean Court of Justice, at 12th inter-sessional meeting of Conference of Heads of Government of the Caribbean Community, within *Caribbean Community (CARICOM, #03476).* Came into force 23 Jul 2003; inaugurated 16 Apr 2005, Port-of-Spain (Trinidad-Tobago). First proposed by *Organization of Commonwealth Caribbean Bar Associations (OCCBA, inactive)*, Mar 1970, and again Apr 1970 at 6th Commonwealth Caribbean Heads of Government, by Jamaican delegation. *West Indian Commission (inactive)* endorsed proposed Caribbean Court of Appeal without qualification, 1989. **Aims** Protect and promote the rule of law as a court of final appeal and as guardian of the Revised Treaty of Chaguaramas by guaranteeing accessibility, fairness, efficiency and transparency, delivering clear and just decisions in a timely manner. **Structure** Court. Judges appointed by *Regional Judicial and Legal Services Commission (RJLSC, #18793).* **Languages** Dutch, English, French. **Finance** Financial sustainability and independence is ensured through a US$ 100,000,000 Trust Fund, currently constituted and managed by a Board of Trustees. **Activities** Politics/policy/regulatory. **Publications** *Caribbean Court of Justice: Issues and Perspectives* – journal. Articles.

Members Agreement is open to all member states of the Caribbean Community and (by invitation of Conference) to any other Caribbean country. Status of the non-independent members of CARICOM in relation to the original jurisdiction of the Court is yet to be decided. The following 12 states, members of CARICOM, are members of the Court:

Antigua-Barbuda, Barbados, Belize, Dominica, Grenada, Guyana, Jamaica, St Kitts-Nevis, St Lucia, St Vincent-Grenadines, Suriname, Trinidad-Tobago.

Bahamas is contemplating participation in the Court; Haiti expected to fully participate as soon as the country's situation resolved; Montserrat awaiting Instruments of Entrustment from Britain to allow involvement in the Court.

IGO Relations *CARICOM Single Market and Economy (CSME, #03575); Caribbean Regional Information and Translation Institute (CRITI, #03548).* **NGO Relations** Represented on CCJ Trust Fund: *Institute of Chartered Accountants of the Caribbean (ICAC, #11245).* [2017.03.22/XF3668/**F***]

♦ Caribbean Customs Law Enforcement Council (CCLEC) 03487

Conférence douanière inter-caraïbe (CDI) – Consejo del Caribe para la Aplicación de las Leyes de Aduaneras (CCALA)

Secretariat 4 Manoel Street, PO Box 1030, Castries, St Lucia. T. +17584532556. Fax +17584532563. E-mail: secretariat@cclec.org.

URL: https://www.cclec.org/

History in the 1970s as an informal association of customs administrations within the Caribbean region, meeting annually to exchange information on smuggling and to help help smaller regional administrations to adjust to the new threat of organized drug trafficking in the region. Has since expanded and diversified. A Memorandum of Understanding (MOU) regarding mutual assistance and cooperation for the prevention and repression of customs offences in the Caribbean zone was agreed by members and signed by 20 countries at Annual Conference, 1989, Miami FL (USA). This created a framework for the business activities of the Council and a legal basis for mutual assistance and exchange of information among members. As of Nov 2002, it has 38 signatories. **Aims** Improve the level of cooperation and information exchange among members; assist members to enhance the professionalism, efficiency, effectiveness and integrity of their organizations, through training, reform and modernization; raise the level of awareness in the Caribbean region of the value and importance of the services provided by customs; provide members with information and enhanced customs systems to allow them to prepare for and meet the challenges of the future. **Structure** Council (highest decision-making organ), meets annually. Executive Committee of 14 members, headed by Chairman. Permanent Secretariat (based in St Lucia), headed by Permanent Secretary, who is assisted by 3 attachés, Administrator Officer, IT specialist and clerical assistant. Joint Intelligence Office (JIO), based in San Juan (Puerto Rico) – cooperative agreement between CCLEC and World Customs Organization. **Languages** English, French, Spanish. **Staff** Secretariat: 3 loaned resources; 2 local, paid. JIO: 4 loaned resources; 1 on temporary assignment. **Finance** Member States' contributions. Other sources: international organizations and donor agencies. **Activities** Strategic priorities: Enhancement of Customs law enforcement cooperation and sharing information; Improvement of human resource management and development within customs; Modernization of customs legislation and procedures; Trade Facilitation, including assistance to members in preparing for *Free Trade Area of the Americas (FTAA, no recent information);* Implementation of measures to fight corruption and enhance integrity; Increase of awareness of CCLEC within the region and internationally. **Events** *Annual Conference* Aruba 2013, *Annual Conference* St Lucia 2012, *Annual Conference* Turks-Caicos 2003, *Annual Conference* 2002, *Annual Conference* Curaçao 2002. **Publications** *CCLEC Newsletter, JIO Enforcement Bulletin* – restricted; *Regional Clearance System Newsletter. CCLEC Strategic Plan 1998-2003.*

Members Customs departments (" indicates countries that have signed the MOU) of 38 countries and territories:

Anguilla, Antigua-Barbuda, Aruba, Bahamas, Barbados, Belize, Bermuda, Canada, Cayman Is, Colombia, Costa Rica, Cuba (*), Dominica, Dominican Rep, France, Grenada, Guatemala, Guyana, Haiti, Honduras, Jamaica, Mexico, Montserrat, Netherlands, Nicaragua (*), Panama, Spain, St Kitts-Nevis, St Lucia, St Vincent-Grenadines, Suriname, Trinidad-Tobago, Turks-Caicos, UK, USA, Venezuela, Virgin Is UK.

IGO Relations Memoranda of Understanding with: *Eastern Caribbean Islands Regional Security System (inactive); Inter-American Drug Abuse Control Commission (#11429); World Customs Organization (WCO, #21350).* **NGO Relations** Memorandum of Understanding with: *Association of Caribbean Commissioners of Police (ACCP, #02403).* [2022/XD4730/**D***]

♦ Caribbean Cytometry and Analytical Society (CCAS) 03488

Sec-Treas address not obtained. T. +12468367227. Fax +12464268406. E-mail: ccassecretariat@gmail.com.

Communications address not obtained.

URL: http://www.caribcas.org/

History 2003. **Structure** Officers; Country representatives. **Events** *Conference* Montego Bay (Jamaica) 2016, *Conference* St Maarten 2014, *Conference* Montego Bay (Jamaica) 2011, *Conference* Bridgetown (Barbados) 2010, *Conference* Frigate Bay (St Kitts-Nevis) 2009.

Members Representatives in 18 countries and territories:

Antigua, Aruba, Bahamas, Barbados, Belize, Dominica, Grenada, Guyana, Haiti, Jamaica, Martinique, Montserrat, St Kitts-Nevis, St Lucia, St Maarten, St Vincent-Grenadines, Suriname, Trinidad-Tobago.

IGO Relations Supporter: *Pan Caribbean Partnership against HIV and AIDS (PANCAP, #18171).* **NGO Relations** Supporter: *Caribbean HIV/AIDS Regional Training Network (CHART, #03515).* [2016/XJ2904/**D**]

♦ Caribbean Democrat Union (CDU) 03489

Contact PO Box 1550, Castries, St Lucia. T. +17587219555. E-mail: caribbeandemocratunion@gmail.com.

Facebook: https://www.facebook.com/CaribbeanDemocratUnion/

History 17 Jan 1986, Kingston (Jamaica). Founded on signature of a Charter known as the *'Kingston Declaration'.* **Aims** Advocate promotion of freedom and an economic system based on a social market economy through consideration of matters of political organization and policies. **Structure** Party Leaders Conference (every 2 years); Executive Committee; Secretariat. Ad hoc groups include Standing Committee on Foreign Affairs. **Staff** 3.00 FTE, paid. **Finance** Members' dues. **Activities** Charter covers: democracy; freedom and the individual; the individual in the community; private property and private enterprise; international relations Programme includes seminars on: environment; drug abuse; training of young leaders; women and development.

Members Political parties in 9 countries and territories:

Anguilla, Belize, Dominica, Grenada, Jamaica, Montserrat, St Kitts-Nevis, St Lucia, St Vincent-Grenadines.

NGO Relations A union with: *Americas Democrat Union (ADU, no recent information); European Democrat Union (EDU, inactive)* and *Asia Pacific Democrat Union (APDU, #01881)*, within *International Democrat Union (IDU, #13147).* [2022/XD1064/**D**]

♦ Caribbean Dermatology Association (CDA) 03490

Contact Ste 20, Seymour Park, 2 Seymour Ave, Kingston 10, Jamaica. T. +18769782276. Fax +18769274199. E-mail: secretariat@caribbeanderm.org.

URL: http://www.caribbeanderm.org/

History Nov 1992, Jamaica. **Aims** Stimulate cooperation of societies of dermatology and cooperation within the field; encourage advancement of dermatology and dermatological science and education throughout the Caribbean. **Structure** Assembly of Delegates; Executive Committee. **Languages** English. **Staff** 4.00 FTE, paid. **Finance** Sources: members' dues. **Activities** Events/meetings. **Events** *Annual Conference* Jamaica 2021, *Annual Conference* Kingston (Jamaica) 2020, *Annual Conference* Port-of-Spain (Trinidad-Tobago) 2019, *Annual Conference* St Vincent-Grenadines 2018, *Annual Conference* Gros-Islet (St Lucia) 2017. **Publications** None.

Members Ordinary; Associate; Honorary; Overseas. Individuals in 21 countries and territories:

Antigua, Aruba, Bahamas, Barbados, Belize, Bermuda, Canada, Cayman Is, Grenada, Guyana, Jamaica, Montserrat, St Kitts-Nevis, St Lucia, St Maarten, St Vincent-Grenadines, Suriname, Trinidad-Tobago, Turks-Caicos, USA, Virgin Is UK.

NGO Relations Member of (1): *International League of Dermatological Societies (ILDS, #14018).* [2020/XD5686/**D**]

♦ Caribbean Desalination Association (CaribDA) 03491

Admin Dir 2409 SE Dixie Hwy, Stuart FL 34996, USA. T. +17727818507. Fax +17724630860. E-mail: admin@caribda.com.

URL: http://www.caribda.com/

History Launched 4 Jun 2008, Curaçao. **Aims** Act as a platform for desalination and *water* reuse owners, designers and operators and others involved or having an interest in desalination and water reuse. **Structure** Board of Directors. **Finance** Members' dues. **Activities** Training/education; events/meetings. **Events** *Biennial Conference* Stuart, FL (USA) 2021, *Workshop* Punta Cana (Dominican Rep) 2017, *Biennial Conference* Port-of-Spain (Trinidad-Tobago) 2016, *Biennial Conference* St Thomas Is (Virgin Is USA) 2014. **Publications** *CaribDA News.* **NGO Relations** Regional Affiliate of: *International Desalination Association (IDA, #13152).* [2017.01.03/XM4290/**D**]

♦ Caribbean Development Bank (CDB) 03492

Banque de développement des Caraïbes – Banco de Desarrollo del Caribe (BDC)

Secretariat PO Box 408, Wildey, St Michael BB11000, ST MICHAEL BB11000, Barbados. T. +12464311600. Fax +12464267269. E-mail: info@caribank.org.

Caribbean Disaster Emergency
03493

alphabetic sequence excludes
For the complete listing, see Yearbook Online at

URL: http://www.caribank.org/
History 18 Oct 1969, Kingston (Jamaica). Established with the assistance of *UNDP (#20292)*, on signature of an agreement which entered into force 26 Jan 1970. An Associate Institution of *Caribbean Community (CARICOM, #03476)*. Former names and other names: *Caribank* – former. **Aims** Contribute to harmonious economic growth and development of member countries in the Caribbean; promote *economic cooperation* and integration among members, with special and urgent regard to the needs of the *less-developed* countries of the region. **Structure** Board of Governors (meets annually), comprises one Governor and one Alternate Governor nominated by each member country (for this purpose Anguilla, British Virgin Islands, Cayman Islands, Montserrat and Turks and Caicos Islands are together regarded as one member). Board of Directors, consisting of 17 Directors, 12 representing regional members and 5 representing non-regional members. President (who is Chairman of the Board of Directors); Vice-President (Operations); Vice-President (Corporate Services) and Bank Secretary. Directors of Departments (6): Economics; Projects; Finance; Legal; Human Resources; Information Technology. Headquarters in St Michael (Barbados). **Languages** English. **Staff** 180.00 FTE, paid. **Finance** Subscribed share capital as at 31 Dec 2011: – US$ 713 million, of which US$ 555.5 million callable and US$ 157.4 million paid-up. Special Funds Resources: US$ 753 million, major contributors being Canada and UK. **Activities** CDB's Charter permits it to make loans to private sector entities without government guarantee and to invest in the equity of enterprises. CDB also gives technical assistance to governments, public and private sector enterprises in Borrowing Member Countries. Sector portfolio: transport, communication and sea defence – 24%; manufacturing and mining – 12% (loans to development corporations for small industrialists, to governments for industrial estates, and to large industrialists); social services – 11%; agriculture, forestry and fishing – 6% (farm improvement credits for small farmers, loans to governments for agricultural infrastructure and to large farmers); power, energy and water – 9% (loans to governments for electric power and water supply); tourism – 2% (loans to governments for tourism infrastructure and to hotel operators); multisector and other – 12% (including the environment, human resource development – loans to governments to be on-lent to students aged 15 and over for university courses, teacher training and technical and vocational training, poverty reduction; institutional strengthening). Of this portfolio, 22% is delivered through financial intermediaries in borrowing member countries. CDB also lends to national development banks and other financial institutions. It seeks to identify projects in productive sectors of the economy in less-developed member countries. *Caribbean Technological Consultancy Services Network (CTCS Network, see: #03492)*, launched 1985, coordinates technical assistance to small and medium-sized manufacturing enterprises. **Events** *Annual Meeting* St George's (Grenada) 2018, *Annual Meeting* Turks-Caicos 2017, *Annual Meeting* Montego Bay (Jamaica) 2016, *Annual Meeting / Board of Governors Annual Meeting* Castries (St Lucia) 2013, *Annual Meeting* Grand Cayman Is (Cayman Is) 2012. **Publications** *CDB News* (4 a year); *CTCS Update* (4 a year). *Policy Sector Papers* – series. *CDB – Its Purpose, Role and Functions*; *Guidelines for Procurement*; *Procedures on the Selection and Engagement of Consultants by Recipients of CDB Financing*. Annual Report; Speciazl Development Fund Annual Report; Board of Governors Summary of Proceedings; development effectiveness review; basic information; statements by the President.
Members Borrowing regional members, 19 countries and territories:
Anguilla, Antigua-Barbuda, Bahamas, Barbados, Belize, Cayman Is, Dominica, Grenada, Guyana, Haiti, Jamaica, Montserrat, St Kitts-Nevis, St Lucia, St Vincent-Grenadines, Suriname, Trinidad-Tobago, Turks-Caicos, Virgin Is UK.
Non-Regional in 5 countries:
Canada, China, Germany, Italy, UK.
Other members in 3 countries:
Colombia, Mexico, Venezuela.
IGO Relations Observer to the Governing Council of: *UNEP (#20299)*. Cooperation Agreement with: *International Fund for Agricultural Development (IFAD, #13692)*. Support from: *International Trade Centre (ITC, #15703)*. Supports: *Caribbean Agricultural Research and Development Institute (CARDI, #03436)*. Participates in the activities of: *UNCTAD (#20285)*. Special agreement with: *ILO (#11123)*; *UNIDO (#20336)*. Accredited by: *United Nations Framework Convention on Climate Change – Secretariat (UNFCCC, #20564)*. Close cooperation with: *Caribbean Export Development Agency (Caribbean Export, #03501)*; *Inter-American Development Bank (IDB, #11427)* – resolution of 1974, entered into force 1977, allows IDB to lend through CDB to all CDB member countries whether or not members of IDB. Under Lom Conventions, links with: *European Commission (EC, #06633)*. Member of: *Committee of International Development Institutions on the Environment (CIDIE, no recent information)*. Observer member of: *Sistema Económico Latinoamericano (SELA, #19294)*. Adheres to: *Global Partnership for Effective Development Co-operation (GPEDC, #10532)*. **NGO Relations** Member of (2): *Association for Human Resources Management in International Organizations (AHRMIO, #02634)*; *Caribbean Digital Library Consortium (no recent information)* (as Founding member of). [2019.11.13/XF4023/**F***]

♦ Caribbean Disaster Emergency Management Agency (CDEMA) 03493

Coordinating Unit Resilience Way, Lower Estate, St Michael, ST MICHAEL, Barbados. T. +12464344880. Fax +12462713660.
URL: http://www.cdema.org/
History Sep 1991, in accordance with 11th Heads of Government meeting of *Caribbean Community (CARICOM, #03476)*, as *Caribbean Disaster Emergency Response Agency (CDERA)*. Present name adopted 1 Sep 2009. **Aims** Play its role as facilitator, driver, coordinator and motivating force for the promotion and engineering of Comprehensive Disaster Management (CDM) in all Participating States. **Structure** Council; Technical Advisory Committee; Coordinating Unit. **Languages** Dutch, English, French. **Finance** Administrative Funds provided by Participating States; each government contributes a specific percentage to the approved annual Administrative Budget of the Agency. Project Funds are provided by Donors to execute specific projects; Donors include government agencies, multilateral agencies – including *European Union (EU, #08967)*, UN agencies, NGOs and private sector firms. Emergency Assistance Fund is a special fund created to help offset the cost of disaster response operations. **Activities** Humanitarian/emergency aid; training/education; knowledgement management/information dissemination; capacity building; awareness raising. **Events** *Caribbean Conference on Comprehensive Disaster Management* Montego Bay (Jamaica) 2012. **Publications** *Caribbean Disaster News* (4 a year). Publishes or contributes to the production of a number of special publications.
Members Participating States (18):
Anguilla, Antigua-Barbuda, Bahamas, Barbados, Belize, Dominica, Grenada, Guyana, Haiti, Jamaica, Montserrat, St Kitts-Nevis, St Lucia, St Vincent-Grenadines, Suriname, Trinidad-Tobago, Turks-Caicos, Virgin Is UK. [2018.06.26/XF5108/**F***]

♦ Caribbean Disaster Emergency Response Agency / see Caribbean Disaster Emergency Management Agency (#03493)
♦ Caribbean Documentation Centre / see Caribbean Knowledge Management Centre (#03521)

♦ Caribbean Electric Utility Services Corporation (CARILEC) 03494

Exec Dir Desir Ave, Sans Soucis, PO Box CP 5907, Castries, St Lucia. T. +7584520140 – +7584520141. Fax +7584520142.
URL: http://www.carilec.org/
History Operations began Jun 1988; formally founded as a common service organization under a 5-year "Cooperative Agreement" signed Aug 1989 between *United States Agency for International Development (USAID)* and 9 Caribbean member utilities. Registered in accordance with the law of St Lucia. **Aims** Improve communication among members; provide technical information, training, capacity building, conference and other services. **Structure** General Meeting (annual); Board of Directors; Committees (4); Secretariat, headed by Executive Director. **Languages** English. **Staff** 13.00 FTE, paid. **Activities** Networking/liaising; knowledge management/information dissemination; training/education; capacity building; events/meetings; advocacy/lobbying/activism; research and development; humanitarian/emergency aid. **Events** *Annual General Meeting* St Thomas (Barbados) 2014, *Annual General Meeting* Jamaica 2013, *Annual General Meeting* St Maarten 2004, *Annual General Meeting* Curaçao 2002. **Publications** *CARILEC Newsletter* (12 a year). Annual Report; industry journal; membership directory. **Members** Full (34); Associate (71); Affiliate (8). Membership countries not specified. **IGO Relations** *Association of Caribbean States (ACS, #02411)*; *Caribbean Community (CARICOM, #03476)*; *Caribbean Disaster Emergency Management Agency (CDEMA, #03493)*; *University of the West Indies (UWI, #20705)*. **NGO Relations** *CANTO (#03416)*; *Caribbean Conservation Association (CCA, #03481)*. [2018.06.01/XF6010/**F**]

♦ Caribbean Employers' Confederation (CEC) 03495

Confédération des employeurs des Caraïbes – Confederación de Empleadores del Caribe
Exec Sec/Treas 17 Samaroo Road, Aranguez Roundabout North, Aranguez, San Juan, PO Box 911, Port-of-Spain, Trinidad-Tobago. T. +18686750273 – +18686752515. Fax +18686754866. E-mail: cecadmin@caribbeanemployers.org.
URL: http://www.caribbeanemployers.org/
History Feb 1960, Port-of-Spain (Trinidad-Tobago). Constitution adopted 1961; revised: Mar 1965; 18 Oct 1968; 27 Oct 1976; Jan 1991; Apr 1994; Apr 2000; Sep 2017. **Aims** Develop and promote good *industrial relations* practices at enterprise and macro-levels with the goal of productivity and prosperity for member countries and the region as a whole. **Structure** General Meeting (annual); Executive Council; Secretariat. **Languages** English. **Staff** 1.00 FTE, paid. **Finance** Members' dues. Project funding. **Activities** Knowledge management/information dissemination; events/meetings; training/education; projects/programmes; advocacy/lobbying/activism. **Events** *Annual General Meeting* Port-of-Spain (Trinidad-Tobago) 2016, *Strengthening Employers' Organizations' Understanding and Application of Research Methodology Workshop* St Lucia 2016, *Annual General Meeting* Christ Church (Barbados) 2015, *Annual General Meeting* Rodney Bay (St Lucia) 2014, *Annual General Meeting* Suriname 2013. **Publications** *CEC Newsletter* (2 a year). Proceedings of meetings; press releases; membership updates; social interest topics.
Members Employers' organizations in 18 countries and territories:
Antigua-Barbuda, Aruba, Bahamas, Barbados, Belize, Bermuda, Cayman Is, Dominica, Grenada, Guyana, Jamaica, Martinique, St Kitts-Nevis, St Lucia, St Maarten, St Vincent-Grenadines, Suriname, Trinidad-Tobago.
Consultative Status Consultative status granted from: *ILO (#11123)* (Regional). **IGO Relations** Caribbean Employers representative on Business Technical Advisory Committee on Labour Matters of: *OAS (#17629)*. Observer at meeting of Standing Committee of Ministers of Labour of *Caribbean Community (CARICOM, #03476)*. **NGO Relations** Consultative Status with: *International Organisation of Employers (IOE, #14428)*. [2020.03.03/XD0211/**D**]

♦ Caribbean Energy Information System (CEIS) 03496

Headquarters Scientific Research Council, PO Box 350, Hope Gardens, Kingston, Jamaica. T. +18099771840. Fax +18099271779. E-mail: ceis@src-jamaica.org.
URL: http://www.ceis-caribenergy.org/
History Established as part of *Caribbean Information System (CIS, inactive)*, by *UNESCO Energy Information Programme (EIP, no recent information)* and *United Nations Economic Commission for Latin America and the Caribbean (ECLAC, #20556)*. As of Oct 2000 "no longer current". **Aims** Facilitate the sharing of information on new and *renewable* sources of energy as well as *petroleum* in the territories of the Caribbean. **Structure** Regional Focal Point is the Scientific Research Council of Jamaica; Subregional Focal Points are Economic Affairs Secretariat in Antigua and Central Secretariat in St Lucia of *Organisation of Eastern Caribbean States (OECS, #17804)*. National Focal Points (12). **Finance** Supported by: *Commonwealth Science Council (CSC, #04361)*; *International Development Research Centre (IDRC, #13162)*. **Activities** Provides: information on energy conservation, new and renewable sources of energy (NRSE) and petroleum in the Caribbean; statistics on energy product flows, prices and sectoral end uses in the Caribbean; information on sources of expertise in energy; reviews of energy from published reports; document delivery services in microfiche; current developments on research in progress in energy. **Events** *Coordinators meeting* Barbados 1992, *Annual meeting* Basseterre (St Kitts-Nevis) 1989.
Members National focal points (12) in 12 countries and territories:
Antigua-Barbuda, Barbados, Dominica, Grenada, Guyana, Jamaica, Montserrat, St Kitts-Nevis, St Lucia, St Vincent-Grenadines, Trinidad-Tobago, Virgin Is UK.
IGO Relations *Caribbean Community (CARICOM, #03476)*; *Caribbean Development Bank (CDB, #03492)*. [2014.01.28/XF0166/**F***]

♦ Caribbean Engineering and Technical Professionals (internationally oriented national body)
♦ Caribbean Environmental Health Institute (inactive)

♦ Caribbean Environment Programme (CEP) 03497

Contact UNEP-CAR/RCU, 14-20 Port Royal Street, Kingston, Jamaica. T. +18769229267. Fax +18769229292. E-mail: unep-cartagenaconvention@un.org.
URL: https://www.unep.org/cep/
History Set up by Caribbean nations in support of *Convention for the Protection and Development of the Marine Environment of the Wider Caribbean Region (Cartagena Convention, 1983)*. Protocols: *Protocol Concerning Cooperation in Combating Oil Spills in the Wider Caribbean Region (1983)*; *Protocol Concerning Specially Protected Areas and Wildlife to the Convention for the Protection and Development of the Marine Environment of the Wider Caribbean Region (1990)*; *Protocol Concerning Pollution from Land-based Sources and Activities (1999)*. **Aims** Promote regional *cooperation* for the *protection* and *development* of the *marine* environment of the Wider Caribbean Region; provide a consolidated legislative, institutional and programmatic framework for cooperation among member countries and organizations concerned with the management of marine and *coastal resources* in the Region; provide effective coordination for implementing the Programme. **Structure** Caribbean Regional Coordinating Unit (CAR/RCU), Kingston (Jamaica), coordinates and implements the Programme and serves as Secretariat. Regional Activity Centres (4): *Regional Marine Pollution Emergency Information and Training Centre – Wider Caribbean (REMPEITC-Carib, #18794)*; Centro de Ingenieria y Manejo Ambiental de Bahamas y Zonas Costeras (LBS RAC-Cimab); Institute of Marine Affairs (LBS RAC-IMA); Plan Mer des Caraïbes (SPAW-RAC). **Languages** English, French, Spanish. **Finance** Funded through contributions to the Caribbean Trust Fund.
Activities Sub-Programmes -
– *'Assessment and Management of Environment Pollution (AMEP)'*: Reducing Pesticide Run-Off to the Caribbean Sea; Planning for Rehabilitation, Environmental Management and Coastal Development in the Wake of Hurricane Mitch; Coastal/Watershed Area Management; Training for Rehabilitation of Contaminated Bays; Land-Based Sources of Marine Pollution; Sewage Collection and Treatment; Sanitation Plan for Whitehorses, Pamphret and Botany Bay (Jamaica); Small Grants Programme – Best Management Practices for Agriculture; Development of National Programmes of Action; Joint Regional Project to Assist Governments of the Wider Caribbean Region in Classifying their Waters so as to Facilitate the Implementation of the LBS Protocol; Joint Regional Project for the Development of Safe Recreational Water Environments.
– *'Specially Protected Areas and Wildlife (SPAW)'*: Strengthening of Protected Areas; Development of Guidelines for Protected Areas and Species Management; Conservation of Threatened and Endangered Species; Conservation and Sustainable Use of Coastal and Marine Ecosystems; International Coral Reef Action Network (ICRAN) in the Wider Caribbean; Training in Protected Areas and Wildlife Management; Sustainable Tourism.
– *'Information Systems for the Management of Marine and Coastal Resources (CEPNET)'*: Strengthening of Secretariat's Information Management Capabilities; CEP Clearinghouse Mechanisms; Spatial Analysis for Decision-Making.
– *'Education, Training and Awareness'*: Promoting Awareness and Understanding of the LBS Protocol; Promotion of the Caribbean Environment Programme and its Sub-Programmes; Distance Learning for Integrated Coastal Management.

Work also covers: mutual combating oil spill; biological diversity conservation; environmental information systems; technical assistance; capacity-building – development and strengthening of regional and national, institutional and legislative frameworks; standardization of approaches and methodologies; encouragement of appropriate research; joint management of shared resources and exchange of relevant information. Organizes meetings (annually or biennially) for monitoring project implementation, efficient functioning of the Programme and administrative purposes. Sub-programmes integrate and implement the *Caribbean Action Plan (CAR, #03432)* and the Cartagena Convention.
IGO Relations Cooperates with: *Convention Concerning the Protection of the World Cultural and Natural Heritage (World Heritage Convention, 1972)*; *Global Programme of Action for the Protection of the Marine Environment from Land-Based Activities (GPA, see: #20299)*; *Secretariat of the Convention of Wetlands (#19200)*; *Secretariat of the Convention on Biological Diversity (SCBD, #19197)*; *Secretariat of the Convention on International Trade in Endangered Species of Wild Fauna and Flora (CITES Secretariat, #19199)*. Works closely with: *International Coral Reef Action Network (ICRAN, #12964)*. Partner of: *International Coral Reef Initiative (ICRI, #12965)*. Close links with: *Intergovernmental Oceanographic Commission (IOC, #11496)*; *UNEP (#20299)*; *Regional Seas Programme (#18814)*. [2022/XE4545/**E***]

♦ Caribbean Epidemiology Centre (inactive)

♦ Caribbean Evaluators International (CEI) 03498

Chair PO Box 2273, Kingston, Jamaica. E-mail: caribbeanevaluatorsinl@gmail.com.
URL: https://www.caribeval.org/

History 25 Feb 2014. Registration: Jamaica. **Aims** Promote excellence in evaluation standards and practices, while strengthening evaluation capacity. **Structure** Board of Directors; Advisory Committee. **Languages** English. **Staff** Voluntary. **Finance** Financed through patronage and service of Sustaining Founding Members. **Activities** Advocacy/lobbying/activism; capacity building; events/meetings; knowledge management/information dissemination; research/documentation; standards/guidelines. **Publications** *Caribbean EvalChat*; *Caribbean Evaluator* – newsletter.
Members Full in 13 countries:
Barbados, Canada, Dominica, Dominican Rep, Guyana, Haiti, India, Jamaica, Netherlands, St Vincent-Grenadines, Trinidad-Tobago, UK, USA.
NGO Relations Member of (1): *International Organisation for Cooperation in Evaluation (IOCE, #14426).*
[2023.02.22/XJ8543/**D**]

♦ Caribbean Evangelical Theological Association (CETA) 03499

Sec/Treas Unit 1153, 3170 Airmans Drive, Fort Pierce FL 34946, USA. T. +17853403266. E-mail: sectres@ceta-edu.org.
Accrediting Coordinator c/o Open Bible Standard Churches, 36-40 Ruth Avenue, San Fernando, Trinidad-Tobago. T. +18686579189.
URL: http://www.cetaonline.org/
History 1973, Trinidad-Tobago. Founded 1973, Arouca (Trinidad-Tobago), as *Caribbean Association of, Bible Colleges (CABC)*. Present name adopted, 1985. **Aims** Promote and facilitate cooperation among persons engaged in provision of evangelical theological education in the Caribbean region. **Structure** Meeting (every 2 years); Executive Committee; Commissions (2); Regional Chapters (7). Major Service Arms (3): Accrediting Commission; Theological Commission; *Caribbean Graduate School of Theology (CGST, no recent information)*. Set up: *Evangelical Association of the Caribbean (EAC, #09210)* with which it now shares a common Theological Commission. **Languages** English, French. **Staff** 2.00 FTE, voluntary. **Finance** Members' dues. **Activities** Training/education; events/meetings. **Events** *Biennial Consultation* Georgetown (Guyana) 2019, *Biennial Consultation* Savanna-la-Mar (Jamaica) 2017, *Biennial Consultation and General Assembly* Haiti 2015, *Biennial Consultation and General Assembly* Puerto Rico 2013, *Biennial consultation and general assembly* Trinidad-Tobago 2011. **Publications** *Caribbean Journal of Evangelical Theology (CJET)* (annual); *CETA News* (periodical). *The Story of Caribbean Evangelical Theological Association, 1973-1993* (1993); *Caribbean Evangelical Theological Association Handbook* (2nd ed 1990); *Standards and Procedures for Accrediting Post-Secondary and Graduate Levels* (3rd ed 1989).
Members Theological schools (48) in 9 countries and territories:
Barbados, Dominican Rep, Grenada, Guyana, Haiti, Jamaica, Puerto Rico, St Vincent-Grenadines, Trinidad-Tobago.
NGO Relations Member of: *Association of Caribbean Tertiary Institutions (ACTI, #02412)*; *Caribbean Area Network for Quality Assurance in Tertiary Education (CANQATE, #03441)*; *Evangelical Association of the Caribbean (EAC, #09210)*; *International Council for Evangelical Theological Education (ICETE, #13020)*; *International Network of Quality Assurance Agencies in Higher Education (INQAAHE, #14312).*
[2019.12.12/XE1752/**E**]

♦ Caribbean Examinations Council (CXC) 03500

Conseil des examens des Caraïbes
Registrar Prince Road, Pine Plantation Road, St Michael BB11091, ST MICHAEL BB11091, Barbados. T. +2462271700. Fax +2464295421.
URL: http://www.cxc.org/
History 20 Apr 1972, Castries (St Lucia). Established as an Associate Institution of *Caribbean Community (CARICOM, #03476)*, on Agreement between 15 English-speaking Caribbean territories, following recommendations, 1964, at 2nd *Conference of Heads of Government of Commonwealth Caribbean Countries*. **Aims** Provide the region with: syllabi of the highest quality; valid and reliable examinations and certificates of international repute for students of all ages, abilities and interests; services to *educational* institutions in the development of syllabi, examinations and examination administration, in the most cost effective way. **Structure** Council (meets annually) of 42 members, including representatives of the teaching profession and of National Committees established in each member State and Vice Chancellors of *University of the West Indies (UWI, #20705)* and University of Guyana. School Examinations Committee (SEC) is the main professional and technical body. Administrative and Finance Committee (AFC); Sub-Committee of School Examinations (SUBSEC). Headquarters located in Barbados; Western Zone office in Jamaica. **Languages** English. **Staff** 132.00 FTE, paid. **Finance** Contributions of participating governments; examination fees; funds from special projects. **Activities** Training/education; certification/accreditation. **Events** *Conference on evaluation in education* St Michael (Barbados) 2003, *Meeting* Belize 1994. **Publications** *Caribbean Examiner* (2 a year) – magazine. Annual Report; syllabi; technical services and associate degree booklets; brochures; newsletters; resource materials.
Members Governments of 16 countries and territories:
Anguilla, Antigua-Barbuda, Barbados, Belize, Cayman Is, Dominica, Grenada, Guyana, Jamaica, Montserrat, St Kitts-Nevis, St Lucia, St Vincent-Grenadines, Trinidad-Tobago, Turks-Caicos, Virgin Is UK.
NGO Relations Support received from examining boards and international agencies, in particular: *Canadian Community Colleges (ACCC)*. Member of: *International Association for Educational Assessment (IAEA, #11861)*. Instrumental in setting up: *Caribbean Association for the Teaching of English (CARATE, inactive).*
[2018/XD5631/**D***]

♦ **Caribbean Export** Caribbean Export Development Agency (#03501)

♦ Caribbean Export Development Agency (Caribbean Export) 03501

Officer in Charge 1st Floor Baobab Tower, Warrens, St Michael BB22026, ST MICHAEL BB22026, Barbados. T. +12464360578. Fax +12464369999. E-mail: info@carib-export.com.
Sub-Regional Office Av Pedro Henriquez Ureña No 150, Torre Diandy XIX, Piso 7, Santo Domingo, Dominican Rep. T. +18095312411. Fax +18094737532.
URL: http://www.carib-export.com/
History Established 1996, by an Inter-Governmental Agreement as the trade promotion Agency of the 15 Member States of *Forum of Caribbean States (CARIFORUM, #09904)*. Successor to *CARICOM Export Development Project (CEDP, inactive)*, set up 1989, Barbados, within the framework of *Caribbean Community (CARICOM, #03476)*. Previously also referred to by the initials *CEDA*. Jul 2005, assumed investment promotion mandate after 14th CARIFORUM Council of Ministers meeting. **Aims** Increase the competitiveness of the Caribbean countries by providing export development and investment promotion services. **Structure** Board of Directors; headquarters in St Michael (Barbados); sub-regional office in Santo Domingo (Dominican Rep). **Languages** English, Spanish. **Staff** 40.00 FTE, paid. **Finance** CARIFORUM countries. Donor agencies, including: *Organisation of African, Caribbean and Pacific States (OACPS, #17796)* BizClim; *Department for International Development (DFID, inactive)*; *European Union (EU, #08967)*; *Deutsche Gesellschaft für Internationale Zusammenarbeit (GIZ)*; cost-sharing of activities with regional institutions in non-traditional manufactured goods and non-tourism sectors. **Activities** Capacity building; financial and/or material support; training/education; networking/liaising; projects/programmes; events/meetings; knowledge management/information dissemination. **Events** *Caribbean Sub-Regional Meeting on Attracting Foreign Direct Investment in the Caribbean* Miami, FL (USA) 2016. **Publications** *TradeWatch* (6 a year) – e-newsletter; *Primed for Success* (annual); *Caribbean Export Outlook*.
Members Covers all CARIFORUM member countries and territories (15):
Antigua-Barbuda, Bahamas, Barbados, Belize, Dominica, Dominican Rep, Grenada, Guyana, Haiti, Jamaica, St Kitts-Nevis, St Lucia, St Vincent-Grenadines, Suriname, Trinidad-Tobago.
IGO Relations Cooperates with: *Caribbean Development Bank (CDB, #03492)*; CARICOM organizations; *Organisation of Eastern Caribbean States (OECS, #17804)*; *Organisation of Eastern Caribbean States/Competitive Business Unit (OECS/CBU, #17805)*. Also cooperates with inter-governmental agencies and regional public sector agencies.
[2019/XK1031/e/**F***]

♦ Caribbean Family Planning Affiliation (CFPA) 03502

Fédération caraïbéenne des associations de planification familiale – Caraïbische Gezinsplanning Affiliatie
Contact Corners of Factory and Airport Roads, PO Box 3386, St John's, St John, Antigua-Barbuda. T. +12687761518 – +12684624170. E-mail: ceo.cfpa@gmail.com.
URL: https://caribbeanfamilyplanning.com/
History 1971. By-laws adopted at 1st General Meeting, 1972. Registration: Government of Anguilla, No/ID: 2455, Start date: 6 Jun 1985, Anguilla, Caribbean. **Aims** Promote Sexual and Reproductive Health in the Caribbean through family planning, considered as a basic human right fashioned from people's right to know, their right to decide and their freedom to act on matters concerning their sexual and reproductive health; represent Member Associations on appropriate international organizations and Councils of the International Planned Parenthood Federation (IPPF). **Structure** General Assembly (annual); Board of Directors; Secretariat. **Languages** Dutch, English, French. **Staff** 2.00 FTE, paid; 12.00 FTE, voluntary. **Finance** Supported by: *International Planned Parenthood Federation (IPPF, #14589)*. **Activities** Advocacy/lobbying/activism; events/meetings; financial and/or material support; knowledge management/information dissemination; projects/programmes; training/education. **Events** *Annual General Meeting* Castries (St Lucia) 2017, *Annual General Assembly* Curaçao 2013, *Annual General Assembly* St Maarten 2008, *Annual General Assembly* Grenada 2006, *Annual General Assembly* St Maarten 2005. **Publications** Books; pamphlets; other publications.
Members Associations in 19 countries and territories:
Anguilla, Antigua-Barbuda, Aruba, Bahamas, Barbados, Belize, Bermuda, Curaçao, Dominica, Grenada, Guadeloupe, Guyana, Haiti, Jamaica, Martinique, St Lucia, St Vincent-Grenadines, Suriname, Trinidad-Tobago.
IGO Relations Associated with Department of Global Communications of the United Nations. **NGO Relations** Affiliated with (1): *International Planned Parenthood Federation (IPPF, #14589)* (Regional).
[2022.10.27/XE0866/**F**]

♦ Caribbean Farmers Network (CaFAN) 03503

Chief Coordinator PO Box 827, New Montrose, Kingstown, St Vincent-Grenadines. T. +17844531004. Fax +17844531239.
History 2004. **Aims** Foster linkages, training and information sharing amongst Caribbean farmers so that they are in a better position to respond to the key challenges facing the agricultural sector in the Caribbean. **Activities** Organizes: training workshops; advocacy; study tours; information sharing; regional planning sessions. Publishing activity.
Members Farmers' associations and NGOs in 13 countries:
Antigua-Barbuda, Bahamas, Barbados, Belize, Dominica, Grenada, Guyana, Jamaica, St Kitts-Nevis, St Lucia, St Vincent-Grenadines, Suriname, Trinidad-Tobago.
NGO Relations Cooperates with: *Global Forum on Agricultural Research (GFAR, #10370).* [2013/XJ1597/**D**]

♦ Caribbean Federation of Aeroclubs (inactive)
♦ Caribbean Federation of Youth Revitalization Committee (inactive)
♦ Caribbean Festival of Arts / see Caribbean Festival of Creative Arts (#03504)

♦ Caribbean Festival of Creative Arts (CARIFESTA) 03504

Contact Ministry of Culture/Sports/Youth, Sky Mall Complex, Haggatt Hall, St Michael, ST MICHAEL, Barbados. T. +12466212700ext721. Fax +12464240141. E-mail: infosecretariat@carifesta.net.
URL: http://www.carifesta.net/
History 1972, Georgetown (Guyana), at 1st festival, under the auspices of *Caribbean Free Trade Association (CARIFTA, inactive)*. Original title: *Caribbean Festival of Arts*. From 1973, responsibility devolved to Secretariat of *Caribbean Community (CARICOM, #03476)*. Objectives redefined, 1993, by Cultural Committee. **Aims** Stage a mega multidisciplinary roving festival that develops Caribbean Arts and *Culture*; position CARIFESTA as a world-renowned, hallmark festival of Caribbean cultural and *artistic* excellence that generates economic benefits, unites the region and excites all people. **Structure** Ministers of the Council of Human and Social Development (COHSOD) responsible for Culture are responsible for all policy-decisions on CARIFESTA, based on technical advice of the CARICOM Secretariat and the Regional Cultural Committee. Planning and organization of each festival carried out by Festival Directorate in close collaboration with host country and sending countries, and under the guidance of CARIFESTA Board. **Finance** Festivals implemented with funding from host country, sending countries and CARICOM Secretariat. **Activities** Initially organized every 4 years, the "New" CARIFESTA model proposes biennial organization with Festival being hosted by CARICOM Member States based on a bidding procedure. **Events** *CARIFESTA* Suriname 2013, *CARIFESTA* Guyana 2008, *CARIFESTA* Trinidad-Tobago 2006, *CARIFESTA* Paramaribo (Suriname) 2003, *CARIFESTA* St Kitts-Nevis 2000. **Members** Participation in CARIFESTA is open to all States in the Region. [2017/XF2530/**F***]

♦ Caribbean Financial Action Task Force (CFATF) 03505

Groupe d'action financière des Caraïbes (GAFIC) – Grupo de Acción Financiera del Caribe
Exec Dir Level 21 Nicholas Tower, 63-65 Independence Square, Port-of-Spain, Trinidad-Tobago. T. +18686239667 – +18686234888 – +18686257665. Fax +18686241297. E-mail: cfatf@cfatf.org.
URL: http://www.cfatf-gafic.org/
History Set up following meetings convened May 1990, Aruba, and Nov 1992, Kingston (Jamaica), when Kingston Declaration was issued, endorsing and affirming a commitment to implement *Financial Action Task Force (FATF, #09765)* and Aruba Recommendations, *OAS (#17629)* Model Regulations and the *United Nations Global Programme Against Money Laundering, Proceeds of Crime and the Financing of Terrorism (GPML, #20568)*, and when the establishment of the Secretariat was mandated. Former names and other names: *Caribbean Financial Action Task Force on Money Laundering* – former. **Aims** Achieve effective implementation of, and compliance with, recommendations to prevent and control money laundering and combat the financing of terrorism. **Structure** Meeting of Ministers in Council (annual); Plenary Meeting of Senior Officials (twice a year); Secretariat located in Port-of-Spain (Trinidad-Tobago). **Languages** English, Spanish. **Staff** 22.00 FTE, paid. **Finance** Sources: contributions of member/participating states. Cooperating and Supporting Nations (COSUNs) which are members of FATF (Canada, France, Mexico, Netherlands, Spain, UK, USA). **Activities** Guidance/assistance/consulting; monitoring/evaluation; politics/policy/regulatory; training/education. **Events** *Joint typologies meeting* Cayman Is 2009, *Plenary Meeting* Willemstad (Curaçao) 2009, *Plenary Meeting* Basseterre (St Kitts-Nevis) 2008, *Plenary Meeting* Port-au-Prince (Haiti) 2008, *Plenary Meeting* Panama 2007.
Members Governments of 25 countries and territories:
Anguilla, Antigua-Barbuda, Aruba, Bahamas, Barbados, Belize, Bermuda, Cayman Is, Curaçao, Dominica, El Salvador, Grenada, Guyana, Haiti, Jamaica, Montserrat, St Kitts-Nevis, St Lucia, St Maarten, St Vincent-Grenadines, Suriname, Trinidad-Tobago, Turks-Caicos, Venezuela, Virgin Is UK.
IGO Relations Observer status with (23):
- *Caribbean Community (CARICOM, #03476)*;
- *Caribbean Customs Law Enforcement Council (CCLEC, #03487)*;
- *Caribbean Development Bank (CDB, #03492)*;
- *Caribbean Regional Technical Assistance Centre (CARTAC, #03550)*;
- *Central American Bank for Economic Integration (CABEI, #03658)*;
- *Committee of Experts on the Evaluation of Anti-Money Laundering Measures and the Financing of Terrorism (MONEYVAL, #04257)*;
- *Commonwealth Secretariat (#04362)*;
- *Eastern and Southern African Anti-Money Laundering Group (ESAAMLG, #05252)*;
- *Eastern Caribbean Central Bank (ECCB, #05231)*;
- *Egmont Group of Financial Intelligence Units (#05396)*;
- *European Commission (EC, #06633)*;
- *Financial Action Task Force (FATF, #09765)*;
- *Forum of Caribbean States (CARIFORUM, #09904)*;
- *Grupo de Acción Financiera de Latinoamérica (GAFILAT, #10799)*;
- *Inter-American Development Bank (IDB, #11427)*;
- *Inter-American Drug Abuse Control Commission (#11429)*;
- *International Criminal Police Organization – INTERPOL (ICPO-INTERPOL, #13110)*;
- *International Monetary Fund (IMF, #14180)*;
- *International Money Laundering Information Network (IMoLIN, #14181)*;
- *Organisation of Eastern Caribbean States (OECS, #17804)*;
- *The World Bank Group (#21218)*;
- *United Nations Office on Drugs and Crime (UNODC, #20596)*;
- *World Customs Organization (WCO, #21350).* [2020.09.17/XF3732/**F***]

♦ Caribbean Financial Action Task Force on Money Laundering / see Caribbean Financial Action Task Force (#03505)

♦ Caribbean Financial Services Corporation (CFSC) 03506

Head Office Radley Court, Collymore Rock, St Michael, ST MICHAEL, Barbados. T. +2464316400. Fax +2464261869. E-mail: cfsc@caribsurf.com.
URL: http://www.cfsc.com.bb/

Activities Provides finance up to the local equivalent of US$ 300,000 for private sector manufacturing, agro-industry, tourism and related enterprises and service sectors with foreign earning potential in English-speaking Caribbean countries, particularly those of the Organisation of Eastern Caribbean States and Barbados.
Members Shareholders (34 as of May 1993) – private sector Caribbean countries and individuals. Membership countries not specified. International shareholders – multinational banks (7, unspecified) and 3 further organizations:
International shareholders – multinational banks (7, unspecified) and 3 further organizations:
CDC Group; DEG – Deutsche Investitions- und Entwicklungsgesellschaft; International Finance Corporation (IFC, #13597).
IGO Relations *Centre for the Development of Enterprise (CDE, inactive).* [2015/XF3003/ey/F]

♦ Caribbean Fisheries Training and Development Institute (CFTDI) . . . 03507
Principal PO Box 1150, Port of Spain Western Main Road, Chaguaramas, Trinidad-Tobago. T. +18686344276 – +18686341635. Fax +18686344405. E-mail: info@cftdi.edu.tt.
Training Officer / Vice Principal 1st Avenue South, Chaguaramas, Trinidad-Tobago. T. +18686341635 – +18686341865. Fax +18686341635 – +18686341865. E-mail: training@cftdi.edu.tt.
URL: http://www.cftdi.edu.tt/
History 1974, as a regional fisheries training institute for the Caribbean by *FAO (#09260)* and the Governments of Barbados, Guyana and Trinidad-Tobago. Since 1983, operated within the framework of *Caribbean Technical Cooperation Network in Artisanal Fisheries and Aquaculture (inactive)* and *FAO Regional Office for Latin America and the Caribbean (FAO/RLC, #09268).* **Aims** Provide maritime and fisheries training in accordance with IMO's STCW Convention and Code for Seafarers and STCW-F for fishing vessel personnel. **Structure** Board of Management. **Finance** Sources: subvention from the Government of Trinidad-Tobago; revenue generated from training activities. **IGO Relations** Formal contact with: *Japan International Cooperation Agency (JICA);* Samuel Jackman Prescod Polytechnic (Barbados). [2018/XF6074/j/E*]

♦ Caribbean Fishery Management Council (CFMC) 03508
Conseil d'administration pour les pêches des Caraïbes – Consejo de Administración Pesquera del Caribe
Exec Dir 268 Muñoz Rivera Ave, 4th Floor, Ste 401, San Juan PR 00918, USA. T. +17877665926. Fax +17877666239.
URL: http://www.caribbeanfmc.com/
History 13 Apr 1976, under the provisions of the 'Magnuson Fishery Conservation and Management Act' (PL-94-265), as one of 8 regional fishery management councils. The Act established a USA national fishery conservancy zone and exclusive USA fishery management authority over fishery resources within that zone except the (migratory) tuna. **Aims** Ensure conservation and orderly utilization of fishery resources of USA in the region. **Events** *Regular meeting* Ponce (Puerto Rico) 2006, *Regular meeting* St Croix (Virgin Is USA) 2006, *Regular meeting* St Croix (Virgin Is USA) 2005, *Regular meeting* St Thomas Is (Virgin Is USA) 2005, *Regular meeting* St Thomas Is (Virgin Is USA) 2005.
Members Unique among the 8 councils in that it does not include one of the 50 states of the Union. Council of 2 territories:
Puerto Rico, Virgin Is USA.
IGO Relations *FAO (#09260).* [2018/XD0496/F*]

♦ Caribbean Food Crops Society (CFCS) 03509
Société Caraïbe des plantes alimentaires – Sociedad Caribeña de Cultivos Alimenticios
Main Office PO Box 9030, Ag Experiment Sta, Mayagüez PR 00681-9030, USA. E-mail: cfcs@cfcs1963.org – ue_wcolon@uagm.edu.
URL: https://www.cfcs1963.org/
History 3 May 1963, San Juan (Puerto Rico). **Aims** Advance and foster Caribbean food production, processing and distribution in all their aspects, so as to help improve the quality of life for the people of the Caribbean; bring together scholars, researchers, extensionists, growers and other professionals associated with food production, distribution and policy. **Structure** Annual Member's Meeting; Board of Directors; Advisory Board; Regional Representatives. **Languages** Dutch, English, French, Spanish. **Finance** Members' dues. **Activities** Events/meetings; training/education. **Events** *CFCS Meeting* St Martin 2021, *Annual Meeting* Gosier (Guadeloupe) 2016, *Annual Meeting* Paramaribo (Suriname) 2015, *Annual Meeting* Virgin Is USA 2014, *Annual Meeting* Trinidad-Tobago 2013. **Publications** *CFCS Newsletter* (3 a year). Meeting proceedings.
Members Active; Life; Honorary; Emeritus. Individuals in 43 countries and territories:
Antigua-Barbuda, Australia, Bahamas, Barbados, Belize, Brazil, Canada, Cayman Is, Colombia, Costa Rica, Côte d'Ivoire, Cuba, Curaçao, Denmark, Dominica, Dominican Rep, El Salvador, France, Grenada, Guadeloupe, Guatemala, Guiana Fr, Guyana, Haiti, Honduras, Jamaica, Martinique, Mexico, Montserrat, Peru, Puerto Rico, Sri Lanka, St Kitts-Nevis, St Lucia, St Vincent-Grenadines, Suriname, Switzerland, Thailand, Trinidad-Tobago, UK, USA, Venezuela, Virgin Is USA.
Consultative Status Consultative status granted from: *ECOSOC (#05331)* (Ros C); *FAO (#09260)* (Liaison Status). [2022/XD4024/v/D]

♦ Caribbean Food and Nutrition Institute (inactive)

♦ Caribbean Football Union (CFU) 03510
Headquarters Barbados Football Association Annex, Garfield Sobers Complex, Wildey, St Michael, ST MICHAEL, Barbados. T. +12465382255. E-mail: info@cfufootball.org.
URL: http://www.cfufootball.org/
History 1978, Trinidad-Tobago. **Aims** Promote, control and develop football in the Caribbean. **Structure** Congress (annual). Executive Committee, comprising President, 1st and 2nd Presidents, 4 members and representatives of the Caribbean Zone before CONCACAF and FIFA. General Secretariat. Standing Committees (8): Finance; Referees; Technical and Development; Sports Medicine; Disciplinary; Protocol; Fair Play and Security; Statutes and Rules. General Secretary. **Languages** English. **Staff** 3.00 FTE, voluntary. **Finance** Members' dues. Levies. **Activities** International Tournaments – Seniors and Juniors in alternate years. **Events** *Annual Congress* Budapest (Hungary) 2012, *Annual Congress* Basseterre (St Kitts-Nevis) 1990, *Annual Congress* Port-of-Spain (Trinidad-Tobago) 1989, *Annual Congress* Anse Mitan (Guadeloupe) 1988, *Executive committee meeting* Port-of-Spain (Trinidad-Tobago) 1987.
Members Full in 30 countries and territories:
Anguilla, Antigua-Barbuda, Aruba, Bahamas, Barbados, Bermuda, Cayman Is, Cuba, Curaçao, Dominica, Dominican Rep, Grenada, Guadeloupe, Guiana Fr, Guyana, Haiti, Jamaica, Martinique, Montserrat, Puerto Rico, St Kitts-Nevis, St Lucia, St Maarten, St Martin, St Vincent-Grenadines, Suriname, Trinidad-Tobago, Turks-Caicos, Virgin Is UK, Virgin Is USA.
NGO Relations Affiliated to: *Confederación Norte-Centroamericana y del Caribe de Fútbol (CONCACAF, #04465).* [2020/XD5571/D]

♦ Caribbean Forest Conservation Association (inactive)
♦ Caribbean Forum / see Forum of Caribbean States (#09904)
♦ Caribbean Forum of ACP States / see Forum of Caribbean States (#09904)
♦ Caribbean Forum for Development (no recent information)

♦ Caribbean Forum of Local Government Ministers (CFLGM) 03511
Secretariat 85 Hagley Park Road, Kingston, Jamaica. T. +187675409929. Fax +18767541000.
History Established Apr 2004, Montego Bay (Jamaica). **Aims** Provide a forum for sharing of knowledge and experiences in regard to local governance and local *democracy;* assist individual member states in the formulation of national policies on local governance and towards strengthening local governance; provide a channel through which support from external parties could be galvanized and channelled to enhance the realization of policy objectives. **Structure** Comprises Ministers responsible for Local Governance and Local Democracy in CARICOM member states. Secretariat. **Languages** English. **Staff** None. Staff support from secretariat of *Caribbean Community (CARICOM, #03476).* **Finance** May raise funds from members as required. **Activities** Instrumental in partnering and obtaining support for the Caribbean Local Economic Development Programme; now a member of the Programme Management and Programme Steering Committees. Regional Policy and Cooperation Framework helps member states formulate their own policies and in seeking assistance to advance local governance and local democracy.
Members Governments of 14 countries:
Antigua-Barbuda, Bahamas, Barbados, Belize, Dominica, Grenada, Guyana, Haiti, Jamaica, St Kitts-Nevis, St Lucia, St Vincent-Grenadines, Suriname, Trinidad-Tobago. [2018.08.28/XM2996/F*]

♦ Caribbean Foundation / see The Caribbean Council (#03482)
♦ Caribbean Free Trade Association (inactive)
♦ Caribbean Group of the American Society for Horticultar Science / see InterAmerican Society of Tropical Horticulture (#11451)

♦ Caribbean Group of Banking Supervisors (CGBS) 03512
Chair 2017 address not obtained. E-mail: igeduld@cbvs.sr.
URL: http://cgbsnet.org/
History Established 1983, under the aegis of *Caribbean Community (CARICOM, #03476)* Committee of Central Bank Governors. **Aims** Enhance and coordinate harmonization of bank supervisory practices in the English speaking Caribbean, so as to bring them in line with internationally accepted practices. **Structure** Rotating Chairmanship.
Members Central banks in 10 countries and territories:
Aruba, Barbados, Belize, Cayman Is, Guyana, Jamaica, St Kitts-Nevis, Suriname, Trinidad-Tobago, Virgin Is UK.
Included in the above, 1 regional Central Bank:
IGO Relations *Caribbean Community (CARICOM, #03476).* [2017/XM5887/E*]

♦ Caribbean Harm Reduction Coalition (CHRC) 03513
Coordinator PO Box 1419, Castries, St Lucia. T. +17587217278. E-mail: chrc@candw.lc.
URL: http://caribbeanharmreductioncoalition.htmlplanet.com/
History 2001. **Aims** Initiate and promote education, intervention and community programmes focusing on reduction of drug related harm; advocate policy change from a judicial to a public health response in addressing the issues around *drug use* and HIV. **Languages** English. **Staff** 4.00 FTE, paid. **Finance** Grants.
Members Full in 5 countries:
Bahamas, Dominican Rep, Jamaica, St Lucia, Trinidad-Tobago.
IGO Relations *Caribbean Community (CARICOM, #03476).* **NGO Relations** *Caribbean Vulnerable Communities Coalition (CVC, #03565); Harm Reduction International (HRI, #10861); International AIDS Society (IAS, #11601); Frontline AIDS (#10007).* [2018.09.05/XM2060/F]

♦ Caribbean Health Research Council (inactive)

♦ Caribbean Herbal Business Association (CHBA) 03514
Contact c/o Inter-American Inst for Cooperation on Agriculture, PO Box 1318, Port-of-Spain, Trinidad-Tobago. T. +18686454555 – +18686455020 – +18686458886. Fax +18686628253.
Structure Executive Committee, comprising President, Vice-President, Treasurer, Secretary and Assistant Secretary; Steering Committee. **Events** *Annual general meeting* St Thomas Is (Virgin Is USA) 2006, *Annual General Meeting* Rodney Bay (St Lucia) 2005. **NGO Relations** Cooperates with: *Caribbean Association of Researchers and Herbal Practitioners Association (CARAPA, no recent information).* [2019/XJ4347/D]

♦ Caribbean HIV/AIDS Regional Training Network (CHART) 03515
Contact c/o UWI HARP, Postgraduate Medical Education Bldg – UHWI, Office of the Vice Chancellor – UWI, Mona, Kingston, Jamaica. T. +18769772717. Fax +18769703243.
URL: http://www.chartcaribbean.org/
History Jun 2001, on request of *Caribbean Community (CARICOM, #03476).* **Aims** Establish training centres for the Caribbean that utilize the cost-effective mechanisms, institutions and concepts for the ongoing training and development of healthcare workers; ensure that transfer of knowledge and technologies support the building of indigenous Caribbean capacity to sustain training competence and responsibility within Caribbean regional and local institutions; serve as a coordinating body and focal point for promoting the unique needs and resources of the Caribbean region. **Structure** Executive Council, comprising Chair, Former Chair and 12 members. Advisory Board. **Finance** Main source: *International Training and Education Center on HIV (I-TECH).* Also funded by US Centres for Disease Control and *United States Agency for International Development (USAID),* with additional support from *Joint United Nations Programme on HIV/AIDS (UNAIDS, #16149).* **IGO Relations** Located at: *University of the West Indies (UWI, #20705).* Collaborating agencies: CARICOM; *Deutsche Gesellschaft für Technische Zusammenarbeit (GTZ, inactive); Japan International Cooperation Agency (JICA).* **NGO Relations** Collaborating agencies: *Caribbean Coalition of National AIDS Programme Coordinator (CCNAPC, #03473); Caribbean Regional Network of People Living with HIV/AIDS (CRN+, #03549); François-Xavier Bagnoud Center for Health and Human Rights;* I-TECH; *Johns Hopkins Program for International Education in Gynecology and Obstetrics (JHPIEGO).* [2013/XM2025/F]

♦ Caribbean Horse Racing Confederation (#04447)
♦ Caribbean Hotel Association / see Caribbean Hotel and Tourism Association (#03516)
♦ Caribbean Hotel Council / see Caribbean Hotel and Tourism Association (#03516)

♦ Caribbean Hotel and Tourism Association (CHTA) 03516
CEO/Dir Gen 501 East Las Olas Blvd, Ste Suite 200/300, Fort Lauderdale FL 33301, USA. T. +13054433040. E-mail: membership@caribbeanhotelandtourism.com – events@caribbeanhotelandtourism.com.
URL: http://www.caribbeanhotelandtourism.com/
History 1959, Santurce (Puerto Rico). Founded following recommendations made at 8th Annual General Meeting of the since superseded *Caribbean Tourism Association (CTA, inactive),* held in 1959, Bogota. Present structure adopted 1962, Barbados. Former names and other names: *Caribbean Hotel Council* – former; *Caribbean Hotel Association (CHA)* – former; *Association hôtelière des Caraïbes* – former; *Asociación de Hoteles del Caribe* – former. Registration: Cayman Is. **Aims** Provide national hotel and tourism associations and members with exceptional value which generates business and advances a sustainable and profitable industry. **Languages** English, French, Spanish. **Activities** Events/meetings. **Events** *CHRIS : Caribbean Hotel and Resort Investment Summit* Coral Gables, FL (USA) 2023, *CHICOS : Caribbean Hotel Investment Conference and Operations Summit* La Romana (Dominican Rep) 2022, *CHICOS : Caribbean Hotel Investment Conference and Operations Summit* Nassau (Bahamas) 2021, *CHICOS : Caribbean Hotel Investment Conference and Operations Summit* Nassau (Bahamas) 2020, *Caribbean Travel Marketplace Conference* Nassau (Bahamas) 2020. **Consultative Status** Consultative status granted from: *OAS (#17629).* [2022/XD0214/D]

♦ Caribbean Human Rights Network 03517
Address not obtained.
History Founded 1 Aug 1987, Georgetown (Guyana). Known as *Caribbean Rights.* **Aims** Disseminate information to national, regional and international organizations; promote human rights at a regional level – this includes embarking on regional campaigns; assist in the coordination of regional human rights action programmes; facilitate the exchange of visits between persons or groups with a human rights interest; mount missions – fact-finding and elections observer missions. **Structure** Executive Committee (meets once a year), consisting of one representative of each affiliate. Liaison Office based in Barbados. **Finance** Funded by church organizations and international foundations in Europe and North America. **Activities** Advocacy/lobbying/activism; awareness raising; capacity building; networking/liaising; Major areas of concern: police brutality; elections and democracy; freedom of expression. Current new programmes: (i) Women's Rights (ii) Death Penalty; (iii) Democracy within the Region; (iv) Documentation; (v) Rights of People with Disabilities; (vi) Monitoring Socio-Economic Conditions and its Negative Impact on Caribbean peoples; (vii) Human Rights Education and Training. **Events** *Annual General Meeting* Bridgetown (Barbados) 2000, *Annual General Meeting* Kingston (Jamaica) 1999, *Annual General Meeting* Bridgetown (Barbados) 1998, *Annual General Meeting* Bridgetown (Barbados) 1997, *Annual General Meeting* Bridgetown (Barbados) 1996. **Publications** Reports; press releases.
Members National human rights bodies in 8 countries:
Bahamas, Belize, Dominican Rep, Haiti, Jamaica, Puerto Rico, St Vincent-Grenadines, Suriname.
Regional Liaison Office in:
Barbados.
NGO Relations Member of: *World Organisation Against Torture (OMCT, #21685).* [2016/XF2013/F]

♦ Caribbean Information Action Group (inactive)

♦ **Caribbean Information System for the Agricultural Sciences (CAGRIS)** 03518
Contact c/o Alma Jordan Library, Univ of the West Indies, St Augustine, Trinidad-Tobago. T. +18686622002ext82261 – +186883594. E-mail: almajordanlibrary@sta.uwi.edu.
URL: https://libraries.sta.uwi.edu/ajl/
History Established within the framework of *Caribbean Information System (CIS, inactive)* of the *United Nations Economic Commission for Latin America and the Caribbean (ECLAC, #20556)*; took over activities of *Caribbean Information System for Agriculture (CARIB/AGRI)*, which was also referred to as *CEPAL/CARIB-AGRI*. Currently coordinated by *University of the West Indies (UWI, #20705)*. **Aims** Support agricultural development by making relevant material available according to existing and potential needs. **Structure** Senior Management Team; Departments (5). **Languages** English. **Staff** Professional: 25 FTE; other: 105 FTE. **Finance** Contribution from the University of the West Indies of a monetary equivalent of staff and material input. **Activities** Access to regional and worldwide information through: AGRIS; CARIS. Participating countries designate national centres to collect, organize and exchange information in the following sectors: plant science and production; plant protection; post-harvest technology; animal production; animal protection; agricultural administration; agricultural legislation; fisheries and aquaculture; forestry; soil science and management; agricultural machinery; water resources, irrigation and drainage; energy; pollution; agricultural economics; rural development; education and extension.
Members Governments of 20 participating countries and territories (" indicates regional coordinating centre):
Anguilla, Antigua-Barbuda, Bahamas, Barbados, Belize, Dominica, Dominican Rep, Grenada, Guadeloupe, Guyana, Haiti, Jamaica, Martinique, Montserrat, St Kitts-Nevis, St Lucia, St Vincent-Grenadines, Trinidad-Tobago (*), Virgin Is USA.
IGO Relations *Caribbean Agricultural Science and Technology Networking System (PROCICARIBE, no recent information)*; *FAO (#09260)*; *International Development Research Centre (IDRC, #13162)*; *International Information System for the Agricultural Sciences and Technology (AGRIS, #13848)*; *OAS (#17629)*; *UNESCO (#20322)*. [2022/XF9788/**F***]

♦ Caribbean Institute for Alcoholism and Drug Abuse / see Caribbean Institute on Alcoholism and Other Drug Problems (#03519)

♦ **Caribbean Institute on Alcoholism and Other Drug Problems (CARIAD)** 03519
Exec Sec 12 Herbert Street, St Clair, Trinidad-Tobago. T. +18096226453. Fax +18096226453.
History Also referred to as *Caribbean Institute for Alcoholism and Drug Abuse*. **Aims** Train professionals in the treatment and prevention of *addictions*. **Activities** Functions as an annual Summer School, through which training is provided. **Publications** Annual Report; reports. **IGO Relations** *Inter-American Drug Abuse Control Commission (#11429)*. [2014/XE2893/j/**E**]

♦ Caribbean Institute of Mass Communications / see Caribbean School of Media and Communication (#03552)
♦ Caribbean Institute of Media and Communication / see Caribbean School of Media and Communication (#03552)

♦ **Caribbean Institute for Meteorology and Hydrology (CIMH)** 03520
Principal PO Box 130, Bridgetown, St Michael, Bridgetown ST MICHAEL, Barbados. T. +12464251362 – +12464251363 – +12464251365. Fax +12464244733. E-mail: cgriffith@cimh.edu.bb.
URL: http://www.cimh.edu.bb/
History 23 Aug 1967, under the name *Caribbean Meteorological Institute (CMI)*, as part of a project – funded by *UNDP (#20292)* – of the *World Meteorological Organization (WMO, #21649)*, under the auspices of *Caribbean Meteorological Organization (CMO, #03524)*. Designated a Regional Meteorological Training Centre by WMO in 1978. Amalgamated, 1985, with *Caribbean Operational Hydrology Institute (COHI, inactive)*, set up 1982, to form CIMH. **Aims** Train personnel in meteorology and hydrology for the governments of the region; conduct research in meteorology, hydrology and allied sciences. **Structure** (a) Principal; (b) Sections (5): Applied Climatology and Meteorology; Meteorology; Instruments; Administrative. **Languages** English. **Staff** 35.00 FTE, paid. **Finance** Budget (annual): Barbados $ 3.6 million. **Activities** Training/education; research/documentation; guidance/assistance/consulting. **Events** *Caribbean conference on meteorology and hydrology* St James (Barbados) 2002, *Caribbean conference on meteorology and hydrology* St James (Barbados) 1997, *Conference* St James (Barbados) 1995, *Conference* St James (Barbados) 1994, *Conference / Caribbean Conference on Meteorology and Hydrology* St James (Barbados) 1993. **Publications** *Climatic Data* (12 a year); *Hydrological Handbook* (annual); *Monthly Weather Review*. Annual Report. Technical reports; research papers. **Information Services** *Hydrological Data* – for several Caribbean Islands; *Meteorological Data* – for several Caribbean Islands.
Members Governments of 16 countries and territories:
Anguilla, Antigua-Barbuda, Barbados, Belize, Cayman Is, Dominica, Grenada, Guyana, Jamaica, Montserrat, St Kitts-Nevis, St Lucia, St Vincent-Grenadines, Trinidad-Tobago, Turks-Caicos, Virgin Is UK. [2015/XE8645/j/**E***]

♦ Caribbean Institute of Perinatology (no recent information)
♦ Caribbean Institute for the Rule of Law (internationally oriented national body)
♦ Caribbean Institute for Socioeconomic Studies / see Network of Institutes for Socioeconomic Studies of the Caribbean Basin
♦ Caribbean Investment Corporation (inactive)
♦ Caribbean Journalists Union (inactive)
♦ Caribbean Judo Confederation (#04452)

♦ **Caribbean Knowledge Management Centre (CKMC)** 03521
Contact c/o ECLAC Subregional Headquarters for the Caribbean, 1 Chancery Lane, PO Box 1113, Port-of-Spain, Trinidad-Tobago. T. +18682248000. E-mail: eclac-library-pos@eclac.org.
URL: https://www.cepal.org/en/library/port-of-spain/
History 1977, Port-of-Spain (Trinidad-Tobago), by *Caribbean Development and Cooperation Committee (CDCC, inactive)*, as a permanent subsidiary body of the *United Nations Economic Commission for Latin America and the Caribbean (ECLAC, #20556)*. Original title: *Caribbean Documentation Centre (CDC) – Centre de documentation des Caraïbes – Centro de Documentación para el Caribe*. Also referred to by acronym *CARIB/DOC*. **Aims** Create a *virtual* library of Caribbean information in order to disseminate and/or facilitate access to information of relevance to development priorities in the region; research and initiate discussion and debate on *information technology* and information delivery issues in the Caribbean region. **Languages** Dutch, English, French, Spanish. **Finance** Source: ECLAC. **Activities** Reference services; inter-library information delivery; literature searches; e-mail query response service; electronic bibliographic catalogue to ECLAC documents. **Publications** *Current Awareness Bulletin (CAB)* (6 a year). **Information Services** *Caribbean Digital Library (CDL)*; *Caribbean Social Statistical Database*; *CARIBTRADE Merchandise Trade and Transportation Database*; *Selected Statistical Indicators*; *Women in Development Bibliography*.
Members Participating countries and territories (21):
Antigua-Barbuda, Aruba, Bahamas, Belize, Cuba, Dominica, Dominican Rep, Grenada, Guyana, Haiti, Jamaica, Montserrat, Neth Antilles, Puerto Rico, St Kitts-Nevis, St Lucia, St Vincent-Grenadines, Suriname, Trinidad-Tobago, Virgin Is UK, Virgin Is USA. [2019.12.13/XE9897/**E***]

♦ **Caribbean Med Labs Foundation (CMLF)** 03522
Dir 63A Petra Str, Woodbrook, Port-of-Spain, Trinidad-Tobago. T. +18686285911 – +18686284765. E-mail: cmedlabsfoundation@gmail.com.
URL: http://cmedlabsfoundation.net/
History Set up following a request from *Caribbean Community (CARICOM, #03476)* Ministers of Health, Jun 2007, at meeting of Council for Human and Social Development (COHSOD). **Aims** Promote and support the achievement of quality *laboratory* services in accordance with appropriate standards, through advocacy, resource mobilisation, collaboration, research and education. **Structure** Board. **Activities** Standards/guidelines; advocacy/lobbying/activism. **Publications** *CMLF News*. **IGO Relations** Partners include: *Pan American Health Organization (PAHO, #18108)*; *Pan Caribbean Partnership against HIV and AIDS (PANCAP, #18171)*; *University of the West Indies (UWI, #20705)*. **NGO Relations** Member of: *International Federation of Biosafety Associations (IFBA, #13373)*. Partners include: *Caribbean Cytometry and Analytical Society (CCAS, #03488)*. [2014/XJ8870/f/**F**]

♦ Caribbean Landslide Working Group (see: #20705)
♦ Caribbean and Latin American Studies Library (internationally oriented national body)

♦ **Caribbean Law Institute (CLI)** 03523
Contact address not obtained. T. +18506443400.
URL: http://www.law.fsu.edu/centers/cli/index.html
History 1988, as a joint project between the *University of the West Indies (UWI, #20705)* and the Florida State University, Tallahassee FL (USA). **Aims** Reform and harmonize the *commercial laws* of the Commonwealth Caribbean. **Publications** *Caribbean Law and Business – vol 1* (1989); *Caribbean Commercial Law Reports – vol 1* (1988). **Members** Membership countries not specified. **IGO Relations** Member of: *Caribbean Community (CARICOM, #03476)*. [2008/XF1502/j/**F**]

♦ Caribbean Management Development Association (inactive)
♦ Caribbean Marine Biology Institute Foundation / see Caribbean Research and Management of Biodiversity
♦ Caribbean Marine Protected Areas Management Network (internationally oriented national body)
♦ Caribbean Media Corporation / see Caribbean Broadcasting Union (#03465)
♦ Caribbean Medical Association (internationally oriented national body)
♦ Caribbean Memorandum of Understanding on Port State Control (1996 treaty)
♦ Caribbean Mesoamerica FRIEND (see: #13826)
♦ Caribbean Meteorological Institute / see Caribbean Institute for Meteorology and Hydrology (#03520)

♦ **Caribbean Meteorological Organization (CMO)** 03524
L'Organisation météorologique des Caraïbes
Coordinating Dir 27 O'Connor Street, Woodbrook, PO Box 461, Port-of-Spain, Trinidad-Tobago. T. +18686224711. Fax +18686220277. E-mail: cmohq@cmo.org.tt.
URL: http://www.cmo.org.tt/
History 19 Oct 1973, Basseterre (St Kitts-Nevis). Established following the Treaty of 4 Jul 1973, Chaguaramas (Trinidad-Tobago). 4th Meeting of Heads of Government of *Caribbean Community (CARICOM, #03476)*, 4-8 Jul 1973, decided that CMO should become a specialized autonomous Institution of the Caribbean Community. **Aims** Promote and coordinate regional activities in the fields of meteorology, allied sciences and operational *hydrology*; provide related support and advice to regional governments. **Structure** Caribbean Meteorological Council (CMC), meeting at least annually; Headquarters Unit; *Caribbean Institute for Meteorology and Hydrology (CIMH, #03520)* in Bridgetown (Barbados). **Languages** English. **Staff** 52.00 FTE, paid. **Finance** Sources: contributions of member/participating states. Expenses borne by Member States as apportioned by the Council. **Activities** Events/meetings; guidance/assistance/consulting; knowledge management/information dissemination; networking/liaising; research/documentation. **Events** *Annual Meeting* Georgetown (Guyana) 2021, *Annual Meeting* Kingstown (St Vincent-Grenadines) 2020, *Annual Meeting* West End (Anguilla) 2019, *Annual Meeting* Basseterre (St Kitts-Nevis) 2018, *Annual Meeting* St John's (Antigua-Barbuda) 2017.
Members Governments of 16 countries and territories:
Anguilla, Antigua-Barbuda, Barbados, Belize, Cayman Is, Dominica, Grenada, Guyana, Jamaica, Montserrat, St Kitts-Nevis, St Lucia, St Vincent-Grenadines, Trinidad-Tobago, Turks-Caicos, Virgin Is UK.
IGO Relations Cooperates with (3): *Group on Earth Observations (GEO, #10735)*; *International Civil Aviation Organization (ICAO, #12581)*; *World Meteorological Organization (WMO, #21649)*. [2021.11.22/XD5659/**D***]

♦ Caribbean MOU – Caribbean Memorandum of Understanding on Port State Control (1996 treaty)

♦ **Caribbean Natural Resources Institute (CANARI)** 03525
Exec Dir 105 Twelfth St, Barataria, Trinidad-Tobago. T. +18686266062. Fax +18686261788. E-mail: communications@canari.org – info@canari.org.
URL: https://canari.org/
History 1977. Founded as a field programme of Caribbean Conservation Association and the University of Michigan (USA). Independent organization since 1986. Former names and other names: *Eastern Caribbean Natural Area Management Programme (ECNAMP)* – former (1977 to 1989). **Aims** Promote and facilitate equitable participation and effective collaboration in the management of natural resources critical to *development* in the Caribbean islands. **Structure** Board of Directors. Operational structure functions as partnership. **Languages** Creoles and pidgins, English, French, Spanish. **Staff** 10.00 FTE, paid. **Finance** Grants; technical assistance contracts. Budget (annual): about US$ 1.5 million. **Activities** Projects/programmes. **Events** *Workshop on managing information for civil society participation in natural resource management* Port-of-Spain (Trinidad-Tobago) 2004, *Workshop on participatory mangrove management* St Lucia 1999, *Workshop on understanding and managing natural resource conflicts* St Lucia 1999, *Workshop on revenue generation for protected areas* Las Palmas de Gran Canaria (Spain) 1997. **Publications** *CANARI Policy Briefs*. *CANARI Guidelines Series*. Technical Reports. See website for more publications. **Members** Not a membership organization. **Consultative Status** Consultative status granted from: *UNEP (#20299)*. **IGO Relations** *Caribbean Community (CARICOM, #03476)*; *Caribbean Community Climate Change Centre (CCCCC, #03477)*; *Caribbean Regional Fisheries Mechanism (CRFM, #03547)*; *Commonwealth Foundation (CF, #04330)*; *Commonwealth Secretariat (#04362)*; *FAO (#09260)*; *Green Climate Fund (GCF, #10714)*; *OAS (#17629)*; *Organisation of Eastern Caribbean States (OECS, #17804)*; *UNDP (#20292)*; *United Nations Economic Commission for Latin America and the Caribbean (ECLAC, #20556)*; *University of the West Indies (UWI, #20705)*; universities. **NGO Relations** *Universities Caribbean (#20694)*; *BirdLife International (#03266)*; *Consortium of Caribbean Universities for Natural Resource Management (CCUNRM, no recent information)*; *Green Economy Coalition (GEC, #10717)*; *International Institute for Environment and Development (IIED, #13877)*; *International Union for Conservation of Nature and Natural Resources (IUCN, #15766)*; Nature Caribe; *Overseas Development Institute (ODI)*; *World Resources Institute (WRI, #21753)*; many Caribbean regional and national organizations. [2020/XF1032/j/**E**]

♦ **Caribbean Netball Association (CNA)** 03526
Pres PO Box 60WR, Welches Road Post Office, St Michael, ST MICHAEL, Barbados.
History 1954, as *West Indies Netball Board of Control*. Present name adopted 1974. **Aims** Foster and develop the game of netball in the Caribbean. **Structure** General Meeting (annual). Council. Executive Committee, comprising President, 2 Vice-Presidents, Secretary, Treasurer and Immediate Past President. **Finance** Members' dues. Other sources: sponsors; donations; tournament fees; contributions. Budget (annual): US$ 200,000. **Activities** Organizes championships, seminars and workshops. **Events** *Annual Conference* Guyana 2006, *Conference* 1998, *Conference / Annual Conference* St Kitts-Nevis 1996.
Members in 17 countries and territories:
Anguilla, Antigua-Barbuda, Bahamas, Barbados, Bermuda, Cayman Is, Dominica, Grenada, Guyana, Jamaica, St Kitts-Nevis, St Lucia, St Maarten, St Vincent-Grenadines, Trinidad-Tobago, Turks-Caicos, Virgin Is UK.
NGO Relations *Americas Federation of Netball Associations (AFNA, #00793)*; *Organización de la Administración Caribeña de Deporte y Educación Fisica (OCASPE, no recent information)*. [2010/XD8983/**D**]

♦ **Caribbean Network of Fisherfolk Organisations (CNFO)** 03527
Coordinator address not obtained.
URL: https://cnfo.fish/
History 2004. Founded with the support from *Caribbean Regional Fisheries Mechanism (CRFM, #03547)*. **Aims** Promote effective ecosystem based management of fisheries resources; secure livelihoods; contribute to food security for Caribbean communities increase their resilience to risk including climate change. **Structure** General Assembly; Board of Directors; Executive. **Publications** *Fisherfolk Net*.
Members National Fisherfolk Organizations in 13 countries:
Antigua-Barbuda, Bahamas, Barbados, Belize, Dominica, Grenada, Guyana, Jamaica, St Kitts-Nevis, St Lucia, St Vincent-Grenadines, Suriname, Trinidad-Tobago.
IGO Relations Observer status with (1): *Caribbean Regional Fisheries Mechanism (CRFM, #03547)*. [2020/AA1264/**F**]

♦ **Caribbean Network for Integrated Rural Development (CNIRD)** 03528
Head Office No 5 Tunapuna Road, Tunapuna, Trinidad-Tobago. T. +18682218497. E-mail: cnird@live.com.
URL: http://www.cnirdregional.org/

History Mar 1988, Jamaica. **Aims** Support and promote rural development issues in the Caribbean via a strategy of information networking; carry out research on the current issues relevant to rural development; coordinate diverse activities aimed at bettering conditions overall in rural areas. **Structure** General Assembly; Executive Committee; Secretariat, managed by Director. **Finance** Sources: international NGOs, including: *Commonwealth Foundation (CF, #04330); Humanistisch Instituut voor Ontwikkelingssamenwerking (Hivos); W K Kellogg Foundation (WKKF); Oxfam GB.* **Activities** Networking/liaising; research/documentation; training/education; advocacy/lobbying/activism. **Events** *Biennial Assembly* Castries (St Lucia) 1998, *Caribbean wide land symposium* Grenada 1995, *Biennial Assembly* St Augustine (Trinidad-Tobago) 1995, *Biennial Assembly* St Augustine (Trinidad-Tobago) 1992, *Biennial assembly* St Augustine (Trinidad-Tobago) 1990. **Publications** *Rural Link Up* – regional newsletter. *Developing the Rural Network – A Directory of Rural Development Resources in the Caribbean; Integrated Rural Development – Caribbean Perspectives; Reaping without Weeping: A Guide to Safe Management and Application of Chemicals in Agriculture.* Reports; directories; surveys. **Information Services** *INCARD* – Database of Rural Development Information of Relevance to the Caribbean; *Network News* – an Update of Acquisitions in INCARD database.
Members National organizations in 6 countries:
Barbados, Belize, Dominica, Grenada, Jamaica, St Vincent-Grenadines.
International organizations (3):
Caribbean Organization of Indigenous Peoples (COIP, #03535); Caribbean Policy Development Centre (CPDC, #03540); Caribbean Youth Environment Network (CYEN, #03570).
Consultative Status Consultative status granted from: *UNEP (#20299).* **IGO Relations** Accredited to the Conference of the Parties of: *Secretariat of the United Nations Convention to Combat Desertification (Secretariat of the UNCCD, #19208).* **NGO Relations** Founding member of: *Caribbean Digital Library Consortium (no recent information).* Member of: *Global Forum on Sustainable Food and Nutritional Security (no recent information).* [2017/XF1268/F]

♦ Caribbean Network of Researchers on Sickle Cell Disease and Thalassemia (CAREST) 03529

Réseau Caraïbéen des Chercheurs/Cliniciens sur la Drépanocytose et les Thalassemies – Red Caribeña de Investigadores/Clinicos sobre la Drepanocitosis y las Talas

Address not obtained.

History Registered in accordance with French law, 26 Sep 2009. **Aims** Promote Sickle Cell Disease and Thalassemia as public health concerns in the region; provide epidemiological and other health data on Sickle Cell Disease and Thalassemia for policymakers; improve the quality of care offered to persons and their families affected with Sickle Cell Disease and Thalassemia by the creation of clinical protocols or standard of care guidelines appropriate to the level of development within each territory; provide a framework for collaborative research on research priorities in the field within the region; act as a technical resource for families, non-governmental organizations and governments in the region. **Structure** Steering Committee. **Events** *Advances in clinical care and research* Kingston (Jamaica) 2016, *Conference* Havana (Cuba) 2013, *Conference* Gosier (Guadeloupe) 2011, *Conference* Guadeloupe 2006. [2012/XJ5359/F]

♦ Caribbean News Agency (CANA) 03530

Admin Officer Caribbean Media Corporation Harbour Industrial Estate, Unit 1B, Building 6A, St Michael BB11145, ST MICHAEL BB11145, Barbados. T. +2464671000. Fax +2464294355. E-mail: lori.weatherhead@cmccaribbean.com – admin@cmccaribbean.com.
URL: http://canananewsonline.com/main/

History 7 Jan 1976, as successor to Reuter's 'Caribbean News Service', with the assistance of *Caribbean Publishing and Broadcasting Association (CPBA, inactive).* From 2000, business operations undertaken by *Caribbean Media Corporation (CMC).* **Aims** Enhance *integration* and understanding among Caribbean peoples and between them and the rest of the world community, with the provision of *information* about the Caribbean media. **Structure** Shareholders: 8 privately-owned media and 4 state-owned public corporations. Board of Trustees; Board of Directors. Company Secretary/General Manager. **Staff** 1.00 FTE, paid. **Finance** Financed by CMC. **Activities** Monitors freedom of the press in the Caribbean; provides a media information service; facilitates training of media personnel; organizes seminars and workshops. **Events** *Caribbean seminar on business reporting* Christ Church (Barbados) 1995.
Members Shareholders in 5 countries:
Barbados, Jamaica, Montserrat, St Vincent-Grenadines, Trinidad-Tobago. [2018/XF7786/e/F]

♦ Caribbean and North American Council for Mission (CANACOM) 03531

Education in Mission Sec 49 Hope Road, Kingston, Jamaica. Fax +18769278829. E-mail: canacom1986@yahoo.com.
URL: http://canacom.org/

History 1986. Founded as a mission partnership of regional churches. **Aims** Challenge, equip and empower one another for creative mission engagement in a local, national and worldwide context. **Structure** Council (meets annually); Administrative Committee; Secretariat. **Languages** English, Old Dutch, Spanish. **Staff** 2.00 FTE, paid. **Finance** Sources: donations; fundraising; grants. **Activities** Projects/programmes; religious activities; training/education. **Events** *Meeting* Willemstad (Curaçao) 2018, *Meeting* Paramaribo (Suriname) 2016, *Meeting* Jamaica 2014, *Meeting* Grenada 2012, *Meeting* Dominican Rep 2011.
Members National churches (14) in 11 countries and territories:
Canada, Cayman Is, Cuba, Curaçao, Dominican Rep, Grenada, Guyana, Jamaica, Suriname, Trinidad-Tobago, USA. [2021.09.02/XE2115/E]

♦ Caribbean Nurses Organization (CNO) 03532

Organisation des infirmières de la Caraïbe

Secretariat c/o Nurses Assoc HQs, Queen Elizabeth Highway, St John's, St John, Antigua-Barbuda. E-mail: cnoconference@gmail.com.
URL: http://www.cnoconference.org/

History 1957, on the initiative of Mavis Harney. **Events** *Biennial Conference* Antigua-Barbuda 2016, *Biennial Conference* Castries (St Lucia) 2014, *Biennial Conference* Paramaribo (Suriname) 2012, *Biennial Conference* Aruba 2010, *Biennial Conference* Gosier (Guadeloupe) 2008. **Members** Membership countries not specified. **IGO Relations** Observer to: *Regional Nursing Body, CARICOM Community (RNB, no recent information).* **NGO Relations** *Commonwealth Nurses and Midwives Federation (CNMF, #04353); International Council of Nurses (ICN, #13054).* [2017/XD9784/D]

♦ Caribbean Ombudsman Association (CAROA) 03533

Pres Office Ombudsman Curaçao, Scharlooweg 41, Scharloo, Willemstad, Curaçao. T. +59994610303. E-mail: info@ombudsman-curacao.cw.
URL: https://www.caribbeanombudsman.com/

History 1998, Antigua (Antigua-Barbuda). Proposed 1998, Antigua. Interim constitution adopted 2000, St Lucia. Final constitution ratified 2002, Trinidad. *CAROA Administration Foundation* set up May 2014, Curaçao. **Aims** Strengthen offices of the Ombudsman in the Caribbean so as to foster cooperative work, harness resources of, network and provide continued enrichment with other offices of the Ombudsman and other similar institutions. **Structure** Council; Board of CAROA Administration Foundation. **Languages** English. **Staff** None. **Finance** Members' dues. Donations. **Activities** Events/meetings; training/education; guidance/assistance/consulting. **Events** *Conference* Southampton (Bermuda) 2019, *Biennial Conference* Bonaire Is (Dutch Caribbean) 2017, *Biennial Conference* Willemstad (Curaçao) 2015, *Biennial Conference* St Maarten 2013, *Biennial Conference* Curaçao 2010.
Members Full in 16 countries and territories:
Antigua-Barbuda, Barbados, Belize, Bermuda, Cayman Is, Curaçao, Grenada, Haiti, Jamaica, Netherlands, St Kitts-Nevis, St Lucia, St Maarten, Trinidad-Tobago, Turks-Caicos, Virgin Is UK.
IGO Relations *Commonwealth Secretariat (#04362); European Court of Human Rights (#06855). UNICEF (#20332).* [2022/XJ7831/D]

♦ Caribbean Oral Health Initiative (COHI) 03534

Iniciativa de Salud Oral del Caribe

Address not obtained.
URL: http://www.cohiweb.org/

History 2012. **Structure** Board of Directors. **Activities** Events/meetings. [2018/AA2223/F]

♦ Caribbean Organization (inactive)

♦ Caribbean Organization of Indigenous Peoples (COIP) 03535

Chairman Santa Rosa First Peoples Community, 7 Paul Mitchell St, Arima, Trinidad-Tobago. T. +18686641897.
URL: http://coipnews.blogspot.com/

History Founded 1987, St Vincent-Grenadines, during a conference funded by *Cuso International* and *Oxfam GB.* **Aims** Enhance opportunities for social and economic development; promote retrieval of indigenous culture; advocate basic human and civil rights; reinforce positive self-image; foster exchanges among members and with other indigenous peoples; correct inequalities traditionally meted out against indigenous peoples and other deprived *minorities.* **Structure** Executive; General Body. **Languages** Arawak, English, Spanish. **Staff** Voluntary. Currently approaching government for assistance for paid staff and office equipment for secretariat. **Finance** Citizen and government assistance. No fixed budget. **Activities** Events/meetings; capacity building; advocacy/lobbying/activism. **Events** *General Assembly* Trinidad-Tobago 2015, *General Assembly / Annual Gathering* Trinidad-Tobago 2014, *General Assembly / Annual Gathering* Trinidad-Tobago 2013, *International Conference* Trinidad-Tobago 2013, *General Assembly / Annual Gathering* Trinidad-Tobago 2012. **Publications** *Indigi-Notes* – newsletter. *KUNUWATON – A Book on the Culture of the First Peoples of Trinidad and Tobago. Newspaper Brochure* (2013, 2014).
Members Grass roots national organizations in 7 countries:
Belize, Dominica, Guyana, Puerto Rico, St Vincent-Grenadines, Suriname, Trinidad-Tobago.
NGO Relations Member of: *Caribbean Network for Integrated Rural Development (CNIRD, #03528); Caribbean Policy Development Centre (CPDC, #03540).* [2018.09.05/XD1967/D]

♦ Caribbean Organization for Rural Development and Education (inactive)

♦ Caribbean Organization of Supreme Audit Institutions (CAROSAI) 03536

Organisation des institutions supérieures de contrôle des finances publiques des Caraïbes – Organización de Entidades Fiscalizadoras Superiores del Caribe – Karibische Organisation der Obersten Rechnungskontrollbehörden

SG c/o Auditor General's Dept, 40 Knutsford Boulevard, PO Box 455, Kingston, Jamaica. T. +18769268309 – +18769265963 – +18769265846. Fax +18769684690. E-mail: carosai@auditorgeneral.gov.jm.
URL: http://www.carosai.org/

History 7 Aug 1988, Port-of-Spain (Trinidad-Tobago). **Aims** Expand training and continuing education between Supreme Audit Institutions (SAIs); render technical assistance and support to members; increase importance of internal audit function in the public sector. **Structure** Congress; Executive Council; Secretariat. **Languages** Dutch, English, French. **Staff** 1.00 FTE, paid. **Finance** Sources: members' dues. **Activities** Events/meetings; knowledge management/information dissemination; training/education. **Events** *Congress* Oranjestad (Aruba) 2022, *Congress* Georgetown (Guyana) 2019, *Congress* Paramaribo (Suriname) 2016, *Congress* Port-of-Spain (Trinidad-Tobago) 2013, *Congress* Belize City (Belize) 2010. **Publications** *CAROSAI 30th Anniversary Commemorative Magazine 1988-2018.* Manuals; guidelines; policies; procedures; reports.
Members Charter; Ordinary; Associate. Members in 23 countries and territories:
Anguilla, Antigua-Barbuda, Aruba, Bahamas, Barbados, Belize, Bermuda, Cayman Is, Curaçao, Dominica, Grenada, Guyana, Haiti, Jamaica, Montserrat, St Kitts-Nevis, St Lucia, St Maarten, St Vincent-Grenadines, Suriname, Trinidad-Tobago, Turks-Caicos, Virgin Is UK.
NGO Relations Cooperates with (1): *International Organization of Supreme Audit Institutions (INTOSAI, #14478).* [2022.10.27/XD1333/D]

♦ Caribbean Organization of Tax Administrators (COTA) 03537

Pres Barbados Revenue Authority, Treasury Bldg, Bridge Street, Bridgetown, St Michael, Bridgetown ST MICHAEL, Barbados.
Contact Caribbean Community Secretariat, Turkeyen, PO Box 10827, Georgetown, Guyana. T. +5922220001 – +5922220075. Fax +5922220155 – +5922220170. E-mail: registry@caricom.org.
URL: http://www.caricom.org/jsp/community/institutions.jsp?menu=community/

History 1971, St Lucia, at a meeting of the Heads of Regional Tax Administration, where Constitution was ratified. **Aims** Improve tax administration within the Caribbean Community (CARICOM); promote closer collaboration with other tax institutions. **Structure** General Assembly (every 2 years); Executive Council. **Languages** English. **Staff** 3.00 FTE, paid. **Finance** Financed through *Caribbean Community (CARICOM, #03476)* Secretariat. **Activities** Training/education; knowledge management/information dissemination; guidance/assistance/consulting. **Events** *Biennial General Assembly and Conference* Trinidad-Tobago 2012, *Biennial General Assembly and Conference* Barbados 2010, *Biennial General Assembly and Conference* Belize 2008, *Biennial General Assembly and Conference* St Lucia 2006, *Biennial general assembly and conference* Nassau (Bahamas) 2004. **Publications** *COTA Newsletter* (2 a year).
Members CARICOM member states (19):
Anguilla, Antigua-Barbuda, Bahamas, Barbados, Belize, Cayman Is, Dominica, Grenada, Guyana, Haiti, Jamaica, Montserrat, St Kitts-Nevis, St Lucia, St Vincent-Grenadines, Suriname, Trinidad-Tobago, Turks-Caicos, Virgin Is UK.
NGO Relations Instrumental in setting up: *Council of Executive Secretaries of Tax Organizations (CESTO, inactive).* [2015.12.08/XD1866/D*]

♦ Caribbean Patent Information Network (no recent information)
♦ Caribbean Peoples Development Agency (no recent information)
♦ Caribbean Pest Information Network (internationally oriented national body)

♦ Caribbean Philanthropy Network (CPN) 03538

Coordinator c/o Community Foundation of the Virgin Is, PO Box 11790, St Thomas VI 00801, USA. T. +13407746031. Fax +13407743852.
Street aAddress 5150 Dronningens Gade, Suite 1, St Thomas VI 00802, USA.
URL: http://www.caribbeanphilanthropy.org/

History May 2003, Anguilla, as *Association of Caribbean Community Foundations (ACCF).* Current title adopted, May 2008, when became a project of Community Foundation of the Virgin Islands (CFVI). **Aims** Link groups and individuals that make grants and provide other resources – community, corporate, private, and family foundations, as well as individual donors – to charitable nonprofit organizations that are working to improve the quality of life for residents of the Caribbean region. **Structure** Advisory Group. **Activities** Organizes symposium. Runs Caribbean Philanthropy Mapping Project. **Events** *Symposium* St Thomas Is (Virgin Is USA) 2010. **NGO Relations** Member of: *Worldwide Initiatives for Grantmaker Support (WINGS, #21926).* [2018.01.18/XM1379/D]

♦ Caribbean Philosophical Association (internationally oriented national body)

♦ Caribbean Plant Health Directors Forum (CPHD Forum) 03539

Contact USDA-APHIS IS Office, Frank Stockdale Bldg, University Campus, St Augustine 685509, Trinidad-Tobago. T. +18686622002.
URL: http://www.cphdforum.org/

History 29 Jul 2014, Grand Cayman (Cayman Is). Charter adopted at 7th Meeting of the CPHD. **Aims** Increase communication and the transparent exchange of sanitary information among Caribbean Countries. **Structure** Forum; Steering Committee. Sub-committees (2): Caribbean Pest Diagnostic Network (CPDN); Technical Comittee on the Formulation and Prioritization of a Regional Pest List. **Activities** Capacity building; events/meetings; research and development; training/education. **Events** *Annual Meeting* St Augustine (Trinidad-Tobago) 2020, *Annual Meeting* Nassau (Bahamas) 2019.
Members National Plant Health Services; regional and international organizations; government entities; universities and reference laboratories. Governmental agencies in 27 countries and territories, as well as 11 organizations:
Anguilla (Associated), Antigua-Barbuda, Aruba, Bahamas, Barbados, Belize, Bermuda (Associated), Cayman Is (Associated), Cuba, Curaçao, Dominica, Dominican Rep, Grenada, Guyana, Haiti, Jamaica, Martinique, Montenegro, St Kitts-Nevis, St Lucia, St Maarten, St Vincent-Grenadines, Suriname, Trinidad-Tobago, Turks-Caicos, Virgin Is UK (Associated), Virgin Is USA.
CABI (#03393); Caribbean Agricultural Research and Development Institute (CARDI, #03436); FAO (#09260); Inter-American Institute for Cooperation on Agriculture (IICA, #11434); International Center for Research and Decision Support of the International Federation of Catholic Universities (CIRAD, #12476); Organisation of Eastern Caribbean States (OECS, #17804); Organismo Internacional Regional de Sanidad Agropecuaria (OIRSA, #17830); United States Department of Agriculture (Animal and Plant Health Inspection Service Greater Caribbean Safeguarding Initiative (USDA/APHIS GCSI)); University of Florida; University of Guyana; *University of the West Indies (UWI, #20705).*

IGO Relations Cooperates with (1): *Caribbean Community (CARICOM, #03476).* [2020/AA1276/y/**F**]

♦ Caribbean Plant Protection Commission (inactive)

♦ Caribbean Policy Development Centre (CPDC) 03540

Mailing Address PO Box 57, Welches Road, St Michael, ST MICHAEL, Barbados. E-mail: cpdc@caribsurf.com.
URL: http://www.cpdcngo.org/

History 1991. Founded within *Caribbean Conference of Churches (CCC, #03479).* Serves as the Policy Secretariat of NGOs and Community Based Organizations throughout the Caribbean. Former names and other names: *Caribbean Policy Unit* – former (1991). Registration: Start date: 1991, Barbados. **Aims** Sensitize NGOs and the general public on key policy issues; foster civil society partnerships with government in the design and implementation of policies that improve the lives of Caribbean people. **Structure** Assembly of Members (every 2 years); Board of Directors; Specialized Committees; Regional Secretariat. **Languages** Creoles and pidgins, Dutch, English, French. **Finance** Members' dues. Grants. **Activities** Projects/programmes; capacity building. **Events** *Alternative development models for caribbean forum* 1995, *Workshop on strategies for influencing public policy* 1994, *Caribbean regional economic education workshop* Santo Domingo (Dominican Rep) 1992. **Publications** *Caribbean Beacon* (annual) – policy magazine; *Just Us Magazine* (annual). *Elements of Regional Integration: The Way Forward* (1998); *Challenges in Caribbean Development* (1992).
Members Membership open to regional organizations; national networks/umbrella organizations; national agencies with regional perspective. Members in 9 countries:
Barbados, Belize, Grenada, Guyana, Haiti, Jamaica, St Vincent-Grenadines, Suriname, Trinidad-Tobago.
Included in the above, 6 organizations listed in this Yearbook:
Caribbean Association for Feminist Research and Action (CAFRA, #03445); Caribbean Conference of Churches (CCC, #03479); Caribbean Network for Integrated Rural Development (CNIRD, #03528); Caribbean Organization of Indigenous Peoples (COIP, #03535); Caribbean Youth Environment Network (CYEN, #03570); Windward Islands Farmers' Association (WINFA, #20966).
Consultative Status Consultative status granted from: *ECOSOC (#05331)* (Special); *UNEP (#20299).* [2022/XF1481/y/**E**]

♦ Caribbean Policy Unit / see Caribbean Policy Development Centre (#03540)

♦ Caribbean Postal Union (CPU) 03541

SG General Post Office, PO Box 413, Castries, St Lucia. T. +17584581787. Fax +17584521543. E-mail: cpuslu@hotmail.com.
URL: http://caribbeanpostalunion.org/

History 5 Sep 1997. Established on official notification of entry into force of convention, as a Restricted Union of *Universal Postal Union (UPU, #20682).* Headquarters in Castries (St Lucia). **Structure** Council of Ministers of Postal Affairs; Management Board. **Languages** English, French, Spanish. **Staff** 2.50 FTE, paid. **Activities** Events/meetings. **Events** *Conference* St Lucia 2021, *Conference* Havana (Cuba) 2019, *Conference* Gros-Islet (St Lucia) 2018, *Conference* Gosier (Guadeloupe) 2017, *Conference* Bridgetown (Barbados) 2016.
Members Postal operators in 29 countries and territories party to the convention:
Anguilla, Antigua, Aruba, Bahamas, Barbados, Belize, Bermuda, Canada, Cayman Is, Cuba, Curaçao, Dominica, Dominican Rep, Grenada, Guyana, Haiti, Jamaica, Montserrat, Netherlands, St Kitts-Nevis, St Lucia, St Maarten, St Vincent-Grenadines, Suriname, Trinidad-Tobago, Turks-Caicos, UK, USA, Virgin Is USA. [2021.11.16/XD6892/**D***]

♦ Caribbean Poultry Association (CPA) 03542

Exec Dir CARIRI, University of the West Indies, St Augustine Campus, St Augustine, Trinidad-Tobago. T. +8686627161. Fax +8686627177.
URL: https://www.caribbeanpoultry.org/

History 1999, Atlanta, GA (USA). Formally incorporated, Apr 2000. **Aims** Promote the development of the Caribbean broiler and table egg industries. **Structure** Officers: President; Vice-President; Treasurer; Corporate Secretary; Executive Director. **Languages** English. **Staff** 3.50 FTE, paid. **Finance** Sources: members' dues. Annual budget: 100,000 USD. **Activities** Advocacy/lobbying/activism; events/meetings. **Events** *Joint meeting on animal disease surveillance and preparedness* Port-of-Spain (Trinidad-Tobago) 2006.
Members Ordinary; Associate; Honorary; Observer. Ordinary members (18) in 8 countries:
Barbados, Belize, Grenada, Guyana, Haiti, Jamaica, St Vincent-Grenadines, Suriname, Trinidad-Tobago.
Associate members (2) in 1 country:
USA.
Honorary members (3) in 2 countries:
Canada, Trinidad-Tobago.
Observers (8) in 8 countries:
Antigua-Barbuda, Dominica, Grenada, Guyana, Haiti, St Lucia, Suriname, USA.
NGO Relations Member of (3): Community Involved in Sustaining Agriculture; *International Poultry Council (IPC, #14628);* Latin American Association for AVIAN Health. [2022/XD8428/**D**]

♦ Caribbean Press Council (inactive)
♦ Caribbean Psychiatric Association (no recent information)

♦ Caribbean Public Finance Association (CaPFA) 03543

Contact Dept Finance Corporate Office, 4th Floor Finance Admin Centre, Pointe Seraphine, Castries, St Lucia. T. +17584685503. Fax +17584526700. E-mail: capfa@gosl.gov.lc.
URL: http://www.cartac.org/capfa/

History Feb 2003, Trinidad-Tobago, as *Public Expenditure Network.* Present name adopted Jun 2003. **Aims** Be the leading organization in promoting development and application of highest standards in public finance management in the Caribbean. **Structure** Board. **Languages** English, French, Spanish. **Staff** Voluntary. **Finance** Establishment support through *Caribbean Regional Technical Assistance Centre (CARTAC, #03550).* **Activities** Standards/guidelines; training/education; events/meetings. **Publications** *CaPFA Newsletter.*
Members Full in 20 countries and territories:
Anguilla, Antigua-Barbuda, Bahamas, Barbados, Belize, Cayman Is, Dominica, Dominican Rep, Grenada, Guyana, Haiti, Jamaica, Montserrat, St Kitts-Nevis, St Lucia, St Vincent-Grenadines, Suriname, Trinidad-Tobago, Turks-Caicos, Virgin Is UK. [2019.11.14/XJ3004/**D**]

♦ Caribbean Public Health Agency (CARPHA) 03544

Exec Dir 16-18 Jamaica Blvd, Federation Park, Newtown 190324, Trinidad-Tobago. T. +18686224261. Fax +18686222792. E-mail: postmaster@carpha.org.
URL: https://carpha.org/

History Dec 2010. Established following recommendation by *Caribbean Community (CARICOM, #03476),* and approval by *Bureau of the Conference of Heads of Government of the Caribbean Community,* Mar 2010. Legally established 2 Jul 2011, by Intergovernmental Agreement. Started operations 2 Jan 2013. Brings together 5 Caribbean Regional Health Institutes (RHIs): *Caribbean Health Research Council (CHRC, inactive); Caribbean Epidemiology Centre (CAREC, inactive); Caribbean Environmental Health Institute (CEHI, inactive); Caribbean Food and Nutrition Institute (CFNI, inactive); CARPHA Drug Testing Laboratory (CRDTL, inactive).* A CARICOM Institution. **Aims** Promote physical and mental health and wellness of people within the Caribbean. **Structure** Heads of Governments; CARICOM Council of Human and Social Development; Executive Board; Technical Advisory Committee. **Languages** English. **Staff** 92.00 FTE, paid. **Finance** Combination of *Caribbean Community (CARICOM, #03476)* Countries quotas and international funding. **Activities** Awareness raising; events/meetings; healthcare; knowledge management/information dissemination; monitoring/evaluation; networking/liaising; research and development; training/education. **Events** *Annual Health Research Conference* Trinidad-Tobago 2021, *Annual Health Research Conference* Port-of-Spain (Trinidad-Tobago) 2019, *Annual Health Research Conference* Frigate Bay (St Kitts-Nevis) 2018, *Annual Health Research Conference* Georgetown (Guyana) 2017, *Annual Health Research Conference* Turks-Caicos 2016. **Publications** *State of Public Health Report* in English. Annual Report; data and statistics; guidelines; manuals; reports.
Members Governments of 26 countries and territories:
Anguilla, Antigua-Barbuda, Aruba, Bahamas, Barbados, Belize, Bermuda, Bonaire Is, Cayman Is, Curaçao, Dominica, Grenada, Guyana, Haiti, Jamaica, Montserrat, Saba, St Eustatius, St Kitts-Nevis, St Lucia, St Maarten, St Vincent-Grenadines, Suriname, Trinidad-Tobago, Turks-Caicos, Virgin Is UK.
IGO Relations Partners include:
– *Organisation of African, Caribbean and Pacific States (OACPS, #17796);*
– *Caribbean Agricultural Research and Development Institute (CARDI, #03436);*
– *Caribbean Community (CARICOM, #03476);*
– *Caribbean Development Bank (CDB, #03492);*
– *Caribbean Disaster Emergency Management Agency (CDEMA, #03493);*
– *Caribbean Tourism Organization (CTO, #03561);*
– *CARICOM Implementation Agency for Crime and Security (IMPACS, #03573);*
– *Department for International Development (DFID, inactive);*
– *Deutsche Gesellschaft für Internationale Zusammenarbeit (GIZ);*
– *European Centre for Disease Prevention and Control (ECDC, #06476);*
– *European Commission (EC, #06633);*
– *FAO Regional Office for Latin America and the Caribbean (FAO/RLC, #09268);*
– *Inter-American Development Bank (IDB, #11427)* (World Bank);
– *Inter-American Institute for Cooperation on Agriculture (IICA, #11434);*
– *International Agency for Research on Cancer (IARC, #11598);*
– *International Bank for Reconstruction and Development (IBRD, #12317);*
– *International Development Law Organization (IDLO, #13161);*
– *Pan American Health Organization (PAHO, #18108);*
– *Pan Caribbean Partnership against HIV and AIDS (PANCAP, #18171);*
– *UNEP (#20299);*
– *UNICEF/UNDP/World Bank/WHO Special Programme for Research and Training in Tropical Diseases (TDR, #20331);*
– *Unitaid (#20493);*
– *University of the West Indies (UWI, #20705);*
– *WHO (#20950).*

NGO Relations Partners include: *Caribbean College of Family Physicians (CCFP, #03474);* Caribbean Health and Education Foundation; *Caribbean Hotel and Tourism Association (CHTA, #03516); Caribbean Med Labs Foundation (CMLF, #03522); Healthy Caribbean Coalition (HCC, #10893); Tulane University School of Public Health and Tropical Medicine; World Diabetes Foundation (WDF, #21359);* national organizations; universities. [2021.03.08/XJ1503/**E***]

♦ Caribbean Public Health Association (no recent information)

♦ Caribbean Public Services Association (CPSA) 03545

Pres c/o PSA Trinidad and Tobago, 89 Abercromby Street, Port-of-Spain, Trinidad-Tobago. E-mail: psa.tnt@gmail.com.
General Sec address not obtained. E-mail: cpsayoungworkers@gmail.com.
Facebook: https://www.facebook.com/CaribbeanPublicServicesAssociation/

History 1970. Former names and other names: *Federation of British Caribbean Civil Service Association* – former. **Events** *Annual Conference* Trinidad-Tobago 2015, *Annual Conference* Guyana 2010, *Annual Conference* Grenada 2009, *Annual Conference* Dominica 2008, *Annual Conference* Barbados 2005. **Members** Public service unions (19). Membership countries not specified. [2020/XD2725/**D**]

♦ Caribbean Publishers Network (CAPNET) 03546

Groupement d'éditeurs des Caraïbes – Red de Editores del Caribe

Secretariat 11 Cunningham Avenue, PO Box 686, Kingston, Jamaica. T. +18769780739. Fax +18769780739.
Pres 97B Saddle Road, Maraval, Port-of-Spain, Trinidad-Tobago. T. +18686283111. Fax +18686283111.

History Jun 2000, Port-of-Spain (Trinidad-Tobago). **Aims** Support creation and development of the publishing industry in the Caribbean; further cooperation and communication among Caribbean publishers. **Structure** Council, including President, Vice-President, Honorary Secretary and Honorary Treasurer. **Finance** Members' dues. **Activities** Organizes: International conference on publishing; annual bookfair. **Events** *Biennial Conference on Publishing* Jamaica 2009, *International forum on publishers against AIDS* Kingston (Jamaica) 2005, *Biennial Conference on Publishing* Curaçao 2003, *Biennial Conference* Willemstad (Curaçao) 2003, *Annual General Meeting* Port-of-Spain (Trinidad-Tobago) 2002.
Members in 21 countries and territories:
Aruba, Barbados, Belize, Canada, Colombia, Cuba, Curaçao, Dominican Rep, Guadeloupe, Haiti, Jamaica, Mexico, Puerto Rico, St Kitts-Nevis, St Lucia, St Maarten, Suriname, Trinidad-Tobago, USA, Venezuela, Virgin Is USA.
IGO Relations *University of the West Indies (UWI, #20705).* [2015/XF6789/**F**]

♦ Caribbean Publishing and Broadcasting Association (inactive)
♦ Caribbean Regional Accident and Incident Investigation Organization (unconfirmed)
♦ Caribbean Regional Badminton Confederation / see Caribbean Badminton Confederation (#03463)
♦ Caribbean Regional Branch of the International Council on Archives (see: #12996)
♦ Caribbean Regional Centre for Collective Management of Copyright / see Association of Caribbean Copyright Societies (#02404)
♦ Caribbean Regional Council for Adult Education (inactive)

♦ Caribbean Regional Fisheries Mechanism (CRFM) 03547

Exec Dir Princess Margaret Drive, Belize City, Belize City, Belize. T. +5012234443. Fax +5012234446. E-mail: communications@crfm.int.
Eastern Caribbean Office 1st Floor TEKA Bldg, Arnos Vale, PO Box 2427, Kingstown VC0100, St Vincent-Grenadines. T. +17844584269 – +17844564628. Fax +17844573475. E-mail: crfmsvg@crfm.int.
URL: https://crfm.int/

History 27 Mar 2003, Belize City (Belize). Officially inaugurated following signing of Agreement Establishing the CRFM, 4 Feb 2002. A *Caribbean Community (CARICOM, #03476)* Institution. **Aims** Promote and facilitate responsible utilization of the region's fisheries and other aquatic resources for the economic and social benefits of the current and future population of the region. **Structure** Ministerial Council, consisting of Ministers responsible for Fisheries in each Member State. Caribbean Fisheries Forum, consisting of one representative from each Member, each Associate Member and each Observer. Technical Unit (Secretariat). **Languages** English. **Activities** Active in: Belize, St Vincent-Grenadines. **Publications** *Newsletter of the Caribbean Regional Fisheries Mechanism.* Technical Reports.
Members Governments (17):
Anguilla, Antigua-Barbuda, Bahamas, Barbados, Belize, Dominica, Grenada, Guyana, Haiti, Jamaica, Montserrat, St Kitts-Nevis, St Lucia, St Vincent-Grenadines, Suriname, Trinidad-Tobago, Turks-Caicos.
Observers (7):
Bermuda.
Caribbean Community (CARICOM, #03476); Caribbean Network of Fisherfolk Organisations (CNFO, #03527); FAO (#09260); OECS Secretariat; *Organisation of Eastern Caribbean States (OECS, #17804); University of the West Indies (UWI, #20705).*
IGO Relations Agreements with: *Intergovernmental Oceanographic Commission (IOC, #11496); United Nations University (UNU, #20642)* – Fisheries Training Programme (UNU-FTP). Partner organizations: *Centre technique de coopération agricole et rurale (CTA, inactive); Network of Aquaculture Centres in Asia-Pacific (NACA, #16991).* **NGO Relations** Partner of (1): *Caribbean Natural Resources Institute (CANARI, #03525).* Instrumental in setting up (1): *Caribbean Network of Fisherfolk Organisations (CNFO, #03527).* [2023.02.13/XJ7911/y/**F***]

♦ Caribbean Regional Information and Translation Institute (CRITI) . . 03548

Institut caribéen et régional de l'information et de la traduction – Instituto de Información y Traducción para la Región del Caribe – Caribisch Regionaal Informatie en Vertaal Instituut

Contact Henck Arronstr 25 – 2nd floor, Paramaribo, Suriname. T. +597474215. Fax +597474259. E-mail: contact@criti.info.
URL: http://criti.info/

History Jan 2008, by *Forum of Caribbean States (CARIFORUM, #09904)* Council of Ministers and with support of *European Commission (EC, #06633).* A Functional Institution of *Caribbean Community (CARICOM, #03476).* **Aims** Foster better regional integration and cooperation and commercial enterprise; provide high quality translation, information and other language services to the entire Caribbean. **Finance** Funded by: *European Union (EU, #08967).* **Activities** Translation services.
Members Member States (16):
Antigua-Barbuda, Bahamas, Barbados, Belize, Cuba, Dominica, Dominican Rep, Grenada, Guyana, Haiti, Jamaica, St Kitts-Nevis, St Lucia, St Vincent-Grenadines, Suriname, Trinidad-Tobago.
IGO Relations Cooperates with: *Caribbean Court of Justice (CCJ, #03486); Dutch Language Union; European Commission (EC, #06633)* – DG Translation; *University of the West Indies (UWI, #20705);* national institutions. [2017/XM6108/j/**D***]

♦ Caribbean Regional Library / see Caribbean and Latin American Studies Library

♦ Caribbean Regional Network of People Living with HIV/AIDS (CRN+) 03549

Sec PO Box 5061, Tragarete Road, Port-of-Spain, Trinidad-Tobago. T. +18686278741 – +18686279620. Fax +18686278741 – +18686279620.
Street address 31 Carlos Street, Woodbrook, Trinidad-Tobago.
URL: http://www.gnpplus.net/

History 28 Sep 1996, Port-of-Spain (Trinidad-Tobago), as the only civil society organization of regional scope, managed by and working directly with the community of people living with HIV/AIDS (PLWHA). Regional network of *Global Network of People Living with HIV/AIDS (GNP+, #10494)*. **Aims** Empower and support persons infected with and affected by HIV/AIDS through advocacy, research, partnership, capacity building and resource mobilization. **Structure** Regional Board; Technical Advisory Committee; Secretariat; National Networks/Members; territories (Dutch, English, French and Spanish). **Finance** Contributions from donor agencies, including: *Global Fund to Fight AIDS, Tuberculosis and Malaria (Global Fund, #10383)*; *International Bank for Reconstruction and Development (IBRD, #12317)* (World Bank); United States Centres for Disease Control. **Activities** Serves as a direct link between the community of people living with HIV/AIDS, local and regional partners and donor agencies; informs, designs and implements programmes aimed at mitigating the impact of HIV/AIDS in the region. Programmes: *'Strengthening the Institutional Response to HIV/AIDS/STIs in the Caribbean (SIRHASC)'* – to provide technical, material and financial support to 5 regional agencies to coordinate, plan, implement and monitor a regional response to the HIV/AIDS epidemic in 15 ACP countries in the Caribbean; *'Institutional Strengthening of PLWHA Network in the Caribbean Region'*; programme to strengthen communications links; project under the Pan Caribbean Partnership (PANCAP) to strengthen management and operational capacity of key regional institutions that support country efforts against HIV/AIDS and to ensure effective and efficient coordination of regional response to provide a favourable environment for further scaling up of country efforts; *'Strengthening the Community of PLWHA and Those Affected by HIV/AIDS in the Caribbean'* – treatment preparedness and adherence, capacity building, advocacy and monitoring and evaluation; *'CRN+/IFRC Anti-Stigma and Discrimination Campaign'*.

Members in the 27 countries and territories:
Antigua-Barbuda, Aruba, Bahamas, Barbados, Bermuda, Bonaire Is, Cayman Is, Cuba, Curaçao, Dominica, Dominican Rep, Grenada, Guadeloupe, Guiana Fr, Guyana, Haiti, Jamaica, Martinique, Neth Antilles, St Kitts-Nevis, St Lucia, St Maarten, St Martin, St Vincent-Grenadines, Suriname, Trinidad-Tobago, Turks-Caicos.

IGO Relations Collaborates with: *Canadian International Development Agency (CIDA, inactive)*; *Caribbean Community (CARICOM, #03476)*; *Department for International Development (DFID, inactive)*; *Deutsche Gesellschaft für Technische Zusammenarbeit (GTZ, inactive)*; *European Commission (EC, #06633)*; *Joint United Nations Programme on HIV/AIDS (UNAIDS, #16149)*; *Pan American Health Organization (PAHO, #18108)*; *Pan Caribbean Partnership against HIV and AIDS (PANCAP, #18171)*; *UNDP (#20292)*; *United States Agency for International Development (USAID)*; *University of the West Indies (UWI, #20705)*; *WHO (#20950)*. **NGO Relations** Collaborates with: *International Federation of Red Cross and Red Crescent Societies (#13526)*; *Frontline AIDS (#10007)*. [2008/XF5669/**F**]

♦ Caribbean Regional Organization of Associations for Science Education (inactive)
♦ Caribbean Regional Shipping Council (inactive)

♦ Caribbean Regional Technical Assistance Centre (CARTAC) 03550

Administration 1st Floor, The Business Centre, Upton, St Michael, ST MICHAEL, Barbados. T. +12464342840. Fax +12464373159.
URL: https://www.cartac.org/

History Established Sep 1999, by *Caribbean Community (CARICOM, #03476)*. Became operational Nov 2001. **Aims** Enhance the institutional and human resource capacities of countries in the Caribbean region to achieve their macroeconomic, fiscal and monetary policy objectives. **Structure** An office of *International Monetary Fund (IMF, #14180)*. Steering Committee. **Languages** English. **Staff** 19.00 FTE, paid. **Finance** Government of Canada through its aid office Global Affairs Canada (GAC) provides largest share of funding. Other contributors include: *Caribbean Development Bank (CDB, #03492)*; *Department for International Development (DFID, inactive)*; *European Union (EU, #08967)*; *International Monetary Fund (IMF, #14180)*. Government of Barbados finances office facilities; other 21 beneficiary countries make annual contributions to operating expenses. **Activities** Guidance/assistance/consulting; training/education. **Publications** *CARTAC News* (4 a year) – newsletter.

Members Governments of 22 countries and territories:
Anguilla, Antigua-Barbuda, Aruba, Bahamas, Barbados, Belize, Bermuda, Cayman Is, Curaçao, Dominica, Grenada, Guyana, Haiti, Jamaica, Montserrat, St Kitts-Nevis, St Lucia, St Vincent-Grenadines, Suriname, Trinidad-Tobago, Turks-Caicos, Virgin Is UK. [2021/XJ0956/**E***]

♦ Caribbean Regional Youth Council (CRYC) 03551

Contact address not obtained. E-mail: timstlucia@gmail.com – info.cryc@gmail.com.
URL: http://caryc.org/

Aims Work towards regional representation, integration and cooperation as a platform for youth development. **Structure** Executive; Management Team. **Activities** Advocacy/lobbying/activism.

Members Full in 13 countries and territories:
Anguilla, Antigua-Barbuda, Bahamas, Barbados, Belize, Dominica, Grenada, Guyana, Jamaica, St Kitts-Nevis, St Lucia, St Vincent-Grenadines, Trinidad-Tobago. [2017/XM5805/**D**]

♦ Caribbean Research and Management of Biodiversity (internationally oriented national body)
♦ Caribbean Rice Association (no recent information)
♦ Caribbean Rice Industry Development Network (no recent information)
♦ Caribbean Rights / see Caribbean Human Rights Network (#03517)

♦ Caribbean School of Media and Communication (CARIMAC) 03552

Dir Univ of West Indies, 3 Sherlock Drive, Mona, Jamaica. T. +18769271481. Fax +18769771597. E-mail: carimac@uwimona.edu.jm.
URL: http://www.carimac.com/

History 1974, under the title *Caribbean Institute of Mass Communications*, as a teaching department of the Faculty of Arts and General Studies of *University of the West Indies (UWI, #20705)*, Mona Campus. Later known as *Caribbean Institute of Media and Communication (CARIMAC)*. 2017, present name adopted. **Aims** Remain in the forefront of changes occurring in the field of communication as a result of technological convergence, the rise of new media and the blurring of boundaries between social, political and cultural spheres globally; demonstrate in theory and practice the unique role of media and communication in the continued evolution and enhancement of Pan-Caribbean culture; provide leadership in the educational, policy planning, research and professional development of media and communication in the wider Caribbean and its diaspora. **Structure** Functions within the Faculty of Humanities and Education at the University of West Indies. Led by Director and Management Team. **Languages** English. **Staff** 60.00 FTE, paid. **Finance** Financed through central government grants to the University of West Indies. **Activities** Training/education; research/documentation; events/meetings; projects/programmes. **Events** *Consultation on the ownership and control in Caribbean media industries* Kingston (Jamaica) 1998, *Caribbean workshop on communications strategies for drug abuse prevention* Kingston (Jamaica) 1993. **Publications** *Cross Over* (3 a year); *CARIMAC Newsletter*. Occasional paper series. **IGO Relations** Cooperates with: *Caribbean Telecommunications Union (CTU, #03560)*. **NGO Relations** Member of: *Caribbean Broadcasting Union (CBU, #03465)*; *International Association for Media and Communication Research (IAMCR, #12022)*. [2018/XE0600/j/**F**]

♦ Caribbean Science and Technology Information Network (inactive)
♦ Caribbean Scientific Community / see Caribbean Scientific Union (#03553)

♦ Caribbean Scientific Union 03553

Comunidad Cientifica del Caribe (CCC)

Exec Dir 112 Las Damas Str – at the corner of El Conde str, Old City, PO Box 932, Santo Domingo, Dominican Rep. T. +18096876315. Fax +18096856443. E-mail: wamello@yahoo.com.
Pres c/o Academia de Ciencias de la Rep Dominicana, Calle Las Damas 112 esq, Del Conde – Zona Colonial, AP 932, Santo Domingo, Dominican Rep. T. +18686622002ext3100. Fax +18686457132.

History 2000. Former names and other names: *Caribbean Scientific Community* – alias. **Aims** Integrate, consolidate and promote the Academies of the Wider Caribbean region and their impact on the strengthening of scientific communities there; increase their impact on local communities. **Structure** Board of Directors, comprising President, Vice-President, Secretary, Treasurer and member. **Events** *General Assembly* Colombia 2012, *Meeting* Santo Domingo (Dominican Rep) 2006. **Publications** *CCC Bulletin*. **NGO Relations** Member of: *InterAmerican Network of Academies of Science (IANAS, #11441)*; *InterAcademy Partnership (IAP, #11376)*. [2013/XJ1838/**D**]

♦ Caribbean Shipping Association (CSA) 03554

Association des armateurs des Caraïbes

General Manager 4 Fourth Avenue, Newport West, Kingston 13, Jamaica. T. +18769233491. Fax +18767571592. E-mail: csa@cwjamaica.com.
Pres address not obtained.
URL: http://www.caribbeanshipping.org/

History 1971. Founded following a series of informal meetings. New constitution adopted 1977, Puerto Rico. **Aims** Promote and foster the highest quality service to the maritime industry through training development; work with all agencies, groups and other associations for the benefit and development of members and the people of the Caribbean region. **Structure** General Meeting (annual). General Council, comprising President, Vice-President, Immediate Past President, Chairmen and 1 representative of each of the 4 Groups, and General Manager. **Languages** English. **Staff** 3.00 FTE, paid. **Finance** Members' dues: Individuals US$ 700; National associations, based on tonnages passing over the port, from US$ 700 to US$ 5,900. **Activities** Organizes: General Meeting (annual, in October); meeting (annual, in May). **Events** *Caribbean Shipping Executives Conference* Kingston (Jamaica) 2021, *General Meeting* Kingston (Jamaica) 2020, *General Meeting* Panama (Panama) 2013, *General Meeting* San Juan (Puerto Rico) 2012, *TOC Americas : terminal operations conference for the Americas* Panama (Panama) 2011. **Publications** *Caribbean Maritime Magazine* (3 a year); *Handbook of Caribbean Ports* (annual).

Members A Ships' Agents and Private Stevedore Contractors and national associations. B Port Owners and Terminal Operators. C Ship Owners/Operators. D. Transportation Intermediaries, Ocean Freight Forwarders or Non-Vessel Operating Common Carriers. Members in 41 countries and territories:
Antigua-Barbuda, Aruba, Austria, Bahamas, Barbados, Belgium, Belize, Bermuda, Canada, Cayman Is, China, Colombia, Costa Rica, Curaçao, Dominica, Dominican Rep, France, Germany, Grenada, Guadeloupe, Guatemala, Guiana Fr, Guyana, Haiti, Jamaica, Martinique, Netherlands, Norway, Panama, Puerto Rico, St Kitts-Nevis, St Lucia, St Maarten, St Vincent-Grenadines, Suriname, Trinidad-Tobago, UK, USA, Venezuela, Virgin Is UK.

Consultative Status Consultative status granted from: *UNCTAD (#20285)* (Special Category). **IGO Relations** Cooperation Agreement with: *Association of Caribbean States (ACS, #02411)*. [2013.06.27/XD6742/**D**]

♦ Caribbean Society of Hotel Association Executives (CSHAE) 03555

Acting CEO/Dir Gen CHTA, 2655 Le Jeune Rd, Ste 800, Coral Gables FL 33134, USA. T. +13054433040. E-mail: greta@marketplaceexcellence.com.
URL: http://www.caribbeanhotelandtourism.com/about-chta/cshae/

History 1985. **Aims** Provide opportunities for discussions, study and conference on subjects of interest to hotel and tourism associations; promote sound policies for marketing, promotion, administration, management procedures and techniques for hotel and tourism associations; cooperate and counsel with CHA. **Structure** General Meeting (annual). Executive Committee, comprising President, 1st and 2nd Vice Presidents, Secretary Treasurer, 4 Directors and Immediate Past President. **Finance** Members' dues (annual): US$ 200. **Activities** Educational seminars; annual Leadership Conference; other meetings. Awards. **Events** *Leadership Conference* Montego Bay (Jamaica) 2014, *Leadership conference* Barbados 2007, *Annual Caribbean sales and marketing strategy conference* Miami, FL (USA) 2006, *Leadership conference* San Juan (Puerto Rico) 2005, *Annual leadership conference* Bonaire Is (Dutch Caribbean) 2003.

Members Regular active industry association executives; Honorary former regular member who served the industry with distinction. Chief executive officers of hotel association members of CHA. Individuals in 33 countries and territories:
Anguilla, Antigua-Barbuda, Aruba, Bahamas, Barbados, Belize, Bermuda, Bonaire Is, Cayman Is, Curaçao, Dominica, Dominican Rep, Grenada, Guadeloupe, Guyana, Haiti, Jamaica, Martinique, Montserrat, Puerto Rico, St Barthélemy, St Croix Is, St Eustatius, St Kitts-Nevis, St Lucia, St Maarten, St Martin, St Thomas Is, St Vincent-Grenadines, Trinidad-Tobago, Turks-Caicos, Venezuela, Virgin Is UK.

NGO Relations Recognized professional body of chief staff executives of hotel association members of: *Caribbean Hotel and Tourism Association (CHTA, #03516)*. [2020/XD1485/**D**]

♦ Caribbean Society of Orthodontists (unconfirmed)

♦ Caribbean Society of Radiologists (CSR) 03556

Secretariat PO Box 577, Kingstown, St Vincent-Grenadines. T. +17844570317. E-mail: csrsecretariat@gmail.com.
URL: http://www.csor.co/

History Founded Jun 1994, Martinique. **Aims** Represent primarily English-speaking radiologists, radiographers and medical physicists in the Caribbean. **Structure** Congress (annual); Executive. **Languages** English. **Staff** 2.00 FTE, paid. **Finance** Congress fees; support from sponsors. **Activities** Events/meetings. **Events** *Annual Congress* Miami, FL (USA) 2017, *Annual Congress* St Vincent-Grenadines 2016, *Annual Congress* Orlando, FL (USA) 2015, *Annual Congress* Montego Bay (Jamaica) 2014, *Annual Congress* Ocho Rios (Jamaica) 1998.

Members Individuals in 27 countries and territories:
Antigua-Barbuda, Aruba, Bahamas, Barbados, Belgium, Belize, Bermuda, Cayman Is, Cuba, Curaçao, Dominica, Dominican Rep, Grenada, Guadeloupe, Guyana, Haiti, Honduras, Jamaica, Martinique, Puerto Rico, St Kitts-Nevis, St Lucia, St Vincent-Grenadines, Suriname, Trinidad-Tobago, USA, Virgin Is UK. [2018.09.07/XM4495/v/**D**]

♦ Caribbean Solar Energy Society (CSES) 03557

Pres Dept of Physics, Univ of the West Indies, St Augustine Campus, 3rd Floor, Natural Sciences Bldg, St Augustine, Trinidad-Tobago. T. +8686622002 ext 83122. Fax +8686629904.

Events *SATIS conference / Meeting* San Juan (Puerto Rico) 1999. **NGO Relations** Member of: *Global Islands Network (GIN, #10437)*. [2017/XD8687/**D**]

♦ Caribbean Spa and Wellness Association (CSWA) 03558

Contact address not obtained. T. +18682998097. E-mail: tomashungria@codetel.net.do – info@caribbeanspawellness.com – cswacaribbean@gmail.com.
URL: http://caribbeanspawellness.com/

History Founded Nov 2005, following first Caribbean Spa and Wellness Conference. Official launch Jul 2006. **Aims** Foster and promote growth of the Caribbean spa and wellness industry. **Structure** Board of Directors. **Languages** English, French, Spanish. **Activities** Events/meetings. **Events** *Conference* Barbados 2009, *Conference* Bayahibe (Dominican Rep) 2006, *Conference* St Lucia 2005. **IGO Relations** Cooperates with: *Caribbean Tourism Organization (CTO, #03561)*. **NGO Relations** Cooperates with: *Caribbean Hotel and Tourism Association (CHTA, #03516)*; *International Spa Association (ISPA)*. [2016/XM4551/**D**]

♦ Caribbean Studies Association (CSA) 03559

Association d'études des Caraïbes – Asociación de Estudios del Caribe

Secretariat c/o SALISES, Univ of the West Indies, St Augustine, Trinidad-Tobago. E-mail: secretariat@caribbeanstudiesassociation.org.
URL: http://www.caribbeanstudiesassociation.org/

History 1974, Puerto Rico. Former names and other names: *Asociación de Estudios Caribeños* – alias; *AEC* – alias. Registration: Puerto Rico. **Aims** Foster Caribbean studies and research from a multidisciplinary, multicultural perspective. **Structure** Executive Council. **Languages** English, French, Spanish. **Staff** 0.50 FTE, paid. **Finance** Sources: donations; fees for services; members' dues; subscriptions. **Activities** Awards/prizes/competitions; events/meetings; training/education. **Events** *Annual Conference* St Croix (Virgin Is USA) 2023, *Annual Conference* Georgetown (Guyana) 2021, *Annual Conference* Guyana 2020, *Annual Conference* Santa Marta (Colombia) 2019, *Annual Conference* Havana (Cuba) 2018. **Publications** *CSA Newsletter* (3 a year) in English, Spanish; *Directory of Caribbeanists* (occasional).

Members Individuals (over 1,100) in 33 countries and territories:
Antigua-Barbuda, Australia, Bahamas, Barbados, Belize, Brazil, Canada, Chile, Colombia, Costa Rica, Cuba, Dominican Rep, France, Germany, Grenada, Haiti, Jamaica, Japan, Mexico, Netherlands, New Zealand, Panama, Puerto Rico, South Africa, Spain, St Kitts-Nevis, St Lucia, Suriname, Sweden, Trinidad-Tobago, UK, USA, Venezuela.

NGO Relations Member of (1): *United Nations Academic Impact (UNAI, #20516)*. [2022.11.10/XD6085/v/**D**]

♦ Caribbean Table Tennis Federation (no recent information)
♦ Caribbean Technological Consultancy Services Network (see: #03492)
♦ Caribbean Telecommunications Council (no recent information)
♦ Caribbean Telecommunications Partnership (unconfirmed)

♦ Caribbean Telecommunications Union (CTU) 03560

Union des télécommunications des Caraïbes

SG 4 Mary Street, St Clair, Port-of-Spain, Trinidad-Tobago. T. +18686280281.
Pres address not obtained.
URL: http://www.ctu.int/

History Mar 1988, in the framework of *Caribbean Community (CARICOM, #03476)*. Inaugurated 20 Jul 1990, Port-of-Spain (Trinidad-Tobago). Constitution amended in 2004 to accept non-governmental members. **Aims** Correlate, plan and assist in development of intra-regional, regional and international telecommunications; promote awareness of telecommunications needs among members; encourage exploitation of telecommunications potential in promoting socio-economic development among Member States; encourage exchange of information and ideas; foster coordination of technical standards and routing plans; encourage adoption of efficient methods; as far as possible, harmonize positions of members in preparation for conferences and meetings; encourage technology transfer; establish links with other telecommunications organizations. **Structure** General Conference (annual). Executive Council (meeting twice a year). Secretariat; Technical Conference. **Languages** English. **Staff** 5.00 FTE, paid. **Finance** Members' dues. Other sources: donations and grants from international bodies. Budget (annual): US$ 300,000. **Activities** Research/documentation; guidance/assistance; events/meetings. **Events** *General conference session* Georgetown (Guyana) 1997, *General conference session* 1992. **Publications** *CTU Nexus* (4 a year) – online newsletter.
Members Member and Associate Member Governments of the Caribbean Community (17):
Anguilla, Antigua-Barbuda, Bahamas, Barbados, Belize, Cayman Is, Dominica, Grenada, Guyana, Jamaica, Montserrat, St Kitts-Nevis, St Lucia, St Vincent-Grenadines, Trinidad-Tobago, Turks-Caicos, Virgin Is UK.
Corporations (5). Membership countries not specified.
IGO Relations Member of (1): *Bureau de développement des télécommunications (BDT, #03358)*. Cooperates with (1): *International Telecommunication Union (ITU, #15673)*. Cooperation agreement with: *Commonwealth Telecommunications Organisation (CTO, #04365)*. **NGO Relations** Affiliate of: *Internet Society (ISOC, #15952)*.
[2014/XD2107/y/**D***]

♦ Caribbean Tourism Association (inactive)

♦ Caribbean Tourism Organization (CTO) 03561

Communications Officer 7th Floor – Baobab Tower, Warrens, St Michael BB22026, ST MICHAEL BB22026, Barbados. T. +12464275242. Fax +12464293065. E-mail: ctobarbados@caribtourism.com.
URL: http://www.onecaribbean.org/

History Jan 1989. Established on merger of *Caribbean Tourism Research and Development Centre (CTRC, inactive)*, set up Sep 1974, as *'Caribbean Tourism Research Centre'* and *Caribbean Tourism Association (CTA, inactive)*, created in 1951, Curaçao. Functions under a Headquarters Agreement with the Government of Barbados. A Functional Institution of *Caribbean Community (CARICOM, #03476)*. Former names and other names: *Caribbean Tourist Association* – former; *Caribbean Travel Association* – former. **Aims** Provide to and through its members the services and information necessary for development of sustainable tourism for the economic and social benefit of the Caribbean people. **Structure** Tourism Ministerial Council; Board of Directors; Executive Sub-Committee. *Caribbean Tourism Organization Foundation (CTO Foundation)*. Headquarters in Barbados. **Languages** English, French, Spanish. **Staff** 18.00 FTE, paid. **Finance** Sources: contributions of member/participating states; fees for services; government support; international organizations; revenue from activities/projects; sale of products. **Activities** Advocacy/lobbying/activism; guidance/assistance/consulting; knowledge management/information dissemination; research/documentation. **Events** *Caribbean Tourism Recovery Forum* 2020, *State of the Tourism Industry Conference* Paradise Is (Bahamas) 2018, *CHICOS : Caribbean Hotel Investment Conference and Operations Summit* Southampton (Bermuda) 2018, *CHICOS : Caribbean Hotel Investment Conference and Operations Summit* Southampton (Bermuda) 2017, *Workshop on Sustainable Tourism Destination* St Lucia 2017. **Publications** *Monthly Tourism Statistical Report* (12 a year); *Quarterly Tourism Statistical Review* (4 a year); *Caribbean Tourism Statistical Report* (annual). Conference proceedings; surveys; economic, environmental, market research and organizational studies, including individual country and special interest market guides; tour operator directory; occasional studies.
Members Government: English, French, Spanish and Dutch speaking territories of the Caribbean. Allied: Companies, corporations, firms, organizations, agencies and individuals providing goods and services to or engaged in the tourism industry. Affiliate: organizations in the tourism industry. Private sector: companies, organizations and persons providing goods and services to the tourism industry. Government members in 26 countries and territories:
Anguilla, Antigua-Barbuda, Bahamas, Barbados, Belize, Cayman Is, Curaçao, Dominica, Grenada, Guyana, Haiti, Jamaica, Martinique, Montserrat, Nevis Is, Puerto Rico, St Eustatius, St Kitts-Nevis, St Lucia, St Maarten, St Martin, St Vincent-Grenadines, Tobago, Trinidad-Tobago, Turks-Caicos, Virgin Is UK.
Affiliate (8):
Association of Caribbean States (ACS, #02411); *Caribbean Community (CARICOM, #03476)*; *Caribbean Congress of Labour (CCL, #03480)*; *Inter-American Institute for Cooperation on Agriculture (IICA, #11434)*; *OAS (#17629)*; *Organisation of Eastern Caribbean States (OECS, #17804)*; *Pan American Health Organization (PAHO, #18108)*; *World Travel and Tourism Council (WTTC, #21871)*.
IGO Relations Affiliate member of: *World Tourism Organization (UNWTO, #21861)*. Collaborates with: *Canadian International Development Agency (CIDA, inactive)*; *Caribbean Action Plan (CAR, #03432)*; *Caribbean Development Bank (CDB, #03492)*; *Commonwealth Fund for Technical Cooperation (CFTC, #04331)*; *Inter-American Development Bank (IDB, #11427)*; *International Bank for Reconstruction and Development (IBRD, #12317)*; *International Development Research Centre (IDRC, #13162)*; *OAS (#17629)*; *Organisation of Eastern Caribbean States (OECS, #17804)*; *UNDP (#20292)*; *United States Agency for International Development (USAID)*; *University of the West Indies (UWI, #20705)*. **NGO Relations** Accredited by (2): *International Committee of Tourism Film Festivals (CIFFT)*; *The Caribbean Council (CC, #03482)*. Partner of (1): *International Institute for Peace through Tourism (IIPT)*. Cooperates with (3): *Caribbean Hotel and Tourism Association (CHTA, #03516)*; *Caribbean Spa and Wellness Association (CSWA, #03558)*; *Inter-American Foundation (IAF, #11431)*.
[2021/XD1294/**D***]

♦ Caribbean Tourism Research and Development Centre (inactive)
♦ Caribbean Tourist Association / see Caribbean Tourism Organization (#03561)
♦ Caribbean Travel Association / see Caribbean Tourism Organization (#03561)

♦ Caribbean Union of Teachers (CUT) 03562

Union des enseignants des Caraïbes

Gen Sec JTA, 97B Church Street, Kingston, Jamaica. T. +187692213857. Fax +18769223257 – +18769484069. E-mail: cutjamaica@gmail.com.
Pres PO Box 452, Marine Villa, St George's, St George, St George's ST GEORGE, Grenada.
URL: http://www.caribbeanteachers.com/

History 1935, Trinidad-Tobago. **Aims** Unite teacher organizations at regional level and provide the framework for cooperation and exchange of knowledge and experiences among workers; promote and support all efforts aimed at uniting the people of the Caribbean; obtain a collective teacher and education worker opinion on matters of an educational, professional, trade union and political nature; work for improvement of education in all its aspects in the Caribbean area and ensure equal opportunity in unit territories; work towards elimination of illiteracy and functional illiteracy in every Caribbean territory; strive for establishment of a new international economic order based on justice, mutual respect, equality of rights, peaceful cooperation and political and economic independence with a view to putting an end to exploitation and under-development and to facilitate economic, social and cultural progress of all peoples of the Caribbean. **Structure** Biennial Conference is the highest decision-making body and elects Officers: President; 1st, 2nd and 3rd Vice-Presidents. Executive Committee (meets at least twice a year), comprising one delegate from each member organization, Officers, Secretariat staff. Trustees (3). **Languages** Creoles and pidgins, English, French. **Staff** 3.00 FTE, paid. **Finance** Members' dues. Other sources: allocation in budget of Education International; sponsorship. **Activities** Encourages adoption of Teacher Codes of Ethics by affiliates and the adherence to the UNESCO/ILO Recommendation on the Status of the Profession; encourages production of indigenous educational material and the use by teachers of modern educational aids (slides, projects, etc) and techniques; provides assistance (material, financial, legal, etc) to affiliates especially at times of industrial action; establishes relationships regionally and internationally with professional and trade union organizations; promotes within the Caribbean the aims, general principles and policies of Education International; monitors the administration and working of the various educational legislation to endeavour to amend their terms and application when educationally desirable and to strive to secure the removal of difficulties, abuses and regulations detrimental to the interests of teachers, other education workers, education and children; encourages the establishment of Teaching Service Commissions in territories where appropriate; encourages all teachers in the Caribbean to obtain professional training and to further support efforts for ongoing training. Organizes: Caribbean/North America Regional Conference (every 3 years); conferences; biennial athletics championships for students ages 8-15 years; consultations. **Events** *Biennial Congress / Biennial Conference* Georgetown (Guyana) 2013, *Biennial congress / Biennial Conference* Barbados 2011, *Biennial congress / Biennial Conference* Grenada 2009, *Biennial Congress* Port-of-Spain (Trinidad-Tobago) 2007, *Biennial Conference* Trinidad-Tobago 2007.
Members Teachers' Unions in 23 countries and territories:
Anguilla, Antigua-Barbuda, Bahamas, Barbados, Belize, Bermuda, Dominica, Grenada, Guadeloupe, Guyana, Haiti, Jamaica, Martinique, Montserrat, Nevis Is, St Croix Is, St Kitts Is, St Lucia, St Maarten, St Vincent-Grenadines, Trinidad-Tobago, Virgin Is UK, Windward Is.
[2013.07.03/XD6094/**D**]

♦ Caribbean Urological Association (CURA) 03563

Sec/Treas Dept of Urology San Fernando General Hosp, Independence Avenue, San Fernando, Trinidad-Tobago. E-mail: admin@curaonline.org.
Pres 10 Bel Air Springs, Georgetown, Guyana.
URL: http://www.curaonline.org

History 17 apr 1999, Port-of-Spain (Trinidad-Tobago). **Aims** Improve urological standards. **Structure** Council; Executive. **Languages** English. **Staff** Voluntary. **Finance** Members' dues. Conference proceeds. **Events** *Annual Conference* San Fernando (Trinidad-Tobago) 2015, *Annual Conference* Montego Bay (Jamaica) 2014, *Annual Conference* San Fernando (Trinidad-Tobago) 2013, *Annual Conference* Nassau (Bahamas) 2012, *Annual Conference* Tobago (Trinidad-Tobago) 2009.
Members Individuals Active; Associate; Honorary. Active and Associate in 7 countries:
Bahamas, Barbados, Curaçao, Haiti, Jamaica, St Lucia, Trinidad-Tobago.
Honorary members in 3 countries:
Trinidad-Tobago, UK, USA.
NGO Relations Affiliate of: *Société Internationale d'Urologie (SIU, #19499)*.
[2015/XJ6875/**D**]

♦ Caribbean Veterinary Medical Association (CVMA) 03564

Sec-Treas PO Box 1829, Wrightson Road, Port-of-Spain, Trinidad-Tobago. E-mail: cbvma.conference@gmail.com.
URL: http://cbvma.org/

History Founded 8 Nov 2012. **Aims** Advance the practice of veterinary medicine in the Caribbean region by providing a forum for integration, communication and continuing education. **Structure** Secretariat rotates with location of forthcoming conference. **Activities** Events/meetings; training/education; awareness raising; networking/liaising. **Events** *Biennial Conference* Georgetown (Guyana) 2016, *Biennial Conference* Grand Cayman Is (Cayman Is) 2014, *Biennial Conference* Port-of-Spain (Trinidad-Tobago) 2012, *Biennial Conference* Ocho Rios (Jamaica) 2010, *Biennial Conference* St Maarten 2008. **Publications** *West Indian Veterinary Journal* (2 a year).
Members Individuals in 17 countries and territories:
Anguilla, Antigua-Barbuda, Bahamas, Barbados, Belize, Bermuda, Cayman Is, Dominica, Grenada, Guyana, Jamaica, Montserrat, St Kitts-Nevis, St Lucia, St Vincent-Grenadines, Trinidad-Tobago, Virgin Is UK.
[2016.02.11/XD7707/v/**D**]

♦ Caribbean Vulnerable Communities Coalition (CVC) 03565

Exec Dir Ste no 1, 1D-1E Braemar Avenue, Kingston, Jamaica. T. +18766317299. Fax +18766317219. E-mail: info@cvccoalition.org.
URL: http://www.cvccoalition.org/

History Dec 2004, Jamaica. **Aims** Address and promote national and regional responses to the human rights challenges in reducing the spread of HIV among vulnerable populations; provide support in facilitating access to stigma- and discrimination-free care and treatment for people living with HIV and AIDS from vulnerable populations; facilitate the prevention of HIV transmission among vulnerable populations. **Activities** Advocacy/lobbying/activism; capacity building. **Events** *International AIDS conference* Washington, DC (USA) 2012, *International AIDS conference* Vienna (Austria) 2010. **NGO Relations** Cooperates with: *Global Coalition on Women and AIDS (GCWA, #10297)*; *ICASO (#11040)*. Member of: *Robert Carr civil society Networks Fund (RCNF, #18956)*.
[2018.09.04/XM2059/**F**]

♦ Caribbean WaterNet 03566

Contact c/o Engineering Inst, Fac of Engineering, UWI, St Augustine, Trinidad-Tobago. T. +18686637383. Fax +18686637383. E-mail: jopadeyi@hotmail.com.

History Also referred to as *Caribbean Water Network*. **Aims** Improve attitudes, improve, share and develop awareness and knowledge, skills/competencies, and capacities in the implementation of integrated water resources management (IWRM) among stakeholders concerned with water and water related development in the Caribbean. **Structure** Members' General Council. Steering Committee. Secretariat. **NGO Relations** Member of: *Network for Capacity Building in Integrated Water Resources Management (CAP-Net, #17000)*.
[2011/XJ2389/**F**]

♦ Caribbean Water Network / see Caribbean WaterNet (#03566)

♦ Caribbean Water and Sewerage Association (CAWASA) 03567

Exec Dir Unit No 15, Orange Park Commercial Ctr, Bois d'Orange, Gros-Islet, St Lucia. T. +17584580601. Fax +17584580191. E-mail: cawasa@candw.lc – info@cawasa.org.
URL: http://www.cawasa.org/

History 1996, Barbados, as *Caribbean Basin Management Project*. Restructured as *Caribbean Basin Water Management Programme (CBWMP)*, 30 Nov 2001, St Lucia. Restructured under current title 27 May 2010. **Aims** Provide for the sustainable growth and development of Caribbean Water Utilities and the promotion of water and water related issues through the delivery of quality training and utilizing collective resources and experiences. **Structure** Board of Directors, comprising President, Vice-President, Secretary, Treasurer, Executive Director and 9 members.
Members Water utilities in 12 countries and territories:
Anguilla, Antigua-Barbuda, Barbados, Cayman Is, Dominica, Grenada, Montserrat, Nevis Is, St Kitts Is, St Lucia, Turks-Caicos, Virgin Is UK.
NGO Relations Member of: *Global Water Operators' Partnerships Alliance (GWOPA, #10652)*.
[2013/XJ6909/**D**]

♦ Caribbean Water and Wastewater Association (CWWA) 03568

Exec Dir c/o Water and Sewerage Authority, Bldg HO12, Farm Road, St Joseph 000000, Trinidad-Tobago. T. +18686458681 – +18686622302 ext 3747. E-mail: cwwattsecretariat@gmail.com.
URL: http://www.cwwa.net/

History 30 Nov 1988, Montserrat. Founded following the activities of the Caribbean Water Engineers Conference. Registration: The Parliament of Trinidad and Tobago, No/ID: Act # 8, Start date: 5 Aug 1991, End date: 31 Dec 2022, Trinidad-Tobago, Caribbean. **Aims** Bring together the water, sanitation and solid waste community in the Caribbean towards protection of public health and promotion of sustainable development. **Structure** Executive Council, headed by President; Secretariat, headed by Executive Director. **Languages** English. **Staff** 2.00 FTE, paid; 8.00 FTE, voluntary. **Activities** Advocacy/lobbying/activism; events/meetings; research and development; training/education. **Events** *Annual Conference* St Joseph (Trinidad-Tobago) 2020, *Annual Conference* St Kitts-Nevis 2019, *Annual Conference* Montego Bay (Jamaica) 2018, *Annual Conference* Georgetown (Guyana) 2017, *Annual Conference* Port-of-Spain (Trinidad-Tobago) 2016.
Members Individuals in 28 countries and territories:
Anguilla, Antigua-Barbuda, Aruba, Bahamas, Barbados, Belize, Canada, Cayman Is, Curaçao, Dominica, Grenada, Guyana, Israel, Italy, Jamaica, Montserrat, Norway, Puerto Rico, South Africa, St Kitts-Nevis, St Lucia, St Vincent-Grenadines, Suriname, Trinidad-Tobago, Turks-Caicos, USA, Venezuela, Virgin Is UK.

IGO Relations Partner of (5): *Caribbean Development Bank (CDB, #03492); Inter-American Development Bank (IDB, #11427); Pan American Health Organization (PAHO, #18108); UNEP (#20299); United Nations Human Settlements Programme (UN-Habitat, #20572).* **NGO Relations** Partner of (5): *Caribbean Desalination Association (CaribDA, #03491); Caribbean Water and Sewerage Association (CAWASA, #03567); Global Water Operators' Partnerships Alliance (GWOPA, #10652); Global Water Partnership (GWP, #10653); Inter-American Association of Sanitary and Environmental Engineering (#11400).* [2021.06.11/XD6273/v/**D**]

♦ Caribbean Women's Association (CARIWA) 03569

Secretariat ANCW, Box 500, The Valley, Anguilla.
History 1970. **Events** *Annual Conference* Anguilla 2008.
Members National organizations in 5 countries and territories:
Anguilla, Antigua-Barbuda, Barbados, Guyana, St Vincent-Grenadines. [2012/XD3100/**D**]

- ♦ Caribbean Women's Cricket Federation (no recent information)
- ♦ Caribbean Young Democrat Union (unconfirmed)
- ♦ Caribbean Youth Committee on Human Environment (inactive)

♦ Caribbean Youth Environment Network (CYEN) 03570

Headquarters PO Box 915, Cheapside, Bridgetown, St Michael BB11000, Bridgetown ST MICHAEL BB11000, Barbados. T. +12462317263. E-mail: executivecoordinator@cyen.org.
URL: http://www.cyen.org/

History 18 Nov 1993, Plymouth (Montserrat). Registration: Corporate Affairs and Intellectual Property Office, Government of Barbados, No/ID: 507, Start date: 14 Sep 2001, Barbados; Registrar of Companies – Government of Grenada, No/ID: 27 of 2014-7092, Start date: 10 Feb 2014, Grenada; Registrar of Companies – Republic of Trinidad and Tobago, No/ID: C2013062704250, Start date: 26 Jun 2013, Trinidad-Tobago; Belize Companies and Corporate Affairs Registry, No/ID: 22873, Start date: 28 Jul 2015, Belize. **Aims** Empower young citizens of Caribbean communities to develop programmes/actions to address socio-economic and environmental issues. **Structure** General Congress (every 2 years); Regional Steering Committee; Office managed by Executive Coordinator. **Languages** English. **Activities** Advocacy/lobbying/activism; awareness raising; training/education. **Publications** *Global Environment Outlook for Youth in the Caribbean* (2008).
Members Organizations and individuals in 18 countries and territories:
Antigua-Barbuda, Barbados, Belize, Cuba, Dominica, Dominican Rep, Grenada, Guyana, Haiti, Jamaica, Montserrat, Puerto Rico, St Eustatius, St Kitts-Nevis, St Lucia, St Vincent-Grenadines, Suriname, Trinidad-Tobago.
IGO Relations Affiliated with (2): *UNICEF (#20332)*; UN Sustainable Development Solutions Network. Accredited to the Conference of the Parties of: *Secretariat of the United Nations Convention to Combat Desertification (Secretariat of the UNCCD, #19208).* **NGO Relations** Member of (3): *Caribbean Network for Integrated Rural Development (CNIRD, #03528); Caribbean Policy Development Centre (CPDC, #03540); Global Water Partnership (GWP, #10653).* Partner of (1): *Global Call for Climate Action (GCCA, inactive).* [2022.02.08/XF3821/**F**]

- ♦ CARIBCAN – Caribbean-Canada Trade Agreement (treaty)
- ♦ **CaribDA** Caribbean Desalination Association (#03491)
- ♦ CARIB/DOC / see Caribbean Knowledge Management Centre (#03521)
- ♦ Caribisch Regionaal Informatie en Vertaal Instituut (#03548)
- ♦ **CARIBISNET** Caribbean Business and Investment Support Network (#03466)
- ♦ CARIBRO – Caribbean Brain Research Organization (inactive)
- ♦ **CaribVET** Caribbean Animal Health Network (#03440)
- ♦ **CARICAD** Caribbean Centre for Development Administration (#03468)
- ♦ **CARICC** Central Asian Regional Information and Coordination Centre for Combating Illicit Trafficking of Narcotic Drugs, Psychotropic Substances and Their Precursors (#03683)
- ♦ CARI – Centre d'actions et de réalisations internationales (internationally oriented national body)
- ♦ CARI – Centre Africain de Recherche Interdisciplinaire (internationally oriented national body)
- ♦ **CARICOM** Caribbean Community (#03476)

♦ CARICOM Competition Commission (CCC) 03571

Exec Dir Hendrikstraat 69, Paramaribo, Suriname. T. +597491439 – +597491455. Fax +597530639.
URL: http://www.caricomcompetitioncommission.com/

History Established by Art 171 of *Treaty of Chaguaramas – Revised (2001)*, as a key institution in support of *CARICOM Single Market and Economy (CSME, #03575).* Inaugurated 18 Jan 2008. A *Caribbean Community (CARICOM, #03476)* Institution. **Aims** Promote and maintain fair competition within the Caribbean Community for the enhancement of economic efficiency and consumer welfare. **Structure** Commissioners; Executive Director. [2017/XM6106/**E***]

♦ CARICOM Development Fund (CDF) 03572

CEO 1st Floor East, SKY Mall, Haggatt Hall, St Michael BB11063, ST MICHAEL BB11063, Barbados. T. +12464361849. Fax +12464354037. E-mail: info@caricomdf.org.
URL: http://www.caricomdevelopmentfund.org/

History Established under Art 158 of *Treaty of Chaguaramas – Revised (2001).* Agreement Relating to the Operations of the Fund signed Jul 2008. Operational since 24 Aug 2009. A *Caribbean Community (CARICOM, #03476)* Institution. **Aims** Assist Member States in maximizing the benefits arising from participation in the CSME, by reducing intra-regional disparities through effective partnerships and the provision of financial and technical assistance. **Structure** Board. **Languages** English.
Members Governments (12):
Antigua-Barbuda, Barbados, Belize, Dominica, Grenada, Guyana, Jamaica, St Kitts-Nevis, St Lucia, St Vincent-Grenadines, Suriname, Trinidad-Tobago. [2021.10.25/XM6107/**F***]

♦ CARICOM Implementation Agency for Crime and Security (IMPACS) 03573

Exec Dir 19 Keate Street, Port-of-Spain, Trinidad-Tobago. T. +18682355511. Fax +18686273064. E-mail: secretariat@carimpacs.org.
URL: http://www.caricomimpacs.org/

History Jul 2006, during 27th Meeting of the Conference of Heads of Government of *Caribbean Community (CARICOM, #03476).* **Aims** Enhance capacity of CARICOM Member States to control crime and participate in international counter crime and security initiatives. **Structure** Headquarters, led by Executive Director; Sub-Agencies (2). **Languages** English. **Staff** 75 FTE and seconded. **Finance** Member and Associate States' contributions. **Activities** Capacity building; training/education; events/meetings; networking/liaising; projects/programmes research and development; standards/guidelines. **IGO Relations** Works closely with: *Caribbean Aviation Safety and Security Oversight System (CASSOS, #03462); Caribbean Centre for Development Administration (CARICAD, #03468); Caribbean Customs Law Enforcement Council (CCLEC, #03487); Caribbean Disaster Emergency Management Agency (CDEMA, #03493); Caribbean Public Health Agency (CARPHA, #03544); European Union (EU, #08967); International Criminal Police Organization – INTERPOL (ICPO-INTERPOL, #13110); OAS (#17629); Organisation of Eastern Caribbean States (OECS, #17804);* SOUTHCOM; *United Nations (UN, #20515).* **NGO Relations** *Asset Recovery Inter-Agency Network for the Caribbean (ARIN-CARIB, #02321); International Committee of the Red Cross (ICRC, #12799).* [2019.12.30/XM2218/**D***]

- ♦ CARICOM Multilateral Air Services Agreement (1996 treaty)

♦ CARICOM Regional Organization for Standards and Quality (CROSQ) 03574

Main Office 2nd Floor, Baobab Towers, Warrens, St Michael, ST MICHAEL, Barbados. T. +12466227670. Fax +12466227677. E-mail: crosq.caricom@crosq.org.
URL: http://www.crosq.org/

History Feb 2002, Belize City (Belize). Feb 2002, Belize (Belize), on signature of an intergovernmental agreement by Conference of Heads of Government of the Caribbean Community. A *Caribbean Community (CARICOM, #03476)* Institution, replacing *Caribbean Common Market Standards Council (CCMSC, inactive)* in the development of *CARICOM Single Market and Economy (CSME, #03575).* **Aims** Establish and harmonize standards to: enhance the efficiency and improve quality in the *production* of goods and services in the Community; protect the *consumer* and the *environment*; improve *trade* within the Community and with third states. **Structure** General Meeting (annually). Council (meets twice a year), consisting of Executive Heads of national standards bodies of the State Parties, and including Chairman and Vice-Chairman. Technical Management Committee; Special Committee; Editorial Committee. Secretariat, headed by Executive Secretary. **Finance** Contributions of State Parties and Associate Members. Donations or grants; fees for services; sales of standards. **Activities** Organizes regional conferences on: Accreditation; Finance; Food and Tourism; Information Technology. Organizes workshop on Labour Related Standards. Major activities: IDB-SME Project; IDB Metrology Project; CDB Regional Building Standards. **Events** *Meeting* Jamaica 2003, *Annual General Meeting* Kingston (Jamaica) 2001. **Publications** *The Standard* (annual) – newsletter. Regional standards.
Members Governments of 15 countries and territories:
Antigua-Barbuda, Bahamas, Barbados, Belize, Dominica, Grenada, Guyana, Haiti, Jamaica, Montenegro, St Kitts-Nevis, St Lucia, St Vincent-Grenadines, Suriname, Trinidad-Tobago.
Associative members (5):
Anguilla, Bermuda, Cayman Is, Turks-Caicos, Virgin Is UK.
IGO Relations Advises: CARICOM Council for Trade and Economic Development (COTED). Formal contacts with: *Bureau international des poids et mesures (BIPM, #03367).* **NGO Relations** Formal links with: *International Code Council (ICC); International Organization for Standardization (ISO, #14473); Pan American Standards Commission (#18133).* [2021/XE4243/**E***]

♦ CARICOM Single Market and Economy (CSME) 03575

Sec 1st Floor, Skye Mall Haggat Hall, St Michael, ST MICHAEL, Barbados. T. +12464296064. Fax +12464372689. E-mail: registry@caricom.org.
URL: http://csmeonline.org/

History 2002. Following a proposal Jul 1989, Grand Anse (Grenada), by Conference of Heads of Government of the Caribbean Community, within the framework of *Caribbean Community (CARICOM, #03476).* Based on 9 Protocols amending the *Treaty of Chaguaramas (1973)*, the first of which came into force on 4 Jul 1997. The last remaining 2 Protocols were signed in early 2000. *Treaty of Chaguaramas – Revised (2001)*, signed Jul 2001, Georgetown, paves the way for CSME, which was institutionalized 16 Nov 2004. CARICOM decided during 18th Inter-Sessional Meeting, St Vincent-Grenadines, Feb 2007, to phase single economy component in between 2009-2015. Phase I: consolidation of the single market and initiation of a single economy implemented no later than 1 Jan 2009. Phase II: consolidation and completion of the single market expected to cover 2009-2015. Replaces and expands the concept of *Caribbean Common Market – Marché commun des Caraïbes – Mercado Común del Caribe.* **Aims** Enable CARICOM to participate in the globalized arena by establishing systems for: hassle-free and unrestricted movement of all citizens, whether visitors, traders, skilled persons, job-seekers or entrepreneurs; unrestricted trade in goods originating from CARICOM; free movement of services; free movement of capital to purchase, sell, trade or negotiate in all legitimate forms across participating member states. **Structure** *Council for Trade and Economic Development (COTED)* is ministerial body with principal responsibility. *Council for Human and Social Development (COHSOD)* also involved in establishment of CSME. *Caribbean Court of Justice (CCJ, #03486)* discharges the functions of an international tribunal in respect of interpretation and application of the Treaty of Chaguaramas. Key institutions include: *CARICOM Development Fund (CDF, #03572); CARICOM Competition Commission (CCC, #03571).* **Activities** Politics/policy/regulatory. **Events** *Prime Ministerial Sub-Committee on the CSME Conference* Bridgetown (Barbados) 2022, *Regional private sector forum* Barbados 2003.
Members Governments of 13 countries:
Antigua-Barbuda, Bahamas, Barbados, Belize, Dominica, Grenada, Guyana, Jamaica, St Kitts-Nevis, St Lucia, St Vincent-Grenadines, Suriname, Trinidad-Tobago.
IGO Relations *Caribbean Export Development Agency (Caribbean Export, #03501); CARICOM Regional Organization for Standards and Quality (CROSQ, #03574).* Works closely with: *Caribbean Centre for Development Administration (CARICAD, #03468).* [2021/XF5457/**F***]

- ♦ **CARIFESTA** Caribbean Festival of Creative Arts (#03504)
- ♦ **CARIFORUM** Forum of Caribbean States (#09904)
- ♦ CARIFTA – Caribbean Free Trade Association (inactive)
- ♦ **CARILEC** Caribbean Electric Utility Services Corporation (#03494)
- ♦ CARIMAC / see Caribbean School of Media and Communication (#03552)
- ♦ **CARIMAC** Caribbean School of Media and Communication (#03552)
- ♦ CARINFO – Caribbean Information Action Group (inactive)
- ♦ Caring and Living As Neighbours (internationally oriented national body)
- ♦ CARIPEDA – Caribbean Peoples Development Agency (no recent information)
- ♦ CariPestNet – Caribbean Pest Information Network (internationally oriented national body)
- ♦ CARIPHA – Caribbean Public Health Association (no recent information)
- ♦ Cariplo Foundation for Initiatives and Studies on Multiethnicity / see ISMU Foundation – Foundation for Initiatives and Studies on Multi-ethnicity

♦ CARIRI – Caribbean Industrial Research Institute 03576

CEO UWI Campus, St Augustine, Trinidad-Tobago. T. +18682990210 – +18682855050. Fax +18686627177. E-mail: mail@cariri.com.
URL: http://www.cariri.com/

History 1970, St Augustine (Trinidad-Tobago), by the Government of Trinidad and Tobago on the campus of *University of the West Indies (UWI, #20705)*, initially assisted by *UNDP (#20292)* with *UNIDO (#20336)* as Executing Agency. **Aims** Be a national and regional focal point for technology and innovation, playing a leadership role in providing value added technological solutions to manufacturing and service sectors, as well as public sector entities, designed to enhance efficiency, competitiveness and viability, foster new business creation, improve quality of life and promote sustainable development. **Activities** Monitoring/evaluation; guidance/assistance/consulting; research and development; training/education. **Events** *International seminar on technological innovation* Port-of-Spain (Trinidad-Tobago) 1988. **Publications** Annual Report. [2017.07.06/XE5481/jt/**E***]

♦ CARISCIENCE 03577

Exec Sec Univ of the West Indies, St Augustine, Trinidad-Tobago. T. +18686622002ext82529 – +18686635812. Fax +18686457132. E-mail: cariscience.org@gmail.com – haroldramkissoon@hotmail.com.
URL: http://www.cariscience.com/

History 1 Jun 1999, Jamaica. **Aims** Upgrade *academic* excellence of graduate, postgraduate, research and development programmes and the quality of *science research* in the *Caribbean.* **Structure** General Meeting (annual). **Languages** English. **Staff** 5.00 FTE, paid. **Finance** Sources: contributions; members' dues. Supported by: *UNESCO (#20322).* **Activities** Awards/prizes/competitions; events/meetings; guidance/assistance/consulting; training/education. **Events** *Annual Meeting* Pointe-à-Pitre (Guadeloupe) 2012, *Annual Meeting* Pointe-à-Pitre (Guadeloupe) 2012, *Annual Meeting* Port-of-Spain (Trinidad-Tobago) 2011, *Annual Meeting* Port-of-Spain (Trinidad-Tobago) 2010, *Annual meeting* Paramaribo (Suriname) 2009. **Publications** *Using Science, Technology and Innovation to Change the Fortunes of the Caribbean Region* (2007). Reports.
Members Research centres in 6 countries and territories:
Barbados, Guadeloupe, Guyana, Jamaica, Suriname, Trinidad-Tobago. [2021.09.11/XJ4489/**F**]

- ♦ Caritas – Africa / see Caritas Internationalis – Africa Region (#03581)
- ♦ Caritas Africa Região / see Caritas Internationalis – Africa Region (#03581)

♦ Caritas Asia 03578

Regional Coordinator 408/42 Phaholyothin Place Bldg, 10th Floor, Phaholyothin Road, Samsennai, Phyathai, Bangkok, 10400, Thailand. T. +6626190634 – +6626190635. Fax +6626190639. E-mail: asiacaritas@caritas.asia.
URL: http://www.caritas.asia/

History 1973. Current name adopted when merged with *'Caritas Asia'*, another association formed in 1999. Former names and other names: *Asia Fund for Human Development* – former (1973); *Asia Partnership for Human Development (APHD)* – former (2007); *Partenariat asiatique pour un développement humain (PADH)* – former (2007). Registration: No/ID: 099-3-00043757-8, Start date: 1 Sep 2019, Thailand, Bangkok. **Aims** Intensify interchange and mutual aid among member organizations in Asia for promotion and harmonization of their work and to achieve the goals pushed in the region by the Caritas Confederation. **Structure** Regional Conference (annual); Regional Commission (meets twice a year); Regional Strategic Priorities (6).

Languages English. **Staff** 6.00 FTE, paid. **Finance** Sources: members' dues. Annual budget: 3,000,000 USD. **Activities** Financial and/or material support. **Events** *General Assembly* Macau (Macau) 2001, *General Assembly* Philippines 1997, *General Assembly* Wattala (Sri Lanka) 1993, *Seminar on women in migration and the sex industry* Hong Kong (Hong Kong) 1992. **Publications** *Link* (4 a year). Annual report; country profile series.

Members Organizations (25) in 24 countries and territories:
Bangladesh, Cambodia, Hong Kong, India, Indonesia, Japan, Kazakhstan, Korea Rep, Kyrgyzstan, Macau, Malaysia, Mongolia, Myanmar, Nepal, Pakistan, Philippines, Singapore, Sri Lanka, Taiwan, Tajikistan, Thailand, Timor-Leste, Uzbekistan, Vietnam. [2022.05.04/XF1908/y/**F**]

- ♦ Caritas Australia (internationally oriented national body)
- ♦ Caritas Christi (religious order)
- ♦ Caritas para la Cooperación Internacional – Caritas Española (internationally oriented national body)

♦ Caritas Europa 03579

SG Rue de la Charité 43, 1210 Brussels, Belgium. T. +3222800280. Fax +3222301658. E-mail: info@caritas.eu.
Sec address not obtained.
URL: http://www.caritas.eu/

History 28 Feb 1985, Brussels (Belgium). Founded within the framework of *Caritas Internationalis (CI, #03580)*. Former names and other names: *Euro-Caritas (EC)* – former. Registration: Banque-Carrefour des Entreprises, No/ID: 0450.716.537, Start date: 19 Jul 1993, Belgium; EU Transparency Register, No/ID: 6082564924-85, Start date: 6 Jan 2009. **Aims** Promote social and environmental justice through inclusion, integration, integral human development and humanitarian response. **Structure** General Assembly (annual); Board of Directors; President Secretariat, headed by Secretary-General; Working Groups (7). **Languages** English, French, German. **Finance** Sources: members' dues. **Activities** Advocacy/lobbying/activism; capacity building; events/meetings; knowledge management/information dissemination; networking/liaising; training/education. **Events** *Annual Conference* Stockholm (Sweden) 2014, *Humanitarian meeting* Brussels (Belgium) 2006, *Regional conference* Barcelona (Spain) 1991, *Meeting* Brussels (Belgium) 1990, *European refugee congress* Strasbourg (France) 1990.

Members 49 in 46 countries:
Albania, Andorra, Armenia, Austria, Azerbaijan, Belarus, Belgium, Bosnia-Herzegovina, Bulgaria, Croatia, Czechia, Denmark, Estonia, Finland, France, Georgia, Germany, Greece, Hungary, Iceland, Ireland, Italy, Kosovo, Latvia, Lithuania, Luxembourg, Malta, Moldova, Monaco, Montenegro, Netherlands, North Macedonia, Norway, Poland, Portugal, Romania, Russia, Serbia, Slovakia, Slovenia, Spain, Sweden, Switzerland, Türkiye, UK, Ukraine.

Consultative Status Consultative status granted from: *Council of Europe (CE, #04881)* (Participatory Status). **IGO Relations** *Council of the European Union (#04895)*; *European Commission (EC, #06633)*; *European Parliament (EP, #08146)*. Participant in Fundamental Rights Platform of: *European Union Agency for Fundamental Rights (FRA, #08969)*. Member of Consultative Forum of: *Frontex, the European Border and Coast Guard Agency (#10005)*. **NGO Relations** Member of (5): *Conference of INGOs of the Council of Europe (#04607)*; *Confédération européenne des ong d'urgence et de développement (CONCORD, #04547)*; *EU Alliance for a democratic, social and sustainable European Semester (EU Semester Alliance, #05565)*; *European Policy Centre (EPC, #08240)*; *SDG Watch Europe (#19162)*. Links with European networks active in the field of social policy and North South solidarity. [2021.09.06/XE1590/**E**]

- ♦ Caritas Internationaal Hulpbetoon (internationally oriented national body)
- ♦ Caritas international (internationally oriented national body)

♦ Caritas Internationalis (CI) 03580

SG Palazzo San Calisto, 00120 Vatican City, Vatican. T. +39669879799. Fax +39669887237. E-mail: caritas.internationalis@caritas.va.
Geneva Delegation Rue de Varembe 1, 1202 Geneva, Switzerland. T. +41227344005 – +41227344007. Fax +41227344006. E-mail: fpolito@caritas-internationalis.com.
New York Delegation 777 United Nations Plaza, Suite S-10G, New York NY 10017, USA.
URL: http://www.caritas.org/

History Founded 1950, Rome (Italy), as *International Caritas Conference (ICC)*, to respond to the need for a high-level global umbrella organization for the various national Catholic humanitarian assistance, social service and development organizations worldwide, many of which use the name "Caritas". Incorporated the already existing 'Caritas Internationalis' based in Lucerne (Switzerland). Statutes were approved and adopted on an "ad experimentum" basis in Sep 1950. Constitutional Assembly took place 12-14 Dec 1951, Rome, and was attended by delegates from national organizations in 13 countries. Current name adopted 4 Nov 1954. Acronym "CI" in official use since Feb 1957. Full title: *Caritas Internationalis – International Confederation of Catholic Organizations for Charitable and Social Action – Confédération internationale d'organismes catholiques d'action charitable et sociale – Confederación Internacional de Organizaciones Católicas de Acción Caritativa y Social.* **Aims** Stimulate and aid national Caritas organizations to facilitate assistance, advancement and integral *development* of the most *underprivileged*, by means of active *charity* in keeping with the teaching and tradition of the *Catholic* Church. **Structure** General Assembly (every 4 years), always in Rome (Italy); Executive Committee (meets at least annually); Bureau (meets at least twice a year); General Secretariat. Commissions (2): Legal Affairs; Finance. Groups (2): Humanitarian Assistance; Theology. Headquarters located at the Vatican City (Vatican). Regional Conferences (7): Africa; MONA (Middle East/North Africa); North America; Latin America and Caribbean; Asia; Oceania; Europe. Regional Commissions, each with a President and Zone Coordinators, including: *Caritas Internationalis – Africa Region (#03581)*; *Caritas Europa (#03579)*. Working Groups at international level (4). Divisions / teams (4): Management and Coordination; Emergency and Humanitarian Response; Building Sustainable Peace; Integral Human Development. Departments (4): International Cooperation; Global Issues; Communications, including Documentation Centre; Finance. International Delegates: Council of Europe – Strasbourg (France); FAO/WFP – Rome; OSCE; OUA/ECA – Addis Ababa (Ethiopia); UNESCO – Paris (France); United Nations – Geneva (Switzerland); United Nations – New York NY (USA); United Nations – Vienna (Austria). **Languages** English, French, Spanish. **Staff** 24.00 FTE, paid. **Finance** Sources: contributions; gifts, legacies; members' dues. Annual budget: 7,000,000 EUR. **Activities** Advocacy/lobbying/activism; knowledge management/information dissemination. **Events** *General Assembly* Rome (Italy) 2019, *General Assembly* Rome (Italy) 2015, *General Assembly* Rome (Italy) 2011, *General Assembly* Rome (Italy) 2007, *Quadrennial General Assembly* Rome (Italy) 2003. **Publications** Annual Report; thematic documents.

Members Autonomous national organizations in 166 countries and territories:
Albania, Algeria, Andorra, Angola, Argentina, Armenia, Australia, Austria, Azerbaijan, Bangladesh, Belarus, Belgium, Benin, Bolivia, Bosnia-Herzegovina, Botswana, Brazil, Bulgaria, Burkina Faso, Burundi, Cambodia, Cameroon, Canada, Cape Verde, Central African Rep, Chad, Chile, Colombia, Comoros, Congo Brazzaville, Congo DR, Costa Rica, Côte d'Ivoire, Croatia, Cuba, Cyprus, Czechia, Denmark, Djibouti, Dominican Rep, Ecuador, Egypt, El Salvador, Equatorial Guinea, Eritrea, Estonia, Eswatini, Ethiopia, Fiji, Finland, France, Gabon, Gambia, Georgia, Germany, Ghana, Greece, Guatemala, Guinea, Guinea-Bissau, Haiti, Honduras, Hong Kong, Hungary, Iceland, India, Indonesia, Iran Islamic Rep, Iraq, Ireland, Israel, Italy, Japan, Jordan, Kazakhstan, Kenya, Kiribati, Korea Rep, Kuwait, Latvia, Lebanon, Lesotho, Liberia, Libya, Lithuania, Luxembourg, Macau, Madagascar, Malawi, Malaysia, Mali, Malta, Marshall Is, Mauritania, Mauritius, Mexico, Micronesia FS, Moldova, Monaco, Mongolia, Montenegro, Morocco, Mozambique, Myanmar, Namibia, Nauru, Nepal, Netherlands, New Zealand, Nicaragua, Niger, Nigeria, North Macedonia, Norway, Pakistan, Palau, Panama, Papua New Guinea, Paraguay, Peru, Philippines, Poland, Portugal, Puerto Rico, Romania, Russia, Rwanda, Samoa, Sao Tomé-Principe, Senegal, Seychelles, Sierra Leone, Singapore, Slovakia, Slovenia, Solomon Is, Somalia, South Africa, Spain, Sri Lanka, Sudan, Sweden, Switzerland, Syrian AR, Taiwan, Tajikistan, Tanzania UR, Thailand, Timor-Leste, Togo, Tokelau, Tonga, Tunisia, Türkiye, Tuvalu, Uganda, UK, Ukraine, Uruguay, USA, Uzbekistan, Vanuatu, Venezuela, Zambia, Zimbabwe.

Included in the above, 9 organizations listed in this Yearbook:
Caritas Australia; *Caritas para la Cooperación Internacional – Caritas Española*; *Catholic Organization for Relief and Development (Cordaid)*; *Catholic Relief Services (CRS, #03608)*; *Conferentia Episcopalis Pacifici (CEPAC, #04659)*; *Development and Peace (CCODP)*; *Scottish Catholic International Aid Fund (SCIAF)*; *Secours catholique – Caritas France*; *Trocaire – Catholic Agency for World Development.*

Consultative Status Consultative status granted from: *ECOSOC (#05331)* (General); *UNESCO (#20322)* (Associate Status); *ILO (#11123)* (Special List); *FAO (#09260)*; *UNICEF (#20332)*; *WHO (#20950)* (Official Relations). **IGO Relations** Associated with Department of Global Communications of the United Nations.

NGO Relations

- *Alliance Against Hunger and Malnutrition (AAHM, no recent information)*;
- *Asian Centre for Organisation Research and Development (ACORD, #01374)*;
- *Caritas Asia (#03578)*;
- *Carrefour de solidarité internationale (CSI)*;
- *Catholic Office for Emergency Relief and Refugees (COERR)*;
- *Centre for Information, Counseling and Training Professions Relating to International Cooperation and Humanitarian Aid (CINFO)*;
- *CHS Alliance (#03911)*;
- *Commission for Justice, Peace and Integrity of Creation – USG/UISG (#04230)*;
- *Committee on Migrant Workers (CMW, #04271)*;
- *Committee of NGOs on Human Rights, Geneva (#04275)*;
- *Conference of European Justice and Peace Commissions (#04596)*;
- *Conference of Non-Governmental Organizations in Consultative Relationship with the United Nations (CONGO, #04635)*;
- *Congregation of Teresian Carmelite Missionaries Sisters*;
- *Control Arms (#04782)*;
- *Cooperation Committee for Cambodia (CCC)*;
- *Council of Catholic Patriarchs of the Orient (CCPO, #04875)*;
- *Council of Non-Governmental Organizations for Development Support (#04911)*;
- *Diakonie Katastrophenhilfe*;
- *EarthAction (EA, #05159)*;
- *Ecumenical Advocacy Alliance (EAA, inactive)*;
- *Environnement et développement du Tiers-monde (enda, #05510)*;
- *eu can aid (ECA, #05570)*;
- *Euro-Children*;
- *Euronet Consulting (#05739)*;
- *Food and Disarmament International (FDI, no recent information)*;
- *Forum of Catholic Inspired NGOs (#09905)*;
- *Franciscan Clarist Congregation*;
- *Franciscans International (FI, #09982)*;
- *Gelbes Kreuz International (no recent information)*;
- *Global Call for Action Against Poverty (GCAP, #10263)*;
- *Global Call for Climate Action (GCCA, inactive)*;
- *GLOBAL RESPONSIBILITY – Austrian Platform for Development and Humanitarian Aid*;
- *Humanitarian Accountability Partnership International (HAP International, inactive)*;
- *CIDSE (CIDSE, #03926)*;
- *International Blue Crescent (IBC)*;
- *International Catholic Centre of Geneva (ICCG, #12449)*;
- *International Catholic Child Bureau (#12450)*;
- *International Catholic Cooperation Centre for UNESCO (CCIC, #12454)*;
- *International Catholic Organizations Information Center (ICO Center)*;
- *International Centre for Earth Construction (#12485)*;
- *International Conference of NGOs (#12883)*;
- *International Council on Alcohol and Addictions (ICAA, #12989)*;
- *International Council of Voluntary Agencies (ICVA, #13092)*;
- *International Federation of Red Cross and Red Crescent Societies (#13526)*;
- *International Organization for the Right to Education and Freedom of Education (#14468)*;
- *Jesuit Refugee Service (JRS, #16106)*;
- *Joint Learning Initiative on Faith and Local Communities (JLI, #16139)*;
- *MISSIO (#16827)*;
- *New York NGO Committee on Drugs (NYNGOC, #17097)*;
- *NGO Committee on Freedom of Religion or Belief, New York NY (#17109)*;
- *NGO Working Group on the Security Council (#17128)*;
- *NGO Committee on UNICEF (#17120)*;
- *Orbi-Pharma (OP)*;
- *Pax Christi – International Catholic Peace Movement (#18266)*;
- *Religious in Europe Networking Against Trafficking and Exploitation (RENATE, #18833)*;
- *Riunione delle Opere per l'Aiuto alle Chiese Orientali (ROACO, see: #04672)*;
- *Rotary International (RI, #18975)*;
- *Social Justice Secretariat*;
- *The Sphere Project (#19918)*;
- *Star of Hope International (SoHI, #19967)*;
- *Steering Committee for Humanitarian Response (SCHR, #19978)*;
- *Symposium of Episcopal Conferences of Africa and Madagascar (SECAM, #20077)*;
- *Transparency, Accountability and Participation Network (TAP Network, #20222)*;
- *Una Terra Mondo di Tutti (UNA)*;
- *UNITED for Intercultural Action – European Network Against Nationalism, Racism, Fascism and in Support of Migrants and Refugees (UNITED, #20511)*;
- *Verband Entwicklungspolitik und Humanitäre Hilfe e.V. (VENRO)*;
- *Vienna NGO Committee on the Family (#20774)*;
- *World Bank – Civil Society Joint Facilitation Committee (JFC, #21217)*;
- *World Catholic Association for Communication (SIGNIS, #21264)*;
- *World Council of Churches (WCC, #21320)*;
- *World Organisation Against Torture (OMCT, #21685)*;
- *World Social Forum (WSF, #21797)*;
- *World Union of Catholic Women's Organisations (WUCWO, #21876)*;
- *WorldFish (#21507)*. [2021.03.05/XB0216/y/**B**]

♦ Caritas Internationalis – Africa Region 03581

Caritas Internationalis – Région Afrique – Caritas Internationalis – Região Africa

Exec Sec 8 BP 8395, Lomé, Togo. T. +22822212937. E-mail: secaf@caritas-africa.org – secaf2007@yahoo.fr.
Nairobi Office Centenary House, Westlands, PO Box 14954, Nairobi, 00800, Kenya. T. +254204442039 – +254204442139. Fax +254204441876. E-mail: mmwaniki@ciaas.org.
URL: https://www.caritas.org/where-caritas-work/africa/

History 1960, as regional organization of national members of *Caritas Internationalis (CI, #03580)*. Also referred to as *Caritas – Africa* and *African Region Caritas – Caritas Région Afrique – Caritas Africa Região.* Current Statutes adopted by Regional Conference, May 2015, Rome (Italy). **Aims** Assist the *Church* in Africa in carrying out its social-pastoral ministry of serving, accompanying and defending the poor and marginalized according to the *Gospel* and teaching of the *Catholic* Church. **Structure** Regional Conference; Regional Chair; Africa Regional Commission; Executive Secretariat; Zonal Coordination. **Languages** English, French, Portuguese. **Staff** 10.00 FTE, paid. **Finance** Sources: Subventions; statutory fees; donations; legacies; collections. Annual budget: about euro 650,000. **Activities** Humanitarian/emergency aid; events/meetings. **Events** *Pan African conference* Addis Ababa (Ethiopia) 1987. **Publications** *Caritas Africa Info.*

Members Caritas organizations in 46 Sub-Saharan countries:
Angola, Benin, Botswana, Burkina Faso, Burundi, Cameroon, Cape Verde, Central African Rep, Chad, Comoros, Congo Brazzaville, Congo DR, Côte d'Ivoire, Equatorial Guinea, Eritrea, Eswatini, Ethiopia, Gabon, Gambia, Ghana, Guinea, Guinea-Bissau, Kenya, Lesotho, Liberia, Madagascar, Malawi, Mali, Mauritius, Mozambique, Namibia, Niger, Nigeria, Rwanda, Sao Tomé-Principe, Senegal, Seychelles, Sierra Leone, South Africa, South Sudan, Sudan, Tanzania UR, Togo, Uganda, Zambia, Zimbabwe. [2018/XE0459/**E**]

- ♦ Caritas Internationalis – International Confederation of Catholic Organizations for Charitable and Social Action / see Caritas Internationalis (#03580)
- ♦ Caritas Internationalis – Região Africa (#03581)
- ♦ Caritas Internationalis – Région Afrique (#03581)
- ♦ Caritas Région Afrique / see Caritas Internationalis – Africa Region (#03581)

♦ Caritas in Veritate Foundation 03582

Fondation Caritas in Veritate (FCIV)

Dir Chemin du Vengeron, 1292 Chambésy GE, Switzerland. T. +41227589820.
Office Grand Place 14, 1700 Fribourg, Switzerland. E-mail: contact@fciv.org.
URL: http://www.fciv.org/

Aims Make the positions of the *Catholic* Church more understandable to third parties and more visible in the open debate held within the United Nations system. **Structure** Board; Strategic Board. **Events** *The right to education – Towards a Renewed Commitment to Education* Geneva (Switzerland) 2019. **NGO Relations** Member of: *Forum of Catholic Inspired NGOs (#09905)*. [2019/XM8825/f/**F**]

- ♦ **CARIWA** Caribbean Women's Association (#03569)
- ♦ CARJJ – Centre Arabe de Recherches Juridiques et Judiciaires (unconfirmed)
- ♦ Carl Friedrich von Weizäcker Centre for Science and Peace Research (internationally oriented national body)

- ♦ Carl Friedrich von Weizsäcker-Zentrum für Naturwissenschaft und Friedensforschung (internationally oriented national body)
- ♦ Carl Rogers Institute for Peace (internationally oriented national body)
- ♦ CARMABI – Caribbean Research and Management of Biodiversity (internationally oriented national body)
- ♦ CARMABI Foundation / see Caribbean Research and Management of Biodiversity
- ♦ Carmelamalhavinte Sabha (religious order)
- ♦ Carmelitane Missionarie (religious order)
- ♦ Carmelitani (religious order)
- ♦ Carmelitani della Beata Vergine Maria Immacolata (religious order)
- ♦ Carmelitani Scalzi (religious order)
- ♦ Carmelitas Misioneras (religious order)
- ♦ Carmelite Fathers – Order of Brothers of the Blessed Virgin Mary of Mount Carmel (religious order)
- ♦ Carmelite Missionaries (religious order)

♦ Carmelite NGO 03583

Contact 1725 General Taylor Street, New Orleans LA 70115, USA. T. +15044583029.
URL: https://carmelitengo.org/

History Set up as project of members of the Carmelite Family worldwide. **Aims** Actively participate in creating a more peaceful, just and loving world, by advocating and caring for the spiritual and human needs of the human family and the environment. **Consultative Status** Consultative status granted from: *ECOSOC (#05331)* (Special); *UNEP (#20299)*. **IGO Relations** Affiliated with (1): *United Nations Framework Convention on Climate Change – Secretariat (UNFCCC, #20564)*. Associated with the Department of Global Communications of the United Nations. [2020.02.14/XM8509/**E**]

- ♦ Carmelite Nuns of the Ancient Observance (religious order)
- ♦ Carmelites of the Blessed Virgin Mary Immaculate (religious order)
- ♦ Carmelite Sisters of Charity, Vedruna (religious order)
- ♦ Carmelite Sisters of the Divine Heart of Jesus (religious order)
- ♦ Carmelite Sisters of Saint Teresa (religious order)
- ♦ Carmélites missionnaires (religious order)
- ♦ Carmélites Missionnaires Terésianes (religious order)
- ♦ Carmélites de la Primitive Observance (religious order)
- ♦ Carmelite Third Order (religious order)
- ♦ **CARMEN** CARMEN – The Worldwide Medieval Network (#03584)

♦ CARMEN – The Worldwide Medieval Network (CARMEN) 03584

Contact address not obtained. E-mail: carmen.medieval@gmail.com.
URL: http://www.carmen-medieval.net/

History Mar 2007, Budapest (Hungary). Set up mar 2007, Budapest (Hungary). CARMEN stands for *Co-operative for the Advancement of Research through a Medieval European Network*. **Aims** Bring medievalists together both with other medievalists and scholars and specialists outside medieval disciplines, to form international collaborative research projects and research-related activities. **Structure** Annual Meeting; Executive Committee. **Languages** English. **Staff** 3.00 FTE, voluntary. **Finance** Members' dues. **Activities** Research/documentation; events/meetings; projects/programmes; guidance/assistance/consulting; awards/prizes/competitions.
Members Participating institutions in 18 countries:
Albania, Australia, Austria, Belgium, China, Denmark, Estonia, Finland, France, Germany, Hungary, Netherlands, Portugal, Romania, Spain, Sweden, UK, USA.
NGO Relations Member of: *European Alliance for the Social Sciences and Humanities (EASSH, #05885)*. [2019.04.23/XM6597/**F**]

- ♦ Carmes de l'Ancienne Observance (religious order)
- ♦ Carmes de la Bienheureuse Vierge Marie Immaculée (religious order)
- ♦ Carmes Déchaussés (religious order)
- ♦ Carmes Déchaux – Carmes Déchaussés (religious order)
- ♦ Carnegie Corporation / see Carnegie Corporation of New York
- ♦ Carnegie Corporation of New York (internationally oriented national body)
- ♦ Carnegie Council on Ethics and International Affairs / see Carnegie Council for Ethics in International Affairs
- ♦ Carnegie Council for Ethics in International Affairs (internationally oriented national body)
- ♦ Carnegie Endowment for International Peace (internationally oriented national body)

♦ Carnegie Europe 03585

Dir Rue du Congrès 15, 1000 Brussels, Belgium. T. +3227355650. Fax +3227366222.
URL: http://carnegieeurope.eu/

History 2007, within *Carnegie Endowment for International Peace (CEIP)*. **Aims** Provide depth of analysis and thoughtful, carefully crafted *policy* recommendations on the *strategic* issues facing the *European Union* and its member states. **NGO Relations** Member of: *Euro-Mediterranean Study Commission (EuroMeSCo, #05727)*. [2021/XM6582/**E**]

- ♦ **CARNET** Cerebral Autoregulation Research Network (#03831)
- ♦ **CAROA** Caribbean Ombudsman Association (#03533)
- ♦ CARO – Computer AntiVirus Research Organization (no recent information)
- ♦ **CAROSAI** Caribbean Organization of Supreme Audit Institutions (#03536)
- ♦ CARPA – Caribbean Psychiatric Association (no recent information)
- ♦ **CAR/PAP** Centre d'activités régionales du programme d'actions prioritaires (#18501)

♦ Carpathian Balkan Geological Association (CBGA) 03586

Association de géologie carpato-balkanique – Karpatho-Balkanische Geologische Assoziation (KBGA)

Sec Geology Dept, Univ St Kliment Ohridski, 15 Tzar Osvoboditel Blvd, 1504 Sofia, Bulgaria.

History 1922, Brussels (Belgium). Founded during the 13th IGC. Activities have currently expanded beyond the original Carpathian and Balkan regions. Former names and other names: *Carpathian Geological Association* – former (1922 to 1958). **Aims** Promote close international collaboration to solve fundamental problems of the geological structure of the region. **Structure** Congress (every 4 years). Council, consisting of one representative of each collective member of CBGA. Board, comprising President, Secretary-General, Vice-President and Past-President. Sections (13), each with Chairman. **Languages** English, French, German, Russian. **Staff** None. **Finance** No fixed finance. Occasional support for congresses from IUGS and national sponsors. **Activities** Programmes carried out through 13 sections: Mineralogy and Geochemistry; Magmatism; Metamorphism; Tectonics; Stratigraphy; Sedimentology; Economic Geology/Ore Deposits; Hydrogeology; Engineering Geology; Geological Map; Isotope Geochronology; Geophysics; Environmental Geology. **Events** *International Congress* Plovdiv (Bulgaria) 2022, *Quadrennial Congress* Salzburg (Austria) 2018, *Quadrennial Congress* Tirana (Albania) 2014, *Quadrennial Congress* Thessaloniki (Greece) 2010, *Quadrennial Congress* Belgrade (Serbia) 2006. **Publications** *CBGA News*; *Geologica Balcanica*; *Geologica Carpathica* – journal. Abstracts of congress papers; background papers.
Members Full in 13 countries:
Albania, Austria, Bulgaria, Czechia, Greece, Hungary, North Macedonia (former Serbia Rep of), Poland, Romania, Serbia, Slovakia, Slovenia, Ukraine.
NGO Relations Affiliated member of: *International Union of Geological Sciences (IUGS, #15777)*. [2021/XD3797/**D**]

- ♦ Carpathian convention – Convention on the Protection and Sustainable Development of the Carpathians (2003 treaty)

♦ Carpathian Ecoregion Initiative (CERI) 03587

Secretariat Podunajska 24, 821 06 Bratislava, Slovakia. T. +421245524019. Fax +421245640201. E-mail: jansef@daphne.sk.
URL: http://www.carpates.org/

History 1999, Danube Carpathian Programme of *World Wide Fund for Nature (WWF, #21922)*. since 2004, separate legal entity, registered in accordance with Slovakian law. Previously known by acronym *CEI*. **Aims** Provide a Carpathian-wide network to support *biodiversity conservation* and *sustainable development* within the framework of the Carpathian Convention. **Structure** General Assembly. Board, comprising 7 national focal point organizations and WWF-DCP. Officers: Chairman; Vice-Chairman. Working Groups. **Activities** Working Groups: Biodiversity; Biodiversity Information System; Communication; Tourism; Environmental and Sustainable Development Education; Environmental Policy and Rural Development; Management Planning. Carpathian Ecological Network; Carpathian Biodiversity Information System. Organizes events. **Events** *General Assembly* Brasov (Romania) 2007, *General Assembly* Poprad (Slovakia) 2006, *General Assembly* Brasov (Romania) 2005, *General Assembly* Serbia-Montenegro 2005. **Publications** *CERI Newsletter*. Reports.
Members Organizations (43) in 7 countries:
Czechia, Hungary, Poland, Romania, Serbia, Slovakia, Ukraine.
Included in the above, 2 organizations listed in this Yearbook:
CEEweb for Biodiversity (#03626); WWF-DCP.
IGO Relations Memorandum of Cooperation with: Interim Secretariat of *Convention on the Protection and Sustainable Development of the Carpathians (Carpathian convention, 2003)* of *UNEP (#20299)*. [2008.07.03/XM2485/**F**]

- ♦ Carpathian Foundation International (see: #05264)
- ♦ Carpathian Geological Association / see Carpathian Balkan Geological Association (#03586)
- ♦ CAR/PB / see Plan Bleu pour l'environnement et le développement en Méditerranée (#18379)
- ♦ **CARP** Caminos de Arte Rupestre Prehistórico (#18478)
- ♦ **CARPE** Consortium on Applied Research and Professional Education (#04735)
- ♦ Carpenter's Tools International / see CTI Music Ministries
- ♦ **CARPHA** Caribbean Public Health Agency (#03544)
- ♦ CARPHA Drug Testing Laboratory (inactive)
- ♦ CARPI – International Conference on Applied Robotics for the Power Industry (meeting series)
- ♦ CARPIN – Caribbean Patent Information Network (no recent information)
- ♦ CARP International – Collegiate Association for the Research of the Principle
- ♦ Carr Center for Human Rights Policy (internationally oriented national body)
- ♦ CAR/RCU / see Caribbean Action Plan (#03432)
- ♦ Carrefour canadien international (internationally oriented national body)
- ♦ Carrefour d'éducation à la solidarité internationale – Québec (internationally oriented national body)
- ♦ Carrefour mondial de l'internet citoyen (internationally oriented national body)
- ♦ Carrefour de solidarité internationale (internationally oriented national body)
- ♦ Carrefour Tiers-monde / see Carrefour d'éducation à la solidarité internationale – Québec

♦ Carsharing Association (CSA) 03588

Exec Dir address not obtained.
URL: http://carsharing.org/

History Incorporated in the State of Illinois (USA). **Aims** Support the sustainability and efficacy of the carsharing industry so as to meet financial, environmental and educational goals based on socially responsible ethics, standards and practices. **Structure** Board of Directors. **Events** *Annual Conference* Vancouver, BC (Canada) 2021, *Annual Conference* Vancouver, BC (Canada) 2020, *Annual Conference* Paris (France) 2018, *Annual Conference* Montréal, QC (Canada) 2017. **Members** Organizations in North and South America, Europe, Asia and Oceania. Membership countries not specified. [2017/XM6318/**D**]

- ♦ **CARSI** Conseil Africain de la recherche scientifique et de l'innovation (#00451)
- ♦ CARSTIN – Caribbean Science and Technology Information Network (inactive)
- ♦ CARS / see World Skate Asia (#21789)
- ♦ **CARTAC** Caribbean Regional Technical Assistance Centre (#03550)
- ♦ Carta de derechos y deberes económicos de los Estados (1974 treaty)
- ♦ Carta de los derechos fundamentales de la Unión Europea (2000 treaty)
- ♦ Carta dos direitos fundamentais da União Europeia (2000 treaty)
- ♦ Carta dei diritti fondamentali dell'Unione Europea (2000 treaty)
- ♦ Carta europea delle autonomie locali (1985 treaty)
- ♦ Carta europea delle lingue regionali o minoritarie (1992 treaty)
- ♦ Carta Europea de les Llengües Regionals o Minoritàries (1992 treaty)
- ♦ Cartagena Agreement – Andean Subregional Integration Agreement (1969 treaty)
- ♦ Cartagena Convention – Convention for the Protection and Development of the Marine Environment of the Wider Caribbean Region (1983 treaty)

♦ Cartagena Group 03589

Groupe de Carthagène – Grupo de Cartagena

Address not obtained.

History 21 Jun 1984, Cartagena de Indias (Colombia). 21-22 Jun 1984, Cartagena de Indias (Colombia), as a permanent regional forum for consultation on debt matters, in particular addressed to securing an efficient exchange of relevant information. Also known as *Group of Eleven – Groupe des onze*, or *Group of 11 – Groupe des 11*. **Aims** Agree on a common strategy for establishing a direct dialogue with the 7 most *industrialized* countries (USA, Japan, Germany, France, UK, Italy, Canada), so as to ensure best possible conditions for re-negotiating terms of external *loans* and to avoid compromising economic *development*. **Structure** Comprises the Ministers of Finance and of Foreign Affairs of the most indebted countries of Latin America. Committee of Surveillance, consisting of 5 members (Argentina, Brazil, Colombia, Mexico and Venezuela).
Members Governments of 11 Latin American countries:
Argentina, Bolivia, Brazil, Chile, Colombia, Dominican Rep, Ecuador, Mexico, Peru, Uruguay, Venezuela. [2010/XF7406/**F***]

♦ Cartagena Network of Engineering (CNE) 03590

Réseau Carthagène d'Ingénierie – Red Cartagena de Ingeniería (RCI)

Administrator Ecole Natl d'Ingénieurs Metz, 1 route d'Ars Laquenexy, CS65820, 57078 Metz CEDEX 3, France. T. +33387344269. Fax +33387346935.

History 19 Sep 2006, Cartagena de Indias (Colombia). **Aims** Establish a multilateral collaboration so as to enhance engineers training in its domains and modernize producing capacities of member countries. **Structure** Direction Committee, including President and Secretary. **Events** *International Congress* Agadir (Morocco) 2012.
Members Academic; Institutional; Industrial. Members in 23 countries:
Albania, Argentina, Austria, Belgium, Benin, Brazil, Canada, China, Colombia, Dominican Rep, El Salvador, France, Germany, Ghana, Guatemala, Mexico, Netherlands, Poland, Romania, Senegal, Spain, Togo, USA. [2013/XJ1442/**E**]

- ♦ Cartagena Protocol on Biosafety (2000 treaty)
- ♦ Carta da Organização dos Estados Americanos (1948 treaty)
- ♦ Carta de la Organización de los Estados Americanos (1948 treaty)
- ♦ Carta de Punta del Este (1961 treaty)
- ♦ Carta sociale europea (1961 treaty)
- ♦ Carta sociale europea – riveduta (1996 treaty)
- ♦ CART – Caribbean Association for Rehabilitation Therapists (inactive)
- ♦ CAR/TDE / see Regional Activity Centre for Information and Communication of the Barcelona Convention (#18745)
- ♦ Cartel international de la paix (inactive)
- ♦ The Carter Center (internationally oriented national body)
- ♦ Carter Center of Emory University / see The Carter Center
- ♦ CARTFund – Caribbean Aid for Trade and Regional Integration Trust Fund (inactive)
- ♦ Carthusian Order (religious order)
- ♦ Cartographie des invertébrés européens (inactive)

♦ Pro Carton / see Association of European Cartonboard and Carton Manufacturers (#02502)

♦ CartONG 03591

Technical Dir 23 boulevard du Musée, 73000 Chambéry, France. T. +33479262882. E-mail: info@cartong.org.
URL: http://www.cartong.org/

History Set up 2006, France. **Aims** Put data at the service of humanitarian, international development and social action projects; further the use of *geographic* and non-geographic information tools and methodologies to improve data gathering and analysis for emergency *relief* and development programmes around the world. **Structure** Board. **Languages** English, French. **Activities** Capacity building; knowledge management/information dissemination; guidance/assistance/support; events/meetings. **Publications** *CartONG Newsletter* (4 a year). **IGO Relations** Partners include: *Agence française de développement (AFD)*; *UNHCR (#20327)*. **NGO Relations** Partners include: *ACAPS (#00044)*; *Action Against Hunger (#00086)*; *Action pour le développement – SOS Faim (SOS Faim)*; Care; *Fondation de France*; *Global Partnership for Sustainable Development Data (Data4SDGS, #10542)*; *Groupe urgence, réhabilitation et développement (Groupe URD)*; *Humanity and Inclusion (HI, #10975)*; *International Committee of the Red Cross (ICRC, #12799)*; *International Rescue Committee (IRC, #14717)*; Médecis sans frontières – Switzerland; *Solidarités International*; *Terre des hommes Foundation (Tdh Foundation, #20132)*. [2019.09.04/XM7204/**F**]

♦ CARTOON – Association européenne du film d'animation (#03592)

♦ CARTOON – European Association of Animation Film (EAAF) 03592

CARTOON – Association européenne du film d'animation (AEFA)

Gen Dir Avenue Huart Hamoir 105, 1030 Brussels, Belgium. T. +3222451200. Fax +3222454689. E-mail: info@cartoon-media.eu.
URL: http://www.cartoon-media.eu/

History Founded 16 Feb 1988, when statutes were adopted, on the initiative of *MEDIA Programme (MEDIA, inactive)* of the European Commission. Registered in accordance with Belgian law. **Aims** Promote the animated film industry in the countries of the European Community; support development of production capacities for cartoons. **Structure** General Assembly (annual); Administrative Council; Board. **Languages** English, French. **Activities** Training/education; events/meetings; knowledge management/information dissemination. **Events** *European Cartoon Movie Forum* Bordeaux (France) 2019, *Cartoon 360 Meeting* Lille (France) 2019, *Cartoon Connection Asia Meeting* Seoul (Korea Rep) 2019, *Cartoon Business Meeting* Tampere (Finland) 2019, *Forum* Toulouse (France) 2019.

Members Covers 30 countries:
Austria, Belgium, Bulgaria, Cyprus, Czechia, Denmark, Estonia, Finland, France, Germany, Greece, Hungary, Iceland, Ireland, Italy, Latvia, Liechtenstein, Lithuania, Luxembourg, Malta, Netherlands, Norway, Poland, Portugal, Slovakia, Slovenia, Spain, Sweden, Switzerland, UK. [2014.10.02/XE1223/**E**]

♦ Cartooning for Peace 03593

Dessins pour la Paix

Contact 12 Cité Malesherbes, 75009 Paris, France. T. +33140232403. E-mail: contact@cartooningforpeace.org.
URL: http://www.cartooningforpeace.org/

History 16 Oct 2006. Founded following the bloody reactions to the publication of the Mohammed cartoons in a Danish newspaper, 30 Sep 2005. Set up as a Foundation, 2009, Switzerland. Registration: Association, France. **Aims** Defend fundamental freedoms and democracy; promote press cartoons and press cartoonists through international meetings, exhibitions; use educational value of press cartoon to free speech and promote debate. **Languages** English, French, Spanish. **Staff** 7.00 FTE, paid. **Activities** Advocacy/lobbying/activism; events/meetings; networking/liaising; training/education. **Members** Press cartoonists (more than 250). Membership countries not specified. [2022.02.09/XJ8906/**F**]

♦ Cartoonists Rights Network International (CRN International) 03594

Exec Dir PO Box 7272, Fairfax Station VA 22039, USA. T. +17035438727.
URL: http://www.cartoonistsrights.com/

Aims Defend the interests of editorial cartoonists worldwide. **Structure** Board of Directors. **Activities** Organizes workshops.

Members National organizations (20) in 20 countries:
Afghanistan, Argentina, Botswana, Bulgaria, Cameroon, Ghana, Iran Islamic Rep, Moldova, Morocco, Nepal, Nigeria, Pakistan, Romania, Serbia, South Africa, Türkiye, Uganda, Ukraine, USA, Zimbabwe.

NGO Relations Member of: *IFEX (#11100)*. [2017/XF6827/**F**]

♦ Cartujos (religious order)
♦ CARU – Comisión Administradora del Rio Uruguay (internationally oriented national body)
♦ CAS / see Center for Pacific and American Studies
♦ Casa Alianza (internationally oriented national body)
♦ Casa de América Latina, Bruxelles (internationally oriented national body)
♦ Casa de las Américas (internationally oriented national body)
♦ Casa Árabe (internationally oriented national body)
♦ Casa Asia (internationally oriented national body)
♦ Casablanca Centre / see Islamic Centre for Development of Trade (#16035)
♦ Casablanca Group – African States of the Casablanca Charter (inactive)
♦ **CASA** Campaign For Safer Alternatives (#03404)
♦ **CASA** Caribbean Area Squash Association (#03442)
♦ CASA – Citizens' Alliance for Saving the Atmosphere and the Earth (internationally oriented national body)
♦ CASA Consortium – Center for Arabic Study Abroad (internationally oriented national body)
♦ **CASA** Contemporary A Cappella Society (#04778)
♦ CASA LATINA – Consejo de Asentamientos Sustentables de América Latina (unconfirmed)
♦ Casa Latinoamericana, Curitiba (unconfirmed)
♦ CASAN – Conseil africain des sciences de l'alimentation et de la nutrition (no recent information)
♦ Casa de la Paz, Santiago de Chile (internationally oriented national body)
♦ CASAS – Centre for Advanced Studies of African Society (internationally oriented national body)
♦ CASAS – Commonwealth Association of Scientific Agricultural Societies (no recent information)
♦ Casa Universal de los Sefardies (inactive)
♦ CASBAA / see Asia Video Industry Association (#02103)
♦ CASB – Centre for African Studies, Basel (internationally oriented national body)
♦ CASB – Confédération africaine des sports boules (inactive)
♦ **CASBIA** Association Coopérative des Automobilistes et des motocyclistes des Secrétariats et Bureaux des organisations Internationales et des institutions Accrédités (#02454)
♦ **CASCADE** Central Asia and South Caucasus Consortium of Agricultural universities for Development (#03685)
♦ CAS – Canadian Association of Slavists (internationally oriented national body)
♦ CAS – Caribbean Academy of Sciences (internationally oriented national body)
♦ CASC – Central American Security Commission (inactive)
♦ CAS – Centre of African Studies, Edinburgh (internationally oriented national body)
♦ CAS – Centre for Asian Studies (internationally oriented national body)
♦ CAS – Centrum för Afrikastudier, Göteborg (internationally oriented national body)
♦ **CASCI** Arab-Swiss Chamber of Commerce and Industry (#01053)
♦ CAS – Committee on Atlantic Studies (no recent information)
♦ **CAS** Commonwealth Africa Initiative (#04298)
♦ CAS – Cooperación Andina en Salud (no recent information)
♦ Cascos Blancos (#20933)
♦ **CAS** Court of Arbitration for Sport (#04933)
♦ **CASDB** Central African States' Development Bank (#03168)
♦ CASE – Council for Advancement and Support of Education (internationally oriented national body)
♦ **CASE** Council of Asian Science Editors (#04868)
♦ CASEIF – Central American Small Enterprise Investment Fund (internationally oriented national body)
♦ CASEIF I / see Central American Small Enterprise Investment Fund
♦ CASEIF II / see Central American Small Enterprise Investment Fund
♦ CASEIF III LP / see Central American Small Enterprise Investment Fund
♦ **CASE-LCA** Central and Southeast Europe LCA Network (#03720)
♦ CASEP – Central American Solar Energy Project (internationally oriented national body)
♦ CaSES – Caribbean Association of Endo-laparoscopic Surgeons (unconfirmed)
♦ CASH / see African Paralympic Committee (#00410)
♦ Cash-on-delivery Agreement (1984 treaty)
♦ **CASHFI** Caribbean Association of Housing Finance Institutions (#03447)
♦ CASHI / see African Paralympic Committee (#00410)
♦ **CASIC** Consejo de Asociaciones de la Industria Cosmética Latinoamericana (#04701)
♦ CASID – Canadian Association for the Study of International Development (internationally oriented national body)
♦ CASIE – Center for the Advancement and Study of International Education (internationally oriented national body)

♦ CASI Institute 03595

SG Av de Tervuren 168, 1150 Brussels, Belgium.
URL: http://www.casi-institute.com/

History 2008. **Aims** Study all problems arising for the industries which produce *Calcium Silicon alloys* all over the world; share information of a non-commercial nature arising within the global Calcium Silicon Industry. **Structure** General Assembly (annual); Board of Directors. **Languages** English, French. **Staff** 3.00 FTE, paid. **Finance** Sources: members' dues.

Members Full in 4 countries:
Argentina, Brazil, France, Slovakia.

NGO Relations Member of (1): *International Council on Mining and Metals (ICMM, #13048)*. [2022.11.04/XJ9975/**E**]

♦ CASLA – Casa Latinoamericana, Curitiba (unconfirmed)
♦ **CASLE** Commonwealth Association of Surveying and Land Economy (#04313)
♦ CASMA – Confédération des associations et sociétés médicales d'Afrique (no recent information)
♦ CASME / see Commonwealth Association of Science, Technology and Mathematics Educators (#04312)
♦ **CASMET** Caribbean Association of Medical Technologists (#03453)
♦ Caspian Economic Cooperation Organization (unconfirmed)

♦ Caspian Environment Programme (CEP) 03596

Contact CaspEco Project Management and Coordination Unit, 7th fl Kazhydromet Bldg, Orynbor St, Nur-Sultan, Kazakhstan, 010000. T. +77172798317.
URL: http://www.caspianenvironment.org/

History May 1998, Ramsar (Iran Islamic Rep). **Aims** Promote *sustainable development* of the Caspian environment. **Structure** Steering Committee, comprising representatives from each of the 5 Caspian and representatives from *International Bank for Reconstruction and Development (IBRD, #12317)* (World Bank), *UNDP (#20292)* and *UNEP (#20299)*. Programme Coordination Unit in Baku (Azerbaijan). **Finance** Funded by: *Global Environment Facility (GEF, #10346)*; *European Commission (EC, #06633)*; private sector. **Activities** Involved in: *Framework Convention for the Protection of the Marine Environment of the Caspian Sea (Tehran Convention, 2003)*. **Events** *International Symposium on Sturgeon* Ramsar (Iran Islamic Rep) 2005.

Members Governments of 5 countries:
Azerbaijan, Iran Islamic Rep, Kazakhstan, Russia, Turkmenistan.

IGO Relations *Regional Seas Programme (#18814)*; *United Nations Office for Project Services (UNOPS, #20602)*. [2012/XE4278/**E***]

♦ CASPT – International Conference on Advanced Systems in Public Transport (meeting series)
♦ Casques blancs (#20933)
♦ CASSAD – Centre for African Settlement Studies and Development (internationally oriented national body)
♦ CASS, Beijing / see Institute of World Economics and Politics
♦ **CASS** Confédération africaine des sports des sourds (#04498)
♦ **CASS** Conseil Arabe pour les Sciences Sociales (#00932)
♦ CASS – Conseil arabe des sciences sociales (inactive)
♦ CASSH – Conseil africain des sciences sociales et humaines (inactive)
♦ **CASSOS** Caribbean Aviation Safety and Security Oversight System (#03462)

♦ CASSS 03597

Exec Dir 5900 Hollis St, Ste R3, Emeryville CA 94608, USA. T. +15104280740. Fax +15104280741.
URL: http://www.casss.org/

History USA, as California Separation Science Society. Registered in accordance with USA law. **Aims** Enable a global community of industry, academic and regulatory professionals to work together to resolve scientific challenges in the field of *biopharmaceutical* development and regulation. **Structure** Board of Directors; Standing Committees. **Activities** Events/meetings; knowledge management/information dissemination. **Events** *Symposium on the Practical Applications of Mass Spectrometry in the Biotechnology Industry* Long Beach, CA (USA) 2022, *Symposium on the Practical Applications of Mass Spectrometry in the Biotechnology Industry* 2021, *Symposium on Analytical Technologies Europe* Lisbon (Portugal) 2020, *CMC Strategy Forum Europe* Stockholm (Sweden) 2020, *CMC Strategy Forum* Tokyo (Japan) 2018. **Members** Industry, academic and public sector professionals (over 4,000) in the field of separation science. Membership countries not specified. [2021/XJ1924/**E**]

♦ CASTAFRICA – Conference of Ministers Responsible for the Application of Science and Technology to Development in Africa (meeting series)
♦ CASTALAC – Conference of Ministers Responsible for the Application of Science and Technology to Development in Latin America and the Caribbean (meeting series)
♦ **CAST** Caribbean Alliance for Sustainable Tourism (#03439)
♦ CAST – Centro per un Appropriato Sviluppo Tecnologico (internationally oriented national body)
♦ CASTer – Conference and Association of European Steel Territories (inactive)

♦ Castings Technology International (Cti) 03598

Contact Advanced Manufacturing Park, Brunel Way, Rotherham, S60 5WG, UK. T. +441142541144. Fax +441142541155. E-mail: info@castingstechnology.com.
URL: http://www.castingstechnology.com/

History 1953, as British Steel Casting Research Association. Subsequently changed title into *SCRATA*, 1968. Current constitution adopted Apr 1996, on merger with *BCIRA (inactive)*, set up 1921 as *'British Cast Iron Research Association'*. **Aims** Provide technical services for casting producers and users worldwide including design, materials, manufacture, use, quality and performance of castings. **Languages** English. **Staff** 80.00 FTE, paid. **Finance** Owned by members. Assets: about pounds12 million; Revenue (annual): about pounds8 million. **Activities** Members have access to: technical advice from qualified and experienced personnel; leading edge technology; independent analysis and testing services; training courses tailored to specific requirements; R and D programmes, including group sponsored research with shared funding; a programme of international conferences, seminars and workshops. **Publications** Technical broadsheets. Information Services: Information and Library Service of casting-related literature.

Members Steel foundries, castings users and suppliers in 35 countries and territories:
Australia, Belgium, Brazil, Canada, Chile, China, Finland, France, Germany, India, Indonesia, Iran Islamic Rep, Ireland, Italy, Japan, Korea Rep, Mexico, Morocco, Netherlands, New Zealand, Norway, Philippines, Portugal, Russia, Saudi Arabia, Singapore, Slovenia, South Africa, Spain, Sweden, Taiwan, Thailand, UK, United Arab Emirates, USA. [2012.06.01/XF3311/**F**]

♦ **CASTME** Commonwealth Association of Science, Technology and Mathematics Educators (#04312)
♦ Castroviejo Society / see Cornea Society
♦ **CATA** Central American Tourism Agency (#03674)
♦ **CATA** Commonwealth Association of Tax Administrators (#04314)

Catalogue international littérature
03598

- Catalogue international de la littérature scientifique (inactive)
- Catalyst 2030 (unconfirmed)
- CATAPA (internationally oriented national body)
- CATBBAS – Controversies, Arts and Technology in Breast and Bodycontouring Aesthetic Surgery (meeting series)
- Catbior – International Congress on Catalysis for Biorefineries (meeting series)
- CATC – Commonwealth Air Transport Council (inactive)
- CAT – Centre for Alternative Technology (internationally oriented national body)
- CAT – Cities after Transition (unconfirmed)
- CaT Coalition against Typhoid (#04049)
- CAT Committee Against Torture (#04241)
- CAT Confederación Americana de Tiro (#04439)
- CAT Confédération Africaine de Tennis (#04507)
- CAT – Conseil africain de télédétection (inactive)
- Catechiste di Maria Vergine e Madre (religious order)
- Catechisti del Sacro Cuore di Gesù (religious order)
- Catechists of the Sacred Heart of Jesus (religious order)
- Catena Blue Mondiale (#21235)
- CATENA International Masonic Union (#14113)
- Catequistas do Sagrado Coração de Jesús (religious order)
- CATF – Clean Air Task Force (internationally oriented national body)
- CATHALAC Centro del Agua del Trópico Húmedo para América Latina y el Caribe (#20824)
- Catholic Agency for Overseas Development (internationally oriented national body)
- Catholic Association for Latin American and Caribbean Communication (see: #21264)

♦ Catholic Biblical Centre for Africa and Madagascar (BICAM) — 03599
Centre biblique catholique pour l'Afrique et Madagascar (CEBAM) – Centro Bíblico Católico para Africa e Madagascar (CEBAM)
Dir SECAM Secretariat, PO Box KIA 9156, 04 Senchi Street, Airport, Accra, Ghana. T. +233302778867 – +233302778868 – +233302778873. Fax +233302772548. E-mail: bicamcebam.dr@gmail.com.
URL: https://www.bicam-cebam.com/
History 1981, by the Committee for the Biblical Apostolate of *Symposium of Episcopal Conferences of Africa and Madagascar (SECAM, #20077)*. **Aims** Make information concerning the Biblical Apostolate available to the Christian faithful; make the Word of God known, loved and lived in the continent of Africa. **Structure** Board is responsible for the Standing Committee of SECAM. Operates under SECAM Department for Evangelization. Advisory Board; Director. **Languages** English, French, Portuguese. **Finance** Budget (annual): US$ 15,000. **Activities** Organizes and assists in the organization of workshops for biblical formation at local and regional levels according to the needs of the different categories of pastoral agents; assists in elaborating programmes and finds out methods in the promotion of biblical apostolate; assists in information exchange and the sharing of experiences through biblical publications; collaborates with other Christian Churches in the translation of the Bible and other inter-confessional Biblical projects. **Events** *Continental workshop* Dar es Salaam (Tanzania UR) 2007, *Pan African meeting* Burkina Faso 1997, *Bible, dialogue for unity and development in Africa towards the third millennium* Nairobi (Kenya) 1997, *Panafrican seminar on the biblical apostolate* Nairobi (Kenya) 1997. **Publications** *BICAM Newsletter* (4 a year) in English, French, Portuguese – electronic and paper; *Biblical Pastoral Bulletin* (2 a year). *The Year of the Bible in Africa* (2007) in English, French; *Directory of Biblical Apostolate in Africa* (2005) in English, French, Portuguese; *Know, Love, Live and Proclaim the Word of God* (2005) in English, French; *Many Parts, Yet One Body* (2005) in English, French; *Reading and Sharing God's Word Daily in the Family or Community* (2005) in English, French; *World of God: A Blessing for All Nations* (2003) in English, French; *The Bible in the New Evangelization in Africa* (1990) in English, French. Workshop proceedings.
Members Covers 53 countries:
Algeria, Angola, Benin, Botswana, Burkina Faso, Burundi, Cameroon, Cape Verde, Central African Rep, Chad, Comoros, Congo Brazzaville, Congo DR, Côte d'Ivoire, Djibouti, Egypt, Equatorial Guinea, Eritrea, Eswatini, Ethiopia, Gabon, Gambia, Ghana, Guinea, Guinea-Bissau, Kenya, Lesotho, Liberia, Madagascar, Malawi, Mali, Mauritania, Mauritius, Morocco, Mozambique, Namibia, Niger, Nigeria, Rwanda, Sao Tomé-Principe, Senegal, Seychelles, Sierra Leone, Somalia, South Africa, South Sudan, Sudan, Tanzania UR, Togo, Tunisia, Uganda, Zambia, Zimbabwe.
[2015/XE0906/E]

♦ Catholic Biblical Federation (CBF) — 03600
Fédération biblique catholique (FBC) – Federación Bíblica Católica (FEBIC) – Katholische Bibelföderation (KBF) – Federação Bíblica Católica (FBC) – Federazione Biblica Cattolica (FBC)
Gen Sec CBF General Secretariat, 86941 St Ottilien, Germany. T. +498193716900. Fax +498193771699. E-mail: gensec@c-b-f.org.
URL: https://www.c-b-f.org/
History 16 Apr 1969, Rome (Italy). Established under the auspices of the Secretariat for Christian Unity, as an international organization functioning within the area of Episcopal Conferences (Vatican II Constitution on Divine Revelation, Ch 6). Recognized by the Holy See, to which it relates through the *Pontifical Council for Promoting Christian Unity (PCPCU, #18446)*. Constitution drafted May 1970; adopted Apr 1972; amended 1978 and 1984; approved by the Holy See 27 Apr 1985; last amended and approved 18 Jun 2015, Nemi. Constitution approved by the Holy See, 19 Oct 2015. Former names and other names: *World Catholic Federation for the Biblical Apostolate (WCFBA)* – former; *Fédération catholique mondiale pour la pastorale biblique* – former; *Federación Bíblica Católica Mundial* – former; *Katholische Welt-Bibelföderation (KWBF)* – former; *Federação Bíblica Católica Mundial* – former; *Federazione Cattolica Mondiale per l'Apostolato Biblico* – former; *Federação Bíblica Católica (FBC)* – former; *Federazione Biblica Cattolica (FBC)* – former. **Aims** Promote the use of Sacred Scripture in all aspects of *evangelization* as the mission of the *Church*. **Structure** Plenary Assembly (every 6 years); Executive Committee; Administrative Board; General Secretary; Regional Coordinators. **Languages** English, French, German, Spanish. **Staff** 2.00 FTE, paid. **Finance** Sources: donations; gifts, legacies; members' dues. **Events** *Plenary assembly* Dar es Salaam (Tanzania UR) 2008, *Plenary Assembly* Tanzania UR 2008, *International Dei Verbum Congress* Rome (Italy) 2005, *International congress on the sacred scripture in the life of the church* Rome (Italy) 2005, *Asia-Oceania biblical congress* Tagaytay (Philippines) 2005. **Publications** *CBF Newsletter* (4 a year) in English, French, German, Spanish; *BDVdigital – Bulletin Dei Verbum* (2 a year) in English, French, German, Spanish. *Audiens et Proclamans*.
Members Full (98) Roman Catholic Episcopal Conferences and national Biblical associations; Associate (246) Religious orders and individual dioceses, publishing houses and Catholic movements; Sponsors (16). Members (for only Associate Membership) in 130 countries and territories:
Angola, Antigua-Barbuda, Argentina, Australia, Austria, Bahamas (*), Bangladesh, Barbados (*), Belgium, Belize (*), Benin (*), Bermuda (*), Bolivia, Botswana, Brazil, Brunei Darussalam, Burkina Faso, Burundi, Cambodia, Cameroon, Canada, Central African Rep, Chad, Chile, Colombia, Congo DR (*), Costa Rica, Côte d'Ivoire, Croatia, Curaçao (*), Czechia, Denmark, Dominica (*), Dominican Rep, Ecuador, Egypt, El Salvador, Fiji (*), Finland, France, French Antilles (*), Gabon, Gambia, Germany, Ghana, Grenada (*), Guadeloupe (*), Guatemala, Guyana (*), Haiti, Holy See, Honduras, Hong Kong, Hungary, Iceland, India, Indonesia, Iran Islamic Rep, Iraq, Ireland, Israel (*), Italy, Jamaica (*), Japan, Kenya, Korea Rep, Lebanon, Lesotho, Liberia, Lithuania, Luxembourg, Macau, Madagascar (*), Malawi, Malaysia, Mali, Malta, Martinique (*), Mexico, Myanmar, Nepal, Netherlands, New Zealand, Nicaragua (*), Niger, Nigeria, Norway, Pakistan, Papua New Guinea, Paraguay, Peru, Philippines, Poland, Portugal (*), Romania, Rwanda, Samoa (*), Sao Tomé-Principe, Serbia, Sierra Leone, Singapore, Slovakia, Slovenia, Solomon Is, South Africa, Spain, Sri Lanka, St Lucia (*), St Vincent-Grenadines (*), Sudan, Suriname (*), Sweden, Switzerland, Syrian AR, Tahiti Is, Taiwan, Tanzania UR, Thailand, Togo, Tonga (*), Trinidad-Tobago (*), Uganda, UK, Uruguay, USA, Venezuela, Vietnam, Zambia, Zimbabwe.
NGO Relations *East Asian Pastoral Institute (EAPI, #05207)* is associate member.
[2022.10.11/XB3954/B]

♦ Catholic Bishops' Conference of Malaysia-Singapore-Brunei (CBC-MSB) — 03601
Conférence épiscopale catholique de Malaisie-Singapour-Brunéi
Contact 528 Jalan Bukit Nanas, 50250 Kuala Lumpur, Malaysia. T. +60320788828. Fax +60320313815. E-mail: adkl.dvsfm@gmail.com.
Sec MAJODI Centre, 2010 Jalan Masai, Plentong, Masai, 81750 Johor Bahru, Johor, Malaysia.
SG Penang Diocesan Centre, 290 Jalan Macalister, 10450 Penang, Malaysia. E-mail: pgdioce@pd.jaring.my.

History 17 Apr 1980. Also referred to by initials *BCMSB*. **Aims** Plan and implement on a regional level whatever documents come from the Holy See, whatever is good and useful regarding *faith* and *morals*, whatever affects the *Christian* faithful in the region. **Structure** Conference comprises President, Vice-President, Episcopal Secretary, Treasurer and 6 members plus Male Religious Brother as Conference Executive Secretary. Episcopal Commissions (13): Biblical; Catechetical; Catholic Charismatic Renewal; Culture; Family Life; Lay Apostolate; Liturgy; Mission Affairs; Pastoral Care of Migrants and Itinerants; Pastoral Health Care; Consecrated Life; Seminaries and Diocesan Priests; Ecumenism and Inter-Religious. Conference of Religious Major Superiors (Men and Women) with its Executive Committee. **Languages** English. **Finance** Members' dues. Budget (annual): Malaysia Ringgit 110,000. **Activities** Conference meets twice a year.
Members Archbishops and Bishops of the dioceses in 3 countries:
Brunei Darussalam, Malaysia, Singapore.
[2012.07.30/XD4258/v/F]

- Catholic Bishops' Conference of Papua New Guinea and Solomon Islands (internationally oriented national body)
- Catholic Central Agency for Development Aid (internationally oriented national body)

♦ Catholic Charismatic Renewal International Service (CHARIS) — 03602
Exec Sec Palazzo San Calisto, Piazza di San Calisto 16, 00153 Rome RM, Italy. T. +390669887126. E-mail: info@charis.international.
URL: https://www.charis.international/
History 29 May 2017, Rome (Italy). Created by the Holy See, through Dicastery for Ality, Family and Life, following request of Pope Francis for *Catholic Fraternity of Charismatic Covenant Communities and Fellowships (inactive)* and *International Catholic Charismatic Renewal Services (ICCRS, inactive)* to create one joint organization. Statutes adopted 8 Dec 2018. Inaugurated 8 June 2019. **Aims** Spread Baptism in the Holy Spirit throughout the Church; work for Christian unity; promote service of the poor. **Structure** General Assembly; International Service of Communion; Continental Services of Communion; Executive Committee; International Office. **Activities** Events/meetings; training/education. **Events** *Worldwide Intercessors' Conference* Yamoussoukro (Côte d'Ivoire) 2023. **Publications** *CHARIS Magazine News.*
[2023/AA3167/F]

- Catholic Church Relief Fund / see Caritas Australia
- Catholic Committee Against Hunger and for Development (internationally oriented national body)
- Catholic Coordinating Committee for the Sending of Technicians (inactive)
- Catholic Daughters of the Americas (internationally oriented national body)
- Catholic European Study and Information Centre / see Jesuit European Social Centre (#16103)

♦ Catholic Evidence Guild (CEG) — 03603
Contact 84 Grove Green Road, London, E11 4EL, UK.
URL: http://www.catholicevidence.org/
History Circa 1921, London (UK), later evolving into a network of independent guilds without any formal links between them. An association of laypersons within the Roman Catholic Church. **Aims** Teach the *Catholic religion* at street corners.
Members Guilds in 3 countries:
Australia, UK, USA.
[2018/XF5853/F]

- Catholic Family and Human Rights Institute / see Center for Family and Human Rights
- Catholic Foreign Missionary Society of America (religious order)
- Catholic Fund for Overseas Development / see Catholic Agency for Overseas Development
- Catholic Grant Foundation for Africans / see Formation de cadres africains
- Catholic Higher Institute of Eastern Africa / see Catholic University of Eastern Africa, The (#03610)

♦ Catholic International Education Office — 03604
Office International de l'Enseignement Catholique (OIEC) – Oficina Internacional de la Enseñanza Católica
SG c/o Casa Generalice La Salle, Via Aurelia 476, 00160 Rome RM, Italy. E-mail: secretaire.general@oiecinternational.com – direction.generale@cucdb.fr.
URL: http://www.oiecinternational.com/
History 20 Sep 1952, Lucerne (Switzerland). Founded following meeting, Nov 1950, of representatives of 6 national Catholic educational organizations. Constitution approved by the Holy See, 28 Dec 1956. Registered Office previously located in Brussels (Belgium); now in Rome (Italy). Former names and other names: *Internationales Katholisches Büro für Unterricht und Erziehung* – former. **Aims** Promote a worldwide Catholic-inspired educational project. **Structure** General Assembly (every 4 years); Council; General Secretariat in Rome (Italy), directed by Secretary General. Regional Secretariats (5): Africa – *Association of Catholic Education for Africa and Madagascar (#02415)*; Americas – *Inter-American Catholic Education Association (ICCE, #11403)*; Europe – *Comité Européen pour l'Enseignement Catholique (CEEC, #04156)*; Asia/Pacific – *Catholic Education Council (CECT)*; Middle East and North Africa (MENA) – headquarters in Lebanon. Permanent Representatives to intergovernmental organizations accredited in Paris (France), Geneva (Switzerland), Rome (Italy), Strasbourg (France) and New York NY (USA). **Languages** English, French, Spanish. **Staff** 2.00 FTE, paid. **Finance** Sources: members' dues. **Activities** Knowledge management/information dissemination; networking/liaising. **Events** *Congress* Marseille (France) 2022, *Quadrennial Congress* New York, NY (USA) 2019, *Quadrennial Congress* Rome (Italy) 2015, *General Assembly* Saragossa (Spain) 2011, *Quadrennial Congress* Saragossa (Spain) 2011. **Publications** *Bulletin de l'OIEC* (4 a year) in English, French, Spanish. *Cahiers pédagogiques*; *Etudes et documents*; *OIEC Tracts*.
Members Constituent: organizations recognized by competent authorities as representing Catholic education in a given country. Associate: organizations with a worldwide vocation which devote a substantial part of their activities to Catholic education. Collaborating (11): similar organizations to associate members but more geographically restricted and actively collaborating individuals. Corresponding (6): all wishing to use OIEC information facilities. Constituent in 111 countries and territories:
Albania, Argentina, Australia, Austria, Bangladesh, Belgium, Benin, Bolivia, Bosnia-Herzegovina, Botswana, Brazil, Burkina Faso, Burundi, Cameroon, Canada, Central African Rep, Chad, Chile, Colombia, Congo Brazzaville, Congo DR, Costa Rica, Côte d'Ivoire, Croatia, Curaçao, Czechia, Denmark, Djibouti, Dominican Rep, Ecuador, Egypt, El Salvador, England, Equatorial Guinea, Eritrea, Eswatini, Ethiopia, France, Gabon, Gambia, Germany, Ghana, Greece, Guatemala, Guinea, Haiti, Honduras, Hong Kong, Hungary, India, Indonesia, Ireland, Israel, Italy, Jordan, Kenya, Lebanon, Lesotho, Lithuania, Luxembourg, Madagascar, Malawi, Malaysia, Mali, Malta, Mauritius, Mexico, Morocco, Namibia, Netherlands, New Zealand, Nicaragua, Niger, Nigeria, Norway, Pakistan, Palestine, Panama, Paraguay, Peru, Philippines, Poland, Portugal, Puerto Rico, Romania, Rwanda, Scotland, Senegal, Sierra Leone, Singapore, Slovakia, Slovenia, South Africa, Spain, Sri Lanka, Sudan, Switzerland, Taiwan, Tanzania UR, Thailand, Togo, Tunisia, Turkey, Uganda, Ukraine, Uruguay, USA, Venezuela, Wales, Zambia, Zimbabwe.
Associate in 3 countries:
France, Italy, Peru.
Included in the above, 6 organizations listed in this Yearbook:
Comité Européen pour l'Enseignement Catholique (CEEC, #04156); *Handmaids of the Sacred Heart of Jesus (ACJ)*; *Institute of the Brothers of the Sacred Heart (Sacred Heart Brothers)*; *Sisters of St Joseph of Cluny (SJC)*; *Society of Mary (Marianists)*; *Soeurs de Notre-Dame de Namur (SNDN)*.
Consultative Status Consultative status granted from: *ECOSOC (#05331)* (Special); *UNESCO (#20322)* (Consultative Status); *UNICEF (#20332)*; *Council of Europe (CE, #04881)* (Participatory Status). **IGO Relations** Close relations with: *FAO (#09260)*; *ILO (#11123)*; *OAS (#17629)*. Accredited by: *United Nations Office at Vienna (UNOV, #20604)*. Associated with Department of Global Communications of the United Nations. **NGO Relations** Member of: *Conference of INGOs of the Council of Europe (#04607)*; *Conference of Non-Governmental Organizations in Consultative Relationship with the United Nations (CONGO, #04635)*; *Forum of Catholic Inspired NGOs (#09905)*; *International Catholic Centre of Geneva (ICCG, #12449)*; *NGO-UNESCO Liaison Committee (#17127)*; *NGO Committee on UNICEF (#17120)*; *Organisation mondiale des anciens élèves de l'enseignement catholique (OMAEC, #17816)*; *UMEC-WUCT (#20280)*.
[2021.03.08/XB0220/y/B]

- Catholic International Union for Social Service (inactive)
- Catholic League (inactive)
- Catholic Lenten Fund (internationally oriented national body)

♦ Catholic Media Council (CAMECO) 03605

Medienplanung für Entwicklungsländer, Mittel- und Osteuropa

Exec Dir Postfach 10 21 04, 52021 Aachen, Germany. T. +492417013120. Fax +4924170131233. E-mail: cameco@cameco.org.
Pres Anton-Kurze-Allee 2, 52064 Aachen, Germany.
URL: https://www.cameco.org/

History 16 Jun 1969. Founded by 3 international catholic media organizations: International Catholic Union of the Press, the current *International Christian Organisation of the Media (ICOM, #12563)*; *International Catholic Organization for Cinema and Audiovisual (OCIC, inactive)*; *Unda, International Catholic Association for Radio and Television (inactive)* – the latter 2 organizations merging to form *World Catholic Association for Communication (SIGNIS, #21264)* – and the German Catholic Bishops' Conference. Commenced activities 15 Jan 1970, Aachen (Germany FR). Full English title: *Catholic Media Council – Consultancy in the field of Communications (CAMECO)*. Registration: North Rhine-Westphalia District court, No/ID: VR 1380, Start date: 28 Aug 1969, Germany, Aachen. **Aims** Empower community and development-oriented media initiatives and strengthen the presence of the Church in the media; enhance the importance of the media within the Church. **Structure** Assembly; Board. **Languages** English, French, German, Portuguese, Russian, Spanish. **Staff** 9.00 FTE, paid. **Finance** Contributions from funding agencies, including the following listed in this Yearbook: *Bischöfliche Aktion ADVENIAT*; *Catholic Lenten Fund*; *German Catholic Bishops' Organisation for Development Cooperation (MISEREOR)*; *MISSIO (#16827)*; *Renovabis – Solidaritätsaktion der deutschen Katholiken mit den Menschen in Mittel- und Osteuropa*; *Broederlijk Delen*; *Stichting Stem van Afrika*; *Holy Childhood*. Assignments on honorary basis. **Activities** Guidance/assistance/consulting; projects/programmes; monitoring/evaluation; financial and/or material support. **Events** *Latin American communication congress* Santo Domingo (Dominican Rep) 2004. **Publications** *CAMECO Update* – newsletter. *CAMECO Practice Series*. *Forum Media and Development (FoME)* – publications.

Members Catholic Funding Agencies, Media Organizations and individual experts. Organizations include the following 7 organizations listed in this Yearbook (" indicates Observer):
Bischöfliche Aktion ADVENIAT; *Catholic Lenten Fund*; *German Catholic Bishops' Organisation for Development Cooperation (MISEREOR)*; *MISSIO (#16827)*; *Pontifical Council for Social Communications (#18447)* (*); *Renovabis – Solidaritätsaktion der deutschen Katholiken mit den Menschen in Mittel- und Osteuropa*; *World Catholic Association for Communication (SIGNIS, #21264)*.

NGO Relations Cooperates with various organizations, including: *Association mondiale des radiodiffuseurs communautaires (AMARC, #02810)*; *Friedrich-Ebert-Stiftung (FES)*; *Global Forum for Media Development (GFMD, #10375)*; *GRET*; *Konrad Adenauer Foundation (KAF)*; *Panos Network (#18183)*; *World Association for Christian Communication (WACC, #21126)*. [2021/XF3647/y/**F**]

♦ Catholic Media Council – Consultancy in the field of Communications / see Catholic Media Council (#03605)
♦ Catholic Medical Mission Board (internationally oriented national body)

♦ Catholic Near East Welfare Association (CNEWA) 03606

Association catholique d'aide à l'Orient – Consociatio Catholica pro Medio Oriente

Pres 1011 First Ave, New York NY 10022-4195, USA. T. +12128261480. Fax +12128381344.
URL: http://www.cnewa.org/

History Founded 10 Mar 1926, by Pope Pius XI. Placed by the Holy See under the episcopal authority of the archbishop of New York, who is ex officio chair and treasurer of CNEWA. **Aims** Build up the church, affirm human dignity, alleviate poverty, encourage dialogue, and inspire hope. **Structure** Board of Trustees, consisting of Chairman and 5 members; administrative headquarters office; national and regional offices (8). **Languages** Amharic, Arabic, English, French, Italian, Malayalam, Tigrinya. **Staff** 65.00 FTE, paid. **Finance** Sources: gifts from individual benefactors; grants from funding organizations, including the following bodies listed in this Yearbook – *German Catholic Bishops' Organisation for Development Cooperation (MISEREOR)*, *MISSIO (#16827)*, legacies and bequests; investment income; contributed services. **Activities** Training/education; religious activities; financial and/or material support; humanitarian/emergency aid; projects/programmes. Active in: Middle East; Northeast Africa; India; Eastern Europe. **Publications** *ONE-TO-ONE* (daily) – log and ONE magazine; *ONE* (4 a year) – magazine, print.

Members Associations in 16 countries and territories:
Armenia, Canada, Egypt, Eritrea, Ethiopia, Georgia, Holy See, India, Iraq, Israel, Jordan, Lebanon, Palestine, Syrian AR, Ukraine, USA.

IGO Relations Associated with Department of Global Communications of the United Nations. **NGO Relations** Member of: *NGO Committee on Freedom of Religion or Belief, New York NY (#17109)*; *Riunione delle Opere per l'Aiuto alle Chiese Orientali (ROACO, see: #04672)*. Partner of: *Congregation for the Oriental Churches (CO, #04672)*; MISSIO. Supports: CO; *Pontifical Council for Promoting Christian Unity (PCPCU, #18446)*. [2015.11.13/XF3790/**F**]

♦ Catholic Office for Emergency Relief and Refugees (internationally oriented national body)
♦ Catholic Organization for Relief and Development (internationally oriented national body)
♦ Catholic Overseas Relief Committee / see Caritas Australia
♦ Catholic Peacebuilding Network (internationally oriented national body)

♦ Catholic Radio and Television Network 03607

Contact Bischof-Kindermann Strasse 23, 61462 Königstein, Germany. T. +496174291432.
URL: http://www.crtn.org/

History Founded 1988, as *Centre Saints Cyrille et Méthode (CSCM)*. **Aims** Specialize in the production and distribution of Catholic television and radio programming. **Languages** English, French, German. **Activities** Awareness raising. **Publications** *CRTN Newsletter*. **NGO Relations** Member of: *Aid to the Church in Need (#00587)*. Cooperates with: *World Catholic Association for Communication (SIGNIS, #21264)*. [2015/XF1735/**F**]

♦ Catholic Relief Services (CRS) 03608

Head Office 228 W Lexington St, Baltimore MD 21201-3413, USA. T. +18882777575. E-mail: info@crs.org.
Geneva Office 11 rue de Cornavin, 1201 Geneva, Switzerland. T. +41227314654. Fax +41227384814.
URL: http://www.crs.org/

History Jan 1943. Founded by Catholic bishops of the United States to assist the poor and disadvantaged outside USA. Former names and other names: *War Relief Services (IVRS National Welfare Conference)* – former (Jan 1943 to 1955); *Catholic Relief Services – National Catholic Welfare Conference* – former (1955 to 23 Mar 1967); *Catholic Relief Services – United States Catholic Conference (CRS-USCC)* – former (23 Mar 1967); *CATHWEL* – alias. Registration: 501c3, No/ID: 13-5563422, USA. **Aims** Promote services and assistance to meet relief, welfare and educational needs created by underdevelopment or arising out of civil strife or natural causes, their incidence and consequences as well as a social and economic development in developing areas, without regard to race, creed, colour or political affiliation. **Structure** Board of Bishops, selected by the Episcopal Conference of the United States. **Finance** Financed by the Catholic community in the United States. **Activities** Humanitarian/emergency aid. **Events** *ICT4D Conference* Abuja (Nigeria) 2020, *ICT4D Non-Conference* London (UK) 2020, *ICT4D Conference* Uganda 2019, *ICT4D Conference* Lusaka (Zambia) 2018, *ICT4D Conference* Hyderabad (India) 2017. **Publications** *The Good Steward* (4 a year); *Annual Public Summary of Activities*; *Latest Wooden Bell* – newsletter. Annual Report.

Members Active in 90 countries and territories:
Afghanistan, Albania, Angola, Argentina, Armenia, Azerbaijan, Bangladesh, Benin, Bolivia, Bosnia-Herzegovina, Brazil, Bulgaria, Burkina Faso, Burundi, Cambodia, Cameroon, Central African Rep, Chad, China, Colombia, Congo Brazzaville, Congo DR, Côte d'Ivoire, Croatia, Cuba, Czechia, Djibouti, Dominican Rep, Ecuador, Egypt, El Salvador, Equatorial Guinea, Eritrea, Ethiopia, Gambia, Georgia, Ghana, Guatemala, Guinea, Guinea-Bissau, Haiti, Honduras, India, Indonesia, Iraq, Jordan, Kenya, Korea DPR, Kosovo, Laos, Lebanon, Lesotho, Liberia, Madagascar, Malawi, Mali, Mexico, Morocco, Myanmar, Nepal, Nicaragua, Niger, Nigeria, North Macedonia, Pakistan, Peru, Philippines, Romania, Russia, Rwanda, Senegal, Serbia, Sierra Leone, Somalia, South Africa, Sri Lanka, Sudan, Syrian AR, Taiwan, Tanzania UR, Timor-Leste, Togo, Türkiye, Uganda, Venezuela, Vietnam, West Bank, West Bank-Gaza, Zambia, Zimbabwe.

Consultative Status Consultative status granted from: *UNICEF (#20332)*. **IGO Relations** Invited to Governing Council sessions of: *International Fund for Agricultural Development (IFAD, #13692)*. Observer to: *International Organization for Migration (IOM, #14454)*. Partner of: *UNHCR (#20327)*. Supports: *International Crops Research Institute for the Semi-Arid Tropics (ICRISAT, #13116)*. Associated with Department of Global Communications of the United Nations. **NGO Relations** Founder member of: *International Catholic Migration Commission (ICMC, #12459)*. Member of:
- *Advocacy Network for Africa (ADNA)*;
- *Alliance to End Hunger*;
- *Alliance for Malaria Prevention (AMP, #00706)*;
- *American Council for Voluntary International Action (InterAction)*;
- *Basic Education Coalition (BEC, #03184)*;
- *Better Than Cash Alliance (#03220)*;
- *Caritas Internationalis (CI, #03580)*;
- *Consortium of Christian Relief and Development Association (CCRDA)*;
- *CORE Group*;
- *Council of Non-Governmental Organizations for Development Support (#04911)*;
- *Early Childhood Development Action Network (ECDAN, #05155)*;
- *Forum of Catholic Inspired NGOs (#09905)*;
- *Gavi – The Vaccine Alliance (Gavi, #10077)* CSO Constituency;
- *Global Education Cluster (#10333)*;
- *Global Innovation Exchange (The Exchange, inactive)*;
- *Global Partnership for the Prevention of Armed Conflict (GPPAC, #10538)*;
- *Global WASH Cluster (GWC, #10651)*;
- *InsideNGO (inactive)*;
- *Inter-African Committee on Traditional Practices Affecting the Health of Women and Children (IAC, #11384)*;
- *Inter-agency Network for Education in Emergencies (INEE, #11387)*;
- *Joint Learning Initiative on Faith and Local Communities (JLI, #16139)*;
- *Millennium Water Alliance (MWA)*;
- *NetHope (#16979)*;
- *NGO Forum on Cambodia (#17124)*;
- *NGO Committee on UNICEF (#17120)*;
- *Start Network (#19969)*.

Stakeholder in: *Child and Youth Finance International (CYFI, inactive)*. Signatory to the 'Publish What You Pay' appeal of: *Publish What You Pay Coalition (PWYP, #18573)*. Supports: *Africare (#00516)*; *Global Network for Good Governance (GNGG, #10490)*; *International Institute of Tropical Agriculture (IITA, #13933)*; *Inter-Regional Meeting of Bishops of Southern Africa (IMBISA, #15971)*; *Southern African Network of AIDS Service Organizations (SANASO, see: #00272)*. Partner of: *1,000 Days*; *Global Health Cluster (GHC, #10401)*; *Global Shelter Cluster (GSC, #10594)*; *Instituto Centroamericano de Estudios Sociales y Desarrollo (INCEDES, #11327)*; *International Centre for Tropical Agriculture (#12527)*; *Helen Keller International (HKI, #10902)*. Instrumental in setting up: *Catholic Peacebuilding Network (CPN)*; *Consortium for Southern Africa Food Security Emergency (C-SAFE, inactive)*; *Inter-Church Response for the Horn of Africa (ICRHA, no recent information)*. Collaborates with: *FHI 360*. [2020/XF0493/**F**]

♦ Catholic Relief Services – National Catholic Welfare Conference / see Catholic Relief Services (#03608)
♦ Catholic Relief Services – United States Catholic Conference / see Catholic Relief Services (#03608)

♦ Catholics for Choice 03609

Pres 1436 U St NW, Ste 301, Washington DC 20009-3997, USA. T. +12029866093. Fax +12023327995. E-mail: cfc@catholicsforchoice.org.
URL: http://www.CatholicsForChoice.org/

History 1973, USA, as *Catholics for a Free Choice (CFFC) – Católicas por el Derecho a Decidir (CDD) – Católicas pelo Direito de Decidir (CDD)*. Sister organizations founded in Argentina in 1987. Current title adopted, 2007. **Aims** Shape and advance *sexual* and *reproductive ethics* that are based on justice, reflect a commitment to *women*'s wellbeing, and respect and affirm the capacity of women and men to make moral decisions about their lives. **Structure** Board of Directors, consisting of Chair, Secretary, Treasurer and members. President. Latin American partner: *Católicas por el Derecho a Decidir (CDD, #03612)*. European Advisory Group. **Finance** Financed primarily through private foundations based in USA. Other sources: support from individuals; sales of publications; subscriptions. **Activities** Programs include activities in USA, Latin America and Europe, and outreach to other countries and organizations around the world. Priority issues: Reproductive Health and Rights; Sex and Sexuality; Catholicism; Catholic Health Care; HIV and AIDS; Public Policy; Bioethics; New Reproductive Health Technologies. Key activities include: publishing and research; communications, especially the media; public speaking, special events and educational events; policy analysis; collaboration with partner organizations worldwide; communication and values-clarification training. Participation in various fora and conferences. **Events** *Christian women in theology meeting* Brazil 1992, *Meeting* New York, NY (USA) 1992. **Publications** *Conscience* (4 a year). Reports. Information Services: Extensive and comprehensive resource center featuring resources on Catholicism, reproductive rights, women's rights, feminism, ethics and bioethics. **Members** Not a membership organization. **Consultative Status** Consultative status granted from: *ECOSOC (#05331)* (Special). **IGO Relations** Consultation Status with: *United Nations Population Fund (UNFPA, #20612)*. Associated with Department of Global Communications of the United Nations. **NGO Relations** European group is member of: *European Network Church-on-the-Move (#07878)*. Member of *Conference of Non-Governmental Organizations in Consultative Relationship with the United Nations (CONGO, #04635)*; *International Consortium for Emergency Contraception (ICEC, #12911)*; *Reproductive Health Supplies Coalition (RHSC, #18847)*. [2010.11.04/XF2967/**F**]

♦ Catholics in Coalition for Justice and Peace (internationally oriented national body)
♦ Catholics for a Free Choice / see Catholics for Choice (#03609)
♦ Catholic Theological Society of Southern Africa (internationally oriented national body)
♦ Catholic Union of International Studies (inactive)

♦ Catholic University of Eastern Africa, The (CUEA) 03610

Université Catholique de l'Afrique de l'Est

Dir PO Box 62157, Nairobi, 00200, Kenya. T. +254202525811 – +254202525815. E-mail: rector@cuea.edu – linkages@cuea.edu – admin@cuea.edu.
URL: http://www.cuea.edu/

History Founded 3 Sep 1984, Nairobi (Kenya), as *Catholic Higher Institute of Eastern Africa (CHIEA)*, by *Association of Member Episcopal Conferences in Eastern Africa (AMECEA, #02805)*. Formally opened, 18 Aug 1985, by Pope John-Paul II. Present name adopted 3 Nov 1992, when the Institute obtained accreditation/Charter from the Government of Kenya. **Aims** Promote excellence in research, teaching and community service by preparing morally upright leaders based on the intellectual tradition of the Catholic Church. **Structure** Rector/Vice-Chancellor; Vice Rector/Deputy Vice-Chancellor Academic Affair; Vice Rector/Deputy Vice-Chancellor Administration; Vice Rector/Deputy Vice-Chancellor Finance; Coordinator of Academic Linkages; Registrar. **Languages** English, French, German, Hebrew, Irish Gaelic, Italian. **Staff** 450.00 FTE, paid. **Finance** Fees; grants. Annual budget: US$ 13,000,000. **Activities** Guidance/assistance/consulting; training/education; events/meetings, sporting activities. **Events** *Annual International Interdisciplinary Conference* Nairobi (Kenya) 2012, *Conference on Religious Mobility in East Africa and South Africa* Nairobi (Kenya) 2012. **Publications** *Eastern Africa Journal of Humanities and Sciences*. *African Christian Studies*.

Members Catholic churches in 9 countries:
Eritrea, Ethiopia, Kenya, Malawi, South Sudan, Sudan, Tanzania UR, Uganda, Zambia.

NGO Relations Member of (2): *International Association of Universities (IAU, #12246)*; *World Conference of Catholic University Institutions of Philosophy (#21297)*. [2016.11.03/XE1948/**E**]

♦ Catholic Women's Movement of Austria (internationally oriented national body)
♦ Catholic Workers' International (inactive)

♦ Catholic Youth Network for Environmental Sustainability in Africa (CYNESA) 03611

Réseau de Jeunes Catholiques pour un Environnement durable en Afrique

Contact PO Box 37434-00100, Nairobi, 00100, Kenya. T. +254700047093. E-mail: info@cynesa.org.
Street address Upendo House, Mountain View off Waiyaki Way, Nairobi, Kenya.
URL: https://cynesa.org/

History Jan 2012. Registration: Start date: Feb 2014, Kenya. **Aims** Offer a platform through which young Catholics across Africa respond to the twin challenges of Environmental Degradation and Climate Change, from the perspective of Catholic social teaching on care for creation, paying attention to the most vulnerable. **Languages** English, French, Portuguese, Swahili. **Staff** 2.00 FTE, paid; 6.00 FTE, voluntary. **Activities** Advocacy/lobbying/activism; awareness raising; networking/liaising; training/education.

Members National chapters in 10 countries:
Cameroon, Congo DR, Ghana, Kenya, Nigeria, Rwanda, South Africa, Tanzania UR, Zambia, Zimbabwe.
Consultative Status Consultative status granted from: *ECOSOC (#05331)* (Special). **IGO Relations** Accredited by (1): *UNEP (#20299)*. Observer status with (1): *Secretariat of the Convention on Biological Diversity (SCBD, #19197)*. *Secretariat of the United Nations Convention to Combat Desertification (Secretariat of the UNCCD, #19208)*; *United Nations Framework Convention on Climate Change – Secretariat (UNFCCC, #20564)*. **NGO Relations** Member of (3): *Forum of Catholic Inspired NGOs (#09905)*; *International Partnership on Religion and Sustainable Development (PaRD, #14524)*; *Laudato Si' Movement (#16403)*. [2023.02.13/XM6052/F]

- CATHWEL / see Catholic Relief Services (#03608)
- **CATI** Conference of African Theological Institutions (#04580)
- **CATIE** Centro Agronómico Tropical de Investigación y Enseñanza (#20246)
- Católicas por el Derecho a Decidir / see Catholics for Choice (#03609)

♦ Católicas por el Derecho a Decidir (CDD) 03612

Latin American Foundation of Catholics for the Right to Decide

Contact Av Hugo Ernst No 6386 – Bajo Seguencoma, Casilla de Correo No 9, La Paz, Bolivia. T. +59122751534. Fax +59122784955.
URL: http://www.catolicasporelderechoadecidir.org/

History 1987. Also known as *Fundación Católicas por el Derecho a Decidir en América Latina*. **Aims** Contribute to ethical reflection on sexuality and procreation, based on justice; sustain the right of women to have at their disposal information on reproductive health, especially focusing on family planning and abortion in Latin America. **Activities** Fora in the field; education programs; exchange of information. Maintains an Information and Documentation Service. **Publications** *Conciencia Latinoamericana* (4 a year). Monographs; pamphlets; articles.
Members Organizations and individuals in 18 countries:
Argentina, Bolivia, Brazil, Chile, Colombia, Costa Rica, Dominican Rep, Ecuador, El Salvador, Guatemala, Honduras, Mexico, Nicaragua, Panama, Paraguay, Peru, Uruguay, Venezuela.
Consultative Status Consultative status granted from: *ECOSOC (#05331)* (Special). **NGO Relations** Partner organization: *Catholics for Choice (#03609)*. [2010/XF3016/f/F]

- Católicas pelo Direito de Decidir / see Catholics for Choice (#03609)
- CATP / see Peace to the Planet
- **CATS** Caribbean Association of Theological Schools (#03461)
- **CATS** Congress of Asian Theologians (#04676)
- **CATTAC** Caribbean Association of Technologists, Technicians and Craftsmen (#03460)
- CATVET – Caribbean Association for Technical and Vocational Education and Training (internationally oriented national body)
- CATVT / see International Training Centre of the ILO (#15717)
- **CATW** Coalition Against Trafficking in Women (#04047)
- Caucasian Institute for Peace, Democracy and Development (internationally oriented national body)

♦ Caucasus Environmental NGO Network (CENN) 03613

Exec Dir 27 Betlemi Str, 0105 Tbilisi, Georgia. T. +99532751903 – +99532751904. Fax +99532751905. E-mail: info@cenn.org.
URL: http://www.cenn.org/

History 1998. Registration: Georgia. **Aims** Work with communities, governments and businesses across the South Caucasus to create sustainable solutions for a healthy environment by fostering modern and sustainable development values, building bridges between communities and developing progressive society which protects the environment. **Structure** General Meeting; Board; Executive Director. Offices: Armenia; Azerbaijan; Georgia. **Languages** English, Georgian. **Staff** 60.00 FTE, paid. **Finance** Funded by multilateral and bilateral donors. Annual budget: euro 1,580,000. **Activities** Events/meetings; advocacy/lobbying/activism; research and development; guidance/assistance/consulting. **Publications** *Caucasus Environment* (4 a year). Annual report; meeting proceedings; brochures. Information Services: Electronic library.
Members Full in 3 countries:
Armenia, Azerbaijan, Georgia.
Consultative Status Consultative status granted from: *ECOSOC (#05331)* (Special). **IGO Relations** Accredited by (2): *Green Climate Fund (GCF, #10714)*; *UNEP (#20299)*. Accredited to the Conference of the Parties of: *Secretariat of the United Nations Convention to Combat Desertification (Secretariat of the UNCCD, #19208)*. Regional Focal Point of *Global Environment Facility (GEF, #10346)*. **NGO Relations** Member of: *Climate and Clean Air Coalition (CCAC, #04010)*; *Eastern Partnership Civil Society Forum (EaP CSF, #05247)*; *GEF CSO Network (GCN, #10087)*; *Global Network of Civil Society Organizations for Disaster Reduction (GNDR, #10485)*; *International Union for Conservation of Nature and Natural Resources (IUCN, #15766)*; *United Nations Global Compact (#20567)*. Partner of: *1% for the Planet*; *Partnership for Clean Fuels and Vehicles (PCFV, #18231)*. [2022/XM3153/F]

- Caucasus Institute for Peace, Democracy and Development / see Caucasian Institute for Peace, Democracy and Development
- **CAU** Confederación Americana de Urologia (#04440)
- CA – UPU Council of Administration (see: #20682)

♦ Caux Round Table, The (CRT) 03614

Global Exec Dir 6 W Fifth St, Ste 300-M, St Paul MN 55102, USA. T. +16512232852. Fax +16512248328. E-mail: steve@cauxroundtable.net.
URL: http://www.cauxroundtable.org/

History 1986, Caux (Switzerland), as an international network of business leaders. **Aims** Promote principled business leadership. **Structure** World Advisory Council; Global Governing Board; Fellows. **Activities** Networking/liaising; events/meetings. **Events** *Conference* Tokyo (Japan) 2018, *Conference* Tokyo (Japan) 2017, *Global Dialogue* Caux (Switzerland) 2015, *Global Dialogue* Caux (Switzerland) 2009, *Global Dialogue* Seattle, WA (USA) 2007. **Publications** *Pegasus* (12 a year) – electronic newsletter. *Handbook on Moral Government*; *Moral Capitalism: Reconciling Private Interest with the Public Good*; *Principles for Business*; *Principles for Governments*; *Principles for NGOs*; *Principles for Ownership of Wealth*; *Principles for Responsible Globalization*. Position papers. **Members** Not a membership organization. **NGO Relations** Member of: *Sustainable Apparel Coalition (SAC)*; *World Benchmarking Alliance (WBA, #21228)*. [2015/XE2113/v/F]

- CAUZ – Consortium of Aquariums, Universities and Zoos (no recent information)
- Cavalieri Ospedalieri del Sovrano Ordine di San Giovanni di Gerusallem Sede di Malta – Ordine Ecumenico (religious order)
- **CAVB** Confédération africaine de volley-ball (#04503)
- CAVS – Controverses et Actualités en Chirurgie vasculaire (unconfirmed)
- **CAWASA** Caribbean Water and Sewerage Association (#03567)
- **CAW** Centre for African Wetlands (#03727)
- CAW – Children and War Foundation (internationally oriented national body)
- **CAW** Committee for Asian Women (#04243)
- CAWES / see Centre for Canadian, US and Latin American Studies, Delhi
- **CAWI** Coalition of Agricultural Workers International (#04050)
- CAWM – College of African Wildlife Management, Mweka (internationally oriented national body)
- CAWP – Caribbean Association of Women Police (inactive)
- CAWS – Council of Australasian Weed Societies (internationally oriented national body)
- CAWST – Centre for Affordable Water and Sanitation Technology (internationally oriented national body)
- **CAWTAR** Center of Arab Women for Training and Research, Tunis (#03637)
- **CAWT** Circle of Concerned African Women Theologians (#03931)
- CAWU – Center for Arab West Understanding (internationally oriented national body)
- **CAYC** Committee for ASEAN Youth Cooperation (#04242)
- CAZALAC – Centro del Agua para Zonas Aridas y Semiaridas de América Latina y el Caribe (internationally oriented national body)
- **CBAA** Cardiac Bioassist Association (#03426)
- CBAAC – Centre for Black and African Arts and Civilization (internationally oriented national body)
- CBAP – Centrum Badan Azji i Pacyfiku (internationally oriented national body)
- CBA / see Public Media Alliance (#18568)
- CBAR – Comité belge d'aide aux réfugiés (internationally oriented national body)
- **CBBA-Europe** Cross Border Benefits Alliance-Europe (#04969)
- CBCA – Commercial Bank Centrafrique (internationally oriented national body)
- CBC – Caribbean Broadcasting Corporation (internationally oriented national body)
- **CBC** Centro de Estudios Regionales Andinos 'Bartolomé de Las Casas' (#03636)
- **CBC** COMESA Business Council (#04124)
- **CBC-MSB** Catholic Bishops' Conference of Malaysia-Singapore-Brunei (#03601)
- **CB** Crossing Borders (#04970)

♦ CBD Alliance 03615

Address not obtained.
URL: http://www.cbdalliance.org/

Aims Enhance cooperation among organizations wishing to have a positive influence in the CBD; increase the general understanding of all relevant issues. **Structure** Board.
Members Civil society organizations, including 1 listed in this Yearbook:
Global Forest Coalition (GFC, #10368).
IGO Relations *Convention on Biological Diversity (Biodiversity convention, 1992)*. [2014/XJ8533/y/E]

- CBD-Habitat – Fundación para la Conservación de la Biodiversidad y su Habitat (internationally oriented national body)
- **CBE** Confédération des Biologistes Européens (#04520)
- CBE – Coopération bancaire pour l'Europe (internationally oriented national body)
- CBE / see Council of Science Editors (#04917)
- CBEES – Centre for Baltic and East European Studies (internationally oriented national body)
- CBE International (internationally oriented national body)
- CBE / see IUBS Commission for Biological Education (#16079)
- CBE JU – European Partnership for a Circular Bio-based Europe (unconfirmed)
- CBFA – Children and Broadcasting Foundation for Africa (internationally oriented national body)
- CBF – Caribbean Biodiversity Fund (unconfirmed)
- **CBF** Catholic Biblical Federation (#03600)
- **CBFP** Congo Basin Forest Partnership (#04662)
- CBF-WJR / see World Jewish Relief (#21600)
- CBF / see World Jewish Relief (#21600)
- CBF World Jewish Relief / see World Jewish Relief (#21600)
- **CBGA** Carpathian Balkan Geological Association (#03586)
- CBHA / see Start Network (#19969)
- CBI / see WorldVenture
- CBI – Centre for the Promotion of Imports from Developing Countries (internationally oriented national body)
- CBI – Combat Blindness International (internationally oriented national body)
- **CBI** Commission baleinière internationale (#15879)
- CBI – Common Bond Institute (internationally oriented national body)
- **CBI** Confédération bouliste internationale (#04579)
- **CBI** Confederazione Boccistica Internazionale (#04579)
- CBIE – Canadian Bureau for International Education (internationally oriented national body)
- CBIF – Caribbean Basin Investment Fund (inactive)
- CBInternational / see WorldVenture
- **CBJO** Coordinating Board of Jewish Organizations (#04813)
- CBL-ACP – Chamber of Commerce, Industry and Agriculture Belgium – Luxembourg – Africa-Caribbean-Pacific (internationally oriented national body)
- **CBLT** Commission du Bassin du Lac Tchad (#16220)
- CBM – Canadian Baptist Ministries (internationally oriented national body)
- CBMC / see The Brewers of Europe (#03324)
- **CBMC** Covered Bond and Mortgage Council (#04940)
- **CBM** Chaîne bleue mondiale: pour la protection des animaux et de la nature (#21235)
- CBM – Christian Blind Mission (internationally oriented national body)
- CBM Christoffel-Blindenmission Christian Blind Mission / see Christian Blind Mission
- CBMC International (internationally oriented national body)
- CBM Global – CBM Global Disability Inclusion (unconfirmed)
- CBM Global Disability Inclusion (unconfirmed)
- CBM International / see Christian Blind Mission
- **CBMP** Circumpolar Biodiversity Monitoring Program (#03941)
- CBMR – Center for Black Music Research (internationally oriented national body)
- **CBMS** Chemical and Biological Microsystems Society (#03858)
- **CBN-E** Climate Broadcasters Network – Europe (#04007)
- **CBOL** Consortium for the Barcode of Life (#04737)

♦ CBR Africa Network (CAN) 03616

Chairman Ntinda Complex Block A Level 3, PO Box 114, Kyambogo, Kampala, Uganda. T. +256414574462. E-mail: info@afri-can.org.
URL: http://www.afri-can.org/

History Jul 2002. Former names and other names: *Community Based Rehabilitation Africa Network* – full title. **Aims** Develop a strong community based *rehabilitation* (CBR) information management capacity; support a strong lobby for the promotion of CBR. **Structure** General Assembly (every 3 years); Executive Committee; Secretariat, headed by Executive Director. **Languages** English. **Staff** 3.00 FTE, paid. **Finance** Funded mainly by CP Charitable Trust (UK). Past funding obtained from: Berkeley Trust; *Christian Blind Mission (CBM)*; *ILO (#11123)*; Norwegian Association of the Disabled (NAD); *UNICEF (#20332)*; *WHO (#20950)*. **Activities** Events/meetings; projects/programmes. **Events** *World Congress* Uganda 2021, *World Congress* Entebbe (Uganda) 2020, *CBR for resilience building and sustainable development – leave no one behind* Lusaka (Zambia) 2018, *Conference* Nairobi (Kenya) 2015, *Conference* Nairobi (Kenya) 2014. **Publications** *CBR Directory for Africa* (2008). **Members** Individuals in 12 countries. Membership countries not specified. **NGO Relations** Member of: *CBR Global Network (#03618)*; *Global Partnership for Disability and Development (GPDD, #10530)*. [2020/XJ2081/F]

- **CBR AP Network** CBR Asia-Pacific Network (#03617)

♦ CBR Asia-Pacific Network (CBR AP Network) 03617

Secretariat c/o APCD, 255 Rajvithi Road, Rajthevi, Bangkok, 10400, Thailand. T. +6623547505. Fax +6623547507. E-mail: cbrapnetwork@apcdfoundation.org.
URL: http://www.cbrasiapacific.net/

History Set up and endorsed by *WHO (#20950)*, 2009. **Aims** Promote and strengthen Community-Based *Rehabilitation* (CBR) across the region and globally; mobilize and support resources and information exchange. **Structure** Regional Council; Executive Committee. Secretariat provided by *Foundation of Asia-Pacific Development Centre on Disability (APCD Foundation, #09941)*. **Events** *Asia-Pacific Community-Based Inclusive Development (AP-CBID) Congress* Phnom Penh (Cambodia) 2023, *Asia-Pacific Community-Based Inclusive Development (AP-CBID) Congress* Ulaanbaatar (Mongolia) 2019, *Asia-Pacific Community-Based Inclusive Development (AP-CBID) Congress* Tokyo (Japan) 2015, *Asia-Pacific Community-Based Inclusive Development (AP-CBID) Congress* Manila (Philippines) 2011, *Asia-Pacific Community-Based Inclusive Development (AP-CBID) Congress* Bangkok (Thailand) 2009.
Members Full in 37 countries and territories:
Afghanistan, Australia, Bangladesh, Brunei Darussalam, Cambodia, China, Cook Is, Fiji, Hong Kong, India, Indonesia, Iran Islamic Rep, Japan, Kiribati, Malaysia, Maldives, Micronesia FS, Mongolia, Myanmar, Nauru, Nepal, New Zealand, Niue, Pakistan, Palau, Palestine, Papua New Guinea, Philippines, Samoa, Solomon Is, Sri Lanka, Thailand, Timor-Leste, Tonga, Tuvalu, Vanuatu, Vietnam.
NGO Relations Member of: *CBR Global Network (#03618)*. [2015/XJ9044/F]

♦ **CBR Global Network** 03618
Pres c/o ADD India, No 4005 – 19th Cross 2nd Stage, Banasankari, Bangalore, Karnataka 560070, Bangalore KARNATAKA 560070, India. T. +919676286388 – +919440686839. E-mail: cbr.inclusion@gmail.com.
URL: https://cbrglobalnetwork.org/
History Nov 2012, Agra (India), at *Community-based Rehabilitation (CBR)* World Congress. **Aims** Improve the quality of life of people with *disabilities*, particularly women and children, who live in the poorest and most marginalized communities, especially in the countries of the South. **Structure** Executive Committee, consisting of representatives of *CBR Africa Network (CAN, #03616), CBR Asia-Pacific Network (CBR AP Network, #03617)* and *CBR Americas Network, Disabled Peoples' International (DPI, #05097), International Disability Alliance (IDA, #13176), International Disability and Development Consortium (IDDC, #13177)* and 2 coopted members. **Languages** English. **Staff** None paid. **Finance** Congress proceeds. **Activities** Advocacy/lobbying/activism; capacity building; networking/liaising. **Events** World Congress Uganda 2021, World Congress Entebbe (Uganda) 2020, World Congress Kuala Lumpur (Malaysia) 2016, *Meeting* Bangkok (Thailand) 2013, *World Congress* Agra (India) 2012. **IGO Relations** WHO *(#20950).* [2015.01.19/XJ9043/y/F]

♦ **CBR Network South Asia** Community-Based Rehabilitation Network – South Asia (#04391)
♦ **CBS** – Confraternity of the Blessed Sacrament (religious order)
♦ **CBS Network International** (internationally oriented national body)
♦ **CBSN International** – CBS Network International (internationally oriented national body)
♦ **CBSS** Council of the Baltic Sea States (#04870)
♦ **CBS** – Sisters of Bon Secours of Paris (religious order)
♦ **CBSWCA** – Committee of Banking Supervisors of West and Central Africa (unconfirmed)
♦ **CBS** West Indies Central Sugar Cane Breeding Station (#20922)
♦ **CBTN** – Children's Brain Tumor Network (internationally oriented national body)
♦ **CBTTC** / see Children's Brain Tumor Network
♦ **CBU** Caribbean Broadcasting Union (#03465)
♦ **CBWAS** / see Banque centrale des Etats de l'Afrique de l'Ouest (#03167)
♦ **CBWMP** / see Caribbean Water and Sewerage Association (#03567)
♦ **CCA** / see Conflict Analysis Research Centre
♦ **CCAAA** Co-ordinating Council of Audiovisual Archives Associations (#04820)
♦ **CCAA** / see Atlantic Cities (#03008)
♦ **CCA** Caribbean Conservation Association (#03481)
♦ **CCAC** / see Climate and Clean Air Coalition (#04010)
♦ **CCAC** Climate and Clean Air Coalition (#04010)
♦ **CCAC** / see European Network for Central Africa (#07874)
♦ **CCA** – Chamber of Commerce of the Americas (inactive)
♦ **CCA** Christian Conference of Asia (#03898)
♦ **CCA** Comisión para la Cooperación Ambiental (#04211)
♦ **CCA** Commonwealth Chess Association (#04317)
♦ **CCA** Confederation of Chess for the Americas (#04516)
♦ **CCA** – Conseil du cyclisme amateur de l'UCI (inactive)
♦ **CCA** Consejo Centroamericano de Acreditación de la Educación Superior (#04703)
♦ **CCA** – Corporate Council on Africa (internationally oriented national body)
♦ **CCAD** Comisión Centroamericana de Ambiente y Desarrollo (#04129)
♦ **CCAE** / see Conseil des communautés africaines en Europe/Belgique
♦ **CCAE/B** – Conseil des communautés africaines en Europe/Belgique (internationally oriented national body)
♦ **CCAE Belgique** / see Conseil des communautés africaines en Europe/Belgique
♦ **CCAE** – Conférence des chefs d'Etat de l'Afrique équatoriale (inactive)
♦ **CCA-Europe** Calcium Carbonate Association – Europe (#03399)
♦ **CCALA** Consejo del Caribe para la Aplicación de las Leyes de Aduaneras (#03487)

♦ **CCAM Association (CCAM)** 03619
Head of Office Av de Cortenbergh 66, 1000 Brussels, Belgium.
URL: https://www.ccam.eu
History 2021. Represents the private side of the CCAM Partnership – co-programmed with *European Commission (EC, #06633)* in the Horizon Europe Framework. Former names and other names: *CONNECTED, COOPERATIVE AND AUTOMATED MOBILITY (CCAM)* – legal name. Registration: Banque-Carrefour des Entreprises, No/ID: 0765.350.982, Start date: 18 Mar 2021, Belgium. **Aims** Promote and facilitate pre-competitive research on connected, cooperative and automated mobility (CCAM) within the European Research Area. **Structure** General Assembly; Administration Board; Executive Group; Partnership Delegation; Secretariat. **Finance** Sources: members' dues. **Events** *European Conference on Connected Automated Driving* Brussels (Belgium) 2023, *European Conference on Results from Road Transport Research in H2020 Projects* Brussels (Belgium) 2023, *European Conference on Results from Road Transport Research in H2020 Projects* Brussels (Belgium) 2022.
Members Stakeholders (over 180) in 23 countries:
Austria, Belgium, Cyprus, Czechia, Denmark, Estonia, Finland, France, Germany, Greece, Hungary, Ireland, Italy, Netherlands, Norway, Poland, Portugal, Slovakia, Slovenia, Spain, Sweden, Türkiye, UK. [2022/AA2955/E]

♦ **CCAM** / see CCAM Association (#03619)
♦ **CCAM** CCAM Association (#03619)
♦ **CCAMLR** Commission for the Conservation of Antarctic Marine Living Resources (#04206)
♦ **CCAMLR** – Convention on the Conservation of Antarctic Marine Living Resources (1980 treaty)
♦ **CCAO** – Chambre de compensation de l'Afrique de l'Ouest (inactive)
♦ **CCAP** – Center for Clean Air Policy (internationally oriented national body)
♦ **CCAR** / see Jimmy and Rosalynn Carter School for Peace and Conflict Resolution
♦ **CCARDESA** Centre for Coordination of Agricultural Research and Development for Southern Africa (#03736)
♦ **CCAS** Caribbean Cytometry and Analytical Society (#03488)
♦ **CCAS** – Center for Contemporary Arab Studies, Washington DC (internationally oriented national body)
♦ **CCAS** – Centre of Central Asian Studies, Srinagar (internationally oriented national body)
♦ **CCAS** – Convention for the Conservation of Antarctic Seals (1972 treaty)
♦ **CCASG** / see Gulf Cooperation Council (#10826)
♦ **CCASIP** Comité de coordination des associations et syndicats internationaux du personnel du système des Nations Unies (#04818)
♦ **CCBA** / see Chamber of Commerce, Industry and Agriculture Belgium – Luxembourg – Africa-Caribbean-Pacific
♦ **CCB** Caribbean Council for the Blind (#03483)
♦ **CCB** CEPI ContainerBoard (#03824)
♦ **CCB** Coalition Clean Baltic (#04053)
♦ **CCBE** Council of Bars and Law Societies of Europe (#04871)
♦ **CCBG** Committee of Central Bank Governors in SADC (#04245)
♦ **CCBLA** Chambre de commerce Belgique-Luxembourg-Pays arabes (#00907)
♦ **CCC** / see Sea Turtle Conservancy
♦ **CCCAN** / see Central American and Caribbean Amateur Swimming Confederation (#03660)
♦ **CCCAN** Confederación Centroamericana y del Caribe de Aficionados a la Natación (#03660)
♦ **CC** The Caribbean Council (#03482)
♦ **CCC-CA** Confederación de Cooperativas del Caribe, Centro y Suramérica (#04445)
♦ **CCC** – Calorie Control Council (internationally oriented national body)
♦ **CCC** Caribbean Conference of Churches (#03479)
♦ **CCC** CARICOM Competition Commission (#03571)
♦ **CCCCC** Caribbean Community Climate Change Centre (#03477)
♦ **CCC** Celtic Conference in Classics (#03631)
♦ **CCC** – Centro de Comunicación Científica con Ibero-América (internationally oriented national body)
♦ **CCC** Clean Clothes Campaign (#03986)

♦ **CCC** Climate Chain Coalition (#04008)
♦ **CCC** COMESA Competition Commission (#04125)
♦ **CCC** Comunidad Científica del Caribe (#03553)
♦ **CCC** / see Confederación de Cooperativas del Caribe, Centro y Suramérica (#04445)
♦ **CCC** – Cooperation Committee for Cambodia (internationally oriented national body)
♦ **CCCCP** – Comité coordonnateur canadien pour la consolidation de la paix (internationally oriented national body)
♦ **CCCE** / see Agence française de développement
♦ **CCCE** Cámara de Comercio del Caribe para Europa (#03471)
♦ **CCCE** Caribbean Chamber of Commerce in Europe (#03471)
♦ **CCCE** Chambre de Commerce et d'Industrie des Caraïbes en Europe (#03471)
♦ **CCCES** – Centre for Climate Change and Environmental Studies (internationally oriented national body)
♦ **CCCET** – Comité catholique de coordination pour l'envoi de techniciens (inactive)
♦ **CCCF** / see Comité Catholique contre la Faim et pour le Développement-Terre Solidaire
♦ **CCCI** / see Cooperation Canada
♦ **CCCI** – Campus Crusade for Christ International (internationally oriented national body)
♦ **CCCI** Coca-Cola Collectors Club International (#04077)
♦ **CCCIV** / see Coordinating Committee for International Voluntary Service (#04819)
♦ **CC** – Climate Cleanup Foundation (internationally oriented national body)
♦ **CCCLP** – Confederación Centroamericana y del Caribe de Levantamiento de Pesas (inactive)
♦ **CCCM Cluster** Global Camp Coordination and Camp Management Cluster (#10268)
♦ **CCC MDTF** / see Connect4Climate (#04680)
♦ **CCCOCYD** / see Eurasian Association of Contitutional Review Bodies (#05602)
♦ **CC** – Conference on Cryocrystals and Quantum Crystals (meeting series)
♦ **CCCU** Caribbean Confederation of Credit Unions (#03478)
♦ **CCCU** – Council for Christian Colleges and Universities (internationally oriented national body)
♦ **CCC/UN** – Communications Coordination Committee for the United Nations (internationally oriented national body)
♦ **CCCW** – Cambridge Centre for Christianity Worldwide (internationally oriented national body)
♦ **CCC** / see World Customs Organization (#21350)
♦ **CCCWU** Consultative Council of Cultural Workers' Unions (#04766)
♦ **CCD** – Council for a Community of Democracies (internationally oriented national body)
♦ **CCDDS** Congregazione per il Culto Divino e la Disciplina dei Sacramenti (#04668)
♦ **CCDHR** – Centre for Citizenship, Development and Human Rights (internationally oriented national body)
♦ **CCDI** – Conseil canadien de droit international (internationally oriented national body)
♦ **CCDLNE** / see Commission for Controlling the Desert Locust in the Central Region (#04208)
♦ **CCDLNWA** / see FAO Commission for Controlling the Desert Locust in the Western Region (#09259)
♦ **CCDP** – Centre on Conflict, Development and Peacebuilding (internationally oriented national body)
♦ **CCD** / see World Customs Organization (#21350)
♦ **CCEA** / see Commonwealth Council for Educational Administration and Management (#04319)
♦ **CCEA** – Consejo Consultivo Empresarial Andino (see: #00817)
♦ **CCEA** – Council on Chiropractic Education Australasia (internationally oriented national body)
♦ **CCEA** Council of Churches of East Asia (#04877)
♦ **CCEAM** Commonwealth Council for Educational Administration and Management (#04319)
♦ **CCEASE** – Conseil Canadien des études sur l'Asie du Sud-Est (internationally oriented national body)
♦ **CCE** Cancer Core Europe (#03412)
♦ **CCE** / see The Caribbean Council (#03482)
♦ **CCE** – Centre de culture européenne, Bruxelles (internationally oriented national body)
♦ **CCE** Comité de Cooperación Económica de Centroamericana (#03667)
♦ **CCE** Commission de coopération environnementale (#04211)
♦ **CCE** – Council for Creative Education (unconfirmed)
♦ **CCE** / see Council of European Municipalities and Regions (#04891)
♦ **CCEE** Consilium Conferentiarum Episcoporum Europae (#04884)
♦ **CCE** / see European Commission (#06633)
♦ **CCEG** Commonwealth Centre for e-Governance (#04316)
♦ **CCEG** Confédération des compagnonnages européens (#04522)
♦ **CCEG** Confederation Europäische Gesellenzünfte (#04522)
♦ **CCEIA** / see Carnegie Council for Ethics in International Affairs
♦ **CCEIA** – Carnegie Council for Ethics in International Affairs (internationally oriented national body)
♦ **CCEI** Councils on Chiropractic Education International (#04916)
♦ **CCELAT** – Canon Collins Educational and Legal Assistance Trust (internationally oriented national body)
♦ **CCEM** – Conference of Commonwealth Education Ministers (meeting series)
♦ **CCEN** Citizens' Climate Engagement Network (#03955)
♦ **CCEO** Council of Caribbean Engineering Organizations (#04874)
♦ **CCETSA** / see Canon Collins Educational and Legal Assistance Trust
♦ **CCEU** / see International Association for Continuing Education and Training
♦ **CCFA** – Caribbean Cane Farmers' Association (inactive)
♦ **CCFA** – Chambre de commerce franco-arabe (internationally oriented national body)
♦ **CCF** – Calmeadow Charitable Foundation (internationally oriented national body)
♦ **CCF** – Cheetah Conservation Fund (internationally oriented national body)
♦ **CCF** / see ChildFund International (#03869)
♦ **CCF** Computational Complexity Foundation (#04423)
♦ **CCFD** / see Comité Catholique contre la Faim et pour le Développement-Terre Solidaire
♦ **CCFD-Terre Solidaire** – Catholic Committee Against Hunger and for Development (internationally oriented national body)
♦ **CCFD-Terre Solidaire** – Comité Catholique contre la Faim et pour le Développement-Terre Solidaire (internationally oriented national body)
♦ **CCfE** Commonwealth Consortium for Education (#04318)
♦ **CCFLA** Cities Climate Finance Leadership Alliance (#03952)
♦ **CCFLH** – Caribbean Council of Forensic Laboratory Heads (inactive)
♦ **CCFP** Caribbean College of Family Physicians (#03474)
♦ **CCFR** / see Chicago Council on Global Affairs
♦ **CCFT** – Consortium for Countering the Financing of Terrorism (internationally oriented national body)
♦ **CCGA** – Caribbean Citrus Growers Association (no recent information)
♦ **CCG** – Center for Constitutional Governance (internationally oriented national body)
♦ **CCG** Conseil de coopération du Golfe (#10826)
♦ **CCGM** Commission de la carte géologique du monde (#04216)
♦ **CCGS** – Commonwealth Consultative Group on Human Settlement (inactive)
♦ **CCGTM** / see Commonwealth Partnership for Technology Management (#04356)
♦ **CCHD** / see Comité Catholique contre la Faim et pour le Développement-Terre Solidaire
♦ **CCHR** / see Centre for Citizenship, Development and Human Rights
♦ **CCHR** – Center for Civil and Human Rights, Notre Dame IN (internationally oriented national body)
♦ **CCHR International** – Citizens Commission on Human Rights International (see: #03922)
♦ **CCHRP** – Carr Center for Human Rights Policy (internationally oriented national body)
♦ **CCI** / see International Trade Centre (#15703)
♦ **CCIA** – Asia-Pacific Cultural Creative Industry Association (internationally oriented national body)
♦ **CCIA** Comité Consultivo Internacional del Algodón (#12979)
♦ **CCIA** – Computer and Communications Industry Association (internationally oriented national body)
♦ **CCIb** – Centro Cochrane Iberoamericano (internationally oriented national body)
♦ **CCIC** / see Consultative Committee on Industrial Change (#04763)
♦ **CCIC** / see Cooperation Canada

♦ CCI – Canadian Crossroads International (internationally oriented national body)
♦ CCI – Carrefour canadien international (internationally oriented national body)
♦ **CCIC** Centre catholique international de coopération avec l'UNESCO (#12454)
♦ **CCIC** Comité consultatif international du coton (#12979)
♦ CCICED – China Council for International Cooperation on Environment and Development (internationally oriented national body)
♦ **CCI** Centro Comum de Investigação (#16147)
♦ **CCI** Centro Común de Investigación (#16147)
♦ CCI – Centro per la Cooperazione Internazionale (internationally oriented national body)
♦ **CCI** Charter for Compassion International (#03855)
♦ **CCI** Childhood Cancer International (#03871)
♦ **CCI** Christian Camping International (#03897)
♦ CCI – Christian Communications International (internationally oriented national body)
♦ CCIC / see International Catholic Cooperation Centre for UNESCO (#12454)
♦ **CCIC** International Catholic Cooperation Centre for UNESCO (#12454)
♦ **CCI** Cleft-Children International (#03994)
♦ CCICMS / see Council for International Organizations of Medical Sciences (#04905)
♦ **CCI** Confraternidad Carcelaria Internacional (#18503)
♦ CCI / see Consumer Co-operatives Worldwide (#04770)
♦ CCI – Cotton Council International (inactive)
♦ CCI – Creative Commons International (internationally oriented national body)
♦ CCID – Community Colleges for International Development (internationally oriented national body)
♦ **CCI Europe** Childhood Cancer International Europe (#03872)
♦ **CCI France International** Chambres de Commerce et d'Industrie Françaises à l'International (#03849)
♦ **CCIG** Centre catholique international de Genève (#12449)
♦ **CCIG** Centro Católico Internacional de Ginebra (#12449)
♦ CCIH – Christian Connections for International Health (internationally oriented national body)
♦ CCI / see International Criminal Court (#13108)
♦ CCIL – Canadian Council on International Law (internationally oriented national body)
♦ CCIN / see Global Cosmetics Cluster (#10309)
♦ CCIR – Comité consultatif international des radiocommunications (inactive)
♦ **CCIRN** Coordinating Committee for Intercontinental Research Networking (#04817)
♦ CCIS – College Consortium for International Studies (internationally oriented national body)
♦ CCISD – Centre de coopération internationale en santé et développement (internationally oriented national body)
♦ **CCISUA** Coordinating Committee for International Staff Unions and Associations of the United Nations System (#04818)
♦ CCITT – Comité consultatif international télégraphique et téléphonique (inactive)
♦ **CCIVS** Coordinating Committee for International Voluntary Service (#04819)
♦ CCIVW / see Coordinating Committee for International Voluntary Service (#04819)
♦ CCI Worldwide / see Christian Camping International (#03897)
♦ CCI WW / see Christian Camping International (#03897)
♦ **CCJA** Conference of Constitutional Jurisdictions of Africa (#04585)
♦ **CCJ** Caribbean Court of Justice (#03486)
♦ **CCJ** Corte Centroamericana de Justicia (#04850)
♦ **CCJE** Consultative Council of European Judges (#04767)
♦ CCJI – Comisión Centroamericana de Juristas de la Integración (no recent information)
♦ CCJP – Catholics in Coalition for Justice and Peace (internationally oriented national body)
♦ CCK Foundation – Chiang Ching-Kuo Foundation for International Scholarly Exchange (internationally oriented national body)
♦ CCLA – Consejo Consultivo Laboral Andino (see: #00817)
♦ CCL / see Association of Caribbean Copyright Societies (#02404)
♦ CCLAT – Convention-cadre de l'OMS pour la lutte antitabac (2003 treaty)
♦ **CCL** Caribbean Congress of Labour (#03480)
♦ **CCL** Center for Creative Leadership (#03638)
♦ **CCL** Commonwealth Countries League (#04320)
♦ **CCLEC** Caribbean Customs Law Enforcement Council (#03487)
♦ CCLEF / see Commonwealth Girls Education Fund (#04334)
♦ **CCLP Worldwide** Chamber of Computer Logistics People Worldwide (#03847)
♦ **CCMA** Comité consultatif mondial des Amis (#10004)
♦ CCMC / see ACCESS Facility (#00048)
♦ CCM – Centre de coopération maritime de la CCI (see: #12534)
♦ **CCM** Centre for Cooperation in the Mediterranean (#03734)
♦ CCM – Comitato Collaboriazione Medica (internationally oriented national body)
♦ **CCM** Consejo Cultural Mundial (#04705)
♦ CCM – Convention on Cluster Munitions (2008 treaty)
♦ **CCME** Churches' Commission for Migrants in Europe (#03912)
♦ CCMI – Central Caribbean Marine Institute (internationally oriented national body)
♦ **CCMI** Commission consultative des mutations industrielles (#04763)
♦ CCMRG – Commonwealth Consultative Group on Mineral Resources and Geology (inactive)
♦ CCMS / see Caribbean Centre for Money and Finance (#03469)
♦ CCM – Senter for Konflikthåndtering, Oslo / see Centre for Peacebuilding and Conflict Management, Oslo
♦ CCMWE / see Churches' Commission for Migrants in Europe (#03912)
♦ CCNA / see Euro Atlantic Partnership Council (#05646)
♦ **CCNAPC** Caribbean Coalition of National AIDS Programme Coordinator (#03473)
♦ CCN – Coastal Conservation Network (internationally oriented national body)
♦ CCN – Communauté du chemin neuf (internationally oriented national body)
♦ CCN – Community of the Cross of Nails (internationally oriented national body)
♦ CCN – Conservation Council of Nations (internationally oriented national body)
♦ CCNI – Commission de coopération notariale internationale (see: #15795)
♦ **CCNR** Central Commission for the Navigation of the Rhine (#03687)
♦ **CCNR** Commission centrale pour la navigation du Rhin (#03687)
♦ CCNSS / see International Federation of Social Science Organizations (#13543)
♦ CCNUCC – Convention-cadre des Nations Unies sur les changements climatiques (1992 treaty)
♦ **CCNUCC** Convention-cadre des nations unies sur les changements climatiques – Secrétariat (#20564)
♦ CCODP / see Development and Peace
♦ CCODP – Development and Peace (internationally oriented national body)
♦ CCOIC / see China International Economic and Trade Arbitration Commission
♦ CCOOACAL – Comisión Coordinadora de Organizaciones de Obreros Agricolas y Campesinos de América Latina (inactive)
♦ CCO – Osho International – Centre for Consciousness in Organizations (see: #17904)
♦ **CCOP** Coordinating Committee for Geoscience Programmes in East and Southeast Asia (#04816)
♦ **CCOS** Caribbean College of Surgeons (#03475)
♦ CCP / see Conflict Analysis Research Centre
♦ CCPA – Commonwealth Conference of Postal Administrations (meeting series)
♦ CCPAL / see Alliance of Presbyterian and Reformed Churches in Latin America (#00713)
♦ CCPAU / see Pan-African Citizens Network (#18044)
♦ CCP – Centre for the Contemporary Pacific (internationally oriented national body)
♦ **CCPCJ** United Nations Commission on Crime Prevention and Criminal Justice (#20530)
♦ **CCP** Comisión Centroamericana Permanente para la Erradicación de la Producción, Trafico, Consumo y Uso Ilicitos de Estupefacientes y Sustancias Psicotrópicas (#04130)
♦ **CCP** Commission de consolidation de la paix (#20606)
♦ CCP – Conférence chrétienne pour la paix (inactive)
♦ CCP – Conferencia Cristiana por la Paz (inactive)
♦ **CCPE** Conseil consultatif de procureurs européens (#04685)
♦ CCPF / see Confederation of European Forest Owners (#04525)
♦ CCPIT – China Council for the Promotion of International Trade (internationally oriented national body)
♦ CCP – Johns Hopkins University Center for Communications Programs (internationally oriented national body)
♦ CCPMO – Comité de Coordinación de los Puertos del Mediterraneo Nord-Occidental (inactive)
♦ **CCPO** Council of Catholic Patriarchs of the Orient (#04875)
♦ **CCPR** Human Rights Committee (#10979)
♦ CCPS – Center for Chemical Process Safety (internationally oriented national body)
♦ **CCPSI** Conseil consultatif professionnel et scientifique international du Programme des Nations Unies pour la prévention du crime et de la justice (#14810)
♦ **CCPT Association** Association of the Compendium of Cultural Policies and Trends (#02442)
♦ **CCPVJ** Coalición Centroamericana para la Prevención de la Violencia Juvenil (#04043)
♦ CCRA / see United Cities and Local Governments of Africa (#20500)
♦ CCR – Canadian Council for Refugees (internationally oriented national body)
♦ **CCR** Centrale Commissie voor de Rijnvaart (#03687)
♦ **CCR** Centre commun de recherche (#16147)
♦ CCR – Centre for Conflict Resolution, Bradford (internationally oriented national body)
♦ CCR – Centre for Conflict Resolution, Cape Town (internationally oriented national body)
♦ **CCR** Centro Comune de Ricerca (#16147)
♦ CCRDA – Consortium of Christian Relief and Development Association (internationally oriented national body)
♦ **CCRE** Conseil des communes et régions d'Europe (#04891)
♦ **CCREEE** Caribbean Centre for Renewable Energy and Energy Efficiency (#03470)
♦ CCRF / see Caritas Australia
♦ **CCRI** Coalition for Climate Resilient Investment (#04054)
♦ CCRRMM – Ordo Clericorum Regularium Minorum (religious order)
♦ CCR-S / see South West Waters Advisory Council (#19896)
♦ CCSA – Carbon Capture and Storage Association (unconfirmed)
♦ CCSBSIF / see Consejo Centroamericano de Superintendentes de Bancos, de Seguros y de Otras Instituciones Financieras (#04704)
♦ **CCSBSO** Consejo Centroamericano de Superintendentes de Bancos, de Seguros y de Otras Instituciones Financieras (#04704)
♦ **CCSBT** Commission for the Conservation of Southern Bluefin Tuna (#04207)
♦ **CCS** Caribbean Cardiac Society (#03467)
♦ CCS – Centre for Conflict Studies, Marburg (internationally oriented national body)
♦ **CCS** Conseil des chefs de secrétariat des organismes des Nations Unies (#20636)
♦ **CCS** Council of Commonwealth Societies (#04878)
♦ **CCSCS** Coordinadora de Centrales Sindicales del Cono Sur (#04805)
♦ **CCSDS** Consultative Committee for Space Data Systems (#04764)
♦ CCSEAS – Canadian Council for Southeast Asian Studies (internationally oriented national body)
♦ CCSEM / see Ettore Majorana Centre for Scientific Culture
♦ CCS – ICC Commercial Crime Services (see: #12534)
♦ CCSP – Centro Camuno di Studi Preistorici (internationally oriented national body)
♦ **CCST** Caribbean Council for Science and Technology (#03485)
♦ **CC SUD** Conseil Consultatif des Eaux Occidentales Australes (#19896)
♦ **CC SUL** Conselho Consultivo para as Águas Ocidentais Austrais (#19896)
♦ **CC SUR** Consejo Consultivo para las Aguas Occidentales Australes (#19896)
♦ **CCSVI** Comité Coordinador del Servicio Voluntario Internacional (#04819)
♦ **CCSVI** Comité de coordination du service volontaire international (#04819)
♦ **CCTA** Collagen Casings Trade Association (#04102)
♦ CCTA – Commission de coopération technique en Afrique au Sud du Sahara (inactive)
♦ **CCTC** Consumer Culture Theory Consortium (#04771)
♦ CCT – Centro Científico Tropical, Costa Rica (internationally oriented national body)
♦ CCT – Confederación Centroamericana de Trabajadores (inactive)
♦ **CCT** Confrérie des Chevaliers du Tastevin (#04661)
♦ **CCT** Consejo Centroamericano de Turismo (#03675)
♦ CCTI – Conseil central du tourisme international (inactive)
♦ CCTR / see Fédération européenne des retraités et des personnes âgées (#09580)
♦ CCTST / see Coordinating Council on Trans-Siberian Transportation (#04821)
♦ CCTT / see Coordinating Council on Trans-Siberian Transportation (#04821)
♦ **CCTT** Coordinating Council on Trans-Siberian Transportation (#04821)
♦ CCU – Circumpolar Conservation Union (internationally oriented national body)
♦ CCULAS – Centre for Canadian, US and Latin American Studies, Delhi (internationally oriented national body)
♦ CCVAH – Consejo Centroamericano de Vivienda y Asentamientos Humanos (inactive)
♦ CCV – Congregacion Hermanas Carmelitas de la Caridad, Vedruna (religious order)
♦ CCV – Convention Internationale Relative au Contrat de Voyage (1970 treaty)
♦ **CCW** Consumer Co-operatives Worldwide (#04770)
♦ CCW – Convention on Prohibitions or Restrictions on the Use of Certain Conventional Weapons Which May be Deemed to be Excessively Injurious or to Have Indiscriminate Effects, with Annexed Protocols (1980 treaty)
♦ CCW – Corpus Christi Watershed (unconfirmed)
♦ CC-WFSRC / see World Futures Studies Federation (#21535)
♦ CCyDEL / see Centro de Investigaciones sobre América y el Caribe (#03810)
♦ **CDAA** Communauté de développement de l'Afrique australe (#19843)
♦ CDAA – Copper Development Association Africa (internationally oriented national body)
♦ **CDA** Caribbean Dermatology Association (#03490)
♦ CDA – Church Development and Aid (internationally oriented national body)
♦ **CDAC Network** Communicating with Disaster Affected Communities Network (#04379)
♦ **CDA** Commonwealth Dental Association (#04321)
♦ CDA Foundation for International Solidarity – Eduardo Frei / see Eduardo Frei Foundation
♦ **CDAP** Centre de développement pour l'Asie et le Pacifique (#01608)
♦ CDAS / see Institute for the Study of International Development
♦ **CDB** Caribbean Development Bank (#03492)
♦ CDC / see PYXERA Global
♦ CDC / see CDC Group
♦ **CDC** Cairo Demographic Centre (#03396)
♦ CDC / see Caribbean Knowledge Management Centre (#03521)
♦ CDC Development Solutions / see PYXERA Global
♦ **CDCF** Community Development Carbon Fund (#04395)
♦ CDC Group (internationally oriented national body)
♦ **CDCJ** Comité européen de coopération juridique (#06655)
♦ **CD** Commission du Danube (#04210)
♦ **CD** Community of Democracies (#04394)
♦ **CD** Conference on Disarmament (#04590)
♦ **CD** Corps diplomatique (#05089)
♦ CDCoSEA / see International Copper Association Southeast Asia
♦ CDCS / see European Committee on Social Cohesion, Human Dignity and Equality (#06667)
♦ CDD / see Catholics for Choice (#03609)
♦ **CDD** Católicas por el Derecho a Decidir (#03612)

♦ CDD – Commission du développement durable des Nations Unies (inactive)
♦ **CdD** Comunidad de las Democracias (#04394)
♦ **CDDECS** European Committee on Social Cohesion, Human Dignity and Equality (#06667)
♦ CDDF Africa – Community Directed Development Foundation (internationally oriented national body)
♦ **CDDF** Cancer Drug Development Forum (#03413)
♦ CDE – Centre for the Development of Enterprise (inactive)
♦ CDE – Centre for Development and Environment, Bern (internationally oriented national body)
♦ CDE – Commission on Development and Exchanges (see: #14121)
♦ CDEG – Comité directeur pour l'égalité entre les femmes et les hommes (inactive)
♦ CDELI – Centro de Dokumentado kaj Esploro pri la Lingvo Internacia (internationally oriented national body)
♦ **CDEMA** Caribbean Disaster Emergency Management Agency (#03493)
♦ CDERA / see Caribbean Disaster Emergency Management Agency (#03493)
♦ CDESCO – Centro Latinoamericano para el Desarrollo y la Comunicación Participativa (internationally oriented national body)
♦ **CDF** CARICOM Development Fund (#03572)
♦ **CDF** Charles Darwin Foundation for the Galapagos Islands (#03852)
♦ CDFI – Christian Democrat Feminine International (inactive)
♦ CDH International (internationally oriented national body)
♦ CDH International – A global initiative to stop Congenital Diaphragmatic Hernia / see CDH International
♦ CDHR – Coalition for the Defense of Human Rights (internationally oriented national body)
♦ **CDIA** Cities Development Initiative for Asia (#03953)
♦ CDI-Bwamanda – Centre de Développement Intégral de Bwamanda (internationally oriented national body)
♦ CDI-Bwamanda – Centrum voor Dorpsintegratie Bwamanda-België (internationally oriented national body)
♦ CDI – Centre for Democratic Institutions (internationally oriented national body)
♦ CDI / see Centrist Democrat International (#03792)
♦ **CDI** Centrist Democrat International (#03792)
♦ CDI / see Cobalt Institute (#04076)
♦ **CDI** Commission du droit international (#14004)
♦ CDI – Community Development International (internationally oriented national body)
♦ **CDI** Conférence douanière inter-caraïbe (#03487)
♦ CDIDD – Centre de droit international du développement durable (internationally oriented national body)
♦ CDIDS – Centro de Derecho Internacional del Desarrollo Sostenible (internationally oriented national body)
♦ CDIL – Center for Development of International Law, New York (internationally oriented national body)
♦ CD – International Conference on Chiroptical Spectroscopy (meeting series)

♦ CDISC 03620

CEO 401 West 15th St, Ste 800, Austin TX 78701, USA.
URL: http://www.cdisc.org/

History Full title: *Clinical Data Interchange Standards Consortium (CDISC)*. Registered in accordance with US law. **Aims** Develop data standards to streamline clinical research and enable connections to healthcare. **Structure** Advisory Council; Board of Directors. **Activities** Healthcare; research and development; standards/guidelines; training/education. **Events** *Europe Interchange Meeting* Austin, TX (USA) 2021, *Europe Interchange Meeting* Berlin (Germany) 2020, *Europe Interchange Meeting* Amsterdam (Netherlands) 2019, *Europe Interchange Meeting* Berlin (Germany) 2018, *Europe Interchange Meeting* London (UK) 2016. **Publications** *CDISC Newsletter*. **Members** Organizations. Membership countries not specified. [2017/XM6072/**C**]

♦ CDISS – Centre for Defence and International Security Studies (internationally oriented national body)
♦ **CDKN** Climate and Development Knowledge Network (#04012)
♦ CDL / see Association européenne des métaux (#02578)
♦ CDLS World – International Federation of National CdLS Support Organizations (unconfirmed)
♦ CDMAC / see Asian Mycological Association (#01545)
♦ **CDN** Cooperation and Development Network Eastern Europe (#04794)
♦ CDNEE / see Cooperation and Development Network Eastern Europe (#04794)
♦ **CDNLAO** Conference of Directors of National Libraries in Asia and Oceania (#04588)
♦ **CDNL** Conference of Directors of National Libraries (#04587)
♦ CDO – Compagnia delle Opere (internationally oriented national body)

♦ CDP 03621

CEO Plantation Place South, 60 Great Tower Street, 4th Floor, London, EC3R 5AD, UK. T. +442038183900.
Global Head of Communications address not obtained.
Exec Dir c/o WeWork, Potsdamer Platz – Kemperplatz 1, 10785 Berlin, Germany. T. +4930629033100. E-mail: cdpeurope@cdp.net.
URL: http://www.cdp.net/

History 4 Dec 2000, London (UK). Founded as a coalition of institutional investors. Former names and other names: *Carbon Disclosure Project (CDP)* – former; *CDP – Driving Sustainable Economies* – full title; *CDP Worldwide* – alias. Registration: Charity Commission, No/ID: 1122330, England and Wales; Companies House, No/ID: 05013650, England and Wales. **Aims** Help *investors* improve their understanding of *climate change risks* and opportunities; encourage development of a common *carbon dioxide emissions measurement* methodology; facilitate its integration into general investment analysis. **Structure** Board; Trustees; Advisors. Offices: Europe; Americas; Asia-Pacific; Middle East and Africa. **Activities** Events/meetings. **Events** *Supply Chain Asia Summit* Tokyo (Japan) 2017, *Meeting on CDP Japan 500 Climate Change Report 2013* Tokyo (Japan) 2013. **Consultative Status** Consultative status granted from: *ECOSOC (#05331)* (Special); *UNEP (#20299)*. **IGO Relations** *Global Alliances for Water and Climate (GAfWaC, #10230)*. **NGO Relations** Member of (13): *Alliance for Water Stewardship (AWS, #00727)*; *Cities Climate Finance Leadership Alliance (CCFLA, #03952)*; *Climate and Clean Air Coalition (CCAC, #04010)*; *Climate Bonds Initiative (#04006)*; *European Public Real Estate Association (EPRA, #08301)*; *Global Commons Alliance*; *International Centre for Earth Simulation (ICES Foundation)*; *Natural Capital Coalition (NCC, #16952)*; *ResponsibleSteel (#18921)*; *Science Based Targets Network*; *United Nations Global Compact (#20567)*; *We Mean Business*; *World Benchmarking Alliance (WBA, #21228)*. Partner of (1): *Tropical Forest Alliance (TFA, #20249)*. Instrumental in setting up (2): *Business Alliance for Water and Climate (BAFWAC)*; *RE100*. [2022/XM1147/**F**]

♦ **CDPC** Comité européen pour les problèmes criminels (#06645)
♦ **CDPC** European Committee on Crime Problems (#06645)
♦ **CDPD** Comité sobre los Derechos de las Personas con Discapacidad (#04284)
♦ CDP – Driving Sustainable Economies / see CDP (#03621)
♦ CDPIAC – Centre de Politique Internationale et d'Analyse des Conflits (internationally oriented national body)
♦ CDPICC / see Centre de recherche en matière pénale – Fernand Boulan
♦ CDPR – Centre for Development Policy and Research, London (internationally oriented national body)
♦ **CDP** United Nations Committee for Development Policy (#20537)
♦ CDP Worldwide / see CDP (#03621)
♦ **CDRAV** Caribbean Coalition for Development and Reduction of Armed Violence (#03472)
♦ **CdR** Comité européen des régions (#06665)
♦ CDRIA – Centre de développement rural intégré pour l'Afrique (no recent information)
♦ **CDRIAP** Centre de développement rural intégré pour l'Asie et le Pacifique (#03750)
♦ CDRI – Coalition for Disaster Resilient Infrastructure (unconfirmed)
♦ CDRPC / see Observatoire des armements / CDRPC
♦ **CDRSEE** Center for Democracy and Reconciliation in Southeast Europe (#03639)
♦ CDS / see Unifob Global
♦ CDS / see PYXERA Global
♦ CDS / see Centre for Global Development, Leeds
♦ **CDSA** Content Delivery and Storage Association (#04779)
♦ CDS – Centre for Defence Studies (internationally oriented national body)
♦ CDS – Centre for Development Studies, Bath (internationally oriented national body)
♦ CDS – Centre for Development Studies, Groningen (internationally oriented national body)
♦ CDS – Centre for Development Studies, Trivandrum (internationally oriented national body)
♦ **CDS** Centre de données astronomiques de Strasbourg (#20003)
♦ CDS – Community Development Society (internationally oriented national body)
♦ CDSO – Commonwealth Defence Science Organization (inactive)
♦ CDSP – Comité européen de la santé (inactive)
♦ CDSR/AA / see ECA Subregional Office for Southern Africa (#05276)
♦ CDSR/AC / see ECA Sub-Regional Office for Central Africa (#05274)
♦ CDSR/AE / see ECA Sub-Regional Office for Eastern Africa (#05275)
♦ CDSR/AN / see ECA Office for North Africa (#05273)
♦ CDSR/AO / see ECA Sub-Regional Office for West Africa (#05277)
♦ CDSS / see Centre for Defence and Security Studies
♦ CDSS – Centre for Defence and Security Studies (internationally oriented national body)
♦ CDSSS – Center for Defence and Security Strategic Studies (internationally oriented national body)
♦ CDS Swansea – Centre for Development Studies, Swansea (internationally oriented national body)
♦ CDT – Center for Democracy and Technology (internationally oriented national body)
♦ **CdT** Centre de traduction des organes de l'Union européenne (#03790)
♦ CDTM – Centre de documentation Tiers-Monde, Montpellier (internationally oriented national body)
♦ CDTM – Centre de documentation Tiers-monde de Paris (internationally oriented national body)
♦ **CDU** Caribbean Democrat Union (#03489)
♦ CDUCE – Christian Democratic Union of Central Europe (inactive)
♦ CDUN / see Democracy Without Borders
♦ **CDWA** Christian Democratic Women of America (#03900)
♦ CDWU / see Centrist Democrat International (#03792)
♦ CEAA – Centre de Estudos Afro-Asiaticos (internationally oriented national body)
♦ CEAA – Centro de Estudios de Asia y Africa, México (internationally oriented national body)
♦ **CEAAL** Consejo de Educación de Adultos de América Latina (#04707)
♦ CEAAS / see European Sulphuric Acid Association (#08854)
♦ **CEABAD** Centro de Estudios Avanzados en Banda Ancha para el Desarrollo (#03797)
♦ **CEA/BSR-AC** CEA bureau sous-régional pour l'Afrique centrale (#05274)
♦ CEA/BSR-AC Yaoundé / see ECA Sub-Regional Office for Central Africa (#05274)
♦ CEA bureau sous-régional pour l'Afrique australe (#05276)
♦ CEA bureau sous-régional pour l'Afrique centrale (#05274)
♦ CEA bureau sous-régional pour l'Afrique de l'Est (#05275)
♦ CEA bureau sous-régional pour l'Afrique de l'Ouest (#05277)
♦ CEAC – Centro de Estudios Americanos y Caribeños (internationally oriented national body)
♦ **CEAC** Confédération Européenne des Anciens Combattants (#04537)
♦ **CEAC** Conférence européenne de l'aviation civile (#06564)
♦ CEAC – Council on East Asian Community (internationally oriented national body)
♦ CEA/CDSR-AA / see ECA Subregional Office for Southern Africa (#05276)
♦ CEA/CDSR-AC / see ECA Sub-Regional Office for Central Africa (#05274)
♦ CEA/CDSR-AE / see ECA Sub-Regional Office for Eastern Africa (#05275)
♦ CEA/CDSR-AN / see ECA Office for North Africa (#05273)
♦ CEA/CDSR-AO / see ECA Sub-Regional Office for West Africa (#05277)
♦ CEA Centre de développement sous-régional pour l'Afrique australe / see ECA Subregional Office for Southern Africa (#05276)
♦ CEA Centre de développement sous-régional pour l'Afrique central / see ECA Sub-Regional Office for Central Africa (#05274)
♦ CEA Centre de développement sous-régional pour l'Afrique de l'Est / see ECA Sub-Regional Office for Eastern Africa (#05275)
♦ CEA Centre de développement sous-régional pour l'Afrique du Nord / see ECA Office for North Africa (#05273)
♦ CEA Centre de développement sous-régional pour l'Afrique de l'Ouest / see ECA Sub-Regional Office for West Africa (#05277)
♦ CEA – Centre for Effective Altruism (unconfirmed)
♦ CEA – Centre d'études asiatiques (internationally oriented national body)
♦ CEA – Centre for European Affairs (internationally oriented national body)
♦ CEA – Centro di Ecologia Alpina (internationally oriented national body)
♦ CEA – Centro d'Estudis Africans, Barcelona (internationally oriented national body)
♦ CEA – Centro de Estudos Africanos, Maputo (internationally oriented national body)
♦ CEA – Centro de Estudos Africanos, São Paulo (internationally oriented national body)
♦ CEA CEPAL – Conferencia Estadística de las Américas (see: #20556)
♦ CEA – Cercle d'Ethique des Affaires (internationally oriented national body)
♦ **CEACM** Central European Association of Computational Mechanics (#03705)
♦ **CEA** Coalition pour l'Éléphant d'Afrique (#00296)
♦ **CEA** Commission économique des Nations Unies pour l'Afrique (#20554)
♦ **CEA** Confederación de Educadores Americanos (#04446)
♦ CEA – Confédération européenne de l'agriculture (inactive)
♦ **CEA** Cour européenne d'arbitrage (#06853)
♦ **CEACS** Central European Association for Canadian Studies (#03704)
♦ **CEADO** Central European Anti-Doping Organization (#03703)
♦ CEADS – Confédération européenne des activités en déchets spéciaux (inactive)
♦ CEAEO / see United Nations Economic and Social Commission for Asia and the Pacific (#20557)
♦ CEAf – Centre d'études africaines, Paris (internationally oriented national body)
♦ CEAF / see European Foundry Association, The (#07352)
♦ CEAIE – China Education Association for International Exchange (internationally oriented national body)
♦ CEA / see Insurance Europe (#11362)
♦ CEALB / see Groupe d'études latino-américaines de l'Institut de sociologie, Bruxelles
♦ **CEAL** Consejo Empresario de América Latina (#16261)
♦ CEAL – Council on East Asian Libraries (internationally oriented national body)
♦ CEAN / see Les Afriques dans le monde
♦ CEAO – Centro de Estudios sobre Asia y Oceania, Habana (internationally oriented national body)
♦ CEAO – Centro de Estudios de Asia Oriental, Madrid (internationally oriented national body)
♦ CEAO – Centro de Estudos Afro-Orientais, Bahia (internationally oriented national body)
♦ CEAO – Communauté économique de l'Afrique de l'Ouest (inactive)
♦ CEAO – Confédération des étudiants d'Afrique occidentale (inactive)
♦ CEAO / see United Nations Economic and Social Commission for Western Asia (#20558)
♦ CEAPAZ – Centro de Estudios y Acción para la Paz, Lima (internationally oriented national body)
♦ **CEA-PME** Confédération Européenne des Associations de Petites et Moyennes Entreprises (#06994)
♦ CEAR – Comisión Española de Ayuda al Refugiado (internationally oriented national body)
♦ CEART / see Joint ILO/UNESCO Committee of Experts on the Application of the Recommendations Concerning Teaching Personnel (#16132)
♦ **CEART** Joint ILO/UNESCO Committee of Experts on the Application of the Recommendations Concerning Teaching Personnel (#16132)
♦ CEASA / see Southern African Project Controls Institute
♦ CEAS – Center for East Asian Studies, Austin TX (internationally oriented national body)
♦ CEAS – Center for East Asian Studies, Lawrence KS (internationally oriented national body)

♦ CEAS – Center for Euro-Atlantic Studies (internationally oriented national body)
♦ CEAs – Centro de Estudos das Americas, Rio de Janeiro (internationally oriented national body)
♦ CEAS / see Council of European Aerospace Societies (#04882)
♦ **CEAS** Council of European Aerospace Societies (#04882)
♦ CEASEE – Camera Europea degli Arbitri Stragiudiziali e degli Esperti d'Europa (internationally oriented national body)
♦ **CEAT** Coordination européenne des Amis de la Terre Europe (#10001)
♦ CEATE / see Confederation of European Environmental Engineering Societies (#04524)
♦ **CEATL** Conseil européen des associations de traducteurs littéraires (#04686)
♦ CEATS Agreement – Agreement Relating to the Provision and Operation of Air Traffic Services and Facilities by EUROCONTROL at the Central European Air Traffic Services Upper Area Control Centre (1997 treaty)
♦ **CEATS** Central European Air Traffic Services (#03702)
♦ CEAU – Central European Association of Urology (no recent information)
♦ CEAUP – Centro de Estudos Africanos da Universidade do Porto (internationally oriented national body)
♦ CEB / see Council of Europe Development Bank (#04897)
♦ CEBA / see Confederation of European Baseball (#04518)
♦ **CEBA** Controlled Environment Building Association (#04783)
♦ **CEBAM** Centre biblique catholique pour l'Afrique et Madagascar (#03599)
♦ **CEBAM** Centro Biblico Católico para Africa e Madagascar (#03599)
♦ **CEB** Banque de développement du Conseil de l'Europe (#04897)
♦ CEBC – Central European Covered Bond Conference (meeting series)
♦ CEBC – Central European Craft Brewers Conference (meeting series)
♦ **CEBC** Consortium of European Building Control (#04739)
♦ CEB – Comité Euro-international du béton (inactive)
♦ CEB – Comité européen des constructeurs de brûleurs (inactive)
♦ CEB – Communauté électrique du Bénin (internationally oriented national body)
♦ **CEB** Confederation of European Baseball (#04518)
♦ **CEB** Confederation of European Biopathologists (#04520)
♦ **CEB** Confédération européenne de baseball (#04518)
♦ **CEB** Confédération Européenne de Billard (#04539)
♦ CEB / see Council of the Baltic Sea States (#04870)
♦ **CEB** Council of Europe Development Bank (#04897)
♦ CEBI – Comité européen des bureaux d'ingénierie (inactive)
♦ **CeBiPE** Information Centre for Bilingual and Plurilingual Education (#11195)
♦ CEBP / see European Confederation of National Bakery and Confectionery Organizations (#06714)
♦ **CEBP** European Confederation of National Bakery and Confectionery Organizations (#06714)
♦ **CEBRA** Central Bank Research Association (#03686)
♦ **CEBR** Council of European BioRegions (#04883)
♦ CEBS – Committee of European Banking Supervisors (inactive)
♦ CEBSD / see European Community Development Network (#06679)
♦ **CEBTS** Consortium of European Baptists Theological Schools (#04738)
♦ CEB / see United Nations System Chief Executives Board for Coordination (#20636)
♦ **CEB** United Nations System Chief Executives Board for Coordination (#20636)
♦ CEC / see Euro-Toques International (#09190)
♦ CECA – Committee of European Coffee Associations (inactive)
♦ CECA – Communauté européenne du charbon et de l'acier (inactive)
♦ CECA – Comunidade Européia do Carvão e do Aço (inactive)
♦ CECA – Comunidad Europea del Carbón y del Acero (inactive)
♦ CECA – Comunità Europea del Carbone e dell'Acciaio (inactive)
♦ CECADI – Centro de Capacitación a Distancia (see: #11434)
♦ CECAFA – Council for East and Central Africa Football Associations (unconfirmed)
♦ **CECAF** Fishery Committee for the Eastern Central Atlantic (#09784)
♦ CECA – ICOM International Committee for Education and Cultural Action (see: #13051)
♦ CECAL – Centre d'échanges et coopération pour l'Amérique latine (internationally oriented national body)
♦ **CECAM** Centre Européen de Calcul Atomique et Moléculaire (#06471)
♦ **CECAPI** Comité européen des constructeurs d'appareillage électrique d'installation (#06646)
♦ **CECAPI** European Committee of Electrical Installation Equipment Manufacturers (#06646)
♦ CECAT – Centro de Estudios de Construcción y Arquitectura Tropical (internationally oriented national body)
♦ CECATEC-RD – Central America – Dominican Republic Apparel and Textile Council (unconfirmed)
♦ CECAVI – Confédération européenne des catégories auxiliaires des activités viti-vinicole (inactive)
♦ CECB – Conseil européen du cuir brut (inactive)
♦ **CEC** Caribbean Employers' Confederation (#03495)
♦ CECC – Central European Conference on Cryptology (meeting series)
♦ CECC – Commonwealth Economic Consultative Council (inactive)
♦ CECC – Communauté européenne de crédit communal (inactive)
♦ **CECC** Conference of European Constitutional Courts (#04594)
♦ **CECC** Coordinación Educativa y Cultural Centroamericana (#04803)
♦ CEC / see CEC European Managers (#03623)
♦ **CEC** Centre européen de la culture (#06472)

♦ Cecchetti International – Classical Ballet (CICB) 03622

Sec 39 Cold Spring Drive, Bloomfield CT 06022, USA. E-mail: secretary@cicb.org.
URL: http://www.cicb.org/

History 1997, to honour the work of ballet dancer and teacher Enrico Cecchetti (1850-1928). Registered in accordance with Canadian law. **Aims** Promote and expand the Cecchetti ballet method of classical ballet. **Structure** Officers: Chair; Vice-Chair; Secretary; Treasurer; Book Keeper. **Languages** English, French, Italian. **Staff** 5.00 FTE, paid.
Members National organizations (7) in 6 countries:
Australia, Canada, Italy, South Africa, UK, USA. [2017.03.09/XM0082/**E**]

♦ **CECCM** Confederation of European Community Cigarette Manufacturers (#04521)
♦ CEC – Collège européen des chirurgiens (inactive)
♦ **CEC** Comité européen de coordination (#04153)
♦ **CEC** Commission for Environmental Cooperation (#04211)
♦ **CEC** Commonwealth Engineers Council (#04324)
♦ **CEC** Confédération européenne des cadres (#03623)
♦ **CEC** Confédération Européenne de l'Industrie de la Chaussure (#04544)
♦ **CEC** Conference of European Churches (#04593)
♦ **CEC** Congregation for Catholic Education – for Seminaries and Educational Institutions (#04665)
♦ CEC – Conseil européen de l'enseignement par correspondance (inactive)
♦ CEC – Coopération par l'éducation et la culture (internationally oriented national body)
♦ CEC / see Coordinación Educativa y Cultural Centroamericana (#04803)
♦ **CEC** Coordinating European Council for the Development of Performance Tests for Transportation Fuels, Lubricants and Other Fluids (#04822)
♦ CEC – Council for Education in the Commonwealth (internationally oriented national body)
♦ CEC – Council for Exceptional Children (internationally oriented national body)
♦ CECD – Comité européen des chevaux de débardage (internationally oriented national body)
♦ CECD – Confédération européenne du commerce de détail (inactive)
♦ **CECDO** Council of European Chief Dental Officers (#04885)
♦ **CECE** Committee for European Construction Equipment (#04254)
♦ CECED / see APPLiA – Home Appliance Europe (#00877)

♦ **C and E** Cereals and Europe (#03829)
♦ CEC / see European Commission (#06633)

♦ CEC European Managers 03623

Confédération européenne des cadres (CEC)

Pres CEC European Secretariat, Rue de la Loi 81a, 1040 Brussels, Belgium. T. +3224201051. E-mail: info@cec-managers.org.
URL: http://www.cec-managers.org/

History 25 Nov 1950, Paris (France). Constituent Congress: 22-23 Sep 1951, Rome (Italy). Former names and other names: *Confédération internationale des cadres (CIC)* – former; *European Confederation of Executives and Managerial Staff (CEC)* – former. Registration: Start date: 26 Dec 1989, France; Banque Carrefour des Entreprises, No/ID: 0474.274.966, Start date: 15 Mar 2001, Belgium; EU Transparency Register, No/ID: 10426402966-04, Start date: 7 Jan 2010. **Aims** Represent managers and managerial staff in Europe. **Structure** General Assembly; Advisory Committee; Executive Board; Standing Committees (2); Ad-hoc Working Groups; European Secretariat. **Languages** English, French. **Staff** 2.50 FTE, paid. **Finance** Sources: members' dues. **Activities** Events/meetings; politics/policy/regulatory. **Events** *Triennial Congress* Mainz (Germany) 2018, *General Assembly and Seminar* Stockholm (Sweden) 2017, *Triennial Congress* Lisbon (Portugal) 2015, *Conference* Cannes (France) 2014, *Conference* Madrid (Spain) 2013. **Publications** *CEC Newsletter* (4 a year); *CEC Activity Report* (every 2 years).
Members National organizations in 15 countries:
Belgium, Denmark, France, Germany, Greece, Italy, Montenegro, Norway, Portugal, Serbia, Slovenia, Spain, Sweden, Switzerland, UK.
European professional federations (8), listed in this Yearbook:
Association Européenne des Cadres de l'Assurance (AECA, #02556); European Federation for Managers in Technologies of Information and Communication (eTIC-CEC, #07163); European Federation of Managerial Staff in the Chemical and Allied Industries (FECCIA, #07160); European Federation of Managers in the Banking Sector (#07161); European Federation of Managers in the Steel Industry (#07162); European Managers in the Transport Industry (#07730); Fédération européenne des cadres de la construction (FECC, #09561); Fédération européenne des cadres de l'énergie et de la recherche (FECER, #09562). [2021.03.03/XD1664/y/**D**]

♦ CECG – Confédération européenne du commerce de la chaussure en gros (inactive)
♦ CECHE – Center for Communications, Health and the Environment (internationally oriented national body)
♦ CECI – Canadian Centre for International Studies and Cooperation (internationally oriented national body)
♦ **CECICN** Conference of European Cross-border and Interregional Cities Network (#04595)
♦ CECID – Centre d'études de la coopération internationale et du développement (internationally oriented national body)
♦ **CECIF** Centre européen du Conseil international des femmes (#06485)
♦ CECIMO / see European Association of the Machine tool Industries and related Manufacturing Technologies (#06113)
♦ **CECIMO** European Association of the Machine tool Industries and related Manufacturing Technologies (#06113)
♦ CECIOS / see European Management Association (#07729)
♦ **CECIP** Comité européen des constructeurs d'instruments de pesage (#04151)
♦ **CECJ** Conseil européen des communautés juives (#06825)
♦ **CeCLAD-M** Centre de coordination pour la lutte anti-drogue en Méditerranée (#03737)
♦ CECL – Centre for European Constitutional Law – Themistokles and Dimitris Tsatsos Foundation (internationally oriented national body)
♦ **CECM** Convention européenne de la construction métallique (#06779)
♦ CECOB – Centro per l'Europa Centro-Orientale e Balcanica (internationally oriented national body)
♦ CECO – Caspian Economic Cooperation Organization (unconfirmed)
♦ **CECOD** Comité de fabricants européens d'installations et de distribution de pétrole (#04167)
♦ CECODEC – Conseil européen des constructeurs de cuisine (no recent information)
♦ CECODE – Centre européen du commerce de détail (inactive)
♦ CECODHAS / see Housing Europe – The European Federation for Public Cooperative and Social Housing (#10956)
♦ CECOF / see The European Committee of Industrial Furnace, Heating and Metallurgical Equipment Associations (#06653)
♦ **CECOF** The European Committee of Industrial Furnace, Heating and Metallurgical Equipment Associations (#06653)
♦ **CECOG** Central European Cooperative Oncology Group (#03706)
♦ CECOMA – Confédération européenne des commerces de mobilier, machines de bureau et accessoires (inactive)
♦ CECOMAF – Comité européen des constructeurs de matériel frigorifique (inactive)
♦ CECOMM – Conference of the European Communications Museums (internationally oriented national body)
♦ CE – Communautés européennes (inactive)
♦ CE – Comunidades Europeas (inactive)
♦ CE – Comunidades Européias (inactive)
♦ CE – Comunità Europee (inactive)
♦ **CE** Conseil de l'Entente (#05491)
♦ **CE** Conseil de l'Europe (#04881)
♦ CECOP / see Confédération européenne des coopératives de travail associé, des coopératives sociales et des entreprises sociales et participatives (#04541)
♦ **CECOP** Confédération européenne des coopératives de travail associé, des coopératives sociales et des entreprises sociales et participatives (#04541)
♦ **CE** Council of Europe (#04881)
♦ CE / see Counterpart Global Network (#04927)
♦ CECPA – Comité européen du commerce des produits amylacés et dérivés (inactive)
♦ **CECPC-CICPC** Consejo de las Asociaciones Profesionales de Ingenieros Civiles de Lengua Oficial Portuguesa y Castellana (#04702)
♦ **CECPC-CICPC** Conselho das Associações Profissionais De Engenheiros Civis dos Paises de Lingua Oficial Portuguesa e Castelhana (#04702)
♦ CECP – Central European Conference on Photochemistry (meeting series)
♦ CECPI / see European Inland Fisheries and Aquaculture Advisory Commission (#07540)
♦ **CE-CPLP** Confederação Empresarial da Comunidade dos Paises de Lingua Portuguesa (#04435)
♦ **CECRA** Conseil européen du commerce et de la réparation automobiles (#06832)
♦ CECRI – Centre d'études des crises et des conflits internationaux (internationally oriented national body)
♦ **CE** Cruise Europe (#04972)
♦ CECSO / see European Association for Coal and Lignite (#05978)
♦ CECT – Comité européen de la chaudronnerie et de la tuyauterie (no recent information)
♦ **CECUA** Confederation of European Computer User Associations (#04523)
♦ CECV – Centre européen de la colonne vertébrale (internationally oriented national body)
♦ CED / see Cercle d'Ethique des Affaires
♦ CEDA / see Caribbean Export Development Agency (#03501)
♦ **CEDA** Central Dredging Association (#03688)
♦ **CEDAG** Comité européen des associations d'intérêt général (#06834)
♦ CEDAM International (internationally oriented national body)
♦ **CEDARE** Centre for Environment and Development for the Arab Region and Europe (#03738)
♦ **CEDAR** European Muslim Professionals Network (#07840)
♦ CEDAR Fund (internationally oriented national body)
♦ **CEDAW** Committee on the Elimination of Discrimination against Women (#04250)
♦ CEDAW – Convention on the Elimination of all Forms of Discrimination Against Women (1979 treaty)

- ♦ CEDAW-OP – Optional Protocol to the Convention on the Elimination of all Forms of Discrimination Against Women (1999 treaty)
- ♦ CED / see Centre for Research and Documentation on World Language Problems (#03780)
- ♦ **CeD** Centre for Research and Documentation on World Language Problems (#03780)
- ♦ **CED** Centro de Esploro kaj Dokumentado pri Mondaj Lingvaj Problemoj (#03780)
- ♦ CED – Centrul Euroregional pentru Democratie (internationally oriented national body)
- ♦ CED – Christian Engineers in Development (internationally oriented national body)
- ♦ CED – Committee for Economic Development (internationally oriented national body)
- ♦ **CED** Committee on Enforced Disappearances (#04252)
- ♦ CED – Communauté européenne de défense (inactive)
- ♦ CED – Confédération européenne de la droguerie (inactive)
- ♦ **CED** Council of European Dentists (#04886)
- ♦ CEDDEC – Confédération européenne des associations de détaillants en chaussures (inactive)
- ♦ **CEDEAO** Communauté économique des Etats de l'Afrique de l'Ouest (#05312)
- ♦ CEDEC – Centre européen de documentation et de compensation (inactive)
- ♦ CEDEC – Centro de Estudos de Cultura Contemporânea (internationally oriented national body)
- ♦ CEDECE / see Association Française d'Études Européennes
- ♦ CEDEC / see European Federation of Local Energy Companies (#07156)
- ♦ **CEDEC** European Federation of Local Energy Companies (#07156)
- ♦ **CEDE** Club européen des diététiciens de l'enfance (#06583)
- ♦ CEDE – Conseil européen du droit de l'environnement (no recent information)
- ♦ **Cedefop** Centre européen pour le développement de la formation professionnelle (#06474)
- ♦ **Cedefop** European Centre for the Development of Vocational Training (#06474)
- ♦ CEDEG – Centre européen de documentation et d'études gérontologiques (inactive)
- ♦ CEDEGE – Communauté européenne des étudiants en sciences économiques (inactive)
- ♦ CEDEI – Centro de Estudios Interamericanos (internationally oriented national body)
- ♦ CEDEM – Centre d'étude de l'ethnicité et des migrations (internationally oriented national body)
- ♦ CEDEPCA – Centro Evangélico de Estudios Pastorales en Centro América (internationally oriented national body)
- ♦ **CEDEP** Comité européen – droit, éthique et psychiatrie (#04154)
- ♦ **CeDePesca** Centro Desarrollo y Pesca Sustenable (#03796)
- ♦ CEDEP / see European Centre for Executive Development (#06479)
- ♦ **CEDEP** European Centre for Executive Development (#06479)
- ♦ CEDES – Centro de Estudios de Estado y Sociedad, Buenos Aires (internationally oriented national body)
- ♦ CEDETIM – Centre d'études et initiatives de solidarité internationale (internationally oriented national body)
- ♦ CEDHA – Centro de Derechos Humanos y Ambiente (internationally oriented national body)
- ♦ CEDHAL – Centro de Estudios de Demografia Histórica de América Latina (internationally oriented national body)
- ♦ CEDHU – Comisión Ecuménica de Derechos Humanos (internationally oriented national body)
- ♦ **CEDIA** Confédération européenne des associations d'ingénieurs agronomes (#04538)
- ♦ CEDIA – Custom Electronic Design and Installation Association (internationally oriented national body)
- ♦ **CED-IADR** Continental European Division of the International Association for Dental Research (#04780)
- ♦ **CEDI** Confédération européenne des indépendants (#06080)
- ♦ CEDIDELP – Centre de documentation internationale pour le développement, les libertés et la paix (internationally oriented national body)
- ♦ **CEDIGAZ** Centre international d'information sur le gaz naturel et tous hydrocarbures gazeux (#13845)
- ♦ CEDIM – Comité européen des fédérations nationales de la maroquinerie, articles de voyages et industries connexes (inactive)
- ♦ CEDIMES – Centre d'études de développement international et des mouvements économiques et sociaux (internationally oriented national body)
- ♦ CEDIME-SE – Centre for Documentation and Information on Minorities in Europe-Southeast Europe (internationally oriented national body)
- ♦ CEDIMOM – Centre européen pour le développement industriel et la mise en valeur de l'outre-mer (inactive)
- ♦ **CEDIP** European Committee of Professional Diving Instructors (#06663)
- ♦ **CEDITH** Cercle Euro-Mediterranean des Dirigeants du Textile, de l'Habillement et des Industries de la mode (#03828)
- ♦ **CEDIVI** Confédération européenne des distilleries vinicoles (#04542)
- ♦ CEDLA – Centro de Estudios para el Desarrollo Laboral y Agrario (internationally oriented national body)
- ♦ CEDLA – Centro de Estudios y Documentación Latinoamericanos (internationally oriented national body)
- ♦ CEDOC-LI – Red de Centros de Documentación de Literatura Infantil y Juvenil (see: #17629)
- ♦ **CEDOI** Conférence épiscopale de l'Océan Indien (#04592)
- ♦ **CEDR** Comité Européen de Droit Rural (#04155)
- ♦ **CEDR** Conference of European Directors of Roads (#04603)
- ♦ **CEDR** Conférence Européenne des directeurs des routes (#04603)
- ♦ CEDRE – Centre de documentation de recherche et d'expérimentations sur les pollutions accidentelles des eaux (internationally oriented national body)
- ♦ CEDROMA – Centre d'études des droits du monde arabe (internationally oriented national body)
- ♦ **CEDT** Confédération européenne des détaillants en tabacs (#06725)
- ♦ CED – World Centre of Excellence for Destinations (internationally oriented national body)
- ♦ CEE / see Ocean Conservancy
- ♦ CEEAB – Central and East European Association of Bioethics (inactive)
- ♦ **CEEAC** Communauté économique des Etats de l'Afrique centrale (#05311)
- ♦ **CEEAC** Comunidad Económica de los Estados del Africa Central (#05311)
- ♦ **CEEAC** Comunidade Economica dos Estados da Africa Central (#05311)
- ♦ CEEA – Centre d'études euro-arabe, Paris (internationally oriented national body)
- ♦ CEEA – Confederation of European Economic Associations (inactive)
- ♦ CEEA – Conseil européen des études africaines (no recent information)
- ♦ CEEAMS – Central and Eastern European Association for Mission Studies (inactive)
- ♦ CEEAN / see International Danube Neurology Association of Central and East Europe (#13134)
- ♦ CEEAS – Centre for European and Euro-Atlantic Studies, Bucharest (internationally oriented national body)
- ♦ **CEEBA** Confederation of Egyptian European Business Associations (#04517)

♦ CEE Bankwatch Network 03624

Exec Dir Hermanova 1088/8, 170 00 Prague 7, Czechia. T. +420777995515. E-mail: main@bankwatch.org.
URL: http://www.bankwatch.org/

History 1995. Registration: EU Transparency Register, No/ID: 93834493808-49. **Aims** Monitor activities of international public finance institutions in central and eastern Europe and the Commonwealth of Independent States. **Structure** Members' Meeting; Executive Committee; Executive Director. **Finance** Sources: donations; grants. Annual budget: 2,400,000 EUR. URL: https://bankwatch.org/about/donors-finances **Activities** Advocacy/lobbying/activism; events/meetings; monitoring/evaluation; training/education. **Events** *Forum on making the EU Budget Work for People and Planet* Brussels (Belgium) 2013. **Publications** *Bankwatch Newsletter* (12 a year) – newsletter. Reports; briefings; policy letters; guidebooks.
Members Environmental organizations in 14 countries:
Bulgaria, Croatia, Czechia, Estonia, Georgia, Hungary, Latvia, Lithuania, North Macedonia, Poland, Russia, Serbia, Slovakia, Ukraine.

IGO Relations Accredited by (2): *Green Climate Fund (GCF, #10714); United Nations Framework Convention on Climate Change – Secretariat (UNFCCC, #20564).* **NGO Relations** Member of (7): *Friends of the Earth International (FoEI, #10002); Global Transparency Initiative (GTI, #10634); NGO Forum on ADB (#17123); SDG Watch Europe (#19162); Spring Alliance (inactive); The Green 10 (#10711); World Social Forum (WSF, #21797).* Supports (1): *Change Partnership.* Signatory to the 'Publish What You Pay' appeal of: *Publish What You Pay Coalition (PWYP, #18573).* Signatory to Founding Statement of: *Alliance for Lobbying Transparency and Ethics Regulation (ALTER-EU, #00705).* [2023.02.16/XF5785/**F**]

- ♦ **CEEB** Centre européen d'études bourguignonnes (#05960)
- ♦ **CEEBP** Fund for Central and East European Book Projects (#10040)
- ♦ **CEECA** Central and Eastern European Copyright Alliance (#03690)
- ♦ CEEC – Central and Eastern Europe Data Protection Authorities (unconfirmed)
- ♦ **CEEC** Comité Européen pour l'Enseignement Catholique (#04156)
- ♦ CEEC – Committee for European Economic Cooperation (inactive)
- ♦ **CEEC** Communion of Evangelical Episcopal Churches (#04385)
- ♦ **CEEC** Conférence européenne sur l'éducation chrétienne (#06732)
- ♦ **CEEC** Conseil européen des économistes de la construction (#06812)
- ♦ CEE – Centre d'études européennes, Lyon (internationally oriented national body)
- ♦ CEE – Centre d'études européennes, Paris (internationally oriented national body)
- ♦ CEE – Centro de Estudios Ecuménicos, México (internationally oriented national body)
- ♦ CEE – Centro de Estudios Europeos, Habana (internationally oriented national body)
- ♦ CEE – Centro de Estudios Europeos – Universidad de Navarra (internationally oriented national body)
- ♦ **CEE CN** Central and Eastern European Citizens Network (#03689)
- ♦ **CEE** Confédération européenne d'escrime (#07239)
- ♦ CEECSDA – Central and Eastern European Central Securities Depositories Association (inactive)
- ♦ CEEES / see Confederation of European Environmental Engineering Societies (#04524)
- ♦ **CEEES** Confederation of European Environmental Engineering Societies (#04524)
- ♦ **CEEF** Claims Conference Central and Eastern European Fund (#03976)
- ♦ **CEE Forum** Central and Eastern European Forum of Young Legal, Political and Social Theorists (#03691)
- ♦ **CEE Gender Network** Central and Eastern European Network for Gender Issues (#03695)
- ♦ **CEE GN** Central and Eastern European Genetic Network (#03692)
- ♦ CEEGS – Central and Eastern European Game Studies Conference (meeting series)
- ♦ CEEH – Confédération européenne pour l'emploi des handicapés (no recent information)
- ♦ CEEI / see Bruegel
- ♦ CEE / see IEC System of Conformity Assessment Schemes for Electrotechnical Equipment and Components (#11096)
- ♦ **CEEI** Réseau européen des centres européens d'entreprise et d'innovation (#06420)
- ♦ **CEEISA** Central and East European International Studies Association (#03700)
- ♦ CEELA / see Centro de Estudios Americanos y Caribeños
- ♦ CEELI / see Central and Eastern European Law Initiative (#03693)
- ♦ **CEELI** Central and Eastern European Law Initiative (#03693)
- ♦ CEEMA – Committee for Engineering Education of Middle Africa (inactive)
- ♦ **CEEMAN** CEEMAN – International Association for Management Development in Dynamic Societies (#03625)

♦ CEEMAN – International Association for Management Development in Dynamic Societies (CEEMAN) 03625

Pres Presernova cesta 33, 4260 Bled, Slovenia. T. +38645792505. Fax +38645792501. E-mail: info@ceeman.org.
Dir address not obtained.
URL: http://www.ceeman.org/

History 1993, Brdo (Slovenia). Originally also referred to as *Central and East European Management Development Network.* Subsequently changed title to *Central and East European Management Development Association.* Current title adopted following increased geographical expansion of membership. **Aims** Foster quality of management development; change processes through development of educational, research, consulting, information, networking support, and other related services for management development institutions and corporations operating in transition and dynamically changing environments. **Structure** General Assembly (annual); Board; Headquarters at *IEDC – Bled School of Management,* Bled (Slovenia). **Languages** English. **Staff** 3.00 FTE, paid. **Finance** Members' dues. Other sources: conference and seminar fees; grants; sponsorships. **Activities** Training/education; events/meetings; research/documentation; standards/guidelines; certification/accreditation. **Events** *Annual Conference* Almaty (Kazakhstan) 2023, *Program Management Seminar* Bled (Slovenia) 2023, *Program Management Seminar* Bled (Slovenia) 2022, *Understanding the Big Picture Surrounding the Future of Management Education* Bled (Slovenia) 2022, *Management Education at the Crossroads* Trieste (Italy) 2021. **Publications** Newsletters; conference proceedings; research and survey reports; books.
Members Institutional; Corporate; Honorary; Individual; Exchange. Members (217) in 54 countries:
Albania, Austria, Azerbaijan, Bahrain, Belarus, Belgium, Brazil, Bulgaria, Canada, China, Congo Brazzaville, Croatia, Czechia, Estonia, Finland, France, Georgia, Germany, Greece, Hungary, Iceland, India, Ireland, Italy, Kazakhstan, Kenya, Kyrgyzstan, Latvia, Lithuania, Malaysia, Mongolia, Netherlands, Norway, Oman, Pakistan, Peru, Philippines, Poland, Qatar, Romania, Russia, Serbia, Singapore, Slovenia, South Africa, Spain, Sweden, Switzerland, Tanzania UR, Türkiye, UK, Ukraine, USA, Zimbabwe.
Included in the above, 18 organizations listed in this Yearbook:
Academy of Business in Society (ABIS, #00032); Association of African Business Schools (AABS, #02351); Association of Management Development Institutions in South Asia (AMDISA, #02792); Baltic Management Development Association (BMDA, #03123); BMI Executive Institute (BMI, #03288); Central Asian Foundation for Management Development (CAMAN, #03682); EFMD – The Management Development Network (#05387); ESMT Berlin; European Academy of Management (EURAM, #05800); European Institute for Advanced Studies in Management (EIASM, #07544); European Retail Academy (ERA, #08386); IEDC – Bled School of Management; International Black Sea University (IBSU); International Management Institute, Kiev (IMI-Kiev); International Management Institute, St Petersburg (IMISP); Latin American Council of Business Schools (#16308); Moscow International Higher Business School (MIRBIS); Riga International School of Economics and Business Administration (RISEBA).
NGO Relations Member of: *European Quality Link (EQUAL, #08314).* Co-convenor and Steering Committee Member of: *Principles for Responsible Management Education (PRME, #18500).* Reciprocal membership with over 20 regional and international partner associations, not specified. [2023/XD3807/y/**D**]

- ♦ **CEEMET** Council of European Employers of the Metal, Engineering and Technology-Based Industries (#04887)
- ♦ CEENASWE – Central and Eastern European Network for the Academic Study of Western Esotericism (unconfirmed)
- ♦ CEENELS – Central and European Network of Legal Scholars (meeting series)
- ♦ CEENet – Central and Eastern European Networking Association (no recent information)
- ♦ **CEENQA** Central and Eastern European Network of Quality Assurance Agencies in Higher Education (#03696)
- ♦ CEEO / see Centro de Estudios Europeos, Habana
- ♦ CEEOA – Central and Eastern European Outsourcing Association (unconfirmed)
- ♦ **CEEOG** Central and East European Oncology Group (#03701)
- ♦ CEE-ONU / see United Nations Economic Commission for Europe (#20555)
- ♦ **CEE-ONU** Commission économique des Nations Unies pour l'Europe (#20555)
- ♦ **CEEO-UNASUR** Centro de Estudios sobre el Esoterismo Occidental de la Unión de Naciones Suramericanas (#03798)
- ♦ CEEPA – Centre for Environmental Economics and Policy in Africa (internationally oriented national body)
- ♦ CEEP – Central Europe Energy Partners (internationally oriented national body)
- ♦ **CEEP** Consortium européen sur l'économie du paysage (#04745)
- ♦ CEEPN – Central and Eastern European Privatization Network (no recent information)

- ♦ CEEP / see SGI Europe (#19253)
- ♦ CEEPUS – Central European Exchange Programme for University Students (internationally oriented national body)
- ♦ CEER – Corporation européenne des ébénistes restaurateurs (internationally oriented national body)
- ♦ **CEER** Council of European Energy Regulators (#04888)
- ♦ **CEEREAL** European Breakfast Cereal Association (#06399)
- ♦ **CEESA** Central and Eastern European Schools Association (#03697)
- ♦ **CEESA** Centre européen d'études pour la santé animale (#03745)
- ♦ CEESA – Conférence des associations européennes d'étudiants ingénieurs (inactive)
- ♦ CEES – Center for European and Eurasian Studies, Los Angeles (internationally oriented national body)
- ♦ **CEES** Centre européen d'études des silicates (#03746)
- ♦ CEES / see European Salt Producers Association (#08425)
- ♦ **CEESS** Central and Eastern European Stroke Society (#03698)
- ♦ CEESTAHC – Central And Eastern European Society Of Technology Assessment In Health Care (internationally oriented national body)
- ♦ **CEETB** Comité européen des équipements techniques du bâtiment (#08879)
- ♦ **CEETRA** Central and Eastern European Travel Retail Association (#03699)
- ♦ CEE Trust – Trust for Civil Society in Central and Eastern Europe (internationally oriented national body)
- ♦ **CEETTAR** Confédération européenne des entrepreneurs de travaux techniques agricoles, ruraux et forestiers (#08105)
- ♦ CEEUN – Central and Eastern European University Network (internationally oriented national body)
- ♦ **CEEV** Comité européen des entreprises vins (#04157)

♦ CEEweb for Biodiversity 03626

Gen Sec Széher ut 40, Budapest 1021, Hungary. T. +3613980135. Fax +3613980136. E-mail: office@ceeweb.org.
URL: http://www.ceeweb.org/

History Jan 1993. Founded with the support of the *European Union (EU, #08967)* and 2 Hungarian NGOs. Former names and other names: *Central and Eastern European Working Group for the Enhancement of Biodiversity (CEEweb for Biodiversity)* – former. **Aims** Identify and change drivers behind biodiversity loss; create common policies and action for enhancement of biodiversity in the Central and East European region; promote enforcement of international conventions for nature and biodiversity conservation, in particular the Convention on Biological Diversity; promote concept and strategies of *sustainable development* and contribute to their implementation; raise public awareness on the importance of biodiversity and its protection. **Structure** Advisory Committee; Working Groups; Board. **Languages** English. **Staff** 7.00 FTE, paid. **Finance** Supported by: *European Commission (EC, #06633)*; national organizations and foundations. **Activities** Advocacy/lobbying/activism; knowledge management/information exchange; capacity building; training/education. Management of treaties and agreements: *Convention on Biological Diversity (Biodiversity convention, 1992)*. **Events** *European Urban Green Infrastructure Conference* London (UK) 2019, *Conference on How People and the Economy Can Benefit from Nature* Brussels (Belgium) 2017, *European Urban Green Infrastructure Conference* Budapest (Hungary) 2017, *European Urban Green Infrastructure Conference* Vienna (Austria) 2015, *Meeting* Dobogókö (Hungary) 2011. **Publications** *Diversity* (14 a year) – newsletter. Conference reports; biennial reports; awareness raising publications.

Members National and regional organizations (64) in 18 countries:
Belarus, Bulgaria, Croatia, Czechia, Estonia, Germany, Hungary, Latvia, Lithuania, Moldova, Montenegro, North Macedonia, Poland, Romania, Serbia, Slovakia, Slovenia, Ukraine.

Included in the above, 5 organizations listed in this Yearbook:
BALKANI Wildlife Society (#03076); *Coalition Clean Baltic (CCB, #04053)*; *Ecological Tourism in Europe (ÖTE)*; *International Scientific Forum 'Danube – River of Cooperation' (ISF "DRC")*; *Youth and Environment Europe (YEE, #22012)*.

Consultative Status Consultative status granted from: *UNEP (#20299)*. **NGO Relations** Member of: *Carpathian Ecoregion Initiative (CERI, #03587)*; *European Environmental Bureau (EEB, #06996)*; *European Habitats Forum (EHF, #07443)*; *SDG Watch Europe (#19162)*. [2020/XF3457/y/**F**]

- ♦ **CEFACD** Comité européen des fabricants d'appareils de chauffage et de cuisine domestique (#04158)
- ♦ CEFACEF – Association européenne des producteurs de matériel de chauffage en fonte (inactive)
- ♦ CEFA – Central European Frisbee Disc Association (inactive)
- ♦ **CEFA** Centre d'études de la famille africaine (#03726)
- ♦ CEFA – Comitato Europeo per la Formazione e l'Agricoltura (internationally oriented national body)
- ♦ **CEFA** Council for Environmentally Friendly Aviation (#04880)
- ♦ **CEFACT-ONU** Centre pour la facilitation du commerce et les transactions électroniques des Nations Unies (#20527)
- ♦ CEFACT / see United Nations Centre for Trade Facilitation and Electronic Business (#20527)
- ♦ CEFAG – Centre européen de formation à la gestion, Bruxelles (no recent information)
- ♦ **CEF** Center of Excellence in Finance (#03640)
- ♦ **CEF** Commission européenne des forêts (#07299)
- ♦ CEF – Commonwealth Equity Fund (inactive)
- ♦ **CEF** Council of European Foresters (#04889)
- ♦ CEF / see Council of Europe Development Bank (#04897)
- ♦ CEFCTU – Central European Federation of Christian Trade Unions (inactive)
- ♦ CEFE – Comité européen des associations des fabricants de produits d'apport de soudage (inactive)
- ♦ CEFEC / see Social Firms Europe (#19338)
- ♦ **CEFEC** Social Firms Europe (#19338)
- ♦ CEFEI / see European Federation of Financial Executives Institutes (#07124)
- ♦ **CEFEP** CEFEP – European Interest Group for FEF and PEF Insulation (#03627)

♦ CEFEP – European Interest Group for FEF and PEF Insulation (CEFEP) 03627

Contact Schildenstr 24, 29221 Celle, Germany. T. +495141889265. Fax +495141889267. E-mail: info@cefep.net.
URL: http://www.cefep.net/

History 2012. **Aims** Demonstrate the contribution of *pipe* insulation regarding energy conservation and system *sustainability* of the entire mechanical system. **Structure** Board. **Activities** Advocacy/lobbying/activism. **NGO Relations** Sector group of: *European Plastics Converters (EuPC, #08216)*. [2017/XM7654/**F**]

- ♦ **CEFIC** Conseil européen de l'industrie chimique (#04687)
- ♦ CEFIR / see Association Rencontre CEFIR
- ♦ **CEFIR** Centro de Formación para la Integración Regional (#20197)
- ♦ **CEFL** Commission on European Family Law (#04212)
- ♦ **CEFLEX** Circular Economy for Flexible Packaging (#03935)
- ♦ CEFODE / see Coopération et Formation au Développement
- ♦ CEFODE – Coopération et Formation au Développement (internationally oriented national body)
- ♦ CEFOR / see Nordic Association of Marine Insurers (#17198)
- ♦ **Cefor** Nordic Association of Marine Insurers (#17198)
- ♦ CEFPI / see Association for Learning Environments
- ♦ CEFPI Australasia / see Learning Environments Australasia
- ♦ CEFRES – Centre européen féminin de recherche sur l'évolution de la société (inactive)
- ♦ **CEFS** Comité européen des fabricants de sucre (#04159)
- ♦ CEFTA – Central European Free Trade Agreement (1992 treaty)
- ♦ CEFTA – Central European Free Trade Association (no recent information)
- ♦ **CEFW** Conseil Européen des Fédérations WIZO (#06850)
- ♦ CEG / see Centre for European Studies
- ♦ CEGAA – Centre for Economic Governance and AIDS in Africa (internationally oriented national body)
- ♦ CEGAM – Confédération européenne des grandes associations musicales (inactive)
- ♦ CEGAN – Comité de Expertos Gubernamentales de Alto Nivel (see: #20556)
- ♦ CEGAP – Komitee der Europäischen Garten- und Landschaftsarchitekten (inactive)
- ♦ CEGA – UC Berkeley Center of Evaluation for Global Action (internationally oriented national body)
- ♦ **CEG** Catholic Evidence Guild (#03603)
- ♦ CEG / see Confederation of European Companions (#04522)
- ♦ CEGESTI (internationally oriented national body)
- ♦ CEGRE – Centro de Estudios Globales y Regionales, Buenos Aires (internationally oriented national body)
- ♦ **CEGROBB** Association européenne des associations du commerce de gros de bière et boissons des pays de l'Europe (#02555)
- ♦ **CEGS** Centre européen de géodynamique et de séismologie (#06481)
- ♦ CEGSS – Central European Group for Separation Sciences (internationally oriented national body)
- ♦ CEHA – Centro de Estudos de História do Atlântico (internationally oriented national body)
- ♦ **CEHA** WHO Regional Centre for Environmental Health Activities (#20942)
- ♦ CEH – Conférence européenne des horaires des trains de voyageurs (inactive)
- ♦ CEHI – Caribbean Environmental Health Institute (inactive)
- ♦ **CEHILA** Comisión de Estudios de Historia de la Iglesia en América Latina (#04133)
- ♦ **C-EHRN** Correlation – European Harm Reduction Network (#04848)
- ♦ CEHURD – Center for Health, Human Rights and Development (internationally oriented national body)
- ♦ CEI / see Carpathian Ecoregion Initiative (#03587)
- ♦ CEI / see African Agency For Integrated Development
- ♦ CEIA – Confédération européenne d'ingénieurs d'agriculture (inactive)
- ♦ **CEIB** Consejo de Empresarios Iberoamericanos (#04708)
- ♦ **CEI Bois** Confédération européenne des industries du bois (#04545)
- ♦ **CEIBS** China-Europe International Business School (#03888)
- ♦ **CEI** Caretakers of the Environment International (#03430)
- ♦ **CEI** Caribbean Evaluators International (#03498)
- ♦ CEIC – Centre for the Study of Education in an International Context (internationally oriented national body)
- ♦ **CEI** Central European Initiative (#03708)
- ♦ CEI – Centre d'échanges internationaux (internationally oriented national body)
- ♦ CEI – Centre d'études interaméricaines (internationally oriented national body)
- ♦ CEI – Centro de Estudios Internacionales, Managua (internationally oriented national body)
- ♦ **CEI** Chambre européenne d'ingénieurs (#06514)
- ♦ CEI – Charity Education International (internationally oriented national body)
- ♦ **CEIC** International Committee on Electronic Information and Communication (#12766)
- ♦ **CEI** Communauté des Etats indépendants (#04341)
- ♦ **CEI** Comunidad de Estados Independientes (#04341)
- ♦ CEI – Confédération européenne de l'immobilier (inactive)
- ♦ **CEI** Conselho Espirita Internacional (#15585)
- ♦ CEIDP – International Conference on Electrical Insulation and Dielectric Phenomena (meeting series)
- ♦ CEIE – Centre d'études internationales et européennes (internationally oriented national body)
- ♦ CEIHD / see Impact Carbon
- ♦ CEIICH – Centro de Investigaciones Interdisciplinarias en Ciencias y Humanidades (internationally oriented national body)
- ♦ CEILA – Centro de Estudios Ibéricos y Latinoamericanos (internationally oriented national body)
- ♦ CEINS / see MCF-B
- ♦ CE International – Childhood Education International (internationally oriented national body)
- ♦ CEIOPS / see European Insurance and Occupational Pensions Authority (#07578)
- ♦ CEIP – Carnegie Endowment for International Peace (internationally oriented national body)
- ♦ CEIP – Chambre européenne des ingénieurs professionnels (no recent information)
- ♦ CEIPES – Centro Internazionale per la Promozione dell'Educazione e lo Sviluppo (internationally oriented national body)
- ♦ CEIPI – Centre d'études internationales de la propriété intellectuelle (internationally oriented national body)
- ♦ CEIR / see European Association for the Taps and Valves Industry (#06246)
- ♦ **CEIR** European Association for the Taps and Valves Industry (#06246)
- ♦ **CEIRPP** United Nations Committee on the Exercise of the Inalienable Rights of the Palestinian People (#20539)
- ♦ **CEISAL** Consejo Europeo de Investigaciones Sociales de América Latina (#04710)
- ♦ **CEIS** Caribbean Energy Information System (#03496)
- ♦ CEIS – Centre for Economic and International Studies (internationally oriented national body)
- ♦ CEIS – Centre for European and International Studies, Kiev (internationally oriented national body)
- ♦ CeIS – Centro Italiano di Solidarieta (internationally oriented national body)
- ♦ CEISE – Centro Europeo de Investigación Social de Situaciones de Emergencia (internationally oriented national body)
- ♦ CEIS / see Middle European Iris Society (#16793)
- ♦ **CEJA** Centro de Estudios de Justicia de las Américas (#16171)
- ♦ **CEJA** Commonwealth Environmental Journalists Association (#04326)
- ♦ **CEJA** Conseil européen des jeunes agriculteurs (#04689)
- ♦ **CEJ** Centres européens de la jeunesse (#09138)
- ♦ CEJ – Collège des études juives (internationally oriented national body)
- ♦ CEJ – Confédération européenne du jouet (inactive)
- ♦ **CEJH** Communauté européenne des jeunes de l'horticulture (#04376)

♦ CEJI 03628

Dir address not obtained. T. +3223443444.
URL: http://www.ceji.org/

History 1991. Legal name changed to acronym, 2011. Former names and other names: *Centre européen juif d'information (CEJI)* – former (1991 to 2011); *Centre for European Jewish Information* – former (1991 to 2011); *CEJI – A Jewish Contribution to an Inclusive Europe* – full title. Registration: Belgium. **Aims** Combat *prejudice* and discrimination; promote social cohesion through training, education, dialogue and advocacy. **Structure** Board. **Languages** English, French. **Activities** Training/education; politics/policy/regulatory; networking/liaising. **Events** *Facing all the Facts Conference* Brussels (Belgium) 2018, *Annual international conference* Brussels (Belgium) 2004, *Annual international conference* Montecatini Terme (Italy) 2003, *Annual international conference* Malaga (Spain) 2002, *Meeting* Antwerp (Belgium) 1999. **Consultative Status** Consultative status granted from: *Council of Europe (CE, #04881)* (Participatory Status). **IGO Relations** Participant in Fundamental Rights Platform of *European Union Agency for Fundamental Rights (FRA, #08969)*. **NGO Relations** Member of (3): *European Network against Racism (ENAR, #07862)*; *European Network for Countering Antisemitism through Education (ENCATE)*; *International Network Against Cyber Hate (INACH, #14229)*. Instrumental in setting up (1): *European Peer Training Organization (EPTO)*. Coordinates: *Facing Facts (#09235)*. [2021/XN4863/**D**]

- ♦ CEJI – A Jewish Contribution to an Inclusive Europe / see CEJI (#03628)
- ♦ **CEJIL** Center for Justice and International Law (#03647)
- ♦ CEJS – Conférence européenne de la jeunesse sportive (inactive)
- ♦ CELAC – Center for Latino, Latin American and Caribbean Studies (internationally oriented national body)
- ♦ **CELAC** Comunidad de Estados Latinoamericanos y Caribeños (#04432)
- ♦ CELA – Centro de Estudios Latinoamericanos 'Justo Arosemena' (internationally oriented national body)
- ♦ CELA – Cirujanos Endovasculares de Latino América (unconfirmed)
- ♦ CELADEC – Comisión Evangélica Latinoamericana de Educación Cristiana (inactive)
- ♦ **CELADE** Centro Latinoamericano y Caribeño de Demografia (#16273)
- ♦ CELADEL – Centro Latinoamericano de Estudios Locales (unconfirmed)

- ♦ CELAG – Centro Latinoamericano de la Globalidad (internationally oriented national body)
- ♦ CELA-IS / see Groupe d'études latino-américaines de l'Institut de sociologie, Bruxelles
- ♦ CELAJU – Centro Latinoamericano sobre Juventud (internationally oriented national body)
- ♦ **CELAM** Consejo Episcopal Latinoamericano (#04709)
- ♦ **CELAP** Centro Latinoamericano de Periodismo (#16345)
- ♦ CELARE – Centro Latinoamericano para les Relaciones con Europa (internationally oriented national body)
- ♦ CELASA – Center for Latino Studies in the Americas (internationally oriented national body)
- ♦ CEL – Association de chefs d'entreprises latines (inactive)
- ♦ CELA / see UWW-Europe (#20739)
- ♦ **CELCAA** Comité européen de liaison des commerces agricoles et agro-alimentaires (#07687)
- ♦ **CELCA** Central European Lung Cancer Association (#03709)
- ♦ **CELC** Confédération européenne du lin et du chanvre (#04546)
- ♦ **CELCIT** Centro Latinoamericano de Creación e Investigación Teatral (#03811)
- ♦ **CEL** Conseil Européen pour les Langues (#07646)
- ♦ C elegans Topic Meeting: NEURONAL DEVELOPMENT, SYNAPTIC FUNCTION & BEHAVIOR (meeting series)
- ♦ CELEI – Centro de Estudios Latinoamericanos de Educación Inclusiva (internationally oriented national body)
- ♦ **CELEP** Coalition of European Lobbies on Eastern African Pastoralism (#04059)
- ♦ **CEL** European Confederation of Laryngectomees (#06709)
- ♦ **CELHTO** Centre d'études linguistiques et historiques par tradition orale (#03771)
- ♦ CELIBRIDE – Comité de liaison international des broderies, rideaux et dentelles (inactive)
- ♦ **CELiège** Confédération européenne du liège (#06798)
- ♦ CELIMAC – Comité européen de liaison des industries de la machine à coudre (inactive)
- ♦ Celim Bergamo – Organisation de volontariat international chrétien (internationally oriented national body)
- ♦ Celim Bergamo – Organizzazione di Volontariato Internazionale Cristiano (internationally oriented national body)
- ♦ CeLiM – Centro Laici Italiani per le Missioni (internationally oriented national body)
- ♦ **CELIMO** Comité européen de liaison des importateurs de machines-outils (#04161)
- ♦ CELINTEX – European Organization for Home Textiles, Laces and Embroideries (no recent information)

♦ Cell Stress Society International (CSSI) 03629

Managing Editor Editorial Office & CSSI, 53 Auburn Road, West Hartford CT 06119, USA.
Sec/Treas address not obtained.
URL: http://www.cellstressresponses.org/

History 1999. Registration: 501(c)(3) organization, No/ID: EIN: 06-1528876, Start date: 1999, USA, Connecticut. **Aims** Promote investigation of stress responses using molecular and cellular approaches, or bridging from molecular and cellular level to organismal biology including studies of natural populations and clinical and environmental applications. **Structure** Council. **Languages** English. **Staff** 1.50 FTE, paid. **Activities** Events/meetings. **Events** *International Symposium on Cellular and Organismal Stress Responses* 2022, *International Symposium on Heat Shock Proteins in Biology and Medicine* 2021, *International Symposium on Cellular and Organismal Stress Responses* 2020, *International Congress on Stress Responses in Biology and Medicine* San Diego, CA (USA) 2019, *International Congress on Stress Responses in Biology and Medicine* Turku (Finland) 2017. **Publications** *Cell Stress and Chaperones* – journal. **Members** (250) in 30 countries. Membership countries not specified. [2022/XM1847/**D**]

♦ Cell Transplant and Regenerative Medicine Society (CTRMS) 03630

Pres c/o TTS, 505 Bd René-Léveque Ouest, Suite 1401, Montréal QC H2Z 7Y7, Canada. T. +15148741717. Fax +15148741716. E-mail: info@tts.org.
URL: http://www.tts.org/ctrms-home/home/

History Set up as *Cell Transplant Society (CTS)*. Section of *The Transplantation Society (TTS, #20224)*. **Aims** Promote and encourage education and research with respect to cellular transplantation. **Structure** Council. **Finance** Members' dues. **Activities** Events/meetings. **Events** *Joint Congress* 2021, *Joint Meeting* 2021, *Joint Congress* San Diego, CA (USA) 2021, *Congress* Lesbos Is (Greece) 2019, *Joint Scientific Meeting* Halifax, NS (Canada) 2017. **Publications** *Cell Transplantation Journal*. [2019/XJ4169/**E**]

- ♦ Cell Transplant Society / see Cell Transplant and Regenerative Medicine Society (#03630)
- ♦ Cellular Agriculture Europe (unconfirmed)
- ♦ **CELRA** Conférence des évêques latins dans les régions arabes (#04604)
- ♦ CEL / see Royal Commonwealth Ex-Services League (#18989)
- ♦ CELSAM – Centro Latinoamericano Salud y Mujer (inactive)
- ♦ CELSIG – European Liaison Committee on Services of General Interest (internationally oriented national body)
- ♦ CELTE – Constructeurs européens de locomotives thermiques et électriques (inactive)

♦ Celtic Conference in Classics (CCC) 03631

Colloque celtique d'études classiques

Dir address not obtained.
URL: http://www.celticconferenceinclassics.org/

History 1998, Wales. **Languages** English, French. **Activities** Events/meetings. **Events** *Conference* Lyon (France) 2021, *Conference* Lyon (France) 2020, *Conference* Coimbra (Portugal) 2019, *Conference* St Andrews (UK) 2018, *Conference* Montréal, QC (Canada) 2017. [2021/AA1601/c/**E**]

♦ Celtic Congress 03632

Congrès celtique – Chòmhdhail Cheilteach – Chomhdhail Cheilteach – Kendalc'h Keltiek – Gyngres Geltaidd – Cuntelles Keltek – Cohaglym Celtiagh

Sec 16 Hilary Road, Isle of Man, Douglas, IM2 3EG, UK.
URL: http://www.celtic-congress.org/

History Founded 1902. Statutes amended 1994. **Aims** Perpetuate the *culture*, ideas and *languages* of the Celtic people; maintain an intellectual contact and close cooperation between the respective Celtic communities. **Structure** General Meeting (annual). International Committee, comprising President, Vice-President, International Secretary, International Treasurer and 12 representatives of the National Committees (6). **Languages** Celtic languages. **Finance** Members' dues. **Activities** Annual congress organized since 1917. **Events** *Annual Congress* Bodmin (UK) 2013, *Annual Congress* Fort William (UK) 2011, *Congress / Annual Congress* Douglas (UK) 2010, *Annual Congress* Isle of Man 2010, *Congress / Annual Congress* Sligo (Ireland) 2009.

Members Individuals in Celtic territories (6):
Bretagne, Ireland, Isle of Man, Scotland, UK (Cornwall), Wales.

NGO Relations *Celtic League (CL, #03633).* [2016/XF0802/cv/**F**]

♦ Celtic League (CL) 03633

Ligue celtique – Conradh Ceilteach – Comunn Ceilteach – Kevre Keltiek – Undeb Celtaidd – Kesunyans Keltek – Commeeys Celtiagh

SG c/o 12 Lon Rhedyn, Lon y Llyn, Caerphilly, CF83 1DR, UK. E-mail: gensec@celticleague.net.
Dir of Communication 11 Cleiy Rhennee, Kirk Michael, IM6 1HT, UK. Fax +441624877918.
American Branch c/o PO Box 20153, Dag Hammarshjold Postal Centre, New York NY 10017, USA.
URL: http://www.celticleague.net/

History 9 Aug 1961, Rhosllannerchrugog (UK). Constitution amended 1972, 1989. **Aims** Contribute to the struggle of the Celtic nations to secure or win political, cultural, social and economic *freedom* by: fostering cooperation among Celtic peoples; developing consciousness of the special relationship and solidarity among them; making their national struggles and achievements better known abroad; campaigning for a formal association of the Celtic nations once two or more have achieved *self-government*; advocating the use of national resources of each Celtic nation for the benefit of all its people. **Structure** General Meeting (annual). General Council. Officers: Chairman/Convenor; General Secretary; Assistant General Secretary; Treasurer; Editor. National branches (6) and international branches (4), each with secretariat. **Languages** Breton, Cornish, English, Irish Gaelic, Manx, Welsh. **Staff** 15.00 FTE, voluntary. **Finance** Members' dues (annual): pounds12 (for UK and Ireland) – pounds15 (for Europe), pounds18 (outside Europe)/ US$ 25. Other sources: donations; sale of magazine. Budget (annual): pounds9,000. **Activities** Campaigns politically on issues affecting Celtic countries, for example: status for the Welsh language; conscription in Brittany; situation in Ulster. In particular monitors military activity. Cooperates with national cultural organizations in promoting Celtic languages and culture, in particular TV and radio language services. Liaises with other groups on environmental matters affecting Celtic areas. **Events** *Annual General Assembly* Venice (Italy) 2010, *Annual General Assembly* Cornwall (UK) 2009, *Annual General Assembly* Wales (UK) 2007, *Annual General Assembly* Brest (France) 2006, *Annual General Assembly* Teangue (UK) 2005. **Publications** *Carn* (4 a year); *Keltoi* (2 a year); *Celtic Calendar* (annual). *Combating Corruption* (2001); *Projects in Celtic Studies at the Berlin University* (1999); *Whose National Identity (Critique of ID Cards)* (1996); *Celtic League Submission to the Forum for Peace and Reconciliation* (1995); *Employment Discrimination in Ulster* (1995); *Human Rights on the Celtic Fringe* (1995); *Promoting National Self Determination* (1995); *RAF Post (Aircraft) Crash Management Techniques* (1994); *Chronicles of the Kings of Man and the Isles* (1988); *For a Celtic Future* (1984); *The Celtic Experience* (1972); *Celtic Unity – 10 Years On* (1971); *The Celt in the Seventies* (1970); *Significance of Freedom* (1969); *Maintaining a National Identity* (1968); *Celtic Advance in the Atomic Age* (1967). Yearbooks; pamphlets. Information Services: Press information service.

Members Individuals in 6 Celtic territories:
Bretagne, Ireland, Isle of Man, Scotland, UK (Cornwall), Wales.
Individuals in 4 countries and territories:
Australia, Canada, England, USA.

Consultative Status Consultative status granted from: *ECOSOC (#05331)* (Ros A). [2012.09.12/XD0227/v/**D**]

- ♦ **CELV** Centre européen pour les langues vivantes (#06491)
- ♦ **CEMAC** Communauté économique et monétaire d'Afrique centrale (#04374)
- ♦ CEMAC Community Court of Justice (#04931)
- ♦ CEMAC-P – Economic and Monetary Community of Central Africa Parliament (no recent information)
- ♦ CEMA / see European Agricultural Machinery Association (#05846)
- ♦ **CEMA** European Agricultural Machinery Association (#05846)
- ♦ CEMAFON / see European Foundry Equipment Suppliers Association, The (#07353)
- ♦ **CEMAFON** European Foundry Equipment Suppliers Association, The (#07353)
- ♦ CEMASTEA – Centre for Mathematics, Science and Technology in Africa (internationally oriented national body)
- ♦ **CEMAT** Centre d'études maghrébines, Tunis (#03740)
- ♦ **CEMAT** Centro Mesoamericano de Estudios sobre Tecnologia Apropiada (#03650)
- ♦ **CEMATEX** Comité européen des constructeurs de matériel textile (#06672)
- ♦ CEMBREU – Centre européen médical bioclimatique de recherche et d'enseignement universitaire (internationally oriented national body)
- ♦ CEMBUREAU – Association européenne du ciment (#03634)
- ♦ **CEMBUREAU** CEMBUREAU – The European Cement Association (#03634)

♦ CEMBUREAU – The European Cement Association (CEMBUREAU) . . 03634

CEMBUREAU – Association européenne du ciment

Chief Exec Rue d'Arlon 55, 1040 Brussels, Belgium. T. +3222341011. Fax +3222304720. E-mail: communications@cembureau.eu – secretariat@cembureau.eu.
URL: http://www.cembureau.eu/

History 1947, Stockholm (Sweden). Secretariat originally located in Malmö (Sweden); transferred: Jan 1966, to Paris (France); Oct 1988, to Brussels (Belgium). Registration: Banque-Carrefour des Entreprises, No/ID: 0454.355.324, Start date: 1 Dec 1994, Belgium; EU Transparency Register, No/ID: 93987316076-63, Start date: 24 Jun 2011. **Aims** Act as spokesperson for the cement industry before EU institutions and other public authorities; communicate the industry's views on all issues and policy developments regarding technical, environmental, energy, employee health and safety and sustainability issues. **Structure** General Assembly (annual, closed); Board; Steering Committee; Working Groups (4); Task Forces; Secretariat in Brussels (Belgium). **Languages** English. **Staff** Paid. **Finance** Sources: members' dues; sale of publications. **Activities** Knowledge management/information dissemination; publishing activities. **Events** *Annual General Assembly* Helsinki (Finland) 2019, *Annual General Assembly* Madrid (Spain) 2018, *Annual General Assembly* Paris (France) 2017, *Concrete Dialogue Conference* Brussels (Belgium) 2016, *Annual General Assembly* Oslo (Norway) 2015. **Publications** *World Statistical Review 2004-2014*. Activity Report; studies; reports; standards.

Members Full: national cement industry associations and cement companies in 27 countries:
Austria, Belgium, Bulgaria, Czechia, Denmark, Estonia, Finland, France, Germany, Greece, Hungary, Ireland, Italy, Latvia, Lithuania, Luxembourg, Netherlands, Norway, Poland, Portugal, Romania, Slovenia, Spain, Sweden, Switzerland, Türkiye, UK.
Associate in 2 countries:
Croatia, Serbia.
Cooperation agreement with 2 countries:
Cyprus, Ukraine.

NGO Relations Member of (7): *Alliance for a Competitive European Industry (ACEI, #00670)*; *Concrete Europe (#04433)*; *Construction 2050 Alliance (#04760)*; *Construction Products Europe AISBL (#04761)*; *European Construction Forum (ECF, #06765)*; *European Network on Silica (NEPSI, #08001)*; *Industry4Europe (#11181)*. [2022.05.11/XD0606/**D**]

- ♦ **CEMCA** Commonwealth Educational Media Centre for Asia (#04322)
- ♦ CEM – Centre Europeen de Musique (unconfirmed)
- ♦ CEM – Centro Educazione alla Mondialità (internationally oriented national body)
- ♦ CEMCI – Centro de Estudios Municipales y de Cooperación Internacional (internationally oriented national body)
- ♦ **CEM** Clean Energy Ministerial (#03988)
- ♦ **CEM** Comité d'état-major du Conseil de sécurité des Nations Unies (#20626)
- ♦ CEM – Confédération européenne des maires (inactive)
- ♦ CEM – Conférence européenne des horaires des trains de marchandises (inactive)
- ♦ CEM / see Council of European Municipalities and Regions (#04891)
- ♦ CEMEA / see International Federation of Training Centres for the Promotion of Progressive Education (#13572)
- ♦ **CEMEC** Centro Europeo per la Medicina delle Catastrofi (#06475)
- ♦ **CEME** Commission des Eglises auprès des migrants en Europe (#03912)
- ♦ **CEMEP** Conférence européenne des associations de musique d'église protestante (#05753)
- ♦ **CEMEP** European Committee of Manufacturers of Electrical Machines and Power Electronics (#06658)
- ♦ **CEMHAL** Centro de Estudios la Mujer en la Historia de América Latina (#03799)
- ♦ CEMI – Centre des Etudes Méditerranéennes et Internationales (internationally oriented national body)
- ♦ CEMI – Committee of the European Hardware, Housewares and Metalworking Industries (inactive)
- ♦ CEMLA – Centro de Estudios Migratorios Latinoamericanos (internationally oriented national body)
- ♦ **CEMLA** Centro de Estudios Monetarios Latinoamericanos (#03648)
- ♦ CEMLAWS Africa – Centre for Maritime Law and Security Africa (internationally oriented national body)
- ♦ CEMM / see European Confederation of Medical Mycology (#06712)
- ♦ Cemnijn Sinzilgeenij Negdsen Institut / see Joint Institute for Nuclear Research (#16134)
- ♦ CEMN / see Organization of Black Sea Economic Cooperation (#17857)
- ♦ **CEMO** Conseil d'Eglises du Moyen-Orient (#16756)
- ♦ CEMPA – Comisión para el Estudio de la Organización de Aguas (no recent information)
- ♦ CEMPE – Commission Europe-Méditerranée de planification pour les problèmes de l'eau (no recent information)
- ♦ **CEMR** Council of European Municipalities and Regions (#04891)
- ♦ CEMS / see CEMS – The Global Alliance in Management Education (#03635)

♦ CEMS – The Global Alliance in Management Education 03635

Exec Dir 1 rue de la Libération, 78350 Jouy-en-Josas, France. T. +33139677457. Fax +33139677481. E-mail: info@cems.org.
URL: http://www.cems.org/

History Dec 1988. Founded on the initiative of 4 European business schools. Former names and other names: *Community of European Management Schools (CEMS)* – former (Dec 1988). **Aims** Promote a pre-experience Master's degree in International Management, based on behavioural, economic, social and cultural dimensions of organizations. **Structure** General Assembly (annual); Executive Board; Task Forces (temporary); Inter-Faculty Teams (14); Head Office located in Jouy-en-Josas (France). **Languages** English. **Staff** 14.70 FTE, paid. **Finance** Members' dues. **Activities** Training/education. **Events** *Annual Meeting* Copenhagen (Denmark) 2021, *Nordic Forum* Copenhagen (Denmark) 2019, *Annual Meeting* Vienna (Austria) 2019, *Nordic Forum* Helsinki (Finland) 2018, *Annual Meeting* St Julian's (Malta) 2018. **Publications** *Student Board Newsletter* (3 a year); *CEMS Magazine* (annual). *CEMS Student Book*; *Graduate CV Book and Directory*; *Student MIM and MBC Guides*. Annual Report; brochures; leaflets; survey reports.

Members Academic: business schools in 31 countries and territories:
Australia, Austria, Belgium, Brazil, Canada, Chile, China, Czechia, Denmark, Egypt, Finland, France, Germany, Hong Kong, Hungary, India, Ireland, Italy, Japan, Korea Rep, Netherlands, Norway, Poland, Portugal, Russia, Singapore, Spain, Sweden, Switzerland, Türkiye, UK.
Corporate partners (over 70); Social Partners (4). Membership countries not specified.

NGO Relations Member of: *EFMD – The Management Development Network (#05387)*; *Principles for Responsible Management Education (PRME, #18500)*. [2021/XF2209/**F**]

- ♦ CEMSI / see Centro Einstein di Studi Internazionali sul Federalismo, la Pace, la Politica del Territorio
- ♦ **CEMT** Confederation of European Maritime Technology Societies (#04526)
- ♦ CEMT / see International Transport Forum (#15725)
- ♦ CEM / see United Nations Security Council Military Staff Committee (#20626)
- ♦ CENAA – Centre for European and North Atlantic Affairs (internationally oriented national body)
- ♦ Cenacle Sisters – Congregation of Our Lady of the Retreat in the Cenacle (religious order)
- ♦ **CENAD** Centre for Experiential Negotiation and Applied Diplomacy (#03747)
- ♦ CENARBICA – Branche régionale du Conseil international des archives pour l'Afrique centrale (see: #12996)
- ♦ **CEN** Comité européen de normalisation (#04162)
- ♦ CENDES – Centro de Estudios del Desarrollo, Caracas (internationally oriented national body)
- ♦ CENEL – Comité européen de coordination des normes électriques (inactive)
- ♦ **CENELEC** Comité européen de normalisation électrotechnique (#06647)
- ♦ **CENELEC** European Committee for Electrotechnical Standardization (#06647)
- ♦ CeNeuro – C elegans Topic Meeting: NEURONAL DEVELOPMENT, SYNAPTIC FUNCTION & BEHAVIOR (meeting series)
- ♦ CENIS – MIT Center for International Studies, Cambridge MA (internationally oriented national body)
- ♦ **CENL** Conference of European National Librarians (#04597)
- ♦ **CENN** Caucasus Environmental NGO Network (#03613)
- ♦ CENPROMYPE / see Centro Regional de Promoción de la MIPYME (#03816)
- ♦ **CENPROMYPE** Centro Regional de Promoción de la MIPYME (#03816)
- ♦ CENSA – Confederation of European National Societies of Anaesthesiologists (inactive)
- ♦ CENSA – Council of European and Japanese National Shipowners' Associations (inactive)
- ♦ **CEN-SAD** Community of Sahel-Saharan States (#04406)
- ♦ **CENS** Central European Neurosurgical Society (#03710)
- ♦ CENSIS – Center for Science and International Security (internationally oriented national body)
- ♦ Centar za Mir, Nenasilje i Ljudska Prava (internationally oriented national body)
- ♦ Center for Advanced Studies for Broadband (#03797)
- ♦ Center for the Advancement and Study of International Education (internationally oriented national body)
- ♦ Center for African Studies, Berkeley CA / see Berkeley Stanford Joint Center for African Studies
- ♦ Center for African Studies, Champaign (internationally oriented national body)
- ♦ Center for African Studies, Gainesville FL (internationally oriented national body)
- ♦ Center for Afrikastudier, København (internationally oriented national body)
- ♦ Center for Afro-Asian Studies (internationally oriented national body)
- ♦ Center of Afro-Oriental Studies, Bahia (internationally oriented national body)
- ♦ Center for American and International Law / see Institute for Transnational Arbitration
- ♦ Center for American Studies / see Institute of European and American Studies, Taiwan
- ♦ Center for American Studies, Tokyo / see Center for Pacific and American Studies
- ♦ Center d'analyse politique des relations internationales (internationally oriented national body)
- ♦ Center for Andean Medicine (internationally oriented national body)

♦ Center for Andean Regional Studies 'Bartolomé de Las Casas' 03636

Centre d'études régionales andines 'Bartolomé de Las Casas' – Centro de Estudios Regionales Andinos 'Bartolomé de Las Casas' (CBC)

SG Centro Bartolomé de las Casas Cusco, Pasaje Pampa de la Alianza Nro 164, Cusco, Peru. T. +5184245415.
URL: http://www.cbc.org.pe/

History 25 May 1974, Cusco (Peru), as *Center for Andean Rural Studies: Bartolomé de Las Casas – Centro de Estudios Rurales Andinos: Bartolomé de Las Casas*. Present name adopted 1989. **Activities** Research/documentation; training/education; guidance/assistance/consulting. **Events** *Identidad y etnicidad en los Andes* Jujuy (Argentina) 1994, *Ethics and democracy in Latin America* Santiago (Chile) 1994. **Publications** *Revista Andina* (2 a year). *Archivos de Historia Andina (Serie 1000)*; *Biblioteca de la Tradición Oral Andina (Serie 2000)*; *Cuadernos de Capacitación Campesina (Serie 5000)*; *Cuadernos para el Debate Regional (Serie 4000)*; *Cuadernos para la Historia de la Evangelización en América Latina*; *Debates Andinos (Serie 3000)*; *Ecologia y Desarrollo (Serie 6000)*. *Monumenta Linguistica Andina*. **IGO Relations** Member of: *Latin American and Caribbean Research Network (#16284)*. **NGO Relations** Member of: *Latin American Network on Environmental Conflicts (no recent information)*; *Consejo Latinoamericano de Ciencias Sociales (CLACSO, #04718)*. [2017/XE0833/**E**]

- ♦ Center for Andean Rural Studies: Bartolomé de Las Casas / see Center for Andean Regional Studies 'Bartolomé de Las Casas' (#03636)
- ♦ Center for Applied Conflict Management (internationally oriented national body)
- ♦ Center for Applied Nonviolent Action and Strategies (internationally oriented national body)
- ♦ Center for Applied Policy Research (internationally oriented national body)
- ♦ Center for Arabic Study Abroad (internationally oriented national body)
- ♦ Center for Arab West Understanding (internationally oriented national body)

♦ Center of Arab Women for Training and Research, Tunis (CAWTAR) 03637

Contact PO Box 105, 1003 Cité El Khadra, 1003 Tunis, Tunisia. T. +21671790511. Fax +21671773611 – +21671780002. E-mail: info@cawtar.org.
URL: http://www.cawtar.org/

History 7 Mar 1993. Former names and other names: *Arab Women Centre for Training and Research, Tunis (AWCTR)* – former. **Aims** Develop and support an Arab women's perspective on changing *gender* roles and the role of *families* in the process of *social change*; raise awareness about the status of the Arab women and her potential contribution to national *development*; collect and analyse gender-specific data; advocate and train on all issues relating to women's participation, or lack thereof, in social, political and economic life in the Arab region. **Activities** Instrumental in setting up: *Arab Network on Gender and Development (ANGAD, no recent information)*. **Publications** *Arab Women Development Reports* (periodical); *Cawtaryet* (periodical) – newsletter. Academic and policy-related reports; paper series. Database of Arab experts and academicians interested in women's issues; Arab women's bibliographic data base. Maintains library.

Members Individuals in 21 countries and territories:
Algeria, Bahrain, Comoros, Djibouti, Eswatini, Iraq, Jordan, Kuwait, Lebanon, Libya, Mauritania, Morocco, Oman, Palestine, Qatar, Saudi Arabia, Somalia, Sudan, Syrian AR, United Arab Emirates, Yemen.

IGO Relations Accredited by (1): *Organisation internationale de la Francophonie (OIF, #17809)*. Memorandum of Understanding with (1): *Arab Women Organization (AWO, #01078)*. Cooperates with (1): *Islamic World Educational, Scientific and Cultural Organization (ICESCO, #16058)*. **NGO Relations** Member of (4): *Euro-Mediterranean Network for Co-operation (Mediter, #05726)*; *Euro-Mediterranean Study Commission (EuroMeSCo, #05727)*; *Euro-Mediterranean Women's Foundation (#05729)* (Founding); *International Federation for Sustainable Development and Fight to Poverty in the Mediterranean-Black Sea (FISPMED, #13562)*. [2021/XG2957/v/**E**]

- ♦ Center for Asian and African Studies, Mexico (internationally oriented national body)
- ♦ Center for Asian and North African Studies, Mexico City / see Center for Asian and African Studies, Mexico
- ♦ Center for Asian and Pacific Studies / see School of Pacific and Asian Studies
- ♦ Center for Asian and Pacific Studies, Eugene OR (internationally oriented national body)
- ♦ Center of Asian and Pacific Studies, Iowa City (internationally oriented national body)
- ♦ Center for Asian Research, Tempe (internationally oriented national body)
- ♦ Center for Asian Studies / see Center for Asian Research, Tempe
- ♦ Center for Black Music Research (internationally oriented national body)
- ♦ Center for Chemical Process Safety (internationally oriented national body)
- ♦ Center for Civil and Human Rights, Notre Dame IN (internationally oriented national body)
- ♦ Center for Civilians in Conflict (internationally oriented national body)
- ♦ Center for Clean Air Policy (internationally oriented national body)
- ♦ Center for Cognitive Studies of the Moving Image / see Society for Cognitive Studies of the Moving Image (#19531)
- ♦ Center for Communications, Health and the Environment (internationally oriented national body)
- ♦ Center for Comparative and International Studies (internationally oriented national body)
- ♦ Center for Conflict Analysis and Resolution / see Jimmy and Rosalynn Carter School for Peace and Conflict Resolution
- ♦ Center for Conservation Peacebuilding (internationally oriented national body)
- ♦ Center for Constitutional Governance (internationally oriented national body)
- ♦ Center for Contemporary Arab Studies, Washington DC (internationally oriented national body)
- ♦ Center of Coordination and Diffusion of Latin American Studies / see Centro de Investigaciones sobre América y el Caribe (#03810)
- ♦ Center for Coordination of the Prevention of Natural Disasters in Central America (#03795)

♦ Center for Creative Leadership (CCL) 03638

Contact Client Services, 1 Leadership Place, Greensboro NC 27410, USA. T. +13365657216. Fax +13362885759.
URL: https://www.ccl.org/

History Founded 1970. **Aims** Advance the understanding, practice and development of leadership for the benefit of society worldwide. **Structure** Board of Trustees; Board of Governors. **Activities** Training/education. [2020/XM8753/**C**]

- ♦ Center for Cultural and Technical Interchange between East and West / see East-West Center (#05263)
- ♦ Center Culturel Esperantist (internationally oriented national body)
- ♦ Center for Defence and Security Strategic Studies (internationally oriented national body)

♦ Center for Democracy and Reconciliation in Southeast Europe (CDRSEE) 03639

Exec Dir Krispou 9, Ano Poli, 546 34 Thessaloniki, Greece. T. +302310960820. Fax +302310960822.
Facebook: https://www.facebook.com/cdrsee/

History Oct 1998, Netherlands. Inaugurated May 2000, Thessaloniki (Greece). **Aims** Foster, within Southeast Europe, democratic, pluralist and peaceful societies; advocate principles of social responsibility, sustainable development and reconciliation among the peoples in the region. **Structure** Board of Directors. **Languages** English, French, German, Irish Gaelic, Serbian. **Staff** 7.00 FTE, paid. **Finance** Donations from the German government and international organizations, including: *Austrian Development Agency (ADA)*; *ERSTE Foundation*; *European Commission (EC, #06633)*; *Fondation Pro Victimis (FPV)*; *Friedrich-Ebert-Stiftung (FES)*; *Open Society Foundations (OSF, #17763)*. **Activities** Advocacy/lobbying/activism; capacity building; events/meetings; networking/liaising; training/education. **Events** *International Conference* Thessaloniki (Greece) 2013, *International Conference* Belgrade (Serbia) 2012, *International Conference* Thessaloniki (Greece) 2010, *International conference* Athens (Greece) 2002, *International conference on national memory in Southeastern Europe* Halki Is (Greece) 1999. **Publications** *Vicinities – First Regional News Talk Show*. *Disclosing Hidden History: Lustration in the Western Balkans*; *Employed, Empowered – Training Manuals* – 8 vols; *JHP History Education Materials* – in 11 languages; *Teaching for Early Learning – A Reference Guide for Pre-School Teachers in Diverse classrooms* – in 2 languages; *Teaching for Learning – A Reference Guide for Results-Oriented Teachers* – in 7 languages. Annual Report; books; studies, surveys; transcripts. [2018/XE3925/**E**]

- ♦ Center for Democracy and Technology (internationally oriented national body)
- ♦ Center for Development of International Law, New York (internationally oriented national body)
- ♦ Center for Development Policy / see International Forum for Innovative Northeast Asia Strategy
- ♦ Center for Development Research, Bonn (internationally oriented national body)
- ♦ Center for Development Studies and Promotion (internationally oriented national body)
- ♦ Center for Earth Jurisprudence / see Earth Law Center
- ♦ Center for East Asian Studies, Austin TX (internationally oriented national body)
- ♦ Center for East Asian Studies, Delhi (internationally oriented national body)
- ♦ Center for East Asian Studies, Lawrence KS (internationally oriented national body)
- ♦ Center for East Asian Studies, Madison WI (unconfirmed)
- ♦ Center for Economic and Policy Research (internationally oriented national body)
- ♦ Center for Economic Research on Africa, Upper Montclair NJ (internationally oriented national body)
- ♦ Center for Economic and Social Rights (internationally oriented national body)
- ♦ Center EMUNI / see Euro-Mediterranean University (#05728)
- ♦ Center for Entrepreneurship in International Health and Development / see Impact Carbon
- ♦ Center for Environmental Education / see Ocean Conservancy
- ♦ Center d'études latinoaméricaines, Pittsburgh (internationally oriented national body)
- ♦ Center for Eurasian, Russian and East European Studies, Washington DC (internationally oriented national body)
- ♦ Center for Euro-Atlantic Studies (internationally oriented national body)
- ♦ Center for European and Eurasian Studies, Los Angeles (internationally oriented national body)
- ♦ Center for European Policy (internationally oriented national body)
- ♦ Center for European Policy Analysis (internationally oriented national body)
- ♦ Center for European and Russian Studies, Los Angeles / see Center for European and Eurasian Studies, Los Angeles
- ♦ Center for European Studies, Cambridge MA (internationally oriented national body)
- ♦ Center for European Studies, Maastricht (internationally oriented national body)
- ♦ Center for European Studies, Madison WI (internationally oriented national body)
- ♦ Center for European Studies, Nagoya (internationally oriented national body)
- ♦ Center for European Studies, Stanford CA / see Forum on Contemporary Europe, Stanford CA
- ♦ Center for European Studies, University of Connecticut (internationally oriented national body)

♦ Center of Excellence in Finance (CEF) 03640

Dir Cankarjeva 18, 1000 Ljubljana, Slovenia. T. +38613696190. Fax +38613696218.
URL: http://www.cef-see.org/

History 2001, by Slovene Government, within the context of *Stability Pact for South Eastern Europe (inactive)*. **Aims** Directly contribute to design and implementation of public financial management, tax policy and administration, and central banking reform efforts. **Structure** Governing Board; Advisory Board; Coordinators; Secretariat. **Languages** English. **Staff** 30.00 FTE, paid. **Finance** Financed by: Government of Slovenia; bilateral and multilateral donors. **Activities** Events/meetings; training/education; networking/liaising; certification/accreditation; knowledge management/information dissemination. **Events** *Workshop on Debt Reduction Strategies and Risk Management* Ljubljana (Slovenia) 2018, *Workshop on Ensuring Fischal Sustainability with Medium-Term Budgeting and Fiscal Rules* Ljubljana (Slovenia) 2018, *Workshop on Mini One-Stop Shop for Cross-Border VAT Compliance* Ljubljana (Slovenia) 2018, *Workshop on Reforms for Accelerating Non-Performing Loans Resolution* Ljubljana (Slovenia) 2018, *Workshop on Training of Trainers on Financial Management and Control* Ljubljana (Slovenia) 2018. **Publications** *Strategic Planning and Budgeting Final Report* (2016); *Strategic Planning and Budgeting Newspaper* (2015). Annual Report; annual learning program brochure; thematic area brochures; comics; reports.
Members Governments of 7 countries:
Albania, Bulgaria, Moldova, Montenegro, North Macedonia, Romania, Slovenia.
CEF Constituency (12):
Albania, Bosnia-Herzegovina, Bulgaria, Croatia, Kosovo, Moldova, Montenegro, North Macedonia, Romania, Serbia, Slovenia, Türkiye. [2017.04.11/XJ7244/**E***]

♦ Center for Family and Human Rights (internationally oriented national body)
♦ Center for Family Planning Program Development / see Guttmacher Institute
♦ Center for Financial Inclusion at Accion (internationally oriented national body)
♦ Center for German and European Studies, Madison WI (internationally oriented national body)
♦ Center for Global Accountabilities, Blacksburg VA (internationally oriented national body)
♦ Center for Global Communications (internationally oriented national body)
♦ Center for Global Communication Studies (internationally oriented national body)
♦ Center on Global Counterterrorism Cooperation / see Global Center on Cooperative Security
♦ Center for Global Development (internationally oriented national body)
♦ Center for Global Development in Europe (internationally oriented national body)

♦ Center for Global Dialogue and Cooperation (CGDC) 03641

Headquarters Route de Florissant 89B, 1206 Geneva, Switzerland. T. +4318900549. Fax +431890054949. E-mail: office@cgdc.eu.
URL: http://www.cgdc.eu/
History 2009, by Petar Stoyanov, Dr Walter Schwimmer, Dr Werner Wasslabend, Stamen Stantchev and Etienne Declerq. **Aims** Support and assist emerging countries to become more capable, stable and trustworthy partners on a global scale. **Structure** International Board. President; Secretary-General; 3 Vice-Presidents. **Languages** English. **Activities** Training/education; meeting activities; networking/liaising. **Events** *Annual Meeting* Vienna (Austria) 2013, *Annual Meeting* Vienna (Austria) 2012, *Meeting on Dialogue and Cooperation for Change* Vienna (Austria) 2012. **Publications** Guides. **IGO Relations** Cooperates with: *UNIDO (#20336)*. [2016/XJ8288/**F**]

♦ Center for Global Education and Experience (internationally oriented national body)
♦ Center for Global Education, Minneapolis / see Center for Global Education and Experience
♦ Center for Global, International and Regional Studies (internationally oriented national body)

♦ Center for Global Nonkilling 03642

Chair 3653 Tantalus Drive, Honolulu HI 96822-5033, USA. T. +18085367442. E-mail: info@nonkilling.org.
Sec address not obtained.
URL: http://www.nonkilling.org/
History 1988. Founded as an exploratory planning project in the *'Spark m Matsunaga Institute of Peace'* at the University of Hawai'i. Became an independent organization, 2 Oct 1994. Former names and other names: *Center for Global Nonviolence, Honolulu HI (CGNK)* – former (Dec 2008). **Aims** Promote change toward the measurable goal of a killing-free world; discover and encourage global nonkilling human capabilities; introduce nonkilling knowledge in global education and policy; apply nonkilling knowledge in global problem-solving; develop and assist nonkilling global leadership; assist institutions and centers for global nonkilling; measure, monitor and disseminate the impact of nonkilling global efforts. **Structure** Governing Council; Leadership Team. **Languages** English, Portuguese, Spanish. **Staff** 7.00 FTE, paid. **Finance** Sources: foundations; donations. Budget (2012) US$ 40,000. **Activities** Training/education; events/meetings; knowledge management/information dissemination. **Events** *Conference on Countries without Armies* Vaasa (Finland) 2019, *Global Nonkilling Leadership Forum* Honolulu, HI (USA) 2007. **Publications** *Global Nonkilling Working Papers* – series. *Nonkilling Psychology* (2012); *Nonkilling Korea: Six Culture Exploration* (2012); *Nonkilling Geography* (2011); *Engineering Nonkilling: Scientific Responsibility and the Advancement of Killing-Free Societies* (2011); *Quest for Gandhi: A Nonkilling Journey* (2010); *Nonkilling Societies* (2010); *Nonkilling History: Shaping Policy with Lesons from the Past* (2010); *Towards a Nonkilling Paradigm* (2009); *Nurturing Nonkilling: A Poetic Plantation* (2009); *Violence and Health* (2009); *Nonkilling Global Political Science* (2009); *Global Nonkilling Leadership* (2008); *Towards a Nonkilling Filipino Society* (2004); *The Frontiers of Nonviolence* (1998); *Gandhi in the Global Village* (1998); *Hawai'i Journeys in Nonviolence: Autobiographical Reflections* (1995); *Islam and Nonviolence* (1993); *To Nonviolent Political Science: From Seasons of Violence* (1993); *Nonviolence Speaks to Power* (1992) by Petra K Kelly; *Nonviolence in Hawaii's Spiritual Traditions* (1991); *Buddhism and Nonviolent Global Problem-Solving: Ulaanbaatar Explorations* (1991).
Members Cooperating individuals in 50 countries:
Australia, Austria, Bangladesh, Belgium, Brazil, Burundi, Canada, Chile, China, Colombia, Congo DR, Costa Rica, Cuba, Denmark, Estonia, Finland, France, Germany, Haiti, Hungary, India, Indonesia, Ireland, Israel, Italy, Japan, Jordan, Korea Rep, Mexico, Mongolia, Nepal, Netherlands, New Zealand, Nigeria, Norway, Pakistan, Philippines, Portugal, Russia, Rwanda, Singapore, South Africa, Spain, Sri Lanka, Sweden, Switzerland, Thailand, Türkiye, UK, USA.
Consultative Status Consultative status granted from: *ECOSOC (#05331)* (Special). **NGO Relations** Member of (1): *Violence Prevention Alliance (VPA, #20781)*. Partner of (1): *International Coalition for the Responsibility to Protect (ICRtoP, #12620)*. [2020/XF3518/v/**E**]

♦ Center for Global Nonviolence, Honolulu HI / see Center for Global Nonkilling (#03642)
♦ Center for Global Peace, Washington DC (internationally oriented national body)
♦ Center for Global Political Economy, Burnaby (internationally oriented national body)
♦ Center for the Global South (internationally oriented national body)
♦ Center for Global Studies, Fairfax VA (internationally oriented national body)
♦ Center for Health and Gender Equity (internationally oriented national body)
♦ Center for Health and the Global Environment (internationally oriented national body)
♦ Center for Health, Human Rights and Development (internationally oriented national body)
♦ Center for Health Science Training, Research and Development International (internationally oriented national body)
♦ Center for Hemispheric Defense Studies (internationally oriented national body)
♦ Center for Humanitarian Outreach and Intercultural Exchange (internationally oriented national body)
♦ Center for Human Rights and Environment (internationally oriented national body)
♦ Center for Human Rights and Humanitarian Law, Washington DC (internationally oriented national body)
♦ Center for Human Services (internationally oriented national body)
♦ Center for Iberian and Latin American Studies (internationally oriented national body)
♦ Center for Indigenous Languages of Latin America (internationally oriented national body)

♦ Center for Information on Migration in Latin America 03643

Centre d'information sur la migration en Amérique latine – Centro de Información sobre Migraciones en América Latina (CIMAL)
Main Office c/o OIM – Oficina Regional para América del Sur, Av Santa Fe 1460, Piso 5, C1060ABN Buenos Aires, Argentina. T. +541148133330 – +541148164596. E-mail: robuepress@iom.int.
URL: http://robuenosaires.iom.int/publicaciones/
History 1983, Santiago (Chile), within *International Organization for Migration (IOM, #14454)*. Previously also referred to in English as *Latin American Information Center on Migration*. **Aims** Act as a specialized information resource on international migration and connected matters in Latin America, the *Caribbean* and other geographical areas, for servicing IOM, the Member States and general public; collect, review, abstract and make available documents written about international migration. **Structure** Attached to IOM Mission in Santiago (Chile). **Staff** 1.00 FTE, paid. **Finance** Members' dues. **Activities** Bibliographic research on specific fields such as migratory legislation, history, politics and programs, theory of migrations, migration trends, migrants, etc. Advise on information systems. Identification of consultants and institutions in the field of international relations. **Publications** *Revista de la OIM sobre Migraciones en América Latina – IOM Latin American Migration Journal* (3 a year) in English, Spanish. Information Services: Database – 9,000 bibliographic records of documents on international migration; CD-ROM published in cooperation with the Bibliographic System of ECLAC/United Nations, including part of CIMAL's database; compact discs on population matters; online international directory of persons and institutions relevant to international migration; news clipping file with news articles about almost all countries.
Members Member States (59):
Albania, Angola, Argentina, Armenia, Australia, Austria, Bangladesh, Belgium, Bolivia, Bulgaria, Canada, Chile, Colombia, Costa Rica, Croatia, Cyprus, Czechia, Denmark, Dominican Rep, Ecuador, Egypt, El Salvador, Finland, France, Germany, Greece, Guatemala, Haiti, Honduras, Hungary, Israel, Italy, Japan, Kenya, Korea Rep, Liberia, Luxembourg, Netherlands, Nicaragua, Norway, Pakistan, Panama, Paraguay, Peru, Philippines, Poland, Portugal, Senegal, Slovakia, Sri Lanka, Sweden, Switzerland, Tajikistan, Thailand, Uganda, Uruguay, USA, Venezuela, Zambia.
Offices in 22 countries and territories:
Belize, Canada, Egypt, France, Holy See, Hong Kong, Indonesia, Japan, Korea Rep, Macau, Malaysia, Malta, Mexico, Pakistan, Philippines, San Marino, Singapore, Spain, Sweden, Taiwan, Türkiye, UK.
IGO Relations Coordinates activities with: *United Nations Economic Commission for Latin America and the Caribbean (ECLAC, #20556)*. Links with various organizations and institutions worldwide. **NGO Relations** Links with various organizations and institutions worldwide. [2017/XE3480/**E***]

♦ Center for Inquiry International / see Center for Inquiry Transnational (#03644)

♦ Center for Inquiry Transnational 03644

Contact PO Box 741, Amherst NY 14226, USA. T. +17166364869. Fax +17166361733. E-mail: info@centerforinquiry.net.
URL: http://www.centerforinquiry.org/
History 1991, Amherst, NY (USA). Founded as (US) Center for Inquiry, as a joint project of *Committee for Skeptical Inquiry (CSI)* and *Council for Secular Humanism*. Former names and other names: *Center for Inquiry International* – former. **Aims** Foster a secular society based on science, reason, freedom of inquiry and *humanist* values. **Finance** Annual budget: 8,000,000 USD. **Events** *World congress* Bethesda, MD (USA) 2009, *World congress* Beijing (China) 2007. **Publications** National centres publish newsletters.
Members Centres (14) in 12 countries:
Egypt, France, Germany, India, Nepal, Netherlands, Nigeria, Peru, Poland, Russia, UK, USA.
Included in the above, 1 centre listed in this Yearbook:
Centre for Inquiry – Europe. [2020.11.16/XM1170/y/**E**]

♦ Center for Integrated Social Development (no recent information)
♦ Center for Inter-American Relations, New York / see Americas Society
♦ Center for Inter-American Studies (internationally oriented national body)
♦ Center for Interdisciplinary Research in Humanities / see Centro de Investigaciones Interdisciplinarias en Ciencias y Humanidades
♦ Center for International Accounting Development (internationally oriented national body)
♦ Center for International Affairs / see Weatherhead Center for International Affairs

♦ Center for International Blood and Marrow Transplant Research (CIBMTR) 03645

Contact Froedtert and the Medical College of Wisconsin, Clinical Cancer Center, 9200 West Wisconsin Ave, Suite C5500, Milwaukee WI 53226, USA. T. +14148050700. E-mail: contactus@cibmtr.org.
Minneapolis Campus National Marrow Donor Program/Be The Match, 500 N 5th St, Minneapolis MN 55401, USA.
URL: http://www.cibmtr.org/
History 1 Jul 2004. Founded as a research collaboration between the Medical College of Wisconsin, Milwaukee WI (USA) and the National Marrow Donor Program/Be The Match, Minneapolis MN (USA). **Aims** Collaborate with the global scientific community to advance hematopoietic cell transplantation (HCT) and cellular therapy research worldwide to increase survival and enrich quality of life for patients. **Structure** Chief Scientific Director, CIBMTR MCW; Chief Scientific Director, CIBMTR NMDP; Senior Scientific Directors. **Languages** English. **Staff** 250.00 FTE, paid. **Finance** Sources: grants; revenue from activities/projects. **Activities** Events/meetings; research and development. **Events** *Tandem Transplantation and Cellular Therapy Meeting* Honolulu, HI (USA) 2025, *Tandem Transplantation and Cellular Therapy Meeting* Aurora, CO (USA) 2024, *Tandem Transplantation and Cellular Therapy Meeting* Orlando, FL (USA) 2023, *Tandem Transplantation and Cellular Therapy Meeting* Salt Lake City, UT (USA) 2022, *Transplantation and Cellular Therapy Meeting* 2021. **Publications** *Newsletter* (4 a year). Articles.
Members Transplant centres (about 330) in 33 countries and territories:
Argentina, Australia, Belgium, Brazil, Canada, Chile, Colombia, Czechia, Denmark, Egypt, Germany, Hong Kong, India, Israel, Japan, Korea Rep, Mexico, Netherlands, New Zealand, Nigeria, Norway, Pakistan, Peru, Saudi Arabia, Singapore, Spain, Sweden, Switzerland, Türkiye, UK, Uruguay, USA, Venezuela.
NGO Relations Member of (2): *Alliance for Harmonisation of Cellular Therapy Accreditation (AHCTA, #00686)*; *Federation of Clinical Immunology Societies (FOCIS, #09472)*. Founding member of: *Worldwide Network for Blood and Marrow Transplantation (WBMT, #21929)*. [2022.05.04/XM2063/**E**]

♦ Center for International Business (internationally oriented national body)
♦ Center for International and Comparative Law (internationally oriented national body)
♦ Center for International Conflict Resolution (internationally oriented national body)
♦ Center for International Cooperation and Development / see Commissione Cooperazione Internazionale per lo Sviluppo
♦ Center on International Cooperation, New York NY (internationally oriented national body)
♦ Center for International Development and Conflict Management (internationally oriented national body)
♦ Center for International and Development Economics Research, Berkeley CA (internationally oriented national body)
♦ Center for International Development, Harvard University (internationally oriented national body)
♦ Center for International Development Research, Durham NC / see Duke Center for International Development
♦ Center for International Disaster Information (internationally oriented national body)
♦ Center for International Earth Science Information Network (internationally oriented national body)
♦ Center for International Economic Collaboration (internationally oriented national body)
♦ Center for International Education (internationally oriented national body)
♦ Center for International Education, Milwaukee WI (internationally oriented national body)
♦ Center for International Environmental Law (internationally oriented national body)
♦ Center for International Environment Information / see World Environment Center (#21386)

♦ Center for International Forestry Research (CIFOR) 03646

Centre de recherche forestière internationale
Headquarters Situ Gede, Bogor Barat, Bogor 16115, Indonesia. T. +62218622622. Fax +62218622100. E-mail: cifor-dgoffice@cgiar.org – cifor@cgiar.org.
URL: http://www.cifor.org/
History May 1993. Founded on signing of Establishment Agreement, as an international institutions within *CGIAR System Organization (CGIAR, #03843)*, sponsored by Australia, Sweden, Switzerland and USA, with *Australian Centre for International Agricultural Research (ACIAR)* acting as the implementing agency during the 2-year development period. Former names and other names: *Centre international pour la recherche forestière* – former. **Aims** Conduct research on the most pressing challenges for forest and landscape management around the world; improve human well-being; protect the environment; increase equity.

Center International Humanitarian
03646

alphabetic sequence excludes
For the complete listing, see Yearbook Online at

Structure Headquarters in Bogor (Indonesia); Offices in 8 countries. **Finance** Sources: over 30 countries and organizations (not specified). **Activities** Research and development. **Events** *Global Landscape Forum* Kyoto (Japan) 2019, *Global Landscapes Forum* Luxembourg (Luxembourg) 2019, *Global Landscapes Forum* Bonn (Germany) 2018, *Global Landscapes Forum* Bonn (Germany) 2017, *Global Landscapes Forum* Paris (France) 2015. **Publications** *CIFOR News* (3 a year). Annual Report. Monographs; occasional papers; special publications. **Members** Not a membership organization.

IGO Relations Observer status with: *FAO (#09260)*. Accredited by: *United Nations Framework Convention on Climate Change – Secretariat (UNFCCC, #20564)*. Member of: *Collaborative Partnership on Forests (CPF, #04100)*; *Congo Basin Forest Partnership (CBFP, #04662)*. Collaborates with:
- *African Timber Organization (ATO, no recent information)*;
- *ASEAN Forest Tree Seed Centre Project (no recent information)*;
- *Asian Forest Cooperation Organization (AFoCO, #01489)*;
- *Bioversity International (#03262)*;
- *CABI (#03393)*;
- *Centre de coopération internationale en recherche agronomique pour le développement (CIRAD, #03733)*;
- *Institut de recherche pour le développement (IRD)*;
- *Inter-American Institute for Cooperation on Agriculture (IICA, #11434)*;
- *International Bank for Reconstruction and Development (IBRD, #12317)*;
- *International Information System for the Agricultural Sciences and Technology (AGRIS, #13848)*;
- *International Tropical Timber Organization (ITTO, #15737)*;
- *Southeast Asian Regional Center for Graduate Study and Research in Agriculture (SEARCA, #19781)*;
- *Secretariat of the Convention on Biological Diversity (SCBD, #19197)*;
- *Southeast Asian Regional Centre for Tropical Biology (SEAMEO BIOTROP, #19782)*;
- *Tropical Agriculture Research and Higher Education Center (#20246)*;
- *UNEP (#20299)*;
- *UNDP (#20292)*;
- *UNESCO (#20322)*;
- *UNESCO Office, Jakarta – Regional Bureau for Sciences in Asia and the Pacific (#20313)*.

NGO Relations Member of: *Climate Knowledge Brokers (CKB, #04016)*; *Global Alliance for Climate-Smart Agriculture (GACSA, #10189)*; *International Foundation for Science (IFS, #13677)*; *International Teak Information Network (TEAKNET, #15665)*; *International Union for Conservation of Nature and Natural Resources (IUCN, #15766)*; *Natural Capital Coalition (NCC, #16952)*; *Planetary Health Alliance (PHA, #18383)*. Affiliate member of: *Global Platform for Sustainable Natural Rubber (GPSNR, #10552)*. Partner of: *Global Partnership on Forest and Landscape Restoration (GPFLR, #10535)*; *Tropical Forest Alliance (TFA, #20249)*. Instrumental in setting up and active collaborator of: *Rights and Resources Initiative (RRI, #18947)*. Instrumental in setting up and leads: *Global Landscapes Forum (GLF, #10451)*. Contacts with: *SYLVA-WORLD for Development and the Protection of Forests and the Environment*. Collaboration with:
- *Asia-Pacific Association of Forestry Research Institutions (APAFRI, #01841)*;
- *European Tropical Forest Research Network (ETFRN, #08950)*;
- *Forest Stewardship Council (FSC, #09869)*;
- *International Centre for Tropical Agriculture (#12527)*;
- *International Food Policy Research Institute (IFPRI, #13622)*;
- *International Institute for Environment and Development (IIED, #13877)*;
- *International Institute of Tropical Agriculture (IITA, #13933)*;
- *International Union of Forest Research Organizations (IUFRO, #15774)*;
- *Rainforest Alliance*;
- *Smithsonian Tropical Research Institute, Panama (STRI)*;
- *Tropenbos International (TBI)*;
- *Tropical Forest Foundation (TFF)*;
- *World Agroforestry Centre (ICRAF, #21072)*;
- *World Forest Institute (WFI)*;
- *World Resources Institute (WRI, #21753)*;
- *World Wide Fund for Nature (WWF, #21922)*;
- *WorldFish (#21507)*.

Also links with a large number of national organizations active or interested in the field (not specified).
[2021/XE3089/**E**]

- ♦ Center for International Humanitarian Cooperation (internationally oriented national body)
- ♦ Center for International Legal Cooperation (internationally oriented national body)
- ♦ Center for International Legal Studies, Salzburg (internationally oriented national body)
- ♦ Center for International Media Assistance (internationally oriented national body)
- ♦ Center for International Peace Operations (internationally oriented national body)
- ♦ Center for International Policy (internationally oriented national body)
- ♦ Center for International Private Enterprise (internationally oriented national body)
- ♦ Center for International and Regional Studies (internationally oriented national body)
- ♦ Center for International Rehabilitation (internationally oriented national body)
- ♦ Center for International Relations, Los Angeles / see Burkle Center for International Relations
- ♦ Center for International Relations/Peace and Conflict Studies (internationally oriented national body)
- ♦ Center for International Relations and Sustainable Development (internationally oriented national body)
- ♦ Center for International Security and Arms Control, Stanford / see Center for International Security and Cooperation
- ♦ Center for International Security and Arms Control Studies (internationally oriented national body)
- ♦ Center for International Security and Cooperation (internationally oriented national body)
- ♦ Center for International and Security Studies at Maryland (internationally oriented national body)
- ♦ Center for International and Strategic Affairs / see Burkle Center for International Relations
- ♦ Center of International Studies / see Institute for Global Studies, Minneapolis
- ♦ Center for International Studies, Los Angeles CA (internationally oriented national body)
- ♦ Center for International Studies, Atlanta GA / see Andrew Young Center For International Affairs
- ♦ Center for International Studies, Durham / see Duke University Center for International and Global Studies
- ♦ Center for International Studies, Inchon / see Inha Center for International Studies
- ♦ Center for International Studies, Ohio University (internationally oriented national body)
- ♦ Center of International Studies, Princeton / see Princeton Institute for International and Regional Studies
- ♦ Center for International Studies and Research (internationally oriented national body)
- ♦ Center for International Trade and Security (internationally oriented national body)
- ♦ Center for International Training and Education (internationally oriented national body)
- ♦ Center for International Virtual Schooling (unconfirmed)

♦ Center for Justice and International Law (CEJIL) 03647

Centre pour la justice et le droit international – Centro por la Justicia y el Derecho Internacional – Centro pela Justiça e o Direito Internacional – Pemonton Kowantok Wacüpe Yuwanin Pataset

Exec Dir 1630 Connecticut Ave NW, Ste 401, Washington DC 20009-1053, USA. T. +12023193000. Fax +12023193019. E-mail: washington@cejil.org.
URL: http://www.cejil.org/

History 1991, Caracas (Venezuela). **Aims** Defend and promote human rights in the American content, litigating before the Inter-American Commission on Human Rights and the Inter-American Court of Human Rights. **Structure** Board of Directors, including Chair, Vice-Chair, Secretary and 6 members. Regional sections (3): CEJIL/Brazil; CEJIL/Meso America; CEJIL/Sur. **Languages** English, Portuguese, Spanish. **Finance** Supported by: *European Commission (EC, #06633)*; *Ford Foundation (#09858)*; *Instituto Interamericano de Derechos Humanos (IIDH, #11334)*; *John Merck Fund*; *MacArthur Foundation*; *German Catholic Bishops' Organisation for Development Cooperation (MISEREOR)*; Open Society Institute; *Swedish International Development Cooperation Agency (Sida)*; national organizations; national organizations. **Activities** Training/education; guidance/assistance/consulting; events/meetings. **Events** *Workshop on the improvement of the regional systems of human rights* Lisbon (Portugal) 2000. **Publications** *CEJIL/Gazette* (6 a year) in English, Portuguese, Spanish. Occasional papers; books; manuals.
Members Organizations in 4 countries:
Argentina, Brazil, Costa Rica, USA.

Consultative Status Consultative status granted from: *African Commission on Human and Peoples' Rights (ACHPR, #00255)* (Observer); *ECOSOC (#05331)* (Special). **IGO Relations** *Inter-American Convention on Human Rights (Pact of San José de Costa Rica, 1969)*. Consultative Status with: *OAS (#17629)*. Monitors: *Inter-American Commission on Human Rights (IACHR, #11411)*; *Corte Interamericana de Derechos Humanos (Corte IDH, #04851)*. **NGO Relations** Member of: *Americas Network on Nationality and Statelessness (Red ANA)*; *Global Campaign for Equal Nationality Rights (#10265)*. [2021/XF3339/**E**]

- ♦ Center for Justice and Peacebuilding (internationally oriented national body)
- ♦ Center for Konfliktløsning (internationally oriented national body)
- ♦ Center for Latin America, Milwaukee WI / see Center for Latin American and Caribbean Studies, Milwaukee WI
- ♦ Center for Latin American and Caribbean Studies, Athens GA / see Latin American and Caribbean Studies Institute
- ♦ Center for Latin American and Caribbean Studies, Bloomington (internationally oriented national body)
- ♦ Center for Latin American and Caribbean Studies, Champaign (internationally oriented national body)
- ♦ Center for Latin American and Caribbean Studies, Michigan (internationally oriented national body)
- ♦ Center for Latin American and Caribbean Studies, Milwaukee WI (internationally oriented national body)
- ♦ Center for Latin American and Caribbean Studies, New York (internationally oriented national body)
- ♦ Center for Latin American and Caribbean Studies, Storrs CT / see El Instituto: Institute of Latina/o, Caribbean and Latin American Studies
- ♦ Center for Latin American and Caribbean Studies, University of Illinois at Urbana-Champaign / see Center for Latin American and Caribbean Studies, Champaign

♦ Center for Latin American Monetary Studies 03648

Centro de Estudios Monetarios Latinoamericanos (CEMLA)

Dir-Gen Durango 54, Cuauhtémoc, Col Roma, 06700 Mexico City CDMX, Mexico. T. +525550616646. E-mail: direccion@cemla.org.
URL: http://www.cemla.org/

History Dec 1949, Santiago (Chile), at 2nd congress of central bank technicians from the American continent and on the initiative of the Bank of Mexico. Statutes approved at 3rd congress, Feb-Mar 1952, Havana (Cuba); amended by Assembly, Sep 1973, Managua (Nicaragua) and Sep 1986, Panama. Formally opened Sep 1952, Mexico City (Mexico). Previously also referred to in French as *Centre d'études monétaires latinoaméricaines*. **Aims** Increase understanding of monetary and central *banking* questions in Latin America, particularly with regard to *financial* policies. **Structure** Assembly (annual); Board of Governors. **Languages** English, Spanish. **Staff** 53.00 FTE, paid. **Finance** Members' dues. **Activities** Training/education; events/meetings; guidance/assistance/consulting. **Events** *Meeting* Madrid (Spain) 2019, *Conference on Financial Education and Inclusion in Latin America and the Caribbean* Mexico City (Mexico) 2019, *Conference on Financial Education and Inclusion in Latin America and the Caribbean* Madrid (Spain) 2018, *Risk Management Conference* Bogota (Colombia) 2016, *Meeting* Brasilia (Brazil) 2016. **Publications** *CEMLA Bulletin* (4 a year) in Spanish; *Monetaria* (2 a year) in English, Spanish. Special reports; books.
Members Associate (regional central banks); Cooperating (non-regional central banks); Founder (7, marked 'F'), in 52 countries and territories:
Antigua-Barbuda, Argentina, Aruba, Bahamas, Barbados, Belize, Bolivia, Brazil, Canada, Cayman Is, Chile (F), Colombia (F), Costa Rica, Cuba (F), Curaçao, Dominica, Dominican Rep, Ecuador (F), El Salvador, France, Germany, Grenada, Guatemala (F), Guyana, Haiti, Honduras (F), Hungary, Italy, Jamaica, Mexico (F), Montserrat, Neth Antilles, Nicaragua, Panama, Paraguay, Peru, Philippines, Portugal, Puerto Rico, Spain, St Kitts-Nevis, St Lucia, St Maarten, St Vincent-Grenadines, Suriname, Sweden, Switzerland, Trinidad-Tobago, Turks-Caicos, Uruguay, USA, Venezuela.
Included in the above, one organization listed in this Yearbook:
Consultative Status Consultative status granted from: *ECOSOC (#05331)* (Ros C); *UNCTAD (#20285)* (General Category). **IGO Relations** Observer to: *International Bank for Reconstruction and Development (IBRD, #12317)* (World Bank); *International Monetary Fund (IMF, #14180)*; *Sistema Económico Latinoamericano (SELA, #19294)*. Full member of: *Irving Fisher Committee on Central Bank Statistics (IFC, #16020)*. Cooperates with: *Central American Bank for Economic Integration (CABEI, #03658)*; *Central American Monetary Council (#03672)*; *Eastern Caribbean Central Bank (ECCB, #05231)*; *Inter-American Development Bank (IDB, #11427)*; *Latin American Reserve Fund (#16367)*. Partner of: *South East Asian Central Banks Research and Training Centre (SEACEN Centre, #19760)*. **NGO Relations** Cooperates in related fields of interest with: *Banco Latinoamericano de Comercio Exterior (BLADEX, #03159)*. [2017.10.25/XF0255/**E**]

- ♦ Center for Latin American Studies, Berkeley CA (internationally oriented national body)
- ♦ Center for Latin American Studies, Gainesville (internationally oriented national body)
- ♦ Center for Latin American Studies of Inclusive Education (internationally oriented national body)
- ♦ Center for Latin American Studies, Pittsburgh (internationally oriented national body)
- ♦ Center for Latin American Studies, San Diego CA (internationally oriented national body)
- ♦ Center for Latin American Studies, Stanford CA (internationally oriented national body)
- ♦ Center for Latin American Studies, Tempe AZ (internationally oriented national body)
- ♦ Center for Latin American Studies, Tucson (internationally oriented national body)
- ♦ Center of Latin American Studies, University of Kansas (internationally oriented national body)
- ♦ Center for Latin American Studies, Washington DC (internationally oriented national body)
- ♦ Center for Latino, Latin American and Caribbean Studies (internationally oriented national body)
- ♦ Center for Latino Studies in the Americas (internationally oriented national body)
- ♦ Center for Management and International Cooperation for Development (internationally oriented national body)
- ♦ Center for Marine Conservation / see Ocean Conservancy

♦ Center for Mediterranean Integration (CMI) 03649

Centre pour l'Intégration en Méditerranée

Senior External Affairs Officer Tour La Marseillaise, 2bis Bd Euromediterranée, Quai d'Arenc, 13002 Marseille, France. E-mail: info@cmimarseille.org.
URL: https://www.cmimarseille.org/

History 2009. Founded as a cooperation based on an organizational arrangement managed by *International Bank for Reconstruction and Development (IBRD, #12317)* (World Bank). Since July 2021, hosted by *United Nations Office for Project Services (UNOPS, #20602)*. Former names and other names: *Marseille Center for Mediterranean Integration (CMI)* – former. **Aims** Provide a platform where international development agencies, governments, local authorities and civil society from around the Mediterranean convene to exchange ideas, discuss public policies and identify regional solutions to address regional challenges in the Mediterranean. **Staff** 41.00 FTE, paid.
Members Governments (11):
Egypt, France (City of Marseille), Greece, Italy, Jordan, Lebanon, Morocco, Palestine, Provence-Alpes-Côte-d'Azur, Spain, Tunisia.
Institutions (2):
European Investment Bank (EIB, #07599); *International Bank for Reconstruction and Development (IBRD, #12317)* (World Bank); *United Nations Human Settlements Programme (UN-Habitat, #20572)*.
Observer:
European External Action Service (EEAS, #07018).
IGO Relations Cooperates with (8): *Agence française de développement (AFD)*; *Deutsche Gesellschaft für Internationale Zusammenarbeit (GIZ)*; *European Bank for Reconstruction and Development (EBRD, #06315)*; *Islamic Development Bank (IsDB, #16044)*; *Islamic World Educational, Scientific and Cultural Organization (ICESCO, #16058)*; *Plan Bleu pour l'environnement et le développement en Méditerranée (Plan Bleu, #18379)*; *UNDP (#20292)*; *Union for the Mediterranean (UfM, #20457)*. **NGO Relations** Cooperates with (1): *Cities Alliance (#03950)*. [2022.02.01/XJ9302/**E***]

- ♦ Center za Mednarodno Sodelovanje in Razvoj (internationally oriented national body)

♦ Center for Meso American Studies on Appropriate Technology 03650

Centre mésoaméricain d'études sur la technologie appropriée – Centro Mesoamericano de Estudios sobre Tecnologia Apropiada (CEMAT)

Pres 2a Avenida 1-66, Zona 16, Concepción Las Lomas, Guatemala, Guatemala. T. +50223640419. Fax +50223640422.
URL: http://www.cemat.org/
Aims Promote and systematize transference of appropriate technology knowledge from other countries, and the local knowledge to other countries; develop and implement appropriate technology projects and training systems for popular groups; promote communication and exchange of experience and information. **Structure** General Assembly; Directive Board; Executive Board; Executive Director; Working Units. **Languages** English, French, Portuguese, Spanish. **Staff** 15.00 FTE, paid. **Finance** Budget (annual): US$ 150,000. **Activities** Advocacy/lobbying/activism; events/meetings. **Publications** *Boletin RED* (4 a year) in English, Spanish. Brochures; monographs; various texts; translations.
Members Individuals and national organizations in 35 countries:
Argentina, Belgium, Belize, Bolivia, Botswana, Brazil, Canada, Chile, China, Colombia, Costa Rica, Denmark, Dominican Rep, Ecuador, El Salvador, France, Germany, Guatemala, Honduras, India, Jamaica, Kenya, Malaysia, Mexico, Netherlands, Nicaragua, Paraguay, Philippines, Sweden, Switzerland, Thailand, UK, Uruguay, USA, Venezuela.
IGO Relations *FAO (#09260)*; *UNICEF (#20332)*; *UNIDO (#20336)*; *WHO (#20950)*. **NGO Relations** Member of: *International Union for Conservation of Nature and Natural Resources (IUCN, #15766)*. [2015/XE6633/**E**]

- ♦ Center for Middle East Development (internationally oriented national body)
- ♦ Center for Middle Eastern and North African Studies, Ann Arbor MI (internationally oriented national body)
- ♦ Center for Middle Eastern Strategic Studies (internationally oriented national body)
- ♦ Center for Middle Eastern Studies, Austin TX (internationally oriented national body)
- ♦ Center for Middle Eastern Studies, Berkeley (internationally oriented national body)
- ♦ Center for Middle Eastern Studies, Cambridge MA (internationally oriented national body)
- ♦ Center for Middle Eastern Studies, University of Arizona (internationally oriented national body)
- ♦ Center for Middle East Peace and Economic Cooperation, Washington DC / see S Daniel Abraham Center for Middle East Peace
- ♦ Center for Migration Studies, New York (internationally oriented national body)
- ♦ Center for Muslim-Christian Understanding – History and International Affairs / see Prince Alwaleed Bin Talal Center for Muslim-Christian Understanding
- ♦ centerNet (unconfirmed)
- ♦ Center for New Creation (internationally oriented national body)
- ♦ Center for Oceanic Awareness, Research and Education (internationally oriented national body)
- ♦ Center for Oceans Law and Policy (internationally oriented national body)
- ♦ Center for OPEC Studies (no recent information)
- ♦ Center for Operations Research and Econometrics (internationally oriented national body)
- ♦ Center for Pacific and American Studies (internationally oriented national body)
- ♦ Center for Pacific Island Studies, Honolulu (internationally oriented national body)
- ♦ Center for Peacebuilding (internationally oriented national body)
- ♦ Center for Peace and Conflict Studies, Detroit (internationally oriented national body)
- ♦ Center for Peace, Conversion and Foreign Policy of Ukraine (internationally oriented national body)
- ♦ Center for Peaceful Change / see Center for Applied Conflict Management
- ♦ Center for Peace Mediation (internationally oriented national body)
- ♦ Center for Peace Studies, Akron / see Centre for Conflict Management, Akron OH
- ♦ Center of the Picture Industry / see Coordination of European Picture Agencies, Press Stock Heritage (#04825)
- ♦ Center for Political and International Studies, Moscow (internationally oriented national body)
- ♦ Center for Population Communications – International / see PCI Media
- ♦ Center for Population Options / see Advocates for Youth, Washington DC
- ♦ Center for Post-Soviet and East European Studies / see Center for Russian, East European and Eurasian Studies, Austin TX
- ♦ Center for Preventive Action (internationally oriented national body)
- ♦ Center for the Progress of Peoples / see Asian Center for the Progress of Peoples
- ♦ Center for the Promotion of MSMEs in Central America (#03816)
- ♦ Center for Psychological Studies in the Nuclear Age / see John E Mack Institute
- ♦ Center for Psychology and Social Change / see John E Mack Institute
- ♦ Center for Reproductive Rights (internationally oriented national body)

♦ Center of Research and Action for Peace (CERAP) 03651

Centre de Recherche et d'Action pour la Paix
Gen Dir 08 BP 2088, Abidjan 08, Côte d'Ivoire. T. +22522404720. Fax +22522448438. E-mail: info@cerap-inades.org – direction.generale@cerap-inades.org.
URL: http://www.cerap-inades.org/
History 4 Dec 1962, Abidjan (Côte d'Ivoire). Founded by *Society of Jesus (SJ)*, following request of *Conférence épiscopale régionale de l'Afrique de l'Ouest francophone (CERAO, inactive)*. Former names and other names: *African Institute for Economic and Social Development* – former; *Institut africain pour le développement économique et social (INADES)* – former. Registration: Côte d'Ivoire. **Aims** Collect information and analyse socio-cultural, economic, political and religious changes which determine the development of peoples and personal decisions in black *Africa*. **Structure** Administrative Council; Jesuit Social and Academic Institute. **Languages** English, French. **Staff** 50.00 FTE, paid. Plus 70 seconded from other institutions. **Finance** Sources: subsidies. Annual budget: 950,000,000,000 XAF. **Activities** Capacity building; conflict resolution; events/meetings; humanitarian/emergency aid; monitoring/evaluation; research/documentation; training/education. **Events** *Atelier sur l'étude de l'audience pour les radios rurales* Ouagadougou (Burkina Faso) 2001. **Publications** *Débat Courrier de l'Afrique de l'Ouest* (11 a year); *Top Management*. Books.
[2021.05.25/XF0972/**E**]

- ♦ Center for Research and Action for Peace (internationally oriented national body)
- ♦ Center for Research and Telecommunication Experimentation for Networked Communities (internationally oriented national body)
- ♦ Center for Russia, East Europe and Central Asia, Madison WI (internationally oriented national body)
- ♦ Center for Russian, East European and Eurasian Studies, Austin TX (internationally oriented national body)
- ♦ Center for Russian and East European Studies, Pittsburgh PA (internationally oriented national body)
- ♦ Center for Science and International Security (internationally oriented national body)
- ♦ Center for Science in the Public Interest (internationally oriented national body)
- ♦ Center for Security Studies (internationally oriented national body)
- ♦ Centers for International Business Education and Research (internationally oriented national body)

♦ Centers for Natural Resources and Development (CNRD) 03652

Coordinator TH Köln – Univ of Applied Sciences, Betzdorfer Str 2, 50679 Cologne, Germany. E-mail: cnrd-admin@th-koeln.de – contact@cnrd.info.
URL: http://www.cnrd.info/
Aims Promote academic exchange and cooperation in the field of natural resource management, particularly with regards to water, land, ecosystems and renewable energy. **Structure** Advisory Board. **Finance** Supported by: *Deutscher Akademischer Austauschdienst (DAAD)*; Federal Ministry for Economic Cooperation and Development (Germany). **Activities** Capacity building; research/documentation; training/education. **Events** *Water Security and Climate Change conference (WSCC)* Hanoi (Vietnam) 2021, *WSCC : Water Security and Climate Change Conference* San Luis Potosí (Mexico) 2019, *WSCC : Water Security and Climate Change Conference* Nairobi (Kenya) 2018, *WSCC : Water Security and Climate Change Conference* Cologne (Germany) 2017, *WSCC : Water Security and Climate Change Conference* Bangkok (Thailand) 2016.
Members Partners in 28 countries:
Bangladesh, Barbados, Brazil, Chile, Colombia, Costa Rica, Ecuador, Egypt, Ethiopia, Germany, Ghana, Indonesia, Iran Islamic Rep, Jordan, Kenya, Mexico, Myanmar, Nepal, Oman, Pakistan, Philippines, Qatar, Sudan, Tanzania UR, Thailand, USA, Vietnam, Zambia. [2021/XM6025/**F**]

- ♦ Center for South Asia, Madison WI (internationally oriented national body)
- ♦ Center for South Asian Studies, Charlottesville VA (internationally oriented national body)
- ♦ Center for South Asian Studies, Honolulu HI (internationally oriented national body)
- ♦ Center for Southeast Asian Studies-Indonesia (internationally oriented national body)
- ♦ Center for Southeast Asian Studies, Madison WI (internationally oriented national body)
- ♦ Center for Strategic and Defense Studies, Budapest (internationally oriented national body)
- ♦ Center for Strategic and International Studies, Washington DC (internationally oriented national body)
- ♦ Center for Studies on Development, Caracas (internationally oriented national body)
- ♦ Center for Studies on the Holocaust / see ADL Braun Holocaust Institute
- ♦ Center for Studies on Labor and Agrarian Development (internationally oriented national body)
- ♦ Center for the Study of Global Change (internationally oriented national body)
- ♦ Center for the Study of Global Christianity (internationally oriented national body)
- ♦ Center for Study of the Global Economy, Havana (internationally oriented national body)
- ♦ Center for the Study of Human Rights, New York / see Institute for the Study of Human Rights, Columbia University
- ♦ Center for the Study of Muslim Networks / see Duke Islamic Studies Center
- ♦ Center for the Study of State and Society, Buenos Aires (internationally oriented national body)
- ♦ Center for the Study of Tropical Construction and Architecture (internationally oriented national body)
- ♦ Center for Sustainable Asian Cities (internationally oriented national body)
- ♦ Center for Sustainable Development in the Americas (internationally oriented national body)
- ♦ Center for Teaching International Relations (internationally oriented national body)
- ♦ Center for Third World Organizing (internationally oriented national body)

♦ Center for United Nations Constitutional Research (CUNCR) 03653

Exec Dir Avenue Franklin Roosevelt 103, 1050 Brussels, Belgium. E-mail: info@cuncr.org.
URL: https://cuncr.org/
History Registration: Banque-Carrefour des Entreprises, No/ID: 0670.457.169, Start date: 27 Jan 2017, Belgium. **Aims** Provide research and policy recommendations concerning the Charter and the structure of the United Nations (UN) in the direction of achieving the Charter Preamble's "we the peoples" ideals and objectives and towards its constitutionalization. **Structure** General Assembly; Board; Advisory Board. **Activities** Guidance/assistance/consulting; networking/liaising; research/documentation; training/education. **Members** Full; Associate. Membership countries not specified. [2022.07.05/AA1191/**E**]

- ♦ Center for UN Reform Education (internationally oriented national body)
- ♦ Center for Urban History of East Central Europe (internationally oriented national body)
- ♦ Center for Victims of Torture (internationally oriented national body)
- ♦ Center for War, Peace and the News Media, New York (internationally oriented national body)
- ♦ Center for War Peace Studies (internationally oriented national body)
- ♦ Center for Western European Studies / see Centro de Estudios Europeos, Habana
- ♦ Center for West European Studies, Pittsburgh PA / see European Studies Center, Pittsburgh PA
- ♦ Center for West European Studies, Seattle WA (internationally oriented national body)
- ♦ Center for Women, the Earth, the Divine (internationally oriented national body)
- ♦ Center for Women's Global Leadership (internationally oriented national body)
- ♦ Center for World Indigenous Studies (internationally oriented national body)

♦ Centesimus Annus Pro Pontifice Foundation (CAPP) 03654

Fondazione Centesimus Annus – Pro Pontifice
Main Office Fondazione Centesimus Annus, 00120 Vatican City, Vatican. T. +39669885752. Fax +39669881971.
CAPP USA 6 Wyndover Ln, Cos Cob CT 06807-1818, USA. E-mail: info@capp-usa.org.
URL: http://www.centesimusannus.org/
History 5 Jun 1993, by Pope John Paul II. Comes within *Administrative Hierarchy of the Roman Catholic Church (#00117)*. **Aims** Promote *Roman Catholic social* teaching, as expressed in the Papal Encyclical 'Centesimus Annus', in the *business* and professional communities. **Structure** Chairman; Board of Directors; Comptrollers; Secretary General. **Events** *International conference on confronting globalization* Rome (Italy) 2004.
[2013/XM4657/f/**F**]

- ♦ CENTICA – Centre for Tourism in Islands and Coastal Areas (internationally oriented national body)
- ♦ CENTO – Central Treaty Organization (inactive)
- ♦ Centraal Comité van Verenigingen van Boseigenaren in de EG / see Confederation of European Forest Owners (#04525)
- ♦ Centraal Europees Instituut voor Neuro-Semantiek / see MCF-B
- ♦ Centra za Antiratnu akciju (internationally oriented national body)
- ♦ CENTRAG – International Centre for Research in Accountability and Governance (unconfirmed)
- ♦ Central Africa Economic and Monetary Community (#04374)
- ♦ Central African Association of Mathematics, Physics and Computer Science (inactive)
- ♦ Central African Clearing House (no recent information)
- ♦ Central African Convention for the Control of Small Arms and Light Weapons, Their Ammunition, Parts and Components That Can be Used for Their Manufacture, Repair and Assembly (2010 treaty)
- ♦ Central African Customs and Economic Union (inactive)
- ♦ Central African Economic Union (#20376)
- ♦ Central African Federation (inactive)
- ♦ Central African Forests Commission (#04214)
- ♦ Central African Mineral Resources Development Centre (no recent information)
- ♦ Central African Missions (internationally oriented national body)
- ♦ Central African Monetary Area / see Union monétaire de l'Afrique centrale (#20463)
- ♦ Central African Monetary Area / see Communauté économique et monétaire d'Afrique centrale (#04374)
- ♦ Central African Monetary System / see Communauté économique et monétaire d'Afrique centrale (#04374)
- ♦ Central African Monetary System / see Union monétaire de l'Afrique centrale (#20463)
- ♦ Central African Monetary Union (#20463)
- ♦ Central African Network of AIDS Service Organizations (see: #00272)

♦ Central African Power Pool (CAPP) 03655

Pool energétique de l'Afrique centrale (PEAC)
Permanent Sec Tour Nabemba, 14ème étage A, Brazzaville, Congo Brazzaville. T. +2425439039. Fax +242810569.
History 12 Apr 2003, Brazzaville (Congo Brazzaville), within *Economic Community of Central African States (ECCAS, #05311)*. **Aims** Study energy potentials in the region. **Finance** Project funding from the US Government.
Members Companies (8) in 8 countries:
Cameroon, Central African Rep, Chad, Congo Brazzaville, Congo DR, Equatorial Guinea, Gabon, Sao Tomé-Principe.
IGO Relations *ECA Sub-Regional Office for Central Africa (ECA/SRO-CA, #05274)*; *Southern African Power Pool (SAPP, #19858)*. **NGO Relations** *Association of Power Utilities in Africa (APUA, #02867)* is member and supporting partner. [2009/XM0736/**F**]

- ♦ Central African States' Development Bank (#03168)

♦ Central Africa Protected Areas Network 03656

Réseau des aires protégées d'Afrique centrale (RAPAC) – Red de las Areas Protegidas del Africa Central – Rede das Areas Prategidas da Africa Central
Exec Sec BP 14533, Libreville, Gabon. T. +241443322. E-mail: secretariat.executif@rapac.org – hakuzadamas@gmail.com.
History Statutes adopted 31 May 2000; Statutes revised 18 Feb 2006, Libreville (Gabon). **Aims** Promote the conservation of the biological diversity and the management of natural resources in and around the protected areas of Central Africa, through the development of an efficient network; promote professional governance, harmonization of policies and management tools. **Languages** English, French, Portuguese, Spanish. **Events** *Extraordinary General Assembly* Libreville (Gabon) 2013, *Extraordinary General Assembly* Libreville (Gabon) 2006. **Publications** *RAPAC Infos* – newsletter. Annual Report.

Members Active; Observer; Honorary; Benefactor. Governmental and non-governmental organizations in 8 countries:
Cameroon, Central African Rep, Chad, Congo Brazzaville, Congo DR, Equatorial Guinea, Gabon, Sao Tomé-Principe.
Consultative Status Consultative status granted from: *UNESCO (#20322)* (Consultative Status). **NGO Relations** Member of (1): *International Union for Conservation of Nature and Natural Resources (IUCN, #15766).* [2017/XM3868/**D**]

♦ Central America – Dominican Republic Apparel and Textile Council (unconfirmed)
♦ Central America and Mexico Migration Alliance (unconfirmed)
♦ Central American Academy, San José (internationally oriented national body)
♦ Central American Agency for Air Navigation Services (see: #04837)
♦ Central American Agreement on the Equalization of Import Charges (1959 treaty)
♦ Central American Agreement on Fiscal Incentives to Industrial Development, 1962 (1962 treaty)
♦ Central American Agreement on Highway Traffic (1958 treaty)
♦ Central American Agreement on Uniform Road Signs (1958 treaty)

♦ Central American Agricultural Council 03657

Consejo Agropecuario Centroamericano (CAC)
Exec Sec 600 Metros Noreste del Cruce de Ipis-Coronado, San Isidro Coronado, San José, San José, San José, Costa Rica. T. +50622160303. Fax +50622160285. E-mail: julio.calderon@yahoo.com – info.cac@sica.int.
URL: http://www.sica.int/cac/
History Jul 1991, within the framework of *Central American Integration System (#03671).* Secretariat based at *Inter-American Institute for Cooperation on Agriculture (IICA, #11434)* and coordinated by *Secretaria Permanente del Tratado General de Integración Económica Centroamericana (SIECA, #19195).* **Aims** Define, coordinate and give direction to policies, programmes, projects and regional activities in the field of agriculture and *agroindustry.* **Structure** Council of Ministers of Agriculture; Regional Technical Commission. **Languages** English, Spanish. **Activities** Guidance/assistance/consulting; projects/programmes.
Members Ministries and Secretariats of Agriculture of 8 countries:
Belize, Costa Rica, Dominican Rep, El Salvador, Guatemala, Honduras, Nicaragua, Panama. [2016.07.14/XD5496/**E***]

♦ Central American Air Safety Services Corporation / see Corporación Centroamericana de Servicios de Navegación Aérea (#04837)
♦ Central American Association for Economy, Health and Environment (internationally oriented national body)
♦ Central American Association of Families of Missing Detainees (no recent information)
♦ Central American Association of Flower Therapists (no recent information)
♦ Central American Association of Medical Schools (no recent information)
♦ Central American Association of Orthotists, Prosthetics, Rehabilitation Professionals and Affiliates (inactive)
♦ Central American Association of Phonographic Producers (no recent information)
♦ Central American Association of Psychiatry (no recent information)

♦ Central American Bank for Economic Integration (CABEI) 03658

Banque centroaméricaine d'intégration économique – Banco Centroamericano de Integración Económica (BCIE)
Exec Pres Apto Postal 772, Tegucigalpa, Francisco Morazán, Honduras. T. +5042402222 – +5042402243. Fax +5042402101 – +5042402185.
URL: http://www.bcie.org/
History Founded 31 May 1961, Tegucigalpa (Honduras), when started operations, following signature of Articles of Agreement, 13 Dec 1960, Managua (Nicaragua), by governments of El Salvador, Guatemala (Guatemala), Honduras and Nicaragua. Costa Rica became a member 23 Sep 1963. A financial institution of *Central American Common Market (CACM, #03666).* Statutes registered in *'UNTS 1/6544'.* **Aims** Implement economic integration and balanced economic growth of member countries; finance projects to further these aims and develop trade in the Central American Common Market; support Central American *free trade* objectives; improve, expand or substitute agricultural activities to establish a regional supply system. **Structure** Assembly of Governors (annual), comprising Ministers of Economics and Presidents of Central Banks of member countries. Board of Directors of up to 9 members (5 from founding countries and 4 from non-regional members). Headed by Executive President/Executive Officer, assisted by Executive Vice-President. Management Divisions (6), each headed by Manager: Business; Credit; Institutional Risk; Financial; Operations; Human Resources. Staff areas (3): Chief Economist; Institutional Relations; Legal Advisor. **Languages** English, Spanish. **Staff** Top management: 6; regional management: 5. **Finance** At the end of fiscal year 2013: total assets – US$ 7,537,000; gross loan portfolio – US$ 5,200,000; total disbursements – US$ 1,444,500; net profit – US$ 118,200,000. **Activities** Principal investment sectors: regional infrastructure projects; long-term investment projects in regional industries; coordinated agricultural projects; enterprises needing to expand or modernize their operations; services necessary for functioning of the Common Market; other projects to create economic coordination among members and increase Central American trade. Concessionary window: *Fondo Especial para la Transformación Social de Centroamérica (FETS, see: #03658).* **Events** *CABEI-Korea Week Meeting* Seoul (Korea Rep) 2019, *Meeting of Board of Governors* Honduras 2011, *Meeting of Board of Governors* Nicaragua 2010, *Meeting of Board of Governors* Honduras 2009, *EEP regional forum* San Pedro Sula (Honduras) 2008. **Publications** *Boletín Estadístico Mensual* (12 a year) in Spanish – in 2 parts; *Carta Informativa* (12 a year); *Tendencias y Perspectivas Económicas de Centroamérica* (4 a year); *Revista de la Integración y el Desarrollo de Centroamérica. Información Financiera* in English, Spanish. Annual Report.
Members Founding members governments of 5 countries:
Costa Rica, El Salvador, Guatemala, Honduras, Nicaragua.
Non-regional members governments of 7 countries and territories:
Argentina, Colombia, Dominican Rep, Mexico, Panama, Spain, Taiwan.
Beneficiary countries governments of 3 countries:
Belize, Dominican Rep, Panama.
IGO Relations Formal agreement with: *UNESCO (#20322).* Member of: *Committee of International Development Institutions on the Environment (CIDIE, no recent information).* Observer member of: *Association of Caribbean States (ACS, #02411); Sistema Económico Latinoamericano (SELA, #19294).* Specialized institution of: *Central American Integration System (#03671).* Accredited by: *United Nations Framework Convention on Climate Change – Secretariat (UNFCCC, #20564).* Special links with: *European Commission (EC, #06633); Inter-American Development Bank (IDB, #11427); OAS (#17629); Secretaria Permanente del Tratado General de Integración Económica Centroamericana (SIECA, #19195).* Extensive cooperation with: *Nordic Investment Bank (NIB, #17327).* Sponsors: *Latin American and Caribbean Institute for Economic and Social Planning (#16279).* Joint projects with: *Comisión Centroamericana de Ambiente y Desarrollo (CCAD, #04129); International Fund for Agricultural Development (IFAD, #13692).* Assists: *Comisión para el Desarrollo Científico y Tecnológico de Centro América y Panama (CTCAP, #04132).* Adheres to: *Global Partnership for Effective Development Co-operation (GPEDC, #10532).* **NGO Relations** Member of: *Asociación Latinoamericana de Instituciones Financieras para el Desarrollo (ALIDE, #02233); International Development Finance Club (IDFC, #13159).* Adhering member of: *Latin American Banking Association (#16254).* Supports: *Centro Latinoamericano para la Competitividad y el Desarrollo Sostenible (CLACDS).* [2017.07.26/XF0230/**F***]

♦ Central American Baseball Confederation (unconfirmed)

♦ Central American Black Organization (CABO) 03659

Organización Negra Centroamericana (ONECA)
Pres 324 East 151 St, Bronx NY 10451, USA. T. +17182135439.
Contact Bo Teodoro Martinez, contiguo laboratorio Talley, Bluefields SOUTH CARIBBEAN, Nicaragua. T. +150525720434. E-mail: francissidney1950@yahoo.com – presidencia.oneca@yahoo.com.
History Aug 1995. **Aims** Protect and defend the rights of Central Americans of African descent. **Structure** General Assembly; Board; Country Chapters. **Languages** English, Garifuna, Spanish. **Staff** None. **Finance** Budget (annual): US$ 50,000. **Events** *Women Conference* Bluefields (Nicaragua) 2015, *Fortalecimiento Afro Meeting on VIH* Colón (Panama) 2015, *General Assembly* Colón (Panama) 2015, *General Assembly / Youth Conference* Dangriga (Belize) 2015, *Sustainable Development Conference* Panama (Panama) 2015.
Members Chapters in 7 countries:
Belize, Costa Rica, Guatemala, Honduras, Nicaragua, Panama, USA.
NGO Relations The Southern Diaspora Research and Development Center. [2015.06.01/XF6015/**F**]

♦ Central American Boxing Federation (#09351)

♦ Central American and Caribbean Amateur Swimming Confederation 03660

Confederación Centroamericana y del Caribe de Aficionados a la Natación (CCCAN)
Pres address not obtained. T. +17875870078.
URL: https://www.teamunify.com/Home.jsp?team=cccan
History 1947. Former names and other names: *Confederación Centro Americana y del Caribe de Aficionados a la Natación (CCCAN)* – former. [2020/XD6712/**D**]

♦ Central American and Caribbean Area Endocrine Association (inactive)

♦ Central American and Caribbean Athletic Confederation (CACAC) . . 03661

Confederación Centroamericana y del Caribe de Atletismo
Pres Féd Haitienne d'Athlétisme Amateur, 48 rue Clerveaux, HT6114 Pétion-Ville, Haiti. T. +50922571039. E-mail: hai@mf.iaaf.org – cacacathletics@yahoo.com.
URL: http://www.cacacathletics.org/
History 1966, San Juan (Puerto Rico). Constitution adopted Aug 1969; amended 16 Jun 1979, Guadalajara (Mexico); 5 Jul 1979, San Juan (Puerto Rico); 22 Aug 1980, Nassau (Bahamas); 11 Jul 1981, Santo Domingo (Dominican Rep); 18 Aug 1998, Maracaibo (Venezuela); 27 Jun 1999, Bridgetown (Barbados); 16 Jul 2000, San Juan (Puerto Rico); 7 Jul 2002, Bridgetown (Barbados). **Languages** English, Spanish. **Staff** Voluntary. **Finance** Budget: US$ 20,000. **Activities** Organizes championships.
Members Organizations in 35 countries and territories:
Anguilla, Antigua-Barbuda, Aruba, Bahamas, Barbados, Belize, Bermuda, Cayman Is, Colombia, Costa Rica, Cuba, Dominica, Dominican Rep, El Salvador, Grenada, Guatemala, Guyana, Haiti, Honduras, Jamaica, Mexico, Montserrat, Neth Antilles, Nicaragua, Panama, Puerto Rico, St Kitts-Nevis, St Lucia, St Vincent-Grenadines, Suriname, Trinidad-Tobago, Turks-Caicos, Venezuela, Virgin Is UK, Virgin Is USA.
NGO Relations Member of: *Asociación Panamericana de Atletismo (APA, #02284).* [2014/XD2208/**D**]

♦ Central American and Caribbean Boxing Federation / see American Boxing Confederation (#00776)

♦ Central American & Caribbean Bridge Federation (CAC) 03662

Pres Lee Green, Warners Terrace, Christ Church BB15077, CHRIST CHURCH BB15077, Barbados. T. +12462305555.
URL: https://www.bridgewebs.com/cacbf/
History 1971. Since 1976, a zone of *World Bridge Federation (WBF, #21246).* **Aims** Organize and govern bridge in Central America and the Caribbean. **Structure** Executive Committee. **Activities** Sporting activities.
Members Organizations in 12 countries and territories:
Barbados, Bermuda, Costa Rica, Cuba, Grenada, Guadeloupe, Guatemala, Jamaica, Martinique, Panama, Suriname, Trinidad-Tobago. [2020/AA0987/**D**]

♦ Central American and Caribbean Confederation of Esports (unconfirmed)
♦ Central American and Caribbean Confederation of Small and Medium Sized Independent Companies (no recent information)
♦ Central American and Caribbean Confederation of Weightlifting (inactive)

♦ Central American and Caribbean Dermatological Society 03663

Sociedad Centroamericana y del Caribe de Dermatologia (SCCAD)
Secretaria de Archivo address not obtained.
URL: http://www.sccad.net/
History Founded 8 Dec 1957, San Salvador (El Salvador), at 1st Central American Congress of Dermatology, as *Central American Dermatological Society – Société dermatologique de l'Amérique centrale – Sociedad Centroamericana de Dermatologia.* **Aims** Promote dermatology of the central and Caribbean countries. **Structure** Secretariat rotates among members, which also organizes the congress; Board. **Languages** Spanish. **Staff** Staff changes, in general, every 2 years; File Secretary changes every 6 years. **Finance** Congress financed by pharmaceutical companies. No annual budget. **Activities** Organizes Congress (every 2 years) in different countries of Central America or Dominican Rep. **Events** *Congress / Biennial Congress* Panama (Panama) 2013, *Congress / Biennial Congress* San José (Costa Rica) 2011, *Congress / Biennial Congress* Nicaragua 2009, *Congress / Biennial Congress* San Pedro Sula (Honduras) 2006, *Congress / Biennial Congress* El Salvador 2004. **Publications** None.
Members Full dermatological societies (426) in 7 countries:
Costa Rica, Dominican Rep, El Salvador, Guatemala, Honduras, Nicaragua, Panama.
NGO Relations *Colegio Ibero-Latinoamericano de Dermatologia (CILAD, #04093); International League of Dermatological Societies (ILDS, #14018).* [2019/XD1081/c/**F**]

♦ Central American, Caribbean and Mexican Association of Laboratory Animals (#02113)
♦ Central American and Caribbean Pharmaceutical Federation (#09301)

♦ Central American and Caribbean Physical Society 03664

Sociedad Centroamericana y del Caribe de Fisica (SOCECAF)
Contact address not obtained. T. +5076219183. E-mail: moreno@cwpanama.net.
URL: http://www.socecaf.org/
History 20 Nov 1965, as *Sociedad Centroamericana de Fisica.* **Aims** Promote and coordinate the development of *physics* in the region. **Structure** Council. Executive Committee, comprising President, Secretary and Treasurer. **Languages** Spanish. **Staff** 4.50 FTE, voluntary. **Finance** Members' dues. Supported by FELASOFI. **Activities** Organizes: *'CURCCAF'* – Central American and Caribean rotary course; seminars and workshops. **Events** *Central American and Caribbean Physical Congress* Panama (Panama) 2001, *Central American and Caribbean Physical Congress* Costa Rica 2000.
Members National organizations (8) in 8 countries:
Costa Rica, Cuba, Dominica, El Salvador, Guatemala, Honduras, Nicaragua, Panama.
NGO Relations Member of: *Federación Latinoamericana de Sociedades de Fisica (FELASOFI, #09370).* [2013/XD8264/**D**]

♦ Central American and Caribbean Society of Classification and Data Analysis (#19352)

♦ Central American and Caribbean Sports Organization (CACSO) 03665

Organisation des sports d'Amérique centrale et des Caraïbes – Organización Deportiva Centroamericana y del Caribe (ODECABE)
Pres Casa Olimpica, Avenida de la Constitución 3, Parada 1, Apartado 902-0008, San Juan PR 00902-0008, USA. T. +17877233890. Fax +17877216805. E-mail: olimpur@coqui.net.
SG Apartado Aéreo 5093, Avenida 68 No 55-65, Bogota, Bogota DC, Colombia. T. +5716300093. Fax +5712314183.
URL: http://www.odecabe.org/
History 1926, Mexico City (Mexico). **Aims** Encourage promotion of sports and Olympic movement in Central America and the Caribbean. **Structure** General Assembly (every 2 years); Executive Committee. **Languages** English, Spanish. **Staff** Voluntary. **Finance** Budget (annual): US$ 100,000. **Activities** Events/meetings. **Events** *Annual Meeting* Cartagena de Indias (Colombia) 2005, *Annual Meeting* Havana (Cuba) 2005, *Annual Meeting* St Croix (Virgin Is USA) 2004, *Meeting / Annual Meeting* San Salvador (El Salvador) 2001, *Annual Meeting* Maracaibo (Venezuela) 1999.
Members Affiliates in 31 countries and territories:
Antigua-Barbuda, Aruba, Bahamas, Barbados, Belize, Bermuda, Cayman Is, Colombia, Costa Rica, Cuba, Dominica, Dominican Rep, El Salvador, Grenada, Guatemala, Guyana, Haiti, Honduras, Jamaica, Mexico, Nicaragua, Panama, Puerto Rico, St Kitts-Nevis, St Lucia, St Vincent-Grenadines, Suriname, Trinidad-Tobago, Venezuela, Virgin Is UK, Virgin Is USA.
NGO Relations Recognized by: *International Olympic Committee (IOC, #14408). Pan American Hockey Federation (PAHF, #18110)* is member. [2014.09.23/XD8566/**D**]

♦ Central American and Caribbean Zone Commission of the Pan American Basketball Confederation (#04146)

- Central American Center for Competitiveness and Sustainable Development (internationally oriented national body)
- Central American Coffee Board (inactive)
- Central American Commission on Environment and Development (#04129)
- Central American Commission of Geography and Cartography (inactive)
- Central American Commission of Maritime Transport (#04131)
- Central American Commission for Migration (no recent information)
- Central American Commission on Population and Environment and Development (inactive)
- Central American Commission of Port Authorities / see Comisión Centroamericana de Transporte Maritimo (#04131)

♦ Central American Common Market (CACM) 03666
Marché commun centroaméricain – Mercado Común Centroamericano (MERCOMUN)
Contact c/o SIECA, Apartado Postal 1237, 4a Avenida 10-25, Zona 14, 01901 Guatemala, Guatemala. T. +50223682151. E-mail: info@sieca.int.
History 1991, replacing a common market of the same name which collapsed in 1969, having been set up 13 Dec 1960, Managua (Nicaragua), under the auspices of *Organization of Central American States (ODECA, inactive)*, through the signature of *General Treaty on Central American Economic Integration, 1960 (1960)*, administered by *Secretaria Permanente del Tratado General de Integración Económica Centroamericana (SIECA, #19195)*, which came into force in Jun 1961. Costa Rica joined in Jul 1962 and the Treaty was ratified by all the five member countries by Sep 1963. Also referred to as *Central American Economic Integration* and by Spanish initials *MCCA*. Treaty was due to expire Jun 1981, but contracting parties agreed, Jul 1980, that it should continue in operation until agreement was reached on a new integration scheme, possibly a *Central American Economic and Social Community (inactive)*. The *Central American Integration System (#03671)* was established 13 Dec 1991, by *Protocol of Tegucigalpa (1991)*, replacing OCAS. MERCOMUN does not yet actually exist. The following paragraphs relate in some cases to the previous Common Market. **Aims** Establish a common market which contributes towards acceleration of economic growth of member countries and facilitates diversification of their production bases towards manufactures; overcome the problems of of small domestic markets; facilitate the process of industrialization. **Structure** expected to be as follows: Tripartite Commission of Ministers and Deputy Ministers of Finance and the Governors of Central Banks. Ministerial Commission, previously *Central American Economic Council (inactive)*, consisting of ministers of economy of member states; Executive Council (one representative and one alternate from each member). *Central American Bank for Economic Integration (CABEI, #03658)*, set up 1961 under a separate agreement, finances directly, and administers funds for, regional projects. Agreement for the establishment of *Central American Monetary Union (inactive)*, now amalgamated with *Central American Monetary Council (#03672)*, became effective Mar 1964, the Central Banks having been meeting regularly since 1952. *Central American Clearing House (CACH, inactive)*, set up 1961, Tegucigalpa (Honduras), joined CACM in 1964.
Activities The first stage of integration was to involve formation of a free trade area, firstly through elimination of trade restrictions on subregional trade in industrial products and secondly through progressive removal of trade restrictions on the remaining (non-industrial) products. The second stage was to be elevation of the free trade area into a customs union, when members adopted a common external tariff. The third and final stage was to be formation of a common market. Despite problems in intra-regional trade, progress has been made in external trade and economic cooperation. '*Central American Tariff System'* approved 1986, implemented 1993 as '*New Central American Tariff System'*. Under the System, the '*Common External Tariff (CET)'* allows for tariff policy based on common criteria and economic principles and is managed by Council; new tariffs replace all fiscal incentives granted earlier in favour of investments. Other initiatives are: the creation of the *Parlamento Centroamericano (PARLACEN, #18201)*; the approval, 1988, of a '*Plan of Immediate Action'* to re-establish a common market in Central America; the signing of cooperation and trade agreements between CACM countries and those of ALADI; the signing of cooperation agreements among CACM countries themselves; establishment, 1986, of *Fund for the Economic and Social Development of Central America (inactive)*, by CABEI, to attract contributions from third countries; signing of economic agreements between CACM and the European Economic Community, Apr 1990, Dublin (Ireland), aimed at removing the main financial constraints on intra-CACM trade; '*Declaration of Guatemala'*, Oct 1993, agreeing to strengthen efforts towards improving free trade and the CET, achieve customs union, enhance free mobility of capital and human resources and seek gradual monetary and financial integration. Institutions include:
– Comisión Centroamericana de Transporte Maritimo (COCATRAM, #04131);
– Corporación Centroamericana de Servicios de Navegación Aérea (COCESNA, #04837);
– INCAE Business School (#11141);
– Confederación Universitaria Centroamericana (CSUCA, #04497);
– Federación de Cámaras y Asociaciones Industriales de Centroamérica y República Dominicana (FECAICA, #09294);
– Institute of Nutrition of Central America and Panama (INCAP, #11285);
– Comisión Técnica Regional de Telecomunicaciones (COMTELCA, #04144).
Publications *Carta Informativa* (12 a year); *Compendio Estadístico* (4 a year); *Anuario Estadístico Centroamericano de Comercio Exterior – Central American Yearbook of International Trade Statistics* (annual); *Estadísticas Macroeconómicas* (annual); *Compendio Estadístico Centroamericano* (every 5 years).
Members Governments of 5 countries:
Costa Rica, El Salvador, Guatemala, Honduras, Nicaragua.
IGO Relations Committee for Economic Cooperation of the Central American Isthmus of the: *United Nations Economic Commission for Latin America and the Caribbean (ECLAC, #20556)* acts as advisor. Links or proposed links with: *Andean Community (#00817)*; *Central American Meeting of Directors of Planning Bodies (no recent information)*; *Group of Four (G-4, #10780)*; *Inter-American Development Bank (IDB, #11427)*; *Latin American Common Market (no recent information)*; *Meeting of Ministers Responsible for the Economic Integration of Central America (ROMRIECA)*; *UNCTAD (#20285)*, *UNIDO (#20336)*. [2008/XF6292/p/**F***]

- Central American Common Market Fund (inactive)
- Central American Confederation of Workers (inactive)
- Central American Convention on the Unification of the Fundamental Norms of Education (1962 treaty)
- Central American Coordination for Human Rights Organizations (inactive)
- Central American Corporation for Air Navigation Services (#04837)
- Central American Council for Education and Cultural Workers (no recent information)
- Central American Council on Housing and Human Settlements (inactive)
- Central American Council of Ministers of Health (#04722)
- Central American Council of Social Security Institutions / see Consejo de Institutos de Seguridad Social de Centroamérica y República Dominicana (#04715)
- Central American Council of Supervisors of Banks, Insurance Companies and other Financial Institutions (#04704)
- Central American Court of Justice (#04850)
- Central American Dairy Federation (#09297)
- Central American Defence Council (inactive)
- Central American Democratic Security Treaty (1995 treaty)
- Central American Dermatological Society / see Central American and Caribbean Dermatological Society (#03663)
- Central American Development Association (no recent information)
- Central American and Dominican Republic Council of Social Security Institutions (#04715)

♦ Central American Economic Cooperation Committee 03667
Comité de Cooperación Económica de Centroamericana (CCE)
Permanent Secretariat c/o CEPAL, Av Presidente Masaryk 29, 11570 Mexico City CDMX, Mexico. T. +525552639600. Fax +525555311151. E-mail: cepalmexico@cepal.org – cepal@un.org.mx.
URL: http://www.cepal.org/
History 27 Aug 1952, at 1st meeting of Ministers of the 5 States comprising *Secretaria Permanente del Tratado General de Integración Económica Centroamericana (SIECA, #19195)*, on establishment of the *Central American Economic Integration Programme*. Also referred to as *Economic Cooperation Committee of the Central American Isthmus – Comité de coopération économique de l'Isthme centroaméricain – Comité de Cooperación Económica del Istmo Centroamericano* and in English as *Committee on Central American Economic Cooperation*. A subsidiary permanent body of *United Nations Economic Commission for Latin America and the Caribbean (ECLAC, #20556)*. **Aims** Act as a consultative and advisory body for the 5 Central American member countries of ECLAC in matters concerning Central American *economic* integration. **Structure** Secretariat provided by ECLAC Subregional Headquarters. **Languages** English, French, Spanish. **Activities** Subcommittees on: trade; statistical coordination; transport; housing; building and planning; electrical power and industrial initiatives; agricultural development. Instrumental in drawing up *General Treaty on Central American Economic Integration, 1960 (1960)*.
Members Governments of 6 countries:
Costa Rica, El Salvador, Guatemala, Honduras, Nicaragua, Panama. [2010.01.19/XE3278/**E***]

- Central American Economic Integration / see Central American Common Market (#03666)
- Central American Economic Integration Programme / see Central American Economic Cooperation Committee (#03667)
- Central American Educational and Cultural Coordination (#04803)
- Central American Education Coordination System / see Coordinación Educativa y Cultural Centroamericana (#04803)
- Central American Energy Commission (inactive)

♦ Central American Engineering Institutions Network (REDICA) 03668
Contact Av 16 Streets 2 and 4, San José, San José, San José, 5117-1000, Costa Rica. T. +50688274514 – +50622289611 – +50622280684. Fax +50622201833. E-mail: redicamerica@gmail.com.
URL: http://redicanetwork.com/
History Founded 1998, as part of a framework for capacity development in sustainable development in Central America. Spanish title: *Red Centroamericana de Instituciones de Ingenieria (REDICA)*. **Aims** Articulate capabilities, resources and efforts in the region to improve the education, research, coverage and service *development* and management of *water resources*, awareness of *climate change* and gender equity, as well as regional and bilateral cooperation with other regional and international organizations; mobilize regional and national capacity through different cooperation mechanisms; promote development and application of engineering disciplines in the solution of social and economical problems of the region; join efforts for improvement of education, research, extension and service delivery in engineering fields; improve regional and bi-lateral cooperation among members and other regional and local organizations. **Structure** General Assembly; Board of Directors; Technical Secretariat on Climate Change. **Languages** English, Portuguese, Spanish. **Staff** 3.00 FTE, paid. **Activities** Capacity building; research/documentation; politics/policy/regulatory.
Members Professional associations, and public and private universities in 8 countries:
Belize, Costa Rica, Dominican Rep, El Salvador, Guatemala, Honduras, Nicaragua, Panama.
NGO Relations Member of: *Network for Capacity Building in Integrated Water Resources Management (CAP-Net, #17000)*. [2014.08.11/XJ2391/**F**]

- Central American Extradition Convention (1934 treaty)
- Central American Federation (inactive)
- Central American Federation of Architects (inactive)
- Central American Federation of Banks (inactive)
- Central American Federation of Export Chambers / see Federación de Camaras y Asociaciones de Exportadores de Centroamérica y el Caribe (#09293)
- Central American Federation of Medical Students (inactive)
- Central American Federation of Non-Governmental Conservation Associations (inactive)

♦ Central American Federation of Pharmaceutical Industries 03669
Fédération centroaméricaine des laboratoires pharmaceutiques – Federación Centroamericana de Laboratorios Farmacéuticos (FEDEFARMA)
Contact 4t Ave, 12-20 Santa Luisa St, Zone 16, 01016 Guatemala, Guatemala. T. +50688196982 – +506(50255108149. E-mail: comunicacion@fedefarma.org.
URL: http://www.fedefarma.org/
History 1965, as *COPACS*. Current title adopted 1980. **Aims** Protect the activities of the foreign pharmaceutical industry operating in Central America. **Structure** General Assembly; Board of Directors. **Languages** English, Spanish. **Staff** 8.00 FTE, paid. **Finance** Members' dues.
Members Pharmaceutical laboratories in 7 countries:
Costa Rica, Dominican Rep, El Salvador, Guatemala, Honduras, Nicaragua, Panama.
NGO Relations Member of: *International Federation of Pharmaceutical Manufacturers and Associations (IFPMA, #13505)*; *Latin American Federation of the Pharmaceutical Industry (#16328)*. [2019.09.17/XD0835/t/**D**]

- Central American Federation of Sports Medicine (#04444)
- Central American Federation of University Women (no recent information)
- Central American Health Institute (#11328)
- Central American Historical Institute, Managua / see Instituto de História de Nicaragua y Centroamérica
- Central American HIV/AIDS Prevention Project (internationally oriented national body)
- Central American Indigenous and Peasant Coordination Association for Community Agroforestry / see Asociación Coordinadora Indigena y Campesina de Agroforesteria Comunitaria (#02120)
- Central American Indigenous and Peasant Coordinator of Communal Agroforestry / see Asociación Coordinadora Indigena y Campesina de Agroforesteria Comunitaria (#02120)
- Central American Institute of Aeronautical Training (see: #04837)
- Central American Institute for Business Administration / see INCAE Business School (#11141)
- Central American Institute for Political Studies (internationally oriented national body)

♦ Central American Institute of Public Administration 03670
Institut centroaméricain d'administration publique – Instituto Centroamericano de Administración Pública (ICAP)
Dir Apartado postal 10025-1000, San José, San José, San José, Costa Rica. T. +50622341011 – +5062254616. Fax +50622252049. E-mail: info@icap.ac.cr.
URL: http://www.icap.ac.cr/
History 1954, San José (Costa Rica), as *Advanced School of Public Administration Central America – Escuela Superior de Administración Pública América Central (ESAPAC)*, by 5 Central American governments (Panama participated from 1961). Reconstituted and present name adopted 17 Feb 1967. **Aims** Support the Central American *integration* process and other efforts for economic and social development in the region; improve and streamline Central American public administration; contribute to development of efficient public service practices in the region. **Structure** General Board. Research department: Integration and Public Administration Studies. **Languages** Spanish. **Staff** 40.00 FTE, paid. **Finance** Main source: member governments. Support from national and international agencies and institutions. **Activities** Research; consulting; Master Degree Programmes in Public Management; Doctoral Programme on Public Management and Business Studies; capacity building; training courses for managers and technical personnel; cooperation. Organizes: international seminars; Directors' Meeting of Civil Services in Central America, Panama and Dominican Rep. **Events** *International seminar* Berlin (Germany) / Bonn (Germany) / Cologne (Germany) / Butzbach (Germany) 2004, *International seminar* Panama (Panama) 2003, *Central American meeting* Guatemala (Guatemala) 1996, *Central American meeting* San José (Costa Rica) 1995, *Latin American meeting* San José (Costa Rica) 1995. **Publications** *Revista Centroamericana de Administración Pública* (2 a year). *Buenas Practicas en la Gestión Pública* (2013); *Función Pública: acceso a la información, transparencia, rendición de cuentas y responsabilidad social* (2012); *Buenas Practicas de Gestión de Calidad* (2011); *Formulación y Evaluación de Proyector* (2008) by R Rosales; *El Proceso Presupuestario en el Sector de Salud Pública – Compilación* (2004); *Finanzas Públicas, Administración Financiera y Descentralización – Compilación* (2003); *Experiencias en Planificación Financiera de Mediano Plazo – Compilación* (2002); *Adquisiciones, Licitaciones, Contrataciones y Concesiones Públicas en Centroamérica, Panama y República Dominicana – Compilación* (2001); *Avances de los Sistemas de Administración Financiera Integrada – Compilación* (2001); *Evaluación de Impacto Ambienta: Metodologia y Alcances – El Método MEL-ENEL* (2001) by M López; *Experiencias del Nuevo Proceso Presupuestario en Centroamérica, Panama y República Dominicana – Compilación* (2001). Special

publications – 9 series; pamphlets. Information Services: Maintains a Documentation Centre, of information and learning resources, containing 25,000 books and 688 periodicals. **Information Services** *Alianza Sistema de Información y Documentación de las Américas (SIDALC/IICA); Database ICAP; Database REVICAP; Database SCOPUS; Database SIABUC9; Database UNPAN; METABASE.*
Members Governments of 6 countries:
Costa Rica, El Salvador, Guatemala, Honduras, Nicaragua, Panama.
IGO Relations Specialized Institute of: *Central American Integration System (#03671).* **NGO Relations** Member of: *Association of University Programs in Health Administration (AUPHA).* [2014.01.09/XD0232/j/**F***]

- ♦ Central American Institute of Social Studies (#11326)
- ♦ Central American Integrated System for Agricultural Technology (no recent information)

♦ Central American Integration System 03671

Sistema de la Integración Centroamericana (SICA)

SG Final Bulevar Cancilleria, Distrito El Espino, Ciudad Merliot, Antiguo Cuscatlan, La Libertad, El Salvador. T. +50322488800. E-mail: info.sgsica@sica.int.
URL: https://www.sica.int/

History 13 Dec 1991. Founded with the signing of the *Protocol of Tegucigalpa (1991)*, which amended the Charter of the *Organization of Central American States (ODECA, inactive)*, 1962. Creation of SICA was supported by the General Assembly of the *United Nations (UN, #20515).* General Secretariat officially established 1 Feb 1993, San Salvador (El Salvador), and *Tratado de Integración Social Centroamericano (1995)* adopted 30 Mar 1995. **Aims** Realize the integration of Central America in order for the Isthmus to become a region of peace, freedom, democracy and development.
Structure Principal organs: Meeting of Presidents; Council of Ministers; Executive Committee; General Secretariat, headed by Secretary-General. Also part of the System: Meeting of Vice-Presidents; *Parlamento Centroamericano (PARLACEN, #18201); Corte Centroamericana de Justicia (CCJ, #04850);* Consultative Committee (CC-SICA). Executive Secretariats (10):
- *Secretaría Permanente del Tratado General de Integración Económica Centroamericana (SIECA, #19195)* (Secretaria de Integración Económica Centroamericana);
- *Coordinación Educativa y Cultural Centroamericana (CECC, #04803);*
- *Central American Monetary Council (#03672);*
- *Consejo de Ministros de Hacienda o Finanzas de Centroamérica y República Dominicana (SE-COSEFIN);*
- *Secretaría de Integración Turística Centroamericana (SITCA, #19193);*
- *Secretaría de Integración Social Centroamericana (SISCA, #19192)* (Consejo de Integración Social);
- *Consejo de Ministros de Salud de Centroamérica (COMISCA, #04722);*
- *Consejo de Ministras de la Mujer de Centroamérica (ST-COMMCA);*
- *Comisión Centroamericana de Ambiente y Desarrollo (CCAD, #04129);*
- *Central American Agricultural Council (#03657).*

Specialized institutions (25):
- *Central American Bank for Economic Integration (CABEI, #03658);*
- *Central American Institute of Public Administration (#03670);*
- *Centro de Coordinación para la Prevención de los Desastres Naturales en América Central (CEPREDENAC, #03795);*
- *Centro Regional de Promoción de la MIPYME (CENPROMYPE, #03816);*
- *Comisión Centroamericana de Estadística del Sistema de la Integración Centroamericana (CENTROESTAD);*
- *Comisión Centroamericana Permanente para la Erradicación de la Producción, Trafico, Consumo y Uso Ilicitos de Estupefacientes y Sustancias Psicotrópicas (CCP, #04130);*
- *Comisión Centroamericana de Transporte Marítimo (COCATRAM, #04131);*
- *Comisión para el Desarrollo Científico y Tecnológico de Centro América y Panama (CTCAP, #04132);*
- *Comisión Regional de Interconexión Eléctrica (CRIE);*
- *Comisión Técnica Regional de Telecomunicaciones (COMTELCA, #04144);*
- *Comité de Cooperación de Hidrocarburos de América Central (CCHAC);*
- *Comité Regional de Recursos Hidraulicos del Istmo Centroamericano (CRRH, #04196);*
- *Commisión Trinacional del Plan Trifinio (CTPT);*
- *Confederación Universitaria Centroamericana (CSUCA, #04497);*
- *Consejo Centroamericano de Protección al Consumidor (CONCADECO);*
- *Consejo Fiscalizador Regional del SICA (CFR-SICA);*
- *Consejo del Istmo Centroamericano de Deportes y Recreación (CODICADER, #04716);*
- *Consejo Registral Inmobiliario de Centroamérica y Panama (CRICAP);*
- *Corporación Centroamericana de Servicios de Navegación Aérea (COCESNA, #04837);*
- *Ente Operador Regional (EOR);*
- *Foro Centroamericano y República Dominicana de Agua Potable y Saneamiento (FOCARD-APS);*
- *Institute of Nutrition of Central America and Panama (INCAP, #11285);*
- *Organización del Sector Pesquero y Acuicola del Istmo Centroamericano, Panama (OSPESCA, #17848);*
- *Secretaria Ejecutiva del Consejo de Electrificación de América Central (SE-CEAC, #19191).*

Languages Spanish. **Staff** 50.00 FTE, paid. **Finance** Members' dues. **Activities** Actions and interactions are intended to ensure the follow up of regional policies and decisions and are carried out by the organs and institutions under principles of coordinated action and respect for their functional autonomy in order to attain the final purpose of the integral development of Central American people. Main activities are developed by the General Secretariat and include: coordination of the political, economic, social, cultural and environmental integration process; enhancement of a community of law in the region; ensuring the region's effective participation in the new international order. **Events** *Meeting* Berlin (Germany) 2014, *Korea-Central America dialogue and cooperation mechanism forum* Jeju (Korea Rep) 2006, *Consultation* Chile 2003, *Regional workshop on environmental management and reducing vulnerability to natural disasters* San Salvador (El Salvador) 1999, *Summit meeting* San Salvador (El Salvador) 1997. **Publications** *Integrandonos* (6 a year) – bulletin; *Memoria de Labores* (annual). **Information Services** *SICA Integrated Portal* – integrates 33 sites (another 2 under construction) of institutions and programmes into one portal in order to provide full and timely progress in the consolidation of the Central American Integration Process.
Members Signatories to the Protocol of Tegucigalpa (8):
Belize, Costa Rica, Dominican Rep, El Salvador, Guatemala, Honduras, Nicaragua, Panama.
Regional Observers (9):
Argentina, Brazil, Chile, Colombia, Ecuador, Mexico, Peru, Uruguay, USA.
Extra regional Observers (10):
Australia, France, Germany, Holy See, Italy, Japan, Korea Rep, Spain, Taiwan, UK.
Extra regional Observer:
European Union (EU, #08967).
IGO Relations Permanent Observer to General Assembly of: *United Nations (UN, #20515).* Member of: *Intergovernmental Organizations Conference (IGO Conference, #11498).* Observer status with: *Sistema Económico Latinoamericano (SELA, #19294).* Permanent observer status with: *ECOSOC (#05331).* Special agreement with: *UNESCO (#20322).* Participates in the activities of: *UNCTAD (#20285).* Cooperates with: *Andean Community (#00817); Association of Caribbean States (ACS, #02411); Caribbean Community (CARICOM, #03476); European Commission (EC, #06633); OAS (#17629); Southern Common Market (#19868);* other integration schemes worldwide such as international institutions. Also established or re-established by the Protocol of Tegucigalpa (Honduras). [2020/XF2858/y/**F***]

- ♦ Central American Interparliamentary Commission (inactive)
- ♦ Central American Isthmus Port Institution Meeting (meeting series)
- ♦ Central American Meeting of Civil Aviation Directors (meeting series)
- ♦ Central American Mission / see CAM International
- ♦ Central American Monetary Agreement (1974 treaty)

♦ Central American Monetary Council 03672

Consejo Monetario Centroamericano (CMCA)

Exec Sec CMCA Executive Secretariat, Apartado Postal 5438-1000, San José, San José, San José, 1000, Costa Rica. T. +50622809522 – +50622806447. Fax +50625241062 – +50625241063. E-mail: secmca@secmca.org.
URL: http://www.secmca.org/

History 20 Mar 1964, on coming into effect of the *Agreement for the Establishment of a Central American Monetary Union* after ratification by signatory central banks, following its signature on 24 Feb 1964. From 25 Oct 1974, this a Agreement was replaced by *Central American Monetary Agreement (1974)*, subsequently modified on 22 Jan 1999. CMCA, which is also referred to as *CONMONECA*, comes within the framework of *Central American Integration System (#03671)* and includes the former *Central American Central Banks System (inactive)* and *Central American Monetary Union (inactive).* **Aims** By a permanent system of consultation, evaluate and coordinate *macroeconomic policies* of member countries, particularly monetary, *credit* and exchange policies which will progressively form the basis of monetary and financial regional integration; contribute to *financial integration*; improve and harmonize economic accounts and implement courses and other activities to enhance central banks' technical capacity. **Structure** Council (meeting 3 times a year) comprises Presidents or alternate representatives of central banks of member countries. President elected annually from within the Council on a rotational basis. Executive Secretariat, headed by Executive Secretary and Executive Sub-Secretary. Advisory Committees of the Council (3), each comprising a representative and an alternate of each central bank: Monetary policy; Capital markets: Legal studies. Special Commissions (4): National Accounts; Monetary Accounts; Balance of Payments; Information and Technology Systems. Technical Committees (2): System of payments; Regional Standards. **Languages** Spanish. **Staff** 17, plus 3 temporary employees. **Finance** Projects (between 8-10 per year) are sponsored by international institutions. **Activities** Working towards a *Central American Common Market (CACM, #03666).* Executive Secretariat prepares technical studies requested by the Council, coordinates activities of the Committees and serves as official liaison between the Council and the other Central American integration entities. Organizes: committee and ad hoc group meetings; seminars; fora. **Events** *Conférence sur l'Amérique Centrale* Antigua (Guatemala) 2002. **Publications** *Notas Económicas* (12 a year); *Reporte Ejecutivo Mensual* (12 a year); *Informe de Coyuntura* (4 a year); *Informe de Riesgo País* (4 a year); *Informe Económico Regional* (annual). Press releases. Information Services: Database of main macroeconomic variables, including monthly information of each of the Central American countries, including Dominican Republic.
Members Presidents of central banks of 6 countries:
Costa Rica, Dominican Rep, El Salvador, Guatemala, Honduras, Nicaragua.
IGO Relations CMCA Secretariat coordinated by: *Secretaría Permanente del Tratado General de Integración Económica Centroamericana (SIECA, #19195).* Full member of: *Irving Fisher Committee on Central Bank Statistics (IFC, #16020). Central American Agricultural Council (#03657); Central American Bank for Economic Integration (CABEI, #03658); Central American Institute of Public Administration (#03670); Consejo Centroamericano de Superintendentes de Bancos, de Seguros y de Otras Instituciones Financieras (CCSBSO, #04704); Consejo Regional de Cooperación Agrícola de Centroamérica, México y la República Dominicana (CORECA, no recent information); Inter-American Development Bank (IDB, #11427); International Bank for Reconstruction and Development (IBRD, #12317); International Monetary Fund (IMF, #14180); UNDP (#20292); United Nations Economic Commission for Latin America and the Caribbean (ECLAC, #20556).* [2010/XE5976/**E***]

- ♦ Central American Monetary Union (inactive)
- ♦ Central American Paediatric Society (inactive)
- ♦ Central American Parliament (#18201)
- ♦ Central American Pedagogical Institute (inactive)
- ♦ Central American Public Health Council (inactive)
- ♦ Central American Regional Water Resources Committee / see Comité Regional de Recursos Hidraulicos del Istmo Centroamericano (#04196)
- ♦ Central American Research Institute for Industry (inactive)
- ♦ Central American Security Commission (inactive)
- ♦ Central American Shipowners Association (no recent information)
- ♦ Central American Small Enterprise Investment Fund (internationally oriented national body)
- ♦ Central American Social Integration Secretariat (#19192)
- ♦ Central American Society of Cardiology (inactive)
- ♦ Central American Society of Pharmacology (inactive)
- ♦ Central American Solar Energy Project (internationally oriented national body)

♦ Central American Table Tennis Confederation (CTIC) 03673

Confederación Centroamérica de Tenis de Mesa (CONCATEME)

Technical Dir FSTM, Alameda Juan Pablo II, Centro de Gobierno, Palacio de los Deportes, San Salvador, El Salvador.
Pres address not obtained.
URL: http://concateme.com/

Members Membership countries not specified. **NGO Relations** Recognized by: *International Table Tennis Federation (ITTF, #15650).* [2017/XD1349/**D**]

- ♦ Central American Tariff and Customs Council (no recent information)
- ♦ Central American Technical Institute, Santa Tecla (internationally oriented national body)
- ♦ Central American Telecommunications Institute (inactive)

♦ Central American Tourism Agency (CATA) 03674

Agencia de Promoción Turistica de Centroamérica

Dir Gen De Donde Fue el Cine Cabreras 2 cuadras al Este, 1/2 al Sur Edificio La Merced, Módulo M 23, Managua, Nicaragua. T. +50522223512. E-mail: karinacanto@catatourismagency.org – info@visitcentroamerica.com.
URL: http://www.visitcentroamerica.com/

History Set up Dec 2002, including by *Federación de Camaras de Turismo de Centroamérica (FEDECATUR, #09295).* Moved from Madrid (Spain) to Managua (Nicaragua) 2015. **Aims** Promote and position Central America as a multi-international tourism destination. **Structure** Governing Board. **Members** Membership countries not specified. **IGO Relations** *Central American Tourism Council (#03675).* [2018/XJ0825/**D**]

♦ Central American Tourism Council 03675

Conseil Centroaméricain de Tourisme – Consejo Centroamericano de Turismo (CCT)

Contact Final Bulevar Cancilleria Distrito El Espino, Ciudad Merliot, Antiguo Cuscatlan, La Libertad, El Salvador. T. +50322488837. E-mail: info.stcct@sica.int.
URL: http://www.sica.int/cct/

History Established 1965, Nicaragua, during the 1st Extraordinary Conference of Ministers of External Relations of Central America, 29 Mar to 2 Apr 1965, San Salvador (El Salvador). A regional organization of *Organization of Central American States (ODECA, inactive).* **Aims** Promote and coordinate actions for the development of tourism in Central America. **Structure** Council of Ministers; Executive Committee; Tourism Marketing Committee (COMECATUR); *Central American Tourism Agency (CATA, #03674); Secretaría de Integración Turística Centroamericana (SITCA, #19193).* **Languages** English, Spanish. **Staff** 4.00 FTE, paid. **Activities** Coordination of regional tourism projects; promotion of Central America as a tourist destination; implementation of Strategic Plan for Tourism Development in Central America (2014-2018). Organizes Annual Centroamerica Travel Market Fair. **Publications** *CCT News Bulletin* (12 a year); *Statistics Bulletin* (annual). Annual Report. Tourism product brochures; reports. **Information Services** *Development and Investigation System (SID); Markets Investigation System (SIM).*
Members Tourism ministries of 8 countries:
Belize, Costa Rica, Dominican Rep, El Salvador, Guatemala, Honduras, Nicaragua, Panama.
NGO Relations *Federación de Camaras de Turismo de Centroamérica (FEDECATUR, #09295).* [2014.01.07/XE5478/**E***]

- ♦ Central American Transport Federation (#09298)
- ♦ Central American Treaty for the Protection of Industrial Property (1968 treaty)
- ♦ Central American Union (unconfirmed)
- ♦ Central American Union (inactive)
- ♦ Central American Union of Associations of Engineers and Architects (inactive)
- ♦ Central American University Confederation (#04497)
- ♦ Central American University José Simeón Cañas (internationally oriented national body)
- ♦ Central American University, Managua (internationally oriented national body)

♦ Central American Water Resource Management Network (CARA) . . 03676

Red Centroamericana de Manejo de Recursos Hidricos

Coordinator Fac of Sciences ES 1040, Univ of Calgary, 2500 Univ Drive NW, Calgary AB T2N 1N4, Canada. T. +4032208029. Fax +4032108105.
URL: http://www.caragua.org/

History 1999, through funding from *Canadian International Development Agency (CIDA, inactive)* University Partnerships and Cooperation Program. **Aims** Act as a water resource training network focusing on building local capacity to improve the management and protection of Central American water resources. **Events** *International conference on hydrogeology and water resource maangement in Central America* Nicaragua 2005.
Members Universities in 7 countries:
Bolivia, Canada, Costa Rica, El Salvador, Guatemala, Honduras, Nicaragua.
NGO Relations Member of: *Network for Capacity Building in Integrated Water Resources Management (CAP-Net, #17000).* [2011/XJ2387/E]

♦ Central American Women's Fund 03677
Fondo Centroamericano de Mujeres (FCAM)
Exec Dir Rotonda El Güegüense 4 cuadras abajo, 1 cuadra al lago, Managua, Nicaragua. T. +50522544981. E-mail: info@fcmujeres.org.
URL: http://www.fcmujeres.org/
History Founded Jul 2003, Managua (Nicaragua). Registered in accordance with the law of Nicaragua, 2006. **Aims** Mobilize resources to strengthen the women's movement and support the initiative of women's groups and organizations, particularly young women's organizations that promote and defend women's *human rights.* **Structure** General Assembly; Board of Directors; Executive Direction; Management Team. **Languages** English, Spanish. **Staff** 16.00 FTE, paid. **Finance** Fund raising; institutional supporters; women's funds and consortia; donations. **Activities** Financial and/or material support; capacity building; networking/liaising; training/education. **Publications** *Ten Year Evaluation of the FCAM, Synthesis Report* (2015); *Sistematization of the FCAM Model*; *Teleidoscopic Model of Planning, Monitoring, Evaluation and Learning.*
Members in 6 countries:
Belize, Costa Rica, El Salvador, Guatemala, Honduras, Nicaragua.
NGO Relations Member of: *Human Rights Funders Network (HRFN)*; *Prospera – International Network of Women's Funds (INWF, #18545)*; *Women's Funding Network.* Links with many foundations including: *Both ENDS (#03307)*; *CALALA – Fondo de Mujeres (Calala)*; *Confederación Latinoamericana y del Caribe de Trabajadoras del Hogar (CONLACTRAHO)*; *Ford Foundation (#09858)*; *Global Fund for Women (GFW, #10384)*; *Humanistisch Instituut voor Ontwikkelingssamenwerking (Hivos)*; *Levi Strauss Foundation (LSF)*; *Mama Cash (#16560)*; *Oak Foundation*; *Open Society Foundations (OSF, #17763)*; *Sigrid Rausing Trust*; *Women Win (#21042).* [2015.09.01/XM2821/f/F]

- ♦ Central American Workers Coordinating Council (no recent information)
- ♦ Central American Zonal Railways Meeting (meeting series)

♦ Central Asia and the Caucasus Association of Agricultural Research Institutions (CACAARI) 03678
Exec Sec c/o ICARDA, Program Facilitation Unit, PO Box 4375, Tashkent, Uzbekistan, 100000. T. +998712372130. Fax +998711207125.
Street Address 6 Osiyo Street, Tashkent, Uzbekistan, 100000.
URL: http://www.cacaari.org/
History 2000, when leaders of the 8 National Agricultural Research Systems (NARS) came together under the aegis of the *CGIAR System Organization (CGIAR, #03843)* CAC Programme facilitated by *International Center for Agricultural Research in the Dry Areas (ICARDA, #12466).* **Aims** Foster development of agricultural research in Central Asia and the Caucasus Region by: promoting exchange of scientific and technical know-how and information in agriculture; encouraging establishment of appropriate cooperative research and training programmes in accordance with identified regional, bilateral or national needs and priorities; assisting in strengthening of research, organizational and management capability of member institutions; strengthening cross-linkages between national, regional and international research centers and organizations, including universities, through involvement in jointly-planned research and training programmes. **Structure** Steering Committee (meets annually). **Finance** Grants and donations from governments, national regional or international organizations, and development banks; proceeds from sale of publications; fees from events. **Activities** Project: Central Asia and the Caucasus Regional Agricultural Information System (CAC-RAIS). Organizes regional consultations, workshops and meetings.
Members Research institutions, universities, NGOs and farmer associations in 8 countries:
Armenia, Azerbaijan, Georgia, Kazakhstan, Kyrgyzstan, Tajikistan, Turkmenistan, Uzbekistan.
IGO Relations Partner of: *International Center for Agricultural Research in the Dry Areas (ICARDA, #12466).* Sponsored by: *FAO (#09260).* **NGO Relations** Instrumental in setting up: *Central Asia and South Caucasus Consortium of Agricultural universities for Development (CASCADE, #03685)*; *Inter-regional Network on Cotton in Asia and North Africa (INCANA, #15972).* Partner of: *Young Professionals for Agricultural Development (YPARD, #21996).* [2015/XJ1702/D]

- ♦ Central Asia-Caucasus Institute and Silk Road Studies Program (internationally oriented national body)
- ♦ Central Asian Association of Rheumatologists (inactive)

♦ Central Asian and Caucasus Regional Fisheries and Aquaculture Commission (CACFish) 03679
Sec Ivedik Cad 55, Yenimahalle, 06170 Ankara/Ankara, Türkiye. E-mail: cacfish-secretariat@fao.org.
URL: https://www.fao.org/fishery/en/organization/24546/en
History 2009. Established under the provisions of Article XIV, paragraph 2, of the *FAO (#09260)* Constitution, upon the approval of the CACFish Agreement by the FAO Council at its 137th Session (Resolution 1/137). CACFish Agreement entered into force 3 Dec 2010. **Aims** Promote the development, conservation, rational management and best utilization of living aquatic resources, as well as the sustainable development of aquaculture in Central Asia and the Caucasus. **Structure** Commission; Secretariat; Technical Advisory Committee. **Languages** English. **Events** *Session* Istanbul (Turkey) 2021, *Session* Izmir (Turkey) 2018, *Session* Tashkent (Uzbekistan) 2016, *Session* Ulaanbaatar (Mongolia) 2015, *Session* Baku (Azerbaijan) 2014.
Members States Parties (5):
Armenia, Azerbaijan, Kyrgyzstan, Tajikistan, Türkiye. [2022/AA1981/E*]

♦ Central Asian Cellular Forum (CACF) 03680
Head Office 13 R Plaza 2nd Floor, F-7 Markaz, Islamabad, Pakistan. T. +92512609324. Fax +92512652519. E-mail: info@3gca.org.
URL: http://3gca.org/
History Current title adopted 2007. Registered in accordance with the law of Pakistan. **Aims** Support the development of mobile *broadband* technologies in the region. **Activities** Guidance/assistance/consulting; advocacy/lobbying/activism; events/meetings; training/education. **Publications** *CACF Newsletter.*
Members Full in 10 countries:
Afghanistan, Armenia, Azerbaijan, Kazakhstan, Kyrgyzstan, Mongolia, Pakistan, Tajikistan, Turkmenistan, Uzbekistan. [2020.02.27/XM4098/F]

- ♦ Central Asian Development and Cooperation Bank (no recent information)

♦ Central Asian Football Association (CAFA) 03681
Pres I37/1 Bokhtar Street, Bokhtar Business Center, 734002 Dushanbe, Tajikistan. T. +9926100081. E-mail: international@the-cafa.com.
URL: http://the-cafa.com/
History Approved Jun 2014, as a regional zone of *Asian Football Confederation (AFC, #01487).* **Aims** Develop football in the region, by promoting an active interchange within Central Asia, strengthening unity and solidarity, and making contributions to peace through football. **Structure** Executive Committee. **Languages** English. **Staff** 2.00 FTE, paid. **Activities** Sporting activities.
Members National associations in 6 countries:
Afghanistan, Iran Islamic Rep, Kyrgyzstan, Tajikistan, Turkmenistan, Uzbekistan. [2021/XJ9407/D]

♦ Central Asian Foundation for Management Development (CAMAN) . 03682
Contact address not obtained. T. +73272423545 – +73272428933. Fax +73272509228.
History Founded Apr 1994. **Aims** Promote and improve management development and management education development. **Staff** 5.00 FTE, paid. **Finance** Members' dues. Project grants. Budget (annual): between US$ 50,000 – 70,000. **Activities** Events/meetings; training/education. **Events** *Methodology of setting and development of career center* Almaty (Kazakhstan) 2003, *Workshop on strategic approaches to ensuring quality of education and international accreditation* Tashkent (Uzbekistan) 2003, *Human resource management – strategy and practice* Almaty (Kazakhstan) 1996. **Publications** *CAMAN Herald* (4 a year) – bulletin.
Members Institutional; Associate; Corporate; Individual. Members (58 Educational Institutions; 5 Training Centres; 13 Business and Public Organizations) in 5 countries:
Kazakhstan, Kyrgyzstan, Tajikistan, Turkmenistan, Uzbekistan.
NGO Relations Member of: *EFMD – The Management Development Network (#05387).* [2015/XD6257/f/F]

- ♦ Central-Asian Institute for Applied Geosciences (internationally oriented national body)
- ♦ Central Asian Regional Environmental Centre / see Regional Environmental Centre for Central Asia

♦ Central Asian Regional Information and Coordination Centre for Combating Illicit Trafficking of Narcotic Drugs, Psychotropic Substances and Their Precursors (CARICC) 03683
Dir 52 Abay Ave, Almaty, Kazakhstan, 050008. T. +77272599990. Fax +77273921554. E-mail: registry@caricc.org.
URL: http://www.caricc.org/
History 4 May 1996, Tashkent (Uzbekistan), based on Memorandum of Understanding and Cooperation between Azerbaijan, Kazakhstan, Kyrgyzstan, Russia, Tajikistan, Turkmenistan and Uzbekistan, on establishment of the Centre. Agreement on establishment of CARICC signed 24 Jul 2006. As of 1 Nov 2007, operating in pilot regime, and as of 1 Jun 2010, officially in normal mode. Established within the framework of UNODC Project AD/RER/H22, "Establishment of Central Asian Regional Information and Coordination Centre". **Aims** Serve as a permanent regional information coordination interstate body to assist in organizing, implementing and coordinating agreed joint international operations to combat illicit drug trafficking; ensure collection, storage, protection, analysis and exchange of information on cross-border crime related to drug trafficking. **Structure** Member States have authorized representatives (liaison officers) at CARICC to communicate between competent authorities of the State and CARICC. **Languages** Russian. **Finance** Supported by: *United Nations Office on Drugs and Crime (UNODC, #20596).* **Activities** Politics/policy/regulatory; knowledge management/information dissemination; networking/liaising; financial and/or material support; events/meetings. **Events** *Meeting* Almaty (Kazakhstan) 2018.
Members Governments of 7 countries:
Azerbaijan, Kazakhstan, Kyrgyzstan, Russia, Tajikistan, Turkmenistan, Uzbekistan.
Observer States (11):
Afghanistan, Austria, Canada, Finland, France, Germany, Italy, Pakistan, Türkiye, UK, USA.
International Observer organizations (3):
International Criminal Police Organization – INTERPOL (ICPO-INTERPOL, #13110); *Southeast European Cooperative Initiative (SECI, #19812)*; *Southeast European Law Enforcement Center (SELEC, #19815).*
IGO Relations Memorandum of Understanding with: *Southeast European Cooperative Initiative (SECI, #19812)* (5 Feb 2010); *UNDP (#20292)* in Kazakhstan (9 Jun 2010); *World Customs Organization (WCO, #21350)* (30 Mar 2010). Letter of intent on cooperation with: *Organization for Security and Cooperation in Europe (OSCE, #17887)* (16 Jul 2010). Protocol of Interaction with: Council of *Commonwealth of Independent States (CIS, #04341)* Border Troops Commanders (21 Apr 2011). [2018.09.12/XJ2145/E*]

- ♦ Central Asian Regional Research Hydrometeorological Institute / see Hydrometeorological Research Institute of Uzhydromet
- ♦ Central Asian Scientific Research Institute for Irrigation / see Central Asia Research Institute for Irrigation

♦ Central Asia Regional Economic Cooperation (CAREC) 03684
Unit Head c/o ADB, CAREC Unit, 6 ADB Avenue, Mandaluyong City, METRO 1550 Manila, Philippines. T. +6326326134. Fax +6326362387. E-mail: info@carecprogram.org.
URL: http://www.carecprogram.org/
Aims Promote development through regional cooperation. **Structure** Ministerial Conference (annual); Coordinating Committees (4); National Focal Points; Asian Development Bank serves as Secretariat. **Languages** English, Russian. **Events** *Workshop on Water-Energy-Food Security Nexus in Central Asia* Vienna (Austria) 2019, *Aviation Consultation Workshop* Singapore (Singapore) 2017, *Annual CAREC Federation of Carrier and Forwarder Associations Meeting* Singapore (Singapore) 2016. **Publications** *CAREC Corridor Performance Measurement and Monitoring* (annual); *CAREC Development Effectiveness Review* (annual); *From Landlocked to Linked In: The Central Asia Regional Economic Cooperation Program* (annual). Studies; reports. **Information Services** *CAREC Institute* – a virtual information hub.
Members Countries (10):
Afghanistan, Azerbaijan, China, Kazakhstan, Kyrgyzstan, Mongolia, Pakistan, Tajikistan, Turkmenistan, Uzbekistan.
IGO Relations *Asian Development Bank (ADB, #01422)*; *Asian Development Bank Institute (ADB Institute, #01423)*; *European Bank for Reconstruction and Development (EBRD, #06315)*; *International Bank for Reconstruction and Development (IBRD, #12317)*; *International Monetary Fund (IMF, #14180)*; *Islamic Development Bank (IsDB, #16044)*; *Transport Corridor from Europe-Caucasus-Asia (TRACECA, #20225)*; *UNDP (#20292).* [2016.06.01/XJ5314/y/E*]

- ♦ Central Asia Research Institute for Irrigation (internationally oriented national body)

♦ Central Asia and South Caucasus Consortium of Agricultural universities for Development (CASCADE) 03685
Exec Sec Kory Niyoziy Street 39, Tashkent, Uzbekistan, 100000. T. +998712371934. Fax +998712375439.
History Initiated by Tashkent Institute of Irrigation and Amelioration, Uzbekistan (TIIM), *Central Asia and the Caucasus Association of Agricultural Research Institutions (CACAARI, #03678)*, *International Center for Agricultural Research in the Dry Areas (ICARDA, #12466)* and Project Facilitation Unit of *CGIAR System Organization (CGIAR, #03843).* **Aims** Improve cooperation and partnership in higher education, research and innovation systems for sustainable agricultural development. **Structure** Steering Committee; Executive Committee.
Members Full in 8 countries:
Armenia, Azerbaijan, Georgia, Kazakhstan, Kyrgyzstan, Tajikistan, Turkmenistan, Uzbekistan.
NGO Relations Member of: *Global Confederation of Higher Education Associations for Agriculture and Life Sciences (GCHERA, #10304).* [2017.12.24/XJ6112/E]

- ♦ Centralasiatisk Selskab (internationally oriented national body)

♦ Central Bank Research Association (CEBRA) 03686
Pres c/o artax Fide Consult AG, Gartenstrasse 95, 4052 Basel BS, Switzerland. E-mail: office@cebra.org.
URL: http://cebra.org/
Aims Encourage applied and theoretical research on topics relevant to central banks, financial regulators, international financial institutions, and fiscal authorities, as well as to connect the research staff of these institutions with academia. **Structure** Senior Council; Executive Officers. Chapters (3): Americas; Asia Pacific; Africa, Europe and the Middle East. **Activities** Events/meetings; research/documentation. **Events** *Annual Meeting* New York, NY (USA) 2023, *Annual Meeting* Barcelona (Spain) 2022, *Annual Meeting* Cambridge, MA (USA) 2021, *Annual Meeting* New York, NY (USA) 2019, *Annual Meeting* Frankfurt-Main (Germany) 2018.
Members Researchers from about 60 central banks, IFIs and academic institutions. Membership countries not specified. [2023.02.15/XM6821/v/C]

- ♦ Central Banks' Bank / see Bank for International Settlements (#03165)
- ♦ Central Banks of Southeast Asia, New Zealand and Australia (meeting series)
- ♦ Central Bank of the States of Equatorial Africa and Cameroon (inactive)
- ♦ Central Bank of the West African States (#03167)

- Central British Fund for German Jewry / see World Jewish Relief (#21600)
- Central British Fund for World Jewish Relief / see World Jewish Relief (#21600)
- Central Bureau for the Prevention of Tuberculosis (inactive)
- Central Bureau for Terrestrial Magnetism / see International Service for Geomagnetic Indices (#14840)
- Central Caribbean Marine Institute (internationally oriented national body)
- Central Commission for Brain Study (inactive)

♦ Central Commission for the Navigation of the Rhine (CCNR) 03687

Commission centrale pour la navigation du Rhin (CCNR) – Zentralkommission für die Rheinschifffahrt (ZKR) – Centrale Commissie voor de Rijnvaart (CCR)

SG Palais du Rhin, 2 place de la République, CS 10023, 67082 Strasbourg CEDEX, France. T. +33388522010. Fax +33388321072. E-mail: l.fahrner@ccr-zkr.org – ccnr@ccr-zkr.org.
URL: https://www.ccr-zkr.org/

History 24 Mar 1815. Established 1815, by the Congress of Vienna (Austria). Its legal foundation is the Revised Convention for Navigation on the Rhine – referred to as the Mannheim Document – of 17 Oct 1868. In its present form it is the result of modifications which came about through the Rhine Navigation Act of Mainz (31 Mar 1831), the revised Convention for Rhine Navigation of Mannheim (17 Oct 1868), and the Treaty of Versailles (1919) Arts 354 to 362. Protocols of adhesion of Netherlands 1921, 1923. Inter-governmental arrangements 1945, 1950. Convention amended 1963, Strasbourg (France). Additional Protocols numbers 1 (1975), 2 (1985), 3 (1982), 4 (1991), 5 (1999), 6 (not yet ratified), 7 (2004). Statutes registered in *'LNTS 1366'*. **Aims** Address effectively all issues concerning inland navigation; play an essential role in regulating navigation on the Rhine; promote development of close cooperation with other international organizations working in the field of European transport policy and with non-governmental organizations active in the field of inland navigation. **Structure** Plenary meetings (twice a year); Committees (12); Working Groups (15); Court of Appeals; Secretariat. **Languages** Dutch, French, German. **Staff** 33.00 FTE, paid. **Finance** Sources: contributions of member/participating states. Annual budget: 2,700,000 EUR. **Activities** Events/meetings; guidance/assistance/consulting; politics/policy/regulatory; research/documentation; standards/guidelines. **Events** *Workshop on Low Water and Effects on Rhine Navigation* Bonn (Germany) 2019, *Workshop on Cybersecurity in Inland Navigation* Bonn (Germany) 2019, *Workshop on River-Sea Transport* Duisburg (Germany) 2019, *Congress* Mannheim (Germany) 2018, *Workshop on Berths as Element for a Future Oriented Inland Navigation* Vienna (Austria) 2018. **Publications** *Market Insight* (2 a year); *Market Observation* (annual). *Police Regulations for the Navigation of the Rhine – RPR*; *Radiotelephony guide for inland navigation*; *Regulations for Rhine navigation personnel*; *Rhine Vessel Inspection Regulations – RVIR*; *RIS Guidelines*; *Stability guide for container transport in inland navigation*; *Unique European vessel identification number – ENI*. Thematic report (annual). Conventions on the CCNR; agreements; reports; statistics; rules of procedure; resolutions.

Members Governments of 5 countries:
Belgium, France, Germany, Netherlands, Switzerland.

IGO Relations Observer status with (1): *UNEP (#20299)*. Cooperates with (2): *ILO (#11123)*; *International Transport Forum (ITF, #15725)*. Provides secretariat for: *Administrative Centre of Social Security for Rhine Boatmen (#00116)*; CDNI; *Comité européen pour l'élaboration de standards dans le domaine de la navigation intérieure (CESNI, #04160)*. [2022.02.01/XD0241/E*]

- Central Committee of the Forest Ownership in the EC / see Confederation of European Forest Owners (#04525)
- Central Council of International Touring (inactive)
- Central Council of the Nordic Farmers' Associations (no recent information)

♦ Central Dredging Association (CEDA) 03688

General Manager Radex Bldg, Rotterdamseweg 183 C, 2629 HD Delft, Netherlands. T. +31152682575. Fax +31152682576. E-mail: ceda@dredging.org.
URL: http://www.dredging.org/

History 12 Jun 1978, Delft (Netherlands). Founded as the regional association for Europe, Africa and the Middle East. Registration: No/ID: KVK 40397215, Netherlands, South Holland. **Aims** Exchange knowledge in those fields which are concerned with dredging in the widest sense of the term; represent the interests of principals of dredging projects, engineering advisors, academic and research establishments, manufacturers and designers of dredging equipment and dredging contractors. **Structure** Board of Directors; national and regional sections. **Languages** English. **Staff** 2.00 FTE, paid. **Finance** Members' dues. Annual budget: euro 150,000. **Activities** Events/meetings. **Events** *World Dredging Congress* Copenhagen (Denmark) 2022, *Dredging Days* Delft (Netherlands) 2021, *Dredging Days* Rotterdam (Netherlands) 2019, *Dredging for sustainable infrastucture* Amsterdam (Netherlands) 2018, *Dredging Days* Rotterdam (Netherlands) 2017. **Publications** *CEDA Newsletter*. Conference and symposium proceedings.

Members Individuals (660) and Corporate (130). Members in 23 countries:
Belgium, Cyprus, Denmark, Egypt, Finland, France, Germany, Greece, Iceland, Ireland, Italy, Kuwait, Latvia, Netherlands, Norway, Portugal, Russia, South Africa, Spain, Sweden, Türkiye, UK, United Arab Emirates.

IGO Relations Observer to: *OSPAR Commission for the Protection of the Marine Environment of the North-East Atlantic (OSPAR Commission, #17905)*. **NGO Relations** Member of: *World Organization of Dredging Associations (WODA, #21688)*. Sister organizations: *Eastern Dredging Association (EADA, #05238)*; *European Dredging Association (EuDA, #06946)*; *Western Dredging Association (WEDA, #20913)*. [2022/XD0238/D]

- Central and Eastern European Association for Mission Studies (inactive)
- Central and Eastern European Bar Association (inactive)
- Central and Eastern European Central Securities Depositories Association (inactive)

♦ Central and Eastern European Citizens Network (CEE CN) 03689

Address not obtained.
URL: https://ceecn.net/

History Aug 2001. Still legally exists but without funding or staff. Registration: Start date: 2005, Slovakia. **Aims** Provide opportunities for grassroots citizens initiatives from CEE region to learn, exchange experiences and ideas as well as enhance their organizational growth through establishing and managing a partner relationship among themselves. **Activities** Organizes the *Citizen Participation University (CPU)*. **Publications** *CEE CN Newsletter*.

Members Full in 19 countries:
Albania, Armenia, Azerbaijan, Belarus, Bosnia-Herzegovina, Bulgaria, Croatia, Czechia, Estonia, Georgia, Hungary, Moldova, Poland, Romania, Russia, Serbia, Slovakia, Slovenia, Ukraine.

Affiliate member:
European Community Organizing Network (ECON, #06681).

NGO Relations Member of: *Pan European eParticipation Network (PEP-NET, inactive)*. Participates in: *Civil Society Europe*. [2022/XJ0968/dy/D]

♦ Central and Eastern European Copyright Alliance (CEECA) 03690

Chairman address not obtained. E-mail: ceeca@t-online.hu.

Consultative Status Consultative status granted from: *World Intellectual Property Organization (WIPO, #21593)* (Observer Status). [2019/XF5882/F]

♦ Central and Eastern European Forum of Young Legal, Political and Social Theorists (CEE Forum) 03691

Contact Univ of Zagreb, Fac of Law, Marshal Tito Square 14, HR-10000 Zagreb, Croatia.
Contact address not obtained.
URL: http://www.cee-forum.org/

History 2009, Katowice (Poland). **Aims** Establish a community able to provide a competitive environment for young scholars in the field of legal, political and social theory in Central and Eastern Europe. **Structure** Coordinators. **Languages** English. **Staff** Voluntary. **Finance** Sources: participation fees; additional funding. **Activities** Events/meetings. **Events** *Conference* Budapest (Hungary) 2022, *Political Imagination and Utopian Energies in Central and Eastern Europe* Prague (Czechia) 2021, *Conference* Vienna (Austria) 2020, *Conference* Bratislava (Slovakia) 2019, *Conference* Timisoara (Romania) 2018. **Publications** *Cenral and Eastern European Forum for Legal, Political and Social Theory Yearbook*. **Members** Not a membership organization. [2022/XJ8295/F]

- Central and Eastern European Game Studies Conference (meeting series)

♦ Central and Eastern European Genetic Network (CEE GN) 03692

Chairman Dept of Molecular Biology, Univ of Gdansk, Wita Stwosza 59, Wita Stwosza 59, 80-308 Gdansk, Poland. T. +48585236024.

History Oct 2003, Cavtat (Croatia). Registration: Start date: 25 Mar 2008, Netherlands. **Aims** Promote research and development of medicines in countries of Central and Eastern Europe; encourage CEE patients involvement and active participation in research into the causes and cures of genetic diseases. **Structure** Board, comprising President, Secretary, Treasurer and 5 members. **Activities** Organizes meetings, workshops and conferences. Participates in EU projects. Collaborates with science and industry. **Events** *Central and Eastern European summit on preconception health and prevention of birth defects* Budapest (Hungary) 2008. **Publications** Statements; position papers.

Members Full in 11 countries:
Bosnia-Herzegovina, Bulgaria, Croatia, Czechia, Hungary, Poland, Romania, Russia, Serbia, Slovenia, Türkiye.

NGO Relations Member of: *EGAN – Patients Network for Medical Research and Health (EGAN, #05394)*. [2012.07.05/XM2882/E]

♦ Central and Eastern European Law Initiative (CEELI) 03693

Exec Dir Havlickovy Sady 58, 120 00 Prague, Czechia. T. +420222520100. Fax +420222518576. E-mail: office@ceeli.eu.
URL: http://ceeliinstitute.org/

History 1990, as *Central and East European Law Initiative (CEELI)*, by the American Bar Association. Also referred to as *ABA CEELI*. Subsequently changed title to *Central European and Eurasian Law Initiative (CEELI)*. Ended formal relationship with ABA and became a free-standing, independent institution, 2004. Registered in accordance with Czech law. **Aims** Develop and train an international network of legal professionals committed to a rule of law. **Structure** Management Board; Supervisory Board. **Languages** Czech, English. **Staff** 9.00 FTE, paid. **Finance** Grants; donations; income generated by use of Villa Grebovka. Budget (annual): about US$ 2 million. **Activities** Training/education; events/meetings. **Events** *Conference of Chief Justices* Tbilisi (Georgia) 2014, *Conference of Chief Justices* Montenegro 2013, *Conference of Chief Justices* Albania 2012, *Central Eastern Europe regional meeting* Prague (Czech Rep) 2007. **Publications** *CEELI Newsletter*. Annual Report; reports; manuals.

Members Organizations and individuals in 24 countries:
Albania, Algeria, Armenia, Azerbaijan, Bahrain, Belarus, Bosnia-Herzegovina, Bulgaria, Croatia, Czechia, Georgia, Jordan, Kazakhstan, Kyrgyzstan, Moldova, Morocco, North Macedonia, Romania, Russia, Serbia, Tajikistan, Turkmenistan, Ukraine, Uzbekistan.

IGO Relations *Organization for Security and Cooperation in Europe (OSCE, #17887)*. **NGO Relations** American Bar Association rule of Law Initiative (ABA ROLI); *International Association of Prosecutors (IAP, #12111)*; *International Bar Association's Human Rights Institute (IBAHRI, #12322)*; *International Legal Assistance Consortium (ILAC, #14025)*; *Siracusa International Institute for Criminal Justice and Human Rights (SII, #19289)*; *Sabre Foundation (inactive)*. [2022/XG7865/E]

♦ Central and Eastern European Media Centre Foundation (EMF-FCP) 03694

Centre de communication pour l'Europe centrale et orientale – Fundacja Centrum Prasowe dla Krajów Europy Srodkowej i Wschodniej

Main Office Nowy Swiat 58, 00-363 Warsaw, Poland. T. +48228261096. Fax +48228268962.

History 7 Dec 1990, Warsaw (Poland), after proposal of association of Polish journalists, *International Federation of Journalists (IFJ, #13462)* and *UNESCO (#20322)*. Also referred to as: *European Media Foundation (EMF)*; *Centre de communication de Varsovie*. **Aims** Support changes in the *mass media* of post-communist countries in line with their transformation from totalitarianism and the moulding of democracy; achieve complete *freedom* of expression, maximum independence and pluralism of the media; empower *journalists* to fulfil their function of providing information, expressing *public opinion*, monitoring performance of government authorities and protecting the values which society considers vital to its freedom and ability to shape the conditions under which it lives. **Structure** Board of Directors, comprising Chairman, Director, Deputy Director and Member of the Board. Foundation Council, consisting of Chairman and 9 members. **Staff** 6.00 FTE, paid. **Finance** Self-financed and sponsoring. **Activities** Monitoring, documenting, and analysing changes within the media and social systems for communication within the countries of the region. Exchange of experiences and ideas between journalists, publishers and the broadcasting media of various countries. Influencing media policies of government and legislation by proposing appropriate action and time tested solutions. Training of journalists and publishers in acquiring and passing on information, modern editorial technologies such as radio and television, media management, marketing, advertising, press law and journalistic ethics and the question of professional protection. Creation of a computerized data base. Meetings, seminars and conferences.

Members No regular membership. Journalists and journalist communities in 10 countries are involved:
Czechia, Estonia, Hungary, Latvia, Lithuania, Poland, Romania, Russia, Serbia, Ukraine.

IGO Relations Formal contacts with: *UNDP (#20292)*; UNESCO. [2015/XE1463/f/F]

- Central and Eastern European Network for the Academic Study of Western Esotericism (unconfirmed)

♦ Central and Eastern European Network for Gender Issues (CEE Gender Network) 03695

Zagreb Office Iblerov trg 9, HR-10000 Zagreb, Croatia. E-mail: ceegendernet@gmail.com.
URL: https://ceegendernetwork.eu/

History 1994. Founded under the auspices of *European Forum for Democracy and Solidarity (EFDS, #07307)*. Began work 1 Feb 1998. **Aims** Promote the empowerment of women and gender equality objectives into mainstream strategies, policies and programs of center-left, progressive and social democratic political parties in Central and Eastern European transition countries. **Structure** International Board; Advisory Council; Management. **Activities** Politics/policy/regulatory; capacity building; awareness raising; advocacy/lobbying/activism; guidance/assistance/consulting. **Publications** *CEE Gender Network Newsletter* (4 a year). Annual Report; books; meeting reports. **NGO Relations** Partner of (1): *Progressive Alliance for Freedom, Justice and Solidarity (Progressive Alliance, #18530)*. Observer member of: *Foundation for European Progressive Studies (FEPS, #09954)*. [2020/XK1874/F]

- Central and Eastern European Networking Association (no recent information)

♦ Central and Eastern European Network of Quality Assurance Agencies in Higher Education (CEENQA) 03696

Contact c/o ASIIN, Mörsenbroicher Weg 200, 40470 Düsseldorf, Germany. E-mail: secretariat@ceenqa.org.
URL: http://www.ceenqa.org/

History 3 Oct 2001, Krakow (Poland). Formally established 19 Oct 2002, Vienna (Austria), succeeding the 'Regional Subnetwork of the International Network of Quality Assurance Agencies in Higher Education', founded 19 Nov 2000, Budapest (Hungary). Registration: Start date: 2011, Germany. **Aims** Foster cooperation in the field of quality assurance. **Structure** General Assembly (annual); Executive Board. **Languages** English. **Staff** 1.00 FTE, paid. **Finance** Sources: members' dues; revenue from activities/projects. **Activities** Events/meetings. **Events** *General Assembly* Kyrenia (Cyprus) 2019, *General Assembly* Tirana (Albania) 2018, *General Assembly* Zagreb (Croatia) 2017, *General Assembly* Krakow (Poland) 2016, *General Assembly* Ljubljana (Slovenia) 2015.

Members National and regional agencies and councils (27) in 22 countries and territories:
Albania, Armenia, Austria, Bosnia-Herzegovina, Bulgaria, Croatia, Czechia, Estonia, Germany, Hungary, Kazakhstan, Kosovo, Kyrgyzstan, Latvia, Lithuania, Moldova, Northern Cyprus, Poland, Romania, Russia, Slovenia, Türkiye.

Included in the above, 1 organization listed in this Yearbook:
Foundation for International Business Administration Accreditation (FIBAA, #09961).

NGO Relations Associate member of: *European Association for Quality Assurance in Higher Education (ENQA, #06183)*. [2020.05.06/XE4443/y/E]

- Central and Eastern European Outsourcing Association (unconfirmed)
- Central and Eastern European Privatization Network (no recent information)
- Central and Eastern European Regional Network (internationally oriented national body)

♦ **Central and Eastern European Schools Association (CEESA)** **03697**

Exec Dir Vocarska 106, HR-10000 Zagreb, Croatia. T. +385911817921. E-mail: office@ceesa.org.
URL: http://www.ceesa.org/

History 1983, as *East European Schools Association (EESA)*. **Aims** Provide a forum for on-going communication, cooperation and growth among member institutions; promote exchanges among *staff* and *students* to foster professionalism, scholarship and understanding; foster exchange of ideas and know-how. **Structure** Board of Directors. **Languages** English. **Staff** 2.00 FTE, paid. **Finance** Members' dues. Other sources: grants; funding from US Department of State. **Activities** Training/education; events/meetings. **Events** *Annual Conference* Budapest (Hungary) 2021, *Annual Conference* Zagreb (Croatia) 2020, *Annual Conference* Warsaw (Poland) 2019, *Annual Conference* Prague (Czechia) 2018, *Annual Conference* Sofia (Bulgaria) 2017. **Publications** *CEESA Newsletter* (3 a year).
Members Full; Provisional; Associate. Members (71) in 23 countries:
Albania, Armenia, Austria, Azerbaijan, Belarus, Bosnia-Herzegovina, Bulgaria, Croatia, Czechia, Estonia, Finland, Georgia, Hungary, Latvia, North Macedonia, Poland, Romania, Russia, Serbia, Slovakia, Slovenia, Türkiye, Ukraine.
Included in the above, 2 organizations listed in this Yearbook:
International Educators Cooperative (no recent information); *International Schools Services (ISS)*.
[2017.03.13/XE1953/y/**E**]

♦ Central And Eastern European Society Of Technology Assessment In Health Care (internationally oriented national body)

♦ **Central and Eastern European Stroke Society (CEESS)** **03698**

Pres Ulica grada Vukovara 271/4, HR-10000 Zagreb, Croatia. E-mail: ceess.org@gmail.com.
Sec Univ Dept of Neurology, Univ Hosp "Sestre milosrdnice", Vinogradska 29, HR-10000 Zagreb, Croatia. T. +38513768282. Fax +38513768282. E-mail: ztrkanj@gmail.com.
URL: http://www.ceess.org/

History 10 Oct 1996. **Aims** Promote organization of modern management of stroke patients; organize stroke units; improve diagnostic procedures; provide evidence based treatment of stroke; comprehensive rehabilitation of stroke patients; monitor quality of stroke care in the region. **Structure** Board; International Committee. **Languages** English. **Staff** No permanent staff. **Finance** Donations; grants. **Activities** Events/meetings; teaching/education. **Events** *Stroke Update Conference* Warsaw (Poland) 2016, *Meeting* Zagreb (Croatia) 2010, *Congress* Warsaw (Poland) 2008, *Summer symposium* Loughborough (UK) 2001, *Congress* Budapest (Hungary) 1999.
Members Full in 22 countries:
Albania, Austria, Belarus, Bosnia-Herzegovina, Bulgaria, Croatia, Czechia, Estonia, Georgia, Germany, Hungary, Latvia, Lithuania, Moldova, North Macedonia, Poland, Romania, Russia, Serbia, Slovakia, Slovenia, Ukraine.
NGO Relations Member of: *World Stroke Organization (WSO, #21831)*. [2018/XD7229/**D**]

♦ **Central and Eastern European Travel Retail Association (CEETRA)** . **03699**

Association du commerce du voyageur pour l'Europe centrale et orientale

Secretariat c/o Hume Brophy, Rue de la Science 41, 1040 Brussels, Belgium. T. +3222346860. E-mail: secretariat@ceetra.org.
URL: http://www.ceetra.org/

History Registered in accordance with Belgian law: 0597 926 905. **Aims** Protect, promote and facilitate the region's travel retail channel by providing the means to obtain the most favourable trading environment for the travel related commerce. **Structure** General Meeting (annual); Board of Directors. **Finance** Members' dues. **Activities** Advocacy/lobbying/activism; networking/liaising.
Members Full in 14 countries:
Albania, Austria, Bulgaria, Croatia, Czechia, Hungary, Kosovo, Montenegro, North Macedonia, Poland, Romania, Serbia, Slovakia, Slovenia.
NGO Relations Member of: *European Travel Retail Confederation (ETRC, #08945)*. [2017/XM6041/**D**]

♦ Central and Eastern European University Network (internationally oriented national body)
♦ Central and Eastern European Working Group for the Enhancement of Biodiversity / see CEEweb for Biodiversity (#03626)
♦ Central and Eastern Europe Data Protection Authorities (unconfirmed)
♦ Central and East European Association of Bioethics (inactive)
♦ Central and East-European Association for Neurology / see International Danube Neurology Association of Central and East Europe (#13134)

♦ **Central and East European International Studies Association (CEEISA)** **03700**

Secretariat Univ of Economics, Jan Masaryk Ctr of Intl Studies, W Churchill Sq 4, 130 67 Prague 3, Czechia. T. +420224095232. Fax +420224095289. E-mail: secretariat@ceeisa.net.
URL: https://www.ceeisa.net/

History Feb 1996, by *International Affairs Network (IAN, inactive)* and St Petersburg State University. **Aims** Enable meetings and exchange of research results of researchers from Central and Eastern Europe; enhance cooperation within the region so as to secure a more tangible IR output to the global scientific community. **Structure** General Assembly; Executive Council; President; Secretariat. **Languages** English. **Staff** 0.50 FTE, voluntary. **Finance** Administrative expenses covered through conference fees. **Activities** Events/meetings. **Events** *Convention* Bratislava (Slovakia) 2022, *The politics of international relations* Ljubljana (Slovenia) 2016, *Convention* Cluj-Napoca (Romania) 2014, *Boundaries in/of international relations* Krakow (Poland) 2012, *Convention* Istanbul (Turkey) 2011. **Publications** *Journal of International Relations and Development*. *CEEISA Book Series*.
Members Individuals in 20 countries:
Austria, Belgium, Canada, Czechia, Denmark, Estonia, France, Germany, Hungary, Italy, Latvia, Netherlands, Poland, Portugal, Russia, Slovenia, Switzerland, Türkiye, UK, USA.
IGO Relations None. **NGO Relations** *Jan Masaryk Centre of International Studies (JMCIS)* is Founding Member. [2022/XD6521/**D**]

♦ Central and East European Law Initiative / see Central and Eastern European Law Initiative (#03693)
♦ Central and East European Management Development Association / see CEEMAN – International Association for Management Development in Dynamic Societies (#03625)
♦ Central and East European Management Development Network / see CEEMAN – International Association for Management Development in Dynamic Societies (#03625)

♦ **Central and East European Oncology Group (CEEOG)** **03701**

Sec Medical Univ Gdansk, Oncology – Radiotherapy, 7 Debinki Street, 80-211 Gdansk, Poland. T. +48585844565. Fax +48583492244.
URL: http://www.ceeog.eu/

History 1983. Former names and other names: *South and East European Oncology Group (SEEOG)* – former. **Aims** Promote research and development of *cancer* treatment methods; manage cancer-related clinical trials. **Structure** Chairman; Vice-Chairman; Treasurer; Registrar; Clinical Trials Coordinator. **Languages** English. **Staff** 1.00 FTE, paid; 25.00 FTE, voluntary. **Finance** Sources: donations; sponsorship. **Activities** Events/meetings; research/documentation. **Events** *Conference* Gdynia (Poland) 2006, *State-of-the-art treatment of breast cancer conference / Conference* Vienna (Austria) 2005, *State-of-the-art treatment of breast cancer conference / Conference* Budapest (Hungary) 2004.
Members Ordinary in 10 countries:
Bosnia-Herzegovina, Croatia, Czechia, Lithuania, Poland, Russia, Serbia, Slovakia, Slovenia, Ukraine.
NGO Relations Member of: *Breast International Group (BIG, #03319)*. [2020.07.06/XJ3520/**D**]

♦ Centrale catholique d'aide au développement (internationally oriented national body)
♦ Centrale Commissie voor de Rijnvaart (#03687)
♦ Centrale latinoaméricaine des travailleurs (inactive)
♦ Centrale sanitaire internationale (inactive)
♦ Central Esperantist Office (inactive)
♦ Centrale des travailleurs chrétiens du Pacifique (inactive)
♦ Central Eurasian Studies Society (internationally oriented national body)

♦ **Central European Air Traffic Services (CEATS)** **03702**

Contact address not obtained. T. +3612972211. Fax +3612972228. E-mail: philippe.debels@eurocontrol.int.
URL: http://www.eurocontrol.int/ceats/public/subsite_homepage/homepage.html

History 27 Jun 1997, Brussels (Belgium), in the framework of *EUROCONTROL (#05667)* through *Agreement Relating to the Provision and Operation of Air Traffic Services and Facilities by EUROCONTROL at the Central European Air Traffic Services Upper Area Control Centre (CEATS Agreement, 1997)*, signed between the National Contracting Parties of Austria, Bosnia-Herzegovina, Croatia, Czech Rep, Hungary, Slovakia, Slovenia and Northern Italy. **Aims** Implement the Central European Air Traffic Services Agreement; create a single, unified air traffic *control* system for the upper *airspace* over 8 nations – Austria, Bosnia and Herzegovina, Croatia, the Czech Republic, Hungary, the northern part of Italy (Padua), the Slovak Republic and Slovenia; manage the upper airspace of the region in much the same way that the Maastricht UAC has directed the skies over Belgium, Luxembourg (Luxembourg), the Netherlands and north-western Germany; maintain or upgrade current *safety* levels, while simultaneously offering increased capacity, efficiency and speed over the present scheme; improve economy of flight operations; support access of *military* users to the *airspace*. **Structure** Programme Directorate (CPD) led by Acting Director and Programme Manager. Management Office (CMO). Units (4): Strategy Planning and Development (CSPDU), Prague (Czech Rep); Research, Development and Simulation Centre (CRDS), Budapest (Hungary); Training Centre (CTC), Forli (Italy), when established; UAC, Vienna (Austria), when established. [2011/XK1241/**E***]

♦ **Central European Anti-Doping Organization (CEADO)** **03703**

Contact Gertrude-Fröhlich-Sandner-Str 13 / Top 6, 1030 Vienna, Austria. T. +4315058035. Fax +431505803535. E-mail: office@ceado.org.
URL: https://www.ceado.org/

History 28 May 2019, Budapest (Hungary). Founded by organizations from Austria, Croatia, Hungary, Poland, Serbia, Slovakia and Slovenia. **Aims** Strengthen and support the Anti-Doping work to the benefit of the clean athletes.
Members Organizations in 8 countries:
Austria, Croatia, Czechia, Hungary, Poland, Serbia, Slovakia, Slovenia.
NGO Relations Memorandum of Understanding with (1): *World Anti-Doping Agency (WADA, #21096)*. Cooperates with (1): *International Testing Agency (ITA, #15678)*. [2022/AA3049/**D**]

♦ **Central European Association for Canadian Studies (CEACS)** **03704**

Association d'études canadiennes en Europe Centrale (AECEC)

Contact address not obtained. E-mail: cecanstud@gmail.com.
URL: http://www.cecanstud.cz/

History Founded summer 2003, as the culmination of regional Canadian Studies activities dating back to May 1995. **Aims** Bring together university teachers, researchers and students from the Central European region who are doing work related to Canada. **Structure** General Meeting; Executive Committee; Advisory Board. **Languages** English, French. **Finance** Sources: members' dues. **Activities** Awards/prizes/competitions; events/meetings; projects/programmes; publishing activities; research/documentation. **Events** *Triennial International Conference* Budapest (Hungary) 2022, *Triennial Conference* Prague (Czechia) 2018. **Publications** *Central European Journal of Canadian Studies* (annual).
Members Full (180) in 9 countries:
Bulgaria, Croatia, Czechia, Hungary, Montenegro, Romania, Serbia, Slovakia, Slovenia.
NGO Relations Member of (1): *International Council for Canadian Studies (ICCS)*. [2022.05.12/XM7952/**D**]

♦ **Central European Association of Computational Mechanics (CEACM)** **03705**

Pres Mechanics Chair UTC, Patriotske lige 30, 71000 Sarajevo, Bosnia-Herzegovina.
URL: https://gf.unsa.ba/web/

History 25 Mar 1992, Leipzig (Germany). Registration: Austria. **Aims** Stimulate and promote education, research and practical applications in the field of computational mechanics; foster exchange of ideas among members; provide a forum for dissemination of knowledge about computational mechanics. **Structure** General Assembly; Executive Committee. **Languages** English. **Staff** 2.00 FTE, voluntary. **Finance** Members' dues. Annual budget: euro 500 and US$ 890. **Activities** Events/meetings; training/education. **Events** *General Assembly* Bosnia-Herzegovina 2021, *General Assembly* Vienna (Austria) 2017, *General Assembly* Opatija (Croatia) 2015, *General Assembly* Vienna (Austria) 2013, *Meeting* Vienna (Austria) 2012. **Publications** *Central European Journal of Computer Assisted Mechanics and Engineering Sciences (CAMES)* (4 a year).
Members Individuals in 8 countries:
Austria, Bosnia-Herzegovina, Croatia, Czechia, Hungary, Poland, Slovakia, Slovenia.
NGO Relations Member of: *European Committee on Computational Methods in Applied Sciences (ECCOMAS, #06644)*; *International Association for Computational Mechanics (IACM, #11800)*. Links with national associations. [2021/XD3380/v/**D**]

♦ Central European Association of Urology (no recent information)
♦ Central European Centre for Health and the Environment / see Center for Communications, Health and the Environment
♦ Central European Conference on Cryptology (meeting series)
♦ Central European Conference on Photochemistry (meeting series)

♦ **Central European Cooperative Oncology Group (CECOG)** **03706**

Contact Schlagergasse 6/6, 1090 Vienna, Austria. T. +4314097725. Fax +4314097726.
URL: http://www.cecog.org/

History 1999, Vienna (Austria). Registered in accordance with Austrian law. **Aims** Promote cooperation among centres dealing with *clinical* oncology in Central Europe; increase standards of clinical research and treatment of patients with cancer in the region. **Structure** Scientific Committee; Advisory Board; Educational Committee. **Events** *International symposium on biological therapy of cancer* Munich (Germany) 2008, *Interconference breast cancer meeting* Sarajevo (Bosnia-Herzegovina) 2007, *Workshop* Vienna (Austria) 2007, *Meeting* Orlando, FL (USA) 2005, *Meeting* New Orleans, LA (USA) 2004. **Publications** *Oncology Newsletter*.
Members Centres in 22 countries:
Austria, Bosnia-Herzegovina, Bulgaria, Croatia, Cyprus, Czechia, Estonia, Hungary, Israel, Latvia, Lebanon, Lithuania, Montenegro, Poland, Portugal, Romania, Russia, Serbia, Slovakia, Slovenia, South Africa, Türkiye.
NGO Relations Member of: *European Thoracic Oncology Platform (ETOP, #08910)*. [2014/XM2129/**F**]

♦ Central European Covered Bond Conference (meeting series)
♦ Central European Craft Brewers Conference (meeting series)

♦ **Central European Diatomists** **03707**

Contact Botanischer Garten und Botanisches Museum Berlin-Dahlem, Königin-Luise-Str 6-8, 14195 Berlin, Germany. T. +493083850142.
URL: http://www.bgbm.org/diatoms/default.htm

History 1987. Former names and other names: *Deutschsprachige Diatomologen mit Internationaler Beteiligung* – former. **Events** *Central European Diatom Meeting* Luxembourg (Luxembourg) 2019, *Meeting* Prague (Czechia) 2017, *Meeting* Budapest (Hungary) 2016, *Meeting* Bremerhaven (Germany) 2015, *Meeting* Zagreb (Croatia) 2014. [2019/XM2114/**D**]

♦ Central European and Eurasian Law Initiative / see Central and Eastern European Law Initiative (#03693)
♦ Central European Exchange Programme for University Students (internationally oriented national body)
♦ Central European Federation of Christian Trade Unions (inactive)
♦ Central European Free Trade Agreement (1992 treaty)
♦ Central European Free Trade Association (no recent information)
♦ Central European Frisbee Disc Association (inactive)
♦ Central European Group for Separation Sciences (internationally oriented national body)

♦ Central European Initiative (CEI) 03708

SG Via Genova 9, 34121 Trieste TS, Italy. T. +39407786777. Fax +3940360640. E-mail: cei@cei.int.
URL: http://www.ceinet.org/

History 11 Nov 1989, Budapest (Hungary), as *Quadrilateral Initiative – Initiative quadrilatérale* or *Quadragonale*, by representatives of Austria, Hungary, Italy and Yugoslavia. When Czechoslovakia joined, May 1990, became *Pentagonal Initiative – Initiative pentagonale*, also referred to as *Pentagonale*, *Pentagon Group* or *Pentagonal Conference*. During 2nd summit meeting, 27 Jul 1991, Dubrovnik (Yugoslavia), when Poland became a member, name changed to *Hexagonal Initiative – Initiative hexagonale* or *Hexagonal – Hexagonale*. Present name adopted 1992, when Croatia, Slovenia and Bosnia-Herzegovina became full members. Nov 2000, Yugoslavia joined (later called Serbia and Montenegro); Jun 2006, when countries split, Montenegro became 18th Member State, with Serbia continuing membership. Also referred to by the French acronyms *ICE* or *INCE*. **Aims** As an intergovernmental forum for concertation and cooperation based on *political decision-making* rather than official international agreements: establish *cohesion* in Europe; strengthen cooperation among member states, participation of all member states in the process of European integration and the transition process of the reform countries. **Structure** Functions through 3 Dimensions. *'Governmental Dimension'*, consisting of Summit of Heads of Government (annual), Meeting of Ministers for Foreign Affairs (annual), other Ministerial meetings, Committee of National Coordinators (CNC) and Network of Focal Points. *'Parliamentary Dimension'*, consisting of *Parliamentary Assembly*, Parliamentary Committee and General Committees (Political and Home Affairs; Economic Affairs; Cultural Affairs). *'Business Dimension'*. Rotating Presidency with meetings held in country holding Presidency. Secretariat, headed by Secretary-General, based in Trieste (Italy). **Languages** English. **Finance** In principle every country finances its own costs. *'CEI Cooperation Fund'* – for the implementation of programmes and projects; *'CEI Solidarity Fund'* – based on voluntary contributions from member states to facilitate participation in CEI events; *'CEI Fund (Trust Fund)'* – at *European Bank for Reconstruction and Development (EBRD, #06315)* and managed by Secretariat for CEI projects. **Activities** Politics/policy/regulatory; events/meetings; awards/prizes/competitions. **Events** *Ministers of Foreign Affairs Meeting* Vienna (Austria) 2014, *Summit economic forum* Bucharest (Romania) 2009, *Summit economic forum* Chisinau (Moldova) 2008, *Summit economic forum* Sofia (Bulgaria) 2007, *Meeting on x-ray emission techniques for forensic applications* Trieste (Italy) 2007. **Publications** *CEI Instrument for the Protection of Minority Rights*; *Political and Economic Documents* – 2 vols published so far; *Towards Sustainable Transport in the CEI Countries*. Reports.

Members Governments of 18 countries:
Albania, Austria, Belarus, Bosnia-Herzegovina, Bulgaria, Croatia, Czechia, Hungary, Italy, Moldova, Montenegro, North Macedonia, Poland, Romania, Serbia, Slovakia, Slovenia, Ukraine.

IGO Relations Parliamentary Dimension is Observer to: *Parliamentary Assembly of the Organization of the Black Sea Economic Cooperation (PABSEC, #18213)*. **NGO Relations** Member of: *International Network for Small and Medium Sized Enterprises (INSME, #14325)*. Partner of: *United Nations Academic Impact (UNAI, #20516)*. Supports: *Association Justice and Environment, z.s. (J&E, #02774)*; *Mladiinfo International (#16834)*. Formal contacts with: *Europe and the Balkans International Network (EBIN, #09150)*.
[2015/XF5087/F*]

♦ Central European Institute of Neuro-Semantics / see MCF-B

♦ Central European Lung Cancer Association (CELCA) 03709

Contact c/o Mondial Congress & Events, Operngasse 20b, 1040 Vienna, Austria. T. +43158804202. E-mail: celca@mondial-congress.com.

Structure Board. **Activities** Events/meetings. **Events** *Central European Lung Cancer Conference* Vienna (Austria) 2021, *Central European Lung Cancer Conference* Prague (Czechia) 2020, *Central European Lung Cancer Conference* Budapest (Hungary) 2019, *Central European Lung Cancer Conference* Novi Sad (Serbia) 2018.
[2022/AA2438/c/D]

♦ Central and European Network of Legal Scholars (meeting series)

♦ Central European Neurosurgical Society (CENS) 03710

Pres UNB Neurochirurgicka Klinika, Pazitkova 4, 821 01 Bratislava, Slovakia.

Aims Increase cooperation between neurosurgeons from Central European countries; disseminate knowledge of neurosciences between the members. **Structure** General Assembly. Board, comprising President, 2 Vice-Presidents, Scientific Secretary and 4 further members. **Languages** English. **Events** *Meeting* Vienna (Austria) 2008, *Meeting* Budapest (Hungary) 2006, *Meeting* Hungary 2004, *Meeting* Ljubljana (Slovenia) 2004, *Meeting* Brno (Czech Rep) 2002.
[2019/XD8205/D]

♦ Central European Opinion Research Group (no recent information)

♦ Central European Police Academy 03711

Mitteleuropäischen Polizeiakademie (MEPA)

Contact Zentrales Koordinationsbüro der MEPA, Bundesministerium für Inneres, Postfach 100, 1014 Vienna, Austria. T. +431531264854. Fax +431531264873. E-mail: mepa@bmi.gv.at.
URL: http://www.mepa.net/

History Founded 1993, Vienna (Austria). **Aims** Contribute to the European *integration* process by helping to create common police standards. **Structure** Board; Coordination Office in Vienna (Austria). **Languages** German. **Staff** 2.00 FTE, paid. **Finance** Members' dues. Support from: Government of Austria and other member states; *European Commission (EC, #06633)*. **Activities** Training/education. **Publications** *MEPA Buch*; *MEPA Fachjournal*.

Members Contact points in 7 countries:
Austria, Czechia, Germany, Hungary, Slovakia, Slovenia, Switzerland.

NGO Relations *Association of European Police Colleges (AEPC, #02531)*; *European Union Agency for Law Enforcement Training (CEPOL, #08970)*.
[2014.11.21/XE3922/E]

♦ Central European Political Science Association (CEPSA) 03712

Pres Univ of Ljubljana, Dept of Politics, Kardeljeva ploscad 5, 1000 Ljubljana, Slovenia.
Gen Sec address not obtained.
URL: http://www.cepsanet.org/

History 1994. Established as a common forum of post-communist Central European political scientists. Founded by six national political science associations from Austria, the Czech Republic, Hungary, Poland, Slovakia and Slovenia. **Aims** Develop links among political scientists from post-communist countries who were making effort to establish political science in their respective countries. **Structure** Officers: President; Vice-President; Secretary General. **Languages** English. **Staff** Voluntary. **Finance** No direct financial sources. **Activities** Events/meetings; publishing activities. **Events** *Annual Conference* Ljubljana (Slovenia) 2021, *Annual Conference* Olsztyn (Poland) 2021, *Annual Conference* Olsztyn (Poland) 2020, *Annual Conference* Pécs (Hungary) 2019, *Annual Conference* Banska Bystrica (Slovakia) 2018. **Publications** *Politicke Vedy* (4 a year); *Politics in Central Europe* (3 a year); *Political Preferences* (2 a year); *Journal of Comparative Politics* (2 a year); *Baltic Journal of Political Science* (annual).

Members National political science associations in 8 countries:
Austria, Croatia, Czechia, Hungary, Lithuania, Poland, Slovakia, Slovenia.

NGO Relations Member of (1): *International Political Science Association (IPSA, #14615)*.
[2021.02.16/XD8435/D]

♦ Central European Pragmatist Forum (CEPF) 03713

Co-Chair Dept of Philosophy and History of Philosophy, Fac of Arts, Comenius Univ, Safarikova nam 6, 818 01 Bratislava, Slovakia.
URL: http://www.cepf.sk/

Structure Board of Directors. **Activities** Events/meetings. **NGO Relations** Member of: *European Pragmatism Association*.
[2016/XM4970/F]

♦ Central European Real Estate Associations Network (CEREAN) 03714

Pres 160 Stirbei Voda Str, Bl 22B – Ap 12, 010121 Bucharest, Romania. T. +40216732178. Fax +40212602665. E-mail: office@cerean.com – cerean@cerean.com.
URL: http://www.cerean.com/

History 10 Jun 1995, Krakow (Poland), following a proposal 1994, during 1st conference of Central European real estate associations. Statutes adopted Jun 2001; Revised: Nov 2003; Nov 2007; Nov 2008. **Aims** Promote ethics and training in the profession of brokers, realtors, appraisals and counsellors in real estate; establish and preserve private property as a fundamental right of citizens living in a democratic system; promote real estate property as a key element of development and safety in a free society; create effective and fair real estate markets. **Structure** Council (meets twice a year). Board of Directors of up to 5 members, including President and Executive Director. **Languages** English. **Staff** 2.00 FTE, paid. **Finance** Members' dues. Other sources: grants; donations; income from conferences and other activities. **Activities** Promotion of European Standard of Real Estate. **Events** *Annual conference* Sofia (Bulgaria) 2011, *Annual Conference* Thessaloniki (Greece) 2009, *Annual Conference* Istanbul (Turkey) 2008, *Annual Conference* Bucharest (Romania) 2007, *Annual Conference* Sofia (Bulgaria) 2006. **Publications** *CEREAN Eurolink*. Annual Yearbook.

Members Full; affiliate; individual. Members in 11 countries:
Armenia, Bulgaria, Czechia, Georgia, Greece, Poland, Romania, Russia, Slovakia, Türkiye, Ukraine.
[2008.11.26/XM0140/F]

♦ Central European Regional Research Organization (no recent information)

♦ Central European Regulatory Forum (CERF) 03715

Contact Natl Media and Infocommuncations Authority 23-25, Ostrom u, Budapest 1015, Hungary.
URL: http://cerfportal.org/

History Set up 15 Dec 2009, when Memorandum of Understanding was signed. **Aims** Enhance cooperation and facilitate the exchange of ideas and best practices among the audiovisual regulatory authorities of Central Europe. **Languages** English. **Staff** None paid. **Finance** No independent budget. Annual meetings finance by event organizer. **Activities** Events/meetings.

Members Regulatory authorities of 8 countries:
Croatia, Czechia, Hungary, Poland, Romania, Serbia, Slovakia, Slovenia.

IGO Relations *European Commission (EC, #06633)*.
[2019.03.22/XM5888/F*]

♦ Central European Research Infrastructure Consortium (CERIC) 03716

Exec Dir SS 14 – Km 163-5 in AREA Science Park, Basovizza, 34149 Trieste TS, Italy. E-mail: secretariat-ga@ceric-eric.eu.
URL: http://www.ceric-eric.eu/

History Awarded the status of *European Research Infrastructure Consortium ERIC*, following which it is also known as *CERIC-ERIC*. **Structure** General Assembly; Board of Directors; International Scientific and Technical Advisory Committee. **Events** *International European Social Survey Conference* Lausanne (Switzerland) 2016.

Members Research centres in 9 countries:
Austria, Croatia, Czechia, Hungary, Italy, Poland, Romania, Serbia, Slovenia.

NGO Relations Member of (1): *Association of European-level Research Infrastructure Facilities (ERF-AISBL, #02518)*.
[2020.11.17/XM5203/E]

♦ Central European Society for Anticancer Drug Research-EWIV (internationally oriented national body)
♦ Central European Turtle and Tortoise Association (no recent information)

♦ Central European University (CEU) 03717

Közép-európai Egyetem

Main Office Quellenstr 51, 1100 Vienna, Austria.
Office in Hungary Nador utca 9, Budapest 1051, Hungary.
URL: https://www.ceu.edu/

History 1989. Founded by *Open Society Foundations (OSF, #17763)*. Charter granted in accordance with laws of the State of New York (USA). Commenced activities in 1991, in Budapest and Prague (Czech Rep). From academic year 2003-2004 onward, operated in Budapest only; in 2019 majority of operations moved to Vienna. Accreditation granted by CHE Middle States Commission on Higher Education, Jun 2004, Philadelphia PA (USA). Recognized as a Hungarian private university, "Kozep-europai Egyetem" (CEU); accredited by the Hungarian Accreditation Committee (MAB), Mar 2005, Budapest (Hungary). Former names and other names: *Central European University Private University (CEU PU)* – legal name (2019). Registration: Austria. **Aims** As an internationally recognized institution of post-graduate education in social sciences and humanities: seek to develop and sustain open societies, democracy, rule of law, free markets, tolerance and political and cultural pluralism in Central and Eastern Europe and the former Soviet Union and other parts of the world experiencing emerging democracy; serve as an advanced centre of research and policy analysis; facilitate academic dialogue and provide an environment in which the region's next generation of leaders and scholars can meet and interact. **Structure** Board of Trustees, comprising Chair and 19 members. Academic Senate, consisting of President/Rector (ex-officio), 11 members and 2 ex-officio members. Includes: *CEU Business School*. **Languages** English. **Staff** Professors: 140; administrative staff: 280. **Finance** 2008: endowment of euro 500 million. Budget (annual): euro 35 million. **Activities** Training/education. **Events** *Budapest CEU Conference on Cognitive Development (BCCCD)* Budapest (Hungary) 2022, *Budapest CEU Conference on Cognitive Development (BCCCD)* Budapest (Hungary) 2021, *Budapest CEU Conference on Cognitive Development (BCCCD)* Budapest (Hungary) 2020, *Workshop on Information and Communications Technologies for Sustainable Development Goals Indicator Monitoring* Budapest (Hungary) 2016, *Conference on Cognitive Development* Budapest (Hungary) 2014. **Publications** *Central European University Press*.

Members Not a membership organization. Students and faculty come from over 100 countries. **Consultative Status** Consultative status granted from: *UNEP (#20299)*.
[2020/XF5067/F]

♦ Central European University Private University / see Central European University (#03717)

♦ Central European Vascular Forum (CEVF) 03718

Admin Sec Ustecka 3041, 272 01 Kladno, Czechia. T. +420731476665.
URL: http://www.cevf.org/

History 24 Oct 1997, Rome (Italy). **Activities** Events/meetings; training/education. **Events** *International Congress* Bratislava (Slovakia) 2020, *International Congress* Palermo (Italy) 2018, *International Congress* Warsaw (Poland) 2016, *International Congress* Rome (Italy) 2014, *International Congress* Prague (Czech Rep) 2012.

Members Individuals in 9 countries:
Austria, Croatia, Czechia, Hungary, Italy, Poland, Romania, Slovakia, Slovenia.
[2022.10.19/XN8991/F]

♦ Central European Workshop on Quantum Optics (meeting series)

♦ Central Europe Center for Research and Documentation (Centropa) 03719

Austria Selzergasse 10, Top 5-8, 1150 Vienna, Austria. T. +4314090971. Fax +43140909714. E-mail: office@centropa.org.
Germany Centropa c/o wework, Axel Springer Platz 3, 20355 Hamburg, Germany. T. +4917645751975. E-mail: ruehle@centropa.org.
URL: http://www.centropa.org/

History Registered in accordance with US, Hungarian and Austrian laws. Registration: 501c3, USA; Hungary; Austria; Hamburg District court, No/ID: VR 23236, Start date: 3 May 2017, Germany, Hamburg. **Aims** Preserve *Jewish* memory in Central and Eastern Europe, the former Soviet Union, the Balkans and the Baltics. **Activities** Events/meetings; training/education. **NGO Relations** Member of (2): *Association of Holocaust Organizations (AHO)*; *European Network for Countering Antisemitism through Education (ENCATE)*.
[2021/XJ1656/F]

♦ Central Europe Energy Partners (internationally oriented national body)
♦ Central Europe Foundation (unconfirmed)
♦ Central Institute of Latin American Studies, Berlin / see Lateinamerika-Institut, Freie Universität Berlin
♦ Centralinstitut for Nordisk Asienforskning / see NIAS-Nordisk Institut for Asienstudier (#17132)
♦ Central International Bureau of Seismology (inactive)
♦ Central Latinoamericana y del Caribe de Trabajadores Jubilados, Pensionados y Adultos Mayores / see Confederación Latinoamericana de Trabajadores Jubilados, Pensionados y Adultos Mayores (#04462)
♦ Central Latinoamericana de Trabajadores (inactive)
♦ Central Latinoamericana dos Trabalhadores (inactive)
♦ Central Meteoric Bureau (inactive)
♦ Central Office of International Associations / see Union of International Associations (#20414)

- ♦ Central Office of the International Pedological Congresses (inactive)
- ♦ Central Office for Maghrebian Compensation (no recent information)
- ♦ Central Office of Nationalities (inactive)
- ♦ Central Office for the National Societies of Roman Catholic Doctors (inactive)
- ♦ Central Office of Women's Documentation (inactive)
- ♦ Central Organization for a Durable Peace (inactive)
- ♦ Central Pan American Bureau of Eugenics and Homiculture (inactive)
- ♦ Central and South American Air School / see Inter-American Air Forces Academy

♦ Central and Southeast Europe LCA Network (CASE-LCA) 03720

Secretariat Univ of Novi Sad, Fac of Technical Sciences, Trg Dositeja Obradovica 6, Novi Sad, PAK 21000, Serbia. T. +381214852255.
URL: http://www.caselca.org/

History Sep 2011, Novi Sad (Serbia). **Aims** Promote *life cycle* thinking at all levels in society; increase awareness of and promote adoption of *environmental* LCA among industry, government, and NGOs; promote networking among LCA practitioners and researchers. **Events** *Meeting* Novi Sad (Serbia) 2013, *Meeting* Poznań (Poland) 2012.
Members Full in 7 countries:
Croatia, Czechia, Hungary, Poland, Serbia, Slovakia, Slovenia.
NGO Relations *Life Cycle Initiative (LCI, #16464).* [2016/XJ7338/**F**]

♦ Central and Southern Europe Central Conference – The United Methodist Church 03721

Contact Central and Southern Europe Area, Badenerstrasse 69, Postfach 2111, 8021 Zurich ZH 1, Switzerland. E-mail: bishop@umc-cse.org.
URL: http://www.umc-cse.org/

History 1954. **Aims** Bring together into one *episcopal* area Methodists from the countries of Central and Eastern Europe. **Languages** English, German. **Staff** 2.80 FTE, paid. **Events** *Session* Zurich (Switzerland) 2017, *Session* Winterthur (Switzerland) 2013, *Session* Bülach (Switzerland) 2009, *Youth meeting* Czech Rep 2006, *Women's seminar* Waldegg (Switzerland) 2006.
Members Full in 12 countries:
Albania, Austria, Belgium, Czechia, France, Hungary, North Macedonia, Poland, Romania, Serbia, Slovakia, Switzerland.
[2022.05.03/XF3072/**F**]

- ♦ Central Treaty Organization (inactive)
- ♦ Centraludvalget for det EØFs Skovbrugsejere / see Confederation of European Forest Owners (#04525)
- ♦ Central Union of Marine Underwriters / see Nordic Association of Marine Insurers (#17198)
- ♦ **CENTR** Council of European National Top-Level Domain Registries (#04892)

♦ Centre for Access to Football in Europe (CAFE) 03722

Managing Dir No 1 Olympic Way, Wembley, London, HA9 0NP, UK. E-mail: info@cafefootball.eu.
URL: http://www.cafefootball.eu/

History Founded 2009, through Monaco Charity Award of *Union of European Football Associations (UEFA, #20386).* UK Registered Charity: 1131339. **Aims** Promote and ensure *inclusiveness* and *equality* across the UEFA region; provide support, guidance and advice to partners and stakeholders; raise disability awareness more widely throughout Europe; empower *disabled* people to exercise their rights; promote equal access to all European football stadiums and their clubs; act as accessible stadia advisors and recognize and share good practice wherever it exists (facilities and services); increase disability and access awareness using the special influence of football; establish a European network of local and national disabled football supporters groups as user-led self-advocates at a local level; enable more disabled people to follow and get involved in football at all levels of the game. **Structure** Board of Directors; Advisory Group. **Languages** Dutch, English, French, German, Italian, Polish, Portuguese, Russian, Spanish, Ukrainian. **Staff** 6.00 FTE, paid. **Finance** *Union of European Football Associations (UEFA, #20386)* – Monaco Award 2009; voluntary contributions and donations; sponsorship. **Activities** Guidance/assistance/consulting; knowledge management/information dissemination; financial and/or material support. **Events** *European conference* London (UK) 2011. **Publications** *CAFE E-newsletter* (12 a year). *Good Practice Guide.* Annual Report. **NGO Relations** Cooperates with: *Comité européen de normalisation (CEN, #04162); Union of European Football Associations (UEFA, #20386)*; European associations; national football associations and their leagues and member clubs; disabled supporter groups; other national and European equality and supporter networks, NGOs and interested organizations. [2014.11.05/XJ0914/**E**]

- ♦ Centre d'action européenne démocratique et laïque / see Mouvement Europe et laïcité
- ♦ Centre d'action européenne fédéraliste (inactive)
- ♦ Centre d'actions et de réalisations internationales (internationally oriented national body)
- ♦ Centre d'Activités Régionales pour les Aires Spécialement Protégées (#18746)
- ♦ Centre d'Activités Régionales pour la Consommation et la Production Durables (#18747)
- ♦ Centre d'Activités Régionales pour l'Information et la Communication de la Convention de Barcelone (#18745)
- ♦ Centre d'activités régionales du programme d'actions prioritaires (#18501)
- ♦ Centre d'activités régionales de télédétection appliquée à l'environnement / see Regional Activity Centre for Information and Communication of the Barcelona Convention (#18745)
- ♦ Centre d'activités régionales pour la télédétection en matière d'environnement / see Regional Activity Centre for Information and Communication of the Barcelona Convention (#18745)
- ♦ Centre administratif permanent pour la sécurité sociale des bateliers rhénans / see Administrative Centre of Social Security for Rhine Boatmen (#00116)
- ♦ Centre administratif de la sécurité sociale pour les bateliers rhénans (#00116)
- ♦ Centre d'administration du développement pour l'Asie et le Pacifique (inactive)
- ♦ Centre for Administrative Innovation in the Euro-Mediterranean Region (internationally oriented national body)
- ♦ Centre for Advanced Legal Studies in International and Public Law, Canberra / see Centre for International and Public Law, Canberra
- ♦ Centre for Advanced Studies of African Society (internationally oriented national body)
- ♦ Centre for the Advanced Study of European and Comparative Law / see Institute of European and Comparative Law, Oxford

♦ Centre for Affordable Housing Finance in Africa (CAHF) 03723

Dir PO Box 72624, Parkview, 2122, South Africa. T. +27114479581. E-mail: info@housingfinanceafrica.org.
URL: http://www.housingfinanceafrica.org/

History Set up as a division of *FinMark Trust (FMT, #09775).* Became an independent organization, May 2014. **Aims** Make Africa's housing finance markets work, with special attention to access to housing finance for the poor. **Languages** English, French, Portuguese. **Staff** 13.00 FTE, paid. **Finance** Grant-funded. Core funders include: *FSD Africa (#10010); Agence française de développement (AFD).* Additional programme and project funding. **Activities** Research/documentation; knowledge management/information dissemination; monitoring/evaluation; events/meetings. **Publications** *Housing Finance in Africa Yearbook.* **NGO Relations** Secretariat for: *African Union for Housing Finance (AUHF, #00491).* [2020.01.15/XM4866/**D**]

- ♦ Centre for Affordable Water and Sanitation Technology (internationally oriented national body)
- ♦ Centre for Africa Democratic Affairs (internationally oriented national body)
- ♦ Centre africain pour les applications de la météorologie au développement (#00242)
- ♦ Centre africain d'assistance et de protection de l'environnement au Sahel (internationally oriented national body)
- ♦ Centre africain pour la démocratie et les études des droits de l'homme (#00239)
- ♦ Centre africain pour le développement des engrais (#00241)
- ♦ Centre Africain de développement minier (unconfirmed)
- ♦ Centre africain pour l'éducation aux droits humains (internationally oriented national body)
- ♦ Centre Africain d'Etudes et de Recherches sur le Terrorisme (#00236)

♦ Centre africain d'études supérieures en gestion (CESAG) 03724

African Centre for Advanced Studies in Management

Dir Gen Bvd du Général De Gaulle x Malick sy, BP 3802, Dakar, Senegal. T. +221338397360. Fax +221338397360. E-mail: courrier@cesag.edu.sn.
URL: http://www.cesag.sn/

History 1983. Established by *Communauté économique de l'Afrique de l'Ouest (CEAO, inactive).* Attached, since 1995, to *Banque centrale des Etats de l'Afrique de l'Ouest (BCEAO, #03167)*, on behalf of *Union économique et monétaire Ouest africaine (UEMOA, #20377).* **Aims** Provide postgraduate, graduate and undergraduate training to *managers* of public and private enterprises, administration and various regional or African organizations; act as university institution; improve the training of and retrain managerial staff in management issues; train trainers in management training in the region; provide consultancy and research. **Structure** Board of Directors (meets twice a year). Specialized Departments (7) Professional Education; Grande école; Banque, Finance, Comptabilité, Contrôle et Audit; Executive Education; Langues; Projects autonomes; SANTE. **Languages** English, French. **Staff** 98.00 FTE, paid. **Finance** Mainly self-funded; some annual support from *Banque centrale des Etats de l'Afrique de l'Ouest (BCEAO, #03167)* and other regional banks. **Activities** Knowledge management/information dissemination; training/education.
Members Governments of 8 countries:
Benin, Burkina Faso, Côte d'Ivoire, Guinea-Bissau, Mali, Niger, Senegal, Togo.
NGO Relations Member of (1): *Agence universitaire de La Francophonie (AUF, #00548).* [2020/XE0840/**E***]

- ♦ Centre africain de formation à l'édition et à la diffusion (internationally oriented national body)
- ♦ Centre africain de formation à l'édition, la diffusion et la distribution du livre, Tunisia / see Centre africain de formation à l'édition et à la diffusion
- ♦ Centre africain de formation à la maintenance des équipements de la micro-informatique (internationally oriented national body)
- ♦ Centre africain de formation en micro-informatique / see Centre africain de formation à la maintenance des équipements de la micro-informatique
- ♦ Centre Africain de Formation et de Recherche Administratives pour le Développement (#00486)
- ♦ Centre Africain pour la Liberté d'Information (#00175)
- ♦ Centre africain des minéraux et des géosciences (#00373)
- ♦ Centre africain de l'Ombudsman / see Association des ombudsmans et médiateurs africains (#02838)
- ♦ Centre africain de perfectionnement des journalistes et communicateurs (internationally oriented national body)
- ♦ Centre Africain de Prévention et Résolution des Conflits (internationally oriented national body)
- ♦ Centre Africain pour la Prévention et la Résolution des Conflits (internationally oriented national body)
- ♦ Centre africain de protection environnementale et pour l'assistance (internationally oriented national body)
- ♦ Centre africain de recherche appliquée et de formation en matière de développement social (#00237)
- ♦ Centre Africain de Recherche Industrielle, Kinshasa / see Centre Africain de Recherche Interdisciplinaire
- ♦ Centre Africain de Recherche Interdisciplinaire (internationally oriented national body)

♦ Centre Africain de Recherches sur Bananiers et Plantains (CARBAP) 03725

Main Office Rue Dinde no 110, Bonanjo, BP 832, Douala, Cameroon. T. +23733425786. Fax +23733425786. E-mail: carbapafrica@gmail.com – yotetang@gmail.com – carbap.njombe@carbapafrica.org.
URL: http://www.carbapafrica.org/

History 25 Oct 1989, as *Centre régional de recherches sur bananiers et plantains (CRBP)*, by the Government of Cameroon and *Centre de coopération internationale en recherche agronomique pour le développement (CIRAD, #03733).* Restructured under present name, 1 Feb 2001, Yaoundé (Cameroon), following intergovernmental agreement signed by Conference of Ministers Responsible for Research and Development of West and Central Africa (COMRED/AOC). Headquarters agreement with government of Cameroon, 30 May 2013. **Aims** Improve production and productivity of plantains and other locally consumed bananas towards maintaining food security and alleviating poverty through sustainable agricultural practices in Central and West Africa. **Structure** Board of Directors; Technical and Scientific Committee; Directorate; National Focal Points. **Languages** English, French. **Staff** 113.00 FTE, paid. **Finance** Members' dues. Other sources: Cameroon Government; *European Commission (EC, #06633); Vlaamse Vereniging voor Ontwikkelingssamenwerking en Technische Bijstand (VVOB).* Additional funding generated through expertise provided to export banana and phytopharmaceutical companies. Also support from: *Pôle régional de recherche appliquée au développement des systèmes agricoles d'Afrique Centrale (PRASAC, #18413); West and Central African Council for Agricultural Research and Development (WECARD, #20907).* **Activities** Projects/programmes; research and development; events/meetings; training/education; capacity building; advocacy/lobbying/activism. **Events** *International symposium on bananas and food security* Douala (Cameroon) 1998. **Publications** *Banana and Plantain e-newsletter for West and Central Africa.* Scientific articles; leaflets; fact sheets; technical guides; posters; research, activity and project reports.
Members Governments (7):
Cameroon, Central African Rep, Chad, Congo Brazzaville, Congo DR, Equatorial Guinea, Gabon.
NGO Relations *Banana Research Network for West and Central Africa (Innovate Plantain)*; Fonds Interprofessionnel pour la Recherche et le Conseil Agricoles (FIRCA); *ProMusa (inactive).* [2016.12.15/XE2944/**E***]

- ♦ Centre Africain de Recherches Forestières Appliquées et de Développement (internationally oriented national body)
- ♦ Centre africain pour les zones humides (#03727)
- ♦ Centre for African Area Studies, Kyoto University (internationally oriented national body)
- ♦ Centre for African, Asian and Latin American Studies / see Centre for African and Development Studies
- ♦ Centre for African and Development Studies (internationally oriented national body)
- ♦ Centre of African and Development Studies, Lisbon / see Centre for African and Development Studies
- ♦ Centre for African Entrepreneurship Research and Development (internationally oriented national body)

♦ Centre for African Family Studies (CAFS) 03726

Centre d'études de la famille africaine (CEFA)

Dir CAFS Centre, Mara Road, Upper Hill, PO Box 60054, Nairobi, 00200, Kenya. T. +254202731479 – +254202725641. Fax +254202731489. E-mail: info@cafs.org.
Lomé Regional Office BP 80529, Lomé, Togo. T. +2282223640 – +2282215452. Fax +2282223587.
URL: http://www.cafs.org/

History Founded 1975, Njoro (Kenya), at the then Egerton Agricultural College, by the African Regional Council of *International Planned Parenthood Federation (IPPF, #14589).* Project temporarily wound up in 1978 and re-established in 1979. The African Regional Council of IPPF passed a formal resolution, 15 Jun 1982, establishing the Centre as an autonomous institution with its own separate constitution and Board of Directors. Registered in accordance with Kenyan law. Initially was operating only Anglophone programmes, but from 1983 operates Francophone programmes as well. West African Sub-Office located in Lomé (Togo). **Aims** Be the leading provider of technical assistance and training in health and development to organizations and individuals for the well-being of African families; forge partnerships to develop, support and improve reproductive health in sub-Saharan Africa. **Structure** Board of Directors. **Languages** English, French. **Finance** Sales of services. Other main funders include: *International Bank for Reconstruction and Development (IBRD, #12317)* (World Bank); *International Planned Parenthood Federation (IPPF, #14589)* – Africa Region; *United Nations Population Fund (UNFPA, #20612); United States Agency for International Development (USAID)*; David and Lucile Packard Foundation. **Activities** Training/education. **Events** *Conference on NGO partnerships for reproductive health in Africa / International Conference* Nairobi (Kenya) 2002, *Conference on NGO partnerships for reproductive health in Africa / International Conference* Nairobi (Kenya) 1999, *Inter-Africa conference on adolescent health* Nairobi (Kenya) 1992, *Population/family planning in Sub-Saharan Africa* Nairobi (Kenya) 1991. **Publications** Annual Report. Course catalogues; CD-ROM on Monograph on East AFrican Family

Transformations. **Consultative Status** Consultative status granted from: *United Nations Population Fund (UNFPA, #20612).* **IGO Relations** *Partners in Population and Development (PPD, #18247).* **NGO Relations** *Africa Liaison Program Initiative (ALPI); African Islamic Organization on Population and Development (#00347); International Council on the Management of Population Programs (ICOMP, #13043); Management Strategies for Africa (MSA, inactive); Pan African Institute for Development (PAID, #18053); Africa Capacity Alliance (ACA, #00160); Regional Centre for Quality of Health Care (RCQHC, inactive).* [2013.07.26/XE0103/E]

♦ Centre for African Settlement Studies and Development (internationally oriented national body)
♦ Centre of African Studies / see Instytut Studiów Regionalnych i Globalnych
♦ Centre for African Studies, Barcelona (internationally oriented national body)
♦ Centre for African Studies, Basel (internationally oriented national body)
♦ Centre of African Studies, Copenhagen (internationally oriented national body)
♦ Centre of African Studies, Edinburgh (internationally oriented national body)
♦ Centre for African Studies, Lisbon (internationally oriented national body)
♦ Centre of African Studies, London (internationally oriented national body)
♦ Centre for African Studies – Politics, Society and International Relations / see Les Afriques dans le monde
♦ Centre of African Studies, Sao Paulo (internationally oriented national body)
♦ Centre of African Studies, University of Cambridge (internationally oriented national body)

♦ Centre for African Wetlands (CAW) 03727

Centre africain pour les zones humides

Contact PO Box LG67, Univ of Ghana, Legon, Accra, Ghana. T. +233209134932. E-mail: info@afriwet.edu.gh.

History Nov 1997. Activities started Dec 1999. Previously also referred to in French as *Centre pour les zones humides africaines.* **Aims** Promote sustainable wetland management in West Africa. **Structure** General Assembly; Board; Steering Committee; Secretariat in Accra (Ghana). **Languages** English, French. **Finance** Supported by the Dutch Government; *International Society for Mangrove Ecosystems (ISME, #15245); International Tropical Timber Organization (ITTO, #15737).* **Activities** Training/education; capacity building; knowledge management/information dissemination; research and development; networking/liaising; advocacy/lobbying/activism; politics/policy/regulatory; monitoring/evaluation; events/meetings. **Publications** Reports. **Information Services** *Global Mangrove Database and Information System (GLOMIS).*

Members in 12 countries:

Benin, Burkina Faso, Cameroon, Cape Verde, Côte d'Ivoire, Ghana, Guinea-Bissau, Liberia, Mali, Mauritania, Nigeria, Senegal. [2016.09.30/XE4577/E]

♦ Centre for Africa Studies, Gothenburg (internationally oriented national body)

♦ Centre Afrika Obota (CAO) 03728

Contact c/o National Secretary Urbain AMEGBEDJI, 03 BP, 1514 Jéricho, C/723 Gbégamey, Cotonou, Benin. T. +22921304210. Fax +22921305271. E-mail: afrikaobota@yahoo.fr.

Facebook: https://www.facebook.com/centreafrikaobotabenin/

History Founded 15 Oct 1989, Cotonou (Benin), by young intellectuals from Benin, Burundi, Burkina Faso and Togo. Pan African organization with a scientific and cultural character. **Aims** Promote *human rights*, democracy, development and solidarity in Africa. **Structure** General Assembly; National Council (NC); National Secretariat; headquarters in Cotonou (Benin); regional offices (4). **Languages** French. **Staff** 20.00 FTE, paid; 150.00 FTE, voluntary. **Activities** Programmes and projects: Programme de Promotion de la Démocratie par Appui aux Organisation de la Societé Civile (ProDOSC); Programme d'Appui Régional à l'Economie Sociale en Afrique (PARESOC); Projet Hydraulique; Observatoire de la Justice; Agenda de la Femme; Projet d'Education Civique. **Publications** *Agenda da la Femme* (annual).

Members National organizations in 6 countries:

Benin, Burkina Faso, Côte d'Ivoire, Mali, Niger, Togo.

Consultative Status Consultative status granted from: *African Commission on Human and Peoples' Rights (ACHPR, #00255)* (Observer). **IGO Relations** *Deutsche Gesellschaft für Internationale Zusammenarbeit (GIZ); UNDP (#20292); United States Agency for International Development (USAID).* **NGO Relations** *Konrad Adenauer Foundation (KAF); Réseau pour l'Intégration des Femmes des Organisations Non Gouvernementales et Associations Africaines (RIFONGA); Social Watch (#19350); Women in Law and Development in Africa-Afrique de l'Ouest (WiLDAF-AO, #21005); WSM;* national embassies. [2016/XJ0838/E]

♦ Centre AGRHYMET / see AGRHYMET Regional Centre (#00565)
♦ Centre for Agricultural Biosciences International / see CABI (#03393)
♦ Centre agronomique tropical de recherche et d'enseignement (#20246)
♦ Centre d'aide au développement dans la liberté et le progrès (internationally oriented national body)
♦ **Centre Aldo Dami** Centre européen de cartographie ethnolinguistique (#03744)
♦ Centre allemand d'opérations de maintien de la paix (internationally oriented national body)
♦ Centre for Alleviation of Poverty through Sustainable Agriculture (inactive)
♦ Centre for Alpine Ecology (internationally oriented national body)
♦ Centre for Alternative Technology (internationally oriented national body)
♦ Centre of American Studies, Rio de Janeiro (internationally oriented national body)
♦ Centre for American and West European Studies, Delhi / see Centre for Canadian, US and Latin American Studies, Delhi
♦ Centre for the Analysis of Conflict – CAC / see Conflict Analysis Research Centre
♦ Centre d'Ankara / see Statistical, Economic and Social Research and Training Centre for Islamic Countries (#19971)
♦ Centre for Anti-War Action, Belgrade (internationally oriented national body)
♦ Centre for Anti-war Activities / see Centre for Anti-War Action, Belgrade
♦ Centre for the Application of Molecular Biology to International Agriculture (internationally oriented national body)
♦ Centre for Applied Research on Population and Development (no recent information)
♦ Centre arabe pour l'arabisation, la traduction, la création et la publication / see Arab Centre for Arabization, Translation, Authorship and Publication (#00914)
♦ Centre arabe d'arabisation, de traduction, de production et d'édition (#00914)
♦ Centre arabe pour l'éducation au droit international humanitaire et aux droits humains (#00915)
♦ Centre arabe pour l'étude des zones arides et des terres sèches (#00918)
♦ Centre Arabe de l'Indépendance des Avocats et de la Magistrature (internationally oriented national body)
♦ Centre Arabe de Recherches Juridiques et Judiciaires (unconfirmed)

♦ Centre for Arab Genomic Studies (CAGS) 03729

Pres PO Box 22252, Dubai, United Arab Emirates. T. +97143986777. Fax +97143980999. E-mail: cags@eim.ae.

Dir address not obtained.

URL: http://www.cags.org.ae/

History 25 Jun 2003, Dubai (United Arab Emirates). **Aims** Characterize, prevent and ameliorate the impact of genetic disorders in the Arab world, in accordance with the recent advances in human genetics, genomics and biotechnology. **Structure** Council; Executive Board; Administrative Office. **Languages** Arabic, English. **Staff** 6.00 FTE, paid. With additional administrative or technical staff. **Finance** Supported by Sheikh Hamdan Bin Rashid Al Maktoum Award for Medical Sciences, Dubai (United Arab Emirates). Annual budget: 2,000,000 USD. **Activities** Knowledge management/information dissemination; events/meetings. **Events** *Pan Arab Human Genetics Conference* Dubai (United Arab Emirates) 2020, *Pan Arab Human Genetics Conference* Dubai (United Arab Emirates) 2018, *Pan Arab Human Genetics Conference* Dubai (United Arab Emirates) 2016, *Pan Arab Human Genetics Conference* Dubai (United Arab Emirates) 2013, *Pan Arab human genetics conference* Dubai (United Arab Emirates) 2011. **Publications** *Genetic Disorders in the Arab World* – 5 vols published to date. Guides; articles; reports. **Information Services** *Catalogue for Transmission Genetics in Arabs Database (CTGA).*

Members Individuals in 12 countries:

Bahrain, Egypt, Jordan, Kuwait, Lebanon, Oman, Palestine, Qatar, Saudi Arabia, Sudan, Tunisia, United Arab Emirates. [2020.05.12/XM2778/E]

♦ Centre for Arab Gulf Studies / see Institute of Arab and Islamic Studies
♦ Centre for Arab and Islamic Studies, Middle East and Central Asia (internationally oriented national body)
♦ Centre for Arab Unity Studies, Beirut (internationally oriented national body)
♦ Centre d'arbitrage et de médiation commercial pour les Amériques (inactive)
♦ Centre des archives d'Outre-mer, Aix-en-Provence / see Archives nationales d'Outre mer
♦ Centre for Arctic Gas Hydrate, Environment and Climate (internationally oriented national body)
♦ Centre for Arctic Medicine, Oulu (internationally oriented national body)

♦ Centre on Asia and Globalisation (CAG) 03730

Dir Lee Kuan Yew School of Public Policy, Nat'l Univ of Singapore, 469C Bukit Timah Rd, 02-03L Wing A Level 2, Oei Tiong Ham Bldg, Singapore 259772, Singapore. T. +6565166796. E-mail: sppkpb@nus.edu.sg – eyeoh@nus.edu.sg.

URL: https://lkyspp.nus.edu.sg/cag/

Aims Through partnerships with pre-eminent institutions: produce policy relevant knowledge on the impact of globalization on Asia and Asia's role in governing an integrated world. **Activities** Investigates the following fields at global, regional, national and sub-national levels: Major power relations in the Asia-Pacific; Regional regimes in the Asia-Pacific; Common-goods issues (energy, food, water and health); New approaches to building markets in Asia. **Events** *Seminar on ASEAN Facing the Future* Singapore (Singapore) 2020, *Seminar on Maintaining Peace in China-India Relations* Singapore (Singapore) 2020, *Seminar on the Anatomy of Meritocracy* Singapore (Singapore) 2020, *Round Table on the Belt and Road Initiative* Singapore (Singapore) 2019, *Seminar on Globalization, Robotics, and the Future of Work in Asia* Singapore (Singapore) 2019. [2020/XJ2110/F]

♦ Centre for Asian Legal Studies, Vancouver (internationally oriented national body)
♦ Centre for Asian Pacific Studies, Hong Kong (internationally oriented national body)
♦ Centre for Asian Studies (internationally oriented national body)
♦ Centre for Asia-Pacific Area Studies (internationally oriented national body)
♦ Centre for Asia-Pacific Initiatives (internationally oriented national body)
♦ Centre for Asia-Pacific Island Studies (internationally oriented national body)

♦ Centre for Asia-Pacific Women in Politics (CAPWIP) 03731

Exec Dir 4227-4229 Tomas Claudio Street, Baclaran, 1700 Parañaque METRO MANILA, Philippines. T. +6328322112 – +6328320680. Fax +6328322263.

URL: http://www.capwip.org/

History 1992. **Structure** Board of Trustees, comprising President, 4 Vice-Presidents, Treasurer, Executive Director, Secretary and Corporate Secretary. Sub-regional groupings (5): Central Asia; East Asia; Pacific; Southeast Asia; South Asia. **Finance** Members' dues. Contributions; grants. **Activities** Instrumental in setting up: *Global Network of Women in Politics (GLOBALNET).* **Events** *Global Congress of Women in Politics and Governance / Conference* Makati (Philippines) 2013, *Asian grassroots women's academy on resilience* Cebu City (Philippines) 2008, *Global congress of women in politics and governance / Conference* Makati (Philippines) 2008, *Asia Pacific congress of women in politics* Makati (Philippines) 2006, *Asia-Pacific congress of women and men in media, and women in politics, governance and decision-making on transformative leadership* Makati (Philippines) 2001. **Publications** *CAPWIP Newsletter.* **NGO Relations** Member of: *Global Gender and Climate Alliance (GGCA, no recent information). IO – Facilitating Space for Feminist Conversations (Io, #16005).* [2013/XE3744/E]

♦ Centre asiatique pour les études théologiques et les missions (internationally oriented national body)
♦ Centre asiatique d'information sur les recherches en communication de masse (#01536)
♦ Centre asiatique de recherche et de développement dans le domaine des végétaux / see AVRDC – The World Vegetable Center (#03051)
♦ Centre asiatique de recherches sur les migrations (internationally oriented national body)
♦ Centre de l'Asie et du Pacifique pour la femme et le développement (inactive)
♦ Centre d'Asie et du Pacifique de transfert de technologie (#01603)
♦ Centre d'Asie et du Pacifique de transfert de technologie des Nations Unies / see Asian and Pacific Centre for Transfer of Technology (#01603)
♦ Centre d'Assistance Technique Financière du Pacifique (#17948)
♦ Centre for Atlantic Historical Studies (internationally oriented national body)
♦ Centre australien de recherche agricole internationale (internationally oriented national body)
♦ Centre for Baltic and East European Studies (internationally oriented national body)
♦ Centre belge d'études slaves (internationally oriented national body)
♦ Centre biblique catholique pour l'Afrique et Madagascar (#03599)
♦ Centre for Black and African Arts and Civilization (internationally oriented national body)
♦ Centre Camuno pour l'étude des arts préhistoriques (internationally oriented national body)
♦ Centre for Canadian, US and Latin American Studies, Delhi (internationally oriented national body)
♦ Centre canadien d'étude et de coopération internationale (internationally oriented national body)
♦ Centre des Caraïbes pour l'administration du développement (#03468)
♦ Centre for Caribbean Studies, Coventry (internationally oriented national body)
♦ Centre catholique de coordination auprès de l'UNESCO / see International Catholic Cooperation Centre for UNESCO (#12454)
♦ Centre catholique international de coopération avec l'UNESCO (#12454)
♦ Centre catholique international de Genève (#12449)
♦ Centre catholique international pour l'UNESCO / see International Catholic Cooperation Centre for UNESCO (#12454)
♦ Centre of Central Asian Studies, Srinagar (internationally oriented national body)
♦ Centre for Citizenship, Development and Human Rights (internationally oriented national body)
♦ Centre for Citizenship and Human Rights / see Centre for Citizenship, Development and Human Rights
♦ Centre for Citizens' Participation on the African Union / see Pan-African Citizens Network (#18044)
♦ Centre for Climate Change and Environmental Studies (internationally oriented national body)
♦ Centre of Collections of Microbial Species (inactive)
♦ Centre de collections de types microbiens (inactive)
♦ Centre du Commerce Africaine (internationally oriented national body)
♦ Centre du commerce international (#15703)
♦ Centre du commerce international CNUCED/GATT / see International Trade Centre (#15703)
♦ Centre du commerce international CNUCED/OMC / see International Trade Centre (#15703)
♦ Centre de communication pour l'Europe centrale et orientale (#03694)
♦ Centre for Communication and Information on Development, Peace and Human Rights (internationally oriented national body)

♦ Centre for Communication Rights 03732

Contact c/o WACC, 308 Main St, Toronto ON M4C 4X7, Canada. T. +14166911999. Fax +14166911997. E-mail: info@waccglobal.org.

URL: http://www.centreforcommunicationrights.org/

History Founded 1996, as *Platform for Communication Rights*, as an informal network coordinated by *World Association for Christian Communication (WACC, #21126)*, as *Platform for Cooperation on Democratization of Communication.* Also referred to as *Platform for Cooperation.* Established as a clearinghouse for materials on the right to communicate, 2006. **Aims** Work for recognition and guarantee of the right to communicate as fundamental to securing human rights based on principles of genuine participation, social justice and diversity. **Structure** Informal network. **Languages** English, French, Spanish. **Staff** through *World Association for Christian Communication (WACC, #21126).* **Activities** Publishing activity; advocacy/lobbying/activism; events/meetings. **Publications** *Handbook on the Right to Communicate.* **Members** Not a membership organization. **NGO Relations** Maintains ongoing relations with civil society organizations and movements working to advance communication rights, democratization of communication and the media, and to strengthen ethical principles of communication practice. [2017.10.30/XF5580/F]

♦ Centre de communication de Varsovie / see Central and Eastern European Media Centre Foundation (#03694)

- ♦ Centre commun de recherche (#16147)
- ♦ Centre for Conflict Analysis / see Conflict Analysis Research Centre
- ♦ Centre on Conflict, Development and Peacebuilding (internationally oriented national body)
- ♦ Centre for Conflict Management, Akron OH (internationally oriented national body)
- ♦ Centre for Conflict Management, Oslo / see Centre for Peacebuilding and Conflict Management, Oslo
- ♦ Centre for Conflict and Peace / see Conflict Analysis Research Centre
- ♦ Centre for Conflict Resolution, Bradford (internationally oriented national body)
- ♦ Centre for Conflict Resolution, Cape Town (internationally oriented national body)
- ♦ Centre for Conflict Studies, Marburg (internationally oriented national body)
- ♦ Centre consultatif sur la législation de l'OMC (#00138)
- ♦ Centre for Contemporary Cultural Studies (internationally oriented national body)
- ♦ Centre for the Contemporary Pacific (internationally oriented national body)
- ♦ Centre continental de brasserie / see European Brewery Convention (#06401)
- ♦ Centre de contrôle de l'espace aérien supérieur, Maastricht (#05670)

♦ Centre de coopération internationale en recherche agronomique pour le développement (CIRAD) 03733

International Cooperation Centre of Agricultural Research for Development

Pres – Managing Dir 42 rue Scheffer, 75116 Paris, France. T. +33153702000. E-mail: presse-com@cirad.fr.

Montpellier Research Centre av Agropolis, 34398 Montpellier CEDEX 5, France. T. +33467615800.

URL: http://www.cirad.fr/

History Established 5 Jun 1984, Paris (France), as a state-owned industrial and commercial body (France), taking over the activities of 8 organizations which formed the previous *Groupement d'études et de recherches pour le développement de l'agronomie tropicale (GERDAT, inactive)*. EU Transparency Register: 36403517495-84. **Aims** Work in partnership with developing countries to generate and pass on new knowledge, support sustainable development and fuel the debate on the main global issues concerning agriculture. **Structure** Management; Scientific Departments (3). **Languages** English, French. **Staff** 1650.00 FTE, paid. **Finance** Budget (annual): about euro 195 million. **Activities** Research and development. **Events** *International Symposium on Cocoa Research* Montpellier (France) 2022, *World Congress of Agroforestry* Montpellier (France) 2019, *International Conference on Sustainable Agriculture* Chiang Mai (Thailand) 2017, *International Conference on Starch Technology* Bangkok (Thailand) 2015, *Regional Advocacy Meeting on Veterinary Epidemiology Capacity Development* Bangkok (Thailand) 2015. **Publications** *Fruitrop* (12 a year); *Bois et forêts des tropiques* (4 a year); *Revue d'élevage et de médecine vétérinaire des pays tropicaux* (4 a year). Papers and other publications in all relevant fields, in English and French. **Information Services** *CIRAD-DELCOM* – comunication service; *CIRAD-DIST* – scientific and technical information service.

Members State-owned body:

France.

French overseas departments and territories (7):

Guadeloupe, Guiana Fr, Martinique, Mayotte, New Caledonia, Polynesia Fr, Réunion.

Other countries (19):

Benin, Brazil, Burkina Faso, Cameroon, Chad, Colombia, Comoros, Congo Brazzaville, Côte d'Ivoire, Gabon, Guinea, Madagascar, Mali, Senegal, South Africa, Thailand, USA, Vanuatu, Vietnam.

IGO Relations Supports: *Africa Rice Center (AfricaRice, #00518)*.

NGO Relations Member of: *Global Alliance for Climate-Smart Agriculture (GACSA, #10189)*; *ORCID (#17790)*. Affiliate member of: *Global Platform for Sustainable Natural Rubber (GPSNR, #10552)*. Charter member of: *Global Landscapes Forum (GLF, #10451)*. Cooperates with:

- *African Coffee Research Network (ACRN, #00253)*;
- *Agence pour l'investissement dans la recherche à l'étranger (AIRE développement, no recent information)*;
- *Agence universitaire de La Francophonie (AUF, #00548)*;
- *AGRINATURA (#00578)*;
- *Agropolis International*;
- *Amazonian Agroforestry Research Centre (no recent information)*;
- *Association of Institutions of Tropical Veterinary Medicine (AITVM, #02648)*;
- *Centre européen de santé humanitaire, Lyon*;
- *Center for International Forestry Research (CIFOR, #03646)*;
- *Coconut Genetic Resources Network (COGENT, #04080)*;
- *Crops For the Future (CFF, #04968)*;
- *Environnement et développement du Tiers-monde (enda, #05510)*;
- *European Conservation Agriculture Federation (ECAF, #06743)*;
- *European Group for Integrated Pest Management in Development Cooperation (IPMEurope, no recent information)*;
- *European Plant Science Organization (EPSO, #08211)*;
- *Forestry Research Network for Sub-Saharan Africa (FORNESSA, #09866)*;
- *Forum for Agricultural Research in Africa (FARA, #09897)*;
- *Fund for Latin American Irrigated Rice (#10041)*;
- *Global Forum on Agricultural Research (GFAR, #10370)*;
- *Global Horticulture Initiative (GlobalHort, #10412)*;
- *GRET*;
- *Groupe d'aquaculture méditerranéenne et tropicale (GAMET, no recent information)*;
- *Groupement d'intérêt scientifique pour l'étude de la mondialisation et du développement (GEMDEV)*;
- *Inland Valley Consortium (IVC, no recent information)*;
- *Institute of Tropical Medicine Antwerp (IMT)*;
- *Inter-Regional Cooperative Research Network on Cotton for the Mediterranean and Middle East Regions (#15968)*;
- *International Centre for Development Oriented Research in Agriculture (ICRA)*;
- *International Centre of Insect Physiology and Ecology (ICIPE, #12499)*;
- *International Centre for Tropical Agriculture (#12527)*;
- *International Council on Archives (ICA, #12996)*;
- *International Food Policy Research Institute (IFPRI, #13622)*;
- *International Foundation for Science (IFS, #13677)*;
- *International Institute of Tropical Agriculture (IITA, #13933)*;
- *International Society for Horticultural Science (ISHS, #15180)*;
- *International Technical Tropical Timber Association (ITTTA, #15668)*;
- *International Union for Conservation of Nature and Natural Resources (IUCN, #15766)*;
- *International Union of Forest Research Organizations (IUFRO, #15774)*;
- *International Water Management Institute (IWMI, #15867)*;
- *Observatoire français de la coopération internationale (OFCI)*;
- *Pasteur Institute*;
- *Plantain and Banana Research and Development Network for Latin America and the Caribbean (#18389)*;
- *Professional Association of Natural Rubber in Africa (ANRA, no recent information)*;
- *Programa de Desarrollo de la Agroindustria Rural de América Latina y el Caribe (PRODAR, no recent information)*;
- *ProMusa (inactive)*;
- *Resilience Alliance (RA, #18911)*;
- *Roundtable on Sustainable Palm Oil (RSPO, #18986)*;
- *Royal Tropical Institute (KIT)*;
- *SYLVA-WORLD for Development and the Protection of Forests and the Environment*;
- *Tropical Science Research Institute (IICT)*;
- *Vétérinaires Sans Frontières International (VSF International, #20760)*;
- *West Indies Central Sugar Cane Breeding Station (CBS, #20922)*;
- *World Agroforestry Centre (ICRAF, #21072)*;
- *World Phosphate Institute (#21728)*;
- *WorldFish (#21507)*;
- *Young Professionals for Agricultural Development (YPARD, #21996)*. [2016.01.28/XE6070/**E***]

- ♦ Centre de coopération internationale en santé et développement (internationally oriented national body)
- ♦ Centre pour la coopération internationale et la technologie appropriée (internationally oriented national body)
- ♦ Centre de coopération maritime de la CCI (see: #12534)

♦ Centre for Cooperation in the Mediterranean (CCM) 03734

Vice-Pres Av Portal de l'Angel 7, 4th Office J-K, 08004 Barcelona, Spain. T. +34933021585. Fax +34933022075. E-mail: mediterraneo@cruzroja.es.

Acting Dir address not obtained.

URL: http://www.mediterraneumrc.org/

History Jul 2005, by the Spanish Red Cross, on an initiative of the Mediterranean Conference. **Aims** Host the Permanent Office for follow-up of the Conference; facilitate follow-up of Conference resolutions; promote interaction among national societies of the Mediterranean, and exchange and sharing of experience contributing to fulfilment of the purposes of the International *Red Cross* and Red Crescent Movement. **Structure** Governing Board. **Events** *Mediterranean Conference of Red Cross and Red Crescent Societies* Cavtat (Croatia) 2010, *Mediterranean Conference of Red Cross and Red Crescent Societies* Athens (Greece) 2007, *Mediterranean Conference of Red Cross and Red Crescent Societies* Cairo (Egypt) 2004, *Mediterranean Conference of Red Cross and Red Crescent Societies* Nice (France) 2000, *Mediterranean Conference of Red Cross and Red Crescent Societies* Tunis (Tunisia) 1997. **Publications** *CCM Newsletter*.

Members Full in 25 countries and territories:

Albania, Algeria, Andorra, Bosnia-Herzegovina, Croatia, Egypt, France, Greece, Israel, Italy, Lebanon, Libya, Malta, Monaco, Montenegro, Morocco, Palestine, Portugal, San Marino, Serbia, Slovenia, Spain, Syrian AR, Tunisia, Türkiye.

NGO Relations Memorandum of Understanding with: *Asociación de las Camaras de Comercio e Industria del Mediterraneo (ASCAME, #02112)*. [2015/XJ9259/**E**]

♦ Centre de coopération pour les recherches scientifiques relatives au tabac (CORESTA) 03735

Cooperation Centre for Scientific Research Relative to Tobacco – Centro de Cooperación para la Investigación Cientifica del Tabaco – Zentrum für Wissenschaftliche Zusammenarbeit in der Tabakforschung

Gen Sec 11 rue du Quatre Septembre, 75002 Paris, France. T. +33158625870. Fax +33158625879. E-mail: ndetervarent@coresta.org.

URL: https://www.coresta.org/

History 25 Apr 1956, Paris (France). Founded following recommendations of the First International Congress on Tobacco, 10 Sep 1955, Paris, organized by SEITA. Registration: French Ministerial Decree, Start date: 21 Jul 1956, France. **Aims** Promote and facilitate cooperation in scientific research relative to tobacco and its derived products by collaborative experimentation, exchange of scientific learnings and development of publically available methods and guides. **Structure** General Assembly (every 2 years, at Scientific Congress); Board; Scientific Commission; Study Groups; Working Groups. **Languages** English. **Staff** 3.50 FTE, paid. **Finance** Sources: members' dues. **Activities** Awards/prizes/competitions; events/meetings; financial and/or material support; research/documentation. **Events** *CROM (Consumer Reported Outcome Measures) Workshop* 2022, *Agro-Phyto Conference* 2021, *CROM (Consumer Reported Outcome Measures) Symposium* 2021, *Smoke Science and Product Technology Conference* Paris (France) 2021, *Consumer Reported Outcome Measures Symposium* Paris (France) 2020. **Publications** *Nicotiana Catalogue*; *Recommended Methods*. Guides; technical reports.

Members Research centres; governmental organizations: monopolies; private institutions or companies; laboratories; universities; associations; consultants. Active members (160) in 38 countries:

Argentina, Austria, Belgium, Brazil, Canada, Chile, China, Costa Rica, Cuba, France, Germany, Greece, India, Indonesia, Iran Islamic Rep, Italy, Japan, Korea Rep, Lebanon, Luxembourg, Malawi, Netherlands, North Macedonia, Paraguay, Philippines, Poland, South Africa, Spain, Sweden, Switzerland, Thailand, Türkiye, UK, United Arab Emirates, Uruguay, USA, Vietnam, Zimbabwe.

Consultative Status Consultative status granted from: *ECOSOC (#05331)* (Ros C); *FAO (#09260)* (Liaison Status). **NGO Relations** Cooperates with (3): Association Française de Normalisation (AFNOR); *Comité européen de normalisation (CEN, #04162)*; *International Organization for Standardization (ISO, #14473)*. [2022.06.15/XB0419/**C**]

- ♦ Centre de coopération régionale pour l'éducation des adultes en Amérique latine dans et les Caraïbes (#03794)

♦ Centre for Coordination of Agricultural Research and Development for Southern Africa (CCARDESA) 03736

Centre de Coordination de la Recherche et du Développement Agricole de l'Afrique Australe – Centro para a Coordenação e Desenvolvimento Agrario na Africa Austral

Exec Dir Ground Fl – Red Brick Bldg, Plot 4701 Station Exit Road, Private Bag 00357, Gaborone, Botswana. T. +2673914997. Fax +2673167211. E-mail: registry@ccardesa.org.

URL: http://www.ccardesa.org/

History Jul 2011, as a Sub-regional Organisation (SRO) in the *Southern African Development Community (SADC, #19843)* region. Charter signed Nov 2010, Windhoek (Namibia). **Aims** Sustainably reduce the food insecurity and poverty in the region. **Structure** Ministers responsible for Agriculture and Food Security in SADC Member States; General Assembly; Board of Directors; Secretariat. **Activities** Politics/policy/regulatory.

Members Governments (15):

Angola, Botswana, Congo DR, Eswatini, Lesotho, Madagascar, Malawi, Mauritius, Mozambique, Namibia, Seychelles, South Africa, Tanzania UR, Zambia, Zimbabwe.

NGO Relations Constituent organization of *Forum for Agricultural Research in Africa (FARA, #09897)*. Cooperates with: *International Centre of Insect Physiology and Ecology (ICIPE, #12499)*. [2015/XJ9321/**E***]

- ♦ Centre de coordination et de diffusion des études latinoaméricaines / see Centro de Investigaciones sobre América y el Caribe (#03810)

♦ Centre de coordination pour la lutte anti-drogue en Méditerranée (CeCLAD-M) 03737

Address not obtained.

History 31 Dec 2008, France.

Members Governments (10):

Algeria, France, Italy, Libya, Malta, Mauritania, Morocco, Portugal, Spain, Tunisia. [2012/XJ5110/**D***]

- ♦ Centre de coordination des oeuvres sociales au Tiers monde / see VIA Don Bosco (#20766)
- ♦ Centre de Coordination de la Recherche et du Développement Agricole de l'Afrique Australe (#03736)
- ♦ Centre de coordination de la recherche de la Fédération Internationale des Universités Catholiques / see International Center for Research and Decision Support of the International Federation of Catholic Universities (#12476)
- ♦ Centre for Coordination of Research of the International Federation of Catholic Universities / see International Center for Research and Decision Support of the International Federation of Catholic Universities (#12476)
- ♦ Centre for Cross-Cultural Research on Women / see International Gender Studies Centre, Oxford
- ♦ Centre for Culture and Development (internationally oriented national body)
- ♦ Centre de culture européenne, Bruxelles (internationally oriented national body)
- ♦ Centre culturel asiatique pour l'UNESCO / see Asia/Pacific Cultural Centre for UNESCO (#01879)
- ♦ Centre culturel de l'Asie-Pacifique pour l'UNESCO (#01879)
- ♦ Centre culturel espérantiste (internationally oriented national body)
- ♦ Centre culturel européen Jean Monnet, Bruxelles (internationally oriented national body)
- ♦ Centre culturel international (internationally oriented national body)
- ♦ Centre culturel international 'Athenaeum' (internationally oriented national body)
- ♦ Centre for Defence and International Security Studies (internationally oriented national body)
- ♦ Centre for Defence and Security Studies (internationally oriented national body)
- ♦ Centre for Defence and Security Studies, Winnipeg / see Centre for Defence and Security Studies
- ♦ Centre for Defence Studies (internationally oriented national body)
- ♦ Centre for Democratic Institutions (internationally oriented national body)
- ♦ Centre d'étude et de recherche en droit international et relations internationales de l'Académie de la Haye (internationally oriented national body)
- ♦ Centre d'études en sciences sociales sur les mondes africains, américains et asiatiques (internationally oriented national body)
- ♦ Centre for Developing Area Studies / see Institute for the Study of International Development
- ♦ Centre for Development Aid with Liberty and Progress (internationally oriented national body)
- ♦ Centre for the Development of Enterprise (inactive)
- ♦ Centre for Development and Environment, Bern (internationally oriented national body)
- ♦ Centre for Development and the Environment, Oslo (internationally oriented national body)

- Centre for Development Information and Education (internationally oriented national body)
- Centre for Development Policy and Research, London (internationally oriented national body)
- Centre for Development Research, Bergen / see Unifob Global
- Centre for Development Studies, Bath (internationally oriented national body)
- Centre for Development Studies, Bergen / see Unifob Global
- Centre for Development Studies, Bhubaneswar (internationally oriented national body)
- Centre for Development Studies, Glasgow (internationally oriented national body)
- Centre for Development Studies, Groningen (internationally oriented national body)
- Centre for Development Studies, Leeds / see Centre for Global Development, Leeds
- Centre for Development Studies, Swansea (internationally oriented national body)
- Centre for Development Studies, Trivandrum (internationally oriented national body)
- Centre de développement pour l'Asie et le Pacifique (#01608)
- Centre de Développement Intégral de Bwamanda (internationally oriented national body)
- Centre du développement international du Japon (internationally oriented national body)
- Centre de développement de l'OCDE (#17692)
- Centre de développement des pêches de l'Asie du Sud-Est (#19767)
- Centre de développement rural intégré pour l'Afrique (no recent information)
- Centre de développement rural intégré pour l'Asie et le Pacifique (#03750)
- Centre pour le dialogue humanitaire (internationally oriented national body)
- Centre for Disarmament Affairs / see United Nations Office for Disarmament Affairs (#20594)
- Centre documentaire catéchétique / see International Centre for Studies in Religious Education (#12519)
- Centre de documentation des Caraïbes / see Caribbean Knowledge Management Centre (#03521)
- Centre de documentation pour un développement solidaire / see Centre de recherche et d'information pour un développement solidaire
- Centre de documentation et d'études (#19241)
- Centre de documentation européenne, Université de Navarre / see Centre for European Studies – University of Navarra
- Centre for Documentation and Exploration of the International Language (internationally oriented national body)
- Centre de documentation sur la guerre aérochimique (inactive)
- Centre de documentation et d'information en matière de brevets (see: #00434)
- Centre for Documentation and Information on Minorities in Europe-Southeast Europe (internationally oriented national body)
- Centre de documentation internationale pour le développement et la libération des peuples / see Centre de documentation internationale pour le développement, les libertés et la paix
- Centre de documentation internationale pour le développement, les libertés et la paix (internationally oriented national body)
- Centre de documentation nordique pour la recherche de communication en masse / see Nordicom (#17374)
- Centre de documentation et de recherche sur l'Asie / see Centre for Asian Studies
- Centre de documentation et de recherche européenne, Lyon / see Centre d'études européennes, Lyon
- Centre de documentation de recherche et d'expérimentations sur les pollutions accidentelles des eaux (internationally oriented national body)
- Centre de documentation, de recherche et d'information des peuples autochtones (internationally oriented national body)
- Centre de documentation et de recherche pour la langue internationale (internationally oriented national body)
- Centre de documentation et de recherche sur la paix et les conflits / see Observatoire des armements / CDRPC
- Centre of Documentation, Research and Experimentation on Accidental Water Pollution (internationally oriented national body)
- Centre for Documentation and Research on Peace and Conflict / see Observatoire des armements / CDRPC
- Centre de documentation Tiers-Monde, Montpellier (internationally oriented national body)
- Centre de documentation Tiers-monde de Paris (internationally oriented national body)
- Centre de données astronomiques de Strasbourg (#20003)
- Centre de données stellaires / see Strasbourg Astronomical Data Centre (#20003)
- Centre de droit international, Bruxelles (internationally oriented national body)
- Centre de droit international du développement durable (internationally oriented national body)
- Centre de droit international et de sociologie appliquée au droit international / see Centre for International Law, Brussels
- Centre de droit pénal international et de criminologie comparée / see Centre de recherche en matière pénale – Fernand Boulan
- Centre pour le droit et les politiques en matière de santé et de reproduction / see Center for Reproductive Rights
- Centre du Droit Privé Européen (internationally oriented national body)
- Centre pour les droit reproductifs (internationally oriented national body)
- Centre pour les droits de l'homme des Nations Unies (inactive)
- Centre for East Asian Studies, Madrid (internationally oriented national body)
- Centre for East Asian Studies, Montreal (internationally oriented national body)
- Centre of East Asian Studies, Warsaw (internationally oriented national body)
- Centre for Eastern Studies, Warsaw (internationally oriented national body)
- Centre for East and Southeast Asian Studies, Lund (internationally oriented national body)
- Centre d'échanges et coopération pour l'Amérique latine (internationally oriented national body)
- Centre d'échanges internationaux (internationally oriented national body)
- Centre d'échanges et promotion des artisans en zones à équiper (internationally oriented national body)
- Centre d'écologie et de toxicologie de l'industrie chimique européenne / see European Centre for Ecotoxicology and Toxicology of Chemicals (#06477)
- Centre écologique européen – Terre vivante (internationally oriented national body)
- Centre for Economic Governance and AIDS in Africa (internationally oriented national body)
- Centre for Economic and International Studies (internationally oriented national body)
- Centre for Economic Policy Research, London (internationally oriented national body)
- Centre for Economic Research on Mediterranean Countries (internationally oriented national body)
- Centre d'éducation sanitaire et technologies appropriées sanitaires (internationally oriented national body)
- Centre d'éducation à la solidarité mondiale (internationally oriented national body)
- Centre for Effective Altruism (unconfirmed)
- Centre for Electoral Promotion and Assistance (see: #11334)
- Centre d'entraide internationale aux populations civiles (inactive)
- Centre for Environmental Economics and Policy in Africa (internationally oriented national body)
- Centre for Environmental Law / see Macquarie University Centre for International and Environmental Law
- Centre for Environmentally Clean Production / see Regional Activity Centre for Sustainable Consumption and Production (#18747)
- Centre for Environmentally Clean Technology / see Regional Activity Centre for Sustainable Consumption and Production (#18747)

♦ Centre for Environment and Development for the Arab Region and Europe (CEDARE) 03738

Exec Dir CEDARE Building, 2 El-Hegaz St, PO Box 1057, Heliopolis Bahary, Cairo, 11737, Egypt. T. +2024513921 – +2024513924. Fax +2024513918. E-mail: email@cedare.int.
URL: http://www.cedare.int/

History 13 Jan 1992, on signature of the Arab convention for establishing CEDARE, Dec 1991. **Aims** Develop coordinated and collaborative programmes and projects to intensify activities in the Arab, developing, Mediterranean and European States to solve environmental problems and promote sustainable development. **Structure** Board of Trustees; Executive Committee; Technical Advisory Committee. Executive Director. **Finance** Ad hoc contributions from financing agencies for specific programmes/projects. Sponsors, including: the Government of Egypt; *Arab Fund for Economic and Social Development (AFESD, #00965)*; *UNDP (#20292)*; IFAD; *Islamic Development Bank (IsDB, #16044)*. **Activities** Research/documentation; knowledge management/information dissemination. **Events** *Arab water forum* Cairo (Egypt) 2011. **Publications** *Chronicle* (6 a year) in Arabic, English; *Directory of Arab Environmental Institutions*; *Directory of Arab Environmental Periodicals*. Information Services: Environmental Information Unit gathers, assesses and makes available environmental data: Environmental Experts; Environmental Events; Remote Sensing Institutions; Environmental Libraries and Information Centres within the CEDARE region; GIS Data holdings. Documentation Unit.
Members Full in 33 countries and territories:
Albania, Algeria, Bahrain, Bosnia-Herzegovina, Chad, Comoros, Croatia, Djibouti, Egypt, France, Greece, Iraq, Italy, Jordan, Kuwait, Lebanon, Libya, Malta, Monaco, Morocco, Oman, Palestine, Qatar, Saudi Arabia, Serbia, Somalia, Spain, Sudan, Syrian AR, Tunisia, Türkiye, United Arab Emirates, Yemen.
IGO Relations *Mediterranean Environmental Technical Assistance Programme (METAP, inactive)*. Accredited to the Conference of the Parties of: *Secretariat of the United Nations Convention to Combat Desertification (Secretariat of the UNCCD, #19208)*. Invited to Governing Council sessions of: *International Fund for Agricultural Development (IFAD, #13692)*. Observer to: *Agricultural and Land and Water Use Commission for the Near East (ALAWUC, #00570)*. Partner of: *Group on Earth Observations (GEO, #10735)*. **NGO Relations** Member of: *International Network for Environmental Compliance and Enforcement (INECE, #14261)*; *International Union for Conservation of Nature and Natural Resources (IUCN, #15766)*; Mediterranean Technical Advisory Committee (MEDTAC) of *Global Water Partnership (GWP, #10653)*. Partner of: *Partnership for Clean Fuels and Vehicles (PCFV, #18231)*; *Rainwater Partnership (no recent information)*; *Sanitation and Water for All (SWA, #19051)*.
[2022/XE2032/**E***]

- Centre for Environment and Sustainable Development (internationally oriented national body)
- Centre d'épidémiologie des Caraïbes (inactive)
- Centre d'Estudis del Transport per a la Mediterrània Occidental (internationally oriented national body)
- Centre de Estudos Afro-Asiaticos (internationally oriented national body)
- Centre d'étude d'Afrique noire / see Les Afriques dans le monde
- Centre d'étude d'Afrique noire de l'Institut d'études politiques de Bordeaux / see Les Afriques dans le monde
- Centre d'étude de l'Amérique latine, Bruxelles / see Groupe d'études latino-américaines de l'Institut de sociologie, Bruxelles
- Centre d'étude sur la communication en Afrique (inactive)
- Centre d'étude et de coopération internationale, Montréal / see Canadian Centre for International Studies and Cooperation
- Centre pour l'étude et le développement des établissements humains en Afrique (internationally oriented national body)
- Centre d'étude de l'Etat et de la société, Buenos Aires (internationally oriented national body)
- Centre d'étude de l'ethnicité et des migrations (internationally oriented national body)
- Centre d'étude latino-américaines de l'Institut de sociologie, Bruxelles / see Groupe d'études latino-américaines de l'Institut de sociologie, Bruxelles
- Centre d'étude et de promotion des relations entre les pays de la CE et de l'Amérique latine / see Centre d'étude et de promotion des relations entre les pays de l'Union européenne et de l'Amérique latine
- Centre d'étude et de promotion des relations entre les pays de l'Union européenne et de l'Amérique latine (internationally oriented national body)

♦ Centre d'étude et de prospective stratégique (CEPS) 03739

Centre for Prospective Strategic Studies

Managing Dir 1 rue de Villersexel, 75007 Paris, France. T. +33153631363. Fax +33153631360. E-mail: ceps@ceps-oing.org.
URL: http://www.ceps-oing.org/

History 1985. **Aims** Determine, analyse and put into perspective technological, economic and financial development factors in order to assist companies, institutions and governments in defining their positions in a global environment. **Structure** Board of Directors. **Languages** English, French. **Staff** 10.00 FTE, paid. **Finance** Members' dues. Other sources: study and research contracts; events; consulting; sponsorship. **Activities** Events/meetings; guidance/assistance/consulting. **Events** *European meeting* Brussels (Belgium) 1996, *Réunion internationale sur la recherche et l'innovation dans l'Europe communautaire* Paris (France) 1990. **Publications** *Strategic Prospective* (4 a year) – review. Editorials, with limited distribution, highlighting the thoughts developed through the work of CEPS; works highlighting strategic issues from diverse areas of activity; reports that address in greater detail innovative perspectives detected by CEPS; investigations of public value carried out at national and international level. **Members** Full (about 1,200). Membership countries not specified. **Consultative Status** Consultative status granted from: *Council of Europe (CE, #04881)* (Participatory Status); *UNESCO (#20322)* (Consultative Status). **IGO Relations** Accredited by (1): *Organisation internationale de la Francophonie (OIF, #17809)*. Partner of (3): *African Development Bank (ADB, #00283)*; *OECD (#17693)*; *UNESCO (#20322)*.
[2019.10.21/XM1395/**E**]

- Centre d'étude et de recherche de droit international et de relations internationales de l'Académie de La Haye / see The Hague Academy Centre for Studies and Research in International Law and International Relations
- Centre d'étude et de recherche pour l'intégration régionale et le développement de l'Afrique (internationally oriented national body)
- Centre d'étude régional pour l'amélioration de l'adaptation à la sécheresse (see: #20907)
- Centre d'étude de la région des grands lacs d'Afrique (internationally oriented national body)
- Centre d'étude sur les régions en développement / see Institute for the Study of International Development
- Centre d'étude et de rencontres francophones (internationally oriented national body)
- Centre d'études africaines de Bâle (internationally oriented national body)
- Centre d'études africaines, Edimbourg (internationally oriented national body)
- Centre d'études Africaines Leiden (internationally oriented national body)
- Centre d'études africaines, Maputo (internationally oriented national body)
- Centre d'études africaines, Paris (internationally oriented national body)
- Centre d'études anti-impérialistes / see Centre d'études et initiatives de solidarité internationale
- Centre d'études asiatiques (internationally oriented national body)
- Centre d'études asiatiques, Tempe (internationally oriented national body)
- Centre d'études de l'Asie de l'Est, Montréal (internationally oriented national body)
- Centre d'études d'Asie et de Pacifique, Havane (internationally oriented national body)
- Centre d'études et de construction d'architecture tropicale (internationally oriented national body)
- Centre d'études de la coopération internationale et du développement (internationally oriented national body)
- Centre d'études des crises et des conflits internationaux (internationally oriented national body)
- Centre d'études de démographie historique de l'Amérique latine (internationally oriented national body)
- Centre d'études du développement, Bath (internationally oriented national body)
- Centre d'études de développement international et des mouvements économiques et sociaux (internationally oriented national body)
- Centre d'études sur le développement à Sri Lanka / see Marga Institute
- Centre d'études du développement, Swansea (internationally oriented national body)
- Centre d'études et de documentation latinoaméricaines (internationally oriented national body)
- Centre d'études des droits du monde arabe (internationally oriented national body)
- Centre d'études euro-arabe, Paris (internationally oriented national body)
- Centre des études européennes, Budapest / see Institute for Social and European Studies

- ♦ Centre d'études européenne – Sciences-Po, Paris / see SciencesPo – Centre d'études européene et de politique comparée
- ♦ Centre d'études européennes, Lyon (internationally oriented national body)
- ♦ Centre d'études européennes, Paris (internationally oriented national body)
- ♦ Centre d'études européennes, Trier (internationally oriented national body)
- ♦ Centre d'études européennes – Université de Navarre (internationally oriented national body)
- ♦ Centre d'études européennes de Waterloo (internationally oriented national body)
- ♦ Centre d'études pour l'évolution humaine (internationally oriented national body)
- ♦ Centre d'études de la famille africaine (#03726)
- ♦ Centre d'études gouvernementales européennes, Edimbourg (internationally oriented national body)
- ♦ Centre d'études et initiatives de solidarité internationale (internationally oriented national body)
- ♦ Centre d'études interaméricaines (internationally oriented national body)
- ♦ Centre d'études internationales, Cambridge MA (internationally oriented national body)
- ♦ Centre d'études internationales et européennes (internationally oriented national body)
- ♦ Centre d'études internationales, México (internationally oriented national body)
- ♦ Centre d'études internationales de la propriété industrielle / see Centre d'études internationales de la propriété intellectuelle
- ♦ Centre d'études internationales de la propriété intellectuelle (internationally oriented national body)
- ♦ Centre d'Études Latino-américaines de l'Éducation Inclusive (internationally oriented national body)
- ♦ Centre d'études latinoaméricaines 'Justo Arosemena' (internationally oriented national body)
- ♦ Centre d'études latinoaméricaines Rómulo Gallegos (internationally oriented national body)
- ♦ Centre d'études linguistiques et historiques par tradition orale (#03771)

♦ Centre d'études maghrébines, Tunis (CEMAT) 03740

Centre for Maghrib Studies, Tunis

Contact 25 rue Fatma Ennachi, Menzah 5, 2080 Tunis, Tunisia. T. +21671232533. E-mail: info@cematmaghrib.org.
URL: https://www.cematmaghrib.org/

History 1985, pursuant an agreement between *American Institute for Maghrib Studies (AIMS)* and the Ministry of Higher Education and Scientific and Technological Research of the Tunisian Government. **Aims** Promote reciprocal research and exchanges between specialists in the various fields of social and human sciences. **Structure** Board of Directors; International Advisory Committee. Officers: President, Vice-President, Secretary and Treasurer. Managing Board, comprising 6 members. **Languages** Arabic, English, French. **Staff** 3.00 FTE, paid. **Finance** Members' dues. Sources: Grants. **Activities** Aids researchers; provides grants; hosts international conference of American Institute for Maghribi Studies; maintains a library. **Events** *Conference on the expansion of the North African city* Tunis (Tunisia) 2005. **Publications** *CEMAT Newsletter* (annual). **Members** Regular; Life; Student; Institutional Members in 4 countries:
Algeria, Morocco, Tunisia, USA. [2018/XE3321/**E**]

- ♦ Centre des Etudes Méditerranéennes et Internationales (internationally oriented national body)
- ♦ Centre d'études sur les migrations, Rome (internationally oriented national body)
- ♦ Centre d'études migratoires (internationally oriented national body)
- ♦ Centre d'études monétaires latinoaméricaines / see Center for Latin American Monetary Studies (#03648)
- ♦ Centre d'études sur le Moyen-Orient, Berkeley (internationally oriented national body)
- ♦ Centre d'études oecuméniques, Strasbourg (#11258)
- ♦ Centre d'études prospectives et d'informations internationales, Paris (internationally oriented national body)
- ♦ Centre d'études, de recherche et d'histoire Compostellanes (internationally oriented national body)
- ♦ Centre d'études et de recherche sur la population pour le développement (no recent information)
- ♦ Centre d'études et de recherches sur la coopération internationale (internationally oriented national body)
- ♦ Centre d'études et de recherches sur le développement international, Clermont-Ferrand (internationally oriented national body)
- ♦ Centre d'études et de recherches internationales (internationally oriented national body)
- ♦ Centre d'études et de recherches internationales et communautaires (internationally oriented national body)
- ♦ Centre d'études et de recherches internationales et communications / see Centre d'études et de recherches internationales et communautaires
- ♦ Centre d'études et de recherches sur les migrations ibériques (internationally oriented national body)
- ♦ Centre d'études et de recherches sur l'urbanisation du monde arabe / see Centre d'études et de recherches sur l'urbanisation du monde arabe – Equipe monde arabe et méditerranée
- ♦ Centre d'études et de recherches sur l'urbanisation du monde arabe – Equipe monde arabe et méditerranée (internationally oriented national body)
- ♦ Centre d'études régionales andines 'Bartolomé de Las Casas' (#03636)
- ♦ Centre d'études des relations internationales / see Centre européen de recherche internationales et stratégiques
- ♦ Centre d'études des relations internationales et stratégiques, Bruxelles / see Centre européen de recherche internationales et stratégiques
- ♦ Centre d'Etudes et de Sauvegarde des Tortues Marines de Méditerranée (internationally oriented national body)
- ♦ Centre d'études sur la sécurité internationale et les coopérations européennes (internationally oriented national body)
- ♦ Centre d'Etudes de Sécurité Internationale et de Maîtrise des Armements (internationally oriented national body)
- ♦ Centre d'études stratégiques de l'Afrique (internationally oriented national body)
- ♦ Centre d'études stratégiques et de défense (internationally oriented national body)
- ♦ Centre d'études stratégiques, Rabat (internationally oriented national body)
- ♦ Centre d'études du Tiers-monde (internationally oriented national body)
- ♦ Centre d'études des transports pour la Méditerranée occidentale (internationally oriented national body)
- ♦ Centre for Euro-Atlantic Studies, Bucharest (internationally oriented national body)
- ♦ Centre euro-atlantique de coordination des réactions en cas de catastrophe (#05644)
- ♦ Centre euro-méditerranéen sur la contamination marine accidentelle / see Euro-Mediterranean Centre on Insular Coastal Dynamics (#05718)
- ♦ Centre euro-méditerranéen sur l'evaluation et la prévention du risque sismique (internationally oriented national body)
- ♦ Centre for European Affairs (internationally oriented national body)
- ♦ Centre for European Constitutional Law – Themistokles and Dimitris Tsatsos Foundation (internationally oriented national body)
- ♦ Centre for European Documentation and Research / see Institute for European Studies, Malta
- ♦ Centre for European Economic Research / see ZEW – Leibniz-Zentrum für Europäische Wirtschaftsforschung
- ♦ Centre for European and Euro-Atlantic Studies, Bucharest (internationally oriented national body)
- ♦ Centre for European Governance / see Centre for European Studies
- ♦ Centre of European Governmental Studies, Edinburgh / see Edinburgh Europa Institute
- ♦ Centre for European History and Civilization, Iasi (internationally oriented national body)
- ♦ Centre for European Integration Research (internationally oriented national body)
- ♦ Centre for European Integration Studies (internationally oriented national body)
- ♦ Centre for European and International Studies, Kiev (internationally oriented national body)
- ♦ Centre for European Jewish Information / see CEJI (#03628)
- ♦ Centre of European Law, London (internationally oriented national body)
- ♦ Centre for European Law, Oslo (internationally oriented national body)
- ♦ Centre for European and North Atlantic Affairs (internationally oriented national body)

♦ Centre for European Policy Studies (CEPS) 03741

Dir Place du Congrès 1, 1000 Brussels, Belgium. T. +3222293938. Fax +3222194151.
CEO address not obtained. T. +3222293956.
URL: http://www.ceps.eu/

History 1983, Brussels (Belgium). Originally managed by *European Cultural Foundation (ECF, #06868)*, the funding structure being provided by *Network of European Foundations (NEF, #17019)*. Registration: Banque-Carrefour des Entreprises, No/ID: 0863.021.173, Start date: 27 Jan 2004, Belgium; EU Transparency Register, No/ID: 206201438220-85, Start date: 2 Jun 2020. **Aims** Carry out state-of-the-art policy research leading to solutions to the challenges facing Europe; achieve high standards of academic excellence and maintain unqualified independence; provide a forum for discussion among all stakeholders in the European policy process; build collaborative networks of researchers, policy-makers and business representatives across Europe; disseminate finding and views through publications and public events. **Structure** General Meeting (annual); Board of Directors; Executive Committee. **Languages** English. **Staff** 70.00 FTE, paid. **Finance** Sources: members' dues. Other sources: project research; foundation grants; conference fees; publication sales. **Activities** Research/documentation; politics/policy/regulatory; knowledge management/information dissemination. **Events** *Cybersecurity Summit* Brussels (Belgium) 2022, *De-Globalisation – A New World Order?* Brussels (Belgium) 2022, *New Dynamics in the EU's Relations with Asia Workshop* Brussels (Belgium) 2022, *Principled Tax Policy* Brussels (Belgium) 2022, *Roma and Memorialization: Advancing Recognition and Remedy for the Dark Chapters of the Past and their Impact on the Present* Brussels (Belgium) 2022. **Publications** *CEPS News* (10 a year). Commentaries; paperbacks; policy briefs; reports; working documents; briefs; essays. **Members** Corporate (123); Institutional (130). Membership countries not specified. **NGO Relations** Member of (1): *Euro-Mediterranean Study Commission (EuroMeSCo, #05727)* (Observer). Cooperates with: *European Capital Markets Institute (ECMI, #06439)*; *European Climate Platform (inactive)*; *European Credit Research Institute (ECRI, #06857)*; *European Network for Better Regulation (ENBR, #07868)*; *European Network of Economic Policy Research Institutes (ENEPRI, #07894)*; *European Policy Institutes Network (EPIN, #08242)*. [2020/XF2989/y/**E**]

- ♦ Centre for European Private Law (internationally oriented national body)
- ♦ Centre for European Progression (internationally oriented national body)
- ♦ Centre for European Reform (internationally oriented national body)
- ♦ Centre for European Regional and Local Studies (internationally oriented national body)
- ♦ Centre for European Regional Studies / see European Institute for Futures Studies (#07556)
- ♦ Centre for European Research Training and Development Projects (internationally oriented national body)
- ♦ Centre for European, Russian, and Eurasian Studies, Toronto (internationally oriented national body)
- ♦ Centre for European Security Studies (internationally oriented national body)
- ♦ Centre for European and Security Studies, Belarus (internationally oriented national body)
- ♦ Centre for European Security Studies, Sofia (internationally oriented national body)

♦ Centre for European Social and Economic Policy (CESEP) 03742

Centre de politique sociale et économique européenne (CePSE)

Dir Rue de la Pacification 67, 1000 Brussels, Belgium. T. +320497659379. E-mail: cesep@skynet.be.
URL: http://cesep.eu/

History 1 Nov 1987, Brussels (Belgium). Registration: No/ID: BE0432544675, Start date: 26 Nov 1987, Belgium. **Aims** Help the work of business, labour, government and international organizations on problems related to European social and economic policy; monitor EU and national socio-economic policies; elaborate economic and statistical indicators. **Structure** Departments (3). **Languages** English, French. **Staff** 2.00 FTE, paid. **Finance** Sources: fees for services. **Activities** Guidance/assistance/consulting; research/documentation. **Publications** *European comparative data on Europe 2020 & People with disabilities* (annual) in English. *European Pillar of Social Rights: Social Scoreboard and Persons with disabilities – Quantitative indicators* in English; *MONITORING & ASSESSING EU POLICIES Europe 2020, Selected UNCRPD Articles & New Challenges* in English – Free; *Sustainable Development in the European Union: EU SDG Indicators and Persons with Disabilities* in English. Studies; reports; research notes. [2022.05.10/XE5908/**E**]

- ♦ Centre for European Sociology (internationally oriented national body)
- ♦ Centre for European Studies / see Wilfried Martens Centre for European Studies (#20962)
- ♦ Centre for European Studies / see European Union Studies Center, New York
- ♦ Centre for European Studies (internationally oriented national body)
- ♦ Centre for European Studies (internationally oriented national body)
- ♦ Centre for European Studies, Ankara (internationally oriented national body)
- ♦ Centre For European Studies, Bangkok (internationally oriented national body)
- ♦ Centre for European Studies, Budapest / see Institute for Social and European Studies
- ♦ Centre for European Studies, Cairo (internationally oriented national body)
- ♦ Centre for European Studies, Chisinau (internationally oriented national body)
- ♦ Centre for European Studies, Delhi (internationally oriented national body)
- ♦ Centre for European Studies, Exeter / see Centre for European Studies
- ♦ Centre of European Studies, Habana (internationally oriented national body)
- ♦ Centre for European Studies, Limerick (internationally oriented national body)
- ♦ Centre for European Studies, Louvain-la-Neuve / see Institute of European Studies, Louvain-la-Neuve
- ♦ Centre for European Studies, Ottawa (internationally oriented national body)
- ♦ Centre for European Studies, Szombathely / see Institute for Social and European Studies
- ♦ Centre for European Studies, Trier (internationally oriented national body)
- ♦ Centre for European Studies – University of Navarra (internationally oriented national body)
- ♦ Centre for European Transformation (internationally oriented national body)
- ♦ Centre for European Union Studies, Hull (internationally oriented national body)

♦ Centre for European Volunteering (CEV) 03743

Dir Av des Arts 7/8, 1210 Brussels, Belgium. T. +32474064353. E-mail: communication@cev.be.
URL: https://www.europeanvolunteercentre.org

History Feb 1992. Former names and other names: *European Volunteer Centre* – former (1 Jul 2020). Registration: Start date: 6 Aug 1992, Belgium; Start date: 22 May 2002, Belgium; EU Transparency Register, No/ID: 65297771902-13. **Aims** Contribute to the creation of an enabling political, social and economic environment in Europe where the full potential of volunteering can be realized. **Structure** General Assembly (twice a year); Executive Board; Secretariat, headed by Director, based in Brussels (Belgium). **Languages** English, French. **Staff** 4.50 FTE, paid. **Finance** Sources: grants; members' dues; revenue from activities/projects. Supported by: *European Commission (EC, #06633)* (Europe for Citizens programme). Annual budget: 216,212 EUR (2020). **Activities** Advocacy/lobbying/activism; capacity building; knowledge management/information dissemination; training/education. **Events** *DYVO Project Final Conference* Brussels (Belgium) 2022, *Service-Learning Upscaling Social Inclusion for Kids (SLUSIK) Project Final Conference* Brussels (Belgium) 2022, *Spring Volunteering Congress* Brussels (Belgium) 2022, *Autumn Volunteering Congress* Gdansk (Poland) 2022, *Autumn Volunteering Congress* Berlin (Germany) 2021. **Publications** *CEV News* (12 a year). *Volunteering Infrastructure in Europe* (2012); *European Elections Manifesto* (2009); *Manifesto for Volunteering in Europe* (2006). *Blueprint for European Volunteering 2030* (2021) in Croatian, English, French, German, Italian, Spanish – The blueprint serves as guidance to CEV and other stakeholders concerned with volunteering, especially policymakers, regarding the steps that need to be taken for volunteering to reach its true potential.. Annual Report; symposia report; fact-sheet; other publications – all online.
Members Organizations (about 100) in 29 countries:
Austria, Belgium, Bosnia-Herzegovina, Bulgaria, Croatia, Cyprus, Denmark, Estonia, Finland, France, Germany, Greece, Hungary, Ireland, Italy, Latvia, Luxembourg, Malta, Netherlands, Poland, Portugal, Romania, Russia, Slovakia, Slovenia, Spain, Sweden, Türkiye, UK.
Included in the above, 4 organizations listed in this Yearbook:
Confederation of European Senior Expert Services (CESES, #04533); *International Communications Volunteers (ICVolunteers, #12817)*; *South East European Youth Network (SEEYN, #19821)*; *Voluntary Service Overseas (VSO)*.

Consultative Status Consultative status granted from: *Council of Europe (CE, #04881)* (Participatory Status). **IGO Relations** Member of (1): *European Economic and Social Committee (EESC, #06963)* (Liaison Group). **NGO Relations** Memorandum of Understanding with (1): *International Association for Volunteer Effort (IAVE, #12260)*. Member of (2): *Civil Society Europe*; *SDG Watch Europe (#19162)*. Supports (2): *European Alliance for the Statute of the European Association (EASEA, #05886)*; *European Citizens' Initiative Campaign (ECI Campaign, #06558)*. [2022.05.04/XF5335/y/**E**]

- Centre européen d'arbitrage / see European Center for Arbitration and Mediation (#06462)
- Centre Européen d'Arbitrage et de Médiation (#06462)
- Centre européen sur les aspects réglementaires liés aux catastrophes / see Higher Institute of Emergency Planning – European Centre Florival
- Centre européen associé de sécurité technologique (internationally oriented national body)
- Centre européen des astronautes (#06287)
- Centre Européen de Calcul Atomique et Moléculaire (#06471)

♦ Centre européen de cartographie ethnolinguistique (Centre Aldo Dami) 03744

European Centre for Ethnolinguistic Cartography

Contact address not obtained. T. +3224285614. Fax +3224285614.

History 20 Dec 1986, Brussels (Belgium), when statutes were adopted. **Aims** Promote, undertake and commission research and study in the domain of the *geography* of *ethnic* and *linguistic* groups in Europe so as to assist the design, realization and publication of *maps* and *atlases*. **Structure** Founder Members propose further members who are approved by General Assembly. Directing Committee of up to 5 members coming from at least 3 countries of the Council of Europe, including President, 2 Vice-Presidents, Scientific Secretary and Treasurer. **Languages** English, French. **Finance** Members' dues. **Events** *Meeting* Poznań (Poland) 2005, *Meeting* Brussels (Belgium) 2003, *Meeting* Birmingham (UK) 2001, *Meeting* Barcelona (Spain) 1999, *Meeting* The Hague (Netherlands) 1997. **Publications** *Report of Geneva Meeting: The Cartographic Representation of Linguistic Data* by Y Peeters and C H Williams.

Members Individuals (maximum 3 per Council of Europe Members States) in 32 countries:
Austria, Belgium, Bulgaria, Cyprus, Czechia, Denmark, Estonia, Finland, France, Germany, Greece, Hungary, Iceland, Ireland, Italy, Liechtenstein, Lithuania, Luxembourg, Malta, Netherlands, Norway, Poland, Portugal, Romania, San Marino, Slovakia, Slovenia, Spain, Sweden, Switzerland, Türkiye, UK. [2013/XF2267/v/**E**]

- Centre européen de la colonne vertébrale (internationally oriented national body)
- Centre européen du commerce de détail (inactive)
- Centre européen du Conseil international des femmes (#06485)
- Centre européen de coordination de recherche et de documentation en sciences sociales (inactive)
- Centre européen de la culture (#06472)
- Centre européen des cultures traditionnelles et régionales / see European Centre for Training and Regional Cooperation (#06503)
- Centre européen pour le développement de la formation professionnelle (#06474)
- Centre européen pour le développement industriel et la mise en valeur de l'outre-mer (inactive)
- Centre européen de documentation et de compensation (inactive)
- Centre européen de documentation et d'études gérontologiques (inactive)
- Centre européen pour le droit et la justice (internationally oriented national body)
- Centre européen sur la dynamique non linéaire et la théorie du risque sismique / see European Centre of New Technologies for the Management of Natural and Technological Major Hazards (#06494)
- Centre européen d'économie internationale / see Bruegel
- Centre européen d'écotoxicologie et de toxicologie des produits chimiques (#06477)
- Centre européen d'éducation permanente (#06479)
- Centre européen pour enfants disparus et exploités / see European Centre for Missing and Sexually Exploited Children
- Centre européen pour enfants disparus et sexuellement exploités (internationally oriented national body)
- Centre européen de l'entreprise publique / see SGI Europe (#19253)
- Centre européen des entreprises à participation publique / see SGI Europe (#19253)
- Centre européen des entreprises à participation publique et des entreprises d'intérêt économique général / see SGI Europe (#19253)
- Centre européen de l'environnement et de la santé de l'OMS (see: #20945)
- Centre européen d'études de l'acide sulfurique / see European Sulphuric Acid Association (#08854)
- Centre européen d'études bourguignonnes (#05960)
- Centre européen d'études burgondo-médianes / see European Association of Burgundy Studies (#05960)
- Centre européen d'études compostellanes, France / see Centre d'études, de recherche et d'histoire Compostellanes

♦ Centre européen d'études pour la santé animale (CEESA) 03745

European Animal Health Study Centre

SG Av de Terveuren 168, 1150 Brussels, Belgium.

History 8 Feb 1983, Brussels (Belgium), as *European Information Bureau for Animal Health Development – Bureau européen d'information pour le développement de la santé animale*, following meeting of manufacturers of ethical animal health products. Statutes adopted 8 Dec 1983. Present name and statutes adopted 1995. Registration: AISBL/IVZW, Belgium. **Aims** Generate tools (economic, epidemiological as well as other scientific studies) to assist animal health industry lobbying efforts in Europe. **Structure** General Assembly (annual). Management Board, consisting of President, Vice-President, General Secretary and Treasurer. **Finance** Members' dues. Contract work. **Events** *Biennial conference* Brussels (Belgium) 1986.

Members Active; Associate; Honorary. Institutions in 16 countries:
Austria, Belgium, Denmark, Finland, France, Germany, Greece, Ireland, Italy, Netherlands, Norway, Portugal, Spain, Sweden, Switzerland, UK. [2019/XD8079/**E**]

- Centre européen d'études de sécurité George C Marshall, Garmisch Partenkirchen (internationally oriented national body)

♦ Centre européen d'études des silicates (CEES) 03746

European Silicates Centre

Secretariat CEFIC, Rue Belliard 40, Box 15, 1040 Brussels, Belgium. T. +3226767288. Fax +3226767475. E-mail: bpi@cefic.be.

URL: http://www.cees-silicates.org/

History 1963, as a sector group of *Conseil européen de l'industrie chimique (CEFIC, #04687)*. **Structure** Heads of Delegation; General Assembly; Technical Committee. **Activities** Sponsors fundamental research. Recent work includes study of the structure of aqueous solutions of alkaline silicates and principles of labelling in conformity with national and European Community regulations on dangerous substances such as risk and safety phrases. Life cycle analysis.

Members Western European manufacturers of silicates (14) in 7 countries:
Belgium, France, Germany, Italy, Netherlands, Spain, Switzerland. [2017/XE0881/**E**]

- Centre européen des fédérations de l'industrie chimique (inactive)
- Centre européen féminin de recherche sur l'évolution de la société (inactive)
- Centre européen de formation d'artisans pour la conservation du patrimoine architectural / see European Centre for Heritage Crafts and Professions (#06484)
- Centre européen de formation sur les désastres naturels (internationally oriented national body)
- Centre européen de formation à la gestion, Bruxelles (no recent information)
- Centre européen de formation interrégional pour les sauveteurs / see European Interregional Scientific and Educational Centre on Major Risk Management
- Centre européen de formation et de recherche en action sociale / see European Centre for Social Welfare Policy and Research (#06500)
- Centre européen de formation des statisticiens économistes des pays en voie de développement / see CESD – statisticiens pour le développement
- Centre européen de géodynamique et de séismologie (#06481)
- Centre européen de gestion des politiques de développement (#06473)
- Centre européen d'information de l'énergie (inactive)
- Centre européen d'information sur la production, le traitement, le transport et le stockage du gaz naturel et autres hydrocarbures gazeux, Reuil Malmaison / see International Information Centre for Natural Gas and Gaseous Hydrocarbons (#13845)
- Centre européen pour l'interdépendance et la solidarité mondiales (#06483)
- Centre européen interrégional de formation sur les risques majeurs (internationally oriented national body)
- Centre européen pour l'irradiation des aliments (inactive)
- Centre européen du journalisme (#07612)
- Centre européen juif d'information / see CEJI (#03628)
- Centre européen de langue française (internationally oriented national body)
- Centre européen pour les langues vivantes (#06491)
- Centre européen pour les langues vivantes du Conseil de l'Europe / see European Centre for Modern Languages (#06491)
- Centre européen de la lutte contre le terrorisme (#06851)
- Centre européen de la magistrature et des professions juridiques (#06488)
- Centre européen pour la médecine des catastrophes (#06475)
- Centre européen médical bioclimatique de recherche et d'enseignement universitaire (internationally oriented national body)
- Centre européen pour les métiers du patrimoine (#06484)
- Centre Europeen de Musique (unconfirmed)
- Centre européen des nouvelles technologies pour la gestion des risques naturel et technologiques majeurs (#06494)
- Centre européen d'opérations spatiales (#08800)
- Centre européen pour la paix et le développement (#06496)
- Centre européen de prévention et de contrôle des maladies (#06476)
- Centre européen pour les prévisions météorologiques à moyen terme (#06490)
- Centre européen pour la promotion des innovations technologiques / see EURO-CHINA (#05658)
- Centre européen pour la recherche, le développement et l'enseignement de la nutrithérapie / see Centre européen pour la recherche, le développement et l'enseignement de la nutrition et de la nutrithérapie
- Centre européen pour la recherche, le développement et l'enseignement de la nutrition et de la nutrithérapie (internationally oriented national body)
- Centre européen de recherche et de documentation parlementaires (#06495)
- Centre européen de recherche en économie du développement (internationally oriented national body)
- Centre européen de recherche et de formation avancée en calcul scientifique (internationally oriented national body)
- Centre européen de recherche internationales et stratégiques (internationally oriented national body)
- Centre européen de recherche en politique sociale (#06500)
- Centre européen de recherche et de prospective politique (unconfirmed)
- Centre européen de recherche des techniques d'information du public en situation d'urgence (internationally oriented national body)
- Centre européen de recherche et de technologie spatiales (#08802)
- Centre Européen de référence pour l'education aux premiers secours (internationally oriented national body)
- Centre européen de réflexion et d'étude en thermodynamique (#06469)
- Centre européen des régions (see: #07569)
- Centre européen pour la réhabilitation des fleuves (#06499)
- Centre européen pour le renseignement stratégique et la sécurité (internationally oriented national body)
- Centre européen sur les risques géo- et morphodynamiques, Strasbourg / see European Centre on Geomorphological Hazards (#06482)
- Centre Européen sur les Risques Géomorphologiques (#06482)
- Centre européen Robert Schuman (internationally oriented national body)
- Centre européen de santé humanitaire, Lyon (internationally oriented national body)
- Centre européen de sécurité des procédés / see European Process Safety Centre (#08279)
- Centre européen des silicones / see CES – Silicones Europe (#03838)
- Centre européen de technologie spatiale / see European Space Research and Technology Centre (#08802)
- Centre Européen des Textiles Innovants (unconfirmed)
- Centre européen de traduction / see Centre de traduction des organes de l'Union européenne (#03790)
- Centre européen de traduction littéraire, Bruxelles (internationally oriented national body)
- Centre européen pour les travailleurs (#06505)
- Centre européen pour la validation des méthodes alternatives (inactive)
- Centre européen de Venise pour les métiers de la conservation du patrimoine architectural / see European Centre for Heritage Crafts and Professions (#06484)
- Centre Europe – Tiers-monde (internationally oriented national body)
- Centre for Europe, University of Warsaw (internationally oriented national body)
- Centre d'excellence pour l'enseignement des mathématiques et des sciences en Afrique (internationally oriented national body)
- Centre for the Exchange and Promotion of Craftsmen in Development Areas (internationally oriented national body)
- Centre for Executive Development / see European Centre for Executive Development (#06479)

♦ Centre for Experiential Negotiation and Applied Diplomacy (CENAD) 03747

Programme Dir/Trainer Rue Abbé Cuypers 3, 1040 Brussels, Belgium. T. +3227412450. Fax +3227347910. E-mail: info@cenad.org.

URL: http://www.cenad.org/

Aims Equip and empower national and institutional public servants, diplomats, civil society and business professionals with the competence, skills and techniques to effectively influence bilateral and multi-party, formal and informal negotiation results, and experience greater "real world" success. **Structure** General Assembly (annual); Board. **Languages** English, French, German. **Activities** Guidance/assistance/consulting; training/education. [2020.05.06/XE4237/**E**]

- Centre pour la facilitation du commerce et les transactions électroniques des Nations Unies (#20527)
- Centre for Facilitation of Procedures and Practices for Administration, Commerce and Transport / see United Nations Centre for Trade Facilitation and Electronic Business (#20527)
- Centre pour la facilitation des procédures et des pratiques dans l'administration, le commerce et le transport / see United Nations Centre for Trade Facilitation and Electronic Business (#20527)
- Centre for Foreign Journalists / see International Center for Journalists
- Centre for Foreign Policy Studies, Halifax (internationally oriented national body)
- Centre for Foreign Relations (internationally oriented national body)
- Centre for Forestry Education Development for Asia and the Southwest Pacific Region / see Training Center for Tropical Resources and Ecosystems Sustainability
- Centre for Forestry Education Research and Development for Asia and the Pacific Regions / see Training Center for Tropical Resources and Ecosystems Sustainability
- Centre de formation pour le développement, Strasbourg / see Coopération et Formation au Développement
- Centre de formation postale pour l'Asie et le Pacifique / see Asian-Pacific Postal College (#01624)
- Centre de formation statistique de l'Afrique de l'Est (#05228)

♦ Centre français sur la population et le développement / see Centre Population et développement
♦ Centre Gandhi au service de l'homme et de la vie (internationally oriented national body)
♦ Centre de Genève pour la gouvernance du secteur de la sécurité (#10121)
♦ Centre de Genève pour la Promotion de l'homme et le Dialogue Global (#10120)
♦ Centre géoscientifique du Pacifique (internationally oriented national body)
♦ Centre for German and European Studies / see BMW Center for German and European Studies
♦ Centre for Global Development, Leeds (internationally oriented national body)
♦ Centre for Global Education (internationally oriented national body)
♦ Centre for Global Environmental Research, Ibaraki (internationally oriented national body)
♦ Centre for Globalization Studies, Teheran (internationally oriented national body)
♦ Centre for Global Mental Health (internationally oriented national body)
♦ Centre for Global Political Economy, Brighton (internationally oriented national body)
♦ Centre for Global Studies, Victoria (internationally oriented national body)
♦ Centre pour la gouvernance du secteur de la sécurité – Genève / see Geneva Centre for Security Sector Governance (#10121)
♦ Centre for Health Education and Appropriate Health Technology, Bologna (internationally oriented national body)
♦ Centre hellénique d'études européennes (internationally oriented national body)
♦ Centre hellénique d'études et de recherches européennes (internationally oriented national body)
♦ Centre Henri Rolin de droit international / see Centre for International Law, Brussels

♦ Centre for Heritage Development in Africa (CHDA) 03748

Dir PO Box 90010-80100, Mombasa, Kenya. T. +254707701761. Fax +254412227985.
Street Address RISSEA Premises, Off Mama Ngina Drive, Next to Mombasa Hosp, Mombasa, Kenya.
URL: http://www.heritageinafrica.org/

History 2000, as *Programme for Museum Development in Africa (PMDA)*. Current title adopted 2005. **Aims** Preserve, manage, develop and promote Africa's heritage through programmes of training and development support services. **Structure** International Board; Director; Programme Coordinators. **Languages** English. **Staff** 4.00 FTE, paid. **Finance** Funding/development partners, including: *British Council*; *Ford Foundation (#09858)*; *Norwegian Agency for Development Cooperation (Norad)*; *Swiss Agency for Development and Cooperation (SDC)*; *UNESCO (#20322)*; governments of Italy, Netherlands, Norway; national and private institutions. **Activities** Training/education; capacity building; projects/programmes. **Events** *Workshop on introduction to museum basics and collection management* Addis Ababa (Ethiopia) 2006. **Publications** *Cultural Heritage Impact Assessment in Africa: An Overview*.

Members Covers 29 countries in English and Portuguese speaking Sub-Saharan Africa:
Angola, Botswana, Cape Verde, Djibouti, Equatorial Guinea, Eritrea, Eswatini, Ethiopia, Gambia, Ghana, Guinea-Bissau, Kenya, Lesotho, Liberia, Malawi, Mauritius, Mozambique, Namibia, Nigeria, Seychelles, Sierra Leone, Somalia, South Africa, South Sudan, Sudan, Tanzania UR, Uganda, Zambia, Zimbabwe.

NGO Relations Sister organization: *School of African Heritage (EPA)*. Instrumental in setting up: *AFRICA 2009 – Conservation of Immovable Cultural Heritage in Sub-Saharan Africa (inactive)*. [2016.01.08/XE4502/**E**]

♦ Centre for History and European History / see Centre for European History and Civilization, Iasi
♦ Centre for the History of Globalization, Moscow (internationally oriented national body)
♦ Centre for Human Evolution Studies (internationally oriented national body)
♦ Centre for Humanitarian Dialogue (internationally oriented national body)
♦ Centre for Humanitarian Leadership (internationally oriented national body)
♦ Centre for Human Rights and Democracy in Africa (unconfirmed)
♦ Centre for Human Rights, Pretoria (internationally oriented national body)
♦ Centre for Iberian and Latin American Studies, Bratislava (internationally oriented national body)

♦ Centre for Indigenous Instrumental Music and Dance Practices of Africa (CIIMDA) 03749

Dir 64 14th Street, Menlo Park, Pretoria, South Africa. T. +27124604839. Fax +27124604800.
URL: http://www.ciimda.org/

History Founded 2004, Pretoria (South Africa), with funding from the Norwegian Foreign Office through Concert Norway (Rikskonsertene); funding ended 2011. **Aims** Promote learning of the philosophy, theory and human meaning of African instrumental music and dance practices in classroom music education in SADC countries. **Structure** Board; Management. **Languages** English. **Staff** 4.00 FTE, voluntary. **Finance** No financing since initial funding which ended Dec 2011. Seeking funding. **Activities** Meeting activities. **Publications** *Modern African Classical Drumming: Performance Pieces for Schools* (2011); *African Classical Ensemble Music – vols 1-3* (2009); *Beyond Memories: An Anthology of Popular Musicians in South Africa, Past and Present* (2008); *Career Choices* (2008); *Contemporary Study of Musical Arts: INformed by African Indigenous Knowledge System – vols 1-5* (2007); *Learning the Musical Arts in Contemporary Africa: Informed by Indigenous Knowledge Systems – vols 1-2* (2006).

Members Full in 7 countries:
Eswatini, Lesotho, Malawi, Mozambique, Namibia, Tanzania UR, Zambia. [2014.06.01/XJ8156/**E**]

♦ Centre d'Informació i Documentació Internacionals a Barcelona (internationally oriented national body)
♦ Centre d'information canadien sur les diplômes internationaux (internationally oriented national body)
♦ Centre d'information et de conseil sur la commercialisation des produits de la pêche dans la région arabe (#03772)
♦ Centre d'information, de conseil et de formation professions de la coopération internationale et de l'aide humanitaire (internationally oriented national body)
♦ Centre for Information, Counseling and Training Professions Relating to International Cooperation and Humanitarian Aid (internationally oriented national body)
♦ Centre d'information et de documentation Amilcar Cabral (internationally oriented national body)
♦ Centre d'information et de documentation sur le Conseil de l'Europe (internationally oriented national body)
♦ Centre d'information et documentation sur le Mozambique et l'Afrique australe / see Alternatives – Action and Communication Network for International Development
♦ Centre d'information sur l'éducation bilingue et plurilingue (#11195)
♦ Centre d'information et d'études sur les migrations internationales (internationally oriented national body)
♦ Centre d'Information et de Formation en matière de Droits Humains en Afrique (internationally oriented national body)
♦ Centre d'information sur le G8 (internationally oriented national body)
♦ Centre d'information inter-peuples, Grenoble (internationally oriented national body)
♦ Centre d'information sur la migration en Amérique latine (#03643)
♦ Centre d'information muséologique UNESCO-ICOM (see: #13051)
♦ Centre d'information des organisations internationales catholiques / see International Catholic Centre of Geneva (#12449)
♦ Centre d'information textile – habillement (internationally oriented national body)
♦ Centre d'information Tiers-monde (internationally oriented national body)
♦ Centre d'initiation pour réfugiés et étrangers / see Coordination et initiatives pour réfugiés et étrangers
♦ Centre d'initiatives Asie-Pacifique (internationally oriented national body)
♦ Centre d'initiatives pour l'europe (internationally oriented national body)
♦ Centre pour l'innovation dans la gouvernance internationale (internationally oriented national body)
♦ Centre for Inquiry – Europe (internationally oriented national body)
♦ Centre of Integrated Geomorphology for the Mediterranean Area (internationally oriented national body)
♦ Centre for Integrated Regional Development Bwamanda-Belgium (internationally oriented national body)
♦ Centre on Integrated Rural Development for Africa (no recent information)

♦ Centre on Integrated Rural Development for Asia and the Pacific (CIRDAP) 03750

Centre de développement rural intégré pour l'Asie et le Pacifique (CDRIAP)

Dir Gen 17 Topkhana Road, GPO Box 2883, Dhaka 1000, Bangladesh. T. +88029558751. Fax +88029562035. E-mail: infocom@cirdap.org.
URL: http://cirdap.org/

History 6 Jul 1979. Foundecd by countries of Asia-Pacific Region at the initiative of *FAO (#09260)*, with support from other UN bodies and donors. New seat in Dhaka (Bangladesh) inaugurated 1 Jan 1985. Statutes registered in *'UNTS 1/17852'*. **Aims** Assist national action and promote regional cooperation relating to integrated rural development through a network of national institutions in Member States in Asia and the Pacific Region, particularly for improving production, income and living conditions of small scale *farmers* and other needy rural groups and encouraging their participation in social and economic life; act as servicing institution for Member States with respect to integrated rural development. **Structure** Governing Council (meets every 2 years); Executive Committee; Technical Committee; Director, assisted by Deputy Director; Divisions (5); Main office in Dhaka (Bangladesh); *'Sub-Regional Office in Southeast Asia (SOCSEA)'* set up 1997, Jakarta (Indonesia). **Languages** English. **Staff** Directorial and professional: 7; local professional: 8; general service staff: 43; temporary staff: 12. **Finance** Contributions from Member countries and donor countries and agencies. Biennial budget: about US$ 2,000,000. **Activities** Projects/programmes; research and development; training/education; knowledge management/information dissemination. **Events** *Workshop on participatory process in project design, implementation, monitoring and evaluation* Bangalore (India) 2000, *Workshop on participatory monitoring and evaluation* Myanmar 2000, *Regional seminar on planning method for integrated local community development* Comilla (Bangladesh) 1998, *Towards gender equity regional workshop* Dhaka (Bangladesh) 1998, *Regional workshop on sustainable development and disaster reduction* Comilla (Bangladesh) 1997. **Publications** *CIRDAP Development Digest (CDD)* (4 a year); *Asia-Pacific Journal of Rural Development* (2 a year). *CIRDAP Action Research Series*; *CIRDAP Study Series*; *CIRDAP Training Series*. *CIRDAP Documentation*. Annual Report; books; case studies; monographs; research reports; brochures.

Members Governments of 15 countries:
Afghanistan, Bangladesh, Fiji, India, Indonesia, Iran Islamic Rep, Laos, Malaysia, Myanmar, Nepal, Pakistan, Philippines, Sri Lanka, Thailand, Vietnam.

IGO Relations Partner of (1): *UNESCO (#20322)* (Regional Unit for Social and Human Sciences for the Asia-Pacific Region). **NGO Relations** Member of: *Transparency, Accountability and Participation Network (TAP Network, #20222)*. Associate member of: *International Initiative for Impact Evaluation (3ie, #13851)*. [2019.07.16/XE2355/**E***]

♦ Centre pour l'Intégration en Méditerranée (#03649)
♦ Centre interaméricain des administrateurs fiscaux / see Inter-American Centre for Tax Administrations (#11405)
♦ Centre interaméricain des administrations fiscales (#11405)
♦ Centre interaméricain pour le développement des archives (inactive)
♦ Centre interaméricain pour le développement intégral des ressources en eau et en terre / see Centro Interamericano de Desarrollo e Investigación Ambiental y Territorial
♦ Centre interaméricain pour le développement et la recherche environnementale et territoriale (internationally oriented national body)
♦ Centre interaméricain des études et des recherches pour la planification et l'éducation (no recent information)
♦ Centre interaméricain d'études de la sécurité sociale (#03803)
♦ Centre interaméricain de formation statistique (no recent information)
♦ Centre interaméricain de promotion des exportations (inactive)
♦ Centre intercontinental d'études de techniques biologiques (inactive)
♦ Centre for Intercultural Music Arts / see Centre for Intercultural Musicology at Churchill College
♦ Centre for Intercultural Musicology at Churchill College (internationally oriented national body)
♦ Centre interculturel rencontre / see Association Rencontre CEFIR
♦ Centre Interculturel Timisoara / see Intercultural Institute Timisoara
♦ Centre interdisciplinaire méditerranéen d'études et de recherches en sciences sociales (internationally oriented national body)
♦ Centre interdisciplinaire de recherche sur la paix et d'études stratégiques (internationally oriented national body)
♦ Centre for Interdisciplinary Research in Sciences and Humanities, Mexico (internationally oriented national body)
♦ Centre interfacultaire de phonétique appliquée / see Centre international de phonétique appliquée
♦ Centre for Intergroup Studies / see Centre for Conflict Resolution, Cape Town
♦ Centre Internacional Escarré per a les Minories Etniques i les Nacions (#05535)
♦ Centre Internacional d'Investigació dels Recursos Costaners (#12480)
♦ Centre international Abdus Salam de physique théorique (#00005)
♦ Centre for International Affairs, Barcelona / see Escuela Superior de Administración y Dirección de Empresas
♦ Centre international d'agriculture tropicale (#12527)
♦ Centre international d'amélioration du maïs et du blé (#14077)
♦ Centre international d'assistance médicale universelle (inactive)
♦ Centre international d'astrophysique, Rome / see International Center for Relativistic Astrophysics (#12474)
♦ Centre international pour l'avancement de la réadaptation à base communautaire (internationally oriented national body)
♦ Centre international bancaja pour la paix et le développement (internationally oriented national body)
♦ Centre for International Briefing / see Farnham Castle International Briefing and Conference Centre
♦ Centre for International Business Research (internationally oriented national body)
♦ Centre international de calcul (#12839)
♦ Centre international catholique de coopération (inactive)
♦ Centre for International Child Health / see UCL Institute for Global Health
♦ Centre for International Child Health (internationally oriented national body)
♦ Centre international chrétien de recherche, d'information et d'analyse de la bande dessinée (#12557)
♦ Centre international des civilisations Bantu (inactive)
♦ Centre for International Climate and Energy Research, Oslo / see Centre for International Climate and Environmental Research, Oslo
♦ Centre for International Climate and Environmental Research, Oslo (internationally oriented national body)
♦ Centre international de codicologie (internationally oriented national body)
♦ Centre international du commerce de gros intérieur et extérieur (inactive)
♦ Centre international de la common law en français, Moncton (internationally oriented national body)
♦ Centre of International Conflicts and Crises Studies (internationally oriented national body)
♦ Centre international pour la conservation du patrimoine (internationally oriented national body)
♦ Centre international de la construction en terre (#12485)
♦ Centre international de la construction en terre – Ecole nationale supérieure d'architecture de Grenoble / see International Centre for Earth Construction (#12485)
♦ Centre international contre la censure / see ARTICLE 19 (#01121)
♦ Centre for International Cooperation and Appropriate Technology (internationally oriented national body)
♦ Centre for International Cooperation and Computerization (internationally oriented national body)
♦ Centre for International Cooperation and Development (internationally oriented national body)
♦ Centre for International Cooperation in Health and Development (internationally oriented national body)
♦ Centre international pour la coopération sud-sud dans le domaine des sciences, de la technologie et de l'innovation, Kuala Lumpur / see International Science, Technology and Innovation Centre for South-South Cooperation under the auspices of UNESCO (#14799)
♦ Centre for International Courts and Tribunals (internationally oriented national body)

♦ Centre international pour le crédit communal (#12501)
♦ Centre international du crédit mutuel (internationally oriented national body)
♦ Centre international de criminologie comparée (#12482)
♦ Centre of International Cultural and Linguistic Exchanges in the Pacific (#03778)
♦ Centre international de culture populaire, Paris (internationally oriented national body)
♦ Centre international de cyto-cybernétique (inactive)
♦ Centre for International and Defence Policy, Kingston ON (internationally oriented national body)
♦ Centre international de déminage humanitaire – Genève (internationally oriented national body)
♦ Centre for International Development Issues, Nijmegen (internationally oriented national body)
♦ Centre for International Development Studies / see Norwegian Centre for International Cooperation in Higher Education
♦ Centre for International Development and Training (internationally oriented national body)
♦ Centre international Développement et Civilisations – Lebret-Irfed / see Centre international LEBRET-IRFED
♦ Centre international de développement des engrais / see International Fertilizer Development Center (#13590)
♦ Centre international pour le développement des politiques migratoires (#12503)
♦ Centre international de développement et de recherche (internationally oriented national body)
♦ Centre international du diaconat (#13167)
♦ Centre international de documentation arachnologique / see International Society of Arachnology (#14935)
♦ Centre international de documentation concernant les expressions plastiques (inactive)
♦ Centre international de documentation et d'échanges de la Francophonie / see Centre international de documentation et d'échanges de la Francophonie – L'Agora francophone internationale
♦ Centre international de documentation et d'échanges de la Francophonie – L'Agora francophone internationale (internationally oriented national body)
♦ Centre international de documentation économique et sociale africaine (inactive)
♦ Centre international de documentation et d'information / see International Young Catholic Students (#15926)

♦ Centre international de documentation Marguerite Yourcenar (Cidmy) 03751

Contact Rue des Minimes 46, 1000 Brussels, Belgium. T. +32473321580. E-mail: michelegoslar@gmail.com.
Contact Archives et Musée de la Littérature (AML), c/o Bibliothèque Royale 3e étage, Blvd de l'Empereur 4, 1000 Brussels, Belgium. T. +32473177585. E-mail: cidmy@skynet.be – marc-etienne@aml.cfwb.be.
URL: http://www.cidmy.be/

History Sep 1989, Brussels (Belgium). Registration: ASBL/VZW, Belgium. **Aims** Collect and disseminate documentation and information on the work of Marguerite Yourcenar; collect her work and bibliography, as well as all works that she could inspire or influence and those which inspired her. **Structure** Management Board, consisting of President, 3 Vice-Presidents, Administrative Delegate, Treasurer and 5 members. Honorary Committee, comprising 4 individual members and 5 bodies. **Languages** French. **Staff** 2.00 FTE, paid. **Finance** Members' dues: Full and Associate – euro 25 in Belgium, euro 30 outside of Belgium. Other sources: subsidies from Belgian governmental regional (francophone) bodies. **Activities** Maintains a library and a videothèque. Assistance to research work. Guided tours (Belgium, France); travels (USA). Colloquia; conferences; lectures; exhibitions. **Events** *Anniversary meeting* Brussels (Belgium) 1999, *Inauguration du passage Marguerite Yourcenar, lieu de passage et de réflexion, citations de "l'Oeuvre au Noir" taillées dans la pierre* Brussels (Belgium) 1998, *Réunion scientifique* Brussels (Belgium) 1997, *Colloque international* Mendoza (Argentina) 1994, *Marguerite Yourcenar et le sacré* Brussels (Belgium) 1992. **Publications** *Cidmy Bulletin* (annual).
Members Individuals in 28 countries and territories:
Argentina, Austria, Belgium, Brazil, Canada, Colombia, Czechia, Finland, France, Germany, Greece, Hungary, Ireland, Italy, Japan, Luxembourg, Netherlands, New Caledonia, Norway, Portugal, Romania, South Africa, Spain, Switzerland, Thailand, Tunisia, UK, USA.
NGO Relations Links with national associations and foundations. [2020/XE1477/v/E]

♦ Centre for International Documentation on Organized and Economic Crime, Cambridge (internationally oriented national body)
♦ Centre international de droit comparé de l'environnement (#12483)
♦ Centre international des droits et des libertés syndicales / see International Centre for Trade Union Rights (#12525)
♦ Centre international pour les droits syndicaux (#12525)
♦ Centre international de l'eau et de l'assainissement / see IRC (#16016)
♦ Centre international d'écologie tropicale (#03805)
♦ Centre for International Economics, Canberra (internationally oriented national body)
♦ Centre for International Economic Studies, Adelaide (internationally oriented national body)
♦ Centre international pour l'éducation et le développement humain (internationally oriented national body)

♦ Centre international pour l'éducation des filles et des femmes en Afrique de l'Union Africaine (UA/CIEFFA) 03752

African Union International Centre for Girls' and Women's Education in Africa (AU/CIEFFA)
Coordinator 01 BP, Ouagadougou 01, Burkina Faso. T. +22650376496. Fax +22650376498. E-mail: au-cieffa@africa-union.org.
URL: http://cieffa.org/

History A specialized institution of *African Union (AU, #00488)*, since 3rd Ordinary Session of the Conference of Heads of States and Governments, Jul 2004, Addis Ababa (Ethiopia), by Decision Assembly AU/DEC 44 (III). Since Oct 2005, a Category 2 Institute under the auspices of *UNESCO (#20322)* (33 C/Resolution 20). **Aims** Build an integrated, prosperous and peaceful Africa by ensuring that all girls and women have the required competencies to respond to life challenges; sustain Africa's sustainable development. Promote girls' and women's education and training in Africa. **Structure** Coordinator. Working groups (9). Secretariat. **Languages** English, French. **Staff** 12; support staff. **Finance** Funding from *African Union (AU, #00488)*; support from government of Burkina Faso. **Publications** *AU/CIEFFA News Bulletin*. Guides; studies; colloquia proceedings.
Members Member states of African Union and UNESCO, not specified. [2018/XJ0959/E*]

♦ Centre international d'éducation ouvrière (inactive)
♦ Centre international des engrais chimiques / see Centre international scientifique des fertilisants (#03767)
♦ Centre international des engrais chimiques et produits chimiques utiles à l'agriculture / see Centre international scientifique des fertilisants (#03767)
♦ Centre international d'enregistrement des publications en série / see ISSN International Centre (#16069)
♦ Centre international pour l'entreprise privée (internationally oriented national body)
♦ Centre international pour les entreprises publiques / see International Centre for Promotion of Enterprises (#12509)
♦ Centre international pour les entreprises publiques dans les pays en développement / see International Centre for Promotion of Enterprises (#12509)
♦ Centre international d'épistémologie génétique (inactive)
♦ Centre internationale de promotion artistique / see Sail For Ethics
♦ Centre international d'étiquetage (inactive)
♦ Centre international d'étude et de documentation – Institut Paul VI (internationally oriented national body)
♦ Centre international d'étude de langues de Strasbourg / see CIEL de Strasbourg
♦ Centre international d'étude des producteurs de tantale / see Tantalum-Niobium International Study Center (#20095)
♦ Centre international d'études sur l'antisémitisme / see Vidal Sassoon International Center for the Study of Antisemitism
♦ Centre international d'études pour la conservation et la restauration des biens culturels (#12521)
♦ Centre international d'études pour le développement local (internationally oriented national body)
♦ Centre international d'études sur la famille (#12492)
♦ Centre international d'études et de formation de l'IPA (#12877)
♦ Centre international d'études de la formation religieuse (#12519)
♦ Centre international d'études des langues, Le Relecq-Kerhuon (internationally oriented national body)
♦ Centre International d'Etudes sur le Linceul de Turin (unconfirmed)
♦ Centre international d'études monétaires et bancaires (#12506)
♦ Centre international d'études pédagogiques, Sèvres (internationally oriented national body)
♦ Centre international d'étude du sport (internationally oriented national body)
♦ Centre international d'études sur le projet urbain (#12520)
♦ Centre international d'études, de recherche et d'action pour le développement / see Centre international d'études, de recherche, d'action pour le développement et prévention des conflicts (#03753)

♦ Centre international d'études, de recherche, d'action pour le développement et prévention des conflicts (CINTERAD-PRECO) 03753

Contact Holleveldweg 52, 1500 Halle, Belgium. T. +3223610072.
Contact Rue Franklin 126A, 1040 Etterbeek, Belgium. T. +32476228921.

History 1981, as *Centre international d'études, de recherche et d'action pour le développement (CINTERAD)*. Registered in accordance with Belgian law. **Aims** Promote the development and *self-development* of the countries of *South* and *North*. **Structure** General Assembly (annual). Board of Management, consisting of President, Vice-President, Secretary and Treasurer. **Finance** Members' dues. Income generated by activities. **Activities** Develops the *Programme international d'information sur le développement*. **Events** *Conference / Meeting* Kinshasa (Congo DR) 2004, *Conference / Meeting* Belgium 2002, *Conference / Meeting* Bamako (Mali) 1999, *Environment and rural development* 1997, *Séminaire / Meeting* Abidjan (Côte d'Ivoire) 1996.
Members Collective (14) in 13 countries:
Belgium, Benin, Burkina Faso, Cameroon, Congo DR, Côte d'Ivoire, France, Mali, Netherlands, Niger, Senegal, Togo, Trinidad-Tobago.
Individuals in 3 countries:
Congo Brazzaville, Germany, Mauritius. [2019/XE0590/F]

♦ Centre international d'études sur le Saint Suaire (#12516)
♦ Centre international d'études supérieures de communication pour l'Amérique latine (#03806)
♦ Centre international d'études sur le transfert de chaleur et de masse (#12496)
♦ Centre international d'étude de tantale et niobium (#20095)
♦ Centre of International and European Economic Law, Thessaloniki (internationally oriented national body)
♦ Centre international du film pour l'enfance et la jeunesse (#12493)
♦ Centre international du film médical et chirurgical (inactive)
♦ Centre international flamand / see KIYO

♦ Centre international pour la formation et les échanges en géosciences (CIFEG) 03754

International Centre for Training and Exchanges in the Geosciences
Contact address not obtained. T. +33238643367. Fax +33238643072.

History 1981, Paris (France). Founded following a call to set up such a centre voiced at 26th International Geological Congress, 1980, Paris. Follows the work of the (France) *Centre d'Etudes Géologiques et Minières (CEGM)*, which had been founded in 1931. Registration: France. **Aims** Develop training and exchanges between geoscientists from all countries, in particular for the benefit of *developing countries*; cooperate with public or private, national and international organizations interested in *earth sciences*, as well as with companies and associations interested in *international cooperation* in the field of *geology*. **Structure** Administrative Council of not more than 14 members. Board, composed of Chairman, Vice-Chairman, Treasurer and Secretary. Director. **Languages** English, French. **Staff** 2.00 FTE, paid. Varying number of voluntary staff. **Finance** French ministries; international organizations. Budget (annual): about euro 325,000. **Activities** Basic CIFEG activities: geoscientific and technical information; scientific exchanges; training. Themes of sustainable development priorities (3): mineral resources; environmental geology; underground water. Projects concerning Africa. **Events** *International symposium in hydrogeology* Djibouti (Djibouti) 2008, *Asia-Pacific conference on computers applied to the mineral industry* Manila (Philippines) 1990, *Seminar on geology and mineral resources of Africa* Nancy (France) 1990. **Publications** *Pangea* (2 a year) in English, French. Occasional publications.
Members Associate membership for individuals and organizations in 46 countries:
Algeria, Angola, Belgium, Benin, Botswana, Burkina Faso, Burundi, Cambodia, Cameroon, Chad, China, Congo DR, Djibouti, Eswatini, Ethiopia, France, Gabon, Ghana, Guinea, Indonesia, Japan, Kenya, Korea Rep, Laos, Lesotho, Madagascar, Malawi, Malaysia, Mali, Mauritania, Morocco, Mozambique, Niger, Papua New Guinea, Philippines, Rwanda, Senegal, Sierra Leone, Tanzania UR, Thailand, Togo, Tunisia, Uganda, Vietnam, Zambia, Zimbabwe.
NGO Relations Affiliated member of: *International Union of Geological Sciences (IUGS, #15777)*. Set up: *Pan African Network for a Geological Information System (PANGIS, no recent information)*; *Southeast Asian Network for a Geological Information System (SANGIS, #19778)*. [2011.09.30/XE3988/E]

♦ Centre international de formation à l'enseignement des droits de l'homme et de la paix, Genève (see: #21184)

♦ Centre international de formation européenne (CIFE) 03755

Dir Gen 81 rue de France, 06000 Nice, France. T. +33493979397. Fax +33493979398. E-mail: cife@cife.eu.
URL: http://www.cife.eu/

History Nov 1954, Nice (France), to organize courses and seminars on matters related to European unity. **Aims** Offer graduate programmes concerning European integration, international relations, energy transition, global governance and federalism. **Structure** Federal Council; Board of Trustees. Departments include: Institut européen (IE) – European Institute (EI). **Languages** English, French, German. **Staff** 25.00 FTE, paid. **Finance** Financed by: registration fees; funding from the European Union and from international organizations; subventions and grants from governments and local or regional collectivities; contributions from foundations and associations. Annual budget: euro 3,000,000. **Activities** Training/education; publishing activities. **Events** *International seminar on citizen's Europe* Berlin (Germany) 1997, *International seminar on European training of teachers* Esneux (Belgium) 1997, *International seminar on European agriculture of the third millennium* Grainau (Germany) 1997, *International seminar on European citizenship at school* Klingenthal (France) 1997, *International seminar on the Euro and the Economic and Monetary Union* Marly-le-Roi (France) 1997. **Publications** *L'Europe en formation* (4 a year). Books; brochures; documents; leaflets; reports.
Members Individuals in 21 countries:
Austria, Belgium, Bulgaria, Canada, Cyprus, Denmark, France, Germany, Hungary, Ireland, Italy, Luxembourg, Moldova, Netherlands, Poland, Romania, Russia, Spain, Switzerland, Tunisia, UK.
NGO Relations Member of: *European Movement International (EMI, #07825)*; *European Network for Education and Training (EUNET, #07899)*; *International Association of Centers for Federal Studies (IACFS, #11761)*. Supports: *European Alliance for the Statute of the European Association (EASEA, #05886)*. Cooperates with: *Association of European Journalists (AEJ, #02516)*; *Association européenne des enseignants (AEDE, #02565)*; *European Academy Berlin*; *Federal Trust for Education and Research*; *Institut für Europäische Politik, Berlin (IEP)*; national organizations and universities; *Observatoire stratégique méditerranéen (no recent information)*; *Trans European Policy Studies Association (TEPSA, #20209)*; *Union of European Federalists, The (UEF, #20385)*; *Universitatea Libera Internationala din Moldova (ULIM)*; *Young European Federalists (#21984)*. [2020/XF0879/v/E]

♦ Centre international de formation de l'OIT (#15717)
♦ Centre international de formation et de recherche sur l'érosion et la sédimentation (#14745)
♦ Centre international de formation et de recherche en sexualité (internationally oriented national body)

- ♦ Centre international de formation sur les statistiques vitales et les statistiques de la santé de l'Asie du Sud-Est (inactive)
- ♦ Centre international de génie génétique et de biotechnologie (#12494)
- ♦ Centre international de gérontologie sociale (inactive)
- ♦ Centre international de gestion des resources aquatiques biologiques / see WorldFish (#21507)
- ♦ Centre for International Governance Innovation (internationally oriented national body)
- ♦ Centre international de la harpe (internationally oriented national body)
- ♦ Centre International de Hautes Etudes Agronomiques Méditerraéennes – Institut Agronomique Méditerranéen de Montpellier / see Mediterranean Agronomic Institute of Montpellier (#16643)
- ♦ Centre international de hautes études agronomiques méditerranéennes (#03927)
- ♦ Centre for International Health, Bergen (internationally oriented national body)
- ♦ Centre for International Health and Development / see UCL Institute for Global Health
- ♦ Centre for International Health Studies / see Institute for Global Health and Development, Edinburgh
- ♦ Centre for International Heritage Activities (internationally oriented national body)
- ♦ Centre for International ICT Policies West and Central Africa (internationally oriented national body)
- ♦ Centre for International Information and Documentation, Barcelona (internationally oriented national body)
- ♦ Centre international d'information sur le gaz naturel et tous hydrocarbures gazeux (#13845)
- ♦ Centre international d'information de la mutualité / see Association internationale de la mutualité (#02721)
- ♦ Centre international pour l'information scientifique et technique (#12514)
- ♦ Centre international d'informations pour le crédit communal / see International Centre for Local Credit (#12501)
- ♦ Centre international d'information des secours par téléphone / see International Federation of Telephone Emergency Services (#13567)
- ♦ Centre international d'information sur les sources de l'histoire balkanique et méditerranéenne / see International Information Centre for Balkan Studies (#13844)
- ♦ Centre international d'information pour la terminologie (#13846)
- ♦ Centre international d'information sur le tsunami (#15740)
- ♦ Centre for International Intellectual Property Studies (internationally oriented national body)
- ♦ Centre International d'Investissement (internationally oriented national body)
- ♦ Centre international d'investissement (internationally oriented national body)
- ♦ Centre international de l'ISSN (#16069)
- ♦ Centre international des jeunes San Lorenzo (internationally oriented national body)
- ♦ Centre international de la jeunesse pour le développement, Bruxelles (internationally oriented national body)
- ♦ Centre international Kofi Annan pour la formation et maintien de la paix (internationally oriented national body)
- ♦ Centre international de langue et civilisation, Saint-Etienne (internationally oriented national body)
- ♦ Centre for International Law, Brussels (internationally oriented national body)

♦ Centre for International Law Research and Policy (CILRAP) 03756

Dir Av des Saisons 100, 1050 Brussels, Belgium. E-mail: info@cilrap.org.
CILRAP Bottega Via San Gallo 135r, 50129 Florence FI, Italy. T. +393474821600.
URL: http://www.cilrap.org/

History 2010. Registration: Banque-Carrefour des Entreprises, No/ID: 0827.424.153, Start date: 2010, Belgium, Brussels. **Aims** Contribute to knowledge generation and dissemination in international law, and to practitioners and policy makers in international law. **Structure** Departments: Case Matrix Network (CMN); *Forum for International Criminal and Humanitarian Law (FICHL, #09921)*; Torkel Opsahl Academic EPublisher (TOAEP). **Languages** Arabic, Chinese, English. **Staff** 20.00 FTE, paid; 50.00 FTE, voluntary. **Activities** Awards/prizes/competitions; events/meetings; research/documentation. **Events** *Religion, Hateful Expression and Violence* Florence (Italy) 2022, *International Conference on Integrity in International Justice* The Hague (Netherlands) 2018. **Publications** *CILRAP Conversations on World Order*; *CILRAP FILM*; *CILRAP Podcast*. Brochure; online symposia. **Members** Individuals. Membership countries not specified.

[2022.07.02/XJ9753/v/**C**]

- ♦ Centre international LEBRET-IRFED (internationally oriented national body)
- ♦ Centre international de liaison des écoles de cinéma et de télévision (#11771)
- ♦ Centre international de liaison des instituts et associations d'études africaines (inactive)
- ♦ Centre international du loup (internationally oriented national body)

♦ Centre international de lutte contre la pollution de l'Atlantique du Nord-Est (CILPAN) 03757

International Action Centre for Pollution Incidents Response in the North-East Atlantic – Centro Internacional de Luta contra a Poluição do Atlântico do Nordeste (CILPAN)

Coordinator Rua Alfredo Magalhães Ramalho No 6, 1495-006 Lisbon, Portugal. T. +351218291000. E-mail: cilpan@dgpm.mam.gov.pt.
URL: http://www.dgpm.mam.gov.pt/Pages/CILPAN.aspx

History 1990, Lisbon (Portugal), to enable parties of *Cooperation Agreement for the Protection of North-East Atlantic Coasts and Waters Against Pollution (Lisbon Agreement, 1990)* to act rapidly and efficiently to pollution incidents. **Aims** Deal with accidental pollution, from *oil* and other harmful substances, caused by *ships* as well as fixed *floating platforms* on North-East Atlantic coasts. **Languages** Arabic, English, French, Portuguese. **Events** *Workshop* Lisbon (Portugal) 2000, *The regime of compensation under the 1992 Civil Liability Convention and the 1992 Fund Convention, its importance for Portugal* Lisbon (Portugal) 1999. **Publications** *CILPAN Information* (4 a year) in French, Portuguese. *Dicionario Técnico de Poluição Maritima*; *Manual de Operações para Navios Tanques e Terminais*; *Manual Sobre Poluição Maritima por Hidrocarbonetos*. Guides; handbooks.
Members Governments of 4 countries signatory to the Agreement:
France, Morocco, Portugal, Spain.
Regional integration EU entity:
European Union (EU, #08967).

[2016.12.14/XE2099/**E***]

- ♦ Centre international des marées terrestres (#12486)
- ♦ Centre international mathématique pour le relèvement de la qualification des cadres scientifiques 'Stefan Banach' (#19981)

♦ Centre international de mathématiques pures et appliquées (CIMPA) 03758

International Centre for Pure and Applied Mathematics

Exec Dir 28 avenue Valrose, Campus Valrose, Bâtiment Dieudonné II, 06108 Nice CEDEX 02, France. E-mail: director@cimpa.info – cimpa@unice.fr – hela@cimpa.info.
URL: http://www.cimpa-icpam.org/

History Founded Oct 1978, Nice (France), following recommendations of UNESCO General Conferences: 1974, Paris (France); 1976, Nairobi (Kenya). Registered in accordance with French law. **Aims** Promote mathematics teaching and research in *developing countries*; contribute to high level training of mathematicians from developing countries; assist these countries in gaining access to mathematical documentation; improve cooperation among mathematicians both between developing and developed countries (North-South dialogue) and among developing countries (South-South dialogue). **Structure** International Executive Council; International Scientific Council; Development and Exchanges Commission; *African Mathematical Union (AMU, #00370)*; *Southeast Asian Mathematical Society (SEAMS, #19773)*; Société Mathématique de France. **Languages** English, French. **Staff** 1.50 FTE, paid; 2.00 FTE, voluntary. 1.5 FTE, paid; 2 FTE, voluntary. **Finance** Budget (annual): euro 510,000. **Activities** Training/education; events/meetings. **Events** *Workshop on geometry and topology of singularities* Cuernavaca (Mexico) 2007, *CARI : African conference on research in computer science* Cotonou (Benin) 2006, *CARI : African conference on research in computer science* Hammamet (Tunisia) 2004, *CARI : African conference on research in computer science* Yaoundé (Cameroon) 2002, *CARI : African conference on research in computer science* Antananarivo (Madagascar) 2000. **Publications** *Annuaire mathématique du Tiers monde* (annual); *Mathématiques et développement* (periodical). *Les cours du CIMPA* – series; *Travaux en cours* – series. Bibliographies.

Members Full in 10 countries:
Chile, China, Côte d'Ivoire, Egypt, France, India, Morocco, Senegal, Tunisia, Vietnam.

[2018/XE0093/**E**]

- ♦ Centre international pour les micro-alges alimentaires contre la malnutrition (internationally oriented national body)
- ♦ Centre for International Migration and Development (internationally oriented national body)
- ♦ Centre International pour la Migration, la Santé, et le Développement (#12502)
- ♦ Centre international de mise en valeur intégrée des montagnes (#12500)
- ♦ Centre for International Mobility (internationally oriented national body)
- ♦ Centre international du mouvement espérantiste neutre (inactive)
- ♦ Centre for International Music Arts / see Centre for Intercultural Musicology at Churchill College
- ♦ Centre international de la musique / see IMZ International Music + Media Centre (#11139)
- ♦ Centre international pour la musique chorale (internationally oriented national body)

♦ Centre international de myriapodologie (CIM) 03759

International Society for Myriapodology

Address not obtained.
URL: https://myriapodology.org/

History 1968, Paris (France). Formally constituted as an international society since 1999. Constitution adopted in 2002, at 12th ICM, Mtuzini (South Africa). **Aims** Provide rapid information on current work and publications on *Myriapoda* and *Onychophora* for myriapodologists and other interested biologists, from study of macromolecules to that of ecosystems and landscape ecology. **Structure** General Assembly (every 2 years, at Congress); International Committee; Executive Committee; Secretariat. **Languages** English, French. **Staff** 3.00 FTE, voluntary. **Finance** Sources: members' dues. **Activities** Events/meetings; projects/programmes. **Events** *International Congress of Myriapodology* Montenegro (Colombia) 2023, *International Congress of Myriapodology* Montenegro (Colombia) 2022, *Triennial Congress* Montenegro (Colombia) 2021, *International Congress of Myriapodology* Budapest (Hungary) 2019, *International Congress of Myriapodology* Krabi (Thailand) 2017. **Publications** *CIM Newsletter*. *Acta Myriapodologica*. Monographs; papers; studies; congress proceedings. Information Services: Library of myriapodology, including books, reprints, papers and research work contributed by members.
Members Active (159); Moral (8); Honorary (11). Myriapodologists and other interested biologists in 61 countries and territories:
Albania, Algeria, Argentina, Australia, Austria, Belarus, Belgium, Bolivia, Bosnia-Herzegovina, Botswana, Brazil, Bulgaria, Cameroon, Canada, China, Costa Rica, Côte d'Ivoire, Croatia, Cuba, Czechia, Denmark, Egypt, Finland, France, Georgia, Germany, Greece, Hungary, India, Ireland, Israel, Italy, Japan, Korea Rep, Luxembourg, Mexico, Morocco, Netherlands, New Zealand, Norway, Pakistan, Poland, Puerto Rico, Romania, Russia, Senegal, Serbia, Slovakia, Slovenia, South Africa, Spain, Sweden, Switzerland, Taiwan, Tunisia, Türkiye, UK, Ukraine, USA, Vietnam, Zimbabwe.
NGO Relations *International Society of Biospeleology (#14975).*

[2020.01.15/XF3387/v/**C**]

- ♦ Centre for International Negotiation / see Centre for Negotiation and Dispute Resolution
- ♦ Centre international ondes courtes de Moyabi (no recent information)
- ♦ Centre International d'Ostéopathie (internationally oriented national body)
- ♦ Centre for International Patent Rights / see Centre d'études internationales de la propriété intellectuelle
- ♦ Centre international de perfectionnement professionnel et technique / see International Training Centre of the ILO (#15717)
- ♦ Centre international de phonétique appliquée (internationally oriented national body)
- ♦ Centre international sur la physiologie et l'écologie des insectes (#12499)
- ♦ Centre international Pierre Monestier (internationally oriented national body)
- ♦ Centre for International Politics, Organization and Disarmament, Delhi (internationally oriented national body)
- ♦ Centre for International Politics, Thessaloniki (internationally oriented national body)
- ♦ Centre international sur la pollution de l'eau et la gestion de ce risque (internationally oriented national body)
- ♦ Centre international de la pomme de terre (#14627)
- ♦ Centre international pour la presse étrangère (internationally oriented national body)
- ♦ Centre international pour la prévention de la criminalité (#12508)
- ♦ Centre international pour la promotion des droits de l'homme aux niveaux local et régional / see European Training- and Research Centre for Human Rights and Democracy
- ♦ Centre international de promotion pour les entreprises (#12509)
- ♦ Centre international de promotion de la qualité (inactive)
- ♦ Centre for International and Public Law, Canberra (internationally oriented national body)
- ♦ Centre for International Public Policy and Administration (internationally oriented national body)
- ♦ Centre international sur les Qanats et les ouvrages historiques hydrauliques, Yazd (#12473)
- ♦ Centre international de radiodiffusion rurale (inactive)
- ♦ Centre international de rayonnement synchrotron pour les sciences expérimentales et appliquées au Moyen-Orient (#20078)
- ♦ Centre international pour la recherche agricole orientée vers le développement (internationally oriented national body)
- ♦ Centre international pour la recherche en agroforesterie – / see World Agroforestry Centre (#21072)
- ♦ Centre International de Recherche et d'Aide à la Décision de la Fédération Internationale des Universités Catholiques (#12476)
- ♦ Centre international de recherche et d'application pour la construction en terre / see International Centre for Earth Construction (#12485)
- ♦ Centre international de Recherche sur le Cancer (#11598)
- ♦ Centre international de recherche et développement en agriculture naturelle / see International Nature Farming Research Center

♦ Centre international de recherche-développement sur l'élevage en zone subhumide (CIRDES) 03760

Contact 01 BP 454, Bobo Dioulasso 01, Burkina Faso. T. +22620972053. Fax +22620972320. E-mail: dgcirdes@fasonet.bf.
URL: http://www.cirdes.org/

History Founded 1972. **Aims** Organize research and development activities to improve the health of domestic animals and to increase their productivity in order to meet increasing needs of the populations and to improve their revenues with respect for ecological balance. **Structure** Council of Ministers; Executive Committee; Scientific Council. **Languages** French. **Staff** 100.00 FTE, paid. **Finance** Members' dues. Other sources: donations; expertise; support from regional and international organizations; foundations. Annual budget: CFA Fr 900 million. **Activities** Research/documentation; training/education; guidance/assistance/consulting; events/meetings; knowledge management/information dissemination. **Events** *Seminar on sustainable crop livestock production for improved livelihoods and natural resources management in West Africa* Nigeria 2001. **Publications** Annual report; technical reports; publications in international scientific journals.
Members Full in 8 countries:
Benin, Burkina Faso, Côte d'Ivoire, Guinea, Guinea-Bissau, Mali, Niger, Togo.
Associate members in 2 countries:
France, Ghana.
IGO Relations Member of: *African and Malagasy Council for Higher Education (#00364). Inter-State School of Veterinary Sciences and Medicine (#15982).*

[2021/XE3647/**E**]

♦ Centre International de Recherche et de Documentation sur les Traditions et les Langues Africaines (CERDOTOLA) 03761

Exec Sec BP 479, Yaoundé, Cameroon. T. +23722207040 – +23722303188. Fax +23722303189. E-mail: contact@cerdotola.org.
URL: http://www.cerdotola.org/

Centre international recherche
03761

alphabetic sequence excludes
For the complete listing, see Yearbook Online at

History 25 Aug 1977, Yaoundé (Cameroon). Former names and other names: *Centre régional de recherche et de documentation sur les traditions orales et pour le développement des langues africaines* – former (1977 to 2010); *Centre for Research and Documentation on Oral Traditions and African Languages* – alias. **Aims** Preserve and diffuse African cultural heritage. **Structure** Board of Directors; Executive Secretary; National Offices. **Languages** English, French. **Staff** 50.00 FTE, paid. **Finance** Sources: contributions of member/participating states. Annual budget: 3,000,000 USD. **Activities** Events/meetings; knowledge management/information dissemination; research/documentation. **Events** *International Conference* Yaoundé (Cameroon) 2022, *Forum Africain de la Musique* Segou (Mali) 2016, *Colloque International sur l'Afrique à la Quête d'un Développement Culturellement Soutenable* Yaoundé (Cameroon) 2015, *Colloque International* Brazzaville (Congo Brazzaville) 2014, *Symposium International sur l'Industrie Musicale Africaine face aux exigences du marché international* Yaoundé (Cameroon) 2012. **Publications** Linguistic atlases and maps; thematic lexicons; children's books; meeting proceedings; reports.
Members Full members in 11 countries:
Angola, Burundi, Cameroon, Central African Rep, Chad, Congo Brazzaville, Congo DR, Equatorial Guinea, Gabon, Rwanda, Sao Tomé-Príncipe. [2022/XE6562/**E***]

- Centre international de recherche sur l'environnement et le développement (internationally oriented national body)
- Centre international pour la recherche forestière / see Center for International Forestry Research (#03646)
- Centre International de Recherche en Infectiologie (internationally oriented national body)
- Centre international de recherches agricoles dans les régions sèches (#12466)
- Centre international de recherches sur l'anarchisme (internationally oriented national body)

♦ Centre international de recherches, d'échanges et de coopération de la Caraïbe et des Amériques (CIRECCA) 03762

Contact address not obtained. T. +596734519. Fax +596605104. E-mail: cireccamartinique@gmail.com.
History 1981, Fort de France (Martinique), under the auspices of *Association des universités partiellement ou entièrement de langue française (AUPELF, inactive)*. Statutes modified: 17-18 May 1984; 31 Oct 1984; 29 Jan 1985; 26 Jan 1988; 27 Jan 1988; 12 Mar 1997. Registered in accordance with French law. **Aims** Promote, by means of the *French language*, the development of international relations and of international exchanges in the Caribbean in the Americas. **Structure** General Assembly (annual ordinary meeting; every 3 years the session takes place in the framework of a Congress). Administrative Board, consisting of 12 members; Bureau of the Administrative Board, consisting of President, Vice-President, Treasurer and 2 other members. International Sponsorship Committee. Secretariat, headed by Director General. **Finance** Members' dues. Other sources: governmental subsidies; subsidies from national and international public and private bodies; donations; grants and bequests. **Activities** Inter-Caribbean and inter-American cooperation. Exchanges of students, professors and researchers. Courses organized together with AUPELF. **Events** *General Assembly* Fort de France (Martinique) 1997, *Colloquium* Marie Galante Is (Guadeloupe) 1993, *General Assembly* Guadeloupe 1991, *General Assembly* Fort de France (Martinique) 1989.
Members Organizations and individuals in 13 countries and territories:
Barbados, Canada, Dominican Rep, Guadeloupe, Guyana, Haiti, Jamaica, Martinique, Neth Antilles, Puerto Rico, St Lucia, Trinidad-Tobago, USA. [2014/XE4016/**E**]

- Centre international de recherches pour l'énergie et le développement économique (internationally oriented national body)
- Centre international de recherches et études transdisciplinaires (#12526)

♦ Centre international de recherches glyptographiques (CIRG) 03763

Internationales Zentrum für Glyptographische Forschungen – Internationaal Centrum voor Onderzoek van Steenmerken
Contact Rue Mathias 13, 1440 Braine-le-Château, Belgium. T. +3223660529. Fax +3223660529. E-mail: cirg@skynet.be.
URL: http://www.cirg.be/
History 6 Apr 1981, when registered in accordance with Belgian law. Referred to in English as *International Center for Glyptics Research*. **Aims** Study stone marks; develop a method of *classification* and a data bank at the disposal of historians, ethnologists, *epigraphists* and *archaeologists*. **Events** *Colloquium* Colmar (France) 2014, *Autour de l'architecture gothique méditerranéenne* Valencia (Spain) 2012, *Colloquium* Krakow (Poland) 2010, *Colloquium* Münsterschwarzach (Germany) 2008, *Colloquium* Córdoba (Spain) 2006. **Publications** *Dictionnaire des signes d'Espagne* (2012); *Dictionnaire des signes de France* (2005). Books; symposia proceedings.
Members Individuals in 15 countries:
Argentina, Australia, Belgium, France, Germany, Greece, Guatemala, Hungary, Ireland, Italy, Netherlands, Spain, Switzerland, UK, USA. [2014.06.24/XE6697/v/**E**]

- Centre international de recherches et d'information sur l'économie collective / see Centre international de recherches et d'information sur l'économie publique, sociale et coopérative (#03764)

♦ Centre international de recherches et d'information sur l'économie publique, sociale et coopérative (CIRIEC) 03764

International Centre of Research and Information on the Public, Social and Cooperative Economy – Internationales Forschungs- und Informationszentrum für Öffentliche Wirtschaft, Sozialwirtschaft und Genossenschaftswesen
Dir c/o HEC-Université de Liège, Rue Saint-Gilles 199, Bât. N3a, 4000 Liège, Belgium. T. +3243662746. Fax +3243662958. E-mail: ciriec@uliege.be.
Pres address not obtained.
URL: http://www.ciriec.uliege.be/
History 12 Feb 1947, Geneva (Switzerland). Founded following efforts of Prof Edgard Milhaud and Swiss national organization. The publication *'Annals of Public and Cooperative Economics'* existed from 1908-1924 as *'Annales de la régie directe'* and from 1925-1974 as *'Annals of Collective Economy'*. Former names and other names: *International Centre of Research and Information on Collective Economy* – former; *Centre international de recherches et d'information sur l'économie collective* – former; *Internationales Forschungs- und Informationszentrum für Öffentliche Wirtschaft und Gemeinwirtschaft (IFIG)* – former; *Annals of Public and Cooperative Economics* – former. Registration: Start date: 27 Jul 1961, Belgium; Start date: 26 Sep 1974, Belgium; Start date: 3 Aug 1995, Belgium; Start date: 26 Apr 2006, Belgium. **Aims** Undertake and promote collection of information, scientific research and publication of works on economic sectors and activities oriented towards service of general and collective interest. **Structure** General Assembly (every 2 years); Board of Directors; International Board; Praesidium; International Scientific Council; International Scientific Commissions (2); International Secretariat, located in Liège (Belgium). **Languages** English, French, German. **Staff** 9.00 FTE, paid. **Finance** Sources: grants; members' dues. **Activities** Events/meetings; research/documentation. **Events** *Biennial Congress and General Assembly* Costa Rica 2024, *International Research Conference on Social Economy* Seoul (Korea Rep) 2023, *Biennial Congress and General Assembly* Valencia (Spain) 2022, *International Research Conference on Social Economy* San José (Costa Rica) 2021, *Biennial General Assembly* Paris (France) 2020. **Publications** *Annals of Public and Cooperative Economics/Les Annales de l'Economie publique, sociale et cooperative* (4 a year). *CIRIEC Studies Series*; *Social Economy and Public Economy*. Books; working papers. **Information Services** *CIRIEC Documentation Centre*.
Members Collective: agencies, enterprises and organizations forming part of the public, cooperative and not-for-profit sectors of the economy; institutions with an interest of a scientific or cultural nature in these problems. Individual membership. National sections in 14 countries:
Argentina, Austria, Belgium, Canada, Colombia, Costa Rica, France, Japan, Mexico, Portugal, Spain, Tunisia, Türkiye, Venezuela.
Associate members in 11 countries:
Brazil, Chile, Cyprus, Ecuador, Germany, Greece, Ireland, Korea Rep, Poland, Romania, Sweden.
Observer members:
European Federation of Local Energy Companies (CEDEC, #07156).
Consultative Status Consultative status granted from: *ILO (#11123)* (Special List). **IGO Relations** Observer status with (1): UK Inter-Agency Task Force on Social and Solidarity Economy (TFSSE).. Works with: *European Commission (EC, #06633)* on various aspects of public, social and cooperative economy; *European Parliament (EP, #08146)*. [2022.11.09/XD1466/**D**]

- Centre international de recherches médicales de Franceville (internationally oriented national body)
- Centre international de recherche sur l'unité humaine (internationally oriented national body)
- Centre for International Reconciliation, Coventry / see International Centre for Reconciliation, Coventry
- Centre international de référence pour l'approvisionnement collectif en eau et l'assainissement / see IRC (#16016)
- Centre international de référence pour l'approvisionnement en eau collective et l'assainissement / see IRC (#16016)
- Centre international de référence Chantal Biya, Yaoundé (unconfirmed)
- Centre international de référence et d'information pédologique / see ISRIC – World Soil Information (#16068)
- Centre international pour la réforme du droit criminel et la politique en matière de justice pénale (internationally oriented national body)
- Centre international réformé John Knox (internationally oriented national body)
- Centre international pour le règlement des différends relatifs aux investissements (#12515)
- Centre of International Relations, Ljubljana (internationally oriented national body)
- Centre for International Relations, Mexico (internationally oriented national body)
- Centre for International Relations, Warszawa (internationally oriented national body)
- Centre international de rencontres mathématiques (internationally oriented national body)

♦ Centre for International Research on Economic Tendency Surveys (CIRET) 03765

Pres c/o KOF Swiss Economic Inst, LEE G 116, Leonhardstrasse 21, 8092 Zurich ZH, Switzerland. T. +41446324239. E-mail: info@ciret.org.
URL: http://www.ciret.org/
History 1960. Forerunner body: *Comité international pour l'étude des méthodes conjoncturelles (CIMCO)*, set up 1952. Former names and other names: *Contact international des recherches économiques tendancielles* – former (1960 to 1971). Registration: Belgium. **Aims** Serve as a forum for leading economists and institutions concerned with analysing and predicting development of the business cycle and the economic and socio-political consequences. **Structure** General Assembly; Council. **Languages** English. **Staff** 3.00 FTE, paid. **Finance** Sources: members' dues. **Activities** Events/meetings; knowledge management/information dissemination; networking/liaising. **Events** *Workshop on the Use of Surveys for Economic Development in Difficult Times* Helsinki (Finland) 2023, *Biennial Conference* Istanbul (Türkiye) 2022, *Biennial Conference* Poznań (Poland) 2021, *Biennial Conference* Poznań (Poland) 2020, *Biennial Conference* Rio de Janeiro (Brazil) 2018. **Publications** *Journal of Business Cycle Research* (3 a year).
Members Individual; Corporate. Members in 30 countries and territories:
Austria, Belgium, Brazil, Canada, China, Croatia, Denmark, Finland, France, Germany, Greece, Hungary, Indonesia, Italy, Japan, Latvia, Liechtenstein, Luxembourg, Netherlands, Poland, Russia, Serbia, South Africa, Sweden, Switzerland, Taiwan, Türkiye, UK, Ukraine, USA.
IGO Relations Joint publication with: *OECD (#17693)*. [2023.02.23/XF1144/**E**]

- Centre of International Research in Human Unity (internationally oriented national body)
- Centre International de Ressources et d'Innovation pour le Développement Durable (internationally oriented national body)
- Centre international de ressources et de valorisation de l'information dans les filières laitières petits ruminants (internationally oriented national body)
- Centre for International Rural Development, Kassel (internationally oriented national body)
- Centre international des sciences biologiques, Caracas (internationally oriented national body)
- Centre international des sciences de l'homme, Byblos (internationally oriented national body)
- Centre international pour les sciences de l'homme et le développement, Byblos / see International Centre for Human Sciences, Byblos

♦ Centre International des Sciences Mécaniques (CISM) 03766

International Centre for Mechanical Sciences
Acting Gen Sec Palazzo del Torso, Piazza Garibaldi 18, 33100 Udine UD, Italy. T. +39432248511. Fax +39432248550. E-mail: cism@cism.it.
URL: http://www.cism.it/
History 6 Dec 1968, Udine (Italy). **Aims** Promote research in mechanical sciences and related multidisciplinary sciences; favour exchange, diffusion and application of the most advanced knowledge in the field; establish active relations with similar national or international institutions; enlist cooperation of qualified scientists and research workers; establish research laboratories and libraries. **Structure** Academic Assembly; Scientific Council; Board of Directors. **Languages** English, Italian. **Staff** 5.00 FTE, paid. **Finance** Funded by: the Friuli Venezia Giulia Region, the City of Udine (Italy); The Friuli Foundation, the University of Udine and local public and private institutions, together with other European institutions. **Activities** Awards/prizes/competitions; events/meetings; training/education. **Events** *Symposium on Theory and Practice of Robots and Manipulations* Moscow (Russia) 2014, *Symposium on robot design, dynamics, and control* Warsaw (Poland) 2006, *Symposium on robot design, dynamics and control* Montréal, QC (Canada) 2004, *Symposium on theory and practice of robots and manipulators* Udine (Italy) 2002, *Symposium on theory and practice of robots and manipulators* Zakopane (Poland) 2000. **Publications** *Mechanics Research Communications* (6 a year). *CISM – Courses and Lectures* – series.
Members Individuals in 11 countries:
Austria, Croatia, France, Germany, Hungary, Italy, Luxembourg, Poland, Portugal, South Africa, Switzerland.
NGO Relations Cooperates with (8): *EUROMECH – European Mechanics Society (#05713)*; *European Committee on Computational Methods in Applied Sciences (ECCOMAS, #06644)*; *Gesellschaft für Angewandte Mathematik und Mechanik (GAMM)*; *International Association for Bridge and Structural Engineering (IABSE, #11737)*; *International Federation for the Promotion of Mechanism and Machine Science (IFToMM, #13519)*; *International Society for the Interaction of Mechanics and Mathematics (ISIMM, #15208)*; *International Union of Theoretical and Applied Mechanics (IUTAM, #15823)*; *Réunion internationale des laboratoires d'essais et de recherches sur les matériaux et les constructions (RILEM, #18930)*. [2022.05.04/XE0276/v/**E**]

- Centre international pour la science et de technologie (#14798)

♦ Centre international scientifique des fertilisants (CIEC) 03767

International Scientific Centre of Fertilizers – Centro Internacional Científico de Abonos – Internationales Wissenschaftliches Zentrum für Düngemittel – Centro Internazionale Scientifico Concimi Chimici – Mezdunarodnyj Naucnyj Centr Udobrenij
SG c/o Julius Kühn-Institut, Bundesallee 69, 38116 Braunschweig, Germany.
Pres address not obtained.
URL: https://ciec.iae.ac.cn/
History Oct 1932, Rome (Italy). Statutes most recently revised Apr 1996. Former names and other names: *Conférence internationale des engrais chimiques (CIEC)* – former (1932 to 1949); *International Centre of Chemical Fertilizers and Products Useful for Agriculture* – former (1949); *Centre international des engrais chimiques et produits chimiques utiles à l'agriculture* – former (1949); *Centre international des engrais chimiques* – former. **Aims** Establish relations and cooperation with other organizations (national and international) and persons interested in the problems of science, technology, production, distribution and application of all types of fertilizer and fertilizing materials; promote and organize international meetings in the field as means for improving yield, crop quality, soil fertility and sustaining management of land use systems; study problems concerning utilization of natural nutrient resources under various ecological and climatic conditions; study effects of fertilization and fertilizer application on the natural environment; carry out activities in the field of recycling nutrients by waste processing, upgrading and evaluation of waste-processed fertilizing materials – *composts* etc; promote research on soil testing and plant analysis methods, assessment of nutrient demand on soil, water and plants; promote methods and initiatives for calibration and control of nutrient content and formulas in fertilizers by legal measures. **Structure** General Assembly/Assembly of Members (every 2 years); General Committee; Praesidium; Advisory Council. International Relations Board, comprising Vice-Presidents (5) for: Europe and Middle East; North America; Central and South America; Africa; Asia and the Pacific. National branches. International Scientific Board. **Languages** English. **Finance** Members' dues, depending on membership category (A, B, C, D). Contributions of organizations and societies. **Activities** Events/meetings; research/documentation. **Events** *Symposium* Cairo (Egypt) 2022, *World Congress* Hohhot

(China) 2022, *Symposium* Athens (Greece) 2020, *Symposium* Quilin (China) 2019, *Impact of anticipating research in the past on research in the future* Braunschweig (Germany) 2018. **Publications** Proceedings of world congresses and symposia.
Members Institutions in 40 countries:
Algeria, Australia, Austria, Belgium, Bosnia-Herzegovina, Brazil, Bulgaria, Croatia, Cuba, Cyprus, Czechia, Egypt, Finland, France, Germany, Greece, Hungary, Israel, Italy, Lithuania, Morocco, Netherlands, New Zealand, Norway, Poland, Portugal, Romania, Russia, Serbia, Slovakia, Slovenia, Spain, Sweden, Syrian AR, Thailand, Trinidad-Tobago, Tunisia, Türkiye, UK, USA.
[2022/XC1482/**C**]

- ♦ Centre for International Security and Strategic Studies, Kiev (internationally oriented national body)
- ♦ Centre for International Security Studies (internationally oriented national body)
- ♦ Centre for International Security Studies, Moscow (internationally oriented national body)
- ♦ Centre international Sivananda de yoga vedanta (#14863)
- ♦ Centre international de solidarité ouvrière (internationally oriented national body)
- ♦ Centre for International Studies, Baku (internationally oriented national body)
- ♦ Centre for International Studies and Diplomacy (internationally oriented national body)
- ♦ Centre for International Studies in Education, Newcastle upon Tyne (internationally oriented national body)
- ♦ Centre for International Studies, Managua (internationally oriented national body)
- ♦ Centre for International Studies, Mexico (internationally oriented national body)
- ♦ Centre for International Studies, Warsaw (internationally oriented national body)
- ♦ Centre for International Studies, Zurich / see Center for Comparative and International Studies
- ♦ Centre for the International Study of Industrial Property / see Centre d'études internationales de la propriété intellectuelle
- ♦ Centre for International Sustainable Development Law (internationally oriented national body)
- ♦ Centre international de sylviculture (inactive)
- ♦ Centre international des systèmes d'éducation (#12487)
- ♦ Centre international des technologies de l'environnement (#13282)
- ♦ Centre for International Trade and Development (internationally oriented national body)
- ♦ Centre for International Trade, Economics and Environment (internationally oriented national body)
- ♦ Centre international de transfert d'innovations et de connaissances en économie sociale et solidaire (#12498)
- ♦ Centre international des travailleurs de solidarité latinoaméricaine (inactive)
- ♦ Centre international de l'UNESCO pour l'enseignement et la formation techniques et professionnels (#20307)
- ♦ Centre for International University Cooperation / see Norwegian Centre for International Cooperation in Higher Education
- ♦ Centre international d'urbanisme et développement régional (inactive)
- ♦ Centre international Vidal Sassoon pour l'étude de l'antisémitisme (internationally oriented national body)
- ♦ Centre international pour la ville, l'architecture et le paysage (internationally oriented national body)
- ♦ Centre international du vitrail (internationally oriented national body)
- ♦ Centre international du vitrail, Chartres / see Centre international du vitrail
- ♦ Centre international de volontaires du Japon (internationally oriented national body)
- ♦ Centre international Wiesenthal / see Simon Wiesenthal Center
- ♦ Centre inter-universitaire des études avancées (#15986)
- ♦ Centre inter-universitaire des études post-universitaires / see Inter-University Centre for Advanced Studies (#15986)
- ♦ Centre interuniversitaire européen pour les droits de l'homme et la démocratisation / see Global Campus of Human Rights (#10269)
- ♦ Centre de Inversiones Internacionales (internationally oriented national body)
- ♦ Centre d'investigació, docència, documentació i divulgació de Relacions Internacionals i Desenvolupament, Barcelona / see Centre for International Information and Documentation, Barcelona
- ♦ Centre d'investissement de la FAO (#09264)
- ♦ Centre of Islamic and Middle Eastern Law, London (internationally oriented national body)
- ♦ Centre islamique pour le développement du commerce (#16035)
- ♦ Centre islamique pour la formation professionnelle et technique et de recherches / see Islamic University of Technology (#16055)
- ♦ Centre islamique international des études et recherches démographiques (#13956)
- ♦ Centre italien de collaboration pour le développement de la construction dans les pays en développement (internationally oriented national body)
- ♦ Centre italien de solidarité (internationally oriented national body)
- ♦ Centre Jacques-Henri Pirenne / see Centre d'études européennes de Waterloo
- ♦ Centre pour la justice et le droit international (#03647)
- ♦ Centre for Latin American Migration Studies (internationally oriented national body)
- ♦ Centre for Latin American Research and Documentation (internationally oriented national body)
- ♦ Centre of Latin American Studies, Cambridge (internationally oriented national body)
- ♦ Centre for Latin American Studies, Eichstätt (internationally oriented national body)
- ♦ Centre for Latin American Studies, Warsaw (internationally oriented national body)
- ♦ Centre for Latin America Studies of the Institute of Sociology, Brussels / see Groupe d'études latino-américaines de l'Institut de sociologie, Bruxelles
- ♦ Centre latinoaméricain d'administration pour le développement (#16294)
- ♦ Centre latinoaméricain et de caraïbes de démographie (#16273)
- ♦ Centre Latinoaméricain et des Caraïbes d'Information dans les Sciences de la Santé (#16267)
- ♦ Centre latinoaméricain de création et de recherches théâtrales (#03811)
- ♦ Centre latinoaméricain de documentation économique et sociale (inactive)
- ♦ Centre latinoaméricain d'écologie sociale (#16292)
- ♦ Centre latinoaméricain d'économie humaine / see Universidad CLAEH (#20688)
- ♦ Centre latinoaméricain d'études en informatique (#16293)
- ♦ Centre Latinoaméricain de Physique (#03815)
- ♦ Centre latinoaméricain de recherches en sciences sociales (inactive)
- ♦ Centre latinoaméricain de technologie éducative pour la santé (inactive)

♦ Centre for the Law of EU External Relations (CLEER) 03768

Contact c/o TMC Asser Inst, PO Box 30461, 2500 GL The Hague, Netherlands. E-mail: info@cleer.eu.
URL: http://www.asser.nl/default.aspx?site_id=26
History Founded 2009. **Aims** Stimulate excellence in research, reflection and teaching in EU external relations studies in higher education institutions within and outside the Union; promote innovative solutions to practical challenges to the external dimension of the EU's legal order. **Structure** Governing Board; Advisory Board; Representatives of Partner Institutions. **Languages** English. **Staff** 1.00 FTE, paid. **Activities** Events/meetings; training/education. **Events** *Conference* The Hague (Netherlands) 2018, *The influence of international organization on the European Union – the EU as an autonomous legal order* The Hague (Netherlands) 2010. **Publications** *CLEER Newsletter* (2 a year); *Working Papers* – students' magazine. Weekly News service. **NGO Relations** *TMC Asser Institute – Centre for International and European Law.*
[2018.01.26/XJ2752/**E**]

- ♦ Centre for Legumes in Mediterranean Agriculture (internationally oriented national body)

♦ Centre de liaison artistique et culturelle en méditerranée 03769

Pres Chambre des Beaux Arts de Tunisie, Résidence le Beau Rivage, Rue IBN Battuta, 2015 Le Kram, Tunis, Tunisia. E-mail: mb.mansi@gmail.com.
History by *Med-Urbs (inactive)* of *European Commission (EC, #06633).*
Members Participating cities in 14 countries:
Algeria, Armenia, Belgium, Egypt, France, Greece, Jordan, Kyrgyzstan, Lebanon, Morocco, Palestine, Russia, Tunisia, Uzbekistan.
NGO Relations Coordinated by: *European Cultural Network for Development Cooperation (#06869).*
[2012/XE0446/**E**]

- ♦ Centre de liaison des industries transformatrices de viandes de la CEE Verbindungsstelle der Fleischverwertungsindustrie der EWG-Länder / see Liaison Centre for the Meat Processing Industry in the EU (#16452)
- ♦ Centre de liaison des industries transformatrices de viandes de l'UE (#16452)
- ♦ Centre of Liaison and Information of Masonic Powers Signatories of Strasbourg Appeal (#03770)

♦ Centre de liaison et d'information des puissances maçonniques signataires de l'Appel de Strasbourg (CLIPSAS) 03770

Centre of Liaison and Information of Masonic Powers Signatories of Strasbourg Appeal – Centro de Enlace e Información de las Potencias Masónicas signatarias del Llamamiento de Estrasburgo
Contact c/o GLMU, 8 rue Voltaire, 93100 Montreuil, France.
URL: https://clipsas.org/
History 22 Jan 1961, by representatives of 11 Grand Lodges. In the press, also referred to as *Comité de liaison et d'information des puissances signataires de l'Appel de Strasbourg.* Comes within the framework of the *Masonic Movement (#16593).* Registration: Start date: 17 Nov 1993, France, Paris. **Aims** Act as a liaison and information centre for national organizations working in accordance with the principles of *humanistic* tradition; defend and represent the members' interests at the level of international governmental organizations and nongovernmental organizations. **Structure** General Assembly (annual). Bureau, consisting of President, 6 Vice-Presidents and Secretary General. **Languages** English, French, Spanish. **Staff** 0.50 FTE, paid; 2.00 FTE, voluntary. **Finance** Members' dues. Budget (annual): euro 28,000. **Activities** Studies issues that determine the future of mankind. **Events** *General Assembly* Brazzaville (Congo Brazzaville) 2021, *General Assembly* Brazzaville (Congo Brazzaville) 2020, *General Assembly* Montréal, QC (Canada) 2019, *General Assembly* Barcelona (Spain) 2018, *Annual Colloquium* Brussels (Belgium) 2014.
Members Grand Lodges (70) in 40 countries and territories:
Argentina, Austria, Belgium, Benin, Bolivia, Brazil, Bulgaria, Cameroon, Canada, Chile, Colombia, Congo Brazzaville, Congo DR, Côte d'Ivoire, Denmark, Ecuador, El Salvador, France, Germany, Greece, Haiti, Italy, Lebanon, Luxembourg, Madagascar, Mexico, Moldova, Morocco, Netherlands, Peru, Portugal, Puerto Rico, Romania, Spain, Sweden, Switzerland, Togo, Türkiye, Uruguay, USA.
Included in the above, 5 regional and international lodges listed in this Yearbook:
Grande loge symbolique masculine d'Afrique (no recent information); Grand Rite Malgache (GRM, see: #16593); Gran Oriente Latinoamericano (GOLA, no recent information); International Masonic Order 'DELPHI' (#14112); Universaler Freimaurer Orden "Humanitas" (no recent information).
Consultative Status Consultative status granted from: *ECOSOC (#05331)* (Special). [2020/XF2665/y/**E**]

- ♦ Centre de Liaison International des Marchands de Machines Agricoles et des Réparateurs (#14034)

♦ Centre for Linguistic and Historical Studies by Oral Tradition 03771

Centre d'études linguistiques et historiques par tradition orale (CELHTO)
Coordinator BP 878, Niamey, Niger. E-mail: celhto@africa-union.org – mariamad@celhto.org.
URL: http://www.celhto.org/
History 1968, Niamey (Niger), on signature of an agreement between the Niger Government and Unesco, as *Regional Documentation Centre on Oral Traditions – Centre regional de documentation sur la tradition orale (CRDTO).* Integrated within *Organization of African Unity (OAU, inactive)* in 1974, when present name was adopted. Currently part of: *African Union (AU, #00488).* **Aims** Contribute to the prestige of African cultures through the valorisation of the oral tradition. **Languages** English, French. **Staff** 16.00 FTE, paid; 1.00 FTE, voluntary. **Finance** Operational budget (annual): US$ 1,000,000; program budget (annual): US$ 600,000. **Publications** *Cahiers du CELHTO* (annual). Monographs; studies; textbooks; dictionaries. Publications in African languages, French, English, in bilingual or trilingual editions.
Members Individuals in 54 member states of the African Union:
Algeria, Angola, Benin, Botswana, Burkina Faso, Burundi, Cameroon, Cape Verde, Central African Rep, Chad, Comoros, Congo Brazzaville, Congo DR, Côte d'Ivoire, Djibouti, Egypt, Equatorial Guinea, Eritrea, Eswatini, Ethiopia, Gabon, Gambia, Ghana, Guinea, Guinea-Bissau, Kenya, Lesotho, Liberia, Libya, Madagascar, Malawi, Mali, Mauritania, Mauritius, Morocco, Mozambique, Namibia, Niger, Nigeria, Rwanda, Sao Tomé-Principe, Senegal, Seychelles, Sierra Leone, Somalia, South Africa, Sudan, Tanzania UR, Togo, Tunisia, Uganda, Zambia, Zimbabwe. [2016.06.01/XE8288/**E***]

- ♦ Centre for Livelihoods, Ecosystems, Energy, Adaptation and Resilience in the Caribbean (internationally oriented national body)
- ♦ Centre L-J Lebret / see Centre international LEBRET-IRFED
- ♦ Centre de lutte biologique pour l'Afrique (see: #13933)
- ♦ Centre maghrébin d'études et de recherches administratives (no recent information)
- ♦ Centre for Maghrib Studies, Tunis (#03740)
- ♦ Centre de Management Europe-Amérique Latine (internationally oriented national body)
- ♦ Centre de management hôtelier international (internationally oriented national body)
- ♦ Centre du manganèse / see International Manganese Institute (#14083)
- ♦ Centre for Maritime Law and Security Africa (internationally oriented national body)

♦ Centre for Marketing Information and Advisory Services for Fishery Products in the Arab Region (INFOSAMAK) 03772

Centre d'information et de conseil sur la commercialisation des produits de la pêche dans la région arabe
Dir 71 Boulevard Rahal El Meskini, BP 16 243, 20 000 Casablanca, Morocco. T. +212225540856. Fax +212222540855. E-mail: info@infosamak.org.
URL: http://www.infosamak.org/
History 1 Mar 1986, as a regional project of *FAO (#09260)* financed by *UNDP (#20292)* and based in Bahrain. Became an independent Arab intergovernmental organization, 24 Jun 1993, when constitution entered into force. Headquarters moved to Casablanca (Morocco), Sep 2000. Also referred to as *Fish Marketing Information, Promotion and Technical Advisory Services for Arab Countries – Service d'information sur la commercialisation, la promotion, et de conseils techniques de la pêche pour les pays arabes.* **Aims** Assist the region's fisheries to develop and adapt to present and future market demand for fishery products; make the most effective use of available fishery resources and *aquaculture* production; contribute to an improved stability in supply and demand for fishery products in the region and so improve *fish* consumption and *food* security; maximize exploitation of all available export opportunities within the Arab region and in world markets to develop trade and create employment opportunities; promote technical and economic cooperation in the fishery sector between Member States. **Structure** General Assembly comprises one representative of each member state, including Chairman and 2 Vice-Chairmen. Managing Director, supported by a team of professional staff in the fields of marketing, fish processing technology and quality assurance. **Languages** Arabic, English, French. **Finance** Contributions of member states; revenue from sales of publications and from consultancy services. Financial support from international agencies; including: *Common Fund for Commodities (CFC, #04293)*; FAO; *International Fund for Agricultural Development (IFAD, #13692).* **Activities** Provides information on marketing opportunities and supply prospects for fishery products within and outside the region; advises the fish processing industry on product specifications, processing methods and quality standards in accordance with market requirements; identifies new niche markets for products from underutilized fishery resources; undertakes research and studies on fish processing and markets; collects and disseminates fish marketing information and prices through a series of publications; provides training in marketing techniques and in quality assurance of fishery products to private sector operators, government institutions and agencies; identifies investment opportunities and prepares investment profiles. Organizes: Annual Buyer-Seller Meeting for importers and exporters of fishery products within and outside the region; regional seminars on quality assurance and food safety for the fish processing industry; fisheries commodity conferences; workshops. Participates in fairs and exhibitions dealing with fishing sector. **Events** *Seafood Mideast conference* Muscat (Oman) 2006, *Seminar on fish quality* Casablanca (Morocco) 2002, *International small pelagic conference* Agadir (Morocco) 2001, *International buyer-seller meeting and seminar* Bahrain 1992. **Publications** *INFOSAMAK AFAK Price* (12 a year); *Infosamak Trade News (ITN)* (12 a year) in Arabic, English; *GLOBEFISH Highlights (GH)* (4 a year); *INFOSAMAK International Magazine* (4 a year) in Arabic, English, French. *Directory of Fish Importers and Exporters.* **Information Services** *Database of Importers and Exporters in the Arab Region*; *GLOBEFISH Database* – fish marketing information, including time-series price data for fishery commodities worldwide.

Members States which have signed or deposited a letter of acceptance of the Centre's constitution, currently 11 Arab countries and territories:
Algeria, Bahrain, Djibouti, Libya, Mauritania, Morocco, Palestine, Sudan, Syrian AR, Tunisia, Yemen.
IGO Relations Cooperation agreement with *FAO (#09260)*. Part of *FAO GLOBEFISH (#09261)*, also comprising: *International Organisation for the Development of Fisheries and Aquaculture in Europe (EUROFISH, #14427)* (Europe); *Intergovernmental Organization for Marketing Information and Technical Advisory Services for Fishery Products in the Asia and Pacific Region (INFOFISH, #11497)* (Asia and the Pacific); *INFOPECHE (#11191)* (Africa); *INFOPESCA (#11192)* (Latin America and the Caribbean); *INFOSA (#11203)* (Southern Africa); *'INFOYU'* (China). Links with Ministries of Fisheries, Chambers of Commerce in different countries. **NGO Relations** Links with fisheries professional organizations, trade associations and different other NGOs in Arab and Non-Arab countries. [2009.01.27/XF0634/**E***]

- ♦ Centre for Mathematics, Science and Technology in Africa (internationally oriented national body)
- ♦ Centre Maurits Coppieters / see Coppieters Foundation (#04831)
- ♦ Centre for Media and Celebrity Studies (unconfirmed)
- ♦ Centre for Mediation in Africa (internationally oriented national body)
- ♦ Centre of Mediterranean and International Studies (internationally oriented national body)
- ♦ Centre for Mediterranean Studies / see Institute of Arab and Islamic Studies
- ♦ Centre de la Méditerranée Moderne et Contemporaine (internationally oriented national body)
- ♦ Centre Méditerranéen de la Communication Audiovisuelle (#16648)
- ♦ Centre for Meeting of Peoples (internationally oriented national body)
- ♦ Centre mésoaméricain d'études sur la technologie appropriée (#03650)
- ♦ Centre for Mesoamerican Research (internationally oriented national body)
- ♦ Centre for Middle Eastern and Central Asian Studies / see Centre for Arab and Islamic Studies, Middle East and Central Asia
- ♦ Centre for Middle Eastern and Islamic Studies / see Institute for Middle Eastern and Islamic Studies, Durham
- ♦ Centre for Middle Eastern and Islamic Studies, Bergen (internationally oriented national body)
- ♦ Centre of Middle Eastern and Islamic Studies, Cambridge / see Prince Alwaleed Bin Talal Centre of Islamic Studies
- ♦ Centre of Middle Eastern Studies, Cambridge / see Prince Alwaleed Bin Talal Centre of Islamic Studies
- ♦ Centre pour la migration internationale et le développement (internationally oriented national body)
- ♦ Centre for Migration Studies, Rome (internationally oriented national body)
- ♦ Centre de mise en valeur des ressources minérales de l'Afrique centrale (no recent information)
- ♦ Centre de mise en valeur des ressources minérales de l'Afrique de l'Est et du Sud / see African Minerals and Geosciences Centre (#00373)
- ♦ Centre Mondial du Cyclisme (internationally oriented national body)
- ♦ Centre mondial de données sur l'écoulement (#10584)
- ♦ Centre mondial de données pour les indices d'activité solaire / see Solar Influences Data Analysis Centre (#19675)
- ♦ Centre Mondial d'Excellende des Destinations (internationally oriented national body)
- ♦ Centre mondial d'information sur l'éducation bilingue / see Information Centre for Bilingual and Plurilingual Education (#11195)
- ♦ Centre mondial d'information sur l'éducation bilingue et plurilingue / see Information Centre for Bilingual and Plurilingual Education (#11195)
- ♦ Centre mondial d'informations et de recherches appliquées aux nuisances urbaines (inactive)
- ♦ Centre mondial des organisations féminines (inactive)
- ♦ Centre mondial de la paix, des libertés et des droits de l'homme (internationally oriented national body)
- ♦ Centre mondial des sciences sociales, Byblos / see International Centre for Human Sciences, Byblos
- ♦ Centre mondial de surveillance continue de la conservation / see UN Environment Programme World Conservation Monitoring Centre (#20295)
- ♦ Centre Moshe Dayan pour les études sur le Moyen-Orient et l'Afrique (internationally oriented national body)
- ♦ Centre for Mountain Studies (internationally oriented national body)
- ♦ Centre multinational de programmation et d'éxécution de projets / see ECA Office for North Africa (#05273)
- ♦ Centre for Municipal Studies and International Cooperation (internationally oriented national body)

♦ Centre Muraz 03773

Gen Dir BP 153, Bobo Dioulasso 01, Burkina Faso. T. +22620970102. Fax +226970457. E-mail: dg.muraz@fasonet.bf.
URL: http://www.centre-muraz.bf/

History 1939, as *Service général autonome de la maladie du sommeil en Afrique occidentale française et au Togo*. Name changed, 1945, to *Service général d'hygiène mobile et de prophylaxie (SGHMP)*. Current name adopted 1956. From 25 Apr 1960 until Dec 2000, acted as headquarters and was a research centre of *Coordination and Cooperation Organization for the Control of the Major Endemic Diseases (OCCGE, inactive)*. Subsequently became public institution, directly linked to the Ministry of Health in Burkina Faso, 2001. **Aims** Combat major *endemic* diseases in *Africa*, with emphasis on: *malaria*; *dracunculosis*; *trypanosomiasis*; *bilharzia*; *sexually transmitted* diseases; *AIDS* and opportunistic diseases, including *tuberculosis*; *vaccinology*. **Structure** Sections (7): Parasitology; Immunochemistry; Biology; Vaccinology; Health Centre; Direction. **Languages** French. **Staff** 100.00 FTE, paid. **Finance** Contributions from Member States. Also various subsidies, mostly from the Ministère de la Coopération et du Développement (France), and from: *Agence universitaire de La Francophonie (AUF, #00548)*; *European Commission (EC, #06633)*; *Joint United Nations Programme on HIV/AIDS (UNAIDS, #16149)*; *UNICEF (#20332)*; *WHO (#20950)*. Budget (annual): CFA Fr 1,500 million. **Activities** Main areas: (1) Research – priority health problems of member states for action development; (2) Training – internships for paramedical workers, doctoral students, post-doctoral researchers; (3) International Technical Support – at member states' request, planning for control programmes, conduct of training workshops, programme evaluation, epidemiology and public health intervention, laboratory quality control; technical support and expertise to international organizations. **Events** *Conference* Bobo Dioulasso (Burkina Faso) 1989, *Seminar on expanded programmes on immunization and epidemiological surveillance* Bobo Dioulasso (Burkina Faso) 1989. **Publications** Scientific publications.
Members Governments of 8 countries:
Benin, Burkina Faso, Côte d'Ivoire, Mali, Mauritania, Niger, Senegal, Togo.
IGO Relations OCCGE research centres and institutes: *Institute for Tropical Ophthalmology in Africa (IOTA, inactive)*; *Pierre Richet Institute (IPR, no recent information)*. **NGO Relations** OCCGE research centres and institutes: *Service d'épidémiologie, de statistique et d'information sanitaire (SESIS, no recent information)*. [2010/XE0028/**E***]

- ♦ Centre national de coopération au développement / see Coalition of the Flemish North South Movement – 11 11 11
- ♦ Centre des Nations Unies pour le développement régional (#20526)
- ♦ Centre des Nations Unies pour les établissements humains / see United Nations Human Settlements Programme (#20572)
- ♦ Centre des Nations Unies pour l'habitation, la construction et la planification (inactive)
- ♦ Centre des Nations Unies pour les ressources naturelles, l'énergie et les transports (inactive)
- ♦ Centre des Nations Unies pour la science et la technique au service du développement (inactive)
- ♦ Centre des Nations Unies sur les sociétés transnationales (inactive)
- ♦ Centre néerlandais pour les peuples autochtones (internationally oriented national body)
- ♦ Centre de négociation internationale (internationally oriented national body)
- ♦ Centre for Negotiation and Dispute Resolution (internationally oriented national body)
- ♦ Centre for Nepal and Asian Studies (internationally oriented national body)
- ♦ Centre neuromusculaire européen (#08042)
- ♦ Centre for Non-Traditional Security Studies (internationally oriented national body)
- ♦ Centre of Non-Western Studies / see Research School of Asian, African and Amerindian Studies
- ♦ Centre nordique pour des journalistes (#17516)
- ♦ **Centre Nord-Sud** Centre européen pour l'interdépendance et la solidarité mondiales (#06483)
- ♦ Centre Nord-Sud du Conseil de l'Europe / see European Centre for Global Interdependence and Solidarity (#06483)
- ♦ Centre Nord-Sud pour l'échange technique et culturel (inactive)
- ♦ Centre of North American Studies / see Centro de Estudos das Americas, Rio de Janeiro
- ♦ Centre for North East and Adriatic Studies (internationally oriented national body)
- ♦ Centre for Northeast Asian Studies, Sendai (internationally oriented national body)
- ♦ Centre oecuménique de documentation et d'information pour l'Afrique australe et du Sud / see Ecumenical Documentation and Information Centre in Southern Africa (#05346)
- ♦ Centre oecuménique de documentation et d'information pour l'Afrique du Sud (#05346)
- ♦ Centre de l'OIT à Turin / see International Training Centre of the ILO (#15717)
- ♦ Centre OMS pour le développement sanitaire, Kobe (see: #20950)
- ♦ Centre for the Opening and Development of Latin America (internationally oriented national body)
- ♦ Centre for Oriental Studies, Vilnius / see Institute of Asian and Transcultural Studies
- ♦ Centre Orient-Occident (#05263)
- ♦ Centre orthodoxe du Patriarcat oecuménique (internationally oriented national body)
- ♦ Centre orthodoxe du Patriarcat œcuménique à Genève / see Orthodox Centre of the Ecumenical Patriarchate
- ♦ Centre for OSCE Research (internationally oriented national body)
- ♦ Centre de la paix mondiale par le droit / see World Jurist Association (#21604)
- ♦ Centre panafricain de formation coopérative / see African University for Cooperative Development (#00494)
- ♦ Centre panaméricain d'études et de recherches géographiques (#18086)
- ♦ Centre panaméricain de la fièvre aphteuse (#18106)
- ♦ Centre du patrimoine mondial (#21566)
- ♦ Centre de patrimoine populaire des pays arabes du Golfe (no recent information)
- ♦ Centre for Peace and Arms Control Studies and Documentation – Archivio Disarmo (internationally oriented national body)
- ♦ Centre for Peace in the Balkans (internationally oriented national body)
- ♦ Centre for Peacebuilding and Conflict Management, Oslo (internationally oriented national body)

♦ Centre for Peace and Conflict Studies (CPCS) 03774

Dir PO Box 93066, Siem Reap, Cambodia. E-mail: centrepeaceconflictstudies@gmail.com.
Street Address Unit 501, Ly Residence, Bakheng Road, Svaydangkum Village, Svaydangkum Commune, Siem Reap 017252, Cambodia.
URL: http://www.centrepeaceconflictstudies.org/

History 2008, Cambodia. Finding its foundations in local peace initiatives such as Alliance for Conflict Transformation (ACT) and *Action Asia*. **Aims** Strengthen strategic intervention into violent conflict with the overall aim of fostering sustainable peace in the Asia region. **Structure** Board. **Languages** English. **Staff** 15.00 FTE, paid. **Finance** Sources: donations; government support. **Activities** Capacity building; conflict resolution; events/meetings; research/documentation; training/education. **Events** *Annual Peace Practitioners Research Conference* Siem Reap (Cambodia) 2014, *Annual Peace Practitioners Research Conference* Siem Reap (Cambodia) 2013, *Annual Peace Practitioners Research Conference* Siem Reap (Cambodia) 2012. **Publications** Annual Report; research papers. **NGO Relations** Member of: *Mediation Support Network (MSN, #16622)*. [2022.05.05/XJ5672/**E**]

- ♦ Centre for Peace and Development, Bangalore (internationally oriented national body)
- ♦ Centre for Peace and Development Studies, Limerick (internationally oriented national body)
- ♦ Centre for Peace and Disarmament for Asia and the Pacific / see United Nations Regional Centre for Peace and Disarmament for Asia and the Pacific (#20617)
- ♦ Centre for Peace and International Relations Studies (internationally oriented national body)
- ♦ Centre for Peace, Non-Violence and Human Rights, Osijek (internationally oriented national body)
- ♦ Centre for Peace Research, Madrid (internationally oriented national body)
- ♦ Centre for Peace Research and Strategic Studies, University of Leuven / see Centre for Research on Peace and Development
- ♦ Centre for Peace Research, University of Leuven / see Centre for Research on Peace and Development
- ♦ Centre for Peace Studies, Hamilton (internationally oriented national body)
- ♦ Centre for Peace Studies, Tromsí (internationally oriented national body)
- ♦ Centre for Peace and War Studies, Athens (unconfirmed)
- ♦ Centre for Pentecostal and Charismatic Studies (internationally oriented national body)
- ♦ Centre de perfectionnement des cadres de l'administration du travail / see African Regional Labour Administration Centre, Yaoundé (#00436)
- ♦ Centre Pew sur les changements climatiques globaux (internationally oriented national body)
- ♦ Centre for Planetarian Education / see Centro Educazione alla Mondialità
- ♦ Centre de PNUD pour le développement des zones arides (inactive)
- ♦ Centre for Political and Constitutional Studies (internationally oriented national body)
- ♦ Centre for Political and Strategic Studies / see Al Ahram Centre for Political and Strategic Studies
- ♦ Centre pour la politique internationale (internationally oriented national body)
- ♦ Centre de Politique Internationale et d'Analyse des Conflits (internationally oriented national body)
- ♦ Centre de politique de sécurité, Genève (internationally oriented national body)
- ♦ Centre sur les politiques internationales des TIC Afrique du centre et de l'ouest (internationally oriented national body)
- ♦ Centre de politique sociale et économique européenne (#03742)
- ♦ Centre Population et développement (internationally oriented national body)
- ♦ Centre population et développement, Paris / see Centre Population et développement
- ♦ Centre for Poverty-Related Communicable Diseases / see Amsterdam Institute for Global Health and Development
- ♦ Centre de prévention des conflits, Vienne (see: #17887)
- ♦ Centre pour la prévention internationale du crime (inactive)
- ♦ Centre pour la promotion du commerce, des investissements et du tourisme en Asie du Sud-Est (#01225)
- ♦ Centre for the Promotion of Imports from Developing Countries (internationally oriented national body)
- ♦ Centre pour la promotion de la paix (internationally oriented national body)
- ♦ Centre for the Promotion of Small and Medium Sized Enterprises in Central America / see Centro Regional de Promoción de la MIPYME (#03816)
- ♦ Centre for Prospective Strategic Studies (#03739)
- ♦ Centre de protection sociale et de développement social pour l'Asie et le Pacifique (inactive)
- ♦ Centre for Public Services / see European Services Strategy Unit
- ♦ Centre Quaker international / see Quaker United Nations Office (#18588)
- ♦ Centre québécois de relations internationales / see École supérieure d'études internationales
- ♦ Centre Raoul Wallenberg pour les droits de la personne (internationally oriented national body)
- ♦ Centre de Recerca en Economia Internacional, Barcelona (internationally oriented national body)
- ♦ Centre de Recherche et d'Action pour la Paix (#03651)
- ♦ Centre de recherche sur l'Amérique latine et les Caraïbes (internationally oriented national body)
- ♦ Centre de recherche sur l'Asie moderne / see Centre for Asian Studies
- ♦ Centre de recherche et de développement sur les légumes en Asie / see AVRDC – The World Vegetable Center (#03051)
- ♦ Centre de recherche et de documentation sur l'Amérique Latine (internationally oriented national body)
- ♦ Centre de recherche et de documentation sur le problème de langues / see Centre for Research and Documentation on World Language Problems (#03780)
- ♦ Centre de recherche et de documentation sur les problèmes de langues (#03780)
- ♦ Centre de recherche en droit international de l'environnement (internationally oriented national body)

- Centre de recherche, d'échanges et de documentation universitaire / see Institut français de recherche en Afrique
- Centre de recherche en économie appliquée pour le développement (internationally oriented national body)
- Centre de recherche sur l'épidémiologie des désastres (#03781)
- Centre de recherche et d'études sur la Méditerranée orientale (#03782)
- Centre de recherche forestière internationale (#03646)
- Centre de recherche pour la gestion des associations et des coopératives, Fribourg / see Institut de recherche pour la gestion des associations et des coopératives, Fribourg
- Centre de recherche – information – action pour le développement en Afrique (internationally oriented national body)
- Centre de recherche – information – action pour le développement en Afrique australe / see Centre de recherche – information – action pour le développement en Afrique
- Centre de recherche et d'information pour le développement, Paris (internationally oriented national body)
- Centre de recherche et d'information pour un développement solidaire (internationally oriented national body)
- Centre de recherche en matière pénale – Fernand Boulan (internationally oriented national body)
- Centre de recherche sur la mondialisation (internationally oriented national body)
- Centre de recherche Ouest Africain (internationally oriented national body)
- Centre de recherche sur la paix, Madrid (internationally oriented national body)
- Centre de recherches africaines / see Institute for Anthropological Research in Africa
- Centre de recherche scientifique et techniques sur les régions arides (internationally oriented national body)
- Centre de recherches pour le développement agricole et économique international, Heidelberg (internationally oriented national body)
- Centre de recherches pour le développement agricole international, Heidelberg / see Forschungsstelle für Internationale Agrar- und Wirtschaftsentwicklung, Heidelberg
- Centre de recherches pour le développement international (#13162)
- Centre de recherches sur le développement social et économique en Asie méridionale (inactive)
- Centre de recherches en économie mondiale (internationally oriented national body)
- Centre de recherches économiques des pays méditerranéens (internationally oriented national body)
- Centre de recherches de Genève (inactive)
- Centre de recherches sur l'histoire, l'art et la culture islamiques (#18852)
- Centre de Recherche sur les sociétés de l'océan Indien (internationally oriented national body)
- Centre de recherches et de promotion pour la sauvegarde des sites et monuments historiques en Afrique (internationally oriented national body)
- Centre de recherches et de publications sur les rapports Nord-Sud / see Europe – Third World Centre
- Centre de recherches et de publications sur les relations entre l'Europe et le Tiers-monde / see Europe – Third World Centre
- Centre de recherches statistiques, économiques et sociales et de formation pour les pays islamiques (#19971)
- Centre de recherches sur les traditions orales et les langues nationales africaines en Afrique orientale (inactive)
- Centre de recherche touristique et de développement des Caraïbes (inactive)
- Centre for Refugee Studies, York (internationally oriented national body)
- Centre régional d'action culturelle / see Institut Régional d'Enseignement Supérieur et de Recherche en Développement Culturel (#11355)
- Centre régional pour les activités d'hygiène de l'environnement / see WHO Regional Centre for Environmental Health Activities (#20942)
- Centre régional africain d'administration du travail, Harare / see African Regional Labour Administration Centre, Harare (#00435)
- Centre régional africain d'administration du travail, Yaoundé (#00436)
- Centre régional africain de conception et de fabrication techniques (no recent information)
- Centre régional africain pour l'énergie solaire (no recent information)
- Centre régional africain de ressources sur la sexualité (internationally oriented national body)
- Centre régional africain pour la science de l'information (#00517)
- Centre régional africain des sciences et technologies de l'espace en langue française /Affilié à l'Organisation des nations unies/ (see: #04277)
- Centre régional africain de technologie (#00432)
- Centre régional AGRHYMET (#00565)
- Centre régional d'alphabétisation fonctionnelle en milieu rural pour les Etats arabes (no recent information)
- Centre régional sur les armes légères et de petit calibre dans la région des Grands Lacs, la corne de l'Afrique et les États limitrophes (#18760)
- Centre Régional pour les Arts Vivants en Afrique (internationally oriented national body)
- Centre régional de biologie tropicale de l'Asie du Sud-Est / see Southeast Asian Regional Centre for Tropical Biology (#19782)
- Centre régional de biologie tropicale de la SEAMEO (#19782)
- Centre regional de documentation sur la tradition orale / see Centre for Linguistic and Historical Studies by Oral Tradition (#03771)
- Centre régional pour l'eau potable et l'assainissement à faible coût / see Water and Sanitation for Africa (#20836)
- Centre régional de l'eau pour les zones arides et semi-arides de l'Amérique latine et des Caraïbes (internationally oriented national body)
- Centre Régional pour les Énergies Renouvelables et le Efficacité Énergétique (#18754)
- Centre régional pour l'enseignement et la formation en biotechnologie, Inde (internationally oriented national body)
- Centre régional pour l'enseignement des sciences et des mathématiques de la SEAMEO (#19172)
- Centre régional pour l'enseignement supérieur et le développement de la SEAMEO (#19174)
- Centre régional pour l'environnement de l'Asia centrale (internationally oriented national body)
- Centre régional pour l'environnement en Europe centrale et en Europe de l'Est (#18782)
- Centre régional des études de population (no recent information)
- Centre régional européen d'écohydrologie, Lodz (#08341)
- Centre régional de formation et d'application en agrométéorologie et hydrologie opérationnelle / see AGRHYMET Regional Centre (#00565)
- Centre régional de formation de bibliothécaires des pays d'Afrique d'expression française / see Ecole de bibliothécaires, archivistes et documentalistes (#05296)
- Centre régional de formation aux techniques des levés aérospatiaux / see African Regional Institute for Geospatial Information Science and Technology (#00433)
- Centre régional francophone pour l'Asie-Pacifique (internationally oriented national body)

♦ Centre régional francophone pour l'Europe centrale et orientale, Sofia (CREFECO)   03775
Contact Léopold Sédar Senghor Street 1, Floor 3, 1618 Sofia, Bulgaria. T. +35929555971 – +35924894845. Fax +35929555977. E-mail: crefeco@francophonie.org.
URL: http://www.crefeco.refer.bg/
History May 2005, Sofia (Bulgaria), by *Organisation internationale de la Francophonie (OIF, #17809)*. **Events** *Semaine de la francophonie* Sofia (Bulgaria) 2016. [2022/XM2309/**E**]

- Centre régional de gestion des eaux urbaines (internationally oriented national body)
- Centre régional d'information des Nations Unies pour l'Europe occidentale (#20621)
- Centre régional d'information sur les ressources d'énergie (#18780)
- Centre régional d'information scientifique et technologique pour l'Amérique latine et les Caraïbes (internationally oriented national body)
- Centre régional pour l'innovation et la technologie en matière d'éducation de la SEAMEO (#19168)
- Centre régional d'intervention pour la coopération, Reggio Calabria (internationally oriented national body)
- Centre régional des langues de la SEAMEO (#19181)
- Centre régional méditerranéen pour l'intervention d'urgence contre la pollution marine accidentelle (#18795)
- Centre régional méditerranéen de lutte contre la pollution par les hydrocarbures / see Regional Marine Pollution Emergency Response Centre for the Mediterranean Sea (#18795)
- Centre régional des Nations Unies pour la paix et le désarmement en Afrique (#20616)
- Centre régional des Nations Unies pour la paix et le désarmement en Asie et dans le Pacifique (#20617)
- Centre régional des Nations Unies pour la paix, le désarmement et le développement en Amérique latine / see United Nations Regional Centre for Peace, Disarmament and Development in Latin America and the Caribbean (#20618)
- Centre régional des Nations Unies pour la paix, le désarmement et le développement en Amérique latine et les Caraïbes (#20618)
- Centre régional pour la promotion du livre en Amérique latine et dans les Caraïbes (#18758)
- Centre régional de radioisotopes du Moyen-Orient pour les pays arabes (#16761)
- Centre régional de recherche et de documentation sur les traditions orales et pour le développement des langues africaines / see Centre International de Recherche et de Documentation sur les Traditions et les Langues Africaines (#03761)
- Centre régional de recherches sur bananiers et plantains / see Centre Africain de Recherches sur Bananiers et Plantains (#03725)
- Centre régional de la réforme agraire et de développement rural au Proche-Orient (#18755)
- Centre régional de séismologie pour l'Amérique du Sud (#03818)
- Centre Régional de Télédétection des Etats de l'Afrique du nord (#18807)
- Centre régional de télédétection, Ouagadougou (inactive)
- Centre régional de topographie, cartographie et télédétection / see Regional Centre for Mapping of Resources for Development (#18757)
- Centre régional de l'UNESCO pour l'enseignement supérieur en Amérique latine et dans les Caraïbes / see UNESCO International Institute for Higher Education in Latin America and the Caribbean (#20309)

♦ Centre for Registration of European Ergonomists (CREE)   03776
Contact ARTEE, c/o Francis Six, 525 rue du Haut, 59283 Moncheaux, France. T. +33557571042. Fax +33556900873. E-mail: fdurocher@free.fr.
URL: http://www.eurerg.org/
Structure Board. **Events** *Conference on Workers Contribution to Safer Workplaces* Brussels (Belgium) 2017, *Meeting* Helsinki (Finland) 2008, *Meeting* Bordeaux (France) 2007, *Meeting* Gothenburg (Sweden) 2007, *Meeting* Naples (Italy) 2006.
Members in 16 countries:
Belgium, Denmark, Finland, France, Germany, Greece, Ireland, Italy, Luxembourg, Netherlands, Norway, Portugal, Spain, Sweden, Switzerland, UK.
NGO Relations *Federation of European Ergonomics Societies (FEES, #09504)*. [2012/XJ3161/**E**]

♦ Centre on Regulation in Europe (CERRE)   03777
Dir Gen Av Louise 475, Box 10, 1050 Brussels, Belgium. T. +3222308360. E-mail: info@cerre.eu – communications@cerre.eu.
URL: http://www.cerre.eu/
History 2010. Registration: Banque-Carrefour des Entreprises, Belgium; EU Transparency Register, No/ID: 041592911733-05. **Aims** Promote robustness and consistency in regulation processes and systems in Europe; clarify the respective roles of market operators, governments and regulatory authorities; recommend and disseminate top quality regulation practices. **Structure** General Assembly; Governing Board; Secretariat; Director General. **Languages** English. **Staff** 11.00 FTE, paid. **Finance** Sources: donations; members' dues; revenue from activities/projects. **Activities** Awareness raising; events/meetings; monitoring/evaluation; politics/policy/regulatory; projects/programmes; publishing activities; research/documentation; standards/guidelines; training/education. **Events** *Digitalisation of the Energy Sector – the Case for Data Sharing* Brussels (Belgium) 2022, *The Energy Crisis and Wholesale Electricity Markets* Brussels (Belgium) 2022, *Towards an EU Regulatory Framework for AI Explainability* Brussels (Belgium) 2022, *Digital Identity Services in the Platform Economy* Brussels (Belgium) 2021, *Conference on a Regulatory Agenda for EU Citizens* Brussels (Belgium) 2019. **Publications** Annual Report; issue papers; reports. [2023/XJ9022/**D**]

- Centre de relations internationales, México (internationally oriented national body)
- Centre religieux d'information et d'analyse de la bande dessinée / see International Christian Centre for Research on Information about and Analysis of the Strip Cartoon (#12557)
- Centre for Religious Movements in Primal Societies / see Centre for Pentecostal and Charismatic Studies

♦ Centre de rencontres et d'échanges internationaux du Pacifique (CREIPAC)   03778
Centre of International Cultural and Linguistic Exchanges in the Pacific
Dir BP 3755, 98846 CEDEX Nouméa, New Caledonia. T. +687254124 – +687274328. Fax +687254058. E-mail: creipac@creipac.nc.
URL: http://www.creipac.nc/
History Founded 5 Feb 1980, Nouméa (New Caledonia), under the auspices of *Association des universités partiellement ou entièrement de langue française (AUPELF, inactive)*, and with the support of: Territory of New Caledonia, French Ministry of Foreign Affairs, French State Secretariat for Overseas Departments and Territories, Vice-Chancellor of New Caledonia and *Conférence permanente des responsables des départements d'études françaises de la région du Pacifique Sud (inactive)*. Became a public institutions, 1992. Registered in accordance with French law. **Aims** Develop cultural, educational and scientific exchange, through the medium of the *French language*, between Pacific countries; develop the *values* of the *Francophonie* in Pacific countries. **Structure** General Assembly (annual); Administration Council. **Languages** French. **Staff** 9.00 FTE, paid. **Finance** Proceeds of activities. Budget (annual): CFP 130 million. **Activities** Training/education; events/meetings. **Events** *General Assembly* Nouméa (New Caledonia) 1987. **Publications** *Dossiers CREIPAC*.
Members Individuals and organizations in 12 countries and territories:
Australia, Fiji, France, Germany, Japan, New Caledonia, New Zealand, Papua New Guinea, Switzerland, Thailand, UK, Vanuatu. [2017/XE8247/**E**]

♦ Centre de rencontres et d'études des dirigeants des administrations fiscales (CREDAF)   03779
SG 86 allée de Bercy, Bâtiment TURGOT Télédoc 908, 75012 Paris, France. T. +33153181100. Fax +33153690423. E-mail: credaf@orange.fr.
URL: http://www.credaf.org/
History 14 May 1982, Yaoundé (Cameroon), at constituent assembly, following meetings of the directors of tax administrations in French-speaking countries, 1972 and 1978, Paris (France), and 1980, Abidjan (Côte d'Ivoire). Registered in accordance with French law. **Aims** Develop international fiscal cooperation between *French-speaking* countries. **Structure** General Assembly; Council of Administration or Bureau; Secretariat, headed by Secretary-General, based in Paris (France). **Languages** French. **Finance** Members' dues. **Activities** Events/meetings; knowledge management/information dissemination; training/education. **Events** *Annual Symposium* Abidjan (Côte d'Ivoire) 2014, *Annual Symposium* Congo DR 2013, *Annual Symposium* Lebanon 2012, *Annual Symposium* Algeria 2011, *Annual Symposium* Senegal 2010. **Publications** *Bulletin de liaison CREDAF*. Audiovisual teaching materials on aspects of taxation. **Information Services** *International Tax Information Service* – databank.
Members Tax administrations of 30 countries:
Algeria, Belgium, Benin, Burkina Faso, Burundi, Cambodia, Cameroon, Canada, Central African Rep, Chad, Comoros, Congo Brazzaville, Congo DR, Côte d'Ivoire, Djibouti, France, Gabon, Guinea, Guinea-Bissau, Haiti, Lebanon, Madagascar, Mali, Mauritania, Morocco, Niger, Sao Tomé-Principe, Senegal, Togo, Tunisia.

IGO Relations *Association of African Tax Administrators (AATA, no recent information); Canadian International Development Agency (CIDA, inactive); European Commission (EC, #06633); Global Forum on Transparency and Exchange of Information for Tax Purposes (#10379); International Monetary Fund (IMF, #14180); OECD (#17693); UNCTAD (#20285).* **NGO Relations** Instrumental in setting up: *Council of Executive Secretaries of Tax Organizations (CESTO, inactive).* [2016.02.26/XF2436/**E**]

- ♦ Centre rennais d'information pour le développement et la libération des peuples (internationally oriented national body)
- ♦ Centre for Reproductive Law and Policy / see Center for Reproductive Rights
- ♦ Centre for Research on the Arab World (internationally oriented national body)
- ♦ Centre for Research Documentation and Experimentation on Accidental Water Pollutions / see Centre of Documentation, Research and Experimentation on Accidental Water Pollution
- ♦ Centre for Research and Documentation on Oral Traditions and African Languages / see Centre International de Recherche et de Documentation sur les Traditions et les Langues Africaines (#03761)
- ♦ Centre for Research and Documentation on the World Language Problem / see Centre for Research and Documentation on World Language Problems (#03780)

♦ Centre for Research and Documentation on World Language Problems (CeD) 03780

Centre de recherche et de documentation sur les problèmes de langues – Centro de Esploro kaj Dokumentado pri Mondaj Lingvaj Problemoj (CED)

Head Office CED, Nieuwe Binnenweg 176, 3015 BJ Rotterdam, Netherlands. T. +31104361044. Fax +31104361751.

Dir 279 Ridgewood Road, West Hartford CT 06107, USA. T. +18607684448.

URL: https://www.esperantic.org/en/research/research-tools/the-centre-for-research-and-documentation-on-world-language-problems/

History 1 Jan 1952, London (UK). Founded as Research and Documentation Centre of *Universal Esperanto Association (UEA, #20676).* Former names and other names: *Centre for Research and Documentation on the World Language Problem (CRD)* – former (1969 to 1975); *Centre de recherche et de documentation sur le problème de langues* – former (1969 to 1975); *Centro de Esploro kaj Dokumentado pri la Monda Lingvo-Problemo (CED)* – former (1969 to 1975). **Aims** Promote *linguistic,* sociological, psychological and policy-oriented studies in order to contribute to the resolution of language problems, particularly in international relations. **Structure** International Steering Committee, consisting of 9 members. **Languages** Esperanto. **Activities** Holds conferences (annually) in conjunction with UEA World Congress. Symposium series named in honour of Inazô Nitobe (Under-Secretary-General of the League of Nations, 1920-1926). **Events** *Annual Conference* Lille (France) 2015, *Annual Conference* Buenos Aires (Argentina) 2014, *Annual Conference* Reykjavik (Iceland) 2013, *Annual Conference* Hanoi (Vietnam) 2012, *Annual Conference* Copenhagen (Denmark) 2011. **Publications** *Language Problems and Language Planning* (3 a year); *Informilo por Interlingvistoj* (periodical). [2021/XE0256/**E**]

- ♦ Centre for Research in Economic Development and International Trade (internationally oriented national body)
- ♦ Centre for Research, Environmental Sustainability and Advancement of Mountain Viticulture (#03819)

♦ Centre for Research on the Epidemiology of Disasters (CRED) 03781

Centre de recherche sur l'épidémiologie des désastres

Contact UCL School of Public Health, Clos Chapelle-aux-Champs, Bte B1/30/15, 1200 Brussels, Belgium. T. +3227643327. Fax +3227643441. E-mail: contact@cred.be.

URL: http://www.cred.be/

History 1973, Brussels (Belgium). Former names and other names: *Association for the Epidemiological Study and Assessment of Disasters in Developing Countries* – former (1973); *Association pour l'étude et l'évaluation épidémiologiques des désastres dans les pays en voie de développement* – former (1973); *Association for the Epidemiology of Disasters* – alias; *Association pour l'épidémiologie des désastres* – alias. Registration: Start date: 23 Mar 1977, Belgium. **Aims** Undertake research and provide an evidence base on the burden of disease and health issues arising from disasters and conflicts to improve needs-based *preparedness* and responses to humanitarian emergencies. **Structure** Functions as part of the Université Catholique de Louvain – Institute of Health and Society. **Languages** English, French. **Activities** Humanitarian/emergency aid; research and development; events/meetings; training/education; guidance/assistance/consulting. **Events** *Conference on Ageing Societies in Europe and Japan* Tokyo (Japan) 2012, *Biennial European conference of the Fourth World people's universities* Brussels (Belgium) 1999. **Publications** Seminar and workshop reports. **Information Services** *International Disaster Database EM-DAT.* **Members** Not a membership organization. **IGO Relations** Collaborates with: United Nations Department for Humanitarian Affairs; *WHO (#20950)* and its regional offices. Partner of: *UNHCR (#20327).* [2020/XF0669/**E**]

- ♦ Centre for Research on Europe, Christchurch / see National Centre for Research on Europe, Christchurch
- ♦ Centre for Research on Globalization (internationally oriented national body)
- ♦ Centre for Research on Globalization and Democratic Governance (internationally oriented national body)
- ♦ Centre for Research – Information – Action for Development in Africa (internationally oriented national body)
- ♦ Centre for Research and Information on Substance (internationally oriented national body)
- ♦ Centre for Research in International Economics (internationally oriented national body)
- ♦ Centre for Research on Latin America and the Caribbean (internationally oriented national body)
- ♦ Centre for Research on Multinational Corporations (internationally oriented national body)
- ♦ Centre for Research on Peace and Development (internationally oriented national body)

♦ Centre of Research and Studies for the Eastern Mediterranean 03782

Centre de recherche et d'études sur la Méditerranée orientale (CREMO)

Contact Univ of the Aegean, University Hill, 811 00 Mytilene, Greece. E-mail: cremo@aegean.gr.

URL: http://www.cremo.edu.gr/

History as the research pillar of Euro-Mediterranean University – *Euro-Mediterranean University (EMUNI, #05728).* Participants sign the Euro-Med Academic Consortium Agreement (EMACA). **Aims** Promote research in the areas of conservation and enhancement of cultural heritage, environment, local and regional security and migration; make proposals on the political and economic dimension of relations between the European Union and its Mediterranean partner countries. **Structure** Steering Committee.

Members Participants include the following organizations listed in this Yearbook:

Community of Mediterranean Universities (CMU, #04403); Institut de relations internationales et stratégiques (IRIS); Institut of International Relations, Athens (IIR); International Telematic University UNINETTUNO. [2010/XJ1535/y/**E**]

- ♦ Centre for Research on Sustainable Agriculture and Rural Development (internationally oriented national body)

♦ Centre for Resilience and Socio-Emotional Health 03783

Dir Room 241 Old Humanities Bldg, Univ of Malta, Msida, MSD 2080, Malta. T. +35623402345. Fax +35621317938.

Research Support Officer Room 105 Guzè Cassar Pullicino Bldg, Univ of Malta, Msida, MSD 2080, Malta. T. +35623403014.

URL: http://www.um.edu.mt/cres/

History Founded 2008, as *European Centre for Educational Resilience and Socio-Emotional Health (EDRES),* at University of Malta. Serves as a regional base for *European Network for Social and Emotional Competence (ENSEC, #08006).* **Aims** Conduct and publish research in the promotion of social and emotional health and resilience and in the prevention of social, emotional and behaviour difficulties in children and young persons through collaborative partnerships with local and international researchers and practitioners in the area. **Structure** Board. **Languages** English. **Staff** 3.00 FTE, paid. **Finance** Funded by: University of Malta; self-generated research projects. **Activities** Research/documentation; training/education. **Publications** *International Journal of Emotional Education* (2 a year). Research reports; manuscripts.

Members Individuals in 4 countries:

Australia, Italy, UK, USA. [2017.11.01/XJ0953/**E**]

- ♦ Centre de ressources sur les entreprises et les droits de l'homme (internationally oriented national body)
- ♦ Centre du riz pour l'Afrique (#00518)
- ♦ Centre Robert Schuman (internationally oriented national body)
- ♦ Centre Robert Schuman pour l'Europe / see Centre Robert Schuman
- ♦ Centre roumain d'études de la mondialisation (internationally oriented national body)
- ♦ Centre for Rural Training and Development / see Centre for International Development and Training
- ♦ Centre russe et est-européen, Oxford / see Russian and Eurasian Studies Centre, Oxford
- ♦ Centre for Russia and Eurasia (internationally oriented national body)
- ♦ Centre for Russian, Central Asian and East European Studies, Delhi (internationally oriented national body)
- ♦ Centre for Russian, Central and East European Studies (internationally oriented national body)
- ♦ Centre for Russian and East European Studies / see Centre for Russian, Central Asian and East European Studies, Delhi
- ♦ Centre for Russian and East European Studies, Los Angeles / see Center for European and Eurasian Studies, Los Angeles
- ♦ Centre for Russian and East European Studies, Birmingham (internationally oriented national body)
- ♦ Centre for Russian and East European Studies, Toronto / see Centre for European, Russian, and Eurasian Studies, Toronto
- ♦ Centre for Safety and Development (internationally oriented national body)
- ♦ Centre Saints Cyrille et Méthode / see Catholic Radio and Television Network (#03607)
- ♦ Centre satellitaire de l'Union européenne (#09015)
- ♦ Centre for Science, Society and Citizenship (internationally oriented national body)

♦ Centre for Science and Technology of the Non-Aligned and Other Developing Countries (NAM S and T Centre) 03784

Centro de Ciencia y Tecnologia de los Paises No Alineados y otros en Desarrollo

Dir Gen c/o India Habitat Centre, Core 6A – 2nd Floor, Lodi Road, Delhi 110003, DELHI 110003, India. T. +911124645134 – +911124644974. Fax +911124644973. E-mail: namstcentre@gmail.com.

URL: http://www.namstct.org/

History Established 1989, as an inter-governmental organization with India as the host country, pursuant to recommendations of various *Conference of Heads of State or Government of Non-Aligned Countries.* **Aims** Promote mutually beneficial cooperation in science and technology among non-aligned and other developing countries; stimulate and promote joint research, development projects and training programmes; act as a clearing house of information regarding technological capabilities of individual countries; maintain a registry of scientific and technological experts of high calibre for utilization of their services by member countries. **Structure** Governing Council (GC); Bureau; Secretariat in Delhi (India). **Languages** Arabic, English, French, Spanish. **Staff** 15.00 FTE, paid. **Finance** Members' dues. Project funding from other organizations. **Activities** Events/meetings; training/education; networking/liaising; projects/programmes. **Events** *International Workshop on Policy Making for Transforming Silo-Based Education to STEM Education* Colombo (Sri Lanka) 2020, *International Workshop on Air Pollution and Public Health* Delhi (India) 2020, *International African Symposium on Lightning* Johannesburg (South Africa) 2020, *International Conference on Dryland Agriculture* Masvingo (Zimbabwe) 2020, *SFSA : Science Forum South Africa* Pretoria (South Africa) 2019. **Publications** *NAM S and T Newsletter* (4 a year). Scientific publications; books; monographs; state-of-art reports.

Members Governments of 47 countries:

Afghanistan, Algeria, Argentina, Bangladesh, Bhutan, Bolivia, Burkina Faso, Cambodia, Colombia, Congo Brazzaville, Cuba, Cyprus, Egypt, Ethiopia, Gabon, Gambia, Guyana, India, Indonesia, Iran Islamic Rep, Iraq, Jordan, Kenya, Korea DPR, Lebanon, Malawi, Malaysia, Malta, Mauritius, Myanmar, Nepal, Nicaragua, Nigeria, Pakistan, Palestine, Serbia, South Africa, Sri Lanka, St Lucia, Syrian AR, Tanzania UR, Togo, Uganda, Venezuela, Vietnam, Zambia, Zimbabwe.

NAM S and T Industry Network Organization members (14) in 5 countries:

Bolivia, Brazil, India, Nigeria, Türkiye.

NGO Relations Member of: *International Network for Sustainable Energy (INFORSE, #14331); World Association of Industrial and Technological Research Organizations (WAITRO, #21145); World Renewable Energy Network (WREN, #21750).* [2019.12.13/XE2494/**E***]

- ♦ Centre for Scientific Cooperation of UNESCO for Latin America / see UNESCO Office, Montevideo – Regional Bureau for Sciences in Latin America and the Caribbean (#20314)
- ♦ Centre for Scientific Research and Middle East Strategic Studies (internationally oriented national body)
- ♦ Centres de documentation européenne (#06937)

♦ Centre for Security Cooperation (RACVIAC) 03785

Sec Stari hrast 53, Rakitje, HR-10437 Bestovje, Croatia. T. +38513330803. Fax +38513330809. E-mail: info@racviac.org.

URL: http://www.racviac.org/

History Oct 2000. Founded within framework of *Stability Pact for South Eastern Europe (inactive),* by bilateral agreement between the Government of the Republic of Croatia and the Federal Republic of Germany, originally signed in Zagreb (Croatia), 8 Mar 2001. Italy acceded 21 Aug 2002; Turkey 15 Sep 2004. Transformation process started 2007 and concluded and signed 14 Apr 2010, Budva (Montenegro), by 9 countries of *South East European Cooperation Process (SEECP, #19811).* New Agreement entered into force 1 Dec 2011, when current title was adopted, and when centre became an independent, regionally owned organization with the status of a diplomatic mission in accordance with *Vienna Convention on Diplomatic Relations (1961).* Former names and other names: *Regional Arms Control Verification and Implementation Assistance Centre* – former (2000 to 2011). **Aims** Foster dialogue and cooperation on critical issues related to peace and security matters in South Eastern Europe (SEE) through a partnership between the countries of the region and their international partners. **Structure** Multinational Advisory Group (MAG); Director (from a member State); Deputy Director (always from Croatia, as host nation). Pillars (3): Cooperative Security Environment; Countering Transnational Security Threats; Security Sector Governance. **Languages** English. **Staff** 28.00 FTE, paid; 4.00 FTE, voluntary. **Finance** Sources: contributions; contributions of member/participating states; government support; in-kind support; international organizations. Supported by: *Organisation for the Prohibition of Chemical Weapons (OPCW, #17823); United States European Command (EUCOM).* Annual budget: 660,000 EUR (2020). **Activities** Awareness raising; capacity building; certification/accreditation; conflict resolution; events/meetings; guidance/assistance/consulting; knowledge management/information dissemination; management of treaties and agreements; monitoring/evaluation; networking/liaising; politics/policy/regulatory; projects/programmes; training/education. Active in all member countries. **Events** *Arms Control Symposium* Bestovje (Croatia) 2022, *Conference on the Implementation of UN SC Resolution 1373 Mechanism in the Western Balkans* Bestovje (Croatia) 2022, *RACVIAC-US DOE Regional Nuclear Security Cooperation Initiative Kick-off Meeting* Bestovje (Croatia) 2022, *Regional Workshop on Ammunition Surveillance.* Podgorica (Montenegro) 2022, *Regional Workshop on Threat Assessment and a Risk Informed Approach for Nuclear and other Radioactive Material out of Regulatory Control* Zagreb (Croatia) 2022. **Publications** *RACVIAC Newsletter* (4 a year); *RACVIAC Catalogue* (annual).

Members Member countries (9):

Albania, Bosnia-Herzegovina, Croatia, Greece, Montenegro, North Macedonia, Romania, Serbia, Türkiye.

Associate countries (14):

Austria, Czechia, Denmark, France, Germany, Hungary, Italy, Netherlands, Norway, Russia, Slovenia, Spain, Sweden, UK.

Observer countries (6):

Canada, Moldova, Poland, Slovakia, Ukraine, USA.

Participant country (1):

Kosovo.

*This designation is without prejudice to positions on status, and is in line with UNSCR 1244 and the ICJ Opinion on the Kosovo Declaration of Independence. (In accordance with Arrangements regarding regional representation and cooperation.).

NGO Relations Partner of (7): *Collège européen de sécurité et de défense (CESD, #04107); Geneva International Centre for Humanitarian Demining (GICHD); George C Marshall European Centre for Security Studies, Garmisch Partenkirchen (GCMC); International Centre for Democratic Transition (ICDT); ITF Enhancing Human Security (ITF); NATO SCHOOL Oberammergau (NSO, #16947); Nordic Centre for Gender in Military Operations (NCGM).* [2022.11.10/XJ2481/**E***]

♦ Centre for Security and Peace Studies (internationally oriented national body)
♦ Centre for Security Studies and Conflict Research / see Center for Security Studies
♦ Centre séismologique international (#14830)
♦ Centres européens de la jeunesse (#09138)
♦ Centre Simon Wiesenthal (internationally oriented national body)
♦ Centre Simon Wiesenthal-Europe (internationally oriented national body)
♦ Centres d'Information des Nations Unies (#20574)
♦ Centre sismologique euro-méditerranéen (#07774)
♦ Centre for Social and Economic Research on the Global Environment (internationally oriented national body)

♦ Centre for Social and Environmental Accounting Research (CSEAR) 03786

Contact School of Management – Univ of St Andrews, The Gateway, North Haugh, St Andrews, KY16 9RJ, UK. E-mail: csear@st-andrews.ac.uk.
URL: https://www.st-andrews.ac.uk/csear/

History 1991, Dundee (UK). Founded by Emeritus Professor Rob Gray, also founder and editor from 1993 to 2007 of the Centre's journal. **Aims** Be a world-recognized, global community of scholars who engage with students, activists, practitioners, policy makers and other interested groups in order to generate and disseminate knowledge on social and environmental accounting and accountability; encourage and facilitate high quality, relevant research, teaching and external engagement with practice and policy through developing knowledge, expertise, resources and a supportive network for mentoring and career development. **Structure** Council; Committee of International Associates. **Activities** Advocacy/lobbying/activism; events/meetings; training/education. Active in: Argentina, Australia, Austria, Bahrain, Belgium, Brazil, Canada, China, Denmark, Egypt, Estonia, Fiji, Finland, France, Germany, Hawaii, Hong Kong, India, Indonesia, Ireland, Italy, Jamaica, Japan, Kenya, Korea Rep, Libya, Malaysia, Malta, Mauritius, Netherlands, New Zealand, Nigeria, Norway, Poland, Portugal, Romania, Serbia, Slovenia, South Africa, Spain, Sweden, Thailand, Trinidad-Tobago, Türkiye, UK, United Arab Emirates, USA, Zimbabwe. **Events** *CSEAR International Congress* St Andrews (UK) 2023, *Emerging Scholars Colloquium* St Andrews (UK) 2023, *Emerging Scholars Colloquium* St Andrews (UK) 2022, *International Congress on Social and Environmental Accounting Research* St Andrews (UK) 2022, *CSEAR Australasian Conference (A-CSEAR)* Hobart, TAS (Australia) 2021. **Publications** *CSEAR E-Newsletter*, *Social and Environmental Accountability Journal*.
Members Members (over 250) in 35 countries. Membership countries not specified.
Partnership in 4 countries:
Brazil, Canada, France, Italy.
[2023.02.21/AA0840/**C**]

♦ Centre for Social Markets (internationally oriented national body)
♦ Centre for social sciences studies on the African, American and Asian worlds (internationally oriented national body)
♦ Centre de sociologie européenne (internationally oriented national body)
♦ Centre de Solidarité Internationale Corcovado (internationally oriented national body)
♦ Centre de solidarité internationale du Saguenay Lac-Saint-Jean (internationally oriented national body)
♦ Centres for South Asian Studies, Clayton / see National Centre for South Asian Studies, Clayton
♦ Centre for South Asian Studies, Edinburgh (internationally oriented national body)
♦ Centre for South Asian Studies, Lahore (internationally oriented national body)
♦ Centre for South, Central South East-Asian and South-West Pacific Studies, Delhi (internationally oriented national body)
♦ Centre for Southeast Asian Social Studies (internationally oriented national body)
♦ Centre of Southeast Asian Studies, Clayton (internationally oriented national body)
♦ Centre for Southeast Asian Studies, Kyoto (internationally oriented national body)
♦ Centre for South South Technical Cooperation / see Non-Aligned Movement Centre for South-South Technical Cooperation (#17147)
♦ Centre for Soviet and East European Studies / see Centre for Russian, Central Asian and East European Studies, Delhi
♦ Centre for Space Science and Technology in Africa, Morocco /Affiliated to the United Nations/ (see: #04277)
♦ Centre for Space Science and Technology Education Africa, Nigeria / see African Regional Centre for Space Science and Technology Education – English (#00431)
♦ Centre for Space Science and Technology Education in Asia and the Pacific /Affiliated to the United Nations/ (see: #04277)
♦ Centre for Space Science and Technology Education in Latin America and the Caribbean /Affiliated to the United Nations/ (see: #04277)
♦ Centre spiritain européen pour la coopération au développement (#16188)

♦ Centres régionaux d'enseignement spécialisé en agriculture (CRESA) 03787

Contact c/o Univ de Dschang, Fac d'Agronomie et des Sciences Agricoles, BP 222, Dschang, Cameroon. E-mail: agro50tenair@gmail.com.
URL: http://www.univ-dschang.org/fasa/

History Abidjan (Côte d'Ivoire), at 'Centre ivorien de recherches économiques et sociales (CIRES)', to coordinate specialized regional centres of *Agence universitaire de La Francophonie (AUF, #00548)* in cooperation with *Comité de programme: enseignement supérieur et recherche (CPESR, inactive)*. **Aims** Provide countries of the South with facilities for *higher education* in the *French language* in the field of *rural development*; promote regional cooperation among these countries; organize cooperation among aid agencies, augmenting currently existing training potential rather than creating new structures. Fields: *economics* and *rural sociology*; *agricultural water resources*; protection of the *environment* and improving systems in the *Sahel*; *irrigation*; *forestry*. **IGO Relations** *Organisation internationale de la Francophonie (OIF, #17809)*. [2016/XE2547/**E**]

♦ Centre of Stellar Data / see Strasbourg Astronomical Data Centre (#20003)
♦ Centre for Strategic and Defence Studies, Africa (internationally oriented national body)
♦ Centre for Strategic and International Studies, Jakarta (internationally oriented national body)
♦ Centre for Strategic Studies / see Institute for Strategic Studies, Ulaanbaatar
♦ Centre for Strategic Studies, Amman (internationally oriented national body)
♦ Centre for Strategic Studies of Defense and Security / see Center for Defence and Security Strategic Studies
♦ Centre for Strategic Studies, New Zealand (internationally oriented national body)
♦ Centre for Strategic Studies, Rabat (internationally oriented national body)
♦ Centre for Strategic Studies and Research (internationally oriented national body)
♦ Centre for Studies on Asia and Oceania, Havana (internationally oriented national body)
♦ Centre for Studies in Diplomacy, International Law and Economics, Delhi (internationally oriented national body)
♦ Centre for Studies on East-Central and Balkan Europe (internationally oriented national body)
♦ Centre for Studies on Ethnicity and Migrations (internationally oriented national body)
♦ Centre for Studies of Multilingualism and the Multicultural Society / see Centre for the Study of Superdiversity
♦ Centre for Studies on New Religions (#03820)
♦ Centre for Studies and Research on International Development, Clermont-Ferrand (internationally oriented national body)
♦ Centre for the Study of African Economies, Oxford (internationally oriented national body)

♦ Centre for the Study of Communication and Culture (CSCC) 03788

Managing Editor CSCC Admin Office, Communication Dept, Santa Clara Univ, 500 E Camino Real, Santa Clara CA 95053, USA. T. +14085544022. Fax +14085544913.
URL: http://cscc.scu.edu/

History Founded 1977, London (UK). Moved to Saint Louis University, St Louis MO (USA) in 1993. Administration moved to Santa Clara University, Santa Clara CA (USA) in 2001. **Aims** Study and reflect on all kinds of communication in a dialogue with scholars and *media* practitioners worldwide, with special emphasis on *religious* communication, *theology* and cultural issues. **Structure** Coordinates: *Consultation of International Christian Communication Organizations (CICCO, no recent information)*. **Languages** English, French, Spanish. **Staff** 1.00 FTE, paid. **Finance** Subscription revenues. **Activities** Publishing activity; events/meetings; training/education; networking/liaising. **Publications** *Communication Research Trends* (4 a year). Book series; books.
Members Individuals in 43 countries and territories:
Australia, Belgium, Bolivia, Brazil, Canada, Chile, Croatia, Ecuador, Finland, France, Germany, Ghana, Holy See, Hong Kong, India, Indonesia, Ireland, Italy, Japan, Kenya, Korea Rep, Lithuania, Malaysia, Malta, Mexico, Netherlands, Nigeria, Norway, Philippines, Poland, Portugal, Russia, Singapore, Slovenia, South Africa, Spain, Sweden, Switzerland, Taiwan, UK, Uruguay, USA, Venezuela.
NGO Relations Member of: *World Catholic Association for Communication (SIGNIS, #21264)*.
[2019.02.11/XE3649/v/**E**]

♦ Centre for the Study of Developing Societies (internationally oriented national body)
♦ Centre for the Study of Education in an International Context (internationally oriented national body)
♦ Centre for the Study of Forced Migration (internationally oriented national body)
♦ Centre for the Study of Global Ethics (internationally oriented national body)
♦ Centre for the Study of Globalization, Aberdeen (internationally oriented national body)
♦ Centre for the Study of Globalization, Athens (internationally oriented national body)
♦ Centre for the Study of Globalization and Regionalization (internationally oriented national body)
♦ Centre for the Study of the Great Lakes Region of Africa (internationally oriented national body)
♦ Centre for the Study of International Cooperation in Education (internationally oriented national body)
♦ Centre for the Study of International Economic Relations, Campinas (internationally oriented national body)
♦ Centre for the Study of International Relations and Strategy, Brussels / see Centre européen de recherche internationales et stratégiques
♦ Centre for the Study of Islam and Democracy (internationally oriented national body)
♦ Centre for the Study of New Religious Movements / see Centre for Pentecostal and Charismatic Studies
♦ Centre for the Study and Promotion of Relations between the EC Countries and those of Latin America / see Centre d'étude et de promotion des relations entre les pays de l'Union européenne et de l'Amérique latine
♦ Centre for the Study and Promotion of Relations between the European Union Countries and those of Latin America (internationally oriented national body)
♦ Centre for the Study of Superdiversity (internationally oriented national body)
♦ Centre for the Study of Violence and Reconciliation (internationally oriented national body)
♦ Centre for the Study of Wars, Armaments and Development / see Forschungsstelle Kriege, Rustung und Entwicklung
♦ Centre for the Study of Women in Latin American History (#03799)
♦ Centre Sud (#19753)
♦ Centre for Supporting Evidence Based Interventions in Livestock (internationally oriented national body)
♦ Centre de surveillance de la conservation mondiale de la nature (#20295)
♦ Centre for Sustainability Studies, Lviv (see: #21583)

♦ Centre for Sustainable Agricultural Mechanization (CSAM) 03789

Contact Room 2060 – 20th Floor, Beijing Sunflower Tower, 37 Maizidian Street, Chaoyang District, 100125 Beijing, China. T. +861082253580. Fax +861082253584. E-mail: escap-csam@un.org.
URL: http://www.un-csam.org/

History Established 26 Nov 2002, as a subsidiary body of *United Nations Economic and Social Commission for Asia and the Pacific (ESCAP, #20557)*. Original title: *Asian and Pacific Centre for Agricultural Engineering and Machinery (APCAEM)*. Replaces *Regional Network for Agricultural Engineering and Machinery (RCAEM, inactive)*. **Aims** Help reduce poverty across Asia and the Pacific by enhancing technical cooperation among UNESCAP member countries. **Structure** Governing Board.
Members Governments of 53 countries:
Afghanistan, Armenia, Australia, Azerbaijan, Bangladesh, Bhutan, Brunei Darussalam, Cambodia, China, Fiji, France, Georgia, India, Indonesia, Iran Islamic Rep, Japan, Kazakhstan, Kiribati, Korea DPR, Korea Rep, Kyrgyzstan, Laos, Malaysia, Maldives, Marshall Is, Micronesia FS, Mongolia, Myanmar, Nauru, Nepal, Netherlands, New Zealand, Pakistan, Palau, Papua New Guinea, Philippines, Russia, Samoa, Singapore, Solomon Is, Sri Lanka, Tajikistan, Thailand, Timor-Leste, Tonga, Türkiye, Turkmenistan, Tuvalu, UK, USA, Uzbekistan, Vanuatu, Vietnam.
Associate members (9):
Cook Is, Guam, Hong Kong, Macau, New Caledonia, Niue, Northern Mariana Is, Polynesia Fr, Samoa USA.
NGO Relations *International Commission of Agricultural and Biosystems Engineering (#12661)*.
[2020/XE4682/**E***]

♦ Centre for Sustainable Development and Education in Africa (unconfirmed)
♦ Centre for Technical and Professional Problems in Archives / see International Institute for Archival Science of Trieste and Maribor (#13862)
♦ Centre technique de coopération agricole et rurale (inactive)
♦ Centre technique international de l'embouteillage / see International Technical Centre for Bottling and Packaging (#15667)
♦ Centre technique international de l'embouteillage et du conditionnement (#15667)
♦ Centre des technologies douces (internationally oriented national body)
♦ Centre for Tourism in Islands and Coastal Areas (internationally oriented national body)

♦ Centre de traduction des organes de l'Union européenne (CdT) 03790

Translation Centre for the Bodies of the European Union
Dir Rue Guillaume Kroll 12 E, L-1882 Luxembourg, Luxembourg. T. +3524217111. E-mail: cdt@cdt.europa.eu.
Sec address not obtained. E-mail: secretariat.direction@cdt.europa.eu.
URL: http://www.cdt.europa.eu/

History 28 Nov 1994. Founded by Council Regulation (EC) 2965/1994, last amended by Council Regulation (EC) 1645/2003 of 18 Jun 2003. A decentralized agency of *European Union (EU, #08967)*. Registered in accordance with European law. Former names and other names: *European Translation Centre* – former; *Centre européen de traduction* – former. **Aims** Provide translation services required by various decentralized European Union agencies; provide services to EU institutions and bodies which already have translation services, in order to absorb any peaks in their workload; participate in the work of the Interinstitutional Committee for Translation and Interpreting, so as to promote inter-service cooperation on the basis of the principle of subsidiarity and economies of scale in the translation field. **Structure** Management Board; Departments (4). **Languages** EU languages. **Staff** 200.00 FTE, paid. **Finance** Sources: fees for services. **Activities** Knowledge management/information dissemination. **Publications** Annual Activity Report; annual Highlights. **NGO Relations** Member of (1): *EU Agencies Network (EUAN, #05564)*. [2021.09.07/XE2993/**E***]

♦ Centre for Training and Networking in Nonviolent Action / see KURVE Wustrow
♦ Centre on Transatlantic Foreign and Security Policy Studies / see Centre for Transnational Relations, Foreign and Security Policy
♦ Centre for Transnational Crime Prevention, University of Wollongong (internationally oriented national body)
♦ Centre for Transnational Relations, Foreign and Security Policy (internationally oriented national body)
♦ Centre tricontinental (internationally oriented national body)
♦ Centre for Tropical Marine Ecology / see Leibniz Centre for Tropical Marine Ecology
♦ Centre for Tropical Medicine, Oxford (internationally oriented national body)
♦ Centre for Tropical and Subtropical Agriculture and Forestry (internationally oriented national body)
♦ Centre for Tropical Veterinary Medicine, Edinburgh (internationally oriented national body)
♦ Centre de Turin / see International Training Centre of the ILO (#15717)
♦ Centre UNESCO de Catalunya (internationally oriented national body)

Centre UNESCO femmes
03790

alphabetic sequence excludes
For the complete listing, see Yearbook Online at

- ♦ Centre UNESCO pour les femmes et la paix dans les Balkans (#20303)
- ♦ Centre universel d'amélioration de la paix et de la violence (internationally oriented national body)
- ♦ Centre universitaire européen pour les biens culturels, Ravello (internationally oriented national body)
- ♦ Centre universitaire de recherches sur la paix, Wien (internationally oriented national body)
- ♦ Centre for University Research, Exchange and Documentation / see Institut français de recherche en Afrique
- ♦ Centre for Urban and Regional Studies (internationally oriented national body)
- ♦ Centre de Vienne – Centre européen de coordination de recherche et de documentation en sciences sociales (inactive)
- ♦ Centre de volontariat international (internationally oriented national body)
- ♦ Centre for Voluntary Aid and Cooperation in Third World Development (internationally oriented national body)
- ♦ Centre of West African Studies, Birmingham (internationally oriented national body)
- ♦ Centre for West Asian and African Studies, Delhi (internationally oriented national body)
- ♦ Centre for Women's Development Studies (internationally oriented national body)
- ♦ Centre for World Biodiversity Information and Assessment / see UN Environment Programme World Conservation Monitoring Centre (#20295)

♦ Centre for World Dialogue 03791

Address not obtained.
URL: http://www.worlddialogue.org/

History 1997. **Aims** Initiate and encourage dialogue on political, social, economic and religious issues of global and regional concern. **Structure** Officers: President; Executive Director. Board of Governors of 18 members. **Finance** Funded through: bank institutions; businesses; independent donations. Budget (annual): US$ 300,000. **Activities** Organizes conferences and seminars. **Publications** *Global Dialogue* (2 a year) – online. Books; occasional papers.

Members Organizations and individuals. Individuals in 45 countries and territories:
Australia, Austria, Azerbaijan, Bahrain, Belgium, Bulgaria, Canada, Cuba, Cyprus, Denmark, Egypt, France, Germany, Greece, Holy See, Hungary, Iceland, India, Indonesia, Iran Islamic Rep, Iraq, Israel, Italy, Japan, Jordan, Kazakhstan, Kuwait, Lebanon, Libya, Monaco, Morocco, Netherlands, Norway, Oman, Pakistan, Palestine, Philippines, Qatar, Saudi Arabia, Sweden, Switzerland, Syrian AR, UK, United Arab Emirates, USA.
Organizations in 14 countries:
Australia, Cyprus, Denmark, France, Germany, Greece, Iran Islamic Rep, Japan, Jordan, Kazakhstan, Sweden, Switzerland, UK, USA. [2013.06.12/XE3661/**E**]

- ♦ Centre on World Economy Studies (internationally oriented national body)
- ♦ Centre for the World Religions, A (internationally oriented national body)
- ♦ Centre for World Solidarity (internationally oriented national body)
- ♦ Centre pour les zones humides africaines / see Centre for African Wetlands (#03727)
- ♦ Centr Informacii po Dvuhjazycnomu Obrazovaniju (#11195)

♦ Centrist Democrat International (CDI) 03792

Internacional Demócrata de Centro (IDC)

Head of Secretariat Rue du Commerce 10, 1000 Brussels, Belgium. T. +3222854145. Fax +3223008013. E-mail: secretariat@idc-cdi.com.
URL: http://www.idc-cdi.com/

History Jun 1961, Santiago (Chile). Founded at 3rd Christian Democratic World Congress, previous congresses having been held: Nov 1954, Paris (France); Jul 1958, Brussels (Belgium). Constitution adopted and World Committee set up Sep 1963, Strasbourg (France). Statutes modified: Jan 1974, Rome (Italy); 1982, Quito (Ecuador); Jun 1986, Lisbon (Portugal); Sep 1989, Guatemala (Guatemala); Mar 1993, Brussels; Jun 1995, Brussels. Former names and other names: *Christian Democratic World Union (CDWU)* – former (Jun 1961); *Union mondiale démocrate chrétienne* – former (Jun 1961); *Unión Mundial Demócrata Cristiana* – former (Jun 1961); *Christlich-Demokratische Weltunion* – former (Jun 1961); *Unione Mondiale Democratica Cristiana (UMDC)* – former (Jun 1961); *World Union of Christian Democrats (WUCD)* – former alias; *Christian Democratic International (CDI)* – former (1982 to 1999); *Internationale démocrate chrétienne (IDC)* – former (1982 to 1999); *Internacional Demócrata Cristiana* – former (1982 to 1999). **Aims** Promote and coordinate international activity of Christian democratic *parties*, ensuring political solidarity; carry out *doctrinal* and *political* research of general interest for Christian democracy; disseminate Christian democratic ideas and promote knowledge of their achievements. **Structure** General Assembly; Executive Committee. Regional entities: *Christian Democratic Organization of America (#03899)*; IDC-CDI Africa; European People's Party (EPP); IDC-CDI Asia-Pacific; IDC-CDI Europe. **Languages** English, French, German, Spanish. **Staff** 8.00 FTE, voluntary. **Finance** Members' dues. **Activities** Events/meetings; advocacy/lobbying/activism; knowledge management/information dissemination; training/education. **Events** *Meeting* Brussels (Belgium) 2019, *Meeting* Budapest (Hungary) 2018, *Meeting* Brussels (Belgium) 2017, *Meeting* Malta 2017, *Meeting* Lisbon (Portugal) 2016. **Publications** *Human Rights* (5 a year) in English, French, Spanish; *DC-Info* (4 a year) in English, French, Spanish – sometimes also in Dutch, German, Hungarian, Italian, Polish, Russian; *Documents* (4 a year) in English, French, Spanish.

Members National Christian democratic parties in 72 countries and territories:
Algeria, Argentina, Armenia, Aruba, Austria, Azerbaijan, Belarus, Belgium, Bolivia, Bonaire Is, Bulgaria, Cameroon, Chile, Colombia, Congo DR, Costa Rica, Croatia, Cuba (in exile), Curaçao, Cyprus, Czechia, Dominica, Dominican Rep, Ecuador, El Salvador, Equatorial Guinea, Estonia, France, Georgia, Germany, Greece, Guatemala, Guyana, Haiti, Honduras, Hungary, Indonesia, Ireland, Italy, Lebanon, Lithuania, Luxembourg, Madagascar, Malta, Mauritius, Mozambique, Netherlands, Nicaragua, Norway, Panama, Paraguay, Peru, Philippines, Poland, Portugal, Romania, Russia, Saba, San Marino, Slovakia, Slovenia, Spain, St Kitts-Nevis, Suriname, Sweden, Switzerland, Taiwan, Uganda, Ukraine, Uruguay, Venezuela.
Observers (3) in 3 countries:
Denmark, Korea Rep, Mexico.
Regional and international organizations (12):
Christian Democratic Organization of America (#03899); Christian Democratic Women of America (CDWA, #03900); Christian Democratic Workers International (CDWI, no recent information); European People's Party (EPP, #08185); Frente de Trabajadores Demócratas Cristianos de América Latina (FETRAL DC, no recent information); Group of the European People's Party (#10774); Group of the European People's Party – Christian Democrats (EPP, #10775).

Consultative Status Consultative status granted from: *ECOSOC (#05331)* (Special); *UNCTAD (#20285)* (General Category). **IGO Relations** *UNESCO (#20322)*. Accredited by: *United Nations Office at Vienna (UNOV, #20604)*. Associated with Department of Global Communications of the United Nations. [2022/XF0266/y/**F**]

- ♦ Centro del Sur (#19753)
- ♦ Centro de Actividad Regional para el Consumo y la Producción Sostenibles (#18747)
- ♦ Centro Africano Dedesenvolvimento de Minerais (unconfirmed)
- ♦ Centro Africano de Investigaciones Aplicadas y de Formación en Materia de Desarrollo Social (#00237)
- ♦ Centro Africano Oriental para la Investigación de las Tradiciones Orales y las Lenguas Nacionales Africanas (inactive)
- ♦ Centro Agronómico Tropical de Investigación y Enseñanza (#20246)
- ♦ Centro del Agua para América Latina y el Caribe (unconfirmed)
- ♦ Centro del Agua del Trópico Húmedo para América Latina y el Caribe (#20824)
- ♦ Centro del Agua para Zonas Aridas y Semiaridas de América Latina y el Caribe (internationally oriented national body)
- ♦ Centro Amazónico de Educación Ambiental e Investigación (internationally oriented national body)
- ♦ Centro de Amigos para la Paz (internationally oriented national body)

♦ Centro de Análise Estratégica da Comunidade dos Países de Língua Portuguesa (CAE/CPLP) 03793

Diretor Rua Aurélio Manave 383, Sommerschield, 0101 Maputo, Cidade de Maputo, Mozambique. T. +25821089743. E-mail: secretaria@caecplp.org.
URL: https://caecplp.org/

History Proposed Jul 1998. Statutes approved 28 May 2002. Headquarters inaugurated 28 Nov 2003. **Aims** Research, study and disseminate knowledge in the field of Strategy so as to contribute to the objectives of the Community of Portuguese Language Countries (CPLP). **Structure** Advisory Board; Director. **Languages** Portuguese. **Finance** Sources: contributions of member/participating states. Annual budget: 43,000 USD. **Activities** Events/meetings; research/documentation. **Publications** *Boletim Estratégico* (4 a year) in Portuguese – CAE/CPLP's newsletter; *Revista Estratégica* (annual) in Portuguese – Scientific Magazine of CAE/CPLP.

Members Full in 9 countries:
Angola, Brazil, Cape Verde, Equatorial Guinea, Guinea-Bissau, Mozambique, Portugal, Sao Tomé-Principe, Timor-Leste.

IGO Relations *Comunidade dos Países de Língua Portuguesa (CPLP, #04430).* [2020.08.27/XM8648/**E***]

- ♦ Centro de Analise e de Operações contra o Narcotrafico Maritimo (#16581)
- ♦ Centro Andino de Acción Popular (internationally oriented national body)
- ♦ Centro para la Apertura y el Desarrollo de América Latina (internationally oriented national body)
- ♦ Centro per un Appropriato Sviluppo Tecnologico (internationally oriented national body)
- ♦ Centro Arabe para el Estudio de las Zonas y Tierras Aridas (#00918)
- ♦ Centro de Arbitraje y Mediación Comercial para las Américas (inactive)
- ♦ Centro de Asesoria Legal en Asuntos de la OMC (#00138)
- ♦ Centro de Asesoria y Promoción Electoral (see: #11334)
- ♦ Centro Biblico Católico para Africa e Madagascar (#03599)
- ♦ Centro Camuno di Studi Preistorici (internationally oriented national body)
- ♦ Centro canadiense de Estudios y Cooperación Internacional (internationally oriented national body)
- ♦ Centro de Capacitación a Distancia (see: #11434)
- ♦ Centro Católico Internacional de Cooperación para la UNESCO (#12454)
- ♦ Centro Católico Internacional de Coordinación ante la UNESCO / see International Catholic Cooperation Centre for UNESCO (#12454)
- ♦ Centro Católico Internacional de Ginebra (#12449)
- ♦ Centro Católico Internacional para la UNESCO / see International Catholic Cooperation Centre for UNESCO (#12454)
- ♦ Centro de Ciencia y Tecnologia de los Paises No Alineados y otros en Desarrollo (#03784)
- ♦ Centro Cientifico Tropical, Costa Rica (internationally oriented national body)
- ♦ Centro Cochrane Iberoamericano (internationally oriented national body)
- ♦ Centro di Collegamento delle Industrie Trasformatrici delle Carni Macellate della CEE / see Liaison Centre for the Meat Processing Industry in the EU (#16452)
- ♦ Centro de Comercio Internacional (#15703)
- ♦ Centro de Comercio Internacional UNCTAD/GATT / see International Trade Centre (#15703)
- ♦ Centro de Comercio Internacional UNCTAD/OMC / see International Trade Centre (#15703)
- ♦ Centro Comum de Investigação (#16147)
- ♦ Centro Comune de Ricerca (#16147)
- ♦ Centro de Comunicación Cientifica con Ibero-América (internationally oriented national body)
- ♦ Centro de Comunicación, Investigación y Documentación entre Europa, España y América / see Fundación CIDEAL de Cooperación e Investigación
- ♦ Centro Común de Investigación (#16147)
- ♦ Centro de Cooperación Internacional en Salud y Desarrollo (internationally oriented national body)
- ♦ Centro de Cooperación para la Investigación Cientifica del Tabaco (#03735)

♦ Centro de Cooperación Regional para la Educación de Adultos en América Latina y el Caribe (CREFAL) 03794

Regional Cooperation Center for Adult Education in Latin America and the Caribbean – Centre de coopération régionale pour l'éducation des adultes en Amérique latine dans et les Caraïbes

Gen Dir and Institutional Office Av Lazaro Cardenas 525, Col Revolución, CP 61609, Patzcuaro, 61609 Michoacan, Mexico. T. +524343428212. Fax +524343428100. E-mail: crefal@crefal.edu.mx.
URL: http://www.crefal.edu.mx/crefal25/

History Established 9 May 1951, Patzcuaro (Mexico), by a resolution of *UNESCO (#20322)*, as an organism functioning under its auspices and with the collaboration of the Mexican government and the *OAS (#17629)*. Since 1990, an autonomous international organization governed by a Board of Directors, composed of member states and representatives of UNESCO and OAS. Previously known as: *Centro Regional de Educación Fundamental para América Latina et el Caribe.* **Aims** Promote cooperation in *adult education* throughout *Latin America* and the *Caribbean*; participate in projects sponsored by intergovernmental and international organizations; provide technical assistance; support training programmes, research, studies and publications. **Structure** Board of Administration, consisting of representatives from the 12 member countries, UNESCO and OAS; headed by Mexico's Secretary of Public Education. **Languages** English, Portuguese, Spanish. **Staff** 128.00 FTE, paid. **Activities** Training/education; events/meetings; guidance/assistance/consulting; networking/liaising. **Events** *Latin American meeting on the training of educators for young people and adults* Patzcuaro (Mexico) 2003. **Publications** *Decisio* – series; *Retablo de Papel* – series; *Revista Interamericana de Educación de Adultos* – series. Courses; monographs; reports and surveys; bibliographies. Information Services: 'Lucas Ortiz Benitez' library of more than 43,000 vols and 30,000 titles, one quarter specialized on adult education. Documentary Center specializing in adult education. **Information Services** *a database on education in general and other topics*; *BIB* – database directory of specialists and institutions related to CREFAL; *EDA* – bibliographical database specialized in adult education; *'Lucas Ortiz Benitez' library of more than 43,000 vols and 30,000 titles, one quarter specialized on adult education.*

Members Governments of 12 countries:
Argentina, Brazil, Cuba, Ecuador, El Salvador, Guatemala, Honduras, Mexico, Nicaragua, Paraguay, Uruguay, Venezuela.

NGO Relations Member of: *EarthAction (EA, #05159)*; *Information Network on Education for Latin America (no recent information).* [2016.02.12/XE4251/**E***]

- ♦ Centro per la Cooperazione Internazionale (internationally oriented national body)
- ♦ Centro para a Coordenação e Desenvolvimento Agrario na Africa Austral (#03736)

♦ Centro de Coordinación para la Prevención de los Desastres Naturales en América Central (CEPREDENAC) 03795

Center for Coordination of the Prevention of Natural Disasters in Central America

Exec Sec Avda Hincapié 21-72, zona 13, Guatemala, Guatemala. T. +50223900200. E-mail: info@cepredenac.org.
URL: http://www.cepredenac.org/

History Nov 1987. **Aims** Foster reduction of natural disaster process in Central America through the exchange of information, experience and technology; analyse common strategic problems and channel external cooperation. **Structure** Representative Council; Board of Directors; Executive Secretariat. National Commissions. **Finance** Financed through the contributions from governments of Central America. Also works as an executive office for external cooperation resources, through projects on natural disaster reduction areas. Budget (annual): US$ 1,600,000. **Activities** *'Regular Program'*: Responds to the regional mandate of CEPREDENAC. Refers mainly to some activities, that in a short time, should be financed by member countries. Activities are focused on the promotion of regional cooperation on issues related to natural disaster reduction process. Also includes efforts in mobilizing international cooperation resources within the countries for preventing and mitigating natural disasters. Under the Regular Programs there are some efforts that are being developing, such as the Regional Plan for Disaster Reduction and *Fuerza Institutional de Solidaridad Centroamericana (FISCA)*. *'Projects'*: Basically referred to the activities related to the services for the countries in project identification, evaluation and execution. **Events** *Central American Expert Meeting on the Use of Space-Based Information in Early Warning Systems* San Salvador (El Salvador) 2014, *Regional Consultation and Dissemination Workshop on Integral Disaster Risk Management in Central America* Panama (Panama) 2013, *Regional conference* San Salvador (El Salvador) 2005. **Publications** *CEPREDENAC Bulletin* (4 a year). **Information Services** *Seismological Data Base for Central America.*

Members National Commissions in 6 countries:
Costa Rica, El Salvador, Guatemala, Honduras, Nicaragua, Panama.

IGO Relations Specialized Institution of: *Central American Integration System (#03671)*. **NGO Relations** Since 1997, an agency involved in: *Regional Disaster Information Center for Latin America and the Caribbean (#18778)*. Member of: *International Recovery Platform (IRP, #14704).* [2017/XE1928/**E**]

- ♦ Centro Coordinador y Difusor de Estudios Latinoamericanos / see Centro de Investigaciones sobre América y el Caribe (#03810)
- ♦ Centro Coordinador de la Investigación de la Federación Internacional de Universidades Católicas / see International Center for Research and Decision Support of the International Federation of Catholic Universities (#12476)
- ♦ Centro Culturale Esperantista (internationally oriented national body)
- ♦ Centro Cultural Encuentro / see Association Rencontre CEFIR
- ♦ Centro Cultural Iberoamericano 'Casa de América', Madrid (internationally oriented national body)
- ♦ Centro Cultural Universitario / see Universidad Iberoamericana, México
- ♦ Centro de Derecho Internacional del Desarrollo Sostenible (internationally oriented national body)
- ♦ Centro de Derechos Humanos y Ambiente (internationally oriented national body)
- ♦ Centro de Derechos Humanos Miguel Agustin Pro Juarez (internationally oriented national body)
- ♦ Centro de Derechos Humanos de las Naciones Unidas (inactive)
- ♦ Centro de derechos reproductivos (internationally oriented national body)

♦ Centro Desarrollo y Pesca Sustenable (CeDePesca) 03796

Exec Dir/Pres Rondeau 361, Mar del Plata, Buenos Aires, Argentina. T. +542234896397. E-mail: info@cedepesca.net.
URL: http://www.cedepesca.net/

History 1997. **Aims** Help Latin American fisheries attain sustainability. **Languages** English, Portuguese, Spanish. **Staff** 7.00 FTE, paid. **Activities** Research and development; training/education.
Members Representatives in 6 countries:
Argentina, Brazil, Chile, Mexico, Panama, Peru.
NGO Relations Member of: *Deep Sea Conservation Coalition (DSCC, #05024)*; *International Union for Conservation of Nature and Natural Resources (IUCN, #15766)*. [2020.04.06/XM6785/**D**]

- ♦ Centro Disegno Urbano / see International Centre for Studies on Urban Design (#12520)
- ♦ Centro de Documentación para el Caribe / see Caribbean Knowledge Management Centre (#03521)
- ♦ Centro de Documentación Europea, Universidad de Navarra / see Centre for European Studies – University of Navarra
- ♦ Centro de Documentación e Información sobre los Derechos Humanos en América Latina (internationally oriented national body)
- ♦ Centro de Documentación, Investigación e Información de los Pueblos Indigenas (internationally oriented national body)
- ♦ Centro de Dokumentado kaj Esploro pri la Lingvo Internacia (internationally oriented national body)
- ♦ Centro di Ecologia Alpina (internationally oriented national body)
- ♦ Centro de Ecologia y Pueblos Andinos (internationally oriented national body)
- ♦ Centro Ecumênico de Documentação e Informação para Africa Austral (#05346)
- ♦ Centro Ecumênico de Documentação e Informação para Africa Austral e Oriental / see Ecumenical Documentation and Information Centre in Southern Africa (#05346)
- ♦ Centro Educazione Mondialità / see Centro Educazione alla Mondialità
- ♦ Centro Educazione alla Mondialità (internationally oriented national body)
- ♦ Centro di Educazione Sanitaria e Tecnologie Appropriate Sanitarie (internationally oriented national body)
- ♦ Centro Einstein di Studi Internazionali sul Federalismo, la Pace, la Politica del Territorio (internationally oriented national body)
- ♦ Centro de Enlace e Información de las Potencias Masónicas signatarias del Llamamiento de Estrasburgo (#03770)
- ♦ Centro de Epidemiologia del Caribe (inactive)
- ♦ Centro Español de Relaciones Internacionales (internationally oriented national body)
- ♦ Centro de Esploro kaj Dokumentado pri Mondaj Lingvaj Problemoj (#03780)
- ♦ Centro de Esploro kaj Dokumentado pri la Monda Lingvo-Problemo / see Centre for Research and Documentation on World Language Problems (#03780)
- ♦ Centro de Estudios y Acción para la Paz, Lima (internationally oriented national body)
- ♦ Centro de Estudios Africanos (internationally oriented national body)
- ♦ Centro de Estudios de América Latina, Bruxelles / see Groupe d'études latino-américaines de l'Institut de sociologie, Bruxelles
- ♦ Centro de Estudios Americanos y Caribeños (internationally oriented national body)
- ♦ Centro de Estudios Americanos y Caribeños Dr Gastón Parra Luzardo / see Centro de Estudios Americanos y Caribeños
- ♦ Centro de Estudios de Asia y Africa, México (internationally oriented national body)
- ♦ Centro de Estudios sobre Asia y Oceania, Habana (internationally oriented national body)
- ♦ Centro de Estudios de Asia Oriental, Madrid (internationally oriented national body)

♦ Centro de Estudios Avanzados en Banda Ancha para el Desarrollo (CEABAD) 03797

Center for Advanced Studies for Broadband

Contact Avenida Bolivar, Complejo TELCOR, Edificio CEABAD, 12001, Managua, Nicaragua. T. +50578262400. E-mail: info.ceabad@ceabad.com.
URL: https://ceabad.com/

History 2014. Founded by Ministry of Science and ICt of Korea Rep, TELCOR (Government of Nicaragua) and *Inter-American Development Bank (IDB, #11427)*. **Aims** Transfer knowledge and increase the capacities of government officials at public institutions. **Structure** Board of Directors; Executive Secretariat. **Activities** Training/education. **IGO Relations** Partner of: *Comisión Técnica Regional de Telecomunicaciones (COMTELCA, #04144)*; *International Telecommunication Union (ITU, #15673)*. **NGO Relations** Member of (1): *Cybersecurity Alliance for Mutual Progress (CAMP, #04987)*. Partner of: *Asociación Interamericana de Empresas de Telecomunicaciones (ASIET, #02160)*; *GSM Association (GSMA, #10813)*; *Internet Corporation for Assigned Names and Numbers (ICANN, #15949)*; *Internet Society (ISOC, #15952)*; national organizations. [2020/AA0212/**E**]

- ♦ Centro de Estudios en Ciencias Sociales sobre los Mundos Africanos, Americanos y Asiáticos (internationally oriented national body)
- ♦ Centro de Estudios Constitucionales / see Centro de Estudios Politicos y Constitucionales
- ♦ Centro de Estudios de Construcción y Arquitectura Tropical (internationally oriented national body)
- ♦ Centro de Estudios de Demografia Histórica de América Latina (internationally oriented national body)
- ♦ Centro de Estudios del Desarrollo, Caracas (internationally oriented national body)
- ♦ Centro de Estudios para el Desarrollo Laboral y Agrario (internationally oriented national body)
- ♦ Centro de Estudios y Documentación Internacionales de Barcelona (internationally oriented national body)
- ♦ Centro de Estudios y Documentación Latinoamericanos (internationally oriented national body)
- ♦ Centro de Estudios Ecuménicos, México (internationally oriented national body)

♦ Centro de Estudios sobre el Esoterismo Occidental de la Unión de Naciones Suramericanas (CEEO-UNASUR) 03798

Dir c/o FILO-UBA, Fac de Filosofia y Letras, Puan 430 – CABA, C1406CQJ Buenos Aires, Argentina.
URL: http://ceeo-unasur.blogspot.be/

History Aug 2011. **Activities** Research/documentation. **Publications** *Melancolia* – review. Newsletter.
Members Full in 6 countries:
Argentina, Brazil, Chile, Colombia, Costa Rica, Mexico.
IGO Relations *Union of South American Nations (#20481)*. **NGO Relations** Affiliated with: *European Society for the Study of Western Esotericism (ESSWE, #08749)*. [2017/XM6371/**E**]

- ♦ Centro de Estudios de Estado y Sociedad, Buenos Aires (internationally oriented national body)
- ♦ Centro de Estudios Europeos, Habana (internationally oriented national body)
- ♦ Centro de Estudios Europeos – Universidad de Navarra (internationally oriented national body)
- ♦ Centro de Estudios Globales y Regionales, Buenos Aires (internationally oriented national body)
- ♦ Centro de Estudios Hemisféricos de Defensa (internationally oriented national body)
- ♦ Centro de Estudios Ibéricos y Latinoamericanos (internationally oriented national body)
- ♦ Centro de Estudios Interamericanos (internationally oriented national body)
- ♦ Centro de Estudios Internacionales, Managua (internationally oriented national body)
- ♦ Centro de Estudios Internacionales, México (internationally oriented national body)
- ♦ Centro de Estudios de Justicia de las Américas (#16171)
- ♦ Centro de Estudios Latinoamericanos (internationally oriented national body)
- ♦ Centro de Estudios Latinoamericanos, Buenos Aires (internationally oriented national body)
- ♦ Centro de Estudios Latinoamericanos y del Caribe / see Latin American and Caribbean Studies Institute
- ♦ Centro de Estudios Latinoamericanos de Educación Inclusiva (internationally oriented national body)
- ♦ Centro de Estudios Latinoamericanos 'Justo Arosemena' (internationally oriented national body)
- ♦ Centro de Estudios Latinoamericanos Rómulo Gallegos (internationally oriented national body)
- ♦ Centro de Estudios Latinoamericanos, Universidad de Varsovia (internationally oriented national body)
- ♦ Centro de Estudios Migratorios (internationally oriented national body)
- ♦ Centro de Estudios Migratorios Latinoamericanos (internationally oriented national body)
- ♦ Centro de Estudios Monetarios Latinoamericanos (#03648)

♦ Centro de Estudios la Mujer en la Historia de América Latina (CEMHAL) 03799

Centre for the Study of Women in Latin American History

Dir Malecón Castilla 106, 04, Lima, Peru. T. +512474567.
URL: http://www.cemhal.org/

History Founded Nov 1998. **Aims** Promote research and studies in the history of women in Latin America. **Structure** Council; Scientific Committee of the Women's History Magazine. **Languages** Spanish. **Staff** Voluntary. **Finance** Members' dues. Other sources: sponsored by *UNESCO (#20322)* for publication of books; University of San Martin de Porres in conducting conferences. **Activities** Research/documentation; publishing activities; knowledge management/information dissemination. **Events** *International Congress* Lima (Peru) 2013, *Symposium* Lima (Peru) 2009, *Symposium* Lima (Peru) 2006, *Congress* 2005, *Symposium* Lima (Peru) 2000. **Publications** *Las mujeres en los procesos de independencia de América Latina* (2014); *Viajeras entre dos mundos* (2012); *Las mujeres en la Independencia de América Latina* (2010); *Escritura de la Historia de las Mujeres en América Latina – El Retorno de la Diosas* (2005); *Historia de las mujeres en América Latina* (2002). Cuadernos de investigacion.
Members Individuals in 31 countries:
Argentina, Australia, Bolivia, Brazil, Canada, Chile, Colombia, Costa Rica, Dominican Rep, Ecuador, El Salvador, France, Germany, Guatemala, Honduras, Hungary, Italy, Mexico, New Zealand, Nicaragua, Panama, Paraguay, Peru, Portugal, Puerto Rico, Spain, Sweden, UK, Uruguay, USA, Venezuela. [2020/XE4471/v/**E**]

- ♦ Centro de Estudios Municipales y de Cooperación Internacional (internationally oriented national body)
- ♦ Centro de Estudios Politicos y Constitucionales (internationally oriented national body)
- ♦ Centro de Estudios y Promoción del Desarrollo (internationally oriented national body)
- ♦ Centro de Estudios Regionales Andinos 'Bartolomé de Las Casas' (#03636)
- ♦ Centro de Estudios Regionales Urbanos y Rurales / see Weitz Center for Development Studies
- ♦ Centro de Estudios Rurales y de Agricultura Internacional (internationally oriented national body)
- ♦ Centro de Estudios Rurales Andinos: Bartolomé de Las Casas / see Center for Andean Regional Studies 'Bartolomé de Las Casas' (#03636)
- ♦ Centro de Estudios y Solidaridad con América Latina / see CESAL
- ♦ Centro de Estudios del Transporte para el Mediterraneo Occidental (internationally oriented national body)
- ♦ Centro de Estudios Urbanos y Regionales (internationally oriented national body)
- ♦ Centro d'Estudis Africans, Barcelona (internationally oriented national body)
- ♦ Centro de Estudos sobre Africa, Asia e América Latina / see Centre for African and Development Studies
- ♦ Centro de Estudos sobre Africa e do Desenvolvimento / see Centre for African and Development Studies
- ♦ Centro de Estudos sobre África e Desenvolvimento (internationally oriented national body)
- ♦ Centro de Estudos Africanos, Lisboa (internationally oriented national body)
- ♦ Centro de Estudos Africanos, Maputo (internationally oriented national body)
- ♦ Centro de Estudos Africanos, São Paulo (internationally oriented national body)
- ♦ Centro de Estudos Africanos da Universidade do Porto (internationally oriented national body)
- ♦ Centro de Estudos Afro-Orientais, Bahia (internationally oriented national body)
- ♦ Centro de Estudos das Americas, Rio de Janeiro (internationally oriented national body)
- ♦ Centro de Estudos de Cultura Contemporânea (internationally oriented national body)
- ♦ Centro de Estudos e Documentação Latinoamericanos (internationally oriented national body)
- ♦ Centro de Estudos Europeus, Lisbon / see Instituto de Estudos Europeus, Lisboa
- ♦ Centro de Estudos de História do Atlântico (internationally oriented national body)
- ♦ Centro de Estudos Latino-Americanos de Educação Inclusiva (internationally oriented national body)
- ♦ Centro de Estudos Norte-Americanos / see Centro de Estudos das Americas, Rio de Janeiro
- ♦ Centro de Estudos de Relações Económicas Internacionais (internationally oriented national body)
- ♦ Centro Euro-Mediterraneo per i Cambiamenti Climatici (internationally oriented national body)
- ♦ Centro Euromediterraneo di Studi Internazionali, Turin / see Centro Einstein di Studi Internazionali sul Federalismo, la Pace, la Politica del Territorio
- ♦ Centro per l'Europa Centro-Orientale e Balcanica (internationally oriented national body)
- ♦ Centro Europa – Tercer Mundo (internationally oriented national body)
- ♦ Centro Europeo de Arbitraje y de Mediación (#06462)
- ♦ Centro Europeo di Arbitrato e di Mediazione (#06462)
- ♦ Centro Europeo del Commercio al Minuto (inactive)
- ♦ Centro Europeo de Coordinación de Investigación y de Documentación en las Ciencias Sociales (inactive)
- ♦ Centro Europeo de la Cultura (#06472)
- ♦ Centro Europeo para el Desarrollo de la Formación Profesional (#06474)
- ♦ Centro Europeo de la Empresa Pública / see SGI Europe (#19253)
- ♦ Centro Europeo de Empresas e Innovación (internationally oriented national body)
- ♦ Centro Europeo de Empresas con Participación Pública / see SGI Europe (#19253)
- ♦ Centro Europeo di Formazione degli Artigiani per la Conservazione del Patrimonio Architettonico / see European Centre for Heritage Crafts and Professions (#06484)
- ♦ Centro Europeo dell'Impresa Pubblica / see SGI Europe (#19253)
- ♦ Centro Europeo delle Imprese a Partecipazione Pubblica / see SGI Europe (#19253)
- ♦ Centro Europeo para la Investigación Nuclear (#08108)
- ♦ Centro Europeo de Investigación Social de Situaciones de Emergencia (internationally oriented national body)
- ♦ Centro Europeo para la Medicina de Catastrofes (#06475)
- ♦ Centro Europeo per la Medicina delle Catastrofi (#06475)
- ♦ Centro Europeo per i Mestieri del Patrimonio (#06484)
- ♦ Centro Europeo para la Paz y el Desarrollo (#06496)
- ♦ Centro Europeo para la Prevención y el Control de las Enfermedades (#06476)
- ♦ Centro Europeo per la Prevenzione e il Controllo delle Malattie (#06476)
- ♦ Centro Europeo per le Previsioni Meteorologiche a Medio Termine (#06490)
- ♦ Centro Europeo de Regiones (see: #07569)
- ♦ Centro Europeo di Studi e Informazioni / see Centro Einstein di Studi Internazionali sul Federalismo, la Pace, la Politica del Territorio
- ♦ Centro Europeo per gli Studi e le Ricerche sul Federalismo (internationally oriented national body)
- ♦ Centro Europeo per lo Sviluppo della Formazione Professionale (#06474)
- ♦ Centro Europeo para la Validación de Métodos Alternativos (inactive)

Centro Europeo Venezia
03799

alphabetic sequence excludes
For the complete listing, see Yearbook Online at

- ♦ Centro Europeo di Venezia per i Mestieri della Conservazione del Patrimonio Architettonico / see European Centre for Heritage Crafts and Professions (#06484)
- ♦ Centro Europeu para o Desenvolvimento da Formação Profissional (#06474)
- ♦ Centro Europeu da Empresa Pública / see SGI Europe (#19253)
- ♦ Centro Europeu das Empresas com Participação Pública / see SGI Europe (#19253)
- ♦ Centro Europeu para a Interdependência e Solidariedade Globais (#06483)
- ♦ Centro Europeu de Prevenção e Controlo das Doenças (#06476)
- ♦ Centro Evangélico de Estudios Pastorales en Centro América (internationally oriented national body)
- ♦ Centro Experimental de Estudios Latinoamericanos / see Centro de Estudios Americanos y Caribeños
- ♦ Centro Extremeño de Estudios y Cooperación con Iberoamérica (internationally oriented national body)
- ♦ Centro Femenino Europeo de Investigación sobre la Evolución de la Sociedad (inactive)
- ♦ Centro Financiero para la Cooperación Sur-Sur (internationally oriented national body)
- ♦ Centro de Formación para la Integración Regional (#20197)
- ♦ Centro di Geomorfologia Integrata per l'Area del Mediterraneo (internationally oriented national body)
- ♦ Centro de Gestión y Cooperación Internacional para el Desarrollo (internationally oriented national body)
- ♦ Centro de Ginebra para la Gobernanza del Sector de la Seguridad (#10121)
- ♦ Centro Giovanile Internazionale San Lorenzo (internationally oriented national body)
- ♦ Centro Holandés para el Estudio del Derecho en el Sudeste de Asia y la Région del Caribe / see Van Vollenhoven Institute for Law, Governance and Development
- ♦ Centro Holandés para los Pueblos Indigenas (internationally oriented national body)
- ♦ Centro Iberoamericano de Cooperación / see Dirección General de Cooperación con Iberoamérica

♦ Centro Iberoamericano de Desarrollo Estratégico Urbano (CIDEU) . . 03800

Iberoamerican Center for Strategic Urban development

SG Calle Avinyó, 15, 08002 Barcelona, Spain. T. +34933427640. Fax +34933427641. E-mail: secretaria@cideu.org.
URL: http://www.cideu.org/

History 1993, Barcelona (Spain). Founded as a programme of cooperation of Ibero-American Summit of Chiefs of State and Government. **Aims** Promote use of strategic planning methods in urban development. **Structure** General Assembly; Governing Council; Permanent Secretariat; Technical Office. **Languages** Spanish. **Activities** Events/meetings; training/education. **Events** *Congress* Bogota (Colombia) 2022, *Public space and urban landscape* Santiago (Chile) 2018, *General Assembly* Oaxaca (Mexico) 2017, *Congress* San Sebastian (Spain) 2016, *General Assembly* Buenos Aires (Argentina) 2015. **Members** Cities (123) in 21 countries. Membership countries not specified. [2023/XE4409/**E**]

- ♦ Centro Iberoamericano de Tercera Edad (internationally oriented national body)
- ♦ Centro de Informação e Documentação Amilcar Cabral (internationally oriented national body)
- ♦ Centro de Informação Europeia Jacques Delors (internationally oriented national body)
- ♦ Centro de Información Bancaria (internationally oriented national body)
- ♦ Centro de Información y Comunicación Ambiental de Norte América (internationally oriented national body)
- ♦ Centro de Información sobre Educación Bilingüe e Plurilingüe (#11195)
- ♦ Centro de Información sobre Migraciones en América Latina (#03643)
- ♦ Centro de Información de las Organizaciones Internacionales Católicas / see International Catholic Centre of Geneva (#12449)
- ♦ Centro d'Informazione, di Consulenza e di Formazione Professioni della Cooperazione Internazionale e dell'Aiuto Umanitario (internationally oriented national body)
- ♦ Centro Informazione e Educazione allo Sviluppo (internationally oriented national body)
- ♦ Centro di Informazione sull' Educazione Bilingua e Plurilingue (#11195)
- ♦ Centro d'Iniciatives per a la Producció Neta / see Regional Activity Centre for Sustainable Consumption and Production (#18747)
- ♦ Centro d'Iniziativa per l'Europa (internationally oriented national body)
- ♦ Centro per l'Innovazione Amministrativa nelle Regione Euro-mediterranea (internationally oriented national body)
- ♦ Centro Interamericano de Administraciones Tributarias (#11405)
- ♦ Centro Interamericano de Administrações Tributarias (#11405)
- ♦ Centro Interamericano de Administradores Tributarios / see Inter-American Centre for Tax Administrations (#11405)

♦ Centro Interamericano de Artesanias y Artes Populares (CIDAP) . . . 03801

Inter-American Center for Crafts and Popular Arts

Contact Hermano Miguel 3-23 y Paseo Tres de Noviembre, Cuenca, Ecuador. T. +59372840919 – +59372829451 – +5937285051. E-mail: cidap@cidap.gob.ec.
URL: http://www.cidap.gob.ec/

History May 1975, Cuenca (Ecuador), within the framework of *OAS (#17629)*, as a project of *Inter-American Council for Education, Science and Culture (inactive)*. **Aims** Preserve popular crafts. **Structure** Board of Directors, including Ecuador's Minister of Industry. Executive Director, in permanent contact with OAS Department of Cultural Affairs. Departments (4, each with its Director): Technical; Administrative; Publishing; Crafts Promotion. **Staff** 35.00 FTE, paid. **Finance** Grants from OAS and Ecuadorian government. **Activities** Training/education; research/documentation; knowledge management/information dissemination. **Publications** *Revista Artesanías de América*. Information bulletins; books.
Members Governments of 35 countries:
Antigua-Barbuda, Argentina, Bahamas, Barbados, Belize, Bolivia, Brazil, Canada, Chile, Colombia, Costa Rica, Cuba, Dominica, Dominican Rep, Ecuador, El Salvador, Grenada, Guatemala, Guyana, Haiti, Honduras, Jamaica, Mexico, Nicaragua, Panama, Paraguay, Peru, St Kitts-Nevis, St Lucia, St Vincent-Grenadines, Suriname, Trinidad-Tobago, Uruguay, USA, Venezuela.
IGO Relations Member of: *Fundación de Etnomusicologia y Folklore (FUNDEF, no recent information)*; *Centro Interamericano de Etnomusicologia y Folklore (CIDEF, inactive)*. [2016/XE5829/**E***]

- ♦ Centro Interamericano de Cooperación y Capacitación (internationally oriented national body)
- ♦ Centro Interamericano de Desarrollo de Archivos (inactive)

♦ Centro Interamericano para el Desarrollo del Conocimiento en la Formación Profesional (OIT/Cinterfor) 03802

Inter-American Centre for Knowledge Development in Vocational Training

Dir Avda Uruguay 1238, CP 11-100, Montevideo, Uruguay. T. +59829020557. Fax +59829021305. E-mail: webmaster@oitcinterfor.org – oitcinterfor@ilo.org.
URL: http://www.oitcinterfor.org/

History 17 Sep 1963, Montevideo (Uruguay), on signature of an Agreement between the Government of Uruguay and *ILO (#11123)*, following Technical Preparatory Meetings, Sep 1962, Bogota, and Jun 1963, Rio de Janeiro (Brazil). A technical services of the ILO. Also referred to in Spanish as *Centro Interamericano de Investigación y Documentación sobre la Formación Profesional* and by the acronym *OIT/Cinterfor*. **Aims** Serve as the core of an integrated system of vocational training entities belonging to ILO Member States in Latin America, the Caribbean, Spain and Germany; contribute to the strategic of goals of ILO and the Decent Work Agenda for the Hemisphere (2006-2015). **Structure** Technical Committee (meets every 2 years), consisting of representatives of national specialized organisms in vocational training and human resources development from American ILO Member States and Europe. **Languages** English, Portuguese, Spanish. **Staff** 20.00 FTE, paid. **Finance** Supported by *ILO (#11123)*, the Government of Uruguay and contributions from member countries and their specialized institutions. Budget (biannual). **Activities** Research/documentation; events/meetings; projects/programmes; training/education. **Events** *Meeting* Montevideo (Uruguay) 2019, *The future of work and the challenges for vocational training* San José (Costa Rica) 2017, *Annual Meeting* Buenos Aires (Argentina) 2015, *Meeting* Port-of-Spain (Trinidad-Tobago) 2013, *Meeting* Panama (Panama) 2011.
Members Contributing Governments of 31 countries and territories:
Argentina, Bahamas, Barbados, Bolivia, Brazil, Chile, Colombia, Costa Rica, Cuba, Dominica, Dominican Rep, Ecuador, El Salvador, Grenada, Guatemala, Guyana, Haiti, Honduras, Jamaica, Mexico, Neth Antilles, Nicaragua, Panama, Paraguay, Peru, Spain, St Lucia, Suriname, Trinidad-Tobago, Uruguay, Venezuela.
IGO Relations United Nations Specialized Agencies (not specified); *UNDP (#20292)*; vocational training institutes (not specified); ministries of labour and of education. Coordinates: *Sistema Regional de Información sobre Formación Profesional (SIRFO, #19296)*. **NGO Relations** Member of: *Information Network on Education for Latin America (no recent information)*. [2021/XD3648/**E***]

- ♦ Centro Interamericano para el Desarrollo Integral de Aguas y Tierras / see Centro Interamericano de Desarrollo e Investigación Ambiental y Territorial
- ♦ Centro Interamericano de Desarrollo e Investigación Ambiental y Territorial (internationally oriented national body)
- ♦ Centro Interamericano de Enseñanza de Estadistica (no recent information)

♦ Centro Interamericano de Estudios de Seguridad Social (CIESS) . . . 03803

Inter-American Center for Social Security Studies – Centre interaméricain d'études de la sécurité sociale

Dir Calle San Ramon s/n, Colonia San Jeronimo Lidice, Delg Magdalena Contreras, CP 10100 Mexico City CDMX, Mexico. T. +525553774705. E-mail: ciess@ciess.org.
URL: http://www.ciess.org.mx/

History Founded 19 Mar 1963, Mexico City (Mexico), as complement to Resolution 58 of *Inter-American Conference on Social Security (ICSS, #11419)*, adopted at 6th meeting of CISS, 1960, Mexico City. CIESS is the educational, training and research body of the Inter-American Conference on Social Security. **Aims** As the educational, teaching and research organ of CISS, contribute to the strengthening of Inter-American social security institutions. **Languages** English, French, Portuguese, Spanish. **Staff** 5.00 FTE, paid. **Activities** Training/education; research/documentation; guidance/assistance/consulting. **Events** *Latin American congress on health services* Sao Paulo (Brazil) 1996. **Publications** *CIESS Bulletin – Boletin CIESS* in English, Spanish. *Documentos Ingresados al Centro de Información* – series.
Members Full in 36 countries and territories:
Anguilla, Antigua-Barbuda, Argentina, Aruba, Bahamas, Barbados, Belize, Bolivia, Brazil, Canada, Chile, Colombia, Costa Rica, Cuba, Dominica, Dominican Rep, Ecuador, El Salvador, Grenada, Guatemala, Haiti, Honduras, Mexico, Neth Antilles, Nicaragua, Panama, Paraguay, Peru, St Kitts-Nevis, St Lucia, St Vincent-Grenadines, Trinidad-Tobago, Turks-Caicos, Uruguay, USA, Virgin Is UK.
NGO Relations Member of: *Education and Solidarity Network (#05374)*. [2014.12.18/XE9070/**E**]

- ♦ Centro Interamericano de Estudios Superiores de Relaciones Públicas y Opinión Pública (internationally oriented national body)
- ♦ Centro Interamericano de Gerencia Politica (internationally oriented national body)
- ♦ Centro Interamericano de Investigación y Documentación sobre la Formación Profesional / see Centro Interamericano para el Desarrollo del Conocimiento en la Formación Profesional (#03802)
- ♦ Centro Interamericano de Investigaciones y Estudios para el Planeamiento de la Educación (no recent information)
- ♦ Centro Interamericano de Promoción de Exportaciones (inactive)
- ♦ Centro Interamericano de Recursos del Agua (#11404)
- ♦ Centro de Intercambios y Cooperación para America Latina (internationally oriented national body)
- ♦ Centro Interdisciplinare di Studi Latinoamericani, Roma (internationally oriented national body)
- ♦ Centro Interdisciplinario de Estudios Latinoamericanos (internationally oriented national body)
- ♦ Centro Interfacoltà per la Cooperazione con i Paesi in Via di Sviluppo / see Commissione Cooperazione Internazionale per lo Sviluppo
- ♦ Centro Internacional de Agricultura Tropical (#12527)
- ♦ Centro Internacional de Arreglo de Diferencias Relativas a Inversiones (#12515)
- ♦ Centro Internacional Bancaja para la Paz y el Desarrollo (internationally oriented national body)
- ♦ Centro Internacional Celso Furtado de Politicas para o Desenvolvimento (internationally oriented national body)
- ♦ Centro Internacional de Ciencias Biológicas (internationally oriented national body)
- ♦ Centro Internacional de Ciencias, Cuernavaca (internationally oriented national body)
- ♦ Centro Internacional Cientifico de Abonos (#03767)
- ♦ Centro Internacional de Civilizaciones Bantu (inactive)
- ♦ Centro Internacional de Civilizações Bantu (inactive)
- ♦ Centro Internacional para la Conservación del Patrimonio (internationally oriented national body)
- ♦ Centro Internacional para el Crédito Comunal (#12501)
- ♦ Centro Internacional de la Democracia para la Mujer (internationally oriented national body)
- ♦ Centro Internacional de Demonstración y Capacitación en Aprovechamiento de Agua de Lluvia (internationally oriented national body)
- ♦ Centro Internacional de Derecho Registral / see IPRA-CINDER – International Property Registries Association (#16012)
- ♦ Centro Internacional para los Derechos Humanos de los Migrantes (internationally oriented national body)
- ♦ Centro Internacional para los Derechos Sindicales (#12525)

♦ Centro Internacional de Desarrollo de Albergues Juveniles de América Latina (CIDAJAL) 03804

International Center for the Development of Youth Hostels in Latin America

Address not obtained.

Structure Secretariat rotates. **Events** *Congress* Costa Rica 1989, *Congress* Costa Rica 1989, *Congress* Colombia 1988, *Congress* Uruguay 1987. **NGO Relations** *Hostelling International (#10950)*. [2008/XF1299/**E**]

- ♦ Centro Internacional para el Desarrollo Humano (internationally oriented national body)
- ♦ Centro Internacional de Direitos Económicos, Sociais e Culturais (internationally oriented national body)
- ♦ Centro Internacional de Documentación e Investigación del Baloncesto (internationally oriented national body)

♦ Centro Internacional de Ecologia Tropical (CIET) 03805

Centre international d'écologie tropicale – International Centre for Tropical Ecology

Dir c/o IVIC, Apdo Postal 20632, Caracas 1020-A DF, Venezuela. E-mail: cietunesco@gmail.com – ciet@ivic.gob.ve.
URL: http://www.ivic.gob.ve/ecologia/CIET/

History Founded 1977, following agreement between the Venezuelan Government and *UNESCO (#20322)*. Also referred to by acronym *CIET/UNESCO*. An autonomous institution serving UNESCO member- or associate member countries in the tropical region. **Aims** Promote and support research projects focused towards *conservation* of ecosystems and sustainable development of natural resources; make governmental and non-governmental organizations aware of the need to preserve tropical biodiversity and the goods and services derived from it for the benefit of human kind. **Structure** Administration Board; Advisory Council. **Languages** English, Spanish. **Staff** 2.00 FTE, paid. **Finance** Operation costs funded by IVIC; projects supported by UNESCO's Participation programmes and other institutions. **Activities** Events/meetings; knowledge management/information dissemination; training/education. **Publications** *Ecologia en breves/Ecology briefs* – bulletin. **Members** Not a membership organization. **IGO Relations** Cooperates with: *International Hydrological Programme (IHP, #13826)*; *Programme on Man and the Biosphere (MAB, #18526)*; *UNESCO Office, Montevideo – Regional Bureau for Sciences in Latin America and the Caribbean (#20314)*. [2015.06.04/XE3227/**E**]

- ♦ Centro Internacional de Educación y Desarrollo Humano (internationally oriented national body)
- ♦ Centro Internacional para la Empresa Privada (internationally oriented national body)
- ♦ Centro Internacional para Empresas Públicas / see International Centre for Promotion of Enterprises (#12509)
- ♦ Centro Internacional para Empresas Públicas de Paises en Desarrollo / see International Centre for Promotion of Enterprises (#12509)
- ♦ Centro Internacional de Estudios para el Desarrollo Local (internationally oriented national body)
- ♦ Centro Internacional de Estudios de la Formación Religiosa (#12519)

♦ Centro Internacional de Estudios Superiores sobre Agronomia Mediterranea / see CIHEAM – International Centre for Advanced Mediterranean Agronomic Studies (#03927)

♦ Centro Internacional de Estudios Superiores de Comunicación para América Latina (CIESPAL) 03806

Centre international d'études supérieures de communication pour l'Amérique latine – International Centre of Advanced Communication Studies for Latin America

Contact Avenida Diego de Almagro N 32-133 y Andrade Marin, Casilla 1701584, Quito, Ecuador. T. +59322548011 – +59322234031. Fax +59322502487. E-mail: info@ciespal.org.
URL: http://www.ciespal.org/

History 9 Oct 1959, Quito (Ecuador). Founded on signature of tripartite convention by *UNESCO (#20322)*, the Government of Ecuador and the Central University of Ecuador. At one time a member of *International Network of Documentation Centres on Communication Research and Policies (COMNET, inactive)*, functions as a regional non-governmental international body registered in accordance with Ecuador law. Agreement with *OAS (#17629)* signed in 1964. **Aims** Provide advanced training in *information* science and scientific *journalism*; carry out scientific research on mass communications; provide specialized *documentation* on radio and television productions, technical equipment and technology. **Languages** English, Portuguese, Spanish. **Staff** 56.00 FTE, paid. **Finance** Grants from Government of Ecuador. Self-sustaining funds and resources from national and foreign NGO's. **Activities** Training/education; events/meetings; financial and/or material support; publishing activities. Offers a variety of quality media products to incorporate into training and events; works on productions in radio and TV. **Events** *Congreso Internacional sobre Comunicacion e Integracion Latinoamericana desde y para el SUR* Quito (Ecuador) 2015, *Congreso Internacional sobre Comunicacion, Decolonizacion y Buen Vivir* Quito (Ecuador) 2015, *Workshop on evaluation strategies for drug abuse communications campaigns* Quito (Ecuador) 1991. **Publications** *Chasqui* (4 a year). Meeting reports; manuals; books. **NGO Relations** Member of: *Asociación Latinoamericana de Investigadores de la Comunicación (ALAIC, #02237)*; *Consejo Latinoamericano de Ciencias Sociales (CLACSO, #04718)*; *Federación Latinoamericana de Facultades de Comunicación Social (FELAFACS, #09353)*; *Redes de Comunicación de América Latina y el Caribe para el Desarrollo (G-8, no recent information).* [2021/XE3205/E]

♦ Centro Internacional del Film para Niños y Jóvenes (#12493)

♦ Centro Internacional de Fisica (CIF) 03807

International Centre of Physics

Dir Cra 30 N 45-03, Univ Nac de Colombia, Ed de Programas Especiales "Manuel Ancizar" Ciudad Universitaria, Bogota, Bogota DC, Colombia. T. +5713681517. Fax +5713681517.

History 4 Dec 1985, Bogota (Colombia). **Aims** Promote scientific and technological development of *Latin America*, particularly of *Andean* and *Caribbean* subregions, and establishment of *high technology industries*. **Structure** Administrative Council; Scientific Council; Executive Director. **Finance** Main source: Government of Colombia. Other sources: support from international, regional and bilateral funding agencies in Canada, Italy, Spain and USA. **Activities** Research and development; training/education; events/meetings. **Events** *Seminar on microprocessors applications in instrumentation* La Paz (Bolivia) 1995. **Publications** Books; articles; proceedings of conferences.

Members Organizations and individuals in 33 countries:
Argentina, Belgium, Bolivia, Brazil, Canada, Chile, China, Colombia, Costa Rica, Cuba, Dominican Rep, Ecuador, El Salvador, France, Germany, Guatemala, Honduras, Israel, Italy, Mexico, New Zealand, Nicaragua, Pakistan, Peru, Russia, Spain, Sudan, Switzerland, Trinidad-Tobago, Ukraine, Uruguay, USA, Venezuela.

IGO Relations Cooperation agreement with: *Andean Community (#00817)*. Affiliated as a Centre of Excellence to: *Commission on Science and Technology for Sustainable Development in the South (COMSATS, #04239)*. **NGO Relations** Member of: *Network of International Science and Technology Centers (#17044)*. [2014/XE1942/E]

♦ Centro Internacional de Fisica y Matematicas Aplicadas / see Centro Internacional de Ciencias, Cuernavaca
♦ Centro Internacional de Fisica y Matematicas Orientadas / see Centro Internacional de Ciencias, Cuernavaca
♦ Centro Internacional de Fisiologia y Ecologia de los Insectos (#12499)
♦ Centro Internacional Flamenco / see KIYO
♦ Centro Internacional de Fonética Aplicada, Mons (internationally oriented national body)
♦ Centro Internacional de Formação dos Trabalhadores da Indústria e Energia (internationally oriented national body)
♦ Centro Internacional de Formación – Aristides Calvani / see Instituto de Formación Demócrata Cristiana
♦ Centro internacional de formación para la enseñanza de los derechos humanos y la paz (see: #21184)
♦ Centro Internacional de Información Cientifica y Técnica (#12514)
♦ Centro Internacional de Información sobre Cultivos de Cobertura (internationally oriented national body)
♦ Centro Internacional de Inovação e Intercâmbio em Administração Pública (internationally oriented national body)
♦ Centro Internacional de Investigación en Agroforesteria / see World Agroforestry Centre (#21072)
♦ Centro Internacional para Investigación en Agrosilvicultura / see World Agroforestry Centre (#21072)
♦ Centro Internacional de Investigación y de Apoyo a la Decisión de la Federación Internacional de Universidades Católicas (#12476)
♦ Centro Internacional de Investigación sobre la Delincuencia, la Marginalidad y las Relaciones Sociales (#12510)
♦ Centro Internacional para la Investigación del Fenómeno de EL Niño (internationally oriented national body)
♦ Centro Internacional Iwokrama para la Conservación y el Desarrollo del Bosque Tropical (internationally oriented national body)
♦ Centro Internacional para la Justicia Transicional (internationally oriented national body)
♦ Centro Internacional de Luta contra a Poluição do Atlântico do Nordeste (#03757)
♦ Centro Internacional de Matematica (internationally oriented national body)
♦ Centro Internacional de Materiales Avanzados y Materias Primas de Castilla y León (internationally oriented national body)
♦ Centro Internacional de Medicina Familiar / see Confederación Iberoamericana de Medicina Familiar (#04450)
♦ Centro Internacional de Mejoramiento de Maiz y Trigo (#14077)
♦ Centro Internacional de Métodos Numéricos en Ingenieria (internationally oriented national body)
♦ Centro Internacional para la Migración, la Salud y el Desarrollo (#12502)
♦ Centro Internacional para la Música Coral (internationally oriented national body)
♦ Centro Internacional de la Papa (#14627)
♦ Centro Internacional de Perfeccionamiento Profesional y Técnico / see International Training Centre of the ILO (#15717)
♦ Centro Internacional de Politica Económica para el Desarrollo Sostenible (internationally oriented national body)
♦ Centro Internacional de Politicas para el Desarrollo / see International Forum for Innovative Northeast Asia Strategy
♦ Centro Internacional para la Prevención de la Criminalidad (#12508)
♦ Centro Internacional para la Promoción de los Derechos Humanos (internationally oriented national body)
♦ Centro Internacional de Promoción de Empresas (#12509)
♦ Centro Internacional de Radiodifusión Rural (inactive)
♦ Centro Internacional de Referencia e Información en Suelos / see ISRIC – World Soil Information (#16068)
♦ Centro Internacional de Sindonologia (#12516)
♦ Centro Internacional de Sismologia (#14830)
♦ Centro Internacional de Toledo para la Paz (internationally oriented national body)
♦ Centro Internacional de Transferencia de Innovaciones y Conociemientos en Economia Social y Solidaria (#12498)
♦ Centro Internationale del Diaconado (#13167)

♦ Centro Internazionale di Animazione Missionaria 03808

Dir Via Urbano VIII 16, 00165 Rome RM, Italy. T. +39669882484. E-mail: segreteria@ciam.va.
URL: http://www.ciam-va.com/

History 31 May 1974. [2017/XE1994/E]

♦ Centro Internazionale per gli Antiparassitari e la Prevenzione Sanitaria (internationally oriented national body)
♦ Centro Internazionale Civiltà dell'Acqua (internationally oriented national body)
♦ Centro Internazionale del Commercio all'Ingrosso ed Estero (inactive)
♦ Centro Internazionale per la Conservazione e lo Sviluppo della Foresta Pluviale (internationally oriented national body)
♦ Centro Internazionale Cooperazione per lo Sviluppo / see Commissione Cooperazione Internazionale per lo Sviluppo
♦ Centro Internazionale Crocevia (internationally oriented national body)
♦ Centro Internazionale di Ipnosi Medica e Psicologica (#15257)
♦ Centro Internazionale per la Pace fra i Popoli (internationally oriented national body)
♦ Centro Internazionale per la Promozione dell'Educazione e lo Sviluppo (internationally oriented national body)
♦ Centro Internazionale di radio comunicazioni mediche / see Fondazione Centro Internazionale Radio Medico
♦ Centro Internazionale di Radiodiffusione Rurale (inactive)
♦ Centro Internazionale di Ricerca Promozione e Sviluppo / see Fondazione Livorno Euro Mediterranea
♦ Centro Internazionale Scientifico Concimi Chimici (#03767)
♦ Centro Internazionale di Sindonologia (#12516)
♦ Centro Internazionale di Studi e Documentazione – Istituto Paolo VI (internationally oriented national body)
♦ Centro Internazionale di Studi sull'Economia Turistica (internationally oriented national body)
♦ Centro Internazionale Studi Famiglia (#12492)
♦ Centro Internazionale per lo Studio dei Papiri Ercolanesi "Marcello Gigante" (internationally oriented national body)
♦ Centro Internazionale di Studi sul Disegno Urbano (#12520)
♦ Centro Internazionale di Sviluppo e Cooperazione Culturale, Roma (internationally oriented national body)
♦ Centro Internazionale 'Universal Medical Assistance' (inactive)

♦ Centro Interuniversitario de Desarrollo (CINDA) 03809

Exec Dir Santa Magdalena 75, Piso 11, Providencia, Santiago, Santiago Metropolitan, Chile. T. +56222339869 – +56222341128. Fax +56222341117. E-mail: cinda@cinda.cl.
URL: http://www.cinda.cl/

History Nov 1971, as *Centro Interuniversitario de Desarrollo Andino*, on signature of an agreement between universities in the Andean region. Later expanded membership to include universities in Latin America and Europe. **Aims** Link member universities and channel, promote and guide their contribution to the *integration* and political, economic, social and cultural development of *Latin America* and Europe; act as a consultant in fields related with university management, quality assurance and policy making in higher education. **Structure** Board of Directors; Executive Board; Network of member universities. **Languages** Spanish. **Finance** Members' dues. Grants from international sources for specific projects, studies and programmes. **Activities** Training/education; projects/programmes. **Events** *Meeting of the innovation and research network* 2010, *International seminar on equity in higher education* Talca (Chile) 2009, *Seminario internacional sobre la desercion y repitencia en Latinoamérica* Talca (Chile) 2005, *International seminar* Santiago (Chile) 1998, *International seminar* Santiago (Chile) 1995. **Publications** *Boletin Informativo CINDA* (periodical). *Colección Gestión Universitaria* – book series; *Educación Superior en Iberoamerica* – series. Reports.

Members Full: universities (39) in 15 countries:
Argentina, Bolivia, Brazil, Chile, Colombia, Costa Rica, Dominican Rep, Ecuador, Italy, Mexico, Panama, Peru, Spain, Uruguay, Venezuela.
Associate: university 1 country:
Paraguay.

IGO Relations *UNESCO (#20322)*. **NGO Relations** Member of: *International Network of Quality Assurance Agencies in Higher Education (INQAAHE, #14312)*; *Red Iberoamericana para el Aseguramiento de la Calidad en la Educación Superior (RIACES, #18657)*. [2020.03.04/XD6066/F]

♦ Centro Interuniversitario de Desarrollo Andino / see Centro Interuniversitario de Desarrollo (#03809)
♦ Centro Interuniversitario de Estudios y Documentación Latinoamericanos / see Centre for Latin American Research and Documentation
♦ Centro Interuniversitario di Ricerca sul Sud Europa (internationally oriented national body)
♦ Centro de Inversiones de la FAO (#09264)
♦ Centro de Investigación para el Desarrollo Económico-Social (no recent information)
♦ Centro de investigación, docencia, documentación y divulgación de Relaciones Internacionales y Desarrollo, Barcelona / see Centre for International Information and Documentation, Barcelona
♦ Centro de Investigación Economica para el Caribe (internationally oriented national body)
♦ Centro de Investigación de Enfermedades Tropicales / see Community Information, Empowerment and Transparency

♦ Centro de Investigaciones sobre América y el Caribe (CIALC) 03810

Admin Sec UNAM Torre II de Hum 8o Piso, Ave Universidad 3000, Ciudad Universitaria, Coyoacan, 04510 Mexico City CDMX, Mexico. E-mail: difusion.cialc@unam.mx.
URL: http://www.cialc.unam.mx/

History Nov 1978, Mexico City (Mexico). Founded on the initiative of *'I Simposio para la Coordinación y Difusión de los Estudios Latinoamericanos'* to develop efforts and projects to better know the region, and later to consolidate its presence and leadership as a research centre. Operations began 13 Dec 1979. Original title: *Center of Coordination and Diffusion of Latin American Studies – Centre de coordination et de diffusion des études latinoaméricaines – Centro Coordinador y Difusor de Estudios Latinoamericanos (CCyDEL)*. Current title adopted in 2007. **Aims** Exchange knowledge of Latin America amongst members, especially in domaines of *human, social* and *political* sciences; contribute towards Latin American *integration*. **Structure** General Assembly. Executive Committee, consisting of 6 members representing different regions of Latin America. Coordinator, assisted by Consultative Council. **Finance** All activities financed by Mexico's National Autonomous University. **Activities** Research/documentation; training/education; networking/liaising; events/meetings. **Publications** *Cuadernos Americanos* (6 a year); *Latinoamérica* (2 a year). *Nuestra América* – research monographs. **Information Services** *Biblioteca Simón Bolivar.*

Members Institutions in 32 countries:
Argentina, Austria, Belgium, Brazil, Chile, Colombia, Costa Rica, Cuba, Dominican Rep, Ecuador, France, Germany, Haiti, Hungary, India, Israel, Italy, Jamaica, Japan, Mexico, Nicaragua, Panama, Peru, Poland, Portugal, Russia, Spain, Switzerland, Trinidad-Tobago, Uruguay, USA, Venezuela.

NGO Relations Coordinates activities of *Federación Internacional de Estudios sobre América Latina y el Caribe (FIEALC, #09338)* and *Sociedad Latinoamericana de Estudios sobre América Latina y el Caribe (SOLAR, #19406)*. [2021/XE4192/E]

♦ Centro de Investigaciones de Economia Internacional, Habana (internationally oriented national body)
♦ Centro de Investigaciones de la Economía Mundial (internationally oriented national body)
♦ Centro de Investigaciones de la Economia Mundial, Habana (internationally oriented national body)
♦ Centro de Investigaciones Económicas Internacionales, La Havana / see Centro de Investigaciones de Economia Internacional, Habana
♦ Centro de Investigaciones y Estudios Familiares / see Instituto de Ciencias Familiares (#11330)

Centro Investigaciones Interdisciplinarias
03810

alphabetic sequence excludes
For the complete listing, see Yearbook Online at

♦ Centro de Investigaciones Interdisciplinarias en Ciencias y Humanidades (internationally oriented national body)
♦ Centro de Investigaciones Interdisciplinarias en Humanidades / see Centro de Investigaciones Interdisciplinarias en Ciencias y Humanidades
♦ Centro de Investigaciones Regionales de Mesoamérica (internationally oriented national body)
♦ Centro de Investigación y Extensión Forestal Andino Patagónico (internationally oriented national body)
♦ Centro de Investigación para la Paz, Madrid (internationally oriented national body)
♦ Centro de Investigación de la Universidad del Pacifico (internationally oriented national body)
♦ Centro Italiano di Collaborazione per lo Sviluppo Edilizio delle Nazioni Emergenti (internationally oriented national body)
♦ Centro Italiano di Formazione Europea (internationally oriented national body)
♦ Centro Italiano di Solidarieta (internationally oriented national body)
♦ Centro por la Justicia y el Derecho Internacional (#03647)
♦ Centro Laici Italiani per le Missioni / see Celim Bergamo – Organizzazione di Volontariato Internazionale Cristiano
♦ Centro Laici Italiani per le Missioni (internationally oriented national body)
♦ Centro Latinoamericano de Administración para el Desarrollo (#16294)
♦ Centro Latinoamericano para Altos Estudios Musicales, Washington DC (internationally oriented national body)
♦ Centro Latinoamericano de Aprendizaje y Servicio Solidario (#16291)
♦ Centro Latinoamericano e do Caribe de Informação em Ciências da Saúde (#16267)
♦ Centro Latinoamericano y del Caribe de Información en Ciencias de la Salud (#16267)
♦ Centro Latinoamericano y Caribeño de Demografia (#16273)
♦ Centro Latinoamericano para la Competitividad y el Desarrollo Sostenible (internationally oriented national body)

♦ Centro Latinoamericano de Creación e Investigación Teatral (CELCIT) 03811

Centre latinoaméricain de création et de recherches théâtrales – Latin American Center for Theater Creation and Research

Dir Moreno 431, 1091 Buenos Aires, Argentina. T. +541143421026. E-mail: correo@celcit.org.ar.
URL: http://www.celcit.org.ar/

History 1977, Caracas (Venezuela). **Aims** Contribute to *Ibero-American* integration through *theatrical* activities and research. **Structure** International Director; National Directors of each Head Office and branches. **Finance** Sources: State grants; self-supportive activities. **Activities** Courses, workshops, seminars, research, publications, play productions. Related to the organization of the festivals of Cadiz (Spain), Córdoba (Argentina), Manizales (Colombia), Porto (Portugal). **Events** *Extraordinary congress* Caracas (Venezuela) 1988. **Publications** *Teatro-CELCIT – Información Boletin* (6 a year). *Colección Premios*; *Cuadernos de Dramaturgia*; *Cuadernos de Investigación Teatral*; *Serie Documentos*. Brochures; leaflets.
Members Head Offices () and branches in 28 countries:
Argentina (*), Bolivia, Brazil, Canada, Chile, Colombia, Costa Rica, Cuba, Dominican Rep, Ecuador, El Salvador, France, Germany, Guatemala, Honduras, Italy, Mexico, Nicaragua, Panama, Paraguay, Peru, Portugal, Puerto Rico, Spain (*), Sweden, Uruguay, USA, Venezuela (*).
IGO Relations *UNESCO (#20322)*. **NGO Relations** *Escuela Internacional de Teatro de la América Latina y el Caribe (EITALC, no recent information).* [2015/XE0109/**E**]

♦ Centro Latinoamericano de Demografia / see Latin American and Caribbean Demographic Centre (#16273)

♦ Centro Latinoamericano de Derechos Humanos (CLADH) 03812

Exec Dir Tierra del Fuego 79, Capital Mendoza, 5500 Mendoza, Argentina. T. +542614242344. E-mail: contacto@cladh.org – idecasas@cladh.org.
URL: http://www.cladh.org/

History 2005, Mendoza (Argentina). **Aims** Promote and protect human rights throughout Latin America. **Structure** Directors. Headquarters in Mendoza (Argentina). Offices in: Santiago (Chile); Asunción (Paraguay); Guatemala City (Guatemala); Mexico City (Mexico). **Languages** Spanish. **Staff** 4.00 FTE, paid; 2.00 FTE, voluntary. **Finance** Proceeds from teaching. Annual budget (2016): about US$ 40,000. **Activities** Advocacy/lobbying/activism; politics/policy/regulatory; publishing activities; training/education. **Publications** *Revista Internacional de Derechos Humanos*. Information Services: Human Rights International Online Program.
Members Full in 5 countries:
Argentina, Chile, Guatemala, Mexico, Paraguay.
Consultative Status Consultative status granted from: *ECOSOC (#05331)* (Special). **IGO Relations** *OAS (#17629)*; *United Nations Economic Commission for Latin America and the Caribbean (ECLAC, #20556)*. **NGO Relations** *Instituto Interamericano de Derechos Humanos (IIDH, #11334)*; *International Service for Human Rights (ISHR, #14841).* [2018.09.12/XM5399/**D**]

♦ Centro Latinoamericano para el Desarrollo y la Comunicación Participativa (internationally oriented national body)

♦ Centro Latinoamericano para el Desarrollo Rural (RIMISP) 03813

Contact Huelén 10, Piso 6, Providencia, Santiago, Santiago Metropolitan, Chile. T. +5622364557. Fax +5622364558. E-mail: rimisp@rimisp.org.
URL: http://www.rimisp.org/

History 1986, as *International Network for Farming Systems Research Methodology – Red Internacional de Metodologia de Investigación de Sistemas de Producción (RIMISP)*. **Aims** Stimulate institutional, economic and social changes to make Latin America a prosperous, fair and sustainable region. **Languages** Spanish. **Staff** 48.00 FTE, paid. **Finance** Funding from international cooperation, including: *Ford Foundation (#09858)*; *ICCO – Interchurch Organization for Development Cooperation*; *International Development Research Centre (IDRC, #13162)*; *International Fund for Agricultural Development (IFAD, #13692)*; New Zealand Aid Programme. **Activities** Events/meetings. **Events** *Latin American symposium on research and extension of agricultural and livestock systems* Santiago (Chile) 2000, *Symposium* Santiago (Chile) 2000. **Publications** *InterCambios Boletin* (12 a year) – electronic; *Equitierra* – magazine. Books; working papers; newsletters.
Members Institutions in 3 countries:
Chile, Ecuador, Mexico. [2014.06.01/XF4246/**F**]

♦ Centro Latinoamericano de Documentación Económica y Social (inactive)
♦ Centro Latinoamericano de Ecologia Social (#16292)
♦ Centro Latinoamericano de Economia Humana / see Universidad CLAEH (#20688)

♦ Centro Latino-Americano em Sexualidade e Direitos Humanos (CLAM) 03814

Latin American Center on Sexuality and Human Rights – Centro Latinoamericano en Sexualidad y Derechos Humanos

Main Office c/o IMS/UERJ, R São Francisco Xavier 524, 6o Andar, BL E, Rio de Janeiro RJ, 20550-013, Brazil. T. +552125680599. E-mail: contatoclam@gmail.com.
URL: http://www.clam.org.br/

History 2002. Founded as a project housed within the Program on Gender, Sexuality and Health, at the State University of Rio de Janeiro's Institute of Social Medicine (IMS/UERJ). **Aims** Produce, organize, and disseminate knowledge about sexuality from a human rights perspective, so as to help fight gender inequality and contribute to the struggle against the discrimination of sexual minorities in the region. **Publications** *Sexualidad, Salud y Sociedad – Revista Latinoamericana.* [2020/XJ5190/**D**]

♦ Centro Latinoamericano de Estudios en Informatica (#16293)
♦ Centro Latinoamericano de Estudios Locales (unconfirmed)
♦ Centro Latinoamericano de Estudios sobre Violencia y Salud 'Jorge Careli' (internationally oriented national body)
♦ Centro Latino-Americano de Estudos sobre Violência e Saúde 'Jorge Careli' (internationally oriented national body)

♦ Centro Latino-Americano de Fisica (CLAF) 03815

Centre Latinoaméricain de Physique – Latin American Centre for Physics

Dir Avda Venceslau Braz 71 – Fundos, Rio de Janeiro RJ, 22290-140 RJ, Brazil. T. +552122955096 – +552122955145 – +552121417267. E-mail: claffisica@gmail.com.
Gen Coordinator address not obtained. E-mail: elenaclaf@cbpf.br.
URL: http://www.claffisica.org.br/

History 26 Mar 1962, Rio de Janeiro (Brazil), on signature by Ambassadors of 15 Latin American countries of an Agreement which entered into force 17 Mar 1965, on its ratification by Brazil, Cuba, Ecuador, Mexico, Nicaragua and Peru. **Aims** Support and promote development of physics and related disciplines in Latin America. **Structure** General Assembly (every 2 years); Governing Board (annual). **Languages** English, French, Portuguese, Spanish. **Staff** 1.50 FTE, paid. **Finance** Contributions from member governments; collaboration with other intergovernmental organizations, scientific institutions; physical societies. **Activities** Events/meetings; financial and/or material support; research/documentation; training/education. **Events** *General Assembly* Brasilia (Brazil) 2014, *Latin American Conference on the Mössbauer Effect* Medellin (Colombia) 2012, *General Assembly* Varadero (Cuba) 2012, *General Assembly* Rio de Janeiro (Brazil) 2010, *ISMANAM – International Symposium on Metastable, Amorphous and Nanostructured Materials* Buenos Aires (Argentina) 2008. **Publications** *CLAF Newsletter* (4 a year) in Portuguese, Spanish.
Members Governments of 14 countries:
Argentina, Bolivia, Brazil, Chile, Costa Rica, Cuba, Ecuador, Mexico, Nicaragua, Panama, Paraguay, Peru, Uruguay, Venezuela.
IGO Relations *Abdus Salam International Centre for Theoretical Physics (ICTP, #00005)*; *European Organization for Nuclear Research (CERN, #08108)*; *UNESCO Office, Montevideo – Regional Bureau for Sciences in Latin America and the Caribbean (#20314).* [2020.02.18/XD2865/**E***]

♦ Centro Latinoamericano de la Globalidad (internationally oriented national body)
♦ Centro Latinoamericano de Información en Ciencias de la Salud / see Latin American and Caribbean Centre on Health Sciences Information (#16267)
♦ Centro Latinoamericano de Investigaciones en Ciencias Sociales (inactive)
♦ Centro Latinoamericano sobre Juventud (internationally oriented national body)
♦ Centro Latinoamericano de Perinatologia y Desarrollo Humano / see Latin American Center for Perinatology/Unit of Woman and Reproductive Health (#16290)
♦ Centro Latinoamericano de Perinatologia/Unidad de Salud de la Mujer y Reproductiva (#16290)
♦ Centro Latinoamericano de Periodismo (#16345)
♦ Centro Latinoamericano de Pesquisas em Ciências Sociais (inactive)
♦ Centro Latino-Americano de Pós-Graduação em Música, Washington DC (internationally oriented national body)
♦ Centro Latinoamericano para les Relaciones con Europa (internationally oriented national body)
♦ Centro Latinoamericano Salud y Mujer (inactive)
♦ Centro Latinoamericano en Sexualidad y Derechos Humanos (#03814)
♦ Centro Latinoaméricano de Tecnologia Educativa para la Salud (inactive)
♦ Centro Legal para Derechos Reproductivos y Politicas Públicas / see Center for Reproductive Rights
♦ Centro de Management Europa-América Latina (internationally oriented national body)
♦ Centro Marino Internazionale (internationally oriented national body)
♦ Centro de Medicina Andina (internationally oriented national body)
♦ Centro Mediterrâneo da Comunicação Audiovisual (#16648)
♦ Centro Mediterraneo de la Comunicación Audiovisual (#16648)
♦ Centro Mesoamericano de Estudios sobre Tecnologia Apropiada (#03650)
♦ CENTROMIDCA – Centro Taller Interamericano de Conservación y Restauración de Libros, Documentos y Material Fotografico (no recent information)
♦ Centro Mondiale di Informazione sull' Educazione Bilingua / see Information Centre for Bilingual and Plurilingual Education (#11195)
♦ Centro Mondiale di Informazione sull' Educazione Bilingua e Plurilingue / see Information Centre for Bilingual and Plurilingual Education (#11195)
♦ Centro Mondialità Sviluppo Reciproco (internationally oriented national body)
♦ Centro Morris E Curiel de Estudios Internacionales, Tel Aviv (internationally oriented national body)
♦ Centro Mundial de Datos de Escorrentia (#10584)
♦ Centro Mundial de Excelencia de Destinos (internationally oriented national body)
♦ Centro Mundial de Información sobre Educación Bilingüe / see Information Centre for Bilingual and Plurilingual Education (#11195)
♦ Centro Mundial de Información sobre Educación Bilingüe e Plurilingüe / see Information Centre for Bilingual and Plurilingual Education (#11195)
♦ Centro de las Naciones Unidas para los Asentamientos Humanos / see United Nations Human Settlements Programme (#20572)
♦ Centro de las Naciones Unidas de Ciencia y Tecnologia para el Desarrollo (inactive)
♦ Centro de las Naciones Unidas para el Desarrollo Regional (#20526)
♦ Centro de las Naciones Unidas sobre las Empresas Transnacionales (inactive)
♦ Centro Neotropical de Entrenamiento en Humedales (internationally oriented national body)
♦ Centro Norte-Sur para Intercambio Técnico y Cultural (inactive)
♦ Centro Norte-Sul do Conselho da Europa / see European Centre for Global Interdependence and Solidarity (#06483)
♦ Centro Nuovo Modello di Sviluppo, Vecchiano (internationally oriented national body)
♦ Centro OIL a Turin / see International Training Centre of the ILO (#15717)
♦ Centro de la OIT en Turin / see International Training Centre of the ILO (#15717)
♦ Centro Orientamento Educativo, Barzio (internationally oriented national body)
♦ **Centropa** Central Europe Center for Research and Documentation (#03719)
♦ Centro Panamericano de Estudios e Investigaciones Geograficas (#18086)
♦ Centro Panamericano de Fiebre Aftosa (#18106)
♦ Centro del Patrimonio Mundial (#21566)
♦ Centro del Patrimonio Popular de los Paises Arabes del Golfo (no recent information)
♦ Centro para la Paz y la Acción para la Transformación de Conflictos (unconfirmed)
♦ Centro para la Paz Mundial Mediante el Derecho / see World Jurist Association (#21604)
♦ CENTROPEC – Center for OPEC Studies (no recent information)
♦ Centro pela Justiça e o Direito Internacional (#03647)
♦ Centro Pew sobre Cambio Climatico Global (internationally oriented national body)
♦ Centro Piemontese di Studi Sul Medio ed Estremo Oriente / see International Institute for Advanced Asian Studies
♦ Centro Popular para América Latina de Comunicación (internationally oriented national body)
♦ Centro Prodh – Centro de Derechos Humanos Miguel Agustin Pro Juarez (internationally oriented national body)
♦ Centro para la Promoción del Comercio, las Inversiones y el Turismo en Asia Sudoriental (#01225)
♦ Centro para la Promoción de la Micro y Pequeña Empresa en Centroamérica / see Centro Regional de Promoción de la MIPYME (#03816)
♦ Centro per la promozione della pace (internationally oriented national body)
♦ Centro de Recursos sobre Empresas y Derechos Humanos (internationally oriented national body)
♦ Centro de Referencia Cientifica y Tecnológica para América Latina y el Caribe (internationally oriented national body)
♦ Centro Regional de Educación Fundamental para América Latina et el Caribe / see Centro de Cooperación Regional para la Educación de Adultos en América Latina y el Caribe (#03794)
♦ Centro Regionale d'Informazione delle Nazioni Unite (#20621)
♦ Centro Regionale d'Intervento per la Cooperazione (internationally oriented national body)
♦ Centro Regional de Enseñanza en Ciencia y Tecnologia Espacial para América Latina y el Caribe (see: #04277)
♦ Centro Regional para el Fomento del Libro en América Latina y el Caribe (#18758)
♦ Centro Regional para o Fomento do Livro na América Latina e o Caribe (#18758)
♦ Centro Regional de Formación y Enseñanza sobre Biotecnologia, India (internationally oriented national body)

♦ Centro Regional de Informação das Nações Unidas (#20621)
♦ Centro Regional de Información sobre Desastres para América Latina y el Caribe (#18778)
♦ Centro Regional de Informaciones Ecuménicas / see Centro de Estudios Ecuménicos, México
♦ Centro Regional de Información de las Naciones Unidas (#20621)
♦ Centro Regional de las Naciones Unidas para la Paz, el Desarme y el Desarrollo en América Latina / see United Nations Regional Centre for Peace, Disarmament and Development in Latin America and the Caribbean (#20618)
♦ Centro Regional de las Naciones Unidas para la Paz, el Desarme y el Desarrollo en América Latina y el Caribe (#20618)

♦ Centro Regional de Promoción de la MIPYME (CENPROMYPE) 03816

Center for the Promotion of MSMEs in Central America

Contact Colonia San Benito, Calle Cirunvalacion 294, San Salvador, El Salvador. T. +50322644965. Fax +50322644965. E-mail: info@cenpromype.org.
URL: http://www.cenpromype.org

History Jun 2001, San Salvador (El Salvador). Former names and other names: *Centro para la Promoción de la Micro y Pequeña Empresa en Centroamérica (CENPROMYPE)* – former; *Centre for the Promotion of Small and Medium Sized Enterprises in Central America* – former. **Aims** Support micro, small and medium enterprises (MSMEs) in Central America. **Languages** Spanish. **Activities** Active in: Belize, Costa Rica, Dominica, El Salvador, Guatemala, Honduras, Nicaragua, Panama. **IGO Relations** *Central American Integration System (#03671).* [2020.05.06/XM2714/E]

♦ Centro Regional para a Salvaguarde do Patrimônio Cultural Imaterial da América Latina (#03817)

♦ Centro Regional para la Salvaguardia del Patrimonio Cultural Inmaterial de América Latina (CRESPIAL) 03817

Centro Regional para a Salvaguarde do Patrimônio Cultural Imaterial da América Latina

Dir Av Brasil A-14, Urbanización Quispicanchi, 08001, Cusco, Peru. T. +5184231191. E-mail: pramos@crespial.org – frubio@crespial.org.
URL: http://www.crespial.org/

History Feb 2006, Paris (France). Founded on signature of the Constitution agreement between *UNESCO (#20322)* and the Government of Peru. A UNESCO Category II Centre. **Aims** Contribute to the achievement of the strategic objectives and the expected results of the UNESCO program in relation to the lines of action in the field of intangible cultural heritage and its safeguard in Latin America. **Structure** Administrative Council; Executive Committee; Technical Secretariat. **Languages** Portuguese, Spanish. **Staff** 10.00 FTE, paid. **Finance** Sources: contributions; government support. Contribution from the Government of Peru. Annual budget: 500,000 USD. **Activities** Advocacy/lobbying/activism; awareness raising; capacity building; events/meetings; guidance/assistance/consulting; knowledge management/information dissemination; networking/liaising; politics/policy/regulatory; publishing activities; research/documentation; standards/guidelines. **Publications** *Looks at the management of the ICH in Latin America: advances and perspectives* (2019). Books; studies; CDs.
Members Full in 16 countries:
Argentina, Bolivia, Brazil, Chile, Colombia, Costa Rica, Cuba, Dominican Rep, Ecuador, El Salvador, Guatemala, Mexico, Paraguay, Peru, Uruguay, Venezuela. [2021.05.27/XM6089/E]

♦ Centro Regional de Sismologia para América del Sur (CERESIS) ... 03818

Centre régional de séismologie pour l'Amérique du Sud – Regional Center for Seismology for South America

Exec Dir Fray Luis de León 921, 41, Lima, Peru. T. +5112256283. Fax +5112245144. E-mail: ceresis.direccionejecutiva@gmail.com.
URL: http://www.ceresis.org/

History May 1966, Lima (Peru), on signature of agreement between Government of Peru and *UNESCO (#20322).* Became an autonomous international organization, Jun 1971, on signature of multinational agreement by the then 9 member governments. Membership open to all countries interested in South America. **Aims** Further seismological activities and research throughout South American region; provide support and promote closer ties between institutions and seismic stations in the region and with international seismological centers; increase capability of member states to cope with seismic events. **Structure** Directive Council, consisting of President and 12 delegates of Member States; Director. **Finance** Annual quotas paid by Member States. Other sources: grants; contracts; donations. **Activities** Research/documentation; guidance/assistance/consulting; monitoring/evaluation; training/education; events/meetings; projects/programmes. **Events** *Meeting / Directive Council Meeting* La Paz (Bolivia) 2013, *Joint assembly* Foz do Iguaçu (Brazil) 2010, *Directive Council Meeting* Lima (Peru) 2009, *Directive Council Meeting* La Paz (Bolivia) 2008, *Directive Council Meeting* Lima (Peru) 2007. **Publications** *Actas de las Sesiones Ordinarias del Consejo Directivo* (every 2 years). *Misiones de Estudio Post-terremoto.* Monographs; maps; catalogues; handbooks. Information Services: Regional databank.
Members Governments of 11 countries:
Argentina, Bolivia, Brazil, Chile, Colombia, Ecuador, Paraguay, Peru, Spain, Uruguay, Venezuela. [2018.11.09/XE0099/E*]

♦ Centro Regional de la UNESCO para la Educación Superior en América Latina y el Caribe / see UNESCO International Institute for Higher Education in Latin America and the Caribbean (#20309)
♦ Centro de Rehabilitación e Investigación para Victimas de la Tortura / see DIGNITY – Danish Institute Against Torture
♦ Centro para las Relaciones Interamericanas, New York / see Americas Society
♦ Centro de Relaciones Internacionales, México (internationally oriented national body)
♦ Centro Ricerche Istituto Europeo di Design (internationally oriented national body)

♦ Centro di Ricerche, Studi e Valorizzazione per la Viticoltura Montana (CERVIM) 03819

Centre for Research, Environmental Sustainability and Advancement of Mountain Viticulture

Sec Fraz Chateau 3, 11010 Aymavilles AO, Italy. T. +39165902451. Fax +39165902451.
URL: http://www.cervim.org/

History 1987, under the auspices of *International Organisation of Vine and Wine (OIV, #14435).* Registered in accordance with Italian law. **Aims** Promote and protect viticulture. **Structure** Assembly (annual). Board of Directors, consisting of 7 up to 15 members. Board of Auditors. Technical-Scientific Committee. Director. **Finance** Members' dues. **Events** *International Congress on Vine-growing in the Mountains and on Steep Slopes / Congress* Lyon (France) 2012, *International Congress on Vine-growing in the Mountains and on Steep Slopes / Congress* Castiglione di Sicilia (Italy) 2010, *International Congress on Vine-Growing in the Mountains and on Steep Slopes / Congress* Monforte de Lemos (Spain) 2008, *Congress* Saint-Vincent (Italy) 2006, *International Congress on Vine-Growing in the Mountains and on Steep Slopes* Saint-Vincent (Italy) 2006. **Publications** *Mountain Vine-Growing* (annual) in English, French, Italian – magazine; *CERVIM Newsletter* – electronic.
Members Category A Regional and Provincial authorities. Category B Local Authorities, Mountain Communities and interprofessional bodies. Category C founder members; wineries; research institutes. Category A members in 5 countries:
Germany, Italy, Portugal, Spain, Switzerland.
Category B members in 6 countries:
Austria, France, Italy, Spain, Switzerland, USA.
Category C members in 8 countries:
Andorra, France, Germany, Italy, Portugal, Spain, Switzerland, USA. [2012/XJ5147/E]

♦ Centro de Servicios de Cooperación para la Desarrollo / see Kepa – the Finnish NGO platform for global development
♦ Centro de Serviçõs de Cooperação para o Desenvolvimento / see Kepa – the Finnish NGO platform for global development
♦ Centro Simon Wiesenthal (internationally oriented national body)
♦ Centro de Solidaridad Sindical de Finlandia (internationally oriented national body)
♦ Centro Studi e Documentazione sulla Pace e sul Controllo degli Armamenti (internationally oriented national body)
♦ Centro Studi Ed Iniziative Europeo / see CESIE
♦ Centro Studi Emigrazione (internationally oriented national body)
♦ Centro Studi Emigrazione, Roma (internationally oriented national body)
♦ Centro Studi per l'Evoluzione Umana (internationally oriented national body)
♦ Centro Studi Iniziative e Informazioni Amilcar Cabral (internationally oriented national body)
♦ Centro Studi Nord Est e Adriatico (internationally oriented national body)

♦ Centro Studi sulle Nuove Religioni (CESNUR International) 03820

Centre for Studies on New Religions

Dir Via Confienza 19, 10121 Turin TO, Italy. T. +3911541950. Fax +3911541905. E-mail: cesnur_to@virgilio.it.
URL: http://www.cesnur.org/

History 1988. **Aims** Promote scholarly research in the field of new religious *consciousness.* **Activities** Events/meetings; research/documentation. **Events** *Annual Conference* Taichung (Taiwan) 2018, *Annual Conference* Jerusalem (Israel) 2017, *Annual Conference* Tallinn (Estonia) 2015, *Annual Conference* Waco, TX (USA) 2014, *Annual Conference* Falun (Sweden) 2013. [2016.12.14/XE3442/E]

♦ Centro di Studio e di Ricerca sulla Comunità Internazionale e le sue Istituzioni, Roma / see Istituto di Studi Giuridici Internazionali
♦ Centro di Studi di Politica Internazionale (internationally oriented national body)
♦ Centro Studi Problemi Internazionali, Milano (internationally oriented national body)
♦ Centro Studi Terzo Mondo (internationally oriented national body)
♦ Centro Taller Interamericano de Conservación y Restauración de Libros, Documentos y Material Fotografico (no recent information)
♦ Centro de Tecnologia Alternativa (internationally oriented national body)
♦ Centro UNESCO Euskal Herria / see Centro UNESCO del Pais Vasco
♦ Centro UNESCO del Pais Vasco (internationally oriented national body)
♦ Centro pro Unione (internationally oriented national body)
♦ Centro Unitario per la Cooperazione Missionaria tra le Chiese (internationally oriented national body)
♦ Centro Universitario Europeo per i Beni Culturali, Ravello (internationally oriented national body)
♦ Centro per il Volontariato e la Cooperazione Internazionale / see Terra Nuova
♦ Centro di Volontariato Internazionale (internationally oriented national body)
♦ Centro Volontari Cooperazione allo Sviluppo (internationally oriented national body)
♦ Centro Volontari Marchigiani / see Comunità Volontari per il Mondo
♦ Centro Volontari per il Mondo / see Comunità Volontari per il Mondo
♦ Centrul Comun de Cercetare (#16147)
♦ Centrul European pentru Prevenirea Adictiilor (internationally oriented national body)
♦ Centrul Euroregional pentru Democratie (internationally oriented national body)
♦ Centrul International de Informare Stiintifica si Tehnica (#12514)
♦ Centrul de Istorie si Civilizatie Europeana, Iasi (internationally oriented national body)
♦ Centrul Roman de Politici Europene (internationally oriented national body)
♦ Centrul Român de Studii Globale (internationally oriented national body)
♦ Centrul de Studii Euro-Atlantice, Bucuresti (internationally oriented national body)
♦ Centrum voor Afrika-onderzoek / see Institute for Anthropological Research in Africa
♦ Centrum för Afrikastudier, Göteborg (internationally oriented national body)
♦ Centrum für angewandte Politikforschung (internationally oriented national body)
♦ Centrum Badan Azji i Pacyfiku (internationally oriented national body)
♦ Centrum voor Dorpsintegratie Bwamanda-België (internationally oriented national body)
♦ Centrum für Europäische Politik (internationally oriented national body)
♦ Centrum für Europäisches Privatrecht (internationally oriented national body)
♦ Centrum Europejskie Uniwersytetu Warszawskiego (internationally oriented national body)
♦ Centrum voor Europese Veiligheids Studies (internationally oriented national body)
♦ Centrum voor Europese Vorming in het Nederlandse Onderwijs / see European Platform – internationalising education
♦ Centrum Historii Meijskiej Europy Srodkow-Wschodniej (internationally oriented national body)
♦ Centrum iberskych a latinskoamerickych stúdii (internationally oriented national body)
♦ Centrum IKO – Centrum International Kinderontvoering (internationally oriented national body)
♦ Centrum Internationale Erfgoedactiviteiten (internationally oriented national body)
♦ Centrum für Internationale Migration and Entwicklung (internationally oriented national body)
♦ Centrum voor Internationale Verenigingen (internationally oriented national body)
♦ Centrum International Kinderontvoering (internationally oriented national body)
♦ Centrum Ontmoeting der Volkeren (internationally oriented national body)
♦ Centrum voor Ontwikkelingssamenwerking / see COS West and Midden Brabant Centrum voor Internationale Samenwerking
♦ Centrum voor Ontwikkelingssamenwerking in Vrijheid en Vooruitgang (internationally oriented national body)
♦ Centrum för Östersjö- och Östeuropaforskning (internationally oriented national body)
♦ Centrum Pre Európske A Severoatlantické Vztahy (internationally oriented national body)
♦ Centrum Stosunków Miedzynarodowych (internationally oriented national body)
♦ Centrum voor Studie en Documentatie van Latijns-Amerika (internationally oriented national body)
♦ Centrum voor de studie van het gebied van de grote meren in Afrika (internationally oriented national body)
♦ Centrum voor Studies van Meertaligheid in de Multiculturele Samenleving / see Centre for the Study of Superdiversity
♦ Centrum Studiów Latynoamerykanskich, Universytet Warszawski (internationally oriented national body)
♦ Centrum tot Bevordering van de Import uit Ontwikkelingslanden (internationally oriented national body)
♦ Centrum voor Vredesonderzoek en Strategische Studies, KU Leuven / see Centre for Research on Peace and Development
♦ Centr po Uprosceniju Procedur i Praktiki v Upravlenii, Torgovle i na Transporte / see United Nations Centre for Trade Facilitation and Electronic Business (#20527)
♦ The Century Foundation (internationally oriented national body)
♦ Century Fund / see The Century Foundation
♦ CENYC – Council of European National Youth Committees (inactive)
♦ CEOAH – Comité européen de l'outillage agricole et horticole (inactive)
♦ CEOC International – International Confederation of Inspection and Certification Organisations (inactive)
♦ **CEO** Collège européen d'orthodontie (#04106)
♦ **CEO** Comité européen de l'outillage (#04163)
♦ **CEOCOR** Comité Européen pour l'etude de la corrosion et la protection des canalisations (#06670)
♦ **CEO** Corporate Europe Observatory (#04839)
♦ Ceolfhoireann Aosóg an Chomhphobail Eorapaigh / see European Union Youth Orchestra (#09024)
♦ **CEOM** Conseil Européen des Ordres des Médecins (#06830)
♦ CEOP – Communauté européenne des organisations de publicitaires (inactive)
♦ CEORG – Central European Opinion Research Group (no recent information)
♦ **CEOS** Committee on Earth Observation Satellites (#04249)
♦ CEPAA / see Social Accountability International
♦ CEPA – Asociación Espirita Internacional (#03821)

♦ CEPA – Associação Espirita Internacional (CEPA) 03821

CEPA – Asociación Espirita Internacional – CEPA – International Spiritist Association

Contact address not obtained. E-mail: seccepa@gmail.com.
URL: http://cepainternacional.org/

CEPAC
03821

alphabetic sequence excludes
For the complete listing, see Yearbook Online at

History Founded 13 Oct 1946, Buenos Aires (Argentina), as *Confederação Espirita Pan-Americana (CEPA)* – *Confederación Espirita Pan-Americano – Pan American Spiritist Confederation*. Current title adopted May 2016. **Aims** Promote and disseminate the ideas and knowledge within *Spiritism*, derived from the works of Allan Kardec, with a secular, *freethinking*, *humanist*, progressive, and pluralistic vision; promote, encourage and follow along all efforts aimed at the continuous updating of Spiritism; promote the integration between spiritists and spiritist institutions from all continents. **Structure** General Assembly; Executive Council. **Languages** English, Portuguese, Spanish. **Staff** Voluntary. **Finance** Members' dues. Donations. **Activities** Events/meetings; publishing activities. **Events** *Congress* 2021, *Congress* Salou (Spain) 2020, *Congress* Rosario (Argentina) 2016, *Congress* Santos (Brazil) 2012, *Congress* San Juan (Puerto Rico) 2008.
[2019.03.02/XM7389/**D**]

♦ CEPAC – Confédération européenne de l'industrie des pâtes, papiers et cartons (inactive)
♦ **CEPAC** Conferentia Episcopalis Pacifici (#04659)
♦ CEPA – Center for European Policy Analysis (internationally oriented national body)
♦ CEPA – Centro de Ecologia y Pueblos Andinos (internationally oriented national body)
♦ CEPA – Centrul European pentru Prevenirea Adictiilor (internationally oriented national body)
♦ CEPA / see CEPA – Associação Espirita Internacional (#03821)
♦ **CEPA** CEPA – Associação Espirita Internacional (#03821)
♦ **CEPA** Comisión Económica de las Naciones Unidas para Africa (#20554)
♦ **CEPA** Confédération européenne des associations de pesticides appliqués (#06717)
♦ **CEPA** Confédération Européenne de Pédiatrie Ambulatoire (#06721)
♦ CEPAD / see European Council for Alkylphenols and Derivatives (#06802)
♦ **CEPAD** European Council for Alkylphenols and Derivatives (#06802)
♦ CEPA – International Spiritist Association (#03821)
♦ CEPALC – Centro Popular para América Latina de Comunicación (internationally oriented national body)
♦ **CEPALC** Commission économique des Nations Unies pour l'Amérique latine et les Caraïbes (#20556)
♦ **CEPAL** Comisión Económica de las Naciones Unidas para América Latina y el Caribe (#20556)
♦ CEPALO / see United Nations Economic and Social Commission for Asia and the Pacific (#20557)
♦ CEPAO / see United Nations Economic and Social Commission for Western Asia (#20558)
♦ **CEPA** United Nations Committee of Experts on Public Administration (#20542)
♦ CEPAZE – Centre d'échanges et promotion des artisans en zones à équiper (internationally oriented national body)
♦ **CEP** Caribbean Environment Programme (#03497)
♦ **CEP** Caspian Environment Programme (#03596)
♦ CEPC – Centro de Estudios Politicos y Constitucionales (internationally oriented national body)
♦ CEP – Centrum für Europäische Politik (internationally oriented national body)
♦ CEP – Centrum für Europäisches Privatrecht (internationally oriented national body)
♦ CEPCEO / see European Association for Coal and Lignite (#05978)
♦ CEP-CMAF / see Social Economy Europe (#19335)
♦ **CEP** Colloque européen des paroisses (#04119)
♦ CEP / see Comité des organisations nationales des importateurs et exportateurs de poisson de l'UE (#04194)
♦ **CEP** Comité des organisations nationales des importateurs et exportateurs de poisson de l'UE (#04194)
♦ CEP / see Confederation of European Probation (#04530)
♦ **CEP** Confederation of European Probation (#04530)
♦ CEP – Confédération européenne d'études phytosanitaires (inactive)
♦ **CEP** Confédération européenne de pétanque (#04548)
♦ **CEP** Congregation for the Evangelization of Peoples (#04670)
♦ CEP – Conseil d'exploitation postale (see: #20682)
♦ **CEPEC** Confédération européenne des professionelles de l'esthétique cosmétique (#04549)
♦ **CEPE** Comisión Económica de las Naciones Unidas para Europa (#20555)
♦ **CEPE** Communion d'églises protestantes en Europe (#04405)
♦ **CEPE** Conseil européen de l'industrie des peintures, des encres d'imprimerie et des couleurs d'art (#04688)
♦ CEPED / see Centre Population et développement
♦ Ceped – Centre Population et développement (internationally oriented national body)
♦ **CEPEIGE** Centro Panamericano de Estudios e Investigaciones Geograficas (#18086)
♦ **CEPEJ** Commission européenne pour l'efficacité de la justice (#04213)
♦ CEPES – Comité européen pour le progrès économique et social (inactive)
♦ **CEPF** Central European Pragmatist Forum (#03713)
♦ **CEPF** Confederation of European Forest Owners (#04525)
♦ **CEPF** Critical Ecosystem Partnership Fund (#04958)
♦ CEPG / see European Association of Geographers (#06054)
♦ **CEPGL** Communauté économique des pays des Grands Lacs (#04375)

♦ Cephalopod International Advisory Council (CIAC) 03822

Pres Dept of Biological Sciences, STG 222, Univ of South Florida St Petersburg, 140 7th Ave South, St Petersburg FL 33701, USA. T. +17278734512.
URL: http://www.cephalopod.wordpress.com/

History 1983. **Aims** Stimulate, accelerate and influence the direction of cephalopod research; provide help and advice on aspects of cephalopod *biology*; spread information on past and current research. **Structure** Council. **Languages** English. **Finance** No operating budget; financed by members and their institutions. **Activities** Events/meetings; knowledge management/information dissemination. **Events** *Cephalopods in the Anthropocene – multiple challenges in a changing ocean* Sesimbra (Portugal) 2022, *International Symposium Cephalopods* Fez (Morocco) 2018, *International Symposium* St Petersburg, FL (USA) 2018, *International Symposium* Hakodate (Japan) 2015, *International Symposium Cephalopods* Zurich (Switzerland) 2014. **Publications** *CIAC Newsletter*. Directory; computerized bibliography; state-of-the-art papers.
Members Individuals in 15 countries and territories:
Australia, Brazil, China, Falklands/Malvinas, France, Germany, Ireland, Italy, Japan, New Zealand, Peru, South Africa, Spain, UK, USA. [2021/XF3545/v/**F**]

♦ CEPI Cartonboard 03823

Manager c/o ARCO Assn Management AG, Postal Box, 8027 Zurich ZH, Switzerland. E-mail: procarton@arco.swiss.
Chairman address not obtained.
URL: http://www.cepicartonboard.com/

History Founded, replacing *Association of Board Manufacturers in the EEC (inactive)*. A legally autonomous industry sector of *Confederation of European Paper Industries (CEPI, #04529)*. Transferred from Brussels (Belgium) to Zurich (Switzerland), 2008. Registration: Swiss Civil Code, Start date: 2008, Switzerland; End date: 2008, Belgium. **Aims** Study economic, technical and statistical and financial issues of the European cartonboard *industry*; promote cooperation among European organizations of *cartonboard* and other paper and board manufacturers. **Structure** General Assembly (annual); Board of Directors. **Languages** English. **Events** *Annual General Assembly* Zurich (Switzerland) 2020, *Annual General Meeting* Barcelona (Spain) 2001, *Annual General Assembly* Oslo (Norway) 1996, *Forum* Oslo (Norway) 1996.
Members Associate European cardboard manufacturers. Members in 13 countries:
Austria, Finland, France, Germany, Greece, Italy, Netherlands, Poland, Slovenia, Spain, Sweden, Türkiye, UK.
[2022.05.09/XE3048/**E**]

♦ **CEPIC** Coordination of European Picture Agencies, Press Stock Heritage (#04825)
♦ CEPI-CEI / see European Association of Real Estate Professions (#06186)
♦ **CEPI** Coalition for Epidemic Preparedness Innovations (#04057)
♦ **CEPI** Confederation of European Paper Industries (#04529)

♦ CEPI ContainerBoard (CCB) 03824

Main Office Avenue Louise 250, 1050 Brussels, Belgium. T. +3226474157. Fax +3226471724. E-mail: info@cepi-containerboard.org.
URL: http://www.cepi-containerboard.org/

History Nov 2001, Brussels (Belgium). Since Apr 2006, a Participating Industry Sector of *Confederation of European Paper Industries (CEPI, #04529)*, under listed title. From 1 Jan 2010, includes the previous *Groupement européen des fabricants de papiers pour ondulé (ONDULE, inactive)*. Former names and other names: *European Containerboard Industry Trade Organization (Kraft Institute)* – former (Nov 2001); *European Containerboard Organization (ECO)* – former. **Aims** Promote the interests of *producers* of corrugated case materials (containerboard). **Structure** General Assembly; Committees (3). **Languages** English. **Activities** Monitoring/evaluation. **Events** *Annual Congress* Nice (France) 2022, *Annual Congress* Rome (Italy) 2021, *Annual Congress* Rotterdam (Netherlands) 2019, *Annual Congress* Vienna (Austria) 2015, *Annual Congress* London (UK) 2013.
Members Full in 16 countries:
Austria, Belgium, Czechia, Finland, France, Germany, Italy, Lithuania, Netherlands, Norway, Russia, Slovakia, Spain, Sweden, Türkiye, UK. [2023.02.15/XD3370/**E**]

♦ **CEPI Eurokraft** European Kraft Paper Producers for the Flexible Packaging Industry (#07630)
♦ CEPI / see European Association of Real Estate Professions (#06186)
♦ **CEPI** European Association of Real Estate Professions (#06186)
♦ CEPI / see European Audiovisual Production (#06295)
♦ **CEPI** European Audiovisual Production (#06295)
♦ CEPII – Centre d'études prospectives et d'informations internationales, Paris (internationally oriented national body)
♦ CEPII's Business Club / see Club du CEPII
♦ CEPIPRINT / see European Association of Graphic Paper Producers (#06060)
♦ **CEPIS** Council of European Professional Informatics Societies (#04893)
♦ CEPIT / see EURO-CHINA (#05658)
♦ **CEPLI** Confédération Européenne des Pouvoirs Locaux Intermédiaires (#06710)
♦ **CEPLIS** Conseil européen des professions libérales (#06828)
♦ CEPMC / see Construction Products Europe AISBL (#04761)
♦ **CEPM** Confédération Européenne de la Production de Maïs (#06711)
♦ CEPM / see European Confederation of Maize Production (#06711)
♦ **CEPMMT** Centre européen pour les prévisions météorologiques à moyen terme (#06490)
♦ CEPOL / see European Union Agency for Law Enforcement Training (#08970)
♦ **CEPOL** European Union Agency for Law Enforcement Training (#08970)
♦ CEPPAF – Comité européen pour la protection des animaux dans un monde meilleur pour tous (no recent information)
♦ **CEPPLE** Conférence des Eglises protestantes des pays latins d'Europe (#04591)
♦ CEPPOL / see Caribbean Action Plan (#03432)
♦ **CEPPs** Childhood and Early Parenting Principles (#03873)
♦ CEPR – Center for Economic and Policy Research (internationally oriented national body)
♦ CEPR – Centre for Economic Policy Research, London (internationally oriented national body)
♦ **CEPREDENAC** Centro de Coordinación para la Prevención de los Desastres Naturales en América Central (#03795)
♦ CEPRIS – Euro-Mediterranean Centre on Evaluation and Prevention of Seismic Risk (internationally oriented national body)
♦ **CEPSA** Central European Political Science Association (#03712)
♦ **CEPS** Centre d'étude et de prospective stratégique (#03739)
♦ **CEPS** Centre for European Policy Studies (#03741)
♦ **CePSE** Centre de politique sociale et économique européenne (#03742)
♦ CEPS / see spiritsEUROPE (#19921)
♦ CEPS – Strategic and Corporate Europlanners Society (inactive)
♦ CEPT – Agreement on the Common Effective Preferential Tariff (1992 treaty)
♦ **CEPT** Conférence européenne des administrations des postes et des télécommunications (#04602)
♦ CERAAS – Centre d'étude régional pour l'amélioration de l'adaptation à la sécheresse (see: #20907)
♦ CERAF – Center for Economic Research on Africa, Upper Montclair NJ (internationally oriented national body)

♦ CERA Global Association (CGA) 03825

Contact c/o Ins and Fac of Actuaries, 1st Floor, Park Central, 40/41 Park End Street, Oxford, OX1 1JD, UK. E-mail: cera.global@actuaries.org.uk.
URL: https://ceraglobal.org/

History Nov 2009. **Aims** Promote and administer the CERA credential worldwide. **Structure** Board. Governed by Treaty with signatories from actuarial professional bodies. **Activities** Events/meetings.
Members Actuarial associations in 26 countries and territories:
Australia, Austria, Belgium, Canada, Croatia, Czechia, Denmark, Finland, France, Germany, Greece, India, Ireland, Israel, Italy, Japan, Netherlands, Norway, Slovenia, South Africa, Spain, Sweden, Switzerland, Taiwan, UK, USA. [2020/AA0370/**B**]

♦ CERAI – Centro de Estudios Rurales y de Agricultura Internacional (internationally oriented national body)
♦ **CERAME-UNIE** European Ceramic Industry Association (#06506)
♦ **CERAO** Conférence épiscopale régionale de l'Afrique de l'Ouest (#18783)
♦ CERAO – Conférence épiscopale régionale de l'Afrique de l'Ouest francophone (inactive)
♦ **CERAP** Center of Research and Action for Peace (#03651)
♦ CER / see Assembly of European Regions (#02316)
♦ CERAV/Afrique – Centre Régional pour les Arts Vivants en Afrique (internationally oriented national body)
♦ CERAW – Centre for Research on the Arab World (internationally oriented national body)
♦ **CERC3** Chairmen of the European Research Councils' Chemistry Committees (#03846)
♦ CERCAL / see Centre d'étude et de promotion des relations entre les pays de l'Union européenne et de l'Amérique latine
♦ CERCAL – Centre d'étude et de promotion des relations entre les pays de l'Union européenne et de l'Amérique latine (internationally oriented national body)
♦ CERCCC / see Chairmen of the European Research Councils' Chemistry Committees (#03846)
♦ CERC – Conférence européenne des radios chrétiennes (no recent information)
♦ CER – Centre for European Reform (internationally oriented national body)
♦ CERCI – Centre d'études et de recherches sur la coopération internationale (internationally oriented national body)

♦ Le Cercle 03826

Address not obtained.

History in the 1950s, by right-wing senior politicians, diplomats and intelligence agents. Initially set up to unite Franco-German relations as a buffer to Soviet aggression during the Cold War, although current remit much wider. Originally referred to as *Pinay Circle* after first chairman, former French Prime Minister Antoine Pinay. **Aims** Provide a confidential forum for discussion – focusing on *foreign affairs* and international *security* – among *right wing* senior *politicians*, diplomats, business men, *polemicists*, personnel of diplomatic and security services and *intelligence agents*. **Activities** Meets twice a year: autumn meeting in Washington DC (USA); spring meeting in another venue as decided. **Events** *Half-Yearly Meeting* Berlin (Germany) 1997, *Half-Yearly Meeting* Washington, DC (USA) 1997, *Half-Yearly Meeting* Amman (Jordan) 1996, *Half-Yearly Meeting* Washington, DC (USA) 1996. **Members** Individuals advocating right-wing causes – politicians, businessmen, polemicists and personnel in diplomatic and security services (about 70 worldwide) in 25 countries. Membership countries not specified. [2019/XF4443/cv/**F**]

♦ Cercle Benelux d'histoire de la pharmacie 03827

Kring voor de Geschiedenis van de Pharmacie in Benelux

Sec and Editor address not obtained. E-mail: info@kringbenelux.eu – redactie@kringbenelux.eu.
Pres address not obtained.
URL: http://www.kringbenelux.eu/

History 18 Apr 1950. **Structure** Officers: President; Vice-President; Treasurer; Editor and Public Relations Officer. **Finance** Members' dues. Budget (annual): euro 5,000. **Activities** Events/meetings. **Events** *De natuur als verzamelobject in de 16e eeuw* Antwerp (Belgium) 1996, *Meeting* Heidelberg (Germany) 1993, *Meeting* Luxembourg (Luxembourg) 1991. **Publications** *Bulletin* (2 a year).
Members Full in 3 countries:
Belgium, Luxembourg, Netherlands.
NGO Relations Member of: *International Society for History of Pharmacy (ISHP, #15173).* [2019/XF2239/F]

♦ Cercle civique européen, Lausanne (unconfirmed)
♦ Cercle d'Ethique des Affaires (internationally oriented national body)

♦ Cercle Euro-Mediterranean des Dirigeants du Textile, de l'Habillement et des Industries de la mode (CEDITH) 03828

Euro-Mediterranean Circle of Textile and Clothing Managers

Pres address not obtained.

History 2004. Registration: Start date: 2004, France. **Aims** Defend and promote the interests of the textile and clothing industry in the Mediterranean area; lobby on European and international levels so as to as to develop and promote the sector. **Structure** President; Vice-President. **Publications** *Textile-Business News* (12 a year). [2020/XJ2170/t/F]

♦ Cercle européen des déontologues / see Cercle d'Ethique des Affaires
♦ Cercle féminin des Nations Unies – Genève (internationally oriented national body)
♦ Cercle féminin des Nations Unies – New York (#20651)
♦ Cercle féminin des Nations Unies de Vienne (internationally oriented national body)
♦ Cercle international d'études hymnologiques (#13213)
♦ Cercle international pour la promotion de la création (#12575)
♦ Cercle international de recherches philosophiques par ordinateur (inactive)
♦ Cercle magique (#16545)
♦ Cercle mondial du consensus / see Consensus for Sustainable People, Organisations and Communities
♦ Cercle odontologique du Sud (inactive)
♦ Cercle des Réseaux Européens (unconfirmed)
♦ Cercle Richelieu Senghor (internationally oriented national body)
♦ **CercleS** Confédération européenne des centres de langues de l'enseignement supérieur (#04540)
♦ Cercle de sociologie et nomologie juridiques / see European Network on Law and Society (#07937)
♦ CER / see Community of European Railway and Infrastructure Companies (#04396)
♦ **CER** Community of European Railway and Infrastructure Companies (#04396)
♦ **CER** Conference of European Rabbis (#04598)
♦ CERD / see Institute for the Study of International Development
♦ **CERD** Committee on the Elimination of Racial Discrimination (#04251)
♦ CERDEN – Centre européen pour la recherche, le développement et l'enseignement de la nutrition et de la nutrithérapie (internationally oriented national body)
♦ CERD / see European Centre on Geomorphological Hazards (#06482)
♦ CERDI – Centre d'études et de recherches sur le développement international, Clermont-Ferrand (internationally oriented national body)
♦ **CERDOTOLA** Centre International de Recherche et de Documentation sur les Traditions et les Langues Africaines (#03761)
♦ **CERDP** Centre européen de recherche et de documentation parlementaires (#06495)

♦ Cereals and Europe (C and E) 03829

Chair Rietgorsweg 1-3, 3350 AA Papendrecht, Netherlands.

History Formal activities launched, Oct 1997. A regional section of *Cereals and Grains Association (#03830).* Former names and other names: *AACC EUROPE SECTION* – alias. Registration: Banque-Carrefour des Entreprises, No/ID: 0832.711.841, Start date: 12 Jan 2011, Belgium. **Aims** Advance understanding and knowledge of cereal grain science and its product development applications through research, leadership, education, technical service and advocacy in Europe. **Structure** Board; Executive Committee. **Languages** English. **Finance** Members' dues. Proceeds from activities. **Activities** Research/documentation; training/education; guidance/assistance/consulting; advocacy/lobbying/activism; events/meetings; networking/liaising. **Events** *Spring Meeting* Thessaloniki (Greece) 2021, *Spring Meeting* Thessaloniki (Greece) 2020, *Spring Meeting* Amsterdam (Netherlands) 2017, *Spring Meeting* Budapest (Hungary) 2015, *European Youth Cereal Scientists and Technologies Workshop* Copenhagen (Denmark) 2015. **Members** About 300. Membership countries not specified. **NGO Relations** Member of: *Federation of European and International Associations Established in Belgium (FAIB, #09508).* [2020/XJ4850/t/E]

♦ Cereals and Grains Association 03830

Contact 3352 Sherman Ct, Ste. 202, St Paul MN 55121-2097, USA. T. +16514547250. Fax +16514540766. E-mail: info@cerealsgrains.org.
Main: https://www.cerealsgrains.org/

History 1915. Former names and other names: *American Association of Cereal Chemists (AACC)* – former (1915 to 2005); *AACC International* – former (2005 to 2019). Registration: 501(c)(3) organization, No/ID: EIN: 41-0777936, Start date: 1949, USA, MN. **Aims** Advance *cereal science* and related technologies; create interpreting and disseminate cereals information; provide personal and professional development opportunities. **Structure** Board of Directors. Ad Hoc Committees; Administrative Committees. Sections include: *Cereals and Europe (C and E, #03829).* **Finance** Sources: members' dues. **Activities** Events/meetings; knowledge management/information dissemination; research/documentation. **Events** *Annual Meeting* St Paul, MN (USA) 2021, *Annual Meeting* St Paul, MN (USA) 2021, *Annual Meeting* St Paul, MN (USA) 2020, *Annual Meeting* Denver, CO (USA) 2019, *Annual Meeting* London (UK) 2018. **Publications** *Cereal Foods World* (6 a year); *Cereal Chemistry*; *New Titles in Food Science. The Eagen Press Handbook Series.* **Information Services** *AACCnet Membership Directory*; *AACCnet Online Symposia.* **Members** Primarily North American membership. **IGO Relations** Participates as observer in the activities of: *Codex Alimentarius Commission (CAC, #04081).* **NGO Relations** Member of (1): *Whole Grain Initiative (WGI, #20939).* Cooperation agreement and joint congress with: *ICC – International Association for Cereal Science and Technology (#11048).* Affiliated with: *American Association for the Advancement of Science (AAAS)*; *AOAC INTERNATIONAL (#00863).* [2021/XG3712/C]

♦ Cereals Network (unconfirmed)
♦ **CEREAN** Central European Real Estate Associations Network (#03714)

♦ Cerebral Autoregulation Research Network (CARNET) 03831

Sec Dept Engineering Science, University of Oxford, Parks Road, Oxford, OX1 3PJ, UK.
URL: http://www.car-net.org/

History Jun 2011. **Aims** Foster collaboration within the diverse research base of cerebral autoregulation. **Structure** Steering Committee, including Chairman, Secretary and 3 Coordinators (Funding, Technical and Projects). **Events** *International Meeting on Cerebral Haemodynamic Regulation / Meeting* Southampton (UK) 2015, *International Conference on Cerebral Autoregulation / Meeting* San Diego, CA (USA) 2014, *International Conference on Cerebral Autoregulation / Meeting* Porto (Portugal) 2013, *International Conference on Cerebral Autoregulation / Meeting* Nijmegen (Netherlands) 2012, *International Conference on Cerebral Autoregulation / Meeting* London (UK) 2011. [2015.08.26/XJ6007/F]

♦ Cerebral Palsy – European Community Association (CP-ECA) 03832

SG address not obtained. E-mail: contact@cp-eca.eu – contact@cpint.org – info@cpint.org.
URL: https://cp-eca.eu/

History Jun 1991. June 1991. Serves as the European arm of *International Cerebral Palsy Society (ICPS, #12531).* **Aims** Stimulate interest in development and improvement of research in the field of cerebral palsy. **Structure** Executive Committee. **Languages** English. **Staff** 1.00 FTE, paid; 0.50 FTE, voluntary. **Finance** Members' dues. Charitable contributions. Budget (annual): euro 11,000. **Activities** Supplies vital expertise, advice, resources and information in the field. **Events** *Meeting* Utrecht (Netherlands) 2009.
Members Organizations; individuals. Organizational members (16) in 14 countries:
Belgium, Cyprus, Denmark, Finland, Germany, Greece, Ireland (2), Italy, Netherlands, Portugal, Slovenia, Spain, Sweden, UK (2).
Associate members (11) in 9 countries:
Belgium, Denmark, France, Greece (2), Luxembourg, Portugal, Spain (2), Sweden, UK.
NGO Relations Full voting member of: *European Disability Forum (EDF, #06929).* [2022/XD4711/D]

♦ Cerebral Palsy International Sports and Recreation Association (CPISRA) 03833

Infirmité motrice cérébrale association internationale pour le sport et la récréation

SG Suite 102, Fullarton House, 4 Fullarton St, Ayr, KA7 1UB, UK. E-mail: info@cpisra.org.
Chief Executive address not obtained.
URL: http://www.cpisra.org/

History 1978. Initially been set up, 1969, as a sub-committee of *International Cerebral Palsy Society (ICPS, #12531).* Registration: Scottish Charitable Incorporated Organisation, No/ID: SC049934, Scotland. **Aims** Provide greater opportunities for people throughout the world who experience cerebral palsy or allied conditions to access sport and enjoy a wide variety of sports and recreational activities at all levels. **Structure** General Assembly; Executive Committee; Committees (4); Secretariat. **Languages** English. **Staff** 0.50 FTE, paid. **Finance** Sources: fundraising; members' dues. Other sources: bid fees; host fees. **Activities** Knowledge management/information dissemination; networking/liaising; training/education. **Events** *General Assembly* Ayr (UK) 2021, *CPISRA International Conference* Sydney, NSW (Australia) 2021, *CPISRA International Conference* Sydney, NSW (Australia) 2020, *General Assembly* Stellenbosch (South Africa) 2008, *General Assembly* Lisbon (Portugal) 2006. **Publications** *CPISRA News* (2 a year). *CPISRA Sports Manual* (10th ed 2009). Symposium reports.
Members National; Associate; Individual. National in 63 countries and territories:
Algeria, Argentina, Armenia, Australia, Austria, Bahrain, Belgium, Brazil, Bulgaria, Canada, Chile, China, Colombia, Croatia, Cyprus, Czechia, Denmark, Egypt, England, Faeroe Is, Finland, France, Germany, Greece, Hong Kong, Hungary, Iceland, Iran Islamic Rep, Iraq, Ireland, Israel, Italy, Japan, Korea Rep, Kuwait, Lithuania, Macau, Malaysia, Mexico, Nepal, Netherlands, New Zealand, Northern Ireland, Norway, Poland, Portugal, Qatar, Russia, Scotland, Singapore, Slovakia, Slovenia, South Africa, Spain, Sweden, Switzerland, Taiwan, Thailand, Tunisia, Türkiye, Ukraine, United Arab Emirates, USA.
Associate in 2 countries:
Germany, Great Britain.
NGO Relations Member of (1): *International Paralympic Committee (IPC, #14512).* [2020/XC3980/C]

♦ Cerebrovascular Research and Education Foundation (unconfirmed)
♦ CERE – Centre for Russia and Eurasia (internationally oriented national body)
♦ **CERE** Consortium of European Research on Emotion (#04741)
♦ **CEREDOC** Confédération européenne d'experts en évaluation et réparation du dommage corporel (#04543)
♦ CEREPPOL – Centre européen de recherche et de prospective politique (unconfirmed)
♦ CERES (internationally oriented national body)
♦ CERES – Center for Eurasian, Russian and East European Studies, Washington DC (internationally oriented national body)
♦ CERES – Centre for European, Russian, and Eurasian Studies, Toronto (internationally oriented national body)
♦ **CERESIS** Centro Regional de Sismologia para América del Sur (#03818)
♦ CERES – Research School for Resource Studies for Development (internationally oriented national body)
♦ **CERET** Centre européen de réflexion et d'étude en thermodynamique (#06469)
♦ CERFACS – Centre européen de recherche et de formation avancée en calcul scientifique (internationally oriented national body)
♦ **CERF** Central European Regulatory Forum (#03715)
♦ CERF – Centre d'étude et de rencontres francophones (internationally oriented national body)
♦ **CERF** Centre européen pour la réhabilitation des fleuves (#06499)
♦ **CERF** Coastal Education and Research Foundation (#04071)
♦ CERF – Coastal Environmental Rights Foundation (internationally oriented national body)
♦ CERF – Coastal and Estuarine Research Federation (internationally oriented national body)
♦ **CERF** United Nations Central Emergency Response Fund (#20525)
♦ **CERG** Centre Européen sur les Risques Géomorphologiques (#06482)
♦ CERGE-EI – Central and Eastern European Regional Network (internationally oriented national body)
♦ CERI / see Centre européen de recherche internationales et stratégiques
♦ **CERI** Carpathian Ecoregion Initiative (#03587)
♦ **CERIC** Central European Research Infrastructure Consortium (#03716)
♦ CERIC – Centre d'études et de recherches internationales et communautaires (internationally oriented national body)
♦ CERI – Centre d'études et de recherches internationales (internationally oriented national body)
♦ CERI – Centro Español de Relaciones Internacionales (internationally oriented national body)
♦ CERI – Centro de Estudos de Relações Económicas Internacionais (internationally oriented national body)
♦ CERIC-ERIC / see Central European Research Infrastructure Consortium (#03716)
♦ CERIDA – Centre d'étude et de recherche pour l'intégration régionale et le développement de l'Afrique (internationally oriented national body)
♦ **CERILH** Comité européen roller in-line hockey (#04165)
♦ CE-RIO – EU-Rio Group Institutionalized Ministerial Meeting (inactive)
♦ CERIS – Centre européen de recherche internationales et stratégiques (internationally oriented national body)
♦ CERIST / see Regional Information Technology and Software Engineering Centre (#18789)
♦ CERLAC – Centre for Research on Latin America and the Caribbean (internationally oriented national body)
♦ **CERLALC** Centro Regional para el Fomento del Libro en América Latina y el Caribe (#18758)
♦ **CERL** Consortium of European Research Libraries (#04742)
♦ CERMI – Centre d'études et de recherches sur les migrations ibériques (internationally oriented national body)
♦ **CERNA** Conférence des évêques de la région du Nord de l'Afrique (#04605)
♦ CERN – Conseil européen pour la recherche nucléaire (inactive)
♦ **CERN** European Organization for Nuclear Research (#08108)

♦ CERN Staff Association 03834

Association du personnel du CERN

Secretariat CERN Bldg 64/R-010, 1211 Geneva 23, Switzerland. T. +41227663738. E-mail: staff.association@cern.ch.
URL: http://staff-association.web.cern.ch/

History Founded Apr 1955, Geneva (Switzerland), to represent staff members of *European Organization for Nuclear Research (CERN, #08108).* Statutes approved 20 nov 2002; amended 26 Mar 2004, 23 Mar 2007, 11 Apr 2008, 20 Apr 2010, 17 Apr 2012, 24 May 2013 and 22 May 2014. **Aims** Promote and defend the interests of CERN staff through collective negotiation; improve the employment, working, safety and welfare conditions for all staff; safeguard the rights and defend the interests of the families of CERN staff; facilitate the integration in the Geneva (Switzerland) area; provide collective and individual representation, consultation and advisory services, social and cultural activities; pursue relations with other associations or unions representing staff of international organizations and of related national institutions. **Structure** General Assembly (annual); Staff Council with 45 staff delegates (elected for a 2-year mandate); Executive Committee; Election Committee; Board of Auditors; Disputes Board. Non-statutory Standing Commissions (7): Employment Conditions; Health

and Safety; Pensions; Social Security; Legal Matters; Information, Training and Actions; Individual Cases. **Languages** English, French. **Finance** Members' voluntary contributions. Budget (annual): Swiss Fr 290,000. **Activities** Advocacy / lobbying / activism; meeting activities; awareness raising. **Events** *Meeting* Paris (France) 2006, *Conference of staff associations of international organizations* Frankfurt-Main (Germany) 2003, *Conference of staff associations of international organizations* London (UK) 2002. **Publications** *ECHO* (bi-weekly) – bulletin. Press releases; circulars.
Members Individuals (1,450) in 21 countries:
Austria, Belgium, Bulgaria, Czechia, Denmark, Finland, France, Germany, Greece, Hungary, Israel, Italy, Netherlands, Norway, Poland, Portugal, Slovakia, Spain, Sweden, Switzerland, UK. [2019/XE1687/v/E]

- ♦ CERP – Comité européen de régulation postale (see: #04602)
- ♦ CERP – Confédération européenne des relations publiques (inactive)
- ♦ CERP Education and Research / see European Public Relations Education and Research Association (#08302)
- ♦ CERPOD – Centre d'études et de recherche sur la population pour le développement (no recent information)
- ♦ **CERRA** International Civil Engineering Risk and Reliability Association (#12583)
- ♦ **CERR** Conférence des Eglises riveraines du Rhin (#04646)
- ♦ **CERRE** Centre on Regulation in Europe (#03777)
- ♦ CERRO – Central European Regional Research Organization (no recent information)
- ♦ Cerro Tololo Inter-American Observatory (internationally oriented national body)
- ♦ CERS / see Center for European and Eurasian Studies, Los Angeles
- ♦ CERS – Centre européen Robert Schuman (internationally oriented national body)
- ♦ **CERS** Confédération Européenne de Roller-Skating (#04550)
- ♦ CERSS – Centre européen pour le renseignement stratégique et la sécurité (internationally oriented national body)
- ♦ **CERT** Canada-Europe Roundtable for Business (#03410)
- ♦ CERT/CC – CERT Coordination Center (internationally oriented national body)
- ♦ CERT Coordination Center (internationally oriented national body)
- ♦ CERTDP – Centre for European Research Training and Development Projects (internationally oriented national body)
- ♦ Certified Color Manufacturers Association / see International Association of Color Manufacturers
- ♦ CERTIL – Confédération européenne des radios et télévisions indépendantes et locales (no recent information)

♦ CertiLingua Network 03835

Chair Ministerium Schule / Weiterbildung Nordrhein-Westfalen, Völklinger Str 49, 40221 Düsseldorf, Germany. T. +49211586740. E-mail: poststelle@msb.nrw.de.
URL: http://www.certilingua.net/

History CertiLingua Label of Excellence initiated and tested 1 Aug 2007 – 31 Jul 2009. **Structure** International Steering Group. **Activities** Certification/accreditation. **Events** *Annual Conference* 2021, *Annual Conference* 2020, *Annual Conference* Eupen (Belgium) 2019, *Annual Conference* Hannover (Germany) 2018, *Annual Conference* Tallinn (Estonia) 2017.
Members Schools (over 200). Representatives in 10 countries:
Austria, Belgium, Czechia, Estonia, Finland, France, Germany, Italy, Russia, Sweden. [2021/XJ9093/F]

- ♦ Certosini (religious order)
- ♦ CERT-TT-M / see European Knowledge and Technology Transfer Society (#07629)
- ♦ CERU – European Centre on Urban Risks (internationally oriented national body)
- ♦ CERUR / see Weitz Center for Development Studies
- ♦ CERV / see Assembly of European Wine Regions (#02317)

♦ Cerveceros Latinoamericanos 03836

Latin American Beer Manufacturers Association

Gen Sec address not obtained.
URL: https://cerveceroslatinoamericanos.com/

History 1959. as *Asociación Latinoamericana de Fabricantes de Cerveza (ALAFACE)*, a sectorial member of *Latin American Industrialists Association (#16341)*. Present name adopted, 2001. **Aims** Protect the interests of the Latin American beer industry. **Structure** Board of Directors elects Executive Committee. **Languages** English, Spanish. **Staff** 6.00 FTE, paid. **Activities** Organizes every 2 years: technical congress; convention. **Events** *Technical Congress* Managua (Nicaragua) 2006, *Technical congress* 2003, *Technical Congress* Guatemala (Guatemala) 2003, *Convention* Miami, FL (USA) 2002, *Convention* Peru 2002. **Publications** *Bulletin* (weekly) – online; *Brauwelt* (4 a year) in Spanish – technical magazine.
Members Active Beer and malting barley manufacturing companies. Members in 15 countries:
Argentina, Bolivia, Chile, Colombia, Dominican Rep, Ecuador, El Salvador, Guatemala, Honduras, Mexico, Panama, Paraguay, Peru, Uruguay, Venezuela.
Affiliate Beer manufacturers outside Latin America. Members in 3 countries:
Canada, Netherlands, USA.
NGO Relations Member of (1): *Worldwide Brewing Alliance (WBA, #21917)*. [2020/XD0460/D]

- ♦ Cervical Spine Research Society (internationally oriented national body)

♦ Cervical Spine Research Society – Europe (CSRS-Europe) 03837

General Manager Lifford Hall, Lifford Lane, Kings Norton, Birmingham, B30 3JN, UK. E-mail: info@csrs-europe.org.
Sec Dept Neurosurgery J11-82, Leiden Univ Medical Ctr, Albinusdreef 2, 2300 RC Leiden, Netherlands.
URL: https://csrs-europe.org/

History Acts as European section of *Cervical Spine Research Society (CSRS)*. Registration: Companies House, No/ID: 05373700, Start date: 23 Feb 2005, England and Wales. **Aims** Develop and exchange ideas and philosophy regarding the diagnosis and treatment of cervical spine injury and disease. **Structure** Board. **Activities** Events/meetings; research/documentation; training/education. **Events** *Annual Meeting* Barcelona (Spain) 2022, *Annual Meeting* Paris (France) 2021, *Annual Meeting* Rome (Italy) 2019. [2022/AA2711/D]

- ♦ **CERVIM** Centro di Ricerche, Studi e Valorizzazione per la Viticoltura Montana (#03819)
- ♦ CES / see Institute for Social and European Studies
- ♦ CES / see European Studies Center, Pittsburgh PA
- ♦ CES / see Forum on Contemporary Europe, Stanford CA
- ♦ CEsA / see Center for African and Development Studies
- ♦ CEsA – Centre for African and Development Studies (internationally oriented national body)
- ♦ CEsA – Centro de Estudos sobre África e Desenvolvimento (internationally oriented national body)
- ♦ CESA – Community of European Shipyards Associations (inactive)
- ♦ **CESA** Comparative Education Society of Asia (#04409)
- ♦ **CESA** Conseil économique et social arabe (#00937)
- ♦ **CESAER** Conference of European Schools for Advanced Engineering Education and Research (#04599)
- ♦ **CESAG** Centre africain d'études supérieures en gestion (#03724)
- ♦ CESAL (internationally oriented national body)
- ♦ **CESAO** Commission économique et sociale des Nations Unies pour l'Asie occidentale (#20558)
- ♦ **CESAP** Commission économique et sociale des Nations Unies pour l'Asie et le Pacifique (#20557)
- ♦ CESAR – Central European Society for Anticancer Drug Research-EWIV (internationally oriented national body)
- ♦ CESASS – Centre for Southeast Asian Social Studies (internationally oriented national body)
- ♦ CESCA – Centre d'étude sur la communication en Afrique (inactive)
- ♦ CESCA – Conference of Eastern, Southern and Central African Heads of Correctional Services (inactive)
- ♦ CESCE – European Committee for Business Support Services (inactive)
- ♦ CES – Center for European Studies, Cambridge MA (internationally oriented national body)
- ♦ CES – Center for European Studies, Maastricht (internationally oriented national body)
- ♦ CES – Center for European Studies, Madison WI (internationally oriented national body)
- ♦ CES – Center for European Studies, University of Connecticut (internationally oriented national body)
- ♦ CES – Centre for European Studies (internationally oriented national body)
- ♦ CES – Centre for European Studies, Ankara (internationally oriented national body)
- ♦ CES – Centre for European Studies, Chisinau (internationally oriented national body)
- ♦ CES – Centre for European Studies, Delhi (internationally oriented national body)
- ♦ CES – Centre for European Studies, Ottawa (internationally oriented national body)
- ♦ CES – Centre for European Studies, Trier (internationally oriented national body)
- ♦ CES / see CES – Silicones Europe (#03838)
- ♦ CESC / see European Council for Modelling and Simulation (#06831)
- ♦ CESCJ / see European Council of Jewish Communities (#06825)
- ♦ **CES** Community Exchange System (#04399)
- ♦ **CES** Confederación Europea de Sindicatos (#08927)
- ♦ **CES** Confédération européenne de scoutisme (#04531)
- ♦ **CES** Confédération européenne des syndicats (#08927)
- ♦ **CES** Confederazione Europea dei Sindacati (#08927)
- ♦ **CES** Conference of European Statisticians (#04600)
- ♦ **CES** Conseil européen de stomathérapie (#06820)
- ♦ **CES** Council for European Studies (#04894)
- ♦ **CESCR** United Nations Committee on Economic, Social and Cultural Rights (#20538)
- ♦ CESD / see CESD – statisticiens pour le développement
- ♦ **CESD** Collège européen de sécurité et de défense (#04107)
- ♦ CESD – Statisticians for Development (internationally oriented national body)
- ♦ CESD – statisticiens pour le développement (internationally oriented national body)
- ♦ **CESE** Comparative Education Society in Europe (#04410)
- ♦ CESEL-ECLAWS – European Committee of Liquid Applied Waterproofing Systems (inactive)
- ♦ CESEM / see European Microscopy Society (#07795)
- ♦ **CESEP** Centre for European Social and Economic Policy (#03742)
- ♦ CESEP – International Conference on Carbon for Energy Storage and Environment Protection (meeting series)
- ♦ **CESES** Confederation of European Senior Expert Services (#04533)
- ♦ CES / see European Economic and Social Committee (#06963)
- ♦ CESG / see European Centre on Geomorphological Hazards (#06482)
- ♦ **CESH** European Committee for Sports History (#06669)
- ♦ CESI / see Centro Einstein di Studi Internazionali sul Federalismo, la Pace, la Politica del Territorio
- ♦ CESICE – Centre d'études sur la sécurité internationale et les coopérations européennes (internationally oriented national body)
- ♦ CESI – Centro Einstein di Studi Internazionali sul Federalismo, la Pace, la Politica del Territorio (internationally oriented national body)
- ♦ CESIE (internationally oriented national body)
- ♦ **CESI** European Confederation of Independent Trade Unions (#06705)
- ♦ CESI / see Inter-American Conference on Social Security (#11419)
- ♦ CESIM – Centre d'Etudes de Sécurité Internationale et de Maîtrise des Armements (internationally oriented national body)
- ♦ **CESIO** Comité européen des agents de surface et leurs intermédiaires organiques (#06660)
- ♦ CESIQ – Carrefour d'éducation à la solidarité internationale – Québec (internationally oriented national body)
- ♦ Ceske Fórum pro Rozvojovou Spolupraci (internationally oriented national body)
- ♦ CESLA – Centro de Estudios Latinoamericanos, Universidad de Varsovia (internationally oriented national body)
- ♦ CESL / see European Trade Union Confederation (#08927)
- ♦ **CESMA** Confederation of European Shipmasters' Associations (#04534)
- ♦ CESMEO – International Institute for Advanced Asian Studies (internationally oriented national body)
- ♦ CESM / see European Microscopy Society (#07795)
- ♦ CESNA / see Centro de Estudos das Americas, Rio de Janeiro
- ♦ CESNERM / see Centre for Pentecostal and Charismatic Studies
- ♦ **CESNI** Comité européen pour l'élaboration de standards dans le domaine de la navigation intérieure (#04160)
- ♦ **CESNI** Europäischer Ausschuss für die Ausarbeitung von Standards im Bereich der Binnenschifffahrt (#04160)
- ♦ **CESNI** European committee for drawing up standards in the field of inland navigation (#04160)
- ♦ **CESNI** Europees Comité voor de opstelling van standaarden voor de binnenvaart (#04160)
- ♦ **CESNUR International** Centro Studi sulle Nuove Religioni (#03820)
- ♦ CESO – Canadian Executive Service Organization (internationally oriented national body)
- ♦ CESPAM – SADC Centre for Specialization in Public Administration and Management (see: #19843)
- ♦ **CESPAO** Comisión Económica y Social de las Naciones Unidas para el Asia Occidental (#20558)
- ♦ **CESPAP** Comisión Económica y Social de las Naciones Unidas para Asia y el Pacifico (#20557)
- ♦ **CESP** Conseil européen des syndicats de police (#06837)
- ♦ **CESP** Consejo Europeo de Sindicatos de Policia (#06837)
- ♦ CESP / see European Academy of Paediatrics (#05811)
- ♦ CeSPI – Centro di Studi di Politica Internazionale (internationally oriented national body)
- ♦ CESPI – Centro Studi Problemi Internazionali, Milano (internationally oriented national body)
- ♦ **CESPU** Committee of the European Starch Potato Producers' Union (#04256)
- ♦ **CESRA** Community of European Solar Radio Astronomers (#04397)
- ♦ CESR – Center for Economic and Social Rights (internationally oriented national body)
- ♦ CESR – Centre d'études stratégiques, Rabat (internationally oriented national body)
- ♦ CESR / see European Securities and Markets Authority (#08457)
- ♦ CESS – Central Eurasian Studies Society (internationally oriented national body)
- ♦ CESS – Centre for European Security Studies (internationally oriented national body)
- ♦ CESS – Confédération Européenne Sport Santé (no recent information)
- ♦ CESSDA / see Consortium of European Social Science Data Archives (#04743)
- ♦ **CESSDA** Consortium of European Social Science Data Archives (#04743)
- ♦ CESSD / see European Strabismological Association (#08840)
- ♦ CESSE – Council of Engineering and Scientific Society Executives (internationally oriented national body)

♦ CES – Silicones Europe 03838

Manager c/o CEFIC, Rue Belliard 40 – bte 15, 1040 Brussels, Belgium. T. +32479687205.
URL: http://www.silicones.eu/

History 1968, Brussels (Belgium). Founded as sector group of *Conseil européen de l'industrie chimique (CEFIC, #04687)*. Former names and other names: *European Silicones Centre* – former (1968); *Centre européen des silicones (CES)* – former (1968). Registration: Banque-Carrefour des Entreprises, No/ID: 0424.123.887, Start date: 15 Jun 1983, End date: 4 Oct 1995. **Aims** Promote joint scientific studies and technical development aimed at improving the environment and the safety of silicones and *organosilanes*. **Structure** Steering Committee; Committees (3); Working Groups (15). **Languages** English. **Finance** Members' dues. **Publications** Fact sheets; industry updates; studies; videos.
Members Full; Associate. Members in 4 countries:
Belgium, France, Germany, Netherlands.
IGO Relations *European Chemicals Agency (ECHA, #06523)*; *European Commission (EC, #06633)* and institutions; national authorities and associations. **NGO Relations** Member of: *Global Silicones Council (GSC, #10600)*. [2021/XE1170/E]

- ♦ CESSMA – Centre d'études en sciences sociales sur les mondes africains, américains et asiatiques (internationally oriented national body)

♦ CESTAS – Centro di Educazione Sanitaria e Tecnologie Appropriate Sanitarie (internationally oriented national body)
♦ CEST – Consortium for European Symposia on Turkey (internationally oriented national body)
♦ CESTMed – Centre d'Etudes et de Sauvegarde des Tortues Marines de Méditerranée (internationally oriented national body)
♦ CESVI / see CESVI Fondazione
♦ CESVI Fondazione (internationally oriented national body)
♦ CES / see Wilfried Martens Centre for European Studies (#20962)
♦ **CETA** Caribbean Evangelical Theological Association (#03499)
♦ Cetacean Alliance (inactive)
♦ Cetacean Freedom Network (internationally oriented national body)
♦ Cetacean Monitoring Unit / see Sea Watch Foundation
♦ Cetacean Society International (internationally oriented national body)
♦ **CETA** Conférence des Eglises de toute l'Afrique (#00640)
♦ **CETAF** Consortium of European Taxonomic Facilities (#04744)
♦ CETASE – Centre d'études de l'Asie de l'Est, Montréal (internationally oriented national body)
♦ CETB – Confédération européenne de twirling bâton (inactive)
♦ CET – Centre for European Transformation (internationally oriented national body)
♦ **CET** Comité Européen de la Tréfilerie (#04166)
♦ **CET** Commission européenne du tourisme (#08943)
♦ **CET** The Commonwealth Education Trust (#04323)
♦ CET – Confédération européen des taxis (inactive)
♦ CETEAM International / see International Institute of Concurrent Engineering
♦ CETELA – Comunidad de Educación Teológica Ecuménica Latinoamericana y Caribeña (unconfirmed)
♦ **CET** European Ceramic Tile Manufacturers' Federation (#06508)
♦ CETI – Centre Européen des Textiles Innovants (unconfirmed)
♦ **CETIE** Centre technique international de l'embouteillage et du conditionnement (#15667)
♦ CETIM – Centre Europe – Tiers-monde (internationally oriented national body)

♦ Cetinje Parliamentary Forum (CPF) 03839

Cetinjski parlamentarni forum (CPF)

Contact Skupština Crne Gore, Bulevar Svetog Petra Cetinjskog broj 10, 81000 Podgorica, Montenegro. T. +38220404558. Fax +38220242192. E-mail: cpf@skupstina.me.
URL: https://www.skupstina.me/en/international-cooperation/cetinje-parliamentary-forum

History Feb 2004, Montenegro. Conceived and launched by the Parliament of the Republic of Montenegro, in cooperation with the Parliament of the State Union of Serbia and Montenegro. **Aims** Encourage and promote parliamentary dialogue among South East European countries. **Activities** Events/meetings. **Events** *Cetinje Parliamentary Forum* Cetinje (Montenegro) 2019, *Cetinje Parliamentary Forum* 2018, *Cetinje Parliamentary Forum* 2017, *Cetinje Parliamentary Forum* 2015, *Cetinje Parliamentary Forum* Cetinje (Montenegro) 2015.
Members Parliamentary representatives from 7 countries:
Albania, Croatia, Kosovo, Montenegro, North Macedonia, Serbia, Slovenia. [2019/AA3039/v/**F**]

♦ Cetinjski parlamentarni forum (#03839)
♦ CETL – Centre européen de traduction littéraire, Bruxelles (internationally oriented national body)
♦ CETMI / see Churches' Commission for Migrants in Europe (#03912)
♦ CETMO – Centre d'études des transports pour la Méditerranée occidentale (internationally oriented national body)
♦ CETOP / see European Fluid Power Committee (#07273)
♦ **CETOP** European Fluid Power Committee (#07273)
♦ CETOS / see OITS/ European Commission for Social Tourism (#17713)
♦ CETP – Caribbean Engineering and Technical Professionals (internationally oriented national body)
♦ CETP – Confédération européenne pour la thérapie physique (inactive)
♦ CETRI – Centre tricontinental (internationally oriented national body)
♦ CeTSAF – Forschungs- und Studienzentrum für Agrar- und Forstwissenschaften der Tropen und Subtropen (internationally oriented national body)
♦ **CETS** Comité européen des traitements de surfaces (#06671)
♦ CETS – Conférence européenne des télécommunications par satellites (inactive)
♦ **CETS** OITS/ European Commission for Social Tourism (#17713)
♦ CETTA – Central European Turtle and Tortoise Association (no recent information)
♦ CEU Business School (internationally oriented national body)
♦ **CEUC** Conference of European University Chaplains (#04601)
♦ **CEU** Central European University (#03717)
♦ CEU – Centro Studi per l'Evoluzione Umana (internationally oriented national body)
♦ **CEUCO** Conseil Européen des Confréries Enogastronomiques (#08076)
♦ **CEU** Council for European Urbanism (#04896)
♦ CEU Graduate School of Business / see CEU Business School
♦ CEU PU / see Central European University (#03717)
♦ CEUR – Centro de Estudios Urbanos y Regionales (internationally oriented national body)
♦ CEUREG Forum (meeting series)
♦ CEUS – Centre for European Studies, Cairo (internationally oriented national body)
♦ CEUS – Centre for European Union Studies, Hull (internationally oriented national body)
♦ CEU – UNWTO Commission for Europe (see: #21861)
♦ CEV / see Comité européen des entreprises vins (#04157)

♦ CEVAA – Communauté d'églises en mission 03840

Main Office CS 49530, 13 rue Louis Perrier, 34961 Montpellier CEDEX 2, France. T. +33467065177. Fax +33467065007. E-mail: secretariat@cevaa.org.
URL: http://www.cevaa.org/

History 30 Oct 1971, Paris (France), as *Evangelical Community for Apostolic Action – Communauté évangélique d'action apostolique.* **Aims** Link mainly French-speaking and English-speaking protestant churches in Africa, the Pacific, Latin America and Europe. **Structure** General Assembly (every 2 years). Executive Council (meets every 8 months). Secretariat, headed by Secretary General. Permanent Coordination on: Animation; Projects. **Staff** 6.00 FTE, paid. **Finance** Members' dues. Private partners. **Activities** Exchange of persons; training; missionary projects and programmes. Supports member activities. International events: training sessions; theological animation; communication. **Events** *General Assembly* Torre Pellice (Italy) 2012, *General assembly / Congress* Libreville (Gabon) 2010, *General assembly / Congress* Neuchâtel (Switzerland) 2008, *General assembly / Congress* Bouznika (Morocco) 2006, *General Assembly / Congress* Strasbourg (France) 2004. **Publications** *La Lettre de la Communauté* (2 a year). Dossiers.
Members Member churches (37) among which associate member churches (2) in 24 countries and territories:
Argentina, Benin, Cameroon, Central African Rep, Congo Brazzaville, Côte d'Ivoire, France, Gabon, Ghana, Italy, Lesotho, Madagascar, Mauritius, Morocco, Mozambique, New Caledonia, Polynesia Fr, Réunion, Rwanda, Senegal, Switzerland, Togo, Uruguay, Zambia. [2017/XF3006/**F**]

♦ **CEV** Centre for European Volunteering (#03743)
♦ **CEV** Confédération européenne de volleyball (#09078)
♦ **CEVF** Central European Vascular Forum (#03718)
♦ **CEVHAP** Coalition to Eradicate Viral Hepatitis in Asia Pacific (#04058)
♦ CEVI – Centro di Volontariato Internazionale (internationally oriented national body)
♦ **CEVI** Confédération Européenne des Vignerons Indépendants (#06706)
♦ **CEVMA** Christian European Visual Media Association (#03902)
♦ CEVNO / see European Platform – internationalising education

♦ CEV Small Countries Association (SCA) 03841

Pres Sport Center Laugardalur, 104 Reykjavik, Iceland. T. +3545144111. E-mail: cevsca@gmail.com.
URL: https://cevsca.com/

History 1984, Cancún (Mexico). Former names and other names: *CEV Small Countries Division (SCD)* – former. **Aims** Promote the sport of *volleyball*. **Structure** General Assembly; Executive Committee. **Languages** English.
Members Federations in 14 countries and territories:
Andorra, Faeroe Is, Gibraltar, Greenland, Iceland, Ireland, Liechtenstein, Luxembourg, Malta, Monaco, Northern Ireland, San Marino, Scotland, Wales.
NGO Relations Affiliated with (2): *European Volleyball Confederation (#09078)*; *Fédération internationale de volleyball (FIVB, #09670).* [2023.03.01/XJ8517/**D**]

♦ CEV Small Countries Division / see CEV Small Countries Association (#03841)
♦ cewas – International Centre for Water Management Services (internationally oriented national body)
♦ **CEWEP** Confederation of European Waste-to-Energy Plants (#04535)
♦ **CEWP** China Europe Water Platform (#03889)
♦ CEWQO – Central European Workshop on Quantum Optics (meeting series)
♦ CEXECI – Centro Extremeño de Estudios y Cooperación con Iberoamérica (internationally oriented national body)
♦ CFA / see African Forestry and Wildlife Commission (#00319)
♦ CFAB – Children and Families Across Borders (internationally oriented national body)
♦ **CFAC** Conferencia de las Fuerzas Armadas de Centroamérica (#04651)
♦ CFA – Circus Federation of Australasia (internationally oriented national body)
♦ **CFA** Commonwealth Forestry Association (#04329)
♦ **CFA** Communauté financière africaine (#04377)
♦ **CFA** Communication Foundation for Asia (#04380)
♦ CFA – Congregatio Fratrum Cellitarum seu Alexianorum (religious order)
♦ CFA – Conservation Finance Alliance (unconfirmed)
♦ CFA – Constituency for Africa (internationally oriented national body)
♦ CFA – Cool Farm Alliance (unconfirmed)
♦ CFACT – Committee for a Constructive Tomorrow (internationally oriented national body)
♦ CFACT Europe – European Committee for a Constructive Tomorrow (internationally oriented national body)
♦ CFAF – Change For Animals Foundation (internationally oriented national body)
♦ CFA Franc Zone (#18270)
♦ CFA – Fundación Cultural de las Américas (internationally oriented national body)
♦ CFA Institute (internationally oriented national body)
♦ C-Fam – Center for Family and Human Rights (internationally oriented national body)
♦ **CFAN** Christ for All Nations (#03895)
♦ **CFAN** Comisión Forestal para América del Norte (#17565)
♦ CFA / see Pan African Women's Organization (#18074)
♦ **CFAP** Child Friendly Asia Pacific (#03867)
♦ **CFAP** Commission des forêts pour l'Asie et le Pacifique (#01909)
♦ **CFATF** Caribbean Financial Action Task Force (#03505)
♦ CFCA / see Unbound
♦ CFCA – Caribbean Forest Conservation Association (inactive)
♦ CFCA – Communications Fraud Control Association (internationally oriented national body)
♦ CFCA / see European Fisheries Control Agency (#07266)
♦ CF – Carpathian Foundation International (see: #05264)
♦ **CFC** Common Fund for Commodities (#04293)
♦ CFC – Congregatio Fratrum Christianorum (religious order)
♦ **CFC** Conseil francophone de la chanson (#04690)
♦ CFCE – Conseil des fédérations commerciales d'Europe (inactive)
♦ CFCF / see Comité français pour la solidarité internationale
♦ CFC Family Network / see CFC International
♦ CF – Cicero Foundation (internationally oriented national body)
♦ CFCI – Congrès Francophone de Cardiologie Interventionnelle (meeting series)
♦ CFC International (internationally oriented national body)
♦ C and FC – International Symposium on Catalysis and Fine Chemicals (meeting series)
♦ CFCMF / see Comité français pour la solidarité internationale
♦ **CFCO** Comisión Forestal para el Cercano Oriente (#16965)
♦ **CF** Commonwealth Foundation (#04330)
♦ CF – Council on Foundations (internationally oriented national body)
♦ **CFCS** Caribbean Food Crops Society (#03509)
♦ CFD / see Agence française de développement
♦ CFD / see Coopération et Formation au Développement
♦ CFD – Caribbean Forum for Development (no recent information)
♦ CFE / see CFE Tax Advisers Europe (#03842)
♦ **CFE** CFE Tax Advisers Europe (#03842)
♦ **CFE** Children's Fashion Europe (#03876)
♦ **CFE** Comisión Forestal Europea (#07299)
♦ CFED / see Training Center for Tropical Resources and Ecosystems Sustainability
♦ CFEM – Comité pour une fédération européenne et mondiale (inactive)
♦ **CFEnetwork** Computational and Financial Econometrics (#04424)
♦ CFEP – Centre for European Progression (internationally oriented national body)
♦ CFERDAP / see Training Center for Tropical Resources and Ecosystems Sustainability
♦ CFES – Center for European Studies, Nagoya (internationally oriented national body)

♦ CFE Tax Advisers Europe (CFE) 03842

Secretariat Av de Tervuren 188a, 1150 Brussels, Belgium. T. +3227610091. Fax +3227610090. E-mail: info@taxadviserseurope.org.
URL: http://taxadviserseurope.org/

History May 1959, Paris (France). Former names and other names: *Confederation of Tax Consultants' Groups in the EEC* – former (1959); *Confédération de groupements de conseils fiscaux européens* – former (1959); *European Tax Confederation* – former; *Vereinigung der Steuerberaterverbände in Europa* – former; *Confédération Fiscale Européenne (CFE)* – former; *European Federation of Tax Advisers* – former. Registration: EU Transparency Register, No/ID: 3543183647-05; Start date: 2011, Belgium; Start date: 9 Nov 1959, France. **Aims** Bring together all tax advisers' organizations of all European States; safeguard the professional interests of tax advisers; assure the quality of tax services provided to the public. **Structure** General Assembly, consisting of up to 6 delegates and observers from each country. Executive Board of 8 members. Committees (2): Fiscal; Professional Affairs. **Languages** English. **Staff** 3.00 FTE, paid. **Finance** Members' dues. **Activities** Guidance/assistance/consulting; politics/policy/regulatory; networking/liaising; events/meetings. **Events** *CFE Forum* Brussels (Belgium) 2022, *CFE Forum* Brussels (Belgium) 2021, *Conference on Tax Advisers Professional Affairs* Brussels (Belgium) 2020, *Forum* Brussels (Belgium) 2019, *Conference on Tax Advisers Professional Affairs* Paris (France) 2019. **Publications** *CEF's Tax Top 5: Key Tax News of the Week* (weekly); *CFE European Tax and Professional Law Report* (12 a year); *European Taxation* (12 a year); *CFE National Report* (3 a year) – two in taxation, one in professional affairs. *Towards Greater Fairness in Taxation: A Model Taxpayer Charter – Final Report* (2016); *CFE Professional Affairs Handbook for Tax Advisers* (2nd ed 2013); *CFE Forum Reports on European Taxation* – 6 eds until 2014.
Members National professional organizations of tax advisers (26), comprising over 200,000 individual members, in 20 countries:
Austria, Belgium, Czechia, Finland, France, Ireland, Italy, Latvia, Luxembourg, Malta, Netherlands, Poland, Portugal, Romania, Slovakia, Slovenia, Spain, Switzerland, UK, Ukraine.
Observers in 1 country:
Russia.
NGO Relations Cooperates with: *International Bureau of Fiscal Documentation (IBFD, #12415).* [2021/XE8499/**D**]

♦ CFE – Treaty on Conventional Armed Forces in Europe (1990 treaty)
♦ **CFEU** Citizens for Europe (#03956)
♦ **CF Europe** Cystic Fibrosis Europe (#04991)
♦ **CFFA** Coalition for Fair Fisheries Agreements (#04060)

- ♦ CFFC / see Catholics for Choice (#03609)
- ♦ **CFF** Commonwealth Fencing Federation (#04328)
- ♦ **CFF** Crops For the Future (#04968)
- ♦ **CFFSA** Comisión Forestal y de la Flora y Fauna Silvestres para Africa (#00319)
- ♦ **CFFSA** Commission des forêts et de la faune sauvage pour l'Afrique (#00319)
- ♦ CFGB – Canadian Foodgrains Bank (internationally oriented national body)
- ♦ CFGS – Centre for Global Studies, Victoria (internationally oriented national body)
- ♦ CFHI – Child Family Health International (internationally oriented national body)
- ♦ CFHTB – Confédération Francophone d'Hypnose et Thérapies brèves (internationally oriented national body)
- ♦ CFI – Center for Financial Inclusion at Accion (internationally oriented national body)
- ♦ CFIC – Filii Immaculatae Conceptionis (religious order)
- ♦ **CFI** Christian Friends of Israel (#03903)
- ♦ CFI – Christliche Fachkräfte International (internationally oriented national body)
- ♦ CFI – Commonwealth Forestry Institute (inactive)
- ♦ CFI – Community Forestry International (internationally oriented national body)
- ♦ CFI – Community Forests International (internationally oriented national body)
- ♦ CFI – Conference on Future Internet Technologies (meeting series)
- ♦ **CFI** Corporación Financiera Internacional (#13597)
- ♦ CFI – Cummings Foundation (internationally oriented national body)
- ♦ CFIEC – Center for International Economic Collaboration (internationally oriented national body)
- ♦ CFI – General Court of the European Communities (inactive)
- ♦ CFIOP / see International Organization of Psychophysiology (#14466)
- ♦ CFJ – Clooney Foundation for Justice (internationally oriented national body)
- ♦ CFJ – Committee For Justice (unconfirmed)
- ♦ CFK – Christliche Friedenskonferenz (inactive)
- ♦ **CFLGM** Caribbean Forum of Local Government Ministers (#03511)
- ♦ CFMAL and El Caribe – Confederación Femenina Metodista América Latina y El Caribe (no recent information)
- ♦ **CFMC** Caribbean Fishery Management Council (#03508)
- ♦ CFM – Council of Foreign Ministers (see: #17813)
- ♦ CFM – Council of Foreign Ministers (inactive)
- ♦ CFME ACTIM / see Agence française pour le développement international des entreprises
- ♦ CFM Europe – Christian Family Movement Europe (see: #12851)
- ♦ CFMSS – Clarist Franciscan Missionaries of the Most Blessed Sacrament (religious order)
- ♦ CFN – Cetacean Freedom Network (internationally oriented national body)
- ♦ **CFN** Choral Festival Network (#03894)
- ♦ CFN – Christ for the Nations (internationally oriented national body)
- ♦ CFNI – Caribbean Food and Nutrition Institute (inactive)
- ♦ CFN / see Niger Basin Authority (#17134)
- ♦ CFNU – Genève – Cercle féminin des Nations Unies – Genève (internationally oriented national body)
- ♦ CFO Forum – European Insurance CFO Forum (unconfirmed)
- ♦ **CFPA** Caribbean Family Planning Affiliation (#03502)
- ♦ CFPA – China Folklore Photographic Association (internationally oriented national body)
- ♦ CFPA – Coalition for Peace Action (internationally oriented national body)
- ♦ **CFPA Europe** Confederation of Fire Protection Associations (#04552)
- ♦ **CFPA-I** Confederation of Fire Protection Associations International (#04553)
- ♦ CFP / see Comptoirs français du pacifique (#04422)
- ♦ **CFP** Comptoirs français du pacifique (#04422)
- ♦ CFP – Congregatio Fratrum Pauperum Sancti Francisci Seraphici (religious order)
- ♦ CFP – Corporate Funding Programme (internationally oriented national body)
- ♦ **CFP-E** Commercial Film Producers Europe (#04202)
- ♦ **CFPI** Commission de la fonction publique internationale (#12587)
- ♦ **CFPO** Commission des forêts pour le Proche-Orient (#16965)
- ♦ CFP / see Peace Quest International (#18282)
- ♦ CFPS – Centre for Foreign Policy Studies, Halifax (internationally oriented national body)
- ♦ CFR – Centre for Foreign Relations (internationally oriented national body)
- ♦ CFR – Council on Foreign Relations (internationally oriented national body)
- ♦ **CfRN** Coalition for Rainforest Nations (#04066)
- ♦ CFSC – Canadian Friends Service Committee (internationally oriented national body)
- ♦ **CFSC** Caribbean Financial Services Corporation (#03506)
- ♦ **CFSC Consortium** Communication for Social Change Consortium (#04383)
- ♦ CFS – Committee on World Food Security (see: #09260)
- ♦ CFS – Congregazione della Fraternità Sacerdotale (religious order)
- ♦ CFSI – Comité français pour la solidarité internationale (internationally oriented national body)
- ♦ CFSI – Community and Family Services International (internationally oriented national body)
- ♦ CFSP / PESC / see European Commission (#06633)
- ♦ **CFTC** Commonwealth Fund for Technical Cooperation (#04331)
- ♦ **CFTDI** Caribbean Fisheries Training and Development Institute (#03507)
- ♦ CFTZ / see African Continental Free Trade Area (#00267)
- ♦ **CFU** Caribbean Football Union (#03510)
- ♦ CFWCC – Children and Families World Community Chest (inactive)
- ♦ **CFW** Cystic Fibrosis Worldwide (#04992)
- ♦ CFX – Congregatio Fratrum a Sancto Francisco Xaverio (religious order)
- ♦ CGACB / see Council of Arab Central Banks and Monetary Agencies' Governors (#04858)
- ♦ **CGACB** Council of Arab Central Banks and Monetary Agencies' Governors (#04858)
- ♦ **CGA** CERA Global Association (#03825)
- ♦ **CGAP** Consultative Group to Assist the Poor (#04768)
- ♦ **CGB** Commonwealth Geographical Bureau (#04333)
- ♦ **CGBS** Caribbean Group of Banking Supervisors (#03512)
- ♦ CGCC / see Global Center on Cooperative Security
- ♦ CGCID – Centro de Gestión y Cooperación Internacional para el Desarrollo (internationally oriented national body)
- ♦ CGCM – Consortium for Globalization of Chinese Medicine (internationally oriented national body)
- ♦ CGCS – Center for Global Communication Studies (internationally oriented national body)
- ♦ CGCTC / see Global Center on Cooperative Security
- ♦ CGDA / see International Game Developers Association
- ♦ **CGDC** Center for Global Dialogue and Cooperation (#03641)
- ♦ CGD – Center for Global Development (internationally oriented national body)
- ♦ CGD – Centre for Global Development, Leeds (internationally oriented national body)
- ♦ CGD Europe – Center for Global Development in Europe (internationally oriented national body)
- ♦ CGE / see Center for Global Education and Experience
- ♦ CGE – Centre for Global Education (internationally oriented national body)
- ♦ CGEE – Center for Global Education and Experience (internationally oriented national body)
- ♦ **CGEF** Commonwealth Girls Education Fund (#04334)
- ♦ CGER – Centre for Global Environmental Research, Ibaraki (internationally oriented national body)
- ♦ CGES – BMW Center for German and European Studies (internationally oriented national body)
- ♦ CGES – Center for German and European Studies, Madison WI (internationally oriented national body)
- ♦ **CGF** Commonwealth Games Federation (#04332)
- ♦ **CGF** The Consumer Goods Forum (#04772)
- ♦ CGFNS International – Commission on Graduates of Foreign Nursing Schools (internationally oriented national body)
- ♦ **CGFS** Committee on the Global Financial System (#04258)
- ♦ CGHH – Coalition for Global Hearing Health (unconfirmed)
- ♦ CGI / see Skylark International
- ♦ CGIAM – Centro di Geomorfologia Integrata per l'Area del Mediterraneo (internationally oriented national body)
- ♦ **CGIAP** Conseil International des Créateurs des Arts Graphiques, Plastiques et Photographiques (#13011)
- ♦ CGIAP / see International Council of Creators of Graphic, Plastic and Photographic Arts (#13011)
- ♦ CGIAR / see CGIAR System Organization (#03843)
- ♦ **CGIAR** CGIAR System Organization (#03843)

♦ CGIAR System Organization (CGIAR) 03843

Exec Dir 1000 av Agropolis, 34394 Montpellier CEDEX 5, France. T. +33467047575. E-mail: contact@cgiar.org.
URL: http://www.cgiar.org/

History May 1971, Washington, DC (USA). Established as an informal network of public and private entities. Reformed 2008, with new name, but acronym was retained as a title. Initially a contractual joint venture set up by the 15 Research Centers, but Agreement Establishing the Consortium as an independent international organization entered into force, 29 Apr 2010. Governance structure revised and current name adopted, 1 Jul 2016. Former names and other names: *Consultative Group on International Agricultural Research (CGIAR)* – former (May 1971 to 2008); *Groupe consultatif pour la recherche agricole internationale* – former (May 1971 to 2008); *Grupo Consultivo sobre Investigación Agrícola Internacional* – former (May 1971 to 2008); *Consortium of International Agricultural Research Centers (CGIAR)* – former (2008 to 1 Jul 2016). **Aims** Advance agri-food science and innovation to enable poor people, especially poor women, to increase *agricultural* productivity and resilience, share in economic growth, better feed themselves and their families, and conserve natural resources in the face of *climate change* and other threats.
Structure CGIAR System Council; CGIAR System Board; System Organization Management Office; General Assembly of the Centers.
Research Centers (15):
- *Africa Rice Center (AfricaRice, #00518)*, Cotonou (Benin);
- *International Centre for Tropical Agriculture (#12527)*, Cali (Colombia);
- *Center for International Forestry Research (CIFOR, #03646)*, Bogor (Indonesia);
- *International Maize and Wheat Improvement Center (#14077)*, El Batan (Mexico);
- *International Potato Center (#14627)*, Lima (Peru);
- *International Center for Agricultural Research in the Dry Areas (ICARDA, #12466)*, Aleppo (Syrian AR);
- *International Crops Research Institute for the Semi-Arid Tropics (ICRISAT, #13116)*, Patancheru (India);
- *International Food Policy Research Institute (IFPRI, #13622)*, Washington DC (USA);
- *International Institute of Tropical Agriculture (IITA, #13933)*, Ibadan (Nigeria);
- *Bioversity International (#03262)*, Rome (Italy);
- *International Livestock Research Institute (ILRI, #14062)* Nairobi (Kenya);
- *International Rice Research Institute (IRRI, #14754)*, Los Baños (Philippines);
- *International Water Management Institute (IWMI, #15867)*, Colombo (Sri Lanka);
- *World Agroforestry Centre (ICRAF, #21072)*, Nairobi (Kenya);
- *WorldFish (#21507)*, Penang (Malaysia).

Languages English. **Staff** 10500.00 FTE, paid. Staff in over 60 countries. **Finance** CGIAR system-wide budget and consolidated Research Programme and Centre reporting services. Fund allocation; annual financing plan and disbursements of funds to Centers. **Activities** Research/ documentation. **Events** *NEXUS Gains Talks 6: Tools for Groundwater Governance* 2022, *Global Landscapes Forum* Bonn (Germany) 2018, *Global Science Conference on Climate Smart Agriculture* Johannesburg (South Africa) 2017, *Asian Maize Conference* Bangkok (Thailand) 2015, *Global Landscapes Forum* Paris (France) 2015. **Publications** *CGIAR Annual Report*; *e-CGIAR News*. *CGIAR Strategy and Results Framework 2016-2030: Harnessing New Opportunties*. Brochures; reports; CGIAR Impact Stories. **IGO Relations** Associated organization within: *The World Bank Group (#21218)*. Contributes to implementation of: *Global Action Plan for Environment and Development in the 21st Century (Agenda 21, inactive)*. Accredited to the Conference of the Parties of: *Secretariat of the United Nations Convention to Combat Desertification (Secretariat of the UNCCD, #19208)*. Cooperates with: *Arab Organization for Agricultural Development (AOAD, #01018)*; *West African Science Service Center on Climate Change and Adapted Land Use (WASCAL, #20897)* through *Climate Change Agriculture and Food Security (CCAFS)*. Set up: *International Network for the Improvement of Banana and Plantain (INIBAP, inactive)*. Instrumental in setting up: *Global Crop Diversity Trust (Crop Trust, #10313)*. Supports: *Africa Rice Center (AfricaRice, #00518)*.
NGO Relations Participates in: *Global Terrestrial Observing Network (GT-Net, no recent information)*. Member of: *Association for Human Resources Management in International Organizations (AHRMIO, #02634)*; *Global Alliance for Climate-Smart Agriculture (GACSA, #10189)*; *Global Open Data for Agriculture and Nutrition (GODAN, #10514)*; *InsideNGO (inactive)*; *Inter-Agency Network for Safety in Biotechnology (IANB, inactive)*; *International Foundation for Science (IFS, #13677)*; *LEDS Global Partnership (LEDS GP, #16435)*.
Instrumental in setting up: *African Highland Initiative Eco-regional Programme (AHI, inactive)*; *Central Asia and the Caucasus Association of Agricultural Research Institutions (CACAARI, #03678)*; *e-Agriculture (#00575)*; *HarvestPlus (#10862)*; *Global Rice Science Partnership (GRiSP, #10580)*; *Inland Valley Consortium (IVC, no recent information)*; *International Centre for Development Oriented Research in Agriculture (ICRA)*; *Rice-Wheat Consortium for the Indo-Gangetic Plains (RWC, #18937)*. Supports: *African Mountain Forum (no recent information)*; *Coconut Genetic Resources Network (COGENT, #04080)*; *Forum for Agricultural Research in Africa (FARA, #09897)*.
Cooperates with: *Alliance of Communicators for Sustainable Development (COMplus, #00669)*; *Bellanet Alliance of Social Entrepreneurs (BASE, #03196)*; *Ford Foundation (#09858)*; *International Centre of Insect Physiology and Ecology (ICIPE, #12499)*; *International Network of Resource Centers on Urban Agriculture and Food Security (RUAF Foundation, #14319)*; *The Rockefeller Foundation (#18966)*; *W K Kellogg Foundation (WKKF)*; *Young Professionals for Agricultural Development (YPARD, #21996)*. [2018.09.05/XE4468/y/**E***]

- ♦ **CGI** Church Growth International (#03913)
- ♦ **CGI** IUGS Commission on Management and Application of Geoscience Information (#16081)
- ♦ CGIRS – Center for Global, International and Regional Studies (internationally oriented national body)
- ♦ CGIUKI – The Chartered Governance Institute of UK and Ireland (internationally oriented national body)
- ♦ **CGLU Afrique** Cités et Gouvernements Locaux Unis d'Afrique (#20500)
- ♦ **CGLU** Organisation mondiale des cités et gouvernements locaux unis (#21695)
- ♦ CGMB – Common Global Ministries Board (internationally oriented national body)
- ♦ CGMH – Centre for Global Mental Health (internationally oriented national body)
- ♦ CGMJCI – Church of God Ministry of Jesus Christ International (religious order)
- ♦ **CGMS** Coordination Group for Meteorological Satellites (#04827)
- ♦ **CGMW** Commission for the Geological Map of the World (#04216)
- ♦ CGNK / see Center for Global Nonkilling (#03642)
- ♦ CGOM – International Workshop on Crystal Growth of Organic Materials (meeting series)
- ♦ CGP – Center for Global Peace, Washington DC (internationally oriented national body)
- ♦ **CGP** Council for Global Problem-Solving (#04898)
- ♦ CGPE – Center for Global Political Economy, Burnaby (internationally oriented national body)
- ♦ CGPE – Centre for Global Political Economy, Brighton (internationally oriented national body)
- ♦ **CGPM** Comisión General de Pesca del Mediterraneo (#10112)
- ♦ **CGPM** Commission générale des pêches pour la Méditerranée (#10112)
- ♦ **CGRFA** Commission on Genetic Resources for Food and Agriculture (#04215)
- ♦ CGRGP – Laurier Centre for Global Relations, Governance and Policy (internationally oriented national body)
- ♦ CGS – Center for the Global South (internationally oriented national body)
- ♦ CGS – Center for Global Studies, Fairfax VA (internationally oriented national body)
- ♦ **CGS** Computer Graphics Society (#04427)
- ♦ **CGS** Confédération générale des syndicats (#10108)
- ♦ CGS – Congregazione di Gesù Sacerdote (religious order)
- ♦ CGSIC – Civil Global Positioning System Service Interface Committee (internationally oriented national body)
- ♦ CGS – International Symposium on Capture Gamma-Ray Spectroscopy and Related Topics (meeting series)
- ♦ CGTA – Conference on Geometry: Theory and Applications (meeting series)

♦ CHA / see Children's Healthcare Australasia

♦ Chabad Lubavitch 03844

Exec Officer 770 Eastern Parkway, Brooklyn NY 11213, USA. T. +17187744000. Fax +17187742718. E-mail: hq@lubavitch.com – info@lubavitch.com.
URL: http://www.lubavitch.com/

History Set up early 1940s, Russia, as *Lubavitch Movement*. Named after Lubavitch (Belarus). Previously also known as *Chabad Movement* and *Chabad Lubavitch Global Network*. **Aims** Proclaim *Judaism* and the observance of the *Torah* worldwide.
Members Centres (approx 4,000) in 68 countries and territories:
Argentina, Armenia, Australia, Austria, Azerbaijan, Belarus, Belgium, Bolivia, Brazil, Bulgaria, Canada, Chile, China, Colombia, Congo DR, Costa Rica, Croatia, Cyprus, Czechia, Denmark, Estonia, Finland, France, Georgia, Germany, Greece, Guatemala, Hungary, India, Ireland, Israel, Italy, Japan, Kazakhstan, Kyrgyzstan, Laos, Latvia, Lithuania, Luxembourg, Moldova, Morocco, Nepal, Netherlands, New Zealand, Norway, Panama, Paraguay, Peru, Poland, Puerto Rico, Romania, Russia, Singapore, Slovakia, South Africa, Spain, Sweden, Switzerland, Thailand, Tunisia, UK, Ukraine, Uruguay, USA, Uzbekistan, Venezuela, Vietnam, Virgin Is USA. [2016.06.27/XN4955/**F**]

♦ Chabad Lubavitch Global Network / see Chabad Lubavitch (#03844)
♦ Chabad Movement / see Chabad Lubavitch (#03844)
♦ CHA / see Caribbean Hotel and Tourism Association (#03516)
♦ CHA – Children's Healthcare Australasia (internationally oriented national body)
♦ CHA – Commission hydrographique sur l'Antarctique (see: #13825)
♦ **CHA** Commonwealth Handball Association (#04335)
♦ CHA – Cotton House Africa (internationally oriented national body)
♦ CHAdeMO (unconfirmed)
♦ CHAFI – Chantiers d'Afrique (internationally oriented national body)
♦ CHAGS – Conference on Hunting and Gathering Societies (meeting series)
♦ CHAIA – Commission hydrographique de l'Afrique et des Iles Australes (see: #13825)
♦ Chaim Herzog Center for Middle East Studies and Diplomacy (internationally oriented national body)
♦ **CHAIN** Community Health and Information Network (#04400)
♦ Chaîne bleue mondiale: pour la protection des animaux et de la nature (#21235)
♦ Chaîne de l'Espoir (internationally oriented national body)
♦ Chaîne de l'espoir – Belgique (internationally oriented national body)
♦ Chaîne des rôtisseurs / see Chaîne des Rôtisseurs – Association Mondiale de la Gastronomie (#03845)

♦ Chaîne des Rôtisseurs – Association Mondiale de la Gastronomie (Chaîne des Rôtisseurs) 03845

Headquarters 111 rue de Longchamp, 75016 Paris, France. T. +33142813012. Fax +33140168185. E-mail: chancellerie@chainehq.org.
URL: http://www.chainedesrotisseurs.com/

History Aug 1950, Paris (France). Established when constitution was adopted. Origins go back to 1248 when Saint Louis, King of France, set up several professional guilds. Registered in accordance with French law. Former names and other names: *Confrérie de la chaîne des rôtisseurs* – former (1950); *Guild of Rôtisseurs* – former; *Chaîne des rôtisseurs* – former; *Cadena de Asadores* – former; *Association mondiale de la gastronomie* – former. Registration: France. **Aims** Bring together professional and non-professional members to celebrate their passion for fine cuisine and wines, promote international fellowship and goodwill, and aid and encourage the development of young chefs and sommeliers worldwide through its national and international competitions as well as provide food support and aid to those in need across the globe thanks to its charitable programmes and food-related initiatives. **Structure** General Assembly (annual); Board of Directors; Conseil Magistral'; Provincial and Local 'Baillages'. Bailli Délégué. Includes *Ordre Mondial des Gourmets Dégustateurs (OMGD)*, set up 1963, as a section. Set up the charity *Association Caritative de la Chaîne des Rôtisseurs (ACCR)*, 2 Jan 2008. **Finance** Sources: members' dues. **Activities** Advocacy/lobbying/activism; awards/prizes/competitions; events/meetings. **Events** *Assemblée générale* Paris (France) 2004, *Assemblée générale* Vienna (Austria) 2000, *Assemblée générale* Trondheim (Norway) 1997, *Assemblée générale* 1996, *Réunion* Bergen (Norway) 1995. **Publications** *Chaîne des rôtisseurs magazine* (2 a year).
Members National 'Bailliages' representing over 25,000 members (25% professional and 75% non-professional) in 69 countries and territories:
Australia, Austria, Bahrain, Belgium, Bermuda, Brunei Darussalam, Cameroon, Canada, China, Colombia, Costa Rica, Côte d'Ivoire, Cyprus, Czechia, Denmark, Egypt, Finland, France, Germany, Greece, Guadeloupe, Guiana Fr, Hong Kong, Hungary, Indonesia, Israel, Italy, Japan, Jordan, Kenya, Korea Rep, Kuwait, Lebanon, Liechtenstein, Lithuania, Luxembourg, Macau, Malaysia, Malta, Mexico, Monaco, Netherlands, New Zealand, Norway, Oman, Philippines, Poland, Portugal, Russia, Saudi Arabia, Singapore, Slovakia, Slovenia, South Africa, Spain, Sri Lanka, Sweden, Switzerland, Syrian AR, Taiwan, Thailand, Tunisia, Türkiye, Uganda, UK, United Arab Emirates, USA, Venezuela. [2022/XF2769/**F**]

♦ **Chaîne des Rôtisseurs** Chaîne des Rôtisseurs – Association Mondiale de la Gastronomie (#03845)
♦ Chain of Hope – Belgium (internationally oriented national body)

♦ Chairmen of the European Research Councils' Chemistry Committees (CERC3) 03846

Contact Dept of Sciences, NWO, PO Box 93223, 2509 AL The Hague, Netherlands.

History 9 Feb 1990, Paris (France). Also referred to as *CERCCC*. **Aims** Increase coordination of national research programmes in chemistry in the European Union in order to achieve a more effective use of both national and international resources and raise the visibility of chemistry research in Europe. **Structure** Executive Group including Chairperson and Past Chairperson. **Languages** English. **Activities** Organizes annual meeting, workshops. **Events** *Young chemists workshop* Netherlands 2006, *Young chemists workshop* Sweden 2006, *Young chemists workshop* Karlsruhe (Germany) 2005, *Young chemists workshop* Sesimbra (Portugal) 2005, *Young chemists workshop* Saint-Malo (France) 2004.
Members Individuals in 16 countries:
Austria, Belgium, Denmark, Finland, France, Germany, Greece, Ireland, Italy, Luxembourg, Netherlands, Portugal, Spain, Sweden, Switzerland (Special Status), UK.
IGO Relations *European Commission (EC, #06633)*. **NGO Relations** Founding member of: *European Federation of Chemical Engineering (EFCE, #07074)*. Member of: *Alliance for Chemical Sciences and Technologies in Europe (AllChemE, #00664)*. [2009/XE4495/**E**]

♦ **Challenges Forum** International Forum for the Challenges of Peace Operations (#13632)
♦ Challenges Worldwide (internationally oriented national body)
♦ Chamber of Commerce of the Americas (inactive)
♦ Chamber of Commerce, Industry and Agriculture Belgium – Luxembourg – Africa-Caribbean-Pacific (internationally oriented national body)
♦ Chamber of Commerce of the United States of America (internationally oriented national body)

♦ Chamber of Computer Logistics People Worldwide (CCLP Worldwide) 03847

Secretariat Gujarat Bhavan, 17 tara chand dutt street, Kolkata, West Bengal, Kolkata WEST BENGAL, India. E-mail: info@cclpworldwide.com.
URL: http://cclpworldwide.com/

History Registration: India; EU Transparency Register, No/ID: 031673743402-23, Start date: 22 Jul 2021. **Aims** Advance effective principled *education* policies in governments, higher education institutes and civil societies so as to improve *sustainable development*. **Structure** International Council; World Council; Advisory Council; Secretariat. **Languages** English, Hindi. **Staff** 5.00 FTE, paid. **Finance** Sources: donations; members' dues. **Activities** Events/meetings; research and development; awards/prizes/competitions; advocacy/lobbying/activism. **Publications** *Education Charter* (4 a year) – magazine. **Consultative Status** Consultative status granted from: *ECOSOC (#05331)* (Special). **NGO Relations** Member of (6): *Conference of Non-Governmental Organizations in Consultative Relationship with the United Nations (CONGO, #04635)*; Network on Education Quality Monitoring in the Asia-Pacific (NEQMAP); *PMNCH (#18410)*; *UNCAC Coalition (#20283)*; *United Nations Academic Impact (UNAI, #20516)*; *United Nations Global Compact (#20567)*. [2021/XJ4548/**F**]

♦ Chamber Orchestra of Europe (COE) 03848

Gen Manager North House, 27 Great Peter St, London, SW1P 3LN, UK. T. +442070703333. Fax +442070703330. E-mail: redbird@coeurope.org.
Registered Office 40 Queen Anne Street, London, W1G 9EL, UK.
URL: http://www.coeurope.org/

History 1981. Founded by Peter Readman and a group of inspired young European musicians with the active support of a number of determined friends. Registration: Companies House, No/ID: 01587684, England and Wales. **Aims** Promote, improve and develop aesthetic education through the medium of *music* by the practice and performance of works of a wide variety of essentially European music. **Structure** Executive Committee. **Languages** Danish, English, Finnish, French, German, Italian, Polish, Spanish, Swedish. **Staff** 4.00 FTE, paid. **Finance** Sources: contributions; international organizations. No public subsidies. **Activities** Events/meetings; training/education. **Publications** *COE Newsletter* (12 a year).
Members Musicians from 16 countries:
Australia, Austria, Canada, Denmark, Finland, France, Germany, Italy, Netherlands, Norway, Poland, Spain, Sweden, Switzerland, UK, USA. [2020.08.28/XF2679/**F**]

♦ Chambre des beaux arts de Méditerranée / see European Cultural Network for Development Cooperation (#06869)
♦ Chambre de Commerce allemande en Belgique / see Chambre de commerce belgo-luxembourgeoise-allemande
♦ Chambre de Commerce allemande à Bruxelles / see Chambre de commerce belgo-luxembourgeoise-allemande
♦ Chambre de commerce des Amériques (inactive)
♦ Chambre de commerce Belgique-Luxembourg-Pays arabes (#00907)
♦ Chambre de commerce belgo-africaine / see Chamber of Commerce, Industry and Agriculture Belgium – Luxembourg – Africa-Caribbean-Pacific
♦ Chambre de Commerce Belgo-allemande / see Chambre de commerce belgo-luxembourgeoise-allemande
♦ Chambre de commerce belgo-luxembourgeoise-allemande (internationally oriented national body)
♦ Chambre de commerce des Etats-Unis (internationally oriented national body)
♦ Chambre de commerce franco-arabe (internationally oriented national body)
♦ Chambre de commerce, d'industrie et d'agriculture Belgique – Luxembourg – Afrique-Caraïbes-Pacifique (internationally oriented national body)
♦ Chambre de Commerce et d'Industrie des Caraïbes en Europe (#03471)
♦ Chambre de commerce internationale (#12534)
♦ Chambre de commerce internationale gaie et lesbienne (no recent information)
♦ Chambre de compensation de l'Afrique centrale (no recent information)
♦ Chambre de compensation de l'Afrique de l'Ouest (inactive)
♦ Chambre économique européenne de commerce, d'artisanat et d'industrie (#06959)
♦ Chambre européenne des arbitres extrajudiciaires et des experts conseillers techniques / see European Chamber of Extrajudicial Adjudicators and Experts of Europe
♦ Chambre européenne des arbitres extrajudiciaires et des experts d'Europe (internationally oriented national body)
♦ Chambre européenne d'ingénieurs (#06514)
♦ Chambre européenne des ingénieurs professionnels (no recent information)
♦ Chambre internationale de droit (inactive)
♦ Chambre internationale des experts-conseils en transport (inactive)
♦ Chambre internationale de film (inactive)
♦ Chambre internationale du film d'enseignement (inactive)
♦ Chambre internationale de la marine marchande (#12535)
♦ Chambre islamique de commerce et d'industrie / see Islamic Chamber of Commerce, Industry and Agriculture (#16036)
♦ Chambre Islamique de Commerce, d'Industrie et d'Agriculture (#16036)
♦ Chambre islamique de commerce, d'industrie et d'échange de marchandises / see Islamic Chamber of Commerce, Industry and Agriculture (#16036)
♦ Chambres de commerce et de l'industrie de l'ANASE (#01151)

♦ Chambres de Commerce et d'Industrie Françaises à l'International (CCI France International) 03849

Dir-Gen 46 avenue de la Grande Argmée, CS 50071, 75858 Paris CEDEX 17, France. T. +33140693704. Fax +33147206128.
URL: http://www.ccifrance-international.org/

History Founded 1907, *Union des chambres de commerce et d'industrie françaises à l'étranger (UCCIFE)*. Present name adopted, 2014. **Aims** Offer support to French companies wishing to import, export and invest in foreign countries; look for reliable business partners; create a forum for contact and communication; represent business interests; foster mutual understanding; promote the image of France abroad; provide companies with relevant assistance and services. **Structure** Board of Directors; Bureau. **Languages** French. **Staff** 8.00 FTE, paid. **Finance** Members' dues (annual). **Activities** Gathers, represents, coordinates and develops the network of members; represents members in France and abroad; disseminates information; promotes members. Meets regularly with national ministers and public institutions in charge of foreign commerce and of French foreign residents. **Events** *Symposium* Abu Dhabi (United Arab Emirates) 2022. **Publications** *UCCIFE Annuaire* (annual); *France Monde Express* (24 a year) – electronic newsletter.
Members French chambers of commerce and industry (111) in 81 countries and territories:
Albania, Algeria, Argentina, Armenia, Australia, Austria, Bangladesh, Belgium, Brazil, Bulgaria, Cambodia, Canada, Chile, China, Colombia, Congo DR, Costa Rica, Côte d'Ivoire, Cuba, Czechia, Denmark, Dominican Rep, Ecuador, Egypt, El Salvador, Finland, Georgia, Germany, Greece, Haiti, Hong Kong, Hungary, India, Indonesia, Iran Islamic Rep, Ireland, Israel, Italy, Japan, Jordan, Korea Rep, Kuwait, Lithuania, Luxembourg, Madagascar, Malaysia, Malta, Mauritius, Mexico, Moldova, Morocco, Myanmar, Netherlands, New Zealand, Nigeria, Norway, Pakistan, Paraguay, Peru, Philippines, Poland, Portugal, Romania, Russia, Serbia, Singapore, Slovakia, South Africa, Spain, Sweden, Switzerland, Taiwan, Thailand, Tunisia, Türkiye, UK, Ukraine, United Arab Emirates, USA, Venezuela, Vietnam.
NGO Relations *International Chamber of Commerce (ICC, #12534)*. [2018/XD8779/t/**D**]

♦ Chambre syndicale des fabricants de compteurs de gaz / see Association of European Manufacturers of Gas Meters, Gas Pressure Regulators, Safety Devices and Stations (#02521)

♦ Chance for Childhood 03850

CEO Westmead House, Westmead, Farnborough, GU14 7LP, UK. T. +441483230250. E-mail: info@chanceforchildhood.org.
Mailing Address PO Box 3030, Romford, RM7 1US, UK.
Registered Address 3 Fairfields, 26 Green Lane, Cobham, KT11 2NN, UK.
URL: http://chanceforchildhood.org/

History 11 Aug 1992, UK. *Street Child Africa (inactive)* merged into Chance for Childhood, 2016. 2020, *Glad's House UK* merged into Chance for Childhood. Former names and other names: *Jubilee Action* – former. Registration: Charity Commission, No/ID: 1013587, Start date: 11 Aug 1992, England and Wales. **Aims** Work in Africa to support the most vulnerable children, often invisible from society, such as street children, disabled children, children affected by conflict and children in conflict with the law. **Structure** Based in UK. **Staff** 15.00 FTE, paid; 2.00 FTE, voluntary. **Finance** Sources: grants; charitable donations. **Activities** Advocacy/lobbying/activism; humanitarian/emergency aid; training/education. Active in: Congo DR, Ghana, Kenya, Rwanda, Uganda. **Members** Not a membership organization. **NGO Relations** Member of: *British Overseas NGO's for Development (BOND)*; *Keeping Children Safe*. [2020.05.18/XF4998/v/**F**]

♦ Change Agents for Peace International (internationally oriented national body)
♦ Change For Animals Foundation (internationally oriented national body)
♦ CHANGE – Center for Health and Gender Equity (internationally oriented national body)
♦ Change Partnership (unconfirmed)
♦ Changing Markets Foundation (#19984)

Channel Swimming Association
03851

alphabetic sequence excludes
For the complete listing, see Yearbook Online at

♦ **Channel Swimming Association (CSA)** **03851**
Sec PO Box 10580, Nottingham, NG5 0JH, UK. T. +441304600610. E-mail: secretary@channelswimmingassociation.com.
Pres 9 Church Crescent, Sproughton, Ipswich, IP8 3BJ, UK. T. +441473743144.
URL: http://www.channelswimmingassociation.com/
History 1927, London (UK). For UK legal purposes, from 1999 owned by 'Channel Swimming Association Ltd'. UK Registered Charity: 3868395. **Aims** Encourage all aspects of open water and sea swimming; assist swimmers to cross the English Channel safely and in compliance with maritime laws applicable to the Dover Strait. **Structure** Officers: Chairman; President; 5 Vice-Presidents; 11 Directors; Treasurer. Network of International Representatives. **Languages** English. **Staff** 0.50 FTE, paid. **Finance** Sources: members' dues. Annual budget: 90,000 GBP. **Activities** Certification/accreditation; events/meetings; guidance/assistance/consulting; sporting activities. **Publications** *Channel Swimming Association Handbook* (regular, latest 2020).
Members Floating membership of swimmers for the current year. Core (permanent) members – individuals in 46 countries:
Argentina, Australia, Bahamas, Bangladesh, Belgium, Brazil, Canada, China, Cyprus, Czechia, Ecuador, Egypt, France, Germany, Greece, Hungary, India, Ireland, Italy, Japan, Kenya, Lithuania, Malaysia, Malta, Mexico, Montenegro, Namibia, Netherlands, New Zealand, Norway, Pakistan, Peru, Serbia, Slovakia, Slovenia, South Africa, Spain, Switzerland, Tunisia, Türkiye, UK, Ukraine, Uruguay, USA, Venezuela, Zimbabwe.
NGO Relations National organizations. [2022.10.23/XE4217/v/**E**]

♦ Chanoines Réguliers de l'Immaculée Conception (religious order)
♦ Chanoines Réguliers du Latran (religious order)
♦ Chanoines Réguliers de Prémontré (religious order)
♦ Chanoines Réguliers de Saint Augustin Confédérés (religious order)
♦ Chanoinesses régulières hospitalières de la miséricorde de Jésus de l'Ordre de St-Augustin (religious order)
♦ Chantiers d'Afrique (internationally oriented national body)
♦ Chantiers jeunes – Chantiers pour le développement / see Quinoa
♦ CHAO – Commission hydrographique de l'Asie orientale (see: #13825)
♦ CHAP – Cultural Heritage Asia Pacific Network (internationally oriented national body)
♦ **CHARIS** Catholic Charismatic Renewal International Service (#03602)
♦ Charities Aid Foundation (internationally oriented national body)
♦ Charities Aid Foundation of America (internationally oriented national body)
♦ Charities Aid Foundation Southern Africa (unconfirmed)
♦ Charity Education International (internationally oriented national body)
♦ Charity Global / see Charity: Water
♦ Charity Global UK Limited / see Charity: Water
♦ Charity Organization / see Human Appeal (#10961)
♦ Charity: Water (internationally oriented national body)

♦ **Charles Darwin Foundation for the Galapagos Islands (CDF)** **03852**
Fondation Charles Darwin pour les Iles Galapagos – Fundación Charles Darwin para las Islas Galapagos
Contact Avenida Charles Darwin S/N, Santa Cruz Is, Galapagos, 090306 Puerto Ayora, Ecuador. T. +59352526146 – +59352527013. E-mail: cdrs@fcdarwin.org.ec.
Registered Office Chaussée de la Hulpe 177 – Bte 20, 1170 Brussels, Belgium.
URL: http://www.darwinfoundation.org/
History Founded 1959, Brussels (Belgium), under the auspices of *UNESCO (#20322)* and *International Union for Conservation of Nature and Natural Resources (IUCN, #15766)*. Registered in accordance with Belgian law. **Aims** Provide knowledge and assistance through scientific research and complementary action to ensure the conservation of the environment, biodiversity and natural resources in the Galapagos Archipelago. **Structure** General Assembly (annual). Board of Directors (meeting twice a year in Ecuador, USA, Europe or elsewhere, alternately). **Languages** English, Spanish. **Staff** About 100 at Research Station in the Galapagos Islands and in Quito (Ecuador). **Finance** Donations. Annual budget: about US$ 5,000,000. **Activities** Research/documentation; knowledge management/information dissemination. **Events** *General Assembly* Quito (Ecuador) 2012, *General Assembly* Galapagos Is (Ecuador) 2011, *General Assembly* Guayaquil (Ecuador) 2010, *General Assembly* Galapagos Is (Ecuador) 2009, *General Assembly* Quito (Ecuador) 2008. **Publications** *Galapagos Research* – information bulletin. Annual Report; e-newsletter; brochures.
Members Governmental or private bodies in 15 countries:
Belgium, Brazil, Canada, Chile, Denmark, Ecuador, France, Germany, Ireland, Japan, Luxembourg, New Zealand, Switzerland, UK, USA.
NGO Relations Memorandum of Understanding signed with: *Alliance for Zero Extinction (AZE, #00730)*. Partner of: *1% for the Planet*. Member of: *GEF CSO Network (GCN, #10087)*. [2020/XF0260/f/**F**]

♦ Charles F Kettering Foundation (internationally oriented national body)
♦ Charles Léopold Mayer Foundation for the Progress of Humankind (#09815)
♦ Charles Léopold Mayer Stiftung für den Fortschritt des Menschen (#09815)

♦ **Charles Rennie Mackintosh Society (CRM Society)** **03853**
Exec Dir/Sec The Mackintosh Church, Queen's Cross, 870 Garscube Road, Glasgow, G20 7EL, UK. T. +441419466600. Fax +441419467276. E-mail: info@crmsociety.com.
URL: http://www.crmsociety.com/
History 1973, Glasgow (UK), to promote awareness of Scottish architect, Charles Rennie Mackintosh. UK Registered Charity. **Aims** Promote and encourage *conservation* and improvement of the condition of buildings and *artifacts* designed by Mackintosh and his associates. **Structure** General Meeting (annual); Council. **Languages** English. **Staff** 2.50 FTE, paid; 4.00 FTE, voluntary. **Finance** Members' dues. Other sources: grants; legacies; corporate donations; shop; architectural tours; weddings. **Activities** Events/meetings; training/education. **Events** *International conference* UK 1990. **Publications** *Charles Rennie Mackintosh Society Journal* (2 a year).
Members Individuals in 25 countries and territories:
Australia, Austria, Bangladesh, Belgium, Canada, Denmark, France, Germany, Hong Kong, Hungary, Iran Islamic Rep, Ireland, Italy, Japan, Netherlands, New Zealand, Norway, Portugal, Slovenia, Spain, Sweden, Switzerland, Trinidad-Tobago, UK, USA.
NGO Relations Member of: *Art Nouveau European Route (#01125)*. [2014.10.28/XE0111/v/**E**]

♦ Charles Stewart Mott Foundation (internationally oriented national body)
♦ CHARM / see Oceania Customs Organisation (#17658)
♦ Charta 77 Foundation / see Foundation for a Civil Society
♦ Charta der grundrechte der Europäischen Union (2000 treaty)
♦ **CHART** Caribbean HIV/AIDS Regional Training Network (#03515)
♦ Charte africaine des droits de l'homme et des peuples (1981 treaty)
♦ Charte de l'aide alimentaire / see Réseau de prévention des crises alimentaires (#18905)
♦ Charte de l'Atlantique (1941 treaty)
♦ Charte communautaire des droits sociaux fondamentaux des travailleurs (1989 treaty)
♦ Charte des droits et devoirs économiques des Etats (1974 treaty)
♦ Charte des droits fondamentaux de l'Union européenne (2000 treaty)
♦ Charte européenne des abbayes cisterciennes / see Charte européenne des Abbayes et Sites Cisterciens (#03854)

♦ **Charte européenne des Abbayes et Sites Cisterciens** **03854**
European Charter of the Cistercian Abbeys and Sites
Contact Hostellerie des Dames de l'Abbaye de Clairvaux, 10310 Ville-sous-la-Ferté, France. T. +33325275255. Fax +33325275255. E-mail: info@cister.net – info@cister.eu.
Pres address not obtained.
URL: http://www.cister.net/
History Original title: *Charte européenne des abbayes cisterciennes*. Registered in accordance with French law. **Aims** Set up a structural link between the owners and/or managers of Cistercian abbeys or sites, which are open to the public, so as to organize common actions (cultural or tourist) and represent its members vis-à-vis local, regional, national and international administration. **Structure** General Meeting. **Finance** Members' dues. **Events** *Annual General Meeting* Troyes (France) 2015.
Members Sites (over 180) in 11 countries:
Belgium, Czechia, Denmark, France, Germany, Italy, Poland, Portugal, Spain, Sweden, Switzerland. [2016/XE2629/**E**]

♦ Charte européenne de l'autonomie locale (1985 treaty)
♦ Charte européenne des langues régionales ou minoritaires (1992 treaty)
♦ Charte européenne des régions de montagne (1995 treaty)
♦ Charte internationale de l'éducation physique et du sport (1978 treaty)
♦ Charte de l'Organisation des Etats américains (1948 treaty)
♦ Charte du Pacifique: traité de défense collective pour l'Asie du Sud-Est (1954 treaty)
♦ Charte de Punta del Este (1961 treaty)

♦ **Charter for Compassion International (CCI)** **03855**
Dir PO Box 10787, Bainbridge Island WA 98110, USA. T. +12068429956.
URL: http://www.charterforcompassion.org/
History Charter unveiled 12 Nov 2009. AS US 501(c)(3) nonprofit organization. **Aims** Bring to life the principles articulated in the Charter for Compassion. **Structure** Global Compassion Council – advisory body; Board of Directors. **Languages** English. **Finance** Members' dues. Other sources: grants; donations. **Activities** Events/meetings; training/education. [2019.03.11/XM5274/**F**]

♦ Charter on Economic Rights and Duties of States (1974 treaty)
♦ Chartered Alternative Investment Analyst Association (internationally oriented national body)
♦ The Chartered Governance Institute of UK and Ireland (internationally oriented national body)
♦ Chartered Institute of Arbitrators (internationally oriented national body)

♦ **Chartered Institute of Logistics and Transport** **03856**
Contact Earlstrees Court, Earlstrees Road, Corby, NN17 4AX, UK. T. +441536740162.
SG address not obtained.
URL: http://www.ciltinternational.org/
History 1919, as *Institute of Transport*. Incorporated in UK, 26 Aug 1920; granted Royal Charter, 26 Nov 1926. Became *Chartered Institute of Transport* 12 Mar 1971, on granting of supplemental charter. Subsequently changed to: *Chartered Institute of Transport in the UK (CIT)*. UK Registered Charity: 313376. **Aims** Promote, encourage and coordinate study and advancement of the science and art of logistics and transport. **Structure** International Council; National Councils; Standing Committees; Special Interest Groups. **Languages** English. **Finance** Members' dues. Educational and development activity. **Activities** Knowledge management/information dissemination; training/education; awards/prizes/competitions; events/meetings. **Events** *International Convention* Perth, WA (Australia) 2022, *TOC Asia : Container Supply Chain Conference* Singapore (Singapore) 2022, *TOC Asia : Container Supply Chain Conference* Singapore (Singapore) 2021, *International Convention* Perth, WA (Australia) 2020, *TOC Asia : Container Supply Chain Conference* Singapore (Singapore) 2020.
Members Managers and professionals in transport and logistics industries; national and local government departments; universities and research establishments. Members in 33 countries and territories:
Australia, Bangladesh, China, Egypt, Ethiopia, Ghana, Hong Kong, India, Indonesia, Ireland, Kenya, Macau, Malawi, Malaysia, Malta, Mauritius, Namibia, New Zealand, Nigeria, Oman, Pakistan, Singapore, South Africa, Sri Lanka, Taiwan, Tanzania UR, Uganda, UK, Ukraine, United Arab Emirates, USA, Zambia, Zimbabwe. [2020/XD1421/j/**F**]

♦ Chartered Institute of Transport / see Chartered Institute of Logistics and Transport (#03856)
♦ Chartered Institute of Transport in the UK / see Chartered Institute of Logistics and Transport (#03856)
♦ Chartered Institution of Water and Environmental Management (internationally oriented national body)
♦ Chartered Society of Designers (internationally oriented national body)
♦ Charter on Euro-Mediterranean Cooperation Concerning the Environment in the Mediterranean Basin (1990 treaty)
♦ Charter of Fundamental Rights of the European Union (2000 treaty)
♦ Charter of the Organization of American States (1948 treaty)
♦ Charter on the Participation of Young People in Municipal and Regional Affairs (1992 treaty)
♦ Charter of Punta del Este (1961 treaty)
♦ Charter Seventy-Seven Foundation / see Foundation for a Civil Society
♦ Charter of Seville – Mediterranean Landscape Charter (1993 treaty)
♦ Charte sociale européenne (1961 treaty)
♦ Charte sociale européenne – révisée (1996 treaty)
♦ Charte urbaine européenne (1992 treaty)
♦ Chart and Nautical Instrument Trade Association (internationally oriented national body)
♦ Châteaux et hôtels de charme (#14063)
♦ Châteaux and Hotels – ILA / see International Lodging Association (#14063)
♦ Chatham House / see Royal Institute of International Affairs
♦ Chatham House Foundation (internationally oriented national body)
♦ CHAtO – Commission hydrographique de l'Atlantique oriental (see: #13825)
♦ CHAtSO – Comisión Hidrografica del Atlantico Sudoccidental (see: #13825)
♦ **CHBA** Caribbean Herbal Business Association (#03514)
♦ CHBP – United Nations Centre for Housing, Building and Planning (inactive)
♦ CHCAP / see Cultural Heritage Asia Pacific Network
♦ CHC – Chaim Herzog Center for Middle East Studies and Diplomacy (internationally oriented national body)
♦ CHC – Congressional Hunger Center (internationally oriented national body)
♦ CHCE / see European Hospital and Healthcare Federation (#07501)
♦ CHCI – Consortium of Humanities Centers and Institutes (internationally oriented national body)
♦ **CHDA** Centre for Heritage Development in Africa (#03748)
♦ CHDS – Center for Hemispheric Defense Studies (internationally oriented national body)
♦ **CHEC** Commonwealth Human Ecology Council (#04339)
♦ Cheetah Conservation Fund (internationally oriented national body)
♦ Cheiron / see CHEIRON – The International Society for the History of Behavioral and Social Sciences (#03857)
♦ Cheiron-Europe / see European Society for the History of the Human Sciences (#08621)

♦ **CHEIRON – The International Society for the History of Behavioral and Social Sciences** **03857**
Contact Center for the History of Psychology, Univ of Akron, 73 College St, Akron OH 44325-4302, USA. T. +13309726096. Fax +13309722093.
Treas Dept of Psychology, Graceland Univ, University Place, Lamoni IA 50065-9761, USA.
URL: http://www.uakron.edu/cheiron/
History 1968, USA, as *International Society of the History of Behavioral and Social Sciences (Cheiron)*. **Aims** Promote international cooperation and multidisciplinary studies in the history of behavioural and social sciences. **Finance** Members' dues. **Activities** Organizes annual meetings (in Jun of each year). **Events** *Annual Meeting* Edmonton, AB (Canada) 2019, *Annual Meeting* Akron, OH (USA) 2018, *Annual Meeting* Starkville, MS (USA) 2017, *Annual Meeting* Barcelona (Spain) 2016, *Annual Meeting* Lawrence, KS (USA) 2015. **Members** Individuals. Membership countries not specified. [2015.08.26/XD8729/v/**F**]

♦ CHEMECA – Australasian Conference on Chemical Engineering (meeting series)

♦ **Chemical and Biological Microsystems Society (CBMS)** **03858**
Contact c/o Preferred Meeting Mgmt Inc, 307 Laurel St, San Diego CA 92101-1630, USA. T. +16192329499. Fax +16192320799. E-mail: info@cbmsociety.org.
URL: http://www.cbmsociety.org/
History USA. Registered as a nonprofit corporation in the State of North Carolina (USA). **Aims** Promote and advance science and engineering in the field of chemical and biological microsystems; stimulate the exchange of ideas and information between academic, industrial and government researchers. **Structure** Board of Directors. **Activities** Awards/prizes/competitions; events/meetings. **Events** *International Conference on Miniaturized Systems for Chemistry and Life Sciences* Hangzhou (China) 2022, *International Conference on Miniaturized Systems for Chemistry and Life Sciences* Palm Springs, CA (USA) 2021, *International Conference on Miniaturized Systems for Chemistry and Life Sciences* San Diego, CA (USA) 2020, *International Conference on Miniaturized Systems for Chemistry and Life Sciences* Basel (Switzerland) 2019, *International Conference on Miniaturized Systems for Chemistry and Life Sciences* Kaohsiung (Thailand) 2018. **Members** Not a membership organization. [2015/XJ9666/**C**]

- ♦ Chemical Industry Association for Scientific Understanding (inactive)
- ♦ Chemical Industry Labour Relations Committee / see International Chemical Employers Labour Relations Committee (#12541)

♦ Chemical Legislation European Enforcement Network (CLEEN) 03859
Co-Sec Kemikalieinspektionen, Swedish Chemicals Agency, Box 2, SE-172 13 Sundbyberg, Sweden. T. +46851941252. Fax +4687357698.
Co-Sec Fed Dept of Home Affairs, Fed Office of Public Health, Consumer Protection Directorate, Div of Chemicals, Schwarzenburgstr 165, 3003 Bern, Switzerland. T. +41584629625.
URL: http://www.cleen-europe.eu/
History Founded 2000, Athens (Greece). **Aims** Coordinate and improve the enforcement of EU chemicals legislation; ensure harmonized enforcement of European chemical legislation. **Structure** Secretariat (rotates every 3 years); Working Groups; Task Forces; National Focal Points. **Languages** English. **Staff** 4.00 FTE, paid. **Finance** No budget. Expenses borne by participating authorities. **Activities** Events/meetings; networking/liaising; knowledge management/information dissemination. **Events** Conference Berlin (Germany) 2018, Conference Dortmund (Germany) 2017, Conference Helsinki (Finland) 2016, Conference Stockholm (Sweden) 2015, Conference / Annual Conference Utrecht (Netherlands) 2014. **Publications** Project reports.
Members Chemical inspectorates in 30 countries:
Austria, Belgium, Bulgaria, Croatia, Cyprus, Czechia, Denmark, Estonia, Finland, France, Germany, Greece, Hungary, Ireland, Italy, Latvia, Lithuania, Luxembourg, Malta, Netherlands, Norway, Poland, Portugal, Romania, Slovakia, Slovenia, Spain, Sweden, Switzerland, UK.
IGO Relations All EU institutions and national competent authorities relevant for EU chemical management.
NGO Relations No formal contacts. [2018.09.18/XM0015/F]

♦ Chemical Recycling Europe (ChemRecEurope) 03860
Gen Sec Avenue de Cortenbergh 71, 1000 Brussels, Belgium. T. +3226691876. E-mail: solutions@chemicalrecyclingeurope.eu.
URL: https://www.chemicalrecyclingeurope.eu/
History 2019. Registration: Banque-Carrefour des Entreprises, No/ID: 0738.628.868, Start date: 2 Dec 2019, Belgium; EU Transparency Register, No/ID: 163494536726-42, Start date: 3 Dec 2019. **Aims** Close the loop for the plastics industry by offering the technology to chemically recycle all plastic waste back into its original components and/or other value-added materials. **NGO Relations** Member of (1): Circular Plastics Alliance (#03936). Partner of (1): European Coalition for Chemical Recycling. [2021/AA2024/D]

♦ Chemical Research Applied to World Needs (CHEMRAWN Committee) 03861
Exec Dir PO Box 13757, Research Triangle Park NC 27709-3757, USA. T. +19194858700. E-mail: secretariat@iupac.org.
URL: http://www.iupac.org/home/about/members-and-committees.html
History 1976, within the framework of International Union of Pure and Applied Chemistry (IUPAC, #15809). **Aims** Identify human needs amenable to solution through chemistry, with particular attention to areas of global or multinational interest; serve as an international body and forum for gathering, discussion, advancement and dissemination of chemical knowledge deemed useful for the improvement of man and his environment; serve as an international nongovernmental source of advice for the benefit of governments and international agencies with respect to chemistry and its application to world needs. **Structure** Committee comprises Chairman, Secretary, 6 members, 6 associate members and the Treasurer of IUPAC ex officio. **Staff** 6.00 FTE, paid. **Finance** Funded through IUPAC. **Activities** Organizes: Chemical Research Applied to World Needs (CHEMRAWN Conference). **Events** CHEMRAWN : Chemical Research Applied to World Needs Conference Dhaka (Bangladesh) 2015, CHEMRAWN : chemical research applied to world needs conference Kuala Lumpur (Malaysia) 2011, CHEMRAWN : chemical research applied to world needs conference Kingston, ON (Canada) 2007, CHEMRAWN : chemical research applied to world needs conference Stellenbosch (South Africa) 2007, CHEMRAWN : chemical research applied to world needs conference / CHEMRAWN Conference Paris (France) 2004.
Members Individuals in 13 countries:
Argentina, Bulgaria, Canada, India, Japan, Korea Rep, Poland, Russia, South Africa, Switzerland, Türkiye, UK, USA. [2012/XE2257/v/E]

- ♦ Chemical Research Applied to World Needs (meeting series)
- ♦ Chemicals, Health and Environment Monitoring Trust / see CHEM Trust
- ♦ Chemical Societies of the Nordic Countries (inactive)

♦ Chemical Society of the South Pacific (CSSP) 03862
Sec School of Biological and Chemical Sciences, Fac of Science/Technology/Environment, Univ of South Pacific, Private Mail Bag, Suva, Fiji. T. +6793232414. Fax +6793231513. E-mail: info@thecssp.org.
URL: http://www.thecssp.org/
History 1985, within Department of Chemistry of University of the South Pacific (USP, #20703). **Aims** Promote chemistry, particularly within the South Pacific region. **Structure** Executive Committee. **Languages** English. **Finance** Sponsorship. **Activities** Awards/prizes/competitions; training/education. **Events** International conference on chemistry, environment and climate change / Conference Suva (Fiji) 2011. **Publications** CSSP e-Newsletter. Course books.
Members Schools in 3 countries:
Solomon Is, Tonga, Vanuatu.
NGO Relations Affiliated to: Federation of Asian Chemical Societies (FACS, #09431). [2014.06.01/XJ2730/E]

- ♦ Chemical Specialties Manufacturers Association / see Consumer Specialty Products Association (#04774)
- ♦ Chemical Weapons Convention Coalition (unconfirmed)
- ♦ **CheMI** European Platform for Chemicals Using Manufacturing Industries (#08223)
- ♦ Chemin Neuf Community (internationally oriented national body)
- ♦ **CHEMRAWN Committee** Chemical Research Applied to World Needs (#03861)
- ♦ CHEMRAWN Conference – Chemical Research Applied to World Needs (meeting series)
- ♦ CHEMREACTOR – International Conference on Chemical Reactors (meeting series)
- ♦ **ChemRecEurope** Chemical Recycling Europe (#03860)
- ♦ ChemSec – International Chemical Secretariat (internationally oriented national body)
- ♦ CHEM Trust (internationally oriented national body)
- ♦ **CHENS** Chiefs of European Navies (#03865)
- ♦ CHEP – International Conference on Computing in High Energy and Nuclear Physics (meeting series)
- ♦ **CHER** Consortium of Higher Education Researchers (#04746)
- ♦ Cherie Blair Foundation for Women (internationally oriented national body)
- ♦ Chernobyl Centre / see International Humanitarian Centre for Rehabilitation of Survivors after Chernobyl Disaster
- ♦ Chernobyl International Laboratory on Radio-Ecology / see International Radioecology Laboratory
- ♦ Cheshire Foundation Homes for the Sick / see Leonard Cheshire Disability (#16443)

♦ Chess Collectors International 03863
Pres 63 Shepherds Lane, Dartford, DA1 2NS, UK.
URL: http://www.ccifrance.com/
History 1984. **Aims** Promote the study of art and history of chess sets and related items. **Languages** English, German. **Staff** None. **Activities** Events/meetings. **Events** Biennial Congress St Louis, MI (USA) 2020, Biennial Congress Prague (Czechia) 2018, Biennial Congress Paris (France) 2016, Biennial Congress Jersey City, NJ (USA) 2014, Biennial Congress Dresden (Germany) 2012. **Publications** CCI-USA (3 a year); Chess Collector (3 a year).
Members Individual collectors of chess-sets and related items in 28 countries:
Argentina, Australia, Austria, Belgium, Canada, Denmark, France, Germany, Hungary, India, Israel, Italy, Japan, Luxembourg, Mexico, Netherlands, New Zealand, Norway, Pakistan, Poland, Russia, South Africa, Spain, Sweden, Switzerland, UK, USA, Venezuela. [2022.10.23/XF4595/F]

- ♦ Chess Confederation of the Americas (inactive)

- ♦ **CHEST** American College of Chest Physicians (#00778)
- ♦ **CHESTRAD** International – Center for Health Science Training, Research and Development International (internationally oriented national body)

♦ Chest Wall International Group (CWIG) 03864
Contact Claus Petersen, Dept of Pediatric Surgery, Hannover Medical School, Carl-Neuberg-Str 1, 30625 Hannover, Germany. T. +495115329040. Fax +495115328052. E-mail: petersen.claus@mh-hannover.de – chestwall@mh-hannover.de.
URL: http://www.chestwall.org/
Structure Executive Committee. **Events** Congress Dubai (United Arab Emirates) 2020, Congress Pretoria (South Africa) 2019, Congress Seoul (Korea Rep) 2018.
Members Individuals in 44 countries and territories:
Albania, Argentina, Australia, Austria, Belgium, Brazil, Brunei Darussalam, Chile, China, Colombia, Costa Rica, Denmark, Ecuador, France, Germany, Hong Kong, India, Iran Islamic Rep, Israel, Italy, Japan, Korea Rep, Maldives, Mexico, Morocco, Netherlands, Peru, Poland, Portugal, Romania, Russia, Saudi Arabia, Serbia, Slovakia, South Africa, Spain, Switzerland, Taiwan, Tunisia, Türkiye, UK, USA, Uzbekistan, Vietnam. [2021/XM8296/v/F]

- ♦ Chevaliers de Colomb (internationally oriented national body)
- ♦ **CHF** / see Cordell Hull Foundation for International Education
- ♦ **CHF** – Chatham House Foundation (internationally oriented national body)
- ♦ **CHF** – Child Health Foundation (internationally oriented national body)
- ♦ **CHF** – Congregation of the Holy Family (religious order)
- ♦ **CHFIE** – Cordell Hull Foundation for International Education (internationally oriented national body)
- ♦ **CHF** International / see Global Communities
- ♦ **CHG** – Centre for the History of Globalization, Moscow (internationally oriented national body)
- ♦ **CHGE** – Center for Health and the Global Environment (internationally oriented national body)
- ♦ **CHGN** – Community Health Global Network (internationally oriented national body)
- ♦ Chiang Ching-Kuo Foundation for International Scholarly Exchange (internationally oriented national body)
- ♦ Chicago Convention – Convention on International Civil Aviation (1944 treaty)
- ♦ Chicago Council on Foreign Relations / see Chicago Council on Global Affairs
- ♦ Chicago Council on Global Affairs (internationally oriented national body)
- ♦ **CHI** Child Helpline International (#03870)
- ♦ **CHI** Christian Hotels/Hospitality International (#13298)
- ♦ **CHI** – Congenital Hyperinsulinism International (internationally oriented national body)
- ♦ **CHI** Co-operative Housing International (#04799)
- ♦ **CHI** – Creating Hope International (internationally oriented national body)
- ♦ **CHI** – Cultural Homestay International (internationally oriented national body)
- ♦ **CHIEA** / see Catholic University of Eastern Africa, The (#03610)
- ♦ Chief Learning Officer Middle East (unconfirmed)

♦ Chiefs of European Navies (CHENS) 03865
Address not obtained.
URL: http://www.chens.eu/
History Set up as an informal, independent and non-political forum. **Aims** Promote understanding between navies of the member countries; examine issues of common and mutual interest; increase awareness of the maritime domain in member countries. **Events** Annual Conference Helsinki (Finland) 2018. **Members** Chiefs of Navy of each European maritime nation that is either a member of NATO or the European Union and has naval armed forces. Membership countries not specified. [2019/XM7923/v/E]

- ♦ Chierici Mariani sotto il titolo dell'Immacolata Concezione della Beata Vergine Maria (religious order)
- ♦ Chierici Regolari della Madre di Dio (religious order)
- ♦ Chierici Regolari Minori (religious order)
- ♦ Chierici Regolari Poveri della Madre di Dio della Scuole Pie (religious order)
- ♦ Chierici Regolari di San Paolo (religious order)
- ♦ Chierici Regolari Teatini (religious order)
- ♦ Chierici di San Viatore (religious order)
- ♦ Chiesa di Dio Ministeriale di Gesù Cristo Internazionale (religious order)
- ♦ Chikyu Kankyo to Taiki Osen wo Kangaeru Zenkoku Shimin Kaigi (internationally oriented national body)
- ♦ Child10 (internationally oriented national body)
- ♦ ChildAid (internationally oriented national body)
- ♦ Childbirth Survival International (internationally oriented national body)
- ♦ Child to Child (internationally oriented national body)
- ♦ Child-to-Child International / see Child to Child
- ♦ Child to Child Movement / see Child to Child
- ♦ Child-to-Child Trust / see Child to Child

♦ Child in the City Foundation 03866
City Community Manager address not obtained.
URL: http://www.childinthecity.org/
Aims Strengthen the position of children in cities; promote and protect their rights; give them space and opportunities to play and enjoy their own social and cultural lives. **Structure** Scientific Program Committee; Board. **Activities** Events/meetings; training/education; research/documentation. **Events** World Conference Dublin (Ireland) 2021, World Conference Dublin (Ireland) 2020, Children in the sustainable city Antwerp (Belgium) 2019, World Conference Vienna (Austria) 2018, Children's play in the urban environment London (UK) 2017. [2019.03.13/XM7363/f/F]

- ♦ Child Family Health International (internationally oriented national body)
- ♦ Child Focus – European Centre for Missing and Sexually Exploited Children (internationally oriented national body)

♦ Child Friendly Asia Pacific (CFAP) 03867
Secretariat Univ of Western Sydney, Locked Bag 1797, Penrith NSW 2751, Australia.
History Former names and other names: Child Friendly Asia Pacific Network – alias; Asia-Pacific Child-Friendly Cities Network – alias. **Events** International Conference on Child Friendly Asia Pacific Surakarta (Indonesia) 2011, Asia Pacific conference Chiba (Japan) 2009. **IGO Relations** UNESCO (#20322). **NGO Relations** European Network Child Friendly Cities (ENCFC, #07877). [2013/XJ6720/F]

- ♦ Child Friendly Asia Pacific Network / see Child Friendly Asia Pacific (#03867)

♦ ChildFund Alliance 03868
Contact 545 Fifth Ave, Ste 1205, New York NY 10017, USA. E-mail: info@childfundalliance.org.
URL: http://www.childfundalliance.org/
History Jun 2002. Registration: No/ID: 0680.416.396, Start date: 15 Jun 2017, Belgium; EU Transparency Register, No/ID: 025312336988-40, Start date: 15 Jan 2020. **Aims** Create sustainable, child-focused, community-based development programmes in areas where children are impacted by war, natural disaster, poverty and global health issues. **Structure** Secretariat, based in New York NY (USA). **Languages** English, French, Japanese, Korean, Spanish, Swedish. **Staff** 6.00 FTE, paid. **Finance** Members' dues.
Members Full in 11 countries:
Australia, Canada, France, Germany, Ireland, Japan, Korea Rep, New Zealand, Spain, Sweden, USA.
Included in the above, 2 organizations listed in this Yearbook:
ChildFund International (#03869); EDUCO.
Consultative Status Consultative status granted from: ECOSOC (#05331) (Special). **NGO Relations** Shareholder in: International Civil Society Centre (#12589). Member of: Accountable Now (#00060); Alliance for Child Protection in Humanitarian Action (The Alliance, #00667); Child Rights Connect (#03884); Confédération européenne des ong d'urgence et de développement (CONCORD, #04547); Global Coalition to End Child Poverty (#10292); Global Partnership to End Violence Against Children (End Violence Against Children, #10533); Keeping Children Safe; Watchlist on Children and Armed Conflict (Watchlist). Supports: Global Call for Action Against Poverty (GCAP, #10263). [2019/XJ0484/y/F]

♦ **ChildFund International** **03869**
Main Office 2821 Emerywood Pkwy, PO Box 26484, Richmond VA 23294, USA. T. +18047562700. Fax +18047562718. E-mail: questions@childfund.org.
URL: http://www.childfund.org/
History 1938. UK Chapter and *European Children's Trust (inactive)* merged in 2001 to form *EveryChild*. Former names and other names: *China's Children Fund* – former (1938 to 1951); *Christian Children's Fund (CCF)* – former (1951 to 2009); *Fonds chrétien pour l'enfance* – former (1951 to 2009); *Fondo Cristiano para Niños* – former (1951 to 2009); *Fundo Cristão para Crianças* – former (1951 to 2009). Registration: USA. **Aims** Assist children and their families through individual sponsorship, focusing on: primary healthcare; nutrition; education; adult literacy; early childhood development; special assistance to children at risk. **Structure** Board of Directors, consisting of Chairman, 1st Vice-Chair, 2nd Vice-Chair, Secretary, Treasurer and 15 other members. Executive Staff of 13. National Offices. **Finance** Sources: revenue from child sponsorship; individual and corporate contributions; grants. Budget (annual): about US$ 213 million. **Activities** Advocacy/lobbying/activism; financial and/or material support. **Events** *Global youth enterprise conference* Washington, DC (USA) 2009, *Children and youth in conflict with the law in the Baltic countries* Riga (Latvia) 1994, *European research convention on environment research* Stuttgart (Germany) 1994, *Meeting* Geneva (Switzerland) 1993, *The future of children with disabilities in the Baltic states* Vilnius (Lithuania) 1993. **Publications** *Childworld* (4 a year). Annual Report.
Members Community organizations 1250 projects coordinated in 30 countries:
Afghanistan, Albania, Angola, Belarus, Bolivia, Brazil, Chad, Dominica, Ecuador, Ethiopia, Gambia, Guatemala, Guinea, Honduras, India, Indonesia, Kenya, Liberia, Mexico, Mozambique, Philippines, Senegal, Sierra Leone, Sri Lanka, St Vincent-Grenadines, Thailand, Timor-Leste, Uganda, USA, Zambia.
International affiliates in 11 countries and territories:
Australia, Canada, China, Denmark, France, Germany, Hong Kong, Japan, Korea Rep, New Zealand, UK.
Consultative Status Consultative status granted from: *UNICEF (#20332)*. **IGO Relations** Partner of (1): *UNHCR (#20327)*. Associated with Department of Global Communications of the United Nations. **NGO Relations** Member of (16): *Advocacy Network for Africa (ADNA)*; *American Council for Voluntary International Action (InterAction)*; *British Overseas NGO's for Development (BOND)*; *ChildFund Alliance (#03868)*; *Child Rights Connect (#03884)*; *Child Rights International Network (CRIN, #03885)*; *CHS Alliance (#03911)*; *Consortium of Christian Relief and Development Association (CCRDA)*; *Council of Non-Governmental Organizations for Development Support (#04911)*; *Early Childhood Development Action Network (ECDAN, #05155)*; *Global Campaign for Education (GCE, #10264)*; *Global Partnership to End Violence Against Children (End Violence Against Children, #10533)*; *IMPACT (#11136)*; *InsideNGO (inactive)*; *NetHope (#16979)*; *NGO Committee on UNICEF (#17120)*. Stakeholder in: *Child and Youth Finance International (CYFI, inactive)*. Also links with a large number of national bodies active in the field. [2020/XF2501/f/**F**]

♦ Child Health Foundation (internationally oriented national body)

♦ **Child Helpline International (CHI)** **03870**
Exec Dir Bruggebouw Suite 5.08, Bos en Lommerplein 280, 1055 RW Amsterdam, Netherlands. E-mail: info@childhelplineinternational.org.
URL: http://www.childhelplineinternational.org/
History 2003, Netherlands. Founded by Jeroo Billimoria. **Aims** Help and support child protection systems globally, regionally and nationally; help members advocate for the rights of children. **Structure** Supervisory Board; Supervisory Committee; Regional Representatives. **Languages** Arabic, English, French, Spanish. **Staff** 4.50 FTE, paid; 6.00 FTE, voluntary. **Finance** Supported by: *European Union (EU, #08967)*; *Oak Foundation*; *UNICEF (#20332)*. **Activities** Events/meetings. **Events** *International Consultation* Stockholm (Sweden) 2022, *International Consultation* Stockholm (Sweden) 2021, *International Consultation* Stockholm (Sweden) 2020, *International Consultation* Toronto, ON (Canada) 2018, *European Regional Consultation* Brussels (Belgium) 2013. **Publications** Annual Report; reports; guides; manuals.
Members Helplines in 145 countries and territories.
Afghanistan, Albania, Algeria, Antigua-Barbuda, Argentina, Armenia, Aruba, Australia, Austria, Azerbaijan, Bahrain, Bangladesh, Belarus, Belgium, Benin, Bhutan, Bolivia, Bosnia-Herzegovina, Botswana, Brazil, Brunei Darussalam, Bulgaria, Burkina Faso, Burundi, Cambodia, Cameroon, Canada, Chile, China, Colombia, Congo DR, Costa Rica, Côte d'Ivoire, Croatia, Curaçao, Cyprus, Czechia, Denmark, Egypt, Estonia, Eswatini, Ethiopia, Fiji, Finland, France, Gambia, Georgia, Germany, Ghana, Greece, Guinea, Haiti, Hong Kong, Hungary, Iceland, India, Indonesia, Iran Islamic Rep, Iraq, Ireland, Israel, Italy, Japan, Jordan, Kazakhstan, Kenya, Kuwait, Kyrgyzstan, Laos, Latvia, Lebanon, Lesotho, Liberia, Libya, Liechtenstein, Lithuania, Luxembourg, Madagascar, Malawi, Malaysia, Maldives, Malta, Mauritania, Mauritius, Moldova, Mongolia, Montenegro, Mozambique, Myanmar, Namibia, Nepal, Netherlands, New Zealand, Nicaragua, Nigeria, North Macedonia, Norway, Pakistan, Palestine, Papua New Guinea, Paraguay, Peru, Philippines, Poland, Portugal, Qatar, Romania, Russia, Saudi Arabia, Senegal, Serbia, Sierra Leone, Singapore, Slovakia, Slovenia, South Africa, South Sudan, Spain, Sri Lanka, St Kitts-Nevis, St Maarten, Sudan, Suriname, Sweden, Switzerland, Syrian AR, Taiwan, Tajikistan, Tanzania UR, Thailand, Togo, Trinidad-Tobago, Türkiye, Uganda, UK, Ukraine, United Arab Emirates, Uruguay, USA, Uzbekistan, Vanuatu, Vietnam, Yemen, Zambia, Zimbabwe.
Consultative Status Consultative status granted from: *ECOSOC (#05331)* (Special); *African Committee of Experts on the Rights and Welfare of the Child (ACERWC, #00257)* (Observer Status); *Council of Europe (CE, #04881)* (Participatory Status). **IGO Relations** Participant in Fundamental Rights Platform of: *European Union Agency for Fundamental Rights (FRA, #08969)*. **NGO Relations** Member of (5): *Child Rights Connect (#03884)*; *Conference of Non-Governmental Organizations in Consultative Relationship with the United Nations (CONGO, #04635)* (as Associate Member of); *End Corporal Punishment (#05457)*; *Global Partnership to End Violence Against Children (End Violence Against Children, #10533)*; *Movimiento Mundial por la Infancia de Latinoamérica y El Caribe (MMI-LAC, #16873)*. [2022/XJ4441/**D**]

♦ **Childhood Cancer International (CCI)** **03871**
Main Office Kraijenhoffstraat 137-A, 1018 RG Amsterdam, Netherlands. E-mail: admin@cci.care.
URL: https://www.childhoodcancerinternational.org/
History 1994. Former names and other names: *International Confederation of Childhood Cancer Parent Organizations (ICCCPO)* – former (1994). Registration: RSIN, No/ID: 855025177, Netherlands; Chamber of Commerce, No/ID: 62945432, Netherlands. **Aims** Share information and experience in order to improve access to the best possible treatment and care for children with cancer everywhere in the world. **Structure** Board; Head Office in the Netherlands. Regions: Africa; Asia; Europe – represented by *Childhood Cancer International Europe (CCI Europe, #03872)*; Latin America; North America; Oceania. **Languages** English. **Staff** 0.25 FTE, paid. Voluntary. **Finance** Sources: members' dues; sponsorship. Annual budget: 90,000 EUR. **Activities** Advocacy/lobbying/activism; events/meetings; guidance/assistance/consulting; networking/liaising. **Events** *International Conference* Ottawa, ON (Canada) 2023, *Asia Conference* Mumbai (India) 2020, *International Conference* Ottawa, ON (Canada) 2020, *International Conference* Lyon (France) 2019, *European Meeting* Prague (Czechia) 2019. **Publications** *A Guide to Clinical Trials – For Young People with Cancer and Their Parents*; *Guidelines for Standards of Treatment and Care for Childhood Cancer* – developed jointly with SIOP; *The Survivorship Passport: An Innovative Solution for Long-term Follow-up*. Handbook.
Members Organizations (177): parent support groups and survivor networks in 90 countries:
Argentina, Armenia, Australia, Austria, Azerbaijan, Bangladesh, Bolivia, Bosnia-Herzegovina, Brazil, Bulgaria, Cameroon, Canada, Chile, China, Colombia, Costa Rica, Croatia, Czechia, Denmark, Dominican Rep, Ecuador, Egypt, Ethiopia, Finland, France, Georgia, Germany, Ghana, Greece, Guatemala, Honduras, Hungary, Iceland, India, Indonesia, Iran Islamic Rep, Iraq, Ireland, Israel, Italy, Japan, Kenya, Korea Rep, Lebanon, Lithuania, Luxembourg, Malawi, Malaysia, Mexico, Montenegro, Morocco, Namibia, Nepal, Netherlands, New Zealand, Nicaragua, Nigeria, North Macedonia, Norway, Pakistan, Palestine, Panama, Paraguay, Peru, Philippines, Portugal, Romania, Russia, Senegal, Serbia, Sierra Leone, Singapore, Slovenia, South Africa, Spain, Sweden, Switzerland, Syrian AR, Tanzania UR, Tonga, Trinidad-Tobago, Türkiye, Uganda, UK, Ukraine, USA, Venezuela, Vietnam, Zambia, Zimbabwe.
Consultative Status Consultative status granted from: *ECOSOC (#05331)* (Special); *WHO (#20950)* (Official Relations). **NGO Relations** Member of (3): *European Cancer Organisation (ECO, #06432)*; *The NCD Alliance (NCDA, #16963)*; *Union for International Cancer Control (UICC, #20415)* (Patient Advisory Committee). [2023/XJ1215/**B**]

♦ **Childhood Cancer International Europe (CCI Europe)** **03872**
Main Office Mooslackengasse 17, 1190 Vienna, Austria. E-mail: europe@cci.care.
URL: https://ccieurope.eu/
History 2015. Parents and Patients Advocacy Committee (PPAC) created within European Network for Cancer Research in Children and Adolescents (ENCCA), including parents and survivors' representatives of *Childhood Cancer International (CCI, #03871)* European members. Since early 2019, officially the European branch of CCI. Registration: EU Transparency Register, No/ID: 682126441400-50, Start date: 2 Mar 2021. **Aims** Cure children and adolescents with childhood cancer with no- or as few as possible long-term health problems and late-effects. **Structure** Committee. **Activities** Awareness raising; events/meetings; projects/programmes. **Events** *Conference* Valencia (Spain) 2023, *Special Europe Policy Seminar* 2022, *Conference* Vienna (Austria) 2022, *Conference* Vienna (Austria) 2021.
Members Full in 33 countries:
Austria, Belgium, Bosnia-Herzegovina, Bulgaria, Croatia, Denmark, Estonia, Finland, France, Georgia, Germany, Greece, Iceland, Ireland, Italy, Lithuania, Luxembourg, Montenegro, Netherlands, North Macedonia, Norway, Poland, Portugal, Romania, Russia, Serbia, Slovakia, Slovenia, Spain, Sweden, Switzerland, UK, Ukraine.
NGO Relations Member of (2): *EURORDIS – Rare Diseases Europe (#09175)*; *Workgroup of European Cancer Patient Advocacy Networks (WECAN, #21054)*. Cooperates with (2): *Pan-European Network for Care of Survivors after Childhood and Adolescent Cancer (PanCare, #18178)*; *SIOP Europe (SIOPE, #19288)*. [2021/AA1439/**E**]

♦ **Childhood and Early Parenting Principles (CEPPs)** **03873**
Contact 101 St Georges Square, London, SW1V 3QP, UK.
Facebook: https://www.facebook.com/CEPPrinciples/
History Registered in the UK: 10725959. **Aims** Support and accelerate implementation of the UN 2030 Agenda; seek CEPPs Statements of Support from civic leaders to commit resources and implement policies consistent; share evidenced-based knowledge and best practice in health and social care; build collaborative multi-sector networks at city, regional and country level, capable of delivering a continuum of care to mothers and young children. **NGO Relations** Member of: *Global Alliance for Maternal Mental Health (GAMMH, #10208)*; *PMNCH (#18410)*. [2019/XM7000/**F**]

♦ Childhood Education International (internationally oriented national body)
♦ Childhood Third World (internationally oriented national body)
♦ CHILDHOPE Europe / see ChildHope UK
♦ ChildHope UK (internationally oriented national body)
♦ ChildKind International (internationally oriented national body)
♦ Child Legacy International (internationally oriented national body)
♦ Childnet International (internationally oriented national body)
♦ **ChildONEurope** European Network of National Observatories on Childhood (#07951)

♦ **ChildPact** **03874**
SG Rotasului 7, 012167 Bucharest, Romania. T. +40744508227. E-mail: info@childpact.org.
URL: http://www.childpact.org/
History 2011, Bucharest (Romania), as an informal coalition. Memorandum of Understanding signed and organizational basis established, 2012. Officially registered as a formal coalition, Jan 2015. Full title: *ChildPact – Regional Coalition for Child Protection*. **Aims** Identify and encourage solutions that prevent and address *child vulnerability* in the wider Black Sea area. **Structure** Steering Committee. **Languages** English. Also languages of members. **Staff** 2.00 FTE, paid; 1.00 FTE, voluntary. **Finance** European and other private grants. **Activities** Advocacy/lobbying/activism; awareness raising; capacity building; knowledge management/information dissemination.
Members National networks focused on child rights in 10 countries:
Albania, Armenia, Azerbaijan, Bosnia-Herzegovina, Bulgaria, Georgia, Kosovo, Moldova, Romania, Serbia.
Consultative Status Consultative status granted from: *Council of Europe (CE, #04881)* (Participatory Status). **IGO Relations** *Parliamentary Assembly of the Organization of the Black Sea Economic Cooperation (PABSEC, #18213)*. **NGO Relations** Member of: *Global Partnership to End Violence Against Children (End Violence Against Children, #10533)*. [2017.06.01/XM5362/**D**]

♦ ChildPact – Regional Coalition for Child Protection / see ChildPact (#03874)
♦ Childreach / see Plan International (#18386)
♦ Childreach International (internationally oriented national body)
♦ Child Redress International (unconfirmed)
♦ Children Around the World (internationally oriented national body)
♦ Children and Broadcasting Foundation for Africa (internationally oriented national body)
♦ Children of the Caribbean Foundation (internationally oriented national body)
♦ Children in Crisis (internationally oriented national body)
♦ Children in Crossfire (unconfirmed)
♦ Children of the Earth (internationally oriented national body)
♦ Children and Families Across Borders (internationally oriented national body)
♦ Children and Families World Community Chest (inactive)
♦ Children of God / see The Family International (#09253)
♦ Children International (internationally oriented national body)
♦ Children Need Arts Foundation (unconfirmed)
♦ Children as the Peacemakers / see Peace to the Planet
♦ Children of Priests International (internationally oriented national body)

♦ **Children of Prisoners Europe (COPE)** **03875**
Dir 8-10 rue Auber, BP 38, 92120 Montrouge, France. E-mail: contact@networkcope.eu.
URL: http://childrenofprisoners.eu/
History 1993. Founded by 4 organizations in France, Belgium and UK. Structure formalized in 2000. Former names and other names: *European Action Research Committee on Children with Imprisoned Parents (EUROCHIPS)* – former (1993 to 2013); *Comité européen de recherche-action pour les enfants de parents emprisonnés* – former (1993 to 2013). **Aims** Safeguard the social, political and judicial inclusion of children with an imprisoned parent, while fostering the pursuit and exchange of knowledge which enhances good practices, and contributes to a better understanding of the psychological, emotional and social development of these children. **Structure** General Assembly (annual); Board of Directors. **Languages** English, French. **Staff** 4.00 FTE, paid. **Finance** Sources: donations; grants; members' dues; private foundations. Supported by: *European Commission (EC, #06633)* (DG Justice and Consumers – operating grant 2020); Porticus Foundation. Annual budget: 380,000 EUR (2022). **Activities** Advocacy/lobbying/activism; events/meetings; research/documentation. Active in: Belgium, Croatia, Czechia, Denmark, Finland, France, Germany, Hungary, Ireland, Italy, Luxembourg, Netherlands, Norway, Poland, Portugal, Romania, Sweden, Switzerland, UK, USA. **Events** *Annual Conference* Cascais (Portugal) 2022, *Annual Conference* Leiden (Netherlands) 2021, *Annual Network Meeting* Montrouge (France) 2021, *Mitigating Uncertainty for Children – From pre-trial procedures to the COVID-19 pandemic* Montrouge (France) 2021, *Annual Network Meeting* Paris (France) 2020. **Publications** *The European Journal of Parental Imprisonment* (annual). Toolkits; guidance documents; reports; stakeholder briefings; videos; books for children and young people. https://childrenofprisoners.eu/resources/network-publications/ **Information Services** *Facts & Figures* in English – Statistics relating to prison populations and children with parents imprisoned across Europe.
Members Full. Organizations (23) in 15 countries:
Belgium, Croatia, Czechia, France, Germany, Ireland, Italy, Luxembourg, Netherlands, Norway, Poland, Romania, Sweden, Switzerland, UK.
Individuals (26) in 11 countries:
Belgium, Croatia, France, Germany, Hungary, Ireland, Luxembourg, Netherlands, Norway, UK, USA.
Applicant organizations (13) in 12 countries:
Bulgaria, Croatia, Czechia, Denmark, Finland, Germany, Ireland, Malta, Norway, Portugal, Romania, UK.
Affiliate. Organizations (20) and individuals (37) in 28 countries:
Australia, Austria, Belgium, Brazil, Canada, Croatia, Cyprus, Czechia, Denmark, France, Germany, Greece, Ireland, Italy, Korea Rep, Latvia, Lithuania, Netherlands, New Zealand, Portugal, Slovenia, Spain, Sweden, Switzerland, Türkiye, UK, USA, Zimbabwe.
Consultative Status Consultative status granted from: *Council of Europe (CE, #04881)* (Participatory Status). **NGO Relations** Member of (4): *Alliance for Childhood European Network Group (AFC-ENG, #00666)*; Child Rights Action Group; *Child Rights Connect (#03884)*; *Eurochild (#05657)*. [2022.05.23/XJ6187/**F**]

♦ Children of Promise International (internationally oriented national body)
♦ Children's Brain Tumor Network (internationally oriented national body)
♦ Children's Brain Tumor Tissue Consortium / see Children's Brain Tumor Network
♦ Children's Care International (internationally oriented national body)

♦ **Children's Fashion Europe (CFE)** **03876**

Contact San Vicente 16-4-1, 46002 Valencia, Spain. T. +34963910334. Fax +34963155484. E-mail: cfe3@childrensfashioneurope.com.

URL: http://cfeurope.wordpress.com/

History Founded 2005. EU Transparency Register: 405215919593-77. **Aims** Enhance the image and prestige of European children's fashion; develop measures in defence of the EU market against unfair competition from abroad. **Structure** General Assembly; Board of Directors. **Languages** English. **Finance** Members' dues. **Members** Children's wear and childcare manufacturers, national associations, technological institutes and universities, from any country of the European Union may become a member. Members in 8 countries:
Belgium, Bulgaria, Finland, France, Germany, Italy, Portugal, Spain.

NGO Relations Member of: *SMEunited (#19327)*. Liaison Organization of: *Comité européen de normalisation (CEN, #04162)*. [2017.03.07/XJ4956/**D**]

♦ Children's Healthcare Australasia (internationally oriented national body)
♦ Children's Heart Fund / see Children's HeartLink
♦ Children's HeartLink (internationally oriented national body)
♦ Children's Helpers Worldwide (internationally oriented national body)
♦ Children's High Level Group / see Lumos Foundation
♦ Children's Hospitals Australasia / see Children's Healthcare Australasia

♦ **Children's Identity and Citizenship European Association (CiCea)** . . **03877**

Mailing Address c/o Behavioural / Social Sciences, Ramsden Building, Queensgate Campus, Huddersfield, HD1 3DH, UK. E-mail: ciceassociation@gmail.com.

URL: http://www.cicea.eu/

History by members of the Children's Identity and Citizenship in Europe Network (CiCe), a European Commission Erasmus Academic Network project set up in 1998. Inaugural meeting took place May 2006, Riga (Latvia). Registration: Charity Commission, No/ID: 1120176, Start date: 2007, England and Wales; Companies House, No/ID: 6290058, UK. **Aims** Promote, strengthen and develop *education* and training for those who will work professionally with children and young people providing citizenship education and education to promote social identity in a European and world context; develop networks of information, research and dissemination; provide a network resource for organizations and individuals in education and training for citizenship. **Structure** General Assembly (annual). Executive, including President, President-Elect, Past President, Secretary and Treasurer; the Executive also coordinates the CiCe Network. European Research Centres (8). **Finance** Members' dues. **Activities** Awards: research support and travel grants to members; Outstanding Publication Award (annual). Promotes and organizes conferences, training and events that develop research and good teaching practice in citizenship education. **Events** *Conference* York (UK) 2020, *Conference* Bruges (Belgium) 2017, *Conference* Madrid (Spain) 2016, *Conference* Olsztyn (Poland) 2014, *Conference* Lisbon (Portugal) 2013. **Publications** *Cicea Newsletter* (6 a year) – electronic; *Citizenship Teaching and Learning* (3 a year) – journal. **Members** Institutional; individual. Membership countries not specified. [2019/XJ1897/**D**]

♦ Children's International Summer Villages / see CISV International (#03949)
♦ Children's Investment Fund Foundation (internationally oriented national body)
♦ Children's Mitochondrial Disease Network / see European Mitochondrial Disease Network (#07809)
♦ The Children's Project International (internationally oriented national body)
♦ Children's Resources International (internationally oriented national body)
♦ Children's Rights Advocacy and Lobby Mission – Africa (internationally oriented national body)

♦ **Children's Rights European Academic Network (CREAN)** **03878**

Coordinator c/o Center for Children's Rights Studies, University of Geneva, Valais Campus, Chemin de l'Institut 18, 1967 Sion VS, Switzerland. T. +41272057306. E-mail: crean@unige.ch.

URL: http://www.crean-network.org/

History Sep 2004, Berlin (Germany). Founded by 5 European universities, with the support of *Rädda Barnen – Save the Children Sweden*. Through EU grant, set up 3-year project *Children's Rights Erasmus Academic Network*, 2012. Following termination of the project, Jul 2015, members of ENMCR and the Erasmus project merged into one single network. In order to ensure the network's sustainability and future development, the CREAN's coordination office has been transferred from the Free University of Berlin to the Centre for Children's Rights Studies at the University of Geneva, 2016. Former names and other names: *European Network of Masters in Children's Rights (ENMCR)* – former (Sep 2004 to 2016). **Aims** Support development of education, research and outreach activities; enhance the academic field of children's rights as an interdisciplinary field of studies; encourage research collaboration between members and exchange of information; support integration of children's rights and childhood studies research in academic teaching and social policy; act as facilitator for policy makers at national and international level. **Structure** General Assembly; Steering Committee; Coordination Office. **Languages** English. **Finance** Sources: government support. Supported by: State Secretariat for Education, Research and Innovation (SERI) (Swiss federal government). **Activities** Events/meetings; publishing activities; research/documentation; training/education. **Events** *Conference* Potsdam (Germany) 2021, *Conference* Potsdam (Germany) 2020, *Symposium* Liverpool (UK) 2019, *Conference* Geneva (Switzerland) 2018, *Symposium* Geneva (Switzerland) 2017. **Publications** *CRnews* (12 a year).

Members Universities. Full in 14 countries:
Belgium, Croatia, Germany, Greece, Italy, Lithuania, Netherlands, Norway, Portugal, Romania, Serbia, Spain, Switzerland, UK.
Associate in 4 countries:
Estonia, Germany, Poland, Serbia.

NGO Relations Member of (3): *Child Rights International Network (CRIN, #03885)*; *Eurochild (#05657)*; *International Childhood and Youth Research Network (ICYRnet, #12549)*. Cooperates with (2): *Red Latinoamericana de Maestrías en Derechos y Políticas Sociales de Infancia y Adolescencia (RMI, #18715)*; *Rädda Barnen – Save the Children Sweden*. [2020.10.27/XJ1080/**F**]

♦ **Children's Rights International (CRI)** **03879**

Chairman address not obtained. E-mail: webmaster@childjustice.org.

URL: http://www.childjustice.org/

History 22 Sep 2001, Bath (UK). Founded during 3rd *World Congress on Family Law and the Rights of Children and Youth (WCFLCR)*. Currently a division of the World Congress on Family Law and Children's Rights Inc. Foundation Committee of international experts oversees establishment of CRI as and independent international non-governmental human rights agency. Former names and other names: *International Children's Rights Protection Network (ICRPN)* – former (2001). **Aims** Promote, protect and advance across the world, the *human rights* of children and without limiting that aim, in particular to promote the meaningful implementation of the United Nations Convention on the Rights of the Child; promote, protect and advance the interests of children by bringing together eminent judges, lawyers, psychologists, medical practitioners, mediators, councillors, mental health workers, media representatives, child carers, teachers and allied professionals to contribute their specialized expertise in a practical manner through education, legal and other advocacy; monitor and encourage the application of the principles of the Convention by relevant laws, policies, treaties, judicial decision-making, legal practice, and by service-delivery, immigration and law enforcement agencies; train and assist relevant persons in children's rights advocacy and in the promotion, protection and advancement of those rights at a regional level; defend where possible pro bono the right of children in particular instances where they might otherwise go unrepresented or where the action may set standards that will protect other children's rights and promote legal reform. **Structure** Managed by Chief Executive Officer who reports to the Board of the World Congress and the Foundation Committee. Advisory Committee, including Founding Patron and 17 members. **Finance** Initial funding from World Congress Inc and Harbinger Foundation. **Events** *International conference on child labour and child exploitation* Cairns, QLD (Australia) 2008, *World Congress* San Francisco, CA (USA) 1997. **Publications** *CRI Journal*. [2017/XF6257/**F**]

♦ Children's Surgery International (internationally oriented national body)

♦ **Children's Tumor Foundation Europe (CTF Europe)** **03880**

Registered Address Av du Port 86C, Box 204, 1000 Brussels, Belgium. T. +32460205252. E-mail: info@ctf.org.

URL: https://www.ctfeurope.org/

History Registration: Banque-Carrefour des Entreprises, No/ID: 0711.985.938, Start date: 23 Oct 2018, Belgium; EU Transparency Register, No/ID: 364424439411-39, Start date: 3 Sep 2020. **Aims** Drive research, expand knowledge and advance care for the neurofibromatosis (NF) community. **Structure** Board of Directors. **Activities** Events/meetings; research/documentation. **NGO Relations** Member of (1): *EURORDIS – Rare Diseases Europe (#09175)* (Associate). [2022.10.18/AA2334/t/**F**]

♦ Children as Teachers of Peace / see Peace to the Planet
♦ Children Unite (internationally oriented national body)
♦ Children and War Foundation (internationally oriented national body)

♦ **Children Without Worms (CWW)** **03881**

Dir c/o Task Force for Global Health, 325 Swanton Way, Decatur GA 30030, USA. T. +14043710466. E-mail: cww@taskforce.org.

URL: http://www.childrenwithoutworms.org/

History 2006. Founded by Johnson and Johnson and *Task Force for Global Health (TFGH, #20098)*. **Aims** Globally control soil-transmitted helminthiasis (STH), commonly known as intestinal worm infection. **Activities** Advocacy/lobbying/activism; healthcare. **Publications** *CWW Newsletter*. **NGO Relations** Member of (1): *Neglected Tropical Diseased NGO Network (NNN, #16969)*. *International Podoconiosis Initiative (Footwork, #14607)*. [2020/XM5860/**E**]

♦ Children and Youth Development Foundation International (internationally oriented national body)
♦ Children and Youth Foundation / see Plan Børnefonden

♦ **Children and Youth International (CYI)** **03882**

Chair 1 Arlington Mews, Brighton, BN2 0AE, UK. T. +441273252929. E-mail: op@unmgcy.org.

URL: https://www.unmgcy.org/cyi

History Apr 2010. Founded as *Rio+twenties*, as the fundraising and legal arm of *UN Major Group of Children and Youth (MGCY)*. Registration: Crossroads Bank for Enterprises, No/ID: 831048686, Start date: 12 Nov 2010, End date: 12 Feb 2018, Belgium; Charity Commission, No/ID: 1163598, England and Wales. **Aims** Advance sustainable development of education. **Structure** Board. **Activities** Advocacy/lobbying/activism; capacity building. **Consultative Status** Consultative status granted from: *UNEP (#20299)*. [2023/XM8513/**E**]

♦ Child Rescue International (see: #16830)
♦ Child Rights Asianet Centre (internationally oriented national body)

♦ **Child Rights Coalition Asia (CRC Asia)** **03883**

Contact Unit 13 Block 5 Romarosa Townhomes, Luzon Avenue, Barangay Matandang Balara, 1119 Quezon City, Philippines. T. +63277792971. E-mail: secretariat@crcasia.org.

URL: http://www.crcasia.org/

History 25 Nov 2008, Pasig City (Philippines). Founded during a meeting convened by *Rädda Barnen – Save the Children Sweden*. Registration: Start date: Aug 2012, Philippines. **Aims** Be a strong voice for child rights by leading in strengthening child rights movements, promoting innovative programs, and advocating better policies for and with children in the region. **Activities** Advocacy/lobbying/activism; networking/liaising; politics/policy/regulatory.

Members Organizations (13) in 13 countries and territories:
Cambodia, Hong Kong, Indonesia, Korea Rep, Laos, Malaysia, Myanmar, Nepal, Pakistan, Philippines, Taiwan, Thailand, Vietnam.

IGO Relations Consultative status with: *ASEAN (#01141)* Intergovernmental Commission on Human Rights (AICHR). **NGO Relations** Member of: *Child Rights Connect (#03884)*; *Global Partnership to End Violence Against Children (End Violence Against Children, #10533)*. [2020.05.06/XJ7705/**F**]

♦ **Child Rights Connect** **03884**

Main Office Rue Varembé 1, 1202 Geneva, Switzerland. T. +41225524130. Fax +41227404683. E-mail: director@childrightsconnect.org – secretariat@childrightsconnect.org.

URL: http://www.childrightsconnect.org/

History 1983, to lobby for and advocate in favour of the drafting of the *United Nations Convention on the Rights of the Child (CRC, 1989)* and to ensure that a number of essential issues were included. Following the adoption of the Convention by the United Nations General Assembly, 20 Nov 1989, the Group has continued to be active in its implementation and a number of thematic Sub-Groups were formed to follow up specific issues. Original title: *NGO Group for the Convention on the Rights of the Child (NGO Group) – Groupe des ONG pour la Convention relative aux droits de l'enfant – Grupo de ONGs para la Convención sobre los Derechos del Niño*. Previously also known as *NGO Group for the CRC*. Present title adopted 2013. Present statutes adopted Mar 2016. **Aims** Empower children's rights defenders, including children, to influence and use the UN human rights system for change at national level; strengthen the UN human rights system to make it a better mechanism for change in children's rights practices. **Structure** General Assembly (annual); Executive Committee; Secretariat, headed by Director. **Languages** English, French, Russian, Spanish. **Staff** 5.00 FTE, paid. **Finance** Members' dues. Other sources: grants from member organizations, governments and foundations. **Activities** Advocacy/lobbying/activism; capacity building; guidance/assistance/consulting; networking/liaising. **Events** *World congress on commercial and other forms of sexual exploitation of children* Yokohama (Japan) 2001, *World conference on commercial and other forms of sexual exploitation of children* Stockholm (Sweden) 1996, *Meeting* Geneva (Switzerland) 1993. **Publications** Guides; case studies; fact sheets; session reports; advocacy materials; publications for children and youth.

Members International and regional organizations, including 53 organizations listed in this Yearbook:

- *African Child Policy Forum (ACPF, #00246)*;
- *Anti-Slavery International (#00860)*;
- *Arigatou International*;
- *Associated Country Women of the World (ACWW, #02338)*;
- *Baha'i International Community (#03062)*;
- *ChildFund Alliance (#03868)*;
- *ChildFund International (#03869)*;
- *Child Helpline International (CHI, #03870)*;
- *Childhood Education International (CE International)*;
- *Children of Prisoners Europe (COPE, #03875)*;
- *Child Rights Coalition Asia (CRC Asia, #03883)*;
- *Child Rights International Network (CRIN, #03885)*;
- *Defence for Children International (DCI, #05025)*;
- *Edmund Rice International (ERI, #05362)*;
- *End Child Prostitution, Child Pornography and Trafficking of Children for Sexual Purposes (ECPAT, #05456)*;
- *End Corporal Punishment (#05457)*;
- *Eurochild (#05657)*;
- *European Association for Children in Hospital (EACH, #05970)*;
- *Fédération internationale des communautés éducatives (FICE-International, #09622)*;
- *Fondazione Marista per la Solidarietà Internazionale Onlus (#09831)*;
- *Franciscans International (FI, #09982)*;
- *Friends World Committee for Consultation (FWCC, #10004)*;
- *Hope and Homes for Children*;
- *Human Rights Watch (HRW, #10990)*;
- *International Association of Youth and Family Judges and Magistrates (IAYFJM, #12283)*;
- *International Baby Food Action Network (IBFAN, #12305)*;
- *International Catholic Child Bureau (#12450)*;
- *International Child Rights Center (InCRC)*;
- *International Council of Women (ICW, #13093)*;
- *International Federation of Social Workers (IFSW, #13544)*;
- *International Foster Care Organization (IFCO, #13663)*;
- *International Inner Wheel (IIW, #13855)*;
- *International Juvenile Justice Observatory (IJJO)*;
- *International Movement ATD Fourth World (#14193)*;
- *International Play Association (IPA, #14604)*;
- *International Social Service (ISS, #14886)*;
- *Internet Watch Foundation (IWF)*;
- *Make Mothers Matter (#16554)*;
- *Plan International (#18386)*;
- *Proyecto Solidario*;

- *Red Latinoamericana de Acogimiento Familiar (RELAF, #18700);*
- *Red Latinoamericana y Caribeña por la Defensa de los Derechos de los Niños, Niñas y Adolescentes (REDLAMYC, #18705);*
- *Save the Children International (#19058);*
- *SOS-Kinderdorf International (#19693);*
- *Terre des Hommes International Federation (TDHIF, #20133);*
- *WAO-Afrique (#20816);*
- *Women's World Summit Foundation (WWSF, #21038);*
- *World Alliance of Young Men's Christian Associations (YMCA, #21090);*
- *World Association of Girl Guides and Girl Scouts (WAGGGS, #21142);*
- *World Organisation Against Torture (OMCT, #21685);*
- *World Vision International (WVI, #21904).*

Consultative Status Consultative status granted from: *ECOSOC (#05331)* (Special). **NGO Relations** Member of: *Fédération des Institutions Internationales établies à Genève (FIIG, #09599); International Coalition for the Optional Protocol to the Convention on the Rights of the Child on a Communications Procedure (Ratify OP3CRC, #12617).*Links indicated by: *UPR Info (#20727).* [2019/XE1429/y/**E**]

♦ Child Rights Information Network / see Child Rights International Network (#03885)

♦ Child Rights International Network (CRIN) 03885

Dir Unit 4, Old Paradise Yard, 20 Carlisle Lane, London, SE1 7LG, UK. E-mail: info@crin.org.
URL: http://www.crin.org/

History Jul 1995. Founded by a group of Child Rights' organizations, including *Rädda Barnen – Save the Children Sweden, Save the Children UK (SC UK), UNICEF (#20332)* and others. Until 2008, hosted by Save the Children UK, when it became independent. Former names and other names: *Child Rights Information Network (CRIN)* – former. Registration: Charities Commission, No/ID: 1125925, England and Wales. **Aims** Monitor patterns of children's rights violations globally; advocate for change; engage relevant professionals. **Structure** Council (Board of Trustees); Director. **Languages** Arabic, English, French, Russian, Spanish. **Staff** 15.00 FTE, paid. **Finance** Donations, including from *Rädda Barnen – Save the Children Sweden*, Norwegian Ministry of Foreign Affairs, *Oak Foundation* and *Swedish International Development Cooperation Agency (Sida).* **Activities** Knowledge management/information dissemination; monitoring/evaluation; advocacy/lobbying/activism; research/documentation. **Events** *Latin American Regional Conference* Buenos Aires (Argentina) 2019, *World Congress on Justice for Children* Paris (France) 2018. **Publications** *CRINmail* (weekly and 12 a year) in Arabic, English, French, Russian, Spanish. Research; policy papers; case studies. **Consultative Status** Consultative status granted from: *Council of Europe (CE, #04881)* (Participatory Status). **IGO Relations** *UNESCO (#20322).* Supports: *United Nations Convention on the Rights of the Child (CRC, 1989).* Participant in Fundamental Rights Platform of: *European Union Agency for Fundamental Rights (FRA, #08969).* **NGO Relations** Member of (4): *EDC Free Europe (#05355); Ethical Journalism Network (EJN, #05554); Global Partnership to End Violence Against Children (End Violence Against Children, #10533); International Coalition for the Optional Protocol to the Convention on the Rights of the Child on a Communications Procedure (Ratify OP3CRC, #12617).* Instrumental in setting up (1): *Global March Against Child Labour (#10463).* Stakeholder in: *Child and Youth Finance International (CYFI, inactive).* Portal for other networks, including: *European Network of Ombudspersons for Children (ENOC, #07959).* [2021/XF4594/**F**]

♦ ChildRights International Research Institute (internationally oriented national body)
♦ Child Rights Network for Southern Africa (unconfirmed)
♦ ChildSafe International (internationally oriented national body)
♦ Child Savings International / see Aflatoun International (#00152)
♦ Child Survival Collaborations and Resources / see CORE Group
♦ Child Survival Partnership / see PMNCH (#18410)

♦ Child Vision Research Society (CVRS) 03886

Events Organizer School of Biomedical Sciences, Ulster Univ, Room G159, Cromore Road, Coleraine, BT5 1SA, UK.
URL: http://www.cvrsoc.org/

History 1987, Oxford (UK). **Structure** Informal structure. **Activities** Biennial meeting. **Events** *Biennial Meeting* Coleraine (UK) 2017, *Biennial Meeting* Prague (Czech Rep) 2015, *Biennial Meeting* Toronto, ON (Canada) 2013, *Biennial Meeting* Huizen (Netherlands) 2011, *Biennial Meeting* Cardiff (UK) 2009. [2017/XJ6669/c/**F**]

♦ Childwatch International Research Network 03887

Secretariat CINDE, Calle 93 No 45A-31, Bogota, Bogota DC, Colombia.
URL: http://www.childwatch.uio.no/

History Jan 1993. **Aims** Promote *capacity building* in inter-disciplinary *child* research in all parts of the world and the use of research based knowledge in policy making and practice for *children.* **Structure** Key Institutions Assembly; Board. Secretariat located at Center for Education and Human Development (CINDE), Bogota (Colombia). **Languages** English. **Staff** 1.00 FTE, paid. **Finance** Part-funding from Norwegian Foreign Ministry. **Activities** Research/documentation; events/meetings; projects/programmes. **Events** *Meeting* Bangkok (Thailand) 2002, *Meeting of child researchers in East/Central Europe* Bratislava (Slovakia) 2002.
Members Institutions (41) in 28 countries and territories:
Australia, Brazil, Canada, Chile, China, Colombia, Costa Rica, Czechia, Hong Kong, India, Ireland, Israel, Italy, Jamaica, Jordan, Mexico, New Zealand, Norway, Palestine, Russia, Slovakia, Spain, Sri Lanka, Thailand, UK, Uruguay, USA, Venezuela.
Included in the above, 5 organizations listed in this Yearbook:
Council for the Development of Social Science Research in Africa (CODESRIA, #04879); Inter-American Children's Institute (IACI, #11406); International Center for Education and Human Development (CINDE); UNICEF (#20332) (Office of Research).
IGO Relations *European Network of National Observatories on Childhood (ChildONEurope, #07951).* **NGO Relations** Member of: *Child Rights International Network (CRIN, #03885).* [2015.06.01/XF0418/y/**F**]

♦ **CHIME Foundation** European Foundation for Chinese Music Research (#07345)
♦ China Association for International Friendly Contact (internationally oriented national body)
♦ China Association for International Science and Technology Cooperation (internationally oriented national body)
♦ China Council for International Cooperation on Environment and Development (internationally oriented national body)
♦ China Council for the Promotion of International Trade (internationally oriented national body)
♦ China Education Association for International Exchange (internationally oriented national body)
♦ China-EU Association (internationally oriented national body)

♦ China-Europe International Business School (CEIBS) 03888

Shanghai Campus 699 Hongfeng Road, Pudong, 201206 Shanghai, China. T. +862128905890. E-mail: info@ceibs.edu.
Zurich Campus Hirsackerstrasse 46, PO Box, 8810 Zurich ZH, Switzerland. T. +41447289944.
Main Website: https://www.ceibs.edu/

History 8 Nov 1994. Set up by agreement between MOFTEC and European Commission. Signing parties: Shanghai Jiao Tong University (China) and *EFMD – The Management Development Network (#05387).* **Aims** Contribute to the economic development of China and its business communities. **Structure** International Advisory Board; Board of Directors; Management Committee. **Finance** Support from *European Commission (EC, #06633)* and the Chinese Ministry of Foreign Trade and Economic Cooperation. **Activities** Training/education. **Events** *China Conference* Beijing (China) 2012, *China Conference* Brussels (Belgium) 2011, *Joint conference* Shanghai (China) 2008. **NGO Relations** Member of: *Asia-Pacific Research and Training Network on Trade (ARTNeT, #02014); Globally Responsible Leadership Initiative (GRLI, #10462); Graduate Management Admission Council (GMAC, #10687); Principles for Responsible Management Education (PRME, #18500).* [2021/XK0653/**E**]

♦ China Europe Water Platform (CEWP) 03889

Europe address not obtained. E-mail: hedis@nst.dk.
China address not obtained.
URL: http://cewp.org/

History Launched Mar 2012, Marseille (France), at 6th World Water Forum. Set up as a regional component of *European Union Water Initiative (EUWI, inactive).* **Aims** Promote policy dialogue, joint research and business development in the water sector. **Structure** Secretariats (2). **Finance** Financed by Chinese Ministry of Water Resources and Danish Ministry of the Environment on behalf of *European Union (EU, #08967)* and its Member States. **Events** *Annual High Level Conference* Turku (Finland) 2017, *Annual High Level Conference* Copenhagen (Denmark) 2015, *Annual Meeting* Beijing (China) 2014. [2015/XM4249/**F**]

♦ China Folklore Photographic Association (internationally oriented national body)
♦ China Inland Mission / see OMF International (#17722)
♦ China Inland Mission Overseas Missionary Fellowship / see OMF International (#17722)
♦ China Institute of Contemporary International Relations (internationally oriented national body)
♦ China Institute for International Strategic Studies (internationally oriented national body)
♦ China Institute of International Studies (internationally oriented national body)
♦ China International Centre for Economic and Technical Exchanges (internationally oriented national body)
♦ China International Council for the Promotion of Multinational Corporations (internationally oriented national body)
♦ China International Economic and Trade Arbitration Commission (internationally oriented national body)
♦ China International Institute of Multinational Corporations / see China International Council for the Promotion of Multinational Corporations
♦ China International Public Relations Association (internationally oriented national body)
♦ China-Mekong Law Center (internationally oriented national body)
♦ China Ministries International (internationally oriented national body)
♦ China Native Evangelistic Crusade / see Partners International
♦ China NGO Network for International Exchanges (internationally oriented national body)

♦ China-Nordic Research Center (CNARC) 03890

Contact Polar Research Inst of China, No 451 Jinqiao Road, Pundong, 2000136 Shanghai, China.
URL: http://www.cnarc.info/

History Founded 10 Dec 2013, Shanghai (China). **Aims** Provide a platform for academic cooperation to increase awareness, understanding and knowledge of the Arctic and its global impacts, as well as to promote cooperation for sustainable development of the Nordic Arctic and coherent development of China in a global context. **Structure** Assembly; Executive Committee; Secretariat. **Activities** Events/meetings; research and development; knowledge management/information dissemination. **Events** *Arctic fisheries, polar Silk Road, and sustainable development practices* Shanghai (China) 2019, *Symposium* Tromsø (Norway) 2018. **Publications** *CNARC Newsletter.*
Members Institutes in 6 countries:
China, Denmark, Finland, Iceland, Norway, Sweden.
Included in the above, 3 organizations listed in this Yearbook:
Arctic Centre, Rovaniemi; Fridtjof Nansen Institute (FNI); NIAS-Nordisk Institut for Asienstudier (NIAS, #17132). [2019/XM8049/y/**D**]

♦ China's Children Fund / see ChildFund International (#03869)
♦ Chinese Association for International Understanding (internationally oriented national body)
♦ Chinese Association for Middle East Studies (internationally oriented national body)
♦ Chinese Education Association for International Exchanges / see China Education Association for International Exchange
♦ Chinese Initiative on International Criminal Justice / see Chinese Initiative on International Law
♦ Chinese Initiative on International Law (internationally oriented national body)
♦ Chinese Medicine and Acupuncture Association of South America (no recent information)
♦ Chinese and Oriental Languages Computer Society (no recent information)

♦ Chinese and Oriental Languages Information Processing Society (COLIPS) 03891

Pres Dept of Mechanical Engineering, National Univ of Singapore, 4 Engineering Drive 3, Singapore 117583, Singapore.
URL: http://www.colips.org/

History 1988. Founded following International Conference on Chinese Computing, 1986, Singapore. Registration: Singapore. **Aims** Promote research on information processing for Chinese and other Asian languages. **Structure** Council. **Languages** Chinese, English. **Staff** Voluntary. **Finance** Members' dues. Other sources: donations; conferences fees. **Activities** Events/meetings; training/education. **Events** *International Conference on Asian Language Processing (IALP)* Shenzhen (China) / Singapore (Singapore) 2022, *International Symposium on Chinese Spoken Language Processing (ISCSLP)* Singapore (Singapore) 2022, *International Conference on Asian Language Processing (IALP)* Singapore (Singapore) 2021, *International Conference on Asian Language Processing* Kuala Lumpur (Malaysia) 2020, *International Conference on Asian Language Processing* Shanghai (China) 2019. **Publications** *International Journal of Asian Language Processing (IJALP).*
Members Full in 10 countries and territories:
China, Hong Kong, India, Indonesia, Japan, Malaysia, Philippines, Singapore, Taiwan, Vietnam.
NGO Relations Founding member of: *Asian Federation of Natural Language Processing (AFNLP, #01467).* [2016.10.27/XJ6811/**D**]

♦ Chinese People's Association for Peace and Disarmament (internationally oriented national body)
♦ Chinese Society for Future Studies (internationally oriented national body)
♦ **ChIN** International Chemical Information Network (#12542)
♦ **CHIR** Commission of History of International Relations (#04217)
♦ Chiropractic Health Bureau / see International Chiropractors Association
♦ CHISA – International Congress of Chemical and Process Engineering (internationally oriented national body)
♦ CHITEL – Congrès des Chimistes Théoriciens d'Expression Latine (meeting series)
♦ CHIYODEVFI – Children and Youth Development Foundation International (internationally oriented national body)
♦ Chlamy – International Conference on the Cell and Molecular Biology of Chlamydomonas (meeting series)
♦ CHL – Centre for Humanitarian Leadership (internationally oriented national body)
♦ CHL – Children's HeartLink (internationally oriented national body)
♦ CHLG / see Lumos Foundation
♦ Chlorine Institute (internationally oriented national body)
♦ CHMAC – Commission hydrographique de la Mésoamérique et de la mer des Caraïbes (see: #13825)
♦ CHMB – Commission hydrographique de la Mer Baltique (see: #13825)
♦ CHMMN – Commission hydrographique de la Méditerranée et de la mer Noire (see: #13825)
♦ CHMN – Commission hydrographique de la Mer du Nord (see: #13825)
♦ CHN – Commission hydrographique nordique (see: #13825)
♦ CHNT – International Conference on Cultural Heritage and New Technologies (meeting series)
♦ the Chocolate Way (unconfirmed)
♦ Choeur mondial des jeunes (#21955)
♦ Choeurs des Communautés européennes / see European Union Choir (#08980)
♦ Choeurs de l'Union européenne (#08980)
♦ **CHOGM** Commonwealth Heads of Government Meeting (#04337)
♦ CHOICE Humanitarian – Center for Humanitarian Outreach and Intercultural Exchange (internationally oriented national body)

♦ Choices International Foundation 03892

Contact Molenweg 18, 7084 AV Breedenbroek, Netherlands. E-mail: info@choicesprogramme.org.
URL: http://www.choicesprogramme.org/

History 2007. **Aims** Support national initiatives for healthier *food* choices by means of actions and policies based on a product group specific multi-level criteria set distinguishing healthier and less-healthy products. **Structure** International Board; International Scientific Committee; National Implementing Platforms. **Languages** English. **Staff** 2.00 FTE, paid. **Activities** Guidance/assistance/consulting; knowledge management/information dissemination; monitoring/evaluation; research and development. **Events** *European nutrition and lifestyle conference* Brussels (Belgium) 2011. **Publications** *Choices*. Scientific papers; articles.
Members Full in 2 countries:
Czechia, Nigeria. [2023.02.15/XJ5360/f/**F**]

- ♦ CHOICE for Youth and Sexuality (unconfirmed)

♦ Choike 03893

Main Office c/o ITEM, Avda 18 de julio 2095/301, 11200 Montevideo, Uruguay. T. +59824031424. E-mail: item@item.org.uy.
URL: http://www.choike.org/

History 1990, as *NGONET* to support NGOs in advance of the 1992 *United Nations Conference on Environment and Development (UNCED)* and beyond. Full implementation since Jun 1991. Project hosted by *Instituto del Tercer Mundo, Montevideo (ITEM)*. **Aims** Improve visibility of work done by *NGOs* and social movements from the South; serve as a platform for citizen groups to disseminate their work while enriching it with information presented from the Southern *civil society* perspective and from various sources. **Structure** Coordinator/Editor-in-Chief; Editors (6); 2 people working in Design and Programming. **Activities** Disseminates NGO actions and campaigns. Search engine for information in the directory's web sites, designed to search the sites selected by Choike on the basis of their quality and relevance. **Publications** *Choike Newsletter* (24 a year) in English, Spanish. [2012/XF1706/**F**]

- ♦ CHOIS – Commission hydrographique de l'Océan Indien Septentrional (see: #13825)
- ♦ Chol-Chol Foundation for Human Development (internationally oriented national body)
- ♦ **CHOLDInet** Global Laboratory Network for Cholera and Other Diarrhoeal Infections (#10444)
- ♦ Chomhairle Eorpach (#06801)
- ♦ An Chomhairle do Mhic Léinn Eachtracha in Eirinn / see Irish Council for International Students
- ♦ An Chomhairle do Mhic Léinn in Eirinn (internationally oriented national body)
- ♦ Chòmhdhail Cheilteach (#03632)
- ♦ CHoPS – International Conference for Conveying and Handling of Particulate Solids (meeting series)
- ♦ CHOPS Syndrome Global (internationally oriented national body)

♦ Choral Festival Network (CFN) 03894

SG Rijsenbergstraat 150, 9000 Ghent, Belgium. E-mail: artisticdirector@choralfestival.org.
Pres Eesti Kooriühing, Roosikrantsi 13, 10119 Tallinn, Estonia. T. +3725144301.
URL: http://www.choralfestivalnetwork.org/

History 2005. **Aims** Be a platform for international choir festivals and competitions. **Structure** Board; Official Seat located in Ghent (Belgium). **Languages** English. **Staff** Voluntary. **Finance** Sources: members' dues. **Members** Membership countries not specified. **NGO Relations** Close cooperation with: *European Choral Association – Europa Cantat (#06541)*. Member of: American Choral Directors' Association (ACDA); *International Federation for Choral Music (IFCM, #13388)*. [2021.09.01/XJ0731/**F**]

- ♦ Chor der Europäischen Gemeinschaften / see European Union Choir (#08980)
- ♦ Chor der Europäischen Union / see European Union Choir (#08980)
- ♦ Chosen People Ministries (internationally oriented national body)
- ♦ CHPA / see Commonwealth Health Professions and Partners Alliance (#04338)
- ♦ **CHPA** Commonwealth Health Professions and Partners Alliance (#04338)
- ♦ CHPSO – Commission hydrographique du pacifique sud-ouest (see: #13825)
- ♦ **CHRA** Commission hydrographique régionale de l'Arctique (#01101)
- ♦ **CHRC** Caribbean Harm Reduction Coalition (#03513)
- ♦ CHRC – Caribbean Health Research Council (inactive)
- ♦ **CHR** Commission internationale de l'hydrologie du bassin du Rhin (#12693)
- ♦ CHRDA – Centre for Human Rights and Democracy in Africa (unconfirmed)
- ♦ Chrétiens pour le Sahel / see Fondation Chrëschte mam Sahel
- ♦ CHRF / see Equitas – International Centre for Human Rights Education
- ♦ **CHRI** Commonwealth Human Rights Initiative (#04340)
- ♦ CHRIE – International Council on Hotel, Restaurant and Institutional Education (internationally oriented national body)

♦ Christ for All Nations (CFAN) 03895

Missionswerk Christus für alle Nationen

Headquarters Postfach 60 05 74, 60335 Frankfurt-Main, Germany. T. +4969478780. Fax +49694787820. E-mail: cfan@bonnke.net.
URL: http://www.cfan.org/

Structure Regional offices (8): Asia/Pacific – Singapore (Singapore); Canada – London (UK); East Africa – Nairobi (Kenya); South Africa – West Beach; South America – Belo Horizonte (Brazil); UK – Halesowen; USA – Orlando FL; West Africa – Lagos (Nigeria). **Events** *Fire conference* Singapore (Singapore) 2006. **Publications** *Impact* – newsletter. **NGO Relations** Support from: *Stamps for Evangelism*. [2009/XN9496/**F**]

- ♦ Christelijke Organisatie voor Internationale Vluchtelingenhulp / see ZOA
- ♦ Christelijke Raad voor Informatie en Analyse van Beeldverhalen / see International Christian Centre for Research on Information about and Analysis of the Strip Cartoon (#12557)
- ♦ Christenen voor Israel / see Christians for Israel International (#03908)
- ♦ Christensen Fund (internationally oriented national body)
- ♦ Christ Espérance – Missionnaires des Malades (religious order)
- ♦ Christian / see AsiaLink
- ♦ Christian Action (internationally oriented national body)
- ♦ Christian Aid (internationally oriented national body)
- ♦ Christian Aid Mission (internationally oriented national body)
- ♦ Christian AIDS Bureau for Southern Africa (internationally oriented national body)
- ♦ Christian Aid USA / see Christian Aid Mission
- ♦ Christian Artists Europe (internationally oriented national body)

♦ Christian Artists International Association 03896

Association internationale des artistes chrétiens

Chairman PO Box 81065, 3009 GB Rotterdam, Netherlands. T. +31104568688. Fax +31104559022. E-mail: info@continentalart.org.
Street Address Continental Arts Centre, Robert Kochplaats 342, 3068 JD Rotterdam, Netherlands.
URL: http://www.christianartists-network.org/

History 1990. Also referred to as *Association of Christian Artists* and *Christian Artists Network*. Registered in accordance with Dutch law. **Aims** Function as umbrella organization for *trade unions* in the arts and artists's associations based on Christian values; promote *lifelong learning*; discuss current *European culture*; develop policy measures. **Structure** Governing Board (4-year term), comprising representatives of all sectors of art and areas of Europe. **Languages** English. **Staff** 16.00 FTE, paid. **Finance** Members' dues. **Activities** Organizes annual *Christian Artists Seminar*, always in Doorn (Netherlands). **Events** *International Christian artists seminar* Doorn (Netherlands) 2010, *International Christian artists seminar* Doorn (Netherlands) 2009, *International Christian artists seminar* Doorn (Netherlands) 2008, *International Christian artists seminar* Doorn (Netherlands) 2007, *International Christian artists seminar* Doorn (Netherlands) 2006. **Publications** *Christian Artists Directory*, *Expression* in Dutch – yearbook; *Signs* in Dutch – magazine. Results of annual seminar debates. **Members** European associations (102). Membership countries not specified. [2012/XD8622/**D**]

- ♦ Christian Artists Network / see Christian Artists International Association (#03896)
- ♦ Christian Associates Europe / see Communitas International (#04388)
- ♦ Christian Associates International / see Communitas International (#04388)
- ♦ Christian Blind Mission (internationally oriented national body)
- ♦ Christian Blind Mission International / see Christian Blind Mission
- ♦ Christian Brothers (religious order)
- ♦ Christian Brothers – Brothers of the Christian Schools (religious order)
- ♦ Christian Business Men's Association International (#13316)
- ♦ Christian Business Men's Committee International / see CBMC International

♦ Christian Camping International (CCI) 03897

Contact Journeys End, Avenue Road, Cranleigh, GU6 7LL, UK. E-mail: info@cciworldwide.org.
USA Office PO Box 62189, Colorado Springs CO 80962, USA.
URL: http://www.cciworldwide.org/

History 1959. Founded following a meeting of 13 Christ-centered camp/conference directors, Nov 1950, California (USA). Former names and other names: *CCI Worldwide (CCI WW)* – alias. **Aims** Support an alliance of internally strong, sustainable and growth-focused associations of Christian camps, conference centres, outdoor activity providers and their leaders. **Structure** An alliance of Christian camping associations. **Languages** English. **Staff** 1.50 FTE, paid. **Finance** Sources: donations. **Activities** Events/meetings; religious activities; training/education. Active in: Albania, Angola, Argentina, Armenia, Australia, Bangladesh, Belarus, Bhutan, Bolivia, Botswana, Brazil, Burundi, Canada, Colombia, Congo DR, Costa Rica, Cuba, Dominican Rep, El Salvador, Estonia, France, Georgia, Ghana, Guatemala, Honduras, Iceland, Ireland, Jamaica, Japan, Kazakhstan, Kenya, Korea Rep, Kyrgyzstan, Latvia, Lesotho, Lithuania, Malaysia, Mexico, Moldova, Mozambique, Myanmar, Namibia, Nepal, Netherlands, New Zealand, Pakistan, Panama, Paraguay, Peru, Philippines, Poland, Portugal, Romania, Russia, Rwanda, Sierra Leone, South Africa, Spain, Sudan, Tanzania UR, Uganda, UK, Ukraine, USA, Uzbekistan, Venezuela, Zambia, Zimbabwe. **Publications** *#together*. **Information Services** *CCI Resource Bank*.
Members National Associations in 22 countries:
Albania, Australia, Brazil, Canada, France, India, Jamaica, Japan, Korea Rep, México, Nepal, Netherlands, New Zealand, Pakistan, Philippines, Poland, Romania, Russia, Spain, UK, Ukraine, USA.
Regional associations (3):
ACC East Africa; CCI Latin America; CCSA Southern Africa. [2022.05.04/XF6905/**F**]

- ♦ Christian Children's Fund / see ChildFund International (#03869)
- ♦ Christian Church (internationally oriented national body)
- ♦ Christian Committee for Human Rights in Latin America (internationally oriented national body)
- ♦ Christian Communications International (internationally oriented national body)

♦ Christian Conference of Asia (CCA) 03898

Conférence chrétienne d'Asie

Gen Sec PO Box 183, Chiang Mai, 50000, Thailand. E-mail: cca@cca.org.hk – ccagensec@gmail.com.
URL: http://www.cca.org.hk/

History 14 May 1959, Malaya Fed. Founded as *East Asia Christian Conference (EACC)*. Constitutional changes: 1964; 1971; 1973 (when present name was adopted); amended: 1981, 1985. Reorganized 1988. Constitution last amended by CCA Extraordinary Assembly, Jun 8-9 1995, Colombo (Sri Lanka). **Aims** Act as a a forum of continuing cooperation among Churches and national Christian bodies in Asia within the framework of the wider ecumenical movement; promote the equal participation of women, men, youth, clergy and laity in church and society. **Structure** General Assembly (every 5 years). General Committee, consisting of: Officers (4 Presidents, Honorary Treasurer and General Secretary); one member from each country represented; up to 5 additional members. Executive Committee, comprising the Officers and 3-5 members. Program Committees (9). **Languages** English. **Staff** 17.00 FTE, paid. **Finance** Contributions from member Councils and Churches in Asia. Donations from Churches and church-related agencies outside Asia. **Activities** Program Units (9), each with its Program Committee: Communications; Development and Service; Education; International Affairs; Mission and Evangelism; Theological Concerns; Urban Rural Mission (URM); Women's Concerns; Youth. Special programs, each with its Working Group: Indo-China Concerns; Migrant Workers, Refugees and Internally Displaced Communities in Asia (MRIA); Joint Program with *Federation of Asian Bishops' Conferences (FABC, #09430)*; Joint Program with *United Nations Economic and Social Commission for Asia and the Pacific (ESCAP, #20557)*; Joint program with *World Student Christian Federation (WSCF, #21833)*. Each of these special programs has its own Working Group. Convenes pan-Asian and sub-regional conferences and seminars. Sponsors: Development Assistance and Rural Youth Development Funds, supporting action programs at national and local levels; Human Rights Fund; Asian Missionary Support Program (AMSP); Asian Ecumenical Course; Asian Ecumenical Educational Exchange (scholarships). *Ecumenical Peace Program in Asia (EPPIA, inactive)* is a project. Together with Office of Human Development of FABC, instrumental in setting up *Asian Committee for People's Organization (ACPO, inactive)*. This was dissolved in Jan 1993, and the work of training trainers and community organizers is currently undertaken by the Urban Rural Mission, CCA-URM. As EACC, instrumental in setting up *Asian Rural Institute – Rural Leaders Training Center (ARI, #01688)*. **Events** *General Assembly* Kovalam (India) 2023, *General Assembly* Kovalam (India) 2020, *Young Ambassadors of Peace in Asia Meeting* Chiang Mai (Thailand) 2017, *General Assembly* Jakarta (Indonesia) 2015, *General Assembly* Kuala Lumpur (Malaysia) 2010. **Publications** *CCA News* (12 a year); *CCA Directory* (annual); *CCA Publications List* (annual). *New CCA Hymnal*. *CCA Brochure*.
Members National Christian Councils and Churches in 18 countries and territories:
Australia, Bangladesh, Cambodia, Hong Kong, India, Indonesia, Japan, Korea Rep, Laos, Malaysia, Myanmar, New Zealand, Pakistan, Philippines, Sri Lanka, Taiwan, Thailand, Timor-Leste.
Consultative Status Consultative status granted from: *ECOSOC (#05331)* (Special).
NGO Relations Ecumenical: *World Council of Churches (WCC, #21320)*. Regional Councils: *All Africa Conference of Churches (AACC, #00640)*; *Caribbean Conference of Churches (CCC, #03479)*; *Conference of European Churches (CEC, #04593)*; *Latin American Council of Churches (LACC, #16309)*; *Pacific Conference of Churches (PCC, #17943)*. Represented in: *Fellowship of the Least Coin (FLC, #09728)*. Far East and Near East regions of *Salvation Army (#19041)* and *Anglican Church in Aotearoa, New Zealand and Polynesia (#00823)* are members. Member of: *Conference of Non-Governmental Organizations in Consultative Relationship with the United Nations (CONGO, #04635)*; *Ecumenical Advocacy Alliance (EAA, inactive)*. Instrumental in setting up: *Documentation for Action Groups in Asia (DAGA)*. Other relations:
- *Anglican Consultative Council (ACC, #00828)*;
- *Asia and Pacific Alliance of YMCAs (APAY, #01826)*;
- *Asia Pacific Baptist Federation (APBF, #01857)*;
- *Asian Christian Art Association (ACAA)*;
- *Asian Conference of Religions for Peace (ACRP, #01400)*;
- *Asian Cultural Forum on Development Foundation (ACFOD, no recent information)*;
- *Asian Health Institute (AHI, #01502)*;
- *Asian-Pacific Christian Peace Conference (APCPC, no recent information)*;
- *Association of Christian Institutes for Social Concern in Asia (ACISCA, #02428)*;
- *Association for Theological Education in South East Asia (ATESEA, #02952)*;
- *Australian and New Zealand Association of Theological Schools (ANZATS, no recent information)*;
- *Baptist World Alliance (BWA, #03176)*;
- *Church World Service (CWS)*;
- *Committee for Asian Women (CAW, #04243)*;
- *Congress of Asian Theologians (CATS, #04676)*;
- *Council for World Mission (CWM, #04925)*;
- *Disciples Ecumenical Consultative Council (DECC, #05100)*;
- *The Lutheran World Federation (LWF, #16532)*;
- *Oikocredit International (Oikocredit, #17704)*;
- *Programme for Theology and Cultures in Asia (PTCA, inactive)*;
- *United Mission to Nepal (UMN)*;
- *World Methodist Council (WMC, #21650)*;
- *World Young Women's Christian Association (World YWCA, #21947)*. [2022/XD0475/**D**]

- ♦ Christian Connections for International Health (internationally oriented national body)
- ♦ Christian Democrat Feminine International (inactive)
- ♦ Christian Democrat Formation Institute (internationally oriented national body)
- ♦ Christian Democrat Group /in the Parliamentary Assembly of the Council of Europe/ / see Group of the European People's Party (#10774)

♦ Christian-Democratic Group / see Group of the European People's Party – Christian Democrats (#10775)
♦ Christian Democratic International / see Centrist Democrat International (#03792)
♦ Christian Democratic International Center (internationally oriented national body)

♦ Christian Democratic Organization of America 03899

Organisation démocrate chrétienne d'Amérique – Organización Demócrata Cristiana de América (ODCA)

Exec Sec Av Paseo de la Reforma 136, Piso 5 oficina A, Col Juarez Del Cuauhtémoc, CP 06600, 06600 Mexico City CDMX, Mexico. T. +525555465234.
Pres address not obtained. E-mail: jocejo43@hotmail.com.
URL: http://www.odca.org.mx/

History 23 Apr 1947, Montevideo (Uruguay). Statutes adopted by 7th Congress, 16-20 Dec 1969 and modified by: 10th Congress, 2-5 Dec 1981, Caracas (Venezuela); 2nd Extraordinary Council, 25 Jul 1983, Caracas. Current Statutes adopted at 13th Congress, 28-30 Nov 1991, Caracas. **Aims** Serve as a link between Christian democratic parties in *Latin America*. **Structure** Congress (every 3 years); Council; Continental areas (4); General Secretariat. **Languages** Spanish. **Finance** Financed mainly by: *Konrad Adenauer Foundation (KAF)*. Budget (annual): about US$ 450,000. **Activities** Knowledge management/information dissemination; research/documentation; networking/liaising. **Events** *Triennial Congress* Mexico City (Mexico) 2013, *Triennial Congress* San Salvador (El Salvador) 2010, *Triennial Congress* Santiago (Chile) 2006, *Triennial Congress* Caracas (Venezuela) 2003, *Triennial Congress* Santiago (Chile) 2000. **Publications** *ODCA Informa* (4 a year) in English, Spanish. Congress reports. Diary press report.
Members Affiliated parties (32) in 28 countries and territories:
Argentina (2), Aruba, Bolivia, Bonaire Is, Chile, Colombia, Costa Rica, Cuba (2), Curaçao, Dominica, Dominican Rep, Ecuador, El Salvador, Guatemala, Guyana, Haiti, Honduras (2), Mexico, Nicaragua, Panama, Paraguay, Peru (2), Saba, St Kitts-Nevis, Suriname, Trinidad-Tobago, Uruguay, Venezuela.
Functional organizations (3):
Christian Democratic Women of America (CDWA, #03900); Frente de Trabajadores Demócratas Cristianos de América Latina (FETRAL DC, no recent information); Young Christian Democrats of America (YCDA, no recent information).
Specialized organizations (4):
Americas People's Parliament (no recent information); Instituto de Formación Demócrata Cristiana (IFEDEC); Movimiento de Parlamentarios Demócrata-Cristianos de América (no recent information); Movimiento de Participación Regional, Municipal y Comunitaria Demócrata-Cristiana de América (no recent information).
NGO Relations Member of: *Centrist Democrat International (CDI, #03792)*. Instrumental in setting up: *Coordinación Parlamentaria Demócrata Cristiana (PARLA-DC, no recent information); International Union of Young Christian Democrats (IUYCD, inactive).* [2014.09.23/XD0264/y/**D**]

♦ Christian Democratic Union of Central Europe (inactive)

♦ Christian Democratic Women of America (CDWA) 03900

Femmes démocrates-chrétiennes d'Amérique – Mujeres Demócrata Cristianas de América (MUDCA)

Pres c/o COPEI, El Bosque, Av Principal El Bosque, cruce con Av Gloria Quinta Cujicito, Chacao, Caracas DF, Venezuela. T. +582127314746. Fax +582127314953.
URL: http://mudca.blogspot.com/

History 23 Sep 1967, Santiago (Chile). 23-24 Sep 1967, Santiago (Chile), at 1st Congress. **Aims** Work for transforming *Latin America* according to the Christian Democratic principles; further and defend the values of the human being and the principles of liberty, democracy, justice and peace; strive to achieve the full promotion of women at all levels of the society, especially in the political field. **Structure** Executive Committee, consisting of President, 4 Vice-Presidents (one for each of the regions of Latin America and the Caribbean: Andean, Caribbean, Central American, South Cone), Secretary-General and one member. **Finance** Financed by OCDA. **Activities** Training courses; fight for the promotion of women; seminars, meetings.
Members Organizations in 22 countries and territories:
Argentina, Aruba, Bolivia, Chile, Colombia, Costa Rica, Cuba, Curaçao, Dominican Rep, Ecuador, El Salvador, Guatemala, Haiti, Honduras, Mexico (observer), Nicaragua, Panama, Paraguay, Peru, Puerto Rico, Uruguay, Venezuela.
NGO Relations Functional organization of: *Christian Democratic Organization of America (#03899)*. Member of: *Centrist Democrat International (CDI, #03792).* [2008/XF0623/**F**]

♦ Christian Democratic World Union / see Centrist Democrat International (#03792)
♦ Christian Democrats / see Group of the European People's Party – Christian Democrats (#10775)
♦ Christian Disaster Response International (internationally oriented national body)
♦ Christian Education Development and Relief / see CEDAR Fund
♦ Christian Endeavor Movement / see World's Christian Endeavor Union (#21768)
♦ Christian Engineers in Development (internationally oriented national body)

♦ Christian Esperanto International Association 03901

Ligue internationale des chrétiens espérantistes – Kristana Esperantista Ligo Internacia (KELI)

Pres 26 rue de Pré Ventenet, 86340 Nouaillé-Maupertuis, France. T. +33549468021.
Sec Lidicka 939/11, 290 01 Podebrady, Czechia.
URL: http://keli.chez.com/

History Founded 25 Aug 1911, Antwerp (Belgium). **Aims** Create effective contacts among Christians worldwide and, by means of Esperanto, make known the good news of *Jesus Christ*. **Structure** Several countries have national sections with their own administrations. **Languages** Esperanto. **Staff** Voluntary. **Finance** Sources: members' dues. **Activities** Events/meetings; publishing activities. **Events** *Congress* Domaszék (Hungary) 2022, *Congress* Legnica (Poland) 2021, *Congress* Révfülöp (Hungary) 2019, *Congress* Podebrady (Czechia) 2018, *Congress* Zöblitz (Germany) 2017. **Publications** *Dia Regno* (6 a year).
Members Individuals either in national sections (which may or may not imply direct membership of KELI) or as direct members of KELI, in 35 countries:
Argentina, Australia, Austria, Belgium, Brazil, Bulgaria, Canada, China, Congo DR, Czechia, Denmark, Estonia, Finland, France, Germany, Greece, Guyana, Hungary, Korea Rep, Lithuania, Netherlands, New Zealand, Nicaragua, Norway, Poland, Romania, Russia, Serbia, Slovakia, Sweden, Switzerland, Tanzania UR, Togo, UK, USA.
NGO Relations *Universal Esperanto Association (UEA, #20676).* [2022/XC0268/**C**]

♦ Christian European Visual Media Association (CEVMA) 03902

Contact c/o IMM, APDO 2010, Alcala De Henares, 28801 Madrid, Spain. T. +39248003805. E-mail: info@cevma.com.
Chair address not obtained.
URL: http://www.cevma.com/

History 1981, Wetzlar (Germany). **Aims** Allow Christians in visual media to meet and exchange views. **Structure** Board. **Languages** English. **Staff** 0.50 FTE, paid. **Finance** Sources: meeting proceeds. **Activities** Events/meetings. **Events** *Annual Conference* Ede (Netherlands) 2022, *Annual Conference* Ede (Netherlands) 2015, *Annual Conference* Saalbach (Austria) 2014, *Annual Conference* Cullera (Spain) 2013, *Annual Conference* Oberägeri (Switzerland) 2012. **Publications** *CEVMA Newsletter*.
Members Individuals in 25 countries:
Albania, Australia, Austria, Belgium, Bulgaria, Canada, Cyprus, Czechia, Denmark, Finland, France, Germany, Ireland, Italy, Netherlands, New Zealand, Norway, Romania, Russia, Slovakia, Spain, Sweden, Switzerland, UK, USA.
[2023.02.14/XD0511/v/**D**]

♦ Christian Family Movement / see International Confederation of Christian Family Movements (#12851)
♦ Christian Family Movement Europe (see: #12851)
♦ Christian Foundation for Aid to the Persecuted for Cause of Conscience / see Dorcas (#05123)
♦ Christian Foundation for Children / see Unbound
♦ Christian Foundation for Children and Aging / see Unbound

♦ Christian Friends of Israel (CFI) 03903

Contact PO Box 1813, 9101701 Jerusalem, Israel. T. +97226233778. Fax +97226233913. E-mail: cfi@cfijerusalem.org.
URL: http://www.cfijerusalem.org/

Aims Comfort and support the people of Israel; inform Christians around the world of God's plan for Israel. **Activities** Events/meetings. **Events** *Annual Conference* Jerusalem (Israel) 2020, *Annual Conference* Jerusalem (Israel) 2018, *Annual Conference* Jerusalem (Israel) 2017, *Annual Conference* Jerusalem (Israel) 2016, *Annual Conference* Jerusalem (Israel) 2015. **Publications** *Israel News Digest* (12 a year); *Watchmans Prayer Letter* (12 a year); *For Zions Sake* (4 a year); *InGathering* (4 a year).
Members Representatives in 21 countries:
Australia, Austria, Belgium, Bulgaria, Canada, France, Germany, Hungary, India, Mexico, New Zealand, Philippines, Poland, Singapore, Slovakia, South Africa, Switzerland, Tanzania UR, UK, USA, Zimbabwe.
NGO Relations Founding member of: *European Coalition for Israel (ECI).* [2017.07.25/XM1774/**E**]

♦ Christian Growth International / see Skylark International
♦ Christian Hotels/Hospitality International (#13298)
♦ Christian Identity (internationally oriented national body)
♦ Christian Institute for the Study of Religion and Society (internationally oriented national body)
♦ Christian International Relief Mission (internationally oriented national body)
♦ Christian International of Wood Workers (inactive)
♦ Christian International of Workers in the Building Trade (inactive)
♦ Christian League (inactive)

♦ Christian Learning Materials Centre, Nairobi (CLMC) 03904

Contact PO Box 24345-00502, Karen-Dagoretti Road, Nairobi, 00502, Kenya. T. +254715838481. Fax +254202673693. E-mail: christianlearningmaterials@gmail.com – director@christianlearning.or.ke.
URL: http://www.christianlearning.or.ke/

History Jun 1981. A project of *Association of Evangelicals in Africa (AEA, #02587)*. **Aims** Provide Christian learning materials that are culturally African, educationally effective and thoroughly biblical to families and local churches all over Africa. **Structure** Board of Directors. **Languages** English. **Staff** 5.00 FTE, paid. **Finance** Sources: sales of publications; donor funding. **Activities** Publishing activities: training/education. **Publications** Sunday School curricula; Bible study guides; games – in English, Kiswahili, French. **NGO Relations** *Compassion International (CI, #04413); Hilfe für Brüder International*; Johnson Jeffery Baptist Church, USA. [2018.09.19/XE5999/**E**]

♦ Christian Life Community (CLC) 03905

Communauté de vie chrétienne (CVX) – Comunidad de Vida Cristiana (CVX)

Exec Sec World Secretariat, Borgo Santo Spirito 4, 00193 Rome RM, Italy. T. +3966869844. E-mail: exsec@cvx-clc.net.
Sec address not obtained.
URL: http://www.cvx-clc.net/

History 1563. Founded at the Congregatio of the Roman College; established canonically Dec 1584, by Pope Gregory XIII, as the Prima Primaria. On 2 Jul 1953, Rome (Italy), on approval of statutes by Pope Pius XII, was formed into *World Federation of the Sodalities of Our Lady – Fédération mondiale des congrégations mariales*. Subsequently, name changed to *World Federation of Christian Life Communities (WFCLC) – Federation mondiale des communautés de vie chrétienne (FMCVX) – Federación Mundial de las Comunidades de Vida Cristiana (FMCVX) – Weltverband der Gemeinschaften Christlichen Lebens – Federazione Mondiale delle Comunità di Vita Cristiana*, and new General Principles adopted 1967, Rome. Present name and revised General Principles adopted by World CLC Assembly, 7 Sep 1990, Guadalajara (Mexico); canonically confirmed by the Holy See, 3 Dec 1990. **Aims** Become committed Christians in bearing witness to those human and Gospel *values* with the Church and society which affect the *dignity* of the person, the welfare of the family and the *integrity* of creation. **Structure** World Assembly (every 5 years); Executive Council (meets annually); Permanent Secretariat. Membership open only through national communities. **Languages** English, French, Spanish. **Staff** 3.00 FTE, paid. **Finance** Sources: contributions. **Activities** Religious activities. **Events** *World Assembly* Buenos Aires (Argentina) 2018, *World Assembly* Beirut (Lebanon) 2013, *World Executive Council Meeting* Rome (Italy) 2012, *World Assembly* Fatima (Portugal) 2008, *World assembly* Nairobi (Kenya) 2003. **Publications** *Progressio* (3 a year) in English, French, Spanish.
Members Groups (about 5,000), totalling about 24,000 individuals, in 64 countries and territories:
Argentina, Australia, Austria, Belgium, Bolivia, Botswana, Brazil, Cameroon, Canada, Chile, Colombia, Congo DR, Côte d'Ivoire, Croatia, Cuba, Dominican Rep, Ecuador, Egypt, El Salvador, England, France, Germany, Guatemala, Hong Kong, Hungary, India, Indonesia, Ireland, Italy, Japan, Kenya, Korea Rep, Latvia, Lebanon, Lesotho, Lithuania, Luxembourg, Madagascar, Malta, Mauritius, Mexico, Nicaragua, Nigeria, Paraguay, Peru, Philippines, Poland, Portugal, Puerto Rico, Rwanda, Slovenia, South Africa, Spain, Sri Lanka, Switzerland, Syrian AR, Taiwan, Uruguay, USA, Venezuela, Vietnam, Wales, Zambia, Zimbabwe.
Consultative Status Consultative status granted from: *ECOSOC (#05331)* (Roster); *UNICEF (#20332)*. **IGO Relations** *United Nations Office at Vienna (UNOV, #20604)*. Associated with Department of Global Communications of the United Nations. **NGO Relations** Member of (2): *Forum of Catholic Inspired NGOs (#09905); Laudato Si' Movement (#16403). Conference of Non-Governmental Organizations in Consultative Relationship with the United Nations (CONGO, #04635); International Catholic Organizations Information Center (ICO Center); Jesuit Conference of Africa and Madagascar (JCAM, #16098); NGO Committee on Freedom of Religion or Belief, New York NY (#17109); Society of Jesus (SJ).* [2023/XB3518/**B**]

♦ Christian Literature Crusade / see CLC International
♦ Christian Michelsen Institute for Science and Intellectual Freedom / see Chr Michelsen Institute – Development Studies and Human Rights
♦ Christian Michelsens Institutt for Videnskap og Andsfrihet / see Chr Michelsen Institute – Development Studies and Human Rights
♦ The Christian Mission / see Salvation Army (#19041)
♦ Christian Mission Aid (internationally oriented national body)
♦ Christian and Missionary Alliance (internationally oriented national body)
♦ Christian Mission to Buddhists (religious order)
♦ Christian Mission to the Communist World / see Release International
♦ Christian Missions to the Communist World / see The Voice of the Martyrs (#20804)
♦ Christian Missions to the Communist World International / see The Voice of the Martyrs (#20804)
♦ Christian Organization for International Refugee Care / see ZOA

♦ Christian Organization Research and Advisory Trust of Africa (CORAT Africa) 03906

Managing dir PO Box 42493, Nairobi, 00100, Kenya. T. +25428891900 – +2542890165. Fax +2542891900. E-mail: corat@coratafrica.com.
URL: http://www.coratafrica.com/

History 1975. Registered in accordance with the law of Kenya. **Aims** Enable *Christian* organizations to improve their *management* capability. **Structure** Board of Directors. **Activities** Training/education; guidance/assistance/consulting; research and development. **Publications** *CORAT AFRICA Newsletter*.
[2014/XF0476/**F**]

♦ Christian Outreach – Relief and Development (internationally oriented national body)
♦ Christian Outreach, UK / see Christian Outreach – Relief and Development
♦ Christian Partners in Africa (internationally oriented national body)
♦ Christian Peace Conference (inactive)
♦ Christian Peacemaker Teams (internationally oriented national body)
♦ Christian Reconstruction in Europe / see Christian Aid
♦ Christian Reformed World Relief Committee / see World Renew
♦ Christian Relief and Development Association / see Consortium of Christian Relief and Development Association
♦ Christian Relief Fund / see Consortium of Christian Relief and Development Association
♦ Christian Relief Fund (internationally oriented national body)
♦ Christian Relief Services (internationally oriented national body)

♦ Christian Research Association (CRA) 03907

Address not obtained.
URL: http://www.christian-research.org.uk/

History 1993, taking over the activities of *MARC Europe (inactive)*. Charity registered in accordance with UK law. **Aims** Give Christian *leaders* the insight and skills required for *strategic planning* for growth. **Structure** Board. Departments (5): Research; Membership Services; Publications; Information Dissemination; Training. **Languages** English. **Staff** 5.50 FTE, paid; 0.50 FTE, voluntary. **Finance** Members' dues. Donations. Budget (annual): pounds250,000. **Activities** Carries out qualitative and quantitative research; runs briefings and seminars for leaders; provides consultancy service; publishes resource material; maintains Church address list; organizes conferences. **Events** *National archdeacons conference* Hoddesdon (UK) 2007, *International Lausanne researchers conference* Limassol (Cyprus) 2005, *National archdeacons conference* Swanwick (UK) 2005, *Senior church leaders conference* Hoddesdon (UK) 2004, *National archdeacons conference* Swanwick (UK) 2003. **Publications** *Quadrant* (6 a year). Booklets; handbooks; books; briefings.
Members Individual and Corporate in 18 countries:
Australia, Eswatini, France, Ghana, Hungary, India, Ireland, Italy, Kenya, Malaysia, Malta, Philippines, Portugal, Spain, Switzerland, Uganda, UK, USA.
NGO Relations Member of: *Global Connections*. [2010/XE1853/**E**]

- ♦ The Christian Revival Association / see Salvation Army (#19041)
- ♦ Christian Rural Fellowship of East Africa (inactive)
- ♦ Christians Abroad (internationally oriented national body)
- ♦ Christians in Action (internationally oriented national body)
- ♦ Christians for Biblical Equality / see CBE International
- ♦ Christian Schools International (internationally oriented national body)

♦ Christians for Israel International 03908

Intl Head Office PO Box 1100, 3860 BC Nijkerk, Netherlands. T. +31332458824. Fax +31332463644. E-mail: info@c4israel.org.
URL: http://www.c4israel.org/

History Founded 1980, Netherlands. Previously also referred to in Dutch as *Christenen voor Israel*. Registered in accordance with Dutch law. **Aims** Bring biblical understanding in the Church and among nations concerning God's purposes for Israel; promote comfort of Israel through prayer and action. **Structure** Board of Directors; Head Office in Nijkerk (Netherlands). **Finance** Contributions from national and regional branches (33%); donors (67%). **Activities** Awareness raising. **Publications** *Israel and Christians Today* (4-6 a year) – newspaper. *Why Israel ?* – DVD teaching series, including study guides. *Israel, the Nations and the Valley of Decision* by Harld Eckert in German – also in 7 other languages; *Why End Times?* by Rev Willem J J Glashouwer in Dutch – also in 8 other languages; *Why Israel ?* by Rev Willem J J Glashouwer in Dutch – also in 32 other languages.
Members Affiliates, partners and representatives in 35 countries:
Australia, Austria, Belgium, Botswana, Cameroon, Canada, Congo Brazzaville, France, Germany, Greece, Hungary, India, Indonesia, Italy, Kenya, Malaysia, Netherlands, New Zealand, Nigeria, Pakistan, Philippines, Poland, Romania, Russia, Rwanda, Singapore, South Africa, South Sudan, Switzerland, Tanzania UR, Uganda, UK, Ukraine, USA, Zambia.
NGO Relations Member of: *European Coalition for Israel (ECI)*. [2018.07.25/XF5933/**F**]

- ♦ Christians Linked in Mission / see International Partners in Mission (#14526)

♦ Christian Solidarity International (CSI) 03909

Solidarité chrétienne internationale

Contact Zelglistrasse 64, 8122 Binz, Switzerland. T. +41449823333. Fax +41449823334. E-mail: info@csi-schweiz.ch.
English: http://www.csi-usa.org/

History 1977, Zurich (Switzerland). **Aims** Promote religious freedom in the framework of the United Nations Charter and Declaration of Human Rights; give legal and material assistance to victims of oppression. **Structure** General Assembly (annual); International Coordinating Council; Regional Offices (5); International Headquarters in Binz (Switzerland). **Languages** Czech, English, French, German, Hungarian, Italian. **Staff** 29.00 FTE, paid; 6.00 FTE, voluntary. **Finance** Individual donations. **Activities** Humanitarian/emergency aid. **Events** *Annual Conference* 2006, *Annual Conference* 2005, *Annual Conference* 2004, *Annual Conference* Zurich (Switzerland) 2000, *Annual Conference* Munich (Germany) 1999. **Publications** *CSI Magazine* (11 a year). Annual Report.
Members Full; Adhering; Honorary. National committees in 7 countries:
Czechia, France, Germany, Hungary, Korea Rep, Switzerland (HQ), USA.
NGO Relations Instrumental in setting up: *CSW*. Member of: *Alliance Against Genocide (AAG, #00655)*.
[2018.09.12/XF0490/**F**]

- ♦ Christian Solidarity Worldwide / see CSW
- ♦ Christianson Syndrome Europe (unconfirmed)
- ♦ Christian Temperance Council for the Nordic Countries (no recent information)
- ♦ Christian Veterinary Mission (internationally oriented national body)
- ♦ Christian World Communion Executives Conference / see Conference of Secretaries of Christian World Communions (#04647)
- ♦ Christian World Service / see Act for Peace
- ♦ Christian World Service (internationally oriented national body)
- ♦ Christian World Service – Action Against Poverty / see Christian World Service
- ♦ Christ the King (religious order)
- ♦ Christlich-Demokratische Weltunion / see Centrist Democrat International (#03792)
- ♦ Christliche Arbeit Jugend – Europa / see JOC Europe (#16118)
- ♦ Christliche Blindenmission / see Christian Blind Mission
- ♦ Christliche Fachkräfte International (internationally oriented national body)
- ♦ Christliche Freundschaft in Europa (inactive)
- ♦ Christliche Friedenskonferenz (inactive)
- ♦ Christ for the Nations (internationally oriented national body)
- ♦ Christoffel-Blindenmission / see Christian Blind Mission
- ♦ Christopher Movement / see Christophers
- ♦ Christophers (internationally oriented national body)
- ♦ Christ-Roi (religious order)
- ♦ Chr Michelsen Institute – Development Studies and Human Rights (internationally oriented national body)
- ♦ Chr Michelsens Institutt – Utviklingsstudier og Menneskerettigheter (internationally oriented national body)
- ♦ **Chromosome 18 Europe** Chromosome 18 Registry and Research Society Europe (#03910)

♦ Chromosome 18 Registry and Research Society Europe (Chromosome 18 Europe) 03910

Sec 14 Main Street, Twechar, G65 9TA, UK.
URL: http://www.chromosome18eur.org/

History Founded Mar 2009, when registered as a Scottish charity. **Aims** Help individuals with chromosome 18 abnormalities overcome the obstacles they face so they might lead healthy, happy and productive lives; bring the latest research to people affected by all chromosome 18 disorders and their families in Europe. **Structure** Management Committee. **Languages** English, French, German, Irish Gaelic, Italian, Polish, Spanish. **Staff** 0.50 FTE, paid. **Finance** Fundraising by members; donations. Budget (annual): less than pounds50,000. **Activities** Organizes family conferences for affected children and adults, parents, siblings, relatives, friends and professionals. **Events** *Conference* Manchester (UK) 2014, *Conference* Milan (Italy) 2012, *Conference* Glasgow (UK) 2010. **Publications** Annual Report.
Members Primarily parents of individuals with a chromosome 18 abnormality. Also affected individuals, extended family members, and professionals. Members in 21 countries:
Australia, Belgium, Denmark, Estonia, Finland, France, Germany, Greece, Hungary, Ireland, Israel, Italy, Latvia, Netherlands, Norway, Poland, Slovakia, Spain, Sweden, UK, USA.
NGO Relations *Chromosome 18 Registry and Research Society*; *EURORDIS – Rare Diseases Europe (#09175)*; national organizations; support groups. [2013.08.21/XJ6571/**D**]

- ♦ Chronic Disease Alliance / see European Chronic Disease Alliance (#06548)
- ♦ CHR – United Nations Centre for Human Rights (inactive)
- ♦ Chrystusowcy – Towarzystwo Chrystusowe dla Polonii Zagranicznej (religious order)
- ♦ CHS² – International Conference on "Hot Sheet Metal Forming of High-Performance Steel" (meeting series)

♦ CHS Alliance 03911

Exec Dir Humanitarian Hub, La Voie-Creuse 16, 1202 Geneva, Switzerland. E-mail: info@chsalliance.org.
London Office Romero House, 55 Westminster Bridge Road, London, SE1 7JB, UK. T. +442034455605.
URL: http://www.chsalliance.org/

History Founded on merger of *Humanitarian Accountability Partnership International (HAP International, inactive)* and *People in Aid (inactive)*. Statutes adopted 9 Jun 2015. Former names and other names: *Core Humanitarian Standard on Quality and Accountability – CHS- Alliance* – full title. Registration: Switzerland. **Aims** Promote respect for the rights and dignity of people and communities *vulnerable* to *risk* and affected by disaster, conflict or poverty and enhance the effectiveness and impact of assistance by building a culture of quality and accountability. **Structure** General Assembly; Governing Board; Standing Committees; Secretariat. **Finance** Sources: international organizations; members' dues. Supported by: *Department for International Development (DFID, inactive)*; *Irish Aid*; *Swedish International Development Cooperation Agency (Sida)*; *Swiss Agency for Development and Cooperation (SDC)*. **Activities** Advocacy/lobbying/activism; capacity building; standards/guidelines; training/education. **Events** *Humanitarian HR Europe Conference* Antwerp (Belgium) 2019, *Humanitarian HR Europe Conference* Helsinki (Finland) 2017.
Members Full; Associate; Supporter. Organizations in 53 countries and territories:
Afghanistan, Angola, Australia, Austria, Bangladesh, Belgium, Brazil, Cambodia, Canada, Costa Rica, Denmark, Ethiopia, Finland, France, Gambia, Germany, Ghana, Greece, Guatemala, Haiti, Hong Kong, India, Indonesia, Ireland, Italy, Japan, Kenya, Lebanon, Liberia, Malawi, Malaysia, Mexico, Mozambique, Nepal, Netherlands, New Zealand, Nigeria, Norway, Pakistan, Philippines, Qatar, Sierra Leone, South Africa, Spain, Sweden, Switzerland, Tanzania UR, Thailand, Türkiye, Uganda, UK, Zambia, Zimbabwe.
Included in the above, 113 organizations listed in this Yearbook:
- *Acceso*;
- *ACORD – Agency for Cooperation and Research in Development (#00073)*;
- *ACT Alliance (#00081)*;
- *Act for Peace*;
- *Action Against Hunger (#00086)*;
- *ActionAid (#00087)* (various national sections);
- *African Network for Prevention and Protection Against Child Abuse and Neglect (ANPPCAN, #00393)*;
- *African Office for Development and Cooperation (OFADEC)*;
- *Aga Khan Foundation (AKF, #00545)*;
- *Agency for Technical Cooperation and Development (ACTED)*;
- *American Refugee Committee (ARC)*;
- *Amnesty International (AI, #00801)*;
- *ARTICLE 19 (#01121)*;
- *Australian Council for International Development (ACFID)*;
- *AVI*;
- *BRAC (#03310)*;
- *British Council*;
- *Bureau international des Médecins sans frontières (MSF International, #03366)* (various national sections);
- *CABI (#03393)*;
- *CARE International (CI, #03429)* (with various national sections);
- *Caritas Internationalis (CI, #03580)*;
- *Catholic Agency for Overseas Development (CAFOD)*;
- *Catholic Organization for Relief and Development (Cordaid)*;
- *Centre for Information, Counseling and Training Professions Relating to International Cooperation and Humanitarian Aid (CINFO)*;
- *Centre for Safety and Development (CSD)*;
- *CESVI Fondazione*;
- *ChildFund International (#03869)*;
- *Christian Aid*;
- *Christian Blind Mission (CBM)*;
- *Christian Outreach – Relief and Development (CORD)*;
- *Christian World Service (CWS)*;
- *Comhlamh*;
- *Community and Family Services International (CFSI)*;
- *Community World Service Asia (#04407)*;
- *Concern Worldwide*;
- *Consortium of Christian Relief and Development Association (CCRDA)*;
- *Cooperation Committee for Cambodia (CCC)*;
- *DANIDA*;
- *Danish Refugee Council (DRC)*;
- *Department for International Development (DFID, inactive)*;
- *Diakonia*;
- *Disasters Emergency Committee (DEC)*;
- *Donkey Sanctuary, The (#05120)*;
- *FilmAid International (FAI)*;
- *Finn Church Aid (FCA)*;
- *Folkekirkens Nødhjaelp (FKN)*;
- *Fred Hollows Foundation*;
- *GOAL*;
- *Greenpeace International (#10727)*;
- *Habitat for Humanity International (HFHI)*;
- *HALO Trust*;
- *HealthNet TPO*;
- *Health Poverty Action (HPA)*;
- *HelpAge International (#10904)*;
- *Human Appeal (#10961)*;
- *Human Relief Foundation (HRF)*;
- *International Aid Services (IAS)*;
- *International Alert (#11615)*;
- *International Federation of Red Cross and Red Crescent Societies (#13526)*;
- *International Medical Corps (IMC)*;
- *International Nepal Fellowship (INF)*;
- *International Rescue Committee (IRC, #14717)*;
- *International Union Against Tuberculosis and Lung Disease (The Union, #15752)*;
- *Islamic Relief Worldwide (IRWW, #16048)*;
- *JAM International (Joint Aid Management)*;
- *Japanese NGO Center for International Cooperation (JANIC)*;
- *Keeping Children Safe*;
- *Leprosy Mission International (TLMI, #16446)*;
- *Lutheran World Relief (LWR)*;
- *Malaria Consortium*;
- *Malteser International*;
- *MEDAIR*;
- *Medical Aid for Palestinians (MAP)*;
- *Medical Teams International (MTI)*;
- *Medica Mondiale*;
- *Mercy Corps International (MCI)*;
- *Mérieux Foundation*;
- *Mines Advisory Group (MAG)*;
- *Mission Aviation Fellowship (MAF, #16829)*;
- *Mission East*;
- *MSI Reproductive Choices*;
- *Muslim Aid*;
- *Muslim Hands*;
- *New World Hope Organization (NWHO)*;
- *Norwegian Church Aid*;
- *Norwegian Refugee Council (NRC)*;
- *Oxfam International (#17922)* (various national sections);

- *People in Need (PIN)*;
- *Plan International (#18386)*;
- *PMU Interlife*;
- *Retrak*;
- *Saferworld*;
- *Save the Children International (#19058)*;
- *Save the Children UK (SC UK)*;
- *SEEDS Asia (#19216)*;
- *Swedish International Development Cooperation Agency (Sida)*;
- *TEAR Australia*;
- *Tearfund, UK*;
- *The Brooke (#03338)*;
- *The Lutheran World Federation (LWF, #16532)*;
- *Transparency International (TI, #20223)*;
- *Trocaire – Catholic Agency for World Development*;
- *UnitingWorld*;
- *Voluntary Service Overseas (VSO)*;
- *War Child International (#20817)* (UK section);
- *Welthungerhilfe*;
- *Womankind Worldwide (#20982)*;
- *Women's Refugee Commission (WRC)*;
- *WorldFish (#21507)*;
- *World Relief*;
- *World Renew*;
- *World Vision International (WVI, #21904)* (including UK Section);
- *ZOA*.

NGO Relations Member of (1): *Active Learning Network for Accountability and Performance in Humanitarian Action (ALNAP, #00101)*. [2019/XM4452/y/**B**]

♦ **CHTA** Caribbean Hotel and Tourism Association (#03516)
♦ CHU / see Hipólito Unanue Agreement (#10921)
♦ Chuo cha Diplomasia (internationally oriented national body)
♦ Church of the Brethren (internationally oriented national body)
♦ Church Development and Aid (internationally oriented national body)

♦ Churches' Commission for Migrants in Europe (CCME) 03912

Commission des Eglises auprès des migrants en Europe (CEME) – Kommission der Kirchen für Migranten in Europa

SG Rue Joseph II 174, 1000 Brussels, Belgium. T. +3222346800. Fax +3222311413. E-mail: info@ccme.be.
Exec Sec address not obtained.
URL: http://www.ccme.eu/

History Mar 1964, Geneva (Switzerland). Independent status acquired Oct 1966, London (UK).Statutes adopted 25-27 Apr 1972, Bossey (Switzerland); came into force in Jun 1973. Offices transferred to Brussels (Belgium), 1978; statutes modified, 21-26 Oct 1984, Strasbourg (France), 2-5 Oct 1999, Järvenpää (Finland). Former names and other names: *Churches Committee on Migrant Workers in Western Europe* – former (1964 to Apr 1972); *Comité des Eglises auprès des travailleurs migrants en Europe occidentale* – former (1964 to Apr 1972); *Ausschuss der Kirchen für Fragen der Ausländischen Arbeitnehmer in Westeuropa* – former (1964 to Apr 1972); *Churches' Committee on Migrant Workers in Europe (CCMWE)* – former (Apr 1972 to 1987); *Comité des Eglises auprès des travailleurs migrants en Europe (CETMI)* – former (Apr 1972 to 1987); *Ausschuss der Kirchen für Fragen Ausländischer Arbeitnehmer in Europa* – former (Apr 1972 to 1987); *Churches' Committee for Migrants in Europe* – former (1987 to 1993); *Comité des Eglises auprès des migrants en Europe* – former (1987 to 1993); *Ausschuss der Kirchen für Ausländerfragen in Europa (AKFA)* – former (1987 to 1993). Registration: Banque-Carrefour des Entreprises, No/ID: 0418.995.755, Start date: 8 Jan 1979, Belgium; EU Transparency Register, No/ID: 01765274994-03, Start date: 14 Jan 2011. **Aims** Promote the vision of an inclusive community through advocating for an adequate policy for migrants, refugees and minority ethnic groups at European and national level. **Structure** General Assembly (every 3 years); Executive Committee (meets twice a year); Secretariat in Brussels (Belgium). **Languages** English, French, German. **Staff** 3.50 FTE, paid. **Finance** Sources: members' dues. Church funds. Annual budget: 400,000 EUR. **Activities** Research/documentation; events/meetings; capacity building. **Events** *General Assembly* Sigtuna (Sweden) 2014, *General Assembly* Bucharest (Romania) 2011, *Meeting* Budapest (Hungary) 2009, *General Assembly* Paralimni (Cyprus) 2008, *General Assembly* Protaras (Cyprus) 2008. **Publications** *Mapping Migration – Mapping Churches' Responses* (2016) – co-published with WCC. Briefing papers; topical brochures.

Members Protestant, Anglican and Orthodox churches, church agencies and ecumenical councils in 20 European countries:
Austria, Belgium, Cyprus, Czechia, Finland, France, Germany, Greece, Hungary, Ireland, Italy, Netherlands, Norway, Portugal, Romania, Slovakia, Spain, Sweden, Switzerland, UK.

Consultative Status Consultative status granted from: *Council of Europe (CE, #04881)* (Participatory Status). **IGO Relations** Member of Consultative Forum of: *Frontex, the European Border and Coast Guard Agency (#10005)*; *European Union Agency for Asylum (EUAA, #08968)*. **NGO Relations** Member of (7): *European Coordination for Foreigners' Right to Family Life (COORDEUROP, #06794)*; *European Network against Racism (ENAR, #07862)*; *European Network on Statelessness (ENS, #08013)*; *European NGO Platform Asylum and Migration (EPAM, #08051)*; *Federation of European and International Associations Established in Belgium (FAIB, #09508)*; *Oikocredit International (Oikocredit, #17704)*; *United4Rescue*. [2020/XD0276/y/**D**]

♦ Churches' Committee for Migrants in Europe / see Churches' Commission for Migrants in Europe (#03912)
♦ Churches' Committee on Migrant Workers in Europe / see Churches' Commission for Migrants in Europe (#03912)
♦ Churches Committee on Migrant Workers in Western Europe / see Churches' Commission for Migrants in Europe (#03912)
♦ Churches International Relief and Rehabilitation Committee / see Act for Peace
♦ Churches for Middle East Peace (internationally oriented national body)
♦ Churches United Against HIV and AIDS (inactive)
♦ Churches United In Christ (internationally oriented national body)
♦ Church of God Ministry of Jesus Christ International (religious order)
♦ Church of God World Missions (internationally oriented national body)

♦ Church Growth International (CGI) 03913

Chairman 11 Floor CCMM Bldg, 12 Yeoido-Dong, Youngdeungpo-Gu, Seoul 150869, Korea Rep. T. +8227839920. Fax +8227841990.
URL: http://churchgrowthint.homestead.com/home.html

History Nov 1976, on the initiative of David Yonggi Cho. **Aims** Promote world church growth, setting an example of success for *pastors* and churches based on the principles of the *Bible*. **Structure** Board of Directors; Chairman. **Languages** English. **Staff** 7.00 FTE, paid. **Finance** Church funding; donations. **Activities** Events/meetings. **Events** *Conference* Seoul (Korea Rep) 2019, *Conference* Seoul (Korea Rep) 2018, *Conference* Seoul (Korea Rep) 2015, *Conference* Kuala Lumpur (Malaysia) 2014, *Conference* Seoul (Korea Rep) 2013. **Publications** *Church Growth* (4 a year); *Church Growth Manual* (2 a year). *Church Growth and the Home Cell System*. **Members** Members in about 181 countries. Membership countries not specified. [2015.08.27/XF1333/**F**]

♦ Churchill Centre, The 03914

Exec Dir PO Box 945, Downers Grove IL 60515-0945, USA. T. +18449721874.
URL: http://www.winstonchurchill.org/

History Founded 1968, to group international Churchill societies in a number of countries. Also referred to as *International Churchill Societies (ICS)*. Merged with *'American Friends of the Churchill Museum'* at Cabinet War Rooms, London (UK), Jan 2008. **Aims** Foster leadership, *statesmanship*, vision and boldness among democratic and freedom-loving peoples worldwide, through the thoughts, words, works and deeds of Winston Spencer Churchill. **Structure** Council of Churchill Societies or Council of Churchill Organizations, an informal body, comprises 15 members, including at least one representative of each country having an international Churchill society (registered charitable associations in Canada, UK and USA, branch in Australia, 3 associated, independent societies in Western Canada). **Languages** English. **Staff** 2.50 FTE, paid. **Finance** Members' dues. Other sources: contributions; programme income. Budget (annual) US$ 1 million. **Activities** Events/meetings; training/education; research/documentation; publishing activity. **Events** *Annual Conference* Washington, DC (USA) 2016, *Annual Conference* Woodstock (UK) 2015, *Annual Conference* New Orleans, LA (USA) 2014, *Annual Conference* Washington, DC (USA) 2013, *Annual conference / Annual International Churchill Conference* Ottawa, ON (Canada) 2012. **Publications** *Chartwell Bulletin* (4 a year) – member periodical; *Finest Hour* (4 a year) – journal; *UK Newsletter* (4 a year). *Churchill Papers* – series. Free teaching aids for teachers; special publications.

Members Individuals, members of one of 7 international societies in 4 countries (marked "). Members in a total of 25 countries:
Australia (*), Austria, Belgium, Canada (*), Denmark, Finland, France, Germany, Hungary, Ireland, Israel, Italy, Kenya, Latvia, Malta, Netherlands, Norway, Portugal, South Africa, Spain, Sweden, Switzerland, UK (*), USA (*), Zimbabwe.
[2016.06.01/XE0230/**E**]

♦ Church of Jesus Christ of the Latter-day Saints 03915

Public Affairs Joseph Smith Memorial Bldg, 15 E South Temple St, 2nd Floor, Salt Lake City UT 84150, USA. T. +80014533860. Fax +80012405551.
URL: http://www.lds.org/

History 6 Apr 1830, USA. 6 Apr 1830, Fayette NY (USA), by Joseph Smith. Also known as *The Mormons*. After several moves following (sometimes violent) opposition, including the assassination of Joseph Smith, finally established in Salt Lake City UT (USA) under the leadership of Brigham Young. **Aims** Bless the children of God, offering the teaching, support and essential ordinances necessary to the *salvation* of each individual. **Structure** First Presidency; Quorum of the Twelve Apostles (Council); the Seventy, serving in Area Presidencies worldwide. Each local congregation (ward) and group of wards (stake) is grouped in an area presided over by a Stake President. Wards and stakes have no paid ministry. Temples of the Church (150). Humanitarian arm: *LDS Charities*. **Finance** Volontary contributions by members. **Activities** Training/education; advocacy/lobbying/activism; humanitarian/emergency aid; religious activities. **Members** Individuals (15.6 million), of whom just under half live in USA, in 169 countries and territories. Membership countries not specified. **NGO Relations** LDS Charities is member of: *NGO Alliance on Global Concerns and Values (NGO Alliance, #17102)*. Partner of: *Adventist Development and Relief Agency International (ADRA, #00131)*. [2016.06.28/XF4240/**F**]

♦ Church Mission Society (internationally oriented national body)
♦ Church of the Movement of Spiritual Inner Awareness / see Movement of Spiritual Inner Awareness

♦ Church and Peace 03916

Eglise et paix – Kirche und Frieden

Sec Mittelstrasse 4, 34474 Diemelstadt, Germany. T. +4956949905506. Fax +4956941532.
URL: http://www.church-and-peace.org/

History 1975. Founded by Mennonites, Quakers and the Church of the Brethren, together with IFOR, as successor organization to *Historic Peace Churches European Continuation Committee (inactive)*. **Aims** Provide a forum of exchange and a theological resource for *Christian* communities, groups, organizations and churches who see the peace witness as essential to the Gospel of Christ, and who wish to explore what it means to be a 'Peace Church'. **Structure** General Assembly (at least annual); Board. **Languages** Bosnian, Croatian, English, French, German, Serbian. **Staff** 1.50 FTE, paid. **Finance** Sources: contributions; donations; members' dues. **Events** *Conference* Berlin (Germany) 2019, *Conference* Pristina (Kosovo) 2015, *Conference / Annual General Assembly* Baarlo (Netherlands) 2014, *Conference / Annual General Assembly* Selbitz (Germany) 2013, *Annual General Assembly* Brussels (Belgium) 2012. **Publications** *Theology and Peace* in Bosnian, Croatian, English, French, German, Serbian – occasional pamphlet series.

Members Corporate (52) in 11 countries and territories:
Belgium, France, Germany, Hungary, Italy, Kosovo, Netherlands, Russia, Serbia, Spain, Switzerland, UK.

Individuals (60) in 9 countries:
Croatia, Czechia, France, Germany, Netherlands, Serbia, Switzerland, UK.

Associate (4) in 4 countries:
Germany, Italy, UK, USA.

Out of founding and corporate members, 5 international and regional organizations listed in this Yearbook:
Anglican Pacifist Fellowship (APF, #00830); *Brethren Volunteer Service (BVS, #03321)*; *Friends World Committee for Consultation (FWCC, #10004)*; *International Christian Peace Service (EIRENE, #12564)*; *International Fellowship of Reconciliation (IFOR, #13586)*.

NGO Relations Member of (4): *Action Committee Service for Peace (AGDF)*; *Conference of European Churches (CEC, #04593)*; *International Network for a Culture of Nonviolence and Peace (#14247)*; *United4Rescue*. Cooperates with (1): *World Council of Churches (WCC, #21320)*. [2019.12.11/XF8580/y/**F**]

♦ Church Peace Union / see Carnegie Council for Ethics in International Affairs

♦ Church of the Province of Central Africa 03917

Primate PO Box 20798, Kitwe, Zambia. T. +2602223264. Fax +2602224778.
Treas address not obtained.
URL: http://www.anglicancommunion.org/

History 1955, as an autonomous member Church of *Anglican Communion (#00827)*.
Members Individual Anglicans (750,000) in 15 Dioceses comprising 400 parishes in 4 countries:
Botswana, Malawi, Zambia, Zimbabwe.

NGO Relations Represented on the: *Anglican Consultative Council (ACC, #00828)*. Every diocese represented at the: *Lambeth Conference of Bishops of the Anglican Communion (#16224)*. Primates meet at: *Primates Meeting of the Anglican Communion (#18497)*. Member of: *World Council of Churches (WCC, #21320)*. [2016/XE2131/**E**]

♦ Church of the Province of Melanesia 03918

Main Office Anglican Church of Melanesia, PO Box 19, Honiara, Guadalcanal, Solomon Is. E-mail: info@acom.org.sb.
URL: http://www.acom.org.sb/

History 1975, on formation of the Province, an Anglican presence having existed in Melanesia since 1849. An autonomous member Church of *Anglican Communion (#00827)*. Former names and other names: *Anglican Church of the Province of Melanesia* – full title.
Members Individuals (132,000), in 100 parishes and districts, with 8 dioceses, in 3 countries and territories:
New Caledonia, Solomon Is, Vanuatu.

NGO Relations Represented on the: *Anglican Consultative Council (ACC, #00828)*. Every diocese represented at the: *Lambeth Conference of Bishops of the Anglican Communion (#16224)*. Primates meet at: *Primates Meeting of the Anglican Communion (#18497)*. [2020/XE1963/**E**]

♦ Church of the Province of New Zealand / see Anglican Church in Aotearoa, New Zealand and Polynesia (#00823)

♦ Church of the Province of South East Asia 03919

Primate 214 Halan Pahang, 53000 Kuala Lumpur, Malaysia. T. +603402432133. Fax +60340323225. E-mail: bishopsecretary.dwm@gmail.com.

History as an autonomous member Church of the *Anglican Communion (#00827)*. **NGO Relations** Represented on the: *Anglican Consultative Council (ACC, #00828)*. Every diocese represented at the: *Lambeth Conference of Bishops of the Anglican Communion (#16224)*. Member of: *Primates Meeting of the Anglican Communion (#18497)*. [2019/XE2718/**E**]

♦ Church of the Province of Southern Africa / see Anglican Church of Southern Africa (#00826)

♦ Church of the Province of West Africa (CPWA) 03920

Provincial Sec PO Box KN 2023, Kaneshie, Accra, Ghana. T. +233302257370. Fax +233302669125.
URL: http://www.anglicancommunion.org/

History 17 Apr 1951, as an autonomous member Church of *Anglican Communion (#00827)*, work having begun in Ghana in 1752 and in other countries of the Province through the Episcopal Church of the USA and *Society for Promoting Christian Knowledge (SPCK, #19624)*. Synod first met Nov 1957. Constitution and canons adopted Aug 1962, Lagos (Nigeria), at 2nd meeting, and came into effect 1 Mar 1963, on approval by the Archbishop of Canterbury. **Aims** Spread the Gospel. **Structure** Provincial Synod comprising 3 Houses: Bishops; Clergy; Laity. **Languages** English, French. **Staff** 4.00 FTE, paid. **Finance** Payment of assessments; external grants. **Events** *Meeting* Cape Coast (Ghana) 2001.

Members Individual Anglicans (1 million) in 16 dioceses comprising 300 churches in 6 countries:
Cameroon, Gambia, Ghana, Guinea, Liberia, Sierra Leone.
NGO Relations Member of: *World Council of Churches (WCC, #21320)*. Represented on the: *Anglican Consultative Council (ACC, #00828)*. Every diocese represented at the: *Lambeth Conference of Bishops of the Anglican Communion (#16224)*. Primates meet at: *Primates Meeting of the Anglican Communion (#18497)*.
[2017/XE2135/**E**]

♦ Church in the Province of the West Indies (CPWI) 03921

Provincial Sec Bamford House, Society Hill, St John BB26028, ST JOHN BB26028, Barbados. T. +1246423842 – +1246423843. Fax +12464230855. E-mail: cpwi.secretariat@gmail.com – cpwi@caribsurf.com.
URL: http://www.anglicancommunion.org/tour/index.cfm
History 1883. Founded on formation of the Province with a Primate and Synod, having existed as Churches in various West Indian territories that became British colonies. An autonomous member Church of *Anglican Communion (#00827)*. **Structure** Dioceses (8); Theological seminaries (2); *United Theological College of the West Indies (UTCWI, #20662)*; Codrington College, Barbados. **Finance** Sources: grants. Assessments on the member Dioceses. Annual budget: 28,300 GBP. **Publications** *Provincial Newsletter* (4 a year).
Members Individuals (770,000) in 8 Dioceses, covering 23 countries and territories:
Anguilla, Antigua, Aruba, Bahamas, Barbados, Barbuda, Belize, Cayman Is, Dominica, Grenada, Guyana, Jamaica, Montserrat, Saba, St Barthélemy, St Eustatius, St Kitts-Nevis, St Lucia, St Martin, St Vincent-Grenadines, Trinidad-Tobago, Turks-Caicos, Windward Is.
NGO Relations Member of (2): *Caribbean Conference of Churches (CCC, #03479)*; *World Council of Churches (WCC, #21320)*. Represented on: *Anglican Consultative Council (ACC, #00828)*. Every diocese represented at: *Lambeth Conference of Bishops of the Anglican Communion (#16224)*. Primates meet at: *Primates Meeting of the Anglican Communion (#18497)*.
[2020.05.21/XE2024/**E**]

♦ Church of Scientology International (CSI) 03922

Eglise de scientologie
Public Affairs Dir 6331 Hollywood Boulevard, Ste 1200, Los Angeles CA 90028, USA. T. +13239603500. Fax +13239603508. E-mail: publicaffairs@churchofscientology.net.
Church of Scientology Intl European Office Director, Rue de la Loi 91, 1040 Brussels, Belgium. T. +3222311596. Fax +3222801540.
Main: http://www.scientology.org/
History Founded Feb 1954, Los Angeles CA (USA), when first Church of Scientology was set up on the research and writings of L Ronald Hubbard, founder of Dianetics and Scientology and a forerunner of scientology, who set up the *Hubbard Association of Scientologists International (HASI) – Association internationale Hubbard des scientologistes*. **Aims** As the mother church of all Scientology, apply the religious philosophy of scientology, as developed by L Ron Hubbard, in the study and handling of the spirit in relationship to itself, universes and other life and the Supreme Being; achieve a renewed awareness of self as a spiritual and immortal being; apply principles of scientology to improve confidence, intelligence, abilities and skills; provide workable solutions to problems faced by people today; promote a world without war, without crime and without insanity through the application of dianetics and scientology. **Structure** International Board of Directors approves international ecclesiastic policy. National and local churches, missions and groups have their own boards of directors. **Languages** English. **Staff** 15000.00 FTE, paid. **Finance** Fixed donations for courses and counselling; book sales. **Activities** Religious activities; guidance/assistance/consulting; training/education. **Events** *Meeting* Paris (France) 2009. **Publications** *Freedom Magazine. Theology and Practice of a Contemporary Religion – Scientology* (1998) by L Ron Hubbard in English – translated in 53 languages; *Works of L Ron Hubbard, in English, translated in 53 languages and including: Dianetics – the Modern Science of Mental Health* (1950) by L Ron Hubbard in English – translated in 53 languages; *Scientology 0-8* by L Ron Hubbard in English – translated in 53 languages; *What is Scientology ?* by L Ron Hubbard in English – translated in 53 languages; *Volunteer Ministers Handbook* by L Ron Hubbard in English – translated in 53 languages; *The Problems of Work* by L Ron Hubbard in English – translated in 53 languages; *The Book of Basics* by L Ron Hubbard in English – translated in 53 languages; *Scientology: The Fundamentals of Thought* by L Ron Hubbard in English – translated in 53 languages; *A New Slant on Life* by L Ron Hubbard in English – translated in 53 languages; *Axioms and Logics* by L Ron Hubbard in English – translated in 53 languages; *Purification: An Illustrated Answer to Drugs* by L Ron Hubbard in English – translated in 53 languages; *Introduction to Scientology Ethics* by L Ron Hubbard in English – translated in 53 languages; *Dianetics: The Modern Science of Mental Health* by L Ron Hubbard in English – translated in 53 languages; *Dianetics: The Evolution of a Science* by L Ron Hubbard in English – translated in 53 languages; *Clear Mind* by L Ron Hubbard in English – translated in 53 languages; *Clear Body* by L Ron Hubbard in English – translated in 53 languages; *Science and Survival* by L Ron Hubbard in English – translated in 53 languages.
Members National and local churches, missions, groups and social betterment organizations (over 4,000), representing about 8 million members, in 116 countries and territories:
Afghanistan, Albania, Algeria, Andorra, Armenia, Australia, Austria, Azerbaijan, Bangladesh, Belarus, Belgium, Bolivia, Bosnia-Herzegovina, Botswana, Brazil, Bulgaria, Cambodia, Cameroon, Canada, Chile, China, Colombia, Congo Brazzaville, Congo DR, Costa Rica, Croatia, Cuba, Cyprus, Czechia, Denmark, Dominican Rep, Ecuador, Egypt, El Salvador, Eritrea, Estonia, Eswatini, Ethiopia, Fiji, Finland, France, Gambia, Georgia, Germany, Ghana, Greece, Guatemala, Guyana, Haiti, Honduras, Hungary, India, Indonesia, Iran Islamic Rep, Ireland, Israel, Italy, Jamaica, Japan, Jordan, Kazakhstan, Kenya, Korea Rep, Kuwait, Kyrgyzstan, Latvia, Lesotho, Liberia, Lithuania, Luxembourg, Malaysia, Marshall Is, Mexico, Moldova, Mozambique, Nepal, Netherlands, New Zealand, Nicaragua, Nigeria, North Macedonia, Norway, Peru, Philippines, Poland, Portugal, Puerto Rico, Romania, Russia, Rwanda, Saudi Arabia, Senegal, Serbia, Sierra Leone, Slovakia, Slovenia, South Africa, Spain, Sudan, Suriname, Sweden, Switzerland, Taiwan, Tajikistan, Thailand, Trinidad-Tobago, Turkmenistan, Uganda, UK, Ukraine, USA, Uzbekistan, Venezuela, Zambia, Zimbabwe.
[2019/XF2468/s/**F**]

♦ Church Women United (internationally oriented national body)
♦ Church of World Messianity (unconfirmed)
♦ Church World Service (internationally oriented national body)
♦ Church World Service-Pakistan/Afghanistan / see Community World Service Asia (#04407)
♦ CHUSC – Commission hydrographique USA/Canada (see: #13825)
♦ Chuto Chosakai (internationally oriented national body)
♦ CHwB – Cultural Heritage without Borders (internationally oriented national body)
♦ CHW – Children's Helpers Worldwide (internationally oriented national body)
♦ **CHZMR** Commission hydrographique de la zone maritime ROPME (#18971)
♦ CIAA – Confederation of the Food and Drink Industries of the EU / see FoodDrinkEurope (#09841)
♦ CIAA – Confédération des industries agro-alimentaires de l'UE / see FoodDrinkEurope (#09841)
♦ CIAA – Confédération internationale des associations d'artistes (inactive)
♦ CIAA – UNICE / see FoodDrinkEurope (#09841)
♦ **CIACA** Corte Internacional de Arbitraje y Conciliación Ambiental (#13096)
♦ **CiA** CAN in Automation (#03411)
♦ **CIAC** Cephalopod International Advisory Council (#03822)
♦ **CIA** Collegium Internationale Allergologicum (#04114)
♦ **CIA** Comité international d'Auschwitz (#12297)
♦ **CIA** Confédération Internationale des Accordéonistes (#12841)
♦ CIA – Confédération internationale de l'agriculture (inactive)
♦ CIADEC – Confédération internationale des associations de diplômés en sciences économiques et commerciales (inactive)
♦ **CIADI** Centro Internacional de Arreglo de Diferencias Relativas a Inversiones (#12515)
♦ **CIAEM** Comité Interamericano de Educación Matematica (#11413)
♦ **CI-AF** Comité Inter-Africain sur les pratiques traditionnelles ayant effet sur la santé des femmes et des enfants (#11384)
♦ CIAF – Confederación Internacional de Apoyo Familiar (inactive)
♦ CIAF – Congrès international des études africaines (inactive)
♦ CIAGA – Confederación Interamericana de Ganaderos y Agricultores (no recent information)
♦ CIAGI / see Arab Investment and Export Credit Guarantee Corporation (#00997)
♦ CIAH – Collectif interafricain des habitants (internationally oriented national body)
♦ CIAI – Comité international d'aide aux intellectuels (inactive)
♦ CIA / see International Council on Archives (#12996)
♦ CIAK / see Kneipp Worldwide (#16197)
♦ **CIALC** Centro de Investigaciones sobre América y el Caribe (#03810)
♦ CIAL – Conseil international des auteurs littéraires (inactive)
♦ CIALP – Conselho Internacional dos Arquitetos de Lingua Portuguesa (internationally oriented national body)
♦ CIALS – Confédération internationale des arts, des lettres et des sciences (inactive)
♦ CIAMAC – Conférence internationale des associations de mutilés de guerre et anciens combattants (inactive)
♦ CIAM – Congrès internationaux d'architecture moderne (inactive)
♦ **CIAM** Conseil International des Créateurs de Musique (#13052)
♦ CIAM / see International Council of Music Authors (#13052)
♦ CIANA – Consejo Iberoamericano de Asociaciones Nacionales de Arquitectos (no recent information)
♦ **C.I.A.N.A.M.** Cámara Interamericana de Asociaciones Nacionales de Agentes Marítimos (#03400)
♦ CIAN – Conseil français des investisseurs en Afrique (internationally oriented national body)
♦ CIAN – Conseil des investisseurs français en Afrique noire / see Conseil français des investisseurs en Afrique
♦ **CIANEA** Community Based Impact Assessment Network for Eastern Africa (#04390)
♦ CIANS – Collegium Internationale Activitatis Nervosae Superioris / see Collegium Internationale Activitatis Nervosae Superioris (#04113)
♦ **CIANS** Collegium Internationale Activitatis Nervosae Superioris (#04113)
♦ CIAO – Conférence internationale des africanistes de l'Ouest (inactive)
♦ **CIAPA** Colectivo Internacional en Apoyo al Pescador Artesanal (#12639)
♦ CIAPA / see International Collective in Support of Fishworkers (#12639)
♦ **CIAP** Conference Interpreters Asia Pacific (#04623)
♦ CIAP – Conseil interafricain de philosophie (no recent information)
♦ CIAPG – Confédération internationale des anciens prisonniers de guerre (inactive)
♦ CIAP – International Centre of Innovation and Exchange in Public Administration (internationally oriented national body)
♦ CIAPP – Congrès international d'anthropologie et d'archéologie préhistoriques (inactive)
♦ CIAP / see Société internationale d'ethnologie et de folklore (#19481)
♦ CIArb – Chartered Institute of Arbitrators (internationally oriented national body)
♦ **CIAR** Colegio Ibero-Americano de Reumatologia (#11020)
♦ CIAS / see California Institute of Integral Studies
♦ CIASC – Confederación Interamericana de Acción Social Católica (inactive)
♦ CIASC – Confédération interaméricaine sociale catholique (inactive)
♦ **CIAS** Conseil international de l'action sociale (#13076)
♦ **CIAS** Conseil international de l'arbitrage en matière de Sport (#12994)
♦ CIAS – Consejo Interamericano de Seguridad (no recent information)
♦ **CIASEM** Comité Interamericano de Sociedades de Microscopia Electrónica (#04171)
♦ **CIAT** Centro Interamericano de Administraciones Tributarias (#11405)
♦ **CIAT** Centro Internacional de Agricultura Tropical (#12527)
♦ **CIAT** Comisión Interamericana del Atún Tropical (#11454)
♦ CIATF / see World Foundry Organization (#21528)
♦ **CIAV** Comité international pour l'architecture vernaculaire de l'ICOMOS (#11069)
♦ CIBA – CILECT Ibero América (see: #11771)
♦ **CIBAFI** General Council for Islamic Banks and Financial Institutions (#10111)
♦ Ciba-Geigy Foundation for Cooperation with Developing Countries / see Novartis Foundation
♦ CIBAL / see International Information Centre for Balkan Studies (#13844)
♦ **CIBAL** International Information Centre for Balkan Studies (#13844)
♦ **CIBAR** Conference of International Broadcasters' Audience Research Services (#04611)
♦ **CIBC** Confédération internationale de la boucherie et de la charcuterie (#12421)
♦ CIB – Center for International Business (internationally oriented national body)
♦ **CIB** Comité international de bioéthique de l'UNESCO (#12348)
♦ CIB – Comité international du bois (inactive)
♦ **CIB** Comité international du bois de l'ICOMOS (#11085)
♦ **CIB** Conférence internationale des barreaux de tradition juridique commune (#04612)
♦ **CIBD** Comité international Buchenwald-Dora et Kommandos (#12749)
♦ **CIBE** International Confederation of European Beet Growers (#12860)
♦ **CIBELAE** Corporación Iberoamericana de Loterias y Apuestas de Estado (#04838)
♦ CIBEP – Association du commerce international de bulbes à fleurs et de plantes (no recent information)
♦ CIBER Network – Centers for International Business Education and Research (internationally oriented national body)
♦ **CIB** ICC Counterfeiting Intelligence Bureau (#11043)
♦ **CIB** International Council for Research and Innovation in Building and Construction (#13069)
♦ CIB / see International Grains Council (#13731)
♦ **CIBJO** CIBJO – The World Jewellery Confederation (#03923)
♦ **CIBJO** Confédération internationale de la bijouterie, joaillerie, orfèvrerie, des diamants, perles et pierres (#03923)

♦ CIBJO – The World Jewellery Confederation (CIBJO) 03923

Confédération internationale de la bijouterie, joaillerie, orfèvrerie, des diamants, perles et pierres (CIBJO) – Internationale Vereinigung Schmuck, Silberwaren, Diamanten, Perlen und Steine – Confederazione Internazionale Oreficeria Gioielleria, Argenteria, Diamanti, Pietre e Perle
Chief Financial Officer Schmiedenplatz 5, Postfach 2237, 3001 Bern 7, Switzerland. T. +41313292072. E-mail: cibjo@cibjo.org.
Pres Viale Berengario 19, 20149 Milan MI, Italy. T. +39249977098. E-mail: communications_1@cibjo.org.
URL: http://www.cibjo.org/
History 1926, Paris (France). Founded to represent and advance the interests of the jewellery trade in Europe. Restructured, 1961. Former names and other names: *Bureau international des associations de fabricants, grossistes et détaillants de bijouterie et argenterie (BIBOA)* – former; *International Bureau of Associations of Manufacturers, Wholesalers and Retailers of Jewellery, Gold and Silver Ware* – former; *Internationales Büro der Fabrikanten-, Grossisten- und Einzelhändlerverbände des Juwelen- und Edelmetallfaches* – former; *Ufficio Internazionale delle Associazioni di Fabbricanti, Grossisti e Dettaglianti di Gioielleria, Oreficeria e Argenteria* – former; *International Confederation of Jewellery, Silverware, Diamonds, Pearls and Stones* – alias. Registration: Switzerland. **Aims** Encourage harmonization, promote international cooperation in the jewellery industry and consider issues which concern the *trade* worldwide, in particular protection of consumer confidence in the industry. **Structure** Assembly of Delegates; Board of Directors; Executive Committee. Sectors (3): Sector A – Gem Materials/Trade/Laboratories; Sector B – Jewellery Distribution; Sector C – Manufacturing/Technology/Precious Metals. Supported by Commissions. **Languages** English. **Staff** Secretariat. **Finance** Sources: meeting proceeds; members' dues. **Activities** Advocacy/lobbying/activism; events/meetings; knowledge management/information dissemination; standards/guidelines. **Events** *Congress* Dubai (United Arab Emirates) 2021, *Congress* Dubai (United Arab Emirates) 2020, *Annual Congress* Manama (Bahrain) 2019, *Annual Congress* Bogota (Colombia) 2018, *Annual Congress* Bangkok (Thailand) 2017. **Publications** *CIBJO Blue Books*.
Members National associations in 38 countries and territories:
Armenia, Australia, Austria, Bahrain, Belgium, Brazil, Canada, China, Cook Is, Denmark, France, Germany, Greece, Hong Kong, India, Israel, Italy, Japan, Korea Rep, Lithuania, Netherlands, New Zealand, Norway, Panama, Peru, Polynesia Fr, Portugal, Russia, Saudi Arabia, Slovenia, South Africa, Sri Lanka, Switzerland, Thailand, UK, Ukraine, United Arab Emirates, USA.
Commercial members in 16 countries and territories:
Australia, Belgium, Canada, China, France, Germany, Hong Kong, Italy, Madagascar, Polynesia Fr, Russia, Taiwan, Türkiye, UK, United Arab Emirates, USA.
Consultative Status Consultative status granted from: *ECOSOC (#05331)* (Special). **NGO Relations** In liaison with technical committees of: *International Organization for Standardization (ISO, #14473)*.
[2022/XD9472/t/**C**]

- ♦ **CIBMTR** Center for International Blood and Marrow Transplant Research (#03645)
- ♦ **CIBP** Confederazione Internazionale delle Banche Popolari (#12867)
- ♦ CIBPD – Centro Internacional Bancaja para la Paz y el Desarrollo (internationally oriented national body)
- ♦ CIBR – Centre for International Business Research (internationally oriented national body)
- ♦ CIBS – Conferencia Interamericana de Bienestar Social (inactive)
- ♦ **CIBV** Consejo Internacional de Buena Vecindad (#13728)
- ♦ **CICAA** Comisión Internacional para la Conservación del Atún Atlantico (#12675)
- ♦ CICA – Centro Internazionale Civiltà dell'Acqua (internationally oriented national body)
- ♦ **CICA** Coloquios Internacionales sobre Cerebro y Agresión (#12653)
- ♦ CICA – Comité international catholique des aveugles (inactive)
- ♦ **CICA** Confederation of International Contractors Associations (#04558)
- ♦ **CICA** Confédération internationale du crédit agricole (#04560)
- ♦ **CICA** Conference on Interaction and Confidence-Building Measures in Asia (#04609)
- ♦ CICA – Conférence internationale des contrôles d'assurance des Etats africains (inactive)
- ♦ **CICAD** Comisión Interamericana para el Control del Abuso de Drogas (#11429)
- ♦ **CICAE** Confédération Internationale des Cinémas d'Art-et-d'Essai (#12847)
- ♦ CICAFOC / see Asociación Coordinadora Indigena y Campesina de Agroforesteria Comunitaria (#02120)
- ♦ **CICAIA** Comité international des associations d'industriels aérospatiaux (#12956)
- ♦ CICA / see International Colloquium on Conflict and Aggression (#12653)
- ♦ CICA International Foundation / see International Colloquium on Conflict and Aggression (#12653)
- ♦ CICAL – Centro de Intercambios y Cooperación para America Latina (internationally oriented national body)
- ♦ **CIC-Angkor** Comité international de coordination pour la sauvegarde et le développement du site historique d'Angkor (#12954)
- ♦ CICAP – Centro Interamericano de Cooperación y Capacitación (internationally oriented national body)
- ♦ **CICAP** Consejo Internacional para la Colaboración en los Analisis de Plaguicidas (#04099)
- ♦ CICAR – Cooperative Investigations of the Caribbean and Adjacent Areas (inactive)
- ♦ **CI** CARE International (#03429)
- ♦ **CI** Caritas Internationalis (#03580)
- ♦ CICAT – Centre for International Cooperation and Appropriate Technology (internationally oriented national body)
- ♦ CICATIRS / see Coatings Societies International (#04075)
- ♦ CICB / see Benelux Inter-Parliamentary Consultative Council (#03201)
- ♦ **CICB** Cecchetti International – Classical Ballet (#03622)
- ♦ CICB – Centro Internacional de Ciencias Biológicas (internationally oriented national body)
- ♦ CICB / see International Union of Building Centres (#15761)
- ♦ **CICCA** Committee for International Cooperation between Cotton Associations (#04265)
- ♦ CIC – Caribbean Investment Corporation (inactive)
- ♦ CICC – Centre for International Cooperation and Computerization (internationally oriented national body)
- ♦ **CICC** Centre international de criminologie comparée (#12482)
- ♦ **CICC** Coalition for the International Criminal Court (#04062)
- ♦ CIC / see CEC European Managers (#03623)
- ♦ CIC – Center on International Cooperation, New York NY (internationally oriented national body)
- ♦ **CIC** Centre international de calcul (#12839)
- ♦ CIC – Centro Internazionale Crocevia (internationally oriented national body)
- ♦ **CIC** Climate Investment Coalition (#04014)
- ♦ **CIC** Comité Intergubernamental Coordinador de los Paises de la Cuenca del Plata (#04172)
- ♦ **CIC** Comité Internacional de Coordinación para la Iniciación a la Ciencia y al Desarrollo de Actividades Cientificas Extraescolares (#12953)
- ♦ CIC – Comité international des camps (no recent information)
- ♦ **CIC** Comité international de coordination pour l'initiation à la science et le développement des activités scientifiques extra-scolaires (#12953)
- ♦ CIC – Confédération internationale d'amateurs et éleveurs de canaris (inactive)
- ♦ CIC – Confédération internationale du cheval (inactive)
- ♦ CIC – Congregation of the Immaculate Conception (religious order)
- ♦ **CIC** Conseil international de la chasse et de la conservation du gibier (#13024)
- ♦ **CIC** Consejo Internacional de Curtidores (#13084)
- ♦ **CIC** Consiglio Internazionale dei Conciatori (#13084)
- ♦ CICD – Campaign for International Cooperation and Disarmament (internationally oriented national body)
- ♦ CICD – Centre for International Cooperation and Development (internationally oriented national body)
- ♦ **CICD** Council for International Congresses of Dipterology (#04899)
- ♦ CICDI – Centre d'information canadien sur les diplômes internationaux (internationally oriented national body)
- ♦ CICD / see International Society for Digestive Surgery (#15060)
- ♦ **CiCea** Children's Identity and Citizenship European Association (#03877)
- ♦ CICEANA – Centro de Información y Comunicación Ambiental de Norte América (internationally oriented national body)
- ♦ CICE – Centre for the Study of International Cooperation in Education (internationally oriented national body)
- ♦ **CICE** Comisión Iberoamericana de Calidad Educativa (#04134)
- ♦ **CICE** Conferencia Internacional Católica de Escultismo (#12453)
- ♦ CICERO – Centre for International Climate and Environmental Research, Oslo (internationally oriented national body)
- ♦ **CICERO** Cicero League of International Lawyers (#03924)
- ♦ Cicero Foundation (internationally oriented national body)

♦ Cicero League of International Lawyers (CICERO) 03924

Contact Pinewood Lodge, Warren Lane, Oxshott, KT22 0ST, UK. T. +441372843078. E-mail: mail@ciceroleague.com.
Registered Office Regent's Court, Princess Street, Hull, HU2 8BA, UK.
URL: https://ciceroleague.com/

History Registered as a company limited by guarantee in England: 8546808. **Structure** Board. **Events** *Biannual Conference* Oslo (Norway) 2019.
Members Full in 40 countries and territories:
Austria, Belgium, Brazil, Bulgaria, Cape Verde, Croatia, Cyprus, Czechia, Denmark, England, France, Germany, Greece, Hungary, Indonesia, Ireland, Isle of Man, Israel, Italy, Jersey, Latvia, Malaysia, Mexico, Netherlands, Norway, Poland, Portugal, Romania, Russia, Scotland, Singapore, Slovakia, South Africa, Spain, Sudan, Sweden, Switzerland, Türkiye, United Arab Emirates, USA.
NGO Relations Member of: *Association of International Law Firm Networks (AILFN, #02753).*
[2019/XM8855/**C**]

- ♦ CICETE – China International Centre for Economic and Technical Exchanges (internationally oriented national body)
- ♦ CIC / see European Theological Libraries (#08906)
- ♦ CIC / see Events Industry Council (#09212)
- ♦ **CICG** Committee of the International Children's Games (#04264)
- ♦ **CICG** Conférence internationale catholique du guidisme (#12452)
- ♦ **CICG** Conferencia Internacional Católica del Guidismo (#12452)
- ♦ CICGH – Confederación Iberoamericana de las Ciencias Genealógica y Heraldica (inactive)
- ♦ CIC / see Global Alliance of National Human Rights Institutions (#10214)
- ♦ CICH / see UCL Institute for Global Health
- ♦ CICH – Centre for International Child Health (internationally oriented national body)
- ♦ **CICH** Comité international de la culture du houblon (#13807)
- ♦ CICH – Confederación Internacional Católica de Hospitales (inactive)
- ♦ Cichlid Science (meeting series)
- ♦ **CICIA** Chambre Islamique de Commerce, d'Industrie et d'Agriculture (#16036)
- ♦ CICIAM / see International Council for Industrial and Applied Mathematics (#13032)
- ♦ **CICIAMS** Comité international catholique des infirmières et des assistantes médico-sociales (#12451)
- ♦ CICIBA – Centre international des civilisations Bantu (inactive)
- ♦ CICIC – Canadian Information Centre for International Credentials (internationally oriented national body)
- ♦ **CICI** Comité Internacional de la Cuarta Internacional (#12771)
- ♦ CICI – Commission internationale de la coopération intellectuelle (inactive)
- ♦ **CICIG** Comisión Internacional contra la Impunidad en Guatemala (#12660)
- ♦ CICIH – Confédération internationale catholique des institutions hospitalières (inactive)
- ♦ CICI / see Islamic Chamber of Commerce, Industry and Agriculture (#16036)
- ♦ CICILS / see Global Pulse Confederation (#10562)
- ♦ **CICIND** Comité international des cheminées industrielles (#04173)
- ♦ CIC – International Commission for the Study of Communication Problems (inactive)
- ♦ CICIR – China Institute of Contemporary International Relations (internationally oriented national body)
- ♦ CI – Civitan International (internationally oriented national body)
- ♦ CICJ – Comité international pour la coopération des journalistes (inactive)
- ♦ CICLEF – Centre international de la common law en français, Moncton (internationally oriented national body)
- ♦ Ciclo Norte-Sur (internationally oriented national body)
- ♦ Ciclovias Unidas de las Américas / see Red de Ciclovias Recreativas de las Américas (#18640)
- ♦ CICM – Centre international du crédit mutuel (internationally oriented national body)
- ♦ **CICM** Commission internationale catholique pour les migrations (#12459)
- ♦ CICM – Congregatio Immaculati Cordis Mariae (religious order)
- ♦ **CICM – Europe** Commission Internationale Catholique pour les Migrations – Europe (#12460)
- ♦ **CI** Cobalt Institute (#04076)
- ♦ CICO – Conference of International Catholic Organizations (inactive)
- ♦ CI – Communication Initiative (internationally oriented national body)
- ♦ CI – Communications International (inactive)
- ♦ **CI** Compassion International (#04413)
- ♦ CIC / OMPO / see Oiseaux migrateurs du paléarctique occidental (#17712)
- ♦ CICONADI – Confederación Iberoamericana de Comités, Consejos y Comisiones Nacionales de Discapacidades (no recent information)
- ♦ CICON – International Cancer Immunotherapy Conference (meeting series)
- ♦ CI – Conservation International (internationally oriented national body)
- ♦ **CI** Consumers International (#04773)
- ♦ CI – Cooperación Internacional (internationally oriented national body)

♦ CICOPA-Américas 03925

Pres CONACOOP, Costado Norte Mall San Pedro, San Pedro de Montes de Oca, San José, San José, San José, Costa Rica. T. +5062535544.
URL: http://www.cicopa.coop/

History Founded Nov 1998, Montevideo (Uruguay), at constituent assembly (the first meeting of producers' cooperatives from the American region), when statutes were approved, Declaration of Principles – *'Charta Montevideo'* – accepted and work plan agreed. A regional committee of *International Organisation of Industrial and Service Cooperatives (CICOPA, #14429).* **Structure** General Assembly. [2016/XE4362/**E**]

- ♦ CICOPA / see International Organisation of Industrial and Service Cooperatives (#14429)
- ♦ **CICOPA** International Organisation of Industrial and Service Cooperatives (#14429)
- ♦ CICOP – Centro Internacional para la Conservación del Patrimonio (internationally oriented national body)
- ♦ CICOPS / see Commissione Cooperazione Internazionale per lo Sviluppo
- ♦ CICOPS – Commissione Cooperazione Internazionale per lo Sviluppo (internationally oriented national body)
- ♦ CICOPS – Committee for International Cooperation and Development (internationally oriented national body)
- ♦ CI – CORD International (internationally oriented national body)
- ♦ **CICOS** Commission internationale du Bassin Congo-Oubangui-Sangha (#12674)
- ♦ CICP – Cambodian Institute for Cooperation and Peace (internationally oriented national body)
- ♦ CICP – Centre international de culture populaire, Paris (internationally oriented national body)
- ♦ CICP – Comité Internacional para la Cooperación de las Periodistas (inactive)
- ♦ CICP / see International Confederation of Popular Banks (#12867)
- ♦ CICPLB / see International Committee for Animal Recording (#12746)
- ♦ CICPMC – China International Council for the Promotion of Multinational Corporations (internationally oriented national body)
- ♦ **CICPP** Commission internationale consultative principe de précaution (#11591)
- ♦ CICP – United Nations Centre for International Crime Prevention, Vienna (inactive)
- ♦ CICR / see Association Rencontre CEFIR
- ♦ **CICR** Comité Internacional de la Cruz Roja (#12799)
- ♦ **CICR** Comité international de la Croix-Rouge (#12799)
- ♦ **CICSAL** Congregation for Institutes of Consecrated Life and Societies of Apostolic Life (#04671)
- ♦ **CICS** Conférence internationale catholique du scoutisme (#12453)
- ♦ CICSE – Comité international de coopération syndicale des enseignants (inactive)
- ♦ CICSENE – Centro Italiano di Collaborazione per lo Sviluppo Edilizio delle Nazioni Emergenti (internationally oriented national body)
- ♦ **CICTA** Commission internationale pour la conservation des thonidés de l'Atlantique (#12675)
- ♦ CICT – Centre for International Courts and Tribunals (internationally oriented national body)
- ♦ CICT – Conférence des Institutions catholiques de Théologie (see: #13381)
- ♦ **CICT** Conseil international du cinéma, de la télévision et de la communication audiovisuelle (#13022)
- ♦ **CICTE** Comité Interamericano Contra el Terrorismo (#11412)
- ♦ CIC / see World Hairdressers' Organization (#21550)
- ♦ CICY – Centre international de cyto-cybernétique (inactive)
- ♦ CICYP – Consejo Interamericano de Comercio y Producción (no recent information)
- ♦ CIDAC – Centro de Informação e Documentação Amilcar Cabral (internationally oriented national body)
- ♦ CIDA – Centro Interamericano de Desarrollo de Archivos (inactive)
- ♦ CIDADEC – Confédération internationale des associations d'experts et de conseils (inactive)
- ♦ Cidades Atlânticas (#03008)
- ♦ CIDA / see International Society of Arachnology (#14935)
- ♦ **CIDAJAL** Centro Internacional de Desarrollo de Albergues Juveniles de América Latina (#03804)
- ♦ CIDALC – Comité international pour la diffusion des arts et des lettres par le cinéma (no recent information)
- ♦ **CIDAPA** Comité Iberoamericano para el Desarrollo y Aplicación de los Plasticos en Agricultura (#04168)
- ♦ **CIDAP** Centro Interamericano de Artesanias y Artes Populares (#03801)
- ♦ CID – Association de consultants internationaux en droits de l'homme (inactive)
- ♦ CIDB – Cooperative Insurance Development Bureau (inactive)
- ♦ CIDC – Canadian International Demining Corps (internationally oriented national body)
- ♦ **CIDC** Centre islamique pour le développement du commerce (#16035)
- ♦ **CIDCDF** Conférence internationale des doyens des facultés de chirurgie dentaire d'expression totalement ou partiellement française (#04615)
- ♦ **CIDCE** Centre international de droit comparé de l'environnement (#12483)

- ♦ CID – Center for International Development, Harvard University (internationally oriented national body)
- ♦ CIDC / see International Association of Legal Science (#11997)
- ♦ CIDCM – Center for International Development and Conflict Management (internationally oriented national body)
- ♦ **CID** Comité international de Dachau (#04174)
- ♦ CID – Comité international des dérivés tensio-actifs (inactive)
- ♦ CID – Commission internationale de diplomatique (see: #12777)
- ♦ **CID** Conseil international de la danse (#13130)
- ♦ CID – Council for International Development (internationally oriented national body)
- ♦ CIDEAL / see Fundación CIDEAL de Cooperación e Investigación
- ♦ CIDEAL Foundation for Cooperation and Research (internationally oriented national body)
- ♦ CIDECALL – Centro Internacional de Demonstración y Capacitación en Aprovechamiento de Agua de Lluvia (internationally oriented national body)
- ♦ CIDECALLI / see Centro Internacional de Demonstración y Capacitación en Aprovechamiento de Agua de Lluvia
- ♦ CIDEC – Confederación Iberoamericana de Estudiantes Católicos (inactive)
- ♦ CIDEC – Conseil international pour le développement du cuivre (inactive)
- ♦ CIDE – Comité international pour la dignité de l'enfant (internationally oriented national body)
- ♦ **CIDE** Commission intersyndicale des déshydrateurs européens (#06896)
- ♦ **CIDE** Conseil international du droit de l'environnement (#13018)
- ♦ **CIDECT** Comité international pour le développement et l'étude de la construction tubulaire (#04266)
- ♦ **CIDECT** Committee for International Development and Education on Construction of Tubular Structures (#04266)
- ♦ CIDEF / see Centre international de documentation et d'échanges de la Francophonie – L'Agora francophone internationale
- ♦ **CIDEFA** Conférence internationale des directeurs et doyens des établissements supérieurs d'expression française des sciences de l'agriculture et de l'alimentation (#04613)
- ♦ CIDEF-AFI – Centre international de documentation et d'échanges de la Francophonie – L'Agora francophone internationale (internationally oriented national body)
- ♦ **CIDEGEF** Conférence internationale des dirigeants des institutions d'enseignements supérieur de gestion d'expression française (#04614)
- ♦ CIDEHUM – Centro Internacional para los Derechos Humanos de los Migrantes (internationally oriented national body)
- ♦ CIDEM – Consejo Interamericano de Música (no recent information)
- ♦ CIDEP – Centre international de documentation concernant les expressions plastiques (inactive)
- ♦ CIDER – Center for International and Development Economics Research, Berkeley CA (internationally oriented national body)
- ♦ CIDESA – Centre international de documentation économique et sociale africaine (inactive)
- ♦ CIDESC – Centro Internacional de Direitos Económicos, Sociais e Culturais (internationally oriented national body)
- ♦ CIDES – Centro de Investigación para el Desarrollo Económico-Social (no recent information)
- ♦ CIDESCO / see Comité international d'esthétique et de cosmétologie (#04175)
- ♦ **CIDESCO** Comité international d'esthétique et de cosmétologie (#04175)
- ♦ **CIDES** Comisión Interamericana de Desarrollo Social (#04135)
- ♦ **CIDEU** Centro Iberoamericano de Desarrollo Estratégico Urbano (#03800)
- ♦ CIDH / see Corte Interamericana de Derechos Humanos (#04851)
- ♦ CIDHAL – Communicación, Intercambio y Desarrollo Humano en América Latina (internationally oriented national body)
- ♦ CIDH – Centro Internacional para el Desarrollo Humano (internationally oriented national body)
- ♦ CIDH – Circulo Internacional de Directores de Hotel (unconfirmed)
- ♦ **CIDH** Comisión Interamericana de Derechos Humanos (#11411)
- ♦ **CIDH** Commission internationale de démographie historique (#12684)
- ♦ CIDIAT – Centro Interamericano de Desarrollo e Investigación Ambiental y Territorial (internationally oriented national body)
- ♦ CIDICCO – Centro Internacional de Información sobre Cultivos de Cobertura (internationally oriented national body)
- ♦ CIDI – Center for International Disaster Information (internationally oriented national body)
- ♦ **CIDI** Consejo Interamericano para el Desarrollo Integral (#11423)
- ♦ CIDIE – Comité des institutions internationales de développement sur l'environnement (no recent information)
- ♦ CIDIE – Committee of International Development Institutions on the Environment (no recent information)
- ♦ CIDI / see International Young Catholic Students (#15926)
- ♦ CIDIN – Centre for International Development Issues, Nijmegen (internationally oriented national body)
- ♦ CIDIP – Conferencia Especializada Interamericana sobre derecho Internacional Privado (meeting series)
- ♦ CIDL – Colloque international sur la didactique des langues secondes (meeting series)
- ♦ CIDMAA / see Alternatives – Action and Communication Network for International Development
- ♦ **CIDMEF** Conférence internationale des doyens des facultés de médecine d'expression française (#04616)
- ♦ **Cidmy** Centre international de documentation Marguerite Yourcenar (#03751)
- ♦ CIDOB Foundation – Centre for International Information and Documentation, Barcelona (internationally oriented national body)
- ♦ CIDOB Research, Teaching, Documentation and Dissemination Centre for International Relations and Development, Barcelona / see Centre for International Information and Documentation, Barcelona
- ♦ CIDOC – Comité international pour la documentation de l'ICOM (see: #13051)
- ♦ CIDO – Centre International d'Ostéopathie (internationally oriented national body)
- ♦ CIDOEC – Centre for International Documentation on Organized and Economic Crime, Cambridge (internationally oriented national body)
- ♦ CIDP – Confédération internationale pour le désarmement et la paix (inactive)
- ♦ **CIDPHARMEF** Conférence internationale des doyens des facultés de pharmacie d'expression française (#04617)
- ♦ CIDR – Centre international de développement et de recherche (internationally oriented national body)
- ♦ **CIDREE** Consortium of Institutions for Development and Research in Education in Europe (#04749)
- ♦ **CIDS** Centre international pour les droits syndicaux (#12525)
- ♦ **CIDS** Centro Internacional para los Derechos Sindicales (#12525)

♦ CIDSE (CIDSE) 03926

Gen Sec Rue Stévin 16, 1000 Brussels, Belgium. T. +3222307722. E-mail: postmaster@cidse.org.
Communications Assistant address not obtained.
URL: http://www.cidse.org/

History 18 Nov 1965, Rome (Italy). Commenced activities 1 Oct 1966. Former names and other names: *International Cooperation for Socio-Economic Development* – former; *Coopération internationale pour le développement et la solidarité* – former; *Cooperación Internacional para el Desarrollo Socio-Económico* – former; *Internationale Arbeitsgemeinschaft für Sozial-Wirtschaftliche Entwicklung* – former; *Coopération internationale pour le développement et la solidarité (CIDSE)* – former (10 Sep 1981); *International Cooperation for Development and Solidarity* – former (10 Sep 1981); *Internationale Arbeitsgemeinschaft für Entwicklung und Solidarität* – former (10 Sep 1981); *Cooperación Internacional para el Desarrollo y la Solidaridad* – former (10 Sep 1981); *International Alliance of Catholic Development Agencies (CIDSE)* – former (2009); *CIDSE – Together for Global Justice* – full title. Registration: Banque-Carrefour des Entreprises, Start date: 16 Jul 1967, Belgium; EU Transparency Register, No/ID: 61263518557-92. **Aims** Work for transformational change to end poverty and inequalities, challenging systemic injustice, inequity, destruction of nature and promoting just and environmentally sustainable alternatives. **Structure** Board of Directors (meets annually); Executive Committee; General Secretariat, headed by Secretary General. **Languages** English, French, German, Spanish. **Staff** 13.70 FTE, paid; 0.00 FTE, voluntary. **Finance** Sources: grants; members' dues. Supported by: *European Commission (EC, #06633)*; *KR Foundation (#16208)*; *Porticus*. Annual budget: 1,534,929 EUR (2021). **Activities** Advocacy/lobbying/activism; awareness raising; events/meetings; projects/programmes. **Events** *Workshop on Climate and Agriculture* Brussels (Belgium) 2016, *Civil society forum* Doha (Qatar) 2008, *International conference for the reform of international institutions* Geneva (Switzerland) 2006, *Meeting on EU-ACP relations / Half-Yearly General Assembly* Brussels (Belgium) 2000, *Joint NGO workshop / Half-Yearly General Assembly* Brussels (Belgium) 1993. **Publications** *CIDSE News* (5 a year). Annual activities report; policy papers.

Members Ordinary members – 18 organizations:
Broederlijk Delen (Broederlijk Delen); *Catholic Agency for Overseas Development (CAFOD)*; *Catholic Lenten Fund*; *Catholic Organization for Relief and Development (Cordaid)*; Christian Children Communities Movement (eRko); *Comité Catholique contre la Faim et pour le Développement-Terre Solidaire (CCFD-Terre Solidaire)*; *Development and Peace (CCODP)*; *Entraide et fraternité*; *Federazione Organismi Cristiani Servizio Internazionale Volontario (Volontari nel Mondo – FOCSIV)*; *Fondation Partage Luxembourg*; Fundação Fé e Cooperação (FEC); *German Catholic Bishops' Organisation for Development Cooperation (MISEREOR)*; *Koordinierungstelle der Österreichischen Bischofskonferenz für Internationale Entwicklung und Mission (KOO)*; *Manos Unidas*; *Maryknoll Office for Global Concern (MOGC)*; *Scottish Catholic International Aid Fund (SCIAF)*; *Trocaire – Catholic Agency for World Development*; Vastenactie.
Permanent observers (2), listed in this Yearbook:
Bischöfliche Aktion ADVENIAT; *Caritas Internationalis (CI, #03580)*.

Consultative Status Consultative status granted from: *ECOSOC (#05331)* (General); *FAO (#09260)* (Liaison Status); *UNCTAD (#20285)* (General Category); *ILO (#11123)* (Special List). **IGO Relations** Accredited by (1): *United Nations Office at Vienna (UNOV, #20604)*. Observer status with (1): *United Nations Framework Convention on Climate Change (UNFCCC, 1992)*. **NGO Relations** Member of (6): *Climate Action Network Europe (CAN Europe, #04001)*; *Confédération européenne des ong d'urgence et de développement (CONCORD, #04547)*; European Laudato Si Alliance – ELSIA; *Forum of Catholic Inspired NGOs (#09905)*; *Laudato Si' Movement (#16403)*; *World Social Forum (WSF, #21797)*. [2023.02.13/XC1708/y/**F**]

- ♦ CIDSE / see CIDSE (#03926)
- ♦ CIDSE – Together for Global Justice / see CIDSE (#03926)
- ♦ CIDSM – Cambridge Italian Dialect Syntax-Morphology Meeting (meeting series)
- ♦ CIDT – Centre for International Development and Training (internationally oriented national body)
- ♦ CIDUI – Congrés Internacional de Docència Universitària i Innovació (meeting series)
- ♦ CIDUI – Congreso Internacional de Docencia Universitaria e Innovación (meeting series)
- ♦ CIE / see Toute l'Europe
- ♦ **CIEA** Conseil international d'éducation des adultes (#12983)
- ♦ **CIEAEM** Commission internationale pour l'étude et l'amélioration de l'enseignement des mathématiques (#12732)
- ♦ CIEAM / see International Commission for the Study and Improvement of Mathematics Teaching (#12732)
- ♦ CIEAMO – Consortium interuniversitaire pour les études arabes et moyen-orientales (internationally oriented national body)
- ♦ **CiE** Association Computability in Europe (#02444)
- ♦ **CIEBP** Centre d'information sur l'éducation bilingue et plurilingue (#11195)
- ♦ CIECA – Centro de Investigación Economica para el Caribe (internationally oriented national body)
- ♦ **CIECA** Commission internationale des examens de conduite automobile (#12678)
- ♦ CIECA / see International Commission for Driver Testing (#12678)
- ♦ **CIECA** International Commission for Driver Testing (#12678)
- ♦ **CIECA** Internationale Kommission für Fahrerlaubnisprüfungen (#12678)
- ♦ CIE – Cartographie des invertébrés européens (inactive)
- ♦ CIEC / see Centre international scientifique des fertilisants (#03767)
- ♦ **CIEC** Centre international scientifique des fertilisants (#03767)
- ♦ **CIEC** Comité international des études créoles (#12757)
- ♦ **CIEC** Commission internationale de l'état civil (#12671)
- ♦ **CIEC** Confederación Interamericana de Educación Católica (#11403)
- ♦ **CIEC** Conseil international d'Eglises chrétiennes (#13005)
- ♦ CIEC – Conseil international des employeurs du commerce (inactive)
- ♦ CIEC – Conseil international d'études canadiennes (internationally oriented national body)
- ♦ CIE – Center for International Education (internationally oriented national body)
- ♦ CIE – Center for International Education, Milwaukee WI (internationally oriented national body)
- ♦ CIE – Centro d'Iniziativa per l'Europa (internationally oriented national body)
- ♦ CIE – Centrum Internationale Erfgoedactiviteiten (internationally oriented national body)
- ♦ **CIE** Comisión Interamericana de Educación (#04136)
- ♦ CIE – Comissão Inter-Africana de Estatistica (inactive)
- ♦ **CIE** Commission Internationale de l'Eclairage (#04219)
- ♦ **CIE** Commission internationale de l'Escaut (#12727)
- ♦ CIE – Confédération internationale des étudiants (inactive)
- ♦ CIE – Conseil international de l'étain (inactive)
- ♦ **CIE** Consejo Internacional de Enfermeras (#13054)
- ♦ **CIE** Cycling Industries Europe (#04988)
- ♦ CIEDEL – Centre international d'études pour le développement local (internationally oriented national body)
- ♦ **CIEE** Consejo Internacional de Educación para la Enseñanza (#13016)
- ♦ **CIEE** Council on International Educational Exchange (#04901)
- ♦ CIEFAP – Centro de Investigación y Extensión Forestal Andino Patagónico (internationally oriented national body)
- ♦ **CIEF** Conseil international d'études francophones (#04691)
- ♦ **CIEF** Financial Inclusion Equity Council (#09766)
- ♦ CIEF / see Instituto de Ciencias Familiares (#11330)
- ♦ **CIEFR** Centre international d'études de la formation religieuse (#12519)
- ♦ CIEH – Comité interafricain d'études hydrauliques (inactive)
- ♦ **CIEHS** Commission internationale des études historiques slaves (#04220)
- ♦ **CIEHV** Conseil international pour l'éducation des handicapés de la vue (#13015)
- ♦ CIEI – Centro de Investigaciones de Economia Internacional, Habana (internationally oriented national body)
- ♦ CIE / see Inter-American Scout Committee (#11445)
- ♦ **CIEIP** Conseil international pour l'étude des îles du Pacifique (#13079)
- ♦ CIEI / see World Environment Center (#21386)
- ♦ CIEJD – Centro de Informação Europeia Jacques Delors (internationally oriented national body)
- ♦ CIEL – Center for International Environmental Law (internationally oriented national body)
- ♦ CIEL – Centre international d'études des langues, Le Relecq-Kerhuon (internationally oriented national body)
- ♦ CIEL de Strasbourg (internationally oriented national body)
- ♦ CIELT – Centre International d'Etudes sur le Linceul de Turin (unconfirmed)
- ♦ **CIEMAL** Consejo de Iglesias Evangélicas Metodistas de América Latina y el Caribe (#04714)
- ♦ CIEM – Centro de Investigaciones de la Economía Mundial (internationally oriented national body)
- ♦ CIEM – Centro de Investigaciones de la Economia Mundial, Habana (internationally oriented national body)
- ♦ **CIEM** Comité international d'études morisques (#12788)
- ♦ **CIEM** Commission internationale de l'enseignement mathématique (#12700)
- ♦ **CIEM** Confédération internationale des éditeurs de musique (#12864)
- ♦ **CIEM** Conseil international pour l'exploration de la mer (#13021)
- ♦ **CIEM** Convention internationale des écoles de marionnettes (#12938)
- ♦ **CIEMEN** Centre Internacional Escarré per a les Minories Etniques i les Nacions (#05535)

♦ CIEMI – Centre d'information et d'études sur les migrations internationales (internationally oriented national body)
♦ CIEM / see International Council for the Exploration of the Sea (#13021)
♦ CIENCE – Commission internationale d'études de normalisation comptable économique (inactive)
♦ CIEN – Comisión Interamericana de Energia Nuclear (inactive)
♦ CIEN – Comissão Interamericana de Energia Nuclear (inactive)
♦ CIEN – Commission interaméricaine de l'énergie nucléaire (inactive)
♦ CIENES – Centro Interamericano de Enseñanza de Estadistica (no recent information)
♦ Los Cien para Seguir Viviendo/Por el Desarme Mundial y la Paz (internationally oriented national body)
♦ CIEPA – Comité international de l'éducation de plein air (inactive)
♦ CIEP – Centre international d'études pédagogiques, Sèvres (internationally oriented national body)
♦ **CIEP** Commission internationale sur l'éducation en physique (#12714)
♦ CIEPI – Comité interprofessionnel européen des professions intellectuelles (inactive)
♦ **CIEPO** Comité international d'études pré-ottomanes et ottomanes (#12795)
♦ **CIEPS** Centre international de l'ISSN (#16069)
♦ CIEPS / see ISSN International Centre (#16069)
♦ **CIEPSS** Conseil international pour l'éducation physique et la science du sport (#13077)
♦ **CIER** Comisión de Integración Energética Regional (#18764)
♦ **CIER** Comissão de Integração Energética Regional (#18764)
♦ CIER – Conseil international des économies régionales (inactive)
♦ **CIEREA** Conférence des institutions d'enseignement et de recherche économiques et de gestion en Afrique (#04608)
♦ CIESC – Comparative and International Education Society of Canada (internationally oriented national body)
♦ CIES – Centre for International Economic Studies, Adelaide (internationally oriented national body)
♦ CIES – Centre international d'étude du sport (internationally oriented national body)
♦ CIES – Centro Informazione e Educazione allo Sviluppo (internationally oriented national body)
♦ CIES – Collège international d'étude de la statique (internationally oriented national body)
♦ CIES – Comparative and International Education Society (internationally oriented national body)
♦ CIES – Congreso Iberoamericano de Energia Solar (meeting series)
♦ CIES – The Food Business Forum / see The Consumer Goods Forum (#04772)
♦ CIESIN – Center for International Earth Science Information Network (internationally oriented national body)
♦ **CIESM** Commission internationale pour l'exploration scientifique de la Mer Méditerranée (#16674)
♦ **CIESM** The Mediterranean Science Commission (#16674)
♦ **CIESPAL** Centro Internacional de Estudios Superiores de Comunicación para América Latina (#03806)
♦ **CIESS** Centro Interamericano de Estudios de Seguridad Social (#03803)
♦ CIESURP – Centro Interamericano de Estudios Superiores de Relaciones Públicas y Opinión Pública (internationally oriented national body)
♦ CIETAC – China International Economic and Trade Arbitration Commission (internationally oriented national body)
♦ CIETB – Centre intercontinental d'études de techniques biologiques (inactive)
♦ **CIET** Centro Internacional de Ecologia Tropical (#03805)
♦ CIET International – Community Information, Empowerment and Transparency (internationally oriented national body)
♦ Ciett / see World Employment Confederation (#21376)
♦ CIET/UNESCO / see Centro Internacional de Ecologia Tropical (#03805)
♦ CIEUA – Congrès international de l'enseignement universitaire pour adultes (inactive)
♦ CIEURP – Conférence internationale pour l'enseignement universitaire des relations publiques (inactive)
♦ **CIFAA** Committee for Inland Fisheries and Aquaculture of Africa (#04261)
♦ **CIFA** Comité international de recherche et d'étude de facteurs de l'ambiance (#12801)
♦ CIFA / see Committee for Inland Fisheries and Aquaculture of Africa (#04261)
♦ **CIFA** Consortium of Institutes on Family in the Asian Region (#04747)
♦ CIFA – Convention of Independent Financial Advisors (internationally oriented national body)
♦ CIFAS – Congrès international francophone sur l'agression sexuelle (meeting series)
♦ CIFCA – Confédération internationale des installateurs de matériel frigorifique et de conditionnement d'air (inactive)
♦ **CIF** Centre international de formation de l'OIT (#15717)
♦ **CIF** Centro Internacional de Fisica (#03807)
♦ **CIF** Climate Investment Funds (#04015)
♦ **CIF** Comité international pour la formation de l'ICOMOS (#11084)
♦ CIF – Confederación Iberoamericana de Fundaciones (no recent information)
♦ CIF – Confédération internationale des fonctionnaires (no recent information)
♦ **CIF** Conseil international des femmes (#13093)
♦ CIF / see Council of International Fellowship (#04902)
♦ **CIF** Council of International Fellowship (#04902)
♦ CIF – Cultural Integration Fellowship (internationally oriented national body)
♦ CIF – Curatio International Foundation (internationally oriented national body)
♦ CIFDHA – Centre d'Information et de Formation en matière de Droits Humains en Afrique (internationally oriented national body)
♦ **CIFDUF** Conférence internationale des facultés de droit ayant en commun l'usage du français (#04618)
♦ **CIFE** Centre international de formation européenne (#03755)
♦ CIFE – Centro Italiano di Formazione Europea (internationally oriented national body)
♦ CIFEDHOP – Centre international de formation à l'enseignement des droits de l'homme et de la paix, Genève (see: #21184)
♦ **CIFEG** Centre international pour la formation et les échanges en géosciences (#03754)
♦ **CIFEJ** Centre international du film pour l'enfance et la jeunesse (#12493)
♦ CIFF – Children's Investment Fund Foundation (internationally oriented national body)
♦ CIF / see Fédération internationale culturelle féminine (#09625)
♦ CIFF / see International Committee for Research and Study of Environmental Factors (#12801)
♦ CIFFT – Comité International des Festivals du Film Touristique (unconfirmed)
♦ CIFFT – International Committee of Tourism Film Festivals (unconfirmed)
♦ CIFF-UK / see Children's Investment Fund Foundation
♦ CIFF-USA / see Children's Investment Fund Foundation
♦ CIF / see Groupe International Francophone pour la Formation aux Classifications du Handicap (#10749)
♦ CIFMA / see Centro Internacional de Ciencias, Cuernavaca
♦ CIFMO / see Centro Internacional de Ciencias, Cuernavaca
♦ **CIFOR** Center for International Forestry Research (#03646)
♦ CIFOTIE – Centro Internacional de Formação dos Trabalhadores da Indústria e Energia (internationally oriented national body)
♦ CIFPCA – Confederación Iberoamericana y Filipina de Productores de Caña de Azúcar (no recent information)
♦ **CIFP** Comité international pour le fair play (#12769)
♦ CIFRES – Centre international de formation et de recherche en sexualité (internationally oriented national body)
♦ CIFS – Copenhagen Institute for Futures Studies (internationally oriented national body)
♦ CIFS / see International Nut and Dried Fruit Council Foundation (#14387)
♦ **CIFTA** Comité international des fédérations théâtrales d'amateurs de culture latine (#04176)
♦ CIFU – Congressus Internationalis Fenno-Ugristarum (meeting series)
♦ **CIGAR** Comparative International Governmental Accounting Research Network (#04411)
♦ **CIGB** Commission internationale des grands barrages (#12696)
♦ **CIGEPS** Comité intergouvernemental pour l'éducation physique et le sport (#11475)
♦ **CIGGB** Centre international de génie génétique et de biotechnologie (#12494)
♦ **CIGH** Confédération internationale de généalogie et d'héraldique (#04561)
♦ CIGI – Centre for International Governance Innovation (internationally oriented national body)
♦ CIG / see International Association of Craniofacial Identification (#11823)
♦ CIG / see International Tar Association (#15655)
♦ **CIGIOC** Coordinamento Internazionale della Gioventù Operaia Cristiana (#12960)
♦ CIGNL – Contractors International Group on Nuclear Liability (internationally oriented national body)
♦ CIGP – Conférence internationale sur la guerre politique (meeting series)
♦ **CIGR** Commission internationale du génie rural (#12661)
♦ **CIGRE** Conseil international des grands réseaux électriques (#13040)
♦ CIGR / see International Commission of Agricultural and Biosystems Engineering (#12661)
♦ CIGS – Centre international de gérontologie sociale (inactive)
♦ **CIGV** Club international des grands voyageurs (#15915)
♦ **CIHA** Comité international d'histoire de l'art (#04177)
♦ **CIHAE** Commission internationale pour l'histoire des assemblées d'Etats (#12689)
♦ CIHC – Center for International Humanitarian Cooperation (internationally oriented national body)
♦ CIH – Centre for International Health, Bergen (internationally oriented national body)
♦ CIHCLB – Congresso Internacional da História da Construção Luso-Brasileira (meeting series)
♦ CIHD / see UCL Institute for Global Health
♦ **CIHEAM** Centre international de hautes études agronomiques méditerranéennes (#03927)
♦ **CIHEAM** CIHEAM – International Centre for Advanced Mediterranean Agronomic Studies (#03927)
♦ CIHEAM-IAMM / see Mediterranean Agronomic Institute of Montpellier (#16643)

♦ CIHEAM – International Centre for Advanced Mediterranean Agronomic Studies (CIHEAM) 03927

Centre international de hautes études agronomiques méditerranéennes (CIHEAM)

Pres 11 rue Newton, 75116 Paris, France. T. +33153239100. E-mail: secretariat@ciheam.org.
URL: http://www.ciheam.org/

History 21 May 1962, Paris (France). Established by signature of an agreement between 7 countries: Portugal, Spain, France, Italy, Yugoslavia, Greece and Turkey, on the initiative of *Council of Europe (CE, #04881)* and *OECD (#17693)*. Former names and other names: *ICAMAS* – alias; *Centro Internacional de Estudios Superiores sobre Agronomia Mediterranea* – former. **Aims** Promote multilateral cooperation in the Mediterranean in the fields of agriculture, food, fishery and rural territories through specialized training, networked research, scientific diplomacy and political partnership. **Structure** Governing Board; Scientific Advisory Board; Institutes (4): *Mediterranean Agronomic Institute of Bari (Bari MAI, #16641)*; *Mediterranean Agronomic Institute of Chania (MAICh, #16642)*; *Mediterranean Agronomic Institute of Montpellier (CIHEAM Montpellier, #16643)*; *Mediterranean Agronomic Institute of Zaragoza (MAIZ, #16644)*. General Secretariat located in Paris (France). **Languages** English, French. **Finance** Sources: members' dues. **Activities** Events/meetings; knowledge management/information dissemination; networking/liaising; politics/policy/regulatory; training/education. **Events** *Subnetwork on Mountain Pastures Meeting* Ballstad (Norway) 2018, *Meeting on Integrated Actions against XF to Protect Olive Trees and International Trade* Bari (Italy) 2018, *Meeting on Enhancing International Cooperation in the Field of Mediterranean Agriculture* Bari (Italy) 2017, *Forum on Sustainable Value Chains* Meknès (Morocco) 2017, *Meeting on Red Palm Weevil Management* Rome (Italy) 2017. **Publications** *Watch Letter* (4 a year); *New Medit – Mediterranean Journal of Economics, Agriculture and Environment* (4 a year); *MediTerra* (every 2 years) – flagship publication. **Information Services** *Banque de données socio-économiques des pays méditerranéens (MEDISTAT)*; *Collaborative Mediterranean Biotechnology Network – COMBINE* – online database; *MEDUSA* – database of useful native Mediterranean plants.

Members Governments of 13 Mediterranean countries:
Albania, Algeria, Egypt, France, Greece, Italy, Lebanon, Malta, Morocco, Portugal, Spain, Tunisia, Türkiye.

IGO Relations
- *Arab Centre for the Studies of Arid Zones and Dry Lands (ACSAD, #00918)*;
- *Arab Organization for Agricultural Development (AOAD, #01018)*;
- *Association of Agricultural Research Institutions in the Near East and North Africa (AARINENA, #02364)*;
- *European Commission (EC, #06633)*;
- *European Initiative for Agricultural Research for Development (EIARD, #07537)*;
- *FAO (#09260)*;
- *General Fisheries Commission for the Mediterranean (GFCM, #10112)*;
- *International Bank for Reconstruction and Development (IBRD, #12317)*;
- *International Center for Agricultural Research in the Dry Areas (ICARDA, #12466)*;
- *International Fund for Agricultural Development (IFAD, #13692)*;
- *International Information System for the Agricultural Sciences and Technology (AGRIS, #13848)*;
- *International Institute of Refrigeration (IIR, #13918)*;
- *International Livestock Research Institute (ILRI, #14062)*;
- *International Olive Council (IOC, #14405)*;
- *Mediterranean Action Plan (MAP, #16638)*;
- *Mediterranean Water Network (MWN, no recent information)*;
- *Regional Centre on Agrarian Reform and Rural Development for the Near East (#18755)*;
- *UNESCO (#20322)*.

NGO Relations Member of (2): *European Forest Institute Mediterranean Facility (EFIMED, #07298)*; *Mountain Partnership (MP, #16862)*. [2020/XF3184/**E***]

♦ CIHEAM MAIM / see Mediterranean Agronomic Institute of Montpellier (#16643)
♦ CIHEAM Montpellier / see Mediterranean Agronomic Institute of Montpellier (#16643)
♦ **CIHEAM Montpellier** Institut agronomique méditerranéen de Montpellier (#16643)
♦ **CIHEAM Montpellier** Mediterranean Agronomic Institute of Montpellier (#16643)
♦ **CIHEC** Commission Internationale d'Histoire et d'Etudes du Christianisme (#04221)
♦ **CIHEF** Commission internationale humanitaire d'établissement des faits (#13820)
♦ **CIHM** Commission internationale d'histoire militaire (#12705)
♦ **CIHRF** Commission internationale d'histoire de la Révolution française (#04222)
♦ **CIHRS** Cairo Institute for Human Rights Studies (#03397)
♦ CIHS / see Institute for Global Health and Development, Edinburgh
♦ **CIHU** Commission internationale pour l'histoire des universités (#04223)
♦ CIIA – Canadian Institute of International Affairs (internationally oriented national body)
♦ CIIA – Commission internationale des industries agricoles et alimentaires (inactive)
♦ CIIAI – Conseil international des industries des aliments infantiles (inactive)
♦ CIIAN – Canadian International Institute of Applied Negotiation (internationally oriented national body)
♦ **CIIC** Concilio Internacional de Iglesias Cristianas (#13005)
♦ **CIIC** Concílio Internacional de Igrejas Cristãs (#13005)
♦ CIIC / see ICOMOS International Committee on Cultural Routes (#11060)
♦ CII – Coady International Institute (internationally oriented national body)
♦ **CII** Conseil international des infirmières (#13054)
♦ **CII** Corporação Interamericana de Investimentos (#11438)
♦ **CII** Corporación Interamericana de Inversiones (#11438)
♦ CII – Council of International Investigators (internationally oriented national body)
♦ **CIID** Commission internationale des irrigations et du drainage (#12694)
♦ CIIFEN – Centro Internacional para la Investigación del Fenómeno de EL Niño (internationally oriented national body)
♦ CIIH / see Centro de Investigaciones Interdisciplinarias en Ciencias y Humanidades
♦ CIIIAP – Centro Internacional de Inovação e Intercâmbio em Administração Pública (internationally oriented national body)
♦ CIIM / see Association internationale de la mutualité (#02721)
♦ CIIMC / see China International Council for the Promotion of Multinational Corporations
♦ CIIM – Cyprus International Institute of Management (internationally oriented national body)
♦ **CIIMDA** Centre for Indigenous Instrumental Music and Dance Practices of Africa (#03749)
♦ **CIIMP** Centro Internazionale di Ipnosi Medica e Psicologica (#15257)

- ♦ CI – Institutum Patrum Josephitarum Gerardimontensium (religious order)
- ♦ CIIO – Canadian Institute for International Order (internationally oriented national body)
- ♦ CIIP – Centre d'information inter-peuples, Grenoble (internationally oriented national body)
- ♦ **CIIQ** Confederación Interamericana de Ingenieria Quimica (#11417)
- ♦ **CIIRC** Centre Internacional d'Investigació dels Recursos Costaners (#12480)
- ♦ CIIS / see World Association of International Studies
- ♦ CIIS – California Institute of Integral Studies (internationally oriented national body)
- ♦ CIIS – China Institute of International Studies (internationally oriented national body)
- ♦ CI – Island Conservation (internationally oriented national body)
- ♦ CIISS – China Institute for International Strategic Studies (internationally oriented national body)
- ♦ CII Suisse – Centre International d'Investissement (internationally oriented national body)
- ♦ CIJA – Commission for International Justice and Accountability (unconfirmed)
- ♦ **CIJC** Conferencia Iberoamericana de Justicia Constitucional (#04652)
- ♦ **CIJ** Comisión Internacional de Juristas (#12695)
- ♦ **CIJ** Commission internationale de juristes (#12695)
- ♦ **CIJ** Corte Internacional de Justicia (#13098)
- ♦ **CIJ** Cour internationale de Justice (#13098)
- ♦ CIJD / see Centro de Informação Europeia Jacques Delors
- ♦ CIJD – Centre international de la jeunesse pour le développement, Bruxelles (internationally oriented national body)
- ♦ CIJE / see Federación Iberoamericana de Jóvenes Empresarios (#09314)
- ♦ **CIJF** Comité international des Jeux de La Francophonie (#04178)
- ♦ CIJF / see European Fruit Juice Association (#07362)
- ♦ **CIJM** Comité International des Jeux Méditerranéens (#12783)
- ♦ **CIJOC** Coordinación Internacional de la Juventud Obrera Cristiana (#12960)
- ♦ **CIJOC** Coordination Internationale de la Jeunesse Ouvrière Chrétienne (#12960)
- ♦ CILAC – Foro Abierto de Ciencias de America Latina y el Caribe (meeting series)
- ♦ **CILAD** Colegio Ibero-Latinoamericano de Dermatologia (#04093)
- ♦ CILAF – Comité international de liaison des associations féminines (internationally oriented national body)
- ♦ **CILANE** Commission d'information et de liaison des associations nobles d'Europe (#06637)
- ♦ CILAS – Center for Iberian and Latin American Studies (internationally oriented national body)
- ♦ CILB / see International Organisation for Biological Control (#14424)
- ♦ CILC – Center for International Legal Cooperation (internationally oriented national body)
- ♦ CILC / see Confédération européenne du lin et du chanvre (#04546)
- ♦ CILC – Confédération internationale du lin et du chanvre (no recent information)
- ♦ **CILEA** Comité de Integración Latino Europa-América (#04169)
- ♦ CILEC – Centre international de langue et civilisation, Saint-Etienne (internationally oriented national body)
- ♦ CILECT Africa Regional Association (see: #11771)
- ♦ CILECT Asia-Pacific Association (see: #11771)
- ♦ **CILECT** Centre international de liaison des écoles de cinéma et de télévision (#11771)
- ♦ CILECT Ibero América (see: #11771)
- ♦ **CILF** Conseil international de la langue française (#04692)
- ♦ CIL / see International Union of Photobiology (#15798)
- ♦ **CILIP ILIG** International Library and Information Group (#14037)
- ♦ CILLA – Center for Indigenous Languages of Latin America (internationally oriented national body)
- ♦ **CILPAN** Centre international de lutte contre la pollution de l'Atlantique du Nord-Est (#03757)
- ♦ **CILPAN** Centro Internacional de Luta contra a Poluição do Atlântico do Nordeste (#03757)
- ♦ CILPE – Conférence internationale de liaison entre producteurs d'énergie électrique (inactive)
- ♦ **CILRAP** Centre for International Law Research and Policy (#03756)
- ♦ CILS – Center for International Legal Studies, Salzburg (internationally oriented national body)
- ♦ **CILSS** Comité permanent inter-Etats de lutte contre la sécheresse dans le Sahel (#04195)
- ♦ CIMA / see Centre for Intercultural Musicology at Churchill College
- ♦ CIMACC – Centre for Intercultural Musicology at Churchill College (internationally oriented national body)
- ♦ **CIMAC** Conseil international des machines à combustion (#04693)
- ♦ CIMA – Center for International Media Assistance (internationally oriented national body)
- ♦ **CIMA** Conférence interafricaine des marchés d'assurances (#11385)
- ♦ CIM – Additional Convention to the International Convention Signed at Rome on 23 Nov 1933 Concerning the Transport of Goods by Rail (1950 treaty)
- ♦ CIMADE (internationally oriented national body)
- ♦ **CIMAL** Centro de Información sobre Migraciones en América Latina (#03643)
- ♦ CIMAM – Centre international pour les micro-alges alimentaires contre la malnutrition (internationally oriented national body)
- ♦ CIMAM – International Committee of ICOM for Museums and Collections of Modern Art (see: #13051)
- ♦ **CIMAP** Commission internationale des méthodes d'analyse des pesticides (#04099)
- ♦ CIMAS / see International Social Security Association (#14885)
- ♦ **CIMB** Centre international d'études monétaires et bancaires (#12506)
- ♦ CIMC – Centre international pour la musique chorale (internationally oriented national body)
- ♦ **CIM** Centre international de myriapodologie (#03759)
- ♦ CIM – Centro Internacional de Matematica (internationally oriented national body)
- ♦ CIM – Centrum für Internationale Migration and Entwicklung (internationally oriented national body)
- ♦ CIMCIM – ICOM Comité internacional para museos y colecciones de instrumentos y de música (see: #13051)
- ♦ CIMCIM – ICOM Comité international pour les musées et collections d'instruments et de musique (see: #13051)
- ♦ CIMCIM – ICOM International Committee of Museums and Collections of Instruments and Music (see: #13051)
- ♦ CIM, CIV – Revision of the International Conventions Concerning the Carriage of Goods by Rail and of Passengers and Luggage by Rail (1952 treaty)
- ♦ **CIM** Coetus Internationalis Ministrantium (#04083)
- ♦ **CIM** Comisión Interamericana de Mujeres (#04137)
- ♦ **CIM** Comité international de Mauthausen (#04179)
- ♦ **CIM** Commission interméditerranéenne (#11521)
- ♦ **CIM** Commission internationale de la Meuse (#12702)
- ♦ CIM – Congregatio Iesu et Mariae (religious order)
- ♦ **CIM** Conseil international de la musique (#14199)
- ♦ **CIM** Consejo Internacional de la Música (#14199)
- ♦ CIM – Convention additionnelle à la Convention internationale signée à Rome le 23 novembre 1933 et concernant le transport des marchandises par chemins de fer (1950 treaty)
- ♦ CIM – Convention internationale concernant le transport des marchandises par chemins de fer (1890 treaty)
- ♦ CIMEA – Comité international des mouvements d'enfants et d'adolescents (inactive)
- ♦ **CIME** Confédération internationale de musique électroacoustique (#12858)
- ♦ **CIME** Conseil international des médias éducatifs (#13014)
- ♦ CIME / see International Organization for Migration (#14454)
- ♦ CIMEL – Centre of Islamic and Middle Eastern Law, London (internationally oriented national body)
- ♦ CIMERSS – Centre interdisciplinaire méditerranéen d'études et de recherches en sciences sociales (internationally oriented national body)
- ♦ CIMF / see Confederación Iberoamericana de Medicina Familiar (#04450)
- ♦ **CIMF** Confederación Iberoamericana de Medicina Familiar (#04450)
- ♦ **CIMH** Caribbean Institute for Meteorology and Hydrology (#03520)
- ♦ **CIMH** Comité international pour la métrologie historique (#12776)
- ♦ CIMH – Consortium for International Maritime Heritage (unconfirmed)
- ♦ **CIMHET** Conferencia de Directores de los Servicios Meteorológicos e Hidrológicos Iberoamericanos (#04586)
- ♦ CIM / see International Organization for Migration (#14454)
- ♦ **CIMM** Comité International de Médecine Militaire (#12785)
- ♦ CIMM / see International Committee of Military Medicine (#12785)
- ♦ **CIMMYT** Centro Internacional de Mejoramiento de Maiz y Trigo (#14077)
- ♦ CIMNE – International Centre for Numerical Methods in Engineering (internationally oriented national body)
- ♦ CIMNI – Centro Internacional de Métodos Numéricos en Ingenieria (internationally oriented national body)
- ♦ CIMO – Centre for International Mobility (internationally oriented national body)
- ♦ CIMODE – Congresso Internazionale di Moda e Design (meeting series)
- ♦ CIMO – European Fresh Produce Importers Association (inactive)
- ♦ **CIMPA** Centre international de mathématiques pures et appliquées (#03758)
- ♦ CIMPA – Connected International Meeting Professionals Association (internationally oriented national body)
- ♦ **CIMP** Commission internationale de la météorologie polaire (#12718)
- ♦ **CIMP** Commission internationale de microflore du paléozoïque (#04225)
- ♦ CIMP – Conférence internationale des matières premières (inactive)
- ♦ CIMP / see International Council for Traditional Music (#13087)
- ♦ CIMPM / see International Committee of Military Medicine (#12785)
- ♦ CIMRI / see International Commission on Couple and Family Relations (#12676)
- ♦ **CIMS** Consociatio Internationalis Musicae Sacrae (#04730)
- ♦ **CIMT** Association for Cancer Immunotherapy (#02399)
- ♦ **CIMT** Comisión Internacional de Medicina del Trabajo (#12709)
- ♦ **CIMT** Conseil international de la musique traditionnelle (#13087)
- ♦ CIMTP – Congrès international de médecine tropicale et de paludisme (meeting series)
- ♦ **CIMU** Consultation internationale sur les maladies urologiques (#12928)
- ♦ CIMUSET – ICOM International Committee for Museums and Collections of Science and Technology (see: #13051)
- ♦ CINA / see NIAS-Nordisk Institut for Asienstudier (#17132)
- ♦ **CinC** Computing in Cardiology (#04429)
- ♦ **CIN** Conseil international de numismatique (#14385)
- ♦ **CINDA** Centro Interuniversitario de Desarrollo (#03809)
- ♦ CINDE – Centro Internacional de Educación y Desarrollo Humano (internationally oriented national body)
- ♦ CINDER / see IPRA-CINDER – International Property Registries Association (#16012)
- ♦ Cinema for Peace Foundation (unconfirmed)
- ♦ Cinema Union of Latin America (no recent information)
- ♦ CINEO – Congrès international de néologie de langues romanes (meeting series)

♦ Cine-Regio 03928

SG c/o VAF, Bischoffsheimlaan 38, 1000 Brussels, Belgium. E-mail: info@cineregio.org.
URL: http://www.cineregio.org/

History 11 May 2005. Former names and other names: *Cine-Regio – European network of regional film funds* – full title. Registration: Banque-Carrefour des Entreprises, Belgium; EU Transparency Register, No/ID: 829063922689-04. **Aims** Exchange views, perspectives, good practice and information for the benefit of the European film industry, including integrating new regional film funds; raise awareness, represent and promote regional audiovisual interests across Europe; strengthen the co-development and co-production of audiovisual products, fusing talents and resources in different regions for a wider market. **Structure** General Assembly (annual, in Cannes, France); Board of Directors. **Languages** English. **Finance** Sources: members' dues. **Activities** Knowledge management/information dissemination; politics/policy/regulatory; projects/programmes. **Events** *KIDS Regio forum* Erfurt (Germany) 2009, *KIDS Regio expert meeting* Malmö (Sweden) 2008. **Publications** Reports.
Members Regional Film Funds (49) in 16 countries:
Austria, Belgium, Denmark, Estonia, Finland, France, Germany, Ireland, Italy, Latvia, Norway, Poland, Spain, Sweden, Switzerland, UK. [2021.02.22/XJ1182/**D**]

- ♦ Cine-Regio – European network of regional film funds / see Cine-Regio (#03928)
- ♦ **CINET** Comité international de l'entretien du textile (#12809)
- ♦ **CINet** Continuous Innovation Network (#04781)
- ♦ **CINETS** Crimmigration Control – International Net of Studies (#04956)
- ♦ CINFO – Centre for Information, Counseling and Training Professions Relating to International Cooperation and Humanitarian Aid (internationally oriented national body)
- ♦ CIN / see International Numismatic Council (#14385)
- ♦ **CINOA** Confédération internationale des négociants en oeuvres d'art (#12848)
- ♦ **CINP** Collegium Internationale Neuropsychopharmacologicum (#04115)
- ♦ CINPE – Centro Internacional de Politica Económica para el Desarrollo Sostenible (internationally oriented national body)
- ♦ Cinquième protocole additionnel à l'Accord général sur les privilèges et immunités du Conseil de l'Europe (1990 treaty)
- ♦ CINRG – Cooperative International Neuromuscular Research Group (internationally oriented national body)
- ♦ CINS / see Canadian Institute for Nordic Studies
- ♦ CINS – Canadian Institute for Nordic Studies (internationally oriented national body)
- ♦ CINS – Cooperazione Italiana Nord-Sud (internationally oriented national body)
- ♦ CINTERAD / see Centre international d'études, de recherche, d'action pour le développement et prévention des conflicts (#03753)
- ♦ **CINTERAD-PRECO** Centre international d'études, de recherche, d'action pour le développement et prévention des conflicts (#03753)
- ♦ CINTERPLAN – Centro Interamericano de Investigaciones y Estudios para el Planeamiento de la Educación (no recent information)
- ♦ CIOA / see Olympic Solidarity (#17721)
- ♦ CIOCM – Centre international ondes courtes de Moyabi (no recent information)
- ♦ **CIO** Comité international olympique (#14408)
- ♦ **CIO** Commission Internationale d'Optique (#12710)
- ♦ CIO / see European Council of Medical Orders (#06830)
- ♦ **CIOFF** Conseil international des organisations de festivals de folklore et d'arts traditionnels (#13058)
- ♦ CIOIC / see International Catholic Centre of Geneva (#12449)
- ♦ CIOMAL / see Campagne Internationale de l'Ordre de Malte contre la lèpre (#03403)
- ♦ **CIOMR** Confédération Interalliée des Officiers Médicaux de Réserve (#04555)
- ♦ **CIOMS** Council for International Organizations of Medical Sciences (#04905)
- ♦ **CIOPF** Conférence internationale des ordres de pharmaciens francophones (#04620)
- ♦ **CIOPORA** Communauté internationale des obtenteurs de plantes ornementales et fruitières à reproduction asexuée (#12821)
- ♦ CIOPORA / see International Community of Breeders of Asexually Reproduced Ornamental and Fruit Varieties (#12821)
- ♦ **CIOR** Confédération interalliée des officiers de réserve (#04557)
- ♦ CIOSL – Confederación Internacional de Organizaciones Sindicales Libres (inactive)
- ♦ **CIOSTA** Commission internationale pour organisation scientifique du travail en agriculture (#04226)
- ♦ CIOS – World Council of Management (inactive)
- ♦ CIP / see Council of International Programs USA
- ♦ CIPA / see Sail For Ethics
- ♦ **CIPAC** Collaborative International Pesticides Analytical Council (#04099)

- ♦ CIPA – Centre international de phonétique appliquée (internationally oriented national body)
- ♦ CIPA / see CIPA Heritage Documentation (#03929)
- ♦ **CIPA** CIPA Heritage Documentation (#03929)
- ♦ CIPACO – Centre for International ICT Policies West and Central Africa (internationally oriented national body)
- ♦ CIPA – Comité Interamericano Permanente Antiacridiano (inactive)
- ♦ CIPA – Comité Interamericano de Protección Agricola (inactive)
- ♦ **CIPA** Comité International des Plastiques en Agriculture (#04185)
- ♦ **CIPA** Comité international de prévention des accidents du travail de la navigation intérieure (#12796)
- ♦ CIPA – Commission internationale permanente des associations agricoles (inactive)
- ♦ CIPA – Council on International and Public Affairs (internationally oriented national body)
- ♦ CIPAD – Coopération internationale de promotion et aides au développement (internationally oriented national body)
- ♦ **CIPAD** Council of International Plastics Associations Directors (#04906)
- ♦ CIPA Documentation du Patrimoine (#03929)

♦ CIPA Heritage Documentation (CIPA) 03929

CIPA Documentation du Patrimoine

Pres PO Box 27281, CY-1643 Nicosia, Cyprus. E-mail: president@cipa.icomos.org.
SG address not obtained. E-mail: secretarygeneral@cipa.icomos.org.
URL: https://www.cipaheritagedocumentation.org/

History 1969. Founded as a joint committee liaising between *International Council on Monuments and Sites (ICOMOS, #13049)* and *International Society for Photogrammetry and Remote Sensing (ISPRS, #15362)*. Most recent statutes adopted Jan 2019. Former names and other names: *Comité international de photogrammétrie architecturale – Comité ICOMOS et ISPRS pour la documentation du patrimoine culturel (CIPA)* – former; *International Committee for Architectural Photogrammetry – ICOMOS and ISPRS Committee for Documentation of Cultural Heritage* – former; *ICOMOS International Committee for Architectural Photogrammetry* – former; *Comité international de photogrammétrie architecturale de l'ICOMOS* – former; *International Committee for Documentation of Cultural Heritage (CIPA)* – alias; *ICOMOS / ISPRS Committee for Documentation of Cultural Heritage* – alias. **Aims** Encourage the development of principles and practices for the recording, documentation and information management for all aspects of cultural heritage; support and encourage the development of specialised tools and techniques in support of these activities. **Structure** Executive Committee; Permanent Commissions. **Languages** English, French, German. **Staff** Voluntary. **Finance** Sources: contributions of member/participating states; meeting proceeds. **Activities** Knowledge management/information dissemination; research and development; events/meetings; training/education. **Events** *International Symposium* Florence (Italy) 2023, *International Symposium* Beijing (China) 2021, *Symposium* Avila (Spain) 2019, *Symposium* Ottawa, ON (Canada) 2017, *Symposium* Taipei (Taiwan) 2015. **Publications** Symposium proceedings. **Members** Individuals Honorary; Executive Board; Expert; Regular. Membership countries not specified. [2023/XE9453/v/**E**]

- ♦ CIPAN – Comisión Internacional de Pesquerias del Atlantico Noroeste (inactive)
- ♦ CIPAN – Commission internationale des pêches de l'Atlantique Nord-Ouest (inactive)
- ♦ CIPAS – California Institute of Pan African Studies (internationally oriented national body)
- ♦ CIPASE – Commission internationale des pêches de l'Atlantique Sud-Est (inactive)
- ♦ CIPASO – Comisión Internacional de Pesquerias del Atlantico Sud-Oriental (inactive)
- ♦ **CIPAT** Conseil international sur les problèmes de l'alcoolisme et des toxicomanies (#12989)
- ♦ CIP – Caribbean Institute of Perinatology (no recent information)
- ♦ CIP – Cartel international de la paix (inactive)
- ♦ **CIPC** Centre international pour la prévention de la criminalité (#12508)
- ♦ **CIPC** Centro Internacional para la Prevención de la Criminalidad (#12508)
- ♦ **CIPC** Comité international Pierre de Coubertin (#04184)
- ♦ CIPCEL – Comité international de la pellicule cellulosique (no recent information)
- ♦ CIP – Center for International Policy (internationally oriented national body)
- ♦ **CIP** Centre international de la pomme de terre (#14627)
- ♦ **CIP** Centro Internacional de la Papa (#14627)
- ♦ CIPCI – Conseil international des praticiens du plan comptable international (inactive)
- ♦ **CIP** Comisión Interamericana de Puertos (#11415)
- ♦ **CIP** Comité Internacional Paralimpico (#14512)
- ♦ **CIP** Comité Internacional de Planificación para la Soberanía Alimentaria (#14365)
- ♦ **CIP** Comité international paralympique (#14512)
- ♦ **CIP** Comité international de planification pour la souveraineté alimentaire (#14365)
- ♦ **CIP** Commission internationale permanente pour l'épreuve des armes à feu portatives (#04227)
- ♦ **CIP** Commission internationale du peuplier (#14619)
- ♦ CIP – Confédération internationale des parents (no recent information)
- ♦ CIP – Congreso Ibérico de Percepción (meeting series)
- ♦ **CIPCRE** Cercle international pour la promotion de la création (#12575)
- ♦ CIPD – Centre for International and Defence Policy, Kingston ON (internationally oriented national body)
- ♦ CIPDD – Caucasian Institute for Peace, Democracy and Development (internationally oriented national body)
- ♦ CIPDH / see Centro Internacional para la Promoción de los Derechos Humanos
- ♦ CIPDH-UNESCO – Centro Internacional para la Promoción de los Derechos Humanos (internationally oriented national body)
- ♦ CIPEC – Conseil intergouvernemental des pays exportateurs de cuivre (inactive)
- ♦ CIPE – Center for International Private Enterprise (internationally oriented national body)
- ♦ CIPE – Centro Interamericano de Promoción de Exportaciones (inactive)
- ♦ CIPE – Collège international de phonologie expérimentale (inactive)
- ♦ **CIPE** Conseil international de la préparation à l'enseignement (#13016)
- ♦ CIPEG – Comité international de l'ICOM pour l'égyptologie (see: #13051)
- ♦ CIPE / see International Commission of the Schelde River (#12727)
- ♦ CIPEL – Commission Internationale pour la Protection des Eaux du Léman (internationally oriented national body)
- ♦ **CIPEM** Comité international permanent des études mycéniennes (#04181)
- ♦ CIPESA – Collaboration on International ICT Policy-Making for East and Southern Africa (internationally oriented national body)
- ♦ **CIPESUR** Federación de Sociedades de Cirurgia Pediatrica del Cono sur de América (#09390)
- ♦ CIPF – Confédération internationale du commerce des pailles, fourrages, tourbes et dérivés (no recent information)
- ♦ CIP-FUHEM – Centre for Peace Research, Madrid (internationally oriented national body)
- ♦ CIP – Global Initiative for Consensus in Pediatrics (unconfirmed)
- ♦ CIPGS – Conseil international pour un progrès global de la santé (no recent information)
- ♦ CIPh – Collège international de philosophie, Paris (internationally oriented national body)
- ♦ **CIPH** Comité international des pharmaciens homéopathes (#04183)
- ♦ **CIPIE** Fundación Iberoamérica Europa Centro de Investigación, Promoción y Cooperación Internacional (#10025)
- ♦ CIP Institute – Complex Interactive Processes Institute (unconfirmed)
- ♦ CIP / see International Federation of Foot and Ankle Societies (#13431)
- ♦ CIP / see International Organization of Psychomotricity and Relaxation (#14465)
- ♦ CIP / see International Union of Photobiology (#15798)
- ♦ **CIPIST** Centre international pour l'information scientifique et technique (#12514)
- ♦ CIPL – Centre for International and Public Law, Canberra (internationally oriented national body)
- ♦ **CIPL** Comité international de paléographie latine (#04180)
- ♦ **CIPL** Comité international permanent des linguistes (#04182)
- ♦ CIPM / see International Commission of the Meuse (#12702)
- ♦ **CIPMS** Commissions internationales pour la protection de la Moselle et de la Sarre (#12729)
- ♦ CIPO / see BirdLife International (#03266)
- ♦ CIPOD – Centre for International Politics, Organization and Disarmament, Delhi (internationally oriented national body)
- ♦ CIPPA – Centre for International Public Policy and Administration (internationally oriented national body)
- ♦ CIPP / see Asia-Pacific Fishery Commission (#01907)
- ♦ CIPP – Congrès international de pneumologie pédiatrique (meeting series)
- ♦ CIPPI – Conseil interétatique pour la protection de la propriété industrielle (inactive)
- ♦ CIPPT – Colloque international de psychodynamique et psychopathologie du travail (meeting series)
- ♦ CIPQ – Centre international de promotion de la qualité (inactive)
- ♦ CIPRA – China International Public Relations Association (internationally oriented national body)
- ♦ CIPRA / see CIPRA International (#03930)

♦ CIPRA International 03930

Dir Kirchstrasse 5, 9494 Schaan, Liechtenstein. T. +4232375353. E-mail: international@cipra.org.
URL: http://www.cipra.org/

History 1952. Former names and other names: *Commission internationale pour la protection des régions alpines* – former; *Commission internationale pour la protection des Alpes (CIPRA)* – full title; *Internationale Alpenschutzkommission* – full title; *Commissione Internazionale per la Protezione delle Alpi* – full title; *Mednarodna komisija za varstvo Alp* – full title; *International Commission for the Protection of the Alps* – former. Registration: Liechtenstein; EU Transparency Register, No/ID: 542073745770-07, Start date: 10 Mar 2022. **Aims** Contribute to solving current problems and upcoming challenges in the Alpine region in order to bring about a sustainable and ecological future for the region. **Structure** Assembly of Delegates; Presiding Committee; CIPRA Youth Council. **Languages** English, French, German, Italian, Slovene. **Staff** 12.00 FTE, paid. **Finance** Annual budget: 2,000,000 USD. **Activities** Advocacy/lobbying/activism; events/meetings; training/education. **Events** *AlpWeek* Brig (Switzerland) 2022, *Annual Conference* Altdorf (Switzerland) 2019, *Annual Conference and General Assembly* Bolzano (Italy) 2013, *AlpWeek* Poschiavo (Switzerland) 2012, *Annual Conference and General Assembly* Poschiavo (Switzerland) 2012. **Publications** *alpMedia* (12 a year) in French, German, Italian, Slovene – newsletter, also 4 a year in English; *AlpsInsight* (1-3 a year) in French, German, Italian, Slovene. *Alpine Reports* in French, German, Italian, Slovene – 3 vols published to date. Conference proceedings; reports.

Members Associations involved in nature management, protection and natural history of alpine regions, in 7 countries:
Austria, France, Germany, Italy, Liechtenstein, Slovenia, Switzerland.

IGO Relations Instrumental in setting up (1): *Alliance in the Alps (#00656)*. **NGO Relations** Member of (2): *International Union for Conservation of Nature and Natural Resources (IUCN, #15766)*; *Mountain Partnership (MP, #16862)*. Instrumental in setting up (1): *Alliance of Central Asian Mountain Communities (AGOCA, #00662)*. [2023.02.14/XD4295/**E**]

- ♦ CIPR – Coalition for Intellectual Property Rights (internationally oriented national body)
- ♦ **CIPR** Commission internationale de protection contre les radiations (#12724)
- ♦ **CIPR** Commission internationale pour la protection du Rhin (#12721)
- ♦ **CIPRES** Conférence interafricaine de la prévoyance sociale (#04610)
- ♦ **CIPS** Confédération internationale de la pêche sportive (#04562)
- ♦ **CIPS** Confederazione Internazionale de la Pesca Sportive (#04562)
- ♦ **CIPSH** Conseil international de la philosophie et des sciences humaines (#13061)
- ♦ **CIPSH** Consejo Internacional de Filosofia y Ciencias Humanas (#13061)
- ♦ **CIPSH** International Council for Philosophy and Human Sciences (#13061)
- ♦ **CIPSH** Internationaler Rat für Philosophie und die Geisteswissenschaften (#13061)
- ♦ **CIPSH** Mezdunarodnyj Sovet po Filosofii i Gumanitarnym Naukam (#13061)
- ♦ CIPSI – Coordinamento di Iniziative Popolari di Solidarietà Internazionale (internationally oriented national body)
- ♦ **CIPT** Centre international Abdus Salam de physique théorique (#00005)
- ♦ CIPT – Centre for International Politics, Thessaloniki (internationally oriented national body)
- ♦ CIPUSA – Council of International Programs USA (internationally oriented national body)
- ♦ **CIPYC** Consejo Iberoamericano para la Productividad y la Competitividad (#04713)
- ♦ CIQ – Confoederatio Internationalis ad Qualitates Plantarum Edulium Perquirendas (inactive)
- ♦ **CIQI** Comité international de la Quatrième internationale (#12771)
- ♦ CIQUIM – Conselho da Indústria Quimica do Mercosul (no recent information)
- ♦ CIR / see Burkle Center for International Relations
- ♦ CIRAC – Circle for International Reflect Action and Communication (internationally oriented national body)
- ♦ CIRA – Centre international de recherches sur l'anarchisme (internationally oriented national body)
- ♦ **CIRA** Centro Interamericano de Recursos del Agua (#11404)
- ♦ CIRA – Comité international pour la réglementation des ascenseurs et monte-charge (inactive)
- ♦ **CIRA** Conseil International sur la Résidence Alternée (#13072)
- ♦ **CIRAD** Centre de coopération internationale en recherche agronomique pour le développement (#03733)
- ♦ **CIRAD** International Center for Research and Decision Support of the International Federation of Catholic Universities (#12476)
- ♦ CIRAF / see World Agroforestry Centre (#21072)
- ♦ CIRCB – Centre international de référence Chantal Biya, Yaoundé (unconfirmed)
- ♦ **CIRC** Centre international de Recherche sur le Cancer (#11598)
- ♦ CIR – Center for International Rehabilitation (internationally oriented national body)
- ♦ CIR – Centre of International Relations, Ljubljana (internationally oriented national body)
- ♦ CIR – Centre for International Relations, Warszawa (internationally oriented national body)
- ♦ **CIRCF** Commission internationale des relations du couple et de la famille (#12676)
- ♦ **CirchNet** Circumpolar Health Research Network (#03942)
- ♦ Circle of Blue (internationally oriented national body)

♦ Circle of Concerned African Women Theologians (CAWT) 03931

Coordinator WCC, 150 Route de Ferney, 1211 Geneva 2, Switzerland. T. +41227916027. Fax +41227916406.

History 1989, Accra (Ghana). Founded on the initiative of Mercy Amba Oduyoye. **Aims** Undertake research and publish theological literature written by African women with special focus on religion and culture. **Structure** General Coordinator; Linguistic and Regional Research Coordinators (7). **Languages** English, French, Portuguese. **Staff** One part-time, paid; voluntary. **Finance** Funding partnership, including with the following organizations: listed in this Yearbook: *The Lutheran World Federation (LWF, #16532)*; Presbyterian Church (Canada and USA); *World Council of Churches (WCC, #21320)*; World Women's Day of Prayer – Germany. Budget (annual): US$ 100,000. **Activities** Conducts scientifically based research; organizes conferences and meetings; disseminates information. **Events** *Regional Meeting* South Africa 2009, *Healing and transformation – a year of celebration* Stellenbosch (South Africa) 2009, *Pan-African conference* Kempton Park (South Africa) 2007, *Pan-African Conference* Yaoundé (Cameroon) 2007, *Regional conference* Maputo (Mozambique) 2005. **Publications** *Circle Newsletter* (2 a year). Directory; books.

Members Individuals (616) in 40 countries:
Angola, Belgium, Benin, Botswana, Burundi, Cameroon, Canada, Central African Rep, Congo DR, Côte d'Ivoire, Egypt, Eritrea, Eswatini, Ethiopia, France, Germany, Ghana, Kenya, Lesotho, Liberia, Madagascar, Malawi, Mozambique, Namibia, Niger, Philippines, Rwanda, Senegal, Sierra Leone, South Africa, Sudan, Sweden, Switzerland, Tanzania UR, Togo, Uganda, UK, USA, Zambia, Zimbabwe.

NGO Relations Affiliate Member of: *International Network of Societies for Catholic Theology (INSeCT, #14328)*. [2013/XJ4001/v/**F**]

- ♦ Circle of Health International (internationally oriented national body)
- ♦ Circle for International Reflect Action and Communication (internationally oriented national body)

♦ **CirclesEurope Association (CirclesEurope)** **03932**

Contact Vivaldiplantsoen 100, 3533 JE Utrecht, Netherlands. E-mail: info@circleseurope.eu.
URL: https://www.circleseurope.eu/

History Nov 2018. The result of Circles4EU, a European project (2013-2014). Launched at conference of *Confederation of European Probation (CEP, #04530)*. Registration: No/ID: RSIN 8588.94.592, Netherlands; Handelsregister, No/ID: KvK 71898190, Netherlands. **Aims** Support, develop and promote Circles of Support and Accountability Services (Circles) across Europe according to the commonly agreed Circles model and with the intention of assisting similar developments elsewhere. **Structure** Board. **Finance** Sources: members' dues.
Members Full; Associate. Full in 6 countries:
Belgium, Ireland, Italy, Netherlands, Spain, UK. [2022/AA2928/**E**]

♦ **CirclesEurope** CirclesEurope Association (#03932)
♦ CIRCM / see Pacific Path Institute
♦ **CIR** Colegio Interamericano de Radiologia (#11409)
♦ **CIRCOM Regional** European Association of Regional Television (#06189)
♦ CIR – Consejo Interuniversitario Regional (inactive)
♦ CIR – Consiglio Italiano Per I Rifugiati (internationally oriented national body)

♦ **Circostrada Network** **03933**

Coordinator c/o ARTCENA, 68 rue de la Folie-Méricourt, 75011 Paris, France. T. +33155281010.
URL: http://www.circostrada.org/

History 1993. Previously listed as full title: *Circostrada Network – Street Arts and Circus Arts – European Platform for Information, Research and Professional Exchanges*. **Aims** As a European platform for the street arts and *circus*, stimulate information, observation and professional exchanges. **Structure** General Meeting; Steering Committee; Work Groups. **Languages** English, French. **Staff** 3.00 FTE, paid. **Activities** Research/documentation; events/meetings; training/education. **Events** *General Meeting* Rotterdam (Netherlands) 2018, *General Meeting* Fossano (Italy) 2017, *General Meeting* Ljubljana (Slovenia) 2017, *General Meeting* London (UK) 2016, *General Meeting* Zagreb (Croatia) 2016.
Members Organizations (about 100) in 33 countries and territories:
Australia, Austria, Belgium, Burkina Faso, Croatia, Czechia, Denmark, Egypt, Estonia, Ethiopia, Finland, France, Germany, Greece, Ireland, Italy, Japan, Latvia, Morocco, Netherlands, Norway, Poland, Portugal, Réunion, Russia, Serbia, Slovakia, Slovenia, Spain, Sweden, Switzerland, Tunisia, UK.
Included in the above, 3 organizations listed in this Yearbook:
CircusNext (#03943); *Fédération européenne des écoles de cirque professionnelles (FEDEC, #09565)*; *International Association for Creation and Training (I-act)*. [2019.06.27/XJ6162/y/**F**]

♦ Circostrada Network – Street Arts and Circus Arts – European Platform for Information, Research and Professional Exchanges / see Circostrada Network (#03933)

♦ **Circuits International** **03934**

Association internationale des circuits permanents (AICP)

Gen Sec AICP Secretariat, c/o Circuit Park Zandvoort, PO Box 132, 2040 AC Zandvoort, Netherlands. T. +31235740741.
URL: https://circuitsinternational.com/

History 1951. **Aims** Optimize the utilization of permanent circuits according to the needs of autocar and *motorcycle* sporting events, by exchanging ideas and experiences, in collaboration with recognized sporting authorities and other relevant organizations. **Languages** English, French. **Activities** Meetings (twice a year). **Publications** *Newsletter* (4 a year).
Members Major motor racing circuits (40) in 17 countries:
Australia, Austria, Belgium, China, Czechia, France, Germany, Ireland, Italy, Japan, Malaysia, Netherlands, Portugal, Spain, Türkiye, UK, USA.
NGO Relations Member of: *Fédération Internationale de Motocyclisme (FIM, #09643)*. Associate member of: *Fédération Internationale de l'Automobile (FIA, #09613)*. [2013/XD4850/**D**]

♦ **Circular Economy for Flexible Packaging (CEFLEX)** **03935**

Communication Watermolen 6, 2661 LA Bergschenhoek, Netherlands. E-mail: info@ceflex.eu.
Coordinator address not obtained.
URL: https://ceflex.eu/

History Former names and other names: *Stichting CEFLEX* – legal name. Registration: Handelsregister, No/ID: KVK 70082510, Netherlands. **Aims** Represent the entire value chain of flexible packaging; work to make all flexible packaging in Europe circular. **Structure** Management Team. **Publications** Ceflex News; guidelines.
NGO Relations Partner of (1): *European Coalition for Chemical Recycling*. [2022/AA2023/**F**]

♦ **Circular Plastics Alliance** **03936**

Secretariat DG for Internal Market, Industry, Entrepreneurship and SMEs, European Commission, 1049 Brussels, Belgium. E-mail: grow-env-rplastics-pledge@ec.europa.eu.
URL: https://ec.europa.eu/growth/industry/policy/circular-plastics-alliance_en

History Dec 2018, Belgium. Launched by *European Commission (EC, #06633)*, as an initiatve under the European Strategy for Plastics (2018). **Aims** Help plastics value chains boost the EU market for recycled plastics to 10 million tonnes by 2025. **Structure** General Assembly; Steering Committee.
Members Signatories of the declaration (currently over 300), include 48 organizations listed in this Yearbook:
– *Association of Cities and Regions for Sustainable Resource Management (ACR+, #02433)*;
– *Association of European Automative and Industrial Battery Manufacturers (EUROBAT, #02498)*;
– *Association of Plastics Manufacturers in Europe (Plastics Europe, #02862)*;
– *Chemical Recycling Europe (ChemRecEurope, #03860)*;
– *Comité européen de normalisation (CEN, #04162)*;
– *Conseil européen de l'industrie chimique (CEFIC, #04687)*;
– *COPA – european farmers (COPA, #04829)*;
– *CropLife Europe (#04965)*;
– *EDANA, the voice of nonwovens (EDANA, #05353)*;
– *EuroCommerce (EC, #05665)*;
– *European Association of Automotive Suppliers (CLEPA, #05948)*;
– *European Association of Flexible Polyurethane Foam Blocks Manufacturers (EUROPUR, #06042)*;
– *European Association of Manufacturers of Moulded Polyurethane Parts for the Automotive Industry (EURO-MOULDERS, #06116)*;
– *European Association of Plastics Recycling and Recovery Organizations (EPRO, #06153)*;
– *European Automobile Manufacturers' Association (ACEA, #06300)*;
– *European Brands Association (#06397)*;
– *European Carpet and Rug Association (ECRA, #06452)*;
– *European Chemical Regions Network (ECRN, #06522)*;
– *European Committee for Electrotechnical Standardization (CENELEC, #06647)*;
– *European Committee of Machinery Manufacturers for the Plastics and Rubber Industries (EUROMAP, #06656)*;
– *European Composites Industry Association (EuCIA, #06692)*;
– *European Composites, Plastics and Polymer Processing Platform (ECP4, #06693)*;
– *European Diisocyanate and Polyol Producers Association (ISOPA, #06926)*;
– *European Extruded Polystyrene Insulation Board Association (EXIBA, #07019)*;
– *European Federation of Waste Management and Environmental Services (#07232)*;
– *European Manufacturers of Expanded Polystyrene (EUMEPS, #07732)*;
– *European Organization for Packaging and the Environment (EUROPEN, #08110)*;
– *European Plastics Converters (EuPC, #08216)*;
– *European Recycling Industries' Confederation (EuRIC, #08335)*;
– *European Resilient Flooring Manufacturers' Institute (ERFMI, #08380)*;
– *European Snacks Association (ESA, #08498)*;
– *European Trade Association of PVC Window System Supplies (EPPA, #08924)*;
– *Extended Producer Responsibility Alliance (EXPRA, #09227)*;
– *Fédération européenne des cadres de la construction (FECC, #09561)*;
– *Fédération européenne des industries de corderie ficellerie et de filets (EUROCORD, #09573)*;
– *Flexible Packaging Europe (FPE, #09794)*;
– *FoodDrinkEurope (#09841)*;
– *General Confederation of Agricultural Cooperatives in the European Union (#10107)*;
– *Industrieverband Kunststoffbahnen (IVK Europe)*;
– *International Association for Soaps, Detergents and Maintenance Products (#12166)*;
– *Municipal Waste Europe (MWE, #16903)*;
– *Natural Mineral Waters Europe (NMWE, #16955)*;
– *PET Container Recycling Europe (Petcore Europe, #18339)*;
– *Plastics Recyclers Europe (PRE, #18394)*;
– *Producer Responsibility Organisations Packaging Alliance (PROsPA, #18508)*;
– *Styrenics Circular Solutions (SCS, #20022)*;
– *The European Plastic Pipes and Fittings Association (TEPPFA, #08215)*;
– *UNESDA Soft Drinks Europe (UNESDA, #20323)*. [2022/AA1036/y/**E**]

♦ Circulo femenino de Naciones Unidas – Ginebra (internationally oriented national body)
♦ Circulo femenino de Naciones Unidas – Nueva York (#20651)
♦ Circulo Femenino de Naciones Unidas de Viena (internationally oriented national body)
♦ Circulo Internacional de Directores de Hotel (unconfirmed)
♦ Circulo Internacional de Reflect (internationally oriented national body)
♦ Circulo Latinoamericano de Estudios Internacionales (internationally oriented national body)

♦ **Circulo Latinoamericano de Fenomenologia (CLAFEN)** **03937**

Latin American Circle of Phenomenology

Sec Depto de Humanidades, Pontificia Universidad Católica del Perú, Apartado 1761, 1, Lima, Peru. E-mail: clafen@pucp.edu.pe.
URL: http://www.clafen.org/

History Founded 18 Aug 1999, Puebla (Mexico). May evolve into *Latin American Society of Phenomenology – Sociedad Latinoamericana de Fenomenologia*. **Aims** Promote research into phenomenology in Latin America. **Structure** Assembly; Board of Directors; Local Coordinators; Secretariat. **Languages** Portuguese, Spanish. **Staff** 6.00 FTE, paid. **Finance** Support from Pontificia Universidad Católica del Perú. **Activities** Events/meetings. **Events** *Latin American Phenomenology Colloquium* Puebla (Mexico) 2019, *Latin American Phenomenology Colloquium* Santiago (Chile) 2012, *Latin American phenomenology colloquium / Latin-American Phenomenology Colloquium* Morelia (Mexico) 2009, *Latin American phenomenology colloquium* Bogota (Colombia) 2007, *Latin-American phenomenological colloquium* Lima (Peru) 2004. **Publications** *Acta Fenomenológica Latinoamericana* – in 6 vols. Phenomenological Bibliography in Spanish; Dictionary. **Information Services** *Husserl Database Homepage*.
Members Associate (43); Assigned (3); Ordinary (85); Collaborators (113). Individuals in 23 countries:
Argentina, Belgium, Bolivia, Brazil, Canada, Chile, Colombia, Costa Rica, Dominican Rep, Ecuador, France, Germany, Guatemala, Italy, Mexico, Peru, Portugal, Romania, Spain, Sweden, Uruguay, USA, Venezuela.
NGO Relations Member of: *Organization of Phenomenological Organizations (OPO, #17883)*. [2018.09.07/XF6013/v/**F**]

♦ **Circulo de Montevideo** **03938**

Coordinator José Luis Zorrilla de San Martin 248, 11300 Montevideo, Uruguay. T. +159827123113. Fax +159827123116.
URL: http://www.circulodemontevideo.org/

History 1996, Uruguay. Founded on the initiative of Julio Maria Sanguinetti. Former names and other names: *Fundación Círculo de Montevideo* – full title. **Aims** Promote wide-ranging *debate* among people, cultures and regions in *Latin America*. **Events** *Reunión Plenaria* Mexico City (Mexico) 2019, *Reunión Plenaria* Bogota (Colombia) 2018, *Reunión Plenaria* Buenos Aires (Argentina) 2017, *Reunión Plenaria* Mexico City (Mexico) 2016, *Reunión Plenaria* Alicante (Spain) 2015. **IGO Relations** *UNDP (#20292)*. [2019/XF5783/**E**]

♦ Circulo Odontológico del Sur (inactive)
♦ Circulo Ornitológico Esperantista (no recent information)

♦ **Circum-Pacific Council (CPC)** **03939**

SG PO Box 6000, 8960 West Saanich Road, Sidney BC V81 4B2, Canada.
Exec Office Moss Landing Marine Labs, 8272 Moss Landing Road, Moss Landing CA 95039, USA. T. +18317714141. E-mail: greene@mlml.calstate.edu.
URL: http://www.circum-pacificcouncil.org/

History 1972, USA. Former names and other names: *Circum-Pacific Council for Energy and Mineral Resources (CPCEMR)* – former (1972). **Aims** Develop and promote research and cooperation among industry, government and academia for *sustainable utilization* of earth resources in the Pacific Region; improve knowledge of earth resources and damaging geological hazards in the region; increase collaboration among geologists, hydrologists, biologists, oceanographers and related scientists; disseminate *earth-science* information. **Structure** Board of Directors. **Languages** English. **Staff** Voluntary. **Finance** Sources: contributions; grants. **Activities** Events/meetings; knowledge management/information dissemination; networking/liaising; training/education. **Events** *Energy summit* 2007, *Geothermal workshop* Santiago (Chile) 2005, *Geology, exploration and development potential of energy and mineral resources of Vietnam and adjoining regions* Hanoi (Vietnam) 1994, *Quadrennial Conference* Santiago (Chile) 1994, *Symposium on Arctic resources* Anchorage, AK (USA) 1993. **Publications** *Circum-Pacific Newsletter*. *Circum-Pacific Map*; *Conference Transactions*; *Earth Science*; *East Asia Geographic and Geotectonic Map*. Conference proceedings.
Members Societies and individuals in 34 countries and territories:
Argentina, Australia, Bolivia, Canada, Chile, China, Colombia, Costa Rica, Ecuador, El Salvador, Fiji, Guatemala, Honduras, Hong Kong, Indonesia, Japan, Malaysia, Mexico, Myanmar, New Caledonia, New Zealand, Nicaragua, Panama, Papua New Guinea, Peru, Philippines, Russia, Singapore, Solomon Is, Thailand, USA, Vanuatu, Venezuela, Vietnam.
IGO Relations *Coordinating Committee for Geoscience Programmes in East and Southeast Asia (CCOP, #04816)*. **NGO Relations** Affiliated with (2): *American Association of Petroleum Geologists (AAPG)*; *International Union of Geological Sciences (IUGS, #15777)*. [2021/XD0156/**C**]

♦ Circum-Pacific Council for Energy and Mineral Resources / see Circum-Pacific Council (#03939)

♦ **Circumpolar Agricultural Association (CAA)** **03940**

Dir c/o Bioforsk Nord, PO BOX 2284, 9269 Tromsø, Norway.

History 1995, Tromsø (Norway). **Aims** Encourage exchange of information, material and technology of agriculture and rural development in circumpolar areas; maintain relations with other organizations active in the field. **Structure** General Assembly (annual). Board of Directors, comprising President and 4 Vice-Presidents. **Languages** English, Russian. **Finance** Subscriptions; income from conferences; donations. **Events** *Conference* Rovaniemi (Finland) 2019, *Conference* Alta (Norway) 2010, *Conference* Canada 2007, *Conference* Happy Valley-Goose Bay, NL (Canada) 2007, *Conference* Umeå (Sweden) 2004.
Members in 9 countries and territories:
Canada, Finland, Greenland, Iceland, Norway, Russia, Sweden, USA. [2012/XD8321/**D**]

♦ **Circumpolar Biodiversity Monitoring Program (CBMP)** **03941**

Program Officer c/o CAFF Intl Secretariat, Borgir, Nordurslod, 600 Akureyri, Iceland. T. +3544623350. E-mail: caff@caff.is.
URL: http://www.cbmp.is/

History Set up as the cornerstone programme of *Conservation of Arctic Flora and Fauna (CAFF, #04728)* and endorsed by *Arctic Council (#01097)*, 2004 (Reykjavik Declaration) and 2006 (Salekhard Declaration). **Aims** As an international network of scientists, governments, indigenous organizations and conservation groups: work to harmonize and integrate efforts to monitor the Arctic's living resources. **Structure** Steering Committees; Secretariat. **Languages** English. **Activities** Monitoring/evaluation; research/documentation. **Events** *International Workshop* Hvalsø (Denmark) 2011. **Publications** *CBMP Newsletter*. *CBMP Monitoring Publications Series*. **Information Services** *Arctic Biodiversity Data Service*.
Members Full in 8 countries:
Canada, Denmark, Finland, Iceland, Norway, Russia, Sweden, USA.
Permanent participants (6):
Aleut International Association (AIA); *Arctic Athabaskan Council (AAC)*; *Gwich'in Council International (GCI)*; *Inuit Circumpolar Council (ICC, #15995)*; *Russian Association of Indigenous Peoples of the North (RAIPON)*; *Saami Council (#19012)*.
IGO Relations Endorsed by: *Arctic Council (#01097)*; *Secretariat of the Convention on Biological Diversity (SCBD, #19197)*. **NGO Relations** Monitoring Network Partners of: *BirdLife International (#03266)*; *INTERACT – International Network for Terrestrial Research and Monitoring in the Arctic (INTERACT, #11377)*; *International Tundra Experiment (ITEX, #15742)*; *Wetlands International (#20928)*. [2015.08.26/XJ2098/y/**E**]

♦ Circumpolar Conservation Union (internationally oriented national body)

♦ Circumpolar Health Research Network (CirchNet) 03942

Pres Natl Inst of Public Health, Univ of Southern Denmark, Øster Farimagsgade 5A, 2nd floor, 1353 Copenhagen K, Denmark. T. +4565507720. E-mail: cll@niph.dk.
URL: http://circhnet.org/
History 2012 on merger of *International Association of Circumpolar Health Publishers (IACHP, inactive)* and *International Network for Circumpolar Health Research (INCHR, inactive)*. Bylaws adopted Aug 2012. **Aims** Promote cooperation and collaboration among health researchers engaged in research in the circumpolar region; facilitate exchange, communication and dissemination of research results and other health data; support training and development of researchers in circumpolar health. **Structure** Board. **Languages** English. **Staff** 0.50 FTE, voluntary. **Finance** Members' dues. Annual budget: about euro 47,500. **Activities** Training/education. **Publications** *International Journal of Circumpolar Health.*
Members Individual (84); Institutional (7). Members in 9 countries and territories:
Canada, Denmark, Finland, Greenland, Norway, Russia, Sweden, UK, USA.
NGO Relations Member of: *International Union for Circumpolar Health (IUCH, #15764).*
[2017.12.04/XJ7457/**D**]

- ♦ Circumpolar Universities Association (inactive)
- ♦ Circus Federation of Australasia (internationally oriented national body)

♦ CircusNext 03943

Contact c/o Parc de La Villette, Cité Administrative – Bât D, 211 Av Jean Jaurès, 75019 Paris, France. T. +33143404860. E-mail: coordination@circusnext.eu – info@circusnext.eu.
URL: http://www.circusnext.eu/
History Set up as *Jeunes Talents Cirque Europe*. Current title adopted 2012. **Aims** Offer optimal conditions to contemporary *circus* authors.
Members Full in 12 countries:
Belgium, Czechia, Finland, France, Germany, Italy, Norway, Poland, Portugal, Spain, Sweden, UK.
IGO Relations *European Commission (EC, #06633).* **NGO Relations** Member of: *Circostrada Network (#03933).* [2020/XJ6163/**F**]

- ♦ CIRDAFRICA – Centre on Integrated Rural Development for Africa (no recent information)
- ♦ **CIRDAP** Centre on Integrated Rural Development for Asia and the Pacific (#03750)
- ♦ **CIRDES** Centre international de recherche-développement sur l'élevage en zone subhumide (#03760)
- ♦ **CIRDI** Centre international pour le règlement des différends relatifs aux investissements (#12515)
- ♦ CIRE / see Coordination et initiatives pour réfugiés et étrangers
- ♦ **CIRECCA** Centre international de recherches, d'échanges et de coopération de la Caraïbe et des Amériques (#03762)
- ♦ CIRE – Coordination et initiatives pour réfugiés et étrangers (internationally oriented national body)
- ♦ CIRED – Centre international de recherche sur l'environnement et le développement (internationally oriented national body)
- ♦ **CIRED** Congrès international des réseaux électriques de distribution (#12879)
- ♦ CIRELFA – Conseil international de réflexion et d'expertise en linguistique fondamentale appliquée (no recent information)
- ♦ CIREM / see Club du CEPII
- ♦ CIRESA / see Agropolis International
- ♦ CIRES – Centro Interuniversitario di Ricerca sul Sud Europa (internationally oriented national body)
- ♦ **CIRET** Centre international de recherches et études transdisciplinaires (#12526)
- ♦ **CIRET** Centre for International Research on Economic Tendency Surveys (#03765)
- ♦ CIRFF – Congrès International des Recherches Féministes dans la Francophonie (meeting series)
- ♦ CIRFS / see CIRFS – European Man-made Fibres Association (#03944)

♦ CIRFS – European Man-made Fibres Association 03944

Dir-Gen 40 rue Belliard, 1040 Brussels, Belgium. T. +3224369635. Fax +3224369638. E-mail: secretariat@cirfs.org.
URL: http://www.cirfs.org/
History Jun 1950, Paris (France). Most recent statutes adopted Dec 1997. Former names and other names: *International Rayon and Synthetic Fibres Committee (IRSFC)* – former (1950 to 2009); *Comité international de la rayonne et des fibres synthétiques (CIRFS)* – former (1950 to 2009). Registration: Belgium. **Aims** Study at scientific, technical and information level, the evolution of the *rayon* and *synthetic* fibre industry; improve, increase and develop the use of rayon, other artificial fibres, synthetic fibres and derived products; coordinate contacts at international level with other international professional and intergovernmental organizations; consider economic policy and its implications for other industries, and make recommendations accordingly. **Structure** General Assembly (twice a year); Board; General Secretariat; Commissions; Special Interest Groups. **Languages** English. **Staff** 7.00 FTE, paid. **Finance** Members' dues. **Activities** Research and development; knowledge management/information dissemination. **Events** *General assembly* Paris (France) 1986. **Publications** *Statistical Booklet* (annual).
Members Full in 18 countries:
Austria, Belarus, Belgium, Czechia, France, Germany, Ireland, Italy, Lithuania, Luxembourg, Netherlands, Portugal, Romania, Slovenia, Spain, Switzerland, Türkiye, UK.
Associate in 2 countries:
Japan, South Africa.
Consultative Status Consultative status granted from: *ECOSOC (#05331)* (Ros C); *UNCTAD (#20285)* (Special Category); *FAO (#09260)* (Liaison Status). **IGO Relations** *European Commission (EC, #06633); European Parliament (EP, #08146).* **NGO Relations** Affiliated with (1): *EMEA Synthetic Turf Council (ESTC, #05436). AEGIS Europe; Bureau international pour la standardisation de la rayonne et des fibres synthétiques (BISFA, #03369); Comité européen de normalisation (CEN, #04162); Conseil européen de l'industrie chimique (CEFIC, #04687); EURATEX – The European Apparel and Textile Confederation (EURATEX, #05616); Federation of European and International Associations Established in Belgium (FAIB, #09508); Industry4Europe (#11181); International Organization for Standardization (ISO, #14473);* national organizations. [2022/XC2400/**D**]

- ♦ CIRG / see Translational Research In Oncology
- ♦ **CIRG** Centre international de recherches glyptographiques (#03763)
- ♦ CIRHU – Centre of International Research in Human Unity (internationally oriented national body)
- ♦ CIRI – Centre International de Recherche en Infectiologie (internationally oriented national body)
- ♦ CIRIDD – Centre International de Ressources et d'Innovation pour le Développement Durable (internationally oriented national body)
- ♦ **CIRIEC** Centre international de recherches et d'information sur l'économie publique, sociale et coopérative (#03764)
- ♦ CIR / see IRC (#16016)
- ♦ CIRMA – Centro de Investigaciones Regionales de Mesoamérica (internationally oriented national body)
- ♦ CIRM – Centre international de rencontres mathématiques (internationally oriented national body)
- ♦ CIRM – Christian International Relief Mission (internationally oriented national body)
- ♦ **CIRM** Comité International Radio-Maritime (#04186)
- ♦ CIRMF / see Centre international de recherches médicales de Franceville
- ♦ CIRMF – Centre international de recherches médicales de Franceville (internationally oriented national body)
- ♦ CIRM – Fondazione Centro Internazionale Radio Medico (internationally oriented national body)
- ♦ **CIRN** Community Informatics Research Network (#04401)
- ♦ CIRP – Collège International pour la Recherche en Productique (#03945)
- ♦ CIRPES – Centre interdisciplinaire de recherche sur la paix et d'études stratégiques (internationally oriented national body)
- ♦ CIRPHO – Cercle international de recherches philosophiques par ordinateur (inactive)

♦ CIRP – The International Academy for Production Engineering 03945

CIRP – Collège International pour la Recherche en Productique – CIRP Internationale Akademie für Produktionstechnik

SG 9 rue Mayran, 75009 Paris, France. T. +33145262180. E-mail: cirp@cirp.net.
URL: https://www.cirp.net/
History 20 Nov 1950, Paris (France). Founded following work of international participants at French national meeting, 1948, Paris; commenced activities Sep 1951, Paris; statutes adopted 1 Dec 1953. Former names and other names: *International Institution for Production Engineering Research* – former; *Internationale Forschungsgemeinschaft für Mechanische Produktions Technik* – former. **Aims** Promote scientific research on the mechanical processing of all *solid materials*, including checks on efficiency and quality of work; establish permanent contacts among research workers, comparing their programmes and exchanging, synthesizing and publishing results of their experiments. **Structure** General Assembly (annual); Council; Committees (8). **Languages** English. **Staff** 2.00 FTE, paid; 1.00 FTE, voluntary. **Finance** Sources: grants; investments; members' dues. **Activities** Awards/prizes/competitions; events/meetings; knowledge management/information dissemination; networking/liaising; research/documentation; standards/guidelines. **Events** *Annual General Assembly* Dublin (Ireland) 2023, *Winter Meetings* Paris (France) 2023, *Annual General Assembly* Bilbao (Spain) 2022, *International Conference on Surface Integrity* Lyon (France) 2022, *Winter Meeting* Paris (France) 2022. **Publications** *CIRP Journal of Manufacturing Science and Technology* (4 a year); *CIRP Annals* (2 a year). *CIRP Encyclopedia of Production Engineering.* Conference proceedings.
Members Fellows and Associate members (450) – researchers chosen by co-option; Corporate members (170) – leading companies and private research institutes; Research Affiliates (100) – young researchers chosen by co-option. Research workers and laboratories in 43 countries and territories:
Australia, Austria, Belgium, Brazil, Canada, China, Croatia, Czechia, Denmark, Egypt, Finland, France, Germany, Greece, Hong Kong, Hungary, India, Ireland, Israel, Italy, Japan, Korea Rep, Malaysia, Mexico, Netherlands, New Zealand, Norway, Poland, Portugal, Romania, Serbia, Singapore, Slovenia, South Africa, Spain, Sri Lanka, Sweden, Switzerland, Taiwan, Türkiye, UK, Ukraine, USA.
NGO Relations Cooperates with (1): *International Organization for Standardization (ISO, #14473).*
[2022.06.16/XC2172/v/**C**]

- ♦ CIRP Internationale Akademie für Produktionstechnik (#03945)
- ♦ CIRPP – Commission internationale de réflexion pédagogique et pastorale (see: #15589)

♦ CIRRUS – Nordic-Baltic Network of Art and Design Education 03946

Coordinator Põhja pst 7, 10412 Tallinn, Estonia. T. +3726267369.
URL: https://cirrus.artun.ee/
History 1990. **Aims** Be a leading design innovator, debater and player on higher education field in the Nordic-Baltic region. **Structure** Board. **Languages** English. **Activities** Events/meetings; projects/programmes; training/education. **Events** *Meeting* Riga (Latvia) 2022, *Meeting* Tallinn (Estonia) 2021, *Meeting* Tallinn (Estonia) 2020, *Meeting* Bergen (Norway) 2019, *Meeting* Oslo (Norway) 2018.
Members Full in 8 countries:
Denmark, Estonia, Finland, Iceland, Latvia, Lithuania, Norway, Sweden. [2020.05.12/XM8063/**F**]

- ♦ CIRS – Center for International and Regional Studies (internationally oriented national body)
- ♦ CIRSD – Center for International Relations and Sustainable Development (internationally oriented national body)
- ♦ **CIRSE** Cardiovascular and Interventional Radiological Society of Europe (#03427)
- ♦ **CIRT** Conseil international de réadaptation pour les victimes de la torture (#14712)
- ♦ **CIRTEF** Conseil international des radios-télévisions d'expression française (#04694)
- ♦ **CIRUISEF** Conférence internationale des responsables des universités et instituts à dominante scientifique et technique d'expression française (#04622)
- ♦ Cirujanos Endovasculares de Latino América (unconfirmed)

♦ Cirujanos Vasculares de Habla Hispana (CVHH) 03947

Technical Secretary address not obtained.
URL: http://www.cvhhispana.org/
Structure Board of Directors, comprising President, President-Elect, Past-President, 2 Vice-Presidents, Secretary-General, Treasurer and 7 members. Committees (2): Scientific; Credentials. **Events** *Congreso* Madrid (Spain) 2017, *Congreso* San Juan (Puerto Rico) 2013, *Congreso / Congress* Granada (Spain) 2011, *Congreso / Congress* Cusco (Peru) 2009, *Congreso / Congress* Monterrey (Mexico) 2007. [2018/XJ7368/**D**]

- ♦ CIRVAL – Centre international de ressources et de valorisation de l'information dans les filières laitières petits ruminants (internationally oriented national body)
- ♦ CIS / see Princeton Institute for International and Regional Studies
- ♦ CIS / see Center for Comparative and International Studies
- ♦ CIS / see Inha Center for International Studies
- ♦ CIS / see Centre for Conflict Resolution, Cape Town
- ♦ CIS-7 Initiative (no recent information)
- ♦ CISA / see Burkle Center for International Relations
- ♦ CISAC / see Center for International Security and Cooperation
- ♦ CISAC – Center for International Security and Cooperation (internationally oriented national body)
- ♦ **CISAC** Confédération internationale des sociétés d'auteurs et compositeurs (#04563)
- ♦ **CISA** Comité Interamericano de Sanidad Avicola (#04170)
- ♦ **CISA** Commission internationale de sauvetage alpin (#12662)
- ♦ **CISA** Confédération internationale des syndicats arabes (#12845)
- ♦ **CISA** Consejo Indio de Sudamérica (#11158)
- ♦ CISAD – Conseil international des services d'aide à domicile (inactive)
- ♦ **CISAL** Confederación de Institutos Seculares en América Latina (#04451)
- ♦ CIS AS – Commonwealth of Independent States Atherosclerosis Society (no recent information)
- ♦ **CIS ATC** Commonwealth of Independent States Anti-Terrorism Center (#04342)
- ♦ CISBH – Comité international de standardisation en biologie humaine (inactive)
- ♦ **CISCA** Commission internationale de surveillance, de contrôle et d'arbitrage (#04228)
- ♦ CISCE – Comité international pour la sécurité et la coopération européennes (inactive)
- ♦ CIS – Center for Comparative and International Studies (internationally oriented national body)
- ♦ CIS – Centre for International Studies, Baku (internationally oriented national body)
- ♦ **CIS** Comité international de Sachsenhausen (#04187)
- ♦ CIS – Comité international du suivi du Sommet francophone (inactive)
- ♦ CIS Committee on Environment and Natural Resources (inactive)
- ♦ **CIS** Commonwealth of Independent States (#04341)
- ♦ CIS – Conference of Internationally-Minded Schools (inactive)
- ♦ **CIS** Council of International Schools (#04907)
- ♦ CISDA – Confederation of International Beverages Associations (inactive)
- ♦ CISD – Centre for International Studies and Diplomacy (internationally oriented national body)
- ♦ CISD – Coalition interagence SIDA et développement (internationally oriented national body)
- ♦ CISDL – Centre for International Sustainable Development Law (internationally oriented national body)
- ♦ CISD – La Loggia – Centro Internazionale di Scrittura Drammaturgica (internationally oriented national body)
- ♦ **CISDU** Centro Internazionale di Studi sul Disegno Urbano (#12520)
- ♦ CISE – Centre for International Studies in Education, Newcastle upon Tyne (internationally oriented national body)
- ♦ **CISE** Centre international des systèmes d'éducation (#12487)
- ♦ **CISEI** Consejo Interamericano Sobre la Espiritualidad Indigena (#11422)
- ♦ CISET – International Centre of Studies on the Tourist Economy (internationally oriented national body)
- ♦ **CISF** Centro Internazionale Studi Famiglia (#12492)
- ♦ **CISH** Comité international des sciences historiques (#12777)
- ♦ CIS – Inha Center for International Studies (internationally oriented national body)
- ♦ CIS Interstate Council for Emergency Situations (inactive)
- ♦ CISIS – International Conference on Complex, Intelligent, and Software Intensive Systems (meeting series)
- ♦ **CISLB** Comité international pour la sauvegarde de la langue bretonne (#12761)
- ♦ CISL – Confédération internationale des syndicats libres (inactive)

♦ **CISM** Centre International des Sciences Mécaniques (#03766)
♦ **CISM** Confédération internationale des sociétés musicales (#12865)
♦ **CISM** Conseil international du sport militaire (#04695)
♦ **CISM** International Confederation of Music Societies (#12865)
♦ **CISM** Internationaler Musikbund (#12865)
♦ CISO – Centre international de solidarité ouvrière (internationally oriented national body)
♦ CISO / see International Council of Onomastic Sciences (#13055)
♦ **CISOR** Confédération Interalliée des Sous-Officiers de Réserve (#04556)
♦ CISP – Comitato Internazionale per lo Sviluppo dei Popoli (internationally oriented national body)
♦ CISPE – Centro Internazionale per lo Studio dei Papiri Ercolanesi "Marcello Gigante" (internationally oriented national body)
♦ CISPP / see International Union of Prehistoric and Protohistoric Sciences (#15801)
♦ CIS – Prince Alwaleed Bin Talal Centre of Islamic Studies (internationally oriented national body)
♦ **CISRI** Collaborative Intergovernmental Scientific Research Institute (#04098)
♦ CISR / see International Society for the Sociology of Religions (#15451)
♦ CISRS – Christian Institute for the Study of Religion and Society (internationally oriented national body)
♦ **CISSA** Committee of Intelligence and Security Service of Africa (#04263)
♦ **CISSCAD** Consejo de Institutos de Seguridad Social de Centroamérica y República Dominicana (#04715)
♦ CISS – Canadian Institute of Strategic Studies (internationally oriented national body)
♦ CISS – Centre for International Security Studies (internationally oriented national body)
♦ CISS – Centre for International Security Studies, Moscow (internationally oriented national body)
♦ **CISS** Comité International des Sports des Sourds (#12805)
♦ **CISS** Conferencia Interamericana de Seguridad Social (#11419)
♦ CISS – Conseil international des sciences sociales (inactive)
♦ CISS – Cooperazione Internazionale Sud-Sud (internationally oriented national body)
♦ CISS / see Inter-American Conference on Social Security (#11419)
♦ CISS / see International Committee of Sports for the Deaf (#12805)
♦ CISSM – Center for International and Security Studies at Maryland (internationally oriented national body)

♦ CIS Society of Allergology and Clinical Immunology 03948

Chairman 4 Ostrovityanova Street, Moscow MOSKVA, Russia, 117513. T. +7957351414. Fax +7957351441. E-mail: info@wipocis.org.
URL: http://www.isir.ru/

History 1992. **Aims** Organize scientific, medical, diagnostic and prophylactic activities leading to: improvement of public health; encouragement of allergology and clinical immunology; consolidation of allergologists and immunologists of countries of the former USSR; creation of regional centres of allergology and clinical immunology; expansion of international contacts. **Events** *European asthma congress* Tbilisi (Georgia) 2004. **Publications** *Allergology and Immunology* (4 a year) – journal; *Asthma* (2 a year) – journal.
Members Organizations in 11 countries:
Armenia, Azerbaijan, Belarus, Georgia, Kazakhstan, Kyrgyzstan, Moldova, Russia, Turkmenistan, Ukraine, Uzbekistan.
NGO Relations Affiliate member of: *European Academy of Allergy and Clinical Immunology (EAACI, #05779).* [2015/XG0323/**D**]

♦ CISSS – Centre for International Security and Strategic Studies, Kiev (internationally oriented national body)
♦ **CIS-Stat** Interstate Statistical Committee of the Commonwealth of Independent States (#15983)
♦ CISTA – Council of International String Teachers Associations (inactive)
♦ **CIST** Centre international pour la science et de technologie (#14798)
♦ **CIST** Commission internationale de la santé du travail (#12709)
♦ Cistercensi della Stretta Osservanza (religious order)
♦ Cistercian Nuns (religious order)
♦ Cistercian Order of the Strict Observance (religious order)
♦ Cisterciennes de l'Ordre de Cîteaux (religious order)
♦ CISTOD – Confederation of International Scientific and Technological Organizations for Development (inactive)
♦ CISU – Chemical Industry Association for Scientific Understanding (inactive)
♦ CISV – Comunità Impegno Servizio Volontariato (internationally oriented national body)

♦ CISV International 03949

Communications Dir MEA House, Ellison Place, Newcastle upon Tyne, NE1 8XS, UK. T. +441912324998. Fax +441912614710. E-mail: international@cisv.org.
URL: http://www.cisv.org/

History 1950, Cincinnati, OH (USA). Founded by Dr Doris Allen. Activities commenced 1951. Constitution for the International Association of CISV: adopted at annual meeting, 1956, Sweden; revised and approved Aug 1991. Latest revision: Aug 2013. Former names and other names: *Children's International Summer Villages (CISV International)* – former; *Villages internationaux d'enfants* – former. Registration: Charity Commission, No/ID: 1073308, England and Wales; Companies House, No/ID: 3672838, England and Wales. **Aims** Educate and inspire people to act for peace through building inter-cultural friendship, cooperation and understanding, starting with children. **Structure** Governing Board; Standing Committees (4); International Junior Branch; Regional Teams; Secretary-General; Senior Management Team; International Office Staff. **Languages** English. **Staff** 8.00 FTE, paid. **Finance** Sources: fundraising. Programme participation fees. **Activities** Projects/programmes; training/education. **Events** *Global Conference* Eindhoven (Netherlands) 2022, *Asia Pacific Regional Conference* Seoul (Korea Rep) 2019, *Global Conference* Eindhoven (Netherlands) 2018, *Global Conference* Oslo (Norway) 2015, *Asia Pacific Regional Workshop* Bangkok (Thailand) 2014. **Publications** Annual Review. https://cisv.org/about-us/annual-reviews/.
Members National Associations (Categories A and B); Associated Organizations (Category C – reserved); Promotional Associations (Categories D, E and F); Former Affiliates (Category G). National and Promotional Associations in 67 countries and territories:
Algeria, Argentina, Australia, Austria, Belarus, Belgium, Brazil, Bulgaria, Canada, Chile, China, Colombia, Costa Rica, Côte d'Ivoire, Croatia, Czechia, Denmark, Ecuador, Egypt, El Salvador, Estonia, Faeroe Is, Finland, France, Georgia, Germany, Great Britain, Greece, Greenland, Guatemala, Honduras, Hong Kong, Hungary, Iceland, India, Indonesia, Israel, Italy, Japan, Jordan, Korea Rep, Latvia, Lebanon, Lithuania, Luxembourg, Mexico, Mongolia, Myanmar, Netherlands, New Zealand, Norway, Peru, Philippines, Poland, Portugal, Romania, Russia, Singapore, Slovenia, Spain, Sweden, Switzerland, Thailand, Türkiye, Uruguay, USA, Vietnam.
Consultative Status Consultative status granted from: *UNESCO (#20322)* (Consultative Partnership); *Council of Europe (CE, #04881)* (Participatory Status). **NGO Relations** Candidate member of: *European Youth Forum (#09140).* [2021.08.31/XD5491/**F**]

♦ **CITAC** Cooperation on International Traceability in Analytical Chemistry (#04797)
♦ CITA – Confederación Interamericana de Transporte Aéreo (inactive)
♦ CITA – Confédération internationale des fabricants de tissus d'ameublement (inactive)
♦ CITA – Confédération internationale des ingénieurs agronomes (inactive)
♦ **CITA** International Motor Vehicle Inspection Committee (#14187)
♦ CITBA – Customs and International Trade Bar Association (internationally oriented national body)
♦ **CIT** Cámara Internacional de la Industria de Transportes (#12536)
♦ CITCE / see International Society of Electrochemistry (#15079)
♦ CIT / see Chartered Institute of Logistics and Transport (#03856)
♦ CITC – International Conference on Construction in the 21st Century (meeting series)
♦ CIT – CODA International Training (internationally oriented national body)
♦ **CIT** Comité international des transports ferroviaires (#04188)
♦ **CIT** Congrès international de télétrafic (#15674)
♦ **CIT** Conseil international des tanneurs (#13084)
♦ CITD – Centre for International Trade and Development (internationally oriented national body)
♦ CITE – Center for International Training and Education (internationally oriented national body)
♦ CITED – Centro Iberoamericano de Tercera Edad (internationally oriented national body)
♦ CITEE – Centre for International Trade, Economics and Environment (internationally oriented national body)
♦ CITEF – Association des fabricants européens de compteurs d'électricité (inactive)
♦ **CITEF** Conférence internationale des formations d'ingénieurs et de techniciens d'expression française (#04619)
♦ CITEJA – Comité international technique d'experts juridiques aériens (inactive)
♦ **CITEL** Comisión Interamericana de Telecomunicaciones (#04138)
♦ **CITELEC** Association européenne des villes intéressées par l'utilisation de véhicules électriques (#05974)
♦ CITEM – Congreso Iberoamericano de Ciencia y Tecnologia de Membranas (meeting series)
♦ CITEN – Comité international de la teinture et du nettoyage à sec (inactive)
♦ CITERES-EMAM – Centre d'études et de recherches sur l'urbanisation du monde arabe – Equipe monde arabe et méditerranée (internationally oriented national body)
♦ CITES – Convention on International Trade in Endangered Species of Wild Fauna and Flora (1973 treaty)
♦ Cités et Gouvernements Locaux Unis d'Afrique (#20500)
♦ Cités des métiers International Network (#18890)
♦ **CITES Secretariat** Secretariat of the Convention on International Trade in Endangered Species of Wild Fauna and Flora (#19199)
♦ CITET – Tunis International Centre for Environmental Technologies (internationally oriented national body)
♦ **CITF** Commission internationale du théâtre francophone (#04229)
♦ CITHA / see European Confederation of International Trading Houses Associations (#06708)
♦ **CITHA** European Confederation of International Trading Houses Associations (#06708)
♦ CITH – Centre d'information textile – habillement (internationally oriented national body)
♦ **CITI** Confédération internationale des travailleurs intellectuels (#04564)
♦ **CITI** Consejo Internacional de los Tratados Indios (#13836)
♦ Citicorp Foundation / see Citi Foundation
♦ Cities after Transition (unconfirmed)

♦ Cities Alliance 03950

Secretariat UN House, Blvd du Régent 37, 1000 Brussels, Belgium. T. +3228804217. E-mail: info@citiesalliance.org.
URL: http://www.citiesalliance.org/

History Founded 19 May 1999, by *The World Bank Group (#21218)* and *United Nations Human Settlements Programme (UN-Habitat, #20572).* **Aims** As a global partnership for *urban poverty* reduction: promote and strengthen the role of cities in *sustainable development.* **Structure** Assembly (meets annually); Management Board; Secretariat in Brussels (Belgium). Hosted by *United Nations Office for Project Services (UNOPS, #20602).* **Languages** English, French, Portuguese, Spanish. **Staff** 20.00 FTE, paid. **Finance** Support from: *Ford Foundation (#09858); Habitat for Humanity International (HFHI); Shack-Slum Dwellers International (SDI, #19255); UNICEF (#20332); United Nations Human Settlements Programme (UN-Habitat, #20572); UNEP (#20299); International Bank for Reconstruction and Development (IBRD, #12317)* (World Bank); *World Organization of United Cities and Local Governments (UCLG, #21695)*; governments of Brazil, Chile, Ethiopia, France, Germany, Ghana, Norway, Philippines, South Africa, Sweden, Switzerland and UK. **Activities** Networking/liaising; financial and/or material support; advocacy/lobbying/activism; guidance/assistance/consulting; events/meetings. **Events** *EMDS : Meeting of Municipalities with Sustainable Development* Brasilia (Brazil) 2017, *Public policy forum* Barcelona (Spain) 2009, *Urban research symposium* Marseille (France) 2009. **Publications** *Cities Alliance in Action*; *eNewsletter*. *Civis Series.* Annual Report; thematic and technical publications. **Members** Full in 34 countries. Membership countries not specified. [2020/XF5597/**F**]

♦ **CITIES** Centre international de transfert d'innovations et de connaissances en économie sociale et solidaire (#12498)

♦ Cities for Children 03951

Project Dir City Hall Stuttgart, Rathaus, Marktplatz 1, 70173 Stuttgart, Germany. T. +4971121660756. Fax +4971121660755.
URL: http://www.citiesforchildren.eu/

History Founded Jun 2007, under the initiative of city of Stuttgart (Germany) and with the support of *Robert Bosch Foundation.* Full title: *European Network Cities for Children.* **Aims** Work on: equality of opportunities through education; affordable housing and space for outdoor activities; health and well-being for every child; work-life balance; local contract between generations; youth participation; children's safety. **Activities** Grants: European Award of Excellence. Thematic Working Groups (7): Education; Affordable Housing and Space for Outdoor Activities; Health; Work-Life Balance; Generation Dialogue – Active Living Together of Old and Young; Youth Participation; Traffic and Safety. **Events** *Annual Conference* Stuttgart (Germany) 2013, *Annual Conference* Stuttgart (Germany) 2012, *Annual conference* Stuttgart (Germany) 2011, *Annual Conference* Stuttgart (Germany) 2010, *Annual Conference* Stuttgart (Germany) 2009. **Publications** Agendas; brochures; conference proceedings.
Members Cities (76) in 32 countries:
Austria, Belgium, Bulgaria, Croatia, Czechia, Denmark, Estonia, Finland, France, Germany, Greece, Hungary, Ireland, Italy, Latvia, Lithuania, Luxembourg, Malta, Netherlands, Norway, Poland, Portugal, Romania, Russia, Serbia, Slovakia, Slovenia, Spain, Sweden, Switzerland, Türkiye, UK.
IGO Relations *European Committee of the Regions (CoR, #06665); Congress of Local and Regional Authorities of the Council of Europe (#04677).* **NGO Relations** *Council of European Municipalities and Regions (CEMR, #04891).* [2013.10.24/XJ1406/**E**]

♦ Cities Climate Finance Leadership Alliance (CCFLA) 03952

Contact address not obtained. E-mail: alliancesecretariat@cpiglobal.org.
URL: http://www.citiesclimatefinance.org/

History Sep 2014, New York, NY (USA). Renewed Sep 2019. **Aims** Deploy finance for city level climate action at scale by 2030. **Structure** Assembly; Steering Committee; Action Groups; Secretariat provided by: *Climate Policy Initiative (CPI, #04020).* **Languages** English. **Activities** Events/meetings. **Events** *Assembly* Heidelberg (Germany) 2019.
Members Public and private institutions include 27 organizations listed in this Yearbook:
– *African Development Bank (ADB, #00283);*
– *Agence française de développement (AFD);*
– *Banque ouest africaine de développement (BOAD, #03170);*
– *C40 (#03391);*
– *CDP (#03621);*
– *Children's Investment Fund Foundation (CIFF);*
– *Cities Development Initiative for Asia (CDIA, #03953);*
– *Climate and Clean Air Coalition (CCAC, #04010);*
– *Climate Bonds Initiative (#04006);*
– *Climate Investment Funds (CIF, #04015);*
– *Climate Policy Initiative (CPI, #04020);*
– *Commonwealth Local Government Forum (CLGF, #04348);*
– *Development Bank of Latin America (CAF, #05055);*
– *European Investment Bank (EIB, #07599);*
– *Global Environment Facility (GEF, #10346);*
– *Global Infrastructure Basel Foundation (GIB Foundation, #10418);*
– *Inter-American Development Bank (IDB, #11427);*
– *Kreditanstalt für Wiederaufbau (KfW);*
– *Local Governments for Sustainability (ICLEI, #16507);*
– *Regions of Climate Action (R20, #18820);*
– *The World Bank Group (#21218);*
– *UNEP (#20299);*
– *United Nations Capital Development Fund (UNCDF, #20524);*
– *United Nations Human Settlements Programme (UN-Habitat, #20572);*
– *World Organization of United Cities and Local Governments (UCLG, #21695);*

Cities Development Initiative
03953

alphabetic sequence excludes
For the complete listing, see Yearbook Online at

– *World Resources Institute (WRI, #21753)*;
– *World Wide Fund for Nature (WWF, #21922)*.
Governments of 4 countries:
Congo DR, France, Germany, USA. [2022/XM6288/**C**]

♦ Cities Development Initiative for Asia (CDIA) 03953

Contact Room 7504-7506, Asian Development Bank Bldg, 6 ADB Avenue, Mandaluyong City, 1550 METRO Manila, Philippines. T. +6326312342 – +6326330520 – +6326332366. E-mail: info@cdia.asia – secretariat@cdia.asia.
URL: http://cdia.asia/

History 2007, by *Asian Development Bank (ADB, #01422)* and the Government of Germany. Registered in accordance with Philippine law. **Aims** Contribute to sustainable and equitable urban development, leading to improved environmental and living conditions for all in Asian cities. **Structure** Board of Trustees; Core Management Team (CMT). **Finance** Funding from: *Asian Development Bank (ADB, #01422)*; *Deutsche Gesellschaft für Internationale Zusammenarbeit (GIZ)*; *Kreditanstalt für Wiederaufbau (KfW)*; governments of Germany, Austria, Sweden, Switzerland and Shanghai Municipal. **Events** *Asia Urban Resilience Finance Forum* Bangkok (Thailand) 2017. **NGO Relations** Member of: *Cities Climate Finance Leadership Alliance (CCFLA, #03952)*. [2017/XJ9618/**E**]

♦ Citi Foundation (internationally oriented national body)
♦ CitiHope International (internationally oriented national body)
♦ CITIM – Centre d'information Tiers-monde (internationally oriented national body)
♦ CIT / see International Chamber of the Transport Industry (#12536)
♦ CIT / see International Grains Council (#13731)
♦ CIT – International Television Committee (inactive)

♦ Citizens Advice International (CAI) 03954

Conseil international aux citoyens

Chairperson CAB-GI, 10 Governor's Lane, Gibraltar, Gibraltar.
Registered Address Rue du Prince Royal 83, 1050 Brussels, Belgium. T. +3225120113.
URL: http://www.citizensadviceinternational.org/

History Mar 2004, London (UK). Registered in accordance with Belgian law. **Aims** Promote free, impartial and confidential advice and information to the public about their rights; represent the interests of member organizations; provide a mechanism for information exchange, cooperation and joint projects among citizens advice organizations. **Structure** General Assembly (annual); Council. **Languages** English. **Events** *European forum of citizens advice services* Brussels (Belgium) 2009.
Members National organizations (12) in 10 countries and territories:
Czechia, Gibraltar, Ireland, Lithuania, New Zealand, Nigeria, Poland, Romania, Slovenia, UK.
NGO Relations Partner of: *European Citizen Action Service (ECAS, #06555)*. [2019/XM0357/**D**]

♦ Citizens' Alliance for Saving the Atmosphere and the Earth (internationally oriented national body)
♦ Citizen Sciences (internationally oriented national body)

♦ Citizens' Climate Engagement Network (CCEN) 03955

Address not obtained.
URL: http://engage4climate.org/

History Foundational meeting 25 Oct 2015, Minneapolis MN (USA). Launched 2 Dec 2015, Paris (France). **Aims** Support and expand direct citizen and stakeholder engagement in the intergovernmental climate negotiating process. **Structure** Advisory Coalition; Secretariat. **Activities** Advocacy/lobbying/activism. **Publications** *CCEN Newsletter*. **NGO Relations** *International Association for the Advancement of Innovative Approaches to Global Challenges (IAAI, #11687)*. [2018/XM6365/**F**]

♦ Citizens Commission on Human Rights International (see: #03922)
♦ Citizens Democracy Corps / see PYXERA Global
♦ Citizens Development Corps / see PYXERA Global

♦ Citizens for Europe (CFEU) 03956

Address not obtained.
URL: https://www.citizensforeurope.eu/

History 2010. No legal structure. **Aims** Create a participatory and democratic Europe. **Finance** Supported by: *Fondation Charles Léopold Mayer pour le progrès de l'homme (FPH, #09815)*. **Activities** Awards/prizes/competitions; networking/liaising.
Members Organizations in 34 countries:
Albania, Austria, Belgium, Bosnia-Herzegovina, Bulgaria, Croatia, Czechia, Denmark, Estonia, Finland, France, Germany, Greece, Hungary, Ireland, Italy, Latvia, Lithuania, Malta, Netherlands, North Macedonia, Poland, Portugal, Romania, Serbia, Slovakia, Slovenia, Spain, Sweden, Switzerland, Türkiye, UK, Ukraine, USA.
Access Info Europe; *AGE Platform Europe (#00557)*; *Alliance for Lobbying Transparency and Ethics Regulation (ALTER-EU, #00705)*; *ASKO Europa-Stiftung (AES)*; *A Soul for Europe (ASF, #19697)*; *Assembly of European Regions (AER, #02316)*; *Association des chambres de commerce et d'industrie européennes (EUROCHAMBRES, #02423)*; *Association des états généraux des étudiants de l'Europe (AEGEE-Europe, #02495)*; *Association internationale de techniciens, experts et chercheurs (AITEC, #02745)*; *Association of European Journalists (AEJ, #02516)*; *Austrian Institute for European Law and Policy*; *Bridging Europe (BREF, #03329)*; *Bruegel*; *European Association for Local Democracy (ALDA, #06110)*; *European Movement International (EMI, #07825)*; *Stand Up for Europe*. [2020/AA1277/y/**F**]

♦ Citizens of Europe (internationally oriented national body)
♦ Citizens' Forum for a Democratic Europe / see European Dialogue
♦ Citizens for Global Solutions (internationally oriented national body)
♦ Citizen's Network / see RCN Justice et Démocratie
♦ Citizens Network for Foreign Affairs / see Cultivating New Frontiers in Agriculture
♦ Citizens Network for Sustainable Development (internationally oriented national body)

♦ Citizens' Pact for South Eastern Europe (CP) 03957

Contact address not obtained. T. +38121452315. Fax +38121613089.
URL: http://www.citizenspact.org/

History Jul 2000. **Aims** Contribute to the development of civil society and stability in South Eastern Europe through strengthening cross-border cooperation and partner relations among local governments and organizations. **Structure** General Assembly (annual). **Activities** Organizes conferences.
Members in 8 countries:
Albania, Bosnia-Herzegovina, Bulgaria, Croatia, Moldova, North Macedonia, Romania, Serbia.
NGO Relations *PAX*. [2010/XF7157/**F**]

♦ Citizens for a Peaceful Planet / see Citizens for a United Earth
♦ Citizens for a United Earth (internationally oriented national body)
♦ **Citizen@Work** European network for health promotion and economic development (#07920)
♦ CITL – Collège international des traducteurs littéraires (internationally oriented national body)
♦ CitNet – Citizens Network for Sustainable Development (internationally oriented national body)
♦ **CITPA** Confédération internationale des transformateurs de papier et carton en Europe (#12866)
♦ **CITPA** International Confederation of Paper and Board Converters in Europe (#12866)
♦ CITpax – Centro Internacional de Toledo para la Paz (internationally oriented national body)
♦ **CITP** Comité international des télécommunications de presse (#14637)
♦ CITS – Center for International Trade and Security (internationally oriented national body)
♦ CITS – Commission internationale technique de sucrerie (inactive)

♦ Cittaslow 03958

Headquarters Comune di Orvieto, via Cipriano Manente 7, 05018 Orvieto PG, Italy. T. +39763341818. Fax +39763394455. E-mail: info@cittaslow.net.
SG address not obtained. E-mail: direttore@cittaslow.net.
URL: http://www.cittaslow.org/

History 1999, Italy. Full title: *Cittaslow International – Rete Internazionale delle città del buon vivere*. Other full titles: *International Network of Cities where living is easy – Réseau international des villes du bien vivre – Red Internacional de Municipios por la calidad de vida – International Vereinigung der Lebenswerten Städte – Rede Internacional de Cidades onde Viver é Facil – Ett Internationellt Nätverk för det goda livet – Internationellt Nätverk för Städer där man lever det goda livet – Internasjonalt Nettverk for Steder hvor det er godt å leve – Internationalt Bynetvaerk for Det gode Liv – Miedzynarodowa Siec Miast Dobrego Zycia – Yasamin Kolay Oldugu Kentlerin Ulusararasi Agi*. **Aims** Promote and spread the culture of good living through research, testing and application of solutions for the city organization. **Structure** International Assembly. International Coordinating Committee, including President and 8 Vice-Presidents. **Languages** English, Italian. **Events** *Assembly* Midden Delfland (Netherlands) 2014, *Korea international assembly* Seoul (Korea Rep) 2010.
Members Cities (147) in 24 countries:
Australia, Austria, Belgium, Canada, China, Denmark, Finland, France, Germany, Hungary, Italy, Korea Rep, Netherlands, New Zealand, Norway, Poland, Portugal, South Africa, Spain, Sweden, Switzerland, Türkiye, UK, USA. [2015/XJ4882/**F**]

♦ Cittaslow International – Rete Internazionale delle città del buon vivere / see Cittaslow (#03958)
♦ City2000 Youth Action International (internationally oriented national body)

♦ City to City Europe 03959

Faciliator address not obtained. E-mail: info@citytocityeurope.com.
URL: http://www.citytocityeurope.com/

Aims Catalyze and serve a Europe wide movement of leaders who create new *churches*, new ventures, and new expressions of the gospel of Jesus Christ for the common good. **Structure** Executive Team. **NGO Relations** *European Evangelical Alliance (EEA, #07010)*. [2015/XJ9165/**F**]

♦ City of Dawn / see Auroville Foundation (#03019)

♦ City Destinations Alliance (CityDNA) 03960

CEO 29D rue de Talant, 21000 Dijon, France. T. +33380560204. Fax +33380560205. E-mail: headoffice@citydna.eu.
URL: https://citydestinationsalliance.eu/

History 1 Jan 2007. Founded by merger of *European Cities Tourism (ECT, inactive)* and *European Federation of Conference Towns (EFCT, inactive)*. Former names and other names: *European Cities Marketing (ECM)* – former (1 Jan 2007 to 31 Mar 2022). **Aims** Provide a platform for convention, leisure and city marketing professionals to exchange knowledge, best practice and widen their network to build new business. **Structure** General Assembly; Board. **Languages** English. **Staff** 4.00 FTE, paid. **Activities** Events/meetings. **Events** *International Conference and General Assembly* Sofia (Bulgaria) 2023, *International Conference and General Assembly* Hamburg (Germany) 2022, *Autumn Conference* Tel Aviv (Israel) 2022, *TourMIS Users Workshop and International Seminar* Vienna (Austria) 2022, *TourMIS Users Workshop and International Seminar* Vienna (Austria) 2021. **Publications** *City Tourism Monitor*; *The European Cities Marketing Benchmarking Report*; *The European Cities Marketing Meetings Statistics Report*.
Members Tourist Offices, Convention Bureaux and City Marketing Organizations (125) in 37 countries and territories:
Austria, Azerbaijan, Belgium, Croatia, Czechia, Denmark, England, Estonia, Finland, France, Germany, Greece, Hungary, Ireland, Israel, Italy, Lithuania, Luxembourg, Malta, Monaco, Netherlands, North Macedonia, Northern Ireland, Norway, Poland, Portugal, Romania, Russia, Scotland, Serbia, Slovakia, Slovenia, Spain, Sweden, Switzerland, Türkiye, Ukraine.
IGO Relations Affiliate member of: *World Tourism Organization (UNWTO, #21861)*. **NGO Relations** Associate member of: *Union of International Associations (UIA, #20414)*. Member of: *Joint Meetings Industry Council (JMIC, #16140)*. [2022/XM2496/**F**]

♦ **CityDNA** City Destinations Alliance (#03960)
♦ **CITYNET** Regional Network of Local Authorities for the Management of Human Settlements (#18799)
♦ City-VITAlity-Sustainability / see CIVITAS (#03972)
♦ Ciudadanos Europeas (internationally oriented national body)
♦ Ciudades Atlanticas (#03008)
♦ **CIUEPS** Consorcio Interamericano de Universidades y Centros de Formación de Personal en Educación para la Salud y Promoción de la Salud (#04731)
♦ CIUP – Centro de Investigación de la Universidad del Pacifico (internationally oriented national body)
♦ CIUPST / see Scientific Committee on Solar-Terrestrial Physics (#19151)
♦ CIUS / see CIUS – European Sugar Users (#03961)

♦ CIUS – European Sugar Users 03961

SG 9-31 Av des Nerviens, 1040 Brussels, Belgium. T. +3225112781. Fax +3225081025. E-mail: cius@cius.org.
URL: http://www.cius.org/

History 1995. Former names and other names: *Committee of International Sugar Users (CIUS)* – former (1995); *European Sugar Users* – alias. Registration: EU Transparency Register, No/ID: 44875424605-90. **Aims** Represent European sugar-using *food* and *beverage industries*; share skills and understanding with all stakeholders and decision-makers interested in sugar so as to contribute to impartial and prospective policies for development of a transparent, competitive and fair sugar market. **Structure** Officers: President; Vice President; Secretary-General; Communications Manager. **Languages** English, French. **Staff** 2.00 FTE, paid. **Publications** Position papers.
Members National and European associations and international industrial companies, in total using almost 70% of the European annual consumption of sugar through incorporation in value-added products, and including 3 organizations listed in this Yearbook:
Association of the Chocolate, Biscuit and Confectionery Industries of the EU (CAOBISCO, #02427); *European Association of Fruit and Vegetable Processors (PROFEL, #06049)*; *UNESDA Soft Drinks Europe (UNESDA, #20323)*. [2022/XM0621/y/**D**]

♦ CIUSS – Catholic International Union for Social Service (inactive)
♦ **CIUTI** Conférence internationale permanente d'instituts universitaires de traducteurs et interprètes (#04621)
♦ CIVA – Centre international pour la ville, l'architecture et le paysage (internationally oriented national body)
♦ CIV – Centre international du vitrail (internationally oriented national body)
♦ CIV – Comité international du vaurien (see: #21760)
♦ **CIV** Commission internationale du verre (#12683)
♦ CIV – Convention internationale concernant le transport des voyageurs et des bagages par chemin de fer, 1961 (1961 treaty)
♦ CIV – Convention internationale concernant le transport des voyageurs et des bagages par chemins de fer (1924 treaty)
♦ **CIVCSVA** Congregazione per gli Istituti di Vita Consacrata e le Società di Vita Apostolica (#04671)
♦ CIVIC / see Center for Civilians in Conflict
♦ CIVIC – Center for Civilians in Conflict (internationally oriented national body)
♦ Civic Life International (internationally oriented national body)

♦ CIVICUS: World Alliance for Citizen Participation 03962

SG 25 Owl Street, 6th Floor, Johannesburg, 2092, South Africa. T. +27118335959. Fax +27118337997. E-mail: info@civicus.org.
URL: https://www.civicus.org/

History 28 May 1993, Barcelona (Spain). Registration: EU Transparency Register, No/ID: 656236835033-67, Start date: 12 Jun 2019. **Aims** Strengthen citizen action and civil society, and monitor state of civil liberties throughout the world, especially in areas where participatory democracy and citizens' freedoms of expression, peaceful assembly, and association are threatened. **Structure** Board of Directors; Executive Committee; Secretariat headed by Secretary General. Also offices in: Geneva (Switzerland); London (UK); New York NY (USA). **Languages** Arabic, English, French, Portuguese, Russian, Spanish. **Staff** 70.00 FTE, paid. **Finance** Sources: government support; members' dues; private foundations. **Activities** Advocacy/lobbying/activism; capacity building; events/meetings. Active in all member countries. **Events** *World Assembly* Belgrade (Serbia) 2019, *World Assembly* Suva (Fiji) 2017, *World Assembly* Bogota (Colombia) 2016, *World Assembly* Johannesburg (South Africa) 2014, *Conference on Building a Global Citizens Movement* Johannesburg (South

Africa) 2013. **Publications** *e-CIVICUS* (weekly) – electronic bulletin; *Civil Society Watch* (12 a year) – bulletin; *CIVICUS Monitor Global Ratings Report* (annual) in Arabic, English, French, Spanish; *State of Civil Society Report* (annual). *The Compendium of International Legal Instruments and Other Intergovernmental Commitments Concerning Core Civil Society Rights* (2010); *From Political Won't to Political Will – Building Support for Participatory Governance* (2009); *CIVICUS Global Survey of the State of Civil Society – vols 1-2* (2007); *Civil Society Index Country Reports* (2003-2006). **Information Services** *CIVICUS Lens* – CIVICUS Lens – Perspectives for a Changing World; *MONITOR – Tracking Civic Space*.
Members Organizations and individuals (over 14,000) in 181 countries and territories:
Afghanistan, Albania, Algeria, Antigua-Barbuda, Argentina, Armenia, Australia, Austria, Azerbaijan, Bahrain, Bangladesh, Barbados, Belarus, Belgium, Belize, Benin, Bhutan, Bolivia, Bosnia-Herzegovina, Botswana, Brazil, Brunei Darussalam, Bulgaria, Burkina Faso, Burundi, Cambodia, Cameroon, Canada, Cape Verde, Central African Rep, Chad, Chile, China, Colombia, Comoros, Congo Brazzaville, Congo DR, Cook Is, Costa Rica, Côte d'Ivoire, Croatia, Cuba, Cyprus, Czechia, Denmark, Djibouti, Dominica, Dominican Rep, Ecuador, Egypt, El Salvador, Equatorial Guinea, Estonia, Eswatini, Ethiopia, Fiji, Finland, France, Gabon, Gambia, Georgia, Germany, Ghana, Greece, Grenada, Guatemala, Guinea, Guinea-Bissau, Guyana, Haiti, Holy See, Honduras, Hungary, Iceland, India, Indonesia, Iraq, Ireland, Italy, Jamaica, Japan, Jordan, Kazakhstan, Kenya, Kiribati, Korea Rep, Kosovo, Kuwait, Kyrgyzstan, Latvia, Lebanon, Lesotho, Liberia, Libya, Luxembourg, Macedonia, Madagascar, Malawi, Malaysia, Maldives, Mali, Marshall Is, Mauritania, Mauritius, Mexico, Micronesia FS, Mongolia, Montenegro, Morocco, Mozambique, Myanmar, Namibia, Nepal, Netherlands, New Zealand, Nicaragua, Niger, Nigeria, Norway, Oman, Pakistan, Palau, Palestine, Panama, Papua New Guinea, Paraguay, Peru, Philippines, Poland, Portugal, Puerto Rico, Qatar, Romania, Russia, Rwanda, Samoa, Saudi Arabia, Senegal, Serbia, Sierra Leone, Singapore, Slovakia, Slovenia, Solomon Is, Somalia, South Africa, South Sudan, Spain, Sri Lanka, St Kitts-Nevis, St Lucia, St Vincent-Grenadines, Sudan, Sweden, Switzerland, Syrian AR, Taiwan, Tajikistan, Tanzania UR, Thailand, Timor-Leste, Togo, Tonga, Trinidad-Tobago, Tunisia, Türkiye, Turkmenistan, Tuvalu, Uganda, UK, Ukraine, United Arab Emirates, Uruguay, USA, Uzbekistan, Vanuatu, Venezuela, Vietnam, Yemen, Zambia, Zimbabwe.
Included in the above, 98 organizations listed in this Yearbook:
- *AARP International*;
- *ACORD – Agency for Cooperation and Research in Development (#00073)*;
- *ActionAid (#00087)*;
- *African Dignity Foundation*;
- *African Women's Development and Communication Network (FEMNET, #00503)*;
- *Andes University (ULA)*;
- *Arab NGO Network for Environment and Development (RAED, #01017)*;
- *Asian Institute for Civil Society Movement, Seoul (no recent information)*;
- *Asia Pacific Public Affairs Forum*;
- *Asia Pacific Socio-Economic Research Institute (APSERI)*;
- *Association for Research on Nonprofit Organizations and Voluntary Action (ARNOVA)*;
- *Association franco-latine pour le développement humain (no recent information)*;
- *Australian Council for International Development (ACFID)*;
- *Big Brothers Big Sisters International (BBBSI)*;
- *Bread for the World Institute (BFW Institute)*;
- *Canada World Youth (JCM)*;
- *Canadian Crossroads International (CCI)*;
- *Canadian International Development Agency (CIDA, inactive)*;
- *Carnegie Corporation of New York*;
- *Carnegie Endowment for International Peace (CEIP)*;
- *Charities Aid Foundation (CAF)*;
- *Charles F Kettering Foundation*;
- *Coady International Institute (CII)*;
- *Commonwealth Foundation (CF, #04330)*;
- *Conrad N Hilton Foundation (CNHF)*;
- *Cooperation Canada*;
- *Council of Women World Leaders (CWWL, #04923)*;
- *Counterpart International (FSP)*;
- *Covenant House*;
- *Disabled Peoples' International (DPI, #05097)*;
- *Eastern African Support Unit for NGOs (EASUN)*;
- *Endowment for Democracy in Eastern Europe (Reichmann Foundation, no recent information)*;
- *Esquel Group Foundation (EGF, inactive)*;
- *European Citizen Action Service (ECAS, #06555)*;
- *European Foundation Centre (EFC, inactive)*;
- *Ford Foundation (#09858)*;
- *Foundation for a Civil Society (FCS)*;
- *Fundação Luso-Americana para o Desenvolvimento (FLAD)*;
- *German Marshall Fund of the United States (GMF)*;
- *Global Fund for Children (GFC)*;
- *Global Fund for Women (GFW, #10384)*;
- *Human Rights Internet (HRI, #10986)*;
- *Initiative for Social Action and Renewal in Eurasia (ISAR, no recent information)*;
- *Institute for Sustainable Communities (ISC)*;
- *Institute of Cultural Affairs International (ICAI, #11251)*;
- *Inter-Africa Group – Centre for Dialogue on Humanitarian, Peace and Development Issues in the Horn of Africa (IAG, #11381)*;
- *Intercultural Development Research Association (IDRA)*;
- *International Association for Community Development (IACD, #11793)*;
- *International Association for Political Science Students (IAPSS, #12095)*;
- *International Association for Transformation (IAT)*;
- *International Association for Volunteer Effort (IAVE, #12260)*;
- *International Center for Not-for-Profit Law (ICNL, #12471)*;
- *International Centre for Development Affairs (ICDA, no recent information)*;
- *International Council for Adult Education (ICAE, #12983)*;
- *International Development Law Organization (IDLO, #13161)*;
- *International Federation of Women Lawyers (FIDA, #13578)*;
- *International Institute of Association and Foundation Lawyers*;
- *International Islamic Charitable Organization (IICO, #13957)*;
- *International Medical Assistance Foundation (AMI)*;
- *International Primate Protection League (IPPL, #14641)*;
- *International Society for Prevention of Child Abuse and Neglect (ISPCAN, #15385)*;
- *International Society for Third-Sector Research (ISTR, #15510)*;
- *International Women's Democracy Center (IWDC)*;
- *International Youth Foundation (IYF)*;
- *Kresge Foundation*;
- *Mentor International (MI, #16716)*;
- *Mercy Corps International (MCI)*;
- *Mweleko wa NGO (MWENGO, no recent information)*;
- *National Council for Voluntary Organizations (NCVO)*;
- *Near East Foundation (NEF)*;
- *Network of European Foundations (NEF, #17019)*;
- *Networks and Development Foundation (no recent information)*;
- *OneWorld International Foundation (OWIF, #17738)*;
- *Pact (#18016)*;
- *Partners of the Americas*;
- *Pathways To Peace (PTP, #18262)*;
- *Philanthropy without Frontiers, Canada*;
- *Raleigh International*;
- *Save the Children Federation (SCF)*;
- *School for International Training (SIT)*;
- *Society for Participatory Research in Asia (PRIA)*;
- *Southern African Non-Governmental Development Organization Network (SANGONeT, #19854)*;
- *Stakeholder Forum for a Sustainable Future (SF)*;
- *The Duke of Edinburgh's International Award Foundation (#05145)*;
- *The Management Centre of the Mediterranean (MC)*;
- *Toyota Foundation*;
- *Transparency International (TI, #20223)*;
- *TVE International*;
- *United Way Worldwide (#20663)*;
- *West Africa Rural Foundation (WARF, #20902)*;
- *Women's World Summit Foundation (WWSF, #21038)*;
- *World Affairs Councils of America (WACA)*;
- *World Association of Girl Guides and Girl Scouts (WAGGGS, #21142)*;
- *World Education (WE)*;
- *World Federation of Friends of Museums (WFFM, #21435)*;
- *World Learning*;
- *World Organization of the Scout Movement (WOSM, #21693)*;
- *World Young Women's Christian Association (World YWCA, #21947)*.

Consultative Status Consultative status granted from: *ECOSOC (#05331)* (General); *Council of Europe (CE, #04881)* (Participatory Status); *United Nations Population Fund (UNFPA, #20612)*; *African Commission on Human and Peoples' Rights (ACHPR, #00255)* (Observer). **IGO Relations** Member of (1): *United Nations Democracy Fund (UNDEF, #20551)*. Cooperates with (1): *Global Partnership for Social Accountability (GPSA, #10541)*. Associated with Department of Global Communications of the United Nations. **NGO Relations** Member of (7): *Accountable Now (#00060)*; *Conference of Non-Governmental Organizations in Consultative Relationship with the United Nations (CONGO, #04635)*; *Global Call for Climate Action (GCCA, inactive)*; *Global Partnership for Sustainable Development Data (Data4SDGS, #10542)*; *Transparency, Accountability and Participation Network (TAP Network, #20222)*; *UNCAC Coalition (#20283)*; *Worldwide Initiatives for Grantmaker Support (WINGS, #21926)*. Partner of (1): *UNLEASH*. Cooperates with (4): *Actions for Genuine Democratic Alternatives (AGENDA, #00097)*; *Arab NGO Network for Development (ANND, #01016)*; *Global Meeting of Generations (GMG)*; *International Communications Volunteers (ICVolunteers, #12817)*. Supports (1): *Global Call for Action Against Poverty (GCAP, #10263)*. Hosts: *Action for Sustainable Development (Action4SD)*. [2022.11.07/XF3276/y/**F**]

♦ CIVIH / see ICOMOS International Committee on Historic Cities, Towns and Villages (#11063)

♦ Civil Air Navigation Services Organisation (CANSO) 03963

Dir Gen c/o LVNL Room B3 33, Stationsplein Zuid-West 1001, 1117 CV Schiphol, Netherlands. T. +31235685380. Fax +31235685389. E-mail: info@canso.org.
URL: http://www.canso.org/

History 1996. **Aims** Be the global voice of air traffic management (ATM) in the transformation of the aviation system; create value for members and stakeholders. **Structure** Annual General Meeting; Executive Committee; Region Directors (5); Secretariat based in Amsterdam (Netherlands). **Languages** English. **Staff** 22.00 FTE, paid. **Activities** Events/meetings; knowledge management/information dissemination. **Events** *World Air Traffic Management (ATM) Congress* Madrid (Spain) 2024, *World Air Traffic Management (ATM) Congress* Madrid (Spain) 2023, *Africa Conference* Dakar (Senegal) 2022, *World Air Traffic Management (ATM) Congress* Madrid (Spain) 2022, *Latin American and Caribbean Conference* Orlando, FL (USA) 2022. **Publications** *ATM News* (weekly); *Airspace* – journal. **Members** Full (86); Associate (87). Membership countries not specified. **IGO Relations** Works closely with: *European Commission (EC, #06633)*; *EUROCONTROL (#05667)*. Liaison office with: *International Civil Aviation Organization (ICAO, #12581)*. **NGO Relations** Works closely with: *International Air Transport Association (IATA, #11614)*; *Airports Council International (ACI, #00611)*. Member of: *Air Transport Action Group (ATAG, #00614)*. [2022.02.07/XM4201/**C**]

♦ Civil Aviation Medical Association (CAMA) 03964

Exec Vice Pres PO Box 823177, Dallas TX 75382, USA. T. +17704870100. Fax +17704870080. E-mail: civilavmed@aol.com.
URL: http://civilavmed.org/

History 1948. Former names and other names: *Airline Medical Examiners Association* – former (1948 to 1955). **Aims** Promote the best methodology for assessment of mental and physical requirements for civil aviation *pilots*; actively enlarge their scientific knowledge; advocate, through continuing education, both basic and advanced civil aeromedical knowledge; promote professional fellowship among colleagues from allied scientific disciplines; unite civil aviation medical examiners into an effective, active medical body to promote aviation safety for the good of the public. **Structure** Officers: President; President-Elect; Secretary-Treasurer; Executive Vice-President; 4 Vice-Presidents (Management, Education, Communications, Representation). **Staff** 1.50 FTE, paid. **Finance** Sources: members' dues. **Activities** Events/meetings; networking/liaising. **Events** *Annual Scientific Meeting* Omaha, NE (USA) 2023, *Annual Scientific Meeting* Albuquerque, NM (USA) 2022, *Annual Scientific Meeting* San Antonio, TX (USA) 2021, *Annual Meeting* Albuquerque, NM (USA) 2020, *Annual Meeting* Cleveland, OH (USA) 2019. **Publications** *CAMA Bulletin* (6 a year); *Flight Physician*.
Members Individuals (850), mainly in the USA but in a total of 79 countries and territories:
Afghanistan, Antigua-Barbuda, Argentina, Australia, Austria, Bahrain, Belgium, Bolivia, Brazil, Bulgaria, Canada, Central African Rep, Chile, China, Colombia, Congo DR, Costa Rica, Croatia, Czechia, Egypt, El Salvador, Ethiopia, France, Gambia, Georgia, Germany, Greece, Guatemala, Honduras, Hungary, India, Indonesia, Iraq, Israel, Italy, Jamaica, Japan, Jordan, Kazakhstan, Kenya, Korea Rep, Kuwait, Laos, Lebanon, Liberia, Malaysia, Malta, Mexico, Nepal, Netherlands, Nicaragua, Nigeria, Norway, Pakistan, Palestine, Panama, Paraguay, Peru, Philippines, Poland, Portugal, Puerto Rico, Qatar, Rwanda, Saudi Arabia, Senegal, Somalia, South Africa, Spain, Suriname, Sweden, Switzerland, Taiwan, Thailand, Trinidad-Tobago, Tunisia, United Arab Emirates, USA, Zambia.
NGO Relations Affiliated with (1): *Aerospace Medical Association (ASMA)*. [2023.02.13/XD2190/v/**F**]

♦ Civil Global Positioning System Service Interface Committee (internationally oriented national body)
♦ Civil GPS Service Interface Committee / see Civil Global Positioning System Service Interface Committee
♦ Civil Initiative International Organization (internationally oriented national body)
♦ Civil Law Convention on Corruption (1999 treaty)

♦ Civil Liberties Union for Europe (Liberties) 03965

Exec Dir Ringbahnstrasse 16-18-20, 3rd Floor, 12099 Berlin, Germany. E-mail: info@liberties.eu.
URL: http://www.liberties.eu/

History Registration: Start date: 2017, Germany, Berlin. **Aims** Promote civil liberties of everyone in the European Union. **Structure** General Assembly; Board. **Languages** English, German. **Staff** 10.00 FTE, paid. **Activities** Knowledge management/information dissemination; advocacy/lobbying/activism.
Members Organizations in 14 countries:
Belgium, Bulgaria, Croatia, Czechia, Estonia, Hungary, Ireland, Italy, Lithuania, Netherlands, Poland, Romania, Slovenia, Spain. [2021/XM6305/**F**]

♦ Civil Peace Service (internationally oriented national body)
♦ Civil Rights Defenders (internationally oriented national body)

♦ Civilscape 03966

Vice-Pres Presidency Headquarters – CIVILSCAPE Bonn Office, Adenauerallee 68, 53113 Bonn, Germany. T. +4922829971100 – +4922829971101. Fax +4922829971109.
SG Secretary General Headquarters – CIVILSCAPE Office Olot, c/o L'Observatori del Paisatge de Catalunya, Carrer Hospici 8, 17800 Olot, Girona, Spain. T. +4922829971113. E-mail: pere.sala@civilscape.eu.
URL: http://www.civilscape.eu/

History 23 Feb 2008, Florence (Italy). Full title: *Civilspace – Non-Governmental Organisations for the European Landscape Convention*. Registered in accordance with Dutch law. EU Transparency Register: 66005431265-06. **Aims** Function as an international network for *nongovernmental organizations* striving to safeguard and improve the quality of *landscape*, in accordance with the European Landscape Convention. **Structure** General Assembly (annual); Executive Board. **Languages** English. **Staff** 1.00 FTE, voluntary. **Finance** Members' dues. **Activities** Events/meetings. **Events** *General Assembly* Marstrand (Sweden) 2014, *General Assembly* Emmeloord (Netherlands) 2013, *General Assembly* Lelystad (Netherlands) 2013, *General Assembly* Königswinter (Germany) 2012, *General Assembly* Florence (Italy) 2011. **Publications** *Civilscape Newsletter*.
Members Full in 16 countries:
Austria, Belgium, Bulgaria, Czechia, Germany, Hungary, Ireland, Italy, Montenegro, Netherlands, Slovakia, Slovenia, Spain, Sweden, Switzerland, UK.
International organizations (2):
European Council for the Village and Small Town (ECOVAST, #06848); *IFLA Europe (#11103)*.
Consultative Status Consultative status granted from: *Council of Europe (CE, #04881)* (Participatory Status). **IGO Relations** *European Landscape Convention (2000)*. Registered as a lobby organization with *European Commission (EC, #06633)*. **NGO Relations** Member of (2): *European Association for Local Democracy (ALDA, #06110)*; *European Heritage Alliance 3.3 (#07477)*. Together with *European Network of Local and Regional Authorities for the Implementation of the European Landscape Convention (RECEP-ENELC, #07939)* and *European Network of Universities for the Implementation of the European Landscape Convention (UNISCAPE, #08030)*, constitutes *European Landscape Network (Eurolandscape, #07644)*. [2019.04.24/XM1578/y/**E**]

♦ **Civil Society Coalition on Climate Change (CSCCC)** **03967**
Contact IPN, 410 Constitution Avenue NE, Washington DC 20002, USA. E-mail: cscccblog@gmail.com.
URL: http://csccc.info/
History As a response to the 2007 report of *Intergovernmental Panel on Climate Change (IPCC, #11499)*. **Aims** Educate the public about climate change issues in an impartial manner. **Members** Organizations (59) in 40 countries and territories:
Argentina, Australia, Austria, Brazil, Bulgaria, Burkina Faso, Canada, Chile, China, Costa Rica, Czechia, Denmark, Ecuador, Georgia, Germany, Ghana, Guatemala, Honduras, Hong Kong, India, Israel, Italy, Lithuania, Malaysia, New Zealand, Nigeria, Pakistan, Panama, Paraguay, Peru, Philippines, Russia, Slovakia, South Africa, Switzerland, Türkiye, UK, Uruguay, USA, Venezuela.
Included in the above, 2 organizations listed in this Yearbook:
European Coalition for Economic Growth (ECEG, #06593); *International Policy Network (IPN)*.
IGO Relations Accredited organization of: *Green Climate Fund (GCF, #10714)*. [2011/XM2617/**F**]

♦ Civil Society Europe (unconfirmed)

♦ **Civil Society Forum on Drugs (CSFD)** **03968**
Contact address not obtained.
URL: http://www.civilsocietyforumondrugs.eu/
History Set up 2007, as an expert group of *European Commission (EC, #06633)*, on the basis of Commission Green Paper. **Aims** Provide a broad platform for a structured dialogue between the Commission and the European civil society which supports drug policy formulation and implementation through practical advice. **Structure** Plenary Meeting; Core Group. Working Groups (4): EU Action Plan on Drugs; Relations with International Institutions; Civil Society Involvement with National Drug Policies; Minimum Quality Standards. **Members** Organizations include 16 listed in this Yearbook:
AIDS Foundation East-West (AFEW); *Association DIOGENIS – Initiative for Drug Policy Dialogue in South East Europe (Association DIOGENIS)*; *Correlation – European Harm Reduction Network (C-EHRN, #04848)*; *DIANOVA International (#05068)*; *European AIDS Treatment Group (EATG, #05850)*; *European Association for Palliative Care (EAPC, #06141)*; *European Cities Against Drugs (ECAD, #06553)*; *European Forum for Urban Security (Efus, #07340)*; *European Institute of Studies on Prevention (IREFREA, #07573)*; *European Treatment Centers for Drug Addiction (EURO-TC, #08947)*; *Harm Reduction International (HRI, #10861)*; *International Drug Policy Consortium (IDPC, #13205)*; *International Network of People who Use Drugs (INPUD, #14301)*; *Médecins du Monde – International (MDM, #16613)*; *World Federation Against Drugs (WFAD, #21408)*; *Youth Organisations for Drug Action (YODA, #22023)*. [2018/XM7749/y/**F**]

♦ **Civil Society and Indigenous Peoples' Mechanism for Relations with the UN Committee on World Food Security (CSM)** **03969**
Coordinator c/o FAO, Viale delle Terme di Caracalle, Room E-128, 00153 Rome RM, Italy. E-mail: cso4cfs@gmail.com.
URL: http://www.csm4cfs.org/
History Proposed 2009 at *Committee on World Food Security (CFS, see: #09260)*. Proposal endorsed Oct 2010, Rome (Italy). Former names and other names: *International Food Security and Nutrition Civil Society Mechanism (CSM)* – former (2009 to 2018). **Aims** Facilitate civil society participation in agriculture, food security and nutrition policy development at national, regional and global levels in the context of the Committee on World Food Security (CFS). **Structure** Coordination Committee, consisting of 41 focal points representing 11 constituencies and 17 sub-regions. Advisory Group. **Activities** Organizes forum at CFS Session. [2021/XJ7219/**E**]

♦ **Civil Society Platform for Peacebuilding and Statebuilding (CSPPS)** **03970**
Plateforme de la Société Civile pour la Consolidation de la Paix et le Renforcement de l'Etat
Coordinator Grote Marktstraat 45, PO Box 16440, 2511 BH The Hague, Netherlands. T. +31641887737. E-mail: info@cspps.org.
URL: http://www.cspps.org/
History First coordinated by *Interpeace (#15962)*. Since 2012 active under current title and coordinated by *Catholic Organization for Relief and Development (Cordaid)*. **Aims** Strengthen the voice and capacity of civil society to effectively engage in, and influence, peacebuilding and statebuilding as a critical contribution to crisis prevention and sustainable peace and development for all. **Structure** Executive Committee; Core Group; Secretariat hosted by *Catholic Organization for Relief and Development (Cordaid)*. **Languages** English, French. **Staff** 2.00 FTE, paid. **Finance** Sources: grants. Budget participation received through Secretariat host organization. Annual budget: 500,000 EUR. **Activities** Advocacy/lobbying/activism; awareness raising; capacity building; conflict resolution; events/meetings; networking/liaising; politics/policy/regulatory; projects/programmes. **Events** *Annual Conference* Berlin (Germany) 2022, *Annual Core Group Meeting* Berlin (Germany) 2016. **Publications** *CSPPS Newsletter*. *The Triple-Nexus and Climate Change in Conflict-Affected Settings: Experiences, Lessons Learned, and Best Practices* (2022) in English; *SDG16+ in Peril: An urgent call-to-action for safeguarding commitments to Peaceful, Just and Inclusive Societies – 2022 Rome Civil Society Declaration* (2020) in Arabic, English, French, Spanish. Annual Report; country reports; meeting reports; advocacy papers; position documents; policy briefs; statements.
Members Organizations in 34 countries:
Afghanistan, Burundi, Cameroon, Central African Rep, Chad, Comoros, Congo Brazzaville, Congo DR, Côte d'Ivoire, Egypt, Ethiopia, Guinea, Guinea-Bissau, India, Kenya, Lebanon, Liberia, Libya, Nepal, Niger, Nigeria, Papua New Guinea, Rwanda, Sao Tomé-Principe, Senegal, Sierra Leone, Solomon Is, Somalia, South Sudan, Timor-Leste, Togo, Uganda, Yemen, Zimbabwe.
Included in the above, 5 organizations listed in this Yearbook:
Centre for Sustainable Development and Education in Africa (CSDEA); *Fellowship of Christian Councils and Churches in West Africa (FECCIWA, #09724)*; *New African Research and Development Agency (NARDA)*; *Réseau des Plate-formes nationales d'ONG d'Afrique de l'Ouest et du Centre (REPAOC, #18902)*; *West Africa Network for Peacebuilding (WANEP, #20878)*.
IGO Relations Cooperates with: *European Commission (EC, #06633)*; *OECD (#17693)* – International Dialogue on Peacebuilding and Statebuilding (IDPS) and International Network on Conflict and Fragility (INCAF); *UNDP (#20292)*. **NGO Relations** Member organizations include: *Alliance for Peacebuilding*; *Arbeitsgemeinschaft Frieden und Entwicklung (FriEnt)*; *Catholic Organization for Relief and Development (Cordaid)*; Council for International Conflict Resolution (RIKO); *Global Partnership for the Prevention of Armed Conflict (GPPAC, #10538)*; *Integrity Action*; *International Alert (#11615)*; *International Budget Partnership (IBP, #12406)*; *Interpeace (#15962)*; *Oxfam Novib*; *Saferworld*; *Search for Common Ground (SFCG)*; *Swisspeace*; *United Network of Young Peacebuilders (UNOY, #20653)*; *World Vision International (WVI, #21904)*. [2022.10.19/XJ8939/y/**F**]

♦ Civil Society for the Renewal of European Democracy (inactive)

♦ **Civil Society Task Force** **03971**
Contact c/o Opinión Sur, Salguero 2835 7B, Buenos Aires, Argentina. T. +541148018616.
Pres 8404 Whitman Drive, Bethesda MD 20817, USA. T. +1202466-2988. Fax +12024662920.
URL: http://www.esquel.org/taskforce.htm
History 1994. Coordinated by *Esquel Group Foundation (EGF, inactive)*. **Aims** Function as a clearinghouse and forum for debate on active citizen participation in the *Americas*, especially within the framework of the Hemispheric Summit process, which emphasizes a *sustainable* and inclusive development process, and as a vehicle to coordinate civil society action on the Miami Process; work with key persons in the Summit of the Americas process to advance civil society participation; generate opportunities for civil society participation on other specific issues/instances at the regional level; increase awareness of the Summit process within governmental and nongovernmental sectors in countries of the region; promote constructive dialogue and collaboration between governmental and nongovernmental sectors in each country; foster implementation of Summit mandates; promote information exchange between civil society and Summit officials at the hemispheric level so as to advance effective participation of civil society in the Summit Process. **Activities** Monitors follow-up from the Hemispheric Summit for Sustainable Development, Dec 1996, Santa Cruz (Bolivia), the Summit of the Americas, Apr 1998, Santiago (Chile), and the Canadian Summit, Mar 2001, Québec (Canada). Participants monitor the work of the Government Committee on Civil Society (GCCS) of *Free Trade Area of the Americas (FTAA, no recent information)* in devising procedures to promote discussions with civil society and are actively engaged in definition of the OAS program 'Inter-American Strategy for Citizen Participation (ISP)' in sustainable development policies in the Americas. *'NGO Working Group on the OAS'*, created Nov 1998, advises several missions on OAS reform, in particular with respect to OAS relationship to civil society; recent efforts focus on an NGO accreditation system within the OAS. *'Sur Norte Inversión y Desarrollo (Sur Norte)'*, created in 1999 in Argentina, promotes solutions to poverty and social exclusion; work focuses on new generation of socially-responsible and environmentally sustainable entrepreneurial support instruments to catalyze local development. Sur Norte works closely with sister organization *'South North Development Initiative'*, based in New York NY (USA). **Publications** *Opinión Sur* (12 a year) – from Sur Norte. *A Country for All: Towards a Fair and Vigorous Development* by Roberto Sansón Mizrahi; *Threads of Disorder: Early Geopolitical Trends in the New Century* by Juan Eugenio Corradi. Information Services: Participant database of over 300 names. **Members** Not a membership organization. Participants include representatives from US and international NGOs, government agencies, multilateral institutions, foundations, academia, the media and private for-profit organizations. [2008.06.01/XF6136/**F**]

♦ Civilspace – Non-Governmental Organisations for the European Landscape Convention / see Civilscape (#03966)
♦ Civil Volunteer Group (internationally oriented national body)
♦ CIV – International Convention Concerning the Carriage of Passengers and Luggage by Rail, 1961 (1961 treaty)
♦ CIV – International Convention Concerning the Carriage of Passengers and Luggage by Rail, with Additional Protocol, 1970 (1970 treaty)
♦ **CIVIS** Association of Non-Governmental Organizations of Southeast Europe (#02825)
♦ Civitan / see Civitan International
♦ Civitan International (internationally oriented national body)
♦ Civitan International Research Center (internationally oriented national body)

♦ **CIVITAS** **03972**
Secretariat c/o Regional Environmental Ctr for Central and Eastern Europe, Ady Endre út 9-11, Szentendre 2000, Hungary. T. +3625504046. Fax +3625311294.
EU Representative EU – DG Mobility and Transport, Unit B-4 – Clean Transport/Urban Transport/Intelligent Transport Systems, Office DM24/127, 1049 Brussels, Belgium. T. +3222971748. Fax +3222964710.
URL: http://www.civitas.eu/
History 2002, as *CIVITAS I* (2002-2006), within 5th Framework Research Programme of *European Commission (EC, #06633)*. *CIVITAS II* (2005-2009) started 2005 within 6th Framework Research Programme. Current *CIVITAS PLUS* (2008-2012) started 2008, within 7th Framework Research Programme. CIVITAS is derived from *CIty-VITAlity-Sustainability*. **Aims** Promote and implement sustainable, clean and (energy) efficient *urban transport* measures; implement integrated packages of technology and policy measures in the field of energy and transport; build up critical mass and markets for innovation. **Structure** Steering Group – Political Advisory Committee. CIVITAS National Networks (5): CIVINET España-Portugal; CIVINET Francophone; CIVINET Italia; CIVINET Slovenija; CIVIT UK and Ireland. **Activities** Grants 'CIVITAS Award'. *CIVITAS FORUM Network* provides a platform for the exchange of ideas and experiences between all the participating CIVITAS I, CIVITAS II and CIVITAS PLUS demonstration cities, and other cities that are committed to introducing ambitious, clean urban transport strategies. **Events** *Urban Mobility Days* Brussels (Belgium) 2020, *Annual Forum Conference* Graz (Austria) 2019, *Urban Freight Conference* Brussels (Belgium) 2018, *Annual Forum Conference* Umeå (Sweden) 2018, *Annual Forum Conference* Ljubljana (Slovenia) 2015.
Members Cities in 15 countries:
Belgium (Ghent), Bulgaria (Gorna Oryahovitsa), Croatia (Zagreb), Czechia (Brno – Usti nad Labem), Denmark (Ålborg), Estonia (Tallinn), Italy (Bologna – Monza – Brescia – Perugia), Netherlands (Utrecht), North Macedonia (Skopje), Poland (Gdansk – Szczecinek), Portugal (Porto – Coimbra), Romania (Iasi – Craiova), Slovenia (Ljubljana), Spain (Donostia-San Sebastian – Vitoria-Gasteiz), UK (Bath – Brighton – Hove). [2013/XJ2401/**E***]

♦ CIVITAS I / see CIVITAS (#03972)
♦ CIVITAS II / see CIVITAS (#03972)

♦ **CIVITAS International** **03973**
Contact c/o Center for Civic Education, 5115 Douglas Fir Rd, Ste J, Calabasas CA 91302, USA. T. +18185919321. Fax +18185919330. E-mail: international@civiced.org.
URL: http://www.civiced.org/programs/civitas
History Jun 1995, Prague (Czechia). Founded at an international conference of civic educators. Former names and other names: *International Consortium for Civic Education* – former (Jun 1995). **Aims** Strengthen effective *education* for informed and *responsible citizenship* in new and established *democracies* worldwide. **Structure** Council; Executive Board, including Steering Committee. Secretariat in Strasbourg (France). **Finance** Members' dues. Other sources: funds; gifts. **Activities** Provides online resources and services for international civic educational audience; maintains a worldwide network; promotes international exchanges; strives to bring the knowledge, skills, and experience of education for democracy to bear on the tasks that confront today's democracies. **Events** *International conference* Mexico 1999, *International congress / International Conference* Palermo (Italy) 1999, *Asia Pacific conference / International Conference* Kuala Lumpur (Malaysia) 1998, *Southern Africa workshop* Maputo (Mozambique) 1998, *Conference on education for democracy / International Conference* Strasbourg (France) 1998. **Publications** *CIVITAS Newsletter*. **Information Services** *Civnet* – website.
Members Organizational; Individual; Associate. Organizational (62) in 35 countries:
Argentina, Australia, Brazil, Bulgaria, Burkina Faso, Canada, Colombia, Côte d'Ivoire, Croatia, Denmark, Ethiopia, France, Georgia, Germany, Ghana, Hungary, Indonesia, Latvia, Lithuania, Mali, Mexico, Moldova, Mongolia, Niger, Nigeria, Panama, Poland, Romania, Russia, Senegal, Tajikistan, Tanzania UR, UK, Ukraine, USA.
Individuals (30) in 24 countries:
Argentina, Bosnia-Herzegovina, Cameroon, Colombia, Croatia, Dominican Rep, Ethiopia, France, India, Indonesia, Italy, Nigeria, Paraguay, Peru, Romania, Senegal, Serbia, South Africa, Tanzania UR, Thailand, Türkiye, Ukraine, USA, Venezuela.
Associate (7) in 7 countries:
Bulgaria, Chile, Croatia, Denmark, Estonia, Israel, North Macedonia.
Included in the above, 3 organizations listed in this Yearbook:
Georg Eckert Institute for International Textbook Research; *Joint Eastern Europe Center for Democratic Education and Governance (Joint Centre, no recent information)*; *Mershon Center for International Security Studies*.
IGO Relations *UNESCO (#20322)*. **NGO Relations** *Asia-Pacific Civic Education Network (APCEN, no recent information)*. [2014/XF4598/y/**F**]

♦ Civitas Nostra – Fédération internationale des quartiers anciens (inactive)
♦ CIVITAS PLUS / see CIVITAS (#03972)

♦ **Civitates** **03974**
Programme Manager c/o Philanthropy House, Rue Royale 94, 1000 Brussels, Belgium. E-mail: secretariat@civitates-eu.org.
Programme Officer address not obtained.
URL: https://civitates-eu.org/
History 2018. Former names and other names: *Civitates – A philanthropic initiative for democracy and solidarity in Europe* – full title. **Aims** Strengthen the capacity of civil society to play its indispensable role in shaping vibrant open European democracies that work for all. **Structure** Steering Committee; Executive Committee; Secretariat. Working Groups. Hosted by *Network of European Foundations (NEF, #17019)*. **Finance** Supported by: *Adessium Foundation*; *Bertelsmann Foundation*; *Charles Stewart Mott Foundation*; *ERSTE Foundation*; *European Cultural Foundation (ECF, #06868)*; *Fondation de France*; Fondation Nicolas Puech; Fondazione Compagnia di San Paolo; Fritt Ord; *King Baudouin Foundation (KBF)*; *Luminate*; *Oak Foundation*; *Open Society Foundations (OSF, #17763)*; *Porticus*; *Robert Bosch Foundation*; Rudolf Augstein Stiftung; Schöpflin Stiftung; Stefan Batory Foundation; *Stiftung Mercator*. Annual budget: 3,000,000 EUR. **Activities** Capacity building; financial and/or material support; networking/liaising. [2023/AA1348/**F**]

♦ Civitates – A philanthropic initiative for democracy and solidarity in Europe / see Civitates (#03974)
♦ CIVJ – Centre international de volontaires du Japon (internationally oriented national body)
♦ **CIVL** Comité international pour un Vietnam libre (#12772)
♦ CIVPOL / see United Nations Police (#20611)
♦ CivSource Africa (unconfirmed)

♦ CIVVIH / see ICOMOS International Committee on Historic Cities, Towns and Villages (#11063)
♦ CIWEM – Chartered Institution of Water and Environmental Management (internationally oriented national body)
♦ **CIWF** Compassion in World Farming (#04414)
♦ CIX – Commercial Internet eXchange Association (inactive)
♦ **CJA** Commonwealth Journalists Association (#04344)
♦ CJBE – Colleagues in Jesuit Business Education (internationally oriented national body)
♦ **CJC** Confederación de Judo del Caribe (#04452)
♦ **CJ-CEMAC** Cour de justice communautaire de la CEMAC (#04931)
♦ **CJCPLP** Conferência das Jurisdições Constitucionais dos Países de Língua Portuguesa (#04653)

♦ CJD International Support Alliance (CJDISA) 03975

Co-Chair c/o JFD Support Group Network, 13 Araluen Place, Glenhaven, Sydney NSW 2156, Australia. E-mail: contactus@cjdsupport.org.au.
Co-Chair address not obtained. E-mail: cjdinsight@gmail.com.
URL: http://cjdisa.com/

Aims Raise awareness of prion *disease*; educate healthcare professionals and the public at large. **Members** Organizations (11). Full in 8 countries:
Australia, Chile, France, Germany, Italy, Japan, UK, USA.
Associate in 3 countries:
Canada, Israel, Mexico. [2016/XM5420/**C**]

♦ **CJDISA** CJD International Support Alliance (#03975)
♦ CJEC / see Court of Justice of the European Union (#04938)
♦ **CJE** Congrès juif européen (#07609)
♦ CJEI – Commonwealth Judicial Education Institute (internationally oriented national body)
♦ **CJEU** Court of Justice of the European Union (#04938)
♦ CJHA / see European Commission (#06633)
♦ CJI – Comité Juridico Interamericano (see: #17629)
♦ **CJIE** Comité des jeux internationaux des écoliers (#04264)
♦ **CJL** Congreso Judio Latinoamericano (#16344)
♦ CJM – Congregation of Jesus and Mary (religious order)
♦ **CJM** Congrès juif mondial (#21599)
♦ CJPA – Coalition for Justice and Peace in Africa (internationally oriented national body)
♦ CJP – Center for Justice and Peacebuilding (internationally oriented national body)
♦ CJP – Commission justice et paix (internationally oriented national body)
♦ **CKB** Climate Knowledge Brokers (#04016)
♦ CKF / see European Society Coudenhove-Kalergi (#08573)
♦ **C-KIN** Cancer and the Kidney International Network (#03414)
♦ **CKMC** Caribbean Knowledge Management Centre (#03521)
♦ CL / see Centre international LEBRET-IRFED
♦ **CLAAF** Comité Latinoamericano de Asuntos Financieros (#16300)
♦ CLA – Association du droit de l'informatique / see International Technology Law Association (#15669)
♦ CLABE – Consejo Latinoamericano de Biomedicina Experimental (no recent information)
♦ CLABIO – Conferencia Latinoamericana en Bioimpedancia (meeting series)
♦ **CLACAI** Consortio Latinoamericano Contra el Aborto Inseguro (#04733)
♦ **CLAC** Comisión Latinoamericana de Aviación Civil (#16297)
♦ **CLAC** Coordinadora Latinoamericana y del Caribe de Pequeños Productores de Comercio Justo (#16282)
♦ CLACDS – Centro Latinoamericano para la Competitividad y el Desarrollo Sostenible (internationally oriented national body)
♦ **CLACIES** Confederación Latinoamericana de Centros de Espiritualidad Ignaciana (#04455)
♦ CLACJ / see Latin American and Caribbean Alliance of YMCAs (#16264)
♦ **CLA** Commonwealth Lawyers Association (#04345)
♦ CLA – Conseil latinoaméricain et des Caraïbes pour l'autogestion (inactive)
♦ **CLACPI** Coordinadora Latinoamericana de Cine et de Comunicación de los Pueblos Indigenas (#04806)
♦ CLACS – Center for Latin American and Caribbean Studies, Bloomington (internationally oriented national body)
♦ CLACS – Center for Latin American and Caribbean Studies, Michigan (internationally oriented national body)
♦ CLACS – Center for Latin American and Caribbean Studies, New York (internationally oriented national body)
♦ **CLACSO** Consejo Latinoamericano de Ciencias Sociales (#04718)
♦ **CLAD** Centro Latinoamericano de Administración para el Desarrollo (#16294)
♦ **CLADEA** Consejo Latinoamericano de Escuelas de Administración (#16308)
♦ **CLADE** Campaña Latinoamericana por el Derecho a la Educación (#03407)
♦ **CLADEC** Conferencia Latino Americana de Compañias Express (#04654)
♦ **CLADE** Consejo Latinoamericano de Estrabismo (#04720)
♦ **CLADEM** Comité de América Latina y el Caribe para la Defensa de los Derechos de la Mujer (#16268)
♦ CLADES – Centro Latinoamericano de Documentación Económica y Social (inactive)
♦ **CLADH** Centro Latinoamericano de Derechos Humanos (#03812)
♦ **CLAEC** Comisión Latinoamericana de Empresarios de Combustibles (#04140)
♦ CLAE – Comité de liaison et d'action des étrangers (internationally oriented national body)
♦ **CLAE** Consorcio Latinoamericano de Anticoncepción de Emergencia (#16306)
♦ CLAEH / see Universidad CLAEH (#20688)
♦ CLAEI – Circulo Latinoamericano de Estudios Internacionales (internationally oriented national body)
♦ **CLAEP** Consejo Latinoamericano de Acreditación de la Educación en Periodismo (#04717)
♦ **CLAES** Centro Latinoamericano de Ecologia Social (#16292)
♦ **CLAF** Centro Latino-Americano de Fisica (#03815)
♦ CLAFE – Consejo Latinoamericano de Fisica del Espacio (inactive)
♦ **CLAFEN** Circulo Latinoamericano de Fenomenologia (#03937)
♦ **CLAFK** Confederación Latinoamericana de Fisioterapia y Kinesiologia (#04458)
♦ CLAG / see Conference of Latin American Geography (#04625)
♦ **CLAG** Conference of Latin American Geography (#04625)
♦ CLAH – Conference on Latin American History (internationally oriented national body)
♦ **CLAI** Consejo Latinoamericano de Iglesias (#16309)
♦ CLAIHR / see Canadian Lawyers for International Human Rights
♦ CLAIHR – Canadian Lawyers for International Human Rights (internationally oriented national body)

♦ Claims Conference Central and Eastern European Fund (CEEF) 03976

Contact PO Box 1215, New York NY 10113, USA. T. +16465369100. E-mail: info@claimscon.org.
URL: http://www.claimscon.org/what-we-do/compensation/background/ceef/

History May 1998. Following an agreement between the Government of Germany and *Conference on Jewish Material Claims Against Germany (Claims Conference, #04624)*. **Aims** Provide justice and care for Jewish Holocaust victims; ensure that future generations learn the lessons of the Holocaust; preserve the memory of the Holocaust victims. **Structure** Board of Directors; Officers. **Activities** Financial and/or material support; advocacy/lobbying/activism. **NGO Relations** Instrumental in setting up: *International Commission on Holocaust Era Insurance Claims (ICHEIC, inactive)*. [2018.06.01/XF5907/f/**F**]

♦ **Claims Conference** Conference on Jewish Material Claims Against Germany (#04624)
♦ **CLAIP** Consejo Latinoamericano de Investigaciones para la Paz (#16310)
♦ CLAIR – Council of Local Authorities for International Relations (internationally oriented national body)
♦ **CLAIRE** Confédération des Laboratoires de Recherche sur l'Intelligence Artificielle en Europe (#04565)
♦ **CLAIRE** Confederation of Laboratories for Artificial Intelligence Research in Europe (#04565)
♦ CLAIU / see Council of Associations of Long Cycle Engineers of a University or Higher School of Engineering of the European Union (#04869)
♦ **CLAIUEU** Council of Associations of Long Cycle Engineers of a University or Higher School of Engineering of the European Union (#04869)
♦ **CLAM** Centro Latino-Americano em Sexualidade e Direitos Humanos (#03814)
♦ CLAM – Comité de liaison de l'agrumiculture méditerranéenne (inactive)
♦ **CLAM** Confederación Latinoamericana Macabea (#04459)
♦ **CLAME** CropLife Africa Middle East (#04963)
♦ CLAMUC – Consejo Latinoamericano de Mujeres Católicas (inactive)
♦ CLAN – Caring and Living As Neighbours (internationally oriented national body)
♦ CLAN / see Club Latinoamericano de Neuroftalmologia (#04036)
♦ **CLAN** Club Latinoamericano de Neuroftalmologia (#04036)
♦ CLANP – Colegio Latinoamericano de Neuropsicofarmacologia (unconfirmed)
♦ CLAO – Consejo Latinoamericano de Oceanografia (inactive)
♦ CLAP – Consejo Latinoamericano de Perfusión (unconfirmed)
♦ CLAP – Conselho Latinoamericano de Perfusão (unconfirmed)
♦ CLAP / see Latin American Center for Perinatology/Unit of Woman and Reproductive Health (#16290)
♦ CLAPN – Comité Latinoamericano de Parques Nacionales (inactive)
♦ **CLAP/SMR** Centro Latinoamericano de Perinatologia/Unidad de Salud de la Mujer y Reproductiva (#16290)
♦ CLAPTUR – Confederación Latinoamericana de Prensa Turistica (no recent information)
♦ **CLAPU** Confederación Latino Americana de Asociaciones de Profesionales Universitarios (#04453)
♦ **CLAP/WR** Latin American Center for Perinatology/Unit of Woman and Reproductive Health (#16290)
♦ CLARA / see Cooperación Latino Americana de Redes Avanzadas (#04790)
♦ Clara Lachmanns Fond för Befrämjande av den Skandinaviska Samkänslan (#03977)

♦ Clara Lachmanns Fund to Promote Inter-Nordic Understanding . . . 03977

Fonds Clara Lachmanns pour promouvoir la compréhension inter-nordique – Clara Lachmanns Fond för Befrämjande av den Skandinaviska Samkänslan

Pres c/o Consensus Asset Management AB, Stiftelsetjänst, Krokslätts Parkgata 4, SE-431 68 Mölndal, Sweden. E-mail: info@claralachmann.org.
URL: http://www.claralachmann.org/

History 12 Jul 1927, Geneva (Switzerland). **Aims** Promote mutual understanding between Denmark, Iceland, Norway and Sweden. **Structure** Governing Board of 9 (Denmark 3, Iceland 1, Norway 2, Sweden 3). [2007/XF0102/f/**F**]

♦ CLAR / see Confederación Caribeña y Latinoamericana de Religiosas y Religiosos (#04442)
♦ **CLAR** Confederación Caribeña y Latinoamericana de Religiosas y Religiosos (#04442)
♦ CLAR – Consejo Latinoamericano de Resucitación (inactive)
♦ CLARe – Corpora for Language and Aging Research (meeting series)
♦ Clarétains – Missionnaires Fils du Coeur Immaculé de Marie (religious order)
♦ Claretiani – Missionari Figli del Cuore Immacolato di Maria (religious order)
♦ Claretianos – Misioneros Hijos del Inmaculado Corazón de Maria (religious order)
♦ Claretians – Missionary Sons of the Immaculate Heart of Mary (religious order)
♦ Claretian Volunteers / see Claretian Volunteers and Lay Missionaries
♦ Claretian Volunteers and Lay Missionaries (internationally oriented national body)
♦ **CLARIN** Common Language Resources and Technology Infrastructure (#04295)
♦ CLARIN ERIC / see Common Language Resources and Technology Infrastructure (#04295)
♦ Clarissan Missionary Sisters of the Blessed Sacrament (religious order)
♦ Clarist Franciscan Missionaries of the Most Blessed Sacrament (religious order)

♦ Clarity 03978

Treas WMU Cooley Law School, 300 S Capitol Avenue, Lansing MI 48933, USA. T. +15173715140. Fax +15173345748.
URL: http://clarity-international.net/

History 1983. Founded on the initiative of John Walton. Former names and other names: *Clarity International* – alias. **Aims** Promote plain legal *language*; promote use of good, clear language by the *legal* profession. **Structure** Committee; President; Editor. **Staff** None. **Finance** Members' dues. Donations. **Activities** Events/meetings. **Events** *International Conference* Tokyo (Japan) 2022, *Biennial International Conference* Montréal, QC (Canada) 2018, *Biennial International Conference* Washington, DC (USA) 2012, *Biennial international conference / Conference* Lisbon (Portugal) 2010, *Biennial international conference / Conference* Mexico City (Mexico) 2008. **Publications** *Clarity* (2 a year) – journal. **Members** Individuals (over 700) in over 25 countries. Membership countries not specified. [2021/XJ8067/v/**F**]

♦ Clarity International / see Clarity (#03978)
♦ **CLASA** Confederación Latinoamericana de Sociedades de Anestesiologia (#16305)
♦ CLAS – Center for Latin American Studies, Berkeley CA (internationally oriented national body)
♦ CLAS – Center for Latin American Studies, Gainesville (internationally oriented national body)
♦ CLAS – Center for Latin American Studies, Pittsburgh (internationally oriented national body)
♦ CLAS – Center for Latin American Studies, Washington DC (internationally oriented national body)
♦ CLAS – Commonwealth Legal Advisory Service (inactive)
♦ CLASEP / see Coordinadora Latinoamericana de Trabajadores de los Servicios Públicos (#04809)

♦ CLASP 03979

Exec Dir 1401 K St NW, Ste 1100, Washington DC 20005, USA. T. +12027505600.
URL: http://www.clas.ngo/

History 1999, through strategic cooperation of *Alliance to Save Energy (ASE)*, *International Institute for Energy Conservation (IIEC, #13875)* and Lawrence Berkeley National Laboratory. Became independent 2005. Full title: *Collaborative Labeling and Appliance Standards Program (CLASP)*. **Aims** Promote *energy efficiency* standards and labels for appliances, equipment and lighting. **Structure** Board. **Finance** Donors include: *Asia-Pacific Economic Cooperation (APEC, #01887)*; *ClimateWorks Foundation (#04024)*; *International Bank for Reconstruction and Development (IBRD, #12317)*; *International Copper Association (ICA, #12962)*; *UNDP (#20292)*; *United Nations Foundation (UNF, #20563)*; *United States Agency for International Development (USAID)*; governmental support from various countries. **NGO Relations** Partner in: *ClimateWorks Foundation (#04024)*. Member of: *LEDS Global Partnership (LEDS GP, #16435)*. [2019.07.16/XJ5895/**E**]

♦ CLASP – Consortium of Latin American Studies Programs (internationally oriented national body)
♦ The Class of 2020 / see The Class Foundation (#03980)

♦ The Class Foundation 03980

Communications Dir P.O. Box 10140, 1001 EC Amsterdam, Netherlands. T. +31611078115. E-mail: info@theclassfoundation.com.
URL: https://www.theclassfoundation.com/

History 2011. Former names and other names: *The Class of 2020* – former. Registration: No/ID: 55876420, Netherlands. **Aims** Advocate for community collaboration and provide thought leadership on the future of university cities. **Structure** Head; Core Team. **Languages** Dutch, English. **Staff** 3.00 FTE, paid. **Activities** Events/meetings; research/documentation; training/education. **Events** *Student Housing Market Update – Central Europe* Amsterdam (Netherlands) 2021, *Student Housing Market Update – Western Europe* Amsterdam (Netherlands) 2021, *Student Housing Market Update* Amsterdam (Netherlands) 2021, *The Class Conference* Amsterdam (Netherlands) 2021, *The Class Conference* Amsterdam (Netherlands) 2020. **NGO Relations** Partner of (3): *Erasmus Student Network (ESN, #05529)*; *Netherlands Organization for International Cooperation in Higher Education (NUFFIC)*; *Urban Land Institute (ULI)*. [2021.03.11/AA0754/**F**]

♦ CLAS, Stanford CA – Center for Latin American Studies, Stanford CA (internationally oriented national body)
♦ CLAT – Central Latinoamericana de Trabajadores (inactive)
♦ **CLATE** Confederación Latinoamericana de Trabajadores Estatales (#16304)
♦ CLATES – Centro Latinoamericano de Tecnologia Educativa para la Salud (inactive)

CLATJUPAM
03980

alphabetic sequence excludes
For the complete listing, see Yearbook Online at

◆ CLATJUPAM / see Confederación Latinoamericana de Trabajadores Jubilados, Pensionados y Adultos Mayores (#04462)
◆ CLATJUP / see Confederación Latinoamericana de Trabajadores Jubilados, Pensionados y Adultos Mayores (#04462)
◆ CLATO Confederación Latinoamericana de Terapeutas Ocupacionales (#16356)
◆ CLATRAMM – Coordinación Latinoamericana de Trabajadores Minero-Metalúrgicos (inactive)
◆ CLATSEP Coordinadora Latinoamericana de Trabajadores de los Servicios Públicos (#04809)
◆ CLAVE Coalición Latinoamericana para la Prevención de la Violencia Armada (#04044)
◆ CLAVES – Centro Latinoamericano de Estudios sobre Violencia y Salud 'Jorge Careli' (internationally oriented national body)

◆ **CLAWAR Association** **03981**
Main Office 57 London Road, High Wycombe, HP11 1BS, UK.
URL: http://www.clawar.org/
History as *CLAWAR Network*. Name derives from the phrase 'Climbing and Walking Robots'. Registered in accordance with UK law. **Aims** Advance education and science for public benefit in the field of *robotics* and associated technologies. **Structure** Board of Trustees; Management Team; Chapter in Kuwait. **Languages** English. **Staff** 6.00 FTE, voluntary. **Finance** Members' dues. Other sources: events; sponsorship donations. **Activities** Events/meetings. **Events** *International Conference on Climbing and Walking Robots and the Support Technologies for Mobile Machines* Kuala Lumpur (Malaysia) 2019, *International Conference on Climbing and Walking Robots and the Support Technologies for Mobile Machines* Panama (Panama) 2018, *International Conference on Climbing and Walking Robots and the Support Technologies for Mobile Machines* Porto (Portugal) 2017, *International Conference on Climbing and Walking Robots and the Support Technologies for Mobile Machines* London (UK) 2016, *International Conference on Climbing and Walking Robots and the Support Technologies for Mobile Machines* Hangzhou (China) 2015. **Publications** *CLAWAR News*. Conference proceedings.
Members Partners in 14 countries:
Belgium, Bulgaria, China, Denmark, France, Germany, Greece, Hungary, Italy, Poland, Portugal, Slovenia, Spain, Sweden.
NGO Relations Member of: *euRobotics (#05649)*.
[2018/XM0136/**F**]

◆ CLAWAR Network / see CLAWAR Association (#03981)
◆ Clay Conference – International Conference on Clays in Natural and Engineered Barriers for Radioactive Waste Confinement (meeting series)

◆ **Clay Minerals Society (CMS)** **03982**
Office Manager 3635 Concorde Pkwy – Ste 500, Chantilly VA 20151-1110, USA. T. +17036529960.
E-mail: cms@clays.org.
URL: http://www.clays.org/
History Incorporated 18 Jul 1962, Washington DC (USA). **Aims** Study clays and clay minerals. **Structure** Council; Executive Committee. **Activities** Events/meetings; research/documentation. **Events** *Annual Meeting* Austin, TX (USA) 2023, *Annual Meeting* Istanbul (Türkiye) 2022, *Annual Meeting* Chantilly, VA (USA) 2021, *Annual Meeting* Richland, WA (USA) 2020, *Annual Meeting* Paris (France) 2019. **Publications** *Clays and Clay Minerals*; *CMS e-News*. **NGO Relations** *Association internationale pour l'étude des argiles (AIPEA, #02688)*; *International Natural Zeolite Association (INZA, #14218)*.
[2019/XM5811/**C**]

◆ CLAYSS Centro Latinoamericano de Aprendizaje y Servicio Solidario (#16291)
◆ CLAYUCA Consorcio Latinoamericano y del Caribe de Apoyo a la Investigación y Desarrollo de la Yuca (#16271)
◆ CLB / see Commonwealth Lawyers Association (#04345)
◆ CLC / see CLC International
◆ CLC Christian Life Community (#03905)
◆ CLC – CLC International (internationally oriented national body)
◆ CLC – Community Learning Centres (see: #02002)
◆ CLC – Consejo Latinoamericano de Cultura (inactive)
◆ CLCCR / see International Association of the Body and Trailer Building Industry (#11727)
◆ CLCCR International Association of the Body and Trailer Building Industry (#11727)
◆ CL Celtic League (#03633)
◆ CLC / see Events Industry Council (#09212)
◆ CLC International (internationally oriented national body)
◆ CLC – International Convention on Civil Liability for Oil Pollution Damage (1969 treaty)
◆ CL Communion and Liberation (#04386)
◆ CLCPANO / see FAO Commission for Controlling the Desert Locust in the Western Region (#09259)
◆ CLCS Commission on the Limits of the Continental Shelf (#04232)
◆ CLDD – Consejo Latinoamericano de Derecho y Desarrollo (inactive)
◆ CLEA Commonwealth Legal Education Association (#04347)
◆ CLEA Coordinadora Latinoamericana de Estudiantes de Arquitectura (#04807)

◆ **Clean Air Asia** **03983**
Exec Dir 3504-05 Robinsons Equitable Tower, ADB Avenue, Ortigas Center, 1605 Pasig City RIZ, Philippines. T. +63286311042. Fax +63286311390. E-mail: center@cleanairasia.org.
URL: http://cleanairasia.org/
History 2001. Founded by *Asian Development Bank (ADB, #01422)*, *International Bank for Reconstruction and Development (IBRD, #12317)* (World Bank) and *United States Agency for International Development (USAID)*, as a regional programme of *Clean Air Initiative for Cities Around the World (CAI, #03984)*. Former names and other names: *CAI-Asia* – alias; *Clean Air Initiative for Asian Cities* – full title. Registration: Philippines. **Aims** Promote better air quality and livable cities by translating knowledge to policies and actions that reduce air pollution and greenhouse gas emissions from transport, energy and other sectors. **Structure** Board of Trustees; Clean Air Asia Partnership Advisory Council; Country Networks. **Activities** Active in: China, India, Indonesia, Nepal, Philippines, Vietnam. **Events** *Better Air Quality Conference* Kuching (Malaysia) 2018, *Better Air Quality Conference* Busan (Korea Rep) 2016, *Better Air Quality Conference* Colombo (Sri Lanka) 2014, *Better Air Quality Conference* Hong Kong (Hong Kong) 2012, *Better Air Quality Conference* Singapore (Singapore) 2010.
Members Networks in 6 countries:
Indonesia, Malaysia, Nepal, Philippines, Sri Lanka, Vietnam.
Partnership members: City members (45); Government agencies (33); NGOs and Academics (115); International development agencies and foundations (17); Private sector (37). Cities in 12 countries:
Bangladesh, Cambodia, China, India, Indonesia, Mongolia, Nepal, Pakistan, Philippines, Sri Lanka, Thailand, Vietnam.
Governmental agencies of 14 countries:
Afghanistan, Bangladesh, Cambodia, China, India, Indonesia, Japan, Malaysia, Maldives, Nepal, Pakistan, Philippines, Thailand, Vietnam.
NGOs include 7 organizations listed in this Yearbook:
Asian Institute of Technology (AIT, #01519); *Asia Pacific Roundtable on Sustainable Consumption and Production (APRSCP, #02017)*; *East-West Center (EWC, #05263)*; *European Federation for Transport and Environment (T and E, #07230)*; *Global Change Impact Studies Centre (GCISC)*; *International Environmental Analysis and Education Center (IEAEC)*; *New World Hope Organization (NWHO)*.
Development agencies include 9 organizations listed in this Yearbook:
Asian Development Bank (ADB, #01422); *Deutsche Gesellschaft für Internationale Zusammenarbeit (GIZ)*; *International Bank for Reconstruction and Development (IBRD, #12317)*; *International Forum for Rural Transport and Development (IFRTD, #13650)*; *International Union for Conservation of Nature and Natural Resources (IUCN, #15766)*; *Swedish International Development Cooperation Agency (Sida)*; *The William and Flora Hewlett Foundation*; *United Nations Centre for Regional Development (UNCRD, #20526)*; *United States Agency for International Development (USAID)*.
Consultative Status Consultative status granted from: *UNEP (#20299)*. **NGO Relations** Member of (5): *Asian Co-Benefits Partnership (ACP, #01382)* (Advisory Group); *Climate and Clean Air Coalition (CCAC, #04010)*; *GEF CSO Network (GCN, #10087)*; *Global Methane Initiative (GMI, #10471)*; *LEDS Global Partnership (LEDS GP, #16435)*. Partner of (2): *Partnership for Clean Fuels and Vehicles (PCFV, #18231)*; *Partnership on Sustainable, Low Carbon Transport Foundation (SLoCaT Foundation, #18244)*.
[2021.09.01/XJ2237/y/**E**]

◆ Clean Air Initiative for Asian Cities / see Clean Air Asia (#03983)

◆ **Clean Air Initiative for Cities Around the World (CAI)** **03984**
Contact IBRD Headquarters, 1818 H St NW, Washington DC 20433, USA. T. +12024580859. Fax +12026760977.
History 1998. **Aims** Improve air quality in cities through partnerships in selected regions of the world by sharing knowledge and experiences. **Activities** Regional programmes in: *Clean Air Asia (#03983)*; Europe and Central Asia; Latin America; Sub-Saharan Africa. Organizes workshops. **IGO Relations** *International Bank for Reconstruction and Development (IBRD, #12317)*.
[2010/XM1524/**F**]

◆ **Clean Air Institute (CAI)** **03985**
Exec Dir c/o 1120 G Str NW, Washington DC 20005, USA. T. +12024645450.
COO address not obtained.
URL: http://cleanairinstitute.org/
History 2006, with the support of *International Bank for Reconstruction and Development (IBRD, #12317)* (World Bank). **Aims** Improve air quality and combat *climate* change caused by global warming. **Structure** Board of Directors. **Staff** 6.00 FTE, paid. **IGO Relations** Member of: *Water Environment Partnership in Asia (WEPA, #20827)*. **NGO Relations** Partner of: *Partnership on Sustainable, Low Carbon Transport Foundation (SLoCaT Foundation, #18244)*.
[2019/XJ8644/j/**E**]

◆ Clean Air Task Force (internationally oriented national body)

◆ **Clean Clothes Campaign (CCC)** **03986**
Campagne vêtements propres: les droits de l'homme dans le travail – Kampagne für Saubere Kleidung – Campaña Ropa Limpia – Schone Kleren Campagne – Kampanjen Rena Kläder
Contact PO Box 11584, 1001 GN Amsterdam, Netherlands. T. +31204122785. Fax +31204122786.
E-mail: info@cleanclothes.org.
URL: https://cleanclothes.org/
History 1990. Comprises a number of national campaigns with titles as listed; but in UK referred to as *Labour behind the Label* and in France as *De l'éthique sur l'étiquette*. Also referred to as *European Project on Clean Clothes* and as *European Clean Clothes Campaign*. **Aims** Improve *labour conditions* of *workers* in the clothing and sportswear industry; raise awareness of workers' *rights*; inform and mobilize *consumers* so they will put pressure on companies to improve labour conditions. **Structure** International coordinating office located in the Netherlands. Autonomous national coalitions of local organizations (NGOs and unions). **Languages** English. **Staff** 11.00 FTE, paid. Voluntary. **Finance** Grants; project subsidies. **Activities** Awareness raising; events/meetings. **Events** *Global Forum* Hong Kong (Hong Kong) 2014, *Forum* Turkey 2010, *International forum* Bangkok (Thailand) 2007. **Publications** Newsletter.
Members Campaigns, comprising over 250 NGOs and trade unions, in 17 countries:
Austria, Belgium (2), Czechia, Denmark, Finland, France, Germany, Ireland, Italy, Netherlands, Norway, Poland, Spain, Sweden, Switzerland, Türkiye, UK.
IGO Relations *European Commission (EC, #06633)*.
[2023/XF3993/**F**]

◆ **Clean Cooking Alliance** **03987**
CEO 1750 Pennsylvania Ave NW, Washington DC 20006, USA. T. +12056505345. Fax +12056505350. E-mail: info@cleancookingalliance.org – cookstoves@unfoundation.org.
URL: http://cleancookstoves.org/
History 21 Sep 2010. Founded as an initiative of *United Nations Foundation (UNF, #20563)*. Since 2012, integrated *Partnership for Clean Indoor Air (PCIA)* (2002-2012). Former names and other names: *Global Alliance for Clean Cookstoves* – former. **Aims** Save lives, improve livelihoods, empower women and protect the *environment* by creating a thriving global market for clean and efficient household cooking solutions. **Structure** Advisory Board; Leadership Council. **Finance** Founding funders are governments of Germany, Norway, Peru and USA and include the following organizations listed in this Yearbook: *Deutsche Gesellschaft für Internationale Zusammenarbeit (GIZ)*; *SNV Netherlands Development Organisation (SNV)*; *Shell Foundation*; *United Nations Foundation (UNF, #20563)*; *United States Agency for International Development (USAID)*. **Events** *Cookstoves Future summit* New York, NY (USA) 2014, *Forum* Phnom Penh (Cambodia) 2013. **NGO Relations** Member of (3): *Climate and Clean Air Coalition (CCAC, #04010)*; *Global Coalition Against Child Pneumonia (#10290)*; *The ICCF Group (#11045)* (Conservation Council). Partners include: *Every Woman Every Child (EWEC, #09215)*; *Energy 4 Impact (#05465)*; *International Federation for Home Economics (IFHE, #13447)*. Supports: *Sustainable Energy for All (SEforALL, #20056)*.
[2020/XJ3095/**E**]

◆ **Clean Energy Ministerial (CEM)** **03988**
Communications Manager c/o IEA, 31-35 rue de la Fédération, 75015 Paris, France. T. +33140576686. E-mail: secretariat@cemsecretariat.org.
URL: http://www.cleanenergyministerial.org/
History Dec 2009, Copenhagen (Denmark). Established at *United Nations Framework Convention on Climate Change (UNFCCC, 1992)* Conference of Parties. **Aims** Promote policies and programmes that advance clean energy technology; share lessons learned and best practices; encourage the transition to a global clean energy economy. **Activities** Advocacy/lobbying/activism; politics/policy/regulatory. Includes: *Global Superior Energy Performance Partnership (GSEP, #10615)*; *International Smart Grid Action Network (ISGAN, #14877)*. **Events** *Meeting* Brazil 2024, *Meeting* India 2023, *Global Clean Energy Action Forum (GCEAF)* Pittsburgh, PA (USA) 2022, *Meeting* Vancouver, BC (Canada) 2019, *Meeting* Copenhagen (Denmark) / Malmö (Sweden) 2018. **Publications** *CEM Newsletter*.
Members Participating governments account for over 80% of global energy consumption and of market for clean energy technologies. Governments (22):
Australia, Brazil, Canada, China, Denmark, Finland, France, Germany, India, Indonesia, Italy, Japan, Korea Rep, Mexico, Norway, Russia, South Africa, Spain, Sweden, UK, United Arab Emirates, USA.
Regional community:
European Union (EU, #08967).
[2022/XJ2647/c/**F***]

◆ Clean Hydrogen Partnership (unconfirmed)
◆ Clean Shipping Alliance (unconfirmed)

◆ **Clean Shipping Coalition (CSC)** **03989**
Pres 2nd floor, Square de Meeûs 18, 1050 Brussels, Belgium. T. +3228510202. Fax +3228510229.
E-mail: info@cleanshipping.org.
URL: http://www.cleanshipping.org/
History Registration: Belgium. **Aims** Improve the environmental performance of international shipping by bringing extensive experience and expertise to bear on relevant international *regulatory* processes. **Structure** Board, comprising President and 7 members.
Members Organizations (8) in 5 countries:
Belgium, Netherlands, Norway, Sweden, USA.
Included in the above, 4 organizations listed in this Yearbook:
European Federation for Transport and Environment (T and E, #07230); *North Sea Foundation*; *Oceana*; *Seas at Risk (SAR, #19189)*.
Consultative Status Consultative status granted from: *International Maritime Organization (IMO, #14102)*.
[2021/XJ6628/y/**C**]

◆ Clean Sky / see Clean Sky Joint Undertaking (#03990)
◆ Clean Sky 2 Joint Undertaking / see Clean Sky Joint Undertaking (#03990)

◆ **Clean Sky Joint Undertaking (Clean Sky JU)** **03990**
Exec Dir White Atrium Bldg T056, 4th Floor, 1049 Brussels, Belgium. T. +3222218152. Fax +3222218150. E-mail: info@cleansky.eu.
Street address Avenue de la Toison d'Or 56-60, 1060 Brussels, Belgium.
URL: http://www.cleansky.eu/

History Set up through *Council of the European Union (#04895)* Regulation No 71/2008, 20 Dec 2007. Clean Sky 2 Joint Undertaking set up through Council Regulation No 558/2014, 6 May 2014. A Public-Private Partnership (PPP) between *European Commission (EC, #06633)* and Europe's aeronatics industry. Manages the *Clean Sky Joint Technology Initiative (CS JTI)*. Will be replaced by *European Partnership for Clean Aviation*. **Aims** Stimultae new research within the framework of a public-private partnership which enables long-term cooperation to take place among European aeronatical stakeholders. **Structure** Governing Board. **Staff** 35.00 FTE, paid. **Finance** Total budget Clean Sky 2 Programme: euro 4,000,000,000. **Activities** Advocacy/lobbying/activism; awards/prizes/competitions; events/meetings; networking/liaising. **Events** *Greener Aviation Conference* Brussels (Belgium) 2016, *Greener Aviation Conference* Brussels (Belgium) 2014.
Members Leaders; Core Partners: Vehicle IADPs (Innovative Aircraft Demonstrator Platform); Large Systems ITD Leaders – Integrated Technology Demonstrator. Membership countries not specified.
European Commission (EC, #06633).
NGO Relations Member of (1): *EU Agencies Network (EUAN, #05564).* [2021/XJ8736/**E**]

♦ **Clean Sky JU** Clean Sky Joint Undertaking (#03990)

♦ Clean Trade 03991

CEO 78 Offord Road, London, N1 1EB, UK. E-mail: cleantradeorg@gmail.com.
URL: http://www.cleantrade.org/
History Registration: Charity, No/ID: 1177571, England and Wales. **Aims** Secure people's rights to their natural resource wealth. **Structure** Board of Trustees. **NGO Relations** Member of (1): *European Responsible Investment Network (ERIN).* [2019/AA0071/**F**]

♦ Clean the World (internationally oriented national body)

♦ Clean Up the World (CUW) 03992

Mailing address 193 Darlinghurst Road, Darlinghurst NSW 2010, Australia. T. +61295526177. E-mail: world@cleanup.com.au.
URL: http://www.cleanuptheworld.org/
History 1993, with the support of *UNEP (#20299)*, after *'Clean Up Australia'* Days had been organized since 1990. Registered in accordance with Australian law. **Aims** Focus international attention on the problems of *rubbish* and *waste* affecting the state of the world's *environment*; bring together citizens from all over the world in a simple activity that will positively assist their *local* environments; share with all nations and cultures the information and practical experience developed by clean-up organizations; create an international media focus for clean-up activities, thus raising awareness of governments, industries and communities about local environmental issues, particularly waste minimization, *recycling* and waste management. **Structure** Headquarters based in Sydney (Australia). **Languages** English, French, Spanish. **Finance** Sponsorships from private firms and government departments. **Activities** Advocacy/lobbying/activism; training/education; networking/liaising. **Events** *Regional workshop for East-Central Europe and Central Asia* Kiev (Ukraine) 2002, *Meeting* 1994, *Meeting* Sydney, NSW (Australia) 1993. **Publications** *Clean Up the World* – newsletter. Annual Activity Report; waste education kit; factsheets.
Members Groups (470) currently participating in 104 countries and territories:
Argentina, Australia, Austria, Bahrain, Bangladesh, Botswana, Brazil, Bulgaria, Cameroon, Canada, Chile, China, Colombia, Congo DR, Costa Rica, Côte d'Ivoire, Cuba, Czechia, Denmark, Ecuador, Egypt, El Salvador, Ethiopia, Fiji, France, Gabon, Georgia, Germany, Ghana, Gibraltar, Greece, Guatemala, Hong Kong, Hungary, India, Indonesia, Ireland, Israel, Italy, Japan, Jordan, Kenya, Kiribati, Korea Rep, Liberia, Lithuania, Luxembourg, Madagascar, Malaysia, Maldives, Mali, Malta, Mauritania, Mexico, Micronesia FS, Morocco, Namibia, Nepal, Neth Antilles, New Zealand, Nicaragua, Nigeria, North Macedonia, Pakistan, Palestine, Panama, Papua New Guinea, Peru, Philippines, Poland, Portugal, Romania, Samoa USA, Saudi Arabia, Senegal, Serbia, Seychelles, Sierra Leone, Slovakia, Solomon Is, South Africa, Spain, Sri Lanka, Sudan, Sweden, Switzerland, Taiwan, Tanzania UR, Thailand, Togo, Tonga, Tunisia, Türkiye, Uganda, UK, Ukraine, United Arab Emirates, Uruguay, USA, Vanuatu, Venezuela, Vietnam, Zambia, Zimbabwe.
Included in the above, 3 organizations listed in this Yearbook:
EcoPeace Middle East (#05325); *Fundación Ecológica Universal (FEU, no recent information)*; UNEP – Africa Regional Office.
Consultative Status Consultative status granted from: *UNEP (#20299).* **IGO Relations** Supported by: *Pacific Community (SPC, #17942).* **NGO Relations** Supported by: *International Federation of Red Cross and Red Crescent Societies (#13526)*; *World Association of Girl Guides and Girl Scouts (WAGGGS, #21142).* [2018/XF2649/**F**]

♦ Clean the World Foundation / see Clean the World
♦ CLEAR Caribbean – Centre for Livelihoods, Ecosystems, Energy, Adaptation and Resilience in the Caribbean (internationally oriented national body)
♦ Clear Path International (internationally oriented national body)

♦ CLECAT 03993

Dir Gen Rue du Commerce 77, 1040 Brussels, Belgium. T. +3225034705. Fax +3225034752. E-mail: info@clecat.org.
URL: https://www.clecat.org/
History 3 Nov 1958, Antwerp (Belgium). Most recent Statutes adopted: 2 Dec 2008. Former names and other names: *European Liaison Committee of Common Market Forwarders* – former; *Comité de liaison européen des commissionnaires et auxiliaires de transports du Marché commun (CLECAT)* – former; *Europäisches Verbindungskomitee des Speditions- und Lagereigewerbes im Gemeinsamen Markt* – former; *Europees Verbindingscomité van Expediteurs en Bemiddelaars bij het Vervoer in de Gemeenschappelijke Markt* – former; *European Association for Forwarding, Transport, Logistics and Customs Services* – full title; *European Liaison Committee of Freight Forwarders* – former. Registration: Belgium; EU Transparency Register, No/ID: 684985491-01, Start date: 28 Jun 2008. **Aims** Strengthen and improve representation of the *logistics*, *freight* forwarding and *customs services* industry in Europe. **Structure** General Assembly (at least annually); Board; Secretariat. **Languages** English. **Staff** 5.00 FTE, paid. **Finance** Sources: members' dues. **Activities** Events/meetings; research/documentation. **Events** *Logistics for Europe Forum* Brussels (Belgium) 2022, *Freight Forwarders Forum* Brussels (Belgium) 2021, *Freight Forwarders Forum* Brussels (Belgium) 2020, *Freight Forwarders Forum* Brussels (Belgium) 2019, *Freight Forwarders Forum* Brussels (Belgium) 2018. **Publications** *CLECAT Newsletter*. Position papers; studies.
Members National federations in 16 countries:
Austria, Belgium, Bulgaria, Croatia, Finland, France, Germany, Italy, Netherlands, Poland, Portugal, Slovakia, Slovenia, Spain, Sweden, UK.
Associate in 2 countries:
North Macedonia, Türkiye.
Observers in 2 countries:
Switzerland, Ukraine.
NGO Relations Member of (3): *European Logistics Platform (ELP, #07711)*; *European Technology Platform ALICE (ALICE, #08888)*; *Federation of European and International Associations Established in Belgium (FAIB, #09508).* Cooperates with (1): *Comité européen de normalisation (CEN, #04162).* [2022/XE0801/**E**]

♦ **CLE** Council of Legal Education (#04908)
♦ **CLEEN** Chemical Legislation European Enforcement Network (#03859)
♦ **CLEEN** Competition Law and Economics European Network (#04416)
♦ **CLEER** Centre for the Law of EU External Relations (#03768)
♦ CLEFA – Conferencia Latinoamericana de Escuelas y Facultades de Arquitectura (meeting series)

♦ Cleft-Children International (CCI) 03994

Founder Asylstrasse 64, 8032 Zurich ZH, Switzerland. E-mail: office.cci@cleft-children.org.
URL: http://www.cleft-children.org/
History Former names and other names: *International Cleft Lip and Palate Foundation* – former; *Helping the World's Cleft Children* – former. **Aims** Promote means of healing patients with *cleft lip*, *palate* and other *craniofacial* anomalies. **Structure** Board; National Branches; Headquarters in Zurich (Switzerland). **Finance** Sources: donations; private foundations; sponsorship. **Activities** Events/meetings; financial and/or material support; healthcare; knowledge management/information dissemination; research and development; training/education. **Events** *World cleft congress* Munich (Germany) 2002, *World cleft congress* Zurich (Switzerland) 2000. **Members** Membership countries not specified. [2021.05.18/XF5900/**F**]

♦ **CLEI** Centro Latinoamericano de Estudios en Informatica (#16293)
♦ **CLEN** Customs Laboratories European Network (#04986)
♦ CLEO – Comité de liaison européen des ostéopathes (inactive)
♦ **CLEO** Consejo Latinoamericano de Ecografia Ocular (#04719)
♦ CLEPA / see European Association of Automotive Suppliers (#05948)
♦ **CLEPA** European Association of Automotive Suppliers (#05948)
♦ Clercs Réguliers Mariens de l'Immaculée Conception de la Bienheureuse Vierge Marie (religious order)
♦ Clercs Réguliers de la Mère de Dieu (religious order)
♦ Clercs Réguliers Mineurs (religious order)
♦ Clercs Réguliers Pauvres de la Mère de Dieu des Ecoles Pies (religious order)
♦ Clercs Réguliers de Saint-Paul (religious order)
♦ Clercs Réguliers Théatins (religious order)
♦ Clercs de Saint-Viateur (religious order)
♦ Clerics Regular Minor (religious order)
♦ Clerics Regular of Somasca (religious order)
♦ Clerics Regular of St Paul (religious order)
♦ Clerics of St Viator (religious order)
♦ Clerks Regular of the Mother of God (religious order)
♦ CLES – International Common Law Exchange Society (inactive)
♦ Clett and A / see Confederación Latinoamericana de Empleo (#04457)
♦ Cleveland International Fellowship / see Council of International Fellowship (#04902)
♦ **CLGE** Comité de liaison des géomètres européens (#04890)
♦ CLG Europe (internationally oriented national body)
♦ **CLGF** Commonwealth Local Government Forum (#04348)
♦ CLIA Asia (inactive)
♦ CLIA Australasia (internationally oriented national body)
♦ CLIA – Consejo Latinoamericano de Información Alimentaria (internationally oriented national body)
♦ **CLIA** Cruise Lines International Association (#04973)

♦ CLIA Europe 03995

SG Rue du Trône 60, 1050 Brussels, Belgium. T. +3227090131. E-mail: info.europe@cruising.org.
URL: https://cruising.org/fr-be
History Became part of *Cruise Lines International Association (CLIA, #04973)*, Dec 2012. Former names and other names: *European Cruise Council (ECC)* – former. Registration: No/ID: 0826.711.402, Start date: 17 Jun 2010, Belgium; EU Transparency Register, No/ID: 69525934310-58, Start date: 7 Oct 2010. **Aims** Promote interests of cruise ship operators within Europe; promote cruising to a wider audience to encourage expansion of the European cruise markets. **Structure** Board; Executive Committee. Sub-Committees (4): Environment; Ports and Destination; Taxation; Tourism and Consumer Affairs. **Events** *Annual Conference* St Petersburg (Russia) 2018, *Annual Conference* Bremerhaven (Germany) 2017, *Workshop on Port Infrastructure* Brussels (Belgium) 2017, *Europe Conference* Brussels (Belgium) 2013, *Annual Conference* Brussels (Belgium) 2012.
Members Full (over 50); Executive Partners (over 340). Membership countries not specified. **IGO Relations** Observer status with (1): *Baltic Marine Environment Protection Commission – Helsinki Commission (HELCOM, #03126).* Cooperates with (3): *European Commission (EC, #06633)*; *European Maritime Safety Agency (EMSA, #07744)*; *European Parliament (EP, #08146).* **NGO Relations** Member of (2): *European Tourism Manifesto (#08921)*; *Network for the European Private Sector in Tourism (NET, #17027).* Cooperates with (2): *European Community Shipowners' Associations (ECSA, #06683)*; *The European Travel Agents' and Tour Operators' Associations (ECTAA, #08942).* [2021.09.07/XJ4685/**D**]

♦ **CLI** Caribbean Law Institute (#03523)
♦ **CLIC** Consortium of Longitudinal Integrated Clerkships (#04752)
♦ **CLI** Climate Ledger Initiative (#04017)
♦ CLI – Cutis Laxa Internationale (internationally oriented national body)
♦ CLIEC / see Confédération Européenne de l'Industrie de la Chaussure (#04544)

♦ ClientEarth 03996

Fundacja ClientEarth
CEO Fieldworks, 274 Richmond Road, London, E8 3QW, UK. T. +442077495970. Fax +442077294568. E-mail: rorlik@clientearth.org – info@clientearth.org.
Brussels Office 60 Rue du Trône Box 11, 1050 Brussels, Belgium.
URL: http://www.clientearth.org/
History Registration: Companies House, No/ID: 02863827, Start date: 19 Oct 1993, England; Charities Commission, No/ID: 1053988, England and Wales; Banque-Carrefour des Entreprises, No/ID: 0714.925.038, Start date: 29 Nov 2018, Belgium; Berlin District court, No/ID: HRB 202487, Start date: 21 Dec 2018, Germany, Charlottenburg; Foundation, No/ID: KRS 0000364218, Poland; 501(c)(3), No/ID: EIN 81-0722756, USA; Subsidiary, No/ID: G1110000MA0095H836, China; EU Transparency Register, No/ID: 96645517357-19, Start date: 21 Dec 2011. **Aims** Secure a healthy planet; create pragmatic solutions to key *environmental* challenges. **Structure** Trustees; Patrons; Offices (7). **Languages** English, French, German, Mandarin Chinese, Polish, Spanish. **Finance** Individuals; foundations; government grants. **Activities** Politics/policy/regulatory; advocacy/lobbying/activism. **Publications** *Client Earth* (2018). **NGO Relations** Member of (11): *Climate Action Network Europe (CAN Europe, #04001)*; *Coalition for Energy Savings (#04056)*; *EDC Free Europe (#05355)*; *European Environmental Bureau (EEB, #06996)*; *European Habitats Forum (EHF, #07443)*; *European Responsible Investment Network (ERIN)*; *North Sea Advisory Council (NSAC, #17603)*; *North Western Waters Advisory Council (NWWAC, #17607)*; *Pesticide Action Network Europe (#18338)*; *Synchronicity Earth*; *World Heritage Watch (WHW).* [2019.10.29/XJ2714/**F**]

♦ Clifford Beers Foundation 03997

Chief Exec Mariazell, 5 Castle Way, Stafford, ST16 1BS, UK.
URL: http://www.cliffordbeersfoundation.co.uk/
History 1996, in honour of Clifford Whittingham Beers (1876-1973), an American humanitarian devoted to the study and advancement of mental hygiene movement. UK Registered Charity: 1057476. **Aims** Improve people's *mental health*. **Structure** Board, including Chair. Includes *Asia Pacific Centre for Mental Health and Wellbeing*, set up 2010. **Activities** *World Congress on the Promotion of Mental Health and the Prevention of Mental and Behavioural Disorders*. **Events** *World Congress on the Promotion of Mental Health and the Prevention of Mental and Behavioural Disorders* Columbia, SC (USA) 2015, *World Congress on the Promotion of Mental Health and the Prevention of Mental and Behavioural Disorders / World Conference* London (UK) 2014, *International conference on the promotion of mental health and wellbeing* Kuching (Malaysia) 2012, *World Conference on the Promotion of Mental Health and the Prevention of Mental and Behavioural Disorders* Perth, WA (Australia) 2012, *World conference on the promotion of mental health and prevention of mental and behavioral disorders* Washington, DC (USA) 2010. **Publications** *Advances in School Mental Health Promotion* (3 a year) – journal; *International Journal of Mental Health Promotion*. **Members** Membership countries not specified. [2015/XJ2668/f/**F**]

♦ CLIMA – Centre for Legumes in Mediterranean Agriculture (internationally oriented national body)
♦ Climate Action (internationally oriented national body)
♦ Climate Action (unconfirmed)

♦ Climate Action Accelerator (CAA) 03998

Dir Chemin des Mines 2, 1202 Geneva, Switzerland. E-mail: contact@climateactionaccelerator.org.
URL: https://climateactionaccelerator.org/
History Registration: EU Transparency Register, No/ID: 424946946188-48, Start date: 21 Apr 2022. **Aims** Mobilize a critical mass of community organizations in order to scale up climate solutions, contain global warming below 2°C and avoid the risk of dangerous runaway climate change. **IGO Relations** Joined the Race to Zero Campaign of *United Nations Framework Convention on Climate Change (UNFCCC, 1992).* [2023.02.14/AA2661/**F**]

♦ Climate Action Network (CAN) 03999

Exec Dir Kaiserstr 201, 53113 Bonn, Germany. E-mail: administration@climatenetwork.org.
URL: http://www.climatenetwork.org/

History Mar 1989, Brussels (Belgium). **Aims** Promote government and individual action to limit human-induced climate change to ecologically sustainable levels. **Structure** An international consortium. Regional Networks (10) include: *Climate Action Network Eastern Europe, Caucasus and Central Asia (#04000)*; *Climate Action Network Europe (CAN Europe, #04001)*; *Climate Action Network Latin America (CANLA, #04002)*; *Pacific Islands Climate Action Network (PICAN, #17965)*; *Climate Action Network South Asia (CANSA, #04003)*; *Climate Action Network South East Asia (CANSEA, #04004)*. National Networks (10). **Languages** English. **Staff** 25.00 FTE, paid. **Activities** Events/meetings; knowledge management/information dissemination. **Events** *Annual Strategy Meeting* Arusha (Tanzania UR) 2020. **Publications** Global and regional newsletters; position papers.

Members Open to any environmental, development or other citizen-based organization subscribing to CAN goals and active on climate-related issues. NGOs (over 1100) in 117 countries and territories:
Afghanistan, Algeria, Argentina, Armenia, Australia, Austria, Azerbaijan, Bahrain, Bangladesh, Barbados, Belarus, Belgium, Benin, Bhutan, Bolivia, Botswana, Bulgaria, Cameroon, Canada, Cape Verde, Chad, Chile, China, Colombia, Congo DR, Côte d'Ivoire, Croatia, Czechia, Denmark, Djibouti, Eswatini, Ethiopia, Fiji, Finland, France, Gambia, Georgia, Ghana, Greece, Guinea, Haiti, Holy See, Honduras, Hungary, Iceland, India, Indonesia, Ireland, Italy, Japan, Jordan, Kazakhstan, Kenya, Kiribati, Kyrgyzstan, Lebanon, Lesotho, Libya, Lithuania, Luxembourg, Malawi, Malaysia, Maldives, Mali, Malta, Mauritania, Mauritius, Mexico, Moldova, Morocco, Mozambique, Namibia, Nepal, Netherlands, New Zealand, Nicaragua, Niger, Nigeria, Norway, Pakistan, Palestine, Paraguay, Peru, Philippines, Poland, Portugal, Romania, Russia, Rwanda, Saudi Arabia, Senegal, Serbia, Slovenia, South Africa, Spain, Sri Lanka, Sudan, Sweden, Switzerland, Taiwan, Tajikistan, Tanzania UR, Thailand, Togo, Tunisia, Türkiye, Tuvalu, Uganda, UK, Ukraine, Uruguay, USA, Uzbekistan, Vanuatu, Venezuela, Zambia, Zimbabwe.

Included in the above, 30 organizations listed in this Yearbook:
- *Action for Solidarity, Equality, Environment and Diversity (A SEED, #00098)*;
- *AFREPREN/FWD (#00153)*;
- *African Centre for Technology Studies (ACTS, #00243)*;
- *African Water Network (AWN, no recent information)*;
- *Alliance Sud, Swiss Alliance of Development Organisations Swissaid – Catholic Lenten Fund – Bread for All – Helvetas – Caritas – Interchurch Aid*;
- *Carbon Market Watch (#03423)*;
- *Center for International Environmental Law (CIEL)*;
- *Center for Sustainable Development in the Americas (CSDA)*;
- *Centre africain de recherche et de promotion environnementale pour le développement durable (CARPE, no recent information)*;
- *Centre on World Economy Studies (CIEM)*;
- *EcoNews Africa (ENA)*;
- *Environment Liaison Centre International (ELCI, no recent information)*;
- *Environnement et développement du Tiers-monde (enda, #05510)*;
- *Friends of the Earth Europe (FoEE, #10001)*;
- *Friends of the Earth International (FoEI, #10002)*;
- *Institute for European Environmental Policy (IEEP, #11261)*;
- *Institute for the Evaluation of Energy and Environment Strategies in Europe (INESTENE, no recent information)*;
- *International Climate Development Institute (ICDI)*;
- *International Energy Initiative (IEI, no recent information)*;
- *International Institute for Energy Conservation – Europe (IIEC-Europe, see: #13875)*;
- *International Institute for Energy Conservation (IIEC, #13875)*;
- *International Society of Doctors for the Environment (ISDE, #15065)*;
- *Local Governments for Sustainability (ICLEI, #16507)* (European Secretariat);
- *Pacific Institute*;
- *Society for Development Alternatives*;
- *Women's Environment and Development Organization (WEDO, #21016)*;
- *World Council of Churches (WCC, #21320)*;
- *World Information Service on Energy (WISE, #21582)* (Paris Office);
- *World Resources Institute (WRI, #21753)*;
- *World Wide Fund for Nature (WWF, #21922)*.

Consultative Status Consultative status granted from: *UNEP (#20299)*. **IGO Relations** Climate Change Secretariat; *Intergovernmental Panel on Climate Change (IPCC, #11499)*. Observer status at meetings of: *United Nations Framework Convention on Climate Change (UNFCCC, 1992)*. Accredited by: *Green Climate Fund (GCF, #10714)*; *United Nations Framework Convention on Climate Change – Secretariat (UNFCCC, #20564)*. **NGO Relations** Member of: *EarthAction (EA, #05159)*; *Global 100% RE (#10160)*. Partner of: *Global Call for Climate Action (GCCA, inactive)*; *Wetlands International (#20928)*. Hosts: *Action for Sustainable Development (Action4SD)*. [2021.09.06/XF1289/y/**F**]

♦ Climate Action Network Central and Eastern Europe / see Climate Action Network Eastern Europe, Caucasus and Central Asia (#04000)

♦ Climate Action Network Eastern Europe, Caucasus and Central Asia 04000

Coordinator address not obtained.
URL: http://infoclimate.org/

History 1994, as *Climate Action Network Central and Eastern Europe (CANCEE)*, as a regional focal point of *Climate Action Network (CAN, #03999)*. Subsequently changed title to *Climate Action Network Eastern Europe and Eurasia (CANEEE)*. **Aims** Promote actions to limit human-induced *climate change* to *ecologically sustainable* levels; bring together views from NGOs across the region and represent their concerns at an international level. **Structure** Board; Coordinator; Secretariat. **Languages** English, Russian. **Finance** Support from: *Friedrich-Ebert-Stiftung (FES)*; Swedish Society for Nature Conservation (SSNC). **Activities** Advocacy/lobbying/activism; events/meetings. **Events** *Meeting* Bonn (Germany) 2002, *Meeting* Delhi (India) 2002. **Publications** *Climate and Energy Bulletin* (4 a year). Position papers.

Members NGOs (48) in 11 countries:
Armenia, Azerbaijan, Belarus, Georgia, Kazakhstan, Kyrgyzstan, Moldova, Russia, Tajikistan, Ukraine, Uzbekistan.

IGO Relations *Kyoto Protocol to the United Nations Framework Convention on Climate Change (1997)*; *United Nations Framework Convention on Climate Change (UNFCCC, 1992)*. **NGO Relations** Works closely with: *Climate Action Network Europe (CAN Europe, #04001)*. [2019.06.27/XK0742/**E**]

♦ Climate Action Network Eastern Europe and Eurasia / see Climate Action Network Eastern Europe, Caucasus and Central Asia (#04000)

♦ Climate Action Network Europe (CAN Europe) 04001

Coordinator Mundo B, Rue d'Edimbourg 26, 1050 Brussels, Belgium. T. +32473170887.
URL: http://www.caneurope.org/

History 1989, as *Climate Network Europe (CNE)*, as a regional network of *Climate Action Network (CAN, #03999)*, being the first Climate Network node originally managed by *Stockholm Environment Institute (SEI, #19993)*. Current title adopted 2002. EU Transparency Register: 55888811123-49. **Aims** Provide a forum for NGOs to share ideas and expertise, strategies and information on *climate change* and to promote actions and link these with wider efforts. **Structure** General Assembly; Board of Directors. **Languages** English. **Staff** 30.00 FTE, paid. **Finance** Supported by: *European Climate Foundation (ECF, #06574)*; *European Commission (EC, #06633)*; *KR Foundation (#16208)*; Minor Foundation for Major Challenges; *Stiftung Mercator*. **Activities** Knowledge management/information dissemination; networking/liaising. Follows international negotiations on *United Nations Framework Convention on Climate Change (UNFCCC, 1992)* and *Kyoto Protocol to the United Nations Framework Convention on Climate Change (1997)*. **Events** *2030 Climate and Energy Framework Workshop* Brussels (Belgium) 2013, *European sustainable energy seminar* Bratislava (Slovakia) 1995. **Publications** Press releases; working papers; review; position papers. Information Services: Information service on climate change issues which includes a library; databank on publications; database on member organizations.

Members Full; Accepted; Observer. NGOs (152) in 32 countries:
Austria, Belgium, Bosnia-Herzegovina, Bulgaria, Croatia, Czechia, Denmark, Finland, France, Germany, Greece, Hungary, Iceland, Ireland, Italy, Latvia, Lithuania, Luxembourg, Malta, Netherlands, North Macedonia, Norway, Poland, Portugal, Romania, Serbia, Slovenia, Spain, Sweden, Switzerland, Türkiye, UK.

Included in the above, 48 organizations listed in this Yearbook:
- *ACT Alliance EU (#00082)*;
- *Alliance Sud, Swiss Alliance of Development Organisations Swissaid – Catholic Lenten Fund – Bread for All – Helvetas – Caritas – Interchurch Aid*;
- *Both ENDS (#03307)*;
- *Brot für die Welt*;
- *Catholic Agency for Overseas Development (CAFOD)*;
- *Change Partnership*;
- *Christian Aid*;
- *CIDSE (CIDSE, #03926)*;
- *ClientEarth (#03996)*;
- *Climate Analytics*;
- *CliMates*;
- *CNCD Opération 11 11 11*;
- *Coalition of the Flemish North South Movement – 11 11 11*;
- *Compassion in World Farming (CIWF, #04414)*;
- *Development Fund*;
- *E3G – Third Generation Environmentalism*;
- *Ecologic Institut (#05303)*;
- *Eco-union*;
- *Environmental Investigation Agency (EIA)*;
- *Folkekirkens Nødhjaelp (FKN)*;
- *Friends of the Earth Europe (FoEE, #10001)*;
- *German Catholic Bishops' Organisation for Development Cooperation (MISEREOR)*;
- *GLOBAL 2000*;
- *Greenpeace International (#10727)* (several units in Europe);
- *Health Care Without Harm (HCWH, #10875)*;
- *Humanistisch Instituut voor Ontwikkelingssamenwerking (Hivos)*;
- *Institute for European Environmental Policy (IEEP, #11261)*;
- *MEDITERRANEAN SOS Network (MEDSOS)*;
- *Norwegian Church Aid*;
- *OroVerde – Die Tropenwaldstiftung (OroVerde)*;
- *Oxfam International (#17922)*;
- *Practical Action (#18475)*;
- *Save the Children Norway (Redd Barna)*;
- *Seas at Risk (SAR, #19189)*;
- *SEE Change Net Foundation*;
- *Suomalaiset Kehitysjärjestöt (Fingo)*;
- *Tearfund, UK*;
- *Third World Solidarity Action (ASTM)*;
- *Transparency International (TI, #20223)*;
- *Trocaire – Catholic Agency for World Development*;
- *Verdens Skove*;
- *Verification Research, Training and Information Centre (VERTIC)*;
- *Welthungerhilfe*;
- *Women Engage for a Common Future (WECF, #20992)*;
- *World Animal Protection (#21092)*;
- *World Council of Churches (WCC, #21320)*;
- *World Future Council Foundation (WFC, #21533)*;
- *World Wide Fund for Nature (WWF, #21922)*.

IGO Relations Accredited by: *European Commission (EC, #06633)*; *European Parliament (EP, #08146)*; *Intergovernmental Panel on Climate Change (IPCC, #11499)*; *United Nations Framework Convention on Climate Change – Secretariat (UNFCCC, #20564)*. **NGO Relations** Member of: *Coalition for Energy Savings (#04056)*; *Eastern Partnership Civil Society Forum (EaP CSF, #05247)*; *GEF CSO Network (GCN, #10087)*; *The Green 10 (#10711)*; *Renewables Grid Initiative (RGI, #18839)*; *SDG Watch Europe (#19162)*. Cooperates with other CAN focal points: CAN-Australia (CANA); CAN Canada (RAC-Canada); CAN-China; Can-Japan (Kiko Network); CAN-Pacific; CAN-Southern Africa (SACAN); *Climate Action Network Eastern Europe, Caucasus and Central Asia (#04000)*: CAN France (RAC France); *Climate Action Network Latin America (CANLA, #04002)*; *Climate Action Network North Africa (RAC Maghreb, inactive)*; Climate Action Network South Africa; *Climate Action Network South Asia (CANSA, #04003)*; *Climate Action Network South East Asia (CANSEA, #04004)*; United States Climate Action Network (USCAN). Partner of: *Global Call for Climate Action (GCCA, inactive)*. Strategic Allies include: *BirdLife International (#03266)*; *CEE Bankwatch Network (#03624)*; *European Environmental Bureau (EEB, #06996)*; *European Federation for Transport and Environment (T and E, #07230)*; *Health and Environment Alliance (HEAL, #10879)*. [2019.12.13/XK1053/y/**E**]

♦ Climate Action Network Latin America (CANLA) 04002

Réseau latinoaméricaine d'action climatique – Red Latinoamericana de Cambio Climatico

Coordinator c/o CEMDA, Atlixco 138, col Condesa Deleg, Cuauhtémoc, Mexico City CDMX, Mexico.
URL: http://www.climatenetwork.org/

History Jun 1992, Rio de Janeiro (Brazil), as a regional network of *Climate Action Network (CAN, #03999)*. **Aims** Collect and disseminate documentation on existing research on *climate change* in the region and follow the international change *negotiation* and *development* process while paying special attention to regional interests. **Events** *Workshop* Santiago (Chile) 1994. **Publications** *CANLA Bulletin*.

Members Organizations in 11 countries:
Argentina, Bolivia, Brazil, Chile, Colombia, Cuba, Ecuador, Mexico, Nicaragua, Peru, Uruguay.

IGO Relations Accredited by: *United Nations Framework Convention on Climate Change – Secretariat (UNFCCC, #20564)*. [2020/XK1046/**E**]

♦ Climate Action Network South Asia (CANSA) 04003

Secretariat Bangladesh Ctr for Advanced Studies, House 10, Road 16A, Gulshan 1, Dhaka 1212, Bangladesh. T. +88028851237 – +88028851986 – +88028852217. Fax +88028851417. E-mail: info@cansouthasia.net.
URL: http://www.cansouthasia.net/

History Apr 1991, as a regional network of *Climate Action Network (CAN, #03999)*. **Aims** Collect and disseminate documentation on existing research on *climate change* in the region and follow the international change negotiation and development process while paying special attention to regional interests. **Structure** Regional Steering Committee. **Activities** Research and development; training/education; events/meetings. **Publications** *Clime Asia* – newsletter.

Members Organizations (about 150) in 7 countries:
Bangladesh, Bhutan, India, Maldives, Nepal, Pakistan, Sri Lanka.

Included in the above, 2 organizations listed in this Yearbook:
International Centre for Climate Change and Development (ICCCAD); *South Asian Forum for Environment (SAFE)*.

IGO Relations Accredited by: *Green Climate Fund (GCF, #10714)*. **NGO Relations** Acts as sub-regional node of: *Asia Pacific Adaptation Network (APAN, #01818)*. [2016/XK1028/**E**]

♦ Climate Action Network South East Asia (CANSEA) 04004

Regional Coordinator address not obtained. T. +60328575113.
URL: http://cansea.net/

History Jan 1992, as a regional network of *Climate Action Network (CAN, #03999)*. **Aims** Create synergy in the matter of doing advocacy work at local and national levels with the area's governments and internationally. Address the socio-political issues associated with the *climate change* debate. **Structure** Steering Committee; Regional Secretariat (rotates every 2 years). **Languages** English. **Staff** 1.00 FTE, voluntary. **Finance** Ad-hoc and occasional project grants. **Activities** Advocacy/lobbying/activism; events/meetings. **Publications** *SEANEWS* (irregular) – newsletter.

Members National core groups in 4 countries:
Indonesia, Malaysia, Philippines, Thailand.

IGO Relations Accredited by: *United Nations Framework Convention on Climate Change – Secretariat (UNFCCC, #20564)*. [2017/XK1081/**E**]

♦ Climate Alliance 04005

Klima-Bündnis – Alianza del Clima – Alleanza per il Clima – Alliance pour le Climat

Exec Dir European Secretariat, Galvanistr 28, 60486 Frankfurt-Main, Germany. T. +49697171390. Fax +496971713993. E-mail: europe@climatealliance.org.
URL: http://www.climatealliance.org

History 1990. Founded by representatives of European municipalities and the indigenous peoples of Amazonia. Formally constituted 1992. Former names and other names: *Climate Alliance of European Cities with Indigenous Rainforest Peoples* – full title; *Alliance pour le Climat entre les Villes Européennes et les Peuples Indigènes des Forêts Tropicales* – full title; *Alianza del Clima de las Ciudades Europeas con los Pueblos Indigenas de los Bosques Tropicales* – full title; *Klima-Bündnis der europäischen Städte mit indigenen Völkern der Regenwälder* – full title. Registration: EU Transparency Register, No/ID: 83923664694-38. **Aims** Reduce CO2 emissions by 10 percent every 5 years, equivalent to the halving of per capita emissions by 2030; strive for a per capita emissions level of 2.5 tonnes CO2 equivalent through energy conservation, energy efficiency and the use of renewable energy; work towards climate justice in partnership with indigenous peoples by supporting their initiatives, raising awareness, and abstaining from the use of unsustainably managed tropical timber. **Structure** Executive Board; European Secretariat; National Coordination Offices. **Languages** English, German, Spanish. **Staff** 40.70 FTE, paid; 3.00 FTE, voluntary. **Finance** Sources: members' dues; revenue from activities/projects. **Activities** Advocacy/lobbying/activism; events/meetings; knowledge management/information dissemination; politics/policy/regulatory; projects/programmes; publishing activities. **Events** *Annual Conference and General Assembly* Barcelona (Spain) 2018, *Annual Conference and General Assembly* Essen (Germany) 2017, *Annual Conference and General Assembly* Krems (Austria) 2016, *Annual Conference and General Assembly* Dresden (Germany) 2015, *Annual Conference and General Assembly* Luxembourg (Luxembourg) 2014. **Publications** *eClimail* (6 a year) – newsletter; *Annual Report* (annual). *Climate Alliance Resolutions.*

Members Local authorities (over 1,800) and associated members in 27 European countries:
Austria, Belgium, Bosnia-Herzegovina, Bulgaria, Croatia, Czechia, Denmark, Finland, France, Georgia, Germany, Greece, Hungary, Ireland, Italy, Luxembourg, Netherlands, North Macedonia, Poland, Portugal, Romania, Slovakia, Slovenia, Spain, Switzerland, UK, Ukraine.
Cooperation partner (1):
Coordinadora de las Organizaciones Indígenas de la Cuenca Amazónica (COICA, #04811).
Consultative Status Consultative status granted from: *UNEP (#20299).* **IGO Relations** Accredited by (1): *Green Climate Fund (GCF, #10714).* Observer status with (2): *Convention on Biological Diversity (Biodiversity convention, 1992); United Nations Framework Convention on Climate Change (UNFCCC, 1992).* **NGO Relations** Member of (2): *European Sustainable Cities and Towns Campaign (#08863)* (Steering Committee); *SDG Watch Europe (#19162).* Supports (1): *Global 100% RE (#10160).* [2021.03.09/XF2519/**F**]

♦ Climate Alliance of European Cities with Indigenous Rainforest Peoples / see Climate Alliance (#04005)
♦ Climate Analytics (internationally oriented national body)
♦ **CLIMATE Asia Pacific** Climate change Learning Initiative Mobilizing Action Transforming Environments in Asia Pacific (#04009)

♦ Climate Bonds Initiative 04006

CEO 40 Bermondsey Str, London, SE1 3UD, UK. T. +447435280312.
Europe Avenue Léon Jourez 34, 1420 Braine-l'Alleud, Belgium.
URL: http://www.climatebonds.net/

History Registration: Charity, No/ID: 1154413, Start date: 30 Nov 2010, England and Wales; No/ID: 0730.588.756, Start date: 11 Jul 2019, Belgium; Eu Transparency Register, No/ID: 124307537876-65, Start date: 17 Apr 2020. **Aims** Promote investment in projects and assets necessary for a rapid transition to a low-carbon and climate resilient economy. **Structure** Advisory Panel; Governors. **Languages** English. **Staff** 10.00 FTE, paid. **Finance** Sources: fees for services; government support; private foundations. Annual budget: 600,000 EUR. **Activities** Awards/prizes/competitions; certification/accreditation; events/meetings; guidance/assistance/consulting. Active in: Australia, Brazil, Canada, China, France, Germany, India, Indonesia, Mexico, Netherlands, Sweden, UK, USA. **Publications** *Bonds and Climate: State of the Market* (annual). Email updates.
Members Organizations, including the following listed in this Yearbook:
CDP (#03621); Partnership on Sustainable, Low Carbon Transport Foundation (SLoCaT Foundation, #18244).
IGO Relations UN Secretary General's Climate Finance Team. **NGO Relations** Member of (3): *Cities Climate Finance Leadership Alliance (CCFLA, #03952); High Level Panel for a Sustainable Ocean Economy (Panel, #10917)* (Advisory Network); *ResponsibleSteel (#18921)* (associate). Subscriber to: *ISEAL (#16026).* [2020/XJ9724/y/**F**]

♦ Climate Broadcasters Network – Europe (CBN-E) 04007

Address not obtained.
History 16 Feb 2007, in the context of the pan-European Climate Change Campaign, launched by *European Commission (EC, #06633)*, May 2006. **Aims** Communicate to citizens the science of *climate change*, its impacts, adaptation and mitigation needs, so as to facilitate a broad understanding of the various issues. **Structure** General Meeting. Core Group of up to 6 members. Presidency (2-year term). Secretariat. **Languages** English. **Finance** Support from *European Commission (EC, #06633)* (DG Environment). **Events** *Annual Meeting* Geneva (Switzerland) 2009, *Annual Meeting* Monte Carlo (Monaco) / Cannes (France) 2008.
Members Full in 23 countries:
Andorra, Austria, Belgium, Bulgaria, Croatia, Czechia, Denmark, Estonia, Finland, France, Germany, Greece, Hungary, Ireland, Italy, Lithuania, Poland, Romania, Slovakia, Slovenia, Spain, Sweden, UK.
NGO Relations Located at: *European Environmental Communication Networks (EECN, #06997).* [2010/XJ0964/**E**]

♦ Climate Centre – Red Cross Red Crescent Climate Centre (internationally oriented national body)

♦ Climate Chain Coalition (CCC) 04008

Co-Chair address not obtained.
Co-Chair address not obtained.
URL: https://www.climatechaincoalition.io/

History Dec 2017, Paris (France). **Aims** Cooperatively support the application of distributed ledger technology ('DLT', including 'the blockchain') and related digital solutions to addressing climate change.
Members Organizations (over 250) in over 50 countries. Membership countries not specified.
Climate Ledger Initiative (CLI, #04017); Deutsche Gesellschaft für Internationale Zusammenarbeit (GIZ); EIT Climate-KIC (#05403); Institute for Social and Environmental Transition–International (ISET-International, #11294); International Association for the Advancement of Innovative Approaches to Global Challenges (IAAI, #11687); IOTA Foundation (#16009).
NGO Relations Member of (1): *International Association of Trusted Blockchain Applications (INATBA).* [2021/AA1978/y/**E**]

♦ Climate change Learning Initiative Mobilizing Action Transforming Environments in Asia Pacific (CLIMATE Asia Pacific) 04009

Address not obtained.
URL: http://climateasiapacific.org/

History Aug 2010, by Center for Environmental Concerns-Philippines, *Asia South Pacific Association for Basic and Adult Education (ASPBAE, #02098)* and *Institut für Internationale Zusammenarbeit des Deutschen Volkshochschul-Verbandes (DVV-International).* **Aims** Work for awareness raising and capacity building of Asia Pacific peoples to understand climate change, its root causes and impact, and people's responses to find appropriate and urgent solutions to the global problem; facilitate dialogues and education programs among people's organizations and social movements in the region for informed engagement with national governments, regional and global platforms towards climate justice; strengthen alliances with people's organizations, labour organizations, peasant organizations, indigenous peoples, women's organizations, environmentalists, social movements and academia to bring about effective elimination of the causes of climate change; ensure that peoples' voices are heard in *policy* development and advocate for better policy on climate change and education in the Asia Pacific region. **Structure** Convenors (7).
Members Organizations (11) in 7 countries:
Bangladesh, Cambodia, India, Korea Rep, Pakistan, Philippines, Samoa. [2012/XJ5402/**E**]

♦ The Climate Change Organisation / see Climate Group (#04013)

♦ Climate and Clean Air Coalition (CCAC) 04010

Secretariat c/o UN Environment, 1 rue Miollis, Bldg VII, 75015 Paris, France. T. +33144371473. Fax +33144371474. E-mail: secretariat@ccacoalition.org.
URL: http://www.ccacoalition.org/en/

History 17 Feb 2012. Launched by governments of Bangladesh, Canada, Ghana, Mexico, Sweden and USA and *UNEP (#20299).* Former names and other names: *Climate and Clean Air Coalition to Reduce Short-Lived Climate Pollutants (CCAC)* – full title. **Aims** As a voluntary international framework for concrete and substantial action: reduce emissions of methane, black carbon and many hydrofluorocarbons (HFCs) in order to protect the *environment* and *public health*; promote food and energy security and address near-term *climate change.* **Structure** High-Level Assembly; Working Group; Steering Committee; Scientific Advisory Panel; Secretariat, hosted by *UNEP (#20299).* **Languages** Arabic, Chinese, English, French, Russian, Spanish. **Finance** Financed by Coalition's Trust Fund. **Activities** Research and development. **Events** *International Day of Clean Air for blue skies* Paris (France) 2020, *High Level Assembly* New York, NY (USA) 2019, *WHO Global Conference on Air Pollution and Health* Geneva (Switzerland) 2018, *Global Methane Forum* Toronto, ON (Canada) 2018, *Working Group Meeting* Toronto, ON (Canada) 2018. **Publications** *Air Pollution in Asia and the Pacific: Science-based solutions* in Chinese, English; *Integrated Assessment of Short-lived Climate Pollutants in Latin America and the Caribbean* in English; *Opportunities for Increasing Ambition of Nationally Determined Contributions through Integrated Air Pollution and Climate Change Planning: A Practical Guidance document* in English.
Members State and REIO Partners in 67 countries:
Argentina, Australia, Bangladesh, Belgium, Benin, Burkina Faso, Cambodia, Canada, Central African Rep, Chad, Chile, Colombia, Congo DR, Costa Rica, Côte d'Ivoire, Denmark, Dominican Rep, Eswatini, Ethiopia, Finland, France, Germany, Ghana, Guinea, India, Iraq, Ireland, Israel, Italy, Japan, Jordan, Kenya, Korea Rep, Laos, Liberia, Luxembourg, Maldives, Mali, Mexico, Moldova, Mongolia, Morocco, Netherlands, New Zealand, Niger, Nigeria, Norway, Pakistan, Panama, Paraguay, Peru, Philippines, Poland, Russia, Rwanda, Spain, Sweden, Switzerland, Thailand, Togo, UK, Ukraine, United Arab Emirates, Uruguay, USA, Vietnam, Zimbabwe.
Included in the above, 2 organizations listed in this Yearbook:
Economic Community of West African States (ECOWAS, #05312); European Commission (EC, #06633).
Non-State Partners (49):
- *Asian Development Bank (ADB, #01422);*
- *Asian Institute of Technology (AIT, #01519);*
- *Bellona Europa;*
- *Business for Social Responsibility (BSR);*
- *C40 (#03391);*
- *Caucasus Environmental NGO Network (CENN, #03613);*
- *CDP (#03621);*
- *Center for Clean Air Policy (CCAP);*
- *Center for Human Rights and Environment (CEDHA);*
- *Clean Air Asia (#03983);*
- *Clean Air Institute (CAI, #03985);*
- *Clean Cooking Alliance (#03987);*
- *Climate Markets and Investment Association (CMIA, #04018);*
- *ClimateWorks Foundation (#04024);*
- *Earthjustice;*
- *Energy and Resources Institute (TERI);*
- *Environmental Defense Fund (EDF);*
- *Environmental Investigation Agency (EIA);*
- *European Investment Bank (EIB, #07599);*
- *Ev-K2-CNR Committee (#16175);*
- *FAO (#09260);*
- *FIA Foundation (#09742);*
- *Institute for Global Environmental Strategies (IGES, #11266);*
- *Institute for Governance and Sustainable Development (IGSD);*
- *Inter-American Institute for Cooperation on Agriculture (IICA, #11434);*
- *International Association of Public Transport (#12118);*
- *International Bank for Reconstruction and Development (IBRD, #12317)* (World Bank);
- *International Centre for Integrated Mountain Development (ICIMOD, #12500);*
- *International Climate Change Partnership (ICCP);*
- *International Council on Clean Transportation (ICCT, #13007);*
- *International Cryosphere Climate Initiative (ICCI, #13119);*
- *International Institute for Sustainable Development (IISD, #13930);*
- *International Network for Environmental Compliance and Enforcement (INECE, #14261);*
- *International Solid Waste Association (ISWA, #15567);*
- *International Union of Air Pollution Prevention and Environmental Protection Associations (IUAPPA, #15753);*
- *Local Governments for Sustainability (ICLEI, #16507);*
- *Nordic Environment Finance Corporation (NEFCO, #17281);*
- *Oxfam International (#17922);*
- *Pure Earth (#18578);*
- *Regional Environmental Centre for Central and Eastern Europe (REC, #18782);*
- *Stockholm Environment Institute (SEI, #19993);*
- *Swisscontact – Swiss Foundation for Technical Cooperation;*
- *UNDP (#20292);*
- *UNEP (#20299);*
- *UNIDO (#20336);*
- *Vital Strategies;*
- *WHO (#20950);*
- *World Resources Institute (WRI, #21753);*
- *Wuppertal Institute for Climate, Environment and Energy.*

NGO Relations *Cities Climate Finance Leadership Alliance (CCFLA, #03952); Every Woman Every Child (EWEC, #09215); Global LPG Partnership (GLPGP, #10461); Global Methane Initiative (GMI, #10471); We Mean Business.* [2020.05.06/XJ7583/y/**E**]

♦ Climate and Clean Air Coalition to Reduce Short-Lived Climate Pollutants / see Climate and Clean Air Coalition (#04010)
♦ Climate Cleanup Foundation (internationally oriented national body)

♦ Climate Counsel 04011

Exec Dir Laan 20, 2512 GN The Hague, Netherlands.
URL: https://www.climatecounsel.org/

History A non-profit outgrowth of Global Diligence LLP. Registration: Handelsregister, No/ID: KVK 77789415, Netherlands. **Aims** Enable international lawyers to help address the climate emergency, by using their expertise in transnational crime and human rights protection. **Structure** Supervisory Board; Panel of Advisors; Counsel; Investigators. Also includes: Ecocide Advice Centre. **Activities** Advocacy/lobbying/activism; guidance/assistance/consulting. **NGO Relations** Partner of (1): *Stop Ecocide International (SEI, #19998).* [2022/AA2671/f/**F**]

♦ Climate and Development Knowledge Network (CDKN) 04012

Alianza Clima y Desarrollo
Head Office c/o SouthSouthNorth, 55 Salt River Road, Salt River, Cape Town, 7925, South Africa. E-mail: cdkn@southsouthnorth.org.
URL: http://cdkn.org/

History 2010. Founded by PwC, *Overseas Development Institute (ODI)*, Lead Pakistan, *Fundación Futuro Latinoamericano (FFLA, #10022), Leadership for Environment and Development (LEAD International, #16416)*, and *SouthSouthNorth (SSN, #19893).* Since 2018, led by South Africa-based *SouthSouthNorth (SSN, #19893)*, working closely with its partners *Fundación Futuro Latinoamericano (FFLA, #10022)* in Quito, *Local Governments for Sustainability (ICLEI, #16507)* South Asia in Delhi, as well as *Overseas Development Institute (ODI)* in London. **Aims** Enhance the quality of life for those most vulnerable to climate change; support decision-makers at different levels to design and deliver climate compatible development; combine knowledge, research and advisory services in support of locally owned and managed policy processes. **Languages** English, Spanish. **Finance** Primary funding from the Dutch Ministry of Foreign Affairs and *International Development Research Centre (IDRC, #13162)* (Canada). **Activities** Awareness raising; capacity building; knowledge management/information dissemination; networking/liaising; projects/programmes. Since 2018, 'Knowledge Accelerator' phase focused on three areas: Knowledge; Engagement; Peer learning. Active in: Bangladesh, Colombia, Ecuador, Ethiopia, Ghana, India, Kenya, Namibia, Nepal, Peru. **Events** *Global Science*

Conference on Climate Smart Agriculture Ede (Netherlands) 2011. **Information Services** *Communicating climate change: A practitioner's guide – Comunicando el cambio climático: una guía para profesionales* by Mairi Dupar in English, Spanish; *How to contribute climate change information to Wikipedia – Cómo contribuir a la información sobre cambio climático en Wikipedia* in English, Spanish; *Weaving knowledge and action on climate change, 2018-2021 – Tejiendo conocimiento y acción sobre el cambio climático, 2018-21.* in English, Spanish. **NGO Relations** Partner of (4): *Fundación Futuro Latinoamericano (FFLA, #10022)*; *Local Governments for Sustainability (ICLEI, #16507)*; *Overseas Development Institute (ODI)*; *SouthSouthNorth (SSN, #19893).* [2022.02.10/XJ7054/y/**F**]

♦ Climate Farmers (unconfirmed)
♦ Climate Foundation (internationally oriented national body)

♦ Climate Group 04013

CEO The Clove Bldg, 4 Maguire Street, London, SE1 2NQ, UK. T. +442079602970. E-mail: info@theclimategroup.org.
URL: https://www.theclimategroup.org/

History 2003. Former names and other names: *The Climate Change Organisation* – alias. Registration: Charity Commission, No/ID: 1102909, England and Wales; Companies House, No/ID: 4964424, Start date: 14 Nov 2003, England and Wales; 501(c)(3) non-profit, No/ID: EIN 43-2073566, USA; EU Transparency Register, No/ID: 166412520967-61, Start date: 29 Mar 2016. **Aims** Advance business and government *leadership* on *climate change.* **Structure** Board of Trustees. **Finance** Supported by a range of organizations, including: *Rockefeller Brothers Fund (RBF).* **Events** *International conference on climate change* Hong Kong (Hong Kong) 2009. **Members** Companies; nongovernmental organization; regional and national governments. Membership countries not specified. **IGO Relations** Accredited by: *United Nations Framework Convention on Climate Change – Secretariat (UNFCCC, #20564).* **NGO Relations** Member of (3): *Global CCS Institute (#10274)*; *ResponsibleSteel (#18921)*; *We Mean Business.* Partner of (1): *Global Alliance for Energy Productivity (#10196).* Instrumental in setting up (1): *RE100.* Agreement with: Climate Initiative of *William J Clinton Foundation.* [2022/XM2096/**F**]

♦ Climate Institute (internationally oriented national body)
♦ Climate Interactive (internationally oriented national body)

♦ Climate Investment Coalition (CIC) 04014

Secretariat address not obtained. E-mail: info@climateinvestmentcoalition.org.
URL: https://www.climateinvestmentcoalition.org/

History Established by Government of Denmark, Insurance & Pension Denmark, *Institutional Investors Group on Climate Change (IIGCC, #11317)* and *World Climate Foundation (WCF).* **Aims** Mobilize ambitious green financial investments; promote green economic regeneration strategies for a post-pandemic economic recovery that ensures climate remains at the forefront of the global agenda and prioritises a just and green energy transition. **Events** *Climate Investment Summit* Copenhagen (Denmark) 2020. [2021/AA1380/**C**]

♦ Climate Investment Funds (CIF) 04015

Head address not obtained. E-mail: cifwebhelpdesk@worldbank.org.
URL: http://www.climateinvestmentfunds.org/

History 2008. **Aims** Help *developing countries* pilot *low-emissions* and climate resilient development. **Structure** Funds (2): *Clean Technology Fund (CTF)*; *Strategic Climate Fund (SCF).* SCF Programs (3): *Pilot Program for Climate Resilience (PPCR)*; *Scaling up Renewable Energy in Low Income Countries Program (SREP)*; *Forest Investment Program (FIP).* Each fund has its own Trust Fund Committee. SCF is subdivided into Sub-Committees to govern each program. **Finance** Budget: over US$ 8,000,000,000. Donor countries: Australia; Canada; Denmark; France; Germany; Japan; Korea Rep; Netherlands; Norway; Spain; Sweden; Switzerland; UK; USA. **Activities** Financial and/or material support. **Events** *CSO Forum* Yokohama (Japan) 2018, *AFIC : African Forestry Investment Conference* Accra (Ghana) 2017, *Adaptation Benefit Mechanism Workshop* London (UK) 2017.

Members Stakeholders: governments; Civil society organizations; indigenous peoples; private sector entities; multilateral development banks; UN and UN agencies. Multilateral Development Banks and Civil society (6): *African Development Bank (ADB, #00283)*; *Asian Development Bank (ADB, #01422)*; *European Bank for Reconstruction and Development (EBRD, #06315)*; *Inter-American Development Bank (IDB, #11427)*; *International Finance Corporation (IFC, #13597)*; *The World Bank Group (#21218).*

Observers (5):
Global Environment Facility (GEF, #10346); *Green Climate Fund (GCF, #10714)*; *UNDP (#20292)*; *UNEP (#20299)*; *United Nations Framework Convention on Climate Change – Secretariat (UNFCCC, #20564).*
NGO Relations Member of: *Cities Climate Finance Leadership Alliance (CCFLA, #03952).*
[2020/XM6568/f/**F**]

♦ Climate-KIC Association / see EIT Climate-KIC (#05403)

♦ Climate Knowledge Brokers (CKB) 04016

Coordination Hub Vienna Intl Centre D-2170, 1400 Vienna, Austria. T. +431260263337.
URL: http://www.climateknowledgebrokers.net/

History 2011, by *Climate and Development Knowledge Network (CDKN, #04012)*, *Deutsche Gesellschaft für Internationale Zusammenarbeit (GIZ)* and *Potsdam Institute for Climate Impact Research (PIK).* **Aims** Improve access to climate information by coordinating and orchestrating the efforts of climate knowledge brokers. **Structure** Steering Group. **Activities** Knowledge management/information dissemination; events/meetings. **Events** *Workshop* Golden, CO (USA) 2016, *Workshop* Copenhagen (Denmark) 2015, *Workshop* Brighton (UK) 2014, *Workshop* Bonn (Germany) 2013, *Workshop* Bonn (Germany) 2012. **Publications** *CKB Newsletter.*

Members Group members include the following 29 organizations listed in this Yearbook:
- *Caribbean Community Climate Change Centre (CCCCC, #03477)*;
- *Center for International Forestry Research (CIFOR, #03646)*;
- *Climate and Development Knowledge Network (CDKN, #04012)*;
- *Commonwealth Secretariat (#04362)*;
- *Deutsche Gesellschaft für Internationale Zusammenarbeit (GIZ)*;
- *European Space Agency (ESA, #08798)*;
- *Global Canopy (#10271)*;
- *Inter-American Development Bank (IDB, #11427)*;
- *International Bank for Reconstruction and Development (IBRD, #12317)*;
- *International Centre for Climate Change and Development (ICCCAD)*;
- *International Centre for Integrated Mountain Development (ICIMOD, #12500)*;
- *International Centre for Tropical Agriculture (#12527)*;
- *International Development Research Centre (IDRC, #13162)*;
- *International Institute for Sustainable Development (IISD, #13930)*;
- *International Renewable Energy Agency (IRENA, #14715)*;
- *Internews*;
- *Internews Europe (#15953)*;
- *Overseas Development Institute (ODI)*;
- *Pacific Community (SPC, #17942)*;
- *Potsdam Institute for Climate Impact Research (PIK)*;
- *REN21 (#18836)*;
- *Renewable Energy and Energy Efficiency Partnership (REEEP, #18837)*;
- *Stockholm Environment Institute (SEI, #19993)*;
- *UNDP (#20292)*;
- *UNEP (#20299)*;
- *United Nations Framework Convention on Climate Change (UNFCCC, 1992)*;
- *United Nations Institute for Training and Research (UNITAR, #20576)*;
- *World Food Programme (WFP, #21510)*;
- *World Wide Fund for Nature (WWF, #21922).* [2016/XM4406/y/**F**]

♦ Climate Ledger Initiative (CLI) 04017

Contact c/o INFRAS, Binzstr 23, 8045 Zurich ZH, Switzerland. T. +41442059595. E-mail: info@climateledger.org.
URL: https://www.climateledger.org/

History Nov 2016, Marrakech (Morocco). Evolved out of a research project of the Zurich-based Cleantech21 (C21) foundation. For 2019-2021, a 2.5-year programme financed by *Swiss Agency for Development and Cooperation (SDC).* Former names and other names: *CarbonBC* – former. **Aims** Accelerate climate action in line with the Paris Climate Agreement and the Sustainable Development Goals (SDGs) through blockchain-based innovation applicable to climate change mitigation, adaptation, and finance. **Structure** Steering Committee; Programme Management Group; Expert Committee. **IGO Relations** *Paris Agreement (2015).* **NGO Relations** Member of (1): *Climate Chain Coalition (CCC, #04008).* [2021.09.24/AA1979/**E**]

♦ Climate Markets and Investment Association (CMIA) 04018

Contact 100 New Bridge Street, London, EC4V 6JA, UK. T. +442074422195. E-mail: info@cmia.net.
URL: http://www.cmia.net/

History 2008. **Aims** Communicate technical expertise to international policy makers, government departments and key law makers to help them develop cost-effective and efficient market based solutions to address *climate change* and resource scarcity. **Structure** Board; Secretariat. **Members** Companies. **IGO Relations** Observer of: *Green Climate Fund (GCF, #10714).* **NGO Relations** Member of: *Climate and Clean Air Coalition (CCAC, #04010).* [2022/XJ7802/**D**]

♦ Climate Network Europe / see Climate Action Network Europe (#04001)

♦ Climate Parliament 04019

Parlement du Climat – Parlamento del Clima

SG Climate Parliament, Kemp House, 152-160 City Road, London, EC1V 2NX, UK. E-mail: info@climateparl.net.
URL: http://www.climateparl.net/

History Founded by an international groups of Members of Parliament and Congress. Original title: *e-Parliament.* Full title: *Climate Parliament – Legislators working worldwide to combat climate change – Le Parlement du Climat – Des législateurs du monde entier combattent ensemble les changements climatiques – Parlamento del Clima – Legisladores trabajando a nivel mundial para combatir el cambio climatico.* UK Registered Charity. **Aims** Link together into a global network Members of Parliament concerned about *climate change*; promote climate action and the shift from fossil fuels to *renewable energy.* **Structure** Board of Trustees; Advisory Committee; Issue Networks. **Languages** Arabic, English, French, Mandarin Chinese, Spanish. **Staff** 20.00 FTE, paid. **Finance** Grants. Budget (2014): about US$ 2 million. **Activities** Capacity building; events/meetings. **Members** Any elected Member of Parliament can participate. Membership countries not specified. **IGO Relations** Partner of: *International Solar Alliance (ISA, #15563).*
[2014.06.01/XF6966/**F**]

♦ Climate Parliament – Legislators working worldwide to combat climate change / see Climate Parliament (#04019)

♦ Climate Policy Initiative (CPI) 04020

Exec Dir 180 Sansome St, Ste 1000, San Francisco CA 94104, USA. T. +14152300795. E-mail: adminsf@cpiglobal.org.
URL: http://climatepolicyinitiative.org/

History Sep 2009. **Aims** Promote low carbon development globally. **Structure** Offices in: Delhi (India); Jakarta (Indonesia); Rio de Janeiro (Brazil); San Francisco CA (USA); Venice (Italy). **Activities** Monitoring/evaluation; research/documentation. **Events** *Geothermal Dialogue* Vienna (Austria) 2015. **Members** Not a membership organization. **IGO Relations** Partner of: *Global Green Growth Forum (3GF).* Associate member of: *NDC Partnership (#16964).* Accredited organization of: *Green Climate Fund (GCF, #10714).* **NGO Relations** Provides Secretariat for: *Cities Climate Finance Leadership Alliance (CCFLA, #03952).* Partners include: *Fondazione Eni Enrico Mattei (FEEM)*; *Tropical Forest Alliance (TFA, #20249).* [2020/XM3876/**F**]

♦ Climate Positive Europe Alliance (CPEA) 04021

SG c/o REHVA, Rue Washington 40, 1050 Brussels, Belgium. T. +4971172232228. E-mail: info@cpea.eu.
URL: https://www.cpea.eu/

History Founded by German Sustainable Building Council DGNB, Austrian Sustainable Building Council ÖGNI, Green Building Council España GBCe and *Federation of European Heating, Ventilation and Air-Conditioning Associations (REHVA, #09507).* Registration: Banque-Carrefour des Entreprises, No/ID: 0772.545.513, Start date: 13 Aug 2021, Belgium; EU Transparency Register, No/ID: 865678148148-67, Start date: 17 Nov 2022. **Aims** Collaboratively accelerate market transformation towards more sustainable market practices by facilitating cross-sectoral dialogue and providing sectoral insights and tangible solutions for the most pressing challenges faced by the construction and real estate stakeholder community. **Structure** Board of Directors.
[2022/AA3024/y/**D**]

♦ Climate Reality Project Europe 04022

Manager Wiedner Hauptstr 120-124, 1050 Vienna, Austria.
URL: https://www.climaterealityeurope.org/

History Set up as the European Branch of The Climate Reality Project, founded by former US vice president Al Gore. Registration: EU Transparency Register, No/ID: 569281438051-07, Start date: 6 May 2020. **Aims** Engage with European communities, empowering them to articulate greater climate ambitions and enabling citizens to co-create responses to the climate crisis, thus generating bottom-up support for the implementation of the Paris Agreement. [2020/AA0083/**F**]

♦ CliMates (internationally oriented national body)

♦ Climate Technology Centre and Network (CTCN) 04023

Secretariat UN City, Marmorvej 51, 2100 Copenhagen, Denmark. T. +4545335372. E-mail: ctcn@unep.org.
URL: http://www.ctc-n.org/

History Operational arm of *United Nations Framework Convention on Climate Change (UNFCCC, 1992)* Technology Mechanism. **Aims** Promote accelerated development and transfer of climate technologies at the request of *developing countries* for energy-efficient, low-carbon and climate-resilient development. **Structure** Hosted by *UNEP (#20299)*, in collaboration with *UNIDO (#20336).* **Finance** Supported by: *UNEP (#20299)*; *UNIDO (#20336)*; governments of Norway, Canada, Switzerland, Germany, Finland, USA, Japan and Ireland; *European Commission (EC, #06633)*; *DANIDA.* **Activities** Guidance/assistance/consulting; networking/liaising; knowledge management/information dissemination; capacity building. **Events** *Regional Forum for Asia* Bangkok (Thailand) 2016, *Regional Forum for Anglophone Africa* Nairobi (Kenya) 2016, *Regional Forum for National Designated Entities* Bangkok (Thailand) 2015.

Members Full (153) in 46 countries:
Australia, Austria, Bangladesh, Belgium, Brazil, Cameroon, Canada, Cape Verde, Chile, Colombia, Costa Rica, Cuba, Denmark, Ecuador, Finland, France, Germany, Guinea, India, Indonesia, Iran Islamic Rep, Iraq, Israel, Italy, Japan, Kazakhstan, Kenya, Korea Rep, Malaysia, Mexico, Nepal, Netherlands, Norway, Pakistan, Peru, Philippines, Samoa, South Africa, Spain, Sudan, Switzerland, Tanzania UR, UK, United Arab Emirates, USA, Vietnam.

Included in the above, 31 organizations listed in this Yearbook:
- *Association pour la Recherche et la Promotion de l'Energie Durable en Afrique Centrale (ARPEDAC)*;
- *Center for Clean Air Policy (CCAP)*;
- *Climate and Development Knowledge Network (CDKN, #04012)*;
- *Consortium for the Sustainable Development of the Andean Ecoregion (#04758)*;
- *ECOWAS Centre for Renewable Energy and Energy Efficiency (ECREEE, #05335)*;
- *European Hydrogen Alliance (EHA, #07511)*;
- *GERES*;
- *Global CCS Institute (#10274)*;
- *Global Enabling Sustainability Initiative (GeSI, #10340)*;
- *Global Environment Centre (GEC)*;
- *Green Cooling Initiative (GCI)*;
- *Institut de recherche pour le développement (IRD)*;
- *International Centre for Integrated Mountain Development (ICIMOD, #12500)*;
- *International Centre for Tropical Agriculture (#12527)*;
- *International Energy Agency (IEA, #13270)*;
- *International Food Policy Research Institute (IFPRI, #13622)*;
- *International Institute for Energy Conservation (IIEC, #13875)*;

– *International Rice Research Institute (IRRI, #14754)*;
– *International Solid Waste Association (ISWA, #15567)*;
– *International Water Management Institute (IWMI, #15867)*;
– *Latin American Energy Organization (#16313)*;
– *LEDS Global Partnership (LEDS GP, #16435)*;
– *Nordic Environment Finance Corporation (NEFCO, #17281)*;
– *Regional Environmental Centre for Central Asia (CAREC)*;
– *REN21 (#18836)*;
– *Renewable Energy and Energy Efficiency Partnership (REEEP, #18837)*;
– *Secretariat of the Pacific Regional Environment Programme (SPREP, #19205)*;
– *SNV Netherlands Development Organisation (SNV)*;
– *World Coal Association (WCA, #21280)*;
– *World Intellectual Property Organization (WIPO, #21593)*;
– *Wuppertal Institute for Climate, Environment and Energy*.

IGO Relations Cooperates with: *Deutsche Gesellschaft für Internationale Zusammenarbeit (GIZ)*; *Tropical Agriculture Research and Higher Education Center (#20246)*; *UNEP (#20299)*; UNEP-DHI Partnership – Centre on Water and Environment; UNEP DTU Partnership; *UNIDO (#20336)*. **NGO Relations** Cooperates with: *Asian Institute of Technology (AIT, #01519)*; *Bariloche Foundation (FB)*; Council for Scientific and Energy Research Centre of the Netherlands; Energy and Resources Institute, India; *Environnement et développement du Tiers-monde (enda, #05510)*; Industrial Research (CSIR), South Africa; National Renewable Energy Laboratory, USA; *World Agroforestry Centre (ICRAF, #21072)*. member of: *International Centre for Earth Simulation (ICES Foundation)*. [2020/XM4404/y/**F**]

♦ Climate Technology Initiative (inactive)

♦ ClimateWorks Foundation 04024

Main Office 235 Montgomery St, Ste 1300, San Francisco CA 94104, USA. T. +14154330500. E-mail: info@climateworks.org.
URL: http://www.climateworks.org/

History 2008, USA. **Aims** Mobilize *philanthropy* to solve the climate crisis and ensure a prosperous future. **Events** *Scenarios Forum for Climate and Societal Futures* Denver, CO (USA) 2019, *Global Climate Action Summit* San Francisco, CA (USA) 2018. **NGO Relations** Partner of (1): *Global Battery Alliance (GBA, #10249)*. [2020/XM3878/fy/**F**]

♦ **Clim-HEALTH Africa** International Network for Climate and Health for Africa (#14244)
♦ **CLIMMAR** Centre de Liaison International des Marchands de Machines Agricoles et des Réparateurs (#14034)
♦ CLIMM / see Mars and Mercury Europe – Industrial and Commercial Circles of Officers and Reserve Officers Inter-Nations Coordination Commission (#16589)
♦ **CLINAM** European Foundation for Clinical Nanomedicine (#07346)
♦ Clingendael Institute for International Relations / see Netherlands Institute of International Relations – Clingendael
♦ Clinical Applications of Cytometry / see International Clinical Cytometry Society
♦ Clinical Data Interchange Standards Consortium / see CDISC (#03620)
♦ Clinical and Laboratory Standards Institute (internationally oriented national body)

♦ Clinical Robotic Surgery Association (CRSA) 04025

Exec Managing Dir Two Prudential Plaza, 180 North Stetson, Suite 3500, Chicago IL 60601, USA.
URL: https://clinicalrobotics.com/

History 2009. **Aims** Spread robotic techniques in general surgery and its related specialties. **Structure** Board of Directors; Executive. **Activities** Events/meetings; knowledge management/information dissemination; networking/liaising; research/documentation; training/education. **Events** *Worldwide Congress* Shanghai (China) 2021, *Worldwide Congress* Durham, NC (USA) 2019, *Worldwide Congress* Hong Kong 2018, *World Congress* Daegu (Korea Rep) 2016. **Publications** *International Journal for Medical Robotics and Computer Assisted Surgery*. [2021/AA2258/**C**]

♦ Clinical RSA Research Network / see International Radiostereometry Society (#14688)
♦ Clinical Trials on Alzheimer's Disease (meeting series)
♦ Cliometric Society (internationally oriented national body)
♦ CLIP – European network of cities for local integration policies for migrants (inactive)
♦ **CLIPSAS** Centre de liaison et d'information des puissances maçonniques signataires de l'Appel de Strasbourg (#03770)
♦ **CLIRSPEC** International Society for Clinical Spectroscopy (#15018)
♦ **CLITRAVI** Centre de liaison des industries transformatrices de viandes de l'UE (#16452)

♦ CLL Advocates Network (CLLAN) 04026

Contact Leukemia Patient Advocates Foundation, POB 453, 3000 Bern 7, Switzerland. E-mail: info@clladvocates.net.

History 2014. CLL stands for Chronic lymphocytic leukaemia. **Aims** Improve CLL patient outcomes as a global network of CLL patient advocates. **Structure** Steering Committee. Hosted by *Leukemia Patient Advocates Foundation (LePAF)*. **Activities** Advocacy/lobbying/activism; events/meetings; training/education. **Events** *CLL Horizons* Edinburgh (UK) 2019. **Members** Full; Associate; Supporters. Membership countries not specified. **NGO Relations** Member of (1): *Workgroup of European Cancer Patient Advocacy Networks (WECAN, #21054)*. [AA0352/**F**]

♦ **CLLAN** CLL Advocates Network (#04026)
♦ CLLSD / see Southeast Asian Center for Lifelong Learning for Sustainable Development
♦ CLM / see Council of Supply Chain Management Professionals
♦ CLM / see Asociación Latinoamericana de Metros y Subterraneos (#02242)
♦ **CLMC** Christian Learning Materials Centre, Nairobi (#03904)
♦ CLMC – Comunità Laici Missionari Cattolici (internationally oriented national body)
♦ CLM / see International Partners in Mission (#14526)
♦ CLMM – Commonwealth Law Ministers' Meeting (meeting series)
♦ CLN – Convention Relating to the Limitation of the Liability of Owners of Inland Navigation Vessels (1973 treaty)
♦ **CLN** Corporate Leaders Network for Climate Action (#04840)
♦ **CLOC** Coordinadora Latinoamericana de Organizaciones del Campo (#04808)
♦ CLO-ME – Chief Learning Officer Middle East (unconfirmed)
♦ Clooney Foundation for Justice (internationally oriented national body)
♦ CLOROSUR / see Latin American Chlor-Alkali and Derivatives Industry Association (#16295)
♦ **CLOROSUR** Latin American Chlor-Alkali and Derivatives Industry Association (#16295)
♦ Close-Up Europe / see International Education Centre of Svendborg
♦ Close the Gap International (internationally oriented national body)
♦ Up Close and Personalized International Congress on Personalized Medicine (meeting series)

♦ Cloud Community Europe 04027

Managing Dir Rue Alcide de Gasperi 7, L-1013 Luxembourg, Luxembourg.
URL: http://www.cloudcommunityeurope.org/

History Previously known as *EuroCloud* and also referred to as *EuroCloud Europe*. Registered in accordance with Luxembourg law: 2013 61 00379. **Aims** As a vendor neutral knowledge sharing network between cloud *computing* customers and providers, start-ups and research centres, maintain a constant open dialogue with all partners to bring IT and *business* together. **Structure** Council; Board. **Activities** Projects/programmes; awards/prizes/competitions; events/meetings. **Events** *European Congress / Forum* Barcelona (Spain) 2015. **Publications** *Cloud Community Europe Newsletter*.
Members Full in 21 countries:
Austria, Croatia, Czechia, France, Germany, Hungary, Italy, Luxembourg, Malta, Monaco, Netherlands, Poland, Portugal, Romania, Serbia, Slovakia, Slovenia, Spain, Sweden, Switzerland, UK. [2018.06.12/XM4613/**D**]

♦ Cloud Security Alliance (internationally oriented national body)

♦ Cloud Security Alliance Asia Pacific (CSA APAC) 04028

Contact 354 Tanglin Road, 01-18/19 Tanglin Intl Ctr, Singapore 247672, Singapore. E-mail: csa-apac-info@cloudsecurityalliance.org.
URL: https://www.csaapac.org/

History A chapter of *Cloud Security Alliance (CSA)*. Former names and other names: *Cloud Security Alliance Asia Pacific Region* – alias. **Activities** Events/meetings; research/documentation; training/education. **Events** *CSA APAC Summit* Singapore (Singapore) 2019.
Members Chapters in 18 countries and territories:
Australia, Bangladesh, Cambodia, China, India, Indonesia, Japan, Korea Rep, Laos, Malaysia, Myanmar, Nepal, Philippines, Singapore, Sri Lanka, Taiwan, Thailand, Vietnam. [2023.02.14/AA2915/**E**]

♦ Cloud Security Alliance Asia Pacific Region / see Cloud Security Alliance Asia Pacific (#04028)
♦ **CLOVE** Colegio Latinoamericano de Oftalmólogos Veterinarios (#04094)

♦ Clowns Without Borders International (CWBI) 04029

Intl Coordinator Pl/ Margarida Xirgu, 1 (ed. Teatre Lliure), 08004 Barcelona, Spain. E-mail: coordination@cwb-international.org – cwbi.coordination@gmail.com.
Sec address not obtained.
URL: https://www.cwb-international.org/

History Registration: Spain. **Aims** Facilitate communication and cooperation between Clowns Without Borders chapters around the world; protect and support the common identity and the quality of the work of existing and future Clowns Without Borders chapters through accountability and governance. **Structure** General Assembly; Board; Steering Committee. **Activities** Projects/programmes.
Members Chapters in 14 countries:
Australia, Belgium, Brazil, Canada, Finland, France, Germany, Ireland, South Africa, Spain, Sweden, Switzerland, UK, USA.
Consultative Status Consultative status granted from: *UNESCO (#20322)* (Consultative Status). [2021/AA1178/**F**]

♦ CLRAE / see Congress of Local and Regional Authorities of the Council of Europe (#04677)
♦ **CLR** European Institute for Construction Labour Research (#07549)
♦ CLSI – Clinical and Laboratory Standards Institute (internationally oriented national body)
♦ CLTC – Confederación Latinoamericana de Trabajadores de Comunicaciones (no recent information)
♦ CLTTC – Confederación Latinoamericana de Trabajadores del Transporte y las Comunicaciones (no recent information)
♦ Club 41 International / see 41 International (#22047)

♦ Club Arc Alpin (CAA) 04030

Dir Anni-Albers-Str.7, 80807 Munich, Germany. T. +498914003648. E-mail: caa@club-arc-alpin.eu.
URL: http://www.club-arc-alpin.eu/

History 18 Nov 1995, Schaan (Liechtenstein). Current constitution adopted 9 Sep 2006; amended 13 Sep 2008, Malbun (Liechtenstein); 2014, Paris (France). Registration: Germany. **Structure** General Assembly; Board; Expert Commissions (3). **Languages** English, German. **Staff** 1.00 FTE, paid. **Events** *AlpWeek* Brig (Switzerland) 2022, *AlpWeek* Poschiavo (Switzerland) 2012.
Members Organizations (8) in 7 countries:
Austria, France, Germany, Italy, Liechtenstein, Slovenia, Switzerland.
NGO Relations Cooperates with (1): *European Union of Mountaineering Associations (EUMA, #09002)*. [2021.09.23/XJ5121/**F**]

♦ Club de las Bahias mas Bellas del Mundo (#16858)

♦ Club of Bologna 04031

Admin Secretariat c/o FEDERUNACOMA, Via Venafro 5, 00165 Rome RM, Italy. T. +39643298253. Fax +3964076370. E-mail: unacoma@unacoma.it.
Pres address not obtained.
URL: http://www.clubofbologna.org/

History 1988. **Aims** Study and define strategies for the development of *agricultural mechanization* worldwide, taking into consideration technical, economic and social advances and changes in agriculture on an international level. **Structure** Management Committee, composed of 16 representatives from 11 Countries (5 European, 2 American, 2 Asian, 1 African, 1 Australian) and 3 International Organisations. Technical Secretariat; Administrative Secretariat. **Finance** Sponsored by UNACOMA (Italian Farm Machinery and Earth Moving Machinery Manufacturers Association). **Activities** Exchange, discussion and confrontation of the experience and knowledge of scientists, researchers, technicians, managers, agricultural machinery manufacturers and farmers who are concerned with the fundamental problems in the field. Information; specific and general studies and analyses. Organizes an annual meeting (always in Bologna, Italy). **Events** *Annual full members meeting* Bologna (Italy) 2005, *Annual full members meeting* Bologna (Italy) 2004, *Annual full members meeting* Bologna (Italy) 2003, *Annual full members meeting* Bologna (Italy) 2002, *Annual full members meeting* Bologna (Italy) 2002. **Publications** Meeting proceedings.
Members Full individuals in 46 countries:
Argentina, Australia, Austria, Belgium, Brazil, Bulgaria, Canada, Chile, China, Czechia, Denmark, Egypt, France, Germany, Greece, Hungary, India, Indonesia, Iran Islamic Rep, Israel, Italy, Japan, Jordan, Korea Rep, Mexico, Morocco, Netherlands, New Zealand, Nigeria, Norway, Philippines, Poland, Portugal, Romania, Russia, Serbia, Slovakia, Spain, Sudan, Thailand, Tunisia, Türkiye, UK, USA, Venezuela, Zimbabwe.
Associate individuals in 16 countries:
Austria, Belgium, Denmark, Finland, France, Germany, Greece, Iran Islamic Rep, Italy, Japan, Netherlands, Pakistan, Portugal, Spain, Switzerland, UK. [2014/XE3044/**E**]

♦ Club of Budapest 04032

Pres Tóth Arpad sétany 29 1/4, Budapest 1014, Hungary. T. +3612129893. E-mail: theclubofbudapest@gmail.com.
Dir address not obtained.
URL: http://www.clubofbudapest.org/

History Nov 1993, Budapest (Hungary), by the Hungarian Cultural Foundation, at the instigation of Ervin Laszló. **Aims** Promote and facilitate a worldwide movement keynoted by the advance from *thinking* in terms of existing limits to growth, to the emerging chances of evolution. **Structure** Responsibility for the twin organizations, Club of Budapest (Hungary) and *Club of Budapest International (COBI, see: #04032)*, resides with the joint President, together with the respective Praesidia (each with 3 members, including President). Officers of the Club of Budapest (Hungary): President, 2 Members of the Praesidium and Deputy to the President. The twin Secretariats (each comprising Deputy to the President, Activities Coordinator and Secretary to the President) are assisted by the Joint Working Group and advised by the International Advisory Board. World Coordination Centre (WCC) in Budapest links Regional Centres for Planetary Consciousness (RCPCs). **Languages** English, Hungarian. **Staff** 1.00 FTE, paid; 3.00 FTE, voluntary. **Activities** Events/meetings; projects/programmes. **Events** *IEC : Integral European Conference* Budapest (Hungary) 2016, *World Thought Leaders Forum* Milan (Italy) 2015, *Anniversary Conference* Budapest (Hungary) 2014, *IEC : Integral European Conference / Integral European Conference* Budapest (Hungary) 2014, *Meeting* Budapest (Hungary) 2009.
Members Leading artists, writers and creative people in various fields of arts and the spiritual domains of culture. Membership categories Honorary; Creative; Supporting; Institutional. Individuals (elected membership in the Club is limited to 100 individuals) in 25 countries:
Austria, Belgium, Canada, Costa Rica, Czechia, Denmark, Finland, France, Germany, Hungary, Iceland, India, Israel, Italy, Japan, Kyrgyzstan, Mexico, Netherlands, Norway, Romania, Russia, Sri Lanka, Switzerland, UK, USA.
Organizations in 24 countries and territories:
Argentina, Australia, Basque Country, Belgium, Brazil, Canada, China, Croatia, Czechia, Denmark, Ethiopia, France, Hungary, Italy, Japan, Malta, Mexico, Netherlands, Pakistan, Russia, Slovakia, Switzerland, UK, USA. [2017.03.09/XF3007/**F**]

♦ Club of Budapest International (see: #04032)
♦ Club du CEPII (internationally oriented national body)

♦ Club des chefs des chefs 04033

Address not obtained.
URL: http://www.chefs-des-chefs.com/

History Founded 1977, France. **Events** *Annual Meeting* Seoul (Korea Rep) 2019, *Annual Meeting* Delhi (India) 2016, *Annual Meeting* Switzerland 2015, *Annual Meeting* London (UK) 2014, *Annual Meeting* USA 2013.
Members The world's most prestigious chefs, in 25 countries:
Canada, China, Denmark, Estonia, Finland, France, Gabon, Germany, Haiti, Iceland, India, Ireland, Israel, Italy, Luxembourg, Monaco, Poland, South Africa, Spain, Sri Lanka, Sweden, Switzerland, Thailand, UK, USA. [2016/XF3335/v/**F**]

Club congrès langue
04033

alphabetic sequence excludes
For the complete listing, see Yearbook Online at

- Club des congrès de langue française / see Coésio – Destinations Francophone de Congrès (#04082)
- Club de Dakar (inactive)
- Club of Dakar (inactive)
- Club of Directors of Banks and Credit Establishments of French-Speaking Africa (#04034)
- Club des dirigeants des banques d'Afrique francophone / see Club des dirigeants des banques et établissements de crédit d'Afrique francophone (#04034)

♦ Club des dirigeants des banques et établissements de crédit d'Afrique francophone 04034

Club of Directors of Banks and Credit Establishments of French-Speaking Africa

Pres c/o Groupe BGFIBank, Blvd Rawiri, BP 25200, Libreville, Gabon. T. +24101441707 – +24107597373. Fax +24101441709.

History 29 Jan 1989, Lomé (Togo), as *Club des dirigeants des banques d'Afrique francophone*. Statutes were adopted. **Aims** Provide information and training to the leaders of *francophone Africa*. **Structure** General Assembly (annual). Bureau, consisting of President, 3 Vice-Presidents and 4 Administrators. Executive Secretary. **Languages** French. **Finance** Members' dues. Income from activities. **Activities** Information; training, including seminars, conferences, study travels. **Events** *Colloque / Colloquium* Nouakchott (Mauritania) 2005, *Annual General Assembly* Dakar (Senegal) 2004, *Colloque / Colloquium* Paris (France) 2004, *Colloquium* Geneva (Switzerland) 2003, *Assemblée générale / Annual General Assembly* Ouagadougou (Burkina Faso) 2003. **Publications** *International Press Review* (5 a year).

Members Full in 28 countries:
Angola, Benin, Burkina Faso, Burundi, Cameroon, Central African Rep, Chad, Comoros, Congo Brazzaville, Congo DR, Côte d'Ivoire, Djibouti, Gabon, Gambia, Guinea, Libya, Madagascar, Mali, Mauritania, Mauritius, Morocco, Mozambique, Niger, Rwanda, Sao Tomé-Principe, Senegal, Togo, Tunisia.
Honorary members in 7 countries:
Burundi, Cameroon, Congo Brazzaville, France, Gabon, Mali, Togo.
Observers in 3 countries:
Côte d'Ivoire, France, Zimbabwe. [2013.09.30/XF4640/F]

- Club Dubois / see European Media Research Organizations (#07759)
- Clube das Mais Lindas Baias do Mundo (#16858)
- Clube de Roma (#04038)
- Club of European Iris Society / see Middle European Iris Society (#16793)
- Club européen des diététiciens de l'enfance (#06583)
- Club européen d'entreprises (internationally oriented national body)
- Club européen des fabricants d'acier utilisant l'énergie nucléaire (inactive)
- Club européen de recherches en pédiatrie (inactive)
- Club européen de la santé / see European network for health promotion and economic development (#07920)
- Club du facteur 10 / see Factor 10 Institute (#09236)
- Club fédéraliste international (inactive)
- Club Francophone des Spécialistes de la Rétine (unconfirmed)
- Club Health Conference – International Conference on Nightlife, Substance Use and Related Health Issues (meeting series)

♦ Clubhouse International 04035

Exec Dir 747 Third Avenue, 2nd Floor, New York NY 10017, USA. T. +12125820343. E-mail: info@clubhouse-intl.org.
URL: http://clubhouse-intl.org/

History 1994. First clubhouse opened 1948, New York NY (USA). Former names and other names: *International Center for Clubhouse Development (ICCD)* – former. **Aims** End social and economic isolation for people with mental illness by growing the number and quality of Clubhouse rehabilitation programs worldwide. **Structure** Board of Directors; Board of Advisors; Executive Leadership Team; Working Groups. **Activities** Advocacy/lobbying/activism; awareness raising; certification/accreditation; research/documentation; training/education. **Events** *World Seminar* Oslo (Norway) 2019, *World Seminar* Oslo (Norway) 2019, *Congress* Stockholm (Sweden) 2011, *Seminar* Helsinki (Finland) 2005. [2020/AA0702/F]

- Club d'information et de réflexion sur l'économie mondiale / see Club du CEPII
- Club Internacional de los Grandes Viajeros (#15915)
- Club Internacional de Guias (inactive)
- Club international des bécassiers du paléarctique occidental / see Fédération des Associations Nationales des Bécassiers du Paléarctique Occidental (#09460)
- Club international des cavaliers de dressage (#13201)
- Club international des cavaliers de saut d'obstacle (#13977)
- Club international des concours hippiques (inactive)
- Club international féminin / see Fédération internationale culturelle féminine (#09625)
- Club international des grands voyageurs (#15915)
- Club international des guides (inactive)
- Club international d'implants oculaires (#13948)
- Club international des ingénieurs et des industriels / see European Society for Engineers and Industrialists
- Club international des technopoles / see International Association of Science Parks and Areas of Innovation (#12151)
- Club Jules Gonin Society / see Jules Gonin Club (#16165)

♦ Club Latinoamericano de Neuroftalmologia (CLAN) 04036

Latin American Club of Neuro Ophthalmology

Contact address not obtained.
URL: http://neuroftalmoclan.blogspot.be/

History Founded 1988, Chile. Previously also referred to as *Latin American Council of Neuro Ophthalmology – Consejo Latino Americano de Neuroftalmologia (CLAN)*. **Aims** Meet and discuss relevant topics; participate with ophthalmologists, neurologists and other related medical areas in courses, meetings and international protocols. **Structure** Annual Meeting. **Staff** None. **Events** *Annual Meeting* Concepción (Chile) 2015, *Annual Meeting* Buenos Aires (Argentina) 2014, *Annual Meeting* Rio de Janeiro (Brazil) 2013, *Annual Meeting* Asunción (Paraguay) 2012, *Annual meeting* Renaca (Chile) 2008.

Members Individuals in 14 countries:
Argentina, Bolivia, Brazil, Chile, Colombia, Dominican Rep, Ecuador, Mexico, Panama, Paraguay, Peru, Uruguay, USA, Venezuela.
NGO Relations Member of: *Pan-American Association of Ophthalmology (PAAO, #18081)*. [2015/XD6802/v/D]

- Club de Londres / see Nuclear Suppliers Group (#17621)
- Club de Madrid / see World Leadership Alliance – Club de Madrid (#21619)
- Club of Madrid / see World Leadership Alliance – Club de Madrid (#21619)
- Club of Mainz / see World Association for Disaster and Emergency Medicine (#21133)
- Club of Mainz for Emergency and Disaster Medicine Worldwide / see World Association for Disaster and Emergency Medicine (#21133)

♦ Club Managers Association of Europe (CMAE) 04037

Manager Rural Innovation Centre, Stoneleigh Park, CV8 2RF, UK. T. +442476692359. Fax +442476414990.
URL: http://www.cmaeurope.org/

History Current constitution adopted, 14 Apr 2010. **Aims** Advance the profession of club management throughout Europe; promote best practice in the club industry; provide a certification programme which recognizes and rewards those club managers that can demonstrate the highest standards of knowledge and competence in club management. **Structure** General Meeting (annual). European Board of Directors. **Staff** 2.00 FTE, paid. **Events** *Conference* Marbella (Spain) 2018, *Conference* Marbella (Spain) 2017, *Annual General Meeting* Rome (Italy) 2013, *Annual General Meeting* Rome (Italy) 2013, *Conference* Rome (Italy) 2013. **Publications** *Clubhouse Europe* (4 a year) – magazine; *CMAE E-newsletter*, *Tribal Tuesday* – best practice articles. [2017.03.07/XJ5149/D]

- Club de Mayence / see World Association for Disaster and Emergency Medicine (#21133)
- Club de Mayence pour la propagation de la médecine d'urgence et des soins intensifs / see World Association for Disaster and Emergency Medicine (#21133)
- Club méditerranéen des brûlures / see Euro-Mediterranean Council for Burns and Fire Disaster (#05719)
- Club méditerranéen des brûlures et désastres du feu / see Euro-Mediterranean Council for Burns and Fire Disaster (#05719)
- Club nordique des cardiologues pour enfants (#17241)
- Club d'oncologie pédiatrique / see International Society of Paediatric Oncology (#15339)
- Club pancréatique européen (#08136)
- Club de Paris / see Paris Club of Industrial Country Creditors (#18199)
- Club des Plus Belles Baies du Monde (#16858)
- Club von Rom (#04038)
- Club de Roma (#04038)
- Club di Roma (#04038)
- Club de Rome (#04038)

♦ Club of Rome (COR) 04038

Club de Rome – Club de Roma – Club von Rom – Club di Roma – Clube de Roma – Rimskij Klub

Main Office Lagerhausstrasse 9, 8400 Winterthur ZH, Switzerland. T. +41522440808. Fax +41522440809.
Co-Pres address not obtained.
URL: http://www.clubofrome.org/

History Founded Apr 1968, Rome (Italy), at a meeting of 30 scientists, educators, economists, humanists, industrialists and national and international civil servants. Registered in accordance with Swiss Civil Code. EU Transparency Register: 806327336072-56. **Aims** Foster understanding of the interdependent economic, political, natural and social components comprising the *global system*; bring this new understanding to the attention of *policy-makers* and the public worldwide; promote new policy initiatives and action; identify a new class of social problems and provide the language, methods and success criteria appropriate for their solution. **Structure** General Assembly; Executive Committee; Secretariat located in Winterthur (Switzerland). **Languages** English, French, German, Russian, Spanish. **Staff** 4.00 FTE, paid. Voluntary. **Finance** Members' dues. Foundation grants. **Activities** Research/documentation; projects/programmes; publishing activities; events/meetings. Instrumental in setting up: *Fondation Forum Humanum Benelux (no recent information)*; *Foundation Reshaping the International Order (RIO, no recent information)*, also referred to as *Rio Foundation*. **Events** *World Conference on Basic Sciences and Sustainable Development* Belgrade (Serbia) 2022, *Global Social Transformations and the Limits to Growth in the 21st Century* 2021, *Annual Conference* Rome (Italy) 2018, *Annual Conference* Vienna (Austria) 2017, *Offshore Arabia Biennial Conference* Dubai (United Arab Emirates) 2011. **Publications** *Factor 5: Transforming the Global Economy through 80% Improvements in Resource Productivity* (2009/2010) by Ernst von Weizsäcker et al; *Limits to Privatization: How to Avoid Too Much of a Good Thing – A Report to the Club of Rome* (2005); *Limits to Grwoth: The 30 Years Update* (2004) by Donella Meadows et al; *Menschlichkeit Gewinnt* (2000) by Reinhard Mohn; *Im Netz: Die Hypnotisierte Gesellschaft* (1999) by Juan Luis Cebrian; *Wie Wir Arbeiten Werden* (1998) by Orio Giarini and Patrick Liedtke; *The Oceanic Circle: Governing the Seas as a Global Resource* (1998) by Elizabeth Mann Borgese; *Factor Four: Doubling Wealth – Halving Resource Use* (1997) by Ernst Ulrich von Weizsäcker et al; *The Limits of Social Cohesion: Conflict and Understanding in a Pluralistic Society* (1997) by Peter L Berger; *The Scandal and the Shame: Poverty and Underdevelopment* (1995) by Bertrand Schneider; *Taking Nature into Account: Towards a Sustainable National Income* (1995); *The Capacity to Govern* (1994) by Yehezkel Dror; *The First Global Revolution* (1991) by Alexander King and Bertrand Schneider; *The Limits to Certainty* (1989-1993) by Orio Giarini and Walter R Stahel; *Africa beyond Famine* (1989) by Aklilu Lemma and Pentti Malaska; *Beyond the Limits to Growth* (1989) by Eduard Pestel; *The Future of the Oceans* (1986) by Elizabeth Mann Borgese; *The Barefoot Revolution* (1985) by Bertrand Schneider; *Le Tiers Monde peut se nourrir* (1984) by René Lenoir; *Microelectronics and Society for Better or Worse* (1982) by A Schaff and G Friedrichs; *L'Impératif de coopération Nord-Sud, la synergie des mondes* (1981) by Jean Saint-Geours; *Road Maps to the Future* (1980) by Bohdan Hawrylyshyn; *Dialogue on Wealth and Welfare* (1980) by Orio Giarini; *Tiers Monde: trois quarts du monde* (1980) by Maurice Guernier; *No Limits to Learning* (1979) by J Botkin et al; *Beyond the Age of Waste* (1978) by D Gabor and U Colombo; *Energy: The Countdown* (1978) by Thierry de Montbrial; *Goals for Mankind* (1977) by Ervin Laszlo et al; *Reshaping the International Order* (1976) by Jan Tinbergen et al; *Mankind at the Turning Point* (1974) by M Mesarovic and E Patel; *The Limits to Growth* (1972) by Dennis L Meadows et al.

Members Honorary; Active; Associate; Institutional. Organizations and individuals (limited to 100) in 47 countries and territories:
Argentina, Australia, Austria, Belgium, Brazil, Bulgaria, Cameroon, Canada, Chile, China, Colombia, Croatia, Czechia, Ecuador, Egypt, Ethiopia, Finland, France, Georgia, Germany, Greece, Hungary, India, Israel, Italy, Japan, Jordan, Kenya, Malaysia, Mexico, Morocco, Netherlands, Peru, Philippines, Poland, Puerto Rico, Romania, Sweden, Switzerland, Taiwan, Tanzania UR, Türkiye, UK, Ukraine, Uruguay, USA, Venezuela.

Consultative Status Consultative status granted from: *UNESCO (#20322)* (Associate Status). **IGO Relations** Observer to: *International Fund for Agricultural Development (IFAD, #13692)*. **NGO Relations** Member of (1): *Wellbeing Economy Alliance (WEAll, #20856)*. Associate member of: *Conference of Non-Governmental Organizations in Consultative Relationship with the United Nations (CONGO, #04635)*. [2019/XF4013/F]

- Club du Sahel / see Sahel and West Africa Club (#19034)
- Club de Sahel et de l'Afrique de l'Ouest (#19034)
- Club of Three / see Institute for Strategic Dialogue (#11296)
- Club Treat Me Nice (#20230)
- Club des vétérans de l'espéranto (#20758)

♦ Club of Vienna 04039

No fixed address address not obtained.

History 7 Dec 1979, Austria. Also referred to as *Vienna Club*.
Members Ministers of the Interior of 5 countries:
Austria, France, Germany, Italy, Switzerland.
IGO Relations *Bern Club (no recent information)*. [2010/XF6197/F*]

- **CLUSTER** Consortium Linking Universities in Science and Technology for Education and Research (#04751)
- Clusterize – Business Roaming Agreement (unconfirmed)
- Cluster sécurité alimentaire (#09849)
- Cluster de Seguridad Alimentaria (#09849)
- CLW – Council for a Livable World (internationally oriented national body)
- CLWR – Canadian Lutheran World Relief (internationally oriented national body)
- **CMA/AOC** Conférence des Ministres de l'Agriculture de l'Afrique de l'Ouest et du Centre (#04631)
- **CMAAO** Confederation of Medical Associations in Asia and Oceania (#04566)
- CMA – Caribbean Medical Association (internationally oriented national body)
- CMA – Centre for Mediation in Africa (internationally oriented national body)
- CMA – Centro de Medicina Andina (internationally oriented national body)
- **C-MAC** European Integrated Center for the Development of new Metallic Alloys and Compounds (#07579)
- CMA – Christian Mission Aid (internationally oriented national body)
- CMA – Christian and Missionary Alliance (internationally oriented national body)
- CMA – Comité mondial pour les apprentissages tout au long de la vie (unconfirmed)
- CMA / see Commonwealth Magistrates' and Judges' Association (#04349)
- **CMA** Commonwealth Medical Association (#04351)
- CMA – Commonwealth Music Association (inactive)
- CMA – Congrès Mondial Amazigh (internationally oriented national body)
- **CMA** Conseil méditerranéen de l'arbitrage (#16645)
- CMA – Conseil des ministres des assurances (see: #11385)
- **CMA** Conseil mondial de l'artisanat (#21342)

♦ CMACP – Conseil mondial pour l'assemblée constituante des peuples (inactive)
♦ **CMAEC** Conseil mondial des associations d'éducation comparée (#21322)
♦ **CMAE** Club Managers Association of Europe (#04037)
♦ CMAEHA – Coalition mondiale pour l'abolition de l'expérimentation sur l'homme et l'animal (inactive)
♦ CMA / see International Confederation of Accordionists (#12841)
♦ CMAM – International Conference "Computational Methods in Applied Mathematics" (meeting series)
♦ CMA / see Multilateral Monetary Area (#16889)
♦ CMAO / see World Crafts Council AISBL (#21342)
♦ CMAS ASIA / see Asian Underwater Federation (#01771)
♦ **CMAS** Confédération mondiale des activités subaquatiques (#21873)
♦ CMAtlv – Comité Mundial para el Aprendizaje a lo Largo de Toda la Vida (unconfirmed)
♦ **CMA/WCA** Conference of Ministers of Agriculture of West and Central Africa (#04631)
♦ **CMBA** Creative Media Business Alliance (#04947)
♦ CMB – Christian Mission to Buddhists (religious order)
♦ **CMB** Conseil mondial de la boxe (#21242)
♦ **CMB** Consejo Mundial de Boxeo (#21242)
♦ **CMCA** Centre Méditerranéen de la Communication Audiovisuelle (#16648)
♦ **CMCA** Comité Mundial de la Consulta de los Amigos (#10004)
♦ **CMCA** Consejo Monetario Centroamericano (#03672)
♦ CMCA – Corporate and Marketing Communication Association (unconfirmed)
♦ CM – Carmelitane Missionarie (religious order)
♦ CMC / see Caribbean Broadcasting Union (#03465)
♦ CMCC – Centro Euro-Mediterraneo per i Cambiamenti Climatici (internationally oriented national body)
♦ CMCC – Centre Mondial du Cyclisme (internationally oriented national body)
♦ CMCC Foundation / see Centro Euro-Mediterraneo per i Cambiamenti Climatici
♦ CMC – Congregation of Mother of Carmel (religious order)
♦ CMC / see Coppieters Foundation (#04831)
♦ CMCD – Comisión Mundial de Cultura y Desarrollo (inactive)
♦ CMCD – Commission mondiale de la culture et du développement (inactive)
♦ CMCE – Conseil musulman de coopération en Europe (no recent information)
♦ CMC / see European Ceramic Tile Manufacturers' Federation (#06508)
♦ CMC – ICC Centre for Maritime Cooperation (see: #12534)
♦ CMCI – Institut de la Méditerranée (internationally oriented national body)
♦ **CMC International Association** Consciousness, Mindfulness, Compassion (#04684)
♦ CM – Congregatio Missionis (religious order)
♦ CMCS – Centre for Media and Celebrity Studies (unconfirmed)
♦ CMCW / see The Voice of the Martyrs (#20804)
♦ CMDC / see Consensus for Sustainable People, Organisations and Communities
♦ **CMDF** Commonwealth Media Development Fund (#04350)
♦ CMDS – International Conference on Coherent Multidimensional Spectroscopy (meeting series)
♦ CMEA – Council for Mutual Economic Assistance (inactive)
♦ CMEAL – Centre de Management Europe-Amérique Latine (internationally oriented national body)
♦ CMEAOC / see Maritime Organization of West and Central Africa (#16582)
♦ **CME** Campagne mondiale pour l'éducation (#10264)
♦ CMECAS / see Centre for Arab and Islamic Studies, Middle East and Central Asia
♦ **CME** Conseil mondial de l'eau (#21908)
♦ **CME** Conseil mondial d'éducation (#21325)
♦ **CME** Conseil mondial de l'énergie (#21381)
♦ CMED – Center for Middle East Development (internationally oriented national body)
♦ CMED – Commission mondiale de l'environnement et du développement (inactive)
♦ CMEE – Conseil mondial des entreprises pour l'environnement (inactive)
♦ CMEF / see Financial Inclusion Equity Council (#09766)
♦ CMEIS / see Prince Alwaleed Bin Talal Centre of Islamic Studies
♦ CMENAS – Center for Middle Eastern and North African Studies, Ann Arbor MI (internationally oriented national body)
♦ CMEP – Churches for Middle East Peace (internationally oriented national body)
♦ CMEPP – RAND Center for Middle East Public Policy (internationally oriented national body)
♦ CMERA – Centre maghrébin d'études et de recherches administratives (no recent information)
♦ **CMER** Communion mondiale d'église réformées (#21289)
♦ CMES – Center for Middle Eastern Studies, Berkeley (internationally oriented national body)
♦ CMES – Center for Middle Eastern Studies, Cambridge MA (internationally oriented national body)
♦ CMES – Center for Middle Eastern Studies, University of Arizona (internationally oriented national body)
♦ CME – UNWTO Commission for the Middle East (see: #21861)
♦ CMF – Cardinal Mindszenty Foundation (internationally oriented national body)
♦ **CMF** Coalition mondiale des forêts (#10368)
♦ **CMF** Conférence ministérielle de la Francophonie (#04630)
♦ **CMFE** Committee for Mapping the Flora of Europe (#04268)
♦ **CMFE** Community Media Forum Europe (#04402)
♦ **CMFI** Comité monétaire et financier international (#14179)
♦ CMFT – Computational Methods and Function Theory (meeting series)
♦ CMG – Color Marketing Group (internationally oriented national body)
♦ CMH – European Center of International Hotel Management (internationally oriented national body)
♦ CMI / see Artsen Zonder Vakantie
♦ CMIA / see Arab Interior Ministers' Council (#00990)
♦ **CMIA** Climate Markets and Investment Association (#04018)
♦ CMI / see Caribbean Institute for Meteorology and Hydrology (#03520)
♦ CMI / see Center for Mediterranean Integration (#03649)
♦ **CMI** Center for Mediterranean Integration (#03649)
♦ CMI – China Ministries International (internationally oriented national body)
♦ CMI – Chr Michelsens Institutt – Utviklingsstudier og Menneskerettigheter (internationally oriented national body)
♦ **CMICI** Concilio Mundial de Iglesias Cristianas Independientes (#21330)
♦ **CMI** COMESA Monetary Institute (#04127)
♦ **CMI** Comité maritime international (#04192)
♦ CMI – Commission mixte internationale (internationally oriented national body)
♦ CMI – Congregatio Fratrum Carmelitarum Beatae Virginis Mariae Immaculatae (religious order)
♦ **CMI** Consejo Mundial de Iglesias (#21320)
♦ CMI – Crisis Management Initiative (internationally oriented national body)
♦ CMIEB / see Information Centre for Bilingual and Plurilingual Education (#11195)
♦ CMIEBP / see Information Centre for Bilingual and Plurilingual Education (#11195)
♦ **CMIR** Comunión Mundial de Iglesias Reformadas (#21289)
♦ CMIRNU – Centre mondial d'informations et de recherches appliquées aux nuisances urbaines (inactive)
♦ CMIS – Centre of Mediterranean and International Studies (internationally oriented national body)
♦ **CMIS** Conferenza Mondiale degli Istituti Secolari (#21299)
♦ **CMJA** Commonwealth Magistrates' and Judges' Association (#04349)
♦ CMJ – Congreso Mundial del Jamón Curado (meeting series)
♦ **CMJPLOP** Conferência de Ministros da Justiça dos Países de Língua Oficial Portuguesa (#04655)

♦ CML Advocacy Network 04040

Co-Founder Leukemia Patient Advocates Foundation, Münzgraben 6, 3000 Bern, Switzerland.
Contact address not obtained.
URL: http://www.cmladvocates.net/

History Set up 2007 as a virtual network. Set up as a legal entity with the title *Leukemia Patient Advocates Foundation*, 2011, Switzerland. **Aims** Foster best practice sharing, education and networking among patient groups supporting leukaemia patients; provide a worldwide web directory of *Chronic Myeloid Leukemia* (CML) *patient* groups and allow patient groups to find national *support* groups in another country; advocate for improving treatment and care of CML patients. **Structure** Steering Committee of 8. **Languages** English. **Staff** 1.00 FTE, paid. Several voluntary. **Events** *International Horizons Conference* Lisbon (Portugal) 2019, *Conference* Belgrade (Serbia) 2014, *Conference* Prague (Czech Rep) 2013, *Conference* Munich (Germany) 2012.

Members Organizations in 66 countries and territories:
Argentina, Australia, Azerbaijan, Bosnia-Herzegovina, Brazil, Bulgaria, Canada, China, Colombia, Costa Rica, Croatia, Czechia, Denmark, Dominican Rep, Ecuador, Estonia, Finland, France, Georgia, Germany, Guatemala, Hong Kong, Hungary, India, Iraq, Ireland, Israel, Italy, Japan, Kazakhstan, Kenya, Korea Rep, Kosovo, Latvia, Lebanon, Lithuania, Malaysia, Morocco, Nepal, Netherlands, New Zealand, Nigeria, North Macedonia, Pakistan, Peru, Philippines, Poland, Portugal, Romania, Russia, Serbia, Slovakia, Slovenia, South Africa, Spain, Sudan, Sweden, Switzerland, Thailand, Tunisia, Türkiye, Uganda, UK, Ukraine, USA, Venezuela.

NGO Relations Member of: *Rare Cancers Europe (RCE, #18620)*. Cooperates with: *European Hematology Association (EHA, #07473)*. [2014.02.21/XJ6438/F]

♦ CML Advocates Network 04041

Exec Dir Leukemia Patient Advocates Foundation, POB 453, 3000 Bern 7, Switzerland. E-mail: info@cmladvocates.net.
URL: https://www.cmladvocates.net/

History 2007. Former names and other names: *CML Advocates Network – For Chronic Myeloid Leukemia Patient Group Advocates* – full title. **Aims** Facilitate and support best practice sharing among patient advocates across the world. **Structure** Steering Committee. Hosted by *Leukemia Patient Advocates Foundation (LePAF)*. **Events** *CML Horizons* Lisbon (Portugal) 2019. **Publications** *CML Advocates Newsletter*.

Members Patient organizations (125) in 90 countries and territories:
Algeria, Argentina, Armenia, Australia, Azerbaijan, Bangladesh, Bolivia, Bosnia-Herzegovina, Brazil, Bulgaria, Cambodia, Canada, Chile, China, Colombia, Costa Rica, Croatia, Czechia, Denmark, Dominican Rep, Ecuador, Egypt, Estonia, Ethiopia, Finland, France, Georgia, Germany, Ghana, Greece, Guatemala, Hong Kong, Hungary, India, Indonesia, Iraq, Ireland, Israel, Italy, Japan, Kazakhstan, Kenya, Korea Rep, Kosovo, Kyrgyzstan, Latvia, Lebanon, Lithuania, Madagascar, Malaysia, Mali, Mexico, Morocco, Nepal, Netherlands, New Zealand, Niger, North Macedonia, Pakistan, Palestine, Panama, Peru, Philippines, Poland, Portugal, Romania, Russia, Saudi Arabia, Senegal, Serbia, Slovakia, Slovenia, South Africa, Spain, Sudan, Sweden, Switzerland, Taiwan, Thailand, Togo, Tunisia, Türkiye, Uganda, UK, Ukraine, USA, Uzbekistan, Vietnam, Yemen, Zimbabwe.

NGO Relations Member of (1): *Workgroup of European Cancer Patient Advocacy Networks (WECAN, #21054)*. [2020/AA0356/F]

♦ CML Advocates Network – For Chronic Myeloid Leukemia Patient Group Advocates / see CML Advocates Network (#04041)
♦ CMLC – China-Mekong Law Center (internationally oriented national body)
♦ **CMLF** Caribbean Med Labs Foundation (#03522)
♦ CMMB – Catholic Medical Mission Board (internationally oriented national body)
♦ CMMC – Centre de la Méditerranée Moderne et Contemporaine (internationally oriented national body)
♦ CMM – Congregatio Fratrum Beatae Mariae Virginis, Matris Misericordiae (religious order)
♦ CMM – Congregatio Missionariorum de Mariannhill (religious order)
♦ CMM – Congregation of the Missionaries of Mariannhill (religious order)
♦ CMMR – International Symposium on Computer Music Multidisciplinary Research (meeting series)
♦ CMNUCC – Convención marco de Naciones Unidas sobre el cambio climatico (1992 treaty)
♦ **CMO** Caribbean Meteorological Organization (#03524)
♦ CMOCDAPUNDHJ – Concile Mondiale de Congrès Diplomatiques des Aumoniers pour la Paix Universelle des Droits Humains et Juridiques (unconfirmed)
♦ CMOPE – Confédération mondiale des organisations de la profession enseignante (inactive)
♦ CMOT – Confédération maghrébine des opérateurs de tourisme (inactive)
♦ CMP – Centre for Meeting of Peoples (internationally oriented national body)
♦ CMPCO – Comité Mixto sobre Programas Cientificos Relacionados con la Oceanografia (inactive)
♦ CMP – Confédération médicale panaméricaine (inactive)
♦ **CMP** Conseil mondial de la paix (#21717)
♦ **CMP** Consejo Mundial de la Paz (#21717)
♦ CMPI – Consejo Mundial de Pueblos Indigenas (inactive)
♦ CMPSC – Consejo Mundial para la Promoción Social de los Ciegos (inactive)
♦ CMPS / see Confédération internationale de la pêche sportive (#04562)
♦ CMP / see World Petroleum Council (#21722)
♦ CMR – Convention on the Contract for the International Carriage of Goods by Road (1956 treaty)
♦ CMR – Convention relative au contrat de transport international de marchandises par route (1956 treaty)
♦ **CMRE** Consejo de Municipios y Regiones de Europa (#04891)
♦ CMR – Protocol to the Convention on the Contract for the International Carriage of Goods by Road (1978 treaty)
♦ CMRSS – Conseil méditerranéen de recherches en sciences sociales (inactive)
♦ **CMRT** Association de la Conférence mondiale sur la recherche dans les transports (#21301)
♦ CMRTV – Conseil mondial pour la radio et la télévision (no recent information)
♦ CMSA – Conference of Major Superiors of the Antilles (inactive)
♦ CMSB – Confédération mondiale des sports de boules (inactive)
♦ CMS – Center for Migration Studies, New York (internationally oriented national body)
♦ CMS – Church Mission Society (internationally oriented national body)
♦ **CMS** Clay Minerals Society (#03982)
♦ CMS – Comboni Missionary Sisters (religious order)
♦ **CMS** Corps mondial de secours (#04845)
♦ CMS – Court of Master Sommeliers (internationally oriented national body)
♦ **CMSEC** Consejo Mundial de Sociedad de Educación Comparada (#21322)
♦ CMSF – Congregatio Missionaria Sancti Francisci Assisiensis (religious order)
♦ CMSR – Center za Mednarodno Sodelovanje in Razvoj (internationally oriented national body)
♦ CMSR – Centro Mondialità Sviluppo Reciproco (internationally oriented national body)
♦ CMST – UNESCO Centre for Membrane Science and Technology (unconfirmed)
♦ CMT / see Solidarité et coopération médicale au Tiers-monde
♦ CMT – Confederación Mundial del Trabajo (inactive)
♦ CMT – Confédération mondiale du travail (inactive)
♦ CMTC-OVM (internationally oriented national body)
♦ **CMU** Community of Mediterranean Universities (#04403)
♦ **CMW** Committee on Migrant Workers (#04271)
♦ CMWR – International Conference on Computational Methods in Water Resources (meeting series)
♦ **CNA** Caribbean Netball Association (#03526)
♦ CNACO – Carbon Neutral Action and Cooperation Organization (unconfirmed)
♦ CNA Foundation – Children Need Arts Foundation (unconfirmed)
♦ CNAJEP – Comité pour les relations nationales et internationales des associations de jeunesse et d'éducation populaire (internationally oriented national body)
♦ **CNARC** China-Nordic Research Center (#03890)
♦ CNAS – Centre for Nepal and Asian Studies (internationally oriented national body)
♦ **CNCA** Carbon Neutral Cities Alliance (#03424)
♦ CNC – Center for New Creation (internationally oriented national body)
♦ CNCD / see Coalition of the Flemish North South Movement – 11 11 11
♦ **CNCD-Africa** Consortium for Non-communicable Diseases Prevention and Control in sub-Saharan Africa (#04754)
♦ CNCD Opération 11 11 11 (internationally oriented national body)
♦ CND – Campaign for Nuclear Disarmament (internationally oriented national body)

- ♦ CNDR – Centre for Negotiation and Dispute Resolution (internationally oriented national body)
- ♦ CNDS – Council of Nordic Dental Students (inactive)
- ♦ CND – Soeurs de la Congrégation de Notre-Dame (religious order)
- ♦ **CND** United Nations Commission on Narcotic Drugs (#20532)
- ♦ CNEAS – Centre for Northeast Asian Studies, Sendai (internationally oriented national body)
- ♦ CNEC / see Partners International
- ♦ **CNE** Cartagena Network of Engineering (#03590)
- ♦ CNE / see Climate Action Network Europe (#04001)
- ♦ **CNE** Cystinosis Network Europe (#04993)
- ♦ CNEH – Centro Neotropical de Entrenamiento en Humedales (internationally oriented national body)
- ♦ CNERT – United Nations Centre for Natural Resources, Energy and Transport (inactive)
- ♦ **CNEWA** Catholic Near East Welfare Association (#03606)
- ♦ CNFA / see Cultivating New Frontiers in Agriculture
- ♦ CNFA – Cultivating New Frontiers in Agriculture (internationally oriented national body)
- ♦ CNF / see Commonwealth Nurses and Midwives Federation (#04353)
- ♦ **CNFO** Caribbean Network of Fisherfolk Organisations (#03527)
- ♦ CNHF – Conrad N Hilton Foundation (internationally oriented national body)
- ♦ CNIE – China NGO Network for International Exchanges (internationally oriented national body)
- ♦ **CNIPA** Committee of National Institutes of Patent Agents (#04274)
- ♦ **CNIRD** Caribbean Network for Integrated Rural Development (#03528)
- ♦ CNIS – Canadian Network for International Surgery (internationally oriented national body)
- ♦ CNITA – Chart and Nautical Instrument Trade Association (internationally oriented national body)
- ♦ CNLM – Common Nordic Labour Market (no recent information)
- ♦ **CNMF** Commonwealth Nurses and Midwives Federation (#04353)
- ♦ **CNO** Caribbean Nurses Organization (#03532)
- ♦ **CNPB** Conseil nordique de la préservation du bois (#17469)
- ♦ CNR – Conseil norvégien pour les réfugiés (internationally oriented national body)
- ♦ **CNRCSA** Confederation of NATO Retired Civilian Staff Associations (#04570)
- ♦ **CNRD** Centers for Natural Resources and Development (#03652)
- ♦ CNS – James Martin Center for Nonproliferation Studies (internationally oriented national body)
- ♦ CNSSC / see International Federation of Social Science Organizations (#13543)
- ♦ CNUAH / see United Nations Human Settlements Programme (#20572)
- ♦ **CNUCED** Conférence des Nations Unies sur le commerce et le développement (#20285)
- ♦ **CNUDCI** Commission des Nations Unies pour le droit commercial international (#20531)
- ♦ **CNUDMI** Comisión de las Naciones Unidas para el Derecho Mercantil Internacional (#20531)
- ♦ **CNUDR** Centre des Nations Unies pour le développement régional (#20526)
- ♦ CNUED – Conférence des Nations Unies sur l'environnement et le développement (meeting series)
- ♦ CNUEH / see United Nations Human Settlements Programme (#20572)
- ♦ CNUE / see Notaries of Europe (#17609)
- ♦ **CNUE** Notaries of Europe (#17609)
- ♦ CNULD – Convención de las Naciones Unidas para la Lucha Contra la Desertificación (1994 treaty)
- ♦ **CO2GeoNet** European Network of Excellence on the Geological Storage of CO2 (#07904)

♦ CO2 Value Europe (CVE) 04042

SG Avenue de Tervuren 188A, 1150 Brussels, Belgium. T. +3227611648. E-mail: contact@co2value.eu.
URL: https://co2value.eu/

History Founded Nov 2017, building on the SCOT – Smart CO2 Transformation project. Registration: Banque-Carrefour des Entreprises, No/ID: 0695.818.117, Start date: 8 May 2018, Belgium; EU Transparency Register, No/ID: 977056531128-71, Start date: 10 Apr 2018. **Aims** Promote the development and market deployment of sustainable industrial solutions that convert CO2 into valuable products, so as to contribute to the net reduction of global CO2 emissions and to the diversification of the feedstock base. **Structure** General Assembly; Board of Directors; Secretariat. Task Forces. **Activities** Events/meetings. **Events** *CO² Value Days* Brussels (Belgium) 2022.
Members Full; Associate. Membership countries not specified. Included in the above, 1 organization listed in this Yearbook:
Included in the above, 1 organization listed in this Yearbook:
ePURE (#05517).
NGO Relations Member of: *Industry4Europe (#11181).* [2022/XM8500/**D**]

- ♦ Coaches Across Continents (internationally oriented national body)
- ♦ **COA** Container Owners Association (#04777)
- ♦ CoA – Council of the Americas (internationally oriented national body)
- ♦ Coady International Institute (internationally oriented national body)

♦ Coalición Centroamericana para la Prevención de la Violencia Juvenil (CCPVJ) 04043

Contact Polideportivo Don Bosco, "Plaza España" Soyapango, Intersección de Carretera a San Miguel y Calle a Tonacatepeque, después de paso a Desnivel de Unicentro Soyapango, San Salvador, El Salvador. T. +50322106600. Fax +50322106672. E-mail: ccpvj.contacto@gmail.com – ccpvj.direccion@gmail.com.
URL: http://ccpvj.com/

History Founded Feb 2005, as a result of the conference "Voces de la Experiencia: Iniciativas Locales y Nuevos Estudios sobre la Violencia de las Pandillas Juveniles en Centro América" organized by Coalición Interamericana para la Prevención de la Violencia (IACPV) together with members of the Washington Office for Latin America (WOLA), Foundation for Due Process, and PAHO-GTZ. **Aims** Work with an integrated approach on the phenomena that cause social suffering among youth from a holistic, rights-based and gender perspective, using the values of justice, harmony, respect, equality, human dignity, solidarity, transparency and loyalty. **Structure** General Assembly; Executive Committee. **Languages** Spanish. **Staff** 7.00 FTE, paid. **Finance** Support from: *Austrian Development Agency (ADA); Catholic Organization for Relief and Development (Cordaid); European Commission (EC, #06633).* Cooperates with: *Central American Integration System (#03671)* – Dirección de Seguridad Democratica (SICA-DSD). **Activities** Guidance/assistance/consulting. **Publications** *Manual para la Construcción de la Cultura de Paz: Herramientas metodologias y conceptuales para la transformación social / Guia a de Facilitación de Justicia y Practicas Restaurativas* (2014).
Members Organizations (over 26) in 5 countries:
Costa Rica, El Salvador, Guatemala, Honduras, Nicaragua.
NGO Relations Member of: *International Centre for the Prevention of Crime (ICPC, #12508).* [2015.02.23/XJ7340/**D**]

- ♦ Coalición contra el Trafico de Mujeres (#04047)
- ♦ Coalición Contra el Trafico de Mujeres – America Latina (#04048)
- ♦ Coalición por la Corte Penal Internacional (#04062)
- ♦ Coalición Europea para la Abolición de los Experimentos con Animales (#06594)
- ♦ Coalición Flamenca para la Cooperación Norte-Sur – 11 11 11 (internationally oriented national body)
- ♦ Coalición por la Igualdad de Derechos (#05519)
- ♦ Coalición internacional para el acceso a la tierra (#13999)
- ♦ Coalición Internacional de Habitat (#10845)
- ♦ Coalición Internacional de Sitios de Conciencia (#12621)

♦ Coalición Latinoamericana para la Prevención de la Violencia Armada (CLAVE) 04044

Contact address not obtained. E-mail: desarme@serpaj.org.ec.
URL: http://www.clave-lat.com/

Members Institutions, including 2 organizations listed in this Yearbook:
Instituto Caribeño para el Estado de Derecho (ICED); Instituto Latinoamericano de Seguridad y Democracia (ILSED, no recent information). [2012/XJ5707/y/**F**]

- ♦ Coalición Mundial por los Bosques (#10368)
- ♦ Coalition pour des accords de pêche équitables (#04060)

♦ Coalition for Advancing Research Assessment (CoARA) 04045

Secretariat c/o ESF Science Connect, 1 quai Lezay-Marnésia, BP 90015, 67080 Strasbourg CEDEX, France. E-mail: info@coara.eu.
URL: https://coara.eu/

History 2022. **Aims** Enable systemic reform on the basis of common principles within an agreed timeframe; facilitate exchanges of information and mutual learning between all those willing to improve research assessment practices. **Structure** General Assembly; Steering Board; Secretariat.
Members Signatories to the Agreement in countries:
Austria, Belgium, Bosnia-Herzegovina, Brazil, Croatia, Czechia, Denmark, Estonia, Finland, France, Germany, Greece, Hungary, Iceland, Ireland, Lithuania, Luxembourg, Moldova, Montenegro, Netherlands, Norway, Poland, Portugal, Romania, Slovakia, Slovenia, Spain, Sweden, Switzerland, Tunisia, Türkiye, UK, Ukraine.
- *Academia Europaea (#00011);*
- *ALLEA – ALL European Academies (#00647);*
- *Association of ERC Grantees (AERG, #02492);*
- *Coimbra Group (#04089);*
- *Conference of European Schools for Advanced Engineering Education and Research (CESAER, #04599);*
- *Digital Research Infrastructure for the Arts and Humanities (DARIAH-EU, #05083);*
- *EUA Council for Doctoral Education (EUA-CDE, #05563);*
- *EU-LIFE (#05586);*
- *European Alliance for the Social Sciences and Humanities (EASSH, #05885);*
- *European Association for the Advancement of Science and Technology (EUROSCIENCE, #05927);*
- *European Association of Research Managers and Administrators (EARMA, #06195);*
- *European Chemical Society (EuCheMS, #06524);*
- *European Commission (EC, #06633);*
- *European Cooperation in Science and Technology (COST, #06784);*
- *European Council of Doctoral Candidates and Junior Researchers (EURODOC, #06815);*
- *European Infrastructure for Translational Medicine (EATRIS, #07536);*
- *European Language Council (ELC, #07646);*
- *European Magnetism Association (EMA, #07725);*
- *European Molecular Biology Laboratory (EMBL, #07813);*
- *European Society for Cognitive and Affective Neuroscience (ESCAN, #08553);*
- *European University Association (EUA, #09027);*
- *European University Hospital Alliance (EUHA, #09032);*
- *European Women Rectors Association (EWORA, #09101);*
- *Global Young Academy (GYA, #10662);*
- *Good Clinical Practice Alliance (GCPA);*
- *Initiative for Science in Europe (ISE, #11214);*
- *International Network of Research Management Societies (INORMS, #14317);*
- *League of European Research Universities (LERU, #16423);*
- *Marie Curie Alumni Association (MCAA, #16576);*
- *Network of Universities from the Capitals of Europe (UNICA, #17061);*
- *Research Data Alliance (RDA, #18853);*
- *Research Software Alliance (ReSA, #18862);*
- *Science Europe (#19139);*
- *SCimPulse Foundation;*
- *SPARC Europe (#19902);*
- *UAS4EUROPE (#20274);*
- *Young Academy of Europe (YAE, #21979);*
- *Young European Research Universities (YERUN, #21988).*

IGO Relations Cooperates with (1): *European Commission (EC, #06633).* **NGO Relations** Cooperates with (2): *European University Association (EUA, #09027); Science Europe (#19139).* [2022/AA3073/y/**C**]

- ♦ Coalition africaine de la société civile contre le SIDA (unconfirmed)
- ♦ Coalition of African Animal Welfare Organisations (internationally oriented national body)
- ♦ Coalition of African Jurists / see Coalition for Justice and Peace in Africa

♦ Coalition of African Lesbians (CAL) 04046

Communications Officer PO Box 31792, Braamfontein, Johannesburg, 2001, South Africa. T. +27114030007.
Registered Address 58 The Valley Rd, Parktown, Johannesburg, 2193, South Africa.
URL: http://www.cal.org.za/

History 2003, Johannesburg (South Africa). Former names and other names: *African Lesbian Alliance* – former (2003 to 2005). **Aims** Advocate and lobby for political, legal social, sexual, cultural and economic rights of African lesbians; eradicate stigma and discrimination against lesbians in Africa; build and strengthen lesbian voices and visibility.
Members in 14 countries:
Botswana, Ghana, Kenya, Liberia, Mozambique, Namibia, Nigeria, Rwanda, Sierra Leone, South Africa, Tanzania UR, Uganda, Zambia, Zimbabwe. [2022/XM0267/**F**]

- ♦ Coalition of African NGOs (unconfirmed)

♦ Coalition Against Trafficking in Women (CATW) 04047

Coalition contre le trafic des femmes – Coalición contra el Trafico de Mujeres

Exec Dir PO Box 7160, Jaf Station, New York NY 10116, USA. Fax +12126439895. E-mail: info@catwinternational.org.
URL: http://www.catwinternational.org/

History 1988, New York NY (USA). **Aims** Bring international attention to all forms of trafficking in women, including prostitution, pornography, sex tourism and mail-order bride selling. **Structure** Board of Directors, representing world regions: Asia; Europe; Africa; North America; Latin America. Co-Executive Directors and Executive Advisory Committee. **Finance** Donations and grants. **Activities** Monitoring/evaluation; events/meetings; advocacy/lobbying/activism; knowledge management/information dissemination. **Events** *Global meeting* Dhaka (Bangladesh) 1999, *Asian conference* Dhaka (Bangladesh) 1998, *Asian conference* Mumbai (India) 1997, *Negociations between Caribbean Community and Lome* Trinidad-Tobago 1997. **Publications** *Coalition Report* (2 a year). Newsletters; bulletins. Information Services: Clearinghouse of information and documentation.
Members Organizations and individuals (" indicates individuals only) in 94 countries and territories:
Algeria (*), Argentina, Australia, Austria, Bangladesh, Barbados (*), Belgium, Belize (*), Bosnia-Herzegovina, Brazil, Cambodia, Canada, Chile, China, Colombia, Costa Rica, Croatia, Cuba, Czechia, Denmark, Dominica, Dominican Rep, Ecuador, Egypt, El Salvador, Ethiopia (*), Fiji (*), Finland, France, Gambia (*), Germany, Greece, Guatemala, Haiti, Honduras, Hong Kong, Hungary, India, Indonesia, Iran Islamic Rep, Ireland, Israel, Italy, Jamaica, Japan, Jordan, Korea Rep, Malawi, Malaysia, Mali, Mauritania, Mauritius, Mexico, Micronesia FS, Morocco (*), Myanmar, Nepal, Netherlands, New Zealand, Nicaragua, Nigeria (*), Norway, Pakistan, Palau (*), Palestine (*), Panama, Paraguay, Peru, Philippines, Poland, Portugal, Puerto Rico, Romania, Russia, Senegal (*), Singapore, Slovakia, South Africa, Spain, Sri Lanka, Sweden, Switzerland, Taiwan, Thailand, Tunisia, Türkiye, Uganda (*), UK, Ukraine (*), Uruguay, USA, Venezuela, Vietnam, Zimbabwe (*).
Consultative Status Consultative status granted from: *ECOSOC (#05331)* (Special). **IGO Relations** *United Nations Commission on Human Rights (inactive); United Nations Commission on the Status of Women (CSW, #20536).* Accredited by: *United Nations Office at Vienna (UNOV, #20604).* Associated with Department of Global Communications of the United Nations. **NGO Relations** Member of: *Conference of Non-Governmental Organizations in Consultative Relationship with the United Nations (CONGO, #04635).* Set up: *Coalition Against Trafficking in Women – Latin America (#04048).* Asia Pacific office links with: *IO – Facilitating Space for Feminist Conversations (Io, #16005).* [2017/XF1491/**F**]

♦ Coalition Against Trafficking in Women – Latin America 04048

Coalición Contra el Trafico de Mujeres – America Latina

Dir Kuis G Vieyra no 23, Depto 3, Col San Miguel Chapultepec, Mexico City CDMX, Mexico. T. +5526141488. Fax +5552721907.
URL: http://www.catwinternational.org/

History Mar 1994, by *Coalition Against Trafficking in Women (CATW, #04047),* as *Latin American and Caribbean Network Against Sexual Exploitation – Red Latinoamericana y del Caribe contra la Explotación Sexual de Mujeres, Niñas y Niños.* Also referred to as *Red Latinoamericana y Caribeña contra la Explotación Sexual de Mujeres y Niñas.* **Aims** Work against all forms of sexual exploitation: pornography, prostitution, strippers, sexual tourism, child prostitution, trafficking, military prostitution, etc. **Activities** Organizes workshops in schools to prevent child prostitution.

Members Full in 50 countries and territories:
Argentina, Australia, Austria, Bangladesh, Belgium, Bolivia, Brazil, Cambodia, Canada, Chile, Colombia, Costa Rica, Curaçao, Dominican Rep, Ecuador, Egypt, El Salvador, Fiji, Finland, France, Germany, Greece, Guatemala, Honduras, India, Indonesia, Israel, Italy, Japan, Korea DPR, Korea Rep, Mali, Mexico, Nepal, New Zealand, Nicaragua, Norway, Pakistan, Peru, Philippines, Puerto Rico, Romania, Singapore, Spain, Sweden, Switzerland, Thailand, UK, Uruguay, Venezuela. [2008/XF4008/**F**]

♦ Coalition against Typhoid (CaT) 04049

Secretariat c/o Sabin Vaccine Inst, 2000 Pennsylvania Ave, Ste 7100, Washington DC 20006, USA. E-mail: cat@sabin.org.
URL: http://www.coalitionagainsttyphoid.org/

Aims Expedite and sustain evidence-based decisions at the global, regional and national levels regarding the use of typhoid *vaccination* to prevent childhood enteric fever. **Structure** Secretariat provided by *Sabin Vaccine Institute (Sabin)*. **Activities** Research and development; advocacy/lobbying/activism. **Events** *Conference on Typhoid and Other Invasive Salmonelloses* Hanoi (Vietnam) 2019, *Conference on Typhoid and Other Invasive Salmonelloses* Kampala (Uganda) 2017. **Publications** *CaT Newsletter*.
Members Organizations (29), including 11 listed in this Yearbook:
Aga Khan University (AKU, #00546); Bill and Melinda Gates Foundation (BMGF); Gavi – The Vaccine Alliance (Gavi, #10077); ICDDR,B (#11051); International Vaccine Institute (IVI, #15839); Mérieux Foundation; PATH (#18260); Sabin Vaccine Institute (Sabin); UNICEF (#20332); Wellcome Trust; WHO (#20950).
NGO Relations Member of: *Developing Countries Vaccine Manufacturers Network (DCVMN, #05052); Gavi – The Vaccine Alliance (Gavi, #10077)* CSO Constituency. [2014/XJ8380/y/**E**]

♦ Coalition of Agricultural Workers International (CAWI) 04050

Secretariat PO Box 1170, 10850 Penang, Malaysia. T. +6046570271. Fax +6046583960. E-mail: secretariat@agriworkers.org.
URL: http://www.agriworkers.org/

History May 2005, Penang (Malaysia). Constitution adopted Sep 2013. **Aims** Aadvance the rights, interests and welfare of agricultural workers. **Structure** Congress; Steering Council; Secretariat.
Members Organizations in countries:
Ghana, India, Indonesia, Malaysia, Pakistan, Philippines, Sri Lanka.
Asian Rural Women's Coalition (ARWC, #01690); PAN Asia and the Pacific (PANAP, #18167).
[2020/AA1210/y/**C**]

♦ Coalition for APP Fairness (unconfirmed)

♦ Coalition of Asia Pacific Regional Networks on HIV/AIDS (Seven Sisters) 04051

Secretariat 12 Jalan 13/48A, The Boulevard Shop Office, Off Jalan Sentul, 51000 Kuala Lumpur, Malaysia. T. +60340451033. Fax +60340449615.
URL: http://www.7sisters.org/

History Feb 2001, Kuala Lumpur (Malaysia). **Structure** Board, comprising 7 permanent representatives from each member network and Secretariat Coordinator.
Members Regional organizations (5):
AIDS Society for Asia and the Pacific (ASAP, #00592); Asian Harm Reduction Network (AHRN, #01501); Asia-Pacific Council of AIDS Service Organizations (APCASO, #01875); Asia-Pacific Network of People Living with HIV/AIDS (APN+, #01973); Asia Pacific Network of Sex Workers (APNSW, #01975). [2012/XM0793/y/**F**]

♦ Coalition of Asia Pacific Tobacco Harm Reduction Advocates (CAPHRA) 04052

Exec Coordinator address not obtained. T. +64272348463. E-mail: admin@caphraorg.net.
URL: https://caphraorg.net/

Aims Educate, advocate and represent the right of adult alternative nicotine consumers to access and use of products that reduce harm from tobacco use. **Structure** Expert Advisory Group. **Publications** *CAPHRA Newsletter*. **Information Services** *APTHRMEDIA*.
Members Full in 11 countries and territories:
Australia, Hong Kong, India, Indonesia, Korea Rep, Malaysia, New Zealand, Pakistan, Philippines, Taiwan, Thailand.
[2023.02.14/AA1323/**D**]

♦ Coalition asiatique des ONG pour la réforme agraire et le développement rural (#01566)
♦ Coalition asiatique des organisations des droits de l'homme (inactive)
♦ Coalition de l'Asie du Sud contre la servitude enfantine (#19725)
♦ Coalition for Children of the Earth / see Children of the Earth

♦ Coalition Clean Baltic (CCB) 04053

Exec Sec Östra Ågatan 53, SE-753 22 Uppsala, Sweden. T. +4618711170. Fax +4618711175. E-mail: secretariat@ccb.se.
URL: http://www.ccb.se/

History Feb 1990, Helsinki (Finland). Current constitution adopted Apr 2018. **Aims** Promote *protection* and improvement of the Baltic Sea *environment* and *natural resources*. **Structure** A network of NGOs in the Baltic Sea area. General Meeting (annual); Board; International Secretariat located in Uppsala (Sweden). **Languages** English. **Finance** Funded by the Swedish Society for Nature Conservation. Project funds received from: *European Commission (EC, #06633)* (DGXI); Government of Sweden; *Nordic Council of Ministers (NCM, #17260)*; Government of Russia; *Swedish International Development Cooperation Agency (Sida)*. **Activities** Events/meetings; advocacy/lobbying/activism; knowledge management/information dissemination; guidance/assistance/consulting; training/education. **Events** *Baltic Sea Conference* Karjaa (Finland) 2008, *Baltic Sea Conference* Rostock (Germany) 2007, *Baltic Sea Conference* Kurzeme (Latvia) 2003, *Annual Baltic sea conference* Lejastiezumi (Latvia) 2003, *Annual Baltic sea conference / Baltic Sea Conference* Palanga (Lithuania) 2002. **Publications** *CCB Newsletter* (4 a year) – electronic; *CCB Yearbook*; *Larus Marinus Adventures in the Baltic Sea* – magazine. *Our Habitat Values* (1999); *Ecotechnology for Wastewater Treatment – Functioning Facilities in the Baltic Sea Region* (1997); *Ecology – An Introduction* (1991); *What is Happening to the Baltic Sea* (1990); *CCB Baltic Sea Action Plan*; *Ecology and Introduction*; *Green Handbook*; *Guide 2000*; *Local Handbook, Sczcecin*; *River Monitoring Handbook*. Booklets; brochures; posters; reports; seminar proceedings; books.
Members Member; Observer Cooperative Partner: national and international organizations. Full (20) and observer (2), comprising over 800,000 individuals in 11 countries:
Belarus, Denmark, Estonia, Finland, Germany, Latvia, Lithuania, Poland, Russia, Sweden, Ukraine.
Cooperative Partners (6) in 4 countries:
Latvia, Netherlands, Poland, Russia.
Included in the above, 5 organizations listed in this Yearbook:
Baltic Fund for Nature (BFN); ECOBALTIC Foundation, Gdansk; Friends of the Earth International (FoEI, #10002) (Swedish section); *Seas at Risk (SAR, #19189); World Wide Fund for Nature (WWF, #21922)* (Swedish section).
IGO Relations Observer to: *Baltic Marine Environment Protection Commission – Helsinki Commission (HELCOM, #03126)*. **NGO Relations** Member of: *Baltic Sea Advisory Council (BSAC, #03139); CEEweb for Biodiversity (#03626); Deep Sea Conservation Coalition (DSCC, #05024); Global Water Partnership (GWP, #10653); International Union for Conservation of Nature and Natural Resources (IUCN, #15766)*. Instrumental in setting up: *European Seas Environmental Cooperation (ESEC, inactive)*. [2022/XF1471/y/**F**]

♦ Coalition for Climate Resilient Investment (CCRI) 04054

Address not obtained.
URL: https://resilientinvestment.org/

History 23 Sep 2019. Launched at *United Nations (UN, #20515)* General Assemly's Climate Action Summit (UNCAS). Conceptualized by Willis Towers Watson, *World Economic Forum (WEF, #21367)*, *Global Commission on Adaptation (#10301)* and UK Government. A multi-industry, multi-region, public/private coalition. **Aims** Create a more resilient global financial industry in which key incentive structures foster an accurate pricing of physical climate risks (PCRs) in investment decision-making, resulting in more resilient economies and communities across the world.
Members Institutional investors; Lending institutions; Credit rating agencies; Engineering construction and infrastructure; Consulting/financial advisory; Insurance industry; Multilateral development institutions; International organizations; Governments; Academic institutions; Legal services; Standards; Advocacy/think tanks; Public institutions; advocacy; Data providers. Governments (6):
Antigua-Barbuda, Canada, Chile, Jamaica, UK, USA (State of California).
Organizations include 11 organizations listed in this Yearbook:
Asian Development Bank (ADB, #01422); Climate Bonds Initiative (#04006); European Bank for Reconstruction and Development (EBRD, #06315); FAO (#09260); Global Center on Adaptation (GCA); Global Water Partnership (GWP, #10653); Green Climate Fund (GCF, #10714); UNDP (#20292); UNEP (#20299) (Finance Initiative); *World Economic Forum (WEF, #21367); World Resources Institute (WRI, #21753).*
NGO Relations Member of (1): *Coalition for Disaster Resilient Infrastructure (CDRI).* [2021/AA2167/y/**E**]

♦ Coalition Coalición Internacional de Preparación paa el Tratamie (#15729)
♦ Coalition contre le trafic des femmes (#04047)
♦ Coalition pour la Cour Pénale Internationale (#04062)
♦ Coalition for the Defense of Human Rights (internationally oriented national body)
♦ Coalition for the Defense of Human Rights Under Islamization / see Coalition for the Defense of Human Rights
♦ Coalition for Democratic World Government (inactive)
♦ Coalition for Disaster Resilient Infrastructure (unconfirmed)
♦ Coalition pour les droits égaux (#05519)
♦ Coalition Eau (internationally oriented national body)

♦ Coalition for an Effective African Court on Human and Peoples' Rights (African Court Coalition) 04055

Exec Sec Mawalla Heritage Park, Plot No 175/20 Mawalla Road, Olasiti, Arusha, Tanzania UR. T. +255732979997. E-mail: executivesecretary@africancourtcoalition.org – info@africancourtcoalition.org.
URL: http://www.africancourtcoalition.org/

History May 2003, Niamey (Niger), during 1st conference for the promotion of the protocol to the African Charter on Human and Peoples' Rights establishing *African Court on Human and Peoples' Rights (AfCHPR, #00278)*. **Aims** Ensure that the African Court on Human and Peoples' Rights is effective, accessible and credible through training, education, information documentation and dissemination, research, advocacy, lobbying and networking. **Structure** General Assembly (every 3 years). Executive Committee, comprising Chairperson, Deputy Chairperson and 7 members. Geographical Focal Points (5): East; Southern; West; Central; North. Thematical Focal Points (2): National Human Rights Institutions; Portuguese-speaking countries. Sub-Committees (3): Finance and Administration; Membership; Legal Affairs. Secretariat. **Events** *Colloquium on Building the Court we Want* Arusha (Tanzania UR) 2015, *General Assembly* Arusha (Tanzania UR) 2015, *General Assembly* Mombasa (Kenya) 2011. **Publications** *Do It Right* (4 a year) in English, French, Portuguese – newsletter.
Members Organizations in 30 countries:
Angola, Botswana, Cameroon, Cape Verde, Congo Brazzaville, Congo DR, Côte d'Ivoire, Egypt, France, Gambia, Ghana, Guinea-Bissau, Kenya, Mauritius, Namibia, Niger, Nigeria, Rwanda, Senegal, Sierra Leone, South Africa, Sudan, Switzerland, Tanzania UR, Togo, Tunisia, Uganda, UK, USA, Zimbabwe.
Included in the above, 25 organizations listed in this Yearbook:
- *Advocates International;*
- *Africa Legal Aid (AFLA, #00186);*
- *Alliances for Africa (AfA);*
- *Anti-Slavery International (#00860);*
- *Arab Centre for the Independence of the Judiciary and the Legal Profession (ACIJLP);*
- *Association africaine de défense des droits de l'homme (ASADHO);*
- *Avocats Sans Frontières (ASF, #03050);*
- *Cairo Institute for Human Rights Studies (CIHRS, #03397);*
- *Centre for Human Rights, Pretoria;*
- *Development Alternatives with Women for a New Era (DAWN, #05054);*
- *East Africa Law Society (EALS, #05173);*
- *Environnement et développement du Tiers-monde (enda, #05510);*
- *Global Alert for Defence of Youth and the Less Privileged (GADYLP);*
- *Institute for Human Rights and Development in Africa (IHRDA);*
- *International Commission of Jurists (ICJ, #12695);*
- *International Federation for Human Rights (#13452);*
- *International Refugee Rights Initiative (IRRI, #14708);*
- *International Service for Human Rights (ISHR, #14841);*
- *Media Institute of Southern Africa (MISA, #16619);*
- *OutRight Action International;*
- *Pan African Development Education and Advocacy Programme (PADEAP);*
- *Pan-African Lawyers Union (PALU, #18054);*
- *Rencontre africaine pour la défense des droits de l'homme (RADDHO);*
- *Southern Africa Litigation Centre (SALC, #19832);*
- *West African Human Rights Defenders' Network (WAHRDN, #20882).* [2017/XJ6551/y/**E**]

♦ Coalition pour l'Éléphant d'Afrique (#00296)

♦ Coalition for Energy Savings 04056

Contact c/o Scheuer Consulting, Rue de Toulouse 49, 1040 Brussels, Belgium. T. +3222352013. Fax +3222352019. E-mail: secretariat@energycoalition.eu.
URL: http://www.energycoalition.eu/

History as a gathering of businesses, professional and civil society associations. Registration: No/ID: 644.403.860, Belgium. **Aims** Make the case for a European energy policy that places a much greater, more meaningful emphasis on energy efficiency and savings. **Structure** General Assembly; Steering Committee; Working Groups; Secretary-General. **Events** *Energy Savings Summit* Brussels (Belgium) 2017, *Meeting on Energy Efficiency and Climate Goals* Brussels (Belgium) 2017, *2030 Climate and Energy Framework Workshop* Brussels (Belgium) 2013. **Publications** *Guidebook for Strong Implementation of the Energy Efficiency Directive*.
Members Businesses, professional and civil society associations which include the following listed in this Yearbook (26):
- *APPLiA – Home Appliance Europe (#00877);*
- *Architects Council of Europe (ACE, #01086);*
- *Buildings Performance Institute Europe (BPIE, #03354);*
- *ClientEarth (#03996);*
- *Climate Action Network Europe (CAN Europe, #04001);*
- *COGEN Europe (#04085);*
- *E3G – Third Generation Environmentalism;*
- *Energy Cities (#05467);*
- *Euroheat and Power (EHP, #05694);*
- *European Alliance of Companies for Energy Efficiency in Buildings (EuroACE, #05865);*
- *European Alliance to Save Energy (EU ASE, #05882);*
- *European Climate Foundation (ECF, #06574);*
- *European Copper Institute (ECI, #06796);*
- *European Council for an Energy Efficient Economy (ECEEE, #06818);*
- *European Environmental Bureau (EEB, #06996);*
- *European Federation of Building and Woodworkers (EFBWW, #07065);*
- *European Federation of Intelligent Energy Efficiency Services (EFIEES, #07145);*
- *European Insulation Manufacturers Association (EURIMA, #07577);*
- *European Partnership for Energy and the Environment (EPEE, #08157);*
- *Federation of European Rigid Polyurethane Foam Associations (PU Europe, #09538);*
- *Friends of the Earth Europe (FoEE, #10001);*
- *Housing Europe – The European Federation for Public Cooperative and Social Housing (Housing Europe, #10956);*
- *LightingEurope (#16472);*
- *Regulatory Assistance Project (RAP);*
- *Royal Institution of Chartered Surveyors (RICS, #18991);*
- *World Wide Fund for Nature (WWF, #21922)* (European Policy Office). [2021/XJ2706/y/**F**]

♦ Coalition for Environmentally Responsible Economies / see CERES

♦ Coalition for Epidemic Preparedness Innovations (CEPI) 04057

Headquarters Postbox 1030 Hoff, 0218 Oslo, Norway.
UK Office Gibbs Building, 215 Euston Rd, London, NW1 2BE, UK.
URL: https://cepi.net/

History Launched 2017, Davos (Switzerland), by governments of Norway and India, *Bill and Melinda Gates Foundation (BMGF)*, *Wellcome Trust* and *World Economic Forum (WEF, #21367)*. **Aims** Stimulate and accelerate the development of vaccines against emerging infectious diseases and enable access to these vaccines for people during outbreaks. **Structure** Board; Scientific Advisory Committee; Joint Coordination Group. **Activities** Research and development. **Events** *Nipah Virus International Conference* Singapore (Singapore) 2019. **NGO Relations** Observer to *Global Research Collaboration for Infectious Disease Preparedness (GLOPID-R, #10573)*. [2021/XM8860/**C**]

♦ Coalition to Eradicate Viral Hepatitis in Asia Pacific (CEVHAP) 04058

Co-Chair Univ of Malaya, Fac of Medicine, Jalan Universiti, 50603 Kuala Lumpur, Malaysia.
Secretariat 20 Upper Circular Road, 02-10/12 The Riverwalk, Singapore 058416, Singapore. E-mail: secretariat@cevhap.org.
URL: http://www.cevhap.org/

History Oct 2010. Registration: Singapore. **Aims** Work with national, regional and global partners to eradicate viral hepatitis and the health, social and economic burdens associated with it in Asia-Pacific by 2050. **Structure** 2 Co-Chairs; Executive Committee. **Languages** English. **Staff** 2.00 FTE, paid. **Finance** Sources: donations. **Activities** Advocacy/lobbying/activism; awareness raising; capacity building; events/meetings; knowledge management/information dissemination. **Publications** *CEVHAP Strategy 2017-2021* (2019); *Situation Analysis of Viral Hepatitis in Indonesia: A Policy Report* (2018); *Viral Hepatitis Policy in Asia Survey* (2016). Reports; peer reviewed articles; other documentation.

Members Mostly in Asia-Pacific region. Members in 50 countries and territories:
Australia, Bangladesh, Bhutan, Brunei Darussalam, Cambodia, China, Cook Is, Fiji, Guam, Hong Kong, India, Indonesia, Japan, Kiribati, Korea DPR, Korea Rep, Laos, Macau, Malaysia, Maldives, Marshall Is, Micronesia FS, Mongolia, Myanmar, Nauru, Nepal, New Caledonia, New Zealand, Niue, Northern Mariana Is, Pakistan, Palau, Papua New Guinea, Philippines, Pitcairn, Polynesia Fr, Samoa, Samoa USA, Singapore, Solomon Is, Sri Lanka, Taiwan, Thailand, Timor-Leste, Tokelau, Tonga, Tuvalu, Vanuatu, Vietnam, Wallis-Futuna.

IGO Relations *WHO (#20950)*. **NGO Relations** Partner of (4): *Asian Pacific Association for the Study of the Liver (APASL, #01602)*; *Australasian Society for HIV, Viral Hepatitis and Sexual Health Medicine (ASHM)*; *European Association for the Study of the Liver (EASL, #06233)*; *World Hepatitis Alliance (WHA, #21564)*. Partner of: national organizations. [2021.06.09/XJ5997/**D**]

♦ Coalition of European Lobbies on Eastern African Pastoralism (CELEP) 04059

Contact Avenue Paul Deschanellaan 36-38, 1030 Brussels, Belgium.
URL: http://www.celep.info/

History Set up as an informal association, 2009. EU Transparency Register: 76932284955-08. **Aims** Work together to lobby national governments, EU bodies as well as other policy formulating bodies/agencies in Europe to explicitly recognize and support pastoralism in the drylands of Eastern Africa. **Structure** Annual General Meeting; rotating Focal Point; Core Team. **Finance** Members' dues. **Activities** Knowledge management/information dissemination; advocacy/lobbying/activism. **Events** *Annual Meeting* London (UK) 2016, *Annual Meeting* The Hague (Netherlands) 2015, *Annual Meeting* Aachen (Germany) 2014, *Annual Meeting* Rome (Italy) 2013, *Annual Meeting* Brussels (Belgium) 2012.

Members Organizations (23) in 8 countries:
Belgium, Denmark, Germany, Ireland, Italy, Netherlands, Switzerland, UK.
Included in the above, 21 organizations listed in this Yearbook:
African Studies Centre Leiden (ASCL); *Association for AgriCulture and Ecology (Agrecol)*; *Catholic Organization for Relief and Development (Cordaid)*; *Concern Worldwide*; *Food and Agricultural Research Management (FARM-Africa)*; *Future Agricultures*; *International Institute for Environment and Development (IIED, #13877)*; *International Union for Conservation of Nature and Natural Resources (IUCN, #15766)* (World Initiative for Sustainable Pastoralism (WISP)); *League for Pastoral Peoples and Endogenous Livestock Development (LPP)*; *Mercy Corps International (MCI)* (European Headquarters); *Minority Rights Group International (MRG, #16820)*; *Netherlands Food Partnership (NFP)*; *Overseas Development Institute (ODI)* (Humanitarian Policy Group); *Oxfam International (#17922)*; *Pastoral and Environmental Network in the Horn of Africa (PENHA)*; *PAX*; *Practical Action (#18475)*; *SNV Netherlands Development Organisation (SNV)*; *Terra Nuova*; *Vétérinaires Sans Frontières International (VSF International, #20760)*. [2016/XM4997/y/**D**]

♦ Coalition européenne contre le cancer du sein (#05745)
♦ Coalition européenne pour mettre fin à l'expérimentation animale (#06594)

♦ Coalition for Fair Fisheries Agreements (CFFA) 04060

Coalition pour des accords de pêche équitables (CAPE)

Coordinator Chaussee de Waterloo 244, 1060 Brussels, Belgium. T. +3226525201. Fax +3226540407. E-mail: cffa.cape@gmail.com.
URL: http://cape-cffa.squarespace.com/

History Dec 1992, Brussels (Belgium). EU Transparency Register: 440395221847-89. **Aims** Work for a fundamental change in European Union policy and practice of the EU-ACP Fisheries Agreements; contribute to the sustainable use and development of fishery resources for the benefit of coastal communities, to the livelihood and *food security* of fishery dependent populations and to the *conservation* of global *fish* stocks for future generations. **Structure** Secretariat in Brussels (Belgium). **Staff** 1.00 FTE, paid. **Finance** Funded exclusively by NGOs participating in CFFA activities. **Activities** Knowledge management/inforation dissemination; guidance/assistance/consulting; advocacy/lobbying/activism. **Publications** *CFFA Newsletter* (4 a year) in English, French. Annual Report. Briefing papers.

Members Covers 8 countries:
Belgium, France, Germany, Ireland, Madagascar, Netherlands, Senegal, UK.

IGO Relations Has participated in meetings of: *Round Table on Sustainable Development at the OECD (see: #17693)*.

NGO Relations Participating organizations:
- *Catholic Agency for Overseas Development (CAFOD)*;
- *Comité Catholique contre la Faim et pour le Développement-Terre Solidaire (CCFD-Terre Solidaire)*;
- *Christian Aid*;
- *Coalition of the Flemish North South Movement – 11 11 11*;
- *Entraide et fraternité*;
- *Fonds voor Ontwikkelingssamenwerking – Socialistische Solidariteit (FOS)*;
- *German Catholic Bishops' Organisation for Development Cooperation (MISEREOR)*;
- *Greenpeace International (#10727)*;
- *International Collective in Support of Fishworkers (ICSF, #12639)*;
- *Oxfam GB*;
- *Practical Action (#18475)*;
- *Progressio (inactive)*;
- *Trocaire – Catholic Agency for World Development*;
- *War on Want*;
- *World Wide Fund for Nature (WWF, #21922)*.

Member of: *Long Distance Advisory Council (LDAC, #16511)*; *Market Advisory Council (MAC, #16584)*. [2016/XE2363/**E**]

♦ Coalition of Faith-Based Organizations (unconfirmed)
♦ Coalition FBOs – Coalition of Faith-Based Organizations (unconfirmed)
♦ Coalition of the Flemish North South Movement – 11 11 11 (internationally oriented national body)
♦ Coalition of Fragile Ecosystems (unconfirmed)
♦ Coalition for Genocide Response (unconfirmed)
♦ Coalition for Global Hearing Health (unconfirmed)

♦ Coalition for Human Rights in Development 04061

Dir address not obtained. E-mail: contact@rightsindevelopment.org.
URL: https://rightsindevelopment.org/

Aims Ensure that development is community-led and that it respects, protects, and fulfills human rights. **Structure** Steering Committee; Secretariat. **Finance** Also from 2 anonymous donors. Supported by: *Charles Stewart Mott Foundation*; *Ford Foundation (#09858)*; *Open Society Foundations (OSF, #17763)*. Annual budget: 830,000 USD (2021).

Members Organizations in 45 countries and territories, including 39 listed in this Yearbook:
Argentina, Armenia, Bangladesh, Bolivia, Brazil, Cambodia, Cameroon, Canada, Chad, Chile, Colombia, Congo DR, Ecuador, Egypt, El Salvador, Fiji, Germany, Guatemala, Honduras, India, Indonesia, Jordan, Kazakhstan, Kenya, Lebanon, Liberia, Mexico, Mongolia, Nepal, Netherlands, Nigeria, Palestine, Panama, Peru, Philippines, Senegal, Sierra Leone, South Africa, Sri Lanka, Switzerland, Thailand, Uganda, UK, USA, Zimbabwe.
- *Accountability Counsel*;
- *African Coalition for Corporate Accountability (ACCA, #00252)*;
- *African Law Foundation (AFRILAW)*;
- *African Network for Environment and Economic Justice (ANEEJ)*;
- *African Resources Watch (AFREWATCH)*;
- *Amnesty International (AI, #00801)*;
- *Arab NGO Network for Development (ANND, #01016)*;
- *Arab Watch Coalition (AWC, #01074)*;
- *ARTICLE 19 (#01121)*;
- *Asia Indigenous Peoples Pact (AIPP, #01282)*;
- *Bank Information Center (BIC)*;
- *Both ENDS (#03307)*;
- *CEE Bankwatch Network (#03624)*;
- *Center for International Environmental Law (CIEL)*;
- *CIVICUS: World Alliance for Citizen Participation (#03962)*;
- *EarthRights International (ERI)*;
- *Forest Peoples Programme (FPP, #09865)*;
- *Front Line Defenders (FLD, #10008)*;
- *Gender Action (#10094)*;
- *Global Initiative for Economic, Social and Cultural Rights (GI-ESCR)*;
- *Global Labor Justice-International Labor Rights Forum (GLJ-ILRF)*;
- *Global Witness (GW)*;
- *Human Rights Watch (HRW, #10990)*;
- *Inclusive Development International (IDI)*;
- *Interamerican Association for Environmental Defense (#11398)*;
- *Internal Displacement Monitoring Centre (IDMC, #11526)*;
- *International Accountability Project (IAP)*;
- *International Disability Alliance (IDA, #13176)*;
- *International Network for Economic, Social and Cultural Rights (ESCR-Net, #14255)*;
- *International Rivers*;
- *Latinoamérica Sustentable (LAS)*;
- *Maryknoll Office for Global Concern (MOGC)*;
- *Minority Rights Group International (MRG, #16820)*;
- *Namati (#16931)*;
- *Natural Justice: Lawyers for Communities and the Environment (Natural Justice, #16954)*;
- *Oxfam International (#17922)*;
- *Protection International (PI, #18548)* (Mesoamerica);
- *Stichting Onderzoek Multinationale Ondernemingen (SOMO)*;
- *Urgewald*. [2022/AA2839/y/**C**]

♦ Coalition for Intellectual Property Rights (internationally oriented national body)
♦ Coalition interagence SIDA et développement (internationally oriented national body)

♦ Coalition for the International Criminal Court (CICC) 04062

Coalition pour la Cour Pénale Internationale – Coalición por la Corte Penal Internacional

Dir c/o HRW IJP, 1275 K St NW, Ste 1100, Washington DC 20005, USA. E-mail: cicc@coalitionfortheicc.org.
Advocacy Officer Bezuidenhoutseweg 99a, 2594 AC The Hague, Netherlands. T. +31703111080. Fax +31703640259.
URL: http://www.coalitionfortheicc.org/

History 1995. Founded to work for the setting up of *International Criminal Court (ICC, #13108)*. Secretariat at *World Federalist Movement – Movement for a Just World Order through a Strengthened United Nations (WFM, #21404)*. Former names and other names: *NGO Coalition for an International Criminal Court* – former; *Coalition des ONG pour la mise en place d'une Cour pénale internationale* – former; *Coalition pour la mise en place d'une Cour pénale internationale* – former. Registration: Handelsregister, No/ID: KVK 27259931, Netherlands; EU Transparency Register, No/ID: 133259443336-02, Start date: 28 Jun 2021. **Aims** Strengthen international cooperation with the ICC; ensure that the Court is fair, effective and independent; make justice both visible and universal; advance stronger national laws that deliver justice to victims of war crimes, crimes against humanity and genocide. **Structure** Headquarters in New York NY (USA) and The Hague (Netherlands). Regional representatives in: Argentina; Benin; Belgium; Cotonou; Peru; Thailand. **Staff** 34.00 FTE, voluntary. Also interns and voluntary. **Finance** Funding from: participating organizations; private individuals; *European Commission (EC, #06633)*; *Ford Foundation (#09858)*; *MacArthur Foundation*. **Activities** Events/meetings; networking/liaising. **Events** *Colloque international sur le rôle des intervenants dans l'abandon des carrières criminelles* Montréal, QC (Canada) 2020, *Colloque international sur le rôle des intervenants dans l'abandon des carrières criminelles* Montréal, QC (Canada) 2020, *Conference on the establishment of an international criminal bar* Paris (France) 2001, *Joint conference* Rome (Italy) 1998. **Publications** *CICC Bulletin* (6 a year); *The Monitor* (annual) in English, French, Spanish. Regional newsletters; media advisories.

Members Organizations (over 2,500) including the following 19 organizations listed in this Yearbook:
Amnesty International (AI, #00801); *Arab Center for the Development of the Rule of Law and Integrity (ACRLI, #00912)*; *Asociación pro Derechos Humanos (APRODEH)*; *Cairo Institute for Human Rights Studies (CIHRS, #03397)*; *Coordinating Board of Jewish Organizations (CBJO, #04813)*; *Human Rights Watch (HRW, #10990)*; *Inter-African Union of Human Rights (IUHR, inactive)*; *International Commission of Jurists (ICJ, #12695)*; *International Committee on Offensive Microwave Weapons (ICOMW)*; *International Federation for Human Rights (#13452)*; *International Society for Traumatic Stress Studies (ISTSS, #15518)*; *Nonviolent Radical Party, Transnational and Transparty (PRNTT, #17154)*; *No Peace Without Justice (NPWJ, #17155)*; *Organisation internationale Post Tenebras Jus (no recent information)*; *Organization for Defending Victims of Violence (ODVV)*; *Parliamentarians for Global Action (PGA, #18208)*; *REDRESS*; *The European Law Students' Association (ELSA, #07660)*; *Unrepresented Nations and Peoples Organization (UNPO, #20714)*; *World Federalist Movement – Movement for a Just World Order through a Strengthened United Nations (WFM, #21404)* (Institute for Global Policy).

NGO Relations Operational collaboration with: *Action Against Hunger (#00086)*. Member of: *Human Rights and Democracy Network (HRDN, #10980)*; *International Criminal Bar (ICB, #13107)*; *New World Hope Organization (NWHO)*; *NGO Working Group on the Security Council (#17128)*. Cooperates with: *Genocide Alert*. [2022/XE2802/y/**E**]

♦ Coalition internationale pour l'accès à la terre (#13999)
♦ Coalition internationale anti-contrefaçon (#11656)
♦ Coalition Internationale de l'Habitat (#10845)
♦ Coalition internationale de la préparation au traitement (#15729)
♦ Coalition internationale pour la santé de la femme (internationally oriented national body)
♦ Coalition Internationale des Sites de Conscience (#12621)
♦ Coalition International SIDA (unconfirmed)
♦ Coalition pour la Justice et la Paix en Afrique (internationally oriented national body)
♦ Coalition for Justice and Peace in Africa (internationally oriented national body)

♦ Coalition of Legal Toothfish Operators (COLTO) 04063

Exec Officer PO Box 280, Mount Hawthorn WA 6915, Australia. T. +6192170100. E-mail: contact@colto.org.
URL: http://www.colto.org/

History 2003. **Aims** Promote legal and sustainable fishing and fisheries of members nationally and internationally; facilitate members working with each other, governments, conservation groups and the general public to eliminate illegal, unreported and unregulated fishing (IUU); be a powerful alliance of toothfish operators; represent the legal toothfish industry to ensure a viable economic future; inform the public about legitimate, sustainable toothfish fisheries; provide effective representation and input at international toothfish management and scientific meetings.

Members in 15 countries and territories:
Argentina, Australia, Canada, Chile, Falklands/Malvinas, France, Japan, Korea Rep, New Zealand, Norway, Singapore, South Africa, Spain, UK, USA. [2022.02.09/XM1751/F]

- ♦ Coalition pour la mise en place d'une Cour pénale internationale / see Coalition for the International Criminal Court (#04062)
- ♦ Coalition mondiale pour l'abolition de l'expérimentation sur l'homme et l'animal (inactive)
- ♦ Coalition mondiale contre la peine de mort (#21281)
- ♦ Coalition mondiale des entreprises contre le SIDA / see GBCHealth
- ♦ Coalition mondiale des forêts (#10368)
- ♦ Coalition du mouvement Nord-Sud en Flandres – 11 11 11 (internationally oriented national body)
- ♦ Coalition for Nuclear Disarmament / see Coalition for Peace Action
- ♦ Coalition des ONG pour la mise en place d'une Cour pénale internationale / see Coalition for the International Criminal Court (#04062)
- ♦ Coalition for Operational Research on Neglected Tropical Diseases (internationally oriented national body)
- ♦ Coalition pour la paix en Afrique (#04064)
- ♦ Coalition panafricaine d'études et d'actions de contrôle de tabac / see Initiative de mobilisation panafricaine de controle de tabac (#11211)
- ♦ Coalition for Peace Action (internationally oriented national body)

♦ Coalition for Peace in Africa (COPA) 04064

Coalition pour la paix en Afrique

Secretariat PO Box 61753, Nairobi, 00200, Kenya. T. +254203866686. E-mail: copa@copafrica.org.
Street Address Dhanjay Apartments room 301, Valley Arcade, Lavington, Nairobi, Kenya.
URL: http://www.copafrica.org/

History 1995/1996. **Aims** Promote peace, justice, human rights and development through capacity building, advocacy, and research and documentation. **Structure** Board. **Languages** English, French. **Activities** Training/education; guidance/assistance/consulting; capacity building; awareness raising; research/documentation. **Publications** News brief; occasional papers; case studies.

Members Individuals and institutions in 20 countries:
Burundi, Congo DR, Eritrea, Ethiopia, Ghana, Kenya, Lebanon, Madagascar, Nigeria, Rwanda, Sierra Leone, Somalia, South Africa, Sudan, Tanzania UR, Uganda, UK, USA, Zambia, Zimbabwe.

NGO Relations Member of: *Global Partnership for the Prevention of Armed Conflict (GPPAC, #10538).* Partner of: *ACTION for Conflict Transformation.* [2017.06.01/XG7477/F]

- ♦ Coalition PLUS – Coalition International SIDA (unconfirmed)
- ♦ Coalition for the Protection of Africa's Genetic Heritage (#04065)

♦ Coalition pour la Protection du Patrimoine Génétique Africain (COPAGEN) 04065

Coalition for the Protection of Africa's Genetic Heritage

Contact Soleil 2 – Villa no 78, Angré-Djibi-Cité Wedouwel, Cocody, Abidjan 06, Côte d'Ivoire. T. +22522504072. E-mail: contact@copagen.org.
URL: http://copagen.org/

History 2004, Grand-Bassam (Côte d'Ivoire). **Aims** Safeguard the African genetic heritage and the sustainable use of African biological resources through the protection of the rights of local communities and farmers, the regulation of access to biodiversity and the management of risks linked to genetic engineering and all other hazardous technologies likely to alienate genetic resources. **Activities** Advocacy/lobbying/activism; awareness raising; events/meetings; knowledge management/information dissemination; research/documentation.

Members Organizations in 9 countries:
Benin, Burkina Faso, Côte d'Ivoire, Guinea, Guinea-Bissau, Mali, Niger, Senegal, Togo.

NGO Relations Member of (1): *Alliance for Food Sovereignty in Africa (AFSA, #00680).* [2020/AA1174/D]

♦ Coalition for Rainforest Nations (CfRN) 04066

Development Dir 52 Vanderbilt Ave, 12th Floor, New York NY 10017, USA. T. +16464486870. Fax +16464486889. E-mail: info@rainforestcoalition.org – giving@cfrn.org.
URL: http://www.rainforestcoalition.org/

History May 2005. Registration: Section 501(c)(3), No/ID: 26-3221530, USA, New York. **Aims** Slow, stop and reverse global deforestation; assist tropical governments, communities and peoples responsibly manage their rainforests. **Languages** English, French, Italian, Spanish. **Staff** 14.00 FTE, paid; 25.00 FTE, voluntary. **Finance** Annual budget: 4,159,123 USD (2021). **Activities** Capacity building; financial and/or material support; knowledge management/information dissemination; networking/liaising; politics/policy/regulatory; training/education.

Members Governments of 55 countries:
Argentina, Bangladesh, Belize, Bolivia, Botswana, Brazil, Cambodia, Cameroon, Central African Rep, China, Congo Brazzaville, Congo DR, Costa Rica, Dominica, Dominican Rep, Ecuador, Equatorial Guinea, Fiji, Gabon, Ghana, Guatemala, Guyana, Honduras, India, Indonesia, Jamaica, Kenya, Laos, Lesotho, Liberia, Madagascar, Malawi, Malaysia, Mali, Mozambique, Namibia, Nicaragua, Nigeria, Pakistan, Panama, Papua New Guinea, Paraguay, Samoa, Sierra Leone, Singapore, Solomon Is, St Lucia, Sudan, Suriname, Thailand, Uganda, Uruguay, Vanuatu, Vietnam, Zambia.

NGO Relations Member of (1): *LEDS Global Partnership (LEDS GP, #16435).* Partner of (3): *Earth Institute at Columbia University; Initiative for Policy Dialogue (IPD);* national organizations. [2022.10.19/XM1649/F*]

♦ Coalition for Religious Equality and Inclusive Development (CREID) 04067

Dir c/o IDS, Library Road, Brighton, BN1 9RE, UK.
URL: https://www.ids.ac.uk/programme-and-centre/creid/

Aims Redress the impact of discrimination on the grounds of religion or belief; tackle poverty and exclusion; promote people's wellbeing and empowerment. **Structure** Led by (UK) Institute of Development Studies. **Finance** Supported by: *Department for International Development (DFID, inactive).* **Activities** Awareness raising; events/meetings; monitoring/evaluation; networking/liaising; research/documentation. **Publications** *Religious Inequalities in Development* – seminar series. Working Papers. **NGO Relations** Partners: Al-Khoei Foundation; *Minority Rights Group International (MRG, #16820).* [2020/AA0033/E]

- ♦ Coalition for Responsible Technology / see International Campaign for Responsible Technology
- ♦ Coalition to Reverse the Nuclear Arms Race / see Coalition for Peace Action

♦ Coalition for Sexual and Bodily Rights in Muslim Societies (CSBR) . 04068

Coordinating Office GAYa NUSANTARA Foundation, Jalan Semolowaru Selatan VI No 9, Surabaya, Indonesia. E-mail: coordinator@csbronline.org.
URL: http://www.csbronline.org/

History Sep 2001, Istanbul (Turkey). **Aims** Advance a holistic approach to sexuality and sexual rights in member countries and at international level through advocacy, capacity-building, research, publications and campaigns; provide information and resource materials to foster national and international level policies and programmes that respect and affirm sexual rights as human rights; stimulate knowledge exchange through regional and global networks to build cross-sector solidarity on sexual health and reproductive rights, LGBTIQ rights, access to justice for gender-based violence and citizenship. **Structure** Coordinating Office. **Languages** English. **Finance** Budget (annual): US$ 90,000.

Members Organizations in 15 countries and territories:
Algeria, Bangladesh, Egypt, Indonesia, Jordan, Lebanon, Malaysia, Morocco, Pakistan, Palestine, Philippines, Sudan, Tunisia, Türkiye, Yemen.

Included in the above, 2 organizations listed in this Yearbook:
Asian-Pacific Resource and Research Centre for Women (ARROW, #01629); International Women's Rights Action Watch Asia Pacific (IWRAW Asia Pacific, #15902).

Consultative Status Consultative status granted from: *United Nations Population Fund (UNFPA, #20612).* [2015.10.19/XJ9293/y/D]

- ♦ Coalition for a Strong United Nations (internationally oriented national body)
- ♦ Coalition for a Sustainable Africa (unconfirmed)

♦ Coalition Theory Network (CTN) 04069

Secretariat c/o CMCC – Ca' Foscari Univ, Edifo Porta dell'Innovazione, Piano 2, Via della Libertà 12, 30175 Venice VE, Italy.
URL: https://www.coalitiontheory.net/

History Founded 1998, Venice (Italy), when CTN was formally founded at 3rd Workshop on theory of coalition forming. **Aims** Advance and diffuse research in the area of *network theory* and coalition formation. **Structure** Scientific Board; Secretariat. **Languages** English. **Staff** None. **Finance** Workshop borne by member institutions on a turn basis. **Activities** Research/documentation; events/meetings. **Events** *Workshop* Barcelona (Spain) 2022, *Workshop* Barcelona (Spain) 2021, *Workshop* Maastricht (Netherlands) 2018, *Workshop* Venice (Italy) 2015, *Workshop* Brussels (Belgium) 2014. **Publications** *CTN Newsletter.* Working papers; books.

Members Educational institutions (9) in 8 countries:
Belgium, France, Italy, Netherlands, Russia, Spain, UK, USA.

NGO Relations Cooperates with: *Association for Public Economic Theory (APET, #02881).* [2017/XJ1254/E]

- ♦ Coalition for the UN We Need (unconfirmed)

♦ Coalition of Women in Africa for Peace and Development (COWAP) 04070

Contact Suite 402C Nawa Complex, Jahi, Abuja 900108, Federal Capital Territory, Nigeria. T. +2348136105628. E-mail: info@cowapafrika.org.
URL: https://cowapafrika.org/

History A project under Engage, Empower, Educate Inititiatve. Former names and other names: *Women in Politics, Wives of Presidents and Vice Presidents in Africa* – alias. **Aims** Harness the experiences of women across all sectors, for positive change by bringing them in contact with other female professionals and women thriving in various fields and contributing to the development of Africa. **Activities** Events/meetings. **Events** *African Women Summit* Kigali (Rwanda) 2022, *African Women Summit* Dubai (United Arab Emirates) 2021. [2022/AA2968/D]

- ♦ Coalizão Internacional de Sites de Consciência (#12621)
- ♦ CoAN – Coalition of African NGOs (unconfirmed)
- ♦ **CoARA** Coalition for Advancing Research Assessment (#04045)
- ♦ **COAR** Confederation of Open Access Repositories (#04573)
- ♦ COARE – Center for Oceanic Awareness, Research and Education (internationally oriented national body)
- ♦ COASP – Comité Ouest-Africain des Semences Paysannes (unconfirmed)
- ♦ Coastal Conservation Network (internationally oriented national body)

♦ Coastal Education and Research Foundation (CERF) 04071

Pres/Exec Dir address not obtained.
URL: http://cerf-jcr.org/

History Founded 1984. **Aims** Help translate and interpret coastal issues for the public; assist in the development of professional coastal research programs. **Structure** Board of Directors. **Activities** Events/meetings; publishing activities; research/documentation. **Events** *Symposium* Seville (Spain) 2021, *Symposium* Seville (Spain) 2020, *Symposium* Busan (Korea Rep) 2018. **Publications** *Journal of Coastal Research (JCR).* [2019/XM8291/f/F]

- ♦ Coastal Environmental Rights Foundation (internationally oriented national body)
- ♦ Coastal and Estuarine Research Federation (internationally oriented national body)
- ♦ Coastal Footprint (internationally oriented national body)

♦ Coastal and Marine Union – EUCC 04072

Dir Gen Rapenburg 8 – room 19, 2311 EV Leiden, Netherlands. T. +31715143719. E-mail: admin@eucc.net.
URL: http://www.eucc.net/

History 1989, as *European Union for Dune Conservation and Coastal Management,* following decision of congress, Sep 1987, Leiden (Netherlands). Title changed to *European Union for Coastal Conservation,* Jun 1991, when scope broadened. Present title adopted 1 Jan 2002. **Aims** Promote *conservation* and wise use of the coast and marine environment in *Europe* and neighbouring regions; stimulate awareness of the importance of the coastal and marine environment and problems associated with its management and conservation; encourage cooperation among governments, organizations and individuals concerned; promote education and disseminate information. **Structure** Council; Executive Committee. EUCC Mediterranean Centre, Barcelona (Spain) inaugurated Nov 2003. EUCC Baltic Office, Klaipeda (Lithuania). International Secretariat, Leiden (Netherlands). **Languages** Dutch, English. **Staff** 25.00 FTE, paid; 6.00 FTE, voluntary. **Finance** Members' dues. Project funds. **Activities** Events/meetings; knowledge management/information dissemination; advocacy/lobbying/activism. Active in: Estonia, Latvia, Lithuania, Poland, Russia, Ukraine. **Events** *LITTORAL : International Symposium on Coastal Zone Research Management and Planning / Congress* Klaipeda (Lithuania) 2014, *LITTORAL : international symposium on coastal zone research management and planning / Congress* London (UK) 2010, *LITTORAL : international symposium on coastal zone research management and planning / Congress* Venice (Italy) 2008, *LITTORAL : international symposium on coastal zone research management and planning / Congress* Gdansk (Poland) 2006, *International conference on nature restoration practices in European coastal habitats* Koksijde (Belgium) 2005. **Publications** *Coastal Guide News* (6 a year); *Coastline* – international magazine; *Journal of Coastal Conservation* – official journal. Documents; studies; conference proceedings. Information Services: Database of 400 institutions involved in coastal research.

Members Individuals (500); organizations (300), in 38 countries:
Albania, Australia, Belgium, Bulgaria, Canada, Croatia, Cyprus, Denmark, Egypt, Estonia, Finland, France, Germany, Greece, Iceland, Ireland, Israel, Italy, Latvia, Lithuania, Malta, Namibia, Netherlands, New Zealand, Norway, Poland, Portugal, Romania, Russia, Saudi Arabia, Slovenia, South Africa, Spain, Sweden, Türkiye, UK, Ukraine, USA.

National branches in 14 countries:
Albania, Belgium, France, Germany, Italy, Latvia, Lithuania, Netherlands, Poland, Portugal, Russia, Spain, UK, Ukraine.

IGO Relations Official observer to: *Baltic Marine Environment Protection Commission – Helsinki Commission (HELCOM, #03126).* **NGO Relations** Member of: *European Network for Sustainable Tourism Development (ECOTRANS, #08018).* Together with: *ECNC – European Centre for Nature Conservation (#05289)* and *Eurosite (#09181),* set up: *EECONET Action Fund (EAF, #05383); NatureNet Europe (#16959).* Together with ECNC, forms *ECNC Group (no recent information).* [2017/XD2856/E]

- ♦ Coastal Oceans Research and Development in the Indian Ocean / see Coastal Oceans Research and Development – Indian Ocean (#04073)

♦ Coastal Oceans Research and Development – Indian Ocean (CORDIO East Africa) 04073

Dir CORDIO East Africa, No 9 Kibaki Flats, Kenyatta Beach, Bamburi Beach, PO Box 10135, Mombasa, 80101, Kenya. T. +254715067417.
Dir address not obtained. T. +254721498713.
URL: https://cordioea.net/

History 1999 as *Coastal Oceans Research and Development in the Indian Ocean (CORDIO),* following the El-Niño related mass bleaching and mortality of corals in the Indian Ocean, 1998. *CORDIO East Africa* formally registered under Kenyan law, 2003. Since Indian Ocean tsunami of 2004, also covered Andaman Sea, and since 2007 also Red Sea/Gulf of Aden and South Asia. Main focus now on Western Indian Ocean (East and Southern Africa). **Aims** Generate and share scientifically sound knowledge and develop solutions to problems and challenges facing coastal and *marine* environments and people in the Western Indian Ocean. **Finance** Funding from various organizations including: *FAO (#09260); International Bank for Reconstruction and Development (IBRD, #12317)* (World Bank); *International Union for Conservation of Nature and Natural Resources (IUCN, #15766); MacArthur Foundation; Norwegian Agency for Development Cooperation (Norad); Swedish International Development Cooperation Agency (Sida); Western Indian Ocean Marine Science Association (WIOMSA, #20916)* – MASMA; *World Wide Fund for Nature (WWF, #21922).* **Publications** *CORDIO Status Report.* Research; surveys. **IGO Relations** Member of: *International Coral Reef Initiative (ICRI, #12965).* **NGO Relations** Member of: *High Level Panel for a Sustainable Ocean Economy (Panel, #10917)* – Advisory Network; *International Union for Conservation of Nature and Natural Resources (IUCN, #15766).* [2019.12.11/XJ2999/E]

Coastal Watershed Institude
04073

alphabetic sequence excludes
For the complete listing, see Yearbook Online at

- ♦ Coastal Watershed Institute (internationally oriented national body)

♦ Coastal Zone Asia-Pacific Association (CZAPA) 04074

Secretariat Coastal Development Ctr, Fac of Fisheries – Kasetsart Univ, 50 Phaholyothin Road, Chatuchak, Bangkok, 10900, Thailand.
URL: http://coastalzoneasiapacific.net/
Events *Oceans to plates* Chiang Mai (Thailand) 2012, *Conference* Bangkok (Thailand) 2010, *Conference* Qingdao (China) 2008, *Conference* Batam (Indonesia) 2006, *Conference* Brisbane, QLD (Australia) 2004. [2013/XJ6643/**E**]

- ♦ Coastlands / see Newfrontiers (#17086)
- ♦ Coastwatch Europe (internationally oriented national body)
- ♦ Coastwatch Europe Network / see Coastwatch Europe
- ♦ COAT – FAO Commission on African Animal Trypanosomiasis (inactive)

♦ Coatings Societies International (CSI) 04075

Pres c/o FPL eV, Allmandring 37, 70569 Stuttgart, Germany. T. +497119793820. E-mail: president@csi-coatings.org – info@csi-coatings.org.
URL: http://www.csi-coatings.org/
History 23 Jun 1979, Paris (France), as *International Committee to Coordinate Activities of Technical Groups in the Coatings Industry (ICCATCI) – Comité international de coordination et d'action des groupements de techniciens des industries de revêtements de surface (CICATIRS)*. Restructured under current title adopted 1985, Australia. **Aims** Advance scientific and technical knowledge related to coatings, *inks, construction materials* and *adhesives*; share information between members for mutual benefit. **Structure** Council; Rotating Secretariat. **Languages** English. **Staff** Provided by host association/federation. **Finance** Sources: members' dues. **Events** *European Technical Coatings Congress* Krakow (Poland) 2022.
Members International organizations (5):
Asociación de Técnicos Andinos en Recubrimientos (STAR, #02302); Asociación Tecnologia Iberoamericana de Pinturas, Adhesivos y Tintas (ATIPAT); Federation of Associations of Technicians for Industry of Paints in European Countries (FATIPEC, #09461); Federation of Scandinavian Paint and Varnish Technologists (#09702); Oil and Colour Chemists' Association (OCCA, #17707). [2022/XD0026/y/**C**]

- ♦ **COBAC** Commission bancaire de l'Afrique centrale (#04204)
- ♦ Cobalt Development Institute / see Cobalt Institute (#04076)

♦ Cobalt Institute (CI) 04076

Communications Manager 18 Jeffries Passage, Guildford, GU1 4AP, UK. T. +441483578877. Fax +441483567042. E-mail: ci@cobaltinstitute.org.
Pres address not obtained.
URL: http://www.cobaltinstitute.org/
History 1957, Brussels (Belgium). Moved to London (UK), 1981. Former names and other names: *Cobalt Development Institute (CDI)* – former; *Cobalt Development Institute* – former. Registration: Companies House, Start date: 1991, UK. **Aims** Promote sustainable and responsible production and use of cobalt in all its forms. **Structure** General Assembly; Board of Directors; Executive Committee; Sub-Committees as required. Wholly owned subsidiary: The Cobalt REACH Consortium Ltd (CoRC). **Languages** English, French. **Staff** 13.00 FTE, paid. **Finance** Sources: members' dues. Annual budget: 3,500,000 GBP. **Activities** Knowledge management/information dissemination; monitoring/evaluation; politics/policy/regulatory. **Events** *Annual Cobalt Conference* Zurich (Switzerland) 2022, *Annual Cobalt Conference* Guildford (UK) 2021, *Annual Cobalt Conference* Madrid (Spain) 2020, *Annual Cobalt Conference* Hong Kong (Hong Kong) 2019, *Annual Cobalt Conference* Las Vegas, NV (USA) 2018. **Publications** *Cobalt News* (4 a year); *Cobalt Facts*. Monograph series: Batteries; Superalloys; Catalyst; Chemicals; Electronics; Medicine; Agriculture and the Environment.
Members Sustaining:
Bahamas, Belgium, Canada, Congo DR, Finland, Japan, Luxembourg, Madagascar, Morocco, Norway, Switzerland.
Supporting:
Belgium, Hong Kong, Sweden, USA.
Affiliate:
Belgium, Denmark, France, Japan, Korea Rep, Spain, Sweden, Türkiye, UK.
Associate:
Australia, Canada, Cook Is, UK, USA.
Institutional:
USA.
NGO Relations Member of (3): *Association européenne des métaux (EUROMETAUX, #02578); International Council on Mining and Metals (ICMM, #13048); ResponsibleSteel (#18921)* (associate). Partner of (1): *Global Battery Alliance (GBA, #10249).* [2022.05.04/XF1918/j/**F**]

- ♦ **COBATY International** International Association of Construction, Urbanism, and Environment and Life Style (#11812)
- ♦ **CoB** Council of Bureaux (#04873)
- ♦ COBEE – International Conference On Building Energy & Environment (meeting series)
- ♦ COBI – Club of Budapest International (see: #04032)
- ♦ **COBIS** Council of British International Schools (#04872)
- ♦ COBISEC / see Council of British International Schools (#04872)
- ♦ **COBSEA** Coordinating Body on the Seas of East Asia (#04814)
- ♦ COCABE – Confederación del Caribe de Béisbol (inactive)

♦ Coca-Cola Collectors Club International (CCCI) 04077

Vice-Pres PMB 609, 4780 Ashford Dunwoody Rd, Suite A, Atlanta GA 30338, USA. E-mail: ccccvp@yahoo.com.
Sec address not obtained.
URL: https://www.cocacolaclub.org/
History 1975. Former names and other names: *The Coke Club* – former; *The Cola Clan* – former. **Aims** Promote collection of memorabilia of the Coca-Cola Company. **Activities** Events/meetings. **Events** *Annual Convention* Kingsport (USA) 2023.
Members Full in 25 countries and territories:
Argentina, Australia, Austria, Belgium, Brazil, Colombia, Finland, France, Germany, Hong Kong, Indonesia, Italy, Japan, Mexico, Netherlands, New Zealand, Norway, Portugal, South Africa, Spain, Sweden, Switzerland, Thailand, UK, USA.
NGO Relations *Nordic Coca-Cola Collectors Club (no recent information).* [2022/XE2334/**E**]

- ♦ **COCAL** Federación de Entidades Organizadoras de Congresos y Afines de América Latina (#09299)
- ♦ **COCATRAM** Comisión Centroamericana de Transporte Marítimo (#04131)
- ♦ COCDYC / see Democrat Youth Community of Europe (#05037)
- ♦ COCEMA – Comité des constructeurs européens de matériel alimentaire et de matériel de conditionnement (inactive)
- ♦ COCENTRA – Coordinadora Centroamericana de Trabajadores (no recent information)
- ♦ **COCERAL** Comité du commerce des céréales, oléagineux, légumineuses, huile d'olive, huiles et graisses, aliments du bétail et agrofournitures de l'UE (#04289)
- ♦ Cocéral / see Committee of the Trade in Cereals, Oilseeds, Pulses, Olive Oil, Oils and Fats, Animal Feed and Agrosupply of the EU (#04289)
- ♦ **COCERAL** Committee of the Trade in Cereals, Oilseeds, Pulses, Olive Oil, Oils and Fats, Animal Feed and Agrosupply of the EU (#04289)
- ♦ **COCESNA** Corporación Centroamericana de Servicios de Navegación Aérea (#04837)

♦ Cochrane Collaboration 04078

Main Office St Albans House, 57-59 Haymarket, London, SW1Y 4QX, UK. T. +442071837503. Fax +442071839163.
General: http://www.cochrane.org/
History Founded 1993, Oxford (UK), at 1st Annual Cochrane Colloquium. **Aims** Collate and review reliable evidence and make it available to *clinicians, patients* and policy-makers; prepare, maintain and promote accessibility of systematic, up-to-date reviews of randomized controlled trials (RCTs) and of reliable evidence from other sources; give *doctors* confidence in *prescribing* on the basis of fact; give patients the information they need to make choices about *health care*. **Structure** Cochrane Centres (14); Centre Branches (17); Review Groups (51); Networks (11); Methods Groups (16). **Languages** Chinese, Croatian, French, German, Japanese, Korean, Malay, Polish, Portuguese, Russian, Spanish, Tamil, Thai. **Staff** 60.00 FTE, paid. **Finance** Supported by centres, foundations, institutes, organizations and universities, including: *British Council; Department for International Development (DFID, inactive); European Commission (EC, #06633); International Bank for Reconstruction and Development (IBRD, #12317); INCLEN Trust International (#11142); Nordic Council of Ministers (NCM, #17260); UNDP (#20292); WHO (#20950).* **Activities** Knowledge management/information dissemination; standards/guidelines. **Events** *Annual International Colloquium* Edinburgh (UK) 2018, *Annual International Colloquium* Seoul (Korea Rep) 2016, *Annual International Colloquium* Vienna (Austria) 2015, *Annual International Colloquium / Annual Colloquium* Hyderabad (India) 2014, *Annual International Colloquium* Québec, QC (Canada) 2013. **Publications** *Cochrane Central Register of Controlled Trials (CCRCT); Cochrane Database of Methodology Reviews (CDMR); Cochrane Database of Systematic Reviews (CDSR); Cochrane Methodology Register (CMR); Database of Abstracts of Reviews of Effects (DARE).* **Information Services** *The Cochrane Library.*
Members (over 37,000) in 120 countries. Centres in 14 countries. Membership countries not specified. Cochrane Review Groups in 11 countries:
Cochrane Review Groups in 11 countries:
Australia, Canada, Denmark, Germany, Italy, Netherlands, New Zealand, Portugal, Spain, UK, USA.
Consultative Status Consultative status granted from: *WHO (#20950)* (Official). **NGO Relations** Member of: *European Alliance for Responsible R and D and Affordable Medicines (#05879); Geneva Global Health Hub (G2H2, #10122).* [2018/XF3708/**F**]

- ♦ COC / see International Coalition of Library Consortia (#12615)
- ♦ COCIR / see European Coordination Committee of the Radiological, Electromedical Healthcare IT Industry (#06792)
- ♦ **COCIR** European Coordination Committee of the Radiological, Electromedical Healthcare IT Industry (#06792)
- ♦ COCIS – Coordinamento delle Organizzazioni Non Governative per la Cooperazione Internazionale allo Sviluppo (internationally oriented national body)
- ♦ COCISS / see Consejo de Institutos de Seguridad Social de Centroamérica y República Dominicana (#04715)

♦ Cocoa Association of Asia (CAA) 04079

Chairman 20 Anson Road, Suite 11-01, Singapore 079912, Singapore. T. +6563035299. E-mail: enquiry@cocoaasia.org.
Dir address not obtained.
URL: http://www.cocoaasia.org/
History 2004, Singapore. **Aims** Serve and promote the interest of the cocoa industry in Asia. **Structure** General Meeting; Council. **Staff** 2.00 FTE, paid. **Finance** Sources: members' dues. **Activities** Events/meetings. **Events** *International Cocoa Conference* Singapore (Singapore) 2022, *International Cocoa Conference* Singapore (Singapore) 2020, *International Cocoa Conference* Singapore (Singapore) 2017, *Annual General Meeting* Singapore (Singapore) 2013. [2022.05.23/XM3468/**D**]

- ♦ COCODEV – Cohesive Communities Development Initiative (internationally oriented national body)
- ♦ COCONA / see Euro Atlantic Partnership Council (#05646)
- ♦ CO – Confoederatio Oratorii Sancti Philippi Nerii (religious order)
- ♦ **CO** Congregation for the Oriental Churches (#04672)

♦ Coconut Genetic Resources Network (COGENT) 04080

Coordinator CIRAD – Bioversity Intl – CIFOR Campus, Jalan CIFOR, Situ Gede, Bogor 16115, Indonesia. T. +6281286504207.
Programme Assistant Bioversity Intl, Parc Scientifique Agropolis II, 34397 Montpellier CEDEX 5, France. T. +33467611302. Fax +33467610334.
URL: http://www.cogentnetwork.org/
History 1992, following recommendations, 1991, of an international workshop. Work commenced 1993. Managed by *Bioversity International (#03262)* through a Coordinator based in Malaysia. **Aims** Promote effective conservation and use of coconut genetic resources developed in consultation with members and partners. **Structure** Steering Committee. **Finance** Several donors, including: *Asian Development Bank (ADB, #01422); CGIAR System Organization (CGIAR, #03843); Department for International Development (DFID, inactive); Deutsche Gesellschaft für Internationale Zusammenarbeit (GIZ); Global Crop Diversity Trust (Crop Trust, #10313); International Development Research Centre (IDRC, #13162); International Fund for Agricultural Development (IFAD, #13692).* **Activities** Capacity building; knowledge management/information dissemination; monitoring/evaluation. **Events** *Meeting* Nadi (Fiji) 2017, *Meeting* Lunuwila (Sri Lanka) 2014, *Meeting* Kochi (India) 2012, *Meeting* Mérida (Mexico) 2003, *International coconut genebank meeting* Kasaragod (India) 2002. **Publications** COGENT strategy; proceedings; manuals; policy briefs; articles. Information Services: Database.
Members Full in 40 countries:
Bangladesh, Benin, Brazil, China, Colombia, Cook Is, Costa Rica, Côte d'Ivoire, Cuba, El Salvador, Fiji, Ghana, Guyana, Haiti, Honduras, India, Indonesia, Jamaica, Kenya, Kiribati, Madagascar, Malaysia, Mexico, Mozambique, Myanmar, Nigeria, Oman, Pakistan, Papua New Guinea, Philippines, Samoa, Seychelles, Solomon Is, Sri Lanka, Tanzania UR, Thailand, Tonga, Trinidad-Tobago, Vanuatu, Vietnam. [2017.03.09/XK0878/**F**]

- ♦ COCOP – Red Latinoamericana de Coordinación y Promoción de Tecnologia Apropiada (inactive)
- ♦ COCOSDA – International Committee for the Coordination and Standardization of Speech Databases and Assessment Techniques for Speech Input-Output (unconfirmed)
- ♦ COCTI – Conference of Catholic Theological Institutions (see: #13381)
- ♦ COCU / see Churches United In Christ
- ♦ CoDa Association – Association for Compositional Data (unconfirmed)
- ♦ CODAC – Community Development and Advocacy Centre (internationally oriented national body)
- ♦ CODA International / see CODA International Training
- ♦ CODA International Training (internationally oriented national body)
- ♦ **CODATA** Committee on Data for Science and Technology (#04247)
- ♦ **CODATU** Coopération pour le développement et l'amélioration des transports urbains et périurbains (#04792)
- ♦ CODE (internationally oriented national body)
- ♦ Codéart – Coopération au développement de l'artisanat (internationally oriented national body)
- ♦ Code Blue (meeting series)
- ♦ Code of Conduct concerning the Repression of Piracy and Armed Robbery against Ships in the Western Indian Ocean and the Gulf of Aden (2009 treaty)
- ♦ Code de conduite de La Haye contre la prolifération des missiles balistiques (treaty)
- ♦ Code européen de sécurité sociale (1964 treaty)
- ♦ Code européen de sécurité sociale, révisé (1990 treaty)
- ♦ CODEFA – Concept pour le Développement du Football Africain (unconfirmed)
- ♦ CODE / see Federation of European Dental Competent Authorities and Regulators (#09501)
- ♦ **CODEGALAC** Comisión de Desarrollo Ganadero para América Latina y el Caribe (#04233)
- ♦ CODEHUCA – Comisión para la Defensa de los Derechos Humanos en Centroamérica (no recent information)
- ♦ **CoDEI** Comité de Dirección Estratégica de los Organismos Iberoamericanos (#04149)
- ♦ Code international de commercialisation des subsituts du lait maternel (1981 treaty)
- ♦ CODE – International Conference on Computational Design in Engineering (meeting series)
- ♦ Code de la normalisation – Accord relatif aux obstacles techniques au commerce (1979 treaty)
- ♦ Code REDD (unconfirmed)
- ♦ Code sanitaire panaméricain (1924 treaty)
- ♦ **CODESRIA** Council for the Development of Social Science Research in Africa (#04879)

♦ Codex Alimentarius Commission (CAC) 04081

Commission du Codex Alimentarius – Comisión del Codex Alimentarius

Sec c/o FAO, Viale delle Terme di Caracalla, 00153 Rome RM, Italy. T. +39657054384. E-mail: codex@fao.org.

URL: http://www.codexalimentarius.org/

History 1962, Rome (Italy), within the framework of *FAO (#09260)* and *WHO (#20950)*, when Statutes and Rules of Procedure established, following recommendations of 11th Session of FAO Conference, 29th Session of WHO Executive Board and a Joint FAO/WHO Conference on Food Standards, to implement the *Joint FAO/WHO Food Standards Programme – Programme mixte FAO/OMS sur les normes alimentaires – Programa Conjunto FAO/OMS sobre Normas Alimentarias.* Statutes revised 1966. Rules of Procedure most recently amended 2015. Also referred to as: *Joint FAO/WHO Codex Alimentarius Commission – Commission mixte FAO/OMS du Codex Alimentarius – Comisión Conjunta FAO/OMS del Codex Alimentarius; ALINORM; FAO/WHO Codex Alimentarius Commission – Commission FAO/OMS du Codex Alimentarius – Comisión FAO/OMS del Codex Alimentarius.* **Aims** Develop harmonized international food standards, which protect consumer health and promote fair practices in food trade. **Structure** Commission (meeting in one regular session annually); Executive Committee; Subsidiary bodies, including: *Joint FAO/WHO Expert Committee on Food Additives (JECFA, #16129).* **Languages** Arabic, Chinese, English, French, Russian, Spanish. **Staff** 18.00 FTE, paid. **Finance** Budget (annual): US$ 4.4 million from budget of *Joint FAO/WHO Food Standards Programme*, administered by FAO on behalf of FAO and WHO, in accordance with the financial regulations of FAO; US$ 3.6 million additional support from governments through hosting of Codex Committees. **Activities** Standards/guidelines; publishing activities. **Events** *Meeting on Antimicrobial Resistance* Goyang (Korea Rep) 2021, *Meeting on Antimicrobial Resistance* Suwon (Korea Rep) 2020, *Session* 2019, *Session* 2019, *Meeting on Antimicrobial Resistance* Pyeongchang (Korea Rep) 2019. **Publications** *Codex Alimentarius Commission* (regular) – session report. Standards; guidelines; codes of practice; advisory texts; meeting reports; documents.

Members Membership open to member nations and associate members of FAO and WHO interested in food standards. Other nations may request or be invited to attend as observers. Current membership: governments of 188 countries which have notified the Directors-General of FAO and WHO of their wish to be considered as members and one Member Organization:

Afghanistan, Albania, Algeria, Angola, Antigua-Barbuda, Argentina, Armenia, Australia, Austria, Azerbaijan, Bahamas, Bahrain, Bangladesh, Barbados, Belarus, Belgium, Belize, Benin, Bhutan, Bolivia, Bosnia-Herzegovina, Botswana, Brazil, Brunei Darussalam, Bulgaria, Burkina Faso, Burundi, Cambodia, Cameroon, Canada, Cape Verde, Central African Rep, Chad, Chile, China, Colombia, Comoros, Congo Brazzaville, Congo DR, Cook Is, Costa Rica, Côte d'Ivoire, Croatia, Cuba, Cyprus, Czechia, Denmark, Djibouti, Dominica, Dominican Rep, Ecuador, Egypt, El Salvador, Equatorial Guinea, Eritrea, Estonia, Eswatini, Ethiopia, Fiji, Finland, France, Gabon, Gambia, Georgia, Germany, Ghana, Greece, Grenada, Guatemala, Guinea, Guinea-Bissau, Guyana, Haiti, Honduras, Hungary, Iceland, India, Indonesia, Iran Islamic Rep, Iraq, Ireland, Israel, Italy, Jamaica, Japan, Jordan, Kazakhstan, Kenya, Kiribati, Korea DPR, Korea Rep, Kuwait, Kyrgyzstan, Laos, Latvia, Lebanon, Lesotho, Liberia, Libya, Lithuania, Luxembourg, Madagascar, Malawi, Malaysia, Maldives, Mali, Malta, Mauritania, Mauritius, Mexico, Micronesia FS, Moldova, Mongolia, Montenegro, Morocco, Mozambique, Myanmar, Namibia, Nauru, Nepal, Netherlands, New Zealand, Nicaragua, Niger, Nigeria, North Macedonia, Norway, Oman, Pakistan, Panama, Papua New Guinea, Paraguay, Peru, Philippines, Poland, Portugal, Qatar, Romania, Russia, Rwanda, Samoa, San Marino, Sao Tomé-Principe, Saudi Arabia, Senegal, Serbia, Seychelles, Sierra Leone, Singapore, Slovakia, Slovenia, Solomon Is, Somalia, South Africa, South Sudan, Spain, Sri Lanka, St Kitts-Nevis, St Lucia, St Vincent-Grenadines, Sudan, Suriname, Sweden, Switzerland, Syrian AR, Tajikistan, Tanzania UR, Thailand, Timor-Leste, Togo, Tonga, Trinidad-Tobago, Tunisia, Türkiye, Turkmenistan, Uganda, UK, Ukraine, United Arab Emirates, Uruguay, USA, Uzbekistan, Vanuatu, Venezuela, Vietnam, Yemen, Zambia, Zimbabwe.

Organizational member:

European Union (EU, #08967).

IGO Relations UN System:

- *International Atomic Energy Agency (IAEA, #12294);*
- *International Trade Centre (ITC, #15703);*
- *Pan American Health Organization (PAHO, #18108);*
- *UNEP (#20299);*
- *UNCTAD (#20285);*
- *UNDP (#20292);*
- *UNIDO (#20336);*
- *United Nations (UN, #20515);*
- *United Nations Economic Commission for Africa (ECA, #20554);*
- *United Nations Economic Commission for Europe (UNECE, #20555);*
- *United Nations Economic Commission for Latin America and the Caribbean (ECLAC, #20556);*
- *United Nations Economic and Social Commission for Asia and the Pacific (ESCAP, #20557);*
- *United Nations Economic and Social Commission for Western Asia (ESCWA, #20558);*
- *World Trade Organization (WTO, #21864).*

Intergovernmental organizations in observer status:

- *Africa Rice Center (AfricaRice, #00518);*
- *Organisation of African, Caribbean and Pacific States (OACPS, #17796);*
- *African Groundnut Council (AGC, #00332);*
- *African Organisation for Standardisation (ARSO, #00404);*
- *African Union (AU, #00488);*
- *Alliance of Cocoa Producing Countries (COPAL, no recent information);*
- *Alliance of Cocoa Producing Countries (COPAL, no recent information);*
- *Alliance of Cocoa Producing Countries (COPAL, no recent information);*
- *Andean Community (#00817);*
- *Arab Industrial Development, Standardization and Mining Organization (AIDSMO, #00981);*
- *Arab Organization for Agricultural Development (AOAD, #01018);*
- *ASEAN (#01141);*
- *International Coconut Community (ICC, #12628);*
- *Bureau international des poids et mesures (BIPM, #03367);*
- *Caribbean Community (CARICOM, #03476);*
- *Caribbean Food and Nutrition Institute (CFNI, inactive);*
- *Comité Regional de Sanidad Vegetal del Cono Sur (COSAVE, #04197);*
- *Common Market for Eastern and Southern Africa (COMESA, #04296);*
- *Community of Sahel-Saharan States (CEN-SAD, #04406);*
- *Council of Europe (CE, #04881);*
- *East African Community (EAC, #05181);*
- *East African Community (EAC, #05181);*
- *Economic Community of West African States (ECOWAS, #05312);*
- *EFTA (#05391);*
- *Eurasian Economic Union (EAEU, #05607);*
- *European and Mediterranean Plant Protection Organization (EPPO, #07773);*
- *Institute of Nutrition of Central America and Panama (INCAP, #11285);*
- *Inter-American Institute for Cooperation on Agriculture (IICA, #11434);*
- *Intergovernmental Authority on Development (IGAD, #11472);*
- *International Cocoa Organization (ICCO, #12627);*
- *International Coffee Organization (ICO, #12630);*
- *International Commission for Food Industries (CIIA, inactive);*
- *International Institute of Refrigeration (IIR, #13918);*
- *International Olive Council (IOC, #14405);*
- *International Organization of Legal Metrology (#14451);*
- *International Organisation of Vine and Wine (OIV, #14435);*
- *International Pepper Community (IPC, #14557);*
- *Latin American Integration Association (LAIA, #16343);*
- *League of Arab States (LAS, #16420);*
- *Nordic-Baltic Committee on Food Analysis (NMKL, #17215);*
- *OAS (#17629);*
- *OECD (#17693);*
- *OIE – World Organisation for Animal Health (#17703);*
- *Organisation africaine et malgache du café (OAMCAF, no recent information);*
- *Pacific Community (SPC, #17942);*
- *Permanent Council of International Convention of Stresa for the Use of Appellations d'Origine and Denominations of Cheeses (no recent information);*
- *Secretaria Permanente del Tratado General de Integración Económica Centroamericana (SIECA, #19195);*
- *Secretaria Permanente del Tratado General de Integración Económica Centroamericana (SIECA, #19195);*
- *Sistema Económico Latinoamericano (SELA, #19294);*
- *South Asian Association for Regional Cooperation (SAARC, #19721);*
- *Southern African Development Community (SADC, #19843);*
- *GCC Standardization Organization (GSO, #10084);*
- *Union économique et monétaire Ouest africaine (UEMOA, #20377);*
- *World Customs Organization (WCO, #21350).*

NGO Relations In liaison with technical committees of: *International Organization for Standardization (ISO, #14473).* Organizations in observer status:

- *Action Against Hunger (#00086);*
- *AgroCare (#00580);*
- *American Oil Chemists' Society (AOCS);*
- *AOAC INTERNATIONAL (#00863);*
- *Asociación Latinoamericana de Avicultura (ALA, #02185);*
- *Asociación Latinoamericana de la Industria Nacional de Agroquimicos (ALINA, #02230);*
- *Association of European Coeliac Societies (AOECS, #02504);*
- *Association of the European Self-Care Industry (#02543);*
- *Association for International Development of Natural Gums (AIDGUM, #02662);*
- *Association for International Promotion of Gums (AIPG, #02759);*
- *Association of Manufacturers and Formulators of Enzyme Products (AMFEP, #02793);*
- *Biotechnology Innovation Organization (BIO);*
- *Bureau Européen des Unions de Consommateurs (BEUC, #03360);*
- *Bureau international des Médecins sans frontières (MSF International, #03366);*
- *Calorie Control Council (CCC);*
- *Centre for Climate Change and Environmental Studies (CCCES);*
- *Cereals and Grains Association (#03830);*
- *COLEACP (#04091);*
- *Collagen Casings Trade Association (CCTA, #04102);*
- *Comité européen des fabricants de sucre (CEFS, #04159);*
- *Comité européen de normalisation (CEN, #04162);*
- *Committee of the Trade in Cereals, Oilseeds, Pulses, Olive Oil, Oils and Fats, Animal Feed and Agrosupply of the EU (COCERAL, #04289);*
- *Conseil européen de l'industrie chimique (CEFIC, #04687);*
- *The Consumer Goods Forum (CGF, #04772);*
- *Consumers International (CI, #04773);*
- *CropLife International (#04966);*
- *CULINARIA EUROPE (#04980);*
- *Enzyme Technical Association (ETA);*
- *EU Specialty Food Ingredients (#09200);*
- *EURACHEM (#05595);*
- *EuroCommerce (EC, #05665);*
- *EUROGLACES – European Ice Cream Association (Euroglaces, #05688);*
- *European Animal Protein Association (EAPA, #05902);*
- *European Association of Polyol Producers (EPA, #06157);*
- *European Cocoa Association (ECA, #06599);*
- *European Committee for Umami (ECU);*
- *European Dairy Association (EDA, #06883);*
- *European Fat Processors and Renderers Association (EFPRA, #07035);*
- *European Federation of Associations of Health Product Manufacturers (EHPM, #07052);*
- *European Federation of Honey Packers and Distributors (#07140);*
- *European Flour Millers' Association (#07272);*
- *European Food Emulsifier Manufacturers' Association (EFEMA, #07281);*
- *European Food and Feed Cultures Association (EFFCA, #07282);*
- *European Food Law Association (EFLA, #07286);*
- *European Plant-Based Foods Association (ENSA, #08210);*
- *European Network of Childbirth Associations (ENCA, #07876);*
- *European Potato Trade Association (EUROPATAT, #08257);*
- *European Salt Producers Association (EUsalt, #08425);*
- *European Society for Paediatric Gastroenterology, Hepatology and Nutrition (ESPGHAN, #08680);*
- *European Specialist Sports Nutrition Alliance (ESSNA, #08810);*
- *European Union Fish Processors Association (#08989);*
- *European Vegetable Protein Association (EUVEPRO, #09047);*
- *Fédération européenne des fabricants d'aliments composés pour animaux (FEFAC, #09566);*
- *FEDIOL – The EU Vegetable Oil and Proteinmeal Industry (#09718);*
- *FIVS (#09789);*
- *Food Industry Asia (FIA);*
- *FoodDrinkEurope (#09841);*
- *FOSFA International (#09935);*
- *Fruit and Vegetable Dispute Resolution Corporation (DRC, #10009);*
- *Global Alliance for Improved Nutrition (GAIN, #10202);*
- *Global Organization for EPA and DHA Omega-3 (GOED, #10517);*
- *Global Pulse Confederation (GPC, #10562);*
- *Global Self-Care Federation (GSCF, #10588);*
- *Grain and Feed Trade Association (GAFTA, #10692);*
- *Greenpeace International (#10727);*
- *Health for Animals (#10870);*
- *Helen Keller International (HKI, #10902);*
- *ICC – International Association for Cereal Science and Technology (#11048);*
- *IFOAM – Organics International (IFOAM, #11105);*
- *Industry Council for Development (ICD, inactive);*
- *Institute of Food Technologists (IFT);*
- *International Accreditation Forum (IAF, #11584);*
- *International Alliance of Dietary Food Supplement Associations (IADSA, #11627);*
- *International Aluminium Institute (IAI, #11643);*
- *International Association of Color Manufacturers (IACM);*
- *International Association of Consumer Food Organizations (IACFO, no recent information);*
- *International Association of Fish Inspectors (IAFI, #11894);*
- *International Baby Food Action Network (IBFAN, #12305);*
- *International Centre of Comparative Environmental Law (#12483);*
- *International Chamber of Commerce (ICC, #12534);*
- *International Chewing Gum Association (ICGA, #12545);*
- *International Commission on Microbiological Specifications for Foods (ICMSF, #12703);*
- *International Commission for Uniform Methods of Sugar Analysis (ICUMSA, #12736);*
- *International Confectionery Association (ICA, #12840);*
- *International Co-operative Alliance (ICA, #12944);*
- *International Council on Amino Acid Science (ICAAS, #12991);*
- *International Council of Beverages Associations (ICBA, #12999);*
- *International Council of Bottled Water Associations (ICBWA, #13001);*
- *International Council of Grocery Manufacturers Associations (ICGMA, #13026);*
- *International Dairy Federation (IDF, #13128);*
- *International Diabetes Federation (IDF, #13164);*
- *International Egg Commission (IEC, #13245);*
- *International Federation of Beekeepers' Associations (APIMONDIA, #13370);*
- *International Federation for Produce Standards (IFPS, #13518);*
- *International Feed Industry Federation (IFIF, #13581);*
- *International Food Additives Council (IFAC);*
- *International Food Authenticity Assurance Organization (IFAAO);*
- *International Food Policy Research Institute (IFPRI, #13622);*
- *International Frozen Food Association (IFFA, #13686);*
- *International Fruit and Vegetable Juice Association (IFU, #13687);*
- *International Glutamate Technical Committee (IGTC, #13722);*
- *International Hydrolyzed Protein Council (IHPC);*
- *International Lactation Consultant Association (ILCA);*
- *International Life Sciences Institute (ILSI, #14044);*
- *International Meat Secretariat (IMS, #14125);*
- *International Nut and Dried Fruit Council Foundation (INC, #14387);*
- *International Organization of the Flavor Industry (IOFI, #14446);*
- *International Organization for Spice Trade Associations (IOSTA);*
- *International Organization for Standardization (ISO, #14473);*
- *International Pectin Producers' Association (IPPA, #14539);*
- *International Poultry Council (IPC, #14628);*
- *International Probiotics Association (IPA, #14645);*
- *International Society of Citriculture (ISC, #15011);*
- *International Special Dietary Food Industries (ISDI, #15576);*

- *International Stevia Council (ISC)*;
- *International Sweeteners Association (ISA, #15639)*;
- *International Union of Food Science and Technology (IUFoST, #15773)*;
- *International Union of Microbiological Societies (IUMS, #15794)*;
- *International Union of Nutritional Sciences (IUNS, #15796)*;
- *International Union of Pure and Applied Chemistry (IUPAC, #15809)*;
- *International Wheat Gluten Association (IWGA)*;
- *Liaison Centre for the Meat Processing Industry in the EU (#16452)*;
- *Liaison Committee of Mediterranean Citrus Producing Countries (CLAM, inactive)*;
- *The Marine Ingredients Organisation (IFFO, #16579)*;
- *Natural Food Colours Association (NATCOL, #16953)*;
- *NSF International*;
- *Oenological Products and Practices (OEnoppia, #17695)*;
- *Organisation des Fabricants de Produits Cellulosiques Alimentaires (OFCA, no recent information)*;
- *Specialised Nutrition Europe (SNE, #19909)*;
- *SSAFE (#19936)*;
- *Working Group on Prolamin Analysis and Toxicity (WGPAT, #21060)*;
- *World Association of Seaweed Processors (MARINALG International, #21185)*;
- *World Federation of Advertisers (WFA, #21407)*;
- *World Obesity (#21678)*;
- *World Processing Tomato Council (WPTC, #21738)*;
- *World Public Health Nutrition Association (WPHNA, #21742)*;
- *World Renderers Association (WRO)*;
- *World Sugar Research Organization (WSRO, #21837)*;
- *World Veterinary Association (WVA, #21901)*. [2020/XE8700/**E***]

♦ CODHO – Comité des observateurs des droits de l'Homme (internationally oriented national body)
♦ CODHy – World Congress on Controversies to Consensus in Diabetes, Obesity and Hypertension (meeting series)
♦ CODIA – Conferencia de Directores Iberoamericanos del Agua (unconfirmed)
♦ **CODICADER** Consejo del Istmo Centroamericano de Deportes y Recreación (#04716)
♦ Codice europeo di sicurezza sociale (1964 treaty)
♦ Codice europeo di sicurezza sociale, riveduto (1990 treaty)
♦ Código internacional de comercialización de substitutos de leche materna (1981 treaty)
♦ Código sanitario panamericano (1924 treaty)
♦ Código sanitario pan-americano (1924 treaty)
♦ CODIP / see The Hague Conference on Private International Law (#10850)
♦ **CODJAJIC** Confederación de Adolescencia y Juventud de Iberoamérica y el Caribe (#04438)
♦ CODMUR – IAGOD Commission on Ore Deposits in Mafic and Ultramafic Rocks (see: #11910)
♦ CoDoCa – Council for Sustainable Development of Central Asia (inactive)
♦ COE – Centro Orientamento Educativo, Barzio (internationally oriented national body)
♦ **COE** Chamber Orchestra of Europe (#03848)
♦ COE – Children of the Earth (internationally oriented national body)
♦ **COE** Les comités olympiques européens (#08083)
♦ **COE** Community of Evaluators in South Asia (#04398)
♦ **COE** Conseil oecuménique des Eglises (#21320)
♦ **COECSA** College of Ophthalmology of Eastern Central and Southern Africa (#04108)
♦ **COEF 5** Communion des oeuvres et des églises dans la francophonie sur les cinq continents (#04387)
♦ COEF 5 International / see Communion des oeuvres et des églises dans la francophonie sur les cinq continents (#04387)
♦ CoEICL – Committee for an Effective International Criminal Law (internationally oriented national body)
♦ CoE / see NGO Forum on Environment (#17125)
♦ COERR – Catholic Office for Emergency Relief and Refugees (internationally oriented national body)
♦ **COESIMA** Coopération européenne des sites majeurs d'accueil (#04795)

♦ Coésio – Destinations Francophone de Congrès 04082

Pres c/o Office de Tourisme, 806 Avenue de Cannes, 06210 Mandelieu-La Napoule, France. T. +33492974832.
SG Bureau des Congrès de Grenoble, 14 rue de la République, 38000 Grenoble, France. T. +33476033756.
URL: http://www.coesiocongres.com/

History Apr 1974, Rouen (France). Founded following preliminary meetings in 1972 and 1973. Former names and other names: *Association internationale des villes francophones de congrès (AIVFC)* – former (1974 to 2018); *International Association of French-Speaking Congress Towns (IAFCT)* – former (1974 to 2018); *Club des congrès de langue française* – former alias. Registration: France. **Aims** Strengthen the natural links which exist between French-speaking towns and regions in a position to organize congresses and rotation of congresses among member towns; assure continuity for organizers of conferences in the French language; promote use of *French language* in international congresses and in general. **Structure** General Assembly; Board of Directors. **Languages** French. **Finance** Members' dues. **Activities** Events/meetings; training/education; research/documentation. **Events** *Forum des Organisateurs* Issy-les-Moulineaux (France) 2019, *Forum des Organisateurs* Paris (France) 2017, *Annual General Assembly* Monte Carlo (Monaco) 2014, *Annual General Assembly* Béziers (France) 2013, *Forum des Utilisateurs des Villes Francophones de Congrès* Paris (France) 2013. **Publications** *File of Francophone Congresses and Associations* (annual).
Members Membership restricted to congress venues capable of accommodating at least 500 participants and organizing at least 15 congresses a year. Congress centres (84) in French-speaking regions in 7 countries:
Andorra, Belgium, Canada, France, Luxembourg, Monaco, Senegal.
NGO Relations Member of: *Association francophone d'amitié et de liaison (AFAL, #02605)*.
[2022/XD5370/**D**]

♦ **CoESS** Confederation of European Security Services (#04532)
♦ **CoESS** Confédération européenne des services de sécurité (#04532)

♦ Coetus Internationalis Ministrantium (CIM) 04083

SG Rue Dewiest 73, 6040 Jumet, Belgium. T. +32496238455.
Pres Trg Slobode 8, PF 98, Zrenjanin, PAK 23001, Serbia. T. +38123534722. Fax +38123528625. E-mail: ordinariatus@yahoo.com.
URL: http://www.minis-cim.net/

History 14 Nov 1960, Altenberg (Germany). 14-16 Nov 1960, Altenberg (German DR). **Aims** Provide contacts between national and diocesan representatives of young *liturgical groups* and *acolytes*; organize the international pilgrimage of altar boys and girls witch takes place every four or five years in Rome. **Events** *General Assembly* Zagreb (Croatia) 2012, *General Assembly* Fatima (Portugal) 2011, *General Assembly* Strasbourg (France) 2010, *General Assembly* Luxembourg (Luxembourg) 2009, *General Assembly* Cluj-Napoca (Romania) 2008.
Members Representatives of groups in 13 countries:
Austria, Belgium, Croatia, France, Germany, Italy, Malta, Poland, Portugal, Romania, Serbia, Spain, Switzerland.
[2019/XF6057/**F**]

♦ A coeur joie international (internationally oriented national body)
♦ CO / see European Cyclists' Federation (#06877)
♦ Coeurs sans frontières / see Euro-Children
♦ COFACE / see COFACE Families Europe (#04084)

♦ COFACE Families Europe 04084

Dir Rue de Londres 17, 1050 Brussels, Belgium. T. +3225114179. Fax +3225144773. E-mail: secretariat@coface-eu.org.
URL: http://www.coface-eu.org/

History 1958, Brussels (Belgium). Founded as a branch of *World Family Organization (WFO, #21399)*. Became more autonomous and set itself up as an independent organization in 1968. In 1979, became legally constituted with emphasis on autonomous and democratic structure, but retaining privileged contacts with IUFO, particularly its European region. Former names and other names: *European Action Committee of the IUFO* – former (1958 to 1968); *Comité d'action européenne de l'UIOF* – former (1958 to 1968); *Committee of Family Organizations in the European Community* – former (1968 to 1979); *Comité des organisations familiales auprès des Communautés européennes* – former (1968 to 1979); *Confederation of Family Organizations in the European Community* – former (1979); *Confédération des organisations familiales de la Communauté européenne* – former (1979); *Confederazione delle Organizzazioni Familiari della Unione Europea* – former; *Confederatie van Gezinsorganisaties in de Europese Unie* – former; *Bund der Familienorganisationen der Europäischen Union* – former; *Confederation of Family Organizations in the European Union* – former; *Confédération des organisations familiales d'Union européenne (COFACE)* – former. Registration: Banque-Carrefour des Entreprises, No/ID: 0420.937.537, Start date: 13 Nov 1980, Belgium; EU Transparency Register, No/ID: 93283396780-85, Start date: 26 Sep 2011. **Aims** Build a Europe more broadly based and permanent than simply a *common market*; represent both *families* and *children* who cannot speak for themselves; safeguard and promote interests of families within the European Union, such that each *household* is free to choose the way it wants to live; promote an EU family policy to provide the social, economic and cultural environment within which families may carry out their human and social responsibilities. **Structure** General Assembly (annual); Administrative Council; Executive Bureau. Secretariat. **Languages** English, French. **Staff** 6.00 FTE, paid. **Finance** Sources: members' dues. Annual budget: 70,000 EUR. **Activities** Events/meetings; knowledge management/information dissemination; projects/programmes; research/documentation. **Events** *General Assembly* Brussels (Belgium) 2021, *General Assembly* Zagreb (Croatia) 2020, *General Assembly* Barcelona (Spain) 2019, *Conference on Child Health and Well-Being* Helsinki (Finland) 2019, *Disability Platform Meeting* Luxembourg (Luxembourg) 2019. **Publications** *COFACE Documents* – series. *COFACE Communiqués* – press-releases. Annual Report.
Members National family organizations (59) in 23 countries:
Austria, Belgium, Bulgaria, Croatia, Cyprus, Finland, France, Germany, Greece, Hungary, Ireland, Italy, Latvia, Luxembourg, Poland, Portugal, Romania, Slovakia, Slovenia, Spain, Sweden, Switzerland, UK.
Consultative Status Consultative status granted from: *ECOSOC (#05331)* (Special). **IGO Relations** Maintains relations with all the institutions of the European Union, particularly through: Consultative Committees of the Common Agricultural Policy; *European Commission (EC, #06633)*; *European Economic and Social Committee (EESC, #06963)*; *European Parliament (EP, #08146)*. Associate member of: *European Consumer Consultative Group (ECCG, #06771)*. **NGO Relations** Member of (8): *European Brain Injury Society (EBIS, #06394)*; *European Disability Forum (EDF, #06929)*; *European Expert Group on the transition from institutional to community-based care (EEG, #07014)*; *European Housing Forum (EHF, #07504)*; *European NGO Platform Asylum and Migration (EPAM, #08051)*; *Permanent Forum of European Civil Society (#18322)*; *SDG Watch Europe (#19162)*; *Social Platform (#19344)* (Associate member). Cooperates with (1): *European Foundation for the Care of Newborn Infants (EFCNI, #07344)*. *Network of European LGBTIQ Families Associations (NELFA, #17021)* is supporting member. [2022/XE0673/**E**]

♦ **COFAHCA** Consejo de Facultades Humanisticas de Centroamérica (#04711)
♦ COFALEC / see Confédération des Fabricants de Levure de l'Union Européenne (#04551)
♦ **COFALEC** Confédération des Fabricants de Levure de l'Union Européenne (#04551)
♦ COFEB – Confédération européenne des fabricants de baignoires (inactive)
♦ COFE – Coalition of Fragile Ecosystems (unconfirmed)
♦ COFE – Council on Forest Engineering (internationally oriented national body)
♦ **COFFI** UNECE Committee on Forests and the Forest Industry (#20294)
♦ COFIDES – Compañia Española de Financiación de Desarrollo (internationally oriented national body)
♦ **COFLAC** Comisión Forestal para America Latina y del Caribe (#16278)
♦ COFLA / see Latin American and Caribbean Forestry Commission (#16278)
♦ COFRASL – Coopération francophone des associations de scoutisme laïque (inactive)
♦ COFTA / see World Fair Trade Organization – Africa (#21397)
♦ **COGECA** Confédération générale des coopératives agricoles de l'Union européenne (#10107)
♦ COGECA – european agri-cooperatives / see General Confederation of Agricultural Cooperatives in the European Union (#10107)
♦ COGECA / see General Confederation of Agricultural Cooperatives in the European Union (#10107)

♦ COGEN Europe 04085

Dir Av des Arts 3/4/5, 1210 Brussels, Belgium. T. +3227728290. Fax +3227725044. E-mail: md@cogeneurope.eu.
Chairman GE Jenbacher GmbH and Co OG, Achenseestrasse 1-3, 6200 Jenbach, Austria. E-mail: info@cogeneurope.eu.
URL: http://www.cogeneurope.eu/

History 1993, as *European Association for the Promotion of Cogeneration*. **Aims** Promote wider use of cogeneration for a *sustainable energy* future in Europe and worldwide. **Structure** Board of Directors. **Languages** English. **Staff** 6.00 FTE, paid. **Activities** Politics/policy/regulatory; events/meetings; knowledge management/information dissemination. **Events** *Annual Conference* Brussels (Belgium) 2020, *Annual Conference* Madrid (Spain) 2019, *Annual Conference* Brussels (Belgium) 2018, *Annual Conference* Brussels (Belgium) 2016, *Annual Conference* Brussels (Belgium) 2013. **Publications** Position papers; press releases; briefing papers; country reports; studies.
Members Businesses, organizations and academic bodies active the European energy sector (over 160). National members in 19 countries:
Austria, Belgium, Croatia, France, Germany, Greece, Hungary, Ireland, Italy, Netherlands, Poland, Portugal, Romania, Serbia, Slovakia, Slovenia, Spain, Türkiye, UK.
Companies and organizations in 28 countries:
Australia, Austria, Belgium, Bulgaria, Croatia, Czechia, Denmark, Finland, France, Germany, Greece, Hungary, Ireland, Italy, Japan, Netherlands, Norway, Poland, Portugal, Romania, Slovakia, Slovenia, Spain, Sweden, Türkiye, UK, Ukraine, USA.
International member:
International District Energy Association (IDEA).
IGO Relations Accredited by: *United Nations Framework Convention on Climate Change – Secretariat (UNFCCC, #20564)*. **NGO Relations** Member of: *Coalition for Energy Savings (#04056)*; *Energy Efficiency Industrial Forum (EEIF, #05470)*; *European Business Council for a Sustainable Energy Future (e5, #06417)*; *World Alliance for Decentralized Energy (WADE, #21081)*. Associate member of: *European Energy Forum (EEF, #06986)*. Associate partner of: *Covenant of Mayors for Climate and Energy (#04939)*. Cooperation agreement with: *European Committee for Electrotechnical Standardization (CENELEC, #06647)*. [2020/XF4040/y/**F**]

♦ **COGENT** Coconut Genetic Resources Network (#04080)
♦ CoGEN – World Congress on Controversies in Preconception, Preimplantation and Prenatal Genetic Diagnosis (meeting series)
♦ COGEODATA / see IUGS Commission on Management and Application of Geoscience Information (#16081)
♦ COGEOINFO / see IUGS Commission on Management and Application of Geoscience Information (#16081)
♦ COGI – World Congress on Controversies in Obstetrics, Gynecology and Infertility (meeting series)

♦ Cognitive Science Society (CSS) 04086

Secretariat c/o Podium Specialists, #124-4730 University Way NE, Ste 104, Seattle WA 98105, USA. E-mail: info@cognitivesciencesociety.org.
URL: http://www.cognitivesciencesociety.org/

History 1979, USA. Registration: USA. **Aims** Promote cognitive science as a discipline; foster scientific interchange among researchers in various areas of study. **Structure** Governing Board. **Activities** Events/meetings. **Events** *Annual Conference* Toronto, ON (Canada) 2022, *Annual Conference* Vienna (Austria) 2021, *Annual Conference* Vienna (Austria) 2020, *Annual Conference* Montréal, QC (Canada) 2019, *Annual Conference* Madison, WI (USA) 2018. **Publications** *Cognitive Science* – journal; *Topics in Cognitive Science (TopiCS)* – journal. [2021/XW1465/**D**]

♦ CoGREE / see Coordinating Group for Religion in Education (#04823)

♦ **CoGREE** Coordinating Group for Religion in Education (#04823)
♦ Cohaglym Celtiagh (#03632)
♦ **COHEHRE** Consortium of Institutes of Higher Education in Health and Rehabilitation in Europe (#04748)

♦ Cohesion Fund 04087

Fonds de cohésion

Contact DG REGIO/02 – Communication, European Commission BU1 0/10, 1049 Brussels, Belgium. T. +3222953258.
URL: http://ec.europa.eu/regional_policy/thefunds/cohesion/index_en.cfm/

History Established 7 Feb 1992, within the framework of *European Communities (EC, inactive) – European Community (inactive)* – and under the terms of the *Treaty on European Union (Maastricht Treaty, 1992)* setting up the *European Union (EU, #08967)*. Normal operations commenced, 16 May 1994, on adoption by *Council of the European Union (#04895)* of the necessary regulation, an interim cohesion instrument having allowed some funding during 1993. Current rules regulated by Regulation (EU) No 1300/2013 of *European Parliament (EP, #08146)* and *Council of the European Union (#04895)*. **Aims** Serve to provide the poorest Member States with a way of developing their infrastructure and meeting EU environmental legislation; working alongside existing Funds, also help beneficiary member states achieve economic convergence with the other *European Union* countries by easing the budgetary constraints associated with their efforts to control budget deficits in accordance with criteria for *economic* and *monetary* union. **Structure** Fund managed by some EU members states and supervised by *European Commission (EC, #06633)* – DG Regional Policy (DG REGIO). **Staff** 650.00 FTE, paid. **Activities** Financial and/or material support. Activities aimed at Member States whose Gross National Income (GNI) per inhabitant is less than 90% of the Community average. Supports projects in 2 domains: trans-European transport network, notably priority projects of European interest; environment, including energy and transport. Projects included: building of key roads and bridges; improvement of rail networks and other public transport modes; expansion of airports; provision of clean drinking water; upgrading treatment of solid waste and waste water. **Publications** *Regio Flash* (12 a year) – electronic newsletter; *Panorama* (4 a year) – brochure.

Members 15 Member States eligible under the Cohesion Fund:
Bulgaria, Croatia, Cyprus, Czechia, Estonia, Greece, Hungary, Latvia, Lithuania, Malta, Poland, Portugal, Romania, Slovakia, Slovenia. [2015.10.05/XK1124/f/**F***]

♦ Cohesive Communities Development Initiative (internationally oriented national body)
♦ COHETA / see Association for Christian Theological Education in Africa (#02431)
♦ **COHETA** Association pour l'Education Théologique Chrétienne en Afrique (#02431)
♦ **COHI** Caribbean Oral Health Initiative (#03534)
♦ COHI – Circle of Health International (internationally oriented national body)
♦ Cohsasa – Council for Health Service Accreditation in Southern Africa (internationally oriented national body)
♦ **COICA** Coordinadora de las Organizaciones Indígenas de la Cuenca Amazónica (#04811)
♦ COIC – Conférence des organisations internationales catholiques (inactive)
♦ COIC – Conferencia de Organizaciones Internacionales Católicas (inactive)
♦ **COICOM** Confederación Iberoamericana de Comunicadores y Medios Masivos Cristianos (#04449)
♦ **COI** Comisión Oceanografica Intergubernamental (#11496)
♦ **COI** Commission de l'Océan Indien (#04236)
♦ **COI** Commission océanographique intergouvernementale (#11496)
♦ **COI** Committee on Information (#04260)
♦ **COI** Conseil oléicole international (#14405)
♦ **COI** Consejo Oleicola Internacional (#14405)
♦ **COI** Consiglio Oleicolo Internazionale (#14405)
♦ COIDIEA – Conseil des organisations internationales directement intéressées à l'enfance et à l'adolescence (inactive)

♦ Coiffure EU 04088

SG Vijfwindgatenstraat 21F, 9000 Ghent, Belgium. T. +3292237124. Fax +3292334219. E-mail: info@coiffure.eu.
URL: http://www.coiffure.eu/

History 21 May 2005, Frankfurt-Main (Germany), as successor to *Confédération européenne des organisations patronales de la coiffure*. **Aims** Promote the interests of member organizations in the field of *hairdressing* artisans and employers in its capacity as a confederation of national employers' organizations. **Structure** General Assembly; Board of Directors. **Languages** English. **Finance** Members' dues.

Members Active; Associate. Members in 20 countries:
Austria, Belgium, Cyprus, Denmark, Finland, France, Germany, Hungary, Ireland, Italy, Lithuania, Luxembourg, Malta, Netherlands, Norway, Poland, Slovenia, Sweden, Switzerland, UK.

IGO Relations *European Commission (EC, #06633)*. **NGO Relations** Member of (2): *Small Business Standards (SBS, #19311)*; *SMEunited (#19327)*. [2017.03.08/XM2718/**D**]

♦ COIL – Congress on Ionic Liquids (meeting series)

♦ Coimbra Group 04089

Groupe Coimbra

Dir c/o Coimbra Group Office, Rue D'Egmont 11, 1000 Brussels, Belgium. T. +3225138332. E-mail: info@coimbra-group.eu.
URL: http://www.coimbra-group.eu/

History 1985, Louvain-la-Neuve (Belgium). Charter drawn up at a meeting, Sep 1987, Pavia (Italy). Structure and organization adopted and approved: Apr 1990; Jun 1991; Jun 1999. Current statutes signed 4 Feb 2002, Brussels (Belgium). New mission statement approved 2011, Padua (Italy). Registration: EU Transparency Register, No/ID: 361887338852-62. **Aims** Create special academic and cultural ties in order to promote, for the benefit of members, internationalization, academic collaboration, excellence in learning and research, and service to society; influence *European education and research* policy; develop best practice through mutual exchange of experience. **Structure** General Assembly (annual); Executive Board; Working Groups (12). **Languages** English, French. **Staff** 4.00 FTE, paid. **Finance** Sources: members' dues. **Activities** Capacity building; events/meetings; networking/liaising; politics/policy/regulatory; projects/programmes; research and development; training/education. **Events** *Annual General Assembly* Padua (Italy) 2022, *Annual General Assembly* 2021, *Annual General Assembly* Brussels (Belgium) 2020, *Annual General Assembly* Krakow (Poland) 2019, *Annual General Assembly* Salamanca (Spain) 2018. **Publications** *Botanical Gardens of the Coimbra Group Universities* (2015); *Negotiating Linguistic Identity: Language and Belonging in Europe* (2014); *Collegiate Learning in the Middle Ages and Beyond* (2012); *Botanical Gardens of the Universities of the Coimbra Group* (2011); *The Forgotten Origins of Universities in Europe* (2011); *Networking across Borders and Frontiers* (2009); *The European Storehouse of Knowledge* (2006); *The Past in the Present – A Multidisciplinary Approach* (2006); *Charters of Foundation and Early Documents of the Universities of the Coimbra Group* (2005); *XX Anniversary Coimbra Group* (2005); *Migration, Minorites, Compensation – Issues of Cultural Identity in Europe* (2001). *Career services in times of Covid-19 – Challenges, Responses and Best Practices* (2021) in English; *PRACTICES AT COIMBRA GROUP UNIVERSITIES IN RESPONSE TO THE COVID-19* (2020) in English. Policy papers.

Members Universities (41) in 23 countries:
Austria, Belgium, Czechia, Denmark, Estonia, Finland, France, Germany, Hungary, Ireland, Italy, Lithuania, Netherlands, Norway, Poland, Portugal, Romania, Russia, Spain, Sweden, Switzerland, Türkiye, UK. [2022.10.19/XE0782/**F**]

♦ An Coimisiún Eorpach (#06633)
♦ COIMR – IAGOD Commission on Industrial Minerals and Rocks (see: #11910)
♦ **COINN** Council of International Neonatal Nurses (#04904)
♦ COINTRA – Coopération internationale des risques aggravés (meeting series)
♦ **COIP** Caribbean Organization of Indigenous Peoples (#03535)
♦ **COIPM** Comité international permanent pour la recherche sur la préservation des matériaux en milieu marin (#18325)
♦ COISTD – Confédération des organisations internationales scientifiques et techniques pour le développement (inactive)
♦ Coiste Eacnamaioch agus Sóisialta na hEorpa (#06963)
♦ Coiste Eorpach na Réigiún (#06665)
♦ **COJE** Conseil oecuménique de la jeunesse en Europe (#05352)
♦ COJEP / see COJEP International – Conseil pour la Justice, l'Egalité et la Paix (#04090)
♦ COJEP France / see COJEP International – Conseil pour la Justice, l'Egalité et la Paix (#04090)
♦ **COJEP International** COJEP International – Conseil pour la Justice, l'Egalité et la Paix (#04090)

♦ COJEP International – Conseil pour la Justice, l'Egalité et la Paix (COJEP International) 04090

Main Office 18 rue du Chemin de Fer, 67200 Strasbourg, France. T. +33388844930. Fax +33388347594. E-mail: cojep.relations.int@gmail.com.
URL: http://cojep.com/

History 1985, France. Former names and other names: *Jeunes Turcs de Belfort* – former; *Fédération nationale des associations omnisports des jeunes Turcs de France* – former; *Conseil de la jeunesse pluriculturelle de France (COJEP France)* – former (1992); *Conseil de la jeunesse pluriculturelle – International (COJEP)* – former (2003). Registration: Start date: 1995, France. **Aims** Work for democracy, prosperity, liberty, human rights, peace and justice, embracing all languages, religions and races worldwide. **Events** *Congress of South East European youth for intercultural dialogue and peace* 2009, *Colloquium on human rights issues in a global world* Geneva (Switzerland) 2009, *Conference on preservation of the cultural heritage in Balkans in post-conflicts periods* Paris (France) 2009, *East-West meeting* Mardin (Turkey) 2008, *Congress of South East European youth for intercultural dialogue and peace* Resen (Macedonia) 2008. **Consultative Status** Consultative status granted from: *ECOSOC (#05331)* (Special); *UNESCO (#20322)* (Consultative Status); *Council of Europe (CE, #04881)* (Participatory Status). **IGO Relations** *European Commission (EC, #06633)*. [2021/XM1545/**E**]

♦ The Coke Club / see Coca-Cola Collectors Club International (#04077)
♦ **COLABIOCLI** Confederación Latinoamericana de Bioquimica Clinica (#04454)
♦ **COLAC** Confederación Latinoamericana de Cooperativas de Ahorro y Crédito (#16302)
♦ The Cola Clan / see Coca-Cola Collectors Club International (#04077)
♦ **COLACOT** Confederación Latinoamericana de Cooperativas y Mutuales de Trabajadores (#04456)
♦ **COLADIC** Consejo Latinoamericano de Estudios de Derecho Internacional y Comparado (#04721)
♦ COLADI / see Consejo Latinoamericano de Estudios de Derecho Internacional y Comparado (#04721)
♦ COLA – International Conference on Laser Ablation (meeting series)
♦ **COLAM** College of the Americas (#04104)
♦ COLAM – Confederación Latinoamericana de Asociaciones de Dirigentes de Empresas (no recent information)
♦ **COLAPOM** Confederación Latinoamericana de Pobladores en la Marginación Social (#04461)
♦ COLATRADE – Comisión Latinoamericana de Trabajadores de la Energia (inactive)
♦ **COL** Commonwealth of Learning (#04346)
♦ COLCS – Chinese and Oriental Languages Computer Society (no recent information)
♦ COLEA / see Coordinadora Latinoamericana de Estudiantes de Arquitectura (#04807)

♦ COLEACP 04091

Head Office 5 Rue de la Corderie, Centra 342, 94586 Rungis CEDEX, France.
Programme Office Rue du Trône 130, 1050 Brussels, Belgium. T. +3225081090. Fax +3225140632.
URL: http://www.coleacp.org/

History 1973, Brussels (Belgium). Former names and other names: *Comité de liaison pour la promotion des fruits tropicaux et légumes de contre-saison originaires des pays africains et malgaches (COLEAMA)* – former; *Comité de liaison pour la promotion des fruits tropicaux et des légumes de contre-saison originaires des Etats ACP* – former; *Comité de liaison EEC – Afrique – Caraïbes – Pacifique pour la promotion des fruits tropicaux, légumes de contre-saison, fleurs, plantes ornementales et épices* – former; *Liaison Committee for the Promotion of Tropical Fruits and Off-Season Vegetables Exported from ACP States* – former; *Comité de liaison Europe – Afrique – Caraïbes – Pacifique pour la promotion des exportations horticoles ACP (COLEACP)* – former; *Comité de liaison Europe – Afrique – Caraïbes – Pacifique pour la promotion des fruits tropicaux, légumes de contre-saison, fleurs, plantes ornementales et épices* – former; *Liaison Committee Europe – Africa – Caribbean – Pacific for the promotion of ACP Horticultural Exports* – former. **Aims** Harmonize relations between producers and exporters of the African, Caribbean and Pacific States and the importers of fresh or processed fruit and vegetables, and of *flowers* and plants. **Structure** General Assembly; Council. **Finance** Members' dues. Additional source: *European Development Fund (EDF, #06914)*. **Activities** Trade information; partnership programmes; pesticides. **Events** *General Assembly* Rungis (France) 2006, *Annual ACP/EC trade conference / Annual ACP EC Trade Conference* Port-of-Spain (Trinidad-Tobago) 1997, *Annual ACP/EEC trade conference / Annual ACP EC Trade Conference* Addis Ababa (Ethiopia) 1995, *Annual ACP/EEC trade conference / Annual ACP EC Trade Conference* Yaoundé (Cameroon) 1994, *Annual ACP EC Trade Conference* Dar es Salaam (Tanzania UR) 1993.

Members ACP producers and exporters; European importers, EU or ACP carriers, forwarding agents and specialized bodies. Institutions and trade associations professionally involved in ACP/EU trade in horticultural produce in 92 countries (77 ACP and 15 EU):
Angola, Antigua-Barbuda, Austria, Bahamas, Barbados, Belgium, Belize, Benin, Botswana, Burkina Faso, Burundi, Cameroon, Cape Verde, Central African Rep, Chad, Comoros, Congo Brazzaville, Congo DR, Cook Is, Côte d'Ivoire, Denmark, Djibouti, Dominica, Dominican Rep, Equatorial Guinea, Eritrea, Eswatini, Ethiopia, Fiji, Finland, France, Gabon, Gambia, Germany, Ghana, Greece, Grenada, Guinea, Guinea-Bissau, Guyana, Haiti, Ireland, Italy, Jamaica, Kenya, Kiribati, Lesotho, Liberia, Luxembourg, Madagascar, Malawi, Mali, Marshall Is, Mauritania, Mauritius, Micronesia FS, Mozambique, Namibia, Nauru, Netherlands, Niger, Nigeria, Niue, Palau, Papua New Guinea, Portugal, Rwanda, Samoa, Sao Tomé-Principe, Senegal, Seychelles, Sierra Leone, Solomon Is, Somalia, South Africa, Spain, St Kitts-Nevis, St Lucia, St Vincent-Grenadines, Sudan, Suriname, Sweden, Tanzania UR, Togo, Tonga, Trinidad-Tobago, Tuvalu, Uganda, UK, Vanuatu, Zambia, Zimbabwe.

IGO Relations Participates as observer in the activities of: *Codex Alimentarius Commission (CAC, #04081)*; *United Nations Economic Commission for Europe (UNECE, #20555)*. [2020/XE6093/**E**]

♦ COLEAMA / see COLEACP (#04091)
♦ Colección de Estudios Latinoamericanos / see Caribbean and Latin American Studies Library
♦ Colectivo Internacional en Apoyo al Pescador Artesanal (#12639)
♦ Colectivo Internacional de Apoyo a los Pescadores Artesanales / see International Collective in Support of Fishworkers (#12639)
♦ Colegio de Abogados Penal Internacional (#13107)
♦ Colegio de las Américas (#04104)
♦ Colégio das Américas (#04104)

♦ Colegio de Compositores Latinoamericanos de Música de Arte 04092

Association of Latin American Composers of Art Music

Pres Universidad Simón Bolívar, Apartado 89000, Cable Unibolivar, Caracas 1010 DF, Venezuela.
Founder Cerro de la Luz 199, Colonia Romero de Terreros, 04310 Coyoacan CHIS, Mexico.
URL: http://www.colegiocompositores-la.org/

History 12 Mar 1999. Established on the initiative of Manuel de Elias.

Members Full; Honorary; Associate; Corresponding. Full (28) in 14 countries:
Argentina, Bolivia, Brazil, Chile, Colombia, Costa Rica, Cuba, El Salvador, Guatemala, Mexico, Peru, Puerto Rico, Uruguay, Venezuela.
Honorary (3) in 3 countries:
Chile, Cuba, Panama.
Associate (1) in 1 country:
Argentina.
Corresponding (4) in 4 countries:
Brazil, Colombia, Ecuador, Mexico. [2021/XJ7898/**D**]

♦ Colegio Ibero-Americano de Reumatologia (#11020)

♦ Colegio Ibero-Latinoamericano de Dermatologia (CILAD) 04093

Ibero-Latin American College of Dermatology – Collège ibéro-latinoaméricain de dermatologie

SG Av Belgrano 1217, Piso 10 Of 104, C1093AAA Buenos Aires, Argentina. E-mail: cilad@cilad.org.
URL: http://www.cilad.org/

History 11 Apr 1948, Havana (Cuba). Re-established 1959, Lisbon (Portugal). **Aims** Promote scientific exchanges and friendly contacts between Spanish or Portuguese-speaking Ibero-Latin American dermatologists. **Structure** Congress (every 2 years). Executive Committee, consisting of President, Vice-Presidents, Secretary-General/Treasurer, Assistant Secretary-General and Editorial Director. **Languages** Portuguese, Spanish. **Staff** Voluntary. **Finance** Members' dues. **Activities** Secures scholarships for specialist studies in other countries; promotes regional meetings. **Events** *Biennial Congress* Buenos Aires (Argentina) 2016, *Symposium* Caracas (Venezuela) 2014, *Biennial Congress* Rio de Janeiro (Brazil) 2014, *Symposium* Santa Cruz (Bolivia) 2014, *Biennial Congress* Seville (Spain) 2012. **Publications** *Medicina Cutanea Ibero-Latinoamericana* (4 a year) in Portuguese, Spanish. Monographs. Congress reports.
Members Doctors specializing in dermatology and allied field (about 1,800) in 26 countries:
Argentina, Bolivia, Brazil, Chile, Colombia, Costa Rica, Cuba, Dominican Rep, Ecuador, El Salvador, France, Guatemala, Haiti, Honduras, Italy, Mexico, Nicaragua, Panama, Paraguay, Peru, Portugal, Puerto Rico, Spain, Uruguay, USA, Venezuela.
NGO Relations Member of: *International League of Dermatological Societies (ILDS, #14018).*
[2014/XD1018/v/**D**]

- ♦ Colegio Interamericano de Defensa (#11426)
- ♦ Colegio Interamericano de Médicos y Cirujanos (#11408)
- ♦ Colegio Interamericano de Radiologia (#11409)
- ♦ Colegio Internacional de Cirujanos (#12650)
- ♦ Colegio Internacional de Medicina Psicosomatica (#12649)
- ♦ Colegio Internacional de Médicos Nucleares (#12646)
- ♦ Colegio Latinoamericano de Neuropsicofarmacologia (unconfirmed)
- ♦ Colégio Latinoamericano de Oftalmologistas Veterinarios (#04094)

♦ Colegio Latinoamericano de Oftalmólogos Veterinarios (CLOVE) . . . 04094

Colégio Latinoamericano de Oftalmologistas Veterinarios
Contact address not obtained. E-mail: secretario@cloveonline.org.
URL: https://cloveonline.com/
History 9 Jun 2000, Rio de Janeiro (Brazil). Originated in *Sociedad Latinoamericana de Oftalmologia Veterinaria (SOLOVE)*, set up 8 Oct 1992, Santiago (Chile). Registration: No/ID: 1553064, Start date: 13 Nov 2000, Brazil. **Structure** Board of Directors; Commissions. **Languages** Portuguese, Spanish. **Activities** Certification/accreditation; events/meetings. **Events** *Congress* Medellin (Colombia) 2019, *Congress* Brasilia (Brazil) 2017, *Congress* Concepción (Chile) 2015, *Congress* Porlamar (Venezuela) 2013, *Congress* Argentina 2011. **Members** Individuals (32). Membership countries not specified. [2021/XJ9073/**D**]

- ♦ Colegio del Mundo Unido del Adriatico (internationally oriented national body)
- ♦ Colegio del Mundo Unido de Africa del Sur Waterford Kamhlaba (internationally oriented national body)
- ♦ Colegio del Mundo Unido del Atlantico / see UWC Atlantic College
- ♦ Colegio del Mundo Unido del Pacifico Lester B Pearson (internationally oriented national body)
- ♦ Colegio del Mundo Unido del Sudeste Asiatico (internationally oriented national body)
- ♦ Colegio Universitario Henry Dunant (#04111)
- ♦ COLIPA / see Cosmetics Europe – The Personal Care Association (#04852)
- ♦ COLIPED – Association of the European Two-Wheeler Parts' and Accessories' Industry (inactive)
- ♦ **COLIPS** Chinese and Oriental Languages Information Processing Society (#03891)
- ♦ CoLIS – Conceptions of Library and Information Science Conference (meeting series)
- ♦ COLISEE – Comité de solidarité avec l'Europe de l'Est (internationally oriented national body)
- ♦ Collaboration on International ICT Policy-Making for East and Southern Africa (internationally oriented national body)
- ♦ Collaboration médicale au tiers-monde / see Solidarité et coopération médicale au Tiers-monde
- ♦ Collaboration of Railway Police and Security Services (#04096)
- ♦ Collaboration Researchers International Working Group (unconfirmed)

♦ Collaboration Researchers International Working Group (CRIWG) . . 04095

Address not obtained.
URL: http://www.criwg.org/
History 1995. **Aims** Support the Conference on Collaboration and Technology which seeks scientific and engineering papers that inform the design, development, deployment, and use of groupware and the work practices they support. **Structure** Steering Committee. **Activities** Events/meetings. **Events** *International Conference on Collaboration and Technology* Lisbon (Portugal) 2018. [2018/XM7825/c/**E**]

- ♦ Collaboration santé internationale (internationally oriented national body)

♦ Collaboration des services de police ferroviaire et de sécurité (COLPOFER) 04096

Collaboration of Railway Police and Security Services – Zusammenarbeit der Bahnpolizei- und Sicherheitsdienste
Secretariat c/o Ferrovie dello Stato, Piazza della Croce Rossa 1, 00161 Rome RM, Italy. T. +39644102580. Fax +39644106410. E-mail: colpofer@fsitaliane.it.
URL: http://www.colpofer.org/
History 1980. A special group of *International Union of Railways (#15813).* **Aims** Promote policy measures to improve the *protection* of persons, installations, objects and valuables on railway premises through the development and strengthening of cooperation between the railway police or the responsible authorities and the railway security services, respecting the responsibilities of the members. **Structure** General Assembly (twice a year); Board; Working Groups. **Languages** English, French, German. **Finance** Sources: members' dues. **Events** *General Assembly* 2021, *General Assembly* Helsinki (Finland) 2020, *General Assembly* Prague (Czechia) 2019, *World forum on security in the railways* Marseille (France) 2004.
Members Railway companies and railway police authorities (32), in 24 countries:
Austria, Belgium, Bosnia-Herzegovina, Croatia, Czechia, Finland, France, Hungary, Italy, Latvia, Lithuania, Luxembourg, Netherlands, Poland, Portugal, Romania, Russia, Serbia, Slovakia, Slovenia, Spain, Sweden, Switzerland, UK.
[2021/XF5593/**F**]

- ♦ Collaboration on University Management – a Bridge between Universities and Scholars in Europe and Latin America / see Institutional Development Programme between European and Latin American Universities (#11316)

♦ Collaborative Africa Budget Reform Initiative (CABRI) 04097

Exec Sec Southdowns Ridge Office Park, Cnr John Vorster and Nellmapius Drive, Centurion, 0062, South Africa. T. +27124920022. E-mail: info@cabri-sbo.org.
URL: http://www.cabri-sbo.org/
History 2004, Maputo (Mozambique). Initially launched as an informal network, 2004. Officially launched 14 May 2008, Maputo (Mozambique). Became a legal and independent membership based organization, 3 Dec 2009, on entering into force of 'International Agreement'. **Aims** Work with African finance and budget ministries to develop and implement reforms that lead to more functional public financial management systems. **Structure** General Assembly. Management Committee. Secretariat. **Languages** English, French, Portuguese. **Staff** 20.00 FTE, paid. **Finance** Members' dues. Donor funding. **Activities** Networking/liaising; knowledge management/information dissemination; capacity building. **Publications** *CABRI Newsletter.* Reports; policy briefs; position papers; case studies; budgets.
Members Governments of 16 countries:
Benin, Burkina Faso, Central African Rep, Côte d'Ivoire, Gambia, Ghana, Guinea, Kenya, Lesotho, Liberia, Mali, Mauritius, Nigeria, Rwanda, Senegal, South Africa.
IGO Relations Collaborates with: *African Development Bank (ADB, #00283); African Union (AU, #00488); International Bank for Reconstruction and Development (IBRD, #12317)* (World Bank); *International Monetary Fund (IMF, #14180); OECD (#17693); United Nations Economic Commission for Africa (ECA, #20554).*
[2019.02.13/XJ6564/**D***]

♦ Collaborative Intergovernmental Scientific Research Institute (CISRI) 04098

Institut pour la coopération intergouvernementale dans la recherche scientifique
SG Via Bonomelli 1, 28100 Novara NO, Italy. T. +3332130340. E-mail: secretary.general@cisri.org.
Contact 144 B-Nord Tevragh Zeina, Nouakchott, Mauritania.
URL: http://www.cisri.org/
History 20 Nov 2000, Rome (Italy). Founded by multilateral agreement and endorsed with Headquarters agreement with Republic of Mauritania, 17 March 2014. **Aims** Conduct study and research focused on international cooperation matters, especially in the field of development of new *agricultural* techniques and *food micro-algae* in new developing countries. **Structure** General Council; Secretariat, headed by Secretary-General; Subsidiary body: *'Intergovernmental Spirulina Programme'.* **Languages** English, French, Spanish. **Activities** Humanitarian/emergency aid; projects/programmes; training/education. Africa and South America. **Publications** *CISRI Bulletin* (4 a year). *The Manual of Humanitarian Aid* (2000) – Edited by CISRI/IEMO Joint Secretariat.
Members Full in 12 countries:
Benin, Burundi, Cameroon, Congo DR, Equatorial Guinea, Gambia, Guinea, Honduras, Madagascar, Mauritania, Sao Tomé-Principe, Somalia.
IGO Relations Observer status with (3): *Common Market for Eastern and Southern Africa (COMESA, #04296); ECOSOC (#05331); UNIDO (#20336).* Member of (1): *Intergovernmental Organizations Conference (IGO Conference, #11498).* Registration by Multilateral Agreement Registered with *United Nations (UN, #20515)* Secretariat, June 2001. [2021.10.22/XE4343/j/**E***]

♦ Collaborative International Pesticides Analytical Council (CIPAC) . . 04099

Commission internationale des méthodes d'analyse des pesticides (CIMAP) – Consejo Internacional para la Colaboración en los Analisis de Plaguicidas (CICAP)
Sec 17 Claygate Avenue,, Herts, AL5 2HE, Harpenden, AL5 2HE, UK. E-mail: cipac@agroscope.admin.ch.
URL: http://www.cipac.org/
History Sep 1957, Hamburg (Germany). Founded at 4th International Congress of Crop Protection. Registration: Companies Act, No/ID: 980476, Start date: 1970, UK. **Aims** Organize collaborative work on methods of analysis for determining the chemical composition and physical properties of materials and their formulations used in crop protection, *insecticides, fungicides, herbicides, rodenticides,* attractants and repellents; promote international agreement on methods for correlating biological efficacy with chemical and physical tests (methods for residue analysis are expressly excluded). **Structure** Annual Meeting. Officers, elected for 2 years: Chairman; Treasurer; Secretary; Assistant Secretary. Regional Centres (3): *Eastern and Southern Africa Centre of International Parasite Control (ESACIPAC, #05250); West African Centre for International Parasite Control (WACIPAC, #20872).* **Languages** English, French. **Staff** None. **Finance** Sources: sale of publications. **Activities** Events/meetings; monitoring/evaluation; research and development; research/documentation. **Events** *Annual Meeting* 2022, *Annual Meeting* 2021, *Virtual Meeting* 2020, *Annual Meeting* Geneva (Switzerland) 2020, *Annual Meeting* Braunschweig (Germany) 2019. **Publications** *CIPAC Handbook* – 10 vols to date; *CIPAC Monographs.*
Members Full in 24 countries:
Belgium, China, Cyprus, Czechia, Denmark, Egypt, El Salvador, France, Germany, Greece, Hungary, Italy, Japan, Netherlands, Portugal, Romania, South Africa, Spain, Switzerland, Thailand, Tunisia, UK, Ukraine, USA.
Consultative Status Consultative status granted from: *ECOSOC (#05331)* (Ros C); *FAO (#09260)* (Special Status); *UNIDO (#20336).* **IGO Relations** Formal contacts with: *WHO (#20950).* **NGO Relations** In liaison with technical committees of: *International Organization for Standardization (ISO, #14473).* Formal contacts with: *AOAC INTERNATIONAL (#00863); CropLife International (#04966); International Union of Pure and Applied Chemistry (IUPAC, #15809).* [2021.02.23/XC0278/**C**]

- ♦ Collaborative Labeling and Appliance Standards Program / see CLASP (#03979)

♦ Collaborative Partnership on Forests (CPF) 04100

Secretariat c/o UNFF Secretariat, 2 United Nations Plaza, CD2-2301, New York NY 10017, USA. T. +12129633401. Fax +19173673186. E-mail: cpf@un.org.
URL: http://www.cpfweb.org/
History Jul 1995, Geneva (Switzerland), as *Inter-Agency Task Force on Forests (ITFF)* by *United Nations Commission on Sustainable Development (CSD, inactive).* Present name adopted Apr 2001, following recommendations of *ECOSOC (#05331).* **Aims** Facilitate collaboration and communication between CPF and other partners; provide a platform for international and regional organizations, non-governmental organizations, indigenous peoples' organizations, private sector entities and other major groups to channel their support for the work of UNFF and to enhance cooperation. **Structure** Secretariat hosted by UNFF; chaired by FAO. **Activities** Reports annually to *United Nations Forum on Forests (UNFF, #20562)* on progress and plans of CPF and its member organizations, focusing on implementation of proposals for action of the *'Intergovernmental Panel on Forests'* and *'Intergovernmental Forum on Forests'.* CPF and member organizations: provide information and technical assistance to countries; facilitate regional and international initiatives; identify and mobilize financial resources; strengthen political support for sustainable forest management; prepare documentation for UNFF sessions; support intersessional activities of UNFF; second staff to the UNFF Secretariat. Joint initiatives: *'CPF Sourcebook on Funding Sustainable Forest Management'; 'CPF Task Force on Streamlining Forest-Related Reporting';* initiative on forest-related definitions. **Events** *Global Landscapes Forum* Paris (France) 2015, *Global Landscapes Forum* Warsaw (Poland) 2013.
Members International forest-related organizations, institutions and convention secretariats (14), listed in this Yearbook:
Center for International Forestry Research (CIFOR, #03646); FAO (#09260); Global Environment Facility (GEF, #10346); International Bank for Reconstruction and Development (IBRD, #12317) (World Bank); *International Tropical Timber Organization (ITTO, #15737); International Union for Conservation of Nature and Natural Resources (IUCN, #15766); International Union of Forest Research Organizations (IUFRO, #15774); Secretariat of the Convention on Biological Diversity (SCBD, #19197); Secretariat of the United Nations Convention to Combat Desertification (Secretariat of the UNCCD, #19208); UNDP (#20292); UNEP (#20299);* UNFF Secretariat; *United Nations Framework Convention on Climate Change – Secretariat (UNFCCC, #20564); World Agroforestry Centre (ICRAF, #21072).*
IGO Relations *United Nations Collaborative Programme on Reducing Emissions from Deforestation and Forest Degradation in Developing Countries (UN-REDD Programme, #20528).* [2013/XE3727/y/**E***]

♦ Collaborative Working Group on Solid Waste Management in Low- and Middle-income Countries (CWG) 04101

Sec c/o Skat, Vadianstrasse 42, 9000 St Gallen, Switzerland. T. +41712285454. Fax +41712285455. E-mail: cwg@skat.ch.
URL: http://www.cwgnet.net/
History as an informal network without legal status. Original framework following workshop 1995, Ittingen (Switzerland). **Aims** Achieve fundamental improvements in the approach to solid waste management in low-and middle-income countries, focusing in particular in improved livelihoods and living conditions for the urban poor. **Structure** Executive Team/CoreGroup of 8 members; Secretariat. **Languages** English, French. **Activities** Events/meetings; guidance/assistance/consulting; knowledge management/information dissemination; networking/liaising. **Events** *Waste governance – sharing burdens, sharing benefits* Istanbul (Turkey) 2011, *Capacity development and advocacy for improved solid waste and resource management* Ouagadougou (Burkina Faso) 2008, *Building sustainable livelihoods – economic aspects of informal sector activities in solid waste management* Gouda (Netherlands) 2007, *Solid waste, health and the millennium development goals* Kolkata (India) 2006, *Workshop* Dar es Salaam (Tanzania UR) 2003. **Publications** *CWG Publication Series.* **Members** No formal membership. **NGO Relations** *Asociación Centroamericana para la Economia, la Salud y el Ambiente (ACEPESA)* is a member. [2021/XJ2206/**F**]

- ♦ CollabTech – International Conference on Collaboration Technologies and Social Computing (meeting series)

♦ Collagen Casings Trade Association (CCTA) 04102

Contact c/o Beiten Burkhardt, Avenue Louise 489, 1050 Brussels, Belgium. E-mail: info@collagencasings.org.
URL: http://www.collagencasings.org/

Aims Advance members' common interests by representing the industry effectively in legislative and administrative matters. **Structure** Management Committee. Sub-committees (2): Food safety and regulatory affairs; Alternative Casings.
Members Full in 5 countries:
Japan, Poland, Spain, UK, USA.
IGO Relations Observer to: *Codex Alimentarius Commission (CAC, #04081).* [2017/XM7041/t/C]

- ♦ Colleagues in Jesuit Business Education (internationally oriented national body)
- ♦ Collectif d'échanges pour la technologie appropriée (internationally oriented national body)
- ♦ Collectif espérantiste communiste / see International Communist Esperantist Collective (#12819)
- ♦ Collectif espérantiste communiste internationale (#12819)
- ♦ Collectif interafricain des habitants (internationally oriented national body)
- ♦ Collectif international d'appui à la pêche artisanale / see International Collective in Support of Fishworkers (#12639)
- ♦ Collectif international d'appui aux travailleurs de la pêche (#12639)
- ♦ Collectif de recherche et d'information sur l'Afrique australe / see Centre de recherche – information – action pour le développement en Afrique
- ♦ Collectif Stratégies Alimentaires (internationally oriented national body)
- ♦ Collectif Tiers-Monde de Poitiers / see Organization for the Research, Communication and Action to further the Sustainable Development between North and South
- ♦ Collection of Bills Agreement (1984 treaty)
- ♦ Collection of Maintenance Allowances (1931 treaty)

♦ Collective Security Treaty Organization (CSTO) 04103

Organisation du Traité de sécurité collective (OTSC)

Address not obtained.
URL: https://en.odkb-csto.org/

History 14 May 2002. Established by decision of the countries of *Traité de Sécurité Collective de la CEI (Traité de Tachkent, 1992)* and as transformation of that Treaty. Develops from previous efforts under the Treaty to set up a *Military Union of the Commonwealth of Independent States*, proposed 16 Mar 1994, Moscow (Russia), by representatives of *Commonwealth of Independent States (CIS, #04341)*, to complement *Inter-State Economic Committee of the Economic Union of the Commonwealth of Independent States (ISEC, no recent information).*
Members Governments of 7 countries:
Armenia, Belarus, Kazakhstan, Kyrgyzstan, Russia, Tajikistan, Uzbekistan.
IGO Relations Permanent Observer to: *ECOSOC (#05331).* Observer member of: *Eurasian Group on Combating Money Laundering and Financing of Terrorism (EAG, #05608).* Observer to General Assembly of: *United Nations (UN, #20515).* **NGO Relations** Cooperates with: *International Federation for Peace and Conciliation (IFPC, #13501); PfP Consortium of Defence Academies and Security Studies Institutes (#18345).* [2021/XJ9199/E*]

- ♦ College of African Wildlife Management, Mweka (internationally oriented national body)
- ♦ College of African Wildlife Management Parks / see College of African Wildlife Management, Mweka
- ♦ Collège américain de médecine thoracique (#00778)

♦ College of the Americas (COLAM) 04104

Collège des Amériques – Colegio de las Américas – Colégio das Américas

Pres Universidad Veracruzana, Lomas del estadio s/n, Edificio A 3er piso, Xalapa, 91000 Veracruz CHIS, Mexico. T. +522288421763 – +522288421762. Fax +522288176370. E-mail: rarias@uv.mx.
Exec Dir a/c Université de Montréal, Bureau 592, CP 6128, succ Centre-ville, Montréal QC H3C 3J7, Canada. T. +15143436980. Fax +15143436454.
Street Address Université de Montréal, 3774 rue Jean-Brillant – local 592, Montréal QC H3T 1P1, Canada.
URL: http://www.oui-iohe.org/webcolam/

History 12 Nov 1997, Brazil. 12 Nov 1997, Salvador de Bahia (Brazil), at biennial congress of *Inter-American Organization for Higher Education (IOHE, #11442)*, as an IOHE programme. **Aims** Contribute to the strengthening of democracy in the continent; promote intercultural understanding; improve the quality and the relevance of university programs in fields of continental interest; encourage research on continental integration; support cooperation between universities and civil society. **Structure** Executive Council, comprising administrators and faculty of IOHE member universities selected on a regionally representative basis. Advisory Council. Administrative Office in Montréal (Canada). Executive Director; Administrative Director. **Finance** IOHE members' contributions. Support from: *Canadian International Development Agency (CIDA, inactive)*; other institutions, governments, agencies and beneficiaries. *'College of the Americas Development Fund'* comprised of members' contributions. **Activities** Promotes: the creation of Inter-American Networks for training and research on themes of continental interest; the establishment of regional centers for the use of distance education and information and communication technologies; the organization of Interamerica Seminars on hemispheric or regional issues for students from various countries and with differing backgrounds. **Events** *Congress on international quality and accreditation in higher distance education* Loja (Ecuador) 2005, *Capacity building workshop* Helsinki (Finland) 2001, *Interamerica seminar on comparative urban planning* Buenos Aires (Argentina) 1999, *Interamerica seminar on women and democracy* Ottawa, ON (Canada) / Kingston, ON (Canada) 1999, *Meeting* Montréal, QC (Canada) 1998. **Publications** *COLAM Newsletter.* Reports. **Members** Member universities of IOHE. **NGO Relations** *Inter-American Centre for Studies on Water Resources (#11404); Inter-American Distance Education Consortium (#11428); Red Interamericana para el Mejoramiento de la Calidad Ambiental (RICA, no recent information).* [2019/XD5959/E]

- ♦ Collège des Amériques (#04104)
- ♦ Collège des chirurgiens de l'Afrique de l'Ouest / see West African College of Surgeons (#20876)
- ♦ College Consortium for International Studies (internationally oriented national body)
- ♦ Collège de défense de l'OTAN (#16944)
- ♦ Collège des études juives (internationally oriented national body)
- ♦ Collège d'Europe (#04105)

♦ College of Europe 04105

Collège d'Europe – Europacollege

Rector Dijver 11, 8000 Bruges, Belgium. T. +3250477111. Fax +3250477110. E-mail: rector@coleurope.eu – communications@coleurope.eu – info@coleurope.eu.
Vice-Rector – Natolin Ul Nowoursynowska 84, Box 120, 02-797 Warsaw, Poland. T. +48225459405. Fax +48226491352.
URL: http://www.coleurope.eu/

History 1949, Bruges (Belgium). Established following resolution, 8-12 Dec 1949, Lausanne (Switzerland), of *'European Cultural Conference'*, organized by *'Research Office for a European Cultural Centre'*, until 2001 *European Centre for Culture (ECC, #06472).* After an experimental session in 1949, programmes were fully launched in 1950. The first institute of European postgraduate studies. Former names and other names: *Europae Collegium* – alias; *Institute of European Postgraduate Studies* – alias. Registration: Banque-Carrefour des Entreprises, Belgium. **Aims** Educate *university graduates* in a way which enables them to function efficiently as leaders in today's European and international affairs environments, in both public and private sectors. **Structure** Administrative Council; Executive Committee; Academic Council;. Locations: Bruges (Belgium) campus; Natolin (Poland) campus, founded Sep 1992 and established permanently in 1994. Includes: *European Training Centre for Railways (ETCR)*; Global Competition Law Centre (GCLC). **Languages** English, French. **Staff** Bruges (Belgium) campus – 152 staff and 210 permanent and visiting professors; Natolin (Poland) campus – 18 staff and 87 visiting professors. **Finance** Sources: national regional and European Union contributions, including student scholarships. **Activities** Events/meetings; knowledge management/information dissemination; research/documentation; training/education. **Events** *Conference on Democracy and Human Rights in the Digital Age* Bruges (Belgium) 2020, *Conference on Sustainability and Competition Policy : Bridging two Worlds to Enable a Fairer Economy* Brussels (Belgium) 2019, *Conference on the EU-China Digital Connectivity* Brussels (Belgium) 2019, *Conference on Trade Policy* Bruges (Belgium) 2013, *Conference on comparing the European Union with other regional organisations* Brussels (Belgium) 2010. **Publications** *College of Europe E-News*; *Collegium* – academic journal. *College of Europe Studies Series.* **Members** National selection committees in 20 countries:
Czechia, Denmark, France, Germany, Greece, Hungary, Ireland, Italy, Latvia, Lithuania, Luxembourg, Malta, Norway, Poland, Portugal, Spain, Sweden, Switzerland, Türkiye, UK.
NGO Relations Ex-students organization: *Association of Alumni of the College of Europe (#02365).* Associate member of: *Trans European Policy Studies Association (TEPSA, #20209).* Member of: *International Forum on Diplomatic Training (IFDT, #13634); University Network of the European Capitals of Culture (UNeECC, #20701).* Library is a member of: *Eurolib (#05703).* Supporting member of: *European Movement International (EMI, #07825).* Partner in: *European Health Parliament (EHP, #07459).* Cooperates with *International Committee of the Red Cross (ICRC, #12799); UNU Institute on Comparative Regional Integration Studies (UNU-CRIS, #20717).* Instrumental in setting up: *Raymond Lemaire International Centre for the Conservation of Historic Towns and Buildings (RLICC).* [2023.02.14/XF2314/y/F]

- ♦ College of Europe Alumni / see Association of Alumni of the College of Europe (#02365)
- ♦ Collège européen des chirurgiens (inactive)
- ♦ Collège européen de neuropsycho-pharmacologie / see European College of Neuropsychopharmacology (#06612)

♦ Collège européen d'orthodontie (CEO) 04106

European Orthodontics College

Contact c/o Colloquium, 2-8 rue Gaston Rebuffat, 75019 Paris, France. E-mail: miquelse@wanadoo.fr.
URL: http://www.ceortho.fr/

History 1967, by Roger X O'Meyer (1911-1987). **Events** *Congrès* Nantes (France) 2019, *Congress* Ischia (Italy) 2006, *Meeting* Stockholm (Sweden) 2004, *Réunion* Angers (France) 1995, *Réunion internationale* Paris (France) 1994. **Publications** *Edgewise Journal*; *International Orthodontics*; *Le Courrier CEO.* [2014.06.01/XN6778/E]

- ♦ Collège européen de police / see European Union Agency for Law Enforcement Training (#08970)

♦ Collège européen de sécurité et de défense (CESD) 04107

European Security and Defence College (ESDC)

Secretariat EEAS, BLMT 10/P003, 1046 Brussels, Belgium. T. +3225846217. E-mail: secretariat-esdc@eeas.europa.eu.
URL: https://esdc.europa.eu

History 29 Jun 2005. Current legal Act: Council Decision (CFSP) 2020/1515. **Aims** Provide training and education in the field of the Union Common Security and Defence Policy (CSDP) in the context of the Common Foreign and Security Policy (CFSP) at the European level in order to develop and promote a common understanding of CSDP among civilian and military personnel; identify and disseminate, through its training and education activities, best practice in relation to various CSDP issues. **Structure** Steering Committee; Executive Academic Board; Head of the ESDC; Secretariat, based in Brussels (Belgium). **Languages** English, French. **Staff** 18.00 FTE, paid. 1 paid intern. **Finance** EU Member States: 80%; EU Budget: 20%. Annual budget: 2,000,000 EUR (2022). **Activities** Awareness raising; capacity building; politics/policy/regulatory; training/education. **Publications** *The European Security and Defence College and its contribution to the Common Security and Defence Culture* (2020) in English – made at the occasion of the 15th anniversary of the College, contains articles on the history of the College and on the development of CSDP in general; *Views on the progress of CSDP* in English – scientific publication based on the research of PhD students who paricipate in the CSDP Doctoral School. Handbooks. **Information Services** *ESDC: Who we are, what we do* in English, French – contains information on the funstioning and organisation of the ESDC.
Members Full members: national institutions; think tanks; NGOs. Members in the 27 EU Member States:
Austria, Belgium, Bulgaria, Croatia, Cyprus, Czechia, Denmark, Estonia, Finland, France, Germany, Greece, Hungary, Ireland, Italy, Latvia, Lithuania, Luxembourg, Malta, Netherlands, Poland, Portugal, Romania, Slovakia, Slovenia, Spain, Sweden.
Associated Network Partners are training providers who do belong to an EU Member State or who have in their decision making body a representative of a non-EU country:
Bosnia-Herzegovina, North Macedonia, Norway, Serbia, UK, Ukraine.
Centre for Security Cooperation (RACVIAC, #03785); Geneva Centre for Security Policy (GCSP); NATO (#16945); Transparency International (TI, #20223); United Nations Institute for Training and Research (UNITAR, #20576). [2022.02.02/XJ3175/E]

- ♦ Collège européen des traducteurs (internationally oriented national body)
- ♦ College for Foreign Affairs, Hanoi / see Diplomatic Academy of Vietnam
- ♦ Collège ibéro-latinoaméricain de dermatologie (#04093)
- ♦ Collège interaméricain de défense (#11426)
- ♦ Collège interaméricain de médecins et de chirurgiens (#11408)
- ♦ Collège international d'angiologie (#12640)
- ♦ Collège international des chirurgiens (#12650)
- ♦ Collège international de chirurgiens-dentistes (#12644)
- ♦ Collège international d'étude de la statique (internationally oriented national body)
- ♦ Collège international de médecine et chirurgie du pied / see International Federation of Foot and Ankle Societies (#13431)
- ♦ Collège international de médecine psychosomatique (#12649)
- ♦ Collège international des officiers de l'Armée du salut (see: #19041)
- ♦ Collège international d'ostéopathie / see Centre International d'Ostéopathie
- ♦ Collège international de philosophie, Paris (internationally oriented national body)
- ♦ Collège international de phonologie expérimentale (inactive)
- ♦ Collège international des sciences (see: #00617)
- ♦ Collège international des traducteurs littéraires (internationally oriented national body)
- ♦ College of Jewish Studies (internationally oriented national body)
- ♦ Collège du monde uni de l'Adriatique (internationally oriented national body)
- ♦ Collège du monde uni de l'Asie du Sud-Est (internationally oriented national body)
- ♦ Collège du monde uni de l'Atlantique / see UWC Atlantic College
- ♦ Collège du monde uni nordique de la Croix-Rouge (internationally oriented national body)
- ♦ Collège du monde uni du Pacifique Lester B Pearson (internationally oriented national body)
- ♦ Collège du monde uni Waterford Kamhlaba de l'Afrique australe (internationally oriented national body)
- ♦ Collège nordique d'écologie (inactive)
- ♦ Collège d'odonto-stomatologie africain et de chirurgie maxillo-faciale (no recent information)

♦ College of Ophthalmology of Eastern Central and Southern Africa (COECSA) 04108

Contact Regent Court, Block A – Ste A7, Argwings Kodhek Road, Hurlingham, PO Box 4539-00506, Nairobi, Kenya. T. +254206009906. E-mail: information@coecsa.org.
URL: http://coecsa.org/

History 2012, resulting from merger between *Eastern Africa College of Ophthalmologists (EACO, inactive)* and *Ophthalmological Society of Eastern Africa (OSEA, inactive).* **Aims** Address the shortage of ophthalmologists in Eastern, Central and Southern Africa; improve the quality of eye care services in the region. **Structure** General Assembly (annual). Council; Executive Committee; Standing Committees; Ad hoc Committees. Secretariat. **Activities** Training/education; research/documentation; advocacy/lobbying/activism. **Events** *Beyond Vision 2020* Nairobi (Kenya) 2021, *Congress* Lilongwe (Malawi) 2020, *Congress* Kigali (Rwanda) 2019, *Congress* Arusha (Tanzania UR) 2016, *Congress* Livingstone (Zambia) 2014. **Publications** *Journal of Ophthalmology of Eastern, Central and Southern Africa (JOECSA).*
Members Institutions (5) in 3 countries:
Kenya, Tanzania UR, Uganda.
NGO Relations Member of: *Middle East African Council of Ophthalmology (MEACO, #16752).* Regional society member of: *College of Ophthalmology of Eastern Central and Southern Africa (COECSA, #04108).* [2014/XJ8817/D]

- ♦ Collège ouest africain des chirurgiens (#20876)
- ♦ Collège ouest africain des médecins (#20875)

♦ College of Pathologists of East Central and Southern Africa (COPECSA) 04109

Contact Plot No 157 Oloirien, Njiro road, PO Box 1009, Arusha, Tanzania UR.
URL: http://copecsa.org/
History Sep 2010, Kampala (Uganda). **Aims** Develop highly competent and ethical specialist workforce in pathology able to provide quality laboratory services for diagnosis, prevention and management of disease and also for research to international standards. **Structure** Executive Committee. **Activities** Training/education.
Members Full in 7 countries:
Botswana, Burundi, Eritrea, Ethiopia, Kenya, Malawi, Mauritius.
NGO Relations *African Strategies for Advancing Pathology (ASAP, #00476)*; *Association of Pathologists of East, Central and Southern Africa (APECSA, #02853).* [2017/XM5512/**D**]

- ♦ Collège scandinave des brasseurs (internationally oriented national body)
- ♦ College of Surgeons of East and Central Africa / see College of Surgeons of East, Central and Southern Africa (#04110)

♦ College of Surgeons of East, Central and Southern Africa (COSECSA) 04110

Contact c/o ECSA-HC, PO Box 1009, Arusha, Tanzania UR. T. +255272508363. Fax +255272504124. E-mail: info@cosecsa.org.
URL: http://www.cosecsa.org/
History Dec 1999 by *Association of Surgeons of East Africa (ASEA, inactive)*, as *College of Surgeons of East and Central Africa*. Current title adopted Dec 2001, Lusaka (Zambia). Since 2003, integrated into *East, Central and Southern African Health Community (ECSA-HC, #05216)*. Merged with ASEA, 2007. **Aims** Promote excellence in surgical care, training and research in East, Central and Southern Africa. **Structure** General Meeting (annual). Council (meets twice a year). Executive Committee, including President, Vice-President, Secretary-General, Treasurer and Chairman. Standing Committees (3). **Events** *Annual General Meeting and Conference* Maputo (Mozambique) 2017, *Annual General Meeting and Conference* Dar es Salaam (Tanzania UR) 2014, *Annual General Meeting* Harare (Zimbabwe) 2013, *Annual General Meeting* Uganda 2010, *Annual General Meeting* Mombasa (Kenya) 2007.
Members Full in 9 countries:
Ethiopia, Kenya, Malawi, Mozambique, Rwanda, Tanzania UR, Uganda, Zambia, Zimbabwe.
NGO Relations Member of: *Global Health Workforce Alliance (GHWA, inactive)*; *International Federation of Surgical Colleges (IFSC, #13560).* [2020/XM2391/**E**]

- ♦ College Theology Society (internationally oriented national body)

♦ Collège universitaire Henry Dunant (CUHD) 04111

Colegio Universitario Henry Dunant (CUHD)
Main Office Ch Pierre-Longue 14, 1212 Geneva, Switzerland. E-mail: info@cuhd.org.
URL: http://www.cuhd.org/
History 1995. Registration: Swiss Civil Code, Switzerland. **Aims** Provide university-level training in human rights issues for non-governmental organization staff, national and international civil servants, activists, lawyers, etc. **Structure** Board. **Languages** English, French, Spanish. **Staff** 2.00 FTE, paid. Several professors and assistants each year during sessions; about 50 professors, experts and speakers of 30 different nationalities take part in training sessions. **Finance** Sources: fees for services; government support. Other sources: institutional. **Activities** Training/education. **Publications** Available on website. **IGO Relations** Cooperates with (2): *International Bureau of Education (IBE, #12413)*; *Office of the United Nations High Commissioner for Human Rights (OHCHR, #17697).* **NGO Relations** Cooperates with (1): *International Organization for the Right to Education and Freedom of Education (#14468).* [2021.06.11/XM3892/**E**]

- ♦ Collegiate Association for the Research of the Principle
- ♦ Collegio del Mondo Unito dell'Adriatico (internationally oriented national body)
- ♦ Collegio Universitario Aspiranti Medici e Missionari / see CUAMM – Medici con l'Africa
- ♦ Collegium for African American Research (internationally oriented national body)
- ♦ Collegium Cultorum Martyrum / see Pontifical Academy Cultorum Martyrum (#18430)
- ♦ Collegium Europaeum pour l'étude de l'évaluation du dommage corporel (inactive)

♦ Collegium International 04112

SG address not obtained. E-mail: collegium@collegium-international.org.
URL: http://www.collegium-international.org/
History Founded 5 Oct 2002, Bled (Slovenia), following initiatives of the co-Presidents (former Prime Minister of France, Michel Rocard and President of Slovenia, Milan Kucan), Mar 2001. Also referred to as *International Ethical Collegium* and *International Ethical, Political and Scientific Collegium*. **Aims** Promote dialogue among leading thinkers and actors in the realms of science, politics and ethical philosophy; produce guidelines for effective action on a global agenda having integrity and political viability; pool the high *ethical* standards of members, their political and scientific wisdom and experience and their diversity so as to provide new and relevant approaches to facing threatened world crises and the increasingly interdependent global society. **Structure** Officers: Honorary President; President; Vice-President; Secretary General; Development Management. **Languages** English, French. **Publications** *White Book Series*.
Members Scientists, philosophers, present and former heads of state or government. Members in 20 countries:
Algeria, Australia, Brazil, Canada, China, Cyprus, Czechia, France, Germany, Indonesia, Ireland, Italy, Japan, Jordan, Mali, Netherlands, Poland, Slovenia, Spain, Switzerland. [2021/XJ3682/**E**]

♦ Collegium Internationale Activitatis Nervosae Superioris (CIANS) 04113

SG c/o Scuola ASIPSE, Via Settembrini 2, 20124 Milan MI, Italy. T. +3922043880. Fax +3922043880.
URL: http://www.cians.org/
History 1958, as a section of *World Psychiatric Association (WPA, #21741)*, formally founded 1960. Became a separate organization from WPA, 1982, Olomouc (Czechoslovakia). New constitution adopted Oct 1989, Osaka (Japan). Full title: *CIANS – Collegium Internationale Activitatis Nervosae Superioris – International Association for Integrative Nervous Functions: Neurobiology of Behaviour and Psychosomatics.* **Aims** Foster interdisciplinary studies on problems of practical importance to *neuroscience*, psychology and biomedical science; emphasize integrative approaches to these problems in order to understand how and through which mechanisms psychosocial factors impact on behaviour and health; support development of health care measures designed to act as adjuncts with other available modalities to decrease death and disability from disease, with special emphasis on behavioural modification of work- and lifestyle-related risk factors, and on positive psychology. **Structure** Executive Committee comprising President, General Secretary, President-Elect, Past-President, Secretary-Treasurer and 4 members. Council (18 members). **Languages** English. **Staff** None. **Finance** Members' dues. **Events** *International Conference* Venice (Italy) 2014, *International Conference* Vysoké Tatry (Slovakia) 2012, *International Conference* Milan (Italy) 2010, *Conference / International Conference* Prague (Czech Rep) 2009, *Conference / International Conference* Smolenice (Slovakia) 2008. **Publications** *Activitas Nervosa Superior Rediviva* – journal. **Members** Founding societies (10); other collective members (2); individuals (185) – neurologists, psychiatrists, neurophysiologists and psychologists. Membership countries not specified. [2013/XD5994/**D**]

♦ Collegium Internationale Allergologicum (CIA) 04114

Pres 555 E Wells St, Ste 1100, Milwaukee WI 53202, USA. T. +14149183018. Fax +14142763349. E-mail: info@ciaweb.org.
URL: http://www.ciaweb.org/
History Founded 15 Oct 1954, London (UK). **Aims** Study scientific and clinical problems in *allergy* and related branches of medicine and *immunology*; promote a humble spirit of scientific enquiry, friendly cooperation, good fellowship and professional relationship in the field of allergy. **Structure** General Meeting (every 2 years); Council. Membership by invitation only. **Languages** English. **Staff** 1.00 FTE, paid. **Finance** Sources: members' dues. Other sources: Grants for symposia. **Events** *Biennial Symposium* Montréal, QC (Canada) 2022, *Biennial Symposium* Montebello, ON (Canada) 2020, *Biennial Symposium* Palma (Spain) 2018, *Biennial Symposium* Charleston, SC (USA) 2016, *Biennial Symposium* Petersberg (Germany) 2014. **Publications** *International Archives of Allergy and Applied Immunology* (periodical). *Allergy Frontiers and Futures*; *From Genes to Phenotypes: The Basis of Future Allergy Management.*
Members Active; Corresponding; Honorary; Lifetime. Individuals in 26 countries:
Australia, Austria, Belgium, Brazil, Canada, Denmark, Finland, France, Germany, Hungary, India, Ireland, Israel, Italy, Japan, Korea Rep, Netherlands, New Zealand, Norway, Portugal, Spain, Sweden, Switzerland, Türkiye, UK, USA. [2020/XC0279/v/**C**]

- ♦ Collegium Internationale Angiologiae (#12640)
- ♦ Collegium Internationale Chirurgiae Digestivae / see International Society for Digestive Surgery (#15060)

♦ Collegium Internationale Neuropsychopharmacologicum (CINP) 04115

International College of Neuropsychopharmacology
Main Office c/o Auditreu, Gonzagagasse 17, 1010 Vienna, Austria. T. +436601258463. Fax +436046811049. E-mail: info@cinp.org.
URL: http://www.cinp.org/
History 2 Sep 1957, Zurich (Switzerland). Founded at 2nd World Congress of Psychiatry. Registration: Switzerland. **Aims** Encourage and provide educational activities in the field of neuropsychopharmacology; advance experimental and clinical aspects of neuropsychopharmacological sciences; facilitate relations between disciplines; consider medico-social problems of psychopharmacology. **Structure** Council; Executive Committee; Constitutional Committees (11); Regional Committees; Head Office. **Languages** English. **Staff** 4.00 FTE, paid. **Finance** Sources: members' dues. **Activities** Awards/prizes/competitions; events/meetings; guidance/assistance/consulting; training/education. **Events** *World Congress* Jerusalem (Israel) 2025, *World Congress* Tokyo (Japan) 2024, *World Congress* Montréal, QC (Canada) 2023, *World Congress* Taipei (Taiwan) 2022, *World Congress* Vienna (Austria) 2021. **Publications** *International Journal of Neuropsychopharmacology* (12 a year); *Neurtransletter*.
Members Founding; Fellows; Emeritus; Honorary; Supporting; Associate. Members in 50 countries and territories:
Argentina, Australia, Austria, Belgium, Bosnia-Herzegovina, Brazil, Canada, Chile, China, Croatia, Czechia, Denmark, Egypt, Finland, France, Germany, Greece, Hong Kong, Hungary, India, Iraq, Ireland, Israel, Italy, Japan, Korea DPR, Korea Rep, Mexico, Morocco, Netherlands, New Zealand, Norway, Pakistan, Peru, Poland, Portugal, Puerto Rico, Romania, Russia, South Africa, Spain, Sweden, Switzerland, Thailand, Türkiye, UK, Ukraine, Uruguay, USA, Venezuela.
Consultative Status Consultative status granted from: *ECOSOC (#05331)* (Ros C). **NGO Relations** Instrumental in setting up (2): *International Society for Neuroimaging in Psychiatry (ISNIP, #15297)*; *Pacific Rim Association for Clinical Pharmacogenetics (PRACP, no recent information).* [2020/XC4449/v/**C**]

- ♦ Collegium Internationale Oris Implantatorum (#12899)
- ♦ Collegium international de radiologie et otorhinolaryngologie (inactive)

♦ Collegium Medicorum Theatri (COMET) 04116

Sec Gen Salzburgerstrasse 7, 5202 Neumarkt am Wallersee, Austria. E-mail: info@comet-collegium.com.
Pres address not obtained.
URL: http://www.comet-collegium.com/
History 14 Aug 1969, Mexico City (Mexico), at 9th International Congress of Otorhinolaryngology, when statutes were adopted. **Aims** Encourage scientific investigation among *laryngologists* of the physiology and pathology of *voice* of singers and actors; further the clinical study of these professional voice users; organize meetings for the exchange of knowledge and ideas; facilitate referral of artists to well-qualified specialists in places where they are to perform; develop educational activities related to the *vocal* problems of singers and actors. **Languages** English. **Finance** Members' dues (annual): US$ 20. **Activities** Congresses, symposia, courses. Liaison with national societies of otorhinolaryngology and phoniatry. **Events** *International Symposium* Salzburg (Austria) 2014, *Annual Congress* Frankfurt-Main (Germany) 2011, *Annual Congress* London (UK) 2010, *Annual Congress* Leuven (Belgium) 2003, *International symposium* Cairo (Egypt) 1990.
Members Full laryngologists connected with major theatres, operas or conservatories, or who have demonstrated special dedication to physiology and pathology of the voice in singers and actors. Associate physicians, scientists, voice coaches and voice pathologists with special qualifications and interest in vocal problems of singers and actors. Members in 24 countries:
Argentina, Australia, Austria, Belgium, Bulgaria, Canada, Denmark, Egypt, Finland, France, Germany, Israel, Italy, Japan, Korea Rep, Mexico, Netherlands, Norway, Spain, Sweden, Switzerland, Taiwan, UK, USA. [2019/XC0280/**D**]

- ♦ Collegium Orbis Radiologiae Docentium (inactive)

♦ Collegium Oto-Rhino-Laryngologicum Amicitiae Sacrum (CORLAS) 04117

Gen Sec ORLHN Surgery, University Hospital, PO Box 263, FI-00029 Helsinki, Finland.
URL: http://www.corlas.org/
History 1926, Groningen (Netherlands). Founded on the initiative of Charles Emile Benjamins and Adriaan De Kleyn. **Structure** Board, comprising President, Vice-President, General Secretary, President-Elect, Treasurer, Vice-President-Elect, 3 Councillors, Editorial Secretary and Second Secretary. **Finance** Members' dues. **Activities** Annual postgraduate course in ear surgery. **Events** *Congress* Santiago (Chile) 2022, *Congress* Santiago (Chile) 2021, *Congress* Santiago (Chile) 2020, *Congress* Bern (Switzerland) 2019, *Congress* Beijing (China) 2018. [2021/XG7031/**D**]

♦ Collegium Palynologicum Scandinavicum (CPS) 04118

Contact LWL-Museum of Natural History, Sentruper Strasse 285, 48161 Münster, Germany. T. +492515916016. E-mail: info@palynology.info.
Chair/Pres Naturhistoriska riksmuseet, Box 50007, SE-104 05 Stockholm, Sweden.
URL: http://www.palynology.info/
History 1969, Stockholm (Sweden). **Aims** Stimulate interest in palynology; coordinate palynological research in the Nordic countries. **Structure** Board. **Languages** Danish, English, Faroese, Finnish, Icelandic, Norwegian, Swedish. **Staff** Voluntary. **Finance** Support from academic and research institutions. **Events** *Annual meeting* Dublin (Ireland) 2018, *Annual Meeting* Bonn (Germany) 2008, *Annual Meeting* Bergen (Norway) 2005, *Annual Meeting* Granada (Spain) 2004, *Annual Meeting* Lund (Sweden) 2003. **Publications** *GRANA* (6 a year) – journal.
Members Full (about 55) in 15 countries:
Albania, Austria, Czechia, Denmark, Finland, Germany, Iceland, Italy, Norway, Philippines, Poland, Romania, Sweden, UK, USA.
NGO Relations Member of (1): *International Federation of Palynological Societies (IFPS, #13498).* Associated with: *Micropalaeontology Society, The (TMS, #16749).* [2022.10.19/XF0889/**F**]

- ♦ Colloque celtique d'études classiques (#03631)
- ♦ Colloque de droit européen (meeting series)
- ♦ Colloque européen des paroisses (#04119)
- ♦ Colloque international de biologie prospective (meeting series)
- ♦ Colloque international sur la didactique des langues secondes (meeting series)
- ♦ Colloque internationale de radioimmunologie de Lyon (meeting series)
- ♦ Colloque international sur les facteurs humains dans les télécommunications (#15642)
- ♦ Colloque international sur le ginseng (meeting series)
- ♦ Colloque international sur les méthodes de calcul scientifique et technique (meeting series)
- ♦ Colloque international sur la pathologie locomotrice (meeting series)
- ♦ Colloque international de prévention des risques professionnels du bâtiment et des travaux publics (meeting series)
- ♦ Colloque international de psychodynamique et psychopathologie du travail (meeting series)
- ♦ Colloque international des universitaires et chercheur-es Sourd-es (meeting series)
- ♦ Colloque judiciaire (meeting series)
- ♦ Colloquies on European Law (meeting series)
- ♦ Colloquium Europäischer Pfarrgemeinden (#04119)
- ♦ Colloquium of European Planetaria (meeting series)
- ♦ Colloquium Spectroscopicum International (meeting series)

♦ Colloquy of European Parishes 04119

Colloque européen des paroisses (CEP) – Coloquio Europeo de Parroquias – Colloquium Europäischer Pfarrgemeinden
Contact Centre d'Estudis Pastorals, Plaça Sant Felip Neri 5, 08002 Barcelona, Spain.

URL: http://www.cep-europa.org/
History 1959, Paris (France). Registered in accordance with French law. **Aims** Group parish priests and lay people interested in pastoral problems or working within parishes to discuss pastoral problems on a European level. **Structure** International Council, consisting of 2 national delegates per country (priest and lay person), Honorary President, General Secretary, a representative of the European Council and 2 permanent specialized advisers. Governing body, comprising President and 2 Vice-Presidents elected from the Council plus General Secretary and an Assistant. **Languages** English, French, German, Italian, Spanish. **Staff** 1.00 FTE, voluntary. **Finance** Members' dues. Donations. **Activities** Events/meetings. **Events** *Biennial Session* Lviv (Ukraine) 2019, *Biennial Session* Barcelona (Spain) 2017, *Biennial Session* Lisieux (France) 2015, *Biennial Session* Mellieha (Malta) 2013, *Biennial Session* Nyiregyhaza (Hungary) 2011. **Publications** Proceedings of Sessions.
Members Individuals (about 400) in 23 European countries:
Austria, Belarus, Belgium, Bosnia-Herzegovina, Bulgaria, Croatia, Czechia, France, Germany, Holy See, Hungary, Italy, Malta, Netherlands, Poland, Portugal, Romania, Russia, Slovakia, Spain, Switzerland, UK, Ukraine.
Consultative Status Consultative status granted from: *Council of Europe (CE, #04881)* (Participatory Status).
[2015/XD6447/v/D]

♦ Colombian Presidential Agency of International Cooperation (internationally oriented national body)
♦ Colombo Plan for Cooperative Economic Development in South and South-East Asia / see Colombo Plan for Cooperative Economic and Social Development in Asia and the Pacific (#04120)

♦ Colombo Plan for Cooperative Economic and Social Development in Asia and the Pacific (CPS) 04120

Plan de Colombo pour la coopération économique et sociale en Asie et dans le Pacifique
Secretariat 556 Bauddhaloka Mawatha, Colombo, 8, Sri Lanka. T. +94112684188. Fax +94112684386. E-mail: info@colombo-plan.org.
URL: http://www.colombo-plan.org/
History May 1950, following a proposal for a *Colombo Plan for Cooperative Economic Development in South and South-East Asia*, put forward by the meeting of Commonwealth and Foreign Ministers, Jan 1950, Colombo. In pursuance of an agreement of this meeting, a Consultative Committee was formed at subsequent meetings in the same year, in Sydney (Australia) and later in London (UK). Technical Cooperation under the Plan commenced Mar 1951; the Plan came into full operation in Jul 1951, with the commencement of capital aid operations and launching of national development plans. Current name adopted Dec 1977. The Plan was initially set up for 6 years; subsequent action by the Consultative Committee extended it from 1957-1961, 1961-1966, 1966-1971, 1971-1976 and 1976-1981; and, at the 28th Meeting of the Consultative Committee in Nov 1980, Jakarta (Indonesia), the Plan was extended indefinitely, its need and relevance henceforth being examined only if considered necessary. **Aims** Promote interest in and support for the economic and social development of Asia and the Pacific; promote technical cooperation and assist in the sharing and transfer of technology among member countries; keep under review relevant information on technical cooperation between member governments, multilateral and other agencies so as to accelerate development through cooperative effort; facilitate transfer and sharing of the developmental experiences among member countries within the region with emphasis on the concept of South-South cooperation. **Structure** Consultative Committee (CCM); Colombo Plan Council; Colombo Plan Secretariat, headed by Secretary-General. Permanent Programmes (4): Drug Advisory Programme (DAP); Programme for Public Administration and Environment (PPA and ENV); Programme for Private Sector Development (PPSD); Long-Term Scholarships Programme (LTSP). *International Centre for Credentialing and Education of Addiction Professionals (ICCE)* serves as training and credentialing arm of DAP. Colombo Plan Gender Affairs Programme (CPGAP). Also includes: *Colombo Plan Staff College (CPSC, #04121)*. **Languages** English. **Staff** 35.00 FTE, paid. **Finance** Administrative costs borne equally by member countries. Training programmes voluntarily funded by donors among member countries as well as by contributions from non-member governments. **Activities** Training/education; events/meetings; politics/policy/regulatory; capacity building. **Events** *Meeting* Manado (Indonesia) 2012, *International conference of Islamic scholars and faith-based organisations in drug demand reduction* Mombasa (Kenya) 2011, *Meeting / Consultative Committee Meeting* Delhi (India) 2010, *Meeting / Consultative Committee Meeting* Kuala Lumpur (Malaysia) 2008, *Meeting / Consultative Committee Meeting* Bhutan 2006. **Publications** *Colombo Plan Focus* (4 a year) – newsletter. Annual report of the Colombo Plan Council; proceedings and conclusions of Consultative Committee meetings.
Members Governments of 27 countries:
Afghanistan, Australia, Bangladesh, Bhutan, Brunei Darussalam, Fiji, India, Indonesia, Iran Islamic Rep, Japan, Korea Rep, Laos, Malaysia, Maldives, Mongolia, Myanmar, Nepal, New Zealand, Pakistan, Papua New Guinea, Philippines, Saudi Arabia, Singapore, Sri Lanka, Thailand, USA, Vietnam.
IGO Relations Cooperates with: *South Asia Cooperative Environment Programme (SACEP, #19714)*. Memorandum of Understanding with: *Economic Cooperation Organization (ECO, #05313)*. **NGO Relations** Member of: *International Federation of Non-Government Organizations for the Prevention of Drug and Substance Abuse (IFNGO, #13490)*. [2017/XC0281/F*]

♦ Colombo Plan International Society (internationally oriented national body)

♦ Colombo Plan Staff College (CPSC) 04121

Dir Gen Block C, DepEd Complex, Meralco Avenue, 1600 Pasig City RIZ, Philippines. T. +6326310991. Fax +6326310996. E-mail: cpsc@cpsctech.org – director-general@cpsctech.org.
URL: http://www.cpsctech.org/
History 5 Dec 1973, Singapore (Singapore). Established at 23rd Consultative Committee Meeting of the Colombo Plan held in Wellington, New Zealand to assist the member countries of *Colombo Plan for Cooperative Economic and Social Development in Asia and the Pacific (CPS, #04120)*. Initially founded as a specialized agency and training center of the Colombo Plan, an international economic organization founded in 1951 to focus on the economic and social development of the nations in the Asia-Pacific region. Became operational, 1974, with the Republic of Singapore serving as the first host Government. Jan 1987, moved to Manila (Philippines), upon the invitation of the Philippine Government. Former names and other names: *Colombo Plan Staff College for Technician Education (CPSC)* – full title. **Aims** Provide courses of further professional education and training to persons responsible for the planning, development, administration, and supervision of technician education and training and persons in key supporting roles; assist in the conduct of projects in the field of staff and curriculum development and other projects aimed at thee effective utilization of resources for learning and teaching; advise and assist member countries in developing their technician teacher education. **Structure** Governing Board; Academic Board; Faculty; Standing Committee; Panel of Advisors. College also has a Liaison Officer in each country. Includes: *Asia Pacific Accreditation and Certification Commission (APACC, #01815)*. **Languages** English. **Finance** Sources: contributions of member/participating states; international organizations. Supported by: *Asian Development Bank (ADB, #01422)*; *Japan International Cooperation Agency (JICA)*; *UNESCO (#20322)*; *United Nations Economic and Social Commission for Asia and the Pacific (ESCAP, #20557)*. **Activities** Events/meetings; guidance/assistance/consulting; knowledge management/information dissemination; networking/liaising; research and development; research/documentation; training/education. Active in all member countries. **Events** *Regional Program and Experts Meeting* Shah Alam (Malaysia) 2022, *Seminar on TVET Education in the Context of COVID-19* Kathmandu (Nepal) 2020, *International conference on technician education and training* Manila (Philippines) 1998, *Regional workshop* Manila (Philippines) 1998, *Regional workshop* Manila (Philippines) 1997. **Publications** *CPSC Quarterly* (4 a year). *Scholarly Training Education Publication Series (STEPS)*. Guidebooks; toolkits; training manuals; research papers; conference proceedings.
Members Participating countries (16):
Afghanistan, Bangladesh, Bhutan, Fiji, India, Malaysia, Maldives, Mongolia, Myanmar, Nepal, Pakistan, Papua New Guinea, Philippines, Singapore, Sri Lanka, Thailand.
Diploma Engineers Association of Nepal; Institute of Diploma Engineers Bangladesh; Technical Vocational Schools and Associations of the Philippines.
NGO Relations Member of (1): *Skillman Network (#19306)*. [2023.02.14/XF9578/F*]

♦ Colombo Plan Staff College for Technician Education / see Colombo Plan Staff College (#04121)
♦ Colonial and Continental Church Society / see Intercontinental Church Society (#11460)
♦ Colonial Institute / see Royal Commonwealth Society (#18990)
♦ Colonial Society / see Royal Commonwealth Society (#18990)
♦ Colonial Waterbird Group / see Waterbird Society
♦ Colonial Waterbird Society / see Waterbird Society
♦ Colonies Françaises du Pacifique / see Comptoirs français du pacifique (#04422)
♦ Coloquio Europeo de Parroquias (#04119)
♦ Coloquios Internacionales sobre Cerebro y Agresión (#12653)
♦ Color Marketing Group (internationally oriented national body)
♦ COLOSS – honey bee research association / see Prevention of Honey Bee COlony LOSSes (#18492)
♦ **COLOSS** Prevention of Honey Bee COlony LOSSes (#18492)
♦ **COLPAR – SIGLO XXI** Confederación Latinoamericana de Paracaidismo (#04460)
♦ COLP – Center for Oceans Law and Policy (internationally oriented national body)
♦ **COLPOFER** Collaboration des services de police ferroviaire et de sécurité (#04096)
♦ COLREG – Convention on the International Regulations for Preventing Collisions at Sea (1972 treaty)
♦ COLSIBA / see Coordinadora Latinoamericano de Sindicatos Bananeros en Agroindustriales (#04810)
♦ **COLSIBA** Coordinadora Latinoamericano de Sindicatos Bananeros en Agroindustriales (#04810)
♦ **COLTO** Coalition of Legal Toothfish Operators (#04063)
♦ Columbian Squires (religious order)
♦ **COLUMBUS Association** Institutional Development Programme between European and Latin American Universities (#11316)
♦ COLUMBUS Programme / see Institutional Development Programme between European and Latin American Universities (#11316)
♦ COLUMBUS Project / see Institutional Development Programme between European and Latin American Universities (#11316)
♦ **COMALEP** Secretaria Permanente del Convenio Multilateral sobre Cooperación y Asistencia Mutua entre las Direcciones Nacionales de Aduanas de América Latina, España y Portugal (#19194)
♦ COMALFA – Comptoir maghrébin de l'alfa (inactive)
♦ COMAP – Comité maghrébin des agrumes et des primeurs (inactive)
♦ **COMARES** Conférence Maghrébine des Responsables des Établissements d'Enseignement Supérieur (#04626)
♦ **COMASSOC** The Commonwealth Association (#04299)
♦ COMAV – Consejo Mundial de Artistas Visuales (no recent information)
♦ Combat Antisemitism Movement (internationally oriented national body)
♦ Combat Blindness Foundation / see Combat Blindness International
♦ Combat Blindness International (internationally oriented national body)
♦ Combating Terrorism Center (internationally oriented national body)
♦ Combined European Bureau for Social Development / see European Community Development Network (#06679)
♦ Combined Orthopaedic Associations Meeting (meeting series)
♦ **CombNet** European Biomass Combustion Network (#06338)
♦ COMBO / see International Council of Multiple Birth Organisations (#13050)

♦ Combois 04122

Executive Manager c/o Sonja Rakete Consulting, Kaiserforst 86, 33378 Rheda-Wiedenbrück, Germany. T. +495242402084. E-mail: info@combois.com.
URL: http://www.combois.com/
History 1967. Also previously referred to as *European Community of Interests – Woodworking and Woodprocessing Machinery – Europäische Interessengemeinschaft Holzbe- und Verarbeitungsmaschinen* and as *Community of Interests of Leading European Woodworking and Wood Processing Machinery Resellers – Interessengemeinschaft der Führenden Holzbe- und Verarbeitungsmaschinen-Grosshändler Europas*. Current full title: *International Organization for Timber Technology Transfer – Internationale Gemeinschaft für Holztechnologie-Transfer (COMBOIS)*. Registered in accordance with German law. **Aims** Exchange technical know-how and practical experience between members; promote members' interests by exchanging technical information, business experience and market information on the *timber* industry. **Structure** General Meeting (annual). Board, comprising Chairman and 2 members. **Languages** English. **Finance** Members' dues. **Activities** Organizes technical conferences, information seminars, fair meetings and annual general meetings. **Events** *Annual General Meeting / General Meeting* Shanghai (China) 2015, *Annual General Meeting* Ålesund (Norway) 2014, *Annual General Meeting* Dresden (Germany) 2013, *Annual general meeting / General Meeting* Sweden 2008, *Annual General Meeting* Milan (Italy) 2007. **Publications** Management reports; technical documentation.
Members Distribution and service companies specializing in woodworking and wood processing machines. Members in 16 countries and territories:
Austria, Belgium, Denmark, Finland, Germany, Hong Kong, Italy, Japan, Netherlands, Norway, Portugal, South Africa, Spain, Sweden, Switzerland, USA. [2015/XF1890/D]

♦ Comboni Missionaries of the Heart of Jesus (religious order)
♦ Comboni Missionary Sisters (religious order)

♦ Combustion Institute 04123

Main Office 5001 Baum Blvd, Ste 644, Pittsburgh PA 15213-1851, USA. T. +14126871366. Fax +14126870340. E-mail: office@combustioninstitute.org.
URL: http://www.combustioninstitute.org/
History 1 Jul 1954, Pittsburgh, PA (USA). Founded during the 5th Combustion Symposium, following the activities of the '*Standing Committee on Combustion Symposia*', founded in 1948. **Aims** Advance research in combustion science. **Structure** Executive Committee; Board of Directors. **Languages** English. **Staff** 5.00 FTE, paid. **Activities** Events/meetings; awards/prizes/competitions. **Events** *International Symposium on Combustion* Milan (Italy) 2024, *International Symposium on Combustion* Vancouver, BC (Canada) 2022, *Biennial Asia-Pacific Conference* 2021, *International Symposium on Combustion* Adelaide, SA (Australia) 2021, *European Combustion Meeting* Naples (Italy) 2021. **Publications** *Combustion and Flame* (12 a year); *Proceedings of The Combustion Institute* (2 a year).
Members Individuals. National or regional sections (35) in (32) countries and territories:
Australia, Belarus, Belgium, Brazil, Canada, Chile, China, Croatia, Egypt, France, Germany, Greece, Hungary, India, Iran Islamic Rep, Ireland, Israel, Italy, Japan, Korea Rep, Mexico, Netherlands, Poland, Portugal, Russia, Spain, Sweden, Switzerland, Taiwan, Türkiye, UK, USA. [2022/XM4500/j/E]

♦ **COMCEC** Standing Committee for Economic and Commercial Cooperation (#19952)
♦ **COMCOL** ICOM International Committee for Collecting (#11055)
♦ **COM** Confédération Ornithologique Mondiale (#04575)
♦ **COMEBA** Confederation of Mediterranean Badminton (#04567)
♦ COMECE / see Commission of the Bishops' Conferences of the European Union (#04205)
♦ **COMECE** Commission of the Bishops' Conferences of the European Union (#04205)
♦ **COMECE** Commission des épiscopats de l'Union européenne (#04205)
♦ **COMECE** Kommission der Bischofskonferenzen der Europäischen Union (#04205)
♦ COMEDA – Conseil mondial d'éthique des droits de l'animal (inactive)
♦ **COMED** Confederación Mundial de Educación (#04464)
♦ **COMELA** Conference on Mediterranean and European Linguistic Anthropology (#04628)
♦ **COMELEC** Comité Maghrébin de l'Electricité (#04191)
♦ COMENER – Comisión Centroamericana de Energia (inactive)
♦ **Comenius Association** European network of teacher training institutes (#18875)
♦ Come Noi (internationally oriented national body)
♦ CoMensha – Coördinatiecentrum Mensenhandel (internationally oriented national body)
♦ COMEP / see Confederación Mundial de Educación (#04464)

♦ COMESA Business Council (CBC) 04124

CEO c/o COMESA Secretariat, Ben Bella Road, PO Box 30051, Lusaka 10101, Zambia. T. +26021122972532. E-mail: info@comesabusinesscouncil.org.
URL: http://comesabusinesscouncil.org/

COMESA Common Market
04124

alphabetic sequence excludes
For the complete listing, see Yearbook Online at

History A private sector institution of *Common Market for Eastern and Southern Africa (COMESA, #04296).* **Aims** Become the leading private sector organization in Africa, that promotes competitive and interconnected industries to actively participate in regional and global markets through advocacy, business facilitation and enterprise development. **Structure** General Assembly; Board; Administrative and Technical Committees; Secretariat. **Finance** Sources: members' dues. **Activities** Advocacy/lobbying/activism; guidance/assistance/consulting; monitoring/evaluation. **Publications** *Biznet Weekly* (weekly). Reports; positions papers; policy briefs; handbooks. **Members** Principal; Honorary/corporate; Associate; Emerging Businesses. Membership countries not specified. [2023.02.14/AA1128/**E**]

♦ **COMESA** Common Market for Eastern and Southern Africa (#04296)

♦ COMESA Competition Commission (CCC) 04125

CEO Kang'ombe House, 5th Floor – West Wing, PO Box 30742, Lilongwe 3, Malawi. T. +2651772466. E-mail: compcom@comesa.int.
URL: https://www.comesacompetition.org/

History 14 Jan 2013. A regional body of and established by *Common Market for Eastern and Southern Africa (COMESA, #04296).* **Aims** Promote competition and protect consumer welfare within the Common Market thereby facilitating regional economic integration. **Structure** Board of Commissioners. Divisions. [2022/AA1129/**E***]

♦ **COMESA Court of Justice** Court of Justice of the Common Market for Eastern and Southern Africa (#04937)

♦ COMESA Federation of National Associations of Women in Business (COMFWB) 04126

CEO Ground Floor – Zimbabwe House, City Centre, 1499, Lilongwe, Malawi. E-mail: info@femcomcomesa.org.
URL: http://www.femcomcomesa.org/

History 28 Jul 1993, Harare (Zimbabwe). Established as an institution of *Preferential Trade Area for Eastern and Southern African States (PTA, inactive).* Currently an institution in the wider framework of *Common Market for Eastern and Southern Africa (COMESA, #04296).* Former names and other names: *Federation of National Associations of Women in Business in Eastern and Southern Africa (FEMCOM)* – former (2020). **Aims** Promote the integration of women into trade and development activities; improve the economic conditions of women in the subregion; increase the awareness of women's issues at the policy level. **Structure** Annual General Meeting; Board; Secretariat. **Events** *General Assembly* Lusaka (Zambia) 1997.
Members Full; Associate. Chapters in 17 countries:
Burundi, Comoros, Congo DR, Eritrea, Eswatini, Ethiopia, Kenya, Libya, Madagascar, Malawi, Mauritius, Rwanda, Seychelles, Sudan, Uganda, Zambia, Zimbabwe. [2020/XD4484/**D**]

♦ COMESA Leather and Leather Products Institute / see Africa Leather and Leather Products Institute (#00185)
♦ COMESA/LLPI / see Africa Leather and Leather Products Institute (#00185)
♦ COMESA Metallurgical Technology Centre (inactive)

♦ COMESA Monetary Institute (CMI) 04127

Dir c/o Kenya School of Monetary Studies, PO Box 65041, Noordin Road, Nairobi, 00618, Kenya. T. +254208646207.
URL: https://cmi.comesa.int/

History Jun 2009, Victoria Falls (Zimbabwe). Established at 13th Summit of *Common Market for Eastern and Southern Africa (COMESA, #04296)* Authority of Heads of State and Government and COMESA Council of Ministers, following a recommendation of Committee of Central Bank Governors, 2008, Cairo (Egypt). **Aims** Undertake all technical preparatory work needed for enhancing monetary cooperation in the region with the aim of establishing a COMESA Monetary Union. **Structure** Committee of Governors of Central Banks; Bureau of COMESA Committee of Governors of Central Banks; Committee on Finance and Monetary Affairs; Secretariat.
Members Central banks of 12 countries:
Burundi, Congo Brazzaville, Egypt, Eswatini, Kenya, Malawi, Mauritius, Rwanda, Sudan, Uganda, Zambia, Zimbabwe.
IGO Relations Partner of (5): *African Development Bank (ADB, #00283); Common Market for Eastern and Southern Africa (COMESA, #04296); International Monetary Fund (IMF, #14180); United Nations Economic Commission for Africa (ECA, #20554); West African Monetary Institute (WAMI, #20888).* [2018/AA1130/**E***]

♦ COMESA Regional Investment Agency (COMESA RIA) 04128

CEO General Authority for Investment Bldg, 3A Salah Salem Road, Nasr City, Cairo, 11562, Egypt. T. +20224055428. Fax +20224055421. E-mail: info@comesaria.org.
URL: http://comesaria.org/

History Jun 2006. Established within *Common Market for Eastern and Southern Africa (COMESA, #04296).* **Aims** Make the COMESA region a viable, attractive destination for regional and international investors. [2021/XJ4671/**E***]

♦ COMESA Reinsurance Company / see PTA Reinsurance Company (#18561)
♦ **COMESA RIA** COMESA Regional Investment Agency (#04128)
♦ COMES – Comunità Europea degli Scrittori (inactive)
♦ **COMESSA** Communauté des états sahelo-sahariens (#04406)
♦ **COMEST** Commission mondiale d'éthique des connaissances scientifiques et des technologies de l'UNESCO (#04235)
♦ **COMET** Collegium Medicorum Theatri (#04116)
♦ COMETEC-GAZ / see Eurogas (#05682)
♦ COMETE international – Communiquer et travailler ensemble (internationally oriented national body)
♦ **COMETH** European Conference of National Ethics Committees (#06734)
♦ **COMFAS** International Association for Comparative Fascist Studies (#11795)
♦ Comfort the Children International (internationally oriented national body)
♦ **COMFWB** COMESA Federation of National Associations of Women in Business (#04126)
♦ **COMHAD** Commonwealth Association for Health and Disability (#04302)
♦ **COMHAFAT** Conférence Ministérielle sur la Coopération Halieutique entre les Etats Africains Riverains de l'Océan Atlantique (#16816)
♦ Comhairle an Aontais Eorpaigh (#04895)
♦ Comhar Eorpach Eagras Poibli / see SGI Europe (#19253)
♦ Comhar Eorpach Eagras le Scar Staitúil / see SGI Europe (#19253)
♦ Comhlamh (internationally oriented national body)
♦ Comhlamh (internationally oriented national body)
♦ Comhlamh – Volunteers and development workers in global solidarity / see Comhlamh
♦ Comhnascas Eorpach der Sheirbhisi Tairgióchta (#07196)
♦ COMIAC – Standing Committee for Information and Cultural Affairs (see: #17813)
♦ **COMIBAM** Cooperación Misionera Iberoamericana (#04791)
♦ COMIBAM Internacional / see Cooperación Misionera Iberoamericana (#04791)
♦ Comic Relief (internationally oriented national body)
♦ COMIDE / see VIA Don Bosco (#20766)
♦ **COMIFAC** Commission des forêts d'Afrique centrale (#04214)
♦ COMIFA – Commission internationale pour l'étude scientifique de la famille (inactive)
♦ COMINAC – Conference of the Information Ministers of Non-Aligned Countries (meeting series)
♦ Cominform – Information Bureau of Communist and Workers' Parties (inactive)
♦ Comintern – Communist International (inactive)
♦ COMIP – Comisión Mixta Argentino-Paraguaya del Rio Parana (internationally oriented national body)
♦ COMISA / see Health for Animals (#10870)
♦ **COMISCA** Consejo de Ministros de Salud de Centroamérica (#04722)
♦ COMISCO / see SOLIDAR (#19680)
♦ COMISCO – Comité international socialiste consultatif (inactive)
♦ Comisia Europeana (#06633)
♦ Comisión de Administración Pública Internacional (#12587)
♦ Comisión Administradora del Rio Uruguay (internationally oriented national body)
♦ Comisión Americana Permanente de Aviación (inactive)
♦ Comisión Andina de Juristas (#00816)
♦ Comisión Arabe Permanente de Correos (#01025)
♦ Comisión Arco Atlantico (#03007)
♦ Comisión Asesora Europea sobre Pesca Continental / see European Inland Fisheries and Aquaculture Advisory Commission (#07540)
♦ Comisión Ballenera Internacional (#15879)
♦ Comisión Católica Internacional de Migración (#12459)

♦ Comisión Centroamericana de Ambiente y Desarrollo (CCAD) 04129

Central American Commission on Environment and Development

Ad Interim Coordinator Bvd Orden de Malta No 470, Antiguo Cuscatlan, La Libertad, El Salvador. T. +50322488843. Fax +50322488899. E-mail: info.ccad@sica.int.
URL: http://www.sica.int/ccad/

History 10 Dec 1989, Coronado (Costa Rica). 10-12 Dec 1989, San Isidro Coronado (Costa Rica), on signature of *Convenio Centroamericano para la Protección del Medio Ambiente (1989)* by the Presidents of Costa Rica, El Salvador, Guatemala (Guatemala), Honduras, Nicaragua, Panama and Minister of Belize (Belize). A commission within the framework of *Central American Integration System (#03671).* **Aims** Contribute to the sustainable development of the Central American region strengthening the cooperation and integration regime of environmental management. **Structure** Council of Ministers, comprising Environmental Authorities of member countries. Presidency, rotating every 6 months among member countries; Executive Secretary; Technical Committees; Executive Secretariat. **Finance** Fund comprising contributions of signatory nations; donations; other sources. **Activities** Acts as a catalyst and facilitator of, and harmonizes and integrates environmental policies in the region. Strategic guidelines of actions carried out by CCAD specified in Central America's Regional Environmental Plan (PARCA), a medium- and long-term strategy that focuses directly on environmental challenges in the region. PARCA 2005-2010 focuses on 2 strategic areas: Pollution control and prevention; Conservation and sustainable use of natural heritage. PARCA III (2010-2015). **Events** *Conférence sur la gestion des problèmes environementaux en Amérique Centrale* Guatemala (Guatemala) 1994.
Members Representatives of 8 countries:
Belize, Costa Rica, Dominican Rep, El Salvador, Guatemala, Honduras, Nicaragua, Panama.
IGO Relations Accredited by: *United Nations Framework Convention on Climate Change – Secretariat (UNFCCC, #20564).* Participates in: *AmeriGEOSS (#00796).* Cooperates with: *United Nations Institute for Training and Research (UNITAR, #20576).* **NGO Relations** Member of: *Alianza por el Agua (no recent information); International Network for Environmental Compliance and Enforcement (INECE, #14261).* Partner of: *Partnership for Clean Fuels and Vehicles (PCFV, #18231).* [2014/XF1464/**E***]

♦ Comisión Centroamericana de Directores de Migración (no recent information)
♦ Comisión Centroamericana de Energia (inactive)
♦ Comisión Centroamericana de Juristas de la Integración (no recent information)

♦ Comisión Centroamericana Permanente para la Erradicación de la Producción, Trafico, Consumo y Uso Ilicitos de Estupefacientes y Sustancias Psicotrópicas (CCP) 04130

Permanent Central American Commission on the Eradication of the Illicit Production, Trafficking, Consumption and Use of Narcotics and Psychotropic Substances

Contact Bulevar Suyapa, Colonia Florencia Norte, Edificio Florencia, Oficina 412, Tegucigalpa, Francisco Morazán, Honduras. T. +50422356349. Fax +50422356349. E-mail: ccp@ccpcentroamerica.org.

History 29 Oct 1993, Guatemala (Guatemala). **IGO Relations** Specialized Institution of: *Central American Integration System (#03671).* [2003/XE3501/**E**]

♦ Comisión Centroamericana de Transporte Maritimo (COCATRAM) .. 04131

Commission centroaméricaine du transport maritime – Central American Commission of Maritime Transport

Exec Dir Apdo Postal 2423, Managua, Nicaragua. T. +50522222754. Fax +50522222759. E-mail: onoack@cocatram.org.ni.
Street Address Frente al Costado Oeste del Hotel Mansión Teodolinda, Managua, Nicaragua.
URL: http://www.cocatram.org.ni/

History 15 Jul 1980. Established by resolution 5-80 of *Meeting of Ministers Responsible for the Economic Integration of Central America (ROMRIECA),* replacing *Comisión Centroamericana de Autoridades Portuarias (COCAAP, inactive),* set up in May 1969 by the then *Central American Economic Council (inactive).* From Feb 1987, within the framework of *Meeting of Ministers Responsible for Transport in Central America (REMITRAN).* Constitution and functioning modified and approved by Special Agreement of REMITRAN, came into force 11 Jul 1991. Currently functions within the framework of *Central American Integration System (#03671);* expected to become an institution of the proposed *Central American Common Market (CACM, #03666).* Former names and other names: *Central American Commission of Port Authorities* – former (1980). **Aims** Adopt policies, measures, recommendations and decisions over different fields of maritime transport to be applied at national and regional level to provide harmonic and effective sub-sector development. **Structure** Meeting of Ministers Responsible for Transport. Board of Directors, comprising a Director and a Deputy Director appointed by each member country and organization, and including President and Vice-President. Secretariat organized in 4 directorates: Executive; Administrative and Finance; Maritime and Ports; Training and Education. **Languages** English, Spanish. **Staff** 12.00 FTE, paid. **Finance** Sources: contributions of member/participating states.
Activities Categories (8): 1. Technical assistance to port administrations, maritime transport authorities, national and private shipping lines, chambers of commerce and any other public or private institution engaged in the field. 2. Courses, lectures and seminars. 3. Maritime and port studies, recommendations and projects tending to solve sector problems and deficiencies. 4. Management of international technical assistance in favour of private and governmental technical institutions, cooperating in performance of technical missions and monitoring implementation of recommendations. 5. Cooperation with public institutions in implementing methodological procedures and systems to improve their administration. 6. Acting as Permanent Secretariat of *Central American Isthmus Port Institution Meeting (REPICA)* (Port meeting of Central America). 7. Acting as Secretariat of *Operational Net of Regional Cooperation of Central American Maritime Authorities (ROCRAMCA, no recent information).* 8. Acting as Secretariat of Statistical Meeting of Central America.
Within these categories, projects include: multimodal transport; direct assistance of ports; maritime ports regional training programme; commercialization and privatization of state ports; strengthening USUARIOS; institutional strengthening COCATRAM itself; quinquennial action plan of REPICA; quinquennial action plan of Central American Isthmus training centres; navigational aids in Central America; maritime freights; informatics growth; dissemination of technical information; Honduras Golf Project and Mapping of the Greater Caribbean Region.
Events *Port meeting of Central America* Belize 2010, *Meeting of maritime authorities* Costa Rica 2010, *Statistical meeting* Costa Rica 2010, *Meeting of maritime authorities* Panama 2010, *Central American isthmus port institution meeting* Panama (Panama) 1997. **Publications** *COCATRAM Bulletin Marport* (quarterly) in Spanish. **Information Services** *Map of Sea Routes; Port Statistics System; Reception of Ship Waste in Central American Ports and Dominican Republic.*
Members Governments of 6 countries:
Costa Rica, El Salvador, Guatemala, Honduras, Nicaragua, Panama.
Regional organizations (3), listed in this Yearbook:
Asociación de Usuarios del Transporte Maritimo, Terrestre y Aéreo del Istmo Centroamericano (USUARIOS, no recent information); Federación de Camaras y Asociaciones de Exportadores de Centroamérica y el Caribe (FECAEXCA, #09293); Federation of Central American Chambers of Commerce (#09470).
IGO Relations Within the United Nations System: *International Maritime Organization (IMO, #14102); UNCTAD (#20285); United Nations Commission on International Trade Law (UNCITRAL, #20531); United Nations Economic Commission for Latin America and the Caribbean (ECLAC, #20556).* Other intergovernmental organizations: *Central American Institute of Public Administration (#03670); Norwegian Agency for Development*

Cooperation (Norad); OAS (#17629); Regional Seas Programme (#18814); Secretaria Permanente del Tratado General de Integración Económica Centroamericana (SIECA, #19195); Sistema Económico Latinoamericano (SELA, #19294). **NGO Relations** *American Association of Port Authorities (AAPA, #00775); Centro de Coordinación para la Prevención de los Desastres Naturales en América Central (CEPREDENAC, #03795).* [2022.10.11/XD2307/y/**E***]

- ♦ Comisión de Ciencia y Tecnologia de Centroamericana y Panama / see Comisión para el Desarrollo Cientifico y Tecnológico de Centro América y Panama (#04132)
- ♦ Comisión del Codex Alimentarius (#04081)
- ♦ Comisión de Comunicaciones Portuarios Intermediterraneas (inactive)
- ♦ Comisión de la Comunidad Andina (#04203)
- ♦ Comisión de las Comunidades Europeas / see European Commission (#06633)
- ♦ Comisión de la Condición Jurídica y Social de la Mujer (#20536)
- ♦ Comisión Conjunta FAO/OMS del Codex Alimentarius / see Codex Alimentarius Commission (#04081)
- ♦ Comisión para la Conservación de los Recursos Vivos Marinos Antarticos (#04206)
- ♦ Comisión de Consolidación de la Paz (#20606)
- ♦ Comisión para la Cooperación Ambiental (#04211)
- ♦ Comisión para la Cooperación Laboral (#04231)
- ♦ Comisión de Cooperación Presbiteriana en América Latina / see Alliance of Presbyterian and Reformed Churches in Latin America (#00713)
- ♦ Comisión Coordinadora de Organizaciones de Obreros Agricolas y Campesinos de América Latina (inactive)
- ♦ Comisión para la Defensa de los Derechos Humanos en Centroamérica (no recent information)

♦ Comisión para el Desarrollo Cientifico y Tecnológico de Centro América y Panama (CTCAP) 04132

Commission pour le développement technologique et scientifique de l'Amérique centrale et du Panama – Commission for the Scientific and Technological Development of Central America and Panama

Contact address not obtained. T. +5032262800. Fax +5032256255. E-mail: crochoa@conacyt.gob.sv.

History Established Jan 1976, under the auspices of *OAS (#17629)*. Comes within the framework of *Central American Integration System (#03671)*. Has been referred to in Spanish as *Comisión de Ciencia y Tecnologia de Centroamericana y Panamá*. **Aims** Foster, facilitate and coordinate joint scientific and technological efforts for development in the countries of Central America and Panama; provide a forum for debate of scientific and technological issues in the region. **Structure** Commission (meeting once or twice a year) comprises national delegates drawn from top echelon of policy-making bodies and from technical personnel involved in science and technology projects in the subregion. **Finance** Mainly supported by OAS but with increasing participation from such other international institutions as: *Central American Bank for Economic Integration (CABEI, #03658); Inter-American Development Bank (IDB, #11427); International Development Research Centre (IDRC, #13162); UNDP (#20292)*. **Activities** Reviews science and technology progress in the area; formulates and follows up joint initiatives.

Members Governments of 6 countries:
Costa Rica, El Salvador, Guatemala, Honduras, Nicaragua, Panama. [2016/XE9620/**E***]

- ♦ Comisión de Desarrollo Ganadero para América Latina y el Caribe (#04233)
- ♦ Comisión Económica de las Naciones Unidas para Africa (#20554)
- ♦ Comisión Económica de las Naciones Unidas para América Latina / see United Nations Economic Commission for Latin America and the Caribbean (#20556)
- ♦ Comisión Económica de las Naciones Unidas para América Latina y el Caribe (#20556)
- ♦ Comisión Económica de las Naciones Unidas para Asia y el Lejano Oriente / see United Nations Economic and Social Commission for Asia and the Pacific (#20557)
- ♦ Comisión Económica de las Naciones Unidas para el Asia Occidental / see United Nations Economic and Social Commission for Western Asia (#20558)
- ♦ Comisión Económica de las Naciones Unidas para Europa (#20555)
- ♦ Comisión Económica y Social de las Naciones Unidas para el Asia Occidental (#20558)
- ♦ Comisión Económica y Social de las Naciones Unidas para Asia y el Pacifico (#20557)
- ♦ Comisión Ecuménica de Derechos Humanos (internationally oriented national body)
- ♦ Comisión Educación para Médicos Graduados en el Extranjero (internationally oriented national body)
- ♦ Comisión Electrotécnica Internacional / see International Electrotechnical Commission (#13255)
- ♦ Comisión Española de Ayuda al Refugiado (internationally oriented national body)
- ♦ Comisión para el Estudio de la Historia de la Iglesia en América Latina y el Caribe / see Comisión de Estudios de Historia de la Iglesia en América Latina (#04133)
- ♦ Comisión para el Estudio de la Organización de Aguas (no recent information)

♦ Comisión de Estudios de Historia de la Iglesia en América Latina (CEHILA) 04133

Commission d'études de l'histoire de l'Eglise en Amérique latine – Commission of Studies for Latin American Church History – Comissão de Estudos de Historia da Igreja na América Latina

Admin Sec 285 Oblate Drive, San Antonio TX 78216, USA. T. +12103411366ext223.
Exec Sec address not obtained. E-mail: glzjudd@gmail.com.
URL: http://www.cehila.org/

History 3 Jan 1973, Quito (Ecuador). Former names and other names: *Comisión para el Estudio de la Historia de la Iglesia en América Latina y el Caribe* – alias. Registration: Start date: 10 Jun 1973, Ecuador. **Aims** Develop formation in and study of Latin American *Christian* history for the benefit of the people; establish scholarly exchanges with academic centres; collaborate in preservation of documents; promote socialization of knowledge. **Structure** General Assembly (every 2 years); Managing Board. **Languages** English, Portuguese, Spanish. **Staff** Voluntary. **Finance** Sources: donations; international organizations; sale of publications. **Activities** Projects/programmes; research/documentation. **Events** *Biennial Symposium* San Salvador (El Salvador) 2015, *Biennial Symposium* Mexico City (Mexico) 2012, *Biennial Symposium* Buenos Aires (Argentina) 2010, *Biennial Symposium* Cuernavaca (Mexico) 2008, *Annual Symposium* Buenos Aires (Argentina) 2006. **Publications** *CEHILANET* – electronic review. *Cristianismos en América Latina: Tiempo presente, historias y memorias* (2013); *Experiencia Religiosa e Identidades en América Latina* (2013); *El Protestantismo en Colombia* (2009); *Otro Mundo y Otra Iglesia son Posibles: un acercamiento al catolicismo centroamericano contemporaneo* (2008); *Protestantismo y Vida Cotidiana en América Latina: un estudio desde la cotidianidad de los sujetos* (2007); *Actores y Dimensión Religiosa en los Movimientos Sociales Latinoamericanos 1960-1992* (2006).

Members Individuals (Founder; Ordinary; Associate) in 25 countries and territories:
Argentina, Bolivia, Brazil, Canada, Chile, Colombia, Costa Rica, Cuba, Dominican Rep, Ecuador, El Salvador, Guatemala, Haiti, Honduras, Mexico, Neth Antilles, Nicaragua, Panama, Paraguay, Peru, Puerto Rico, Spain, Uruguay, USA, Venezuela.

NGO Relations Member of (1): *Conference on Latin American History (CLAH)*. [2021.03.20/XD4342/v/**E**]

- ♦ Comisión Europea (#06633)
- ♦ Comisión Europea de Agricultura (#06634)
- ♦ Comisión Evangélica Latinoamericana de Educación Cristiana (inactive)
- ♦ Comisión FAO/OMS del Codex Alimentarius / see Codex Alimentarius Commission (#04081)
- ♦ Comisión Forestal para América Latina y del Caribe (#16278)
- ♦ Comisión Forestal para América del Norte (#17565)
- ♦ Comisión Forestal para Asia y el Pacifico (#01909)
- ♦ Comisión Forestal para el Cercano Oriente (#16965)
- ♦ Comisión Forestal Europea (#07299)
- ♦ Comisión Forestal y de la Flora y Fauna Silvestres para Africa (#00319)
- ♦ Comisión Forestal Latinoamericana / see Latin American and Caribbean Forestry Commission (#16278)
- ♦ Comisión Forestal Latinoamericana y del Caribe / see Latin American and Caribbean Forestry Commission (#16278)
- ♦ Comisión General de Pesca del Mediterraneo (#10112)
- ♦ Comisión Hidrografica del Atlantico Sudoccidental (see: #13825)
- ♦ Comisión Huevera Internacional (#13245)

♦ Comisión Iberoamericana de Calidad Educativa (CICE) 04134

General Coordinator address not obtained. E-mail: enlace.cice@gmail.com – editorial.descubriendo@gmail.com.
URL: http://comisioniberoamericana.org/

History Set up following a congress held Mar 2012, Mérida (Mexico). **Aims** Contribute to education in Latin America to improve the living conditions of people in the areas where they work. **Structure** Officers. **Languages** Spanish. **Finance** Sources: revenue from activities/projects. **Activities** Events/meetings; guidance/assistance/consulting; humanitarian/emergency aid; networking/liaising; projects/programmes; research and development; training/education. **Events** *Congress* Oaxaca (Mexico) 2023, *Congress* Yucatán (Mexico) 2022, *Congress* Monterrey (Mexico) 2019, *Congress* Campeche (Mexico) 2018, *Congress* Barcelona (Spain) 2017.

Members Full in 8 countries:
Argentina, Bolivia, Brazil, Chile, Colombia, Mexico, Panama, Spain.

NGO Relations Academic foundations; institutions of higher learning. [2023.02.27/XJ7085/**D**]

- ♦ Comisión Iberoamericana de Seguridad Social / see Ibero-American Social Security Organization (#11028)
- ♦ Comisión de Integración Eléctrica Regional / see Regional Commission for Power Integration (#18764)
- ♦ Comisión de Integración Energética Regional (#18764)
- ♦ Comisión Interamericana de Arbitraje Comercial (#11410)
- ♦ Comisión Interamericana del Atún Tropical (#11454)
- ♦ Comisión Interamericana para el Control del Abuso de Drogas (#11429)
- ♦ Comisión Interamericana de Derechos Humanos (#11411)

♦ Comisión Interamericana de Desarrollo Social (CIDES) 04135

Inter-American Committee on Social Development

Contact Unit for Social Development, Education and Culture, OAS, 1889 F St NW, GSB-120 A, Washington DC 20006, USA. T. +12024583010.
URL: http://oas.org/

History 1996. **Aims** Strengthen and reinforce Inter-American dialogue in order to support the creation of policies and develop collaborative actions in the area of social development that fight poverty and discrimination. **Events** *Meeting* Washington, DC (USA) 2010, *Meeting* Washington, DC (USA) 2007, *Meeting* Santiago (Chile) 2004. **IGO Relations** *OAS (#17629)*. [2017/XJ4197/**E***]

♦ Comisión Interamericana de Educación (CIE) 04136

Inter-American Commission on Education

Dir Office of Education and Culture, OAS, General Services Bldg (GSB) room 775, 1889 F St NW, GSB-120 A, Washington DC 20006, USA. T. +12024583368. E-mail: education@oas.org.
URL: http://www.oas.org/sedi/dec/

History 2002, by *OAS (#17629)*. **Aims** Supports the efforts of Member States to improve the quality and equity of education and to enhance and highlight the contribution of their diverse cultures to economic, social and human development. **Activities** Promotes inter-American dialogue on policy and practice in the fields of education and culture, through meetings of Ministers, Inter-American Committees and knowledge-sharing seminars and workshops; assists in knowledge transfer and capacity building through the design and implementation of multi-country projects in education and culture; supports networks of policy makers, researchers, practitioners, and international governmental and non-governmental organizations on key education and culture topics. **Events** *Plenary Meeting* Washington, DC (USA) 2013, *Meeting of the Authorities* Washington, DC (USA) 2012, *Meeting of the Authorities* Washington, DC (USA) 2011, *Meeting of the authorities* Washington, DC (USA) 2010, *Meeting of the authorities* Washington, DC (USA) 2009. [2010.12.09/XJ4196/**E***]

- ♦ Comisión Interamericana de Energia Nuclear (inactive)

♦ Comisión Interamericana de Mujeres (CIM) 04137

Commission interaméricaine des femmes – Inter-American Commission of Women

Secretariat c/o OAS, 1889 F St NW, Washington DC 20006, USA. T. +12024586084. Fax +12024586094. E-mail: cim@oas.org.
URL: http://www.oas.org/CIM/

History 18 Feb 1928, Havana (Cuba), at VI International Conference of American States, pursuant to Resolution LXI. Became a permanent inter-governmental agency through the adoption of Resolution XXIII of VIII International Conference of American States, 1938, Lima (Peru). Resolution XXI of IX International Conference of American States, 1948, Bogota, and Resolution XXVIII, authorized the Secretary General of OAS to organize the Permanent Secretariat of the Commission. In Jun 1953 a formal Agreement between the Council of *OAS (#17629)* and the Commission was signed, which recognizes the Commission as a permanent inter-American Specialized Agency. In 1976 the XVIII Assembly of Delegates reformed the Statute which was modified again in 1986 by XXIII Assembly of Delegates and in 1988 by XXIV Assembly of Delegates. **Aims** Formulate strategies, propose solutions to bring about a new concept of the roles of men and women in the new social structure, considering them as beings of equal worth, equally responsible for the fate of humanity; analyse problems of women in the *Americas*; mobilize, train and organize women for effective, conscious and continuing participation in the process of planning and executing development programmes. **Structure** Commission consists of one Principal Delegate for each member State, appointed by the respective Government; Alternates and Advisors. Delegates, with Committees of Cooperation, carry out the work of Commission in their respective countries. Executive Committee, composed of President, Vice-President and Representatives of 5 member countries, elected for 2-year terms. OAS appoints Executive Secretary and Permanent Secretariat. Assembly (biennial and special). **Languages** English, French, Portuguese, Spanish. **Finance** Maintenance of Commission and Permanent Secretariat included in the budget of OAS. Expenses of Delegates met by their Governments. **Activities** Conventions; treaties; resolutions; recommendations. studies, surveys and reports; technical meetings; leadership training. Courses, seminars, forums, round tables and conferences of local, national, hemispheric or international scope. Developed: *Inter-American Convention on the Prevention, Punishment and Eradication of Violence Against Women (Convention of Belém do Para, 1994)*, adopted by OAS General Assembly in 1994; *Inter-american Programme on the Promotion of Women's Human Rights and Gender Equity and Equality*, adopted by OAS General Assembly in 2000. **Events** *Anti-trafficking in persons conference* Washington, DC (USA) 2005, *Caribbean regional anti-trafficking in persons conference* Washington, DC (USA) 2005, *Biennial Assembly* Washington, DC (USA) 2004, *Meeting of ministers or of the highest-ranking authorities responsible for policies on women in the member states* Washington, DC (USA) 2004, *Meeting on gender and education* Washington, DC (USA) 2003. **Publications** Technical studies; directories; pamphlets; comparative charts; maps on the status of women; surveys; working papers and documentation for biennial Assemblies and other meetings.

Members Governments of 35 countries (since 1962, the Government of Cuba has been suspended from participation in the inter-American system):
Antigua-Barbuda, Argentina, Bahamas, Barbados, Belize, Bolivia, Brazil, Canada, Chile, Colombia, Costa Rica, Cuba (*), Dominica, Dominican Rep, Ecuador, El Salvador, Grenada, Guatemala, Guyana, Haiti, Honduras, Jamaica, Mexico, Nicaragua, Panama, Paraguay, Peru, St Kitts-Nevis, St Lucia, St Vincent-Grenadines, Suriname, Trinidad-Tobago, Uruguay, USA, Venezuela.

IGO Relations Agreements of cooperation with: *Inter-American Children's Institute (IACI, #11406); Inter-American Indian Institute (IAII, inactive); Inter-American Institute for Cooperation on Agriculture (IICA, #11434); Pan American Health Organization (PAHO, #18108)*. **NGO Relations** Member of: *Association for Women's Rights in Development (AWID, #02980)*. Partner of: *Global Forum on Law, Justice and Development (GFLJD, #10373)*. [2017/XE1058/**E***]

- ♦ Comisión Interamericana de Paz (inactive)
- ♦ Comisión Interamericana de Puertos (#11415)
- ♦ Comisión Interamericana de Soluciones Pacificas (inactive)

♦ Comisión Interamericana de Telecomunicaciones (CITEL) 04138

Commission interaméricaine de télécommunications – Inter-American Telecommunication Commission

Secretariat c/o OAS, 1889 F St NW, Ste 348, Washington DC 20006, USA. T. +12024583004. Fax +12024586854. E-mail: citel@oas.org.

URL: http://www.citel.oas.org/

History 2 May 1923. Established by resolution of 13th session of the International Conference of the American States, currently *OAS (#17629)*. Former names and other names: *Inter-American Electrical Communication Commission* – former (2 May 1923); *Commission on Inter-American Telecommunications* – former. **Aims** Facilitate and promote the continuing development of telecommunication in the western hemisphere; organize and promote meetings of telecommunications experts.
Structure Assembly (every 4 years) comprises all member countries. Permanent Executive Committee (COM/CITEL) comprises representatives of Brazil, Canada, Colombia, Granada, Honduras, Mexico, Paraguay, USA and Uruguay, plus Ecuador (site of 2nd Regular Assembly) and Argentina (site of 3rd Regular Assembly). Working Groups of COM/CITEL (5):
- Development of Human Resources;
- Strategic Plan of CITEL;
- Meetings of the Council of the International Telecommunication Union (ITU);
- 2002 Plenipotentiary Conference;
- Cooperative Agreements.

Ad Hoc Groups of COM/CITEL (2):
- Draft Plan of Action for the Telecommunications Sector (to be presented at 3rd Summit of the Americas);
- Improvement in the Working Methods of CITEL.

Permanent Consultative Committees (PCCs). Steering Committee, composed of Chair and Vice-Chair of COM/CITEL and Chairs of the PCCs. Joint Working Group on Legal Matters and Administrative Procedures of the PCCs.
Finance Sources: OAS; voluntary contributions from Associate Members (private sector).
Activities Events/meetings. Plan af action addresses: cooperation between member administrations and harmonization of their actions; participation by non-administration entities and organizations in the activities of the PCCs; coordination with world and other regional intergovernmental and nongovernmental organizations in the Americas concerned with telecommunications; information exchange with ITU Members and with wider telecommunications community.
Permanent Consultative Committees (PCCs):
'PCC I – Public Telecommunication Services', including:
- Working Group on Standards Coordination;
- Working Group on Basic and Universal Telecommunications Services;
- Working Group on Certification Processes and Mutual Recognition Agreements;
- Working Group on the Promotion of the Global Information Infrastructure;
- Working Group on Economic Issues and Tariff Principles within the Telecommunication Sector in the Americas;
- Ad Hoc Group for the Preparation for the ITU World Telecommunication Standardization Assembly;
- Ad Hoc Group to Study and Define an Approach to Telecommunication Services that Use IP Technology.

'PCC II – Broadcasting', including:
- Working Group on Digital Sound Broadcasting;
- Working Group on the Coordination of Incompatibilities of 1981 Rio de Janeiro (Brazil) Plan;
- Working Group to Study Broadcasting Issues at Future Regional and World Radio Communication Conferences;
- Working Group on the Review of the Mandate and Working Methods to Develop a Future Vision for PCC II;
- Working Group on Broadband Wireless Systems in a Fixed Service Operating on Frequency Bands above 20 GHz in Radio Broadcasting;
- Working Group to Study the Implementation of the Digital Television Service.

'PCC III – Radiocommunications', including:
- Working Group on Terrestrial Wireless Access;
- Working Group Relative to CITEL's Preparation for Regional and World Radiocommunication Conferences;
- Working Group on Broadband Wireless Systems in the Fixed Service Operating;
- Ad-Hoc Group to Examine Procedures for Submitting Joint Proposals to the ITU-R;
- Working Group relative to Satellite Systems to Provide Fixed and Mobile Services.

Events *Broadband wireless access seminar* San Salvador (El Salvador) 2003, *Quadrennial Assembly* Washington, DC (USA) 2002, *Quadrennial Assembly* Quito (Ecuador) 1998, *Meeting of senior telecommunication officials of the Americas* Washington, DC (USA) 1996, *Seminar on signalisation and radiodiffusion* Ottawa, ON (Canada) 1994. **Publications** *CITEL Magazine*. Reports of meetings; special studies.
Members Governments of 35 countries:
Antigua-Barbuda, Argentina, Bahamas, Barbados, Belize, Bolivia, Brazil, Canada, Chile, Colombia, Costa Rica, Cuba, Dominica, Dominican Rep, Ecuador, El Salvador, Grenada, Guatemala, Guyana, Haiti, Honduras, Jamaica, Mexico, Nicaragua, Panama, Paraguay, Peru, St Kitts-Nevis, St Lucia, St Vincent-Grenadines, Suriname, Trinidad-Tobago, Uruguay, USA, Venezuela.
Associate Members (from the private sector) in 10 countries:
Argentina, Brazil, Canada, Chile, Colombia, Dominican Rep, Mexico, Nicaragua, USA, Venezuela.
IGO Relations Agreement with: *Conférence européenne des administrations des postes et des télécommunications (CEPT, #04602)*. [2023.02.20/XF1041/**E***]

- ♦ Comisión Intergubernamental para la Eliminación de Triatoma Infestans (no recent information)
- ♦ Comisión Intermediterranea (#11521)
- ♦ Comisión Internacional del Alamo (#14619)
- ♦ Comisión Internacional del Arroz (inactive)
- ♦ Comisión Internacional de Capellanes Generales de Prisión / see International Commission of Catholic Prison Pastoral Care (#12670)
- ♦ Comisión Internacional para la Conservación del Atún Atlantico (#12675)
- ♦ Comisión Internacional contra la Impunidad en Guatemala (#12660)
- ♦ Comisión Internacional contra la Pena de Muerte (#12659)
- ♦ Comisión Internacional de los Derechos Humanos para Gays y Lesbianes / see OutRight Action International
- ♦ Comisión Internacional de Educación Matematica (#12700)
- ♦ Comisión Internacional de Electricidad Atmosférica (#12665)
- ♦ Comisión Internacional para la Exploración Cientifica del Mar Mediterraneo (#16674)
- ♦ Comisión Internacional de Historia Militar (#12705)
- ♦ Comisión Internacional de las Industrias Agricolas y Alimentarias (inactive)
- ♦ Comisión Internacional de Ingenieria Rural (#12661)
- ♦ Comisión Internacional de la Irrigación y el Saneamiento (#12694)
- ♦ Comisión Internacional de Juristas (#12695)
- ♦ Comisión Internacional de Medicina del Trabajo (#12709)
- ♦ Comisión Internacional de Numismatica / see International Numismatic Council (#14385)
- ♦ Comisión Internacional para las Ordenes de Caballeria (#12711)
- ♦ Comisión Internacional de la Pastoral Penitenciaria Católica (#12670)
- ♦ Comisión Internacional de Pesca del Mar Baltico (internationally oriented national body)
- ♦ Comisión Internacional para la Pesca del Salmón en el Pacifico (inactive)
- ♦ Comisión Internacional de Pesquerias del Atlantico Noroeste (inactive)
- ♦ Comisión Internacional de Pesquerias del Atlantico Sud-Oriental (inactive)
- ♦ Comisión Internacional para la Prevención del Alcoholismo (#12719)
- ♦ Comisión Internacional de Protección Radiológica (#12724)
- ♦ Comisión Internacional para la Tecnologia del Azúcar (inactive)
- ♦ Comisión Internacional del Vidrio (#12683)
- ♦ Comisión International sobre Comunicación, Información e Informatica (no recent information)
- ♦ Comisión International del Hipogloso en el Pacifico (internationally oriented national body)
- ♦ Comisión Interparlamentaria Centroamericana (inactive)
- ♦ Comisión de las Islas (#16061)

♦ Comisión Juridica para el Autodesarrollo de los Pueblos Originarios Andinos (CAPAJ) 04139

Legal Commission for the Self-Development of the Indigenous Peoples of the Andes – Commission juridique pour l'auto-développement des peuples autochtones des Andes

Pres Av 2 de Mayo 644, 1er piso-A, Tacna, Peru. T. +5152242601. E-mail: capaj_internacional@yahoo.com.

URL: http://www.capaj.org/

History Founded 2 Dec 1993, Tacna (Peru). **Aims** Contribute to combating *discrimination* or other acts that threaten *indigenous peoples* and their *fundamental rights* as contained in the constitutions of their countries and in the Universal Declaration of the Human Rights. **Activities** Guidance/assistance/consulting.
Members Founding members in 3 countries:
Bolivia, Chile, Peru.
Consultative Status Consultative status granted from: *ECOSOC (#05331)* (Special). **NGO Relations** Proposes setting up: *Academia Andina de Derecho Internacional Público (AADIP, no recent information)*.
[2015/XE2981/**E**]

- ♦ Comisión Justicia, Paz, Integridad de la Creación de las Uniones de Superiores Generales – USG/UISG (#04230)
- ♦ Comisión Latinoamericana de Aviación Civil (#16297)

♦ Comisión Latinoamericana de Empresarios de Combustibles (CLAEC) 04140

Permanent Secretariat c/o UNVENU, R Felix M Olmedo 3520, 11700 Montevideo, Uruguay. Fax +59823095778 – +59823073167. E-mail: info@unvenu.org.uy.

URL: http://www.claecomb.com.br/

History 1995. **Events** *Meeting / Congress* Dominican Rep 2009, *Meeting / Congress* Guanajuato (Mexico) 2009, *Meeting / Congress* San José (Costa Rica) 2008, *Meeting / Congress* Valencia (Venezuela) 2008, *Meeting / Congress* Paipa (Colombia) 2007. [2015/XE4355/**E**]

- ♦ Comisión Latinoamericana de Servidores Públicos / see Coordinadora Latinoamericana de Trabajadores de los Servicios Públicos (#04809)
- ♦ Comisión Latinoamericana de Trabajadores de la Energia (inactive)
- ♦ Comisión para la Lucha contra la Langosta del Desierto en Asia Sudoccidental (#04209)
- ♦ Comisión para la Lucha contra la Langosta del Desierto en el Cercano Oriente / see Commission for Controlling the Desert Locust in the Central Region (#04208)
- ♦ Comisión para la Lucha contra la Langosta del Desierto en la Región Oriental de su Area de Distribución del Asia Sudoccidental / see Commission for Controlling the Desert Locust in South-West Asia (#04209)
- ♦ Comisión del Mar del Norte (#17604)
- ♦ Comisión Mixta Argentino-Paraguaya del Rio Parana (internationally oriented national body)
- ♦ Comisión Mixta Permanente Uruguay, Paraguay, Bolivia (inactive)
- ♦ Comisión Mundial de Cultura y Desarrollo (inactive)
- ♦ Comisión de las Naciones Unidas para el Derecho Mercantil Internacional (#20531)
- ♦ Comisión de las Naciones Unidas de Prevención del Delito y Justicia Penal (#20530)
- ♦ Comisión de las Naciones Unidas sobre la Utilización del Espacio Ultraterrestre con Fines Pacificos / see Committee on the Peaceful Uses of Outer Space (#04277)
- ♦ Comisión Oceanografica Intergubernamental (#11496)
- ♦ Comisión de la OMT para Africa (see: #21861)
- ♦ Comisión de la OMT para las Américas (see: #21861)
- ♦ Comisión de la OMT para Asia Meridional (see: #21861)
- ♦ Comisión de la OMT para Asia Oriental y Pacifico (see: #21861)
- ♦ Comisión de la OMT para Europa (see: #21861)
- ♦ Comisión de la OMT para el Oriente Medio (see: #21861)
- ♦ Comisión de Organismos de Supervisión y Fiscalización Bancaria de América Latina y el Caribe / see Association of Supervisors of Banks of the Americas (#02944)
- ♦ Comisión Panamericana de Atletismo / see Asociación Panamericana de Atletismo (#02284)
- ♦ Comisión Panamericana de Cooperación Intermunicipal / see Organización Iberoamericana de Cooperación Intermunicipal (#17839)
- ♦ Comisión Panamericana de Normas Técnicas (#18133)
- ♦ Comisión Permanente Internacional del Acetileno, la Soldadura Autógena y las Industrias Afines / see European Industrial Gases Association (#07525)

♦ Comisión Permanente del Pacifico Sur (CPPS) 04141

Commission permanente du Pacifique Sud – Permanent Commission for the South Pacific – Comissão Permanente do Pacifico Sul

Contact Av Carlos Julio Arosemena, km 2-5, Edificio Classic – piso 2, Guayaquil, Ecuador. T. +59342221202. E-mail: sgeneral@cpps-int.org – comunicaciones@cpps-int.org – sistemas@cpps-int.org.

URL: http://www.cpps-int.org/

History Established 18 Aug 1952, Santiago (Chile), by *'Declaration of Santiago (Declaration on the Maritime Zone) – Declaración de Santiago (Declaración sobre la Zona Maritima)'*, signed and ratified by the Governments of Chile, Ecuador, and Peru during *'First Conference for the Exploitation and Conservation of Marine Resources in the South Pacific'*. Also referred to as *Permanent Southeast Pacific Commission*. Legal capacity established through an Agreement signed 14 Jan 1966. On 9 Aug 1979, Quito (Ecuador), the Government of Colombia signed an Incorporation Convention to join the *System of the South Pacific*, adhering to the Declaration of Santiago and other related regional conventions. Declarations of the Ministers of Foreign Affairs: 24 Jan 1981 – *'Declaration of Cali – Declaración de Cali'*; 10 Feb 1984 – *'Declaration of Viña del Mar – Declaración de Viña del Mar'*; 10 Dec 1987 – *'Declaration of Quito – Declaración de Quito'*; 4 Mar 1993 – *'Declaration of Lima – Declaración de Lima'*; 4 Aug 1997 – *'Declaration of Bogota – Declaración de Bogota'*; 14 Aug 2000 – *'Declaration of Santiago – Declaración de Santiago'*; 14 Aug 2002 – *'Declaration of Santiago – Declaración de Santiago'*. Statutes registered in *'UNTS 1/16890'*. **Aims** Promote, protect and encourage research on the rational and *sustainable* exploitation of living *marine resources*; promote research on the interaction of *ocean* and *atmosphere* and its social and economic effects; preserve the marine and *coastal environment*; promote and protect development of maritime law; promote economic interests of the member countries. **Structure** Commission, integrated by representatives of member states, meets twice a year. General Secretariat (chief executive organ), rotates every 4 years among member countries and consists of Secretary General, Under-Secretary, Director of Scientific Affairs and Director of Economic Affairs (each from different countries) and Technical Regional Coordinator on *Action Plan for the Protection of the Marine Environment and Coastal Areas in the South East Pacific (SE/PCF, #00095)*. Since the Meeting of Foreign Ministers, Aug 2000, Santiago (Chile), Headquarters permanently located in Guayaquil (Ecuador). National Sections are presided over by a high ranking officer of the Ministry of Foreign Affairs in each country and coordinate activities of General Secretariat with their national authorities. **Languages** English, Spanish. **Staff** 14.00 FTE, paid. **Finance** Members' dues.
Activities Since Declaration of Santiago, 1952, coordinates member states' policies for preservation of the marine environment and efforts against marine pollution, including: scientific research on the interaction among ocean, atmosphere and climate and their variations; ordering and development of the coastal zones and jurisdictional maritime areas; protection and preservation of the marine environment; utilization of non-living maritime resources (minerals and energy); ordering and development of fishing and other living maritime resources. Acts as Regional Coordinating Unit for South East Pacific Action Plan, which includes marine biodiversity, ecosystems of the Peruvian and Humboldt current and transzonal and highly migratory species. Events/meetings.
Management of treaties and agreements:
- *Convention on Biological Diversity (Biodiversity convention, 1992)*;
- *Declaration of Santiago on the Maritime Zone (1952)*, 18 Aug 1952, Santiago (Chile);
- *Agreement on Special Maritime Border Zone (1954)*, 4 Dec 1954, Lima (Peru);
- *Agreement on Regional Cooperation in Combating Pollution of the South-East Pacific by Hydrocarbons or other Harmful Substances in Cases of Emergency (1981)*, 12 Nov 1981, Lima;
- *Convention for the Protection of the Marine Environment and Coastal Area of the Southeast Pacific (Lima Convention, 1981)*, 12 Nov 1981, Lima;
- *Complementary Protocol to the Agreement on Regional Cooperation in Combating Pollution of the Southeast Pacific by Hydrocarbons and other Harmful Substances (1983)*, 22 Jul 1983, Quito (Ecuador);
- *Protocol for the Protection of the Southeast Pacific Against Pollution from Land-based Sources (1983)*, 22 Jul 1983, Quito;

- *Protocol for the Conservation and Management of Protected Marine and Coastal Areas of the Southeast Pacific (1989)*, 21 Sep 1989, Paipa (Colombia);
- *Protocol for the Protection of the South East Pacific Against Radioactive Contamination (1989)*, 21 Sep 1989, Paipa (Colombia);
- Protocol on the *Programa para el Estudio Regional del Fenómeno El Niño en el Pacífico Sudeste (ERFEN, #18523)*, 6 Nov 1992, Callao (Peru);
- Framework Agreement for the Conservation of Live Marine Resources in the High Seas of the Southeast Pacific "Galapagos Agreement", 14 aug 2000, Santiago de Chile.

Events *Ordinary Assembly* Puerto Ayora (Ecuador) 2015, *Ordinary Assembly* Guayaquil (Ecuador) 2014, *Extraordinary Assembly* Guayaquil (Ecuador) 2012, *Ordinary assembly* Guayaquil (Ecuador) 2006, *Extraordinary Assembly* Quito (Ecuador) 2006. **Publications** *Boletín de Alerta Climatico – BAC* (12 a year); *Boletín de Estadísticas Pesqueras del Pacífico Sudeste* (several a year, irregular) in English, Spanish; *Pacífico Sur* – journal.
Members Governments of 5 countries:
Chile, Colombia, Ecuador, Panama, Peru.
IGO Relations Cooperation agreements or notes of understanding signed with: *Agency for the Prohibition of Nuclear Weapons in Latin America and the Caribbean (#00554)*; *FAO (#09260)*; *Intergovernmental Oceanographic Commission (IOC, #11496)*; *International Maritime Organization (IMO, #14102)*; *UNIDO (#20336)*; *World Meteorological Organization (WMO, #21649)*; Secretariat of the 3rd United Nations Conference on the Law of the Sea; ECLAC/UNDP Programme on Resources of the Sea and Regional Development. For matters of a technical nature, maintains relations with: *Inter-American Tropical Tuna Commission (IATTC, #11454)*; Accredited by: *United Nations Framework Convention on Climate Change – Secretariat (UNFCCC, #20564)*. Invited to sessions of: Intergovernmental Council of *International Programme for the Development of Communication (IPDC, #14651)*; *South Pacific Regional Fisheries Management Organisation (SPRFMO, #19889)*. [2021/XD2685/**D***]

- ♦ Comisión de Pesca para Asia-Pacifico (#01907)
- ♦ Comisión de Pesca para el Atlantico Centro-Occidental (#20911)

♦ Comisión de Pesca Continental y Acuicultura para América Latina y el Caribe (COPESCAALC) 04142

Commission for Inland Fisheries and Aquaculture of Latin America and the Caribbean – Comissão de Pesca Continental e Aquiculture para América Latina e o Caribe

Sec FAO Regional Office for Latin America and the Caribbean RLC, Casilla 10095, Av Dag Hammarskjold 3241, Vitacura, Santiago, Santiago Metropolitan, Chile. T. +56229232170. E-mail: alejandro.flores@fao.org.
URL: http://www.fao.org/fishery/rfb/copescal/en/

History 1976, Rome (Italy), within the framework of *FAO (#09260)*, by the FAO Council at its 70th Session. (Article VI-1 of the FAO Constitution). Original title: *Comisión de Pesca Continental para América Latina (COPESCAL) – Commission des pêches intérieures pour l'Amérique latine – Commission for Inland Fisheries of Latin America*. Statutes revised 2009; Statutes and current title adopted, Dec 2010. **Aims** Promote management and sustainable development of inland fisheries and aquaculture in accordance with the principles and rules of the Code of Conduct for Responsbile Fisheries of FAO. **Structure** Commission; Secretariat provided by FAO. **Languages** English, French, Spanish. **Finance** Financial sources: FAO Regular Programme; government contributions. **Activities** Research/documentation; training/education; events/meetings; knowledge management/information dissemination; advocacy/lobbying/activism. **Events** *Session* Lima (Peru) 2016, *Session* Buenos Aires (Argentina) 2014, *Session* Cuernavaca (Mexico) 2011, *Session* Panama (Panama) 2005, *Session* San Salvador (El Salvador) 2003. **Publications** *COPESCAL Occasional Series*; *COPESCAL Technical Series*.
Members Open to all Member Nations and Associate Members of FAO serviced by the Regional Office for Latin America and the caribbean. Current members are the governments of 21 countries:
Argentina, Bolivia, Brazil, Chile, Colombia, Costa Rica, Cuba, Dominican Rep, Ecuador, El Salvador, Guatemala, Honduras, Jamaica, Mexico, Nicaragua, Panama, Paraguay, Peru, Suriname, Uruguay, Venezuela.
IGO Relations *FAO Regional Office for Latin America and the Caribbean (FAO/RLC, #09268)*; *Inter-American Development Bank (IDB, #11427)*; *Sistema Económico Latinoamericano (SELA, #19294)*; *UNDP (#20292)*.
NGO Relations Latin American organizations. [2016.06.01/XE9953/**E***]

- ♦ Comisión de Pesca Continental para América Latina / see Comisión de Pesca Continental y Acuicultura para América Latina y el Caribe (#04142)
- ♦ Comisión de Pesca del Indo-Pacifico / see Asia-Pacific Fishery Commission (#01907)
- ♦ Comisión de Pesquerias del Atlantico Nordeste (#17581)
- ♦ Comisión de Prevención del Delito y Justicia Penal / see United Nations Commission on Crime Prevention and Criminal Justice (#20530)
- ♦ Comisión de Producción y Sanidad Pecuarias para Asia, el Lejano Oriente y el Sudoeste del Pacifico (#00839)
- ♦ Comisión de Protección Fitosanitaria para el Caribe (inactive)
- ♦ Comisión Regional de la FAO de Producción y Sanidad Pecuarias para Asia, el Lejano Oriente y el Sudoeste del Pacifico / see Animal Production and Health Commission for Asia and the Pacific (#00839)
- ♦ Comisión de Seguridad de Centroamérica (inactive)
- ♦ Comisión Sericicola Internacional (#14837)
- ♦ Comisión sobre la Sociedad, el Desarrollo y la Paz del Consejo Mundial de Iglesias y la Comisión Pontificia Justicia y Paz (inactive)

♦ Comisión Sudamericana para la Lucha contra la Fiebre Aftosa (COSALFA) 04143

Commission sud-américaine de lutte contre la fièvre aphteuse – South American Commission for the Control of Foot-and-Mouth Disease – Comissão Sul-Americana para a Luta contra a Febre Aftosa

Contact c/o PANAFTOSA, Governador Leonel de Moura Brizola 7778, São Bento, Duque de Caxias RJ, 25040-002, Brazil. T. +552136619023. Fax +552136619001. E-mail: panaftosa@paho.org.
URL: https://www.paho.org/es/panaftosa/cosalfa

History 26 Feb 1973, Rio de Janeiro (Brazil). Statutes adopted 1973; modified 1983. Secretariat located at *Pan American Foot-and-Mouth Disease Center (PAFMDC, #18106)* of the *Pan American Health Organization (PAHO, #18108)*. **Aims** Foster the advance of programs for the control of foot-and-mouth disease establishing, as a final goal, eradication of this disease in South America; assure coordination in formulation, implementation and evaluation, at regional level, of national programs for control of foot-and-mouth disease; further and provide advisory assistance to programs intended for the investigation of foot-and-mouth disease and contribute towards the interchange of results obtained; see that any emergency situation which may eventually affect cattle raising in South America is promptly dealt with further the development of systems for prevention and early detection of any exotic disease in South America, and organization of control programs in case of introduction of any of these diseases; recommend adoption of such measures as are designed to support the international trade of animals and animal products which are related to the problem of foot-and-mouth disease and exotic diseases. **Structure** Presided over by representative of one of the member countries according to alphabetic order of countries. Director of PAFMDC is ex officio Secretary. **Languages** English, Portuguese, Spanish. **Finance** Member countries pay their representatives' expenses. PAHO funds the Secretariat. Other financing determined by specific circumstances. **Activities** Regular annual meetings at COSALFA Office; special meetings when necessary. **Events** *Annual Meeting* Georgetown (Guyana) 2010, *Annual Meeting* Santiago (Chile) 2003, *Annual meeting* Buenos Aires (Argentina) 2000, *Annual meeting* Rio Grande do Sul (Brazil) 1999, *Annual meeting* Mato Grosso do Sul (Brazil) 1998. **Publications** *Situation of the Foot-and-Mouth Disease Control Programs, South America* (annual). Final report on meetings (annual).
Members Highest ranking veterinarian of the animal health services of the Ministry of Agriculture, or the entity to which these functions have been delegated, in 11 countries:
Argentina, Bolivia, Brazil, Chile, Colombia, Ecuador, Guyana, Paraguay, Peru, Uruguay, Venezuela. [2018/XD8477/**D***]

♦ Comisión Técnica Regional de Telecomunicaciones (COMTELCA) . . . 04144

Exec Sec Col Altos de Miramontes, Calle Principal, Edif Miramontes, Plaza no 1583, MDC 11101 Tegucigalpa, Francisco Morazán, Honduras. E-mail: sec@comtelca.org.
URL: http://www.comtelca.hn/

History 26 Apr 1966, Managua (Nicaragua). Set up within the framework of *Central American Common Market (CACM, #03666)*. Based on the *Central American Telecommunications Agreement*. A specialized institution of *Central American Integration System (#03671)*. Former names and other names: *Technical Commission for Telecommunications in Central America* – former; *Comisión Técnica de las Telecomunicaciones de Centroamérica* – former; *Comisión de Telecomunicaciones de Centroamérica (COMTELCA)* – former; *Commission de télécommunications de l'Amérique centrale* – former; *Commission de télécommunications de l'Amérique centrale* – former. **Aims** Coordinate activities and optimize exploitation of the Central American Telecommunication Network; approve improvement and expansion plans and supervise their execution; set and improve international *tariffs* in the region; elaborate regional and/or national feasibility projects; realize tasks needed to obtain necessary assistance for member administrations; assist regulatory members in training and harmonization matters; set other resolutions according to the Agreement and necessary to achieve its aims. **Structure** Board of Directors; Regulatory Subcommission; Networks and Services Subcommission. Executive Secretary. **Languages** English, Spanish. **Staff** 10.00 FTE, paid. **Finance** Members' dues. **Activities** Events/meetings; guidance/assistance/consulting. **Events** *General Assembly* Seville (Spain) 1992, *Extraordinary meeting* Tegucigalpa (Honduras) 1992.
Members Telecommunication entities of 7 countries:
Costa Rica, Dominican Rep, El Salvador, Guatemala, Honduras, Nicaragua, Panama.
IGO Relations *Comisión Interamericana de Telecomunicaciones (CITEL, #04138)*; *International Telecommunication Union (ITU, #15673)*, especially its Radiocommunication Sector; *OAS (#17629)*. [2019/XD5972/**E***]

- ♦ Comisión Técnica de las Telecomunicaciones de Centroamérica / see Comisión Técnica Regional de Telecomunicaciones (#04144)
- ♦ Comisión de Telecomunicaciones de Centroamérica / see Comisión Técnica Regional de Telecomunicaciones (#04144)
- ♦ Comisión Trilateral (#20237)

♦ Comisión Trinacional para el Desarrollo de la Cuenca del Rio Pilcomayo 04145

Tripartite Commission for the Development of the River Basin of Rio Pilcomayo

Head Office Cecilio Avila Nº 3820, 001229 Asunción, Paraguay. T. +59521604588. E-mail: dectn@pilcomayo.net.
URL: http://www.pilcomayo.net/

History 9 Feb 1995, La Paz (Bolivia). Founded following up on and complying with the Joint Declaration of Formosa-Argentina, 26 April 1994, signed by governments of Argentina, Bolivia and Paraguay. **Aims** Promote integral development of the Pilcomayo river basin based on economic progress, environmental sustainability and equity through rational use of its natural resources and equitable management of water resources. **Structure** Council of Delegates; Executive Directorate; Trinational Coordination Committee. **Languages** Spanish. **Staff** 11.00 FTE, paid. **Finance** Sources: members' dues. **Activities** Knowledge management/information dissemination; monitoring/evaluation; research/documentation.
Members Governments of 3 countries:
Argentina, Bolivia, Paraguay. [2022.02.24/XE4281/**E***]

- ♦ Comisión sobre la Utilización del Espacio Ultraterrestre con Fines Pacificos (#04277)

♦ Comisión de la Zona Centroamericana y del Caribe de la Confederación Panamericana de Basquetbol (CONCENCABA) 04146

Commission de la zone de l'Amérique centrale et des Caraïbes de la Confédération panaméricaine de basketball – Central American and Caribbean Zone Commission of the Pan American Basketball Confederation

Contact PO Box 8925, Fernandez Juncos Station, Santurce PR 00910, USA. T. +17879774999. Fax +17879774007. E-mail: info-americas@fiba.com.
URL: http://www.fibaamericas.com/

History as a continental zone commission of *FIBA Americas (#09745)* of *Fédération internationale de basketball (FIBA, #09614)*. **Structure** Officers: President; Vice-President. **Languages** English, Spanish. **Staff** 7.00 FTE, paid. **Activities** Sporting activities.
Members National federations (members of FIBA) in 32 countries and territories:
Antigua-Barbuda, Aruba, Bahamas, Barbados, Belize, Cayman Is, Costa Rica, Cuba, Dominica, Dominican Rep, El Salvador, Grenada, Guatemala, Guyana, Haiti, Honduras, Jamaica, Mexico, Montserrat, Neth Antilles, Nicaragua, Panama, Puerto Rico, St Kitts-Nevis, St Lucia, St Martin, St Vincent-Grenadines, Suriname, Trinidad-Tobago, Turks-Caicos, Virgin Is UK, Virgin Is USA. [2016.06.01/XE2770/**E**]

- ♦ Comissão Arco Atlântico (#03007)
- ♦ Comissão das Comunidades Européias / see European Commission (#06633)
- ♦ Comissão de Estudos de Historia da Igreja na América Latina (#04133)
- ♦ Comissão Européia (#06633)
- ♦ Comissão do Golfo da Guiné (#10829)
- ♦ Comissão das Ilhas (#16061)
- ♦ Comissão de Integração Elétrica Regional / see Regional Commission for Power Integration (#18764)
- ♦ Comissão de Integração Energética Regional (#18764)
- ♦ Comissão Inter-Africana de Estatistica (inactive)
- ♦ Comissão Interamericana de Arbitragem Comercial (#11410)
- ♦ Comissão Interamericana para o Controle do Abuso de Drogas (#11429)
- ♦ Comissão Interamericana de Direitos Humanos (#11411)
- ♦ Comissão Interamericana de Energia Nuclear (inactive)
- ♦ Comissão Intermediterranica (#11521)
- ♦ Comissão Internacional das Industrias Agricolas e Alimentares (inactive)
- ♦ Comissão Latino-Americana de Aviação Civil (#16297)
- ♦ Comissão Mar do Norte (#17604)
- ♦ Comissão Panamericana de Normas Técnicas (#18133)
- ♦ Comissão Permanente do Pacifico Sul (#04141)
- ♦ Comissão de Pesca Continental e Aquiculture para América Latina e o Caribe (#04142)
- ♦ Comissão Regional da Africa Austral para a Conservação e a Utilização do Solo (inactive)
- ♦ Comissão Sub-Regional das Pescas (#20026)
- ♦ Comissão Sul-Americana para a Luta contra a Febre Aftosa (#04143)
- ♦ Comitas Gentium (#04200)
- ♦ Comitati Privati Internazionali per la Salvaguardia di Venezia (#02758)
- ♦ Comitato delle Associazioni di Armatori delle Comunità Europee / see European Community Shipowners' Associations (#06683)
- ♦ Comitato delle Associazioni di Designers Europei / see Bureau of European Design Associations (#03359)
- ♦ Comitato delle associazioni europee di design (#03359)
- ♦ Comitato delle Associazioni dei Trasformatori di Materie Plastiche dell' Europa Occidentale (inactive)
- ♦ Comitato di Basilea per la Vigilanza Bancaria (#03183)
- ♦ Comitato Centrale Proprietà Forestale della CE / see Confederation of European Forest Owners (#04525)
- ♦ Comitato Collaboriazione Medica (internationally oriented national body)
- ♦ Comitato di Collegamento dei Costruttori di Componenti e Parti per Autoveicoli / see European Association of Automotive Suppliers (#05948)
- ♦ Comitato di Collegamento dei Costruttori di Componenti e Ricambi / see European Association of Automotive Suppliers (#05948)
- ♦ Comitato di Collegamento della Costruzione di Carrozzerie e Rimorchi / see International Association of the Body and Trailer Building Industry (#11727)
- ♦ Comitato del Commercio dei Cereali e degli Alimenti per Animali della CE / see Committee of the Trade in Cereals, Oilseeds, Pulses, Olive Oil, Oils and Fats, Animal Feed and Agrosupply of the EU (#04289)

Comitato Coordinamento Associazioni
04146

alphabetic sequence excludes
For the complete listing, see Yearbook Online at

- ♦ Comitato di Coordinamento della Associazioni dei Costruttori di Apparecchiature elettriche industriali dell'Unione Europea / see European Coordinating Committee of Manufacturers of Electrical Switchgear and Controlgear (#06790)
- ♦ Comitato di Coordinamento delle Organizzazioni per il Servizio Volontario (internationally oriented national body)
- ♦ Comitato di Coordinazione delle Associazioni dei Costruttori di Apparecchiature Industriali Elettriche del Mercato Comune / see European Coordinating Committee of Manufacturers of Electrical Switchgear and Controlgear (#06790)
- ♦ Comitato Economico e Sociale / see European Economic and Social Committee (#06963)
- ♦ Comitato Economico e Sociale delle Comunità Europee / see European Economic and Social Committee (#06963)
- ♦ Comitato Economico e Sociale Europeo (#06963)
- ♦ Comitato Europeo delle Associazioni dei Costruttori di Macchinario Agricolo / see European Agricultural Machinery Association (#05846)
- ♦ Comitato Europeo delle Associazioni d'Interesse Generale / see European Council for Non-Profit Organizations (#06834)
- ♦ Comitato Europeo delle Aziende Vini (#04157)
- ♦ Comitato Europeo del Commercio e de la Riparazione Automotoristica / see European Council for Motor Trades and Repairs (#06832)
- ♦ Comitato Europeo di Cooperazione tra Industrie delle Macchine Utensili / see European Association of the Machine tool Industries and related Manufacturing Technologies (#06113)
- ♦ Comitato Europeo di Coordinamento delle Industrie Radiologiche ed Elettromedicali / see European Coordination Committee of the Radiological, Electromedical Healthcare IT Industry (#06792)
- ♦ Comitato Europeo dei Costruttori di Apparecchiature Aerauliche (inactive)
- ♦ Comitato Europeo dei Costruttori di Macchinario per Lavanderia e Lavaggio a Secco (no recent information)
- ♦ Comitato Europeo dei Costruttori di Macchinario Tessile (#06672)
- ♦ Comitato Europeo dei Costruttori di Macchine da Cantiere e per Movimento di Terra (#04254)
- ♦ Comitato Europeo Costruttori Macchine per Materie Plastiche e Gomma (#06656)
- ♦ Comitato Europeo dei Costruttori di Materiale Frigorifero (inactive)
- ♦ Comitato Europeo dei Costruttori di Strumenti per la Pesatura (#04151)
- ♦ Comitato Europeo per l'Educazione dei Fangiulii ed Adolescenti Precoci, Super Dotati, Talentati / see European Committee Promoting the Education of Gifted and Talented Young People (#06664)
- ♦ Comitato Europeo delle Federazioni Nazionali della Pelletteria, Articoli da Viaggio ed Industrie Affini (inactive)
- ♦ Comitato Europeo di Formazione Agraria / see Comitato Europeo per la Formazione e l'Agricoltura
- ♦ Comitato Europeo per la Formazione e l'Agricoltura (internationally oriented national body)
- ♦ Comitato Europeo fra i Costruttori di Macchine Grafiche e Cartotecniche (#06661)
- ♦ Comitato Europeo dei Gruppi Professionali di Importatori e Distributori di Prodotti Alimentari (inactive)
- ♦ Comitato Europeo dei Materiali e Prodotti per la Fonderia / see European Foundry Equipment Suppliers Association, The (#07353)
- ♦ Comitato Europeo delle Organizzazioni Nazionali di Negozianti di Macchine per l'Edilizia e per la Manipolazione dei Prodotti (no recent information)
- ♦ Comitato Europeo per il Progresso Economico e Sociale (inactive)
- ♦ Comitato europeo delle regioni (#06665)
- ♦ Comitato Europeo Sviluppo Piombo (inactive)
- ♦ Comitato dei Fabbricanti di Lievito per Panificazione della CEE / see Confédération des Fabricants de Levure de l'Union Européenne (#04551)
- ♦ Comitato Generale della Cooperazione Agricola della Comunità Europea / see General Confederation of Agricultural Cooperatives in the European Union (#10107)
- ♦ Comitato Generale della Cooperazione Agricola dell' UE / see General Confederation of Agricultural Cooperatives in the European Union (#10107)
- ♦ Comitato delle Industrie del Cotone e delle Fibre Connesse della CE / see European Federation of Cotton and Allied Textiles Industries (#07093)
- ♦ Comitato Internazionale Anticaccia (internationally oriented national body)
- ♦ Comitato Internazionale Anticaccia Protezione Animale e Natura / see International Anti-Hunting Committee
- ♦ Comitato Internazionale di Collegamento Cattolico-Ebraico (#12458)
- ♦ Comitato Internazionale di Collegamento delle Industrie del Ricamo, del Tendaggio e del Pizzo (inactive)
- ♦ Comitato Internazionale per la Difesa della Lingua Bretone (#12761)
- ♦ Comitato Internazionale Fenomeni Fluttuanti / see International Committee for Research and Study of Environmental Factors (#12801)
- ♦ Comitato per un' Internazionale dei Lavoratori (#04290)
- ♦ Comitato Internazionale degli Scambi (inactive)
- ♦ Comitato Internazionale per lo Sviluppo dei Popoli (internationally oriented national body)
- ♦ Comitato Internazionale dei Trasporti per Ferrovia / see Comité international des transports ferroviaires (#04188)
- ♦ Comitato di Lavoro delle Malterie della CEE / see Working Committee of the Malting Industry of the EU (#21055)
- ♦ Comitato di Lavoro delle Malterie della UE (#21055)
- ♦ Comitato delle Organizzazioni Professionali Agricole della CE / see COPA – european farmers (#04829)
- ♦ Comitato delle Organizzazioni Professionali Agricole dell'Unione Europea / see COPA – european farmers (#04829)
- ♦ Comitato Permanente del Catasto nell'Unione Europea (#18319)
- ♦ Comitato Permanente delle Industrie del Vetro della CEE / see Glass Alliance Europe (#10156)
- ♦ Comitato Permanente delle Industrie del Vetro Europea / see Glass Alliance Europe (#10156)
- ♦ Comitato Permanente dei Medici della CE / see Standing Committee of European Doctors (#19955)
- ♦ Comitato Permanente per il Partenariato Euromediterraneo dei Poteri Locali e Regionali (#19954)
- ♦ Comitato per la Regolamentazione Bancaria e le Procedure di Vigilanza / see Basel Committee on Banking Supervision (#03183)
- ♦ Comitato Scientifico Internazionale Ricerca Alpina (#14804)
- ♦ Comitato Tecnico Internazionale di Prevenzione ed Estinzione Incendi / see CTIF International Association of Fire and Rescue Services (#04979)
- ♦ Comité de 5 nations / see 6 Nations Committee (#22052)
- ♦ Comité des 6 nations (#22052)
- ♦ Comité Académico Técnico de Asesoramiento a Problemas Ambientales / see CATAPA
- ♦ Comité de Acción para los Estados Unidos de Europa (inactive)
- ♦ Comité de Acción para la Integración de América Latina (inactive)
- ♦ Comité de l'ACI pour les coopératives des consommateurs / see Consumer Co-operatives Worldwide (#04770)
- ♦ Comité de ACJs del Medio Oriente (#16755)
- ♦ Comité acteurs interprètes (no recent information)
- ♦ Comité d'action pour les Etats-Unis d'Europe (inactive)
- ♦ Comité d'action européenne de l'UIOF / see COFACE Families Europe (#04084)
- ♦ Comité d'action pour l'intégration de l'Amérique latine (inactive)
- ♦ Comité d'action service pour la paix (internationally oriented national body)
- ♦ Comité administrative de coordination / see United Nations System Chief Executives Board for Coordination (#20636)
- ♦ Comité africain pour la coordination des moyens d'information (inactive)
- ♦ Comité Africain de Métrologie (#00258)
- ♦ Comité agricole de l'ACI / see International Co-operative Agricultural Organisation (#12943)
- ♦ Comité de l'aide alimentaire (inactive)
- ♦ Comité d'aide aux calaminois du Tiers-Monde (internationally oriented national body)
- ♦ Comité d'aide au développement de l'OCDE (see: #17693)
- ♦ Comité d'aide médicale et de parrainage sans frontières (internationally oriented national body)
- ♦ Comité d'Al-Quds (#00749)
- ♦ Comité de América Latina y el Caribe para la Defensa de los Derechos de la Mujer (#16268)
- ♦ Comité des anciens fonctionnaires de l'UNESCO / see Association of Former UNESCO Staff Members (#02601)

♦ Comité Andino de Autoridades de Transporte Acuatico (CAATA) . . . 04147

Andean Committee of Maritime Transport Authorities

Contact Carrera 54 N°. 26-50 CAN, Bogota, Bogota DC, Colombia.
URL: http://www.comunidadandina.org/

History by *Andean Community (#00817)*. **Aims** Establish and propose objectives, policies and actions for increment, development and facilitation of water transport in the Sub region. **Structure** Committee President; Technical Secretary. **Languages** Spanish. **Staff** 1.00 FTE, paid. **Finance** Supported by: *Andean Community (#00817)*. **Activities** Events/meetings; politics/policy/regulatory. **Events** *Meeting* La Paz (Bolivia) 2015. **Publications** Annual Report; statistics.

Members Members in 4 countries:
Bolivia, Colombia, Ecuador, Peru.

IGO Relations Agreement with: *OAS (#17629)*. [2021/XE2381/**E**]

♦ Comité pour l'annulation de la dette du Tiers-monde (CADTM) 04148

Committee for the Abolition of Third World Debt – Comite por Anulación de la Deuda del Tercer Mundo – Komittee voor de Opheffing van de Derde Wereld Schuld (KODEWES)

Contact Place De Bronckart 2, 4000 Liège, Belgium. T. +3242266285. E-mail: info@cadtm.org – international@cadtm.org.
URL: http://www.cadtm.org/

History 15 Mar 1990, Belgium. Also referred to as *Committee for the Cancellation of the Third World Debt*. **Aims** Develop and implement radical alternatives that would contribute to maintenance and retrieval of fundamental *human rights* all over the world. **Publications** *CADTM Newsletter*. *Your Money or Your Life* by Eric Toussaint.

Members Full in 31 countries:
Algeria, Belgium, Brazil, Canada, Colombia, Congo Brazzaville, Congo DR, Czechia, Denmark, France, Hungary, India, Italy, Luxembourg, Mexico, Morocco, Netherlands, Nicaragua, Poland, Portugal, Russia, Senegal, Spain, Sri Lanka, Switzerland, Togo, Tunisia, Uganda, UK, Uruguay, USA.

NGO Relations Member of: *Fédération francophone et germanophone des associations de coopération au développement (ACODEV, #09587)*; *World Social Forum (WSF, #21797)*. Instrumental in setting up: *Worldwide Campaign – World Bank, IMF, WTO – Enough (no recent information)*. Signatory to: *Alter Summit*. Supports: *Global Call for Action Against Poverty (GCAP, #10263)*. [2016.02.04/XN4490/**F**]

- ♦ Comite por Anulación de la Deuda del Tercer Mundo (#04148)
- ♦ Comité arabe des sept (no recent information)
- ♦ Comité des armateurs européens (inactive)
- ♦ Comité asiatique pour la normalisation des tests d'aptitude physique (inactive)
- ♦ Comité de Asociaciones Europeas de Diseño (#03359)
- ♦ Comité des associations d'armateurs des Communautés européennes / see European Community Shipowners' Associations (#06683)
- ♦ Comité des associations d'armateurs du Marché commun / see European Community Shipowners' Associations (#06683)
- ♦ Comité des associations européennes de fonderie / see European Foundry Association, The (#07352)
- ♦ Comité d'associations européennes de médecins catholiques (inactive)
- ♦ Comité des associations d'importateurs et d'emballeurs de miel d'Europe (inactive)
- ♦ Comité des associations nationales d'armateurs d'Europe (inactive)
- ♦ Comité des associations de transformateurs de matières plastiques de l'Europe occidentale (inactive)
- ♦ Comité de Ayuda Alimentaria (inactive)
- ♦ Comité de Bâle sur le contrôle bancaire (#03183)
- ♦ Comité belge d'aide aux réfugiés (internationally oriented national body)
- ♦ Comité van Beroepsverenigingen van Kunststofverwerkers in West-Europa (inactive)
- ♦ Comité des bourses de la Communauté économique européenne / see Federation of European Securities Exchanges (#09542)
- ♦ Comité de Bretton Woods (internationally oriented national body)
- ♦ Comité van Broodgistfabrikanten van de EEG / see Confédération des Fabricants de Levure de l'Union Européenne (#04551)
- ♦ Comité sobre el Capital de los Trabajadores (#10639)
- ♦ Comité sur le capital des travailleurs du groupement Global Unions (#10639)
- ♦ Comité catholique contre la faim / see Comité Catholique contre la Faim et pour le Développement-Terre Solidaire
- ♦ Comité catholique contre la Faim et pour le Développement / see Comité Catholique contre la Faim et pour le Développement-Terre Solidaire
- ♦ Comité Catholique contre la Faim et pour le Développement-Terre Solidaire (internationally oriented national body)
- ♦ Comité catholique de coordination pour l'envoi de techniciens (inactive)
- ♦ Comité central bancaire de l'ACI / see International Cooperative Banking Association (#12945)
- ♦ Comité central des banques coopératives de l'Alliance coopérative internationale / see International Cooperative Banking Association (#12945)
- ♦ Comité central de la propriété forestière de la CE / see Confederation of European Forest Owners (#04525)
- ♦ Comité CFFSA/CEF/CFPO des questions forestières méditerranéennes – Silva Mediterranea (#00542)
- ♦ Comité chargé des négociations avec les institutions intergouvernementales (#20544)
- ♦ Comité des chefs d'état-major du Conseil de sécurité des Nations Unies / see United Nations Security Council Military Staff Committee (#20626)
- ♦ Comité chrétien pour les droits humains en Amérique latine (internationally oriented national body)
- ♦ Comite Científico Internacional de Paisajes Culturales (#11059)
- ♦ Comité Científico Internacional del Patrimonio del Siglo XX (see: #13049)
- ♦ Comité COI-OMM-PNUE pour le Système mondial d'observation de l'océan / see Intergovernmental Committee for the Global Ocean Observing System (#11473)
- ♦ Comité de collaboration nordique pour la recherche médicale arctique (inactive)
- ♦ Comité de collaboration pour la recherche forestière nordique (#17296)
- ♦ Comité pour les colloques européens de biologie marine (#04255)
- ♦ Comité du commerce / see Steering Committee on Trade Capacity and Standards (#19979)
- ♦ Comité du commerce des céréales et des aliments du bétail de la CE / see Committee of the Trade in Cereals, Oilseeds, Pulses, Olive Oil, Oils and Fats, Animal Feed and Agrosupply of the EU (#04289)
- ♦ Comité du commerce des céréales, aliments du bétail, oléagineux, huile d'olive, huiles et graisses, et agrofournitures de l'UE / see Committee of the Trade in Cereals, Oilseeds, Pulses, Olive Oil, Oils and Fats, Animal Feed and Agrosupply of the EU (#04289)
- ♦ Comité du commerce des céréales, oléagineux, légumineuses, huile d'olive, huiles et graisses, aliments du bétail et agrofournitures de l'UE (#04289)
- ♦ Comité des commissaires aux comptes de l'Organisation des Nations Unies (#20523)
- ♦ Comité de la Communauté économique européenne des industries et du commerce des vins, vins mousseux, vins de liqueur, vins aromatisés et autres produits de la vigne / see Comité européen des entreprises vins (#04157)
- ♦ Comité commun pour le désarmement des organisations chrétiennes internationales (inactive)
- ♦ Comité pour communications des Eglises luthériennes minoritaires d'Europe (#16205)
- ♦ Comité commun nordique pour la coopération économique (inactive)
- ♦ Comité commun scandinave des associations des travailleurs de l'industrie du papier (inactive)

♦ Comité conjoint des conseils nordiques de la recherche pour les sciences humaines et sociales (#17530)
♦ Comité conjoint OIT/UNESCO d'experts sur l'application des recommandations concernant le personnel enseignant (#16132)
♦ Comité des Conseillers juridiques sur le droit international public (#04267)
♦ Comité des consommateurs de l'ACI / see Consumer Co-operatives Worldwide (#04770)
♦ Comité des constructeurs européens de matériel alimentaire et de matériel de conditionnement (inactive)
♦ Comité consultatif des Caraïbes orientales (inactive)
♦ Comité consultatif du Commonwealth pour la recherche spatiale (inactive)
♦ Comité consultatif commun des organisations internationales non-gouvernementales dans les domaines de la bibliothéconomie, de la documentation et de l'archivistique (inactive)
♦ Comité consultatif de continuation pour la coopération entre la jeunesse juive à travers le monde (inactive)
♦ Comité consultatif économique et industriel auprès de l'OCDE (#03385)
♦ Comité consultatif de l'EEE (#05378)
♦ Comité consultatif international du coton (#12979)
♦ Comité consultatif international des radiocommunications (inactive)
♦ Comité consultatif international télégraphique et téléphonique (inactive)
♦ Comité consultatif juridique Afrique-Asie / see Asian-African Legal Consultative Organization (#01303)
♦ Comité consultatif pour la lecture des prisonniers et internés de guerre (inactive)
♦ Comité consultatif mondial des Amis (#10004)
♦ Comité consultatif mondial de la société des Amis / see Friends World Committee for Consultation (#10004)
♦ Comité consultatif permanent des Nations Unies chargé des questions de sécurité en Afrique centrale (#20632)
♦ Comité consultatif sur la pollution des mers / see Advisory Committee on Protection of the Sea (#00139)
♦ Comité consultatif sur la protection des mers (#00139)
♦ Comité consultatif pour les questions de télévision (inactive)
♦ Comité Consultivo Internacional del Algodón (#12979)
♦ Comité Consultivo Internacional de Radiocomunicaciones (inactive)
♦ Comité Consultivo Internacional Telegrafico y Telefónico (inactive)
♦ Comité Consultivo Mundial de la Sociedad de los Amigos / see Friends World Committee for Consultation (#10004)
♦ Comité contra la Desaparición Forzada (#04252)
♦ Comité contra el Terrorismo (#04928)
♦ Comité contra la Tortura (#04241)
♦ Comité contre le terrorisme (#04928)
♦ Comité contre la torture (#04241)
♦ Comité de contrôle de la zone internationale de Tanger (inactive)
♦ Comité de Cooperación Económica de Centroamericana (#03667)
♦ Comité de Cooperación Económica del Istmo Centroamericano / see Central American Economic Cooperation Committee (#03667)
♦ Comité de Cooperación Internacional entre Asociaciones Algodoneras (#04265)
♦ Comité de coopération pour le Cambodge (internationally oriented national body)
♦ Comité de coopération des conseils nordiques de la recherche en sciences naturelles (#17529)
♦ Comité de coopération douanière ACP-CE (inactive)
♦ Comité de coopération économique de l'Isthme centroaméricain / see Central American Economic Cooperation Committee (#03667)
♦ Comité pour la coopération internationale entre les associations cotonnières (#04265)
♦ Comité de coopération internationale en sociologie rurale (inactive)
♦ Comité de coopération médicale / see Comitato Collaboriazione Medica
♦ Comité pour la coopération musicale nordique (inactive)
♦ Comité de coopération des organisations pour aveugles dans les pays nordiques (inactive)
♦ Comité de coopération des pépinières nordiques (inactive)
♦ Comité de coopération scandinave baptiste (inactive)
♦ Comité de coopération scandinave pour l'éducation en économie familiale (no recent information)
♦ Comité de coopération sur la technologie maritime nordique (inactive)
♦ Comité de Coordinación de Organizaciones Judias (#04813)
♦ Comité de Coordinación de los Puertos del Mediterraneo Nord-Occidental (inactive)
♦ Comité Coordinador Interuniversitario de los Estudios Orientales en América Latina (inactive)
♦ Comité Coordinador de Organizaciones Psicoanaliticas de América Latina / see Federación Psicoanalitica de America Latina (#09386)
♦ Comité Coordinador del Servicio Voluntario Internacional (#04819)
♦ Comité Coordinador de las Sociedades Iberoamericanas de Inteligencia Artificial / see Iberoamerican Society of Artificial Intelligence (#11029)
♦ Comité de coordination des associations de constructeurs d'appareillage électrique industriel de l'Union Européenne / see European Coordinating Committee of Manufacturers of Electrical Switchgear and Controlgear (#06790)
♦ Comité de coordination des associations de constructeurs d'appareillage industriel électrique du Marché commun / see European Coordinating Committee of Manufacturers of Electrical Switchgear and Controlgear (#06790)
♦ Comité de coordination des associations et syndicats internationaux du personnel du système des Nations Unies (#04818)
♦ Comité de coordination de l'axe Lagos-Tanger (inactive)
♦ Comité de coordination des chantiers internationaux de volontaires / see Coordinating Committee for International Voluntary Service (#04819)
♦ Comité de coordination pour le développement de la statistique en Afrique (inactive)
♦ Comité de coordination européen sur la documentation des droits de l'homme (#06791)
♦ Comité de coordination des hauts fonctionnaires des transports et communications de Sud-Est asiatique (inactive)
♦ Comité de coordination internationale pour la profession de comptable (inactive)
♦ Comité de coordination de normalisation des Nations Unies (inactive)
♦ Comité de coordination d'organisations juives (#04813)
♦ Comité de coordination des organisations de service volontaire (internationally oriented national body)
♦ Comité de coordination de l'OUA sur l'assistance aux réfugiés (no recent information)
♦ Comité de coordination des peuples autochtones d'afrique (#11163)
♦ Comité de coordination des ports de la Méditerranée Nord-occidentale (inactive)
♦ Comité pour la coordination de la prospection commune des ressources minérales au large des côtes de l'Asie / see Coordinating Committee for Geoscience Programmes in East and Southeast Asia (#04816)
♦ Comité de coordination du service volontaire international (#04819)
♦ Comité de coordination des travailleurs retraités / see Fédération européenne des retraités et des personnes âgées (#09580)
♦ Comité coordonnateur canadien pour la consolidation de la paix (internationally oriented national body)
♦ Comité de la crise démographique / see PAI (#18025)
♦ Comité de la Crisis Demografica / see PAI (#18025)
♦ Comité Cristiano por los Derechos Humanos en Latinoamérica (internationally oriented national body)
♦ Comité de Datos para la Ciencia y la Tecnologia (#04247)
♦ Comité Denâ (inactive)
♦ Comité de Derechos Económicos, Sociales y Culturales (#20538)
♦ Comité sobre los Derechos de las Personas con Discapacidad (#04284)
♦ Comité du désarmement / see Conference on Disarmament (#04590)
♦ Comité de désarmement des organisations internationales des étudiants (inactive)
♦ **Comité para el Desarrollo** Comité Ministerial Conjunto de las Juntas de Gobernadores del Banco y del Fondo para la Transferencia de Recursos Reales a los Paises en Desarrollo (#16141)
♦ Comité para el Desarrollo Económico (internationally oriented national body)
♦ **Comité du développement** Comité ministériel conjoint des conseils des gouverneurs de la Banque mondiale et du Fonds monétaire international sur le transfert de ressources réelles aux pays en voie de développement (#16141)
♦ Comité pour le développement économique (internationally oriented national body)

♦ Comité de Dirección Estratégica de los Organismos Iberoamericanos (CoDEI) 04149

Address not obtained.

History 24 Feb 2015. On establishment of CoDEI, mandate of XXIV Ibero-American Summit of Heads of State and Government, held Dec 2014, was fulfilled, with agreements reached between the 5 Ibero-American IGOs put into effect. **Aims** Shape the Ibero-American system by establishing direct functional relations between all the Ibero-American organizations and the bodies of the Summit of Heads of State and Government; establish mechanisms to ensure a common strategy and planning, greater transparency with member countries, increased visibility and more efficent use of availabe sources. **Structure** Committee, consisting of General Secretaries of member organizations.
Members Organizations (5):
Conferencia de Ministros de Justicia de los Países Iberoamericanos (COMJIB, #04656); Ibero-American General Secretariat (#11024); Ibero-American Social Security Organization (#11028); Ibero-American Youth Organization (#11036); Organization of Ibero-American States for Education, Science and Culture (#17871).
[2020/AA1237/**E***]

♦ Comité directeur des capacités et des normes commerciales (#19979)
♦ Comité directeur pour l'égalité entre les femmes et les hommes (inactive)
♦ Comité de Directores de Institutos Geograficos de Sur América, España y Portugal (#04248)
♦ Comité des disparitions forcées (#04252)
♦ Comité de la distinction Nansen pour les réfugiés (internationally oriented national body)
♦ Comité des donateurs pour la développement de l'enterprise (#05122)
♦ Comité pour les données scientifiques et technologiques (#04247)
♦ Comité des droits économiques, sociaux et culturels (#20538)
♦ Comité des droits de l'enfant (#04283)
♦ Comité des droits de l'homme (#10979)
♦ Comité des droits des personnes handicapées (#04284)
♦ Comité Económico y Social / see European Economic and Social Committee (#06963)
♦ Comité Económico e Social / see European Economic and Social Committee (#06963)
♦ Comité Económico y Social de Comunidades Europeas / see European Economic and Social Committee (#06963)
♦ Comité Económico e Social dos Comunidades Européias / see European Economic and Social Committee (#06963)
♦ Comité Económico y Social Europeo (#06963)
♦ Comité Económico e Social Europeu (#06963)
♦ Comité économique interétatique CEI de l'Union économique (no recent information)
♦ Comité économique et social des Communautés européennes / see European Economic and Social Committee (#06963)
♦ Comité économique et social européen (#06963)
♦ Comité voor een Arbeidersinternationale (#04290)
♦ Comité des Eglises auprès des migrants en Europe / see Churches' Commission for Migrants in Europe (#03912)
♦ Comité des Eglises auprès des travailleurs migrants en Europe / see Churches' Commission for Migrants in Europe (#03912)
♦ Comité des Eglises auprès des travailleurs migrants en Europe occidentale / see Churches' Commission for Migrants in Europe (#03912)
♦ Comité para el Ejercicio de los Derechos Inalienables del Pueblo Palestino (#20539)
♦ Comité para la Eliminación de la Discriminación Racial (#04251)
♦ Comité pour l'élimination de la discrimination à l'égard des femmes (#04250)
♦ Comité pour l'élimination de la discrimination raciale (#04251)
♦ Comité de Enlace de Organizaciones Femeninas Internacionales (inactive)
♦ Comité de Enlace de los Paises Citricolas del Mediterraneo (inactive)
♦ Comité d'entente des fédérations internationales du personnel enseignant (inactive)
♦ Comité d'entente des grandes associations internationales (inactive)
♦ Comité Especial de Descolonización (#19906)
♦ Comité Especial encargado de investigar las practicas israelies que afecten a los derechos humanos del pueblo palestino y otros habitantes arabes de los territorios ocupado (#20627)
♦ Comité de Estudios Atlanticos (no recent information)
♦ Comité de Estudios de los Productores de Carbón de la Europa Occidental / see European Association for Coal and Lignite (#05978)
♦ Comité d'état-major du Conseil de sécurité des Nations Unies (#20626)
♦ Comité d'étude de la corrosion et de la protection des canalisations / see European Committee for the study of corrosion and protection of pipes and pipeline systems (#06670)
♦ Comité d'étude des producteurs de charbon d'Europe occidentale / see European Association for Coal and Lignite (#05978)
♦ Comité des études atlantiques (no recent information)
♦ Comité d'études économiques de l'industrie du gaz / see Eurogas (#05682)
♦ Comité d'étude sur le statut juridique des organisations non-gouvernementales (inactive)
♦ Comité Euro-international du béton (inactive)
♦ Comité Europea de Maquinaria de Construcción y Obras Públicas (#04254)

♦ Comité européen d'action spécialisée pour l'enfant et la famille dans leur milieu de vie (EUROCEF) 04150

European Committee for Home-based Priority Action for the Child and the Family

Sec 73 avenue Princesse, 78110 Le Vésinet, France. T. +33681403359. E-mail: contact@eurocef.eu.
Registered Office Maison des Associations, 1A place des Orphelins, 67000 Strasbourg, France.
URL: http://www.eurocef.eu/

History Sep 1988. Constitution adopted, Nov 1989, Geneva (Switzerland). Registered in accordance with French law. **Aims** Develop, in the member countries of the Council of Europe, social and educational home-based assistance for the child and the family. **Structure** General Assembly (annually). Board, consisting of up to 2 persons per member country. Board. Executive Committee, comprising Chairperson, Vice-Chairperson, Secretary, Treasurer and 3 members. **Finance** Members' dues. **Activities** Meetings; Congresses; research; consultations; recommendations; publications. **Events** *INNOV meeting* Paris (France) 2010.
Members Full in 12 countries:
Belgium, Estonia, France, Germany, Greece, Italy, Luxembourg, Portugal, Romania, Spain, Switzerland, UK.
Consultative Status Consultative status granted from: *Council of Europe (CE, #04881)* (Participatory Status).
[2019/XE2628/**E**]

♦ Comité européen des agents de surface et leurs intermédiaires organiques (#06660)
♦ Comité européen d'agriculture / see European Commission on Agriculture (#06634)
♦ Comité européen d'architectes d'intérieurs (inactive)
♦ Comité européen des architectes paysagistes (inactive)
♦ Comité européen des associations de constructeurs d'engrenages et d'éléments de transmission (#06643)
♦ Comité européen des associations de constructeurs de moteurs à combustion interne (inactive)

Comité européen associations
04150

alphabetic sequence excludes
For the complete listing, see Yearbook Online at

- ♦ Comité européen des associations des fabricants de produits d'apport de soudage (inactive)
- ♦ Comité européen des associations de fonderies / see European Foundry Association, The (#07352)
- ♦ Comité européen des associations d'intérêt général (#06834)
- ♦ Comité européen des associations techniques de l'environnement / see Confederation of European Environmental Engineering Societies (#04524)
- ♦ Comité européen des assurances / see Insurance Europe (#11362)
- ♦ Comité européen des bureaux d'ingénierie (inactive)
- ♦ Comité européen de la chaudronnerie et de la tuyauterie (no recent information)
- ♦ Comité européen des chevaux de débardage (internationally oriented national body)
- ♦ Comité européen pour la cohésion sociale / see European Committee on Social Cohesion, Human Dignity and Equality (#06667)
- ♦ Comité européen des combustibles solides / see European Association for Coal and Lignite (#05978)
- ♦ Comité européen du commerce des produits amylacés et dérivés (inactive)
- ♦ Comité européen du commerce et de la réparation automobiles / see European Council for Motor Trades and Repairs (#06832)
- ♦ Comité européen des constructeurs d'appareillage électrique d'installation (#06646)
- ♦ Comité européen des constructeurs de brûleurs (inactive)
- ♦ Comité européen des constructeurs de compresseurs, pompes à vide et outils à air comprimé (#06657)
- ♦ Comité Européen des Constructeurs de Fours et d'Equipements thermiques industriels / see The European Committee of Industrial Furnace, Heating and Metallurgical Equipment Associations (#06653)
- ♦ Comité européen des constructeurs de grands ensembles industriels (no recent information)

♦ Comité européen des constructeurs d'instruments de pesage (CECIP) 04151

European Committee of Constructors of Weighing Instruments – Europäisches Komitee der Waagenhersteller – Comitato Europeo dei Costruttori di Strumenti per la Pesatura – Europees Comité van Fabrikanten van Weeginstrumenten

SG Bluepoint Bldg, Bd A Reyers 80, 1030 Brussels, Belgium. T. +3227068215. Fax +3227068210. E-mail: info@cecip.eu.
URL: http://www.cecip.eu/

History 26 May 1959. Founded by professional organizations in the field. Current statutes adopted by General Assembly, 26 May 1975; amended 22 May 1998, 21 May 2004. Registration: EU Transparency Register, No/ID: 48444564134-24; France. **Aims** Contribute to improvement in the quality of legislation and standards, providing safety and quality to both consumers and users of weighing instruments. **Structure** General Assembly (annual); Board; Secretariat. Groups (3): Legal Metrology; Business and Trade; International Cooperation. **Languages** English, French. **Staff** 1.00 FTE, paid. **Finance** Members' dues. **Activities** Knowledge management/information dissemination; standards/guidelines. **Events** *International Conference of Weighing* Berlin (Germany) 2023, *Annual General Assembly* London (UK) 2021, *Annual General Assembly* London (UK) 2020, *Annual General Assembly* Bratislava (Slovakia) 2019, *Annual General Assembly* Évian (France) 2018. **Publications** *Lettre d'information CECIP* (6 a year). General Assembly minutes.
Members National professional organizations (one per country) in 13 countries:
Austria, Czechia, France, Germany, Hungary, Italy, Netherlands, Poland, Russia, Slovakia, Spain, Switzerland, UK.
IGO Relations Recognized by: *European Commission (EC, #06633)*. Contacts with: *EFTA (#05391)*; *International Organization of Legal Metrology (#14451)*. **NGO Relations** Member of: *Industry4Europe (#11181)*. [2020/XD0657/D]

♦ Comité européen des constructeurs de machines à bois (EUMABOIS) 04152

European Committee of Woodworking Machinery Manufacturers – Europäisches Komitee der Holzbearbeitungsmaschinenhersteller

Contact c/o ACIMALL, Centro Direzionale Milanfiori, 1a Strada, Palazzo F3, 20090 Assago MI, Italy. T. +39289210200. Fax +3928259009. E-mail: info@eumabois.com.
Registered Office Bluepoint, Bld Reyers 80, 1030 Brussels, Belgium.
URL: http://www.eumabois.com/

History 22 Jan 1960, Neuilly-sur-Seine (France). Registered in accordance with Belgian law. Registration: Belgium. **Aims** Study of problems common to woodworking machinery manufacturers of member countries. **Structure** General Meeting (annual). Governing Board, comprising President, Vice President and 3 members. Secretariat. **Languages** English. **Activities** Sub-Committees: Economic (agreements between manufacturers); Technical (recommendations for standardization); Public Relations (fairs and publicity). **Events** *Annual Meeting* Jyväskylä (Finland) 2013, *Annual Meeting* Istanbul (Turkey) 2012, *Annual Meeting* Valencia (Spain) 2011, *Annual Meeting* Vienna (Austria) 2010, *Annual Meeting* Munich (Germany) 2009. **Publications** *EUMABOIS Link* – newsletter.
Members National associations in 13 countries:
Austria, Czechia, Denmark, Finland, France, Germany, Italy, Poland, Portugal, Russia, Slovakia, Spain, Switzerland.
IGO Relations Recognized by: *European Commission (EC, #06633)*. **NGO Relations** In liaison with technical committees of: *Comité européen de normalisation (CEN, #04162)*; *International Organization for Standardization (ISO, #14473)*. Member of: *Wood Technology Club (#21047)*. [2020/XD0658/D]

- ♦ Comité européen des constructeurs de machines pour les industries graphiques et papetières (#06661)
- ♦ Comité européen des constructeurs de machines pour plastiques et caoutchouc (#06656)
- ♦ Comité européen des constructeurs de matériel aéraulique (inactive)
- ♦ Comité européen des constructeurs de matériel de blanchisserie et de nettoyage à sec (no recent information)
- ♦ Comité européen des constructeurs de matériel frigorifique (inactive)
- ♦ Comité européen des constructeurs de matériel d'incendie et de secours (#06659)
- ♦ Comité européen des constructeurs de matériel pour l'industrie chimique / see European Committee for Process Equipment and Plant Manufacturers (#06662)
- ♦ Comité européen des constructeurs de matériel textile (#06672)
- ♦ Comité européen de contrôle laitier-beurrier / see International Committee for Animal Recording (#12746)
- ♦ Comité européen de coopération des industries de la machine-outil / see European Association of the Machine tool Industries and related Manufacturing Technologies (#06113)
- ♦ Comité européen de coopération juridique (#06655)
- ♦ Comité européen des coopératives ouvrières de production / see Confédération européenne des coopératives de travail associé, des coopératives sociales et des entreprises sociales et participatives (#04541)
- ♦ Comité européen des coopératives de production et de travail / see Confédération européenne des coopératives de travail associé, des coopératives sociales et des entreprises sociales et participatives (#04541)
- ♦ Comité européen des coopératives de production et de travail associé / see Confédération européenne des coopératives de travail associé, des coopératives sociales et des entreprises sociales et participatives (#04541)

♦ Comité européen de coordination (CEC) 04153

Dir Chaussée de Boondael 6, Bte 14, 1050 Brussels, Belgium. T. +3226491413. Fax +3226488340. E-mail: cecedbe@gmail.com.
URL: http://www.cecasbl.org/

History 1995. Registration: No/ID: 0471.915.094, Start date: 1 Mar 2000, Belgium; EU Transparency Register, No/ID: 052588323201-74, Start date: 31 Aug 2016. **Aims** Promote social and professional integration of groups in difficulty. **Languages** English, French, Spanish. **Staff** 2.00 FTE, paid. **Finance** Annual budget: 120,000 EUR. **Activities** Projects/programmes; networking/liaising. **Events** *Un emploi pour tous* Brussels (Belgium) 2009, *Séminaire OSS* Brussels (Belgium) 2008, *Insertion – a European challenge* Le Havre (France) 2000.
Members Partners in 14 countries:
Belgium, Bulgaria, Cyprus, France, Germany, Greece, Hungary, Italy, Poland, Portugal, Romania, Serbia, Slovakia, Spain. [2020/XE3934/E]

- ♦ Comité européen de coordination des associations d'amitié avec le monde arabe (inactive)
- ♦ Comité européen de coordination de l'habitat social / see Housing Europe – The European Federation for Public Cooperative and Social Housing (#10956)
- ♦ Comité européen de coordination des industries radiologiques et électromédicales / see European Coordination Committee of the Radiological, Electromedical Healthcare IT Industry (#06792)
- ♦ Comité européen de coordination des normes / see Comité européen de normalisation (#04162)
- ♦ Comité européen de coordination des normes électriques (inactive)
- ♦ Comité européen de coordination du tourisme social / see OITS/ European Commission for Social Tourism (#17713)
- ♦ Comité européen de la culture du houblon / see International Hop Growers' Convention (#13807)

♦ Comité européen – droit, éthique et psychiatrie (CEDEP) 04154

Sec 61 ave de Saint Mandé, 75012 Paris, France. E-mail: info@cedep-europe.eu.
URL: http://www.cedep-europe.eu/

History 1989. Registered in accordance with French law. **Aims** Think, act and influence the political, ethical, law and rights issues in the field of mental health in Europe. **Structure** General Assembly; Executive Committee; Bureau. **Activities** Organizes seminars. **Events** *Des changements qui nous contraignent aux changements que nous voulons* St Cyprien (France) 2014, *Seminar* Paris (France) 2013, *Seminar* Aix-les-Bains (France) 2012, *Seminar* Brussels (Belgium) 2011, *Taking care of the human aspect – individual, legal practices and human rights in mental health* St Paul's Bay (Malta) 2010. [2017/XE2739/E]

♦ Comité Européen de Droit Rural (CEDR) 04155

European Council for Rural Law – Europäisches Gesellschaft für Agrarrecht und das Recht des Ländlichen Raumes – Comité Europeo de Derecho Rural

SG Av des Chasseurs 7-11, 75017 Paris, France.
URL: http://www.cedr.org/

History 30 Oct 1957, Paris (France). Registration: RNA, No/ID: W751048577, Start date: 4 Mar 1958, France; EU Transparency Register, No/ID: 121769913563-50, Start date: 29 Apr 2014. **Aims** Study and develop social Rural Law, in a wide sense, covering all aspects related to *agriculture* – production, environment, food, energy, consumption, trade and economics – at national, regional, European and international levels. **Structure** General Assembly (every 2 years); Board of Management; Executive Council. **Languages** English, French, German. **Staff** Voluntary. **Finance** Sources: members' dues. **Activities** Awards/prizes/competitions; events/meetings; guidance/assistance/consulting. **Events** *Biennial Congress* Poznań (Poland) 2019, *Biennial Congress* Lille (France) 2017, *Biennial Congress* Potsdam (Germany) 2015, *Biennial Congress* Lucerne (Switzerland) 2013, *Biennial Congress* Bucharest (Romania) 2011. **Publications** *CEDR Journal of Rural Law*. Congress Acts; meeting reports in English, French, German.
Members Organizational in 20 countries:
Austria, Belgium, Estonia, Finland, France, Germany, Hungary, Italy, Latvia, Luxembourg, Netherlands, Norway, Poland, Portugal, Romania, Russia, Slovakia, Spain, Switzerland, UK.
Associate and Individual in 13 countries:
Australia, Brazil, Bulgaria, Canada, China, Colombia, Comoros, Côte d'Ivoire, Czechia, Israel, Japan, Kyrgyzstan, USA.
Consultative Status Consultative status granted from: *FAO (#09260)* (Special Status). **NGO Relations** Cooperates with: Mouvement européen de la ruralité (MER); *Rurality – Environment – Development (RED, #19003)*. [2020.06.28/XD0133/D]

- ♦ Comité européen des droits sociaux (#06668)
- ♦ Comité européen pour l'éducation des enfants et adolescents précoces: doués, talentueux et désavantagés, pour filles et garçons / see European Committee Promoting the Education of Gifted and Talented Young People (#06664)
- ♦ Comité européen pour l'éducation des enfants et adolescents précoces surdoués, talentueux / see European Committee Promoting the Education of Gifted and Talented Young People (#06664)
- ♦ Comité européen pour l'éducation des enfants et adolescents précoces surdoués et talentueux (#06664)

♦ Comité Européen pour l'Enseignement Catholique (CEEC) 04156

European Committee for Catholic Education – Comité Europeo para la Enseñanza Católica – Europäisches Komitee für das Katholische Schulwesen – Europees Comité voor het Katholiek Onderwijs

SG Ave Emmanuel Mounier 100, 1200 Brussels, Belgium. T. +3222567078. E-mail: geraldine.vallee@ceec.be – ceec@ceec.be.
URL: http://www.ceec.be/

History Founded 1974, Brussels (Belgium), as regional committee of *Catholic International Education Office (#03604)*. Opening Congress: 1977, Strasbourg (France). An international association since 1997. New statutes adopted, 18 Mar 2005. Registered in accordance with Belgian law. **Aims** Act as a meeting point for heads of Catholic education networks in Central, Eastern and Western Europe; be a study and information centre; promote free Catholic education. **Structure** General Assembly; Executive Board; General Secretariat. **Languages** Dutch, English, French, German, Italian, Spanish. **Staff** 1.00 FTE, paid. **Finance** Members' dues. **Activities** Networking/liaising; training/education. **Events** *International Colloquium* Brussels (Belgium) 2019, *General Assembly* Berlin (Germany) 2018, *General Assembly* Glasgow (UK) 2018, *General Assembly* Ljubljana (Slovenia) 2017, *General Assembly* Tirana (Albania) 2017. **Publications** *Catholic Schools in Europe – Innovation is our Tradition* (2014). Congress proceedings.
Members Networks of Catholic schools (29) representing about 35,000 schools and more than 8 million pupils, in 27 countries (indicates 2 networks per country):
Albania, Austria, Belgium (*), Bosnia-Herzegovina, Croatia, Czechia, Denmark, France, Germany, Greece, Hungary, Ireland, Italy, Lithuania, Malta, Netherlands, Norway, Poland, Portugal, Romania, Slovakia, Slovenia, Spain, Sweden, Switzerland, UK (*), Ukraine.
Associate members:
European Union of Former Pupils of Catholic Education (#08992).
NGO Relations Member of: *Forum of Catholic Inspired NGOs (#09905)*. [2019/XD8522/y/E]

♦ Comité européen des entreprises vins (CEEV) 04157

European Committee of Wine Companies – Comité Europeo de las Empresas Vinos – Europäischer Ausschuss der Unternehmen aus dem Weinsektor – Comitato Europeo delle Aziende Vini

Main Office c/o Comité Vins, Av des Arts 43 5e, 1040 Brussels, Belgium. T. +3222309970. Fax +3225130218. E-mail: ceev@ceev.eu.
URL: http://www.ceev.eu/

History 21 May 1959, Brussels (Belgium). Former names and other names: *EEC Committee for the Wine, Aromatized Wine, Sparkling Wine and Liqueur Wine Industries and Trade* – former (21 May 1959); *Comité de la Communauté économique européenne des industries et du commerce des vins, vins mousseux, vins de liqueur, vins aromatisés et autres produits de la vigne* – former (21 May 1959); *Comité Europeo de las Empresas Vinos* – former (21 May 1959); *Europäischer Ausschuss der Unternehmen aus dem Weinsektor* – former (21 May 1959); *Comitato Europeo delle Aziende Vini* – former (21 May 1959); *Comité vins* – alias; *CEV* – former. Registration: Banque-Carrefour des Entreprises, Belgium; EU Transparency Register, No/ID: 2663914841-28. **Aims** Promote a social, economic and legal environment that favours sustainable and responsible development of a competitive EU Wine sector; enhance the legitimate place of wine and its culture in Europe and in the world. **Structure** General Assembly (annual); Management Board; General Secretariat, headed by Secretary General. **Languages** English, French. **Staff** 5.00 FTE, paid; 1.00 FTE, voluntary. **Finance** Sources: members' dues. **Activities** Advocacy/lobbying/activism; events/meetings; knowledge management/information dissemination; networking/liaising. **Events** *General Assembly* Brussels (Belgium) 2014, *General Assembly* Brussels (Belgium) 2013, *General Assembly* Brussels (Belgium) 2012, *General Assembly* Brussels (Belgium) 2011, *General Assembly* Paris (France) 2009.
Members National organizations in 16 countries:
Austria, Belgium, Croatia, France, Germany, Greece, Italy, Luxembourg, Netherlands, Portugal, Romania, Slovenia, Spain, Switzerland, UK, Ukraine.

IGO Relations Recognized by: *European Commission (EC, #06633).* **NGO Relations** Member of: *European Liaison Committee for Agricultural and Agri-Food Trades (#07687); Wine in Moderation (WIM, #20967).* [2022.05.04/XE0491/**E**]

- ♦ Comité européen des équipements techniques du bâtiment (#08879)
- ♦ Comité Européen pour l'etude de la corrosion et la protection des canalisations (#06670)
- ♦ Comité Européen pour l'etude de la corrosion et la protection des canalisations – Eaux potables, Eaux usées, Gaz et Pétrole / see European Committee for the study of corrosion and protection of pipes and pipeline systems (#06670)
- ♦ Comité européen d'étude du sel / see European Salt Producers Association (#08425)
- ♦ Comité européen des études de normalisation en électronique (inactive)

♦ Comité européen des fabricants d'appareils de chauffage et de cuisine domestique (CEFACD) 04158

European Committee of Manufacturers of Domestic Heating and Cooking Appliances – Europäischer Ausschuss der Heiz- und Kochgeräte-Industrie

SG address not obtained. T. +31653300216. E-mail: cefacd@cpartner.nl.

URL: http://www.cefacd.eu/

History 28 May 1951, Paris (France). Registration: France; Start date: 28 Nov 2011, Germany, Frankfurt-Main. **Aims** Represent and promote efficient and environmentally friendly individual heating appliances and cooking appliances; safeguard the supranational interests of members as appropriate; represent and promote members' common economic, technical and political interests before the European Commission, European Council, European Parliament and other European and international bodies. **Structure** General Assembly (annual); Technical Commission (meets twice a year). Membership open. Meetings closed. **Languages** English, French, German, Spanish. **Finance** Sources: members' dues. **Activities** Networking/liaising; standards/guidelines.

Members National organizations in 9 countries:

Austria, Belgium, France, Germany, Netherlands, Norway, Spain, Sweden, UK. [2021/XD0646/t/**D**]

- ♦ Comité européen des fabricants de récipients en verre (inactive)

♦ Comité européen des fabricants de sucre (CEFS) 04159

European Association of Sugar Producers – Verband der europäischen Zuckerfabrikanten

Dir Gen Av de Tervuren 268, 1150 Brussels, Belgium. T. +3227620760. E-mail: cefs@cefs.org.

Assistant to Dir Gen address not obtained.

URL: http://www.cefs.org/

History 2 Mar 1954, Paris (France). Former names and other names: *European Committee of Sugar Manufacturers* – former. Registration: French Ministerial Decree, Start date: 2 Mar 1954; Banque-Carrefour des Entreprises, No/ID: 0436.324.311, Start date: 18 May 1989; EU Transparency Register, No/ID: 49679062863-35, Start date: 21 Dec 2009. **Aims** Liaise between national organizations of sugar manufacturers; collect statistics and documentation; research agricultural and food problems at the European level; ensure representation vis-à-vis international institutions. **Structure** General Assembly; Board of Directors; Praesidium. Permanent Secretariat. **Languages** English, French, German. **Staff** 7.50 FTE, paid. **Finance** Sources: members' dues. **Activities** Events/meetings; guidance/assistance/consulting; knowledge management/information dissemination. **Events** *Annual General Assembly* Brussels (Belgium) 2013, *Meeting* Brussels (Belgium) 2013, *Annual General Assembly* Prague (Czech Rep) 2012, *Annual General Assembly* Amsterdam (Netherlands) 2011, *Congress / Annual General Assembly* Amsterdam (Netherlands) 2011. **Publications** Statistical booklet; statistical and other surveys (about 1 a year).

Members National associations of sugar manufacturers in 20 countries:

Austria, Belgium, Croatia, Czechia, Denmark, Finland, France, Germany, Greece, Hungary, Italy, Lithuania, Netherlands, Poland, Romania, Slovakia, Spain, Sweden, Switzerland, UK.

Consultative Status Consultative status granted from: *ECOSOC (#05331)* (Ros C); *UNCTAD (#20285)* (Special Category); *FAO (#09260)* (Liaison Status). **IGO Relations** Recognized by: *European Commission (EC, #06633).* Participates as observer in the activities of: *Codex Alimentarius Commission (CAC, #04081).* **NGO Relations** Member of (4): *European Bioeconomy Alliance (EUBA, #06334); FoodDrinkEurope (#09841); Primary Food Processors (PFP, #18496)* (as Affiliated member of); *Sugarmark International (no recent information).* Liaison Committee with: *International Confederation of European Beet Growers (CIBE, #12860).* Liaison Organization of: *Comité européen de normalisation (CEN, #04162).* [2022.11.22/XD0653/**D**]

- ♦ Comité européen des fédérations nationales de la maroquinerie, articles de voyages et industries connexes (inactive)
- ♦ Comité européen de formation agricole / see Comitato Europeo per la Formazione e l'Agricoltura
- ♦ Comité européen pour la formation et l'agriculture (internationally oriented national body)
- ♦ Comité européen pour les futurs accélérateurs (#06650)
- ♦ Comité européen de la grande chasse (inactive)
- ♦ Comité européen des groupements de constructeurs du machinisme agricole / see European Agricultural Machinery Association (#05846)
- ♦ Comité européen des groupements professionnels des importateurs et distributeurs grossistes en alimentation (inactive)
- ♦ Comité européen d'hygiène mentale (inactive)
- ♦ Comité européen des importateurs de machines à bois (inactive)
- ♦ Comité européen de l'industrie de la robinetterie / see European Association for the Taps and Valves Industry (#06246)
- ♦ Comité européen des industries textiles du coton et des fibres connexes / see European Federation of Cotton and Allied Textiles Industries (#07093)
- ♦ Comité européen des ingénieurs agronomes / see Confédération européenne des associations d'ingénieurs agronomes (#04538)
- ♦ Comité européen des ingénieurs agronomes de la CE / see Confédération européenne des associations d'ingénieurs agronomes (#04538)
- ♦ Comité Européen Interprofessionnel du Thon Tropical (#08951)
- ♦ Comité européen des jeunes agriculteurs et des 4H clubs / see Rural Youth Europe (#19007)

♦ Comité européen pour l'élaboration de standards dans le domaine de la navigation intérieure (CESNI) 04160

European committee for drawing up standards in the field of inland navigation (CESNI) – Europäischer Ausschuss für die Ausarbeitung von Standards im Bereich der Binnenschifffahrt (CESNI) – Europees Comité voor de opstelling van standaarden voor de binnenvaart (CESNI)

CESNI Secretariat c/o CCNR, Palais du Rhin, 2 place de la République, CS 10023, 67082 Strasbourg CEDEX, France. E-mail: info@cesni.eu.

URL: https://www.cesni.eu/

History Jun 2015. Established following Resolution of *Central Commission for the Navigation of the Rhine (CCNR, #03687)*, adopted at its Plenary Session. **Aims** Adopt technical standards in various fields, in particular as regards vessels, information technology and crew to which the respective regulations at the European and international level, including those of the European Union and the CCNR, may refer with a view to their application; deliberate on the uniform interpretation and application of the said standards, on the method for applying and implementing the corresponding procedures, on procedures for exchanging information, and on the supervisory mechanisms among the Member States; deliberate on derogations and equivalences of technical requirements for a specific craft; deliberate on priority topics regarding safety of navigation, protection of the environment, and other areas of inland navigation. **Structure** Chair; Vice-Chair; Secretariat. **Languages** Dutch, English, French, German. **Activities** Events/meetings; politics/policy/regulatory; standards/guidelines. **Events** *Meeting of the Examination Commissions* Strasbourg (France) 2021, *Workshop on Accidents* Strasbourg (France) 2020, *Workshop on Collisions* Strasbourg (France) 2019, *Workshop on Accommodations of Inland Navigation Vessels* Strasbourg (France) 2018, *Conference of the Inspection Bodies in Inland Navigation* Vienna (Austria) 2018.

Members States (28):

Austria, Belgium, Bulgaria, Croatia, Cyprus, Czechia, Denmark, Estonia, Finland, France, Germany, Greece, Hungary, Ireland, Italy, Latvia, Lithuania, Luxembourg, Malta, Netherlands, Poland, Portugal, Romania, Slovakia, Slovenia, Spain, Sweden, Switzerland.

Observer States (3):

Serbia, UK, Ukraine. [2023.02.14/XM7989/**E***]

- ♦ Comité européen de liaison des associations nationales d'agences de voyages (inactive)
- ♦ Comité européen de liaison pour la cellulose et le papier (#07688)
- ♦ Comité européen de liaison des commerces agricoles et agro-alimentaires (#07687)
- ♦ Comité européen de liaison des commerces agro-alimentaires / see European Liaison Committee for Agricultural and Agri-Food Trades (#07687)

♦ Comité européen de liaison des importateurs de machines-outils (CELIMO) 04161

European Liaison Committee of Machine Tools Importers

Main Office c/o MTA, 62 Bayswater Road, London, W2 3PS, UK. T. +44272986400. Fax +44272986430. E-mail: celimo@mta.org.uk.

History 1971. **Aims** Establish, at European level, contacts between national trade associations of distributors of machine tools and equipment for the purpose of exchanging views. **Structure** Executive Board; Council, comprising representatives of national associations. **Languages** Dutch, English, French, German, Italian. **Events** *Meeting* Biarritz (France) 2005, *Meeting* Helsinki (Finland) 2004, *Meeting* London (UK) 2004, *Annual meeting / Meeting* Naples (Italy) 2003, *Annual meeting / Meeting* Istanbul (Turkey) 2002. **Publications** *CELIMO Directory* (annual).

Members National trade associations in 13 countries:

Austria, Belgium, Finland, France, Germany, Italy, Netherlands, Norway, Spain, Sweden, Switzerland, Türkiye, UK. [2011/XD6775/**E**]

- ♦ Comité européen de liaison des industries de la machine à coudre (inactive)
- ♦ Comité européen de liaison des pédiatres / see European Academy of Paediatrics (#05811)
- ♦ Comité européen de liaison sur les services d'intérêt général (internationally oriented national body)
- ♦ Comité européen de in-line hockey / see Comité européen roller in-line hockey (#04165)
- ♦ Comité européen des luttes associées / see UWW-Europe (#20739)
- ♦ Comité européen des matériaux de génie civil (#04254)
- ♦ Comité européen des matériels et produits pour la fonderie / see European Foundry Equipment Suppliers Association, The (#07353)
- ♦ Comité européen de mécanique / see EUROMECH – European Mechanics Society (#05713)
- ♦ Comité européen des métiers d'art et de création (inactive)
- ♦ Comité européen pour le moulage sous pression (#08268)
- ♦ Comité européen du mouton (inactive)
- ♦ Comité européenne de constructeurs de machines électriques et d'électronique de puissance (#06658)

♦ Comité européen de normalisation (CEN) 04162

European Committee for Standardization – Europäisches Komitee für Normung

Dir Gen Rue de la Science 23, 1040 Brussels, Belgium. T. +3225500811. Fax +3225500819. E-mail: esantiago@cencenelec.eu – info@cencenelec.eu.

Pres address not obtained.

URL: https://www.cencenelec.eu/

History Mar 1961, Paris (France). Founded in succession to *Common Market and Free Trade Area Committee* set up in Oct 1957. Reconstituted 13 June 1975, Brussels (Belgium). Former names and other names: *European Standards Coordinating Committee* – former (Mar 1961 to Jun 1975); *Comité européen de coordination des normes* – former (Mar 1961 to Jun 1975). Registration: Banque-Carrefour des Entreprises, No/ID: 0415.455.651, Start date: 13 Jun 1975; EU Transparency Register, No/ID: 63623305522-13, Start date: 18 Mar 2011. **Aims** Facilitate the exchange of goods and services for the benefit of both society and the economy and supporting the realization of the European Single Market and the removal of technical barriers to trade by developing and harmonizing standards for products, production processes, services or methods. **Structure** General Assembly; Presidential Committee; Administrative Board; Technical Board; Technical Bodies; Working Groups; Management Centre headed by Director General. **Languages** English, French, German. **Staff** 69.00 FTE, paid. **Finance** Sources: members' dues. Other sources: contracts with *European Commission (EC, #06633)* and *EFTA (#05391).* **Activities** Events/meetings; networking/liaising; politics/policy/regulatory; standards/guidelines. **Events** *Hearing for life – How Can Hearing Protection Support?* Brussels (Belgium) 2022, *Highlights in Circular Economy standardization in CEN and CENELEC* Brussels (Belgium) 2022, *The potential of European Standards to Support the European Strategy towards a Green and Sustainable Environment* Brussels (Belgium) 2022, *Trusted Chips: The Standardization Landscape and Opportunities for Europe* Brussels (Belgium) 2022, *Workshop on Personal Protective Equipment (PPE), Medical Devices (MD) Dual Use Products* Brussels (Belgium) 2022. **Publications** *CEN Catalogue of European Standards and their national implementations.* Annual Report; annual work programme; brochures; booklets; online documents.

Members National: national standards organizations in 34 countries of the European Union, the European Free Trade Association and the Central and East European countries:

Austria, Belgium, Bulgaria, Croatia, Cyprus, Czechia, Denmark, Estonia, Finland, France, Germany, Greece, Hungary, Iceland, Ireland, Italy, Latvia, Lithuania, Luxembourg, Malta, Netherlands, North Macedonia, Norway, Poland, Portugal, Romania, Serbia, Slovakia, Slovenia, Spain, Sweden, Switzerland, Türkiye, UK.

Associate: broad-based European organizations (9) representing particular sectors of industry as well as consumers, environmentalists, workers, and small and medium-sized enterprises:

Association européenne pour la coordination de la représentation des consommateurs pour la normalisation (ANEC, #02561); Environmental Coalition on Standards (ECOS, #05499); European Construction Industry Federation (#06766); European Federation of Railway Trackworks Contractors (EFRTC, #07205); European Trade Union Confederation (ETUC, #08927); European Trade Union Institute (ETUI, #08928); European Water and Wastewater Industry Association (Aqua Europa, #09087); MedTech Europe (#16692); Orgalim – Europe's Technology Industries (#17794); Small Business Standards (SBS, #19311).

Affiliates: national standards bodies which are members of ISO, and are the standardization body from an EU neighboring country having links with the EU or EFTA. Affiliates in 15 countries:

Albania, Armenia, Azerbaijan, Bosnia-Herzegovina, Egypt, Georgia, Israel, Jordan, Lebanon, Moldova, Montenegro, Morocco, Serbia, Tunisia, Ukraine.

IGO Relations Memorandum of Understanding with (5): *African Organisation for Standardisation (ARSO, #00404); Arab Industrial Development, Standardization and Mining Organization (AIDSMO, #00981); EuroAsian Interstate Council for Standardization, Metrology and Certification (EASC, #05639); GCC Standardization Organization (GSO, #10084); Southern Common Market (#19868)* (Association for Standardization). Cooperates with governmental bodies and other authorities, including: *ASEAN (#01141); EFTA (#05391); European Commission (EC, #06633).* Signatory to the 'Code of Good Practice for the Preparation, Adoption and Application of Standards' of: *World Trade Organization (WTO, #21864).*

Technical Committee Liaison Organizations:

- *Association of European Public Postal Operators (PostEurop, #02534);*
- *Committee for Medicinal Products for Human Use (CHMP);*
- *Eureka Association (Eureka, #05621);*
- *European Union Aviation Safety Agency (EASA, #08978);*
- *European Committee for Postal Regulation (CERP, see: #04602);*
- *European Defence Agency (EDA, #06895);*
- *EUROCONTROL (#05667);*
- *Group on Earth Observations (GEO, #10735);*
- *ILO (#11123);*
- *International Energy Agency (IEA, #13270);*
- *International Institute of Refrigeration (IIR, #13918);*
- *International Organization of Legal Metrology (#14451);*
- *International Organisation of Vine and Wine (OIV, #14435);*
- *Nordic-Baltic Committee on Food Analysis (NMKL, #17215);*
- *OECD (#17693);*
- *Universal Postal Union (UPU, #20682);*
- *WHO (#20950);*
- *World Meteorological Organization (WMO, #21649).*

NGO Relations Memorandum of Understanding with (1): *Pan American Standards Commission (#18133).*

Agreement for technical cooperation with: *International Organization for Standardization (ISO, #14473)*. Associated Standards Bodies: *ASD-STAN Standardization (ASD-STAN, #01132)*; *European Committee for Iron and Steel Standardization (ECISS, inactive)*. Cooperates with Partner Standardization Bodies which are national standards bodies in Australia and Mongolia. Cooperates closely with: *Association européenne pour la coordination de la représentation des consommateurs pour la normalisation (ANEC, #02561)*; *European Cooperation for Space Standardization (ECSS, #06785)*; *European Telecommunications Standards Institute (ETSI, #08897)*. Technical Committee Liaison Organizations (European trade or professional organizations):
- *European Federation of National Associations of Measurement, Testing and Analytical Laboratories (EUROLAB, #07168)*;
- *Aerospace and Defence Industries Association of Europe (ASD, #00146)*;
- *All Terrain Vehicle Industry European Association (ATVEA, #00739)*;
- *Alliance for Beverage Cartons and the Environment (ACE, #00658)*;
- *APPLiA – Home Appliance Europe (#00877)*;
- *ASIS International*;
- *Association of the Chocolate, Biscuit and Confectionery Industries of the EU (CAOBISCO, #02427)*;
- *European Automobile Manufacturers' Association (ACEA, #06300)*;
- *Association des constructeurs européens de motocycles (ACEM, #02450)*;
- *Association for Cooperative Operations Research and Development (ACORD, #02456)*;
- *Association for Emissions Control by Catalyst (AECC, #02486)*;
- *Association of the European Heating Industry (EHI, #02514)*;
- *Association of European Manufacturers of Fire and Security Systems (EURALARM, #02520)*;
- *Association of European Refrigeration Component Manufacturers (ASERCOM, #02537)*;
- *Association européenne de fabricants de compteurs d'eau et d'énergie thermique (AQUA, #02567)*;
- *Association des fabricants européens d'appareils de contrôle et de régulation (AFECOR, #02592)*;
- *Association of Issuing Bodies (AIB, #02768)*;
- *Association of Plastics Manufacturers in Europe (Plastics Europe, #02862)*;
- *BIPAR – European Federation of Insurance Intermediaries (#03263)*;
- *buildingSMART International (bSI, #03353)*;
- *Bureau international du béton manufacturé (BIBM, #03363)*;
- *European Agricultural Machinery Association (CEMA, #05846)*;
- *CEMBUREAU – The European Cement Association (CEMBUREAU, #03634)*;
- *Centre de coopération pour les recherches scientifiques relatives au tabac (CORESTA, #03735)*;
- *Children's Fashion Europe (CFE, #03876)*;
- *CIRFS – European Man-made Fibres Association (#03944)*;
- *CLECAT (#03993)*;
- *Comité européen des constructeurs de machines à bois (EUMABOIS, #04152)*;
- *Comité européen des fabricants de sucre (CEFS, #04159)*;
- *Comité de fabricants européens d'installations et de distribution de pétrole (CECOD, #04167)*;
- *Comité international des cheminées industrielles (CICIND, #04173)*;
- *Committee for European Construction Equipment (CECE, #04254)*;
- *Confederation of European Paper Industries (CEPI, #04529)*;
- *Confederation of European Security Services (CoESS, #04532)*;
- *Confédération européenne des industries du bois (CEI Bois, #04545)*;
- *Confédération internationale des agents en douanes (CONFIAD, #04559)*;
- *Confederation of National Associations of Hotels, Restaurants, Cafés and Similar Establishments in the European Union and European Economic Area (HOTREC, #04569)*;
- *Conseil européen de l'industrie chimique (CEFIC, #04687)*;
- *Conseil européen de l'industrie des peintures, des encres d'imprimerie et des couleurs d'art (CEPE, #04688)*;
- *Construction Products Europe AISBL (#04761)*;
- *Cosmetics Europe – The Personal Care Association (#04852)*;
- *Council of European Dentists (CED, #04886)*;
- *Council of European Professional Informatics Societies (CEPIS, #04893)*;
- *Digital Trusts and Compliance Europe (DTCE, #05085)*;
- *DIGITALEUROPE (#05073)*;
- DRIVER Project;
- *ECO Platform (#05326)*;
- *EDANA, the voice of nonwovens (EDANA, #05353)*;
- Eden Project;
- *EN13606 Association (inactive)*;
- *ePURE (#05517)*;
- *ESSA – The International Security Association (ESSA, #05547)*;
- *Euroheat and Power (EHP, #05694)*;
- *EuropeActive (#05772)*;
- *Aggregates Europe (UEPG, #00558)*;
- *European Aluminium (#05893)*;
- *European Asphalt Pavement Association (EAPA, #05920)*;
- *European Association of Air Heater Manufacturers (EURO-AIR, #05933)*;
- *European Association of Automotive Suppliers (CLEPA, #05948)*;
- *European Association of Bioindustries (EuropaBio, #05956)*;
- *European Association for External Thermal Insulation Composite Systems (EAE, #06035)*;
- *European Association of Internal Combustion Engine Manufacturers (EUROMOT, #06090)*;
- *European Association of Mining Industries, Metal Ores and Industrial Minerals (EUROMINES, #06122)*;
- *European Association for Panels and Profiles (PPA-Europe, #06142)*;
- *European Association for Passive Fire Protection (EAPFP, #06143)*;
- *European Association of Plaster and Plaster Product Manufacturers (EUROGYPSUM, #06152)*;
- *European Association of Producers of Steel for Packaging (#06167)*;
- *European Association for Professions in Biomedical Science (EPBS, #06170)*;
- *European Association of Pump Manufacturers (EUROPUMP, #06182)*;
- *European Association of Small and Medium sized Enterprises (SME Safety, #06207)*;
- *European Association for the Streamlining of Energy Exchange-gas (EASEE-gas, #06224)*;
- *European Association for the Taps and Valves Industry (CEIR, #06246)*;
- *European Autoclaved Aerated Concrete Association (EAACA, #06297)*;
- *European Balloon and Party Council (EBPC, #06308)*;
- *European Bentonite Producers Association (EUBA, #06328)*;
- *European Biodiesel Board (EBB, #06333)*;
- *European Bioplastics (#06342)*;
- *European Bitumen Association (EUROBITUME, #06348)*;
- *European Cabin Crew Association (EurECCA, #06428)*;
- *European Calcium Silicate Producers Association (ECSPA, #06430)*;
- *European Cellulose Insulation Association (ECIA, #06460)*;
- *European Central Council of Homeopaths (ECCH, #06467)*;
- *European Ceramic Industry Association (CERAME-UNIE, #06506)*;
- *European Chimneys Association (ECA, #06536)*;
- *European Coal Combustion Products Association (ECOBA, #06588)*;
- *European Cockpit Association (ECA, #06598)*;
- *European Cocoa Association (ECA, #06599)*;
- *European Coil Coating Association (ECCA, #06601)*;
- *European Committee for Homeopathy (ECH, #06651)*;
- *European Committee of the Manufacturers of Fire Protection Equipment and Fire Fighting Vehicles (#06659)*;
- *European Consortium of Anchors Producers (ECAP, #06749)*;
- *European Convention for Constructional Steelwork (ECCS, #06779)*;
- *European Copper Institute (ECI, #06796)*;
- *European Council for Motor Trades and Repairs (#06832)*;
- *European Cyclists' Federation (ECF, #06877)*;
- *European Cylinder Makers Association (ECMA, #06878)*;
- *European E-Invoicing Service Providers Association (EESPA, #06971)*;
- *European e-Skills Association (EeSA, #08489)*;
- *European Expanded Clay Association (EXCA, #07013)*;
- *European Federation of Associations of Locks and Builders Hardware Manufacturers (ARGE, #07054)*;
- *European Federation of Campingsite Organisations and Holiday Park Assocations (EFCO and HPA, #07066)*;
- *European Federation of Clinical Chemistry and Laboratory Medicine (EFLM, #07080)*;
- *European Federation of Concrete Admixtures Associations (EFCA, #07085)*;
- *European Federation for Cosmetic Ingredients (EFfCI, #07092)*;
- *European Federation of Engineering Consultancy Associations (EFCA, #07109)*;
- *European Federation of Food, Agriculture and Tourism Trade Unions (EFFAT, #07125)*;
- *European Federation of Funeral Services (EFFS, #07131)*;
- *European Federation of Intelligent Energy Efficiency Services (EFIEES, #07145)*;
- *European Federation for Non-Destructive Testing (EFNDT, #07179)*;
- *European Federation of Railway Trackworks Contractors (EFRTC, #07205)*;
- *European Federation of Tourist Guide Associations (#07228)*;
- *European Federation for Welding, Joining and Cutting (EWF, #07233)*;
- *European Fertiliser Blenders Association (EFBA, #07241)*;
- *European Fire Sprinkler Network (EFSN, #07262)*;
- *European Garage Equipment Association (EGEA, #07377)*;
- *European Garden Machinery Industry Federation (EGMF, #07379)*;
- *European General Galvanizers Association (EGGA, #07383)*;
- *European Group of Organisations for Fire Testing, Inspection and Certification (EGOLF, #07427)*;
- *European Group for Rooflights and Smoke-Ventilation (EUROLUX, #07434)*;
- *European Industrial Gases Association (EIGA, #07525)*;
- *European Institute for Fire Protection (EIFP, #07555)*;
- *European Institute for Wood Preservation (WEI-IEO, #07575)*;
- *European Insulation Manufacturers Association (EURIMA, #07577)*;
- *European Lift and Lift Component Association (ELCA, #07696)*;
- *European Lift Association (ELA, #07695)*;
- *European Lime Association (EuLA, #07699)*;
- *European Managers in the Transport Industry (#07730)*;
- *European Manufacturers of Expanded Polystyrene (EUMEPS, #07732)*;
- *European Manufacturers of Feed Minerals Association (EMFEMA, #07733)*;
- *European Mortar Industry Organization (EMO, #07822)*;
- *European Network of Forensic Science Institutes (ENFSI, #07910)*;
- *European Nursery Products Confederation (ENPC, #08061)*;
- *European Operating Room Nurses Association (EORNA, #08087)*;
- *European Organization for Packaging and the Environment (EUROPEN, #08110)*;
- *European Organization for Quality (EOQ, #08112)*;
- *European Partnership for Energy and the Environment (EPEE, #08157)*;
- *European Phenolic Foam Association (EPFA, #08199)*;
- *The European Plastic Pipes and Fittings Association (TEPPFA, #08215)*;
- *European Plastics Converters (EuPC, #08216)*;
- *European Racking Federation (ERF, inactive)*;
- *European Ready Mixed Concrete Organization (ERMCO, #08330)*;
- *European Recovered Fuel Organisation (ERFO, #08334)*;
- *European Salt Producers Association (EUsalt, #08425)*;
- *European Society of Aerospace Medicine (ESAM, #08509)*;
- *European Society of Pathology (ESP, #08689)*;
- *European Society on Tattoo and Pigment research (ESTP, #08756)*;
- *Solar Heat Europe (SHE, #19674)*;
- *European Steel Association (EUROFER, #08835)*;
- *European Textile Services Association (ETSA, #08904)*;
- *European Transport Workers' Federation (ETF, #08941)*;
- *European Tyre and Rubber Manufacturers' Association (ETRMA, #08963)*;
- *European Union of Swimming Pool and Spa Associations (EUSA, #09019)*;
- *European Vending and Coffee Service Association (EVA, #09049)*;
- *European Water Association (EWA, #09080)*;
- *European Water Treatment Association (EWTA, #09086)*;
- *European Waterproofing Association (EWA, #09084)*;
- *European Writing Instrument Manufacturer's Association (EWIMA, #09125)*;
- *EUROSLAG*;
- *EuroWindoor (#09196)*;
- eVACUATE Project;
- eWall Project;
- *Federation of European Data & Marketing (FEDMA, #09499)*;
- *Federation of European Heating, Ventilation and Air-Conditioning Associations (REHVA, #09507)*;
- *Federation of European Rigid Polyurethane Foam Associations (PU Europe, #09538)*;
- *Fédération Européenne des Aérosols (FEA, #09557)*;
- *Fédération européenne de l'industrie des aliments pour animaux familiers (FEDIAF, #09571)*;
- *Fédération européenne des industries de colles et adhésifs (FEICA, #09572)*;
- *European Materials Handling Federation (#07752)*;
- *Fédération européenne des producteurs d'enveloppes (FEPE, #09578)*;
- *Fédération de l'industrie dentaire en Europe (FIDE, #09595)*;
- *Fédération internationale des grossistes importateurs et exportateurs en fournitures automobiles (FIGIEFA, #09635)*;
- *Fédération Internationale de Motocyclisme (FIM, #09643)*;
- *FEFANA – EU Association of Specialty Feed Ingredients and their Mixtures (#09720)*;
- FoFam Project;
- *FoodDrinkEurope (#09841)*;
- *Gas Infrastructure Europe (GIE, #10073)*;
- *Glass for Europe (#10157)*;
- *Global Cabin Air Quality Executive (GCAQE, #10262)*;
- *Global Network for B2B Integration in High Tech Industries (EDIFICE, #10481)*;
- *GlobalPlatform (#10551)*;
- *GS1 (#10809)*;
- *GS1 in Europe (#10810)*;
- *IGI – The Global Wallcoverings Association (IGI, #11107)*;
- *Industrial Minerals Association – Europe (IMA Europe, #11179)*;
- *International Association of Oil and Gas Producers (IOGP, #12053)*;
- *International Association of Public Transport (#12118)*;
- *International Association for Soaps, Detergents and Maintenance Products (#12166)*;
- *International Council on Monuments and Sites (ICOMOS, #13049)*;
- *International Dairy Federation (IDF, #13128)*;
- *International Federation of Clinical Chemistry and Laboratory Medicine (IFCC, #13392)*;
- *International Society of Hair Restoration Surgery (ISHRS)*;
- *International Sustainability and Carbon Certification (ISCC)*;
- *International Tennis Federation (ITF, #15676)*;
- *International Water Mist Association (IWMA, #15868)*;
- *International Wool Textile Organisation (IWTO, #15904)*;
- iSTRESS Project;
- LEADing Practice;
- *LightingEurope (#16472)*;
- *Liquid Gas Europe (#16488)*;
- *MARCOGAZ – Technical Association of the European Natural Gas Industry (#16572)*;
- *Methanol Institute (MI)*;
- NaNoDefine Project;
- NaNoREG Project;
- NaNoRem Project;
- *Nanotechnology Industries Association (NIA, #16933)*;
- *NATRUE (#16950)*;
- *Near Field Communication Forum (NFC Forum, #16968)*;
- *NGVA Europe (#17130)*;
- *Nickel Institute (#17133)*;
- *Oil Companies' European Association for Environment, Health and Safety in Refining and Distribution (CONCAWE, #17708)*;
- *Open Pan European Public Procurement Online (OpenPEPPOL, #17761)*;
- *Osteopathic European Academic Network (OSEAN, #17909)*;
- POLYGRAPH Project;
- SETNanoMetro Project;
- *spiritsEUROPE (#19921)*;
- *Starch Europe (#19966)*;
- T-REX Project;
- *Toy Industries of Europe (TIE, #20179)*;
- *Union européenne du commerce du bétail et de la viande (UECBV, #20394)*;
- *Association of the European Rail Supply Industry (UNIFE, #02536)*;
- *International Union of Wagon Keepers (#15827)*;
- *UPEI – The voice of Europe's independent fuel suppliers (#20726)*;
- *Vacuum Insulation Panel Association (VIPA International, #20742)*;
- *VGB PowerTech (VGB, #20764)*;
- VISA EUROPE;
- Vocational Training Charitable Institute;
- *Water Quality Association (WQA)*;
- *World Association of Manufacturers of Bottles and Teats (WBT, #21159)*;
- *World Federation of the Sporting Goods Industry (WFSGI, #21487)*;
- *World Rugby (#21757)*.

[2023.02.14/XD0631/y/**D**]

♦ Comité européen de normalisation électrotechnique (#06647)

- Comité européen pour les normes des laboratoires cliniques (inactive)
- Comité européen orchidées / see European Orchid Council (#08093)
- Comité européen des organisations nationales d'importateurs-négociants de matériel de travaux publics et de manutention (no recent information)

♦ Comité européen de l'outillage (CEO) 04163

European Tool Committee – Europäisches Werkzeugkomitee

SG Elberfelder Str 77, 42853 Remscheid, Germany. T. +49219143827. Fax +49219143879. E-mail: ceo@ceo-tools.com.

URL: http://www.ceo-tools.com/

History 3 Jul 1959, Paris (France). General Assembly of 30 Jun 1972, Gothenburg (Sweden), formalized the existence of CEO. **Aims** Study, in a spirit of free cooperation, the problems arising in the tool trade (especially technical and economic problems), the solutions likely to promote progress in manufacture, the expansion of the European market and the opportunities for export; facilitate exchanges by removing obstacles; achieve good relations between firms; agree on economic and social objectives; seek to maintain fair competition; give a better service to customers. **Structure** Plenary Meeting; Board of Management; Economic Committee. **Languages** English, French, German. **Staff** 1.00 FTE, paid. **Finance** Members' dues. Budget (annual): about euro 100,000. **Events** *General Assembly* Lausanne (Switzerland) 2021, *General Assembly* Remscheid (Germany) 2020, *Congress / Annual Congress* Taormina (Italy) 2013, *Annual plenary meeting / Annual Congress* Lisbon (Portugal) 2006, *Annual Congress* Prague (Czech Rep) 2005. **Publications** Circular letters. Annual report.

Members European Associations in 10 countries:
Austria, Belgium, France, Germany, Italy, Netherlands, Spain, Sweden, Switzerland, UK.
Individual Member Companies in 9 countries:
Denmark, France, Germany, Italy, Liechtenstein, Portugal, Slovenia, Sweden, UK.

IGO Relations Recognized by: *European Commission (EC, #06633).* **NGO Relations** Associate Member of: *Construction Products Europe AISBL (#04761).* [2019/XD3637/**D**]

- Comité européen de l'outillage agricole et horticole (inactive)
- Comité européen permanent de recherches pour la protection des populations contre les risques d'intoxication à long terme (inactive)

♦ Comité européen pour la prévention de la torture et des peines ou traitements inhumains ou dégradants (CPT) 04164

European Committee for the Prevention of Torture and Inhuman or Degrading Treatment or Punishment

Exec Sec c/o Conseil de l'Europe, 67075 Strasbourg CEDEX, France. T. +33388412000. Fax +33388412772. E-mail: cptdoc@coe.int.

URL: http://www.cpt.coe.int/

History 26 Jun 1987. Founded in the framework of *Council of Europe (CE, #04881)*, with entry into force of *European Convention for the Prevention of Torture and Inhuman or Degrading Treatment or Punishment (1987).* Operations started Nov 1989. **Aims** As a fact-finding body, forestall possible acts or practices of torture or inhuman or degrading treatment; discover whether, in places of *detention*, general or specific conditions or circumstances are likely to lead to such treatment. **Structure** Plenary Meeting; Committee; Bureau; Secretariat, headed by Executive Secretary. **Languages** English, French. **Staff** 25.00 FTE, paid. **Finance** Through Ordinary Budget of *Council of Europe (CE, #04881).* Annual budget: 5,497,000 EUR (2020). **Activities** Events/meetings; monitoring/evaluation. **Events** *Plenary Meeting* Strasbourg (France) 2004, *Plenary Meeting* Strasbourg (France) 2003, *Plenary Meeting* Strasbourg (France) 2003, *Plenary Meeting* Strasbourg (France) 2003, *Plenary Meeting* Strasbourg (France) 2002. **Publications** Annual General Report; visit reports; factsheets.

Members Independent experts elected in respect of the 47 Council of Europe countries:
Albania, Andorra, Armenia, Austria, Azerbaijan, Belgium, Bosnia-Herzegovina, Bulgaria, Croatia, Cyprus, Czechia, Denmark, Estonia, Finland, France, Georgia, Germany, Greece, Hungary, Iceland, Ireland, Italy, Latvia, Liechtenstein, Lithuania, Luxembourg, Malta, Moldova, Monaco, Montenegro, Netherlands, North Macedonia, Norway, Poland, Portugal, Romania, Russia, San Marino, Serbia, Slovakia, Slovenia, Spain, Sweden, Switzerland, Türkiye, UK, Ukraine.

IGO Relations Cooperates with (3): *Committee Against Torture (CAT, #04241)*; Sub-Committee on Prevention of Torture (SPT); *UNHCR (#20327).* **NGO Relations** Cooperates with (1): *International Committee of the Red Cross (ICRC, #12799).* [2022.02.15/XK0267/**E***]

- Comité européen pour les problèmes criminels (#06645)
- Comité européen des professeurs de l'enseignement supérieur du paysage (inactive)
- Comité européen pour le progrès économique et social (inactive)
- Comité européen pour la protection des animaux dans un monde meilleur pour tous (no recent information)
- Comité européen de recherche-action pour les enfants de parents emprisonnés / see Children of Prisoners Europe (#03875)
- Comité européen pour la recherche scientifique des origines et des conséquences de la deuxième guerre mondiale (inactive)
- Comité européen des régions (#06665)
- Comité européen sur des règlements et usages du commerce intereuropéen de pommes de terre (#06666)
- Comité européen de régulation postale (see: #04602)

♦ Comité européen roller in-line hockey (CERILH) 04165

Contact address not obtained. E-mail: bdarlet.cerilh@gmail.com.

URL: http://www.cerilh.com/

History Set up as a European Technical Committee of *Confédération Européenne de Roller-Skating (CERS, #04550).* Previously also referred to as *Comité européen de in-line hockey.* Serves as CERS In-Line Hockey Committee. **Aims** Develop and structure the *sport* of roller in-line hockey. **Structure** Committee. **Languages** English, French. **Activities** Sporting activities. [2019.09.03/XE3292/**E**]

- **Comité européen RUCIP** Comité européen sur des règlements et usages du commerce intereuropéen de pommes de terre (#06666)
- Comité européen de la santé (inactive)
- Comité européen des sciences spatiales (see: #08441)
- Comité européen pour la sécurité routière dans les forces armées / see European Commission for Road Safety in Armed Forces (#06638)
- Comité européen des services de soutien aux entreprises (inactive)
- Comité européen des systèmes d'étancheite liquide (inactive)
- Comité européen de technologie agricole / see European Commission on Agriculture (#06634)
- Comité européen du thé (inactive)
- Comité européen des traitements de surfaces (#06671)
- Comité européen des transmissions oléohydrauliques et pneumatiques / see European Fluid Power Committee (#07273)

♦ Comité Européen de la Tréfilerie (CET) 04166

Europenan Committee for Wire Drawing

Sec UK Steel, Broadway House, Tothill Street, London, SW1H 9NQ, UK. T. +442076541550. Fax +447554457819.

URL: http://www.wiredrawing-europe.org/

History 1970. EU Transparency Register: 923907935533-61. **Aims** Promote the interests of the manufacturers of wire and wire products in Europe; exchange market research information on wire and wire products; safeguard common interests vis-à-vis national governments and the European Commission as well as other political and non-political institutions; represent its members to the scientific and technical organizations which deal directly or indirectly with problems relating to wire and wire products; discuss questions of overall interest to the whole wire industry. **Structure** Committees (3): President's; Economic; Technical. Officers: Chairman; General Secretary. **Events** *International technical conference* Stresa (Italy) 2003.

Members Full in 13 countries:
Belgium, Czechia, France, Germany, Hungary, Italy, Netherlands, Poland, Portugal, Slovakia, Spain, Sweden, UK.
Associate in 2 countries:
France, Türkiye. [2020/XE4735/**E**]

- Comité Européen pour l'Umami (unconfirmed)
- Comité européen du verre domestique / see European Domestic Glass (#06938)
- Comité Europeo de Asociaciones de Constructores de Maquinaria Agricola / see European Agricultural Machinery Association (#05846)
- Comité Europeo de Asociaciones de Empresas de Ingenieria (inactive)
- Comité Europeo de Asociaciones de Interés General / see European Council for Non-Profit Organizations (#06834)
- Comité Europeo de Combustibles Sólidos / see European Association for Coal and Lignite (#05978)
- Comité Europeo de Constructores de Maquinaria para Plasticos y Caucho (#06656)
- Comité Europeo de los Constructores de Maquinaria Textil (#06672)
- Comité Europeo de Cooperación de las Industrias de la Maquina-Herramienta / see European Association of the Machine tool Industries and related Manufacturing Technologies (#06113)
- Comité Europeo de Coordinación de las Industrias Radiológicas y Electromédicas / see European Coordination Committee of the Radiological, Electromedical Healthcare IT Industry (#06792)
- Comité Europeo de Derecho Rural (#04155)
- Comité Europeo para la Educación de Alumnos Superdotados y con Talento (#06664)
- Comité Europeo para la Educación de Niños y Adolescentes Precoces, Super Dotatos y Talentosos / see European Committee Promoting the Education of Gifted and Talented Young People (#06664)
- Comité Europeo de las Empresas Vinos (#04157)
- Comité Europeo de Enlace para la Pasta y el Papel (#07688)
- Comité Europeo para la Enseñanza Católica (#04156)
- Comité Europeo de ONGs sobre Drogas y Desarrollo / see European Coalition for Just and Effective Drug Policies (#06596)
- Comité Europeo de Organizaciones de Jóvenes Agricultores y 4H Clubs / see Rural Youth Europe (#19007)
- Comité Europeo de las Regiones (#06665)
- Comité Europeu das Associações de Interesse Geral / see European Council for Non-Profit Organizations (#06834)
- Comité Europeu de Cooperação das Indústrias da Maquina-Ferramenta / see European Association of the Machine tool Industries and related Manufacturing Technologies (#06113)
- Comité exécutif international de l'Ordre de Malte pour l'assistance aux lépreux / see Campagne Internationale de l'Ordre de Malte contre la lèpre (#03403)
- Comité exécutif des organisations non gouvernementales associées au Département de l'information des Nations Unies / see Global NGO Executive Committee (#10507)
- Comité exécutif pour la préparation des congrès internationaux d'aveugles (inactive)
- Comité de Expertos sobre la Gestión Mundial de la Información Geoespacial (#20540)
- Comité de Expertos Gubernamentales de Alto Nivel (see: #20556)
- Comité de Expertos en Transporte de Mercancias Peligrosas y en el Sistema Globalmente Armonizado de Clasificación y Etiquetado de Productos Quimicos (#20543)
- Comité d'experts de la coopération internationale en matière fiscale (#20541)
- Comité d'experts sur l'évaluation des mesures de lutte contre le blanchiment des capitaux et le financement du terrorisme (#04257)
- Comité d'experts des Nations Unies sur la gestion de l'information géospatiale à l'échelle mondiale (#20540)
- Comité d'experts du transport des marchandises dangereuses et du Système général harmonisé de classification et d'étiquetage des produits chimiques (#20543)

♦ Comité de fabricants européens d'installations et de distribution de pétrole (CECOD) 04167

Committee of European Manufacturers of Petroleum Measuring and Distributing Equipment – Komitee der Europäischen Hersteller von Einrichtungen zur Messung und Verteilung von Flüssigen Brennstoffen

Main Office c/o Syndicat de la Mesure, 39-41 rue Louis Blanc, 92400 Courbevoie, France. T. +33143347681. Fax +33143347682. E-mail: cecod@syndicat-mesure.fr.

URL: http://www.cecod.eu/

History 1969. Registration: EU Transparency Register, No/ID: 58060715856-43. **Aims** Allow members to present and compare points of view on common technical problems; study other matters of common interest in technical and industrial fields; offer assistance in the unification of European weights and measures and safety regulations. **Structure** General Assembly (annual); Executive Board; Secretariat; Technical Committee; Study Groups; Special Missions. **Languages** English, French, German. **Finance** Members' dues. **Events** *General Assembly* Taormina (Italy) 2002, *General Assembly* Hamburg (Germany) 2001, *General Assembly* Lisbon (Portugal) 2000, *General Assembly* Beaune (France) 1999, *General Assembly* Dublin (Ireland) 1997.

Members Full and associate. Companies (36) in 12 countries:
Czechia, Denmark, Finland, France, Germany, Italy, Netherlands, Portugal, Spain, Sweden, Switzerland, UK.

NGO Relations Cooperates with (2): *Comité européen de normalisation (CEN, #04162); Comité européen des constructeurs d'instruments de pesage (CECIP, #04151).* [2020/XD3667/**D**]

- Comité des fabricants de levure de panification de la CEE / see Confédération des Fabricants de Levure de l'Union Européenne (#04551)
- Comité des fabricants de levure de panification de l'Union européenne / see Confédération des Fabricants de Levure de l'Union Européenne (#04551)
- Comité Pro-Federación Latinoamericana de Trabajadores del Comercio (inactive)
- Comité Pro-Federación Latinoamericana de Trabajadores del Espectaculo Público (inactive)
- Comité pour une fédération européenne et mondiale (inactive)
- Comité pro-fédération latinoaméricaine des travailleurs du commerce (inactive)
- Comité pro-fédération latinoaméricaine des travailleurs des spectacles publics (inactive)
- Comité des femmes socialistes de l'Europe de l'Est (inactive)
- Comité pour la fondation de l'Organisation internationale de psychophysiologie / see International Organization of Psychophysiology (#14466)
- Comité pour un fonds international des bourses (inactive)
- Comité français pour la campagne mondiale contre la faim / see Comité français pour la solidarité internationale
- Comité français contre la faim / see Comité français pour la solidarité internationale
- Comité français pour la solidarité internationale (internationally oriented national body)
- Comité général de la coopération agricole de la Communauté européenne / see General Confederation of Agricultural Cooperatives in the European Union (#10107)
- Comité général de la coopération agricole de l'UE / see General Confederation of Agricultural Cooperatives in the European Union (#10107)
- Comité général de presse estudiantine (inactive)
- Comité des gouverneurs des banques centrales des Etats membres de la Communauté économique européenne (inactive)
- Comité van de Graan- en Veevoederhandel in de EG / see Committee of the Trade in Cereals, Oilseeds, Pulses, Olive Oil, Oils and Fats, Animal Feed and Agrosupply of the EU (#04289)
- Comité grec pour la détente internationale et la paix (internationally oriented national body)
- Comité Hospitalario de la Comunidad Europea / see European Hospital and Healthcare Federation (#07501)
- Comité hospitalier de la Communauté européenne / see European Hospital and Healthcare Federation (#07501)

♦ Comité Iberoamericano para el Desarrollo y Aplicación de los Plasticos en Agricultura (CIDAPA) 04168

Address not obtained.

URL: http://www.cidapa.com/

History 1997, Santa Cruz de la Sierra (Bolivia). **Structure** Assembly (annual). Executive Committee, comprising President, 1st and 2nd Vice-Presidents, Secretary-General, Treasurer and 9 members. **Events** *Congress* Concepción (Chile) 2022, *Congress* Concepción (Chile) 2020, *Congress* Concepción (Chile) 2019, *Congress* Saltillo, COAH (Mexico) 2015, *Congress* Campinas (Brazil) 2011.
Members Full in 21 countries:
Argentina, Bolivia, Brazil, Chile, Colombia, Costa Rica, Cuba, Dominican Rep, Ecuador, El Salvador, Guatemala, Honduras, Mexico, Nicaragua, Panama, Paraguay, Peru, Portugal, Spain, Uruguay, Venezuela. [2010/XJ1275/**D**]

♦ Comité des Indes occidentales (#20920)
♦ Comité de la Industria Algodonera y Fibras afines de la CE / see European Federation of Cotton and Allied Textiles Industries (#07093)
♦ Comité das Industrias de Algodão e Fibras afins da CE / see European Federation of Cotton and Allied Textiles Industries (#07093)
♦ Comité de l'industrie hôtelière et de la restauration de la Communauté européenne / see Confederation of National Associations of Hotels, Restaurants, Cafés and Similar Establishments in the European Union and European Economic Area (#04569)
♦ Comité des industries du coton et des fibres connexes de la CE / see European Federation of Cotton and Allied Textiles Industries (#07093)
♦ Comité de l'industrie textile cotonnière européenne / see European Federation of Cotton and Allied Textiles Industries (#07093)
♦ Comité de Información (#04260)
♦ Comité de l'information (#04260)
♦ Comité de l'information des Nations Unies / see Committee on Information (#04260)
♦ Comité des institutions internationales de développement sur l'environnement (no recent information)

♦ Comité de Integración Latino Europa-América (CILEA) 04169

Latin Europe-America Integration Committee

Contact Piazza della Repubblica 59, 00185 Rome RM, Italy. T. +39647863317. E-mail: cilea@commercialisti.it.
URL: http://www.cilea.info/

History 6 Aug 1997, Buenos Aires (Argentina). Registered in accordance with Italian law, 2003. **Aims** Bring together professional organizations in the field of economic and *accounting* services from Latin countries. **Structure** General Assembly; Executive Council; Permanent Secretary; Executive Secretary. **Languages** French, Italian, Portuguese, Romanian, Spanish. **Activities** Events/meetings. **Events** *Fiscalidad y tributacion de las PYMES en los paises del CILEA y presentacion de proyectos internacionales para PYMES* Manizales (Colombia) 2014, *La contabilidad como factor de informacion para las PYMES* Aveiro (Portugal) 2013, *Seminar* Bogota (Colombia) 2013, *Seminar / International Seminar* Braga (Portugal) 2012, *Seminar / International Seminar* Sucre (Bolivia) 2012. **Publications** *CILEA International Studies Series.*
Members Professional organizations (19) in 16 countries and territories:
Argentina, Bolivia, Brazil, Colombia, Ecuador, France, Guatemala, Italy, Paraguay, Peru, Portugal, Romania, San Marino, Spain, Uruguay, Venezuela. [2017.06.01/XJ3343/**E**]

♦ Comité interafricain d'études hydrauliques (inactive)
♦ Comité interafricain sur l'océanographie, la pêche maritime et continentale (no recent information)
♦ Comité interafricain sur les plantes médicinales et médecines traditionnelles africaines (inactive)
♦ Comité Inter-Africain sur les pratiques traditionnelles ayant effet sur la santé des femmes et des enfants (#11384)
♦ Comité interafricain de statistique (inactive)
♦ Comité interaméricain d'éducation mathématique (#11413)
♦ Comité interaméricain pour l'établissement pacifique (inactive)
♦ Comité interaméricain des industries laitières (inactive)
♦ Comité interaméricain permanent antiacridien (inactive)
♦ Comité interaméricain de protection agricole (inactive)
♦ Comité interaméricain pour les questions financières et économiques (inactive)
♦ Comité interaméricain de scoutisme (#11445)
♦ Comité Interamericano Contra el Terrorismo (#11412)
♦ Comité Inter-Americano de Educação Matematica (#11413)
♦ Comité Interamericano de Educación Matematica (#11413)
♦ Comité Interamericano Permanente Antiacridiano (inactive)
♦ Comité Interamericano de Proteção Agricola (inactive)
♦ Comité Interamericano de Protección Agricola (inactive)
♦ Comité Interamericano para la Reducción de Desastres Naturales (#11414)

♦ Comité Interamericano de Sanidad Avicola (CISA) 04170

Inter-American Committee on Avian Health

Coordinator OIE Americas Office, Paseo Colón 315 – 5/D, C1063ACD Buenos Aires, Argentina. T. +541143313919. Fax +541143315162. E-mail: rr.americas@oie.int.
URL: http://www.rr-americas.oie.int/es/proyectos/es_cisa.htm

History 19 Nov 2004, Panama, by Americas Commission of *OIE – World Organisation for Animal Health (#17703)*. **Aims** Obtain greater transparency in the definition of sanitary situations by facilitating fulfillment of member countries' notifications to the OIE: coordinate technical information related to *epidemiology* of *poultry diseases*; promote coordinated *sanitary* programmes to prevent, control and eradicate agents or pathologies affecting poultry production and public health; exchange information; analyse and propose modifications and updates to OIE norms, *regulations* and international *standards*; promote generation and update of censuses, registries and sanitary controls of establishments of poultry industry and production in member countries; improve health, quality and control of poultry production by promoting educational programmes in member countries and facilitating access to information so as to develop members' knowledge of techniques and scientific advances in health, technical quality and controls of production; cooperate with all sectors involved in poultry industry and production so as to harmonize technical mechanisms that favour development of sanitary quality and prophylactic measures, promoting greater exchange of such among member countries. **Structure** Meeting (at least annual). Executive Committee (2-year terms), comprising President (public sector), Vice-President (private sector), 2 public sector representatives and 2 private sector representatives, all representing different countries. Coordinator, designated by Executive Committee. Regional Representative of Americas Commission of OIE acts as Secretary (ex-officio). **Finance** Members' dues. Other sources: support from OIE; contributions from public and private sector. **Activities** Identifies reference laboratories and collaborating centres of the OIE; analyses and makes proposals to the codes and manuals of Standards for Avian Influenza and ENC; establishes protocol for recognition of countries or regions free of diseases; contributes to official legislation of member countries with respect to avian diseases; carries out risk analysis; works to improve systems of communication and notification; organizes periodic meetings and seminars.
Members Representatives of official veterinary services responsible for poultry health and of recognized associations in the poultry industry and production in countries of the Americas (one representative for the public sector and one for the private sector in each country). Collaborator members international and regional organizations; official regulatory institutions; research universities and institutes in member countries of OIE; centres collaborating with OIE. OIE countries in the Americas (29):
Argentina, Bahamas, Barbados, Belize, Bolivia, Brazil, Canada, Chile, Colombia, Costa Rica, Cuba, Dominican Rep, Ecuador, El Salvador, Guatemala, Guyana, Haiti, Honduras, Jamaica, Mexico, Nicaragua, Panama, Paraguay, Peru, Suriname, Trinidad-Tobago, Uruguay, USA, Venezuela. [2008/XJ3858/**E**]

♦ Comité Interamericano de Sociedades de Microscopia Electrónica (CIASEM) 04171

Inter-American Committee of Societies for Electron Microscopy – Comité Interamericano das Sociedades de Microscopia

Treas Univ of Buenos Aires, Viamonte 430, 1053 Buenos Aires, Argentina. E-mail: admin@ciasem.com.
URL: http://www.ciasem.com/

History 1991. Founded as a regional committee of *International Federation of Societies for Microscopy (IFSM, #13550)*. Registration: Start date: 2001, Mexico. **Aims** Increase and diffuse, for scientific and educational goals, the science, practice and instrumentation of microscopy on the American continent. **Structure** General Assembly; Executive Council. **Languages** English, Portuguese, Spanish. **Staff** Voluntary. **Activities** Events/meetings. **Events** *Congress* 2022, *Congress* Mexico 2021, *Congress* Buenos Aires (Argentina) 2019, *Congress* Varadero (Cuba) 2017, *Congress* Porlamar (Venezuela) 2015. **Publications** *Acta Microscopica.*
Members Organizations in 11 countries:
Argentina, Brazil, Canada, Chile, Colombia, Cuba, Ecuador, Mexico, Peru, USA, Venezuela. [2021/XE3749/**E**]

♦ Comité Interestatal Permanente de Lucha contra la Sequia en el Sahel (#04195)
♦ Comité intergouvernemental chargé de l'application de la Convention internationale sur la reconnaissance des études, diplômes et des grades de l'enseignement supérieur dans les Etats arabes et les Etats européens riverains de la Méditerranée (inactive)
♦ Comité intergouvernemental de la Convention internationale de Rome sur la protection des artistes interprètes ou exécutants, des producteurs de phonogrammes et des organismes de radiodiffusion (#11474)
♦ Comité intergouvernemental de la convention universelle sur le droit d'auteur (#11478)
♦ Comité intergouvernemental pour l'éducation physique et le sport (#11475)
♦ Comité intergouvernemental pour les migrations / see International Organization for Migration (#14454)
♦ Comité intergouvernemental pour les migrations européennes / see International Organization for Migration (#14454)
♦ Comité intergouvernemental des pays du Bassin de la Plata (#04172)
♦ Comité intergouvernemental pour la promotion du retour de biens culturels à leur pays d'origine ou de leur restitution en cas d'appropriation illégale (#11476)
♦ Comité intergouvernemental pour la protection du patrimoine culturel et naturel de valeur universelle exceptionnelle / see World Heritage Committee (#21567)
♦ Comité intergouvernemental pour la protection du patrimoine mondial culturel et naturel / see World Heritage Committee (#21567)
♦ Comité intergouvernemental provisoire pour les mouvements migratoires d'Europe / see International Organization for Migration (#14454)
♦ Comité intergouvernemental pour les réfugiés (inactive)
♦ Comité intergouvernemental de sauvegarde du patrimoine culturel immatériel (#11477)
♦ Comité Intergovernamental Coordenador dos Paises da Bacia do Plata (#04172)
♦ Comité Intergubernamental de la Convención Universal sobre Derecho de Autor (#11478)
♦ Comité Intergubernamental Coordinador de la Cuenca del Plata / see Comité Intergubernamental Coordinador de los Paises de la Cuenca del Plata (#04172)

♦ Comité Intergubernamental Coordinador de los Paises de la Cuenca del Plata (CIC) 04172

Comité Intergovernamental Coordenador dos Paises da Bacia do Plata – Intergovernmental Committee of the River Plate Basin Countries – Comité intergouvernemental des pays du Bassin de la Plata

Secretariat Paraguay 755, Piso 2, 1057 Buenos Aires, Argentina. T. +541143122506. Fax +541143122272. E-mail: secretaria@cicplata.org.
URL: http://www.cicplata.org/

History Established following ratification of the *River Plate Basin Treaty – Traité du Bassin du Rio de la Plata – Tratado de la Cuenca de la Plata*, opened for signing 23 Apr 1969, Brasilia (Brazil); ratified, 1972. Former names and other names: *Comité Intergubernamental Coordinador de la Cuenca del Plata (CABEI)* – former (Apr 1969); *River Plate Basin System* – alias. **Aims** Promote and support development programmes for the area covered by the River Plate and its affluents, including questions of water resources and navigation, soils conservation and improvement, transports, health, education, environment. **Structure** Committee responsible for implementing the decisions of the Foreign Ministers of the member countries who normally celebrate the *Reunión de Cancilleres de los Paises de la Cuenca del Plata* (once a year), and for promoting and coordinating assistance from international institutions. Commission of Delegates, assisted by Executive Secretary. **Languages** Portuguese, Spanish. **Finance** Contributions of member governments. Annual budget: US$ 261,700. **Activities** Research and development; projects/programmes; events/meetings. **Events** *Water for life forum* Foz do Iguaçu (Brazil) 2005, *Meeting / Meeting of Chancellors of River Plate Basin Countries* Punta del Este (Uruguay) 1992, *Meeting / Meeting of Chancellors of River Plate Basin Countries* Asunción (Paraguay) 1991, *Meeting of Chancellors of River Plate Basin Countries* Brasilia (Brazil) 1989, *Meeting* Brasilia (Brazil) 1988.
Members Governments of 5 countries:
Argentina, Bolivia, Brazil, Paraguay, Uruguay.
IGO Relations Observer to: *Sistema Económico Latinoamericano (SELA, #19294)*. Instrumental in setting up: *Fondo Financiero para el Desarrollo de la Cuenca del Plata (FONPLATA, #09833)*. **NGO Relations** *Regional Commission for Power Integration (#18764); Latin American Railways Association (#16365)*.
[2021/XD4499/**D***]

♦ Comité Intergubernamental para la Educación Física y el Deporte (#11475)
♦ Comité Intergubernamental para Fomentar el Retorno de los Bienes Culturales a sus Paises de Origen o su Restitución en caso de Apropiación Ilicita / see Intergovernmental Committee for Promoting the Return of Cultural Property to its Countries of Origin or its Restitution in case of Illicit Appropriation (#11476)
♦ Comité Intergubernamental para las Migraciones / see International Organization for Migration (#14454)
♦ Comité Intergubernamental para las Migraciones Europeas / see International Organization for Migration (#14454)
♦ Comité Intergubernamental para la Promoción del Retorno de Bienes Culturales hacia sus Paises de Origen o su Restitución en Caso de Apropiación Ilicita (#11476)
♦ Comité Intergubernamental de Protección del Patrimonio Cultural y Natural de Valor Universal Excepcional / see World Heritage Committee (#21567)
♦ Comité Intergubernamental de Protección del Patrimonio Mundial Cultural y Natural / see World Heritage Committee (#21567)
♦ Comité Intergubernamental para la Salvaguardia del Patrimonio Cultural Inmaterial (#11477)
♦ Comité intérimaire pour le brevet communautaire (inactive)
♦ Comité intérimaire du Conseil des gouverneurs du Fonds monétaire international sur le système monétaire international / see International Monetary and Financial Committee (#14179)
♦ Comité intérimaire pour la coordination des études sur le bassin inférieur du Mekong (inactive)
♦ Comité intérimaire / see International Monetary and Financial Committee (#14179)
♦ Comité intérimaire des organisations non gouvernementales jouissant du statut consultatif (inactive)
♦ Comité inter-mouvement auprès des évacués / see CIMADE
♦ Comité Internacional de Auschwitz (#12297)
♦ Comité Internacional Católico de Enfermeras y Asistentas Médico-Sociales (#12451)
♦ Comité Internacional de Ciencias Históricas (#12777)
♦ Comité Internacional para el Control de la Producción Lechera del Ganado / see International Committee for Animal Recording (#12746)
♦ Comité Internacional para la Cooperación de las Periodistas (inactive)
♦ Comité Internacional de Coordinación / see Global Alliance of National Human Rights Institutions (#10214)
♦ Comité Internacional de Coordinación para la Iniciación a la Ciencia y al Desarrollo de Actividades Cientificas Extraescolares (#12953)
♦ Comité Internacional de Coordinación de las Instituciones Nacionales para la Promoción y Protección de los Derechos Humanos / see Global Alliance of National Human Rights Institutions (#10214)
♦ Comité Internacional de la Cruz Roja (#12799)
♦ Comité Internacional de la Cuarta Internacional (#12771)

- Comité Internacional ICOMOS de Asuntos Legales, Administrativos y Financieros (#11077)
- Comité Internacional para los Indios de las Américas / see International Committee for the Indigenous Peoples of the Americas
- Comité Internacional de Intercambios (inactive)
- Comité Internacional de Itinerarios Culturales (#11060)
- Comité Internacional de Itinerarios Culturales ICOMOS / see ICOMOS International Committee on Cultural Routes (#11060)
- Comité Internacional para las Libertades Etnicas / see Internacia Komitato por Etnaj Liberecoj (#11523)
- Comité Internacional de Medicina Militar / see International Committee of Military Medicine (#12785)
- Comité Internacional de Movimientos Infantiles y de Adolescentes (inactive)
- Comité Internacional de los Museos Conmemorativos de las Victimas de Crimenes Públicos (#12784)
- Comité Internacional para los Museos Regionales (see: #13051)
- Comité Internacional Paralimpico (#14512)
- Comité Internacional Pierre de Coubertin (#04184)
- Comité Internacional de Planificación para la Soberanía Alimentaria (#14365)
- Comité Internacional de Plasticos para la Agricultura (#04185)
- Comité Internacional para los Pueblos Indigenas de las Américas (internationally oriented national body)
- Comité Internacional Radio-Maritimo (#04186)
- Comité Internacional de Rescate (#14717)
- Comité Internacional por las Residencias Históricas-Museo (#11057)
- Comité Internacional para la Salvaguardia de la Lengua Bretona (#12761)
- Comité Internacional sobre los Sistemas Mundiales de Navegación por Satélite (#12775)
- Comité Internacional de Sociedades con Sucursales / see The Consumer Goods Forum (#04772)
- Comité Internacional de la Tintura y Limpieza (inactive)
- Comité international d'action démocratique (inactive)
- Comité international pour l'Afrique noire / see Conseil français des investisseurs en Afrique
- Comité international d'aide aux intellectuels (inactive)
- Comité international sur l'alcool, les drogues et la sécurité routière (#12990)
- Comité international de l'alimentation pour les petites démocraties (inactive)
- Comité international pour l'analyse et la restauration des structures du patrimoine architectural de l'ICOMOS (#11072)
- Comité international sur les animaux de laboratoire / see International Council for Laboratory Animal Science (#13039)
- Comité international d'anthropologie de l'alimentation et des habitudes d'alimentation (inactive)
- Comité international anti-chasse (internationally oriented national body)
- Comité international de l'approvisionnement (inactive)
- Comité international pour l'architecture vernaculaire de l'ICOMOS (#11069)
- Comité international pour l'art rupestre de l'ICOMOS (#11066)
- Comité international des arts et traditions populaires (#14447)
- Comité international d'assistance publique et privée (inactive)
- Comité international des associations d'industriels aérospatiaux (#12956)
- Comité international des associations techniques de fonderie / see World Foundry Organization (#21528)
- Comité international des assurances sociales (inactive)
- Comité international Atlantique (inactive)
- Comité international d'Auschwitz (#12297)
- Comité international de bactériologie systématique / see International Committee on Systematics of Prokaryotes (#12807)
- Comité international des banques coopératives / see International Cooperative Banking Association (#12945)
- Comité international des bibliothécaires agricoles (inactive)
- Comité international de biochimie (inactive)
- Comité international de bioéthique de l'UNESCO (#12348)
- Comité international du bois (inactive)
- Comité international du bois de l'ICOMOS (#11085)
- Comité international Buchenwald-Dora et Kommandos (#12749)
- Comité international des camps (no recent information)
- Comité international des camps de concentration de Buchenwald / see International Committee Buchenwald Dora and Commandos (#12749)
- Comité international du carbure et de l'acétylène (inactive)
- Comité international catholique des associations d'infirmières / see International Catholic Committee of Nurses and Medico-social Assistants (#12451)
- Comité international catholique des aveugles (inactive)
- Comité international catholique des infirmières et des assistantes médico-sociales (#12451)
- Comité international catholique de liaison pour les organisations agricoles et rurales / see International Catholic Rural Association (#12461)

♦ Comité international des cheminées industrielles (CICIND) 04173

International Committee on Industrial Chimneys – Internationaler Ausschuss für Industrieschornsteine

Address not obtained.
URL: http://www.cicind.org/

History Founded 1973, Paris (France). **Aims** Promote knowledge about the design, construction and use of chimneys; stimulate the harmonization of national chimney design codes; sponsor research. **Structure** General Assembly (annual, during Spring Meeting); Governing Body; Technical Committees. **Languages** English. **Staff** 7.00 FTE, voluntary. **Finance** Members' dues. **Activities** Research/documentation; events/meetings. **Events** *Meeting* Rotterdam (Netherlands) 2021, *Meeting* Edinburgh (UK) 2019, *Meeting* Madrid (Spain) 2019, *Meeting* Graz (Austria) 2018, *Meeting* Montréal, QC (Canada) 2018. **Publications** *CICIND Report* – journal. *CICIND Chimney Book*; *History of CICIND – 1973-2008*; *Technical Manual*. Model Codes; manuals; recommendations; CD. **Members** Individuals (230) from companies and organizations in 37 countries. Membership countries not specified. **NGO Relations** Cooperates with: *Comité européen de normalisation (CEN, #04162)*. [2017.03.13/XE2338/tv/**E**]

- Comité international pour la chimie et la technologie de l'extraction des solvants (#12804)
- Comité international du cinéma d'enseignement et de la culture (inactive)
- Comité international du commerce des vins, cidres, spiritueux et liqueurs (inactive)
- Comité international pour une conférence mondiale sur les droits de l'homme (inactive)
- Comité international pour les congrès horticoles (inactive)
- Comité international des congrès internationaux du libre-échange (inactive)
- Comité international du Congrès des peuples contre l'impérialisme (inactive)
- Comité international pour la conservation de la mosaïque (#12755)
- Comité international pour la conservation du patrimoine industriel (#12754)
- Comité international de continuation vers le désarment (inactive)
- Comité international contre la maladie mentale (#12742)
- Comité international contre le rhumatisme / see International League of Associations for Rheumatology (#14016)
- Comité international pour le contrôle des collectes de dons (inactive)
- Comité international pour le contrôle des performances en élevage (#12746)
- Comité international pour le contrôle de la productivité laitière du bétail / see International Committee for Animal Recording (#12746)
- Comité international de la coopération agricole / see International Co-operative Agricultural Organisation (#12943)
- Comité international pour la coopération des journalistes (inactive)
- Comité international de coopération syndicale des enseignants (inactive)
- Comité international des coopératives de production et de service industrielles et artisanales / see International Organisation of Industrial and Service Cooperatives (#14429)
- Comité international de coordination / see Global Alliance of National Human Rights Institutions (#10214)
- Comité international de coordination et d'action des groupements de techniciens des industries de revêtements de surface / see Coatings Societies International (#04075)
- Comité international de coordination des associations d'analystes financiers / see International Council of Investment Associations (#13034)
- Comité international de coordination des associations de bibliothèques de théologie catholique / see European Theological Libraries (#08906)
- Comité international de coordination des forces pacifiques (inactive)
- Comité international de coordination d'immunologie de la reproduction (#12958)
- Comité international de coordination pour l'initiation à la science et le développement des activités scientifiques extra-scolaires (#12953)
- Comité international de coordination des institutions nationales pour la promotion et la protection des droits de l'homme / see Global Alliance of National Human Rights Institutions (#10214)
- Comité international de coordination pour la sauvegarde et le développement du site historique d'Angkor (#12954)
- Comité international de courses en montagne / see World Mountain Running Association (#21659)
- Comité international de la Croix-Rouge (#12799)
- Comité international de la culture du houblon (#13807)

♦ Comité international de Dachau (CID) 04174

International Dachau Committee – Mezdunarodnyj Komitet Byvsih Uznikov Dahau

SG Lichtaartseweg 202, 2200 Herentals, Belgium. T. +3214213827.
Pres address not obtained.
Administrator address not obtained.
URL: http://www.comiteinternationaldachau.com/

History 20 Dec 1958, Brussels (Belgium). Registered in accordance with Belgian law. **Aims** Encourage remembrance and defence under all circumstances of the respect due to the *memory* of the *victims* of Dachau and other *concentration camps*; in agreement with the Bavarian Government, arrange and maintain the *camp* in the state in which it was found in 1945 and establish there a documentation centre and museum; defend the rights of *ex-inmates* and their organizations with regard to *reparations* to *war victims* and their dependents; campaign against anything which might contribute to the rebirth of such camps and their horrors. **Structure** General Assembly, composed of 2 delegates per organization; Executive Committee, consisting of President, 2 Vice-Presidents, Secretary-General, Treasurer and 2 other members. **Languages** French, German. **Finance** Members' dues. Grants. **Activities** Annual Ceremony (at Dachau). Set up *Fondation internationale de Dachau (FID, inactive)*. **Events** *Meeting* Dachau (Germany) 1996, *Meeting* Dachau (Germany) 1995, *Annual meeting* Dachau (Germany FR) 1990, *Annual meeting* Dachau (Germany FR) 1989, *Annual meeting* Dachau (Germany FR) 1988. **Publications** *Dachauer Hefte/Cahiers de Dachau*; *Histoire officielle de Dachau 1933-1945* by Paul Berben in English, French, Spanish; *Le Camp de concentration de Dachau* in English, French, German, Italian – photographic catalogue.

Members National associations in 21 countries:
Albania, Austria, Belgium, Bulgaria, Czechia, Denmark, France, Germany, Hungary, Israel, Italy, Lithuania, Luxembourg, Netherlands, Norway, Poland, Romania, Russia, Slovenia, Ukraine, USA.

IGO Relations Working relations with: *UNESCO (#20322)*. [2018/XE1782/**E**]

- Comité international pour la défense des intérêts de l'industrie huilière en Europe (inactive)
- Comité International pour les Demeures Historiques- Musée (#11057)
- Comité international des dérivés tensio-actifs (inactive)
- Comité international pour la dermatopathologie (#12762)
- Comité international de développement du caoutchouc (inactive)
- Comité international pour le développement du commerce (inactive)
- Comité international pour le développement et l'étude de la construction tubulaire (#04266)
- Comité international pour développer le libre échange (inactive)
- Comité international pour la diffusion des arts et des lettres par le cinéma (no recent information)
- Comité international pour la dignité de l'enfant (internationally oriented national body)
- Comité international des directeurs de vente des journaux et publications (inactive)
- Comité international pour la documentation de l'ICOM (see: #13051)
- Comité international de droit comparé / see International Association of Legal Science (#11997)
- Comité international des échanges (inactive)
- Comité international des écoles de service social / see International Association of Schools of Social Work (#12149)
- Comité international sur l'économie de la conservation de l'ICOMOS (#11062)
- Comité international de l'éducation de plein air (inactive)
- Comité international de Eger sur les villes historiques / see ICOMOS International Committee on Historic Cities, Towns and Villages (#11063)
- Comité internationale des musées et collections d'armes et d'histoire militarie (#12790)
- Comité international d'enregistrement des fréquences (inactive)
- Comité international des enseignants pour la lutte contre le racisme, l'antisémitisme et l'apartheid (inactive)
- Comité international de l'enseignement philosophique / see Association internationale des professeurs de philosophie (#02732)
- Comité international d'entente des associations de foyers adoptifs (inactive)
- Comité international des entreprises à succursales / see The Consumer Goods Forum (#04772)
- Comité international de l'entretien du textile (#12809)
- Comité pour une Internationale ouvrière (#04290)

♦ Comité international d'esthétique et de cosmétologie (CIDESCO) .. 04175

Exec Dir Waidstrasse 4a, 8037 Zurich ZH, Switzerland. T. +41444482200. Fax +41444482201. E-mail: info@cidesco.com.
URL: http://www.cidesco.com/

History Founded 27 Dec 1946, Brussels (Belgium). Normally referred to simply by French acronym *'CIDESCO'*. **Aims** Promote aesthetics and cosmetology (skin and body therapy) on an international level; promote education and training in aesthetics and cosmetology; coordinate and support the professional activities of members; accredit institutions that meet CIDESCO Standards. **Structure** General Assembly of national delegates (annual, usually at CIDESCO World Congress); Board of Directors of 6 members; head office in Zurich (Switzerland). **Languages** English. **Staff** 141.00 FTE, paid. **Finance** Quotas based on national membership. **Activities** Awards/prizes/competitions; certification/accreditation; events/meetings. **Events** *World Congress* Chicago, IL (USA) 2019, *World Congress* Stockholm (Sweden) 2018, *World Congress* Mumbai (India) 2017, *World Congress* Dublin (Ireland) 2016, *World Congress* Johannesburg (South Africa) 2015. **Publications** *CIDESCO Link* (4 a year).

Members National associations in 31 countries:
Australia, Austria, Canada, China, Cyprus, Denmark, Estonia, Finland, France, Germany, Greece, Iceland, India, Indonesia, Ireland, Israel, Italy, Japan, Korea Rep, Latvia, Malaysia, Netherlands, New Zealand, Norway, Russia, Singapore, Slovenia, South Africa, Sweden, Switzerland, USA. [2020/XC1575/**C**]

- Comité international des Etats-Unis du monde (inactive)
- Comité international d'étude pour l'aide aux marins (inactive)
- Comité international pour l'étude des bauxites, de l'alumine et de l'aluminium (#12806)
- Comité international pour l'étude en commun de la lutte contre le doryphore (inactive)
- Comité international pour l'étude et de la conservation de l'architecture de terre de l'ICOMOS / see ICOMOS International Committee on Earthen Architectural Heritage (#11061)
- Comité international pour l'étude et le développement de la construction tubulaire / see Committee for International Development and Education on Construction of Tubular Structures (#04266)
- Comité international d'étude des géants processionnels (inactive)

- ♦ Comité international pour l'études des argiles / see Association internationale pour l'étude des argiles (#02688)
- ♦ Comité international d'études des associations catholiques d'infirmières / see International Catholic Committee of Nurses and Medico-social Assistants (#12451)
- ♦ Comité international des études créoles (#12757)
- ♦ Comité international pour les études d'esthétique (inactive)
- ♦ Comité international des études françaises et du dialogue des cultures / see Centre international de documentation et d'échanges de la Francophonie – L'Agora francophone internationale
- ♦ Comité international d'études morisques (#12788)
- ♦ Comité international d'études pré-ottomanes et ottomanes (#12795)
- ♦ Comité international d'études soviétiques et est-européennes / see International Council for Central and East European Studies (#13002)
- ♦ Comité international d'études du vol sans moteur (inactive)
- ♦ Comité international d'experts pour la lutte contre la renaissance du néo-nazisme et de l'antisémitisme (inactive)
- ♦ Comité international des fabricants de panneaux décoratifs stratifiés (#12760)
- ♦ Comité international pour le fair play (#12769)
- ♦ Comité international de la fatigue du dessin aéronautique / see International Committee on Aeronautical Fatigue and Structural Integrity (#12741)

♦ Comité international des fédérations théâtrales d'amateurs de culture latine (CIFTA) 04176

Pres 7 rue Suffren Reymond, 98000 Monte Carlo, Monaco. T. +37793302788. E-mail: studiomc@libello.com.
Contact Lieu-dit Rieucau, 46400 Saint-Vincent-du-Pendit, France. T. +33612511160.
URL: http://www.aitaiata.org/

History 1947, Versailles (France). Also referred to as *Comité international des fédérations de théâtre amateur de culture latine* or *Conseil international des fédérations théâtrales amateurs de culture latine*. **Aims** Provide a network and ease the exchange of opinions and information between members; coordinate international activity for members. **Structure** General Assembly. Administration Council, consisting of President, one or more Vice-Presidents, Secretary-General, Treasurer, Archivist and Delegate at IATA. **Languages** French, Italian, Spanish. **Staff** Voluntary. **Finance** Members' dues: euro 200. **Activities** Organizes: international festival of amateur theatre (annually) on the occasion of CIFTA's meeting; *'Estivades'* (every 3 years, in Marche-en-Famenne, Belgium) – international festival of theatre creation with a common theme reserved to member federations. Plays an active role in the organisation of the *'Mondial de Théâtre'* (every 4 years, in Monaco). **Events** *Congrès annuel* Neuchâtel (Switzerland) 2008, *Congrès annuel* Monte Carlo (Monaco) 1997. **Publications** *Info CIFTA* (annual) – newsletter.
Members Federations (15), comprising more than 10,000 groups, in 9 countries and territories:
Belgium, Canada (Québec), France, Italy, Monaco, Morocco, Spain, Switzerland, Tunisia.
IGO Relations Recognized by: *UNESCO (#20322)*. **NGO Relations** Regional Committee of: *International Amateur Theatre Association (AITA/IATA, #11647)*. [2015/XE0579/**E**]

- ♦ Comité international des fédérations théâtrales d'amateurs de langue française (inactive)
- ♦ Comité international des fédérations de théâtre amateur de culture latine / see Comité international des fédérations théâtrales d'amateurs de culture latine (#04176)
- ♦ Comité International des Festivals du Film Touristique (unconfirmed)
- ♦ Comité international pour la formation de l'ICOMOS (#11084)
- ♦ Comité international futuribles / see Futuribles International (#10052)
- ♦ Comité international pour les futurs accélérateurs (#12774)
- ♦ Comité international de la gauche pour la paix au Moyen-Orient (inactive)
- ♦ Comité international pour la Géorgie (inactive)
- ♦ Comité international de la gestion du patrimoine archéologique de l'ICOMOS / see ICOMOS International Scientific Committee on Archaeological Heritage Management (#11073)

♦ Comité international d'histoire de l'art (CIHA) 04177

International Committee for the History of Art
Address not obtained.
URL: http://www.ciha.org/

History Sep 1930, Paris (France). Founded during 12th International Congress on the History of Art, the 1st Congress having been held in 1873. **Aims** Support collaboration between scholars across the world to promote scientific study of the history of art. **Structure** International Congress (every 4 years); International Colloquium (every 2 years); International Committee (annual); Board; Bureau. **Languages** English, French, German, Italian, Spanish. **Finance** Sources: members' dues. **Events** *Quadrennial Congress* Lyon (France) 2024, *Quadrennial Congress* Sao Paulo (Brazil) 2021, *Motion – Migrations (Second Part)* Sao Paulo (Brazil) 2020, *Quadrennial Congress* Florence (Italy) 2019, *Toward the future – museums and art history in East Asia* Tokyo (Japan) 2019. **Publications** Reports; proceedings; minutes.
Members National Committees in 18 countries:
Argentina, Australia, Austria, Belgium, Brazil, Colombia, France, Holy See, Hungary, India, Italy, Japan, Norway, Poland, Slovenia, Spain, Switzerland, UK.
IGO Relations *UNESCO (#20322)*. [2020/XD1636/**C**]

- ♦ Comité international d'histoire des sciences / see International Academy of History of Science (#11550)
- ♦ Comité international des hôpitaux (inactive)
- ♦ Comité international d'hygiène mentale (inactive)
- ♦ Comité international de l'ICOM pour l'architecture et les techniques muséographiques (see: #13051)
- ♦ Comité international de l'ICOM pour l'audiovisuel et les nouvelles technologies de l'image et du son (see: #13051)
- ♦ Comité international de l'ICOM pour la conservation (see: #13051)
- ♦ Comité international de l'ICOM pour les échanges d'expositions (see: #13051)
- ♦ Comité international de l'ICOM pour l'éducation et l'action culturelle (see: #13051)
- ♦ Comité international de l'ICOM pour l'égyptologie (see: #13051)
- ♦ Comité international de l'ICOM pour la formation du personnel (see: #13051)
- ♦ Comité international de l'ICOM pour les musées et collections d'art moderne (see: #13051)
- ♦ Comité international de l'ICOM pour les musées et collections du costume (see: #13051)
- ♦ Comité international de l'ICOM pour les musées et collections du verre (see: #13051)
- ♦ Comité international de l'ICOM pour les musées littéraires (see: #13051)
- ♦ Comité international de l'ICOM pour les musées régionaux (see: #13051)
- ♦ Comité international de l'ICOM pour la muséologie (see: #13051)
- ♦ Comité international de l'ICOMOS pour les questions de droit, d'administration et de finances (#11077)
- ♦ Comité international de l'ICOM pour la sécurité dans les musées (see: #13051)
- ♦ Comité international pour les Indiens des Amériques / see International Committee for the Indigenous Peoples of the Americas
- ♦ Comité international pour l'ingéniérie cryogénique (#13118)
- ♦ Comité international de l'inspection technique automobile (#14187)
- ♦ Comité international sur l'interpretation et présentation de l'ICOMOS (#11065)
- ♦ Comité international des itinéraires culturels (#11060)
- ♦ Comité international des itinéraires culturels de l'ICOMOS / see ICOMOS International Committee on Cultural Routes (#11060)
- ♦ Comité international pour les jardins historiques-paysages culturels / see ICOMOS – IFLA International Scientific Committee on Cultural Landscapes (#11059)
- ♦ Comité international pour les jardins et les sites historiques / see ICOMOS – IFLA International Scientific Committee on Cultural Landscapes (#11059)
- ♦ Comité international pour les jeunes malentendants / see International Federation of Hard-of-Hearing Young People (#13436)

♦ Comité international des Jeux de La Francophonie (CIJF) 04178

International Committee of the Francophone Games
Dir ad interim Org Int'l de la Francophonie, 19-21 ave Bosquet, 75007 Paris, France. T. +33144373356. Fax +33144373254. E-mail: vuth@francophonie.org – cijf@francophonie.org.
URL: http://www.jeux.francophonie.org/

History 1988, by *Conférence des ministres de la jeunesse et des sports de la Francophonie (CONFEJES, #04634)*, following granting of mandate by *Conférence au sommet des chefs d'Etat et de gouvernement des pays ayant le français en partage (Sommet de la Francophonie, #04648)* to implement Francophone Games, Sep 1987, Québec (Canada). Subsidiary organ of *Organisation internationale de la Francophonie (OIF, #17809)*. **Aims** Ensure general supervision and auditing of the organization of *Francophone Games*. **Structure** Steering Committee, consisting of 16 ministers (8 in charge of sports and 8 in charge of culture) of the States and governments member of the OIF, the General Administrator of the OIF and the Secretary General of CONFEJES. **Languages** French. **Activities** Awards/prizes/competitions; sporting events. **Publications** *Lettre des Jeux de la Francophonie* (6 a year) – online. Sports results; press releases; brochures.
Members Covers OIF governments (54):
Albania, Andorra, Armenia, Belgium, Belgium/Wallonia Region, Benin, Bulgaria, Burkina Faso, Burundi, Cambodia, Cameroon, Canada, Cape Verde, Central African Rep, Chad, Comoros, Congo Brazzaville, Congo DR, Côte d'Ivoire, Djibouti, Dominica, Egypt, Equatorial Guinea, France, Gabon, Greece, Guinea, Guinea-Bissau, Haiti, Laos, Lebanon, Luxembourg, Madagascar, Mali, Mauritania, Mauritius, Moldova, Monaco, Morocco, New Brunswick, Niger, North Macedonia, Québec, Romania, Rwanda, Sao Tomé-Principe, Senegal, Seychelles, St Lucia, Switzerland, Togo, Tunisia, Vanuatu, Vietnam.
Associate governments (3):
Cyprus, Ghana, Qatar.
Observer states (23):
Austria, Bosnia-Herzegovina, Costa Rica, Croatia, Czechia, Dominican Rep, Estonia, Georgia, Hungary, Kosovo, Latvia, Lithuania, Mexico, Montenegro, Mozambique, Poland, Serbia, Slovakia, Slovenia, Thailand, Ukraine, United Arab Emirates, Uruguay. [2019/XE2476/**E**]

- ♦ Comité International des Jeux Méditerranéens (#12783)
- ♦ Comité international laitier (inactive)
- ♦ Comité international de liaison des associations féminines (internationally oriented national body)
- ♦ Comité international de liaison catholique-juif (#12458)
- ♦ Comité international de liaison juif-catholique / see International Catholic-Jewish Liaison Committee (#12458)
- ♦ Comité international pour les libertés ethniques / see Internacia Komitato por Etnaj Liberecoj (#11523)
- ♦ Comité international de la lumière / see International Union of Photobiology (#15798)
- ♦ Comité international de la lumière (inactive)
- ♦ Comité international de lutte contre le charlatanisme (inactive)

♦ Comité international de Mauthausen (CIM) 04179

International Mauthausen Committee (IMC) – Internationales Mauthausen Komitee (IMK)
Pres Westbahnstr 5/9, 1070 Vienna, Austria. T. +352621255607.
SG address not obtained. T. +4313300215-15 – +431(436767015577.
URL: http://www.cim-info.org/

History 1953, Mauthausen (Austria), as successor to an illegal committee set up in Apr 1945. **Aims** Safeguard the interests of former prisoners of the Mauthausen *concentration camp*, and their families; oppose *fascism* and *nazism* in all forms. **Structure** Annual Meeting; Executive Commission (meets annually in May, a few days before the liberation ceremony in Mauthausen). **Languages** English, French, German, Russian, Spanish. **Finance** Members' dues. Donations. **Activities** Collaborates with International Committees of other Nazi concentration camps. **Events** *Annual executive meeting / Meeting* Ljubljana (Slovenia) 2010, *Executive meeting / Meeting* Barcelona (Spain) 2009, *Executive meeting / Meeting* Milan (Italy) 2008, *Executive meeting / Meeting* Budapest (Hungary) 2007, *Executive meeting / Meeting* Vienna (Austria) 2006.
Members National associations in 21 countries:
Albania, Austria, Belarus, Belgium, Bulgaria, Czechia, France, Germany, Greece, Hungary, Italy, Luxembourg, Netherlands, Poland, Russia, Serbia, Slovakia, Slovenia, Spain, Ukraine, USA. [2018/XE2248/**E**]

- ♦ Comité international de médecine d'assurances sur la vie / see International Committee for Insurance Medicine (#12780)
- ♦ Comité International de Médecine Militaire (#12785)
- ♦ Comité International de Médecine et de Pharmacie Militaires / see International Committee of Military Medicine (#12785)
- ♦ Comité international pour la métrologie historique (#12776)
- ♦ Comité international de microbiologie et d'hygiène alimentaires (#12770)
- ♦ Comité international des mouvements d'enfants et d'adolescents (inactive)
- ♦ Comité international des mouvements pour l'unité européenne / see European Movement International (#07825)
- ♦ Comité international pour les musées et collections d'archéologie et d'histoire (see: #13051)
- ♦ Comité international pour les musées à la mémoire des victimes de crimes publics (#12784)
- ♦ Comité international de nomenclature bactériologique / see International Committee on Systematics of Prokaryotes (#12807)
- ♦ Comité international pour la normalisation des tests de l'aptitude physique / see International Council for Physical Activity and Fitness Research (#13062)
- ♦ Comité international de l'olivier (inactive)
- ♦ Comité international olympique (#14408)
- ♦ Comité international de l'Ordre de Malte / see Campagne Internationale de l'Ordre de Malte contre la lèpre (#03403)
- ♦ Comité international d'organisation des trophées du fair play Pierre de Coubertin / see International Committee for Fair Play (#12769)
- ♦ Comité international de paléographie / see Comité international de paléographie latine (#04180)

♦ Comité international de paléographie latine (CIPL) 04180

SG Dept of Language and Communication Studies, Section for Romance and Classical Languages, Univ of Jyväskylä, Bldg F, PO Box 35 (F), FI-40014 Jyväskylä, Finland.
URL: http://www.palaeographia.org/cipl.htm

History Founded 1953, Paris (France), as *Comité international de paléographie*. Underwent reorganization and adopted current name and statutes, 20 Sep 1985. Since 1987, an internal committee of *International Committee of Historical Sciences (ICHS, #12777)*. **Aims** Promote international cooperation in the field of palaeography, including codicology. **Structure** General Assembly (at least every 5 years); Bureau of 9 members (meets annually). **Languages** English, French, German, Italian, Spanish. **Staff** None. **Finance** Members' dues. **Activities** Research/documentation; standards/guidelines; knowledge management/information dissemination; events/meetings. **Events** *L'émergence des écrits en langue vulgaire* Florence (Italy) 2020, *Colloque* New Haven, CT (USA) 2017, *Colloque* Berlin (Germany) 2015, *Scriptoria in the Middle Ages* St Gallen (Switzerland) 2013, *Les autographes du Moyen Age* Ljubljana (Slovenia) 2010. **Publications** *Catalogues de manuscrits datés (CMD)* – by country, each having a national team responsible: Austria; *Lexique international de codicologie* – volumes of French, Italian, Romanian and Spanish terms. Colloquium proceedings.
Members Individuals in 28 countries:
Australia, Austria, Belgium, Canada, Czechia, Denmark, Finland, France, Germany, Holy See, Hungary, Iceland, Ireland, Israel, Italy, Lithuania, Netherlands, Norway, Poland, Portugal, Russia, Slovakia, Slovenia, Spain, Sweden, Switzerland, UK, USA.
[2018.09.06/XD2751/v/**D**]

- ♦ Comité international de papyrologie (inactive)
- ♦ Comité international paralympique (#14512)
- ♦ Comité international de la parole (inactive)
- ♦ Comité international sur le patrimoine de l'architecture de terre de l'ICOMOS (#11061)
- ♦ Comité international sur le patrimoine culturel immatériel (#11064)
- ♦ Comité international sur le patrimoine culturel sous-marin de l'ICOMOS (#11068)
- ♦ Comité international pour le patrimoine historique polaire de l'ICOMOS (#11071)
- ♦ Comité international pour les paysages culturels d'ICOMOS-IFLA / see ICOMOS – IFLA International Scientific Committee on Cultural Landscapes (#11059)

♦ Comité international des peintures murales de l'ICOMOS / see ICOMOS International Scientific Committee on Mural Paintings (#11078)
♦ Comité international de la pellicule cellulosique (no recent information)
♦ Comité international permanent des anciens combattants (inactive)
♦ Comité international permanent du carbone carburant (inactive)
♦ Comité international permanent des congrès de génétique / see International Genetics Federation (#13711)
♦ Comité international permanent d'éducation physique (inactive)

♦ Comité international permanent des études mycéniennes (CIPEM) . 04181

Permanent International Committee for Mycenaean Studies

SG Fac de Filologia, Univ of Basque Country, Apartado Postal 2111, 01080 Vitoria-Gasteiz, Álava, Spain. T. +34945139811. Fax +34945138227.

History Founded 1956. Former title in English: *International Standing Committee for Mycenaean Studies.* **Aims** Propagate study of Linear B texts. **Structure** Committee. Secretary-General; Deputy Secretary-General. **Languages** English, French. **Staff** 1.00 FTE, voluntary. **Finance** No financial support. **Events** *Colloquium / International Colloquium* Paris (France) 2010, *International Colloquium* Rome (Italy) 2006, *Colloquium* Rome (Italy) / Naples (Italy) 2005, *Colloquium / International Colloquium* Austin, TX (USA) 2000, *Colloquium / International Colloquium* Salzburg (Austria) 1995. **Publications** Colloquium proceedings.

Members Full in 17 countries:
Austria, Belgium, Cyprus, Czechia, Denmark, France, Germany, Greece, Ireland, Italy, Netherlands, North Macedonia, Spain, Sweden, Switzerland, UK, USA.

NGO Relations Member of: *Fédération internationale des associations d'études classiques (FIEC, #09607).* [2015/XD3768/**D**]

♦ Comité international permanent pour l'exécution de la carte photographique du ciel (inactive)

♦ Comité international permanent des linguistes (CIPL) 04182

Permanent International Committee of Linguists

SG PO Box 3023, 2301 DA Leiden, Netherlands. T. +31715141648.
URL: https://ciplnet.com/

History Apr 1928, The Hague (Netherlands). Statutes revised: 6 Jun 1964, Amsterdam (Netherlands); 1977. Current Statutes adopted: 2 Sep 1982, Tokyo (Japan); 14 Aug 1987, Berlin (German DR). **Aims** Promote linguistic science and cooperation among linguists. **Structure** General Assembly; Congress; Executive Committee. **Languages** English, French. **Staff** 2.00 FTE, paid. **Finance** Sources: government support; grants; members' dues. Supported by: *UNESCO (#20322).* **Activities** Knowledge management/information dissemination; networking/liaising; projects/programmes. **Events** *International Congress of Linguists (ICL)* Poznań (Poland) 2024, *International Congress of Linguists (ICL)* Kazan (Russia) 2023, *International Congress of Linguists (ICL)* Cape Town (South Africa) 2018, *International Congress of Linguists (ICL)* Geneva (Switzerland) 2013, *International Congress of Linguists (ICL)* Seoul (Korea Rep) 2008. **Publications** *Linguistic Bibliography* (annual). Congress reports.

Members National representatives of organizations in 37 countries and territories:
Australia, Austria, Belgium, Brazil, Canada, China, Cuba, Czechia, Finland, France, Georgia, Germany, Hungary, Indonesia, Ireland, Israel, Italy, Japan, Korea Rep, Latvia, Lithuania, Netherlands, Nigeria, Norway, Poland, Portugal, Romania, Russia, Serbia, South Africa, Spain, Switzerland, Taiwan, Türkiye, UK, Ukraine, USA.
Included in the above 3 international organizations:
International Congress of Celtic Studies (ICCS); *Societas Linguistica Europaea (SLE, #19448); Société Internationale de Dialectologie et Géolinguistique (SIDG, #19477).*

NGO Relations Member of (1): *International Council for Philosophy and Human Sciences (CIPSH, #13061).* In liaison with technical committees of: *International Organization for Standardization (ISO, #14473).* Close cooperation with: *World-Wide Network on Endangered Languages (no recent information).* Links with Project focal points: *Institut für Afrikanistik, Köln (no recent information); Research School of Pacific and Asian Studies, Canberra (RSPAS); Society for the Study of the Indigenous Languages of the Americas (SSILA).* [2022.06.24/XC3124/y/**C**]

♦ Comité international permanent pour la recherche sur la préservation des matériaux en milieu marin (#18325)
♦ Comité international de pétrographie des charbons (#12750)
♦ Comité international pour les Peuples Autochtones des Amériques (internationally oriented national body)

♦ Comité international des pharmaciens homéopathes (CIPH) 04183

International Committee of Homeopathic Pharmacists

Contact 20 rue de la Libération, 69110 Sainte Foy-lès-Lyon, France.

History 1955. Also referred to as *International Organization of Homeopathic Dispensing Chemists.* **Aims** Promote exchange of information between countries on the subject of homeopathy. **Structure** General Assembly (annual). **Languages** English, French, German. **Staff** 3.00 FTE, voluntary. **Finance** Members' dues. **Activities** Carries out scientific work on a European Homeopathy Pharmacopoeia. **Events** *Annual General Assembly* Capri (Italy) 1996, *Annual General Assembly* Venice (Italy) 1992, *Annual General Assembly* Cologne (Germany) 1991, *Annual General Assembly* Brussels (Belgium) 1988, *Annual General Assembly* Strasbourg (France) 1987.

Members Individuals in 19 countries and territories:
Australia, Austria, Belgium, Brazil, Canada, Chile, England, France, Germany, Greece, India, Israel, Italy, Netherlands, New Zealand, Romania, Scotland, Switzerland, USA.

NGO Relations *Liga Medicorum Homoeopathica Internationalis (LMHI, #16471).* [2011/XD3795/v/**E**]

♦ Comité international de photobiologie / see International Union of Photobiology (#15798)
♦ Comité international de photogrammétrie architecturale – Comité ICOMOS et ISPRS pour la documentation du patrimoine culturel / see CIPA Heritage Documentation (#03929)
♦ Comité international de photogrammétrie architecturale de l'ICOMOS / see CIPA Heritage Documentation (#03929)
♦ Comité international de photosynthèse / see International Society of Photosynthesis Research (#15363)

♦ Comité international Pierre de Coubertin (CIPC) 04184

International Pierre de Coubertin Committee – Comité Internacional Pierre de Coubertin

SG c/o Hôtel Continental, Place de la Gare 2, 1001 Lausanne VD, Switzerland. T. +41215574030. Fax +41216910888. E-mail: contact@coubertin.org.
URL: http://coubertin.org/

History 1975, Switzerland. **Aims** Promote the ideals of Pierre de Frédy, Baron de Coubertin (1863-1937), commonly referred to as Pierre de Coubertin. **Structure** Assembly; Executive Office. **Languages** English, French. **Staff** None. **Finance** Grants; activity revenue. **Activities** Events/meetings; awards/prizes/competitions. **Events** *Assembly* Lausanne (Switzerland) 2015, *Youth Forum* Piestany (Slovakia) 2015, *Youth Forum* Lillehammer (Norway) 2013, *Youth Forum* Beijing (China) 2011, *General Meeting* Strasbourg (France) 2010. **Publications** *Information Letter* (2 a year).

Members Schools named after Pierre de Coubertin, in 14 countries:
Australia, Austria, China, Czechia, Estonia, France, Germany, Greece, Italy, Mexico, Russia, Slovakia, Tunisia, UK.

NGO Relations Consultative status with: *International Olympic Committee (IOC, #14408)* and its Culture and Education Commissions. [2022/XE2828/**E**]

♦ Comité international pour la pierre de l'ICOMOS / see ICOMOS International Scientific Committee for Stone (#11082)
♦ Comité international pour le placement des intellectuels émigrés (inactive)
♦ Comité international de planification pour la souveraineté alimentaire (#14365)

♦ Comité International des Plastiques en Agriculture (CIPA) 04185

International Committee for Plastics in Agriculture – Comité Internacional de Plasticos para la Agricultura

SG 125 rue Aristide Briand, 92300 Levallois-Perret, France. T. +33144011649.
URL: http://cipa-plasticulture.com/

History 1959. First Congress 5 May 1964, Avignon (France). Former names and other names: *ICPA* – alias. Registration: Start date: 18 Jul 1969, End date: 2007, France; Start date: 2007, Spain. **Aims** Liaise between the various established National Committees (NCPA); promote the formation of new committees; provide information to producers, converters and users worldwide on research and studies relating to the use of plastic materials in agriculture; encourage, in the widest economic sense, solutions to scientific and technical problems in the field of plastics in agriculture, through international harmonization; promote international standardization of plastics in agriculture and their experimentation in order to encourage creation of quality standard, subjected to CIPA assessment; study and analyse problems relating to plastics in agriculture and the environment. **Structure** General Assembly; Administrative Council; Executive Council, comprising 4 officers and representatives of International Technical Commissions. **Languages** English, French, Spanish. **Staff** 1.00 FTE, paid. **Finance** Members' dues. **Activities** Knowledge management/information dissemination; networking/liaising; standards/guidelines; research and development. **Events** *Congress* Beijing (China) 2024, *Congress* Shanghai (China) 2021, *Triennial Congress* Arcachon (France) 2018, *Triennial Congress* Saltillo, COAH (Mexico) 2015, *Triennial Congress* Tel Aviv (Israel) 2012. **Publications** *Plasticulture* (annual) in English, French, Spanish.

Members National committees in 8 countries:
Algeria, Argentina, Egypt, France, Germany, Israel, Mexico, Spain.

Consultative Status Consultative status granted from: *ECOSOC (#05331)* (Ros C); *UNIDO (#20336).* **IGO Relations** Accredited by: *United Nations Office at Vienna (UNOV, #20604).* [2021/XC3976/**D**]

♦ Comité international sur la préparation aux risques de l'ICOMOS / see ICOMOS International Scientific Committee on Risk Preparedness (#11080)
♦ Comité international de prêtres abstinents (inactive)
♦ Comité international de prévention des accidents du travail de la navigation intérieure (#12796)
♦ Comité international pour la protection des cables (#12423)
♦ Comité international pour la protection des oiseaux / see BirdLife International (#03266)
♦ Comité international provisoire d'organisation des trophées du fair play Pierre de Coubertin / see International Committee for Fair Play (#12769)
♦ Comité international de psychiatrie infantile / see International Association for Child and Adolescent Psychiatry and Allied Professions (#11766)
♦ Comité international de psychologie pédagogique (inactive)
♦ Comité international de psychologie scolaire / see International School Psychology Association (#14788)
♦ Comité international de psychomotricité / see International Organization of Psychomotricity and Relaxation (#14465)
♦ Comité international de publication des tables annuelles de constantes de chimie, de physique, de biologie et de technologie (inactive)
♦ Comité international de la Quatrième internationale (#12771)
♦ Comité international aux questions légales, administratives et financiers de l'ICOMOS / see ICOMOS International Scientific Committee on Legal, Administrative and Financial Issues (#11077)
♦ Comité international de la radio-électricité (inactive)

♦ Comité International Radio-Maritime (CIRM) 04186

International Association for Marine Electronics Companies – Comité Internacional Radio-Maritimo – Internationaler Seefunk-Ausschuss

Sec 71-75 Shelton Street, London, WC2H 9JQ, UK. T. +442034118345. E-mail: office@cirm.org.
URL: http://www.cirm.org/

History 10 Sep 1928, San Sebastian (Spain). Founded by radio companies engaged in application of radio to maritime service. Reconstituted, and new statutes formulated, 1947. Registered by Belgian Royal Decree, 25 Feb 1947. Registration: Companies House, No/ID: 02494458, Start date: 20 Apr 1990, England and Wales. **Aims** Enhance safety of life at sea and the safe and timely conduct of *shipping* by fostering efficient application of technology to maritime communications and *navigation*; advance maritime *telecommunications* and radio navigation services in the most scientific and efficient manner for the benefit of all concerned with maritime matters; represent the interests of the industry by providing a link between members and international authorities; provide a forum for coordination, information exchange and discussion among member companies. **Structure** General Meeting (annual); Board of Directors (meets twice a year). Technical Committee (meets twice a year). Secretariat in London (UK). Working groups as required. **Languages** English. **Staff** 2.00 FTE, paid. Consultants. **Finance** Sources: members' dues. **Activities** Certification/accreditation; events/meetings; standards/guidelines. **Events** *Annual Conference* St Julian's (Malta) 2022, *Annual Conference* St Julian's (Malta) 2020, *Annual Conference* Vouliagmeni (Greece) 2019, *Annual Conference* San Sebastian (Spain) 2018, *Annual Conference* Singapore (Singapore) 2017. **Publications** *An Introduction to CIRM* – brochure; *CIRM News*; *Code of Business Practice for Maritime Accounting Authorities.* Technical papers – for members only; recommended specifications for maritime radio and navigation equipment. Information Services: Obtains and provides information as required by members and responds to specific questions through specialist experts and extensive library of key documentation; regular dissemination of key papers and technical summaries (about 100 a year).

Members Full; Associate. Marine electronic companies, including manufacturers, suppliers, system operators and service providers in 26 countries:
Australia, Austria, Canada, China, Cyprus, Denmark, Finland, France, Germany, Greece, India, Italy, Japan, Korea Rep, Netherlands, New Zealand, Norway, Russia, Singapore, South Africa, Spain, Sweden, UK, Ukraine, United Arab Emirates, USA.

Consultative Status Consultative status granted from: *ECOSOC (#05331)* (Ros C); *International Maritime Organization (IMO, #14102); World Meteorological Organization (WMO, #21649).* **IGO Relations** Working relations with: *International Telecommunication Union (ITU, #15673)*, especially its Radiocommunication Sector (previously CCIR) and Telecommunication Standardization Sector (previously CCITT). **NGO Relations** Member of (2): *International Association of Institutes of Navigation (IAIN, #11965); Radio Technical Commission for Maritime Services (RTCM)* (Observer). In liaison with technical committees of: *International Organization for Standardization (ISO, #14473).* [2022/XC2239/**C**]

♦ Comité international de la rayonne et des fibres synthétiques / see CIRFS – European Man-made Fibres Association (#03944)
♦ Comité international de recherche sur la biocinétique des chocs / see International Research Council on the Biomechanics of Injury (#14723)
♦ Comité international de la recherche charbonnière (no recent information)
♦ Comité international de recherche et d'étude de facteurs de l'ambiance (#12801)
♦ Comité international pour la réglementation des ascenseurs et monte-charge (inactive)
♦ Comité international sur les relations publiques dans le domaine de la réadaptation (inactive)
♦ Comité international de rhéologie (#12802)

♦ Comité international de Sachsenhausen (CIS) 04187

International Sachsenhausen Committee – Internationales Sachsenhausen-Komitee (ISK)

Contact 77 av Jean Jaurès, 75019 Paris, France. T. +33686684420. E-mail: sachsenhausen@orange.fr.
SG Grüner Weg 54a, 15754 Senzig, Germany. T. +493375902096. Fax +493375954963.
URL: https://www.internationales-sachsenhausen-komitee.eu

History 20 May 1964, Berlin (Germany). Founded following up the activities of a secret committee set up at the camp in 1936. **Aims** Commemorate the victims of the *concentration camp* at Sachsenhausen; promote peace and friendship between peoples so as to avoid all return to *fascism.* **Structure** International Committee (European); Meeting (Praesidium) (at least annually): Permanent Secretariat. **Languages** English, French, German, Russian. **Finance** Member's dues. **Activities** Awareness raising. **Events** *Meeting* Oranienburg (Germany) 2005, *Meeting* Prague (Czech Rep) 2005, *Meeting* Oranienburg (Germany) 2004, *Meeting* Oranienburg (Germany) 2003, *Meeting* Oranienburg (Germany) 2002. **Publications** *Bulletin international Sachsenhausen* (annual).

Members National associations and individuals in 17 countries:
Austria, Belarus, Belgium, Czechia, Denmark, France, Germany, Hungary, Israel, Kazakhstan, Luxembourg, Netherlands, Norway, Poland, Russia, UK, Ukraine. [2016.11.16/XE9463/**E**]

- ♦ Comité international pour la santé mentale d'occupation (inactive)
- ♦ Comité international des sapeurs-pompiers / see CTIF International Association of Fire and Rescue Services (#04979)
- ♦ Comité international pour la sauvegarde de la langue bretonne (#12761)
- ♦ Comité international pour la sauvegarde de Tyr / see International Association to Save Tyre (#12144)
- ♦ Comité international de sauvetage / see International Rescue Committee (#14717)
- ♦ Comité International de Saxophone (#14784)
- ♦ Comité international des sciences historiques (#12777)
- ♦ Comité international des sciences onomastiques / see International Council of Onomastic Sciences (#13055)
- ♦ Comité international des sciences et techniques alimentaires (inactive)
- ♦ Comité international de secours (#14717)
- ♦ Comité international de secours aux militaires blessés / see International Committee of the Red Cross (#12799)
- ♦ Comité international pour la sécurité et la coopération européennes (inactive)
- ♦ Comité international des services des eaux du bassin rhénan (#13215)
- ♦ Comité international sur la situation des minorités et des droits de l'homme en URSS (inactive)
- ♦ Comité international socialiste consultatif (inactive)
- ♦ Comité international des sociétés de contrôle de la contamination / see International Confederation of Contamination Control Societies (#12855)
- ♦ Comité international des sports silencieux / see International Committee of Sports for the Deaf (#12805)
- ♦ Comité International des Sports des Sourds (#12805)
- ♦ Comité international pour la standardisation anthropologique synthétique (inactive)
- ♦ Comité international de standardisation en biologie humaine (inactive)
- ♦ Comité international de standardization en hématologie / see International Council for Standardization in Haematology (#13078)
- ♦ Comité international du sucre (inactive)
- ♦ Comité international du suivi du Sommet francophone (inactive)
- ♦ Comité international des syndicats du spectacle et des médias (inactive)
- ♦ Comité international sur les systèmes mondiaux de navigation par satellite (#12775)
- ♦ Comité international de taxonomie des virus (see: #15794)
- ♦ Comité international technique d'experts juridiques aériens (inactive)
- ♦ Comité international de la teinture et du nettoyage à sec (inactive)
- ♦ Comité international des télécommunications de presse (#14637)
- ♦ Comité international de télévision (inactive)
- ♦ Comité international du thé (#15664)
- ♦ Comité international sur le théorie et philosophie de la conservation et de la restauration de l'ICOMOS (#11067)
- ♦ Comité international de thermodynamique et de cinétique électrochimiques / see International Society of Electrochemistry (#15079)
- ♦ Comité international du tourisme culturel de l'ICOMOS / see ICOMOS International Cultural Tourism Committee (#11070)
- ♦ Comité international des transformateurs de papier et carton dans la Communauté européenne / see International Confederation of Paper and Board Converters in Europe (#12866)
- ♦ Comité international des transports par chemins de fer / see Comité international des transports ferroviaires (#04188)

♦ Comité international des transports ferroviaires (CIT) 04188

International Rail Transport Committee – Internationales Eisenbahntransportkomitee

Dep SG CIT Secretariat, Weltpoststrasse 20, 3015 Bern, Switzerland. T. +41313500190 – +41313500197. Fax +41313500199. E-mail: info@cit-rail.org.
SG address not obtained. T. +41313500190 – +41313500193.
URL: http://www.cit-rail.org/

History Founded 1902, Vienna (Austria), originally having French title *Comité international des transports par chemins de fer*, as the organ of railway and other transport undertakings adhering to *International Convention Concerning the Carriage of Goods by Rail (CIM, 1890)*, signed 14 Oct 1890, Bern (Switzerland). Previously also referred to in Italian as *Comitato Internazionale dei Trasporti per Ferrovia*. Terms of reference and activities extended, 23 Oct 1924, by *International Convention Concerning the Carriage of Passengers and Luggage by Rail (CIV, 1924)* and subsequently by supplementary provisions to these conventions: *Additional Convention to the International Convention Signed at Rome on 23 Nov 1933 Concerning the Transport of Goods by Rail (CIM, 1950)*; *Revision of the International Conventions Concerning the Carriage of Goods by Rail and of Passengers and Luggage by Rail (CIM, CIV, 1952)*; *International Convention Concerning the Carriage of Passengers and Luggage by Rail, 1961 (CIV, 1961)*; *International Convention Concerning the Carriage of Passengers and Luggage by Rail, with Additional Protocol, 1970 (CIV, 1970)*. A following convention, signed 9 may 1980, entered into force 1 May 1985 and suspended 30 Jun 2006, is *Convention Concerning International Carriage by Rail, 1980 (COTIF, 1980)*, which fundamentally reformed the structure of the previous conventions, separating provisions (which appear in the Convention paper) from rules on the Contract of Carriage. These latter appear in the two appendices, *'A – Règles uniformes concernant le contrat de transport international ferroviaire des voyageurs et des bagages (CIV)'* and *'B – Règles uniformes concernant le contrat de transport international ferroviaire des marchandises (CIM)'*. The current version of COTIF, *Convention Concerning International Carriage by Rail, 1999 (COTIF, 1999)*, extending its application, simplifying rules and adapting them to liberalization of the international market, was adopted by OTIF General Assembly, 26 May – 4 Jun 1999, Vilnius (Lithuania), and entered into force 1 Jul 2006. It contains the new appendices RID (Appendix C), CUV Uniform Rules for the contract of use of vehicles (Appendix D), CUI Uniform Rules for the contract of Use of Infrastructure (Appendix E), APTU Uniform Rules concerning the validation of Technical Standards (Appendix F) and ATMF Uniform Rules concerning the Technical Admission of Railway Material (Appendix G). Due to a declaration of non-application requested for by *European Commission (EC, #06633)*, 8 Member States do not apply CUI, APTU and ATMF Uniform Rules as from 1 Jul 2006; 3 more from 1 Jan 2008; 2 more from 1 Jan 2009. Under revised statutes adopted, effective 1 Jan 2004, CIT assumes an independent legal personality with power to conclude contracts and defend the interests of the Association as plaintiff and defendant. **Aims** Develop international law relating to rail transport on the basis of the COTIF Convention and its Appendices; adopt standard instructions for the implementation of the international rail transport law, in particular COTIF, and its consistent application; develop relationship between members and represent their interest in the face of liberalization of the *railway* industry and extension of the substantive area of application of COTIF. **Structure** General Assembly (annual); Executive Committee; Committees; Working Groups; Secretariat. **Languages** English, French, German. **Staff** 9.00 FTE, paid. **Finance** Costs distributed among members according to a formula based on equal shares as well as on freight and passenger traffic volume. **Activities** Networking/liaising; politics/policy/regulatory. **Events** *Workshop with NEBs on Rail Passengers Rights* Brussels (Belgium) 2013, *Plenary Session* Bern (Switzerland) 2011, *Plenary Session* Bern (Switzerland) 2010, *Seminar on strengthening cooperation at railway border crossings in Central Asia* Balkanabat (Turkmenistan) 2009, *Plenary Session* Bern (Switzerland) 2009. **Publications** *CIT-Infos* in English, French, German – information bulletin. Annual Report; manuals; texts of Agreements.

Members Railways undertakings and shipping companies (130 in their own right plus 80 linked indirectly) in 42 countries and territories:
Albania, Austria, Azerbaijan, Belgium, Bosnia-Herzegovina, Bulgaria, Croatia, Czechia, Denmark, Finland, France, Germany, Greece, Hungary, Iran Islamic Rep, Iraq, Ireland, Italy, Kosovo, Latvia, Lithuania, Luxembourg, Montenegro, Morocco, Netherlands, North Macedonia, Norway, Poland, Portugal, Romania, Russia, Serbia, Slovakia, Slovenia, Spain, Sweden, Switzerland, Syrian AR, Tunisia, Türkiye, UK, Ukraine. [2020.03.03/XC2394/**C**]

- ♦ Comité international de l'Union des porteurs de valeurs mobilières (inactive)
- ♦ Comité international du vaurien (see: #21760)
- ♦ Comité international pour un Vietnam libre (#12772)
- ♦ Comité international sur les villes historiques de l'ICOMOS / see ICOMOS International Committee on Historic Cities, Towns and Villages (#11063)
- ♦ Comité international des villes et villages historiques de l'ICOMOS / see ICOMOS International Committee on Historic Cities, Towns and Villages (#11063)
- ♦ Comité international pour le vitrail de l'ICOMOS / see ICOMOS International Scientific Committee for the Conservation of Stained Glass (#11074)
- ♦ Comité interprofessionnel européen des professions intellectuelles (inactive)
- ♦ Comité inter-secrétariats sur les programmes scientifiques liés à l'océanographie (inactive)
- ♦ Comité Interuniones para la Atribución de Frecuencias / see Scientific Committee on Frequency Allocations for Radio Astronomy and Space Science (#19148)
- ♦ Comité inter-unions pour l'attribution de fréquences / see Scientific Committee on Frequency Allocations for Radio Astronomy and Space Science (#19148)
- ♦ Comité interuniversitaire de coordination des études orientales en Amérique latine (inactive)
- ♦ Comité inter-universités pour l'Afrique orientale (inactive)
- ♦ Comité islamo-catholique de liaison (see: #09682)
- ♦ Comité de Jérusalem / see Al-Quds Committee (#00749)
- ♦ Comité de la jeunesse des Caraïbes pour l'environnement humain (inactive)
- ♦ Comité des jeux internationaux des écoliers (#04264)
- ♦ Comité de jonction des congrès internationaux de sténographie (inactive)
- ♦ Comité juif international pour les consultations interreligieuses (#13970)
- ♦ Comité Juridico Interamericano (see: #17629)
- ♦ Comité juridique interaméricain (see: #17629)
- ♦ Comité juridique international de l'aviation (inactive)
- ♦ Comité pour la justice sociale (internationally oriented national body)
- ♦ Comité latinoaméricain de coordination et de promotion de la technologie appropriée (inactive)
- ♦ Comité latinoaméricain des parcs nationaux (inactive)
- ♦ Comité Latinoamericano de Asuntos Financieros (#16300)
- ♦ Comité Latinoamericano de Cine de Pueblos Indigenas / see Coordinadora Latinoamericana de Cine et de Comunicación de los Pueblos Indigenas (#04806)
- ♦ Comité Latinoamericano de Decanos de Escuelas de Administración / see Latin American Council of Business Schools (#16308)
- ♦ Comité Latinoamericano para la Defensa de los Derechos de la Mujer / see Latin American and Caribbean Committee for the Defense of Women's Rights (#16268)

♦ Comité Latinoamericano para la Difusión del Derecho Romano 04189

Permanent Sec c/o Fac de Derecho, Univ Veracruzana, Circuito Gonzalo Aguirre Beltran S/N, Centro, Xalapa, 91000 Veracruz CHIS, Mexico. T. +522288421755. E-mail: lucuevas@uv.mx.

History 1972, Xalapa (Mexico), by Universidad Veracruzana. **Languages** Italian, Portuguese, Spanish. **Events** *Congress* Panama (Panama) 2013, *Congress* Lima (Peru) 2011, *Congress* Buenos Aires (Argentina) 2004, *Congress* Brasilia (Brazil) 1983, *Congress* Xalapa (Mexico) 1978.

Members Professors in Latin American and European Universities in 14 countries:
Argentina, Bolivia, Brazil, Chile, Colombia, Costa Rica, Dominica, France, Italy, Mexico, Peru, Spain, Switzerland, Venezuela.
International organizational member (1):
Asociación de Estudios Sociales Latinoamericanos (ASSLAF, no recent information). [2013/XD8532/**D**]

- ♦ Comité Latinoamericano de Parques Nacionales (inactive)
- ♦ Comitê Latino-Americano de Tratamento e Pesquisa em Esclerose Múltipla (#04190)

♦ Comité Latinoamericano para el Tratamiento y la Investigación en Esclerosis Múltiple (LACTRIMS) 04190

Latin American Committee on Treatment and Research of Multiple Sclerosis – Comitê Latino-Americano de Tratamento e Pesquisa em Esclerose Múltipla

Pres c/o FLENI, Montañeses 2325, Buenos Aires, Argentina.

History 11 Oct 1999, Cartagena de Indias (Colombia). **Structure** Executive Committee. **Events** *Congress* Buenos Aires (Argentina) 2016, *Congress* Lima (Peru) 2014, *Congress* Rio de Janeiro (Brazil) 2012, *Congress* Santiago (Chile) 2010, *Joint Meeting* Montréal, QC (Canada) 2008. [2016/XE4529/**D**]

- ♦ Comité de liaison et d'action des étrangers (internationally oriented national body)
- ♦ Comité de liaison de l'agrumiculture méditerranéenne (inactive)
- ♦ Comité de liaison des associations européennes de l'industrie de la parfumerie, des produits cosmétiques et de toilette / see Cosmetics Europe – The Personal Care Association (#04852)
- ♦ Comité de liaison d'associations d'ingénieurs universitaires de la Communauté européenne / see Council of Associations of Long Cycle Engineers of a University or Higher School of Engineering of the European Union (#04869)
- ♦ Comité de liaison des associations internationales de génie civil (#16453)
- ♦ Comité de liaison des associations internationales relevant de l'eau (#15869)
- ♦ Comité de liaison de la construction de carrosseries et de remorques / see International Association of the Body and Trailer Building Industry (#11727)
- ♦ Comité de liaison de la construction d'équipement et de pièces d'automobiles / see European Association of Automotive Suppliers (#05948)
- ♦ Comité de liaison de la construction d'équipements et de pièces d'automobiles / see European Association of Automotive Suppliers (#05948)
- ♦ Comité de liaison EEC – Afrique – Caraïbes – Pacifique pour la promotion des fruits tropicaux, légumes de contre-saison, fleurs, plantes ornementales et épices / see COLEACP (#04091)
- ♦ Comité de liaison entr'aide et action (inactive)
- ♦ Comité de liaison Europe – Afrique – Caraïbes – Pacifique pour la promotion des exportations horticoles ACP / see COLEACP (#04091)
- ♦ Comité de liaison Europe – Afrique – Caraïbes – Pacifique pour la promotion des fruits tropicaux, légumes de contre-saison, fleurs, plantes ornementales et épices / see COLEACP (#04091)
- ♦ Comité de liaison européen des commissionnaires et auxiliaires de transports du Marché commun / see CLECAT (#03993)
- ♦ Comité de liaison européen des ostéopathes (inactive)
- ♦ Comité de liaison des femmes pour la coopération internationale (inactive)
- ♦ Comité de liaison des géomètres de la CEE / see Council of European Geodetic Surveyors (#04890)
- ♦ Comité de liaison des géomètres européens (#04890)
- ♦ Comité de liaison des géomètres-experts européens / see Council of European Geodetic Surveyors (#04890)
- ♦ Comité de liaison des grandes organisations féminines internationales (inactive)
- ♦ Comité de liaison des industries européennes de la chaussure / see Confédération Européenne de l'Industrie de la Chaussure (#04544)
- ♦ Comité de liaison des industries européennes de l'estampage et de la forge (#06649)
- ♦ Comité de liaison des industries de métaux non-ferreux de la Communauté européenne / see Association européenne des métaux (#02578)
- ♦ Comité de liaison et d'information des puissances signataires de l'Appel de Strasbourg / see Centre de liaison et d'information des puissances maçonniques signataires de l'Appel de Strasbourg (#03770)
- ♦ Comité de liaison des ingénieurs agronomes des pays membres des Communautés économiques européennes / see Confédération européenne des associations d'ingénieurs agronomes (#04538)
- ♦ Comité de liaison international des broderies, rideaux et dentelles (inactive)
- ♦ Comité de liaison international des groupes d'amitié judéo-chrétienne / see International Council of Christians and Jews (#13006)
- ♦ Comité de liaison ONG-UNESCO (#17127)
- ♦ Comité de liaison des praticiens de l'art dentaire des pays de la CEE / see Council of European Dentists (#04886)
- ♦ Comité de liaison des praticiens de l'art dentaire des pays de l'Union européenne / see Council of European Dentists (#04886)
- ♦ Comité de liaison pour la promotion des fruits tropicaux et des légumes de contre-saison originaires des Etats ACP / see COLEACP (#04091)

♦ Comité de liaison pour la promotion des fruits tropicaux et légumes de contre-saison originaires des pays africains et malgaches / see COLEACP (#04091)
♦ Comité de liaison des sages-femmes européennes / see European Midwives Association (#07800)
♦ Comité de liaison des sages-femmes des pays du Marché commun / see European Midwives Association (#07800)
♦ Comité de liaison des secrétaires des groupes d'amitié judéo-chrétiennes / see International Council of Christians and Jews (#13006)
♦ Comité de liaison des vétérinaires de la CEE / see Federation of Veterinarians of Europe (#09713)
♦ Comité de libération de l'Ouest arabe (inactive)
♦ Comité maghrébin des agrumes et des primeurs (inactive)

♦ Comité Maghrébin de l'Electricité (COMELEC) 04191

Maghreb Electricity Committee

Contact 02 Bd Krim Belkacem, Algiers, Algeria. T. +21321724348. Fax +21321724335.
URL: http://comelec-net.org/

History Creation approved 1974, by Ministers of Economy of the Maghreb. Statutes adopted 1975. Inactive 1975-1988. Reactivated Oct 1988. **Structure** Steering Committee; Secretariat General. **Events** *Conference* Rabat (Morocco) 2015, *Conference* Tripoli (Libyan AJ) 2009.
Members Companies in 5 countries:
Algeria, Libya, Mauritania, Morocco, Tunisia.
NGO Relations Member of: *MEDELEC (#16614).* [2015/XM4257/**D**]

♦ Comité du marché commun de travail nordique (inactive)

♦ Comité maritime international (CMI) 04192

Admin Assistant c/o Royal Belgian Shipowners' Association, Ernest Van Dijckkaai 8, 2000 Antwerp, Belgium. E-mail: admin-antwerp@comitemaritime.org.
SG 20/29 Temperley Street, Nicholls, Canberra ACT 2913, Australia. T. +61262427531. E-mail: secretary-general@comitemaritime.org.
URL: http://www.comitemaritime.org/

History 1897, Brussels (Belgium). Statutes revised: 27 Jun 1992. Although only the French title is approved by the organization, other bodies sometimes refer to it unofficially in English as *International Maritime Committee. Diplomatic Conference of International Maritime Law (inactive)*, first held 1905, Brussels (Belgium), following the drawing up of a draft convention by CMI, continued as a series until 1979, when many issues that it used to handle were transferred to IMO. **Aims** Contribute by all appropriate means and activities to unification of maritime law and maritime commercial law, maritime customs, usages and practices; promote establishment of national associations of maritime law; cooperate with other international associations or organizations having the same objectives. **Structure** Assembly (annual); Executive Council; Standing Committees; International Working Groups. **Languages** English, French. **Staff** 1.00 FTE, paid. **Finance** Sources: contributions of member/participating states; meeting proceeds; sale of publications. **Activities** Events/meetings; knowledge management/information dissemination; management of treaties and agreements. Other activities cover: revision on general average; definition of certain terms in Charter-parties; arrest of ocean-going ships; international shipping legislation; sea terminals; arbitration; arrest of ships; carriage of goods by sea; classification societies; collision; piracy; finance; general average; cross border insolvencies; judicial sale of ships; Lex Maritima; limitation of liability; marine insurance; promotion of maritime conventions; offshore activities; places of refuge; oil pollution from ships;polar shipping; salvage; pandemic response at sea; ship nomenclature; marine autonomous surface ships. Manages the following treaties/agreements: *International Convention for the Unification of Certain Rules Relating to Arrest of Sea-going Ships (1952); International Convention for the Unification of Certain Rules Relating to Maritime Liens and Mortgages, 1926 (1926); International Convention for the Unification of Certain Rules Relating to the Immunity of State-owned Vessels (1926); International Convention for the Unification of Certain Rules Relative to Maritime Liens and Mortgages, 1967 (1967); International Convention on Maritime Liens and Mortgages (1993).* **Events** *Conference* Tokyo (Japan) 2025, *Conference* Tokyo (Japan) 2021, *Conference* Tokyo (Japan) 2020, *Colloquium* Mexico City (Mexico) 2019, *Assembly* London (UK) 2018. **Publications** *CMI Newsletter* (3 a year); *CMI Yearbook/Annuaire CMI* (annual). *EU Maritime Law Reports.* Conference proceedings; surveys; reports. **Information Services** *CML – CMI Database of Judicial Decisions on International Conventions.*
Members National associations of maritime law in 52 countries and territories (Australia and New Zealand comprising one association):
Argentina, Australia, Belgium, Brazil, Cameroon, Canada, Chile, China, Colombia, Congo DR, Croatia, Denmark, Ecuador, Finland, France, Germany, Greece, Hong Kong, India, Indonesia, Ireland, Israel, Italy, Japan, Korea DPR, Korea Rep, Malaysia, Malta, Mexico, Netherlands, New Zealand, Nigeria, Norway, Panama, Peru, Philippines, Poland, Romania, Senegal, Singapore, Slovenia, South Africa, Spain, Sweden, Switzerland, Tanzania UR, Türkiye, UK, Ukraine, Uruguay, USA, Venezuela.
Regional association:
The Eastern Africa Maritime Law Association.
Consultative members (27):
- Arab Society of Maritime and Commercial Law (ASMCL);
- *Association mondiale de dispacheurs (AMD, #02809);*
- *BIMCO (#03236)* (Baltic and International Maritime Conference (BIMCO));
- *Fédération internationale des associations de transitaires et assimilés (FIATA, #09610);*
- *IMO International Maritime Law Institute (IMLI, #11134);*
- *Instituto Iberoamericano de Derecho Maritimo (IIDM);*
- International Association for the Representation of the Mutual Interest of the Inland Shipping and the Insurance and for the Keeping the Register of Inland Vessels in Europe (IVR);
- *International Association for the Representation of the Mutual Interests of the Inland Shipping and the Insurance and for Keeping the Register of Inland Vessels in Europe (#12131);*
- *International Association of Classification Societies (IACS, #11778);*
- *International Association of Independent Tanker Owners (INTERTANKO, #11959);*
- *International Association of Ports and Harbors (IAPH, #12096);*
- *International Bar Association (IBA, #12320);*
- *International Chamber of Commerce (ICC, #12534);*
- *International Chamber of Shipping (ICS, #12535);*
- *International Group of P and I Clubs (#13751);*
- *International Maritime Industries Forum (IMIF, inactive);*
- *International Maritime Organization (IMO, #14102);*
- *International Oil Pollution Compensation Funds (IOPC Funds, #14402);*
- *International Salvage Union (ISU, #14779);*
- *International Transport Workers' Federation (ITF, #15726);*
- *International Union of Marine Insurance (IUMI, #15789);*
- National Industrial Transportation League (NITL);
- *Nautical Institute;*
- *Pacific International Maritime Law Association (PIMLA, #17956);*
- *World Shipping Council (WSC, #21781).*

Consultative Status Consultative status granted from: *International Maritime Organization (IMO, #14102); UNCTAD (#20285)* (Special Category). **IGO Relations** Observer status with (1): *International Oil Pollution Compensation Funds (IOPC Funds, #14402).* Cooperates with (1): *International Institute for the Unification of Private Law (UNIDROIT, #13934).* [2020.08.27/XC2243/**C**]

♦ Comité Ministerial Conjunto de las Juntas de Gobernadores del Banco y del Fondo para la Transferencia de Recursos Reales a los Paises en Desarrollo (#16141)
♦ Comité ministériel conjoint des conseils des gouverneurs de la Banque mondiale et du Fonds monétaire international sur le transfert de ressources réelles aux pays en voie de développement (#16141)
♦ Comité ministériel nordique pour la coordination de l'assistance au développement (inactive)
♦ Comité des Ministres du Conseil de l'Europe (#04273)
♦ Comité mixte EEE (#05381)
♦ Comité mixte FAO/OMS d'experts des additifs alimentaires (#16129)
♦ Comité mixte nordique des techniciens forestiers (inactive)
♦ Comité mixte des organisations scandinaves de jeunes faucons / see Arbetarrörelsens Barnorganisationer i Norden (#01084)
♦ Comité Mixto FAO/OMS de Expertos en Aditivos Alimentarios (#16129)
♦ Comité Mixto sobre Programas Cientificos Relacionados con la Oceanografia (inactive)
♦ Comité mondial des Amis / see Friends World Committee for Consultation (#10004)
♦ Comité mondial pour les apprentissages tout au long de la vie (unconfirmed)
♦ Comité mondial du Congrès mondial des partisans de la paix (inactive)
♦ Comité mondial contre la guerre et le fascisme (inactive)
♦ Comité mondial d'éthique du tourisme (#21287)
♦ Comité mondial des étudiants contre la guerre et le fascisme (inactive)
♦ Comité mondial des femmes contre la guerre et le fascisme (inactive)
♦ Comité mondial pour la radiodiffusion chrétienne (inactive)
♦ Comité mondial pour des recherches comparatives sur la leucémie / see International Association for Comparative Research on Leukemia and Related Diseases (#11799)
♦ Comité monétaire et financier international (#14179)
♦ Comité monétaire interétatique (inactive)

♦ Comité monétaire de la Zone franc 04193

Monetary Committee of the Franc Zone

Secretariat c/o Banque de France, DG Etudes/Relations Internationales, Service de la Zone Franc, 39 rue des Croix-des-Petits-Champs, 75001 Paris, France. T. +33142925988. Fax +33142923988. E-mail: comozof@banque-france.fr.
URL: http://www.banque-france.fr/fr/eurosys/zonefr/zonefr.htm

History 5 Feb 1952, Paris (France), by French ministerial decree no 52-154, following the creation of a technical committee in 1951. **Aims** Improve *monetary cooperation* between France and the African countries of the Zone franc. **Structure** Each year the Governor of the Bank of France presents a report in the name of the *Secrétariat du Comité monétaire de la Zone franc.* However, this is actually edited by a specialized service of the Bank of France, the *Service de la Zone franc et du financement du développement,* which is also in charge of bilateral relations of the Bank of France with the countries of the Franc Zone, servicing the twice-yearly *Conférence des ministres des finances des pays de la Zone franc (#04633),* organizing non-periodic meetings of the Governors of Central Banks of the Zone and providing information through conferences, receiving visitors and so on. **Activities** The *Zone franc (#22037),* originally established in 1939 on a provisional basis, includes the countries of *Banque centrale des Etats de l'Afrique de l'Ouest (BCEAO, #03167)* and *Banque des Etats de l'Afrique centrale (BEAC, #03169)* as well as France, its overseas territories and Comoros. Local currencies continue to exist within the Zone, but are freely convertible with fixed parity levels. Operations carried out by the central bank of each member country are registered in the treasury records of the reference country, which guarantees unlimited convertibility to the issues of these banks. The issuing institutions each directly manages a float of foreign currency and converts the balance into the reference currency. **Events** *Half-yearly meeting of the ministers of finance* Ouagadougou (Burkina Faso) 2009, *Half-yearly meeting of the ministers of finance* Paris (France) 2009, *Half-yearly meeting of the ministers of finance* Paris (France) 2008, *Half-yearly meeting of the ministers of finance* Yaoundé (Cameroon) 2008, *Half-yearly meeting of the ministers of finance* Lomé (Togo) 2007. **Publications** *Rapports de la Zone franc* (annual). Studies; research articles.
Members Member States (16):
Benin, Burkina Faso, Cameroon, Central African Rep, Chad, Comoros, Congo Brazzaville, Côte d'Ivoire, Equatorial Guinea, France, Gabon, Guinea-Bissau, Mali, Niger, Senegal, Togo. [2013.06.01/XE1202/**E***]

♦ Comité Mundial para el Aprendizaje a lo Largo de Toda la Vida (unconfirmed)
♦ Comité Mundial de la Consulta de los Amigos (#10004)
♦ Comité Mundial de Etica del Turismo (#21287)
♦ Comité de las Naciones Unidas contra la Tortura / see Committee Against Torture (#04241)
♦ Comité de las Naciones Unidas para la Eliminación de la Discriminación Racial / see Committee on the Elimination of Racial Discrimination (#04251)
♦ Comité Nansen / see Nansen Refugee Award Committee
♦ Comité des Nations Unies contre la torture / see Committee Against Torture (#04241)
♦ Comité des Nations Unies pour l'élimination de la discrimination raciale / see Committee on the Elimination of Racial Discrimination (#04251)
♦ Comité des Nations Unies pour l'exercice des droits inaliénables du peuple palestinien (#20539)
♦ Comité des Nations Unies des utilisations pacifiques de l'espace extra-atmosphérique / see Committee on the Peaceful Uses of Outer Space (#04277)
♦ Comité de no intervención (inactive)
♦ Comité de non-intervention dans les affaires espagnoles (inactive)
♦ Comité nordique des Arboreta (#17491)
♦ Comité nordique d'associations pédagogiques de travailleurs (#17377)
♦ Comité nordique des communications (inactive)
♦ Comité nordique commun pour les problèmes militaires de l'ONU (inactive)
♦ Comité nordique de contact des écoles gardiennes et de centres de récréation (inactive)
♦ Comité nordique de coopération pour le commerce des métaux précieux (inactive)
♦ Comité nordique de coopération pour l'industrie des bateaux (inactive)
♦ Comité nordique de coopération pour l'industrie du verre (inactive)
♦ Comité nordique de détaillants de la branche alimentaire (inactive)
♦ Comité nordique des écoles de service social / see Nordic Association of Schools of Social Work (#17204)
♦ Comité nordique des étrangers (#17315)
♦ Comité nordique d'étude des techniques du bois (inactive)
♦ Comité nordique pour une formation forestière intégrée (inactive)
♦ Comité nordique de hauts fonctionnaires pour les problèmes du transport (inactive)
♦ Comité nordique de laboratoires pharmaceutiques (inactive)
♦ Comité nordique pour la législation sur la circulation routière (inactive)
♦ Comité nordique sur la loi pénale (inactive)
♦ Comité nordique des maîtres cordonniers et négociants en chaussures (inactive)
♦ Comité nordique des médicaments (inactive)
♦ Comité nordique mixte des administrateurs hospitaliers (inactive)
♦ Comité nordique mixte des employés du commerce et de l'administration (inactive)
♦ Comité nordique pour la recherche en matière d'alcool et de stupéfiants (inactive)
♦ Comité nordique pour la recherche sur les pays de l'Est (inactive)
♦ Comité nordique pour la recherche de sûreté nucléaire (#17517)
♦ Comité nordique sur les règlements dans le domaine des bâtiments (inactive)
♦ Comité nordique des sports pour les handicapés (inactive)
♦ Comité nordique pour les statistiques sociales (#17409)
♦ Comité nordique des syndicats des femmes (inactive)
♦ Comité nordique de technologie biomédicale (inactive)
♦ Comité des observateurs des droits de l'Homme (internationally oriented national body)
♦ Comité Olimpico Internacional (#14408)
♦ Comité des ONG pour le désarmement / see NGO Committee for Disarmament, Geneva (#17105)
♦ Comité des ONG pour le développement à Genève (#17104)
♦ Comité des ONG pour le développement à Vienne (#17119)
♦ Comité des ONG sur les questions de la famille / see Vienna NGO Committee on the Family (#20774)
♦ Comité des ONG s'intéressant aux personnes âgées, Genève (see: #04635)
♦ Comité des ONG s'intéressant aux personnes âgées, New York (#17103)
♦ Comité des ONG s'intéressant aux personnes âgées, Vienne (see: #04635)
♦ Comité des organisations d'auberges de jeunesse des pays nordiques (no recent information)
♦ Comité des organisations des entrepreneurs de travaux agricoles de la CEE / see European Organization of Agricultural and Rural Contractors (#08105)
♦ Comité des organisations familiales auprès des Communautés européennes / see COFACE Families Europe (#04084)

♦ Comité des organisations nationales des importateurs et exportateurs de poisson de l'UE (CEP) 04194

EU Federation of National Organizations of Importers and Exporters of Fish

SG c/o Kellen, Av de Tervuren 188A, Box 4, 1150 Brussels, Belgium. T. +3227611649. Fax +3227611699. E-mail: aipce@kellencompany.com.

URL: http://www.aipce-cep.org/

History 20 Sep 1963. Original title: *Federation of National Organizations of EEC Fish Wholesalers, Importers and Exporters – Fédération des organisations nationales des grossistes, importateurs et exportateurs en poisson de la CEE (CEP) – Vereinigung der Fischgrosshändler, Importeure und Exporteure von Fischen der EWG – Federatie van Nationale Organisaties van Groothandelaren, Importeurs en Exporteurs van Vis van de EEG.* Subsequently changed title to *Federation of National Organizations Fish Wholesalers, Importers and Exporters of the European Union – Fédération des organisations nationales des grossistes, importateurs et exportateurs en poisson de l'Union Européenne (CEP) – Vereinigung der Fischgrosshändler, Importeure und Exporteure von Fischen der Europäischen Union – Federatie van Nationale Organisaties van Groothandelaren, Importeurs en Exporteurs van Vis van de Europese Unie.* **Aims** Study problems raised by EU treaties in the field; coordinate actions of national federations of fish industries; ensure a link with EU institutions. **Structure** Officers: President; 1st and 2nd Vice-Presidents; Secretary General. **Finance** Members' dues. **Activities** Events/meetings.

Members National organizations in 6 countries:
Denmark, France, Germany, Ireland, Netherlands, Spain.

IGO Relations Recognized by: *European Commission (EC, #06633).* **NGO Relations** Shares secretariat with: *European Union Fish Processors Association (#08989).* Member of: *Baltic Sea Advisory Council (BSAC, #03139); Market Advisory Council (MAC, #16584).* Observer member of: *European Salmon Smokers Association (ESSA, #08424).* [2019.12.11/XE3637/**E**]

- ♦ Comité des organisations non-gouvernementales sur le désarmement, New York NY / see NGO Committee on Disarmament, Peace and Security, New York NY (#17106)
- ♦ Comité d'organisations non-gouvernementales auprès de l'UNICEF / see NGO Committee on UNICEF (#17120)
- ♦ Comité des organisations professionnelles agricoles de la CE / see COPA – european farmers (#04829)
- ♦ Comité des organisations professionnelles agricoles de l'UE / see COPA – european farmers (#04829)
- ♦ Comité de Organizaciones de Albergues de Juventud de los Paises Nórdicos (no recent information)
- ♦ Comité des Organizaciones Profesionales Agrarias de la Unión Europea / see COPA – european farmers (#04829)
- ♦ Comité ornithologique international / see International Ornithologists' Union (#14487)
- ♦ Comité Orthodoxe des amitiés françaises dans le monde (internationally oriented national body)
- ♦ Comité Ouest-Africain des Semences Paysannes (unconfirmed)
- ♦ Comité pour la paix et le désarmement créé par les organisations féminines internationales (inactive)
- ♦ Comité panaméricain de financement des grandes routes (inactive)
- ♦ Comité panaméricain des transports par chemin de fer (inactive)
- ♦ Comité Panamericano de Normas Técnicas / see Pan American Standards Commission (#18133)
- ♦ Comité Panamericano de Transporte Integral (unconfirmed)
- ♦ Comite paralympique africaine / see African Paralympic Committee (#00410)
- ♦ Comité parlementaire nordique pour des communications plus libres (inactive)
- ♦ Comité de parlementaires des pays de l'AELE (#04269)
- ♦ Comité parlement mixte de l'EEE (#05382)
- ♦ Comité pour les Partenariats avec l'Europe Continentale (internationally oriented national body)
- ♦ Comité du patrimoine mondial (#21567)
- ♦ Comité del Patrimonio Mundial (#21567)
- ♦ Comité por la Paz de Finlandia (internationally oriented national body)
- ♦ Comité des pêches pour l'Atlantique centre-Est (#09784)
- ♦ Comité PECO – Comité pour les Partenariats avec l'Europe Continentale (internationally oriented national body)
- ♦ Comité permanent de l'AELE (#19953)
- ♦ Comité permanent du cadastre dans l'Union européenne (#18319)
- ♦ Comité permanent de la chaîne alimentaire et de la santé publique (#19956)
- ♦ Comité permanent des communautés ethniques de langue française / see Conférence des peuples de langue française (#04640)
- ♦ Comité permanent de la Conférence internationale d'embryologie (inactive)
- ♦ Comité permanent des conférences internationales de génétique et de l'hybridation / see International Genetics Federation (#13711)
- ♦ Comité permanent des conférences internationales du service social / see International Council on Social Welfare (#13076)
- ♦ Comité Permanent des Congrès d'Actuaires / see International Actuarial Association (#11586)
- ♦ Comité permanent des congrès d'espéranto (inactive)
- ♦ Comité permanent des congrès internationaux des actuaires / see International Actuarial Association (#11586)
- ♦ Comité permanent des congrès internationaux pour l'amélioration du sort des sourds-muets (inactive)
- ♦ Comité permanent des congrès internationaux pour l'apostolat des laïcs (inactive)
- ♦ Comité permanent des congrès internationaux de l'aviation sanitaire (inactive)
- ♦ Comité permanent des congrès internationaux des chambres de commerce et des associations commerciales et industrielles (inactive)
- ♦ Comité permanent des congrès internationaux de gynécologie et d'obstétrique (inactive)
- ♦ Comité permanent des congrès internationaux des habitations à bon marché (inactive)
- ♦ Comité permanent des congrès internationaux d'hygiène scolaire (inactive)
- ♦ Comité permanent des congrès internationaux de médecine et de pharmacie militaires / see International Committee of Military Medicine (#12785)
- ♦ Comité permanent des congrès internationaux de neurologie (inactive)
- ♦ Comité permanent des congrès internationaux de philosophie (inactive)
- ♦ Comité permanent des Congrès internationaux de psychologie / see International Union of Psychological Science (#15807)
- ♦ Comité permanent des congrès internationaux de zoologie / see International Society of Zoological Sciences (#15552)
- ♦ Comité permanent pour les congrès latinoaméricains de zoologie (inactive)
- ♦ Comité permanent des congrès physiologiques internationaux (inactive)
- ♦ Comité permanent consultatif du Maghreb (inactive)
- ♦ Comité permanent de la Convention de Berne relative à la conservation de la vie sauvage et du milieu naturel de l'Europe (#19949)
- ♦ Comité permanent pour la coopération avec les conseils nationaux de sciences sociales et organismes similaires / see International Federation of Social Science Organizations (#13543)
- ♦ Comité permanent pour la coopération économique et commerciale entre les Etats membres de l'OCI (#19952)
- ♦ Comité permanent pour la coopération économique et commerciale de l'Organisation de la conférence islamique / see Standing Committee for Economic and Commercial Cooperation (#19952)
- ♦ Comité Permanente sobre el Catastro en la Unión Europea (#18319)
- ♦ Comité Permanente para los Congresos Latinoamericanos de Zoologia (inactive)
- ♦ Comité Permanente para la Infrastructura de Datos Geoespaciales de las Américas / see Regional Committee of the UN on Global Geospatial Information Management for the Americas (#18765)
- ♦ Comité Permanente Interamericano de Seguridad Social (see: #11419)
- ♦ Comité Permanente de Médicos de la CE / see Standing Committee of European Doctors (#19955)
- ♦ Comité Permanente dos Médicos da CE / see Standing Committee of European Doctors (#19955)
- ♦ Comité Permanente de Nutrición del Sistema de las Naciones Unidas (inactive)
- ♦ Comité Permanente de los Sindicatos de la Industria Grafica (inactive)
- ♦ Comité permanent des hôpitaux de l'Union européenne / see European Hospital and Healthcare Federation (#07501)
- ♦ Comité permanent des industries du verre de la CEE / see Glass Alliance Europe (#10156)
- ♦ Comité permanent des industries du verre européennes / see Glass Alliance Europe (#10156)
- ♦ Comité permanent des infirmières en liaison avec la CEE / see European Federation of Nurses Associations (#07180)
- ♦ Comité permanent des infirmiers/infirmières de la CE / see European Federation of Nurses Associations (#07180)
- ♦ Comité permanent des infirmiers/infirmières de l'UE / see European Federation of Nurses Associations (#07180)
- ♦ Comité permanent interaméricain de sécurité sociale (see: #11419)

♦ Comité permanent inter-Etats de lutte contre la sécheresse dans le Sahel (CILSS) 04195

Permanent Interstate Committee for Drought Control in the Sahel – Comité Interestatal Permanente de Lucha contra la Sequia en el Sahel

Mailing Address BP 7049, Ouagadougou 03, Burkina Faso. T. +22650374125 – +22650374126. Fax +226374132. E-mail: administration.se@cilss.int – secilss@cilss.int.

URL: http://www.cilss.int/

History 12 Sep 1973. Established on signature of Convention by Heads of State of Chad, Mali, Mauritania, Niger, Senegal and Upper Volta (currently Burkina Faso). Gambia joined Dec 1973 at meeting of Ministerial Council. The Convention entered into force 1 Jul 1974. Convention revised by 11th Conference of the Heads of State and Government, 22 Apr 1994, Praia (Cape Verde), when the Institution was re-structured. Former names and other names: *Intergovernmental Committee to Combat Desertification in the Sudano-Sahelian Region* – alias; *ICDCS* – alias. **Aims** Research obstacles to achievement of food security and enhanced natural resources management in the Sahel, to better define appropriate strategies and effective policies for sustainable development of the region; coordinate, at the subregional and regional levels, reflection and action to ascertain food, ecological and demographic constraints hampering sustainable economic growth; collect, process and disseminate quantitative and qualitative data to inform and sensitize member states and the international community with regard to ecological and human problems relating to development of the region; contribute to coordination of development, research and training policies implemented to combat the effects of drought and desertification; promote the implementation of activities of subregional, inter-state and regional interests, contributing to strengthening cooperation among member states in their joint efforts to combat effects of drought and desertification, and monitor activities that should contribute to regional integration; contribute to coordination of emergency aid obtained in regional or subregional contexts to promote its use as a factor of development. **Structure** Organs: (a) Conference of the Heads of State and Government (every 3 years). (b) Council of Ministers of Agriculture and/or Rural Development (meets annually). (c) Regional Programming and Monitoring Committee (RPMC) (meets annually); (d) Executive Secretariat headed by Executive Secretary, supported by 4 Advisers in charge of: – Natural Resources Management/ Desertification Control, – Food Security, – Planning, – Communication. Administrative and Financial Officer; Internal Auditor. Managing Committee (meets twice a year). Specialized institutions. **Languages** Arabic, English, French, Portuguese. **Staff** 138.00 FTE, paid. **Finance** Member States' contributions. Other sources: financial contributions from partners; subsidies; publications; grants; donations. **Activities** Policy Major Programmes (2): Policy Major Programme on Natural Resource Management/Desertification Control; Policy Major Programme on Food Security. Technical Major Programmes of the *AGRHYMET Regional Centre (#00565)*, Bamako (Mali) (2): Technical Major Programme on Information; Technical Major Programme on Training. Technical Major Programmes of the *Institut du Sahel (INSAH, #11357)*, Niamey (Niger) (2): Technical Major Programme on Agro-socio-economic Research; Technical Major Programme on Population/ Development. *Sahel and West Africa Club (SWAC, #19034)*, set up Mar 1976, Dakar (Senegal), acts as an organ of information to the international community. **Events** *Rencontre de haut-niveau des Ministres de l'Irrigation des pays du Sahel* Niamey (Niger) 2022, *Session* Bamako (Mali) 2004, *Biennial conference of heads of state and government* Nouakchott (Mauritania) 2004, *Session* Nouakchott (Mauritania) 2003, *Session* Bamako (Mali) 2001. **Publications** *Reflets saheliens* (4 a year). Monographs; pamphlets; reports.

Members Governments of 9 countries:
Burkina Faso, Cape Verde, Chad, Gambia, Guinea-Bissau, Mali, Mauritania, Niger, Senegal.

IGO Relations Special agreement with: *UNESCO (#20322); UNIDO (#20336).* Relationship agreement with: *Africa Rice Center (AfricaRice, #00518); FAO (#09260).* Cooperation Agreement with: *International Fund for Agricultural Development (IFAD, #13692).* Cooperates with: *West African Science Service Center on Climate Change and Adapted Land Use (WASCAL, #20897).* Observer to: *UNEP (#20299)* Governing Council. Accredited by: *United Nations Framework Convention on Climate Change – Secretariat (UNFCCC, #20564).* Accredited to the Conference of the Parties of: *Secretariat of the United Nations Convention to Combat Desertification (Secretariat of the UNCCD, #19208).* Agreement with: *Disaster Management Training Programme (DMTP, inactive).* Instrumental in setting up: *Centre for Applied Research on Population and Development (CERPOD, no recent information); Centre régional d'énergie solaire (CRES, inactive); Sahelian Scientific and Technological Information and Documentation Network (RESADOC, no recent information).* **NGO Relations** Member of: *ICSC – World Laboratory (#11088).* Partner of: *Global Resilience Partnership (GRP, #10577).* Instrumental in setting up: *Ministerial Lobby Group (no recent information); Réseau de prévention des crises alimentaires (RPCA, #18905).* [2021/XD4566/**D***]

- ♦ Comité permanent international des architectes (inactive)
- ♦ Comité permanent international du Congrès international de la reproduction animale (#15598)
- ♦ Comité permanent international du Congrès international de la reproduction animale et de l'insémination artificielle / see International Standing Committee of the International Congress on Animal Reproduction (#15598)
- ♦ Comité permanent international des congrès internationaux d'hygiène et de démographie (inactive)
- ♦ Comité permanent international pour l'enseignement médical complémentaire (inactive)
- ♦ Comité permanent international pour l'étude de la médecine des accidents de travail (inactive)
- ♦ Comité permanent international des mères (inactive)
- ♦ Comité permanent international des techniques et de l'urbanisme souterrain et spatial (inactive)
- ♦ Comité Permanent Inter-Organisations (#11393)
- ♦ Comité permanent de juristes pour l'unification des lois civiles et commerciales américaines (inactive)
- ♦ Comité permanent de liaison des organisations, syndicats, associations et unions de journalistes des pays européens (inactive)
- ♦ Comité permanent de liaison des orthophonistes-logopèdes de l'Union européenne / see European Speech and Language Therapy Association (#08812)
- ♦ Comité permanent des médecins de la CE / see Standing Committee of European Doctors (#19955)
- ♦ Comité permanent des médecins européens (#19955)
- ♦ Comité permanent Ministériel de l'OIC pour la Coopération Scientifique et Technologique (#17702)
- ♦ Comité permanent des Nations Unies sur la nutrition (inactive)
- ♦ Comité permanent des ONG / see NGO-UNESCO Liaison Committee (#17127)
- ♦ Comité permanent pour le partenariat euroméditerranéen des pouvoirs locaux et régionaux (#19954)
- ♦ Comité permanent des peuples de langue française / see Conférence des peuples de langue française (#04640)
- ♦ Comité permanent des quincailliers nordiques (inactive)
- ♦ Comité permanent spécial de la conférence internationale de la police (inactive)
- ♦ Comité permanent des statisticiens des Caraïbes (#19950)
- ♦ Comité permanent des syndicats de l'industrie graphique (inactive)
- ♦ Comité phytosanitaire pour la région de l'Asie du Sud-Est et du Pacifique / see Asia and Pacific Plant Protection Commission (#01997)
- ♦ Comité des politiques de développement (#20537)
- ♦ Comité pontifical pour les congrès eucharistiques internationaux (#18442)
- ♦ Comité du Prix de littérature du Conseil nordique (#00114)
- ♦ Comité del Programa y de la Coordinación (#20546)
- ♦ Comité du programme et de la coordination (#20546)

- Comité para la Promoción de la Ayuda a las Cooperativas / see Committee for the Promotion and Advancement of Cooperatives (#04279)
- Comité para la Promoción y el Progreso de las Cooperativas (#04279)
- Comité de promotion de l'action volontaire dans les pays d'Europe / see Volonteurope (#20807)
- Comité pour la promotion de l'aide aux coopératives / see Committee for the Promotion and Advancement of Cooperatives (#04279)
- Comité pour la promotion et l'avancement des coopératives (#04279)
- Comité pour la promotion et le progrès des coopératives / see Committee for the Promotion and Advancement of Cooperatives (#04279)
- Comité pour la protection des journalistes (#04280)
- Comité protestant des amitiés françaises à l'étranger (internationally oriented national body)
- Comité Protestant évangélique pour la Dignité Humaine (internationally oriented national body)
- Comité protestant de propagande française à l'étranger / see Comité protestant des amitiés françaises à l'étranger
- Comité provisoire international de cristallographie / see International Union of Crystallography (#15768)
- Comité de rapprochement belgo-néerlando-luxembourgeois (inactive)
- Comité pour la recherche spatiale (#04287)
- Comité van Rederverenigingen van de Europese Gemeenschappen / see European Community Shipowners' Associations (#06683)
- Comité das Regiões Europeu (#06665)
- Comité Régional Centroaméricain de Ressources Hydrauliques (#04196)
- Comité régional de la COI pour l'Atlantique du Centre-Est (inactive)
- Comité régional de la COI pour l'océan Indien central (see: #11496)
- Comité régional de la COI pour l'océan Indien occidental (inactive)
- Comité régional de la Convention sur la reconnaissance des études et des diplômes relatifs à l'enseignement supérieur dans les Etats de la Région Europe (inactive)
- Comité régional d'éducation pour le développement international de Lanaudière (internationally oriented national body)
- Comité Regional de las Naciones Unidas sobre la Gestión Global de Información Geoespacial para las Américas (#18765)
- Comité régional des pêches du Golfe de Guinée (#18785)

♦ Comité Regional de Recursos Hidraulicos del Istmo Centroamericano (CRRH) 04196

Comité Régional Centroaméricain de Ressources Hydrauliques – Regional Committee on Hydraulic Resources of Water Resources Committee of the Central American Isthmus

Exec Sec Apartado Postal 1527-1200, Pavas, San José, San José, San José, Costa Rica. T. +50622964641. Fax +50622960047. E-mail: secretaria@recursoshidricos.org.

URL: http://recursoshidricos.org/

History 9 Sep 1966, as a regional body. Became an intergovernmental organization in 1975. Serves as a technical institution of *Central American Integration System (#03671)*. Also referred to in English as *Central American Regional Water Resources Committee.* **Aims** Coordinate activities of the region in the fields of *meteorology, hydrology, oceanography,* climate and climate change, with a special commitment regarding *water* and water resources management, and increased *vulnerability* due to *climate change.* **Structure** Presidential Council, comprising Chairmen of national committees of meteorology, hydrology and water resources of member countries. President. Executive Secretariat. **Activities** Carries out studies on the El Niño and La Niña phenomena and other research projects. Organizes training courses, fora, discussions and exchange of experience. Currently developing: indices for analysing environmental vulnerability; Central American meteorological and oceanographical networks; hydrometeorological support centre; *Plan Centroamerican para la Gestión Integrada del Recurso Hidricos (PACAGIRH)* – acting as secretariat of the consultative group on water. **Events** *Central America regional consultation forum toward the 5th world water forum* San Salvador (El Salvador) 2008, *Water information summit* San Salvador (El Salvador) 2008. **Information Services** *Centro Integración de Actividades Meteorológicas e Hidrológicas en America Central (CIMHAC)* – regional climate database.

Members Governments of 7 countries:
Belize, Costa Rica, El Salvador, Guatemala, Honduras, Nicaragua, Panama.

IGO Relations Cooperative projects with: *Comisión Centroamericana de Ambiente y Desarrollo (CCAD, #04129); Department for International Development Cooperation; Inter-American Development Bank (IDB, #11427); Intergovernmental Panel on Climate Change (IPCC, #11499); International Bank for Reconstruction and Development (IBRD, #12317)* (World Bank); *OAS (#17629); UNDP (#20292); UNEP (#20299); United States Agency for International Development (USAID); World Meteorological Organization (WMO, #21649);* governments of Finland, Japan, Sweden, Taiwan and USA. [2021/XE9680/**E***]

- Comité Regional de Salud Animal (no recent information)

♦ Comité Regional de Sanidad Vegetal del Cono Sur (COSAVE) 04197

Southern Cone Regional Phytosanitary Committee

Main Office Av La Molina 1915, Distrito La Molina, 15026, Lima, Peru. T. +513133300. E-mail: cosave@cosave.org.

URL: http://www.cosave.org/

History 21 Nov 1991, Piriapolis (Uruguay). Created through an Agreement signed 9 Mar 1989, Montevideo (Uruguay). Agreement entered into force 1990. Former names and other names: *Comité Regional de Sanidad Vegetal de los Paises del Cono Sur* – alias. **Aims** Harmonize plant protection requirements and procedures in member countries. **Structure** Council of Ministers; Steering Committee; Executive Committee (meets 4 times a year) rotates place of meeting among the 5 countries; Coordination Secretariat; Technical Secretariat; Permanent Working Groups (11). **Finance** Sources: contributions of member/participating states. Annual budget: 330,000 USD. **Activities** Events/meetings; standards/guidelines; training/education. **Events** *Regional Plant Protection Organizations (RPPOs) Annual Technical Consultation* London (UK) 2022, *Regional Plant Protection Organizations (RPPOs) Annual Technical Consultation* Rome (Italy) 2021, *Regional Plant Protection Organizations (RPPOs) Annual Technical Consultation* Rome (Italy) 2020, *Regional Plant Protection Organizations (RPPOs) Annual Technical Consultation* Abuja (Nigeria) 2019, *Regional Plant Protection Organizations (RPPOs) Annual Technical Consultation* Lima (Peru) 2018.

Members Governments of 7 countries:
Argentina, Bolivia, Brazil, Chile, Paraguay, Peru, Uruguay.

IGO Relations Serves as one of 10 Regional Plant Protection Organizations (RPPOs) of *International Plant Protection Convention, 1951 (IPPC, 1951).* Participates as observer in the activities of: *Codex Alimentarius Commission (CAC, #04081).* Instrumental in setting up: *Grupo Interamericano de Coordinación en Sanidad Vegetal (GICSV, no recent information).* [2020/XF2845/**F***]

- Comité Regional de Sanidad Vegetal de los Paises del Cono Sur / see Comité Regional de Sanidad Vegetal del Cono Sur (#04197)
- Comité des régions des Communautés européennes / see European Committee of the Regions (#06665)
- Comité des régions de l'Union européenne / see European Committee of the Regions (#06665)
- Comité van de Regio's van de Europese Unie / see European Committee of the Regions (#06665)
- Comité des règles et pratiques de contrôle bancaire / see Basel Committee on Banking Supervision (#03183)
- Comité de Relaciones Internacionales de Bordados, Visillos y Encajes (inactive)
- Comité pour les relations nationales et internationales des associations de jeunesse et d'éducation populaire (internationally oriented national body)
- Comité des relations avec le pays hôte (#20547)
- Comité des représentants permanents auprès des Communautés européennes / see Committee of Permanent Representatives to the European Union (#04278)
- Comité des représentants permanents de l'Union européenne (#04278)
- Comité des réunions des travailleurs de l'Amérique latine (inactive)
- Comités, associations et organisations privés pour la sauvegarde de Venise / see Association of International Private Committees for the Safeguarding of Venice (#02758)
- Comité sur les satellites d'observation de la terre (#04249)
- Comité scandinave des brevets (inactive)
- Comité scandinave de recherche sur les matériaux (inactive)
- Comité scandinave de recherche sur les techniques de production (inactive)
- Comité pour la science et la liberté (inactive)
- Comité Scientifico para la Atribución de Frecuencias (#19148)
- Comité scientifique de l'architecture et urbanisme coloniaux partagés de l'ICOMOS / see ICOMOS International Scientific Committee on Shared Built Heritage (#11081)
- Comité scientifique pour l'attribution de fréquences à la radioastronomie et à la recherche spatiale (#19148)
- Comité scientifique du Commonwealth (#04361)
- Comité scientifique d'une histoire des civilisations de l'Asie centrale (no recent information)
- Comité scientifique international pour la conservation des vitraux (#11074)
- Comité scientifique international sur le patrimoine du XXe siècle (see: #13049)
- Comité Scientifique International de Paysages Culturels (#11059)
- Comité scientifique international de recherche alpine (#14804)
- Comité scientifique international de recherches et de lutte contre la trypanosomiase (#14809)
- Comité scientifique des Nations Unies pour l'étude des effets des rayonnements ionisants (#20624)
- Comité scientifique de la physique solaire et terrestre / see Scientific Committee on Solar-Terrestrial Physics (#19151)
- Comité scientifique sur les problèmes de l'environnement (#19150)
- Comité scientifique pour les recherches antarctiques (#19147)
- Comité scientifique pour les recherches océaniques (#19149)
- Comité Scout Interamericano (#11445)
- Comité de la sécurité mondiale (see: #09260)
- Comité de Seguridad Alimentaria Mundial (see: #09260)
- Comité du service unitaire du Canada / see SeedChange
- Comité Sindical Europeo de Servicios Públicos / see European Federation of Public Service Unions (#07202)
- Comités nationaux olympiques d'Océanie (#17667)
- Comité de solidarité avec l'Europe de l'Est (internationally oriented national body)
- Les comités olympiques européens (#08083)
- Comité de soutien aux orphelins du Viêt-nam / see Partage – avec les enfants du monde
- Comité spécial chargé d'enquêter sur les pratiques israéliennes affectant les droits de l'homme du peuple palestinien et des autres Arabes des territoires occupés (#20627)
- Comité spécial de la Charte des Nations Unies et du raffermissement du rôle de l'Organisation (#19905)
- Comité spécial de la décolonisation (#19906)
- Comité spécialisé des coopératives agricoles des pays de la CEE pour les engrais et pesticides / see General Confederation of Agricultural Cooperatives in the European Union (#10107)
- Comité spécial des ONG pour le désarmement, Genève (#17105)
- Comité spécial des ONG pour les droits de l'homme, Genève (#04275)
- Comité spécial des ONG internationales pour les droits de l'homme / see Committee of NGOs on Human Rights, Geneva (#04275)
- Comité spécial des opérations de maintien de la paix (#20628)
- Comité spécial des Vingt-Quatre / see Special Committee on Decolonization (#19906)
- Comité sportif des armées amies (inactive)
- Comité sportif international du travail / see International Workers and Amateurs in Sports Confederation (#15905)
- Comité sportif nordique pour les mal-voyants (inactive)
- Comité suisse contre la torture / see Association for the Prevention of Torture (#02869)
- Comité des Superviseurs de Banque de l'Afrique de l'Ouest et du Centre (unconfirmed)
- Comité syndical européen de l'éducation (#08926)
- Comité syndical européen des personnels enseignants (inactive)
- Comité syndical européen des services publics / see European Federation of Public Service Unions (#07202)

♦ Comité syndical francophone de l'éducation et de la formation (CSFEF) 04198

SG c/o CSQ, 9405 rue Sherbrooke Est, Montréal QC H1L 6P3, Canada. T. +15143568888. Fax +15143569393.

Pres c/o Syndicat natl des enseignements de second degré (SNES)/FSU, 46 av d'Ivry, 75647 Paris CEDEX 13, France. T. +33140632900. Fax +33140632968. E-mail: president@csfef.org.

URL: http://www.csfef.org/

History Founded 1987, Québec (Canada). Following meeting of representatives of 32 teaching unions from 22 countries. *'Charter of Ottawa'* (constitutional charter) adopted 1993. **Aims** Design and adapt policies to ensure education is taken into account as a priority element; as a representative of *trade union* expression, affirm active recognition of the need to develop education; commit trade unions of French language regions to support for diversity, solidarity and pursuit of social justice and democracy; see the *French-speaking* community as a privileged solidarity network; reaffirm commitment for human rights, against inequality and for better quality of training and education for all; reaffirm common union commitment within the framework of the democratic trade union movement. **Structure** Functions as a network liaison committee. **Languages** French. **Staff** 7.50 FTE, voluntary. **Finance** Budget: administration and meetings: Canadian$ 25,000; projects: Canadian$ 40,000. **Activities** Projects/programmes; events/meetings; networking/liaising. **Events** *Meeting* Tunis (Tunisia) 2020, *Meeting* Paris (France) 2018, *Meeting* Montréal, QC (Canada) 1997, *Meeting* Carthage (Tunisia) 1996. **Publications** *Francophonie Syndicale.*

Members Committee comprises representatives of national trade union organizations in 8 countries:
Canada, Congo DR, France, Madagascar, Moldova, Senegal, Switzerland, Tunisia.

Corresponding members in 24 countries:
Albania, Benin, Bulgaria, Burkina Faso, Cambodia, Central African Rep, Chad, Congo DR, Gabon, Guinea, Guinea-Bissau, Haiti, Laos, Lebanon, Madagascar, Mauritania, Mauritius, Morocco, Niger, Romania, Senegal, Togo, Tunisia, Vietnam.

Consultative Status Consultative status granted from: *Organisation internationale de la Francophonie (OIF, #17809).* **IGO Relations** *Conférence des ministres de l'éducation des Etats et gouvernements de la Francophonie (CONFEMEN, #04632).* [2015.09.14/XE2340/**E**]

- Comité syndical international de la jeunesse et l'éducation ouvrière (inactive)
- Comité syndical international des travailleuses (inactive)
- Comité syndical des transports dans la Communauté européenne / see European Transport Workers' Federation (#08941)
- Comité Technique International du Glutamate (#13722)
- Comité technique international de la maçonnerie, du béton armé et du gros oeuvre dans la construction moderne (inactive)
- Comité technique international de prévention et d'extinction du feu / see CTIF International Association of Fire and Rescue Services (#04979)
- Comité technique international du vanadium (#20746)
- Comité Técnico Internacional del Vanadio (#20746)
- Comité Técnico para la Transferencia de Tecnologia Agricola entre América Latina y el Caribe (inactive)
- Comité de Trabajo de las Malterias de la UE (#21055)

♦ Comité transnational des géotechniciens d'Afrique (CTGA) 04199

Trans-national Committee of African Geotechnical Engineers

Contact 5 Rue Monseigneur Graffin, 20369, Yaoundé, Cameroon. T. +237699500510 – +237697189923. Fax +237222303006. E-mail: info@ctgaafrique.org.

URL: http://ctgaafrique.org/
History Dec 1995, Marrakech (Morocco). **Aims** Maintain and develop friendly and cultural relations between members; encourage scientific and technical exchanges; promote study and research, directly or indirectly related to geotechnology (ie, soil mechanics, rock mechanics, engineering geology, foundations engineering, environment). **Structure** General Assembly (annual). Board, comprising President, Vice-President, Secretary General and 3 Assessors. **Finance** Members' dues. **Activities** Organizes international congress. **Events** *JAG : Journées Africaines de la Géotechnique* Niamey (Niger) 2019, *JAG : Journées Africaines de la Géotechnique* Abidjan (Côte d'Ivoire) 2018, *JAG : Journées Africaines de la Géotechnique* Lomé (Togo) 2017, *JAG : Journées Africaines de la Géotechnique* Douala (Cameroon) 2016, *JAG : Journées Africaines de la Géotechnique* Ouagadougou (Burkina Faso) 2015. **Publications** *Bulletin de Liaison ALBTP-CTGA* (2 a year).
Members Collective; Individuals geotechnical engineers operating in building laboratories, public works and the private sector (schools, universities, etc). Individuals in 20 countries:
Algeria, Angola, Benin, Burkina Faso, Burundi, Cameroon, Central African Rep, Chad, Congo Brazzaville, Congo DR, Côte d'Ivoire, Djibouti, Gabon, Guinea, Mali, Mauritania, Morocco, Niger, Senegal, Togo.
NGO Relations Affiliated to: *International Society for Soil Mechanics and Geotechnical Engineering (ISSMGE, #15452).* Member of: *Union internationale des associations et organismes scientifiques et techniques (UATI, #20421).* [2019/XE4665/**E**]

- ♦ Comité des transports ferroviaires du Maghreb (#18609)
- ♦ Comité des transports intérieurs (#04262)
- ♦ Comité des travailleurs européens contre la remilitarisation de l'Allemagne (inactive)
- ♦ Comité des travailleurs migrants (#04271)
- ♦ Comité de travail des malteries de la CEE / see Working Committee of the Malting Industry of the EU (#21055)
- ♦ Comité de travail des malteries de l'UE (#21055)
- ♦ Comité Trilateral de Conservación y Manejo de Vida Silvestre y Ecosistemas (#20238)
- ♦ Comité trilatéral de conservation et de gestion des espèces sauvages et des écosystèmes (#20238)
- ♦ Comitetul Economic si Social Europea (#06963)
- ♦ Comitetul European al Regiunilor (#06665)
- ♦ Comité des UCJG du Proche orient (#16755)
- ♦ Comité por una Internacional de los Trabajadores (#04290)
- ♦ Comité universitaire francophone pour le développement des échanges scientifiques (internationally oriented national body)
- ♦ Comité des utilisations pacifiques de l'espace extra-atmosphérique (#04277)
- ♦ Comité vétérinaire permanent de l'Union européenne / see Standing Committee on the Food Chain and Animal Health (#19956)
- ♦ Comité de Vienne des ONG sur les questions de la famille (#20774)
- ♦ Comité de Vienne des ONG sur les stupéfiants (#20773)
- ♦ Comité de vigilance pour les Conseils européens (internationally oriented national body)
- ♦ Comité vins / see Comité européen des entreprises vins (#04157)

♦ Comity of Nations 04200

Courtoisie internationale – Comitas Gentium
Address not obtained.
History Not a legal agreement but a set of rules of conduct for states having international relations which are not legally binding, although failure to abide by them may be considered an unfriendly act. They include immunity from customs search and customs duties of Heads of State and diplomatic agents. [2008/XF3447/**F**]

- ♦ **COMIUCAP** Conférence Mondiale des Institutions Universitaires Catholiques de Philosophie (#21297)
- ♦ **COMJIB** Conferencia de Ministros de Justicia de los Países Iberoamericanos (#04656)
- ♦ COMLA – Commonwealth Library Association (no recent information)
- ♦ COMMACT – COMMACT – Commonwealth Network for People-Centred Development (inactive)
- ♦ COMMACT – Commonwealth Network for People-Centred Development (inactive)
- ♦ Commandement allié en Europe / see Allied Command Operations (#00731)
- ♦ Commandement suprême des forces alliées en Europe / see Supreme Headquarters Allied Powers Europe (#20039)
- ♦ **Commat** Commonwealth Medical Trust (#04352)
- ♦ Commeeys Celtiagh (#03633)
- ♦ CommerceNet Consortium (internationally oriented national body)
- ♦ Commercial Arbitration and Mediation Center for the Americas (inactive)

♦ Commercial Aviation Association of Southern Africa (CAASA) 04201

Office Manager CAASA House, Gate 9, Lanseria International Airport, Johannesburg, 1748, South Africa. T. +270637173460. E-mail: louise@caasa.co.za.
URL: http://www.caasa.co.za/
History 1944. **Aims** Serve, promote, watch over, advance and protect the interests of persons engaged in aviation; act as a link between such persons and the South African government and other public bodies. **Structure** Board of Directors; semi-autonomous Divisions; Committees. **Finance** Sources: members' dues. Annual budget: 300,000 ZAR. **Activities** Events/meetings; knowledge management/information dissemination. **Publications** *Membership Directory.*
Members Full in 3 countries:
Namibia, South Africa, Zimbabwe.
Affiliated associations (8) of which 2 are listed in this Yearbook:
Association of Aviation Maintenance Organizations (AMOSA, no recent information); Helicopter Association of Southern Africa (no recent information).
NGO Relations Member of (3): *Chartered Institute of Transport in Southern Africa (CITSA, no recent information); Southern African Aerospace Council (SAAC, no recent information); Southern African Aviation Safety Council (SAASCo, no recent information).* [2022.05.04/XF5012/**F**]

- ♦ Commercial Bank Centrafrique (internationally oriented national body)
- ♦ Commercial Convention (1923 treaty)

♦ Commercial Film Producers Europe (CFP-E) 04202

Chief Exec c/o APA, 47 Beak St, London, W1F 9SE, UK. T. +442074342651. Fax +442074349002. E-mail: info@a-p-a.net.
Pres address not obtained.
URL: http://www.cfp-e.com/
Activities Established 'Young Director Award' to support and promote creative talent in commercial film production worldwide. **Events** *Conference* Athens (Greece) 2014.
Members National associations in 14 countries:
Austria, Belgium, Czechia, Denmark, Finland, France, Germany, Italy, Netherlands, Norway, Spain, Sweden, Switzerland, UK.
NGO Relations *World Federation of Advertisers (WFA, #21407).* [2018/XF6466/**F**]

- ♦ Commercial Internet eXchange Association (inactive)
- ♦ Commercial Patent Services Group / see Patent Committee (#18258)
- ♦ Commercial Real Estate Finance Council Europe / see CREFC Europe
- ♦ Commissie van de Europese Gemeenschappen / see European Commission (#06633)
- ♦ Commissie van de Katoen-en Aanverwante Vezels Verwerkende Nijverheden van de EG / see European Federation of Cotton and Allied Textiles Industries (#07093)
- ♦ Commissio Episcopatuum Communitatis Europensis (#04205)
- ♦ Commission aéronautique permanente américaine (inactive)
- ♦ Commission pour les affaires africaines (see: #15795)
- ♦ Commission pour les affaires européennes (see: #15795)
- ♦ Commission africaine de l'aviation civile (#00248)
- ♦ Commission africaine des droits de l'homme et des peuples (#00255)
- ♦ Commission africaine de l'energie (#00298)
- ♦ Commission africaine des promoteurs de la santé et des droits de l'homme (internationally oriented national body)
- ♦ Commission for African Affairs (see: #15795)
- ♦ Commission d'Afrique australe pour le transport et les communications (no recent information)
- ♦ Commission on Air Pollution Prevention of VDI and DIN – Standards Committee (internationally oriented national body)
- ♦ Commission alliée pour l'Autriche (inactive)
- ♦ Commission américaine permanente de l'aviation (inactive)
- ♦ Commission américaine des territoires non autonomes (inactive)
- ♦ Commission for American Affairs (see: #15795)

♦ Commission of the Andean Community 04203

Commission de la Communauté andine – Comisión de la Comunidad Andina
Contact Paseo de la República 3895, esq Aramburú, San Isidro, 27, Lima, Peru. T. +511411400. Fax +5112213329. E-mail: correspondencia@comunidadandina.org.
URL: http://www.comunidadandina.org/
History within the framework of *Andean Community (#00817)*, as the main policy-making of the *Sistema Andino de Integración (SAI, #19292)*, replacing *Commission of the Cartagena Agreement – Commission de l'Accord de Carthagène – Comisión del Acuerdo de Cartagena.* **Aims** Make, implement and evaluate Andean subregional integration *policy* in the areas of *trade* and *investment*; adopt measures necessary for attaining the objectives of the Cartagena Agreement and for implementing the Guidelines of the Andean Presidential Council; coordinate the joint position of member countries in international fora and negotiations within its area of responsibility. **Structure** Commission consists of a plenipotentiary representative from each member country of the Andean Community. Legislative role, expressed through the adoption of Decisions, is shared with with the *Andean Council of Foreign Ministers (#00818).* **Activities** At the request of a Member Country or of the SAI General Secretariat, the Commission's Chairman may call the Commission to meet as an Enlarged Commission, in order to address sectoral issues, consider provisions for coordinating development plans and harmonizing economic policies of member countries and take cognizance of and settle all other matters of common interest.
Members Ministers of Trade or Integration of the Andean Community:
Bolivia, Colombia, Ecuador, Peru.
IGO Relations Relevant treaty: *Andean Subregional Integration Agreement (Cartagena Agreement, 1969).*
NGO Relations *Consejo Consultivo Empresarial Andino (CCEA, see: #00817); Andean Labor Advisory Council (CCLA, see: #00817).* [2008.09.23/XE3583/**E***]

- ♦ Commission andine des juristes (#00816)
- ♦ Commission arabe des droits humains (#00924)
- ♦ Commission arabe permanente des postes (#01025)
- ♦ Commission de l'Arc Atlantique (#03007)
- ♦ Commission for Art Recovery (internationally oriented national body)
- ♦ Commission Asie-Pacifique des pêches (#01907)
- ♦ Commission athlétique panaméricaine / see Asociación Panamericana de Atletismo (#02284)
- ♦ Commission on Atmospheric Chemistry and Global Pollution of the International Association of Meteorology and Atmospheric Physics / see International Commission on Atmospheric Chemistry and Global Pollution (#12664)
- ♦ Commission on Atmospheric Chemistry and Radioactivity / see International Commission on Atmospheric Chemistry and Global Pollution (#12664)
- ♦ Commission baleinière internationale (#15879)

♦ Commission bancaire de l'Afrique centrale (COBAC) 04204

General Secretariat BP 1917, Yaoundé, Cameroon. T. +2372234030 – +2372234060. Fax +2372238216 – +2372238256.
History 16 Oct 1990, when Convention was signed by 6 member governments. A principal organ of *Communauté économique et monétaire d'Afrique centrale (CEMAC, #04374).* **Aims** Inspect operating conditions of credit and microfinance institutions. **Structure** Commission of 12 members. Presidency assured by Governor of *Banque des Etats de l'Afrique centrale (BEAC, #03169).* General Secretariat, headed by Secretary-General, assisted by Deputy Secretary-General. **Staff** provided by BEAC. **Finance** Funded by BEAC. **Publications** *COBAC Bulletin* (2 a year). Annual activity report.
Members Governments of the 6 member states of CEMAC:
Cameroon, Central African Rep, Chad, Congo Brazzaville, Equatorial Guinea, Gabon.
IGO Relations Member of: *Committee of Banking Supervisors of West and Central Africa (CBSWCA).* Partner of: *Organisation pour l'Harmonisation en Afrique du Droit des Affaires (OHADA, #17806).* Close cooperation with: *Union monétaire de l'Afrique centrale (UMAC, #20463).* [2008/XE4626/**E***]

- ♦ Commission du bassin des lacs Tanganika et Kivu (inactive)
- ♦ Commission du Bassin du Lac Tchad (#16220)
- ♦ Commission biblique pontificale (#18436)
- ♦ Commission of the Bishops' Conferences of the European Community / see Commission of the Bishops' Conferences of the European Union (#04205)

♦ Commission of the Bishops' Conferences of the European Union (COMECE) 04205

Commission des épiscopats de l'Union européenne (COMECE) – Kommission der Bischofskonferenzen der Europäischen Union (COMECE) – Commissio Episcopatuum Communitatis Europensis
SG Square de Meeûs 19, 1050 Brussels, Belgium. T. +3222303510. Fax +3222303334. E-mail: comece@comece.eu.
URL: http://www.comece.eu/
History 3 Mar 1980, Brussels (Belgium). Former names and other names: *Commission of the Bishops' Conferences of the European Community* – former; *Commission des épiscopats de la Communauté européenne (COMECE)* – former; *Kommission der Bischofskonferenzen der Europäischen Gemeinschaft* – former. Registration: Belgium; EU Transparency Register, No/ID: 47350036909-69, Start date: 7 Oct 2011. **Aims** Promote closer cooperation among Bishops' Conferences in European Union countries and between them and the Holy See in pastoral questions that concern the European Union. **Structure** Commission (meets twice a year); Executive Committee; Secretariat. **Languages** English, French, German, Italian. **Staff** 11.00 FTE, paid. **Finance** Sources: members' dues. **Activities** Events/meetings; training/education. **Events** *The Experience of Women in Times of Pandemic* Brussels (Belgium) 2022, *Conference on the Future of Europe* Brussels (Belgium) 2021, *Plenary Assembly* Brussels (Belgium) 2018, *Plenary Assembly* Brussels (Belgium) 2017, *Meeting on Fighting against Trafficking in Human Beings* Brussels (Belgium) 2014. **Publications** Circulars; summaries.
Members Bishops' Conferences of 27 countries:
Austria, Belgium, Bulgaria, Croatia, Cyprus, Czechia, Denmark, Estonia, France, Germany, Greece, Hungary, Ireland, Italy, Latvia, Lithuania, Luxembourg, Malta, Netherlands, Norway, Poland, Portugal, Romania, Slovakia, Slovenia, Spain, Sweden.
NGO Relations Member of (2): *European NGO Platform Asylum and Migration (EPAM, #08051); European Policy Centre (EPC, #08240).* Cooperates with (1): *International Federation of ACLI (#13336).* Supports (1): *European Sunday Alliance (#08856).* Instrumental in setting up (1): *Coordination et promotion de l'enseignement de la religion en Europe (COOPERE, no recent information).* [2022.10.19/XD8980/**D**]

- ♦ Commission BITS Union Européenne / see OITS/ European Commission for Social Tourism (#17713)
- ♦ Commission des Caraïbes (inactive)
- ♦ Commission des Caraïbes orientales (inactive)
- ♦ Commission de la carte géologique de l'Europe / see Commission for the Geological Map of the World (#04216)
- ♦ Commission de la carte géologique du monde (#04216)
- ♦ Commission centrale pour la navigation du Rhin (#03687)
- ♦ Commission centrale pour les recherches du cerveau (inactive)
- ♦ Commission centroaméricaine de l'énergie (inactive)
- ♦ Commission centroaméricaine pour la migration (no recent information)

- Commission centroaméricaine du transport maritime (#04131)
- Commission du Codex Alimentarius (#04081)
- Sous-Commission de la COI pour l'Afrique et les États insulaires adjacents (see: #11496)
- Sous-commission de la COI pour la mer des Caraïbes et les régions adjacentes (#16003)
- Sous-commission de la COI pour le Pacifique occidental (see: #11496)
- Commission du Commonwealth pour les tombes de guerre / see Commonwealth War Graves Commission (#04367)
- Commission de la Communauté andine (#04203)
- Commission des Communautés européennes / see European Commission (#06633)
- Commission commune luthérienne-orthodoxe (#16530)
- Commission commune des ouvriers du bâtiment et du bois dans la CEE / see European Federation of Building and Woodworkers (#07065)
- Commission des communications portuaires interméditerranéennes (inactive)
- Commission de compensation de l'ONU / see United Nations Compensation Commission (#20548)
- Commission de conciliation des Nations Unies pour la Palestine (no recent information)

♦ Commission for the Conservation of Antarctic Marine Living Resources (CCAMLR) 04206

Commission pour la conservation de la faune et la flore marines de l'Antarctique – Comisión para la Conservación de los Recursos Vivos Marinos Antarticos – Komissija po Sohraneniju Morskih Zivyh Resursov Antarktiki

Exec Sec 181 Macquarie Street, Hobart TAS 7000, Australia. T. +61362101111. Fax +61362248744. E-mail: ccamlr@ccamlr.org.
Street address 181 Macquarie St, Hobart TAS 7000, Australia.
URL: https://www.ccamlr.org/

History 7 Apr 1982, Canberra, ACT (Australia). Established upon entering into force of *Convention on the Conservation of Antarctic Marine Living Resources (CCAMLR, 1980)*, and following conclusion of convention negotiations on 20 May 1980, Canberra. **Aims** Conserve the Antarctic marine *ecosystem* while allowing for rational use of resources. **Structure** Includes Scientific Committee for the Conservation of Antarctic Marine Living Resources; Secretariat. **Languages** English, French, Russian, Spanish. **Staff** 26.00 FTE, paid. **Finance** Annual budget: 6,500,000 AUD. **Activities** Events/meetings; politics/policy/regulatory. **Events** *Annual Meeting* Hobart, TAS (Australia) 2022, *Annual Meeting* Hobart, TAS (Australia) 2021, *Annual Meeting* Hobart, TAS (Australia) 2021, *Annual Meeting* Hobart, TAS (Australia) 2020, *Annual Meeting* Hobart, TAS (Australia) 2020. **Publications** *CCAMLR Science*; *CCAMLR Statistical Bulletin*. Reports of Annual Meetings; schedule of conservation measures in force; basic documents; Fishery Reports.
Members Governments of 26 countries:
Argentina, Australia, Belgium, Brazil, Chile, China, Ecuador, France, Germany, India, Italy, Japan, Korea Rep, Namibia, Netherlands, New Zealand, Norway, Poland, Russia, South Africa, Spain, Sweden, UK, Ukraine, Uruguay, USA.
Regional integration entity (1), listed in this Yearbook:
European Union (EU, #08967).
IGO Relations Observer status with (3): *Antarctic Treaty (AT, #00850)*; *Commission for the Conservation of Southern Bluefin Tuna (CCSBT, #04207)*; Southern Indian Ocean Fisheries Agreement (SIOFA).
[2022.11.29/XE1160/y/**E***]

- Commission pour la conservation de la faune et la flore marines de l'Antarctique (#04206)
- Commission for the Conservation and Management of Highly Migratory Fish Stocks in the Western and Central Pacific Ocean / see Western and Central Pacific Fisheries Commission (#20912)

♦ Commission for the Conservation of Southern Bluefin Tuna (CCSBT) 04207

Exec Sec 81A Denison St, Deakin ACT 2600, Australia. T. +61262828396. Fax +61261009461.
Contact address not obtained.
URL: http://www.ccsbt.org/

History 20 May 1994, when the *Convention for the Conservation of Southern Bluefin Tuna (1993)* came into force. **Aims** Ensure conservation and optimum utilization of southern bluefin tuna. **Structure** Officers: Executive Secretary; Deputy Executive Secretary; Database Manager. Administrative Officer. **Languages** English, Japanese. **Staff** 5.00 FTE, paid. **Finance** Members' dues. Annual budget: Australian $ 2,900,000. **Events** *Operating Model Scientific Technical Group Meeting* Incheon (Korea Rep) 2015, *Annual Meeting* Yeosu (Korea Rep) 2015, *Special Meeting* Sydney, NSW (Australia) 2011, *Ecologically related species working group meeting* Busan (Korea Rep) 2009, *Conference* Jeju (Korea Rep) 2009.
Members Governments of 7 states, fishing entities and/or Regional Economic Integration Organizations:
Australia, Indonesia, Japan, Korea Rep, New Zealand, South Africa, Taiwan.
Regional entity:
European Union (EU, #08967).
IGO Relations Observers at meetings include: *Agreement on the Conservation of Albatrosses and Petrels (ACAP, 2001)*; *Commission for the Conservation of Antarctic Marine Living Resources (CCAMLR, #04206)*; *Indian Ocean Tuna Commission (IOTC, #11162)*; *Inter-American Tropical Tuna Commission (IATTC, #11454)*; *International Commission for the Conservation of Atlantic Tunas (ICCAT, #12675)*; *Western and Central Pacific Fisheries Commission (WCPFC, #20912)*. **NGO Relations** Observers at meetings include: *BirdLife International (#03266)*; *Humane Society International (HSI, #10966)*; *TRAFFIC International (#20196)*; WWF Australia.
[2018.06.01/XE3354/**E***]

- Commission de consolidation de la paix (#20606)
- Commission consultative des barreaux de la Communauté européenne / see Council of Bars and Law Societies of Europe (#04871)
- Commission consultative européenne (inactive)
- Commission consultative internationale pour la protection de la nature (inactive)
- Commission consultative des mutations industrielles (#04763)

♦ Commission for Controlling the Desert Locust in the Central Region (CRC) 04208

Exec Sec c/o FAO/RNE, PO Box 2223, 11 El Eslah, El Zeraist, Dokki, Cairo, Egypt. T. +20233316000 ext2516. Fax +20237616804.
URL: http://desertlocust-crc.org/

History 1965, as a regional commission of *FAO Regional Office for the Near East and North Africa (#09269)* within the framework of *FAO (#09260)*, by Article XIV of FAO Constitution, at 44th session of FAO Council, under the authority of 11th session of the Conference, 1961, and on the recommendation of a special conference, 1965, Beirut (Lebanon). Agreement for establishment came into force 21 Feb 1967; amended 1977. First session: Feb 1969. Original title: *Commission for Controlling the Desert Locust in the Near East – Commission de lutte contre le criquet pèlerin au Proche-Orient – Comisión para la Lucha contra la Langosta del Desierto en el Cercano Oriente.* Name changed, Dec 1994, to *Commission for Controlling the Desert Locust in the Near East (CCDLNE)*. Present name adopted 1998. **Aims** Carry out measures to control desert locust plagues and reduce *crop damage* in the *Near East* region, by: maintaining permanent locust information, reporting and control services; encouraging and supporting training, surveys and research (including maintenance of national desert locust research stations); holding reserves and facilitating storage, export, import and freedom of movement of anti-locust equipment and *insecticides*. **Structure** Commission (meets every 2 years); Executive Committee; Secretariat. **Languages** Arabic, English. **Staff** 3.00 FTE, paid. **Finance** Member States' contributions. Annual budget: US$ 532,000. **Activities** Research/documentation; training/education; capacity building. **Events** *Session* Dubai (United Arab Emirates) 2014, *Session* Jeddah (Saudi Arabia) 2012, *Session* Beirut (Lebanon) 2010, *Session* Doha (Qatar) 2006, *Annual meeting* Khartoum (Sudan) 2005. **Publications** *A Celebration of 50 Years of Service, 1967-2017.* Annual Report; fact sheets; flyer; brochure; guidelines; standard operating procedures; field guides.
Members Representatives of 16 governments:
Bahrain, Djibouti, Egypt, Eritrea, Ethiopia, Iraq, Jordan, Kuwait, Lebanon, Oman, Qatar, Saudi Arabia, Sudan, Syrian AR, United Arab Emirates, Yemen.
[2019.02.12/XE9590/**E***]

- Commission for Controlling the Desert Locust in the Eastern Region of its Distribution Area in South West Asia / see Commission for Controlling the Desert Locust in South-West Asia (#04209)
- Commission for Controlling the Desert Locust in the Near East / see Commission for Controlling the Desert Locust in the Central Region (#04208)

♦ Commission for Controlling the Desert Locust in South-West Asia (SWAC) 04209

Commission de lutte contre le criquet pèlerin en Asie du Sud-Ouest – Comisión para la Lucha contra la Langosta del Desierto en Asia Sudoccidental

Contact c/o FAO – DLIS, Viale delle Terme di Caracalla, 00153 Rome RM, Italy. T. +39657051. E-mail: eclo@fao.org.
URL: http://www.fao.org/ag/locusts/SWAC/

History Established 15 Dec 1964, as *Commission for Controlling the Desert Locust in the Eastern Region of its Distribution Area in South West Asia – Commission de lutte contre le criquet pèlerin dans la partie orientale de son aire de répartition en Asie du Sud-Ouest – Comisión para la Lucha contra la Langosta del Desierto en la Región Oriental de su Area de Distribución del Asia Sudoccidental*, within the framework of *FAO (#09260)*, by Article XIV of FAO Constitution, upon the coming into force of Agreement for Establishment, as approved by the Conference at its 12th session, 1963, following recommendations of meetings of the concerned States and of *FAO Desert Locust Control Committee*. Agreement amended 1977. First session Dec 1964. Current name adopted in 2000. Also referred to as *SWAC*. **Aims** Carry out measures for early warning and preventive control of desert locust plagues and reduce *crop* damage in the region, by: maintaining permanent locust information, reporting and control services; holding reserves of *insecticides* and application equipment; encouraging and supporting training, surveys, planning and use of new technologies; participating in implementation of common locust control or prevention policies approved by the Commission; facilitating storage, export, import and freedom of movement of anti-locust equipment and insecticides. **Structure** Session (every 2 years). Executive Committee, consisting of one representative per member. **Languages** English. **Finance** Includes members' contributions. **Activities** Monitors vegetation development and locust situation; promotes national surveys and joint surveys in border areas, seasonal border meetings, the use of new technologies, and data management and analysis; coordinates increased survey efforts when there is threat of desert locust invasion; establishes training priorities and Master Trainers; maintains updated contingency plans; translates technical material into local languages. **Events** *Session* Teheran (Iran Islamic Rep) 2014, *Session* 2000, *Session* Teheran (Iran Islamic Rep) 2000, *Session* Teheran (Iran Islamic Rep) 1994, *Session* Rome (Italy) 1993.
Members Governments of 4 countries:
Afghanistan, India, Iran Islamic Rep, Pakistan.
[2016.06.01/XE9706/**E***]

- Commission de coopération dans le domaine du travail (#04231)
- Commission de coopération environnementale (#04211)
- Commission de coopération multilatérale des Académies de sciences des pays socialistes – Economie et politique des pays en développement (inactive)
- Commission de coopération notariale internationale (see: #15795)
- Commission de coopération technique en Afrique / see African Union Scientific Technical Research Commission (#00493)
- Commission de coopération technique en Afrique au Sud du Sahara (inactive)
- Commission de coordination nordique en matière d'énergie atomique (inactive)
- Commission on Crime Prevention and Criminal Justice / see United Nations Commission on Crime Prevention and Criminal Justice (#20530)

♦ Commission du Danube (CD) 04210

Danube Commission – Donaukommission (DK) – Dunajskaja Komissija (DK)

Gen Dir Benczur utca 25, Budapest 1068, Hungary. T. +3614618015. Fax +3613521839. E-mail: secretariat@danubecommission.org.
URL: http://www.danubecommission.org/

History Established 18 Aug 1948, Belgrade (Yugoslavia), by *Convention Concerning the Regime of Navigation on the Danube (1948)*, signed by Bulgaria, Czechoslovakia, Hungary, Romania, Ukraine, USSR, Yugoslavia, which entered into force 11 May 1949. Austria joined, 1960; Croatia, Germany, Moldova, 1999. Since 1957, at the invitation of the Commission's Secretariat, experts of Ministry of Transport of the Federal Republic of Germany took part in the work of the Commission. **Aims** Provide and develop free navigation on the Danube for commercial vessels flying the flat of all states in accordance with interests and sovereign rights of the Member States of the Belgrade Convention; strengthen and develop economic and cultural relations of the said states among themselves and with the other countries. **Structure** Ordinary Sessions (twice a year) always in Budapest (Hungary); Extraordinary Sessions as necessary; Working Groups. **Languages** French, German, Russian. **Staff** 30.00 FTE, paid. **Finance** Members States' contributions. Voluntary contributions from observer states. **Activities** Guidance/assistance/consulting; events/meetings. **Events** *Half-yearly session* Budapest (Hungary) 2006, *International conference on the conservation and sustainable development of the Danube delta* Odessa (Ukraine) 2006, *Half-yearly session* Budapest (Hungary) 2005, *Half-yearly session* Budapest (Hungary) 2005, *Half-yearly session* Budapest (Hungary) 2004. **Publications** *Catalogue of Publications of the Danube Commission*; *Handbook on radiocommunication for Inland Navigation.* Books; maps; CD-ROMs. Information Services: E-library.
Members Countries (11) to the Convention:
Austria, Bulgaria, Croatia, Germany, Hungary, Moldova, Romania, Russia, Serbia, Slovakia, Ukraine.
Observers in 10 countries:
Belgium, Cyprus, Czechia, France, Georgia, Greece, Montenegro, Netherlands, North Macedonia, Türkiye.
International observers:
Association for European Inland Navigation and Waterways (VBW); *Central Commission for the Navigation of the Rhine (CCNR, #03687)*; Danube Day; *European Commission (EC, #06633)* (Directorate General for Energy and Transport); *International Association for the Representation of the Mutual Interests of the Inland Shipping and the Insurance and for Keeping the Register of Inland Vessels in Europe (#12131)*; *International Commission for the Protection of the Danube River (ICPDR, #12720)*; *International Sava River Basin Commission (#14783)*; *Moselle Commission (#16857)*; *Organization of Black Sea Economic Cooperation (BSEC, #17857)* (RAINWAT Committee); *United Nations Economic Commission for Europe (UNECE, #20555).*
IGO Relations Cooperates with: *International Maritime Organization (IMO, #14102)*; *International Sava River Basin Commission (#14783)*; *Organization of Black Sea Economic Cooperation (BSEC, #17857)*. **NGO Relations** Cooperates with: *European Federation of Inland Ports (EFIP, #07144).*
[2018.09.18/XD0464/**E***]

- Commission de défense des droits humains en Amérique centrale (no recent information)
- Commission for the Defense of Human Rights in Central America (no recent information)
- Commission du désarmement des Nations Unies (#20552)
- Commission des détroits (inactive)
- Commission on Development and Exchanges (see: #14121)
- Commission du développement durable des Nations Unies (inactive)
- Commission pour le développement technologique et scientifique de l'Amérique centrale et du Panama (#04132)
- Commission du droit international (#14004)
- Commissione dell'Arco Atlantico (#03007)
- Commissione Cattolica Internazionale per le Migrazioni (#12459)
- Commissione delle Comunità Europee / see European Commission (#06633)
- Commission économique des Nations Unies pour l'Afrique (#20554)
- Commission économique des Nations Unies pour l'Amérique latine / see United Nations Economic Commission for Latin America and the Caribbean (#20556)
- Commission économique des Nations Unies pour l'Amérique latine et les Caraïbes (#20556)
- Commission économique des Nations Unies pour l'Asie et l'Extrême-Orient / see United Nations Economic and Social Commission for Asia and the Pacific (#20557)
- Commission économique des Nations Unies pour l'Asie occidentale / see United Nations Economic and Social Commission for Western Asia (#20558)
- Commission économique des Nations Unies pour l'Europe (#20555)
- Commission économique et sociale des Nations Unies pour l'Asie occidentale (#20558)

Commission économique sociale
04210

alphabetic sequence excludes
For the complete listing, see Yearbook Online at

- ♦ Commission économique et sociale des Nations Unies pour l'Asie et le Pacifique (#20557)
- ♦ Commissione Cooperazione Internazionale per lo Sviluppo (internationally oriented national body)
- ♦ Commissione Europea (#06633)
- ♦ Commissione Giustizia, Pace, Integrità del Creato delle Unioni dei Superiori Generali – USG/UISG (#04230)
- ♦ Commission des Eglises auprès des migrants en Europe (#03912)
- ♦ Commissione Interdicasteriale Permanente per la Chiesa in Europa Orientale (#18323)
- ♦ Commissione Intermediterranea (#11521)
- ♦ Commissione Internazionale di Numismatica / see International Numismatic Council (#14385)
- ♦ Commissione Internazionale di Polizia Criminale / see International Criminal Police Organization – INTERPOL (#13110)
- ♦ Commissione Internazionale per la Protezione delle Acque del Lago di Costanza dall'Inquinamento / see Internationale Gewässerschutzkommission für den Bodensee (#13244)
- ♦ Commissione Internazionale per la Protezione delle Alpi / see CIPRA International (#03930)
- ♦ Commissione Internazionale per la Protezione del Lago di Costanza (#13244)
- ♦ Commissione Internazionale per la Sicurezza Elettromagnetica (#12680)
- ♦ Commissione Internazionale di Storia Militare (#12705)
- ♦ Commissione Internazionale per lo studio degli Ordini Cavallereschi (#12711)
- ♦ Commissione Internazionale dell' Unificazione dei Metodi di Analisi delle Derrate Alimentari (inactive)
- ♦ Commissione Intersindicale dei Disidratatori Europei (#06896)
- ♦ Commissione delle Isole (#16061)
- ♦ Commission électrotechnique africaine de normalisation (#00295)
- ♦ Commission électrotechnique internationale (#13255)
- ♦ Commissione del Mar del Nord (#17604)

♦ Commission for Environmental Cooperation (CEC) 04211

Commission de coopération environnementale (CCE) – Comisión para la Cooperación Ambiental (CCA)

Exec Dir 700 de la Gauchetière St West, Suite 1620, Montréal QC H3B 5M2, Canada. T. +15143504300. Fax +15143504314. E-mail: info@cec.org.
URL: http://www.cec.org/

History 1 Jan 1994. Established upon entry into force of the *North American Agreement for Environmental Cooperation (NAAEC, 1993).* Complements environmental provisions established in *NAFTA Secretariat (#16927).* **Aims** Support the cooperative environmental agenda of Canada, Mexico and the USA to green North America's economy; set strategic priorities to address climate change by promoting a low-carbon economy; protect the environment and the health of citizens; enhance compliance with, and promote enforcement of, environmental laws; bring together governments, civil society and businesses to develop innovative North American solutions to regional environmental challenges. **Structure** Council, representing the governments of NAAEC member countries; Joint Public Advisory Committee (JPAC); Secretariat. **Languages** English, French, Spanish. **Staff** 50.00 FTE, paid. **Finance** Equal contributions of Parties. Budget (annual): US$ 9 million. **Activities** Annual work programme covers 3 general areas: Healthy Communities and Ecosystems; Climate Change – Low Carbon Economy; Greening the Economy in North America. Reviews and addresses citizen submissions on enforcement matters on issues relating to a resident of North America's allegation(s) of a failure by any member country to enforce its environmental laws; prepares independent reports on important environmental issues; organizes conferences, workshops and other meetings. Grant programme: North American Partnership for Environmental Community Action (NAPECA). **Events** *Annual Council Session* Mérida (Mexico) 2022, *Annual Council Session* Montréal, QC (Canada) 2021, *Annual Council Session* Montréal, QC (Canada) 2020, *Public meeting of the North American PRTR Initiative* Montréal, QC (Canada) 2020, *Annual Council Session* Mexico City (Mexico) 2019. **Publications** *North American Environmental Law and Policy* – series. *Continental Pollutant Pathways*; *Electricity and the Environment*; *Environmental Hazards of Transborder Lead Battery Recycling*; *Environmental Legislation in North America: Experiences and Best Practices for Its Implementation and Adjudication*; *Green Building*; *Maize and Biodiversity*; *North American Conservation Action Plans*; *North American Environmental Atlas*; *Ribbon of Life*; *Silva Reservoir*; *Sustainable Freight Transportation*; *Taking Stock*; *The North American Mosaic: An Overview of Key Environmental Issues.* Studies; reports; research material.

Members Governments of 3 countries:
Canada, Mexico, USA.

IGO Relations Accredited by: *United Nations Framework Convention on Climate Change – Secretariat (UNFCCC, #20564).* **NGO Relations** Supports: *Center for International Earth Science Information Network (CIESIN).* Member of: *International Network for Environmental Compliance and Enforcement (INECE, #14261).*
[2022/XE2969/**E***]

- ♦ Commission des épidémies (inactive)
- ♦ Commission des épiscopats de la Communauté européenne / see Commission of the Bishops' Conferences of the European Union (#04205)
- ♦ Commission des épiscopats de l'Union européenne (#04205)
- ♦ Commissione per i Rapporti Religiosi con l'Ebraismo (#04238)
- ♦ Commission espagnole d'aide aux réfugiés (internationally oriented national body)
- ♦ Commissione Teologica Internazionale (#15684)
- ♦ Commission pour l'étude des Communautés européennes / see Association Française d'Études Européennes
- ♦ Commission d'études de l'histoire de l'Eglise en Amérique latine (#04133)
- ♦ Commission for European Affairs (see: #15795)
- ♦ Commission of the European Communities / see European Commission (#06633)

♦ Commission on European Family Law (CEFL) 04212

Chair Bucerius Law School, Jungiusstraae 6, 20355 Hamburg, Germany. E-mail: webmaster@ceflonline.net.
URL: http://www.ceflonline.net/

History Founded 1 Sep 2001. **Aims** Launch a pioneering theoretical and practical exercise in relation to the harmonization and/or unification of substantive family and succession law in Europe. **Structure** Organizing Group; Expert Group. **Languages** English. **Staff** 31.00 FTE, voluntary. **Finance** Grants from *European Commission (EC, #06633).* Universities involved carry most of the costs. **Events** *Family law in Europe – new developments, challenges and opportunities* Bonn (Germany) 2013, *The future of family property in Europe* Cambridge (UK) 2010, *European challenges in contemporary family law* Oslo (Norway) 2007, *Conference* Utrecht (Netherlands) 2004, *Conference* Utrecht (Netherlands) 2002. **Publications** National reports.

Members Full in 28 countries:
Austria, Belgium, Bulgaria, Croatia, Czechia, Denmark, Estonia, Finland, France, Germany, Greece, Hungary, Ireland, Italy, Latvia, Lithuania, Luxembourg, Netherlands, Norway, Poland, Portugal, Russia, Slovakia, Slovenia, Spain, Sweden, Switzerland, UK.
[2015.09.08/XM3742/**E**]

- ♦ Commission européenne (#06633)
- ♦ Commission européenne d'agriculture (#06634)
- ♦ Commission européenne consultative pour les pêches dans les eaux intérieures / see European Inland Fisheries and Aquaculture Advisory Commission (#07540)
- ♦ Commission européenne contre le racisme et l'intolérance (see: #04881)
- ♦ Commission européenne pour la démocratie par le droit (#06636)
- ♦ Commission européenne des droits de l'homme (inactive)

♦ Commission européenne pour l'efficacité de la justice (CEPEJ) ... 04213

European Commission for the Efficiency of Justice

Sec c/o Council of Europe, DG Human Rights and Legal Affairs, Justice Div, 67075 Strasbourg CEDEX, France. T. +33388413412. Fax +33388413743. E-mail: cepej@coe.int.
Assistant address not obtained.
URL: http://www.coe.int/cepej/

History 18 Sep 2002. Founded by *Council of Europe (CE, #04881),* as a Committee under the authority of *Committee of Ministers of the Council of Europe (#04273).* **Aims** Improve efficiency and functioning of the justice system of member states, thereby generating increased confidence of the citizens in justice; prevent appeals to the European Convention of Human Rights, based on Article 6; enable a better implementation of the CoE's relevant instruments. **Structure** Plenary meeting (twice a year). Intergovernmental Commission of members appointed by the 47 member States (officials, judges, academicians). Bureau; working parties on specialized subjects; Network of pilot courts; Network of national correspondents; Secretariat. **Languages** English, French. **Activities** Monitoring/evaluation; events/meetings; awards/prizes/competitions; research/documentation. **Events** *Network of Pilot Courts Plenary Meeting* Kristiansand (Norway) 2017, *Plenary Meeting* Strasbourg (France) 2009, *Plenary meeting* Strasbourg (France) 2009, *Plenary Meeting* Strasbourg (France) 2008, *Plenary Meeting* Strasbourg (France) 2008.

Members Participating states: all members of the Council of Europe (47):
Albania, Andorra, Armenia, Austria, Azerbaijan, Belgium, Bosnia-Herzegovina, Bulgaria, Croatia, Cyprus, Czechia, Denmark, Estonia, Finland, France, Georgia, Germany, Greece, Hungary, Iceland, Ireland, Italy, Latvia, Liechtenstein, Lithuania, Luxembourg, Malta, Moldova, Monaco, Montenegro, Netherlands, North Macedonia, Norway, Poland, Portugal, Romania, Russia, San Marino, Serbia, Slovakia, Slovenia, Spain, Sweden, Switzerland, Türkiye, UK, Ukraine.

Observers: governments of 10 countries:
Canada, Guatemala, Holy See, Israel, Japan, Kazakhstan, Mexico, Morocco, Tunisia, USA.

IGO Relations Participants: *European Commission (EC, #06633)* and General Secretariat of *Council of the European Union (#04895)*; *The Hague Conference on Private International Law (HCCH, #10850)*; *International Bank for Reconstruction and Development (IBRD, #12317)* (World Bank); *OECD (#17693).* Represented on: *Consultative Council of European Judges (CCJE, #04767)*; *European Committee on Legal Cooperation (#06655).* Also cooperates with: *European Judicial Network in Civil and Commercial Matters (#07616).* **NGO Relations** Observer status granted to: American Bar Association (ABA); *Association of European Administrative Judges (AEAJ, #02497)*; *Council of Bars and Law Societies of Europe (CCBE, #04871)*; *European Association of Judges (EAJ, #06100)*; *European Judicial Training Network (EJTN, #07617)*; *European Network of Councils for the Judiciary (ENCJ, #07886)*; *European Union of Rechtspfleger (#09012)*; *European Expertise and Expert Institute (EEEI, #07015)*; *International Consortium for Court Excellence (ICCE, #12908)*; *International Mediation Institute (IMI, #14129)*; *International Union of Judicial Officers (#15785)*; *Magistrats européens pour la démocratie et les libertés (MEDEL, #16546)*; *Siracusa International Institute for Criminal Justice and Human Rights (SII, #19289).*
[2021/XJ3114/**E***]

- ♦ Commission européenne des forêts (#07299)
- ♦ Commission européenne de lutte contre la fièvre aphteuse (#06635)
- ♦ Commission européenne de pharmacopée (#08198)
- ♦ Commission européenne du régime du Danube (inactive)
- ♦ Commission européenne du tourisme (#08943)
- ♦ Commission Europe-Méditerranée de planification pour les problèmes de l'eau (no recent information)
- ♦ Commission évangélique latinoaméricaine d'éducation chrétienne (inactive)
- ♦ Commission exécutive pour CEE de la Fédération européenne de l'industrie de la brosserie et pinceauterie / see European Brushware Federation (#06406)
- ♦ Commission de l'Extrême-Orient (inactive)
- ♦ Commission FAO/OMS du Codex Alimentarius / see Codex Alimentarius Commission (#04081)
- ♦ Commission financière internationale (inactive)
- ♦ Commission du fleuve Niger / see Niger Basin Authority (#17134)
- ♦ Commission de la fonction publique internationale (#12587)
- ♦ Commission des forêts pour l'Afrique / see African Forestry and Wildlife Commission (#00319)

♦ Commission des forêts d'Afrique centrale (COMIFAC) 04214

Central African Forests Commission

Mailing Address BP 20 818, Yaoundé, Cameroon. T. +2372213510. Fax +2372213512. E-mail: comifac2005@yahoo.fr.
URL: http://www.comifac.org/

History 6 Dec 2000, Yaoundé (Cameroon). Convergence Plan adopted Feb 2005; revised 2014 with provision for a second Convergence Plan (2015-2025). Former names and other names: *Conference of Ministers for the Forests of Central Africa* – former; *Conférence des ministres en charge des forêts d'Afrique centrale* – former. **Aims** Promote conservation, sustainment and joint management of forest ecosystems in Central Africa. **Structure** Summit of Chiefs Heads of State; Council of Ministers; Executive Secretariat, headquartered in Yaoundé (Cameroon). **Languages** English, French, Portuguese, Spanish. **Staff** Executive Secretariat: 4; technical staff; support staff. **Finance** International partners and donors include: *African Development Bank (ADB, #00283)*; *Cooperation Canada*; *Deutsche Gesellschaft für Internationale Zusammenarbeit (GIZ)*; *FAO (#09260)*; *International Bank for Reconstruction and Development (IBRD, #12317)* (World Bank); *International Union for Conservation of Nature and Natural Resources (IUCN, #15766)*; *Japan International Cooperation Agency (JICA)*; *UNEP (#20299)*; *UNDP (#20292)*; *World Wide Fund for Nature (WWF, #21922).* **Activities** Monitoring/evaluation. **Events** *RRI Dialogue on Forests, Governance and Climate Change* Yaoundé (Cameroon) 2013, *Central Africa heads of state summit on conservation and sustainable management of forests ecosystems* Brazzaville (Congo Brazzaville) 2005, *Conference* Libreville (Gabon) 2004, *Extraordinary conference / Meeting* Libreville (Gabon) 2004, *Extraordinary conference* Yaoundé (Cameroon) 2004.

Members Governments of 10 countries:
Burundi, Cameroon, Central African Rep, Chad, Congo Brazzaville, Congo DR, Equatorial Guinea, Gabon, Rwanda, Sao Tomé-Principe.

IGO Relations *Congo Basin Forest Partnership (CBFP, #04662)*; *ECA Sub-Regional Office for Central Africa (ECA/SRO-CA, #05274)*; *Group on Earth Observations (GEO, #10735)*; *Lake Chad Basin Commission (LCBC, #16220)*; Organization for the Conservation of Wild Fauna in Africa (OCFSA); *Secretariat of the United Nations Convention to Combat Desertification (Secretariat of the UNCCD, #19208).* **NGO Relations** *Confédération des ONG d'environnement et de développement de l'Afrique centrale (CONGAC, #04572).*
[2019.11.11/XF7133/**F***]

- ♦ Commission des forêts pour l'Amérique latine / see Latin American and Caribbean Forestry Commission (#16278)
- ♦ Commission des forêts pour l'Amérique latine et les Caraïbes (#16278)
- ♦ Commission des forêts pour l'Amérique du Nord (#17565)
- ♦ Commission des forêts pour l'Asie et le Pacifique (#01909)
- ♦ Commission des forêts et de la faune sauvage pour l'Afrique (#00319)
- ♦ Commission des forêts pour le Proche-Orient (#16965)
- ♦ Commission frontalière internationale (inactive)
- ♦ Commission of the Fruit and Vegetable Juice Industry of the EEC / see European Fruit Juice Association (#07362)
- ♦ Commission générale des pêches pour la Méditerranée (#10112)

♦ Commission on Genetic Resources for Food and Agriculture (CGRFA) 04215

Sec Natural Resources, FAO, Viale delle Terme di Caracalla, 00100 Rome RM, Italy. T. +39657054981. Fax +39657055246. E-mail: cgrfa@fao.org.
URL: http://www.fao.org/nr/cgrfa/en/

History 1983, by resolution 1/85 of the 85th Session of the Council of *FAO (#09260),* following recommendations of Conference 1983 (Resolution 9/83). Original title: *FAO Commission on Plant Genetic Resources.* Mandate broadened and current title adopted, Oct 1995, Rome (Italy), at 28th FAO conference. Previously also referred to as *FAO Commission on Plant Genetic Resources for Food and Agriculture (CPGRFA).* Originally set up as a basic institutional component of *Global System for the Conservation and Sustainable Utilization of Plant Genetic Resources for Food and Sustainable Agriculture (inactive).* Adopted its own Rules of Procedures, 2009. **Aims** Revised mandate, 1995: cover all aspects of genetic resources relevant to food and agriculture so as to deal in an integrated manner with agro-*biodiversity* issues, including follow-up of *Agenda 21,* and reach international consensus in areas of global interest; keep under continuous review all matters relating to policy, programmes and activities of *FAO* in the area of such resources, including their *conservation* and *sustainable* use and the fair and equitable sharing of benefits derived from their use; recommend measures to ensure development of comprehensive global system(s) on such resources; monitor operation of such system(s) in harmony with the Convention on biological diversity; provide an *intergovernmental* forum to negotiate and oversee other relevant international instruments; facilitate and oversee cooperation between the FAO and other international intergovernmental or nongovernmental bodies dealing with conservation and sustainable use of genetic resources; respond to requests from the *'Conference of Parties to the Convention on biological diversity'* and provide information and other services, especially in the areas of early warning systems, global assessment and clearing house facilities. **Structure** Commission meets every 2 years; Secretariat, headed by Secretary; Working Group (meeting annually) comprising 23 member countries and Chair; possible further working groups and interim expert working groups. **Languages** Arabic, Chinese, English, French, Russian, Spanish. **Activities** Sessions in Rome (Italy) at meetings of Committee on Agriculture (COAG) include both donors and users of germplasm, funds and technology, with attendance of relevant technical assistance agencies, intergovernmental organizations, development banks, non-governmental organizations and private foundations. International agreements being negotiated through the Commission: *International Code of Conduct for Plant Germplasm Collecting and Transfer*, *Code of Conduct for Biotechnology*; basic agreements on genebanks. Global mechanisms being developed: network of *'ex situ'* base collections (with technical assistance of IBPGR); network of areas established or demarcated for *'in situ'* conservation of genetic resources. Other activities: preparation of a code of conduct for international collectors; active monitoring of new biotechnologies; adoption of an agreed interpretation of the *International Undertaking on Plant Genetic Resources*; draft resolution on farmers' rights; structural and legal gaps of animal genetic resource activities; support for adoption of *Convention on Biological Diversity (Biodiversity convention, 1992)*. **Events** *Session* Rome (Italy) 2015, *Session* Rome (Italy) 2015, *Session* Rome (Italy) 2013, *Session* Rome (Italy) 2013, *Session* Rome (Italy) 2011. **Publications** *Report on the State of the World's Plant Genetic Resources for Food and Agriculture* (updated periodically). *The State of the World's Animal Genetic Resources for Food and Agriculture* (2007).

Members Membership open to all members and associate members of FAO desiring to be considered; as of Apr 2016, governments of 178 countries:
Afghanistan, Albania, Algeria, Angola, Antigua-Barbuda, Argentina, Armenia, Australia, Austria, Azerbaijan, Bahamas, Bangladesh, Barbados, Belarus, Belgium, Belize, Benin, Bhutan, Bolivia, Bosnia-Herzegovina, Botswana, Brazil, Bulgaria, Burkina Faso, Burundi, Cambodia, Cameroon, Canada, Cape Verde, Central African Rep, Chad, Chile, China, Colombia, Comoros, Congo Brazzaville, Congo DR, Cook Is, Costa Rica, Côte d'Ivoire, Croatia, Cuba, Cyprus, Czechia, Denmark, Dominica, Dominican Rep, Ecuador, Egypt, El Salvador, Equatorial Guinea, Eritrea, Estonia, Eswatini, Ethiopia, Fiji, Finland, France, Gabon, Gambia, Georgia, Germany, Ghana, Greece, Grenada, Guatemala, Guinea, Guinea-Bissau, Guyana, Haiti, Honduras, Hungary, Iceland, India, Indonesia, Iran Islamic Rep, Iraq, Ireland, Israel, Italy, Jamaica, Japan, Jordan, Kazakhstan, Kenya, Korea DPR, Korea Rep, Kuwait, Kyrgyzstan, Laos, Latvia, Lebanon, Lesotho, Liberia, Libya, Lithuania, Luxembourg, Madagascar, Malawi, Malaysia, Maldives, Mali, Malta, Marshall Is, Mauritania, Mauritius, Mexico, Moldova, Mongolia, Montenegro, Morocco, Mozambique, Myanmar, Namibia, Nepal, Netherlands, New Zealand, Nicaragua, Niger, Nigeria, North Macedonia, Norway, Oman, Pakistan, Palau, Panama, Papua New Guinea, Paraguay, Peru, Philippines, Poland, Portugal, Qatar, Romania, Russia, Rwanda, Samoa, San Marino, Sao Tomé-Principe, Saudi Arabia, Senegal, Serbia, Seychelles, Sierra Leone, Slovakia, Slovenia, Solomon Is, South Africa, Spain, Sri Lanka, St Kitts-Nevis, St Lucia, St Vincent-Grenadines, Sudan, Suriname, Sweden, Switzerland, Syrian AR, Tajikistan, Tanzania UR, Thailand, Togo, Tonga, Trinidad-Tobago, Tunisia, Türkiye, Uganda, UK, Ukraine, United Arab Emirates, Uruguay, USA, Vanuatu, Venezuela, Vietnam, Yemen, Zambia, Zimbabwe.
Member Organization (1):
European Union (EU, #08967).
NGO Relations Member of: *Inter-Agency Network for Safety in Biotechnology (IANB, inactive)*.
[2010.09.01/XE6950/**E***]

- ♦ Commission géodésique nordique (#17304)
- ♦ Commission for the Geological Map of Europe / see Commission for the Geological Map of the World (#04216)

♦ Commission for the Geological Map of the World (CGMW) 04216

Commission de la carte géologique du monde (CCGM)

Head Office 77 rue Claude Bernard, 75005 Paris, France. T. +33147072284. E-mail: ccgm@sfr.fr.
URL: http://www.ccgm.org/

History Founded during the 2nd International Geological Congress (IGC), 1881, Bologna (Italy), when a small group of European geologists was officially constituted to propose a standard legend and draft a Geological Map of Europe. Originally comprised all geological surveys of Europe. The idea of enlarging the Commission to representatives of all countries first postulated in 1910 at the 11th IGC. Officially became a Commission during the 12th IGS, 1913, Toronto ON (Canada). Current Statutes adopted 15 Jul 1980, Paris (France). Former names and other names: *Commission for the Geological Map of Europe* – former (1881 to 1913); *Commission de la carte géologique de l'Europe* – former (1881 to 1913). **Aims** Promote and coordinate preparation and publication of printed and digital *earth science* maps of continents, oceans, major regions of the earth at small scale and develop *cartography* in the earth sciences field. **Structure** General Assembly (every 2 years); Bureau; Subcommissions; General Secretariat, located in Paris (France). **Languages** English, French, Spanish. **Staff** 2.00 FTE, paid. **Finance** Sources: members' dues. Other sources: subsidy from the French government (BRGM); UNESCO and private industry funding for specific projects. **Activities** Events/meetings; knowledge management/information dissemination; publishing activities. **Events** *Biennial General Assembly* Delhi (India) 2020, *Biennial General Assembly* Paris (France) 2018, *Biennial General Assembly* Cape Town (South Africa) 2016, *Biennial General Assembly* Paris (France) 2014, *Biennial General Assembly* Brisbane, QLD (Australia) 2012. **Publications** *CGMW Bulletin* (every 1-2 years). Stratigraphic charts; maps; booklets; atlases; catalogue.

Members Statutory: national organizations responsible for solid earth science mapping of all the countries or territories of the world which adhere to CGMW; public or private organizations interested in and supportive of CGMW (accepted on the recommendation of a Vice-President and with the approval of Bureau). Members in 107 countries:
Albania, Algeria, Angola, Argentina, Australia, Austria, Bangladesh, Belgium, Benin, Botswana, Brazil, Bulgaria, Burkina Faso, Burundi, Cameroon, Canada, Central African Rep, Chad, Chile, China, Colombia, Congo Brazzaville, Congo DR, Costa Rica, Côte d'Ivoire, Croatia, Czechia, Denmark, Djibouti, Ecuador, Egypt, Eritrea, Estonia, Eswatini, Ethiopia, Finland, France, Gabon, Gambia, Germany, Ghana, Greece, Guinea, Guinea-Bissau, Hungary, Iceland, India, Iran Islamic Rep, Iraq, Ireland, Israel, Italy, Japan, Kenya, Latvia, Lebanon, Lesotho, Liberia, Libya, Liechtenstein, Lithuania, Luxembourg, Madagascar, Malawi, Malaysia, Mali, Mauritania, Mauritius, Mexico, Morocco, Mozambique, Namibia, Niger, Nigeria, Norway, Paraguay, Peru, Philippines, Poland, Portugal, Romania, Russia, Rwanda, Senegal, Sierra Leone, Slovakia, Slovenia, Somalia, South Africa, Spain, Sudan, Suriname, Sweden, Switzerland, Tanzania UR, Thailand, Togo, Trinidad-Tobago, Tunisia, Türkiye, Uganda, UK, Uruguay, USA, Venezuela, Zambia, Zimbabwe.
Associate member (1). Membership country not specified.
NGO Relations Member of: *International Union of Geodesy and Geophysics (IUGG, #15776)*; *International Union of Geological Sciences (IUGS, #15777)*. [2020.02.25/XB9351/**B**]

- ♦ Commission on Graduates of Foreign Nursing Schools (internationally oriented national body)
- ♦ Commission des grands lacs (internationally oriented national body)
- ♦ Commission d'histoire de l'historiographie / see International Commission for the History and Theory of Historiography (#12690)
- ♦ Commission of the History of Historiography / see International Commission for the History and Theory of Historiography (#12690)

♦ Commission of History of International Relations (CHIR) 04217

SG Univ degli Studi di Milan, Centro per gli Studi di Politica Estera e Opinione Pubblica, Via Festa del Perdono 7, 20122 Milan MI, Italy. T. +39250312623. Fax +39250312997. E-mail: chir@unimi.it.
URL: http://www.comintrel.com/

History Oct 1981, Milan (Italy), and recognized by ICHS as an 'internal' organism. Became, Sep 1997, an affiliated organization with right to vote at ICHS General Assembly. Also referred to as *International Commission of History of International Relations – Commission internationale d'histoire des relations internationales*. **Aims** Develop the study of the history of international relations by periodically organizing meetings between members, by giving information concerning the activities in this field of the history and by publication of scientific documents useful for the historical research in this field. **Structure** General Assembly; Bureau; Secretariat. **Languages** English, French. **Staff** 3.00 FTE, paid. **Finance** Members' dues. Other sources: publications; subsidies from scientific, governmental and private institutions. Annual budget: about US$ 25,000. **Activities** Events/meetings; publishing activities. **Events** *International Colloquium* Paris (France) 2019, *International Conference* Amsterdam (Netherlands) 2010, *International Conference* Madrid (Spain) 2009, *International Conference* Tokyo (Japan) 2009, *International Conference* Cologne (Germany) 2008. **Publications** *CHIR Newsletter* (annual). Books; reports; proceedings of colloquia.

Members Individuals in 48 countries:
Albania, Argentina, Australia, Austria, Belgium, Bosnia-Herzegovina, Brazil, Bulgaria, Cameroon, Canada, Chile, China, Colombia, Croatia, Czechia, Denmark, Egypt, Finland, France, Germany, Greece, Hungary, India, Israel, Italy, Japan, Luxembourg, Malta, Mexico, Moldova, Netherlands, Nigeria, Norway, Peru, Poland, Portugal, Romania, Russia, Singapore, Slovakia, Spain, Sweden, Switzerland, Tunisia, UK, Uruguay, USA, Venezuela.
NGO Relations Affiliate member of: *International Committee of Historical Sciences (ICHS, #12777)*.
[2018.06.21/XE0402/v/**E**]

- ♦ Commission for Humanity / see World Humanity Commission
- ♦ Commission hydrographique de l'Afrique et des Iles Australes (see: #13825)
- ♦ Commission hydrographique sur l'Antarctique (see: #13825)
- ♦ Commission hydrographique de l'Asie orientale (see: #13825)
- ♦ Commission hydrographique de l'Atlantique oriental (see: #13825)
- ♦ Commission hydrographique de l'atlantique sud-ouest (see: #13825)
- ♦ Commission hydrographique de la Méditerranée et de la mer Noire (see: #13825)
- ♦ Commission hydrographique de la Mer Baltique (see: #13825)
- ♦ Commission hydrographique de la Mer du Nord (see: #13825)
- ♦ Commission hydrographique de la Mésoamérique et de la mer des Caraïbes (see: #13825)
- ♦ Commission hydrographique nordique (see: #13825)
- ♦ Commission hydrographique de l'Océan Indien Septentrional (see: #13825)
- ♦ Commission hydrographique du Pacifique sud-est (see: #13825)
- ♦ Commission hydrographique du pacifique sud-ouest (see: #13825)
- ♦ Commission hydrographique régionale de l'Arctique (#01101)
- ♦ Commission hydrographique USA/Canada (see: #13825)
- ♦ Commission hydrographique de la zone maritime ROPME (#18971)
- ♦ Commission des îles (#16061)
- ♦ Commission d'indemnisation de l'ONU (#20548)
- ♦ Commission Indo-Pacifique des pêches / see Asia-Pacific Fishery Commission (#01907)
- ♦ Commission de l'industrie des jus de fruits et de légumes de la CEE / see European Fruit Juice Association (#07362)
- ♦ Commission des industries agro-alimentaires de l'Union des industries de la Communauté économique européenne / see FoodDrinkEurope (#09841)
- ♦ Commission d'information et de liaison des associations nobles d'Europe (#06637)
- ♦ Commission for Inland Fisheries and Aquaculture of Latin America and the Caribbean (#04142)
- ♦ Commission for Inland Fisheries of Latin America / see Comisión de Pesca Continental y Acuicultura para América Latina y el Caribe (#04142)
- ♦ Commission d'intégration électrique régionale / see Regional Commission for Power Integration (#18764)
- ♦ Commission interaméricaine d'administration territoriale (inactive)
- ♦ Commission interaméricaine d'arbitrage commercial (#11410)
- ♦ Commission interaméricaine de développement (inactive)
- ♦ Commission interaméricaine des droits de l'homme (#11411)
- ♦ Commission interaméricaine de l'énergie nucléaire (inactive)
- ♦ Commission interaméricaine des femmes (#04137)
- ♦ Commission interaméricaine de lutte contre l'abus des drogues (#11429)
- ♦ Commission interaméricaine de la paix (inactive)
- ♦ Commission interaméricaine de télécommunications (#04138)
- ♦ Commission on Inter-American Telecommunications / see Comisión Interamericana de Telecomunicaciones (#04138)
- ♦ Commission interdicastérielle permanente pour l'Eglise en Europe de l'Est (#18323)
- ♦ Commission intereuropéenne Eglise et école (#11469)
- ♦ Commission intergouvernementale de coopération des pays socialistes dans le domaine de la technologie de l'ordinateur (inactive)
- ♦ Commission for Inter-Mediterranean Port Communication (inactive)
- ♦ Commission interméditerranéenne (#11521)
- ♦ Commission internationale sur l'acoustique / see International Commission for Acoustics (#12658)
- ♦ Commission internationale de l'agriculture (inactive)
- ♦ Commission internationale anglicane – catholique romaine (#00831)
- ♦ Commission internationale pour les applications de la météorologie à la navigation aérienne (inactive)
- ♦ Commission internationale des arts et traditions populaires / see Société internationale d'ethnologie et de folklore (#19481)
- ♦ Commission internationale sur l'astrophysique / see IUPAP Commission on Astrophysics (#16082)
- ♦ Commission internationale des aumôniers généraux de prison / see International Commission of Catholic Prison Pastoral Care (#12670)
- ♦ Commission internationale des aumôniers des prisons / see International Commission of Catholic Prison Pastoral Care (#12670)
- ♦ Commission internationale du Bassin Congo-Oubangui-Sangha (#12674)
- ♦ Commission internationale de botanique apicole / see International Commission for Plant-Pollinator Relationships (#12716)
- ♦ Commission internationale des cartes botaniques (inactive)
- ♦ Commission internationale catholique pour les migrations (#12459)
- ♦ Commission Internationale Catholique pour les Migrations – Europe (#12460)
- ♦ Commission internationale catholique romaine-évangélique luthérienne (#16531)
- ♦ Commission internationale de certification de conformité de l'équipement électrique / see IEC System of Conformity Assessment Schemes for Electrotechnical Equipment and Components (#11096)
- ♦ Commission internationale de chimie atmosphérique et de pollution globale (#12664)
- ♦ Commission internationale de chimie atmosphérique et de pollution globale de l'AIMPA / see International Commission on Atmospheric Chemistry and Global Pollution (#12664)
- ♦ Commission internationale des congrès des associations agricoles et de démographie rurale (inactive)
- ♦ Commission internationale des congrès d'éducation familiale (inactive)
- ♦ Commission internationale des congrès européens de mycologie (inactive)
- ♦ Commission internationale pour la conservation des thonidés de l'Atlantique (#12675)
- ♦ Commission internationale consultative principe de précaution (#11591)
- ♦ Commission internationale de la coopération intellectuelle (inactive)
- ♦ Commission internationale de coordination pour l'agriculture (inactive)

♦ Commission internationale pour la couleur dans la mode et le textile (INTERCOLOR) 04218

International Commission for Fashion and Textile Colours – Internationale Kommission für Mode- und Textilfarben

Gen Sec 12 rue du Sentier, 75002 Paris, France. E-mail: contact@intercolor.nu.
URL: http://www.intercolor.nu/

History 9 Sep 1963, Paris (France). Founded at first meeting, under the name *International Commission for the Standardization of Colours for the Fashion and Textile Industries – Commission internationale de normalisation des coloris pour les industries textiles et mode*. Current name adopted at General Assembly, 1 Aug 1972, Paris. Articles amended 27 Jan 1978. Registered in accordance with French law. Registration: Start date: 30 Aug 1973, France. **Structure** General Assembly (annual); Management Committee; Experts' Committee. **Languages** English, French, German. **Finance** Members' dues. **Activities** Events/meetings. **Events** *Meeting* Paris (France) 2021, *Meeting* Copenhagen (Denmark) 2020, *Meeting* Cologne (Germany) 2019, *Meeting* Orlando, FL (USA) 2019, *Meeting* Marseille (France) 2018.

Members National coordinating bodies in 17 countries:
China, Denmark, Finland, France, Germany, Hungary, Indonesia, Italy, Japan, Korea Rep, Portugal, Spain, Switzerland, Thailand, Türkiye, UK, USA. [2020/XD4559/**D**]

- ♦ Commission internationale du Danube (inactive)

Commission Internationale Définition
04218
alphabetic sequence excludes
For the complete listing, see Yearbook Online at

- Commission Internationale pour la Définition des Caractéristiques Microbiologiques des Aliments (#12703)
- Commission internationale de démographie historique (#12684)
- Commission internationale de diplomatique (see: #12777)
- Commission internationale pour les droits des gais et des lesbiennes / see OutRight Action International
- Commission internationale pour les droits des peuples indigènes (#12726)

♦ Commission Internationale de l'Eclairage (CIE) 04219

International Commission on Illumination – Internationale Beleuchtungskommission

Gen Sec Babenbergerstrasse 9/9A, 1010 Vienna, Austria. T. +4317143187. E-mail: ciecb@cie.co.at.
URL: http://www.cie.co.at/

History 1900, Paris (France). Former names and other names: *Commission internationale de photométrie* – former (1900 to 1913). **Aims** Provide an international forum for the discussion of all matters relating to science, technology and art in the fields of *light* and *lighting*; develop basic standards and procedures of metrology; provide guidance in the application of the basic principles and procedures to the development of international and national standards; prepare and publish reports, recommendations and standards and maintain liaison and technical interaction with other international organizations concerned with matters relating to science, technology and art in the fields of light and lighting. **Structure** General Assembly; Board of Administration; Central Bureau. Divisions (6) with Technical Committees (about 100). Meetings open. **Languages** English, French, German. **Staff** 3.00 FTE, paid. Many voluntary. **Finance** Sources: members' dues. **Activities** Events/ meetings; research/documentation; standards/guidelines. **Events** *Quadriennial Session and Conference* Ljubljana (Slovenia) 2023, *Quadrennial Plenary Session* Washington, DC (USA) 2019, *Midterm Meeting* Jeju (Korea Rep) 2017, *Quadrennial Plenary Session* Manchester (UK) 2015, *Symposium on Measurement Uncertainties in Photometry and Radiometry for Industry* Vienna (Austria) 2014. **Publications** *CIE News* (4 a year). *International Lighting Vocabulary* – in 9 languages. Technical reports; Standards; Session proceedings.
Members National committees in 36 countries and territories:
Australia, Austria, Belgium, Brazil, Bulgaria, Canada, China, Czechia, Denmark, Finland, France, Germany, Greece, Hong Kong, Hungary, Israel, Italy, Japan, Korea Rep, Malaysia, Netherlands, New Zealand, Norway, Poland, Romania, Russia, Serbia, Slovakia, Slovenia, South Africa, Spain, Sweden, Switzerland, Türkiye, UK, USA.
Association national members in 2 countries and territories:
Saudi Arabia, Taiwan.
Associate members in 17 countries:
Belarus, Botswana, Congo Brazzaville, Eritrea, Ethiopia, Grenada, Jordan, Kenya, Moldova, Nigeria, Rwanda, Seychelles, St Lucia, Thailand, Uganda, United Arab Emirates, Uruguay.
Consultative Status Consultative status granted from: *ECOSOC (#05331)* (Ros C); *ILO (#11123)* (Special List); *International Civil Aviation Organization (ICAO, #12581)*. **IGO Relations** Cooperates with (1): *United Nations Economic Commission for Europe (UNECE, #20555)*. Associated with Department of Global Communications of the United Nations. **NGO Relations** Member of (1): *International Science Council (ISC, #14796)*. In liaison with technical committees of: *International Electrotechnical Commission (IEC, #13255)*; *International Organization for Standardization (ISO, #14473)*. Liaises with: *IAU Commission on Protection of Existing and Potential Observatory Sites*; *International Association of Marine Aids to Navigation and Lighthouse Authorities (IALA, #12013)*; *International Astronomical Union (IAU, #12287)*; *International Colour Association (AIC, #12655)*; *International Commission for Optics (ICO, #12710)*; *International Council for Research and Innovation in Building and Construction (CIB, #13069)*; *International Union of Pure and Applied Physics (IUPAP, #15810)*.
[2022/XC1561/**C**]

- Commission internationale pour l'édition des sources de l'histoire européenne (no recent information)
- Commission internationale de l'éducation par le cinématographe et la radiodiffusion (inactive)
- Commission internationale sur l'éducation en physique (#12714)
- Commission internationale sur les effets biologiques du bruit (#12668)
- Commission internationale de l'Elbe (inactive)
- Commission internationale de l'Electricité Atmosphérique (#12665)
- Commission internationale de l'électricité atmosphérique de l'AIMPA / see International Commission on Atmospheric Electricity (#12665)
- Commission internationale sur l'électronique quantique / see International Commission on Laser Physics and Photonics (#12697)
- Commission internationale pour l'embellissement de la vie rurale (inactive)
- Commission internationale pour l'emploi de l'anglais dans la liturgie (#12681)
- Commission internationale d'enquête des Nations Unies sur les livraisons d'armes illicites dans la région des Grands Lacs (inactive)
- Commission internationale de l'enseignement agricole (inactive)
- Commission internationale de l'enseignement en biologie / see IUBS Commission for Biological Education (#16079)
- Commission internationale de l'enseignement mathématique (#12700)
- Commission internationale de l'Escaut (#12727)
- Commission internationale des étalons de radium (inactive)
- Commission internationale de l'état civil (#12671)
- Commission internationale pour l'étude et l'amélioration de l'enseignement des mathématiques (#12732)
- Commission internationale pour l'étude et l'amélioration des mathématiques / see International Commission for the Study and Improvement of Mathematics Teaching (#12732)
- Commission internationale pour l'étude chimique du sol (inactive)
- Commission internationale pour l'étude mécanique du sol (inactive)
- Commission internationale d'étude des problèmes de la communication (inactive)
- Commission internationale pour l'étude scientifique de la famille (inactive)

♦ Commission internationale des études historiques slaves (CIEHS) . 04220

International Commission of Slavic Historical Studies

SG c/o GWZO, Specks Hof – Eingang A, Reichsstrasse 4-6, 04109 Leipzig, Germany. T. +493419735572.
Pres Univ of Milan, Via Festa del Perdono 7, 20122 Milan MI, Italy.

History 13 Jun 1952, Brussels (Belgium), as a commission of ICHS. Also referred to as *International Commission for Slavonic Studies – Commission internationale des études slaves*. **Aims** Encourage research into the history and culture of the Slavs in Central and Eastern Europe and their relations with other parts of the world. **Structure** General Assembly (every 5 years at Conference); Bureau. **Languages** English, French. **Staff** Voluntary. **Finance** Members' fees. Occasional subventions from research institutions for selected events and publications. **Activities** Events/meetings; training/education. **Events** *Conference* Milan (Italy) 2018, *Meeting* Oslo (Norway) 2000, *Meeting* Vienna (Austria) 1998, *The consequences of the partitions of Poland and the Slavic world before 1918* Montréal, QC (Canada) 1995, *The nations of East-Central Europe in the 19th and 20th centuries; coexistence, tension and conflict* Poznań (Poland) 1992. **Publications** *Approaches to Slavic Unity: Austro-Slavism, Pan-Slavism, Neo-Slavism, and Solidarity Among the Slavs Today* (2013); *Rewriting Slavic History* (2009). **Members** Specialists in the history and culture of the Slavs with a regional focus on Central and Eastern Europe. Membership countries not specified. **NGO Relations** Affiliate member of: *International Committee of Historical Sciences (ICHS, #12777)*. [2019/XD1528/v/**E**]

- Commission internationale d'études de normalisation comptable économique (inactive)
- Commission internationale des études slaves / see Commission internationale des études historiques slaves (#04220)
- Commission internationale des examens de conduite automobile (#12678)
- Commission internationale pour l'exploration scientifique de l'Atlantique (inactive)
- Commission internationale pour l'exploration scientifique de la Mer Méditerranée (#16674)
- Commission internationale du flétan du Pacifique (internationally oriented national body)
- Commission internationale du génie rural (#12661)
- Commission internationale de géographie historique (inactive)
- Commission internationale des glaciers (inactive)
- Commission internationale des grands barrages (#12696)
- Commission internationale pour l'histoire des assemblées d'Etats (#12689)
- Commission Internationale d'Histoire Ecclésiastique Comparée / see Commission Internationale d'Histoire et d'Etudes du Christianisme (#04221)

♦ Commission Internationale d'Histoire et d'Etudes du Christianisme (CIHEC) 04221

Pres CTR, Lund Univ, Box 192, SE-221 00 Lund, Sweden. T. +46462229037 – +4646(46317780701.
URL: http://www.cihec.org/

History Originally set up in 1930s, but activities ceased because of World War II. Refounded 1955, Rome (Italy), when it became affiliated to *International Committee of Historical Sciences (ICHS, #12777)*. Original title: *Commission Internationale d'Histoire Ecclésiastique Comparée*. **Aims** Facilitate contact and exchange of information between historians of Christianity working in different countries. **Structure** International Bureau. **Languages** English, French, German, Spanish. **Staff** 12.00 FTE, paid. **Finance** Members' dues. **Activities** Events/meetings. **Events** *General Assembly* Jinan (China) 2015, *Conference* Ljubljana (Slovenia) 2015, *Conference* Trogir (Croatia) 2014, *Conference* Vilnius (Lithuania) 2013, *Conference* Tartu (Estonia) 2012.
Members National commissions in 33 countries:
Australia, Austria, Belarus, Belgium, Croatia, Cyprus, Czechia, Denmark, Estonia, Finland, France, Germany, Holy See, Hungary, Ireland, Israel, Italy, Lithuania, Netherlands, Norway, Poland, Portugal, Romania, Russia, Slovakia, Slovenia, South Africa, Spain, Sweden, Switzerland, UK, Ukraine, USA.
NGO Relations Affiliated to: *International Committee of Historical Sciences (ICHS, #12777)*.
[2017.01.07/XD7861/**E**]

- Commission internationale d'Histoire littéraire moderne / see International Federation for Modern Languages and Literatures (#13480)
- Commission internationale d'histoire des littératures modernes / see International Federation for Modern Languages and Literatures (#13480)
- Commission internationale d'histoire militaire (#12705)
- Commission internationale d'histoire militaire comparée / see International Commission of Military History (#12705)
- Commission internationale d'histoire des relations internationales / see Commission of History of International Relations (#04217)

♦ Commission internationale d'histoire de la Révolution française (CIHRF) 04222

International Commission for the History of the French Revolution

SG/Treas Uni Leipzig – Global and Eur Studies Inst, Emil-Fuchs-Str 1, 04105 Leipzig, Germany.
Pres Hitotsubashi Univ, 2-1 Naka, Kunitachi, Tokyo, 186-8601 Japan. E-mail: kyamaz@xb3.so-net.ne.jp.
URL: http://www.cihrf.org/

History Aug 1975, San Francisco CA (USA), as *Commission internationale de la Révolution française*. Statutes revised 30 Aug 1985, Stuttgart (Germany FR); 2006. **Aims** Study revolutions all over the world, particularly the revolutions which took place in France between 1780 and 1830. **Structure** Bureau. **Languages** English, French. **Finance** Members' dues. **Activities** Projects/programmes. **Events** *Colloquium* Jinan (China) 2015, *Colloquium* Vizille (France) 2014, *Colloquium* Amsterdam (Netherlands) 2010, *Colloquium* Grenoble (France) / Leipzig (Germany) 2009, *De la guerre et du droit pendant la Révolution française (1789-1802)* Sydney, NSW (Australia) 2005. **Publications** *The Routledge Companion to the French Revolution in World History* (2015); *Révolution française – French Revolution – Französische Revolution*. Meeting reports.
Members Individuals in 16 countries:
Australia, Austria, Belgium, Canada, China, France, Germany, Italy, Japan, Mexico, Norway, Russia, Spain, Sweden, UK, USA.
NGO Relations Member of: *International Committee of Historical Sciences (ICHS, #12777)*.
[2018.09.05/XD8471/v/**E**]

- Commission internationale pour l'histoire de la Révolution d'octobre en Russie / see International Commission on the History of the Russian Revolution (#12688)
- Commission internationale pour l'histoire de la Révolution russe (#12688)
- Commission internationale d'histoire des sciences géologiques (#12685)

♦ Commission internationale pour l'histoire des universités (CIHU) .. 04223

International Commission for the History of Universities

SG CP 8888 Succ Centre-Ville, Montréal QC H3C 3P8, Canada. T. +15149873000ext8457.
Pres CA Inst of Technology, Humanities / Social Sciences, MC 101-40, Pasadena CA 91125, USA. T. +16263958696.
URL: http://www.cihu-ichu.org/

History Founded 1960, Stockholm (Sweden), by S Stelling-Michaud. **Aims** Promote all forms of historical research on universities and to ensure international coordination of the same, in conjunction with the International Committee of Historical Sciences. **Structure** Commission comprises 1 to 4 representatives of each member country, depending on size of country. **Languages** English. **Finance** Members' dues. **Activities** Events/meetings. **Events** *Meeting* Copenhagen (Denmark) 2015, *Meeting* Messina (Italy) 2014, *Meeting* St Andrews (UK) 2012, *Meeting* Oslo (Norway) 2011, *Meeting* Budapest (Hungary) 2010. **Publications** Bibliographies (irregular).
Members Individuals in 23 countries and territories:
Austria, Belgium, Canada, Czechia, Denmark, Finland, France, Hungary, Iceland, Ireland, Italy, Mexico, Netherlands, Norway, Portugal, Romania, Russia, Spain, Sweden, Switzerland, Taiwan, UK, USA. [2017.03.09/XE7820/v/**E**]

- Commission internationale pour l'histoire des villes (#12691)
- Commission internationale sur l'histoire du voyage et du tourisme (#12692)
- Commission internationale humanitaire d'établissement des faits (#13820)
- Commission internationale de l'hydrologie du bassin du Rhin (#12693)
- Commission internationale des industries agricoles et alimentaires (inactive)
- Commission internationale des irrigations et des canaux / see International Commission on Irrigation and Drainage (#12694)
- Commission internationale des irrigations et du drainage (#12694)
- Commission internationale de juristes (#12695)
- Commission internationale de lutte biologique contre les ennemis des cultures / see International Organisation for Biological Control (#14424)
- Commission internationale sur magnétisme (#12699)

♦ Commission internationale de marketing 04224

International Marketing Commission

Address not obtained.

History 1971, Paris (France). **Structure** Executive Committee, appointed by Senate, comprising representatives of member organizations. Regional Directors, appointed by Executive Council. **Languages** English, French. **Finance** Members' dues. **Activities** Organizes World Economic Development Congress. **Events** *Congress* Washington, DC (USA) 1993, *International marketing, technology and industrial innovation, worldwide cooperation between enterprises and research institutions* Shanghai (China) 1991. **Publications** *Journal of International Marketing and Marketing Research*.
Members Full in 51 countries and territories:
Argentina, Australia, Belgium, Brazil, Canada, China, Croatia, Czechia, Denmark, Egypt, Estonia, Finland, France, Germany, Greece, Guatemala, Hong Kong, Hungary, India, Indonesia, Iran Islamic Rep, Ireland, Italy, Japan, Kenya, Korea Rep, Kuwait, Luxembourg, Malaysia, Netherlands, New Zealand, Norway, Pakistan, Peru, Philippines, Poland, Portugal, Romania, Russia, Serbia, Singapore, Slovenia, South Africa, Spain, Sweden, Switzerland, Türkiye, UK, Uruguay, USA, Venezuela.
NGO Relations *European Marketing Association (EMA, #07746)* is a member. [2010.06.01/XE1611/**E**]

- Commission internationale de la météorologie de l'atmosphère haute / see International Commission on Middle Atmosphere Science (#12704)
- Commission internationale de la météorologie de l'atmosphère haute de l'AIMPA / see International Commission on Middle Atmosphere Science (#12704)
- Commission internationale de la météorologie dynamique (#12679)
- Commission internationale de la météorologie dynamique de l'AIMSA / see International Commission on Dynamical Meteorology (#12679)

- Commission internationale de météorologie maritime (inactive)
- Commission internationale de la météorologie polaire (#12718)
- Commission internationale de la météorologie polaire de l'AOMPA / see International Commission on Polar Meteorology (#12718)
- Commission internationale des méthodes d'analyse des pesticides (#04099)
- Commission internationale de la Meuse (#12702)

♦ Commission internationale de microflore du paléozoïque (CIMP) .. 04225

International Commission on Palaeozoic Microflora

Pres GeoResources STC, Hansastr 1, 69181 Leimen, Germany.

Dir at Large School of Earth and Environmental Sciences, Burnaby Bldg, Burnaby Road, Portsmouth, PO1 3QL, UK.

URL: https://cimp.weebly.com/

History 1958, Heerlen (Netherlands), by *International Congress of Carboniferous and Permian Stratigraphy and Geology* and Commission of Carboniferous Stratigraphy. **Aims** Constitute a forum for Palaeozoic *Palynology*. **Structure** Board, comprising President, Secretary General, Treasurer, Webmaster and 2 IFPS Officers. Subcommissions (3): Acritarch; Chitinozoa; Spores and Pollen. **Languages** English, French. **Staff** 6.00 FTE, voluntary. **Finance** Members' dues. **Activities** Organizes conferences and symposia. **Events** *Meeting* Nottingham (UK) 2017, *Meeting* Bergen (Norway) 2015, *General Meeting* Warsaw (Poland) / Kielce (Poland) 2010, *Session / Meeting* Bonn (Germany) 2008, *Joint meeting* Lisbon (Portugal) 2007. **Publications** *CIMP Newsletter*, *GeoArabia*; *Pal 3* – Palaeogeography, Palaeoclimatology, Palaeoecology; *Review of Palaeontology and Palynology*.

Members Individuals in 61 countries and territories:
Algeria, Argentina, Australia, Austria, Belarus, Belgium, Bolivia, Botswana, Brazil, Bulgaria, Canada, China, Czechia, Denmark, Egypt, Estonia, Finland, France, Germany, Ghana, Hungary, India, Indonesia, Iran Islamic Rep, Iraq, Ireland, Israel, Italy, Japan, Latvia, Libya, Madagascar, Malaysia, Mexico, Morocco, Netherlands, New Zealand, Nigeria, Norway, Oman, Pakistan, Poland, Qatar, Romania, Russia, Saudi Arabia, Slovakia, South Africa, Spain, Sudan, Sweden, Switzerland, Taiwan, Tunisia, Türkiye, UK, Ukraine, United Arab Emirates, Uruguay, USA, Venezuela.

NGO Relations Affiliated as a constituent body of: *International Federation of Palynological Societies (IFPS, #13498)*. [2020/XE5544/v/**E**]

- Commission internationale de la Moselle / see Moselle Commission (#16857)
- Commission internationale de natation travailliste (inactive)
- Commission internationale de navigation aérienne (inactive)
- Commission internationale pour la navigation sur le Congo (inactive)
- Commission internationale pour la nomenclature des espèces végétales cultivées (see: #15760)
- Commission internationale de nomenclature zoologique (#12737)
- Commission internationale de normalisation des coloris pour les industries textiles et mode / see Commission internationale pour la couleur dans la mode et le textile (#04218)
- Commission internationale des nuages (inactive)
- Commission internationale des nuages et des précipitations (#12672)
- Commission internationale de numismatique / see International Numismatic Council (#14385)
- Commission internationale de l'Oder (inactive)
- Commission internationale des oeufs (#13245)
- Commission Internationale d'Optique (#12710)

♦ Commission internationale pour organisation scientifique du travail en agriculture (CIOSTA) 04226

International Committee of Work Study and Labour Management in Agriculture

Pres 2009-2011 DiSTAfA, Località Feo di Vito, 89122 Calabria IM, Italy. E-mail: gzimbalatti@unirc.it.

History 1950, Paris (France). **Aims** Develop the agricultural economy with a view to augmenting agricultural production, yield and quality, safety and ergonomics in agriculture. **Structure** General Assembly (every 2 years, at Congress). President and Secretariat rotate with Congress. **Languages** English. **Staff** 19.00 FTE, paid. **Finance** Congress expenses assumed by the national host group. **Activities** are related to the biennial Congress. Research groups: work science in agriculture; farm and agro-food logistics; food processing and storage; safety and ergonomics in agriculture, landscaping; organic farming; precision agriculture; decision support systems for farmers; agro-food traceability; machinery and robotics in agriculture. Education and advisory working groups. **Events** *Congress* St Petersburg (Russia) 2015, *Efficient and safe production processes in sustainable agriculture and forestry* Vienna (Austria) 2011, *Congress* Calabria (Italy) 2009, *Congress* Nitra (Slovakia) 2007, *Increasing work efficiency in agriculture, horticulture and forestry* Stuttgart (Germany) 2005. **Publications** *Index on Farm Work Science* (annual) – with CIGR. Congress reports.

Members Associations of specialists in 41 countries:
Austria, Belgium, Brazil, Bulgaria, Canada, China, Colombia, Cuba, Czechia, Denmark, Estonia, Finland, France, Germany, Hungary, India, Indonesia, Iran Islamic Rep, Ireland, Israel, Italy, Japan, Korea Rep, Netherlands, Nigeria, Norway, Poland, Portugal, Russia, Serbia, Slovakia, Slovenia, South Africa, Spain, Sweden, Switzerland, Türkiye, Uganda, UK, USA, Zimbabwe.

NGO Relations Joint publication with: *International Commission of Agricultural and Biosystems Engineering (#12661)*. [2011/XD1616/**F**]

- Commission internationale de l'ozone (#14495)
- Commission internationale de l'ozone de l'AIMSA / see International Ozone Commission (#14495)
- Commission internationale pour la paix dans l'esprit des hommes (no recent information)
- Commission internationale sur les particules et champs (#12712)
- Commission internationale de la pastorale catholique des prisons (#12670)
- Commission internationale des pêcheries de saumon du Pacifique (inactive)
- Commission internationale des pêches de l'Atlantique Nord-Ouest (inactive)
- Commission internationale des pêches de l'Atlantique Sud-Est (inactive)
- Commission internationale des pêches de la Baltique (internationally oriented national body)
- Commission internationale des pêches du Pacifique Nord (inactive)
- Commission internationale pénale et pénitentiaire (inactive)
- Commission internationale permanente des associations agricoles (inactive)
- Commission internationale permanente des congrès d'archivistes et de bibliothécaires (inactive)
- Commission internationale permanente des congrès internationaux d'électrologie et de radiologie médicales (inactive)
- Commission internationale permanente des congrès internationaux des sciences administratives (inactive)

♦ Commission internationale permanente pour l'épreuve des armes à feu portatives (CIP) 04227

Permanent International Commission for the Proof of Small Arms

Sec Ecole Royale Militaire, Avenue de la Renaissance 30, 1000 Brussels, Belgium. T. +3224413929. Fax +3224439182.

URL: http://www.cip-bobp.org/

History 1914, Liège (Belgium), on the initiative of Joseph Fraikin. **Aims** Compare *firearms* to determine specifications for small arms; determine the number, type and characteristics of tests needed to establish each category of small arms; study related issues. **Structure** Permanent Bureau. **Events** *Biennial plenary session* Lyon (France) 2018, *Biennial Plenary Session* Santiago (Chile) 2016, *Biennial plenary session* Brussels (Belgium) 2014, *Biennial plenary session* Moscow (Russia) 1998, *Biennial plenary session* Ischia (Italy) 1996.

Members Individuals in 13 countries:
Austria, Belgium, Chile, Czechia, Finland, France, Germany, Hungary, Italy, Russia, Slovakia, Spain, UK.

NGO Relations In liaison with technical committees of: *International Organization for Standardization (ISO, #14473)*. [2018/XF2870/v/**F**]

- Commission internationale permanente pour l'étude des maladies professionnelles / see International Commission on Occupational Health (#12709)
- Commission internationale permanente pour l'étude des problèmes concernant l'enfant et le cinéma (inactive)
- Commission internationale permanente d'études de matériel sanitaire (inactive)
- Commission internationale permanente d'études des ordres de chevalerie (#12711)
- Commission internationale permanente pour la médecine du travail / see International Commission on Occupational Health (#12709)
- Commission internationale permanente pour la reproduction des manuscrits, des médailles et des sceaux (inactive)
- Commission internationale permanente de viticulture (inactive)
- Commission internationale du pétrole (inactive)
- Commission internationale du peuplier (#14619)
- Commission internationale du phare du Cap Spartel (inactive)
- Commission internationale de photométrie / see Commission Internationale de l'Eclairage (#04219)
- Commission internationale de photométrie (inactive)
- Commission internationale sur la physique atomique, moléculaire et optique (#12666)
- Commission internationale sur la physique atomique et moléculaire et la spectroscopie / see International Commission on Atomic, Molecular and Optical Physics (#12666)
- Commission internationale sur la physique pour le développement (#12713)
- Commission internationale sur la physique mathématique (#12701)
- Commission internationale sur la physique nucléaire (#12708)
- Commission internationale sur la physique des plasmas (#12717)
- Commission internationale sur la physique des très basses températures (#12698)
- Commission internationale de la phytopharmacie (inactive)
- Commission internationale de police criminelle / see International Criminal Police Organization – INTERPOL (#13110)
- Commission internationale pour la prévention de l'alcoolisme (#12719)
- Commission internationale pour la protection des Alpes / see CIPRA International (#03930)
- Commission internationale pour la protection contre les mutagènes et les carcinogènes présents dans l'environnement (inactive)
- Commission internationale de protection contre les radiations (#12724)
- Commission internationale de protection contre les rayonnements non-ionisants (#12707)
- Commission internationale pour la protection des eaux du lac de Constance contre la pollution / see Internationale Gewässerschutzkommission für den Bodensee (#13244)
- Commission Internationale pour la Protection des Eaux du Léman (internationally oriented national body)
- Commission internationale pour la protection de l'Escaut / see International Commission of the Schelde River (#12727)
- Commission internationale pour la protection du lac de Constance (#13244)
- Commission internationale pour la protection de la Meuse / see International Commission of the Meuse (#12702)
- Commission internationale pour la protection de la Moselle (inactive)
- Commission internationale pour la protection de l'Oder (#13250)
- Commission internationale pour la protection des planètes contre les microbes de la terre (inactive)
- Commission internationale de protection en radiologie / see International Commission on Radiological Protection (#12724)
- Commission internationale pour la protection des régions alpines / see CIPRA International (#03930)
- Commission internationale pour la protection du Rhin (#12721)
- Commission internationale pour la protection du Rhin contre la pollution / see International Commission for the Protection of the Rhine (#12721)
- Commission internationale pour la protection de la Sarre (inactive)
- Commission internationale des radiations (#14684)
- Commission internationale des radiations de l'AIMPA / see International Radiation Commission (#14684)
- Commission internationale de la radiation solaire (inactive)
- Commission internationale sur les rayons cosmiques / see International Commission on Astroparticle Physics (#12663)
- Commission internationale de réflexion pédagogique et pastorale (see: #15589)
- Commission internationale de réglementation en vue de l'approbation de l'équipement électrique / see IEC System of Conformity Assessment Schemes for Electrotechnical Equipment and Components (#11096)
- Commission internationale des relations du couple et de la famille (#12676)
- Commission internationale sur la relativité générale et la gravitation (#15138)
- Commission internationale pour la revision décennale des nomenclatures nosologiques (inactive)
- Commission internationale pour la révision de la nomenclature des causes de décès (inactive)
- Commission internationale de la Révolution française / see Commission internationale d'histoire de la Révolution française (#04222)
- Commission internationale du riz (inactive)
- Commission internationale de la santé du travail (#12709)
- Commission internationale de sauvetage alpin (#12662)
- Commission internationale sur les semiconducteurs (#12728)
- Commission internationale de standardisation du matériel sanitaire (inactive)
- Commission internationale sur la structure et la dynamique de la matière condensée (#12731)

♦ Commission internationale de surveillance, de contrôle et d'arbitrage (CISCA) 04228

International Supervision, Control and Arbitration Commission

Pres Universidade do Minho, Pavilhao Desportivo Universitario, Campus de Gualtar, 4710 Braga, Portugal. T. +351253604122. Fax +351253678956.

NGO Relations *International University Sports Federation (FISU, #15830)*. [2010/XE0293/**E**]

- Commission internationale sur les symboles, les unités, la nomenclature, les masses atomiques et les constantes fondamentales (#12733)
- Commission internationale technique de sucrerie (inactive)
- Commission internationale de télégraphie météorologique (inactive)
- Commission internationale de télégraphie sans fil / see Union radio-scientifique internationale (#20475)
- Commission internationale des Tests / see International Test Commission (#15677)

♦ Commission internationale du théâtre francophone (CITF) 04229

General Secretariat 62 rue Beaubourg, 75003 Paris, France. E-mail: focuscitf@gmail.com.

URL: http://www.citf-info.net/

History 1987. **Aims** Support French-speaking artistic and theatrical projects. **Structure** Co-Presidency; General Secretariat rotates between members. **Languages** French. **Staff** None. **Finance** Support from: Canada; France; Luxembourg; Québec (Canada); Valais (Switzerland); Wallonie-Bruxelles (Belgium). **Activities** Events/meetings; projects/programmes. **Events** *Meeting* Liège (Belgium) 1992.

Members Full in 5 countries:
Belgium, Canada, France, Luxembourg, Switzerland. [2019.12.12/XF3507/**F**]

- Commission internationale pour la traduction des chefs d'oeuvres (inactive)
- Commission internationale de la trichinellose (#12735)
- Commission internationale pour l'unification de la cartographie agrogéologique (inactive)
- Commission internationale d'unification des méthodes d'analyse des denrées alimentaires (inactive)
- Commission internationale pour l'unification des méthodes d'analyse du sucre (#12736)
- Commission internationale des unités et des mesures de radiation (#12722)
- Commission internationale d'utilisation du bois (inactive)
- Commission internationale du verre (#12683)
- Commission international de l'histoire et de la théorie de l'historiographie (#12690)
- Commission for International Justice and Accountability (unconfirmed)
- Commission for International Notarial Cooperation (see: #15795)

- ♦ Commission interparlementaire centroaméricaine (inactive)
- ♦ Commission intersyndicale des déshydrateurs européens (#06896)
- ♦ Commission jumelée pour la classification de la littérature agricole (inactive)
- ♦ Commission juridique pour l'auto-développement des peuples autochtones des Andes (#04139)
- ♦ Commission justice et paix (internationally oriented national body)
- ♦ Commission justice, paix, intégrité de la création des Unions des supérieurs généraux – USG/UISG (#04230)
- ♦ Commission for Justice and Peace (internationally oriented national body)
- ♦ Commission for Justice, Peace, Integrity of Creation of the Unions of Superiors General – USG/UISG / see Commission for Justice, Peace and Integrity of Creation – USG/UISG (#04230)

♦ Commission for Justice, Peace and Integrity of Creation – USG/UISG 04230

Commission justice, paix, intégrité de la création des Unions des supérieurs généraux – USG/UISG – Comisión Justicia, Paz, Integridad de la Creación de las Uniones de Superiores Generales – USG/UISG – Commissione Giustizia, Pace, Integrità del Creato delle Unioni dei Superiori Generali – USG/UISG

Main Office CPPS, Via Aurelia 476, CP 9099 Aurelio, 00167 Rome RM, Italy. T. +3966622929. Fax +3966622929. E-mail: secretariat@jpicroma.org – jpic.roma@gmail.com.
URL: https://jpicroma.org/

History 1974. Founded as a *'Joint Working Group for Justice and Peace'*, by *International Union of Superiors General (#15820)* and *Union of Superiors General (#20484)*. Became more formalized and adopted the title *Justice and Peace Commission of the USG/UISG* in 1982; subsequently re-organized in 1987 and 1992. Current title adopted 2002. Former names and other names: *Commission for Justice, Peace, Integrity of Creation of the Unions of Superiors General – USG/UISG (JPIC)* – former (1974); *Joint Working Group for Justice and Peace* – former; *Justice and Peace Commission of the USG/UISG* – former. **Aims** Provide information, resources, and opportunities for USG and UISG members in their efforts to educate their members in the values of justice, peace and integrity of creation and how to integrate them into training programmes; facilitate mutual sharing, express solidarity with and assist in network building among *religious congregations* and institutes which require support; encourage and facilitate corporate action on justice, peace, integrity of creation concerns initiated by JPIC promoters, individual congregations as well as the Unions themselves. **Structure** Commission (meets twice a year). **Languages** English, French, Italian, Portuguese, Spanish. **Staff** 2.00 FTE, paid. Voluntary. **Finance** Members' dues. **Activities** Knowledge management/information dissemination; publishing activities; events/meetings; training/education. **Publications** *JPIC Newsbriefs* (10 a year) in English, Spanish; *JPIC E-News* in English, Spanish – weekly.

Members The two Unions for whom the Commission works count over 2,000 Orders, Congregations and Religious Institutes, which represent about 1 million religious worldwide. Generalates of Congregations, Religious Orders and Religious Institutes are located in 152 countries and territories:
Albania, Algeria, Angola, Argentina, Armenia, Australia, Austria, Bangladesh, Belgium, Benin, Bolivia, Bosnia-Herzegovina, Botswana, Brazil, Bulgaria, Burkina Faso, Burundi, Cambodia, Cameroon, Canada, Cape Verde, Central African Rep, Chad, Chile, China, Colombia, Comoros, Congo Brazzaville, Congo DR, Costa Rica, Côte d'Ivoire, Croatia, Cuba, Cyprus, Czechia, Denmark, Dominica, Dominican Rep, Ecuador, Egypt, El Salvador, Equatorial Guinea, Eritrea, Estonia, Eswatini, Ethiopia, Fiji, Finland, France, Gabon, Gambia, Germany, Ghana, Greece, Guatemala, Guinea, Guinea-Bissau, Guyana, Haiti, Honduras, Hong Kong, Hungary, Iceland, India, Indonesia, Iran Islamic Rep, Iraq, Ireland, Israel, Italy, Jamaica, Japan, Jordan, Kenya, Korea Rep, Laos, Lebanon, Lesotho, Liberia, Luxembourg, Madagascar, Malawi, Malaysia, Mali, Malta, Marshall Is, Mauritania, Mexico, Micronesia FS, Mongolia, Morocco, Mozambique, Myanmar, Namibia, Nepal, Netherlands, New Zealand, Nicaragua, Niger, Nigeria, North Macedonia, Norway, Pakistan, Palestine, Panama, Papua New Guinea, Paraguay, Peru, Philippines, Poland, Portugal, Puerto Rico, Romania, Russia, Rwanda, Samoa, Sao Tomé-Principe, Senegal, Serbia, Seychelles, Sierra Leone, Singapore, Slovakia, Slovenia, Solomon Is, Somalia, South Africa, Spain, Sri Lanka, Sudan, Suriname, Sweden, Switzerland, Syrian AR, Taiwan, Tanzania UR, Thailand, Togo, Tonga, Trinidad-Tobago, Tunisia, Türkiye, Uganda, UK, Uruguay, USA, Vanuatu, Venezuela, Vietnam, Zambia, Zimbabwe. [2022/XE7739/**E**]

♦ Commission for Labor Cooperation 04231

Commission de coopération dans le domaine du travail – Comisión para la Cooperación Laboral

Contact address not obtained. T. +12024641107 – +12024641100. Fax +12024649490.
URL: http://www.naalc.org/

History following the signing of *North American Agreement on Labour Cooperation (NAALC, 1993)*. **Aims** Provide information and promote wider understanding of North American labour matters. **Structure** Secretariat; Ministerial Council. **Languages** English, French, Spanish. **Finance** Members' dues. **Activities** Undertakes research and analysis; prepares public reports; organizes seminars. **Publications** *North American Labor Markets – a Comparative Profile* (2nd ed 2001); *North American Labor Relations Law – a Comparative Guide to the Labor Relations Laws in Canada, Mexico and the United States* (2nd ed 2000); *Guide to Labor and Employment Laws for Migrant Workers in North America*. Annual Report; research reports; conference proceedings; books.

Members Full in 3 countries:
Canada, Mexico, USA. [2008/XE3843/**E**]

- ♦ Commission of Latin American and Caribbean Banking Supervisory and Inspection Organizations / see Association of Supervisors of Banks of the Americas (#02944)
- ♦ Commission latinoaméricaine des fonctionnaires des services publics / see Coordinadora Latinoamericana de Trabajadores de los Servicios Públicos (#04809)
- ♦ Commission latinoaméricaine des travailleurs de l'énergie (inactive)
- ♦ Commission de liaison des associations et organismes de prévention routière / see La Prévention Routière Internationale (#18493)
- ♦ Commission de Liaison Inter-Nations Mars et Mercure / see Mars and Mercury Europe – Industrial and Commercial Circles of Officers and Reserve Officers Inter-Nations Coordination Commission (#16589)
- ♦ Commission de liaison des OINGs dotées du statut participatif auprès du Conseil de l'Europe / see Conference of INGOs of the Council of Europe (#04607)
- ♦ Commission de liaison des ONGs dotées du statut consultatif auprès du Conseil de l'Europe / see Conference of INGOs of the Council of Europe (#04607)
- ♦ Commission de liaison des ONGs dotées du statut participatif auprès du Conseil de l'Europe / see Conference of INGOs of the Council of Europe (#04607)

♦ Commission on the Limits of the Continental Shelf (CLCS) 04232

Contact Dir of Div for Ocean Affairs / Law of the Sea, Office of Legal Affairs, Two UN Plaza Room DC2-0450, United Nations, New York NY 10017, USA. T. +12129633962. Fax +19173670560. E-mail: doalos@un.org.
URL: http://www.un.org/Depts/los/clcs_new/clcs_home.htm

History Established under *United Nations Convention on the Law of the Sea (UNCLOS, 1982)*, in conformity with annex II to the Convention. **Aims** As a technical body of experts, consider data and other material submitted by *coastal* states concerning the outer limits of the continental shelf in areas where those limits extend beyond 200 nautical miles, and make recommendations in accordance with article 76 of UNCLOS and the Statement of Understanding adopted on 29 Aug 1980 by Third United Nations Conference on the Law of the Sea; provide scientific and technical advice, if requested by the coastal states concerned during the preparation of the above-mentioned data. **Structure** Sessions (3 a year, at United Nations Headquarters, New York NY, USA) – work is also carried out between sessions. Expert body of 21 members, elected for 5 years by States Parties to UNCLOS. Members are eligible for re-election and serve in their personal capacity. Chairperson; 4 Vice-Chairpersons. Committees (2): Confidentiality; Scientific and Technical Advice to Coastal States. Sub-Commissions of 7 members, established to examine data and other material submitted by coastal states and provide its recommendations to the Commission. Secretariat provided by United Nations Secretary-General. **Languages** Arabic, Chinese, English, French, Russian, Spanish. **Finance** Expenses of the members while in performance of Commission duties are defrayed by the state party which submitted the nomination of the member. Coastal State concerned shall defray expenses incurred in respect of scientific and technical advice provided to it by the Commission. **Events** *Session* New York, NY (USA) 2020, *Session* New York, NY (USA) 2019, *Session* New York, NY (USA) 2019, *Session* New York, NY (USA) 2019, *Session* New York, NY (USA) 2018. **Members** Experts (21), functioning in a personal capacity. [2021.09.20/XE2943/**E***]

♦ Commission on Livestock Development in Latin America and the Caribbean (LDAC) 04233

Comisión de Desarrollo Ganadero para América Latina y el Caribe (CODEGALAC)

Contact FAORLC, Av Dag Hammarskjöld 3241, Vitacura, Santiago, Santiago Metropolitan, Chile.
URL: http://www.rlc.fao.org/

History 1987, by the Council of *FAO (#09260)* at its 92nd Session Resolution 1/92. **Aims** Recommend animal production and *animal health* policies; plan and promote action for improvement of animal production; plan and promote action for survey and control of animal diseases and recommend common standards and practices for this purpose; plan and promote action for transfer and adaptation of *biotechnology* in livestock development and to establish research and educational programmes to meet the needs of the animal industry; determine, in consultation with members concerned, the nature and extent of assistance needed to implement national livestock development programmes; appraise progress reports on implementation and development of the programme. **Structure** Commission (meets every 2 years). **Languages** English, Spanish. **Events** *Biennial Session* Asunción (Paraguay) 2012, *Biennial Session* Panama (Panama) 2011, *Biennial Session* Panama (Panama) / Lima (Peru) / Montevideo (Uruguay) 2001, *Biennial Session* Santiago (Chile) 1998, *Session / Biennial Session* San José (Costa Rica) 1996.

Members Open to all members and associate members of the FAO in Latin America and the Caribbean. Currently the governments of 25 countries:
Argentina, Bahamas, Barbados, Belize, Bolivia, Brazil, Chile, Colombia, Costa Rica, Cuba, Dominican Rep, Ecuador, El Salvador, Guatemala, Haiti, Honduras, Jamaica, Mexico, Nicaragua, Paraguay, Peru, Trinidad-Tobago, Uruguay, USA, Venezuela. [2012/XE1391/**E***]

♦ Commission for Looted Art in Europe 04234

Co-Chair 76 Gloucester Place, London, W1U 6HJ, UK. T. +442074873401. Fax +442074874211.
Co-Chair address not obtained.
General: http://www.lootedartcommission.com/

History Mar 1999, London (UK), as *European Commission on Looted Art*, resulting from the 1998 'Washington Conference on Holocaust-Era Assets'. **Aims** Research, identify and recover looted property on behalf of families, communities, institutions and governments worldwide; negotiate restitution policies and procedures. **Languages** Dutch, English, French, German, Italian, Spanish. **Staff** 8.00 FTE, paid. **Finance** Donations. **Activities** Knowledge management/information dissemination. **Events** *International Conference* London (UK) 2017. **Publications** *Looted Art Newsletter* (weekly) – online. **IGO Relations** *European Commission (EC, #06633)*. [2019.12.11/XE3788/**E**]

- ♦ Commission de lutte contre le criquet pèlerin en Asie du Sud-Ouest (#04209)
- ♦ Commission de lutte contre le criquet pèlerin dans la partie orientale de son aire de répartition en Asie du Sud-Ouest / see Commission for Controlling the Desert Locust in South-West Asia (#04209)
- ♦ Commission de lutte contre le criquet pèlerin au Proche-Orient / see Commission for Controlling the Desert Locust in the Central Region (#04208)
- ♦ Commission de la Méditerranée / see The Mediterranean Science Commission (#16674)
- ♦ Commission de la Mer baltique (#03141)
- ♦ Commission de la Mer du Nord (#17604)
- ♦ Commission mixte des associations des employeurs nordiques (inactive)
- ♦ Commission mixte FAO/OMS du Codex Alimentarius / see Codex Alimentarius Commission (#04081)
- ♦ Commission mixte internationale (internationally oriented national body)
- ♦ Commission mixte internationale du Canada et des Etats-Unis / see International Joint Commission
- ♦ Commission mixte internationale du dialogue entre l'Eglise catholique et la Communion anglicane / see Anglican-Roman Catholic International Commission (#00831)
- ♦ Commission mixte internationale pour la protection des lignes de télécommunications et des canalisations souterraines (inactive)
- ♦ Commission mixte nigéro-nigériane de coopération (internationally oriented national body)
- ♦ Commission mixte permanente Uruguay, Paraguay, Bolivie (inactive)
- ♦ Commission mixte prévue par l'Accord sur les transports routiers entre le Benelux et les Etats baltes (no recent information)
- ♦ Commission mixte sur la radioactivité appliquée (inactive)
- ♦ Commission mixte des stations de recherches en hautes altitudes (inactive)
- ♦ Commission mondiale de la culture et du développement (inactive)
- ♦ Commission mondiale de l'environnement et du développement (inactive)

♦ Commission mondiale d'éthique des connaissances scientifiques et des technologies de l'UNESCO (COMEST) 04235

UNESCO World Commission on the Ethics of Scientific Knowledge and Technology

Main Office Bioethic Ethics of Science Section, 7 place Fontenoy, UNESCO, 75007 Paris, France. T. +33145681000. E-mail: comest@unesco.org.
URL: https://en.unesco.org/themes/ethics-science-and-technology/comest

History 1997. Established by *UNESCO (#20322)*. Statutes adopted at 154th session of UNESCO Executive Board, 7 May 1998. **Aims** Advise UNESCO on the promotion of ethical principles pertaining to scientific and technological progress; raise international awareness and understanding and promote a dialogue between the scientific communities, decision makers and the public at large. **Structure** World Commission comprises 18 eminent scientists and personalities appointed by the Director-General of UNESCO. Bureau, comprising President, 2 Vice-Presidents and Rapporteur. Director-General; Executive Secretary. Observers: intergovernmental and international nongovernmental organizations; member and associate member states of UNESCO are also entitled to attend as observers as are (at the invitation of the Director-General) other member countries of UN System organizations. **Languages** English, French. **Staff** 4.00 FTE, paid. **Finance** Extra-budgetary contributions of UNESCO member countries; private firms. **Activities** Standards/guidelines; research/documentation. **Events** *Ordinary Session* Bratislava (Slovakia) 2013, *Réunion sur l'éthique des nanotechnologies* Brussels (Belgium) 2011, *Ordinary session* Doha (Qatar) 2011, *Extraordinary session* Paris (France) 2010, *Réunion sur l'environnement* Paris (France) 2010. **Publications** *Ethics of Energy: a Framework for Action*; *Ethics of Freshwater Use: a Survey*; *Ethics of Space Policy*; *Nanotechnology, Ethics and Policy*; *Teaching of Ethics*. Reports; brochures; proceedings.

Members Individuals (18) in the field of science, professional engineering, law, philosophy, culture, religion or politics. Members in 16 countries:
Argentina, Belgium, Canada, China, Ethiopia, Germany, Korea Rep, Madagascar, Palestine, Philippines, Qatar, Senegal, Slovakia, Slovenia, USA, Venezuela.

IGO Relations Organizations invited to participate in the work of the Commission: *European Space Agency (ESA, #08798)*; *Intergovernmental Oceanographic Commission (IOC, #11496)*; *International Geoscience Programme (IGCP, #13715)*; *International Hydrological Programme (IHP, #13826)*; *Management of Social Transformations (MOST, #16562)*. **NGO Relations** Organizations invited to participate in the work of the Commission: *International Council for Philosophy and Human Sciences (CIPSH, #13061)*; *International Council for Science (ICSU, inactive)*; *Pugwash Conferences on Science and World Affairs (#18574)*. [2021/XE3796/v/**E**]

- ♦ Commission mondiale pour l'infirmité motrice cérébrale / see International Cerebral Palsy Society (#12531)
- ♦ Commission de la Moselle (#16857)
- ♦ Commission on Multilateral Cooperation of Academies of Sciences of Socialist Countries – Economy and Politics of Developing Countries (inactive)
- ♦ Commission des Nations Unies de la condition de la femme (#20536)
- ♦ Commission des Nations Unies du développement social (#20535)
- ♦ Commission des Nations Unies pour le droit commercial international (#20531)
- ♦ Commission des Nations Unies de la population / see United Nations Commission on Population and Development (#20533)
- ♦ Commission des Nations Unies de la population et du développement (#20533)
- ♦ Commission des Nations Unies pour la prévention du crime et la justice pénale (#20530)
- ♦ Commission des Nations Unies de la science et de la technique au service du développement (#20534)

- Commission des Nations Unies de statistique (#20633)
- Commission on Nomenclature and Taxonomy / see International Committee on Systematics of Prokaryotes (#12807)
- Commission nordique de la marche à pied (inactive)
- Commission for North Africa and Near East / see Organisation régionale pour les pays d'Afrique du Nord et du Proche-Orient (#17824)

♦ Commission de l'Océan Indien (COI) 04236

Indian Ocean Commission (IOC)

SG Blue Tower – 3ème étage, Rue de l'Institut, Ebene, Mauritius. T. +2304026100. Fax +2304656798. E-mail: communication@coi-ioc.org.

URL: http://www.commissionoceanindien.org/

History 21 Dec 1982, Port Louis (Mauritius). Established, by the Ministers of Foreign Affairs of Madagascar, Mauritius and Seyehelles. General Cooperation Agreement signed 10 Jan 1984, Victoria (Seychelles). Comoros and France (for the overseas department of Réunion) subsequently joined the Commission on signature of protocols to the agreement, 7 Jan 1986, Port Louis (Mauritius). Additional protocol to the Victoria agreement signed 14 Apr 1989, Victoria (Seychelles). **Aims** Strengthen links among people of the South West Indian Ocean; improve their quality of life by developing cooperation, especially in diplomatic, economic development, social, cultural and technical sectors. **Structure** Council – *Conseil de la Commission de l'Océan Indien*, prior to 1989 referred to as Meeting of Ministers – meets annually in ordinary session and comprises one representative or his designate of each Member State, appoints Secretary-General. Presidency (1-year) rotates among member countries. Permanent liaison organization in each Member State: Committee of Permanent Liaison Officers meets twice a year. Meeting of Experts (twice a year). Secretary-General. Technical Committees. **Languages** English, French. **Staff** 18.00 FTE, paid. **Finance** Development projects financed mainly by *European Union (EU, #08967)* through *European Development Fund (EDF, #06914)*. Other partners: *Common Market for Eastern and Southern Africa (COMESA, #04296)*; *Southern African Development Community (SADC, #19843)*; *United Nations Economic Commission for Africa (ECA, #20554)*; *UNDP (#20292)*; *UNEP (#20299)*; *UNIDO (#20336)*; *UNESCO (#20322)*; World Bank – through *Global Environment Facility (GEF, #10346)*; contributions from governments of France, Canada and Australia. **Events** *Summit of heads of state and government* Comoros 1999, *Summit of Heads of State and Government* Comoros 1998, *Council Meeting* Mauritius 1998, *Conference of ministers responsible for youth / Council Meeting* Mahe Is (Seychelles) 1997, *Council Meeting* Mahe Is (Seychelles) 1997. **Publications** *Bulletin statistiques de la Commission de l'Océan Indien*; *Guide import/export de la Commission de l'Océan Indien.*

Members Governments of 5 countries:

Comoros, France (for Réunion), Madagascar, Mauritius, Seychelles.

IGO Relations Observer status with (2): *ECOSOC (#05331)*; *United Nations (UN, #20515)*. Member of: *Intergovernmental Organizations Conference (IGO Conference, #11498)*. Memorandum of Understanding with: *International Maritime Organization (IMO, #14102)*. Observer to: *Secretariat for Eastern African Coastal Area Management (SEACAM, no recent information)*. Cooperation agreement with: *Organisation internationale de la Francophonie (OIF, #17809)*. **NGO Relations** Participates in: *Global Island Partnership (GLISPA, #10436)*. Cooperates with: *International Spill Accreditation Association (ISAA)*; *Rainwater Partnership (no recent information)*. Instrumental in setting up: *Cap Business Océan Indien (#03419)*. [2023/XD6438/**D***]

- Commission océanographique intergouvernementale (#11496)
- Commission oecuménique pour la coopération européenne (inactive)
- Commission oecuménique pour les satellites (inactive)
- Commission for Olympic Solidarity / see Olympic Solidarity (#17721)
- Commission de l'OMT pour l'Afrique (see: #21861)
- Commission de l'OMT pour les Amériques (see: #21861)
- Commission de l'OMT pour l'Asie de l'Est et le Pacifique (see: #21861)
- Commission de l'OMT pour l'Asie du Sud (see: #21861)
- Commission de l'OMT pour l'Europe (see: #21861)
- Commission de l'OMT pour le Moyen-Orient (see: #21861)
- Commission d'Oslo (inactive)
- **Commission OSPAR** Commission OSPAR pour la protection du milieu marin de l'Atlantique du Nord-Est (#17905)
- Commission OSPAR pour la protection du milieu marin de l'Atlantique du Nord-Est (#17905)
- Commission Ouest-Africaine de Drogues (#20877)
- Commission du Pacifique Sud / see Pacific Community (#17942)
- Commission du Pacifique Sud pour les géosciences appliquées (inactive)
- Commission Palme sur les problèmes du désarmement et de la sécurité (inactive)
- Commission panaméricaine de conservation du sol (inactive)
- Commission panaméricaine de normalisation (#18133)
- Commission pour le partenariat scientifique aves les pays en développement (internationally oriented national body)
- Commission des pêches pour l'Atlantique centre-Ouest (#20911)
- Commission des pêches de l'Atlantique Nord-Est (#17581)
- Commission des pêches intérieures pour l'Amérique latine / see Comisión de Pesca Continental y Acuicultura para América Latina y el Caribe (#04142)
- Commission des pêches pour le sud-ouest de l'océan indien (#19894)
- Commission permanente et Association internationale pour la médecine de travail / see International Commission on Occupational Health (#12709)
- Commission permanente des congrès internationaux d'apiculture (inactive)
- Commission permanente des congrès internationaux de l'histoire des religions (inactive)
- Commission permanente des congrès internationaux d'hygiène de l'habitation (inactive)
- Commission permanente des congrès internationaux de médecine (inactive)
- Commission permanente des congrès internationaux de médecine vétérinaire (inactive)
- Commission permanente des congrès internationaux de photographie scientifique et appliquée (inactive)
- Commission permanente des congrès internationaux de physiothérapie (inactive)
- Commission permanente des congrès séricoles internationaux / see International Sericultural Commission (#14837)
- Commission permanente de la Convention internationale des pêches de 1946 (inactive)
- Commission permanente pour la coopération afro-arabe (no recent information)
- Commission permanente des dirigeants territoriaux européens / see Union of Local Authority Chief Executives of Europe (#20454)
- Commission permanente internationale de l'acétylène, de la soudure autogène et des industries qui s'y rattachent / see European Industrial Gases Association (#07525)
- Commission permanente internationale européenne des gaz industriels et du carbure de calcium / see European Industrial Gases Association (#07525)
- Commission permanente du Pacifique Sud (#04141)
- Commission permanente du Répertoire bibliographique des sciences mathématiques (inactive)
- Commission permanente des transports et des voyages (inactive)
- Commission du phoque à fourrure /otarie/ du Pacifique Nord (inactive)
- Commission phytosanitaire pour l'Asie et le Pacifique (#01997)
- Commission phytosanitaire interafricaine / see Inter-African Phytosanitary Council (#11386)
- Commission des poissons anadromes du Pacifique Nord (#17600)
- Commission polaire internationale (inactive)
- Commission pontificale pour l'Amérique latine (#18440)
- Commission pontificale d'archéologie sacrée (#18441)
- Commission pontificale pour les biens culturels de l'Eglise (#18438)
- Commission pontificale pour la conservation du patrimoine artistique et historique de l'Eglise / see Pontifical Commission for the Cultural Patrimony of the Church (#18438)
- Commission pontificale "Ecclesia Dei" (#18439)
- Commission préparatoire de l'Organisation du traité d'interdiction complète des essais nucléaires (#18482)
- Commission pour la prévention du crime et la justice pénale / see United Nations Commission on Crime Prevention and Criminal Justice (#20530)
- Commission pour la Prévention du Crime et la Justice Pénale (#20549)
- Commission pour la production et la diffusion de radio-télévision et cinéma d'expression française (inactive)
- Commission de la production et de la santé animales pour l'Asie, l'Extrême-Orient et le Pacifique Sud-Ouest (#00839)
- Commission de propagande touristique des pays alpins / see Alpine Tourist Commission (#00745)

♦ Commission on the Protection of the Black Sea Against Pollution (Black Sea Commission) 04237

Exec Dir Maslak Mahallesi, Büyükdere Caddesi, No 265, Sariyer, 34398 Istanbul/Istanbul, Türkiye. T. +902122992940 – +902122992946. Fax +902122992944. E-mail: secretariat@blacksea-commission.org.

URL: http://www.blacksea-commission.org/

History in implementation of *Convention on the Protection of the Black Sea Against Pollution (Bucharest convention, 1992)*, signed 21 Apr 1992, Bucharest (Romania). Sometimes referred to as *Istanbul Commission*. Also known under the acronym *BSC*. **Aims** Combat pollution from land-based sources and maritime transport; achieve sustainable management of marine living resources; pursue sustainable human development. **Structure** Commission comprises 1 representative of each of the Contracting Parties. Chairmanship rotates. Permanent secretariat located in Istanbul (Turkey). **Languages** English. **Staff** 4.00 FTE, paid. **Finance** Contracting Parties. **Activities** Monitoring/evaluation.

Members Governments of 6 countries:

Bulgaria, Georgia, Romania, Russia, Türkiye, Ukraine.

IGO Relations Observer to: *European Commission (EC, #06633)* (DG Environment); *UNDP (#20292)*; *UNEP (#20299)*. Memorandum of Understanding with: *Agreement on the Conservation of Cetaceans of the Black Sea, Mediterranean Sea and contiguous Atlantic Area (ACCOBAMS, 1996)*; *European Environment Agency (EEA, #06995)*; *General Fisheries Commission for the Mediterranean (GFCM, #10112)*; *IAEA Environment Laboratories (IAEA-EL, #11004)* *International Commission for the Protection of the Danube River (ICPDR, #12720)*; *International Maritime Organization (IMO, #14102)*; *Organization of Black Sea Economic Cooperation (BSEC, #17857)*. Partner of: *Group on Earth Observations (GEO, #10735)*. Close cooperation with: *Baltic Marine Environment Protection Commission – Helsinki Commission (HELCOM, #03126)*; UNEP Regional Seas Programme. [2017.06.01/XJ3857/**E***]

- Commission pour la protection de l'environnement marin de la Mer Baltique (#03126)
- Commission de la protection des plantes des Caraïbes (inactive)
- Commission provisoire de coordination des ententes internationales relatives aux produits de base (inactive)
- Commission RAMOGE / see Accord RAMOGE (#00057)
- Commission de recherches scientifiques et techniques de l'Organisation de l'unité africaine / see African Union Scientific Technical Research Commission (#00493)
- Commission régionale de l'Afrique méridionale pour la conservation et l'utilisation du sol (inactive)
- Commission régionale conjointe FAO/OMS/OUA pour l'alimentation et la nutrition en Afrique (inactive)
- Commission régionale de contrôle des assurances dans les Etats africains (see: #11385)
- Commission régionale FAO de la production et de la santé animales pour l'Asie, l'Extrême-Orient et le Pacifique Sud-Ouest / see Animal Production and Health Commission for Asia and the Pacific (#00839)
- Commission of Regional Electrical Integration / see Regional Commission for Power Integration (#18764)
- Commission sous-régionale des pêches (#20026)
- Commission régionale des politiques économiques et sociales au Proche-Orient (inactive)
- Commission pour les relations religieuses avec le judaïsme (#04238)

♦ Commission for Religious Relations with the Jews 04238

Commission pour les relations religieuses avec le judaïsme – Commissione per i Rapporti Religiosi con l'Ebraismo

Contact c/o Pontifical Council for Promoting Christian Unity, 00120 Vatican City, Vatican. T. +39669884386 – +39669883071. Fax +39669885365. E-mail: office@christianunity.va.

URL: http://www.vatican.va/roman_curia/index.htm

History 22 Oct 1974, distinct from but attached to the *Pontifical Council for Promoting Christian Unity (PCPCU, #18446)*. [2015/XE4700/**E**]

- Commission for Research Partnerships with Developing Countries (internationally oriented national body)
- Commission du réseau et de la météorologie polaire mondiale (inactive)
- Commission on the Responsibilities of the Authors of the War and on the Enforcement of Penalties for Violations of the Laws and Customs of War (inactive)
- Commission de la science et de la technique au service du développement / see United Nations Commission on Science and Technology for Development (#20534)
- Commission on Science and Technology for Development / see United Nations Commission on Science and Technology for Development (#20534)

♦ Commission on Science and Technology for Sustainable Development in the South (COMSATS) 04239

Address not obtained.

URL: http://www.comsats.org/

History 4 Oct 1994, Islamabad (Pakistan). Established at founding meeting organized by Ministry of Science and Technology of Pakistan, in collaboration with *Consortium on Science, Technology and Innovation for the South (COSTIS, no recent information)* and *TWAS (#20270)*. **Aims** Sensitize the countries of the South to the centrality of science and technology in the development process, to the adequate allocation of resources for research and development, and to the integration of science and technology in the national and regional development plans; support initiatives designed to promote indigenous capacity building in science and technology for science-led sustainable development and help mobilize long-term financial support from international donor agencies and from governments / institutions in the North and the South, to supplement the financing of international scientific projects in the South; provide leadership and support for major North-South and South-South cooperative schemes in education, training and research; support programmes and initiatives of major international organizations working for the development and promotion of science and technology in the South. **Structure** Commission of Heads of State and Government. *Network of International Science and Technology Centers (#17044)*. Secretariat, headed by Executive Director. Board of Management COMSATS Internet Services (CIS); Management Committee; Board of Governors COMSATS Institute of Information Technology (CIIT). Chairperson is the Prime Minister of Pakistan. **Finance** Members' dues. Other sources: income from services; donations. Supported by the Government of Pakistan and *UNESCO (#20322)*. **Activities** Ongoing projects: Institute of Information Technology (CIIT); Internet Services (CIS); Tele-Health Services; Syrian-COMSATS-COMSTECH Information Technology Centre (SCCITC), Damascus (Syrian AR); Islamic World Science Net (IWSN) Web-portal. **Events** *International Workshop on Applications of ICTs in Education, Healthcare and Agriculture* Amman (Jordan) 2016, *Coordinating Council Meeting* Bogota (Colombia) 2011, *Coordinating Council Meeting* Trieste (Italy) 2010, *International seminar on physics in developing countries* Islamabad (Pakistan) 2005, *International conference on importance of human resource development in the fields of S and T for sustainable development* Pathum Thani (Thailand) 2005. **Publications** *COMSATS Newsletter* (6 a year); *Science Vision* (2 a year) – journal. Scientific publications and proceedings.

Members Focal points – usually state/government bodies/ministries responsible for science and technology resource management – in 21 countries:

Bangladesh, China, Colombia, Egypt, Ghana, Iran Islamic Rep, Jamaica, Jordan, Kazakhstan, Korea Rep, Nigeria, Pakistan, Philippines, Senegal, Sri Lanka, Sudan, Syrian AR, Tanzania UR, Tunisia, Uganda, Zimbabwe.

Affiliated through the Network of Centres of Excellence, centres (17) in 16 countries:
Bangladesh, Bolivia, Brazil, China, Colombia, Egypt, Ghana, Iran Islamic Rep, Jamaica, Jordan, Nigeria, Pakistan, Sudan, Syrian AR, Tanzania UR, Türkiye.
Included in the above, 3 centres listed in this Yearbook:
Centro Internacional de Fisica (CIF, #03807); International Centre for Environmental and Nuclear Sciences (ICENS); International Centre of Climate and Environmental Sciences (ICCES).
IGO Relations Memorandum of understanding with: *Centre for Science and Technology of the Non-Aligned and Other Developing Countries (NAM S and T Centre, #03784); International Centre for Genetic Engineering and Biotechnology (ICGEB, #12494); International Development Research Centre (IDRC, #13162); Islamic World Educational, Scientific and Cultural Organization (ICESCO, #16058); UNIDO (#20336).* Working Relations with: *Abdus Salam International Centre for Theoretical Physics (ICTP, #00005); OIC Ministerial Standing Committee on Scientific and Technological Cooperation (COMSTECH, #17702); UNESCO (#20322).* **NGO Relations** Memorandum of Understanding with: *Asian Institute of Technology (AIT, #01519); Consortium on Science, Technology and Innovation for the South (COSTIS, no recent information); TWAS (#20270).* Working relationships with: *International Centre for Integrated Mountain Development (ICIMOD, #12500).* Member of: *International Network for Small and Medium Sized Enterprises (INSME, #14325).* [2021/XE2153/y/**E***]

- ♦ Commission for the Scientific and Technological Development of Central America and Panama (#04132)
- ♦ Commission scientifique, technique et de la recherche de l'Organisation de l'unité africaine / see African Union Scientific Technical Research Commission (#00493)
- ♦ Commissions culturelles nordiques (inactive)
- ♦ Commissions pour le dialogue interreligieux monastique / see Monastic Interreligious Dialogue (#16849)
- ♦ Commission on Security and Cooperation in Europe (internationally oriented national body)
- ♦ Commission Séismologique Européenne (#08461)
- ♦ Commission sur les semiconducteurs – UIPPA / see International Commission on Semiconductors (#12728)
- ♦ Commission on Semiconductors – IUPAP / see International Commission on Semiconductors (#12728)
- ♦ Commission séricicole internationale (#14837)
- ♦ Commission des services financiers postaux européens (inactive)
- ♦ Commissions internationales pour la protection de la Moselle et de la Sarre (#12729)
- ♦ Commissions internationales pour la protection de la Moselle et de la Sarre contre la pollution / see International Commissions for the Protection of the Moselle and Saar (#12729)
- ♦ Commission pour la société, le développement et la paix du Conseil oecuménique des églises et de la Commission pontificale Justice et paix (inactive)
- ♦ Commission solaire internationale (inactive)
- ♦ Commission pour la solidarité olympique / see Olympic Solidarity (#17721)
- ♦ Commission des statistiques agricoles pour l'Afrique (#00254)
- ♦ Commission des statistiques agricoles pour l'Asie et le Pacifique (#01873)
- ♦ Commission of Studies for Latin American Church History (#04133)
- ♦ Commission des stupéfiants des Nations Unies – Comisión de Estupefacientes de las Naciones Unidas (#20532)
- ♦ Commission sud-américaine de lutte contre la fièvre aphteuse (#04143)
- ♦ Commission suisse pour le partenariat scientifique aves les pays en développement / see Commission for Research Partnerships with Developing Countries
- ♦ Commission syndicale consultative auprès de l'OCDE (#20186)
- ♦ Commission syndicale consultative auprès de l'Organisation de coopération et de développement économiques / see Trade Union Advisory Committee to the OECD (#20186)
- ♦ Commission for Technical Cooperation in Africa / see African Union Scientific Technical Research Commission (#00493)
- ♦ Commission for Technical Cooperation in Africa South of the Sahara (inactive)
- ♦ Commission technique permanente commune pour les eaux du Nil (#18327)
- ♦ Commission technique permanente du régime des eaux du Danube (inactive)
- ♦ Commission de télécommunications de l'Amérique centrale / see Comisión Técnica Regional de Telecomunicaciones (#04144)
- ♦ Commission théologique internationale (#15684)
- ♦ Commission des thons de l'océan Indien (#11162)
- ♦ Commission Tiers-Monde de l'Eglise catholique, Genève (internationally oriented national body)
- ♦ Commission pour les tombes de guerre du Commonwealth (#04367)
- ♦ Commission trilatérale (#20237)
- ♦ Commission tripartite pour la restitution de l'or monétaire (inactive)
- ♦ Commission de l'UA sur les réfugiés (inactive)
- ♦ Commission de l'UEMOA (see: #20377)
- ♦ Commission de l'UIPPA sur l'astrophysique (#16082)
- ♦ Commission de l'UIPPA sur l'éducation en physique / see International Commission on Physics Education (#12714)
- ♦ Commission de l'UIPPA sur l'électronique quantique / see International Commission on Laser Physics and Photonics (#12697)
- ♦ Commission de l'UIPPA sur magnétisme / see International Commission on Magnetism (#12699)
- ♦ Commission de l'UIPPA sur les particules et champs / see International Commission on Particles and Fields (#12712)
- ♦ Commission de l'UIPPA sur la physique atomique et moléculaire et la spectroscopie / see International Commission on Atomic, Molecular and Optical Physics (#12666)
- ♦ Commission de l'UIPPA sur la physique pour le développement / see International Commission on Physics for Development (#12713)
- ♦ Commission de l'UIPPA sur la physique mathématique / see International Commission on Mathematical Physics (#12701)
- ♦ Commission de l'UIPPA sur la physique nucléaire / see International Commission on Nuclear Physics (#12708)
- ♦ Commission de l'UIPPA sur la physique des plasmas / see International Commission on Plasma Physics (#12717)
- ♦ Commission de l'UIPPA sur la physique des très basses températures / see International Commission on Low Temperature Physics (#12698)
- ♦ Commission de l'UIPPA sur les rayons cosmiques / see International Commission on Astroparticle Physics (#12663)
- ♦ Commission de l'UIPPA sur la structure et la dynamique de la matière condensée / see International Commission on the Structure and Dynamics of Condensed Matter (#12731)
- ♦ Commission de l'UIPPA sur les symboles, les unités, la nomenclature, les masses atomiques et les constantes fondamentales / see International Commission on Symbols, Units, Nomenclature, Atomic Masses and Fundamental Constants (#12733)
- ♦ Commission UISB de l'enseignement en biologie (#16079)
- ♦ **Commission de Venise** Commission européenne pour la démocratie par le droit (#06636)
- ♦ Commission de Venise du Conseil de l'Europe / see European Commission for Democracy through Law (#06636)
- ♦ Commission on Voluntary Service and Action (internationally oriented national body)
- ♦ Commission for the World Polar Meteorological Network (inactive)
- ♦ Commission on Youth Service Projects / see Commission on Voluntary Service and Action
- ♦ Commission de la zone de l'Amérique centrale et des Caraïbes de la Confédération panaméricaine de basketball (#04146)
- ♦ Commissio Pontificia de Re Biblica / see Pontifical Biblical Commission (#18436)
- ♦ Commissio Theologica Internationalis (#15684)
- ♦ Committee of 100 for Tibet (internationally oriented national body)

♦ Committee of 200 (C200) 04240

Dir 980 N Michigan Ave, Ste 1575, Chicago IL 60611, USA. T. +13122550296ext102. Fax +13122550789. E-mail: info@c200.org.
URL: http://www.c200.org/

History 1982, USA, as a USA organization. Became international, 1997, on opening divisions in Europe (UK) and Asia (Hong Kong). **Aims** Function as an organization for senior *women executives* and *entrepreneurs.* **Finance** Members' dues.
Members Business women (485) who are corporate executives or who run their own firms, responsible for a minimum annual sales. Members in 3 countries and territories:
Hong Kong, UK, USA. [2017/XE3594/v/**E**]

- ♦ Committee for the Abolition of Third World Debt (#04148)
- ♦ Committee for Academic Freedom in Africa (internationally oriented national body)
- ♦ Committee of African Road Associations (inactive)
- ♦ Committee Against Bird Slaughter (internationally oriented national body)

♦ Committee Against Torture (CAT) 04241

Comité contre la torture – Comité contra la Tortura

Sec c/o OHCHR – Human Rights Treaties Branch, Palais Wilson, Rue de Pâquis 52, 1201 Geneva 10, Switzerland. T. +41229179220. E-mail: ohchr-registry@un.org.
URL: https://www.ohchr.org/en/treaty-bodies/cat

History 26 Nov 1987, Geneva (Switzerland). Established within the framework of *United Nations (UN, #20515)*, by states party to the *Convention Against Torture and other Cruel, Inhuman or Degrading Treatment or Punishment (1984).* Managed by *Office of the United Nations High Commissioner for Human Rights (OHCHR, #17697)* at *United Nations Office at Geneva (UNOG, #20597).* Former names and other names: *United Nations Committee Against Torture* – alias; *Comité des Nations Unies contre la torture* – alias; *Comité de las Naciones Unidas contra la Tortura* – alias. **Aims** Monitor implementation of provisions of the Convention against torture in states party to the Convention. **Structure** Session (three a year) in Geneva (Switzerland); Committee of 10 experts; Bureau; Secretariat. **Languages** English, French, Spanish. **Finance** On Regular Budget of *United Nations (UN, #20515).* **Activities** Events/meetings; knowledge management/ information dissemination; politics/policy/regulatory. **Events** *Session* Geneva (Switzerland) 2023, *Session* Geneva (Switzerland) 2023, *Session* Geneva (Switzerland) 2022, *Session* Geneva (Switzerland) 2022, *Session* Geneva (Switzerland) 2022. **Publications** Report to the UN General Assembly (annual).
Members Experts from 10 countries (term of expiry indicated between brackets):
China (2025), France (2023), Japan (2025), Latvia (2023), Mexico (2023), Moldova (2023), Morocco (2025), Russia (2025), Türkiye (2023), USA (2025).
State Parties to the Convention (173 as at 17 February 2023):
Afghanistan, Albania, Algeria, Andorra, Angola, Antigua-Barbuda, Argentina, Armenia, Australia, Austria, Azerbaijan, Bahamas, Bahrain, Bangladesh, Belarus, Belgium, Belize, Benin, Bolivia, Bosnia-Herzegovina, Botswana, Brazil, Bulgaria, Burkina Faso, Burundi, Cambodia, Cameroon, Canada, Cape Verde, Central African Rep, Chad, Chile, China, Colombia, Comoros, Congo Brazzaville, Congo DR, Costa Rica, Côte d'Ivoire, Croatia, Cuba, Cyprus, Czechia, Denmark, Djibouti, Dominican Rep, Ecuador, Egypt, El Salvador, Equatorial Guinea, Eritrea, Estonia, Eswatini, Ethiopia, Fiji, Finland, France, Gabon, Gambia, Georgia, Germany, Ghana, Greece, Grenada, Guatemala, Guinea, Guinea-Bissau, Guyana, Holy See, Honduras, Hungary, Iceland, Indonesia, Iraq, Ireland, Israel, Italy, Japan, Jordan, Kazakhstan, Kenya, Kiribati, Korea Rep, Kuwait, Kyrgyzstan, Laos, Latvia, Lebanon, Lesotho, Liberia, Libya, Liechtenstein, Lithuania, Luxembourg, Madagascar, Malawi, Maldives, Mali, Malta, Marshall Is, Mauritania, Mauritius, Mexico, Moldova, Monaco, Mongolia, Montenegro, Morocco, Mozambique, Namibia, Nauru, Nepal, Netherlands, New Zealand, Nicaragua, Niger, Nigeria, North Macedonia, Norway, Oman, Pakistan, Palestine, Panama, Paraguay, Peru, Philippines, Poland, Portugal, Qatar, Romania, Russia, Rwanda, Samoa, San Marino, Sao Tomé-Principe, Saudi Arabia, Senegal, Serbia, Seychelles, Sierra Leone, Slovakia, Slovenia, Somalia, South Africa, South Sudan, Spain, Sri Lanka, St Kitts-Nevis, St Vincent-Grenadines, Sudan, Suriname, Sweden, Switzerland, Syrian AR, Tajikistan, Thailand, Timor-Leste, Togo, Tunisia, Türkiye, Turkmenistan, Uganda, UK, Ukraine, United Arab Emirates, Uruguay, USA, Uzbekistan, Vanuatu, Venezuela, Vietnam, Yemen, Zambia. [2023.02.17/XE6050/v/**E***]

- ♦ Committee of Agricultural Organizations in the EC / see COPA – european farmers (#04829)
- ♦ Committee of Agricultural Organizations in the EU / see COPA – european farmers (#04829)
- ♦ Committee of the Agriculture and Food Industries of the Union of Industries of the European Economic Community / see FoodDrinkEurope (#09841)

♦ Committee for ASEAN Youth Cooperation (CAYC) 04242

SG c/o Malaysian Youth Council, Wisma MBM, 1 Jalan Tasik Permaisuri 2, Bandar Tun Razak, 56000 Kuala Lumpur, Malaysia. T. +60391732761 – +60391732763. Fax +60391732759. E-mail: cayc.sec.gen@gmail.com.
URL: https://www.facebook.com/AseanYouthVolunteers/

History 15 Sep 1975, Jakarta (Indonesia). Founded 15-17 Sep 1975, Jakarta (Indonesia). **Aims** Widen and promote the sense of ASEAN identity and cultivate *friendship* and solidarity; promote greater cooperation and foster regional and *international understanding* and respect; promote and facilitate joint youth programmes concerning youth involvement and participation in national development effort. **Structure** Management Committee (meets annually). **Languages** English. **Staff** 1.00 FTE, paid. **Finance** Members' dues. Grant from the Ministry of Youth and Sports (Malaysia). **Activities** Projects/programmes; events/meetings; networking/ liaising. **Events** *Workshop on youth interpreneurial development* Malaysia 1992.
Members National Youth Committees/Bodies in 8 countries:
Brunei Darussalam, Cambodia, Indonesia, Malaysia, Philippines, Singapore, Thailand, Vietnam.
Consultative Status Consultative status granted from: *ASEAN (#01141).* [2015.11.17/XE0548/**E**]

♦ Committee for Asian Women (CAW) 04243

Secretariat 386/58 Soi Ratchadaphisek 42, Ratchadaphisek Road, Ladyao, Jatujak, Bangkok, 10900, Thailand. T. +6629305634 – +6629305635. Fax +6629305633. E-mail: theintcawinfo@gmail.com.
URL: https://caw-asia.net/

History 1981, as a joint programme of *Christian Conference of Asia (CCA, #03898)* and *Federation of Asian Bishops' Conferences (FABC, #09430).* Independent since 1992. **Aims** Assist in *consciousness-raising* among women *workers* in formal and informal sector in Asia towards realization of the commonalities of their situations, problems and analyses; support the organizing efforts of the organized women workers to effect favourable changes in their lives; facilitate networking and linkages amongst women workers and related groups within and outside Asia for solidarity and support. **Structure** Executive Committee of 9 women: 6 from the 3 sub-regions and 3 experts. Sub-regions: East Asia; Southeast Asia; South Asia. **Activities** Women workers exchange programmes; joint local programmes like national workshops; guided training programmes; sub-regional workshops; regional consultations; publications; documentation and research; urgent appeals and solidarity support for women workers' actions. **Events** *Triennial Meeting* 1998, *Triennial Meeting* 1995. **Publications** *Asian Women Workers Newsletter* (4 a year). Books; studies; articles; manuals; workshop reports.
Members Organizational members (46) in 14 countries and territories:
Bangladesh, China, Hong Kong, India, Indonesia, Japan, Korea Rep, Malaysia, Nepal, Pakistan, Philippines, Sri Lanka, Taiwan, Thailand.
NGO Relations Member of: *United for Foreign Domestic Workers' Rights (UFDWR, #20510).* Instrumental in setting up: *Asian Domestic Workers Network (ADWN, #01430).* [2012.08.29/XF0466/**F**]

- ♦ Committee of Asia/Pacific Societies for Electron Microscopy / see Committee of Asia/Pacific Societies for Microscopy (#04244)

♦ Committee of Asia/Pacific Societies for Microscopy (CAPSM) 04244

Contact Fac of Health Sciences – Natl Univ of Malaysia, School of Diagnostics and Applied Health Sciences, 50300 Kuala Lumpur, Malaysia. T. +61392897175.
URL: https://www.capsm.org/

History as a regional committee of *International Federation of Societies for Microscopy (IFSM, #13550),* under the title *Committee of Asia/Pacific Societies for Electron Microscopy (CAPSEM).* **Aims** Promote microscopy in the Asia-Pacific region. **Structure** President; Vice-President, Secretary-Treasurer; Representative of each member society. **Languages** English. **Staff** Voluntary. **Finance** Conference proceeds. **Events** *Asia Pacific Microscopy Conference (APMC 2024)* Brisbane, QLD (Australia) 2024, *East-Asia Microscopy Conference (EAMC)* Taipei (Taiwan) 2021, *Quadrennial Conference* Hyderabad (India) 2020, *East-Asia Microscopy Conference (EAMC)* Taipei (Taiwan) 2020, *East-Asia Regional Microscopy Conference (EAMC)* Busan (Korea Rep) 2017.

Members Individuals in 16 countries and territories:
Australia, China, Hong Kong, India, Indonesia, Japan, Korea Rep, Malaysia, New Zealand, Pakistan, Philippines, Singapore, Taiwan, Thailand, USA, Vietnam. [2020/XE2004/v/E]

♦ Committee of Associations of European Foundries / see European Foundry Association, The (#07352)
♦ Committee of the Associations of Honey Imports and Packers of Europe (inactive)
♦ Committee on Atlantic Studies (no recent information)
♦ Committee of Baker's Yeast Manufacturers of the EEC / see Confédération des Fabricants de Levure de l'Union Européenne (#04551)
♦ Committee on Banking Regulations and Supervisory Practices / see Basel Committee on Banking Supervision (#03183)
♦ Committee of Banking Supervisors of West and Central Africa (unconfirmed)
♦ Committee for the Cancellation of the Third World Debt / see Comité pour l'annulation de la dette du Tiers-monde (#04148)
♦ Committee on Central American Economic Cooperation / see Central American Economic Cooperation Committee (#03667)

♦ Committee of Central Bank Governors in SADC (CCBG) 04245

Main Office c/o SARB, PO Box 427, Pretoria, 0001, South Africa. E-mail: sadc-ccbg@resbank.co.za.
Contact SADC, Private Bag 0095, Gaborone, Botswana.
URL: http://www.sadcbankers.org/

History 1995, by *Southern African Development Community (SADC, #19843)*. also referred to as *SADC Association of Central Banks* and *Committee of Central Banks in SADC*. **Activities** Together with SADC Committee of Stock Exchanges, coordinates regional developments in the financial markets. **IGO Relations** Close links with: *Southern African Development Community (SADC, #19843)*. **NGO Relations** Close links with: *Committee of SADC Stock Exchanges (CoSSE, #04285)*. [2015/XE3871/E]

♦ Committee of Central Bank Governors in the Southern African Development Community 04246

Secretariat PO Box 427, Pretoria, 0001, South Africa. T. +27123134374 – +27123133353. Fax +27123134177. E-mail: sadc-ccbg@resbank.co.za.
URL: http://www.sadcbankers.org/

History Aug 1995, within the ambit of the Trade, Industry, Finance and Investment Directorate of *Southern African Development Community (SADC, #19843)*. Inaugural meeting: 24 Nov 1995. Terms of reference approved, Jul 1996, by Committee of Ministers of Finance. **Aims** Contribute to the process of regional *economic cooperation* and integration through closer cooperation among central banks of the Community in the areas of: monetary *policy*; monetary policy instruments; bank supervision; money and capital markets; international *financial* relations; payment, clearing and settlement systems; training; *money laundering*. Assist central bank governors and officials in gaining better insight into each others' economies and monetary policies. **Structure** Committee of Governors (meets twice a year) chaired by the Governor of the South African Reserve Bank, assisted by the Secretariat of the Committee of Central Bank Governors (CCBG). Committee of Officials (meeting 2 days prior to meetings of Governors) comprises senior officials of member central banks, chaired by the Head of the CCBG Secretariat; it prepares the meeting of Governors. Secretariat in International Economic Relations and Policy Department, South African Reserve Bank, assisted by Working Group comprising representatives of 3 other central banks on a rotational basis. **Activities** Meetings of Governors discuss recent economic developments in member states. Projects: development of a statistical database; development of a data bank on SADC financial systems – policies, structures and markets; payment, clearing and settlement systems project; coordination of training of central bank officials; legal and operational frameworks of SADC central banks; cooperation in information technology; banking supervision; economic convergence and financial markets. **Members** Central bank governors of all SADC countries. [2014.02.07/XE3591/E*]

♦ Committee of Central Banks in SADC / see Committee of Central Bank Governors in SADC (#04245)
♦ Committee of Cereals, Oilseeds, Animal Feed, Olive Oil, Oils and Fats, and Agro-Supply Trade in the EU / see Committee of the Trade in Cereals, Oilseeds, Pulses, Olive Oil, Oils and Fats, Animal Feed and Agrosupply of the EU (#04289)
♦ Committee on the Christian Responsibility for European Cooperation (inactive)
♦ Committee of the Cider and Fruit Wine Industry of the EEC / see Association des Industries des Cidres et Vins de Fruits de l'UE (#02643)
♦ Committee for a Constructive Tomorrow (internationally oriented national body)
♦ Committee of Control of the International Zone of Tangier (inactive)
♦ Committee for Cooperation between Nordic Hospital Administrators (inactive)
♦ Committee for Coordination of Joint Prospecting for Mineral Resources in Asian Offshore Areas / see Coordinating Committee for Geoscience Programmes in East and Southeast Asia (#04816)
♦ Committee of the Cotton and Allied Textile Industries of the EC / see European Federation of Cotton and Allied Textiles Industries (#07093)

♦ Committee on Data for Science and Technology (CODATA) 04247

Comité pour les données scientifiques et technologiques – Comité de Datos para la Ciencia y la Tecnologia

Exec Dir 5 rue Auguste Vacquerie, 75016 Paris, France. T. +33145250496. Fax +33142881466.
URL: http://www.codata.org/

History Jan 1966, Mumbai (India). Founded by 11th General Assembly of *International Council for Science (ICSU, inactive)*. Following the merger of ICSU with ISSC, CODATA is currently an Interdisciplinary Committee of the *International Science Council (ISC, #14796)*. Constitution (statutes & by-laws) updated 2020. **Aims** Strengthen international science for the benefit of society by promoting improved scientific and technical data management and use. **Structure** General Assembly (every 2 years). Executive Committee. **Languages** English, French. **Staff** 2.00 FTE, paid. Network of 400 scientists. **Finance** Members' dues. Other sources: *International Atomic Energy Agency (IAEA, #12294)*; *Japan Association for International Chemical Information (JAICI)*; *UNESCO (#20322)*; contracts; grants. Budget (annual): US$ 300,000. **Activities** Knowledge management/information dissemination. Instrumental in setting up: *Species 2000 (#19914)*. **Events** *SCIDATACON : International Conference on Data Sharing and Integration for Global Sustainability* Seoul (Korea Rep) 2022, *SCIDATACON : International Conference on Data Sharing and Integration for Global Sustainability* Seoul (Korea Rep) 2021, *Workshop on Big Data and Systems Analysis* Vienna (Austria) 2020, *International Conference* Beijing (China) 2019, *International workshop on Fair RDM in Institutions* Helsinki (Finland) 2019. **Publications** *CODATA Bulletins*; *Special Reports*. Books; monographs; conference proceedings.

Members National associations in 21 countries and territories:
Australia, Brazil, Canada, China, France, Georgia, Germany, India, Indonesia, Ireland, Israel, Japan, Korea Rep, Poland, Russia, South Africa, Taiwan, Thailand, UK, Ukraine, USA.

Union members of ISC (13):
International Astronomical Union (IAU, #12287); *International Geographical Union (IGU, #13713)*; *International Union for Pure and Applied Biophysics (IUPAB, #15808)*; *International Union of Basic and Clinical Pharmacology (IUPHAR, #15758)*; *International Union of Biological Sciences (IUBS, #15760)*; *International Union of Crystallography (IUCr, #15768)*; *International Union of Geodesy and Geophysics (IUGG, #15776)*; *International Union of Geological Sciences (IUGS, #15777)*; *International Union of Microbiological Societies (IUMS, #15794)*; *International Union of Nutritional Sciences (IUNS, #15796)*; *International Union of Psychological Science (IUPsyS, #15807)*; *International Union of Pure and Applied Chemistry (IUPAC, #15809)*; *International Union of Pure and Applied Physics (IUPAP, #15810)*; *International Union of Soil Sciences (IUSS, #15817)*.

Co-opted Delegates (3):
International Council for Scientific and Technical Information (ICSTI, #13070); *ISC World Data System (ISC-WDS, #16024)*; *World Federation for Culture Collections (WFCC, #21424)*.

IGO Relations *Bureau international des poids et mesures (BIPM, #03367)*. Partner of: *Group on Earth Observations (GEO, #10735)*. Links with Directorate-General for Science, research and Development of: *European Commission (EC, #06633)*. [2021/XE0319/y/E]

♦ Committee for a Democratic United Nations / see Democracy Without Borders
♦ Committee for the Development of Mycology in Asian Countries / see Asian Mycological Association (#01545)

♦ Committee of Directors of Geographic Institutes of South American Countries, Spain and Portugal (DIGSA) 04248

Comité de Directores de Institutos Geograficos de Sur América, España y Portugal

Dir Gen Instituto Geografico Português, Rua de Artilharia 1, no 107, 1099-052 Lisbon, Portugal. T. +351213819600. Fax +351213819699.

History 1978. **Aims** Function as a meeting of policy-makers; ease exchange of information among members; stimulate formation of common policy in specific areas for mutual benefit. **Structure** General Assembly (annual). President; Executive Secretary. **Languages** Portuguese, Spanish. **Activities** Priority areas: standards and data infrastructures; licensing; copyright; training policies; digital data production, maintenance and quality. *South American System of Geocentric Reference (SIRGAS)*, unique geodetic reference system for South America, also used to standardize aeronautical data. **Events** *Meeting* Lisbon (Portugal) 2004, *Meeting* Peru 2003, *Meeting* Ecuador 2002, *Meeting* Spain 2001, *Meeting* Portugal 1999.

Members Heads of national mapping institutions in 10 countries:
Argentina, Bolivia, Brazil, Chile, Ecuador, Peru, Portugal, Spain, Uruguay, Venezuela. [2008.07.14/XF5830/F]

♦ Committee on Disarmament / see Conference on Disarmament (#04590)
♦ Committee of Donor Agencies for Small Enterprise Development / see Donor Committee for Enterprise Development (#05122)

♦ Committee on Earth Observation Satellites (CEOS) 04249

Comité sur les satellites d'observation de la terre

CEO address not obtained.
CEO Europe and Africa ESA/ESRIN, Earth Observation Directorate, Via Galileo Galilei, 00044 Frascati RM, Italy. T. +39694180567. Fax +39694180353.
URL: https://ceos.org/

History 1984. Founded by *Asian-Pacific Regional Research and Training Centre for Integrated Fish Farming (IFFC, #01628)*, at the request of the *Panel of Experts on Satellite Remote Sensing of the Economic Summit of Industrialized Nations Working Group on Growth, Technology and Employment*, combining previously existing groups for Coordination on Ocean Remote-Sensing Satellites (CORSS) and Coordination on Land Observing Satellites (CLOS). Subsequently absorbed *International Forum on Earth Observation Using Space Stations Elements (IFEOS, inactive)* and *International Polar Orbiting Meteorological Satellites Group (IPOMS, inactive)*. Former names and other names: *International Earth Observations Satellite Committee (IEOSC)* – former. **Aims** Collaborate internationally among space systems and EO missions; optimize benefits of space-borne Earth observations through cooperation of its Members in mission planning and in development of compatible data products, formats, services, applications, and policies; serve as a focal point for international coordination of space-related Earth observation activities; exchange policy and technical information to encourage complementarity and compatibility of observation and data exchange systems. **Structure** Plenary Session (annual); Strategic Implementation Team. Standing Secretariat maintained by: ESA; EUMETSAT; NASA; NOAA; MEXT/JAXA. Working Groups (3); ad-hoc working groups. **Finance** No centralized budget. **Activities** Projects/programmes; standards/guidelines; management of treaties and agreements. **Events** *Plenary* Silver Spring, MD (USA) 2020, *Plenary* Hanoi (Vietnam) 2019, *Plenary Meeting* Brussels (Belgium) 2018, *Technical Workshop* Darmstadt (Germany) 2018, *Meeting* Ispra (Italy) 2018. **Publications** *CEOS Newsletter* (2 a year); *CEOS Yearbook*. *Data Principles for Global Change Research*; *Data Principles for Operational Environmental Use for the Public Benefit*. *Resources in Earth Observation* (1999) – CD-ROM (4th ed). Annual Report; brochure. **Information Services** *CEOS Database*; *CEOS Disaster Information Server (NOAA)*; *CEOS Information Locator System (CILS)*; *International Directory Network* – online.

Members Full (31) national and international governmental organizations in 22 countries:
Argentina, Australia, Belgium, Brazil, Canada, China, France, Germany, India, Italy, Japan, Korea Rep, Netherlands, Nigeria, Russia, South Africa, Spain, Thailand, Türkiye, UK, USA, Vietnam.

Included in the above, 4 organizations listed in this Yearbook:
Commonwealth Scientific and Industrial Research Organization (CSIRO); *European Commission (EC, #06633)*; *European Organisation for the Exploitation of Meteorological Satellites (EUMETSAT, #08096)*; *European Space Agency (ESA, #08798)*.

Associates (28) in 18 countries:
Australia, Austria, Belgium, Canada, France, Gabon, India, Italy, Kenya, Malaysia, Mexico, New Zealand, Norway, South Africa, Sweden, Switzerland, Thailand, UK.

Included in the above, 16 organizations listed in this Yearbook:
FAO (#09260); *Global Climate Observing System (GCOS, #10289)*; *Global Geodetic Observing System (GGOS, see: #11914)*; *Global Ocean Observing System (GOOS, #10511)*; *Global Terrestrial Observing System (GTOS, #10626)*; *Intergovernmental Oceanographic Commission (IOC, #11496)*; *International Council for Science (ICSU, inactive)*; *International Geosphere-Biosphere Programme (IGBP, inactive)*; *International Ocean Colour Coordinating Group (IOCCG, #14392)*; *International Society for Photogrammetry and Remote Sensing (ISPRS, #15362)*; *UNEP (#20299)*; *UNESCO (#20322)*; *United Nations Economic and Social Commission for Asia and the Pacific (ESCAP, #20557)*; *United Nations Office for Outer Space Affairs (UNOOSA, #20601)*; *World Climate Research Programme (WCRP, #21279)*; *World Meteorological Organization (WMO, #21649)*.

IGO Relations Observer status with: *Committee on the Peaceful Uses of Outer Space (COPUOS, #04277)*. Member of: IGOS Partnership. Participates in: *Group on Earth Observations (GEO, #10735)* with *AmeriGEOSS (#00796)* and *AmeriGEOSS (#00796)*. Collaborates with: *WMO Space Programme (see: #21649)*. **NGO Relations** In liaison with technical committees of: *International Organization for Standardization (ISO, #14473)*. Member of: *International Centre for Earth Simulation (ICES Foundation)*. [2020/XE1457/y/E]

♦ Committee for Economic Development (internationally oriented national body)
♦ Committee for an Effective International Criminal Law (internationally oriented national body)

♦ Committee on the Elimination of Discrimination against Women (CEDAW) 04250

Comité pour l'élimination de la discrimination à l'égard des femmes

Sec UNOG-OHCHR, Palais des Nations, 1211 Geneva 10, Switzerland. T. +41229179000. Fax +41229179008. E-mail: ohchr-cedaw@un.org.
Street address c/o Human Rights Treaties Div – OHCHR, Palais Wilson, Rue des Pâquis 52, 1201 Geneva, Switzerland.
URL: http://www.ohchr.org/en/hrbodies/cedaw/pages/cedawindex.aspx

History 1982. Established in accordance with *Convention on the Elimination of all Forms of Discrimination Against Women (CEDAW, 1979)*, as adopted by resolution 34/180 of the General Assembly of the *United Nations (UN, #20515)*, 18 Dec 1979. Serviced by *Office of the United Nations High Commissioner for Human Rights (OHCHR, #17697)* at *United Nations Office at Geneva (UNOG, #20597)*. **Aims** During its sessions: review initial and periodic reports, address concerns and recommendations in the form of concluding observations to the State that are party to the Convention in order to assess their progress in eliminating all forms of discrimination against women – defined in the Convention as any distinction, exclusion or restriction made on the basis of sex which has the effect or purpose of impairing or nullifying the recognition, enjoyment or exercise by women, irrespective of their marital status, on a basis of equality of men and women, of *human rights* and fundamental *freedoms* in the political, economic, social, cultural, civil or any other field – and to promote *equal rights* of women and men. **Structure** Committee (meeting 3 times a year in sessions of up to 3 or 4 weeks); Bureau; Secretariat. The Committee on the Elimination of Discrimination against Women (CEDAW) is the body of independent experts that monitors implementation of the Convention on the Elimination of All Forms of Discrimination against Women. The CEDAW Committee consists of 23 experts on women's rights from around the world. **Languages** Arabic, Chinese, English, French, Russian, Spanish. **Staff** 6.00 FTE, paid. **Finance** On the regular budget of the United Nations. **Activities** Events/meetings; guidance/assistance/consulting. Countries who have become party to the treaty (States parties) are obliged to submit regular reports to the Committee on how the rights of the Convention are implemented. **Events** *Session* Geneva (Switzerland) 2022, *Session* Geneva (Switzerland) 2022, *Session* Geneva (Switzerland) 2022, *Session* Geneva (Switzerland) 2021, *Session* Geneva (Switzerland) 2021. **Publications** *Joint CRC/CEDAW/Special Rapporteur on the rights of persons with disabilities Statement: Taking action to eliminate gender-based violence against women and girls with disabilities* (2021) in English; *Joint CEDAW/CRC statement calling on the Taliban to protect the human rights of women and children in Afghanistan* (2021); *Statement of the Committee on the Elimination of Discrimination against Women on Virtual Sessions* (2021) – https://www.ohchr.org/Documents/

HRBodies/CEDAW/Statements/CEDAW_Statement_Virtual_Sessions.docx; *Statement of the Committee on the Elimination of Discrimination against Women – Turkey* (2021); *Call by the Committee on the Elimination of Discrimination against Women to release all detained women human rights defenders, including Saudi women's rights activist Loujain Al-Hathloul, in the wake of International Women Human Rights Defenders Day* (2020); *Global anti-racism protests must herald a new era in human rights, social and gender justice* (2020); *Spain must tackle obstertic violence* (2020); *Statement on the occasion of International Human Rights Day 2020: 20th anniversary of the Optional Protocol to CEDAW: A universal instrument for upholding the rights of women and girls and for their effective access to justice* (2020); *Women's activism in political processes* (2020); *CEDAW 40th Anniversary* (2019); *Five UN human rights treaty bodies issue a joint statement on human rights and climate change, 16 Sept 2019* (2019); *Compendium of International Conventions concerning the Status of Women; The Work of CEDAW* – in 2 vols.
Members States party to the Convention on the Elimination of All Forms of Discrimination against Women (189 as of 7 Jan 2019):
Afghanistan, Albania, Algeria, Andorra, Angola, Antigua-Barbuda, Argentina, Armenia, Australia, Austria, Azerbaijan, Bahamas, Bahrain, Bangladesh, Barbados, Belarus, Belgium, Belize, Benin, Bhutan, Bolivia, Bosnia-Herzegovina, Botswana, Brazil, Brunei Darussalam, Bulgaria, Burkina Faso, Burundi, Cambodia, Cameroon, Canada, Cape Verde, Central African Rep, Chad, Chile, China, Colombia, Comoros, Congo Brazzaville, Congo DR, Cook Is, Costa Rica, Côte d'Ivoire, Croatia, Cuba, Cyprus, Czechia, Denmark, Djibouti, Dominica, Dominican Rep, Ecuador, Egypt, El Salvador, Equatorial Guinea, Eritrea, Estonia, Eswatini, Ethiopia, Fiji, Finland, France, Gabon, Gambia, Georgia, Germany, Ghana, Greece, Grenada, Guatemala, Guinea, Guinea-Bissau, Guyana, Haiti, Honduras, Hungary, Iceland, India, Indonesia, Iraq, Ireland, Israel, Italy, Jamaica, Japan, Jordan, Kazakhstan, Kenya, Kiribati, Korea DPR, Korea Rep, Kuwait, Kyrgyzstan, Laos, Latvia, Lebanon, Lesotho, Liberia, Libya, Liechtenstein, Lithuania, Luxembourg, Madagascar, Malawi, Malaysia, Maldives, Mali, Malta, Marshall Is, Mauritania, Mauritius, Mexico, Micronesia FS, Moldova, Monaco, Mongolia, Montenegro, Morocco, Mozambique, Myanmar, Namibia, Nauru, Nepal, Netherlands, New Zealand, Nicaragua, Niger, Nigeria, North Macedonia, Norway, Oman, Pakistan, Palestine, Panama, Papua New Guinea, Paraguay, Peru, Philippines, Poland, Portugal, Qatar, Romania, Russia, Rwanda, Samoa, San Marino, Sao Tomé-Principe, Saudi Arabia, Senegal, Serbia, Seychelles, Sierra Leone, Singapore, Slovakia, Slovenia, Solomon Is, South Africa, South Sudan, Spain, Sri Lanka, St Kitts-Nevis, St Lucia, St Vincent-Grenadines, Suriname, Sweden, Switzerland, Syrian AR, Tajikistan, Tanzania UR, Thailand, Timor-Leste, Togo, Trinidad-Tobago, Tunisia, Türkiye, Turkmenistan, Tuvalu, Uganda, UK, Ukraine, United Arab Emirates, Uruguay, Uzbekistan, Vanuatu, Venezuela, Vietnam, Yemen, Zambia, Zimbabwe.
Committee members from 23 countries (term of expiry indicated in brackets):
Algeria (2022), Australia (2024), Azerbaijan (2022), Bahamas (2024), Bulgaria (2022), Burkina Faso (2022), China (2024), Egypt (2022), France (2024), Georgia (2022), Ghana (2024), Japan (2022), Lebanon (2024), Lithuania (2024), Mauritius (2022), Mexico (2024), Nepal (2024), Netherlands (2024), Peru (2022), Philippines (2024), Saudi Arabia (2022), Spain (2022), Trinidad-Tobago (2022). [2022.10.17/XE6009/**E***]

♦ Committee on the Elimination of Racial Discrimination (CERD) 04251

Comité pour l'élimination de la discrimination raciale – Comité para la Eliminación de la Discriminación Racial

Mailing Address c/o UNOG-OHCHR, 8-14 Avenue de la Paix, 1211 Geneva 10, Switzerland. T. +41229179614. Fax +41229179029. E-mail: ohchr-cerd@un.org.
URL: https://www.ohchr.org/en/treaty-bodies/cerd
History 1969. Established as a committee of *United Nations (UN, #20515)*, on entry into force of *International Convention on the Elimination of all Forms of Racial Discrimination (1965)*, in accordance with article 8 of that Treaty. Managed by *Office of the United Nations High Commissioner for Human Rights (OHCHR, #17697)* at *United Nations Office at Geneva (UNOG, #20597)*. Former names and other names: *United Nations Committee on the Elimination of Racial Discrimination* – former; *Comité des Nations Unies pour l'élimination de la discrimination raciale* – former; *Comité de las Naciones Unidas para la Eliminación de la Discriminación Racial* – former. **Aims** Monitor compliance of states parties with the Convention, under which they are obliged to pursue by all appropriate means and without delay a policy of eliminating discrimination in all its forms on grounds of race, descent or national or ethnic origin; undertake and adopt immediate and positive measures to eradicate all incitement to or acts of racial discrimination; guarantee the equal enjoyment by everyone without discrimination of all human rights. **Structure** Committee comprises 18 experts, elected in their personal capacity for 4-year terms by secret ballot at meetings of states party to the Convention. Bureau; Secretariat in Geneva (Switzerland), headed by Secretary. **Languages** Arabic, Chinese, English, French, Russian, Spanish. **Staff** 4.00 FTE, paid. **Finance** Comes under UN regular budget. **Activities** Sessions (2 a year, each lasting 3 weeks) are held at UNOG, in Geneva (Switzerland). **Events** *Session* Geneva (Switzerland) 2022, *Session* Geneva (Switzerland) 2022, *Session* Geneva (Switzerland) 2022, *Session* Geneva (Switzerland) 2021, *Session* Geneva (Switzerland) 2021. **Publications** Annual Report to UN General Assembly.
Members Independent experts of 18 countries (term of expiry indicated in brackets):
Algeria (2022), Belgium (2022), Brazil (2022), China (2024), Côte d'Ivoire (2022), Germany (2024), Greece (2024), Hungary (2022), Jamaica (2024), Japan (2022), Korea Rep (2022), Mauritania (2024), Mauritius (2022), Peru (2024), Qatar (2024), Senegal (2024), South Africa (2024), Türkiye (2022).
States parties to the Convention as at 13 Aug 2013 (176):
Afghanistan, Albania, Algeria, Andorra, Angola, Antigua-Barbuda, Argentina, Armenia, Australia, Austria, Azerbaijan, Bahamas, Bahrain, Bangladesh, Barbados, Belarus, Belgium, Belize, Benin, Bolivia, Bosnia-Herzegovina, Botswana, Brazil, Bulgaria, Burkina Faso, Burundi, Cambodia, Cameroon, Canada, Cape Verde, Central African Rep, Chad, Chile, China, Colombia, Comoros, Congo Brazzaville, Congo DR, Costa Rica, Côte d'Ivoire, Croatia, Cuba, Cyprus, Czechia, Denmark, Djibouti, Dominica, Dominican Rep, Ecuador, Egypt, El Salvador, Equatorial Guinea, Eritrea, Estonia, Eswatini, Ethiopia, Fiji, Finland, France, Gabon, Gambia, Georgia, Germany, Ghana, Greece, Grenada, Guatemala, Guinea, Guinea-Bissau, Guyana, Haiti, Holy See, Honduras, Hungary, Iceland, India, Indonesia, Iran Islamic Rep, Iraq, Ireland, Israel, Italy, Jamaica, Japan, Jordan, Kazakhstan, Kenya, Korea Rep, Kuwait, Kyrgyzstan, Laos, Latvia, Lebanon, Lesotho, Liberia, Libya, Liechtenstein, Lithuania, Luxembourg, Madagascar, Malawi, Maldives, Mali, Malta, Marshall Is, Mauritania, Mauritius, Mexico, Moldova, Monaco, Mongolia, Montenegro, Morocco, Mozambique, Namibia, Nepal, Netherlands, New Zealand, Nicaragua, Niger, Nigeria, North Macedonia, Norway, Oman, Pakistan, Palestine, Panama, Papua New Guinea, Paraguay, Peru, Philippines, Poland, Portugal, Qatar, Romania, Russia, Rwanda, San Marino, Sao Tomé-Principe, Saudi Arabia, Senegal, Serbia, Seychelles, Sierra Leone, Singapore, Slovakia, Slovenia, Solomon Is, Somalia, South Africa, Spain, Sri Lanka, St Kitts-Nevis, St Lucia, St Vincent-Grenadines, Sudan, Suriname, Sweden, Switzerland, Syrian AR, Tajikistan, Tanzania UR, Thailand, Timor-Leste, Togo, Tonga, Trinidad-Tobago, Tunisia, Türkiye, Turkmenistan, Uganda, UK, Ukraine, United Arab Emirates, Uruguay, USA, Uzbekistan, Venezuela, Vietnam, Yemen, Zambia, Zimbabwe.
States parties recognizing the competence of CERD in accordance with article 14 of the Convention (53):
Algeria, Andorra, Argentina, Australia, Austria, Azerbaijan, Belgium, Bolivia, Brazil, Bulgaria, Chile, Costa Rica, Cyprus, Czechia, Denmark, Ecuador, Finland, France, Georgia, Germany, Hungary, Iceland, Ireland, Italy, Kazakhstan, Korea Rep, Liechtenstein, Luxembourg, Malta, Mexico, Monaco, Montenegro, Morocco, Netherlands, North Macedonia, Norway, Peru, Poland, Portugal, Romania, Russia, San Marino, Senegal, Serbia, Slovakia, Slovenia, South Africa, Spain, Sweden, Switzerland, Ukraine, Uruguay, Venezuela.
NGO Relations Links with several organizations, including: *The International Movement Against All Forms of Discrimination and Racism (IMADR, #14191)*; *International Federation for Human Rights (#13452)*; *Amnesty International (AI, #00801)*; *European Roma Rights Centre (ERRC, #08401)*; *Human Rights Watch (HRW, #10990)*; *International Commission of Jurists (ICJ, #12695)*; *International League for Human Rights (ILHR, inactive)*. [2022/XE1310/**E***]

♦ Committee to encourage Unpaid Volunteer Action in Countries of Europe / see Volonteurope (#20807)

♦ Committee on Enforced Disappearances (CED) 04252

Comité des disparitions forcées – Comité contra la Desaparición Forzada

Secretariat UNOG-OHCHR, 1211 Geneva 10, Switzerland. T. +41229179256. Fax +41229179008. E-mail: ced@ohchr.org – ohchr-ced@un.org.
Street Address Human Rights Treaties Div, OHCHR, Palais Wilson, Rue des Pâquis 52, 1201 Geneva, Switzerland.
URL: http://www.ohchr.org/EN/HRBodies/ced/Pages/CEDIndex.aspx
History Set up within the framework of *United Nations (UN, #20515)*, by states party to the *International Convention for the Protection of all Persons from Enforced Disappearance (2006)*. Managed by *Office of the United Nations High Commissioner for Human Rights (OHCHR, #17697)* at *United Nations Office at Geneva (UNOG, #20597)*. **Structure** Committee of 10 independent experts. Secretary-General. **Events** *Session* Geneva (Switzerland) 2021, *Session* Geneva (Switzerland) 2021, *Session* Geneva (Switzerland) 2020, *Session* Geneva (Switzerland) 2020, *Session* Geneva (Switzerland) 2019.
Members Experts from 10 countries (term of expiry indicated in brackets):
Argentina (2021), France (2023), Germany (2023), Japan (2021), Morocco (2021), Peru (2023), Senegal (2023), Serbia (2021), Spain (2023), Tunisia (2021).
States Parties (63) as at Aug 2020:
Albania, Argentina, Armenia, Austria, Belgium, Belize, Benin, Bolivia, Bosnia-Herzegovina, Brazil, Burkina Faso, Cambodia, Central African Rep, Chile, Colombia, Costa Rica, Cuba, Czechia, Dominica, Ecuador, Fiji, France, Gabon, Gambia, Germany, Greece, Honduras, Iraq, Italy, Japan, Kazakhstan, Lesotho, Lithuania, Malawi, Mali, Malta, Mauritania, Mexico, Mongolia, Montenegro, Morocco, Netherlands, Niger, Nigeria, Norway, Oman, Panama, Paraguay, Peru, Portugal, Samoa, Senegal, Serbia, Seychelles, Slovakia, Spain, Sri Lanka, Switzerland, Togo, Tunisia, Ukraine, Uruguay, Zambia. [2020/XJ7173/**E***]

♦ Committee for Engineering Education of Middle Africa (inactive)

♦ Committee on Environmental Policy 04253

Contact Land Management Div UNECE, Palais des Nations, 1211 Geneva 10, Switzerland. T. +41229172370. Fax +41229170107.
URL: http://www.unece.org/env/cep/welcome.html
History Jun 1994, Geneva (Switzerland), as a sectoral committee of *United Nations Economic Commission for Europe (UNECE, #20555)*. Successor to *Senior Advisers to ECE Governments on Environmental and Water Problems*. Also referred to as *UNECE Committee on Environmental Policy*. **Aims** Provide environmental policy guidance for UNECE region; promote policy instruments to strengthen capabilities of member countries, in particular countries of EECCA and SEE, to integrate environmental considerations into other sectors; promote environmental protection and sustainable development in the light of Agenda 21 and the plan of implementation of the Johannesburg (South Africa) Summit; develop international environmental legal instruments and promote their implementation; coordinate environment-related programmes in the UNECE region and issues on sustainable development within the Commission and encourage public participation in environmental decision-making. **Structure** UNECE member states may participate in Plenary Sessions. Bureau, consisting of 8 member countries. Working Groups and ad hoc expert groups are set up when needed, currently: Ad Hoc Expert Group on Environmental Performance Reviews (EPR Expert Group); Working Group on Environmental Monitoring and Assessment. **Languages** English, French, Russian. **Finance** Main source: UN regular budget. Trust funds (2) for: travel costs for representatives of countries in transition and consultants; Environment for Europe process and Environmental Performance Reviews; Environmental Monitoring and Assessment. **Activities** Programme of work covers 'Environment for Europe' process, including implementation of decisions of last Ministerial Conference and preparation for the next; preparation of environmental performance reviews of EECCA and SEE; preparation and implementation of regional environmental conventions and protocols: *Convention on Access to Information, Public Participation in Decision-making and Access to Justice in Environmental Matters (Århus Convention, 1998)*; *Convention on Environmental Impact Assessment in a Transboundary Context (Espoo Convention, 1991)*; *Convention on the Protection and Use of Transboundary Watercourses and International Lakes (1992)*; *Convention on the Transboundary Effects of Industrial Accidents (1992)*; *Convention on Long-range Transboundary Air Pollution (#04787)*; and protocols related to the above mentioned conventions. Annual sessions and special sessions. **Events** *Ministerial Conference* Belgrade (Serbia) 2007, *Session* Geneva (Switzerland) 2005, *Session* Geneva (Switzerland) 2004, *Session* Geneva (Switzerland) 2003, *Special session* Geneva (Switzerland) 2003. **Publications** UNECE environmental conventions and protocols; environmental performance reviews.
Members UN/ECE member countries (56).
Albania, Andorra, Armenia, Austria, Azerbaijan, Belarus, Belgium, Bosnia-Herzegovina, Bulgaria, Canada, Croatia, Cyprus, Czechia, Denmark, Estonia, Finland, France, Georgia, Germany, Greece, Hungary, Iceland, Ireland, Israel, Italy, Kazakhstan, Kyrgyzstan, Latvia, Liechtenstein, Lithuania, Luxembourg, Malta, Moldova, Monaco, Montenegro, Netherlands, North Macedonia, Norway, Poland, Portugal, Romania, Russia, San Marino, Serbia, Slovakia, Slovenia, Spain, Sweden, Switzerland, Tajikistan, Türkiye, Turkmenistan, UK, Ukraine, USA, Uzbekistan. [2010/XE3246/**E***]

♦ Committee of European Associations of Catholic Doctors (inactive)
♦ Committee of European Banking Supervisors (inactive)
♦ Committee of European Coffee Associations (inactive)

♦ Committee for European Construction Equipment (CECE) 04254

Comité européen des matériaux de génie civil – Comité Europea de Maquinaria de Construcción y Obras Públicas – Europäisches Baumaschinen Komitee – Comitato Europeo dei Costruttori di Macchine da Cantiere e per Movimento di Terra

SG BluePoint Bldg, Bd Reyers 80, 1030 Brussels, Belgium. T. +3227068226. Fax +3227068210. E-mail: info@cece.eu – sg@cece.eu.
URL: http://www.cece.eu/
History Legal Status: Articles of Association not registered. Registration: EU Transparency Register, No/ID: 60534525900-25. **Aims** Represent and promote the European construction equipment and related industries, coordinating the views of national associations and their members by influencing European and national institutions and other organizations worldwide to achieve a fair, competitive environment via harmonized standards and regulations. **Structure** General Meeting (annual); Presidents Committee; Executive Committee; General Secretariat; Technical Secretariat; Technical Commission plus Intercontinental Technical Liaison Group; Main Statistical Committee plus Intercontinental Statistical Liaison Group; Sections; Technical Working Groups; Statistical Working Groups. **Languages** English. **Staff** 6.00 FTE, paid. **Finance** Sources: members' dues. **Activities** Events/meetings; knowledge management/information dissemination; politics/policy/regulatory; standards/guidelines. **Events** *Congress* Chamonix (France) 2023, *Summit* Brussels (Belgium) 2021, *Congress* Stockholm (Sweden) 2020, *Summit* Brussels (Belgium) 2019, *Building customer loyalty through a common vision* Rome (Italy) 2018. **Publications** European standards; illustrated terminologies.
Members National committees representative of their countries' manufacturers in 13 countries:
Austria, Belgium, Czechia, Finland, France, Germany, Italy, Netherlands, Russia, Spain, Sweden, Türkiye, UK.
Consultative Status Consultative status granted from: *ECOSOC (#05331)* (Ros A). **IGO Relations** Recognized by: *European Commission (EC, #06633)*. **NGO Relations** Member of (4): *Alliance for Internet of Things Innovation (AIOTI, #00697)*; *Construction 2050 Alliance (#04760)*; *European Council for Construction Research, Development and Innovation (ECCREDI, #06813)*; *Industry4Europe (#11181)*. In liaison with technical committees of: *Comité européen de normalisation (CEN, #04162)*; *International Organization for Standardization (ISO, #14473)*. [2023.02.14/XD0290/**D**]

♦ Committee of the European Cotton Industry / see European Federation of Cotton and Allied Textiles Industries (#07093)
♦ Committee for European Economic Cooperation (inactive)
♦ Committee of European Electron Microscopy Societies / see European Microscopy Society (#07795)
♦ Committee of European Environmental Engineering Societies / see Confederation of European Environmental Engineering Societies (#04524)
♦ Committee of European Financial Executives Institutes / see European Federation of Financial Executives Institutes (#07124)
♦ Committee of European Foundry Associations / see European Foundry Association, The (#07352)
♦ Committee of the European Hardware, Housewares and Metalworking Industries (inactive)
♦ Committee of European Insurance and Occupational Pensions Supervisors / see European Insurance and Occupational Pensions Authority (#07578)
♦ Committee of European Jesuit Provincials / see Jesuit Conference of European Provincials (#16100)
♦ Committee of European Manufacturers of Petroleum Measuring and Distributing Equipment (#04167)

♦ Committee for European Marine Biology Symposia (EMBS) 04255

Comité pour les colloques européens de biologie marine

Contact c/o MARS Network, Marine Biological Assoc, Citadel Hill, Plymouth, PL1 2PB, UK. E-mail: secretariat@marinestations.org.
URL: https://www.marinestations.org/embs-european-marine-biology-symposium/
History Sep 1966, Germany FR. Founded at 1st European Symposium of Marine Biology, following a series of Symposia in Germany begun in 1960. **Aims** Serve as permanent mechanism for establishing, maintaining and deepening professional, institutional and personal contacts among European marine biologists and *ecologists*. **Structure** Committee, representing European marine biologists, meets at annual Symposium. **Finance** Meeting financed by hosting institute. **Events** *European Marine Biology Symposium (EMBS)* Reykjavik (Iceland) 2023, *European Marine Biology Symposium (EMBS)* Gdansk (Poland) 2022, *European Marine Biology Symposium* Bilbao (Spain) 2021, *European Marine Biology Symposium* Gdansk (Poland) 2020, *European Marine Biology Symposium* Dublin (Ireland) 2019. **Publications** Symposium proceedings. **Members** Not a membership organization. **NGO Relations** Supported by: *European Network of Marine Research Institutes and Stations (MARS Network, #07941)*. Recognized by: *International Association of Biological Oceanography (IABO, #11726)*. [2022/XD0291/**E**]

♦ Committee of European National Shipowners' Associations (inactive)
♦ Committee of European Securities Regulators / see European Securities and Markets Authority (#08457)

♦ Committee of European Shipowners (inactive)
♦ Committee of European Societies for Electron Microscopy / see European Microscopy Society (#07795)
♦ Committee of European Societies for Microscopy / see European Microscopy Society (#07795)
♦ Committee of European Starch Potato Producers / see Committee of the European Starch Potato Producers' Union (#04256)

♦ Committee of the European Starch Potato Producers' Union (CESPU) 04256

SG c/o Union der Deutschen kartoffelenschaft – UNIKA, Schumannstrasse 5 D, 10117 Berlin, Germany. T. +4930657993-83. Fax +493065799385. E-mail: cespu@unika-ev.de.
History Brussels (Belgium). Former names and other names: *Committee of European Starch Potato Producers* – former. **Aims** Defend rights and interests of starch potato producers. **Structure** President; General Secretary. **Languages** English, French, German. **Finance** Sources: members' dues.
Members Full in 7 countries:
Austria, Denmark, Finland, France, Germany, Netherlands, Sweden. [2022.05.17/XE3936/**E**]

♦ Committee for European Studies on Norms for Electronics (inactive)
♦ Committee for European and World Federation (inactive)
♦ Committee of Experts on Children and Families (inactive)
♦ Committee of Experts on the Evaluation of Anti-Money Laundering Measures / see Committee of Experts on the Evaluation of Anti-Money Laundering Measures and the Financing of Terrorism (#04257)

♦ Committee of Experts on the Evaluation of Anti-Money Laundering Measures and the Financing of Terrorism (MONEYVAL) 04257

Comité d'experts sur l'évaluation des mesures de lutte contre le blanchiment des capitaux et le financement du terrorisme
Sec c/o Council of Europe, Palais de l'Europe, 67075 Strasbourg CEDEX, France. T. +33388412930. Fax +33390215073. E-mail: moneyval@coe.int.
URL: http://www.coe.int/moneyval/
History Established 1997, by *Council of Europe (CE, #04881)*, under the authority of *European Committee on Crime Problems (CDPC, #06645)*. Original title: *Committee of Experts on the Evaluation of Anti-Money Laundering Measures*. **Aims** Review anti-money laundering measures and measures to counter the financing of *terrorism* in Council of Europe member states which are not members of the Financial Action Task Force (FATF) and in Israel, Holy See (including Vatican City State), and the UK Crown Dependencies of Guernsey, Jersey and the Isle of Man. **Structure** Plenary meetings (3-4 a year); Bureau; Secretariat. **Languages** English, French. **Finance** General budget of: *Council of Europe (CE, #04881)*; voluntary contributions. **Activities** Monitoring/evaluation; events/meetings; research/documentation. **Events** *Plenary Meeting* Strasbourg (France) 2010, *Plenary Meeting* Strasbourg (France) 2010, *Plenary Meeting* Strasbourg (France) 2010, *Typologies meeting* Cyprus 2009, *Plenary Meeting* Strasbourg (France) 2009.
Members States and territories evaluated by MONEYVAL (33):
Albania, Andorra, Armenia, Azerbaijan, Bosnia-Herzegovina, Bulgaria, Croatia, Cyprus, Czechia, Estonia, Georgia, Guernsey, Holy See, Hungary, Isle of Man, Israel, Jersey, Latvia, Liechtenstein, Lithuania, Malta, Moldova, Monaco, Montenegro, North Macedonia, Poland, Romania, Russia, San Marino, Serbia, Slovakia, Slovenia, Ukraine.
FATF countries appointed for 2-year periods (2):
Austria, UK.
Observers in 5 countries:
Canada, Holy See, Israel, Mexico, USA.
Observer organization (1):
Group of International Finance Centre Supervisors (GIFCS, #10782).
IGO Relations Member of: *Asia/Pacific Group on Money Laundering (APG, #01921)*; *Eurasian Group on Combating Money Laundering and Financing of Terrorism (EAG, #05608)*. Cooperates with: *Commonwealth Secretariat (#04362)*; *Counter-Terrorism Committee (CTC, #04928)*; *Egmont Group of Financial Intelligence Units (#05396)*; *European Bank for Reconstruction and Development (EBRD, #06315)*; *European Commission (EC, #06633)*; *European Council (#06801)*; *Financial Action Task Force (FATF, #09765)*; *International Bank for Reconstruction and Development (IBRD, #12317)* (World Bank); *International Criminal Police Organization – INTERPOL (ICPO-INTERPOL, #13110)*; *International Monetary Fund (IMF, #14180)*; *United Nations Office on Drugs and Crime (UNODC, #20596)*. [2014.12.08/XJ4112/**E***]

♦ **Committee of Experts on TDG and GHS** United Nations Committee of Experts on the Transport of Dangerous Goods and on the Globally Harmonized System of Classification and Labelling of Chemicals (#20543)
♦ Committee of Family Organizations in the European Community / see COFACE Families Europe (#04084)
♦ Committee of Former UNESCO Staff Members / see Association of Former UNESCO Staff Members (#02601)
♦ Committee for the Foundation of the International Organization of Psychophysiology / see International Organization of Psychophysiology (#14466)

♦ Committee on the Global Financial System (CGFS) 04258

Address not obtained.
URL: http://www.bis.org/cgfs/
History 1971, as *Euro-Currency Standing Committee*, within the framework of *Bank for International Settlements (BIS, #03165)*. Present name adopted Feb 1999. **Aims** Monitor and examine broad issues relating to financial *markets* and systems with a view to elaborating appropriate *policy* recommendations to support central *banks* in the fulfillment of their responsibilities for monetary and financial stability. **Structure** Regular Committee; Working Groups. Secretariat. **Languages** English. **Staff** 7.00 FTE, paid. **Activities** Monitoring/evaluation. **Publications** Reports; reviews; notes.
Members Deputy Governors and senior officials of central banks of advanced and emerging market economies in 21 countries and territories, and the Economic Adviser of Bank for International Settlements:
Australia, Belgium, Brazil, Canada, China, France, Germany, Hong Kong, India, Italy, Japan, Korea Rep, Luxembourg, Mexico, Netherlands, Singapore, Spain, Sweden, Switzerland, UK, USA.
Included in the above, 1 organization listed in this Yearbook:
European Central Bank (ECB, #06466).
IGO Relations Member of: *Financial Stability Board (FSB, #09770)*. [2017/XE4143/**E**]

♦ Committee of Governors of the Central Banks of the Member States of the European Economic Community (inactive)
♦ Committee of High-Level Government Experts (see: #20556)
♦ Committee of the Hotel and Restaurant Industry in the European Community / see Confederation of National Associations of Hotels, Restaurants, Cafés and Similar Establishments in the European Union and European Economic Area (#04569)

♦ Committee on Housing and Land Management 04259

Dir Environment/Housing and Land Management Div, UNECE, Palais des Nations, 1211 Geneva 10, Switzerland. T. +41229172370. Fax +41229170107. E-mail: housing.landmanagement@unece.org.
URL: http://www.unece.org/env/
History 1947, Geneva (Switzerland), as *Committee on Human Settlements*, as a sectoral committee of *United Nations Economic Commission for Europe (UNECE, #20555)*. Also referred to as *UNECE Committee on Human Settlements*. **Aims** Assist countries with reforming the housing sector through providing good examples with socially oriented housing programmes and spatial planning practices, with a particular focus on partnerships between all levels of government and the private sector and promoting modern cadastre and land registration systems as a basis for economically, socially and environmentally sound urban and rural development. **Structure** Annual Plenary Session; Bureau; Advisory Board (HUMAN); Subsidiary Body – Working Party on Land Administration. **Languages** English, French, Russian. **Finance** On regular UN budget; Trust Fund on Human Settlements. **Activities** Research/documentation; knoweldge management/information dissemination; guidance/assistance/consulting; events/meetings; politics/policy/regulatory; standards/guidelines. **Events** *Workshop on enhancing urban performance* Prague (Czech Rep) 2010, *Joint workshop on spatial information management toward environmental management of mega cities* Valencia (Spain) 2008, *Annual plenary session* Geneva (Switzerland) 2005, *Annual plenary session* Geneva (Switzerland) 2004, *Annual plenary session* Geneva (Switzerland) 2003. **Publications** *Country Profile on Housing* – series.
Members Government officials in the field of housing, urban and regional planning and land administration in 56 UNECE countries:
Albania, Andorra, Armenia, Austria, Azerbaijan, Belarus, Belgium, Bosnia-Herzegovina, Bulgaria, Canada, Croatia, Cyprus, Czechia, Denmark, Estonia, Finland, France, Georgia, Germany, Greece, Hungary, Iceland, Ireland, Israel, Italy, Kazakhstan, Kyrgyzstan, Latvia, Liechtenstein, Lithuania, Luxembourg, Malta, Moldova, Monaco, Montenegro, Netherlands, North Macedonia, Norway, Poland, Portugal, Romania, Russia, San Marino, Serbia, Slovakia, Slovenia, Spain, Sweden, Switzerland, Tajikistan, Türkiye, Turkmenistan, UK, Ukraine, USA, Uzbekistan. [2016.10.26/XE3247/**E***]

♦ Committee on Human Settlements / see Committee on Housing and Land Management (#04259)

♦ Committee on Information (COI) 04260

Comité de l'information – Comité de Información
Chair United Nations, Room M-16019, 380 Madison Ave, New York NY 10017, USA. T. +2129636555. Fax +2129631893.
URL: https://www.un.org/en/ga/coi/
History 18 Dec 1978, New York, NY (USA). Established, within the framework of *United Nations (UN, #20515)*, by UN General Assembly resolution 33/115 C, as a subsidiary body of the UN General Assembly. Present name adopted by resolution 34/182 of 18 Dec 1979 of the General Assembly. Former names and other names: *Committee to Review United Nations Public Information Policies and Activities* – former (1978 to 1979); *Committee on Information of the United Nations* – former; *Comité de l'information des Nations Unies* – former. **Aims** Continue to examine United Nations public information policies and activities, in the light of the evolution of international relations, particularly during the past two decades, and of the imperatives of the establishment of the new international economic order and of a new world information and communication order; evaluate and follow up the efforts made and the progress achieved by the United Nations system in the field of information and communications; promote the establishment of a new, more just and more effective world information and communication order intended to strengthen peace and international understanding and based on the free circulation and wider and better-balanced dissemination of information and to make recommendations thereon to the General Assembly. **Structure** Annual General Debate; Bureau. **Languages** Arabic, Chinese, English, French, Russian, Spanish. **Finance** United Nations General Assembly. **Activities** Guidance/assistance/consulting; monitoring/evaluation. Responsible for overseeing the work of the UN Department of Global Communications. **Events** *Annual Session* New York, NY (USA) 2011, *Annual Session* New York, NY (USA) 2010, *Annual Session* New York, NY (USA) 2009, *Annual Session* New York, NY (USA) 2007, *Annual Session* New York, NY (USA) 2006. **Publications** Annual Report.
Members Member States (113):
Algeria, Angola, Antigua-Barbuda, Argentina, Armenia, Austria, Azerbaijan, Bangladesh, Belarus, Belgium, Belize, Benin, Bolivia, Brazil, Bulgaria, Burkina Faso, Burundi, Cape Verde, Chile, China, Colombia, Congo Brazzaville, Congo DR, Costa Rica, Côte d'Ivoire, Croatia, Cuba, Cyprus, Czechia, Denmark, Dominican Rep, Ecuador, Egypt, El Salvador, Ethiopia, Finland, France, Gabon, Georgia, Germany, Ghana, Greece, Guatemala, Guinea, Guyana, Hungary, Iceland, India, Indonesia, Iran Islamic Rep, Iraq, Ireland, Israel, Italy, Jamaica, Japan, Jordan, Kazakhstan, Kenya, Korea DPR, Korea Rep, Lebanon, Liberia, Libya, Luxembourg, Madagascar, Malta, Mexico, Moldova, Monaco, Mongolia, Morocco, Mozambique, Nepal, Netherlands, Niger, Nigeria, Oman, Pakistan, Paraguay, Peru, Philippines, Poland, Portugal, Qatar, Romania, Russia, Saudi Arabia, Senegal, Sierra Leone, Singapore, Slovakia, Solomon Is, Somalia, South Africa, Spain, Sri Lanka, St Vincent-Grenadines, Sudan, Suriname, Switzerland, Syrian AR, Tanzania UR, Thailand, Togo, Trinidad-Tobago, Tunisia, Türkiye, UK, Ukraine, Uruguay, USA, Vietnam, Yemen, Zambia, Zimbabwe.
Observers (6):
Holy See, Palestine.
European Union (EU, #08967); *League of Arab States (LAS, #16420)*; *Organisation internationale de la Francophonie (OIF, #17809)*; *UNESCO (#20322)*. [2019/XE0536/**E***]

♦ Committee on Information of the United Nations / see Committee on Information (#04260)
♦ Committee for Inland Fisheries of Africa / see Committee for Inland Fisheries and Aquaculture of Africa (#04261)

♦ Committee for Inland Fisheries and Aquaculture of Africa (CIFAA) 04261

Contact c/o FAO Regional Office, PO Box 1628, Accra, Ghana.
URL: http://www.fao.org/fishery/rfb/cifaa/
History 1971, as *Committee for Inland Fisheries of Africa (CIFA)*, within the framework of *FAO (#09260)*, by Article VI-2 of its Constitution, following decision of 56th Session of FAO Council and coordinated by its Fisheries Division. First Session: Nov-Dec 1972. Based at *FAO Regional Office for Africa (FAO/RAF, #09265)*. **Aims** Promote, coordinate and assist national and regional fishery surveys and research and development designed to utilize rationally inland fishery resources; assist member states in establishing the scientific basis for regulatory and other measures; assist in development of fish culture and stock improvement; promote the use of the most effective fishing craft, gear and techniques; encourage education and training; assist members in formulating programmes to help achieve the objectives referred to in the statutes. **Structure** Sub-Committees for Lake Tanganika. **Languages** English, French. **Activities** Organizes symposia. Sub-Committees involved in setting up *'Lake Victoria Fisheries Commission'* and propose setting up *Lake Tanganika Fisheries Commission (no recent information)* and endorse *'Indicative Action Plan for Aquaculture Research in Sub-Saharan Africa'*. **Events** *Session* Bujumbura (Burundi) 2006, *Session* Entebbe (Uganda) 2004, *Session* Yaoundé (Cameroon) 2002, *Session* Abuja (Nigeria) 2000, *Session* Akosombo (Ghana) 1997. **Publications** *Chlorinated Hydrocarbon Substances in the African Aquatic Environment*; *Source Book for African Inland Fisheries (SIFRA)*. **Information Services** *Database for African Inland Fisheries (DIFRA)*.
Members FAO African Member Nations and Associate Members selected by the Director General. Governments of 36 African countries:
Benin, Botswana, Burkina Faso, Burundi, Cameroon, Central African Rep, Chad, Congo Brazzaville, Congo DR, Côte d'Ivoire, Egypt, Eritrea, Eswatini, Ethiopia, Gabon, Gambia, Ghana, Guinea, Kenya, Lesotho, Madagascar, Malawi, Mali, Mauritius, Niger, Nigeria, Rwanda, Senegal, Sierra Leone, Somalia, Sudan, Tanzania UR, Togo, Uganda, Zambia, Zimbabwe.
Observer: government of 1 country:
UK. [2012/XE0139/**E***]

♦ Committee on Inland Transport 04262

Comité des transports intérieurs (ECE/TRANS)
Contact Director UNECE Sustainable Transport Division, Office 424, Palais des Nations, 1211 Geneva 10, Switzerland. T. +41229172400. Fax +41229170039.
URL: http://www.unece.org/trans/main/itc/itc.html
History Set up as a committee of *United Nations Economic Commission for Europe (UNECE, #20555)*. Former names and other names: *Inland Transport Committee (ITC)* – former; *Comité des transports intérieurs (ECE/TRANS)* – former; *UNECE Inland Transport Committee* – alias; *ONU-CEE Comité des transports intérieurs* – alias. **Aims** Harmonize standards and regulations in the field of inland transport including vehicle construction, road *traffic* safety and transport of dangerous goods; facilitate border crossing; develop a coherent transport system in Europe with harmonized transport infrastructures in rail, road, inland waterways and combined transport. **Structure** Bureau. Working Parties and Groups of Experts. **Languages** English, French, Russian. **Finance** Activities of the Committee and its secretariat financed through the regular budget of UNECE. **Activities** Politics/policy/regulatory. **Events** *Annual Session* Geneva (Switzerland) 2023, *Annual Session* Geneva (Switzerland) 2022, *Annual Session* Geneva (Switzerland) 2021, *Annual Session* Geneva (Switzerland) 2020, *Annual Session* Geneva (Switzerland) 2019. **Publications** Conventions/Agreements on transport matters; statistical bulletins; regulations on the construction of vehicles; recommendations on the transport of dangerous goods; special reports on items in the work programme.
Members UNECE member countries (56):
Albania, Andorra, Armenia, Austria, Azerbaijan, Belarus, Belgium, Bosnia-Herzegovina, Bulgaria, Canada, Croatia, Cyprus, Czechia, Denmark, Estonia, Finland, France, Georgia, Germany, Greece, Hungary, Iceland, Ireland, Israel, Italy, Kazakhstan, Kyrgyzstan, Latvia, Liechtenstein, Lithuania, Luxembourg, Malta, Moldova, Monaco, Montenegro, Netherlands, North Macedonia, Norway, Poland, Portugal, Romania, Russia, San Marino, Serbia, Slovakia, Slovenia, Spain, Sweden, Switzerland, Tajikistan, Türkiye, Turkmenistan, UK, Ukraine, USA, Uzbekistan.
IGO Relations Links include:
– *Agreement Concerning the Adoption of Uniform Conditions for Periodical Technical Inspections of Wheeled Vehicles and the Reciprocal Recognition of Such Inspections (1997)*;

Committee Integrating Forestry
04262

alphabetic sequence excludes
For the complete listing, see Yearbook Online at

- *Agreement concerning the Adoption of Harmonized Technical United Nations Regulations for Wheeled Vehicles, Equipment and Parts which can be Fitted and/or be Used on Wheeled Vehicles and the Conditions for Reciprocal Recognition of Approvals Granted on the Basis of these United Nations Regulations (1958)*;
- *Central Commission for the Navigation of the Rhine (CCNR, #03687)*;
- *Commission du Danube (CD, #04210)*;
- *Commonwealth of Independent States (CIS, #04341)*;
- *Council of Europe (CE, #04881)*;
- *ECOSOC (#05331)*;
- *European Commission (EC, #06633)*;
- *International Institute for the Unification of Private Law (UNIDROIT, #13934)*;
- *International Transport Forum (ITF, #15725)*;
- *OECD (#17693)*;
- *Organization of Black Sea Economic Cooperation (BSEC, #17857)*;
- *Organisation for Cooperation between Railways (OSJD, #17803)*;
- *Trans-European North-South Motorway Project (TEM, #20208)*;
- *Trans-European Railway Project (TER, #20210)*;
- *UNEP (#20299)*;
- *UNCTAD (#20285)*;
- *United Nations Economic Commission for Africa (ECA, #20554)*;
- *United Nations Economic Commission for Latin America and the Caribbean (ECLAC, #20556)*;
- *United Nations Economic and Social Commission for Asia and the Pacific (ESCAP, #20557)*;
- *United Nations Economic and Social Commission for Western Asia (ESCWA, #20558)*;
- *WHO (#20950)*;
- *WHO Regional Office for Europe (#20945)*.

NGO Relations Links with organizations in consultative status with ECOSOC, including: *Liquid Gas Europe (#16488)*; *Fédération Internationale de l'Automobile (FIA, #09613)*; *International Organization of Motor Vehicle Manufacturers (#14455)*; *International Road Transport Union (IRU, #14761)*; *European Association of Automotive Suppliers (CLEPA, #05948)*. [2022/XE1684/**E***]

♦ Committee for Integrating Forestry Training in the Northern Countries (inactive)

♦ Committee of Intelligence and Security Service of Africa (CISSA) . . 04263

Secretariat PO Box 3290, Addis Ababa, Ethiopia. T. +251113712006. Fax +251113716154. E-mail: info@cissaau.org.
Street Address Nifas Silk Lafto Sub City, Kebele 3, Around AU Chair Person Residence, Behind Iranian Embassy, Addis Ababa, Ethiopia.
URL: https://cissaau.org/

History Established 26 Aug 2004, Abuja (Nigeria) by Heads of Intelligence and Security Services of Africa. Endorsed by *African Union (AU, #00488)* Assembly Decision 62. A Specialized Agency of AU. **Aims** Coordinate intelligence as well as promote cooperation, confidence building measures and capacity building among intelligence and security services of Africa. **Structure** Conference; Bureau; Troika; Panel of Experts; Secretariat.
Members Intelligence and Security Services signatory to the Constitutive Memorandum of Understanding (51):
Algeria, Angola, Benin, Botswana, Burkina Faso, Burundi, Cameroon, Cape Verde, Central African Rep, Comoros, Congo Brazzaville, Congo DR, Côte d'Ivoire, Djibouti, Egypt, Equatorial Guinea, Eswatini, Ethiopia, Gabon, Gambia, Ghana, Guinea, Guinea-Bissau, Kenya, Lesotho, Liberia, Libya, Madagascar, Malawi, Mali, Mauritania, Mauritius, Mozambique, Namibia, Niger, Nigeria, Rwanda, Sahara West, Sao Tomé-Principe, Senegal, Sierra Leone, Somalia, South Africa, South Sudan, Sudan, Tanzania UR, Togo, Tunisia, Uganda, Zambia, Zimbabwe.
IGO Relations Partners *African Union Scientific Technical Research Commission (AU STRC, #00493)*; *International Conference on the Great Lakes Region (ICGLR, #12880)*. [2019/XM8549/**E***]

♦ Committee of the International Children's Games (CICG) 04264

Comité des jeux internationaux des écoliers (CJIE) – Komitee der internationalen Schülerspiele
SG Heidelberger Landstrasse 270 A, 64297 Darmstadt, Germany. T. +496151152153. Fax +496151152155.
URL: http://international-childrens-games.org/

History Founded 1968. Statutes amended 17 Feb 1998, Darmstadt (Germany); 12 Jun 1997; Jul 2005, Coventry (UK). **Aims** Enable, develop and advance the meeting, understanding and friendship of students from different countries; advance the *Olympic* ideal. **Structure** General Assembly (every 2 years); Office; Committees (4); Seat located in Lausanne (Switzerland). **Languages** English, French, German. **Staff** Voluntary. **Finance** Funded by IOC. **Activities** Events/meetings. **Events** *General assembly / General Assembly and Games* UK 2011, *General Assembly and Games* Manama (Bahrain) 2010, *General Assembly and Games* Athens (Greece) 2009, *General Assembly and Games* San Francisco, CA (USA) 2008, *General assembly / General Assembly and Games* Reykjavik (Iceland) 2007.
Members Cities, being members and organizers of the International Children's Games; individuals, organizations or cities who recognize the goals of the International Children's Games. Members in 22 countries and territories:
Andorra, Austria, Canada, Czechia, France, Germany, Greece, Hungary, Iceland, Italy, Monaco, Poland, Romania, Slovakia, Slovenia, Spain, Switzerland, Taiwan, Thailand, UK, Ukraine, USA. [2016.10.19/XE1933/**E**]

♦ Committee for International Conferences on Industrial and Applied Mathematics / see International Council for Industrial and Applied Mathematics (#13032)

♦ Committee for International Cooperation between Cotton Associations (CICCA) 04265

Comité pour la coopération internationale entre les associations cotonnières – Comité de Cooperación Internacional entre Asociaciones Algodoneras
Secretariat 6th Floor, Walker House, Exchange Flags, Liverpool, L2 3YL, UK. T. +441512366041.
URL: http://www.cicca.info/

History 1978. **Aims** Provide a representative and influential organization by seeking to develop its infrastructure to assist the industry to prosper in an increasingly competitive and technological environment. **Structure** Plenary Meeting (annual); Working Groups. **Languages** English. **Staff** Voluntary. **Finance** Members' dues. **Activities** Guidance/assistance/consulting. **Publications** Directory.
Members National associations in 16 countries:
Australia, Belgium, Brazil, China, Egypt, France, Germany, India, Italy, Japan, Pakistan, Poland, Spain, Türkiye, UK, USA.
Regional organization (1):
African Cotton Association (#00270).
Consultative Status Consultative status granted from: *UNCTAD (#20285)* (Special Category). **IGO Relations** Regular relations with: *International Cotton Advisory Committee (ICAC, #12979)*. **NGO Relations** Secretariat located at: *International Cotton Association (ICA, #12980)*. [2021/XD8546/**D**]

♦ Committee for International Cooperation and Development (internationally oriented national body)
♦ Committee for International Cooperation in Rural Sociology (inactive)

♦ Committee for International Development and Education on Construction of Tubular Structures (CIDECT) 04266

Comité international pour le développement et l'étude de la construction tubulaire (CIDECT)
Pres c/o IBK, Fachbereich Stahl-, Holz- und Verbundbau ETH Zürich, Stefano-Franscini-Platz 5, 8093 Zurich ZH, Switzerland. E-mail: info@cidect.com.
URL: http://www.cidect.org/

History 1962, with English title *International Committee for Research and Technical Support for Hollow Section Structures*. Also referred to as *Comité international pour l'étude et le développement de la construction tubulaire*. **Aims** Expand knowledge, by means of research and studies, of steel hollow sections and their application in steel construction and engineering. **Structure** President; Vice-President/Treasurer; Committee Chairmen (Technical; Promotion). **Events** *International symposium on tubular structures* Hong Kong (Hong Kong) 2010.
Members Full in 5 countries:
Finland, Germany, Kenya, Spain, UK. [2022/XU8318/**D**]

♦ Committee of International Development Institutions on the Environment (no recent information)
♦ Committee for International Olympic Aid / see Olympic Solidarity (#17721)
♦ Committee of International Sugar Users / see CIUS – European Sugar Users (#03961)
♦ Committee of Islamic Solidarity with the Peoples of the Sahel (inactive)
♦ Committee For Justice (unconfirmed)
♦ Committee of Latin American Workers Conferences (inactive)

♦ Committee of Legal Advisers on Public International Law (CAHDI) . 04267

Comité des Conseillers juridiques sur le droit international public
Contact Public Int Law Div and Treaty Office, Dir Legal Advice and Public Intl Law, Council of Europe, Avenue de l'Europe, 67075 Strasbourg CEDEX, France. T. +33388412092. E-mail: cahdi@coe.int.
URL: http://www.coe.int/cahdi/

History 1991, within the framework of *Council of Europe (CE, #04881)*, on adoption of mandate by *Committee of Ministers of the Council of Europe (#04273)* (renewed every 2 years). **Aims** Examine questions related to public international law; conduct exchanges and coordinate views of member States and provide opinions at the request of the Committee of Ministers or at the request of other Steering Committees or Ad hoc Committees, transmitted via the Committee of Ministers. **Structure** Committee (meeting twice a year, generally in Strasbourg – France), comprising Legal Advisers of Ministries of Foreign Affairs of Member States of the Council of Europe, as well as of Observer States and international organizations. Committee is directly responsible to the Committee of Ministers. **Languages** English, French. **Staff** Provided by Council of Europe. **Finance** Budget of Council of Europe. **Activities** Politics/policy/regulatory. **Events** *Meeting* Helsinki (Finland) 2018, *Meeting* Strasbourg (France) 2004. **Publications** *The CAHDI Contribution to the Development of Public International Law* (2016); *The Judge and International Custom* (2016); *State Practice Regarding State Immunities* (2006); *Treaty Making – Expression of Consent by States to be Bound by a Treaty* (2001); *Implications of the European Convention on Human Rights* (2000); *State Practice Regarding State Succession and Issues of Recognition* (1999); *Immunities of Special Missions*.
Members Participating states – all 47 members of the Council of Europe:
Albania, Andorra, Armenia, Austria, Azerbaijan, Belgium, Bosnia-Herzegovina, Bulgaria, Croatia, Cyprus, Czechia, Denmark, Estonia, Finland, France, Georgia, Germany, Greece, Hungary, Iceland, Ireland, Italy, Latvia, Liechtenstein, Lithuania, Luxembourg, Malta, Moldova, Monaco, Montenegro, Netherlands, North Macedonia, Norway, Poland, Portugal, Romania, Russia, San Marino, Serbia, Slovakia, Slovenia, Spain, Sweden, Switzerland, Türkiye, UK, Ukraine.
Observers – governments of 9 countries:
Australia, Belarus, Canada, Holy See, Israel, Japan, Mexico, New Zealand, USA.
International Observers (10), listed in this Yearbook:
Asian-African Legal Consultative Organization (AALCO, #01303); *European Organization for Nuclear Research (CERN, #08108)*; *European Union (EU, #08967)*; *International Committee of the Red Cross (ICRC, #12799)*; *International Criminal Police Organization – INTERPOL (ICPO-INTERPOL, #13110)*; *NATO (#16945)*; *OECD (#17693)*; *Organization for Security and Cooperation in Europe (OSCE, #17887)*; *The Hague Conference on Private International Law (HCCH, #10850)*; *United Nations (UN, #20515)* (and its specialized agencies).
IGO Relations *International Criminal Court (ICC, #13108)*; *International Law Commission (ILC, #14004)*; Sixth Committee of United Nations General Assembly (UNGA). [2019.12.18/XK1837/y/**E***]

♦ Committee for Mapping the Flora of Europe (CMFE) 04268

Atlas Florae Europaeae (AFE)
Sec Botanical Museum, Finnish Museum of Natural History, Unioninkatu 44, PO Box 7, FI-00014 Helsinki, Finland. T. +358504486231.
URL: https://www.luomus.fi/en/atlas-florae-europaeae-afe-distribution-vascular-plants-europe

History 10 Aug 1965, Aarhus (Denmark). Founded at 4th Flora Europaea Symposium. **Aims** Offer complementary maps with *taxonomic* notes of *species* and subspecies for the Flora Europaea. **Structure** Secretariat in Helsinki (Finland). **Languages** English, French, German, Russian, Swedish. **Staff** 3.00 FTE, paid. **Finance** Financed by the University of Helsinki (Finland). **Activities** Knowledge management/information dissemination. **Events** *Chorological problems in the European flora* Helsinki (Finland) 1997. **Publications** *Atlas Florae Europaeae* (about every 3 years).
Members Individuals in 40 countries:
Albania, Austria, Belarus, Belgium, Bosnia-Herzegovina, Bulgaria, Croatia, Czechia, Denmark, Estonia, Finland, France, Germany, Greece, Hungary, Iceland, Ireland, Italy, Kazakhstan, Latvia, Lithuania, Luxembourg, Moldova, Montenegro, Netherlands, North Macedonia, Norway, Poland, Portugal, Romania, Russia, Serbia, Slovakia, Slovenia, Spain, Sweden, Switzerland, Türkiye, UK, Ukraine. [2014.06.01/XE1354/v/**E**]

♦ Committee of Mediterranean Forestry Questions / see AFWC/EFC/NEFC Committee on Mediterranean Forestry Questions – Silva Mediterranea (#00542)

♦ Committee of Members of Parliament of EFTA Countries (EFTA CMP) 04269

Comité de parlementaires des pays de l'AELE
Contact EFTA Secretariat, Rue Joseph II 12-16, 1000 Brussels, Belgium. T. +3222861724. Fax +3222861750. E-mail: mail.bxl@efta.int.
URL: http://secretariat.efta.int/

History 1977, following 15 years of informal meetings of parliamentarians of the countries of *EFTA (#05391)*. In connection with the agreement on *European Economic Area (EEA, #06957)*, complemented, since 1992, by *Committee of Members of Parliament of the EFTA States Party to the EEA (EFTA MPS, #04270)*. **Structure** CMP Committee (meeting 4-5 times a year); Bureau. **Activities** Guidance/assistance/consulting. **Events** *Annual meeting* Helsinki (Finland) 1994, *Annual meeting* Bergen (Norway) 1993, *Colloque à l'intention de l'Europe orientale* Geneva (Switzerland) 1993, *Parliamentary colloquium with Central and East European countries* Geneva (Switzerland) 1993, *Parliamentary colloquium with Central and East European countries* Geneva (Switzerland) 1993.
Members Parliamentarians from 4 countries:
Iceland, Liechtenstein, Norway, Switzerland.
IGO Relations Organizes parliamentary colloquia with parliamentarians from the CEECs. Also contacts with: *Nordic Council (NC, #17256)*; other inter-parliamentary organizations (not specified). [2015.09.24/XE0832/**E***]

♦ Committee of Members of Parliament of the EFTA States Party to the EEA (EFTA MPS) 04270

Officer EEA Coordination Rue Joseph II 12-16, 1000 Brussels, Belgium. T. +3222861710 – +3222861711. E-mail: mail.bxl@efta.int.
URL: http://www.efta.int/advisory-bodies/parliamentary-committee/

History 20 May 1992, Reykjavik (Iceland). Founded by Member States of *EFTA (#05391)*, in connection with the Agreement on *European Economic Area (EEA, #06957)*. Constituting meeting 24 Jan 1994, Brussels (Belgium). Complements *Committee of Members of Parliament of EFTA Countries (EFTA CMP, #04269)*. **Aims** Survey EEA-related work of EFTA. **Structure** Committee (meeting 4-5 times a year) comprises parliamentarians from Iceland, Liechtenstein and Norway. Switzerland has observer status. **Activities** Serves as consultative body to *Standing Committee of the EFTA States (#19953)* (in the EEA) and as an information channel between EFTA and national parliaments of member countries on EEA matters. Committee Members comprise the EFTA component of: *EEA Joint Parliamentary Committee (EEA JPC, #05382)*, the remaining members being members of the European Parliament.
Members Open only to EFTA States which are contracting parties to the Agreement on the European Economic Area. Currently 4 States:
Iceland, Liechtenstein, Norway, Switzerland. [2020.09.21/XE2527/**E***]

♦ Committee on Migrant Workers (CMW) 04271

Comité des travailleurs migrants
Secretariat UNOG-OHCHR, United Nations Office, Av de la Paix 8-14, 1211 Geneva 10, Switzerland. T. +41229179273. Fax +41229179008. E-mail: cmw@ohchr.org.
URL: http://www.ohchr.org/EN/HRBodies/CMW/Pages/CMWIndex.aspx

History 2004. Established within the framework of *United Nations (UN, #20515)*, by the States parties to the *International Convention on the Protection of the Rights of all Migrant Workers and Members of Their Families (1990)*. Managed by *Office of the United Nations High Commissioner for Human Rights (OHCHR, #17697)* at *United Nations Office at Geneva (UNOG, #20597)*. Former names and other names: *Committee* *on the Protection of the Rights of All Migrant Workers and Members of their Families* – full title. **Aims** Monitor implementation of the provisions of the Convention. **Structure** Committee of 14 members; Bureau; Secretariat, headed by Secretary. Secretariat provided by Human Rights Treaties Branch of *Office of the United Nations High Commissioner for Human Rights (OHCHR, #17697)*. **Languages** English, French, Spanish. **Staff** 3.00 FTE, paid. **Finance** Regular budget approved by General Assembly. **Activities** States having ratified the Convention report to the Committee within 1 year of entry into force and then at 5-year intervals, providing information including the principal legislative, judicial, administrative or other measures taken to give effect to the provisions of the Convention. Organizes 2 annual sessions in Geneva (Switzerland). **Events** *Session* Geneva (Switzerland) 2019, *Session* Geneva (Switzerland) 2019, *Session* Geneva (Switzerland) 2018, *Session* Geneva (Switzerland) 2018, *Session* Geneva (Switzerland) 2017.

Members Experts of 14 States Parties (term of expiry in brackets):
Albania (2021), Algeria (2023), Azerbaijan (2021), Bangladesh (2021), Burkina Faso (2023), Colombia (2021), Guatemala (2023), Mauritania (2023), Mexico (2023), Morocco (2023), Niger (2021), Senegal (2021), Sri Lanka (2021), Türkiye (2023).
States Parties to the Convention (56 as at Dec 2020):
Albania, Algeria, Argentina, Azerbaijan, Bangladesh, Belize, Benin, Bolivia, Bosnia-Herzegovina, Burkina Faso, Cape Verde, Chile, Colombia, Congo Brazzaville, Ecuador, Egypt, El Salvador, Fiji, Gambia, Ghana, Guatemala, Guinea, Guinea-Bissau, Guyana, Honduras, Indonesia, Jamaica, Kyrgyzstan, Lesotho, Libya, Madagascar, Mali, Mauritania, Mexico, Morocco, Mozambique, Nicaragua, Niger, Nigeria, Paraguay, Peru, Philippines, Rwanda, Sao Tomé-Principe, Senegal, Seychelles, Sri Lanka, St Vincent-Grenadines, Syrian AR, Tajikistan, Timor-Leste, Togo, Türkiye, Uganda, Uruguay, Venezuela.

IGO Relations United Nations specialized agencies, including: *ILO (#11123)*; *International Organization for Migration (IOM, #14454)*; *UNHCR (#20327)*. [2021.03.11/XM2805/**E***]

♦ Committee for Mineral Reserves International Reporting Standards (CRIRSCO) 04272

Chairperson address not obtained.
Sec address not obtained.
URL: http://www.crirsco.com/

History 1994, as an informal alliance of National Reporting Organizations. Evolved into a more constituted committee. Since 2007, a Task Force of *International Council on Mining and Metals (ICMM, #13048)*. **Activities** Events/meetings; standards/guidelines. **Events** *Annual Meeting* Jaipur (India) 2016, *Annual Meeting* Brasilia (Brazil) 2015, *Annual Meeting* Ulaanbaatar (Mongolia) 2014, *Annual Meeting* Bogota (Colombia) 2013, *Annual Meeting* London (UK) 2012.

Members Full in 9 countries:
Australia, Brazil, Canada, Chile, Kazakhstan, Mongolia, Russia, South Africa, USA.
Regional member in Europe.

IGO Relations *United Nations Economic Commission for Europe (UNECE, #20555)*. **NGO Relations** Recognized by: *International Accounting Standards Board (IASB, #11583)*. [2016/XM5519/**C**]

♦ Committee of Ministers of the Council of Europe 04273

Comité des Ministres du Conseil de l'Europe

Chair Conseil de l'Europe, Palais de l'Europe, 67075 Strasbourg CEDEX, France. T. +33388412000. Fax +33388413777. E-mail: cm@coe.int.
URL: http://www.coe.int/t/cm/

History 1949, Strasbourg (France). Established within the framework of *Council of Europe (CE, #04881)*, as its decision-making body. **Aims** Discuss national approaches to European problems on an equal terms footing; find collective responses to these challenges; guard the Council's fundamental values; monitor member states' compliance with their undertakings. **Structure** Ministers (meeting annually); Rotating Chairmanship. Meetings held in Strasbourg (France), with decision taken by two-third majority and unanimity required for some major issues. Secretariat of the Committee of Ministers (SECCM) comprises some 22 members of the General Secretariat, headed by Secretary to the Committee of Ministers who has rank of Director General. **Languages** English, French. **Finance** Sources: government support. **Activities** Politics/policy/regulatory. **Events** *Session* Germany 2021, *Session* Madrid (Spain) 2009, *Session* Strasbourg (France) 2008, *Session* Strasbourg (France) 2007, *Session* Strasbourg (France) 2006. **Publications** *Decisions adopted by the Committee of Ministers of the Council of Europe*; *Programme and Budget of the Council of Europe*.

Members Foreign Ministers of 47 countries:
Albania, Andorra, Armenia, Austria, Azerbaijan, Belgium, Bosnia-Herzegovina, Bulgaria, Croatia, Cyprus, Czechia, Denmark, Estonia, Finland, France, Georgia, Germany, Greece, Hungary, Iceland, Ireland, Italy, Latvia, Liechtenstein, Lithuania, Luxembourg, Malta, Moldova, Monaco, Montenegro, Netherlands, North Macedonia, Norway, Poland, Portugal, Romania, Russia, San Marino, Serbia, Slovakia, Slovenia, Spain, Sweden, Switzerland, Türkiye, UK, Ukraine.
Observer States (5):
Canada, Holy See, Japan, Mexico, USA.

IGO Relations *European Union (EU, #08967)* (special status providing for participation in all meetings of the Committee of Ministers and its subsidiary bodies). Relations with: *Congress of Local and Regional Authorities of the Council of Europe (#04677)*; *European Court of Human Rights (#06855)*. [2021.10.28/XE8838/**E***]

♦ Committee of National Institutes of Patent Agents (CNIPA) 04274

Pres Keil und Schaafhausen Patent- und Rechtsanwälte PartGmbB, Friedrichstrasse 2-6, 60323 Frankfurt-Main, Germany.
Vice-Pres Sonn und Partner Patentanwälte, Riemergasse 14, 1010 Vienna, Austria. T. +4315128405. Fax +4315129805. E-mail: office@sonn.at.
URL: http://www.cnipa.eu/

History 26 Mar 1956, Munich (Germany). 26-27 Mar 1956, Munich (Germany FR), by the German, Dutch, and British national institutes. New terms of reference adopted 12 Nov 1985, Munich. **Aims** Promote cooperation among member institutes and associations; facilitate exchange of opinions and of information as to laws and practices in other countries; promote agreement on matters of interest; arrange representation to governmental or other bodies with regard to matters of common interest, including improvements in law and practices. **Structure** Committee (meets at least once a year), of comprising 1 to 3 representatives per member institute; Secretary-General. Meetings closed. **Languages** English. **Staff** 1.00 FTE, voluntary. 1 voluntary. **Finance** Members' dues according to expenses incurred. **Activities** Organizes fora.

Members Institutes in 14 countries:
Austria, Belgium, Czechia, France, Germany, Ireland, Italy, Lithuania, Netherlands, Poland, Portugal, Spain, Sweden, UK.

Consultative Status Consultative status granted from: *World Intellectual Property Organization (WIPO, #21593)* (Permanent Observer Status). **IGO Relations** Observer to: *Union internationale pour la protection des obtentions végétales (UPOV, #20436)*. Cooperates with: *European Union Intellectual Property Office (EUIPO, #08996)*. **NGO Relations** Cooperates in related fields with: *European Federation of Agents of Industry in Industrial Property (#07042)*; *Institute of Professional Representatives before the European Patent Office (epi, #11288)*. [2022/XD0311/**D**]

♦ Committee of NGOs on Human Rights, Geneva 04275

Comité spécial des ONG pour les droits de l'homme, Genève

Contact c/o Pax Romana, ICMICA/MIIC, Rue de Varembé 3, 4th Floor, CP 161, 1211 Geneva, Switzerland. T. +41228230707.
URL: http://www.ngocongo.org/ngosubs/index.htm

History as *Special Committee of International NGOs on Human Rights – Comité spécial des ONG internationales pour les droits de l'homme*, 13 Nov 1969, Geneva (Switzerland), following recommendations of *Conference of Non-Governmental Organizations in Consultative Relationship with the United Nations (CONGO, #04635)* and the work of an ad hoc committee of its members. Constitution amended 22 Jun 1998. **Aims** Promote knowledge and more effective application of the rights enunciated in the Universal Declaration of Human Rights. **Structure** A special committee of NGOs reporting to CONGO but with independent status. Bureau consisting of Chairman, 3 Vice-Chairmen, Rapporteur/Secretary and Treasurer. Committee: *NGO Committee on Freedom of Religion or Belief, Geneva (see: #04275)*. **Languages** English, French. **Staff** Part-time, voluntary. **Finance** Members' dues. Budget (annual): Swiss Fr 14,000. **Activities** Priorities include: ratification of human rights conventions and covenants; promotion of human rights teaching in universities and schools; establishment of procedures for petitions on human rights matters at the United Nations and of regional conventions on human rights. Organizes symposia, seminars and conferences. **Events** *Meeting on how the UN human rights system functions* Geneva (Switzerland) 2005, *Meeting on universality of human rights* Geneva (Switzerland) 1998, *Seminar on human rights and national sovereignty* Marly-le-Roi (France) 1992, *International NGO seminar on education against apartheid* Geneva (Switzerland) 1989, *Conférence internationale des ONG pour combattre le racisme et la discrimination raciale durant la deuxième décennie des Nations Unies* Geneva (Switzerland) 1988.

Members NGOs, members of CONGO, interested in human rights problems (70):
- *African Association of Education for Development (ASAFED, no recent information)*;
- *Afro-Asian Peoples' Solidarity Organization (AAPSO, #00537)*;
- *All India Women's Conference (AIWC, #00737)*;
- *Arab Lawyers' Union (ALU, #01002)*;
- *Association for World Education (AWE, #02983)*;
- *Association internationale pour la défense de la liberté religieuse (AIDLR, #02681)*;
- *Baha'i International Community (#03062)*;
- *Brahma Kumaris World Spiritual University (BKWSU, #03311)*;
- *Caritas Internationalis (CI, #03580)*;
- Centre Unesco de Catalunya;
- *Conference of European Churches (CEC, #04593)*;
- *Defence for Children International (DCI, #05025)*;
- *Education International (EI, #05371)*;
- *European Union of Women (EUW, #09022)*;
- *Federation of American Women's Clubs Overseas (FAWCO, #09416)*;
- *Federation of Associations of Former International Civil Servants (FAFICS, #09457)*;
- *France Libertés – Fondation Danielle Mitterrand*;
- *General Arab Women Federation (GAWF, no recent information)*;
- *General Conference of Seventh-Day Adventists (SDA, #10109)*;
- *Graduate Women International (GWI, #10688)*;
- *Inter-African Committee on Traditional Practices Affecting the Health of Women and Children (IAC, #11384)*;
- *International Alliance of Women (IAW, #11639)*;
- *International Association for Counselling (IAC, #11821)*;
- *International Association for Religious Freedom (IARF, #12130)*;
- *International Association of Democratic Lawyers (IADL, #11837)*;
- *International Catholic Migration Commission (ICMC, #12459)*;
- *International Christian Organisation of the Media (ICOM, #12563)*;
- *International Commission of Jurists (ICJ, #12695)*;
- *International Council of Jewish Women (ICJW, #13036)*;
- *International Council of Nurses (ICN, #13054)*;
- *International Council of Women (ICW, #13093)*;
- *International Council on Social Welfare (ICSW, #13076)*;
- *International Federation of Business and Professional Women (BPW International, #13376)*;
- *International Federation of Social Workers (IFSW, #13544)*;
- *International Inner Wheel (IIW, #13855)*;
- *International Organization for the Elimination of All Forms of Racial Discrimination (EAFORD, #14445)*;
- *International Press Institute (IPI, #14636)*;
- *International Service for Human Rights (ISHR, #14841)*;
- *International Trade Union Confederation (ITUC, #15708)* (replacing World Confederation of Labour WCL);
- *Medical Women's International Association (MWIA, #16630)*;
- *Movement Against Racism and for Friendship between Peoples (MRAP)*;
- *Muslim World League (MWL, #16917)*;
- *Organisation mondiale des anciens élèves de l'enseignement catholique (OMAEC, #17816)*;
- *Pan Pacific and South East Asia Women's Association (PPSEAWA, #18186)*;
- *Pax Christi – International Catholic Peace Movement (#18266)*;
- *Pax Romana, International Catholic Movement for Intellectual and Cultural Affairs (ICMICA, #18267)*;
- *Socialist International Women (SIW, #19341)*;
- *Soroptimist International (SI, #19686)*;
- *Terre des Hommes International Federation (TDHIF, #20133)*;
- *The Lutheran World Federation (LWF, #16532)*;
- *The World Veterans Federation (WVF, #21900)*;
- *Unis pour l'Equite et la Fin du Racisme (UFER, #20490)*;
- *United Nations Watch (UN Watch)*;
- *Women's International League for Peace and Freedom (WILPF, #21024)*;
- *Women's International Zionist Organization (WIZO, #21030)*;
- *Women's World Summit Foundation (WWSF, #21038)*;
- *World Alliance of Young Men's Christian Associations (YMCA, #21090)*;
- *World Association of Girl Guides and Girl Scouts (WAGGGS, #21142)*;
- *World Council of Churches (WCC, #21320)* (Commission of the Churches on International Affairs of);
- *World Federation for Mental Health (WFMH, #21455)*;
- *World Federation of Methodist and Uniting Church Women (WFM and UCW, #21457)*;
- *World Federation of United Nations Associations (WFUNA, #21499)*;
- *World Jewish Congress (WJC, #21599)*;
- *World Psychiatric Association (WPA, #21741)*;
- *World Student Christian Federation (WSCF, #21833)*;
- *World Union of Catholic Women's Organisations (WUCWO, #21876)*;
- *World Vision International (WVI, #21904)*;
- *World Young Women's Christian Association (World YWCA, #21947)*;
- *Zonta International (#22038)*.

NGO Relations Sister committee: *CONGO Committee on Human Rights (#04663)*. *World Family Organization (WFO, #21399)*. [2010/XE6390/y/**E**]

♦ Committee of Non-governmental Organizations on the Family / see Vienna NGO Committee on the Family (#20774)
♦ Committee on Non-Intervention in Spanish Affairs (inactive)
♦ Committee of Nordic Industrial Property Agents / see Committee of Nordic Intellectual Property Attorneys (#04276)

♦ Committee of Nordic Intellectual Property Attorneys (CONOPA) 04276

SG Heinänen Oy Patent Agency, Airport Plaza, Äyritie 8-D, FI-01510 Vantaa, Finland.
URL: http://www.conopa.com/

History as *Council of Nordic Patent Agents*, later known as *Committee of Nordic Patent Agents*; also referred to as *Committee of Nordic Industrial Property Agents*. **Events** *Congress* Finland 2011, *Congress* Copenhagen (Denmark) 2008, *Congress* Norway 2005, *Congress* Uppsala (Sweden) 2002, *Congress* Reykjavik (Iceland) 1999. [2010/XE4384/**E**]

♦ Committee of Nordic Patent Agents / see Committee of Nordic Intellectual Property Attorneys (#04276)
♦ Committee of Occupational Therapists for the European Communities / see Council of Occupational Therapists for the European Countries (#04912)

♦ Committee on the Peaceful Uses of Outer Space (COPUOS) 04277

Comité des utilisations pacifiques de l'espace extra-atmosphérique – Comisión sobre la Utilización del Espacio Ultraterrestre con Fines Pacificos

Contact Office for Outer Space Affairs, United Nations Office at Vienna, PO Box 500, 1400 Vienna, Austria. T. +431260604950. Fax +431260605830. E-mail: oosa@unoosa.org.
URL: http://www.unoosa.org/

History 12 Dec 1959, New York, NY (USA). Established within the framework of *United Nations (UN, #20515)*, by UN General Assembly resolution 1472A (XIV), an ad hoc committee of the same name having previously been established by resolution 1348 (XIII) of 1958. Since 1993, based at and serviced by *United Nations Office for Outer Space Affairs (UNOOSA, #20601)* – – also referred to as *UN-OOSA* – at *United Nations Office at Vienna (UNOV, #20604)*. Former names and other names: *United Nations Committee on the Peaceful Uses of Outer Space (UNCOPUOS)* – alias; *Comité des Nations Unies des utilisations pacifiques de l'espace extra-atmosphérique* – alias; *Comisión de las Naciones Unidas sobre la Utilización del Espacio Ultraterrestre con Fines Pacificos* – alias. **Aims** Review the scope of international cooperation in the peaceful uses of outer space; bring the benefits of space applications to humankind; promote capacity building efforts on the use of space technologies for development. **Structure** Annual Session; Scientific and Technical Subcommittee; Legal Subcommittee; Secretariat provided by the *'Office for Outer Space Affairs (OOSA)'*. Reports to Fourth Committee of the UN General Assembly. **Languages** Arabic, Chinese, English, French, Russian, Spanish. **Staff** 23.00 FTE, paid. **Activities** Advocacy/lobbying/activism; events/meetings; guidance/assistance/consulting; management of treaties and agreements; research/documentation; training/education.

Management of treaties and agreements: *'The Space Millennium: Vienna (Austria) Declaration of Space and Human Development'* (1999). Manages the following treaties/agreements: *Agreement Governing the Activities of States on the Moon and other Celestial Bodies (1979)* (1979); *Agreement on the Rescue of Astronauts, the Return of Astronauts and the Return of Objects Launched into Outer Space (1968)* (1968); *Convention on Registration of Objects Launched into Outer Space (1974)* (1975); *Convention on the International Liability for Damage Caused by Space Objects (1972)* (1972); *Declaration of Legal Principles Governing the Activities of States in the Exploration and Use of Outer Space (1963)* (1963); *Declaration on International Cooperation in the Exploration and Use of Outer Space for the Benefit and in the Interest of all States, Taking into Particular Account the Needs of Developing Countries (1996)* (1996); *Principles Governing the Use by States of Artificial Earth Satellites for International Direct Television Broadcasting (1982)* (1982); *Principles Relating to Remote Sensing of the Earth from Outer Space (1986)* (1986); *Principles Relevant to the Use of Nuclear Power Sources in Outer Space (1992)* (1992); *Treaty on Principles Governing the Activities of States in the Exploration and Use of Outer Space, Including the Moon and other Celestial Bodies (1967)* (1967). **Events** *Annual Session* Vienna (Austria) 2022, *Annual Session* Vienna (Austria) 2021, *Session* Vienna (Austria) 2021, *Session* Vienna (Austria) 2021, *Annual Session* Vienna (Austria) 2020. **Publications** Studies; reports.

Members As of Jan 2022, UN Member States (100):

Albania, Algeria, Angola, Argentina, Armenia, Australia, Austria, Azerbaijan, Bahrain, Bangladesh, Belarus, Belgium, Benin, Bolivia, Brazil, Bulgaria, Burkina Faso, Cameroon, Canada, Chad, Chile, China, Colombia, Costa Rica, Cuba, Cyprus, Czechia, Denmark, Dominican Rep, Ecuador, Egypt, El Salvador, Ethiopia, Finland, France, Germany, Ghana, Greece, Hungary, India, Indonesia, Iran Islamic Rep, Iraq, Israel, Italy, Japan, Jordan, Kazakhstan, Kenya, Korea Rep, Kuwait, Lebanon, Libya, Luxembourg, Malaysia, Mauritius, Mexico, Mongolia, Morocco, Netherlands, New Zealand, Nicaragua, Niger, Nigeria, Norway, Oman, Pakistan, Panama, Paraguay, Peru, Philippines, Poland, Portugal, Qatar, Romania, Russia, Rwanda, Saudi Arabia, Senegal, Sierra Leone, Singapore, Slovakia, Slovenia, South Africa, Spain, Sri Lanka, Sudan, Sweden, Switzerland, Syrian AR, Thailand, Tunisia, Türkiye, UK, Ukraine, United Arab Emirates, Uruguay, USA, Venezuela, Vietnam.

IGO Relations Affiliated with (1): *United Nations (UN, #20515)*. Instrumental in setting up (5): *African Regional Centre for Space Science and Technology Education – English (ARCSSTE-E, #00431)*; *Centre for Space Science and Technology Education in Asia and the Pacific /Affiliated to the United Nations/ (CSSTEAP, see: #04277)*; *Centre for Space Science and Technology Education in Latin America and the Caribbean /Affiliated to the United Nations/ (CSSTE-LAC, see: #04277)*; *Centre régional africain des sciences et technologies de l'espace en langue française /Affilié à l'Organisation des nations unies/ (CRASTE-LF, see: #04277)*; *Regional Centre for Space Science and Technology Education for Western Asia (see: #04277)*. Observer status granted to: *Asia-Pacific Space Cooperation Organization (APSCO, #02051)*; *Association of Remote Sensing Centres in the Arab World*. *European Organization for Astronomical Research in the Southern hemisphere (ESO, #08106)*; *European Space Agency (ESA, #08798)*; *European Telecommunications Satellite Organization (EUTELSAT IGO, #08896)*; *European Union (EU, #08967)*; *Inter-Islamic Network on Space Sciences and Technology (ISNET, #11511)*; International Institute for the Unification of Private Law (UNIDROIT); *International Mobile Satellite Organization (IMSO, #14174)*; *International Telecommunications Satellite Organization (ITSO, #15670)*; *Intersputnik International Organization of Space Communications (#15976)*; *Regional Remote Sensing Centre for North African States (#18807)*; Square Kilometre Array Observatory.

NGO Relations Observer status granted to:

- *African Association of Remote Sensing of the Environment (AARSE, #00216)*;
- *Association of Space Explorers (ASE, #02927)*;
- CANEUS-International
- *Committee on Earth Observation Satellites (CEOS, #04249)*;
- *Committee on Space Research (COSPAR, #04287)*;
- *Eurisy (#05625)*;
- *European Space Policy Institute (ESPI, #08801)*;
- European Science Foundation (ESF), represented by the European Space Sciences Committee;
- *For all Moonkind*;
- *Instituto Iberoamericano de Derecho Aeronautico y del Espacio y de la Aviación Comercial (#11332)*;
- *International Academy of Astronautics (IAA, #11536)*;
- *International Air Transport Association (IATA, #11614)*;
- *International Association for the Advancement of Space Safety (IAASS, #11689)*;
- *International Astronautical Federation (IAF, #12286)*;
- *International Astronomical Union (IAU, #12287)*;
- *International Institute for Applied Systems Analysis (IIASA, #13861)*;
- *International Institute of Space Law (IISL, #13926)*;
- *International Law Association (ILA, #14003)*;
- *International Organization for Standardization (ISO, #14473)*;
- *International Society for Photogrammetry and Remote Sensing (ISPRS, #15362)*;
- *International Space University (ISU, #15575)*;
- Moon Village Association;
- National Space Society (NSS);
- Open Lunar Foundation;
- *Planetary Society (PS)*;
- Prince Sultan Bin Abdulaziz International Prize for Water (PSIPW);
- *Scientific Committee on Solar-Terrestrial Physics (SCOSTEP, #19151)*;
- Secure World Foundation (SWF);
- *Space Generation Advisory Council in Support of the United Nations Programme on Space Applications (SGAC, #19898)*;
- *University Space Engineering Consortium (UNISEC-Global, #20704)*;
- *World Space Week Association (WSWA)*. [2022.10.17/XE0535/**E***]

♦ Committee of Permanent Representatives to the European Communities / see Committee of Permanent Representatives to the European Union (#04278)

♦ Committee of Permanent Representatives to the European Union .. 04278

Comité des représentants permanents de l'Union européenne (COREPER)

Contact Council of the European Union, Bât Justus Lipsius, Rue de la Loi 175, 1048 Brussels, Belgium.
URL: http://www.consilium.europa.eu/

History 25 Jan 1958, Brussels (Belgium), within the framework of *Council of the European Union (#04895)*, as part of the *European Communities (EC, inactive)* system, to advise in deliberations of the *'European Economic Community (EEC)'* – currently *European Community (inactive)* – and *European Atomic Energy Community (Euratom, inactive)*. Institutionalized and mandate confirmed under the 'Merger' Treaty of 8 Apr 1965, which came into force in Jul 1967. Originally referred to as *Committee of Permanent Representatives to the European Communities – Comité des représentants permanents auprès des Communautés européennes*, COREPER became an institution of *European Union (EU, #08967)* under the *Treaty on European Union (Maastricht Treaty, 1992)*, signed 7 Feb 1992. **Aims** Prepare the work of the Council and carry out Council's instructions. **Structure** Comprises one permanent representative and one deputy permanent representative for each member state of the European Union, these meeting as Part 1 – *Coreper I* (Deputy Permanent Representatives) and Part 2 – *Coreper II* (Ambassadors) of COREPER in order to cover the work entrusted to it. Coreper I and II meet every week. Work is prepared by Antici Group (for Coreper II) and Mertens Group (for Coreper I). **Activities** Coordinates and prepares work of various Council configurations; ensures consistency of EU policies; works out agreements and compromises which are then submitted for adoption by the Council. **Events** *COREPER I* Brussels (Belgium) 2010, *COREPER II* Brussels (Belgium) 2010, *COREPER I* Helsinki (Finland) 1999.

Members Representatives of governments of the 27 EU countries:

Austria, Belgium, Bulgaria, Croatia, Cyprus, Czechia, Denmark, Estonia, Finland, France, Germany, Greece, Hungary, Ireland, Italy, Latvia, Lithuania, Luxembourg, Malta, Netherlands, Poland, Portugal, Romania, Slovakia, Slovenia, Spain, Sweden.

IGO Relations *Council for Mediterranean Countries (MEDA, no recent information)*; *European Commission (EC, #06633)*; *European Monitoring Centre for Drugs and Drug Addiction (EMCDDA, #07820)*. **NGO Relations** *CLECAT (#03993)*; *Conseil européen de l'industrie chimique (CEFIC, #04687)*. [2016/XE4101/**E***]

♦ The Committee of PET Manufacturers in Europe / see PET EUROPE – Producers' Association (#18340)
♦ Committee of Plastic Converters Associations of Western Europe (inactive)
♦ Committee of Professional Agricultural Organizations in the EU / see COPA – european farmers (#04829)

♦ Committee for the Promotion and Advancement of Cooperatives (COPAC) 04279

Comité pour la promotion et l'avancement des coopératives – Comité para la Promoción y el Progreso de las Cooperativas

Contact 1775 Eye St NW, 8th Floor, Washington DC 20006, USA. T. +12023835481. E-mail: copac@copac.coop.
URL: http://www.copac.coop/

History Mar 1971, Rome (Italy). Founded as a liaison body of United Nations agencies and international non-governmental organizations, following exploratory meeting, Dec 1967, Paris (France). Secretariat transferred from Rome (Italy) to Geneva (Switzerland) 1996. COPAC Secretariat transferred, 1996, to Geneva (Switzerland). Former names and other names: *Joint Committee for the Promotion of Agricultural Cooperatives* – former; *Committee for the Promotion of Aid to Cooperatives* – former; *Comité pour la promotion de l'aide aux coopératives* – former; *Comité para la Promoción de la Ayuda a las Cooperativas* – former; *Comité pour la promotion et le progrès des coopératives* – former. **Aims** Promote and advocate for people-centred, self-sustaining cooperative enterprises, guided by the principles of economically, socially and environmentally sustainable development. **Structure** Board (meets annually); Committee, headed by rotating Chair; Secretariat, managed by Coordinator. **Languages** English, French, Italian, Spanish. **Staff** 0.50 FTE, paid. **Finance** Members' dues. **Activities** Awareness raising; capacity building; politics/policy/regulatory; knowledge management/information dissemination; events/meetings. **Events** *Meeting of agencies involved in cooperative development* Colombo (Sri Lanka) 2006, *Cooperatives and fair trade* Berlin (Germany) 2005, *Forum* Geneva (Switzerland) 2000, *Successful cooperatibe development models in East and Central Europe* 1999, *International technical meeting* Rome (Italy) 1995. **Publications** Digital library. **IGO Relations** *FAO (#09260)*; *ILO (#11123)*; United Nations Department of Economics and Social Affairs (DESA)/Division of Social Policy and Development (DSPD). [2017.04.21/XE4642/y/**E**]

♦ Committee for the Promotion of Aid to Cooperatives / see Committee for the Promotion and Advancement of Cooperatives (#04279)
♦ Committee on the Protection of the Rights of All Migrant Workers and Members of their Families / see Committee on Migrant Workers (#04271)

♦ Committee to Protect Journalists (CPJ) 04280

Comité pour la protection des journalistes

Exec Dir 330 Seventh Avenue, 11th Floor, New York NY 10001, USA. T. +12124651004. Fax +12124659568. E-mail: info@cpj.org.
URL: http://www.cpj.org/

History Jan 1981, New York NY (USA). **Aims** Document and protest *violations* of *press freedom* worldwide. **Structure** Board of Directors, consisting of 38 journalists, publishers and news executives. Delegations conduct fact-finding missions, respond to emergencies. **Languages** Arabic, Croatian, English, French, German, Hebrew, Irish Gaelic, Italian, Russian, Serbian, Spanish, Ukrainian. **Staff** 25.00 FTE, paid. **Finance** Members' dues. Contributions from foundations, individuals and corporations. Budget (annual): US$ 3.6 million. **Activities** Casework; Information service; Missions. Investigations of censorship and harassment of press worldwide. Publications of annual survey of press freedom violations worldwide with documented lists of imprisoned and killed journalists. Publishing activity. **Events** *International Symposium on Investigative Journalism in the Regions of Asia* Tokyo (Japan) 2017. **Publications** *Dangerous Assignments* (2 a year); *Attacks on the Press* (annual). Country reports; news alerts; press releases; bulletins. **Members** Full journalists; departments of journalism; students. 'Friends of CPJ' non-journalists. Membership countries not specified. **Consultative Status** Consultative status granted from: *ECOSOC (#05331)* (Special); *UNESCO (#20322)* (Associate Status). **IGO Relations** Agreement with: *Council of Europe (CE, #04881)*. **NGO Relations** Links with press freedom, human rights and journalism organizations worldwide (not specified). [2012/XE0241/**E**]

♦ Committee on Publication Ethics (COPE) 04281

Main Office New Kings Court, Tollgate, Chandler's Ford, Eastleigh, SO53 3LG, UK. E-mail: cope_assistant@publicationethics.org.
URL: http://publicationethics.org/

History Apr 1997. Founded by a small group of medical journal editors in the UK. Registration: Charity Commission, No/ID: 1123023, England and Wales; Companies House, No/ID: 6389120, England and Wales. **Aims** Provide advice to editors and publishers on all aspects of publication ethics and, in particular, how to handle cases of research and publication misconduct. **Structure** Annual General Meeting; Council. **Activities** Events/meetings. Guidance/assistance/consulting; standards/guidelines. **Publications** *Ethical Editing Newsletter*. **Members** Full (over 9000). Membership countries not specified. **NGO Relations** *European Association of Science Editors (EASE, #06201)*; *International Society of Managing and Technical Editors (ISMTE, #15244)*; *International Society for Medical Publication Professionals (ISMPP)*; *World Association of Medical Editors (WAME, #21162)*; *World Conferences on Research Integrity Foundation (WCRI, #21300)*; national associations. [2022/XJ9857/**C**]

♦ Committee of Racial Equality / see Congress of Racial Equality
♦ Committee on Recent Ostracoda / see International Research Group on Ostracoda (#14730)
♦ Committee of the Regions of the European Communities / see European Committee of the Regions (#06665)
♦ Committee of the Regions of the European Union / see European Committee of the Regions (#06665)

♦ Committee of Religious NGOs at the United Nations (CRNGOs) 04282

Address not obtained.
URL: https://rngos.wordpress.com/

History Following regular meetings since 1972. **Aims** Serve as a forum to inform and educate members about global challenges and the constructive role the United Nations can play in addressing those issues; serve as a forum for exchanging and promoting shared religious and ethical values, facilitate productive relationships between the UN and the faith-based NGO community. **Structure** Officers: President; 2 Vice-Presidents; Secretary; Treasurer and 2 members-at-large. **Finance** Members' dues. **Activities** Meeting activities. **Publications** *Answering the Call* (2 a year); *Survey of Activities of Religious NGOs at the United Nations* (every 2 years).

Members Organizations accredited to the United Nations including 16 organizations listed in this Yearbook:

Baha'i International Community (#03062); *Baptist World Alliance (BWA, #03176)*; *B'nai B'rith International (BBI, #03290)*; *Brahma Kumaris World Spiritual University (BKWSU, #03311)*; *International Mahavira Jain Mission (IMJM)*; *International Shinto Foundation (ISF)*; *Pax Christi – International Catholic Peace Movement (#18266)*; *Religions for Peace (RfP, #18831)*; *Salvation Army (#19041)*; *Soka Gakkai International (SGI, #19672)*; *Temple of Understanding (ToU, #20124)*; *Unitarian Universalist Association (UUA, #20494)*; *Won Buddhism International*; *World Council of Churches (WCC, #21320)*; *World Council of Conservative/Masorti Synagogues (#21323)*; *World Peace Prayer Society*.

IGO Relations *United Nations (UN, #20515)*. [2015/XE4426/y/**E**]

♦ Committee for the Rescue of Israel's Babies / see EFRAT – International Organization for Saving Jewish Babies (#05389)
♦ Committee on Research Materials on Southeast Asia (internationally oriented national body)
♦ Committee to Review United Nations Public Information Policies and Activities / see Committee on Information (#04260)

♦ Committee on the Rights of the Child 04283

Comité des droits de l'enfant

Secretariat c/o UNOG-OHCHR, United Nations Office, 1211 Geneva 10, Switzerland. T. +41229179220. Fax +41229179008. E-mail: ohchr-crc@un.org – ohchr-petitions@un.org.
URL: http://www.ohchr.org/EN/HRBodies/CRC/Pages/CRCIndex.aspx

History Established within the framework of *United Nations (UN, #20515)*, by the States party to the *United Nations Convention on the Rights of the Child (CRC, 1989)*. Managed by *Office of the United Nations High Commissioner for Human Rights (OHCHR, #17697)* at *United Nations Office at Geneva (UNOG, #20597)*. Former names and other names: *United Nations Committee on the Rights of the Child* – alias. **Aims** Monitor implementation of the provisions of the Convention on the Rights of the Child as well as the Optional Protocols to the Convention on the involvement of children in armed conflict, on the sale of children, child prostitution and child pornography, and on a communications procedure. **Structure** Committee of 18 members. Bureau, comprising Chairperson and 4 Vice-Chairs, of which one is Rapporteur. Secretariat, headed by Secretary.

Secretariat services provided by the Human Rights Treaties Branch of *Office of the United Nations High Commissioner for Human Rights (OHCHR, #17697).* **Languages** English, French, Spanish. **Staff** 8.00 FTE, paid. **Finance** Regular sessions financed by regular budget of OHCHR; other meetings financed by voluntary contributions. **Activities** States having ratified or acceded to the Convention report to the Committee within 2 years of entry into force and then at 5-year intervals, providing information including the principal legislative, judicial, administrative or other measures in force, on: general measures taken to implement the Convention; definition of a child under their laws and regulations; application of the general principles of non-discrimination, best interests of the child, right to life, survival and development and respect for views of the child; civil rights and freedoms; violence against children; family environment and alternative care; basic health and welfare; education, leisure and cultural activities; special protection measures for children in situations of emergency, children in conflict with the law, children in situation of exploitation and children belonging to a minority or an indigenous group. States having ratified or acceded to the Optional Protocol on the involvement of children in armed conflict or the Optional Protocol on the sale of children, child prostitution and child pornography shall submit a report to the Committee on implementation of the provisions of the Optional Protocol within 2 years of entry into force. Thereafter, States Parties shall include in their periodic reports to the Committee regarding the Convention on the Rights of the Child any further information with respect to implementation of the Optional Protocol. States party to the Optional Protocol(s), but not party to the Convention, shall submit a report every 5 years, after submission of the initial report on the Optional Protocol. Organizes: Session (three times a year) in Geneva (Switzerland); Day of General Discussion on the Right of the Child to Be Heard, (biennial) in Geneva. **Events** *Session* Geneva (Switzerland) 2021, *Session* Geneva (Switzerland) 2021, *Session* Geneva (Switzerland) 2021, *Session* Geneva (Switzerland) 2020, *Session* Geneva (Switzerland) 2020.

Members Committee members from 16 countries (term of expiry in brackets):
Austria (2021), Bahrain (2021), Barbados (2023), Bulgaria (2021), Egypt (2023), Ethiopia (2021), Iceland (2023), Japan (2021), Morocco (2023), Niger (2023), Samoa (2023), South Africa (2021), Switzerland (2023), Togo (2023), Venezuela (2023), Zambia (2021).

States having ratified or acceded to the Convention on the Rights of the Child, 196 as at Aug 2021:
Afghanistan, Albania, Algeria, Andorra, Angola, Antigua-Barbuda, Argentina, Armenia, Australia, Austria, Azerbaijan, Bahamas, Bahrain, Bangladesh, Barbados, Belarus, Belgium, Belize, Benin, Bhutan, Bolivia, Bosnia-Herzegovina, Botswana, Brazil, Brunei Darussalam, Bulgaria, Burkina Faso, Burundi, Cambodia, Cameroon, Canada, Cape Verde, Central African Rep, Chad, Chile, China, Colombia, Comoros, Congo Brazzaville, Congo DR, Cook Is, Costa Rica, Côte d'Ivoire, Croatia, Cuba, Cyprus, Czechia, Denmark, Djibouti, Dominica, Dominican Rep, Ecuador, Egypt, El Salvador, Equatorial Guinea, Eritrea, Estonia, Eswatini, Ethiopia, Fiji, Finland, France, Gabon, Gambia, Georgia, Germany, Ghana, Greece, Grenada, Guatemala, Guinea, Guinea-Bissau, Guyana, Haiti, Holy See, Honduras, Hungary, Iceland, India, Indonesia, Iran Islamic Rep, Iraq, Ireland, Israel, Italy, Jamaica, Japan, Jordan, Kazakhstan, Kenya, Kiribati, Korea DPR, Korea Rep, Kuwait, Kyrgyzstan, Laos, Latvia, Lebanon, Lesotho, Liberia, Libya, Liechtenstein, Lithuania, Luxembourg, Madagascar, Malawi, Malaysia, Maldives, Mali, Malta, Marshall Is, Mauritania, Mauritius, Mexico, Micronesia FS, Moldova, Monaco, Mongolia, Montenegro, Morocco, Mozambique, Myanmar, Namibia, Nauru, Nepal, Netherlands, New Zealand, Nicaragua, Niger, Nigeria, Niue, North Macedonia, Norway, Oman, Pakistan, Palau, Palestine, Panama, Papua New Guinea, Paraguay, Peru, Philippines, Poland, Portugal, Qatar, Romania, Russia, Rwanda, Samoa, San Marino, Sao Tomé-Principe, Saudi Arabia, Senegal, Serbia, Seychelles, Sierra Leone, Singapore, Slovakia, Slovenia, Solomon Is, Somalia, South Africa, South Sudan, Spain, Sri Lanka, St Kitts-Nevis, St Lucia, St Vincent-Grenadines, Sudan, Suriname, Sweden, Switzerland, Syrian AR, Tajikistan, Tanzania UR, Thailand, Timor-Leste, Togo, Tonga, Trinidad-Tobago, Tunisia, Türkiye, Turkmenistan, Tuvalu, Uganda, UK, Ukraine, United Arab Emirates, Uruguay, Uzbekistan, Vanuatu, Venezuela, Vietnam, Yemen, Zambia, Zimbabwe.

IGO Relations Member of (1): *Interagency Panel on Juvenile Justice (IPJJ, #11390).* Links with other United Nations specialized agencies and bodies (not specified). **NGO Relations** Numerous NGOs at national level participate in and contribute to the work of CRC through: *Child Rights Connect (#03884).*
[2021.08.31/XE1444/**E***]

♦ Committee on the Rights of Persons with Disabilities (CRPD) 04284

Comité des droits des personnes handicapées – Comité sobre los Derechos de las Personas con Discapacidad (CDPD)

Mailing Address UNOG-OHCHR, Av de la Paix 8-14, 1211 Geneva 10, Switzerland. E-mail: ohchr-crpd@un.org.
Street Address Human Rights Treaties Div (HRTD), OHCHR, Palais Wilson, Rue des Pâquis 52, 1201 Geneva, Switzerland.
URL: http://www.ohchr.org/EN/HRBodies/CRPD/Pages/CRPDIndex.aspx

History Set up within the framework of *United Nations (UN, #20515),* by states party to the *Convention on the Rights of Persons with Disabilities (CRPD, 2006).* Managed by *Office of the United Nations High Commissioner for Human Rights (OHCHR, #17697)* at *United Nations Office at Geneva (UNOG, #20597).* **Aims** Promote, protect and ensure the full and equal enjoyment of all human rights and fundamental freedoms by all persons with disabilities; promote respect for their inherent dignity. **Structure** Committee of 18 members; Conference of States parties. **Languages** English, Russian, Spanish. **Staff** 5.00 FTE, paid. **Finance** Funding from *Office of the United Nations High Commissioner for Human Rights (OHCHR, #17697).* **Activities** Events/meetings; monitoring/evaluation. **Events** *Session* Geneva (Switzerland) 2021, *Session* Geneva (Switzerland) 2021, *Session* Geneva (Switzerland) 2020, *Session* Geneva (Switzerland) 2019, *Session* Geneva (Switzerland) 2019. **Publications** *From Exclusion to Equality: Realizing the Rights of Persons with Disabilities* (2007).

Members Experts from 18 countries (term of expiry indicated in brackets):
Australia (2022), Brazil (2022), Ghana (2022), Hungary (2020), Indonesia (2022), Japan (2020), Kenya (2020), Korea Rep (2022), Lithuania (2022), Mexico (2022), New Zealand (2020), Nigeria (2022), Russia (2020), Saudi Arabia (2020), Switzerland (2022), Thailand (2020), Tunisia (2020), Uganda (2020).

State Parties to the Convention, as at Aug 2020 (182):
Afghanistan, Albania, Algeria, Andorra, Angola, Antigua-Barbuda, Argentina, Armenia, Australia, Austria, Azerbaijan, Bahamas, Bahrain, Bangladesh, Barbados, Belarus, Belgium, Belize, Benin, Bolivia, Bosnia-Herzegovina, Botswana, Brazil, Brunei Darussalam, Bulgaria, Burkina Faso, Burundi, Cambodia, Canada, Cape Verde, Central African Rep, Chad, Chile, China, Colombia, Comoros, Congo Brazzaville, Congo DR, Cook Is, Costa Rica, Côte d'Ivoire, Croatia, Cuba, Cyprus, Czechia, Denmark, Djibouti, Dominica, Dominican Rep, Ecuador, Egypt, El Salvador, Estonia, Eswatini, Ethiopia, Fiji, Finland, France, Gabon, Gambia, Georgia, Germany, Ghana, Greece, Grenada, Guatemala, Guinea, Guinea-Bissau, Guyana, Haiti, Honduras, Hungary, Iceland, India, Indonesia, Iran Islamic Rep, Iraq, Ireland, Israel, Italy, Jamaica, Japan, Jordan, Kazakhstan, Kenya, Kiribati, Korea DPR, Korea Rep, Kuwait, Kyrgyzstan, Laos, Latvia, Lesotho, Liberia, Libya, Lithuania, Luxembourg, Madagascar, Malawi, Malaysia, Maldives, Mali, Malta, Marshall Is, Mauritania, Mauritius, Mexico, Micronesia FS, Moldova, Monaco, Mongolia, Montenegro, Morocco, Mozambique, Myanmar, Namibia, Nauru, Nepal, Netherlands, New Zealand, Nicaragua, Niger, Nigeria, North Macedonia, Norway, Oman, Pakistan, Palau, Palestine, Panama, Papua New Guinea, Paraguay, Peru, Philippines, Poland, Portugal, Qatar, Romania, Russia, Rwanda, Samoa, San Marino, Sao Tomé-Principe, Saudi Arabia, Senegal, Serbia, Seychelles, Sierra Leone, Singapore, Slovakia, Slovenia, Somalia, South Africa, Spain, Sri Lanka, St Kitts-Nevis, St Lucia, St Vincent-Grenadines, Sudan, Suriname, Sweden, Switzerland, Syrian AR, Tanzania UR, Thailand, Togo, Trinidad-Tobago, Tunisia, Türkiye, Turkmenistan, Tuvalu, Uganda, UK, Ukraine, United Arab Emirates, Uruguay, Vanuatu, Venezuela, Vietnam, Yemen, Zambia, Zimbabwe.
[2022/XJ0351/v/**E***]

♦ Committee of SADC Stock Exchanges (CoSSE) 04285

Chairman c/o JSE, Private Bag X991174, Johannesburg, 2146, South Africa.
URL: http://www.african-exchanges.org/about-cosse/contact-cosse/

History Jan 1997, as *SADC Committee of Stock Exchanges,* a private sector initiative within the framework of *Southern African Development Community (SADC, #19843).* **Aims** While retaining autonomous national markets, find ways of using technology, skill-sharing, dual listings and *cross-border investment* in the region to combine forces and speed development. **Activities** Research and development; monitoring/evaluation. **Events** *Meeting* Mauritius 1999.

Members National stock exchanges of the 9 SADC countries having such exchanges (" indicates in the process of foundation):
Botswana, Eswatini, Lesotho (*), Malawi, Mauritius, Namibia, South Africa, Zambia, Zimbabwe.

NGO Relations *Committee of Central Bank Governors in SADC (CCBG, #04245).* [2013/XE3866/**E**]

- ♦ Committee on Science and Freedom (inactive)
- ♦ Committee for the Scientific Investigation of Claims of the Paranormal / see Committee for Skeptical Inquiry

♦ Committee of Senior Officials of the Nordic Countries, Estonia, Latvia and Lithuania in the Field of Food Issues (CSO-NB8-Food) 04286

Address not obtained.

History 15 Sep 1980, Oslo (Norway), by *Nordic Council of Ministers (NCM, #17260).* Statutes adopted 25 Nov 1981, when working procedures approved. Responsible to the Council of Ministers (Agriculture, Fisheries, Forestry and Foodstuffs). Original title: *Standing Nordic Committee on Food – Permanente Nordiske Utvalg for Naeringsmiddelspørsmål (PNUN)*; also previously referred to as *Permanent Nordic Committee on Food and Nutrition Policy – Permanenta Nordiska Utskottet för Livsmedelsfrågor.* Name changed, 8 May 1989, to *Nordic Committee of Senior Officials for Food Issues – Nordiska Ämbetsmannakommittén för Livsmedelsfrågor (ÄK-LIVS) – Pohjoismainen Elintarvikeasiain Virkamieskomitea,* when working procedures were approved. Also referred to in English as *Nordic Committee on Food Questions.* **Aims** Coordinate and harmonize food *legislation,* food *control* and food and nutrition policy within Nordic countries; protect the *consumer* by ensuring safety and wholesomeness of foods and fair practices within the food trade; reduce trade barriers between Nordic countries and on a broad international basis; rationalize the work of the authorities through coordination of administrative arrangements and procedures; enable more effective utilization of scientific and economic resources; further development and strengthening of sectors within the foodstuffs field; develop and strengthen inter-Nordic contact, mutual exchange of information and sharing of experience. **Structure** Committee, comprising 1 or 2 representatives per member country. Working Groups (5): Toxicology and risk assessment; Microbiology and risk assessment; Foodstuffs inspection; Foodstuffs regulations and legislation; Diet and nutrition. **Languages** Danish, Faroese, Icelandic, Norwegian, Swedish. **Finance** Source: Governments of the Nordic countries. Budget (annual): Danish Kr 3.4 million. **Activities** Meetings of researchers and administrators initiate and carry through projects to harmonize legislation, food control systems, etc. Main areas of concern: (1) *'Prevention of diet-related health problems'* – ongoing activities aim at reduction of non-tariff barriers and include review of rules and procedures on: labelling of pre-packaged foods, food additives and food contaminants; control of imported foods; use of drugs in food-producing animals. Future concerns include: food safety and fair practices in the food trade; relationships between diet and health; significance and consequences of biotechnology in the food sector; differences in food law and administrative practices, in the context of EFTA and EEC cooperation and other relevant international fora such as *Codex Alimentarius Commission (CAC, #04081). Nordic Working Group on Nutrition – Nordisk Arbeidsgruppe for Kost- og Ernaeringsspørsmål (NKE)* acts as scientific advisory body. (2) *'Evaluation of harmful substances in food'* – aims for more uniform assessment both of hazards to health caused by individual substances and of total load and overall risk to which the population is subjected. *Nordic Working Group on Food Toxicology – Nordisk Arbeidsgruppe for Naeringsmiddeltoksikologi (NNT)* promotes cooperation and coordination for uniform assessment of health risks. (3) *'Food control and methods of analysis'* – priorities include surveillance and control of imported food, guidelines for laboratory services and development of control and analytical methods. NNK also links the methods committees, channelling NNT and NNK requests for services and studies to NMKL. **Events** *Meeting* Iceland 2004, *Joint meeting* Sweden 2003, *Meeting* Sweden 2003, *Meeting* Stockholm (Sweden) 1991, *Meeting* Copenhagen (Denmark) 1990. **Publications** *Nordisk Samarbeidsprogram på Naeringsmiddelområdet – Pohjoismainen Elintarvikealan Yhteistyöohjelma – Nordic Programme of Cooperation in the Field of Foodstuffs.* ÄK-LIVS reports and handbooks on food regulations, diet, nutrition. Reports published in the Nordic Official Report Series – NORD and Tema Nord.

Members Governments of 5 countries:
Denmark, Finland, Iceland, Norway, Sweden. [2011.10.03/XD5162/**E***]

- ♦ Committee of Shipowners' Associations of the European Communities / see European Community Shipowners' Associations (#06683)
- ♦ Committee for Skeptical Inquiry (internationally oriented national body)
- ♦ Committees for Monastic Interreligious Dialogue / see Monastic Interreligious Dialogue (#16849)
- ♦ Committee on Society, Development and Peace of the World Council of Churches and the Pontifical Commission Justice and Peace (inactive)
- ♦ Committee on South Pacific Trade / see Pacific Islands Forum Secretariat (#17970)

♦ Committee on Space Research (COSPAR) 04287

Comité pour la recherche spatiale

Associate Dir c/o CNES, 2 place Maurice Quentin, 75039 Paris CEDEX 01, France. E-mail: cospar@cosparhq.cnes.fr.
URL: https://cosparhq.cnes.fr/

History 2 Oct 1958, Washington, DC (USA). Founded by *International Council for Science (ICSU, inactive)* at 8th General Assembly. Charter and by-laws adopted 11-13 Nov 1959, Amsterdam (Netherlands); revised 1986 and Aug 1992. New Charter and by-laws adopted Aug 1998; approved by ICSU, Oct 1998. **Aims** Promote, on an international level, scientific research in space with emphasis on exchange of results, information and opinions; provide a forum, open to all scientists, for discussion of problems that may affect scientific space research. **Structure** Council (meets every 2 years); Bureau; Secretariat. Scientific Commissions (8); Panels (12); Task Groups (6); Individual Associates (about 12,000); Industry Partners (2); Associate Supporter Programme (5). **Languages** English, French. **Staff** 4.00 FTE, paid. **Finance** Sources: grants; meeting proceeds; members' dues; sale of publications. **Activities** Knowledge management/information dissemination. **Events** *Scientific Assembly* Busan (Korea Rep) 2024, *Symposium on Space Science with Small Satellites* Singapore (Singapore) 2023, *Scientific Assembly* Athens (Greece) 2022, *Scientific Assembly* Sydney, NSW (Australia) 2021, *Scientific Assembly* Sydney, NSW (Australia) 2020. **Publications** *COSPAR News* (6 a year); *Life Sciences in Space Research (LSSR)* (4 a year); *Space Research Today* (3 a year); *Advances in Space Research (ASR)* (24 a year). *COSPAR Scientific Roadmaps.*

Members National scientific institutions in 46 countries and territories:
Argentina, Australia, Austria, Belgium, Brazil, Canada, China, Cyprus, Czechia, Denmark, Egypt, Ethiopia, Finland, France, Germany, Ghana, Greece, Hungary, India, Indonesia, Israel, Italy, Japan, Korea Rep, Malaysia, Mexico, Netherlands, New Zealand, Pakistan, Poland, Portugal, Romania, Russia, Saudi Arabia, Slovakia, South Africa, Spain, Sweden, Switzerland, Taiwan, Thailand, Türkiye, UK, Ukraine, United Arab Emirates, USA.

International Scientific Unions (13), listed in this Yearbook:
International Astronomical Union (IAU, #12287); International Mathematical Union (IMU, #14121); International Society for Photogrammetry and Remote Sensing (ISPRS, #15362); International Union of Biochemistry and Molecular Biology (IUBMB, #15759); International Union of Biological Sciences (IUBS, #15760); International Union of Crystallography (IUCr, #15768); International Union of Geodesy and Geophysics (IUGG, #15776); International Union of Geological Sciences (IUGS, #15777); International Union of Physiological Sciences (IUPS, #15800); International Union of Pure and Applied Chemistry (IUPAC, #15809); International Union of Pure and Applied Physics (IUPAP, #15810); International Union of Theoretical and Applied Mechanics (IUTAM, #15823); Union radio-scientifique internationale (URSI, #20475).

Consultative Status Consultative status granted from: *ECOSOC (#05331)* (Ros C). **IGO Relations** Observer status with (1): *Committee on the Peaceful Uses of Outer Space (COPUOS, #04277).* Member of (1): *International Committee on Global Navigation Satellite Systems (ICG, #12775).* Regular relations with: *European Space Agency (ESA, #08798); UNESCO (#20322); World Meteorological Organization (WMO, #21649).* Working relations with: *International Telecommunication Union (ITU, #15673)* and its Radiocommunication Sector; *UNEP (#20299).* Collaborates with: *WMO Space Programme (see: #21649).* **NGO Relations** Member of (2): *Scientific Committee on Problems of the Environment (SCOPE, #19150); Scientific Committee on Solar-Terrestrial Physics (SCOSTEP, #19151).* Represented in: *Scientific Committee on Oceanic Research (SCOR, #19149).* Liaison member of: *Consultative Committee for Space Data Systems (CCSDS, #04764).* Official association with: *International Academy of Astronautics (IAA, #11536).* Regular relations with: *World Climate Research Programme (WCRP, #21279).* Collaborates with: *International Association of Meteorology and Atmospheric Sciences (IAMAS, #12031); International Astronautical Federation (IAF, #12286); Space Agency Forum (SAF, no recent information).* In liaison with technical committees of: *International Organization for Standardization (ISO, #14473).* [2022.10.19/XE0323/y/**E**]

- ♦ Committee of Stock Exchanges in the European Economic Community / see Federation of European Securities Exchanges (#09542)
- ♦ Committee on the Study of Corrosion and Protection of Canalizations / see European Committee for the study of corrosion and protection of pipes and pipeline systems (#06670)
- ♦ Committee on the Study of Corrosion and Protection of Pipes / see European Committee for the study of corrosion and protection of pipes and pipeline systems (#06670)
- ♦ Committee for the Study of Corrosion and the Protection of Pipework / see European Committee for the study of corrosion and protection of pipes and pipeline systems (#06670)

♦ Committee for Study and Research in Comparative Adult Education / see International Society for Comparative Adult Education (#15022)

♦ Committee on Sustainable Energy 04288

Sec Sustainable Energy Div – Room 380, Palais des Nations, 1211 Geneva 10, Switzerland. T. +41229172462. Fax +41229170038. E-mail: info.energy@unece.org.
URL: http://www.unece.org/energy/se/com.html

History Nov 1990, Geneva (Switzerland), as a Sectoral Committee of *United Nations Economic Commission for Europe (UNECE, #20555)*. Also referred to as *UNECE Committee on Sustainable Energy*. **Aims** Provide UNECE Member States with a platform for international dialogue and cooperation; carry out a programme of work in the field of sustainable energy with a view to providing access to affordable and clean energy to all, in line with the 2030 Agenda, and help reduce greenhouse gas emissions and the carbon footprint of the energy sector. **Structure** Bureau; Subsidiary Bodies (6). **Languages** English, French, Russian. **Staff** 16.00 FTE, paid. **Finance** Regular UN budget; extrabudgetary contributions. **Events** *Annual Session* Geneva (Switzerland) 2022, *Annual Session* Geneva (Switzerland) 2021, *Annual Session* Geneva (Switzerland) 2020, *Annual Session* Geneva (Switzerland) 2019, *Annual Session* Geneva (Switzerland) 2018. **Publications** Reports; analyses.
Members Representatives from energy sectors of UNECE member countries (56):
Albania, Andorra, Armenia, Austria, Azerbaijan, Belarus, Belgium, Bosnia-Herzegovina, Bulgaria, Canada, Croatia, Cyprus, Czechia, Denmark, Estonia, Finland, France, Georgia, Germany, Greece, Hungary, Iceland, Ireland, Israel, Italy, Kazakhstan, Kyrgyzstan, Latvia, Liechtenstein, Lithuania, Luxembourg, Malta, Moldova, Monaco, Montenegro, Netherlands, North Macedonia, Norway, Poland, Portugal, Romania, Russia, San Marino, Serbia, Slovakia, Slovenia, Spain, Sweden, Switzerland, Tajikistan, Türkiye, Turkmenistan, UK, Ukraine, USA, Uzbekistan.
IGO Relations United Nations bodies and specialized agencies: *European Bank for Reconstruction and Development (EBRD, #06315)*; *Global Environment Facility (GEF, #10346)*; *International Atomic Energy Agency (IAEA, #12294)*; *International Bank for Reconstruction and Development (IBRD, #12317)* (World Bank); *ILO (#11123)*; *UNCTAD (#20285)*; *UNDP (#20292)*; United Nations Department for Economic and Social Affairs (UN/DESA); *UNIDO (#20336)*; *United Nations Economic and Social Commission for Asia and the Pacific (ESCAP, #20557)*; Interim Secretariat of *United Nations Framework Convention on Climate Change (UNFCCC, 1992)*; *United Nations Fund for International Partnerships (UNFIP, #20565)*; *World Meteorological Organization (WMO, #21649)*. Other organizations: *Energy Charter Conference (#05466)*; *Eurasian Economic Community (EurAseC, inactive)*; *European Commission (EC, #06633)*; *International Energy Agency (IEA, #13270)*; *International Renewable Energy Agency (IRENA, #14715)*; *Inter-State Economic Committee of the Economic Union of the Commonwealth of Independent States (ISEC, no recent information)*; *NATO (#16945)*; *Organization of Black Sea Economic Cooperation (BSEC, #17857)*; *Organization of the Petroleum Exporting Countries (OPEC, #17881)*. **NGO Relations** *International Energy Foundation (IEF, #13273)*. Links with organizations in consultative status with ECOSOC: *International Organization for Standardization (ISO, #14473)*; *Liquid Gas Europe (#16488)*; *World Business Council for Sustainable Development (WBCSD, #21254)*; *World Coal Association (WCA, #21280)*. [2021/XE3241/**E***]

♦ Committee on Trade / see Steering Committee on Trade Capacity and Standards (#19979)

♦ Committee of the Trade in Cereals, Oilseeds, Pulses, Olive Oil, Oils and Fats, Animal Feed and Agrosupply of the EU (COCERAL) 04289

Comité du commerce des céréales, oléagineux, légumineuses, huile d'olive, huiles et graisses, aliments du bétail et agrofournitures de l'UE (COCERAL)

SG Rue Montoyer 23, 1000 Brussels, Belgium. T. +3225020808. E-mail: secretariat@coceral.com.
URL: http://www.coceral.com/

History 17 May 1958, Belgium. Founded following the Treaty of Rome establishing the European Economic Community (25 March 1957), by several personalities from the European Cereals Trade to represent interests of cereals and feedstuffs traders. Enlarged as an organisation in parallel to the development of the European Community. In 1997, formed a new structure with *Association du Négoce des Graines Oléagineuses, Huiles et Graisses Animales et Végétales et leurs Dérivés de la Communauté Economique Européenne* (ANGO) and *Union du Commerce des Engrais et Produits Phytosanitaires de la Communauté Européenne* (UCEPPCE), in order to meet new trends in Commission policy. Hosts secretariats of *Unistock Europe (#20492)* and *Working Committee of the Malting Industry of the EU (#21055)* in order to form closer synergies on the Brussels scene. Former names and other names: *Grain and Feed Trade Committee of the EC* – former; *Comité du commerce des céréales et des aliments du bétail de la CE (Cocéral)* – former; *Komitee des Getreide- und Futtermittelhandels in der EG* – former; *Comitato del Commercio dei Cereali e degli Alimenti per Animali della CE* – former; *Comité van de Graan- en Veevoederhandel in de EG* – former; *European Union for Grain, Oilseed and Fodder Trades and Derivatives* – former; *Union européenne des commerces des grains, graines oléagineuses, aliments du bétail et dérivés* – former; *Unión Europea de Comercios de Semillas, Semillas Oleaginosas, Alimentos del Ganado y Derivados* – former; *Europäische Vereinigung des Getreide-, Futter- und Düngemittelhandels* – former; *Committee of Cereals, Oilseeds, Animal Feed, Olive Oil, Oils and Fats, and Agro-Supply Trade in the EU (COCERAL)* – former; *Comité du commerce des céréales, aliments du bétail, oléagineux, huile d'olive, huiles et graisses, et agrofournitures de l'UE* – former; *Komittee des Handels mit Getreide, Futtermitteln, Ölsaaten, Olivenöl, Ölen und Fetten und Landwirtschaftlichen Betriebsmitteln in der EU* – former. Registration: Banque-Carrefour des Entreprises, No/ID: 0453.103.430, Start date: 12 Aug 1994, Belgium; EU Transparency Register, No/ID: 2050009628-31, Start date: 10 Nov 2008. **Aims** Study from scientific, technical and institutional viewpoints, all problems concerning trade and related matters as well as international economic integration, particularly within the EU, in order to seek out and apply the corresponding solutions; represent interests of its members towardst he European Union Institutions and other professional organizations; ensure respect for the commercial function in the different sectors of the cereals, oil seeds, animal feed, pulses, olive oil, oils and fats and agrosupply trade. **Structure** General Assembly (annual); Board; Committes; Secretariat. **Languages** English. **Staff** 6.00 FTE, paid. **Finance** Sources: members' dues. **Activities** Events/meetings; knowledge management/information dissemination; networking/liaising. **Events** *Congress* Sofia (Bulgaria) 2019, *Congress* Brussels (Belgium) 2018, *Congress* Athens (Greece) 2013, *Congress* Brussels (Belgium) 2012, *Congress* Geneva (Switzerland) 2011. **Members** Full members; associate members (non-EU member countries); extraordinary members; individual companies. Membership countries not specified. **IGO Relations** Recognized by: *European Commission (EC, #06633)*. Participates as observer in the activities of: *Codex Alimentarius Commission (CAC, #04081)*. **NGO Relations** Member of (5): *Agri-Food Chain Coalition (AFCC, #00577)*; *European Feed Ingredients Platform (EFIP, #07237)*; *European Liaison Committee for Agricultural and Agri-Food Trades (#07687)*; *Federation of European and International Associations Established in Belgium (FAIB, #09508)*; *International Grain Trade Coalition (IGTC, #13732)*. *Unistock Europe (#20492)* is full member. [2022.02.01/XE1001/ty/**E**]

♦ Committee of Transport Workers' Unions in the European Community / see European Transport Workers' Federation (#08941)
♦ Committee for the USA of the Mission to Lepers in India and the East / see American Leprosy Missions

♦ Committee for a Workers' International (CWI) 04290

Comité pour une Internationale ouvrière – Komitee für eine Arbeiterinternationale – Comité por una Internacional de los Trabajadores – Comitato per un' Internazionale dei Lavoratori – Comité voor een Arbeidersinternationale

Contact PO Box 3688, London, E11 1YE, UK. T. +442089888760. Fax +442089888793. E-mail: cwi@worldsoc.co.uk.
URL: http://www.socialistworld.net/

History 1974. Founded as a campaigning international socialist organization. **Aims** Work to end poverty and oppression; overthrow the rule of big *business* and global *capitalism*; promote a *democratic socialist* society internationally. **Structure** World Congress (every 4 years); Secretariat. **Staff** 7.00 FTE, paid. **Finance** Supported by members and supporters in socialist and workers' movements around the world. **Activities** Advocacy/lobbying/activism. **Publications** *A Socialist World is Possible*; *Marxism in Today's World*. Online publications; pamphlets.
Members Affiliate; Member; Supporter. Members in 44 countries and territories:
Argentina, Australia, Austria, Belarus, Belgium, Bolivia, Brazil, Canada, Chile, China, Côte d'Ivoire, Cyprus, Czechia, Denmark, Finland, France, Germany, Greece, Hong Kong, India, Ireland, Israel, Italy, Japan, Kazakhstan, Lebanon, Malaysia, Netherlands, New Zealand, Nigeria, Pakistan, Poland, Portugal, Romania, Russia, South Africa, Spain, Sri Lanka, Sweden, Taiwan, Tunisia, UK, USA, Venezuela. [2014.07.02/XE4547/**E**]

♦ Committee on World Food Security (see: #09260)
♦ Committee of Youth Hostel Organizations in the Nordic Countries (no recent information)

♦ Common Access to Biological Resources and Information (CABRI) . 04291

Chair Technical Committee IRCCS Ospedale Policlinico San Martino, Largo Rosanna Benzi 10, 16132 Genoa GE, Italy.
URL: http://www.cabri.org/

History Set up as a project 1996, which lasted until 1999, when collection was made public. **Aims** Provide quality biological products to the scientific community and quality guidelines to ensure use of specific technical procedures; expand resources with other centres having acceptable quality standards. **Structure** Scientific Committee; Technical Committee. **Languages** Dutch, English, French, German, Italian. **Staff** None. **Finance** Initially co-funded by a grant from DG XII of *European Commission (EC, #06633)*; currently maintained by partners. **Activities** Knowledge management/information dissemination. **Publications** Journal papers; catalogues. Information Services: Maintains database.
Members in 6 countries:
Belgium, France, Germany, Italy, Netherlands, UK.
IGO Relations Partner collections include: *CABI (#03393)*. [2019.02.12/XF6884/**F**]

♦ Common Action Forum (CAF) 04292

CEO Calle Claudio Coello 5, 28001 Madrid, Spain. T. +34910175850. E-mail: caf@commonactionforum.net.
URL: http://commonactionforum.net/

History 2015, Madrid (Spain). **Aims** Establish and encourage independent platforms of cooperation, research, innovation and advisory in order to shape alternative solutions and empower citizens to address today's challenges, such as the rise of neo-fascist politics, the increase of economic inequalities, the social impacts of technology and the environmental limits of the planet. **Structure** Advisory Board; Board of Trustees; Board of Directors; Executive Office. **Activities** Events/meetings. **Events** *OCTAGON Conference* Madrid (Spain) 2019, *OCTAGON Conference* Madrid (Spain) 2019. [2019/AA0583/**F**]

♦ **CommonAge** Commonwealth Association for the Ageing (#04300)
♦ Common Bond Institute (internationally oriented national body)
♦ **COMMON Europe** Association of IBM Computer Users (#02639)
♦ Common Foreign and Security Policy / see European Commission (#06633)

♦ Common Fund for Commodities (CFC) 04293

Fonds commun pour les produits de base

Managing Dir PO Box 74656, 1070 BR Amsterdam, Netherlands. T. +31205754949. Fax +31206760231. E-mail: managing.director@common-fund.org.
Street address Rietlandpark 301, 1019 DW Amsterdam, Netherlands.
URL: http://www.common-fund.org/

History 27 Jun 1980, Geneva (Switzerland). Established following negotiations within the *UNCTAD (#20285)*, on signature of an agreement which entered into force 19 Jun 1989. Commenced activities 15 Sep 1989. **Aims** Enhance socio-economic development of commodity producers; contribute to development of society as a whole. **Structure** Governing Council (meets annually); Executive Board; Managing Director is CEO; Consultative Committee; Headquarters in Amsterdam (Netherlands). **Languages** Arabic, Chinese, English, French, Russian, Spanish. **Staff** 19.00 FTE, paid. **Finance** Capital subscriptions from member states and voluntary contributions from various sources, including member states. **Activities** Events/meetings; knowledge management/information dissemination; research and development. **Events** *Annual Meeting of Governing Council* The Hague (Netherlands) 2022, *Annual Meeting of Governing Council* Amsterdam (Netherlands) 2021, *Annual Meeting of Governing Council* Amsterdam (Netherlands) 2020, *Meeting* Amsterdam (Netherlands) 2019, *Annual Meeting of Governing Council* The Hague (Netherlands) 2019. **Publications** *Common Fund for Commodities Newsletter*. *Commodity Development in Latin America* – series. Annual Report; Technical Papers; press releases; conference and workshop proceedings.
Members Governments of 101 countries:
Afghanistan, Algeria, Angola, Argentina, Bangladesh, Benin, Bhutan, Botswana, Brazil, Bulgaria, Burkina Faso, Burundi, Cameroon, Cape Verde, Central African Rep, Chad, China, Colombia, Comoros, Congo Brazzaville, Congo DR, Costa Rica, Côte d'Ivoire, Cuba, Denmark, Djibouti, Ecuador, Egypt, Equatorial Guinea, Eswatini, Ethiopia, Finland, Gabon, Gambia, Germany, Ghana, Greece, Guatemala, Guinea, Guinea-Bissau, Haiti, Honduras, India, Indonesia, Iraq, Ireland, Italy, Jamaica, Kenya, Korea DPR, Korea Rep, Kuwait, Laos, Lesotho, Madagascar, Malawi, Malaysia, Maldives, Mali, Mauritania, Mexico, Morocco, Mozambique, Myanmar, Nepal, Netherlands, Nicaragua, Niger, Nigeria, Norway, Pakistan, Papua New Guinea, Peru, Philippines, Portugal, Russia, Rwanda, Samoa, Sao Tomé-Principe, Saudi Arabia, Senegal, Sierra Leone, Singapore, Somalia, Spain, Sri Lanka, Sudan, Sweden, Syrian AR, Tanzania UR, Thailand, Togo, Trinidad-Tobago, Tunisia, Uganda, UK, United Arab Emirates, Venezuela, Yemen, Zambia, Zimbabwe.
Plus the following regional members, who ratified the Agreement Establishing the Common Fund – capital equivalent to about US$ 370.78 million of the Directly Contributed Capital of the Fund. These organizations have no financial obligations to the Fund and hold no vote. Organizations (9) listed in this Yearbook:
African Union (AU, #00488); *Andean Community (#00817)*; *Caribbean Community (CARICOM, #03476)*; *Common Market for Eastern and Southern Africa (COMESA, #04296)*; *East African Community (EAC, #05181)*; *Economic Community of West African States (ECOWAS, #05312)*; *European Union (EU, #08967)*; *Southern African Development Community (SADC, #19843)*; *Union économique et monétaire Ouest africaine (UEMOA, #20377)*.
IGO Relations Consultative Status with: *ECOSOC (#05331)* (observer status). Accredited to the Conference of the Parties of: *Secretariat of the United Nations Convention to Combat Desertification (Secretariat of the UNCCD, #19208)*. Designated International Commodity Bodies (ICBs):
- *Industrial Development Fund (IDF, #11173)*;
- *Intergovernmental Group on Bananas and on Tropical Fruits (#11486)*;
- *Intergovernmental Group on Citrus Fruit (#11487)*;
- *Intergovernmental Group on Grains (#11488)*;
- *Intergovernmental Group on Hard Fibres (IGG on Hard Fibres, #11489)*;
- *Intergovernmental Group on Meat and Dairy Products (#11491)*;
- *Intergovernmental Group on Oilseeds, Oils and Fats (#11492)*;
- *Intergovernmental Group on Rice (#11493)*;
- *Intergovernmental Group on Tea (#11494)*;
- *Intergovernmental Sub-Group on Hides and Skins (#11502)*;
- Intergovernmental Sub-Committee on Fish Trade – FAO;
- *International Cocoa Organization (ICCO, #12627)*;
- *International Coffee Organization (ICO, #12630)*;
- *International Copper Study Group (ICSG, #12963)*;
- *International Cotton Advisory Committee (ICAC, #12979)*;
- *International Grains Council (IGC, #13731)*;
- *International Lead and Zinc Study Group (ILZSG, #14012)*;
- *International Network for Bamboo and Rattan (INBAR, #14234)*;
- *International Nickel Study Group (INSG, #14370)*;
- *International Olive Council (IOC, #14405)*;
- *International Rubber Study Group (IRSG, #14772)*;
- *International Sugar Organization (ISO, #15623)*;
- *International Tropical Timber Organization (ITTO, #15737)*.

Cooperation Agreement with: *International Fund for Agricultural Development (IFAD, #13692)*. Supports: *Africa Rice Center (AfricaRice, #00518)*; *CABI (#03393)*; *Caribbean Agricultural Research and Development Institute (CARDI, #03436)*; *International Crops Research Institute for the Semi-Arid Tropics (ICRISAT, #13116)*; *Lake Victoria Fisheries Organization (LVFO, #16222)*. Observer to General Assembly of: *United Nations (UN, #20515)*. **NGO Relations** Cooperates with (2): *European Cooperative for Rural Development (EUCORD, #06788)*; *International Fertilizer Development Center (IFDC, #13590)*. Supports (2): *International Centre for Tropical Agriculture (#12527)*; *International Institute of Tropical Agriculture (IITA, #13933)*. [2022.02.09/XF9551/fy/**F***]

♦ Common Global Ministries Board (internationally oriented national body)

♦ Common Goal 04294

Address not obtained.
URL: https://www.common-goal.org/

Aims United the global *football* community in tackling today's greatest *social* challenges. **Structure** Steering Board; Core Team.
Members Individuals (642) and organizations (135) pledging 1% of their income. Members in 34 countries and territories:
Andorra, Argentina, Australia, Brazil, Canada, Colombia, Croatia, Czechia, Denmark, Faeroe Is, France, Germany, Ghana, Iceland, Italy, Japan, Kenya, Lesotho, Mexico, Netherlands, Nicaragua, Nigeria, North Macedonia, Norway, Portugal, Slovenia, Spain, Sweden, Türkiye, Uganda, UK, USA, Venezuela, Zambia.
NGO Relations *King Baudouin Foundation (KBF)*; *Transnational Giving Europe (TGE, #20218)*.
[2019/XM8612/**F**]

♦ Common Ground Research Networks (unconfirmed)
♦ Commonland Foundation (internationally oriented national body)

♦ Common Language Resources and Technology Infrastructure (CLARIN) 04295

Contact c/o Utrecht Univ, Drift 10, 3512 BS Utrecht, Netherlands. T. +31302536378. Fax +31302536000. E-mail: clarin@clarin.eu.
URL: http://www.clarin.eu/
History Founded 29 Feb 2012, by decision of *European Commission (EC, #06633)*, and awarded status of *European Research Infrastructure Consortium (ERIC)*, following which it is also known as *CLARIN ERIC*. Current statutes updated and approved by European Commission, 4 Apr 2018. **Aims** Create and maintain an infrastructure to support the sharing, use and sustainability of language data and tools for research in the humanities and social sciences. **Structure** General Assembly; Board of Directors; Office; Scientific Advisory Board. **Activities** Knowledge management/information dissemination; research/documentation. **Events** *Annual Conference* Leipzig (Germany) 2019, *Annual Conference* Pisa (Italy) 2018, *Annual Conference* Budapest (Hungary) 2017, *Annual Conference* Aix-en-Provence (France) 2016. **Publications** Articles.
Members Members and observers can be countries or intergovernmental organizations, which in turn set up a national consortium. Participating consortia set up by members in 18 countries:
Austria, Bulgaria, Croatia, Cyprus, Czechia, Denmark, Estonia, Finland, Germany, Greece, Hungary, Italy, Latvia, Lithuania, Netherlands, Norway, Poland, Portugal, Slovenia, Sweden.
Included in the above, 1 organization listed in this Yearbook:
Dutch Language Union.
Consortia set up by observers in 4 countries:
France, Iceland, South Africa, UK.
Consultative Status Consultative status granted from: *World Intellectual Property Organization (WIPO, #21593)* (Observer Status). **IGO Relations** *European Commission (EC, #06633)*. **NGO Relations** Memorandum of Understanding with (1): *Association of European Research Libraries (#02540)*. Member of (1): *EUDAT Collaborative Data Infrastructure (EUDAT CDI, #05580)*. *Cracking the Language Barrier (#04942)*; *European Alliance for the Social Sciences and Humanities (EASSH, #05885)*; *Europeana Foundation (#05839)*.
[2019/XM5206/**E**]

♦ Common Market for Eastern and Southern Africa (COMESA) 04296

Marché commun de l'Afrique de l'Est et de l'Afrique australe – Mercado Común para Africa Orientale e Austral

SG COMESA Centre, Ben Bella Road, PO Box 30051, Lusaka 10101, Zambia. T. +260211229725 – +260211229726 – +260211229732. Fax +260211225107. E-mail: secgen@comesa.int – info@comesa.int.
URL: http://www.comesa.int/
History 8 Dec 1994. Established on ratification of the *'Treaty establishing the Common Market for Eastern and Southern Africa (COMESA)'* by the requisite number of states, the Treaty having been signed, 5 Nov 1993, Kampala (Uganda), by Heads of State and Government and plenipotentiaries of 15 countries. COMESA is the successor to *Preferential Trade Area for Eastern and Southern African States (PTA, inactive)*, which had been established, 22 Dec 1981, Lusaka (Zambia), and was dissolved by the COMESA Treaty. An ultimate objective is the setting up of an *African Economic Community (AEC, #00290)* through implementation of provisions of *Treaty Establishing the African Economic Community (Abuja treaty, 1991)*. Together with other regional economic groups in Africa, COMESA and AEC negotiated and concluded, 25 Feb 1998, a Protocol on relations between AEC and the regional economic communities; and would convert into an organic entity of AEC at the time the Continental Common Market is established through consolidation of regional common markets. The 2 member countries of *Southern African Customs Union (SACU, #19842)* which are members of PTA and which have signed the COMESA Treaty – Namibia and Swaziland – are exempt from full membership obligations pending the completion of the renegotiation process of SACU Agreement. **Aims** As defined in the COMESA Treaty and its Protocols: (a) attain sustainable growth and development of member states by promoting a more balanced and harmonious development of production and marketing structures; promote joint development in all fields of economic activity and the joint adoption of macro-economic policies and programmes in order to raise the standard of living of the peoples in, and to foster closer relations among, member states; cooperate in the creation of an enabling environment for foreign, cross-border and domestic investment, including joint promotion of research and adaptation of science and technology for development; cooperate in the promotion of peace, security and stability among member states in order to enhance the economic development of the region; cooperate in strengthening the relations between the Common Market and the rest of the world and adopt common positions in international fora; contribute towards the establishment, progress and the realization of the objectives of the African Economic Community.
Structure Main organs:
- COMESA Authority – Heads of State and Government: supreme policy organ, consisting of all Heads of State and Government; decisions by consensus;
- Council of Ministers: decisions by consensus, or – failing that – by two thirds majority.

Supporting organizations: *COMESA Committee of Central Bank Governors*; *Intergovernmental Committee*; Technical Committees. Overal coordination through Secretariat, based in Lusaka (Zambia). Secretariat, consisting of Divisions, Units and Projects. Secretariat Divisions (4): Infrastructure Development; Industry and Agriculture; Trade and Customs; Gender and Social Affairs.
COMESA Institutions:
- *Court of Justice of the Common Market for Eastern and Southern Africa (COMESA Court of Justice, #04937)* – replacing PTA Tribunal (inactive) and PTA Administrative Appeals Board;
- *COMESA Business Council (CBC, #04124)*;
- *Trade and Development Bank (TDB, #20181)*, Nairobi;
- *COMESA Regional Investment Agency (COMESA RIA, #04128)*;
- *Africa Leather and Leather Products Institute (ALLPI, #00185)*, Addis Ababa (Ethiopia);
- *African Trade Insurance Agency (ATI, #00485)*;
- *COMESA Competition Commission (CCC, #04125)*;
- *PTA Reinsurance Company (ZEP-RE, #18561)*, Nairobi (Kenya);
- *COMESA Monetary Institute (CMI, #04127)*;
- *COMESA Federation of National Associations of Women in Business (COMFWB, #04126)*;
- *Regional Association of Energy Regulators for Eastern and Southern Africa (RAERESA, #18751)*.

Specialized agency: *Alliance for Commodity Trade in Eastern and Southern Africa (ACTESA, #00668)*.
Languages Arabic, English, French. **Staff** Over 200: 3 Executive Management; Professional staff (39%); General Service staff (61%). **Finance** Sources: members' dues. Budget (2011): US$ 11 million (from member States) plus US$ 70 million. Supported by: *African Development Bank (ADB, #00283)*; *African Development Fund (ADF, #00285)*; *European Union (EU, #08967)*; *International Bank for Reconstruction and Development (IBRD, #12317)*; *United States Agency for International Development (USAID)*. **Activities** Politics/policy/regulatory. Priority areas: A Free Trade Area; Customs Union; Trade Promotion. Together with *East African Community (EAC, #05181)* and *Southern African Development Community (SADC, #19843)*, announced setting up of *African Continental Free Trade Area (AfCFTA, #00267)*, Oct 2008. Instrumental in setting up: *Association of Regulators of Information and Communications for Eastern and Southern Africa (ARICEA, no recent information)*. **Events** *Annual Summit* Lusaka (Zambia) 2018, *Workshop for validation of the COMESA Time Release Study (TRS) Report* Lusaka (Zambia) 2017, *Annual Summit* Antananarivo (Madagascar) 2016, *TGAIS : Global African Investment Summit* Kigali (Rwanda) 2016, *Annual Summit* Addis Ababa (Ethiopia) 2015. **Publications** *eCOMESA Newsletter* (weekly); *COMESA – Quarterly Newsletter* (4 a year). Annual Report. Pre- and Post Summit publications. Briefs; reports; various publications.
Members Governments of 21 countries:
Burundi, Comoros, Congo DR, Djibouti, Egypt, Eritrea, Eswatini, Ethiopia, Kenya, Libya, Madagascar, Malawi, Mauritius, Rwanda, Seychelles, Somalia, Sudan, Tunisia, Uganda, Zambia, Zimbabwe.
IGO Relations Relationship agreement signed with: *FAO (#09260)*; *UNIDO (#20336)*. Under Lom Conventions, links with: *European Commission (EC, #06633)*. Member of: *Africa Partnership Forum (APF, #00510)*; *Common Fund for Commodities (CFC, #04293)*. Regional Economic Community of: *African Union (AU, #00488)*. Cooperates with: *International Civil Aviation Organization (ICAO, #12581)*. Observer to: *Codex Alimentarius Commission (CAC, #04081)*. Supports: *Eastern Africa Power Pool (EAPP, #05226)*. Memorandum of Understanding with: *International Centre for Migration Policy Development (ICMPD, #12503)*. Adherest to: *Global Partnership for Effective Development Co-operation (GPEDC, #10532)*. Special relations with the following multilateral financing institutions:
- *African Development Bank (ADB, #00283)*;
- *African Development Bank Group (ADB Group, #00284)*;
- *Commonwealth Secretariat (#04362)*;
- *East African Development Bank (EADB, #05183)*;
- *International Bank for Reconstruction and Development (IBRD, #12317)*;
- *International Development Research Centre (IDRC, #13162)*;
- *International Finance Corporation (IFC, #13597)*;
- *International Fund for Agricultural Development (IFAD, #13692)*;
- *International Trade Centre (ITC, #15703)*;
- *Investment Climate Facility for Africa (ICF, #15998)*;
- *UNCTAD (#20285)*;
- *UNDP (#20292)*;
- *United Nations Economic Commission for Africa (ECA, #20554)*;
- *The World Bank Group (#21218)*.

Cordial relations with:
- *Communauté économique des pays des Grands Lacs (CEPGL, #04375)*;
- *East African Community (EAC, #05181)*;
- *Eastern and Southern African Management Institute (ESAMI, #05254)*;
- *Economic Community of West African States (ECOWAS, #05312)*;
- *Commission de l'Océan Indien (COI, #04236)*;
- *Inter-Governmental Standing Committee on Shipping (ISCOS, #11501)*;
- *Organization for the Management and Development of the Kagera River Basin (KBO, no recent information)*;
- *Port Management Association of Eastern and Southern Africa (PMAESA, #18462)*;
- *Southern African Transport and Communications Commission (SATCC, no recent information)*;
- *Tanzania-Zambia Railway Authority (TAZARA, no recent information)*.

Cooperation with:
- *African Foundation for Research and Development (AFRAND, no recent information)*;
- *African Regional Intellectual Property Organization (ARIPO, #00434)*;
- *Canadian International Development Agency (CIDA, inactive)*;
- *Department for International Development Cooperation*;
- *International Monetary Fund (IMF, #14180)*;
- *Norwegian Agency for Development Cooperation (Norad)*;
- *Southern African Development Community (SADC, #19843)*;
- *United States Agency for International Development (USAID)*.

Links with: *Commonwealth Fund for Technical Cooperation (CFTC, #04331)*; *International Red Locust Control Organization for Central and Southern Africa (IRLCO-CSA, no recent information)*; *Maritime Organization of West and Central Africa (MOWCA, #16582)*; *United Nations Commission on International Trade Law (UNCITRAL, #20531)*.
NGO Relations Instrumental in setting up (1): *Association of Regulators of Information and Communications for Eastern and Southern Africa (ARICEA, no recent information)*. Cooperates with: *African Centre for Resources and Environment (ACRE, no recent information)*; *African Technology Policy Studies Network (ATPS, #00481)*; *Eastern and Southern African Business Organization (ESABO, no recent information)*; *International Chamber of Commerce (ICC, #12534)*; *International Fertilizer Development Center (IFDC, #13590)*; *International Institute of Tropical Agriculture (IITA, #13933)*. Formal relations with: *Association of Power Utilities in Africa (APUA, #02867)*. Links with various other organizations, including the following listed in this Yearbook: *African Airlines Association (AFRAA, #00200)*; *Ford Foundation (#09858)*; *Institute of Law and International Relations, Warsaw (no recent information)*; *Organisation of African Trade Union Unity (OATUU, #17798)*. [2020/XF3162/**F***]

♦ Common Market Group of Ceramic Tile Producers / see European Ceramic Tile Manufacturers' Federation (#06508)
♦ Common Market Reinsurance Company / see PTA Reinsurance Company (#18561)
♦ Common Market of the South / see Southern Common Market (#19868)
♦ Common Monetary Area / see Multilateral Monetary Area (#16889)
♦ Common Nordic Labour Market (no recent information)
♦ Common Seas (internationally oriented national body)
♦ Common Sense Environmental Fund (unconfirmed)
♦ Commons Network (unconfirmed)

♦ Common Wadden Sea Secretariat (CWSS) 04297

Sec Virchowstrasse 1, 26382 Wilhelmshaven, Germany. T. +49442191080. E-mail: info@waddensea-secretariat.org.
URL: http://www.waddensea-worldheritage.org/
History 1987. Established by the Governments of Denmark, Germany and the Netherlands. **Aims** Support, facilitate and coordinate activities of the Trilateral Cooperation of Denmark, Germany and the Netherlands on the Protection of the Wadden Sea (Trilateral Wadden Sea Cooperation (TWSC); collect and assess information with regard to Wadden Sea protection, management and monitoring. **Structure** Organizes *Wadden Sea Conference*. Serves as Secretariat to Trilateral Wadden Sea Cooperation (TWSC). **Languages** Danish, Dutch, English, German. **Staff** 7.00 FTE, paid. 4 temporary. **Finance** Sources: government support. through the 3 partner countries – Germany, Denmark and the Netherlands. Annual budget: 672,600 EUR (2013). **Activities** Events/meetings; monitoring/evaluation; networking/liaising; projects/programmes. **Events** *East Atlantic Flyway Youth Forum* Wilhelmshaven (Germany) 2022, *Trilateral Governmental Conference on the protection of the Wadden Sea* Wilhelmshaven (Germany) 2022, *International Scientific Wadden Sea Symposium* Büsum (Germany) 2021, *Trilateral governmental Wadden Sea conference* Leeuwarden (Netherlands) 2018, *Trilateral governmental Wadden Sea conference* Tinder (Denmark) 2014. **Publications** *Wadden Sea Newsletter* (6 a year) in English – The Wadden Sea Newsletter specifically addresses the various stakeholders of the Trilateral Wadden Sea Cooperation (TWSC). With it, we want to keep you informed about the recent activities and publications as well as upcoming events. It is intended as additional means parallel to our website to point you to the newest developments of our Cooperation. The newsletter is published regularly every other month.; *Trilateral Wadden Sea Cooperation – Annual Report 2020* (annual) in English – The report is a product of the Common Wadden Sea Secretariat and gives an overview of the activities of the past year within the Trilateral Wadden Sea Cooperation.; *Wadden Sea Quality Status Report* (every 3-4 years) in English – The Wadden Sea Quality Status Report (QSR) is a conglomeration of thematic reports on the Wadden Sea, including islands and offshore areas.. *Wadden Sea Ecosystem* in English – Irregular publication. Each edition focuses on a specific scientific field, e.g. trends of breeding birds in the Wadden Sea.. Reports on various issues in connection to the protection of the Wadden Sea.
Members in 3 countries:
Denmark, Germany, Netherlands. [2021.11.12/XE3798/**E***]

♦ Common Wagon Pool (inactive)
♦ Commonweal (internationally oriented national body)
♦ Commonwealth Advisory Aeronautical Research Council (internationally oriented national body)

♦ Commonwealth Africa Initiative (CAS) 04298

Secretariat address not obtained. E-mail: secretariat@commonwealthafrica.com.
URL: http://www.commonwealthafrica.com/
Aims Promote the interest of the African bloc of the Commonwealth of Nations; foster more opportunities for Commonwealth Citizens from Africa. **Structure** Advisory Board; International Office Management Team; Youth Advisory Board; Council of Expert and Eminent Professionals. **Activities** Capacity building; research/documentation; training/education. **Events** *Commonwealth Africa Summit* London (UK) 2022, *Africa Forum Singapore* Singapore (Singapore) 2021, *Annual Commonwealth Africa Summit* London (UK) 2019, *Africa Forum New York* New York, NY (USA) 2018, *Africa Forum Canada* Toronto, ON (Canada) 2018. **IGO Relations** *Commonwealth Secretariat (#04362)*. [2022/AA1998/**E**]

Commonwealth Agricultural Bureaux
04298

alphabetic sequence excludes
For the complete listing, see Yearbook Online at

♦ Commonwealth Agricultural Bureaux (inactive)
♦ Commonwealth Air Transport Council (inactive)
♦ Commonwealth Arts Organization (inactive)
♦ Commonwealth Asia Alliance of Young Entrepreneurs (unconfirmed)

♦ The Commonwealth Association (COMASSOC) 04299

Social Sec 72 Redcliffe Close, 274 Old Brompton Road, London, SW5 9HZ, UK.

History 2001, London (UK), as a staff alumni association. **Aims** Support the *values* of the Commonwealth of Nations; support the work of the Commonwealth Secretariat and other Commonwealth associations; promote the discussion of subjects of Commonwealth interest; provide a social and cultural forum for the pursuit of common interests. **Structure** Committee, comprising Chairperson, Vice-Chairperson, Secretary, Treasurer, Membership and Social Secretary, 4 members and 2 co-opted members. **Finance** Members' dues.
Members Former staff of:
Commonwealth Countries League (CCL, #04320); Commonwealth Foundation (CF, #04330); Commonwealth Fund for Technical Cooperation (CFTC, #04331); Commonwealth of Learning (COL, #04346); Commonwealth organizations accredited by the Commonwealth Secretariat; *Commonwealth Youth Programme (CYP, #04372)* (and its regional centres).
IGO Relations Accredited by: *Commonwealth Secretariat (#04362).* [2018/XJ0999/vy/**E**]

♦ Commonwealth Association for the Ageing (CommonAge) 04300

Chairman address not obtained.
URL: http://www.commage.org/

History Officially launched, Nov 2013, Melbourne (Australia). **Aims** Advance the interests of older peoples throughout the Commonwealth by building capability and capacity in health and aged care services. **Structure** Board. **NGO Relations** Partners include: *International Association of Homes and Services for the Ageing (IAHSA, #11938); International Institute on Ageing, United Nations – Malta (INIA, #13860).* [2015/XM4329/**C**]

♦ Commonwealth Association of Architects (CAA) 04301

Association des architectes du Commonwealth

Exec Dir 65-B Shamshad Haider Rd, Gulberg II, Lahore 54600, Pakistan. T. +924235762076 – +924235711288 – +924235712956. E-mail: comarchitect.org@gmail.com – admin@comarchitect.org.
Pres address not obtained.
URL: http://www.comarchitect.org/

History Jul 1965, Malta. Founded when constitution was adopted, following decision, 25 Jul 1963, London (UK), of a conference of Commonwealth architects. Registration: Charity Commission, No/ID: 288022, Start date: 18 Oct 1983, England and Wales. **Aims** Further advancement of architecture throughout the Commonwealth; further acquisition of knowledge of various arts and sciences connected therewith. **Structure** General Assembly (every 2-3 years, at Pan-Commonwealth Conference); Council; Administration Committee. Secretariat, headed by Executive Director. **Languages** English. **Staff** 1.00 FTE, paid. **Finance** Sources: contributions; grants; international organizations; members' dues. Other sources: bequests. Supported by: *Commonwealth Foundation (CF, #04330).* **Activities** Certification/accreditation; events/meetings; training/education. **Events** *General Assembly* London (UK) 2015, *General Assembly* Dhaka (Bangladesh) 2013, *General Assembly* Colombo (Sri Lanka) 2010, *Annual conference on humane habitat* Mumbai (India) 2009, *Annual conference on humane habitat* Mumbai (India) 2008. **Publications** *CAA E-Journal* (irregular).
Members Societies, institutes and associations, totalling over 32,000 architects, in 31 countries and territories:
Bahamas, Bangladesh, Barbados, Bermuda, Botswana, Cyprus, Fiji, Ghana, Guyana, Hong Kong, India, Jamaica, Kenya, Lesotho, Malawi, Malaysia, Malta, Namibia, New Zealand, Nigeria, Papua New Guinea, South Africa, Sri Lanka, St Lucia, Tanzania UR, Tonga, Trinidad-Tobago, Uganda, UK, Zambia, Zimbabwe.
IGO Relations *Commonwealth Secretariat (#04362).* [2021/XC0360/**C**]

♦ Commonwealth Association of Armed Forces Lawyers (no recent information)
♦ Commonwealth Association for Corporate Governance (inactive)
♦ Commonwealth Association for Development (no recent information)
♦ Commonwealth Association for Education in Journalism and Communication (no recent information)
♦ Commonwealth Association for the Education and Training of Adults (inactive)

♦ Commonwealth Association for Health and Disability (COMHAD) . . 04302

Pres Gaurav Child Clinic, G-12 – FF – Anjuman Complex, Sadar, Nagpur, Maharashtra 440001, Nagpur MAHARASHTRA 440001, India. T. +917122584060.
Honorary SG Krishnakung, Khare Town, Dharampeth, Nagpur, Maharashtra 440010, Nagpur MAHARASHTRA 440010, India.
URL: http://www.comhad.com/

History Founded Jan 1983, Sheffield (UK), as *Commonwealth Association for Mental Handicap and Developmental Disabilities (CAMHADD).* Current title adopted 16 Aug 2008. **Aims** Provide education and research in health and disability for quality of life by raising awareness for prevention of disease and disabilities and promoting health care for low and middle income groups of the community in urban settings. **Structure** General Assembly; Executive Committee; Executive Board; Editorial Board; National Chapters (2). **Languages** English. **Staff** None paid. **Finance** Funded by *Commonwealth Foundation (CF, #04330).* At present no grant. **Activities** Advocacy/lobbying/activism; events/meetings; guidance/assistance/consulting; knowledge management/information dissemination; networking/liaising. **Events** *Conference* Nagpur (India) 2021, *Conference* Karnataka (India) 2018, *Conference* Nagpur (India) 2015, *African Regional Workshop* Cape Town (South Africa) 1998, *Asian Regional Workshop* Dhaka (Bangladesh) 1997. **Publications** *COMHAD Newsletter* (2 a year); *COMHAD Members Directory.* Proceedings; recommendations.
Members Individual professional and non-professional members in Commonwealth Countries; Individual professional and non-professional members from national organizations in Commonwealth countries; Affiliated member organizations in Commonwealth countries. Members in 50 countries and territories:
Antigua-Barbuda, Australia, Bahamas, Bangladesh, Barbados, Botswana, Canada, Chad, Colombia, Dominica, Eswatini, Ethiopia, Grenada, Guyana, Hong Kong, India, Jamaica, Kenya, Kiribati, Lesotho, Malawi, Malaysia, Maldives, Mauritius, Mozambique, Namibia, Nauru, Nigeria, Pakistan, Papua New Guinea, Seychelles, Singapore, Solomon Is, South Africa, Sri Lanka, St Kitts-Nevis, St Lucia, Suriname, Sweden, Switzerland, Tanzania UR, Tonga, Trinidad-Tobago, Tuvalu, Uganda, UK, USA, Vanuatu, Zambia, Zimbabwe.
IGO Relations Cooperates with: *IMPACT – International Initiative Against Avoidable Disablement (#11137); UNICEF (#20332); United Nations Population Fund (UNFPA, #20612).* Observer status with: Commonwealth Health Ministers' Meeting (CHMM); Meeting of Commonwealth Representatives Prior to the World Health Assembly. *Commonwealth Secretariat (#04362); East, Central and Southern African Health Community (ECSA-HC, #05216); Swedish International Development Cooperation Agency (Sida); West African Health Organization (WAHO, #20881).* **NGO Relations** Member of: *Commonwealth Health Professions and Partners Alliance (CHPA, #04338); Commonwealth HIV and AIDS Action Group (Para55, no recent information); NGO Forum for Health (inactive).* [2022/XD8092/**C**]

♦ Commonwealth Association of Indigenous Peoples (internationally oriented national body)

♦ Commonwealth Association of Law Reform Agencies (CALRAs) . . . 04303

Honorary Gen Sec 18 Manor Way, Onslow Village, Guildford, GU2 7RN, UK. T. +441483575366.
URL: http://www.calras.org/

History 2003. **Aims** Encourage international cooperation on law reform. **Structure** General Meeting; Executive Committee. **Languages** English. **Staff** 0.50 FTE, voluntary. **Finance** Members' dues: pounds3,000-pounds6,000. **Activities** Research/documentation; training/education. **Events** *Conference* Livingstone (Zambia) 2019, *Conference* Melbourne, VIC (Australia) 2017, *Conference* Edinburgh (UK) 2015, *Conference* South Africa 2013, *Conference* Hyderabad (India) 2011. **Publications** Guide.
Members Law reform agencies in 22 countries and territories:
Australia, Canada, England, Ghana, India, Ireland, Kenya, Lesotho, Malawi, Mauritius, Namibia, New Zealand, Nigeria, Northern Ireland, Scotland, Sierra Leone, South Africa, Sri Lanka, Tanzania UR, Trinidad-Tobago, Virgin Is UK, Wales.
Individual members in 3 countries and territories:
Bahamas, Canada, England.
IGO Relations *Commonwealth Secretariat (#04362); Commonwealth Foundation (CF, #04330).* [2015.02.09/XM3718/**C**]

♦ Commonwealth Association of Legislative Counsel (CALC) 04304

Sec Parliamentary Counsel Office, PO Box 18 070, Wellington 6160, New Zealand.
URL: http://www.calc.ngo/

History 21 Sep 1983, Hong Kong, during 7th Commonwealth Law Conference. **Aims** Improve legislative drafting *standards* and promote cooperation in matters of professional interest by encouraging sharing among members of information on preparation and publication of legislation, on recruitment and training of legislative counsel, and of preparation and publication of comparative *legal* materials and precedents. **Structure** General Meeting, normally biennial and held immediately before or after *Commonwealth Law Conference*; Council. **Languages** English. **Staff** Voluntary. **Finance** Operating expenses met by various legislative drafting offices, including Australian Commonwealth Office of Parliamentary Counsel. Other sources: advertising charges; sale of merchandise; conference registration fees. **Events** *General Meeting and Conference* Livingstone (Zambia) 2019, *General Meeting and Conference* Melbourne, VIC (Australia) 2017, *General Meeting and Conference* Edinburgh (UK) 2015, *General Meeting and Conference* Cape Town (South Africa) 2013, *General Meeting and Conference* Hyderabad (India) 2011. **Publications** *CALC Newsletter*, *The Loophole* – journal.
Members Open to all individuals in the Commonwealth who are or have been engaged in legislative drafting or related training. Members in 70 Commonwealth countries and territories:
Anguilla, Antigua-Barbuda, Australia, Bahamas, Bangladesh, Barbados, Belize, Bermuda, Botswana, Brunei Darussalam, Canada, Cayman Is, Cook Is, Cyprus, Czechia, Dominica, Eswatini, Falklands/Malvinas, Fiji, France, Ghana, Gibraltar, Grenada, Guernsey, Guyana, Hong Kong, India, Isle of Man, Jamaica, Jersey, Kenya, Kiribati, Lesotho, Malawi, Malaysia, Malta, Mauritius, Mozambique, Namibia, Nauru, New Zealand, Nigeria, Pakistan, Papua New Guinea, Qatar, Rwanda, Samoa, Seychelles, Sierra Leone, Singapore, Solomon Is, South Africa, Spain, Sri Lanka, St Helena, St Kitts-Nevis, St Lucia, St Vincent-Grenadines, Sudan, Tanzania UR, Tonga, Trinidad-Tobago, Turks-Caicos, Tuvalu, Uganda, UK, Vanuatu, Virgin Is UK, Zambia, Zimbabwe.
Associate members in 14 countries:
Angola, Gambia, Greece, Ireland, Israel, Liberia, Netherlands, Oman, Poland, Portugal, Puerto Rico, Sweden, Switzerland, USA.
IGO Relations Formally approved for accreditation to: *Commonwealth Secretariat (#04362).* [2019.12.11/XF6139/v/**F**]

♦ Commonwealth Association for Mental Handicap and Developmental Disabilities / see Commonwealth Association for Health and Disability (#04302)

♦ Commonwealth Association of Museums (CAM) 04305

Association des musées du Commonwealth

SG 10023 93 Street, Edmonton AB T5H 1W6, Canada. T. +17804242229.
Pres International Slavery Museum, National Museums Liverpool, Albert Dock, Liverpool, L3 4AQ, UK. T. +441514784574.
URL: http://www.maltwood.uvic.ca/cam/

History Founded Jun 1974, Copenhagen (Denmark), at a conference of *International Council of Museums (ICOM, #13051)*, with support from the *Commonwealth Foundation (CF, #04330).* Registered in accordance with Canadian law. **Aims** Focus on postcolonial museology, human rights and social justice; maintain and strengthen links between members of the museum profession within the Commonwealth; encourage and assist members to obtain additional training and experience by a distance learning programme and other means, and to attend appropriate seminars and conferences; encourage establishment of regional museum associations. **Structure** General Assembly; Council. **Languages** English. **Staff** Paid; voluntary. **Finance** Sources: grants; members' dues. Other sources: programme registration fees. **Activities** Events/meetings; knowledge management/information dissemination; projects/programmes; standards/guidelines. **Events** *Triennial Conference* Cape Town (South Africa) 2020, *Migration:Cities Workshop* Athens (Greece) 2017, *Triennial Conference* Okotoks, AB (Canada) 2017, *Triennial Conference* Glasgow (UK) 2014, *Workshop* Nassau (Bahamas) 2013. **Publications** *CAM Bulletin* (6 a year); *CAM Journal. Access in Museums in South Asia* (2016). Conference proceedings.
Members Institutional and individual in 46 countries and territories:
Antigua-Barbuda, Australia, Bahamas, Bangladesh, Barbados, Belize, Botswana, Brazil, Cameroon, Canada, Cayman Is, Cook Is, Eswatini, Fiji, France, Ghana, Grenada, Guyana, India, Italy, Kenya, Kiribati, Malawi, Mozambique, Namibia, Nauru, New Zealand, Nigeria, Pakistan, Philippines, Samoa, Seychelles, Sierra Leone, Singapore, Solomon Is, South Africa, St Kitts-Nevis, St Lucia, Tanzania UR, Turks-Caicos, Uganda, UK, USA, Vanuatu, Zambia, Zimbabwe.
NGO Relations Member of (2): *Commonwealth Consortium for Education (CCfE, #04318); International Council of Museums (ICOM, #13051).* [2020/XD4792/**C**]

♦ Commonwealth Association of Paediatric Gastroenterology and Nutrition (CAPGAN) 04306

Pres Dept Pediatric Gastroenterology/Hepatology/Liver Transplantation, Medanta – The Medicity Hosp, Sector 38, Gurugram, Haryana, Gurugram HARYANA, India.
Sec address not obtained.
URL: http://capgan.info/

History Founded 1984. **Aims** Promote knowledge of and training in paediatric gastroenterology, hepatology and nutrition throughout the Commonwealth but especially amongst developing countries; foster collaborative research in these fields. **Structure** General Meeting (every 2 years, in conjunction with Congress); General Council; Executive Committee; Working Groups. **Languages** English. **Staff** 2.00 FTE, paid. **Finance** Members'dues, mainly collected as part of registration fee for Congress. **Activities** Events/meetings. **Events** *Commonwealth Congress on Diarrhoea and Malnutrition* Toronto, ON (Canada) 2019, *Commonwealth Congress on Diarrhoea and Malnutrition* Lusaka (Zambia) 2017, *Commonwealth Congress on Diarrhoea and Malnutrition* Delhi (India) 2015, *Commonwealth Congress on Diarrhoea and Malnutrition* Colombo (Sri Lanka) 2013, *Commonwealth Congress on Diarrhoea and Malnutrition* London (UK) 2011. **Members** Active (about 200); Honorary (1); Emeritus. Membership countries not specified. **NGO Relations** Member of: *Commonwealth Health Professions and Partners Alliance (CHPA, #04338); Commonwealth HIV and AIDS Action Group (Para55, no recent information); Paediatric Radiation Oncology Society (PROS, #18019).* Links with international societies of paediatric gastroenterology (not specified). [2017.10.09/XD8128/**D**]

♦ Commonwealth Association of Planners (CAP) 04307

Association des urbanistes du Commonwealth

Administrator c/o RTPI Scotland, 18 Atholl Crescent, Edinburgh, EH3 8HQ, UK. T. +441312299628.
URL: http://www.commonwealth-planners.org/

History 197079, London (UK). Founded Oct 1971, London (UK). Inaugural conference, 1973, Delhi (India). **Aims** Focus and develop the skills of urban and regional planners across the Commonwealth to meet the challenges of urbanization and sustainable development of human settlements. **Structure** Conference of Delegates (at least every 2 years); Executive Committee. **Languages** English. **Staff** 0.50 FTE, paid. **Finance** Sources: contributions; grants; international organizations; members' dues. Other sources: bequests. Supported by: *Commonwealth Foundation (CF, #04330).* Annual budget: 20,000 GBP. **Activities** Events/meetings; networking/liaising; research/documentation; training/education. **Events** *Conference* Singapore (Singapore) 2014, *International Forum on City Planning* Singapore (Singapore) 2014, *Conference* London (UK) 2012, *Conference* Montréal, QC (Canada) 2010, *Conference* Montréal, QC (Canada) 2010. **Publications** Conference proceedings; reports.
Members Professional physical planning organizations, comprising 40,000 qualified physical planners, in 27 countries:
Australia, Bangladesh, Barbados, Belize, Brunei Darussalam, Canada, Cyprus, Dominica, Ghana, India, Jamaica, Kenya, Malawi, Malaysia, Malta, Mauritius, Namibia, New Zealand, Nigeria, Singapore, South Africa, Sri Lanka, St Lucia, Tanzania UR, Trinidad-Tobago, Uganda, UK, Zambia.
NGO Relations Instrumental in setting up: *African Planning Association (no recent information); Built Environment Professions in the Commonwealth (BEPIC).* Partner of: *World Urban Campaign (WUC, #21893).* Member of: *Global Planners Network (GPN, #10548).* [2019.06.04/XC3958/**C**]

♦ Commonwealth Association of Polytechnics in Africa (CAPA) 04308

Association des instituts polytechniques africains du Commonwealth

SG PO Box 52428, Nairobi, 00200, Kenya. T. +25420341639 – +25420343672. E-mail: info@capa-sec.org.
Street Address 4th Floor – Administrative Block, Technical Univ of Kenya, Haile Selassie Avenue, Nairobi, Kenya.
URL: http://www.capa-sec.org/

History Founded Dec 1978, Nairobi (Kenya). **Aims** Undertake advocacy and provide leadership and support in development of adequate technical manpower for economic and industrial development of African Commonwealth countries; study and improve teaching content and methods in polytechnics and comparable institutions and associated curricula, syllabuses and examinations; help students and trainees to move between countries and institutions for courses not available at home; stimulate exchanges of experience and ideas; provide a forum for discussion of matters of common interest; study and improve the the organization management of polytechnics and comparable institutions. **Structure** General Conference (every 3 years); Executive Board (meets annually); Secretariat, headed by Secretary-General. **Languages** English. **Staff** 7.00 FTE, paid. **Finance** Members' dues. Other sources: programme grants from international agencies and foundations; subsidies from Commonwealth African governments. **Activities** Major Programmes: CAPA Entrepreneurship Education; CAPA Women in Technical Education; CAPA Senior Management Development; CAPA Instructional Materials and Textbook Development Project; CAPA Constituency Support and Consolidation Project: Maintenance Management. Organizes colloquia, symposia and training workshops. **Events** *Meeting* Freetown (Sierra Leone) 2007, *Meeting* Lilongwe (Malawi) 2006, *Meeting* Livingstone (Zambia) 2006, *Meeting* Mombasa (Kenya) 2005, *Entrepreneurship – small scale (micro) enterprise development training* Blantyre (Malawi) 2000. **Publications** *CAPA Newsletter* (2 a year); *CAPA Journal of Technical Education and training* (annual).
Members Polytechnics and technical, business and management institutions (150) in 16 African Commonwealth countries:
Botswana, Eswatini, Ghana, Kenya, Lesotho, Malawi, Mauritius, Namibia, Nigeria, Seychelles, Sierra Leone, South Africa, Tanzania UR, Uganda, Zambia, Zimbabwe.
NGO Relations Member of: *Commonwealth Consortium for Education (CCfE, #04318)*; *World Federation of Colleges and Polytechnics (WFCP, #21421).* [2017/XD8293/**D**]

♦ Commonwealth Association of Professional Centres (CAPC) 04309

Contact address not obtained. T. +61293316920. Fax +61293317296. E-mail: info@commonwealth.int.
History within *Commonwealth Secretariat (#04362).* **Aims** Foster international relationships with professional and association members in other countries through exchange programmes. [2012/XM3620/t/**E**]

♦ Commonwealth Association of Public Accounts Committees (unconfirmed)

♦ Commonwealth Association for Public Administration and Management (CAPAM) 04310

Exec Dir/CEO 291 Dalhousie Street, Ste 202, Ottawa ON K1N 7E5, Canada. T. +18199567953. Fax +16137014236.
URL: http://www.capam.org/
History Founded 1994, London (UK), by Commonwealth countries, on the initiative of *Commonwealth Secretariat (#04362).* Groundwork for the Association laid down by the Harare Commonwealth Declaration, 1991. **Aims** Strengthen governments and improve public policy and effectiveness of services in response to citizen needs. **Structure** General Members Meeting (annual); International Board of Directors. **Languages** English. **Staff** 5.00 FTE, paid. Project managers and others on contractual basis as needed. **Finance** Sources: donations; meeting proceeds; members' dues. Other sources: training programmes. Annual budget: 1,500,000 USD. **Activities** Awards/prizes/competitions; events/meetings; knowledge management/information dissemination; training/education. **Events** *Biennial Conference* Georgetown (Guyana) 2018, *Biennial Conference* Port-of-Spain (Trinidad-Tobago) 2016, *Biennial Conference* Putrajaya (Malaysia) 2014, *Biennial Conference* Delhi (India) 2012, *Biennial Conference* St Julian's (Malta) 2010. **Publications** *Commonwealth Innovations Review* (4 a year). Featured CAPAM Reports. **Members** Institutional: ministry, department of agency within any level of government and private sector organizations or corporations. Individual: public servants and former public servants of any level of government and consultants, researchers or other interested parties who have a professional interest in public service at all levels of government. Membership countries not specified. **NGO Relations** Member of: *International Institute of Administrative Sciences (IIAS, #13859).* [2018/XD2687/**C**]

♦ Commonwealth Association of Public Sector Lawyers 04311

Acting Chair/Sec PO Box 403, Mosman NSW 2088, Australia. T. +61292653070 – +6120413544106. Fax +61299682542 – +61292615918. E-mail: capsl@bigpond.com.
URL: http://www.capsl.org/
History Founded Aug 1996, Vancouver BC (Canada), by *Commonwealth Lawyers Association (CLA, #04345),* following a proposal, May 1993, Nicosia (Cyprus). **Aims** Work closely with Commonwealth Lawyers Association to raise profile of public sector law and public sector lawyers within the Commonwealth; provide a focus and forum for exchange of information and ideas; support public sector lawyers in carrying out their professional duties and in providing efficient and professional legal services to governments. **Structure** Officers: Chair; Secretary; Treasurer (presently vacant). **Languages** English. **Staff** 1.00 FTE, voluntary. **Finance** Grant; sponsorship. **Events** *General Meeting* Cape Town (South Africa) 2013, *General Meeting* London (UK) 2005, *General Meeting* Melbourne, VIC (Australia) 2003, *General Meeting* Harare (Zimbabwe) 2001, *General Meeting* Kuala Lumpur (Malaysia) 1999. **Publications** *Newsletter of the Commonwealth Association of Public Sector Lawyers* (irregular) – electronic.
Members Organizations in 13 countries and territories:
Australia, Canada, Fiji, Ghana, Jamaica, Kiribati, Malaysia, Mauritius, New Zealand, South Africa, St Vincent-Grenadines, UK, Virgin Is UK.
Individuals in 30 countries and territories:
Australia, Bahamas, Bermuda, Canada, Cayman Is, Cook Is, Fiji, Guyana, Hong Kong, India, Jamaica, Jersey, Malawi, Malaysia, Mauritius, Namibia, New Zealand, Nigeria, Pakistan, Singapore, South Africa, Sri Lanka, St Kitts-Nevis, St Vincent-Grenadines, Trinidad-Tobago, Turks-Caicos, Uganda, UK, Virgin Is UK, Zambia.
IGO Relations *Commonwealth Secretariat (#04362)* – Legal Division. **NGO Relations** *Commonwealth Lawyers Association (CLA, #04345).* [2016/XD5932/**D**]

♦ Commonwealth Association of Science and Mathematics Educators / see Commonwealth Association of Science, Technology and Mathematics Educators (#04312)

♦ Commonwealth Association of Science, Technology and Mathematics Educators (CASTME) 04312

Contact 92 Welley Rd, Wraysbury, TW19 5EP, UK. T. +441784482001. E-mail: castmeuk@gmail.com – margaret-lenton@btconnect.com.
URL: http://castme.online/
History Founded 14 Oct 1974, London (UK), as *Commonwealth Association of Science and Mathematics Educators (CASME),* following a meeting of representatives of 17 Commonwealth countries, Apr 1973, Kingston (Jamaica). Present name adopted 1982. **Aims** Foster links between those concerned with education in science, technology and mathematics with special reference to the social significance of these subjects and their relationship to community education; help in the process of integrating studies of science and mathematics into existing cultures, customs and developing technology of a country. **Structure** Governing Council. **Languages** English. **Staff** 0.50 FTE, paid. **Finance** Members' dues. Supported by Commonwealth Foundation. **Activities** Knowledge management/information dissemination; projects/programmes; awards/prizes/competitions. **Events** *Biennial meeting / Triennial Meeting* Mauritius 2011, *Triennial Meeting* Ghana 2007, *Triennial Conference* Winneba (Ghana) 2007, *Critical thinking workshop* Cape Town (South Africa) 2006, *European conference* Malta 2006. **Publications** *The Castme Yearbook.*
Members Institutions and organizations (about 200). Council members in 13 countries:
Australia, Bahamas, Barbados, Canada, Ghana, Jamaica, Malta, Mauritius, Nigeria, Papua New Guinea, Sierra Leone, Uganda, UK.
Other membership countries not specified.
NGO Relations Member of: *Commonwealth Consortium for Education (CCfE, #04318)*; *Commonwealth HIV and AIDS Action Group (Para55, no recent information).* [2020/XC4545/**D**]

♦ Commonwealth Association of Scientific Agricultural Societies (no recent information)

♦ Commonwealth Association of Surveying and Land Economy (CASLE) 04313

Association de géodésie et d'économie foncière du Commonwealth
SG Fac of Environment and Technology, Univ of the West of England, Coldharbour Lane, Bristol, BS16 1QY, UK. T. +441173283036.
URL: http://www.casle.org/
History Founded 1 Sep 1969, London (UK), following preliminary conference, Aug 1968, London. **Aims** Represent surveying and land economy in Commonwealth countries. **Structure** General Assembly (at least every 3 years); Management Board. The former *Commonwealth Board of Surveying Education (CBSE, inactive)* is now incorporated within the work of the Management Board. Regions (5): Africa; Asia; Atlantic; Europe; Pacific. **Languages** English. **Staff** 0.50 FTE, paid. **Finance** Sources: contributions; grants; members' dues. **Activities** Events/meetings; monitoring/evaluation; research/documentation; standards/guidelines. **Events** *General Assembly and Conference* London (UK) 2019, *Developing a sustainable professionalism in surveying and relevant education in the commonwealth* Lusaka (Zambia) 2018, *Conference* Dar es Salaam (Tanzania UR) 2017, *General Assembly* Secondi-Takoradi (Ghana) 2015, *General Assembly* St Julian's (Malta) 2011. **Publications** *Survey Review* (6 a year); *CASLE Newsletter* (4 a year). *A Guide to Dispute Resolution* (2013); *An Introduction to Building Maintenance Management* (2002). Technical books; manuals.
Members Professional Societies; Correspondents in 39 Commonwealth countries:
Antigua-Barbuda, Bahamas, Barbados, Botswana, Brunei Darussalam, Canada, Dominica, Eswatini, Ghana, Grenada, Guyana, India, Jamaica, Japan, Kenya, Malawi, Malaysia, Maldives, Mauritius, Namibia, New Zealand, Nigeria, Pakistan, Papua New Guinea, Samoa, Singapore, Solomon Is, South Africa, Sri Lanka, St Kitts-Nevis, St Lucia, St Vincent-Grenadines, Tanzania UR, Tonga, Trinidad-Tobago, Uganda, UK, Vanuatu, Zambia.
Consultative Status Consultative status granted from: *ECOSOC (#05331)* (Special). **NGO Relations** Instrumental in setting up: *Built Environment Professions in the Commonwealth (BEPIC)*; *International Fire Safety Standards Coalition (IFSS Coalition, #13606).* Member of: *International Cost Management Standard Coalition (ICMS Coalition, #12978)*; *International Ethics Standards Coalition (IES Coalition, #13307)*; International Land Measurement Standards Coalition; *International Property Measurement Standards Coalition (IPMSC, #14656).* [2019.04.24/XC0361/**C**]

♦ Commonwealth Association of Tax Administrators (CATA) 04314

Exec Dir Marlborough House, Pall Mall, London, SW1Y 5HX, UK. T. +442077476473 – +442077476474. Fax +4420777476225. E-mail: cata@commonwealth.int.
Pres Mauritius Revenue Authority, 5th Floor, Ehram Court, Cnr Mgr Gonin and Sir Virgil Nez Street, Port Louis, Mauritius.
URL: http://catatax.org/
History 23 May 1978, London (UK). Founded on adoption of Constitution implementing agreement reached at meeting of Commonwealth Finance Ministers, 1977, Barbados. By-laws adopted 26 Oct 1979, Singapore (Singapore). **Aims** Improve tax administration in all its aspects within the Commonwealth, with particular emphasis on developing countries. **Structure** Management Committee. **Languages** English. **Staff** 2.00 FTE, paid. **Finance** Sources: members' dues. **Activities** Events/meetings; knowledge management/information dissemination; research/documentation; training/education. **Events** *Annual Technical Conference* Abuja (Nigeria) 2022, *Annual Technical Conference* 2021, *Annual Technical Conference* Penang (Malaysia) 2019, *Annual Technical Conference* Nadi (Fiji) 2018, *Triennial General Meeting* Nadi (Fiji) 2018. **Publications** *CATA Newsletter* (4 a year). *Examination of Accounts for Tax Auditing*; *Implementing Computerisation and Information Technology for Tax Administrations*; *Implementing Large Taxpayer Units*; *Tax Audit Techniques in Cash Based Economies – A Practical Guide*; *Tax Evasion and Avoidance – Strategies used to Combat these Problems*; *The Tax Audit of Cross-Border Business Transactions.* Reports on Annual Technical Conferences.
Members Tax administrators of 46 countries and territories:
Australia, Bahamas, Bangladesh, Barbados, Belize, Botswana, Brunei Darussalam, Cameroon, Canada, Cyprus, Eswatini, Fiji, Gambia, Ghana, Grenada, Guyana, India, Isle of Man, Jamaica, Kenya, Kiribati, Lesotho, Malawi, Malaysia, Malta, Mauritius, Namibia, New Zealand, Nigeria, Pakistan, Papua New Guinea, Rwanda, Samoa, Seychelles, Sierra Leone, Singapore, Sri Lanka, St Kitts-Nevis, St Lucia, Tanzania UR, Tonga, Trinidad-Tobago, Tuvalu, Uganda, UK, Zambia. [2021.06.18/XC8308/v/**C**]

♦ Commonwealth Broadcasting Association / see Public Media Alliance (#18568)
♦ Commonwealth Broadcasting Conference / see Public Media Alliance (#18568)

♦ Commonwealth Business Women Leaders Network 04315

Chairman The Hour Glass, 302 Orchard Road, Ste 11-01 Tong Bldg, Singapore 238862, Singapore. T. +6567872288. Fax +6567328683.
History Also referred to as *Commonwealth Business Women's Network.* [2007/XM3312/**F**]

♦ Commonwealth Business Women's Network / see Commonwealth Business Women Leaders Network (#04315)
♦ Commonwealth Caribbean Government Statisticians Conference (meeting series)
♦ Commonwealth Centre for Electronic Governance / see Commonwealth Centre for e-Governance (#04316)

♦ Commonwealth Centre for e-Governance (CCEG) 04316

CEO B 5/2 2nd Floor, Model Town-I, Delhi 110009, DELHI 110009, India. T. +919810063137.
Chief Exec/Chair 1601-85 Bronson Avenue, Ottawa ON K1R 6G7, Canada. T. +16132378828.
URL: http://www.electronicgov.net
History as a Commonwealth professional association. Previously referred to as *Commonwealth Centre for Electronic Governance.* **Aims** Assist transition to electronic government and electronic *democracy*; promote good practice, enhance sharing of learning experience, dissemination of information and management of knowledge in electronic government and electronic democracy among human and institutional networks and communities in the *Commonwealth* and beyond. **Structure** International Advisory Council. Executive Director; Chief Operations Officers; Researcher. **Languages** English. **Staff** 2.00 FTE, paid. **Finance** Proceeds from activities. **Activities** Provides seminars, conferences and workshops. **Events** *Seminar on electronic governance* Ottawa, ON (Canada) 2000. **Publications** Papers. **IGO Relations** *Commonwealth Secretariat (#04362).* [2014/XE4127/**E**]

♦ Commonwealth Chess Association (CCA) 04317

Chairman 5588 Basant Lane, Paharganj, Delhi 110055, DELHI 110055, India.
Gen Sec 107/6 Piyadasa Sirisena Mawatha, Colombo, 10, Sri Lanka. T. +94715397829. E-mail: godigamu@yahoo.com.
Facebook: https://www.facebook.com/Commonwealthchess/
History 1980. **Aims** Further the development of chess in the Commonwealth; give opportunities for competitive chess, in particular by planning and holding annual Commonwealth Chess *Championships.* **Structure** Meeting of representatives of member federations (every 2 years) decides policy. **Finance** Sources: members' dues. **Activities** Organizes chess events; assists in training and provision of international masters to run seminars in developing countries; supplies materials and grants to enable players from other Commonwealth countries to take part in British Chess Championship. **Events** *Meeting* Thessaloniki (Greece) 1994, *Meeting* Toronto, ON (Canada) 1986. **Publications** *Chess Trainer* (4 a year).
Members Full national chess federations in 36 countries and territories:
Antigua-Barbuda, Australia, Bahamas, Bahrain, Bangladesh, Barbados, Bermuda, Botswana, Brunei Darussalam, Canada, Cyprus, England, Fiji, Ghana, Guyana, Hong Kong, India, Jamaica, Kenya, Malaysia, Malta, Mauritius, New Zealand, Nigeria, Northern Ireland, Papua New Guinea, Scotland, Seychelles, Singapore, Sri Lanka, Trinidad-Tobago, Uganda, Virgin Is UK, Wales, Zambia, Zimbabwe.
IGO Relations *Commonwealth Secretariat (#04362).* [2021/XD0373/**C**]

♦ Commonwealth Conference of Postal Administrations (meeting series)

♦ Commonwealth Consortium for Education (CCfE) 04318

Contact c/o Association of Commonwealth Universities, Woburn House, 20-24 Tavistock Square, London, WC1H 9HF, UK. T. +447815784409. E-mail: secretary@commonwealtheducation.org.
URL: http://www.commonwealtheducation.org/

History Founded 2001, by a group of education-related Commonwealth NGOs. Formally constituted in 2003. Received formal accreditation to the Commonwealth, Dec 2004. **Aims** Coordinate efforts of education-related Commonwealth NGOs on behalf of Commonwealth education; stimulate more coherence in their work; provide a collective mechanism for interaction with ministries and official Commonwealth organizations; promote development of education throughout the Commonwealth; provide analysis to support formulation of policies on Commonwealth educational cooperation; assist Commonwealth inter-governmental agencies to draw on CSO resources and expertise; develop and disseminate models of good practice in education; constitute a forum which will promote cooperation by members. **Structure** General Meeting (every 3 years); Executive Committee. **Languages** English. **Staff** 5.00 FTE, voluntary. **Finance** Members' dues (annual). **Activities** Advocacy/lobbying/activism; events/meetings; projects/programmes. Regular contact with policy makers and submissions to Commonwealth ministerial meetings. **Events** *Conference of Commonwealth Education Ministers and General Meeting* Nairobi (Kenya) 2021, *Conference of Commonwealth Education Ministers and General Meeting* Nadi (Fiji) 2018, *Conference of Commonwealth Education Ministers and General Meeting* Paradise Is (Bahamas) 2015, *Conference and General Meeting* Nassau (Bahamas) 2012, *Conference of Commonwealth Education Ministers and General Meeting* Pailles (Mauritius) 2012. **Publications** *Quarterly Commonwealth Education Calendar*. *Commonwealth Education Directory*. Analysis of Commonwealth education issues; briefing notes; ministerial submissions; annual reports.

Members Full, international organizations (17):

Association for Commonwealth Literature and Language Studies (ACLALS, #02439); Association of Commonwealth Examination and Accreditation Bodies (ACEAB, #02438); Association of Commonwealth Universities, The (ACU, #02440); Commonwealth Association of Museums (CAM, #04305); Commonwealth Association of Polytechnics in Africa (CAPA, #04308); Commonwealth Association of Science, Technology and Mathematics Educators (CASTME, #04312); Commonwealth Council for Educational Administration and Management (CCEAM, #04319); Commonwealth Countries League (CCL, #04320) (Education Fund (CCLEF)); *Commonwealth Human Ecology Council (CHEC, #04339); Commonwealth Legal Education Association (CLEA, #04347); Commonwealth Youth Exchange Council (CYEC); Council for Education in the Commonwealth (CEC); English-Speaking Union (ESU, #05482); Link Community Development (Link, #16483).*

Associate International Organizations (2):

Royal Commonwealth Society (RCS, #18990); Royal Over-Seas League (ROSL).

Special members (3):

Commonwealth Foundation (CF, #04330); Commonwealth of Learning (COL, #04346); Commonwealth Secretariat (#04362).

IGO Relations Accredited to: Commonwealth. Observer status with: *Conference of Commonwealth Education Ministers (CCEM)*. Accredited status at: *Commonwealth Heads of Government Meeting (CHOGM, #04337)*. Reciprocal 'Special Membership' by CCfE's constitution with: *Commonwealth Foundation (CF, #04330); Commonwealth of Learning (COL, #04346); Commonwealth Secretariat (#04362)*. Participates actively in consultations organized by the intergovernmental bodies and has been represented on official working groups and advisory committees planning, monitoring and in some cases implementing Commonwealth activities, including the Commonwealth Teacher Recruitment Protocol, the Commonwealth post-2015 Education Framework, the Commonwealth Education Hub and CCEMs/Stakeholder Forums. **NGO Relations** Close relations with wider network of Commonwealth Accredited Organizations. [2016.06.01/XM1079/y/**F**]

- ♦ Commonwealth Consultative Group on Human Settlement (inactive)
- ♦ Commonwealth Consultative Group on Mineral Resources and Geology (inactive)
- ♦ Commonwealth Consultative Group on Technology Management / see Commonwealth Partnership for Technology Management (#04356)
- ♦ Commonwealth Consultative Space Research Committee (inactive)
- ♦ Commonwealth and Continental Church Society / see Intercontinental Church Society (#11460)
- ♦ Commonwealth Council for Educational Administration / see Commonwealth Council for Educational Administration and Management (#04319)

♦ Commonwealth Council for Educational Administration and Management (CCEAM) 04319

Admin Office 350 Erbsville Road, Unit 30, Waterloo ON N2T 2P7, Canada. E-mail: cceamfuture@gmail.com.
URL: http://cceam.net/

History Aug 1970, Armidale, NSW (Australia). Founded at 2nd *International Intervisitation Programme (IIP)*. Former names and other names: *Commonwealth Council for Educational Administration (CCEA)* – former (Aug 1970). **Aims** Foster links and exchanges in education administration, management and leadership; encourage development of national associations; organize and support regional and international conferences; promote international understanding and collaboration; encourage study, practice and preparation of education leaders. **Structure** General Meeting (every 2 years); Board; Executive Committee. **Languages** English. **Staff** 0.50 FTE, paid. **Finance** Sources: grants; members' dues; sale of publications; sponsorship. Grants from Commonwealth Foundation and other agencies for specific projects. Supported by: *Commonwealth Foundation (CF, #04330)*. **Activities** Events/meetings; knowledge management/information dissemination. **Events** *International Conference* Liverpool (UK) 2022, *International Conference* Kuala Lumpur (Malaysia) 2021, *International Conference* Kuala Lumpur (Malaysia) 2020, *International Conference* Valletta (Malta) 2018, *International Conference* Udaipur (India) 2016. **Publications** *International Studies in Educational Administration* (3 a year).

Members National and regional affiliated groups; individual members; life members; institutional subscribers. Members (1,938). National and regional affiliated groups in 20 countries:
Australia, Barbados, Cameroon, Canada, Cyprus, Fiji, India, Kenya, Malaysia, Malta, Namibia, New Zealand, Nigeria, Papua New Guinea, Seychelles, South Africa, St Vincent-Grenadines, Tonga, Uganda, UK.
Individuals in 6 countries:
Israel, Netherlands, Nigeria, Sweden, UK, USA.
Life members in 15 countries and territories:
Australia, Bangladesh, Bhutan, Canada, China, Cook Is, India, Malaysia, New Zealand, Pakistan, Papua New Guinea, Taiwan, UK, USA, Vanuatu.
Institutional subscribers in 11 countries and territories:
Australia, Canada, Cyprus, Germany, Korea Rep, Netherlands, New Zealand, Sweden, Taiwan, UK, USA.

IGO Relations Observer status with (2): *Commonwealth Heads of Government Meeting (CHOGM, #04337); Conference of Commonwealth Education Ministers (CCEM)*. Formal relations with: *Commonwealth Secretariat (#04362)* and *Commonwealth Foundation (CF, #04330)*. **NGO Relations** Member of (1): *Commonwealth Consortium for Education (CCfE, #04318)*. Cooperates with (1): *University Council for Educational Administration (UCEA)*. Cooperates with: national organizations interested in the field. [2021.06.15/XC4608/**C**]

♦ Commonwealth Countries League (CCL) 04320

Ligue des pays du Commonwealth

Hon Sec address not obtained. E-mail: cclenquiries@yahoo.co.uk.
URL: http://www.the-ccl.org/

History 1925, as *British Commonwealth League*. Present name adopted 1965. UK Registered Charity: 1159625. **Aims** Advance the well-being, friendship and networking of Commonwealth citizens, in particular Commonwealth *women* and *children*, to facilitate *equality* between women and men. **Structure** Annual General Meeting; Executive Committee; Board of Trustees. **Languages** English. **Staff** Voluntary. **Finance** Members' dues. Other sources: fund raising through *Commonwealth Girls Education Fund (CGEF, #04334)*; donations. **Activities** Training/education; events/meetings. **Events** *Annual General Meeting* London (UK) 2003, *Annual conference* London (UK) 1994, *Annual Conference* London (UK) 1992, *Annual Conference* London (UK) 1991, *Annual Conference* London (UK) 1990. **Publications** *CCL Newsletter*. Annual Report. Brochures. **Members** Affiliated societies constituted on national, state or district basis; Individuals. Membership countries not specified. **IGO Relations** *Commonwealth Secretariat (#04362)*. **NGO Relations** Member of: *The Commonwealth Association (COMASSOC, #04299); Commonwealth Consortium for Education (CCfE, #04318); Federation of International Women's Associations in London (FIWAL)*. [2016.06.01/XC0367/v/**E**]

- ♦ Commonwealth Countries League Education Fund / see Commonwealth Girls Education Fund (#04334)
- ♦ Commonwealth Defence Conference (inactive)
- ♦ Commonwealth Defence Science Organization (inactive)

♦ Commonwealth Dental Association (CDA) 04321

Association dentaire du Commonwealth

Admin 64 Wimpole St, London, W1G 8YS, UK. T. +442075634133. Fax +442075634556. E-mail: administrator@comdental.org – info@comdental.org.
URL: http://www.comdental.org/

History Inaugural meeting, 24-25 Apr 1991, Kuala Lumpur (Malaysia). **Aims** Improve oral health in Commonwealth countries; provide opportunities for the exchange of information, experience and expertise. **Structure** General Meeting. Regions (6): Europe; Caribbean; East, Central and Southern Africa; Southeast Asia; West Africa; Pacific. **Languages** English. **Staff** 0.50 FTE, paid. **Finance** Sources: members' dues. **Activities** Events/meetings; training/education. **Events** *Triennial Conference* Cape Town (South Africa) 2012, *Triennial Conference and Workshop* Kuching (Malaysia) 2012, *Triennial conference and workshop / Triennial Conference* Singapore (Singapore) 2009, *Triennial conference and workshop / Triennial Conference* Colombo (Sri Lanka) 2006, *Triennial conference and workshop / Triennial Conference* Nairobi (Kenya) 2003. **Publications** *CDA News* (periodical).

Members National Dental Associations; CDA Friends – corporate and individual. Members in 35 countries:
Australia, Bahamas, Bangladesh, Barbados, Botswana, Cyprus, Eswatini, Ghana, Guyana, India, Kenya, Malawi, Malaysia, Maldives, Malta, Mauritius, Namibia, New Zealand, Nigeria, Pakistan, Seychelles, Sierra Leone, Singapore, South Africa, Sri Lanka, St Kitts-Nevis, St Vincent-Grenadines, Tanzania UR, Tonga, Trinidad-Tobago, Tuvalu, Uganda, UK, Zambia, Zimbabwe.

IGO Relations Observer status with: Commonwealth Health Ministers' Meeting (CHMM); Meeting of Commonwealth Representatives Prior to the World Health Assembly. **NGO Relations** Member of: *Commonwealth Health Professions and Partners Alliance (CHPA, #04338); Commonwealth HIV and AIDS Action Group (Para55, no recent information); FDI – World Dental Federation (#09281).* [2021/XD2334/**C**]

- ♦ Commonwealth Development Corporation / see CDC Group
- ♦ Commonwealth Economic Consultative Council (inactive)

♦ Commonwealth Educational Media Centre for Asia (CEMCA) 04322

Dir 7/8 Sarv Priya Vihar, Delhi 110016, DELHI 110016, India. E-mail: admin@cemca.org.
URL: http://www.cemca.org/

History Jul 1994, Delhi (India). Former names and other names: *Commonwealth Educational Media Cooperative for Asia* – former. **Aims** Promote cooperation and collaboration in the use of *electronic media* resources for *distance education*; serve as regional electronic media resource centre; facilitate exchange of information and *radio* and *television* programmes. **Structure** Advisory Council, comprising representatives of major distance education institutions in the region. **Finance** Sources: grants. Supported by: *Commonwealth of Learning (COL, #04346)*. Annual budget: 565,000 CAD. **Activities** Operates as a regional media service. Services: stock-footage; value-added information on technological developments and application; audio-visual programme dubbing and translation; customized package for broadcast and non-broadcast use; computer software. Holds regional seminars and workshops (not on a regular basis). International training programmes. **Events** *Conference on the use of multi-media in distance education* 1997, *Workshop on management of non-print media resources* Delhi (India) 1996. **Publications** *CEMCA Newsletter* (4 a year). Reports; papers.

Members Activities cover 8 countries:
Bangladesh, Brunei Darussalam, India, Malaysia, Maldives, Pakistan, Singapore, Sri Lanka.

IGO Relations Member of (1): *Asia-Pacific Institute for Broadcasting Development (AIBD, #01934).* [2022/XK1250/**E**]

- ♦ Commonwealth Educational Media Cooperative for Asia / see Commonwealth Educational Media Centre for Asia (#04322)

♦ The Commonwealth Education Trust (CET) 04323

Contact 7-14 Great Dover Street, London, SE1 4YR, UK. T. +442030967721. E-mail: hello@commonwealtheducationtrust.org.
URL: http://www.commonwealtheducationtrust.org

History 1887, London (UK). Established as a charitable trust by the countries of the Commonwealth, and as successor to the Commonwealth Institute. The Institute was itself the successor trust to the Imperial Institute which had its origins in a fund raised in 1886 to celebrate Queen Victoria's Golden Jubilee. Registration: Charity Commission, No/ID: 1119647, England and Wales. **Aims** Advance education in the Commonwealth with a focus on supporting teacher professional development. **Structure** Corporate Trustee (1); Advisory Trustees (3). **Languages** English. **Staff** 2.00 FTE, paid. **Finance** Trust fund and fundraising. **Activities** Projects/programmes; training/education. The Commonwealth of Nations. **Events** *Cultural identity in the modern Commonwealth* London (UK) 1989, *Studies of the Commonwealth in British higher education* London (UK) 1989, *Women writers workshop* London (UK) 1989, *Conference on Pacific writing* London (UK) 1988, *Women writers workshop* London (UK) 1988. **Publications** *Give the Ball to the Poet: A New Anthology of Caribbean Poetry* (2014); *A River of Stories: Tales and Poems from Across the Commonwealth* (2006) – in 4 vols. [2022.05.10/XE5519/**E**]

- ♦ Commonwealth Engineering Conference / see Commonwealth Engineers Council (#04324)

♦ Commonwealth Engineers Council (CEC) 04324

Conseil des associations d'ingénieurs du Commonwealth

SG c/o Inst of Civil Engineers, One Great George Street, London, SW1P 3AA, UK. T. +442076652348. Fax +442072330267.
Chair address not obtained.
URL: http://cec.ice.org.uk/

History Founded Sep 1946, London (UK), at 1st meeting (held at the invitation of 3 British engineering institutions), as *Conference of Engineering Institutions of the British Commonwealth*. Sometimes referred to as *Commonwealth Engineering Conference*. Present name adopted 1975. **Aims** Advance the common aims of participating institutions; cooperate with other international organizations and support or supplement their work in the engineering field; encourage engineering education and training in the Commonwealth and achieve parity of engineering qualifications. **Structure** Primarily a virtual organization. Secretariat lies with the Institution of Civil Engineers, London (UK). **Languages** English. **Staff** 0.25 FTE, paid. **Finance** Sources: members' dues. **Activities** Advocacy/lobbying/activism; events/meetings; training/education. **Events** *Biennial Conference* Japan 2015, *Biennial Conference* Paris (France) 2014, *Biennial Conference* London (UK) 2012, *Biennial Conference* London (UK) 2010, *Conference on coasts, marine structures and breakwaters* Edinburgh (UK) 2009. **Publications** *CEC Newsletter* (2 a year).

Members Presidents and Secretaries of engineering institutions in 44 Commonwealth countries and territories:
Australia, Bahamas, Bangladesh, Barbados, Botswana, Brunei Darussalam, Cameroon, Canada, Cyprus, Eswatini, Fiji, Ghana, India, Ireland, Jamaica, Kenya, Kiribati, Lesotho, Malawi, Malaysia, Maldives, Malta, Mauritius, Namibia, New Zealand, Nigeria, Pakistan, Papua New Guinea, Samoa, Seychelles, Sierra Leone, Singapore, Solomon Is, South Africa, Sri Lanka, Tanzania UR, Tonga, Trinidad-Tobago, Tuvalu, Uganda, UK, Vanuatu, Zambia, Zimbabwe.

NGO Relations Instrumental in setting up: *Built Environment Professions in the Commonwealth (BEPIC).* [2019.04.25/XC0368/**C**]

♦ Commonwealth Enterprise and Investment Council (CWEIC) 04325

Contact North Wing Guildhall, Gresham Street, London, EC2V 7HH, UK.
URL: http://www.cweic.org/

History Jul 2014. **Aims** Facilitate increased *trade* and investment across the Commonwealth. **Structure** Advisory Board. **Events** *Commonwealth Trade and Investment Summit* London (UK) 2021, *CBF : Commonwealth Business Forum* St Julian's (Malta) 2015. **IGO Relations** *Commonwealth Secretariat (#04362).* [2022/XM5316/**C**]

♦ Commonwealth Environmental Journalists Association (CEJA) 04326

Address not obtained.

History Oct 1998, Colombo (Sri Lanka). **Aims** Create and promote greater awareness of environmental issues among people and journalists in Commonwealth member countries. **Structure** General Body (every 2 years). Executive Committee, comprising Chairman, 3 Vice-Chairmen, Secretary General, Assistant Secretary and 5 further members. **Activities** Organizes conferences, workshops, seminars, round tables and training programmes. **Events** *APFEJ annual congress* Aluthgama (Sri Lanka) 2002, *APFEJ annual congress* Manila (Philippines) 2001, *APFEJ annual congress* Suva (Fiji) 2000, *Commonwealth Congress of Environmental Journalists* Suva (Fiji) 2000. **Publications** *CEJA Newsletter* (2 a year). **Members** in 19 countries. Membership countries not specified. **NGO Relations** *Asia-Pacific Forum of Environmental Journalists (APFEJ, #01910)*. *Asian Media Information and Communication Centre (AMIC, #01536)* is founding member. [2012/XD7747/**D**]

♦ The Commonwealth Equality Network (TCEN) 04327

Secretariat c/o Kaleidoscope Trust, Print House Studio, 18 Ashwin Street, London, E8 3DL, UK. T. +442081336460. E-mail: info@commonwealthequality.org.
URL: https://www.commonwealthequality.org/

History Founded 2013. Current constitution adopted Nov 2016. UK Registered Company: 09193283. **Aims** Give a voice to *LGBTI* communities across the Commonwealth; support joint advocacy in identifying a Commonwealth solution to a Commonwealth problem. **Structure** Management Committee. **Activities** Advocacy/lobbying/activism.
Members Organizations in 30 countries:
Australia, Bangladesh, Barbados, Belize, Botswana, Canada, Côte d'Ivoire, Cyprus, Dominica, Eswatini, Ghana, Jamaica, Kenya, Malawi, Malaysia, Malta, Mauritius, Namibia, Nigeria, Pakistan, Seychelles, Singapore, South Africa, Sri Lanka, St Lucia, Tanzania UR, Trinidad-Tobago, Uganda, UK, Zambia.
Included in the above, 7 organizations listed in this Yearbook:
Asia Pacific Coalition on Male Sexual Health (APCOM, #01872); *Commonwealth Human Rights Initiative (CHRI, #04340)*; *Eastern Caribbean Alliance for Diversity and Equality (ECADE, #05230)*; *Human Dignity Trust*; *Kaleidoscope Trust*; *Pacific Sexual and Gender Diversity Network (PSGDN)*; *Royal Commonwealth Society (RCS, #18990)*. [2019/XM8660/y/**C**]

♦ Commonwealth Equity Fund (inactive)
♦ Commonwealth Ex-Services League / see Royal Commonwealth Ex-Services League (#18989)

♦ Commonwealth Fencing Federation (CFF) 04328

Pres 64 Princes St, Williamstown VIC 3016, Australia. T. +61414781137. E-mail: president@commonwealthfencing.org.
Sec/Treas 22A Commercial Rd, Prahran VIC 3181, Australia. E-mail: sectreas@commonwealthfencing.org.
URL: http://www.commonwealthfencing.org/

History Fencing was included in the programme of the Commonwealth Games from 1950 (then the Empire Games) and then dropped in 1974, although Fencing remains a Recognized Sport of the Commonwealth Games Federation, and may be included on the programme of future Commonwealth Games. CFF maintains the tradition of competition between Commonwealth fencing nations, which underlies the objective of the Federation. Statutes amended 2014; 2017. Former names and other names: *Empire Fencing Federation* – former; *British Commonwealth Fencing Federation* – former (1978 to 1982). Registration: Australia. **Aims** Encourage development of fencing within the Commonwealth; regain inclusion of fencing on the Commonwealth Games programme. **Structure** General Assembly (known as Elective Congress, every 4 years); Executive Committee. **Languages** English. **Staff** Voluntary. **Finance** Sources: members' dues. **Activities** Events/meetings; sporting activities. **Events** *Congress* London (England) 2022, *Congress* 2020, *Congress* Largs (UK) 2014, *Congress* Paris (France) 2013, *Congress* Melbourne, VIC (Australia) 2010.
Members National governing bodies of fencing in 40 Commonwealth countries and territories:
Australia, Bahamas, Bangladesh, Barbados, Belize, Bermuda, Botswana, Brunei Darussalam, Cameroon, Canada, Cyprus, Dominica, England, Ghana, Gibraltar, Guernsey, Guyana, India, Isle of Man, Jamaica, Jersey, Kenya, Malaysia, Malta, Mauritius, Namibia, Nepal, New Zealand, Nigeria, Northern Ireland, Pakistan, Papua New Guinea, Rwanda, Samoa, Scotland, Sierra Leone, Singapore, South Africa, Sri Lanka, Wales. [2022.05.11/XD9143/**D**]

♦ Commonwealth Finance Ministers Meeting (meeting series)

♦ Commonwealth Forestry Association (CFA) 04329

Exec Dir The Crib, Dinchope, Craven Arms, SY7 9JJ, UK. T. +441588672868. Fax +4415880116645. E-mail: cfa@cfa-international.org.
URL: http://www.cfa-international.org/

History 1921, London (UK). Founded following resolution at 1st Empire Forestry Conference, Jul 1920, London. Incorporated by Royal Charter, Nov 1921; and by Supplemental Royal Charters: 1962, when present title was adopted, and 1981. Former names and other names: *Empire Forestry Association* – former (1921 to 1962). **Aims** Promote for public benefit the science and practice of forestry; advance education in the value of trees and forests for the conservation of wildlife, soil and water resources, amenity and recreation; promote research into efficient and sustained production of timber resources, and interrelationships between trees and site fertility, for both forestry and agriculture; stimulate general recognition of beneficial influence of forests over climate; provide means of communication for those concerned with forestry and forest problems. **Structure** Governing Council (meets annually); Executive Committee. **Languages** English, French, Spanish. **Staff** 1.50 FTE, paid. **Finance** Sources: members' dues. **Activities** Events/meetings; knowledge management/information dissemination; publishing activities. **Events** *Commonwealth Forestry Conference* Vancouver, BC (Canada) 2021, *Commonwealth Forestry Conference* Dehra Dun (India) 2017, *Annual General Meeting* Fremantle, WA (Australia) 2001, *Annual general meeting / Annual Meeting* Oxford (UK) 2000, *Annual Meeting* Broughton (UK) 1999. **Publications** *CFA Newsletter* (4 a year); *International Forestry Review* (4 a year).
Members Foresters, forest and wood scientists, timber merchants, ecologists, resource managers and conservationists: Ordinary; Life; Associate; Affiliated (Institutions, Corporations, Firms). Members (about 800) in 87 countries (including 41 – marked " – outside the Commonwealth):
Argentina (*), Australia, Austria (*), Bahamas, Bangladesh, Barbados, Belgium (*), Belize, Bhutan, Bolivia (*), Brazil (*), Brunei Darussalam, Bulgaria, Cameroon, Canada, Chile (*), China (*), Colombia (*), Costa Rica (*), Côte d'Ivoire (*), Croatia, Cuba (*), Cyprus, Czechia (*), Denmark (*), Dominica, Eswatini, Ethiopia (*), Fiji, Finland (*), France (*), Germany (*), Ghana, Greece (*), Grenada, Guatemala (*), Guyana, Honduras (*), Hong Kong, India, Indonesia, Iran Islamic Rep (*), Israel (*), Italy (*), Jamaica, Japan (*), Kenya, Laos, Lesotho, Liberia (*), Madagascar (*), Malawi, Malaysia, Malta, Mexico (*), Nepal (*), Netherlands (*), New Zealand, Niger (*), Nigeria, Norway (*), Pakistan, Papua New Guinea, Philippines (*), Poland (*), Portugal (*), Samoa, Singapore, Solomon Is, South Africa (*), Spain (*), Sri Lanka, Sudan, Sweden (*), Switzerland (*), Taiwan (*), Tanzania UR, Trinidad-Tobago, Türkiye, Uganda, UK, USA (*), Vanuatu, Venezuela, Vietnam, Windward Is, Zimbabwe.
NGO Relations Member of (1): *International Society of Tropical Foresters (ISTF, #15522)*. Close cooperation with the previous *Commonwealth Forestry Institute (CFI, inactive)*, currently *'Oxford Forestry Institute'*. [2023.02.20/XC4552/**C**]

♦ Commonwealth Forestry Institute (inactive)

♦ Commonwealth Foundation (CF) 04330

Fondation du Commonwealth

Dir Marlborough House, Pall Mall, London, SW1Y 5HY, UK. T. +442079303783. Fax +442078398157. E-mail: foundation@commonwealth.int.
Chair address not obtained.
URL: http://www.commonwealthfoundation.com/

History Set up as a Charity under English law, 1965. Reconstituted as an intergovernmental organization, 1982. At *Commonwealth Heads of Government Meeting (CHOGM, #04337)*, 2009, Port-of-Spain (Trinidad-Tobago), Heads of Government committed to reform of Commonwealth institutions. Foundation relaunched 1 Nov 2012. Registered as a UK Registered Charity, 15 Dec 1966. **Aims** Develop the capacity of *civil society* to act together and learn from each other to engage with institutions that shape people's lives. **Structure** Board of Governors, comprising representatives of Commonwealth governments and High Commissioners based in London, civil society representatives and Secretary-General of *Commonwealth Secretariat (#04362)*. Chair. Executive Committee, includes Grants Committee; Civil Society Advisory Committee. **Languages** English. **Staff** 20.00 FTE, paid. **Finance** Member governments' assessed contributions; project specific grants. **Activities** Awards/prizes/competitions; capacity building; events/meetings; knowledge management/information dissemination; networking/liaising; projects/programmes. **Events** *Commonwealth Civil Society Forum* Geneva (Switzerland) 2015, *Commonwealth People's Forum – CPF* Malta 2015, *Commonwealth People's Forum* Mdina (Malta) 2015, *MenEngage Africa symposium* Johannesburg (South Africa) 2009, *Commonwealth people's forum* Port-of-Spain (Trinidad-Tobago) 2009.

Members Membership is voluntary, open to all Commonwealth governments. Current members: governments of 46 countries:
Antigua-Barbuda, Australia, Bahamas, Bangladesh, Barbados, Belize, Botswana, Brunei Darussalam, Cameroon, Canada, Cyprus, Dominica, Eswatini, Ghana, Grenada, Guyana, India, Jamaica, Kenya, Kiribati, Lesotho, Malawi, Malaysia, Maldives, Malta, Mauritius, Mozambique, Namibia, New Zealand, Nigeria, Pakistan, Papua New Guinea, Rwanda, Seychelles, Sierra Leone, Solomon Is, South Africa, Sri Lanka, St Lucia, St Vincent-Grenadines, Tanzania UR, Tonga, Trinidad-Tobago, Uganda, UK, Zambia.
Associate (1):
Gibraltar.
IGO Relations One of the Commonwealth's 3 IGOs alongside: *Commonwealth of Learning (COL, #04346)*; *Commonwealth Secretariat (#04362)*. [2016.01.21/XF0369/f/**F***]

♦ Commonwealth Freedom of Movement Organisation / see CANZUK International (#03417)
♦ The Commonwealth Fund (internationally oriented national body)
♦ Commonwealth Fund of New York / see The Commonwealth Fund

♦ Commonwealth Fund for Technical Cooperation (CFTC) 04331

Fonds du Commonwealth pour la coopération technique

Chief of Staff Commonwealth Sec, Marlborough House, Pall Mall, London, SW1Y 5HX, UK. T. +442077476500. Fax +442079300827. E-mail: technicalassistance@commonwealth.int – info@commonwealth.int.
URL: http://www.thecommonwealth.org/

History 1 Apr 1971, as an integral part of *Commonwealth Secretariat (#04362)*, following *Commonwealth Heads of Government Meeting (CHOGM, #04337)*, Jan 1971, Singapore (Singapore). **Aims** As a source of assistance for *sustainable development* and *poverty* eradication: contribute to development efforts of member states; promote economic and social development and alleviation of poverty in Commonwealth countries; provide technical assistance (advice, experts and training) to meet priority needs of Commonwealth developing countries; support development cooperation activities of the Commonwealth by enabling each country to draw on the variety of skills available in the Commonwealth and to offer its own skills to others. **Structure** Board of Governors (meets annually), consisting of all eligible members. Executive Committee of 16 members: 8 largest contributors to the overall resources of the various Commonwealth Funds for the past 3 years; 8 regional representatives with 2 from each region (Africa; Caribbean; Europe/Asia; Pacific). **Languages** English. **Finance** Governments subscribe annually on a voluntary basis. **Activities** Differs from traditional aid agencies by operating on a system of mutual assistance whereby member governments contribute financing on a voluntary basis and obtain technical assistance as required. Supports development cooperation by enabling each member country to draw on the variety of skills in the Commonwealth with developed and developing countries contributing resources. Largely demand-driven, responds to requests from governments and supports programmes through the provision of technical assistance. Programme priorities (2008-2012): Peace and Democracy; Pro-Poor Growth and Sustainable Development; Mainstreamed Issues (Gender, Youth and Human Rights). **Events** *Workshop on groundwater modeling* Nairobi (Kenya) 1992, *International seminar on environmental management* Halifax, NS (Canada) 1990, *Workshop for Commonwealth South Pacific countries on young people, enterprise and employment* Honiara (Solomon Is) 1990, *Meeting* Bridgetown (Barbados) 1987, *Meeting* London (UK) 1987.
Members Governments of 53 countries:
Antigua-Barbuda, Australia, Bahamas, Bangladesh, Barbados, Belize, Botswana, Brunei Darussalam, Cameroon, Canada, Cyprus, Dominica, Eswatini, Fiji, Ghana, Grenada, Guyana, India, Jamaica, Kenya, Kiribati, Lesotho, Malawi, Malaysia, Maldives, Malta, Mauritius, Mozambique, Namibia, Nauru, New Zealand, Nigeria, Papua New Guinea, Rwanda, Samoa, Seychelles, Sierra Leone, Singapore, Solomon Is, South Africa, Sri Lanka, St Kitts-Nevis, St Lucia, St Vincent-Grenadines, Tanzania UR, Tonga, Trinidad-Tobago, Tuvalu, Uganda, UK, Vanuatu, Zambia, Zimbabwe.
IGO Relations Permanent observer status with: *World Intellectual Property Organization (WIPO, #21593)*.
Works with the following regional organizations:
- *Asia-Pacific Institute for Broadcasting Development (AIBD, #01934)*;
- *Caribbean Centre for Development Administration (CARICAD, #03468)*;
- *Caribbean Community (CARICOM, #03476)* Secretariat;
- *Caribbean Development Bank (CDB, #03492)*;
- *Caribbean Tourism Organization (CTO, #03561)*;
- *Common Market for Eastern and Southern Africa (COMESA, #04296)*;
- *Eastern Caribbean Central Bank (ECCB, #05231)*;
- *Eastern and Southern African Management Institute (ESAMI, #05254)*;
- *Organisation of Eastern Caribbean States (OECS, #17804)*;
- *Pacific Community (SPC, #17942)*;
- *Pacific Islands Forum Fisheries Agency (FFA, #17969)*;
- *Pacific Islands Forum Secretariat (#17970)*;
- *Southern African Development Community (SADC, #19843)*;
- *University of the South Pacific (USP, #20703)*;
- *University of the West Indies (UWI, #20705)*;
- *West African Health Organization (WAHO, #20881)*.

NGO Relations Gives support to training activities of Commonwealth and other bodies, including:
- *African Association for Public Administration and Management (AAPAM, #00215)*;
- *Commonwealth Association for Health and Disability (COMHAD, #04302)*;
- *Commonwealth Association of Polytechnics in Africa (CAPA, #04308)*;
- *Commonwealth Association of Science, Technology and Mathematics Educators (CASTME, #04312)*;
- *Commonwealth Association of Surveying and Land Economy (CASLE, #04313)*;
- *Commonwealth Association of Tax Administrators (CATA, #04314)*;
- *Commonwealth-India Metrology Centre (no recent information)*.

Also funds: *Commonwealth Partnership for Technology Management (CPTM, #04356)*. Former staff members can join: *The Commonwealth Association (COMASSOC, #04299)*. [2018/XF3936/f/**F***]

♦ Commonwealth Games Federation (CGF) 04332

Fédération des jeux du Commonwealth

CEO Commonwealth House, 55-58 Pall Mall, London, SW1Y 5JH, UK. T. +442077476427. E-mail: info@thecgf.com.
URL: http://www.thecgf.com/

History Aug 1932, Los Angeles CA (USA), as *British Empire Games Federation*, following first British Empire Games, 1930, Hamilton (Canada), where 11 countries sent 400 athletes to take part in 6 sports and 59 events. Since then, the Games have been conducted every 4 years, except for 1942 and 1946 due to World War II. The Games were known as the British Empire Games from 1930 to 1950. Subsequent name changes: *British Empire and Commonwealth Games Federation* in 1952 – held the Games under the name British Empire and Commonwealth Games from 1954 to 1966; *British Commonwealth Games Federation* in 1966 – held the Games under the name British Commonwealth Games from 1970 to 1974. Present name of the Federation adopted 1974; holds the Games under the name Commonwealth Games, since 1978. **Aims** Organize a unique, world class, multi-sports event, often referred to as the 'Friendly Games'; encourage and assist education via *sport* development and physical education as a means of improving society and the general well being of the people of the Commonwealth. **Structure** General Assembly (annual); Executive Board; Sub-Committees. **Languages** English. **Staff** 6.00 FTE, paid. **Finance** Rights' fees and television and sponsorship revenues. **Activities** Organizes: Commonwealth Games (every 4 years); Commonwealth Youth Games (every 4 years); Annual General Assembly. **Events** *General Assembly* Edmonton, AB (Canada) 2016, *General Assembly* Auckland (New Zealand) 2015, *Commonwealth Youth Games* Samoa 2015, *Commonwealth Games* Glasgow (UK) 2014, *Meeting* Kuala Lumpur (Malaysia) 2011.
Members Commonwealth Games Associations; National Olympic Committees. Members – divided into 5 regions – in 70 countries and territories:
Anguilla, Antigua-Barbuda, Australia, Bahamas, Bangladesh, Barbados, Belize, Bermuda, Botswana, Brunei Darussalam, Cameroon, Canada, Cayman Is, Cook Is, Cyprus, Dominica, England, Eswatini, Falklands/Malvinas, Ghana, Gibraltar, Grenada, Guernsey, Guyana, India, Isle of Man, Jamaica, Jersey, Kenya, Kiribati, Lesotho, Malawi, Malaysia, Maldives, Malta, Mauritius, Montserrat, Mozambique, Namibia, Nauru, New Zealand, Niue, Norfolk Is, Northern Ireland, Pakistan, Papua New Guinea, Rwanda, Samoa, Scotland, Seychelles, Sierra Leone, Singapore, Solomon Is, South Africa, Sri Lanka, St Helena, St Kitts-Nevis, St Lucia, St Vincent-Grenadines, Tanzania UR, Tonga, Trinidad-Tobago, Turks-Caicos, Tuvalu, Uganda, Vanuatu, Virgin Is UK, Wales, Zambia, Zimbabwe.
IGO Relations *Commonwealth Secretariat (#04362)*.
NGO Relations Member of (2): *Council of Commonwealth Societies (CCS, #04878)*; *Olympic Movement (#17719)*. Partner of (1): *Global ESports Federation (GEF, #10348)*.

Commonwealth Geographical Bureau
04333

alphabetic sequence excludes
For the complete listing, see Yearbook Online at

Recognized by: *International Olympic Committee (IOC, #14408)*. Contacts with:
- *Badminton World Federation (BWF, #03060)*;
- *Commonwealth Fencing Federation (CFF, #04328)*;
- *Fédération internationale de basketball (FIBA, #09614)*;
- *Fédération internationale d'escrime (FIE, #09629)*;
- *Fédération internationale de gymnastique (FIG, #09636)*;
- *World Athletics (#21209)*;
- *International Boxing Association (IBA, #12385)*;
- *International Canoe Federation (ICF, #12437)*;
- *International Cricket Council (ICC, #13105)*;
- *International Judo Federation (IJF, #13975)*;
- *World Netball (WN, #21668)*;
- *International Paralympic Committee (IPC, #14512)*;
- *World Rowing (#21756)*;
- *International Shooting Sport Federation (ISSF, #14852)*;
- *World Aquatics (#21100)*;
- *International Table Tennis Federation (ITTF, #15650)*;
- *International Tennis Federation (ITF, #15676)*;
- *World Triathlon (#21872)*;
- *International Weightlifting Federation (IWF, #15876)*;
- *Union Cycliste Internationale (UCI, #20375)*;
- *United World Wrestling (UWW, #20665)*;
- *World Archery (#21105)*;
- *International Bowling Federation (IBF, #12384)*;
- *World Bowls (WB, #21240)*;
- *World Confederation of Billiards Sports (WCBS, #21291)*;
- *World Rugby (#21757)*;
- *World Sailing (#21760)*;
- *World Squash Federation (WSF, #21826)*. [2018/XC0198/**C**]

♦ Commonwealth Geographical Bureau (CGB) 04333

Bureau des géographes du Commonwealth

Pres Univ of the West Indies, PO Box 105, Mona Campus, Kingston, Jamaica. T. +8769781111. E-mail: elizabeth.thomashope@uwimona.edu.jm – ethomashope@hotmail.com.
Sec Dept Geography, Bayero Univ, PMB 3011, Kano, Nigeria. T. +2348032638229.
URL: http://www.commonwealthgeography.org/

History 30 Nov 1968, Delhi (India). Current constitution adopted Sep 1970, Ghana; most recently amended Aug 2008, Tunis (Tunisia), at 9th General Assembly. **Aims** Promote study and practice of geography at all levels within the Commonwealth, especially in developing countries; disseminate information. **Structure** General Assembly, the Meeting of Commonwealth Geographers (every 4 years, in conjunction with IGU meeting); Committee of Management; Officers: President (CEO), 2 Honorary Vice Presidents, Secretary, Treasurer. **Languages** English. **Staff** 3.00 FTE, voluntary. **Activities** Events/meetings. **Events** *Workshop* Kingston (Jamaica) 2015, *Quadrennial General Assembly* Cologne (Germany) 2012, *Workshop* Freetown (Sierra Leone) 2011, *Workshop* Cape Town (South Africa) 2009, *Quadrennial General Assembly* Tunis (Tunisia) 2008.
Members National associations; individual geographers. Members in 52 Commonwealth countries and territories:
Antigua-Barbuda, Australia, Bahamas, Bangladesh, Barbados, Belize, Botswana, Cameroon, Canada, Cyprus, Eswatini, Fiji, Ghana, Grenada, Guyana, Hong Kong, India, Jamaica, Kenya, Kiribati, Lesotho, Malawi, Malaysia, Malta, Mozambique, Namibia, New Zealand, Nigeria, Pakistan, Papua New Guinea, Samoa, Seychelles, Sierra Leone, Singapore, Solomon Is, South Africa, South Sudan, Sri Lanka, St Kitts-Nevis, St Lucia, St Vincent-Grenadines, Sudan, Tanzania UR, Tokelau, Tonga, Trinidad-Tobago, Tuvalu, Uganda, UK, Vanuatu, Zambia, Zimbabwe.
IGO Relations *Commonwealth Secretariat (#04362)*. **NGO Relations** *Association of Commonwealth Universities, The (ACU, #02440)*; Hungry Cities Partnership. Member of: *Commonwealth HIV and AIDS Action Group (Para55, no recent information)*. [2022/XE0370/**E**]

♦ Commonwealth Girls Education Fund (CGEF) 04334

Admin Sec 56 Morant Place, Commerce Road, London, N22 8HT, UK. T. +442088887115. E-mail: adminsec@cgefund.org.
URL: http://cgefund.org/

History Set up 1967, as the fundraising arm of *Commonwealth Countries League (CCL, #04320)*, with the title *Commonwealth Countries League Education Fund (CCLEF)*. Since 1982, a UK Registered Charity: 1048908. **Aims** Sponsor girls' secondary education across the Commonwealth. **Structure** Board of Trustees; Trustees. **Languages** English. **Activities** Training/education; financial and/or material support; events/meetings. [2018/XM5556/f/**F**]

♦ Commonwealth Handball Association (CHA) 04335

Contact 21 Parakou Crescent, Wuse II, Abuja, Federal Capital Territory, Nigeria. T. +23493140514 – +23497731970. Fax +2345224555. E-mail: chasecretariat@yahoo.com.
Facebook: https://www.facebook.com/Commonwealth-Handball-Association-CHA

History 1985, Salford (UK). Moved to Abuja, Dec 1989. **Aims** Attain greater recognition for the English language speaking nations within the IHF; represent the interest of Commonwealth nations within the IHF; develop technical expertise through coaching and refereeing; promote friendship through competitions; promote handball throughout the Commonwealth; get handball into the Commonwealth Games as a team sports. **Structure** Congress (every 2 years;. Executive Council; Executive Committee; Secretariat. **Languages** English. **Staff** 3.00 FTE, voluntary. **Finance** Sources: donations; members' dues; sponsorship. **Activities** Projects/programmes; sporting activities. **Events** *Biennial Congress* Egypt 2004, *Annual Congress* Auckland (New Zealand) 1990, *Annual Congress* Minna (Nigeria) 1989, *Annual Congress* Seoul (Korea Rep) 1988, *Annual Congress* Nicosia (Cyprus) 1987. **Publications** Information sheet (2 a year).
Members Full in 34 countries and territories:
Australia, Bangladesh, Barbados, Cameroon, Canada, Cook Is, Cyprus, England, Ghana, Grenada, India, Isle of Man, Jamaica, Kenya, Lesotho, Malawi, Malaysia, Mauritius, Mozambique, Namibia, New Zealand, Nigeria, Pakistan, Samoa, Scotland, Sierra Leone, South Africa, St Lucia, St Vincent-Grenadines, Tanzania UR, Trinidad-Tobago, Uganda, Zambia, Zimbabwe.
NGO Relations Affiliate member with observer status of: *International Handball Federation (IHF, #13771)*. [2019/XD1702/**D**]

♦ Commonwealth Hansard Editors Association 04336

Sec Dept of Official Report, 1st Floor, House of Commons, London, SW1 0AA, UK. T. +442072193388. Fax +442072192261.
URL: http://www.commonwealth-hansard.org/

History Jul 1984, London (UK). **Aims** Improve *parliamentary* verbatim reporting; give Hansard editors the opportunity to get to know colleagues, exchange experience and discuss problems. **Languages** English. **Staff** Voluntary Secretary, President and accountant. **Finance** Members' dues; pounds50 per year. **Activities** Technical discussions. **Events** *Conference* London (UK) 2022, *Conference* London (UK) 2018, *Conference* Halifax, NS (Canada) 2015, *Triennial Conference* Port-of-Spain (Trinidad-Tobago) 2011, *Triennial Conference* London (UK) 2008.
Members Commonwealth parliamentary editors in 45 countries and territories:
Australia, Bahamas, Bangladesh, Barbados, Belize, Bermuda, Botswana, Canada, Cayman Is, Cook Is, Dominica, Eswatini, Falklands/Malvinas, Fiji, Ghana, Gibraltar, Grenada, Guyana, India, Jamaica, Kenya, Kiribati, Lesotho, Malawi, Malaysia, Malta, Nauru, New Zealand, Pakistan, Papua New Guinea, Samoa, Singapore, Solomon Is, Sri Lanka, St Kitts-Nevis, St Lucia, Tonga, Trinidad-Tobago, Tuvalu, Uganda, UK, Vanuatu, Virgin Is UK, Zambia, Zimbabwe.
Associates: parliamentary editors in 2 European countries:
Germany, Netherlands.
IGO Relations *Commonwealth Secretariat (#04362)*; *European Parliament (EP, #08146)*. [2018/XD7368/**C**]

♦ Commonwealth Heads of Government Meeting (CHOGM) 04337

Contact c/o Commonwealth Secretariat, Marlborough House, Pall Mall, London, SW1Y 5HX, UK. T. +442078393411. Fax +442079300827. E-mail: info@commonwealth.int.
URL: http://www.thecommonwealth.org/

History Organized and serviced by *Commonwealth Secretariat (#04362)*. Former names and other names: *Imperial Conference* – former (1944); *Prime Ministers Meetings* – former (1944 to 1971); *Imperial Conference of the British Empire* – former. **Aims** Promote common understanding of policies, and common approaches to possible solutions to world problems, by informal exchange of views on major trends in political and economic affairs and on particular problems. **Structure** A series of meetings (every 2 years). The Chairperson of each CHOGM plays a representational role, especially with other intergovernmental organizations, in the period between meetings.
Activities Decisions are reached by consensus and have provided the impetus for the most significant joint Commonwealth activities. Meetings have resulted in: the *Declaration of Commonwealth Principles*, 1971, Singapore (Singapore); the *Gleneagles Agreement*, 1977, to prevent sporting contacts with South Africa so long as that country continues its apartheid policies; the *Lusaka Declaration on Racism and Racial Prejudice*, 1979; the *Melbourne Declaration on International Economic Justice*, 1981; the *Goa Declaration on International Security*, 1983; the *Delhi Statement on Economic Action*, 1983; the *Commonwealth Accord on Southern Africa*, 1985, Nassau (Bahamas); the *Vancouver Declaration on World Trade* and the Okanagan Statement and Programme of Action, 1987; the Kuala Lumpur (Malaysia) Statement, 'Southern Africa: the Way Ahead' and the Langkawi Declaration on Environment, 1989; the Harare (Zimbabwe) Commonwealth Declaration (1991). Britain dissented from parts of the Okanagan and Kuala Lumpur Statements including the establishment of a Committee of Foreign Ministers to provide high level guidance in furtherance of the objectives of the Okanagan Statement (1987) and the agreement to tighten sanctions (1989). A *'Commonwealth Ministerial Action Group'*, set up Nov 1995, Auckland (New Zealand), by the Heads of Government, addresses serious and persistent violations of the principles of the 1991 Harare Declaration. The 1999 CHOGM, Durban (South Africa), adopted the Fancourt Commonwealth Declaration on Globalization and People-Centred Development, spelling out the challenge of how to channel the forces of globalization for the elimination of poverty and empowerment of human beings to lead fulfilling lives; it also decided that a High Level Group should be established to review the role of the Commonwealth and advise on how best it could respond to the challenges of the new century. The Group comprises 10 Heads of Government, including the President of South Africa who chairs the Group. It reported to the next CHOGM in 2001, Australia.
Instrumental in setting up such Commonwealth bodies as: *Centre for Research into Economics and Finance in Southern Africa (CREFSA, inactive)*; *Commonwealth Business Council (CBC, inactive)*; *Commonwealth Committee on Southern Africa (CCSA, inactive)*; *Commonwealth Foundation (CF, #04330)*; *Commonwealth Health Development Programme (CHDP, inactive)*; *Commonwealth Intergovernmental Group on Refugees and Displaced Persons (IGRDP, inactive)*; *Commonwealth of Learning (COL, #04346)*; *Commonwealth Media Development Fund (CMDF, #04350)*; *Commonwealth Ministerial Action Group on the Harare Declaration (CMAG)*; *Commonwealth Nassau Fellowships Scheme (inactive)*; *Commonwealth Private Investment Initiative (CPII, #04359)*; *Commonwealth Women's Affairs Ministers Meeting (WAMM)*.
Events *Biennial meeting* Apia (Samoa) 2024, *Biennial Meeting* Kigali (Rwanda) 2022, *Biennial meeting* Kigali (Rwanda) 2021, *Biennial meeting* Kigali (Rwanda) 2020, *Biennial meeting* London (UK) / Windsor (UK) 2018. **Publications** *The Commonwealth at the Summit, Vol 2 – Communiqués of Commonwealth Heads of Government Meetings 1987-1995* (1997); *Commonwealth Declarations* (1993); *The Commonwealth at the Summit – Communiqués of Commonwealth Heads of Government Meetings 1944-1986* (1987).
Members Heads of Government of all Commonwealth members (except special members – currently only Tuvalu -, Pakistan, which was suspended from councils of the Commonwealth following unconstitutional overthrow of the democratically elected government, 12 Oct 1999, and Fiji, which was also suspended from councils of the Commonwealth since 29 May 2000, following the attempted overthrow of 19 may 2000 and the displacement of its democratically elected government). Governments of 50 countries:
Antigua-Barbuda, Australia, Bahamas, Bangladesh, Barbados, Belize, Botswana, Brunei Darussalam, Cameroon, Canada, Cyprus, Dominica, Eswatini, Ghana, Grenada, Guyana, India, Jamaica, Kenya, Kiribati, Lesotho, Malawi, Malaysia, Maldives, Malta, Mauritius, Mozambique, Namibia, Nauru, New Zealand, Nigeria, Papua New Guinea, Samoa, Seychelles, Sierra Leone, Singapore, Solomon Is, South Africa, Sri Lanka, St Kitts-Nevis, St Lucia, St Vincent-Grenadines, Tanzania UR, Tonga, Trinidad-Tobago, Uganda, UK, Vanuatu, Zambia, Zimbabwe. [2022/XF3257/c/**F***]

♦ Commonwealth Health Professions Alliance / see Commonwealth Health Professions and Partners Alliance (#04338)

♦ Commonwealth Health Professions and Partners Alliance (CHPA) .. 04338

Sec Chinese Univ of Hong Kong, Shatin NT, Hong Kong, Central and Western, Hong Kong. E-mail: secretary@chpa.co – enquiry@chpa.co.
URL: http://www.chpa.co/

History May 2009, Geneva (Switzerland). Founded as an alliance of Commonwealth accredited health professional associations. Former names and other names: *Commonwealth Health Professions Alliance (CHPA)* – former (2009 to 2020). **Aims** Represent and support health professionals in Commonwealth countries; promote high standards of care and equity in access to care for Commonwealth peoples. **Structure** Officers: Chairperson; Deputy Chairperson; Secretary; Treasurer. **Languages** English. **Staff** Voluntary. **Finance** Members' dues. Grants. **Activities** Events/meetings. **Events** *Civil Society Forum* Geneva (Switzerland) 2016, *Commonwealth Civil Society Forum* Geneva (Switzerland) 2015. **Publications** Debates; papers; summary reports.
Members Organizations (7):
Commonwealth Association for Health and Disability (COMHAD, #04302); *Commonwealth Association of Paediatric Gastroenterology and Nutrition (CAPGAN, #04306)*; *Commonwealth Dental Association (CDA, #04321)*; Commonwealth HIV and AIDS Action Group (CHAAG); *Commonwealth Medical Association (CMA, #04351)*; *Commonwealth Nurses and Midwives Federation (CNMF, #04353)*; *Commonwealth Pharmacists Association (CPA, #04357)*.
IGO Relations Formal contacts with: *Commonwealth Foundation (CF, #04330)*; *Commonwealth Secretariat (#04362)*. **NGO Relations** Works closely with other Commonwealth accredited civil society organizations and with national member health professional associations. [2022/XJ0250/ty/**E**]

♦ Commonwealth Heraldry Board (inactive)
♦ Commonwealth Heritage Forum (internationally oriented national body)

♦ Commonwealth Human Ecology Council (CHEC) 04339

Conseil du Commonwealth pour l'écologie humaine – Consejo de Ecologia Humana del Commonwealth

Contact 4 Hurlingham Studios, Ranelagh Gardens, London, SW6 3PA, UK. T. +442036890979. E-mail: contact@checinternational.org.
URL: http://www.checinternational.org/

History 1969, as a British Charitable Organization, having evolved from *Committee on Nutrition in the Commonwealth*, set up 1952 jointly, London (UK), by the *'London School of Hygiene and Tropical Medicine'*. UK Registered Charity: 272018. **Aims** Raise awareness, realize human potential and encourage communities and institutions to work together for environmental, social and human betterment. **Structure** Board; National Chapters; International Headquarters in London (UK). **Languages** English. **Staff** 2.00 FTE, paid. Voluntary. **Finance** Sources: grants; international organizations; members' dues. Supported by: *Department for International Development (DFID, inactive)* (grant); Human Ecology Foundation (grant). **Activities** Events/meetings; guidance/assistance/consulting; projects/programmes; training/education. **Events** *Pre-CHOGM Meeting* Trinidad-Tobago 2009, *Pre-CHOGM Meeting* Kampala (Uganda) 2007, *Pre-CHOGM Meeting* Malta 2005, *Conference / Pre-CHOGM Meeting* Abuja (Nigeria) 2003, *Conference / Pre-CHOGM Meeting* Brisbane, QLD (Australia) 2001. **Publications** *Human Ecology* (annual) – journal; *CHEC Points* (occasional). Annual Report; conference proceedings; occasional papers. **Members** Individual; Corporate; governments; CHEC Chapters; universities and university departments. Members in 47 Commonwealth countries and territories. Membership countries not specified. **Consultative Status** Consultative status granted from: *ECOSOC (#05331)* (Special). **IGO Relations** Working relations with: *UNEP (#20299)*; *United Nations Human Settlements Programme (UN-Habitat, #20572)*. Affiliated with: *United Nations Commission on Sustainable Development (CSD, inactive)*. **NGO Relations** Full member of: *British Overseas NGO's for Development (BOND)*. Member of: *Commonwealth Consortium for Education (CCfE, #04318)*; *Conference of Non-Governmental Organizations in Consultative Relationship with the United Nations (CONGO, #04635)*. Informal networking and partnerships with groups at all levels in Commonwealth and other countries. [2018.12.06/XC3937/**C**]

♦ Commonwealth Human Rights Initiative (CHRI) 04340

Intl Dir 55-A III Floor, Sidhartha Chambers, Kalu Sarai, Delhi 110016, DELHI 110016, India. T. +911143180201 – +911143180200. Fax +911126864688. E-mail: info@humanrightsinitiative.org.
URL: http://www.humanrightsinitiative.org/

History 1987, UK. Set up and supported by: *Public Media Alliance (PMA, #18568); Commonwealth Journalists Association (CJA, #04344); Commonwealth Lawyers Association (CLA, #04345); Commonwealth Legal Education Association (CLEA, #04347); Commonwealth Medical Association (CMA, #04351); Commonwealth Parliamentary Association (CPA, #04355); CPU Media Trust (#04941).* Moved to Delhi (India), 1993. Registration: Charity, No/ID: 803235, England and Wales. **Aims** Ensure the practical realization of human rights in the countries of the Commonwealth through raising awareness of and adherence to internationally recognized human rights instruments and declarations made by Commonwealth Heads of Governments, especially those embodied in the Harare (Zimbabwe) Principles. **Structure** Patron; International Advisory Commission; Executive Committee; Trustee Committee; Head Office in Delhi (India); Offices in London (UK) and Accra (Ghana). **Finance** Funders include: *Commonwealth Foundation (CF, #04330); Department for International Development (DFID, inactive); Ford Foundation (#09858); Friedrich Naumann Foundation for Freedom; New Zealand Ministry of Foreign Affairs and Trade – New Zealand Aid Programme; Swiss Agency for Development and Cooperation (SDC).* **Activities** Knowledge management/information dissemination. **Events** *Consultative constitution making* Delhi (India) 2000, *Conference* Harare (Zimbabwe) 1991, *Meeting* Delhi (India) 1990. **Publications** *CHRI News.* Reports.

Members All 52 Commonwealth countries:
Antigua-Barbuda, Australia, Bahamas, Bangladesh, Barbados, Belize, Botswana, Brunei Darussalam, Cameroon, Canada, Cyprus, Dominica, Eswatini, Fiji, Ghana, Grenada, Guyana, India, Jamaica, Kenya, Kiribati, Lesotho, Malawi, Malaysia, Maldives, Malta, Mauritius, Mozambique, Namibia, Nauru, New Zealand, Nigeria, Pakistan (suspended), Papua New Guinea, Samoa, Seychelles, Sierra Leone, Singapore, Solomon Is, South Africa, Sri Lanka, St Kitts-Nevis, St Lucia, St Vincent-Grenadines, Tanzania UR, Tonga, Trinidad-Tobago, Tuvalu (*), Uganda, UK, Vanuatu, Zambia.

Consultative Status Consultative status granted from: *African Commission on Human and Peoples' Rights (ACHPR, #00255)* (Observer); *ECOSOC (#05331)* (Special). **IGO Relations** Cooperates with: *Commonwealth Heads of Government Meeting (CHOGM, #04337).* **NGO Relations** Member of (5): *Freedom of Information Advocates Network (FOIAnet, #09985); International Dalit Solidarity Network (IDSN, #13129); International Network for Economic, Social and Cultural Rights (ESCR-Net, #14255); The Commonwealth Equality Network (TCEN, #04327); UNCAC Coalition (#20283).* [2020/XF0062/**F**]

♦ Commonwealth of Independent States (CIS) 04341

Communauté des Etats indépendants (CEI) – Comunidad de Estados Independientes (CEI) – Gemeinschaft der Unabhängigen Staaten (GUS) – Sodruzestvo Nezavissimyh Gosudarstv (SNG)

Chairman Kirov Street 17, 220030 Minsk, Belarus. T. +375172223434 – +375172223517. Fax +375173272339. E-mail: cr@cis.minsk.by – info@e-cis.info.
URL: http://www.cis.minsk.by/

History 8 Dec 1991, Belarus. 8 Dec 1991, Visculi (Belarus), by Belarus, Russia and Ukraine. The other countries of the former *Union of Soviet Socialist Republics (USSR, inactive)* – except Estonia, Georgia, Latvia, Lithuania – joined 21 Dec 1991, Almaty. Subsequently Georgia joined CIS. **Structure** Council of CIS Heads of State (meets annually); Council of CIS Heads of Government (meets 2 times a year); Council of Ministers for Foreign Affairs (meets 2 times a year); Executive Secretariat. Other bodies: *Interparliamentary Assembly of Member Nations of the Commonwealth of Independent States (IPA CIS, #15958); Economic Court of the Commonwealth of Independent States (#05315).* **Activities** Management of treaties and agreements: *Traité de Sécurité Collective de la CEI (Traité de Tachkent, 1992),* signed May 1992, Tashkent, by 6 members, and subsequently by Belarus. In accordance with the treaty, *Collective Security Treaty Organization (CSTO, #04103)* was set up 14 May 2002. Setting up a *Customs Union (inactive)* agreed 28 Jan 1995, Moscow (Russia), on signature of a pact by leaders of Belarus, Russia and Ukraine; first stages commenced in the first half of 1995; open to other CIS members, Kyrgyzstan and Tadjikistan joining later. Customs Union was transformed into *Eurasian Economic Community (EurAseC, inactive)* in Oct 2000, which was superseded by *Eurasian Economic Union (EAEU, #05607),* 1 Jan 2015. *Treaty on Cooperation among States Members of the Commonwealth of Independent States in Combating Terrorism (1999)* signed 4 Jun 1999, Minsk (Belarus). **Events** *Meeting of Speakers of Eurasian Countries Parliaments* Seoul (Korea Rep) 2017, *Railwaycouncil Network Meeting* Helsinki (Finland) 2011, *Workshop on national accounts* Geneva (Switzerland) 2001, *Seminar on framework for private sector development, industrial cooperation and direct investments in the CIS countries* Minsk (Belarus) 1996, *Summit* Minsk (Belarus) 1992. **Publications** *CIS Information Bulletin.*

Members Governments of 11 States:
Armenia, Azerbaijan, Belarus, Kazakhstan, Kyrgyzstan, Moldova, Russia, Tajikistan, Turkmenistan, Ukraine, Uzbekistan.

IGO Relations Special links with: *ECOSOC (#05331).* Cooperation agreements with: *International Organization for Migration (IOM, #14454).* Participates in the activities of: *UNCTAD (#20285).* Permanent observer status with: *World Intellectual Property Organization (WIPO, #21593).* Observer member of: *Eurasian Group on Combating Money Laundering and Financing of Terrorism (EAG, #05608).* Observer to General Assembly of: *United Nations (UN, #20515). United Nations Office at Geneva (UNOG, #20597).* [2022/XF2417/**F***]

♦ Commonwealth of Independent States Anti-Terrorism Center (CIS ATC) 04342

Contact 5 Khrushchevsky Pereulok, Bld 3, Moscow MOSKVA, Russia, 119034. T. +74959870444. Fax +74959870411. E-mail: info@cisatc.org.
URL: http://www.cisatc.org/

History Established pursuent to Decision of the Council of the Heads of State of CIS member states, 21 Jun 2000. A permanent specialized institution of *Commonwealth of Independent States (CIS, #04341).* **Aims** Provide coordination of cooperation of the CIS competent authorities in the field of combating international terrorism and other violent manifestations of extremism. **Structure** Head; 3 Deputy Heads. **Languages** Russian. **Activities** Politics/policy/regulatory; knowledge management/information dissemination.

Members CIS Member States (11):
Armenia, Azerbaijan, Belarus, Kazakhstan, Kyrgyzstan, Moldova, Russia, Tajikistan, Turkmenistan, Ukraine, Uzbekistan.

IGO Relations Cooperates with *Commonwealth of Independent States (CIS, #04341)* statutory institutions, including *Interparliamentary Assembly of Member Nations of the Commonwealth of Independent States (IPA CIS, #15958).* Working contacts with various organizations including: *Central Asian Regional Information and Coordination Centre for Combating Illicit Trafficking of Narcotic Drugs, Psychotropic Substances and Their Precursors (CARICC, #03683); Collective Security Treaty Organization (CSTO, #04103); Eurasian Group on Combating Money Laundering and Financing of Terrorism (EAG, #05608); Global Initiative to Combat Nuclear Terrorism (GICNT, #10424); International Criminal Police Organization – INTERPOL (ICPO-INTERPOL, #13110); Organization for Security and Cooperation in Europe (OSCE, #17887); Shanghai Cooperation Organization (SCO, #19256) – RATS; United Nations Office on Drugs and Crime (UNODC, #20596); United Nations Security Council (UNSC, #20625).* [2019/XM5891/**D***]

♦ Commonwealth of Independent States Atherosclerosis Society (no recent information)
♦ Commonwealth of Independent States' Collective Security Treaty (1992 treaty)
♦ Commonwealth Industries Association (inactive)
♦ Commonwealth Institute / see The Commonwealth Education Trust (#04323)
♦ Commonwealth and International Conference on Sport, Physical Education, Recreation and Dance (meeting series)

♦ Commonwealth Jewish Council 04343

CEO BCM Box 6871, London, WC1N 3XX, UK. T. +442033699369. E-mail: info@cjc.org.uk – anna@cjc.org.uk.
URL: https://cjc.org.uk/

History Nov 1982, London (UK). Founded at a meeting of Jewish leaders from 16 Commonwealth countries. Formally inaugurated Jul 1983, London. Former names and other names: *Commonwealth Jewish Trust* – legal name. Registration: Charity Commission, No/ID: 287564, England and Wales. **Aims** Link Commonwealth Jewish communities and seek ways to strengthen them in accordance with their special individual needs and wishes; provide mutual help and cooperation; act as the central representative voice for matters affecting Commonwealth Jews, in particular for preservation of their religious and cultural heritage. **Structure** Board of Trustees; Regional Areas (4); Headquarters in London (UK). Includes: *Commonwealth Jewish Women's Network (CJWN).* **Languages** English. **Staff** 1.00 FTE, paid. **Finance** Sources: donations; meeting proceeds. **Activities** Events/meetings; financial and/or material support; guidance/assistance/consulting; networking/liaising. **Events** *Biennial Conference* Cape Town (South Africa) 2005, *Biennial Conference* London (UK) 2003, *Biennial Conference* Ottawa, ON (Canada) 2001, *Biennial Conference* London (UK) 1999, *Biennial Conference* Gibraltar 1997. **Publications** *News Update* (2 a year). *Shared Values Common Causes.* Briefing papers.

Members Bodies; individuals. Members in 36 countries and territories:
Antigua-Barbuda, Australia, Bahamas, Barbados, Belize, Botswana, Canada, Cayman Is, Cyprus, Eswatini, Gibraltar, Grenada, Hong Kong, India, Isle of Man, Jamaica, Kenya, Lesotho, Malaysia, Malta, Mauritius, Mozambique, Namibia, New Zealand, Nigeria, Seychelles, Singapore, South Africa, Sri Lanka, St Kitts-Nevis, St Lucia, Trinidad-Tobago, Turks-Caicos, UK, Zambia, Zimbabwe.

Observer Status in 3 countries and territories:
Hong Kong, Seychelles, Zimbabwe.

IGO Relations Accreditation to: *Commonwealth Secretariat (#04362).* [2022/XC3672/**C**]

♦ Commonwealth Jewish Trust / see Commonwealth Jewish Council (#04343)

♦ Commonwealth Journalists Association (CJA) 04344

Association des journalistes du Commonwealth

Mailing address c/o Canadian Newspaper Assoc, 890 Yonge St, Ste 200, Toronto ON M4W 3P4, Canada. T. +16478275058.
URL: http://commonwealthjournalists.org/

History 16 Sep 1978, Toronto, ON (Canada). Draft Constitution was approved and adopted at first Conference, 1983, Cyprus. **Aims** Support a free and independent news media throughout the Commonwealth; advocate for journalistic freedom; promote professional standards for journalists; ensure those in power are called to account; provide a platform for exchange of information and views between Commonwealth countries and their media. **Structure** Executive Committee. **Languages** English. **Staff** 0.50 FTE, paid. **Finance** Sources: grants; members' dues. **Activities** Advocacy/lobbying/activism; events/meetings; training/education. **Events** *Conference* London (UK) 2016, *Conference* St Julian's (Malta) 2012, *Conference* Kuching (Malaysia) 2008, *Conference* Dhaka (Bangladesh) 2003, *Conference* Abuja (Nigeria) 2001. **Publications** *CJA Newsletter* (3 a year).

Members Individual journalists, citizens of Commonwealth countries; Commonwealth journalists' associations. Members in 33 countries and territories:
Australia, Bangladesh, Barbados, Canada, Cyprus, Dominica, Ghana, Gibraltar, Grenada, India, Kenya, Lesotho, Malawi, Malaysia, Malta, Mauritius, Namibia, Nigeria, Pakistan, Papua New Guinea, Samoa, Sierra Leone, South Africa, Sri Lanka, St Vincent-Grenadines, Tanzania UR, Tonga, Trinidad-Tobago, Uganda, UK, Vanuatu, Zambia, Zimbabwe.

NGO Relations Member of (2): *Commonwealth HIV and AIDS Action Group (Para55, no recent information); Commonwealth Human Rights Initiative (CHRI, #04340).* Cooperates with (2): *CPU Media Trust (#04941); Public Media Alliance (PMA, #18568).* [2022/XD1667/**C**]

♦ Commonwealth Judicial Education Institute (internationally oriented national body)
♦ Commonwealth Law Conference (meeting series)
♦ Commonwealth Law Ministers' Meeting (meeting series)

♦ Commonwealth Lawyers Association (CLA) 04345

SG c/o Godfrey Wilson Ltd, 5th Floor Mariner House, 62 Prince Street, Bristol, BS1 4QD, UK. E-mail: info@commonwealthlawyers.com.
URL: http://www.commonwealthlawyers.com/

History 1 Jan 1969. Founded following a Meeting of Commonwealth Lawyers, 1968, London (UK). Reconstituted under present title at Commonwealth Law Conference, 1983, Hong Kong. Constitution formally adopted at Commonwealth Law Conference, Sep 1986, Jamaica. Former names and other names: *Commonwealth Legal Bureau (CLB)* – former (1968 to 1983). Registration: Companies House, No/ID: 06868881, Start date: 3 Apr 2009, England and Wales. **Aims** Maintain and promote the rule of law throughout the Commonwealth. **Structure** General Meeting; Council; Executive Committee; Secretariat. **Languages** English. **Staff** 3.00 FTE, paid. **Finance** Sources: members' dues. **Activities** Capacity building; events/meetings; knowledge management/information dissemination. **Events** *Biennial Conference* Goa (India) 2023, *LAWASIA Alternative Dispute Resolution Conference* Denarau (Fiji) 2022, *Biennial Conference* Nassau (Bahamas) 2021, *Biennial Conference* Livingstone (Zambia) 2019, *Biennial Conference* Melbourne, VIC (Australia) 2017. **Publications** *The Commonwealth Lawyer* (3 a year) – journal.

Members Individual Commonwealth lawyers and Commonwealth bars and law societies in 61 countries and territories:
Antigua-Barbuda, Australia, Bahamas, Bangladesh, Barbados, Belize, Bermuda, Botswana, Brunei Darussalam, Cameroon, Canada (and North America), Cayman Is, Cyprus, Dominican Rep, England, Eswatini, Fiji, Gambia, Ghana, Grenada, Guyana, Hong Kong, India, Isle of Man, Jamaica, Kenya, Kiribati, Lesotho, Malawi, Malaysia, Maldives, Malta, Mauritius, Montserrat, Mozambique, Namibia, Nauru, New Zealand, Nigeria, Pakistan, Papua New Guinea, Rwanda, Samoa, Scotland, Sierra Leone, Singapore, Solomon Is, South Africa, Sri Lanka, St Kitts-Nevis, St Lucia, St Vincent-Grenadines, Tanzania UR, Tonga, Trinidad-Tobago, Turks-Caicos, Tuvalu, Uganda, UK, Vanuatu, Zambia.

IGO Relations Cooperates with (1): *Commonwealth Heads of Government Meeting (CHOGM, #04337).* **NGO Relations** Cooperates with (3): *Commonwealth Law Conference; Commonwealth Legal Education Association (CLEA, #04347); Commonwealth Magistrates' and Judges' Association (CMJA, #04349).* Instrumental in setting up (1): *Commonwealth Association of Public Sector Lawyers (#04311).* [2022.06.16/XD5238/**C**]

♦ Commonwealth of Learning (COL) 04346

Contact 4710 Kingsway, Ste 2500, Burnaby BC V5H 4M2, Canada. T. +16047758200. Fax +16047758210. E-mail: info@col.org.
URL: http://www.col.org/

History Sep 1988, London (UK). Established on signing of a Memorandum of Understanding, 1987, Vancouver BC (Canada), at the instigation of *Commonwealth Heads of Government Meeting (CHOGM, #04337),* and following recommendations of an Expert Group, 1987. Commenced activities 14 Nov 1988. **Aims** Help governments, institutions and organizations expand the scale, efficiency and quality of learning by using appropriate open, distance and technology-based approaches. **Structure** Board of Governors. **Languages** English. **Staff** 35.00 FTE, paid. **Finance** Sources: contributions of member/participating states; donations; revenue from activities/projects. **Activities** Events/meetings; knowledge management/information dissemination. **Events** *Pan-Commonwealth Forum on Open Learning* Calgary, AB (Canada) 2022, *Pan-Commonwealth Forum on Open Learning* Edinburgh (UK) 2019, *Pan-Commonwealth Forum on Open Learning* Kuala Lumpur (Malaysia) 2016, *High Level Policy Forum* Sun City (South Africa) 2015, *Regional Symposium on Open Educational Resources* Penang (Malaysia) 2014. **Publications** *Connections. Knowledge Series; Perspectives Series.* Books; reports; consultants' reports; toolkits; manuals; brochures and leaflets.

Members Participants are member countries of the Commonwealth (54), through their governments:
Antigua-Barbuda, Australia, Bahamas, Bangladesh, Barbados, Belize, Botswana, Brunei Darussalam, Cameroon, Canada, Cyprus, Dominica, Eswatini, Fiji, Gambia, Ghana, Grenada, Guyana, India, Jamaica, Kenya, Kiribati, Lesotho, Malawi, Malaysia, Maldives, Malta, Mauritius, Mozambique, Namibia, Nauru, New Zealand, Nigeria, Pakistan, Papua New Guinea, Rwanda, Samoa, Seychelles, Sierra Leone, Singapore, Solomon Is, South Africa, Sri Lanka, St Kitts-Nevis, St Lucia, St Vincent-Grenadines, Tanzania UR, Tonga, Trinidad-Tobago, Tuvalu, Uganda, UK, Vanuatu, Zambia.

IGO Relations Observer status with (1): *World Intellectual Property Organization (WIPO, #21593).* Cooperates with (2): *Commonwealth Telecommunications Organisation (CTO, #04365); UNHCR (#20327).* Supports (1): *Bioversity International (#03262).* Instrumental in setting up (1): *Southeast Asian Ministers of Education Organization (SEAMEO, #19774).* **NGO Relations** Member of (1): *Open Education Consortium (#17751).* Instrumental in setting up (3): *Association of Chief Education Officers in the Caribbean (ACCEO, no recent information); Global Access Television Service (WETV Initiative, no recent information); Pacific Islands Regional Association for Distance Education (PIRADE, no recent information).* [2022.11.29/XF1309/**F***]

♦ Commonwealth Legal Advisory Service (inactive)
♦ Commonwealth Legal Bureau / see Commonwealth Lawyers Association (#04345)

♦ Commonwealth Legal Education Association (CLEA) 04347

Association du Commonwealth pour l'enseignement du droit

Admin c/o Legal and Constitutional Affairs Div – ComSec, Marlborough House, Pall Mall, London, SW1Y 5HX, UK. T. +442077476415. Fax +442077476406. E-mail: clea@commonwealth.int.
Pres Univ of KwaZulu Natal, King George V Ave, Durban, 4001, South Africa. E-mail: mcquoidm@ukzn.ac.za.
URL: http://www.clea-web.com/

History Founded Dec 1971, London (UK), following 4th Commonwealth Law Conference, 1971, Delhi (India). **Aims** Improve and study legal education and research in Commonwealth countries; encourage and strengthen contacts between individuals and organizations concerned; disseminate information and literature and conduct research; facilitate interchange of teachers and exchange of students; facilitate exchange of legal materials among institutions concerned; foster and promote programmes of continuing legal education.

Structure General Meeting (every 2 years at Conference); Executive Committee; Regional Chapters (7). Book recovery programme with: *Commonwealth Lawyers Association (CLA, #04345)*. **Languages** English. **Staff** 2.50 FTE, paid. **Finance** Sources: meeting proceeds; members' dues. **Activities** Awards/prizes/competitions; awareness raising; events/meetings; guidance/assistance/consulting; training/education. **Events** *Conference* Lusaka (Zambia) 2019, *Conference* Melbourne, VIC (Australia) 2017, *Conference* Glasgow (UK) 2015, *Biennial Conference / Conference* Durban (South Africa) 2013, *Biennial Conference / Conference* Bangalore (India) 2011. **Publications** *CLEA Journal* (1-2 a year). Abstracts; teaching resources.
Members Institutional; Individual (mainly), in 52 countries and territories:
Antigua-Barbuda, Australia, Bahamas, Bangladesh, Barbados, Belize, Botswana, Brunei Darussalam, Cameroon, Canada, Cyprus, Dominica, Eswatini, Fiji, Ghana, Grenada, Guyana, Hong Kong, India, Jamaica, Kenya, Kiribati, Lesotho, Malawi, Malaysia, Maldives, Malta, Mauritius, Mozambique, Namibia, Nauru, New Zealand, Nigeria, Pakistan, Papua New Guinea, Samoa, Seychelles, Sierra Leone, Singapore, Solomon Is, South Africa, Sri Lanka, St Kitts-Nevis, St Lucia, St Vincent-Grenadines, Tanzania UR, Tuvalu, Uganda, UK, Vanuatu, Zambia, Zimbabwe.
IGO Relations Consulted by: *Commonwealth Secretariat (#04362)* on behalf of Commonwealth governments. Operates out of ComSec. **NGO Relations** Member of: *Commonwealth Consortium for Education (CCfE, #04318)*. Formal contacts with: Commonwealth associations of law teachers. [2018.06.01/XC4550/**C**]

♦ Commonwealth Library Association (no recent information)

♦ Commonwealth Local Government Forum (CLGF) 04348

Main Office Golden Cross House, 8 Duncannon St, London, WC2N 4JF, UK. E-mail: info@clgf.org.uk.
URL: http://www.clgf.org.uk/
History 22 Feb 1994, Harare (Zimbabwe). Founded at first meeting of the Interim Board. Launched 23 Mar 1994, London (UK). First full meeting, Sep 1995. **Aims** Promote and strengthen effective *democratic* local government throughout the Commonwealth; facilitate the exchange of good practice in local government structures and services. **Structure** General meeting; Board, including members from all regions of the Commonwealth; Executive Committee. **Finance** Sources: donations; members' dues. Project and other activity funding from multilateral donor agencies and other relevant partners. **Activities** Advocacy/lobbying/activism; capacity building; events/meetings; networking/liaising; projects/programmes. **Events** *Conference on Improving Local Government* Kigali (Rwanda) 2023, *Conference on Improving Local Government* Valletta (Malta) 2017, *Conference on Improving Local Government* Gaborone (Botswana) 2015, *Conference on Improving Local Government* Kampala (Uganda) 2013, *Conference on improving local government* Cardiff (UK) 2011. **Publications** *CLGF e-news* (10 a year); *CLGF Bulletin* (3 a year); *Commonwealth e-journal of Local Governance* (2 a year); *The Commonwealth Local Government Handbook* (annual). Workshop, seminar and research reports.
Members Full: national local government associations, individual municipalities and ministries of local government and other governmental institutions in Commonwealth countries; Associate: professional/employers' associations, local government trade unions, training and research institutions (including university departments) promoting local democracy in the Commonwealth. Members (over 150) in 49 Commonwealth countries and territories:
Angola, Antigua-Barbuda, Australia, Bahamas, Bangladesh, Barbados, Belize, Botswana, Brunei Darussalam, Cameroon, Canada, Cyprus, Eswatini, Ghana, Gibraltar, Guyana, India, Kenya, Kiribati, Lesotho, Malawi, Malaysia, Maldives, Malta, Mauritius, Mozambique, Namibia, Nauru, New Zealand, Nigeria, Pakistan, Papua New Guinea, Samoa, Seychelles, Sierra Leone, Solomon Is, South Africa, Sri Lanka, St Kitts-Nevis, St Lucia, St Vincent-Grenadines, Tanzania UR, Tonga, Trinidad-Tobago, Tuvalu, Uganda, UK, Vanuatu, Zambia.
IGO Relations Observer status with (1): *Congress of Local and Regional Authorities of the Council of Europe (#04677)*. **NGO Relations** Member of (3): *Cities Climate Finance Leadership Alliance (CCFLA, #03952)*; *Council of Commonwealth Societies (CCS, #04878)*; *Global Taskforce of Local and Regional Governments (Global Taskforce, #10622)*. [2022/XF3085/**F**]

♦ Commonwealth Magistrates' Association / see Commonwealth Magistrates' and Judges' Association (#04349)

♦ Commonwealth Magistrates' and Judges' Association (CMJA) 04349

Association des magistrats et juges du Commonwealth
SG Uganda House, 58-59 Trafalgar Square, London, WC2N 5DX, UK. T. +442079761007. E-mail: info@cmja.org.
URL: http://www.cmja.org/
History Aug 1970, London (UK). Founded at inaugural Conference (London and Oxford). Former names and other names: *Commonwealth Magistrates' Association (CMA)* – former. **Aims** Advance administration of the law by promoting the independence of the *judiciary*; promote education in *law*, administration of justice, treatment of offenders and prevention of crime within the Commonwealth; disseminate information and literature on matters concerning the legal process; effect closest possible links between members. **Structure** General Assembly (at least every 4 years); Council. **Languages** English. **Staff** 1.00 FTE, paid. **Finance** Sources: donations; grants; members' dues. **Activities** Advocacy/lobbying/activism; events/meetings; networking/liaising; training/education. **Events** *Triennial Conference* Accra (Ghana) 2022, *Annual Virtual Conference* London (UK) 2021, *Parliamentary Democracy and the Role of the Judiciary* Port Moresby (Papua New Guinea) 2019, *Triennial Conference* Brisbane, QLD (Australia) 2018, *Annual Conference* Dar es Salaam (Tanzania UR) 2017. **Publications** *CMJA Newsletter*; *Commonwealth Judicial Journal*; *Gender Newsletter*.
Members Associations of magistrates and/or judges; judicial bodies (national and regional); individual members of the judiciary. Members in 59 Commonwealth countries and territories:
Anguilla, Antigua-Barbuda, Australia, Bangladesh, Barbados, Belize, Bermuda, Botswana, Brunei Darussalam, Canada, Cayman Is, Cook Is, Cyprus, Dominica, England, Eswatini, Falklands/Malvinas, Fiji, Ghana, Gibraltar, Grenada, Guyana, India, Isle of Man, Jamaica, Jersey, Kenya, Kiribati, Malawi, Malaysia, Maldives, Malta, Mauritius, Montserrat, Nauru, New Zealand, Nigeria, Pakistan, Papua New Guinea, Rwanda, Samoa, Scotland, Seychelles, Sierra Leone, Singapore, Solomon Is, Sri Lanka, St Helena, St Lucia, St Vincent-Grenadines, Tanzania UR, Tonga, Trinidad-Tobago, Turks-Caicos, Tuvalu, Uganda, Vanuatu, Wales, Zambia. [2022.06.20/XC4569/**C**]

♦ Commonwealth Media Development Fund (CMDF) 04350

Project Manager ComSec Public Affairs, Marlborough House, Pall Mall, London, SW1Y 5HX, UK. T. +442077476357. Fax +442078399081. E-mail: info@commonwealth.int.
URL: http://www.thecommonwealth.org/subhomepage/166227/
History 1980, as *Commonwealth Media Exchange Fund*, administered by Information Division of *Commonwealth Secretariat (#04362)*, and arising from the *Commonwealth Media Exchange Scheme* approved by *Commonwealth Heads of Government Meeting (CHOGM, #04337)*, Aug 1979, Lusaka (Zambia). **Activities** Assists in the training of media staff through workshops and in-house instruction. **NGO Relations** *Commonwealth Association for Education in Journalism and Communication (CAEJAC, no recent information)*; *Commonwealth Journalists Association (CJA, #04344)*; *CPU Media Trust (#04941)*. [2009.01.10/XF1839/f/**F***]

♦ Commonwealth Media Exchange Fund / see Commonwealth Media Development Fund (#04350)

♦ Commonwealth Medical Association (CMA) 04351

Association médicale du Commonwealth
Vice-Pres Nigerian Medical Assc, No 8 Benghazi Street, Wuse Zone 4, Abuja, Federal Capital Territory, Nigeria. E-mail: nationalnma@yahoo.com.
Sec Ghana Medical Assc, Korle-bu, Accra, Ghana. T. +23330266458.
URL: http://commonwealthdoctors.org/
History 24 Nov 1962, Colombo (Sri Lanka), to continue the work of Commonwealth Medical Conferences and on the initiative of the British Medical Association. New constitutions adopted: 1972; Jul 1989, London (UK); Nov 1992, Jamaica. **Aims** Exchange information among member associations; provide technical cooperation and advice to member associations in *developing countries*; formulate and maintain a code of ethics; provide continuing education programmes, including distance learning and low cost medical journal and book programmes for doctors in developing countries; develop and promote health education programmes; participate actively in the work of UN, WHO and Commonwealth Health Ministers. **Structure** Council (meets every 3 years), comprises representatives of national medical associations in the Commonwealth. Executive comprises President, Immediate Past President, Treasurer, Secretary and 6 Regional Vice-Presidents: Canadian/Caribbean; European; Central Asia; Southeast Asia/Australasia; Central/East Africa; West Africa. Charitable activities carried out by *Commonwealth Medical Trust (COMMAT)*. **Languages** English. **Staff** 2.00 FTE, paid. **Finance** Members' dues, depending on membership numbers. Contributions from member associations; support from: *Commonwealth Foundation (CF, #04330)*; *Ford Foundation (#09858)*. **Activities** Advises national medical associations and arranges training courses and workshops for their officers and officials. Organizes international conferences and joint activities with other professional associations. Participates with other professional associations in joint projects. Current programmes: 1. *'Reproductive Health and Safe Motherhood'* – training workshops in all Commonwealth regions except Europe; workshops in connection with international conferences. 2. *'Advocacy for Women's Health'* – ensures that women's health concerns are fully addressed at UN international conferences. 3. *'Adolescent Health and Sexuality'*. 4. *'The Role of Medical Ethics in the Protection of Human Rights'* – through training sessions, provides doctors practising in developing Commonwealth countries with guiding principles on medical ethics aligned with internationally recognized human rights instruments. **Events** *Triennial Council Meeting* Colombo (Sri Lanka) 2016, *Triennial Council Meeting* Port-of-Spain (Trinidad-Tobago) 2013, *Triennial council meeting* Ghana 2003, *Triennial council meeting* Penang (Malaysia) 2001, *Triennial Council Meeting* London (UK) 1998. **Publications** *CMA Newsletter* – internet.
Members National medical associations in 35 countries:
Bahamas, Bangladesh, Barbados, Belize, Bermuda, Botswana, Cameroon, Dominica, Eswatini, Ghana, Grenada, Guyana, India, Jamaica, Kenya, Lesotho, Malawi, Malaysia, Malta, Mauritius, Nigeria, Pakistan, Papua New Guinea, Samoa, Sierra Leone, Singapore, St Lucia, St Vincent-Grenadines, Tanzania UR, Thailand, Tonga, Trinidad-Tobago, Uganda, UK, Zimbabwe.
Consultative Status Consultative status granted from: *UNICEF (#20332)*. **IGO Relations** *Commonwealth Secretariat (#04362)*. Consultation Status with: *United Nations Population Fund (UNFPA, #20612)*. Accredited by: *United Nations Office at Vienna (UNOV, #20604)*. Associated with Department of Global Communications of the United Nations. **NGO Relations** Member of: *Commonwealth Health Professions and Partners Alliance (CHPA, #04338)*; *Commonwealth HIV and AIDS Action Group (Para55, no recent information)*; *Framework Convention Alliance (FCA, #09981)*; *NGO Committee on UNICEF (#17120)*. Founder member of the steering group of: *Commonwealth Human Rights Initiative (CHRI, #04340)*. [2013/XC0371/**C**]

♦ Commonwealth Medical Conference (meeting series)

♦ Commonwealth Medical Trust (Commat) 04352

Dir Ullyett Cottage, Old School Mews, Sandgate Hill, Folkestone, CT20 3ST, UK. T. +447767313032. E-mail: mh@commat.org – office@commat.org.
Street Address BMA House, Tavistock Square, London, WC1H 9JP, UK.
URL: http://ngosbeyond2014.org/
History Registered in accordance with the laws of England and Wales. **Aims** Promote health; prevent disease and disability; advance human rights and medical ethics, particularly for the poor, vulnerable and marginalized groups in developing countries. **Structure** Board of Trustees. **Languages** English. **Staff** 1.00 FTE, paid; 1.00 FTE, voluntary. **Finance** Sources: donations; grants. Annual budget: 50,000 GBP. **Activities** Advocacy/lobbying/activism. **Members** Not a membership organization. **Consultative Status** Consultative status granted from: *ECOSOC (#05331)* (Special). [2020.04.02/XM3703/**C**]

♦ Commonwealth Ministers of Employment / Labour Meeting (meeting series)
♦ Commonwealth Music Association (inactive)
♦ Commonwealth NGO Forum (meeting series)
♦ Commonwealth Nurses Federation / see Commonwealth Nurses and Midwives Federation (#04353)

♦ Commonwealth Nurses and Midwives Federation (CNMF) 04353

Exec Sec c/o Intl Office, Royal College of Nursing, 20 Cavendish Square, London, W1G 0RN, UK. T. +4461438647252.
URL: http://www.commonwealthnurses.org/
History 1973, London (UK), as *Commonwealth Nurses Federation (CNF)*. Constitution revised: 30 Apr 2011, St Julian's (Malta); 7 Mar 2014, London (UK), when present name adopted; 9 Mar 2018, London (UK). Registered under UK law. **Aims** Influence health policy throughout the Commonwealth; develop nursing networks; enhance nursing education; improve nursing standards and competence; strengthen nursing leadership; contribute to quality care for Commonwealth citizens. **Structure** Meeting (every 2 years); Governing Board. Regions: East, Central and Southern Africa; West Africa; Atlantic; Pacific; Asia; Europe. Head Office in London (UK). **Languages** English. **Staff** 0.30 FTE, paid. **Finance** Sources: grants; members' dues. Other sources: consultancies. **Activities** Politics/policy/regulatory; projects/programmes; standards/guidelines; training/education. **Events** *Biennial Meeting* London (UK) 2020, *Commonwealth Nurses Conference* London (UK) 2020, *Commonwealth Nurses Conference* London (UK) 2016, *Commonwealth Nurses Conference* London (UK) 2014, *Inaugural Commonwealth Nurses Conference* London (UK) 2012. **Publications** *CNMF eNews* (12 a year); *The Commonwealth Nurse* (2 a year) – journal. Regional reports of seminars and workshops. **Members** Full: national nursing and midwifery associations; Affiliate: specialist nursing and midwifery associations; Associate: regional and international health associations; Individual. Membership countries not specified. **IGO Relations** Accredited as a Commonwealth Civil Society Organization by: *Commonwealth Secretariat (#04362)*. Works closely with: *Commonwealth Foundation (CF, #04330)*. **NGO Relations** Member of: *Commonwealth Health Professions and Partners Alliance (CHPA, #04338)*; *Commonwealth HIV and AIDS Action Group (Para55, no recent information)*. [2019.05.15/XC4568/**C**]

♦ Commonwealth Organisation for Social Work (COSW) 04354

Contact Marlborough House, Pall Mall, London, SW1Y 5HX, UK. E-mail: info@commonwealth.int.
URL: http://thecommonwealth.org/organisation/commonwealth-organisation-social-work- cosw/
Aims Promote and support communication and collaboration between social workers and social work associations of Commonwealth countries; uphold and promote the code of ethics of the International Federation of Social Workers. **Structure** Committee, including 2 Co-Chairs and Honorary Secretary-General. **Publications** *COSW Newsletter*. **IGO Relations** *Commonwealth Secretariat (#04362)*. **NGO Relations** Member of: *Commonwealth HIV and AIDS Action Group (Para55, no recent information)*. [2015/XM3699/**C**]

♦ Commonwealth Parliamentary Association (CPA) 04355

Association parlementaire du Commonwealth
SG CPA Headquarters Secretariat, c/o Richmond House, Houses of Parliament, London, SW1A 0AA, UK. T. +442077991460. E-mail: hq.sec@cpahq.org.
URL: http://www.cpahq.org/
History 1911, London (UK). Originally administered by the UK branch. Evolving with the Commonwealth, the Association adopted its present name and changed its rules to enable all member branches to participate in CPA management. Present statutes adopted 1993. Former names and other names: *Empire Parliamentary Association* – former (1911 to 1948). Registration: Charity Commission, No/ID: 263147, England and Wales. **Aims** Promote knowledge and education about the *constitutional*, *legislative*, economic, social and cultural systems within a parliamentary *democratic* framework, with particular reference to the countries of the Commonwealth of Nations and to other countries having close historical and parliamentary associations with it; foster understanding and cooperation among Members of Commonwealth Parliaments; promote the study of and respect for parliamentary institutions. **Structure** General Assembly of delegates (meets annually, at Commonwealth Parliamentary Conference); Executive Committee (meets twice a year), includes Chairperson of *Commonwealth Women Parliamentarians (CWP, #04369)* and Chairperson of CPA Small Branches; Autonomous Branches (about 180); Headquarters in London (UK). **Languages** English. **Staff** 18.00 FTE, paid. **Finance** Sources: contributions of member/participating states; investments; members' dues. **Activities** Capacity building; events/meetings; financial and/or material support; networking/liaising; research/documentation; training/education. Active in all member countries. **Events** *Annual Plenary Conference* Halifax, NS (Canada) 2022, *Annual Plenary Conference* Halifax, NS (Canada) 2021, *Annual Plenary Conference* Kampala (Uganda) 2019, *Annual Plenary Conference* Dhaka (Bangladesh) 2017, *Annual Plenary Conference* London (UK) 2016. **Publications** *CPA Order Paper e-newsletter* (4 a year); *The Parliamentarian, Journal of Commonwealth Parliaments* (4 a year). Annual Report; reports of conferences and general meetings; specialized information and memoranda for members; guides; books; tool kits.
Members Branches, comprising about 17,000 members of national, state, provincial and territorial Parliaments and Legislatures in the 56 countries of the Commonwealth:
Antigua-Barbuda, Australia, Bahamas, Bangladesh, Barbados, Belize, Botswana, Brunei Darussalam, Cameroon, Canada, Cyprus, Dominica, Eswatini, Fiji, Gabon, Gambia, Ghana, Grenada, Guyana, India, Jamaica, Kenya, Kiribati, Lesotho, Malawi, Malaysia, Maldives, Malta, Mauritius, Mozambique, Namibia, Nauru, New Zealand, Nigeria, Pakistan, Papua New Guinea, Rwanda, Samoa, Seychelles, Sierra Leone, Singapore, Solomon Is, South Africa, Sri Lanka, St Kitts-Nevis, St Lucia, St Vincent-Grenadines, Tanzania UR, Togo, Tonga, Trinidad-Tobago, Tuvalu, Uganda, UK, Vanuatu, Zambia.
NGO Relations Member of (1): *Council of Commonwealth Societies (CCS, #04878)*. Extends observer status to other interparliamentary organizations (not specified). Also links with various Commonwealth regional parliamentary and professional organizations. [2023.02.15/XC0372/**C**]

♦ Commonwealth Partnership for Technology Management (CPTM) .. 04356

Registered Office 10 Orange Street, London, WC2H 7DQ, UK. T. +442077982500 – +447802234943. E-mail: info@cptm.org.
URL: http://www.cptm.org/

History 1984 as *Science Management and Organisation Programme* of Commonwealth Science Council, followed by transformation in Oct 1989, Kuala Lumpur (Malaysia), by *Commonwealth Heads of Government Meeting (CHOGM, #04337)*, as an intergovernmental organization with a Support Unit located with the *Commonwealth Secretariat (#04362)*. Original title: *Commonwealth Consultative Group on Technology Management (CCGTM)*. *'CCGTM/Private Sector Partnership (CCGTM/PSP)'* was launched in Feb 1993, Kuala Lumpur, on the initiative of CHOGM. Current status and title adopted Jun 1995, London (UK), when registered under UK law as a not-for-profit company limited by guarantee independent of ComSec. Currently fully operational as a networking organization, officially launched as CPTM Ltd by CHOGM, Nov 1995, Auckland (New Zealand). New transformation phase initiated Feb 2019. **Aims** Promote a global cooperative approach to the harnessing of technology management for development through formal and informal smart partnerships between public and private sectors, binding Commonwealth governments and private sector companies in networking operations of mutual benefit; respond quickly to requests from Commonwealth governments. **Structure** Distributed networks and mission-oriented and customer-driven body with a self-organizing network undertaking hands-on management by participants. **Languages** English. **Staff** 2.00 FTE, paid; 14.00 FTE, voluntary. **Finance** Voluntary contributions from Commonwealth governments and public/private sector corporate members. Annual budget: 700 GBP. **Activities** Capacity building; events/meetings; guidance/assistance/consulting; networking/liaising. **Events** *Southern Africa international dialogue* Kampala (Uganda) 2001, *International dialogue* Langkawi (Malaysia) 2000, *Southern Africa international dialogue* Maputo (Mozambique) 2000, *Langkawi international dialogue* Langkawi (Malaysia) 1999, *Southern Africa international dialogue* Victoria Falls (Zimbabwe) 1999. **Publications** Confidential advisory reports to governments; high-level briefing reports to senior officials; annual report; prospectuses; reports of meetings/seminars/workshops/roundtables; manuals; technical publications.

Members Commonwealth Governments, private and public sector corporate institutions and individual professionals in 52 countries:
Antigua-Barbuda, Australia, Bahamas, Bangladesh, Barbados, Belize, Botswana, Brunei Darussalam, Cameroon, Canada, Cyprus, Dominica, Eswatini, Fiji, Ghana, Grenada, Guyana, India, Jamaica, Kenya, Kiribati, Lesotho, Malawi, Malaysia, Maldives, Malta, Mauritius, Mozambique, Namibia, Nauru, New Zealand, Nigeria, Pakistan (suspended), Papua New Guinea, Samoa, Seychelles, Sierra Leone, Singapore, Solomon Is, South Africa, Sri Lanka, St Kitts-Nevis, St Lucia, St Vincent-Grenadines, Tanzania UR, Tonga, Trinidad-Tobago, Tuvalu (*), Uganda, UK, Vanuatu, Zambia.

IGO Relations
- *African Development Bank (ADB, #00283)*;
- *African Regional Centre of Technology (ARCT, #00432)*;
- *Australian Aid (inactive)*;
- *Canadian International Development Agency (CIDA, inactive)*;
- *Caribbean Community (CARICOM, #03476)*;
- *Caribbean Development Bank (CDB, #03492)*;
- *Commonwealth Fund for Technical Cooperation (CFTC, #04331)*;
- *European Commission (EC, #06633)*;
- *ILO (#11123)*;
- *International Bank for Reconstruction and Development (IBRD, #12317)*;
- *International Development Research Centre (IDRC, #13162)*;
- *OAS (#17629)*;
- *OECD (#17693)*;
- UK Department of Trade and Industry;
- *UNCTAD (#20285)*;
- *UNDP (#20292)*;
- *UNESCO (#20322)*;
- *UNIDO (#20336)*;
- *United States Agency for International Development (USAID)*.

NGO Relations Links with a number of bodies including the following international or internationally-oriented organizations: *American Association for the Advancement of Science (AAAS)*; *Carnegie Corporation of New York*; *Club of Rome (COR, #04038)*; *Commonwealth Human Ecology Council (CHEC, #04339)*; *Consortium on Science, Technology and Innovation for the South (COSTIS, no recent information)*; *Institute for Managing Development (IMD, no recent information)*; *International Centre for Protected Landscapes (ICPL, no recent information)*; *International Institute for Environment and Development (IIED, #13877)*; *International Science Policy Foundation (inactive)*; *International Organization for Standardization (ISO, #14473)*; *Royal Institute of International Affairs (RIIA)*. [2022.10.27/XE1465/**F**]

♦ Commonwealth Pharmaceutical Association / see Commonwealth Pharmacists Association (#04357)

♦ Commonwealth Pharmacists Association (CPA) 04357

Secretariat 66-68 East Smithfield, London, E1W 7AW, UK. T. +442032856652.
URL: https://commonwealthpharmacy.org/

History 1 Jan 1970, London (UK). Inaugural meeting held in London (UK), 16-20 June 1969. Constitution formally adopted 1970. Former names and other names: *Commonwealth Pharmaceutical Association* – former. Registration: Charity Commission, No/ID: 1176132, England and Wales. **Aims** Advance health and education for the public benefit; empower pharmacists at all levels to improve health and wellbeing throughout the Commonwealth. **Structure** Council (meets every 2 years); Board of Trustees; Regional Council (Executive). **Languages** English. **Staff** 1.00 FTE, paid. Several voluntary. **Finance** Sources: contributions; donations; gifts, legacies; grants; members' dues. Annual budget: 209,600 GBP (2020). **Activities** Advocacy/lobbying/activism; awareness raising; capacity building; certification/accreditation; guidance/assistance/consulting; healthcare; knowledge management/information dissemination; networking/liaising; projects/programmes; publishing activities; research and development; research/documentation; training/education. **Events** *Biennial Conference* Sydney, NSW (Australia) 2017, *Biennial Conference* Nassau (Bahamas) 2013, *Biennial conference / Conference* Durban (South Africa) 2011, *Biennial conference / Conference* Accra (Ghana) 2009, *Biennial conference / Conference* Kuala Lumpur (Malaysia) 2007. **Publications** *CPA Newsletter* (6 a year). Policy documents; working party reports; e-mail statements; press releases.

Members National pharmaceutical associations (or equivalent body where no such association exists) in 36 countries and territories:
Antigua-Barbuda, Australia, Bahamas, Bangladesh, Barbados, Botswana, Cameroon, Canada, Dominica, Eswatini, Fiji, Gambia, Ghana, Grenada, Guyana, India, Jamaica, Kenya, Lesotho, Malta, Mauritius, Nigeria, Northern Ireland, Pakistan, Rwanda, Sierra Leone, South Africa, Sri Lanka, St Lucia, St Vincent-Grenadines, Tanzania UR, Trinidad-Tobago, Uganda, UK, Zambia, Zimbabwe.

Consultative Status Consultative status granted from: *ECOSOC (#05331)* (Ros C); *WHO (#20950)* (Official Relations). **IGO Relations** Collaborates in Health Programme of: *Commonwealth Secretariat (#04362)*. Supported by: *Commonwealth Foundation (CF, #04330)*. Observer to: Commonwealth Health Ministers' Meeting (CHMM); Meeting of Commonwealth Representatives Prior to the World Health Assembly. Associated with Department of Global Communications of the United Nations. **NGO Relations** Member of: *Commonwealth Health Professions and Partners Alliance (CHPA, #04338)*; *Commonwealth HIV and AIDS Action Group (Para55, no recent information)*; *International Pharmaceutical Federation (#14566)*. [2023/XC3880/**C**]

♦ Commonwealth Police Association (unconfirmed)
♦ Commonwealth Policy Studies Unit (internationally oriented national body)

♦ Commonwealth Powerlifting Federation (CPF) 04358

Gen Sec address not obtained.
URL: https://commonwealthpowerlifting.com/

Structure Executive. **Activities** Sporting activities.

Members National members in 24 countries and territories:
Australia, Cameroon, Canada, England, Ghana, Guyana, India, Kiribati, Namibia, Nauru, New Zealand, Nigeria, Niue, Northern Ireland, Pakistan, Papua New Guinea, Samoa, Scotland, Sierra Leone, South Africa, Trinidad-Tobago, Tuvalu, Uganda, Wales.

NGO Relations Affiliated with (1): *International Powerlifting Federation (IPF, #14630)*. [2021/AA2500/**C**]

♦ Commonwealth Press Union / see CPU Media Trust (#04941)

♦ Commonwealth Private Investment Initiative (CPII) 04359

Contact Marlborough House, Pall Mall, London, SW1Y 5HX, UK. T. +442077476385 – +442077476386. Fax +442079300827 – +442078399081. E-mail: info@commonwealth.int.

History Sep 1995, Kingston (Jamaica), at *Commonwealth Finance Ministers Meeting*; endorsed by *Commonwealth Heads of Government Meeting (CHOGM, #04337)*, Nov 1995, Auckland (New Zealand). Developed in partnership with *CDC Group*, which provides management. **Aims** Provide long-term investment capital through private equity funds for *commercial* ventures for the *private sector*, fund privatization of public enterprises in *developing countries* of the Commonwealth; encourage mobilization of additional investment capital for both the above purposes. **Activities** Private equity funds are set up and initial seed capital provided by CDC. Successor funds for the following 3 funds with similar aims are being mobilized for continuing investment, under the CPII framework, in 2003. *Kula II Fund for the Pacific Region (see: #04359)*, capitalized at US$ 20 million, launched 2005; *South Asia Regional Fund (SARF, no recent information)*, capitalized at US$ 108.25 million, launched Feb 1998; Malaysia Fund, set up 2007; Brunei Fund, set up Jan 2008; Africa fund, set up Aug 2008. **Members** in all Commonwealth countries. **IGO Relations** *Commonwealth Secretariat (#04362)*. [2010/XF3695/f/**F***]

♦ Commonwealth Producer's Organization (inactive)
♦ Commonwealth Regional Health Community / see East, Central and Southern African Health Community (#05216)
♦ Commonwealth Regional Health Community Secretariat for East, Central and Southern Africa / see East, Central and Southern African Health Community (#05216)
♦ Commonwealth Relations Trust (internationally oriented national body)
♦ Commonwealth Rowing Association (internationally oriented national body)

♦ Commonwealth Scholarship Commission in the United Kingdom (CSC) 04360

Contact Woburn House, 20-24 Tavistock Square, London, WC1H 9HF, UK. T. +442073806700. Fax +442073872655.
URL: http://www.dfid.gov.uk/cscuk/

History 1959. Established by an Act of Parliament. **Aims** Manage Britain's contribution to the Commonwealth Scholarship and Fellowship Plan (CSFP). **Structure** Members appointed in line with the Code of Practice of the Office of the Commissioner for Public Appointments. Secretariat provided by *Association of Commonwealth Universities, The (ACU, #02440)*; overseas services provided by *British Council*. **Languages** English. **Staff** 0.50 FTE, paid; 6.50 FTE, voluntary. **Finance** Awards are funded by *Department for International Development (DFID, inactive)* (for developing Commonwealth countries) and Department for Business, Innovation and Skills and the Scottish Government (for developed Commonwealth countries), in conjunction with UK universities. **Activities** Makes available 7 types of awards: Scholarships for PhD research; Scholarships for Master's study; Shared Scholarships with UK universities in support of Master's programmes; Academic Fellowships for staff serving in developing country universities; Split-site Scholarships for PhD students to spend up to one year in the UK; Professional Fellowships for mid-career professionals in developing countries; Distance Learning Scholarships for developing country students to study UK Master's degree courses while living in their own countries. Nominates UK students for scholarships to study in other Commonwealth countries. Since establishment of the CSC, nearly 24,000 Commonwealth citizens have held awards in the UK. **Publications** *Commonwealth Scholarships News* (2 a year) – alumni magazine. **Members** Not a membership organization. **NGO Relations** Secretariat provided by: *Association of Commonwealth Universities, The (ACU, #02440)*. [2022/XM3822/**F***]

♦ Commonwealth Science Council (CSC) 04361

Comité scientifique du Commonwealth

Contact c/o Commonwealth Secretariat, Marlborough House, Pall Mall, London, SW1Y 5HX, UK. T. +442077476385 – +442077476386. Fax +442078399081. E-mail: info@commonwealth.int.

History Established 1946, as *Standing Committee of the British Commonwealth Scientific Official Conference*; renamed *British Commonwealth Scientific Committee* in 1958 and *Commonwealth Scientific Committee* in 1964. Present name adopted 1975. CSC Secretariat forms part of the Science and Technology Division of *Commonwealth Secretariat (#04362)*. **Aims** Increase capabilities of individual nations to generate and use science and *technology* for their economic, social and environmental development through collaboration between member countries of the Commonwealth, by networking and promoting cooperative projects and information exchange on issues of scientific or technological concern. **Structure** Governing Council (meets every 3 years) of representatives of national ministries for science and technology or research councils of all member countries. Chairman (3-year terms) selected from members on a rotating basis. Executive Committee. Secretariat. **Activities** Areas: Water and Mineral Resources; Biodiversity and Genetic Resources; Chemical Research and Environmental Needs; Scientific Networking through Commonwealth Knowledge Network. **Events** *Biennial Meeting* Port-of-Spain (Trinidad-Tobago) 2000, *Workshop on environmental control in mining* Darwin, NT (Australia) 1998, *Workshop on monitoring heavy metals, pesticides, PCB, dyes and pigments* Islamabad (Pakistan) 1998, *Conference on clean air and environment* Melbourne, VIC (Australia) 1998, *Workshop on acid rain monitoring and atmospheric modelling* Peradeniya (Sri Lanka) 1998. **Publications** *Earth Sciences Programme Newsletter*, *Science and Technology News*. Reports of specialist conferences; directories of research; manuals; seminar proceedings; technical publications; biennial reports.

Members Governments of 35 Commonwealth countries (Pakistan was suspended from councils of the Commonwealth following unconstitutional overthrow of the democratically elected government, 12 Oct 1999):
Australia, Bahamas, Bangladesh, Barbados, Botswana, Brunei Darussalam, Cameroon, Cyprus, Dominica, Eswatini, Ghana, Grenada, Guyana, India, Jamaica, Kenya, Lesotho, Malawi, Malaysia, Malta, Mauritius, Namibia, New Zealand, Papua New Guinea, Seychelles, Sierra Leone, South Africa, Sri Lanka, St Lucia, Tanzania UR, Trinidad-Tobago, Uganda, UK, Zambia, Zimbabwe. [2013/XE0375/**E***]

♦ Commonwealth Scientific Committee / see Commonwealth Science Council (#04361)
♦ Commonwealth Scientific and Industrial Research Organization (internationally oriented national body)

♦ Commonwealth Secretariat 04362

Secrétariat pour les pays du Commonwealth – Secretaria del Commonwealth

SG Marlborough House, Pall Mall, London, SW1Y 5HX, UK. T. +442077476500. Fax +442079300827. E-mail: info@commonwealth.int.
URL: http://www.thecommonwealth.org/

History 1965, London (UK), by decision of Commonwealth Heads of Government. The Commonwealth Secretariat, previously also referred by the initials *CS*, operates as an international organization at the service of all Commonwealth countries. Internally referred to as *ComSec*.

Origins lie in 'London Declaration' of Apr 1949, which leaders from Australia, Canada, India, New Zealand, Pakistan, South Africa, Ceylon and UK adopted and through which member countries no longer owed allegiance to the British Crown, but recognized British head as the symbol of their 'free and equal' association. It marked the end of colonial 'British Commonwealth' and the start of the 'modern Commonwealth', an association of independent countries without a written constitution. Practice is for new members to be admitted only by the consent of all other members, and after showing their commitment for the association's core values.

Having no formal charter, the Commonwealth has, instead, a series of declarations, largely emanating from Commonwealth Heads of Government Meetings (CHOGMs), to which all member countries voluntarily subscribe. Key declarations are: Declaration of Commonwealth Principles, 1971, Singapore (Singapore); Harare Commonwealth Declaration, 1991; Millbrook Action Programme on the Harare Declaration, 1995 (New Zealand), when *'Commonwealth Ministerial Action Group'*, was set up to address serious or persistent violations of the Commonwealth's fundamental values; Trinidad and Tobago Affirmation on Commonwealth Values and Principles, Nov 2009. Other pioneering commitments include: commitment to the 'separation of powers' between legislature, judiciary and executive' – known as Latimer House Principles, 2003; extension of democratic principles to local government and grassroots civil society organizations, known as Aberdeen Principles, 2003. Other key declaration issued at CHOGMs, include: Langkawi Declaration on Environment, 1989; Valletta Statement on Multilateral Trade, 2005; Gozo Statement on Vulnerable Small States, 2005; Lake Victoria Commonwealth Climate Change Action Plan, 2007; Investing in Young People – A Declaration on young people by Commonwealth Heads of Government, 2009.

Aims As an informal grouping, the Commonwealth has no statutory objectives. However, the Declaration of Commonwealth Principles, agreed 1971, Singapore (Singapore) and reaffirmed in the Harare (Zimbabwe) Commonwealth Declaration, 1991, sets out the fundamental political values underpinning the Commonwealth: democracy and good *governance*; respect for human rights and gender equality; the rule of law; sustainable economic and social development. Mission statement: work as a trusted partner for all Commonwealth people as: a force for peace, democracy, equality and good governance; a catalyst for global consensus-building; a source of assistance for sustainable development and poverty eradication. In general, aims are to: act as a bridge between races and religions and between rich and poor, enabling them to discuss common problems and work together for solutions; promote international peace and order, equal rights for all citizens and the liberty of the individual; oppose colonial domination and racial oppression; help to achieve a fairer global society. The common heritage shared by member states in many fields, including a common language, enables them to work together in an atmosphere of cooperation and understanding. The aims of the Secretariat are to: facilitate joint consultation and cooperation among member countries and collect and disseminate information for their use; organize meetings and conferences in areas of common concern and put into effect decisions for collective Commonwealth action. **Structure** Head is HM Queen Elizabeth II, with choice of successive Heads made collectively by Commonwealth leaders. *Commonwealth Heads of Government Meeting (CHOGM, #04337)* (every 2 years). Secretary-General; Deputy Secretary-General. Ministerial Action Group (CMAG); Board of Governors; Chair-in-Office. Secretariat. Divisions and Units (10): Communications and Public Affairs (CPAD); Corporate Services (CSD); Economic Affairs (EAD); Human Rights (HRU); Legal and Constitutional Affairs (LCAD); Political Affairs; Special Advisory Services (SASD); Strategic Planning and Evaluation (SPED); Social Transformation Programmes (STPD); Youth Affairs (YAD) – *Commonwealth Youth Programme (CYP, #04372)*, including: *Commonwealth Youth Programme South Pacific Regional Centre (CYP-SPRC, see: #04362)*; *Commonwealth Youth Programme – Caribbean Centre (CYPCC, see: #04362)*; *African Centre of the Commonwealth Youth Programme (no recent information)*; *Asia Centre of the Commonwealth Youth Programme (CYP Asia Centre, see: #04362)*. Regular conferences include: *Commonwealth Law Ministers' Meeting (CLMM)*; *Conference of Commonwealth Education Ministers (CCEM)*; *Commonwealth Women's Affairs Ministers Meeting (WAMM)*; *Commonwealth Youth Ministers Meeting (CYMM)*. **Languages** English. **Staff** 380.00 FTE, paid. **Finance** Contributions are made to general Secretariat budget on an agreed scale from member governments. **Activities** Projects/programmes. **Events** *Biennial Commonwealth Law Ministers Meeting* Balaclava (Mauritius) 2022, *Biennial Commonwealth Law Ministers Meeting* 2021, *Conference of Commonwealth Education Ministers and General Meeting* Nairobi (Kenya) 2021, *Commonwealth Sports Ministers Meeting* Tokyo (Japan) 2020, *Biennial Commonwealth Law Ministers Meeting* Colombo (Sri Lanka) 2019. **Publications** *Commonwealth Law Bulletin* (4 a year); *Report of the Commonwealth Fund for Technical Cooperation* (annual); *Report of the Commonwealth Secretary-General* (every 2 years); *Commonwealth Discussion Papers*. *Commonwealth Secretariat Trade Hot Topics* – pamphlet series. Secretariat publishes about 25 freestanding priced publications annually. **Information Services** *Commonwealth News* – in-depth coverage of Commonwealth activities; *Commonwealth Secretariat Archives* – about 1,800 records in the public domain dating from 1965; *Commonwealth Secretariat Online Picture Library* – contemporary and historical photographs; *Commonwealth Secretariat Reference Library* – 35,000 books and official publications.

Members Heads of Government meeting in 2007, Kampala (Uganda), reviewed core criteria for Commonwealth membership. Applicant countries: should have had a historic constitutional association with an existing Commonwealth member, with applications to be considered on a case-by-case basis for exceptional circumstances; should accept and comply with the Commonwealth's fundamental values and principles set out in Declarations; must demonstrate commitment to: democracy and democratic processes, including free and fair elections and representative legislatures; rule of law and independence of the judiciary; good governance, including a well-trained public service and transparent public accounts; protection of human rights, freedom of expression and equality of opportunity; should accept Commonwealth norms and conventions, such as use of English language and acknowledgement of Queen Elizabeth II as Head of the Commonwealth. New members: should be encouraged to joint Commonwealth Foundation and promote civil society and business organizations with their countries; are required to augment the existing budget of the Secretariat. Existing members do not need re-apply for Commonwealth membership following changing its formal constitutional status, provided continuation to meet all membership criteria. Current members are the governments of 53 countries, representing over 2,000 million people. Through Commonwealth Ministerial Action Group (CMAG): Zimbabwe was suspended, Mar 2002 and withdrew Dec 2003; Fiji was suspended from the Councils of the Commonwealth, Dec 2006, and fully suspended from membership, Sep 2009; Gambia withdrew in 2013. Governments (53):

Current members are the governments of 53 countries, representing over 2,000 million people. Through Commonwealth Ministerial Action Group (CMAG): Zimbabwe was suspended, Mar 2002 and withdrew Dec 2003; Fiji was suspended from the Councils of the Commonwealth, Dec 2006, and fully suspended from membership, Sep 2009; Gambia withdrew in 2013. Governments (53):

Antigua-Barbuda, Australia, Bahamas, Bangladesh, Barbados, Belize, Botswana, Brunei Darussalam, Cameroon, Canada, Cyprus, Dominica, Eswatini, Fiji (suspended), Ghana, Grenada, Guyana, India, Jamaica, Kenya, Kiribati, Lesotho, Malawi, Malaysia, Maldives, Malta, Mauritius, Mozambique, Namibia, Nauru, New Zealand, Nigeria, Pakistan, Papua New Guinea, Rwanda, Samoa, Seychelles, Sierra Leone, Singapore, Solomon Is, South Africa, Sri Lanka, St Kitts-Nevis, St Lucia, St Vincent-Grenadines, Tanzania UR, Tonga, Trinidad-Tobago, Tuvalu, Uganda, UK, Vanuatu, Zambia.

Associated states and overseas territories: 'Australian External Territories': Ashmore and Cartier Islands; Australian Antarctic Territory; Christmas Is; Cocos-Keeling Is; Coral Sea Islands Territory; Heard Is; McDonald Is; Norfolk Is.

'Australian External Territories': Ashmore and Cartier Islands; Australian Antarctic Territory; Christmas Is; Cocos-Keeling Is; Coral Sea Islands Territory; Heard Is; McDonald Is; Norfolk Is. 'New Zealand Self-governing countries': Cooks Is; Niue.

'New Zealand Self-governing countries': Cooks Is; Niue. 'New Zealand External Territories': Ross Dependency; Tokelau.

'New Zealand External Territories': Ross Dependency; Tokelau. 'UK Overseas Territories': Anguilla; Bermuda; British Antarctic Territory; British Indian Ocean Territory; Virgin Is UK; Cayman Is; Falklands; Gibraltar; Montserrat; Pitcairn; St Helena and dependencies (Ascension; Tristan da Cunha); South Georgia; South Sandwich Islands; Turks-Caicos.

'UK Overseas Territories': Anguilla; Bermuda; British Antarctic Territory; British Indian Ocean Territory; Virgin Is UK; Cayman Is; Falklands; Gibraltar; Montserrat; Pitcairn; St Helena and dependencies (Ascension; Tristan da Cunha); South Georgia; South Sandwich Islands; Turks-Caicos.

IGO Relations Active Strategic Relationships with a large number of international and regional (integration) partners, including: *African Union (AU, #00488)*, and especially African Union Commission; *Caribbean Community (CARICOM, #03476)*; *Commonwealth Telecommunications Organisation (CTO, #04365)*; *European Union (EU, #08967)* and especially *European Commission (EC, #06633)*; *Pacific Community (SPC, #17942)*; *United Nations (UN, #20515)* General Assembly and UN agencies; *World Trade Organization (WTO, #21864)*. Sister organizations: *Commonwealth Foundation (CF, #04330)*; *Commonwealth of Learning (COL, #04346)*. Non-accredited organizations: *Commonwealth Conference of Postal Administrations (CCPA)*; *Conference of Commonwealth Auditors General*.

NGO Relations The Commonwealth has a network of over 90 civil society organizations (CSOs), ranging from professional associations to business organizations, trade unions, and organizations of elected bodies such as parliamentarians and local government authorities. Civil society relations with the Commonwealth have grown in breadth and depth over time, following, part, from the recommendations of the 2002 High Level Review Group, presenting its report at the Coolum (Australia) CHOGM and recommending strengthening links with the non-governmental Commonwealth. Additional strengthening and continued development of relations occurred following decision to grant CSOs Commonwealth accreditation, 2003. Minimum criteria for accreditation include: commitment to the Commonwealth's fundamental values; representation of the diversity of Commonwealth countries; principles of transparency and openness to all members. Accreditation provides CSOs with 'observer status' enabling them to attend Commonwealth Ministerial and other meetings. Accredited civil society organizations associated with the Commonwealth:

- *Association of Commonwealth Archivists and Records Managers (ACARM, inactive)*;
- *Association for Commonwealth Literature and Language Studies (ACLALS, #02439)*;
- *Association of Commonwealth Universities, The (ACU, #02440)*;
- *ComHabitat (inactive)*;
- *The Commonwealth Association (COMASSOC, #04299)*;
- *Commonwealth Association of Architects (CAA, #04301)*;
- *Commonwealth Association for Health and Disability (COMHAD, #04302)*;
- *Commonwealth Association of Law Reform Agencies (CALRAs, #04303)*;
- *Commonwealth Association of Museums (CAM, #04305)*;
- *Commonwealth Association of Paediatric Gastroenterology and Nutrition (CAPGAN, #04306)*;
- *Commonwealth Association of Planners (CAP, #04307)*;
- *Commonwealth Association for Public Administration and Management (CAPAM, #04310)*;
- *Commonwealth Association of Science, Technology and Mathematics Educators (CASTME, #04312)*;
- *Commonwealth Association of Tax Administrators (CATA, #04314)*;
- *Commonwealth Business Council (CBC, inactive)*;
- *Commonwealth Consortium for Education (CCfE, #04318)*;
- *Commonwealth Council for Educational Administration and Management (CCEAM, #04319)*;
- *Commonwealth Countries League (CCL, #04320)*;
- *Commonwealth Dental Association (CDA, #04321)*;
- *The Commonwealth Education Trust (CET, #04323)*;
- *Commonwealth Engineers Council (CEC, #04324)*;
- *Commonwealth Forestry Association (CFA, #04329)*;
- *Commonwealth Games Federation (CGF, #04332)*;
- *Commonwealth Geographical Bureau (CGB, #04333)*;
- *Commonwealth Human Ecology Council (CHEC, #04339)*;
- *Commonwealth Human Rights Initiative (CHRI, #04340)*;
- *Commonwealth Journalists Association (CJA, #04344)*;
- *Commonwealth Judicial Education Institute (CJEI)*;
- *Commonwealth Lawyers Association (CLA, #04345)*;
- *Commonwealth Legal Education Association (CLEA, #04347)*;
- *Commonwealth Local Government Forum (CLGF, #04348)*;
- *Commonwealth Magistrates' and Judges' Association (CMJA, #04349)*;
- *Commonwealth Medical Association (CMA, #04351)*;
- *Commonwealth Medical Trust (Commat, #04352)*;
- *Commonwealth Nurses and Midwives Federation (CNMF, #04353)*;
- *Commonwealth Organisation for Social Work (COSW, #04354)*;
- *Commonwealth Parliamentary Association (CPA, #04355)*;
- *Commonwealth Pharmacists Association (CPA, #04357)*;
- *Commonwealth Policy Studies Unit (CPSU)*;
- *Commonwealth Youth Exchange Council (CYEC)*;
- *Conference of Commonwealth Meteorologists (#04584)*;
- *Council for Education in the Commonwealth (CEC)*;
- *Institute of Commonwealth Studies, London (ICWS)*;
- *NGO Commonwealth Women's Network (CWN, #17122)*;
- *Public Media Alliance (PMA, #18568)*;
- *Royal Agricultural Society of the Commonwealth (RASC, #18987)*;
- *Royal Commonwealth Ex-Services League (RCEL, #18989)*;
- *Royal Commonwealth Society (RCS, #18990)*;
- *Royal Over-Seas League (ROSL)*;
- *Sightsavers International (#19270)*.

Other Accredited CSOs:

- *African Centre for Democracy and Human Rights Studies (ACDHRS, #00239)*;
- *BasicNeeds*;
- *Building Understanding through International Links for Development (BUILD)*;
- *CIVICUS: World Alliance for Citizen Participation (#03962)*;
- *Commonwealth HIV and AIDS Action Group (Para55, no recent information)*;
- *Corona Worldwide (#04836)*;
- *Forum of Federations*;
- *International Council on Social Welfare (ICSW, #13076)*;
- *International Federation for Human Rights (#13452)*;
- *International Trade Union Confederation (ITUC, #15708)*;
- *Pacific Foundation for the Advancement of Women (PACFAW, #17950)*;
- *Pacific Islands Association of Non-Governmental Organizations (PIANGO, #17961)*;
- *Soroptimist International (SI, #19686)* Commonwealth Group;
- *Transparency International (TI, #20223)*;
- *World Vision International (WVI, #21904)*.

Non-accredited organizations:

- *Commonwealth Association of Indigenous Peoples (CAIP)*;
- *Commonwealth Association of Professional Centres (CAPC, #04309)*;
- *Commonwealth Association of Scientific Agricultural Societies (CASAS, no recent information)*;
- *Commonwealth Jewish Council (#04343)*;
- *Commonwealth Library Association (COMLA, no recent information)*;
- *Commonwealth Partnership for Technology Management (CPTM, #04356)*;
- *Commonwealth Relations Trust*;
- *Commonwealth Society for the Deaf (Sound Seekers, inactive)*;
- *Commonwealth Veterinary Association (CVA, #04366)*;
- *CPU Media Trust (#04941)*;
- *Eastern Africa Centre for Constitutional Development (Kituo Cha Katiba, #05220)*;
- *English-Speaking Union (ESU, #05482)*;
- *Victoria League for Commonwealth Friendship*.

[2020/XC0376/**C***]

♦ Commonwealth Society for the Deaf (inactive)

♦ Commonwealth Students' Association (CSA) 04363

Coordinator Commonwealth Secretariat, Marlborough House, Pall Mall, London, SW1Y 5HX, UK. T. +442077476462. E-mail: youth@commonwealth.int – csa@commonwealth.int.
URL: http://www.commonwealthstudent.org/

Aims Raise the profile of student associations and bodies across the Commonwealth. **Structure** Steering Committee. **NGO Relations** Member of (1): *Global Student Forum (GSF, #10614)*. Partner of (1): *100 Million (#22042)*. [2021/AA1589/**C**]

♦ Commonwealth Studies Center / see Duke University Center for International and Global Studies
♦ Commonwealth Sugar Exporters Association (inactive)
♦ Commonwealth Survey Officers' Conference / see Cambridge Conference for National Mapping Organizations (#03401)
♦ Commonwealth Table Tennis Association / see Commonwealth Table Tennis Federation (#04364)

♦ Commonwealth Table Tennis Federation (COMTAB) 04364

Chair Conifers, Church Lane, Ormesby, TS7 9AU, UK.
Hon Sec TTA of Malaysia, Penthouse – 4th Floor, 23-35 Jalan Jejaka 7, Taman Maluri, 55100 Kuala Lumpur, Malaysia. T. +60392811497. Fax +60392811520.
URL: http://comtt.org/

History Founded Mar 1969, as *Commonwealth Table Tennis Association (CTTA)*, at meeting of Commonwealth country representatives. **Aims** Provide a table tennis championship for members of the Commonwealth. **Structure** Board of Directors; Committees (2). **Languages** English. **Staff** Voluntary. **Finance** Members' dues. Annual budget: about pounds1,000. **Activities** Sporting activities. **Events** *Meeting / Biennial General Meeting* Jaipur (India) 2007, *Biennial General Meeting* Bremen (Germany) 2006, *Biennial General Meeting* Shanghai (China) 2005, *Biennial General Meeting* Kuala Lumpur (Malaysia) 2004, *Biennial General Meeting* Paris (France) 2003.

Members Associations in 46 countries and territories:
Anguilla, Australia, Bangladesh, Barbados, Bermuda, Botswana, Brunei Darussalam, Canada, Cyprus, Dominica, England, Fiji, Gambia, Ghana, Guernsey, Guyana, India, Isle of Man, Jamaica, Jersey, Kenya, Kiribati, Malawi, Malaysia, Maldives, Malta, Mauritius, Mozambique, New Zealand, Nigeria, Northern Ireland, Pakistan, Papua New Guinea, Scotland, Seychelles, Sierra Leone, Singapore, South Africa, Sri Lanka, St Kitts-Nevis, St Lucia, Trinidad-Tobago, Uganda, Vanuatu, Wales, Zimbabwe.

NGO Relations Recognized by: *International Table Tennis Federation (ITTF, #15650)*.

[2018.10.04/XD6720/y/**D**]

♦ Commonwealth Telecommunications Board / see Commonwealth Telecommunications Organisation (#04365)
♦ Commonwealth Telecommunications Council / see Commonwealth Telecommunications Organisation (#04365)

♦ Commonwealth Telecommunications Organisation (CTO) 04365

SG 64-66 Glenthorne Road, London, W6 0LR, UK. T. +442086003800. Fax +442086003819. E-mail: info@cto.int.
URL: http://www.cto.int/

History Established 1928, as *Imperial Communications Advisory Committee*. Reconstituted 1944, as *Commonwealth Telecommunications Council*; 31 May 1949, as *Commonwealth Telecommunications Board*, following signature of *Commonwealth Telegraphs Agreement, 1948 (1948)*, 1948. Constituted under present title, 1966. Financial Agreement, *CTOFA 1983*, concluded 30 Mar 1983, replaces 10-year Agreement of 30 Mar 1973, *Commonwealth Telecommunications Organisation Financial Agreement (CTOFA)*, itself replacing the Commonwealth telegraphs agreements of 1948 and 1963. A *Commonwealth Cable Management Committee (CCMC)* organized and exploited the cable systems linking Commonwealth countries prior to 1966. **Aims** As a development partnership between Commonwealth and non-Commonwealth governments, business and civil society organizations, provide the international community with effective means to help bridge the *digital* divide and achieve social and economic development, by delivering research, consultancy, conferences and knowledge-sharing programmes in the use of Information and Communication Technologies in the specific areas of Telecommunications, IT, Broadcasting and the *Internet*, that emancipate, enrich, equalize and empower. **Structure** *Council of the Commonwealth Telecommunications Organisation*, consisting of representatives appointed by Full Member countries (meets once a year) and elects a Chairperson and 2 Vice-Chairpersons. Executive Committee, comprising Chairperson, Vice Chairpersons, 2 members elected by the ICT Sector Members, Chairperson of the Programme for Development and Training and the Secretary-General, oversees affairs of the organisation between Council meetings. Two-tier membership structure consisting of Full Member countries (those Commonwealth countries that contribute to the management budget of the organization) and ICT Sector Members (private sector, non-Commonwealth countries and civil society). **Languages** English. **Staff** 22.00 FTE, paid. **Finance** Contributions from members governments, telecommunications businesses and other sources. Budget (annual): US$ 5 million. **Activities** Capacity building; events/meetings; guidance/assistance/consulting; research/documentation. **Events** *Meeting* Apia (Samoa) 2021, *Annual Forum* Yaoundé (Cameroon) 2020, *Meeting* Yaoundé (Cameroon) 2020, *Meeting* Dhaka (Bangladesh) 2019, *Annual Forum* Freetown (Sierra Leone) 2019.

Members Governments of 32 Commonwealth countries signatory to 1983 Agreement:
Bangladesh, Barbados, Botswana, Cameroon, Cyprus, Eswatini, Fiji, Ghana, Guyana, India, Jamaica, Kenya, Lesotho, Malawi, Malaysia, Malta, Mauritius, Mozambique, Nigeria, Pakistan, Papua New Guinea, Seychelles, Sierra Leone, Solomon Is, South Africa, Sri Lanka, Tanzania UR, Trinidad-Tobago, Uganda, UK, Vanuatu, Zambia.

IGO Relations Cooperation agreements with: *African Telecommunications Union (ATU, #00482)*; *Asia-Pacific Telecommunity (APT, #02064)*; *Caribbean Telecommunications Union (CTU, #03560)*; *Commonwealth of Learning (COL, #04346)*; *Commonwealth Secretariat (#04362)*; *International Maritime Organization (IMO, #14102)*; *International Multilateral Partnership Against Cyber Threats (IMPACT, #14196)*; *International Telecommunication Union (ITU, #15673)*; *International Telecommunications Satellite Organization (ITSO, #15670)*; *Organisation of Caribbean Utility Regulators (OOCUR, #17800)*. **NGO Relations** Cooperation agreement with: *Communications Regulators' Association of Southern Africa (CRASA, #04384)*; *East African Communications Organisation (EACO, #05180)*; *Pacific Islands Telecommunications Association (PITA, #17979)*; *West Africa Telecommunications Regulators Association (WATRA, #20903)*. Member of: *Alliance for Affordable Internet (A4AI, #00651)*. Supports: *African Forum for Utility Regulators (AFUR, #00324)*; *AFRINIC (#00533)*; *Association of Regulators of Information and Communications for Eastern and Southern Africa (ARICEA, no recent information)*; *CANTO (#03416)*; *Global Alliance for ICT and Development (GAID, #10200)*; *International Cyber Security Protection Alliance (ICSPA)*; *Southern Africa Telecommunications Association (SATA, #19867)*.
[2020/XC0382/**C***]

- ♦ Commonwealth Telegraphs Agreement, 1948 (1948 treaty)
- ♦ Commonwealth Telegraphs Agreement, 1963 (1963 treaty)
- ♦ Commonwealth Tourism Centre (internationally oriented national body)
- ♦ Commonwealth Trade Union Council (inactive)

♦ Commonwealth Veterinary Association (CVA) 04366

Association vétérinaire du Commonwealth

Sec Central Veterinary Lab, Mandela Road, PO Box 9254, Dar es Salaam, Tanzania UR. T. +255222861152. Fax +255222864369. E-mail: hbudodi@yahoo.com.
Pres 20 Rapanea Street, Canberra ACT 2611, Australia. T. +61417880672.
URL: http://www.commonwealthvetassoc.com/

History Founded Sep 1967. Previously sometimes referred to as *CwVA*. **Aims** Promote the veterinary profession within the Commonwealth. **Structure** Executive Council; Regional Committees (6). **Languages** English. **Staff** All voluntary (honorary). **Finance** Sources: members' dues. **Activities** Knowledge management/information dissemination; networking/liaising; projects/programmes; training/education. **Events** *Pan Commonwealth Conference / Pan-Commonwealth Conference* Kuala Lumpur (Malaysia) 2015, *Regional Meeting / Pan-Commonwealth Conference* Bangalore (India) 2014, *Regional Meeting* Nadi (Fiji) 2013, *Pan Commonwealth conference / Pan-Commonwealth Conference* Accra (Ghana) 2011, *Regional meeting* Apia (Samoa) 2008. **Publications** *CVA e-Newsletter* (12 a year). *Commonwealth Veterinary Association Handbook*.

Members Regular; Honorary; Associate; Corporate. National associations in 55 countries and territories:
Afghanistan, Antigua-Barbuda, Australia, Bahamas, Bangladesh, Barbados, Belize, Botswana, Cameroon, Canada, Cayman Is, Cook Is, Cyprus, Dominica, Eswatini, Falklands/Malvinas, Fiji, Ghana, Grenada, Guyana, India, Jamaica, Kenya, Kiribati, Lesotho, Malawi, Malaysia, Malta, Mauritius, Mozambique, New Zealand, Nigeria, Pakistan, Papua New Guinea, Samoa, Sierra Leone, Singapore, Solomon Is, South Africa, Sri Lanka, St Kitts-Nevis, St Lucia, St Maarten, St Vincent-Grenadines, Sudan, Tanzania UR, Timor-Leste, Tonga, Trinidad-Tobago, Turks-Caicos, Uganda, UK, Vanuatu, Virgin Is UK, Zambia.
Included in the Regional associate members, 1 organization listed in this Yearbook:
Pacific Community (SPC, #17942).

NGO Relations Member of: *World Veterinary Association (WVA, #21901)*. [2019.07.04/XC4319/y/**C**]

♦ Commonwealth War Graves Commission (CWGC) 04367

Commission pour les tombes de guerre du Commonwealth

Dir-Gen 2 Marlow Road, Maidenhead, SL6 7DX, UK. T. +441628634221. Fax +441628771208. E-mail: enquiries@cwgc.org.
URL: http://www.cwgc.org/

History 1917, London (UK). Established by Royal Charter. Responsibilities extended to the fallen of the Second World War by Supplemental Charter of 1940. Further supplemental Charter, adopted 1964, when the Commission assumed its current functions and name. Former names and other names: *Imperial War Graves Commission* – former (1917 to 1964); *Commission du Commonwealth pour les tombes de guerre* – alias. **Aims** Ensure permanent *commemoration* of the 1,7 million members of the forces of the Commonwealth who died during the two *world wars*, by marking and maintaining their graves or by building and maintaining *memorials* to those who have no known grave; keep records and registers of those who died, including Commonwealth civilians who died in World War II. **Structure** Commission (meets quarterly in the UK). Joint Committees (5): Belgian; French; German-French; Italian; Netherlands. **Languages** English. **Staff** 1250.00 FTE, paid. **Finance** Funds provided by the 6 partner governments in proportion to the number of graves of their dead. Financial assistance also provided by governments or authorities in several other countries. **Activities** War graves and memorials in more than 150 countries maintained either by Commission staff or by agreement with governments or other authorities. Agreements with the governments of Kenya, Malawi, Sri Lanka, Tanzania UR, Uganda, Zambia and Zimbabwe. Active in (under agreement with the governments concerned):. Active in: Belgium, Czechia, Denmark, Egypt, Ethiopia, France, Germany, Greece, Indonesia, Iraq, Italy, Japan, Netherlands, Thailand, Türkiye. **Publications** *For the Fallen*; *The CWGC Somme Companion*. *The Unending Vigil* (1985). *A Debt of Honour* – DVD. Annual Report; cemetery and memorial registers; information sheets; fact sheets on various memorials and cemeteries.

Members Representatives of each of the partner governments and not more than 9 others appointed by Royal Warrant. Representatives of 6 governments (" indicates partner government):
Australia, Canada, India, New Zealand, South Africa, UK (*). [2022/XC0383/**F***]

♦ Commonwealth Weightlifting Federation (CWF) 04368

Fédération haltérophile du Commonwealth

Gen Sec PO Box 9167, Scoresby, Melbourne VIC 3179, Australia. T. +61397648622. E-mail: owf@bigpond.com.
Assistant Gen Sec Mail Point A6, 22nd Floor, One Churchill Place, Canary Wharf, London, E14 5LN, UK.
URL: http://www.commonwealthweightlifting.com/

History 15 Aug 1948, London (UK). Founded at the 1948 Olympic Games. Former names and other names: *British Empire and Commonwealth Weightlifting Council* – former (1948); *British Commonwealth Weightlifting Federation (BCWLF)* – former. **Aims** Recognize, by the award of certificates, Commonwealth weightlifting champions; help in the promotion of the *championships* whenever possible; establish lists of senior and junior Commonwealth records; receive reports from member associations and distribute information for the purposes of improving weightlifting techniques and knowledge for the mutual benefit of all affiliated member associations. **Structure** Congress (every 4 years); Committee. **Languages** English. **Staff** 6.00 FTE, voluntary. **Finance** Sources: members' dues. **Activities** Awards/prizes/competitions; events/meetings; knowledge management/information dissemination. **Events** *Congress* Glasgow (UK) 2014, *Congress* Penang (Malaysia) 2013, *Congress* London (UK) 2012, *Congress* Cape Town (South Africa) 2011, *Congress* Delhi (India) 2010. **Publications** *WCF Bulletin* (4 a year).

Members National associations in 54 countries and territories:
Australia, Bahamas, Bangladesh, Barbados, Belize, Bermuda, Botswana, Brunei Darussalam, Cameroon, Canada, Cook Is, Cyprus, Eswatini, Fiji, Ghana, Guernsey, Guyana, Hong Kong, India, Isle of Man, Jamaica, Jersey, Kenya, Kiribati, Lesotho, Malawi, Malaysia, Maldives, Malta, Mauritius, Namibia, Nauru, New Zealand, Nigeria, Niue, Northern Ireland, Pakistan, Papua New Guinea, Samoa, Saudi Arabia, Scotland, Seychelles, Sierra Leone, Singapore, Solomon Is, Sri Lanka, St Lucia, St Vincent-Grenadines, Tanzania UR, Tonga, Tuvalu, Uganda, UK, Vanuatu, Zambia, Zimbabwe. [2022/XC0199/**C**]

♦ Commonwealth Women Parliamentarians (CWP) 04369

Headquarters c/o Commonwealth Parliamentary Assn, Richmond House, London, SW1P 0AA, UK. T. +442077991460. Fax +442072226073. E-mail: hq.sec@cpahq.org.
URL: http://www.cpahq.org

History Nov 1989, Bridgetown (Barbados). Founded during 35th Commonwealth Parliamentary Conference, as an informal group. **Aims** Improve representation for Commonwealth Women in Parliament and for Women Parliamentarians in the CPA; encourage women to stand for election to representative bodies by advocating the removal of barriers to their participation and facilitating their professional contribution as Members; ensure that *gender* continues to be mainstreamed across all activities to assist Parliaments and Legislatures to exceed the Commonwealth Heads of Government target of having women occupying no less than 30 percent of decision-making positions. **Structure** CWP Business Meeting (takes place at triennial conference); CWP Chairperson (elected for three-year term); CWP President; CWP Steering Committee. Located at *Commonwealth Parliamentary Association (CPA, #04355)*. **Languages** English. **Activities** Awareness raising; capacity building; events/meetings; guidance/assistance/consulting; knowledge management/information dissemination; monitoring/evaluation; networking/liaising; politics/policy/regulatory; projects/programmes; research and development; research/documentation; standards/guidelines. 54 countries of the Commonwealth (180 Commonwealth Parliaments and Legislatures including national, subnational and territorial). **Events** *Plenary Conference* Kampala (Uganda) 2019, *Plenary Conference* Yaoundé (Cameroon) 2014, *Plenary Conference* Cape Town (South Africa) 2013, *Plenary Conference* Colombo (Sri Lanka) 2012, *Plenary Conference* London (UK) 2011. **Publications** A wide range of publications and toolkits. **Members** CWP is linked to CPA Branches, comprising women Members of national, state, provincial and territorial Parliaments and Legislatures in 54 countries and 180 jurisdictions of the Commonwealth. Membership countries not specified. **NGO Relations** Extends observer status to other interparliamentary organizations (not specified). [2022.05.11/XM0335/**D**]

- ♦ Commonwealth Women's Affairs Ministers Meeting (meeting series)
- ♦ Commonwealth Women's Network / see NGO Commonwealth Women's Network (#17122)
- ♦ Commonwealth Youth Climate Change Network / see Commonwealth Youth Climate Initiative (#04370)

♦ Commonwealth Youth Climate Initiative 04370

Contact Youth Affairs Division YAD, Commonwealth Secretariat, Marlborough House, Pall Mall, London, SW1Y 5HX, UK. T. +442077476589.
URL: http://youthclimate.org.uk/

History 2009, London (UK), at Young Commonwealth Climate Summit. Also referred to as *Commonwealth Youth Climate Network (CYCN)* and *Commonwealth Youth Climate Change Network (CYCN)*. **Events** *Young Commonwealth climate summit* London (UK) 2009. **IGO Relations** *Commonwealth Secretariat (#04362)*.
[2018/XJ1258/**E**]

- ♦ Commonwealth Youth Climate Network / see Commonwealth Youth Climate Initiative (#04370)

♦ Commonwealth Youth Council (CYC) 04371

Contact c/o Youth Division, Commonwealth Secretariat, Marlborough House, Pall Mall, London, SW1 5HX, UK. T. +442077476388. Fax +442077476579. E-mail: cyc@commonwealth.int.
URL: http://www.commonwealthyouthcouncil.com/

History Establishment endorsed by *Commonwealth Secretariat (#04362)* – Heads of Government, Nov 2011. Replaces *Pan-Commonwealth Youth Caucus (PCYC, inactive)*. **Aims** Empower and engage young people in sustainable development, democracy and the values of the Commonwealth. **Structure** General Assembly; Executive. **Events** *Youth Forum* Qawra (Malta) 2015. **NGO Relations** *World Youth Foundation (WYF)* is full member. [2016/XM5315/**C**]

- ♦ Commonwealth Youth Exchange Council (internationally oriented national body)
- ♦ Commonwealth Youth Ministers Meeting (meeting series)
- ♦ Commonwealth Youth Peace Ambassadors Network (unconfirmed)

♦ Commonwealth Youth Programme (CYP) 04372

Programme du Commonwealth pour la jeunesse

Dir/Head of Youth Affairs Youth Affairs Div – ComSec, Marlborough House, Pall Mall, London, SW1Y 5HX, UK. T. +442077476462. Fax +442077476549.
URL: http://www.thecommonwealth.org/

History 1973, Ottawa (Canada), by Commonwealth Heads of Government, following discussions in 1969, Singapore (Singapore), and a programme drafted at a special Ministerial meeting, 1973, Lusaka (Zambia). An integral part of *Commonwealth Secretariat (#04362)*. **Aims** Support and assist Commonwealth governments in the development of policies and programmes to increase the participation of *young people* in society; promote participation of youth in the process of national *development*; recognize their contribution to the economic, social and cultural development of their societies. **Structure** *Commonwealth Youth Ministers Meeting (CYMM)* (currently meets every 4 years), elects Committee of Management. Commonwealth Secretary-General charged with overall responsibility for administration. Headquarters are at ComSec in London (UK), originally under the *'Human Resource Development Division'*; merged into a composite *'Women and Youth Affairs Division (WYAD)'* in 1993. Currently administered by the Youth Affairs Department of the renamed *'Gender and Youth Affairs Division (GYAD)'*. Regional centres (4): *Commonwealth Youth Programme South Pacific Regional Centre (CYP-SPRC, see: #04362)*; *Commonwealth Youth Programme – Caribbean Centre (CYPCC, see: #04362)*; *African Centre of the Commonwealth Youth Programme (no recent information)*; *Asia Centre of the Commonwealth Youth Programme (CYP Asia Centre, see: #04362)*. **Finance** Funded by Commonwealth member governments. **Activities** Training/education; events/meetings; projects/programmes. **Events** *Asian regional symposium on CYCI micro-credit management systems* India 1998, *Session of youth ministers* Kuala Lumpur (Malaysia) 1998, *Asia regional workshop on human resource development* Chandigarh (India) 1996, *Session of youth ministers* Port-of-Spain (Trinidad-Tobago) 1995, *Regional conference on Pacific youth* Rarotonga Is (Cook Is) 1994. **Publications** *In Common* (3 a year) – newsletter. *Cross Reference Series*. *Youth Empowerment in the New Millennium* (1998); *Studies in Youth and Development*; *Youth and Community Work Practice*. Newsletters of regional centres; training materials.

Members Ministries responsible for youth affairs in the 52 Commonwealth countries (Pakistan was suspended from councils of the Commonwealth following unconstitutional overthrow of the democratically elected government, 12 Oct 1999):
Antigua-Barbuda, Australia, Bahamas, Bangladesh, Barbados, Belize, Botswana, Brunei Darussalam, Cameroon, Canada, Cyprus, Dominica, Eswatini, Fiji, Ghana, Grenada, Guyana, India, Jamaica, Kenya, Kiribati, Lesotho, Malawi, Malaysia, Maldives, Malta, Mauritius, Mozambique, Namibia, Nauru, New Zealand, Nigeria, Papua New Guinea, Samoa, Seychelles, Sierra Leone, Singapore, Solomon Is, South Africa, Sri Lanka, St Kitts-Nevis, St Lucia, St Vincent-Grenadines, Tanzania UR, Tonga, Trinidad-Tobago, Tuvalu, Uganda, UK, Vanuatu, Zambia, Zimbabwe.
Associated territories (7):
Anguilla (Bahamas), Bermuda, Montserrat (Spain), Niue, Tokelau, Turks-Caicos, Virgin Is UK.

IGO Relations *Commonwealth of Learning (COL, #04346)*; *Pacific Community (SPC, #17942)*; *University of the South Pacific (USP, #20703)*. **NGO Relations** Major youth NGOs and those concerned with economic and social issues; including: *Asian Centre for Organisation Research and Development (ACORD, #01374)*; *International Lesbian, Gay, Bisexual, Transgender, Queer and Intersex Youth and Student Organization (IGLYO, #14032)*. Former staff members can join: *The Commonwealth Association (COMASSOC, #04299)*. [2012/XF2059/**F***]

- ♦ Commonwealth Youth Programme – Caribbean Centre (see: #04362)
- ♦ Commonwealth Youth Programme South Pacific Regional Centre (see: #04362)
- ♦ A Common Word Among the Youth (unconfirmed)
- ♦ Communautair Bureau voor Plantenrassen (#04404)

♦ Communauté africaine de culture 04373

SG 25bis rue des Ecoles, 75005 Paris, France. T. +33143541374. Fax +33143259667. E-mail: presaf@club-internet.fr.
Pres address not obtained.

History 9 May 1957, Paris (France). Founded, following a resolution of 1st Congress of Negro Writers and Artists, Sep 1956, Paris. Former names and other names: *Society of African Culture (SAC)* – former; *Société africaine de culture (SAC)* – former. **Aims** Affirm, defend and enrich members' national cultures; increase awareness of members' responsibilities first to their own cultures and then to a universal culture; promote increased communication so as to eliminate misunderstanding and prejudice. **Structure** General Assembly (every 2 years); Executive Council; Executive Committee; Bureau. **Languages** English, French. **Finance** Grants; gifts. **Activities** Events/meetings. **Events** *La jeunesse, le livre et le développement* Port-au-Prince (Haiti) 1991, *La jeunesse, le livre et le développement* Cotonou (Benin) 1990, *Colloquium on the family in black Africa* Yaoundé (Cameroon) 1986. **Publications** *Présence africaine* (periodical); *Cahiers: Présence africaine*. Paperbacks; books for young people.
Members Full National associations and individuals in 44 countries and territories:
Angola, Benin, Brazil, Burkina Faso, Burundi, Cameroon, Central African Rep, Chad, Comoros, Congo Brazzaville, Congo DR, Côte d'Ivoire, Ethiopia, France, Gabon, Gambia, Ghana, Guadeloupe, Guiana Fr, Guinea, Guinea-Bissau, Guyana, Haiti, Jamaica, Kenya, Liberia, Madagascar, Mali, Martinique, Mauritania, Mauritius, Mozambique, Niger, Nigeria, Rwanda, Senegal, Sierra Leone, Somalia, Sudan, Tanzania UR, Togo, Uganda, USA, Zambia.
Associate members in 4 countries:
Belgium, France, Italy, UK.
Consultative Status Consultative status granted from: *UNESCO (#20322)* (Consultative Status). **NGO Relations** *Institute for Black Peoples (IBP, no recent information)*. [2014.11.12/XD3237/**F**]

- ♦ Communauté de l'Afrique orientale – 1967 (inactive)
- ♦ Communauté andine (#00817)
- ♦ Communauté asiatique et pacifique de la noix de coco / see International Coconut Community (#12628)
- ♦ Communauté des associations d'éditeurs de journaux de la CEE / see European Newspaper Publishers' Association (#08048)
- ♦ Communauté des béatitudes (religious order)
- ♦ Communauté des Caraïbes (#03476)
- ♦ Communauté du chemin neuf (internationally oriented national body)
- ♦ Communauté chrétienne rurale de l'Afrique orientale (inactive)
- ♦ Communauté de développement de l'Afrique australe (#19843)
- ♦ Communauté économique africaine (#00290)
- ♦ Communauté économique de l'Afrique de l'Ouest (inactive)
- ♦ Communauté économique des Etats de l'Afrique centrale (#05311)
- ♦ Communauté économique des Etats de l'Afrique de l'Ouest (#05312)

♦ Communauté économique et monétaire d'Afrique centrale (CEMAC) 04374

Central Africa Economic and Monetary Community (CAEMC)

Pres Avenue des martyrs, BP 969, Bangui, Central African Rep. T. +236612179 – +236614781 – +23675099901. Fax +236612135. E-mail: dyingra@yahoo.fr – secemac@hotmail.com.
Facebook: https://www.facebook.com/Page.Commission.Cemac/

History 16 Mar 1994, Ndjamena (Chad). Established on signature of a treaty by heads of member states, following a study proposed by the Council of Heads of State of *Union douanière et économique de l'Afrique centrale (UDEAC, inactive)*, Dec 1991. Retains the principles inherent in the creation of UDEAC and of Union monétaire de l'Afrique centrale (UMAC), set up 22 Nov 1972, Brazzaville (Congo Brazzaville), by 5 Central African states and by Government of France and of which Equatorial Guinea became a member as from 1 Jan 1985. UMAC is also referred to in English as *'Central African Monetary System'* and *'Central African Monetary Area (CAMA)'*, and in French as *'Zone monétaire centrafricaine'*. UMAC was absorbed into CEMAC, which took over the activities of UDEAC through a transition formalized in an agreement signed by the UDEAC Council on 5 Feb 1997, Libreville (Gabon), effective 1 Jan 1998. CEMAC comes within the framework of *Pays africains de la Zone franc (PAZF, #18270)*, having the common currency – *'CFA franc'* – of the *Communauté financière africaine (CFA, #04377)*. All relevant treaties and conventions are deposited in the state of Chad. **Aims** Cooperate in the joint development of human resources and natural resources of member states in the framework of economic and monetary union; on the basis of already existing cooperation, abolish the division between monetary and economic management and relaunch a policy of economic and social integration; consolidate members' experience in economic and monetary cooperation through reinforcement of common currency; order macro-economic policies; set up a regional legal framework for investment and growth; achieve a single market; set up common sectoral policies; act as the institution in charge of currency issues and harmonization of monetary policies of member countries.
Structure Comprises 4 institutions, each the subject of a convention:
- *Union économique de l'Afrique centrale (UEAC, #20376)*, which is gradually taking over the activities of UDEAC;
- *Union monétaire de l'Afrique centrale (UMAC, #20463)*;
- *Economic and Monetary Community of Central Africa Parliament (CEMAC-P, no recent information)* (proposed);
- *Cour de justice communautaire de la CEMAC (CJ-CEMAC, #04931)*, comprising a judicial chamber and a court of auditors whose composition, function and competence are covered in the convention setting up UEAC.

Principal organs:
- Conference of Heads of State;
- Council of Ministers of UEAC, comprising 3 ministers of each member state;
- Ministerial Committee of UMAC (meeting at least once a year), comprising Ministers of Finance and Economic Affairs of member states;
- Executive Secretariat;
- Inter-state Committee;
- *Banque des Etats de l'Afrique centrale (BEAC, #03169)*;
- *Commission bancaire de l'Afrique centrale (COBAC, #04204)*;
- *Institution de financement et développement.*

Languages French. **Finance** Contributions from member states (annual). **Activities** Groups and integrates the sectors previously covered by UMAC, UDEAC and the Central Bank. Includes: *Ecole Inter-Etats des Douanes de la CEMAC (EIED, #05297)*; *Economic and Statistical Observatory for Sub-Saharan Africa (AFRISTAT, #05321)*, which assists in harmonizing consumer price indexes in member countries. Organizes field-days involving industrial and commercial displays. **Events** *Summit of heads of state and government* Yaoundé (Cameroon) 2008, *Summit of heads of state and government* Ndjamena (Chad) 2007, *Summit of heads of state and government* Congo Brazzaville 2004, *Summit of heads of state and govenrment* Malabo (Equatorial Guinea) 1999. **Information Services** *Investir en Zone franc (IZFnet)* – for all countries of the Franc Zone.
Members Open to any African state sharing the ideals of the founders and subject to their approval. Founding states (6):
Cameroon, Central African Rep, Chad, Congo Brazzaville, Equatorial Guinea, Gabon.
IGO Relations Formal agreement with: *UNESCO (#20322)*; *FAO (#09260)*. Participates in the activities of: *UNCTAD (#20285)*. Memorandum of Understanding with: *World Customs Organization (WCO, #21350)*. Permanent observer status with: *World Intellectual Property Organization (WIPO, #21593)*. *Union of African Shippers' Councils (UASC, #20348)* participates in activities. Accredited by: *Secretariat of the United Nations Convention to Combat Desertification (Secretariat of the UNCCD, #19208)*; *United Nations Framework Convention on Climate Change – Secretariat (UNFCCC, #20564)*. Partner of: *Inter-African Conference on Insurance Markets (#11385)*; *Organisation pour l'Harmonisation en Afrique du Droit des Affaires (OHADA, #17806)*. **NGO Relations** Observer member of: *Assemblée parlementaire de la Francophonie (APF, #02312)*. Member of: *Association des hautes juridictions de cassation des pays ayant en partage l'usage du Français (AHJUCAF, #02629)*. Parliament is member of: *Inter-Parliamentary Union (IPU, #15961)*. [2011.01.20/XF3714/**F***]

♦ Communauté économique des pays des Grands Lacs (CEPGL) 04375

Economic Community of the Great Lakes Countries – Comunidad Económica de los Paises de los Grandes Lagos

Exec Sec POB 58, Gisenyi, Rwanda. T. +25040228. Fax +25040785.

History 20 Sep 1976, Gisenyi (Rwanda), on signature of agreement by Heads of State of member countries, to re-establish on new foundations the traditional economic links which existed prior to the independence of Burundi, Rwanda and Zaire. Amendments to the Agreement: 9 Sep 1977, Bujumbura (Burundi); 7 Dec 1980, Bujumbura; 17 Jun 1984, Bujumbura; 9 Nov 1986, Gbadolite (Zaire). Statutes registered in *'UNTS 1/16748'*. **Aims** Bring about *economic integration* and ensure the security of member States; create a framework for coordination and harmonization in the various areas of social, economic, commercial, scientific, cultural, political, military, financial, technical and touristic developments in the region; promote and intensify *commercial exchanges* and the free movement of persons and goods; pursue objectives consistent with the United Nations Charter and the Charter of the Organization of African Unity (OAU). **Structure** Conference of Heads of State (annual); Council of Ministers and State Commissioner (meeting twice a year); Permanent Executive Secretariat; Arbitration Commission. **Languages** French. **Finance** Contributions from Member States. **Activities** Monetary Arrangement among central banks signed Mar 1981, superseding that of 1978. Social Security Convention signed Sep 1978. Agreements on specific arrangements within this convention on free movement of officials and businessmen and on postal organization, signed 1980. Specialized Technical Commissions (5): Political and Juridical Matters; Social and Cultural Matters; Planning, Industry, Agriculture and Natural Resources; Commerce, Finance, Immigration and Tourism; Public Works, Transport and Energy. Bodies created by CEPGL: *Energy Organization of the Great Lakes Countries (EGL, no recent information)*, integrated within the Community, 1980, Bujumbura (Burundi), having been set up 20 Aug 1974, and known under the present title since 9 Dec 1979; *Banque de développement des Etats des Grands Lacs (BDEGL, inactive)*, formed 9 Sep 1977; *Institute of Agricultural and Zootechnical Research (IRAZ, no recent information)*, set up 9 Dec 1979, Gitega (Burundi). Also instrumental in setting up *ECA Sub-Regional Office for Eastern Africa (SRO-EA Kigali, #05275)*. **Events** *Workshop on definition and adoption of industrial products standard in CEPGL countries* Bujumbura (Burundi) 1996, *Seminar for economic operators in countries interested in forming joint transport company for Lakes Kivu and Tanganyika* Kinshasa (Zaire) 1996, *Session ordinaire de la conférence des recteurs d'université des états membres* Bujumbura (Burundi) 1989, *Seminar on malaria* Gisenyi (Rwanda) 1989, *Ordinary session of the conference of heads of states / Conference of Heads of State of CEPGL* Kinshasa (Zaire) 1989. **Publications** *Journal officiel de la CEGL* (annual); *CEPGL Quarterly Review*. *Revue Grands Lacs* (1996).
Members Governments of 3 countries:
Burundi, Congo DR, Rwanda.
IGO Relations Relationship agreement with: *FAO (#09260)*. Participates in the activities of: *UNCTAD (#20285)*. Permanent observer status with: *World Intellectual Property Organization (WIPO, #21593)*. Close cooperation with:.
- *ASEAN (#01141)*;
- *Economic Community of Central African States (ECCAS, #05311)*;
- *Economic Community of West African States (ECOWAS, #05312)*;
- *European Development Fund (EDF, #06914)*;
- *ILO (#11123)*;
- *International Telecommunication Union (ITU, #15673)*;
- *UNDP (#20292)*;
- *UNIDO (#20336)*;
- *United Nations Economic Commission for Africa (ECA, #20554)* – and its
- *ECA Sub-Regional Office for Eastern Africa (SRO-EA Kigali, #05275)*;
- *WHO (#20950)*;
- *World Customs Organization (WCO, #21350)*.

Under Lomé Conventions, links with: *European Commission (EC, #06633)*.
NGO Relations *International Social Security Association (ISSA, #14885)*. [2011.12.23/XF5516/**F***]

- ♦ Communauté électrique du Bénin (internationally oriented national body)
- ♦ Communauté de l'Emmanuel (religious order)
- ♦ Communauté engagement service volontariat (internationally oriented national body)
- ♦ Communauté des Etats indépendants (#04341)
- ♦ Communauté des Etats Latino-américains et Caraïbéens (#04432)
- ♦ Communauté des états sahelo-sahariens (#04406)
- ♦ Communauté européenne (inactive)
- ♦ Communauté européenne des associations du commerce gros de bière des pays membres de la CEE / see Association européenne des associations du commerce de gros de bière et boissons des pays de l'Europe (#02555)
- ♦ Communauté européenne du charbon et de l'acier (inactive)
- ♦ Communauté européenne des coopératives de consommateurs (#06678)
- ♦ Communauté européenne de crédit communal (inactive)
- ♦ Communauté Européenne des Cuisiniers / see Euro-Toques International (#09190)
- ♦ Communauté européenne de défense (inactive)
- ♦ Communauté européenne des écrivains (inactive)
- ♦ Communauté européenne de l'énergie atomique (inactive)
- ♦ Communauté européenne des étudiants en sciences économiques (inactive)

♦ Communauté européenne des jeunes de l'horticulture (CEJH) 04376

European Community of Young Horticulturists – Arbeitsgemeinschaft Europäischer Junggärtner

SG Giessener Strasse 47, 35305 Grünberg, Germany. T. +496401910150. Fax +496401910176. E-mail: cejh.board@outlook.com.
URL: http://www.cejh.org/

History 23 Jan 1965, Paris (France). Statutes adopted 21 Sep 1976, Guernsey (UK); most recent amendments 8 Jul 1988. **Aims** Support collaboration among European young horticulturist organizations; represent interests and relevance of European youth connected with horticultural professions; enable responsible action of young horticulturists through support for their education and development; support protection of the environment. **Structure** General Meeting (at least annually, usually at congress); Managing Board. **Languages** English. **Staff** 0.50 FTE, voluntary. **Finance** Sources: members' dues. **Activities** Events/meetings. **Events** *Annual Congress* Essen (Germany) 2021, *Annual Congress* Essen (Germany) 2020, *Annual Congress* Riga (Latvia) / Tallinn (Estonia) 2019, *Annual Congress* Malmö (Sweden) 2018, *Annual Congress* Bolzano (Italy) 2017. **Publications** *Grow Young*. Local papers for young gardeners.
Members National organizations representing 7,000 members in 13 countries:
Austria, Belgium, Denmark, Estonia, Finland, Germany, Italy, Latvia, Luxembourg, Norway, Poland, Slovakia, Sweden.
NGO Relations *International Association of Horticultural Producers (#11940)*. [2020/XD0681/**D**]

- ♦ Communauté européenne des organisations de publicitaires (inactive)
- ♦ Communauté Européenne du rail / see Community of European Railway and Infrastructure Companies (#04396)
- ♦ Communauté Européenne du rail et des compagnies d'infrastructure / see Community of European Railway and Infrastructure Companies (#04396)
- ♦ Communauté européenne de recherche en matière d'écoulement, de turbulence et de combustion (#08361)
- ♦ Communauté européenne de travail Eglise et société industrielle / see European Contact Group – Ecumenical Network for Economic and Social Action (#06773)
- ♦ Communauté évangélique d'action apostolique / see CEVAA – Communauté d'églises en mission (#03840)

♦ Communauté financière africaine (CFA) 04377

African Financial Community
Address not obtained.
URL: http://www.banque-france.fr/fr/eurosys/zonefr/zonefr.htm
History as *Communauté franco-africaine*, to group African member countries of *Banque centrale des Etats de l'Afrique de l'Ouest (BCEAO, #03167)* within the wider framework of the *Zone franc (#22037)*, and whose currency, the 'franc de la Communauté financière africaine' (CFA franc), is linked to the French franc. Together with countries of *Banque des Etats de l'Afrique centrale (BEAC, #03169)* and 'Banque centrale des Comores', members comprise *Pays africains de la Zone franc (PAZF, #18270)*. [2008/XF0749/F*]

- ♦ Communauté financière du Pacifique / see Comptoirs français du pacifique (#04422)
- ♦ Communauté française (inactive)
- ♦ Communauté franco-africaine / see Communauté financière africaine (#04377)
- ♦ Communauté des industries européennes de la serrurerie et des ferrures / see European Federation of Associations of Locks and Builders Hardware Manufacturers (#07054)
- ♦ Communauté d'intérêts des anciens résistants dans les pays occupés par le fascisme (inactive)
- ♦ Communauté Internationale Baha'ie (#03062)
- ♦ Communauté internationale des femmes vivant avec le VIH/SIDA (#12826)
- ♦ Communauté internationale des hommes d'affaires du plein Evangile (#10015)
- ♦ Communauté internationale des obtenteurs de plantes ornementales et fruitières de reproduction asexuée / see International Community of Breeders of Asexually Reproduced Ornamental and Fruit Varieties (#12821)
- ♦ Communauté internationale des obtenteurs de plantes ornementales et fruitières à reproduction asexuée (#12821)
- ♦ Communauté internationale des obtenteurs de plantes ornementales de reproduction asexuée / see International Community of Breeders of Asexually Reproduced Ornamental and Fruit Varieties (#12821)
- ♦ Communauté internationale du poivre (#14557)
- ♦ Communauté internationale de volontaires laïcs / see Lay Volunteers International Association
- ♦ Communauté des jeunes chrétiens populaires / see Democrat Youth Community of Europe (#05037)
- ♦ Communauté de la jeunesse démocrate de l'Europe / see Democrat Youth Community of Europe (#05037)
- ♦ Communauté de Marie et des Saints Apôtres de Jésus (religious order)
- ♦ Communauté du moindre sou (#09728)
- ♦ Communauté des organisations suisses de développement / see Alliance Sud, Swiss Alliance of Development Organisations Swissaid – Catholic Lenten Fund – Bread for All – Helvetas – Caritas – Interchurch Aid
- ♦ Communauté ouest africaine pour la santé (inactive)
- ♦ Communauté du Pacifique (#17942)
- ♦ Communauté des pays de langue portugaise (#04430)
- ♦ Communauté promotion et développement (internationally oriented national body)
- ♦ Communauté régionale des postes et télécommunications (#18767)
- ♦ Communauté des régions jurassiennes / see Conférence TransJurassienne
- ♦ Communauté du Sacré-Coeur (inactive)
- ♦ Communauté de Sant'Egidio (religious order)
- ♦ Communautés européennes (inactive)
- ♦ Communautés Laïques Marianistes (see: #21334)
- ♦ Communauté de Taizé (religious order)
- ♦ Communauté von Taizé (religious order)
- ♦ Communauté des télévisions francophones (inactive)
- ♦ Communauté de travail Alpes-Adriatique / see Alps-Adriatic-Alliance (#00747)
- ♦ Communauté de travail des brasseurs du Marché commun / see The Brewers of Europe (#03324)
- ♦ Communauté de travail du Jura / see Conférence TransJurassienne
- ♦ Communauté de travail des pays du Danube (#21056)
- ♦ Communauté de travail des Pyrénées (#21057)
- ♦ Communauté de travail Swissaid – Action de carême – Pain pour le prochain – Helvetas – Caritas / see Alliance Sud, Swiss Alliance of Development Organisations Swissaid – Catholic Lenten Fund – Bread for All – Helvetas – Caritas – Interchurch Aid
- ♦ Communauté de travail Swissaid – Action de carême – Pain pour tous – Helvetas / see Alliance Sud, Swiss Alliance of Development Organisations Swissaid – Catholic Lenten Fund – Bread for All – Helvetas – Caritas – Interchurch Aid
- ♦ Communauté des universités méditerranéennes (#04403)
- ♦ Communauté de vie chrétienne (#03905)

♦ COMMUNIA 04378

Contact c/o Organisation Development Support, Rue Joseph II 20, 1000 Brussels, Belgium. E-mail: communia@communia-association.org.
URL: http://www.communia-association.org/
History 2012. Building on a project funded by *European Commission (EC, #06633)* (2007-2011). Former names and other names: *COMMUNIA International Association on the Public Domain* – full title. Registration: No/ID: 0843.824.873, Start date: 21 Feb 2012, Belgium; EU Transparency Register, No/ID: 003277719548-45, Start date: 16 Nov 2015. **Aims** Foster, strengthen and enrich the *Public Domain*; raise awareness in, educate about, advocate for, offer expertise on and research about the Public Domain in the *digital age* within society and with policy-makers, at the EU level and worldwide. **Staff** 2.00 FTE, paid; 10.00 FTE, voluntary. **Publications** Blog posts; policy papers.
Members Institutions and individuals. Institutions in 9 countries:
France, Germany, Greece, Netherlands, North Macedonia, Poland, Slovenia, UK, USA.
Consultative Status Consultative status granted from: *World Intellectual Property Organization (WIPO, #21593)* (Permanent Observer). [2023.02.13/XJ8344/F]

- ♦ COMMUNIA International Association on the Public Domain / see COMMUNIA (#04378)
- ♦ Communicación, Intercambio y Desarrollo Humano en América Latina (internationally oriented national body)
- ♦ Communicating the Arts (meeting series)

♦ Communicating with Disaster Affected Communities Network (CDAC Network) 04379

Dir 27 Dingley Place, London, EC1V 8BR, UK. T. +442037738691. E-mail: info@cdacnetwork.org.
URL: http://www.cdacnetwork.org/
History 2009. Registration: UK Legal Entity, No/ID: 10571501, Start date: 2007; UK Registered Charity, No/ID: 1178168, Start date: 2018. **Aims** Bring together diverse local, regional and global actors to catalyze communities' ability to connect, access information and have a voice in humanitarian emergencies. **Structure** General Assembly; Board of Trustees; Secretariat. **Languages** English. **Staff** Fewer than 10. **Finance** Sources: donations; members' dues. **Activities** Advocacy/lobbying/activism; capacity building; events/meetings; knowledge management/information dissemination; networking/liaising; research/documentation; training/education. **Publications** Tools and guidance; training resources; case studies; papers and articles; seminar reports.
Members Full: organizations (29) including 20 which are listed in this Yearbook:
ActionAid (#00087); Development and Humanitarian Learning in Action (Dahlia); Fondation Hirondelle – Media for Peace and Human Dignity; International Committee of the Red Cross (ICRC, #12799); International Media Support (IMS, #14128); International Organization for Migration (IOM, #14454); International Shopfitting Organisation (ISO, inactive); Internews Europe (#15953); Norwegian Refugee Council (NRC); Plan International (#18386); Save the Children International (#19058); Thomson Reuters Foundation (TRF); Translators without Borders (#20216); UNHCR (#20327); UNICEF (#20332); United Nations Office for the Coordination of Humanitarian Affairs (OCHA, #20593); United Nations Population Fund (UNFPA, #20612); WHO (#20950); World Food Programme (WFP, #21510); World Vision International (WVI, #21904).
Affiliate (5) include 3 organizations listed in this Yearbook:
Development Media International (DMI); FilmAid International (FAI); Lifeline Energy.
NGO Relations Member of: *Emergency Telecommunications Cluster (ETC, #05438).* [2020.05.14/XJ8594/y/F]

- ♦ Communicating and Working Together (internationally oriented national body)
- ♦ Communication for Climate Change Multi Donor Trust Fund / see Connect4Climate (#04680)
- ♦ Communication Committee for Lutheran Minority Churches in Europe (#16205)

♦ Communication Foundation for Asia (CFA) 04380

Exec Dir 4427 Old Santa Mesa Road, Sta Mesa, 1016 Manila, Philippines. T. +6327132981 – +6327132982 – +6327132985. Fax +6327132736.
URL: http://cfamedia.org/
History Founded May 1968, Manila (Philippines), as *Social Communication Center – Development Research Foundation (SCC-DRF)*, by Cornelio Lagerwey. Current title adopted 1973. **Aims** Harness the power of communication in order to promote *Christian* values and empower people in need towards social transformation. **Structure** Board of Trustees; Departments (8). **Languages** English, Filipino. **Staff** 100.00 FTE, paid. **Finance** Sale of regular publications and other products (books, catechetical materials and audiovisual productions); fees from training programmes; rentals of TV and radio studios and training facilities; project grants. **Activities** Training/education; projects/programmes; publishing activities. **Publications** *Gospel Komiks* (5 a year) in English, Filipino; *Gospel Komiks Magazine for High School* (5 a year) in English; *Gospel Now* (5 a year) in English; *Jesus Magazine* (5 a year) in English. *Film and Faith* – book series. Teaching materials. [2015.12.14/XF0261/f/F]

- ♦ Communication Initiative (internationally oriented national body)

♦ Pro Communicatio Nordica (PCN) 04381

Nordic Foundation for Communication
Contact Resurscenter Mo Gård, SE-612 93 Finspång, Sweden.
URL: http://www.stiftelsen-pcn.net/
History Registered in accordance with Swedish law. **Aims** Increase *cooperation* between the Nordic countries. **Structure** Board of Directors. **Events** *Conference* Turku (Finland) 2008.
Members in 4 countries:
Denmark, Finland, Norway, Sweden. [2010/XM3652/f/F]

♦ Communication Policy Research Latin America (CPRLATAM) 04382

Secretariat Univ of Brasilia, Campus Univ Darcy Ribeiro, Caixa Postal 04413, Brasilia DF, 70910-900, Brazil. E-mail: iorio@ccom.unb.br.
URL: http://cprlatam.org/
History 2007. Former names and other names: *Americas Communication Research Network (ACORN)* – former; *Red Americana de Investigación en Información y Comunicación (REDECOM)* – former; *Rede Americana de Pesquisa em Informação e Comunicação (REDECOM)* – former; *CPRLatam* – former. **Aims** Provide training and consulting services for scholars, private sector and government officers on ICT policy; hold an annual conference to increase awareness regarding ICT policy issues. **Structure** Board of Directors. A cross-disciplinary academic network of research centers. **Languages** English, Portuguese, Spanish. **Finance** Undisclosed. **Activities** Awareness raising; events/meetings; networking/liaising; research/documentation. **Events** *Annual Conference* Mexico City (Mexico) 2022, *Annual Conference* Mexico City (Mexico) 2021, *Annual Conference* Córdoba (Argentina) 2019, *Annual Conference* Varadero (Cuba) 2018, *Annual Conference* Cartagena de Indias (Colombia) 2017. **Publications** Proceedings.
Members Centres in 10 countries:
Argentina, Brazil, Canada, Chile, Colombia, Ecuador, Mexico, Peru, USA, Venezuela. [2022.10.25/XJ5105/F]

- ♦ Communications Convention (1907 treaty)
- ♦ Communications Coordination Committee for the United Nations (internationally oriented national body)
- ♦ Communications Fraud Control Association (internationally oriented national body)
- ♦ Communications International (inactive)

♦ Communication for Social Change Consortium (CFSC Consortium) 04383

Consortium de la communication pour le changement social – Consorcio de Comunicación para el Cambio Social
Pres/CEO 14 South Orange Ave, Ste 2F, South Orange NJ 07079, USA. T. +19737631115. Fax +19737628267. E-mail: info@communicationforsocialchange.org.
CFSC Europe 49 Queen Victoria Street, Ste 69, London, EC4N 4SA, UK.
URL: http://www.communicationforsocialchange.org/
History 2000, USA, following activity begun in 1997 by the Rockefeller Foundation. 29 Aug 2008, European branch established as a UK Registered Charity: 1125636. **Aims** Improve the life of poor and historically marginalized communities by increased use of innovative communication processes. **Structure** Board of Directors. **Activities** Practitioner Network. Includes: *CFSC Europe*. **Publications** *MAZI* – online report. [2008/XM0422/F]

♦ Communications Regulators' Association of Southern Africa (CRASA) 04384

Exec Sec Plot 143 – Unit 2, Gaborone Intl Finance Park, PO Box AD 135 ADD, Gaborone, Botswana. T. +2673158468. Fax +2673181171.
URL: http://www.crasa.org/
History 15 Sep 1997, Dar es Salaam (Tanzania UR), as *Telecommunications Regulators' Association of Southern Africa (TRASA)*. Current title adopted, Feb 2006. Set up within the framework of *Southern African Development Community (SADC, #19843)* Protocol on Transport, Communications and Meteorology. Takes over activities of *Conference of Southern African Telecommunication Administrations (SATA, inactive)*. **Aims** Position ICT and Postal Sectors as catalysts for socio economic development, through developing and implementing harmonized regulations that make the SADC region the preferred choice for investment. **Structure** General Meeting (annual); Executive Committee; Specialized Committees; Secretariat. **Languages** English, French, Portuguese. **Staff** 3.00 FTE, paid. **Finance** Members' dues. **Activities** Politics/policy/regulatory; capacity building; events/meetings. **Events** *Annual General Meeting* Maseru (Lesotho) 2003. **Publications** Annual Report; guidelines; brochures.
Members in 13 countries:
Angola, Botswana, Congo DR, Eswatini, Lesotho, Malawi, Mauritius, Mozambique, Namibia, South Africa, Tanzania UR, Zambia, Zimbabwe.
IGO Relations Cooperation agreement with: *Commonwealth Telecommunications Organisation (CTO, #04365)*. Restricted union of: *Universal Postal Union (UPU, #20682)*. **NGO Relations** Member of: *Alliance for Affordable Internet (A4AI, #00651)*. [2019/XD7545/D]

- ♦ Communication Technique en Europe (#20116)
- ♦ Communion ecclésiale de Leuenberg / see Community of Protestant Churches in Europe (#04405)
- ♦ Communion d'églises protestantes en Europe (#04405)

♦ Communion of Evangelical Episcopal Churches (CEEC) 04385

Gen Sec 902 Spring Valley Roa, Altamonte Springs FL 32714, USA. T. +14073890314. E-mail: bds@thecoc.us – theceec@gmail.com.
International Presiding Archbishop address not obtained.
URL: http://www.theceec.org/
History late 1980s, as *Evangelical Episcopal Church (EEC)*. **Aims** As Historic Apostolic Succession through Catholic, Orthodox and Anglican Apostolic lines, believing that the fullness of *Christian worship* and *spirituality* is found in the convergence of streams in the Body of Christ: pursue a mission that is evangelical, spirit-filled and the liturgical/sacramental; function as a contemporary church rooted in the ancient realities of the faith, while reaching into the twenty-first century in a relevant way to meet the needs of the saved and the unsaved with the Good News of Jesus Christ and glorifying God on earth. **Structure** General Convocation (every 5 years). International House of Bishops, represented by Presiding Bishop. General Secretary. Includes:

Episcopal Relief and Development, as the primary means for Episcopalians to express their compassion for people in need; *Order of Saint John the Beloved (no recent information)*. **Activities** Training/education. In the context of *Domestic and Foreign Missionary Society of the Protestant Episcopal Church (DFMS)*, *Episcopal Migration Ministries (EMM)* advocate protection for the world's refugees and provide the protection afforded by third country resettlement. **Events** *General Convocation* Oklahoma City, OK (USA) 1997. **Publications** *Christianity Today* (periodically); *First Things Magazine* – published by the Institute on Religion and Public Life. Collection of ancient Christian liturgies. Information Services: Online conference room; on-line catalogue index for Episcopal, Anglican and Catholic supplies and furnishings. **Information Services** *Anglicans and Episcopalians Online Discussion* – about orthodoxy, women in priesthood, traditionalism, new music forms; *Christianity-Net* – website produced by 'Christianity Today' evangelical magazine; *Christian Literature* – on the Internet; *Christian Recovery Network Online* – resources and services; *Internet for Christians*; *Marriage Encounter* – worldwide contacts list; *Propertalk* – email-based, user-friendly online lectionary study group. **Members** Membership countries not specified. **NGO Relations** Special relationship with: *Anglican Communion (#00827)*. [2010.06.01/XF4571/F]

♦ Communion and Liberation (CL) 04386

Comunión y Liberación – Comunione e Liberazione

International Office Via Malpighi 2, 00161 Rome RM, Italy. T. +39644252752. Fax +39644252544. E-mail: centroint@comunioneliberazione.org.
URL: http://www.comunione-liberazione.org/

History 1954, by Luigi Giussani. An ecclesiastical movement. **Aims** Educate people to the *Christian Catholic* faith. **Activities** Movement present in over 70 countries. **Publications** *Tracce* (12 a year) in English, French, German, Hungarian, Italian, Japanese, Polish, Portuguese, Russian, Spanish – magazine.
Members Offices in 29 countries:
Argentina, Austria, Belgium, Brazil, Canada, Chile, Colombia, France, Germany, Ireland, Italy, Japan, Kenya, Mexico, Netherlands, Nigeria, Paraguay, Peru, Poland, Portugal, Romania, Russia, Spain, Switzerland, Uganda, UK, Uruguay, USA, Venezuela. [2020/XF6229/F]

♦ Communion mondiale d'église réformées (#21289)

♦ Communion des oeuvres et des églises dans la francophonie sur les cinq continents (COEF 5) 04387

Fellowship of Francophone Organizations and Churches on the Five Continents

Contact address not obtained. T. +33467722767. Fax +33467722767.

History 15 Jul 1992. Also referred to as *COEF 5 International*. **Aims** Promote interaction between *Christian* organizations throughout the Francophone world. **Events** *Leadership conference* Montréal, QC (Canada) 2007, *Conférence internationale / Global Conference* Montpellier (France) 2000, *Conférence mondiale chrétienne francophone / Global Conference* Ouagadougou (Burkina Faso) 1999, *Conférence chrétienne régionale pour l'Afrique Centrale / Global Conference* Libreville (Gabon) 1998, *Conférence chrétienne francophone pour l'Afrique de l'Ouest* Cotonou (Benin) 1997. **Publications** *Signe dans la francophonie* (4 a year); *Perspectives* – newsletter.
Members National committees and organizations in 33 countries:
Algeria, Belgium, Benin, Bulgaria, Burkina Faso, Burundi, Cambodia, Cameroon, Canada, Central African Rep, Chad, Congo Brazzaville, Congo DR, Côte d'Ivoire, Egypt, France, Gabon, Guinea, Haiti, Israel, Lebanon, Madagascar, Mali, Mauritius, Niger, Romania, Rwanda, Senegal, Seychelles, South Africa, Switzerland, Togo, UK. [2009/XF4238/F]

♦ Communion of Protestant Churches in Europe / see Community of Protestant Churches in Europe (#04405)
♦ Communiquer et travailler ensemble (internationally oriented national body)
♦ Communist Esperantist Collective / see International Communist Esperantist Collective (#12819)
♦ Communist International (inactive)
♦ Communist League (inactive)
♦ Communist Youth International (inactive)

♦ Communitas International 04388

Pres US Operations Office, 2221 E Arapahoe Rd, Suite 3338, Centennial CO 80161, USA. E-mail: usoffice@gocommunitas.org.
Europe Operations Office address not obtained. E-mail: euoffice@gocommunitas.org.
URL: http://www.christianassociates.org/

History Founded by Linus Morris, following the activities of the Los Angeles CA based "Jesus Christ Light & Power House". Former names and other names: *Christian Associates International (CAI)* – legal name; *Christian Associates Europe* – alias. **Events** *Conference* Kirchheim unter Teck (Germany) 2010, *Staff conference* Dalfsen (Netherlands) 2006. [2022/XF5937/F]

♦ Communities of Sustainable Europe (CoSE) 04389

Contact De Houtmanstraat 18, 6826 PJ Arnhem, Netherlands. T. +31263629962.
URL: http://communities-of-sustainable.eu/

History Currently (2018) dormant.
Members Villages and neighbourhoods in 6 countries:
Austria, France, Luxembourg, Netherlands, Poland, UK.
IGO Relations *European Commission (EC, #06633)*. **NGO Relations** Associate partner of: *Covenant of Mayors for Climate and Energy (#04939)*. [2018.09.05/XJ7601/d/F]

♦ Community Action in Europe Network (inactive)

♦ Community Based Impact Assessment Network for Eastern Africa (CIANEA) 04390

Contact CIANEA Uganda, PO Box 10478, Kampala, Uganda.

Aims Understand and assess the *environmental* impacts of community driven development projects. **Activities** Provides a venue for members to share their research, find out about new developments and studies concerning community based EIA, disseminate and exchange information and work in partnership with other stakeholders; provides capacity building on community based EIA through training of trainers and community participation. **Members** Researchers, community groups, government agencies, donors and individuals. Membership countries not specified. **NGO Relations** *Capacity Development and Linkages for Environmental Assessment in Africa (CLEAA, no recent information)*; *End Water Poverty (EWP, #05464)*. [2014.01.29/XJ0198/D]

♦ Community Based Rehabilitation Africa Network / see CBR Africa Network (#03616)

♦ Community-Based Rehabilitation Network – South Asia (CBR Network South Asia) 04391

Main Office c/o Ctr for Adv Studies, 134 I Block 6th Main, Banashankari III Stage, Bangalore, Karnataka 560 085, Bangalore KARNATAKA 560 085, India. T. +918026724273.

Events *Conference* Kabul (Afghanistan) 2010, *Conference* Kathmandu (Nepal) 2007, *Conference* Dhaka (Bangladesh) 1997. **NGO Relations** Member of: *Global Partnership for Disability and Development (GPDD, #10530)*. [2009/XM3505/F]

♦ Community of the Beatitudes (religious order)
♦ Community Charter of Fundamental Social Rights for Workers (1989 treaty)

♦ Community of Christ 04392

Pres Community of Christ Auditorium and Temple, 1001 W Walnut, Independence MO 64050-3562, USA. T. +18168331000.
URL: http://www.cofchrist.org/

History 6 Apr 1830, USA. Founded 6 Apr 1830, Fayette NY (USA), by Joseph Smith Jr, on whose death in 1844 the church was dispersed into widely scattered groups. Joseph Smith III succeeded his father and was ordained prophet-president of the church on 6 Apr 1860, when the Church became organized under the title *Reorganized Church of Jesus Christ of Latter Day Saints*. Current title adopted, 6 Apr 2001. **Aims** Proclaim Jesus Christ and promote communities of joy, hope, love and peace. **Structure** Council of Twelve Apostles, comprising 12 high priests; First Presidency; Presiding Bishopric; Presiding Evangelist; Leadership Ministries. **Activities** Networking/liaising; events/meetings. **Publications** *10 Minute News Report* (12 a year). **Members** About 250,000 in over 50 countries (not specified). [2014.12.04/XM0875/F]

♦ Community Colleges for International Development (internationally oriented national body)
♦ Community-COST Concertation Agreement on a Concerted Action Project on the Effects of Processing on the Physical Properties of Foodstuffs (1980 treaty)
♦ Community-COST Concertation Agreement on a Concerted Action Project in the Field of Analysis of Organic Micro-pollutants in Water (1980 treaty)
♦ Community-COST Concertation Agreement on a Concerted Action Project in the Field of Physico-chemical Behaviour of Atmospheric Pollutants (1980 treaty)
♦ Community-COST Concertation Agreement on a Concerted Action Project in the Field of Teleinformatics (1981 treaty)
♦ Community-COST Concertation Agreement on a Concerted Action Project in the Field of Treatment and Use of Sewage Sludge (1979 treaty)

♦ Community Court of Justice 04393

Cour de justice de la communauté

Pres Plot 1137, Dar es Salaam Crescent, Off Aminu Kano Crescent, Wuse II, Abuja, Federal Capital Territory, Nigeria. T. +23495240780. Fax +23495240780.
URL: http://www.ecowas.int/

History 6 Jul 1991, Abuja (Nigeria), when Protocol was signed. Part of an agreement to rationalize subregional institutions in West Africa within the framework of *Economic Community of West African States (ECOWAS, #05312)* so that ECOWAS would eventually become the sole economic community of the West African region. Protocol entered into force 5 Nov 1996. **Structure** The Court consists of President, Vice-President and 5 further judges appointed from member states of ECOWAS. **Members** Membership countries not specified. [2008/XF7200/F*]

♦ Community of the Cross of Nails (internationally oriented national body)

♦ Community of Democracies (CD) 04394

Comunidad de las Democracias (CdD)

Main Office al Ujazdowksie 41, 00-540 Warsaw, Poland. T. +48223195620. Fax +48223195628. E-mail: info@community-democracies.org.
URL: http://www.community-democracies.org/

History First meeting held Jun 2000, Warsaw (Poland), when "Warsaw Declaration Towards a Community of Democracies" was signed. Permanent Secretariat set up 2009 and structural reformed conducted 2011. **Aims** Support democratic transition and consolidation worldwide; help bridge the gap between principles of democracy and universal human rights and their practice by assisting societies in the development and strengthening of democratic institutions and values, identifying, alerting and responding to threats to democracy so as to assist states to remain on the path to democracy, supporting and defending civil society in all countries, advancing broad-based participation in democratic governance, and giving a voice to those working peacefully for democracy in all countries. **Structure** Presidency; Governing Council; Permanent Secretariat; *International Steering Committee of the Community of Democracies (ISC/CD)*. Executive Secretariat. **Languages** English. **Staff** 14.00 FTE, paid. **Finance** Funded through core and project-oriented funding from Governing Council Member States. **Events** *Ministerial Conference* 2021, *Ministerial Meeting* Ulaanbaatar (Mongolia) 2013, *Ministerial Meeting* Vilnius (Lithuania) 2011, *Ministerial Meeting* Mali 2007, *Ministerial conference / Ministerial Meeting* Santiago (Chile) 2005. **Publications** Case studies; handbooks; reports.
Members Governing Council (27):
Canada, Cape Verde, Chile, Costa Rica, El Salvador, Estonia, Finland, Guatemala, Hungary, India, Italy, Japan, Korea Rep, Lithuania, Mali, Mexico, Mongolia, Morocco, Nigeria, Philippines, Poland, Portugal, Romania, South Africa, Sweden, Uruguay, USA.
IGO Relations Supported by: *International Institute for Democracy and Electoral Assistance (International IDEA, #13872)*; *OAS (#17629)*; *United States Agency for International Development (USAID)*. Close relations with: *Council of Europe (CE, #04881)*; *OSCE – Office for Democratic Institutions and Human Rights (OSCE/ODIHR, #17902)*; *United Nations (UN, #20515)*. **NGO Relations** Supported by: *Council for a Community of Democracies (CCD)*; *Westminster Foundation for Democracy (WFD)*. Partner of: *World Leadership Alliance – Club de Madrid (WLA-CdM, #21619)*. Cooperates with various NGOs, including: *CIVICUS: World Alliance for Citizen Participation (#03962)*; *Commonwealth Human Rights Initiative (CHRI, #04340)*; *Freedom House*; *International Centre for Democratic Transition (ICDT)*; *International Service for Human Rights (ISHR, #14841)*. [2022/XJ1033/F*]

♦ Community Development and Action International / see CODA International Training
♦ Community Development and Advocacy Centre (internationally oriented national body)

♦ Community Development Carbon Fund (CDCF) 04395

Contact IBRD Headquarters, Carbon Finance Unit, 1818 H St NW, Washington DC 20433, USA. T. +12024771234. Fax +12024776391.
URL: http://carbonfinance.org/

History 2 Sep 2002, as a joint initiative of *International Emissions Trading Association (IETA, #13262)*, *United Nations Framework Convention on Climate Change – Secretariat (UNFCCC, #20564)* and *International Bank for Reconstruction and Development (IBRD, #12317)*. Operational as of Mar 2003, within IBRD. **Aims** Provide carbon finance, particularly to small scale projects located in the poorest areas of the developing world, including countries designated as Least Developed Countries (LDCs) or that qualify for lending from lending from the International Development Association, and that generate both CDM compliant green house gas emission reductions through investments in clean technologies and measurable benefits for local communities. **Structure** Administered by *International Bank for Reconstruction and Development (IBRD, #12317)* (World Bank), as part of Carbon Finance Unit. **Activities** As of 1 Oct 2007, signed 20 Emissions Reduction Purchase Agreements (ERPA) for the purchase of a total of 7.10 million tons of carbon dioxide equivalent for a value of US$ 60.1 million. **Publications** Annual Report. Reports.
Members Governments (9); private firms (16). Governmental members in 7 countries:
Austria, Belgium, Canada, Italy, Luxembourg, Netherlands, Spain. [2010.08.23/XF6756/f/F]

♦ Community Development International (internationally oriented national body)
♦ Community Development Society (internationally oriented national body)
♦ Community Directed Development Foundation (internationally oriented national body)
♦ Community Empowerment Initiative / see African Agency For Integrated Development
♦ Community Engagement Voluntary Service (internationally oriented national body)
♦ Community of European Lock and Fitting Industries / see European Federation of Associations of Locks and Builders Hardware Manufacturers (#07054)
♦ Community of European Management Schools / see CEMS – The Global Alliance in Management Education (#03635)

♦ Community of European Railway and Infrastructure Companies (CER) 04396

Exec Dir Av des Arts 53, 1000 Brussels, Belgium. T. +3222130870. Fax +3225125231. E-mail: contact@cer.be.
URL: https://www.cer.be/

History 1988. Founded to represent the railways vis-à-vis the EU institutions and political, economic and social interest groups in Europe. Former names and other names: *Community of European Railways (CER)* – former; *Communauté Européenne du rail (CER)* – former; *Gemeinschaft der Europäischen Bahnen (GEB)* – former; *Communauté Européenne du rail et des compagnies d'infrastructure (CER)* – former; *Gemeinschaft der Europäischen Bahnen und Infrastrukturgesellschaften (GEB)* – former. Registration: Banque-Carrefour des Entreprises, Belgium; EU Transparency Register, No/ID: 7574621118-27. **Aims** Represent interests of members towards EU policy makers and transport stakeholders; advocate rail as the backbone of a competitive and sustainable transport system in Europe. **Structure** General Assembly; Management Committee; Secretariat in Brussels (Belgium), headed by Executive Director. **Languages** English. **Staff** 20.00 FTE, paid. **Finance** By member companies. **Events** *TEN-T Conference* Brussels (Belgium) 2022, *CER – EU Presidency Round Table* Brussels (Belgium) 2021, *Conference on Mobility as a Service* Brussels (Belgium) 2019, *Round Table on Rail Europe's Climate Solution* Brussels (Belgium) 2018, *Round Table on the Future of Transport Investments* Brussels (Belgium) 2018. **Publications** Annual Report; newsletters; reports; position papers.

Members Railway undertakings, their national associations as well as infrastructure managers and vehicle leasing companies. Members/partners in 37 countries:
Albania, Austria, Belgium, Bosnia-Herzegovina, Bulgaria, Croatia, Czechia, Denmark, Estonia, Finland, France, Georgia, Germany, Greece, Hungary, Ireland, Israel, Italy, Latvia, Lithuania, Luxembourg, Moldova, Montenegro, Netherlands, North Macedonia, Norway, Poland, Portugal, Romania, Serbia, Slovakia, Slovenia, Spain, Sweden, Switzerland, UK, Ukraine.
NGO Relations Member of (2): *European Logistics Platform (ELP, #07711)*; *Federation of European and International Associations Established in Belgium (FAIB, #09508).* [2022.02.15/XF0818/v/F]

♦ Community of European Railways / see Community of European Railway and Infrastructure Companies (#04396)
♦ Community of European Shipyards Associations (inactive)

♦ Community of European Solar Radio Astronomers (CESRA) 04397

Chair School of Physics and Astronomy, Univ of Glasgow, Glasgow, G12 8QQ, UK. T. +441413302499.
URL: http://cesra.net/
History 1972, Zurich (Switzerland). **Aims** Promote studies of the radio emission of the Sun and related topics including solar-like stars; promote new instrumental developments; facilitate contacts between observers at different wavelengths; stimulate collaboration between observers and theoreticians and solar and stellar physicists; encourage young scientists in the field of solar radio physics. **Structure** Board. **Activities** Events/meetings. **Events** *Workshop on the Sun and the Inner Heliosphere* Potsdam (Germany) 2019, *European Solar Physics Meeting* Budapest (Hungary) 2017, *Workshop on Solar Radio Physics from the Chromosphere to near Earth* Orléans (France) 2016, *New eyes looking at solar activity – challenges for theory and simulations* Prague (Czech Rep) 2013, *Workshop* La Roche-en-Ardenne (Belgium) 2010. **Publications** *Solar Physics Topical Issue*; *Solar Radio Science Highlights.*
Members Individuals in 20 countries:
Belgium, Brazil, China, Croatia, Czechia, Denmark, Finland, France, Germany, Greece, Israel, Italy, Japan, Netherlands, Portugal, Russia, Switzerland, UK, Ukraine, USA. [2018.06.01/XF4573/v/F]

♦ Community of Evaluators in South Asia (COE) 04398

Pres IPID, No 23, P Ruban Peiris Mawatha, Kalubowila, Dehiwela, Sri Lanka.
Sec address not obtained.
URL: http://www.communityofevaluators.org/
History Founded Oct 2008, as part of the project Advancing Evaluation Theory and Practices in South Asia. **Aims** Promote and enhance the quality of the theory and practice of evaluation in South Asia and contribute to the same, particularly from a South Asian perspective, globally. **Events** *Evaluation Conclave Meeting* Kathmandu (Nepal) 2013, *Making evaluation matter* Delhi (India) 2010.
Members Full (36) in 6 countries:
Afghanistan, Bangladesh, India, Nepal, Pakistan, Sri Lanka.
IGO Relations Major support provided by *International Development Research Centre (IDRC, #13162).* **NGO Relations** Member of: *International Organisation for Cooperation in Evaluation (IOCE, #14426).* Cooperates with: *EvalPartners (#09208).* [2018/XJ8280/E]

♦ Community Exchange System (CES) 04399

Co-founder/Dir PO Box 30196, Tokai, Cape Town, 7966, South Africa. T. +27216854741. E-mail: info@community-exchange.org.
URL: https://www.community-exchange.org/
History 1 Feb 2003, Cape Town (South Africa). Former names and other names: *Cape Town Talent Exchange* – former. Registration: Section 21, Start date: Oct 2008, South Africa. **Aims** As a global, *Internet*-based *trading network*, allow participants to exchange goods and services without using *money*; focus on providing and requesting what is really needed; create an environment of openness and transparency; promote equality, fairness and balance; assist in respecting the environment; bring the advantages of a trading network to those unable to get *credit* or loans by traditional methods; enable marginalized and independent communities to become *self-sustaining*. **Structure** 1210 exchange groups (May 2021). **Staff** 4.00 FTE, paid. **Finance** Self-funded. **Activities** Advocacy/lobbying/activism; awareness raising; capacity building; events/meetings; guidance/assistance/consulting; knowledge management/information dissemination; networking/liaising; projects/programmes. Active in all member countries.
Members Communities (1210) in 104 countries and territories:
Argentina, Australia, Austria, Belgium, Bolivia, Botswana, Brazil, Bulgaria, Cameroon, Canada, Chile, China, Colombia, Costa Rica, Croatia, Curaçao, Cyprus, Czechia, Denmark, Dominican Rep, Ecuador, Egypt, Estonia, Eswatini, Ethiopia, Fiji, Finland, France, Germany, Ghana, Gibraltar, Greece, Grenada, Guatemala, Honduras, Hong Kong, Hungary, India, Indonesia, Iran Islamic Rep, Ireland, Israel, Italy, Jordan, Kenya, Latvia, Lebanon, Lesotho, Liberia, Lithuania, Luxembourg, Madagascar, Malaysia, Mauritius, Mexico, Moldova, Namibia, Nepal, Netherlands, New Zealand, Nicaragua, Nigeria, North Macedonia, Norway, Pakistan, Palestine, Panama, Paraguay, Peru, Philippines, Poland, Portugal, Puerto Rico, Qatar, Réunion, Romania, Russia, Saudi Arabia, Serbia, Slovenia, South Africa, Spain, St Maarten, Sudan, Sweden, Switzerland, Taiwan, Tanzania UR, Thailand, Trinidad-Tobago, Tunisia, Türkiye, Turks-Caicos, Uganda, UK, Ukraine, United Arab Emirates, Uruguay, USA, Vanuatu, Venezuela, Virgin Is USA, Zambia, Zimbabwe. [2021.05.20/XJ7903/F]

♦ Community and Family Services International (internationally oriented national body)
♦ Community Fisheries Control Agency / see European Fisheries Control Agency (#07266)
♦ Community Forestry International (internationally oriented national body)
♦ Community Forests International (internationally oriented national body)
♦ Community of French-Language Television Programmes (inactive)
♦ Community of Friends in Need (internationally oriented national body)
♦ Community Health Global Network (internationally oriented national body)

♦ Community Health and Information Network (CHAIN) 04400

Exec Dir Gayaza Zirobwe Road, Kiwenda, PO Box 16051, Kampala, Uganda. T. +256787499087 – +256787(256752693774. E-mail: regina@chainproject.co.ug.
Program Manager address not obtained. T. +256782304880.
URL: http://www.chainproject.co.ug/
History 1998. **Aims** Promote the empowerment of people living with *HIV* and *AIDS*; galvanise key stakeholders in the struggle against HIV and AIDS; focus on *capacity building* and strengthening networks and partnerships of *grass roots* NGOs operating in the HIV and AIDS sector in *Africa*. **Structure** Offices in Kigali (Rwanda) and Kampala (Uganda). **Activities** Runs national HIV and AIDS, TB, Malaria and NCD's health programmes, with emphasis on engagement with the community, in particular with community leaders, youth, women, OVC and their guardians, in all stages of the project cycle (needs assessment, design, implementations and evaluation). Main areas: HIV prevention; treatment and care; policy development; treatment advocacy; supporting orphans and vulnerable children (OVC); monitoring and evaluation. Works in Kenya, Uganda, Tanzania UR, Congo DR, Rwanda and Burundi. **NGO Relations** Member of: *International Alliance of Patients' Organizations (IAPO, #11633).* [2008/XM1077/E]

♦ Community Informatics Research Network (CIRN) 04401

Sec Centre for Community Networking Research, Monach Univ, PO Box 197, Caulfield VIC EAST 3145, Australia. T. +61399031801.
Aims Promote and represent community informatics research internationally; act as a research forum for researchers and practitioners in the community informatics and community networking fields. **Finance** Members' dues. **Events** *Annual conference* Cape Town (South Africa) 2005, *Annual conference* Prato, RN (Italy) 2004. **Publications** *Journal of Community Informatics* – electronic newsletter.
Members in 7 countries:
Australia, Canada, Italy, Russia, South Africa, UK, USA. [2014/XJ4383/F]

♦ Community Information, Empowerment and Transparency (internationally oriented national body)
♦ Community Information and Epidemiological Technologies / see Community Information, Empowerment and Transparency
♦ Community of Interests of Leading European Woodworking and Wood Processing Machinery Resellers / see Combois (#04122)
♦ Community of Latin American and Caribbean States (#04432)
♦ Community Learning Centres (see: #02002)

♦ Community Media Forum Europe (CMFE) 04402

Pres Rue de la Linière 11, 1060 Brussels, Belgium. E-mail: info@cmfe.eu.
Sec address not obtained.
URL: http://www.cmfe.eu/
History 5 Nov 2004, Halle (Saale) (Germany). Registration: Banque-Carrefour des Entreprises, No/ID: 0822.992.342, Start date: 9 Feb 2010, Belgium; EU Transparency Register, No/ID: 40306691699-12, Start date: 15 May 2009. **Aims** Strengthen participation of the Community Media Sector ("Third Media Sector") in European discussion and decision-making processes at a moment when freedom of expression and free access to information are increasingly endangered by the consequences of concentration in the media field. **Structure** Annual General Assembly; Board of Directors. **Languages** English. **Staff** 2.00 FTE, voluntary. **Finance** Sources: members' dues. **Activities** Advocacy/lobbying/activism; events/meetings; projects/programmes; publishing activities; research/documentation. **Events** *General Assembly* Brussels (Belgium) 2022, *Annual Conference* Hamburg (Germany) 2021, *Annual Conference* Luxembourg (Luxembourg) 2020, *Annual Conference* Siena (Italy) 2019, *Annual Conference* Sheffield (UK) 2018. **Publications** *CMFE newsletter* (12 a year); *The Radio Journal.*
Members Individual (45); Organizational (61). Organizations in 24 countries:
Austria, Belgium, Bosnia-Herzegovina, Croatia, Cyprus, Czechia, Denmark, Finland, France, Germany, Hungary, Ireland, Italy, Montenegro, Netherlands, Norway, Poland, Romania, Slovenia, Spain, Sweden, Switzerland, Türkiye, UK.
Included in the above, 1 organization listed in this Yearbook:
Association mondiale des radiodiffuseurs communautaires (AMARC, #02810) (Europe).
Affiliate (18) in 5 countries:
Bangladesh, Canada, Nepal, Pakistan, USA.
Consultative Status Consultative status granted from: *Council of Europe (CE, #04881)* (Participatory Status). **NGO Relations** Member of (2): *AMARC Europe (#00764)*; *Digital Radio Mondiale Consortium (DRM, #05082).* [2022.10.21/XJ6886/y/F]

♦ Community of Mediterranean Universities (CMU) 04403

Communauté des universités méditerranéennes (CUM) – Comunità delle Università Mediterranee (CUM)
Pres Villa La Rocca, Via Celso Ulpiani 27, 70126 Bari BA, Italy. E-mail: presidente@cum.uniba.it.
URL: http://www.cmungo.eu/
History 6 Sep 1983, Bari (Italy). Sep 1983, Bari (Italy), by meeting of Rectors of Universities of the Mediterranean Basin. Functions as a component network of *UNESCO Mediterranean Programme (inactive)*, based on *International Convention on the Recognition of Studies, Diplomas and Degrees in Higher Education in the Arab States and European States Bordering on the Mediterranean (1976).* **Aims** Promote scientific and cultural cooperation in the Mediterranean region; reaffirm the role of culture and of scientific and technical research in solving the complex problems posed by its development; promote scientific research employing the competences and resources possessed of each CMU adhering university, taking into account their features. **Structure** General Assembly (every 2 years); Council; President; General Secretary; College of Auditors; Field Offices (2); Main Office in Bari (Italy). **Languages** Arabic, English, French. **Staff** Paid; voluntary. **Finance** Members' dues. Projects. **Activities** Research and development; meeting activities; training/education; awards/prizes/competitions. **Events** *General Assembly and Workshop / Biennial General Assembly* Trabzon (Turkey) 2015, *Biennial General Assembly* Istanbul (Turkey) 2012, *Mediterranean photonics conference* Ischia (Italy) 2008, *Biennial General Assembly* Izmir (Turkey) 2006, *Forum on the Mediterranean higher education area* Izmir (Turkey) 2006. **Publications** *The Mediterranean – La Méditerranée* (periodical). *Collection CMU Series.* Student reference guide; assembly proceedings.
Members Universities (about 170) in 21 countries and territories of the Mediterranean region:
Albania, Algeria, Croatia, Cyprus, Egypt, France, Greece, Israel, Italy, Lebanon, Libya, Malta, Mauritania, Montenegro, Morocco, Palestine, Portugal, Spain, Syrian AR, Tunisia, Türkiye.
Consultative Status Consultative status granted from: *UNESCO (#20322)* (Consultative Status). **IGO Relations** Observers from: *CIHEAM – International Centre for Advanced Mediterranean Agronomic Studies (CIHEAM, #03927).* Links within the framework of UNESCO's Mediterranean Programme: *Arab League Educational, Cultural and Scientific Organization (ALECSO, #01003)*; *Institut du monde arabe (IMA, #11324)*; *Council of Europe (CE, #04881)*; *OECD (#17693).* **NGO Relations** Observers from national organizations and from: *Centre of Integrated Geomorphology for the Mediterranean Area (CGIAM).* Instrumental in setting up: *United Nations Academic Impact (UNAI, #20516).* Founding member of: *Centre of Research and Studies for the Eastern Mediterranean (#03782)*; *Euro-Mediterranean University (EMUNI, #05728).* Member of: *EuroMed Permanent University Forum (EPUF, #05731)*; *Programme for Palestinian-European-American Cooperation in Education (PEACE Programme, #18527)*; *Réseau méditerranéen des écoles d'ingénieurs (RMEI, #18899)*; *United Nations Academic Impact (UNAI, #20516).* Instrumental in setting up: *Avicenna Project (inactive).* Links within the framework of UNESCO's Mediterranean Programme: *Centre for Mediterranean and International Studies, Tunis (no recent information).* Founding member: *Euro-Mediterranean University (EMUNI, #05728).* [2022/XF8299/F]

♦ Community Organized Relief Effort (internationally oriented national body)
♦ Community Parliament / see Parliament of the Economic Community of West African States (#18221)
♦ Community Partners International (internationally oriented national body)
♦ Community Patent Interim Committee (inactive)

♦ Community Plant Variety Office (CPVO) 04404

Office communautaire des variétés végétales (OCVV) – Oficina Comunitaria de Variedades Vegetales – Gemeinschaftliches Sortenamt – Instituto Comunitario das Variedades Vegetais – Ufficio Comunitario delle Varietà Vegetali – Communautair Bureau voor Plantenrassen – Gemenskapens Växtsortsmyndighet – EF-Sortsmyndigheden – Yhteisön Kasvilajikevirasto – Kinotiko Grafio Fitikon Pikilion – Odrudovy úrad Spolecenstvi – Urad Spolocenstva pre Odrody Rastlin – Közösségi Növényfajta Hivatal – Wspólnotowy Urzad Odmian Roslin – Urad Skupnosti za Rastlinske Sorte – Ühenduse Sordiamet – Kopienas Augu Skirnu Birojs – Bendrijos Augalu Veisliu Tarnyba – L-Uffiċċju Komunitarju tal-Varjetajiet ta' Pjanti – Ured Zajednice za Zastitu Biljnih Sorti
Pres 3 bd Maréchal Foch, CS 10121, 49101 Angers CEDEX 2, France. T. +33241256400. Fax +33241256410. E-mail: cpvo@cpvo.europa.eu.
URL: http://cpvo.europa.eu/
History 27 Apr 1995, Brussels (Belgium). Established pursuant to proposal of *European Commission (EC, #06633)*, following adoption of Regulation (EC) No 2100/94 by *Council of the European Union (#04895)*, 27 Jul 1994. One of the decentralized agencies set up by the *European Union (EU, #08967)* to carry out specialized technical or scientific work on a wide range of subjects. **Aims** Deliver and promote an efficient property rights system that supports creation of new plant varieties for the benefit of society; implement the system of *European Union* plant variety *rights*, the sole and exclusive form of *intellectual property* rights for plant varieties, valid throughout the EU. **Structure** Administrative Council, consisting of representatives of each Member State of the European Union and a representative of the European Commission. Office is managed by President (nominated by Council of the European Union), assisted by Vice-President, and consists of 3 separate units (Technical; Administration; Legal), and 4 supporting services (IT; Human Resources; Quality Audit; PR). Board of Appeal, comprising Chairman and alternate, and members chosen by Chairman from a list depending on the cases under consideration. National plant variety offices act as Examination Offices. Reports to: *European Court of Auditors (#06854).* **Languages** Czech, Danish, Dutch, English, Estonian, Finnish, French, German, Hungarian, Irish Gaelic, Italian, Latvian, Lithuanian, Maltese, Polish, Portuguese, Slovakian, Slovene, Spanish, Swedish. **Staff** 50.00 FTE, paid. **Finance** Self-financing through fees. **Activities** Processes technical examination in relation to and decides on applications for Community plant variety rights. Examination reports of responsible authorities may be considered in the case of technical examinations already carried out or being carried out for official purposes in a European Union Member State. Decides on proposals for variety denominations. Promotes PVR in Europe and internationally. Cooperates with bodies related to enforcement such as the EUIPO Observatory, EUROPPOL, CEPOL and other law professionals. **Events** *Regional seminar on enforcement of plant variety in rights* Madrid (Spain) 2007, *Regional seminar on enforcement of plant variety in rights* Warsaw (Poland) 2006, *Regional seminar on enforcement of plant variety in rights* Brussels (Belgium) 2005. **Publications** *Official Gazette of the Community Plant Variety Office* (6 a year); *CPVO Newsletter* (2 a year). Annual Report; explanatory booklet.
Members Member States of the European Union (27):

Austria, Belgium, Bulgaria, Croatia, Cyprus, Czechia, Denmark, Estonia, Finland, France, Germany, Greece, Hungary, Ireland, Italy, Latvia, Lithuania, Luxembourg, Malta, Netherlands, Poland, Portugal, Romania, Slovakia, Slovenia, Spain, Sweden.
IGO Relations EU Agencies and Institutions; *European Patent Office (EPO, #08166)*; *European Union Intellectual Property Office (EUIPO, #08996)* Observatory; *Union internationale pour la protection des obtentions végétales (UPOV, #20436)*. **NGO Relations** Member of (1): *EU Agencies Network (EUAN, #05564)*.
[2019.12.17/XE2347/**E***]

♦ Community of Portuguese-Speaking Countries (#04430)
♦ Community of Practice for Caribbean Immigrant Entrepreneurs (unconfirmed)

♦ Community of Protestant Churches in Europe (CPCE) 04405

Communion d'églises protestantes en Europe (CEPE) – Gemeinschaft Evangelischer Kirchen in Europa (GEKE)

Main Office Severin-Schreiber-Gasse 3, 1180 Vienna, Austria. T. +4314791523900. Fax +4314791523110. E-mail: geke@leuenberg.eu.
URL: http://www.leuenberg.eu/

History Mar 1973, Leuenberg (Switzerland). Founded when Agreement between the Reformation Churches in Europe (Leuenberg Agreement) was signed. Former names and other names: *Leuenberg Church Fellowship* – former (Mar 1973 to 2003); *Communion ecclésiale de Leuenberg* – former (Mar 1973 to 2003); *Leuenberger Kirchengemeinschaft* – former (Mar 1973 to 2003); *Communion of Protestant Churches in Europe* – alias. **Aims** Promote unity and community of Protestant churches through common witness and service, especially joint theological doctrinal conversations and common statements. **Structure** General Assembly (every 6 years); Praesidium; Council; Regional groups, including: *Conference of Rhine Churches (#04646)*. **Languages** English, French, German. **Staff** 7.00 FTE, paid. **Finance** Members' dues. **Events** *General Assembly* Basel (Switzerland) 2018, *Meeting* Estonia 2012, *General assembly* Florence (Italy) 2012, *Meeting / General Assembly* Florence (Italy) 2012, *Meeting* Florence (Italy) 2011. **Publications** *CPCE Focus* (4 a year). *Leuenberger Texte/Leuenberg Documents* – book series. Songbook; publications on ethical matters.
Members Churches (945) in 31 countries:
Argentina, Austria, Belgium, Croatia, Czechia, Denmark, Ecuador, Estonia, France, Germany, Greece, Hungary, Ireland, Italy, Latvia, Liechtenstein, Lithuania, Luxembourg, Netherlands, Norway, Poland, Portugal, Romania, Russia, Serbia, Slovakia, Slovenia, Spain, UK, Ukraine, Uruguay.
Participating churches (4) in 3 countries:
Finland, Iceland, Sweden.
[2021/XM3286/**D**]

♦ Community of the Regions of Jura / see Conférence TransJurassience

♦ Community of Sahel-Saharan States (CEN-SAD) 04406

Communauté des états sahelo-sahariens (COMESSA)

SG Interim address not obtained. E-mail: censad_sg@yahoo.com.
URL: http://www.censad.org/

History Feb 1998, at the initiative of the Government of Libyan AJ. Secretariat will be set up in Bamako (Mali). **Aims** Promote economic, political and cultural integration in the region. **Structure** Organs (5): Conference of the Heads of States (meets annual); Executive Council (meets twice a year); Secretariat General, headed by Secretary General; African Bank for Development and Trade; Economic, Social and Cultural Council. Includes: *Organisation ferroviaire régionale de la CEN-SAD (see: #04406)*. **Finance** Main support from the Government of Libyan AJ. **Events** *Summit* Ndjamena (Chad) 2013, *High-Level Meeting* Rabat (Morocco) 2013, *Assemblée générale constitutive* Tripoli (Libyan AJ) 2005, *Réunion sur le transport ferroviaire et les chemins de fer dans les pays membres de la CEN-SAD* Tripoli (Libyan AJ) 2005, *Session / Conference of the Heads of States* Bamako (Mali) 2004.
Members Governments of 21 countries:
Benin, Burkina Faso, Central African Rep, Chad, Côte d'Ivoire, Djibouti, Egypt, Eritrea, Gambia, Guinea-Bissau, Liberia, Libya, Mali, Morocco, Niger, Nigeria, Senegal, Somalia, Sudan, Togo, Tunisia.
IGO Relations Accredited to the Conference of the Parties of: *Secretariat of the United Nations Convention to Combat Desertification (Secretariat of the UNCCD, #19208)*. Member of: *Africa Partnership Forum (APF, #00510)*; *Observatoire du Sahara et du Sahel (OSS, #17636)*. Regional Economic Community of: *African Union (AU, #00488)*. Cooperation agreement with: *Organisation internationale de la Francophonie (OIF, #17809)*; *UNESCO (#20322)*. Permanent Observer to: *ECOSOC (#05331)*. Observer to General Assembly of: *United Nations (UN, #20515)*. Observer to: *Codex Alimentarius Commission (CAC, #04081)*; *International Organization for Migration (IOM, #14454)*.
[2015/XD7706/**D***]

♦ Community of Sant'Egidio (religious order)
♦ Community Service Volunteers / see Volunteering Matters

♦ Community World Service Asia 04407

Karachi Office PO Box 20048, Karachi, Pakistan. T. +922134390541. Fax +922134390922. E-mail: info@communityworldservice.asia.
URL: https://communityworldservice.asia/

History 1954, Pakistan. Former names and other names: *Church World Service-Pakistan/Afghanistan* – former. Registration: Pakistan. **Aims** Implement *humanitarian* and development initiatives in Asia. **Activities** Humanitarian/emergency aid; training/education. **NGO Relations** Member of (8): *ACT Alliance (#00081)*; *Active Learning Network for Accountability and Performance in Humanitarian Action (ALNAP, #00101)*; *Asian Disaster Reduction and Response Network (ADRRN, #01428)*; *CHS Alliance (#03911)*; *Global Network of Civil Society Organizations for Disaster Reduction (GNDR, #10485)*; *Global NPO Coalition on FATF (#10508)*; *International Council of Voluntary Agencies (ICVA, #13092)*; *Start Network (#19969)*.
[2023/XM4449/**F**]

♦ **COMNAP** Council of Managers of National Antarctic Programs (#04910)
♦ **CoMO** Confederation of Meningitis Organisations (#04568)
♦ COMODIA – International Conference on Modeling and Diagnostics for Advanced Engine (meeting series)
♦ COmON Foundation (internationally oriented national body)
♦ COmON Stichting (internationally oriented national body)
♦ COMPACI / see Cotton House Africa
♦ Compagnia di Gesù (religious order)
♦ Compagnia di Maria (religious order)
♦ Compagnia di Maria per l'Educazione dei Sordomuti (religious order)
♦ Compagnia delle Opere (internationally oriented national body)
♦ Compagnia dei Sacerdoti di Santo Sulpizio (religious order)
♦ Compagnia di San Paolo (religious order)
♦ Compagnia di Santa Orsola (religious order)
♦ Compagnia di Santa Teresa di Gesù (religious order)
♦ Compagnie arabe de transports maritimes pétroliers (see: #17854)
♦ Compagnie des Filles de la Charité de Saint Vincent de Paul (religious order)
♦ Compagnie inter-arabe pour la garantie des investissements / see Arab Investment and Export Credit Guarantee Corporation (#00997)
♦ Compagnie de Jésus (religious order)
♦ Compagnie de Marie pour l'Education des Sourds-Muets (religious order)
♦ Compagnie des Prêtres de Saint-Sulpice (religious order)
♦ Compagnie de réassurance de la ZEP-RE / see PTA Reinsurance Company (#18561)
♦ Compagnie de réassurance de la Zone d'échanges préférentiels (#18561)
♦ Compagnie de Sainte-Thérèse de Jésus (religious order)
♦ Compagnie de Sainte-Ursule (religious order)
♦ Compagnie de Saint Paul (religious order)
♦ Compagnonnages européens / see Confederation of European Companions (#04522)
♦ Compagnons de l'éducation nouvelle / see World Education Fellowship (#21370)
♦ Compañeros de las Américas (internationally oriented national body)
♦ Companheiros das Américas (internationally oriented national body)
♦ Compañia Española de Financiación de Desarrollo (internationally oriented national body)
♦ Compañia de las Hijas de la Caridad de San Vicente de Paúl (religious order)
♦ Compañia de Jesús (religious order)
♦ Compañia Latinoamericana de Garantias de Inversiones (no recent information)
♦ Compañia de Maria (religious order)
♦ Companions in Work (internationally oriented national body)
♦ Company of the Daughters of Charity of St Vincent de Paul (religious order)

♦ Company for Habitat and Housing in Africa (Shelter-Afrique) 04408

Société pour l'habitat et le logement territorial en Afrique

Managing Dir Shelter Afrique Centre, Longonot Road, PO Box 41479, Nairobi, Kenya. T. +254204978000. E-mail: info@shelterafrique.org.
URL: http://www.shelterafrique.org/

History 8 Dec 1982, Nairobi (Kenya). 8-9 Dec 1982, Nairobi (Kenya), with the assistance of African Development Bank, at 1st General Meeting when Board of Directors was appointed. First preparatory meeting had been held Sep 1981, Arusha (Tanzania UR); constituent charter approved May 1982, Lusaka (Zambia). Commenced operations 19 Oct 1983. Headquarters in Nairobi. **Aims** Identify, finance and implement housing and related urban infrastructure projects to achieve the goal of housing for all. **Structure** Limited company, owned by African governments and regional agencies ADB and Africa-RE. General Meeting of the Shareholders (annual); Board of Directors; Managing Director/Chief Executive, assisted by Directors and Heads of Department. **Languages** English, French. **Finance** Authorized share capital: US$ 1,000,000,000. **Activities** Capacity building; guidance/assistance/consulting. **Events** *Annual General Meeting* Marrakech (Morocco) 2019, *Annual General Meeting* Nairobi (Kenya) 2018, *Annual General Meeting* Nairobi (Kenya) 2002, *Annual General Meeting* Banjul (Gambia) 2001, *Annual General Meeting* Nairobi (Kenya) 2000. **Publications** *Housing the New Africa: Challenges and Opportunities for the Future* (2015). White paper; studies.
Members Class "A": Member States; Class "B": organizations and institutions. Charter signed by 36 States:
Algeria, Benin, Botswana, Burkina Faso, Burundi, Cameroon, Cape Verde, Central African Rep, Congo Brazzaville, Djibouti, Gabon, Gambia, Guinea, Guinea-Bissau, Kenya, Liberia, Madagascar, Malawi, Mali, Mauritania, Mauritius, Morocco, Namibia, Niger, Nigeria, Sao Tomé-Principe, Senegal, Seychelles, Sierra Leone, Somalia, Tanzania UR, Togo, Tunisia, Uganda, Zambia, Zimbabwe.
Class "B" Shareholders (2):
African Development Bank (ADB, #00283); *African Reinsurance Corporation (AFRICA RE, #00438)*.
NGO Relations Partner of: *UNLEASH*. Instrumental in setting up: *African Housing Fund (AHF, no recent information)*; Pan-African Housing Fund.
[2018.08.20/XM1024/e/**F***]

♦ Company of Mary for the Education of Deaf-Mutes (religious order)
♦ Company of St Paul (religious order)
♦ Company of St Ursula (religious order)
♦ Comparative Education Society / see Comparative and International Education Society

♦ Comparative Education Society of Asia (CESA) 04409

Société d'éducation comparée en Asie

Japan Office Kyushu Univ, Dept of Education, 744 Motooka, Nishi Ward, Fukuoka, 819-0395 Japan. E-mail: cesa.secretariat@gmail.com.
URL: https://cesa.jp/

History Founded May 1995. Previously referred to as *Asian Society for Comparative Education (ASCE)*. **Aims** Promote comparative education as a scholarly field across Asia. **Structure** Board; Officers. **Languages** English, Japanese. **Staff** 2.00 FTE, paid. **Activities** Events/meetings. **Events** *Biennial Conference* Hiroshima (Japan) 2023, *Biennial Conference* Siem Reap (Cambodia) 2018, *Biennial Conference* Manila (Philippines) 2016, *Biennial Conference* Hangzhou (China) 2014, *Conference* Bangkok (Thailand) 2012. **NGO Relations** Member of: *World Council of Comparative Education Societies (WCCES, #21322)*.
[2022/XD7668/**D**]

♦ Comparative Education Society in Europe (CESE) 04410

Association d'éducation comparée en Europe – Gesellschaft für Vergleichende Erziehungswissenschaft in Europa

Sec-Treas Education Dept EUC, 6 Diogenes St, PO Box 22006, CY-1516 Nicosia, Cyprus.
URL: http://www.cese-europe.org/

History 6 May 1961, London (UK). Registered in accordance with Belgian law. **Aims** Encourage and promote comparative education and international studies in education. **Structure** General Meeting (every 2 years); Executive Committee, of 7 members; Secretary/Treasurer. **Languages** English, French, German. **Finance** Members' dues: euro 30. Sale of publications. **Events** *Biennial Congress* Freiburg-Breisgau (Germany) 2014, *Biennial Congress* Salamanca (Spain) 2012, *Biennial Congress* Uppsala (Sweden) 2010, *Biennial congress* Athens (Greece) 2008, *Biennial Congress* Granada (Spain) 2006. **Publications** *CESE Newsletter* in English, French. Conference proceedings (every 2 years).
Members University professors and research workers (including a limited number of Honorary members) in 49 countries:
Algeria, Argentina, Austria, Bahrain, Belgium, Brazil, Canada, Chile, Congo DR, Cyprus, Czechia, Denmark, Egypt, Finland, France, Germany, Greece, Hungary, Iceland, India, Iran Islamic Rep, Iraq, Ireland, Israel, Italy, Japan, Jordan, Korea Rep, Lebanon, Luxembourg, Morocco, Netherlands, Norway, Philippines, Poland, Portugal, Romania, Saudi Arabia, Serbia, South Africa, Spain, Sweden, Switzerland, Tunisia, Türkiye, UK, USA, Venezuela, Vietnam.
[2019/XD0388/v/**D**]

♦ Comparative and International Education Society (internationally oriented national body)
♦ Comparative and International Education Society of Canada (internationally oriented national body)

♦ Comparative International Governmental Accounting Research Network (CIGAR) 04411

Chairman Reggio Emilia Univ, Fac of Business and Economics, Via Berengario 51, 41100 Modena MO, Italy. T. +39592056711. Fax +39592056917.
URL: http://www.cigar-network.net/

History 1987, Chicago IL (USA). **Aims** Promote worldwide discussion and research on comparative governmental accounting. **Structure** Board, including Chairman. **Activities** Organizes biennial conference and biennial workshop. **Events** *Biennial Congress* Tokyo (Japan) 2023, *Preliminary Session on Comparative Governmental Accounting in Asia* Tokyo (Japan) 2022, *Biennial Congress* Valletta (Malta) 2015, *Biennial Conference* Birmingham (UK) 2013, *Conference* Cairo (Egypt) 2013. **Publications** *CIGAR Newsletter*.
[2011/XJ4174/**F**]

♦ Comparative Research Programme on Poverty (CROP) 04412

Interim Dir PO Box 7802, 5020 Bergen, Norway. T. +4755589744. E-mail: gripinequality@uib.no.
URL: http://www.crop.org/

History Dec 1992, Paris (France), at 19th General Assembly of *International Social Science Council (ISSC, inactive)*, when Programme was endorsed and Scientific Committee approved, the proposal having been endorsed in May 1991 by ISSC Executive Committee. CROP Secretariat opened, 2 Jun 1993. Agreement between ISSC and University of Bergen (Norway) incorporating CROP into the university's academic and administrative environment. Until 2017, used title of *ISSC Comparative Research Programme on Poverty (CROP)*. Transitioned into a new programme of University of Norway and *International Science Council (ISC, #14796)*, 2019. **Aims** Work in collaboration with knowledge networks, institutions and scholars to build independent and critical knowledge on poverty, and help shape policies for preventing and eradicating poverty. **Structure** Scientific Committee; Secretariat. **Languages** English. **Staff** 2.50 FTE, paid. **Finance** Institutional sponsors: University of Bergen; *International Science Council (ISC, #14796)*. **Activities** Events/meetings; research/documentation; awards/prizes/competitions. **Events** *International Workshop on Poverty and Peasant Persistence* Mexico City (Mexico) 2012, *World social science forum* Bergen (Norway) 2009. **Publications** *CROP Newsletter* (2 a year). *CROP International Studies in Poverty Research* – series. Books. Annual Report. Working Papers.
[2019/XK0591/**E**]

♦ Compartamos (internationally oriented national body)
♦ Compassion Africa Aged Foundation (internationally oriented national body)

♦ Compassion International (CI) 04413

Pres 12290 Voyager Pkwy, Colorado Springs CO 80921, USA. T. +17194877000. Fax +17194815805.
Mailing Address Compassion International, Colorado Springs CO 80997, USA.

URL: http://www.compassion.com/
History 1952, USA, by Rev Everett Swanson (1914-1965), as Everett Swanson Evangelistic Association. 1963, present name adopted. **Aims** Minister to needy *children*, releasing them from spiritual, economic, social and physical *poverty* and enabling them to become responsible and fulfilled *Christian* adults. Through support, education, training and guidance enable them to: be Christian in faith and deed; be responsible members of their families, churches and communities; support themselves and share with others in need; maintain their physical *wellbeing*. **Structure** Board of Directors consisting of: Chairman, Vice-Chairman, Secretary, Treasurer, 7 Directors, 4 Directors Emeritus. **Finance** Public support and revenue: contributions; child programme contributions from affiliated organizations and investment/bequest income. **Activities** Works through local churches in poor communities to foster the spiritual, physical, economic and social development of over 1.3 million children. **Events** *North Korea Ministry Summit* Seoul (Korea Rep) 2015. **Publications** *Compassion Magazine* (3 a year). Annual Report.
Members Active (assisting children and their families) in 26 countries:
Bangladesh, Bolivia, Brazil, Burkina Faso, Colombia, Dominican Rep, Ecuador, El Salvador, Ethiopia, Ghana, Guatemala, Haiti, Honduras, India, Indonesia, Kenya, Mexico, Nicaragua, Peru, Philippines, Rwanda, Sri Lanka, Tanzania UR, Thailand, Togo, Uganda.
Affiliated with organizations in 10 countries:
Australia, Canada, France, Germany, Italy, Korea Rep, Netherlands, New Zealand, Switzerland, UK.
NGO Relations Member of: *Accord Network*; *NetHope (#16979)*. Associate Member of: *World Evangelical Alliance (WEA, #21393)*. Australian branch is member of: *South Pacific Evangelical Alliance (SPEA, #19886)*.
[2017/XF3499/**F**]

♦ Compassion in World Farming (CIWF) 04414

Main Office River Court, Mill Lane, Godalming, GU7 1EZ, UK. T. +441483521950. Fax +441483861639. E-mail: compassion@ciwf.org.uk.
EU Office Place du Luxembourg 12, 1050 Brussels, Belgium.
URL: http://www.ciwf.org/
History 20 Oct 1967, Petersfield (UK). Former names and other names: *Compassion in World Farming International* – former. Registration: Charity Commission, No/ID: 1095050, England and Wales; EU Transparency Register, No/ID: 26535516539-45, Start date: 2011. **Aims** End factory farming; advance the well-being of farm *animals* worldwide. **Structure** A single charitable entity (as of 2006). **Languages** Dutch, English, French, Italian, Polish. **Staff** 86.00 FTE, paid. **Finance** Sources: donations; fundraising; gifts, legacies; subscriptions. Annual budget: 6,000,000 GBP. **Activities** Advocacy/lobbying/activism; awareness raising; research/documentation; training/education. **Events** *Extinction or Regeneration Conference* London (UK) 2023, *Extinction and Livestock Conference* London (UK) 2017, *Meeting on Ensuring Fair Food and Farming for the Future* Brussels (Belgium) 2012, *Conference on global trade and farm animal welfare* Brussels (Belgium) 2009, *International forum on global aspects of farm animal welfare* Brussels (Belgium) 2008. **Publications** *Farm Animal Voice* (3 a year) – magazine. Research and campaigning literature; films.
Members Offices in 6 countries:
France, Italy, Netherlands, Poland, UK, USA.
Representatives in 4 countries:
China, Czechia, South Africa, Ukraine.
Consultative Status Consultative status granted from: *UNEP (#20299)*. **NGO Relations** Member of (2): *Climate Action Network Europe (CAN Europe, #04001)*; *European Environmental Bureau (EEB, #06996)*.
[2023/XF3043/**F**]

♦ Compassion in World Farming International / see Compassion in World Farming (#04414)
♦ Compatible Technology International / see Bountifield International

♦ Compete Caribbean 04415

Exec Dir Inter-American Development Bank, 'Hythe' Welches, Maxwell Main Road, Bridgetown, St Michael BB17068, Bridgetown ST MICHAEL BB17068, Barbados. T. +12466278500. Fax +12464298869. E-mail: competecaribbean@iadb.org.
URL: http://competecaribbean.org/
History A project supported by *Inter-American Development Bank (IDB, #11427)*, *Department for International Development (DFID, inactive)* and the Foreign Affairs, Trade and Development Canada (DFATD). Projects in OECS countries executed in partnership with *Caribbean Development Bank (CDB, #03492)*. **Aims** Provide technical assistance grants and *investment* funding to support *business* climate reforms, clustering initiatives, innovation within firms, and research on private sector development across CARIFORUM states. **Structure** Program Advisory Group; Executive Committee; Programme Coordination Unit. **Languages** English, Spanish. **Staff** 11.50 FTE, paid. **Finance** Funded by *Inter-American Development Bank (IDB, #11427)*, *Department for International Development (DFID, inactive)* and DFATD. Estimated value: US$ 40 million. **Activities** Financial and/or material support. **Publications** *Compete Caribbean* (12 a year) – newsletter; *Compete Caribbean* – magazine. Documentation; studies; data. **Members** Not a membership organization. **IGO Relations** Cooperates with: *Caribbean Development Bank (CDB, #03492)*. **NGO Relations** Supporting institution of *Inter-American Competitiveness Network (#11416)*.
[2015.02.10/XJ9108/**E**]

♦ Competition Law and Economics European Network (CLEEN) 04416

Address not obtained.
URL: https://www.macci-mannheim.eu/macci-mannheim-centre-for-competition-and-innovation/events/cleen-workshop
History 2007. **Activities** Events/meetings; knowledge management/information dissemination. **Events** *Workshop* 2021, *Workshop* Bonn (Germany) 2016, *Workshop* Tilburg (Netherlands) 2015, *Workshop* Norwich (UK) 2014, *Workshop* Bergen (Norway) 2013.
Members Institutions (8) in 5 countries:
France, Germany, Netherlands, Norway, UK.
[2021/AA2016/**F**]

♦ Competitive African Cotton Initiative / see Cotton House Africa

♦ Competitiveness Research Network (CompNet) 04417

Contact Kleine Märkerstr 8, 06108 Halle (Saale), Germany. T. +493457753709. Fax +493457753820. E-mail: secretariat@comp-net.org.
Chairman address not obtained.
URL: https://www.comp-net.org/
History 2012. Founded by *European System of Central Banks (ESCB, #08870)*. Since 2017, an independently funded and regulated network. **Aims** Provide a forum for high level research and policy analysis in the areas of competitiveness and productivity. **Structure** Steering Committee; Advisory Board; Executive Committee. **Activities** Events/meetings; knowledge management/information dissemination; research/documentation. **Events** *CompNet-EIB-ENRI Annual Conference* Luxembourg (Luxembourg) 2022, *Comparative Analysis of Enterprise Data (CAED) Conference* Coimbra (Portugal) 2021, *Annual CompNet Conference* Paris (France) 2021, *CompNet Annual Conference* 2020, *CompNet Annual conference* Luxembourg (Luxembourg) 2019.
Members European and national Partner institutions:
France, Germany, Netherlands.
European Bank for Reconstruction and Development (EBRD, #06315); *European Central Bank (ECB, #06466)*; *European Commission (EC, #06633)* (DG EcFin and DG GROW); *European Investment Bank (EIB, #07599)*; *European Stability Mechanism (ESM, #08829)*.
Data Providers: national statistical institutes, national central banks and governmental research institutions.
Czechia, Denmark, Finland, France, Germany, Hungary, Italy, Latvia, Malta, Netherlands, Poland, Portugal, Slovakia, Sweden, Switzerland.
[2021/AA1999/y/**F**]

♦ Complementary Act to the 1925 Hague Agreement Concerning the International Deposit of Industrial Design (1967 treaty)
♦ Complementary and Alternative Medicine / see CAMDOC Alliance (#03402)
♦ Complementary and Alternative Medicine / see EUROCAM (#05653)
♦ Complementary Protocol to the Agreement on Regional Cooperation in Combating Pollution of the Southeast Pacific by Hydrocarbons and other Harmful Substances (1983 treaty)
♦ Complementary Protocol to the Agreement on Regional Cooperation in Combating Pollution of the Southeast Pacific by Oil and other Harmful Substances in Cases of Emergency (1983 treaty)
♦ COMPLES – Organisation mondiale de la coopération méditerranéenne pour l'énergie solaire (inactive)
♦ Complexe international de recherche et d'enseignement supérieur / see Agropolis International
♦ Complex Interactive Processes Institute (unconfirmed)
♦ Complex Networks – International Conference on Complex Network and their Applications (meeting series)

♦ Complex Systems Society (CSS) 04418

Pres address not obtained. E-mail: css@cssociety.org.
URL: http://cssociety.org/
History 7 Dec 2004, Turin (Italy). Former names and other names: *European Complex Systems Society (ECSS)* – former. Registration: Start date: 2004, France. **Aims** Promote development of all aspects of complex systems science in the countries of Europe, as well as the whole international scientific community. **Structure** Council; Executive Committee, including President, 2 Vice-Presidents, Secretary and Treasurer; Committees (9). **Finance** Sources: members' dues. **Events** *Conference on Complex Systems* Palma (Spain) 2022, *Conference on Complex Systems* Lyon (France) 2021, *Conference on Complex Systems* Palma (Spain) 2020, *Conference on Complex Systems* Singapore (Singapore) 2019, *Conference on Complex Systems* Thessaloniki (Greece) 2018.
[2022.11.11/XM0216/**D**]

♦ **COMplus** Alliance of Communicators for Sustainable Development (#00669)
♦ **CompNet** Competitiveness Research Network (#04417)
♦ Component Obsolescence Group / see International Institute of Obsolescence Management (#13905)
♦ Compostela groupe d'universités (#04419)

♦ Compostela Group of Universities 04419

Compostela groupe d'universités – Grupo Compostela de Universidades
Main Office c/o Casa da Cuncha, Rúa da Conga 1, 15782 Santiago de Compostela, La Coruña, Spain. T. +34881812931. Fax +34881812932. E-mail: grupo.compostela@usc.es.
URL: http://www.gcompostela.org/
History 3 Sep 1994, Santiago de Compostela (Spain). Registered in accordance with Spanish law. **Aims** Strengthen channels of communication between member universities, facilitating cohesion, quality teaching and research exchange; encourage mobility among university members as a basis for a deeper knowledge and understanding of languages, culture and sciences. **Structure** General Assembly (annual); General Council; Executive Committee, comprising President, and Executive Secretary. **Finance** Members' dues. Other sources: regional, national and European funds. **Activities** Organizes: forums for the study and debate of European questions; courses; conferences. Awards *'Compostela-Xunta Prize'*. **Events** *Global University Forum* Santiago de Compostela (Spain) 2018, *General Assembly* Santiago de Compostela (Spain) 2015, *Annual Assembly* Poznań (Poland) 2014, *Annual Assembly* Nantes (France) 2013, *Annual Assembly* Oulu (Finland) 2012. **Publications** *Compostela* – newsletter.
Members Universities (83) in 22 countries and territories:
Australia, Belgium, Czechia, Denmark, Finland, France, Greece, Hungary, Italy, Kosovo, Luxembourg, Malta, Netherlands, Norway, Poland, Portugal, Russia, Slovakia, Spain, Sweden, Switzerland, UK.
NGO Relations Member of: *Euro-Mediterranean University (EMUNI, #05728)*. Partner of: *United Nations Academic Impact (UNAI, #20516)*.
[2021/XE2895/**E**]

♦ Comprehensive Nuclear-Test-Ban Treaty (1996 treaty)

♦ Comprehensive Nuclear-Test-Ban Treaty Organization (CTBTO) 04420

Exec Sec Preparatory Commission for CTBTO, Vienna Intl Centre, PO Box 1200, 1400 Vienna, Austria. T. +431260306200. Fax +431260305823. E-mail: ctbto.public.information@ctbto.org – info@ctbto.org.
URL: http://www.ctbto.org/
History Established under Article II of *Comprehensive Nuclear-Test-Ban Treaty (CTBT, 1996)*, preparation underway through *Preparatory Commission for the Comprehensive Nuclear-Test-Ban Treaty Organization (CTBTO, #18482)*. Organization will come into existence upon the entry into force of the Treaty, which will happen 180 days after the signing and ratification of the Treaty by the 44 States listed in annex 2 to the Treaty. Seat in Vienna (Austria). **Aims** Ensure implementation of the Treaty's provisions and provide a forum for consultation and cooperation. **Structure** To comprise 3 organs: Conference of the States Parties (meeting annually), will as the principal organ oversee the Treaty's implementation and the activities of the other two organs; Executive Council, the principal decision-making body of the Organization and responsible for supervising activities of the Technical Secretariat, will comprise representatives of 51 states party to the Treaty, including 10 from Africa, 7 from Eastern Europe, 9 from Latin America and the Caribbean, 7 from the Middle East and South Asia, 10 from North America and Western Europe and 8 from Southeast Asia, the Pacific and the Far East. Technical Secretariat, headed by a Director-General, will assist States parties to implement the Treaty, carry out verification and other functions and will supervise and coordinate the operation of the International Monitoring System (IMS) and operate the International Data Centre (IDC) at Vienna (Austria). **Events** *Infrasound Technology Workshop* Daejeon (Korea Rep) 2012, *International Seminar* Daejeon (Korea Rep) 2012, *International Noble Gas Experiment Workshop* Mito (Japan) 2012, *International Hydroacoustics Workshop* Yokohama (Japan) 2012, *The way forward workshop* Vienna (Austria) 2002. **IGO Relations** Cooperation agreement with: *World Meteorological Organization (WMO, #21649)*. Observer member of: *Parliamentary Assembly of the Mediterranean (PAM, #18212)*. Supported by: *Agency for the Prohibition of Nuclear Weapons in Latin America and the Caribbean (#00554)*; *World Weather Watch (WWW, #21910)*. **NGO Relations** Member of: *International Committee for Radionuclide Metrology (ICRM, #12798)*; *International Federation of Digital Seismograph Networks (FDSN, #13407)*; *United Nations Evaluation Group (UNEG, #20560)*. Associate Member of: *Federation of International Civil Servants' Associations (FICSA, #09603)*.
[2019.02.25/XF5828/p/**F***]

♦ Comprehensive and Progressive Agreement for Trans-Pacific Partnership (2018 treaty)

♦ Comprehensive System International Rorschach Association (CSIRA) 04421

Association Rorschach Internationale pour le Système Intégré (ARISI)
Contact 8 rue Claude-Pouillet, 75017 Paris, France. E-mail: arisi@orange.fr.
URL: https://www.csira-arisi.org/
History 1989, as *European Rorschach Association for the Comprehensive System (ERA)* – *Association Européenne du Rorschach pour le Système Intégré (AER)*. Current title adopted 2013. Registered in accordance with French law. **Aims** Study and develop the Rorschach Comprehensive System. **Structure** General Assembly; Council of Administration; Executive Board. **Activities** Events/meetings; training/education. **Events** *Congress* Paris (France) 2019, *Conference* Paris (France) 2012, *International Congress* Paris (France) 2012, *Conference* Prague (Czech Rep) 2009, *Conference* Padua (Italy) 2006.
[2020/XJ7406/**C**]

♦ Comptoir maghrébin de l'alfa (inactive)

♦ Comptoirs français du pacifique (CFP) 04422

French-Pacific Banking Agreement
Address not obtained.
URL: http://www.ieom.fr/
History 1967, as *Communauté financière du Pacifique (CFP)*, a grouping of countries in the area using the franc as currency. Prior to 1967, known as *Colonies Françaises du Pacifique*.
Members Governments of 3 territories using the Pacific franc as a currency unit:
French Southern and Antarctic Terr, New Caledonia, Wallis-Futuna.
[2008/XF0739/**F***]

♦ Compton Foundation (internationally oriented national body)
♦ CompuMentor / see TechSoup Global (#20122)

♦ Computational Complexity Foundation (CCF) 04423

Sec C and O and IQC, Univ of Waterloo, 200 University Ave W, Waterloo ON N2L 3G1, Canada. T. +15198884567 ext 43601. E-mail: secretary@computationalcomplexity.org.
URL: http://computationalcomplexity.org/foundation/

History 2015, USA. Set up to take over organization of the conference previously organized by *Institute of Electrical and Electronics Engineers (IEEE, #11259)* – Computer Society Technical Committee on Mathematical Foundations of Computing. Registration: USA, New Jersey. **Aims** Advance research and education in the subject within computer science and mathematics known as computational complexity theory. **Structure** Board of Trustees. **Activities** Events/meetings; publishing activities. **Events** *Computational Complexity Conference* Philadelphia, PA (USA) 2022, *Computational Complexity Conference* Toronto, ON (Canada) 2021, *Computational Complexity Conference* Saarbrücken (Germany) 2020, *Computational Complexity Conference* New Brunswick, NJ (USA) 2019, *Computational Complexity Conference* San Diego, CA (USA) 2018. **Publications** Special issue journal. Conference proceedings. **Members** Full in over 20 countries. Membership countries not specified. [2021.05.21/XM5421/cf/F]

♦ Computational and Financial Econometrics (CFEnetwork) 04424

Coordinator address not obtained. E-mail: info@cfenetwork.org.
URL: http://www.cfenetwork.org/

Aims Consolidate the research in computational and financial econometrics that is scattered throughout Europe; provide researches with a network from which they can obtain information about the most recent developments in computational and financial econometrics as well as its applications. **Structure** Coordinators; Advisory Board. **Activities** Events/meetings. **Events** *International Conference on Computational and Financial Econometrics* London (UK) 2022, *International Conference on Computational and Financial Econometrics* London (UK) 2020, *International Conference on Computational and Financial Econometrics* London (UK) 2019, *International Conference on Econometrics and Statistics (EcoSta)* Taichung (Taiwan) 2019, *International Conference on Econometrics and Statistics (EcoSta)* Taichung (Taiwan) 2018. **Publications** *Annals of Computational and Financial Econometrics* – supplement to Econometrics and Statistics (journal).

Members Individuals in 61 countries and territories:
Algeria, Argentina, Armenia, Australia, Austria, Belgium, Brazil, Canada, Chile, China, Colombia, Cyprus, Czechia, Denmark, Egypt, Estonia, Eswatini, Finland, France, Germany, Greece, Hong Kong, India, Indonesia, Iran Islamic Rep, Israel, Italy, Japan, Kazakhstan, Korea Rep, Latvia, Lithuania, Luxembourg, Malaysia, Mexico, Morocco, Netherlands, New Zealand, Nigeria, Norway, Pakistan, Philippines, Poland, Portugal, Qatar, Romania, Russia, Saudi Arabia, Singapore, Slovenia, South Africa, Spain, Sri Lanka, Sweden, Switzerland, Taiwan, Tunisia, Türkiye, UK, United Arab Emirates, USA. [2020/AA0300/v/F]

♦ Computational Methods and Function Theory (meeting series)

♦ Computer Aided Architectural Design Research in Asia (CAADRIA) . 04425

Admin Officer School of Architecture, Lee Shau Kee Architecture Bldg, Chinese Univ of Hong Kong, Hong Kong, Central and Western, Shatin, Hong Kong. E-mail: i@caadria.org.
Pres address not obtained. E-mail: president@caadria.org.
URL: http://www.caadria.org/

History 26 Apr 1996. **Aims** Promote learning, teaching and research in computer-aided architectural design (CAAD). **Structure** Steering Committee. **Languages** English. **Staff** Voluntary. **Finance** Sources: members' dues. **Events** *Annual Conference* Ahmedabad (India) 2023, *Annual Conference* Sydney, NSW (Australia) 2022, *Annual Conference* Hong Kong (Hong Kong) 2021, *Annual Conference* Daegu (Korea Rep) 2015, *Annual Conference* Kyoto (Japan) 2014. **Publications** Conference proceedings.

Members Covers 36 countries and territories:
Argentina, Australia, Austria, Bangladesh, Belgium, Bolivia, Brazil, Canada, Chile, China, Czechia, Denmark, Germany, Greece, Hong Kong, India, Italy, Japan, Korea Rep, Malaysia, Mexico, Netherlands, New Zealand, Pakistan, Poland, Russia, Singapore, Slovenia, Sweden, Switzerland, Taiwan, Thailand, UK, United Arab Emirates, USA, Vietnam. [2022.10.18/XD5871/D]

♦ Computer Aided Manufacturing International / see Consortium for Advanced Management – International (#04734)
♦ Computer Aid International (internationally oriented national body)
♦ Computer AntiVirus Research Organization (no recent information)
♦ Computer Applications and Quantitative Methods in Archaeology (unconfirmed)
♦ Computer and Communications Industry Association (internationally oriented national body)

♦ Computer Coupling of Phase Diagrams and Thermochemistry (CALPHAD) 04426

Chairman address not obtained. E-mail: calphadeditor@gmail.com.
URL: http://www.calphad.org/

History 1973. **Aims** Promote computational *thermodynamics* through: developing models to represent thermodynamic properties for various phases which permit prediction of properties of multicomponent systems from those of binary and ternary subsystems, critical assessment of data and their incorporation into self-consistent databases; developing *software* to optimize and derive thermodynamic parameters; developing and using *databanks* for calculations to improve understanding of various industrial and technological processes. **Structure** Advisory Board; Editorial Board. **Activities** Grants awards. **Events** *Annual Conference* 2036, *Annual Conference* 2035, *Annual Conference* 2034, *Annual Conference* 2033, *Annual Conference* 2032. **Publications** *CALPHAD Journal.* [2015/XJ6409/F]

♦ Computer Emergency Response Team / see CERT Coordination Center
♦ Computer Game Developers Association / see International Game Developers Association

♦ Computer Graphics Society (CGS) 04427

Contact address not obtained. E-mail: admin@cgs-network.org.
URL: https://cgs-network.org/

History 1992, Geneva (Switzerland). **Aims** Promote advances in computer graphics by exchanging ideas to find innovative solutions. **Structure** Steering Committee; Board. **Activities** Events/meetings. **Events** *International Conference on Computer Animation and Social Agents* Paris (France) 2019, *Computer graphic international conference* Singapore (Singapore) 2010, *International conference in Central Europe on computer graphics, visualization and computer vision* Pilsen (Czech Rep) 2005, *Computer graphic international conference* Hong Kong (Hong Kong) 2001. **Publications** *Computer Animation and Virtual Worlds*; *The Visual Computer.* [2019/AA0914/C]

♦ Computer Law Association / see International Technology Law Association (#15669)
♦ Computer Professionals Forum for Peace and Social Responsibility (internationally oriented national body)
♦ Computers 4 Africa (internationally oriented national body)
♦ Computers in Cardiology / see Computing in Cardiology (#04429)
♦ Computer Section – Printing Industries of America / see International Digital Enterprise Alliance (#13175)

♦ Computers, Privacy and Data Protection (CPDP) 04428

Dir address not obtained. E-mail: info@cpdpconferences.org.
URL: http://www.cpdpconferences.org/

History 2007, Belgium. Founded as a non-profit platform. **Aims** Offer an arena to exchange ideas and discuss the latest emerging issues and trends in legal, regulatory, academic and technological development in privacy and data protection. **Structure** Committees (3): Core Programming; Extended Programming; Scientific. **Events** *International Conference* Brussels (Belgium) 2022, *International Conference* Brussels (Belgium) 2021, *International Conference* Brussels (Belgium) 2020, *International Conference* Brussels (Belgium) 2019, *International Conference* Brussels (Belgium) 2018. [2022.06.15/XJ9136/F]

♦ Computing in Cardiology (CinC) 04429

Contact address not obtained. E-mail: president@cinc.org – contact@cinc.org.
URL: https://www.cinc.org/

History 1978. Founded as an annual international scientific conference. Former names and other names: *Computers in Cardiology* – former. **Aims** Promote the understanding of the application of computational techniques in the field of cardiology. **Structure** Board of Directors. **Languages** English. **Finance** Sources: meeting proceeds; sponsorship. **Activities** Awards/prizes/competitions; events/meetings; training/education. **Events** *CinC : International Conference on Computing in Cardiology* Karlsruhe (Germany) 2024, *CinC : International Conference on Computing in Cardiology* Atlanta, GA (USA) 2023, *CinC : International Conference on Computing in Cardiology* Tampere (Finland) 2022, *CinC : International Conference on Computing in Cardiology* Brno (Czechia) 2021, *CinC : International Conference on Computing in Cardiology* Rimini (Italy) 2020. **Publications** *Proceedings of Computing in Cardiology* (Annual, latest edition 2022). [2022.06.19/XM7812/c/F]

♦ **COMSAM** Conference of Major Superiors of Africa and Madagascar (#04627)
♦ **COMSATS** Commission on Science and Technology for Sustainable Development in the South (#04239)
♦ ComSec / see Commonwealth Secretariat (#04362)
♦ **COMSTECH** Comité permanent Ministériel de l'OIC pour la Coopération Scientifique et Technologique (#17702)
♦ **COMSTECH** OIC Ministerial Standing Committee on Scientific and Technological Cooperation (#17702)
♦ **COMTAB** Commonwealth Table Tennis Federation (#04364)
♦ **COMTA** Consejo de le Música de las Tres Américas (#04723)
♦ COMTELCA / see Comisión Técnica Regional de Telecomunicaciones (#04144)
♦ **COMTELCA** Comisión Técnica Regional de Telecomunicaciones (#04144)
♦ Comunautat de Trabalh dels Pirenèus (#21057)
♦ Comunidad Andina (#00817)
♦ Comunidad de las Bienaventuranzas (religious order)
♦ Comunidad del Caribe (#03476)
♦ Comunidad Cientifica del Caribe (#03553)
♦ Comunidad Cientifica Internacional de Control de Infecciones Nosocomiales (#14376)
♦ Comunidad de las Democracias (#04394)
♦ Comunidade das Beatitudes (religious order)
♦ Comunidad Economica de Africa Occidental (inactive)
♦ Comunidad Económica de los Estados del Africa Central (#05311)
♦ Comunidad Economica de los Estados de Africa Occidental (#05312)
♦ Comunidad Económica de los Paises de los Grandes Lagos (#04375)
♦ Comunidade de Desenvolvimento da Africa Austral (#19843)
♦ Comunidad de Educación Teológica Ecuménica Latinoamericana y Caribeña (unconfirmed)
♦ Comunidade Economica dos Estados da Africa Central (#05311)
♦ Comunidade dos Estados Latino-Americanos e Caribenhos (#04432)
♦ Comunidade Européia (inactive)
♦ Comunidade Européia do Carvão e do Aço (inactive)
♦ Comunidade Européia dos Cozinheiros / see Euro-Toques International (#09190)
♦ Comunidade Européia de Energia Atómica (inactive)
♦ Comunidade Latino Americana de Objetos de Aprendizagem (#16301)
♦ Comunidad del Emmanuel (religious order)

♦ Comunidade dos Paises de Lingua Portuguesa (CPLP) 04430

Community of Portuguese-Speaking Countries – Communauté des pays de langue portugaise

Exec Sec Palacio Conde de Penafiel, Rua de S Mamede 21, 1100-533 Lisbon, Portugal. T. +35113928560. Fax +35113928588. E-mail: comunicacao@cplp.org – philbav@cplp.org – imprensa@cplp.org.
URL: http://www.cplp.org/

History 17 Jul 1996, Lisbon (Portugal). Founded on signature of an agreement by Heads of State and Government of 7 countries. Headquarters in Lisbon. **Aims** Consolidate the national and multinational cultural identity of Portuguese-speaking countries; reflect the special character of their relationship and the experience of their fruitful concerted action and cooperation; enhance a progressively international assertion of Portuguese-speaking countries which, although geographically discontinuous, are identified by their common language; encourage development of parliamentary, economic and entrepreneurial cooperation; give new impetus to academic cooperation; mobilize efforts and resources to assist reconstruction and rehabilitation programmes; promote coordination of activities of public agencies and NGOs; promote measures to overcome problems of immigrant communities, to protect and preserve the environment and achieve sustainable development, to ensure full respect for human rights, to eradicate racism, racial discrimination and xenophobia, to improve living conditions of children, to strengthen the social condition of women and recognize their crucial role in society and to foster exchange of young people; reinforce linguistic, cultural and business links and promote political cooperation. **Structure** Conference of Heads of State and Government (highest organ; meets every 2 years); Council of Ministers (meeting once a year) comprises Foreign Affairs and/or External Relations Ministers of all member states; Executive Secretariat. In 2002 were added: Sectoral Ministerial Meetings; Copoeration Focal Points Meeting. Since 2005, also includes: *Instituto Internacional de Lingua Portuguesa (IILP, #11339)*. Established 2007: *Assembleia Parlamentar da Comunidade dos Países de Língua Portuguesa (AP-CPLP, #02315)*. **Languages** Portuguese. **Staff** 30.00 FTE, paid. **Finance** Sources: contributions of member/participating states. Annual budget: 2,734,731 EUR (2017). **Activities** Advocacy/lobbying/activism; capacity building; events/meetings; politics/policy/regulatory. **Events** *Conference of Heads of State and Government* Luanda (Angola) 2021, *Conference of Heads of State and Government* Brasilia (Brazil) 2016, *Symposium on South-South and Triangular Cooperation* Brussels (Belgium) 2016, *Conference of Heads of State and Government* Dili (Timor-Leste) 2014, *Conference of Heads of State and Government* Maputo (Mozambique) 2012. **Publications** *Noticias CPLP* (2 a year). Anniversary publications.

Members Governments of 9 countries:
Angola, Brazil, Cape Verde, Equatorial Guinea, Guinea-Bissau, Mozambique, Portugal, Sao Tomé-Principe, Timor-Leste.

Associate observer states (10):
Czechia, Georgia, Hungary, Japan, Mauritius, Namibia, Senegal, Slovakia, Türkiye, Uruguay.

IGO Relations Accredited by (1): *Secretariat of the United Nations Convention to Combat Desertification (Secretariat of the UNCCD, #19208)* (Conference of the Parties). Observer status with (4): *ECOSOC (#05331)* (Permanent); *International Organization for Migration (IOM, #14454)*; *UNCTAD (#20285)*; *World Intellectual Property Organization (WIPO, #21593)* (Permanent). Member of (2): *Intergovernmental Organizations Conference (IGO Conference, #11498)*; *United Nations Alliance of Civilizations (UNAOC, #20520)*. Cooperates with (1): *International Fund for Agricultural Development (IFAD, #13692)*. Observer to General Assembly of: *United Nations (UN, #20515)*. Cooperative agreements with: *UNESCO (#20322)*; *FAO (#09260)*. [2022/XD5661/D*]

♦ Comunidades Europeas (inactive)
♦ Comunidades Européias (inactive)

♦ Comunidade Sindical dos Paises de Lingua Portuguesa (CSPLP) ... 04431

Trade Unions' Portuguese Speaking Countries Community (PSCC)

Contact c/o UGT, Av Alm Gago Coutinho 132, 1700-033 Lisbon, Portugal. E-mail: geral@csplp.pt.
URL: http://csplp.org/

History May 1998, Lisbon (Portugal), by 13 trade union federations from Portuguese-speaking countries, when statutes and constitution were approved. **Aims** Straighten the political, cultural, economic, social and trade unionist ties that unite the Portuguese speaking countries. **Structure** Executive Committee, comprising President, 3 Vice-Presidents, 3 Secretaries and 3 members of the Advisory Board. **Events** *Conference* Lisbon (Portugal) 2014, *Conference* Maputo (Mozambique) 2012, *Conference* Brasilia (Brazil) 2002, *Conference* Maputo (Mozambique) 2000.

Members Trade unions in 7 countries:
Angola, Brazil, Cape Verde, Guinea-Bissau, Mozambique, Portugal, Sao Tomé-Principe.

Observers in 4 countries and territories:
Macau, Mozambique, Spain, Timor-Leste.

NGO Relations *International Confederation of Free Trade Unions (ICFTU, inactive)*; *International Federation of Workers' Education Associations (IFWEA, #13580)*; *World Confederation of Labour (WCL, inactive).* [2015/XE3216/t/E]

♦ Comunidades Laicas Marianistas (see: #21334)
♦ Comunidad de Estados Independientes (#04341)

♦ Comunidad de Estados Latinoamericanos y Caribeños (CELAC) ... 04432

Community of Latin American and Caribbean States – Communauté des Etats Latino-américains et Caraïbéens – Comunidade dos Estados Latino-Americanos e Caribenhos

Contact calle Teatinos 180, Piso 14, Santiago, Santiago Metropolitan, Chile. T. +50625395438 – +50622576997. E-mail: cabarca@minrel.gov.cl – cllanos@minrel.gov.cl – jafernandez@minrel.gov.cl.
Contact c/o PARLATINO, Av Principal de Amador, Edif 1111 y 1113 Apartado Zona 4, Panama Ministerio RREE, casilla 1527, Panama, Panamá, Panama PANAMá, Panama. T. +5075128500. Fax +5075128523.

URL: http://www.parlatino.org/en/proyecto-de-la-celac.html
History 22 Feb 2010, Mexico. 22-23 Feb 2010, Mexico, by Heads of State and Government of the countries of Latin America and the Caribbean. Replaces *Permanent Mechanism for Consultation and Political Coordination (Rio Group, inactive)*. **Events** *EU-CELAC Senior Officials Meeting* Brussels (Belgium) 2016, *EU-CELAC Foreign Ministers Meeting* Dominican Rep 2016, *CELAC-EU Summit* Brussels (Belgium) 2015, *EU-CELAC Academic Summit* Brussels (Belgium) 2015, *Summit* Havana (Cuba) 2014.
Members Governments (33):
Antigua-Barbuda, Argentina, Bahamas, Barbados, Belize, Bolivia, Brazil, Chile, Colombia, Costa Rica, Cuba, Dominica, Dominican Rep, Ecuador, El Salvador, Grenada, Guatemala, Guyana, Haiti, Honduras, Jamaica, Mexico, Nicaragua, Panama, Paraguay, Peru, St Kitts-Nevis, St Lucia, St Vincent-Grenadines, Suriname, Trinidad-Tobago, Uruguay, Venezuela.
[2014/XJ5092/**E***]

♦ Comunidade Sul-Americana de Nações / see Union of South American Nations (#20481)
♦ Comunidad Europea (inactive)
♦ Comunidad Europea del Carbón y del Acero (inactive)
♦ Comunidad Europea de Cocineros / see Euro-Toques International (#09190)
♦ Comunidad Europea de Energia Atómica (inactive)
♦ Comunidad Iberoamericana de Naciones (unconfirmed)
♦ Comunidad Internacional Baha'i (#03062)
♦ Comunidad Internacional Emisaria / see Emissaries of Divine Light (#05442)
♦ Comunidad Internacional de Fitomejoradores de Plantas Ornamentales y Frutales de Reproducción Asexuada (#12821)
♦ Comunidad Internacional de Mujeres con VIH/SIDA (#12826)
♦ Comunidad International de los Obtentores de Plantas Ornementales y Frutales de Reproducción Asexuada / see International Community of Breeders of Asexually Reproduced Ornamental and Fruit Varieties (#12821)
♦ Comunidad Latinoamericana de Objetos de Aprendizaje (#16301)
♦ Comunidad Misionera Alemana (internationally oriented national body)
♦ Comunidad de las Regiones del Jura / see Conférence TransJurassience
♦ Comunidad Sudamericana de Naciones / see Union of South American Nations (#20481)
♦ Comunidad de Taizé (religious order)
♦ Comunidad de Trabajo de Holandeses Latinoamericanistas y del Caribe / see Netherlands Association of Latin American and Caribbean Studies
♦ Comunidad de Trabajo de los Pirineos (#21057)
♦ Comunidad de Vida Cristiana (#03905)
♦ Comunione e Liberazione (#04386)
♦ Comunión y Liberación (#04386)
♦ Comunión Mundial de Iglesias Reformadas (#21289)
♦ Comunità delle Beatitudini (religious order)
♦ Comunità Ecumenica 'Cardinale Mercier' (religious order)
♦ Comunità Europea (inactive)
♦ Comunità Europea delle Associazioni del Commercio all'Ingrosso di Birra dei Paesi Membri della CEE (#02555)
♦ Comunità Europea del Carbone e dell'Acciaio (inactive)
♦ Comunità Europea dei Cuochi / see Euro-Toques International (#09190)
♦ Comunità Europea dell'Energia Atomica (inactive)
♦ Comunità Europea delle Organizzazioni di Pubblicitari (inactive)
♦ Comunità Europea degli Scrittori (inactive)
♦ Comunità Europee (inactive)
♦ Comunità delle Federazioni di Editori di Giornali della CEE / see European Newspaper Publishers' Association (#08048)
♦ Comunità Impegno Servizio Volontariato (internationally oriented national body)
♦ Comunità Internazionale de Ottenitori di Piante Ornamentali e Fruttifere a Riproduzione Asessuata (#12821)
♦ Comunità Internazionale Volontari Laici / see Lay Volunteers International Association
♦ Comunità Laici Missionari Cattolici (internationally oriented national body)
♦ Comunità di Lavoro Alpe-Adria / see Alps-Adriatic-Alliance (#00747)
♦ Comunità di Lavoro dei Länder, dei Comitati, delle Regioni e delle Repubbliche delle Alpi Orientali / see Alps-Adriatic-Alliance (#00747)
♦ Comunità di Lavoro delle Regioni Alpine (#01081)
♦ Comunità di Lavoro delle Regioni Europee di Confine (#02499)
♦ Comunità Promozione e Sviluppo (internationally oriented national body)
♦ Comunità delle Regioni del Giura / see Conférence TransJurassience
♦ Comunità di Sant'Egidio (religious order)
♦ Comunità di Sant'Egidio – ACAP (internationally oriented national body)
♦ Comunità di Taizé (religious order)
♦ Comunitatea de Lucru a Statelor Dunarene (#21056)
♦ Comunitat de Treball dels Pirineus (#21057)
♦ Comunità delle Università Mediterranee (#04403)
♦ Comunità Volontari per il Mondo (internationally oriented national body)
♦ Comunn Ceilteach (#03633)
♦ COMUVIR / see Académie d'environnement d'expression francophone, philosophique et scientifique
♦ COMy – World Congress on Controversies in Multiple Myeloma (meeting series)
♦ CONAFCO – Confederation of North American Corporate Football (unconfirmed)
♦ **CONAHEC** Consorcio para la Colaboración de la Educación Superior en América del Norte (#04756)
♦ **CONAHEC** Consortium pour la collaboration dans l'enseignement supérieur en Amérique du nord (#04756)
♦ **CONAHEC** Consortium for North American Higher Education Collaboration (#04756)
♦ Cónaidhm Inneatóiri Teileachumarsaide an Chomhphobail Eorphaigh (#09597)
♦ Cónaidhm Thairgeoiri Uiseshaothraithe na hEorpa / see Federation of European Aquaculture Producers (#09491)
♦ **CONAMA** Confederation of African Midwives Associations (#04506)
♦ CONASS – Convenio andino de seguridad social (no recent information)
♦ **CONCACAF** Confederación Norte-Centroamericana y del Caribe de Fútbol (#04465)
♦ **CONCACFUTSAL** Confederation of North, Central American and the Caribbean Futsal (#04571)
♦ CONCAP – Consejo de Iglesias Luteranas en Centroamérica y Panama (inactive)
♦ CONCAPE – Confederación Centroamericana y del Caribe de la Pequeña y Mediana Empresa (no recent information)
♦ CONCATEC – Consejo Centroamericano de los Trabajadores de la Educación y la Cultura (no recent information)
♦ **CONCATEME** Confederación Centroamérica de Tenis de Mesa (#03673)
♦ **CONCAWE** Oil Companies' European Association for Environment, Health and Safety in Refining and Distribution (#17708)
♦ CONCEBE – Confederación Centroamericana de Béisbol (unconfirmed)
♦ CONCECARES – Confederación Centroamericana y del Caribe de Esports (unconfirmed)
♦ Conceive Design Implement Operate / see Worldwide CDIO Initiative (#21919)
♦ **CONCENCABA** Comisión de la Zona Centroamericana y del Caribe de la Confederación Panamericana de Basquetbol (#04146)
♦ Concept pour le Développement du Football Africain (unconfirmed)
♦ Conceptionistes – Fils de l'Immaculée-Conception (religious order)
♦ Conceptionists – Sons of the Immaculate Conception (religious order)
♦ Conceptions of Library and Information Science Conference (meeting series)
♦ Concern America (internationally oriented national body)
♦ Concern for Development Initiatives in Africa (internationally oriented national body)
♦ Concerned Philosophers for Peace (internationally oriented national body)
♦ Concern Universal / see United Purpose
♦ Concern Worldwide (internationally oriented national body)
♦ Concertation chrétienne pour l'Afrique centrale (CCAC) / see European Network for Central Africa (#07874)
♦ Concerted Action for African Development (inactive)
♦ Concerted Action on Congenital Anomalies and Twins / see EUROCAT – European Surveillance of Congenital Anomalies (#05655)
♦ Concert of Europe (inactive)
♦ Concezionisti – Figli dell'Immacolata Concezione (religious order)
♦ CONCFBP – Confederación Norte y Centroamericana de Béisbol (no recent information)
♦ Conchological Society of Southern Africa (internationally oriented national body)
♦ Concile Mondiale de Congrès Diplomatiques des Aumoniers pour la Paix Universelle des Droits Humains et Juridiques (unconfirmed)
♦ Conciliation and Arbitration Convention (1925 treaty)
♦ Conciliation and Arbitration Rules of Investment Disputes (1968 treaty)
♦ Conciliation internationale (inactive)
♦ Conciliation Resources (internationally oriented national body)
♦ Concilio Internacional de Agencias de Acreditación / see International Council for Evangelical Theological Education (#13020)
♦ Concilio Internacional de Iglesias Cristianas (#13005)
♦ Concílio International de Igrejas Cristãs (#13005)
♦ Concilio Mundial de Iglesias Cristianas Independientes (#21330)
♦ Concilium Bibliographicum (inactive)
♦ Concilium Ophthalmologicum Universale (#13057)
♦ Concilium Sanctum Mundi (inactive)
♦ Concordat de Bâle – Principes pour le contrôle des établissements des banques à l'étranger (1983 treaty)
♦ **CONCORD** Confédération européenne des ong d'urgence et de développement (#04547)
♦ Concordia (internationally oriented national body)
♦ Concordia (internationally oriented national body)
♦ Concordia – International Society of Study, Correspondence and Exchange (inactive)
♦ Concordis International (internationally oriented national body)

♦ Concrete Europe 04433

Sec Rue d'Arlon 55, 1040 Brussels, Belgium. T. +3222341046. E-mail: info@concrete-europe.eu.
URL: https://www.concrete-europe.eu
History Set up by *Bureau international du béton manufacturé (BIBM, #03363)*, *CEMBUREAU – The European Cement Association (CEMBUREAU, #03634)*, *European Federation of Concrete Admixtures Associations (EFCA, #07085)* and *European Ready Mixed Concrete Organization (ERMCO, #08330)*. Former names and other names: *European Concrete Platform (ECP)* – former (31 Dec 2022). Registration: Banque Carrefour des Entreprises, No/ID: 0894.653.467, Start date: 4 Jan 2008, Belgium; EU Transparency Register, No/ID: 875740128184-88, Start date: 31 Aug 2017. **Aims** Promote concrete as the material of choice providing building solutions for sustainable development and *sustainable construction*. **Languages** English. **Finance** Sources: members' dues. **Activities** Knowledge management/information dissemination; standards/guidelines. **Events** *Marketing concrete in the changing world* Brussels (Belgium) 2012. **Publications** Position papers.
Members Organizations (4):
Bureau international du béton manufacturé (BIBM, #03363); CEMBUREAU – The European Cement Association (CEMBUREAU, #03634); European Federation of Concrete Admixtures Associations (EFCA, #07085); European Ready Mixed Concrete Organization (ERMCO, #08330).
NGO Relations Member of (3): *Construction Products Europe AISBL (#04761); European Construction Forum (ECF, #06765); Fire Safe Europe (FSEU, #09780).* [2023.02.14/XM0536/y/**E**]

♦ Concrete Institute / see Institution of Structural Engineers (#11322)

♦ Concrete Reinforcing Steel Institute (CRSI) 04434

Pres Robert J Risser, 933 North Plum Grove Rd, Schaumburg IL 60173-4758, USA. T. +184751200ext17. Fax +18475171206. E-mail: info@crsi.org.
URL: http://www.crsi.org/
History 1924. **Events** *Winter technical meeting* Chicago, IL (USA) 2001, *World of concrete seminar* Las Vegas, NV (USA) 2001, *Annual Convention* Palm Springs, CA (USA) 2001, *Fall business meeting* Chicago, IL (USA) 2000.
Members Companies in 9 countries:
Australia, Canada, Germany, Indonesia, Italy, Qatar, Saudi Arabia, United Arab Emirates, USA. [2015/XE3498/j/**E**]

♦ Concrete Society (internationally oriented national body)
♦ Concrete Society of Southern Africa (internationally oriented national body)
♦ CONCUR – International Conference on Concurrency Theory (meeting series)
♦ CONDECA – Consejo de Defensa Centroamericana (inactive)
♦ **CONDESAN** Consorcio para el Desarrollo Sostenible de la Ecoregión Andina (#04758)
♦ **CONEBI** Confederation of the European Bicycle Industry (#04519)
♦ Conectando Culturas (internationally oriented national body)
♦ Conectas Direitos Humanos (internationally oriented national body)
♦ Conectas Human Rights (internationally oriented national body)
♦ **CONECTUS** Consortium of European Companies Determined to Use Superconductivity (#04740)
♦ **CONELA** Confraternidad Evangélica Latinoamericana (#04660)
♦ CONFECAMARAS – Confederación de Camaras de Comercio del Grupo Andino (no recent information)
♦ Confederação da América do Sul e Central de Handebol (#04443)

♦ Confederação Empresarial da Comunidade dos Paises de Lingua Portuguesa (CE-CPLP) 04435

Secretariat Rua Manuel da Silva Gaio 2, 2795-132 Linda-a-Velha, Portugal. T. +351215850367. E-mail: secretariadogeral@cecplp.org.
URL: http://www.cecplp.org/
History 4 Jun 2004, Lisbon (Portugal). **Aims** Facilitate and strengthen business relations between associations and business entities, increasing business, imports and exports. **Structure** General Assembly; Direction; Fiscal Council; Executive Commission. **Events** *Business Summit* Sao Tomé (Sao Tomé-Principe) 2022, *Business Summit* Malabo (Equatorial Guinea) 2021.
Members Full in 9 countries:
Angola, Brazil, Cape Verde, Equatorial Guinea, Guinea-Bissau, Mozambique, Portugal, Sao Tomé-Principe, Timor-Leste.
Observers in 6 countries:
Georgia, Japan, Mauritania, Namibia, Senegal, Türkiye.
IGO Relations Recognized by: *Comunidade dos Paises de Lingua Portuguesa (CPLP, #04430).*
[2022/XM5696/**E**]

♦ Confederação Espirita Pan-Americana / see CEPA – Associação Espirita Internacional (#03821)
♦ Confederação Européia das Indústrias de Pasta, Papel e Cartão (inactive)
♦ Confederação Européia dos Presidentes das Camaras Municipais (inactive)
♦ Confederação Ibero-Americana das Associações Cientificas e Académicas de Comunicação (#04448)
♦ Confederação Iberoamericana de Fundações (no recent information)
♦ Confederação Interamericana de Educação Católica (#11403)
♦ Confederação Interamericana de Engenharia Quimica (#11417)
♦ Confederação Interamericana de Relações Públicas (#11418)

♦ Confederação Interamericana de Relações Públicas (CONFIARP) .. 04436

Confederación Interamericana de Relaciones Públicas – Interamerican Confederation of Public Relations

Secretariat c/o Independencia 39, Int 304-A, esq Alemania, Col Independencia, 03630 Mexico City CDMX, Mexico. E-mail: confiarpsecretariageneral@gmail.com.
URL: http://confiarp.com/

History 2003, when a group of 5 member countries of *Inter-American Confederation of Public Relations (#11418)* separated. Operates under the same name. **Structure** General Assembly. Officers: President; 3 Vice-Presidents; Treasurer; 4 Directors. **Events** *Congress* Medellin (Colombia) 2015, *Congress* Acapulco (Mexico) 2013, *Biennial congress / Congress* Santa Cruz (Bolivia) 2006, *General Assembly* Guadalajara (Mexico) 2005, *General assembly / Congress* Guadalajara (Mexico) 2004.
Members Institutions in 6 countries:
Argentina, Bolivia, Ecuador, Mexico, Panama, Peru. [2015/XJ4163/**D**]

- ♦ Confederação Latinoamericana das de Associações Cristãos de Moços / see Latin American and Caribbean Alliance of YMCAs (#16264)
- ♦ Confederação Latinoamericana e do Caribe de Associações Cristãos de Moços / see Latin American and Caribbean Alliance of YMCAs (#16264)
- ♦ Confederação Latinoamericana da Industria Grafica (#16303)
- ♦ Confederação Latinoamericana Macabi (#04459)
- ♦ Confederação Latinoamericana dos Religiosos (#04442)
- ♦ Confederação Mundial da Educação (#04464)
- ♦ Confederação Mundial de Ensino Privado / see Confederación Mundial de Educación (#04464)

♦ Confederação das Organizações de Produtores Familiares do Mercosul Ampliado (COPROFAM) 04437

Confederation of Family Producer Organizations of the Expanded Mercosur – Confederación de Organizaciones de Productores Familiares del Mercosur Ampliado

Address not obtained.
URL: https://coprofam.org/

History 1994, Porto Alegre (Brazil). **Aims** Represent the interests of associated organizations, family farmers, peasants and indigenous people of the countries of the expanded Mercosur. **Structure** General Assembly; Board of Directors; Executive Secretariat.
Members National organizations (9) in 7 countries:
Argentina, Bolivia, Brazil, Chile, Paraguay, Peru, Uruguay.
NGO Relations Affiliated with (1): *International Land Coalition (ILC, #13999).* [2022/AA2965/**D**]

- ♦ Confederação de Organizações Turisticas da América Latina (#04466)
- ♦ Confederação Pan-Americana de Desporto do Trabalhador / see Confederación Panamericana del Deporte de los Trabajadores (#04473)
- ♦ Confederação Panamericana para Fornecedores da Industria Grafica (no recent information)
- ♦ Confederação Parlamentar das Américas (#04479)
- ♦ Confederação Sulamericana de Esportes (#19711)

♦ Confederación de Adolescencia y Juventud de Iberoamérica y el Caribe (CODJAJIC) 04438

Contact address not obtained. E-mail: codajic2002@gmail.com.
URL: http://www.codajic.org/

History Proposed Aug 2000, Belo Horizonte (Brazil). Statutes provisionally adopted Oct 2002, Havana (Cuba). **Structure** Executive Council.
Members Full in 20 countries:
Argentina, Bolivia, Brazil, Chile, Colombia, Costa Rica, Cuba, Dominican Rep, Ecuador, El Salvador, Honduras, Italy, Mexico, Panama, Paraguay, Peru, Portugal, Spain, Uruguay, Venezuela. [2018/XM6575/**C**]

- ♦ Confederación Africana de Asociaciones Cooperativas de Ahorro y Crédito (#00261)
- ♦ Confederación de Ajedrez para las Américas (#04516)
- ♦ Confederación de Ajedrez de las Américas (inactive)
- ♦ Confederación Americana de Boxeo (#00776)
- ♦ Confederación Americana de Empleados Bancarios (inactive)

♦ Confederación Americana de Tiro (CAT) 04439

Shooting Confederation of the Americas

Pres Avenida de La Reforma 15-54, zona 9 – Apto 1203, 01009 Guatemala, Guatemala. T. +50223343958. Fax +50222300201. E-mail: cat@conatiro.org – infocat@conatiro.org.
SG address not obtained.
URL: https://www.conatiro.org/

History 4 Apr 1973, Mexico City (Mexico). A continental confederation of *International Shooting Sport Federation (ISSF, #14852).* Former names and other names: *American Shooting Confederation* – former. **Structure** General Assembly; Executive Committee; Committees. **Events** *Meeting* Mexico City (Mexico) 1988.
Members Shooting federations in 254 countries and territories:
Argentina, Aruba, Barbados, Bolivia, Brazil, Canada, Chile, Colombia, Costa Rica, Cuba, Dominican Rep, Ecuador, El Salvador, Guatemala, Honduras, Mexico, Nicaragua, Panama, Paraguay, Peru, Puerto Rico, Trinidad-Tobago, Uruguay, USA, Venezuela.
NGO Relations Member of (1): *Asociación de Confederaciones Deportivas Panamericanas (ACODEPA, #02119).* Recognized by: *International Shooting Sport Federation (ISSF, #14852); Panam Sports Organization (Panam Sports, #18138).* [2023/XD0839/**D**]

- ♦ Confederación Americana de Triatlón / see Americas Triathlon (#00795)

♦ Confederación Americana de Urologia (CAU) 04440

Registered Seat Pasaje de la Carcova 3526, C1172AAB Buenos Aires, Argentina. T. +541149623977. Fax +541149637941.
URL: http://www.caunet.org/

History 1935, Brazil. Registered in accordance with Brazilian law, 9 Mar 1970. **Structure** Executive Committee, comprising Secretary General, Vice-Secretary General, Treasurer and 2 members. **Events** *Congress* Guayaquil (Ecuador) 2020, *Congress* Buenos Aires (Argentina) 2019, *Congress* Punta Cana (Dominican Rep) 2018, *Congress* Santa Cruz (Bolivia) 2017, *Congress* Panama (Panama) 2016. **Publications** *Evolucau* – electronic bulletin.
Members National associations in 19 countries:
Argentina, Bolivia, Brazil, Chile, Colombia, Costa Rica, Cuba, Dominican Rep, Ecuador, El Salvador, Guatemala, Mexico, Panama, Paraguay, Peru, Portugal, Spain, Uruguay, Venezuela.
NGO Relations Represented on the Executive of: *International Consultation on Urological Diseases (ICUD, #12928).* [2013/XM3044/**D**]

- ♦ Confederación Anti-Comunista Latinoamericana (inactive)
- ♦ Confederación Asiatica de Patinaje / see World Skate Asia (#21789)
- ♦ Confederación de Asociaciones Americanas para la Producción de la Agricultura Sostenible (#04508)
- ♦ Confederación de Asociaciones de Empresas de Comercio Internacional / see European Confederation of International Trading Houses Associations (#06708)
- ♦ Confederación de Asociaciones de Heladeros Artesanos de la Comunidad Europea (#04514)
- ♦ Confederación de Asociaciones Internacionales de Contratistas (#04558)
- ♦ Confederación de Asociaciones Nacionales de Curtidores y Peleteros de la Comunidad Europea (#04515)

♦ Confederación Atlética del Istmo Centroamericano (CADICA) 04441

Athletic Confederation of the Central American Isthmus

Pres c/o Federacion Nacional Hondureña de Atletismo, Complejo Deportivo Jose Simon Azcona de Hoyo No 3492, Villa Olimpica, Tegucigalpa, Francisco Morazán, Honduras. T. +50487924589. Fax +50487924589. E-mail: calixto80@hotmail.com.
Members Membership countries not specified. **NGO Relations** *World Athletics (#21209).* [2015/XD7880/**D**]

- ♦ Confederación de Camaras de Comercio del Grupo Andino (no recent information)
- ♦ Confederación del Caribe de Béisbol (inactive)
- ♦ Confederación Caribeña de Cooperativas de Ahorro y Crédito (#03478)

♦ Confederación Caribeña y Latinoamericana de Religiosas y Religiosos (CLAR) 04442

Latin American Confederation of Religious Orders – Confédération latinoaméricaine des religieux – Confederação Latinoamericana dos Religiosos – Confederazione Latinoamericana dei Religiosi

Main Office Calle 64 No 10 – 45 Piso 5, Bogota 110231, Bogota DC, Colombia. T. +5719272889. E-mail: clar@clar.org.
URL: http://www.clar.org/

History 16 Nov 1958, Rome (Italy). Founded at 1st Assembly of National Conferences of Superiors General of Latin American Religious Orders. Recognized by the Holy See and first Statutes adopted 2 Mar 1959. New Statutes approved 12 Dec 2009. Former names and other names: *Confederación Latinoamericana de Religiosos (CLAR)* – former. **Aims** Coordinate the common initiatives and services of the national conferences of Superiors Mayor of Latin American religious orders, respecting their autonomy; promote cooperation among institutes of *monks* and *nuns* and of the societies of apostolic life existing in Latin America; cooperate with related bodies and with the bishops. **Structure** General Assembly (every 3 years); Governing Board; Presidency; Council of Economic Service. **Languages** English, French, Portuguese, Spanish. **Staff** 9.00 FTE, paid. **Finance** Sources: grants; meeting proceeds; sale of publications. **Activities** Financial and/or material support; research/documentation. **Events** *Triennial General Assembly* Rionegro (Colombia) 2022, *Triennial General Assembly* Medellin (Colombia) 2018, *Congress of Consecrated Life* Bogota (Colombia) 2015, *Triennial General Assembly* Bogota (Colombia) 2015, *Triennial General Assembly* Quito (Ecuador) 2012. **Publications** *Magazzine CLAR* (4 a year).
Members National Conferences. Federations or Councils of religious orders, representing about 160,486 individuals, in 35 countries and territories:
Antigua-Barbuda, Argentina, Bahamas, Barbados, Belize, Bermuda, Bolivia, Brazil, Chile, Colombia, Costa Rica, Cuba, Curaçao, Dominica, Dominican Rep, Ecuador, El Salvador, Grenada, Guatemala, Guyana, Haiti, Honduras, Jamaica, Mexico, Nicaragua, Panama, Paraguay, Peru, Puerto Rico, St Kitts-Nevis, St Lucia, St Vincent-Grenadines, Trinidad-Tobago, Uruguay, Venezuela. [2022.11.11/XD2869/**D**]

♦ Confederación de Sur y Centro America de Balonmano (Coscabal) . 04443

Confederação da América do Sul e Central de Handebol – Confederation of South and Central America of Handball

Pres address not obtained. E-mail: info@handballsca.tv.
URL: https://handballsca.com/

History 1 Jul 2019, Gothenburg (Sweden). Together with *North America and the Caribbean Handball Confederation (NACHC, #17557),* supersedes *Pan American Team Handball Federation (PATHF, inactive).* Former names and other names: *South and Central America Handball Confederation (SCAHC)* – alias. **Structure** Congress; Council; Executive Committee; Permanenet Commissions. **Activities** Sporting activities; training/education.
Members Federations in 19 countries and territories:
Argentina, Belize, Bolivia, Brazil, Chile, Colombia, Costa Rica, Ecuador, El Salvador, Guatemala, Guiana Fr, Guyana, Honduras, Nicaragua, Panama, Paraguay, Peru, Uruguay, Venezuela.
NGO Relations Member of (1): *Asociación de Confederaciones Deportivas Panamericanas (ACODEPA, #02119).* Regional federation of *International Handball Federation (IHF, #13771).* [2023/AA3094/**D**]

- ♦ Confederación Centroamericana de Béisbol (unconfirmed)
- ♦ Confederación Centro Americana y del Caribe de Aficionados a la Natación / see Central American and Caribbean Amateur Swimming Confederation (#03660)
- ♦ Confederación Centroamericana y del Caribe de Aficionados a la Natación (#03660)
- ♦ Confederación Centroamericana y del Caribe de Atletismo (#03661)
- ♦ Confederación Centroamericana y del Caribe de Esports (unconfirmed)
- ♦ Confederación Centroamericana y del Caribe de Levantamiento de Pesas (inactive)
- ♦ Confederación Centroamericana y del Caribe de la Pequeña y Mediana Empresa (no recent information)

♦ Confederación Centroamericana de Medicina del Deporte 04444

Central American Federation of Sports Medicine – Fédération centroaméricaine de médecine sportive

Contact address not obtained. T. +5062378956. Fax +5062378956.
History 1986, as the Central American group of *International Federation of Sports Medicine (#13554).*
Members National associations (7) in 7 Central American countries:
Belize, Costa Rica, El Salvador, Guatemala, Honduras, Nicaragua, Panama.
NGO Relations *Pan American Confederation of Sports Medicine (COPAMEDE, no recent information).* [2010/XE0996/**E**]

- ♦ Confederación Centroamericana de Trabajadores (inactive)
- ♦ Confederación Centroamérica de Tenis de Mesa (#03673)

♦ Confederación de Cooperativas del Caribe, Centro y Suramérica (CCC-CA) 04445

Secretariat Apdo Postal 3658-1000, San José, San José, San José, Costa Rica. T. +5062404641. Fax +5062404284. E-mail: info@ccc-ca.com.
URL: http://www.ccc-ca.com/

History 1957, as *Confederation of Cooperatives of the Caribbean (CCC).* Reactivated in 1979; reorganized and current title adopted 1980. Registration: Costa Rica. **Aims** Foster and encourage development, integration, consolidation, representation and defence of cooperatives in the region; by this means achieve structural change in the countries concerned, so they can democratize their political, social and economic life within a concept of justice, participation and peace. **Structure** General Assembly (every 2 years). Board of Directors (meets at least twice a year), consisting of one representative of each national committee of members. Executive Committee, comprising President, Vice-President, Secretary and 2 members. Supervision Committee of 5 members, elected at General Assembly. Executive Director and Deputy Director. **Languages** English, French, Spanish. **Staff** 8.00 FTE, paid; 2.00 FTE, voluntary. 3 consultants. **Finance** Members' dues. Other sources: support from international organizations; technical assistance services; training activities. **Activities** Organizes about 150 national and regional events annually. Sets out strategic guidelines for a common agenda under the heading: integration; development; inter-cooperation; solidarity; representation and defence; institutional consolidation; social justice. Programmes: education and training; strategic planning; research; communication; commercialization; development of sectors; business development; information; organization and development. Policies relate to participation of women and youth and environmental issues. **Events** *General Meeting* Panama 2006, *Extraordinary general assembly* Panama (Panama) 1997, *Regional conference on cooperative education* San Juan (Puerto Rico) 1997, *Regional assembly of cooperative women* San Pedro Sula (Honduras) 1997, *Regional conference on agricultural cooperation* San Pedro Sula (Honduras) 1997. **Publications** *Dialogo Cooperativo Regional* (12 a year); *Memoria CCC-CA* (annual) in English, Spanish. Other publications (6-8 a year) in Spanish include country statistics.
Members National confederations, sectoral federations, cooperative education centres, governmental institutes and grassroots cooperatives, in total representing over 10,000 cooperatives (" indicates State Cooperative Development National Institutes are also members) in 13 countries:
Colombia, Costa Rica (*), Cuba, Dominican Rep (*), El Salvador, Guatemala, Haiti (*), Honduras, Neth Antilles, Nicaragua, Panama (*), Puerto Rico (*), Venezuela.
NGO Relations Affiliated organization of: *Fundación para la Cooperación y el Desarrollo del Caribe y Centro América (FUNCOODE, no recent information).* [2020/XD1617/**D**]

♦ Confederación de Educadores Americanos (CEA) 04446

Confédération des enseignants américains – Confederation of American Educators

SG SNTE, Venezuela 44, Centro Histórico, 06020 Mexico City CDMX, Mexico. E-mail: secretariogeneralceamexico@gmail.com.

Pres address not obtained.
URL: http://www.ceasubsede.com.uy/
History 1929. Also known under the name *Confederation of Latin American Teachers.* **Events** *Triennial Congress* Sao Paulo (Brazil) 2011, *Congress / Triennial Congress* Cochabamba (Bolivia) 2004, *Triennial Congress* Bogota (Colombia) 1988, *Triennial Congress* Managua (Nicaragua) 1985, *Triennial Congress* Mexico City (Mexico) 1982.
Members Full in 19 countries and territories:
Bolivia, Brazil, Canada, Chile, Colombia, Costa Rica, Cuba, Ecuador, El Salvador, Guatemala, Honduras, Jamaica, Martinique, Mexico, Nicaragua, Panama, Puerto Rico, USA, Venezuela.
NGO Relations *World Confederation of Organizations of the Teaching Profession (WCOTP, inactive); Fédération internationale syndicale de l'enseignement (FISE, #09662).* [2014/XD0393/D]

- ♦ Confederación de Empleadores del Caribe (#03495)
- ♦ Confederación Endodóntica Mundial (inactive)
- ♦ Confederación de Entidades Organizadoras de Congresos y Afines de América Latina / see Federación de Entidades Organizadoras de Congresos y Afines de América Latina (#09299)
- ♦ Confederación Espirita Pan-Americano / see CEPA – Associação Espirita Internacional (#03821)
- ♦ Confederación Europea de los Alcaldes (inactive)
- ♦ Confederación Europea de Antiguos Alumnos de Jesuitas (#04536)
- ♦ Confederación Europea de Asociaciones de Protección contra Incendios / see Confederation of Fire Protection Associations (#04552)
- ♦ Confederación Europea de Billar (#04539)
- ♦ Confederación Europea de Excombatientes (#04537)
- ♦ Confederación Europea de Fisioterapia (inactive)
- ♦ Confederación Europea de la Industria del Calzado (#04544)
- ♦ Confederación Europea de la Industria de Pastas, Papel y Cartón (inactive)
- ♦ Confederación Europea de los Laringectomizados (#06709)
- ♦ Confederación Europea de Sindicatos (#08927)
- ♦ Confederación Europea de Sindicatos Independientes (#06705)
- ♦ Confederación de los Fabricantes de Levadura de la Unión Europea (#04551)
- ♦ Confederación Femenina Metodista América Latina y El Caribe (no recent information)
- ♦ Confederación General de las Cooperativas Agrarias de la Unión Europea (#10107)

♦ Confederación Hipica del Caribe 04447

Caribbean Horse Racing Confederation
Contact Edificio de Pista y Caballeriza, Planta Baja, Sector de Caballerizas, Hipódromo La Rinconada, Caracas 1090 DF, Venezuela. T. +582126810493. Fax +582126817821. E-mail: confederacion-hipicadelcaribe@yahoo.com.
URL: http://confederacionhipicadelcaribe.org/
History 30 Nov 1974, San Juan (Puerto Rico). **Structure** Assembly; Board of Directors. **Activities** Awards/prizes/competitions.
Members Full in 7 countries and territories:
Dominican Rep, Jamaica, Mexico, Panama, Puerto Rico, Trinidad-Tobago, Venezuela.
NGO Relations Member of: *International Federation of Horseracing Authorities (IFHA, #13449).* [2021/XD7155/D]

♦ Confederación Iberoamericana de Asociaciones Científicas y Académicas de la Comunicación (CONFIBERCOM) 04448

Confederação Ibero-Americana das Associações Cientificas e Académicas de Comunicação
Contact address not obtained.
URL: http://confibercom.com/
History 18 Apr 2009, Funchal (Portugal). **Structure** General Assembly; Board of Directors. **Events** *Congress* Madrid (Spain) 2016, *Congress* Braga (Portugal) 2014, *Congress* Sao Paulo (Brazil) 2011.
Members Affiliated organizations (15) in 10 countries:
Argentina, Bolivia, Brazil, Chile, Colombia, Ecuador, Mexico, Portugal, Spain, Venezuela.
Asociación Latinoamericana de Investigadores de la Comunicación (ALAIC, #02237); Associação Ibero-Americana de Comunicação (ASSIBERCOM, #02328); Federação de Associações Lusófonas de Ciências da Comunicação (LUSOCOM); Federación Latinoamericana de Facultades de Comunicación Social (FELAFACS, #09353); Unión Latina de Economía Política de la Información, la Comunicación ya la Cultura (ULEPICC, #20447). [2020/XJ5098/y/D]

- ♦ Confederación Iberoamericana de las Ciencias Genealógica y Heraldica (inactive)
- ♦ Confederación Iberoamericana de Comités, Consejos y Comisiones Nacionales de Discapacidades (no recent information)

♦ Confederación Iberoamericana de Comunicadores y Medios Masivos Cristianos (COICOM) 04449

Ibero-American Confederation of Christian Communicators, Mass Media, Pastors and Leaders
Contact 1315 Campo Sano Ave, Miami FL 33146, USA. E-mail: coicom.info@gmail.com.
URL: https://www.coicom.org/
History Founded 1992, Santa Cruz (Bolivia). **Aims** Equip, train, mobilize, motivate and challenge Christian communicators to take the *Gospel* to the ends of the earth. **Structure** Annual Convention (rotates between countries); Board of Directors. **Languages** Spanish. **Staff** 250.00 FTE, paid. **Activities** Events/meetings; religious activities. **Events** *Congress* 2020, *Congress* San Salvador (El Salvador) 2019, *Congress* Miami, FL (USA) 2017, *Congress* Honduras 2012, *Congress* Paraguay 2011. **Publications** *Weekly E-mail Bulletin.*
Members Individuals (about 500). Membership countries not specified. [2021.09.01/XJ7843/D]

- ♦ Confederación Iberoamericana de Estudiantes Católicos (inactive)
- ♦ Confederación Iberoamericana y Filipina de Productores de Caña de Azúcar (no recent information)
- ♦ Confederación Iberoamericana de Fundaciones (no recent information)
- ♦ Confederación Iberoamericana de Jóvenes Empresarios / see Federación Iberoamericana de Jóvenes Empresarios (#09314)

♦ Confederación Iberoamericana de Medicina Familiar (CIMF) 04450

Iberoamerican Confederation of Family Medicine
Pres address not obtained. E-mail: contacto@cimfwonca.org.
URL: http://cimfwonca.org/
History Aug 1981, as *International Center for Family Medicine (ICFM) – Centro Internacional de Medicina Familiar (CIMF).* Present name and structure adopted, 1996. **Aims** Promote better health systems in Ibero America through family medicine and primary health care. **Structure** Board of Directors; Executive Committee. **Languages** English, Portuguese, Spanish. **Activities** Research and development; events/meetings; knowledge management/information dissemination; training/education; networking/liaising; guidance/assistance/consulting. **Events** *Ibero American Regional Conference* Tijuana (Mexico) 2019, *Ibero American Regional Conference* Cali (Colombia) 2018, *Ibero American Regional Conference* Lima (Peru) 2017, *Ibero American Regional Conference* San José (Costa Rica) 2016, *Ibero American Regional Conference* Montevideo (Uruguay) 2015. **Publications** *V Cumbre Iberoamericana de Medicina Familiar.*
Members National societies and colleges of family medicine in 20 countries:
Argentina, Bolivia, Brazil, Chile, Colombia, Costa Rica, Cuba, Dominican Rep, Ecuador, El Salvador, Mexico, Nicaragua, Panama, Paraguay, Peru, Portugal, Puerto Rico, Spain, Uruguay, Venezuela.
NGO Relations Regional member of: *World Organization of Family Doctors (WONCA, #21690).* [2022/XE0837/D]

♦ Confederación de Institutos Seculares en América Latina (CISAL) . 04451

Federation of Secular Institutes in Latin America – Confédération des instituts séculiers d'Amérique latine
Pres Urbanización Palomino B-2, Dpto 31, Lima, Peru. E-mail: lfloresg2000@yahoo.com.
URL: http://congresocisal.blogspot.com/
History 1982, as *Secretariado de Institutos Seculares en América Latina (SISAL).* With the approval of *Congregation for Institutes of Consecrated Life and Societies of Apostolic Life (CICSAL, #04671),* changed to current title, 1996. **Structure** Executive Council. **Events** *Convention* Quito (Ecuador) 2002, *Convention* Asunción (Paraguay) 1998, *Quadrennial Convention* Asunción (Paraguay) 1998, *Convention* Quito (Ecuador) 1994. **Publications** *Boletin del CISAL.*
Members Secular institutes (about 150), representing about 10.000 individuals. Federated and non-federated members in 23 countries:
Argentina, Bolivia, Brazil, Canada, Chile, Colombia, Costa Rica, Cuba, Dominican Rep, Ecuador, El Salvador, Guatemala, Haiti, Honduras, Mexico, Nicaragua, Panama, Paraguay, Peru, Puerto Rico, Uruguay, USA, Venezuela.
NGO Relations Close links with: *Consejo de Institutos de Seguridad Social de Centroamérica y República Dominicana (CISSCAD, #04715). Faithful Servants of Jesus* is a member. [2014/XF6508/F]

- ♦ Confederación Interamericana de Acción Social Católica (inactive)
- ♦ Confederación Interamericana de Educación Católica (#11403)
- ♦ Confederación Interamericana de Ganaderos y Agricultores (no recent information)
- ♦ Confederación Interamericana de Ingenieria Quimica (#11417)
- ♦ Confederación Interamericana de Relaciones Públicas (#11418)
- ♦ Confederación Interamericana de Relaciones Públicas (#04436)
- ♦ Confederación Interamericana de Trabajadores / see Confederación Sindical de Trabajadores y Trabajadoras de las Américas (#04480)
- ♦ Confederación Interamericana de Transporte Aéreo (inactive)
- ♦ Confederación Internacional de Agentes de Aduanas (#04559)
- ♦ Confederación Internacional de Apoyo Familiar (inactive)
- ♦ Confederación Internacional de Asociaciones de Expertos y de Consultores (inactive)
- ♦ Confederación Internacional de Bancos Populares (#12867)
- ♦ Confederación Internacional Católica de Hospitales (inactive)
- ♦ Confederación Internacional de los Comerciantes de Obras de Arte (#12848)
- ♦ Confederación Internacional del Comercio e Industrias de Legumbres Secas / see Global Pulse Confederation (#10562)
- ♦ Confederación Internacional del Crédito Agricola (#04560)
- ♦ Confederación Internacional de Crédito Popular / see International Confederation of Popular Banks (#12867)
- ♦ Confederación Internacional de Empresas de Trabajo Temporal / see World Employment Confederation (#21376)
- ♦ Confederación Internacional de Ex Prisoneros de Guerra (inactive)
- ♦ Confederación Internacional de Funcionarios (no recent information)
- ♦ Confederación Internacional de Ingenieros Agrónomos (inactive)
- ♦ Confederación Internacional para la Juventud (inactive)
- ♦ Confederación Internacional de Matronas (#12863)
- ♦ Confederación Internacional de la Medida (#14124)
- ♦ Confederación Internacional de Movimientos Familiares Cristianos (#12851)
- ♦ Confederación Internacional de Organizaciones Católicas de Acción Caritativa y Social / see Caritas Internationalis (#03580)
- ♦ Confederación Internacional de Organizaciones Sindicales Libres (inactive)
- ♦ Confederación Internacional del Peinado / see World Hairdressers' Organization (#21550)
- ♦ Confederación Internacional de Sociedades de Autores y Compositores (#04563)
- ♦ Confederación Internacional de los Trabajadores Intelectuales (#04564)
- ♦ Confederación internacional de los Transformadores de Papel y Cartón en Europa (#12866)
- ♦ Confederación International de los Remolacheros Europeos / see International Confederation of European Beet Growers (#12860)

♦ Confederación de Judo del Caribe (CJC) 04452

Caribbean Judo Confederation – Confédération Caraïbe de judo
Pres c/o FEDOJUDO, Av Máximo Gómez con 27 de Febrero, Santo Domingo, Dominican Rep. E-mail: secretaria@fedojudo.org.
History 1984. Dormant between 1989-2005. Reactivated and new statutes approved 10 Nov 2005, San José (Costa Rica). **NGO Relations** *Pan American Judo Union (PJU, #18115).* [2017/XM4060/D]

- ♦ Confederación Latinoamericana de Asociaciones de Dirigentes de Empresas (no recent information)

♦ Confederación Latino Americana de Asociaciones de Profesionales Universitarios (CLAPU) 04453

Latin American Confederation of Associations of University Professionals
Contact address not obtained. Fax +541145136417. E-mail: info@cgpra.org.ar.
URL: http://cgp-ra.org/clapu/
History Sep 1971, Lima (Peru). Set up during Primer Congreso Latinoamericano de Instituciones de Profesionales Universitarios. Also referred to as *Confederación Latinoamericana y del Caribe de Asociaciones de Profesionales Universitarios.* Statutes adopted, 21 Oct 1972, Rio de Janeiro (Brazil). **Aims** Seek consensus and integration based on principles of inclusion and equality of justice to enable distributing the products of the national effort and the social, economic and cultural rights for all citizens to ensure the strengthening of democratic institutions. **Structure** Executive Committee, comprising President, 1st, 2nd and 3rd vice-Presidents, Secretary-General, Treasurer, 3 Directors and 3 Alternate Directors. **Languages** Portuguese. **Staff** 12.00 FTE, paid. **Finance** Members' dues.
Members Full in 4 countries:
Argentina, Brazil, Uruguay, Venezuela.
NGO Relations Member of: *World Union of Professions (WUP, #21882).* [2021/XD3995/t/D]

♦ Confederación Latinoamericana de Bioquimica Clinica (COLABIOCLI) 04454

Latin American Confederation of Clinical Biochemistry – Confédération latinoaméricaine de biochimie clinique
Contact Calle Antezana 847, Edificio Torre Atlanta, Piso 4 – Of 11, Cochabamba, Bolivia. E-mail: colabiocli2019.2021bol@gmail.com.
URL: https://colabiocli.com/
History 1968. **Aims** Upgrade the quality of analytical clinical chemistry; stimulate research and development in clinical laboratory sciences. **Structure** Council; Executive Board. **Languages** Portuguese, Spanish. **Staff** 1.00 FTE, paid; 2.00 FTE, voluntary. **Finance** Sources: members' dues. Annual budget: 20,000 USD. **Activities** Events/meetings; training/education. **Events** *Congress* León (Mexico) 2022, *Biennial Congress* Panama (Panama) 2019, *Biennial Congress* Punta del Este (Uruguay) 2017, *Biennial Congress* Quito (Ecuador) 2015, *Biennial Congress* Lima (Peru) 2013. **Publications** *Acta Bioquimica Clinica Latinoamericana* (periodical).
Members National societies in 22 countries:
Argentina, Bolivia, Brazil, Chile, Colombia, Costa Rica, Cuba, Dominican Rep, Ecuador, El Salvador, Guatemala, Honduras, Mexico, Nicaragua, Panama, Paraguay, Peru, Portugal, Puerto Rico, Spain, Uruguay, Venezuela.
IGO Relations Official relations with: *Pan American Health Organization (PAHO, #18108).* [2021/XD3274/D]

- ♦ Confederación Latinoamericana y del Caribe de Asociaciones Cristianas de Jóvenes / see Latin American and Caribbean Alliance of YMCAs (#16264)
- ♦ Confederación Latinoamericana y del Caribe de Asociaciones de Profesionales Universitarios / see Confederación Latino Americana de Asociaciones de Profesionales Universitarios (#04453)
- ♦ Confederación Latinoamericana y Caribeña de Pequeña y Mediana Empresa (no recent information)
- ♦ Confederación Latinoamericana y del Caribe de Trabajadoras del Hogar (unconfirmed)

♦ Confederación Latinoamericana de Centros de Espiritualidad Ignaciana (CLACIES) 04455

Latin American Confederation of Centres of Ignatian Spirituality
Main Office c/o CPAL, Avda Fulgencio Valdez 780, Breña 05 0052, 5, Lima, Peru. T. +5114438110. E-mail: espiritualidad@cpalsj.org – secretario@cpalsj.org.

History Also referred to as *Confederación Latinoamericana de Centros Ignacianos de Espiritualidad*. **Events** *Meeting* Santiago (Chile) 2011, *Meeting* San Miguel (El Salvador) 2001. **Members** Centres (21) in 15 countries. Membership countries not specified. **NGO Relations** *Conferencia de Provinciales Jesuitas de América Latina y El Caribe (CPAL, #04658)*. [2011/XJ5561/**D**]

♦ Confederación Latinoamericana de Centros Ignacianos de Espiritualidad / see Confederación Latinoamericana de Centros de Espiritualidad Ignaciana (#04455)
♦ Confederación Latinoamericana de Cooperativas de Ahorro y Crédito (#16302)

♦ Confederación Latinoamericana de Cooperativas y Mutuales de Trabajadores (COLACOT) 04456

Confédération latinoaméricaine de coopératives des travailleurs – Latin American Confederation of Cooperative Workers

Pres Edificio UTAL – Planta Baja, San Antonio de Los Altos 1204 MI, Venezuela. T. +582128334090. Fax +582123721798. E-mail: presidenciacolacot@yahoo.com.

History Jun 1975, Caracas (Venezuela). Maintains *Centro Latinoamericano de Economia del Trabajo (CELATET)*. **Aims** Promote the development of the cooperative movement rooted into the Latin American reality, able to act as a major agent within the process of economic and social reorientation of the region. **Structure** Latin American Congress; Executive Committee, consisting of President, Vice President, Secretary General, Assistant Secretary General; Executive Secretaries (8). **Languages** Spanish. **Staff** Voluntary. **Finance** Members' dues. **Events** *Congreso internacional sobre globalizacion mundial y el rol del cooperativismo financiero* Bogota (Colombia) 1993, *Congress* Bogota (Colombia) 1993, *Congress* Buenos Aires (Argentina) 1992, *Congreso internacional de economia solidaria* Córdoba (Argentina) 1992, *Joint international conference* San José (Costa Rica) 1992. **Publications** *Nueva Dimensión* (4 a year).

Members Affiliate organizations (80) in 23 countries and territories:
Argentina, Bolivia, Brazil, Chile, Colombia, Costa Rica, Dominican Rep, Ecuador, El Salvador, Guatemala, Haiti, Honduras, Jamaica, Mexico, Neth Antilles, Nicaragua, Panama, Paraguay, Peru, Puerto Rico, St Lucia, Uruguay, Venezuela.

NGO Relations Affiliate organization of: *Confederación de Cooperativas del Caribe, Centro y Suramérica (CCC-CA, #04445)*; *International Trade Union Confederation (ITUC, #15708)*. Member of: *América Cooperativa y Mutual (Red AMEC, #00773)*. [2019.04.24/XD2629/**D**]

♦ Confederación Latinoamericana de Empleo 04457

World Employment Confederation Latin America

Head Office Cr 45 (Autopista Norte, costado oriental), No 103 – 34 Of 312, Bogota, Bogota DC, Colombia. T. +5716016680. E-mail: prensa@acoset.org.
URL: http://www.weclatinamerica.org/

History Set up as *Confederación Latinoamericana de Empresas de Trabajo Temporario y Actividades Afines (Clett and A)*. Current title adopted Sep 2016. A regional association of *World Employment Confederation (WEC, #21376)*.

Members Full in 7 countries:
Argentina, Brazil, Chile, Colombia, Mexico, Peru, Uruguay. [2016/XM5268/**D**]

♦ Confederación Latinoamericana de Empresas de Trabajo Temporario y Actividades Afines / see Confederación Latinoamericana de Empleo (#04457)

♦ Confederación Latinoamericana de Fisioterapia y Kinesiologia (CLAFK) 04458

Latin American Physiotherapy and Kinesiology Confederation

Sec Rue Bento Gonçalves 183, Sala 903, Florianópolis SC, CEP 88010-080 SC, Brazil. E-mail: fernandasvguimaraes@gmail.com.

Languages Spanish. **Staff** Voluntary. **Events** *Quadrennial congress / Congress* Santiago (Chile) 2010, *Congress* Bogota (Colombia) 2006, *Quadrennial Congress* Bogota (Colombia) 2006, *Quadrennial congress / Congress* Santiago (Chile) 1994.

Members Full in 11 countries:
Argentina, Bolivia, Brazil, Chile, Colombia, Ecuador, Mexico, Paraguay, Peru, Uruguay, Venezuela.

NGO Relations *World Confederation for Physical Therapy (WCPT, #21293)*. [2013/XD2186/**D**]

♦ Confederación Latinoamericana de la Industria Grafica (#16303)

♦ Confederación Latinoamericana Macabea (CLAM) 04459

Latin American Maccabi Confederation – Confederação Latinoamericana Macabi

Contact Estadio Israelita Maccabi, Av Las Condes 8361, 7560171 Santiago, Santiago Metropolitan, Chile.
URL: http://www.clamweb.net

History Founded 1950. **Structure** Executive Committee, including President, Secretary-General and Treasurer. **Activities** Sponsors Pan American Maccabi Games (every 4 years).

Members Full in 14 countries and territories:
Argentina, Bolivia, Brazil, Chile, Colombia, Costa Rica, Guatemala, Mexico, Panama, Paraguay, Peru, Uruguay, USA, Venezuela.

NGO Relations Member of: *Maccabi World Union (MWU, #16537)*; *JCC Global (#16093)*. [2017/XD4822/**D**]

♦ Confederación Latinoamericana de Organizadores de Congresos y Afines / see Federación de Entidades Organizadoras de Congresos y Afines de América Latina (#09299)

♦ Confederación Latinoamericana de Paracaidismo (COLPAR – SIGLO XXI) 04460

Confédération latinoaméricaine de parachutisme

Address not obtained.
URL: http://www.colpar.org/

Structure Executive Council.

Members Federations in 12 countries:
Argentina, Brazil, Chile, Colombia, Costa Rica, Cuba, El Salvador, Panama, Paraguay, Peru, Uruguay, Venezuela. [2015/XD6224/**D**]

♦ Confederación Latinoamericana de Pobladores en la Marginación Social (COLAPOM) 04461

Latin American Confederation of People in Social Marginality – Confédération latinoaméricaine de personnes en marginalité sociale

Contact address not obtained. T. +582125420534. Fax +58212720463 – +58212721729.

Events *Congress* Caracas (Venezuela) 2004. **Members** Full in 18 countries. Membership countries not specified. [2010/XE1648/**E**]

♦ Confederación Latinoamericana de Prensa Turistica (no recent information)
♦ Confederación Latinoamericana de Religiosos / see Confederación Caribeña y Latinoamericana de Religiosas y Religiosos (#04442)
♦ Confederación Latinoamericana de Sociedades de Anestesia / see Latin American Confederation of Societies of Anesthesiology (#16305)
♦ Confederación Latinoamericana de Sociedades de Anestesiologia (#16305)
♦ Confederación Latinoamericana de Terapeutas Ocupacionales (#16356)
♦ Confederación Latinoamericana de Trabajadores de Comunicaciones (no recent information)
♦ Confederación Latinoamericana de Trabajadores Estatales (#16304)
♦ Confederación Latinoamericana de Trabajadores Jubilados y Pensionados / see Confederación Latinoamericana de Trabajadores Jubilados, Pensionados y Adultos Mayores (#04462)

♦ Confederación Latinoamericana de Trabajadores Jubilados, Pensionados y Adultos Mayores 04462

Latin American Confederation of Retired Workers, Pensioners and Senior Citizens

Pres Calle A No 21 Nordesa III, Santo Domingo, Dominican Rep. E-mail: jose.gomezc@claro.net.do.
URL: http://academiahumanista.org/adultos-mayores/

History Founded, 5 Apr 1987, as *Confederación Latinoamericana de Trabajadores Jubilados y Pensionados (CLATJUP)*. Name changed to *Central Latinoamericana y del Caribe de Trabajadores Jubilados, Pensionados y Adultos Mayores (CLATJUPAM)*, 2011. Current title adopted 2018. **Aims** Inform, guide and educate the elderly of Latin America and the Caribbean. **Structure** Executive Committee; President. **Languages** French, Portuguese, Spanish. **Staff** Voluntary. **Finance** Members' dues. **Events** *Congress* Santo Domingo (Dominican Rep) 2014, *Congress* Caracas (Venezuela) 2002. **Publications** *Adultos Mayores* (2 a year) – bulletin. **Members** National organizations in 18 countries. Membership countries not specified. **NGO Relations** Member of: [2018.09.05/XD2245/v/**D**]

♦ Confederación Latinoamericana de Trabajadores del Transporte y las Comunicaciones (no recent information)

♦ Confederación Médica Latinoamericana y del Caribe (CONFEMEL) . 04463

Latin American and Caribbean Medical Confederation

Admin Secretariat Br Artigas 1515, PO Box 10-601, 11200 Montevideo, Uruguay. T. +59824014701 ext125. Fax +59824091603. E-mail: confemel@mednet.org.uy.
URL: http://www.confemel.com/

History 1997, Santa Cruz (Bolivia). **Events** *Annual General Assembly* Mexico City (Mexico) 2013, *Extraordinary General Assembly* Lima (Peru) 2010, *General Assembly* San José (Costa Rica) 2010, *General Assembly* Guatemala 2009, *General Assembly* Buenos Aires (Argentina) 2008.

Members in 19 countries:
Argentina, Bolivia, Brazil, Chile, Colombia, Costa Rica, Dominican Rep, Ecuador, El Salvador, Guatemala, Haiti, Honduras, Nicaragua, Panama, Paraguay, Peru, Puerto Rico, Uruguay, Venezuela.

NGO Relations Collaborates with: *World Medical Association (WMA, #21646)*. [2022/XD7099/**D**]

♦ Confederación Médica Panamericana (inactive)
♦ Confederación Mundial de Actividades Subacuaticas (#21873)
♦ Confederación Mundial de Béisbol Softbol (#21222)

♦ Confederación Mundial de Educación (COMED) 04464

World Confederation of Education – Confédération Mondiale de l'Education – Confederação Mundial da Educação

Pres 90 Chacabuco St, 3rd Floor, PO Box 1069AAB, Buenos Aires, Argentina. T. +541143427788. Fax +541143428604. E-mail: ezequiel.martinich@uai.edu.ar.
URL: http://www.comep.org/

History Proposed Jul 1989, San José (Costa Rica), during IV Latin American Seminar on Private Education. Constituted 16 Nov 1989. Declaration of San José serves as Foundational Act. Former names and other names: *Confederación Mundial de Enseñanza Privada (COMEP)* – former; *World Confederation of Private Education* – former; *Confédération Mondiale de l'Enseignement Privé* – former; *Confederação Mundial de Ensino Privado* – former; *World Confederation of Private Teaching* – former. **Aims** Bring together associations and federations of private education from all over the world, so as to promote the exercise and implementation of the right to education respecting pluralism and the right of parents to choose the type of education their children will receive, whatever the religious, philosophical or social principles may be, so long as they conform to those principles stated in the Universal Declaration of Human Rights. **Structure** Officers. **Languages** English, Portuguese, Spanish. **Staff** 42.00 FTE, voluntary. **Finance** Members' dues. **Activities** Events/meetings. Active in: Argentina, Bolivia, Brazil, Chile, China, Colombia, Costa Rica, Ecuador, El Salvador, Honduras, Indonesia, Jamaica, New Zealand, Paraguay, Peru, Puerto Rico, South Africa, Spain, Uruguay, USA, Venezuela. **Events** *World Education Congress* Lisbon (Portugal) 2015, *World Education Congress* Bali (Indonesia) 2013, *World Education Congress* Madrid (Spain) 2012, *World education congress* Valencia (Spain) 2008, *World Education Congress* Madrid (Spain) 2004.

Members Organizations in 18 countries:
Argentina, Bolivia, Brazil, Chile, Colombia, Costa Rica, Ecuador, El Salvador, Honduras, Jamaica, New Zealand, Paraguay, Peru, South Africa, Spain, Uruguay, USA, Venezuela.
Founder member:
Federación de Asociaciones Educativas de América Latina y el Caribe (FAELA, #09289).

Consultative Status Consultative status granted from: *UNESCO (#20322)* (Consultative Status). [2018.03.07/XU1421/y/**D**]

♦ Confederación Mundial de Enseñanza Privada / see Confederación Mundial de Educación (#04464)
♦ Confederación Mundial de la Gastronomia (no recent information)
♦ Confederación Mundial de Organizaciones de Profesionales de la Enseñanza (inactive)
♦ Confederación Mundial del Trabajo (inactive)
♦ Confederación Norteamérica y Caribe de Balonmano (#17557)
♦ Confederación Norte, Centroamerica y Caribe de Fútbol de Salón (#04571)
♦ Confederación Norte y Centroamericana de Béisbol (no recent information)

♦ Confederación Norte-Centroamericana y del Caribe de Fútbol (CONCACAF) 04465

Confederation of North and Central American and Caribbean Association Football – Confédération d'Amérique du Nord, d'Amérique centrale et des Caraïbes de football

Gen Sec 161 NW 6th Street, Suite 1100, Miami FL 33136, USA. T. +13057043232. Fax +13053978813. E-mail: contact@concacaf.org.
Pres address not obtained.
URL: https://www.concacaf.com/

History 1961. Continental confederation of: *International Federation of Association Football (#13360)*. Former names and other names: *North and Central American and Caribbean Football Confederation* – former. **Aims** Promote and minister the *sport* of football in North America, Central America and the Caribbean. **Structure** Congress; Executive Committee; General Secretariat. Emergency Committee. Committees (4): Competitions Group; Public Affairs Group; Technical Group; Legal And Finance Group. Standing Commissions (19). **Languages** English, French, Spanish. **Staff** 33.00 FTE, paid. **Finance** Sources: members' dues. **Activities** Events/meetings; sporting activities. **Events** *Congress* Toronto, ON (Canada) 2007, *Extraordinary congress* Munich (Germany) 2006, *Congress* St George's (Grenada) 2004, *Congress* Miami, FL (USA) 2002, *Congress* Nassau (Bahamas) 2000. **Publications** *CONCACAF News* (4 a year).

Members National Associations in 39 countries and territories:
Anguilla, Antigua-Barbuda, Aruba, Bahamas, Barbados, Belize, Bermuda, Canada, Cayman Is, Costa Rica, Cuba, Dominica, Dominican Rep, El Salvador, Grenada, Guatemala, Guyana, Haiti, Honduras, Jamaica, Mexico, Montserrat, Neth Antilles, Nicaragua, Panama, Puerto Rico, St Kitts-Nevis, St Lucia, St Vincent-Grenadines, Suriname, Trinidad-Tobago, Turks-Caicos, USA, Virgin Is UK, Virgin Is USA.
Associate members (5):
Guadeloupe, Guiana Fr, Martinique, St Maarten, St Martin.

NGO Relations Member of (1): *Asociación de Confederaciones Deportivas Panamericanas (ACODEPA, #02119)*. [2023/XD3003/**D**]

♦ Confederación Nortecentroamericana y del Caribe de Vóleibol (#17576)
♦ Confederación Odontológica Regional Andina (inactive)
♦ Confederación de Organizaciones de Productores Familiares del Mercosur Ampliado (#04437)

♦ Confederación de Organizaciones Turisticas de la América Latina (COTAL) 04466

Confédération des organisations touristiques de l'Amérique latine – Latin American Confederation of Tourism Organizations – Confederação de Organizações Turisticas da América Latina (COTAL) – Verband der Latein-amerikanischen Fremdenverkehrsorganisationen

Vice-Pres Viamonte 640, Piso 3, 1053 Buenos Aires, Argentina. T. +5491134361966. E-mail: info@cotalamerica.org.
URL: http://www.cotalamerica.org/

History 22 Apr 1957, Mexico City (Mexico). Founded during 1st Congress. **Aims** Group national associations of travel agents of Latin America; unify all travel agencies within their own national associations; encourage activities of national associations and protect their members' professional interests; improve facilities and working conditions; promote tourism exchanges; assist in improving hotels, restaurants, means of transport, facilitation of customs and immigration requirements, tourist attractions and native arts and crafts, and the teaching of tourism; establish rules of professional ethics; cooperate with regional and international tourist organizations. **Structure** General Assembly elects Executive Committee and Boards of Directors, comprising 11 members. **Languages** English, Portuguese, Spanish. **Staff** 3.00 FTE, paid. **Finance** Members' dues. Profit of annual Congresses and COTAL magazine. **Activities** Congresses (every year). Lobbies governmental bodies; provides advice on tourist development projects and joint venture possibilities. Training of management staff through COTAL's *Latin American Institute of Tourist Studies (no recent information)*. **Events** *Annual Congress* Acapulco (Mexico) 2015, *Annual Congress* Buenos Aires (Argentina) 2014, *Annual Congress* Panama (Panama) 2013, *Annual Congress* Lima (Peru) 2010, *Annual Congress* Torremolinos (Spain) 2009. **Publications** *Revista COTAL* (6 a year) in Spanish.
Members Membership represents over 12,000 travel agents – retailers, wholesalers and tour operators included – in addition to major hotels, car rental and road transportation companies and airlines. Active members national associations in 21 countries:
Argentina, Bolivia, Brazil, Chile, Colombia, Costa Rica, Cuba, Dominican Rep, Ecuador, El Salvador, Guatemala, Haiti, Honduras, Mexico, Nicaragua, Panama, Paraguay, Peru, Puerto Rico, Uruguay, Venezuela.
Affiliate members in 18 countries:
Canada, China, Cuba, Egypt, France, Germany, Greece, Haiti, Hong Kong, India, Italy, Japan, Jordan, Portugal, Spain, Türkiye, UK, USA.
Consultative Status Consultative status granted from: *ECOSOC (#05331)* (Ros A). **IGO Relations** Cooperation with: *OAS (#17629)*. Accredited by: *United Nations Office at Vienna (UNOV, #20604)*. [2017/XD0396/**D**]

♦ Confederación Panafricana de Empleadores / see Business Africa (#03377)
♦ Confederación Panamericana de Agentes Comerciales (inactive)

♦ Confederación Panamericana de Badminton (PABC) 04467

Badminton Pan American Confederation (BPAC)
COO Calle Recavarren 111, Ovic 601, Miraflores, 15000, Lima, Peru. T. +5115877268. E-mail: bpac@badmintonpanam.org – panambadminton@gmail.com.
Pres address not obtained. T. +8769906305. Fax +8769849556.
URL: http://www.badmintonpanam.org/
History 13 Feb 1976, Mexico City (Mexico). In abeyance between 1981-1986. New Rules and Regulations drafted in Jun 1987. Former names and other names: *Pan American Badminton Confederation (PBC)* – former. **Aims** Promote badminton throughout the region. **Structure** Meeting of delegates of member national associations (annual, on the occasion of the Pan American Badminton Championship); Executive Committee. Regions: North America; South America; Central America; Caribbean. **Languages** English, Spanish. **Staff** 7.50 FTE, paid. **Finance** Sources: members' dues. Some funding received from IBF. **Activities** Sporting activities; training/education; events/meetings. **Events** *Meeting* San Jose, CA (USA) 1988, *Meeting* Seoul (Korea Rep) 1988. **Publications** *Panamerican Badminton Family* (3 a year) – magazine.
Members Associations in 37 countries and territories:
Argentina, Aruba, Barbados, Bermuda, Bolivia, Brazil, Canada, Cayman Is, Chile, Colombia, Costa Rica, Cuba, Curaçao, Dominican Rep, Ecuador, El Salvador, Falklands/Malvinas, Grenada, Guadeloupe, Guatemala, Guiana Fr, Guyana, Haiti, Honduras, Jamaica, Martinique, Mexico, Panama, Paraguay, Peru, Puerto Rico, St Lucia, Suriname, Trinidad-Tobago, Uruguay, USA, Venezuela.
NGO Relations Member of (2): *Asociación de Confederaciones Deportivas Panamericanas (ACODEPA, #02119)*; *Badminton World Federation (BWF, #03060)*. [2021/XD9629/**D**]

♦ Confederación Panamericana de Baloncesto / see FIBA Americas (#09745)

♦ Confederación Panamericana de Béisbol (COPABE) 04468

Pan American Baseball Confederation
Pres Estadio La Normal, Ave V Centenario, Villa Consuelo, Santo Domingo, Dominican Rep. T. +50670107273. E-mail: beisbol@copabe.org – coordinaciocopabe@americas.wbsc.org.
URL: https://www.wbscamericas.org/
History Continental confederation of: *World Baseball Softball Confederation (WBSC, #21222)*. **Publications** *Boletin de COPABE*.
Members National baseball associations in 28 countries and territories:
Argentina, Aruba, Bahamas, Bolivia, Brazil, Canada, Chile, Colombia, Costa Rica, Cuba, Dominican Rep, Ecuador, El Salvador, Guatemala, Honduras, Jamaica, Mexico, Neth Antilles, Nicaragua, Panama, Peru, Puerto Rico, Suriname, Uruguay, USA, Venezuela, Virgin Is UK, Virgin Is USA.
NGO Relations Member of: *Asociación de Confederaciones Deportivas Panamericanas (ACODEPA, #02119)*. [2022/XD2112/**D**]

♦ Confederación Panamericana de Billar (CPB) 04469

Pan American Billiards Confederation
Pres Kilómetro 3/5 Carretera Norte, Edificio INPASA, Managua, Nicaragua. T. +50522493792. E-mail: presidente@cpbillar.net – ceerre@inpasa.com.
URL: http://www.cpbillar.net/
History Registration: No/ID: 5274-2012, Nicaragua. **Structure** Executive Committee.
Members Full in 20 countries and territories:
Argentina, Aruba, Bonaire Is, Brazil, Chile, Colombia, Costa Rica, Curaçao, Ecuador, Guadeloupe, Guatemala, Honduras, Mexico, Nicaragua, Panama, Peru, Trinidad-Tobago, Uruguay, USA, Venezuela.
NGO Relations Member of (1): *Asociación de Confederaciones Deportivas Panamericanas (ACODEPA, #02119)*. *Asociación Iberoamericana de Billar (AIB, no recent information)*; *Asociación de Confederaciones Deportivas Sudamericanas (ACODESU, no recent information)*; *International Billiards and Snooker Federation (IBSF, #12340)*; *World Confederation of Billiards Sports (WCBS, #21291)*; *World Pool-Billiard Association (WPA, #21733)*. [2023/XD5091/**D**]

♦ Confederación Panamericana de Bochas (CPB) 04470

Contact Adolfo Alsina 1450 1o Piso, CIUDAD CP C1088AAL Buenos Aires, Argentina. T. +541143830904. E-mail: cpanamericanadebochas@gmail.com.
URL: http://cpdebochas.wixsite.com/bochas
History *Confederación Sudamericana de Bochas (inactive)* merged with CPB, 2014. **Structure** Officers.
Members Affiliates in 13 countries:
Argentina, Bolivia, Brazil, Canada, Chile, Dominican Rep, Haiti, Mexico, Paraguay, Peru, Uruguay, USA, Venezuela.
NGO Relations Affiliated organization of: *South American Sports Organization (SASO, #19708)*. [2017/XM6690/**D**]

♦ Confederación Panamericana de Canoas (COPAC) 04471

Pan American Canoe Federation
Pres International Canoe Federation, Avenue de Rhodanie 54, 1007 Lausanne VD, Switzerland. T. +41216120290. Fax +41216120291.
Facebook: https://www.facebook.com/COPACOnline/
History Aug 1991. **Structure** Executive Committee; Commissions (6).
Members National federations in 21 countries:
Argentina, Bolivia, Brazil, Canada, Chile, Costa Rica, Cuba, Dominican Rep, Ecuador, El Salvador, Guatemala, Guyana, Mexico, Neth Antilles, Paraguay, Peru, Puerto Rico, Suriname, Uruguay, USA, Venezuela.
NGO Relations Member of (1): *Asociación de Confederaciones Deportivas Panamericanas (ACODEPA, #02119)*. Supported by: *International Canoe Federation (ICF, #12437)*. [2022/XM3586/**D**]

♦ Confederación Panamericana de Ciclismo (#18092)

♦ Confederación Panamericana de Deportes de Montaña y Escalada (UPAME) 04472

Pan-American Confederation of Mountain Sports and Climbing
Pres PO Box 1596, San José, San José, San José, 2150, Costa Rica. T. +50683308929. E-mail: info@upame.org.
URL: http://www.upame.org/
History 1976, as *Pan-American Union of Mountains Associations – Union Panamericana de Asociaciones de Montañismo (UPAM)*. Subsequently changed title to *Union Panamericana de Asociaciones de Montañismo y Escalada*, Jun 1996. Current title with previous acronym adopted 2012. **Aims** Integrate American countries in development and diffusion of mountaineering, climbing, trail and sky running. **Structure** General Assembly; Executive Board; Commissions (4). **Languages** English, Spanish. **Staff** 8.00 FTE, paid. **Activities** Events/meetings; sporting activities; training/education. **Events** *Plenary Assembly* Quito (Ecuador) 2016, *Plenary Assembly* Antigua (Guatemala) 2015, *Mountain Meeting* Uruguay 2015, *Mountain Meeting* Ecuador 2014, *General Assembly / Plenary Assembly* San José (Costa Rica) 2014.
Members National mountaineering and climbing associations (over 50) in 14 countries:
Argentina, Bolivia, Brazil, Chile, Colombia, Costa Rica, Ecuador, El Salvador, Guatemala, Mexico, Panama, Peru, Uruguay, Venezuela.
Permanent Advisor Member in 1 country:
Spain.
NGO Relations Member of: *Union internationale des associations d'alpinisme (UIAA, #20420)*. [2021/XD4056/**D**]

♦ Confederación Panamericana del Deporte de los Trabajadores (COPADET) 04473

Contact Av Ricardo Flores Magon 44, 4 Piso Col Guerrero, DF 06300 Mexico City CDMX, Mexico. T. +525536129924. Fax +525536129925.
History 21 Aug 1993. Previously also referred to as *Confederação Pan-Americana de Desporto do Trabalhador*. **Aims** Promote sports among workers and their families, so as to develop an awareness of the great benefits of regular physical activity. **Structure** Officers: President; 4 Vice-Presidents (North-America, Central America, South America, Caribbean); Secretary-General; 3 members. **Languages** English, French, Portuguese, Spanish. **Activities** Events/meetings.
Members Full in 15 countries and territories:
Argentina, Brazil, Canada, Chile, Costa Rica, Cuba, Dominican Rep, Ecuador, Honduras, Mexico, Panama, Peru, Puerto Rico, USA, Venezuela.
NGO Relations Continental member of: *International Workers and Amateurs in Sports Confederation (#15905)*. [2016/XJ2152/**D**]

♦ Confederación Panamericana de Educación Vial (inactive)
♦ Confederación Panamericana de Escuelas de Hosteleria y Turismo / see Confederación Panamericana de Escuelas de Hoteleria, Gastronomia y Turismo (#04474)

♦ Confederación Panamericana de Escuelas de Hoteleria, Gastronomia y Turismo (CONPEHT) 04474

Pan American Federation of Hotel, Gastronomy and Tourism Schools
Pres Escuela de Turismo, Univ Dominicana O and M, Calle Santiago, Santo Domingo, Dominican Rep. T. +18095334551 – +18096856543. E-mail: bolivar.troncoso@dominicana.net.do.
URL: http://www.conpeht.com/
History 1991, Mexico City (Mexico). Previously referred to as *Confederación Panamericana de Escuelas de Hosteleria y Turismo – Pan American Federation of Hotel and Tourism Schools*. **Activities** Awards 'Medal of Honor in Tourism'. **Events** *Congress* Punta Cana (Dominican Rep) 2013, *Congress* Rio de Janeiro (Brazil) 2012, *Congress* Bucaramanga (Colombia) 2010, *Congress* La Paz (Bolivia) 2009, *Congress* Acapulco (Mexico) 2007.
Members in 14 countries:
Argentina, Bolivia, Canada, Chile, Colombia, Cuba, Dominican Rep, Ecuador, Mexico, Nicaragua, Paraguay, Peru, USA, Venezuela. [2013/XD4317/**D**]

♦ Confederación Panamericana de Esgrima (CPE) 04475

Pan American Fencing Confederation
Pres Sala de Esgrima – Pal de los Deportes, Centro de Gobierno, San Salvador, El Salvador. T. +5215521066216. E-mail: esgrimacpe@yahoo.com – contacto@cpe-fie.com.
Exec Sec address not obtained.
History 8 Mar 1951, Buenos Aires (Argentina). **Structure** Executive Committee. Commissions (4): Development of Fencing and Propaganda; Medical; Rules and Judges; Statutes. **Languages** English, Spanish. **Activities** Sporting activities. **Events** *Annual Congress* Santiago (Chile) 2002.
Members National organizations in 26 countries and territories:
Argentina, Aruba, Bolivia, Brazil, Canada, Chile, Colombia, Costa Rica, Cuba, Ecuador, El Salvador, Guatemala, Haiti, Honduras, Jamaica, Mexico, Neth Antilles, Nicaragua, Panama, Paraguay, Peru, Puerto Rico, Uruguay, USA, Venezuela, Virgin Is USA.
NGO Relations Member of (1): *Asociación de Confederaciones Deportivas Panamericanas (ACODEPA, #02119)*. Recognized by: *Panam Sports Organization (Panam Sports, #18138)*. [2022/XD9016/**D**]

♦ Confederación Panamericana de Fútbol de Salón (#18112)
♦ Confederación Panamericana de Futsal / see Pan American Indoor Football Confederation (#18112)
♦ Confederación Panamericana de Ingenieria Mecanica, Eléctrica y Ramas Afines (#18089)

♦ Confederación Panamericana de Judo (CPJ) 04476

Pan-American Judo Confederation (PJC)
Pres Arenal 507-8, Arenal Tepepan, 14610 Mexico City CDMX, Mexico. T. +5531842279 – +55315534323160. E-mail: contact@panamericanjudo.com – presidente@panamjudo.org.
Gen Sec c/o Judo Canada, 4141 avenue Pierre De Coubertin, Montréal QC H1V 3N7, Canada. T. +15142555836.
URL: https://panamjudo.org/es
History 2009. Founded following a split within *Pan American Judo Union (PJU, #18115)*. **Structure** Board. **Languages** English, Spanish.
Members Full in 32 countries and territories:
Argentina, Aruba, Bahamas, Barbados, Belize, Bolivia, Brazil, Canada, Chile, Colombia, Costa Rica, Cuba, Dominican Rep, Ecuador, El Salvador, Guatemala, Guyana, Haiti, Honduras, Mexico, Nicaragua, Panama, Paraguay, Peru, Puerto Rico, St Lucia, Suriname, Trinidad-Tobago, Uruguay, USA, Venezuela, Virgin Is UK.
NGO Relations Member of (2): *Asociación de Confederaciones Deportivas Panamericanas (ACODEPA, #02119)*; *International Judo Federation (IJF, #13975)*. [2023/XM4059/**D**]

♦ Confederación Panamericana de Levantamiento de Pesas (#18137)
♦ Confederación Panamericana de Lucha Olímpica (#20666)
♦ Confederación Pan Americana de Medicina del Deporte (no recent information)
♦ Confederación Panamericana de Mini-fútbol / see Confederación Panamericana de Minifutbol (#04477)

♦ Confederación Panamericana de Minifutbol (CPM) 04477

Pan-American Minifootball Confederation
Pres address not obtained. E-mail: info@minifutbolamericas.com.
URL: http://minifutbolamericas.com/
History Also referred to as *Confederación Panamericana de Mini-fútbol*. Regional federation of *World Minifootball Federation (WMF, #21652)*.
Members Federations in 9 countries:
Bolivia, Brazil, Canada, Colombia, Ecuador, El Salvador, Mexico, Peru, USA.
NGO Relations *Asian Minifootball Confederation (AMC, #01541)*; *European Minifootball Federation (EMF, #07808)*; *Oceania Mini Football Federation (OMF, #17666)*. [2020/XJ9002/**D**]

♦ Confederación Panamericana de Pelota Vasca (unconfirmed)
♦ Confederación Panamericana de Productores de Seguros (#18088)
♦ Confederación Panamericana para Proveedores de la Industria Grafica (no recent information)
♦ Confederación Panamericana de Racquetball (#18123)

♦ Confederación Panamericana de Remo (COPARE) 04478

Pan-American Rowing Confederation
Pres Mariano Uriarte 6120, CP 11600, Montevideo, Uruguay. T. +59894873723. E-mail: copare.presidencia@gmail.com.
Facebook: https://www.facebook.com/Confederaci%C3%B3n-Panamericana-de-Remo-323705644329726/

History 28 Jul 1945, Rio de Janeiro (Brazil). Reorganized under current title, 18 Mar 1995, Mar del Plata (Argentina). Current Statutes adopted 1997. Former names and other names: *Confederación Sudamericana de Remo (CSAR)* – former. **Aims** Develop and promote rowing in South America. **Structure** Congress; Executive Board. **Languages** English, Spanish. **Staff** 1.00 FTE, paid. **Finance** Sources: members' dues. Budget depends on activities. **Activities** Sporting activities.
Members Affiliated associations and federations in 29 countries:
Argentina, Bahamas, Barbados, Bermuda, Bolivia, Brazil, Canada, Chile, Colombia, Costa Rica, Cuba, Dominican Rep, Ecuador, El Salvador, Guatemala, Haiti, Honduras, Jamaica, Mexico, Nicaragua, Panama, Paraguay, Peru, Puerto Rico, St Vincent-Grenadines, Trinidad-Tobago, Uruguay, USA, Venezuela.
NGO Relations Member of (2): *Asociación de Confederaciones Deportivas Panamericanas (ACODEPA, #02119); Asociación de Confederaciones Deportivas Sudamericanas (ACODESU, no recent information).*
[2021/XD5065/**D**]

♦ Confederación Panamericana de Softbol Amateur / see WBSC Americas Softball (#20840)
♦ Confederación Panamericana de Taekwondo (no recent information)
♦ Confederación Panamericana de Tiro con Arco / see World Archery Americas (#21106)
♦ Confederación Panamericana de Triathlon / see Americas Triathlon (#00795)

♦ Confederación Parlamentaria de las Américas (COPA) 04479

Parliamentary Confederation of the Americas – Confédération parlementaire des Amériques – Confederação Parlamentar das Américas

Québec Secretariat 1050 rue des Parlementaires, 4e étage, Québec QC G1A 1A3, Canada. T. +14186442888. Fax +14186431865. E-mail: copa@assnat.qc.ca.
Executive Secretary Congress of the State of Mexico, Plaza Hidalgo s/n Colonia Centro, CP 50000 Toluca MEX, Mexico. T. +5217222796400. E-mail: secretaria_ejecutivamexico@hotmail.com.
URL: http://www.copa.qc.ca/

History Sep 1997, Québec, QC (Canada). Former names and other names: *Parliamentary Conference of the Americas* – former (Sep 1997); *Conférence parlementaire des Amériques* – former (Sep 1997); *Conferencia Parlamentaria de las Américas (COPA)* – former (Sep 1997); *Conferência Parlamentar das Américas* – former (Sep 1997). **Aims** Serve as a forum for parliamentary assemblies of the Americas; foster dialogue on issues related to Inter-American cooperation; foster the adoption of measures to ensure a peaceful zone founded on the principles of representative and participative democracy and social justice, the protection of individual rights and gender equity. **Structure** General Assembly; Executive Committee of 13 members. Permanent Committees (6): Human Rights, Aboriginal Peoples and Citizen Security; Environment and Sustainable Development; Economy, Trade, Labour and Trading Blocs; Democracy and Peace; Education, Culture, Science and Technology; Health and Social Protection. *Network of Women Parliamentarians of the Americas (#17065).* Secretariats (2): Mexico; Québec (Canada). **Languages** English, French, Portuguese, Spanish. **Staff** 5.00 FTE, paid. **Finance** Contributions from member parliaments. **Events** *General Assembly* San Juan (Puerto Rico) 2020, *General Assembly* Guanajuato (Mexico) 2015, *General Assembly* Asunción (Paraguay) 2014, *General Assembly* Brasilia (Brazil) 2013, *General Assembly* Québec, QC (Canada) 2011.
Members Congresses and parliamentary assemblies of the unitary, federal and federated States of the Americas; regional parliaments and interparliamentary organizations in 35 countries:
Antigua-Barbuda, Argentina, Bahamas, Barbados, Belize, Bolivia, Brazil, Canada, Chile, Colombia, Costa Rica, Cuba, Dominica, Dominican Rep, Ecuador, El Salvador, Grenada, Guatemala, Guyana, Haiti, Honduras, Jamaica, Mexico, Nicaragua, Panama, Paraguay, Peru, St Kitts-Nevis, St Lucia, St Vincent-Grenadines, Suriname, Trinidad-Tobago, Uruguay, USA, Venezuela.
IGO Relations Cooperates with: *Andean Parliament (#00820); Parlamento Centroamericano (PARLACEN, #18201); Parlamento Latinoamericano (PARLATINO, #18203); Unión de Parlamentarios Sudamericanos y del MERCOSUR (UPSM, #20472)*; national organizations. **NGO Relations** Observer status with: *Assemblée parlementaire de la Francophonie (APF, #02312); Inter-Parliamentary Union (IPU, #15961).*
[2020/XF6242/**F***]

♦ Confederación Sindical Internacional (#15708)
♦ Confederación Sindical Mundial de la Enseñanza (inactive)
♦ Confederación Sindical de los Trabajadores de América Latina (inactive)

♦ Confederación Sindical de Trabajadores y Trabajadoras de las Américas (CSA) 04480

Trade Union Confederation of the Americas (TUCA)

SG Rua Formosa 367 – 4o andar, Centro, Sao Paulo SP, CEP 01049-000, Brazil. T. +551121040750. E-mail: sede@csa-csi.org.
URL: http://www.csa-csi.org/

History 8 Jan 1951, Mexico City (Mexico), as Regional Secretariat of *International Confederation of Free Trade Unions (ICFTU, inactive)*, by major democratic labour centres of the Western Hemisphere. Previously operated as *Confederación Interamericana de Trabajadores*, set up 10 Jan 1948, Lima (Peru). Subsequent name change: *Organización Regional Interamericana de Trabajadores (ORIT) – Organisation régionale interaméricaine des travailleurs – ICFTU Inter-American Regional Organization of Workers.* Merged, Nov 2006, with *World Confederation of Labour (WCL, inactive)* into *International Trade Union Confederation (ITUC, #15708).* Unification of ORIT and CLAT took place in 2008, Panama (Panama), when current name adopted. **Aims** Promote respect for human rights in general, and in particular trade union and labour rights of all persons; foster gender equality and equity at all levels of the trade union mouvement; improve working conditions and raise the quality of life of affiliates and their dependents; encourage solidarity between workers and between their organizations from their workplace and the community where they reside up to the global level; strengthen processes of trade union unity; form strategic agreements and alliances with other mouvements and related sociopolitical actors to build the necessary power to be able to defend and make the demands of workers and community, and bring about social justice; promote political, social, labour and economic democracy based on popular sovereignty and enriched with mechanisms and instances of effective participation and social dialogue; strengthen the Social Rule of Law as a fundamental pillar for democratic development and social justice; encourage economic, social, cultural and supportive integration of the nations of the region for balanced and sustainable development with a strong social and participatory dimension that enables the fusion of resources and efforts to eliminate serious existing asymmetries and foster productive development with an increasing added value, while protecting the environment; promote peace and free self-determination of the people and therefore against any form of subjugation that impedes the emancipation of all workers. **Structure** Congress (every 4 years). Executive Council and Secretariat of 17 members. Departments (4). Resident representative in Brazil and Costa Rica. **Languages** English, Portuguese, Spanish. **Staff** 20.00 FTE, paid. **Finance** Members' dues (about 50%). TUCA contributions. Budget (annual): about US$ 400,000. **Activities** Provides services through 4 Departments: Education; Social and Economic Affairs; Human and Trade Union Rights; Working Women. Conducts international seminars; sponsors workers educational and training courses on behalf of affiliates; collaborates with International Trade Secretariats operating in Latin America. Areas of activity: working youth; informal economy; child labour; integration; environmental policies; communication; migration; union self-reform. **Events** *Quadrennial Continental Congress* Foz do Iguaçu (Brazil) 2012, *European Union – Latin America and the Caribbean trade union summit* Madrid (Spain) 2010, *Quadrennial Congress / Quadrennial Continental Congress* Panama 2008, *Quadrennial Congress* Brasilia (Brazil) 2005, *EU-Latin American and Caribbean trade union summit* Mexico City (Mexico) 2004. **Publications** *Américas Info* in English, Portuguese, Spanish; *Boletin Secretaria Politicas Sociales.* Various online documents; meeting and event proceedings; podcasts.
Members Trade Unions (59 affiliates full members), totalling about 50 million individual members, in 26 countries and territories:
Argentina, Aruba, Barbados, Bonaire Is, Brazil, Canada, Chile, Colombia, Costa Rica, Curaçao, Dominica, Dominican Rep, Ecuador, El Salvador, Guatemala, Haiti, Honduras, Mexico, Nicaragua, Panama, Peru, St Lucia, Suriname, Trinidad-Tobago, USA, Venezuela.
Consultative Status Consultative status granted from: *ILO (#11123)* (Regional); *OAS (#17629).* **IGO Relations** Contacts with such organizations as: *OAS (#17629).* **NGO Relations** Member of: *World Social Forum (WSF, #21797).* Close links with: *Coordinadora de Centrales Sindicales Andinas (CCSA); Coordinadora de Centrales Sindicales del Cono Sur (CCSCS, #04805).*
[2017/XE1096/ty/**E**]

♦ Confederación Sudamericana de Actividades Subacuaticas (no recent information)
♦ Confederación Sudamericana de Atletismo (#19701)

♦ Confederación Sudamericana de Badminton (COSUBA) 04481

South American Badminton Confederation

Contact address not obtained. E-mail: presidencia@badminton.org.br.

Activities Organizes championships. **Members** Membership countries not specified. **NGO Relations** Member of: *Asociación de Confederaciones Deportivas Sudamericanas (ACODESU, no recent information).*
[2010/XD5093/**D**]

♦ Confederación Sudamericana de Básquetbol (CONSUBASQUET) . . . 04482

Pres address not obtained. E-mail: prensa@consubasquet.com.
URL: https://consubasquet.com/

History Founded as a continental confederation of *Fédération internationale de basketball (FIBA, #09614).* Part of *FIBA Americas (#09745).* Former names and other names: *Asociación del Basquetbol Sudamericano (ABASU)* – former. **Languages** Spanish. **Staff** 3.00 FTE, paid. **Activities** Events/meetings; sporting activities.
Members National federations (members of FIBA) in 10 countries:
Argentina, Bolivia, Brazil, Chile, Colombia, Ecuador, Paraguay, Peru, Uruguay, Venezuela.
[2021/XE0632/**E**]

♦ Confederación Sudamericana de Béisbol (inactive)
♦ Confederación Sudamericana de Billar (inactive)
♦ Confederación Sudamericana de Bochas (inactive)

♦ Confederación Sudamericana de Bowling 04483

South American Bowling Confederation

Contact c/o Fedecobol, Avda calle 63 No 68-99, 2o piso Bolera, Bogota, Bogota DC, Colombia. Fax +5712501525. E-mail: fedecobol@hotmail.com.
URL: http://www.csbowling.com/

Members Membership countries not specified. **NGO Relations** Member of (1): *Asociación de Confederaciones Deportivas Sudamericanas (ACODESU, no recent information).* Affiliated with (1): *South American Sports Organization (SASO, #19708).*
[2021/XD5089/**D**]

♦ Confederación Sudamericana de Bridge (CSB) 04484

Sec Av Ramón Cruz 1176 Of 409, Ñuñoa, 776 0566 Santiago, Santiago Metropolitan, Chile. T. +56222064020.
Pres address not obtained.
URL: http://csbnews.org/

History 1955. A zone of *World Bridge Federation (WBF, #21246).* **Aims** Administer bridge in the South American countries. **Activities** Events/meetings.
Members Full in 10 countries:
Argentina, Bolivia, Brazil, Chile, Colombia, Ecuador, Paraguay, Peru, Uruguay, Venezuela.
[2020/AA0984/**D**]

♦ Confederación Sudamericana de Canotaje 04485

Contact Monsenhor Celso 231 – 7o andar, Curitiba PR, 80010-922, Brazil. E-mail: presidencia@canoagem.org.br.
URL: http://www.suramericanacanotaje.org/

Members Membership countries not specified.
[2021/XD5088/**D**]

♦ Confederación Sudamericana de Ciclismo (inactive)

♦ Confederación Sudamericana de Esgrima 04486

South American Fencing Confederation

Main Office Acesso dos Jacarandas 118, Barrio Santa Teresa, Porto Alegre RS, 90843-110, Brazil. T. +555130280270. Fax +555130280271.
Pres Tarapaca 739, Santiago, Santiago Metropolitan, Chile. T. +5626395089 – +5626646409. Fax +5626395089. E-mail: rmoreno@bancoestado.cl.
URL: http://www.esgrimasudamericana.com/

History Founded 3 Dec 1945, Montevideo (Uruguay). **Members** Membership countries not specified. **NGO Relations** Member of: *Asociación de Confederaciones Deportivas Sudamericanas (ACODESU, no recent information).* Affiliated to: *South American Sports Organization (SASO, #19708).*
[2015/XD5086/**D**]

♦ Confederación Sudamericana de Fútbol (CONMEBOL) 04487

Main Office Autopista Silvio Pettirossi y Valois Rivarola, Luque, Asunción, Paraguay. T. +595215172000.
URL: http://www.conmebol.com/

History 9 Jul 1916, Buenos Aires (Argentina). Statutes revised: 3 Nov 1962, Lima (Peru); May 1964, Lima; Mar 1964, Santiago (Chile). A continental confederation of: *International Federation of Association Football (#13360).* Former names and other names: *CSF* – alias. **Structure** Congress (every 2 years); Executive Committee. **Languages** English, French, Portuguese, Spanish. **Staff** 18.00 FTE, paid. **Finance** Members' dues. **Activities** Sporting activities. **Events** *Congress* Asunción (Paraguay) 2004, *Congress* Asunción (Paraguay) 2002, *Congress* Asunción (Paraguay) 2000, *Congress* Asunción (Paraguay) 1998, *Congress* Asunción (Paraguay) 1997. **Publications** *CONMEBOL Noticias/News* (6 a year) in English, Spanish.
Members National associations in 10 countries:
Argentina, Bolivia, Brazil, Chile, Colombia, Ecuador, Paraguay, Peru, Uruguay, Venezuela.
NGO Relations Member of (2): *Asociación de Confederaciones Deportivas Panamericanas (ACODEPA, #02119); Asociación de Confederaciones Deportivas Sudamericanas (ACODESU, no recent information).*
[2023/XD3250/**D**]

♦ Confederación Sudamericana de Fútbol Corporativo (unconfirmed)
♦ Confederación Sudamericana de Futsal (no recent information)

♦ Confederación Sudamericana de Gimnasia 04488

South American Gymnastics Confederation

Pres Av Del Aire 950, San Luis, Lima, Peru.
URL: http://consugi.com/

Members Membership countries not specified. **NGO Relations** Member of: *Asociación de Confederaciones Deportivas Sudamericanas (ACODESU, no recent information).* Affiliated to: *South American Sports Organization (SASO, #19708).*
[2014/XD5066/**D**]

♦ Confederación Sudamericana de Golf (no recent information)
♦ Confederación Sudamericana de Handball (no recent information)
♦ Confederación Sudamericana de Judo (#19704)

♦ Confederación Sudamericana de Karate (CSK) 04489

South American Karate Confederation

Pres Luque 203 y Pedro Carbo, 2do piso Of 27, Guayaquil, Ecuador.
URL: http://www.sudamericakarate.com/

Members Membership countries not specified. **NGO Relations** Member of: *Asociación de Confederaciones Deportivas Sudamericanas (ACODESU, no recent information).* Affiliated to: *South American Sports Organization (SASO, #19708).*
[2019/XD5084/**D**]

♦ Confederación Sudamericana de Levantamiento de Pesas (inactive)

♦ Confederación Sudamericana de Lucha 04490

South American Wrestling Confederation

Contact c/o FEDENALOCH, Av Ramón Cruz Montt 1176, Oficina 506, Nuñoa, Santiago, Santiago Metropolitan, Chile.

Members Membership countries not specified. **NGO Relations** Member of: *Asociación de Confederaciones Deportivas Sudamericanas (ACODESU, no recent information).* Affiliated to: *South American Sports Organization (SASO, #19708).*
[2014/XD5083/**D**]

♦ Confederación Sudamericana de Lucha de Brazo (inactive)

♦ Confederación Sudamericana de Natación (CONSANAT) 04491

South American Swimming Confederation – Confédération sud-américaine de natation

Pres Calle 56 No 4A-26, Oficina 202, Bogota, Bogota DC, Colombia. T. +5712483547. Fax +5712493966. E-mail: secretarioconsanat@gmail.com.
URL: http://www.consanat.com/

History 1929. **Structure** Assembly. Executive Committee, comprising President, 1st and 2nd Vice-Presidents and Secretary-Treasurer. Commissions (9): Swimming; Diving; Water Polo; Synchronized Swimming; Open Water Swimming; Open Water Swimming; Master; Judging; Rules and Regulations; Medical. **Languages** Spanish. **Finance** Maintenance fees; sponsorship. **Activities** Organizes South American Swimming Championship. **Publications** Circulars. **Members** Membership countries not specified. **NGO Relations** Member of: *Asociación de Confederaciones Deportivas Sudamericanas (ACODESU, no recent information).* Affiliated to: *South American Sports Organization (SASO, #19708).* [2014/XD3020/**D**]

- ♦ Confederación Sudamericana de Panathlon (inactive)
- ♦ Confederación Sudamericana de Patin / see World Skate America (#21788)
- ♦ Confederación Sudamericana de Pelota (inactive)

♦ Confederación Sudamericana de Pentatlon Moderno (CSPM) 04492

South American Modern Pentathlon Confederation

Pres Ayala 754, L6300DLM Santa Rosa, Argentina. T. +5492954551432. Fax +542954418017.

History Former names and other names: *Modern Pentathlon Sudamerica* – alias. **Structure** Congress; Executive Committee. **Activities** Sporting activities.
Members National federations in 11 countries:
Argentina, Bolivia, Brazil, Chile, Colombia, Ecuador, Panama, Paraguay, Peru, Uruguay, Venezuela.
NGO Relations Continental federation of *World Penthathlon (UIPM, #21720).* [2019/AA2272/**D**]

- ♦ Confederación Sudamericana de Remo / see Confederación Panamericana de Remo (#04478)
- ♦ Confederación Sud Americana de Rugby / see Sudamérica Rugby (#20030)
- ♦ Confederación Sudamericana de Sociedades de Pediatria / see Latin American Pediatric Association (#16360)
- ♦ Confederación Sudamericana de Softbol (no recent information)
- ♦ Confederación Sudamericana de Squash Racket (#19702)
- ♦ Confederación Sudamericana de Tenis (#19709)

♦ Confederación Sudamericana de Tenis de Mesa (CONSUTEME) 04493

South American Table Tennis Confederation – Confédération sud-américaine de tennis de table

Sec/Treas address not obtained. E-mail: consuteme@hotmail.com.
Technical Dir address not obtained.
URL: http://consuteme.org/

History 12 Dec 1943, Buenos Aires (Argentina). **Aims** Promote and develop table tennis in all countries of South America; ensure the application of the official regulations at all events in the area; encourage friendship and cooperation between members. **Structure** Congress (annual); Executive Committee; Commissions. **Languages** Spanish. **Staff** 1.50 FTE, voluntary. **Finance** Sources: members' dues. Championships' registration fees. **Publications** *South American Bulletin* (4 a year); *Calendar of Events* (annual); *South American Championship Abstract* (annual); *The Book of the South American Championships* (annual). *CSTM Laws and Rules.* Reports. Information Services: Databases of participants, competitions, results and statistics of the South American Championships.
Members Associations in 10 countries:
Argentina, Bolivia, Brazil, Chile, Colombia, Ecuador, Paraguay, Peru, Uruguay, Venezuela.
NGO Relations Recognized by: *International Table Tennis Federation (ITTF, #15650); Unión Latinoamericana de Tenis de Mesa (ULTM, #20453).* Member of: *Asociación de Confederaciones Deportivas Sudamericanas (ACODESU, no recent information).* [2023/XD7820/**D**]

♦ Confederación Sudamericana de Tiro (CST) 04494

Sec FA de Tiro, Calle Moreno 1270, 1o Piso Of 109, 1091 Buenos Aires, Argentina.
URL: https://www.facebook.com/confederacionsudamericanadetiro/

History Founded 5 Sep 1959, Lake Forest CA (USA). **Languages** Portuguese, Spanish. **Members** Membership countries not specified. **NGO Relations** Member of: *Asociación de Confederaciones Deportivas Sudamericanas (ACODESU, no recent information).* [2015/XD5136/**D**]

- ♦ Confederación Sudamericana de Triatlón (#19710)
- ♦ Confederación Sudamericana Universitaria de Deportes (#19711)
- ♦ Confederación Sudamericana de Vela (#19706)

♦ Confederación Sudamericana de Voleibol (CSV) 04495

South American Volleyball Confederation – Confédération sudaméricaine de volley

Contact Avenida Visconde de Piraja 433 – sala 904, Ipanema, Rio de Janeiro RJ, 22410-003, Brazil. T. +552121327857 – +552121327255. E-mail: info@voleysur.org.
URL: http://www.voleysur.org/

History 1946, Buenos Aires (Argentina). Set up as a confederation of *Fédération internationale de volleyball (FIVB, #09670).* **Aims** Disseminate the *sport* of volleyball; encourage establishment of national federations and their affiliation with IVBF; organize continental *championship.* **Structure** Congress (at least every 4 years); Board of Administration; Executive Committee; Standing Commissions (5). **Languages** Portuguese, Spanish. **Staff** 5.00 FTE, paid. **Activities** Sporting events; events/meetings. **Events** *Ordinary Congress* Rio de Janeiro (Brazil) 2014, *Ordinary Congress* Rio de Janeiro (Brazil) 2001.
Members Affiliated national federations in 12 countries and territories:
Argentina, Bolivia, Brazil, Chile, Colombia, Ecuador, Guiana Fr, Guyana, Paraguay, Peru, Uruguay, Venezuela.
NGO Relations Member of: *Asociación de Confederaciones Deportivas Sudamericanas (ACODESU, no recent information).* [2016.12.19/XE3785/**E**]

♦ Confederación de Tenis de Centroamérica y el Caribe (COTECC) . . . 04496

Exec Dir address not obtained. T. +15032228-0542. E-mail: cotecc@cotecc.org.sv.
Pres Parque del Este, av Boulevard del Faro, 11604 Santo Domingo, Dominican Rep.
URL: https://cotecc.org.sv/

History 1992, La Romana (Dominican Rep). **Aims** Encourage, direct, organize, regulate, govern and disseminate the practice of tennis. **Structure** Board of Directors. **Languages** English, Spanish. **Staff** 5.00 FTE, paid. **Finance** Supported by: *International Tennis Federation (ITF, #15676).* Annual budget: 1,700,000 USD. **Activities** Sporting activities.
Members Federations in 34 countries and territories:
Anguilla, Antigua-Barbuda, Aruba, Bahamas, Barbados, Belize, Bermuda, Bonaire Is, Cayman Is, Costa Rica, Cuba, Curaçao, Dominican Rep, El Salvador, Grenada, Guadeloupe, Guatemala, Guiana Fr, Guyana, Haiti, Honduras, Jamaica, Martinique, Mexico, Nicaragua, Panama, Puerto Rico, St Kitts-Nevis, St Lucia, St Vincent-Grenadines, Suriname, Trinidad-Tobago, Virgin Is UK, Virgin Is USA.
NGO Relations Member of (2): *Asociación de Confederaciones Deportivas Panamericanas (ACODEPA, #02119); International Tennis Federation (ITF, #15676).* [2023/XD3586/**D**]

- ♦ Confederación de Trabajadores de América Latina (inactive)

♦ Confederación Universitaria Centroamericana (CSUCA) 04497

Confédération universitaire centroaméricaine – Central American University Confederation

SG Avenida Las Américas, 1-03 zona 14, Int Club Los Arcos, 01014 Guatemala, Guatemala. T. +5023671899 – +5023671833. Fax +5023669781 – +5023674517. E-mail: sg@csuca.org.
Sec address not obtained. E-mail: margarita@csuca.org.
URL: http://www.csuca.org/

History 9 Dec 1948, San Salvador (El Salvador). Permanent secretariat set up May 1959; moved to Guatemala (Guatemala) Jul 2002. Statutes modified: 1 Jun 1972; 1995. Also referred to as *Confederation of Central American Universities – Confédération des universités de l'Amérique centrale* and *Consejo Superior Universitario Centroamericano (CSUCA).* **Aims** Integrate higher education in Central America by developing a Central American university structure and securing basic unity of curricula in the various faculties; promote exchange of students, professors and publications; set up regional research institutes. **Structure** *Central American University Council – Conseil supérieur universitaire centroaméricain – Consejo Superior Universitario Centroamericano,* comprising 16 members (8 university rectors and 8 presidents of national students unions) convened 3 times a year. General Secretariat (rotating every 4 years). **Languages** English, Spanish. **Staff** 14.00 FTE, paid. **Finance** Members' dues. **Activities** Assists professional training programmes; encourages creation of regional institutions; coordinates meetings and information exchange; runs secretariat for student affairs, 'Secretaria Adjunta'. Programmes (3): Central American Teaching; *Central American Research Programme (no recent information);* Central American Autonomy. Data Bases (4): Bibliographic, Documentation on Higher Education in Central America (EDSUP); Research in Progress in Central American Universities (INVES); Investigations (ESPEC); Research Centres in Central American Universities (UNINV). Responsible for *Editorial Universitaria Centroamericana (EDUCA, no recent information)* and *Central American Center for Economic and Social Documentation (CEDESC, no recent information).* Instrumental in setting up: *Central American Health Programme (inactive); Central American Social Science Programme (inactive); Consejo Centroamericano de Acreditación de la Educación Superior (CCA, #04703).* **Events** *Central American seminar on information and studies on higher education* Guatemala (Guatemala) 2005, *Encuentro centroamericano sobre tratados de libre comercio e integracion regional* Guatemala (Guatemala) 2003, *Congress* Guatemala (Guatemala) 1988, *Central American seminar on environmental and development with emphasis on agrochemicals* Guatemala (Guatemala) 1986. **Publications** *Carta Informativa de la Secretaria General* (4 a year); *Estudios Sociales Centroamericanos* (4 a year); *Estadisticas Universitarias* (2 a year).
Members National universities (16) in 7 countries:
Belize, Costa Rica, El Salvador, Guatemala, Honduras, Nicaragua, Panama.
IGO Relations Specialized Institution of: *Central American Integration System (#03671).* **NGO Relations** Member of: *Conference of the Americas on International Education (CAIE, #04581); Consejo Universitario Iberoamericano (CUIB, #04727); Environment Liaison Centre International (ELCI, no recent information); Inter-American Organization for Higher Education (IOHE, #11442); Red Iberoamericana para el Aseguramiento de la Calidad en la Educación Superior (RIACES, #18657).* Council is member of: *Asociación Universitaria Iberoamericana de Postgrado (AUIP, #02307); Earth Council Alliance (ECA, inactive); Latin American Programme of Population Activities (no recent information).* [2017/XD3305/**D**]

- ♦ Confederatie van Gezinsorganisaties in de Europese Unie / see COFACE Families Europe (#04084)
- ♦ Confederatie van Kleinhandelaren in Wild en Gevogelte in de EEG Landen / see European Poultry, Egg and Game Association (#08258)

♦ Confederation of Africa Deaf Sports (CADS) 04498

Confédération africaine des sports des sourds (CASS)

Pres c/o KSFD, PO Box 46437, GPO 00100, Nairobi, Kenya.
Facebook: https://www.facebook.com/Cads.Africa.Deafsports/

History 1997. Former names and other names: *African Deaf Sports Federation* – former; *Confederation of African Deaf Sports (CADS)* – former. **Aims** Promote sports for the Deaf athletes in Africa. **Structure** General Assembly elects Executive Board, comprising 6 members. Administered by Secretary General/ Chief Executive. **Languages** Arabic, English, French, International Sign Language. **Staff** Voluntary. **Finance** Self-funded. **Activities** Events/meetings; networking/liaising; sporting activities; training/education. **Events** *African regional seminar for deaf sports leadership and strategic planning* Lagos (Nigeria) 2007, *General Assembly* Nairobi (Kenya) 2006.
Members Full: National Deaf Sports Federations in 18 countries:
Algeria, Cameroon, Egypt, Eswatini, Gambia, Ghana, Guinea, Kenya, Mali, Nigeria, Senegal, Sierra Leone, South Africa, Tanzania UR, Tunisia, Uganda, Zambia, Zimbabwe.
NGO Relations Accredited by (1): *International Committee of Sports for the Deaf (ICSD, #12805).* Affiliated with (2): *Association of African Sports Confederations (AASC, #02360); Association of National Olympic Committees of Africa (ANOCA, #02820).* [2022/XD7222/**D**]

- ♦ Confédération africain de boxe (#00228)
- ♦ Confédération africaine d'athlétisme (#04504)
- ♦ Confédération africaine d'athlétisme amateur / see Confederation of African Athletics (#04504)
- ♦ Confédération africaine de canoë (#04505)

♦ Confédération africaine de cyclisme (CAC) 04499

Pres c/o Egyption Cycling Federation, PO Box 1630, Cairo, Egypt. T. +20222630791. Fax +20224016968. E-mail: egypt_cycling@hotmail.com.
URL: http://www.cac-conf.com/

History Jan 1973, Lagos (Nigeria). **Aims** Develop and promote cyclism in Africa. **Structure** General Assembly (every 2 years); Executive Bureau (annual) composed of: President, 2 Vice-Presidents, Secretary-General, President of the Continental Communication Commission, President of the Continental Technical Commission, Vice-Presidents of Zones (7). **Languages** English, French. **Staff** 2.00 FTE, paid. **Finance** Members' dues. **Events** *General Assembly* Algeria 1996, *General Assembly* Abidjan (Côte d'Ivoire) 1990, *Meeting* Algiers (Algeria) 1990, *Statutory congress / Congress* Algiers (Algeria) 1989, *Seminar / Meeting* Annecy (France) / Chambéry (France) 1989. **Publications** *Afrique Cycliste Information* (4 a year) in English, French.
Members Associations in 155 countries:
Albania, Algeria, Andorra, Angola, Antigua-Barbuda, Argentina, Armenia, Australia, Austria, Azerbaijan, Bahamas, Bahrain, Bangladesh, Barbados, Belarus, Belgium, Belize, Bolivia, Bosnia-Herzegovina, Brazil, Brunei Darussalam, Bulgaria, Burkina Faso, Burundi, Cameroon, Canada, Cape Verde, Central African Rep, Chile, China, Colombia, Congo DR, Costa Rica, Côte d'Ivoire, Croatia, Cuba, Cyprus, Czechia, Denmark, Dominica, Dominican Rep, Ecuador, Egypt, El Salvador, Eritrea, Estonia, Ethiopia, Fiji, Finland, France, Gabon, Georgia, Germany, Greece, Guam, Guatemala, Guyana, Haiti, Holy See, Honduras, Hong Kong, Hungary, India, Indonesia, Iran Islamic Rep, Iraq, Ireland, Israel, Italy, Jamaica, Japan, Jordan, Kazakhstan, Kenya, Korea DPR, Korea Rep, Kuwait, Kyrgyzstan, Laos, Latvia, Lebanon, Libya, Liechtenstein, Lithuania, Luxembourg, Macau, Madagascar, Malaysia, Mali, Malta, Mauritius, Mexico, Moldova, Monaco, Mongolia, Morocco, Myanmar, Namibia, Nepal, Netherlands, New Zealand, Nigeria, North Macedonia, Norway, Oman, Pakistan, Panama, Paraguay, Peru, Philippines, Poland, Portugal, Puerto Rico, Romania, Russia, Rwanda, Samoa, San Marino, Saudi Arabia, Senegal, Serbia, Seychelles, Singapore, Slovakia, Slovenia, South Africa, Spain, Sri Lanka, St Lucia, St Vincent-Grenadines, Sweden, Switzerland, Syrian AR, Taiwan, Tanzania UR, Thailand, Togo, Trinidad-Tobago, Tunisia, Türkiye, Turkmenistan, UK, Ukraine, United Arab Emirates, Uruguay, USA, Uzbekistan, Vanuatu, Venezuela, Vietnam, Virgin Is USA, Yemen, Zambia, Zimbabwe.
NGO Relations Continental confederation of: *Union Cycliste Internationale (UCI, #20375).* [2013/XD1880/**D**]

- ♦ Confédération africaine des échecs (#00244)
- ♦ Confédération africaine d'escrime (no recent information)

♦ Confédération africaine de football (CAF) 04500

Contact 3 Abdel Khalek Sarwat St, El Hay El Motamayez, October City, 6th, Egypt. E-mail: info@cafonline.com.
URL: http://www.cafonline.com/

History Feb 1957, Khartoum (Sudan). Statutes adopted 6-7 Jul 1966, London (UK), at 5th Extraordinary Congress. Also referred to in English as *African Football Confederation* and *Confederation of African Football.* **Aims** Promote football in Africa. **Structure** General Assembly (every 2 years); Executive Committee; Emergency Committee; Standing Committees (11). **Languages** Arabic, English, French. **Staff** 40.00 FTE, paid. **Finance** Members' dues. Other sources: percentages; entry fees. **Activities** Sporting events; training/ education; awards/prizes/competitions. **Events** *General Assembly* Lagos (Nigeria) 2009, *General Assembly* Accra (Ghana) 2008, *General Assembly* Khartoum (Sudan) 2007, *General Assembly* Cairo (Egypt) 2006, *General Assembly* Tunis (Tunisia) 2004. **Publications** *CAF Flash* (4 a year); *CAF News* (4 a year) in English, French. Directory of addresses; technical reports of Cup of Nations and Youth Tournaments; statutes and regulations.
Members National associations in 56 countries:
Algeria, Angola, Benin, Botswana, Burkina Faso, Burundi, Cameroon, Cape Verde, Central African Rep, Chad, Comoros, Congo Brazzaville, Congo DR, Côte d'Ivoire, Djibouti, Egypt, Equatorial Guinea, Eritrea, Eswatini, Ethiopia, Gabon, Gambia, Ghana, Guinea, Guinea-Bissau, Kenya, Lesotho, Liberia, Libya, Madagascar, Malawi, Mali, Mauritania, Mauritius, Morocco, Mozambique, Namibia, Niger, Nigeria, Réunion, Rwanda, Sao Tomé-Principe, Senegal, Seychelles, Sierra Leone, Somalia, South Africa, South Sudan, Sudan, Tanzania UR, Togo, Tunisia, Uganda, Zambia, Zimbabwe.
NGO Relations Continental confederation of: *International Federation of Association Football (#13360).* [2019/XD0019/**D**]

- ♦ Confédération africaine de football corporatif (unconfirmed)
- ♦ Confédération Africaine de Futsal (unconfirmed)

♦ Confédération africaine de golf (#00329)

♦ **Confédération Africaine de Handball (CAHB)** **04501**

Pres 08 BP 1518, Abidjan 08, Côte d'Ivoire. T. +2252722406280 – +2252722406281. Fax +2252722406281. E-mail: info@cahbonline.info.
URL: https://cahbonline.info

History 15 Jan 1973, Lagos (Nigeria). **Aims** Promote the practice of handball in Africa; organize training and retraining courses for coaches, referees, players and officials; encourage and help African countries to found national associations. **Structure** Congress; Executive Council; Executive Committee. Zones (7); Specialized Commissions (5). **Languages** English, French. **Finance** Sources: donations; gifts, legacies; meeting proceeds; members' dues; subsidies. **Activities** Awards/prizes/competitions; events/meetings; sporting activities; training/education. **Publications** *AFRICAHAND* (4 a year).
Members National Associations in 53 countries:
Algeria, Angola, Benin, Botswana, Burkina Faso, Burundi, Cameroon, Cape Verde, Central African Rep, Chad, Comoros, Congo Brazzaville, Congo DR, Côte d'Ivoire, Djibouti, Egypt, Equatorial Guinea, Eswatini, Ethiopia, Gabon, Gambia, Ghana, Guinea, Guinea-Bissau, Kenya, Lesotho, Liberia, Libya, Madagascar, Malawi, Mali, Mauritania, Mauritius, Morocco, Mozambique, Namibia, Niger, Nigeria, Rwanda, Sao Tomé-Principe, Senegal, Seychelles, Sierra Leone, Somalia, South Africa, South Sudan, Sudan, Tanzania UR, Togo, Tunisia, Uganda, Zambia, Zimbabwe.
NGO Relations Regional federation of: *International Handball Federation (IHF, #13771).* [2022.05.23/XD1697/**D**]

♦ **Confédération africaine de natation amateur (CANA)** **04502**

Gen Sec/Treas 124 Van Beek St, North Wing Ground Floor, Johannesburg Stadium, New Doornfontein, Johannesburg, South Africa. T. +27114042480. E-mail: canazone4secretariat@gmail.com.
URL: http://canaswim.com/

History Dec 1970, Cairo (Egypt). **Structure** General Assembly. **Members** in 30 countries. Membership countries not specified. **NGO Relations** Member of: *World Aquatics (#21100).* [2017/XD3593/**D**]

♦ Confédération africaine de rugby / see Rugby Africa (#18996)
♦ Confédération africaine de rugby amateur / see Rugby Africa (#18996)
♦ Confédération africaine des sports boules (inactive)
♦ Confédération africaine des sports pour handicapés – Comité paralympique africaine / see African Paralympic Committee (#00410)
♦ Confédération africaine des sports pour handicapés et inadaptés / see African Paralympic Committee (#00410)
♦ Confédération africaine des sports des sourds (#04498)
♦ Confédération Africaine de Tennis (#04507)
♦ Confédération africaine des travailleurs croyants d'Afrique équatoriale (inactive)
♦ Confédération africaine des travailleurs croyants d'Afrique occidentale (inactive)

♦ **Confédération africaine de volley-ball (CAVB)** **04503**

African Volleyball Confederation

Pres 26 Rue Ahmed Taiseer, Marwa Héliopolis, Cairo, Egypt. T. +20224144852 – +20224192735. Fax +20224173368. E-mail: presidency@cavb.org – info@cavb.org.
URL: http://www.cavb.org/

History 1965, Brazzaville (Congo Brazzaville), as a confederation of *Fédération internationale de volleyball (FIVB, #09670).* **Aims** Disseminate the *sport* of volleyball; encourage establishment of national federations and their affiliation with IVBF; organize continental *championships.* **Structure** Congress (meets at least every 2 years); Board of Administration; Executive Committee; Standing Commissions. **Finance** Members' dues. Other sources: participation fees to the competitions; competition marketing right; sponsoring right; FIVB annual contribution. **Activities** Runs Development Centres in Tunisia, Senegal, Sudan and Zambia; sets up the *'Sport Aids Programme'.* Runs the *'African volleyball project'*, set up 2003. Organizes: continental championships; African Qualification Tournament for the African and Olympic Games; seminars. **Events** *Extraordinary Congress* Cairo (Egypt) 2012, *Congress* Khartoum (Sudan) 2011, *International refereeing seminar* Cairo (Egypt) 2010. **Publications** *Africa Volleyball Express* (4 a year) – newspaper.
Members National Federations in 53 countries:
Algeria, Angola, Benin, Botswana, Burkina Faso, Burundi, Cameroon, Cape Verde, Central African Rep, Chad, Comoros, Congo Brazzaville, Congo DR, Côte d'Ivoire, Djibouti, Egypt, Equatorial Guinea, Eritrea, Eswatini, Ethiopia, Gabon, Gambia, Ghana, Guinea, Guinea-Bissau, Kenya, Lesotho, Liberia, Libya, Madagascar, Malawi, Mali, Mauritania, Mauritius, Morocco, Mozambique, Namibia, Niger, Nigeria, Rwanda, Sao Tomé-Principe, Senegal, Seychelles, Sierra Leone, Somalia, South Africa, Sudan, Tanzania UR, Togo, Tunisia, Uganda, Zambia, Zimbabwe.
IGO Relations Contacts with: *Conférence des ministres de la jeunesse et des sports de la Francophonie (CONFEJES, #04634); Organisation internationale de la Francophonie (OIF, #17809).* **NGO Relations** Contacts with: *International Olympic Committee (IOC, #14408).* [2019/XE3781/**E**]

♦ **Confederation of African Athletics (CAA)** **04504**

Confédération africaine d'athlétisme (CAA)

Head Office Hanne Mariste Cite Som, Bloc C, BP 88, Dakar, Senegal. T. +221338328397. Fax +221338328402.
URL: http://www.webcaa.org/

History 17 Jan 1973, Lagos (Nigeria), as a continental association of: *World Athletics (#21209).* Original title: *African Amateur Athletic Confederation (AAAC) – Confédération africaine d'athlétisme amateur (CAAA).* **Aims** Manage, organize and supervise athletic activities on the African continent. **Structure** General Congress. Council of 23 members, comprising President, 4 Vice-Presidents, 5 Regional Presidents, Treasurer, IAAF Council Representative for Africa and Council members from Africa, and ordinary members. Regional Councils (5). **Languages** English, French. **Staff** 10.00 FTE, paid. **Finance** Subsidies from IAAF; sponsors. **Events** *Congress* Abidjan (Côte d'Ivoire) 2019, *Congress* Dakar (Senegal) 2007.
Members National associations in 53 countries:
Algeria, Angola, Benin, Botswana, Burkina Faso, Burundi, Cameroon, Cape Verde, Central African Rep, Chad, Comoros, Congo Brazzaville, Congo DR, Côte d'Ivoire, Djibouti, Egypt, Equatorial Guinea, Eritrea, Eswatini, Ethiopia, Gabon, Gambia, Ghana, Guinea, Guinea-Bissau, Kenya, Lesotho, Liberia, Libya, Madagascar, Malawi, Mali, Mauritania, Mauritius, Morocco, Mozambique, Namibia, Niger, Nigeria, Rwanda, Sao Tomé-Principe, Senegal, Seychelles, Sierra Leone, Somalia, South Africa, Sudan, Tanzania UR, Togo, Tunisia, Uganda, Zambia, Zimbabwe. [2010/XD6484/**D**]

♦ **Confederation of African Canoeing (CAC)** **04505**

Confédération africaine de canoë

SG address not obtained. E-mail: cac.secgen@gmail.com.
URL: http://www.kayakafrica.org/

History 2000, Casablanca (Morocco). **Aims** Develop the Olympic sport of canoeing and all its disciplines throughout Africa; support cooperation among African national canoeing federations. **Structure** Executive Committee, comprising President, 2 Vice-Presidents, Secretary-General and Treasurer. **Languages** Arabic, English, French. **Staff** Volunteers. **Finance** Members' fees. Grant from *International Canoe Federation (ICF, #12437).* Budget (annual): euro 20,000. **Activities** Commissions (5): Media Marketing and Promotion; Medical; Statutes and Development; Technical Events and Umpiring; Women Youth and Masters. Organizes: championships (every 2 years); biennial Ordinary Congress; Coaching Seminars; Best Athletes and Coaches Award Ceremony. **Events** *Ordinary Congress* Côte d'Ivoire 2009. **Publications** *CAC Newsletter* (12 a year).
Members National federation in 28 countries:
Algeria, Angola, Burkina Faso, Burundi, Cameroon, Côte d'Ivoire, Egypt, Equatorial Guinea, Ethiopia, Ghana, Guinea-Bissau, Kenya, Liberia, Libya, Morocco, Mozambique, Namibia, Nigeria, Sao Tomé-Principe, Senegal, Seychelles, Somalia, South Africa, Sudan, Togo, Tunisia, Uganda, Zambia. [2017/XM2053/**D**]

♦ Confederation of African Corporate Football (unconfirmed)
♦ Confederation of African Deaf Sports / see Confederation of Africa Deaf Sports (#04498)
♦ Confederation of African Football / see Confédération africaine de football (#04500)
♦ Confederation of African Medical Associations and Societies (no recent information)

♦ **Confederation of African Midwives Associations (CONAMA)** **04506**

Sec address not obtained. E-mail: kande1954@yahoo.com.
Pres address not obtained.

History Set up Jul 2013, Nairobi (Kenya), during 3rd Africa Regional Conference of *International Confederation of Midwives (ICM, #12863).* **Aims** Improve reproductive, newborn and child health in Africa by advocating for and strengthening individual country midwifery associations to promote quality education, regulation and midwifery practice. **Structure** Council; Board; Secretariat.
Members Full in 21 countries:
Burkina Faso, Burundi, Chad, Congo Brazzaville, Congo DR, Eswatini, Ethiopia, Gabon, Ghana, Kenya, Lesotho, Madagascar, Malawi, Mauritania, Nigeria, Senegal, Sierra Leone, South Sudan, Sudan, Uganda, Zimbabwe.
NGO Relations *Lugina Africa Midwives Research Network (LAMRN, #16522).* [2013/XJ8951/**D**]

♦ Confédération africano-levantine de billard (inactive)

♦ **Confederation of African Tennis** **04507**

Confédération Africaine de Tennis (CAT)

General Manager and CEO BP 315, El Menzah, 1004 Tunis, Tunisia. T. +21671846960. Fax +21671841045. E-mail: cat@cattennis.com.
URL: http://www.cattennis.com/

History Jan 1973, Lagos (Nigeria). Revived 27 Dec 1989, Abidjan (Côte d'Ivoire). **Aims** Administer and develop tennis in Africa by planning, coordinating and promoting the game for both men and women; ensure effective participation of African countries in international tennis events and tournaments; standardize the game in all its fields: training, competing, coaching and officiating. **Structure** Executive Committee; Committees (2); Commissions (2). **Languages** English, French. **Staff** 5.00 FTE, paid. **Finance** Members' dues. Other sources: contributions from ITF; sponsorship; profits from events and competitions; donations and legacies. **Activities** Events/meetings; sporting activities. **Events** *Annual General Assembly* Tunis (Tunisia) 2020, *Annual General Assembly* Antananarivo (Madagascar) 2019, *Annual General Assembly* Kigali (Rwanda) 2018, *Annual General Assembly* Tunis (Tunisia) 2017, *Annual General Assembly* Pretoria (South Africa) 2016. **Publications** *CAT Tennis News* (3 a year) in English, French; *CAT Yearbook.*
Members National associations in 52 countries:
Algeria, Angola, Benin, Botswana, Burkina Faso, Burundi, Cameroon, Cape Verde, Central African Rep, Chad, Comoros, Congo Brazzaville, Congo DR, Côte d'Ivoire, Djibouti, Egypt, Equatorial Guinea, Eritrea, Eswatini, Ethiopia, Gabon, Gambia, Ghana, Guinea, Guinea-Bissau, Kenya, Lesotho, Liberia, Libya, Madagascar, Malawi, Mali, Mauritania, Mauritius, Morocco, Mozambique, Namibia, Niger, Nigeria, Rwanda, Senegal, Seychelles, Sierra Leone, Somalia, South Africa, Sudan, Tanzania UR, Togo, Tunisia, Uganda, Zambia, Zimbabwe.
NGO Relations Member of: *Association of African Sports Confederations (AASC, #02360).* Regional association of: *International Tennis Federation (ITF, #15676).* [2021/XD3841/**D**]

♦ Confédération américaine des employés de banques (inactive)

♦ **Confederation of American Associations for the Production of Sustainable Agriculture (CAAPAS)** **04508**

Confederación de Asociaciones Americanas para la Producción de la Agricultura Sostenible – Confederation de Associações Americanas para a Produção da Agricultura Sustentavel

Pres 18 de Julio 291, CP 75000, Mercedes, Soriano, Uruguay. T. +59845324567. E-mail: ausid@ausid.com.uy.
URL: http://www.caapas.org/

Languages English, Spanish. **Events** *World congress* Foz do Iguaçu (Brazil) 2010, *World congress on conservation agriculture* Foz do Iguaçu (Brazil) 2003.
Members National organizations (8) in 8 countries:
Argentina, Bolivia, Brazil, Chile, Mexico, Paraguay, Uruguay, USA. [2015.02.28/XJ3771/**D**]

♦ Confederation of American Educators (#04446)
♦ Confédération d'Amérique du Nord, d'Amérique centrale et des Caraïbes de football (#04465)
♦ Confédération anti-communiste latinoaméricaine (inactive)
♦ Confédération arabe des sports (inactive)

♦ **Confederation of ASEAN Journalists (CAJ)** **04509**

Confédération des journalistes de l'ANASE

Contact 538/1 Samsen Road, Dusit, Bangkok, Thailand. E-mail: caj.bangkok@gmail.com.
URL: http://cajnet.org/

History 11 Mar 1975, Jakarta (Indonesia). Current Constitution adopted 25 Nov 1987, Manila (Philippines). **Aims** Cooperate fully in advancing journalism; promote free and responsible *press* in ASEAN countries; promote dialogue, discussion and cooperation with journalists, scholars and professionals worldwide. **Structure** General Assembly (every 2 years, at ASEAN Press Convention). Board of Directors (meets annually); Board of Advisors; Permanent Secretariat. **Languages** English. **Staff** Voluntary. **Finance** Fundraising by affiliates finances activities at national and regional levels. **Activities** Events/meetings; training/education. **Events** *General Assembly* Bangkok (Thailand) 2018, *Biennial General Assembly* Vientiane (Laos) 2007, *Biennial general assembly* Bangkok (Thailand) 2005, *ASEAN press convention* Hanoi (Vietnam) 2003, *Europe-Asia round table on media and sustainable development* Singapore (Singapore) 2003. **Publications** *ASEAN Press Agenda Program Book* (2 a year). *Press Laws and Systems in ASEAN States* (1985).
Members National organizations, totalling nearly 50,000 working journalists in 7 countries:
Indonesia, Laos, Malaysia, Philippines, Singapore, Thailand, Vietnam.
IGO Relations *ASEAN (#01141); ILO (#11123); International Rice Research Institute (IRRI, #14754); Swedish International Development Cooperation Agency (Sida); UNICEF (#20332); United Nations University (UNU, #20642).* [2018/XE0141/**E**]

♦ **Confederation of Asian Futsal (CAFS)** **04510**

Contact No 220 Gongguan Rd, Beitou Dist, Taipei 112, Taiwan. T. +886937869038. E-mail: amftaiwan2013@gmail.com.

History 12 Apr 2013. **Aims** Play a leading role of futsal promotion. **Structure** Congress; Executive Committee; Committees. Secretariat.
Members Federations in 11 countries and territories:
Bangladesh, China, India, Japan, Korea Rep, Macau, Malaysia, Nepal, Pakistan, Taiwan, Vietnam.
NGO Relations *World Futsal Association (#21532).* [2014/XJ9000/**D**]

♦ **Confederation of Asian and Pacific Accountants (CAPA)** **04511**

Secretariat B-9-2 Tower B, Atria Suites, Jalan SS 22/23 Damansara Jaya, Petaling Jaya, 47400 Shah Alam, Selangor, Malaysia. T. +60377318892. E-mail: admin@capa.com.my.
URL: http://www.capa.com.my/

History 1957. Formal charter adopted 23 Sep 1976, Hong Kong; latest amendments 2017, Hong Kong. Incorporated in Hong Kong, Sep 2001. **Aims** Enhance value of the accountancy profession in the region. **Structure** Assembly (twice a year); Board; Committees; Task Forces; Secretariat in Malaysia, headed by Chief Executive. **Languages** English. **Finance** Members' dues. **Activities** Events/meetings; capacity building; monitoring/evaluation; guidance/assistance/consulting. **Events** *Conference* Seoul (Korea Rep) 2015, *Annual General Meeting* Tokyo (Japan) 2015, *Conference* Brisbane, QLD (Australia) 2011, *Annual General Meeting* Seoul (Korea Rep) 2011, *Conference* Osaka (Japan) 2007. **Publications** Annual Review/Reports; guides; case studies.
Members Member; Associate; Affiliate. Members in 18 countries:
Australia, Bangladesh, Canada, China, Fiji, India, Japan, Korea Rep, Mongolia, Nepal, New Zealand, Pakistan, Papua New Guinea, Philippines, Samoa, Sri Lanka, USA, Vietnam.
Associate in 4 countries:
Afghanistan, Korea DPR, Russia, Solomon Is.
Affiliate in 2 countries:
France, UK.
NGO Relations Strategic partners and stakeholders: *Accountancy Europe (#00061); African Organisation of English-speaking Supreme Audit Institutions (AFROSAI-E, #00403); ASEAN Federation of Accountants (AFA, #01171); Asian Organization of Supreme Audit Institutions (ASOSAI, #01594); Inter-American Accounting Association (IAA, #11395); International Accounting Education Standards Board (IAESB, #11582); International Accounting Standards Board (IASB, #11583); International Auditing and Assurance Standards Board (IAASB, #12296); International Federation of Accountants (IFAC, #13335); International Financial Reporting Standards Foundation (IFRS Foundation, #13603); International Forum of Independent Audit Regulators (IFIAR, #13639);*

International Integrated Reporting Council (IIRC, inactive); International Public Sector Accounting Standards Board (IPSASB, #14673); Pacific Association of Supreme Audit Institutions (PASAI, #17935); Pan African Federation of Accountants (PAFA, #18050); South Asian Federation of Accountants (SAFA, #19727). [2020.03.05/XD1563/**D**]

♦ Confederation of Asia-Pacific Chambers of Commerce and Industry (CACCI) 04512

Confédération des chambres de commerce et d'industrie d'Asie et du Pacifique

Dir-Gen 7F-2 No 760, Section 4, Bade Road, Songshan District, Taipei 10567, Taiwan. T. +886227601139. Fax +886227607569. E-mail: cacci@cacci.biz.
URL: http://www.cacci.biz/

History 1966, Taipei (Taiwan). Founded when constitution and by-laws were ratified, as the result of the work of a Select Committee set up Feb 1965, Manila (Philippines), at 1st Conference. **Aims** Promote regional economic growth through business activities by enabling free movement of goods and investments. **Structure** Council (meets annually); Product and Service Councils (13); Secretariat. **Languages** English. **Staff** 7.00 FTE, paid; 200.00 FTE, voluntary. **Finance** Sources: donations; members' dues. **Activities** Advocacy/lobbying/activism; events/meetings; networking/liaising; politics/policy/regulatory; projects/programmes; research/documentation; training/education. **Events** *Sustainable and Resilient Growth Through a Robust World Trade* 2021, *Achieving Sustainable Growth in a Turbulent and Disruptive Global Market* Taipei (Taiwan) 2020, *Conference* Dhaka (Bangladesh) 2019, *Conference* Istanbul (Turkey) 2018, *Conference* Sydney, NSW (Australia) 2017. **Publications** *CACCI Profile* (12 a year); *Journal of Commerce and Industry* (2 a year).
Members Primary (27): national chambers of commerce and industry; Affiliate (20): other chambers of commerce or associations of business interests; Special (over 300): companies, firms and individuals. Primary in 25 countries and territories:
Australia, Azerbaijan, Bangladesh, Cambodia, Georgia, Hong Kong, India, Iran Islamic Rep, Japan, Korea Rep, Mongolia, Nepal, New Zealand, Pakistan, Papua New Guinea, Philippines, Russia, Singapore, Sri Lanka, Taiwan, Tajikistan, Timor-Leste, Türkiye, Uzbekistan, Vietnam.
Affiliate in 10 countries and territories:
Australia, China, Georgia, Japan, Korea Rep, Malaysia, Nepal, Philippines, Russia, Taiwan.
Special in 24 countries and territories:
Australia, Bangladesh, Brunei Darussalam, Cambodia, Georgia, Hong Kong, India, Indonesia, Japan, Korea Rep, Malaysia, Mongolia, Nepal, Pakistan, Papua New Guinea, Philippines, Russia, Saudi Arabia, Singapore, Sri Lanka, Switzerland, Taiwan, Türkiye, Ukraine.
Consultative Status Consultative status granted from: *ECOSOC (#05331)* (Ros A). **IGO Relations** Accredited by (1): *United Nations Office at Vienna (UNOV, #20604).* **NGO Relations** Member of (1): *Conference of Non-Governmental Organizations in Consultative Relationship with the United Nations (CONGO, #04635).* [2022.05.11/XD0390/t/**D**]

♦ Confederation of Asia-Pacific Employers (CAPE) 04513

Pres c/o Malaysian Employers Federation, 3A06-3A07 Block A, Pusat Dagangan Phileo Damansara II, No 15, Jalan 16/11, Off Jalan Damansara, 46350 Petaling Jaya, Selangor, Malaysia. T. +60379557778. Fax +60379559008 – +60379556808. E-mail: shamsuddin@mef.org.my.
SG address not obtained.
URL: http://www.cape-emp.org/

History 27 Aug 2001. **Aims** Promote mutual understanding and cooperation on issues concerning labour, the economy, social policy and labour-management relations; facilitate regular exchange of information among members with specific data relevant to the region; enhance communication among members through joint activities; strive to achieve unity of purpose and action among members. **Structure** General Council; Executive Board. **Languages** English. **Finance** Subscriptions.
Members National organizations (21) in 21 countries:
Australia, Bangladesh, Cambodia, China, Fiji, India, Indonesia, Iran Islamic Rep, Japan, Korea Rep, Malaysia, Mongolia, Nepal, New Zealand, Pakistan, Papua New Guinea, Philippines, Singapore, Sri Lanka, Thailand, Vietnam.
Consultative Status Consultative status granted from: *ILO (#11123)* (Regional). [2017.10.13/XD8922/**D**]

- ♦ Confederation Asia of Roller Skating / see World Skate Asia (#21789)
- ♦ Confederation Asia of Roller Sports / see World Skate Asia (#21789)
- ♦ Confédération asiatique de badminton / see Badminton Asia (#03056)
- ♦ Confédération asiatique de billard (inactive)
- ♦ Confédération asiatique de football (#01487)
- ♦ Confédération asiatique de thérapie physique (#01398)
- ♦ Confédération d'Asie et du Pacifique du génie chimique (#01605)
- ♦ Confederation, Assistance and Defence Treaty (1674 treaty)
- ♦ Confederation de Associações Americanas para a Produção da Agricultura Sustentavel (#04508)

♦ Confédération des associations des artisans glaciers de la Communauté européenne (ARTGLACE) 04514

Confederación de Asociaciones de Heladeros Artesanos de la Comunidad Europea

Contact Via del Parco 3, 32013 Longarone BL, Italy. T. +39437577577. Fax +39437770340.
URL: http://www.artglace.com/

History 29 Nov 1989, Paris (France). Founded taking over the activities of *Association of Independent Manufacturers of Ice Cream and Allied Products, and Manufacturers of Ice Cream Equipment for the EEC and Applicant Countries (inactive).* **Aims** Promote and develop links between national or regional associations; defend and represent the interests of members with European Community authorities. **Structure** Maintains the *Institut européen en recherche technologique d'ARTGLACE.* **Languages** Dutch, English, French, German, Italian, Spanish. **Staff** 2.00 FTE, paid. **Finance** Members' dues. Annual budget: euro 2,100.
Members National organizations in 8 countries:
Belgium, France, Germany, Italy, Netherlands, Portugal, Spain, UK. [2018.12.02/XD2314/**E**]

- ♦ Confédération des associations économiques européennes (inactive)
- ♦ Confederation des associations des facteurs d'instruments de musique de la CEE / see Confederation of European Music Industries (#04527)
- ♦ Confédération des associations internationales d'entrepreneurs (#04558)
- ♦ Confédération des associations kurdes en Europe / see European Kurdish Democratic Societies Congress (#07632)
- ♦ Confédération des associations médicales de l'Asie et de l'Océanie (#04566)
- ♦ Confédération des associations nationales de l'hôtellerie et de la restauration de la Communauté européenne (#04569)

♦ Confédération des associations nationales de tanneurs et mégissiers de la Communauté européenne (COTANCE) 04515

Confederation of National Associations of Tanners and Dressers of the European Community – Confederación de Asociaciones Nacionales de Curtidores y Peleteros de la Comunidad Europea

SG Rue Washington 40, 1050 Brussels, Belgium. T. +3225127703. E-mail: cotance@euroleather.com.
URL: http://www.euroleather.com/

History 8 Mar 1957, Paris (France). Name and statutes adopted by General Assembly, 8 May 1981, Milan (Italy). Statutes most recently amended 24 Feb 2022, Milan (Italy). Former names and other names: *Study Group of Tanners and Dressers in the EEC* – former; *Groupe d'étude des tanneurs et mégissiers de la CEE* – former; *European Leather Association* – alias. Registration: Banque Carrefour Entreprises, No/ID: 445496848, Start date: 7 Nov 1991, Belgium. **Aims** Group associations of tanners and dressers in member countries of the *European Union* in order to maintain and develop among them solidarity links; act with institutions of the EC/EU and, whenever necessary, other international bodies, as an authorized spokesman of tanners and dressers for all problems of general interest to their industry. **Structure** Assembly General (at least annual); Council; Secretariat headed by Secretary General. **Languages** English, French. **Staff** 2.00 FTE, paid. **Finance** Sources: members' dues. Annual budget: 250,000 EUR. **Activities** Networking/liaising; research and development; training/education.
Members Associations in 11 countries:
Austria, Denmark, France, Germany, Hungary, Italy, Netherlands, Portugal, Spain, Sweden, UK.

IGO Relations Observer status with (1): *Intergovernmental Sub-Group on Hides and Skins (#11502).* Recognized by: *European Commission (EC, #06633).* **NGO Relations** Member of (2): *European Platform for Chemicals Using Manufacturing Industries (CheMI, #08223); Federation of European and International Associations Established in Belgium (FAIB, #09508).* [2022.05.04/XE0958/**E**]

- ♦ Confédération des associations de résidents à l'étranger de la Communauté européenne / see Europeans throughout the World (#08839)
- ♦ Confédération des associations et sociétés médicales d'Afrique (no recent information)
- ♦ Confédération bénédictine (religious order)
- ♦ Confédération des Biologistes Européens (#04520)
- ♦ Confédération bouliste internationale (#04579)
- ♦ Confédération des brasseurs du Marché commun / see The Brewers of Europe (#03324)
- ♦ Confederation of the Canons Regular of Saint Augustine (religious order)
- ♦ Confédération Caraïbe de judo (#04452)
- ♦ Confederation of Central African NGOs / see Confédération des ONG d'environnement et de développement de l'Afrique centrale (#04572)
- ♦ Confederation of Central American Universities / see Confederación Universitaria Centroamericana (#04497)
- ♦ Confédération centroaméricaine de travailleurs (inactive)
- ♦ Confederation of Chambers of Commerce of the Andean Group (no recent information)
- ♦ Confédération de chambres de commerce du Groupement Andin (no recent information)
- ♦ Confédération des chambres de commerce et d'industrie d'Asie et du Pacifique (#04512)

♦ Confederation of Chess for the Americas (CCA) 04516

Confederación de Ajedrez para las Américas

Pres Zempoala 415, Col Narvarte Deleg Benito Juarez, CP 03020, Mexico City CDMX, Mexico. T. +5255555433436. E-mail: ccamerica@prodigy.net.mx.
Gen Sec 42 Sparrow Avenue, Bataria, Trinidad-Tobago.
URL: http://www.fideamerica.com/

Structure Officers: President; Deputy President; Treasurer; Director; General Secretary. **Events** *General Assembly* Cali (Colombia) 2015, *General Assembly* Norway 2014, *Extraordinary Assembly* Tallinn (Estonia) 2013, *General Assembly* Istanbul (Turkey) 2012, *General Assembly* Cali (Colombia) 2011. **NGO Relations** Cooperates with: *Fédération internationale des échecs (FIDE, #09627).* [2015/XD8465/**D**]

- ♦ Confederation of Common Market Breweries / see The Brewers of Europe (#03324)
- ♦ Confédération des compagnonnages européens (#04522)
- ♦ Confederation of Cooperatives of the Caribbean / see Confederación de Cooperativas del Caribe, Centro y Suramérica (#04445)
- ♦ Confédération des coopératives d'épargne et de crédit d'Asie (#02377)
- ♦ Confédération des coopératives d'épargne et de crédit des Caraïbes (#03478)
- ♦ Confédération des détaillants en volaille et gibier des pays de la CEE / see European Poultry, Egg and Game Association (#08258)

♦ Confederation of Egyptian European Business Associations (CEEBA) 04517

SG 21 Soliman Abaza St, Cairo, Egypt. T. +20233338484. Fax +20233368786. E-mail: info@ceeba.org.
URL: http://www.ceeba.org/

History Founded 10 May 2004, Egypt, by the British-Egyptian, the French, the German-Arab Chamber and the Italian Chamber of Commerce. **Aims** Create a powerful advocacy network of all Egyptian-European associations. **Structure** Board; Advisory Council. Chairmanship rotates every 6 months. **Languages** Arabic, English, German. **Activities** Networking/liaising; advocacy/lobbying/activism; events/meetings; capacity building. **Events** *Standards and specifications in Eygpt and the EU* Cairo (Egypt) 2004.
Members Founding members associations (4) in 4 countries:
France, Germany, Italy, UK. [2018.09.06/XJ3765/**D**]

- ♦ Confederation of Employers' Organizations of the Indian Ocean Islands (no recent information)
- ♦ Confédération des employeurs de l'ANASE (#01158)
- ♦ Confédération des employeurs des Caraïbes (#03495)
- ♦ Confédération des enseignants américains (#04446)
- ♦ Confederation of Environmental and Development NGOs of Central Africa (#04572)
- ♦ Confédération des étudiants d'Afrique occidentale (inactive)
- ♦ Confederation Europäische Gesellenzünfte (#04522)
- ♦ Confederation of European Aerospace Societies / see Council of European Aerospace Societies (#04882)

♦ Confederation of European Baseball (CEB) 04518

Confédération européenne de baseball (CEB)

SG Savska cesta 137, HR-10000 Zagreb, Croatia. T. +38515615227. E-mail: office@baseballeurope.com.
Pres address not obtained.
URL: http://www.baseballeurope.com/

History 27 Apr 1953, Paris (France). Since 2019, a judicial organization within *World Baseball Softball Confederation Europe (WBSC Europe, #21223).* Former names and other names: *European Baseball Federation* – former (1953); *Fédération européenne de baseball (FEB)* – former (1953); *European Amateur Baseball Confederation* – former (1972); *Confédération européenne de baseball amateur (CEBA)* – former (1972); *European Baseball Confederation* – former (1993). **Aims** Promote, encourage, develop and control baseball in Europe. **Structure** General Assembly; Executive Committee. **Languages** English, French. **Staff** 1.00 FTE, paid. **Finance** Members' dues. **Activities** Sporting activities. **Events** *Joint Congress* Vilnius (Lithuania) 2020, *Joint Congress* Athens (Greece) 2019, *Joint Congress* Paris (France) 2018, *Joint Congress* Belgrade (Serbia) 2017, *Joint Congress* Hoofddorp (Netherlands) 2016. **Publications** *CEBA Newsletter.* Annual review.
Members Baseball federations and clubs in 39 countries:
Austria, Belarus, Belgium, Bulgaria, Croatia, Cyprus, Czechia, Denmark, Estonia, Finland, France, Georgia, Germany, Great Britain, Greece, Hungary, Iceland, Ireland, Israel, Italy, Latvia, Lithuania, Malta, Moldova, Netherlands, Norway, Poland, Portugal, Romania, Russia, San Marino, Serbia, Slovakia, Slovenia, Spain, Sweden, Switzerland, Türkiye, Ukraine. [2021/XD7390/**E**]

- ♦ Confederation of European Bath Manufacturers (inactive)

♦ Confederation of the European Bicycle Industry (CONEBI) 04519

Gen Manager Avenue Marnix 17, 1000 Brussels, Belgium.
Pres address not obtained.
URL: http://www.conebi.eu/

History 19 Nov 2014. Founded on merger of *Association of the European Two-Wheeler Parts' and Accessories' Industry (COLIPED, inactive)* and *Comité de liaison des fabricants européens de bicyclettes (COLIBI, inactive).* Registration: Banque-Carrefour des Entreprises, No/ID: 0476.852.097, Start date: 29 Nov 2001, Belgium; EU Transparency Register, No/ID: 677937617205-76, Start date: 4 May 2015. **Aims** Support growth of the bicycle, electronically power assisted cycle (EPAC) and parts and accessories industries, as well as cycling culture in Europe. **Structure** General Assembly; Board of Directors; Working Groups. **Activities** Advocacy/lobbying/advocacy; monitoring/evaluation; research/documentation; events/meetings. **NGO Relations** Member of (2): *AEGIS Europe; Industry4Europe (#11181).* Cooperates with (1): *Cycling Industries Europe (CIE, #04988).* [2021/XM4370/t/**D**]

♦ Confederation of European Biopathologists (CEB) 04520

Confédération des Biologistes Européens (CBE)

Secretariat 11 rue de Fleurus, 75006 Paris, France. T. +33153638503. Fax +33153638501.
Pres address not obtained.

History 1987. Founded on the initiative of Charles Mazzoni. Previously also referred to in English as *European Confederation of Biologists*. Also referred to as *Confederation of the European Biopathologists and Specialists in Laboratory Medicine*. **Aims** Bring together all biopathologists and directors of laboratories working in the private sector; examine and study the requirements to practice medical biology in Europe and strengthen cooperation and friendship between private professionals. **Structure** Board, comprising Chairman, Vice-President, Secretary, Treasurer and 4 members. **Events** *Meeting* Paris (France) 2011, *Meeting* Paris (France) 2010, *Meeting* Paris (France) 2009, *Meeting* Paris (France) 2008, *Meeting* Paris (France) 2007. **NGO Relations** Member of: *European Council of Liberal Professions (#06828)*. [2011.10.28/XD7463/**D**]

♦ Confederation of the European Biopathologists and Specialists in Laboratory Medicine / see Confederation of European Biopathologists (#04520)

♦ Confederation of European Community Cigarette Manufacturers (CECCM) 04521

Chairman Av Louise 375 – bte 9, 1050 Brussels, Belgium. T. +3225410034. Fax +3225410035. E-mail: ceccm@ceccm.eu.
URL: http://www.ceccm.eu/

History Founded 1989, when registered in accordance with UK law; liquidated 2007. Registered in accordance with Belgian law, 2005: 0879 438 919. EU Transparency Register: 1496873833-97. **Aims** Coordinate and represent views of members on EU tobacco related legislation. **Structure** General Assembly; Board; Executive Committee; Working Groups. **Languages** English. **Staff** 5.00 FTE, paid. **Finance** Members' dues. **Activities** Politics/policy/regulatory.
Members Full (3); Associate. National Manufacturers' Associations (13) in 13 countries:
Belgium, Denmark, Estonia, Finland, Germany, Greece, Ireland, Lithuania, Luxembourg, Netherlands, Spain, Sweden, UK.
Observers (2) in 2 countries:
Luxembourg, USA.
NGO Relations Member of: *American European Community Association (AECA)*; EU Observatory on Infringements of Intellectual Property Rights; *European Policy Centre (EPC, #08240)*; *Federation of European and International Associations Established in Belgium (FAIB, #09508)*. [2016.10.19/XE1491/**E**]

♦ Confederation of European Companions 04522

Confédération des compagnonnages européens (CCEG) – Confederation Europäische Gesellenzünfte (CCEG)
Registered Office 7 rue Petit, 75019 Paris, France.
URL: http://www.cceg.eu/

History 1968, Tours (France), as *Compagnonnages européens – Europäische Gesellenzünfte (CEG)*, two previous joint meetings having been held between 1951 and 1963. Present name and Statutes adopted at 7th Meeting, 21 May 1983, Brussels (Belgium). Registered in accordance with Dutch law. **Aims** Establish or strengthen ties between the various societies of 'companions' and their members, who remain companions once they have finished travelling, whatever their professional or social circumstances; promote the corporative and historical traditions of the 'companions'; promote contacts and understanding among young Europeans through occupational ties; facilitate exchanges of *itinerant workers* who are members of the federated societies. **Structure** General Assembly (annual). Committee, consisting of President, Vice-President, Secretary, Assistant Secretary, Treasurer, Assistant Treasurer, one representative from each member Society and one representative of itinerant companions. Executive Committee, comprising President, 1st and 2nd Vice-Presidents, 1st and 2nd Secretaries, 1st and 2nd Treasurers and 3 Editors. Europe Representative. **Languages** French, German. **Staff** Voluntary. **Finance** Members' dues. **Events** *General Assembly / Annual General Assembly* Kiel (Germany) 2012, *General Assembly / Annual General Assembly* Mouchard (France) 2011, *Annual General Assembly* Heidelberg (Germany) 2010, *General Assembly* Schriesheim (Germany) 2010, *General Assembly / Annual General Assembly* Lüdersburg (Germany) 2009. **Publications** *CCEG Bulletin* (2 a year) in French, German.
Members Societies, representing one or more groups of 'Companions', in 17 countries and territories:
Argentina, Australia, Austria, Belgium, Canada, Chile, Denmark, France, Germany, Netherlands, New Zealand, Norway, Scotland, South Africa, Sweden, Switzerland, USA.
Consultative Status Consultative status granted from: *Council of Europe (CE, #04881)* (Participatory Status).
NGO Relations *Foreningen for Berejste Skandinaviske Håndvaerkere (FBSH, no recent information)*. [2020/XD6459/**D**]

♦ Confederation of European Computer User Associations (CECUA) 04523

Confédération Européenne des Associations d'Utilisateurs des Technologies de l'Information
Vice-Pres/Interim Pres Rue Washington 40, 1050 Brussels, Belgium. E-mail: cecuamedia@aol.com.
URL: https://cecua1.wixsite.com/cecua

History 16 Feb 1978, Brussels (Belgium). Founded as an International Association with Scientific Objectives. Since 2014, operates as a virtual association. Registration: Banque-Carrefour des Entreprises, No/ID: 0423.719.655, Start date: 16 Feb 1983, Belgium. **Aims** Identify hurdles for citizens (private and corporate) to join the Information Society; raise awareness about those hurdles with appropriate authorities; recommend remedies; work with national, European and international bodies on Internet governance issues. **Structure** General Assembly; Board of Directors. **Languages** English. **Staff** Voluntary. **Finance** Voluntary contributions. **Activities** Events/meetings; advocacy/lobbying/activism. **Events** *Conference on the citizen and global information societies* Brussels (Belgium) 1998, *Conference on the citizen and the global information society* Reykjavik (Iceland) 1998, *European congress on electronic data processing* Graz (Austria) 1987, *International congress on electronic data processing in Europe* Vienna (Austria) 1987. **Publications** *The Users: Hostages of the Free Market ?*. Reports. **Members** National Associations; individuals. Membership countries not specified. **IGO Relations** Accredited to: *European Union Agency for Network and Information Security (ENISA, #08971)*; World Summit on the Information Society. [2018/XD8150/**D**]

♦ Confederation of European Economic Associations (inactive)

♦ Confederation of European Environmental Engineering Societies (CEEES) 04524

Secretariat c/o ASTE, Le Central Gare, 1 place Charles de Gaulle, 78180 Montigny-le-Bretonneux, France.
Registered Office Bovenbosstraat 77, 3053 Haasrode, Belgium.
URL: http://www.ceees.org/

History As *Committee of European Environmental Engineering Societies (CEEES) – Comité européen des associations techniques de l'environnement (CEATE)*. Registered in accordance with Belgian law. **Aims** Promote the advancement of science and technology in the field of environmental engineering and related branches of science. **Structure** General Assembly, Secretariat and Advisory Boards. Officers: President, Vice-President and Treasurer. Each member society successively holds Presidency and Secretariat for 2 years. **Languages** English. **Staff** 2.00 FTE, paid; 2.00 FTE, voluntary. **Finance** Members' dues. **Activities** Knowledge management/information dissemination; events/meetings. **Events** *General Assembly* Leuven (Belgium) 2014, *General Assembly* Bratislava (Slovakia) 2013, *General Assembly* Rotterdam (Netherlands) 2012, *International symposium on ultrafine particles* Karlsruhe (Germany) 2007, *General Assembly* Ostend (Belgium) 2007. **Publications** *CEEES Newsletter*.
Members National organizations (12) in 12 countries:
Austria, Belgium, Czechia, Finland, France, Germany, Italy, Netherlands, Portugal, Sweden, Switzerland, UK. [2019/XE3182/**D**]

♦ Confederation of European Firms, Employment Initiatives and Cooperatives for Psychically Disabled / see Social Firms Europe (#19338)

♦ Confederation of European Forest Owners (CEPF) 04525

Confédération européenne des propriétaires forestiers – Zentralverband der Europäischen Waldbesitzer
SG European Forestry House, Rue du Luxembourg 66, 1000 Brussels, Belgium. T. +3222392307. Fax +3222192191. E-mail: office@cepf-eu.org.
URL: http://www.cepf-eu.org/

History 1961. Former names and other names: *Central Committee of the Forest Ownership in the EC* – former; *Comité central de la propriété forestière de la CE (CCPF)* – former; *Zentralausschuss der Waldbesitzerverbände der EG* – former; *Comitato Centrale Proprietà Forestale della CE* – former; *Centraal Comité van Verenigingen van Boseigenaren in de EG* – former; *Centraludvalget for det EØFs Skovbrugsejere* – former. Registration: EU Transparency Register, No/ID: 3647455667-08. **Aims** Promote values of *sustainable* forest management, private property ownership and economic viability of the forest sector. **Structure** Board; Secretariat. A network of forest owner associations. **Languages** English. **Staff** 4.00 FTE, paid. **Finance** Sources: members' dues. **Activities** Events/meetings; monitoring/evaluation; politics/policy/regulatory. **Events** *General Assembly* Brussels (Belgium) 2021, *General Assembly* Hämeenlinna (Finland) 2020, *General Assembly* Lisbon (Portugal) 2019, *General Assembly* Vienna (Austria) 2018, *General Assembly* Zagreb (Croatia) 2015.
Members National organizations in 20 countries:
Austria, Croatia, Czechia, Denmark, Estonia, Finland, France, Germany, Greece, Hungary, Italy, Latvia, Lithuania, Luxembourg, Norway, Portugal, Slovenia, Spain, Sweden, Switzerland.
Consultative Status Consultative status granted from: *ECOSOC (#05331)* (Ros A). **IGO Relations** Accredited by (1): *United Nations Framework Convention on Climate Change – Secretariat (UNFCCC, #20564)*. Observer status with (1): *Intergovernmental Negotiating Committee for a Legally Binding Agreement on Forests in Europe (INC-Forests, inactive)*. Cooperates with (3): *European Community (inactive)*; *European Economic and Social Committee (EESC, #06963)*; *European Parliament (EP, #08146)*. **NGO Relations** Member of (4): *European Bioeconomy Alliance (EUBA, #06334)*; *International Family Forestry Alliance (IFFA, #13329)*; *International Union for Conservation of Nature and Natural Resources (IUCN, #15766)*; *PEFC Council (#18288)*. Together with: *Confederation of European Paper Industries (CEPI, #04529)* and *Confédération européenne des industries du bois (CEI Bois, #04545)*, instrumental in setting up: *Forest-Based Sector Technology Platform (FTP, #09861)*. [2022.02.02/XE0242/**E**]

♦ Confederation of European Laryngectomees / see European Confederation of Laryngectomees (#06709)

♦ Confederation of European Maritime Technology Societies (CEMT) 04526

Sec c/o Royal Institution of Naval Architects, 8-9 Northumberland Street, London, WC2N 5DA, UK.
URL: http://www.cemt.eu/

History Founded 1971, as *West European Confederation of Maritime Technology Societies (WEMT)*. Present name adopted 2003. **Aims** Provide a forum for exchange of information and views by constituent societies on matters relating to the education and professional development of *naval* architects, marine engineers and others in the field or maritime technology; provide a link between members and the European Union in order for the constituent societies to be informed on the above; provide advice, when requested by any body of the European Union, on matters relating to the education and professional development of the above. **Structure** Council (meets twice a year). **Languages** English. **Staff** 0.50 FTE, voluntary. **Finance** Members' dues. **Activities** Knowledge management/information dissemination; publishing activities; events/meetings; awards/prizes/competitions. **Events** *Conference* Naples (Italy) 2012, *Conference* London (UK) 2004, *Conference* Naples (Italy) 2002, *Conference* London (UK) 2000, *Conference* Rotterdam (Netherlands) 1998.
Members Professional institutions involved in education and professional development and learned societies facilitating exchange of information, in European Union member countries (available to non-European Union member countries upon invitation). Societies of naval architects and marine engineers and technologists in 12 countries:
Denmark, France, Germany, Greece, Italy, Netherlands, Poland, Portugal, Serbia, Spain, Türkiye, UK.
Consultative Status Consultative status granted from: *ECOSOC (#05331)* (Special). **NGO Relations** Cooperates with: *Maritime Industries Forum (MIF, no recent information)*. [2017.10.18/XD7621/**D**]

♦ Confederation of European Music Industries (CAFIM) 04527

Contact c/o BDMH, Brunnenstr 31, 65191 Wiesbaden, Germany. T. +496119545886. Fax +496119545885.
URL: http://cafim.org/

History 5 May 1977, Frankfurt-Main (Germany). 5 May 1977, Frankfurt (Germany), as *Musiqueurope*. Later known as *Confederation des associations des facteurs d'instruments de musique de la CEE (CAFIM)*. Present name adopted, 2000.
Members National associations in 8 countries:
Austria, Czechia, France, Germany, Norway, Slovenia, Spain, Switzerland. [2017/XM4622/t/**D**]

♦ Confederation of European National Societies of Anaesthesiologists (inactive)
♦ **Confederation of European ORL-HNS** Confederation of European Otorhinolaryngology – Head and Neck Surgery (#04528)

♦ Confederation of European Otorhinolaryngology – Head and Neck Surgery (Confederation of European ORL-HNS) 04528

Verband der Europäischen Otorhinolaryngologie, Kopf- und Halschirurgie
Exec Officer c/o Mondial Congress, Operngasse 20b, 1040 Vienna, Austria. T. +34618533894. Fax +43158804185.
URL: http://www.ceorlhns.org/

History Jul 2011. Founded as the umbrella organization for *European Federation of Otorhinolaryngological Societies (EUFOS, inactive)*, *European Academy of Otorhinolaryngology, Head and Neck Surgery (EAORL-HNS, inactive)* and *European Union of Medical Specialists (UEMS, #09001)* ORL Section and Board. Registration: ZVR-Zahl, No/ID: 344666629, Austria. **Aims** Facilitate continuing medical education and professional development; maintain and improve the welfare of ORL-HNS specialists in Europe. **Structure** General Assembly; Presidential Council. **Languages** English. **Finance** Sources: members' dues. **Activities** Events/meetings; projects/programmes. **Events** *Congress* Gothenburg (Sweden) 2026, *Congress* Dublin (Ireland) 2024, *Congress* Milan (Italy) 2022, *Congress* Milan (Italy) 2021, *Congress* Brussels (Belgium) 2019.
Members Regroups membership of the former EAORL-HNS, former EUFOS and UEMS ORL Section. International organizations (14):
European Academy of Allergy and Clinical Immunology (EAACI, #05779) (ENT Section); *European Academy of Facial Plastic Surgery (EAFPS, #05792)*; *European Academy of Otology and Neuro-Otology (EAONO, #05809)*; *European Academy of Sleep Medicine (EASM, no recent information)*; *European Federation of Audiology Societies (EFAS, #07058)*; *European Head and Neck Society (EHNS, #07452)*; *European Laryngological Society (ELS, #07653)*; *European Rhinologic Society (ERS, #08388)*; *European Skull Base Society (ESBS, #08492)*; *European Society for Swallowing Disorders (ESSD, #08755)*; *European Society of Pediatric Otorhinolaryngology (ESPO, #08692)*; *European Study Group for Rehabilitation and Functional Surgery Following Laryngectomy (EGFL, #08852)*; Multidisciplinary Salivary Gland Society (MSGS).
National societies in 41 countries:
Albania, Austria, Azerbaijan, Belarus, Belgium, Bosnia-Herzegovina, Bulgaria, Croatia, Cyprus, Czechia, Denmark, Estonia, Finland, France, Germany, Greece, Hungary, Iceland, Ireland, Israel, Italy, Lithuania, Luxembourg, Malta, Moldova, Netherlands, North Macedonia, Norway, Poland, Portugal, Romania, Russia, Serbia, Slovakia, Slovenia, Spain, Sweden, Switzerland, Türkiye, UK, Ukraine. [2022/XJ5364/y/**D**]

♦ Confederation of European Paper Industries (CEPI) 04529

Confédération des industries papetières européennes
Dir-Gen Av Louise 250, Bte 80, 1050 Brussels, Belgium. T. +3226274919. E-mail: mail@cepi.org.
URL: http://www.cepi.org/

History 1 Jan 1992. Founded by merger of *European Confederation of Pulp, Paper and Board Industries (CEPAC, inactive)* and *European Paper Institute (EPI, inactive)*, following a meeting, 27 Nov 1991, London (UK). Also referred to as *Confederation of European Pulp and Paper Industries*. Statutes: adopted 25 Oct 1991, Brussels (Belgium); modified 12 May 1995, Brussels and 27 Nov 2007. Registration: Banque-Carrefour des Entreprises, No/ID: 0447.185.143, Start date: 25 Oct 1991, Belgium; EU Transparency Register, No/ID: 72279144480-58, Start date: 5 Nov 2010. **Aims** Regroup the European pulp and paper industry and champion the industry's achievements and the benefits of its products; promote the business sector by monitoring and analyzing activities and initiatives in the areas of industry, environment, energy, forestry, recycling and competitiveness in general. **Structure** General Assembly (annual); Board; Steering Committee; CEOs Forum; Standing Committees (4). **Languages** English. **Staff** 16.00 FTE, paid. **Finance** Members' dues. **Activities** Networking/liaising; knowledge management/information dissemination; events/meetings. **Events** *Paper and*

Beyond Conference Brussels (Belgium) 2022, *Paper and Beyond Conference* Brussels (Belgium) 2021, *Annual European Paper Week* Brussels (Belgium) 2020, *Paper and Beyond Conference* Brussels (Belgium) 2020, *Annual European Paper Week* Brussels (Belgium) 2019. **Publications** *Sustainability Report* (every 2 years); *CEPI Focus Newsletter* (regular); *Key Statistics* (regular).
Members National associations of pulp, paper and cardboard manufacturers in 18 countries:
Austria, Belgium, Czechia, Finland, France, Germany, Hungary, Italy, Netherlands, Norway, Poland, Portugal, Romania, Slovakia, Slovenia, Spain, Sweden, UK.
Consultative Status Consultative status granted from: *ECOSOC (#05331)* (Ros A). **IGO Relations** *European Committee of the Regions (CoR, #06665); Council of Europe (CE, #04881); European Commission (EC, #06633); European Economic and Social Committee (EESC, #06963); European Parliament (EP, #08146); Statistical Office of the European Union (Eurostat, #19974).* World-wide: *FAO (#09260); United Nations Economic Commission for Europe (UNECE, #20555); OECD (#17693).* Observer to: *Intergovernmental Negotiating Committee for a Legally Binding Agreement on Forests in Europe (INC-Forests, inactive); OSPAR Commission for the Protection of the Marine Environment of the North-East Atlantic (OSPAR Commission, #17905).* Accredited by: *United Nations Framework Convention on Climate Change – Secretariat (UNFCCC, #20564).* **NGO Relations** Europe: *BUSINESSEUROPE (#03381).* Member of: *Alliance for a Competitive European Industry (ACEI, #00670); European Policy Centre (EPC, #08240); European Shippers' Council (ESC, #08477); Federation of European and International Associations Established in Belgium (FAIB, #09508); Industry4Europe (#11181); International Council of Forest and Paper Associations (ICFPA, #13023); PEFC Council (#18288).* Signatory to Declaration of on Paper Recovery, maintained by *European Paper Recycling Council (EPRC, #08139).* In liaison with technical committees of: *Comité européen de normalisation (CEN, #04162); International Organization for Standardization (ISO, #14473).* Together with: *Confederation of European Forest Owners (CEPF, #04525)* and *Confédération européenne des industries du bois (CEI Bois, #04545),* instrumental in setting up: *Forest-Based Sector Technology Platform (FTP, #09861).* Partner of: *World Business Council for Sustainable Development (WBCSD, #21254).* Participating Industry Sectors: *Association of European Cartonboard and Carton Manufacturers (PRO CARTON, #02502); CEPI Cartonboard (#03823); CEPI ContainerBoard (CCB, #03824); European Association of Graphic Paper Producers (EURO GRAPH, #06060); European Carton Makers Association (ECMA, #06453); European Tissue Symposium (ETS, #08917);* ICFPA; *Pulp and Paper Products Council (PPPC, #18577); Speciality Paper Manufacturers Association (PaperImpact, inactive); European Paper Merchants Association (Eugropa, #08138).* [2021/XD2872/ty/**D**]

♦ Confederation of European Probation (CEP) 04530

Confédération européenne de la probation

Exec Officer Postbus 8215, 3503 RE Utrecht, Netherlands. T. +31302324900. E-mail: secr@cep-probation.org.
URL: http://www.cep-probation.org/

History 1981. Former names and other names: *Permanent European Conference on Probation and Aftercare* – former; *Conférence permanente européenne de la probation* – former; *Ständige Europäische Konferenz für Straffälligen- und Bewährungshilfe* – former; *European Organisation for Probation (CEP)* – former; *Organisation européenne de la probation* – former; *Europäische Bewährungshilfeorganisation* – former. Registration: Handelsregister, No/ID: KVK 40217639, Netherlands; EU Transparency Register, No/ID: 126774441461-62, Start date: 16 Feb 2021. **Aims** Unite public and private institutions and organizations in Europe that have as their objective the provision of probation services, including *assistance* to *accused persons* both before and after sentence; promote professionalism in the field of probation in Europe via international cooperation and exchange; enhance the profile of probation at both national and European levels. **Structure** General Assembly (every 3 years); Electronic Monitoring conference (every 2 years); Board and Presidium; Expert Groups; workshops and webinars. **Languages** English. **Staff** 6.00 FTE, paid. **Finance** Sources: grants; members' dues. Supported by: *European Commission (EC, #06633).* **Activities** Awareness raising; events/meetings; guidance/assistance/consulting; knowledge management/information dissemination; networking/liaising; projects/programmes. **Events** *European Electronic Monitoring Conference* Helsinki (Finland) 2022, *International Correctional Research Symposium (CRS)* Porto (Portugal) 2021, *European Electronic Monitoring Conference* Helsinki (Finland) 2020, *European Electronic Monitoring Conference* Zagreb (Croatia) 2018, *Conference of Directors General of Probation* Brussels (Belgium) 2017. **Publications** *CEP Newsletter* (6 a year); *Eurovista – Probation and Community Justice* – journal. *Probabation in Europe* (2015-2018); *Probation and Probation Services – A European Perspective* (2000). Seminar and workshop reports.
Members Full; Associate ; Individual. Members in 41 countries and territories:
Albania, Armenia, Austria, Belgium, Bulgaria, Croatia, Czechia, Denmark, England and Wales, Estonia, Finland, France, Georgia, Germany, Hungary, Ireland, Italy, Jersey, Kosovo, Latvia, Liechtenstein, Lithuania, Luxembourg, Malta, Moldova, Montenegro, Netherlands, North Macedonia, Northern Ireland, Norway, Portugal, Romania, Scotland, Slovakia, Slovenia, Spain, Sweden, Switzerland, Türkiye, UK, Ukraine.
Affiliate partners in 4 countries:
Australia, Canada, Netherlands, USA.
Consultative Status Consultative status granted from: *Council of Europe (CE, #04881)* (Participatory Status). [2023.02.14/XF0388/y/**F**]

♦ Confederation of European Pulp and Paper Industries / see Confederation of European Paper Industries (#04529)

♦ Confederation of European Scouting 04531

Confédération européenne de scoutisme (CES) – Bund Europäischer Pfadfinder – Confederazione Europea Scoutismo

Registered Office Ch de Mons 13, 7090 Braine-le-Comte, Belgium.
URL: http://ces-scout.eu/

History 12 Nov 1978, Brussels (Belgium), following an ideological schism with *Union Internationale des Guides et Scouts d'Europe – Fédération du Scoutisme Européen (UIGSE-FSE, #20426).* Registered in accordance with Belgian law, 5 Dec 1979. **Aims** Promote and practice scouting faithful (in a European spirit) to the educational principles of Baden-Powell in the full; respect others' convictions; secure exchanges between groups from different countries in order to increase effects of educational work; prepare members for fully United Europe. **Structure** Confederal Board, consisting of President, Vice-President, Secretary and 2 members. Confederal Council, composed of 4 members from each national member federation. **Languages** English, French. **Events** *Meeting: Eurojam – Euro-Jamboree* Bad Bergzabern (Germany) 2006, *Eurojam : European jamboree* Chelmsford (UK) 2005, *Eurojam : European jamboree / Meeting: Eurojam – Euro-Jamboree* Ollerton (UK) 2001, *Eurojam : European jamboree* Bassano del Grappa (Italy) 1997, *Eurojam : European jamboree / Meeting: Eurojam – Euro-Jamboree* Olloy-sur-Viroin (Belgium) 1993. **Publications** *CES-Flash.*
Members National federations in 6 countries:
Belgium, Germany, Italy, Netherlands, Spain, UK. [2018/XD7488/**D**]

♦ Confederation of European Security Services (CoESS) 04532

Confédération européenne des services de sécurité (CoESS)

Officer Av des Arts 56, 1000 Brussels, Belgium. T. +32473836359. E-mail: catherine@coess.eu.
URL: http://www.coess.org/

History Founded by a joint initiative of several national associations of private security companies belonging to EU Member States. Statutes adopted, 26 Oct 1989, Rome. Most recent statutes adopted during Extraordinary General Assembly, 27 Sep 2002, Istanbul (Turkey); revised, 26 Sep 2003, Corfu (Greece). Former names and other names: *Confédération européenne des sociétés de sécurité* – former. Registration: Banque-Carrefour des Entreprises, Start date: 2016, Belgium; EU Transparency Register, No/ID: 61991787780-18. **Aims** Defend the interests of the private security services industry in Europe. **Structure** General Meeting (at least annual); Board of Directors; Executive Committee; Working Committees (7). **Languages** English. **Staff** 3.00 FTE, paid. **Finance** Sources: members' dues. **Activities** Events/meetings; politics/policy/regulatory. **Events** *Annual General Meeting* Brussels (Belgium) 2022, *Annual General meeting* Leuven (Belgium) 2021, *Annual General Meeting* 2020, *European Summit* Rome (Italy) 2019, *European Summit* Berlin (Germany) 2015. **Publications** *CoESS Newsletter. Linkedin* in English.
Members Active: national organizations (normally accepts only one body per State) in 21 countries:
Austria, Belgium, Bulgaria, Croatia, Estonia, Finland, France, Germany, Greece, Italy, Luxembourg, Netherlands, North Macedonia, Portugal, Romania, Slovenia, Spain, Sweden, Switzerland, Türkiye, UK.
Associated: national organizations in 2 countries:
Norway, Serbia.

Corresponding members (2), listed in this Yearbook:
Aviation Security Services Association – International (ASSA-I, #03046); European Security Transport Association (ESTA, #08458).
IGO Relations Cooperates with (1): *European Commission (EC, #06633).* **NGO Relations** Member of (1): *European Business Services Alliance (EBSA, #06426).* Cooperates with (1): *Comité européen de normalisation (CEN, #04162).* Technical Liaison Partner with: *European Committee for Electrotechnical Standardization (CENELEC, #06647).* [2022.05.10/XD9477/y/**D**]

♦ Confederation of European Senior Expert Services (CESES) 04533

Gen Sec Rue d'Edimbourg 26, 1050 Brussels, Belgium. T. +32475660591. E-mail: info@ceses.net.
Pres address not obtained.
URL: https://www.ceses.eu/

History Dec 1989, Brussels (Belgium). Former names and other names: *Association of Seniors of the European Community* – former (Dec 1989); *Association de seniors de l'Europe communautaire* – former (Dec 1989); *Association of Senior European Counsellors (ASEC)* – former; *Association de seniors européens conseillers* – former. Registration: Crossroads Bank for Enterprises, No/ID: 0440.143.141, Start date: 1 Mar 1990, Belgium; EU Transparency Register, No/ID: 18460992206-03, Start date: 2 Sep 2009. **Aims** Represent member associations vis-a-vis the European Union institutions to foster all activities in favour of economic, social, cultural, technological or scientific development of Small and Medium-sized enterprises in developing countries. **Structure** General Assembly; Board of Directors; Executive Committee. **Languages** English. **Staff** 0.50 FTE, voluntary. **Finance** Sources: fees for services; members' dues. Annual budget: 75,000 EUR (2011). **Activities** Knowledge management/information dissemination. **Publications** *CESES Bulletin.*
Members Effective; Associate: associations (17) in 12 EU Member States:
Austria, Belgium, Denmark, Finland, France, Germany, Italy, Luxembourg, Netherlands, Portugal, Spain, Switzerland.
Included in the above, 3 organizations listed in this Yearbook:
Association générale des intervenants retraités (AGIRabcd); ECTI – Professionnels Seniors Bénévoles; Technical Office for International Studies and Cooperation (OTECI).
NGO Relations Member of (2): *Centre for European Volunteering (CEV, #03743); Federation of European and International Associations Established in Belgium (FAIB, #09508).* [2022/XF1432/y/**F**]

♦ Confederation of European Shipmasters' Associations (CESMA) ... 04534

Secretariat Muntplein 10, 1012 WR Amsterdam, Netherlands. E-mail: cesma-eu@introweb.nl.
URL: http://www.cesma-eu.org/

History 1995. **Aims** Promote high professional maritime standards; improve maritime safety; protect the marine environment; represent EU shipmasters in the European Commission and European Parliament. **Structure** General Assembly (annual); Council; Board. **Languages** English. **Events** *Annual General Assembly* Antwerp (Belgium) 2019, *Annual General Assembly* Kotor (Montenegro) 2018, *Annual General Assembly* Riga (Latvia) 2017, *Annual General Assembly* Cork (Ireland) 2016, *Annual General Assembly* Viareggio (Italy) 2015. **Publications** *CESMA Newsletter* (4 a year).
Members Associations (18) in 13 countries:
Belgium, Bulgaria, Croatia, Finland, France, Germany, Ireland, Italy, Latvia, Netherlands, Portugal, Slovenia, Spain.
IGO Relations Represented in a number of programmes of *European Commission (EC, #06633).* **NGO Relations** Involved in: *Maritime Industries Forum (MIF, no recent information).* [2019.11.06/XM3343/**D**]

♦ Confederation of European Social Firms, Employment Initiatives and Social Cooperatives / see Social Firms Europe (#19338)
♦ Confederation of European Specialists in Paediatrics / see European Academy of Paediatrics (#05811)

♦ Confederation of European Waste-to-Energy Plants (CEWEP) 04535

Managing Director Peter-Müller-Str 16a, 40468 Düsseldorf, Germany. E-mail: info@cewep.eu.
European Office Av de Tervuren 113, 1040 Brussels, Belgium. T. +3227706311.
URL: https://www.cewep.eu/

History 28 May 2002, Würzburg (Germany). Founded 2002, during 1st Congress. Registration: Bavaria District court, No/ID: VR 2136, Start date: 24 Nov 2004, Germany, Würzburg; EU Transparency Register, No/ID: 7899845424-69, Start date: 24 Sep 2008. **Aims** Boost sustainable energy from waste; work towards reducing dependence on landfilling and fossil fuels; promote quality *recycling*; move towards a level playing field for waste treatment; promote public participation; promote exchange of experience, research and development. **Structure** General Assembly. Officers: President; Deputy-Presidents; Vice-Presidents; Managing Director. **Languages** English. **Staff** 5.50 FTE, paid. **Finance** Sources: members' dues. **Activities** Networking/liaising; politics/policy/regulatory; research/documentation. **Events** *Biennial Congress* Berlin (Germany) 2023, *Biennial Congress* Berlin (Germany) 2022, *Biennial Congress* Prague (Czechia) 2021, *Biennial Congress* Prague (Czechia) 2020, *Biennial Congress* Bilbao (Spain) 2018.
Members Waste-to-Energy Plants (about 400) in 23 countries:
Andorra, Austria, Belgium, Czechia, Denmark, Finland, France, Germany, Hungary, Ireland, Italy, Lithuania, Luxembourg, Netherlands, Norway, Poland, Portugal, Slovakia, Spain, Sweden, Switzerland, Türkiye, UK.
NGO Relations Member of (1): *International Solid Waste Association (ISWA, #15567).* Associate member of: *European Energy Forum (EEF, #06986).* Associated expert of: *Business and Industry Advisory Committee to the OECD (BIAC, #03385).* [2022.10.18/XM0047/**D**]

♦ Confederation of European Yeast Producers (#04551)
♦ Confédération européen de marketing (#07747)
♦ Confédération européenne des activités en déchets spéciaux (inactive)
♦ Confédération européenne des agences privées pour l'emploi / see World Employment Federation Europe (#21377)
♦ Confédération européenne de l'agriculture (inactive)

♦ Confédération européenne des Anciens et Anciennes Elèves des établissements de la Compagnie de Jésus 04536

European Confederation of Jesuit Alumni/ae (ECJA) – Confederación Europea de Antiguos Alumnos de Jesuitas – Europäische Konföderation der Jesuitenaltschüler – Confederazione Europea Ex Alunni dei Padri Gesuiti – Europese Confederatie van oud-leerlingen van jezuïetencolleges

Contact address not obtained. E-mail: secretary@jesuit-alumni.eu.
Registered Office c/o Collège Saint-Michel, Boulevard Saint-Michel 24-26, 1040 Brussels, Belgium.
URL: http://www.jesuit-alumni.eu/

History Sep 1954, Rome (Italy), at a meeting of presidents of national associations. Registered in accordance with Belgian law, 1990. Also referred to as *European Confederation of Jesuit Alumni.* Registration: ASBL/VZW, Belgium. **Aims** Continue the training activity of Jesuit Fathers by means of the *continuing education* of the former students; collaborate with the Society of Jesus in its social and spiritual *educational* action; promote links and ensure mutual assistance between former students in various European countries. **Structure** General Assembly; Council. **Finance** Members' dues. All the Delegates are financed by their national or local associations. **Activities** Organizes (every 3 years) a Congress. Encourages each local or national association to engage in projects which raise the public's awareness of the plight of refugees, and to support the poor, be they homeless, refugees, sick or disadvantaged in some other way. **Events** *Congress* Budapest (Hungary) 2011, *Presidents Meeting / Congress* Turin (Italy) 2008, *Congress* Lisbon (Portugal) 2005, *Congress* Birkirkara (Malta) 2001, *Congress* Malta 2001.
Members Ordinary individuals; Full federations of associations of former students of the Society of Jesus. National federations (14) in 13 countries and territories:
Austria, Belgium (2), England, France, Germany, Hungary, Ireland, Italy, Lebanon, Malta, Netherlands, Portugal, Spain.
NGO Relations Member of (1): *World Union of Jesuit Alumni and Alumnae (WUJA, #21877). Society of Jesus (SJ).* Member of European Section of: *Organisation mondiale des anciens élèves de l'enseignement catholique (OMAEC, #17816).* [2020/XE7348/**E**]

♦ Confédération européenne des anciens et anciennes élèves des Pères jésuites / see Confédération européenne des Anciens et Anciennes Elèves des établissements de la Compagnie de Jésus (#04536)

Confédération Européenne Anciens
04537

alphabetic sequence excludes
For the complete listing, see Yearbook Online at

♦ Confédération Européenne des Anciens Combattants (CEAC) 04537

European War Veterans' Confederation – Confederación Europea de Excombatientes

Contact 49 Rue Belair, L-4514 Differdange, Luxembourg. T. +35226580367.
Head Office c/o Union fédérale, 1 rue de Brissac, 75004 Paris, France. T. +33144542270. Fax +33148876874. E-mail: ufafacvg@wanadoo.fr.
URL: http://www.union-federale.com/

History Founded 1961, Paris (France), in succession to a 'Comité d'entente' set up after World War II. Previously also referred to in French as *Fédération européenne des vétérans de guerre*. Registration: France. **Aims** Group associations of veterans and victims of the war in order to cooperate for preserving peace and ensuring the improvement of their living conditions; promote the idea of a united Europe; defend fundamental human rights; favour European solidarity and defend Western civilization; combat false and tendentious information as well as actions opposed to the unity of veterans serving Europe. **Structure** General Assembly (annual). Director's Board (twice a year). Managers' Meeting. Officers: President, Deputy President, Secretary General and General Treasurer. Honorary Committee. **Languages** French. **Finance** Sources: grants; members' dues. **Activities** Events/meetings. **Events** *General Assembly* Paris (France) 2009, *General Assembly* Tallinn (Estonia) 2008, *General Assembly* London (UK) 2007, *Annual general assembly / General Assembly* Perpignan (France) 2006, *Annual general assembly / General Assembly* London (UK) 2005. **Publications** *Lettre de la CEAC* (4 a year).

Members National sections, gathering about 700,000 members, in 11 countries and territories:
Albania, Belgium, Estonia, France, Germany, Italy, Kosovo, Luxembourg, Netherlands, Spain, UK.

NGO Relations Member of (2): *European Movement International (EMI, #07825)*; *Permanent Forum of European Civil Society (#18322)*. Together with: *International Confederation of Former Prisoners of War (ICFPW, inactive)*, *International Federation of Resistance Movements (#13529)*, *The World Veterans Federation (WVF, #21900)*, instrumental in setting up *Coordinating Committee of 4 International Veterans Organizations*.
[2011/XD4525/**D**]

- ♦ Confédération européenne de l'artisanat, des petites et moyennes entreprises du bâtiment / see European Builders Confederation (#06408)
- ♦ Confédération Européenne des Associations d'Administrateurs (#06702)
- ♦ Confédération européenne des associations de détaillants en chaussures (inactive)
- ♦ Confédération européenne des associations de fabricants de peintures, d'encres d'imprimerie et de couleurs d'art / see Conseil européen de l'industrie des peintures, des encres d'imprimerie et des couleurs d'art (#04688)
- ♦ Confédération Européenne d'associations de fabricants de produits de santé (#07052)
- ♦ Confédération européenne des associations de familles de traumatisés crâniens (#03314)

♦ Confédération européenne des associations d'ingénieurs agronomes (CEDIA) 04538

European Confederation of Agronomist Associations

Pres address not obtained. T. +353868595890.
Registered Office c/o KU LEUVEN Fac L and TBW, Kasteelpark Arenberg 20, 3001 Heverlee, Belgium.
URL: http://www.cedia.eu/

History 23 Jun 1987, Brussels (Belgium), as *European Committee for EC Agricultural Engineers – Comité européen des ingénieurs agronomes de la CE – Europäischer Ausschuss der Diplom-Agraringenieure der Europäischen Gemeinschaft*, previously a *Liaison Committee of Agricultural Engineers for the EEC Countries – Comité de liaison des ingénieurs agronomes des pays membres des Communautés économiques européennes – Verbindungs-Ausschuss der Diplom-Landwirte der Mitgliedstaaten der Europäischen Wirtschaftsgemeinschaften* having been formed, Jun 1963, Brussels. Subsequently name changed to *European Committee of Agronomists – Comité européen des ingénieurs agronomes – Europäischer Ausschuss der Diplom-Agraringenieure*. Current name adopted 13 Oct 1996. Registered in accordance with Belgian law. EU Transparency Register: 562390824467-13. **Aims** Ensure the *protection* and *conservation* of the *environment*; promote the European integration, inter alia, by developing the collaboration between its members and the institutions offering university-level education in agriculture within the *European Union* member countries; promote the general and specific interests of members with EC/EU authorities and other communities and bodies. **Structure** General Assembly (annual). Praesidium, consisting of President, 2 Vice-Presidents and one representative per country. Working Groups. **Languages** English, French. **Finance** Members' dues. **Activities** Networking/liaising; knowledge management/information dissemination. **Events** *Conference / Meeting* Brussels (Belgium) 2014, *General Assembly* Dublin (Ireland) 2011, *Conference / Meeting* Leuven (Belgium) 2009, *Conference on irrigation in Southern Europe countries* Lisbon (Portugal) 2008, *General Assembly* Lisbon (Portugal) 2008. **Publications** *Newsletter CEDIA*. Conference reports.

Members National professional bodies for agricultural engineers in 11 countries:
Belgium, Cyprus, Denmark, France, Germany, Greece, Ireland, Italy, Portugal, Sweden, Switzerland.
Candidate in one territory:
Northern Ireland.

IGO Relations Contacts with: *European Commission (EC, #06633)*; *European Parliament (EP, #08146)*. **NGO Relations** Member of: *World Association of Agronomists (WAA, #21115)*. [2019/XE2921/**E**]

- ♦ Confédération européenne des associations de pesticides appliqués (#06717)
- ♦ Confédération Européenne des Associations de Petites et Moyennes Entreprises (#06994)
- ♦ Confédération européenne des associations de protection contre les incendies / see Confederation of Fire Protection Associations (#04552)
- ♦ Confédération Européenne des Associations d'Utilisateurs des Technologies de l'Information (#04523)
- ♦ Confédération européenne de baseball (#04518)
- ♦ Confédération européenne de baseball amateur / see Confederation of European Baseball (#04518)

♦ Confédération Européenne de Billard (CEB) 04539

European Billiards Confederation – Confederación Europea de Billar – Europäische Billard Konföderation

SG Mont-Cenis-Str 562 b, 44627 Herne, Germany. T. +492323961727. Fax +492323961728.
Pres Ernst-Moritz-Arndt-Str 9, 46240 Bottrop, Germany. T. +4920417064588. Fax +4920417064591.
URL: http://www.eurobillard.org/

History 12 Jul 1958, Geneva (Switzerland). 12-13 Jul 1958, Geneva (Switzerland), on merger of *International Union of Amateur Billiards Federations (inactive)* and *International Billiards Federation (inactive)*. **Aims** Fix rules; officiate at international *games*; study and decide all questions of interest to international billiards and ratify international results and records. **Structure** General Assembly (every 2 years); Committee. **Languages** English, French, German. **Staff** 1.00 FTE, paid. **Finance** Members' dues. **Activities** Events/meetings. **Events** *General Assembly* Terneuzen (Netherlands) 2014, *General Assembly* Brandenburg (Germany) 2013, *General Assembly* Famagusta (Cyprus) 2011, *General Assembly* Cairo (Egypt) 2009, *General Assembly* Famagusta (Cyprus) 2007.

Members Affiliated federations in 29 countries and territories:
Albania, Austria, Belgium, Bulgaria, Croatia, Cyprus, Czechia, Denmark, Finland, France, Germany, Greece, Hungary, Israel, Italy, Lithuania, Luxembourg, Montenegro, Netherlands, Northern Cyprus, Norway, Portugal, Russia, San Marino, Slovakia, Spain, Sweden, Switzerland, Türkiye. [2014.09.06/XD0594/**D**]

- ♦ Confédération européenne des cadres (#03623)
- ♦ Confédération européenne des catégories auxiliaires des activités viti-vinicole (inactive)

♦ Confédération européenne des centres de langues de l'enseignement supérieur (CercleS) 04540

European Confederation of Language Centres in Higher Education – Europäischer Verband der Hochschulsprachenzentren

SG Univ de Lorraine, UFR Lansad, CLSH – 23 bd Albert 1er – BP 60546, 54001 Nancy, France. T. +33372743187. E-mail: generalsecretariat@cercles.org.
Pres Univ of Zurich, Language Center of UZH and ETH Zurich, Rämistrasse 71, 8006 Zurich ZH, Switzerland. T. +41446345280.
URL: http://www.cercles.org/

History 1991, Strasbourg (France). **Aims** Support language centres in European institutes of higher education; promote research in foreign language learning; encourage cooperation between language centres. **Structure** General Meeting; Coordinating Committee; Executive Committee. **Languages** English, French, German. **Finance** Sources: members' dues. **Activities** Events/meetings. **Events** *Biennial Conference* Porto (Portugal) 2022, *Biennial Conference* Brno (Czechia) 2020, *Biennial Conference* Poznań (Poland) 2018, *Biennial Conference* Rende (Italy) 2016, *Biennial Conference* Fribourg (Switzerland) 2014. **Publications** *Language Learning in Higher Education* (2 a year).

Members Language centres, departments, institutes, faculties and schools in higher education. National associations (390 institutions) in 15 countries:
Austria, Belgium, Czechia, Finland, France, Germany, Ireland, Italy, Netherlands, Poland, Portugal, Slovakia, Spain, Switzerland, UK.
Associate member institutions (24) in 14 countries and territories:
Bangladesh, Belgium, Bulgaria, Cyprus, Greece, Hong Kong, Hungary, Iceland, Israel, North Macedonia, Romania, Russia, Spain, Sweden.

NGO Relations Member of: *WorldCALL (#21256)*. [2022.02.27/XD8345/**D**]

- ♦ Confédération européenne du commerce de la chaussure en gros (inactive)
- ♦ Confédération européenne du commerce de cuir en gros (inactive)
- ♦ Confédération européenne du commerce de détail (inactive)
- ♦ Confédération européenne du commerce de la quincaillerie en gros (inactive)
- ♦ Confédération européenne des commerces de mobilier, machines de bureau et accessoires (inactive)
- ♦ Confédération européenne des coopératives de production et de travail associé, des coopératives sociales et des entreprises participatives / see Confédération européenne des coopératives de travail associé, des coopératives sociales et des entreprises sociales et participatives (#04541)

♦ Confédération européenne des coopératives de travail associé, des coopératives sociales et des entreprises sociales et participatives (CECOP) 04541

European Confederation of Worker Cooperatives, Social Cooperatives and Social and Participative Enterprises

SG c/o European Coop House, Av Milcamps 105, 1030 Brussels, Belgium. T. +3225431033. E-mail: cecop@cecop.coop – communication@cecop.coop.
URL: http://www.cecop.coop/

History 1979, Manchester (UK). Secretariat in Brussels (Belgium) set up 1984. Former names and other names: *European Committee of Workers Cooperative Productive Societies* – former (1979 to 1989); *Comité européen des coopératives ouvrières de production* – former (1979 to 1989); *Comité européen des coopératives de production et de travail* – alias; *European Committee of Workers' Cooperatives* – former (1989 to 1997); *Comité européen des coopératives de production et de travail associé* – former (1989 to 1997); *European Confederation of Workers' Cooperatives, Social Cooperatives Participative Enterprises* – former (1997); *Confédération européenne des coopératives de production et de travail associé, des coopératives sociales et des entreprises participatives (CECOP)* – former (1997); *Europäische Konföderation der Produktivgenossenschaften, der Sozialgenossenschaften und Beteiligungsunternehmen* – former (1997). Registration: Belgium; EU Transparency Register, No/ID: 774917716472-20. **Aims** Represent members, provide permanent liaison between them and coordinate and service their projects; promote European workers' cooperative movement to the wider public. **Structure** General Assembly; Board of Directors; Executive Committee; Permanent Secretariat. **Languages** English, French. **Finance** Sources: fees for services; members' dues; revenue from activities/projects; sale of publications. **Activities** Capacity building; events/meetings; networking/liaising; publishing activities. **Events** *Lights On* Brussels (Belgium) 2021, *All in One Conference* Brussels (Belgium) 2020, *European Forum on Social Entrepreneurship* Plovdiv (Bulgaria) 2016, *Conference on How to Promote Sustainable Tourism Experiences through the European Route of Cooperative Culture* Brussels (Belgium) 2015, *European Forum on Social Entrepreneurship* Plovdiv (Bulgaria) 2015. **Publications** Books; studies; documents.

Members Full; Associate. Workers cooperative organizations; social economy enterprises; social economy organizations; participative enterprises; participative organizations; productive societies. Full in in 13 countries:
Bulgaria, Czechia, Denmark, Finland, France, Italy, Malta, Poland, Portugal, Romania, Slovakia, Spain, UK.
Associated in 4 countries:
Belgium, France, Italy, Sweden.

IGO Relations Recognized by European Institutions. Maintains relations with: *European Economic and Social Committee (EESC, #06963)*; think tanks; research institutes. **NGO Relations** Member of: *Cooperatives Europe (#04801)*; *Réseau Européen des Villes and Régions de l'Économie Sociale (REVES, #18880)*; *Social Platform (#19344)*. Acts as European committee of: *International Organisation of Industrial and Service Cooperatives (CICOPA, #14429)*. Maintains relations with: *European Trade Union Confederation (ETUC, #08927)*.
[2022.10.19/XE8289/**E**]

- ♦ Confédération européenne des détaillants en tabacs (#06725)

♦ Confédération européenne des distilleries vinicoles (CEDIVI) 04542

Pres Pol Industrial Emilio Castro, Avda Tecnología 25 Oficina 11, 13600 Alcázar de San Juan, Ciudad Real, Spain. T. +34926588635. E-mail: adevin@infonegocio.com – adevin@adevin.es.
URL: https://cedivi.info/

History 16 Dec 1996. Founded on approval of statutes by founder members at 1st General Assembly. Registration: Belgium; EU Transparency Register, No/ID: 77387528902-68. **Aims** Promote scientific research, exchange of scientific methods and their application in the *European Union* region; represent the wine distillery sector with European institutions and defend the common interests of *manufacturers* of *spirits* and *'eaux-de-vie'* derived from grapes; analyse members' problems arising from the Treaty of Rome (Italy), the agricultural market and directives of the Council of the European Union; research and generate solutions, acting as a forum for discussion and research in the sector. **Structure** General Assembly (annual); Council. **Finance** Sources: members' dues. **Publications** General Assembly proceedings. **Members** Membership countries not specified. [2021/XD6578/**D**]

- ♦ Confédération européenne des distributeurs d'énergie publics communaux / see European Federation of Local Energy Companies (#07156)
- ♦ Confédération européenne des distributeurs d'équipements (no recent information)
- ♦ Confédération européenne des distributeurs, producteurs et importateurs de plantes médicinales (inactive)
- ♦ Confédération européenne de la droguerie (inactive)
- ♦ Confédération européenne pour l'emploi des handicapés (no recent information)
- ♦ Confédération européenne des entrepreneurs pharmaceutiques (#06718)
- ♦ Confédération européenne des entrepreneurs de travaux techniques agricoles et ruraux / see European Organization of Agricultural and Rural Contractors (#08105)
- ♦ Confédération européenne des entrepreneurs de travaux techniques agricoles, ruraux et forestiers (#08105)
- ♦ Confédération européenne des entreprises locales d'énergie / see European Federation of Local Energy Companies (#07156)
- ♦ Confédération européenne d'escrime (#07239)
- ♦ Confédération européenne d'études phytosanitaires (inactive)

♦ Confédération européenne d'experts en évaluation et réparation du dommage corporel (CEREDOC) 04543

European Confederation of Medical Experts in the Assessment and Compensation of Physical Injury

SG Via Natisone 18, 56122 Pisa PI, Italy. T. +39508756850. Fax +39508756859. E-mail: info@ceredoc.eu.
URL: http://www.ceredoc.eu/

History 1997, Paris (France). **Aims** Develop a common European culture in the field of insurance medicine; bring together national associations of medical experts who work in the judicial and insurance fields in Europe. **Structure** Meeting (annual); Board of Directors; Executive Committee; Study groups (4). **Languages** French. **Activities** Research/documentation; events/meetings; training/education; networking/liaising; knowledge management/information dissemination; projects/programmes. **Events** *Meeting* Pisa (Italy) 2008, *Congrès mondial d'évaluation du dommage corporel / Congress* Buenos Aires (Argentina) 2006, *International meeting / Meeting* Pisa (Italy) 2006, *International meeting / Meeting* Pisa (Italy) 2005.
Members National organizations in 7 countries:
Belgium, France, Germany, Italy, Portugal, Spain, Switzerland.
NGO Relations *Institut européen de formation continue en réparation et évaluation du dommage corporel (IFREDOC).* [2019.04.29/XD9345/**D**]

- ♦ Confédération européenne des fabricants de baignoires (inactive)
- ♦ Confédération européenne des grandes associations musicales (inactive)
- ♦ Confédération européenne des grossistes en peintures, revêtements de sols et de murs (inactive)
- ♦ Confédération européenne de l'immobilier (inactive)
- ♦ Confédération européenne des indépendants (#06080)

♦ Confédération Européenne de l'Industrie de la Chaussure (CEC) ... 04544

European Confederation of the Footwear Industry – Confederación Europea de la Industria del Calzado – Europäische Konfederation der Schuhindustrie – Confederazione Europea dell' Industria Calzaturiera – Europese Confederatie van de Schoenindustrie
Gen Sec Square de Meeûs, 37, 1000 Brussels, Belgium. T. +3227917905. E-mail: info@cec-footwearindustry.eu.
Pres address not obtained.
URL: http://cec-footwearindustry.eu/
History 5 Mar 1958, Paris (France). Former names and other names: *Comité de liaison des industries européennes de la chaussure (CLIEC)* – former (1958 to 1973). **Aims** Promote interests and values of the European footwear industry vis-à-vis EU institutions and international organizations; support research and innovation; foster employment and development of necessary skills, as well as the attractiveness of the sector to the young; serve as a platform and communication channel for all footwear stakeholders. **Structure** General Assembly; Board; President; General Secretary. **Languages** English, French. **Staff** 2.00 FTE, paid. **Finance** Sources: fees for services; meeting proceeds; members' dues; revenue from activities/projects. **Activities** Events/meetings; politics/policy/regulatory. **Events** *International Footwear Forum* 2021, *World Footwear Congress* Naples (Italy) 2019, *International Footwear Forum* Milan (Italy) 2015, *World Footwear Congress* León (Mexico) 2014, *World Footwear Congress* Rio de Janeiro (Brazil) 2011.
Members Organizations in 10 countries:
Czechia, Finland, France, Greece, Hungary, Italy, Poland, Portugal, Spain, Sweden.
Observers in 3 countries:
Türkiye, UK, Ukraine.
IGO Relations Recognized by European institutions and other public authorities. **NGO Relations** Member of (2): *AEGIS Europe*; *Industry4Europe (#11181).* [2023.02.14/XD2909/t/**D**]

- ♦ Confédération européenne de l'industrie des pâtes, papiers et cartons (inactive)

♦ Confédération européenne des industries du bois (CEI Bois) 04545

European Confederation of Woodworking Industries – Zentralverband der Europäischen Holzindustrie
SG Rue Montoyer 24, 1000 Brussels, Belgium. T. +3225562585. Fax +3222870875. E-mail: info@cei-bois.org.
URL: http://www.cei-bois.org/
History 29 Sep 1952, Paris (France). Registration: Start date: 1954, France; EU Transparency Register, No/ID: 470333818389-37, Start date: 31 Jul 2015. **Aims** Further the interests of the European wood sector; influence EU policy-making. **Structure** General Assembly (annual); Managing Board; Secretariat; Specialized commissions. Meetings closed. **Languages** English, French, German. **Staff** 4.00 FTE, paid. **Finance** Sources: members' dues. **Events** *Building with Wood Conference* Brussels (Belgium) 2017, *International conference on carbon storage in wood products* Brussels (Belgium) 2009, *General Assembly* Brussels (Belgium) 2008, *General Assembly* Guimarães (Portugal) 2007, *Forest-based sector technology platform conference / Conference* Hannover (Germany) 2007.
Members National organizations in 14 countries:
Austria, Belgium, Croatia, Denmark, Estonia, Finland, Germany, Netherlands, Norway, Portugal, Slovenia, Sweden, Switzerland, UK.
European sector federations (4):
European Institute for Wood Preservation (WEI-IEO, #07575); European Organization of the Sawmill Industry (EOS, #08114); European Timber Trade Federation (ETTF, #08915); Fédération européenne des fabricants de palettes et emballages en bois (FEFPEB, #09567).
Consultative Status Consultative status granted from: *ECOSOC (#05331)* (Roster). **IGO Relations** Observer Status with: *Intergovernmental Negotiating Committee for a Legally Binding Agreement on Forests in Europe (INC-Forests, inactive).* Recognized by: *European Commission (EC, #06633).* Accredited by: *United Nations Framework Convention on Climate Change – Secretariat (UNFCCC, #20564); United Nations Office at Vienna (UNOV, #20604).* Cooperates with: *European State Forest Association (EUSTAFOR, #08832).* **NGO Relations** Member of (8): *AEGIS Europe; Construction Products Europe AISBL (#04761); European Platform for Chemicals Using Manufacturing Industries (CheMI, #08223); Industry4Europe (#11181); International Council of Forest and Paper Associations (ICFPA, #13023); PEFC Council (#18288); Woodrise Alliance (#21045); Wood Sector Alliance for the New European Bauhaus (Wood4Bauhaus, #21046)* (Founding). Together with: *Confederation of European Forest Owners (CEPF, #04525)* and *Confederation of European Paper Industries (CEPI, #04529),* instrumental in setting up: *Forest-Based Sector Technology Platform (FTP, #09861).* Also instrumental in setting up: *European Moulding Manufacturers Association (EMMA, inactive).* In liaison with technical committees of: *Comité européen de normalisation (CEN, #04162).* [2022/XD0693/ty/**D**]

- ♦ Confédération européenne d'ingénieurs d'agriculture (inactive)
- ♦ Confédération européenne des ingénieurs experts et arbitres (inactive)
- ♦ Confédération européenne des instituts d'audit interne (#06707)
- ♦ Confédération européenne du jouet (inactive)
- ♦ Confédération européenne des laryngectomisés (#06709)
- ♦ Confédération européenne du liège (#06798)

♦ Confédération européenne du lin et du chanvre (CELC) 04546

European Confederation of Flax and Hemp
Gen Sec Masters of Linen, 15 rue du Louvre, Bat 3A 4e étage, 75001 Paris, France. T. +33142210235. Fax +33142214822. E-mail: communication@europeanflax.com.
URL: http://www.mastersoflinen.com/
History 20 Apr 1950, Paris (France), at the instigation of Textiles Committee of the then OEEC, currently *OECD (#17693)*, when registered by French Ministerial Decree. Originally referred to as *Confédération internationale du lin et du chanvre (CILC) – International Linen and Hemp Confederation.* Current title adopted Mar 1995, when a new *Confédération internationale du lin et du chanvre (CILC, no recent information)* was set up to carry out extra-European activities, the two confederations sharing the same secretariat. **Aims** Encourage collaboration in technical, commercial and scientific matters with a view to improving production and reducing costs, increasing freedom of trade and developing new markets; represent the industries at the West European level. **Structure** Congress (annual); specialized sections. **Languages** French. **Finance** Members' dues. **Activities** Awards a mark of quality indicating linen derived from West European member countries. **Events** *International Congress* Madrid (Spain) 2016, *Annual Congress* Sainte-Maxime (France) 2007, *Annual Congress* Prague (Czech Rep) 2006, *Annual Congress* Brighton (UK) 2005, *Annual Congress* Ghent (Belgium) 2004.
Members National organizations and individual members in 13 countries:
Austria, Belgium, Finland, France, Germany, Hungary, Italy, Lithuania, Netherlands, Portugal, Spain, Switzerland, UK.
IGO Relations Recognized by: *European Commission (EC, #06633).* [2019/XD2234/**D**]

- ♦ Confédération européenne des maires (inactive)
- ♦ Confédération européenne de mycologie médicale / see European Confederation of Medical Mycology (#06712)
- ♦ Confédération européenne du négoce de la décoration, peintures, revêtements muraux et de sol (inactive)
- ♦ Confédération européenne des négociants en combustibles et carburants (#06703)

♦ Confédération européenne des ong d'urgence et de développement (CONCORD) 04547

European NGO Confederation for Relief and Development
Dir Rue de l'Industrie 10, 1000 Brussels, Belgium. T. +3227438760. E-mail: secretariat@concordeurope.org.
URL: http://www.concordeurope.org/
History 30 Jan 2003. Takes over activities of *Liaison Committee of Development NGOs to the European Union (NGDO-EU Liaison Committee, inactive).* **Aims** Enhance the impact of European NGOs in influencing European institutions. **Structure** General Assembly (annual); Board. **Languages** English, French. **Staff** 9.00 FTE, paid. **Finance** Members' dues. Supported by: *European Commission (EC, #06633).* **Activities** Advocacy/lobbying/activism; events/meetings. **Events** *AidEx : Europe's Leading Humanitarian and Development Aid Conference* Brussels (Belgium) 2018, *AidEx : Europe's Leading Humanitarian and Development Aid Conference* Brussels (Belgium) 2017, *AidWatch Group Conference* Brussels (Belgium) 2016, *HUB3 Meeting* Brussels (Belgium) 2016, *Stand up for a better future for all* Brussels (Belgium) 2016. **Publications** *CONCORD Flash* – newsletter; *Working Groups Newsletter.* Annual Report; reports; manifesto.
Members Represents over 1,600 European NGOs in the field of development or humanitarian aid, grouped in 28 National Platforms and 18 networks in 28 countries:
Austria, Belgium, Bulgaria, Croatia, Cyprus, Czechia, Denmark, Estonia, Finland, France, Germany, Greece, Hungary, Ireland, Italy, Latvia, Lithuania, Luxembourg, Malta, Netherlands, Poland, Portugal, Romania, Slovakia, Slovenia, Spain, Sweden, UK.
Included in the above, 4 organizations listed in this Yearbook:
Ceske Fórum pro Rozvojovou Spolupraci (FoRS); Coordination SUD; GLOBAL RESPONSIBILITY – Austrian Platform for Development and Humanitarian Aid; Globalt Fokus.
Network members (17):
ACT Alliance (#00081); ActionAid (#00087); Adventist Development and Relief Agency International (ADRA, #00131); CARE International (CI, #03429); Caritas Europa (#03579); Christian Blind Mission (CBM); CIDSE (CIDSE, #03926); European Christian Organisations in Relief and Development (EU-CORD, #06545); Humanity and Inclusion (HI, #10975); International Planned Parenthood Federation (IPPF, #14589) (Europe); *Islamic Relief Worldwide (IRWW, #16048); Oxfam International (#17922); Plan International (#18386); Save the Children International (#19058); SOLIDAR (#19680); SOS-Kinderdorf International (#19693); World Vision International (WVI, #21904).*
Associate members (3):
European Association for Local Democracy (ALDA, #06110); European Association for the Education of Adults (EAEA, #06018); World Wide Fund for Nature (WWF, #21922).
Consultative Status Consultative status granted from: *UNCTAD (#20285)* (General Category). **NGO Relations** Founding member of: *Spring Alliance (inactive).* Member of: *Civil Society Europe*; Contact Civil Society Group; *Transparency, Accountability and Participation Network (TAP Network, #20222).* Supports: *Global Call for Action Against Poverty (GCAP, #10263).* [2015/XD9230/y/**D**]

- ♦ Confédération européenne des organisations des centres de jeunes (#06727)
- ♦ Confédération européenne des organisations de conservateurs-restaurateurs (#06701)
- ♦ Confédération européenne des organisations des détaillants en tabacs / see European Confederation of Tobacco Retailers (#06725)
- ♦ Confédération européenne des organisations des entrepreneurs de travaux techniques agricoles et ruraux / see European Organization of Agricultural and Rural Contractors (#08105)
- ♦ Confédération Européenne de Pédiatrie Ambulatoire (#06721)

♦ Confédération européenne de pétanque (CEP) 04548

SG Karadicova 1, 811 09 Bratislava, Slovakia. T. +421257205210. Fax +421257205218. E-mail: secretary@cep-petanque.com – cep.secretaire@gmail.com.
Pres address not obtained. E-mail: president@cep-petanque.com.
URL: http://www.cep-petanque.com/
Structure Executive Committee, comprising President, Vice-President/Treasurer, Secretary General and 7 members.
Members National organizations in 31 countries and territories:
Andorra, Austria, Belgium, Bulgaria, Czechia, Denmark, England, Estonia, Finland, France, Germany, Hungary, Ireland, Israel, Italy, Luxembourg, Monaco, Netherlands, Norway, Poland, Portugal, Russia, San Marino, Scotland, Slovakia, Slovenia, Spain, Sweden, Switzerland, Türkiye, Wales. [2016/XM2923/**D**]

- ♦ Confédération européenne de la plasturgie (#08216)
- ♦ Confédération Européenne des Pouvoirs Locaux Intermédiaires (#06710)
- ♦ Confédération européenne de la probation (#04530)
- ♦ Confédération européenne des producteurs de maïs / see European Confederation of Maize Production (#06711)
- ♦ Confédération européenne des producteurs de spiritueux / see spiritsEUROPE (#19921)
- ♦ Confédération Européenne de la Production de Maïs (#06711)

♦ Confédération européenne des professionelles de l'esthétique cosmétique (CEPEC) 04549

European Association of Professional Beauticians
Pres c/o CNA Estetica, Piazza M Armellini 9A, 00161 Rome RM, Italy. T. +396441881.
URL: http://www.cna.it/
NGO Relations Sectoral member of: *SMEunited (#19327).* [2019/XD5954/t/**D**]

- ♦ Confédération européenne des propriétaires forestiers (#04525)
- ♦ Confédération européenne des propriétaires de maisons de repos (#06700)
- ♦ Confédération européenne des radios et télévisions indépendantes et locales (no recent information)
- ♦ Confédération européenne des relations publiques (inactive)

♦ Confédération Européenne de Roller-Skating (CERS) 04550

European Confederation of Roller Skating
Pres Rua António Pinto Machado 60 – 3o, 4100-068 Porto, Portugal. T. +351222430637. E-mail: cers@cerskating.eu.
SG address not obtained.
URL: https://cerskating.eu/
History 1976, as continental federation of *World Skate (#21786).* **Aims** Organize, promote and control *rink hockey* and *in-line hockey*, artistic and speed roller skating, in-line skating and roller acrobatic skating in Europe. **Structure** General Assembly; Central Committee; Technical Committees (5): Artistic; Freestyle; In-Line Hockey – *Comité européen roller in-line hockey (CERILH, #04165)*, Rink Hockey; Speed. **Languages** English, French. **Finance** Members' dues. Other sources: governmental subsidies; income from competitions. **Activities** Events/meetings; sporting activities. **Publications** Information bulletins; circulars.
Members Affiliated National Federations in 29 countries:
Andorra, Austria, Belgium, Croatia, Czechia, Denmark, Estonia, Finland, France, Germany, Great Britain, Hungary, Ireland, Israel, Italy, Latvia, Liechtenstein, Netherlands, Norway, Poland, Portugal, Romania, Russia, Slovakia, Slovenia, Spain, Sweden, Switzerland, Ukraine. [2022/XD1550/**E**]

- ♦ Confédération européenne de scoutisme (#04531)
- ♦ Confédération européenne des services de sécurité (#04532)
- ♦ Confédération européenne des sociétés de sécurité / see Confederation of European Security Services (#04532)
- ♦ Confédération européenne des spécialistes en pédiatrie / see European Academy of Paediatrics (#05811)
- ♦ Confédération Européenne Sport Santé (no recent information)
- ♦ Confédération européenne des syndicats (#08927)

Confédération européenne syndicats
04550

alphabetic sequence excludes
For the complete listing, see Yearbook Online at

- ♦ Confédération européenne des syndicats indépendants (#06705)
- ♦ Confédération européenne des syndicats libres dans la Communauté / see European Trade Union Confederation (#08927)
- ♦ Confédération européenne des syndicats nationaux et associations professionnelles de pédiatres / see European Academy of Paediatrics (#05811)
- ♦ Confédération européenne pour la thérapie physique (inactive)
- ♦ Confédération européenne de twirling bâton (inactive)
- ♦ Confédération européenne des universités du Rhin supérieur / see Eucor – The European Campus (#05578)
- ♦ Confédération Européenne des Vignerons Indépendants (#06706)
- ♦ Confédération européenne de volleyball (#09078)
- ♦ Confédération européen des taxis (inactive)

♦ Confédération des Fabricants de Levure de l'Union Européenne (COFALEC) 04551

Confederation of European Yeast Producers – Kommittee der Hefehersteller der Europäischen Union – Confederación de los Fabricantes de Levadura de la Unión Europea

Main Office 9 blvd Malesherbes, 75008 Paris, France. T. +33145085482.
URL: http://www.cofalec.com/

History 4 Nov 1959, Paris (France). Former names and other names: *Committee of Baker's Yeast Manufacturers of the EEC* – former (4 Nov 1959); *Comité des fabricants de levure de panification de la CEE* – former (4 Nov 1959); *Ausschuss der Bäckerhefersteller in der EWG* – former (4 Nov 1959); *Comitato dei Fabbricanti di Lievito per Panificazione della CEE* – former (4 Nov 1959); *Comité van Broodgistfabrikanten van de EEG* – former (4 Nov 1959); *Udvalget for det EØFs Fabrikanter af Gaer til Brødfremstilling* – former (4 Nov 1959); *Comité des fabricants de levure de panification de l'Union européenne (COFALEC)* – former (2009); *Bakery Yeast Manufacturers Committee of the European Union* – former (2009); *Komitee der Hefeindustrie in der Europäische Union* – former (2009). Registration: EU Transparency Register, No/ID: 2073390649-79; France. **Aims** Represent the EU yeast industry. **Structure** Board, comprising President, Treasurer and 3 members. Secretary-General. **Events** *Annual General Meeting* Tallinn (Estonia) 2015, *Annual General Meeting* Lisbon (Portugal) 2014, *Annual General Meeting* Krakow (Poland) 2013, *Annual General Meeting* Siena (Italy) 2012, *Annual General Meeting* Madrid (Spain) 2011.
Members Organizations (5) and companies (27) in 23 countries:
Austria, Belgium, Croatia, Czechia, Denmark, Estonia, Finland, France, Germany, Greece, Hungary, Ireland, Italy, Latvia, Lithuania, Netherlands, Poland, Portugal, Slovakia, Slovenia, Spain, Sweden, UK.
IGO Relations Recognized by: *European Commission (EC, #06633)*. **NGO Relations** Member of: *FoodDrinkEurope (#09841)*. Advisory member of: *Oenological Products and Practices (OEnoppia, #17695)*.
[2020/XE0298/**E**]

- ♦ Confederation of Family Organizations in the European Community / see COFACE Families Europe (#04084)
- ♦ Confederation of Family Organizations in the European Union / see COFACE Families Europe (#04084)
- ♦ Confederation of Family Producer Organizations of the Expanded Mercosur (#04437)

♦ Confederation of Fire Protection Associations (CFPA Europe) 04552

Chairman c/o DBI, Jernholmen 12, 2650 Hvidovre, Denmark. T. +4536349000. Fax +45366349001. E-mail: jd@dbi-net.dk.
Dir 9 Cotebrook Drive, Chester, CH2 1RA, UK. T. +447950294146.
URL: http://www.cfpa-e.eu/

History Apr 1974, Paris (France). Current statutes approved 22 May 2014. Former names and other names: *European Confederation of Fire Protection Associations* – alias; *Confédération européenne des associations de protection contre les incendies* – alias; *Confederación Europea de Asociaciones de Protección contra Incendios* – alias. **Aims** Link nationally independent recognized organizations working with fire prevention and protection, safety and security, and natural hazards. **Structure** General Meeting (annual); Management Committee; Committees; Working Groups. **Languages** English. **Staff** 1.00 FTE, paid. Several voluntary. **Finance** Sources: members' dues. Annual budget: 60,000 EUR. **Activities** Events/meetings; guidance/assistance/consulting; knowledge management/information dissemination; training/education. **Events** *Annual General Meeting* 2020, *Annual General Meeting* Stockholm (Sweden) 2019, *Annual General Meeting* Helsinki (Finland) 2018, *Annual General Meeting* Lisbon (Portugal) 2017, *Annual General Meeting* Madrid (Spain) 2016. **Publications** *CFPA Europe Newsletter*. Guidelines; folders; leaflets. **Members** Organizations in 25 countries. Membership countries not specified. **NGO Relations** Cooperates with (7): *Comité européen de normalisation (CEN, #04162)*; *CTIF International Association of Fire and Rescue Services (#04979)*; *European Committee for Electrotechnical Standardization (CENELEC, #06647)*; *European Fire and Security Group (EFSG, #07259)*; *European Group of Organisations for Fire Testing, Inspection and Certification (EGOLF, #07427)*; *Eurosafe (#09178)*; *Federation of the European Union Fire Officer Associations (FEU, #09555)*.
[2021.06.09/XD3138/**D**]

♦ Confederation of Fire Protection Associations International (CFPA-I) 04553

Chairman c/o Egyptian Fire Protection Association, 24 B Anwer El Mofty Street, Nasr City, Cairo, 11321, Egypt.
URL: http://www.cfpa-i.org/

History 1965, London (UK), as *Conference of Fire Protection Associations*. **Aims** Maximize the effectiveness of fire *prevention* and protection and foster improved international fire *safety* codes and *standards* through sharing experience, research, technical know-how and fire statistics. **Structure** Meeting (every 3 years). Executive Committee, comprising Chair, Vice-Chair, Treasurer and 4 Directors. Administrator. **Activities** Triennial General Assembly. **Events** *Meeting* Los Angeles, CA (USA) 1997.
Members Full in 25 countries:
Australia, Austria, Belgium, China, Denmark, Egypt, Finland, France, Germany, Indonesia, Italy, Korea Rep, Malaysia, New Zealand, Nigeria, Norway, Pakistan, Serbia, Slovenia, South Africa, Spain, Sweden, Switzerland, UK, USA.
Consultative Status Consultative status granted from: *ECOSOC (#05331)* (Ros A). [2019/XG2371/**B**]

- ♦ Confédération Fiscale Européenne / see CFE Tax Advisers Europe (#03842)
- ♦ Confederation of the Food and Drink Industries of the EU / see FoodDrinkEurope (#09841)
- ♦ Confédération Francophone d'Hypnose et Thérapies brèves (internationally oriented national body)
- ♦ Confédération générale des coopératives agricoles de l'Union européenne (#10107)
- ♦ Confédération générale des syndicats (#10108)
- ♦ Confédération de groupements de conseils fiscaux européens / see CFE Tax Advisers Europe (#03842)
- ♦ Confédération d'haltérophilie de l'Amérique centrale et des Caraïbes (inactive)
- ♦ Confédération ibéroaméricaine des étudiants catholiques (inactive)
- ♦ Confédération ibéroaméricaine et philippine des cultivateurs de la canne à sucre (no recent information)

♦ Confederation of Independent Football Associations (CONIFA) 04554

Pres Strömnäsbacken 2, 94150 Piteå, Germany. T. +46730637920. E-mail: president@conifa.org.
URL: http://www.conifa.org/

History 6 Jul 2013. Registration: Swedish Tax Agency, No/ID: 802473-7572, Start date: 16 Aug 2013, Sweden, Norrbotten. **Aims** Build bridges between people, nations, minorities and isolated regions all over the world through friendship, culture and the joy of playing football. **Structure** Annual General Meeting; Global Executive Committee; Subcommittees; Members. **Languages** English. **Staff** Voluntary. **Finance** Sources: members' dues; sponsorship. Annual budget: 35,000 EUR (2022). URL: https://www.conifa.org/en/event/annual-general-meeting-2022/ **Activities** Events/meetings; sporting activities. **Events** *Annual General Meeting* Piteå (Sweden) 2022, *Football Strategy Days* Sabbioneta (Italy) 2022, *Annual General Meeting* Bergamo (Italy) 2016, *Annual General Meeting* Skopje (Macedonia) 2015, *Annual General Meeting* Cologne (Germany) 2014. **Publications** *CONIFA Newsletter*. **Members** Football associations (55) outside FIFA, from nations, de-facto nations, regions, minority people and sportingly isolated territories. Membership countries not specified. **IGO Relations** None. **NGO Relations** None. [2022.02.02/XM4903/**C**]

- ♦ Confédération des industries agro-alimentaires de l'UE / see FoodDrinkEurope (#09841)
- ♦ Confédération des industries papetières européennes (#04529)
- ♦ Confédération des instituts séculiers d'Amérique latine (#04451)

♦ Confédération Interalliée des Officiers Médicaux de Réserve (CIOMR) 04555

Interallied Confederation of Medical Reserve Officers

Assistant SG address not obtained. E-mail: sg@ciomr.org – asg@ciomr.org – webmaster@ciomr.org.
Media and Communications Officer 32 Melton Drive East, Rockville Centre NY 11570, USA. T. +15165363287.
URL: http://www.ciomr.org/

History 1947, Brussels (Belgium). Founded as the official organization of medical reserve officers in *NATO (#16945)* Reserve Forces. Current statutes adopted Feb 1997, Brussels. **Aims** Establish close relationships with medical reserve personnel and services within the alliance; study and discuss subjects which are of military importance; promote effective cooperation with the medical services of the active forces by providing information and feedback through its civilian medical expertise. **Structure** Presidential Team (rotating every 2 years); Executive Committee; Secretary General. **Languages** English, French. **Staff** 0.00 FTE, paid; 100.00 FTE, voluntary. **Finance** Sources: members' dues. **Activities** Advocacy/lobbying/activism; awards/prizes/competitions; awareness raising; certification/accreditation; events/meetings; humanitarian/emergency aid; knowledge management/information dissemination; monitoring/evaluation; networking/liaising; politics/policy/regulatory; training/education. **Events** *CIOMR/CIOR/CISOR Summer Congress* Athens (Greece) 2022, *Winter Meeting* Liège (Belgium) 2022, *CIOR and CIOMR Joint Summer Congress* Prague (Czechia) 2017, *Winter Meeting* Brussels (Belgium) 2016, *Congress* Madrid (Spain) 2016.
Members National Reserve Officers Associations (or equivalent) of NATO countries. Delegates are physicians, dentists, pharmacists, veterinarians, nurses, technicians and medical service corps officers. Full in 19 countries:
Belgium, Bulgaria, Canada, Denmark, Estonia, France, Germany, Greece, Italy, Latvia, Lithuania, Netherlands, North Macedonia, Norway, Poland, Slovenia, Spain, UK, USA.
Associate in 4 countries:
Austria, Singapore, South Africa, Switzerland.
NGO Relations Associated with: *Confédération interalliée des officiers de réserve (CIOR, #04557)*.
[2022.05.14/XD1041/**D**]

♦ Confédération interalliée des officiers de réserve (CIOR) 04557

Interallied Confederation of Reserve Officers

Main Office c/o NATO HQ, Office I-324, IMS, Plans and Capabilities Division, Bd Leopold III, 1110 Brussels, Belgium. E-mail: mail@cior.net.
Permanent Representative address not obtained. E-mail: permrep@cior.net.
URL: http://www.cior.net/

History Nov 1948, Brussels (Belgium). Established by reserve officers' associations of Belgium, France and Netherlands. **Aims** Contribute to defence capacity of *NATO* countries; develop uniformity in the duties and rights of *servicemen*; improve motivation, capabilities, interoperability and mutual confidence of reserve forces in member countries; establish and strengthen contacts among reserve officers, inculcating and maintaining an inter-allied spirit among them and providing information on NATO developments and activities. **Structure** Annual Summer Meeting. Executive Committee, comprising: President and Secretary General (elected for 2 years) and both are members of the same national association; 18 Vice-Presidents (delegates elected by National Reserve Officer Associations); up to 4 other delegates from each national association. Permanent Commissions (4); Legal Committee. **Languages** English, French. **Staff** Unpaid. **Finance** Sources: gifts, legacies; members' dues. Annual budget: 50,000 EUR. **Activities** Awards/prizes/competitions; events/meetings; networking/liaising. **Events** *CIOMR/CIOR/CISOR Summer Congress* Athens (Greece) 2022, *CIOR and CIOMR Joint Summer Congress* Prague (Czechia) 2017, *Annual Summer Congress* Madrid (Spain) 2016, *Annual Summer Meeting* Sofia (Bulgaria) 2015, *Annual Summer Congress* Fulda (Germany) 2014.
Members Affiliated national associations (34), representing 800,000 reserve officers, in 32 countries:
Albania, Austria, Belgium, Bulgaria, Canada, Croatia, Czechia, Denmark, Estonia, Finland, France, Germany, Greece, Hungary, Italy, Latvia, Lithuania, Luxembourg, Netherlands, North Macedonia, Norway, Poland, Portugal, Romania, Slovakia, Slovenia, Spain, Sweden, Switzerland, Türkiye, UK, USA.
International organizational member (1):
Confédération Interalliée des Officiers Médicaux de Réserve (CIOMR, #04555). [2022.02.15/XC0105/y/**D**]

♦ Confédération Interalliée des Sous-Officiers de Réserve (CISOR) .. 04556

Interallied Confederation of Reserve Non Commissioned Officers

Gen Sec c/o Association de réservistes, Chaindon 30, 2732 Reconvilier BE, Switzerland. E-mail: office@cisor.info.
URL: http://cisor.info/

History 1 Jun 1963, Toulon (France). Former names and other names: *Association Européenne des Sous-Officiers de Réserve (AESOR)* – former; *European Association of Reserve Non Commissioned Officers* – former. **Aims** Safeguard the prestige of NCOs, bringing to light their merits, spreading a positive image and promoting their growth in a joint context, involving all *military* staff. **Structure** Central Committee, constituting General Assembly; Central Office; Technical Committee; Commission for Legal Affairs. **Languages** English, French. **Staff** Voluntary. **Finance** Sources: members' dues. **Activities** Awards/prizes/competitions; events/meetings. **Events** *CIOMR/CIOR/CISOR Summer Congress* Athens (Greece) 2022, *Biennial Congress* Rovaniemi (Finland) 2018, *Biennial Congress* Helsinki (Finland) 2016, *Biennial Congress* Maribor (Slovenia) 2014, *Biennial Congress* Strasbourg (France) 2012.
Members National organizations in 15 countries:
Albania, Austria, Belgium, Bulgaria, Denmark, Finland, France, Germany, Italy, Luxembourg, Netherlands, Poland, Slovenia, Spain, Switzerland. [2022/XD1122/**D**]

- ♦ Confédération interaméricaine pour la défense du continent contre le communisme (inactive)
- ♦ Confédération interaméricaine des éleveurs (no recent information)
- ♦ Confédération interaméricaine de l'enseignement catholique (#11403)
- ♦ Confédération Interaméricaine de Génie Chimique (#11417)
- ♦ Confédération interaméricaine de relations publiques (#11418)
- ♦ Confédération interaméricaine sociale catholique (inactive)
- ♦ Confédération interaméricaine des transports aériens (inactive)
- ♦ Confederation of International Beverages Associations (inactive)

♦ Confederation of International Contractors Associations (CICA) ... 04558

Confédération des associations internationales d'entrepreneurs – Confederación de Asociaciones Internacionales de Contratistas – Konföderation der Internationalen Unternehmervereinigungen

Dir Gen 3 rue de Berri, 75008 Paris, France. T. +33144133713. Fax +33144139889.
URL: http://www.cica.net/

History 13 Apr 1974, Tokyo (Japan), during 13th Convention of the International Federation of Asian and Western Pacific Contractors' Associations (IFAWPCA). **Aims** Gather and defend the concerns of the *construction* industry worldwide. **Structure** General Assembly (annual); Board. **Languages** English. **Staff** 2.00 FTE, paid. **Finance** Sources: members' dues. **Activities** Events/meetings. **Events** *General Assembly* Brasilia (Brazil) 2020, *General Assembly* Paris (France) 2019, *General Assembly* Seoul (Korea Rep) 2019, *General Assembly* Mexico City (Mexico) 2018, *General Assembly* Paris (France) 2018. **Publications** *CICA Newsletter*. Position papers.
Members International and national organizations of contractors in the construction industry in 49 countries:
Argentina, Austria, Belgium, Bolivia, Brazil, Bulgaria, Canada, Chile, Colombia, Costa Rica, Cyprus, Czechia, Denmark, Dominica, Ecuador, El Salvador, Estonia, Finland, France, Germany, Greece, Guatemala, Honduras, Hungary, Ireland, Italy, Japan, Korea Rep, Luxembourg, Mexico, Netherlands, Nicaragua, Norway, Panama, Paraguay, Peru, Poland, Portugal, Romania, Slovakia, Slovenia, Spain, Sweden, Switzerland, Türkiye, UK, Uruguay, USA, Venezuela.
Included in the above, 2 regional organizations listed in this Yearbook:
European Construction Industry Federation (#06766); *Federación Interamericana de la Industria de la Construcción (FIIC, #09333)*. [2020/XC4381/y/**C**]

- ♦ Confédération Internationale des Accordéonistes (#12841)
- ♦ Confédération internationale des administrateurs de biens immobiliers / see Fédération internationale des professions immobilières (#09653)

- ♦ Confédération internationale des agences d'emploi privé / see World Employment Confederation (#21376)
- ♦ Confédération internationale des agences privées pour l'emploi / see World Employment Confederation (#21376)

♦ Confédération internationale des agents en douanes (CONFIAD) . . . 04559

Confederación Internacional de Agentes de Aduanas

Pres c/o De Gregorio srl, Via S Carlo 26, 80133 Naples NA, Italy. T. +39815520776.
Vice-Pres c/TLF, Immeuble Diapason, 218 avenue Jean Jaurès, 75019 Paris, France. T. +33153684040. Fax +33153684099.
URL: http://www.confiad.org/

History 14 May 1982. Also referred to as *Confiad Paneuropean Network*. EU Transparency Register: 900179622923-45. **Activities** General Assembly. **Events** *Meeting* Paris (France) 2015, *Extraordinary General Assembly* Naples (Italy) 2013, *Meeting* Naples (Italy) 2013, *General Assembly* Warsaw (Poland) 2013, *Meeting* Warsaw (Poland) 2013. **NGO Relations** Liaison Organization of: *Comité européen de normalisation (CEN, #04162)*. Cooperates with: *Professional Customs Brokers Association of the Americas (#18512)*; *International Federation of Customs Brokers Associations (IFCBA, #13400)*. [2015/XD8004/**D**]

- ♦ Confédération internationale de l'agriculture (inactive)
- ♦ Confédération internationale d'amateurs et éleveurs de canaris (inactive)
- ♦ Confédération internationale d'analyse thermique et calorimétrie (#12871)
- ♦ Confédération internationale des anciens prisonniers de guerre (inactive)
- ♦ Confédération internationale des arts, des lettres et des sciences (inactive)
- ♦ Confédération internationale des associations d'artistes (inactive)
- ♦ Confédération internationale des associations de diététique (#12856)
- ♦ Confédération internationale des associations de diplômés en sciences économiques et commerciales (inactive)
- ♦ Confédération internationale des associations d'experts et de conseils (inactive)
- ♦ Confédération internationale des associations de francophones (inactive)
- ♦ Confédération internationale des associations Kneipp / see Kneipp Worldwide (#16197)
- ♦ Confédération internationale des banques populaires (#12867)
- ♦ Confédération internationale des betteraviers européens (#12860)
- ♦ Confédération internationale de la bijouterie, joaillerie, orfèvrerie, des diamants, perles et pierres (#03923)
- ♦ Confédération internationale de la boucherie et de la charcuterie (#12421)
- ♦ Confédération internationale des cadres / see CEC European Managers (#03623)
- ♦ Confédération internationale des cadres fonctionnaires (inactive)
- ♦ Confédération internationale catholique des institutions hospitalières (inactive)
- ♦ Confédération internationale du cheval (inactive)
- ♦ Confédération internationale pour la chirurgie plastique, reconstructrice et esthétique (inactive)
- ♦ Confédération Internationale des Cinémas d'Art-et-d'Essai (#12847)
- ♦ Confédération internationale de la coiffure / see World Hairdressers' Organization (#21550)
- ♦ Confédération internationale du commerce et des industries des légumes secs / see Global Pulse Confederation (#10562)
- ♦ Confédération internationale du commerce des pailles, fourrages, tourbes et dérivés (no recent information)

♦ Confédération internationale du crédit agricole (CICA) 04560

International Confederation for Agricultural Credit – Confederación Internacional del Crédito Agricola – Internationale Vereinigung für Landwirtschaftskredit – Confederazione Internazionale del Credito Agrario

Gen Secretariat Tödistrasse 48, 8002 Zurich ZH, Switzerland. T. +41442910575. Fax +41442910766.
URL: http://www.cica.ws/

History Oct 1932, Rome (Italy). Founded at 4th International Congress of Agricultural Instruction. Present name adopted 11-13 May 1950, Zurich (Switzerland). Former names and other names: *International Agricultural Credit Conference* – former (Oct 1932 to May 1950); *Conférence internationale du crédit agricole* – former (Oct 1932 to May 1950); *Conferencia Internacional para el Crédito Agrícola* – former (Oct 1932 to May 1950); *Internationale Agrarkredit-Konferenz* – former (Oct 1932 to May 1950); *Conferenza Internazionale del Credito Agrario* – former (Oct 1932 to May 1950). **Aims** Represent agricultural credit institutions at the international level; coordinate relevant activities. **Structure** General Assembly (every 2 years). Board. Central Committee, comprising: Honorary President; Honorary Members (9); President; Secretary-General; Vice-Presidents (8); Members (45). Control Commission. CICA-CEA Working Group. Instrumental in setting up: *Common Market Group of the International Confederation of Agricultural Credit (inactive)*. **Languages** English, French, German, Italian, Spanish. **Staff** 1.00 FTE, paid; 1.00 FTE, voluntary. **Finance** Sources: members' dues. **Events** *World Congress on Agricultural and Rural Finance* Morelia (Mexico) 2022, *General Assembly* Paris (France) 2021, *World Congress on Agricultural and Rural Finance* New Delhi (India) 2019, *Rencontres* Bern (Switzerland) 2018, *Rencontres* Québec, QC (Canada) 2017. **Publications** *CICA Information Bulletin* (12 a year); *Bulletin de la CICA* (4 a year) in French. Assembly and Congress reports.

Members Institutes and banks in 40 countries:
Afghanistan, Algeria, Austria, Belgium, Brazil, Canada, China, Congo DR, Côte d'Ivoire, Denmark, Dominica, Egypt, Finland, France, Germany, Ghana, Greece, Hungary, Ireland, Israel, Italy, Liberia, Libya, Luxembourg, Madagascar, Morocco, Netherlands, Niger, Norway, Peru, Poland, Portugal, Senegal, Spain, Sweden, Switzerland, Tunisia, Türkiye, UK, USA.

Consultative Status Consultative status granted from: *ECOSOC (#05331)* (Ros C); *FAO (#09260)* (Liaison Status). **IGO Relations** Working relationship with: *International Bank for Reconstruction and Development (IBRD, #12317)*; *ILO (#11123)*; *OECD (#17693)* Recognized by: *European Commission (EC, #06633)*. **NGO Relations** *Asociación Latinoamericana de Instituciones Financieras para el Desarrollo (ALIDE, #02233)*. [2021/XC1647/y/**C**]

- ♦ Confédération internationale du crédit populaire / see International Confederation of Popular Banks (#12867)
- ♦ Confédération internationale de la critique dramatique et musicale (inactive)
- ♦ Confédération internationale pour le désarmement et la paix (inactive)
- ♦ Confédération internationale des éditeurs de musique (#12864)
- ♦ Confédération internationale des entreprises de travail temporaire / see World Employment Confederation (#21376)
- ♦ Confédération internationale des étudiants (inactive)
- ♦ Confédération internationale des fabricants de tissus d'ameublement (inactive)
- ♦ Confédération internationale des fédérations de fonctionnaires et du personnel des services publics / see Public Services International (#18572)
- ♦ Confédération internationale des fonctionnaires (no recent information)

♦ Confédération internationale de généalogie et d'héraldique (CIGH) . 04561

International Confederation of Genealogy and Heraldry (ICGH)

Pres Via Battisti 3, 40123 Bologna BO, Italy. E-mail: cigh1971@gmail.com.
SG Ginsterweg 12, 30880 Laatzen, Germany.
URL: http://www.cigh.org/

History 13 Nov 1971, Brussels (Belgium), having been reconstituted in 1970, in conjunction with *International Congress of Genealogical and Heraldic Sciences*, from an organization of the same title set up 1901. Previous statutes adopted 29 Nov 1980, Luxembourg; current statutes adopted 3 May 2000, Besançon (France). Registered in accordance with Swiss law. **Aims** Promote international cooperation and collaboration among interested bodies; create and maintain links among national associations and federations; support these organizations in their relations with official national bodies; represent genealogy and heraldry with international organizations. **Structure** General Assembly of members (annual, every other year at International Congress of Genealogical and Heraldic Sciences), comprises 3 delegates for each federation and one delegate for each association. Executive Council. Governing Board, consisting of President, 2 Vice-Presidents, Secretary-General/Treasurer, Comptroller, Legal Adviser and 2 Councillors. **Languages** English, French, German, Spanish. **Staff** 1.50 FTE, voluntary. **Finance** Members' contributions. **Activities** Specific topics considered include: use of pedigrees in demography; computerization of heraldic content; support of heraldry to museological identifications; establishment of guides, repertories, card indexes. Organizes joint international congresses and colloquia with other organizations in the field, notably *Bureau permanent des congrès internationaux des sciences généalogique et héraldique (#03372)*. Awards several prizes. **Events** *Congrès* Madrid (Spain) 2021, *Congrès* Madrid (Spain) 2020, *Congrès* Arras (France) 2018, *Congrès* Glasgow (UK) 2016, *Congrès* Oslo (Norway) 2014. **Publications** *CIGH Bulletin* (2 a year). *General Index of International Congresses, 1928-1982*; *International Heraldic Dictionary*; *World List of Genealogical and Heraldic Associations*.

Members National federations; Associations. Members in 45 countries:
Andorra, Argentina, Australia, Austria, Belgium, Brazil, Bulgaria, Canada, Chile, Costa Rica, Croatia, Czechia, Denmark, Dominican Rep, Ecuador, El Salvador, Finland, France, Germany, Greece, Holy See, Hungary, Ireland, Italy, Luxembourg, Mexico, Morocco, Netherlands, New Zealand, Paraguay, Portugal, Romania, Russia, Serbia, Slovakia, Slovenia, South Africa, Spain, Sweden, Switzerland, UK, Ukraine, Uruguay, USA, Venezuela.

International and regional organizations (4):
Académie internationale de généalogie (AIG, #00028); *Australasian Federation of Family History Organizations (AFFHO)*; *Instituto Internacional de Genealogia y Heraldica (no recent information)*; *International Academy of Heraldry (#11549)*. [2018/XD9773/y/**C**]

- ♦ Confédération internationale des industries techniques du cinéma (inactive)
- ♦ Confédération internationale des ingénieurs agronomes (inactive)
- ♦ Confédération internationale des installateurs de matériel frigorifique et de conditionnement d'air (inactive)
- ♦ Confédération internationale pour la jeunesse (inactive)
- ♦ Confédération internationale du lin et du chanvre / see Confédération européenne du lin et du chanvre (#04546)
- ♦ Confédération internationale du lin et du chanvre (no recent information)
- ♦ Confédération internationale de la mesure (#14124)
- ♦ Confédération internationale des mouvements des familles chrétiennes (#12851)
- ♦ Confédération internationale des musées d'architecture (#12846)
- ♦ Confédération internationale des musiciens (inactive)
- ♦ Confédération internationale de musique électroacoustique (#12858)
- ♦ Confédération internationale des négociants en oeuvres d'art (#12848)
- ♦ Confédération internationale d'organismes catholiques d'action charitable et sociale / see Caritas Internationalis (#03580)
- ♦ Confédération internationale des parents (no recent information)

♦ Confédération internationale de la pêche sportive (CIPS) 04562

International Angling Confederation – Confederazione Internazionale de la Pesca Sportive (CIPS)

SG Viale Tiziano 70, 00196 Rome RM, Italy. T. +396879805147. Fax +39687980087. E-mail: segreteriainternazionale@fipsas.it – cipssecretariat@cips-fips.com.
URL: http://www.cips-fips.com/

History 22 Feb 1952, Rome (Italy). Former names and other names: *Confédération mondiale de la pêche sportive (CMPS)* – alias. **Aims** Promote the sport of amateur angling and casting; foster understanding and friendship among members. **Structure** Congress (annual). Praesidium, comprising President, 2 Vice-Presidents, Presidents of CIPS International Federations, Treasurer and General Secretary. Commissions; Board of Auditors; Secretariat. Includes: *International Federation of Angling in Fresh Waters (FIPSed, see: #04562)*; *FIPS Casting (see: #04562)*; *International Sea Sportfishing Federation (FIPS-M, see: #04562)*; *Fédération internationale de pêche sportive mouche (FIPS Mouche, see: #04562)*. **Languages** English, French, German. **Finance** Sources: members' dues. **Events** *Congress* 2023, *Congress* Acapulco (Mexico) 2022, *Congress* Stenico (Italy) 2021, *Annual Congress* Acapulco (Mexico) 2020, *Annual Congress* Almaty (Kazakhstan) 2019.

Members National federations in 65 countries:
Andorra, Angola, Australia, Austria, Belarus, Belgium, Bosnia-Herzegovina, Brazil, Bulgaria, Canada, Channel Is, Chile, China, Croatia, Czechia, Denmark, Egypt, England, Estonia, Eswatini, Finland, France, Germany, Gibraltar, Greece, Hungary, India, Ireland, Italy, Japan, Kazakhstan, Kuwait, Latvia, Lithuania, Luxembourg, Malta, Mexico, Moldova, Montenegro, Namibia, Netherlands, New Zealand, North Macedonia, Norway, Poland, Portugal, Romania, Russia, San Marino, Saudi Arabia, Scotland, Senegal, Serbia, Slovakia, Slovenia, South Africa, Spain, Sweden, Switzerland, Tunisia, Ukraine, USA, Venezuela, Wales, Zimbabwe.

IGO Relations Observer status with: *International Commission for the Conservation of Atlantic Tunas (ICCAT, #12675)*. **NGO Relations** Member of (4): *Alliance of Independent recognised Members of Sport (AIMS, #00690)*; *Long Distance Advisory Council (LDAC, #16511)*; *Mediterranean Advisory Council (MEDAC, #16639)*; *Olympic Movement (#17719)*. Cooperates with (1): *International Testing Agency (ITA, #15678)*. Recognized by: *International Olympic Committee (IOC, #14408)*. [2021/XD1654/**C**]

- ♦ Confédération internationale des sages-femmes (#12863)
- ♦ Confédération internationale de la Société de Saint Vincent-de-Paul (#12870)

♦ Confédération internationale des sociétés d'auteurs et compositeurs (CISAC) 04563

International Confederation of Societies of Authors and Composers – Confederación Internacional de Sociedades de Autores y Compositores

Dir Gen 20-26 bvd du Parc, 92200 Neuilly-sur-Seine, France. T. +33155620850. E-mail: info@cisac.org.
URL: http://www.cisac.org/

History 15 Jun 1926, Paris (France). Founded by 18 authors' societies from 18 countries, mainly representing the dramatic arts. Inspired by the ideas of universal peace and cooperation that had arisen after World War I, the founders' goal was to unite authors and composers from around the world. They intended to coordinate the work of their societies, to improve national and international copyright law, to foster diffusion of creative works and, in general, to attend to all common problems of creation in its widest sense. Present title adopted 1928, Rome (Italy).
Initially consisted of 5 federations for dramatic performing rights, public performing rights, mechanical rights, literary rights and film rights, namely: *Federation of Societies for Rights of Representation (inactive)*; *Writers and Directors Worldwide (see: #04563)*; *Federation of Societies for Rights of Performance (inactive)*; *International Bureau of the Societies Administering the Rights of Mechanical Recording and Reproduction (#12416)*; *'Fédération internationale des sociétés professionnelles des gens de lettres'*, subsequently *International Institute of Arts and Letters (IIAL, inactive)*; *International Federation of Screen and Television Writers' Associations (inactive)*. In 1966, the 5 federations were united to form the Confederation and lay the foundations of the current structure. In Oct 2004, at the General Assembly in Seoul (Korea Rep), significant amendments to the statutes were adopted; Jun 2007, Professional Rules for Authors' Societies were adopted. **Aims** Strengthen and develop the international network of *copyright* societies; secure a position for creators and their collective management organizations in the international scene; adopt and implement quality and technical efficiency criteria to increase copyright societies' interoperability; support societies' strategic development in each region and in each repertoire; retain a central database allowing societies to exchange information efficiently; participate in improving national and international copyright laws and practices. **Structure** General Assembly (annual); Board of Directors; Executive Governance Committee; Presidency; Secretariat, based at headquarters in Paris (France). Regional offices (4): Africa – Burkina Faso; Latin America and the Caribbean – Chile; Asia-Pacific – China; Europe – Hungary. International Council of Creators: *International Council of Music Authors (#13052)*; *International Council of Creators of Graphic, Plastic and Photographic Arts (#13011)*; *Writers and Directors Worldwide (see: #04563)*. Technical Committees (4): Information Services; Business; Media; Dramatic, Literary and Audivisual. Regional Committees (5): African (CAF); Asia-Pacific (CAP); Canada/USA (CCU); European (EC); Latin American and Caribbean (CLC). **Languages** English, French, Spanish. **Staff** 20.00 FTE, paid. **Finance** Sources: members' dues. Entry fees of new members. **Activities** Advocacy/lobbying/activism; knowledge management/information dissemination; politics/policy/regulatory. **Events** *General Assembly* Neuilly-sur-Seine (France) 2022, *General Assembly* Neuilly-sur-Seine (France) 2021, *General Assembly* Neuilly-sur-Seine (France) 2020, *Meeting* Berlin (Germany) 2019, *General Assembly* Tokyo (Japan) 2019. **Publications** Annual Report; annual royalties report. **Information Services** *Audio-Visual Index (AV INDEX)*; *CIS Net*; *Common Information System (CIS)* – including databases and

identifiers of works; *Interested Parties Information (IPI)*; *International Documentation on Audio-visual Works (IDA)*; *International Standard Audio-visual Number (ISAN)* – overseen by ISAN International Agency (ISANIA); *International Standard Musical Works Code (ISWC)* – overseen by ISWC International Agency; *International Standard Textual Code (ISTC)* – overseen by ISTC Consortium; *Musical Works Information Database (WID)*; *Society Information System (SIS)*; *Territory Information System (TIS)*.
Members Categories: Member; Associate; Provisional. Authors' societies (228) in 121 countries. Full in 108 countries and territories:
Algeria, Angola, Argentina, Australia, Austria, Azerbaijan, Barbados, Belarus, Belgium, Belize, Benin, Bolivia, Bosnia-Herzegovina, Brazil, Bulgaria, Burkina Faso, Cameroon, Canada, Chile, China, Colombia, Congo Brazzaville, Costa Rica, Côte d'Ivoire, Croatia, Cuba, Czechia, Denmark, Dominican Rep, Ecuador, Egypt, El Salvador, Estonia, Finland, France, Georgia, Germany, Greece, Guatemala, Guinea, Honduras, Hong Kong, Hungary, Iceland, Ireland, Israel, Italy, Jamaica, Japan, Kazakhstan, Korea Rep, Kyrgyzstan, Latvia, Lithuania, Luxembourg, Macau, Madagascar, Malawi, Malaysia, Mali, Mauritius, Mexico, Moldova, Montenegro, Morocco, Mozambique, Namibia, Netherlands, Niger, Nigeria, North Macedonia, Norway, Panama, Paraguay, Peru, Philippines, Poland, Portugal, Romania, Russia, Serbia, Seychelles, Singapore, Slovakia, Slovenia, South Africa, Spain, St Lucia, Suriname, Sweden, Switzerland, Taiwan, Tanzania UR, Thailand, Togo, Trinidad-Tobago, Tunisia, Türkiye, Uganda, UK, Ukraine, Uruguay, USA, Uzbekistan, Venezuela, Vietnam, Zambia, Zimbabwe.
Associate in 15 countries:
Australia, Belgium, Canada, Cuba, Ecuador, Finland, France, Holy See, Indonesia, Japan, Nepal, Trinidad-Tobago, Uruguay, USA, Venezuela.
Included in the above, 2 organizations listed in this Yearbook:
European Grouping of Societies of Authors and Composers (#07422); *European Visual Artists (EVA, #09071)*.
Provisional in 28 countries:
Albania, Andorra, Angola, Australia, Azerbaijan, Brazil, Cape Verde, Colombia, Czechia, Djibouti, Ghana, Greece, Japan, Kazakhstan, Korea Rep, Mexico, Mongolia, Nepal, Poland, Romania, Russia, Rwanda, Senegal, Serbia, Slovenia, South Africa, Tanzania UR, Ukraine.
Consultative Status Consultative status granted from: *UNESCO (#20322)* (Consultative Status); *World Intellectual Property Organization (WIPO, #21593)* (Permanent Observer Status). **IGO Relations** In liaison with: *Council of Europe (CE, #04881)*; *European Commission (EC, #06633)*. Observer to: *Intergovernmental Committee of the Universal Copyright Convention (IGC, #11478)*; *Bern Convention for the Protection of Literary and Artistic Works, 1886 (1886)*; *International Convention for the Protection of Performers, Producers of Phonograms and Broadcasting Organizations (Rome Convention, 1961)*. **NGO Relations** Member of (1): *Linked Content Coalition (LCC)*. In liaison with: *International Organization for Standardization (ISO, #14473)*. *Southern African Music Rights Organizations (SAMRO, #19851)* is member. Together with: *Association for the International Collective Management of Audiovisual Works (AGICOA, #02658)* and *International Federation of Film Producers' Associations (#13429)*, set up: *ISAN International Agency (ISAN-IA, #16023)*.
[2022/XB1673/y/**B**]

- Confédération internationale des sociétés coopératives agricoles (inactive)
- Confédération internationale des sociétés musicales (#12865)
- Confédération internationale des sociétés populaires de musique / see International Confederation of Music Societies (#12865)
- Confédération internationale des syndicats agricoles (inactive)
- Confédération internationale des syndicats arabes (#12845)
- Confédération internationale des syndicats de cheminots et de constructeurs de matériel de transport (#12869)
- Confédération internationale des syndicats libres (inactive)
- Confédération internationale des transformateurs de papier et carton dans la Communauté européenne / see International Confederation of Paper and Board Converters in Europe (#12866)
- Confédération internationale des transformateurs de papier et carton en Europe (#12866)

♦ Confédération internationale des travailleurs intellectuels (CITI) . . . 04564

International Confederation of Professional and Intellectual Workers – Confederación Internacional de los Trabajadores Intelectuales – Internationaler Verband der Geistesarbeiter
SG rue du Général Faidherbe 35, 94130 Nogent-sur-Marne, France. T. +33148732992.
History 1923, Paris (France), as *European Secretariat of Social Independent Professions – Secrétariat européen des professions indépendantes sociales (SEPIS) – Internationaler Verband der Geistesarbeiter*. Statutes adopted and registered in accordance with French law, 5 Jul 1955. **Aims** Defend cultural and intellectual work in all its forms; improve the general spiritual and social wellbeing of intellectual workers; encourage international intellectual cooperation. **Structure** General Assembly (annual); Executive Committee (meets at least once a year). **Languages** French. **Staff** 0.50 FTE, paid. **Activities** Sections on: arts and letters; liberal professions; young intellectual workers. **Events** *General assembly* Paris (France) 1992, *General Assembly* Paris (France) 1985. **Publications** Newsletter. Congress reports. **Members** International organizations (5); individuals in 8 countries. Membership countries not specified. **Consultative Status** Consultative status granted from: *World Intellectual Property Organization (WIPO, #21593)* (Permanent Observer Status); *Council of Europe (CE, #04881)* (Participatory Status). **IGO Relations** *UNESCO (#20322)*; *ILO (#11123)*. Observer to: *Intergovernmental Committee of the International Convention of Rome for the Protection of Performers, Producers of Phonograms and Broadcasting Organizations (#11474)*. [2019/XD1671/ty/**D**]

- Confédération internationale des universités populaires (inactive)
- Confédération internationale de voyages pour étudiants (inactive)
- Confederation of International Scientific and Technological Organizations for Development (inactive)
- Confederation of International Trading Houses Associations / see European Confederation of International Trading Houses Associations (#06708)
- Confédération des journalistes de l'ANASE (#04509)
- Confederation of Kurdish Associations in Europe / see European Kurdish Democratic Societies Congress (#07632)
- Confédération des Laboratoires de Recherche sur l'Intelligence Artificielle en Europe (#04565)

♦ Confederation of Laboratories for Artificial Intelligence Research in Europe (CLAIRE) 04565

Confédération des Laboratoires de Recherche sur l'Intelligence Artificielle en Europe (CLAIRE)
Contact The Hague Humanity Hub, Fluwelen Burgwal 58, 2511 CJ The Hague, Netherlands. E-mail: office-netherlands@claire-ai.org.
URL: https://claire-ai.org/
History 18 Jun 2018. Initiated by Holger Hoos, professor in Machine Learning at Universiteit Leiden (The Netherlands), Morten Irgens, Vice Rector at Oslo Metropolitan University (Norway), and Philipp Slusallek, Scientific Director at the German Research Center for Artificial Intelligence (Germany). Headquarters in the Hague (Netherlands) announced at the 2nd CLAIRE Symposium in Rome, 26 Feb 2019. Registration: Banque-Carrefour des Enterprises (BCE), No/ID: 0752.562.127., Start date: 31 Jan 2020, Belgium, Brussels-Capital. **Aims** Establish a pan-European network of Centres of Excellence in AI, strategically located throughout Europe, and a new, central facility with state-of-the-art, "Google-scale", CERN-like infrastructure – the CLAIRE Hub – that will promote new and existing talent and provide a focal point for exchange and interaction of researchers at all stages of their careers, across all areas of AI. **Structure** General Assembly; Board of Directors; Supervisory Board; Informal Advisory Board; International Advisory Groups. Offices: The Hague (Netherlands); Saarbrücken (Germany); Oslo (Norway); Prague (Czech Rep); Rome (Italy); Zurich (Switzerland); Brussels (Belgium); Paris (France). **Languages** Czech, Dutch, English, French, German, Italian, Norwegian, Portuguese. **Activities** Advocacy/lobbying/activism; awareness raising; events/meetings; guidance/assistance/consulting; knowledge management/information dissemination; networking/liaising; projects/programmes; research/documentation.
Members Laboratories, research groups and institutions that conduct research in AI (over 430) in 36 countries:
Argentina, Australia, Austria, Belgium, Bulgaria, Canada, Cyprus, Czechia, Denmark, Finland, France, Germany, Greece, Hungary, Ireland, Israel, Italy, Latvia, Lithuania, Luxembourg, Netherlands, Norway, Poland, Portugal, Romania, Russia, Serbia, Singapore, Slovakia, Slovenia, Spain, Sweden, Switzerland, Türkiye, UK, USA.
For-profit companies, SMEs and start-ups that develop or apply AI (10) in 6 countries:
Czechia, France, Germany, Italy, Netherlands, Switzerland. [2022.02.15/AA0064/**D**]

- Confederation of Latin American Congress Organizing Entities and Related Activities / see Federación de Entidades Organizadoras de Congresos y Afines de América Latina (#09299)
- Confederation of Latin American Teachers / see Confederación de Educadores Americanos (#04446)
- Confederation of Latin American Workers (inactive)
- Confédération latinoaméricaine des associations unions chrétiennes de jeunes gens / see Latin American and Caribbean Alliance of YMCAs (#16264)
- Confédération latinoaméricaine de biochimie clinique (#04454)
- Confédération latinoaméricaine des coopératives d'épargne et de crédit (#16302)
- Confédération latinoaméricaine de coopératives des travailleurs (#04456)
- Confédération latinoaméricaine de l'industrie graphique (#16303)
- Confédération latinoaméricaine de l'industrie de la pulpe et du papier (no recent information)
- Confédération latinoaméricaine de parachutisme (#04460)
- Confédération latinoaméricaine de personnes en marginalité sociale (#04461)
- Confédération latinoaméricaine de la presse touristique (no recent information)
- Confédération latinoaméricaine des religieux (#04442)
- Confédération latinoaméricaine des sociétés d'anesthésie / see Latin American Confederation of Societies of Anesthesiology (#16305)
- Confédération Latinoaméricaine des Sociétés d'Anesthésiologie (#16305)
- Confédération latinoaméricaine des travailleurs des communications (no recent information)
- Confédération latinoaméricaine des travailleurs de l'Etat (#16304)
- Confédération du liège de la CEE: Industrie et commerce / see European Cork Federation (#06798)
- Confédération maghrébine des opérateurs de tourisme (inactive)

♦ Confederation of Medical Associations in Asia and Oceania (CMAAO) . . . 04566

Confédération des associations médicales de l'Asie et de l'Océanie
SG JMA Intl Affairs, 2-28-16 Honkomagome, Bunkyo-ku, Tokyo, 113-8621 Japan. T. +81339462121. Fax +81339466295. E-mail: jmaintl@po.med.or.jp.
URL: http://www.cmaao.org/
History Apr 1956, Manila (Philippines), as *Asian Confederation of Medical Associations*, preliminary conferences having been held in 1950, 1951, and 1954. Previously also referred to in French as *Confédération des associations médicales de l'Asie et de l'Océanie*. **Aims** Raise the standard of medical ethics; implement medical education and health care while maintaining the medical ethics and the professional standards of physicians. **Structure** Congress; Council; Secretariat. **Languages** English. **Staff** of Japan Medical Association. **Finance** Members' dues. **Activities** Organizes Mid-Term Council Meeting and Congress (alternatively every other year). **Events** *Congress* Taipei (Taiwan) 2021, *Meeting* Taipei (Taiwan) 2021, *Congress* Taipei (Taiwan) 2020, *Meeting* Taipei (Taiwan) 2020, *Congress* Goa (India) 2019.
Members Associations in 16 countries and territories:
Australia, Bangladesh, Cambodia, Hong Kong, India, Indonesia, Japan, Korea Rep, Macau, Malaysia, Nepal, New Zealand, Philippines, Singapore, Taiwan, Thailand.
NGO Relations Affiliated with: *World Medical Association (WMA, #21646)*. [2013/XD1975/**D**]

- Confédération médicale panaméricaine (inactive)

♦ Confederation of Mediterranean Badminton (COMEBA) . . . 04567

SG FIBA, Viale Tiziano 70, 00196 Rome RM, Italy. T. +39636858743. Fax +39636858235. E-mail: info@comeba.org.
Pres Adnan Menderes Mahallesi, 1047 Sokak. No : 1, Keçiören-Aktep, 06300 Ankara/Ankara, Türkiye.
URL: http://www.comeba.org/
History 9 Sep 1995. Became dormant in 2005; formally reconstituted 29 Jul 2006 with new Statutes and Board of Directors. New Statutes adopted 29 Jul 2006, Casablanca (Morocco). Former names and other names: *Mediterranean Badminton Confederation* – former (9 Sep 1995). **Aims** Encourage respect of the Badminton World Federation, formerly International Badminton Federation, principles; develop and promote the practice of badminton in the countries of the Mediterranean basin; work for the introduction and maintenance of badminton in the programme of the Mediterranean Games; develop the spirit of friendship and mutual aid among members; strive for continuous development of the badminton technical level and the spreading of this sport in the countries of the Mediterranean basin; promote sports competition in a friendly spirit and elimination of all unfair practices; offer support and supervision to organization of competitions. **Structure** General Assembly (held in odd years). Board of Directors (serving 4-year terms), comprising President, 2 Vice-Presidents, Secretary General, Treasurer and 2 Councillors. Headquarters located at the offices of the National Badminton Association of the current President. Committees. **Languages** Arabic, English, French. **Staff** None. Italian Badminton Federation provides office secretarial and ancillary services. Board is voluntary. **Finance** Sources: members' dues. Participation fees for competitions. **Activities** Committees for technical, development and youth issues, formulate projects for future implementation. **Events** *General Assembly* Nanning (China) 2019, *Mediterranean Cup* Sicily (Italy) 2008, *COMEBA Cup* Spain 2008.
Members Badminton Associations in the countries of the Mediterranean Basin who are also members of the Badminton World Federation. Member associations in 13 countries and territories:
Croatia, Cyprus, Egypt, France, Gibraltar, Greece, Italy, Lebanon, Malta, Morocco, Spain, Syrian AR, Türkiye.
NGO Relations Member of (1): *Badminton World Federation (BWF, #03060)*. [2022/XD6743/**D**]

♦ Confederation of Meningitis Organisations (CoMO) . . . 04568

Manager Newminster House, Baldwin Street, Bristol, BS1 1LT, UK. T. +443334056264. E-mail: info@comomeningitis.org.
Pres address not obtained.
URL: http://www.comomeningitis.org/
History Sep 2004. Founded during 1st World Congress of Meningitis Organizations. Registration: Register of Charities, No/ID: 1167023, England and Wales. **Aims** Work to reduce the incidence and impact of meningitis worldwide. **Structure** Steering Committee. **Languages** English. **Staff** 3.50 FTE, paid. **Finance** Sources: sponsorship. **Activities** Advocacy/lobbying/activism; awareness raising; events/meetings; research and development. **Events** *Global Member Conference* London (UK) 2019, *Global Member Conference* Singapore (Singapore) 2018, *Asia Pacific Regional Conference* Bangkok (Thailand) 2016, *Europe Africa Regional Conference* Brussels (Belgium) 2016, *Americas Regional Conference* Orlando, FL (USA) 2016.
Members National organizations (59) and individuals (19) in 33 countries and territories:
Australia, Belgium, Brazil, Cameroon, Canada, Czechia, Denmark, France, Germany, Ghana, Guinea, Hong Kong, Ireland, Italy, Japan, Korea Rep, Malawi, Malaysia, Mexico, Nepal, Netherlands, New Zealand, Nigeria, Peru, Philippines, Poland, Rwanda, Spain, Sweden, Taiwan, Türkiye, UK, USA.
NGO Relations Member of (1): *International Alliance of Patients' Organizations (IAPO, #11633)*.
[2020.06.26/XM2691/**D**]

- Confédération mondiale de l'accordéon / see International Confederation of Accordionists (#12841)
- Confédération mondiale des activités subaquatiques (#21873)
- Confédération mondiale des centres communautaires juifs / see JCC Global (#16093)
- Confédération Mondiale de l'Education (#04464)
- Confédération mondiale d'endodontique (inactive)
- Confédération Mondiale de l'Enseignement Privé / see Confederación Mundial de Educación (#04464)
- Confédération mondiale des experts-comptables sans frontières (no recent information)
- Confédération mondiale de l'industrie de la santé animale / see Health for Animals (#10870)
- Confédération mondiale des organisations de la profession enseignante (inactive)
- Confédération mondiale de la pêche sportive / see Confédération internationale de la pêche sportive (#04562)
- Confédération mondiale pour les relations diplomatiques et de la presse (inactive)
- Confédération mondiale de la science sur la productivité (#21294)
- Confédération mondiale des sports de boules (inactive)
- Confédération mondiale pour la thérapie physique (#21293)
- Confédération mondiale du travail (inactive)

♦ Confederation of National Associations of Hotels, Restaurants, Cafés and Similar Establishments in the European Union and European Economic Area (HOTREC) 04569

Confédération des associations nationales de l'hôtellerie et de la restauration de la Communauté européenne (HOTREC)

Office Manager Rue Dautzenberg 36-38, 1050 Brussels, Belgium. T. +3225136323. Fax +3225024173. E-mail: fanny.bloy@hotrec.eu.
URL: http://www.hotrec.eu/

History 12 Aug 1982, Paris (France). Moved to Brussels (Belgium) in 1991. Former names and other names: *Committee of the Hotel and Restaurant Industry in the European Community* – former; *Comité de l'industrie hôtelière et de la restauration de la Communauté européenne* – former; *Confederation of National Hotel and Restaurant Associations in the European Community* – former. Registration: Banque-Carrefour des Entreprises, No/ID: 0451.258.945, Start date: 4 Nov 1993, Belgium; EU Transparency Register, No/ID: 7955861942-03, Start date: 8 Jan 2009. **Aims** Link employers' organizations of the hotel, restaurant and *catering industry* of the European Community; promote cooperation and make representations on their behalf to Community institutions; coordinate action. **Structure** General Assembly (2 a year, in the country to hold EU presidency in the forthcoming 6 months); Executive Committee; Permanent Secretariat, headed by Chief Executive. **Languages** English, French. **Staff** 6.00 FTE, paid. **Finance** Sources: members' dues. **Activities** Advocacy/lobbying/activism; events/meetings; politics/policy/regulatory. **Events** *Half-Yearly General Assembly and Seminar* Prague (Czechia) 2022, *Half-Yearly General Assembly and Seminar* Stockholm (Sweden) 2022, *Half-Yearly General Assembly and Seminar* Lyon (France) 2021, *Half-Yearly General Assembly and Seminar* Brussels (Belgium) 2020, *Half-Yearly General Assembly and Seminar* Krakow (Poland) 2018. **Publications** Brochures; code of conduct; seminar reports.

Members Full; Associate; Observer. Members (45) in 33 countries:
Austria, Azerbaijan, Belgium, Bulgaria, Croatia, Czechia, Denmark, Estonia, Finland, France, Georgia, Germany, Greece, Hungary, Iceland, Ireland, Italy, Latvia, Liechtenstein, Lithuania, Luxembourg, Malta, Netherlands, Norway, Poland, Serbia, Slovakia, Slovenia, Spain, Sweden, Switzerland, Türkiye, UK.

IGO Relations Recognized by: *European Commission (EC, #06633)*. Representation with: *European Economic and Social Committee (EESC, #06963)*. Affiliate member of: *World Tourism Organization (UNWTO, #21861)*. **NGO Relations** Member of (3): *European Tourism Manifesto (#08921)*; *Hotel Technology Next Generation (HTNG, #10952)*; *Network for the European Private Sector in Tourism (NET, #17027)*. Partner of (1): *Wine in Moderation (WIM, #20967)*. In liaison with technical committees of: *Comité européen de normalisation (CEN, #04162)*; *International Organization for Standardization (ISO, #14473)*. [2023/XE4159/**E**]

- ♦ Confederation of National Associations of Tanners and Dressers of the European Community (#04515)
- ♦ Confederation of National Hotel and Restaurant Associations in the European Community / see Confederation of National Associations of Hotels, Restaurants, Cafés and Similar Establishments in the European Union and European Economic Area (#04569)

♦ Confederation of NATO Retired Civilian Staff Associations (CNRCSA) 04570

Sec NATO Staff Centre, NATO HQ, 1110 Brussels, Belgium. T. +3227072688. E-mail: confed@cnrcsa.nato.int.
URL: http://www.cnrcsa.nato.int/

History 2002. Founded on approval of Articles of Association. **Aims** Defend the interests of the NATO retired Civilian Staff and their dependents. **Structure** Chairperson; Vice Chair; Executive Secretary; Treasurer. **Languages** English, French. **Staff** 1.00 FTE, paid. **Finance** Sources: members' dues.

Members Constituent organizations (4):
Association internationale des anciens agents, retraités de l'OTAN et de leurs ayants-droits (ARO, #02665) (based at NATO HQ, Belgium); Association of NATO/ACE Retired Civilian Personnel (ANARCP), based at SHAPE HQ, Belgium; Association of Retirees of NATO in France (AROF) based at STO CSO, France; NSPA Former Staff Association (NFSA) based at NATO Support and Procurement Agency (NSPA), Luxembourg.
Members in over 30 countries. Membership countries not specified.

NGO Relations *Association des agents pensionnés des organisations coordonnées et de leurs ayants droit (AAPOCAD, #02363)*. [2020.05.14/XJ9980/**E**]

- ♦ Confédération Nord-centrale américaine et des Caraïbes de volley-ball (#17576)
- ♦ Confederation of the Norden Associations (#09859)
- ♦ Confederation of Nordic Bank Employees' Unions (inactive)
- ♦ Confederation of the Nordic Bank, Finance and Insurance Unions / see Nordic Financial Unions (#17292)
- ♦ Confédération nordique des cadres, techniciens et autres responsables du travail (inactive)
- ♦ Confederation of North American Corporate Football (unconfirmed)
- ♦ Confederation of North and Central American and Caribbean Association Football (#04465)

♦ Confederation of North, Central American and the Caribbean Futsal (CONCACFUTSAL) 04571

Confederación Norte, Centroamerica y Caribe de Fútbol de Salón

Headquarters Larahaweg 9, Willemstad, Curaçao. T. +59994614074. Fax +59994650197. E-mail: concacfutsal@hotmail.com.
URL: http://concacfutsal.com/

History 13 Oct 2000, Mexico, when incorporated under the laws of Mexico. **Aims** Promote and support the playing of futsal. **Structure** Board. **Activities** Events/meetings. **Events** *Congress* Willemstad (Curaçao) 2011, *Congress* Willemstad (Curaçao) 2006, *Congress* Mexico City (Mexico) 2000.

Members Full in 13 countries and territories:
Aruba, Bonaire Is, Canada, Colombia, Costa Rica, Curaçao, El Salvador, Mexico, Puerto Rico, St Martin, Suriname, USA, Venezuela.

NGO Relations Recognized by: *World Futsal Association (#21532)*. [2015/XJ9241/**D**]

- ♦ Confédération océanienne de football (#17662)
- ♦ Confédération odontologique de la région andine (inactive)

♦ Confédération des ONG d'environnement et de développement de l'Afrique centrale (CONGAC) 04572

Confederation of Environmental and Development NGOs of Central Africa

Exec Sec BP 6912, Douala, Cameroon. T. +237699891193. E-mail: congacsige@yahoo.fr.
URL: http://www.congac.org/

History 25 Sep 1992, Douala (Cameroon), at constituent assembly, following *United Nations Conference on Environment and Development (UNCED)*, Jun 1992, Rio de Janeiro (Brazil). Also referred to as *Confederation of Central African NGOs* and as *Confédération des organisations non-gouvernementales de l'Afrique centrale*. **Aims** Provide a framework for mutual support and cooperation among voluntary development organizations and nongovernmental environment and development organizations in Central Africa; promote popular participation in efforts to protect the environment for sustainable development; contribute to waste management and to combating desertification; organize local and village committees for control and preservation of natural resources; assist in identifying and mobilizing self-help resources. **Structure** General Assembly (every 2 years); Administrative Council; Expert Group; Information and Training Centre; Executive Secretariat. **Languages** English, French. **Staff** 5.00 FTE, paid; 5.00 FTE, voluntary. **Finance** Members' dues. Other sources: United Nations; *FAO (#09260)*; *International Bank for Reconstruction and Development (IBRD, #12317)*; *Commission des forêts d'Afrique centrale (COMIFAC, #04214)*; *African Development Bank (ADB, #00283)*; *TerrAfrica (#20127)*; governments of Cameroon, Central African Rep and France; NGOs. Annual budget: CFA Fr 36,650,000. **Activities** Events/meetings; projects/programmes; training/education. **Events** *Volleyball medicine congress* Bled (Slovenia) 2011, *International workshop on regional integration in Africa* Accra (Ghana) 1996, *Mise en oeuvre de la convention de lutte contre la désertification en Afrique Centrale* Cameroon 1996, *Les industries, les déchets urbains, l'assainissement et la santé des populations* Douala (Cameroon) 1995. **Publications** *Enviro-vision* (12 a year). Guides. Information Services: Resource centre gathers and disseminates environmental information.

Members Full (120); Affiliate (1,100); Honorary (15). Full national networks of NGOs in 11 countries:
Angola, Burundi, Cameroon, Central African Rep, Chad, Congo Brazzaville, Congo DR, Equatorial Guinea, Gabon, Rwanda, Sao Tomé-Principe.

IGO Relations Accredited to the Conference of the Parties of: *Secretariat of the United Nations Convention to Combat Desertification (Secretariat of the UNCCD, #19208)*. **NGO Relations** Member of: *EarthAction (EA, #05159)*. Instrumental in setting up: *Réseau environnement des jeunes francophones (no recent information)*. [2019.06.25/XD2804/**D**]

♦ Confederation of Open Access Repositories (COAR) 04573

Office Manager c/o Göttingen State and Univ Library, Platz der Göttingen Sieben 1, 37073 Göttingen, Germany. T. +495513922215. Fax +49551395222. E-mail: office@coar-repositories.org.
Exec Dir address not obtained.
URL: http://www.coar-repositories.org/

History Oct 2009. Articles adopted 29 Mar 2011, Debrecen (Hungary); revised 21 May 2014, Athens (Greece). Registration: Start date: 23 Jun 2010, Germany. **Aims** Facilitate greater visibility and application of research outputs through global networks of open access repositories based on interoperability and international cooperation. **Structure** General Assembly; Executive Board; Strategic Committee. **Languages** English, German, Portuguese, Spanish. **Staff** 1.30 FTE, paid. **Finance** Sources: contributions; members' dues. Other sources: EC project funding. **Activities** Advocacy/lobbying/activism; events/meetings; guidance/assistance/consulting; standards/guidelines. Active worldwide. **Events** *Annual Meeting* Costa Rica 2023, *Annual Meeting* Madrid (Spain) 2022, *Annual Meeting* Göttingen (Germany) 2020, *Annual Meeting* Lyon (France) 2019, *Annual Meeting* Hamburg (Germany) 2018. **Publications** *COAR Roadmap: Future Directions for Repository Interoperability* (2015); *Promoting Open Knowledge and Open Science* (2015); *Incentives, Integration, and Mediation: Sustainable Practices for Populating Repositories* (2013) in English, Spanish; *Open Access Clauses in Publishers' Licenses – Current State and Lessons Learned* (2013); *The Current State of Open Access Repository Interoperability* (2012); *The Case for Interoperability of Open Access Repositories* (2011).

Members Public and private universities, research institutions and national agencies, in 36 countries:
Argentina, Austria, Belgium, Brazil, Bulgaria, Canada, Chile, China, Colombia, Cyprus, Denmark, Ecuador, France, Germany, Greece, Hungary, Italy, Japan, Kenya, Lithuania, Luxembourg, Mexico, Netherlands, Norway, Peru, Poland, Portugal, South Africa, Spain, Sri Lanka, Sweden, Switzerland, Türkiye, UK, Uruguay, USA.
Cooperación Latino Americana de Redes Avanzadas (RedCLARA, #04790); *Middle East Technical University (METU)*.

IGO Relations Cooperates with (3): *European Organization for Nuclear Research (CERN, #08108)*; *International Bank for Reconstruction and Development (IBRD, #12317)* (World Bank); *WHO (#20950)*. **NGO Relations** Cooperates with (3): *Association of European Research Libraries (#02540)*; *euroCRIS (#05672)*; *SPARC Europe (#19902)*. Also links with national bodies. [2021.06.16/XJ7072/y/**C**]

- ♦ Confédération de l'Oratoire de Saint Philippe Neri (religious order)
- ♦ Confederation of the Oratory of St Philip Neri (religious order)
- ♦ Confédération des organisations européennes de phèrologie (inactive)
- ♦ Confédération des organisations familiales de la Communauté européenne / see COFACE Families Europe (#04084)
- ♦ Confédération des organisations familiales d'Union européenne / see COFACE Families Europe (#04084)
- ♦ Confédération des organisations internationales scientifiques et techniques pour le développement (inactive)
- ♦ Confédération des organisations nationales de la boulangerie, pâtisserie, glacerie, chocolaterie, confiserie de la CEE / see European Confederation of National Bakery and Confectionery Organizations (#06714)
- ♦ Confédération des organisations non-gouvernementales de l'Afrique centrale / see Confédération des ONG d'environnement et de développement de l'Afrique centrale (#04572)
- ♦ Confédération des organisations touristiques de l'Amérique latine (#04466)

♦ Confederation of Organizations in Road Transport Enforcement (CORTE) 04574

CEO Rue des Deux Eglises 37, 1000 Brussels, Belgium. T. +3222868032. Fax +3222868037. E-mail: secretariat@corte.be.
URL: http://www.corte.be/

History Nov 2004. Registered in accordance with Belgian law. EU Transparency Register: 667657822548-49. **Aims** Provide a platform for mutual consultation in road transport. **Structure** General Assembly (annual); Management Board; Executive Board; Secretariat. Internal Committees. **Languages** English. **Staff** 2.50 FTE, paid. **Activities** Monitoring/evaluation; projects/programmes. **Publications** *CORTE eNewsletter* (weekly).

Members Full in 28 countries:
Austria, Belgium, Bulgaria, Croatia, Cyprus, Czechia, Denmark, Finland, France, Hungary, Ireland, Kosovo, Latvia, Malta, Montenegro, Netherlands, North Macedonia, Norway, Poland, Portugal, Romania, Serbia, Slovakia, Slovenia, Spain, Sweden, Switzerland, UK.
Associate in 4 countries:
Denmark, Italy, Russia, Türkiye.
Associate – regional associations (6):
European Automobile Manufacturers' Association (ACEA, #06300); *European Transport Workers' Federation (ETF, #08941)*; *European Union Road Federation (ERF, #09014)*; *International Cooperation on Theories and Concepts in Traffic Safety (ICTCT, #12942)*; *International Road Transport Union (IRU, #14761)*; *International Union of Professional Drivers (#15802)*.
Observers. Membership countries not specified.

NGO Relations Member of: *European Organisation for Security (EOS, #08102)*; *European Union Road Federation (ERF, #09014)*. [2020/XM0367/y/**D**]

♦ Confédération Ornithologique Mondiale (COM) 04575

Gen Pres Rua Maria da Paz Varzim 111, 4° andar poente, 4490-658 Póvoa de Varzim, Portugal. T. +351969011071.
SG 23 chemin du Vieux Four, 83150 Bandol, France. T. +33494291221.
URL: http://www.conforni.org/

History 10 Nov 1956, Rome (Italy). Founded on merger of *Association ornithologique internationale (inactive)* and *Confédération internationale d'amateurs et éleveurs de canaris (CIC, inactive)*. Current statutes adopted Jan 2019, Zwolle (Netherlands). Registration: EU Transparency Register, No/ID: 219575239045-56, Start date: 22 Jul 2020. **Structure** Board of Directors. **Languages** French. **Activities** Events/meetings. **Publications** *Les Nouvelles* (2 a year) in French.

Members Full in 48 countries:
Albania, Argentina, Austria, Belgium, Bosnia-Herzegovina, Brazil, Bulgaria, Canada, Chile, Colombia, Costa Rica, Croatia, Cyprus, Czechia, Denmark, Egypt, France, Germany, Greece, Hungary, Iran Islamic Rep, Ireland, Israel, Italy, Korea Rep, Lebanon, Luxembourg, Malta, Mexico, Montenegro, Morocco, Netherlands, North Macedonia, Palestine, Peru, Poland, Romania, Serbia, Slovakia, Slovenia, Spain, Switzerland, Tunisia, Türkiye, UK, Ukraine, Uruguay, USA. [2020/AA0994/**C**]

- ♦ Confédération panafricaine des employeurs / see Business Africa (#03377)
- ♦ Confédération panaméricaine des assureurs (#18088)
- ♦ Confédération panaméricaine d'éducation routière (inactive)
- ♦ Confédération panaméricaine pour les fournisseurs de l'industrie graphique (no recent information)
- ♦ Confédération panaméricaine des grandes voies de communications (inactive)
- ♦ Confédération panaméricaine d'haltérophilie (#18137)
- ♦ Confédération panaméricaine des voyageurs de commerce (inactive)
- ♦ Confédération parlementaire des Amériques (#04479)

♦ Confederation of Rightholders' Societies of Europe and Asia (CRSEA) 04576

SG Bol'shoy Savvinskiy, Pereulok 9-2, Moscow MOSKVA, Russia, 119435. T. +74952253616. E-mail: info@crsea.one.
URL: http://crsea.one/

Aims Form and develop the institution of collective management in the territories of the member countries of the Eurasian Economic Union and the Commonwealth of Independent States. **Structure** Presidium. **Events** *Culture and Creative Industries in Russia* Moscow (Russia) 2021.
Members Full in 8 countries:
Armenia, Azerbaijan, Belarus, Kazakhstan, Kyrgyzstan, Moldova, Russia, Türkiye.
Consultative Status Consultative status granted from: *World Intellectual Property Organization (WIPO, #21593)* (Observer Status). [2022/XM8478/**D**]

- ♦ Confederation of Small Peoples and Ethnic Groups (inactive)
- ♦ Confederation of the Socialist Parties in the European Community / see Party of European Socialists (#18249)
- ♦ Confederation of South and Central America of Handball (#04443)
- ♦ Confédération spirite européenne (inactive)
- ♦ Confédération sportive internationale du travail / see International Workers and Amateurs in Sports Confederation (#15905)
- ♦ Confédération Sportive Internationale Travailliste et Amateur (#15905)
- ♦ Confédération sudaméricaine d'athlétisme (#19701)
- ♦ Confédération sudaméricaine de billard (inactive)
- ♦ Confédération sud-américaine de natation (#04491)
- ♦ Confédération sud-américaine des sociétés de pédiatrie / see Latin American Pediatric Association (#16360)
- ♦ Confédération sud-américaine de tennis de table (#04493)
- ♦ Confédération sudaméricaine de volley (#04495)
- ♦ Confédération syndicale africaine (inactive)
- ♦ Confédération syndicale européenne (no recent information)
- ♦ Confédération syndicale internationale (#15708)
- ♦ Confédération syndicale mondiale de l'enseignement (inactive)
- ♦ Confédération syndicale des travailleurs d'Amérique latine (inactive)
- ♦ Confederation of Tax Consultants' Groups in the EEC / see CFE Tax Advisers Europe (#03842)
- ♦ Confédération des travailleurs de l'Amérique latine (inactive)

♦ Confederation of Unions of Workers in Commerce, Restaurants, Consumers' Cooperatives and Various Forms of Business 04577

Pres 64 Zemlianoy Val, Moscow MOSKVA, Russia, 109004. T. +7959152038. Fax +7959153479. E-mail: kpt@kpt.org.ru.
URL: http://www.kpt.org.ru/
History Founded 22 Jan 1992. **Activities** Events/meetings. **Events** *Congress* Moscow (Russia) 2007.
Members Trade unions in 14 countries:
Armenia, Azerbaijan, Belarus, Georgia, Kazakhstan, Kyrgyzstan, Latvia, Lithuania, Moldova, Russia, Tajikistan, Turkmenistan, Ukraine, Uzbekistan.
NGO Relations Member of: *General Confederation of Trade Unions (GCTU, #10108).* [2014/XM2476/**D**]

- ♦ Confédération universitaire centroaméricaine (#04497)
- ♦ Confédération des universités de l'Amérique centrale / see Confederación Universitaria Centroamericana (#04497)

♦ Confederation of University and College Sports Associations (CUCSA) 04578

Contact c/o Private Bag X 1, Matieland, 7602, South Africa. E-mail: secretary@cucsa.net – info@cucsa.net.
URL: https://cucsa.net/
History 18 Aug 1990, Lusaka (Zambia). Founded under the auspices of Sports Development Zone for Southern African Countries (Zone VI) of *Supreme Council for Sport in Africa (SCSA, inactive).* **Aims** Develop and promote sports at colleges and universities in the member countries. **Structure** General Assembly (every 2 years); Executive Committee. **Languages** English. **Activities** Events/meetings.
Members Organizations (10) in 10 countries:
Angola, Botswana, Eswatini, Lesotho, Malawi, Mozambique, Namibia, South Africa, Zambia, Zimbabwe. [2020/XJ3040/**D**]

- ♦ Confederazione delle Associazioni dei Cittadini all'Estero della Comunità Europea / see Europeans throughout the World (#08839)
- ♦ Confederazione Benedettina (religious order)

♦ Confederazione Boccistica Internazionale (CBI) 04579

Confédération bouliste internationale (CBI)
Pres Mesrutiyet Cad 31/3 Kocatepe Mah, Cankaya, 06420 Ankara/Ankara, Türkiye. E-mail: info@cbi-prv.org.
Head Office Via Bossi 23, 6830 Chiasso TI, Switzerland. T. +41916952777. Fax +41916829805. E-mail: info@cbi-prv.org.
URL: https://cbi-prv.org/
History 1983, Chiasso (Switzerland). Founded by 20 National Federations. **Aims** Encourage and expand international amateur *sport* activity among affiliated National Federations active in the field of synthetic bowl games, on smooth and marked off ground, played with punto, raffa and volo systems. **Structure** Executive Committee; Board of Directors. Committees (4): Auditors; International Technical; Discipline; Medical and Antidoping. **Languages** English, Italian. **Finance** Sources: members' dues. Clearance shares for international competitions.
Members National Federations in 64 countries and territories:
Algeria, Argentina, Australia, Austria, Azerbaijan, Bosnia-Herzegovina, Brazil, Brunei Darussalam, Bulgaria, Burkina Faso, Cameroon, Canada, Chile, China, Congo Brazzaville, Croatia, Cuba, Czechia, Djibouti, Dominican Rep, Egypt, France, Germany, Ghana, Haiti, Hong Kong, Hungary, India, Iran Islamic Rep, Italy, Japan, Latvia, Libya, Liechtenstein, Luxembourg, Malaysia, Mali, Malta, Mauritania, Mongolia, Montenegro, Morocco, Nepal, Niger, Nigeria, Pakistan, Paraguay, Peru, Poland, Portugal, Russia, San Marino, Serbia, Slovakia, Slovenia, South Africa, Sudan, Switzerland, Taiwan, Tunisia, Türkiye, Uruguay, USA, Venezuela.
NGO Relations Instrumental in setting up (1): *Confédération mondiale des sports de boules (CMSB, inactive).* [2022/XD4932/**C**]

- ♦ Confederazione Europea delle Categorie Ausiliarie delle Attività Vitivinicole (inactive)
- ♦ Confederazione Europea dei Commercianti di Calzature (inactive)
- ♦ Confederazione Europea del Commercio all'Ingrosso di Calzature (inactive)
- ♦ Confederazione Europea dei Distributori Comunali d'Energia / see European Federation of Local Energy Companies (#07156)
- ♦ Confederazione Europea Ex Alunni dei Padri Gesuiti (#04536)
- ♦ Confederazione Europea del Giocattolo (inactive)
- ♦ Confederazione Europea dell' Industria Calzaturiera (#04544)
- ♦ Confederazione Europea dell'Industria delle Paste, Carte e Cartoni (inactive)
- ♦ Confederazione Europea dei Laringectomizzati (#06709)
- ♦ Confederazione Europea dei Lavoratori Autonomie (#06080)
- ♦ Confederazione Europea di Musicoterapia (#07838)
- ♦ Confederazione Europea delle Radio e Televisioni Indipendenti e Locali (no recent information)
- ♦ Confederazione Europea di Relazioni Pubbliche (inactive)
- ♦ Confederazione Europea Scoutismo (#04531)
- ♦ Confederazione Europea dei Sindacati (#08927)
- ♦ Confederazione Europea dei Sindacati Indipendenti (#06705)
- ♦ Confederazione Europea di Sindaci (inactive)
- ♦ Confederazione Generale delle Cooperative Agricole dell'Unione Europea (#10107)
- ♦ Confederazione Internazionale delle Banche Popolari (#12867)
- ♦ Confederazione Internazionale dei Bieticoltori Europei (#12860)
- ♦ Confederazione Internazionale del Commercio delle Paglie, Foraggi, Torbe e Derivati (no recent information)
- ♦ Confederazione Internazionale del Credito Agrario (#04560)
- ♦ Confederazione Internazionale del Credito Popolare / see International Confederation of Popular Banks (#12867)
- ♦ Confederazione Internazionale Dottori in Scienze Agrarie (inactive)
- ♦ Confederazione Internazionale degli ex Prigionieri di Guerra (inactive)
- ♦ Confederazione Internazionale dei Fabbricanti di Tessuti per Arredamento (inactive)
- ♦ Confederazione Internazionale dei Movimenti delle Famiglie Cristiane (#12851)
- ♦ Confederazione Internazionale Oreficeria Gioielleria, Argenteria, Diamanti, Pietre e Perle (#03923)
- ♦ Confederazione Internazionale de la Pesca Sportive (#04562)
- ♦ Confederazione Internazionale Unione Apostolica del Clero (#12844)
- ♦ Confederazione Latinoamericana dei Religiosi (#04442)
- ♦ Confederazione dell'Oratorio di San Filippo Neri (religious order)
- ♦ Confederazione delle Organizzazioni Familiari della Unione Europea / see COFACE Families Europe (#04084)
- ♦ Confederazione dei Rivenditori di Pollame e Selvaggina dei Paesi della CEE / see European Poultry, Egg and Game Association (#08258)
- ♦ **CONFEJES** Conférence des ministres de la jeunesse et des sports de la Francophonie (#04634)
- ♦ **CONFEMEL** Confederación Médica Latinoamericana y del Caribe (#04463)
- ♦ **CONFEMEN** Conférence des ministres de l'éducation des Etats et gouvernements de la Francophonie (#04632)
- ♦ conferêcia dos Jesuitas de África e Madagascar (#16098)
- ♦ Conférence des administrations nationales de tourisme des pays socialistes (meeting series)
- ♦ Conférence des administrations postales du Commonwealth (meeting series)
- ♦ Conférence des administrations des postes et télécommunications de l'Afrique centrale / see Conference of Posts and Telecommunications of Central Africa (#04642)
- ♦ Conférence des administrations des postes et télécommunications des Etats de l'Afrique de l'Ouest (#04641)
- ♦ Conférence africaine des tarifs aériens (no recent information)
- ♦ Conférence africaine des théologiens du Tiers-Monde / see Conference of African Theological Institutions (#04580)
- ♦ Conference of African Agricultural Research Managers / see West and Central African Council for Agricultural Research and Development (#20907)
- ♦ Conference of African Demographers (inactive)
- ♦ Conference of African Ministers on the Environment / see African Ministerial Conference on the Environment (#00374)
- ♦ Conference of African Ministers Responsible for Human Development (inactive)
- ♦ Conference of African Ministers Responsible for Sustainable Development and the Environment (inactive)
- ♦ Conference of African Ministers Responsible for Trade, Regional Cooperation and Integration and Tourism (inactive)
- ♦ Conference of African Ministers of Transport, Communications and Planning (meeting series)
- ♦ Conference of African Planners (inactive)
- ♦ Conference of African Socialist Parties (meeting series)
- ♦ Conference of African Statisticians (inactive)

♦ Conference of African Theological Institutions (CATI) 04580

Conférence des institutions théologiques africaines
Exec Sec c/o PCG, PO BOX OS 568, Osu, Accra, Ghana. Fax +23321782515. E-mail: info@pcgonline.org.
Head of IT c/o Presbyterian Church of Ghana, PO Box GP 1800, Accra, Ghana. E-mail: presbyitunit@gmail.com.
History Mar 1980, Mbabane (Eswatini). Founded following consultations, Dec 1976, on the dissolution of the Theological Education Fund of the World Council of Churches and following the setting up, 1977, of the Programme on Theological Education. Former names and other names: *Conférence africaine des théologiens du Tiers-Monde* – former. **Aims** Provide the leadership needed to foster the mission of the Church and to be of service to the theological associations, institutions and Churches in Africa; encourage study and practice of relevant spirituality as an integral part of theological education in Africa, stimulating change and growth; encourage theological institutions in Africa to become a part of this fellowship through the member associations; coordinate on-going research programmes of theological institutions in Africa; exchange and encourage the flow of information between institutions, associations and churches; encourage and facilitate exchange of staff and students; foster ecumenical perspectives and commitments through theological education; establish meaningful relationships between theological institutions and related agencies, within and outside Africa. **Structure** General Meeting (every 3 years); Executive Committee; Secretariat. **Finance** Sources: grants; members' dues. Grants for special purposes from Programme on Theological Education and other ecumenical partners. **Activities** Knowledge management/information dissemination; training/education.
Members Full: associations of theological institutions operating in Africa and Madagascar. Associate: organizations and bodies engaged in promoting theological education in Africa. Members in 28 countries:
Angola, Benin, Botswana, Burundi, Cameroon, Central African Rep, Chad, Congo DR, Côte d'Ivoire, Eswatini, Ethiopia, Ghana, Kenya, Lesotho, Liberia, Madagascar, Malawi, Mozambique, Namibia, Nigeria, Rwanda, Senegal, Sierra Leone, South Africa, Tanzania UR, Uganda, Zambia, Zimbabwe.
Full members (4):
Association of Christian Lay Centres in Africa (ACLCA, #02429); Association of Theological Institutions in Southern and Central Africa (ATISCA, no recent information); Association of Theological Teachers in Madagascar; *West African Association of Theological Institutions (WAATI, no recent information).*
Associate members (2):
All Africa Conference of Churches (AACC, #00640) (Theology Department); *Council of African Instituted Churches (no recent information).*
NGO Relations Member of (1): *World Conference of Associations of Theological Institutions (WOCATI, #21296).* [2021.05.19/XF1063/y/**F**]

- ♦ Conference of African Women / see Pan African Women's Organization (#18074)

♦ Conference of the Americas on International Education (CAIE) 04581

Congrès des Amériques sur l'éducation internationale (CAEI) – Congreso de las Américas sobre la Educación Internacional (CAEI) – Congresso das Américas sobre Educação Internacional (CAEI)
Contact c/o OUI-IOHE, 3744 rue Jean-Brillant, bureau 592, Montréal QC H3T 1P1, Canada. T. +15143436980. E-mail: caei@oui-iohe.org.
URL: http://www.caie-caei.org/
History 2009. **Aims** Bring together the main actors and decision-makers related to the internationalization of higher education in the Americas to strengthen contacts, exchange experiences, and chart the future of the academic cooperation in the region. **Structure** Steering Committee; Advisory Committee; Academic Committee; National Committee; Conference Secreteriat, housed at the Inter-American Organization for Higher Education. **Languages** English, French, Portuguese, Spanish. **Activities** Awards/prizes/competitions; events/meetings; knowledge management/information dissemination; networking/liaising. **Events** *Conference of the Americas on International Education* 2023, *Conference of the Americas on International Education / Congrès des Amériques sur l'éducation internationale / Congreso de las Américas sobre Educación Internacional* Santiago (Chile) 2021, *Conference of the Americas on International Education* Bogota (Colombia) 2019, *Conference of the Americas on International Education* Montréal, QC (Canada) 2017, *Conference of the Americas on International Education* Quito (Ecuador) 2015. **Publications** *CAIE Newsletter.*
Members Higher-education associations including 11 organizations listed in this Yearbook:
Agence universitaire de La Francophonie (AUF, #00548); Association of International Education Administrators (AIEA); Canadian Bureau for International Education (CBIE); Community Colleges for International Development (CCID); Confederación Universitaria Centroamericana (CSUCA, #04497); Consortium for North American Higher Education Collaboration (CONAHEC, #04756); Inter-American Organization for Higher Education (IOHE, #11442); International Institute of Entomology (IIE, inactive); Laspau Inc.; *Latin American Council of Business Schools (#16308); Mexican Association for International Education (AMPEI).* [2021.03.18/XM6263/cy/**F**]

♦ Conference on Asian Affairs / see Council on International and Public Affairs
♦ Conference of Asian Foundations and Organizations (unconfirmed)
♦ Conference on Asian History (internationally oriented national body)
♦ Conference on Asian Linguistic Anthropology / see Global Council for Anthropological Linguistics (#10310)
♦ Conference of Asian and Pacific Labour Ministers (meeting series)
♦ Conference of Asia Pacific Express Carriers (internationally oriented national body)
♦ Conférence d'Asie pour la religion et la paix (#01400)

♦ Conférence des assemblées législatives régionales d'Europe (CALRE) 04582

Conference of the European Regional Legislative Parliaments – Conferencia de Asambleas Regionales Europeas – Konferenz der Europäischen Regionalen Gesetzgebenden Parlamente – Conferência das Assembleias Legislativas Regionais da União Europeia – Conferenza della Assemblee Legislative Regionale Europee – Conferentie van de Europese Regionale Wetgevende Parlementen – Nätverket för Regionala Lagstiftande Församlingar

Pres Via S Trinità 14, 38100 Trento TN, Italy. E-mail: calre2020@parcan.es.
URL: http://www.calrenet.eu/

History 6 Oct 1997, Brussels (Belgium). 6-7 Oct 1997, Brussels (Belgium), at meeting of over 60 presidents, following recommendations of a seminar, 5-7 May 1997, Stuttgart. Previously referred to as *Conference of Presidents of the European Regional Legislative Assemblies – Conférence des présidents des assemblées législatives régionales européennes – Konferenz der Präsidenten der Regionalen Gesetzgebenden Versammlungen in der Europäischen Union* and *Conference of European Regional Legislative Assemblies*. **Aims** Enhance regional *parliamentary* control of European affairs; entrust the task of monitoring and evaluating sector-based programmes to special committees responsible for European affairs within each assembly; encourage exchange of information among regional legislative assemblies and between them and national parliaments and the European Parliament. **Structure** Plenary session of presidents. Standing Committee, comprising 6 presidents. Headquarters at *European Parliament (EP, #08146)* in Brussels (Belgium). **Languages** Dutch, French, German, Italian, Portuguese, Spanish. **Activities** Institutional meetings; computer networking; exchange secondments of civil servants. Participates in meetings of the Committee on Regional Policy of the European Parliament. **Events** *Conference* Barcelona (Spain) 2005. **Publications** *European Regional Parliaments* – directory.

Members Regional legislative assemblies (74) in 8 countries and territories:
Åland, Austria, Azores, Belgium, Germany, Italy, Madeira, Spain.

IGO Relations Member of: *Congress of Local and Regional Authorities of the Council of Europe (#04677)*. Agreement with: *Council of Europe (CE, #04881)*. Cooperates with: *European Committee of the Regions (CoR, #06665)*. [2021/XF5697/**F***]

♦ Conference and Association of European Steel Territories (inactive)
♦ Conférence des associations européennes d'étudiants ingénieurs (inactive)
♦ Conférence et association des zones sidérurgiques (inactive)
♦ Conference of the Atlantic Arc Cities / see Atlantic Cities (#03008)
♦ Conférence des autorités ibéroaméricaines en matière d'informatique (#04606)
♦ Conference of Balkan Democratic Parties (meeting series)
♦ Conference of Balkan Foreign Ministers (meeting series)
♦ Conférence baltique des ministres des transports (meeting series)
♦ Conference of Biological Editors / see Council of Science Editors (#04917)
♦ The Conference Board (internationally oriented national body)

♦ The Conference Board in Europe 04583

Managing Dir Chée de la Hulpe 178, 6th Floor, 1170 Brussels, Belgium. T. +3226755405.
URL: http://www.conference-board.org/

History Founded 1978, as European Division of *The Conference Board*, set up in 1916. **Aims** Create and disseminate knowledge about *management* and the *marketplace* to help *businesses* strengthen their performance and better serve society. **Structure** Regional Directors in 5 areas of Europe; International Counsellors in Europe. Councils: Corporate Governance; Environment and Product Stewardship; Corporate Communications; Risk Management; Corporate Responsibility and Sustainability; Chief Audit Executives; Financial Executives and Controllers; Chief Financial Officers; Economists; Tax; Investor Relations; Mergers and Acquisitions; Treasury; Procurement Leadership; Innovation; Shared Services; health and Safety; Compensation and Benefits; Human Resources Executives; HR Operations; Pensions; Legal; Diversity in Business; Leadership, Talent and Learning; Strategic Workforce Planning. Academies: Governance; Health and Safety; Diversity; Strategic Workforce Planning; Coaching. **Languages** English. **Staff** 30.00 FTE, paid. **Finance** Members' dues (annual) on a sliding scale. Fees from councils, academies, executive and experiential programmes. **Activities** Research/documentation; publishing activity; networking/liaising; events/meetings. **Events** *Building sustainable enterprises forum* Brussels (Belgium) 2005, *Annual shared services conference* Brussels (Belgium) 2004, *Meeting* Barcelona (Spain) 2003, *Meeting* Dublin (Ireland) 2003, *Corporate image conference* London (UK) 2003.

Members Associates in 27 countries:
Austria, Bahrain, Belgium, Czechia, Denmark, Finland, France, Germany, Greece, Hungary, Ireland, Italy, Kuwait, Luxembourg, Malta, Netherlands, Norway, Oman, Poland, Russia, Saudi Arabia, Spain, Sweden, Switzerland, Türkiye, UK, United Arab Emirates. [2014.10.03/XF8628/**E**]

♦ Conférence de Cambridge des géomètres et des fonctionnaires des instituts géographiques nationaux du monde (#03401)
♦ Conference of Catholic Theological Institutions (see: #13381)
♦ Conference of Central American Armed Forces (#04651)
♦ Conference of Chambers of Commerce and Industry of the Island Regions of the European Union (meeting series)
♦ Conférence des chefs d'Etat de l'Afrique équatoriale (inactive)
♦ Conférence des chefs d'Etat et de gouvernement des pays ayant en commun l'usage du français / see Conférence au sommet des chefs d'Etat et de gouvernement des pays ayant le français en partage (#04648)
♦ Conférence des chemins de fer du Moyen-Orient (meeting series)
♦ Conference of Chief Executives of ECA-Sponsored Regional and Sub-Regional Institutions (meeting series)
♦ Conférence chrétienne d'Asie (#03898)
♦ Conférence chrétienne pour la paix (inactive)
♦ Conférence circumpolaire inuit / see Inuit Circumpolar Council (#15995)
♦ Conférence des commissions Justice et paix d'Europe (#04596)
♦ Conference of Commonwealth Auditors General (meeting series)
♦ Conference of Commonwealth Education Ministers (meeting series)

♦ Conference of Commonwealth Meteorologists 04584

Contact International Relations – Met Office, FitzRoy Road, Exeter, EX1 3PB, UK. T. +441392886784. E-mail: commonwealth@metoffice.gov.uk.
URL: http://thecommonwealth.org/organisation/conference-commonwealth-meteorologists -ccm/

Aims Enhance the benefits of meteorology to society though increased cooperation between NMHS, governments and other organizations including the private sector. **Structure** Informal network of representatives from National Meteorological and Hydrological Services (NMHS) of Commonwealth countries. **Events** *Conference* Exeter (UK) 2005, *Conference* Reading (UK) 2001, *Conference* Reading (UK) 1997, *Conference* Reading (UK) 1993. **IGO Relations** *Commonwealth Secretariat (#04362)*. [2016.11.01/XS3298/c/**C**]

♦ Conference of Commonwealth Surveyors / see Cambridge Conference for National Mapping Organizations (#03401)
♦ Conférence des communautés ethniques de langue française (meeting series)
♦ Conference of Community and European Affairs Committees of Parliaments of the European Union / see Conférence des Organes Parlementaires Spécialisés dans les Affaires de l'Union des Parlements de l'Union Européenne (#04637)

♦ Conference on Computation, Communication, Aesthetics and X (meeting series)
♦ Conférence des conseils nationaux de sciences sociales et organismes similaires / see International Federation of Social Science Organizations (#13543)
♦ Conference of Constitutional Control Organs of the Countries of Young Democracy / see Eurasian Association of Contitutional Review Bodies (#05602)

♦ Conference of Constitutional Jurisdictions of Africa (CCJA) 04585

Conférence des Juridictions Constitutionelles Africaines

SG CCJA HQ, Boulevard of 11 December 1960, El Biar, Algiers, Algeria. T. +21321922841. Fax +21323253836. E-mail: contact@cjca-conf.org.
URL: http://www.cjca-conf.org/

History May 2011, Algeria. Decision to create an African Constitutional Justice space adopted Jul 2010, Kampala (Uganda), at 15th session of Conference of Heads of State and Government of *African Union (AU, #00488)*. Constitutive Congress held at the headquarters of the Constitutional Council of Algeria, where Statute was adopted and 1st Executive Bureau elected. Agreement on Headquarters signed Oct 2015, and set in Algiers (Algeria). **Aims** Bring together, in a common African framework, African jurisdictions responsible for ensuring compliance with the Constitution; promote constitutional justice in Africa; promote solidarity and mutual aid; promote the sharing of experiences and information in constitutional jurisprudence; establish links with the legal community, in particular academia; develop relations of exchange and cooperation worldwide; offer the contribution of Africa at international level in the area of constitutional justice. **Structure** Executive Bureau. **Languages** Arabic, English, French, Portuguese. **Staff** Voluntary. **Finance** Sources: contributions; grants. Contributions of members jurisdictions; annual grant of Algerian government. **Activities** Events/meetings. **Events** *Congress* Rabat (Morocco) / Fez (Morocco) 2022, *Congress* Luanda (Angola) 2019, *Strengthening the independence of the judiciary and respect for the rule of law* Cape Town (South Africa) 2017, *Constitutional court and regulatory function* Libreville (Gabon) 2015, *Congress* Cotonou (Benin) 2013. **Publications** Compendium; proceedings.

Members Courts of 44 countries and territories:
Algeria, Angola, Benin, Botswana, Burkina Faso, Burundi, Cameroon, Cape Verde, Central African Rep, Chad, Comoros, Congo Brazzaville, Congo DR, Côte d'Ivoire, Djibouti, Egypt, Equatorial Guinea, Eswatini, Ethiopia, Gabon, Gambia, Ghana, Guinea, Guinea-Bissau, Kenya, Madagascar, Mali, Mauritania, Mozambique, Namibia, Niger, Nigeria, Rwanda, Sahara West, Sao Tomé-Principe, Senegal, Seychelles, Sierra Leone, South Africa, Sudan, Tanzania UR, Togo, Zambia, Zimbabwe.
Observers (2):
Morocco, Russia.

IGO Relations Observer status with (1): *African Union (AU, #00488)*. Cooperation agreement with: *European Commission for Democracy through Law (Venice Commission, #06636)*. Participates with: *World Conference on Constitutional Justice (WCCJ, #21298)*. [2021.08.30/XM4276/**D***]

♦ Conférence continentale des supérieurs-es majeurs-es pour l'Afrique et Madagascar (#04627)
♦ Conférence de coordination du développement de l'Afrique australe (inactive)
♦ Conference on Coordination of Research in the Arctic / see International Arctic Social Sciences Association (#11669)
♦ Conférence des cours constitutionnelles européennes (#04594)
♦ Conference on Cryocrystals and Quantum Crystals (meeting series)
♦ Conférence de défense du Commonwealth (inactive)
♦ Conférence des démographes africains (inactive)
♦ Conférence du désarmement (#04590)
♦ Conference on Detection of Intrusions and Malware and Vulnerability Assessment (meeting series)
♦ Conférence diplomatique de droit maritime international (inactive)
♦ Conférence des directeurs généraux des chemins de fer membres de l'OSJD (see: #17803)
♦ Conférence des directeurs des monnaies (#16822)
♦ Conférence des Directeurs des Services Météorologiques et Hydrologiques Nationaux de l'Afrique de l'Ouest (#04589)

♦ Conference of Directors of the Ibero American Meteorological and Hydrological Services 04586

Conferencia de Directores de los Servicios Meteorológicos e Hidrológicos Iberoamericanos (CIMHET)

Secretariat Agencia Estatal de Meteorologia, C/ Leonardo Prieto Castro 8, Ciudad Universitaria, 28071 Madrid, Spain.
Technical Secretariat Agencia Estatal de Meteorologia, Regional Office for Valencian Community, C/Botanico Cavanilles 3, 46010 Valencia, Spain.
URL: http://www.cimhet.org/

History 19 Nov 2003, Antigua (Guatemala). Founded during meeting of Ibero American National Meteorological Services (IA NMS). **Aims** Strengthen cooperation between IA-NMSs, so as to improve their institutional and operating capacities, growth in the safety of their societies and rise in the profitability of using weather and climate information. **Structure** Directors. Secretariat provided by *World Meteorological Organization (WMO, #21649)* and Agencia Estatal de Meteorologia (AEMET, Spain). **Languages** Spanish. **Finance** Financed by State Meteorological Agency of Spain through Trust Fund created by AEMET with *World Meteorological Organization (WMO, #21649)*. **Activities** Programmes; meeting activities; education. **Events** *Meeting* Cartagena de Indias (Colombia) 2015, *Meeting* Boadilla del Monte (Spain) 2012, *Meeting* Madrid (Spain) 2012, *Meeting* Curitiba (Brazil) 2011, *Iberoamerican workshop on generation of regionalised climate change* Lima (Peru) 2011.

Members National meteorological services in 21 Ibero American countries:
Argentina, Bolivia, Brazil, Chile, Colombia, Costa Rica, Cuba, Dominican Rep, Ecuador, El Salvador, Guatemala, Honduras, Mexico, Nicaragua, Panama, Paraguay, Peru, Portugal, Spain, Uruguay, Venezuela.

NGO Relations *Conference of Directors of the West African National Meteorological and Hydrological Services (AFRIMET, #04589)*. [2020/XJ4679/**F**]

♦ Conference of Directors of National Libraries (CDNL) 04587

Chair c/o KB, Prins Willem-Alexanderhof 5, 2595 BE The Hague, Netherlands. E-mail: cdnl@kb.nl.
URL: http://cdnl.info/

History 1974, Ottawa (Canada). Statutes approved Aug 1990; revised 1999, 2008. **Aims** Facilitate discussion and promote understanding and cooperation on matters of common interest to national libraries worldwide. **Structure** Executive; Secretariat. **Languages** English. **Staff** 1.00 FTE, paid. **Finance** Member libraries fund their own participation in CDNL meetings and activities. Financial responsibility for the Secretariat rests with the Chairperson. **Activities** Events/meetings; research and development; knowledge management/ information dissemination. **Events** *Annual Meeting* Athens (Greece) 2019, *Annual Meeting* Kuala Lumpur (Malaysia) 2018, *Annual Meeting* Wroclaw (Poland) 2017, *Annual Meeting* Columbus, OH (USA) 2016, *Annual Meeting* Cape Town (South Africa) 2015. **Members** Chief executives (or their representatives) of national libraries worldwide are eligible to attend meetings. Membership countries not specified. [2019.11.27/XF2987/v/**F**]

♦ Conference of Directors of National Libraries in Asia and Oceania (CDNLAO) 04588

Contact Branch Libraries and Cooperation Div, Admin Dept – Natl Diet Library, 1-10-1 Nagata-cho Chiyoda-ku, Tokyo, 100-8924 Japan. E-mail: kokusai@ndl.go.jp.
URL: https://www.ndl.go.jp/en/cdnlao/index.html

Aims Exchange information and promote cooperation for development of libraries in Asia and Oceania; assist libraries through cooperation; understand the state of the art of library development among libraries in Asia and Oceania. **Languages** English. **Events** *Meeting* Bali (Indonesia) 2020, *Meeting* Singapore (Singapore) 2019, *Meeting* Nay Pyi Taw (Myanmar) 2018, *Meeting* Beijing (China) 2017, *Adding value through international cooperation* Wellington (New Zealand) 2016. **Publications** *CDNLAO Newsletter*. **Members** National Libraries in Asia and Oceania. Membership countries not specified. [2022/XF6237/**F**]

♦ Conference of Directors of the West African National Meteorological and Hydrological Services (AFRIMET) 04589

Conférence des Directeurs des Services Météorologiques et Hydrologiques Nationaux de l'Afrique de l'Ouest – Conferencia de Directores de los Servicios Meteorológicos e Hidrológicos Nacionales del Africa del Oeste

Contact Agencia Estatal de Meteorologia, C/ Leonardo Prieto Castro 8, Ciudad Universitaria, 28071 Madrid, Spain. E-mail: secretariat@afrimet.org.
Secretariat Agencia Estatal de Meteorologia, Regional Office for Catalonia, Carrer de l'Arquitecte Sert 1, 08071 Barcelona, Spain. E-mail: dtcat@aemet.es.
URL: http://www.afrimet.org/

History Set up following a meeting, 17-19 Oct 2007, Las Palmas de Gran Canaria (Spain), attended by Directors of the National Meteorological and Hydrological Services (NMHS) of the region, *Economic Community of West African States (ECOWAS, #05312)*, *African Union (AU, #00488)*, *AGRHYMET Regional Centre (#00565)*, *African Centre of Meteorological Applications for Development (ACMAD, #00242)* and representatives from European meteorological services. Functions as a programme of cooperation carried out through *World Meteorological Organization (WMO, #21649)*. Original title: *Forum of Directors of the West African National Meteorological and Hydrological Services (AFRIMET) – Forum des Directeurs des Services Météorologiques et Hydrologiques de l'Afrique d'Ouest – Foro de Directores de los Servicios Meteorológicos e Hidrológicos del Africa del Oeste.* **Aims** Facilitate multilateral cooperation in meteorology and hydrology among NMHSs in the West African region in order to build capacity towards operational climate and weather information services, and contribute products and services to sustainable development. **Structure** Forum, composed of Directors of participating NMHSs and *World Meteorological Organization (WMO, #21649)*. Secretariat provided by: WMO and Agencia Estatal de Meteorologia (AEMET) (Spain). **Languages** English, French, Spanish. **Finance** Financed by State Meteorological Agency of Spain (AEMET), through Trust Fund created with *World Meteorological Organization (WMO, #21649)*. **Activities** Projects/programmes; training/education. **Events** *Meeting* Madrid (Spain) 2012, *Conference* Cape Verde 2011, *Conference* Banjul (Gambia) 2010, *Conference* Niamey (Niger) 2008, *Conference* Las Palmas de Gran Canaria (Spain) 2007. **Publications** *AFRIMET Newsletter*. Brochures.

Members National meteorological and hydrological services in 17 countries:
Benin, Burkina Faso, Cape Verde, Côte d'Ivoire, Gambia, Ghana, Guinea, Guinea-Bissau, Liberia, Mali, Mauritania, Niger, Nigeria, Senegal, Sierra Leone, Spain, Togo.

IGO Relations Cooperates with: *African Centre of Meteorological Applications for Development (ACMAD, #00242)*; *Agency for the Safety of Aerial Navigation in Africa and Madagascar (#00556)*; *AGRHYMET Regional Centre (#00565)*; *European Organisation for the Exploitation of Meteorological Satellites (EUMETSAT, #08096)*; *WHO (#20950)*; *World Meteorological Organization (WMO, #21649)* SDS-WAS. **NGO Relations** *Conference of Directors of the Ibero American Meteorological and Hydrological Services (#04586)*; *International Research Institute for Climate and Society (IRI)*. [2019.10.31/XJ1602/**E**]

♦ Conference on Disarmament (CD) 04590

Conférence du désarmement – Conferencia de Desarme

Secretariat Office for Disarmament Affairs, Geneva Branch, Ste 161, 1211 Geneva 10, Switzerland. T. +41229172275. Fax +41229170034. E-mail: cd@un.org.
URL: http://www.unog.ch/disarmament/

History 1978, as *Committee on Disarmament – Comité du désarmement*, resulting from 1st Special Session on Disarmament (SSOD I), of *United Nations (UN, #20515)* General Assembly. Succeeded other Geneva-based negotiating fora, including: *Ten-Nation Committee on Disarmament* (1960); *Eighteen Nations Committee on Disarmament* (1961-1968); *Conference of the Committee on Disarmament* (1969-1978). Started working under current title, 1984. Originally constituted with 40 members; membership gradually expended (and reduced) to 65 countries. Based at *United Nations Office at Geneva (UNOG, #20597)*. **Aims** Act as the single multilateral disarmament negotiating forum of the international community. **Structure** Conference, meeting annually for 24 weeks. Rotating Presidency among Member States (based on English alphabetical order). Conference conducts work by consensus. Plenary meetings open to public; meeting of ad hoc subsidiary bodies closed, with non-member states participating as observers by invitation. **Languages** Arabic, Chinese, English, French, Russian, Spanish. **Staff** Staff from Geneva branch of the UN Office for Disarmement Affairs (UNODA). **Finance** Expenses covered by United Nations regular budget. **Activities** Meeting activities. Negotiated multilateral arms limitation and disarmament agreements including: *Treaty on the Non-proliferation of Nuclear Weapons (NPT, 1968)*; *Convention on the Prohibition of Military or Any other Hostile Use of Environmental Modification Techniques (ENMOD Convention, 1976)*; Seabed treaties; *Convention on the Prohibition of the Development, Production, Stockpiling and Use of Chemical Weapons and on Their Destruction (CWC, 1992)*; *Convention on the Prohibition of the Development, Production and Stockpiling of Bacteriological – Biological – and Toxin Weapons and on Their Destruction (1972)*; *Comprehensive Nuclear-Test-Ban Treaty (CTBT, 1996)*. **Events** *Plenary session* Geneva (Switzerland) 2011, *Plenary session* Geneva (Switzerland) 2010, *Plenary session* Geneva (Switzerland) 2010, *Plenary session* Geneva (Switzerland) 2010, *Plenary session* Geneva (Switzerland) 2009. **Publications** *Report of the Conference on Disarmament to the General Assembly of the United Nations* (annual).

Members As of Jan 2017 governments of 65 countries:
Algeria, Argentina, Australia, Austria, Bangladesh, Belarus, Belgium, Brazil, Bulgaria, Cameroon, Canada, Chile, China, Colombia, Congo DR, Cuba, Ecuador, Egypt, Ethiopia, Finland, France, Germany, Hungary, India, Indonesia, Iran Islamic Rep, Iraq, Ireland, Israel, Italy, Japan, Kazakhstan, Kenya, Korea DPR, Korea Rep, Malaysia, Mexico, Mongolia, Morocco, Myanmar, Netherlands, New Zealand, Nigeria, Norway, Pakistan, Peru, Poland, Romania, Russia, Senegal, Slovakia, South Africa, Spain, Sri Lanka, Sweden, Switzerland, Syrian AR, Tunisia, Türkiye, UK, Ukraine, USA, Venezuela, Vietnam, Zimbabwe.

IGO Relations Close working relationships with: *United Nations (UN, #20515)* General Assembly; First Committee; *United Nations Disarmament Commission (#20552)*; *United Nations Office for Disarmament Affairs (UNODA, #20594)*. [2019.02.12/XE6548/**F***]

- ♦ Conférence douanière inter-caraïbe (#03487)
- ♦ Conference on the Early Neolithic of Europe (meeting series)
- ♦ Conference of East, Central and Southern African Ministers of Health, Chief Medical Officers and Advisers (meeting series)
- ♦ Conference of Eastern, Southern and Central African Heads of Correctional Services (inactive)
- ♦ Conference on East-West Cross-Cultural Relations (meeting series)
- ♦ Conférence des écoles à esprit international (inactive)
- ♦ Conference of Education Ministers of Socialist Countries (meeting series)
- ♦ La Conférence de l'Eglise Méthodiste de la Caraïbe et les Amériques La Conferencia de la Iglesia Metodista en el Caribe y las Americas (#04629)
- ♦ Conférence des Eglises de la Caraïbe (#03479)
- ♦ Conférence des Eglises européennes (#04593)
- ♦ Conférence des eglises du pacifique (#17943)

♦ Conférence des Eglises protestantes des pays latins d'Europe (CEPPLE) 04591

Conference of Protestant Churches in the Latin Countries of Europe

Contact EPUdF – relations internationales, 47 rue de Clichy, 75311 Paris CEDEX 09, France. E-mail: jguy@bluewin.ch.
URL: http://www.cepple.eu/

History Founded 1950. Since Oct 2014, recognized as the Latin Region of Communion of Protestant Churches in Europe. **Aims** Propose to member Churches a platform of dialogue and shared reflection, inciting them to state their identity and their own vocation. **Structure** General Assembly (every 4 years); Continuation Team. **Languages** French. **Finance** Members' dues. **Activities** Events/meetings; networking/liaising. **Events** *Quadrennial General Assembly / Quadrennial Assembly* Malaga (Spain) 2014, *Quadrennial Assembly* Lyon (France) 2010, *Quadrennial Assembly* Brussels (Belgium) 2006, *Quadrennial general assembly / Quadrennial Assembly* Switzerland 2002, *Quadrennial General Assembly* Rome (Italy) 1998. **Publications** Conference proceedings.

Members Protestant Churches (20) in 6 countries:
Belgium, France, Italy, Portugal, Spain, Switzerland. [2014.11.17/XE4516/**E**]

- ♦ Conférence des Eglises riveraines du Rhin (#04646)
- ♦ Conférence des Eglises de toute l'Afrique (#00640)
- ♦ Conference of Engineering Institutions of the British Commonwealth / see Commonwealth Engineers Council (#04324)
- ♦ Conférence des enseignants du génie civil de la moyenne Afrique (inactive)
- ♦ Conférence épiscopale des Antilles (#00856)
- ♦ Conférence épiscopale catholique de Malaisie-Singapour-Bruneï (#03601)

♦ Conférence épiscopale de l'Océan Indien (CEDOI) 04592

Episcopal Conference of the Indian Ocean

Contact 232 Route Royale, Rose-Hill, Moroni, Comoros. T. +2304661757. E-mail: cedoi1986@gmail.com.
Pres Cathedral of St Louis, Mgr Gonin Street, Port Louis, Mauritius.

History 1986, having previously existed as *Zone pastorale d'Océan Indien.* **Aims** Strengthen the links between Catholic dioceses of the South-West islands of Indian Ocean. **Structure** President from among those responsible for the churches. **Languages** English, French. **Events** *Annual Assembly* Mauritius 2012, *Annual Assembly* Réunion 2011, *Annual Assembly* Seychelles 2011, *Annual Assembly* Rodriguez Is (Mauritius) 2009, *Annual Assembly* Souillac (Mauritius) 2008.

Members Dioceses of 5 countries and territories:
Comoros, Mauritius, Réunion, Rodriguez Is, Seychelles.

NGO Relations Member of: *Symposium of Episcopal Conferences of Africa and Madagascar (SECAM, #20077)*. [2014/XD1984/**D**]

- ♦ Conférence épiscopale panafricaine (inactive)
- ♦ Conférence épiscopale régionale de l'Afrique de l'Ouest (#18783)
- ♦ Conférence épiscopale régionale de l'Afrique de l'Ouest francophone (inactive)
- ♦ Conférence épiscopale régionale du Nord de l'Afrique / see Conférence des évêques de la région du Nord de l'Afrique (#04605)
- ♦ Conférence épiscopale scandinave (#17498)
- ♦ Conférence épiscopal latinoaméricain / see Consejo Episcopal Latinoamericano (#04709)
- ♦ Conférence des Etats africains indépendants (inactive)
- ♦ Conférence des états parties de l'Organisation pour l'interdiction des armes chimiques (see: #17823)

♦ Conference of European Churches (CEC) 04593

Conférence des Eglises européennes – Konferenz Europäischer Kirchen (KEK)

Address not obtained.
URL: http://www.ceceurope.org/

History Oct 1964. Founded on MV "Bornholm" in Kattegat, on adoption of Constitution, following assemblies in 1959, 1960 and 1964, Nyborg (Denmark). Constitutional changes: 1971, Nyborg (Denmark); 1974, Engelberg (Switzerland); 1986, Stirling (UK); 1992, Prague (Czech Rep); 2003, Trondheim (Norway); 2009, Lyon (France). New constitution adopted 2013, Budapest (Hungary). *Church and Society Commission of the Conference of European Churches (inactive)* merged into CEC, Dec 2014. Former names and other names: *Konferencija Evropejskih Cerkvej (KEC)* – former; *Conferencia de Iglesias Europeas* – alias. Registration: Banque-Carrefour des Entreprises, No/ID: 0422.232.783, Start date: 26 Nov 1981, Belgium; EU Transparency Register, No/ID: 55481528937-66, Start date: 8 Jun 2012. **Aims** Establish contacts between *Christian* Churches in all parts of Europe – Anglicans, Protestants, Orthodox and Old Catholics, committed to live and witness together in a spirit of *ecumenism*, sharing, understanding and mutual respect; promote unity of the Church, building bridges between minority and majority churches, between generations, between women and men, between Christians of different confessions; present a common Christian witness to the people of Europe. **Structure** General Assembly (every 6 years); Governing Board; Budget Committee; Offices (2): Brussels (Belgium), Strasbourg (France). **Languages** English, French, German, Russian. **Staff** 11.00 FTE, paid. **Finance** Contributions and donations of member churches. Development and Compensation Fund (Solidarity Fund) expresses solidarity with churches unable to pay full fees and ensures their full participation. Annual budget: euro 2,000,000. **Activities** Advocacy/lobbying/activism; networking/liaising; events/meetings. **Events** *General Assembly* Tallinn (Estonia) 2023, *Conference on the Future of Europe* Brussels (Belgium) 2021, *Joint Meeting on Exploring the Europe 2020 Strategy* Brussels (Belgium) 2012, *European ecumenical assembly* Sibiu (Romania) 2007, *European meeting of the delegates of churches, bioshops'conferences, ecumenical bodies and movements* Rome (Italy) 2006. **Publications** *Ecumenical News International* – jointly with WCC, LWF, WCRC; *Official Study Documents and Ongoing Studies of European Churches* in English, French, German. Annual report. Assembly reports; occasional papers; reports on European Ecumenical Encounters with CCEE; leaflets; handbooks; other publications.

Members Members include Protestant, Anglican, Old Catholic and Orthodox Churches. Member Churches, National Councils of Churches and Associated Organizations. Member Churches in 39 countries:
Albania, Armenia, Austria, Belgium, Bulgaria, Croatia, Cyprus, Czechia, Denmark, Estonia, Finland, France, Georgia, Germany, Greece, Hungary, Iceland, Ireland, Italy, Latvia, Liechtenstein, Lithuania, Luxembourg, Montenegro, Netherlands, North Macedonia, Norway, Poland, Portugal, Romania, Russia, Serbia, Slovakia, Slovenia, Spain, Sweden, Switzerland, UK, Ukraine.
Included in the above, 2 organizations listed in this Yearbook:
Council of African and Afro-Caribbean Churches (no recent information); *Euro-Asian Federation of the Unions of the Evangelical Christians-Baptists (no recent information)*.
International members (4), listed in this Yearbook:
Ecumenical Patriarchate of Constantinople (#05349); *European Continental Province of the Moravian Church (#06777)*; *Salvation Army (#19041)*; *The United Methodist Church (UMC, #20514)*.
National Councils of Churches in 25 countries:
Austria, Belgium, Czechia, Denmark, Estonia, Finland, France, Germany, Hungary, Ireland, Italy, Lithuania, Montenegro, Netherlands, Norway, Poland, Portugal, Romania, Serbia, Slovakia, Slovenia, Spain, Sweden, Switzerland, UK.
Observer organization (1), listed in this Yearbook:
Religious Society of Friends (Quakers, #18834).
Partnership organizations (36) in 20 countries:
Belgium, Bulgaria, Czechia, Estonia, Finland, France, Germany, Greece, Hungary, Ireland, Italy, Netherlands, Norway, Portugal, Romania, Slovakia, Spain, Sweden, Switzerland, UK.
Included in the above, 11 organizations listed in this Yearbook:
Church and Peace (#03916); *Churches' Commission for Migrants in Europe (CCME, #03912)*; *Church Mission Society (CMS)*; *Ecumenical Forum of European Christian Women (EFECW, #05347)*; *Ecumenical Youth Council in Europe (EYCE, #05352)*; *European Baptist Federation (EBF, #06316)*; *European Contact Group – Ecumenical Network for Economic and Social Action (ECG, #06773)*; *European Federation for Diaconia (Eurodiaconia, #07099)*; *European Forum of Christian Men (no recent information)*; *Evangelische Arbeitsgemeinschaft für Erwachsenenbildung in Europa (EAEE, inactive)*; *World Student Christian Federation (WSCF, #21833)*.

Consultative Status Consultative status granted from: *ECOSOC (#05331)* (Special); *Council of Europe (CE, #04881)* (Participatory Status). **IGO Relations** *UNHCR (#20327)*, through *European Churches' Working Group on Asylum and Refugees (ECWGAR)*. Accredited by: *United Nations Office at Vienna (UNOV, #20604)*. Participant in Fundamental Rights Platform of: *European Union Agency for Fundamental Rights (FRA, #08969)*. Associated with Department of Global Communications of the United Nations. **NGO Relations** Member of (11): *Committee of NGOs on Human Rights, Geneva (#04275)*; *Conference of Non-Governmental Organizations in Consultative Relationship with the United Nations (CONGO, #04635)*; *European Council on Refugees and Exiles (ECRE, #06839)*; *European Network on Religion and Belief (ENORB, #07985)*; *European Sunday Alliance (#08856)*; *Human Rights and Democracy Network (HRDN, #10980)*; *NGO Committee for Disarmament, Geneva (#17105)*; *NGO Committee on Disarmament, Peace and Security, New York NY (#17106)*; *NGO Committee on the Status of Women, Geneva (#17117)*; *Societas Oecumenica – European Society for Ecumenical Research (#19450)*; *United4Rescue*. Cooperates with (5): *ACT Alliance EU (#00082)*; *Asian Buddhist Conference for Peace (ABCP, no recent information)*; *International Interchurch Film Organization (INTERFILM, #13943)*; *The Lutheran World Federation (LWF, #16532)*; *World Fellowship of Orthodox Youth (Syndesmos, #21504)*. Special links with: *Conférence des Eglises protestantes des pays latins d'Europe (CEPPLE, #04591)*. Close cooperation with: *European Young Women's Christian Association (The European YWCA, #09135)*; *World Council of Churches (WCC, #21320)*. Coordinates: *European Christian Environmental Network (ECEN, #06543)*. [2021/XD0401/y/**F**]

- ♦ Conference of the European Communications Museums (internationally oriented national body)

♦ Conference of European Constitutional Courts (CECC) 04594

Conférence des cours constitutionnelles européennes – Konferenz der Europäischen Verfassungsgerichte – Conferentie van Europese Grondwettelijke Hoven

Address not obtained.

URL: http://www.confcoconsteu.org/

History 1972, Dubrovnik (Yugoslavia), by the constitutional courts of Austria, Germany, Italy and Yugoslavia. **Aims** Promote the exchange of information on the working methods and constitutional case-law of member courts together with the exchange of opinions on institutional, structural and operational issues as regards public-law and constitutional jurisdiction; enhance the independence of constitutional courts as an essential factor in guaranteeing and implementing democracy and the rule of law, in particular with a view to securing protection of human rights. **Structure** Circle of Presidents, composed of the Presidents of the courts and institutions with full member status. Congress. Secretariat provided by the Court organizing the next congress. **Finance** Contributions of members. **Events** *Triennial Conference* Vienna (Austria) 2014, *Preparatory meeting to the 15th conference of European Constitutional courts* Vienna (Austria) 2012, *Triennial Conference* Bucharest (Romania) 2011, *Triennial conference* Vilnius (Lithuania) 2008, *Triennial Conference* Nicosia (Cyprus) 2005.

Members Full constitutional courts of 41 countries:

Albania, Andorra, Armenia, Austria, Azerbaijan, Belgium, Bosnia-Herzegovina, Bulgaria, Croatia, Cyprus, Czechia, Denmark, Estonia, France, Georgia, Germany, Hungary, Ireland, Italy, Latvia, Liechtenstein, Lithuania, Luxembourg, Malta, Moldova, Monaco, Montenegro, Netherlands, North Macedonia, Norway, Poland, Portugal, Romania, Russia, Serbia, Slovakia, Slovenia, Spain, Switzerland, Türkiye, Ukraine.

Associate constitutional court in 1 country:

Belarus.

IGO Relations *European Commission for Democracy through Law (Venice Commission, #06636)*; *World Conference on Constitutional Justice (WCCJ, #21298).* [2014/XF7068/c/**F***]

♦ Conference of European Cross-border and Interregional Cities Network (CECICN) 04595

Address not obtained.

URL: http://www.cecicn.eu/

History 23 Apr 2010, Santiago (Chile). **Aims** Boost territorial cooperation among border cities in Europe; reinforce the message concerning the importance of territorial cooperation.

Members Cities (over 500) in Europe. Membership countries not specified. Networks (5):

Networks (5):

Atlantic Cities (#03008); *Forum of Adriatic and Ionian Cities (FAIC, #09892)*; *MEDCITIES Network (#16610)*; Mission Opérationnelle Transfrontalière (MOT); *Union of the Baltic Cities (UBC, #20366).* [2012/XJ2077/y/**F**]

- ♦ Conference of European Directors of Roads (#04603)
- ♦ Conference of European Engineering Students' Associations (inactive)

♦ Conference of European Justice and Peace Commissions 04596

Conférence des commissions Justice et paix d'Europe

Sec Square de Meeux 19, 1050 Brussels, Belgium. T. +3222350517. Fax +3222350517. E-mail: secretary@jupax-europa.org.

URL: http://www.juspax-eu.org/

History 1971, as *European Conference Justitia et Pax – Conférence européenne Justitia et Pax – Conferencia Europea Justitia et Pax – Europäische Konferenz Justitia et Pax.* Also referred to as *Justitia et Pax European Conference.* **Aims** Bring together the various Justice and Peace Commissions in Europe to promote Church commitment to development, justice, human rights and peace. **Structure** General Assembly. *Executive Committee of the Conference of European Justice and Peace Commissions – Comité exécutif de la Conférence des commissions Justice et paix d'Europe* consists of 8 delegates, headed by President. Presidency and Secretariat rotate among member commissions. **Languages** English. **Staff** 2.50 FTE, paid. **Finance** Contributions of member commissions. **Activities** Events/meetings; training/education. **Events** *General Assembly* Luxembourg (Luxembourg) 2016, *General Assembly* Copenhagen (Denmark) / Malmö (Sweden) 2015, *General Assembly* Athens (Greece) 2014, *General Assembly* Berlin (Germany) 2013, *General Assembly* Rabat (Malta) 2012. **Publications** *INFO Newsletter.* Pamphlets; working papers.

Members Justice and Peace Commissions in 31 countries and territories:

Albania, Austria, Bosnia-Herzegovina, Croatia, Czechia, Denmark, England (with Wales), Flanders, France, Germany, Greece, Hungary, Ireland, Italy, Lithuania, Luxembourg, Malta, Netherlands, Norway, Poland, Portugal, Romania, Scotland, Serbia, Slovakia, Slovenia, Spain, Sweden, Switzerland, Ukraine, Wallonia.

Included in the above, one organization listed in this Yearbook:

Commission justice et paix (CJP).

Correspondents in 25 countries:

Argentina, Australia, Brazil, Cameroon, Canada, Chile, Colombia, Congo DR, Cuba, Egypt, Ghana, Guatemala, Holy See, Japan, Korea Rep, Madagascar, Namibia, New Zealand, Pakistan, Panama, Philippines, South Africa, Thailand, USA, Zimbabwe.

Consultative Status Consultative status granted from: *Council of Europe (CE, #04881)* (Participatory Status).

NGO Relations Member of: *Laudato Si' Movement (#16403).* [2021/XF0339/**F**]

- ♦ Conference of European Ministers Responsible for Family Affairs (meeting series)
- ♦ Conference of European Ministers of Social Affairs (meeting series)

♦ Conference of European National Librarians (CENL) 04597

Chair c/o Nationalbibliothek, Adickesallee 1, 60322 Frankfurt-Main, Germany.

URL: http://www.cenl.org/

History 1987. Registration: Netherlands. **Aims** Make the rich cultural and heritage collections of Europe's national libraries known and available to all. **Structure** Board (meets annually); Executive Committee; Working Groups. **Languages** English. **Staff** Voluntary. **Finance** Members' dues. Voluntary contributions. **Activities** Financial and/or material support; knowledge management / information dissemination. **Events** *Annual General Meeting* 2024, *Annual General Meeting* Paris (France) 2023, *Annual Meeting* Vienna (Austria) 2016, *Annual Meeting / Annual General Assembly* Bern (Switzerland) 2015, *Annual Meeting / Annual General Assembly* Moscow (Russia) 2014.

Members National library executives (49) in 46 countries:

Albania, Armenia, Austria, Azerbaijan, Belgium, Bosnia-Herzegovina, Bulgaria, Croatia, Cyprus, Czechia, Denmark, Estonia, Finland, France, Georgia, Germany, Greece, Holy See, Hungary, Iceland, Ireland, Italy, Latvia, Liechtenstein, Lithuania, Luxembourg, Malta, Moldova, Montenegro, Netherlands, North Macedonia, Norway, Poland, Portugal, Romania, Russia, San Marino, Serbia, Slovakia, Slovenia, Spain, Sweden, Switzerland, Türkiye, UK, Ukraine.

NGO Relations Cooperates with (1): *Federation of European Publishers (FEP, #09536).* [2022/XF5786/**F**]

- ♦ Conference of European Provincials – SJ / see Jesuit Conference of European Provincials (#16100)

♦ Conference of European Rabbis (CER) 04598

Conférence des rabbins européens associées

CEO PO Box 71 04 08, 81454 Munich, Germany. T. +498948002906. Fax +498948002909. E-mail: info@rabbiscer.org.

Headquarters Friedastrasse 3, 81479 Munich, Germany.

Representative Rue Joseph Dupont 2, 1000 Brussels, Belgium.

URL: http://rabbiscer.org/

History 1957, Amsterdam (Netherlands). Former names and other names: *Conference of European Rabbis and Associated Religious Organizations* – former (1957); *Conférence des rabbins européens et des organisations religieuses associées* – former (1957). **Aims** As a combination of rabbinic and synagogal bodies, offer a platform for mutual strengthening of orthodox *Jewish* life, with the *Synagogue* as its focal point. **Structure** Standing Committee (meets twice a year); Executive Council; Praesidium; President. **Languages** English, French, German, Hebrew, Russian. **Staff** 10.00 FTE, paid. **Finance** Voluntary subscriptions from member organizations and supporters. **Activities** Events/meetings; networking/liaising; politics/policy/regulatory; research and development; training/education. **Events** *Conference / Convention* Munich (Germany) 2022, *Conference / Convention* Munich (Germany) 2021, *Biennial Conference* Antwerp (Belgium) 2019, *Biennial Conference* Berlin (Germany) 2013, *Biennial Conference* Warsaw (Poland) 2011. **Publications** *CER Newsletter* (4 a year); *Sridim* (2 a year). Annual Review.

Members Organizations and individuals in 46 countries:

Armenia, Australia, Austria, Azerbaijan, Belarus, Belgium, Bosnia-Herzegovina, Bulgaria, Croatia, Czechia, Denmark, Estonia, Finland, France, Georgia, Germany, Greece, Hungary, Ireland, Israel, Italy, Kazakhstan, Latvia, Liechtenstein, Lithuania, Luxembourg, Malta, Montenegro, Netherlands, Norway, Poland, Portugal, Romania, Russia, Serbia, Slovakia, Slovenia, Spain, Sweden, Switzerland, Tajikistan, Türkiye, UK, Ukraine, USA, Uzbekistan.

Consultative Status Consultative status granted from: *Council of Europe (CE, #04881)* (Participatory Status).

NGO Relations Member of (1): *World Jewish Restitution Organization (WJRO, #21601).* [2022/XD0403/**D**]

- ♦ Conference of European Rabbis and Associated Religious Organizations / see Conference of European Rabbis (#04598)
- ♦ Conference of European Regional Legislative Assemblies / see Conférence des assemblées législatives régionales d'Europe (#04582)
- ♦ Conference of the European Regional Legislative Parliaments (#04582)

♦ Conference of European Schools for Advanced Engineering Education and Research (CESAER) 04599

Address not obtained.

URL: http://www.cesaer.org/

History 10 May 1990, Leuven (Belgium). Registered in accordance with Belgian law. EU Transparency Register: 484959115993-15. **Aims** Provide high quality engineering education in Europe; encourage the training of engineers with broader educational experience; increase the awareness of engineering graduates to the specific needs and opportunities of future European industrial and economic cooperation; maintain the advantageous diversity and the standards of the highest levels of engineering education in Europe; secure international validation and acceptance of the qualification of university educated engineers; promote collaboration in engineering education, research and development between leading European universities. **Structure** General Assembly (annual); Board of Directors; Management Committee, comprising President, Vice-President, Secretary and Treasurer. **Languages** English. **Staff** 1.00 FTE, paid. **Finance** Members' dues. Sponsors. Budget (annual): euro 200,000. **Activities** Maintains consultations between the members on a regular basis concerning the aims of the Conference. Develops and implements programmes of multinational engineering education at undergraduate, postgraduate and professional levels. Cooperates with European and national governmental institutions, agencies and other university networks. Working groups (3): Bologna and academic engineering education; Accreditation of engineering curricula; PhD in Engineering. **Events** *European Convention of Engineering Deans* Enschede (Netherlands) 2023, *European Convention of Engineering Deans* Madrid (Spain) 2021, *European Convention of Engineering Deans* Madrid (Spain) 2020, *European Convention of Engineering Deans* Leuven (Belgium) 2019, *European Convention of Engineering Deans* Trondheim (Norway) 2018. **Publications** Biennial reports. Conference reports.

Members Schools (57) in 23 countries:

Austria, Belgium, Czechia, Denmark, Finland, France, Germany, Greece, Hungary, Ireland, Italy, Lithuania, Netherlands, Norway, Poland, Portugal, Romania, Russia, Spain, Sweden, Switzerland, Türkiye, UK.

Associate members in 1 country:

Israel.

IGO Relations *European Commission (EC, #06633)* (DG XXII). [2019/XD5488/**D**]

♦ Conference of European Statisticians (CES) 04600

Conférence des statisticiens européens – Konferencija Evropejskih Statistikov

Dir Statistical Div, UNECE, Palais des Nations, 1211 Geneva 10, Switzerland. T. +41229171772. Fax +41229170040. E-mail: support.stat@unece.org.

URL: http://www.unece.org/stats/

History Jun 1953, Geneva (Switzerland). A Principal Subsidiary Body of *United Nations Economic Commission for Europe (UNECE, #20555)* and the United Nations Statistical Commission. **Aims** Improve national statistics of UNECE member countries and their international comparability; promote close coordination of statistical activities in Europe and North America undertaken by international organizations; respond to any emerging need for international statistical cooperation arising out of transition, integration and other processes of cooperation; discuss and adopt statistical standards in the UNECE region. **Structure** Plenary Session (annual). Bureau, consisting of 8 member countries, plus Director of UN Statistics Division, New York NY (USA), Head of OECD Statistics Directorate, Director-General of Eurostat, Director of UNECE Statistical Division, Director of IMF Statistics Department, Chairman of Interstate Statistical Committee of CIS, Chairman of OECD Statistical Committee, and Director of the Development Data Group of the World Bank. **Languages** English, French, Russian. **Staff** 29.00 FTE, paid. **Finance** On Regular UN budget.

Activities Programme of work covers the whole field of national statistics (economic statistics; social and demographic statistics; environmental and sustainable development statistics) as well as the study of problems related to information technology and other cross-cutting issues and organization and operation of statistical services. Special attention paid to harmonization of statistical concepts and methodologies. Programme also includes technical assistance projects designed to develop the capacities of countries in transition in different statistical areas, eg national accounts, population censuses, data collection and dissemination. Includes:

- Group of Experts Meeting on Measuring Violence Against Women;
- Group of Experts on National Accounts;
- Joint UNECE/Eurostat/OECD Task Force on the Impact of Globalization on National Accounts;
- Joint UNECE/ILO Meeting on Consumer Price Indices;
- Work Session on Business Registers;
- Joint UNECE/Eurostat Meeting on Population and Housing Censuses;
- Joint UNECE/WHO Meeting on Measurement of Health Status;
- Joint UNECE/UNODC Meeting on Crime Statistics;
- Work Session on Gender Statistics;
- Work Session on Migration Statistics;
- Work Session on Demographic Projections;
- Work Session on Quality of Employment;
- Joint UNECE/Eurostat/OECD Task Force on Measuring Sustainable Development;
- Meeting on the Management of Statistical Information Systems;
- Regional Meeting on MDG Indicators;
- UNECE Intersectoral Task Force on Environmental Indicators;
- Work Session on Statistical Data Confidentiality;
- Work Session on Statistical Metadata;
- Work Session on Statistical Dissemination and Communication;
- Workshop on Human Resources Management and Training.

Events *Annual Plenary Session* Paris (France) 2016, *Annual Plenary Session* Geneva (Switzerland) 2015, *Annual Plenary Session* Paris (France) 2014, *Annual Plenary Session* Geneva (Switzerland) 2013, *Annual Plenary Session* Paris (France) 2012. **Publications** *Statistical Standards and Studies* – (irregular) series containing methodological studies.

Members Directors of national statistical offices of UNECE member countries (56) and OECD member countries (5, indicated by ") and others, totalling 65 countries:

Albania, Andorra, Armenia, Australia (*), Austria, Azerbaijan, Belarus, Belgium, Bosnia-Herzegovina, Brazil, Bulgaria, Canada, Chile, China, Croatia, Cyprus, Czechia, Denmark, Estonia, Finland, France, Georgia, Germany, Greece, Hungary, Iceland, Ireland, Israel, Italy, Japan (*), Kazakhstan, Korea Rep (*), Kyrgyzstan, Latvia, Liechtenstein, Lithuania, Luxembourg, Malta, Mexico (*), Moldova, Monaco, Montenegro, Netherlands, New Zealand (*), North Macedonia, Norway, Poland, Portugal, Romania, Russia, San Marino, Serbia, Slovakia, Slovenia, South Africa, Spain, Sweden, Switzerland, Tajikistan, Türkiye, Turkmenistan, UK, Ukraine, USA, Uzbekistan.

NGO Relations *International Association for Official Statistics (IAOS, #12052)*; *International Statistical Institute (ISI, #15603).* [2010.12.22/XE5349/**E***]

♦ Conference of European University Chaplains (CEUC) 04601

Chair address not obtained. E-mail: secretary@ceuc.org.

URL: http://www.ceuc.org/

History 2002, UK. A Christian ecumenical organization open to all faith groups who have university campus recognition. **Aims** Promote communication and networking between university chaplains in Europe; represent concerns and interests of university chaplains to international institutions and Church bodies. **Structure** General Assembly (annual); Board. **Languages** English. **Events** *Truth in transformation* Neuendettelsau (Germany) 2019, *Our Ancient Future* Dublin (Ireland) 2018, *Rock and Oil: The Hard and the Smooth of Chaplaincy Work Today* Aberdeen (UK) 2017, *Space for spirit* Soesterberg (Netherlands) 2015, *Conference* Ariano Irpino (Italy) 2014. [2022.07.07/XJ4292/**F**]

♦ Conférence européenne (meeting series)

♦ Conférence européenne des administrations des postes et des télécommunications (CEPT) 04602

European Conference of Postal and Telecommunications Administrations – Europäische Konferenz der Verwaltungen für Post und Telekommunikation

Dir c/o ECO, Nyropsgade 37-4, 1602 Copenhagen, Denmark. T. +4533896300. Fax +4533896330. E-mail: ceptpresidency@cept.org.
URL: http://www.cept.org/

History 26 Jun 1959, Montreux (Switzerland). Since Sep 1992 reorganization, CEPT comprises the national authorities and bodies responsible for postal and telecommunications policy and regulatory affairs of the European countries. CEPT is a regional organization within the meaning of the basic instruments of *Universal Postal Union (UPU, #20682)* and *International Telecommunication Union (ITU, #15673)*. **Aims** Strengthen relations between member Administrations; promote their cooperation; contribute to creating a dynamic market in the field of European posts and telecommunications. **Structure** Presidency; Business Committees: *Electronic Communications Committee (ECC, see: #04602)*; *European Committee for Postal Regulation (CERP, see: #04602)* (CERP); Committee for ITU Policy (Com-ITU). *European Communications Office (ECO, #06676)* acts as permanent office. **Languages** English, French, German. **Activities** Events/meetings. Operational postal affairs formerly carried out by CEPT now come under POSTEUROP and CSFPE – these include the following, which were set up, 1988, under the auspices of CEPT: *Express Mail Service (EMS, inactive)*; *International Post Corporation (IPC, #14624)*. Telecommunications operators have set up *European Telecommunications Network Operators' Association (ETNO, #08895)*. CEPT member governments set up, May 1963, Paris (France), *European Conference on Satellite Communications (CETS, inactive)*, which ceased activity in 1970 but was historically a forerunner of *European Space Agency (ESA, #08798)*. CEPT was also instrumental in setting up: *Association of European Public Postal Operators (PostEurop, #02534)*; *European Telecommunications Satellite Organization (EUTELSAT IGO, #08896)*; *European Telecommunications Standards Institute (ETSI, #08897)*. **Events** *ECC Meeting* 2021, *ECC Meeting* 2021, *ECC Meeting* Berlin (Germany) 2020, *ECC Meeting* Copenhagen (Denmark) 2020, *ECC Meeting* Tallinn (Estonia) 2020.

Members National authorities and bodies responsible for postal and telecommunications policy and regulatory affairs in 46 countries:
Albania, Andorra, Austria, Azerbaijan, Belgium, Bosnia-Herzegovina, Bulgaria, Croatia, Cyprus, Czechia, Denmark, Estonia, Finland, France, Georgia, Germany, Greece, Holy See, Hungary, Iceland, Ireland, Italy, Latvia, Liechtenstein, Lithuania, Luxembourg, Malta, Moldova, Monaco, Montenegro, Netherlands, North Macedonia, Norway, Poland, Portugal, Romania, San Marino, Serbia, Slovakia, Slovenia, Spain, Sweden, Switzerland, Türkiye, UK, Ukraine.

IGO Relations Agreement of cooperation with: *African Telecommunications Union (ATU, #00482)*; *Arab Telecommunication and Information Council of Ministers (#01054)* of the League of Arab States; *Asia-Pacific Telecommunity (APT, #02064)*; *European Commission (EC, #06633)*; *Comisión Interamericana de Telecomunicaciones (CITEL, #04138)*; *International Maritime Organization (IMO, #14102)*; *Regional Commonwealth in the Field of Communications (RCC, #18767)*; *Universal Postal Union (UPU, #20682)*. [2022.10.11/XD0696/**D***]

♦ Conférence européenne des associations des industries des télécommunications (inactive)
♦ Conférence européenne des associations de musique d'église protestante (#05753)
♦ Conférence européenne des associations de radio et d'équipement électronique (inactive)
♦ Conférence européenne de l'aviation civile (#06564)
♦ Conférence européenne de biologie moléculaire (#07812)
♦ Conférence européenne des Cartes jeunes / see European Youth Card Association (#09137)
♦ Conférence européenne des comités nationaux d'éthique (#06734)

♦ Conférence Européenne des directeurs des routes (CEDR) 04603

Conference of European Directors of Roads (CEDR)

SG Av d'Auderghem 22-28, 1040 Brussels, Belgium. T. +3227712478. E-mail: information@cedr.eu.
URL: http://www.cedr.eu/

History 18 Sep 2003, Vienna (Austria). Founded as follow-up organization to *Western European Road Directors (WERD) – Directeurs des routes d'europe de l'ouest (DREO)* and *Deputy European Road Directors (DERD) – Directeurs adjoints réseau routiers européen (DARRE)*, founded in 1988. Registration: EU Transparency Register, No/ID: 485630615462-79. **Aims** Ensure a high level of common information among road directors on political and technical developments in the field of road transport in Europe; strengthen the role of national road administrations in discussions with the European Commission, relevant European and international interest groups and the industry; contribute to the ongoing debate on European transport policy and harmonization. **Structure** Presidency rotates every year among members. **Languages** Bosnian, English, French, Greek, Spanish. **Staff** 4.00 FTE, paid. Also contract staff. **Finance** Sources: members' dues. Annual budget: 600,000 EUR. **Activities** Events/meetings; knowledge management/information dissemination; standards/guidelines. **Events** *Meeting* Basel (Switzerland) 2020, *TRA – European Transport Research Arena Conference* Helsinki (Finland) 2020, *Meeting* Lucerne (Switzerland) 2020, *Meeting* Brussels (Belgium) 2019, *Workshop on Powering Future Transport* Gothenburg (Sweden) 2019.

Members Full in 29 countries and territories:
Austria, Belgium/Flemish Region, Belgium/Wallonia Region, Bulgaria, Cyprus, Czechia, Denmark, Estonia, Finland, Germany, Greece, Hungary, Iceland, Ireland, Italy, Latvia, Liechtenstein, Lithuania, Luxembourg, Malta, Netherlands, Norway, Poland, Slovenia, Spain, Sweden, Switzerland, UK.

NGO Relations Memorandum of Understanding with (2): *European Rail Infrastructure Managers (EIM, #08324)*; *World Road Association (PIARC, #21754)*. [2022.02.16/XD5431/**D**]

♦ Conférence européenne de l'Economie sociale (meeting series)
♦ Conférence européenne sur l'éducation chrétienne (#06732)
♦ Conférence européenne des enseignants de gestion (inactive)
♦ Conférence européenne des horaires des trains de marchandises (inactive)
♦ Conférence européenne des horaires des trains de voyageurs (inactive)
♦ Conférence européenne de l'industrie des condensateurs électriques (inactive)
♦ Conférence européenne sur les interactions entre le laser et la matière (meeting series)
♦ Conférence européenne de la jeunesse sportive (inactive)
♦ Conférence européenne Justitia et Pax / see Conference of European Justice and Peace Commissions (#04596)
♦ Conférence européenne des ministres des transports / see International Transport Forum (#15725)
♦ Conférence européenne des ordres et des organismes d'attributions similaires / see European Council of Medical Orders (#06830)
♦ Conférence européenne permanente des coopératives, mutualités, associations et fondations / see Social Economy Europe (#19335)
♦ Conférence européenne pour les problèmes économiques et sociaux des régions de montagne / see Euromontana (#05737)
♦ Conférence européenne sur les propriétés thermophysiques (#14484)
♦ Conférence européenne des radios chrétiennes (no recent information)
♦ Conférence européenne des régions viticoles / see Assembly of European Wine Regions (#02317)
♦ Conférence européenne de soutien et de solidarité avec le peuple sahraoui / see Coordination des comités européens de soutien au peuple sahraoui (#04824)
♦ Conférence européenne des télécommunications par satellites (inactive)
♦ Conference of Evangelical Missions / see Arbeitsgemeinschaft Evangelikaler Missionen
♦ Conférence des évêques catholiques de l'Afrique méridionale (#19838)
♦ Conférence des évêques latins du Proche-Orient / see Conférence des évêques latins dans les régions arabes (#04604)

♦ Conférence des évêques latins dans les régions arabes (CELRA) .. 04604

Conference of Latin Bishops in Arab Regions

SG Notre Dame Center, POB 20531, 9120402 Jerusalem, Israel. T. +97226288554. Fax +97226288555. E-mail: evcat@catholicchurch-holyland.com.
URL: http://catholicchurch-holyland.com/

History 7 Nov 1962, Rome (Italy), during 2nd Vatican Council. Statutes adopted 31 Mar 1967. Previously also referred to as *Conférence des évêques latins du Proche-Orient*. **Aims** Coordinate activities of Latin *Catholic* dioceses in Near-Eastern Arab countries. **Structure** Episcopal Permanent Council; Episcopal Commissions; Presidency; Headquarters located in Jerusalem (Israel). **Languages** Arabic, English, French, Italian. **Staff** 2.00 FTE, paid. **Finance** Members' dues. **Activities** Religious activities. **Events** *Annual Meeting* Rome (Italy) 2022, *Annual Meeting* Abu Dhabi (United Arab Emirates) 2021, *Plenary Assembly* Rome (Italy) 2020, *Annual Meeting* Cairo (Egypt) 2019, *Annual General Assembly* Amman (Jordan) 2018. **Publications** *Jerusalem* (6 a year).

Members Individual membership in 17 countries and territories:
Bahrain, Cyprus, Djibouti, Egypt, Iraq, Israel, Jordan, Kuwait, Lebanon, Oman, Palestine, Qatar, Saudi Arabia, Somalia, Syrian AR, United Arab Emirates, Yemen. [2022/XD9103/v/**D**]

♦ Conférence des évêques du Pacifique (#04659)

♦ Conférence des évêques de la région du Nord de l'Afrique (CERNA) 04605

Regional Episcopal Conference of North Africa

SG 1 rue Hadj Mohammed Riffai, BP 258 RP, 1001 Rabat, Morocco. T. +212537709232.
Pres address not obtained.

History 27 Feb 1967, when provisional statutes were adopted, as *Conférence épiscopale régionale du Nord de l'Afrique*. **Languages** French. **Staff** 3.00 FTE, paid. **Activities** Events/meetings. **Events** *Conference* Tangiers (Morocco) 2016, *Conference* Rome (Italy) 2015, *Meeting* Tunis (Tunisia) 1998, *Plenary Assembly* Algiers (Algeria) 1993.

Members Roman Catholic bishops in 4 countries:
Algeria, Libya, Morocco, Tunisia.

NGO Relations Member of: *International Catholic Migration Commission (ICMC, #12459)*. [2018/XE4023/**D**]

♦ Conférence des évêques du Sénégal, de la Mauritanie, du Cap-Vert et de Guinée-Bissau (no recent information)
♦ Conférence des facultés et des écoles de médecine d'Amérique latine (meeting series)
♦ Conférence des femmes africaines / see Pan African Women's Organization (#18074)
♦ Conférence des femmes d'Asie (inactive)
♦ Conférence des femmes de l'Eglise d'Asie (#01377)
♦ Conférence des femmes de l'Inde (#00737)
♦ Conference on Fetal Breathing / see Fetal and Neonatal Physiological Society (#09740)
♦ Conference of Fire Protection Associations / see Confederation of Fire Protection Associations International (#04553)
♦ Conference of Foreign Ministers of Non-Aligned Countries (meeting series)
♦ Conférence Francophone sur l'Eco-conception en Génie Electrique (meeting series)
♦ Conférence Francophone en Gestion et Ingénierie des Systèmes Hospitaliers (meeting series)
♦ Conference of French-Speaking Ethnic Communities (meeting series)
♦ Conference of French-speaking Peoples (#04640)
♦ Conference on Future Internet Technologies (meeting series)
♦ Conference of General Directors of OSJD Railways (see: #17803)
♦ Conférence générale des adventistes du septième jour (#10109)
♦ Conférence générale de la nouvelle Eglise (inactive)
♦ Conference of General Secretaries of Christian World Communions / see Conference of Secretaries of Christian World Communions (#04647)
♦ Conférence des géomètres et des fonctionnaires du cadastre du Commonwealth / see Cambridge Conference for National Mapping Organizations (#03401)
♦ Conference on Geometry: Theory and Applications (meeting series)
♦ Conférence sur la Gestion de Données – Principes, Technologies et Applications (meeting series)
♦ Conference of Governors of Southeast Asian Central Banks (meeting series)
♦ Conference of Gulf States Ministers of Agriculture (meeting series)
♦ Conférence de La Haye de droit international privé (#10850)
♦ Conference of Heads of State of Equatorial Africa (inactive)
♦ Conference of Heads of State or Government of Non-Aligned Countries (meeting series)
♦ Conférence hémisphérique des assurances / see Federación Interamericana de Empresas de Seguros (#09331)
♦ Conference on Human Tumor Cloning (meeting series)
♦ Conference on Hunting and Gathering Societies (meeting series)

♦ Conference of Iberoamerican Authorities on Informatics 04606

Conférence des autorités ibéroaméricaines en matière d'informatique – Conferencia de Autoridades Iberoamericanas de Informatica (CAIBI)

Exec Sec Ministerio de Administraciones Públicas, Maria de Molina 50 – Oficina 314-A, 28071 Madrid, Spain. T. +34915862948. Fax +34915862904.

History 1970, as *Conference of Latin American Authorities on Informatics – Conferencia de Autoridades Latinoamericanas de Informatica (CALAI)*, also referred to in English as *Conference of Latin American Data-Processing Authorities*. Present name and new statutes adopted 1994. **Aims** Promote knowledge and application of information *technology* in all the member countries; promote exchange of experiences related to informatics policies and network use; act as a consulting body for international organizations; implement international technical cooperation programmes; carry out human resources training projects. **Structure** Secretariat. **Events** *Conference* Santo Domingo (Dominican Rep) 2001, *Conference* Panama 2000, *Conference* Mexico 1999, *Conference* Portugal 1998, *Conference* Peru 1997.

Members Full in 21 countries:
Argentina, Bolivia, Brazil, Chile, Colombia, Costa Rica, Cuba, Dominican Rep, Ecuador, El Salvador, Guatemala, Honduras, Mexico, Nicaragua, Panama, Paraguay, Peru, Portugal, Spain, Uruguay, Venezuela.

Consultative Status Consultative status granted from: *UNCTAD (#20285)* (General Category). [2018/XF2366/c/**F**]

♦ Conference of Ibero-American Cinematographic Authorities (no recent information)
♦ Conference of Independent African States (inactive)
♦ Conference on Industrial Computed Tomography (meeting series)
♦ Conference of the Information Ministers of Non-Aligned Countries (meeting series)

♦ Conference of INGOs of the Council of Europe 04607

Conférence des OINGs du Conseil de l'Europe

Pres c/o Council of Europe, DG of Democracy – Div of Civil Society, Avenue de l'Europe, 67075 Strasbourg CEDEX, France. E-mail: ngo-unit@coe.int.
URL: https://www.coe.int/en/web/ingo

History 25 Jan 1977, Strasbourg (France). Founded following meetings in 1976 of a Liaison Committee of representatives of *Council of Europe (CE, #04881)* and NGOs. Change from consultative status to participatory status in 2003. Former names and other names: *Liaison Committee of NGOs enjoying Consultative Status with the Council of Europe* – former; *Commission de liaison des ONGs dotées du statut consultatif auprès du Conseil de l'Europe* – former; *Liaison Committee of NGOs enjoying Participatory Status with the Council of Europe* – former (2003); *Commission de liaison des ONGs dotées du statut participatif auprès du Conseil de l'Europe* – former (2003); *Liaison Committee of INGOs Enjoying Participatory Status with the Council of Europe* – former; *Commission de liaison des OINGs dotées du statut participatif auprès du Conseil de l'Europe* – former; *Liaison Committee of International Non-Governmental Organizations Enjoying Participatory Status with the Council of Europe* – former. **Aims** Represent INGOs with participatory status, and be the voice of organized civil society at the Council of Europe. **Structure** General Assembly; Standing Committee; Bureau; Thematic Committees; Expert Council on NGO Law; Vice-President in charge of Equality. **Languages** English, French. **Activities** Events/meetings; knowledge management/information dissemination; training/education. **Events** *Forum on the universality of human rights* Oslo (Norway) 2010, *Plenary Conference* Strasbourg (France) 2010, *Plenary Conference* Strasbourg (France) 2010, *Plenary Conference* Strasbourg (France) 2010, *Plenary Conference* Strasbourg (France) 2009. **Publications** Activity reports; Code of Good Practice; reports of Expert Council. **Members** All INGOs (currently 327) enjoying participatory status with Council of Europe. **IGO Relations** Participant in Fundamental Rights Platform of: *European Union Agency for Fundamental Rights (FRA, #08969)*. **NGO Relations** Links with all INGOs with participatory status with the Council of Europe and with civil society in Council of Europe member States. [2022.05.06/XE0001/y/**E**]

♦ Conférence des Institutions catholiques de Théologie (see: #13381)

♦ **Conférence des institutions d'enseignement et de recherche économiques et de gestion en Afrique (CIEREA)** 04608
Contact UFR SEG, Université de Ouaga II, 03 BP 7164, Ouagadougou 03, Burkina Faso. T. +22625301408. E-mail: secretariat@cierea-ptci.com.
URL: http://cierea-ptci.com/
History 13 Feb 1986, Ouagadougou, as an international association of African economic research institutes. Registered in accordance with the law of Burkina Faso, 7 Dec 1990. **Aims** Contribute to the progress and development of education and research in economic sciences and management in Africa; develop cooperation and concentration between all institutions of economic education, research and management in Africa without discrimination; elaborate and manage education and research programmes. **Structure** General Assembly. Executive Committee, comprising President, Vice-President, Executive Secretary, Treasurer, Responsables for Regional Sections, Programme Directors. **Finance** Members' dues. Other sources: subsidies; donations; funds. Budget (annual): CFA Fr 1,350 million. **Activities** Organizes conferences and seminars. Works towards the harmonization of education and research programmes. Exchanges educators, researchers and students. Runs: 'Programme de Troisième Cycle Interuniversitaire (PTCI)'; 'Programmes Doctoral Interuniversitaire de Gestion (PDIG)'. **Publications** CIEREA Bulletin (3 a year); PTCI Bulletin (3 a year). **Members** Active; Associate; Honorary. Membership countries not specified. **NGO Relations** Member of: International Center for Economic Growth (ICEG, inactive).
[2020/XF3573/F]

♦ Conférence des institutions théologiques africaines (#04580)

♦ **Conference on Interaction and Confidence-Building Measures in Asia (CICA)** 04609
Exec Dir 55/20, Mangilik Yel ave., Nur-Sultan, Kazakhstan. T. +77172576510. E-mail: s-cica@s-cica.kz.
Deputy Exec Dir address not obtained.
URL: http://www.s-cica.org/
History Founding documents: Declaration on the Principles Guiding Relations among the CICA Member States, adopted at 1st Meeting of Ministers of Foreign Affairs, 14 Sep 1999, Almaty (Kazakhstan); Almaty Act, adopted at 1st Summit Meeting, 4 Jun 2002, Almaty (Kazakhstan). Secretariat officially set up 17 Jun 2006. **Aims** Enhance cooperation towards promoting peace, security and stability in Asia through dialogue, interaction and confidence building measures. **Structure** Meeting of Heads of State and Government (every 4 years); Meeting of Ministers of Foreign Affairs (every 2 years); Committee of Senior Officials; Special Working Groups; Secretariat in Astana (Kazakhstan). **Languages** English, Russian. **Staff** 26.00 FTE, paid. **Finance** Member States' contributions. **Activities** Events/meetings; networking/liaising; training/education. **Events** Summit Nur-Sultan (Kazakhstan) 2022, Summit Dushanbe (Tajikistan) 2019, Summit Shanghai (China) 2014, Summit Istanbul (Turkey) 2010, Summit Almaty (Kazakhstan) 2006.
Members Governments of 26 countries and territories, having at least part of their territories in Asia:
Afghanistan, Azerbaijan, Bahrain, Bangladesh, Cambodia, China, Egypt, India, Iran Islamic Rep, Iraq, Israel, Jordan, Kazakhstan, Korea Rep, Kyrgyzstan, Mongolia, Pakistan, Palestine, Qatar, Russia, Tajikistan, Thailand, Türkiye, United Arab Emirates, Uzbekistan, Vietnam.
Observers: governments of 8 countries:
Belarus, Indonesia, Japan, Malaysia, Philippines, Sri Lanka, Ukraine, USA.
International observers (5):
International Organization for Migration (IOM, #14454); League of Arab States (LAS, #16420); Organization for Security and Cooperation in Europe (OSCE, #17887); Parliamentary Assembly of Turkic Speaking Countries (TURKPA).
IGO Relations Permanent Observer to: International Organization for Migration (IOM, #14454); United Nations (UN, #20515). Memorandum of Understanding with: Assembly of People of Kazakhstan (APK); Economic Cooperation Organization (ECO, #05313); Eurasian Economic Community (EurAseC, inactive); International Organization for Migration (IOM, #14454); Shanghai Cooperation Organization (SCO, #19256) Regional Anti-Terrorist Structure; United Nations Office on Drugs and Crime (UNODC, #20596). **NGO Relations** CICA Non-Governmental Forum, China.
[2022/XJ0398/y/F*]

♦ Conférence interafricaine des marchés d'assurances (#11385)

♦ **Conférence interafricaine de la prévoyance sociale (CIPRES)** 04610
Exec Sec 1 BP 1228, Lomé, Togo. T. +22822211794 – +22822212045 – +22822212085. Fax +22822214189. E-mail: cipres.org@gmail.com.
URL: http://www.lacipres.org/
History Founded on signature of a treaty, 21 Sep 1993, Abidjan (Côte d'Ivoire), by Ministers of Finance and their colleagues responsible for social providence of 14 African countries. Treaty entered into force 10 Oct 1995. Registration: Togo. **Aims** Set common rules of management; institute a control on the management of organizations responsible for social providence; harmonize legislative and lawful provisions; ensure a policy of initial and permanent training. **Structure** Council of Ministers; Monitoring Commission; Regional Social Welfare Inspection; Secretariat. **Languages** French. **Staff** 1614.00 FTE, paid. **Finance** Members' dues. Subsidies. **Activities** Events/meetings; training/education. **Events** Ordinary Session Abidjan (Côte d'Ivoire) 2014, Extraordinary Session / Extra-ordinary Session Geneva (Switzerland) 2014, Ordinary Session Brazzaville (Congo Brazzaville) 2013, Extra-ordinary Session Geneva (Switzerland) 2013, Extra-ordinary Session Geneva (Switzerland) 2012. **Publications** Le Courrier de la CIPRES (4 a year). Annual Report.
Members Full in 15 countries:
Benin, Burkina Faso, Cameroon, Central African Rep, Chad, Comoros, Congo Brazzaville, Congo DR, Côte d'Ivoire, Equatorial Guinea, Gabon, Mali, Niger, Senegal, Togo.
IGO Relations Partner of: Inter-African Conference on Insurance Markets (#11385); Organisation pour l'Harmonisation en Afrique du Droit des Affaires (OHADA, #17806); Union économique et monétaire Ouest africaine (UEMOA, #20377).
[2021/XF5618/F]

♦ Conférence interaméricaine d'assistance sociale (inactive)
♦ Conférence interaméricaine des ministres du travail (no recent information)
♦ Conférence interaméricaine pour la protection des végétaux (inactive)
♦ Conférence interaméricaine de sécurité sociale / see Inter-American Conference on Social Security (#11419)

♦ **Conference of International Broadcasters' Audience Research Services (CIBAR)** 04611
Contact c/o Deutsche Welle, Market and Media Research, Kurt-Schumacher-Str 3, 53110 Bonn, Germany. E-mail: info@cibar.org.
URL: https://www.cibar.org/
History 2006, Melbourne, VIC (Australia). **Aims** Promote a deeper understanding of audience research among International broadcasters; strengthens practives and value of audience research and audience relations activities. **Structure** Executive Committee. **Events** Annual Conference London (UK) 2019.
Members Full (17). Countries include:
Australia, Canada, France, Germany, Japan, Netherlands, Romania, UK, USA.
Radio France internationale (RFI); Radio Free Asia (RFA); Radio Free Europe/Radio Liberty (RFE/RL); Radio Veritas Asia (#18604); Trans World Radio (TWR); TV5Monde (TV5, #20269).
[2019/AA0316/y/F]

♦ Conference of International Catholic Organizations (inactive)
♦ The Conference – International Conference of Funeral Service Examining Boards (internationally oriented national body)
♦ Conférence internationale des africanistes de l'Ouest (inactive)
♦ Conférence internationale des armateurs / see International Chamber of Shipping (#12535)
♦ Conférence Internationale sur les Aspects Théoriques de la Catalyse (meeting series)
♦ Conférence internationale des associations de mutilés de guerre et anciens combattants (inactive)
♦ Conférence internationale des associations patronales catholiques / see International Christian Union of Business Executives (#12566)

♦ **Conférence internationale des barreaux de tradition juridique commune (CIB)** 04612
Acting Gen Sec 41 av de Friedland, 75008 Paris, France. T. +33188401920. Fax +33153431578. E-mail: contact@cib-avocats.org.
Exec Dir address not obtained.
URL: http://www.cib-avocats.org/
History 29 Nov 1985, Paris (France). Registration: Start date: Dec 1998, France. **Aims** Promote cooperation among bars of common legal tradition in French-speaking countries. **Structure** Board of Directors. President; Secretary General; Treasurer. **Finance** Sources: members' dues. Supported by: Organisation internationale de la Francophonie (OIF, #17809). **Events** Congress Libreville (Gabon) 2021, Congress N'Djamena (Chad) 2019, Congress Kigali (Rwanda) 2012, Colloquium / Meeting Conakry (Guinea) 2010, Congress / Meeting Kinshasa (Congo DR) 2010.
Members Bars in 48 countries and territories:
Algeria, Armenia, Belgium, Benin, Bulgaria, Burkina Faso, Burundi, Cambodia, Cameroon, Canada, Central African Rep, Chad, Comoros, Congo Brazzaville, Congo DR, Côte d'Ivoire, Djibouti, Egypt, France, Gabon, Guadeloupe, Guinea, Guinea-Bissau, Guyana, Haiti, Kosovo, Laos, Libya, Luxembourg, Madagascar, Mali, Martinique, Mauritania, Mauritius, Morocco, Niger, Romania, Rwanda, Senegal, Spain, St Barthélemy, St Martin, Switzerland, Syrian AR, Togo, Tunisia, USA, Vietnam.
NGO Relations Member of (1): World Coalition Against the Death Penalty (#21281). Instrumental in setting up (1): Avocats Sans Frontières (ASF, #03050).
[2022.10.19/XF6915/F]

♦ Conférence internationale des bassins d'essais de carènes (#15698)
♦ Conférence internationale catholique du guidisme (#12452)
♦ Conférence internationale catholique du scoutisme (#12453)
♦ Conférence internationale des contrôles d'assurance des Etats africains (inactive)
♦ Conférence internationale du court métrage (#14854)
♦ Conférence internationale du crédit agricole / see Confédération internationale du crédit agricole (#04560)
♦ Conférence internationale sur les cyclotrons et leurs applications (meeting series)
♦ Conférence internationale des directeurs et doyens des établissements d'enseignement supérieur et facultés d'expression française des sciences de l'agriculture et de l'alimentation au sein de l'UREF-AUPELF / see Conférence internationale des directeurs et doyens des établissements supérieurs d'expression française des sciences de l'agriculture et de l'alimentation (#04613)

♦ **Conférence internationale des directeurs et doyens des établissements supérieurs d'expression française des sciences de l'agriculture et de l'alimentation (CIDEFA)** 04613
Pres c/o Ecole Supérieure des Sciences Agronomiques (ESSA), BP 175, Campus Universitaire d'Ambohitsaina – Université d'Antananarivo, 101 Antananarivo, Madagascar. T. +261202222867. Fax +261202227926.
Sec c/o Centre International de Recherche-Développement sur l'Elevage en Zone Subhumide (CIRDES), 01 BP 454, Bobo Dioulasso 01, Burkina Faso.
URL: http://www.cidefa.org/
History 4 May 1990, at constituent Assembly. An institutional network of Agence universitaire de La Francophonie (AUF, #00548), specifically Université des réseaux d'expression française (UREF, inactive). Also referred to as: Conférence internationale des directeurs et doyens des établissements d'enseignement supérieur et facultés d'expression française des sciences de l'agriculture et de l'alimentation au sein de l'UREF-AUPELF. Registered in accordance with French law. Registered office at AUPELF (AGROPOLIS international, Montpellier, France). **Aims** Improve training in agricultural and alimentary sciences; promote scientific and technological research in these areas; reinforce inter-university cooperation in concerned establishments; reinforce logistical possibilities permitting a more widespread use of the French language while respecting everyone's cultural identity; facilitate exploitation of resources offered by bi- and multi-lateral technical cooperation agencies; contribute to harmonizing the needs, means and possible benefits of scientific and technological cooperation; contribute to inventorying support of actions undertaken; study and promote all forms of cooperation by developing efforts so that this structure of concertation and coordination dialogue is recognized by all international organizations; support conventions and teams of cooperation on the basis of functional and organic relationship to the proper authorities of the countries concerned. **Structure** General Assembly (every 3 years). Permanent Bureau (meets annually) of 12 members, elected by General Assembly for 3-year terms, ensuring where possible equitable geographical representation, and comprising President, 3 Vice-Presidents, Secretary and Treasurer. Composed of Directors and Deans of superior French-language establishments of agricultural and alimentary sciences. **Languages** French. **Finance** Members' dues. Subventions from AUF. Budget (annual): euro 80,000. **Events** General Assembly Dakar (Senegal) 2005, Journée d'études sur les nouvelles voies d'accès à l'information scientifique et technique Rabat (Morocco) 1995, Journées d'études 1992.
Members Schools in 28 countries:
Algeria, Belgium, Benin, Burkina Faso, Burundi, Cameroon, Canada, Central African Rep, Chad, Congo Brazzaville, Congo DR, Côte d'Ivoire, France, Gabon, Haiti, Lebanon, Madagascar, Mali, Mauritania, Morocco, Niger, Rwanda, Senegal, Switzerland, Syrian AR, Togo, Tunisia, Vietnam.
Included in the above, 1 organization listed in this Yearbook:
Agropolis International.
IGO Relations Cooperates with: CIHEAM – International Centre for Advanced Mediterranean Agronomic Studies (CIHEAM, #03927).
[2008/XF1661/y/F]

♦ **Conférence internationale des dirigeants des institutions d'enseignements supérieur de gestion d'expression française (CIDEGEF)** 04614
SG 52 rue de Hastings, 14000 Caen, France. T. +33231862175. Fax +33231382197.
URL: http://www.cidegef.refer.org/
History 5 Oct 1994, Paris (France), when statutes were adopted. An institutional network of Agence universitaire de La Francophonie (AUF, #00548), specifically Université des réseaux d'expression française (UREF, inactive). Also referred to as: Conférence internationale des dirigeants des institutions d'enseignements supérieur et de recherche de gestion d'expression française; Conférence internationale des doyens de facultés et des directeurs d'écoles de gestion. **Aims** Promote: a French-speaking management culture; mobility of individuals and ideas in the framework of inter-institutional projects; regional exchanges; circulation of information on training and research; mutual assistance in educational, research and administrative matters. **Structure** General Assembly (every 3 years). Board (meets annually), comprising 6 to 10 members, including President. Secretary General. **Finance** Members' dues. **Activities** Publishes and disseminates scientific and technical information and other publications in French; creates links with other international French-speaking associations; organizes seminars, colloquia, summer school and study days; supports training of teachers and librarians. **Events** Colloque international / Meeting Liège (Belgium) 2007, Rencontres internationales sur la démocratie et le management local Douala (Cameroon) 2006, Séminaire Saint Louis (Senegal) 2006, Séminaire Alexandria (Egypt) 2005, Assemblée générale Beirut (Lebanon) 2004.
Members Universities, higher education establishments and research establishments in 9 countries:
Canada, France, Lebanon, Mauritius, Morocco, Romania, Senegal, Switzerland, Vietnam.
[2016/XF4057/F]

♦ Conférence internationale des dirigeants des institutions d'enseignements supérieur et de recherche de gestion d'expression française / see Conférence internationale des dirigeants des institutions d'enseignements supérieur de gestion d'expression française (#04614)
♦ Conférence internationale des doyens chirurgiens dentistes de langue partiellement ou totalement française / see Conférence internationale des doyens des facultés de chirurgie dentaire d'expression totalement ou partiellement française (#04615)
♦ Conférence internationale des doyens des facultés de chirurgie dentaire d'expression française / see Conférence internationale des doyens des facultés de chirurgie dentaire d'expression totalement ou partiellement française (#04615)

Conférence internationale doyens
04615
alphabetic sequence excludes
For the complete listing, see Yearbook Online at

♦ Conférence internationale des doyens des facultés de chirurgie dentaire d'expression totalement ou partiellement française (CIDCDF) 04615

Main Office MDEN, Ave Hippocrate 10, bte B2-5721, 1200 Brussels, Belgium.
Registered Office 4 Place de la Sorbonne, 75005 Paris, France.
URL: http://cid-cdf.com/

History 1992, as an institutional network of *Agence universitaire de La Francophonie (AUF, #00548)*, specifically *Université des réseaux d'expression française (UREF, inactive)*. Also referred to as *Conférence internationale des doyens des facultés de chirurgie dentaire d'expression française* and as *Conférence internationale des doyens chirurgiens dentistes de langue partiellement ou totalement française*. **Aims** Promote the *odontological* training and research in the *Francophone* countries. **Structure** Board, consisting of President, 2 Vice-Presidents, Secretary-Treasurer and 6 members. **Events** *General Assembly* Beirut (Lebanon) 1995. **NGO Relations** Member of: *Administration universitaire francophone et européenne en médecine et odontologie (AUFEMO, #00115)*; *Conférence Maghrébine des Responsables des Établissements d'Enseignement Supérieur (COMARES, #04626)*. [2015/XF3872/v/F]

- ♦ Conférence internationale des doyens de facultés et des directeurs d'écoles de gestion / see Conférence internationale des dirigeants des institutions d'enseignements supérieur de gestion d'expression française (#04614)

♦ Conférence internationale des doyens des facultés de médecine d'expression française (CIDMEF) 04616

International Conference of Deans of French-Speaking Faculties of Medicine
SG Fac de Médicine, 10 bd Tonnellé, BP 3223, 37032 Tours CEDEX 1, France.
URL: http://www.cidmef.u-bordeaux2.fr/

History Jan 1981, Abidjan (Côte d'Ivoire), as an institutional network of *Agence universitaire de La Francophonie (AUF, #00548)*, specifically *Université des réseaux d'expression française (UREF, inactive)*. Registered in accordance with French law. **Aims** Improve *medical* and *public health* training; promote medical research and public health research; strengthen *inter-university* medical cooperation. **Structure** General Assembly (every 3 years). Board of Directors, consisting of not less than 10 and not more than 20 members. Officers: President and 3 Vice-President. Networks (6): *Administration universitaire francophone et européenne en médecine et odontologie (AUFEMO, #00115)*; *French Language Network for International Clinical Epidemiology (#09992)*; *Groupe des radiologistes enseignants d'expression française (GREF, #10768)*; Réseau d'appui spécialisé en dermatologie; *Réseau des enseignants francophones de thérapeutique et pharmacologie (REFTEP, no recent information)*; *Réseau francophone d'HTA (RFHTA, no recent information)*. **Languages** French. **Events** *Plenary Meeting* Algiers (Algeria) 2009, *Journées universitaires francophones de pédagogie médicale* Nancy (France) 2003, *Plenary Meeting* Phnom Penh (Cambodia) 2003, *Journées universitaires francophones de pédagogie médicale* Ouagadougou (Burkina Faso) 2001, *Plenary Meeting* Tours (France) 2001. **Publications** *Revue d'éducation médicale* (4 a year).
Members Deans in 38 countries and territories:
Albania, Algeria, Angola, Belgium (Francophone), Benin, Bulgaria, Burkina Faso, Burundi, Cambodia, Cameroon, Canada, Central African Rep, Chad, Congo Brazzaville, Congo DR, Côte d'Ivoire, France, Gabon, Guinea, Haiti, Laos, Lebanon, Madagascar, Mali, Mauritania, Mauritius, Moldova, Morocco, Niger, North Macedonia, Québec, Romania, Rwanda, Senegal, Switzerland (Francophone), Togo, Tunisia, Vietnam. [2009/XF2725/v/F]

♦ Conférence internationale des doyens des facultés de pharmacie d'expression française (CIDPHARMEF) 04617

Pres Fac de Pharmacie, Université Laval, Pavillon Ferdinand-Vandry, Local 2698, 1050 avenue de la Médecine, Québec QC G1V 0A6, Canada. T. +14186562131. Fax +14186562305.
Registered Office Fac de Pharmacie, 8 ave Rockefeller, 69373 Lyon CEDEX 08, France.
URL: http://cidpharmef.org/

History 2002, Bordeaux (France). Registered in accordance with French law. **Structure** General Assembly. **Events** *Conference* Cluj-Napoca (Romania) 2015, *Conference* Rabat (Morocco) 2013, *Conference* Beirut (Lebanon) 2012, *Conference* Lyon (France) 2011, *Conference* Ouagadougou (Burkina Faso) 2010. **NGO Relations** Institutional network member of *Agence universitaire de La Francophonie (AUF, #00548)*. [2019/XM1550/E]

- ♦ Conférence internationale de l'éducation (meeting series)
- ♦ Conférence internationale sur l'éducation des adultes (meeting series)
- ♦ Conférence internationale sur l'électrostatique (meeting series)
- ♦ Conférence internationale des engrais chimiques / see Centre international scientifique des fertilisants (#03767)
- ♦ Conférence internationale pour l'enseignement de l'histoire (inactive)
- ♦ Conférence internationale pour l'enseignement universitaire des relations publiques (inactive)
- ♦ Conférence internationale pour l'étude et l'encouragement de la philanthropie / see International Standing Conference on Philanthropy (#15600)
- ♦ Conférence internationale des évêques vieux-catholiques (#14403)
- ♦ Conférence internationale des experts des assurances sociales (inactive)

♦ Conférence internationale des facultés de droit ayant en commun l'usage du français (CIFDUF) 04618

SG CTHDIP Univ Toulouse, 1 Capitole, 2 rue du Doyen-Gabriel-Marty, 31042 Toulouse CEDEX 9, France.
Pres Faculté de droit, Univ de Toulouse I, Sciences Sociales, place Anatole France, 31042 Toulouse CEDEX, France. T. +33161633526. Fax +33161633898.
URL: http://www.cifduf.refer.org/

History Apr 1991. An institutional network of *Agence universitaire de La Francophonie (AUF, #00548)*, specifically *Université des réseaux d'expression française (UREF, inactive)*. **Aims** Contribute to the development of higher education in Francophone countries in the juridical, political, economic and management fields. **Structure** Board, consisting of President, 3 Vice-Presidents and 6 members. **Activities** Setting up a data bank on legal education in French speaking countries. **Events** *Colloque sur la diversité culturelle* Paris (France) 2004.
Members Full (40) in 18 countries:
Algeria, Belgium, Benin, Burkina Faso, Cambodia, Congo Brazzaville, Congo DR, Côte d'Ivoire, France, Gabon, Lebanon, Madagascar, Mauritius, Morocco, Niger, Senegal, Sweden, Tunisia.
NGO Relations Instrumental in setting up: *Institut pour le développement de l'enseignement supérieur francophone, Bordeaux (IDESUF)*. [2011.10.04/XF0612/F]

- ♦ Conférence internationale sur les fondements scientifiques des services de santé (meeting series)

♦ Conférence internationale des formations d'ingénieurs et de techniciens d'expression française (CITEF) 04619

Pres 4 place de la Sorbonne, 75005 Paris, France. T. +33555434416.
URL: http://www.reseau-citef.org/

History Apr 1986, Rabat (Morocco). Activities commenced Jan 1988. Also referred to as *Conférence internationale des responsables d'établissements formant des techniciens supérieurs et ingénieurs d'expression française*. An institutional network member of *Agence universitaire de La Francophonie (AUF, #00548)* and its *Université des réseaux d'expression française (UREF, inactive)*. **Events** *General Assembly* Bayreuth (Germany) 2002, *Assemblée générale / General Assembly* Phnom Penh (Cambodia) 1996, *Joint meeting* Tunis (Tunisia) 1992. **Members** Membership countries not specified. [2019/XF2153/F]

- ♦ Conférence internationale du goudron / see International Tar Association (#15655)
- ♦ Conférence internationale du goudron pour routes / see International Tar Association (#15655)
- ♦ Conférence internationale des grands réseaux électriques / see International Council on Large Electric Systems (#13040)
- ♦ Conférence internationale des grands réseaux électriques à haute tension / see International Council on Large Electric Systems (#13040)
- ♦ Conférence internationale sur la guerre politique (meeting series)
- ♦ Conférence internationale des historiennes et historiens du mouvement ouvrier / see International Conference of Labour and Social History (#12881)
- ♦ Conférence internationale des historiens des mouvements ouvriers / see International Conference of Labour and Social History (#12881)
- ♦ Conférence internationale sur l'immunofluorescence, immunoenzymes et techniques voisines (meeting series)
- ♦ Conférence internationale des industries de procédés (meeting series)
- ♦ Conférence internationale des jeunes agents des oeuvres sociales (inactive)
- ♦ Conférence internationale de liaison entre producteurs d'énergie électrique (inactive)
- ♦ Conférence internationale des ligues sociales d'acheteurs (inactive)
- ♦ Conférence internationale sur l'urbanisation durable au Canada, en Chine et en Afrique (#12876)
- ♦ Conférence internationale des matières premières (inactive)
- ♦ Conférence internationale sur la Mer du Nord (meeting series)
- ♦ Conférence internationale de la mesure / see International Measurement Confederation (#14124)
- ♦ Conférence internationale sur la métrologie et les propriétés de surface (meeting series)
- ♦ Conférence Internationale sur la Modélisation par Bilans de Population (meeting series)
- ♦ Conférence internationale de la mutualité et des assurances sociales / see International Social Security Association (#14885)
- ♦ Conférence internationale des ONG (#12883)
- ♦ Conférence internationale des ordres et des organismes d'attributions similaires / see European Council of Medical Orders (#06830)

♦ Conférence internationale des ordres de pharmaciens francophones (CIOPF) 04620

Pres 4 av Ruysdaël, 75379 Paris CEDEX 08, France. T. +33156213532. Fax +33156213479. E-mail: sg-international@ordre.pharmacien.fr – contact@ciopf.org.
URL: http://www.ciopf.org/

History 4 Nov 1994, Paris (France). **Aims** Facilitate: *professional* contacts among Francophone pharmacists, while respecting professional ethics and deontology; mutual enrichment of participants through a better knowledge of working conditions and professional ethics in each country; development of French culture and language; collating of results of campaigns launched in various French-speaking countries; the role of Francophone pharmacists in improving public health. **Structure** General Assembly (annual); Executive Committee. **Languages** French. **Finance** Members' dues. **Events** *Annual General Assembly* Paris (France) 2014, *Annual General Assembly* Paris (France) 2013, *Annual General Assembly* Paris (France) 2012, *Annual General Assembly* Paris (France) 2011, *Annual General Assembly* Paris (France) 2010.
Members Councils or associations in 33 countries and territories:
Algeria, Belgium, Benin, Burkina Faso, Burundi, Cambodia, Cameroon, Central African Rep, Chad, Comoros, Congo Brazzaville, Congo DR, Côte d'Ivoire, France, Gabon, Guinea, Haiti, Lebanon, Madagascar, Mali, Mauritania, Monaco, Morocco, New Caledonia, Niger, Polynesia Fr, Québec, Senegal, Switzerland, Syrian AR, Togo, Tunisia, Vietnam. [2014.11.21/XF4239/F]

- ♦ Conférence internationale pour la perception et la cognition musicale (meeting series)
- ♦ Conférence internationale permanente de directeurs d'instituts universitaires pour la formation de traducteurs et d'interprètes / see Conférence internationale permanente d'instituts universitaires de traducteurs et interprètes (#04621)
- ♦ Conférence internationale permanente des inspections centrales et générales de l'éducation / see Standing International Conference of Inspectorates (#19963)
- ♦ Conférence internationale permanente des inspections de l'éducation (#19963)

♦ Conférence internationale permanente d'instituts universitaires de traducteurs et interprètes (CIUTI) 04621

SG KU Leuven Campus Brussel, Warmoesberg 26, 1000 Brussels, Belgium.
URL: http://www.ciuti.org/

History 1961, Heidelberg (Germany). Founded following a first contact meeting held in 1960, Basel (Switzerland). Former names and other names: *Conférence internationale permanente de directeurs d'instituts universitaires pour la formation de traducteurs et d'interprètes* – former (1961). Registration: Start date: 1994, Belgium. **Aims** Offer assistance for curriculum development; provide opportunities for research cooperation; offer an international forum for quality enhancement and assurance and for the elaboration of quality standards. **Structure** General Assembly (annual); Administrative Council. **Languages** English, French. **Staff** None. **Finance** Members' dues. **Activities** Events/meetings; training/education; awards/prizes/competitions. **Events** *Conference* Lima (Peru) 2022, *Annual General Assembly* Madrid (Spain) 2014, *Annual Forum* Geneva (Switzerland) 2013, *Annual General Assembly* Madrid (Spain) 2013, *Annual General Assembly* Antwerp (Belgium) 2012. **Publications** Forum proceedings.
Members University Institutes (53) in 23 countries:
Australia, Austria, Belarus, Belgium, Canada, China, Czechia, Denmark, France, Germany, Italy, Korea Rep, Lebanon, Norway, Peru, Poland, Russia, Slovenia, Spain, Switzerland, Türkiye, UK, USA.
NGO Relations Member of: *European Language Council (ELC, #07646)*; *International Federation of Translators (#13574)*. Associate member of: *European Legal Interpreters and Translators Association (EULITA, #07678)*. [2021/XD4555/F]

- ♦ Conférence internationale permanente pour la philanthropie (#15600)
- ♦ Conférence internationale de police (inactive)
- ♦ Conférence internationale des producteurs de benzol (inactive)
- ♦ Conférence internationale sur la région des Grands Lacs (#12880)
- ♦ Conférence internationale des responsables d'établissements formant des techniciens supérieurs et ingénieurs d'expression française / see Conférence internationale des formations d'ingénieurs et de techniciens d'expression française (#04619)
- ♦ Conférence internationale des responsables de la formation des fonctionnaires supérieurs (meeting series)

♦ Conférence internationale des responsables des universités et instituts à dominante scientifique et technique d'expression française (CIRUISEF) 04622

Pres 118 route de Narbonne, 31062 Toulouse CEDEX 9, France.
URL: http://www.ciruisef.com/

History 1988, Bordeaux (France). An institutional network member of *Agence universitaire de La Francophonie (AUF, #00548)*. Current statutes adopted 21 Mar 2003, Dakar (Senegal). Former names and other names: *Conférence internationale des responsables des universités et instituts scientifiques et techniques d'expression française* – alias; *Conférence internationale des responsables des universités et instituts scientifiques d'expression française* – alias. Registration: France. **Aims** Disseminate information among scientific member bodies; promote cooperation in the field of research carried out by deans; promote training activities. **Structure** General Assembly. Officers: President; 2 Vice-Presidents; Secretary; Treasurer. **Languages** French. **Finance** Members' dues. **Activities** Organizes: Colloquia; scientific symposia. **Events** *Colloquium* 2020, *Seminar* Tunisia 2019, *Colloquium* Abidjan (Côte d'Ivoire) 2017, *Colloquium* Marseille (France) 2016, *Colloquium* Rabat (Morocco) 2014. **Publications** *La Lettre de la CIRUISEF* (2 a year). *La structuration de la recherche scientifique: fragmentation ou intégration?* (2011) by E Garnier-Zarli; *Travailler en interdisciplinarité dans la Recherche en Sciences et Technologie* (2011) by E Garnier-Zarli; *Le Doctorat scientifique dans le monde francophone* (2010) by E Garnier-Zarli; *La Licence scientifique dans l'espace francophone: essai de référentiel de connaissances et compétences* by E Garnier-Zarli. Colloquium proceedings.
Members Departments of Science (over 40) in 25 countries:
Algeria, Belgium, Benin, Burundi, Cameroon, Canada, Central African Rep, Chad, Congo Brazzaville, Congo DR, Côte d'Ivoire, France, Gabon, Haiti, Lebanon, Luxembourg, Madagascar, Mali, Morocco, Niger, Rwanda, Senegal, Switzerland, Syrian AR, Tunisia.
IGO Relations *School of Mining Industry and Geology (#19132)*. **NGO Relations** Universities worldwide. [2020/XF1649/c/F]

♦ Conférence internationale des responsables des universités et instituts scientifiques d'expression française / see Conférence internationale des responsables des universités et instituts à dominante scientifique et technique d'expression française (#04622)
♦ Conférence internationale des responsables des universités et instituts scientifiques et techniques d'expression française / see Conférence internationale des responsables des universités et instituts à dominante scientifique et technique d'expression française (#04622)
♦ Conférence internationale des sciences sociales et de la médecine (meeting series)
♦ Conférence internationale du scoutisme catholique / see International Catholic Conference of Scouting (#12453)
♦ Conférence internationale de sociologie des religions / see International Society for the Sociology of Religions (#15451)
♦ Conférence internationale sur les systèmes et les technologies de l'enveloppe du bâtiment (meeting series)
♦ Conférence internationale des unions nationales de sociétés mutuelles et de caisses d'assurance-maladie / see International Social Security Association (#14885)
♦ Conférence internationale des unions nationales de sociétés mutuelles et de caisses d'assurance-maladie (inactive)
♦ Conférence internationale pour l'unité technique des chemins de fer (inactive)
♦ Conférence internationale des universités (inactive)
♦ Conference of Internationally-Minded Schools (inactive)
♦ Conference of International Non-Governmental Organizations in Consultative Relations – Categories A and B – with UNESCO / see International Conference of NGOs (#12883)
♦ Conference of International Non-Governmental Organizations in Consultative Relations with UNESCO / see International Conference of NGOs (#12883)
♦ Conference of International Non-Governmental Organizations in Official Relations with UNESCO / see International Conference of NGOs (#12883)
♦ Conférence international sur la science nucléaire dans la matière condensée (meeting series)
♦ Conférence interparlementaire / see Inter-Parliamentary Union (#15961)

♦ Conference Interpreters Asia Pacific (CIAP) 04623

Contact Promsak Mansion 405, 5 soi Promsak, Bangkok, 10110, Thailand. T. +33620881250. E-mail: kobine@ciap.net – info@ciap.net.
URL: http://www.ciap.net/

History 1990. **Aims** Promote communication between people of different languages by organizing and providing teams of professional conference interpreters. **Structure** Loose network. **Languages** Arabic, Chinese, English, French, German, Indonesian, Japanese, Korean, Russian, Spanish, Thai, Vietnamese. All main Asian and Western languages. **Staff** 0.50 FTE, voluntary. **Finance** Sources: members' dues. **Activities** Events/meetings; guidance/assistance/consulting. **Publications** *InterpretAsia* (annual).
Members Individuals in 8 countries and territories:
Australia, China, Korea Rep, Malaysia, New Zealand, Singapore, Taiwan, Thailand. [2021.02.17/XD7841/**D**]

♦ Conférence interuniversitaire pour les sciences agronomiques et les disciplines connexes en Europe / see Association for European Life Science Universities (#02519)
♦ Conference of Islamic Kings and Heads of State and Government / see Islamic Summit of Kings and Heads of States and Governments (#16053)
♦ Conférence des Jésuites d'Afrique et Madagascar (#16098)
♦ Conference of Jesuit Provincials in Latin America (#04658)

♦ Conference on Jewish Material Claims Against Germany (Claims Conference) 04624

Contact 1359 Broadway, Room 2000, New York NY 10018, USA. T. +16465369100. E-mail: info@claimscon.org.
Israel Contact Ha'arbaa Street 8, 64739 Tel Aviv, Israel. T. +97235194400. Fax +97235100906. E-mail: infodesk@claimscon.org.
Germany Contact Sophienstrasse 26, 60487 Frankfurt-Main, Germany. Fax +496997070811. E-mail: info@claims-frankfurt.de.
URL: http://www.claimscon.org/

History Founded 1951. **Aims** Represent world Jewry in negotiations with German and Austrian governments and other entities; distribute funds for victims of Nazi persecution; recover Jewish property and allocate funds to institutions that provide social welfare services to Holocaust survivors. **Publications** Annual Report. **NGO Relations** Member of: *World Jewish Restitution Organization (WJRO, #21601).* [2015/XF2099/**F**]

♦ Conférence des Jurisdictions Constitutionelles Africaines (#04585)
♦ Conference of Kings and Heads of State and Governments of Islamic Countries / see Islamic Summit of Kings and Heads of States and Governments (#16053)
♦ Conference on Lasers in the Conservation of Artworks (meeting series)
♦ Conference of Latin American Authorities on Informatics / see Conference of Iberoamerican Authorities on Informatics (#04606)
♦ Conference of Latin American Data-Processing Authorities / see Conference of Iberoamerican Authorities on Informatics (#04606)
♦ Conference of Latin American Faculties and Schools of Medicine (meeting series)

♦ Conference of Latin American Geography (CLAG) 04625

Conferencia de Geografía Latinoamericana

Exec Dir c/o Cal Poly – Geography Dept, Building 5 – 150, 3801 West Temple Ave, Pomona CA 91768, USA. E-mail: communications@clagscholar.org – executive.director@clagscholar.org.
URL: http://clagscholar.org/

History 1970. Founded as the first independent regional specialist group of the *Association of American Geographers (AAG).* Former names and other names: *Conference of LatinAmericanist Geographers (CLAG)* – former; *Conferencia de Geógrafos Latinoamericanistas* – former; *Asociación de Geógrafos Latinoamericanistas* – former. **Aims** Foster geographic education and research in Latin America; facilitate communication among individuals, universities and organizations interested in Latin America; promote interest in Latin America. **Structure** Board of Directors. **Languages** English, French, Portuguese, Spanish. **Staff** 0.50 FTE, paid; 1.00 FTE, voluntary. **Finance** Sources: members' dues. Other sources: income generated by Project MUSE downloads. **Activities** Events/meetings. **Events** *Conference* Tucson, AZ (USA) 2022, *Conference* Antigua (Guatemala) 2020, *Conference* San José (Costa Rica) 2018, *Conference* New Orleans, LA (USA) 2017, *All aspects of geographical analysis* Fortaleza (Brazil) 2015. **Publications** *Journal of Latin American Geography* (3 a year); *CLAG Newsletter* (2 a year). Several irregular special editions.
Members Individuals and organizations in 26 countries and territories:
Argentina, Austria, Bolivia, Brazil, Canada, Chile, Colombia, Costa Rica, Dominican Rep, Ecuador, France, Germany, Guatemala, Honduras, Italy, Jamaica, Mexico, Norway, Peru, Portugal, Puerto Rico, Spain, Sweden, UK, USA, Venezuela. [2021.08.31/XF0520/c/**F**]

♦ Conference on Latin American History (internationally oriented national body)
♦ Conference of LatinAmericanist Geographers / see Conference of Latin American Geography (#04625)
♦ Conference of Latin Bishops in Arab Regions (#04604)
♦ Conference of Local Authorities of Europe / see Congress of Local and Regional Authorities of the Council of Europe (#04677)
♦ Conference of Local and Regional Authorities of Europe / see Congress of Local and Regional Authorities of the Council of Europe (#04677)

♦ Conférence Maghrébine des Responsables des Établissements d'Enseignement Supérieur (COMARES) 04626

Secretariat BP 8962 – Agdal, 10100 Rabat, Morocco. T. +212537683289. E-mail: maghreb@auf.org.
Street Address Annexe Souissi II Fac des Sciences, Univ Mohammed V-Agdal, Rabat, Morocco.
URL: http://www.comares.org/

History Proposed by Maghreb Bureau of *Agence universitaire de La Francophonie (AUF, #00548)*, Jun 2012. Formally set up 2 Sep 2013. Statutes and internal rules adopted, 10 Feb 2014, Tunis (Tunisia). **Structure** General Assembly; Board. **Activities** Awards/prizes/competitions. **Events** *Assemblée Générale* Oran (Algeria) 2016, *Assemblée Généraleérale* Marrakech (Morocco) 2015, *Assemblée Générale* Tunis (Tunisia) 2014.
Members Educational institutes in 3 countries:
Algeria, Morocco, Tunisia.
Included in the above, 1 institute listed in this Yearbook:
Conférence internationale des doyens des facultés de chirurgie dentaire d'expression totalement ou partiellement française (CIDCDF, #04615).
IGO Relations *Agence universitaire de La Francophonie (AUF, #00548).* [2016/XM4723/**D**]

♦ Conference of Major Superiors of Africa and Madagascar (COMSAM) 04627

Conférence continentale des supérieurs-es majeurs-es pour l'Afrique et Madagascar (COSMAM)

Main Office PO Box 14091, Yaoundé, Cameroon.

History 8 May 2005, Cotonou (Benin). **Structure** Bureau, comprising President, Vice-President and 5 further members; General Assembly.
Members in 19 countries:
Algeria, Angola, Benin, Burkina Faso, Cameroon, Chad, Congo Brazzaville, Congo DR, Côte d'Ivoire, Ghana, Madagascar, Mali, Niger, Nigeria, Senegal, Sierra Leone, South Africa, Tunisia, Uganda. [2018/XM1428/**F**]

♦ Conference of Major Superiors of the Antilles (inactive)
♦ Conference of Major Superiors of the Assistancy of Africa and Madagascar / see Jesuit Conference of Africa and Madagascar (#16098)
♦ Conférence maritime baltique et internationale / see BIMCO (#03236)
♦ Conférence médicale du Commonwealth (meeting series)

♦ Conference on Mediterranean and European Linguistic Anthropology (COMELA) 04628

Head of Communications Nat'l and Kapodistrian Univ of Athens, Panepistimiou 30, 106 79 Athens, Greece. E-mail: comela2021@comela.me.
Main Website: https://comela.me/

History 2016, Australia. Registration: No/ID: 42937047321, Start date: 2016, Australia. **Aims** Redefine scholarship on Mediterranean and European language and society. **Structure** Directorship; Communications; Administration; Scientific Committee. **Languages** English. **Staff** 4.00 FTE, paid; 10.00 FTE, voluntary. **Finance** Sources: contributions; grants; meeting proceeds. Annual budget: 55,000 EUR. **Activities** Advocacy/lobbying/activism; awards/prizes/competitions; awareness raising; capacity building; events/meetings; financial and/or material support; guidance/assistance/consulting; knowledge management/information dissemination; networking/liaising; publishing activities; research/documentation; training/education. **Events** *Annual Conference* Athens (Greece) 2022, *Annual Conference* Athens (Greece) 2021, *Annual Conference* Athens (Greece) 2020.
Members Full (66) in 27 countries and territories:
Australia, Cambodia, China, Egypt, Greece, Hong Kong, India, Indonesia, Ireland, Italy, Japan, Korea Rep, Malaysia, Netherlands, Pakistan, Philippines, Qatar, Romania, Saudi Arabia, Singapore, Spain, Sweden, Taiwan, Thailand, UK, USA, Vietnam.
Individuals (122) in 25 countries and territories:
Argentina, Australia, Belgium, Cambodia, Canada, Cyprus, France, Greece, Hong Kong, India, Italy, Japan, Malaysia, Netherlands, Portugal, Qatar, Romania, Saudi Arabia, Singapore, Sweden, Switzerland, Taiwan, Thailand, UK, USA, Vietnam.
NGO Relations Constitutes *Global Network in Linguistic Anthropology*, together with *Global Council for Anthropological Linguistics (GLOCAL, #10310), South and Central American Assembly on Linguistic Anthropology (SCAALA, #19752), Conference on Oceanian Linguistic Anthropology (COOLA, #04636), Middle Eastern Association of Linguistic Anthropology (MEALA, #16760)* and *African Assembly of Linguistic Anthropology (AFALA, #00204).* [2020.04.29/XM8714/c/**F**]

♦ Conference of Members of Parliament from the NATO Member Countries / see NATO Parliamentary Assembly (#16946)
♦ Conférence des membres des Parlements des pays de l'OTAN / see NATO Parliamentary Assembly (#16946)
♦ Conférence mennonite mondiale (#16713)
♦ Conference on Metal Toxicity and Carcinogenesis (meeting series)

♦ The Conference of the Methodist Church in the Caribbean and the Americas (MCCA) 04629

La Conférence de l'Eglise Méthodiste de la Caraïbe et les Amériques La Conferencia de la Iglesia Metodista en el Caribe y las Americas – De Conferentie van de Methodische Kerk en het Caribisch Gebied, Midden en Zuid Amerika

Connexional Pres Scott's Hill, Belmont, PO Box 9, St John's, St John, Antigua-Barbuda. T. +12684605777. Fax +12684605776.
URL: http://www.mccalive.org/

History Started 1760 as a mission of British Methodism. Became autonomous May 1967, Antigua. **Aims** Spread the good news of Jesus Christ throughout the world in creative and meaningful ways. **Structure** Connexional Conference (every 3 years), comprises Representative and Ministerial Sessions and includes President of Conference (MCCA Executive Head), Vice-President, Treasurer, Secretary and elected representatives of the 8 Districts. Connexional Council (meets annually between Conferences). District conferences convened at least annually. **Languages** Creoles and pidgins, Dutch, English, French, Papiamento, Spanish. **Staff** Superannuated: 39 Presbyters; 8 Deacons. Active work: 183 Presbyters; 18 Deacons. Total Ministers: 248. **Finance** Contributions from member churches and specific project grants from various bodies. **Activities** Sponsors and supports: 3 clinics; 2 deaconess centres; an agricultural station; theological seminary; 11 high schools; 9 vocational schools; 41 primary schools; *'Gilbert Ecumenical Centre'* – residential centre for regional and international groups holding seminars, conferences and workshops. **Events** *Conference / Connexional Conference* Grand Turk Is (Turks-Caicos) 2012, *Conference / Connexional Conference* Barbados 2009, *Annual conference / Connexional Conference* Antigua-Barbuda 2006, *Conference / Connexional Conference* Jamaica 2003, *Annual conference / Connexional Conference* Belize City (Belize) 2000. **Publications** *MCCA Year Book.* Conference Minutes. **Members** Communicants (56,751); In training (10,809); Adherents (over 300,000), organized into 8 Districts in 29 countries. Membership countries not specified. **NGO Relations** Branch of: *World Methodist Council (WMC, #21650).* Member of: *Caribbean Conference of Churches (CCC, #03479); Consejo de Iglesias Evangélicas Metodistas de América Latina y el Caribe (CIEMAL, #04714); World Council of Churches (WCC, #21320).* [2012.08.30/XD4265/**F**]

♦ Conference on Methods and Applications in Fluorescence (meeting series)
♦ Conference of the Middle European Cooperation in Statistical Physics (meeting series)
♦ Conférence ministérielle africaine sur l'environnement (#00374)
♦ Conférence Ministérielle Africaine sur la Météorologie (#00375)
♦ Conférence Ministérielle sur la Coopération Halieutique entre les Etats Africains Riverains de l'Océan Atlantique (#16816)

♦ Conférence ministérielle de la Francophonie (CMF) 04630

Contact c/o Organisation internationale de la francophonie, 19-21 av Bosquet, 75007 Paris, France. T. +33144373300. Fax +33145791498.
URL: http://www.francophonie.org/

History 21 Nov 1991, Paris (France). A common organ of the Sommet and of *Organisation internationale de la Francophonie (OIF, #17809)* (formerly *Agence intergouvernementale de La Francophonie (inactive)*), being "General Conference" of the latter. Set up by resolution of *Conférence au sommet des chefs d'Etat et de gouvernement des pays ayant le français en partage (Sommet de la Francophonie, #04648).* First conference: 7-9 Dec 1992, Paris. **Aims** Ensure political continuity between the Summits. **Structure** Comprises ministers of foreign affairs or of the French-speaking community of governments and States represented in the *'Sommet francophone'*, meets annually. President is minister representing the country having held the previous summit and responsible for the follow-up. President of *Conseil permanent de la Francophonie (CPF,*

#04697) participates fully and acts as consultant at all meetings. Special links with: *Conférence des ministres de l'éducation des Etats et gouvernements de la Francophonie (CONFEMEN, #04632)*. **Activities** Acting on decisions of the Summit: assures political follow-up and preparation of Francophone Summits; oversees coordination; is responsible for programmes and budgets. **Events** *Session* Antananarivo (Madagascar) 2016, *Session* Paris (France) 2013, *Session* Kinshasa (Congo DR) 2012, *Session* Paris (France) 2011, *Session* Montreux (Switzerland) 2010. **IGO Relations** Instrumental in setting up: *Institut de la Francophonie numérique (IFN, inactive)*. **NGO Relations** *Assemblée parlementaire de la Francophonie (APF, #02312)*. Instrumental in setting up: *Comité de liaison de la Conférence biennale des organisations non gouvernementales oeuvrant dans l'espace francophone (inactive)*; *Université virtuelle francophone (UVF, inactive)*. [2021/XF5124/c/**F***]

♦ Conférence Ministérielle pour la protection des forêts en Europe (#16817)

♦ Conference of Ministers of Agriculture of West and Central Africa (CMA/WCA) 04631

Conférence des Ministres de l'Agriculture de l'Afrique de l'Ouest et du Centre (CMA/AOC)

Coordinator 7 Avenue Bourguiba prolongé, BP 15799 Dakar, Senegal. T. +221338691190. Fax +221338691193.

History Mar 1991, Dakar (Senegal). **Aims** Promote and develop intra-regional exchanges by creating a regional market for agricultural products; improve competitiveness and harmonize agricultural policy at the regional level. **Structure** Conference of Ministers (every 2 years). Bureau, consisting of 10 ministers in charge of cooperation. Technical Committee. **Languages** English, French. **Staff** 13.00 FTE, paid. **Finance** Support from governments of France, UK, Canada, the European Union and the following international organizations: *African Development Bank (ADB, #00283)*; *International Bank for Reconstruction and Development (IBRD, #12317)*; *International Fund for Agricultural Development (IFAD, #13692)*; *Centre technique de coopération agricole et rurale (CTA, inactive)*; *United States Agency for International Development (USAID)*. **Activities** Biennial Programme (2010-2012) comprises 12 special fields of activity. Multi Donor Child Trust Fund for CAADP Pillar II activities. **Events** *Atelier sur l'appui aux pays africains face aux futures négociations internationales* Dakar (Senegal) 2000, *Biennial ministers conference* Abidjan (Côte d'Ivoire) 1999, *Meeting* Abidjan (Côte d'Ivoire) 1999, *Meeting* Dakar (Senegal) 1998. **Publications** *Integration* (4 a year). *Agriveil*; *Agrovision*.

Members Governments of 20 countries:
Benin, Burkina Faso, Cameroon, Cape Verde, Central African Rep, Chad, Congo Brazzaville, Côte d'Ivoire, Equatorial Guinea, Gabon, Gambia, Ghana, Guinea, Guinea-Bissau, Mali, Mauritania, Niger, Nigeria, Senegal, Togo. [2011.08.16/XF4577/**F***]

♦ Conference of Ministers of Economic Affairs of the Maghreb Countries (meeting series)
♦ Conference of Ministers of Education of African States (meeting series)
♦ Conference of Ministers of Education in French Speaking Countries / see Conférence des ministres de l'éducation des Etats et gouvernements de la Francophonie (#04632)
♦ Conference of Ministers of Education of Member States of the Europe Region (meeting series)
♦ Conference of Ministers of Education and Those Responsible for Economic Planning in Arab States (meeting series)
♦ Conference of Ministers of Education and Those Responsible for Economic Planning in Latin America and Caribbean (meeting series)
♦ Conference of Ministers of Finance of Franc Zone Countries (#04633)
♦ Conference of Ministers for the Forests of Central Africa / see Commission des forêts d'Afrique centrale (#04214)
♦ Conference of Ministers and Heads of Planning of Latin America and the Caribbean (see: #16279)
♦ Conference of Ministers of Health of East, Central and Southern Africa (meeting series)
♦ Conference of Ministers of Higher Education of the Socialist Countries (meeting series)
♦ Conference of Ministers of Justice of French-Speaking Countries (meeting series)
♦ Conference of Ministers of Public Health of French-Speaking Countries (meeting series)
♦ Conference of Ministers Responsible for the Application of Science and Technology to Development in Africa (meeting series)
♦ Conference of Ministers Responsible for the Application of Science and Technology to Development in Latin America and the Caribbean (meeting series)
♦ Conference of Ministers of Youth and Sports of the Francophonie (#04634)
♦ Conférence des ministres des affaires étrangères des pays balkaniques (meeting series)
♦ Conférence des Ministres de l'Agriculture de l'Afrique de l'Ouest et du Centre (#04631)
♦ Conférence des ministres de l'agriculture des pays du Golfe (meeting series)
♦ Conférence des ministres en charge des forêts d'Afrique centrale / see Commission des forêts d'Afrique centrale (#04214)
♦ Conférence des ministres chargés de l'application de la science et de la technologie au développement en Amérique latine et dans les Caraïbes (meeting series)
♦ Conférence des ministres chargés de l'environnement des pays ayant en commun l'usage du français (meeting series)
♦ Conférence des ministres de l'économie du Maghreb (meeting series)

♦ Conférence des ministres de l'éducation des Etats et gouvernements de la Francophonie (CONFEMEN) 04632

SG BP 3220, Dakar, Senegal. T. +221338592979 – +221338592991. Fax +221338251770. E-mail: confemen@confemen.org.
URL: http://www.confemen.org/

History 1960. Permanent ministerial conference of 'La Francophonie', in the framework of *Organisation internationale de la Francophonie (OIF, #17809)*, formerly *Agence intergouvernementale de La Francophonie (inactive)*. Former names and other names: *Conférence des ministres de l'éducation des pays ayant en commun l'usage du français* – former (1960); *Conférence des ministres de l'éducation des pays ayant le français en partage* – former; *Conference of Ministers of Education in French Speaking Countries* – former. Registration: France. **Aims** Contribute to a proper integration of national educational systems into the process of economic and social development. **Structure** Ministerial Conference (session usually every 2 years); Bureau; Permanent Technical Secretariat, located in Dakar (Senegal); Network of National Correspondents; Technical Commissions (3); Working Groups. **Languages** French. **Staff** 22.00 FTE, paid. **Finance** Sources: members' dues. **Activities** Events/meetings; knowledge management/information dissemination; monitoring/evaluation. **Events** *Biennial Ministerial Conference* Bathurst, NB (Canada) 2018, *Conférence Internationale sur la Relance de l'EPS à l'Ecole: Education physique et sportive* Benin 2018, *Biennial Ministerial Conference* Libreville (Gabon) 2016, *Ministerial Conference* Abidjan (Côte d'Ivoire) 2014, *Biennial ministerial conference* Niamey (Niger) 2006. **Publications** *CONFEMEN Info* (4 a year). *Documents de réflection et d'orientation*. School manuals; official texts; acts and reports; studies. **Information Services** *Database on education systems in French-speaking countries and information on education worldwide*; *Information and Documentation Centre (CID)*.

Members Participating States and territories (44):
Belgium, Benin, Bulgaria, Burkina Faso, Burundi, Cambodia, Cameroon, Canada, Cape Verde, Central African Rep, Chad, Comoros, Congo Brazzaville, Congo DR, Côte d'Ivoire, Djibouti, Egypt, France, Gabon, Guinea, Guinea-Bissau, Haiti, Laos, Lebanon, Luxembourg, Madagascar, Mali, Mauritania, Mauritius, Morocco, New Brunswick, Niger, North Macedonia, Québec, Romania, Rwanda, Sao Tomé-Principe, Senegal, Seychelles, Switzerland, Togo, Tunisia, Vanuatu, Vietnam.

IGO Relations Special agreement with: *UNESCO (#20322)*. Special links with: *Conférence ministérielle de la Francophonie (CMF, #04630)*; *Conférence des ministres de la jeunesse et des sports de la Francophonie (CONFEJES, #04634)*. Set up: *African and Malagasy Council for Higher Education (#00364)* Information and Documentation Centre. [2021.09.06/XF3673/**F***]

♦ Conférence des ministres de l'éducation des Etats members de la région Europe (meeting series)
♦ Conférence des ministres de l'éducation et des ministres chargés de la planification économique dans les Etats arabes (meeting series)
♦ Conférence des ministres de l'éducation et des ministres chargés de la planification économique des Etats members d'Afrique (meeting series)
♦ Conférence des ministres de l'éducation et des ministres chargés de la planification économique dans les Etats membres d'Amérique latine et des Caraïbes (meeting series)
♦ Conférence des ministres de l'éducation des pays ayant en commun l'usage du français / see Conférence des ministres de l'éducation des Etats et gouvernements de la Francophonie (#04632)
♦ Conférence des ministres de l'éducation des pays ayant le français en partage / see Conférence des ministres de l'éducation des Etats et gouvernements de la Francophonie (#04632)
♦ Conférence des ministres de l'éducation des pays socialistes (meeting series)
♦ Conférence des ministres européens chargés des affaires familiales (meeting series)

♦ Conférence des ministres des finances des pays de la Zone franc . 04633

Conference of Ministers of Finance of Franc Zone Countries

Secretariat c/o Banque de France, Service de la Zone franc, 39 rue des Croix des Petits Champs, 75001 Paris, France. T. +33142924292.
URL: http://www.banque-france.fr/

History 1964, Paris (France), at the request of African members of the Franc Zone. **Structure** Series of conferences; not an organization. Secretariat functions performed by the *Service de la Zone franc et du financement du développement* of the Bank of France, acting for the now defunct but still theoretically existing Secretariat of *Comité monétaire de la Zone franc (#04193)*. The *Zone franc (#22037)* includes all countries and groups of countries whose currencies are linked with the euro at a fixed rate of exchange; and who agree to hold their reserves mainly in the form of euros on a specific account opened in the books of the French Treasury. Unit of currency, *'CFA franc'*, is used in member countries of *Pays africains de la Zone franc (PAZF, #18270)*. These include those of *Union économique et monétaire Ouest africaine (UEMOA, #20377) – Communauté financière africaine (CFA, #04377)*, and of *Communauté économique et monétaire d'Afrique centrale (CEMAC, #04374) – Coopération financière en Afrique centrale*. **Activities** Ministers of Economy and Finance of the Franc Zone member countries meet twice a year to survey matters of common interest (usually in spring in the capital of an African country and in September in Paris). **Events** *Meeting* Ouagadougou (Burkina Faso) 2009, *Meeting* Paris (France) 2009, *Meeting* Paris (France) 2008, *Meeting* Yaoundé (Cameroon) 2008, *Meeting* Paris (France) 2007. **Information Services** *IZF-net* – for all countries of the Franc Zone.

Members Countries of the Franc Zone (" – includes Mayotte, St Pierre-Miquelon and the Overseas Departments and Territories). Government ministers of 16 countries, including all countries previously constituting French West and Equatorial Africa, except Guinea and Mauritania, and also including (since Jan 1985) Equatorial Guinea, previously a Spanish colony:
Benin, Burkina Faso, Cameroon, Central African Rep, Chad, Comoros, Congo Brazzaville, Côte d'Ivoire, Equatorial Guinea, France (*), Gabon, Guinea-Bissau, Mali, Niger, Senegal, Togo. [2009.11.03/XF6184/**F***]

♦ Conférence des ministres de la jeunesse et des sports de la Francophonie (CONFEJES) 04634

Conference of Ministers of Youth and Sports of the Francophonie – Conferencia de Ministros de la Juventud y los Deportes de los Paises de Habla Francesa

SG Av Cheikh Anta Diop, Stèle Mermz, BP 3314, Dakar, Senegal. T. +221338592709. Fax +2218598099. E-mail: secretariat.general@confejes.org.
URL: http://www.confejes.org/

History Established Dec 1969, Paris (France), at first Conference, following initiatives of the then annual Conference of Ministers of National Education of French-Speaking African and Malagasy countries, 10 Feb 1968, Libreville (Gabon), and modifications Jan 1969, Kinshasa (Congo DR). Statutes of Conference and Secretariat agreed at 2nd session, 1971, Dakar (Senegal); Secretariat set up at 3rd session, 1972, Paris; formal title adopted at 4th session, Nov 1973, Abidjan (Côte d'Ivoire); draft agreement ratified by member states at 6th session, 23 Aug 1975, Kigali (Rwanda); statutes adopted at 17th session, 19 Jan 1987, Ouagadougou, when agreement ratified by Senegal. A permanent ministerial conference of 'La Francophonie', in the framework of *Organisation internationale de la Francophonie (OIF, #17809)*, previously *Agence intergouvernementale de La Francophonie (inactive)*. Original title: *Conférence des ministres de la jeunesse et des sports des pays d'expression française*. **Aims** Ensure application of Conference resolutions and recommendations, maintaining the necessary liaison between member states; cooperate with appropriate specialized bodies for research on educational and technical questions; encourage young people to become active in and take a leading, responsible role in their countries' development. **Structure** Conference (every 2 years) comprises ministers or representatives of member states. Board, comprising President in Office and 14 members from 5 groups: Europe and North America (5); West Africa (3); Central Africa and the Great Lakes (2); North Africa, the Mediterranean and Central Europe (2); Indian Ocean, Asia and Caribbean (2). Committee of Experts. Office of the Secretary General. **Languages** French. **Staff** 21.00 FTE, paid. **Finance** Obligatory contributions from each member country; voluntary contributions to the Common Fund. **Activities** Projects/programmes; training/education; sporting activities. **Events** *Session* Marrakech (Morocco) 2019, *Conférence Internationale sur la Relance de l'EPS à l'Ecole: Education physique et sportive* Benin 2018, *Session* Cotonou (Benin) 2017, *Session* Kinshasa (Congo DR) 2015, *Session* Niamey (Niger) 2013. **Publications** *Lettre d'Information de la CONFEJES*; *Sport Francophone Infos*.

Members Governments of 43 countries and territories:
Belgium/Wallonia Region, Benin, Bulgaria, Burkina Faso, Burundi, Cambodia, Cameroon, Canada, Cape Verde, Central African Rep, Chad, Comoros, Congo Brazzaville, Congo DR, Côte d'Ivoire, Djibouti, Egypt, Equatorial Guinea, France, Gabon, Greece, Guinea, Guinea-Bissau, Haiti, Lebanon, Luxembourg, Madagascar, Mali, Mauritania, Mauritius, Morocco, New Brunswick, Niger, North Macedonia, Québec, Romania, Rwanda, Senegal, Seychelles, Switzerland, Togo, Tunisia, Vietnam.

IGO Relations Special agreement with: *UNESCO (#20322)*. [2022/XF3299/c/**F***]

♦ Conférence des ministres de la jeunesse et des sports des pays d'expression française / see Conférence des ministres de la jeunesse et des sports de la Francophonie (#04634)
♦ Conférence des ministres de la justice des pays d'expression française (meeting series)
♦ Conférence des ministres de la santé de l'Afrique orientale, centrale et australe (meeting series)
♦ Conférence des ministres de la santé publique des pays d'expression française (meeting series)
♦ Conférence mondiale des capitales nationales et régionales sur la ville et la paix (meeting series)
♦ Conférence mondiale de l'énergie / see World Energy Council (#21381)
♦ Conférence mondiale sur la foi et la constitution de l'Eglise (inactive)
♦ Conférence Mondiale des Institutions Universitaires Catholiques de Philosophie (#21297)
♦ Conférence mondiale des instituts séculiers (#21299)
♦ Conférence mondiale sur les juifs soviétiques (meeting series)
♦ Conférence mondiale des religions pour la paix / see Religions for Peace (#18831)
♦ Conférence mondiale de la société civile (meeting series)
♦ Conference of National Social Science Councils and Analogous Bodies / see International Federation of Social Science Organizations (#13543)
♦ Conference of National Tourist Administrations of Socialist Countries (meeting series)
♦ Conférence des Nations Unies sur le commerce et le développement (#20285)
♦ Conférence des Nations Unies sur l'environnement et le développement (meeting series)
♦ Conference of Non-Aligned Countries / see Coordinating Bureau of the Non-Aligned Countries (#04815)

♦ Conference of Non-Governmental Organizations in Consultative Relationship with the United Nations (CONGO) 04635

Conférence des organisations non-gouvernementales ayant des relations consultatives avec les Nations Unies

Pres CP 50, 1211 Geneva 20, Switzerland. T. +41223011000. Fax +41223012000. E-mail: firstvp@ngocongo.org – infonews@ngocongo.org – president@ngocongo.org.
Street Address Crets de Pregny 27, Grand Saconnex, 1218 Geneva, Switzerland.
URL: http://www.ngocongo.org/

History May 1948, Geneva (Switzerland). Founded when *Interim Committee of the Consultative Non-Governmental Organizations (inactive)* organized First Conference of Non-Governmental Organizations in Consultative Status with the United Nations Economic and Social Council (Conférence des organisations non-gouvernementales ayant le statut consultatif auprès du Conseil économique et social des Nations Unies). Present name adopted by 20th General Assembly, Nov 1997, Geneva. Present Statutes adopted by 27th General Assembly, December 2021, New York. Based near *United Nations Office at Geneva (UNOG, #20597)*. **Aims** Ensure that nongovernmental organizations in consultative relationship enjoy the fullest opportunities and all appropriate facilities for performing their consultative functions; foster cooperation and dialogue among all *NGOs* related to the *UN system*; provide a forum for exchange of views on matters relating to the consultative process and on strengthening of the relationship between NGOs and the United Nations, including the contributions which NGOs in consultative relationship can make to promoting the principles, purposes and effectiveness of the UN and its related agencies and programmes; mobilize public opinion in support of the aims and principles of the United Nations; promote education about the UN with special emphasis on the contribution which NGOs make to its work; convene meetings of NGOs for exchange of views on matters of common interest.

Structure General Assembly (every 3-4 years); Board; Secretariat at Geneva, New York and Vienna offices. NGO Substantive Committees which function under the auspices of CONGO, generally with no fixed secretariat, their activities being carried out by member organizations, especially by the organizations of the officers -

(a) New York NY (USA):
- *Alliance of NGOs on Crime Prevention and Criminal Justice (#00709)*;
- *CONGO Committee on Human Rights (#04663)*;
- *NGO Committee on Ageing, New York (#17103)*;
- NGO Committee on Disarmament, New York
- *NGO Committee on Education, Learning and Literacy, New York*;
- *NGO Committee on Financing for Development, New York (#17108)*;
- *NGO Committee on Freedom of Religion or Belief, New York NY (#17109)*;
- *NGO Committee on Human Settlements (#17110)*;
- *NGO Committee on the Rights of Indigenous Peoples (#17114)*;
- *NGO Committee on Mental Health, New York NY (#17111)*;
- *NGO Committee on Migration, New York (#17112)*;
- *NGO Committee for Rare Diseases, New York*;
- *NGO Committee on Social Development (#17115)*;
- *NGO Committee on the Status of Women, New York NY (see: #04635)*;
- *NGO Committee on Sustainable Development, New York (#17118)*;
- *NGO Committee on the Family, New York NY (#17107)*;
- *New York NGO Committee on Drugs (NYNGOC, #17097)*.

(b) Geneva (Switzerland):
- *NGO Committee on the Status of Women, Geneva (#17117)*;
- *NGO Committee on Ageing, Geneva (see: #04635)*;
- *NGO Committee on Development, Geneva (#17104)*;
- *NGO Committee for Disarmament, Geneva (#17105)*;
- *Committee of NGOs on Human Rights, Geneva (#04275), NGO Committee on Freedom of Religion or Belief, Geneva (see: #04275)*.

(c) Vienna (Austria):
- *Vienna NGO Committee on the Status of Women (#20775)*;
- *NGO Committee on Ageing, Vienna (see: #04635)*;
- *NGO Committee on Sustainable Development, Vienna (#17119)*;
- *Vienna NGO Committee on Drugs (VNGOC, #20773)*;
- *NGO Committee on Peace, Vienna (#17113)*.

Languages English, French. **Staff** 5.00 FTE, voluntary. **Finance** Sources: members' dues. Many Substantive Committees associated with the Conference assess an annual fee from their members to cover running costs. Funds from approved sources. UN Secretariat sometimes supports activities by providing meeting facilities, services and resource materials. **Activities** Advocacy/lobbying/activism; capacity building; events/meetings; guidance/assistance/consulting; monitoring/evaluation; networking/liaising. **Events** *General Assembly* New York, NY (USA) 2021, *Meeting* Bangkok (Thailand) 2020, *General Assembly* Geneva (Switzerland) 2018, *Meeting on Peace Building and Education for the SDGs* New York, NY (USA) 2018, *Diversity unites! Governments and NGOs – together against radicalization* Vienna (Austria) 2017. **Publications** *CoNGO Newsletter* – electronic. *COVID-19 Recovery. Building Back Better.* – Statement; *Declaration for the UN 75th Anniversary.*. Assembly Report; member directories; forum and other event reports.

Members (a) Membership in the Conference is open to NGOs having consultative status with the United Nations through the Economic and Social Council (ECOSOC), and which accept the aims set forth under rule 2 ('aims'). (b) Associate membership in the Conference is open to all NGOs having other types of working or operational relationships with the United Nations – including NGOs affiliated with the Department of Gobal Communications, NGOs accredited to United Nations Conferences, and NGOs accredited to treaty bodies – and which accept the aims set forth under rule 2 ('aims'). Associate member organizations shall not have the right to vote. Membership in 70 countries and territories:

Algeria, Angola, Argentina, Australia, Austria, Bangladesh, Belgium, Benin, Bosnia-Herzegovina, Brazil, Burundi, Cameroon, Canada, China, Côte d'Ivoire, Cuba, Czechia, Denmark, Egypt, Ethiopia, Finland, France, Germany, Ghana, Greece, Hong Kong, Hungary, India, Indonesia, Iran Islamic Rep, Ireland, Israel, Italy, Jamaica, Japan, Jordan, Kenya, Korea Rep, Lebanon, Malaysia, Mali, Malta, Nepal, Netherlands, New Zealand, Nicaragua, Niger, Nigeria, Pakistan, Philippines, Portugal, Romania, Russia, Saudi Arabia, Slovakia, South Africa, Spain, Suriname, Sweden, Switzerland, Taiwan, Thailand, Togo, Tunisia, Türkiye, UK, Uruguay, USA, Venezuela, Zimbabwe.

Full members include the following 272 organizations listed in this Yearbook:
- *AARP International*;
- *Academy for Future Science (AFFS)*;
- *ActionAid (#00087)*;
- *African Services Committee (ASC)*;
- *African Women's Development and Communication Network (FEMNET, #00503)*;
- *Afro-Asian Peoples' Solidarity Organization (AAPSO, #00537)*;
- *Åland Islands Peace Institute*;
- *All India Women's Conference (AIWC, #00737)*;
- *All Pakistan Women's Association (APWA)*;
- *Altrusa International (AI, #00757)*;
- *American Council for Voluntary International Action (InterAction)*;
- *Anglican Consultative Council (ACC, #00828)*;
- *Arab Centre for the Independence of the Judiciary and the Legal Profession (ACIJLP)* ;
- *Arab Council for Childhood and Development (ACCD, #00929)*;
- *Arab Lawyers' Union (ALU, #01002)*;
- *Armenian Relief Society (ARS, #01111)*;
- *Art of Living Foundation*;
- *Asian Forum for Human Rights and Development (FORUM-ASIA, #01491)*;
- *Asian Forum of Parliamentarians on Population and Development (AFPPD, #01493)*;
- *Asian-Pacific Resource and Research Centre for Women (ARROW, #01629)*;
- *Asian Partnership for the Development of Human Resources in Rural Asia (AsiaDHRRA, #01654)*;
- *Asia South Pacific Association for Basic and Adult Education (ASPBAE, #02098)*;
- *Associated Country Women of the World (ACWW, #02338)*;
- *Association culturelle d'aide à la promotion éducative et sociale (ACAPES)*;
- *Association for Progressive Communications (APC, #02873)*;
- *Association internationale pour la défense de la liberté religieuse (AIDLR, #02681)* ;
- *Baha'i International Community (#03062)*;
- *Baptist World Alliance (BWA, #03176)*;
- *Brahma Kumaris World Spiritual University (BKWSU, #03311)*;
- *Brothers of Charity (FC)*;
- *Buddha's Light International Association (BLIA, #03346)*;
- *Building and Wood Workers' International (BWI, #03355)*;
- *Caritas Internationalis (CI, #03580)*;
- *Catholic International Education Office (#03604)*;
- *Catholic Lenten Fund*;
- *Catholics for Choice (#03609)*;
- *Center for International Humanitarian Cooperation (CIHC)*;
- *Center for Women's Global Leadership (CWGL)*;
- *Centre Africain de Recherche Interdisciplinaire (CARI)*;
- *Centre de recherches et de promotion pour la sauvegarde des sites et monuments historiques en Afrique*;
- *Centre UNESCO de Catalunya (UNESCOCAT)*;
- *Chinese Association for International Understanding (CAFIU)*;
- *Chinese People's Association for Friendship with Foreign Countries (CPAFFC, no recent information)*;
- *Chinese People's Association for Peace and Disarmament (CPAPD)*;
- *Christian Conference of Asia (CCA, #03898)*;
- *Christian Life Community (CLC, #03905)*;
- *Church Women United (CWU)*;
- *Church World Service (CWS)*;
- *CIVICUS: World Alliance for Citizen Participation (#03962)*;
- *Coalition Against Trafficking in Women (CATW, #04047)*;
- *Commonwealth Human Ecology Council (CHEC, #04339)*;
- *Communications Coordination Committee for the United Nations (CCC/UN)*;
- *Confederation of Asia-Pacific Chambers of Commerce and Industry (CACCI, #04512)*;
- *Confederation of Associations Working for World Peace (no recent information)*;
- *Conference of European Churches (CEC, #04593)*;
- *Conscience and Peace Tax International (CPTI, #04683)*;
- *Consultative Council of Jewish Organizations (CCJO, no recent information)*;
- *Coordinating Board of Jewish Organizations (CBJO, #04813)*;
- *David M Kennedy Center for International Studies*;
- *Defence for Children International (DCI, #05025)*;
- *Development Alternatives with Women for a New Era (DAWN, #05054)*;
- *DEVNET International (#05059)*;
- *Dhaka Ahsania Mission (DAM)*;
- *DIANOVA International (#05068)*;
- *Dzeno Association*;
- *Education International (EI, #05371)*;
- *Emmaus International (#05445)*;
- *Environment Liaison Centre International (ELCI, no recent information)*;
- *Equality Fund (EF)*;
- *European Union of Women (EUW, #09022)*;
- *European Women's Lobby (EWL, #09102)*;
- *European Youth Forum (#09140)*;
- *Europe – Third World Centre (CETIM)*;
- *Families of the Missing (FOM)*;
- *Federal Union of European Nationalities (FUEN, #09396)*;
- *Federation of American Women's Clubs Overseas (FAWCO, #09416)*;
- *Federation of Associations of Former International Civil Servants (FAFICS, #09457)* ;
- *Femmes Africa solidarité (FAS, #09732)*;
- *Femmes chefs d'entreprises mondiales (FCEM, #09733)*;
- *Franciscans International (FI, #09982)*;
- *Fraternité Notre Dame (FND)*;
- *Friedrich-Ebert-Stiftung (FES)*;
- *Fundación Promoción Social*;
- *General Board of Church and Society of the United Methodist Church (GBCS)*;
- *Global Cooperation Society (GCS International)*;
- *Global Ecovillage Network (GEN, #10331)*;
- *Global Foundation for Democracy and Development (GFDD)*;
- *Global Ministries of The United Methodist Church (GM-UMC)*;
- *Good Neighbors International*;
- *Graduate Women International (GWI, #10688)*;
- *Greek Orthodox Archdiocesan Council of America (GOAC, #10708)*;
- *Hadassah*;
- *HelpAge International (#10904)*;
- *Humanists International (#10972)*;
- *Initiatives of Change International – Caux (IofC, #11213)*;
- *Institute for Planetary Synthesis (IPS, #11287)*;
- *Inter-African Committee on Traditional Practices Affecting the Health of Women and Children (IAC, #11384)*;
- *Interfaith International*;
- *International Alliance of Women (IAW, #11639)*;
- *International Association for Counselling (IAC, #11821)*;
- *International Association for Media and Communication Research (IAMCR, #12022)*;
- *International Association for Religious Freedom (IARF, #12130)*;
- *International Association for the Protection of Intellectual Property (#12112)*;
- *International Association for Volunteer Effort (IAVE, #12260)*;
- *International Association IUS Primi Viri (IPV)*;
- *International Association of Applied Psychology (IAAP, #11705)*;
- *International Association of Gerontology and Geriatrics (IAGG, #11920)*;
- *International Association of Jewish Lawyers and Jurists (IJL, #11977)*;
- *International Association of Judges (IAJ, #11978)*;
- *International Association of Schools of Social Work (IASSW, #12149)*;
- *International Association of Universities (IAU, #12246)*;
- *International Association of University Presidents (IAUP, #12248)*;
- *International Bureau for Epilepsy (IBE, #12414)*;
- *International Christian Organisation of the Media (ICOM, #12563)*;
- *International Commission of Jurists (ICJ, #12695)*;
- *International Co-operative Alliance (ICA, #12944)*;
- *International Corrections and Prisons Association for the Advancement of Professional Corrections (ICPA, #12970)*;
- *International Council of Jewish Women (ICJW, #13036)*;
- *International Council of Management Consulting Institutes (ICMCI, #13042)*;
- *International Council of Nurses (ICN, #13054)*;
- *International Council of Psychologists (ICP, #13065)*;
- *International Council of Women (ICW, #13093)*;
- *International Council on Archives (ICA, #12996)*;
- *International Council on Jewish Social and Welfare Services (INTERCO, #13035)*;
- *International Council on Social Welfare (ICSW, #13076)*;
- *International Federation for Home Economics (IFHE, #13447)*;
- *International Federation of Business and Professional Women (BPW International, #13376)*;
- *International Federation of Library Associations and Institutions (IFLA, #13470)*;
- *International Federation of Little Brothers of the Poor (IFLBP, #13471)*;
- *International Federation of Settlements and Neighbourhood Centres (IFS, #13538)*;
- *International Federation of Social Workers (IFSW, #13544)*;
- *International Federation of Training and Development Organizations (IFTDO, #13573)* ;
- *International Federation of Women in Legal Careers (IFWLC, #13579)*;
- *International Federation of Women Lawyers (FIDA, #13578)*;
- *International Fellowship of Reconciliation (IFOR, #13586)*;
- *International Human Rights Observer (IHRO)*;
- *International Inner Wheel (IIW, #13855)*;
- *International Institute for Peace through Tourism (IIPT)*;
- *International Islamic Relief Organization (IIRO)*;
- *International Movement ATD Fourth World (#14193)*;
- *International Multiracial Shared Cultural Organization (IMSCO)*;
- *International Network for the Prevention of Elder Abuse (INPEA, #14307)*;
- *International Organization for the Elimination of All Forms of Racial Discrimination (EAFORD, #14445)*;
- *International Peace Bureau (IPB, #14535)*;
- *International Peace Research Association (IPRA, #14537)*;
- *International Petroleum Industry Environmental Conservation Association (IPIECA, #14562)*;
- *International Platform for Black, Migrant and Refugee Women's Organizations (TIYE International)*;
- *International Presentation Association (IPA, #14635)*;
- *International Progress Organization (IPO, #14653)*;
- *International Psychoanalytical Association (IPA, #14662)*;
- *International Public Policy Institute (IPPI)*;
- *International Real Estate Institute (IREI)*;
- *International Road Transport Union (IRU, #14761)*;
- *International Service for Human Rights (ISHR, #14841)*;
- *International Shinto Foundation (ISF)*;
- *International Social Service (ISS, #14886)*;
- *International Society for Traumatic Stress Studies (ISTSS, #15518)*;
- *International Trade Union Confederation (ITUC, #15708)*;
- *International Union for Health Promotion and Education (IUHPE, #15778)*;
- *International Union of Marine Insurance (IUMI, #15789)*;
- *International Union of Muslim Women (inactive)*;
- *International Women's Year Liaison Group (no recent information)*;
- *Inuit Circumpolar Council (ICC, #15995)*;
- *IPS – Inter Press Service International Association (#16013)*;
- *Islamic Relief Worldwide (IRWW, #16048)*;
- *Islamic World Studies Centre (IWSC, no recent information)*;
- *Junior Chamber International (JCI, #16168)*;
- *Kitakyushu Forum on Asian Women (KFAW)*;
- *KOLPING INTERNATIONAL (#16203)*;
- *Korea International Volunteer Organization (KVO International)*;

- *La Leche League International (LLLI, #16433)*;
- *Legion of Good Will (LGW)*;
- *Life for Relief and Development*;
- *Lions Clubs International (LCI, #16485)*;
- *Lucis Trust (LT, #16519)*;
- *Make Mothers Matter (#16554)*;
- *Marangopoulos Foundation for Human Rights (MFHR)*;
- *Medical Care Development International (MCDI)*;
- *Medical Mission Sisters*;
- *Medical Women's International Association (MWIA, #16630)*;
- *Mercy-USA for Aid and Development (MUSA)*;
- *Muslim World League (MWL, #16917)*;
- *Nonviolent Peaceforce (NP, #17153)*;
- *Organisation mondiale des anciens élèves de l'enseignement catholique (OMAEC, #17816)* ;
- *Organización de Entidades Mutuales de las Américas (ODEMA, #17836)*;
- *Organization for Defending Victims of Violence (ODVV)*;
- *Organization of Islamic Capitals and Cities (OICC, #17875)*;
- *Pan African Women's Organization (PAWO, #18074)*;
- *Pan Pacific and South East Asia Women's Association (PPSEAWA, #18186)*;
- *Pax Christi – International Catholic Peace Movement (#18266)*;
- *Pax Romana, International Catholic Movement for Intellectual and Cultural Affairs (ICMICA, #18267)*;
- *PCI Media*;
- *Public Services International (PSI, #18572)*;
- *Religions for Peace (RfP, #18831)*;
- *Right to Energy – SOS Future*;
- *RI Global (#18948)*;
- *Rotary International (RI, #18975)*;
- *Russian Peace Foundation (RPF)*;
- *Salvation Army (#19041)*;
- *Save Africa Concerts Foundation (SAC)*;
- *Save the Children International (#19058)*;
- *School Sisters of Notre Dame (SSND)*;
- *Service and Research Institute on Family and Children (SERFAC, #19243)*;
- *Simply Help*;
- *Sisters of Our Lady of Charity of the Good Shepherd*;
- *Socialist International Women (SIW, #19341)*;
- *Society for Psychological Study of Social Issues (SPSSI)*;
- *Soeurs de Notre-Dame de Namur (SNDN)*;
- *Soka Gakkai International (SGI, #19672)*;
- *Soroptimist International (SI, #19686)*;
- *SOS-Kinderdorf International (#19693)*;
- *Sovereign Military Order of the Temple of Jerusalem (SMOTJ)*;
- *Sri Aurobindo Society*;
- *Sulabh International Social Service Organization*;
- *Susila Dharma International Association (SDIA, #20048)*;
- *Temple of Understanding (ToU, #20124)*;
- *Teresian Association*;
- *Terre des Hommes International Federation (TDHIF, #20133)*;
- *The Mothers' Union (#16860)*;
- *The World Veterans Federation (WVF, #21900)*;
- *To Love Children Educational Foundation International*;
- *Union of Arab Doctors in Europe (#20352)*;
- *Union of International Associations (UIA, #20414)*;
- *Unis pour l'Equite et la Fin du Racisme (UFER, #20490)*;
- *United Nations Watch (UN Watch)*;
- *United Schools International (USI, #20660)*;
- *Universal Esperanto Association (UEA, #20676)*;
- *Universal Peace Federation (UPF International, #20681)*;
- *Verification Research, Training and Information Centre (VERTIC)*;
- *Voices of African Mothers (VAM)*;
- *Volontariato Internazionale Donna Educazione Sviluppo (VIDES, #20806)*;
- *Women First International Fund (#20996)*;
- *Women's Environment and Development Organization (WEDO, #21016)*;
- *Women's Federation for World Peace International (WFWPI)*;
- *Women's International Democratic Federation (WIDF, #21022)*;
- *Women's International League for Peace and Freedom (WILPF, #21024)*;
- *Women's International Zionist Organization (WIZO, #21030)*;
- *Workability International (#21049)*;
- *World Alliance of Young Men's Christian Associations (YMCA, #21090)*;
- *World Animal Protection (#21092)*;
- *World Association for Psychosocial Rehabilitation (WAPR, #21178)*;
- *World Association of Girl Guides and Girl Scouts (WAGGGS, #21142)*;
- *World Association of Industrial and Technological Research Organizations (WAITRO, #21145)*;
- *World Blind Union (WBU, #21234)*;
- *World Council of Arameans – Syriacs (WCA, #21318)*;
- *World Council of Churches (WCC, #21320)* (Commission of the Churches on International Affairs of);
- *World Council of Muslim Communities*;
- *World Federalist Movement – Movement for a Just World Order through a Strengthened United Nations (WFM, #21404)*;
- *World Federation for Mental Health (WFMH, #21455)*;
- *World Federation of Democratic Youth (WFDY, #21427)*;
- *World Federation of Khoja Shia Ithna-Asheri Muslim Communities (World Federation of KSIMC, #21449)*;
- *World Federation of Methodist and Uniting Church Women (WFM and UCW, #21457)*;
- *World Federation of Scientific Workers (WFSW, #21480)*;
- *World Federation of Trade Unions (WFTU, #21493)*;
- *World Federation of Ukrainian Women's Organizations (WFUWO, #21496)*;
- *World Federation of United Nations Associations (WFUNA, #21499)*;
- *World Islamic Call Society (WICS, inactive)*;
- *World Jewish Congress (WJC, #21599)*;
- *World Muslim Congress (WMC, #21664)*;
- *World Organisation Against Torture (OMCT, #21685)*;
- *World Organization of the Scout Movement (WOSM, #21693)*;
- *World Psychiatric Association (WPA, #21741)*;
- *World Safety Organization (WSO, #21759)*;
- *World Society for Ekistics (WSE, #21801)*;
- *World Student Christian Federation (WSCF, #21833)*;
- *World Union for Progressive Judaism (WUPJ, #21883)*;
- *World Union of Catholic Women's Organisations (WUCWO, #21876)*;
- *World Vision International (WVI, #21904)*;
- *Worldwide Organization for Women (WOW)*;
- *World Young Women's Christian Association (World YWCA, #21947)*;
- *Youth with a Mission (YWAM, #22020)*;
- *Zonta International (#22038)*.

Associate members include 22 organizations listed in this Yearbook:

- *African Citizens Development Foundation (ACDF)*;
- *Ambedkar Center for Justice and Peace (ACJP, #00769)*;
- *Ananda Marga Universal Relief Team (AMURT, #00811)*;
- *Asian Federation Against Involuntary Disappearances (AFAD, #01453)*;
- *Association of African Women for Research and Development (AAWORD, #02362)*;
- *Ateliers pour les initiatives de développement (AID, no recent information)*;
- *Autistic Minority International*;
- *Chamber of Computer Logistics People Worldwide (CCLP Worldwide, #03847)*;
- *Child Helpline International (CHI, #03870)*;
- *Club of Rome (COR, #04038)*;
- *Democracy Coalition Project (DCP, no recent information)*;
- *Diplomatic Society of St Gabriel (DSSG)*;
- *Environmental Ambassadors for Sustainable Development (Environmental Ambassadors)* ;
- *Europe Against Drugs (EURAD, #05774)*;
- *Global Marshall Plan Initiative (#10466)*;
- *Ingénieurs du monde (IdM)*;
- *Institute of International Humanitarian Affairs (IIHA)*;
- *International Catholic Centre of Geneva (ICCG, #12449)*;
- *International Mahavira Jain Mission (IMJM)*;
- *People to People International (PTPI, #18300)*;
- *The Grail – International Movement of Christian Women (#10689)*;
- *World Evangelical Alliance (WEA, #21393)*.

Consultative Status Consultative status granted from: *ECOSOC (#05331)* (General). **NGO Relations** Partner of (1): *United Nations Informal Regional Network of Non-Governmental Organizations (UN-NGO-IRENE, #20573)*. [2022.10.24/XE0409/y/**E**]

♦ Conférence nordique de volley-ball (meeting series)
♦ Conférence des notariats de l'Union Européenne / see Notaries of Europe (#17609)

♦ Conference on Oceanian Linguistic Anthropology (COOLA) 04636

Address not obtained.

Aims Redefine the way Oceanian language and society is viewed. **Languages** English. **Staff** 4.00 FTE, paid; 10.00 FTE, voluntary. **Activities** Events/meetings. **Publications** *The Journal of Oceanian Linguistic Anthropology (COOLA Journal)*. **NGO Relations** Constitutes *Global Network in Linguistic Anthropology*, together with *Global Council for Anthropological Linguistics (GLOCAL, #10310)*, *Conference on Mediterranean and European Linguistic Anthropology (COMELA, #04628)*, *South and Central American Assembly on Linguistic Anthropology (SCAALA, #19752)*, *Middle Eastern Association of Linguistic Anthropology (MEALA, #16760)* and *African Assembly of Linguistic Anthropology (AFALA, #00204)*. [2020.05.02/XM8716/c/**F**]

♦ Conférence des OINGs du Conseil de l'Europe (#04607)
♦ Conférence de l'ONU sur les questions de désarmement (meeting series)
♦ Conference of Orders and Assimilated Bodies of Dental Practitioners in Europe / see Federation of European Dental Competent Authorities and Regulators (#09501)
♦ Conférence des ordres et organismes assimilés des praticiens de l'art dentaire européens / see Federation of European Dental Competent Authorities and Regulators (#09501)

♦ Conférence des Organes Parlementaires Spécialisés dans les Affaires de l'Union des Parlements de l'Union Européenne (COSAC) 04637

Conference of Parliamentary Committees for Union Affairs of Parliaments of the European Union

Secretariat European Parliament, WIE 05 U 041, Rue Wiertz 50, 1047 Brussels, Belgium. T. +3222843776. Fax +3222844925. E-mail: secretariat@cosac.eu.
URL: http://www.cosac.eu/

History May 1989, Madrid (Spain), as *Conférence des organes spécialisés en affaires européennes des pays membres de l'Union et du Parlement européen – Conference of Community and European Affairs Committees of Parliaments of the European Union*. Formally recognized in a protocol to *Treaty of Amsterdam (1997)*, that was concluded by Heads of Government, Jun 1997. *Protocol on the Role of National Parliaments in the European Union* came into force 1 May 1999. Superseding treaty – *Treaty of Lisbon (2007)* – came into force 1 Dec 2009. **Aims** Allow representatives of parliaments of member states of the *European Union*, together with those of the European Parliament, to exchange information on progress in European Union affairs. **Structure** Meets twice a year in the country having at that time the Presidency of the Union. Each Parliament is represented by 6 members. Secretariat, composed of officials from the Parliaments of the Presidential Troika, and a Permanent Member. **Events** *Conference* Helsinki (Finland) 2019, *Meeting* Athens (Greece) 2014, *Meeting* Dublin (Ireland) 2013, *Meeting* Lithuania 2013, *Meeting* Denmark 2012. **IGO Relations** *Baltic Sea Parliamentary Conference (BSPC, #03146)*. [2018/XS0187/c/**E***]

♦ Conférence des organes spécialisés en affaires européennes des pays membres de l'Union et du Parlement européen / see Conférence des Organes Parlementaires Spécialisés dans les Affaires de l'Union des Parlements de l'Union Européenne (#04637)
♦ Conférence des organisations internationales catholiques (inactive)
♦ Conférence des organisations internationales non gouvernementales entretenant des relations de consultation – catégories A et B – avec l'UNESCO / see International Conference of NGOs (#12883)
♦ Conférence des organisations internationales non gouvernementales entretenant des relations de consultation avec l'UNESCO / see International Conference of NGOs (#12883)
♦ Conférence des organisations internationales non gouvernementales entretenant des relations officielles avec l'UNESCO / see International Conference of NGOs (#12883)
♦ Conférence des organisations non-gouvernementales ayant des relations consultatives avec les Nations Unies (#04635)
♦ Conférence parlementaire des Amériques / see Confederación Parlamentaria de las Américas (#04479)
♦ Conférence parlementaire internationale du commerce (inactive)
♦ Conférence des parlementaires de l'OTAN / see NATO Parliamentary Assembly (#16946)
♦ Conference of Parliamentary Committees for Union Affairs of Parliaments of the European Union (#04637)
♦ Conférence des partis socialistes africains (meeting series)
♦ Conference on Peace Research in History / see Peace History Society
♦ Conference of Peripheral Maritime Regions of the EC / see Conference of Peripheral Maritime Regions of Europe (#04638)

♦ Conference of Peripheral Maritime Regions of Europe (CPMR) 04638

Conférence des régions périphériques maritimes d'Europe (CRPM) – Conferencia de las Regiones Periféricas Maritimas de Europa (CRPM) – Konferenz der Peripheren Küstenregionen Europas (KPKR) – Conferência das Regiões Periféricas Maritimas da Europa (CRPM) – Conferenza delle Regioni Periferiche Marittime d'Europa (CRPM) – Conferentie van de Perifere Maritieme Regios van Europa – Konferensen för Europas Perifera Maritima Regioner – Konferansen for Europas Maritime Utkantregioner – Konferencen for Perifere Maritime Regioner i Europa – Euroopa Mereliste Äärealade Konverents – Euroopan Peripfeeristen Merellisten Alueiden Konferenssi – Eiropas Perifero Piejuras Regionu Konference – Konferencja Peryferycznych Regionów Morskich – Konferencija Primorskih Okrainov v Evrope – Diaskepsi ton Periferiakon Paraktion Periohon tis Evropis (DPPP)

SG Rond Point Schuman 14, 1040 Brussels, Belgium. T. +3226121700. Fax +3222802765. E-mail: info@crpm.org.
Contact 6 rue St Martin, 35700 Rennes, France. T. +33299354050. Fax +33299350919.
URL: https://cpmr.org/

History 21 Jun 1973, Saint-Malo (France). *Declaration of Saint Malo'* adopted Oct 1983. Statutes modified, 18 Oct 2019. Former names and other names: *Conference of Peripheral Maritime Regions of the EC* – former (Jun 1973); *Conférence des régions périphériques maritimes de la CE* – former (Jun 1973); *Conferencia de las Regiones Periféricas Maritimas de la CE* – former (Jun 1973); *Konferenz von Periphären Küstenregionen der EG* – former (Jun 1973); *Conferência das Regiões Periféricas Maritimas de la CE* – former (Jun 1973); *Conferenza delle Regioni Periferiche Marittime della CE* – former (Jun 1973); *Diaskepsi ton Periferiakon Paraktion Periohon tis EK* – former (Jun 1973). Registration: EU Transparency Register, No/ID: 5546423688-07; France. **Aims** Promote better cooperation between peripheral regions and European institutions and organizations and influence European policy-making in areas of interest to the region; promote the concept of a more balanced and poly-centric development in which creation of competitive territories in maritime areas on the basis of large macro-areas contributes to a better balance and overall development of the European region as a whole; protect and improve regional potentials linked with sea and coast; put forward proposals in the context of negotiations on European Structural Funds; encourage inter-regional and transnational networking, particularly through cooperation programmes. **Structure** General Assembly (annual). Political Bureau (meets twice a year), Including Executive Board. Geographical Commissions General Secretariat. Treasurer, assisted by Financial Committee. Geographical Commissions (6): *Atlantic Arc Commission (#03007)*; *Balkan and Black Sea Regional Commission (BBSC, #03068)*; *Baltic Sea Commission (BSC, #03141)*; *Intermediterranean Commission (IMC, #11521)*; *Islands Commission (#16061)*; *North Sea Commission (NSC, #17604)*. **Languages** English, French, German, Irish Gaelic, Italian, Portuguese, Spanish. **Staff** 30.00 FTE, paid. **Finance** Members' dues based on number of inhabitants. Annual budget: euro 3 million. **Activities** Advocacy/lobbying/activism; projects/programmes; research and development. **Events**

General Assembly Agios Nikolaos (Greece) 2022, *Joint Meeting on the Role of Oceran Literacy and Responsible Research and Innovation in Supporting Effective Ocean Governance* Brussels (Belgium) 2019, *General Assembly* Gdansk (Poland) 2019, *Future of Europe Conference* Lahti (Finland) 2019, *International Seminar on Circular Economy* Lahti (Finland) 2019. **Publications** *Objectif 2009: Un Grand Pas pour l'Europe* (2004) by Xavier Gizard in English, French, German, Italian, Spanish; *Euroland / Civiland: Europe in Wonderland* (1998) by Xavier Gizard and Philippe Cichowlaz in English, French. Working and information documents on meetings; technical studies; discussion papers.
Members Peripheral or maritime regions (160 regional authorities) in 25 countries:
Albania, Bulgaria, Cyprus, Denmark, Estonia, Finland, France, Germany, Greece, Ireland, Italy, Malta, Moldova, Morocco, Netherlands, Norway, Poland, Portugal, Romania, Spain, Sweden, Tunisia, Türkiye, UK, Ukraine.
IGO Relations Close cooperation: *European Committee of the Regions (CoR, #06665)*; *European Commission (EC, #06633)*; *European Parliament (EP, #08146)*; *OECD (#17693)*. Observer to: *Baltic Marine Environment Protection Commission – Helsinki Commission (HELCOM, #03126)*; *Congress of Local and Regional Authorities of the Council of Europe (#04677)*; *International Oil Pollution Compensation Funds (IOPC Funds, #14402)*. Memorandum of Understanding with: *FAO (#09260)*; *UNDP (#20292)*. Also relations with relevant national institutions. **NGO Relations** Member of: *European Centre for Information on Marine Science and Technology (EurOcean)*. Supports: *European Alliance for the Statute of the European Association (EASEA, #05886)*.
[2022/XD6554/F]

- ♦ Conférence permanente africaine sur le contrôle bibliographique (inactive)
- ♦ Conférence permanente de l'audiovisuel méditerranéen (#18320)
- ♦ Conférence permanente des bibliothèques universitaires africaines (no recent information)
- ♦ Conférence permanente des chambres de commerce et de l'industrie de la CEE / see Association des chambres de commerce et d'industrie européennes (#02423)

♦ Conférence Permanente des Chambres Consulaires Africaines et Francophones (CPCCAF) 04639

General Delegate 6/8 av de la Porte Champerret, 75017 Paris, France. T. +33155653527. Fax +33155653940. E-mail: cpccaf@cci-paris-idf.fr.
URL: http://www.cpccaf.org/
History 1973. **Aims** Advocate for African consular chambers for development of the private sector and the market for economic growth. **Structure** General Assembly; Permanent Delegation; Bureau. **Languages** French. **Staff** 2.00 FTE, paid. **Activities** Events/meetings; networking/liaising; projects/programmes. **Events** *General Assembly* Yaoundé (Cameroon) 2022, *General Assembly* Benin 2011, *RIFE : rencontre internationale de la francophonie économique* Québec, QC (Canada) 2008. **Publications** *Baromètre de l'Opinion des Entreprises Africaines 2019*.
Members Full in 28 countries:
Belgium, Benin, Burkina Faso, Burundi, Cameroon, Canada, Cape Verde, Central African Rep, Chad, Comoros, Congo Brazzaville, Congo DR, Côte d'Ivoire, Equatorial Guinea, France, Gabon, Guinea, Guinea-Bissau, Madagascar, Mali, Mauritania, Mauritius, Morocco, Niger, Rwanda, Senegal, Togo, Tunisia.
Associate in 3 countries:
Andorra, Haiti, Morocco.
Regional associate members:
Communauté économique et monétaire d'Afrique centrale (CEMAC, #04374) (Conférence des Chambres consulaires); *Union économique et monétaire Ouest africaine (UEMOA, #20377)* (Chambre consulaire régional).
IGO Relations Accredited by (1): *Organisation internationale de la Francophonie (OIF, #17809)*.
[2021/XJ4903/y/C]

- ♦ Conférence permanente des délégués des fédérations nationales de basketball de l'Europe / see FIBA-Europe (#09747)
- ♦ Conférence permanente des écoles africaines de bibliothéconomie, d'archivistique and de sciences de l'information (inactive)
- ♦ Conférence permanente européenne des associations de professeurs de géographie / see European Association of Geographers (#06054)
- ♦ Conférence Permanente Européenne des Associations de Professeurs d'Histoire / see European Association of History Educators (#06069)
- ♦ Conférence permanente européenne de la probation / see Confederation of European Probation (#04530)
- ♦ Conférence permanente des fédérations nationales de basketball de l'Europe / see FIBA-Europe (#09747)
- ♦ Conférence permanente des fédérations professionnelles internationales (inactive)
- ♦ Conférence permanente des hautes études internationales (inactive)
- ♦ Conférence permanente de l'industrie européenne productrice d'articles émaillés (inactive)
- ♦ Conférence permanente internationale des centres du bâtiment / see International Union of Building Centres (#15761)
- ♦ Conférence permanente internationale des organisations privées pour la protection des migrants (inactive)
- ♦ Conférence permanente des notariats de la Communauté européenne / see Notaries of Europe (#17609)
- ♦ Conférence permanente pour l'organisation universelle de la communauté de la jeunesse pour la paix (inactive)
- ♦ Conférence permanente des partis politiques d'Amérique latine et le caraïbe (#04657)
- ♦ Conférence permanente des responsables des départements d'études françaises de la région du Pacifique Sud (inactive)
- ♦ Conférence des peuples africains (inactive)

♦ Conférence des peuples de langue française (CPLF) 04640

Conference of French-speaking Peoples
Contact Maison de la Francité, Rue Joseph II 18, 1000 Brussels, Belgium. T. +3225333011. Fax +3225360131.
URL: http://www.peuplesdelanguefrancaise.org/
History 16 Apr 1971, Geneva (Switzerland). 16-17 Apr 1971, Geneva (Switzerland), as *Comité permanent des communautés ethniques de langue française*, when the first *Conférence des minorités ethniques de langue française* was organized, subsequently referred to as *Conférence des communautés ethniques de langue française*. Later became *Comité permanent des peuples de langue française*. Current statutes adopted 6 Jun 1992, Brussels (Belgium). Present name adopted 1993. **Aims** Affirm the values of democracy and freedom as fundamental components of *French-speaking* people's *identity*; defend these principles wherever necessary; promote the idea that individual rights must correspond to the rights of people; participate in the development and continuity of French as a modern and universal language of communication and civilization; provide the means for mutual political help among movements wishing to render French-speaking people more autonomous with respect to external decision-making; contribute to the full integration of French-speaking people in a world searching for new balance and express the will to build joint destinies around common values; increase exchanges among French-speaking people; coordinate internationally information related to their movements and to their research and documentation centres. **Structure** Standing Committee (meeting twice a year) comprises 4 representatives and 4 deputies of each member and includes the President, 2 Vice-Presidents, Secretary-General and Treasurer. **Languages** French. **Finance** Contributions of member movements. **Events** *Biennial Conference* Québec, QC (Canada) 2008, *Biennial Conference* Sète (France) 2005, *Biennial Conference* Jonquière, QC (Canada) 1997, *Biennial Conference* Liège (Belgium) 1995, *Biennial Conference* Delémont (Switzerland) 1993. **Publications** Conference proceedings.
Members Ethnic movements in 5 countries:
Belgium (Brussels – Wallonia), Canada (Acadia – New Brunswick – Québec), France, Italy (Aosta), Switzerland (Jura – Romandy).
[2013/XD0320/F]

- ♦ Conference of Philosophical Societies (internationally oriented national body)
- ♦ Conférence des planificateurs africains (inactive)

♦ Conference of Postal and Telecommunications Administrations of the States of West Africa 04641

Conférence des administrations des postes et télécommunications des Etats de l'Afrique de l'Ouest (CAPTEAO)
Address not obtained.
History 4 Mar 1971, Nouakchott (Mauritania), on signing of an Agreement; commenced activities 1 Jan 1972. Took over activities of *Union des postes et télécommunications des Etats de l'Afrique de l'Ouest (UPTEAO)*, set up 1959, Dakar (Senegal), which came under the Convention of 18 Jan 1962, Cotonou (Benin); this Convention now having been replaced by the 1971 Agreement. **Structure** No permanent secretariat; coordinated and executed by member states in rotation, each of which in turn nominates Secretary General. Members (representatives of member states' postal and telecommunications administrations) meet annually under the presidency of the host country.
Members Postal and telecommunications administration of 7 countries:
Benin, Burkina Faso, Côte d'Ivoire, Mali, Mauritania, Niger, Senegal.
[2008/XF0516/F*]

- ♦ Conférence des Postes des Etats de l'Afrique de l'Ouest (#20893)
- ♦ Conférence des postes et télécommunications de l'Afrique centrale (#04642)
- ♦ Conference of Posts and Telecommunications Administrations of Central Africa / see Conference of Posts and Telecommunications of Central Africa (#04642)

♦ Conference of Posts and Telecommunications of Central Africa ... 04642

Conférence des postes et télécommunications de l'Afrique centrale (COPTAC) – Conferencia de Correos y Telecomunicaciones de Africa Central
Secretariat c/o Ministère des Postes et des Télécommunications, Yaoundé, Cameroon. T. +23722233625. Fax +23722233625.
History Established 30 Oct 1975, Kinshasa (Congo DR), as *Conference of Posts and Telecommunications Administrations of Central Africa – Conférence des administrations des postes et télécommunications de l'Afrique centrale (COPTAC) – Conferencia de Administraciones de Correos y Telecomunicaciones de Africa Central*. New structure adopted 26 Oct 1984, Brazzaville (Congo Brazzaville), by Convention signed by plenipotentiaries of 7 countries. Original acronym was *CAPTAC*. Dissolved and then re-established under current acronym, Oct 1998. A Restricted Union of *Universal Postal Union (UPU, #20682)*. **Aims** Improve, promote and develop post and telecommunication services in the Central African region. **Structure** Plenary Assembly, comprising Ministers of Posts and Telecommunications of countries of the sub-region. Specialized Commissions (3): Posts; Telecommunications; Regulations. **Languages** French. **Finance** Contributions of Member States. **Events** *Regular Session* Ndjamena (Chad) 1995, *Regular session* Kigali (Rwanda) 1993, *Conference* Brazzaville (Congo Brazzaville) 1984, *Conference* Libreville (Gabon) 1984, *Conference* Brazzaville (Congo Brazzaville) 1983.
Members Governments of 9 countries:
Burundi, Cameroon, Central African Rep, Chad, Congo Brazzaville, Congo DR, Equatorial Guinea, Gabon, Rwanda.
IGO Relations *African Postal Union (APU, no recent information)*; *Arab Permanent Postal Commission (APPC, #01025)*; *Asian-Pacific Postal Union (APPU, #01625)*; *Associação dos Operadores de Correios e Telecomunicações dos Países e Territórios de Língua Oficial Portuguesa (AICEP, #02333)*; *Association of European Public Postal Operators (PostEurop, #02534)*; *Baltic Postal Union (BPU, #03137)*; *Caribbean Postal Union (CPU, #03541)*; *Conférence européenne des administrations des postes et des télécommunications (CEPT, #04602)*; *International Telecommunication Union (ITU, #15673)*; *Nordic Postal Union (NPU, #17391)*; *Pan African Postal Union (PAPU, #18060)*; *Postal Union of the Americas, Spain and Portugal (PUASP, #18466)*.
[2014.01.07/XD9097/D*]

- ♦ Conférence des présidents des assemblées législatives régionales européennes / see Conférence des assemblées législatives régionales d'Europe (#04582)
- ♦ Conference of the Presidents of Bar Associations in Asia / see Presidents of Law Associations in Asia (#18486)
- ♦ Conference of Presidents of the European Regional Legislative Assemblies / see Conférence des assemblées législatives régionales d'Europe (#04582)
- ♦ Conférence de présidents des parlements du Commonwealth (#04649)
- ♦ Conférence des présidents des parlements de l'Union européenne (meeting series)
- ♦ Conference of Presidents of Regions with Legislative Power / see REGLEG (#18823)
- ♦ Conference of Principal Bars of Europe / see European Bars Federation (#06320)
- ♦ Conference on Process Integration for Energy Saving and Pollution Reduction (meeting series)
- ♦ Conference of Protestant Churches in the Latin Countries of Europe (#04591)
- ♦ Conférence des provinciaux européens – SJ / see Jesuit Conference of European Provincials (#16100)
- ♦ Conference on Quantum Cryptography (meeting series)
- ♦ Conference on Quantum Thermodynamics (meeting series)
- ♦ Conférence des rabbins européens associées (#04598)
- ♦ Conférence des rabbins européens et des organisations religieuses associées / see Conference of European Rabbis (#04598)
- ♦ Conférence rail tourisme (inactive)
- ♦ Conference on Recrystallization and Grain Growth (meeting series)

♦ Conférence des Recteurs et Présidents de la Région du Moyen-Orient (CONFREMO) 04643

Contact AUF Bureau Moyen-Orient, Rue de Damas, Villa F, Cité Bounoure Inst français du Liban, Beirut, Lebanon. T. +9611420270. Fax +9611615884. E-mail: confremo@auf.org.
URL: http://www.confremo.org/
History 19 Jul 2007, Aleppo (Syrian AR), under the aegis of *Agence universitaire de La Francophonie (AUF, #00548)*. Current statutes adopted during 2nd General Assembly, Oct 2008. **Structure** General Assembly. Board. **Languages** Arabic, French.
Members Universities in 12 countries:
Cyprus, Djibouti, Egypt, Iran Islamic Rep, Iraq, Jordan, Lebanon, Pakistan, Palestine, Syrian AR, United Arab Emirates, Yemen.
Included in the above, 1 university listed in this Yearbook:
Beirut Arab University (BAU).
[2021/XJ7348/y/E]

- ♦ Conférence de recteurs d'universités africaines (meeting series)
- ♦ Conférence des recteurs des universités francophones d'Afrique / see Conférence des recteurs des universités francophones d'Afrique et de l'Océan indien (#04644)

♦ Conférence des recteurs des universités francophones d'Afrique et de l'Océan indien (CRUFAOCI) 04644

Main Office c/o CAMES, 01 BP 134, Ouagadougou 01, Burkina Faso. T. +22650368146. Fax +22650368573. E-mail: afriqueouest@crufaoci.org.
URL: http://crufaoci-afric-west.org/
History 29 Mar 1978, Abidjan (Côte d'Ivoire), as *Conférence des recteurs des universités francophones d'Afrique (CRUFA)*. **Structure** General Assembly; Executive Committee. **Finance** Members' dues. Subsidies. **Activities** Programmes (3): *'Bourses de mobilité'* – assists in developing research and academic capacity of teaching staff through a programme of exchanges; *'Bourses d'encouragement à la recherche'* and *'Subvention aux revues scientifiques'* (not yet functioning); *'Création des centres d'excellence'* – comprising centres, laboratories and schools the quality of whose programmes, whose infrastructure and high level of personnel attracts research teaching staff and doctoral students. There are currently 2 such centres, including *Inter-State School of Veterinary Sciences and Medicine (#15982)*. **Events** *Assemblée générale* Saint Louis (Senegal) 2010, *General Assembly* Saint Louis (Senegal) 2010, *General Assembly* Yaoundé (Cameroon) 2009, *Assemblée générale / General Assembly* Ouagadougou (Burkina Faso) 2008, *Assemblée générale / General Assembly* Niamey (Niger) 2005.
Members Rectors of French-speaking universities in 16 countries:
Benin, Burkina Faso, Burundi, Cameroon, Central African Rep, Congo Brazzaville, Congo DR, Côte d'Ivoire, Gabon, Guinea, Madagascar, Mali, Mauritania, Niger, Rwanda, Togo.
IGO Relations *UNESCO (#20322)*. **NGO Relations** *Association des universités partiellement ou entièrement de langue française (AUPELF, inactive)*. Members are eligible to join: *Université virtuelle francophone (UVF, inactive)*.
[2017/XD8033/D]

Conference Rectors African
04644

alphabetic sequence excludes
For the complete listing, see Yearbook Online at

- ♦ Conference of Rectors of African Universities (meeting series)
- ♦ Conférence régionale sur les femmes de l'Amérique Latine et des Caraïbes (#18770)
- ♦ Conférence régionale sur l'intégration de la femme au développement économique et sociale de l'Amérique latine et des Caraïbes / see Regional Conference on Women in Latin America and the Caribbean (#18770)
- ♦ Conférence régionale des ministres de l'éducation et des ministres chargés de la planification économique en d'Asie et dans le Pacifique (meeting series)
- ♦ Conférence régionale du Service volontaire international / see International Forum for Volunteering in Development (#13659)

♦ Conference of the Regional and Local Authorities for the Eastern Partnership (CORLEAP) 04645

Secretariat c/o European Committee of the Regions, Rue Belliard 99-101, 1040 Brussels, Belgium. E-mail: corleap@cor.europa.eu.
URL: https://cor.europa.eu/en/our-work/Pages/CORLEAP.aspx

History Set up 2011, by *European Committee of the Regions (CoR, #06665)*. **Aims** Coordinate the representation of the local and regional authorities within the Eastern Partnership; complement and support the effort by the EU institutions and other participating stakeholders in delivering the *European Neighbourhood* Policy; spread the concepts that will bring partner countries closer to the *EU* and foster the internal reform and capacity building at the local and regional level. **Structure** Annual Meeting. Composition: 18 members of CoR and 18 representatives from the Eastern partner countries (3 seats per partner country). Bureau; Co-chaired by CoR President and a representative from partner countries. EU seats distributed among 5 political groups: *Group of the European People's Party in the Committee of the Regions (EPP-CoR, #10776)*; *Party of European Socialists (PES, #18249)*; *Renew Europe – Committee of the Regions (Renew Europe, #18841)*; *European Conservatives and Reformists Group – Committee of the Regions (ECR-CoR, #06746)*. **Languages** English, Russian. **Staff** 2.00 FTE, paid. **Finance** No budget. *European Committee of the Regions (CoR, #06665)* contributes to financing activities and reimburses participation expenses of members. **Activities** Knowledge management/information dissemination; politics/policy/regulatory. **Events** *Annual Meeting* Turku (Finland) 2019, *Annual Meeting* Kiev (Ukraine) 2018. **Publications** *CORLEAP digest* (3 a year) – electronic newlsetter.
Members Eastern partner countries (6):
Armenia, Azerbaijan, Belarus, Georgia, Moldova, Ukraine.
NGO Relations *Eastern Partnership Civil Society Forum (EaP CSF, #05247)*; *European Association for Local Democracy (ALDA, #06110)*. [2018.12.03/XM7076/**E***]

- ♦ Conférence des régions de l'Europe du Nord-Ouest (inactive)
- ♦ Conference of Regions of North-West Europe (inactive)
- ♦ Conférence des régions périphériques maritimes de la CE / see Conference of Peripheral Maritime Regions of Europe (#04638)
- ♦ Conférence des régions périphériques maritimes d'Europe (#04638)
- ♦ Conférence des responsables de recherche agronomique africains / see West and Central African Council for Agricultural Research and Development (#20907)
- ♦ Conférence des responsables de la recherche agronomique africains et français / see West and Central African Council for Agricultural Research and Development (#20907)
- ♦ Conference to Review and Extend the Non-Proliferation Treaty / see Abolition 2000 – Global Network to Eliminate Nuclear Weapons (#00006)

♦ Conference of Rhine Churches 04646

Conférence des Eglises riveraines du Rhin (CERR) – Konferenz der Kirchen Am Rhein
Contact 1 bis quai Saint-Thomas, BP 80022, 67081 Strasbourg CEDEX, France. T. +33388259058.
URL: http://www.leuenberg.net/

History 1960. As of 2008, a regional group of *Community of Protestant Churches in Europe (CPCE, #04405)*. **Aims** Act as an informal meeting for discussing contemporary European problems. **Structure** No formal structure. **Languages** English, French, German. **Finance** Member Churches' contributions. **Activities** Events/meetings. **Events** *International Soil Conference* Phetchaburi (Thailand) 2015, *Annual conference* Goersdorf (France) 2004, *Annual Conference* Strasbourg (France) 2003, *Annual Conference* Goersdorf (France) 1997, *Annual conference* Goersdorf (France) 1996. **Publications** *CERR Newsletter*.
Members Churches in 5 countries:
Austria, France, Germany, Netherlands, Switzerland.
IGO Relations Adviser to Ecumenical Secretariat of: *Council of Europe (CE, #04881)*. **NGO Relations** Instrumental in setting up *Protestant Churches' Secretariat for the Council of Europe (inactive)*.
[2019.11.11/XF0070/c/**F**]

- ♦ Conférence sanitaire internationale (inactive)
- ♦ Conférences des associations industrielles nordiques (meeting series)
- ♦ Conferences of the Baltic Chambers of Commerce (meeting series)
- ♦ Conférences des commissaires aux comptes généraux du Commonwealth (meeting series)
- ♦ Conferences on the Development and the Planning of Urban Transport in Developing Countries / see Cooperation for the Continuing Development of Urban and Suburban Transportation (#04792)
- ♦ Conférences sur le développement et l'aménagement des transports urbains dans les pays en développement / see Cooperation for the Continuing Development of Urban and Suburban Transportation (#04792)

♦ Conference of Secretaries of Christian World Communions (CS/CWC) 04647

Address not obtained.

History 1957. Founded as an informal ecumenical forum. Former names and other names: *Christian World Communion Executives Conference* – alias; *Conference of General Secretaries of Christian World Communions* – alias. **Aims** Share information, Christian fellowship and review current issues. **Structure** A global forum composed of most of the large world families of Christian communions and churches. **Finance** None. Members pay their own expenses. **Events** *Annual Conference* Hendersonville, NC (USA) 2002, *Annual Conference* Geneva (Switzerland) 2001, *Annual Conference* Johannesburg (South Africa) 2000, *Annual Conference* Jerusalem (Israel) 1999, *Annual Conference* UK 1998. **Publications** Conference proceedings. **NGO Relations** Churches belonging to the Methodist/Wesleyan tradition represented by: *World Methodist Council (WMC, #21650)*. [2019/XF5855/c/**F**]

- ♦ Conférence sur la sécurité et la coopération en Europe / see Organization for Security and Cooperation in Europe (#17887)
- ♦ Conference on Security Cooperation in the Asia Pacific (meeting series)
- ♦ Conference on Security and Cooperation in Europe / see Organization for Security and Cooperation in Europe (#17887)
- ♦ Conference for Security and Cooperation in Europe / see Finnish Committee for European Security
- ♦ Conference on Security, Stability, Development and Cooperation in Africa (inactive)
- ♦ Conférence des services de traduction des états européens (#04650)
- ♦ Conférences intercitoyennes européennes (meeting series)
- ♦ Conférences internationales sur l'avenir de l'environnement (meeting series)
- ♦ Conference on Small Animal Precision Image-Guided Radiotherapy (meeting series)
- ♦ Conférence socialiste d'Asie (inactive)
- ♦ Conférence des sociétés d'ingénieurs de l'Europe occidentale et des Etats-Unis d'Amérique (inactive)
- ♦ Conference of Societies for the History of Pharmacy (inactive)

♦ Conférence au sommet des chefs d'Etat et de gouvernement des pays ayant le français en partage (Sommet de la Francophonie) 04648

Contact c/o OIF, 19-21 avenue Bosquet, 75007 Paris, France. T. +33144373300. Fax +33145791498.
Contact c/o AIF, 13 quai André-Citroën, 75015 Paris, France. T. +33144373300. Fax +33145791498.
URL: https://www.francophonie.org/le-sommet-84

History 1986. Established when the first Summit was held. Former names and other names: *Conférence des chefs d'Etat et de gouvernement des pays ayant en commun l'usage du français (Sommet de la Francophonie)* – former (1986). **Aims** Fundamental objectives for *multilateral francophone cooperation* as laid down by the Paris (France) (Chaillot) Summit of Nov 1991 concern: culture and communication; education, youth and sport; science; environment and development; commitment to development and democracy. **Structure** The supreme organ of the French-speaking world, the Summit comprises a biennial conference series originally prepared and followed up by *Comité international de préparation du Sommet francophone (CIP, inactive)* and *Comité international du suivi du Sommet francophone (CIS, inactive)*, these two committees having been replaced, 21 Nov 1991, by *Conseil permanent de la Francophonie (CPF, #04697)*. Principal operator of Summits: *Organisation internationale de la Francophonie (OIF, #17809)*, formerly *Agence intergouvernementale de La Francophonie (inactive)*. Operator of higher education and research aspects: *Agence universitaire de La Francophonie (AUF, #00548)*. Operator of audiovisual aspects: *TV5Monde (TV5, #20269)*. *Association Internationale des Maires et responsables des capitales et métropoles partiellement ou entièrement Francophones (AIMF, #02715)* and *Université internationale de langue française au service du développement africain à Alexandrie d'Egypte (Université Senghor, #20691)* also implement Summit decisions. Common organ with OIF: *Conférence ministérielle de la Francophonie (CMF, #04630)*. **Activities** Instigated, 1986, Paris (France) and formalized, 14-16 Nov 1997, Hanoi (Vietnam), the existence of 'La Francophonie'. **Events** *Sommet* Djerba (Tunisia) 2021, *Sommet* Tunis (Tunisia) 2020, *Sommet* Yerevan (Armenia) 2018, *Sommet* Antananarivo (Madagascar) 2016, *Femmes et jeunes en francophonie – vecteurs de paix, acteurs de développement* Dakar (Senegal) 2014.
Members Heads of State and Government of 53 countries and territories:
Albania, Andorra, Belgium, Belgium/Wallonia Region, Benin, Bulgaria, Burkina Faso, Burundi, Cambodia, Cameroon, Canada, Cape Verde, Central African Rep, Chad, Comoros, Congo Brazzaville, Congo DR, Côte d'Ivoire, Djibouti, Dominica, Egypt, Equatorial Guinea, France, Gabon, Greece, Guinea, Guinea-Bissau, Haiti, Laos, Lebanon, Luxembourg, Madagascar, Mali, Mauritania, Mauritius, Moldova, Monaco, Morocco, New Brunswick, Niger, North Macedonia, Québec, Romania, Rwanda, Sao Tomé-Principe, Senegal, Seychelles, St Lucia, Switzerland, Togo, Tunisia, Vanuatu, Vietnam.
Observer states (10):
Armenia, Austria, Croatia, Czechia, Georgia, Hungary, Lithuania, Poland, Slovakia, Slovenia.
IGO Relations Instrumental in setting up: *Conférence des ministres de la jeunesse et des sports de la Francophonie (CONFEJES, #04634)*; *Fonds francophone d'intervention pour l'enseignement supérieur (no recent information)*; *Fonds francophone de la recherche (FFR, inactive)*; *Observatoire du traitement avancé du français et des langues nationales partenaires (OTAF, no recent information)*; *TV5MONDE Europe (see: #20269)*.
NGO Relations Instrumental in setting up:
- *Assemblée parlementaire de la Francophonie (APF, #02312)*;
- *Association internationale des éditeurs africains francophones (AIEAF, no recent information)*;
- *Association internationale des libraires francophones (AILF, #02712)*;
- *Comité pour le français dans les organisations internationales (inactive)*;
- *Comité international des Jeux de La Francophonie (CIJF, #04178)*;
- *Comité de liaison de la Conférence biennale des organisations non gouvernementales oeuvrant dans l'espace francophone (inactive)*;
- *Conseil francophone de la chanson (CFC, #04690)*;
- *Consortium international francophone de formation à distance (CIFFAD, inactive)*;
- *Fondation internationale de l'enseignement supérieur et de la recherche (FIESR, no recent information)*;
- *Fonds francophone universitaire de l'information (FFI, inactive)*;
- *Forum francophone des affaires (FFA, #09916)*;
- *International Francophone Institute (IFI, #13682)*;
- *Réseau francophone de l'ingénierie de la langue (FRANCIL, inactive)*;
- *UNISAT (inactive)*;
- *Université des réseaux d'expression française (UREF, inactive)*;
- *École supérieure de la francophonie pour l'administration et le management (ESFAM, #05298)*. [2016/XF1536/c/**F***]

- ♦ Conference of Southeast Asian Historians (inactive)
- ♦ Conference of Southeast Asian Librarians / see Congress of Southeast Asian Librarians (#04679)
- ♦ Conference of Speakers of the European Union Parliaments (meeting series)

♦ Conference of Speakers and Presiding Officers of the Commonwealth (CSPOC) 04649

Conférence de présidents des parlements du Commonwealth
Sec 131 Queen Street, 4th Floor, Parliament of Canada, Ottawa ON K1A 0A6, Canada. T. +16139436703. Fax +16139955357. E-mail: cspoc@parl.gc.ca.
URL: http://www.cspoc.org/

History Founded 12 Sep 1969, Ottawa (Canada), at 1st Conference of Commonwealth Speakers and Presiding Officers, as *Conference of Speakers and Presiding Officers of Commonwealth Parliaments*. **Aims** Maintain, foster and encourage impartiality and fairness of the part of Speakers and Presiding Officers of Parliaments; promote knowledge and understanding of parliamentary democracy in its various forms; develop parliamentary institutions. **Structure** Conference (every 2 years); Standing Committee (meets in intervening years). **Languages** English. **Staff** No full-time staff. Conference staff provided by the Parliament hosting conference. Secretary provided by House of Commons of Canada. **Finance** No operating budget. The travel and accommodation expenses of Conference delegates are paid by their own Parliaments. The host Parliament pays administration and certain ancillary costs. **Events** *Conference* Uganda 2024, *Conference* Canberra, ACT (Australia) 2023, *Conference* Ottawa, ON (Canada) 2020, *Conference* Victoria (Seychelles) 2018, *Conference* Kota Kinabalu (Malaysia) 2016. **Publications** Conference proceedings.
Members Speakers and Presiding Officers of Upper and Lower Chambers of fully sovereign Commonwealth Parliaments (54):
Antigua-Barbuda, Australia, Bahamas, Bangladesh, Barbados, Belize, Botswana, Cameroon, Canada, Cook Is, Cyprus, Dominica, Eswatini, Fiji, Ghana, Grenada, Guyana, India, Jamaica, Kenya, Kiribati, Lesotho, Malawi, Malaysia, Maldives, Malta, Mauritius, Mozambique, Namibia, Nauru, New Zealand, Nigeria, Niue, Pakistan, Papua New Guinea, Rwanda, Samoa, Seychelles, Sierra Leone, Singapore, Solomon Is, South Africa, Sri Lanka, St Kitts-Nevis, St Lucia, St Vincent-Grenadines, Tanzania UR, Tonga, Trinidad-Tobago, Tuvalu, Uganda, UK, Vanuatu, Zambia. [2021/XC4534/v/**C**]

- ♦ Conference of Speakers and Presiding Officers of Commonwealth Parliaments / see Conference of Speakers and Presiding Officers of the Commonwealth (#04649)
- ♦ Conférences Pugwash sur la science et les problèmes internationaux (#18574)
- ♦ Conference of States Parties of the Organization for the Prohibition of Chemical Weapons (see: #17823)
- ♦ Conférence des statisticiens africains (inactive)
- ♦ Conférence des statisticiens du Commonwealth (meeting series)
- ♦ Conférence des statisticiens européens (#04600)
- ♦ Conference on Stochastic Weather Generators (meeting series)
- ♦ Conférence des supérieurs principaux des Antilles (inactive)
- ♦ Conference on the Theory of Quantum Computation, Communication and Cryptography (meeting series)
- ♦ Conférence sur la toxicité et la carcinogenèse des métaux (meeting series)
- ♦ Conférence TransJurassienne (internationally oriented national body)
- ♦ Conférence TransJurassienne – L'Arc jurassien franco-suisse / see Conférence TransJurassience

♦ Conference of Translation Services of European States (COTSOES) 04650

Conférence des services de traduction des états européens (CST) – Konferenz der Übersetzungsdienste Europäischer Staaten (KÜDES)
Pres Communications Dept, Language Services, Ministry for Foreign Affairs, SE-103 39 Stockholm, Sweden.
URL: http://www.cotsoes.org/

History Jun 1980, The Hague (Netherlands), as *Conference of Translation Services of West European States*. Present name adopted 1992. **Aims** Increase cooperation between the central government translation and terminology services in European countries. **Structure** Assembly (every 2 years); Presidency; Working Groups (4). **Languages** English, French, German. **Staff** No permanent staff. **Finance** None. **Activities** Knowledge management/information dissemination; networking/liaising. **Events** *Assembly* Stockholm (Sweden) 2016, *Assembly* Fribourg (Switzerland) 2014, *Assembly* Paris (France) 2012, *Assembly* Bonn (Germany) 2010, *Assembly* The Hague (Netherlands) 2006. **Publications** *COTSOES Recommendations for Terminology Work* (3rd ed revised 2014).

Members Services in 17 countries:
Austria, Belgium, Finland, France, Germany, Iceland, Ireland, Italy, Latvia, Lithuania, Netherlands, Portugal, Spain, Sweden, Switzerland, Türkiye, UK.
IGO Relations *European Commission (EC, #06633); Nordic Council (NC, #17256).* [2016.12.23/XM2845/**F**]

♦ Conference of Translation Services of West European States / see Conference of Translation Services of European States (#04650)
♦ Conférence de l'union européenne (meeting series)
♦ Conference of University Professors of Civil Engineering of Central Africa (meeting series)
♦ Conference of Vice-Chancellors, Presidents and Rectors of Institutions of Higher Learning in Africa (meeting series)
♦ Conférence des Villes de l'Arc Atlantique / see Atlantic Cities (#03008)
♦ Conference on Visual Literacy / see International Visual Literacy Association
♦ Conference on Web and Internet Economics (meeting series)
♦ Conference on Wind energy and Wildlife impacts (meeting series)
♦ Conference on World Affairs / see Council on International and Public Affairs
♦ Conferencia de Administraciones de Correos y Telecomunicaciones de Africa Central / see Conference of Posts and Telecommunications of Central Africa (#04642)
♦ Conferencia de Asambleas Regionales Europeas (#04582)
♦ Conferência das Assembleias Legislativas Regionais da União Europeia (#04582)
♦ Conferencia de Autoridades Cinematograficas de Iberoamérica (no recent information)
♦ Conferencia de Autoridades Iberoamericanas de Informatica (#04606)
♦ Conferencia de Autoridades Latinoamericanas de Informatica / see Conference of Iberoamerican Authorities on Informatics (#04606)
♦ Conferência dos Chefes de Polícia das Capitais Europeias (meeting series)
♦ Conferência das Cidades do Arco Atlântico / see Atlantic Cities (#03008)
♦ Conferencia Circumpolar Inuit / see Inuit Circumpolar Council (#15995)
♦ Conferencia de las Ciudades del Arco Atlantico / see Atlantic Cities (#03008)
♦ Conferencia de Compañias Express de Latinoamérica y el Caribe / see Conferencia Latino Americana de Compañias Express (#04654)
♦ Conferencia de Correos y Telecomunicaciones de Africa Central (#04642)
♦ Conferencia Cristiana por la Paz (inactive)
♦ Conferencia de Desarme (#04590)
♦ Conferencia de Directores de Ceca (#16822)
♦ Conferencia de Directores Iberoamericanos del Agua (unconfirmed)
♦ Conferencia de Directores de los Servicios Meteorológicos e Hidrológicos Iberoamericanos (#04586)
♦ Conferencia de Directores de los Servicios Meteorológicos e Hidrológicos Nacionales del Africa del Oeste (#04589)
♦ Conferencia Episcopal Latinoamericana / see Consejo Episcopal Latinoamericano (#04709)
♦ Conferencia Especializada Interamericana sobre derecho Internacional Privado (meeting series)
♦ Conferencia Estadistica de las Américas (see: #20556)
♦ Conferencia de los Estados Partes de la Organización para la Prohibición de las Armas Quimicas (see: #17823)
♦ Conferencia Europea Justitia et Pax / see Conference of European Justice and Peace Commissions (#04596)
♦ Conferencia Europea de las Regiones Vinicolas / see Assembly of European Wine Regions (#02317)
♦ Conferência Europeia das Regiões Vinicolas / see Assembly of European Wine Regions (#02317)
♦ Conferencia de Facultades y Escuelas de Medicina de América Latina (meeting series)

♦ Conferencia de las Fuerzas Armadas de Centroamérica (CFAC) . . . 04651

Conference of Central American Armed Forces

SG KM 5 1/2 Carretera a Santa Tecla, Frente a Centro de Convenciones, San Salvador, El Salvador. T. +50322500005. Fax +50322500255. E-mail: sgcfac.es2016@gmail.com.
URL: https://www.conferenciafac.org/

History 12 Nov 1997. Established upon the signing of an accord by the Presidents of 4 Central American countries. **Aims** Operate as a permanent system of cooperation, coordination and mutual support; promote security, development and military integration of Central America and the Caribbean; promote research of common interests; provide an optimal level of defense against threats to democracy, peace and freedom. **Languages** English, Spanish.
Members Governments of 5 countries:
Dominican Rep, El Salvador, Guatemala, Honduras, Nicaragua.
NGO Relations Cooperation agreement with: *International Committee of the Red Cross (ICRC, #12799).* [2016.07.27/XF6365/**F***]

♦ Conferencia de Geografía Latinoamericana (#04625)
♦ Conferencia de Geógrafos Latinoamericanistas / see Conference of Latin American Geography (#04625)
♦ Conferencia de La Haya de Derecho Internacional Privado / see The Hague Conference on Private International Law (#10850)
♦ Conferencia Hemisférica de Seguros / see Federación Interamericana de Empresas de Seguros (#09331)
♦ Conferência ibero-americana de Justiça Constitucional (#04652)

♦ Conferencia Iberoamericana de Justicia Constitucional (CIJC) 04652

Ibero-American Conference on Constitutional Justice – Conferência ibero-americana de Justiça Constitucional

Main Office c/o Tribunal Constitucional, Domenico Scarlatti 6, 28003 Madrid, Spain. E-mail: cijc@tribunalconstitucional.es.
URL: http://www.cijc.org/

History Oct 2005, Seville (Spain), following earlier meeting activities. Statutes adopted, Oct 2006, Santiago (Chile). **Events** *Conference* Bogota (Colombia) 2020, *Conference* Panama (Panama) 2018, *Conference* Lima (Peru) 2016, *Conference* Santo Domingo (Dominican Rep) 2014, *Conference* Cadiz (Spain) 2012.
Members Tribunals, courts and constitutional chambers of 22 countries:
Andorra, Argentina, Bolivia, Brazil, Chile, Colombia, Costa Rica, Dominican Rep, Ecuador, El Salvador, Guatemala, Honduras, Mexico, Nicaragua, Panama, Paraguay, Peru, Portugal, Puerto Rico, Spain, Uruguay, Venezuela.
IGO Relations *European Commission for Democracy through Law (Venice Commission, #06636); World Conference on Constitutional Justice (WCCJ, #21298).* [2020/XJ8260/**D***]

♦ Conferencia de Iglesias del Caribe (#03479)
♦ Conferencia de Iglesias Europeas / see Conference of European Churches (#04593)
♦ Conferencia de las Instituciones Católicas de Teologia (see: #13381)
♦ Conferencia Interamericana de Bienestar Social (inactive)
♦ Conferencia Interamericana de Ministros de Trabajo (no recent information)
♦ Conferencia Interamericana de Ministros do Trabalho (no recent information)
♦ Conferência Interamericana de Seguridade Social / see Inter-American Conference on Social Security (#11419)
♦ Conferencia Interamericana de Seguridad Social (#11419)
♦ Conferencia Internacional Católica de Escultismo (#12453)
♦ Conferencia Internacional Católica del Guidismo (#12452)
♦ Conferencia Internacional para el Crédito Agricola / see Confédération internationale du crédit agricole (#04560)
♦ Conferencia Internacional sobre Educación de Adultos (meeting series)
♦ Conferencia Internacional sobre Ventilación Mecanica (meeting series)

♦ Conferência das Jurisdições Constitucionais dos Paises de Lingua Portuguesa (CJCPLP) 04653

Presidency Tribunal Constitucional, Rua de "O Século" nº 111, 1249-117 Lisbon, Portugal. T. +351213233600. E-mail: gabinete.presidente@tribconstitucional.pt.
URL: https://cjcplp.tribunalconstitucional.pt/cjcplp/

History 2008, Brasilia (Brazil). Established when Constitutive Declaration was signed. Statutes approved during 1st Assembly, May 2010, Lisbon (Portugal). **Aims** Promote *human rights*; defend democracy and *judicial independence*; foster cooperation. **Structure** Assembly; Council of Presidents. **Events** *Assembly* Lisbon (Portugal) 2022, *Assembly* Brasilia (Brazil) 2016, *Assembly* Luanda (Angola) 2014, *Assembly* Maputo (Mozambique) 2012, *Assembly* Lisbon (Portugal) 2010.
Members Constitutional courts of 8 countries and territories:
Angola, Brazil, Cape Verde, Guinea-Bissau, Mozambique, Portugal, Sao Tomé-Principe, Timor-Leste.
IGO Relations Participates in: *World Conference on Constitutional Justice (WCCJ, #21298).* [2022/XJ9009/**C***]

♦ Conferencia Latinoamericana en Bioimpedancia (meeting series)

♦ Conferencia Latino Americana de Compañias Express (CLADEC) . . 04654

Latin American Association of Express Companies

Exec Dir 777 Brickell Ave, Ste 500, Miami FL 33131, USA. T. +13055734775.
Co-Exec Dir address not obtained. E-mail: maria@cvoxgroup.com.
URL: http://www.cladec.org/

History 1991. Previously referred to as *Conferencia Latinoamericana de Empresas Courier*. Also referred to as *Conferencia de Compañias Express de Latinoamérica y el Caribe.* **Structure** Executive Committee of 7 members. **Activities** Annual meeting. **Events** *Symposium of the Americas customs/trade/finance* Miami, FL (USA) 2005.
Members National trade associations (22) and express delivery companies in 24 countries and territories:
Argentina, Bahamas, Barbados, Bolivia, Brazil, Chile, Colombia, Costa Rica, Dominican Rep, Ecuador, El Salvador, Guatemala, Honduras, Jamaica, Mexico, Nicaragua, Panama, Paraguay, Peru, Trinidad-Tobago, Uruguay, USA, Venezuela.
IGO Relations *Secretaria Permanente del Convenio Multilateral sobre Cooperación y Asistencia Mutua entre las Direcciones Nacionales de Aduanas de América Latina, España y Portugal (COMALEP, #19194).* **NGO Relations** Affiliated member of: *Global Express Association (GEA, #10351).* [2016/XD4727/**D**]

♦ Conferencia Latinoamericana de Empresas Courier / see Conferencia Latino Americana de Compañias Express (#04654)
♦ Conferencia Latinoamericana de Escuelas y Facultades de Arquitectura (meeting series)
♦ Conferencia Latinoamericana de Facultades y Escuelas de Ingenieria de Sistemas y Ciencias de la Computación (meeting series)
♦ Conferencia de Ministros de Educación de América Latina y el Caribe (meeting series)
♦ Conferencia de Ministros y Jefes de Planificación de América Latina y el Caribe (see: #16279)

♦ Conferência de Ministros da Justiça dos Países de Língua Oficial Portuguesa (CMJPLOP) 04655

Address not obtained.
URL: https://dgpj.justica.gov.pt/Relacoes-Internacionais/Cooperacao-internacional/Conferencia-de-Ministros-da-Justica-dos-Paises-de-Lingua-Oficial-Portuguesa

History Established by Cooperation Agreement, signed Sep 1992, Sao Tomé-Principe. **Structure** Plenary Session; Commissions; Secretariat. **Events** *Conference* Luanda (Angola) 2022, *Conference* Cape Verde 2019.
Members Governments of 8 countries:
Angola, Brazil, Cape Verde, Guinea-Bissau, Mozambique, Portugal, Sao Tomé-Principe, Timor-Leste. [2022/AA2813/c/**F***]

♦ Conferencia de Ministros de Justicia de los Países Iberoamericanos (COMJIB) 04656

SG Paseode Recoletos 8, 28001 Madrid, Spain. T. +34915753624.
URL: https://comjib.org/

History 1992. Established by the "Madrid Treaty", bringing together Ministries of Justice and similar institutions of the 22 countries of the Ibero-American Community. One of 5 organizations within *Comité de Dirección Estratégica de los Organismos Iberoamericanos (CoDEI, #04149).* **Aims** Strengthen cooperation in the field of justice in the Ibero-American community, promoting processes of institutional transformation and development of public policies for justice, contributing to the social welfare of the region. **Structure** Plenary Assembly; Delegate Commission; Deputy General Secretariats; National Coordinators. **Events** *Plenary Assembly* Colombia 2019. **IGO Relations** Observer status with (1): *United Nations (UN, #20515)* (General Assembly). Cooperates with (4): *Ibero-American General Secretariat (#11024); Ibero-American Social Security Organization (#11028); Ibero-American Youth Organization (#11036); Organization of Ibero-American States for Education, Science and Culture (#17871).* **NGO Relations** Instrumental in setting up (1): *Red Iberoamericana de Cooperación Jurídica Internacional (IberRed, #18662).* [2020/AA1014/**F***]

♦ Conferencia de Ministros de la Juventud y los Deportes de los Paises de Habla Francesa (#04634)
♦ Conferencia Mundial de Comunidades Terapéuticas (meeting series)
♦ Conferencia Mundial de la Religión por la Paz / see Religions for Peace (#18831)
♦ Conferencia Mundial de la Sociedad Civil (meeting series)
♦ Conferencia de las Naciones Unidas sobre Comercio y Desarrollo (#20285)
♦ Conferencia de Organizaciones Internacionales Católicas (inactive)
♦ Conferencia Panindia de Mujeres (#00737)
♦ Conferência Parlamentar das Américas / see Confederación Parlamentaria de las Américas (#04479)
♦ Conferencia Parlamentaria de las Américas / see Confederación Parlamentaria de las Américas (#04479)
♦ Conferencia de Parlamentarios de Asia-Pacifico sobre Medio Ambiente y Desarrollo (#01621)
♦ Conferencia Permanente de Academias Juridicas de Iberoamérica (unconfirmed)
♦ Conferencia Permanente de Partidos Politicos de América Latina / see Conferencia Permanente de Partidos Políticos de América Latina y el Caribe (#04657)

♦ Conferencia Permanente de Partidos Políticos de América Latina y el Caribe (COPPPAL) 04657

Permanent Conference of Political Parties of Latin America and the Caribbean – Conférence permanente des partis politiques d'Amérique latine et le caraïbe

Acting Pres Ezequiel Montes 99, Colonia Tabacalera, Cuauhtémoc, CP 06030, 06030 Mexico City CDMX, Mexico. T. +525556834603. E-mail: secretariaejecutiva@copppal.org.
URL: http://www.copppal.org/

History 12 Oct 1979, Oaxaca (Mexico). Established at the instigation of the Institutional Revolutionary Party of Mexico (PRI) by standing group of Latinoamerican and Caribean leaders. Former names and other names: *Conferencia Permanente de Partidos Politicos de América Latina* – former. **Aims** Defend development of democracy and legal and political institutions; strengthen the principle of self-determination of the peoples of Latin America; promote regional integration; support any initiative for disarmament; encourage defence, sovereignty and better utilization of natural resources of each country in the region; promote regional organizations and joint actions that will enable establishment of a more just international economic order; defend and promote respect for human rights. **Structure** President; Vice Predident; Executive Secretariat; Assistant Executive Secretaries; Work Commissions. **Languages** English, Spanish. **Activities** Events/meetings; politics/policy/regulatory; publishing activities; research/documentation. **Events** *Plenary Meeting* Mexico City (Mexico) 2020, *Plenary Meeting* Managua (Nicaragua) 2019, *Plenary Meeting* Panama (Panama) 2018, *Plenary Meeting* Tegucigalpa (Honduras) 2017, *Plenary Meeting* Managua (Nicaragua) 2014. **Publications** *Boletin Informativo de la COPPPAL.*
Members Political parties (over 60) in 32 countries and territories:
Argentina, Aruba, Belize, Bolivia, Bonaire Is, Brazil, Canada, Chile, Colombia, Costa Rica, Cuba, Curaçao, Dominica, Dominican Rep, Ecuador, El Salvador, Guatemala, Haiti, Honduras, Jamaica, Mexico, Nicaragua, Panama, Paraguay, Peru, Puerto Rico, St Lucia, St Maarten, St Vincent-Grenadines, Suriname, Uruguay, Venezuela. [2021.03.05/XD4981/**D**]

♦ Conferencia de Presidentes de Parlamentos Iberoamericanos (meeting series)

♦ Conferencia de Provinciales Jesuitas de América Latina y El Caribe (CPAL) 04658

Conference of Jesuit Provincials in Latin America

Sec Av Fulgencio Valdez 780, Breña 05 0052, 5, Lima, Peru. T. +5114438110. E-mail: secretario@cpalsj.org.
Pres address not obtained.
URL: http://www.jesuitas.lat/

History 27 Nov 1999, by *Society of Jesus (SJ)*. **Aims** Foster unity, communication and a common view among the Jesuits in Latin America. **Structure** Assembly (meets twice a year); Council; Committees; Head Office. **Languages** English, Portuguese, Spanish. **Staff** 7.00 FTE, paid. **Finance** Annual budget: US$ 276,674. **Activities** Events/meetings; religious activities; training/education. **Events** *Reunion de sectores educativos* Córdoba (Argentina) 2005. **Publications** *CPAL Bulletin* (26 a year and 12 a year). *La Compañia de Jesús y el derecho universal a una Educación de calidad* (2019); *Colaboración en el corazón de la misión* (2018); *Cuadernos del CIF (Centro Interprovincial de Formación en Teologia)* (2018); *Somos un cuerpo para la misión* (2017); *Ejercicios Espirituales en América Latina* (2010) in Portuguese, Spanish; *CPAL 10 años al servicio de la misión* (2009); *Disponer la Vida para la Misión* (2009) in Spanish; *Programa de Formación Política y Cuidadana* (2009) in Portuguese, Spanish; *Projyecto Educativo Común de la Compañia de Jesús en América Latina (PEC): Textos y comentarios* (2006) in Spanish – with CD-ROM; *Manual de Pastoral Vocacional de la Compañía de Jesús para América Latina* (2005) in Spanish; *Proyecto Educativo Común de la Compañia de Jesús en America Latina (PEC)* (2005) in Portuguese, Spanish; *Hacia un Proyecto Educativo Común* (2004) by Andrea Ramal in Spanish; *Transparencia en la Vida Religiosa* (2003) in Portuguese, Spanish; *Apostolado Social: Sector y Dimensión Apostólica* (2003) by Ricardo Antoncich in Portuguese, Spanish; *Viento en Popa a Toda Vela* (2003) by Francisco Ivern in Portuguese, Spanish; *Principio y Horizonte de Nuestra Misión en América Latina* (2002) in English, Portuguese, Spanish; *Caracteristicas de la Parroquia Jesuita en la A Latina de Hoy* (2002) in Portuguese, Spanish; *Colaboración con los Laicos en la Misión* (2001) in Portuguese, Spanish. CD-ROMs.
Members Individuals (2,072) in 19 countries and territories:
Argentina, Bolivia, Brazil, Chile, Colombia, Costa Rica, Cuba, Dominican Rep, Ecuador, El Salvador, Guatemala, Honduras, Mexico, Nicaragua, Panama, Paraguay, Peru, Uruguay, Venezuela.
Invited members in 3 countries:
Guyana, Haiti, Jamaica. [2019.12.13/XF6825/v/**F**]

- ♦ Conferência das Regiões Periféricas Marítimas de la CE / see Conference of Peripheral Maritime Regions of Europe (#04638)
- ♦ Conferência das Regiões Periféricas Marítimas da Europa (#04638)
- ♦ Conferencia Regional para la Integración de la Mujer en el Desarrollo Económico y Social de América Latina y el Caribe / see Regional Conference on Women in Latin America and the Caribbean (#18770)
- ♦ Conferencia Regional sobre Migración (#18769)
- ♦ Conferencia Regional sobre la Mujer de América Latina y el Caribe (#18770)
- ♦ Conferencia de las Regiones Periféricas Marítimas de la CE / see Conference of Peripheral Maritime Regions of Europe (#04638)
- ♦ Conferencia de las Regiones Periféricas Marítimas de Europa (#04638)
- ♦ Conferencia y Unión de los Distritos Siderúrgicos de Europa (inactive)
- ♦ Conferencia Veterinaria Latinoamericana (meeting series)

♦ Conferentia Episcopalis Pacifici (CEPAC) 04659

Conférence des évêques du Pacifique – Episcopal Conference of the Pacific

Pres CEPAC Secretariat, PO Box 289, 14 Williamson Road, Suva, Fiji. T. +679300340. Fax +679303143. E-mail: cepac@connect.com.fj.
URL: http://www.gcatholic.org/dioceses/conference/037.htm/

History Mar 1968, Suva (Fiji), when the status of Mission territories was changed to Dioceses and Archdioceses from former status of Vicariate Apostolic. A grouping of Roman Catholic bishops of the South Pacific area. **Aims** Provide a forum in which bishops of certain Pacific Island dioceses and ordinaries of other Ecclesiastical jurisdictions exercise their pastoral office through forms and programmes of the apostolate which are adapted to the present circumstances and needs of the Pacific Islands. **Structure** Plenary Assembly (in principle annually). The Conference functions under the directive of President, in his absence of Vice-President, assisted by permanent Secretary. Standing Committee of Bishops forms Seminary Senate (meeting twice a year), to handle matters concerning *Pacific Regional Seminary of St Peter Chanel* in Suva (Fiji). **Languages** English, French. **Staff** 2.00 FTE, paid. **Finance** Members' dues. Budget (annual): US$ 64,000. **Activities** Commissions (4): Communications; Mission and Unity; Justice and Development; Matrimonial Tribunal of Second Instance. Many programs implemented on a sub-regional rather than regional level. Sub-regions (3): Northern region (Micronesia); French speaking region; "Polynesian" region. **Events** *Plenary Assembly* Rome (Italy) 1998, *Plenary Assembly* Rome (Italy) 1998, *Plenary Assembly* Hagatna (Guam) 1996, *Plenary Assembly* Auckland (New Zealand) 1994, *Plenary Assembly* Rome (Italy) 1993.
Members Archdioceses (1, in Agana, Nouméa, Papeete, Suva, Samoa-Apia), with 5 Archdioceses, 9 Dioceses, 1 Prefect Apostolic, 2 Missions 'Sui Juris' (Tuvalu), covering 19 countries and territories:
Cook Is, Fiji, Guam, Kiribati, Marshall Is, Micronesia FS (Carolines), Nauru, New Caledonia, Niue, Northern Mariana Is, Palau, Polynesia Fr, Samoa, Samoa USA, Tokelau, Tonga, Tuvalu, Vanuatu, Wallis-Futuna.
IGO Relations *Pacific Community (SPC, #17942)*. **NGO Relations** Member of: *Caritas Internationalis (CI, #03580)*; *Federation of Catholic Bishops' Conferences of Oceania (FCBCO, #09467)*. *Pacific Regional Seminary (PRS, #17995)*. [2020/XD8498/**D**]

- ♦ Conferentia Episcopalis Scandiae (#17498)
- ♦ Conferentie van Caraïbische Kerken (#03479)
- ♦ Conferentie van Europese Grondwettelijke Hoven (#04594)
- ♦ Conferentie van de Europese Regionale Wetgevende Parlementen (#04582)
- ♦ De Conferentie van de Methodische Kerk en het Caribisch Gebied, Midden en Zuid Amerika (#04629)
- ♦ Conferentie van de Perifere Maritieme Regios van Europa (#04638)
- ♦ Conferentie voor Regionale Ontwikkeling in Noord-West Europa (inactive)
- ♦ Conferenza della Assemblee Legislative Regionale Europee (#04582)
- ♦ Conferenza ed Associazione delle Aree Siderurgiche in Europa (inactive)
- ♦ Conferenza ecumenica internazionale permanente per i religiosi (#18326)
- ♦ Conferenza Europea degli Orari dei Treni Merci (inactive)
- ♦ Conferenza Internazionale del Credito Agrario / see Confédération internationale du crédit agricole (#04560)
- ♦ Conferenza Mondiale degli Istituti Secolari (#21299)
- ♦ Conferenza delle Regioni Periferiche Marittime della CE / see Conference of Peripheral Maritime Regions of Europe (#04638)
- ♦ Conferenza delle Regioni Periferiche Marittime d'Europa (#04638)
- ♦ **CONFIAD** Confédération internationale des agents en douanes (#04559)
- ♦ Confiad Paneuropean Network / see Confédération internationale des agents en douanes (#04559)
- ♦ **CONFIARP** Confederação Interamericana de Relações Públicas (#04436)
- ♦ **CONFIARP** Confederación Interamericana de Relaciones Públicas (#11418)
- ♦ **CONFIBERCOM** Confederación Iberoamericana de Asociaciones Científicas y Académicas de la Comunicación (#04448)
- ♦ CONFINTEA – Conférence internationale sur l'éducation des adultes (meeting series)
- ♦ Conflict Analysis Research Centre (internationally oriented national body)
- ♦ Conflict Prevention Centre, Vienna (see: #17887)
- ♦ Conflict Research Consortium (internationally oriented national body)
- ♦ Conflict Resolution Consortium / see Conflict Research Consortium
- ♦ Conflict Resolution Network (internationally oriented national body)
- ♦ Confluence Philanthropy (internationally oriented national body)
- ♦ Confoederatio Benedictina (religious order)
- ♦ Confoederatio Internationalis ad Qualitates Plantarum Edulium Perquirendas (inactive)
- ♦ Confoederatio Oratorii Sancti Philippi Nerii (religious order)
- ♦ Confraternidad Carcelaria Internacional (#18503)

♦ Confraternidad Evangélica Latinoamericana (CONELA) 04660

Confraternity of Evangelicals in Latin America – Fraternité évangélique latinoaméricaine

Pres c/o OneHope, 600 SW 3rd St, Pompano Beach FL 33060, USA.

History 1982. **Aims** Unite Spanish-speaking and Portuguese-speaking *Protestants* in the Caribbean, Central America, Latin America, Canada and USA. **Structure** Officers: President, 2 Vice-Presidents, Secretary, Treasurer, Executive Secretary. **Languages** Portuguese, Spanish. **Finance** Members' dues. **Events** *Quadrennial plenary assembly* San José (Costa Rica) 1994, *Quadrennial plenary assembly* Querétaro (Mexico) 1990, *Consultation on ethics in communications* Guatemala (Guatemala) 1988, *Meeting on evangelizing the Spanish world* Los Angeles, CA (USA) 1988, *Meeting on social responsibility of the Evangelical Church in Latin America* Santa Cruz (Bolivia) 1988. **Publications** *NotiCONELA*.
Members National organizations in 23 countries:
Argentina, Bolivia, Brazil, Chile, Colombia, Costa Rica, Dominican Rep, Ecuador, El Salvador, Germany, Guatemala, Haiti, Honduras, Jamaica, Mexico, Nicaragua, Panama, Paraguay, Peru, Puerto Rico, Spain, Uruguay, Venezuela.
NGO Relations *Latin Evangelical Alliance (#16397)*. [2014/XF0148/**F**]

- ♦ Confraternità del Santissimo Sacramento (religious order)
- ♦ Confraternité de Notre Dame du Mont Carmel (religious order)
- ♦ Confraternity of the Blessed Sacrament (religious order)
- ♦ Confraternity of Evangelicals in Latin America (#04660)
- ♦ Confraternity of the Holy Ghost (religious order)
- ♦ Confraternity of Ladies of Charity / see Association Internationale des Charités (#02675)
- ♦ Confraternity of the Most Holy Rosary (religious order)
- ♦ Confraternity of Our Lady of Mount Carmel (religious order)
- ♦ CONFREGE – Conférence Francophone sur l'Eco-conception en Génie Electrique (meeting series)
- ♦ **CONFREMO** Conférence des Recteurs et Présidents de la Région du Moyen-Orient (#04643)
- ♦ Confrérie de la chaîne des rôtisseurs / see Chaîne des Rôtisseurs – Association Mondiale de la Gastronomie (#03845)

♦ Confrérie des Chevaliers du Tastevin (CCT) 04661

SG 2 rue de Chaux, 21701 Nuits-Saint-Georges CEDEX, France. T. +33380610712. Fax +33380623709.
URL: http://www.tastevin-bourgogne.com/

History Founded 16 Nov 1934, Nuits-Saint-Georges (France). Registered in accordance with French law. **Aims** Make the *Burgundy* region and its *wine* more widely known. **Languages** English, French. **Staff** 20.00 FTE, paid. **Finance** Members' dues. **Activities** Organizes 'Tastevinage' and receptions. **Publications** *Tastevin en Main* (2 a year). *Le Guide des Vins Tastevinés*.
Members Branches in 19 countries and territories:
Australia, Bermuda, Brazil, Canada, China, Côte d'Ivoire, France, Hong Kong, Japan, Mauritius, Mexico, Morocco, New Zealand, Puerto Rico, Senegal, Singapore, Tahiti Is, USA, Venezuela. [2014.06.01/XF7215/**F**]

- ♦ Confrérie internationale de poésie (inactive)
- ♦ Confrérie du Rosaire (religious order)
- ♦ Confrérie du Saint-Sacrement (religious order)
- ♦ Confrontations for a European Participative Democracy (internationally oriented national body)
- ♦ Confrontations Europe – Confrontations for a European Participative Democracy (internationally oriented national body)
- ♦ Conf-SFE / see European Public Service Union (#08303)
- ♦ **CONGAC** Confédération des ONG d'environnement et de développement de l'Afrique centrale (#04572)
- ♦ **CONGAD** Conseil des organisations non-gouvernementales d'appui au développement (#04911)
- ♦ CONGDE – Coordinadora de Organizaciones No Gubernamentales para el Desarrollo, España (internationally oriented national body)
- ♦ Congenital Hyperinsulinism International (internationally oriented national body)
- ♦ Congé solidaire (internationally oriented national body)

♦ Congo Basin Forest Partnership (CBFP) 04662

Partenariat pour les forêts du Bassin du Congo (PFBC)

Communications Officer address not obtained. E-mail: info@pfbc-cbfp.org.
URL: http://www.pfbc-cbfp.org/

History Established Sep 2002, Johannesburg (South Africa), during World Summit on Sustainable Development. **Aims** Promote *sustainable* management of Congo Basin Forest *ecosystems* and *wildlife*; improve the lives of people living in the region. **Structure** Located at: *Commission des forêts d'Afrique centrale (COMIFAC, #04214)*. **Events** *Séminaire sur l'état des forêts d'Afrique centrale* Kinshasa (Congo DR) 2006, *Partnership meeting* Paris (France) 2006, *Partnership meeting / Meeting* Brazzaville (Congo Brazzaville) 2004, *Partnership meeting / Meeting* Paris (France) 2003.
Members Governments of 21 countries:
Belgium, Burundi, Cameroon, Canada, Central African Rep, Chad, Congo Brazzaville, Congo DR, Equatorial Guinea, France, Gabon, Germany, Japan, Netherlands, Norway, Rwanda, Sao Tomé-Principe, South Africa, Spain, UK, USA.
International organizations, listed in this Yearbook (39):
- *African Development Bank (ADB, #00283)*;
- *African Model Forest Network (AMFN, #00377)*;
- *African Wildlife Foundation (AWF, #00498)*;
- *Center for International Forestry Research (CIFOR, #03646)*;
- *Centre de coopération internationale en recherche agronomique pour le développement (CIRAD, #03733)*;
- *Commission des forêts d'Afrique centrale (COMIFAC, #04214)*;
- *Conservation International (CI)*;
- *Department for International Development (DFID, inactive)*;
- *Deutsche Gesellschaft für Internationale Zusammenarbeit (GIZ)*;
- *European Commission (EC, #06633)*;
- *FAO (#09260)*;
- *Forest Stewardship Council (FSC, #09869)*;
- *Forest Trends (#09870)*;
- Global Mechanism and Secretariat of the United Nations Convention to Combat Desertification (Secretariat of the UNCCD);
- *Great Apes Survival Project (GRASP, #10699)*;
- *International Bank for Reconstruction and Development (IBRD, #12317)* (World Bank);
- *International Tropical Timber Organization (ITTO, #15737)*;
- *International Union for Conservation of Nature and Natural Resources (IUCN, #15766)*;
- *Jane Goodall Institute (JGI, #16089)*;
- *Japan International Cooperation Agency (JICA)*;
- *Joint Research Centre (JRC, #16147)*;
- *PEFC Council (#18288)*;
- *Rainforest Alliance*;
- *Secretariat of the Convention on Biological Diversity (SCBD, #19197)*;
- *Secretariat of the Convention on the Conservation of Migratory Species of Wild Animals (UNEP/CMS, #19198)*;
- *SNV Netherlands Development Organisation (SNV)*;
- *The Nature Conservancy (TNC)*;
- *TRAFFIC International (#20196)*;
- *Transparency International (TI, #20223)*;
- *UNDP (#20292)*;
- *UNEP (#20299)*;
- *UNESCO (#20322)*;
- *United States Agency for International Development (USAID)*;
- *West and Central African Council for Agricultural Research and Development (WECARD, #20907)*;
- *Wildlife Conservation Society (WCS)*;
- *World Agroforestry Centre (ICRAF, #21072)*;
- *World Resources Institute (WRI, #21753)*;
- *World Wide Fund for Nature (WWF, #21922)*. [2016/XF7131/y/**F***]

- ♦ CONGO Committee on Ageing, New York / see NGO Committee on Ageing, New York (#17103)

♦ CONGO Committee on Human Rights **04663**

Pres Pax Romana, Rue de Varembé 3 – 4th Floor, CP 161, 1211 Geneva 20, Switzerland. T. +41228230707.

URL: http://www.ngocongo.org/committees/

History as a Committee of *Conference of Non-Governmental Organizations in Consultative Relationship with the United Nations (CONGO, #04635).* Original title: *International Non-governmental Organizations Committee on Human Rights.* Previously also referred to as *NGO Committee on Human Rights.* **Aims** Raise human rights as a priority in the *United Nations*; enable *NGO* representatives to represent their organizations more effectively in the field of human rights. **Structure** Bureau, comprising Chair, Vice-Chair, Secretary, Treasurer and 3 Members-at-large. Includes: Sub-Committee on the World Conference against Racisme; Sub-Committee on Immigration and Refugees. **Finance** Members' dues. **Activities** Makes no statements in its own name but provides a forum for discussion and education about human rights issues, especially as they relate to the work of the United Nations. **Events** *Meeting* Geneva (Switzerland) 2010, *Meeting* Geneva (Switzerland) 2010. **Members** NGOs in consultative status with ECOSOC. **IGO Relations** *ECOSOC (#05331).* **NGO Relations** *Economists for Peace and Security (EPS, #05322)* is member. *International Institute for Non-Aligned Studies (IINS, #13904)* was instrumental in the setting up of the Committee. [2011/XE1381/E]

♦ CONGO Committee on Narcotic, Drugs and Psychotropic Substances / see Vienna NGO Committee on Drugs (#20773)
♦ **CONGO** Conference of Non-Governmental Organizations in Consultative Relationship with the United Nations (#04635)
♦ Congodorpen – Centre for Integrated Regional Development Bwamanda-Belgium (internationally oriented national body)
♦ Congregação para a Doutrina da Fé (#04669)
♦ Congregação dos Missionarios de São Carlos, Escalabrinianos (religious order)
♦ Congregación Carmelitas Misioneras Teresianas (religious order)
♦ Congregación para el Clero (#04667)
♦ Congregación para la Doctrina de la Fe (#04669)
♦ Congregación para la Educación Católica (#04665)
♦ Congregación para la Evangelización de los Pueblos (#04670)
♦ Congregación de la Fraternidad Sacerdotal (religious order)
♦ Congregacion Hermanas Carmelitas de la Caridad, Vedruna (religious order)
♦ Congregación de las Hermanas de Jesuscristo Crucificado (religious order)
♦ Congregación para los Institutos de Vida Consagrada y las Sociedades de Vida Apostólica (#04671)
♦ Congregación de los Legionarios de Cristo Legionari di Cristo (religious order)
♦ Congregación de los Misioneros de San Carlos, Scalabrinianos (religious order)
♦ Congregación Pias Discipulas del Divino Maestro (religious order)
♦ Congregación de San Pedro ad-Vincula (religious order)
♦ Congregación del Santisimo Sacramento (religious order)
♦ Congregatie van het Onbevlekt Hart van Maria (religious order)
♦ Congregatie Onze-Lieve-Vrouw Visitatie (religious order)
♦ Congregatio Augustinianorum ab Assumptione (religious order)
♦ Congregatio de Causis Sanctorum (#04666)
♦ Congregatio pro Clericis (#04667)
♦ Congregatio Clericorum Marianorum ab Immaculata Conceptione Beatissimae Virginis Mariae (religious order)
♦ Congregatio Clericorum Parochialium seu Catechistarum Sancti Viatoris (religious order)
♦ Congregatio Clericorum Regularium Sancti Pauli (religious order)
♦ Congregatio Cooperatorum Parochialium Christi Regis (religious order)
♦ Congregatio de Cultu Divino et Disciplina Sacramentorum (#04668)
♦ Congregatio pro Doctrina Fidei (#04669)
♦ Congregatio pro Ecclesia Orientali / see Congregation for the Oriental Churches (#04672)
♦ Congregatio pro Ecclesiis Orientalibus (#04672)
♦ Congregatio pro Episcopis (#04664)
♦ Congregatio Eremitarum Camaldulensium Montis Coronae (religious order)
♦ Congregatio Filiorum Beatae Virginis Mariae Immaculatae (religious order)
♦ Congregatio Filiorum a Caritate (religious order)
♦ Congregatio Filiorum Mariae Immaculatae (religious order)
♦ Congregatio Filiorum Sanctae Mariae Immaculatae (religious order)
♦ Congregatio Fratrum Adunationis Tertii Regularis Ordinis Sancti Francisci (religious order)
♦ Congregatio Fratrum Beatae Mariae Virginis, Matris Misericordiae (religious order)
♦ Congregatio Fratrum Carmelitarum Beatae Virginis Mariae Immaculatae (religious order)
♦ Congregatio Fratrum Cellitarum seu Alexianorum (religious order)
♦ Congregatio Fratrum Christianorum (religious order)
♦ Congregatio Fratrum Immaculatae Conceptionis Beatae Mariae Virginis (religious order)
♦ Congregatio Fratrum Pauperum Sancti Francisci Seraphici (religious order)
♦ Congregatio Fratrum a Sancto Aloysio Gonzaga (religious order)
♦ Congregatio Fratrum a Sancto Francisco Xaverio (religious order)
♦ Congregatio Fratrum a Sancto Ioseph Benedicto Cottolengo (religious order)
♦ Congregatio Fratrum a Sancto Patricio (religious order)
♦ Congregatio Fratrum Servorum Mariae Immaculatae (religious order)
♦ Congregatio Fratrum Tertiariorum Franciscalium a Mountbellew (religious order)
♦ Congregatio pro Gentium Evangelizatione (#04670)
♦ Congregatio Iesu et Mariae (religious order)
♦ Congregatio Iesu Sacerdotis (religious order)
♦ Congregatio Immaculati Cordis Mariae (religious order)
♦ Congregatio de Institutione Catholica – de Seminariis atque Studiorum Institutis (#04665)
♦ Congregatio pro Institutis Vitae Consacratae et Societatibus Vitae Apostolicae (#04671)
♦ Congregatio Legionariorum Christi (religious order)
♦ Congregatio Missionaria Sancti Francisci Assisiensis (religious order)
♦ Congregatio Missionariorum a Divina Redemptione (religious order)
♦ Congregatio Missionariorum Filiorum Immaculati Cordis Beatae Virginis Mariae (religious order)
♦ Congregatio Missionariorum Immaculatae Conceptionis Beatae Mariae Virginis (religious order)
♦ Congregatio Missionariorum de Mariannhill (religious order)
♦ Congregatio Missionariorum Oblatorum Beatae Mariae Virginis Immaculatae (religious order)
♦ Congregatio Missionariorum Pretiosissimi Sanguinis (religious order)
♦ Congregatio Missionariorum a Sacra Familia (religious order)
♦ Congregatio Missionariorum a Sancto Carolo (religious order)
♦ Congregatio Missionariorum Servorum Pauperum (religious order)
♦ Congregatio Missionariorum Servorum Sanctissimae Trinitatis (religious order)
♦ Congregatio Missionariorum a SS Cordium Jesu et Mariae (religious order)
♦ Congregatio Missionis (religious order)
♦ Congregational Council for World Mission / see Council for World Mission (#04925)
♦ Congregation of the Apostles of the Sacred Heart of Jesus (religious order)
♦ Congregation of the Apostolic Carmel (religious order)
♦ Congregation of the Archangel St Michael (religious order)
♦ Congrégation des Auxiliaires du Sacerdoce (religious order)
♦ Congregation of Bethlehemite Religious Women, Daughters of the Sacred Heart (religious order)

♦ Congregation for Bishops **04664**

Congrégation pour les évêques – Congregazione per i Vescovi – Congregatio pro Episcopis

Sec Piazza Pio XII 10, 00120 Vatican City, Vatican. T. +39669884271. Fax +39669885303. E-mail: vati076@cbishops.va.

Prefect address not obtained.

URL: http://www.vatican.va/roman_curia/congregations/cbishops/

History within the framework of *Administrative Hierarchy of the Roman Catholic Church (#00117).* Previously referred to *Sacred Congregation for Bishops.* **Structure** A branch of the *'Roman Curia'*, the Central Administrative Body of the Roman Catholic Church. **Activities** Under the authority of the Pope, coordinates matters regarding: (1) the establishment of Dioceses, their division, unification, suppression and other changes; (2) the procedure for nomination of Bishops in the Latin Rite (apart from those Dioceses which come under the competence of the Secretariat of State or the Congregation for the Evangelization of Peoples). Attends to what concerns the right exercise of the apostolic office of the episcopacy, collaborating with Bishops in their pastoral ministry and for the good of local churches; coordinates the periodic visits to Rome (Italy) made by the Bishops of the world ("ad limina" visits) and assists Bishops in the course of these; studies diocesan quinquennial reports; oversees matters pertaining to erection and activity of Military Ordinariates; facilitates the establishment of Episcopal Conferences and any revision of their statutes, studies their acts and decrees and gives to the decrees the necessary approval. [2018.06.19/XF1110/E]

♦ Congregation of the Blessed Sacrament (religious order)
♦ Congregation of the Brothers of the Immaculate Conception of the Blessed Virgin Mary (religious order)
♦ Congrégation Carmelites Missionnaires Thérésiennes (religious order)

♦ Congregation for Catholic Education – for Seminaries and Educational Institutions (CEC) **04665**

Congrégation pour l'éducation catholique – Congregación para la Educación Católica – Kongregation für das Katholische Bildungswesen – Congregazione per l'Educazione Cattolica – Congregatio de Institutione Catholica – de Seminariis atque Studiorum Institutis

Main Office Piazza Pio XII 3, 00120 Vatican City, Vatican. E-mail: vidim@cec.va.

URL: http://www.educatio.va/

History 1588. Founded by Pope Sixtus V, as *Congregatio pro Universitate Studii Romani.* Title changed to *Congregatio Studiorum* in 1824, when competence extended by Pope Leo XII to cover all educational institutions of the Pontifical State. Restructured in 1915 by Pope Benedict XV, as *Sacra Congregatio de Seminariis et Studiorum Universitatibus*, within the framework of *Administrative Hierarchy of the Roman Catholic Church (#00117)*, joining the *Congregatio Studiorum*, created 1824, and having authority over all Catholic universities, with the Office of Seminaries within the Sacred Consistorial Congregation. In Aug 1967, under the title *Sacra Congregatio pro Institutione Catholica*, adopted a new constitution which extended authority to cover primary and secondary schools responsible to the Ecclesiastical Authorities. Present name adopted, 1988, by Apostolic Constitution *'Pastor Bonus'* of Pope John-Paul II. Since the Congregation is a department of the Pope's Roman Curia for the government of the Universal Church, it is similar to a state's Department for Education and/or Culture and as such may be considered a governmental institution of the Holy See. **Aims** Provide care and give directives and norms to diocesan seminaries through which individual bishops provide for training the clergy of their dioceses; develop and assist Catholic universities, faculties, institutes and colleges of higher education; promote worldwide the presence of Catholic schools for elementary and secondary education. **Structure** Governed by a body of 31 Cardinals, Archbishops and Bishops represented by the Prefect, Secretary and Under-Secretary. Offices (3) each with a Head of Office: Office for Seminaries; Office for Universities; Office for Catholic Schools. **Staff** 25.00 FTE, paid. **Finance** Funded by the financial administration of the Holy See. **Activities** Organizes meetings, congresses and inquiries in the field. **Events** *Conférence internationale* Rome (Italy) 2002. **Publications** *Seminarium* (4 a year). Statistics. [2021/XF0540/E]

♦ Congregation for the Causes of Saints **04666**

Congrégation pour les causes des saints – Congregazione delle Cause dei Santi – Congregatio de Causis Sanctorum

Sec Via della Conciliazione 5-7, 00120 Vatican City, Vatican.

URL: http://www.vatican.va/roman_curia/congregations/csaints/

History within the framework of *Administrative Hierarchy of the Roman Catholic Church (#00117).* [2019/XF1114/E]

♦ Congrégation pour les causes des saints (#04666)
♦ Congregation of Cellites (religious order)
♦ Congrégation pour le clergé (#04667)

♦ Congregation for the Clergy **04667**

Congrégation pour le clergé – Congregación para el Clero – Congregazione per il Clero – Congregatio pro Clericis

Sec Palazzo delle Congregazioni, Piazza Pio XII 3, 00193 Rome RM, Italy. T. +39669884137 – +39669884136. Fax +39669884845.

URL: http://www.clerus.org/

History within the framework of *Administrative Hierarchy of the Roman Catholic Church (#00117).* **Structure** Consultative council of the Congregation: *Consiglio Internazionale per la Catechesi (COINCAT).* **Events** *International meeting of priests* Valletta (Malta) 2004, *International Meeting of Priests* Rome (Italy) 2000, *International meeting of priests* Rome (Italy) 2000, *International meeting of priests* Jerusalem (Israel) 1999, *International meeting of priests* Mexico City (Mexico) 1998. **NGO Relations** *Pontifical Commission for the Cultural Patrimony of the Church (#18438)* was originally attached to the Congregation under the title: *Commission pontificale pour la conservation du patrimoine artistique et historique de l'Eglise – Pontificia Commissione per la Conservazione del Patrimonio Artistico e Storico.* [2021/XF0724/E]

♦ Congrégation du Coeur Immaculé de Marie (religious order)
♦ Congrégation pour le culte divin et la discipline des sacrements (#04668)
♦ Congregation of Daughters of Divine Charity (religious order)
♦ Congregation of the Daughters of Jesus (religious order)
♦ Congregation of the Daughters of Mary Immaculate (religious order)

♦ Congregation for Divine Worship and the Discipline of the Sacraments **04668**

Congrégation pour le culte divin et la discipline des sacrements – Congregazione per il Culto Divino e la Disciplina dei Sacramenti (CCDDS) – Congregatio de Cultu Divino et Disciplina Sacramentorum

Address not obtained.

URL: http://www.vatican.va/roman_curia/congregations/ccdds/index.htm

History Founded within the framework of *Administrative Hierarchy of the Roman Catholic Church (#00117).* Former names and other names: *Sacred Congregation for the Sacraments and Divine Worship* – alias; *Congregation for the Sacraments and Divine Worship* – alias. **Activities** Accountable to the Congregation: *Consociatio Internationalis Musicae Sacrae (CIMS, #04730).* [2008.07.28/XF1116/E]

♦ Congregation for the Doctrine of the Faith **04669**

Congrégation pour la Doctrine de la Foi – Congregación para la Doctrina de la Fe – Kongregation für die Glaubenslehre – Congregazione per la Dottrina della Fede – Congregação para a Doutrina da Fé – Kongregacji Nauki Wiary – Congregatio pro Doctrina Fidei

Secretariat Palazzo del Sant'Uffizio, 00120 Vatican City, Vatican.

URL: https://www.vatican.va/roman_curia/congregations/cfaith/index.htm

History 1542, when instituted by Pope Paul III, as *Sacred Roman and Universal Inquisition* or *Sacred Congregation of the Universal Inquisition – Congregatio Romanae et universalis Inquisitionis.* Congregation reorganized by St Pius X, 29 Jun 1908, when name changed to *Sacred Congregation of the Holy Office.* Further reformed, 7 Dec 1965, by Pope Paul VI, when current title adopted, methods of doctrinal examination updated and preservation and promotion of the faith given priority over the punitive function of condemnation. Function, responsibilities and norms governing the Congregation most recently specified, 28 Jun 1988, on reorganization of the Roman Curia by Pope John Paul II. Comes within the framework of *Administrative Hierarchy of the Roman Catholic Church (#00117).* **Aims** Promote and safeguard the Doctrine of the faith and morals throughout the *Catholic* world; foster studies to deepen understanding of the faith and ensure response in the light of faith to new questions arising from progress in human knowledge and culture; assist

Congrégation Doctrine Foi
04669

alphabetic sequence excludes
For the complete listing, see Yearbook Online at

Bishops in the exercise of their responsibilities as authentic teachers and masters of the faith. **Structure** College of Cardinals and Bishops, headed by Cardinal Prefect, assisted by Secretary, Under Secretary and Promote of Justice. Offices (3), each with a Head and comprising Officials: Doctrinal; Disciplinary; Matrimonial. Special Official for dispensations related to the priesthood. Consultors (meeting weekly to examine specific cases). Experts. Cardinal Prefect acts as President of *Pontifical Biblical Commission (#18436), International Theological Commission (#15684)* and *Pontifical Commission "Ecclesia Dei" (#18439).* **Activities** Areas of competence include: all questions regarding Catholic teaching on faith and morals; examination of new theories in dogmatic and moral theology; warning against and possible condemnation of teachings which are contrary to the principles of the faith; pre-publication examination of documents of other Dicasteries with respect to the competence of the Congregation; examination of crimes against faith, morals or celebration of the sacraments; judgement of cases concerning *'privilegium fidei'*; promotion and organization of studies and congresses. Offices follow questions under the competence of the Congregation and attend to its duties. The task of updating the list of prohibited books compiled by the Inquisition was entrusted to *Congregation for the Reform of the Index of Forbidden Books (inactive)* from 1571 until its suppression in 1917. **Events** *Plenary Assembly* Vatican City (Vatican) 2006, *Plenary Assembly* Vatican City (Vatican) 2004. **Publications** *Index of Forbidden Books* (last ed 1948) – has now been abolished. [2019/XK0871/**E**]

- ♦ Congrégation pour la Doctrine de la Foi (#04669)
- ♦ Congrégation Dominicaine de Sainte Catherine-de-Sienne d'Etrépagny (religious order)
- ♦ Congrégation des Dominicaines du Coeur Immaculée de Marie (religious order)
- ♦ Congrégation des dominicaines de Notre-Dame du Très Saint Rosaire de Monteils (religious order)
- ♦ Congregation for the Eastern Churches / see Congregation for the Oriental Churches (#04672)
- ♦ Congrégation pour l'éducation catholique (#04665)
- ♦ Congrégation pour les Eglises orientales (#04672)
- ♦ Congrégation de l'Enfant Jésus (religious order)
- ♦ Congrégation pour l'évangélisation des peuples (#04670)

♦ Congregation for the Evangelization of Peoples (CEP) 04670

Congrégation pour l'évangélisation des peuples – Congregación para la Evangelización de los Pueblos – Congregazione per l'Evangelizzazione dei Popoli – Congregatio pro Gentium Evangelizatione

Contact Piazza di Spagna 48, 00187 Rome RM, Italy. E-mail: segreteria@propagandafide.va.
URL: http://www.vatican.va/roman_curia/congregations/cevang/index.htm

History 22 Jun 1622, as *De Propagande Fide*, within the framework of the *Administrative Hierarchy of the Roman Catholic Church (#00117).* Previously also referred to as *Sacred Congregation for the Evangelization of Peoples (SCEP).* **Structure** Ecclesiastical circumscriptions (1,082) in Africa, America, Asia and Oceania. **Events** *Plenary Assembly* Vatican City (Vatican) 2009, *Symposium of African and European bishops* Rome (Italy) 2004, *Plenary Assembly* Rome (Italy) 2003, *International meeting of priests* Yamoussoukro (Côte d'Ivoire) 1997, *International meeting of priests* Fatima (Portugal) 1996. **NGO Relations** Instrumental in setting up: *Congregation for the Oriental Churches (CO, #04672); Federation of Catholic Bishops' Conferences of Oceania (FCBCO, #09467); Ordo Sanctissimi Salvatoris (Bridgettines); Pontificia Universitas Urbaniana (PUU, #18454).* [2008/XF2610/**E**]

- ♦ Congrégation pour les évêques (#04664)
- ♦ Congrégation des filles de Jésus (religious order)
- ♦ Congrégation de la Fraternité Sacerdotale (religious order)
- ♦ Congrégation des Frères de l'Immaculée Conception de la Sainte Vierge Marie (religious order)
- ♦ Congregation of Holy Cross (religious order)
- ♦ Congregation of the Holy Family (religious order)
- ♦ Congregation of the Holy Spirit (religious order)
- ♦ Congrégation Hospitalière Missionnaire des Filles de Notre-Dame des Douleurs (religious order)
- ♦ Congregation of the Immaculate Conception (religious order)
- ♦ Congregation of the Immaculate Heart of Mary (religious order)

♦ Congregation for Institutes of Consecrated Life and Societies of Apostolic Life (CICSAL) 04671

Congrégation pour les instituts de vie consacrée et les sociétés de vie apostolique – Congregación para los Institutos de Vida Consagrada y las Sociedades de Vida Apostólica – Congregazione per gli Istituti di Vita Consacrata e le Società di Vita Apostolica (CIVCSVA) – Congregatio pro Institutis Vitae Consecratae et Societatibus Vitae Apostolicae

Contact Palazzo delle Congregazioni, Piazza Pio XII 3, 00193 Rome RM, Italy. E-mail: civcsva.pref@ccscrlife.va – civcsva.segr@ccscrlife.va.
URL: http://www.congregazionevitaconsacrata.va/

History as *Sacred Congregation of Religious (SCR)*, within the framework of *Administrative Hierarchy of the Roman Catholic Church (#00117).* **Publications** *Informationes* (2 a year). [2017/XF1115/**E**]

- ♦ Congrégation pour les instituts de vie consacrée et les sociétés de vie apostolique (#04671)
- ♦ Congrégation de Jésus et Marie (religious order)
- ♦ Congregation of Jesus and Mary (religious order)
- ♦ Congregation of the Marian Clerics of the Immaculate Conception of the Most Blessed Virgin Mary (religious order)
- ♦ Congrégation de la Mère de Dieu (religious order)
- ♦ Congregation of the Mission (religious order)
- ♦ Congregation of the Missionaries of the Holy Family (religious order)
- ♦ Congregation of the Missionaries of Mariannhill (religious order)
- ♦ Congregation of the Missionaries of St Charles, Scalabrinians (religious order)
- ♦ Congregation of the Most Holy Redeemer (religious order)
- ♦ Congregation of Mother of Carmel (religious order)
- ♦ Congrégation de Notre-Dame (religious order)
- ♦ Congrégation Notre-Dame Chanoinesses de Saint-Augustin (religious order)
- ♦ Congrégation de Notre-Dame-de-Fidélité (religious order)
- ♦ Congrégation Notre-Dame de Sion (religious order)
- ♦ Congregation of the Oblates of St Joseph (religious order)
- ♦ Congrégation des Oblats de Saint Joseph (religious order)

♦ Congregation for the Oriental Churches (CO) 04672

Congrégation pour les Eglises orientales – Congregazione per le Chiese Orientali – Congregatio pro Ecclesiis Orientalibus

Main Office Palazzo dei Convertendi, Via della Conciliazione 34, 00193 Rome RM, Italy. T. +39669884282. Fax +39669885938. E-mail: cco@orientchurch.va.
URL: https://www.orientchurch.va/

History 1862. Founded by the Roman Catholic Church on the initiative of Pope Pius IX. Originally aligned with *Congregation for the Evangelization of Peoples (CEP, #04670)*, known then as 'De Propagande Fide'. Made independent by Pope Benedict XV in 1917. Administered within the framework of *Administrative Hierarchy of the Roman Catholic Church (#00117).* Former names and other names: *Congregation for the Eastern Churches* – alias; *Congregatio pro Ecclesia Orientali* – former (1917 to 1967). **Aims** Maintain relations of the Holy See with Eastern Catholic Churches. **Structure** Includes *Riunione delle Opere per l'Aiuto alle Chiese Orientali (ROACO, see: #04672).* **Publications** *Congregazione per le Chiese Orientali – Oriente Cattolico* (5th ed 2017). **NGO Relations** Supported by: *Catholic Near East Welfare Association (CNEWA, #03606).* [2018.09.13/XK0288/**E**]

- ♦ Congregation of Our Lady – Canonesses of Saint Augustine (religious order)
- ♦ Congregation of Our Lady of Charity of the Good Shepherd (religious order)
- ♦ Congregation Our Lady of Fidelity (religious order)
- ♦ Congregation of Our Lady of the Retreat in the Cenacle (religious order)
- ♦ Congregation of Our Lady of Sion (religious order)
- ♦ Congrégation des Ouvriers Chrétiens de Saint Joseph Calasanz (religious order)
- ♦ Congregation of the Passion (religious order)
- ♦ Congrégation de la Passion de Jésus-Christ (religious order)
- ♦ Congrégation Pie IX de l'Immaculée-Conception (religious order)
- ♦ Congrégation des Prêtres des Ecoles de Charité (religious order)
- ♦ Congrégation des Prêtres de la Mission (religious order)
- ♦ Congregation of Regular Clerics (religious order)
- ♦ Congrégation des Religieuses de l'Ange-Gardien (religious order)
- ♦ Congrégation de la Résurrection du Notre Seigneur Jésus Christ (religious order)
- ♦ Congregation of the Resurrection of our Lord Jesus Christ (religious order)
- ♦ Congregation of La Retraite (religious order)
- ♦ Congrégation de la Retraite (religious order)
- ♦ Congregation of the Sacerdotal Fraternity (religious order)
- ♦ Congregation for the Sacraments and Divine Worship / see Congregation for Divine Worship and the Discipline of the Sacraments (#04668)
- ♦ Congrégation du Sacré-Coeur de Jésus (religious order)
- ♦ Congrégation du Sacré-Coeur de Jésus (religious order)
- ♦ Congregation of the Sacred-Heart of Jesus (religious order)
- ♦ Congregation of the Sacred Hearts of Jesus and Mary (religious order)
- ♦ Congregation of the Sacred Stigmata (religious order)
- ♦ Congrégation des Sacrés-Coeurs de Jésus et de Marie (religious order)
- ♦ Congrégation de Sainte-Croix (religious order)
- ♦ Congrégation de la Sainte-Famille (religious order)
- ♦ Congrégation de la Sainte Famille de Bergame (religious order)
- ♦ Congrégation de la Sainte Famille de Nazareth (religious order)
- ♦ Congrégation de Sainte-Marie (religious order)
- ♦ Congrégation du Saint-Esprit (religious order)
- ♦ Congrégation de la Sainte-Union des Sacrés-Coeurs (religious order)
- ♦ Congrégation Saint Jean (religious order)
- ♦ Congregation of Saint John the Baptist Precursor (religious order)
- ♦ Congrégation de Saint Michel Archange (religious order)
- ♦ Congrégation de Saint Pierre aux Liens (religious order)
- ♦ Congrégation du Saint-Sacrement (religious order)
- ♦ Congregation of the Sister Disciples of the Divine Master (religious order)
- ♦ Congregation of Sisters of the Divine Saviour (religious order)
- ♦ Congregation of the Sister Servants of the Most Sacred Heart of Jesus (religious order)
- ♦ Congregation of the Sisters of Jesus Crucified (religious order)
- ♦ Congregation of the Sisters of Nazareth (religious order)
- ♦ Congregation of the Sisters of Our Lady of Sorrows (religious order)
- ♦ Congregation of the Sisters of Our Lady of the Visitation (religious order)
- ♦ Congregation of Sisters of St Agnes (religious order)
- ♦ Congregation of the Sisters of St Dorothea of Frassinetti (religious order)
- ♦ Congregation of Sisters of St Felix of Cantalice (religious order)
- ♦ Congregation of the Sisters of St John the Baptist (religious order)
- ♦ Congrégation des Soeurs des Coopérateurs Paroissiaux du Christ-Roi (religious order)
- ♦ Congrégation des Soeurs Disciples du Divin Maître (religious order)
- ♦ Congrégation des Soeurs de Marie Auxiliatrice (religious order)
- ♦ Congrégation des Soeurs de Sainte Dorothée de la Frassinetti (religious order)
- ♦ Congrégation des Soeurs de Sainte-Marie (religious order)
- ♦ Congrégation des Soeurs de Sainte-Marthe de Périgueux (religious order)
- ♦ Congrégation des Soeurs de Saint Félix de Cantalice (religious order)
- ♦ Congrégation des Soeurs de Saint Jean-Baptiste (religious order)
- ♦ Congrégation des Soeurs des Saints Coeurs de Jésus et de Marie (religious order)
- ♦ Congrégation des Soeurs des Saints-Coeurs de Jésus et de Marie (religious order)
- ♦ Congrégation des Soeurs du Très Saint Sauveur (religious order)

♦ Congregations of St Joseph (CSJs) 04673

Contact 246 E 46th Str, Suite 1F, New York NY 10017, USA. E-mail: csjunngo@gmail.com.
URL: http://csj-unngo.org/

Aims Live and work so that all may be one. **Structure** A cooperation of 4 national organizations (Canada; France; Italy; USA), congregation of Argentina, and 3 international congregations: *Soeurs de Saint Joseph de Lyon; Arab Postal Faculty, Damascus (inactive); Sisters of St Joseph of Annecy.* **Members** Individuals (over 10,000) in 49 countries. Membership countries not specified. **Consultative Status** Consultative status granted from: *ECOSOC (#05331)* (General). **NGO Relations** Member of (1): *Forum of Catholic Inspired NGOs (#09905).* [2020/XM8827/**E**]

- ♦ Congregation of St Basil (religious order)
- ♦ Congregation of St Peter in Chains (religious order)
- ♦ Congregation of Teresian Carmelite Missionaries Sisters (religious order)
- ♦ Congrégation du Très Saint Rédempteur (religious order)
- ♦ Congrégation Vincentienne de Malabar (religious order)
- ♦ Congregatio Oblatorum Beatae Mariae Virginis (religious order)
- ♦ Congregatio Oblatorum Sancti Ioseph, Astae Pompejae (religious order)
- ♦ Congregatio pro Operariis Christianis a Sancto Iosepho Calasanctio (religious order)
- ♦ Congregatio Passionis Jesu Christi (religious order)
- ♦ Congregatio Patrum Doctrinae Christianae (religious order)
- ♦ Congregatio Pauperum Servorum Divinae Providentiae (religious order)
- ♦ Congregatio Piarum Matrum Nigritiae (religious order)
- ♦ Congregatio Piorum Operariorum Catechistarum Ruralium (religious order)
- ♦ Congregatio Presbyterorum a Sancta Maria de Tinchebray (religious order)
- ♦ Congregatio Religiosorum Sancti Vincentii a Paulo, Patrum et Fratrum (religious order)
- ♦ Congregatio a Resurrectione Domini Nostri Jesu Christi (religious order)
- ♦ Congregatio Rogationistarum a Corde Iesu (religious order)
- ♦ Congregatio Romanae et universalis Inquisitionis / see Congregation for the Doctrine of the Faith (#04669)
- ♦ Congregatio Sacerdotum a Sacro Corde Iesu (religious order)
- ♦ Congregatio Sacrae Familiae a Nazareth (religious order)
- ♦ Congregatio a Sacra Familia (religious order)
- ♦ Congregatio Sacratissimi Cordis Jesu (religious order)
- ♦ Congregatio Sacrorum Cordium Jesu et Mariae necnon Adorationis Perpetuae Sacratissimi Sacramenti Altaris (religious order)
- ♦ Congregatio a Sancta Cruce (religious order)
- ♦ Congregatio Sancti Iohannis Baptistae Praecursoris (religious order)
- ♦ Congregatio Sancti Ioseph (religious order)
- ♦ Congregatio Sancti Michaelis Archangeli (religious order)
- ♦ Congregatio Sancti Spiritus sub Tutela Immaculati Cordis Beatissimae Virginis Mariae (religious order)
- ♦ Congregatio Sanctissimi Redemptoris (religious order)
- ♦ Congregatio Sanctissimi Sacramenti (religious order)
- ♦ Congregatio a Sancto Petro in Vinculis (religious order)
- ♦ Congregatio Scholarum Charitatis (religious order)
- ♦ Congregatio Servorum a Charitate (religious order)
- ♦ Congregatio Sororum Missionariarum a Nostra Domina Sancti Rosarii (religious order)
- ♦ Congregatio a SS Stigmatibus Domini Nostri Jesu Christi (religious order)
- ♦ Congregatio Studiorum / see Congregation for Catholic Education – for Seminaries and Educational Institutions (#04665)

♦ Congregatio pro Universitate Studii Romani / see Congregation for Catholic Education – for Seminaries and Educational Institutions (#04665)
♦ Congregatio Vincentiana (religious order)
♦ Congregazione Carmelitane Missionarie Teresiane (religious order)
♦ Congregazione delle Cause dei Santi (#04666)
♦ Congregazione per le Chiese Orientali (#04672)
♦ Congregazione per il Clero (#04667)
♦ Congregazione per il Culto Divino e la Disciplina dei Sacramenti (#04668)
♦ Congregazione del Cuore Immacolato di Maria (religious order)
♦ Congregazione per la Dottrina della Fede (#04669)
♦ Congregazione per l'Educazione Cattolica (#04665)
♦ Congregazione degli Eremiti Camaldolesi di Monte Corona (religious order)
♦ Congregazione per l'Evangelizzazione dei Popoli (#04670)
♦ Congregazione dei Fratelli dell'Immacolata Concezione della Beata Vergine Maria di Maastricht (religious order)
♦ Congregazione della Fraternità Sacerdotale (religious order)
♦ Congregazione di Gesù e Maria (religious order)
♦ Congregazione di Gesù Sacerdote (religious order)
♦ Congregazione per gli Istituti di Vita Consacrata e le Società di Vita Apostolica (#04671)
♦ Congregazione della Madre di Dio (religious order)
♦ Congregazione dei Missionari di San Carlo, Scalabriniani (religious order)
♦ Congregazione della Missione (religious order)
♦ Congregazione di Nostra Signora Canonichesse di Santo Agostino (religious order)
♦ Congregazione di Nostra Signora di Sion (religious order)
♦ Congregazione degli Oblati di Maria Vergine (religious order)
♦ Congregazione degli Operai Cristiani di San Giuseppe Calasanzio (religious order)
♦ Congregazione della Passione di Gesù Cristo (religious order)
♦ Congregazione delle Pie Discepole del Divin Maestro (religious order)
♦ Congregazione della Retraite (religious order)
♦ Congregazione della Risurrezione di Nostro Signore Gesù Cristo (religious order)
♦ Congregazione della Sacra Famiglia di Bergamo (religious order)
♦ Congregazione della Sacra Famiglia di Nazareth di Padre Giovanni Piamarta (religious order)
♦ Congregazione delle Sacre Stimmate di Nostro Signore Gesù Cristo (religious order)
♦ Congregazione dei Sacri Cuori (religious order)
♦ Congregazione del Sacro Cuore (religious order)
♦ Congregazione del Sacro Cuore di Gesù (religious order)
♦ Congregazione di San Giovanni Battista Precursore (religious order)
♦ Congregazione di San Giuseppe (religious order)
♦ Congregazione di San Michele Archangelo (religious order)
♦ Congregazione di San Pietro in Vincoli (religious order)
♦ Congregazione di Santa Croce (religious order)
♦ Congregazione del Santissimo Redentore (religious order)
♦ Congregazione del Santissimo Sacramento (religious order)
♦ Congregazione delle Scuole di Carità (religious order)
♦ Congregazione dello Spirito Santo (religious order)
♦ Congregazione delle Suore di San Felice da Cantalice (religious order)
♦ Congregazione delle Suore di San Giovanni Battista (religious order)
♦ Congregazione delle Suore di Santa Dorotea della Frassinetti (religious order)
♦ Congregazione per i Vescovi (#04664)
♦ Congregazione Vincenziana Malabarese (religious order)
♦ Congrès des Amériques sur l'éducation internationale (#04581)
♦ Congrès des assurances de l'Asie de l'Est (meeting series)
♦ Congrès des bibliothécaires de l'Asie du Sud-Est (#04679)
♦ Congrès cardiologique de langue française (meeting series)
♦ Congrès celtique (#03632)
♦ Congrès des Chimistes Théoriciens d'Expression Latine (meeting series)
♦ Congrès des dermatologistes et syphiligraphes de langue française (meeting series)
♦ Congrès de l'égalité raciale (internationally oriented national body)
♦ Congrès européen des communautés de base (meeting series)
♦ Congrès féminin ouvrier international (inactive)
♦ Congrès Francophone de Cardiologie Interventionnelle (meeting series)
♦ Congrès francophone de chirurgie digestive et hépato-bilio-pancréatique (meeting series)
♦ Congrès Francophone Fragilité du Sujet Agé Le Vieillissement en Santé Prévention de la Perte d'Autonomie (meeting series)
♦ Congrès géologique international (meeting series)
♦ Congrès Internacional de Docència Universitària i Innovació (meeting series)
♦ Congrès international d'acarologie (meeting series)
♦ Congrès international des américanistes (#12890)
♦ Congrès international d'anthropologie et d'archéologie préhistoriques (inactive)
♦ Congrès international d'archéologie chrétienne (meeting series)
♦ Congrès international de botanique (meeting series)
♦ Congrès international de bouchers / see International Butchers' Confederation (#12421)
♦ Congrès International de Catalyse pour les Bioraffineries (meeting series)
♦ Congrès international des chrétiens libéraux et d'autres libre-croyants / see International Association for Religious Freedom (#12130)
♦ Congrès international de la cinématographie et ses applications (inactive)
♦ Congrès international contre la poliomyélite (inactive)
♦ Congrès international des critiques d'art / see Association internationale des critiques d'art (#02680)
♦ Congrès international sur les décharges dans les gaz et leurs applications (meeting series)
♦ Congrès international de dermatologie (meeting series)
♦ Congrès international des droguistes (inactive)
♦ Congrès international des écrivains pour la défense de la culture (inactive)
♦ Congrès international des éditeurs / see International Publishers Association (#14675)
♦ Congrès international de l'éducation morale (inactive)
♦ Congrès international de l'emploi des mathématiques en génie civil (meeting series)
♦ Congrès international de l'enseignement universitaire pour adultes (inactive)
♦ Congrès international des études africaines (inactive)
♦ Congrès international des études asiatiques et nord-africaines (#12891)
♦ Congrès international des étudiants de l'Amérique centrale (inactive)
♦ Congrès international des fabricants de meubles (meeting series)
♦ Congrès international francophone sur l'agression sexuelle (meeting series)
♦ Congrès international de la gestion d'information (inactive)
♦ Congrès international des herbages (meeting series)
♦ Congrès international des historiens de la comptabilité (meeting series)
♦ Congrès international d'horticulture (meeting series)
♦ Congrès international de l'hygiène des villes (inactive)
♦ Congrès international des implantologistes de la bouche (#12899)
♦ Congrès international sur les jumeaux (meeting series)
♦ Congrès international des machines à combustion / see Conseil international des machines à combustion (#04693)

♦ Congrès international de médecine légale et de médecine sociale de langue française 04674

International French-Language Congress of Forensic and Social Medicine

Contact CHU Saint-Etienne – Hôpital Bellevue, Service de Médecine Légale, 42055 Saint-Étienne CEDEX 2, France. T. +33477120523. Fax +33477120462.

History 29 May 1911, Paris (France). 29-30 May 1911, Paris (France), at 1st Congress. **Aims** Organize an annual congress, in French, for forensic and social medicine. **Structure** Permanent Committee; Working Groups. Permanent Secretariat is *'Société de médecine légale et de criminologie de France'*. **Events** *Congress* Lille (France) 2009, *Congress* Saint-Étienne (France) 2007, *Congress* Angers (France) 2004, *Congress* Limoges (France) 2001, *Congress* Lille (France) 1998. [2009/XF0171/F]

♦ Congrès international de médecine légale, de médecine sociale et de médecine du travail (inactive)
♦ Congrès international de médecine tropicale et de paludisme (meeting series)
♦ Congrès international des métaux légers (meeting series)
♦ Congrès international des musées maritimes (#12896)
♦ Congrès international de néologie de langues romanes (meeting series)
♦ Congrès international pour une nouvelle évangélisation (meeting series)
♦ Congrès international d'ophtalmologie (meeting series)
♦ Congrès international des orientalistes / see International Congress of Asian and North African Studies (#12891)
♦ Congrès international du paludisme (inactive)
♦ Congrès international de pneumologie pédiatrique (meeting series)
♦ Congrès international de radiologie (meeting series)
♦ Congrès International des Recherches Féministes dans la Francophonie (meeting series)
♦ Congrès international des religions / see Parliament of the World's Religions (#18222)
♦ Congrès international des réseaux électriques de distribution (#12879)
♦ Congrès international des sciences humaines en Asie et en Afrique du Nord / see International Congress of Asian and North African Studies (#12891)
♦ Congrès international de sciences préhistoriques et protohistoriques / see International Union of Prehistoric and Protohistoric Sciences (#15801)
♦ Congrès international de télétrafic (#15674)
♦ Congrès international de traitement de l'information et d'ingénierie chimique (meeting series)
♦ Congrès international pour l'unité de la science, 1934 (inactive)
♦ Congrès internationaux d'architecture moderne (inactive)
♦ Congrès internationaux sur la communication de la culture par l'architecture, les arts et les mass media (inactive)
♦ Congrès internationaux des mathématiciens (inactive)
♦ Congrès juif européen (#07609)
♦ Congrès juif latinoaméricain (#16344)
♦ Congrès juif mondial (#21599)
♦ Congrès latinoaméricain sur les minorités juives en URSS (meeting series)
♦ Congrès latin de rhumatologie (meeting series)
♦ Congrès magique international (inactive)
♦ Congrès médical homéopathique panaméricain (meeting series)
♦ Congrès médical international de l'assurance maladie invalidité (inactive)
♦ Congrès minier mondial (#21654)
♦ Congrès du monde islamique (#21664)
♦ Congrès mondial Alternatives et développement (meeting series)
♦ Congrès Mondial Amazigh (internationally oriented national body)
♦ Congrès mondial arménien (meeting series)
♦ Congrès mondial de cardiologie pédiatrie (meeting series)
♦ Congrès mondial de la harpe (#21553)
♦ Congrès Mondial du Jamboc Sec (meeting series)
♦ Congrès mondial macédonien de la jeunesse
♦ Congrès Mondial Ouïghour (#21896)
♦ Congrès mondial de la presse (inactive)
♦ Congrès mondial des religions ethniques / see European Congress of Ethnic Religions (#06740)
♦ Congrès mondial des ukrainiens libres (#21305)
♦ Congrès mondiaux du pétrole / see World Petroleum Council (#21722)
♦ Congrès des municipalités d'Asie et du Pacifique (meeting series)
♦ Congrès des nationalités européennes (inactive)
♦ Congrès de la navigation fluviale (inactive)
♦ Congrès de la navigation maritime (inactive)
♦ Congrès neurologique international / see World Federation of Neurology (#21461)
♦ Congrès nordique de cosmétologie (meeting series)
♦ Congreso de las Américas sobre la Educación Internacional (#04581)
♦ Congrès des officiers nordiques de marine (#17407)
♦ Congreso Ibérico de Percepción (meeting series)
♦ Congreso Iberoamericana de Egiptologia (meeting series)
♦ Congreso Iberoamericano ArTechnologia (meeting series)
♦ Congreso Iberoamericano de Ciencia y Tecnologia de Membranas (meeting series)
♦ Congreso Iberoamericano de Energia Solar (meeting series)
♦ Congreso Iberoamericano de Nefrologia (meeting series)
♦ Congreso Iberoamericano de Sensores (meeting series)
♦ Congreso de Igualdad Racial (internationally oriented national body)
♦ Congreso Interamericano de Ministros y Altas Autoridades de Turismo (see: #11423)
♦ Congreso Internacional de Americanistas (#12890)
♦ Congreso Internacional de Dermatologia (meeting series)
♦ Congreso Internacional de Docencia Universitaria e Innovación (meeting series)
♦ Congreso Internacional de Escritores para la Defensa de la Cultura (inactive)
♦ Congreso Internacional de Fabricantes de Muebles (meeting series)
♦ Congreso Internacional de Literatura Chicana y Estudios Latinos (meeting series)
♦ Congreso Internacional de Medicina Tropical y Paludismo (meeting series)
♦ Congreso Internacional de Minificción (meeting series)
♦ Congreso Internacional de Neologia en las lenguas romanicas (meeting series)
♦ Congreso Internacional Ornitológico (#14486)
♦ Congreso Internacional de Quimicos Teóricos de Expresión Latina (meeting series)
♦ Congreso Internacional de Teletrafico (#15674)
♦ Congreso Internacional de Tintorerias (#13207)
♦ Congreso Judio Latinoamericano (#16344)
♦ Congreso Judio Mundial (#21599)
♦ Congreso Latinoamericano de Botanica / see Asociación Latinoamericana de Paleobotanica y Palinologia (#02249)
♦ Congreso Latinoamericano sobre las Minorias Judias en la URSS (meeting series)
♦ Congreso Médico Homeopatico Panamericano (meeting series)
♦ Congreso Mundial del Jamón Curado (meeting series)
♦ Congreso Mundial de la Juventud de Macedonia
♦ Congreso Mundial Menonita (#16713)
♦ Congreso Mundial de Mineria (#21654)
♦ Congreso Mundial de Ucranios Libres (#21305)
♦ Congreso Mundial Uigur (#21896)
♦ Congreso Panamericano de Educación Fisica (meeting series)
♦ Congreso Permanente de Unidad Sindical de los Trabajadores de América Latina (inactive)
♦ Congreso de los Pueblos (internationally oriented national body)

- ♦ Congreso Sobre Relaciones Culturales Este-Oeste (meeting series)
- ♦ Congreso de Reumatologia del Cono Sur (meeting series)
- ♦ Congrès ornithologique international (#14486)
- ♦ Congreso Sudamericano de Ferrocarriles – Asociación Internacional Permanent / see Pan American Railway Congress Association (#18124)
- ♦ Congreso de Trabajadores del Caribe (#03480)
- ♦ Congrès panafricain, 1919 (inactive)
- ♦ Congrès panafricain de Préhistoire et d'études du Quaternaire / see Pan-African Archaeological Association (#18035)
- ♦ Congrès permanent de l'unité syndicale des travailleurs d'Amérique latine (inactive)
- ♦ Congrès du peuple européen (inactive)
- ♦ Congrès des peuples (internationally oriented national body)
- ♦ Congrès des pouvoirs locaux et régionaux du Conseil de l'Europe (#04677)
- ♦ Congrès des pouvoirs locaux et régionaux de l'Europe / see Congress of Local and Regional Authorities of the Council of Europe (#04677)
- ♦ Congrès des psychanalystes de langue française (meeting series)

♦ Congrès de psychiatrie et de neurologie de langue française (CPNLF) 04675

SG CHRU – Hôp Fontan, 6 rue du Pr Laguesse, 59037 Lille CEDEX, France.
Registered Office Hôp Sainte Anne, Bibliothèque, 1 rue Cabanis, 75014 Paris, France.
URL: http://www.cpnlf.fr/

History 1889, France. Registered in accordance with French law. Statutes renewed 1981. **Aims** Organize annual congresses in a French-speaking country, with a view to discussing problems in the field of psychiatry, neurology and assistance. **Structure** General Assembly (annual); Administrative Council; Board. **Finance** Members' dues. **Events** *Annual Plenary Session* La Rochelle (France) 2021, *Congress* Lille (France) 2020, *Annual Plenary Session* Beirut (Lebanon) 2019, *Annual Plenary Session* Bastia (France) 2018, *Annual Plenary Session* Dijon (France) 2017. **Publications** Annual report.
Members Individuals in 29 countries:
Albania, Algeria, Andorra, Argentina, Cameroon, Canada, Côte d'Ivoire, Djibouti, France, Germany, Greece, Guyana, Hungary, Italy, Lebanon, Luxembourg, Mauritania, Monaco, Morocco, Niger, Poland, Portugal, Romania, Senegal, Spain, Switzerland, Tunisia, Türkiye, USA. [2015/XF0977/v/**F**]

- ♦ Congress of Arabic and Islamic Studies / see European Union of Arabists and Islamicists (#08976)

♦ Congress of Asian Theologians (CATS) 04676

Congrès des théologiens asiatiques
Exec Sec c/o Payap University, Chiang Mai, 5000, Thailand. T. +6653243906. Fax +6653247303.
Mailing Address c/o Christian Conference of Asia, PO Box 183, Chiang Mai, 5000, Thailand.
URL: http://www.cca.org.hk

History 1 Jun 1997, Suwon (Korea Rep). **Aims** Promote theological studies in the region; provide a platform for professional exchange. **Structure** Congress; Continuation Committee; Working Groups. **Finance** Members' dues. Other sources: CCA funding partners and ecumenical partners; congress fees. No annual budget. **Events** *Biennial Congress* Korea Rep 2013, *Biennial Congress* Seoul (Korea Rep) 2012, *Biennial Congress* Iloilo (Philippines) 2009, *Biennial Congress* Hong Kong (Hong Kong) 2006, *Biennial Congress* Chiang Mai (Thailand) 2003. **Publications** *CTC Bulletin*. **Members** Asian Theologians throughout Asia and worldwide (countries not specified). **NGO Relations** Supported by and cooperates with: *Asian Christian Art Association (ACAA)*; *Association for Theological Education in South East Asia (ATESEA, #02952)*; *Christian Conference of Asia (CCA, #03898)*; *Federation of Asian Bishops' Conferences (FABC, #09430)*; *North East Asia Association of Theological Schools (NEAATS, no recent information)*; *Programme for Theology and Cultures in Asia (PTCA, inactive)*; *South Asia Theological Research Institute, Bangalore (SATHRI)*. [2015/XD5916/c/**F**]

- ♦ Congrès scientifique panaméricain (inactive)
- ♦ Congress of European Nationalities (inactive)
- ♦ Congress of French-Speaking Dermatologists and Syphiligraphers (meeting series)
- ♦ Congress of International Vertebrate Morphologists (meeting series)
- ♦ Congressional Hunger Center (internationally oriented national body)
- ♦ Congress on Ionic Liquids (meeting series)

♦ Congress of Local and Regional Authorities of the Council of Europe 04677

Congrès des pouvoirs locaux et régionaux du Conseil de l'Europe – Kongress der Gemeinden und Regionen des Europarates
SG c/o Conseil de l'Europe, 67075 Strasbourg CEDEX, France. T. +33388412248 – +33388412110. Fax +33388412751 – +33388413747. E-mail: congress.adm@coe.int.
URL: https://www.coe.int/en/web/congress/home

History 1994, Strasbourg (France). Established by *Committee of Ministers of the Council of Europe (#04273)*, as a organ representing regions and municipalities of the Member States of the *Council of Europe (CE, #04881)*, replacing *Standing Conference of Local and Regional Authorities of Europe – Conférence permanente des pouvoirs locaux et régionaux de l'Europe – Ständige Konferenz der Gemeinden und Regionen Europas*, set up 12 Jan 1957, Strasbourg. Former names and other names: *Congress of Local and Regional Authorities of Europe (CLRAE)* – former; *Congrès des pouvoirs locaux et régionaux de l'Europe (CPLRE)* – former; *Kongress der Gemeinden und Regionen Europas (KGRE)* – former; *Conference of Local Authorities of Europe* – former (1957 to 1975); *Conference of Local and Regional Authorities of Europe* – former (1975 to 1983); *Standing Conference of Local and Regional Authorities of Europe (CLRAE)* – former (1983 to 1994). **Aims** Ensure participation of regional and local authorities in the process of European unity and in the work of the Council of Europe; promote and monitor functioning of local and regional democracy in the larger Europe; strengthen trans-frontier and inter-regional cooperation; deal with all questions of policy affecting local and regional authorities, including local and regional self-government, rural and urban development; advise and provide expertise to national authorities on issues relating to local and regional democracy. **Structure** Congress, consisting of 2 Chambers: Chamber of Local Authorities and Chamber of Regions. Assembly; Bureau; President; Secretariat. Committees (3): Monitoring; Governance; Current Affairs. Statutory Forum. **Languages** English, French, German, Italian, Russian, Turkish. **Staff** 53.00 FTE, paid. **Finance** On the general budget of the Council of Europe. Annual budget: 6,000,000 EUR.
Activities Politics/policy/regulatory; events/meetings; monitoring/evaluation; networking/liaising; awards/prizes/competitions. Management of treaties and agreements:
European Outline Convention on Transfrontier Cooperation between Territorial Communities or Authorities (1980) and protocols *Additional Protocol to the European Outline Convention on Transfrontier Cooperation between Territorial Communities or Authorities (1995)* and *Protocol no 2 to the European Outline Convention on Transfrontier Cooperation between Territorial Communities or Authorities Concerning Interterritorial Cooperation (1998)*; *European Charter of Local Self-government (1985)*; *Charter on the Participation of Young People in Municipal and Regional Affairs (1992)*; *European Charter for Regional or Minority Languages (ECRML, 1992)*; *Convention on the Participation of Foreigners in Public Life at Local Level (1992)*; *European Urban Charter (1992)*; draft *European Charter on Mountain Regions (1995)*; *European Landscape Convention (2000)*; Draft European Charter of Regional Democracy. Instrumental in setting up: *Adriatic Ionian Euroregion (AIE, #00120)*; *Black Sea Euroregion (BSER, #03275)*; *European Network of Training Organizations for Local and Regional Authorities (ENTO, #08023)* for staff of local and regional authorities; *European Association for Local Democracy (ALDA, #06110)*, as part of the peace process in the former Yugoslavia.
Events *Plenary Session* Strasbourg (France) 2022, *Plenary Session* Strasbourg (France) 2022, *Plenary Session – First Part* Strasbourg (France) 2021, *Plenary Session – Second Part* Strasbourg (France) 2021, *Plenary Session* Strasbourg (France) 2021. **Publications** *Local and Regional Authorities in Europe* – study series; *Official Reports of Debates* in English, French; *Official Reports of Texts Adopted* in English, French. Annual Activity Report; surveys; reports; thematic publications.
Members Elected local and regional councillors (648) representing 47 countries:
Albania, Andorra, Armenia, Austria, Azerbaijan, Belgium, Bosnia-Herzegovina, Bulgaria, Croatia, Cyprus, Czechia, Denmark, Estonia, Finland, France, Georgia, Germany, Greece, Hungary, Iceland, Ireland, Italy, Latvia, Liechtenstein, Lithuania, Luxembourg, Malta, Moldova, Monaco, Montenegro, Netherlands, North Macedonia, Norway, Poland, Portugal, Romania, Russia, San Marino, Serbia, Slovakia, Slovenia, Spain, Sweden, Switzerland, Türkiye, UK, Ukraine.

Observers (26): international associations of local and regional authorities:
- *Arab Towns Organization (ATO, #01059)*;
- *Assembly of European Regions (AER, #02316)*;
- *Association of European Border Regions (AEBR, #02499)*;
- Association of Kosovo Municipalities;
- Association of Palestinian Local Authorities (APLA);
- *Association of Working Communities of the Alpine Regions (AWCAR, #02981)*;
- *Commonwealth Local Government Forum (CLGF, #04348)*;
- *Conférence des assemblées législatives régionales d'Europe (CALRE, #04582)*;
- *Conference of Peripheral Maritime Regions of Europe (CPMR, #04638)*;
- *Council of European Municipalities and Regions (CEMR, #04891)*;
- *Council of Local Authorities for International Relations (CLAIR)*;
- *European Association of Elected Representatives from Mountain Regions (#06021)*;
- *European Centre for the Regions, Barcelona (ECR, see: #07569)*;
- *European Grouping of Territorial Cooperation – Twinned Cities and Areas in the Mediterranean (EGTC – AMPHICTYONY, #07423)*;
- European Network of Training Organizations for Local and Regional Authorities;
- *European Roma and Travellers Forum (ERTF, #08402)*;
- *Fondation pour l'économie et le développement durable des régions d'Europe (FEDRE, #09817)*;
- Lev Sapieha Foundation;
- Local Authorities Confronting Disasters and Emergencies (LACDE);
- *Network of Associations of Local Authorities of South-East Europe (NALAS, #16997)*;
- *Standing Committee Euro-Mediterranean Partnership of the Local and Regional Authorities (#19954)*;
- Union of Local Authorities in Israel;
- *Union of Local Authority Chief Executives of Europe (#20454)*;
- *Union of the Baltic Cities (UBC, #20366)*;
- *World Mountain People Association (WMPA, #21658)*;
- *World Organization of United Cities and Local Governments (UCLG, #21695)*. [2021/XE1645/y/**F***]

- ♦ Congress of Local and Regional Authorities of Europe / see Congress of Local and Regional Authorities of the Council of Europe (#04677)
- ♦ Congresso das Américas sobre Educação Internacional (#04581)
- ♦ Congresso Ebraico Mondiale (#21599)
- ♦ Congresso Internacional da História da Construção Luso-Brasileira (meeting series)
- ♦ Congresso Internazionale di Moda e Design (meeting series)
- ♦ Congresso degli Italianisti Scandinavi (meeting series)
- ♦ Congresso Judaico Latino Americano (#16344)
- ♦ Congresso Judaico Mundial (#21599)
- ♦ Congresso Latino di Reumatologia (meeting series)
- ♦ Congresso Mundial dos Ucranianos Livres (#21305)
- ♦ Congress of the People of Europe (inactive)

♦ Congress of Political Economists, International (COPE) 04678

Main Office c/o Wilkes Univ Business Div, 84 W South St, Wilkes-Barre PA 18766, USA. E-mail: congofpoli@gmail.com.
URL: http://www.copeintl.org/

History 1990. Also referred to as *COPE International*. **Aims** Encourage worldwide discussion about the theory, principles and problems of economics, with special emphasis on economic policy. **Structure** Officers: President; Honorary President; President-Elect; Executive Director. Directors. **Finance** Members' dues. **Events** *Annual Convention* Rome (Italy) 2019, *Annual Convention* Jakarta (Indonesia) 2018, *Annual Convention* Madrid (Spain) 2016, *Annual Convention* Toronto, ON (Canada) 2015, *Annual Convention* Zurich (Switzerland) 2014. **Publications** Congress proceedings. [2019/XS0111/c/**F**]

- ♦ Congress of Racial Equality (internationally oriented national body)
- ♦ Congress on Regional Geological Cartography and Information Systems (meeting series)
- ♦ Congress of Romance Language Psychoanalysts (meeting series)

♦ Congress of Southeast Asian Librarians (CONSAL) 04679

Congrès des bibliothécaires de l'Asie du Sud-Est
SG Library and Info Center, Vietnam National Univ, 144 Xuan Thuy St, Cau Giay District, Hanoi, Vietnam. T. +84437546558. Fax +84437687900. E-mail: dzuong@gmail.com.
URL: http://www.consalxvii.org/

History Aug 1970, Singapore (Singapore), as *Conference of Southeast Asian Librarians*, during 1st Conference of Southeast Asian Librarians. Present name adopted, under a revised constitution, during 3rd Conference, 1975, Jakarta (Indonesia). Secretariat established, Apr 2000, Singapore. **Aims** Establish and strengthen relations among librarians, libraries, library schools, library associations and related organizations in the region; promote cooperation in the region and cooperate with other regional and international organizations and institutions in the fields of librarianship, library and information sciences, documentation, information and related activities in the region. **Structure** Conference (meets once every 3 years). Council of Chief Librarians. Executive Board, comprising Chairman, Vice-Chairman, Secretary, Treasurer, 3 members from each member country and Secretary-General. **Languages** English. **Finance** Ad hoc grants. **Activities** Conferences (held every 2 or 3 years). Master List of Southeast Asian Microfilms (a union catalogue project). *SARBICA-CONSAL Regional Microfilm Clearinghouse*. CONSAL Outstanding Librarian Award (annually). Collaborative Projects (5): Resource Sharing and Legal Depository; Copyright; Preservation and Conservation; Translation of Materials; Training Coordination. **Events** *ASEAN aspirations – libraries for sustainable advancement* Bangkok (Thailand) 2015, *Congress* Bangkok (Thailand) 2013, *National heritage – preservation and dissemination* Bali (Indonesia) 2012, *Towards dynamic libraries and information services in Southeast Asian countries* Hanoi (Vietnam) 2009, *CONSAL at the crossroads – challenges for greater regional cooperation* Manila (Philippines) 2006. **Publications** *CONSAL Bulletin*; *CONSAL Newsletter*. Directories; conference proceedings.
Members National; associate (libraries and related organizations and individuals). National members in 10 countries:
Brunei Darussalam, Cambodia, Indonesia, Laos, Malaysia, Myanmar, Philippines, Singapore, Thailand, Vietnam. [2017/XD5455/**D**]

- ♦ Congress of Thoracic and Cardiovascular Surgeons of Asia (meeting series)
- ♦ Congress on Tooth Transplantation (meeting series)
- ♦ Congressus Internationalis Fenno-Ugristarum (meeting series)
- ♦ Congressus internationalis Limitis Romani studiosorum (meeting series)
- ♦ Congressus Internationalis Ornithologicus (#14486)
- ♦ Congress of Vienna Decision on Rhine Navigation (1815 treaty)
- ♦ Congrès des théologiens asiatiques (#04676)
- ♦ Congrès du travail des Caraïbes (#03480)
- ♦ **CONHU** Convenio Hipólito Unanue (#10921)
- ♦ **CONIFA** Confederation of Independent Football Associations (#04554)
- ♦ CONLACTRAHO – Confederación Latinoamericana y del Caribe de Trabajadoras del Hogar (unconfirmed)
- ♦ CONLATI – Conferencia Latinoamericana de Facultades y Escuelas de Ingenieria de Sistemas y Ciencias de la Computación (meeting series)
- ♦ **CONLATINGRAF** Confederación Latinoamericana de la Industria Grafica (#16303)
- ♦ **CONMEBOL** Confederación Sudamericana de Fútbol (#04487)
- ♦ Connect (internationally oriented national body)
- ♦ Connect 4 Climate / see Connect4Climate (#04680)

♦ Connect4Climate 04680

Contact c/o World Bank Group, 1818 H Str NW, Washington DC 20433, USA. T. +12024731000. E-mail: connect4climate@worldbank.org.
URL: http://www.connect4climate.org/

History Jan 2009. Founded by Lucia Grenna (d 2017) at *The World Bank Group (#21218)*. Former names and other names: *Communication for Climate Change Multi Donor Trust Fund (CCC MDTF)* – former; *Connect 4 Climate* – alias. **Aims** Raise awareness about *climate change* and its impact at various levels, but particularly with young people; promote commitment among the public, private sector and policy-makers to take action and to encourage lifestyle change; build coalitions for further advocacy efforts. **Finance** Sources: government support. Support from governments of Italy and Germany. **Activities** Advocacy/lobbying/activism; awards/prizes/competitions; events/meetings. **IGO Relations** *United Nations (UN, #20515)* **NGO Relations** *Wild for Life Campaign (Wild for Life, #20958).* [2022.06.10/XM5105/**E**]

♦ CONNECTED, COOPERATIVE AND AUTOMATED MOBILITY / see CCAM Association (#03619)
♦ Connected International Meeting Professionals Association (internationally oriented national body)

♦ Connected Vehicle Systems Alliance (COVESA) 04681

Exec Dir 5000 Executive Parkway, Suite 302, San Ramon CA 94583, USA. T. +19252756634. E-mail: help@covesa.global.
URL: https://www.covesa.global/

History 2009. Former names and other names: *GENIVI Alliance* – former (2021). **Aims** Develop open standards and technologies that accelerate innovation for connected vehicle systems, resulting in a more diverse, sustainable and integrated mobility ecosystem. **Structure** Board. **Activities** Projects/programmes. **Events** *All Member Meeting* Leipzig (Germany) 2022, *Meeting* Seoul (Korea Rep) 2017, *Meeting* Seoul (Korea Rep) 2015. [2021/AA2309/**C**]

♦ Connecting Cultures (internationally oriented national body)
♦ CONNECT International (unconfirmed)

♦ Connective Tissue Oncology Society (CTOS) 04682

Admin Office PO Box 320574, Alexandria VA 22320, USA. T. +13015027371. Fax +13015484882. E-mail: ctos@ctos.org.
URL: http://www.ctos.org/

History 1995. Registered in the State of Illinois. **Aims** Advance care of patients with connective tissue tumors; increase knowledge of all aspects of the biology of connective tissue tumors. **Structure** Board of Directors. Executive Committee, comprising President, Vice-President, Past President, Secretary and Treasurer. Standing Committees (6): Executive; Nominating; Membership; Bylaws; Programme; Fundraising. **Finance** Members' dues. **Events** *Annual Meeting* San Diego, CA (USA) 2024, *Annual Meeting* Dublin (Ireland) 2023, *Annual Meeting* Vancouver, BC (Canada) 2022, *Annual Meeting* Alexandria, VA (USA) 2021, *Annual Meeting* Alexandria, VA (USA) 2020.
Members Individuals in 23 countries:
Australia, Belgium, Brazil, Canada, China, Denmark, France, Germany, Greece, Israel, Italy, Japan, Korea Rep, Netherlands, Norway, Portugal, Slovakia, Spain, Sweden, Switzerland, Türkiye, UK, USA. [2014/XD8794/**D**]

♦ Connect Worldwide / see Connect
♦ **CONOPA** Committee of Nordic Intellectual Property Attorneys (#04276)
♦ CONPASA / see WBSC Americas Softball (#20840)
♦ **CONPEHT** Confederación Panamericana de Escuelas de Hoteleria, Gastronomia y Turismo (#04474)
♦ CONRAD (internationally oriented national body)
♦ Conrad Grebel College Institute of Peace and Conflict Studies (internationally oriented national body)
♦ Conradh Ceilteach (#03633)
♦ Conrad N Hilton Foundation (internationally oriented national body)
♦ **CONSAL** Congress of Southeast Asian Librarians (#04679)
♦ **CONSANAT** Confederación Sudamericana de Natación (#04491)
♦ **CONSCERT** European Group for the Certification of Constructional Steels (#07418)
♦ Conscience mondiale (inactive)
♦ Conscience – the Peace Tax Campaign (internationally oriented national body)

♦ Conscience and Peace Tax International (CPTI) 04683

Sec/Treas 1b Waterlow Road, London, N19 5NJ, UK. T. +441380812294. E-mail: cpti@cpti.ws.
URL: http://www.cpti.ws/

History 17 Sep 1994, Hondarribia (Spain). Registered in accordance with Belgian law, 20 Mar 1996, Brussels (Belgium); dissolved as a Belgian association 30 Jun 2013, when became registered in accordance with English law. **Aims** Obtain recognition that the right of *conscientious objection* to military service includes conscientious objecting to paying for *armaments, war* preparation and war conduct by means of taxes. **Structure** General Meeting (every 2 years). **Languages** English. **Staff** 10.00 FTE, voluntary. **Finance** Individual donations; trusts; foundations. **Activities** Advocacy/lobbying/activism. **Events** *International Conference on War Tax Resistance and Peace Tax Campaigns / Biennial International Conference* Bogota (Colombia) 2013, *International conference on war tax resistance and peace tax campaigns / Biennial International Conference* Sandefjord (Norway) 2010, *International conference on war tax resistance and peace tax campaigns / Biennial International Conference* Manchester (UK) 2008, *International conference on war tax resistance and peace tax campaigns / Biennial International Conference* Woltersdorf (Germany) 2006, *International conference on war tax resistance and peace tax campaigns / Biennial International Conference* Brussels (Belgium) 2004. **Publications** *CPTI Bulletin* (occasional). Study.
Members Organizations and individuals in 15 countries and territories:
Belgium, Canada, Colombia, Denmark, Germany, Italy, Japan, Netherlands, Norway, Palestine, Spain, Sweden, Switzerland, UK, USA.
Included in the above, 1 organization listed in this Yearbook:
Conscience – the Peace Tax Campaign.
Consultative Status Consultative status granted from: *ECOSOC (#05331)* (Special). **NGO Relations** Member of: *Conference of Non-Governmental Organizations in Consultative Relationship with the United Nations (CONGO, #04635).* [2014.11.01/XF4107/y/**F**]

♦ Consciousness, Mindfulness, Compassion (CMC International Association) 04684

Contact address not obtained. E-mail: info@cmc-ia.org.
URL: http://www.cmc-ia.org/

Aims Investigate consciousness, mindfulness, empathy, mental states, self-reference and related aspects, with the integration of multiple areas of expertise, approaches, methods and paradigms. **Structure** Assembly; Board of Directors; Advisory Board. **Activities** Events/meetings; training/education. **Events** *International Conference on Mindfulness* Auckland (New Zealand) 2019, *International Conference on Mindfulness* Amsterdam (Netherlands) 2018. [2019/XM8020/**D**]

♦ Conseil d'administration pour les pêches des Caraïbes (#03508)
♦ Conseil africain de l'arachide (#00332)
♦ Conseil africain de la comptabilité (no recent information)
♦ Conseil africain pour le développement soutenable de santé (#00277)
♦ Conseil africain d'enseignement de la communication (#00273)
♦ Conseil africain et malgache pour l'enseignement supérieur (#00364)
♦ Conseil africain et malgache du sucre (inactive)
♦ Conseil africain et mauricien pour l'enseignement supérieur / see African and Malagasy Council for Higher Education (#00364)
♦ Conseil africain de la musique (#00379)
♦ Conseil Africain de la recherche scientifique et de l'innovation (#00451)
♦ Conseil africain des sciences de l'alimentation et de la nutrition (no recent information)
♦ Conseil africain des sciences sociales et humaines (inactive)
♦ Conseil africain de télédétection (inactive)
♦ Conseil agro-commercial international du centre des Etats-Unies / see Food Export Association of the Midwest USA
♦ Conseil de l'alimentation halal d'Europe (internationally oriented national body)
♦ Conseil allié pour le Japon (inactive)
♦ Conseil andin des ingénieurs (inactive)
♦ Conseil de l'ANZUS (#00862)
♦ Conseil arabe de défense commune (no recent information)
♦ Conseil arabe de l'enfance et le développement (#00929)
♦ Conseil Arabe pour les Sciences Sociales (#00932)
♦ Conseil arabe des sciences sociales (inactive)
♦ Conseil de l'Archevêché orthodoxe grec d'Amérique (#10708)
♦ Conseil de l'Archevêché orthodoxe grec d'Amérique du Nord et du Sud / see Greek Orthodox Archdiocesan Council of America (#10708)
♦ Conseil des Architectes d'Europe (#01086)
♦ Conseil des architectes de l'Europe Centrale et de l'Est (no recent information)
♦ Conseil des arts du Pacifique / see Pacific Cultural Council (#17944)
♦ Conseil asiatique d'analystes financiers / see Asian Securities and Investments Federation (#01695)
♦ Conseil asiatique pour le développement industriel (inactive)
♦ Conseil asiatique de l'environnement (no recent information)
♦ Conseil asiatique de la jeunesse (#01788)
♦ Conseil asiatique de recherche sur la paix (inactive)
♦ Conseil de l'Asie et du Pacifique (inactive)
♦ Conseil d'assistance économique mutuelle (inactive)
♦ Conseil des Associations de Football d'Afrique de l'Est et Centrale (unconfirmed)
♦ Conseil des associations d'ingénieurs du Commonwealth (#04324)
♦ Conseil des associations d'ingénieurs de cycle long d'université ou d'école d'ingénieurs de l'union européenne (#04869)
♦ Conseil des associations nationales d'armateurs d'Europe et du Japon (inactive)
♦ Conseil atlantique pour la coopération internationale (internationally oriented national body)
♦ Conseil Atlantique des Etats-Unis / see Atlantic Council
♦ Conseil de l'Atlantique nord (#17572)
♦ Conseil pour l'avancement et support de l'éducation (internationally oriented national body)
♦ Conseil de la Baltique / see Baltic Council (#03108)
♦ Conseil baltique (#03108)
♦ Conseil des barreaux de la Communauté européenne / see Council of Bars and Law Societies of Europe (#04871)
♦ Conseil des barreaux européens (#04871)
♦ Conseil des bâtiments élevés et de l'habitat urbain (#04921)
♦ Conseil des Bois du Nord (inactive)
♦ Conseil des bureaux (#04873)
♦ Conseil des bureaux d'assureurs / see Council of Bureaux (#04873)
♦ Conseil de la calotte polaire (#17545)
♦ Conseil canadien pour la coopération internationale / see Cooperation Canada
♦ Conseil canadien de droit international (internationally oriented national body)
♦ Conseil Canadien des études sur l'Asie du Sud-Est (internationally oriented national body)
♦ Conseil canadien pour les réfugiés (internationally oriented national body)
♦ Conseil caraïbe d'éducation supérieure en agriculture (#03484)
♦ Conseil des Caraïbes (#03482)
♦ Conseil des Caraïbes pour l'Europe / see The Caribbean Council (#03482)
♦ Conseil des Caraïbes pour la science et la technologie (#03485)
♦ Conseil central des associations nordiques des fermiers (no recent information)
♦ Conseil central du tourisme international (inactive)
♦ Conseil centroaméricain des surintendants de banques, de compagnies d'assurances et autres institutions financières (#04704)
♦ Conseil Centroaméricain de Tourisme (#03675)
♦ Conseil des chefs de secrétariat des organismes des Nations Unies (#20636)
♦ Conseil des chefs de secrétariat des organismes des Nations Unies pour la coordination / see United Nations System Chief Executives Board for Coordination (#20636)
♦ Conseil des chirurgiens-dentistes Européens (#04886)
♦ Conseil chrétien anti-alcoolique des pays nordiques (no recent information)
♦ Conseil circumpolaire inuit (#15995)
♦ Conseil du Commonwealth pour les échanges de jeunes (internationally oriented national body)
♦ Conseil du Commonwealth pour l'écologie humaine (#04339)
♦ Conseil des communautés africaines en Europe / see Conseil des communautés africaines en Europe/Belgique
♦ Conseil des communautés africaines en Europe/Belgique (internationally oriented national body)
♦ Conseil des Communautés européennes / see Council of the European Union (#04895)
♦ Conseil des communes d'Europe / see Council of European Municipalities and Regions (#04891)
♦ Conseil des communes et régions d'Afrique / see United Cities and Local Governments of Africa (#20500)
♦ Conseil des communes et régions d'Europe (#04891)
♦ Conseil commun des fédérations nordiques des industries (inactive)
♦ Conseil de concertation pour l'approvisionnement en eau et l'assainissement (inactive)
♦ Conseil des conférences centrales méthodistes en Europe (inactive)
♦ Conseil des conférences épiscopales d'Europe (#04884)
♦ Conseil pour les congrès internationaux d'entomologie (#04900)
♦ Conseil consultatif africain de population (inactive)
♦ Conseil consultatif pour l'Assemblée constituante mondiale (inactive)
♦ Conseil Consultatif des Eaux Occidentales Australes (#19896)
♦ Conseil Consultatif pour les Eaux Occidentales Septentrionales (#17607)
♦ Conseil consultatif économique du Commonwealth (inactive)
♦ Conseil consultatif pour l'égalité entre les femmes et les hommes (unconfirmed)
♦ Conseil consultatif européen pour les échanges technologiques / see EURO-CHINA (#05658)
♦ Conseil consultatif de juges européens (#04767)
♦ Conseil consultatif maghrébin / see Consultative Council of the Arab Maghreb Union (#04765)
♦ Conseil Consultatif de Pêche Lointaine (#16511)

♦ Conseil consultatif de procureurs européens (CCPE) 04685

Consultative Committee of European Prosecutors

Contact DG – Human Rights – Law, Justice Division, Av de l'Europe, 67075 Strasbourg CEDEX, France. T. +33388413412.
URL: http://www.coe.int/CCPE/

History 13 Jul 2005, by the Committee of Ministers of *Council of Europe (CE, #04881)*, to institutionalize the annual *Conference of Prosecutors General of Europe (CPGE)*. Former names and other names: *Consultative Council of European Prosecutors* – alias. **Aims** Prepare opinions for the European Committee on crime problems, and on difficulties concerning the implementation of Recommendation Rec (2000) 19; promote implementation of this recommendation; collect information about the functioning of prosecution services in Europe. **Structure** Board (meets twice a year), comprising President, Vice-President and 2 members. Working Group (meets twice a year). **Events** *Meeting* Moscow (Russia) 2006. **Members** All Council of Europe member states may be represented on the Committee. [2021/XJ0931/**E***]

♦ Conseil consultatif professionnel et scientifique international du Programme des Nations Unies pour la prévention du crime et de la justice (#14810)
♦ Conseil consultatif de la recherche aéronautique pour le Commonwealth (internationally oriented national body)
♦ Conseil consultatif de la recherche ferroviaire européenne (#08325)
♦ Conseil consultatif de l'Union du Maghreb arabe (#04765)
♦ Conseil de coopération arabe CCA (inactive)
♦ Conseil de coopération des associations nordiques de juristes (meeting series)
♦ Conseil de coopération douanière / see World Customs Organization (#21350)

- ♦ Conseil de coopération économique du Pacifique (#17947)
- ♦ Conseil de coopération des Etats arabes du Golfe / see Gulf Cooperation Council (#10826)
- ♦ Conseil de coopération des fonctionnaires des pays nordiques (no recent information)
- ♦ Conseil de coopération du Golfe (#10826)
- ♦ Conseil de coopération du Golfe arabe / see Gulf Cooperation Council (#10826)
- ♦ Conseil de coopération des institutions nordiques de crédit immobilier (inactive)
- ♦ Conseil de coopération Nord-Atlantique / see Euro Atlantic Partnership Council (#05646)
- ♦ Conseil de coopération régionale (#18773)
- ♦ Conseil de coordination des associations aéroportuaires (inactive)
- ♦ Conseil pour la coordination des congrès internationaux des sciences médicalesi / see Council for International Organizations of Medical Sciences (#04905)
- ♦ Conseil de coordination islamique d'Asie (inactive)
- ♦ Conseil de coordination nordique en matière de criminologie (#17493)
- ♦ Conseil de Coordination du Personnel d'ONUG (#20712)
- ♦ Conseil de coordination des syndicats d'Afrique australe (#19865)
- ♦ Conseil coordonnateur des organisations des travailleurs agricoles et des paysans d'Amérique latine (inactive)
- ♦ Conseil cultural du Comité Nordkallot (inactive)
- ♦ Conseil culturel mondial (#04705)
- ♦ Conseil du cyclisme amateur de l'UCI (inactive)
- ♦ Conseil du cyclisme professionnel de l'UCI (inactive)
- ♦ Conseil danois pour les réfugiés (internationally oriented national body)
- ♦ Conseil de défense de l'Afrique équatoriale (inactive)
- ♦ Conseil de défense de l'Amérique centrale (inactive)
- ♦ Conseil des dentistes Européens / see Council of European Dentists (#04886)
- ♦ Conseil pour le développement de la recherche économique et sociale en Afrique / see Council for the Development of Social Science Research in Africa (#04879)
- ♦ Conseil pour le développement de la recherche en sciences sociales en Afrique (#04879)
- ♦ Conseil des droits de l'homme des Nations Unies (#20571)
- ♦ Conseil économique du bassin du Pacifique (#17938)
- ♦ Conseil économique et social arabe (#00937)
- ♦ Conseil économique et social des Nations Unies (#05331)
- ♦ Conseil de l'éducation des adultes de l'Amérique latine (#04707)
- ♦ Conseil pour l'éducation et le développement Europe (internationally oriented national body)
- ♦ Conseil de l'EEE (#05379)
- ♦ Conseil des Eglises luthériennes en Amérique centrale et au Panama (inactive)
- ♦ Conseil d'Eglises du Moyen-Orient (#16756)
- ♦ Conseil de l'enseignement du droit (#04908)
- ♦ Conseil de l'Entente (#05491)
- ♦ Conseil épiscopal latinoaméricain (#04709)
- ♦ Conseil des Etats baltes / see Baltic Council (#03108)
- ♦ Conseil des Etats de la Mer baltique / see Council of the Baltic Sea States (#04870)
- ♦ Conseil de l'euro / see Eurogroup (#05689)
- ♦ Conseil euro-jeunes sourds / see European Union of Deaf Youth (#08986)
- ♦ Conseil euro-marocain du développement de coopération et d'échanges socioculturels (internationally oriented national body)
- ♦ Conseil de l'Europe (#04881)
- ♦ Conseil européen (#06801)
- ♦ Conseil européen de l'arboriculture (#05911)
- ♦ Conseil Européen d'Archéologie (#05746)
- ♦ Conseil européen de l'artisanat et des petites et moyennes entreprises (inactive)
- ♦ Conseil européen des artistes (#06805)
- ♦ Conseil européen des associations nationales d'écoles indépendantes (#06833)

♦ Conseil européen des associations de traducteurs littéraires (CEATL) 04686

European Council of Literary Translators' Associations

Pres Maison des Auteurs, Rue Prince Royal 87, 1050 Brussels, Belgium. E-mail: info@ceatl.eu – president@ceatl.eu.

URL: http://www.ceatl.eu/

History 17 Nov 1993. Registration: Banque-Carrefour des Entreprises, Belgium; EU Transparency Register, No/ID: 65913704675-82. **Aims** Promote quality of translation of literary works in Europe; work towards improving the social, moral, legal and economic status of the literary translator; exchange information and best practices between member associations. **Structure** General Meeting (annual); Steering Committee; Working Groups. **Languages** English, French. **Staff** None. **Finance** Sources: members' dues. Annual budget: 20,000 EUR. **Activities** Advocacy/lobbying/activism; awareness raising; knowledge management/information dissemination; networking/liaising; training/education. **Publications** *Counterpoint* (2 a year) – e-magazine.

Members National organizations (34) in 28 countries:

Austria, Belgium, Bulgaria, Croatia, Czechia, Denmark, Finland, France, Germany, Hungary, Iceland, Ireland, Italy, Lithuania, Netherlands, North Macedonia, Norway, Poland, Portugal, Romania, Serbia, Slovakia, Slovenia, Spain, Sweden, Switzerland, Türkiye, UK.

NGO Relations Member of (2): *Culture Action Europe (CAE, #04981)*; *International Authors Forum (IAF, #12298)*. [2022.05.11/XD6228/**D**]

- ♦ Conseil européen des associations d'utilisateurs des télécommunications (inactive)
- ♦ Conseil européen de certification logistique (inactive)
- ♦ Conseil européen des chambres de commerce américaines / see European Council of American Chambers of Commerce (#06803)
- ♦ Conseil européen du Codex Alimentarius (inactive)
- ♦ Conseil européen des comités nationaux de jeunesse (inactive)
- ♦ Conseil européen du commerce et de la réparation automobiles (#06832)
- ♦ Conseil européen des communautés juives (#06825)
- ♦ Conseil Européen des Confréries Enogastronomiques (#08076)
- ♦ Conseil européen des constructeurs d'appareillage électro-domestique / see APPLiA – Home Appliance Europe (#00877)
- ♦ Conseil européen des constructeurs d'appareils domestiques / see APPLiA – Home Appliance Europe (#00877)
- ♦ Conseil européen des constructeurs de cuisine (no recent information)
- ♦ Conseil européen de coordination pour le développement des essais de performance des combustibles, lubrifiants et autres fluides utilisés dans les transports (#04822)
- ♦ Conseil européen de coordination pour le développement des essais de performance des lubrifiants et des combustibles pour moteurs / see Coordinating European Council for the Development of Performance Tests for Transportation Fuels, Lubricants and Other Fluids (#04822)
- ♦ Conseil européen du cuir brut (inactive)
- ♦ Conseil européen des doctorants et jeunes docteurs (#06815)
- ♦ Conseil européen du droit de l'environnement (no recent information)
- ♦ Conseil européen des écoles internationales / see Educational Collaborative for International Schools (#05365)
- ♦ Conseil européen des économistes de la construction (#06812)
- ♦ Conseil européen des églises méthodistes (#07787)
- ♦ Conseil européen de l'enseignement par correspondance (inactive)
- ♦ Conseil européen de l'équipement naval (inactive)
- ♦ Conseil européen des études africaines (no recent information)
- ♦ Conseil européen d'études à domicile (inactive)
- ♦ Conseil européen des fédérations de l'industrie chimique / see Conseil européen de l'industrie chimique (#04687)
- ♦ Conseil Européen des Fédérations WIZO (#06850)
- ♦ Conseil européen de l'industrie de la bande magnétique (inactive)

♦ Conseil européen de l'industrie chimique (CEFIC) 04687

European Chemical Industry Council

Dir Gen Rue Belliard 40 – bte 15, 1040 Brussels, Belgium. T. +3224369300. E-mail: mail@cefic.be.

URL: http://www.cefic.org/

History 6 Oct 1972. Founded as *European Council of Chemical Manufacturers' Federations – Conseil européen des fédérations de l'industrie chimique* by merger of *European Centre of Chemical Manufacturers' Federations (inactive)*, set up 28 Apr 1959, and *International Secretariat of Professional Groups in the Chemical Industry of the European Community Countries (inactive)*. Statutes revised: 12 Dec 1990 (when current title adopted); 26 Nov 1997, Brussels (Belgium) – approved by Royal Decree, 18 Mar 1998, following approval by the General Assembly of a new "3 pillar" structure; Jun 2001, Helsinki (Finland). Registration: Banque-Carrefour des Entreprises, No/ID: 0412.849.915, Start date: 5 Jan 1973, Belgium; EU Transparency Register, No/ID: 64879142323-90, Start date: 24 Sep 2009. **Aims** Be the forum and voice of the chemical industry in Europe. **Structure** General Assembly (annual). Board, including Executive Committee. Boards (2): National Associations; Industry Sectors. Leadership Team; International Chemicals Management (ICM) unit. Programme Councils (6): Communications; Energy, HSE and Logistics; Industrial Policy; Legislation and Institutional Affairs; Product Stewardship; Research and Innovation. Industry Sectors (3): Speciality Chemicals; *Petrochemicals Europe (#18342)*; Halogens/ *Euro Chlor (#05659)*. *'Speciality Chemicals'*, comprising the following sector groups:

- *European Biocidal Product Forum (EBPF, #06332)*;
- Formaldehyde Biocides Interest Group (FABI);
- *Microbial Control Executive Council – MCEC*;
- *Peracetic Acid Registration Group (PAR)*;
- *Sorbic Acid BPD Registration Group (SARG)*;
- Sodium Chlorite/Chlorie Dioxide BPD Registration Group (SC BPD RG);
- *Active Pharmaceutical Ingredients Committee (APIC, #00102)*;
- Calcium Chloride;
- Cyanides;
- *European Fine Chemicals Group (EFCG, #07257)*;
- *European Soda Ash Producers Association (ESAPA, #08791)*;
- *Chemical Vitamin E Producers (CVEP)*;
- *European Fermentation Group (EFG, #07240)*;
- *European Polymer Dispersion and Latex Association (EPDLA)*;
- *Food Contact Additives (FCA)*;
- *Gelatin Manufacturers Association of Europe (GME, #10090)*;
- *Inorganic Feed Phosphates (IFP, #11226)*;
- *Phosphoric Acid and Phosphates Producers Association (PAPA, #18363)*, including *European Oleochemicals and Allied Products Group (APAG, #08081)*;
- *European Committee of Organic Surfactants and their Intermediates (#06660)*;
- Environmental Risk Assessment and Management;
- *Association of Synthetic Amorphous Silica Producers (ASASP, #02946)*;
- *European Catalyst Manufacturers Association (ECMA, #06457)*;
- *European Producers of Specialty Aluminas (EPSA, #08282)*;
- *Pigments, Dyes and Fillers Producers (Eurocolour)*;
- *Titanium Dioxide Manufacturers' Association (TDMA, #20168)*;
- *Sodium Sulphate Producers Association (SSPA, #19667)*;
- *European Plasticisers (#08214)*;
- *European Light Stabilisers and Antioxidants Association (ELiSANA)*;
- *European Rubber Chemicals Association (ERCA, #08410)*;
- *European Stabiliser Producers Association (ESPA, #08827)*;
- *Phosphorus, Inorganic and Nitrogen Flame Retardants Association (pinfa, #18364)*;
- *CES – Silicones Europe (#03838)*;
- *European Melamine Producers Association (EMPA, #07775)*;
- *Formacare (#09871)*;
- *Hydrocarbon and Rosin Resins Producers Association (HARRPA, #10996)*;
- *Polyester Powder Resin Manufacturers (PPRM)*;
- *Solvent Resin Manufacturers (SRM)*;
- *UV/EB Acrylate Sector Group*;
- *Activated Carbons Producers Association (#00099)*;
- *Centre européen d'études des silicates (CEES, #03746)*;
- *European Council for Alkylphenols and Derivatives (CEPAD, #06802)*;
- *European Phosphonates Association (EPA)*;
- *European Zeolites Producers Association (EUZEPA, #09148)*;
- *European Inorganic Coagulants Producers Association (INCOPA, #07542)*;
- *Peroxygens*;
- *Synthetic Organic Ion Exchangers and Adsorbents (SOIA, #20084)*.

'Petrochemistry'

Petrochemicals Europe (#18342), including the following Sector Groups:

- *Acetyls Sector Group (ASG)*;
- *European Basic Acrylic Monomer Group (EBAM)*;
- Acrylonitrile Group (ACN);
- *Amines Sector Group*;
- *Aromatics Producers' Association (APA, #01113)*;
- *Automotive Grade Urea (AGU)*;
- *BDO and Derivatives Sector Group*;
- *Coal Chemicals (CCSG)*;
- *Ethylene Oxide and Derivates Producers Association (EO and Glycols, #05556)*;
- *Sustainable Fuels (#20060)*;
- *Lower Olefins Sector Group (LOSG)*, including *Methacrylates Sector Group (MSG)*;
- *Methanol Sector Group*;
- *Phenol and Acetone Sector Group (PASG)*;
- *Propylene Oxide and Glycols Sector Group (PO and Glycols)*;
- *European Solvents Industry Group (ESIG, #08796)*;
- *European UP/VE Resin Association (#09038)*.

'Halogens'

Euro Chlor (#05659), including the following sector Groups:

- *European Fluorocarbons Technical Committee (EFCTC, #07274)*;
- *Global Fluorocarbon Producers Forum (GFPF, #10364)*;
- *European Sulphuric Acid Association (ESA, #08854)*;
- *EUROFLUOR (#05681)*.

Other groups not listed above, include:

- *European Aliphatic Isocyanates Producers Association (ALIPA)*;
- *European Citric Acid Manufacturers Association (ECAMA, #06561)*;
- *European Extruded Polystyrene Insulation Board Association (EXIBA, #07019)*;
- *Association of Synthetic Amorphous Silica Producers (ASASP, #02946)*;
- *European Chlorinated Solvent Association (ECSA, #06540)*;
- European Sulphuric Acid Association (ESA);
- *Fluorspar*;
- *Acrylonitrile Producers' Association (see: #04687)*;
- *Flame Retardants Europe (FRE, #09791)*;
- *European Phenolic Resins Association (EPRA, #08200)*;
- *European Solvents VOC Co-ordination Group (ESVOCG)*;
- *Hydrocarbon Solvents Producers Association (HSPA, #10997)*;
- *Oxygenated Solvents Producers Association (OSPA, #17923)*.

Languages English. **Staff** Central Activities: about 100; Sectoral Activities: 87. **Finance** Members' dues. **Activities** Networking/liaising. **Events** *European Conference* Amsterdam (Netherlands) 2020, *LRI Human Health Progress Review and Scoping Meeting* Brussels (Belgium) 2020, *LRI Human Health Progress Review and Scoping Meeting* Brussels (Belgium) 2019, *Global Chemical Industry European Convention* Helsinki (Finland) 2019, *European Conference* Prague (Czechia) 2019. **Publications** *Facts and Figures 2013*.

Members Members: Corporate (ACOM); Federation (AFEM); Business (ABM). Partners: associated companies; affiliated associations; partners. Corporate: major multinational chemical corporations. Members in 12 countries:

Austria, Belgium, Finland, France, Germany, Hungary, Italy, Netherlands, Spain, Sweden, Switzerland, UK.
Federation: national federations representing the chemical industry in European countries. Members in 22 countries:
Austria, Belgium, Czechia, Denmark, Finland, France, Germany, Greece, Hungary, Ireland, Italy, Netherlands, Norway, Poland, Portugal, Slovakia, Slovenia, Spain, Sweden, Switzerland, Türkiye, UK.
Business: companies (over 500) engaged in chemical manufacturing in CEFIC countries. Membership countries not specified. Associated National Federations in 8 countries:
Associated National Federations in 8 countries:
Bulgaria, Croatia, Estonia, Latvia, Lithuania, Romania, Russia, Ukraine.
Associated Companies: companies engaged in the production of chemicals in countries outside Europe. Membership countries not specified. Affiliated associations: European chemical associations (23):
Affiliated associations: European chemical associations (23):
- *Association of European Manufacturers of Sporting Ammunition (#02522);*
- *Association of Plastics Manufacturers in Europe (Plastics Europe, #02862);*
- British Association of Chemical Specialities (BACS);
- *CIRFS – European Man-made Fibres Association (#03944);*
- *Conseil européen de l'industrie des peintures, des encres d'imprimerie et des couleurs d'art (CEPE, #04688);*
- *CropLife Europe (#04965);*
- *Ecological and Toxicological Association of Dyes and Organic Pigments Manufacturers (ETAD, #05302);*
- *Euro Chlor (#05659);*
- *European Diisocyanate and Polyol Producers Association (ISOPA, #06926);*
- *European Federation for Construction Chemicals (EFCC, #07088);*
- *European Industrial Gases Association (EIGA, #07525);*
- *European Industrial Nitrocellulose Association (EINA, #07528);*
- *European Phenolic Resins Association (EPRA, #08200);*
- *European Photocatalysis Federation (EPF, #08203);*
- *European Resin Manufacturers' Association (ERMA, #08381);*
- *Fédération européenne des industries de colles et adhésifs (FEICA, #09572);*
- *Fédération européenne du commerce chimique (Fecc, #09563);*
- *Federation of European Explosives Manufacturers (FEEM, #09505);*
- *Fertilizers Europe (#09738);*
- *GlassFibreEurope (#10158);*
- *International Association for Soaps, Detergents and Maintenance Products (#12166);*
- *International Fragrance Association (IFRA, #13680);*
- *Technical Committee of Petroleum Additive Manufacturers in Europe (ATC, #20115).*

Partners: European non-chemical companies and associations, including the following 3 listed in this Yearbook:
European Chemical Society (EuCheMS, #06524); European Panel Federation (EPF, #08137); International Antimony Association (i2a, #11657).
Consultative Status Consultative status granted from: *ECOSOC (#05331)* (Ros C); *UNCTAD (#20285)* (General Category); *World Intellectual Property Organization (WIPO, #21593)* (Permanent Observer Status); *International Maritime Organization (IMO, #14102); UNEP (#20299).* **IGO Relations** Other main external contacts in Europe: *Council of the European Union (#04895); European Economic and Social Committee (EESC, #06963); European Commission (EC, #06633); European Parliament (EP, #08146).* Other main external contacts worldwide: *FAO (#09260); ILO (#11123); International Civil Aviation Organization (ICAO, #12581); UNIDO (#20336); United Nations Economic Commission for Europe (UNECE, #20555); WHO (#20950).* Observer to: *International Oil Pollution Compensation Funds (IOPC Funds, #14402); OSPAR Commission for the Protection of the Marine Environment of the North-East Atlantic (OSPAR Commission, #17905).* Accredited by: *United Nations Framework Convention on Climate Change – Secretariat (UNFCCC, #20564).* Participates as observer in the activities of: *Codex Alimentarius Commission (CAC, #04081).* Cooperates with: *European Union Intellectual Property Office (EUIPO, #08996).* Associated with Department of Global Communications of the United Nations. **NGO Relations** Member of (15): *Alliance for a Competitive European Industry (ACEI, #00670); Alliance for Chemical Sciences and Technologies in Europe (AllChemE, #00664); Alliance for Chemical Sciences and Technologies in Europe (AllChemE, #00664); Circular Plastics Alliance (#03936); Covenant of Mayors for Climate and Energy (#04939)* (Associate); *European Energy Forum (EEF, #06986)* (Associate); *European Factories of the Future Research Association (EFFRA, #07023); European Policy Centre (EPC, #08240); European Shippers' Council (ESC, #08477); European Technology Platform ALICE (ALICE, #08888); European Technology Platform for Sustainable Chemistry (SusChem, #08893)* (Founding); *EU Specialty Food Ingredients (#09200); Federation of European and International Associations Established in Belgium (FAIB, #09508); Industry4Europe (#11181); Knowledge4Innovation (K4I, #16198).*
Liaison Organization of: *Comité européen de normalisation (CEN, #04162).* Associate expert of: *Business and Industry Advisory Committee to the OECD (BIAC, #03385).* Close links and maintains secretariat for: *International Council of Chemical Associations (ICCA, #13003).* Affiliate organisation: *Association of Plastics Manufacturers in Europe (Plastics Europe, #02862).* In liaison with technical committees of: *International Organization for Standardization (ISO, #14473).* Close cooperation with other representative organizations: *International Chamber of Commerce (ICC, #12534).* Partner of: *European Partnership for Alternative Approaches to Animal Testing (EPAA, #08155).* Works with: *European Chemical Regions Network (ECRN, #06522); International Chewing Gum Association (ICGA, #12545).*
Sectoral related associations:
- *Association européenne des métaux (EUROMETAUX, #02578);*
- *BUSINESSEUROPE (#03381);*
- *CEMBUREAU – The European Cement Association (CEMBUREAU, #03634);*
- *Confederation of European Paper Industries (CEPI, #04529);*
- *Cosmetics Europe – The Personal Care Association (#04852);*
- *EURATEX – The European Apparel and Textile Confederation (EURATEX, #05616);*
- *European Association of Bioindustries (EuropaBio, #05956);*
- *European Centre for Ecotoxicology and Toxicology of Chemicals (ECETOC, #06477);*
- *Orgalim – Europe's Technology Industries (#17794);*
- *European Federation of Pharmaceutical Industries and Associations (EFPIA, #07191);*
- *European Petrochemical Association, The (EPCA, #08192);*
- *European Steel Association (EUROFER, #08835);*
- *European Tyre and Rubber Manufacturers' Association (ETRMA, #08963);*
- *FoodDrinkEurope (#09841);*
- *FuelsEurope (#10014);*
- *Oil Companies' European Association for Environment, Health and Safety in Refining and Distribution (CONCAWE, #17708).*

[2020/XD0615/ty/**D**]

♦ Conseil européen de l'industrie des peintures, des encres d'imprimerie et des couleurs d'art (CEPE) 04688

European Council of the Paint, Printing Ink and Artists' Colours Industry
Managing Dir Bd du Triomphe 172, 4th Floor, 1160 Brussels, Belgium. T. +3228972020. E-mail: secretariat@cepe.org.
URL: http://www.cepe.org/
History Nov 1951, Paris (France). New statutes adopted 19 Mar 1998, when restructured. Former names and other names: *Liaison Bureau of Paint and Printing Ink Manufacturers' Associations of the Common Market Countries* – former (1953 to 1990); *Bureau de liaison des associations de fabricants de peintures et d'encres d'imprimerie des pays du Marché commun* – former (1953 to 1990); *European Confederation of Paint, Printing Ink and Artists' Colours Manufacturers' Associations* – former (1990 to 1998); *Confédération européenne des associations de fabricants de peintures, d'encres d'imprimerie et de couleurs d'art* – former (1990 to 1998); *Europäischer Vereinigung der Verbände der Lack-, Druckfarben- und Künstlerfarbenfabrikanten* – former (1990 to 1998). Registration: Banque-Carrefour des Entreprises, No/ID: 0419.271.810, Start date: 22 May 1979, Belgium; Start date: 1953, End date: 1979, France; EU Transparency Register, No/ID: 47031804648-91, Start date: 1 Dec 2010. **Aims** Represent paint, printing ink and artists colours industries and associated products. **Structure** Consultative Assembly: Board. Manages: *European Artists' Association (EuACA, #05917); European Printing Ink Association (EuPIA, #08275).* **Languages** English, French, German. **Staff** 9.00 FTE, paid. **Finance** Sources: contributions. **Activities** Guidance/assistance/consulting; knowledge management/information dissemination; standards/guidelines. **Events** *Annual Conference and General Assembly* Madrid (Spain) 2022, *General Assembly* 2021, *Annual Conference and General Assembly* St Julian's (Malta) 2019, *Annual Conference and General Assembly* Belgrade (Serbia) 2018, *Annual Conference and General Assembly* Athens (Greece) 2017. **Publications** *CEPE Annual Review.*
Members Company members (about 900) with membership in a national association. Direct members via national associations in 17 countries:
Austria, Belgium, Denmark, Finland, France, Germany, Greece, Hungary, Ireland, Italy, Netherlands, Norway, Poland, Portugal, Romania, Spain, Sweden, Switzerland, UK.
IGO Relations Recognized by: *European Commission (EC, #06633).* Participates in the work of: *United Nations Economic Commission for Europe (UNECE, #20555).* **NGO Relations** Member of (7): *Conseil européen de l'industrie chimique (CEFIC, #04687)* (Affiliate); *Downstream Users of Chemicals Co-ordination group (DUCC, #05127); European Biocidal Product Forum (EBPF, #06332); Federation of European and International Associations Established in Belgium (FAIB, #09508); Industry4Europe (#11181); Metal Packaging Europe (MPE, #16736)* (Associate); *World Coatings Council (#21283)* (Founder). Liaises with: *BUSINESSEUROPE (#03381).* In liaison with technical committees of: *Comité européen de normalisation (CEN, #04162); International Organization for Standardization (ISO, #14473).* Involved in the work of: *European Organisation for Technical Assessment (EOTA, #08103).* [2022.10.27/XD0651/t/**D**]

- ♦ Conseil Européen de l'information sur l'alimentation (#07284)
- ♦ Conseil européen d'information du plomb (inactive)
- ♦ Conseil européen des ingénieurs civils (#06810)

♦ Conseil européen des jeunes agriculteurs (CEJA) 04689

European Council of Young Farmers – Consejo Europeo de los Jóvenes Agricultores – Europäischer Rat der Junglandwirte – Conselho Europeu dos Jovens Agricultores – Consiglio Europeo dei Giovani Agricoltori – Europese Raad voor Jonge Landbouwers – Europaeisk Råd for Unge Landmaend – Evropaiko Simvulio Neon Agroton
Main Office Rue de la Loi 67, 1040 Brussels, Belgium. T. +3222304210. E-mail: info@ceja.eu.
URL: http://www.ceja.eu/
History 12 Dec 1958, Rome (Italy). Established as a Liaison Committee of Agricultural Trade Union Youth Organizations by organizations representing young farmers from the six founding members of the European Economic Community. **Aims** Promote a younger and more innovative agricultural sector across the EU-27; create good working and living conditions for young people setting up in farming and those who are already "young farmers". **Structure** General Assembly; Praesidium; Presidency; Working Groups; Secretariat based in Brussels (Belgium). **Languages** English, French, German, Italian, Spanish. **Staff** 5.00 FTE, paid; 5.00 FTE, voluntary. **Finance** Sources: members' dues. Activities co-financed by: *European Commission (EC, #06633).* **Activities** Advocacy/lobbying/activism; events/meetings; knowledge management/information dissemination; networking/liaising; projects/programmes; training/education. **Events** *Round Table on Enhancing Youth Employment in Agriculture for a More Sustainable Europe* Brussels (Belgium) 2013, *Conference on Generational Renewal in Agriculture* Brussels (Belgium) 2011, *General Assembly* Brussels (Belgium) 2011, *General Assembly* Brussels (Belgium) 2010, *Conference on the future of young farmers* Rome (Italy) 2003. **Publications** Annual Activity Report; briefings; documents; position papers; press releases.
Members Full: national organizations (32) in 22 countries:
Austria, Belgium, Cyprus, Czechia, Denmark, Estonia, Finland, France, Germany, Ireland, Italy, Latvia, Lithuania, Luxembourg, Malta, Netherlands, Poland, Portugal, Slovakia, Slovenia, Spain, Sweden.
Associate in 2 countries:
Serbia, UK.
IGO Relations Cooperates with (6): *European Commission (EC, #06633); European Committee of the Regions (CoR, #06665); European Council (#06801); European Economic and Social Committee (EESC, #06963); European Parliament (EP, #08146); FAO (#09260).* Consulted by 18 advisory groups of the European Commission and by DG AGRI. **NGO Relations** Observer status with (1): *European Youth Forum (#09140).* Member of (2): *TP Organics – European Technology Platform (TP Organics, #20180); World Farmers' Organisation (WFO, #21401).* Partner of (1): *IFOAM Organics Europe (#11104).* [2022.05.04/XE2922/**E**]

- ♦ Conseil européen de la jeunesse méthodiste / see European Methodist Youth and Children's Council (#07788)
- ♦ Conseil Européen pour les Langues (#07646)
- ♦ Conseil européen des luttes associées / see UWW-Europe (#20739)
- ♦ Conseil européen du marketing (inactive)
- ♦ Conseil européen de mécanique / see EUROMECH – European Mechanics Society (#05713)
- ♦ Conseil européen des médecins pour le pluralisme thérapeutique (#06816)
- ♦ Conseil européen de la musique (#07837)
- ♦ Conseil européen de l'optométrie et de l'optique (#06835)
- ♦ Conseil Européen des Ordres des Médecins (#06830)
- ♦ Conseil européen des organisations de conscrits (inactive)
- ♦ Conseil européen des phénols alkylés et dérivés / see European Council for Alkylphenols and Derivatives (#06802)
- ♦ Conseil européen des pouvoirs municipaux et régionaux / see Council of European Municipalities and Regions (#04891)
- ♦ Conseil Européen des Producteurs de Matériaux de Construction / see Construction Products Europe AISBL (#04761)
- ♦ Conseil européen des professionnels de la construction (inactive)
- ♦ Conseil européen des professions immobilières / see European Association of Real Estate Professions (#06186)
- ♦ Conseil européen des professions libérales (#06828)
- ♦ Conseil européen de la recherche en équipements sous pression (#08269)
- ♦ Conseil européen pour la recherche nucléaire (inactive)
- ♦ Conseil européen de recherches sociales sur l'Amérique latine (#04710)
- ♦ Conseil européen sur les réfugiés et les exilés (#06839)
- ♦ Conseil européen des routes de vin (inactive)
- ♦ Conseil européen pour la sécurité des transports (#08940)
- ♦ Conseil européen des services communautaires juifs / see European Council of Jewish Communities (#06825)
- ♦ Conseil européen de stomathérapie (#06820)
- ♦ Conseil européen des syndicats de police (#06837)
- ♦ Conseil européen des systèmes de paiement (inactive)
- ♦ Conseil européen du tourisme social / see OITS/ European Commission for Social Tourism (#17713)
- ♦ Conseil européen des urbanistes (#06843)
- ♦ Conseil européen de la vie étudiante (#06845)
- ♦ Conseil européen pour le village et la petite ville (#06848)
- ♦ Conseil d'évaluation éducationnelle du Pacifique du Sud (inactive)
- ♦ Conseil des examens de l'Afrique occidentale (inactive)
- ♦ Conseil des examens des Caraïbes (#03500)
- ♦ Conseil d'exploitation postale (see: #20682)
- ♦ Conseil des fédérations commerciales d'Europe (inactive)
- ♦ Conseil des fédérations nordiques des commerçants en gros (inactive)
- ♦ Conseil FIABCI Communauté économique européenne / see European Association of Real Estate Professions (#06186)
- ♦ Conseil finlandais pour les réfugiés (internationally oriented national body)
- ♦ Conseil des fondations américaines de développement (#04712)
- ♦ Conseil français des investisseurs en Afrique (internationally oriented national body)

♦ Conseil francophone de la chanson (CFC) 04690

Contact address not obtained. T. +14509737675. Fax +14509736672.
URL: http://www.conseilfrancophone.org/
History 1986, Brussels (Belgium). Founded following recommendations of a colloquium, 1985, Wégimont (Belgium). Former names and other names: *Conseil international de la chanson* – former. Registration: Banque-Carrefour des Entreprises, No/ID: 0430.478.476, Start date: 24 Feb 1987, Belgium. **Aims** Unite professional singers and others active in creation, production and dissemination in French-speaking areas; support international cooperation and exchange; promote integral development of *singing* and *music* in

French-speaking areas. **Structure** General Assembly (every 2 years); Board (meets annually); Executive Committee. **Activities** Training/education; events/meetings; awards/prizes/competitions; advocacy/lobbying/activism. **Publications** *Rythmes* (4 a year) – bulletin. *Droits d'auteur et droits voisins dans les pays d'Afrique francophone* (1995); *La chanson dans l'espace francophone* (1989). Guides; proceedings.
Members Liaison bureaux in 8 countries:
Belgium, Cameroon, Canada, Congo Brazzaville, Congo DR, France, Switzerland, Togo.
Active members in 20 countries and territories:
Belgium, Benin, Burkina Faso, Burundi, Cameroon, Canada, Central African Rep, Chad, Comoros, Congo Brazzaville, Congo DR, Côte d'Ivoire, France, Gabon, Madagascar, Mali, Réunion, Senegal, Switzerland, Togo.
Consultative Status Consultative status granted from: *World Intellectual Property Organization (WIPO, #21593)* (Observer Status). [2020/XD4570/**D**]

- Conseil général des assemblées de Dieu (#10110)
- Conseil général des pêches pour la Méditerranée / see General Fisheries Commission for the Mediterranean (#10112)
- Conseil général du quart monde (#09978)
- Conseil homéopathique international (inactive)
- Conseil pour l'homologation des établissements théologiques en Afrique / see Association for Christian Theological Education in Africa (#02431)
- Conseil de l'Inde pour les affaires mondiales (internationally oriented national body)
- Conseil indien sudaméricain (#11158)
- Conseil Indo-Pacifique des pêches / see Asia-Pacific Fishery Commission (#01907)
- Conseil interafricain de philosophie (no recent information)
- Conseil interaméricain de commerce et de la production (no recent information)
- Conseil interaméricain pour le développement intégré (#11423)
- Conseil interaméricain des jurisconsultes (inactive)
- Conseil interaméricain de la musique (no recent information)
- Conseil interaméricain de sécurité (no recent information)
- Conseil interétatique pour la protection de la propriété industrielle (inactive)
- Conseil intergouvernemental des pays exportateurs de cuivre (inactive)
- Conseil international de l'action sociale (#13076)
- Conseil international des agences accréditantes / see International Council for Evangelical Theological Education (#13020)
- Conseil international des agences bénévoles (#13092)
- Conseil international pour l'arbitrage commercial (#13010)
- Conseil international de l'arbitrage en matière de Sport (#12994)
- Conseil international d'archéozoologie (#12995)
- Conseil international des architectes de langue officielle portugaise (internationally oriented national body)
- Conseil international des architectes de monuments historiques (inactive)
- Conseil international des archives (#12996)
- Conseil international des associations de bibliothèques de théologie / see European Theological Libraries (#08906)
- Conseil international des associations chimiques (#13003)
- Conseil international des associations de design graphique / see International Council of Design (#13013)
- Conseil international d'associations graphiques / see International Council of Design (#13013)
- Conseil international des associations des industries nautiques (#13044)
- Conseil international des associations de négociants en cuirs et peaux (#13029)
- Conseil international des associations de propriétaires et pilotes d'aéronefs (#12988)
- Conseil international des associations de la transformation des métaux en feuilles (#13073)
- Conseil international des auteurs des arts graphiques et plastiques et des photographes / see International Council of Creators of Graphic, Plastic and Photographic Arts (#13011)
- Conseil international des auteurs et compositeurs dramatiques / see Société des auteurs et compositeurs dramatiques
- Conseil international des auteurs et compositeurs de musique / see International Council of Music Authors (#13052)
- Conseil international des auteurs littéraires (inactive)
- Conseil international pour l'avenir de l'université (inactive)
- Conseil international de l'aviation d'affaires (#12418)
- Conseil international 'Band of Hope' (inactive)
- Conseil International du Bâtiment pour la recherche, l'étude et la documentation / see International Council for Research and Innovation in Building and Construction (#13069)
- Conseil international du blé / see International Grains Council (#13731)
- Conseil international du bon voisinage (#13728)
- Conseil international des centres commerciales (#13074)
- Conseil international des céréales (#13731)
- Conseil international de la chanson / see Conseil francophone de la chanson (#04690)
- Conseil international de la chasse / see International Council for Game and Wildlife Conservation (#13024)
- Conseil international de la chasse et de la conservation du gibier (#13024)
- Conseil international de la chasse et du tir / see International Council for Game and Wildlife Conservation (#13024)
- Conseil international du cinéma et de la télévision / see International Council for Film, Television and Audiovisual Communication (#13022)
- Conseil international du cinéma, de la télévision et de la communication audiovisuelle (#13022)
- Conseil international aux citoyens (#03954)
- Conseil international pour les communautés solidaires (internationally oriented national body)
- Conseil international des compositeurs (inactive)
- Conseil international congrégationaliste (inactive)
- Conseil international pour la coopération économique et sociale (inactive)
- Conseil international pour la coordination des services aux gens de mer (inactive)
- Conseil international de la corrosion (#12973)
- Conseil International des Créateurs des Arts Graphiques, Plastiques et Photographiques (#13011)
- Conseil International des Créateurs de Musique (#13052)
- Conseil international de la crevette (inactive)
- Conseil international de cricket féminin (inactive)
- Conseil international de la danse (#13130)
- Conseil international pour la danse de salon / see World Dance Council (#21353)
- Conseil international du design (#13013)
- Conseil international de design industriel / see World Design Organization (#21358)
- Conseil international pour le développement du cuivre (inactive)
- Conseil international pour le développement de l'éducation (inactive)
- Conseil international du diamant (#13170)
- Conseil international des doyens des beaux arts (internationally oriented national body)
- Conseil international du droit de l'environnement (#13018)
- Conseil international pour l'Echange international chrétien de jeunesse / see International Cultural Youth Exchange (#13122)
- Conseil international des économies régionales (inactive)
- Conseil internationale de cricket (#13105)
- Conseil international pour l'édition des oeuvres complètes d'Erasme (#13066)
- Conseil international d'éducation des adultes (#12983)
- Conseil international pour l'éducation des handicapés de la vue (#13015)
- Conseil international pour l'éducation physique et la science du sport (#13077)
- Conseil international pour l'éducation physique et le sport / see International Council of Sport Science and Physical Education (#13077)
- Conseil international d'Eglises chrétiennes (#13005)
- Conseil international des Eglises chrétiennes, Alliance européenne (inactive)
- Conseil international de l'électrodéposition (no recent information)
- Conseil international des employeurs du commerce (inactive)
- Conseil international de l'enseignement par correspondance / see International Council for Open and Distance Education (#13056)
- Conseil international de l'enseignement à distance / see International Council for Open and Distance Education (#13056)
- Conseil international d'esthétique industriel / see World Design Organization (#21358)
- Conseil international de l'étain (inactive)
- Conseil international des éthologie (#13019)
- Conseil international pour l'étude des îles du Pacifique (#13079)
- Conseil international d'études canadiennes (internationally oriented national body)
- Conseil international d'études de l'Europe centrale et orientale (#13002)

♦ Conseil international d'études francophones (CIEF) 04691

International Council for Francophone Studies
Exec Dir Université Laurentienne, Département d'études francophones, Campus de Sudbury, E-230E Pavilion Alphonse Raymond, Sudbury ON P3E 2C6, Canada. E-mail: directeur@cief.org.
Co-Dir College of Humanities and Social Sciences, 402 Bartow Ave, MD 2201, Kennesaw GA 30339, USA. T. +17704236124. E-mail: codirecteur@cief.org.
URL: http://secure.cief.org/wp/

History 1987, Lafayette, LA (USA). Founded by Maurice Cagnon. Registration: USA, Louisiana. **Aims** Promote multidisciplinary studies, research and publications on *French-speaking* cultures and literatures. **Structure** General Assembly; Management Committee; Continental Representatives (5). **Languages** French. **Staff** 5.00 FTE, voluntary. **Finance** Sources: members' dues. Subventions from French-speaking governments and organizations, including the following listed in this Yearbook: *Agence universitaire de La Francophonie (AUF, #00548)*; *Organisation internationale de la Francophonie (OIF, #17809)*. **Activities** Awards/prizes/competitions; events/meetings; knowledge management/information dissemination; research/documentation. **Events** *Congress* Hammamet (Tunisia) 2023, *Congress* Trento (Italy) 2022, *Congress* 2021, *Congress* Gdansk (Poland) 2020, *Congress* Ottawa, ON (Canada) 2019. **Publications** *Nouvelles Etudes Francophones* (2 a year) – journal; *Bulletin du CIEF*.
Members Individuals (about 400) in 52 countries and territories:
Algeria, Argentina, Australia, Austria, Belgium, Brazil, Burundi, Cambodia, Cameroon, Canada, China, Colombia, Congo Brazzaville, Congo DR, Costa Rica, Côte d'Ivoire, Denmark, Djibouti, Egypt, Equatorial Guinea, France, Gabon, Germany, Guiana Fr, Guinea, Haiti, Italy, Japan, Korea Rep, Luxembourg, Madagascar, Mali, Mauritania, Mauritius, Mexico, Morocco, Netherlands, New Zealand, Nigeria, Norway, Polynesia Fr, Puerto Rico, Senegal, Spain, Sudan, Sweden, Switzerland, Tunisia, UK, USA, Venezuela, Vietnam. [2022/XF1338/v/**F**]

- Conseil international d'études soviétiques et est-européennes / see International Council for Central and East European Studies (#13002)
- Conseil international des excipients pharmaceutiques (#14565)
- Conseil international pour l'exploration de la mer (#13021)
- Conseil international des fédérations théâtrales amateurs de culture latine / see Comité international des fédérations théâtrales d'amateurs de culture latine (#04176)
- Conseil international des femmes (#13093)
- Conseil international des femmes juives (#13036)
- Conseil international des femmes social-démocrates / see Socialist International Women (#19341)
- Conseil international du film d'enseignement / see International Council for Educational Media (#13014)
- Conseil international de fruits secs / see International Nut and Dried Fruit Council Foundation (#14387)
- Conseil international des grands réseaux électriques (#13040)
- Conseil international habitat / see Habitat International Coalition (#10845)
- Conseil international des industries des aliments infantiles (inactive)
- Conseil international des industries de jouets (#13086)
- Conseil international des infirmières (#13054)
- Conseil international pour l'information scientifique et technique (#13070)
- Conseil international pour les initiatives écologiques locales / see Local Governments for Sustainability (#16507)
- Conseil international des jeux (#13004)
- Conseil international des jeux et jouets / see International Council for Children's Play (#13004)
- Conseil International pour les Jeux et Sports Traditionnels (#13088)

♦ Conseil international de la langue française (CILF) 04692

International Council of the French Language
Pres 11 rue de Navarin, 75009 Paris, France. T. +33148787395. E-mail: cilf75@gmail.com.
URL: http://www.cilf.org/

History Jul 1967, Paris (France), on adoption of Constitution by Constitutive Assembly. Registered in accordance with French law, 20 Dec 1972, Paris. **Aims** Enrich the French language, promote its influence and administer its resources; consider all problems involving the French language and its relations with other languages, including educational aspects. **Structure** Plenary Assembly (annual), composed of full members representing States where French is the national, official or cultural language. **Languages** French. **Staff** 4.00 FTE, paid. **Finance** Members' dues: associates' subscriptions. Contracts. **Activities** Organizes symposia and conferences; maintains *Institut de recherches interculturelles (see: #04692)*, including 'Château de la Bûcherie' conference centre in Saint-Cyr-en-Arthies (France); produces publications on terminology, linguistics, architecture, oral dialogue, agronomy, mechanics. Specific tasks carried out by scientific commissions. Instrumental in setting up: Formation postuniversitaire interculturelle (FPI). Offers *'Humblet Prize'* (every 2 years) to encourage works concerning the French language in general, or concerning relations between French speaking people, their exchanges, their similarities and their common actions. **Events** *Entretiens européens* Cluny (France) 1990, *Seminar* Heidelberg (Germany FR) 1988, *International colloquium* Paris (France) 1987. **Publications** *La banque des mots* (2 a year); *Le français moderne* (2 a year). *Dictionnaire d'agriculture* (1999); *Dictionnaire de spatiologie – Tome 1 – Termes et définitions* (most recent ed 1998); *Le potager tropical* (3rd ed 1998) by Charles-Marie Messiaen; *Dictionnaire de spatiologie – Tome 2 – Lexique multilingue* (most recent ed 1998) in English, French, German, Italian, Russian, Spanish; *Dictionnaire commercial* (1998) in English, French, German; *Dictionnaire juridique: Terminologie du contrat* (1998) in English, French, German; *Dictionnaire multilingue de l'aménagement de l'espace* (1993) in English, French, German, Spanish; *Dictionnaire normand-français* (1993); *Wörterbuch für Industrie und Technik* (1993) in French, German; *Dictionnaire des noms d'agents pathogènes* (1992) in English, French; *Dictionnaire quadrilingue de la presse et des médias* (1991) in French, Italian, Portuguese, Spanish; *Dictionnaire d'histoire et de géographie agraires* (1991) by Paul Fénelon in English, French, German, Italian, Spanish; *Thésaurus de l'éducation* (1991) in Arabic, French; *Dictionnaire de génétique* (1991); *Dictionnaire de la photographie* (1990) in English, French, German; *Dictionnaire de l'océan* (1990) in English, French, German, Spanish; *Dictionnaire encyclopédique d'agrométéorologie* (1990) in English, French, Spanish; *L'Absolu, ses réalités humains: Les aspects scientifiques, philosophiques et sociologiques de l'Environnement* (1989) by Jean A Ternisien; *Francophonie et codéveloppement* (1989) by Tabi Manga; *Simulation de modèles linguistiques et enseignement assisté par ordinateur de l'arabe* (1989); *Terminologie diachronique* (1989); *Dictionnaire français-arabe de la presse et des médias* (1989); *Dictionnaire d'histoire et de géographie agraire* (1989); *Dictionnaire des chanteurs francophones de 1900 à nos jours* (1989) by Alain-Pierre Noyer; *Pour l'harmonisation orthographique des dictionnaires* (1988); *Anthologie de l'oeuvre de Victor Hugo* (1987) by Colette Murcia; *Dictionnaire des industries* (1986) in English, French; *Anthologie du roman maghrébin, négro-africain, antillais et réunionnais d'expression française, de 1945 à nos jours* (1986) by Denise Brahimi-Chapuis and Gabriel Belloc ; *Terminologie cotonnière* (1986) in English, French, Spanish; *Termes et définitions utilisés en soudage et techniques connexes* (1986); *Médecins arabes anciens – Xe et XIe siècles* (1986) by Jean-Charles

Sournia; *Lexique de météorologie* (1986) in English, French, Indonesian; *Le Savouron, petit dictionnaire gourmand* (1986); *Dictionnaire pratique arabe-français* (1986); *Dictionnaire pratique français-arabe* (1985); *Dictionnaire de la plongée sous-marine* (1985) in English, French, German, Italian, Spanish; *Dictionnaire d'agriculture français-arabe-anglais* (1984); *Dictionnaire des secours d'urgence en cas de catastrophe* (1984); *Langues arabes et langues africaines* (1983); *Vocabulaire technique du tabac* (1982); *Dictionnaire des termes nouveaux des sciences et des techniques* (1982); *Chrétiens et musulmans, que croyons-nous* (1982); *Petit guide de la néologie* (1981) by C Murcia et al; *La technologie vue par l'enfant* (1981); *Vocabulaire de la micrographie* (1980); *Vocabulaire d'astronomie* (1980); *Vocabulaire de la topographie* (1980); *Manuel pratique de terminologie* (1980) by Robert Dubuc; *Le livre dans la vie quotidienne de l'enfant* (1979); *Vocabulaire de la radiographie* (1979); *Vocabulaire d'écologie* (1979); *Vocabulaire de la géomorphologie* (1979); *Petit vocabulaire memento de l'olivier* (1978); *Vocabulaire de l'administration* (1978); *Répertoire des dictionnaires scientifiques et techniques (1950-1975)* (1978); *Vocabulaire de l'hydrologie et de la météorologie* (1978); *Vocabulaire des sciences et techniques spatiales* (1978); *Vocabulaire des relations culturelles internationales* (1977); *Enrichissement de la langue française* (1976); *Vocabulaire de l'environnement* (1976); *Dictionnaire forestier multilingue* (1976); *Textes et civilisations* – collection; *Techniques vivantes* – collection; *Dictionnaire d'anesthésie, réanimation, urgences*; *Dictionnaire du génie civil* in English, French; *Manuel terminologique didactique de télédétection et photogrammétrie* in English, French; *Dictionnaire d'aéronautique*; *Dictionnaire de gynécologie-obstétrique*; *Dictionnaire d'urologie*; *Dictionnaire de microbiologie*; *Dictionnaire de l'imagerie médicale*; *Dictionnaire de l'aéronautique et de l'espace* – Vol 1 English/French 1984, Vol 2 French/English 1986; *Dictionnaire de l'appareil moteur*; *Dictionnaire d'otorhinolaryngologie*; *Dictionnaire de génie civil*; *Fleuve et flamme* – collection; *Index espagnole du dictionnaire des industries*; *Dictionnaire de psychiatrie*; *Index portugais du dictionnaire des industries*; *Dictionnaire de dermatologie*; *Langue française et francophonie: Répertoire des organisations pour la promotion de la langue française*; *Dictionnaire des identités culturelles de la francophonie*; *Dictionnaire d'ophtalmologie, appareil digestif et neurologie*; *Dictionnaire de médecine ORL*; *Dictionnaire du radiodiagnostic industriel: Techniques et moyens d'acquisition de l'information* in English, French; *Mille mots du français mauricien: Réalités lexicales et francophonie à l'île Maurice*; *Dictionnaire de biologie*. Dictionaries on CD-ROM; colloquium proceedings. Information Services: Documentation centre. **Information Services** *ORTHONET*; *ORTHOTEL* – orthogrammatical databank.

Members Full in 28 countries and territories:
Belgium, Benin, Burkina Faso, Cameroon, Canada, Chad, Congo Brazzaville, Côte d'Ivoire, Djibouti, France, Gabon, Guadeloupe, Guinea, Haiti, Luxembourg, Madagascar, Mali, Martinique, Mauritius, Monaco, Morocco, Niger, Polynesia Fr, Rwanda, Senegal, Switzerland, Togo, Tunisia.
Associate in 18 countries and territories:
Abu Dhabi, Algeria, Bahrain, Brazil, Burundi, Canada, Congo DR, Egypt, Guinea-Bissau, Libya, Mauritania, Qatar, Réunion, Saudi Arabia, Seychelles, Sudan, Syrian AR, USA. [2020/XC1761/**C**]

♦ Conseil international des machines à combustion (CIMAC) 04693

International Council on Combustion Engines

SG c/o VDMA, Lyoner Strasse 18, 60528 Frankfurt-Main, Germany. T. +496966031353. Fax +496966032353. E-mail: cimac@vdma.org.
URL: http://www.cimac.com/

History Founded 1951, Paris (France), as *International Congress on Combustion Engines – Congrès international des machines à combustion*, when 1st International Congress decided to set up a Permanent Committee. Statutes accepted, 13 Mar 1952; current statutes adopted May 2014. **Aims** Promote improved technical and scientific knowledge; improve understanding between manufacturers, users and suppliers. **Structure** Congress (every 3 years); Council; Executive Board; Technical Programme Group; Working Groups (8); Financial Committee; Secretariat. Meetings closed. **Languages** English. **Staff** Secretariat, paid. **Finance** Members' dues. **Activities** Research/documentation; standards/guidelines. **Events** *Triennial Congress* Busan (Korea Rep) 2023, *Triennial Congress* Busan (Korea Rep) 2022, *Triennial Congress* Vancouver, BC (Canada) 2019, *CASCADES Seminar* Helsinki (Finland) 2017, *Triennial Congress* Helsinki (Finland) 2016. **Publications** Recommendations; guidelines; congress proceedings.

Members National associations in 14 countries:
Austria, China, Denmark, Finland, France, Germany, Greece, India, Japan, Korea Rep, Netherlands, Norway, Switzerland, USA.
Corporate members in 13 countries:
Belgium, Brazil, Canada, Croatia, Czechia, Greece, Italy, Monaco, Poland, Russia, Singapore, Spain, Sweden.
NGO Relations Cooperates with: *International Organization for Standardization (ISO, #14473)*. [2018.07.20/XC1767/**D**]

♦ Conseil international de médecine botanique (inactive)
♦ Conseil international des médecins homéopathes (inactive)
♦ Conseil international des médias éducatifs (#13014)
♦ Conseil international des métaux et de l'environnement (inactive)
♦ Conseil international des missions (inactive)
♦ Conseil international des missions (inactive)
♦ Conseil international des monuments et des sites (#13049)
♦ Conseil international des moyens d'enseignement / see International Council for Educational Media (#13014)
♦ Conseil international des moyens du film d'enseignement / see International Council for Educational Media (#13014)
♦ Conseil international des musées (#13051)
♦ Conseil international des musées africains (#12986)
♦ Conseil international de la musique (#14199)
♦ Conseil international de la musique populaire / see International Council for Traditional Music (#13087)
♦ Conseil international de la musique traditionnelle (#13087)
♦ Conseil international des navigateurs aériens (inactive)
♦ Conseil international des normes comptables (#11583)
♦ Conseil international pour de nouvelles initiatives de coopération Est-Ouest / see International Vienna Council (#15853)
♦ Conseil international de numismatique (#14385)
♦ Conseil international des organisations de communication technique (inactive)
♦ Conseil international des organisations de festivals de folklore / see International Council of Organizations for Folklore Festivals and Folk Art (#13058)
♦ Conseil international des organisations de festivals de folklore et d'arts traditionnels (#13058)
♦ Conseil international de la philosophie et des sciences humaines (#13061)
♦ Conseil international des praticiens du plan comptable international (inactive)
♦ Conseil international de la préparation à l'enseignement (#13016)
♦ Conseil international pour la préservation des oiseaux / see BirdLife International (#03266)
♦ Conseil international sur les problèmes de l'alcool et de l'alcoolisme / see International Council on Alcohol and Addictions (#12989)
♦ Conseil international sur les problèmes de l'alcoolisme et des toxicomanies (#12989)
♦ Conseil international pour un progrès global de la santé (no recent information)
♦ Conseil international pour la qualité de la vie professionnelle (inactive)

♦ Conseil international des radios-télévisions d'expression française (CIRTEF) 04694

French-Speaking Radio and Television International Council

SG c/o RTBF, Local 2C35, Boulevard Auguste Reyers 52, 1044 Brussels, Belgium. T. +3227368958 – +3227324585. Fax +3227326240. E-mail: cirtef@rtbf.be.
URL: http://cirtef.com/

History 19 Jun 1978, Montréal, QC (Canada). 19-23 Jun 1978, Montréal (Canada), following a meeting of 46 organizations of radio and television from Africa, America, Caribbean, Europe and Asia organized on the initiative of *Agence intergouvernementale de La Francophonie (inactive)*, 1977, Montréal. Statutes most recently modified Apr 1997. **Aims** Enhance: professional exchange; mutual help in technical training, production and programming; multilateral cooperation among all radio and television organizations which produce wholly or partly – nation or region-wide – French programmes; maintain continuing dialogue between these organizations; promote the role of radio and television as means of collective development; improve knowledge, appreciation and respect for cultures and aspirations of members' countries. **Structure** General Conference (every 2 years); Bureau; Executive Committee; Commissions (4); General Secretariat in Brussels (Belgium), headed by Secretary-General. **Languages** French. **Staff** 5.00 FTE, paid. **Finance** Annual budget: 1,900,000 EUR. **Activities** Events/meetings; knowledge management/information dissemination; training/education. **Events** *Annual SEFOR Seminar* Bujumbura (Burundi) 2012, *Annual SEFOR Seminar* Niamey (Niger) 2011, *Biennial general conference* Paris (France) 2011, *Annual SEFOR Seminar* Cotonou (Benin) 2009, *Biennial general conference* Hanoi (Vietnam) 2009. **Publications** *Bulletin CIRTEF*; *Le CIRTEF en Bref*. **Information Services** *Vidéothèque* – bank of TV programmes, mainly from countries of the south, financed by the Agence intergouvernementale de la francophonie.

Members Organizations in 33 countries:
Belgium, Benin, Burkina Faso, Burundi, Cameroon, Canada, Central African Rep, Chad, Comoros, Congo Brazzaville, Congo DR, Côte d'Ivoire, Djibouti, France, Gabon, Guinea, Haiti, Lebanon, Libya, Madagascar, Mali, Mauritania, Mauritius, Morocco, Niger, Rwanda, Senegal, Seychelles, Switzerland, Togo, Tunisia, Vanuatu, Vietnam.
Internationally oriented organizations (3):
Radio France internationale (RFI); TV5 Europe Satellimage; TV5 Québec/Canada.
Consultative Status Consultative status granted from: *UNESCO (#20322)* (Consultative Status). **IGO Relations** Comes within the network of: *TV5Monde (TV5, #20269)*, acting as partner of *TV5MONDE Europe (see: #20269)* and, through SEFOR seminars, supporting *TV5MONDE Afrique (see: #20269)*. Invited to sessions of Intergovernmental Council of: *International Programme for the Development of Communication (IPDC, #14651)*. Institutional relations with: *Arab States Broadcasting Union (ASBU, #01050)*. **NGO Relations** Member of: *International Conference of NGOs (#12883)*; *NGO-UNESCO Liaison Committee (#17127)*. Institutional relations with: *Radios francophones publiques (RFP, inactive)*. [2017.10.24/XC7500/**C**]

♦ Conseil international de réadaptation pour les victimes de la torture (#14712)
♦ Conseil international pour la recherche en agroforesterie / see World Agroforestry Centre (#21072)
♦ Conseil international de recherche sur le caoutchouc (inactive)
♦ Conseil international de la recherche et du développement sur le caoutchouc / see International Rubber Research and Development Board (#14771)
♦ Conseil international pour la recherche en sociologie de la coopération (inactive)
♦ Conseil international de réflexion et d'expertise en linguistique fondamentale appliquée (no recent information)
♦ Conseil international de reprographie (inactive)
♦ Conseil International sur la Résidence Alternée (#13072)
♦ Conseil international des ressources phytogénétiques / see Bioversity International (#03262)
♦ Conseil international pour la santé, l'éducation physique et la récréation / see International Council for Health, Physical Education, Recreation, Sport and Dance (#13028)
♦ Conseil international pour la santé, l'éducation physique, la récréation, le sport et la dance (#13028)
♦ Conseil international des sapeurs-pompiers (inactive)
♦ Conseil international pour la science (inactive)
♦ Conseil international des sciences de l'aéronautique (#12985)
♦ Conseil international des sciences de l'animal de laboratoire (#13039)
♦ Conseil international des sciences sociales (inactive)
♦ Conseil international scientifique agricole (inactive)
♦ Conseil international de secours alimentaire (inactive)
♦ Conseil international des services d'aide à domicile (inactive)
♦ Conseil international des services juifs de bienfaisance et d'assistance sociale (#13035)
♦ Conseil international des services médicaux pénitentiaires (no recent information)
♦ Conseil international des sociétés de design industriel / see World Design Organization (#21358)
♦ Conseil international des sociétés de pathologie (no recent information)
♦ Conseil international pour le soutien à des procès équitables et aux droits de l'homme (#13081)

♦ Conseil international du sport militaire (CISM) 04695

International Military Sports Council – Consejo Internacional del Deporte Militar

SG/CEO Rue J Jordaens 26, 1000 Brussels, Belgium. T. +3226500271 – +32497712511.
Dir address not obtained. T. +3226476852. Fax +3226475387.
URL: http://www.milsport.one/

History Founded 18 Feb 1948, Nice (France), in succession to *Inter-Allied Council for Sport – Conseil des sports des forces alliées*, set up 1945, Frankfurt-Main (Germany FR). Previous statutes approved by: 43rd General Assembly, 10-14 Apr 1988, Paramaribo (Suriname), and amended by 45th General Assembly, 4-10 May 1990, Lusaka (Zambia); 56th General Assembly, May 2001, Algiers (Algeria). Current statutes approved by 62nd General Assembly, 21-27 May 2007, Ouagadougou (Burkina Faso). Registered in accordance with Belgian law, 9 Jan 1989, Brussels (Belgium). **Aims** Encourage military physical and sporting activities; develop friendly relations among *armed forces* and uniformed services of member countries; develop mutual technical assistance between member countries; contribute to progressive, balanced development of youth and to the worldwide effort for universal peace. **Structure** General Assembly (annual); Board of Directors (meets 3 times a year); General Secretariat; Liaison Offices (meet once a year); Commissions (annual). **Languages** Arabic, English, French, Spanish. **Staff** 6 civilian; 12 military. **Finance** Members' dues in accordance with the UN list of national gross income up to about euro 15,000 (annual). Total annual budget: about euro 800,000. **Activities** Events/meetings; sporting activities. **Events** *Annual General Assembly* Nairobi (Kenya) 2020, *Annual General Assembly* Ho Chi Minh City (Vietnam) 2019, *Annual General Assembly* Punta Cana (Dominican Rep) 2018, *Annual General Assembly* Athens (Greece) 2017, *Annual General Assembly* Tartu (Estonia) 2016. **Publications** *CISM Directory* (2 a year) in English, French – a list of CISM delegations for internal use; *CISM Digest* (annual); *CISM Year Book* (annual); *CISM Magazine*. Annual report.

Members Armed forces of 138 countries and territories:
Afghanistan, Albania, Algeria, Angola, Argentina, Armenia, Austria, Azerbaijan, Bahrain, Bangladesh, Barbados, Belarus, Belgium, Benin, Bolivia, Bosnia-Herzegovina, Botswana, Brazil, Bulgaria, Burkina Faso, Burundi, Cameroon, Canada, Cape Verde, Central African Rep, Chad, Chile, China, Colombia, Comoros, Congo Brazzaville, Congo DR, Côte d'Ivoire, Croatia, Cyprus, Czechia, Denmark, Djibouti, Dominican Rep, Ecuador, Egypt, Equatorial Guinea, Eritrea, Estonia, Eswatini, Finland, France, Gabon, Gambia, Georgia, Germany, Ghana, Greece, Guatemala, Guinea, Guinea-Bissau, Hungary, India, Indonesia, Iran Islamic Rep, Iraq, Ireland, Italy, Jamaica, Jordan, Kazakhstan, Kenya, Korea DPR, Korea Rep, Kuwait, Kyrgyzstan, Latvia, Lebanon, Lesotho, Libya, Lithuania, Luxembourg, Madagascar, Malawi, Mali, Malta, Mauritania, Monaco, Mongolia, Montenegro, Morocco, Myanmar, Namibia, Nepal, Netherlands, Niger, Nigeria, North Macedonia, Norway, Oman, Pakistan, Palestine, Paraguay, Peru, Philippines, Poland, Portugal, Qatar, Romania, Russia, Rwanda, Saudi Arabia, Senegal, Serbia, Sierra Leone, Slovakia, Slovenia, South Africa, Spain, Sri Lanka, Sudan, Suriname, Sweden, Switzerland, Syrian AR, Tanzania UR, Thailand, Togo, Trinidad-Tobago, Tunisia, Türkiye, Turkmenistan, Uganda, Ukraine, United Arab Emirates, Uruguay, USA, Uzbekistan, Venezuela, Vietnam, Yemen, Zambia, Zimbabwe.
Consultative Status Consultative status granted from: *ECOSOC (#05331)* (Special). **IGO Relations** *Council of Europe (CE, #04881)*; *International Committee of Military Medicine (ICMM, #12785)*; *UNESCO (#20322)*; United Nations. **NGO Relations** Member of (4): *Federation of European and International Associations Established in Belgium (FAIB, #09508)*; *International Committee for Fair Play (#12769)*; *International Council of Sport Science and Physical Education (ICSSPE, #13077)*; *Olympic Movement (#17719)*. Recognized by: *International Olympic Committee (IOC, #14408)*. [2018.09.27/XB2262/**B**]

♦ Conseil international de standardisation en hématologie (#13078)
♦ Conseil international du sucre (inactive)
♦ Conseil international des tanneurs (#13084)
♦ Conseil international de la technologie de chaudrons sous pression (#13064)
♦ Conseil international temporaire pour le relèvement de l'éducation (inactive)
♦ Conseil international de tennis professionnel hommes (inactive)
♦ Conseil international des traités indiens (#13836)
♦ Conseil international de Vienne (#15853)
♦ Conseil interparlementaire consultatif de Benelux (#03201)
♦ Conseil islamique de l'Europe (no recent information)
♦ Conseil de la Jeunesse Arabe et Africaine (#00894)
♦ Conseil de la jeunesse des bons templiers de l'Europe centrale (inactive)
♦ Conseil de la jeunesse océanienne (#18013)
♦ Conseil de la jeunesse oecuménique d'Europe / see Ecumenical Youth Council in Europe (#05352)

- ♦ Conseil de la jeunesse pluriculturelle de France / see COJEP International – Conseil pour la Justice, l'Egalité et la Paix (#04090)
- ♦ Conseil de la jeunesse pluriculturelle – International / see COJEP International – Conseil pour la Justice, l'Egalité et la Paix (#04090)
- ♦ Conseil des jeux du Pacifique (#17951)
- ♦ Conseil des jeux du Pacifique Sud / see Pacific Games Council (#17951)
- ♦ Conseil juif mondial pour les migrations (inactive)
- ♦ Conseil latinoaméricain et des Caraïbes pour l'autogestion (inactive)
- ♦ Conseil latinoaméricain de culture (inactive)
- ♦ Conseil latinoaméricain des écoles d'administration (#16308)
- ♦ Conseil latinoaméricain des Eglises (#16309)
- ♦ Conseil latinoaméricain des femmes catholiques (inactive)
- ♦ Conseil latinoaméricain pour la loi et le développement (inactive)
- ♦ Conseil latinoaméricain d'océanographie (inactive)
- ♦ Conseil latinoaméricain pour la physique de l'espace (inactive)
- ♦ Conseil latinoaméricain de recherches sur la paix (#16310)
- ♦ Conseil latinoaméricain de sciences sociales (#04718)
- ♦ Conseillers pour les centres de conférences internationales (inactive)
- ♦ Conseillers volontaires canadiens à l'entreprise / see Canadian Executive Service Organization
- ♦ Conseil de la liberté des Etats baltiques (inactive)
- ♦ Conseil de licence industrielle d'Afrique orientale (inactive)
- ♦ Conseil maritime baltique et international / see BIMCO (#03236)
- ♦ Conseil méditerranéen de l'arbitrage (#16645)
- ♦ Conseil méditerranéen de recherches en sciences sociales (inactive)
- ♦ Conseil méthodiste mondial (#21650)
- ♦ Conseil des ministres / see Council of the European Union (#04895)
- ♦ Conseil des Ministres ACP-CE / see ACP-EU Council of Ministers (#00076)
- ♦ Conseil des Ministres ACP-UE (#00076)
- ♦ Conseil des ministres des affaires étrangères (inactive)
- ♦ Conseil des ministres africains chargés de l'eau (#00376)
- ♦ Conseil des Ministres arabes de l'habitat / see Council of Arab Ministers for Housing and Reconstruction (#04862)
- ♦ Conseil des ministres arabes de la justice (no recent information)
- ♦ Conseil des ministres arabes de la santé (#04861)
- ♦ Conseil des ministres des assurances (see: #11385)
- ♦ Conseil des ministres baltes (#03109)
- ♦ Conseil des ministres des Communautés européennes / see Council of the European Union (#04895)
- ♦ Conseil des ministres pour la coopération économique en Asie (inactive)
- ♦ Conseil des ministres des Etats associés des Caraïbes (inactive)
- ♦ Conseil des ministres de l'intérieur arabes (#00990)
- ♦ Conseil des ministres nordiques de l'éducation et de la culture (inactive)
- ♦ Conseil des ministres des pays nordiques (#17260)
- ♦ Conseil des ministres de l'Union européenne / see Council of the European Union (#04895)
- ♦ Conseil mixte de l'Afrique (inactive)
- ♦ Conseil mondial de l'artisanat (#21342)
- ♦ Conseil mondial pour l'assemblée constituante des peuples (inactive)
- ♦ Conseil mondial des associations d'éducation comparée (#21322)
- ♦ Conseil mondial de la boxe (#21242)
- ♦ Conseil mondial des clubs d'entraide (no recent information)
- ♦ Conseil mondial des coopératives d'épargne et de crédit (#21324)
- ♦ Conseil mondial de l'eau (#21908)
- ♦ Conseil mondial d'éducation (#21325)
- ♦ Conseil mondial de l'éducation chrétienne (inactive)
- ♦ Conseil mondial pour l'émancipation coloniale (inactive)
- ♦ Conseil mondial de l'énergie (#21381)
- ♦ Conseil mondial des entreprises pour l'environnement (inactive)
- ♦ Conseil mondial de l'environnement et des ressources (inactive)
- ♦ Conseil mondial estonien (#05550)
- ♦ Conseil mondial d'éthique des droits de l'animal (inactive)
- ♦ Conseil mondial de la famille marianiste (#21334)
- ♦ Conseil mondial de la gastronomie (no recent information)
- ♦ Conseil mondial de l'hindouisme (internationally oriented national body)
- ♦ Conseil Mondial des Instituts Paulo Freire (unconfirmed)
- ♦ Conseil mondial de management (inactive)
- ♦ Conseil mondial de la paix (#21717)
- ♦ Conseil mondial des peuples indigènes (inactive)
- ♦ Conseil mondial de la race Hereford (#21565)
- ♦ Conseil mondial pour la radio et la télévision (no recent information)
- ♦ Conseil mondial de sécurité des femmes (unconfirmed)
- ♦ Conseil mondial solaire (#10609)
- ♦ Conseil mondial suprême des mosquées (no recent information)
- ♦ Conseil mondial des synagogues massort (#21323)
- ♦ Conseil mondial de la tomate transformée (#21738)
- ♦ Conseil mondial des travailleurs du nucléaire (inactive)
- ♦ Conseil des municipalités du Commonwealth (inactive)
- ♦ Conseil de la musique du Nordkallotten (inactive)
- ♦ Conseil musulman de coopération en Europe (no recent information)
- ♦ Conseil des Nations Unies pour la Namibie (inactive)
- ♦ Conseil nordique (#17256)
- ♦ Conseil nordique des académies de musique (#02830)
- ♦ Conseil nordique des acteurs (#17166)
- ♦ Conseil nordique des administrations de douanes (#17497)
- ♦ Conseil nordique anti-alcoolique (inactive)
- ♦ Conseil nordique de l'artisanat (inactive)
- ♦ Conseil nordique des associations diaconales (inactive)
- ♦ Conseil nordique des bateaux (#17221)
- ♦ Conseil nordique des bons templiers (#17483)
- ♦ Conseil nordique pour la boulangerie (inactive)
- ♦ Conseil nordique du commerce de détail (inactive)
- ♦ Conseil nordique du commerce des parfums (inactive)
- ♦ Conseil nordique pour le commerce du verre et de la porcelaine (inactive)
- ♦ Conseil nordique des détaillants en parfumerie (inactive)
- ♦ Conseil nordique des écoles de ski (inactive)
- ♦ Conseil nordique de l'Eglise pour les gens de la mer (no recent information)
- ♦ Conseil nordique de l'élevage ovin et caprin (inactive)
- ♦ Conseil nordique d'études fiscales (#17443)
- ♦ Conseil nordique des étudiants en dentisterie (inactive)
- ♦ Conseil nordique des étudiants en médecine (inactive)
- ♦ Conseil nordique des fabricants de meubles (inactive)
- ♦ Conseil nordique du film pour enfants (inactive)
- ♦ Conseil nordique de management (inactive)
- ♦ Conseil nordique des marchands de papier (inactive)
- ♦ Conseil nordique de missions à domicile (inactive)
- ♦ Conseil nordique pour la musique des chemins de fer (no recent information)
- ♦ Conseil nordique pour la musique d'Eglise (#17257)
- ♦ Conseil nordique d'océanographie physique (inactive)
- ♦ Conseil nordique d'orientation (no recent information)
- ♦ Conseil nordique de la pharmacopée (inactive)
- ♦ Conseil nordique de plantations de semences à usage forestier (inactive)
- ♦ Conseil nordique de la préservation du bois (#17469)
- ♦ Conseil nordique de la presse professionnelle (inactive)
- ♦ Conseil nordique pour la protection des animaux (inactive)
- ♦ Conseil nordique des publications en sciences naturelles (inactive)
- ♦ Conseil nordique pour la recherche et le développement ferroviaires (inactive)
- ♦ Conseil nordique de la recherche économique (inactive)
- ♦ Conseil nordique de recherches sur l'alcool (inactive)
- ♦ Conseil nordique des recherches anthropologiques (inactive)
- ♦ Conseil nordique de recherches sur les drogues (inactive)
- ♦ Conseil nordique de recherches sur la nature (#17262)
- ♦ Conseil nordique pour la reliure des livres (inactive)
- ♦ Conseil nordique des sociétés de recherches sur la musique (inactive)
- ♦ Conseil nordique pour les sourds (#05126)
- ♦ Conseil nordique du théâtre d'amateurs (#17172)
- ♦ Conseil nordique de tourisme (no recent information)
- ♦ Conseil norvégien pour les réfugiés (internationally oriented national body)
- ♦ Conseil des notariats de l'Union Européenne / see Notaries of Europe (#17609)
- ♦ Conseil oecuménique du christianisme pratique (inactive)
- ♦ Conseil oecuménique des Eglises (#21320)
- ♦ Conseil oecuménique de la jeunesse en Europe (#05352)
- ♦ Conseil oléicole international (#14405)
- ♦ Conseil olympique d'Asie (#17718)
- ♦ Conseil optique nordique (#17376)
- ♦ Conseil des organisations d'action contre le SIDA en Afrique (#00272)
- ♦ Conseil des organisations internationales directement intéressées à l'enfance et à l'adolescence (inactive)
- ♦ Conseil des organisations internationales des sciences médicales (#04905)
- ♦ Conseil des organisations non-gouvernementales d'appui au développement (#04911)
- ♦ Conseil Ouest et Centre Africain pour la Recherche et le Développement Agricoles (#20907)
- ♦ Conseil panafricain pour la protection de l'environnement et le développement (inactive)
- ♦ Conseil panafricain de la reconciliation / see Pan-African Reconciliation Council (#18063)
- ♦ Conseil panaméricain pour les aveugles (inactive)
- ♦ Conseil panaméricain d'odontologie infantile (inactive)

♦ Conseil parlementaire interrégional (CPI) 04696

Interregionaler Parlamentarier-Rat (IPR) – Interregional Parliamentary Council

Secretariat 23 rue du Marché-aux-Herbes, Chambre des Députés, L-1728 Luxembourg, Luxembourg. T. +352466966338. Fax +352466966209.

URL: https://cpi-ipr.eu/

History 17 Feb 1986, Metz (France). Established when Convention was signed. Convention modified: 17 Apr 1989, Arlon (Belgium). **Aims** Encourage harmonious development of the 'Grande Région' by studying and encouraging adoption of legal and technical mechanisms adapted to cross-border realities and evolution in a European and international context; support development of bilingualism so as to increase the intellectual and physical mobility of students and businesses. **Structure** Council, comprising representatives of regional parliaments and headed alternately by the President of each Member Assembly. Standing Committee, consisting of 2 representatives of each regional parliament. Commissions (5): Economic Affairs; Social Affairs; Transport and Communications; Environment and Agriculture; Education, Training, Research and Culture. Permanent Secretariat, headed by Permanent Secretary. Honorary President. Official Observers. **Activities** Participates in activities to reinforce cooperation between the different regional or national executives, towns and consultant and professional bodies; expresses opinions by means of resolutions addressed to regional and national executives. **Events** *Session plénière / Plenary Assembly* Metz (France) 2004, *Session plenière / Plenary Assembly* Kirkel (Germany) 2003, *Plenary Assembly* Metz (France) 2003, *Plenary Assembly* Saarbrücken (Germany) 2003, *Session plenière / Plenary Assembly* Otzenhausen (Germany) 2002.

Members Regions in 4 countries:

Belgium (French Community – Wallonia Region – German Community), France (Lorraine), Germany (Rhineland-Palatinate – Saarland), Luxembourg.

IGO Relations Observer: *Benelux Inter-Parliamentary Consultative Council (Benelux Parliament, #03201).*

[2022/XF3667/**F***]

- ♦ Conseil de partenariat euro-atlantique (#05646)
- ♦ Conseil des Patriarches catholiques d'Orient (#04875)
- ♦ Conseil paysan international (inactive)
- ♦ Conseil permanent de la Convention internationale de Stresa sur l'emploi des appellations d'origine et dénominations de fromages (no recent information)
- ♦ Conseil permanent pour la coopération internationale des compositeurs (inactive)

♦ Conseil permanent de la Francophonie (CPF) 04697

Pres s/c OIF, 19-21 avenue Bosquet, 75007 Paris, France. T. +33144373300. Fax +33145791498.

URL: http://www.francophonie.org/

History 21 Nov 1991, Paris (France), by resolution of *Conférence au sommet des chefs d'Etat et de gouvernement des pays ayant le français en partage (Sommet de la Francophonie, #04648)*, as a common organ of the Sommet and of *Agence intergouvernementale de La Francophonie (inactive)*, being Administration Council of the latter, to replace *Comité international du suivi du Sommet francophone (CIS, inactive)* and *Comité international de préparation du Sommet francophone (CIP, inactive)*. Currently an institution of *Organisation internationale de la Francophonie (OIF, #17809)*. **Aims** Ensure the cohesion of the pluralistic community whose common denominator is the sharing of the *French language* while respecting the specific ethnic and cultural characteristics of each; enliven and coordinate the partners and institutional activities of the francophone community. **Structure** Council meets at least 4 times a year and comprises permanent representatives of 18 Heads of State and Government who are members of the Sommet francophone, together with representatives appointed by the other member states. Headed by Secretary-General. Presidency is held by the host State or Government in whose country the previous summit was held and is in charge of follow-up, then by the country in which the next summit will be held. The President participates fully and acts as consultant at all meetings of *Conférence ministérielle de la Francophonie (CMF, #04630)*.

Activities Programmes operated by OIF and *Agence universitaire de La Francophonie (AUF, #00548)*. As the enlarged Bureau of OIF, CPF carries out the tasks set out in the Charter and regulations of that body.

Following on from the *'Comité de suivi'*, as follow-up to the Sommet francophone: Actuates, arbitrates and settles political, economic and cooperative aspects; examines and approves projects; processes evaluations; reports to the ministerial conference. Defines programme priorities and passes their execution to chosen agencies. Examines the respective roles of the OIF, networks and other francophone organizations. Negotiates the setting up and management of multilateral funds: (i) a permanent multilateral common fund for financing projects in every sector of cooperation among countries which have in common their use of the French language. (ii) Funds for specific objectives of the OIF (iii) 2 funds dealing with the objectives of other organizations: *Centre d'échanges multilatéraux d'actualités francophones (CEMAF, no recent information)*.

Coordinates the work of networks and their harmonization: I. *'Agriculture and the Protection of the Environment'* comprising a technical committee and working groups (4) which carry out specific projects – Regional Training and Specialized Training Centres; Cooperative Networks and Research; Pisciculture and Biotechnology Research; Limiting Post-Harvest Losses. Cooperative research programme with *Communauté économique des pays des Grands Lacs (CEPGL, #04375)* and *West and Central African Council for Agricultural Research and Development (WECARD, #20907)*. Includes setting up of *Institut international de recherche pour le développement, Adiopodoumé (no recent information)*, Côte d'Ivoire. II. *'Energy'* Consultative Committee

on Energy of experts from 13 countries develops programmes such as: Diffusion of Knowledge; Energy Management; Electrification. Includes projects such as *Institut de la Francophonie pour le développement durable (IFDD, #11305)*, seminars and training programmes. III. *'Culture and Communication'* Under 'Culture', includes projects on: low-priced paperbacks; free circulation of books in francophone areas; rural centres for reading and cultural activities; book fairs; festivals of cinema; African languages and civilizations; databank on cultural property. Under 'Communication', includes projects concerning: *TV5Monde (TV5, #20269)* and its *TV5MONDE Europe (see: #20269)*, *TV5-Québec*, *TV5MONDE Latin America (see: #20269)* and *TV5MONDE Afrique (see: #20269)*; co-production of television programmes; creation of *Agence international de commercialisation et de promotion des produits des industries francophones d'enregistrement sonore (inactive)*; development of rural radio; exchange of personnel among francophone radio and television; setting up of *Agence des télécommunications de la francophonie (no recent information)*. IV. *'Scientific Information and Technological Development'* Projects: Diffusion of scientific publications; *Banque internationale d'information sur les Etats francophones (BIEF, inactive)*; review of informatics and telematics reception infrastructure; Network service centres; informatics and education; university and higher education projects. V. *'French-language Industries'* Projects: computer-assisted translation of technical terms; software for industrial use; courses and training information; inventory of available resources in the French language; linguistic development and transfer of terminology; training. VI. *'Education of French-speaking Children'*.
Events *Session* Antananarivo (Madagascar) 2016, *Session* Paris (France) 2013, *Session* Paris (France) 2013, *Session* Paris (France) 2013, *Session* Paris (France) 2013.
Members Representatives of 15 of the governments taking part in the Sommet francophone. Current membership:
Belgium, Benin, Burundi, Cameroon, Canada, Côte d'Ivoire, Egypt, France, Laos, Liberia, Mali, Mauritius, Québec, Rwanda, Senegal.
NGO Relations *Assemblée parlementaire de la Francophonie (APF, #02312)*; *Association Internationale des Maires et responsables des capitales et métropoles partiellement ou entièrement Francophones (AIMF, #02715)*. Instrumental in setting up: *Comité pour le français dans les organisations internationales (inactive)*.
[2021/XE3041/**E***]

- Conseil permanent international pour l'exploration de la mer / see International Council for the Exploration of the Sea (#13021)
- Conseil permanent des sept Patriarches catholiques de l'Orient / see Council of Catholic Patriarchs of the Orient (#04875)
- Conseil permanent des sept Patriarches catholiques de l'Orient; Conseil des sept Patriarches catholiques de l'Orient. / see Council of Catholic Patriarchs of the Orient (#04875)
- Conseil permanent des traducteurs européens (inactive)
- Conseil du Personnel de la Banque africaine de développement (#19943)
- Conseil phytosanitaire interafricain (#11386)
- Conseil pontifical pour les communications sociales (#18447)
- Conseil pontifical de la culture (#18443)
- Conseil pontifical pour le dialogue interreligieux (#18444)
- Conseil pontifical pour le dialogue avec les non-croyants (inactive)
- Conseil pontifical pour l'interprétation des textes législatifs / see Pontifical Council for Legislative Texts (#18445)
- Conseil pontifical pour la promotion de l'unité des chrétiens (#18446)
- Conseil pontifical pour les textes législatifs (#18445)
- Conseil de la population (#18458)
- Conseil portugais pour les refugiés (internationally oriented national body)
- Conseil présidentiel andin (see: #00817)
- Conseil professionnel nordique (inactive)
- Conseil promotionnel pour l'action des jeunes en Afrique (unconfirmed)
- Conseil quaker pour les affaires européennes (#18587)
- Conseil pour le recensement des oiseaux d'Europe (#06347)
- Conseil de la recherche médicale d'Afrique orientale (inactive)
- Conseil de recherches sur les ressources naturelles d'Afrique orientale (inactive)
- Conseil de reconciliation Panafricain (#18063)
- Conseil régional des architectes d'Asie (#01087)
- Conseil régional pour l'éducation et l'alphabétisation des adultes en Afrique (no recent information)

♦ Conseil régional de l'épargne publique et des marchés financiers (CREPMF) 04698

Regional Council for Public Savings and Financial Markets
Contact 01 BP 1878, Abidjan 01, Côte d'Ivoire. T. +22520215742 – +22520215768. Fax +22520332304 – +22520221657. E-mail: sg@crepmf.org – presidence@crepmf.org.
URL: http://www.crepmf.org/
History 3 Jul 1996, within *Union monétaire Ouest africaine (UMOA, inactive)*. **Aims** Protect savings invested in securities and any other placement leading to a procedure of public appeal for savings in all the Member States of the West Africa Economic and Monetary Union. **Structure** A representative of each Member State, appointed by the Council of Ministers of UEMOA; the Governor of Central Bank of the West African States or his representative; the President of the Commission of UEMOA or his representative; a magistrate specialized in financial matters, appointed by the Council of Ministers of UEMOA; an accountant expert witness, appointed by the Council of Ministers of UEMOA. **Finance** Financed through commissions, royalties or any other income from its activities. **Publications** Annual Report.
[2011/XM2058/**E***]

- Conseil régional européen de la Fédération mondiale pour la santé mentale / see Mental Health Europe (#16715)
- Conseil régional européen de la FMSM / see Mental Health Europe (#16715)

♦ Conseil Régional de Formation des Institutions Supérieures de Contrôle des Finances Publiques de l'Afrique Francophone Subsaharienne (CREFIAF) 04699

Contact BP 376, Yaoundé, Cameroon. T. +23722220182. Fax +23722234403.
URL: http://www.crefiaf.org/
History 1997, Yaoundé (Cameroon), at the instigation of *International Organization of Supreme Audit Institutions (INTOSAI, #14478)* Development Initiative (IDI). **Aims** Strengthen the capacity of of the Supreme Audit Institutions (SAIs) in the Francophone Subsaharan region. **Structure** General Assembly; Regional Committee of Institutional Reinforcement; Technical Commissions. **Languages** French. **Staff** 1.00 FTE, paid. **Activities** Training/education.
Members SAIs of 23 countries:
Benin, Burkina Faso, Burundi, Cameroon, Cape Verde, Central African Rep, Chad, Comoros, Congo Brazzaville, Congo DR, Côte d'Ivoire, Djibouti, Equatorial Guinea, Gabon, Guinea, Guinea-Bissau, Madagascar, Mali, Niger, Rwanda, Sao Tomé-Principe, Senegal, Togo.
IGO Relations *African Development Bank (ADB, #00283)*; *Canadian International Development Agency (CIDA, inactive)*; *Deutsche Gesellschaft für Internationale Zusammenarbeit (GIZ)*; *International Bank for Reconstruction and Development (IBRD, #12317)* (World Bank). **NGO Relations** *African Organization of Supreme Audit Institutions (AFROSAI, #00406)*; *International Organization of Supreme Audit Institutions (INTOSAI, #14478)*.
[2018.02.13/XM5890/**D**]

- Conseil régional interuniversitaire (inactive)
- Conseil régional islamique Da'wah de l'Asie du Sud-Est et du Pacifique (#18792)
- Conseil régional de la marine marchande dans les Caraïbes (inactive)
- Conseil régional du tourisme pour l'Afrique australe (inactive)
- Conseil des régions d'Europe / see Assembly of European Regions (#02316)
- Conseil Same (#19012)
- Conseil Same nordique / see Saami Council (#19012)
- Conseil pour la santé publique d'Amérique centrale (inactive)
- Conseil de Saskatchewan pour la coopération internationale (internationally oriented national body)
- Conseil scandinave de l'habillement (inactive)
- Conseil scientifique pour l'Afrique au Sud du Sahara (inactive)
- Conseil de sécurité des Nations Unies (#20625)
- Conseil de Senlis / see ICOS (#11086)
- Conseil des sept Patriarches catholiques de l'Orient / see Council of Catholic Patriarchs of the Orient (#04875)
- Conseils oecuméniques (meeting series)
- Conseil solaire méditerranéen (no recent information)
- Conseil de solidarité de Moyen-Orient (no recent information)
- Conseil spirituel mondial (inactive)
- Conseil des sports des forces alliées / see Conseil international du sport militaire (#04695)
- Conseil du sport de l'Union Africaine (unconfirmed)
- Conseil pour la stratégie paneuropéenne de la diversité biologique et paysagère (inactive)
- Conseil supérieur des Ecoles européennes (#03295)
- Conseil supérieur du sport en Afrique (inactive)
- Conseil syndical du Commonwealth (inactive)
- Conseil syndical des travailleurs andins (inactive)
- Conseil des syndicats nordiques (#17158)
- Conseil des syndicats nordiques des professeurs (#17444)
- Conseil des télécommunications du Pacifique (#18007)
- Conseil sur les tensions mondiales (inactive)
- Conseil de la Toison d'Or / see Fondation Toison d'Or – Académie Européenne d'Histoire (#09830)
- Conseil des traducteurs nordiques (inactive)
- Conseil du transport aérien du Commonwealth (inactive)
- Conseil du transport aérien du Pacifique Sud (inactive)
- Conseil de travailleurs de la Caribe (no recent information)
- Conseil de tutelle des Nations Unies (#20639)
- Conseil de l'Union européenne (#04895)
- Conseil de l'unité économique arabe (#04859)
- Conseil universitaire interaméricain pour le développement économique et social (no recent information)
- Conseil universitaire pour le système des Nations Unies (#00020)
- Conseil pour l'urbanisme européen (#04896)
- Conseil Wallonie Bruxelles de la coopération internationale (internationally oriented national body)
- Consejeria en Proyectos (#18532)
- Consejeria en Proyectos para Refugiados Latinoamericanos / see Project Counselling Service (#18532)
- Consejo Académico para el Sistema de las Naciones Unidas (#00020)
- Consejo de Administración Fiduciaria de las Naciones Unidas (#20639)
- Consejo de Administración Pesquera del Caribe (#03508)
- Consejo Africano de Organizaciones al Servicio del SIDA (#00272)
- Consejo Agropecuario Centroamericano (#03657)
- Consejo Andino de Ingenieria (inactive)
- Consejo Andino de Ministros de Relaciones Exteriores (#00818)
- Consejo Arancelario y Aduanero Centroamericano (no recent information)
- Consejo Argentino para las Relaciones Internacionales (internationally oriented national body)

♦ Consejo de Armonización de Normas Electrotécnicas de las Naciones en las Américas (CANENA) 04700

Council for Harmonization of Electrotechnical Standards of the Nations in the Americas (CANENA)
Contact National Electrical Manufacturers Assoc, 1300 N 17th St, Ste 900, Rosslyn VA 22209, USA. T. +17038413267. Fax +17038413367.
URL: http://www.canena.org/
History 1992. Founded by electro-industry manufacturers' associations of North America. Registration: Section 501(c)(6), Start date: 13 Jun 1995, USA. **Aims** Advance regional trade through harmonization of electrotechnical product safety standards for equipment intended for use in the North American-type distribution system. **Structure** Council; Executive Committee; Audit Committee; Planning Committee; Operations Committee; Marketing Committee. **Languages** English, Spanish. **Staff** None. **Finance** None. **Activities** Knowledge management/information dissemination; networking/liaising; publishing activities; standards/guidelines. **Events** *Annual General Meeting* Mexico City (Mexico) 2023, *Annual General Meeting* Mexico City (Mexico) 2019, *Annual Meeting* San José (Costa Rica) 2015, *General Meeting* Arlington, VA (USA) 2014, *Annual Meeting* Washington, DC (USA) 2014. **Publications** Electrotechnical safety standards.
Members Electro-industry organizations including standards developers, conformity assessment testing laboratories, regulators, and other interested parties, in 4 countries:
Canada, Costa Rica, Mexico, USA.
IGO Relations Association for Standardization of: *Southern Common Market (#19868)*. **NGO Relations** Association for Standardization of: *Canadian Standards Association (CSA International)*; *European Committee for Electrotechnical Standardization (CENELEC, #06647)*; *International Electrotechnical Commission (IEC, #13255)*; *Pan American Standards Commission (#18133)*; national organizations.
[2022/XE3519/**E**]

- Consejo del Arzobispado Ortodoxo Griego de América (#10708)
- Consejo del Arzobispado Ortodoxo Griego de América del Norte y del Sur / see Greek Orthodox Archdiocesan Council of America (#10708)
- Consejo de Asentamientos Sustentables de América Latina (unconfirmed)
- Consejo de Asia-Pacifico de Organizaciones al Servicio del SIDA (#01875)

♦ Consejo de Asociaciones de la Industria Cosmética Latinoamericana (CASIC) 04701

Exec Sec Avda Italia 6101, 11500 Montevideo, Uruguay. T. +59826040464. Fax +59826040495. E-mail: casic@casic-la.org.
URL: http://www.casic-la.org/
History 17 Nov 1999, Santiago (Chile). **Structure** General Assembly; Board; Executive Commission. **Events** *General Assembly* Paraguay 2014.
Members Associations in 14 countries:
Argentina, Brazil, Chile, Colombia, Costa Rica, Dominican Rep, Ecuador, El Salvador, Mexico, Panama, Paraguay, Peru, Uruguay, Venezuela.
[2014/XJ8709/t/**D**]

- Consejo de Asociaciones Nacionales Europeas y Japoneses de Armadores (inactive)

♦ Consejo de las Asociaciones Profesionales de Ingenieros Civiles de Lengua Oficial Portuguesa y Castellana (CECPC-CICPC) 04702

Conselho das Associações Profissionais De Engenheiros Civis dos Paises de Lingua Oficial Portuguesa e Castelhana (CECPC-CICPC)
Contact Av António Augusto de Aguiar 3D, 1069-030 Lisbon, Portugal. T. +351213132600. E-mail: cecpc@ordemdosengenheiros.pt.
URL: http://www.cicpc-civil.org/
History 2007, Brazil. Registered in accordance with Portuguese law. **Aims** Satisfy basic needs and improve living conditions; promote globalization and recognition of the skills of civil engineers. **Structure** General Assembly; Board of Directors; Secretary General. **Languages** Portuguese, Spanish. **Activities** Training/education; events/meetings; monitoring/evaluation; politics/policy/regulatory; standards/guidelines. **Events** *General Assembly* Madrid (Spain) 2016.
Members Full in 31 countries and territories:
Andorra, Angola, Argentina, Bolivia, Brazil, Cape Verde, Chile, Colombia, Costa Rica, Cuba, Dominican Rep, Ecuador, El Salvador, Equatorial Guinea, Guatemala, Guinea-Bissau, Honduras, Macau, Mexico, Mozambique, Nicaragua, Panama, Paraguay, Peru, Portugal, Puerto Rico, Sao Tomé-Principe, Spain, Timor-Leste, Uruguay, Venezuela.
International organizations (6):

European Council of Civil Engineers (ECCE, #06810); *Fédération Européenne d'Associations Nationales d'Ingénieurs (FEANI, #09558)*; *Latin American Engineering Association for Labour Security (#16314)*; *Unión Panamericana de Asociaciones de Ingenieros (UPADI, #20469)*; *World Council of Civil Engineers (WCCE, #21321)*; *World Federation of Engineering Organizations (WFEO, #21433)*. [2016.07.29/XM4941/y/**D**]

♦ Consejo para el Avance y Apoyo a la Educación (internationally oriented national body)
♦ Consejo de Ayuda Mutua Económica (inactive)
♦ Consejo del Caribe (#03482)
♦ Consejo del Caribe para la Aplicación de las Leyes de Aduaneras (#03487)
♦ Consejo del Caribe para Europea / see The Caribbean Council (#03482)
♦ Consejo Caribeño de Educación Superior en Agricultura (#03484)

♦ Consejo Centroamericano de Acreditación de la Educación Superior (CCA) 04703

Pres Instituto de Cooperación y Desarrollo, Edificio Roque Ramos, Universidad Pedagógica Francisco Morazan, Tegucigalpa, Francisco Morazán, Honduras.
Exec Dir Costa Rican Institute of Technology, Escuele de Ingenieria en Seguridad Laboral e Higiene Ambiental, Cartago, Cartago, 30101, Costa Rica. E-mail: cca@ucr.ac.cr.
URL: http://www.ccacreditacion.org/

History Founded 19 Nov 2003, by *Confederación Universitaria Centroamericana (CSUCA, #04497)*. **Aims** Promote improvement of the quality and integration of superior *education* in Central America through national or regional agencies of *accreditation* properly recognized by CCA. **Structure** Council (meets 2 times a year); Technical Secretariat; Forum (meets every 3 years). **Languages** Spanish. **Finance** Principal support from University of Costa Rica. Other sources: contributions from participating universities and the Confederation of University Professional Organizations in Central America. **Activities** Certification/accreditation; training/education. **Events** *Forum* Panama (Panama) 2003.
Members in 7 countries:
Belize, Costa Rica, El Salvador, Guatemala, Honduras, Nicaragua, Panama.
NGO Relations Member of: *Red Iberoamericana para el Aseguramiento de la Calidad en la Educación Superior (RIACES, #18657)*. [2015/XJ3245/**E**]

♦ Consejo Centroamericano de Instituciones de Seguridad Social / see Consejo de Institutos de Seguridad Social de Centroamérica y República Dominicana (#04715)
♦ Consejo Centroamericano de la Salud Pública (inactive)

♦ Consejo Centroamericano de Superintendentes de Bancos, de Seguros y de Otras Instituciones Financieras (CCSBSO) 04704

Conseil centroaméricain des surintendants de banques, de compagnies d'assurances et autres institutions financières – Central American Council of Supervisors of Banks, Insurance Companies and other Financial Institutions

Exec Sec c/o Superintendencia de Bancos de Panama, Ave Samuel Lewis, Torre Banistmo – Mezzanine, Bella Vista, Panama, Panamá, Panama PANAMá, Panama. T. +5075067750. Fax +5075067705. E-mail: contacto@ccsbso.org.
URL: http://www.ccsbso.org/

History Jul 1976. Previously also known under the acronym *CCSBSIF*. Current statutes revised Apr 2009. **Aims** Promote cooperation and exchange of information between members. **Structure** General Assembly. President; Vice-President; Executive Secretary. **Languages** Spanish. **Staff** Superintendency that holds the Presidency and Executive Secretariat uses own staff to fulfil the duties of the Council. **Finance** Members' dues. **Activities** Technical staff of each Superintendency hold periodic working sessions known as Technical Committees to develop regional supervisory best practices as well as to integrate supervisory framework. Superintendents of banks: meet to approve results of the Technical Committees; revise execution of regional projects; give instructions to the Committees on principal matters of work. Organizes; conferences and seminars; events in coordination and cooperation with the US Treasury and FMI. **Events** *Annual Meeting* Tegucigalpa (Honduras) 2011. **Publications** Public information related to regional financial statistics published on website.
Members Individuals in 7 countries:
Costa Rica, Dominican Rep, El Salvador, Guatemala, Honduras, Nicaragua, Panama.
IGO Relations *Central American Bank for Economic Integration (CABEI, #03658)*; *Central American Monetary Council (#03672)*. Participates in the activities of: *UNCTAD (#20285)*. **NGO Relations** *Association of Supervisors of Banks of the Americas (ASBA, #02944)*. [2019/XD9761/v/**D***]

♦ Consejo Centroamericano de los Trabajadores de la Educación y la Cultura (no recent information)
♦ Consejo Centroamericano de Turismo (#03675)
♦ Consejo Centroamericano de Vivienda y Asentamientos Humanos (inactive)
♦ Consejo de Ciencia y Tecnologia para el Caribe (#03485)
♦ Consejo de los Comités Nacionales Europeos de Juventud (inactive)
♦ Consejo de las Comunidades Europeas / see Council of the European Union (#04895)
♦ Consejo para las Conferencias Interamericanas sobre Educación en Fisica / see Inter-American Council on Physics Education (#11424)
♦ Consejo Consultivo para las Aguas Noroccidentales (#17607)
♦ Consejo Consultivo para las Aguas Occidentales Australes (#19896)
♦ Consejo Consultivo Empresarial Andino (see: #00817)
♦ Consejo Consultivo de Flota de Larga Distancia en Aguas No Comunitarias (#16511)
♦ Consejo Consultivo Laboral Andino (see: #00817)
♦ Consejo de Control de Calorías (internationally oriented national body)
♦ Consejo Coordinador de Asociaciones Aeroportuarias (inactive)
♦ Consejo Coordinador Internacional de Asociaciones de Industrias Aeroespaciales (#12956)

♦ Consejo Cultural Mundial (CCM) 04705

Conseil culturel mondial – World Cultural Council

Contact Case Postale 373, 1630 Bulle FR, Switzerland. E-mail: info@consejoculturalmundial.org – nominations@consejoculturalmundial.org.
URL: https://www.consejoculturalmundial.org

History 1981, Monterrey (Mexico). **Aims** Increase efficient and positive use of knowledge and promote *fraternity* among men, nations and governments; establish relations with scientific, cultural and social institutions throughout the world. **Structure** Directive Board; Interdisciplinary Committee; International Arts and Education Jury. **Languages** English, French, Spanish. **Staff** 3.00 FTE, paid; 15.00 FTE, voluntary. **Finance** Sources: donations; fundraising; grants. Major universities collaborate each year to host Awarding Ceremony. **Activities** Awards/prizes/competitions; events/meetings. **Events** *Summit* Dundee (UK) 2015, *Summit* Espoo (Finland) 2014, *Annual Awarding Ceremony* Toluca (Mexico) 2010, *Annual Awarding Ceremony* Liège (Belgium) 2009, *Annual Awarding Ceremony* Princeton, NJ (USA) 2008.
Members Individuals in 64 countries:
Algeria, Argentina, Australia, Austria, Bahrain, Bangladesh, Belgium, Benin, Bolivia, Brazil, Canada, Chile, China, Colombia, Costa Rica, Cyprus, Czechia, Denmark, Egypt, Estonia, Finland, France, Germany, Ghana, Greece, Hungary, Iceland, India, Indonesia, Ireland, Israel, Italy, Japan, Kenya, Kuwait, Malaysia, Malta, Mexico, Morocco, Nepal, Netherlands, New Zealand, Norway, Pakistan, Peru, Philippines, Poland, Romania, Russia, Saudi Arabia, Serbia, South Africa, Spain, Sri Lanka, Sweden, Switzerland, Syrian AR, Thailand, Tunisia, Türkiye, UK, USA, Venezuela, Vietnam. [2023.02.15/XF0073/v/**F**]

♦ Consejo Danés para Asistencia a los Refugiados (internationally oriented national body)
♦ Consejo de Defensa Centroamericana (inactive)
♦ Consejo para el Desarrollo de la Investigación Económica y Social de Africa / see Council for the Development of Social Science Research in Africa (#04879)

♦ Consejo de Directores de Carreteras de Iberia e Iberoamérica (DIRCAIBEA) 04706

Council of Directors of Highways of Iberia and Ibero-America

Pres address not obtained. E-mail: presidencia2016-2019@dircaibea.com.
URL: http://dircaibea.org/

History 7 Sep 1995, Montréal, QC (Canada). 7 Sept 1995, Montréal (Canada), during 20th World Road Conference of *World Road Association (PIARC, #21754)*. **Aims** Promote cooperation among member *highway administrations*; improve the technical level of highway administrations through exchange of experience and dissemination of knowledge; promote the use of *Spanish language* in international bodies within the highway engineering field; act as a permanent forum for dialogue among directors; serve as a joint representative to international organizations and institutions. **Structure** Meeting of Directors; Meeting of Assistants to the Directors. President; 2 Vice-Presidents. **Events** *Meeting* Seville (Spain) 2019, *International Seminar on Bridges Rehabilitation and Sustainable Technology in Bridges* Campeche (Mexico) 2018, *Meeting* Campeche (Mexico) 2018, *Meeting* Guatemala (Guatemala) 2018, *Meeting* Lisbon (Portugal) 2017.
Members National highways administrations in 22 countries and territories:
Argentina, Bolivia, Brazil, Chile, Colombia, Costa Rica, Cuba, Dominican Rep, Ecuador, El Salvador, Guatemala, Honduras, Mexico, Nicaragua, Panama, Paraguay, Peru, Portugal, Puerto Rico, Spain, Uruguay, Venezuela. [2019/XD6842/**D**]

♦ Consejo de Ecologia Humana del Commonwealth (#04339)
♦ Consejo Económico y Social de las Naciones Unidas (#05331)

♦ Consejo de Educación de Adultos de América Latina (CEAAL) 04707

Conseil de l'éducation des adultes de l'Amérique latine – Latin American Council of Adult Education

SG Aptdo Postal 0831-00817, Estafeta Paitilla, Panama, Panamá, Panama PANAMá, Panama. Fax +5072701084 – +5072701085. E-mail: info@ceaal.org.
Street Address Via Cincuentenario 84B, Coco del Mar, Corregimiento de San Francisco, Panama, Panamá, Panama PANAMá, Panama.
URL: http://www.ceaal.org/

History 1981, as regional council of *International Council for Adult Education (ICAE, #12983)*. Statutes adopted 3 Sep 1983. Also referred to as *Latin American Adult Education Council*. **Aims** Promote adult education in Latin America and the *Caribbean*. **Structure** General Assembly (every 4 years); Executive Committee; Steering Committee; General Secretariat, headed by Secretary General. Networks and Working Groups: *Red de Educación Popular entre Mujeres de América Latina y el Caribe (REPEM LAC, #18647)*, created 1982 and supporting the grass roots women's movement. (2) *'Popular Education (REPPOL)'* in conjunction with *Popular Education Coordinated Regional Program (#18456)*. (3) *Red Latinoamericana de Educación para la Paz y los Derechos Humanos (REPDH, no recent information)*; (4) *'Literacy'*, supporting efforts of NGOs and based on participation in CREFAL. (5) *'Systematization'*. **Languages** Portuguese, Spanish. **Staff** Paid. **Finance** Source: DVV Deutscher Volkshochschulverband; *Oxfam Novib*; various foundations. **Activities** Training/education; knowledge management/information dissemination. **Events** *General Assembly* El Salvador 2010, *General Assembly* San Salvador (El Salvador) 2010, *General Assembly* Cochabamba (Bolivia) 2008, *Regional conference in Latin America and the Caribbean on literacy* Mexico City (Mexico) 2008, *General Assembly* Recife (Brazil) 2004. **Publications** *La Piragua* (2 a year); *La Carta* (56 a year). Books. Information Services: Documentation, Information and Publications Center.
Members Groups or Organizations and Individuals Full; Fraternal; Honorary; Invited. Organizations in 21 countries:
Argentina, Bolivia, Brazil, Chile, Colombia, Costa Rica, Cuba, Dominican Rep, Ecuador, El Salvador, Guatemala, Haiti, Honduras, Mexico, Nicaragua, Panama, Paraguay, Peru, Puerto Rico, Uruguay, Venezuela.
Included in the above, the following 11 organizations listed in this Yearbook:
Casa de las Américas; *Centro Andino de Educación y Promoción 'José Maria Arguedas', Cusco (CADEP-JMA, no recent information)*; *Centro de Investigación y Promoción Amazónica (CIPA, no recent information)*; *Centro de Medicina Andina (CMA)*; *Centro Latinoamericano de Apoyo al Saber y la Educación Popular (CLASEP, no recent information)*; *Centro Popular para América Latina de Comunicación (CEPALC)*; *Commission for the Defense of Human Rights in Central America (CODEHUCA, no recent information)*; *Inter-American Cooperative Institute (ICI, #11420)*; *Latin American Institution of Communications Pedagogy (no recent information)*; Programa Regional Coordinado de Educación Popular (ALFORJA); *Servicio Paz y Justicia en América Latina (SERPAJ-AL, #19247)*.
Consultative Status Consultative status granted from: *ECOSOC (#05331)* (Ros C). **IGO Relations** Working agreements with: *Centro de Cooperación Regional para la Educación de Adultos en América Latina y el Caribe (CREFAL, #03794)*; *International Development Research Centre (IDRC, #13162)*; *OAS (#17629)*. **NGO Relations** Member of: *Global Campaign for Education (GCE, #10264)*; *Mesa de Articulación de Asociaciones Nacionales y Redes de ONGs de América Latina y el Caribe (La Mesa de articulación, #16727)*; *World Social Forum (WSF, #21797)*. Affiliated with: *Corporation for Cultural and Social Development (no recent information)*. Working agreements with: *CODE*; *Comité Catholique contre la Faim et pour le Développement-Terre Solidaire (CCFD-Terre Solidaire)*. On Steering Committee of: *Campaña Latinoamericana por el Derecho a la Educación (CLADE, #03407)*. [2018/XD4156/y/**E**]

♦ Consejo Empresario de América Latina (#16261)

♦ Consejo de Empresarios Iberoamericanos (CEIB) 04708

Ibero-American Business Council

Permanent Sec c/o CEOE, Calle Diego de Léon 50, 28006 Madrid, Spain. T. +34915663400. Fax +34915622562. E-mail: ceib@ceoe.org.
URL: http://www.empresariosiberoamericanos.org/

History 2015. Founded at 26th meeting of Presidents of Ibero-American Business Organizations, as an initiative supported by *International Organisation of Employers (IOE, #14428)*, entity to which the most representative business organization in Latin America, Spain and Portugal belong. **Aims** Give value to the common competitiveness factors among Ibero-American employers and improve their contributions towards the economic and social *development* of the countries in the region. **Structure** Council of Presidents (every 2 years); Presidency; Permanent Secretariat; Directors. **Languages** Portuguese, Spanish. **Staff** 4.00 FTE, voluntary. **Activities** Events/meetings; guidance/assistance/consulting; projects/programmes; training/education. **Events** *Encuentro Empresarial Iberoamericano* Andorra la Vella (Andorra) 2021, *SMEs Business Forum* Buenos Aires (Argentina) 2019, *Iberoamerican Open Innovation Forum* Madrid (Spain) 2019, *SMEs Business Forum* Madrid (Spain) 2019, *Encuentro Empresarial Iberoamericano* Antigua (Guatemala) 2018.
Members Full in 21 countries:
Andorra, Argentina, Bolivia, Brazil, Chile, Colombia, Costa Rica, Dominican Rep, Ecuador, El Salvador, Guatemala, Honduras, Mexico, Nicaragua, Panama, Paraguay, Peru, Portugal, Spain, Uruguay, Venezuela. [2022/XM6529/**E**]

♦ Consejo Episcopal Latinoamericano / see Consejo Episcopal Latinoamericano (#04709)

♦ Consejo Episcopal Latinoamericano (CELAM) 04709

Conseil épiscopal latinoaméricain – Latin American Episcopal Council – Conselho Episcopal Latinoamericano

Gen Sec Carrera 5 No 118-31, Bogota 110111, Bogota DC, Colombia. T. +5715879710 ext 207. Fax +5715879717. E-mail: celam@celam.org – secretariadogeneral@celam.org.
Pres address not obtained.
URL: http://www.celam.org/

History 2 Nov 1955, Rio de Janeiro (Brazil). Statutes approved 9 Nov 1974; revised 2005. Former names and other names: *Latin American Episcopal Council* – former; *Conseil épiscopal latinoaméricain* – former; *Consejo Episcopal Latinoamericano* – former; *Conselho Episcopal Latinoamericano* – former; *Latin American Episcopal Conference* – former; *Conférence épiscopal latinoaméricain* – former; *Conferencia Episcopal Latinoamericana* – former; *Conferência Episcopal Latinoamericana* – former. **Aims** Act as contact, reflection and cooperation body for the Episcopal Conferences of Latin America, which are represented therein by their Presidents and delegates; study problems of interest to the Church in Latin America, with a view to finding appropriate solutions; coordinate Catholic activities in the continent to ensure maximum efficiency; promote and maintain, directly or indirectly, initiatives and activities of common interest. **Structure** Assembly (every 2 years); Board; Specialized Departments and Centres (10). **Languages** Portuguese, Spanish. **Staff** Regular paid contracts. **Finance** Sources: contributions from national Episcopal Conferences; grants. **Events** *Assembly* Managua (Nicaragua) 2009, *General conference* Aparecida (Brazil) 2007, *Assembly* Havana (Cuba) 2007, *Meeting* Bogota (Colombia) 2006, *Meeting on new religious movements and postoral plans for the bishops of continental Amazon region* Manaus (Brazil) 2006. **Publications** *Medellin* (4 a year). Theological articles and researches.
Members Bishops (1,312), representing a total of 974 diocese in 22 Bishops Conferences, in 20 countries and territories:

Argentina, Bolivia, Brazil, Chile, Colombia, Costa Rica, Cuba, Dominican Rep, Ecuador, El Salvador, Guatemala, Haiti, Honduras, Mexico, Nicaragua, Panama, Peru, Puerto Rico, Uruguay, Venezuela.
Also in 16 countries of the Antilles (not specified).
NGO Relations Member of (1): *Foro Latinoamericano de Juventud (FLAJ, #09881).* Instrumental in setting up (3): *Instituto Teológico Pastoral para América Latina (ITEPAL, #11350)* (Centro Biblico); Observatorio Pastoral de Latinoamérica; *Red Informatica de la Iglesia en América Latina (RIIAL, #18689).* [2021/XD2874/v/**D**]

- Consejo de Europa (#04881)
- Consejo Europeo (#06801)
- Consejo Europeo de Asociaciones Nacionales de Escuelas Independientes (#06833)
- Consejo Europeo de Cofradias Enogastronómicas (#08076)
- Consejo Europeo de Idiomas (#07646)
- Consejo Europeo de Información sobre la Alimentación (#07284)

♦ Consejo Europeo de Investigaciones Sociales de América Latina (CEISAL) 04710

European Council for Social Research on Latin America – Conseil européen de recherches sociales sur l'Amérique latine – Europäischer Rat für Sozialwissenschaftliche Forschung über Lateinamerika
Pres School of Global Studies – Univ of Gothenburg, Box 700, SE-405 30 Gothenburg, Sweden. T. +46317864923. E-mail: ceisaloficial@gmail.com.
URL: https://rediceisal.hypotheses.org/
History 1 Feb 1980, Vienna (Austria). Registered office located at Austrian Latin America Institute. Current Statutes adopted Sep 1998, Halle (Germany). Presidency located in Gothenburg (Sweden). **Aims** Contribute to and support a closer cooperation among European associations which deal with Latin America; promote the cooperation of these associations with equivalent Latin American bodies and carry out analytical studies mainly on critical problems of Latin American societies; emphasize especially the contribution of social sciences to a better knowledge of present Latin America, with its regions and as a whole; strengthen, as far as possible, the interest of Europe for Latin America. **Structure** General Assembly; Managing Board; Working Groups (8). **Languages** English, French, Portuguese, Spanish. **Staff** Voluntary. **Finance** Sources: grants; international organizations; members' dues. Support from European public and private bodies. **Activities** Events/meetings; networking/liaising; research/documentation. **Events** *Congress* Helsinki (Finland) 2022, *Congress* Bucharest (Romania) 2019, *European Congress of Latinoamericanists* Salamanca (Spain) 2016, *General Assembly / European Congress of Latin-Americanists* St Petersburg (Russia) 2015, *General Assembly* Paris (France) 2014.
Members Ordinary Category 'A' national and European research associations; Category 'B' research institutions; Category 'C' researchers who live in Europe. Associated and invited institutions. Members in 21 countries:
Austria, Belgium, Bulgaria, Croatia, Denmark, Finland, France, Germany, Hungary, Ireland, Israel, Italy, Netherlands, Poland, Portugal, Russia, Slovakia, Slovenia, Spain, Sweden, UK.
Included in the above, 10 associations and institutions listed in this Yearbook:
Asociación Española de Americanistas; *Centre for Latin American Research and Documentation (CEDLA)*; *Groupe d'études latino-américaines de l'Institut de sociologie, Bruxelles (GELA-IS)*; *Institut des hautes études de l'Amérique latine (IHEAL)*; *Latin American Research Group (no recent information)*; *Netherlands Association of Latin American and Caribbean Studies (NALACS)*; *Nordic Institute of Latin American Studies (NILAS)*; *Polish Society for Latin American Studies (no recent information)*; *Red Europea de Información y Documentación sobre América Latina (REDIAL, #18652)*; *Society for Latin American Studies (SLAS).*
Consultative Status Consultative status granted from: *UNESCO (#20322)* (Consultative Status).
[2022.05.12/XD8907/y/**D**]

- Consejo Europeo de los Jóvenes Agricultores (#04689)
- Consejo Europeo Medico para la Pluralidad Medica (#06816)
- Consejo Europeo de las Rutas del Vino (inactive)
- Consejo Europeo de Sindicatos de Policia (#06837)

♦ Consejo de Facultades Humanisticas de Centroamérica (COFAHCA) 04711

Council of Central American Humanities Faculties
Pres c/o Universidad Estatal a Distancia, De la Rotonda La Betania 500m al este, Carretera a Sabanilla, Mercedes de Montes de Oca, San José, San José, 474 2050, Costa Rica. T. +50625272000.
History 1993, Heredia (Costa Rica). **Activities** General Assembly. **Publications** *Identidad Centroamericana* (periodical). [2015/XE4314/**E**]

- Consejo de Federaciones Comerciales de Europa (inactive)

♦ Consejo de Fundaciones Americanas de Desarrollo (SOLIDARIOS) . 04712

Conseil des fondations américaines de développement – SOLIDARIOS, Council of American Development Foundations – Rat der Amerikanischen Entwicklungsstiftungen – Conselho de Fundações Americanas de Desenvolvimento – Raad der Amerikaanse Ontwikkelingsstichtingen
Secretariat Aptdo Postal 620, Calle Regina Koenig 10, Ensanche Paraiso, Santo Domingo, Dominican Rep. T. +18095495111. Fax +18095440550. E-mail: info@redsolidarios.org – secretaria.solidarios@gmail.com.
URL: http://www.redsolidarios.org/
History Oct 1972, Guatemala (Guatemala). Founded at a meeting held by representatives of American national development foundations. Incorporated in the Dominican Republic by Presidential Decree 4259, 29 Jan 1974, as a civil and non-profit association. Registration: Start date: Jan 1974, Dominican Rep. **Aims** Exercise multinational representation of members when they act jointly; assist and support individual and collective work of members; coordinate joint programmes; stimulate participation of the *Latin American* private sector in *social development* activities in their respective countries; make available the necessary information to extend and improve members' work; administer funds for members' *development projects.* **Structure** General Assembly (annual); Executive Committee of 5. Executive Committee designates Secretary General. **Languages** Spanish. **Staff** 5.00 FTE, paid. **Finance** Members' dues. Donations. Specific programmes are financed by contributions and loans from international organizations. **Activities** Training/education; guidance/assistance/consulting. **Events** *Annual meeting* Rye, NY (USA) 1998, *Annual meeting* Coral Gables, FL (USA) 1997, *Fundraising* Mexico City (Mexico) 1997, *Annual Meeting* Washington, DC (USA) 1996, *South American fundraising seminar for NGOs* Buenos Aires (Argentina) 1995. **Publications** *Catalogo de Instituciones sin Fines de Lucro en Latinoamérica y el Caribe*; *Rural Development Policies* by Rodolfo Martinez Ferraté; *Short Course in Development Training* by David Macarov and Frandkin Gershon. Seminar documents and reports.
Members Development foundations in 10 countries:
Bolivia, Colombia, Costa Rica, Dominican Rep, Ecuador, Honduras, Mexico, Paraguay, Peru, Venezuela.
IGO Relations Cooperates with: *OAS (#17629).* Associated general collaboration agreement with joint program of: *Inter-American Institute for Cooperation on Agriculture (IICA, #11434).* [2021/XD0154/**D**]

- Consejo General de Pesca del Mediterraneo / see General Fisheries Commission for the Mediterranean (#10112)
- Consejo Iberoamericano de Asociaciones Nacionales de Arquitectos (no recent information)

♦ Consejo Iberoamericano para la Productividad y la Competitividad (CIPYC) 04713

Dir Principe de Vergara 187, 28002 Madrid, Spain.
URL: http://cipyc.org/
History Founded 2015. Registered in accordance with Spanish law. **Aims** Promote dialogues; analyse problems; make proposals to promote increases in competitiveness and productivity in Ibero-American countries. **Structure** General Assembly; Board of Directors. **Events** *Meeting* Madrid (Spain) 2018. **Publications** *Pódium* – review.
Members Full in 10 countries:
Argentina, Brazil, Colombia, Honduras, Mexico, Panama, Peru, Portugal, Spain, Uruguay. [2018/XM7677/**D**]

♦ Consejo de Iglesias Evangélicas Metodistas de América Latina y el Caribe (CIEMAL) 04714

Council of Evangelical Methodist Churches of Latin America and the Caribbean – Conselho das Igrejas Evangélicas Metodistas da América Latina e do Caribe
SG Jr Nicolas de Piérola 250, Bellavista, Callao-02, Lima, Peru.
URL: http://www.ciemal.net
History 1969, Santiago (Chile). **Aims** Promote close relationship and communication between Methodist Churches in Latin America as well as *ecumenical* links with other *Christian* organizations. **Structure** Assembly (every 4 years); Executive Commission. Working Commissions (4): Witness and Evangelization; Education and Training; Human Promotion; Finance. **Finance** Contributions from Latin American Methodist Churches in accordance with their membership. Financial assistance from Churches in Europe and USA. **Activities** Advocacy/lobbying/activism. **Events** *General assembly / Quinquennial General Assembly* Havana (Cuba) 1993, *General assembly / Quinquennial General Assembly* Quito (Ecuador) 1988. **Publications** *Boletin de CIEMAL* (2 a year).
Members Methodist Churches in 13 countries:
Argentina, Bolivia, Brazil, Chile, Costa Rica, Cuba, Dominican Rep, Ecuador, Guatemala, Mexico, Panama, Peru, Uruguay.
Regional Methodist Church (1):
The Conference of the Methodist Church in the Caribbean and the Americas (MCCA, #04629).
NGO Relations *World Council of Churches (WCC, #21320).* [2020/XF0963/y/**F**]

- Consejo de Iglesias Luteranas en Centroamérica y Panama (inactive)
- Consejo Indio de Sudamérica (#11158)

♦ Consejo de Institutos de Seguridad Social de Centroamérica y República Dominicana (CISSCAD) 04715

Central American and Dominican Republic Council of Social Security Institutions
Exec Dir Barrio Bajo 555, 10th Floor, Tegucigalpa, Francisco Morazán, Honduras. T. +5042228414.
URL: http://www.cisscad.org/
History 9 Dec 1992, Panama. Founded 9-12 Dec 1992, Panama, at 13th Meeting of Central American Presidents, the previous *Association of Social Security Institutions of Central America and Panama (AISSCAP, inactive)* having been dissolved, 10 Oct 1992, Honduras. Original title: *Consejo Centroamericano de Instituciones de Seguridad Social (COCISS) – Central American Council of Social Security Institutions.* Comes within the framework of *Central American Integration System (#03671).* **Aims** Integrate and strengthen work among social security institutions of Central America. **Languages** Spanish. **Activities** Knowledge management/information dissemination; monitoring/evaluation; standards/guidelines; capacity building; projects/programmes. **Events** *Triennial international conference on fracture mechanics of concrete and concrete structures* Jeju (Korea Rep) 2010, *High level seminar on social security techniques* Belize City (Belize) 2001, *High-level seminar on actuarial and financial techniques of social security* San José (Costa Rica) 1999, *High-level seminar on actuarial techniques* 1997, *High-level seminar on actuarial techniques* Panama (Panama) 1996. **Publications** *COCISS – Boletin Informativo. Register of Medicaments in the Central American Countries*; *Social Security in Central America.* Information Services: *Central American Information Network on Health and Social Security (no recent information).*
Members Social security institutions of 6 countries:
Costa Rica, El Salvador, Guatemala, Honduras, Nicaragua, Panama. [2014/XD2784/**D**]

- Consejo Interamericana sobre Educación en Fisica (#11424)
- Consejo Interamericano de las Autoridades Regulatorias de Valores (#04918)
- Consejo Interamericano de Comercio y Producción (no recent information)
- Consejo Interamericano para el Desarrollo Integral (#11423)
- Consejo Interamericano de Escultismo / see Inter-American Scout Committee (#11445)
- Consejo Interamericano Sobre la Espiritualidad Indigena (#11422)
- Consejo Interamericano de Música (no recent information)
- Consejo Interamericano de Seguridad (no recent information)
- Consejo Intergubernamental de Paises Exportadores de Cobre (inactive)
- Consejo Internacional de Archivos (#12996)
- Consejo Internacional de los Arquitectos de Monumentos Históricos (inactive)
- Consejo Internacional de Asociaciones de Comerciantes de Cueros y Pieles (#13029)
- Consejo Internacional de Asociaciones de Fabricantes de Productos Quimicos (#13003)
- Consejo Internacional de Asociaciones de Imprentas Metalúrgicas (#13073)
- Consejo Internacional de Asociaciones de Industrias Nauticas (#13044)
- Consejo Internacional de Asociaciones de Propietarios y Pilotos de Aeronaves (#12988)
- Consejo Internacional de Aviación de Asuntos (#12418)
- Consejo Internacional de Bienestar Social (#13076)
- Consejo Internacional de Buena Vecindad (#13728)
- Consejo Internacional para la Calidad de la Vida Laboral (inactive)
- Consejo Internacional de Cereales (#13731)
- Consejo Internacional para la Ciencia del Deporte y la Educación Fisica (#13077)
- Consejo Internacional de Ciencias Sociales (inactive)
- Consejo Internacional para la Colaboración en los Analisis de Plaguicidas (#04099)
- Consejo Internacional de Creadores de Artes Graficas, Plasticas y Fotograficas (#13011)
- Consejo Internacional de Creadores de Música (#13052)
- Consejo Internacional de Cricket Femenino (inactive)
- Consejo Internacional de Cristianos y Judios (#13006)
- Consejo Internacional de Curtidores (#13084)
- Consejo Internacional del Deporte Militar (#04695)
- Consejo Internacional sobre el Derecho del Medio Ambiente (#13018)
- Consejo Internacional para el Desarrollo de la Educación (inactive)
- Consejo Internacional de las Economias Regionales (inactive)
- Consejo Internacional de Educación de Adultos (#12983)
- Consejo Internacional de Educación para la Enseñanza (#13016)
- Consejo Internacional para la Educación Fisica y el Deporte / see International Council of Sport Science and Physical Education (#13077)
- Consejo Internacional de Enfermeras (#13054)
- Consejo Internacional de la Enseñanza por Correspondencia / see International Council for Open and Distance Education (#13056)
- Consejo Internacional de la Enseñanza a Distancia / see International Council for Open and Distance Education (#13056)
- Consejo Internacional para la Exploración del Mar / see International Council for the Exploration of the Sea (#13021)
- Consejo Internacional de Filosofia y Ciencias Humanas (#13061)
- Consejo Internacional de los Frutos Secos / see International Nut and Dried Fruit Council Foundation (#14387)
- Consejo Internacional de los Grupos de Amistad Judeocristianos / see International Council of Christians and Jews (#13006)
- Consejo Internacional de la Industria de Alimentos Infantiles (inactive)
- Consejo Internacional de Industrias de Buena Voluntad / see Goodwill Industries International
- Consejo Internacional para las Iniciativas Ambientales Locales / see Local Governments for Sustainability (#16507)
- Consejo Internacional para Investigación en Agrosilvicultura / see World Agroforestry Centre (#21072)
- Consejo Internacional para los Juegos Tradicionales y Deportes (#13088)
- Consejo Internacional de Medios Educativos (#13014)
- Consejo Internacional de Metales y Medio Ambiente (inactive)
- Consejo Internacional de Monumentos y Sitios (#13049)
- Consejo Internacional de Mujeres Judias (#13036)
- Consejo Internacional de Mujeres Social-Demócratas / see Socialist International Women (#19341)

- ♦ Consejo Internacional de Museos (#13051)
- ♦ Consejo Internacional de la Música (#14199)
- ♦ Consejo Internacional de Música Popular / see International Council for Traditional Music (#13087)
- ♦ Consejo Internacional de Música Tradicional (#13087)
- ♦ Consejo Internacional de Navegadores de Lineas Aéreas (inactive)
- ♦ Consejo Internacional de Numismatica (#14385)
- ♦ Consejo Internacional de Organizaciones Voluntarias (#13092)
- ♦ Consejo Internacional de Organización de Festivales de Folklore y Arte Popular / see International Council of Organizations for Folklore Festivals and Folk Art (#13058)
- ♦ Consejo Internacional de Organización de Festivales de Folklore y Arte Tradicional (#13058)
- ♦ Consejo Internacional de los Practicos del Plan Contable Internacional (inactive)
- ♦ Consejo Internacional para la Preservación de las Aves / see BirdLife International (#03266)
- ♦ Consejo Internacional sobre el Problema del Alcoholismo y las Toxicomanias / see International Council on Alcohol and Addictions (#12989)
- ♦ Consejo Internacional de Recursos Fitogenéticos / see Bioversity International (#03262)
- ♦ Consejo Internacional para Salud, Educación Fisica, Recreación, Deporte y Baile (#13028)
- ♦ Consejo Internacional de los Servicios Judios de Previsión y Asistencia Social (#13035)
- ♦ Consejo Internacional de Sociedades de Diseño Industrial / see World Design Organization (#21358)
- ♦ Consejo Internacional de Telecomunicaciones de Prensa (#14637)
- ♦ Consejo Internacional de los Tratados Indios (#13836)
- ♦ Consejo Internacional del Trigo / see International Grains Council (#13731)
- ♦ Consejo Interstatal sobre la Protección de la Propiedad Industrial (inactive)
- ♦ Consejo Interuniversitario Regional (inactive)

♦ Consejo del Istmo Centroamericano de Deportes y Recreación (CODICADER) 04716

Sport and Recreation Council of the Central American Isthmus

Permanent Secretariat c/o SISCA, Av R F Chiari y Calle G W Goethal, Edificio 711, Balboa, Panama, Panamá, Panama PANAMá, Panama.
URL: https://sisca.int/codicader

History 6 Oct 1992, San Salvador (El Salvador), within the framework of *Central American Integration System (#03671)*. **Aims** Reinforce integration, solidarity and peace among peoples of Central America by means of *sport, physical education* and *recreational* activities. **Structure** General Assembly; Executive Committee; Directive Advice; Technical Commission; functional committees; permanent Technical Secretary. **Activities** Promotes horizontal cooperation programmes between member countries; exchanges information and creates an information system; encourages scientific and technical research related to the practice of sports, physical and recreational activities; organizes regional meetings.
Members Governmental sports organizations in 7 countries:
Belize, Costa Rica, El Salvador, Guatemala, Honduras, Nicaragua, Panama.
IGO Relations *Secretaria de Integración Social Centroamericana (SISCA, #19192)* provides Permanent Secretariat since 2009. [2020/XE2871/**E***]

- ♦ Consejo Laboral para el Adelanto del Obrero Latino-Americano (internationally oriented national body)

♦ Consejo Latinoamericano de Acreditación de la Educación en Periodismo (CLAEP) 04717

Latin American Council for Journalism Education Accreditation

Exec Dir c/o Inter American Press Assoc, 3511 NW 91 Avenue, Miami FL 33172, USA. T. +13056342465 – +13058604264. E-mail: info@sipiapa.org.
Pres Southen Methodist Univ, PO Box 750113, Dallas TX 75275, USA. T. +12147683969 – +12147683307.
URL: http://www.claep.org

Aims Foster and promote excellence in professional education in journalism. **Structure** Council comprises President, Vice-President, 4 Academic Members, 4 Professional Members and 2 Expert Members. 5 members are professional journalists from the Inter American Press Association, 5 are scholars of journalism, and 2 are general members. **Activities** Promotes effective journalism training programmes; assists in the relationship between journalistic training and the needs of professional practice; defines and gains acceptance of standards for journalism training; acts as an agency for accreditation of journalism training programmes. [2016/XJ1218/**F**]

- ♦ Consejo Latinoamericano de Biomedicina Experimental (no recent information)
- ♦ Consejo Latinoamericano y Caribeño de Organizaciones No Gubernamentales con Servicio en VIH/Sida (#16272)

♦ Consejo Latinoamericano de Ciencias Sociales (CLACSO) 04718

Latin American Social Sciences Council – Conseil latinoaméricain de sciences sociales – Conselho Latinoamericano de Ciencias Sociais

Exec Sec Estados Unidos 1168, C110AAX, Buenos Aires, Argentina. T. +541143049145. Fax +541143050875. E-mail: clacsoinst@clacso.edu.ar.
URL: http://www.clacso.org/

History Oct 1967, Bogota (Colombia). Founded following 2nd Conference of Latin American Centres and Institutes for Research on Development. Restructured following General Assembly, Dec 1994, Caracas (Venezuela). **Aims** Contribute to development of social sciences in Latin America, strengthening research and training institutions and improving training of researchers. **Structure** General Assembly (every 2 to 3 years); Steering Committee; Working Groups; Executive Secretariat. **Languages** Portuguese, Spanish. **Staff** 18.00 FTE, paid. **Finance** Sources: members' dues. Other sources: foundation support; project and program activities; sale of publications and services. Major institutional/program funders: Government of Argentina; IDRC; *Inter-American Foundation (IAF, #11431); Ford Foundation (#09858); Andrew W Mellon Foundation; Swedish International Development Cooperation Agency (Sida)*; UNDP; UNESCO. Annual budget: Programmes US$ 800,000; Executive Secretariat US$ 150,000. **Activities** Knowledge management/information dissemination; research/documentation; training/education. **Events** *Latin American and Caribbean Conference on Social Sciences* Mexico City (Mexico) 2022, *General Assembly* Buenos Aires (Argentina) 2018, *Latin American and Caribbean Social Sciences Conference* Buenos Aires (Argentina) 2018, *General Assembly* Medellin (Colombia) 2015, *Latin American and Caribbean Social Sciences Conference* Medellin (Colombia) 2015. **Publications** *Carta de CLACSO* (6 a year); *David y Goliath* (periodical). Books; studies; documents; proceedings; CD-ROM of Latin American Social Sciences.
Members Full; Associate Partner Institutions; Associate Partner Networks. Full in 22 countries and territories:
Argentina, Bolivia, Brazil, Chile, Colombia, Costa Rica, Cuba, Dominican Rep, Ecuador, El Salvador, Guatemala, Haiti, Honduras, Mexico, Nicaragua, Panama, Paraguay, Peru, Puerto Rico, Trinidad-Tobago, Uruguay, Venezuela.
Regional centres and institutes of FLACSO, ILET and other regional institutes, including 15 organizations listed in this Yearbook:
Andean Center of Popular Action (CAAP); Center for Andean Regional Studies 'Bartolomé de Las Casas' (#03636); Center for the Study of State and Society, Buenos Aires (CEDES); Centre de Estudos Afro-Asiaticos (CEAA); Centro de Estudios Latinoamericanos de Educación Inclusiva (CELEI); Centro de Estudios para el Desarrollo Laboral y Agrario (CEDLA); Centro de Investigaciones de Economia Internacional, Habana (CIEI); Centro Internacional de Estudios Superiores de Comunicación para América Latina (CIESPAL, #03806); Instituto de Estudios Politicos y Relaciones Internacionales, Bogota (IEPRI); Instituto Paulo Freire (IPF); International Relations Institute, Rio de Janeiro (IRI); Latin American Faculty of Social Sciences (#16316); Latin American Studies Center 'Justo Arosemena' (CELA); Memoria Popular Latinoamericana (MEPLA); Universidad CLAEH (#20688).
Associate partner institutions in 26 countries and territories:
Australia, Austria, Belgium, Cameroon, China, Ethiopia, Finland, France, Gabon, Germany, Guinea-Bissau, Italy, Korea Rep, Lebanon, Norway, Palestine, Poland, Portugal, Russia, South Africa, Spain, Sweden, Switzerland, Thailand, UK, USA.
Associate partner networks in 16 countries:
Argentina, Brazil, Canada, Chile, Colombia, Costa Rica, Ecuador, Guatemala, Mexico, Norway, Panama, Peru, Spain, St Lucia, USA, Venezuela.
Included in the above, 4 organizations listed in this Yearbook:
International Federation of Fe y Alegria (FIFyA, #13425); Middle Atlantic Council of Latin American Studies (MACLAS); Red Europea de Información y Documentación sobre América Latina (REDIAL, #18652); Water Center for the Humid Tropics of Latin America and the Caribbean (#20824).
Consultative Status Consultative status granted from: *ECOSOC (#05331)* (Ros C); *UNESCO (#20322)* (Associate Status). **IGO Relations** Cooperative relations with: *ILO (#11123); International Development Research Centre (IDRC, #13162); OECD Development Centre (#17692); UNEP (#20299); UNDP (#20292); United Nations Economic Commission for Latin America and the Caribbean (ECLAC, #20556); United Nations University (UNU, #20642)*. **NGO Relations** Member of: *Alianza Social Continental (ASC, #00635); Globalization Studies Network (GSN, #10440); International Science Council (ISC, #14796); NGO-UNESCO Liaison Committee (#17127); World Forum for Alternatives (WFA, #21513); World Social Forum (WSF, #21797)*. Actively involved with: *Latin American Programme of Population Activities (no recent information).* [2022/XD4250/y/**D**]

- ♦ Consejo Latinoamericano de Cine et de Comunicación de los Pueblos Indigenas / see Coordinadora Latinoamericana de Cine et de Comunicación de los Pueblos Indigenas (#04806)
- ♦ Consejo Latinoamericano de Cultura (inactive)
- ♦ Consejo Latinoamericano de Derecho y Desarrollo (inactive)

♦ Consejo Latinoamericano de Ecografia Ocular (CLEO) 04719

Latin American Council of Ultrasound in Ophthalmology

Pres Bacaflor 430 33, Lima, Peru. T. +5113721117. E-mail: mariodlt@gmail.com.
Vice-Pres Calle 145 A No 21-20 Apto 401, Bogota, Bogota DC, Colombia. T. +5718049246. Fax +5718049246. E-mail: ramiroprada@yahoo.com.

Aims Spread ocular ultrasound among members; promote continuous education of members. **Languages** English, Portuguese, Spanish. **Activities** Events/meetings; training/education; networking/liaising. **Members** in 20 countries. Membership countries not specified. **NGO Relations** Member of: *Pan-American Association of Ophthalmology (PAAO, #18081).* [2019.06.03/XD6803/**D**]

- ♦ Consejo Latinoamericano de Escuelas de Administración (#16308)

♦ Consejo Latinoamericano de Estrabismo (CLADE) 04720

Latin American Council of Strabismus – Conselho Latino-americano de Estrabismo

SG Boston 99, Col Nochebuena, Benito Juarez, 03720 Mexico City CDMX, Mexico. E-mail: mearroyo1@gmail.com – castella60@yahoo.com.
URL: http://www.cladeweb.com/

History 1965, Mendoza (Argentina). **Aims** Prevent, diagnose, treat and conduct research on strabismus. **Languages** Portuguese, Spanish. **Finance** Members' dues. Full: US$ 20; Associate: US$ 10. **Events** *Congress / Biennial International Meeting* Punta Cana (Dominican Rep) 2015, *Congress* Rio de Janeiro (Brazil) 2013, *Biennial International Meeting* Rio de Janeiro (Brazil) 2012, *Congress / Biennial International Meeting* Cancún (Mexico) 2010, *Congress / Biennial International Meeting* Buenos Aires (Argentina) 2008. **Publications** *CLADE Journal* (3 a year).
Members Principle (482) and Associate. Members in 13 countries:
Argentina, Bolivia, Brazil, Chile, Colombia, Ecuador, Guatemala, Mexico, Panama, Paraguay, Peru, Uruguay, Venezuela.
NGO Relations Member of: *International Pediatric Ophthalmology and Strabismus Council (IPOSC, #14544)*. Affiliated member of: *Pan-American Association of Ophthalmology (PAAO, #18081).* [2014/XD6801/v/**D**]

- ♦ Consejo Latinoamericano de Estudiantes del Derecho Internacional / see Consejo Latinoamericano de Estudios de Derecho Internacional y Comparado (#04721)

♦ Consejo Latinoamericano de Estudios de Derecho Internacional y Comparado (COLADIC) 04721

SG address not obtained. E-mail: infocoladic@gmail.com.
URL: http://www.coladic-rd.org/

History Founded May 1994, Mexico City (Mexico), as *Consejo Latinoamericano de Estudiantes del Derecho Internacional (COLADI)*. Present name adopted, 1997. **Aims** Promote the study of International and Comparative Law through international and local academic projects. **Structure** Board of Directors; International Secretary; Chapters (Division). **Languages** English, French, Spanish. **Staff** Board of Directors and CEO (Executive Director) paid; Corps of Volunteers. **Activities** Organizes: International Congress; seminars; conferences. Oversees international competences. **Events** *Congress* Santo Domingo (Dominican Rep) 2010, *Congress* Santiago (Chile) 2009, *Congress* Santo Domingo (Dominican Rep) 2008, *International congress / Congress* Mendoza (Argentina) 2007, *International congress / Congress* Guayaquil (Ecuador) 2006. **Publications** *Boletin COLADIC-RD*; *Revista de Derecho Internacional y Comparado (REDIC).*
Members in 11 countries:
Argentina, Chile, Colombia, Costa Rica, Dominican Rep, Ecuador, El Salvador, Guatemala, Mexico, Panama, Venezuela.
NGO Relations *The European Law Students' Association (ELSA, #07660); International Law Institute, Washington DC (ILI); International Law Students Association (ILSA).* [2021/XD8937/**D**]

- ♦ Consejo Latinoamericano de Fisica del Espacio (inactive)
- ♦ Consejo Latinoamericano de Iglesias (#16309)
- ♦ Consejo Latinoamericano de Información Alimentaria (internationally oriented national body)
- ♦ Consejo Latinoamericano de Investigaciones para la Paz (#16310)
- ♦ Consejo Latinoamericano de Mujeres Católicas (inactive)
- ♦ Consejo Latino Americano de Neuroftalmologia / see Club Latinoamericano de Neuroftalmologia (#04036)
- ♦ Consejo Latinoamericano de Oceanografia (inactive)
- ♦ Consejo Latinoamericano de Perfusión (unconfirmed)
- ♦ Consejo Latinoamericano de Resucitación (inactive)
- ♦ Consejo de la Media América para el Comercio Agricola Internacional / see Food Export Association of the Midwest USA

♦ Consejo de Ministros de Salud de Centroamérica (COMISCA) 04722

Central American Council of Ministers of Health

Exec Sec Final Bulevar Cancilleria, Distrito El Espino, Ciudad Merliot, San Salvador, El Salvador. T. +150322486901. Fax +150322486914.
URL: http://www.sica.int/comisca/

History The Council of Ministers of Health of Central America, COMISCA, has its genesis and raison d'être framed juridically and institutionally by the Declaration of San Salvador, the Protocol of Tegucigalpa and the Treaty of the Social Integration of Central America, TISCA, adopted by the Presidents of Central America at the X Summit held from Jul 15 to 17, 1991 in El Salvador, XI Summit held on December 12 and 13, 1991 in Honduras and the XVI Summit held on March 30, 1995 in San Salvador, respectively. **Aims** Support member states in their role of guaranteeing citizens' rights for access, universal coverage and quality of health services. **Languages** English, Spanish. **Staff** 6.00 FTE, paid. **Finance** International cooperations. **Events** *Meeting* Panama (Panama) 2014, *Meeting* Managua (Nicaragua) 2012, *Meeting* Honduras 2005, *Meeting* Tegucigalpa (Honduras) 2005, *Meeting* Guatemala 2004.
Members Member States (8):
Belize, Costa Rica, Dominican Rep, El Salvador, Guatemala, Honduras, Nicaragua, Panama.
IGO Relations Executive Secretariat is part of: *Central American Integration System (#03671).* [2018.07.03/XE4736/**E***]

- ♦ Consejo Monetario Centroamericano (#03672)
- ♦ Consejo Mundial del Agua (#21908)
- ♦ Consejo Mundial de Artesanias (#21342)
- ♦ Consejo Mundial de Artes y Oficios / see World Crafts Council AISBL (#21342)
- ♦ Consejo Mundial de Artistas Visuales (no recent information)
- ♦ Consejo Mundial pro Asamblea Constituyente de los Pueblos (inactive)
- ♦ Consejo Mundial de Boxeo (#21242)
- ♦ Consejo Mundial de Cooperativas de Ahorro y Crédito (#21324)
- ♦ Consejo Mundial de Educación (#21325)
- ♦ Consejo Mundial de Educación para los Medios (no recent information)
- ♦ Consejo Mundial de la Energia (#21381)

- ♦ Consejo mundial de Enlace sobre Resucitación (#14036)
- ♦ Consejo Mundial de la Familia Marianista (#21334)
- ♦ Consejo Mundial de Gestión (inactive)
- ♦ Consejo Mundial de Iglesias (#21320)
- ♦ Consejo Mundial de Institutos Paulo Freire (unconfirmed)
- ♦ Consejo Mundial del Medio Ambiente y los Recursos Naturales (inactive)
- ♦ Consejo Mundial del Niño Dotado y Talentoso (#21328)
- ♦ Consejo Mundial de la Paz (#21717)
- ♦ Consejo Mundial para la Promoción Social de los Ciegos (inactive)
- ♦ Consejo Mundial de Pueblos Indigenas (inactive)
- ♦ Consejo Mundial de Sociedad de Educación Comparada (#21322)
- ♦ Consejo Mundial de Synagogas Masorti (#21323)
- ♦ Consejo de Municipios de Europa / see Council of European Municipalities and Regions (#04891)
- ♦ Consejo de Municipios y Regiones de Europa (#04891)

♦ Consejo de le Música de las Tres Américas (COMTA) 04723

Music Council of the Three Americas

Chair 1 W 4th St, Ste 1550, Cincinnati OH 45202, USA. T. +18885125278. E-mail: comta@imc-cim.org.

History 1995, Seoul (Korea Rep), as an informal regional group of *International Music Council (IMC, #14199)*. Legalized as an independent non-profit Jun 2013. **Structure** General Assembly; Board. [2018.09.26/XM4248/**E**]

- ♦ Consejo Musulman de Cooperación en Europa – Islamischer Kooperatiosrat in Europa (no recent information)
- ♦ Consejo Naviero Regional del Caribe (inactive)
- ♦ Consejo Nórdico (#17256)
- ♦ Consejo Nordico de la Madera (inactive)
- ♦ Consejo Nórdico de Ministros (#17260)
- ♦ Consejo Nórdico Same / see Saami Council (#19012)
- ♦ Consejo Norteamericano de Organizaciones al Servicio del SIDA (internationally oriented national body)
- ♦ Consejo Oleicola Internacional (#14405)
- ♦ Consejo Olimpico de Asia (#17718)
- ♦ Consejo de Organizaciones Internacionales de las Ciencias Médicas (#04905)
- ♦ Consejo Panamericano Pro-Ciegos (inactive)
- ♦ Consejo Panamericano de Educación en las Ciencias Veterinarias (#18091)
- ♦ Consejo de Población (#18458)
- ♦ Consejo Presidencial Andino (see: #00817)
- ♦ Consejo Regional para la Educación y la Alfabetización de Adultos en Africa (no recent information)

♦ Consejo Regional de Ingeniería Biomédica para América Latina (CORAL) 04724

Sec address not obtained.
Pres address not obtained.
URL: http://coralbiomedica.org/

History 1989. **Structure** Administrative Council. **Events** *CLAIB: Congreso Latinoamericano de Ingeniería Biomédica* Florianópolis (Brazil) 2022, *CLAIB: Congreso Latinoamericano de Ingeniería Biomédica* Cancún (Mexico) 2019, *Congreso Latinoamericano de Ingeniería Biomédica (CLAIB)* Bucaramanga (Colombia) 2016, *Congreso Latinoamericano de Ingeniería Biomédica (CLAIB)* Paraná (Argentina) 2014, *Congreso Latinoamericano de Ingeniería Biomédica (CLAIB)* Havana (Cuba) 2011.
Members Full in 12 countries:
Argentina, Brazil, Chile, Colombia, Costa Rica, Cuba, Ecuador, El Salvador, Mexico, Panama, Peru, Uruguay.
NGO Relations Member of (1): *International Federation for Medical and Biological Engineering (IFMBE, #13477)* (Affiliated). [2022/AA3221/**D**]

♦ Consejo Regional de Planificación (CRP) 04725

Regional Council for Planning

Contact c/o ILPES, Edificio ONU, Avda Dag Hammarskjöld 3477, Vitacura, Santiago, Santiago Metropolitan, Chile. T. +5622102630. Fax +5622066104.

History 1974, as the guiding intergovernmental body of *Latin American and Caribbean Institute for Economic and Social Planning (#16279)*. A permanent subsidiary body of *United Nations Economic Commission for Latin America and the Caribbean (ECLAC, #20556)*, its resolutions being ratified at ECLAC Sessions. **Structure** Council meets every 4 years at level of Ministers or Heads of National Planning Bodies of all member governments and, more frequently, as the Presiding Officers of the Regional Council for Planning – *Mesa Directiva del Consejo Regional de Planificación (MD/CRP)*, comprising 10 members chosen by CRP plus a representative of the country of ILPES Headquarters (Chile). **Events** *Meeting* Brasilia (Brazil) 2013, *Conference of Ministers and Heads of Planning of Latin America and the Caribbean* Spain 2002, *Conference of Ministers and Heads of Planning of Latin America and the Caribbean* Chile 1998, *Session* Santiago (Chile) 1998, *Presiding officers meeting* 1994.
Members Governments of 40 countries and territories:
Antigua-Barbuda, Argentina, Aruba, Bahamas, Barbados, Belize, Bolivia, Brazil, Chile, Colombia, Costa Rica, Cuba, Dominica, Dominican Rep, Ecuador, El Salvador, Grenada, Guatemala, Guyana, Haiti, Honduras, Jamaica, Mexico, Montserrat, Neth Antilles, Nicaragua, Panama, Paraguay, Peru, Puerto Rico, Spain, St Kitts-Nevis, St Lucia, St Vincent-Grenadines, Suriname, Trinidad-Tobago, Uruguay, Venezuela, Virgin Is UK, Virgin Is USA.
IGO Relations Instrumental in setting up: *Conference of Ministers and Heads of Planning of Latin America and the Caribbean (see: #16279)*. [2008/XE5998/**E***]

- ♦ Consejo de las Regiones de Europa / see Assembly of European Regions (#02316)
- ♦ Consejo Same (#19012)
- ♦ Consejo de Seguridad de las Naciones Unidas (#20625)
- ♦ Consejo de Senlis / see ICOS (#11086)
- ♦ Consejo Sindical de Trabajadores Andinos (inactive)
- ♦ Consejo de Sindicatos Nordicos de Profesores (#17444)

♦ Consejo Sudamericano de Deportes (CONSUDE) 04726

No fixed address address not obtained.

History Established 1993, Asunción (Paraguay). Most recent status agreed 2002, Belém (Brazil), at regular congress. Treaty signed 25 Aug 2003, in force 5 Nov 2003. **Structure** Officers (4); Technical Commission. **Activities** Regulates South American Games, including all sports popular in schools of the region.
Members Ministers or Secretaries for Sport in 10 countries:
Argentina, Bolivia, Brazil, Chile, Colombia, Ecuador, Paraguay, Peru, Uruguay, Venezuela.
NGO Relations Agreement signed with: *South American University Sports Confederation (#19711)*. [2018/XD5096/**D***]

- ♦ Consejo Superior Universitario Centroamericano / see Confederación Universitaria Centroamericana (#04497)
- ♦ Consejo de Telecomunicaciones del Caribe (no recent information)
- ♦ Consejo de Telecomunicaciones del Pacifico (#18007)
- ♦ Consejo de Trabajadores del Caribe (no recent information)
- ♦ Consejo de Transporte Aéreo del Pacifico Meridional (inactive)
- ♦ Consejo le la Unión Europea (#04895)

♦ Consejo Universitario Iberoamericano (CUIB) 04727

Secretariat Plaza de las Cortes 2, 7a planta, 28014 Madrid, Spain. T. +34913601200. Fax +34913601201.
URL: http://www.cuib.org/

History 21 Nov 2002, Cartagena de Indias (Colombia). **Publications** *CUIB Noticias*.
Members Full organizations (23) in 21 countries:
Argentina, Bolivia, Brazil, Chile, Colombia, Costa Rica, Cuba, Dominican Rep, Ecuador, El Salvador, Guatemala, Honduras, Mexico, Nicaragua, Panama, Paraguay, Peru, Portugal, Spain, Uruguay, Venezuela.
Associate national organization in 1 country:
Uruguay.
Regional associated organizations (3):
Association of Universities of Latin America and the Caribbean (#02970); *Confederación Universitaria Centroamericana (CSUCA, #04497)*; *Universities Caribbean (#20694)*. [2014/XM1873/y/**E**]

- ♦ Consejo Universitario Interamericano para el Desarrollo Económico y Social (no recent information)
- ♦ Conselho Africano de Pequisa Cientifica e Inovação (#00451)
- ♦ Conselho das Associações Profissionais De Engenheiros Civis dos Paises de Lingua Oficial Portuguesa e Castelhana (#04702)
- ♦ Conselho das Comunidades Européias / see Council of the European Union (#04895)
- ♦ Conselho Consultivo para as Águas Ocidentais Austrais (#19896)
- ♦ Conselho de Coordenação dos Sindicatos da Africa Austral (#19865)
- ♦ Conselho Coordenador das Organizações Psicanaliticas da América Latina / see Federación Psicoanalitica de América Latina (#09386)
- ♦ Conselho para o Desenvolvimento da Pequina em Ciências Sociais na Africa (#04879)
- ♦ Conselho dos Desportos da União Africana (unconfirmed)
- ♦ Conselho de Empresarios da América Latina (#16261)
- ♦ Conselho Episcopal Latinoamericano (#04709)
- ♦ Conselho Espirita Internacional (#15585)
- ♦ Conselho Europeu (#06801)
- ♦ Conselho Europeu das Associações Nacionais de Escolas Independentes (#06833)
- ♦ Conselho Europeu de Confrarias Enogastronômicas (#08076)
- ♦ Conselho Europeu dea Rotas do Vinho (inactive)
- ♦ Conselho Europeu dos Jovens Agricultores (#04689)
- ♦ Conselho de Fundações Americanas de Desenvolvimento (#04712)
- ♦ Conselho das Igrejas Evangélicas Metodistas da América Latina e do Caribe (#04714)
- ♦ Conselho da Indústria Quimica do Mercosul (no recent information)
- ♦ Conselho Interamericano de Música (no recent information)
- ♦ Conselho Internacional dos Arquitetos de Lingua Portuguesa (internationally oriented national body)
- ♦ Conselho Internacional de Esportes e Jogos Tradicionais (#13088)
- ♦ Conselho Latino-Americano e do Caribe de Organizações Nã Governamentais com Serviço em VIH/Aids (#16272)
- ♦ Conselho Latinoamericano de Ciencias Sociais (#04718)
- ♦ Conselho Latino-americano de Estrabismo (#04720)
- ♦ Conselho Latinoamericano de Igrejas (#16309)
- ♦ Conselho Latinoamericano de Perfusão (unconfirmed)
- ♦ Conselho dos Municipios e Regiões da Europa (#04891)
- ♦ Conselho Português para os Refugiados (internationally oriented national body)
- ♦ Conselho de Reguladores de Valores Mobiliarios das Américas (#04918)
- ♦ Conselho da União Europeia (#04895)
- ♦ Conselho da Vida Familiar (religious order)
- ♦ Consensus for Self Sustaining People, Organisations and Communities / see Consensus for Sustainable People, Organisations and Communities
- ♦ Consensus for Sustainable People, Organisations and Communities (internationally oriented national body)
- ♦ Conservation Agriculture Network / see Social Agriculture Network (#19333)

♦ Conservation of Arctic Flora and Fauna (CAFF) 04728

Exec Dir Borgir, Nordurslod, 600 Akureyri, Iceland. E-mail: caff@caff.is.
URL: https://www.caff.is/

History Established Jun 1991, Rovaniemi (Finland), by ministerial declaration, within the framework of *Arctic Environmental Protection Strategy (AEPS, inactive)*. Since 1997, biodiversity working group of *Arctic Council (#01097)*. **Aims** Address the conservation of Arctic *biodiversity*, and communicate findings to the governments and residents of the Arctic, helping to promote practices which ensure the sustainability of the Arctic's living resources; serve as a vehicle to cooperate on species and habitat management and utilization, to share information on management techniques and regulatory regimes, and to facilitate more knowledgeable decision-making; provide a mechanism to develop common responses on issues of importance for the Arctic ecosystem such as development and economic pressures, conservation opportunities and political commitments. **Structure** Management Board (meets twice a year); Chair; International Secretariat. Operates by the Arctic Council Rules of Procedures. Includes: *Circumpolar Biodiversity Monitoring Program (CBMP, #03941)*. **Staff** 5.00 FTE, paid. **Activities** Monitoring/evaluation; knowledge management/information dissemination; politics/policy/regulatory; projects/programmes. **Events** *Arctic Migratory Birds Initiative Workshop* Singapore (Singapore) 2017, *Meeting* Kirkenes (Norway) 2016, *Meeting* Tromsø (Norway) 2015, *Symposium on Assessing Vulnerability of Flora and Fauna in Polar Areas* Tromsø (Norway) 2014, *Arctic Biodiversity Congress* Trondheim (Norway) 2014. **Publications** *Administrative Series*; *Assessment Series*; *Educational Series*; *Expert Group Series*; *Monitoring Series*; *Proceedings Series*; *Strategies Series*.
Members National representatives assigned by each of the 8 Arctic Council Member States; representatives of indigenous people's organizations that are Permanent Participants to the Council; Arctic Council observer countries and organizations. Designated agencies and national contacts representing Governments of 8 countries:
Canada, Denmark (with Greenland), Finland, Iceland, Norway, Russia, Sweden, USA.
Permanent Participant Organizations (6):
Aleut International Association (AIA); *Arctic Athabaskan Council (AAC)*; *Gwich'in Council International (GCI)*; *Inuit Circumpolar Council (ICC, #15995)*; *Russian Association of Indigenous Peoples of the North (RAIPON)*; *Saami Council (#19012)*.
Observers countries (12):
China, France, Germany, India, Italy, Japan, Korea Rep, Netherlands, Poland, Singapore, Spain, UK.
Observer organizations (12):
Circumpolar Conservation Union (CCU); *Global Resource Information Database (GRID, #10578)*; *International Arctic Science Committee (IASC, #11668)*; *International Market Research Association (IMRA, inactive)*; *International Union for Conservation of Nature and Natural Resources (IUCN, #15766)*; *Nordic Council of Ministers (NCM, #17260)*; North American Marine Mammal Commission; *Northern Forum, The (#17592)*; *Secretariat of the Convention on the Conservation of Migratory Species of Wild Animals (UNEP/CMS, #19198)*; *Standing Committee of Parliamentarians of the Arctic Region (SCPAR, #19958)*; *UN Environment Programme World Conservation Monitoring Centre (UNEP-WCMC, #20295)*.
IGO Relations Cooperates with:
- *African-Eurasian Migratory /Water Bird/ Agreement (AEWA, 1995)*;
- *Arctic Contaminants Action Program (ACAP, see: #01097)*;
- *Arctic Monitoring and Assessment Programme (AMAP, #01100)*;
- *Convention on Biological Diversity (Biodiversity convention, 1992)*;
- *Emergency, Prevention, Preparedness and Response (EPPR, #05437)*;
- *European Environment Agency (EEA, #06995)*;
- *European Union (EU, #08967)*;
- *Global Resource Information Database (GRID, #10578)*;
- *Nordic Council of Ministers (NCM, #17260)*;
- *OSPAR Commission for the Protection of the Marine Environment of the North-East Atlantic (OSPAR Commission, #17905)*;
- *Protection of the Arctic Marine Environment (PAME, #18547)*;
- *Secretariat of the Convention on Biological Diversity (SCBD, #19197)*;
- *Secretariat of the Convention on the Conservation of Migratory Species of Wild Animals (UNEP/CMS, #19198)*;
- *Secretariat of the Convention of Wetlands (#19200)*;
- *Standing Committee of Parliamentarians of the Arctic Region (SCPAR, #19958)*;
- *UN Environment Programme World Conservation Monitoring Centre (UNEP-WCMC, #20295)*;
- *UNESCO (#20322)*;
- *Working Group on Sustainable Development (SDWG, #21061)*.

NGO Relations Cooperates with: *Association of Polar Early Career Scientists (APECS, #02864); Association of World Reindeer Herders (WRH, #02985); East Asian – Australasian Flyway Partnership (EAAFP, #05198); International Arctic Science Committee (IASC, #11668); International Association for Vegetation Science (IAVS, #12253); International Union for Conservation of Nature and Natural Resources (IUCN, #15766); Wetlands International (#20928); World Wide Fund for Nature (WWF, #21922)* Arctic. [2015.10.08/XK0713/y/**E***]

- ♦ Conservation Council of Nations (internationally oriented national body)
- ♦ Conservation Finance Alliance (unconfirmed)
- ♦ Conservation, Food and Health Foundation (internationally oriented national body)

♦ Conservation Force 04729

Contact 3240 S I-10 Service Rd W, Ste 200, Metairie LA 70001-6911, USA. T. +15048371233. Fax +15048371145. E-mail: cf@conservationforce.org.
URL: http://www.conservationforce.org/

History A US 501(c)(3) not-for-profit organization. **Aims** Expand and secure conservation of *wildlife*, wild places and the outdoor way of life. **Structure** Board of Directors. **Activities** Advocacy/lobbying/activism; awards/prizes/competitions. **Publications** *World Conservation Force Bulletin* (12 a year). **Consultative Status** Consultative status granted from: *ECOSOC (#05331)* (Special). **IGO Relations** International observer of: *Convention on Biological Diversity (Biodiversity convention, 1992); Convention on International Trade in Endangered Species of Wild Fauna and Flora (CITES, 1973).* **NGO Relations** Member of: *International Council for Game and Wildlife Conservation (#13024); International Union for Conservation of Nature and Natural Resources (IUCN, #15766); World Forum on Shooting Activities (WFSA, #21523).* Associate member of: *Federation of Associations for Hunting and Conservation of the EU (#09459).* [2018/XM6786/**F**]

- ♦ The Conservation Foundation, UK (internationally oriented national body)
- ♦ Conservation International (internationally oriented national body)
- ♦ Conservation Through Public Health (unconfirmed)
- ♦ Conservation, Research and Education Opportunities International (internationally oriented national body)
- ♦ Conservation Volunteers Greece / see ELIX – Conservation Volunteers Greece
- ♦ Conservative Baptist Foreign Mission Society / see WorldVenture
- ♦ Conservative and Christian Democrat Youth Community / see Democrat Youth Community of Europe (#05037)
- ♦ Conserve Africa Foundation (internationally oriented national body)
- ♦ Conserve Africa International / see Conserve Africa Foundation
- ♦ Consiglio dei Comuni d'Europa / see Council of European Municipalities and Regions (#04891)
- ♦ Consiglio dei Comuni e delle Regioni d'Europa (#04891)
- ♦ Consiglio delle Comunità Europee / see Council of the European Union (#04895)
- ♦ Consiglio delle Conferenze Episcopali d'Europa (#04884)
- ♦ Consiglio Europeo (#06801)
- ♦ Consiglio Europeo di Confraternite Enogastronomiche (#08076)
- ♦ Consiglio Europeo dei Costruttori di Apparecchi Domestici / see APPLiA – Home Appliance Europe (#00877)
- ♦ Consiglio Europeo del Cuoio Grezzo (inactive)
- ♦ Consiglio Europeo degli Enti Regolatori delle Professioni Infermieristiche / see European Nursing Council (#08063)
- ♦ Consiglio Europeo dei Giovani Agricoltori (#04689)
- ♦ Consiglio Europeo delle Lingue (#07646)
- ♦ Consiglio Europeo delle Strade del Vino (inactive)
- ♦ Consiglio Internazionale degli Architetti di Monumenti Storici (inactive)
- ♦ Consiglio Internazionale dei Conciatori (#13084)
- ♦ Consiglio Internazionale della Frutta Secca / see International Nut and Dried Fruit Council Foundation (#14387)
- ♦ Consiglio Internazionale di Numismatica (#14385)
- ♦ Consiglio Internazionale Ragazzi per la Pace (internationally oriented national body)
- ♦ Consiglio Italiano Per I Rifugiati (internationally oriented national body)
- ♦ Consiglio Oleicolo Internazionale (#14405)
- ♦ Consiglio delle Regioni d'Europa / see Assembly of European Regions (#02316)
- ♦ Consiglio Superiore delle Scuole Europee (#03295)
- ♦ Consiglio dell'Unione Europea (#04895)
- ♦ Consiliul European (#06801)
- ♦ Consiliul Uniunii Europene (#04895)
- ♦ Consilium Conferentiarum Episcoporum Europae (#04884)
- ♦ Consilium Europaeum Strabismi Studio Deditum / see European Strabismological Association (#08840)
- ♦ Consociatio Catholica pro Medio Oriente (#03606)

♦ Consociatio Internationalis Musicae Sacrae (CIMS) 04730

Gen Sec Piazza S. Agostino 20 A, 00186 Rome RM, Italy. E-mail: info@cims-roma.org.
Permanent Address Via di Torre Rossa 21, 00165 Rome RM, Italy.
Chairman Institut für Hymnologische und, Musikethnologische Studien e.V. der CIMS, Drususgasse 7-11, 50667 Cologne, Germany. E-mail: info@cims-institut.de.
Main Website: https://cims-roma.org

History 22 Nov 1963. Founded when canonically established in Rome (Italy) by Pope Paul VI. Exercises its apostolic activity by mandate of the hierarchy. Approbation of statutes by Pope John-Paul II, 16 Jan 1979. Registration: End date: 1977, Germany. **Aims** Preserve and develop the musical treasury of the Roman *Catholic Church*. **Structure** Subject to *Congregation for Divine Worship and the Discipline of the Sacraments (#04668).* General Assembly (meets every 5 years); Board of Directors; Board of Moderators; Special Committees (7); Secretariat based in Rome (Italy). **Languages** English, French, German, Italian. **Finance** Sources: donations. **Activities** Events/meetings; research/documentation. **Events** *General Assembly* Lyon (France) / Triors (France) 2019, *General Assembly* Rome (Italy) 2005, *L'oeuvre musicale, réflexions musicologiques et conséquences pour le droit d'auteur* Kaslik (Lebanon) 2004, *International Congress of Sacred Music* Lebanon 2004, *Symposium / International Congress of Sacred Music* Lublin (Poland) 2003. **Publications** *Musicae Sacrae Ministerium* (every 2 years); *Musicae Aptatio.* Congress and symposia proceedings. Information Services: Establishing a Central Musical Archive.
Members Corporate approved national church music organizations and institutions; Individuals, including Honorary Members (250). Members in 36 countries:
Argentina, Australia, Austria, Belgium, Bosnia-Herzegovina, Brazil, Cameroon, Canada, Croatia, Czechia, El Salvador, France, Germany, Holy See, Hungary, Indonesia, Ireland, Italy, Japan, Kenya, Korea Rep, Lebanon, Luxembourg, Malta, Mexico, Netherlands, Nigeria, Poland, Portugal, Senegal, Slovenia, Spain, Switzerland, Tanzania UR, UK, USA.
[2021.06.09/XF9271/**F**]

- ♦ Consociatio Internationalis Studio Iuris Canonici Promovendo (#12193)
- ♦ Consolata Fathers – Institute of Consolata Missionaries (religious order)
- ♦ Consolata Missionary Sisters (religious order)
- ♦ Consorcio para la Atención Postaborto / see Abortion and Postabortion Care Consortium (#00007)
- ♦ Consorcio para la Colaboración de la Educación Superior en América del Norte (#04756)
- ♦ Consorcio de Comunicación para el Cambio Social (#04383)
- ♦ Consorcio para el Desarrollo Sostenible de la Ecoregión Andina (#04758)
- ♦ Consórcio Iberoamericano para la Educação em Ciência e Tecnologia (#11027)
- ♦ Consorcio Iberoamericano para la Educación en Ciencia y Tecnologia (#11027)

♦ Consorcio Interamericano de Universidades y Centros de Formación de Personal en Educación para la Salud y Promoción de la Salud (CIUEPS) 04731

Office Escuela de Salud Pública, Recinto de Ciencias Médicas, Univ de Puerto Rico, PO Box 365067, San Juan PR 00936-5067, USA. T. +17872740582 – +17877582525. Fax +17877546621 – +17877596719. E-mail: consorcio.rcm@upr.edu.
URL: http://www.ciueps.org/

Events *General Assembly* Medellin (Colombia) 2009, *General Assembly* San José (Costa Rica) 2008, *General Assembly* Sao Paulo (Brazil) 2006, *General Assembly* Rio de Janeiro (Brazil) 2005, *General Assembly* Sao Paulo (Brazil) 2002. [2012/XJ0676/**F**]

- ♦ Consorcio Internacional del Aborto con Medicamentos (inactive)
- ♦ Consorcio Internacional de Gestión Financiera Gubernamental (#12915)
- ♦ Consorcio de Inter-Universidades para el Desarrollo Social Internacional / see International Consortium for Social Development (#12922)
- ♦ Consorcio Latinoamericano de Anticoncepción de Emergencia (#16306)
- ♦ Consorcio Latinoamericano y del Caribe de Apoyo a la Investigación y Desarrollo de la Yuca (#16271)

♦ Consorcio Latinoamericano de Libertad Religiosa 04732

Latin American Consortium for Religious Liberty

Contact address not obtained. E-mail: contacto@libertadreligiosa.org.
URL: http://libertadreligiosa.org/

History 22 Sep 2000, Lima (Peru). **Aims** Provide a permanent forum for reflection, research and promotion of the right to religious freedom, the legal regulation of the religious phenomenon and the legal relations that must exist between religious denominations and the States. **Structure** Board of Directors. **Activities** Events/meetings. **Events** *Colloquium* Bogota (Colombia) 2019, *Colloquium* Rio de Janeiro (Brazil) 2018.
Members Individuals in 15 countries:
Argentina, Brazil, Chile, Colombia, Cuba, Dominican Rep, Italy, Mexico, Paraguay, Peru, Poland, Spain, UK, Uruguay, USA.
NGO Relations Cooperates with (1): *G20 Interfaith Forum Association (IF20, #10055).* [2019/AA0116/v/**D**]

- ♦ Consorcio-Red de Educación a Distancia (#11428)
- ♦ Consórcio-Rede de Educação à Distância (#11428)
- ♦ Consorcio TICCA (#11041)

♦ Consortio Latinoamericano Contra el Aborto Inseguro (CLACAI) . . . 04733

Latin American and Caribbean Consortium against Unsafe Abortion

Coordinator Promsex, Av José Pardo 601, oficina 604, Miraflores, 18, Lima, Peru.
URL: http://www.clacai.org/

History May 2006, Lima (Peru) at first General Meeting, following earlier discussions, Oct 2004, Johannesburg (South Africa). Previously a regional network of *International Consortium for Medical Abortion (ICMA, inactive);* currently *International Campaign for Women's Right to Safe Abortion (#12430).* **Aims** Promote access to innovative technologies that could improve the safety and quality of abortion care in the region. **Structure** Coordinating Committee. **Events** *Regional Conference* Lima (Peru) 2014, *Regional Conference* Bogota (Colombia) 2012, *Regional Conference / Conference* Lima (Peru) 2009.
Members Full in 11 countries:
Argentina, Bolivia, Brazil, Colombia, Costa Rica, Cuba, Guatemala, Mexico, Peru, Uruguay, USA.
NGO Relations Member of: *Reproductive Health Supplies Coalition (RHSC, #18847).* Partner of: *International Campaign for Women's Right to Safe Abortion (#12430).* Supports: *Equipo Latinoamericano de Justicia y Género (ELA).* [2019/XJ1243/**E**]

♦ Consortium for Advanced Management – International (CAM-I) . . . 04734

Pres 108 Wild Basin Rd South, Ste 250, Austin TX 78746, USA. T. +15126176428.
URL: https://www.cam-i.net/

History 1972, USA. A not-for-profit research and development corporation owned by members and supported by industrial, governmental and educational organizations worldwide. Former names and other names: *Computer Aided Manufacturing International* – former (1972); *Consortium for Advanced Manufacturing – International (CAM-I)* – former. **Aims** Further the cooperative research and development efforts of companies with common interests in advanced management and manufacturing systems, technology and standards. **Structure** Board of Directors. Project and Committee representatives meet on a regular basis. **Activities** Research and development programs; workshops and training courses. Contact office for Library Catalogue.
Members Industrial, governmental, educational, research and service organizations (50) in 13 countries:
Australia, Belgium, Canada, Finland, France, Germany, Italy, Japan, Netherlands, Norway, Sweden, UK, USA.
NGO Relations In liaison with technical committees of: *International Organization for Standardization (ISO, #14473).* [2022/XF5336/**F**]

- ♦ Consortium for Advanced Manufacturing – International / see Consortium for Advanced Management – International (#04734)
- ♦ Consortium d'Afrique australe pour le pilotage de la qualité de l'éducation (#19871)
- ♦ Consortium APAC (#11041)

♦ Consortium on Applied Research and Professional Education (CARPE) 04735

Contact address not obtained. E-mail: carpe@hu.nl.
URL: https://carpenetwork.org/

History 2011, Utrecht (Netherlands). Launched by 4 universities from Germany, Netherlands, Finland and Spain. **Aims** Encourage cooperation in European research programmes and jointly develop educational programmes. **Structure** Steering Committee. Special Interest Groups. **Languages** English. **Activities** Events/meetings; research/documentation. **Events** *Conference* Debrecen (Hungary) 2021, *Conference* Valencia (Spain) 2019, *Conference* Hamburg (Germany) 2017, *Conference* Turku (Finland) 2015, *Conference* 2013.
Members Universities in 7 countries and territories:
Finland, Germany, Hungary, Netherlands, Portugal, Scotland, Spain. [2023.02.16/AA2470/**D**]

- ♦ Consortium of Aquariums, Universities and Zoos (no recent information)

♦ Consortium for Asian and African Studies (CAAS) 04736

Executive Coordinator Office for Intenational Affairs, Tokyo University of Foreign Studies, 3-11-1 Asahi-cho, Fuchu-shi, Tokyo, 183-8534 Japan. T. +81423305594. E-mail: intl-service@tufs.ac.jp.
URL: http://www.tufs.ac.jp/ofias/caas/

History Mar 2007. **Aims** Strengthen collaboration in research and education activities. **Languages** English. **Activities** Events/meetings; networking/liaising; research/documentation; training/education. **Events** *International Conference* London (UK) 2021, *International Conference* Shanghai (China) 2019, *International Conference* Paris (France) 2018, *International Conference* Leiden (Netherlands) 2017, *International Conference* Tokyo (Japan) 2016.
Members Institutions (7) in 7 countries:
China, France, Japan, Korea Rep, Netherlands, UK, USA. [2022/XM8441/**C**]

♦ Consortium for the Barcode of Life (CBOL) 04737

Exec Dir Museum of Natural History, Smithsonian Institution, PO Box 37012, MRC-105, Washington DC 20013-7012, USA. T. +12026330812. Fax +12026332938.
URL: http://www.barcodeoflife.org/

History 25 May 2004, Washington DC (USA). **Aims** Explore and develop the potential of DNA barcoding as a practical tool for species identification in taxonomic research, biodiversity studies and conservation, and diverse applications that use taxonomic information in service to science and society. **Structure** Executive Committee of 6 members. **Events** *International Barcode of Life Conference* Kunming (China) 2013, *European Conference for the Barcode of Life* Brussels (Belgium) 2012, *International Barcode of Life Conference* Adelaide, SA (Australia) 2011, *International barcode of life conference* Mexico City (Mexico) 2009, *International barcode conference* Taipei (Taiwan) 2007.
Members Centres, institutes, universities and organizations (46) in 22 countries and universities:
Argentina, Australia, Belgium, Brazil, Canada, China, Colombia, Costa Rica, Denmark, France, Ghana, Hong Kong, Iran Islamic Rep, Italy, Mexico, Morocco, Netherlands, New Zealand, South Africa, Spain, UK, USA.
Included in the above, 4 organizations listed in this Yearbook:
BioNET INTERNATIONAL – Global Network for Taxonomy (BI, #03253); Commonwealth Scientific and Industrial Research Organization (CSIRO); International Centre for Genetic Engineering and Biotechnology (ICGEB, #12494); Ocean Genome Legacy (OGL).
IGO Relations Member of: *Global Biodiversity Information Facility (GBIF, #10250).* [2014/XJ4308/y/**F**]

♦ Consortium de bibliothèques de recherche européennes (#04742)
♦ Consortium of British Humanitarian Agencies / see Start Network (#19969)
♦ Consortium of Christian Relief and Development Association (internationally oriented national body)
♦ Consortium pour la collaboration dans l'enseignement supérieur en Amérique du nord (#04756)
♦ Consortium de la communication pour le changement social (#04383)
♦ Consortium for Conservation Medicine / see EcoHealth Alliance
♦ Consortium of Consortia / see International Coalition of Library Consortia (#12615)
♦ Consortium for Countering the Financing of Terrorism (internationally oriented national body)
♦ Consortium for Emergency Contraception / see International Consortium for Emergency Contraception (#12911)

♦ Consortium of European Baptists Theological Schools (CEBTS) 04738

Contact address not obtained. T. +420296392300. E-mail: clerk@cebts.eu – info@cebts.eu.
URL: http://www.cebts.eu/

History Sep 2001. **Activities** Training/education; events/meetings; knowledge management/information dissemination.
Members Schools (over 25) in 22 countries:
Armenia, Belarus, Bosnia-Herzegovina, Bulgaria, Czechia, Estonia, Germany, Hungary, Israel, Jordan, Lebanon, Lithuania, Netherlands, Norway, Poland, Portugal, Romania, Russia, Spain, Sweden, UK, Ukraine.
Included in the above, 1 organization listed in this Yearbook:
International Baptist Theological Study Centre, Amsterdam (IBTSC, #12319).
NGO Relations *European Baptist Federation (EBF, #06316).* [2016/XM5213/E]

♦ Consortium of European Building Control (CEBC) 04739

SG c/o Registered Office, Duncan and Toplis, 18 Northgate, Seaford, NG34 7BJ, UK. E-mail: secretary.general@cebc.eu.
Pres address not obtained. E-mail: president@cebc.eu.
URL: http://www.cebc.eu/

History 1989. Current statutes adopted 13 Oct 2015. Registered in accordance with UK law. **Aims** Be the voice of European building control; safeguard building control activities; promote their significance within a rapidly changing Europe. **Structure** General Assembly (twice a year); Policy Committee; Officers. **Languages** English. **Staff** 0.50 FTE, paid. **Finance** Member's dues. **Events** *Business Meeting* Milan (Italy) 2015, *Business Meeting* Reykjavik (Iceland) 2015, *Business Meeting* Frankfurt-Main (Germany) 2014, *Business Meeting* Izmir (Turkey) 2014, *Business Meeting* Jerusalem (Israel) 2013. **Publications** *Access for All in Europe*; *Building Control Systems in Europe*; *Self Confirmation across Europe.*
Members National bodies or government bodies. Members in 23 countries:
Austria, Belgium, Croatia, Cyprus, Denmark, Estonia, Finland, France, Germany, Hungary, Iceland, Ireland, Israel, Italy, Netherlands, Norway, Poland, Romania, Slovenia, Spain, Sweden, Türkiye, UK.
IGO Relations *European Commission (EC, #06633).* **NGO Relations** Member of: *International Fire Safety Standards Coalition (IFSS Coalition, #13606).* [2015.10.21/XM0743/F]

♦ Consortium of European Companies Determined to Use Superconductivity (CONECTUS) 04740

Company Sec c/o Bock SuperConductors Consulting, Am Burgfeld 51, 50374 Erftstadt, Germany. T. +492235465933.
URL: http://www.conectus.org/

History 2 Aug 1994. Registered in accordance with UK law. EU Transparency Register: 80327962885-40. **Aims** Strengthen the basis for commercial applications of superconductivity in Europe. **Structure** Council; Secretary. **Languages** English.
Members Full in 4 countries:
Czechia, Finland, Germany, Italy.
NGO Relations *European Society for Applied Superconductivity (ESAS, #08522).* [2018.10.12/XJ6840/D]

♦ Consortium of European Research on Emotion (CERE) 04741

Address not obtained.
URL: http://www.cere-emotionconferences.org/

History An informal organization. **Activities** Events/meetings. **Events** *Conference* Granada (Spain) 2020, *Conference* Glasgow (UK) 2018, *Conference* Leiden (Netherlands) 2016, *Conference* Berlin (Germany) 2014, *Conference* Canterbury (UK) 2012. [2020/AA2009/c/D]

♦ Consortium of European Research Libraries (CERL) 04742

Consortium de bibliothèques de recherche européennes

Sec 40 Bowling Green Lane, London, EC1R 0NE, UK. T. +442074157134. E-mail: secretariat@cerl.org.
URL: http://www.cerl.org/

History 1992; incorporated in 1993. **Aims** Improve access to, and exploitation and preservation of European printed heritage in the *hand-press* period (up to about 1850). **Structure** Board of Directors; Coordinating Committee. **Languages** Dutch, English, French, German, Italian. **Staff** 3.00 FTE, paid. **Finance** Members' dues. Grants. **Activities** Research/documentation; events/meetings; knowledge management/information dissemination. **Events** *Annual Meeting* 2020, *Annual Meeting* Göttingen (Germany) 2019, *Annual Meeting* Venice (Italy) 2018, *Seminar* Zurich (Switzerland) 2018, *Annual Meeting* Amsterdam (Netherlands) 2017. **Publications** *CERL Papers* – series. **Information Services** *15cBOOKTRADE Project*; *CERL Portal*; *CERL Thesaurus*; *Heritage of the Printed Book Database*; *Material Evidence in Incunabula (MEI) Database*; *PATRIMONil.*
Members Full; Group; Special; Cluster. Members in 35 countries:
Argentina, Austria, Belgium, Bolivia, Brazil, Chile, Cuba, Czechia, Denmark, Dominican Rep, El Salvador, Estonia, Finland, France, Germany, Greece, Guatemala, Holy See, Hungary, Ireland, Italy, Latvia, Liechtenstein, Lithuania, Luxembourg, Mexico, Netherlands, Norway, Poland, Spain, Sweden, Switzerland, UK, USA, Venezuela. [2018.06.01/XF3350/F]

♦ Consortium of European Social Science Data Archives (CESSDA) ... 04743

Dir Parkveien 20, 5007 Bergen, Norway. T. +4740100964. E-mail: cessda@cessda.eu.
URL: https://www.cessda.eu/

History 1976. Founded as an informal umbrella organisation for European national social science data archives. Main office is located in Bergen (Norway). Former names and other names: *Council of European Social Science Data Archives (CESSDA)* – former. Registration: European Commission, No/ID: OJ L 149, Start date: 9 Jun 2017, Norway; Start date: 2013, Norway. **Aims** Provide a full scale sustainable research infrastructure enabling the research community to conduct high-quality research in social sciences contributing to production of effective solutions to major challenges facing society today and to facilitate teaching and learning in the social sciences. **Structure** General Assembly; Director; Scientific Advisory Board; Service Providers Forum. **Languages** English. **Staff** 11.00 FTE, paid. **Finance** Financed by member states' ministries of research or delegated institutions. **Activities** Capacity building; networking/liaising; research and development; training/education. **Events** *Joint Meeting* Stockholm (Sweden) 2021. **Information Services** *CESSDA Data Catalogue*; *CESSDA Data Management Expert Guide*; *Zenodo Community.*
Members Members in 20 countries:
Austria, Belgium, Croatia, Czechia, Denmark, Finland, France, Germany, Greece, Hungary, Lithuania, Netherlands, North Macedonia, Norway, Portugal, Serbia, Slovakia, Slovenia, Sweden, UK.
Observer in 1 country:
Switzerland. [2022/XD5855/D]

♦ Consortium for European Symposia on Turkey (internationally oriented national body)

♦ Consortium of European Taxonomic Facilities (CETAF) 04744

Gen Sec c/o Inst of Natural Sciences, Rue Vautier 29, 1000 Brussels, Belgium. E-mail: info@cetaf.org.
URL: http://cetaf.org/

History Dec 1996. Founded, when 10 European national history museums and botanical gardens signed Memorandum of Understanding to establish CETAF. Legal body set up during 2009. 2012, established General Secretariat at the Royal Belgian Institute of Natural Sciences in Brussels (Belgium). Continued the work of *ESF Network on Systematic Biology (inactive).* Registration: Start date: 13 Mar 2009, Belgium. **Aims** Promote collection-based research into biodiversity and geodiversity, training in systematic biosciences and paleobiology, and open up access and sharing of biodiversity data and collections with the taxonomic expertise of member institutions across Europe. **Structure** General Meeting; Executive Committee; General Secretariat. **Languages** English. **Staff** 4.00 FTE, paid; 1.00 FTE, voluntary. **Finance** Sources: members' dues. **Activities** Knowledge management/information dissemination; research/documentation. **Events** *General Meeting* 2021, *General Meeting* Paris (France) 2021, *General Meeting* Bratislava (Slovakia) 2018, *General Meeting* London (UK) 2018, *General Meeting* Madrid (Spain) 2016. **Publications** *European Journal of Taxonomy.* Policy and position papers. **Information Services** *CETAF Code of Conduct and Best Practices* in English – Best Practcice on Access and Benefit-Sharing.
Members Full (33) in 20 countries:
Austria, Belgium, Bulgaria, Czechia, Denmark, Estonia, Finland, France, Germany, Greece, Hungary, Italy, Netherlands, Norway, Poland, Slovakia, Spain, Sweden, Switzerland, UK. [2021.09.08/XF4718/F]

♦ Consortium européen sur l'économie du paysage (CEEP) 04745

European Consortium on Landscape Economics

Contact address not obtained. E-mail: walid.ouestlati@univ-angers.fr.

History Founded Sep 2005. **Aims** Develop a common research platform on various aspects of landscape economics. **Structure** Coordinating Committee. **Events** *International conference on landscape economics* Vienna (Austria) 2009, *Workshop* Paris (France) 2008, *Workshop* Montpellier (France) 2007, *Workshop* Angers (France) 2006. [2011/XM2974/D]

♦ Consortium européen pour la recherche en communication / see European Communication Research and Education Association (#06675)
♦ Consortium européen de recherches en sciences politiques (#06762)
♦ Consortium on Gender, Security & Human Rights (internationally oriented national body)
♦ Consortium for Global Commerce / see World Chambers Network (#21270)
♦ Consortium for Globalization of Chinese Medicine (internationally oriented national body)

♦ Consortium of Higher Education Researchers (CHER) 04746

Gen Sec Rua 1o de Dezembro 399, 4450-227 Matosinhos, Portugal. T. +351229398790. E-mail: cher@cipes.up.pt.
URL: http://www.cher-highered.org/

History 24 Nov 1988, Kassel (Germany). Founded at 1st Conference. Became a foundation registered in accordance with Dutch law, 1993. **Aims** Develop activities in the field of research in higher education; stimulate cooperation in research projects; further develop internationalization of higher education research; stimulate development of an international training programme on higher education in Europe. **Structure** Board of Governors. **Languages** English. **Finance** Sources: gifts, legacies; members' dues; revenue from activities/projects; subsidies. **Activities** Events/meetings. **Events** *Annual Conference* Jyväskylä (Finland) 2022, *Annual Conference* Hong Kong (Hong Kong) 2021, *Annual Conference* Rijeka (Croatia) 2020, *Annual Conference* Kassel (Germany) 2019, *Annual Conference* Moscow (Russia) 2018. **Publications** *CHER Newsletter*. *Higher Education in the 21st Century* – book series.
Members Individuals, both active researchers in higher education and doctoral students, in 43 countries and territories:
Australia, Austria, Brazil, Bulgaria, Canada, Chile, China, Croatia, Cyprus, Denmark, Finland, France, Germany, Hong Kong, Hungary, Iceland, India, Ireland, Israel, Italy, Japan, Kazakhstan, Korea DPR, Korea Rep, Luxembourg, Malaysia, Netherlands, New Zealand, Norway, Poland, Portugal, Russia, Serbia, Singapore, Slovenia, South Africa, Spain, Sweden, Switzerland, Taiwan, Turkey, UK, USA.
IGO Relations *Council of Europe (CE, #04881)*; *European Commission (EC, #06633)*; *International Bank for Reconstruction and Development (IBRD, #12317)*; *OECD (#17693)*; *TEMPUS IV (inactive)*; *UNESCO (#20322).* [2022.10.21/XF5260/v/F]

♦ Consortium of Humanities Centers and Institutes (internationally oriented national body)
♦ Consortium pour les infrastructures en Afrique (#11206)

♦ Consortium of Institutes on Family in the Asian Region (CIFA) 04747

Contact Portion B, 21/F Wofoo Commercial Bldg, 574-576 Nathan Road, Kowloon, Hong Kong. T. +85223630700. Fax +85223633010. E-mail: cifasecretariat@gmail.com.
URL: http://www.cifa-net.org/

History 24 Jan 2008. Registration: Hong Kong. **Aims** Strengthen family functioning and promote family health in the region while contributing to the body of knowledge in relationship science in the international arena. **Structure** General Meeting; Council; Secretariat. Committees (5): Research & Training; Promotion & Fundraising; Web-based Exchange Platform Development; 3A Project; Memberhsip. **Activities** Events/meetings; research/documentation; training/education. **Events** *Symposium* Taiwan 2021, *Symposium* Taiwan 2020, *Symposium* Seoul (Korea Rep) 2016, *Symposium* Shanghai (China) 2014, *Symposium* Singapore (Singapore) 2012.
Members Agencies in 8 countries and territories:
China, Hong Kong, Japan, Korea Rep, Macau, Malaysia, Singapore, Taiwan. [2021/AA2003/D]

♦ Consortium of Institutes of Higher Education in Health and Rehabilitation in Europe (COHEHRE) 04748

Contact Voetweg 66, 9000 Ghent, Belgium. T. +3292347191. Fax +3292347001. E-mail: administration.cohehre@arteveldehs.be.
URL: https://www.cohehre.com/

History 9 Feb 1990, Ghent (Belgium). Founded by 8 European institutions. Registration: Belgium. **Aims** Enhance the quality of training for health care *professionals* through international cooperation among institutes of higher education in the field; promote qualitative reinforcement of the respective curricula, mutual recognition and exchange of educational programmes, joint development and dissemination of new programmes. **Structure** General Assembly (annual); Consortium Council; Executive Board. **Staff** 0.50 FTE, paid. **Finance** Members' dues: euro 850 (full); euro 500 (associate). Established with the financial support of *European Commission (EC, #06633).* Budget (annual): euro 10,000. **Events** *Annual Conference* Rotterdam (Netherlands) 2022, *Annual Conference* Rotterdam (Netherlands) 2021, *Annual Conference* Rotterdam (Netherlands) 2020, *Annual Conference* Vic (Spain) 2019, *Annual Conference* Ghent (Belgium) 2018. **Publications** *COHEHRE Newsletter* (4 a year).
Members Full; Associate. Public agencies, organizations and institutions in 14 countries and territories:
Belgium, Czechia, Denmark, Finland, France, Germany, Greece, Netherlands, Norway, Palestine, Poland, Portugal, Sweden, UK. [2021/XF2389/F]

♦ Consortium of Institutions for Development and Research in Education in Europe (CIDREE) 04749

Secretariat c/o SKBF, Entfelderstrasse 61, 5000 Aarau AG, Switzerland. E-mail: secretariat@cidree.org.
URL: http://www.cidree.org/

History Dec 1989. **Aims** Promote exchange of information and expertise among professionals of member institutions, hence contributing to organization development. **Structure** General Assembly (annual); Board; Secretariat. **Languages** English. **Staff** 1.00 FTE, voluntary. **Finance** Sources: members' dues. **Activities** Events/meetings; networking/liaising. **Events** *Annual General Assembly* Oslo (Norway) 2022, *Annual General Assembly* Amersfoort (Netherlands) 2021, *Annual General Assembly* Aarau (Switzerland) 2020, *Annual General Assembly* Ljubljana (Slovenia) 2019, *Annual General Assembly* Walferdange (Luxembourg) 2018. **Publications** *CIDREE Yearbook.* Special reports of seminars, workshops and projects.
Members Educational organizations in 19 countries and territories:
Albania, Belgium, Bosnia-Herzegovina, Estonia, Finland, France, Hungary, Ireland, Kosovo, Luxembourg, Montenegro, Netherlands, Norway, Scotland, Serbia, Slovenia, Sweden, Switzerland, Wales. [2023.02.08/XF3407/F]

♦ Consortium of International Agricultural Research Centers / see CGIAR System Organization (#03843)
♦ Consortium international pour la contraception d'urgence (#12911)
♦ Consortium international de coopération sur le Nil (#12907)
♦ Consortium for International Earth Science Information Network / see Center for International Earth Science Information Network
♦ Consortium international sur la gestion financière gouvernementale (#12915)

♦ Consortium for International Maritime Heritage (unconfirmed)

♦ Consortium for International Pacific Education and Communication Experiments by Satellite (PEACESAT) 04750

Program Dir Univ of HI, 2424 Maile Way, Saunders Hall Room 713, Honolulu HI 96822, USA. T. +18089568848. Fax +18089568019.

History 1973. Founded by agreement between Wellington (New Zealand) Polytechnic (New Zealand) and the University of Hawaii (USA). "PEACESAT" derives from "Pan-Pacific Education and Communication Experiments by Satellite". Former names and other names: *International PEACESAT Consortium* – former; *PEACESAT Consortium* – former. **Aims** Coordinate cooperation in improving two-way communications among *health* education and *community services* in the Pacific Basin and worldwide; support long-range planning to improve communication concerning such services in areas inadequately served by *telecommunication* resources. **Structure** Council.

Members Council members include individuals from the following countries (4):
Fiji, New Zealand, Papua New Guinea, USA. [2018/XF1720/**F**]

♦ Consortium interuniversitaire pour les études arabes et moyen-orientales (internationally oriented national body)
♦ Consortium interuniversitaire pour les recherches politiques et sociales (internationally oriented national body)
♦ Consortium of Latin American Studies Programs (internationally oriented national body)

♦ Consortium Linking Universities in Science and Technology for Education and Research (CLUSTER) 04751

Coopération liant les universités en science et technologie pour l'enseignement et la recherche

Coordinator Electrical Eng TUE, PO Box 513, 5600 MB Eindhoven, Netherlands.
URL: http://www.cluster.org/

History 1990. Previously also referred to as *Cooperative Link Between Universities in Science and Technology for Education and Research.* **Aims** Be the leading university network of technology for research, education and innovation in Europe. **Structure** General Assembly (annual). Steering Committee. **Languages** English. **Staff** 1.00 FTE, paid. **Finance** Members' dues. Co-financing from member universities and externally funded projects. **Activities** Exchange of experience; enhanced student mobility with full recognition; Mutual recognition of degrees; joint EU proposals; network of Dual Degrees; relations with industry and EU bodies. **Events** *Seminar on university management* Darmstadt (Germany) 2009, *General Assembly* Lisbon (Portugal) 2009, *General Assembly* Helsinki (Finland) 2008, *General Assembly* Barcelona (Spain) 2007, *General Assembly* Stockholm (Sweden) 2006.

Members Universities and polytechnics in 12 countries:
Belgium, Finland, France, Germany, Ireland, Italy, Netherlands, Portugal, Spain, Sweden, Switzerland, UK.
Associate (6) in 6 non-European countries. Membership countries not specified. [2015/XF3100/**F**]

♦ Consortium of Longitudinal Integrated Clerkships (CLIC) 04752

Address not obtained.
URL: https://clicmeded.com/

Structure International Planning Committee. **Activities** Events/meetings. **Events** *Returning to Our Roots – Vision and Values* Stellenbosch (South Africa) 2021, *Conference* Vancouver, BC (Canada) 2019, *Conference* Singapore (Singapore) 2017, *Conference* Asheville, NC (USA) / Durham, NC (USA) 2015, *Conference* Ayers Rock, NT (Australia) 2014. [2021/AA2010/c/**E**]

♦ Consortium for the Maintenance of the Text Encoding Initiative (TEI Consortium) 04753

Board Member 30 Addison St, Arlington MA 02476, USA. E-mail: chair@tei-c.org – martina.scholger@uni-graz.at.
Board Member address not obtained.
URL: http://www.tei-c.org/

History Dec 2000. **Aims** Sustain and develop the Text Encoding Initiative (TEI). **Structure** Council; Board of Directors (7 to 9 members). Officers: Chair; Vice-Chair; Secretary; Treasurer. **Finance** Members' dues. Grants from research funds. **Activities** The Text Encoding Initiative was launched in 1987. **Events** *Annual Conference and General Meeting* Newcastle upon Tyne (UK) 2022, *Conference and Members' Meeting* USA 2021, *Annual Members Meeting* Graz (Austria) 2019, *Annual Members Meeting* Tokyo (Japan) 2018, *Annual Members Meeting* Victoria, BC (Canada) 2017. **Publications** *TEI P5: Guidelines for Electronic Text Encoding and Interchange* (2007); *TEI P4: Guidelines for Electronic Text Encoding and Interchange* (2002).

Members Full in 21 countries and territories:
Australia, Austria, Belgium, Bulgaria, Canada, Croatia, Czechia, Denmark, France, Germany, Hungary, Ireland, Italy, Netherlands, New Zealand, Norway, Slovenia, Sweden, Taiwan, UK, USA. [2022/XE4756/**E**]

♦ Consortium for Non-communicable Diseases Prevention and Control in sub-Saharan Africa (CNCD-Africa) 04754

Coordinator c/o AIHD, Commodore Office Stes, Kindaruma Raod, 7th Floor – Ste B, PO Box 45259-00100, Nairobi, Kenya. T. +254203873385 – +25420(254727850851. E-mail: cncdafrica@aihdint.org – info@aihdint.org.
Sec address not obtained.
URL: http://www.aihdint.org/cncd/

History Founded Jul 2009, Entebbe (Uganda), following an NCD Prevention and Health Promotion Advocacy Meeting, 30-31 Aug 2008, Bagamoyo (Tanzania UR), initiated by the Department of Health UK in partnership with *International Union for Health Promotion and Education (IUHPE, #15778)* and *African Institute for Health and Development (AIHD).* The meeting brought together 55 experts on various aspects of NCD from 10 African countries (Kenya, Uganda, Tanzania UR, Seychelles, Ghana, Nigeria, Benin, Cameroon, Zambia and South Africa), participants from IUHPE, WHO, Department of Health UK, US Centres for Disease Control and Prevention (CDC), several universities in Africa, Europe and America, and several international/regional associations. **Aims** Provide a framework for engaging in a joint dialogue in addressing NCDs in the Sub-Saharan African Region; synergize on-going NCD prevention and control activities in the region with a view to increasing the coherence, overall impact and visibility of actions undertaken in the region; build a platform for members to support development of comprehensive and multisectoral policies, standards, guidelines and protocols, and to mobilize resources for addressing NCDs in the region; create a forum for networking and partnership that builds on the capacities and expertise of members in the areas of health care, surveillance, policy, advocacy and implementation of NCD interventions and evaluation; identify and define the unique circumstances that drive the NCD burden in the region with a view to developing context-relevant strategies; articulate regional issues at the global level with a view to ensuring that NCD interventions in sub-Saharan Africa are highly visible, relevant, effective, efficient and sustainable. **Structure** Steering Committee. **Languages** English, French. **Staff** 4.00 FTE, paid. **Finance** Initial funding through *International Union for Health Promotion and Education (IUHPE, #15778).* **Activities** Research; education; training; knowledge generation and sharing; networking platform; policy advocacy; awareness creation. **Publications** *CNCD-Africa Newsletter.* **Information Services** *Mapping of NCD Activities* – database of actors.

Members Institutional; Individual; Honorary; Trustee. Members, comprising CSOs, NGOs, institutions and individuals, in 22 countries:
Afghanistan, Antigua-Barbuda, Botswana, Cameroon, Denmark, Egypt, Ethiopia, Gambia, Ghana, Kenya, Mauritania, Nigeria, Philippines, Seychelles, South Africa, Switzerland, Tanzania UR, Togo, Uganda, UK, USA, Zambia.
Included in the above, 5 organizations listed in this Yearbook:
African Field Epidemiology Network (AFENET, #00315); African Institute for Health and Development (AIHD); African Tobacco Control Alliance (ATCA, #00484); Arab Medical Association Against Cancer (AMAAC, #01006); Pan African Society of Cardiology (PASCAR, #18066). [2013.11.20/XJ6272/y/**D**]

♦ Consortium of Non-Traditional Security Studies in Asia (NTS-Asia) . 04755

SG Ctr for Non-Traditional Security (NTS) Studies, S Rajaratnam School of Intl Studies, Nanyang Technological Univ, Blk S4 Level B4, 50 Nanyang Ave, Singapore 639798, Singapore. T. +6567905886. Fax +6567932991. E-mail: ismsembiring@ntu.edu.sg.
URL: http://www.rsis-ntsasia.org/

History 9 Jan 2007, Singapore (Singapore). Founded following a series of plenary meetings on non-traditional security issues conducted from 2003 to 2006. Relaunched 2016. **Aims** Develop a platform for networking and exchange between regional NTS scholars and analysts; build regional capacity for research on NTS; mainstream and advance the field of *non-traditional security* studies; collate and manage a regional database of publications and resources. **Structure** Secretariat based at *Centre for Non-Traditional Security Studies (NTS Centre).* **Languages** English. **Staff** 1.00 FTE, paid. **Activities** Events/meetings. **Events** *Annual Conference* Singapore (Singapore) 2022, *Annual Conference* Singapore (Singapore) 2021, *Annual Conference* Singapore (Singapore) 2020, *COVID-19 and Economic Crisis – Mitigating Impact and Sustaining Development in Asia* Singapore (Singapore) 2020, *COVID-19 and its Impacts on the Women of Southeast Asia* Singapore (Singapore) 2020. **Publications** Books; working papers; articles; conference reports. Information Services: Online Resource Database of publications, activities and experts.

Members Research institutes (32), including the following 14 listed in this Yearbook:
Asian Research Centre for Migration (ARCM); Asia-Pacific Centre for the Responsibility to Protect (#01868); Center for Southeast Asian Studies-Indonesia (CSEAS-Indonesia); Centre for International Security Studies (CISS); Centre for Non-Traditional Security Studies (NTS Centre); Centre for Strategic and International Studies, Jakarta (CSIS); Council for Security Cooperation in the Asia Pacific (CSCAP, #04919); Institute for Strategic and Development Studies, Quezon City (ISDS); Institute of Strategic and International Studies, Malaysia (ISIS); Institute of World Economics and Politics (IWEP); International Rice Research Institute (IRRI, #14754); Regional Centre for Strategic Studies, Colombo (RCSS); Women in Security, Conflict Management and Peace (WISCOMP); WorldFish (#21507). [2023.02.14/XM2594/y/**F**]

♦ Consortium for North American Higher Education Collaboration (CONAHEC) 04756

Consortium pour la collaboration dans l'enseignement supérieur en Amérique du nord (CONAHEC) – Consorcio para la Colaboración de la Educación Superior en América del Norte (CONAHEC)

Exec Dir Univ of Arizona, 1430 E 2nd St., PO Box 210069, Tucson AZ 85721-0300, USA. T. +15202013949. Fax +15206262675. E-mail: membership@conahec.org.
Main Website: https://www.conahec.org/

History 1994. Founded by *Mexican Association for International Education (AMPEI)* and (US) Western Interstate Commission for Higher Education. Registration: Internal Revenue Service, USA. **Aims** Enhance mutual understanding and cooperation by: fostering collaboration between institutions of higher education in Canada, Mexico and the USA and select Affiliate members outside the North American region; offer international education mobility programs for students, faculty and staff; organize conferences and events to promote collaboration among our member higher education institutions; work with governments and policy makers on issues relating to international higher education on behalf of membership. **Structure** General Assembly; Executive Committee; Advisory Board. **Languages** English, French, Portuguese, Spanish. **Staff** 1.50 FTE, paid. **Finance** Sources: government support; grants; members' dues. Funded from a variety of sources, including: Lumina Foundation for Education; University of Arizona (USA). **Activities** Events/meetings; networking/liaising; research/documentation. **Events** *Conference of the Americas on International Education / Congrès des Amériques sur l'éducation internationale / Congreso de las Américas sobre Educación Internacional* Santiago (Chile) 2021, *North American Higher Education Conference* USA 2020, *Conference of the Americas on International Education* Bogota (Colombia) 2019, *North American Higher Education Conference* Las Cruces, NM (USA) 2019, *Conference of the Americas on International Education* Montréal, QC (Canada) 2017. **Publications** *Understanding the Differences* (annual).

Members Colleges, universities and organizations (168) in 18 countries:
Argentina, Brazil, Burkina Faso, Canada, Chile, Colombia, Costa Rica, Dominican Rep, Ecuador, France, Guatemala, Honduras, Iceland, Korea Rep, Mexico, Puerto Rico, Spain, USA.
Included in the above, 10 organizations listed in this Yearbook:
Association of International Education Administrators (AIEA); Canadian Bureau for International Education (CBIE); Council for Advancement and Support of Education (CASE); Institute of International Education (IIE); Inter-American Organization for Higher Education (IOHE, #11442); Inter-American University of Puerto Rico; Laspau Inc.; Mexican Association for International Education (AMPEI); Texas A and M International University; Universidad Iberoamericana, México (UIA).

NGO Relations Founding member of: *Network of International Education Associations (NIEA, #17042).* Member of: *Conference of the Americas on International Education (CAIE, #04581); Global University Network for Innovation (GUNI, #10641); International Association of Universities (IAU, #12246).* Sister organization: *Asia-Pacific Association for International Education (APAIE, #01844).* [2022.05.04/XF4888/y/**F**]

♦ Consortium pour la recherche économique en Afrique (#00292)
♦ Consortium-réseau d'éducation à distance (#11428)
♦ Consortium of South Asian Think Tanks (unconfirmed)

♦ Consortium for Southeast Asian Studies in Asia (SEASIA) 04757

Contact Natl Chengchi Univ, No 64 Wanshou Rd, Weshan Dist, Taipei CITY 116, Taiwan. E-mail: museiniir@gmail.com.

History 2015. **Aims** Promote region-based Southeast Asian studies. **Structure** Governing Board; Executive Committee. Secretariat, headed by Executive Director. Committees (3): Conference; Education and Training; Research and Project. **Languages** English. **Staff** 4.00 FTE, paid. **Finance** Sponsored by governments and universities. **Activities** Events/meetings. **Events** *International Conference* Jakarta (Indonesia) 2022, *International Conference* Jakarta (Indonesia) 2021, *International Conference* Taipei (Taiwan) 2019, *International Conference* Bangkok (Thailand) 2017, *International Conference* Kyoto (Japan) 2015.

Members Institutions in 9 countries and territories:
Brunei Darussalam, China, Hong Kong, Indonesia, Japan, Philippines, Singapore, Taiwan, Thailand.
Included in the above, 5 organizations listed in this Yearbook:
Asia Research Institute (ARI); Centre for Asia-Pacific Area Studies (CAPAS); Centre for Southeast Asian Studies, Kyoto (CSEAS); ISEAS – Yusof Ishak Institute (ISEAS); School of International Studies, Beijing (SIS). [2022/XM7858/y/**D**]

♦ Consortium for Street Children (internationally oriented national body)
♦ Consortium for the Study of European Transition (no recent information)

♦ Consortium for the Sustainable Development of the Andean Ecoregion 04758

Consorcio para el Desarrollo Sostenible de la Ecoregión Andina (CONDESAN)

Coordinator Av La Molina 1895, Puesta No3 del Centro Internacional de la Papa, La Molina, Lima, Peru. T. +5116189400. Fax +5116189415. E-mail: condesan@condesan.org.
URL: http://www.condesan.org/

History Founded 1993, Lima (Peru), by *International Development Research Centre (IDRC, #13162), International Potato Center (#14627), CGIAR System Organization (CGIAR, #03843)* and other institutions from the Andean eco-region. **Aims** Mobilize the wealth of the Andes, so as to overcome poverty and social exclusion; create and share information and knowledge about the environment in Andean rural societies; promote policy dialogues with local actors, national governments and regional organisms; strengthen Andean human and institutional capital so as to promote new leaders for sustainable development in the Andes. **Structure** General Assembly. Steering Committee; Management Committee. Executive Director; Thematic Areas Coordinator. **Languages** English, Spanish. **Staff** 26.00 FTE, paid. **Finance** Government grants from European Union, Canada, Denmark, Germany, Netherlands, Spain, Switzerland. Also grant from: *International Bank for Reconstruction and Development (IBRD, #12317)* (World Bank); *Global Environment Facility (GEF, #10346); Deutsche Gesellschaft für Internationale Zusammenarbeit (GIZ); International Development Research Centre (IDRC, #13162); FAO (#09260).* **Activities** Advocacy/lobbying/activism; projects/programmes. **Events** *World Congress on Terraced Landscapes* Cusco (Peru) 2014, *Global Workshop on Long-Term Observatories of Mountain Social-Ecological Systems* Reno, NV (USA) 2014, *Workshop on experiences in the management of biosphere reserves in mountainous regions of Latin America* 1998, *Policy and rural development in the high Andes* Lima (Peru) 1996. **Publications** Books. **Information Services** *INFOANDINA* – electronic communications system to support research on natural resources management.

Members Partners in 7 countries:

Argentina, Bolivia, Chile, Colombia, Ecuador, Peru, Venezuela.
NGO Relations Hosts: *Mountain Forum (MF, #16861).* Member of: *Climate Technology Centre and Network (CTCN, #04023); International Mountain Society (IMS, #14190); Mountain Partnership (MP, #16862); Red de Bosques Andinos (#18637).* [2014/XD4750/F]

- ♦ Consortium for Sustainable Village-Based Development / see Village Earth
- ♦ Consortium of Universities for Global Health (internationally oriented national body)
- ♦ The Consortium / see World Chambers Network (#21270)
- ♦ Consorzeio CTM Altromercato – Consorzio 'Cooperazione Terzo Mondo' Altromercato (internationally oriented national body)
- ♦ Consorzio 'Cooperazione Terzo Mondo' Altromercato (internationally oriented national body)
- ♦ Consorzio Internazionale di Astrofisica Relativistica / see International Center for Relativistic Astrophysics (#12474)
- ♦ Consorzio Italiano di Solidarietà (internationally oriented national body)
- ♦ Constituency for Africa (internationally oriented national body)
- ♦ Constructeurs européens de locomotives thermiques et électriques (inactive)

♦ Constructing the Peace 04759

Contact Article 12, PO Box 7182, Montrose, DD10 9WW, UK. T. +441674674086. Fax +441674671227. E-mail: admin@article12.org.
History 2005, Melilla (Spain), following SALTO Euromed Peace Education Seminar. An alliance of civil society organizations. **Aims** Build a culture of freedom, justice, democracy and peace. **Activities** International Seminar. **IGO Relations** *Anna Lindh Euro-Mediterranean Foundation for the Dialogue between Cultures (Anna Lindh Foundation, #00847).* [2009/XM2318/F]

♦ Construction 2050 Alliance 04760

Contact c/o CECE, BluePoint, Boulevard August Reyers 80, 1030 Brussels, Belgium.
URL: https://euconstruction2050.eu/
History 17 Jun 2020, Belgium. Launched during 8th High Level Forum of Construction, organised by DG GROW of *European Commission (EC, #06633).* Set up on an initiative by *European Construction Industry Federation (#06766), European Builders Confederation (EBC, #06408), Construction Products Europe AISBL (#04761)* and *Committee for European Construction Equipment (CECE, #04254).* **Aims** Advance the needs and priorities of the wider construction and built-environment sector at EU level. **Structure** Steering Group.
Members EU associations (49):
- *Aggregates Europe (UEPG, #00558);*
- *Association of Plastics Manufacturers in Europe (Plastics Europe, #02862);*
- *Build Europe (#03350);*
- *Bureau international du béton manufacturé (BIBM, #03363);*
- *CEMBUREAU – The European Cement Association (CEMBUREAU, #03634);*
- *Committee for European Construction Equipment (CECE, #04254);*
- *Construction Products Europe AISBL (#04761);*
- *European Alliance of Companies for Energy Efficiency in Buildings (EuroACE, #05865);*
- *European Aluminium (#05893);*
- *European Asphalt Pavement Association (EAPA, #05920);*
- *European Association for External Thermal Insulation Composite Systems (EAE, #06035);*
- *European Association for Panels and Profiles (PPA-Europe, #06142);*
- *European Association of Plaster and Plaster Product Manufacturers (EUROGYPSUM, #06152);*
- *European Builders Confederation (EBC, #06408);*
- *European Calcium Silicate Producers Association (ECSPA, #06430);*
- *European Ceramic Industry Association (CERAME-UNIE, #06506);*
- *European Construction Industry Federation (#06766);*
- *European Council of Civil Engineers (ECCE, #06810);*
- *European Demolition Association (EDA, #06902);*
- *European Expanded Clay Association (EXCA, #07013);*
- *European Federation for Construction Chemicals (EFCC, #07088);*
- *European Federation of Associations of Locks and Builders Hardware Manufacturers (ARGE, #07054);*
- *European Federation of Building and Woodworkers (EFBWW, #07065);*
- *European Federation of Concrete Admixtures Associations (EFCA, #07085);*
- *European Federation of Engineering Consultancy Associations (EFCA, #07109);*
- *European Floor Coverings Association (EUFCA, #07271);*
- *European General Galvanizers Association (EGGA, #07383);*
- *European Heat Pump Association (EHPA, #07469);*
- *European Insulation Manufacturers Association (EURIMA, #07577);*
- *European Lime Association (EuLA, #07699);*
- *European Mortar Industry Organization (EMO, #07822);*
- *European Panel Federation (EPF, #08137);*
- *European Plastics Converters (EuPC, #08216);*
- *European Ready Mixed Concrete Organization (ERMCO, #08330);*
- *European Rental Association (ERA, #08358);*
- *European Trade Association of PVC Window System Supplies (EPPA, #08924);*
- *EuropeOn (#09166);*
- *Fédération européenne des industries de colles et adhésifs (FEICA, #09572);*
- *Federation of European Rigid Polyurethane Foam Associations (PU Europe, #09538);*
- *GCP Europe (#10085);*
- *Glass for Europe (#10157);*
- *Housing Europe – The European Federation for Public Cooperative and Social Housing (Housing Europe, #10956);*
- *International Union of Property Owners (#15804);*
- *METALS FOR BUILDINGS (#16737);*
- *Royal Institution of Chartered Surveyors (RICS, #18991);*
- *SolarPower Europe (#19676);*
- *The European Plastic Pipes and Fittings Association (TEPPFA, #08215);*
- *Union internationale des entrepreneurs de peinture (UNIEP, #20425);*
- *VinylPlus (#20780).*

[2022/AA1290/y/E]

♦ Construction Products Europe AISBL 04761

Office Manager Bd du Souverain 68, Box 1, 1170 Brussels, Belgium. T. +3224634957. E-mail: info@construction-products.eu.
Dir Gen address not obtained.
URL: https://www.construction-products.eu/
History 1988. Former names and other names: *Council of European Producers of Materials for Construction (CEPMC)* – former; *Conseil Européen des Producteurs de Matériaux de Construction* – former; *Vereinigung Europäischer Baustoffhersteller* – former. Registration: Banque Carrefour des Entreprises, No/ID: 0465.221.205, Start date: 26 Aug 1998, Belgium; EU Transparency Register, No/ID: 48010783162-91, Start date: 1 Feb 2010. **Aims** Facilitate sustainable competitive growth of the European construction products industry by promoting efficient *housing* and *infrastructure* solutions through consensus and dialogue with European institutions and societal stakeholders. **Structure** General Assembly; Executive Board. **Languages** English. **Staff** 3.00 FTE, paid. **Finance** Sources: members' dues. Annual budget: 500,000 EUR (2021). **Activities** Events/meetings. **Events** *Digital Construction – Back to basics* Brussels (Belgium) 2022, *Digital Construction* Brussels (Belgium) 2022, *Leveraging Our EU Representation for a More Competitive Construction Industry* Brussels (Belgium) 2022, *Taxonomy Regulation and Construction* Brussels (Belgium) 2021. **Publications** *Newsletter* (10 a year). File Status Reports; position papers; information documents.
Members Full national federations in 12 countries:
Austria, Belgium, Denmark, Finland, France, Germany, Ireland, Netherlands, Norway, Sweden, Switzerland, UK.
Full organizations listed in this Yearbook (8):
CEMBUREAU – The European Cement Association (CEMBUREAU, #03634); Concrete Europe (#04433); European Autoclaved Aerated Concrete Association (EAACA, #06297); European Calcium Silicate Producers Association (ECSPA, #06430); European Ceramic Industry Association (CERAME-UNIE, #06506); European Floor Coverings Association (EUFCA, #07271); European Insulation Manufacturers Association (EURIMA, #07577); METALS FOR BUILDINGS (#16737).
Associate Members (35):
- *Aggregates Europe (UEPG, #00558);*
- *Association of Plastics Manufacturers in Europe (Plastics Europe, #02862);*
- *Bureau international du béton manufacturé (BIBM, #03363);*
- *Comité européen de l'outillage (CEO, #04163);*
- *Confédération européenne des industries du bois (CEI Bois, #04545);*
- *European Aluminium (#05893);*
- *European Association for External Thermal Insulation Composite Systems (EAE, #06035);*
- *European Association for Panels and Profiles (PPA-Europe, #06142);*
- *European Association for Passive Fire Protection (EAPFP, #06143);*
- *European Association of Plaster and Plaster Product Manufacturers (EUROGYPSUM, #06152);*
- *European Cellulose Insulation Association (ECIA, #06460);*
- *European Consortium of Anchors Producers (ECAP, #06749);*
- *European Copper Institute (ECI, #06796);*
- *European Council of Vinyl Manufacturers (ECVM, #06849);*
- *European Expanded Clay Association (EXCA, #07013);*
- *European Extruded Polystyrene Insulation Board Association (EXIBA, #07019);*
- *European Federation for Construction Chemicals (EFCC, #07088);*
- *European Federation of Associations of Locks and Builders Hardware Manufacturers (ARGE, #07054);*
- *European Federation of Concrete Admixtures Associations (EFCA, #07085);*
- *European Federation of Fibre-Cement Manufacturers (EFFCM, #07120);*
- *European Lime Association (EuLA, #07699);*
- *European Manufacturers of Expanded Polystyrene (EUMEPS, #07732);*
- *European Mortar Industry Organization (EMO, #07822);*
- *European Panel Federation (EPF, #08137);*
- *European Phenolic Foam Association (EPFA, #08199);*
- *European Plastics Converters (EuPC, #08216);*
- *European Steel Association (EUROFER, #08835);*
- *European Trade Association of PVC Window System Supplies (EPPA, #08924);*
- *European Waterproofing Association (EWA, #09084);*
- *Fédération européenne des industries de colles et adhésifs (FEICA, #09572);*
- *Federation of European Rigid Polyurethane Foam Associations (PU Europe, #09538);*
- *Glass for Europe (#10157);*
- International Zinc Association Europe (IZA-Europe);
- *Orgalim – Europe's Technology Industries (#17794);*
- *The European Plastic Pipes and Fittings Association (TEPPFA, #08215).*

NGO Relations Member of (2): *Construction 2050 Alliance (#04760); Industry4Europe (#11181).* Cooperates with (1): *Covenant of Mayors for Climate and Energy (#04939).* [2022.07.07/XD2792/y/D]

- ♦ Construction Sector Transparency Initiative / see CoST – the Infrastructure Transparency Initiative (#04855)
- ♦ CONSUASA – Confederación Sudamericana de Actividades Subacuaticas (no recent information)
- ♦ **CONSUBASQUET** Confederación Sudamericana de Básquetbol (#04482)
- ♦ CONSUBE – Confederación Sudamericana de Béisbol (inactive)
- ♦ **CONSUDATLE** Confederación Sudamericana de Atletismo (#19701)
- ♦ **CONSUDE** Consejo Sudamericano de Deportes (#04726)

♦ CONSULEGIS – International Network of Law Firms 04762

Managing Dir Poststrasse 14/16 III, 20354 Hamburg, Germany. T. +4915236381171. E-mail: office@consulegis.com.
URL: http://www.consulegis.com/
History Founded 1990, Germany, as a *European Economic Interest Grouping (EEIG, #06960).* **Aims** Offer members and their clients effective hands-on support, collaboration and networks across the world. **Structure** General Meeting (annual); Board; Practice, Sector and Regional Groups; Committees. **Languages** English, German, Italian, Spanish. **Staff** 2.00 FTE, paid; 10.00 FTE, voluntary. **Finance** Sources: members' dues. **Activities** Events/meetings; guidance/assistance/consulting; knowledge management/information dissemination; networking/liaising. **Events** *European Regional Meeting* Bordeaux (France) 2020, *Autumn Conference* Asunción (Paraguay) 2019, *Annual General Meeting and Spring Conference* Madrid (Spain) 2019, *European Regional Meeting* Mainz (Germany) 2019, *Autumn Conference* Prague (Czechia) 2018. **Publications** *Class Actions Around the World by Consulegis ILASG* (2019) in English – Welcome to the latest edition of the Newsletter of the CONSULEGIS International Litigation and Arbitration Specialist Group ("ILASG"). We hope you will find useful the articles from around the world on Class Actions.; *Director's liability in 14 jurisdictions by Consulegis ILASG* (2019) in English – We are pleased to share with you the latest Newsletter of the Consulegis International Litigation and Arbitration Specialist Group ("ILASG").; *Corporate Q&As.* Investors guides; press releases; articles; interviews. **Members** Over 90 member firms totaling about 1,900 lawyers in 46 countries. Membership countries not specified. **NGO Relations** Fundación Solidaridad (Paraguay). [2021.09.01/XM3846/F]

- ♦ Consultation on Church Union / see Churches United In Christ
- ♦ Consultation européenne sur les réfugiés et les exilés / see European Council on Refugees and Exiles (#06839)
- ♦ Consultation of Heads of Water Management Organizations (meeting series)
- ♦ Consultation internationale sur les maladies urologiques (#12928)
- ♦ Consultation mondiale de l'industrie de la santé animale / see Health for Animals (#10870)
- ♦ Consultative Committee of the Bars and Law Societies of the European Community / see Council of Bars and Law Societies of Europe (#04871)
- ♦ Consultative Committee of Bars and National Associations of the Six States of the EEC / see Council of Bars and Law Societies of Europe (#04871)
- ♦ Consultative Committee of European Prosecutors (#04685)

♦ Consultative Committee on Industrial Change 04763

Commission consultative des mutations industrielles (CCMI)
Pres c/o EESC, Rue Belliard 99, 1040 Brussels, Belgium. T. +3225469432. E-mail: ccmi2@eesc.europa.eu.
URL: http://eesc.europa.eu/sections/ccmi/index_en.asp
History 24 Oct 2002, by *European Economic and Social Committee (EESC, #06963).* Continues the work of *Consultative Committee of the European Coal and Steel Community (inactive),* not limited to the coal and steel sectors but encompasses all aspects relating to industrial change. Previously also known under the English acronym *CCIC.* **Aims** With a special emphasis on anticipation, pre-emption and analysis, ensure positive common approaches to the management of industrial change from an economic, social, territorial and environmental point of view; promote coordination and coherence of Community action in relation to the main industrial changes in the context of the enlarged EU; ensure balance between the need for socially acceptable change and the retention of a competitive edge for EU industry. **Structure** Committee, comprising 48 EESC members and 48 external delegates. Bureau, including Chairman (EESC member) and Co-Chairman (delegate).
Members Representatives in the 27 member countries of the European Union:
Austria, Belgium, Bulgaria, Cyprus, Czechia, Denmark, Estonia, Finland, France, Germany, Greece, Hungary, Ireland, Italy, Latvia, Lithuania, Luxembourg, Malta, Netherlands, Poland, Portugal, Romania, Slovakia, Slovenia, Spain, Sweden, UK.
[2018/XE4594/t/E*]

- ♦ Consultative Committee for Reading Facilities for Prisoners of War and Internees (inactive)

♦ Consultative Committee for Space Data Systems (CCSDS) 04764

Contact address not obtained. E-mail: secretariat@mailman.ccsds.org.
URL: http://public.ccsds.org/
History Founded 1982. **Aims** Serve as forum for discussion of common problems in the development and operation of space data systems. **Structure** Management Council; Engineering Steering Group. **Languages** English. **Activities** Networking/liaising; events/meetings. **Events** *Fall Meeting* Berlin (Germany) 2018, *Plenary Meeting* Pasadena, CA (USA) 2015, *Plenary Meeting* London (UK) 2014, *Plenary Meeting* Noordwijkerhout (Netherlands) 2014, *Plenary Meeting* Bordeaux (France) 2013. **Publications** Recommended standards; recommended practices; information reports.
Members Full; observer; commercial; liaison. Space agencies, organizations and institutes (157) in 26 countries:
Australia, Austria, Belgium, Brazil, Canada, China, Denmark, France, Germany, Greece, Hungary, India, Israel, Italy, Japan, Korea Rep, Norway, Pakistan, Russia, South Africa, Spain, Sweden, Switzerland, Taiwan, UK, USA.

Included in the above, 5 organizations listed in this Yearbook:
Committee on Space Research (COSPAR, #04287); Commonwealth Scientific and Industrial Research Organization (CSIRO); European Space Operations Centre (ESOC, #08800); European Telecommunications Satellite Organization (EUTELSAT IGO, #08896); World Meteorological Organization (WMO, #21649).
[2017/XJ4407/y/**E**]

♦ Consultative Council of the Arab Maghreb Union 04765

Conseil consultatif de l'Union du Maghreb arabe

SG Villa Bouguerra, 54 ave Franklin Roosevelt, Algiers, Algeria. T. +21321230028. Fax +21321230027.
URL: http://www.maghrebarabe.org/

History Founded 17 Feb 1989, within the framework of *Arab Maghreb Union (AMU, #01004)*. Also referred to in French as *Conseil consultatif maghrébin*; *Parlement de l'Union du Maghreb*. **Aims** Contribute to the construction of UMA; promote unification of community *legislation* in Maghreb countries. **Structure** General Assembly; Bureau; Standing Committees (6). Includes Children's Parliament of the Maghreb, set up 12 Jul 2008. **Languages** Arabic. **Staff** 15.00 FTE, paid. **Finance** Members' dues. **Activities** Guidance/assistance/consulting; events/meetings. **Events** *Session* Algiers (Algeria) 2010, *Session* Algiers (Algeria) 2008, *Conference* Tripoli (Libyan AJ) 2008, *Conference* Algiers (Algeria) 2007, *Conference* Nouakchott (Mauritania) 2007. **Publications** Conference reports.
Members Full; Associate (5); Observer. Full in 5 countries:
Algeria, Libya, Mauritania, Morocco, Tunisia.
Observers (7):
African Parliamentary Union (APU, #00412); Arab Inter-Parliamentary Union (Arab IPU, #00995); Arab Parliament (#01023) (transitional); *Association of Senates, Shoora and Equivalent Councils in Africa and the Arab World (ASSECAA, #02913); Inter-Parliamentary Union (IPU, #15961); Parliamentary Assembly of the Mediterranean (PAM, #18212); Parliamentary Union of the OIC Member States (PUIC, #18220).*
IGO Relations *European Parliament (EP, #08146); European Union (EU, #08967).* **NGO Relations** *Association of Secretaries General of Parliaments (ASGP, #02911).* [2018.09.18/XE3026/y/**E**]

- ♦ Consultative Council of Cultural Workers of the CIS / see Consultative Council of Cultural Workers' Unions (#04766)

♦ Consultative Council of Cultural Workers' Unions (CCCWU) 04766

Gen Sec Zemlianoy Val 64-2, Office 703, Moscow MOSKVA, Russia, 109004. T. +74959150479. Fax +74959150479. E-mail: consind.cultura@gmail.com.

History Jan 1992, as *Consultative Council of Cultural Workers' Unions of Independent States*, by national workers' unions of 10 CIS republics. Also known as *Consultative Council of Cultural Workers of the CIS*. Statutes revised 16 Jun 1999, when current title was adopted. Registered in accordance with Russian law. **Aims** As an international *trade union* association: act as a permanent forum for exchange of experience and information; preserve and promote relations among trade unions of workers in the cultural sector; consolidate their activities on the basis of mutual recognition of state sovereignty, equality and furtherance of mutually beneficial cooperation; protect and further cultural workers' professional, economic and social rights and interests; ensure dissemination of progressive experience of such protection among affiliated unions; represent affiliates in international institutions; assist affiliated unions in establishing and developing contacts and joining kindred international and regional trade union federations. **Structure** Conference of Cultural Workers' Union of Independent States (every 5 years); Council; Permanent Head Office in Moscow (Russia). **Languages** Russian. **Staff** 2.00 FTE, paid. **Finance** Members' dues. Support for events from: sister trade union federations; European Commission; *Friedrich-Ebert-Stiftung (FES)*; Union to Union Foundation (Sweden). **Activities** Events/meetings; training/education. **Events** *Conference of cultural workers unions of independent states* Moscow (Russia) 2004.
Members National Cultural Workers' Unions (11) in 11 countries:
Armenia, Azerbaijan, Belarus, Georgia, Kazakhstan, Kyrgyzstan, Lithuania, Moldova, Russia, Tajikistan, Ukraine.
IGO Relations *Council of Europe (CE, #04881); European Commission (EC, #06633).* **NGO Relations** Member of: *General Confederation of Trade Unions (GCTU, #10108).* Cooperates with: *International Federation of Actors (#13337); International Federation of Musicians (#13486); UNI Global Union (#20338).*
[2019.02.18/XD6171/**D**]

- ♦ Consultative Council of Cultural Workers' Unions of Independent States / see Consultative Council of Cultural Workers' Unions (#04766)

♦ Consultative Council of European Judges (CCJE) 04767

Conseil consultatif de juges européens

Main Office c/o Council of Europe, DG Human Rights – Rule of Law, Avenue de l'Europe, 67075 Strasbourg CEDEX, France.
URL: http://www.coe.int/ccje/

History 2000. Established by *Council of Europe (CE, #04881)* as a consultative body to *Committee of Ministers of the Council of Europe (#04273)*. **Aims** Act as advisory body to the Committee of Ministers in preparing opinions for that Committee on general questions concerning independence, impartiality and competence of judges. **Structure** Consultative Council (meets at annual Plenary Meeting); Bureau; Secretariat. **Languages** English, French. **Activities** Contributes to the implementation of the framework global action plan for judges in Europe. Provides practical assistance to enable States to comply with CoE standards concerning judges. Prepares texts or opinions at the request of the Committee of Ministers or other CoE bodies. Encourages partnerships in the judicial field involving courts, judges and judges' associations. **Events** *Plenary Meeting* London (UK) 2015, *Conference of the Presidents of the Courts of Appeal of the European Union* Turku (Finland) 2015, *Plenary Meeting* Strasbourg (France) 2014, *Plenary Meeting* Strasbourg (France) 2013, *Plenary Meeting* Paris (France) 2012.
Members Participating states: all members states of the Council of Europe (47):
Albania, Armenia, Austria, Azerbaijan, Belgium, Bosnia-Herzegovina, Bulgaria, Croatia, Cyprus, Czechia, Denmark, Estonia, Finland, France, Georgia, Germany, Greece, Hungary, Iceland, Ireland, Italy, Latvia, Liechtenstein, Lithuania, Luxembourg, Malta, Moldova, Monaco, Montenegro, Netherlands, North Macedonia, Norway, Poland, Portugal, Romania, Russia, Serbia, Slovakia, Slovenia, Spain, Sweden, Switzerland, Türkiye, UK, Ukraine.
Observers: governments of 2 countries:
Canada, Japan.
Observers (5):
Association of European Administrative Judges (AEAJ, #02497); Council of Bars and Law Societies of Europe (CCBE, #04871); European Judicial Training Network (EJTN, #07617); European Network of Councils for the Judiciary (ENCJ, #07886); Magistrats européens pour la démocratie et les libertés (MEDEL, #16546).
IGO Relations *European Commission (EC, #06633)* and General Secretariat of *Council of the European Union (#04895)* may take part. [2023/XJ3990/**E***]

- ♦ Consultative Council of European Prosecutors / see Conseil consultatif de procureurs européens (#04685)
- ♦ Consultative Council to the World Constitutional Convention (inactive)

♦ Consultative Group to Assist the Poor (CGAP) 04768

Groupe consultatif d'assistance aux plus pauvres – Grupo Consultativo de Ayuda a la Población Mas Pobre

Main Office 1818 H Street NW, 7th Floor, MSN F3K-306, Washington DC 20006, USA. E-mail: cgap@worldbank.org.
URL: http://www.cgap.org/

History Jun 1995. Former names and other names: *Consultative Group to Assist the Poorest* – former. **Aims** Improve the lives of poor people by spurring innovations and advancing knowledge and solutions that promote responsible, sustainable, inclusive *financial* markets. **Structure** Council of Governors; Executive Committee; Operational Team. **Staff** 49.00 FTE, paid. **Events** *Annual Meeting* Urubamba (Peru) 2014, *Annual Meeting* Urubamba (Peru) 2014, *Annual Meeting* Amsterdam (Netherlands) 2013, *Annual Meeting* Hyderabad (India) 2008, *Annual Meeting* Hyderabad (India) 2008. **Publications** *CGAP Newsletter*.
Members Organizations and government ministries (37):
Australia, Canada, Denmark, Germany, Italy, Japan, Luxembourg, Netherlands.

- *African Development Bank (ADB, #00283);*
- *Agence française de développement (AFD);*
- *Bill and Melinda Gates Foundation (BMGF);*
- *CDC Group;*
- Credit Suisse;
- *Deutsche Gesellschaft für Internationale Zusammenarbeit (GIZ);*
- *European Bank for Reconstruction and Development (EBRD, #06315);*
- *European Commission (EC, #06633);*
- Flourish;
- IDB Lab;
- *ILO (#11123);*
- *Inter-American Development Bank (IDB, #11427);*
- *International Finance Corporation (IFC, #13597);*
- *International Fund for Agricultural Development (IFAD, #13692);*
- *Investeringsfonden for Udviklingslande (IFU);*
- Jersey Overseas Aid;
- *Korea International Cooperation Agency (KOICA);*
- *Kreditanstalt für Wiederaufbau (KfW);*
- *Mastercard Foundation;*
- *Norwegian Agency for Development Cooperation (Norad);*
- Platform of Inclusive Finance;
- *Swedish International Development Cooperation Agency (Sida);*
- *Swiss Agency for Development and Cooperation (SDC);*
- *The World Bank Group (#21218);*
- *UNDP (#20292);*
- *United Nations Capital Development Fund (UNCDF, #20524);*
- *United States Agency for International Development (USAID).*

IGO Relations *Arab Monetary Fund (AMF, #01009); Global Partnership for Effective Development Co-operation (GPEDC, #10532).* **NGO Relations** Member of (1): *European Microfinance Platform (E-MFP, #07793).* Partner of (2): *Access to Insurance Initiative (A2ii, #00051)* (Founding); *Responsible Finance Forum (RFF).*
[2020/XJ9436/y/**E**]

- ♦ Consultative Group to Assist the Poorest / see Consultative Group to Assist the Poor (#04768)
- ♦ Consultative Group on International Agricultural Research / see CGIAR System Organization (#03843)
- ♦ Consultative Group on International Economic and Monetary Affairs / see Group of Thirty (#10790)
- ♦ Consultative Group of Nordic Cooperatives / see Föreningarna Nordens Förbund (#09859)
- ♦ Consultative Meeting of Contracting Parties to the London Convention / see Consultative Meeting of Contracting Parties to the London Convention/Meeting of Contracting Parties to the London Protocol (#04769)

♦ Consultative Meeting of Contracting Parties to the London Convention/Meeting of Contracting Parties to the London Protocol 04769

Secretariat Office London Convention/Protocol and Ocean Affairs, c/o IMO, 4 Albert Embankment, London, SE1 7SR, UK. T. +442077357611. Fax +442075873210. E-mail: olcp@imo.org.
URL: https://www.imo.org/en/OurWork/Environment/Pages/London-Convention-Protocol.aspx

History 18 Dec 1975, London (UK). Established as governing body of *Convention on the Prevention of Marine Pollution by Dumping of Wastes and other Matter (LDC, 1972)*, London Convention 1972. Since 30 Oct 2006, governing body of *1996 Protocol to the Convention on the Prevention of Marine Pollution by Dumping of Wastes and other Matter (LC Prot 1996, 1996)* (London Protocol). Former names and other names: *Consultative Meeting of Contracting Parties to the London Convention* – former. **Aims** Prevent and control marine pollution caused by dumping of wastes and other matter at sea. **Structure** Consultative Meeting of Contracting Parties (annual, in London), since Convention came into force, 30 Aug 1975. Meeting of Contracting Parties to the Protocol (annual), since it came into force, 24 Mar 2006. Standing Scientific Groups, one for convention and protocol. Compliance Group is set up under the Protocol. Secretariat maintained by *International Maritime Organization (IMO, #14102).* **Languages** Arabic, Chinese, English, French, Russian, Spanish. **Staff** 3.00 FTE, paid. **Finance** All work carried out within the framework of both instruments is, upon request of the governing bodies, carried out by IMO and covered by IMO budget. Special projects and technical cooperation activities funded by voluntary contributions from Contracting Parties and occasionally provided by IMO Integrated Technical Cooperation Programme. **Activities** Monitoring/evaluation; networking/liaising; politics/policy/regulatory. **Events** *Joint Consultative Meeting of Contracting Parties to the London Convention, and Meeting of Contracting Parties to the London Protocol* London (UK) 2022, *Annual Consultative Meeting* London (UK) 2021, *Meeting of Contracting Parties* London (UK) 2021, *Annual Consultative Meeting* London (UK) 2020, *Meeting of Contracting Parties* London (UK) 2020. **Publications** Reports (available from IMO) of governing bodies or scientific groups.
Members Contracting Parties to Convention, governments of 87 countries:
Afghanistan, Antigua-Barbuda, Argentina, Australia, Azerbaijan, Barbados, Belarus, Belgium, Benin, Bolivia, Brazil, Bulgaria, Canada, Cape Verde, Chile, China, Congo DR, Costa Rica, Côte d'Ivoire, Croatia, Cuba, Cyprus, Denmark, Dominican Rep, Egypt, Equatorial Guinea, Finland, France, Gabon, Germany, Greece, Guatemala, Haiti, Honduras, Hungary, Iceland, Iran Islamic Rep, Ireland, Italy, Jamaica, Japan, Jordan, Kenya, Kiribati, Korea Rep, Libya, Luxembourg, Malta, Mexico, Monaco, Montenegro, Morocco, Nauru, Netherlands, New Zealand, Nigeria, Norway, Oman, Pakistan, Panama, Papua New Guinea, Peru, Philippines, Poland, Portugal, Russia, Serbia, Seychelles, Sierra Leone, Slovenia, Solomon Is, South Africa, Spain, St Lucia, St Vincent-Grenadines, Suriname, Sweden, Switzerland, Syrian AR, Tanzania UR, Tonga, Tunisia, UK, Ukraine, United Arab Emirates, USA, Vanuatu.
Contracting Parties to the Protocol, governments of 53 countries:
Angola, Antigua-Barbuda, Australia, Barbados, Belgium, Bulgaria, Canada, Chile, China, Congo Brazzaville, Denmark, Egypt, Estonia, Finland, France, Georgia, Germany, Ghana, Guatemala, Guyana, Iceland, Iran Islamic Rep, Ireland, Italy, Japan, Kenya, Korea Rep, Luxembourg, Madagascar, Marshall Is, Mexico, Morocco, Netherlands, New Zealand, Nigeria, Norway, Peru, Philippines, Saudi Arabia, Sierra Leone, Slovenia, South Africa, Spain, St Kitts-Nevis, Suriname, Sweden, Switzerland, Tonga, Trinidad-Tobago, UK, Uruguay, Vanuatu, Yemen.
IGO Relations Observer status with (10): *Baltic Marine Environment Protection Commission – Helsinki Commission (HELCOM, #03126); Comisión Permanente del Pacífico Sur (CPPS, #04141); European Commission (EC, #06633); International Atomic Energy Agency (IAEA, #12294); International Bank for Reconstruction and Development (IBRD, #12317)* (World Bank); *International Council for the Exploration of the Sea (ICES, #13021); OECD (#17693); OSPAR Commission for the Protection of the Marine Environment of the North-East Atlantic (OSPAR Commission, #17905); Secretariat of the Pacific Regional Environment Programme (SPREP, #19205); United Nations (UN, #20515).* **NGO Relations** Observer status with (3): *BIMCO (#03236); Oil Companies International Marine Forum (OCIMF, #17709); Pew Charitable Trusts.* [2022.10.24/XF9896/**F***]

- ♦ Consultative Sub-Committee on the Economic Aspects of Rice / see Intergovernmental Group on Rice (#11493)
- ♦ Consulting Engineers in the Nordic Countries (no recent information)
- ♦ Consumer Cooperative International / see Consumer Co-operatives Worldwide (#04770)

♦ Consumer Co-operatives Worldwide (CCW) 04770

Secretariat Rue du Trône 4, 1000 Brussels, Belgium.
URL: http://www.ccw.coop/en/

History 1969, as *ICA Consumer Committee – Comité des consommateurs de l'ACI*, also referred to as *ICA Committee for Consumer Co-operatives – Comité de l'ACI pour les coopératives des consommateurs.* Subsequently referred to as *International Consumer Co-operatives Organization.* Title again changed, Aug 1999, to *International Cooperatives Consumer Organization (ICCO)*, when merged with *International Organization for Consumer Cooperative Distributive Trade (INTER-COOP, inactive).* Later known as *Consumer Cooperative International (CCI).* A specialized body of *International Co-operative Alliance (ICA, #12944).* Registered in accordance with Belgian law. **Aims** Initiate discussion on the crucial problems of cooperative consumer policy; communicate information to ICA members and to organizations outside the cooperative movement; advise on consumer matters to new consumer cooperatives; cooperate with other ICA specialized bodies; represent cooperative consumer interests to other international organizations within or outside the cooperative movement; collaborate with governmental and nongovernmental agencies for consumer affairs; provide information on matters of interest to consumers, such as consumer *protection*, through the press and other media. **Structure** General Assembly; Executive Committee. **Languages** English. **Finance** Members' dues: Swiss Fr 500 – 2,000. **Activities** Events/meetings; training/education. **Events** *General Meeting* Cartagena de Indias (Colombia) 2005, *Successful consumer cooperatives competing on our cooperative values* Cartagena de Indias (Colombia) 2005, *Annual Seminar* Warsaw (Poland) 2005, *Annual seminar* Warsaw (Poland) 2004, *Annual seminar* Oslo (Norway) 2003. **Publications** *CCW Newsletter*.

Members Cooperative organizations in 29 countries:
Argentina, Brazil, Bulgaria, Canada, China, Cyprus, Czechia, Denmark, Finland, France, Germany, Hungary, Iceland, India, Israel, Italy, Japan, Korea Rep, Norway, Portugal, Romania, Russia, Slovakia, Spain, Sri Lanka, Sweden, UK, Ukraine, USA.
[2016/XE1340/**E**]

♦ Consumer Culture Theory Consortium (CCTC) 04771

Secretariat address not obtained. E-mail: cctexecsec@gmail.com.
URL: http://cctweb.org/

History Current constitution and bylaws adopted May 2020. Registration: 501(c)(3), USA. **Aims** Promote research, education, and other activities that contribute to the understanding of consumer culture in business and society. **Structure** Board of Directors. **Finance** Sources: members' dues. **Activities** Awards/prizes/competitions; events/meetings; research/documentation. **Events** *Conference* Montréal, QC (Canada) 2019.
[2020/AA0405/**C**]

♦ The Consumer Goods Forum (CGF) 04772

Communications Dir 47-53 Rue Raspail, 92300 Levallois-Perret, France. T. +33182009595. Fax +33182009596.
URL: http://www.theconsumergoodsforum.com/

History 1953, Ostend (Belgium). Current title adopted when *Global Commerce Initiative (GCI, inactive)* merged into the organization. Former names and other names: *International Association of Chain Stores* – former; *Comité international des entreprises à succursales* – former; *Comité Internacional de Sociedades con Sucursales* – former; *Internationale Vereinigung der Filialbetriebe* – former; *CIES – The Food Business Forum* – former; *The Consumer Goods Forum – The Global Network Serving Shopper and Consumer Needs* – full title (Jun 2009). Registration: France. **Aims** Bring consumer goods retailers and manufacturers together globally; help the world's retailers and consumer goods manufacturers to collaborate, alongside other key stakeholders, to secure consumer trust and drive positive change, including greater efficiency; drive positive change and help address key challenges impacting the industry, including environmental and social sustainability, health, food safety and product data accuracy. **Structure** General Assembly (every 2 years); Board of Directors. Regional Offices (4): Americas; Asia-Pacific; China; Latin America. **Languages** Chinese, English, French, German, Japanese, Spanish. **Staff** 40.00 FTE, paid. **Finance** Sources: meeting proceeds; members' dues; sponsorship. **Activities** Awareness raising; capacity building; certification/accreditation; events/meetings; knowledge management/information dissemination; networking/liaising; projects/programmes; standards/guidelines. **Events** *Conference* Atlanta, GA (USA) 2023, *Global Summit* Kyoto (Japan) 2023, *GFSI : Global Food Safety Initiative Conference* Barcelona (Spain) 2022, *Future Leaders Congress* New York, NY (USA) 2021, *Sustainable Retail Summit* Paris (France) 2021. **Publications** *Positive Actions* (6 a year). Annual Report; reports; studies; booklets; brochures; infographics; videos. more details: https://www.theconsumergoodsforum.com/news-resources/. **Information Services** *Media Centre.*

Members Association; educational institution; manufacturer; retailer – wholesaler; service providers. Members in 48 countries and territories:
Argentina, Australia, Austria, Belgium, Bermuda, Bolivia, Canada, China, Colombia, Croatia, Denmark, Dominican Rep, Egypt, Finland, France, Germany, Honduras, Hong Kong, Indonesia, Ireland, Israel, Italy, Japan, Korea Rep, Kuwait, Luxembourg, Mexico, Netherlands, New Zealand, Paraguay, Peru, Philippines, Poland, Portugal, Russia, Saudi Arabia, Singapore, Slovenia, South Africa, Spain, Sri Lanka, Sweden, Switzerland, Thailand, Türkiye, UK, United Arab Emirates, USA.
Included in the above, 9 organizations listed in this Yearbook:
amfori (#00797); Consumer Specialty Products Association (CSPA, #04774); EuroCommerce (EC, #05665); European Brands Association (#06397); European Federation of Corrugated Board Manufacturers (#07091); FoodDrinkEurope (#09841); Food Industry Asia (FIA); GS1 (#10809); International Egg Commission (IEC, #13245).

IGO Relations Observer status with (1): *Codex Alimentarius Commission (CAC, #04081).* **NGO Relations** Member of (2): *ECR Community (#05340); International Accreditation Forum (IAF, #11584).* Partnerships in Asia with: China Chain Store and Franchise Association (CCFA); Japan Chain Stores Association (JCA).
[2023.01.18/XC1261/y/**C**]

♦ The Consumer Goods Forum – The Global Network Serving Shopper and Consumer Needs / see The Consumer Goods Forum (#04772)

♦ Consumers International (CI) 04773

Dir Gen 24 Highbury Crescent, London, N5 1RX, UK. T. +442072266663. Fax +442073540607. E-mail: consint@consint.org.
URL: http://www.consumersinternational.org/

History 1 Apr 1960, The Hague (Netherlands). Constitution amended: Mar 1975; Jul 1984. Former names and other names: *International Office of Consumers Unions* – former (1 Apr 1960); *International Organization of Consumers Unions (IOCU)* – former (Jan 1995); *Organisation internationale des unions de consommateurs* – former (Jan 1995); *Organización Internacional de Asociaciones de Consumidores* – former (Jan 1995). Registration: Netherlands. **Aims** Promote a fairer society by defending *rights* of all consumers, especially the poor, marginalized and disadvantaged; support and strengthen members and the consumer movement in general; campaign at international level for policies that respect consumer concerns, focusing on specific areas such as food, standards and trade; seek full incorporation of consumer policy into *trade* and development agreements negotiated at international and regional levels. Promote basic consumer rights to: basic needs; safety; information; choice; representation; redress; education; a healthy environment. **Structure** General Assembly, consisting of one voting delegate from each full member, elects Council, comprising 20 full members. Executive Committee. Regional Offices (4): Accra (Ghana); Kuala Lumpur (Malaysia); Santiago (Chile); London (UK). **Languages** English, French, Spanish. **Staff** 50.00 FTE, paid. **Finance** Sources: grants; international organizations; members' dues; sale of publications. Special grants from member organizations of: Belgium; Australia; UK; USA; Netherlands. Supported by: *Christian Aid; DANIDA; Department for International Development (DFID, inactive); European Commission (EC, #06633); Ford Foundation (#09858); Fundação Luso-Americana para o Desenvolvimento (FLAD); Humanistisch Instituut voor Ontwikkelingssamenwerking (Hivos); Japan Foundation; Nordic Council of Ministers (NCM, #17260); Oxfam Novib; Swedish International Development Cooperation Agency (Sida); The African Capacity Building Foundation (ACBF, #00233); The Rockefeller Foundation (#18966); UNEP (#20299); UNESCO (#20322); WHO (#20950).* Annual budget: 3,000,000 USD. **Activities** Works with consumer organizations at national, regional and international levels; carries out research, facilitates partnerships and exchange of information and provides information, education, training, technical assistance, community development, seed grants and support in policy development. Main areas of concern: trade; food/nutrition; regional development (Agenda 21). Specific working fields: trade and economics; food; technical standard; utilities; environment; health. Regional offices develop and implement programmes and activities in: trade and economics; food safety and security; sustainable consumption and production; health; product safety; issues related to consumer education, information and legislation. Current programmes include: Unethical Marketing; Food Safety; Sustainable Consumption; Consumer Protection. **Events** *Quadrennial World Congress* Estoril (Portugal) 2019, *Quadrennial World Congress* Brasilia (Brazil) 2015, *International Conference on Consumer Protection in the Digital Age* Chiang Mai (Thailand) 2014, *Quadrennial World Congress* Hong Kong (Hong Kong) 2011, *Financial education summit* Singapore (Singapore) 2009. **Publications** *World Consumer Rights Day Kit* (annual) in English, French, Spanish. *Policy Briefing Papers.* Annual Report. Issue-specific reports; conference proceedings; briefing papers.

Members Consumer associations; government-financed consumer councils; consumer bodies supported by family organizations, labour unions and similar groups. Full; Affiliate; Government Affiliate. Full (82) in 65 countries and territories:
Argentina, Australia, Austria, Bangladesh, Belgium, Bolivia, Brazil, Burkina Faso, Chad, China, Cyprus, Czechia, Denmark, Ecuador, El Salvador, Fiji, Finland, France, Germany, Greece, Guyana, Hong Kong, Hungary, Iceland, India, Indonesia, Ireland, Israel, Italy, Jamaica, Japan, Jordan, Kenya, Korea Rep, Lebanon, Luxembourg, Malawi, Malaysia, Mali, Malta, Mauritius, Mexico, Netherlands, New Zealand, North Macedonia, Norway, Pakistan, Peru, Philippines, Poland, Portugal, Russia, Seychelles, Slovakia, Slovenia, South Africa, Spain, Switzerland, Taiwan, Thailand, Tunisia, UK, USA, Zimbabwe.
Included in the above, 1 organization listed in this Yearbook:
European Research into Consumer Affairs (ERICA, #08363).
Affiliate (116) in 71 countries and territories:
Albania, Argentina, Armenia, Azerbaijan, Bangladesh, Belarus, Benin, Bolivia, Brazil, Bulgaria, Burundi, Cameroon, Canada, Chile, Costa Rica, Côte d'Ivoire, Croatia, Cuba, Denmark, Dominican Rep, Estonia, Ethiopia, Finland, France, Georgia, Germany, Ghana, Greece, Honduras, Hungary, India, Indonesia, Italy, Jamaica, Japan, Kazakhstan, Kenya, Korea Rep, Malaysia, Mali, Martinique, Mongolia, Morocco, Mozambique, Nepal, Nicaragua, Nigeria, Norway, Panama, Peru, Philippines, Poland, Romania, Senegal, Singapore, Slovakia, South Africa, Spain, Sweden, Switzerland, Taiwan, Thailand, Togo, Türkiye, Uganda, UK, Uruguay, USA, Vietnam, Yemen, Zambia.
Included in the above, 3 organizations listed in this Yearbook:
Association européenne pour la coordination de la représentation des consommateurs pour la normalisation (ANEC, #02561); Bureau Européen des Unions de Consommateurs (BEUC, #03360); Environnement et développement du Tiers-monde (enda, #05510).
Government Affiliate (37) in 34 countries:
Australia, Botswana, Canada, Chile, China, Dominican Rep, Fiji, Hungary, India, Israel, Kiribati, Latvia, Lesotho, Macau, Mexico, New Zealand, Nigeria, Panama, Papua New Guinea, Philippines, Portugal, Romania, Russia, Samoa, South Africa, Spain, Sri Lanka, St Lucia, Sweden, Thailand, Trinidad-Tobago, UK, Zambia, Zimbabwe.

Consultative Status Consultative status granted from: *FAO (#09260)* (Special Status); *WHO (#20950)* (Official Relations); *UNCTAD (#20285)* (General Category); *UNICEF (#20332); UNIDO (#20336); World Intellectual Property Organization (WIPO, #21593)* (Observer Status); *UNEP (#20299); ECOSOC (#05331)* (General).

IGO Relations
- *ASEAN (#01141);*
- *Codex Alimentarius Commission (CAC, #04081);*
- *Economic Community of West African States (ECOWAS, #05312);*
- *European Commission (EC, #06633);*
- *Foro Iberoamericano de Agencias Gubernamentales de Protección al Consumidor (FIAGC, #09877);*
- *Joint FAO/WHO Expert Committee on Food Additives (JECFA, #16129);*
- *Latin American Integration Association (LAIA, #16343);*
- *OECD (#17693);*
- *Parlamento Latinoamericano (PARLATINO, #18203);*
- *United Nations Commission on the Status of Women (CSW, #20536);*
- *United Nations Commission on Sustainable Development (CSD, inactive);*
- *United Nations Conference on Environment and Development (UNCED);*
- *United Nations Economic Commission for Latin America and the Caribbean (ECLAC, #20556);*
- *United Nations Economic and Social Commission for Asia and the Pacific (ESCAP, #20557);*
- *United Nations Office at Vienna (UNOV, #20604);*
- *World Trade Organization (WTO, #21864).*

Associated with Department of Global Communications of the United Nations.

NGO Relations
- *Alliance for Affordable Internet (A4AI, #00651);*
- *Arab Federation for the Consumer (AFC, #00942);*
- *Asia-Pacific Research Network (APRN, #02013);*
- *Association of European Consumers (AEC, no recent information);*
- *Consumer Co-operatives Worldwide (CCW, #04770);*
- *Consumer Unity and Trust Society (CUTS);*
- *Development Innovations and Networks (#05057);*
- *Earth Council Alliance (ECA, inactive);*
- *EarthAction (EA, #05159);*
- *Environment Liaison Centre International (ELCI, no recent information);*
- *Framework Convention Alliance (FCA, #09981);*
- *Global Call for Climate Action (GCCA, inactive);*
- *Global Forum on Sustainable Food and Nutritional Security (no recent information);*
- *Global Reporting Initiative (GRI, #10567);*
- *Green Economy Coalition (GEC, #10717);*
- *Health Action International (HAI, #10868);*
- *International Association for Consumer Law (IACL, #11814);*
- *International Baby Food Action Network (IBFAN, #12305);*
- *International Breast Feeding Action Group (no recent information);*
- *International Centre for Trade and Sustainable Development, Geneva (ICTSD, #12524);*
- *International Electrotechnical Commission (IEC, #13255);*
- *International Organization for Standardization (ISO, #14473);*
- *International People's Health Council (IPHC);*
- *ISEAL (#16026);*
- *NGO Committee on the Status of Women, New York NY (see: #04635);*
- *Pan-African Alliance for Environment and Development (no recent information);*
- *Partnership for Education and Research about Responsible Living (PERL, #18234);*
- *People's Alliance for Social Development (no recent information);*
- *People's Health Movement (PHM, #18305);*
- *Pesticide Action Network (PAN, #18336);*
- *Privacy International (PI, #18504);*
- *South Asia Watch on Trade, Economics and Environment (SAWTEE, #19749);*
- *Transatlantic Consumer Dialogue (TACD, #20203);*
- *Vienna NGO Committee on the Family (#20774);*
- *World Alliance for Breastfeeding Action (WABA, #21079).*

Links indicated bu: *International Consumer Research and Testing (ICRT, #12931).* [2021/XB2321/y/**B**]

♦ Consumer Specialty Products Association (CSPA) 04774

Pres / CEO 1667 K St NW, Ste 300, Washington DC 20006, USA. T. +12028728110. Fax +12022232636.
URL: http://www.cspa.org/

History Founded 1914, as *Chemical Specialties Manufacturers Association (CSMA).* Present name adopted Dec 2000. **Aims** Represent the household and institutional products industry; provide consistent value for members by fostering high standards to maximize the safety, performance and sustainability of members' products; influence and proactively address legislative and regulatory challenges; advise these outcomes at federal, state and international levels; enhance business opportunities for members. **Structure** Board of Directors, consisting of Chairman, 1st Vice-Chairman, 2nd Vice-Chairman, Treasurer, President and other members. **Staff** 24.00 FTE, paid. **Finance** Budget (annual): US$ 4-5 million. **Activities** Carries out surveys. Organizes: Mid-Year Meeting (annual, in May) in Chicago IL (USA); Annual Meeting (in Dec) in Ft Lauderdale FL (USA); meetings; conferences; webinars. Divisions (7): Aerosol Products; Air Care Products; Antimicrobial Products; Cleaning Products; Industrial and Automotive Products; Pest Management Products; Polishes and Floor Maintenance. **Events** *Mid-year meeting* Chicago, IL (USA) 2004, *New horizons meeting* Lake George, NY (USA) 2004, *International regulatory conference* Washington, DC (USA) 2004, *Annual meeting* Fort Lauderdale, FL (USA) 2003, *Annual meeting* Fort Lauderdale, FL (USA) 2002. **Publications** *Cleaning Products Compendium: Consumer Product Ingredients Dictionary* (2012); *Aerosol Guide: Aerosol Pressurized Products Survey* (2011); *Aerosol Propellants Safety Manual* (2010).

Members Manufacturers of chemical specialties (mostly in USA) in 7 countries:
Australia, Canada, Germany, Italy, Switzerland, UK, USA.

NGO Relations Corresponding member of: *Fédération Européenne des Aérosols (FEA, #09557).* Member of: *The Consumer Goods Forum (CGF, #04772).* [2016/XF3095/**F**]

♦ Consumer Unity and Trust Society (internationally oriented national body)
♦ CONSUR / see Sudamérica Rugby (#20030)
♦ **CONSUTEME** Confederación Sudamericana de Tenis de Mesa (#04493)

♦ Contact-2103 04775

SG Rue du Maraîcher 9, 1082 Brussels, Belgium. T. +32477347756.
Facebook: https://www.facebook.com/Contact-2103-506222839432699/

History 1998. Registered in accordance with Belgian law. Also referred to as *Coordination européenne des maisons de jeunes et de la culture 'Youthclubs and Youth Associations; European Coordination of MJC, Youthclubs and Youth Associations – Coordination européenne de MJC, Youthclubs and Youth Associations.* **Aims** Promote dialogue with all socio-cultural and education organizations respecting individuals and differences in Europe and the world. **Structure** General Assembly. Board of Directors, including President, Treasurer and Secretary. General Secretary. **Finance** Co-funded by: *European Commission (EC, #06633).*

Members Full in 14 countries:
Belgium, Estonia, France, Germany, Greece, Hungary, Italy, Latvia, Netherlands, Poland, Portugal, Romania, Spain, Sweden.

NGO Relations Member of: *European Civic Forum (ECF, #06563).* [2018/XJ0439/**F**]

- ♦ Contact Center Network / see Action Without Borders
- ♦ ContactCenterWorld – Global Association for Contact Center & Customer Engagement Best Practices (unconfirmed)
- ♦ Contact International (inactive)
- ♦ Contact international des recherches économiques tendancielles / see Centre for International Research on Economic Tendency Surveys (#03765)
- ♦ Contact universitaire pour l'enseignement de l'administration des entreprises (inactive)

♦ Contadora Parliament 04776

Address not obtained.

History 1986. **IGO Relations** Member of: *Intergovernmental Organizations Conference (IGO Conference, #11498).* **NGO Relations** Cooperates with: *UCODEP.* [2009/XF5447/F*]

♦ Container Owners Association (COA) 04777

Gen Sec Suite 3, Charter House, 26 Claremont Road, Surbiton, KT6 4QU, UK. T. +447770636613. E-mail: secretary@containerownersassociation.org.
URL: https://www.containerownersassociation.com/

History Nov 2004. Registration: Companies House, No/ID: 05346179, Start date: 28 Jan 2005, England and Wales. **Aims** Promote the quality and utilization of ISO type containers used in the *freight* transport industry throughout the supply chain. **Structure** General Assembly; Board of Directors; Working Groups. **Languages** English. **Activities** Events/meetings. **Events** *General Meeting* Rotterdam (Netherlands) 2019, *General Meeting* Shanghai (China) 2019, *General Meeting* Rotterdam (Netherlands) 2018, *General Meeting* Singapore (Singapore) 2018, *General Meeting* Rotterdam (Netherlands) 2017.
Members Full; Associate; Group. Membership countries not specified. Partner members include:
Partner members include:
Bureau international des containers et du transport intermodal (BIC, #03364). [2022/XJ6452/C]

- ♦ Contemplatives Passionistes (religious order)

♦ Contemporary A Cappella Society (CASA) 04778

Main Office 237 Kearny St, Suite 9227, San Jose CA 94108, USA. T. +17708470814. E-mail: contact@casa.org.
URL: http://www.casa.org/

History 1990, USA. Founded by Deke Sharon. **Aims** Foster and promote 'a cappella' *music* of all styles. **Structure** A Cappella Ambassadors; President; Officers. **Finance** Sources: members' dues. **Activities** Events/meetings; training/education. **Events** *Summit / International Acappella Summit* Boston, MA (USA) 2000. **Publications** *Contemporary A Cappella News* (6 a year). Booklets. **Information Services** *Recording Resource Database* – Central reference for studios, engineers and producers.
Members Groups, individual singers and persons who enjoy a cappella music. Organizations in 59 countries and territories:
Albania, Armenia, Australia, Austria, Belgium, Brazil, Bulgaria, Canada, Chile, Colombia, Costa Rica, Croatia, Cuba, Czechia, Denmark, Ecuador, Fiji, Finland, France, Germany, Greece, Hong Kong, Hungary, Iceland, Indonesia, Ireland, Israel, Italy, Japan, Liechtenstein, Lithuania, Mexico, Netherlands, New Zealand, Norway, Panama, Philippines, Poland, Puerto Rico, Russia, Samoa, Saudi Arabia, Serbia, Singapore, Slovenia, South Africa, Spain, Sri Lanka, Sweden, Switzerland, Taiwan, Thailand, Tonga, Türkiye, UK, Ukraine, United Arab Emirates, USA, Vietnam. [2020.05.06/XE3621/E]

- ♦ Contemporary Theatre for Young Audiences (#18879)

♦ Content Delivery and Storage Association (CDSA) 04779

Pres 39 N Bayles Ave, Port Washington, New York NY 11050, USA. T. +15167676720. Fax +15168835793.
Exec Dir address not obtained. T. +19175135963.
URL: http://www.cdsaonline.org/

History 21 Jul 1970, New York NY (USA), as *International Tape Association.* In 1980 became *International Tape/Disc Association*, occasionally referred to as *ITDA.* Although subsequently again referred to under original title, the name *International Association of Magnetic and Optical Media Manufacturers and Related Industries* was adopted, 1990, for official purposes. In 1995 became *ITA, International Recording Media Association.* Name changed to *International Recording Media Association (IRMA)*, 1 Jan 1999, to reflect representation of a range of recording media. **Aims** Advocate the growth and development of all *recording media*; serve as the industry forum for *information* exchange regarding global trends and innovations. **Languages** English. **Staff** 5.00 FTE, paid. **Finance** Members' dues. Sources: Seminar registration fees; trade show exhibits. Budget (annual): over 2 million. **Activities** Organizes annual conference, regional seminars, trade shows (several each year) and statistical programmes. **Events** *Annual Content Protection Summit* Los Angeles, CA (USA) 2013, *Annual REPLItech North America* Los Angeles, CA (USA) 2002, *Annual replitech North America meeting* Los Angeles, CA (USA) 2002, *Annual marketing summit* New York, NY (USA) 2002, *Annual Conference* Tucson, AZ (USA) 2002. **Publications** *Buyers Guide of the Magnetic and Optical Recording Media Industries*; *International Source Directory.*
Members Manufacturers, suppliers and users of recording media (about 80 percent in North America) in 48 countries and territories:
Argentina, Australia, Austria, Belgium, Brazil, Canada, Chile, China, Colombia, Costa Rica, Denmark, Ecuador, Egypt, El Salvador, France, Germany, Ghana, Greece, Guatemala, Hong Kong, India, Ireland, Italy, Japan, Korea Rep, Liechtenstein, Luxembourg, Malaysia, Mexico, Netherlands, New Zealand, Norway, Panama, Peru, Philippines, Portugal, Puerto Rico, Singapore, South Africa, Spain, Sri Lanka, Sweden, Switzerland, Taiwan, Thailand, Türkiye, UK, Venezuela. [2020/XD3845/D]

- ♦ Continence Club / see International Continence Society (#12934)
- ♦ Continental Advertising Association (inactive)
- ♦ Continental Automated Building Association (internationally oriented national body)
- ♦ Continental Billiards and Snooker Association (inactive)
- ♦ Continental Brewery Centre / see European Brewery Convention (#06401)
- ♦ Continental Common Market / see African Economic Community (#00290)

♦ Continental European Division of the International Association for Dental Research (CED-IADR) 04780

Sec KUL – Dentristy, Kapucijnenvoer 7, Block A Box 7001, 3000 Leuven, Belgium.
URL: http://www.ced-iadr.eu/

History Serves as the European Branch of *International Association for Dental Research (IADR, #11838).* Previously known as *International Association for Dental Research – Pan European Federation (IADR-PER).* **Aims** Promote high quality oral health research in Europe. **Structure** Board, comprising President, President Elect, Past President, Secretary, and Treasurer Secretary and 5 members. Councillors (3). **Finance** Contributions from constituent divisions; sponsorship and support from industry. Also possible funding from IADR. **Activities** Offers: CED-IADR Robert Frank Awards; CED-IADR Travel Stipends; CED-IADR Visiting Scholar Stipends; IADR/Unilever Hatton Divisional Award. **Events** *PER-IADR Oral Health Research Congress* Marseille (France) 2022, *CED-IADR/ NOF Oral Health Research Congress* Brussels (Belgium) 2021, *PER-IADR Oral Health Research Congress* Marseille (France) 2020, *CED-IADR/ NOF Oral Health Research Congress* Madrid (Spain) 2019, *Pan European Regional Congress* London (UK) 2018.
Members in 33 countries:
Albania, Austria, Belarus, Belgium, Bosnia-Herzegovina, Bulgaria, Croatia, Czechia, Denmark, Estonia, France, Germany, Greece, Hungary, Italy, Latvia, Liechtenstein, Lithuania, Luxembourg, Moldova, Montenegro, Netherlands, North Macedonia, Poland, Portugal, Romania, Serbia, Slovakia, Slovenia, Spain, Switzerland, Türkiye, Ukraine.
NGO Relations Member of: *Initiative for Science in Europe (ISE, #11214).* [2016/XD8347/E]

- ♦ Continental Europe Rifle Association (inactive)
- ♦ Continental Europe Simulation Council / see European Council for Modelling and Simulation (#06831)
- ♦ Continental Free Trade Zone / see African Continental Free Trade Area (#00267)
- ♦ Continental Law Foundation (internationally oriented national body)
- ♦ Continental Organization of Latin American and Caribbean Students (#17834)
- ♦ Continental Tournaments Players Association (inactive)
- ♦ Continuing Committee of the World Futures Studies Research Conferences / see World Futures Studies Federation (#21535)
- ♦ Continuing Consultative Committee for Cooperation among World Jewish Youth (inactive)

♦ Continuous Innovation Network (CINet) 04781

Sec Fac of Technology and Management, Univ Twente, Postbus 217, 7500 AE Enschede, Netherlands.
URL: http://www.continuous-innovation.net/

History A continuation of *EuroCINet (inactive)*, founded 1994. **Structure** Annual General Meeting. **Activities** Organizes PhD Seminar; conferences; supervisors workshop. **Events** *International Conference* Stockholm (Sweden) 2015, *International conference / Conference* Zurich (Switzerland) 2010, *International conference / Conference* Brisbane, QLD (Australia) 2009, *International conference / Conference* Valencia (Spain) 2008, *International conference* Gothenburg (Sweden) 2007. **Publications** *Research in Continuous Innovation* – series. **Members** Membership countries not specified. [2012/XF6923/F]

- ♦ Contra Cancrum Mammarium (inactive)
- ♦ Contractors International Group on Nuclear Liability (internationally oriented national body)
- ♦ Controinformazione Terzo Mondo – Servizio Internazionale Volontario (internationally oriented national body)

♦ Control Arms 04782

Contact 223 W 38th St, no 1091, New York NY 10018, USA. T. +16237765727. E-mail: raluca.muresan@controlarms.org – info@controlarms.org.
URL: http://www.controlarms.org/

History 2003. Launched as a campaign gathering support for *Arms Trade Treaty (ATT, 2013).* **Aims** Ensure that governments effectively implement the Arms Trade Treaty, that more States join the Treaty to advance universalization and that the first Conference of States Parties is a success in establishing high international norms for treaty adherence. **Structure** Steering Board; Secretariat. **Languages** Arabic, English, French, Spanish. **Staff** 4.00 FTE, paid. **Finance** Sources: donations; government support. **Activities** Advocacy/lobbying/activism; awareness raising; projects/programmes; research/documentation. **Publications** *ATT Monitor.*
Members Members includes 29 organizations listed in this Yearbook:
- *Africa Peace Forum (APFO);*
- *Amnesty International (AI, #00801);*
- *Arias Foundation for Peace and Human Progress;*
- *Article 36;*
- *Atlas Alliance;*
- *Caribbean Coalition for Development and Reduction of Armed Violence (CDRAV, #03472);*
- *Caritas Internationalis (CI, #03580);*
- *Comité Catholique contre la Faim et pour le Développement-Terre Solidaire (CCFD-Terre Solidaire);*
- *Forum for Development and Environment (ForUM);*
- *Global Potential (GP);*
- *International Action Network on Small Arms (IANSA, #11585);*
- *International Peace Bureau (IPB, #14535);*
- *International Physicians for the Prevention of Nuclear War (IPPNW, #14578);*
- *Landmine Survivors Network (LSN);*
- *Latin American Circle for International Studies (LACIS);*
- *Nonviolence International (NI, #17152);*
- *Oxfam International (#17922);*
- *Parliamentarians for Global Action (PGA, #18208);*
- *PAX;*
- *Pax Christi – International Catholic Peace Movement (#18266);*
- *Permanent Peace Movement (PPM);*
- *Project Ploughshares;*
- *Saferworld;*
- *Servicio Tercer Mundo (SETEM);*
- *Southern African Centre for the Constructive Resolution of Disputes (SACCORD);*
- *The Eastern African Sub-Regional Support Initiative for the Advancement of Women (EASSI, #05225);*
- *Vision GRAM-International;*
- *West Africa Action Network on Small Arms (WAANSA, #20863);*
- *West Africa Network for Peacebuilding (WANEP, #20878).*

IGO Relations *UN Women (#20724)*; *UNDP (#20292)*; United Nations Office for Disarmament Affairs (UNODA); United Nations Office of Legal Affairs (UNOLA); *United Nations Regional Centre for Peace and Disarmament in Africa (UNREC, #20616)*; *United Nations Regional Centre for Peace, Disarmament and Development in Latin America and the Caribbean (UNLIREC, #20618).* [2023.02.27/XJ7671/y/E]

- ♦ Control Ciudadano (#19350)

♦ Controlled Environment Building Association (CEBA) 04783

Exec Vice-Pres c/o GCCA, 241 18th Street South, Ste 620, Arlington VA 22202, USA. E-mail: email@gcca.org.
URL: http://www.gcca.org/

History 1978, as (USA) National Association of Cold Storage Insulation Contractors. Statutes amended and name changed to *International Association of Cold Storage Contractors (IACSC)*, 1987. 2002, name changed to *International Association for Cold Storage Construction (IACSC).* 2018, present name adopted. **Aims** Promote standards, professional education and the interests of the cold storage *construction* industry. **Structure** Board of Directors, comprising Chairman, Vice Chairman, Treasurer, Immediate Past Chairman and 5 members. President/CEO. European Division, headed by Executive Secretary in UK. **Staff** 2.00 FTE, paid. **Activities** Organizes: annual conference and exposition; technical seminars. Maintains IACSC library. **Events** *Annual Conference* Las Vegas, NV (USA) 2011, *Annual Conference* Las Vegas, NV (USA) 2008, *Annual Conference* Los Cabos (Mexico) 2006, *Annual Conference* Miami, FL (USA) 2004, *Annual Conference* Tucson, AZ (USA) 2003. **Publications** *Cold Talk* (2 a year). *Annual Membership and Services Directory*; *Statistical Report.*
Members Companies, mostly in USA, but in a total of 7 countries:
Australia, China, Mexico, Trinidad-Tobago, UK, United Arab Emirates, USA.
NGO Relations Core Partner in: *Global Cold Chain Alliance (GCCA, #10299).* [2022/XD8317/D]

♦ Controlled Release Society (CRS) 04784

COO 1120 Route 73, Suite 200, Mount Laurel NJ 08054, USA. T. +18563806910. Fax +18564390525. E-mail: info@controlledreleasesociety.org.
URL: http://www.controlledreleasesociety.org/

History Incorporated 1978. Previously also referred to as *International Controlled Release Society.* Constitution revised 1999. Registered in the State of Ohio (USA). **Aims** Advance all aspects of delivery science and technology, including biological, physiological, preclinical, clinical and development aspects; maintain a core focus in physical science-based aspects such as formulation, processing, synthetic chemistry and characterization. **Structure** Business Meeting (annual). Board of Governors. Board of Scientific Advisors. Committees (6): Nominating; Membership and Development; Marketing; Annual Meetings; Publications; Awards Coordinating. Ad-hoc Committees. **Languages** English. **Staff** 14.00 FTE, paid. **Finance** Members' dues. **Events** *Annual Meeting* Montréal, QC (Canada) 2022, *Annual Meeting* Mount Laurel, NJ (USA) 2021, *Annual Meeting* Mount Laurel, NJ (USA) 2020, *Annual Meeting* Valencia (Spain) 2019, *Annual Meeting* New York, NY (USA) 2018. **Publications** *Drug Delivery and Translational Research* (6 a year) – journal; *CRS Newsletter* (irregular); *Journal of Controlled Release.* **Members** Full; Student; Honorary; Institutional. Full (2,500) representing industry, academia and government in over 55 countries. Membership countries not specified. [2020/XD4767/F]

- ♦ Controller Verein / see Internationaler Controller Verein (#13292)
- ♦ Control System Cyber Security Association International (internationally oriented national body)
- ♦ Controverses et Actualités en Chirurgie vasculaire (unconfirmed)
- ♦ Controversies, Arts and Technology in Breast and Bodycontouring Aesthetic Surgery (meeting series)
- ♦ Controversies and Updates in Vascular Surgery (unconfirmed)
- ♦ Convenção sobre agentes consulares (1928 treaty)
- ♦ Convenção sobre asilo, 1928 (1928 treaty)
- ♦ Convenção sobre aviação comercial (1928 treaty)
- ♦ Convenção de Belém do Para – Convenção interamericana para prevenir, punir e erradicar a violência contra a mulher (1994 treaty)
- ♦ Convenção sobre condição dos estrangeiros (1928 treaty)

♦ Convenção contra a tortura e outors tratamentos ou penas cruéis, desumanos ou degradantes (1984 treaty)
♦ Convenção para coordenar, ampliar e assegurar a observância dos tratados existentes entre os Estados americanos (1936 treaty)
♦ Convenção sobre criação do passaporte pan-americano de turismo e de passaporte de trânsito para veiculos (1935 treaty)
♦ Convenção sobre direito internacional (1906 treaty)
♦ Convenção de direito internacional privado (1928 treaty)
♦ Convenção sobre direitos e deveres dos Estados (1933 treaty)
♦ Convenção sobre o ensino da história (1933 treaty)
♦ Convenção sobre o exercicio de profissões liberais, 1902 (1902 treaty)
♦ Convenção sobre extradição (1933 treaty)
♦ Convenção sobre facilidades aos filmes educativos ou de propaganda (1936 treaty)
♦ Convenção sobre facilidades para exposições artisticas (1936 treaty)
♦ Convenção fixando a condição dos cidadões naturalizados que renovam a sua residência no pais de origem (1906 treaty)
♦ Convenção para a formação de códigos de direito internacional público e privado (1902 treaty)
♦ Convenção general de conciliação Interamericana (1929 treaty)
♦ Convenção geral Interamericana de proteção de proteção de marcas de fabrica e proteção comercial (1929 treaty)
♦ Convenção interamericana sobre assistencia mútua em matéria penal (1992 treaty)
♦ Convenção interamericana de comunicações elétricas (1924 treaty)
♦ Convenção Interamericana Contra o Racismo e Toda Forma de Discriminação a Intolerância (unconfirmed)
♦ Convenção interamericana para facilitar a assistência em casos de desastre (1991 treaty)
♦ Convenção interamericana para prevenir, punir e erradicar a violência contra a mulher (1994 treaty)
♦ Convenção interamericana para prevenir e punir a tortura (1985 treaty)
♦ Convenção interamericana sobre radiocomunicações, 1937 (1937 treaty)
♦ Convenção sobre intercâmbio de publicações (1936 treaty)
♦ Convenção de Kampala – Convenção de União Africana sobre a Protecção e Assistência as Pessoas Deslocadas Internamente em África (2009 treaty)
♦ Convenção sobre manutenção, garantia e restabelecimento de paz (1936 treaty)
♦ Convenção sobre marcas de fabrica e de comércio (1910 treaty)
♦ Convenção sobre nacionalidade (1933 treaty)
♦ Convenção sobre a nacionalidade da mulher (1933 treaty)
♦ Convenção sobre neutralidade maritima (1928 treaty)
♦ Convenção de Niamey – Convenção da União Africana sobre Cooperação Transfronteiriça (2014 treaty)
♦ Convenção sobre os deveres e direitos dos Estados nos casos de lutas civis (1928 treaty)
♦ Convenção sobre patentes, de invenção, desenhos e modelos industriais (1910 treaty)
♦ Convenção sobre patentes de invenção, desenhos e modelos industriais, marcas de fabrica e comércio, e propriedade literaria e artistica (1906 treaty)
♦ Convenção sobre a permuta de publicações oficiais, cientificas, literarias e industriais (1902 treaty)
♦ Convenção para promover as relações culturais Interamericanas, 1936 (1936 treaty)
♦ Convenção sobre propriedade literaria e artistica, 1910 (1910 treaty)
♦ Convenção para e proteção de marcas de fabrica, comércio e agricultura e nomes comerciais (1923 treaty)
♦ Convenção para a proteção das obras literarias e artisticas, 1902 (1902 treaty)
♦ Convenção sobre a publicidade de documentos aduaneiros (1923 treaty)
♦ Convenção sobre reclamações pecuniarias, 1906 (1906 treaty)
♦ Convenção sobre reclamações pecuniarias, 1910 (1910 treaty)
♦ Convenção regional de radio de América Central, Panama e Zona do Canal (1938 treaty)
♦ Convenção relativa ao transito de aviões (1935 treaty)
♦ Convenção sobre repressão de contrabando (1935 treaty)
♦ Convenção do trafego automotor (1930 treaty)
♦ Convenção sobre tratados (1928 treaty)
♦ Convenção da União Africana sobre Cibersegurança e Protecção de Dados Pessoais (2014 treaty)
♦ Convenção da União Africana sobre Cooperação Transfronteiriça (2014 treaty)
♦ Convenção de União Africana sobre a Protecção e Assistência as Pessoas Deslocadas Internamente em África (2009 treaty)
♦ Convenção sobre uniformidade de nomenclatura para a classificação de mercadorias (1923 treaty)
♦ Convención de adopción del manual interamericano de dispositivos para el control del transito en calles y carreteras (1979 treaty)
♦ Convención sobre agentes consulares (1928 treaty)
♦ Convención sobre asilo, 1928 (1928 treaty)
♦ Convención sobre asilo, 1933 (1933 treaty)
♦ Convención sobre asilo diplomatico (1954 treaty)
♦ Convención sobre aviación comercial (1928 treaty)
♦ Convención de Belém do Para – Convención interamericana para prevenir, sancionar y erradicar la violencia contra la mujer (1994 treaty)
♦ Convención sobre canje de publicaciones oficiales, cientificas, literarias e industriales (1902 treaty)
♦ Convención sobre condiciones delos extranjeros (1928 treaty)
♦ Convención contra la tortura y otros tratos o penas crueles, inhumanos o degradantes (1984 treaty)
♦ Convención para coordinar, ampliar y asegurar el cumplimiento de los tratados existentes entre los Estados americanos (1936 treaty)
♦ Convención sobre deberes y derechos de los Estados en caso de luchas civiles (1928 treaty)
♦ Convención sobre defensa del patrimonio arqueológico, histórico y artistico de las Naciones Americanas (1976 treaty)
♦ Convención sobre derecho internacional (1906 treaty)
♦ Convención sobre derecho internacional privado (1928 treaty)
♦ Convención sobre derechos y deberes de los Estados (1933 treaty)
♦ Convención sobre los derechos de las personas con discapacidad (2006 treaty)
♦ Convención sobre el ejercicio de profesiones liberales, 1889 (1889 treaty)
♦ Convención sobre el ejercicio de profesiones liberales, 1902 (1902 treaty)
♦ Convención sobre el ejercicio de profesiones liberales, 1939 (1939 treaty)
♦ Convención sobre la enseñanza de la historia (1933 treaty)
♦ Convención sobre extradición (1933 treaty)
♦ Convención sobre facilidades a exposiciones artisticas (1936 treaty)
♦ Convención sobre facilidades a las peliculas educativas o de propaganda (1936 treaty)
♦ Convención sobre el Fomento de las Relaciones Culturales Interamericanas (1954 treaty)
♦ Convención para el fomento de las relaciones culturales Interamericanas, 1936 (1936 treaty)
♦ Convención para la formación de códigos de derecho internacional público y privado (1902 treaty)
♦ Convención general de conciliación Interamericana (1929 treaty)
♦ Convención general Interamericana de protección marcaria y comercial (1929 treaty)
♦ Convención interamericana sobre arbitraje comercial internacional (1975 treaty)
♦ Convención interamericana sobre asistencia mutua en materia penal (1992 treaty)
♦ Convención interamericana sobre la competencia en la esfera interamericana para la eficacia extraterritorial de las sentencias extranjeras (1984 treaty)
♦ Convención interamericana de comunicaciones eléctricas (1924 treaty)
♦ Convención interamericana sobre la concesión de derechos civiles a la mujer (1948 treaty)
♦ Convención interamericana sobre conflicto de leyes en materia de adopción de menores (1984 treaty)
♦ Convención interamericana sobre conflicto de leyes en materia de letras de cambio, pagaros y facturas (1975 treaty)
♦ Convención interamericana sobre conflicto de leyes en materia de sociedades mercantiles (1979 treaty)
♦ Convención interamericana sobre conflictos de leyes en materia de cheques, 1975 (1975 treaty)
♦ Convención interamericana sobre conflictos de leyes en materia de cheques, 1979 (1979 treaty)
♦ Convención interamericana contra la fabricación y el trafico ilicitos de armas de fuego, municiones, explosivos y otros materiales relacionados (1997 treaty)
♦ Convención Interamericana contra el lavado de dinero (unconfirmed)
♦ Convención Interamericana Contra el Racismo y Toda Forma de Discriminación e Intolerancia (unconfirmed)
♦ Convención interamericana sobre contratación de transporte internacional de mercaderia por carreteras (1989 treaty)
♦ Convención interamericana contra al terrorismo (2002 treaty)
♦ Convención interamericana para el cumplimiento de condenas penales en el extranjero (1993 treaty)
♦ Convención interamericana sobre derecho aplicable a contratos internacionales (1994 treaty)
♦ Convención interamericana de derechos humanos (1969 treaty)
♦ Convención interamericana sobre de los derechos politicos a la mujer (1948 treaty)
♦ Convención interamericana sobre desaparición forzada de personas (1994 treaty)
♦ Convención interamericana sobre domicilio de las personas fisicas en el derecho internacional privado (1979 treaty)
♦ Convención interamericana sobre eficacia extraterritorial de sentencias y laudos arbitrales extranjeros (1979 treaty)
♦ Convención interamericana para la eliminación de todas las formas de discriminación contra las personas con discapacidad (1999 treaty)
♦ Convención interamericana sobre exhortos y cartas rogatorias (1975 treaty)
♦ Convención interamericana de extradición (1981 treaty)
♦ Convención interamericana para facilitar la asistencia en casos de desastre (1991 treaty)
♦ Convención interamericana sobre normas generales de derecho internacional privado (1979 treaty)
♦ Convención interamericana sobre obligaciones alimentarias (1989 treaty)
♦ Convención interamericana sobre permiso internacional de radioaficionados (1995 treaty)
♦ Convención interamericana sobre personalidad y capacidad de personas juridicas en el derecho internacional privado (1984 treaty)
♦ Convención interamericana para prevenir, sancionar y erradicar la violencia contra la mujer (1994 treaty)
♦ Convención interamericana para prevenir y sancionar la tortura (1985 treaty)
♦ Convención interamericana de pruebas e información acerca del derecho extranjero (1979 treaty)
♦ Convención interamericana sobre radiocomunicaciones, 1937 (1937 treaty)
♦ Convención interamericana sobre recepción de pruebas en el extranjero (1975 treaty)
♦ Convención interamericana sobre el régimen legal de poderes para ser utilizados en el extranjero (1975 treaty)
♦ Convención interamericana sobre restitución internacional de menores (1989 treaty)
♦ Convención interamericana sobre transparencia en las adquisiciones de armas convencionales (1999 treaty)
♦ Convención interamericano contra la corrupción (1996 treaty)
♦ Convención interamericano sobre servicio de radioaficionados (1987 treaty)
♦ Convención sobre intercambio de publicaciones (1936 treaty)
♦ Convención internacional contra el dopaje en el deporte (2005 treaty)
♦ Convención internacional del cumplimiento de ejecución de medidas preventivas (1979 treaty)
♦ Convención internacional para la seguridad de la vida humana en el mar, 1960 (1960 treaty)
♦ Convención internacional de Torremolinos para la seguridad de los buques pesqueros (1978 treaty)
♦ Convención sobre mantenimiento, afianzamiento y restablecimiento de la paz (1936 treaty)
♦ Convención sobre marcas de fabrica y comercio (1910 treaty)
♦ Convención marco de Naciones Unidas sobre el cambio climatico (1992 treaty)
♦ Convención sobre Municiones en Racimo (2008 treaty)
♦ Convención sobre nacionalidad (1933 treaty)
♦ Convención sobre nacionalidad de la mujer (1933 treaty)
♦ Convención de la Naciones Unidas contra la delincuencia organizada transnacional (2000 treaty)
♦ Convención de las Naciones Unidas contra el Tráfico Ilícito de Estupefacientes y Sustancias Sicotrópicas (1988 treaty)
♦ Convención de las Naciones Unidas sobre letras de cambio internacionales y pagares internacionales (1988 treaty)
♦ Convención de las Naciones Unidas para la Lucha Contra la Desertificación (1994 treaty)
♦ Convención sobre neutralidad maritima (1928 treaty)
♦ Convención sobre la orientación pacifica de la enseñanza (1936 treaty)
♦ Convención sobre patentes de invención, dibujos y modelos industriales (1910 treaty)
♦ Convención sobre patentes de invención, dibujos y modelos industriales, marcas de fabrica y comercio, y propiedad literaria y artistica (1906 treaty)
♦ Convención del Patrimonio Mundial – Convención sobre la protección del patrimonio mundial cultural y natural (1972 treaty)
♦ Convención para prevenir y sancionar actos de terrorismo (1971 treaty)
♦ Convención para la protección de marcas de fabrica, comercio y agricultura y nombres comerciales (1923 treaty)
♦ Convención para la protección de las obras literarias y artisticas, 1902 (1902 treaty)
♦ Convención sobre la protección del patrimonio cultural subacuatico (2001 treaty)
♦ Convención sobre la protección del patrimonio mundial cultural y natural (1972 treaty)
♦ Convención sobre publicidad de documentos aduaneros (1923 treaty)
♦ Convención que fija la condición de ciudadanos naturalizados que renuevan su residencia en el pais du su origen (1906 treaty)
♦ Convención sobre reclamaciones pecuniarias, 1906 (1906 treaty)
♦ Convención sobre reclamaciones pecuniarias, 1910 (1910 treaty)
♦ Convención regional de radio de Centro América, Panama y Zona del Canal (1938 treaty)
♦ Convención sobre la reglamentación del trafico automotor (1930 treaty)
♦ Convención relativa a la creación del pasaporte panamericano de turismo y del pasaporte de transito para vehiculos (1935 treaty)
♦ Convención sobre represión del contrabando (1935 treaty)
♦ Convención para la salvaguardia del patrimonio cultural inmaterial (2003 treaty)
♦ Convención sobra la conservación de las especies migratorias de animales silvestres (1979 treaty)
♦ Convención sobre trafico internacional de menores (1994 treaty)
♦ Convención sobre transito de aviones (1935 treaty)
♦ Convención sobre tratados (1928 treaty)
♦ Convención sobre uniformidad de nomenclatura para la clasificación de Mercaderias (1923 treaty)
♦ Convenio acerca de las medidas para prohibir y empedir importación exportación y transferencia de la propiedad cultural (1970 treaty)
♦ Convenio acerca de la nomenclatura para la clasificación de mercancias en los aranceles aduaneros (1950 treaty)
♦ Convenio acerca de la responsabilidad civil en materia de energia nuclear (1960 treaty)
♦ Convenio acerca del valor en aduana de mercancias (1950 treaty)
♦ Convenio sobre acuerdos de elección del fuero (1965 treaty)
♦ Convenio sobre la administración del trabajo: cometido, funciones y organización (1978 treaty)
♦ Convenio aduanero acerca de importación de material profesional (1961 treaty)
♦ Convenio aduanero acerca de la importación temporaria de embalajes (1960 treaty)
♦ Convenio aduanero acerca de la importación temporaria de material cientifico (1968 treaty)
♦ Convenio aduanero sobre el carnet ATA para la admisión temporaria de mercancias (1961 treaty)
♦ Convenio aduanero de los carnets para muestras comerciales (1956 treaty)
♦ Convenio aduanero sobre contenedores, 1956 (1956 treaty)

Convenio aduanero contenedores
04784

alphabetic sequence excludes
For the complete listing, see Yearbook Online at

♦ Convenio aduanero sobre contenedores, 1972 (1972 treaty)
♦ Convenio aduanero relativo a la importación temporaria a uso privado de embarcaciones y de aeronaves (1956 treaty)
♦ Convenio aduanero relativo a la importación temporaria de vehiculos comerciales de carretera (1956 treaty)
♦ Convenio aduanero relativo a la importación de vehiculos de carretera privados (1954 treaty)
♦ Convenio aduanero relativo al transito internacional de mercancias (1971 treaty)
♦ Convenio aduanero relativo al transporte internacional de mercancias bajo carnet TIR (1959 treaty)
♦ Convenio sobre las agencias de empleo privadas (1997 treaty)
♦ Convenio de alta mar (1958 treaty)
♦ Convenio andino de seguridad social (no recent information)
♦ **Convenio Andrés Bello** Convenio Andrés Bello de integración educativa, cientifica y cultural de América Latina y España (#04785)

♦ Convenio Andrés Bello de integración educativa, cientifica y cultural de América Latina y España (Convenio Andrés Bello) 04785

Andrés Bello convention for the educational, scientific and cultural integration of Latin America and Spain (Andrés Bello Convention)

Exec Sec Calle 94 No 14-48 Oficina 201, Bogota, Bogota DC, Colombia. T. +576449292. Fax +576449292. E-mail: comunicaciones@convenioandresbello.org.
URL: http://www.convenioandresbello.org/

History 31 Jan 1970, Bogota (Colombia), on adoption of the Convention by the Governments of Bolivia, Chile, Colombia, Ecuador, Peru and Venezuela, as a cooperation organism of the *Andean Subregional Integration Agreement (Cartagena Agreement, 1969)*. The Convention entered into force on 24 Nov 1970. Panama adhered to the Convention on 2 Feb 1980, Spain on 9 Jul 1982 and Cuba on 23 Apr 1998. The Convention was originally referred to as *Convenio Andrés Bello de integración educativa, cientifica y cultural de los paises de la Región Andina* and is currently also referred to by the initials *CAB*. It functions as a *'Social Agreement'* of *Sistema Andino de Integración (SAI, #19292)*, within the framework of *Andean Community (#00817)*. *Secretaria Ejecutiva del Convenio Andrés Bello (SECAB) – Secretariat of the Andrés Bello Agreement – Secrétariat de la Convention Andrés Bello* was set up 30 Mar 1972, Quito (Ecuador), by Resolution No 24 of the 3rd Meeting of Ministers of Education of signatory countries (REMECAB III); the permanent head office of the secretariat is in Bogota. The *Organización del Convenio Andrés Bello de Integración Educativa, Cientifica, Tecnológica y Cultural (no recent information)* was approved by 15th Meeting of Ministers of Education, 27 Nov 1990, Madrid (Spain), on amendment of the Convention, which was ratified by all member countries. **Aims** Promote integration, mutual knowledge and brotherhood among the countries of Latin America; complement integration efforts in the economic and trade sectors with action in the fields of educational, scientific and cultural integration; contribute to the achievement of an adequate balance in educational, scientific, technical and cultural development; secure joint efforts through education, science, technology and culture in favour of the integral development of nations involved; apply science and technology to improve living standards of the peoples in the region. **Structure** Organs of the Agreement: International Level – – *Reunión de Ministros de Educación del Convenio Andrés Bello (REMECAB)*; -Executive Secretariat – SECAB, with permanent head office in Bogota (Colombia); -Principal Advisory Commission; -Technical Committee of Education, Science and Technology; -Technical Committee of Culture; -Special Entities: – *International Integration Institute of the Andrés Bello Convention (#13940)*, Bolivia, – *Andean Institute of Popular Arts (IADAP, no recent information)*, Ecuador, – *Institute of Appropriate Technology Transfer to Marginal Sectors of the Andrés Bello Convention (#11242)*, Peru. National Level – -Ministers of Education; -National Commissions (offices for international cooperation of Ministries of Education); -National Secretariats. **Languages** Spanish. **Staff** 50.00 FTE, paid. **Finance** Main source: *Fondo de Financiamiento del Convenio Andrés Bello*, to which all member countries contribute. Other sources: national and international cooperation; own incomes. **Activities** Carries out programmes, projects and plans in the fields of: education; science and technology; culture; cultural heritage; communication and information for integration. Organizes contests and awards: Social Appropriation of the Cultural and Natural Heritage, 1977; Latin American Thinking, 1998. **Events** *International conference on European-Latin American cultural cooperation* Cartagena de Indias (Colombia) 2001, *Meeting of the ministers of education / Meeting of the Ministers of Education – REMECAB* Cochabamba (Bolivia) 1998, *Meeting of the Ministers of Education – REMECAB* Quito (Ecuador) 1995, *Meeting of ministers of education* Bogota (Colombia) 1994, *Meeting of the Ministers of Education – REMECAB* Cartagena de Indias (Colombia) 1994. **Publications** *Pensamiento Latinoamericano* – series. *Somos Patrimonio: Experiencias de los Paises del Convenio Andrés Bello en Apropiación Social del Patrimonio Cultural y Natural para el Desarrollo Comunitario* (1999); *De los Medios a las Mediaciones: Comunicación, Cultura y Hegemonia* (5th ed 1998) by Jésus Martin-Barbero; *Otro Territorio: Ensayos sobre el Mundo Contemporaneo* (2nd ed 1998) by Renato Ortiz; *Periodismo Cultural y Cultura del Periodismo* (1993); *Periodismo Cultural en los Paises del Convenio Andrés Bello* (1991). *Legislación Cultural de los Paises del Convenio Andrés Bello* – on the Internet. Other publications in the fields mentioned above: monographs; guides; pamphlets; studies. Information Services: Documentation Centre.
Members Signatory governments, represented by their Ministers of Education, of 9 countries:
Bolivia, Chile, Colombia, Cuba, Ecuador, Panama, Peru, Spain, Venezuela.
IGO Relations Special agreement with: *Development Bank of Latin America (CAF, #05055)*; *OAS (#17629)*; *UNESCO (#20322)*. Instrumental in setting up: *Andean Management School (no recent information)*; *Red Andina de Información sobre Artes Populares (RADIAP, no recent information)*. **NGO Relations** Supports: *Federación Latinoamericana de Facultades de Comunicación Social (FELAFACS, #09353)*. Member of: *Red de Centros Culturales de América y Europa (RCCAE, #18639)*. [2016/XD4506/F*]

♦ Convênio sobre a aplicação da clausula de nação mais favorecida (1934 treaty)
♦ Convenio sobre aplicación de la clausula de la nación mas favorecida (1934 treaty)
♦ Convenio sobre arreglo de diferencias relativas a inversiones entre Estados y nacionales de otros Estados (1965 treaty)
♦ Convenio sobre asilo territorial (1954 treaty)
♦ Convenio de Atenas relativo al transporte de pasajeros y sus equipajes por mar (1974 treaty)
♦ Convenio de Atenas relativo al transporte de pasajeros y sus equipajes por mar, 1976 (1976 treaty)
♦ Convenio de Atenas relativo al transporte de pasajeros y sus equipajes por mar, 1990 (1990 treaty)
♦ Convenio de Atenas relativo al transporte de pasajeros y sus equipajes por mar, 2002 (2002 treaty)
♦ Convenio sobre la aviación civil internacional (1944 treaty)
♦ Convenio de Basilea sobre el control de los movimientos transfronterizos de los desechos peligrosos y su eliminación (1989 treaty)
♦ Convenio de Berne para la Protección de las Obras Literarias y Artisticas (1886 treaty)
♦ Convenio sobre el bienestar de la gente de mar en el mar y en puerto (1987 treaty)
♦ Convenio centroamericano sobre equiparación de gravamenes a la importación (1959 treaty)
♦ Convenio centroamericano de incentivos fiscales al desarrollo industrial, 1962 (1962 treaty)
♦ Convenio Centroamericano para la Protección del Medio Ambiente (1989 treaty)
♦ Convenio sobre el comercio internacional de especies de fauna y flora silvestres amenzadas de extincción (1973 treaty)
♦ Convenio complementario al Convenio de Paris acerca de responsabilidad civil en materia de daños nucleares (1963 treaty)
♦ Convenio complementario al Convenio de Varsovia para la unificación de ciertas reglas relativas al transporte aéreo internacional por un transportador no contractual (1961 treaty)
♦ Convenio sobre las condiciones de trabajo en los hoteles, restaurantes y establecimientos similares (1991 treaty)
♦ Convenio para la conservación de la biodiversidad y protección de areas silvestres prioritarias en America Central (1992 treaty)
♦ Convenio sobre la conservación de la fauna y la flora en el Antartico (1980 treaty)
♦ Convenio sobre consultas tripartitas para promover la aplicación de las normas internacionales des trabajo (1976 treaty)
♦ Convenio sobre contaminación atmosférica transfronteriza o larga distancia / see Convention on Long-range Transboundary Air Pollution (#04787)
♦ Convenio sobre la continuidad del empleo de la gente de mar (1976 treaty)
♦ Convenio sobre el desempleo (1919 treaty)
♦ Convenio destinado a solventar ciertos conflictos de leyes en materia de cheques (1931 treaty)
♦ Convenio destinado a solventar ciertos conflictos de leyes en materia de letras de cambio y pagares (1930 treaty)
♦ Convenio sobre la distribución de señales portadoras de programas transmitidas por satélite (1974 treaty)
♦ Convenio sobre la diversidad biológica (1992 treaty)
♦ Convenio sobre los documentos de identidad de la gente de mar (2003 treaty)
♦ Convenio sobre duración del trabajo y periodos de descanso en los transportes por carretera (1979 treaty)
♦ Convenio económico de Bogota (1948 treaty)
♦ Convenio sobre la edad minima de admisión al empleo (1973 treaty)
♦ Convenio sobre el empleo y condiciones de trabajo y de vida del personal de enfermeria (1977 treaty)
♦ Convenio sobre el establecimiento de un sistema internacional para la conservación de los derechos en materia de seguridad social (1982 treaty)
♦ Convenio sobre estadisticas del trabajo (1985 treaty)
♦ Convenio de Estocolmo Sobre Contaminantes Organicos Persistentes (2001 treaty)
♦ Convenio europeo sobre arbitraje comercial internacional (1961 treaty)
♦ Convenio sobre facilidades aduaneras para el turismo (1954 treaty)
♦ Convenio para facilitar el trafico maritimo internacional (1965 treaty)
♦ Convenio sobre factoring internacional (1988 treaty)
♦ Convenio sobre el fomento del empleo y la protección contra el desempleo (1988 treaty)
♦ Convenio sobre el fomento de la negociación colectiva (1981 treaty)
♦ Convenio Hipólito Unanue (#10921)
♦ Convenio sobre la igualdad de oportunidades y de trato entre trabajadores y trabajadoras: trabajadores con responsabilidades familiares (1981 treaty)
♦ Convenio sobre infracciones y otros actos cometidos a bordo de aeronaves (1963 treaty)
♦ Convenio sobre a la inspección de las condiciones de vida y de trabajo de la gente de mar (1996 treaty)
♦ Convenio instituyendo ley uniforme de cheques (1931 treaty)
♦ Convenio de Integración Cinematografica Iberoamericana (1989 treaty)
♦ Convenio de Integración Socio-Laboral Simón Rodriguez / see Simón Rodriguez Agreement (#19284)
♦ Convenio interamericano para facilitar el transporte acuatico interamericano (1963 treaty)
♦ Convênio interamericano sobre o serviço de radioamadores (1987 treaty)
♦ Convenio internacional del aceite de oliva y las aceitunas de mesa, 2005 (2005 treaty)
♦ Convenio internacional sobre arqueo de buques (1969 treaty)
♦ Convenio internacional de asistencia administrativa mutual para prevenir, buscar, reprimir infracciones aduaneras (1977 treaty)
♦ Convenio internacional sobre búsqueda y salvamento maritimos (1979 treaty)
♦ Convenio internacional del café de 2001 (2000 treaty)
♦ Convênio internacional do café de 2001 (2000 treaty)
♦ Convenio internacional para facilitar la importación de muestras comerciales y material publicitario (1955 treaty)
♦ Convenio internacional para facilitar la importación de muestras y material publicitario (1952 treaty)
♦ Convenio internacional para facilitar el pasaje a las fronteras de las mercancias transportadas por via férrea (1952 treaty)
♦ Convenio internacional para facilitar el pasaje de las fronteras de viajeros y equipajes por via férrea (1952 treaty)
♦ Convenio internacional sobre harmonización de los controles de mercancias a las fronteras (1982 treaty)
♦ Convenio internacional sobre lineas de carga (1966 treaty)
♦ Convenio internacional para prevenir la contaminación de las aguas del mar por hidrocarburos (1954 treaty)
♦ Convenio internacional para prevenir la contaminación por los buques (1973 treaty)
♦ Convenio internacional sobre la protección de los artistas intérpretes o ejecutantes, los productores de fonógramas y los organismos de radiodifusión (1961 treaty)
♦ Convenio internacional para la protección de las obtenciones vegetales, 1961 (1961 treaty)
♦ Convenio internacional para la protección de pajaros (1950 treaty)
♦ Convenio internacional para la protección de vegetales (1951 treaty)
♦ Convenio internacional para la reglementación de la caza de la ballena (1946 treaty)
♦ Convenio internacional relativo a la intervención en alta mar en casos de accidentes que causen una contaminación por hidrocarburos (1969 treaty)
♦ Convenio internacional para la represión de los actos de terrorismo nuclear (2005 treaty)
♦ Convenio internacional sobre la responsabilidad civil nacida de daños debidos a contaminación por hidrocarburos (1969 treaty)
♦ Convenio internacional para la seguridad de los buques pesqueros (1977 treaty)
♦ Convenio internacional sobre la seguridad de los contenedores (1972 treaty)
♦ Convenio internacional para la seguridad de la vida humana en el mar, 1948 (1948 treaty)
♦ Convenio internacional para la seguridad de la vida humana en el mar en su forma enmendada, 1974 (1974 treaty)
♦ Convenio internacional de telecomunicaciones, 1982 (1982 treaty)
♦ Convenio internacional de telecomunicaciones, 1989 (1989 treaty)
♦ Convenio internacional del trigo (1986 treaty)
♦ Convenio internacional para la unificación de certas reglas relativas a las immunidades de navios de Estado (1927 treaty)
♦ Convenio internacional para la unificación de certas reglas relativas a las inmunidades de navios de Estado (1926 treaty)
♦ Convenio sobre el leasing internacional (1988 treaty)
♦ Convenio sobre la ley aplicable a contratos de venta internacional de mercancias (1986 treaty)
♦ Convenio sobre limitación de la responsabilidad nacida de reclamaciones de derecho maritimo (1976 treaty)
♦ Convenio sobre la Marcación de Explosivos Plasticos para los fines de Detección (1991 treaty)
♦ Convenio sobre el marco promocional para la seguridad y salud en el trabajo (2006 treaty)
♦ Convenio del metro (1875 treaty)
♦ Convenio sobre las migraciones en condiciones abusivas y la promoción de la igualdad de oportunidades y de trato de los trabajadores migrantes (1975 treaty)
♦ Convenio de Minamata sobre el Mercurio (2013 treaty)
♦ Convenio multilateral sobre cooperación y asistencia mutua entre las direcciones nacionales de aduanas (1981 treaty)
♦ Convenio de las Naciones Unidas acerca de las condiciones de matriculación de navios (1986 treaty)
♦ Convenio de las Naciones Unidas sobre el derecho del mar (1982 treaty)
♦ Convenio de las Naciones Unidas sobre el transporte de mercancias por mar (1978 treaty)
♦ Convenio sobre las normas minimas en la marina mercante (1976 treaty)
♦ Convenio sobre la obtención de pruebas al extranjero en materia civil o commercial (1970 treaty)
♦ Convenio sobre las organizaciones de trabajadores rurales y su función en el desarrollo económico y social (1975 treaty)
♦ Convenio sobre la orientación profesional y la formación profesional en el desarrollo de los recursos humanos (1975 treaty)
♦ Convenio sobre pesca y conservación de riquezas biológicas en alta mar (1958 treaty)
♦ Convenio de la plataforma continental (1958 treaty)
♦ Convenio postal universal, 1984 (1985 treaty)
♦ Convenio sobre la prescripción en materia de venta internacional de mercancias (1974 treaty)
♦ Convenio sobre la prevención de accidentes industriales mayores (1993 treaty)

♦ Convenio sobre la prevención de la contaminación del mar por vertimiento de desechos y otras materias (1972 treaty)
♦ Convenio sobre la prevención y el control de los riesgos profesionales causados por las sustancias o agentes cancerigenos (1974 treaty)
♦ Convenio sobre la prohibición de las peores formas de trabajo infantil y la acción inmediata para su eliminación (1999 treaty)
♦ Convenio para la protección de la capa de ozono (1985 treaty)
♦ Convenio sobre la protección de los créditos laborales en caso de insolvencia del empleador (1992 treaty)
♦ Convenio sobre la protección del derecho de sindicación y los procedimientos para determinar las condiciones de empleo en la administración pública (1978 treaty)
♦ Convenio para la protección de los productores de fonogramas contra la reproducción no autorizada de sus fonogramas (1971 treaty)
♦ Convenio sobre la protección de la salud y la asistencia médica de la gente de mar (1987 treaty)
♦ Convenio sobre la protección de los trabajadores contra los riesgos profesionales debidos a la contaminación del aire, el ruido y las vibraciones en el lugar de trabajo (1977 treaty)
♦ Convenio sobre pueblos indigenas y tribales en paises independientes (1989 treaty)
♦ Convenio por el que sa garantizan indemnizaciones o subsidios a los desempleados involuntarios (1934 treaty)
♦ Convenio por el que se fija la edad de admisión de los niños a los trabajos industriales, 1937 (1937 treaty)
♦ Convenio por el que se fija la edad minima de admisión de los menores al trabajo en calidad de pañoleros o fogoneros (1921 treaty)
♦ Convenio por el que se fija la edad minima de admisión de los niños al trabajo maritimo (1920 treaty)
♦ Convenio por el que se fija la edad minima de admisión de los niños al trabajo maritimo, 1936 (1936 treaty)
♦ Convenio por el que se fija la edad minima de admisión de los niños a los trabajos industriales (1919 treaty)
♦ Convenio por el que se limitan las horas de trabajo en las empresas industriales a ocho horas diarias y cuarenta y ocho semanales (1919 treaty)
♦ Convenio por el que se limitan las horas de trabajo en las minas de carbón, 1931 (1931 treaty)
♦ Convenio por el que se limitan las horas de trabajo en las minas de carbón, 1935 (1935 treaty)
♦ Convenio por el que se revisan parcialmente los convenios adoptados por la conferencia general de la Organización Internacional del Trabajo (1961 treaty)
♦ Convenio sobre la readaptación profesional y el empleo de personas invalidas (1983 treaty)
♦ Convenio sobre el reconocimiento y ejecución de las sentencias arbitrales extranjeras (1958 treaty)
♦ Convenio sobre el régimen de industrias centroamericanas de integración (1958 treaty)
♦ Convenio regional sobre cooperación pesquera entre los estados Africanos ribereños del Océano Atlantico (1991 treaty)
♦ Convenio regional para el manejo y conservación de los ecosistemas naturales forestales y el desarrollo de plantaciones forestales (1993 treaty)
♦ Convênio regional Norte-Americano de radiodifusão, 1937 (1937 treaty)
♦ Convenio regional norteamericano de radiodifusión, 1937 (1937 treaty)
♦ Convenio sobre el registro de objectos lanzados al espacio ultraterrestre (1974 treaty)
♦ Convenio sobre el reglamento internacional para prevenir los abordajes (1972 treaty)
♦ Convenio para el reglamento pacifico de conflictos internacionales (1899 treaty)
♦ Convenio relativo a la abolición de las sanciones penales por incumplimiento del contrato de trabajo por parte de los trabajadores indigenas (1955 treaty)
♦ Convenio relativo a la abolición del trabajo forzoso (1957 treaty)
♦ Convenio relativo a las agencias retribuidas de colocación, 1933 (1933 treaty)
♦ Convenio relativo a las agencias retribuidas de colocación, 1949 (1949 treaty)
♦ Convenio relativo a la alimentación y al servicio de fonda a bordo de los buques (1946 treaty)
♦ Convenio relativo al alojamiento a bordo de los barcos pesqueros (1966 treaty)
♦ Convenio relativo al alojamiento de la tripulación a bordo, 1946 (1946 treaty)
♦ Convenio relativo al alojamiento de la tripulación a bordo, 1949 (1949 treaty)
♦ Convenio relativo al alojamiento de la tripulación a bordo, 1970 (1970 treaty)
♦ Convenio relativo a la aplicación del descanso semanal en las empresas industriales (1921 treaty)
♦ Convenio relativo a la aplicación de normas internacionales de trabajo en los territorios no metropolitanos (1947 treaty)
♦ Convenio relativo a la aplicación de los principios del derecho de sindicación y de negociación colectiva (1949 treaty)
♦ Convenio relativo a la asistencia médica y a las prestaciones monetarias de enfermedad (1969 treaty)
♦ Convenio relativo al certificado de aptitud de los cocineros de buque (1946 treaty)
♦ Convenio relativo al certificado de marinero preferente (1946 treaty)
♦ Convenio relativo a los certificados de competencia de pescadores (1966 treaty)
♦ Convenio relativo a las clausulas de trabajo en los contratos celebrados por las autoridades públicos (1949 treaty)
♦ Convenio relativo a un código de conducta de las conferencias maritimas (1974 treaty)
♦ Convenio relativo a la colocación de la gente de mar (1920 treaty)
♦ Convenio relativo a las condiciones de empleo de los trabajadores de las plantaciones (1958 treaty)
♦ Convenio relativo a la conservación de la fauna y flora al estado natural (1933 treaty)
♦ Convenio relativo a la contratación y la colocación de la gente de mar (1996 treaty)
♦ Convenio relativo al contrato de enrolamiento de la gente de mar (1926 treaty)
♦ Convenio relativo al contrato de enrolamiento de los pescadores (1959 treaty)
♦ Convenio relativo al contrato de transporte internacional de mercancias por carretera (1956 treaty)
♦ Convenio relativo al contrato de transporte internacional de viajeros y equipajes por carretera (1973 treaty)
♦ Convenio relativo al derecho de asociación y a la solución de los conflictos de trabajo en los territorios no metropolitanos (1947 treaty)
♦ Convenio relativo a los derechos de asociación y de coalición de los trabajadores agricolas (1921 treaty)
♦ Convenio relativo al derecho de sello en materia de cheques (1931 treaty)
♦ Convenio relativo al derecho de sello en materia de letras de cambio y pagares (1930 treaty)
♦ Convenio relativo derecho de sello en materia de letras de cambio y pagares (1930 treaty)
♦ Convenio relativo al descanso semanal en el comercio y en las oficinas (1957 treaty)
♦ Convenio relativo a la discriminación en materia de empleo y ocupación (1958 treaty)
♦ Convenio relativo a los documentos nacionales de identidad de la gente de mar (1958 treaty)
♦ Convenio relativo a la duración maxima de los contratos de trabajo de los trabajadores indigenas (1947 treaty)
♦ Convenio relativo a la edad de admisión de los niños al trabajo agricola (1921 treaty)
♦ Convenio relativo e la edad de admisión de los niños a los trabajos no industriales, 1932 (1932 treaty)
♦ Convenio relativo a la edad de admisión de los niños a los trabajos no industriales, 1937 (1937 treaty)
♦ Convenio relativo a la edad minima de admisión al trabajo de los pescadores (1959 treaty)
♦ Convenio relativo a la edad minima de admisión al trabajo subterraneo en las minas (1965 treaty)
♦ Convenio relativo al empleo de la cerusa en la pintura (1921 treaty)
♦ Convenio relativo al empleo de las mujeres antes y después del parto (1919 treaty)
♦ Convenio relativo al empleo de las mujeres en los trabajos subterraneos de toda clase de minas (1935 treaty)
♦ Convenio relativo al establecimiento de métodos para la fijación de salarios minimos (1928 treaty)
♦ Convenio relativo a las estadisticas de salarios y horas de trabajo en las industrias principales mineras y manufacturas, en la edificación y la construcción y en la agricultura (1938 treaty)
♦ Convenio relativo al examen médico de aptitud para el empleo de los menores en la industria (1946 treaty)
♦ Convenio relativo al examen médico de aptitud para el empleo de los menores en trabajos no industriales (1946 treaty)
♦ Convenio relativo al examen médico de aptitud de los menores para el empleo en trabajos subterraneos en las minas (1965 treaty)
♦ Convenio relativo al examen médico de la gente de mar (1946 treaty)
♦ Convenio relativo al examen médico obligatorio de los menores empleados a bordo de los buques (1921 treaty)
♦ Convenio relativo al examen médico de los pescadores (1959 treaty)
♦ Convenio relativo a las facilidades concedidas a la importación de mercancias destinadas a ser presentadas o utilizadas en muestras, ferias, congresos o manifestaciones similares (1961 treaty)
♦ Convenio relativo a la fijación de salarios minimos, con especial referencia a los paises en vias de desarrollo (1970 treaty)
♦ Convenio relativo a la higiene en el comercio y en las oficinas (1964 treaty)
♦ Convenio relativo a las horas de trabajo a bordo y a la dotación (1936 treaty)
♦ Convenio relativo a las horas de trabajo a bordo y la dotación de los buques (1996 treaty)
♦ Convenio relativo a las horas de trabajo y al descanso en el transporte por carretera (1939 treaty)
♦ Convenio relativo a las horas de trabajo en la fabricación automatica de vidrio plano (1934 treaty)
♦ Convenio relativo a la igualdad de remuneración entre la mano de obra masculina y la mano de obra femenina por un trabajo de igual valor (1951 treaty)
♦ Convenio relativo a la igualdad de trato entre los trabajadores extranjeros y nacionales en materia de indemnización por accidentes del trabajo (1925 treaty)
♦ Convenio relativo a la igualdad de trato de nacionales y extranjeros en materia de seguridad social (1962 treaty)
♦ Convenio relativo a la indemnización por accidentes del trabajo (1925 treaty)
♦ Convenio relativo a la indemnización por accidentes del trabajo en la agricultura (1921 treaty)
♦ Convenio relativo a la indemnización de desempleo en caso de pérdida por naufragio (1920 treaty)
♦ Convenio relativo a la indemnización por enfermedades profesionales, 1925 (1925 treaty)
♦ Convenio relativo a la indemnización por enfermedades profesionales, 1934 (1934 treaty)
♦ Convenio relativo a la indicación del peso en los grandes fardos transportados por barco (1929 treaty)
♦ Convenio relativo a la inscripción de derechos relativos a los navios en construcción (1967 treaty)
♦ Convenio relativo a la inspección del trabajo en la agricultura (1969 treaty)
♦ Convenio relativo a la inspección del trabajo en la industria y el comercio (1947 treaty)
♦ Convenio relativo a la inspección del trabajo en los territorios no metropolitanos (1947 treaty)
♦ Convenio relativo a la ley aplicable al trust y a su reconocimiento (1985 treaty)
♦ Convenio relativo a la libertad sindical y a la protección del derecho de sindicación (1948 treaty)
♦ Convenio relativo a la licencia pagada de estudios (1974 treaty)
♦ Convenio relativo a la limitación del trabajo nocturno de los menores en trabajo no industriales (1946 treaty)
♦ Convenio relativo a los métodos para la fijación de salarios minimos en la agricultura (1951 treaty)
♦ Convenio relativo al minimo de capacidad profesional de los capitanes y oficiales de la marina mercante (1936 treaty)
♦ Convenio relativo a la norma minima de la seguridad social (1952 treaty)
♦ Convenio relativo a las normas y objetivos basicos de la politica social (1962 treaty)
♦ Convenio relativo a las obligaciones del armador en caso de enfermedad, accidente o muerte de la gente de mar (1936 treaty)
♦ Convenio relativo a la organización de un régimen internacional para la conservación de los derechos del seguro de invalidez, vejez y muerte (1936 treaty)
♦ Convenio relativo a la organización del servicio del empleo (1948 treaty)
♦ Convenio relativo a las pensiones de la gente de mar (1946 treaty)
♦ Convenio relativo al peso maximo de la carga que puede ser transportada por un trabajador (1967 treaty)
♦ Convenio relativo a la politica del empleo (1964 treaty)
♦ Convenio relativo a la politica social en los territorios no metropolitanos (1947 treaty)
♦ Convenio relativo a las prescripciones de seguridad en la industria de la edificación (1937 treaty)
♦ Convenio relativo a las prestaciones en caso de accidentes del trabajo y enfermedades profesionales (1964 treaty)
♦ Convenio relativo a las prestaciones de invalidez, vejez y sobrevivientes (1967 treaty)
♦ Convenio relativo a la prevención de los accidentes del trabajo de la gente de mar (1970 treaty)
♦ Convenio relativo a la procedura civil, 1954 (1954 treaty)
♦ Convenio relativo a la protección contra los accidentes de los trabajadores empleados en la carga y descarga de los buques, 1932 (1932 treaty)
♦ Convenio relativo a la protección contra los accidentes de los trabajadores empleados en la carga y descargo de los buques (1929 treaty)
♦ Convenio relativo a la protección contra los riesgos de intoxicación por el benceno (1971 treaty)
♦ Convenio relativo a la protección y facilidades que deben otorgarse a los representantes de los trabajadores en la empresa (1971 treaty)
♦ Convenio relativo a la protección e integración de las poblaciones indigenas y de otras poblaciones tribuales y semitribuales en los paises independientes (1957 treaty)
♦ Convenio relativo a la protección de la maquinaria (1963 treaty)
♦ Convenio relativo a la protección de la maternidad (1952 treaty)
♦ Convenio relativo a la protección del salario (1949 treaty)
♦ Convenio relativo a la protección de los trabajadores contra las radiaciones ionizantes (1960 treaty)
♦ Convenio relativo al reclutamiento, colocación y condiciones de trabajo de los trabajadores migrantes (1939 treaty)
♦ Convenio relativo al reconocimiento de la personalidad juridica de sociedades, asociaciones y fundaciones extranjeras (1956 treaty)
♦ Convenio relativo a la reducción de las horas de trabajo a cuarenta por semana (1935 treaty)
♦ Convenio relativo a la reducción de las horas de trabajo en las fabricas de botellas (1935 treaty)
♦ Convenio relativo a la reducción de las horas de trabajo en la industria textil (1937 treaty)
♦ Convenio relativo a la reducción de las horas de trabajo en las obras públicas (1936 treaty)
♦ Convenio relativo al régimen fiscal de vehiculos de carretera efectuando transportes internacionales de mercancias (1956 treaty)
♦ Convenio relativo al régimen fiscal de vehiculos de carretera efectuando transportes internacionales de viajeros (1956 treaty)
♦ Convenio relativo al régimen fiscal de vehiculos de carretera a uso privado en circulación internacional (1956 treaty)
♦ Convenio relativo a la reglamentación de ciertos sistemas especiales de reclutamiento de trabajadores (1936 treaty)
♦ Convenio relativo a la reglamentación de los contratos escritos de trabajo de los trabajadores indigenas (1939 treaty)
♦ Convenio relativo a la reglamentación de las horas de trabajo en el comercio y las oficinas (1930 treaty)
♦ Convenio relativo a la repatriación de la gente de mar, 1926 (1926 treaty)
♦ Convenio relativo a la responsabilidad en la esfera del transporte maritimo de materiales nucleares (1971 treaty)
♦ Convenio relativo a la responsabilidad de explotadores de navios nucleares (1962 treaty)
♦ Convenio relativo a la revisión del Convenio sobre la protección de la maternidad (2000 treaty)
♦ Convenio relativo a los salarios, las horas de trabajo a bordo y la dotación, 1946 (1946 treaty)
♦ Convenio relativo a los salarios, las horas de trabajo a bordo y la dotación, 1949 (1949 treaty)

- ♦ Convenio relativo a salarios, horas de trabajo a bordo y dotación, 1958 (1958 treaty)
- ♦ Convenio relativo a las sanciones penales contra los trabajadores indigenas por incumplimiento del contrato de trabajo (1939 treaty)
- ♦ Convenio relativo a la seguridad social de la gente de mar, 1946 (1946 treaty)
- ♦ Convenio relativo al seguro de enfermedad de la gente de mar (1936 treaty)
- ♦ Convenio relativo al seguro de enfermedad de los trabajadores agricolas (1927 treaty)
- ♦ Convenio relativo al seguro de enfermedad de los trabajadores de la industria, del comercio y del servicio doméstico (1927 treaty)
- ♦ Convenio relativo al seguro obligatorio de invalidez de los asalariados en las empresas agricolas (1933 treaty)
- ♦ Convenio relativo al seguro obligatorio de invalidez de los asalariados en las empresas industriales y comerciales, en las profesiones liberales, en el trabajo a domicilio y en el servicio doméstico (1933 treaty)
- ♦ Convenio relativo al seguro obligatorio de muerte de los asalariados en las empresas industriales y comerciales, en las profesiones liberales, en el trabajo a domicilio y en el servicio doméstico (1933 treaty)
- ♦ Convenio relativo al seguro obligatorio de vejez de los asalariados en las empresas agricolas (1933 treaty)
- ♦ Convenio relativo al seguro obligatorio de vejez de los asalariados en las empresas industriales y comerciales, en las profesiones liberales, en el trabajo a domicilio y en el servicio doméstico (1933 treaty)
- ♦ Convenio relativo a la simplificación de la inspección de los emigrantes a bordo de los buques (1926 treaty)
- ♦ Convenio relativo a los trabajadores migrantes (1949 treaty)
- ♦ Convenio relativo al trabajo forzoso u obligatorio (1930 treaty)
- ♦ Convenio relativo al trabajo nocturno de los menores en la industria (1919 treaty)
- ♦ Convenio relativo al trabajo nocturno de los menores en la industria, 1948 (1948 treaty)
- ♦ Convenio relativo al trabajo nocturno de las mujeres (1919 treaty)
- ♦ Convenio relativo al trabajo nocturno de las mujeres, 1934 (1934 treaty)
- ♦ Convenio relativo al trabajo nocturno de las mujeres empleadas en la industria (1948 treaty)
- ♦ Convenio relativo al trabajo nocturno el las panaderias (1925 treaty)
- ♦ Convenio relativo a transportes internacionales ferroviarios, 1980 (1980 treaty)
- ♦ Convenio relativo a transportes internacionales ferroviarios, 1999 (1999 treaty)
- ♦ Convenio relativo a las vacaciones anuales pagadas (1970 treaty)
- ♦ Convenio relativo a las vacaciones anuales pagadas, 1936 (1936 treaty)
- ♦ Convenio relativo a las vacaciones anuales pagadas de la gente de mar, 1936 (1936 treaty)
- ♦ Convenio relativo a las vacaciones pagadas en la agricultura (1952 treaty)
- ♦ Convenio relativo a las vacaciones pagadas de la gente de mar, 1946 (1946 treaty)
- ♦ Convenio relativo a las vacaciones pagadas de la gente de mar, 1949 (1949 treaty)
- ♦ Convenio relativo a las zonas húmedas de importancia internacional y en particular en habitats de salvajina (1971 treaty)
- ♦ Convenio sobre la repatriación de la gente de mar, 1987 (1987 treaty)
- ♦ Convenio sobre las repercusiones sociales de los nuevos métodos de manipulación de cargas en los puertos (1973 treaty)
- ♦ Convenio sobre representación en materia de venta internacional de mercancias (1983 treaty)
- ♦ Convenio para la represión de actos ilicitos dirigidos contra la seguridad de la aviación civil (1971 treaty)
- ♦ Convenio para la Represión de Actos Ilicitos Relacionados con la Aviación Civil Internacional (2010 treaty)
- ♦ Convenio para la represión del apoderamiento ilicito de aeronaves (1970 treaty)
- ♦ Convenio sobre responsabilidad por daños causados por aeronaves a terceros en la superficie (1952 treaty)
- ♦ Convenio sobre la responsabilidad internacional por daños causados por objectos espaciales (1972 treaty)
- ♦ Convenio sobre la revisión de los articulos finales (1946 treaty)
- ♦ Convenio sobre seguridad e higiene en los trabajos portuarios (1979 treaty)
- ♦ Convenio sobre la seguridad y la salud en la agricultura (2001 treaty)
- ♦ Convenio sobre seguridad y salud en la construcción (1988 treaty)
- ♦ Convenio sobre seguridad y salud en las minas (1995 treaty)
- ♦ Convenio sobre seguridad y salud de los trabajadores y medio ambiente de trabajo (1981 treaty)
- ♦ Convenio sobre la seguridad social de la gente de mar, 1987 (1987 treaty)
- ♦ Convenio sobre la seguridad en la utilización de los productos quimicos en el trabajo (1990 treaty)
- ♦ Convenio sobre los servicios de salud en el trabajo (1985 treaty)
- ♦ Convenio Simón Rodriguez (#19284)
- ♦ Convenio sobre simplificación u harmonización de regimenes aduaneros (1973 treaty)
- ♦ Convenio sobre la terminación de la relación de trabajo por iniciativa del empleador (1982 treaty)
- ♦ Convenio sobre el trabajo a domicilio (1996 treaty)
- ♦ Convenio sobre el trabajo maritimo (2006 treaty)
- ♦ Convenio sobre el trabajo nocturno (1990 treaty)
- ♦ Convenio sobre el trabajo a tiempo parcial (1994 treaty)
- ♦ Convenio sobre el transporte multimodal international de mercancias (1980 treaty)
- ♦ Convenio para la unificación de ciertas reglas en materia de transporte de equipajes de pasajeros por mar (1967 treaty)
- ♦ Convenio para unificación de ciertas reglas en materia de transporte de pasajeros por mar (1961 treaty)
- ♦ Convenio sobre unificación de ciertas reglas en matiera de transportes aéreos internacionales, 1929 (1929 treaty)
- ♦ Convenio para la unificación de ciertas reglas relativas a privilegios y hipotecas, 1926 (1926 treaty)
- ♦ Convenio para la unificación de ciertas reglas relativas a privilegios y hipotecas maritimas (1967 treaty)
- ♦ Convenio sobre utilización del asbesto en condiciones de seguridad (1986 treaty)
- ♦ Convenio sobre las vacaciones anuales pagadas de la gente de mar (1976 treaty)
- ♦ Convenio de Viena relativo a la responsabilidad civil en materia de daños nucleares (1963 treaty)
- ♦ Convention of 6 Feb 1931 Containing Certain Provisions of Private International Law Regarding Marriage, Adoption and Guardianship (1953 treaty)
- ♦ Convention du 6 février 1931 contenant certaines dispositions de droit international privé sur le mariage, l'adoption et la tutelle (1953 treaty)
- ♦ Convention Abolishing the Legalization of Documents in the Member States of the European Communities (1987 treaty)
- ♦ Convention Abolishing the Requirement of Legalisation for Certain Documents (1977 treaty)
- ♦ Convention Abolishing the Requirement of Legalisation for Foreign Public Documents (1961 treaty)
- ♦ Convention sur l'accès à l'information, la participation du public au processus décisionnel et l'accès à la justice en matière d'environnement (1998 treaty)
- ♦ Convention on Access to Information, Public Participation in Decision-making and Access to Justice in Environmental Matters (1998 treaty)
- ♦ Convention sur les accords d'élection de for (1965 treaty)
- ♦ Convention sur les accords d'élections de for (2005 treaty)
- ♦ Convention ACP-CEE (1975 treaty)
- ♦ Convention for the Adaptation of the Principles of the Geneva Convention to Maritime War (1907 treaty)
- ♦ Convention additionnelle de l'Acte de navigation de l'Elbe (1923 treaty)
- ♦ Convention additionnelle à la Convention internationale signée à Rome le 23 novembre 1933 et concernant le transport des marchandises par chemins de fer (1950 treaty)
- ♦ Convention additionnelle modifiant la Convention au sujet du traitement réciproque des successions (1936 treaty)
- ♦ Convention additionnelle relative à la responsabilité du chemin de fer pour la mort et les blessures des voyageurs (1966 treaty)
- ♦ Convention sur l'administration provisoire des colonies et des possessions européennes d'Amérique (1940 treaty)
- ♦ Convention pour l'adoption d'un système uniforme de jaugeage des navires (1947 treaty)
- ♦ Convention sur l'affacturage international (1988 treaty)
- ♦ Convention Affecting the Nationality of Arabs Resident in Countries to Which They Are Not Related by Origin (1952 treaty)
- ♦ Convention africaine pour la conservation de la nature et des ressources naturelles (1968 treaty)
- ♦ Convention on the African Migratory Locust (1962 treaty)
- ♦ Convention Against Discrimination in Education (1960 treaty)

♦ Convention against Torture Initiative (CTI) 04786

Head Secretariat Nations Business Centre, Rue du Pré-de-la-bichette 1, 1202 Geneva, Switzerland. T. +41225921419. E-mail: info@cti2024.org.
URL: http://www.cti2024.org/

History 3 Mar 2014, Geneva (Switzerland). Launched at a high level meeting during 25th session of the *United Nations Human Rights Council (HRC, #20571)*, by Foreign Ministers of Chile, Denmark, Ghana, Indonesia and Morocco, to promote *Convention Against Torture and other Cruel, Inhuman or Degrading Treatment or Punishment (1984)*. **Aims** Achieve universal ratification and implementation of the UN Convention against Torture by 2024. **Structure** Core Group; Secretariat; Group of Friends. **Languages** English. **Staff** 3.00 FTE, paid. **Finance** Supported by: *Association for the Prevention of Torture (APT, #02869)*. **Activities** Advocacy/lobbying/activism; events/meetings; knowledge management/information dissemination; training/education. **Events** *Annual Forum* Geneva (Switzerland) 2021, *Workshop for Pacific States* Geneva (Switzerland) 2021, *Regional Technical Workshop for the Commonwealth Caribbean* Geneva (Switzerland) 2020, *Cooperation and Innovation* Copenhagen (Denmark) 2019, *Seminar* Nusa Dua (Indonesia) 2019. **Publications** *CTI Newsletter*. Training material; videos.

Members Core group of 6 governments:
Chile, Denmark, Fiji, Ghana, Indonesia, Morocco.
Group of Friends States (43):
Albania, Argentina, Australia, Austria, Bahamas, Bosnia-Herzegovina, Brazil, Burkina Faso, Canada, Costa Rica, Egypt, Finland, France, Gambia, Georgia, Germany, Grenada, Guatemala, Honduras, Iraq, Italy, Jordan, Luxembourg, Moldova, Montenegro, Myanmar, New Zealand, North Macedonia, Norway, Peru, Poland, Sierra Leone, Slovenia, Spain, Sweden, Switzerland, Togo, Tunisia, Türkiye, Uganda, UK, Uruguay, USA.
NGOs include 8 listed in this Yearbook:
Amnesty International (AI, #00801); *Center for Victims of Torture (CVT)*; *DIGNITY – Danish Institute Against Torture*; *International Bar Association (IBA, #12320)*; *International Commission of Jurists (ICJ, #12695)*; *International Federation of ACATs – Action by Christians for the Abolition of Torture (#13334)*; *Penal Reform International (PRI, #18290)*; *REDRESS*.
[2023.03.03/XM4870/**E***]

- ♦ Convention Against Torture and other Cruel, Inhuman or Degrading Treatment or Punishment (1984 treaty)
- ♦ Convention on Agency in the International Sale of Goods (1983 treaty)
- ♦ Convention Allied Surveillance of the Siberian Railways (1919 treaty)
- ♦ Convention alpine – Convention pour la protection des Alpes (1991 treaty)
- ♦ Convention for the Amelioration of the Condition of the Wounded in Armies in the Field, 1864 (1864 treaty)
- ♦ Convention on Anti-diphtheritic Serum (1930 treaty)
- ♦ Convention on the Application of Standards of the Council for Mutual Economic Assistance (1974 treaty)
- ♦ Convention sur les Armes Légères et de Petit Calibre, leurs Munitions et Autres Matériels Connexes (2006 treaty)
- ♦ Convention sur les armes à sous-munitions (2008 treaty)
- ♦ Convention sur l'asile, 1928 (1928 treaty)
- ♦ Convention sur l'asile politique, 1933 (1933 treaty)
- ♦ Convention sur les aspects civils de l'enlèvement international d'enfants (1980 treaty)
- ♦ Convention sur l' assistance en cas d' accident nucléaire ou de situation d' urgence radiologique (1986 treaty)
- ♦ Convention on Assistance in the Case of Nuclear Accident or Radiological Emergency (1986 treaty)
- ♦ Convention d'assistance mutuelle (1914 treaty)
- ♦ Convention d'assistance mutuelle en matière de perception des impôts sur le chiffre d'affaires, de la taxe de transmission et des impôts analogues (1964 treaty)
- ♦ Convention d'assistance sociale et médicale (1949 treaty)
- ♦ Convention assurant aux chômeurs involontaires des indemnités ou des allocations (1934 treaty)
- ♦ Convention on Asylum, 1928 (1928 treaty)
- ♦ Convention d'Athènes relative au transport par mer de passagers et leurs bagages (1974 treaty)
- ♦ Convention sur l'aviation commerciale (1928 treaty)
- ♦ Convention on the Avoidance of Double Taxation on the Income and Property of Corporate Bodies (1978 treaty)
- ♦ Convention on the Avoidance of Double Taxation on Personal Income and Property (1977 treaty)
- ♦ Convention for the avoidance of double taxation with respect to taxes on inheritances and gifts (1989 treaty)
- ♦ Convention de Bâle sur le contrôle des mouvements transfrontières de déchets dangereux et de leur élimination (1989 treaty)
- ♦ Convention to Ban the Importation into Forum Island Countries of Hazardous Wastes and Radioactive Wastes and to Control the Transboundary Movement and Management of Hazardous Wastes within the South Pacific (1995 treaty)
- ♦ Convention on the Ban of the Import of Hazardous Wastes into Africa and on the Control of Their Transboundary Movements within Africa (1991 treaty)
- ♦ Convention de Belém do Para – Convention interaméricaine pour la prévention, la sanction et l'élimination de la violence contre la femme (1994 treaty)
- ♦ Convention of Belém do Para – Inter-American Convention on the Prevention, Punishment and Eradication of Violence Against Women (1994 treaty)
- ♦ Convention Benelux Concernant la Coopération Transfrontalière entre Collectivités ou Autorités Territoriales (1986 treaty)
- ♦ Convention Benelux en matière de chasse et de protection des oiseaux (1970 treaty)
- ♦ Convention Benelux en matière de conservation de la nature et de protection des paysages (1982 treaty)
- ♦ Convention Benelux en matière de dessins ou modèles (1966 treaty)
- ♦ Convention Benelux en matière de marques de produits (1962 treaty)
- ♦ Convention Benelux en Matière de Propriété Intellectuelle (2005 treaty)
- ♦ Convention Benelux portant loi uniforme relative à l'astreinte (1973 treaty)
- ♦ Convention Benelux relative à l'assurance obligatoire de la responsabilité civile en matière de véhicules automoteurs (1966 treaty)
- ♦ Convention Benelux relative aux comourants (1972 treaty)
- ♦ Convention de Berne – Convention relative à la conservation de la vie sauvage et du milieu naturel de l'Europe (1979 treaty)
- ♦ Convention de Berne pour la protection des oeuvres littéraires et artistiques, 1886 (1886 treaty)
- ♦ Convention on Biological Diversity (1992 treaty)
- ♦ Convention sur le brevet eurasien (1994 treaty)
- ♦ Convention sur le brevet européen – Convention sur la délivrance de brevets européens (1973 treaty)
- ♦ Convention sur les brevets d'invention, les dessins et modèles industriels, les marques de fabrique et de commerce et la propriété littéraire et artistique (1906 treaty)

articles and prepositions
http://www.brill.com/yioo

Convention concernant navigation
04786

♦ Convention sur brevets d'invention, patentes de dessins et de modèles industriels (1910 treaty)
♦ Convention-cadre du Conseil de l'Europe sur la valeur du patrimoine culturel pour la société (2005 treaty)
♦ Convention-cadre européenne sur la coopération transfrontalière des collectivités ou autorités territoriales (1980 treaty)
♦ Convention-cadre des Nations Unies sur les changements climatiques (1992 treaty)
♦ Convention-cadre des nations unies sur les changements climatiques – Secrétariat (#20564)
♦ Convention-cadre de l'OMS pour la lutte antitabac (2003 treaty)
♦ Convention sur le cadre promotionnel pour la sécurité et la santé au travail (2006 treaty)
♦ Convention-cadre pour la protection des minorités nationales (1995 treaty)
♦ Convention on the Canalization of the Moselle (1956 treaty)
♦ Convention on Celebration and Recognition of the Validity of Marriages (1978 treaty)
♦ Convention sur la célébration et la reconnaissance de la validité des mariages (1978 treaty)
♦ Convention on Central American Tariff and Customs Regulations (1984 treaty)
♦ Convention centroaméricaine pour l'unification des normes fondamentales de l'enseignement (1962 treaty)
♦ Convention centroaméricaine sur l'uniformisation des droits à l'importation (1959 treaty)
♦ Convention on Certain Questions Relating to the Conflict of Nationality Laws (1930 treaty)
♦ Convention on the Choice of Court (1965 treaty)
♦ Convention on Choice of Court Agreements (2005 treaty)
♦ Convention sur le chômage (1919 treaty)
♦ Convention sur la circulation routière, 1949 (1949 treaty)
♦ Convention sur la circulation routière, 1968 (1968 treaty)
♦ Convention on the Civil Aspects of International Child Abduction (1980 treaty)
♦ Convention civile sur la corruption (1999 treaty)
♦ Convention on Civil Liability for Damage Caused During Carriage of Dangerous Goods by Road, Rail and Inland Navigation Vessels (1989 treaty)
♦ Convention on Civil Liability for Damage Resulting from Activities Dangerous to the Environment (1993 treaty)
♦ Convention on Civil Liability for Oil Pollution Damage Resulting from Exploration for and Exploitation of Seabed Mineral Resources (1977 treaty)
♦ Convention on Cluster Munitions (2008 treaty)
♦ Convention on a Code of Conduct for Liner Conferences (1974 treaty)
♦ Convention sur le commerce international des espèces de faune et de flore sauvages menacées d'extinction (1973 treaty)
♦ Convention on Commercial Aviation (1928 treaty)
♦ Convention commerciale (1923 treaty)
♦ Convention on a Common Transit Procedure (1987 treaty)
♦ Convention commune sur la sûreté de la gestion du combustible usé et sur la sûreté de la gestion des déchets radioactifs (1997 treaty)
♦ Convention sur la compétence du for contractuel en cas de vente à caractère international d'objets mobiliers corporels (1958 treaty)
♦ Convention complémentaire à la Convention de Paris sur la responsabilité civile dans le domaine de l'énergie nucléaire (1963 treaty)
♦ Convention, complémentaire à la Convention de Varsovie, pour l'unification de certaines règles relatives au transport aérien international effectué par une personne autre que le transporteur contractuel (1961 treaty)
♦ Convention concernant l'abolition des capitulations en Egypte (1937 treaty)
♦ Convention concernant l'abolition des sanctions pénales pour manquements au contrat de travail de la part des travailleurs indigènes (1955 treaty)
♦ Convention concernant l'abolition du travail forcé (1957 treaty)
♦ Convention concernant l'administration du travail: rôle, fonctions et organisation (1978 treaty)
♦ Convention concernant l'âge d'admission des enfants au travail dans l'agriculture (1921 treaty)
♦ Convention concernant l'âge d'admission des enfants aux travaux non industriels, 1932 (1932 treaty)
♦ Convention concernant l'âge d'admission des enfants aux travaux non industriels, 1937 (1937 treaty)
♦ Convention concernant l'âge minimum d'admission à l'emploi (1973 treaty)
♦ Convention concernant l'âge minimum d'admission au travail des pêcheurs (1959 treaty)
♦ Convention concernant l'âge minimum d'admission aux travaux souterrains dans les mines (1965 treaty)
♦ Convention concernant les agences d'emploi privées (1997 treaty)
♦ Convention concernant l'alimentation et le service de table à bord des navires (1946 treaty)
♦ Convention concernant l'application de la législation d'assurance-accidents des différents pays dans les cas où un employeur de l'un des pays contractants exerce une activité ou occupe des travailleurs dans un autre de ces pays (1937 treaty)
♦ Convention concernant l'application de normes internationales du travail aux territoires non métropolitains (1947 treaty)
♦ Convention concernant l'application des principes du droit d'organisation et de négociation collective (1949 treaty)
♦ Convention concernant l'application du repos hebdomadaire dans les établissements industriels (1921 treaty)
♦ Convention concernant l'assistance administrative mutuelle en matière fiscale (1988 treaty)
♦ Convention concernant l'assurance-décès obligatoire des salariés des entreprises agricoles (1933 treaty)
♦ Convention concernant l'assurance-décès obligatoire des salariés des entreprises industrielles et commerciales, des professions libérales, ainsi que des travailleurs à domicile et des gens de maison (1933 treaty)
♦ Convention concernant l'assurance-invalidité obligatoire des salariés des entreprises agricoles (1933 treaty)
♦ Convention concernant l'assurance-invalidité obligatoire des salariés des entreprises, industrielles et commerciales, des professions libérales, ainsi que des travailleurs à domicile et des gens de maison (1933 treaty)
♦ Convention concernant l'assurance-maladie des gens de mer (1936 treaty)
♦ Convention concernant l'assurance-maladie des travailleurs agricoles (1927 treaty)
♦ Convention concernant l'assurance-maladie des travailleurs de l'industrie et du commerce et des gens de maison (1927 treaty)
♦ Convention concernant l'assurance-vieillesse obligatoire des salariés des entreprises agricoles (1933 treaty)
♦ Convention concernant l'assurance-vieillesse obligatoire des salariés des entreprises industrielles et commerciales, des professions libérales, ainsi que des travailleurs à domicile et des gens de maison (1933 treaty)
♦ Convention concernant le bien-être des gens de mer, en mer et dans les ports (1987 treaty)
♦ Convention concernant les brevets de capacité des pêcheurs (1966 treaty)
♦ Convention concernant les bureaux de placement payants, 1933 (1933 treaty)
♦ Convention concernant les bureaux de placement payants, 1949 (1949 treaty)
♦ Convention concernant certaines questions relatives au conflit de loi sur la nationalité (1930 treaty)
♦ Convention concernant les certificats de capacité de matelot qualifié (1946 treaty)
♦ Convention concernant la cessation de la relation de travail à l'initiative de l'employeur (1982 treaty)
♦ Convention concernant les clauses de travail dans les contrats passés par une autorité publique (1949 treaty)
♦ Convention concernant la compétence des autorités et la loi applicable en matière de protection des mineurs (1961 treaty)
♦ Convention concernant la compétence des autorités, la loi applicable et la reconnaissance des décisions en matière d'adoption (1965 treaty)
♦ Convention concernant la compétence judiciaire et l'exécution des décisions en matière civile et commerciale (1968 treaty)
♦ Convention concernant la compétence, la loi applicable, la reconnaissance, l'exécution et la coopération en matière de responsabilité parentale et de mesures de protection des enfants (1996 treaty)
♦ Convention concernant les conditions d'emploi des travailleurs des plantations (1958 treaty)
♦ Convention concernant les conditions de travail dans les hôtels, restaurants et établissements similaires (1991 treaty)
♦ Convention concernant les conflits de lois relatifs aux effets du mariage sur les droits et les devoirs des époux dans leurs rapports personnels et sur les biens des époux (1905 treaty)
♦ Convention concernant le congé-éducation payé (1974 treaty)
♦ Convention concernant les congés annuels payés (1970 treaty)
♦ Convention concernant les congés annuels payés, 1936 (1936 treaty)
♦ Convention concernant les congés annuels payés des marins, 1936 (1936 treaty)
♦ Convention concernant les congés payés dans l'agriculture (1952 treaty)
♦ Convention concernant les congés payés annuels des gens de mer (1976 treaty)
♦ Convention concernant les congés payés des marins, 1946 (1946 treaty)
♦ Convention concernant les congés payés des marins, 1949 (1949 treaty)
♦ Convention concernant la conservation de la biodiversité et la protection des aires forestières prioritaires de l' Amérique centrale (1992 treaty)
♦ Convention concernant la conservation des ressources d'anadromes (1992 treaty)
♦ Convention concernant les consultations tripartites destinées à promouvoir la mise en oeuvre des normes internationales du travail (1976 treaty)
♦ Convention concernant la continuité de l'emploi des gens de mer (1976 treaty)
♦ Convention concernant le contrat d'engagement des pêcheurs (1959 treaty)
♦ Convention concernant la coopération pour la protection et l' utilisation durable du Danube (1994 treaty)
♦ Convention concernant le diplôme de capacité professionnelle des cuisiniers de navires (1946 treaty)
♦ Convention concernant la discrimination en matière d'emploi et de profession (1958 treaty)
♦ Convention concernant la distribution de signaux porteurs de programmes transmis par satellite (1974 treaty)
♦ Convention concernant le droit d'association et le règlement des conflits du travail dans les territoires non métropolitains (1947 treaty)
♦ Convention concernant les droits d'association et de coalition des travailleurs agricoles (1921 treaty)
♦ Convention concernant la durée maximum des contrats de travail des travailleurs indigènes (1947 treaty)
♦ Convention concernant la durée du travail à bord des navires et les effectifs (1936 treaty)
♦ Convention concernant la durée du travail des gens de mer et les effectifs des navires (1996 treaty)
♦ Convention concernant la durée du travail et les périodes de repos dans les transports routiers (1979 treaty)
♦ Convention concernant la durée du travail et les repos dans les transports par route (1939 treaty)
♦ Convention concernant la durée du travail dans les verreries à vitres automatiques (1934 treaty)
♦ Convention concernant les échanges entre Etats de publications officielles et documents gouvernementaux (1958 treaty)
♦ Convention concernant les échanges internationaux de publications (1958 treaty)
♦ Convention concernant l'égalité de chances et de traitement pour les travailleurs des deux sexes: travailleurs ayant des responsabilités familiales (1981 treaty)
♦ Convention concernant l'égalité de rémunération entre la main-d'oeuvre masculine et la main-d'oeuvre féminine pour un travail de valeur égale (1951 treaty)
♦ Convention concernant l'égalité de traitement des nationaux et des non-nationaux en matière de sécurité sociale (1962 treaty)
♦ Convention concernant l'égalité de traitement des travailleurs étrangers et nationaux en matière de réparation des accidents du travail (1925 treaty)
♦ Convention concernant l'emploi de la céruse dans la peinture (1921 treaty)
♦ Convention concernant l'emploi et les conditions de travail et de vie du personnel infirmier (1977 treaty)
♦ Convention concernant l'emploi des femmes avant et après l'accouchement (1919 treaty)
♦ Convention concernant l'emploi des femmes aux travaux souterrains dans les mines de toutes catégories (1935 treaty)
♦ Convention concernant l'emploi de la radiodiffusion dans l'intérêt de la paix (1936 treaty)
♦ Convention concernant l'établissement d'un régime international de conservation des droits à l'assurance-invalidité-vieillesse-décès (1936 treaty)
♦ Convention concernant l'établissement d'un système international de conservation des droits en matière de sécurité sociale (1982 treaty)
♦ Convention concernant l'examen médical d'aptitude des adolescents à l'emploi aux travaux souterrains dans les mines (1965 treaty)
♦ Convention concernant l'examen médical d'aptitude à l'emploi dans l'industrie des enfants et des adolescents (1946 treaty)
♦ Convention concernant l'examen médical d'aptitude à l'emploi aux travaux non industriels des enfants et des adolescents (1946 treaty)
♦ Convention concernant l'examen médical des gens de mer (1946 treaty)
♦ Convention concernant l'examen médical obligatoire des enfants et des jeunes gens employés à bord des bateaux (1921 treaty)
♦ Convention concernant l'examen médical des pêcheurs (1959 treaty)
♦ Convention concernant les expositions internationales (1928 treaty)
♦ Convention concernant la fixation des salaires minima, notamment en ce qui concerne les pays en voie de développement (1970 treaty)
♦ Convention concernant l'hygiène dans le commerce et les bureaux (1964 treaty)
♦ Convention concernant l'indemnité de chômage en cas de perte par naufrage (1920 treaty)
♦ Convention concernant l'indication du poids sur les gros colis transportés par bateau (1929 treaty)
♦ Convention concernant l'inspection des conditions de travail et de vie des gens de mer (1996 treaty)
♦ Convention concernant l'inspection du travail dans l'agriculture (1969 treaty)
♦ Convention concernant l'inspection du travail dans l'industrie et le commerce (1947 treaty)
♦ Convention concernant l'inspection du travail dans les territoires non métropolitains (1947 treaty)
♦ Convention concernant l'institution de méthodes de fixation des salaires minima (1928 treaty)
♦ Convention concernant l'interdiction et les mesures de protection analogues (1905 treaty)
♦ Convention concernant l'interdiction des pires formes de travail des enfants et l'action immédiate en vue de leur élimination (1999 treaty)
♦ Convention concernant la liberté syndicale et la protection du droit syndical (1948 treaty)
♦ Convention concernant la limitation du travail de nuit des enfants et adolescents dans les travaux non industriels (1946 treaty)
♦ Convention concernant le logement à bord des bateaux de pêche (1966 treaty)
♦ Convention concernant le logement de l'équipage à bord, 1946 (1946 treaty)
♦ Convention concernant le logement de l'équipage à bord, 1949 (1949 treaty)
♦ Convention concernant la lutte contre la discrimination dans le domaine de l'enseignement (1960 treaty)
♦ Convention concernant les mesures à prendre pour interdire et empêcher l'exportation, l'importation et le transfert de propriété illicites des biens culturels (1970 treaty)
♦ Convention concernant les méthodes de fixation des salaires minima dans l'agriculture (1951 treaty)
♦ Convention concernant le minimum de capacité professionnelle des capitaines et officiers de la marine marchande (1936 treaty)
♦ Convention concernant les monnaies divisionnaires d'argent, 1885 (1885 treaty)
♦ Convention concernant la navigabilité et l'équipement des navires (1926 treaty)
♦ Convention concernant la navigation sur le lac de Constance (1973 treaty)

Convention concernant norme
04786

alphabetic sequence excludes
For the complete listing, see Yearbook Online at

- ♦ Convention concernant la norme minimum de la sécurité sociale (1952 treaty)
- ♦ Convention concernant les normes minima à observer sur les navires marchands (1976 treaty)
- ♦ Convention concernant les objectifs et les normes de base de la politique sociale (1962 treaty)
- ♦ Convention concernant les obligations de l'armateur en cas de maladie ou de décès des gens de mer (1936 treaty)
- ♦ Convention concernant l'organisation du service de l'emploi (1948 treaty)
- ♦ Convention concernant les organisations de travailleurs ruraux et leur rôle dans le développement économique et social (1975 treaty)
- ♦ Convention concernant les pensions des gens de mer (1946 treaty)
- ♦ Convention concernant les peuples indigènes et tribaux dans les pays indépendants (1989 treaty)
- ♦ Convention concernant les pièces d'identité nationales des gens de mer (1958 treaty)
- ♦ Convention concernant le placement des marins (1920 treaty)
- ♦ Convention concernant les placements en emprunts de guerre (1922 treaty)
- ♦ Convention concernant le poids maximum des charges pouvant être transportées par un seul travailleur (1967 treaty)
- ♦ Convention concernant la politique de l'emploi (1964 treaty)
- ♦ Convention concernant la politique sociale dans les territoires non métropolitains (1947 treaty)
- ♦ Convention concernant les prescriptions de sécurité dans l'industrie du bâtiment (1937 treaty)
- ♦ Convention concernant les prestations d'invalidité, de vieillesse et de survivants (1967 treaty)
- ♦ Convention concernant la prévention des accidents industriels majeurs (1993 treaty)
- ♦ Convention concernant la prévention des accidents du travail des gens de mer (1970 treaty)
- ♦ Convention concernant la prévention et le contrôle des risques professionnels causés par les substances et agents cancérogènes (1974 treaty)
- ♦ Convention concernant la promotion de l'emploi et la protection contre le chômage (1988 treaty)
- ♦ Convention concernant la promotion de la négociation collective (1981 treaty)
- ♦ Convention concernant la protection contre les risques d'intoxication dus au benzène (1971 treaty)
- ♦ Convention concernant la protection des créances des travailleurs en cas d'insolvabilité de leur employeur (1992 treaty)
- ♦ Convention concernant la protection du droit d'organisation et les procédures de détermination des conditions d'emploi dans la fonction publique (1978 treaty)
- ♦ Convention concernant la protection de l' environnement marin et des aires côtières du Pacifique du Sud-Est (1981 treaty)
- ♦ Convention concernant la protection et l'intégration des populations aborigènes et autres populations tribales et semi-tribales dans les pays indépendants (1957 treaty)
- ♦ Convention concernant la protection des machines (1963 treaty)
- ♦ Convention concernant la protection de la maternité (1952 treaty)
- ♦ Convention concernant la protection du patrimoine mondial culturel et naturel (1972 treaty)
- ♦ Convention concernant la protection des représentants des travailleurs dans l'entreprise et les facilités à leur accorder (1971 treaty)
- ♦ Convention concernant la protection de la santé et les soins médicaux des gens de mer (1987 treaty)
- ♦ Convention concernant la protection des travailleurs contre les radiations ionisantes (1960 treaty)
- ♦ Convention concernant la protection des travailleurs contre les risques professionnels dus à la pollution de l'air, au bruit et aux vibrations sur les lieux de travail (1977 treaty)
- ♦ Convention concernant la protection des travailleurs occupés au chargement ou au déchargement des bateaux contre les accidents, 1929 (1929 treaty)
- ♦ Convention concernant la protection des travailleurs occupés au chargement et au déchargement des bateaux contre les accidents, 1932 (1932 treaty)
- ♦ Convention concernant la publicité des documents douaniers (1923 treaty)
- ♦ Convention concernant la réadaptation professionnelle et l'emploi des personnes handicapées (1983 treaty)
- ♦ Convention concernant la reconnaissance et l'exécution des décisions en matière d'obligations alimentaires envers les enfants (1958 treaty)
- ♦ Convention concernant la reconnaissance et l'exécution de décisions relatives aux obligations alimentaires (1973 treaty)
- ♦ Convention concernant la reconnaissance et l'exécution des jugements rendus en matière civile (1977 treaty)
- ♦ Convention concernant la reconnaissance de la personnalité juridique des sociétés, associations et fondations étrangères (1956 treaty)
- ♦ Convention concernant le recrutement, le placement et les conditions de travail des travailleurs migrants (1939 treaty)
- ♦ Convention concernant le recrutement et le placement des gens de mer (1996 treaty)
- ♦ Convention concernant la réduction de la durée du travail dans l'industrie textile (1937 treaty)
- ♦ Convention concernant la réduction de la durée du travail à quarante heures par semaine (1935 treaty)
- ♦ Convention concernant la réduction de la durée du travail dans les travaux publics (1936 treaty)
- ♦ Convention concernant la réduction de la durée du travail dans les verreries à bouteilles (1935 treaty)
- ♦ Convention concernant le régime des détroits (1923 treaty)
- ♦ Convention concernant la réglementation de certains systèmes particuliers de recrutement des travailleurs (1936 treaty)
- ♦ Convention concernant la réglementation des contrats de travail écrits des travailleurs indigènes (1939 treaty)
- ♦ Convention concernant la réglementation de la durée du travail dans le commerce et dans les bureaux (1930 treaty)
- ♦ Convention concernant la réglementation des prélèvements d'eau opérés dans le lac de Constance (1966 treaty)
- ♦ Convention concernant le règlement de diverses catégories de pensions qui n'ont pas été réglées par la Convention de Rome (1922 treaty)
- ♦ Convention concernant le règlement des pensions provinciales, communales et de districts (1923 treaty)
- ♦ Convention concernant les règles adoptées en matière de sauvetage de torpilles automobiles (1934 treaty)
- ♦ Convention concernant la réparation des accidents du travail (1925 treaty)
- ♦ Convention concernant la réparation des accidents du travail dans l'agriculture (1921 treaty)
- ♦ Convention concernant la réparation des maladies professionnelles, 1925 (1925 treaty)
- ♦ Convention concernant la réparation des maladies professionnelles, 1934 (1934 treaty)
- ♦ Convention concernant les répercussions sociales des nouvelles méthodes de manutention dans les ports (1973 treaty)
- ♦ Convention concernant le repos hebdomadaire dans le commerce et les bureaux (1957 treaty)
- ♦ Convention concernant la révision de la Convention sur la protection de la maternité (2000 treaty)
- ♦ Convention concernant le rôle de l'orientation et de la formation professionnelles dans la mise en valeur des ressources humaines (1975 treaty)
- ♦ Convention concernant les salaires, la durée du travail à bord et les effectifs, 1946 (1946 treaty)
- ♦ Convention concernant les sanctions pénales pour manquements au contrat de travail de la part des travailleurs indigènes (1939 treaty)
- ♦ Convention concernant la sécurité et l'hygiène du travail dans les manutentions portuaires (1979 treaty)
- ♦ Convention concernant la sécurité et la santé dans la construction (1988 treaty)
- ♦ Convention concernant la sécurité et la santé dans les mines (1995 treaty)
- ♦ Convention concernant la sécurité, la santé des travailleurs et le milieu de travail (1981 treaty)
- ♦ Convention concernant la sécurité sociale des gens de mer, 1946 (1946 treaty)
- ♦ Convention concernant la sécurité dans l'utilisation de l'amiante (1986 treaty)
- ♦ Convention concernant la sécurité dans l'utilisation des produits chimiques au travail (1990 treaty)
- ♦ Convention concernant les services de santé au travail (1985 treaty)
- ♦ Convention concernant la simplification de l'inspection des émigrants à bord des navires (1926 treaty)
- ♦ Convention concernant les soins médicaux et les indemnités de maladies (1969 treaty)
- ♦ Convention concernant les stagiaires (1950 treaty)
- ♦ Convention concernant les statistiques des salaires et des heures de travail dans les principales industries minières et manufacturières, y compris le bâtiment et la construction, et dans l'agriculture (1938 treaty)
- ♦ Convention concernant le statut des réfugiés provenant d'Allemagne (1938 treaty)
- ♦ Convention concernant le transfert du contrôle des personnes vers les frontières extérieures du territoire du Benelux (1960 treaty)
- ♦ Convention concernant le transfert à l'Etat français de la propriété des emplacements des monuments britanniques commémoratifs de la guerre 1914-1918 (1938 treaty)
- ♦ Convention concernant le travail à domicile (1996 treaty)
- ♦ Convention concernant le travail forcé ou obligatoire (1930 treaty)
- ♦ Convention concernant les travailleurs frontaliers (1950 treaty)
- ♦ Convention concernant les travailleurs migrants (1949 treaty)
- ♦ Convention concernant le travail de nuit dans les boulangeries (1925 treaty)
- ♦ Convention concernant le travail de nuit des enfants dans l'industrie (1919 treaty)
- ♦ Convention concernant le travail de nuit des enfants dans l'industrie, 1948 (1948 treaty)
- ♦ Convention concernant le travail de nuit des femmes (1919 treaty)
- ♦ Convention concernant le travail de nuit des femmes, 1934 (1934 treaty)
- ♦ Convention concernant le travail de nuit des femmes occupées dans l'industrie (1948 treaty)
- ♦ Convention concernant le travail à temps partiel (1994 treaty)
- ♦ Convention Concerning the Abolition of Forced Labour (1957 treaty)
- ♦ Convention Concerning the Abolition of Penal Sanctions for Breaches of Contract of Employment by Indigenous Workers (1955 treaty)
- ♦ Convention Concerning Accommodation on Board Fishing Vessels (1966 treaty)
- ♦ Convention Concerning Accommodation of Crews, 1970 (1970 treaty)
- ♦ Convention Concerning the Age for Admission of Children to Employment in Agriculture (1921 treaty)
- ♦ Convention Concerning the Age for Admission of Children to Non-industrial Employment, 1932 (1932 treaty)
- ♦ Convention Concerning the Age for Admission of Children to Non-industrial Employment, 1937 (1937 treaty)
- ♦ Convention Concerning Annual Holidays with Pay (1970 treaty)
- ♦ Convention Concerning Annual Holidays with Pay, 1936 (1936 treaty)
- ♦ Convention Concerning Annual Holidays with Pay for Seamen, 1936 (1936 treaty)
- ♦ Convention Concerning Annual Leave with Pay for Seafarers (1976 treaty)
- ♦ Convention Concerning the Application of the Principles of the Right to Organize and to Bargain Collectively (1949 treaty)
- ♦ Convention Concerning the Application of the Weekly Rest in Industrial Undertakings (1921 treaty)
- ♦ Convention Concerning Artistic Exhibitions (1936 treaty)
- ♦ Convention Concerning Basic Aims and Standards of Social Policy (1962 treaty)
- ♦ Convention Concerning Benefits in the Case of Employment Injury (1964 treaty)
- ♦ Convention Concerning the Certification of Able Seamen (1946 treaty)
- ♦ Convention Concerning the Certification of Ships' Cooks (1946 treaty)
- ♦ Convention Concerning Compulsory Invalidity Insurance for Persons Employed in Agricultural Undertakings (1933 treaty)
- ♦ Convention Concerning Compulsory Invalidity Insurance for Persons Employed in Industrial or Commercial Undertakings, in the Liberal Professions, and for Outworkers and Domestic Servants (1933 treaty)
- ♦ Convention Concerning the Compulsory Medical Examination of Children and Young Persons Employed at Sea (1921 treaty)
- ♦ Convention Concerning Compulsory Old-age Insurance for Persons Employed in Agricultural Undertakings (1933 treaty)
- ♦ Convention Concerning Compulsory Old-age Insurance for Persons Employed in Industrial or Commercial Undertakings, in the Liberal Professions, and for Outworkers and Domestic Servants (1933 treaty)
- ♦ Convention Concerning Compulsory Widows' and Orphans' Insurance for Persons Employed in Agricultural Undertakings (1933 treaty)
- ♦ Convention Concerning Compulsory Widows' and Orphans' Insurance for Persons Employed in Industrial or Commercial Undertakings, in the Liberal Professions and for Outworkers and Domestic Servants (1933 treaty)
- ♦ Convention Concerning Conditions of Employment of Plantation Workers (1958 treaty)
- ♦ Convention Concerning Continuity of Employment of Seafarers (1976 treaty)
- ♦ Convention Concerning Cooperation with Regard to Customs and Excise (1952 treaty)
- ♦ Convention Concerning Cooperation in the Regulation of Imports, Exports and Transit Traffic (1961 treaty)
- ♦ Convention Concerning Courts Jurisdiction and the Enforcement of Judgements in Civil and Commercial Matters (1968 treaty)
- ♦ Convention Concerning the Creation of Minimum Wage-fixing Machinery (1928 treaty)
- ♦ Convention Concerning Crew Accommodation on Board Ship, 1946 (1946 treaty)
- ♦ Convention Concerning Crew Accommodation on Board Ship, 1949 (1949 treaty)
- ♦ Convention Concerning Customs Clearance for the International Transport of Goods by Road Vehicle (1965 treaty)
- ♦ Convention Concerning Customs Facilities for Touring (1954 treaty)
- ♦ Convention Concerning Discrimination in Respect of Employment and Occupation (1958 treaty)
- ♦ Convention Concerning Employment and Conditions of Work and Life of Nursing Personnel (1977 treaty)
- ♦ Convention Concerning Employment Policy (1964 treaty)
- ♦ Convention Concerning Employment Promotion and Protection Against Unemployment (1988 treaty)
- ♦ Convention Concerning the Employment of Women before and After Childbirth (1919 treaty)
- ♦ Convention Concerning Employment of Women During the Night, 1919 (1919 treaty)
- ♦ Convention Concerning Employment of Women During the Night, 1934 (1934 treaty)
- ♦ Convention Concerning the Employment of Women on Underground Work in Mines of all Kinds (1935 treaty)
- ♦ Convention Concerning Equality of Treatment for National and Foreign Workers as Regards Workmen's Compensation for Accidents (1925 treaty)
- ♦ Convention Concerning Equality of Treatment of Nationals and Non-nationals in Social Security (1962 treaty)
- ♦ Convention Concerning Equal Opportunities and Equal Treatment for Men and Women Workers: Workers with Family Responsibilities (1981 treaty)
- ♦ Convention Concerning Equal Remuneration for Men and Women Workers for Work of Equal Value (1951 treaty)
- ♦ Convention Concerning the Establishment of an International Scheme for the Maintenance of Rights under Invalidity, Old-age and Widows' and Orphans' Insurance (1936 treaty)
- ♦ Convention Concerning the Establishment of an International System for the Maintenance of Rights in Social Security (1982 treaty)
- ♦ Convention Concerning the Exchange of Official Publications and Government Documents between States (1958 treaty)
- ♦ Convention Concerning Facilities for Educational and Publicity Films (1936 treaty)
- ♦ Convention Concerning Fee-charging Employment Agencies, 1933 (1933 treaty)
- ♦ Convention Concerning Fee-charging Employment Agencies, 1949 (1949 treaty)
- ♦ Convention Concerning Fishermen's Articles of Agreement (1959 treaty)
- ♦ Convention Concerning Fishermen's Certificates of Competency (1966 treaty)

articles and prepositions
http://www.brill.com/yioo
Convention Conduct Fishing
04786

- Convention Concerning Fishing in the Black Sea (1959 treaty)
- Convention Concerning Fishing in the Waters of the Danube (1958 treaty)
- Convention Concerning Food and Catering for Crews on Board Ship (1946 treaty)
- Convention Concerning Forced or Compulsory Labour (1930 treaty)
- Convention Concerning Freedom of Association and Protection of the Right to Organize (1948 treaty)
- Convention Concerning Frontier Workers (1950 treaty)
- Convention Concerning German Tourist Traffic with Belgium and the Grand Duchy of Luxembourg (1939 treaty)
- Convention Concerning the Guarding of Machinery (1963 treaty)
- Convention Concerning Health Protection and Medical Care for Seafarer (1987 treaty)
- Convention Concerning Holidays with Pay in Agriculture (1952 treaty)
- Convention Concerning Home Work (1996 treaty)
- Convention Concerning Hours of Work on Board Ship and Manning (1936 treaty)
- Convention Concerning Hours of Work and Rest Periods in Road Transport (1979 treaty)
- Convention Concerning Hygiene in Commerce and Offices (1964 treaty)
- Convention Concerning Indigenous and Tribal Peoples in Independent Countries (1989 treaty)
- Convention Concerning the Inspection of Seafarers' Working and Living Conditions (1996 treaty)
- Convention Concerning the International Administration of the Estates of Deceased Persons (1973 treaty)
- Convention Concerning International Carriage by Rail, 1980 (1980 treaty)
- Convention Concerning International Carriage by Rail, 1999 (1999 treaty)
- Convention Concerning International Cooperation Regarding Administrative Assistance to Refugees (1985 treaty)
- Convention Concerning the International Exchange of Information Relating to Civil Status (1958 treaty)
- Convention Concerning the International Exchange of Publications (1958 treaty)
- Convention Concerning Invalidity, Old-age and Survivors' Benefits (1967 treaty)
- Convention Concerning the Issuance of a Certificate of Matrimonial Capacity (1980 treaty)
- Convention Concerning the Issue of Certain Extracts from Civil Status Records to be Sent Abroad (1956 treaty)
- Convention Concerning the Issue of Plurilingual Extracts from Civil Status Records (1976 treaty)
- Convention Concerning Labour Administration: Role, Functions and Organization (1978 treaty)
- Convention Concerning Labour Clauses in Public Contracts (1949 treaty)
- Convention Concerning Labour Inspection in Agriculture (1969 treaty)
- Convention Concerning Labour Inspection in Industry and Commerce (1947 treaty)
- Convention Concerning Labour Inspectorates in Non-metropolitan Territories (1947 treaty)
- Convention Concerning Labour Standards in Non-metropolitan Territories (1947 treaty)
- Convention Concerning Labour Statistics (1985 treaty)
- Convention Concerning the Legal Status, Privileges and Immunities of Inter-state Economic Organizations Active in Certain Spheres of Cooperation (1980 treaty)
- Convention Concerning the Liability of the Shipowner in Case of Sickness, Injury or Death of Seamen (1936 treaty)
- Convention Concerning the Marking of the Weight on Heavy Packages Transported by Vessels (1929 treaty)
- Convention Concerning Maternity Protection (1952 treaty)
- Convention Concerning the Maximum Length of Contracts of Employment of Indigenous Workers (1947 treaty)
- Convention Concerning the Maximum Permissible Weight to be Carried by One Worker (1967 treaty)
- Convention Concerning Medical Care and Sickness Benefits (1969 treaty)
- Convention Concerning Medical Examination of Children and Young Persons for Fitness for Employment in Non-industrial Occupations (1946 treaty)
- Convention Concerning the Medical Examination of Fishermen (1959 treaty)
- Convention Concerning Medical Examination for Fitness for Employment in Industry of Children and Young Persons (1946 treaty)
- Convention Concerning the Medical Examination of Seafarers (1946 treaty)
- Convention Concerning Medical Examination of Young Persons for Fitness for Employment Underground in Mines (1965 treaty)
- Convention Concerning Migration for Employment (1949 treaty)
- Convention Concerning Migrations in Abusive Conditions and the Promotion of Equality of Opportunity and Treatment of Migrant Workers (1975 treaty)
- Convention Concerning Minimum Age for Admission to Employment (1973 treaty)
- Convention Concerning the Minimum Age for Admission to Employment as Fishermen (1959 treaty)
- Convention Concerning the Minimum Age for Admission to Employment Underground in Mines (1965 treaty)
- Convention Concerning the Minimum Requirement of Professional Capacity for Masters and Officers on Board Merchant Ships (1936 treaty)
- Convention Concerning Minimum Standards in Merchant Ships (1976 treaty)
- Convention Concerning Minimum Standards of Social Security (1952 treaty)
- Convention Concerning Minimum Wage Fixing Machinery in Agriculture (1951 treaty)
- Convention Concerning Minimum Wage Fixing, with Special Reference to Developing Countries (1970 treaty)
- Convention Concerning Mutual Relief to Indigent Citizens of the Respective Countries (1928 treaty)
- Convention Concerning Navigation on Lake Constance (1973 treaty)
- Convention Concerning Night Work (1990 treaty)
- Convention Concerning Night Work in Bakeries (1925 treaty)
- Convention Concerning Night Work of Women Employed in Industry (1948 treaty)
- Convention Concerning the Night Work of Young Persons Employed in Industry, 1919 (1919 treaty)
- Convention Concerning the Night Work of Young Persons Employed in Industry, 1948 (1948 treaty)
- Convention Concerning Occupational Health Services (1985 treaty)
- Convention Concerning Occupational Safety and Health in Dock Work (1979 treaty)
- Convention Concerning Occupational Safety and Health and the Working Environment (1981 treaty)
- Convention Concerning the Organization of the Employment Service (1948 treaty)
- Convention Concerning Organizations of Rural Workers and Their Role in Economic and Social Development (1975 treaty)
- Convention Concerning Paid Educational Leave (1974 treaty)
- Convention Concerning the Partial Revision of the Conventions Adopted by the General Conference of the International Labour Organisation (1961 treaty)
- Convention Concerning Part-time Work (1994 treaty)
- Convention Concerning Peaceful Orientation of Public Instruction (1936 treaty)
- Convention Concerning Penal Sanctions for Breaches of Contracts of Employment by Indigenous Workers (1939 treaty)
- Convention Concerning the Powers of Authorities and the Law Applicable in Respect of the Protection of Infants (1961 treaty)
- Convention Concerning Prevention and Control of Occupational Hazards Caused by Carcinogenic Substances and Agents (1974 treaty)
- Convention Concerning Prevention and Control of Occupational Hazards Caused by Carcinogenic Substances and Agents (1974 treaty)
- Convention Concerning the Prevention of Occupational Accidents to Seafarers (1970 treaty)
- Convention Concerning Private Employment Agencies (1997 treaty)
- Convention Concerning the Prohibition and Immediate Action for the Elimination of the Worst Forms of Child Labour (1999 treaty)
- Convention Concerning the Promotion of Collective Bargaining (1981 treaty)
- Convention Concerning the Protection Against Accidents of Workers Employed in Loading or Unloading Ships, 1929 (1929 treaty)
- Convention Concerning Protection Against Hazards of Poisoning Arising from Benzene (1971 treaty)
- Convention Concerning Protection and Facilities to be Afforded to Workers' Representatives in the Undertaking (1971 treaty)
- Convention Concerning the Protection and Integration of Indigenous and other Tribal and Semi-tribal Populations in Independent Countries (1957 treaty)
- Convention Concerning Protection of the Rights to Organize and Procedures for Determining Conditions of Employment in the Public Service (1978 treaty)
- Convention Concerning the Protection of Wages (1949 treaty)
- Convention Concerning the Protection of Workers Against Ionising Radiations (1960 treaty)
- Convention Concerning the Protection of Workers Against Occupational Hazards in the Working Environment Due to Air Pollution, Noise and Vibration (1977 treaty)
- Convention Concerning the Protection of Workers' Claims in the Event of the Insolvency of Their Employer (1992 treaty)
- Convention Concerning the Protection of the World Cultural and Natural Heritage (1972 treaty)
- Convention Concerning the Reciprocal Grant of Assistance to Distressed Persons (1951 treaty)
- Convention Concerning the Recognition and Enforcement of Decisions Relating to Maintenance Obligations Towards Children (1958 treaty)
- Convention Concerning the Recognition and Enforcement of Judgements Rendered in Civil Matters (1977 treaty)
- Convention Concerning the Recognition of the Legal Personality of Foreign Companies, Associations and Institutions (1956 treaty)
- Convention Concerning the Recovery of Maintenance Contributions (1962 treaty)
- Convention Concerning the Recruitment and Placement of Seafarers (1996 treaty)
- Convention Concerning the Recruitment, Placing and Conditions of Labour of Migrants for Employment (1939 treaty)
- Convention Concerning the Reduction of Hours of Work to Forty a Week (1935 treaty)
- Convention Concerning the Reduction of Hours of Work in Glass-bottle Works (1935 treaty)
- Convention Concerning the Reduction of Hours of Work on Public Works (1936 treaty)
- Convention Concerning the Reduction of Hours of Work in the Textile Industry (1937 treaty)
- Convention Concerning the Regime of Navigation on the Danube (1948 treaty)
- Convention Concerning the Regulation of Certain Special Systems of Recruiting Workers (1936 treaty)
- Convention Concerning the Regulation of Hours of Work in Commerce and Offices (1930 treaty)
- Convention Concerning the Regulation of Hours of Work and Rest Periods in Road Transport (1939 treaty)
- Convention Concerning the Regulation of Written Contracts of Employment of Indigenous Workers (1939 treaty)
- Convention Concerning the Repatriation of Seafarers, 1987 (1987 treaty)
- Convention Concerning the Repatriation of Seamen, 1926 (1926 treaty)
- Convention Concerning the Restriction of Night Work of Children and Young Persons in Non-industrial Occupations (1946 treaty)
- Convention Concerning the Revision of the Maternity Protection Convention (2000 treaty)
- Convention Concerning the Right of Association and the Settlement of Labour Disputes in Non-metropolitan Territories (1947 treaty)
- Convention Concerning the Rights of Association and Combination of Agricultural Workers (1921 treaty)
- Convention Concerning Safety and Health in Construction (1988 treaty)
- Convention Concerning Safety and Health in Mines (1995 treaty)
- Convention Concerning Safety Provisions in the Building Industry (1937 treaty)
- Convention Concerning Safety in the Use of Asbestos (1986 treaty)
- Convention Concerning Safety in the Use of Chemicals at Work (1990 treaty)
- Convention Concerning Seafarers' Hours of Work and the Manning of Ships (1996 treaty)
- Convention Concerning Seafarers' National Identity Documents (1958 treaty)
- Convention Concerning Seafarers' Pensions (1946 treaty)
- Convention Concerning Seafarers' Welfare at Sea and in Port (1987 treaty)
- Convention Concerning Seamen's Articles of Agreement (1926 treaty)
- Convention Concerning the Seaworthiness and the Equipment of Ships (1926 treaty)
- Convention Concerning the Settlement of Various Classes of Pensions Which Were Not Regulated by the Rome Convention (1922 treaty)
- Convention Concerning Sickness Insurance for Agricultural Workers (1927 treaty)
- Convention Concerning Sickness Insurance for Seamen (1936 treaty)
- Convention Concerning Sickness Insurance for Workers in Industry and Commerce and Domestic Servants (1927 treaty)
- Convention Concerning the Simplification of the Inspection of Emigrants on Board Ship (1926 treaty)
- Convention Concerning Small Silver Currency, 1885 (1885 treaty)
- Convention Concerning Social Policy in Non-metropolitan Territories (1947 treaty)
- Convention Concerning the Social Repercussions of New Methods of Cargo Handling in Docks (1973 treaty)
- Convention Concerning Social Security for Seafarers, 1946 (1946 treaty)
- Convention Concerning Social Security for Seafarers, 1987 (1987 treaty)
- Convention Concerning Statistics of Wages and Hours of Work in the Principal Mining and Manufacturing Industries, Including Building and Construction, and in Agriculture (1938 treaty)
- Convention Concerning the Status of Refugees Coming from Germany (1938 treaty)
- Convention Concerning Student Employees (1950 treaty)
- Convention Concerning Termination of Employment at the Initiative of the Employer (1982 treaty)
- Convention Concerning the Transfer to the French State of the Property in the Sites of British Monuments (1938 treaty)
- Convention Concerning the Transit of Animals, Meat and other Products of Animal Origin (1935 treaty)
- Convention Concerning Tripartite Consultations to Promote the Implementation of International Labour Standards (1976 treaty)
- Convention Concerning Unemployment (1919 treaty)
- Convention Concerning Unemployment Indemnity in Case of Loss or Foundering of the Ship (1920 treaty)
- Convention Concerning the Unification of Road Signals (1931 treaty)
- Convention Concerning the Use of Broadcasting in the Cause of Peace (1936 treaty)
- Convention Concerning the Use of White Lead in Painting (1921 treaty)
- Convention Concerning Vacation Holidays with Pay for Seafarers, 1946 (1946 treaty)
- Convention Concerning Vacation Holidays with Pay for Seafarers, 1949 (1949 treaty)
- Convention Concerning Vocational Guidance and Vocational Training in the Development of Human Resources (1975 treaty)
- Convention Concerning Vocational Rehabilitation and Employment (1983 treaty)
- Convention Concerning Wages, Hours of Work on Board Ship and Manning, 1946 (1946 treaty)
- Convention Concerning Wages, Hours of Work on Board Ship and Manning, 1949 (1949 treaty)
- Convention Concerning Wages, Hours of Work on Board Ship and Manning, 1958 (1958 treaty)
- Convention Concerning Weekly Rest in Commerce and Offices (1957 treaty)
- Convention Concerning Working Conditions in Hotels, Restaurants and Similar Establishments (1991 treaty)
- Convention Concerning the Working Environment (1989 treaty)
- Convention Concerning Workmen's Compensation for Accidents (1925 treaty)
- Convention Concerning Workmen's Compensation in Agriculture (1921 treaty)
- Convention Concerning Workmen's Compensation for Occupational Diseases, 1925 (1925 treaty)
- Convention Concerning Workmen's Compensation for Occupational Diseases, 1934 (1934 treaty)
- Convention de conciliation et d'arbitrage (1925 treaty)
- Convention on Conciliation and Arbitration within the CSCE (1992 treaty)
- Convention sur la condition des étrangers (1928 treaty)
- Convention on the Conduct of Fishing Operations in the North Atlantic (1967 treaty)

Convention Conflicts Laws
04786
alphabetic sequence excludes
For the complete listing, see Yearbook Online at

- ♦ Convention on the Conflicts of Laws Relating to the Form of Testamentary Dispositions (1961 treaty)
- ♦ Convention sur les conflits de lois en matière de forme des dispositions testamentaires (1961 treaty)
- ♦ Convention du Conseil de l'Europe sur l'accès aux documents publics (2009 treaty)
- ♦ Convention du Conseil de l'Europe sur la contrefaçon des produits médicaux et les infractions similaires menaçant la santé publique (2011 treaty)
- ♦ Convention du Conseil de l'Europe contre le trafic d'organes humains (2015 treaty)
- ♦ Convention du Conseil de l'Europe sur la lutte contre la traite des êtres humains (2005 treaty)
- ♦ Convention du Conseil de l'Europe sur la manipulation de compétitions sportives (2014 treaty)
- ♦ Convention du Conseil de l'Europe sur la prévention des cas d'apatridie en relation avec la succession d'états (2006 treaty)
- ♦ Convention du Conseil de l'Europe sur la prévention et la lutte contre la violence à l'égard des femmes et la violence domestique (2011 treaty)
- ♦ Convention du Conseil de l'Europe pour la prévention du terrorisme (2005 treaty)
- ♦ Convention du Conseil de l'Europe sur la protection des enfants contre l'exploitation et les abus sexuels (2007 treaty)
- ♦ Convention du Conseil de l'Europe relative au blanchiment, au dépistage, à la saisie et à la confiscation des produits du crime et au financement du terrorisme (2005 treaty)
- ♦ Convention on Consent to Marriage, Minimum Age for Marriage and Registration of Marriages (1962 treaty)
- ♦ Convention for the Conservation of Anadromous Stocks in the North Pacific Ocean (1992 treaty)
- ♦ Convention on the Conservation of Antarctic Marine Living Resources (1980 treaty)
- ♦ Convention for the Conservation of Antarctic Seals (1972 treaty)
- ♦ Convention for the Conservation of the Biodiversity and the Protection of Wilderness Areas in Central America (1992 treaty)
- ♦ Convention sur la conservation des espèces migratrices appartenant à la faune sauvage (1979 treaty)
- ♦ Convention on the Conservation of European Wildlife and Natural Habitats (1979 treaty)
- ♦ Convention sur la conservation de la faune et la flore marines de l'Antarctique (1980 treaty)
- ♦ Convention on the Conservation of the Living Resources of the Southeast Atlantic (1969 treaty)
- ♦ Convention on the Conservation and Management of Fishery Resources in the South-East Atlantic Ocean (2001 treaty)
- ♦ Convention on the Conservation and Management of Highly Migratory Fish Stocks in the Western and Central Pacific Ocean (2000 treaty)
- ♦ Convention on the Conservation and Management of the High Seas Fisheries Resources in the North Pacific Ocean (2012 treaty)
- ♦ Convention on the Conservation and Management of High Seas Fishery Resources in the South Pacific Ocean (2009 treaty)
- ♦ Convention on the Conservation and Management of Pollock in the Central Bering Sea (1994 treaty)
- ♦ Convention for the Conservation and Management of the Vicuña (1979 treaty)
- ♦ Convention on the Conservation of Migratory Species of Wild Animals (1979 treaty)
- ♦ Convention on Conservation of Nature in the South Pacific (1976 treaty)
- ♦ Convention for the Conservation of the Red Sea and Gulf of Aden Environment (1982 treaty)
- ♦ Convention sur la conservation des ressources biologiques de l'Atlantique sud-est (1969 treaty)
- ♦ Convention for the Conservation of Salmon in the North Atlantic Ocean (1982 treaty)
- ♦ Convention for the Conservation of Southern Bluefin Tuna (1993 treaty)
- ♦ Convention on Consular Agents (1928 treaty)
- ♦ Convention on Contact Concerning Children (2003 treaty)
- ♦ Convention Containing Certain Provisions of Private International Law Regarding Marriage, Adoption and Guardianship (1931 treaty)
- ♦ Convention contenant certaines dispositions de droit international privé sur le mariage, l'adoption et la tutelle (1931 treaty)
- ♦ Convention on the Continental Shelf (1958 treaty)
- ♦ Convention on the Contract for the Carriage of Goods by Inland Waterway (1999 treaty)
- ♦ Convention on the Contract for the International Carriage of Goods by Road (1956 treaty)
- ♦ Convention on the Contract for the International Carriage of Passengers and Luggage by Inland Waterway (1976 treaty)
- ♦ Convention on the Contract for the International Carriage of Passengers and Luggage by Road (1973 treaty)
- ♦ Convention sur le contrat d'engagement des marins (1926 treaty)
- ♦ Convention contre le cybercriminalité (2001 treaty)
- ♦ Convention contre le dopage (1989 treaty)
- ♦ Convention contre la torture et autres peins ou traitements cruels, inhumains ou dégradants (1984 treaty)
- ♦ Convention on the Control and Marking of Articles of Precious Metals (1972 treaty)
- ♦ Convention for the Control of the Trade in Arms and Ammunition (1919 treaty)
- ♦ Convention for Cooperation in the Protection and Development of the Marine and Coastal Environment of the West and Central African Region (1981 treaty)
- ♦ Convention for Cooperation in the Protection and Sustainable Development of the Marine and Coastal Environment of the Northeast Pacific (2002 treaty)
- ♦ Convention on Cooperation for the Protection and Sustainable Use of the Danube River (1994 treaty)
- ♦ Convention sur la coopération pour l'utilisation des brise-glace (1961 treaty)
- ♦ Convention to Coordinate, Extend and Assure the Fulfillment of the Existing Treaties between the American States (1936 treaty)
- ♦ Convention pour coordonner, développer et assurer l'application des traités conclus entre les Etats américains (1936 treaty)
- ♦ Convention créant un livret de famille international (1974 treaty)
- ♦ Convention for the creation of an international criminal court (inactive)
- ♦ Convention for the Creation of Pan American Commercial Committees (1935 treaty)
- ♦ Convention sur le crédit-bail international (1988 treaty)
- ♦ Convention sur le criquet migrateur africain (1962 treaty)
- ♦ Convention culturelle européenne (1954 treaty)
- ♦ Convention on Customs Treatment of Pool Containers Used in International Transport (1994 treaty)
- ♦ Convention on Cybercrime (2001 treaty)
- ♦ Convention on Damage Caused by Foreign Aircraft to Third Parties on the Surface (1952 treaty)
- ♦ Convention on Decisions to Rectify Civil Status Certificates (1964 treaty)
- ♦ Convention on the Declaration of Death of Missing Persons, 1950 (1950 treaty)
- ♦ Convention on the Declaration of Death of Missing Persons, 1967 (1967 treaty)
- ♦ Convention for the Definition of Aggression, 3 July 1933 (1933 treaty)
- ♦ Convention for the Definition of Aggression, 4 July 1933 (1933 treaty)
- ♦ Convention de définition de l'agression, 3 juillet 1933 (1933 treaty)
- ♦ Convention de définition de l'agression, 4 juillet 1933 (1933 treaty)
- ♦ Convention sur la délivrance de brevets européens (1973 treaty)
- ♦ Convention destinée à régler certains conflits de lois en matière de chèques (1931 treaty)
- ♦ Convention destinée à régler certains conflits de lois en matière de lettres de change et de billets à ordre (1930 treaty)
- ♦ Convention sur les devoirs et droits des Etats en cas de luttes civiles (1928 treaty)
- ♦ Convention on Diplomatic Asylum (1954 treaty)
- ♦ Convention sur la diversité biologique (1992 treaty)
- ♦ Convention douanière sur le carnet ATA pour l'admission temporaire de marchandises (1961 treaty)
- ♦ Convention douanière sur les carnets ECS pour échantillons commerciaux (1956 treaty)
- ♦ Convention douanière relative aux containers, 1956 (1956 treaty)
- ♦ Convention douanière relative aux conteneurs, 1972 (1972 treaty)
- ♦ Convention douanière relative aux facilités accordées pour l'importation des marchandises destinées à être présentées ou utilisées à une exposition, une foire, un congrès ou une manifestation similaire (1961 treaty)
- ♦ Convention douanière relative à l'importation temporaire des emballages (1960 treaty)
- ♦ Convention douanière relative à l'importation temporaire de matériel pédagogique (1970 treaty)
- ♦ Convention douanière relative à l'importation temporaire de matériel professionnel (1961 treaty)
- ♦ Convention douanière relative à l'importation temporaire de matériel scientifique (1968 treaty)
- ♦ Convention douanière relative à l'importation temporaire pour usage privé des embarcations de plaisance et des aéronefs (1956 treaty)
- ♦ Convention douanière relative à l'importation temporaire des véhicules routiers (1956 treaty)
- ♦ Convention douanière relative à l'importation temporaire des véhicules routiers privés (1954 treaty)
- ♦ Convention douanière relative au matériel de bien-être destiné aux gens de mer (1964 treaty)
- ♦ Convention douanière relative aux pièces de rechange utilisées pour la réparation des wagons EUROP (1958 treaty)
- ♦ Convention douanière relative au transit international des marchandises (1971 treaty)
- ♦ Convention douanière relative au transport international de marchandises sous le couvert de carnets tir (1975 treaty)
- ♦ Convention douanière relative au transport international de marchandises sous le couvert de carnets TIR, 1959 (1959 treaty)
- ♦ Convention sur le droit international (1906 treaty)
- ♦ Convention sur le droit international privé (1928 treaty)
- ♦ Convention sur le droit relatif aux utilisation des cours d' eau internationaux à des fins autres que la navigation (1997 treaty)
- ♦ Convention sur les droits et les devoirs des Etats (1933 treaty)
- ♦ Convention sur les droits de l'enfant (1989 treaty)
- ♦ Convention sur les droits des personnes handicapées (2006 treaty)
- ♦ Convention sur les droits politiques de la femme (1953 treaty)
- ♦ Convention de Dublin (1990 treaty)
- ♦ Convention on Duties and Rights of States in the Event of Civil Strife (1928 treaty)
- ♦ Convention on Early Notification of a Nuclear Accident (1986 treaty)
- ♦ Convention sur l'échange de publications (1936 treaty)
- ♦ Convention pour l'échange des publications officielles, scientifiques, littéraires et industrielles (1902 treaty)
- ♦ Convention of Economic Rapprochement (1930 treaty)
- ♦ Convention sur les effets transfrontières des accidents industriels (1992 treaty)
- ♦ Convention on the Elaboration of a European Pharmacopoeia (1964 treaty)
- ♦ Convention on the Elimination of all Forms of Discrimination Against Women (1979 treaty)
- ♦ Convention sur l'élimination de toutes les formes de discrimination à l'égard des femmes (1979 treaty)
- ♦ Convention sur l'enseignement de l'histoire (1933 treaty)
- ♦ Convention sur l'enseignement technique et professionnel (1989 treaty)
- ♦ Convention Ensuring Benefit or Allowances to the Involuntarily Unemployed (1934 treaty)
- ♦ Convention on Environmental Impact Assessment (1990 treaty)
- ♦ Convention on Environmental Impact Assessment in a Transboundary Context (1991 treaty)
- ♦ Convention for Establishing Facilities for Finding Employment for Seamen (1920 treaty)
- ♦ Convention Establishing the Status of Naturalized Citizens Who Again Take up Their Residence in the Country of Their Origin (1906 treaty)
- ♦ Convention for the Establishment of Free Trade, 1911 (1911 treaty)
- ♦ Convention for the Establishment of Free Trade, 1923 (1923 treaty)
- ♦ Convention for the establishment of international commissions of inquiry (inactive)
- ♦ Convention for the Establishment of Permanent Central American Commissions (1923 treaty)
- ♦ Convention for the Establishment of a Postal and Telegraph Money Order Service (1912 treaty)
- ♦ Convention on the Establishment of a Scheme of Registration of Wills (1972 treaty)
- ♦ Convention on the Establishment of a Security Control in the Field of Nuclear Energy (1957 treaty)
- ♦ Convention for the Establishment of Stations for Agricultural Experiments and Animal Industries (1923 treaty)
- ♦ Convention établissant le statut définitif du Danube (1921 treaty)
- ♦ Convention sur l' établissement d'un contrôle de sécurité dans le domaine de l' énergie nucléaire (1957 treaty)
- ♦ Convention entre les Etats parties au Traité de l'Atlantique Nord sur le statut de leurs forces (1951 treaty)
- ♦ Convention européenne sur l'arbitrage commercial international (1961 treaty)
- ♦ Convention européenne d'assistance sociale et médicale (1953 treaty)
- ♦ Convention européenne de brasserie (#06401)
- ♦ Convention européenne sur certains aspects internationaux de la faillite (1990 treaty)
- ♦ Convention européenne sur la classification internationale des brevets d'invention (inactive)
- ♦ Convention européenne sur la computation des délais (1974 treaty)
- ♦ Convention européenne concernant des questions de droit d'auteur et de droits voisins dans le cadre de la radiodiffusion transfrontière par satellite (1994 treaty)
- ♦ Convention européenne de la construction métallique (#06779)
- ♦ Convention européenne sur le contrôle de l'acquisition et la détention d'armes à feu par des particuliers (1978 treaty)
- ♦ Convention européenne sur la coproduction cinématographique (1992 treaty)
- ♦ Convention européenne dans le domaine de l'information sur le droit étranger (1968 treaty)
- ♦ Convention européenne sur les effets internationaux de la déchéance du droit de conduire un véhicule à moteur (1976 treaty)
- ♦ Convention européenne d'entraide judiciaire en matière pénale (1959 treaty)
- ♦ Convention européenne sur l'équivalence des périodes d'études universitaires (1956 treaty)
- ♦ Convention européenne sur l'équivalence des périodes d'études universitaires (1990 treaty)
- ♦ Convention européenne d'établissement (1955 treaty)
- ♦ Convention européenne d'établissement des sociétés (1966 treaty)
- ♦ Convention Européenne sur L'exécution des Peines (1991 treaty)
- ♦ Convention européenne sur l'exercice des droits des enfants (1996 treaty)
- ♦ Convention européenne des exportateurs du bois (inactive)
- ♦ Convention européenne d'extradition (1957 treaty)
- ♦ Convention européenne sur les fonctions consulaires (1967 treaty)
- ♦ Convention européenne sur l'immunité des états (1972 treaty)
- ♦ Convention européenne sur l'imprescriptibilité des crimes contre l'humanité et des crimes de guerre (1974 treaty)
- ♦ Convention européenne sur les infractions visant des biens culturels (1985 treaty)
- ♦ Convention européenne en matière d'adoption des enfants (1967 treaty)
- ♦ Convention européenne en matière d'adoption des enfants – révisée (2008 treaty)
- ♦ Convention européenne sur la nationalité (1997 treaty)
- ♦ Convention européenne sur la notification à l'étranger des documents en matière administrative (1977 treaty)
- ♦ Convention européenne sur l'obtention à l'étranger d'informations et de preuves en matière administrative (1978 treaty)
- ♦ Convention européenne du paysage (2000 treaty)
- ♦ Convention européenne portant loi uniforme en matière d'arbitrage (1966 treaty)
- ♦ Convention européenne pour la prévention de la torture et des peines ou traitements inhumains et dégradants (1987 treaty)
- ♦ Convention européenne sur la promotion d'un service volontaire transnational a long terme pour les jeunes (2000 treaty)
- ♦ Convention européenne sur la protection des animaux d'abattage (1979 treaty)
- ♦ Convention européenne pour la protection des animaux de compagnie (1987 treaty)
- ♦ Convention européenne sur la protection des animaux dans les élevages (1976 treaty)
- ♦ Convention européenne sur la protection des animaux en transport international (1968 treaty)

- ♦ Convention européenne sur la protection des animaux en transport international – révisée (2003 treaty)
- ♦ Convention européenne sur la protection des animaux vertébrés utilisés à des fins expérimentales ou à d'autres fins scientifiques (1986 treaty)
- ♦ Convention européenne sur la protection juridique des services à accès conditionnel et des services d'accès conditionnel (2001 treaty)
- ♦ Convention européenne pour la protection du patrimoine archéologique (1969 treaty)
- ♦ Convention européenne pour la protection du patrimoine archéologique, révisée (1992 treaty)
- ♦ Convention européenne de radiodiffusion (1933 treaty)
- ♦ Convention européenne sur le rapatriement des mineurs (1970 treaty)
- ♦ Convention européenne sur la reconnaissance académique des qualifications universitaires (1959 treaty)
- ♦ Convention européenne sur la reconnaissance et l'exécution des décisions en matière de garde des enfants et le rétablissement de la garde des enfants (1980 treaty)
- ♦ Convention européenne sur la reconnaissance de la personnalité juridique des organisations internationales non gouvernementales (1986 treaty)
- ♦ Convention européenne pour le règlement pacifique des différends (1957 treaty)
- ♦ Convention européenne relative à l'assurance obligatoire de la responsabilité civile en matière de véhicules automoteurs (1959 treaty)
- ♦ Convention européenne relative au dédommagement des victimes d'infractions violentes (1983 treaty)
- ♦ Convention européenne relative à l'équivalence des diplômes donnant accès aux établissements universitaires (1953 treaty)
- ♦ Convention européenne relative aux formalités prescrites pour les demandes de brevets (1953 treaty)
- ♦ Convention européenne relative au lieu de paiement des obligations monétaires (1972 treaty)
- ♦ Convention européenne relative aux obligations en monnaie étrangère (1967 treaty)
- ♦ Convention européenne relative à la protection du patrimoine audiovisuel (2001 treaty)
- ♦ Convention européenne relative à la protection sociale des agriculteurs (1974 treaty)
- ♦ Convention européenne relative au régime douanier des palettes utilisées dans les transports internationaux (1960 treaty)
- ♦ Convention européenne relative au statut juridique du travailleur migrant (1977 treaty)
- ♦ Convention européenne relative à la suppression de la légalisation des actes établis par les agents diplomatiques ou consulaires (1968 treaty)
- ♦ Convention européenne pour la répression des infractions routières (1964 treaty)
- ♦ Convention européenne pour la répression du terrorisme (1977 treaty)
- ♦ Convention européenne sur la responsabilité civile en cas de dommages causés par des véhicules automoteurs (1973 treaty)
- ♦ Convention européenne sur la responsabilité du fait des produits en cas de lésions corporelles ou de décès (1977 treaty)
- ♦ Convention européenne de sécurité sociale (1972 treaty)
- ♦ Convention européenne sur le statut juridique des enfants nés hors mariage (1975 treaty)
- ♦ Convention européenne pour la surveillance des personnes condamnées ou libérées sous condition (1964 treaty)
- ♦ Convention européenne sur la télévision transfrontière (1989 treaty)
- ♦ Convention européenne sur la transmission des procédures répressives (1972 treaty)
- ♦ Convention européenne sur la valeur internationale des jugements répressifs (1970 treaty)
- ♦ Convention européenne sur violence et les débordements de spectateurs lors de manifestations sportives et notamment de matches de football (1985 treaty)
- ♦ Convention sur l'évaluation de l' impact sur l' environnement dans un contexte transfrontière (1991 treaty)
- ♦ Convention for the Exchange of Information as to the Antecedents of Persons Dangerous to Society (1905 treaty)
- ♦ Convention on the Exchange of Information Regarding the Acquisition of Nationality (1964 treaty)
- ♦ Convention for the Execution of Foreign Arbitral Awards (1927 treaty)
- ♦ Convention pour l'exécution des sentences arbitrales étrangères (1927 treaty)
- ♦ Convention pour l'exercice des professions libérales, 1902 (1902 treaty)
- ♦ Convention sur l'exercice des professions libérales, 1939 (1939 treaty)
- ♦ Convention sur l'exercise de la pêche dans l'Atlantique Nord (1967 treaty)
- ♦ Convention on the Exercise of Professional Occupations and Recognition of University Studies (1962 treaty)
- ♦ Convention on Export of Guano, 1857 (1857 treaty)
- ♦ Convention to Extend and Coordinate Social Security Schemes in Their Application to the Nationals of the Parties to the Brussels Treaty (1949 treaty)
- ♦ Convention Extending the Competence of Authorities Qualified to Record the Affiliation of Illegitimate Children (1961 treaty)
- ♦ Convention for the Extension to Certain Protectorates and Mandated Territories of the Treaty of December 12 1891 (1930 treaty)
- ♦ Convention for the Extension of the Extradition Treaty of October 3 1904, to Certain Protectorates and Mandated Territories (1930 treaty)
- ♦ Convention pour l'extension du Traité d'extradition du 3 octobre 1904 à certains protectorats et territoires sous mandat (1930 treaty)
- ♦ Convention sur l'extradition (1933 treaty)
- ♦ Convention on Extradition (1933 treaty)
- ♦ Convention d'extradition, 1907 (1907 treaty)
- ♦ Convention to Facilitate the Celebration of Marriages Abroad (1964 treaty)
- ♦ Convention for Facilitating the International Circulation of Films of an Educational Character (1933 treaty)
- ♦ Convention for Facilitating Trade Exchange and the Regulation of Transit Trade between States of the Arab League (1953 treaty)
- ♦ Convention on the Facilitation of Border Crossing Procedures for Passengers, Luggage and Load-luggage Carried in International Traffic by Rail (2019 treaty)
- ♦ Convention on Facilitation of International Maritime Traffic (1965 treaty)
- ♦ Convention pour faciliter la circulation internationale des films ayant un caractère éducatif (1933 treaty)
- ♦ Convention sur les Facilités et le Développement des échanges Commerciaux (1981 treaty)
- ♦ Convention sur les facilités douanières en faveur du tourisme (1954 treaty)
- ♦ Convention on fisheries and the conservation of living marine resources in the Black Sea (unconfirmed)
- ♦ Convention on Fishing and Conservation of the Living Resources in the Baltic Sea and the Belts (1973 treaty)
- ♦ Convention on Fishing and Conservation of the Living Resources of the High Seas (1958 treaty)
- ♦ Convention fixant l'âge minimum d'admission des enfants au travail maritime (1920 treaty)
- ♦ Convention fixant l'âge minimum d'admission des enfants au travail maritime, 1936 (1936 treaty)
- ♦ Convention fixant l'âge minimum d'admission des enfants aux travaux industriels (1919 treaty)
- ♦ Convention fixant l'âge minimum d'admission des enfants aux travaux industriels, 1937 (1937 treaty)
- ♦ Convention fixant l'âge minimum d'admission des jeunes gens au travail en qualité de soutiers ou chauffeurs (1921 treaty)
- ♦ Convention fixant le statut des citoyens naturalisés qui rétablissent leur résidence dans leur pays d'origine (1906 treaty)
- ♦ Convention Fixing the Minimum Age for Admission of Children to Employment at Sea, 1920 (1920 treaty)
- ♦ Convention Fixing the Minimum Age for the Admission of Children to Employment at Sea, 1936 (1936 treaty)
- ♦ Convention Fixing the Minimum Age for Admission of Children to Industrial Employment, 1919 (1919 treaty)
- ♦ Convention Fixing the Minimum Age for Admission of Children to Industrial Employment, 1937 (1937 treaty)
- ♦ Convention Fixing the Minimum Age for the Admission of Young Persons to Employment as Trimmers or Stokers (1921 treaty)
- ♦ Convention sur les fonctionnaires diplomatiques (1928 treaty)
- ♦ Convention sur les formalités de chasse applicables aux touristes entrant dans les pays du Conseil de l' entente (1976 treaty)
- ♦ Convention for the Formation of Codes on Public and Private International Law (1902 treaty)
- ♦ Convention on the Free Issue of Certificates of Civil Status and Exemption from the Need for Legislation (1957 treaty)
- ♦ Convention sur la future coopération multilatérale dans les pêches de l'Atlantique du Nord-Est, 1980 (1980 treaty)
- ♦ Convention sur la future coopération multilatérale dans les pêches de l'Atlantique Nord-Ouest, 1978 (1978 treaty)
- ♦ Convention on Future Multilateral Cooperation in North-East Atlantic Fisheries, 1980 (1980 treaty)
- ♦ Convention on Future Multilateral Cooperation in the Northwest Atlantic Fisheries, 1978 (1978 treaty)
- ♦ Convention on the Game Hunting Formalities Applicable to Tourists Entering Countries in the Conseil de L'entente (1976 treaty)
- ♦ Convention générale de conciliation interaméricaine (1929 treaty)
- ♦ Convention générale interaméricaine pour la protection des marques de fabrique et commerciale (1929 treaty)
- ♦ Convention de Genève pour l'amélioration du sort des blessés et des malades dans les armées en campagne, 1929 (1929 treaty)
- ♦ Convention de Genève pour l'amélioration du sort des blessés et des malades dans les forces armées en campagne, 1949 (1949 treaty)
- ♦ Convention de Genève pour l'amélioration du sort des blessés, des malades et des naufragés des forces armées sur mer (1949 treaty)
- ♦ Convention de Genève – Convention de Genève pour la protection des blessés dans les armées en campagne, 1864 (1864 treaty)
- ♦ Convention de Genève – Convention de Genève pour la Protection des Blessés dans les Armées en Campagne, 1906 (1906 treaty)
- ♦ Convention de Genève pour la protection des blessés dans les armées en campagne, 1864 (1864 treaty)
- ♦ Convention de Genève pour la Protection des Blessés dans les Armées en Campagne, 1906 (1906 treaty)
- ♦ Convention de Genève relative à la protection des personnes civiles en temps de guerre (1949 treaty)
- ♦ Convention de Genève relative au traitement des prisonniers de guerre (1949 treaty)
- ♦ Convention on the Grant of European Patents (1973 treaty)
- ♦ Convention sur la haute mer (1958 treaty)
- ♦ Convention on the High Seas (1958 treaty)
- ♦ Convention Hipólito Unanue (#10921)
- ♦ Convention sur l'immatriculation des objets lancés dans l'espace atmosphérique (1974 treaty)
- ♦ Convention sur l'imprescriptibilité des crimes de guerre et des crimes contre l'humanité (1968 treaty)
- ♦ Convention for the Improvement of Sea Communications (1912 treaty)
- ♦ Convention of Independent Financial Advisors (internationally oriented national body)
- ♦ Convention Industry Council / see Events Industry Council (#09212)
- ♦ Convention sur l'information et la coopération juridique concernant les "services de la société de l'information" (2001 treaty)
- ♦ Convention on Information and Legal Cooperation Concerning "Information Society Services" (2001 treaty)
- ♦ Convention on Insider Trading (1989 treaty)
- ♦ Convention Instituting the Definitive Statute of the Danube (1921 treaty)
- ♦ Convention Instituting an International Family Carnet (1974 treaty)
- ♦ Convention Instituting the Statute of Navigation of the Elbe (1922 treaty)
- ♦ Convention interaméricaine des communications électriques (1924 treaty)
- ♦ Convention interaméricaine contre le racisme et toutes les formes de discrimination et d'intolérance (unconfirmed)
- ♦ Convention interaméricaine des droits de l'homme (1969 treaty)
- ♦ Convention interaméricaine sur l'entraide en matière pénale (1992 treaty)
- ♦ Convention interaméricaine pour la prévention et la répression de la torture (1985 treaty)
- ♦ Convention interaméricaine pour la prévention, la sanction et l'élimination de la violence contre la femme (1994 treaty)
- ♦ Convention interaméricaine des radiocommunications, 1937 (1937 treaty)
- ♦ Convention interaméricaine des radiocommunications, 1940 (1940 treaty)
- ♦ Convention interaméricaine visant à faciliter l'apport d'assistance dans les cas de catastrophes (1991 treaty)
- ♦ Convention on Interchange of Publications (1936 treaty)
- ♦ Convention sur l'interdiction de l'emploi, du stockage, de la production et du transfert des mines antipersonnel et sur leur destruction (1997 treaty)
- ♦ Convention sur l' interdiction d' importer en Afrique des déchets dangereux et sur le contrôle des mouvements transfrontières (1991 treaty)
- ♦ Convention to Interdiction and Like Measures of Protection (1905 treaty)
- ♦ Convention sur l'interdiction ou la limitation de l'emploi de certaines armes classiques qui peuvent être considérées comme produisant des effets traumatiques excessifs ou comme frappant sans discrimination, et protocoles annexes (1980 treaty)
- ♦ Convention sur l'interdiction de la mise au point, de la fabrication et du stockage des armes bactériologiques – biologiques – ou à toxines et sur leur destruction (1972 treaty)
- ♦ Convention sur l'interdiction de la mise au point, de la fabrication, du stockage et de l'emploi des armes chimiques et sur leur destruction (1992 treaty)
- ♦ Convention pour l'interdiction de la pêche au filet maillant dérivant de grande dimension dans le Pacifique Sud (1989 treaty)
- ♦ Convention sur l'interdiction d'utiliser des techniques de modification de l'environnement à des fins militaires ou toutes autres fins hostiles (1976 treaty)
- ♦ Convention intérimaire sur la conservation des phoques à fourrure du Pacifique nord (1957 treaty)
- ♦ Convention on the International Access to Justice (1980 treaty)
- ♦ Convention on International Civil Aviation (1944 treaty)
- ♦ Convention internationale de 1996 sur la responsabilité et l' indemnisation pour les dommages liés au transport par mer de substances nocives et potentiellement dangereuses (1996 treaty)
- ♦ Convention internationale pour l'abolition des prohibitions et restrictions à l'importation et à l'exportation (1927 treaty)
- ♦ Convention internationale sur l'assistance (1989 treaty)
- ♦ Convention internationale d'assistance mutuelle administrative en vue de prévenir, de rechercher et de réprimer les infractions douanières (1977 treaty)
- ♦ Convention internationale pour le catalogue international de la littérature scientifique (inactive)
- ♦ Convention internationale concernant l'entretien de certains phares de la Mer rouge (1962 treaty)
- ♦ Convention internationale concernant les pêcheries hauturières de l'Océan Pacifique Nord (1952 treaty)
- ♦ Convention internationale concernant les statistiques économiques, 1928 (1928 treaty)
- ♦ Convention internationale concernant le transport des marchandises par chemins de fer (1890 treaty)
- ♦ Convention internationale concernant le transport des marchandises par chemins de fer, 1924 (1927 treaty)
- ♦ Convention internationale concernant le transport des marchandises par chemins de fer, 1961 (1961 treaty)

Convention internationale concernant
04786

alphabetic sequence excludes
For the complete listing, see Yearbook Online at

- ♦ Convention internationale concernant le transport des marchandises par chemins de fer, 1970 (1970 treaty)
- ♦ Convention internationale concernant le transport des voyageurs et des bagages par chemin de fer, 1961 (1961 treaty)
- ♦ Convention internationale concernant le transport des voyageurs et des bagages par chemins de fer (1924 treaty)
- ♦ Convention internationale concernant le transport des voyageurs et des bagages par chemins de fer, 1927 (1927 treaty)
- ♦ Convention internationale concernant le transport des voyageurs et des bagages par chemins de fer, 1970 (1970 treaty)
- ♦ Convention internationale contre l'apartheid dans les sports, 1985 (1985 treaty)
- ♦ Convention internationale contre l'apartheid dans les sports, 1988 (1988 treaty)
- ♦ Convention internationale contre le dopage dans le sport (2005 treaty)
- ♦ Convention internationale contre la prise d'otages (1979 treaty)
- ♦ Convention internationale pour le contrôle permanent des foyers d'origine du criquet nomade (1949 treaty)
- ♦ Convention internationale des écoles de marionnettes (#12938)
- ♦ Convention internationale sur l'élimination et la répression du crime d'apartheid (1973 treaty)
- ♦ Convention internationale sur l'élimination de toutes les formes de discrimination raciale (1965 treaty)
- ♦ Convention internationale pour faciliter le franchissement des frontières aux marchandises transportées par voie ferrée (1952 treaty)
- ♦ Convention internationale pour faciliter le franchissement des frontières aux voyageurs et aux bagages transportés par voie ferrée (1952 treaty)
- ♦ Convention internationale pour faciliter l'importation des échantillons commerciaux et du matériel publicitaire (1952 treaty)
- ♦ Convention internationale sur l'harmonisation des contrôles des marchandises aux frontières (1982 treaty)
- ♦ Convention internationale d'héraldique (inactive)
- ♦ Convention internationale sur l'intervention en haute mer en cas d'accident entraînant ou pouvant entraîner une pollution par les hydrocarbures (1969 treaty)
- ♦ Convention internationale sur le jaugeage des navires (1969 treaty)
- ♦ Convention internationale sur les lignes de charge (1930 treaty)
- ♦ Convention internationale sur les lignes de charge (1966 treaty)
- ♦ Convention internationale pour la lutte contre les maladies contagieuses des animaux (1935 treaty)
- ♦ Convention internationale pour le marquage des oeufs dans le commerce internationale (1931 treaty)
- ♦ Convention internationale sur les normes de formation des gens de mer, de délivrance des brevets et de veille (1978 treaty)
- ♦ Convention internationale de l'opium, 1925 (1925 treaty)
- ♦ Convention internationale de l'opium, 1946 (1946 treaty)
- ♦ Convention internationale pour les pêcheries de l'Atlantique nord-ouest (1949 treaty)
- ♦ Convention internationale pour la prévention de la pollution des eaux de la mer par les hydrocarbures (1954 treaty)
- ♦ Convention internationale pour la prévention de la pollution par les navires (1973 treaty)
- ♦ Convention internationale pour la prévention de la pollution par les navires telle que modifiée par le Protocole de 1978 (1978 treaty)
- ♦ Convention internationale sur la protection des artistes interprètes ou exécutants, des producteurs de phonogrammes et des organismes de radiodiffusion (1961 treaty)
- ♦ Convention internationale sur la protection des droits de tous les travailleurs migrants et des membres de leur famille (1990 treaty)
- ♦ Convention internationale sur la protection mutuelle contre la fièvre dengue (1934 treaty)
- ♦ Convention internationale pour la protection des obtentions végétales, 1961 (1961 treaty)
- ♦ Convention internationale pour la protection des oiseaux (1950 treaty)
- ♦ Convention internationale pour la protection de toutes les personnes contre les disparitions forcée (2006 treaty)
- ♦ Convention internationale pour la protection des végétaux, 1929 (1929 treaty)
- ♦ Convention internationale pour la protection des végétaux, 1951 (1951 treaty)
- ♦ Convention internationale sur la recherche et le sauvetage maritimes (1979 treaty)
- ♦ Convention internationale sur la reconnaissance des études, des diplômes et des grades de l'enseignement supérieur dans les Etats arabes et les Etats européens riverains de la Méditerranée (1976 treaty)
- ♦ Convention Internationale sur le Régime des Cabarets Flottants (1887 treaty)
- ♦ Convention internationale pour la réglementation de la chasse à la baleine (1946 treaty)
- ♦ Convention Internationale pour la Réglementation des Pêches en Mer du Nord (1882 treaty)
- ♦ Convention internationale relative à la circulation automobile (1926 treaty)
- ♦ Convention internationale relative à la circulation routière (1926 treaty)
- ♦ Convention Internationale Relative au Contrat de Voyage (1970 treaty)
- ♦ Convention internationale relative au régime des sucres (1902 treaty)
- ♦ Convention internationale relative à la répression de la traite des blanches, 1910 (1910 treaty)
- ♦ Convention internationale relative à la répression de la traite des femmes majeures (1933 treaty)
- ♦ Convention internationale pour la répression des actes de terrorisme nucléaire (2005 treaty)
- ♦ Convention internationale pour la répression des attentats terroristes à l'explosif (1997 treaty)
- ♦ Convention internationale pour la répression du financement du terrorisme (1999 treaty)
- ♦ Convention internationale pour la répression de la traite des femmes et des enfants (1921 treaty)
- ♦ Convention internationale sur la responsabilité civile pour les dommages dus à la pollution par les hydrocarbures (1969 treaty)
- ♦ Convention Internationale sur la Responsabilité et L'indemnisation pour les Dommages Liés au Transport par Mer de Substances Nocives et Potentiellement Dangereuses (1996 treaty)
- ♦ Convention internationale sur la saisie conservatoire des navires (1999 treaty)
- ♦ Convention internationale pour la sauvegarde de la vie humaine en mer, 1933 (1929 treaty)
- ♦ Convention internationale pour la sauvegarde de la vie humaine en mer, 1948 (1948 treaty)
- ♦ Convention internationale pour la sauvegarde de la vie humaine en mer, 1960 (1960 treaty)
- ♦ Convention internationale pour la sauvegarde de la vie humaine en mer, 1974 (1974 treaty)
- ♦ Convention internationale sur la sécurité des conteneurs (1972 treaty)
- ♦ Convention internationale sur la sécurité des navires de pêche (1977 treaty)
- ♦ Convention internationales sur le Système harmonisé de désignation et de codification des marchandises (1983 treaty)
- ♦ Convention internationale des télécommunications, 1973 (1973 treaty)
- ♦ Convention internationale des télécommunications, 1982 (1982 treaty)
- ♦ Convention internationale des télécommunications, 1982 (1982 treaty)
- ♦ Convention internationale des télécommunications, 1989 (1989 treaty)
- ♦ Convention internationale pour l'unification de certaines règles concernant les immunités des navires d'Etat (1926 treaty)
- ♦ Convention internationale pour l'unification de certaines règles concernant la limitation de la responsabilité des propriétaires de navires de mer (1924 treaty)
- ♦ Convention internationale pour l'unification de certaines règles en matière d'abordage et protocole de signature (1910 treaty)
- ♦ Convention internationale pour l'unification de certaines règles en matière de connaissement (1924 treaty)
- ♦ Convention internationale pour l'unification de certaines règles relatives à la compétence civile en matière d'abordage (1952 treaty)
- ♦ Convention internationale pour l'unification de certaines règles relatives à la compétence pénale en matière d'abordage et autres événements de navigation (1952 treaty)
- ♦ Convention internationale pour l'unification de certaines règles relatives aux privilèges et hypothèques maritimes, 1926 (1926 treaty)
- ♦ Convention internationale pour l'unification de certaines règles sur la saisie conservatoire des navires de mer (1952 treaty)
- ♦ Convention internationale pour l'unification des méthodes d'analyse et d'appréciation des vins (1954 treaty)
- ♦ Convention internationale pour l'unification des méthodes de prélèvement des échantillons et d'analyse des fromages (1934 treaty)
- ♦ Convention internationale pour l'unification de la présentation des résultats d'analyse des matières destinées à l'alimentation de l'homme et des animaux (1931 treaty)
- ♦ Convention on International Factoring (1988 treaty)
- ♦ Convention on International Financial Leasing (1988 treaty)
- ♦ Convention on International Law (1906 treaty)
- ♦ Convention on the International Liability for Damage Caused by Space Objects (1972 treaty)
- ♦ Convention on the International Protection of Adults (2000 treaty)
- ♦ Convention on the International Recognition of Rights in Aircraft (1948 treaty)
- ♦ Convention on the International Recovery of Child Support and other Forms of Family Maintenance (2007 treaty)
- ♦ Convention for the International Registration of Trade Marks (1911 treaty)
- ♦ Convention on the International Regulations for Preventing Collisions at Sea (1972 treaty)
- ♦ Convention on the International Right of Correction (1953 treaty)
- ♦ Convention on International Trade in Endangered Species of Wild Fauna and Flora (1973 treaty)
- ♦ Convention on Inventions, Patents, Designs and Industrial Models (1910 treaty)
- ♦ Convention sur les Investissements dans les Pays Arabes (1980 treaty)
- ♦ Convention on the Issue of a Certificate of Multiple Surnames (1982 treaty)
- ♦ Convention d'Istanbul – Convention relative à l'admission temporaire (1990 treaty)
- ♦ Convention on Jurisdiction, Applicable Law and Recognition of Decrees Relating to Adoptions (1965 treaty)
- ♦ Convention on Jurisdiction, Applicable Law, Recognition, Enforcement and Cooperation in Respect of Parental Responsibility and Measures for the Protection of Children (1996 treaty)
- ♦ Convention on Jurisdiction and the Enforcement of Judgements in Civil and Commercial Matters (1988 treaty)
- ♦ Convention on jurisdiction and the recognition and enforcement of judgments in civil and commercial matters (2007 treaty)
- ♦ Convention on the Jurisdiction of the Selected Forum in the Case of International Sales of Goods (1958 treaty)
- ♦ Convention de Kampala – Convention de l'Union Africaine sur la protection et l'assistance aux personnes déplacées en Afrique (2009 treaty)
- ♦ Convention on Laundering, Search, Seizure and Confiscation of the Proceeds from Crime (1990 treaty)
- ♦ Convention on the Law Applicable to Agency (1978 treaty)
- ♦ Convention on the Law Applicable to Certain Rights in Respect of Securities Held with an Intermediary (2002 treaty)
- ♦ Convention on the Law Applicable to Contracts for the International Sale of Goods (1986 treaty)
- ♦ Convention on the Law Applicable to Contractual Obligations (1980 treaty)
- ♦ Convention on the Law Applicable to International Sales of Goods (1955 treaty)
- ♦ Convention on the Law Applicable to Maintenance Obligations (1973 treaty)
- ♦ Convention on the Law Applicable to Maintenance Obligations Towards Children (1956 treaty)
- ♦ Convention on the Law Applicable to Matrimonial Property Regimes (1978 treaty)
- ♦ Convention on the Law Applicable to Products Liability (1973 treaty)
- ♦ Convention on the Law Applicable to Succession to the Estates of Deceased Persons (1989 treaty)
- ♦ Convention on the Law Applicable to Surnames and First Names (1980 treaty)
- ♦ Convention on the Law Applicable to Traffic Accidents (1971 treaty)
- ♦ Convention on the Law Applicable to Trusts and on Their Recognition (1985 treaty)
- ♦ Convention on the Law Governing Transfer of Title in International Sales of Goods (1958 treaty)
- ♦ Convention on the Law of the Non-navigational Uses of International Watercourses (1997 treaty)
- ♦ Convention sur la légitimation par mariage (1970 treaty)
- ♦ Convention on Legitimation by Marriage (1970 treaty)
- ♦ Convention on the Liability of Hotel-keepers Concerning the Property of Their Guests (1962 treaty)
- ♦ Convention on the Liability of Operators of Nuclear Ships (1962 treaty)
- ♦ Convention Liaison Committee / see Events Industry Council (#09212)
- ♦ Convention Liaison Council / see Events Industry Council (#09212)
- ♦ Convention limitant la durée du travail dans les mines de charbon, 1931 (1931 treaty)
- ♦ Convention limitant la durée du travail dans les mines de charbon, 1935 (1935 treaty)
- ♦ Convention for the Limitation of Armaments (1923 treaty)
- ♦ Convention on Limitation of Liability for Maritime Claims (1976 treaty)
- ♦ Convention on the Limitation Period in the International Sale of Goods (1974 treaty)
- ♦ Convention sur la limitation de la responsabilité en matière de créances maritimes (1976 treaty)
- ♦ Convention sur la limitation de la responsabilité des propriétaires des navires de mer (1957 treaty)
- ♦ Convention pour limiter la fabrication et règlementer la distribution des stupéfiants (1931 treaty)
- ♦ Convention Limiting Hours of Work in Coal Mines, 1931 (1931 treaty)
- ♦ Convention Limiting Hours of Work in Coal Mines, 1935 (1935 treaty)
- ♦ Convention Limiting the Hours of Work in Industrial Undertakings to Eight in the Day and Forty-eight in the Week (1919 treaty)
- ♦ Convention for Limiting the Manufacture and Regulating the Distribution of Narcotic Drugs (1931 treaty)
- ♦ Convention for Limiting the Manufacture and Regulating the Distribution of Narcotic Drugs, 1946 (1946 treaty)
- ♦ Convention on Literary and Artistic Copyright, 1902 (1902 treaty)
- ♦ Convention on Literary and Artistic Copyright, 1910 (1910 treaty)
- ♦ Convention sur le logement des équipages, 1970 (1970 treaty)
- ♦ Convention sur la loi applicable à certains droits sur des titres détenus auprès d'un intermédiaire (2002 treaty)
- ♦ Convention sur la loi applicable aux contrats intermédiaires et à la représentation (1978 treaty)
- ♦ Convention sur la loi applicable aux contrats de vente internationale de marchandises (1986 treaty)
- ♦ Convention sur la loi applicable en matière d'accidents de la circulation routière (1971 treaty)
- ♦ Convention sur la loi applicable aux obligations alimentaires (1973 treaty)
- ♦ Convention sur la loi applicable aux obligations alimentaires envers les enfants (1956 treaty)
- ♦ Convention sur la loi applicable aux régimes matrimoniaux (1978 treaty)
- ♦ Convention sur la loi applicable à la responsabilité du fait des produits (1973 treaty)
- ♦ Convention sur la loi applicable aux successions à cause de mort (1989 treaty)
- ♦ Convention sur la loi applicable au transfert de la propriété en cas de vente à caractère international d'objets mobiliers corporels (1958 treaty)
- ♦ Convention sur la loi applicable aux ventes à caractère international d'objets mobiliers corporels (1955 treaty)
- ♦ Convention de Lomé – Convention ACP-CEE (1975 treaty)
- ♦ Convention de Londres sur la pêche (1964 treaty)

♦ Convention on Long-range Transboundary Air Pollution 04787

Convention sur la pollution atmosphérique transfrontière à longue distance

Contact c/o UNECE – Environment Div, Palais des Nations, Avenue de la Paix 8-14, 1211 Geneva 10, Switzerland. T. +41229070621. Fax +41229070107. E-mail: air.env@unece.org.

URL: https://treaties.un.org/

History 13 Nov 1979. Established on signature of the Convention, as a result of a High-level Meeting within the framework of the *United Nations Economic Commission for Europe (UNECE, #20555)* on the Protection of Environment; in force since 16 Mar 1983. Convention has been followed by: *Protocol to the 1979 Convention on Long Range Transboundary Air Pollution on Long-term Financing of the Cooperative Programme for Monitoring and Evaluation of the Long-range Transmission of Air-pollutants in Europe (1984 EMEP protocol, 1984)*, adopted 28 Sep 1984, Geneva (Switzerland), and entered into force on 28 Jan 1988; *Protocol to the 1979 Convention on Long Range Transboundary Air Pollution on the Reduction of Sulphur Emissions or Their Transboundary Fluxes by at Least 30 per Cent (1985 Sulphur protocol, 1985)*, adopted 8 Jul 1985, Helsinki (Finland), and entered into force on 2 Sep 1987; *Protocol to the 1979 Convention on Long Range Transboundary Air Pollution Concerning the Control of Nitrogen Oxides Emissions or Their Transboundary Fluxes (1988 NOx protocol, 1988)*, adopted 31 Oct 1988, Sofia (Bulgaria), and entered into force on 14 Feb 1991; *Protocol to the 1979 Convention on Long Range Transboundary Air Pollution Concerning the Control of Emissions of Volatile Organic Compounds on Their Transboundary Fluxes (1991 VOC protocol, 1991)*, adopted 18 Nov 1991, Geneva, and entered into force 29 Sep 1997; *Protocol to the 1979 Convention on Long Range Transboundary Air Pollution on Further Reduction of Sulphur Emissions (1994)*, adopted 14 Jun 1994, Oslo (Norway), and entered into force 5 Aug 1998; *Protocol to the Convention on Long-range Transboundary Air Pollution on Heavy Metals (1998)*, adopted 24 Jun 1998, Århus (Denmark), and entered into force 29 Dec 2003; *Protocol to the Convention on Long Range Transboundary Air Pollution on Persistent Organic Pollutants (POP protocol, 1998)*, adopted 24 Jun 1998, Århus, and entered into force 23 Oct 2003; *Protocol to the 1979 Convention on Long-range Transboundary Air Pollution to Abate Acidification, Eutrophication and Ground-level Ozone (1999)*, adopted 30 Nov 1999, Gothenburg (Sweden), and entered into force 17 May 2005. Entered into force on 16 Mar 1983. Former names and other names: *Convenio sobre contaminación atmosférica transfronteriza o larga distancia* – former; *LRTAP Convention* – former. **Aims** Limit and, as far as possible, generally reduce and prevent air pollution, especially long-range transboundary air pollution. **Structure** Executive Body (meets annually). Bureau. Secretariat. Subsidiary bodies: Working Group on Effects; Steering Body to the *Cooperative Programme for Monitoring and Evaluation of the Long-range Transmission of Air Pollutants in Europe (EMEP, #04800)*; Working Group on Strategies and Review. Implementation Committee. Task Forces. Groups of governmentally designated experts. International Cooperative Programmes. **Languages** English, French, Russian. **Staff** 6 member of UNECE staff provide Secretariat, some part-time. **Finance** Sources: UNECE budget; contributions (mandatory and voluntary) to the *'UN Trust Fund for Implementation of the Convention on Long-Range Transboundary Air Pollution'*; voluntary counterpart contributions in kind by Governments. **Events** *Annual Session* Geneva (Switzerland) 2011, *Annual Session* Geneva (Switzerland) 2010, *Workshop* Stockholm (Sweden) 2009, *Annual Session of the Executive Body* Geneva (Switzerland) 2008, *Annual Session of the Executive Body* Geneva (Switzerland) 2007. **Publications** *National Strategies and Policies for Air Pollution Abatement* (every 4 years). *Air Pollution Studies Series* (annual). Reports of the sessions of the Executive Body.

Members As of Apr 2021, 51 Signatory Parties:
Albania, Armenia, Austria, Azerbaijan, Belarus, Belgium, Bosnia-Herzegovina, Bulgaria, Canada, Croatia, Cyprus, Czechia, Denmark, Estonia, Finland, France, Georgia, Germany, Greece, Hungary, Iceland, Ireland, Italy, Kazakhstan, Kyrgyzstan, Latvia, Liechtenstein, Lithuania, Luxembourg, Malta, Moldova, Monaco, Montenegro, Netherlands, North Macedonia, Norway, Poland, Portugal, Romania, Russia, Serbia, Slovakia, Slovenia, Spain, Sweden, Switzerland, Türkiye, UK, Ukraine, USA.
European Union (EU, #08967).

NGO Relations Accredited organizations: *European Federation of Clean Air and Environmental Protection Associations (EFCA, #07079); International Union of Air Pollution Prevention and Environmental Protection Associations (IUAPPA, #15753).* [2021/XD9557/**F***]

- ♦ Convention for the Maintenance, Preservation and Reestablishment of Peace (1936 treaty)
- ♦ Convention pour le maintien, la préservation et le rétablissement de la paix (1936 treaty)
- ♦ Convention on Maritime Neutrality (1928 treaty)
- ♦ Convention on the Marking of Plastic Explosives for the Purpose of Identification (1991 treaty)
- ♦ Convention sur le marquage des explosifs plastiques et en feuille aux fins de détection (1991 treaty)
- ♦ Convention sur les marques de fabrique et de commerce (1910 treaty)
- ♦ Convention en matière de coopération, préparation et intervention contre la pollution par les hydrocarbures (1990 treaty)
- ♦ Convention on the Means of Prohibiting and Preventing the Illicit Import, Export and Transfer of Ownership of Cultural Property (1970 treaty)
- ♦ Convention on the Measurement of Inland Navigation Vessels (1966 treaty)
- ♦ Convention between the Member States of the European Communities on Double Jeopardy (1987 treaty)
- ♦ Convention sur la mer territoriale et la zone contiguë (1958 treaty)
- ♦ Convention du mètre (1875 treaty)
- ♦ Convention sur les migrations dans des conditions abusives et sur la promotion de l'égalité de chances et de traitement des travailleurs migrants (1975 treaty)
- ♦ Convention de Minamata sur le mercure (2013 treaty)
- ♦ Convention mondiale des Eglises du Christ (#21315)
- ♦ Convention monétaire, 1873 (1873 treaty)
- ♦ Convention monétaire, 1879 (1879 treaty)
- ♦ Convention multilatérale tendant à éviter la double imposition des redevances de droits d'auteur et protocole additionnel (1979 treaty)
- ♦ Convention of Mutual Assistance in Respect of the Collection of the Turnover Tax, the Purchase Tax and other Similar Taxes (1964 treaty)
- ♦ Convention on Mutual Legal Assistance in Criminal Matters between the Member States of the European Union (2000 treaty)
- ♦ Convention for the Mutual Recognition of Inspections in Respect of the Manufacture of Pharmaceutical Products (1970 treaty)
- ♦ Convention of Mutual Relief (1914 treaty)

♦ Convention of National Associations of Electrical Engineers of Europe (EUREL) 04788

Fédération des Associations Nationales des Ingénieurs Electriciens de l'Europe – Föderation der Nationalen Elektrotechnischen Vereinigungen Europas

Pres Florida Int Univ, Dp Electrical and Computer Engineering, c/o ISTEC, 10555 W Flagler St Room ECE 3944, Miami FL 33174, USA. T. +13053484943. Fax +13053483707.
URL: http://www.eurel.org/

History 24 Nov 1972, Zurich (Switzerland), as *Convention of National Societies of Electrical Engineers of Western Europe – Convention des sociétés nationales d'électriciens de l'Europe occidentale – Föderation der Nationalen Elektrotechnischen Vereinigungen Westeuropas.* Subsequently known as *Convention of National Societies of Electrical Engineers of Europe (EUREL) – Fédération des Sociétés Nationales des Ingénieurs Electriciens de l'Europe.* Previously also referred to in French as *Convention des sociétés nationales d'électriciens de l'Europe.* **Aims** Facilitate communication and exchange of information; foster a wider dissemination of scientific, technical and related knowledge relevant to electrical engineering in its widest sense, including *electronics, informatics* and related subjects; represent members with regional, national and European institutions. **Structure** General Assembly (annual). Board of Directors. Executive Committee. Secretary-General. Committees; Working Groups. **Languages** English. **Finance** Members' dues. Secretariat expense borne by member associations. **Activities** Meeting activities. **Events** *International symposium on electromagnetic compatibility* Barcelona (Spain) 2006, *International Conference on Architecture of Computing Systems* Frankfurt-Main (Germany) 2006, *EMC Europe: workshop on electromagnetic compatibility of wireless systems* Rome (Italy) 2005, *European wireless conference* Barcelona (Spain) 2004, *Wroclaw biennial international symposium on electromagnetic compatibility* Wroclaw (Poland) 2004.

Members National associations (9) in 9 countries:
Austria, Bulgaria, Germany, Israel, Poland, Portugal, Romania, Sweden, Switzerland.

NGO Relations Instrumental in setting up: *European Specialized Technical Societies (ESTES, inactive).* [2014/XD4356/**F**]

- ♦ Convention sur la nationalité (1933 treaty)
- ♦ Convention sur la nationalité de la femme (1933 treaty)
- ♦ Convention sur la nationalité de la femme mariée (1957 treaty)
- ♦ Convention on Nationality (1933 treaty)
- ♦ Convention on the Nationality of Married Women (1957 treaty)
- ♦ Convention on the Nationality of Women (1933 treaty)
- ♦ Convention of National Societies of Electrical Engineers of Europe / see Convention of National Associations of Electrical Engineers of Europe (#04788)
- ♦ Convention of National Societies of Electrical Engineers of Western Europe / see Convention of National Associations of Electrical Engineers of Europe (#04788)
- ♦ Convention des Nations-Unies sur les conditions d'immatriculation des navires (1986 treaty)
- ♦ Convention des Nations Unies contre la criminalité transnationale organisée (2000 treaty)
- ♦ Convention des Nations Unies contre le trafic illicite de stupéfiants et de substances psychotropes (1988 treaty)
- ♦ Convention des Nations Unies sur le droit de la mer (1982 treaty)
- ♦ Convention des Nations Unies sur les lettres de change internationales et les billets à ordre internationaux (1988 treaty)
- ♦ Convention des Nations Unies sur la lutte contre la désertification (1994 treaty)
- ♦ Convention des Nations-Unies sur le transport de marchandises par mer (1978 treaty)
- ♦ Convention des Nations Unies sur le transport multimodal international des marchandises (1980 treaty)
- ♦ Convention on Nature Protection and Wild Life Preservation in the Western Hemisphere (1940 treaty)
- ♦ Convention sur la neutralité maritime (1928 treaty)
- ♦ Convention de Niamey – Convention de l'Union Africaine sur la coopération transfrontalière (2014 treaty)
- ♦ Convention on the Nomenclature for the Classification of Goods in Customs Tariffs (1950 treaty)
- ♦ Convention sur la nomenclature pour la classification des marchandises dans les tarifs douaniers (1950 treaty)
- ♦ Convention on the Non-applicability of Statutory Limitations to War Crimes and Crimes Against Humanity (1968 treaty)
- ♦ Convention nordique sur la protection de l'environnement (1974 treaty)
- ♦ Convention sur la notification rapide d' un accident nucléaire (1986 treaty)
- ♦ Convention on Nuclear Safety (1994 treaty)
- ♦ Convention sur l'obtention des preuves à l'étranger en matière civile ou commerciale (1970 treaty)
- ♦ Convention on Offences and Certain other Acts Committed on Board Aircraft (1963 treaty)
- ♦ Convention sur les opérations financières des "initiés" (1989 treaty)
- ♦ Convention of the Organization of the Islamic Conference on Combating International Terrorism (1999 treaty)
- ♦ Convention sur l'orientation pacifiste de l'enseignement (1936 treaty)
- ♦ Convention d'Oslo – Convention pour la prévention de la pollution marine par les opérations d'immersion effectuées par les navires et aéronefs (1972 treaty)
- ♦ Convention de l'OUA régissant les aspects propres aux problèmes des réfugiés en Afrique (1969 treaty)
- ♦ Convention for the Pacific Settlement of International Disputes, 1907 (1907 treaty)
- ♦ Convention for the Pacific Settlements of International Conflicts, 1899 (1899 treaty)
- ♦ Convention de paix et d'arbitrage (1902 treaty)
- ♦ Convention on the Pan American Highway (1936 treaty)
- ♦ Convention on the Pan American Union (1928 treaty)
- ♦ Convention de Paris – Convention pour la prévention de la pollution marine d'origine tellurique (1974 treaty)
- ♦ Convention de Paris pour la protection de la propriété industrielle, 1883 (1883 treaty)
- ♦ Convention de Paris sur la responsabilité civile dans la domaine de l'énergie nucléaire (1960 treaty)
- ♦ Convention sur la participation des étrangers à la vie publique au niveau local (1992 treaty)
- ♦ Convention on the Participation of Foreigners in Public Life at Local Level (1992 treaty)
- ♦ Convention on Patents of Invention, Drawings and Industrial Models, Trademarks, and Literary and Artistic Property (1906 treaty)
- ♦ Convention du patrimoine mondial – Convention concernant la protection du patrimoine mondial culturel et naturel (1972 treaty)
- ♦ Convention of Peace and Arbitration (1902 treaty)
- ♦ Convention sur la pêche et la conservation des ressources biologiques de la haute mer (1958 treaty)
- ♦ Convention sur la pêche et la conservation des ressources biologiques dans la mer Baltique et les Belts (1973 treaty)
- ♦ Convention sur les pêcheries de l'Atlantique du Nord-Est (1959 treaty)
- ♦ Convention on Pecuniary Claims, 1906 (1906 treaty)
- ♦ Convention on Pecuniary Claims, 1910 (1910 treaty)
- ♦ Convention pénale sur la corruption (1999 treaty)
- ♦ Convention on the Physical Protection of Nuclear Material (1979 treaty)
- ♦ Convention phytosanitaire pour l' Afrique (1967 treaty)
- ♦ Convention phytosanitaire pour l'Afrique au Sud du Sahara (1954 treaty)
- ♦ Convention sur les pièces d'identité des gens de mer (2003 treaty)
- ♦ Convention sur le plateau continental (1958 treaty)
- ♦ Convention de police (1920 treaty)
- ♦ Convention on Political Asylum, 1933 (1933 treaty)
- ♦ Convention on the Political Rights of Women (1953 treaty)
- ♦ Convention sur la pollution atmosphérique transfrontière à longue distance (#04787)
- ♦ Convention portant dispense de légalisation pour certains actes et documents (1977 treaty)
- ♦ Convention portant loi uniforme sur les chèques (1931 treaty)
- ♦ Convention portant loi uniforme sur la formation des contrats de vente internationale des objets mobiliers corporels (1964 treaty)
- ♦ Convention portant loi uniforme sur les lettres de change et billets à ordre (1930 treaty)
- ♦ Convention portant loi uniforme sur la vente internationale des objets mobiliers corporels (1964 treaty)
- ♦ Convention portant réglementation de la navigation aérienne (1919 treaty)
- ♦ Convention portant révision des articles finals (1946 treaty)
- ♦ Convention portant unification des droits d'accise et de la rétribution pour la garantie des ouvrages en métaux précieux (1950 treaty)
- ♦ Convention postale pour l'Asie et l'Océanie (1961 treaty)
- ♦ Convention postale universelle, 1906 (1906 treaty)
- ♦ Convention postale universelle, 1920 (1920 treaty)
- ♦ Convention postale universelle, 1924 (1924 treaty)
- ♦ Convention postale universelle, 1929 (1929 treaty)
- ♦ Convention postale universelle, 1952 (1952 treaty)
- ♦ Convention postale universelle, 1957 (1957 treaty)
- ♦ Convention postale universelle, 1964 (1964 treaty)
- ♦ Convention postale universelle, 1974 (1974 treaty)
- ♦ Convention postale universelle, 1979 (1979 treaty)
- ♦ Convention postale universelle, 1984 (1985 treaty)
- ♦ Convention on the Practice of Learned Professions, 1889 (1889 treaty)
- ♦ Convention on the Practice of Learned Professions, 1902 (1902 treaty)
- ♦ Convention on the Practice of Learned Professions, 1939 (1939 treaty)
- ♦ Convention on the Practice of Liberal Professions (1923 treaty)
- ♦ Convention sur la prescription en matière de vente internationale de marchandises (1974 treaty)
- ♦ Convention pour la préservation des animaux sauvages, des oiseaux et des poissons en Afrique (1900 treaty)
- ♦ Convention for the Preservation of Wild Animals, Birds and Fish in Africa (1900 treaty)

Convention prestations cas
04788

alphabetic sequence excludes
For the complete listing, see Yearbook Online at

- Convention sur les prestations en cas d'accidents du travail et de maladies professionelles (1964 treaty)
- Convention on the Prevention of Major Industrial Accidents (1993 treaty)
- Convention for the Prevention of Marine Pollution by Dumping from Ships and Aircraft (1972 treaty)
- Convention on the Prevention of Marine Pollution by Dumping of Wastes and other Matter (1972 treaty)
- Convention on the Prevention of Marine Pollution from Land-based Sources (1974 treaty)
- Convention pour la prévention de la pollution marine par les opérations d'immersion effectuées par les navires et aéronefs (1972 treaty)
- Convention pour la prévention de la pollution marine d'origine tellurique (1974 treaty)
- Convention sur la prévention de la pollution des mers résultant de l'immersion de déchets (1972 treaty)
- Convention on the Prevention and Punishment of the Crime of Genocide (1948 treaty)
- Convention on the Prevention and Punishment of Crimes Against Internationally Protected Persons, Including Diplomatic Agents (1973 treaty)
- Convention pour la prévention et la répression du crime de génocide (1948 treaty)
- Convention sur la prévention et la répression du terrorisme (1937 treaty)
- Convention for the Prevention of Terrorism and Punishment of Terrorism (1937 treaty)
- Convention to Prevent and Punish the Acts of Terrorism Taking the Form of Crimes Against Persons and Related Extortion That Are of International Significance (1971 treaty)
- Convention on Private International Law (1928 treaty)
- Convention sur les privilèges et immunités des institutions spécialisées (1947 treaty)
- Convention sur les privilèges et immunités des Nations-Unies (1946 treaty)
- Convention of the Privileges and Immunities of the League of Arab States (1953 treaty)
- Convention on the Privileges and Immunities of the Specialized Agencies (1947 treaty)
- Convention on the Privileges and Immunities of the United Nations (1946 treaty)
- Convention on the Prohibition of the Development, Production and Stockpiling of Bacteriological – Biological – and Toxin Weapons and on Their Destruction (1972 treaty)
- Convention on the Prohibition of the Development, Production, Stockpiling and Use of Chemical Weapons and on Their Destruction (1992 treaty)
- Convention for the Prohibition of Fishing with Long Driftnets in the South Pacific (1989 treaty)
- Convention on the Prohibition of Military or Any other Hostile Use of Environmental Modification Techniques (1976 treaty)
- Convention on Prohibitions or Restrictions on the Use of Certain Conventional Weapons Which May be Deemed to be Excessively Injurious or to Have Indiscriminate Effects, with Annexed Protocols (1980 treaty)
- Convention on the Prohibition of the Use, Stockpiling, Production and Transfer of Anti-personnel Mines and on Their Destruction (1997 treaty)
- Convention pour la Promotion et le Développement de L'industrie des Assurances dans les Pays Africains (1990 treaty)
- Convention for the Promotion of Inter-American Cultural Relations, 1936 (1936 treaty)
- Convention for the Promotion of Inter-American Cultural Relations, 1954 (1954 treaty)
- Convention sur la propriété artistique et littéraire, 1910 (1910 treaty)
- Convention for the Protection of Agriculture (1913 treaty)
- Convention pour la protection des Alpes (1991 treaty)
- Convention for the Protection of the Alps (1991 treaty)
- Convention on the Protection of the Archeological, Historical and Artistic of the American Nations (1976 treaty)
- Convention for the Protection of the Architectural Heritage of Europe (1985 treaty)
- Convention pour la protection des biens culturels en cas de conflit armé (1954 treaty)
- Convention for the Protection of Birds Useful to Agriculture (1902 treaty)
- Convention on the Protection of the Black Sea Against Pollution (1992 treaty)
- Convention on Protection of Children and Cooperation in Respect of Intercountry Adoption (1993 treaty)
- Convention for the Protection of Commercial, Industrial, and Agricultural Trade Marks and Commercial Names (1923 treaty)
- Convention pour la protection de la couche d'ozone (1985 treaty)
- Convention for the Protection of Cultural Property in the Event of Armed Conflict (1954 treaty)
- Convention for the Protection and Development of the Marine Environment of the Wider Caribbean Region (1983 treaty)
- Convention pour la protection des Droits de l'Homme et de la dignité de l'être humain à l'égard des applications de la biologie et de la médecine: Convention sur les Droits de l'Homme et la biomédecine (1997 treaty)
- Convention sur la protection des enfants et la coopération en matière d'adoption internationale (1993 treaty)
- Convention on Protection of the Environment through Criminal Law (1998 treaty)
- Convention on the Protection of the Environment between Denmark, Finland, Norway and Sweden (1974 treaty)
- Convention sur la protection de l'environnement par le droit pénal (1998 treaty)
- Convention pour la protection de la flore, de la faune et des beautés panoramiques naturelles des pays de l'Amérique (1940 treaty)
- Convention pour la protection, la gestion et la mise en valeur du milieu marin et des zones côtières de la région de l'Afrique orientale (1985 treaty)
- Convention for the Protection of Human Rights and Dignity of the Human Being with regard to the Application of Biology and Medicine: Convention on Human Rights and Biomedicine (1997 treaty)
- Convention for the Protection of Human Rights and Fundamental Freedoms (1950 treaty)
- Convention for the Protection of Individuals with Regard to Automatic Processing of Personal Data (1981 treaty)
- Convention sur la protection internationale des adultes (2000 treaty)
- Convention for the Protection, Management and Development of the Marine and Coastal Environment of the Eastern African Region (1985 treaty)
- Convention on the Protection of the Marine Environment of the Baltic Sea Area (1974 treaty)
- Convention on the Protection of the Marine Environment of the Baltic Sea Area, 1992 (1992 treaty)
- Convention on the Protection of the Marine Environment of the Baltic Sea Area, 1999 (1999 treaty)
- Convention for the Protection of the Marine Environment and Coastal Area of the Southeast Pacific (1981 treaty)
- Convention for the Protection of the Marine Environment and the Coastal Region of the Mediterranean (1976 treaty)
- Convention for the Protection on the Marine Environment for the North-East Atlantic (1992 treaty)
- Convention pour la protection des marques de fabrique, de commerce, d'agriculture et de noms commerciaux (1923 treaty)
- Convention pour la protection de la mer Méditerranée contre la pollution (1976 treaty)
- Convention sur la protection de la Mer noire contre la pollution (1992 treaty)
- Convention pour la protection du milieu marin de l' Atlantique du nord-est (1992 treaty)
- Convention pour la protection du milieu marin dans la zone de la mer Baltique (1974 treaty)
- Convention pour la protection du milieu marin dans la zone de la mer Baltique (1992 treaty)
- Convention pour la protection et la mise en valeur du milieu marin dans la région des Caraïbes (1983 treaty)
- Convention for the Protection of the Natural Resources and Environment of the South Pacific Region (1986 treaty)
- Convention sur la protection de la nature dans le Pacifique Sud (1976 treaty)
- Convention pour la protection des oeuvres littéraires et artistiques, 1902 (1902 treaty)
- Convention pour la protection des oiseaux utiles à l' agriculture (1902 treaty)
- Convention for the Protection of Patents of Invention, Designs and Industrial Models (1910 treaty)
- Convention sur la protection du patrimoine culturel subaquatique (2001 treaty)
- Convention pour la protection des personnes à l'égard du traitement automatisé des données à caractère personnel (1981 treaty)
- Convention pour la protection des phoques de l'Antarctique (1972 treaty)
- Convention sur la protection physique des matières nucléaires (1979 treaty)
- Convention for the Protection of Producers of Phonograms Against Unauthorized Duplication of Their Phonograms (1971 treaty)
- Convention pour la protection des productions de phonogrammes contre la reproduction non autorisée de leurs phonogrammes (1971 treaty)
- Convention on the Protection and Promotion of the Diversity of Cultural Expressions (2005 treaty)
- Convention sur la protection des ressources naturelles et de l'environnement de la région du Pacifique sud (1986 treaty)
- Convention on the Protection of the Rhine (1999 treaty)
- Convention for the Protection of the Rhine Against Chemical Pollution (1976 treaty)
- Convention for the Protection of the Rhine from Pollution by Chlorides Modified by Exchanges of Letters (1976 treaty)
- Convention sur la protection du salaire (1949 treaty)
- Convention for the Protection of Submarine Cables (1884 treaty)
- Convention on the Protection and Sustainable Development of the Carpathians (2003 treaty)
- Convention on the Protection of Trade Marks (1910 treaty)
- Convention on the Protection of the Underwater Cultural Heritage (2001 treaty)
- Convention on the Protection and Use of Transboundary Watercourses and International Lakes (1992 treaty)
- Convention sur la protection et l'utilisation des cours d'eau transfrontières et des lacs internationaux (1992 treaty)
- Convention Providing a Uniform Law for Bills of Exchange and Promissory Notes (1930 treaty)
- Convention Providing a Uniform Law for Cheques (1931 treaty)
- Convention Providing a Uniform Law on the Form of an International Will (1973 treaty)
- Convention on the Provisional Administration of European Colonies and Possessions in the Americas (1940 treaty)
- Convention on Psychotropic Substances (1971 treaty)
- Convention on Publicity of Customs Documents (1923 treaty)
- Convention radiotélégraphique internationale (1906 treaty)
- Convention radiotélégraphique internationale (1912 treaty)
- Convention sur le rapatriement des marins, 1926 (1926 treaty)
- Convention sur le rapatriement des marins, 1987 (1987 treaty)
- Convention de rapprochement économique (1930 treaty)
- Convention for Reciprocal Exchange of Central American Students (1923 treaty)
- Convention for the Reciprocal Recognition of Proof Marks on Small Arms (1969 treaty)
- Convention sur les réclamations pécuniaires, 1906 (1906 treaty)
- Convention sur les réclamations pécuniaires, 1910 (1910 treaty)
- Convention on the Recognition of Decisions Relating to the Marriage Bond (1967 treaty)
- Convention on the Recognition of Divorces and Legal Separations (1970 treaty)
- Convention on the Recognition and Enforcement of Decisions Relating to Maintenance of Obligations (1973 treaty)
- Convention on the Recognition and Enforcement of Foreign Arbitral Awards (1958 treaty)
- Convention on the Recognition and Enforcement of Foreign Judgements in Civil or Commercial Matters (2019 treaty)
- Convention on the Recognition and Enforcement of Foreign Judgements in Civil and Commercial Matters (1971 treaty)
- Convention on the Recognition of Qualifications Concerning Higher Education in the European Region (1997 treaty)
- Convention on the Recognition of Studies, Diplomas and Degrees in Higher Education in the Arab States (1978 treaty)
- Convention on the Recognition of Studies, Diplomas and Degrees in Higher Education in the States Belonging to the Europe Region (1979 treaty)
- Convention sur la reconnaissance des décisions relatives au lien conjugal (1967 treaty)
- Convention sur la reconnaissance des divorces et des séparations de corps (1970 treaty)
- Convention sur la reconnaissance des études et des diplômes de l'enseignement supérieur dans les Etats arabes (1978 treaty)
- Convention sur la reconnaissance des études et des diplômes relatifs à l'enseignement supérieur dans les Etats de la région Europe (1979 treaty)
- Convention sur la reconnaissance et l'exécution des jugements étrangers en matière civile et commerciale (1971 treaty)
- Convention pour la reconnaissance et l'exécution des sentences arbitrales étrangères (1958 treaty)
- Convention sur la reconnaissance des qualifications relatives à l'enseignement supérieur dans la région européenne (1997 treaty)
- Convention pour la reconnaissance réciproque des poinçons d'épreuves des armes à feu portatives (1969 treaty)
- Convention sur le recouvrement des créances alimentaires (1962 treaty)
- Convention on the Recovery Abroad of Maintenance (1956 treaty)
- Convention pour la rédaction de codes de droit international public et de droit international privé (1902 treaty)
- Convention sur la réduction des cas d'apatridie (1961 treaty)
- Convention on Reduction of Cases of Multiple Nationality and Military Obligations in Cases of Multiple Nationality (1963 treaty)
- Convention sur la réduction des cas de pluralité de nationalités et sur les obligations militaires en cas de pluralité de nationalités (1963 treaty)
- Convention on the Reduction of the Number of Cases of Statelessness (1973 treaty)
- Convention on the Reduction of Statelessness (1961 treaty)
- Convention Regarding the Abolition of the Capitulations in Egypt (1937 treaty)
- Convention Regarding Bankruptcy between Nordic States (1933 treaty)
- Convention Regarding Booklets of Travellers' Postal Vouchers in the Relations between Denmark, Finland, Iceland, Norway and Sweden (1937 treaty)
- Convention Regarding Inheritance and the Settlement of the Devolution of Property (1934 treaty)
- Convention Regarding International Exhibitions (1928 treaty)
- Convention Regarding Investments in War-loans (1922 treaty)
- Convention Regarding the Measurement and Registration of Vessels Employed in Inland Navigation (1956 treaty)
- Convention Regarding the Measurement of Vessels Employed in Inland Navigation (1925 treaty)
- Convention Regarding Mutual Payment of Old-age Pensions (1949 treaty)
- Convention Regarding the Organization of the Campaign Against Locusts (1920 treaty)
- Convention Regarding the Recognition and Enforcement of Judgments (1932 treaty)
- Convention Regarding the Recognition and Enforcement of Judgments in Criminal Matters (1948 treaty)
- Convention sur le régime fiscal des véhicules (1931 treaty)
- Convention sur le régime des spiritueux en Afrique (1919 treaty)
- Convention régionale de l'Amérique du Nord sur la radiodiffusion, 1937 (1937 treaty)
- Convention régionale concernant la conservation de l'environnement de la Mer Rouge et du Golf d'Aden (1982 treaty)
- Convention régionale concernant la gestion et la conservation des écosystèmes forestiers naturels et le développement des plantations forestières (1993 treaty)
- Convention régionale européenne du service mobile radio-maritime (1948 treaty)

- ♦ Convention régionale du Koweït relative à la coopération dans le domaine de la protection du milieu marin contre la pollution (1978 treaty)
- ♦ Convention régionale de la radio pour l'Amérique centrale, Panama et la Zone du Canal (1938 treaty)
- ♦ Convention régionale sur la reconnaissance des études et des certificats, diplômes, grades et autres titres de l'enseignement supérieur dans les Etats d'Afrique (1981 treaty)
- ♦ Convention régionale sur la reconnaissance des études et des diplômes de l'enseignement supérieur en Amérique latine et dans la région des Caraïbes (1974 treaty)
- ♦ Convention régionale sur la reconnaissance des études, des diplômes et des grades de l'enseignement supérieur en Asie et dans le Pacifique (1983 treaty)
- ♦ Convention régionale relative à la coopération halieutique entre les Etats africains riverains de l'Océan Atlantique (1991 treaty)
- ♦ Convention on the Registration of Inland Navigation Vessels (1965 treaty)
- ♦ Convention on Registration of Objects Launched into Outer Space (1974 treaty)
- ♦ Convention réglementant les transports routiers (1970 treaty)
- ♦ Convention sur la réglementation des activités relatives aux ressources minérales de l'Antarctique (1988 treaty)
- ♦ Convention pour la réglementation de la chasse à la baleine (1931 treaty)
- ♦ Convention sur la réglementation de la circulation automobile (1930 treaty)
- ♦ Convention pour la réglementation du maillage des filets de pêches et des tailles limites des poissons (1946 treaty)
- ♦ Convention pour le règlement des différends relatifs aux investissements entre Etats et ressortissants d'autres Etats (1965 treaty)
- ♦ Convention sur le règlement international de 1972 pour prévenir les abordages en mer (1972 treaty)
- ♦ Convention pour le règlement pacifique des conflits internationaux (1899 treaty)
- ♦ Convention pour le règlement du transit et des communications sur le réseau de la Compagnie des chemins de fer Danube-Save-Adriatique (1923 treaty)
- ♦ Convention sur le règlement par voie d'arbitrage des contestations de droit civil découlant des relations de coopération économique, scientifique et technique (1972 treaty)
- ♦ Convention pour régler les conflits entre la loi nationale et la loi du domicile (1955 treaty)
- ♦ Convention pour régler les conflits de lois et de juridictions en matière de divorce et de séparations de corps (1902 treaty)
- ♦ Convention pour régler les conflits de lois en matière de mariage (1902 treaty)
- ♦ Convention pour régler la tutelle des mineurs (1902 treaty)
- ♦ Convention Regulating Provincial, Communal and District Pensions (1923 treaty)
- ♦ Convention Regulating Road Transport (1970 treaty)
- ♦ Convention Regulating the Withdrawal of Water from Lake Constance (1966 treaty)
- ♦ Convention on the Regulation of Antarctic Mineral Resource Activities (1988 treaty)
- ♦ Convention on the Regulation of Automotive Traffic (1930 treaty)
- ♦ Convention for the Regulation of Hours of Work in Automatic Sheet-glass Works (1934 treaty)
- ♦ Convention on the Regulation of Inter-American Automotive Traffic (1943 treaty)
- ♦ Convention for the Regulation of the Meshes of Fishing Nets and the Size Limits of Fish (1946 treaty)
- ♦ Convention for the Regulation of Transit and Communications on the System of the Danube-Save-Adriatic Railway Company (1923 treaty)
- ♦ Convention for the Regulation of the Unified Central American Consular Service (1912 treaty)
- ♦ Convention for the Regulation of Whaling (1931 treaty)
- ♦ Convention Relating to the Authentication of Certain Deaths (1966 treaty)
- ♦ Convention Relating to Changes of Surname and First Name (1958 treaty)
- ♦ Convention Relating to Civil Liability in the Field of Maritime Carriage of Nuclear Material (1971 treaty)
- ♦ Convention Relating to Civil Procedure, 1905 (1905 treaty)
- ♦ Convention Relating to Civil Procedure, 1954 (1954 treaty)
- ♦ Convention Relating to Conflicts of Laws with Regard to the Effects of Marriage on the Rights and Duties of the Spouses in Their Personal Relationship and with Regard to Their Estates (1905 treaty)
- ♦ Convention Relating to Deprivation of Civil Rights and Similar Measures of Protection (1905 treaty)
- ♦ Convention Relating to the Designation of Names in Civil Registration Records (1973 treaty)
- ♦ Convention Relating to the Development of Hydraulic Power Affecting More Than One State (1923 treaty)
- ♦ Convention Relating to the Distribution of Programme-carrying Signals Transmitted by Satellite (1974 treaty)
- ♦ Convention Relating to the Establishment of the Maternity of Illegitimate Children (1962 treaty)
- ♦ Convention Relating to the International Status of Refugees (1933 treaty)
- ♦ Convention Relating to the Limitation of the Liability of Owners of Inland Navigation Vessels (1973 treaty)
- ♦ Convention Relating to the Liquor Traffic in Africa (1919 treaty)
- ♦ Convention Relating to the Regime of the Straits (1923 treaty)
- ♦ Convention Relating to Registration of Rights in Respect of Vessels under Construction (1967 treaty)
- ♦ Convention Relating to the Regulation of Aerial Navigation (1919 treaty)
- ♦ Convention Relating to the Salvage of Torpedoes (1934 treaty)
- ♦ Convention Relating to the Settlement of the Conflict of Laws Concerning Marriage (1902 treaty)
- ♦ Convention Relating to the Settlement of the Conflict of Laws and Jurisdictions as Regards to Divorce and Separation (1902 treaty)
- ♦ Convention Relating to the Settlement of the Conflicts between the Law of Nationality and the Law of Domicile (1955 treaty)
- ♦ Convention Relating to the Settlement of Guardianship of Minors (1902 treaty)
- ♦ Convention Relating to the Simplification of Customs Formalities (1923 treaty)
- ♦ Convention Relating to the Status of Refugees (1951 treaty)
- ♦ Convention Relating to the Status of Stateless Persons (1954 treaty)
- ♦ Convention Relating to Stops on Bearer Securities in International Circulation (1970 treaty)
- ♦ Convention Relating to the Tonnage Measurement of Merchant Ships (1934 treaty)
- ♦ Convention Relating to the Transit of Airplanes (1935 treaty)
- ♦ Convention Relating to the Transmission in Transit of Electric Power (1923 treaty)
- ♦ Convention Relating to the Unification of Certain Rules Concerning Collisions in Inland Navigation (1960 treaty)
- ♦ Convention Relating to the Unification of Excise Duties and of Fees for the Warranty of Articles of Precious Metals (1950 treaty)
- ♦ Convention Relating to a Uniform Law on the Formation of Contracts for the International Sale of Goods (1964 treaty)
- ♦ Convention Relating to a Uniform Law on the International Sale of Goods (1964 treaty)
- ♦ Convention sur les relations personnelles concernant les enfants (2003 treaty)
- ♦ Convention relative à l'admission temporaire (1990 treaty)
- ♦ Convention relative à l'aide alimentaire, 1986 (1986 treaty)
- ♦ Convention relative à l'aménagement des forces hydrauliques intéressant plusieurs Etats (1923 treaty)
- ♦ Convention relative à l'application à certains protectorats et territoires sous mandat du Traité d'extradition du 17 décembre 1891 (1930 treaty)
- ♦ Convention relative à l'application des normes du Conseil d'aide économique mutuelle (1974 treaty)
- ♦ Convention relative à l'assistance mutuelle aux indigents des pays respectifs (1928 treaty)
- ♦ Convention relative à l'assistance réciproque en cas de maternité (1953 treaty)
- ♦ Convention relative à l'assistance réciproque en matière de recouvrement de créances fiscales (1952 treaty)
- ♦ Convention relative à l'aviation civile internationale (1944 treaty)
- ♦ Convention relative au blanchiment, au dépistage, à la saisie et à la confiscation des produits du crime (1990 treaty)
- ♦ Convention Relative to the Canalisation of the Main (1906 treaty)
- ♦ Convention relative aux carnets de bons postaux de voyage dans les rapports entre le Danemark, la Finlande, l'Islande, la Norvège et la Suède (1937 treaty)
- ♦ Convention Relative to Certain Restrictions on the Rights of Capture in Maritime War (1907 treaty)
- ♦ Convention relative aux circuits télégraphiques et téléphoniques entre Bujumbura et Kigali (1970 treaty)
- ♦ Convention Relative to the Circulation of Automobiles (1909 treaty)
- ♦ Convention relative à un code de conduite des conférences maritimes (1974 treaty)
- ♦ Convention Relative à la Collecte, au Dépôt et à la Réception des Déchets Survenant en Navigation Rhenane et Intérieure (1996 treaty)
- ♦ Convention relative à la conservation de la faune et de la flore à l'état naturel (1933 treaty)
- ♦ Convention relative à la conservation du saumon dans l'Atlantique-nord (1982 treaty)
- ♦ Convention relative à la conservation de la vie sauvage et du milieu naturel de l'Europe (1979 treaty)
- ♦ Convention relative à la constatation de certains décès (1966 treaty)
- ♦ Convention relative au contrat de transport international de marchandises par route (1956 treaty)
- ♦ Convention relative au contrat de transport international de voyageurs et de bagages par route (1973 treaty)
- ♦ Convention relative au contrat de transport de marchandises en navigation intérieure (1999 treaty)
- ♦ Convention relative au contrôle du commerce des armes et munitions (1919 treaty)
- ♦ Convention Relative to the Conversion of Merchant-ships into War-ships (1907 treaty)
- ♦ Convention relative à la coopération en matière de douanes et d'accises (1952 treaty)
- ♦ Convention relative à la coopération en matière de protection et de mise en valeur du milieu marin et des zones côtières de la région de l' Afrique de l' Ouest et du Centre (1981 treaty)
- ♦ Convention relative à la coopération en matière de réglementation des importations, des exportations et du transit (1961 treaty)
- ♦ Convention Relative to the Creation of a Pan American Tourist Passport and of a Transit Passport for Vehicles (1935 treaty)
- ♦ Convention relative à la création du passeport panaméricain du tourisme et du passeport de transit pour les véhicules (1935 treaty)
- ♦ Convention relative au dédouanement dans le cas des transports internationaux de marchandises par véhicules (1965 treaty)
- ♦ Convention relative à la délivrance de certains extraits d'actes de l'état civil destinés à l'étranger (1956 treaty)
- ♦ Convention relative à la délivrance d'extraits plurilingues d'actes de l'état civil (1976 treaty)
- ♦ Convention relative aux dommages causés aux tiers à la surface par des aéronefs étrangers (1952 treaty)
- ♦ Convention relative au droit international de rectification (1953 treaty)
- ♦ Convention relative aux droits et aux devoirs des puissances neutres en cas de guerre maritime (1907 treaty)
- ♦ Convention relative au droit de timbre en matière de lettres de change et de billets à ordre (1930 treaty)
- ♦ Convention relative au droit de timbre en matières de chèques (1931 treaty)
- ♦ Convention relative à l'élaboration d'une pharmacopée européenne (1964 treaty)
- ♦ Convention relative à l'esclavage, 1926 (1926 treaty)
- ♦ Convention relative à l'établissement et à la compétence judiciaire (1923 treaty)
- ♦ Convention relative à l'établissement d'un système d'inscription des testaments (1972 treaty)
- ♦ Convention Relative to the Exchange of Official, Scientific, Literary and Industrial Publications (1902 treaty)
- ♦ Convention relative à l'exercice des professions universitaires et à la reconnaissance des études universitaires (1962 treaty)
- ♦ Convention relative à la fourniture réciproque d'une assistance aux indigents (1951 treaty)
- ♦ Convention relative à l'héritage et à la liquidation des successions (1934 treaty)
- ♦ Convention Relative to Hospital Ships (1904 treaty)
- ♦ Convention relative à l'indication des noms et prénoms dans les registres de l'état civil (1973 treaty)
- ♦ Convention relative aux infractions et à certains autres actes survenant à bord des aéronefs (1963 treaty)
- ♦ Convention relative à l'inscription des droits relatifs aux navires en construction (1967 treaty)
- ♦ Convention relative au jaugeage des bâteaux de navigation intérieure (1925 treaty)
- ♦ Convention relative au jaugeage des navires de commerce (1934 treaty)
- ♦ Convention Relative to the Laying of Automatic Submarine Contact Mines (1907 treaty)
- ♦ Convention relative à la loi applicable au trust et à sa reconnaissance (1985 treaty)
- ♦ Convention relative à la marine marchande du Commonwealth britannique (1931 treaty)
- ♦ Convention Relative to the Monetary System, Customs, Weights and Measures, Fiscal Laws, International Trade and the Consular Service (1909 treaty)
- ♦ Convention relative à l'octroi d'avantages réciproques en cas de réduction de la capacité de travail (1953 treaty)
- ♦ Convention relative à l'octroi réciproque de pensions de vieillesse (1949 treaty)
- ♦ Convention relative à l'opposition sur titres au porteur à circulation internationale (1970 treaty)
- ♦ Convention relative à l'organisation de la lutte contre les sauterelles (1920 treaty)
- ♦ Convention relative au passage des membres d'une caisse-maladie et l'un des pays signataires à une caisse-maladie de l'un des autres pays et concernant l'assistance-maladie à l'occasion de séjours temporaires dans l'un des pays susvisés (1953 treaty)
- ♦ Convention relative à la pêche dans le Danube (1958 treaty)
- ♦ Convention Relative to the Preparation of Projects of Electoral Legislation (1923 treaty)
- ♦ Convention Relative to the Preservation of Fauna and Flora in Their Natural State (1933 treaty)
- ♦ Convention relative à la procédure civile, 1905 (1905 treaty)
- ♦ Convention relative à la procédure civile, 1954 (1954 treaty)
- ♦ Convention relative à la protection du Rhin (1999 treaty)
- ♦ Convention relative à la protection du Rhin contre la pollution chimique (1976 treaty)
- ♦ Convention relative à la protection du Rhin contre la pollution par les chlorures modifiée par échanges de lettres (1976 treaty)
- ♦ Convention relative à la reconnaissance et à l'exécution des décisions judiciaires en matière pénale (1948 treaty)
- ♦ Convention relative à la reconnaissance et à l'exécution des jugements (1932 treaty)
- ♦ Convention relative à la reconnaissance internationale des droits sur aéronef (1948 treaty)
- ♦ Convention relative au recouvrement de pensions alimentaires (1931 treaty)
- ♦ Convention relative au régime douanier des conteneurs utilisés en transport international dans le cadre d'un pool (1994 treaty)
- ♦ Convention relative au régime fiscal des véhicules routiers effectuant des transports internationaux de marchandises (1956 treaty)
- ♦ Convention relative au régime fiscal des véhicules routiers effectuant des transports internationaux de voyageurs (1956 treaty)
- ♦ Convention relative au régime fiscal des véhicules routiers à usage privé en circulation internationale (1956 treaty)
- ♦ Convention relative au régime des industries centroaméricaines d'intégration économique (1958 treaty)
- ♦ Convention relative au régime de la navigation sur le Danube (1948 treaty)
- ♦ Convention relative au régime des patentes de bateliers du Rhin (1923 treaty)
- ♦ Convention Relative to the Regulations for Rhine Navigation Certificates (1923 treaty)
- ♦ Convention relative à la responsabilité civile dans le domaine du transport maritime de matières nucléaires (1971 treaty)
- ♦ Convention relative à la responsabilité des exploitants des navires nucléaires (1962 treaty)
- ♦ Convention Relative to the Rights of Aliens (1902 treaty)
- ♦ Convention relative à la sécurité sociale (1955 treaty)
- ♦ Convention relative à la sécurité sociale dans les pays nordiques (1981 treaty)

Convention relative sépultures
04788

alphabetic sequence excludes
For the complete listing, see Yearbook Online at

♦ Convention relative aux sépultures militaires (1935 treaty)
♦ Convention relative au sérum antidiphtérique (1930 treaty)
♦ Convention relative à la signification et à la notification à l'étranger des actes judiciaires et extrajudiciaires en matière civile ou commerciale (1965 treaty)
♦ Convention relative à la simplification et à l'harmonisation des régimes douaniers (1973 treaty)
♦ Convention relative au statut des apatrides (1954 treaty)
♦ Convention relative au statut international des réfugiés (1933 treaty)
♦ Convention relative au statut légal et aux privilèges et immunités des organisations économiques inter états actives dans certains domaines de coopération (1980 treaty)
♦ Convention relative au statut des réfugiés (1951 treaty)
♦ Convention relative au tourisme allemand vers la Belgique et le Grand-Duché de Luxembourg (1939 treaty)
♦ Convention relative au traitement des prisonniers de guerre (1929 treaty)
♦ Convention relative au transfert dans l'Etat dont ils sont ressortissants, pour y subir leur peine, de condamnés à l'emprisonnement (1978 treaty)
♦ Convention relative aux transports internationaux ferroviaires, 1980 (1980 treaty)
♦ Convention relative aux transports internationaux ferroviaires, 1999 (1999 treaty)
♦ Convention relative au transport en transit de l'énergie électrique (1923 treaty)
♦ Convention Relative to the Treatment of Prisoners of War (1929 treaty)
♦ Convention relative à l'unification de certaines règles en matière d'abordage en navigation intérieure (1960 treaty)
♦ Convention relative à l'unification des formalités de rédaction et de présentation des demandes de brevet d'invention (1975 treaty)
♦ Convention relative à l'unification des formalités de rédaction et de présentation des demandes d'obtention de brevets d'invention (1975 treaty)
♦ Convention relative à l'unification du territoire douanier Benelux (1969 treaty)
♦ Convention relative à 'unité technique dans le domaine des chemins de fer (1882 treaty)
♦ Convention relative aux zones humides d'importance internationale particulièrement comme habitats de la sauvagine (1971 treaty)
♦ Convention sur le représentation en matière de vente internationale de marchandises (1983 treaty)
♦ Convention sur la répression des actes illicites dirigés contre l'aviation civile internationale (2010 treaty)
♦ Convention pour la répression d'actes illicites dirigés contre la sécurité de l'aviation civile (1971 treaty)
♦ Convention pour la répression de la capture illicite d'aéronefs (1970 treaty)
♦ Convention pour la répression de la circulation du trafic des publications obscènes (1923 treaty)
♦ Convention sur la répression de la contrebande (1935 treaty)
♦ Convention pour la répression de la contrebande des marchandises alcooliques (1925 treaty)
♦ Convention pour la répression du faux monnayage (1929 treaty)
♦ Convention sur la répression des infractions contre les personnes jouissant d'une protection internationale y compris les agents diplomatiques (1973 treaty)
♦ Convention on the Repression of Smuggling (1935 treaty)
♦ Convention pour la répression de la traite des êtres humains et de l'exploitation de la prostitution d'autrui (1949 treaty)
♦ Convention Respecting Annual Reports to be Presented to Centro-American Conferences (1912 treaty)
♦ Convention Respecting the Application of the Accident Insurance Laws of the Various States to Cases Where an Employer in One of the Contracting States Carries on a Business or Employs Workers in Another of the Said States (1937 treaty)
♦ Convention Respecting Central American Commerce (1910 treaty)
♦ Convention Respecting Conditions of Residence and Business and Jurisdiction (1923 treaty)
♦ Convention Respecting the Conflict of Laws in Matters of Succession and Wills (1905 treaty)
♦ Convention Respecting the Consular Service (1910 treaty)
♦ Convention Respecting the Free Navigation of the Suez Canal (1888 treaty)
♦ Convention Respecting International Exhibitions (1912 treaty)
♦ Convention Respecting the Liquor Traffic in Africa (1906 treaty)
♦ Convention Respecting Measures for the Preservation and Protection Fur Seals in the North Pacific Ocean (1911 treaty)
♦ Convention Respecting the Prohibition of Night Work for Women in Industrial Employment (1906 treaty)
♦ Convention Respecting the Reciprocal Payment of Child Allowances (1951 treaty)
♦ Convention Respecting Reciprocity in the Granting of Benefits for Reduced Working Capacity (1953 treaty)
♦ Convention Respecting Reciprocity in the Granting of Maternity Assistance (1953 treaty)
♦ Convention Respecting the Rights and Duties of Neutral Powers in Maritime War (1907 treaty)
♦ Convention Respecting the Rights and Duties of Neutral Powers and Persons in War on Land, 1901 (1901 treaty)
♦ Convention Respecting the Rights and Duties of Neutral Powers and Persons in War on Land, 1907 (1907 treaty)
♦ Convention Respecting Sabotage (1911 treaty)
♦ Convention Respecting Social Security (1955 treaty)
♦ Convention Respecting Transfers of Insured Persons from One Sick Fund to Another and Respecting Sickness Benefit During Temporary Residence (1953 treaty)
♦ Convention sur la responsabilité civile des dommages resultant d'activités dangereuses pour l'environnement (1993 treaty)
♦ Convention sur la responsabilité pour les dommages de pollution par les hydrocarbures résultant de la recherche et de l'exploitation des ressources minérales du sous-sol marin (1977 treaty)
♦ Convention sur la responsabilité des hôteliers quant aux objets apportés par les voyageurs (1962 treaty)
♦ Convention sur la responsabilité internationale pour les dommages causés par des objets spaciaux (1972 treaty)
♦ Convention pour la révision partielle des conventions adoptées par la Conférence générale de l'Organisation internationale du travail (1961 treaty)
♦ Convention on Rights and Duties of States (1933 treaty)
♦ Convention on the Rights of Persons with Disabilities (2006 treaty)
♦ Convention on Road Signs and Signals (1968 treaty)
♦ Convention on Road Traffic, 1949 (1949 treaty)
♦ Convention on Road Traffic, 1968 (1968 treaty)
♦ Convention on Road Traffic Concerning the Dimensions and Weights of Vehicles Permitted to Travel on Certain Roads (1950 treaty)
♦ Convention de Rotterdam sur la procédure de consentement préalable en connaissance de cause applicable a certains produits chimiques et pesticides dangereux qui font l'objet d' un commerce international (1998 treaty)
♦ Convention for the Safeguarding of Intangible Cultural Heritage (2003 treaty)
♦ Convention on the Safety of United Nations and Associated Personnel (1994 treaty)
♦ Convention sur les salaires, la durée du travail à bord et les effectifs, 1949 (1949 treaty)
♦ Convention sur les salaires, la durée du travail à bord et les effectifs, 1958 (1958 treaty)
♦ Convention Sales Professionals International (internationally oriented national body)
♦ Convention sanitaire, 1852 (1852 treaty)
♦ Convention sanitaire, 1903 (1903 treaty)
♦ Convention sanitaire, 1904 (1904 treaty)
♦ Convention sanitaire, 1905 (1905 treaty)
♦ Convention sanitaire internationale, 1900 (1900 treaty)
♦ Convention sanitaire internationale, 1912 (1912 treaty)
♦ Convention sanitaire internationale, 1914 (1914 treaty)
♦ Convention sanitaire internationale, 1926 (1926 treaty)
♦ Convention sanitaire internationale, 1944 (1944 treaty)
♦ Convention sanitaire internationale pour la navigation aérienne, 1933 (1933 treaty)
♦ Convention sanitaire internationale pour la navigation aérienne, 1944 (1944 treaty)
♦ Convention of San Salvador – Convention on the Protection of the Archeological, Historical and Artistic of the American Nations (1976 treaty)
♦ Convention de sauvegarde des droits de l'homme et des libertés fondamentales (1950 treaty)
♦ Convention pour la sauvegarde du patrimoine architectural de l'Europe (1985 treaty)
♦ Convention pour la sauvegarde du patrimoine culturel immateriel (2003 treaty)
♦ Convention de Schengen (1990 treaty)
♦ Conventions sur la défense du patrimoine archéologique, historique et artistique des nations américaines (1976 treaty)
♦ Convention sur la sécurité et la santé dans l'agriculture (2001 treaty)
♦ Convention sur la sécurité sociale des gens de mer, 1987 (1987 treaty)
♦ Convention on the Service Abroad of Judicial and Extrajudicial Documents in Civil or Commercial Matters (1965 treaty)
♦ Convention on the Settlement by Arbitration of Civil Law Disputes Arising out of Economic, Scientific and Technical Cooperation Relationships (1972 treaty)
♦ Convention for the Settlement of Certain Conflicts of Laws in Connection with Bills of Exchange and Promissory Notes (1930 treaty)
♦ Convention for the Settlement of Certain Conflicts of Laws in Connection with Cheques (1931 treaty)
♦ Convention on the Settlement of Investment Disputes between States and Nationals of other States (1965 treaty)
♦ Convention for the Settlement of Payments of Current Transaction and the Movements of Capital between States of the Arab League (1953 treaty)
♦ Convention sur la signalisation routière (1968 treaty)
♦ Convention Simón Rodriguez (#19284)
♦ Convention pour la simplification des formalités douanières (1923 treaty)
♦ Convention on the Simplification of Formalities in Trade in Goods (1987 treaty)
♦ Convention SNPD – Convention Internationale sur la Responsabilité et L'indemnisation pour les Dommages Liés au Transport par Mer de Substances Nocives et Potentiellement Dangereuses (1996 treaty)
♦ Convention on Social and Medical Assistance (1949 treaty)
♦ Convention des sociétés nationales d'électriciens de l'Europe / see Convention of National Associations of Electrical Engineers of Europe (#04788)
♦ Convention des sociétés nationales d'électriciens de l'Europe occidentale / see Convention of National Associations of Electrical Engineers of Europe (#04788)
♦ Convention on Special Missions (1969 treaty)
♦ Convention on the Stamp Laws in Connection with Bills of Exchange and Promissory Notes (1930 treaty)
♦ Convention on the Stamp Laws in Connection with Cheques (1931 treaty)
♦ Convention on Standards of Democratic Elections, Electoral Rights and Freedoms in Member Nations of the Commonwealth of Independent States (2002 treaty)
♦ Convention sur les statistiques du travail (1985 treaty)
♦ Convention on the Status of Aliens (1928 treaty)
♦ Convention and Statute on Freedom of Transit (1921 treaty)
♦ Convention and Statute on the International Régime of Maritime Ports (1923 treaty)
♦ Convention and Statute on the International Régime of Railways (1923 treaty)
♦ Convention and Statute on the Regime of Navigable Waterways of International Concern (1921 treaty)
♦ Convention et statut sur la liberté de transit (1921 treaty)
♦ Convention sur le statut de l'Organisation du Traité de l'Atlantique Nord, des représentants nationaux et du personnel international (1951 treaty)
♦ Convention et statut sur le régime international des ports maritimes (1923 treaty)
♦ Convention et statut sur le régime international des voies ferrées (1923 treaty)
♦ Convention et statut sur le régime des voies navigables d'intérêt international (1921 treaty)
♦ Convention de Stockholm sur les polluants organiques persistants (2001 treaty)
♦ Convention on Stolen or Illegally Exported Cultural Objects (1995 treaty)
♦ Convention au sujet de la canalisation de la Moselle (1956 treaty)
♦ Convention supplémentaire relative à l'abolition de l'esclavage, de la traite des esclaves et des institutions et pratiques analogues à l'esclavage (1956 treaty)
♦ Convention on Supplementary Compensation for Nuclear Damage (1997 treaty)
♦ Convention Supplementary to the Paris Convention on Third Party Liability in the Field of Nuclear Energy (1963 treaty)
♦ Convention Supplementary to the Statute of Navigation of the Elbe (1923 treaty)
♦ Convention, Supplementary to the Warsaw Convention, for the Unification of Certain Rules Relating to International Carriage by Air Performed by a Person other Than the Contracting Carrier (1961 treaty)
♦ Convention for the Suppression of the Circulation of and Traffic in Obscene Publications (1923 treaty)
♦ Convention for the Suppression of the Contraband Traffic in Alcoholic Liquors (1925 treaty)
♦ Convention for the Suppression of Counterfeiting Currency (1929 treaty)
♦ Convention for the Suppression of the Illicit Traffic in Dangerous Drugs, 1936 (1936 treaty)
♦ Convention for the Suppression of the Illicit Traffic in Dangerous Drugs, 1946 (1946 treaty)
♦ Convention for the Suppression of the Traffic in Persons and of the Exploitation of the Prostitution of Others (1949 treaty)
♦ Convention for the Suppression of the Traffic in Women and Children (1947 treaty)
♦ Convention for the Suppression of the Traffic in Women of Full Age (1947 treaty)
♦ Convention pour la suppression du trafic illicite des drogues nuisibles, 1936 (1936 treaty)
♦ Convention for the Suppression of Unlawful Acts Against the Safety of Civil Aviation (1971 treaty)
♦ Convention for the Suppression of Unlawful Acts Against the Safety of Maritime Navigation (1988 treaty)
♦ Convention on the Suppression of Unlawful Acts Relating to International Civil Aviation (2010 treaty)
♦ Convention for the Suppression of Unlawful Seizure of Aircraft (1970 treaty)
♦ Convention supprimant l'exigence de la légalisation des actes publics étrangers (1961 treaty)
♦ Convention sur la sûreté nucléaire (1994 treaty)
♦ Convention on the Taking of Evidence Abroad in Civil or Commercial Matters (1970 treaty)
♦ Convention on the Taxation of Foreign Motor Vehicles (1931 treaty)
♦ Convention on the Taxation of Road Vehicles Engaged in International Goods Transport (1956 treaty)
♦ Convention on the Taxation of Road Vehicles Engaged in International Passenger Transport (1956 treaty)
♦ Convention on the Taxation of Road Vehicles for Private Use in International Traffic (1956 treaty)
♦ Convention on the Teaching of History (1933 treaty)
♦ Convention on Technical and Vocational Education (1989 treaty)
♦ Convention on Temporary Admission (1990 treaty)
♦ Convention tendant à établir la réciprocité en matière d'allocations familiales (1951 treaty)
♦ Convention tendant à étendre et à coordonner l'application des législations de sécurité sociale aux ressortissants des Parties contractantes du Traité de Bruxelles (1949 treaty)
♦ Convention tendant à éviter les doubles impositions en matière d'impôts sur le revenu et la fortune des personnes physiques (1977 treaty)
♦ Convention tendant à éviter les doubles impositions en matière d'impôts sur le revenu et le patrimoine des personnes morales (1978 treaty)
♦ Convention tendant à faciliter l'accès international à la justice (1980 treaty)
♦ Convention tendant à limiter à huit heures par jour et à quarante-huit heures par semaine le nombre des heures de travail dans les établissements industriels (1919 treaty)
♦ Convention tendant à réduire le nombre des cas d'apatridie (1973 treaty)
♦ Convention on Territorial Asylum (1954 treaty)

- ♦ Convention on the Territorial Sea and the Contiguous Zone (1958 treaty)
- ♦ Convention de tir – Convention douanière relative au transport international de marchandises sous le couvert de carnets tir (1975 treaty)
- ♦ Convention TIR – Convention douanière relative au transport international de marchandises sous le couvert de carnets TIR, 1959 (1959 treaty)
- ♦ Convention sur les traités (1928 treaty)
- ♦ Convention on the Transboundary Effects of Industrial Accidents (1992 treaty)
- ♦ Convention on the Transfer of Control of Persons to the External Frontiers of Benelux Territory (1960 treaty)
- ♦ Convention sur le transfèrement des personnes condamnées (1983 treaty)
- ♦ Convention on the Transfer of Sentenced Persons (1983 treaty)
- ♦ Convention on the Transfer to the State of Which They Are Citizens, to Serve Their Sentence, of Persons Condemned to Emprisonment (1978 treaty)
- ♦ Convention sur le transit d'avions (1935 treaty)
- ♦ Convention on Transit Trade of Land-locked States (1965 treaty)
- ♦ Convention sur le travail de nuit (1990 treaty)
- ♦ Convention on Treaties (1928 treaty)
- ♦ Convention on the Unification of the Benelux Customs Area (1969 treaty)
- ♦ Convention pour l'unification de certaines règles en matière de transport de bagages de passagers par mer (1967 treaty)
- ♦ Convention pour l'unification de certaines règles en matière de transport de passagers par mer (1961 treaty)
- ♦ Convention pour l'unification de certaines règles relatives aux privilèges et hypothèques maritimes (1967 treaty)
- ♦ Convention pour l'unification de certaines règles relatives à la saisie conservatoire des aéronefs (1933 treaty)
- ♦ Convention pour l'unification de certaines règles relatives au transport aérien international, 1929 (1929 treaty)
- ♦ Convention pour l'unification de certaines règles relatives au transport aérien international, 1999 (1999 treaty)
- ♦ Convention on the Unification of Certain Points of Substantive Law on Patents for Invention (1963 treaty)
- ♦ Convention for the Unification of Certain Rules for International Carriage by Air, 1999 (1999 treaty)
- ♦ Convention for the Unification of Certain Rules Regarding International Carriage by Air, 1929 (1929 treaty)
- ♦ Convention for the Unification of Certain Rules Relating to the Precautionary Attachment of Aircraft (1933 treaty)
- ♦ Convention sur l'unification de certains éléments du droit des brevets d'invention (1963 treaty)
- ♦ Convention for the Unification for the Law of Bills of Exchange and Cheques (1912 treaty)
- ♦ Convention pour l'unification des méthodes d'analyse des aliments (1912 treaty)
- ♦ Convention of the Unification of Methods of Analysis of Human and Animal Foods (1912 treaty)
- ♦ Convention for the Unification of the Monetary System (1910 treaty)
- ♦ Convention sur l'unification des poids et mesures (1910 treaty)
- ♦ Convention for the Unification of Primary and Secondary Instruction in Central America (1911 treaty)
- ♦ Convention for the Unification of Protective Laws for Workmen and Laborers (1923 treaty)
- ♦ Convention for the Unification of the Rules Relating to Collisions at Sea (1910 treaty)
- ♦ Convention sur l'unification de la signalisation routière (1931 treaty)
- ♦ Convention for the Unification of Weights and Measures (1910 treaty)
- ♦ Convention sur l'uniformité de nomenclature pour la classification des marchandises (1923 treaty)
- ♦ Convention on Uniformity of Nomenclature for the Classification of Merchandise (1923 treaty)
- ♦ Convention for a Uniform System of Tonnage Measurement of Ships (1947 treaty)
- ♦ Convention de l'Union Africaine sur la coopération transfrontalière (2014 treaty)
- ♦ Convention de l'Union Africaine sur la cybersécurité et la protection des données a caractère personnel (2014 treaty)
- ♦ Convention de l'Union Africaine sur la prévention et la lutte contre la corruption (2003 treaty)
- ♦ Convention de l'Union Africaine sur la protection et l'assistance aux personnes déplacées en Afrique (2009 treaty)
- ♦ Convention unique sur les stupéfiants, 1961 (1961 treaty)
- ♦ Convention unique sur les stupéfiants, de 1961, telle que modifiée par le Protocole portant amendement de la Convention unique sur les stupéfiants de 1961 (1975 treaty)
- ♦ Convention universelle sur le droit d'auteur, 1952 (1952 treaty)
- ♦ Convention universelle sur le droit d'auteur, 1971 (1971 treaty)
- ♦ Convention sur la valeur en douane des marchandises (1950 treaty)
- ♦ Convention on the Valuation of Goods for Customs Purposes (1950 treaty)
- ♦ Convention de Vienne sur le droit des traités (1969 treaty)
- ♦ Convention de Vienne sur le droit des traités entre Etats et organisations internationales ou entre organisations internationales (1986 treaty)
- ♦ Convention de Vienne sur les relations consulaires (1963 treaty)
- ♦ Convention de Vienne sur les relations diplomatiques (1961 treaty)
- ♦ Convention de Vienne relative à la responsabilité civile en matière de dommages nucléaires (1963 treaty)
- ♦ Convention de Vienne sur la représentation des Etats dans leurs relations avec les organisations internationales de caractère universel (1975 treaty)
- ♦ Convention de Vienne sur la succession d'Etats en matière de biens, archives et dettes d'Etat (1983 treaty)
- ♦ Convention visant à faciliter le trafic maritime international (1965 treaty)
- ♦ Convention on the Voluntary Recognition of Children Born out of Wedlock (1980 treaty)
- ♦ Convention en vue d'accorder des facilités aux expositions artistiques (1936 treaty)
- ♦ Convention en vue d'accorder des facilités aux films éducatifs ou de propagande (1936 treaty)
- ♦ Convention en vue d'encourager les relations culturelles interaméricaines, 1936 (1936 treaty)
- ♦ Convention on Wetlands – Convention on Wetlands of International Importance Especially as Waterfowl Habitat (1971 treaty)
- ♦ Convention on Wetlands of International Importance Especially as Waterfowl Habitat (1971 treaty)
- ♦ Convention sur une zone nucléaire libre dans le Pacifique sud (1985 treaty)
- ♦ Convenzione concernente l'elaborazione di una farmacopea europea (1964 treaty)
- ♦ Convenzione del Consiglio d'Europa sulla lotta contro la tratta degli esseri umani (2005 treaty)
- ♦ Convenzione del Consiglio d'Europa sulla prevenzione della condizione di apolide in relazione alla successione di stati (2006 treaty)
- ♦ Convenzione del Consiglio d'Europa per la prevenzione del terrorismo (2005 treaty)
- ♦ Convenzione del Consiglio d'Europa sul riciclaggio, la ricerca, il sequestro e la confisca dei proventi di reato e sul finanziamento del terrorismo (2005 treaty)
- ♦ Convenzione sulla criminalità informatica (2001 treaty)
- ♦ Convenzione culturale europea (1954 treaty)
- ♦ Convenzione sulla diminuzione dei casi di doppia nazionalità e sugli obblighi militari in caso di doppia nazionalità (1963 treaty)
- ♦ Convenzione sull'elaborazione di un sistema di iscrizione dei testamenti (1972 treaty)
- ♦ Convenzione europea sull'adozione dei minori (1967 treaty)
- ♦ Convenzione europea su alcuni aspetti internazionali del fallimento (1990 treaty)
- ♦ Convenzione europea sull'assicurazione obbligatoria della responsabilità civile in materia di veicoli a motori (1959 treaty)
- ♦ Convenzione europea di assistenza giudiziaria in materia penale (1959 treaty)
- ♦ Convenzione europea di assistenza sociale e medica (1953 treaty)
- ♦ Convenzione europea sulla classificazione internazionale dei brevetti di invenzione (inactive)
- ♦ Convenzione europea sulla coproduzione cinematografica (1992 treaty)
- ♦ Convenzione europea sulla costituzione delle società (1966 treaty)
- ♦ Convenzione europea sull'efficacia internazionale delle sentenze penali (1970 treaty)
- ♦ Convenzione europea sull'equivalenza generale dei periodi di studi universitari (1990 treaty)
- ♦ Convenzione europea sull'equivalenza dei periodi di studi universitari (1956 treaty)
- ♦ Convenzione europea sull'esercizio dei diritti dei minori (1996 treaty)
- ♦ Convenzione europea di estradizione (1957 treaty)
- ♦ Convenzione europea sulle funzioni consolari (1967 treaty)
- ♦ Convenzione europea sull'immunità degli stati (1972 treaty)
- ♦ Convenzione europea sull'imprescrittibilità dei crimini contro l'umanità e dei crimini di guerra (1974 treaty)
- ♦ Convenzione europea dell'informazione giuridica concernente i "servizi della società di informazione" (2001 treaty)
- ♦ Convenzione europea sulle infrazioni coinvolgenti i beni culturali (1985 treaty)
- ♦ Convenzione europea sulla legislazione uniforme in materia di arbitrato (1966 treaty)
- ♦ Convenzione europea sulla nazionalità (1997 treaty)
- ♦ Convenzione europea nel campo dell'informazione sul diritto estero (1968 treaty)
- ♦ Convenzione europea sulla notificazione all'estero dei documenti in materia amministrativa (1977 treaty)
- ♦ Convenzione europea per la prevenzione della tortura e delle pene o trattamenti inumani o degradanti (1987 treaty)
- ♦ Convenzione europea sulla promozione del servizio di volontariato transnazionale a lungo termine per i giovani (2000 treaty)
- ♦ Convenzione europea sulla protezione degli animali negli allevamenti (1976 treaty)
- ♦ Convenzione europea per la protezione degli animali da compagnia (1987 treaty)
- ♦ Convenzione europea sulla protezione degli animali da macello (1979 treaty)
- ♦ Convenzione europea sulla protezione degli animali nel trasporto internazionale (1968 treaty)
- ♦ Convenzione europea sulla protezione degli animali nel trasporto internazionale – riveduta (2003 treaty)
- ♦ Convenzione europea sulla protezione degli animali vertebrati utilizzati a fini sperimentali o ad altri fini scientifici (1986 treaty)
- ♦ Convenzione europea sulla protezione giuridica dei servizi a accesso condizionato e di accesso condizionato (2001 treaty)
- ♦ Convenzione europea per la protezione del patrimonio archeologico, riveduta (1992 treaty)
- ♦ Convenzione europea sulla protezione sociale degli agricoltori (1974 treaty)
- ♦ Convenzione europea sulle questioni di diritto d'autore e dei diritti vicini nel quadro delle radiodiffusioni transfrontaliere via satellite (1994 treaty)
- ♦ Convenzione europea relativa all'equipollenza dei diplomi per l'ammissione alle università (1953 treaty)
- ♦ Convenzione europea relativa alle formalità prescritte per le domande dei brevetti (1953 treaty)
- ♦ Convenzione europea relativa al luogo di pagamento delle obbligazioni monetarie (1972 treaty)
- ♦ Convenzione europea relativa alle obbligazioni in valuta estera (1967 treaty)
- ♦ Convenzione europea relativa alla protezione del patrimonio audiovisivo (2001 treaty)
- ♦ Convenzione europea relativa al risarcimento delle vittime di reati violenti (1983 treaty)
- ♦ Convenzione europea per la repressione delle infrazioni stradali (1964 treaty)
- ♦ Convenzione europea per la repressione del terrorismo (1977 treaty)
- ♦ Convenzione europea sulla responsabilità civile in caso di danni causati da veicoli a motore (1973 treaty)
- ♦ Convenzione europea sulla responsabilità derivante dai prodotti in caso di lesioni corporali o di decessi (1977 treaty)
- ♦ Convenzione europea per la risoluzione pacifica delle controversie (1957 treaty)
- ♦ Convenzione europea di Sicurezza sociale (1972 treaty)
- ♦ Convenzione europea sulla soppressione della legalizzazione di atti compilati dagli agenti diplomatici o consolari (1968 treaty)
- ♦ Convenzione europea sulla sorveglianza delle persone condannate o liberate sotto condizione (1964 treaty)
- ♦ Convenzione europea di stabilimento (1955 treaty)
- ♦ Convenzione europea sugli effetti internazionali della decadenza del diritto di condurre un veicolo a motore (1976 treaty)
- ♦ Convenzione europea sul computo dei termini (1974 treaty)
- ♦ Convenzione europea sul conseguimento all'estero d'informazioni e di prove in materia amministrativa (1978 treaty)
- ♦ Convenzione europea sul controllo dell'acquisto e detenzione di armi da fuoco (1978 treaty)
- ♦ Convenzione europea sullo status giuridico dei minori nati al di fuori del matrimonio (1975 treaty)
- ♦ Convenzione europea sullo statuto giuridico dei lavoratori emigranti (1977 treaty)
- ♦ Convenzione europea sul riconoscimento accademico delle qualifiche universitarie (1959 treaty)
- ♦ Convenzione europea sul riconoscimento e l'esecuzione delle decisioni in materia di affidamento dei minori e sulla ristabilimento dell'affidamento dei minori (1980 treaty)
- ♦ Convenzione europea sul riconoscimento della personalità giuridica alle organizzazioni internazionale non governative (1986 treaty)
- ♦ Convenzione europea sul rimpatrio dei minori (1970 treaty)
- ♦ Convenzione europea sul trasferimento delle procedure penali (1972 treaty)
- ♦ Convenzione europea sulla televisione transfrontaliera (1989 treaty)
- ♦ Convenzione sull'insider trading (1989 treaty)
- ♦ Convenzione sulla partecipazione degli stranieri alla vita pubblica a livello locale (1992 treaty)
- ♦ Convenzione sulla protezione delle persone rispetto al trattamento automatizzato di dati a carattere personale (1981 treaty)
- ♦ Convenzione quadro del Consiglio d'Europa sul valore del patrimonio culturale per la società (2005 treaty)
- ♦ Convenzione-quadro europea sulla cooperazione transfrontaliera delle collettività e autorità territoriali (1980 treaty)
- ♦ Convenzione-quadro per la protezione delle minoranze nazionali (1995 treaty)
- ♦ Convenzione sulla reciproca assistenza in materia fiscale (1988 treaty)
- ♦ Convenzione relativa all'opposizione sui titoli al portatore a circolazione internazionale (1970 treaty)
- ♦ Convenzione sulle relazioni personali riguardanti i fanciulli (2003 treaty)
- ♦ Convenzione sulla responsabilità degli albergatori per i beni di proprietà dei viaggiatori (1962 treaty)
- ♦ Convenzione per la salvaguardia dei diritti dell'uomo e delle libertà fondamentali (1950 treaty)
- ♦ Convenzione sul riciclaggio, la ricerca, il sequestro e la confisca dei proventi di reato (1990 treaty)
- ♦ Convenzione sul riconoscimento delle qualifiche relative all'insegnamento superiore nella regione europea (1997 treaty)
- ♦ Convenzione sul trasferimento delle persone condannate (1983 treaty)
- ♦ Convenzione sull'unificazione di taluni elementi del diritto dei brevetti d'invenzione (1963 treaty)
- ♦ Convergence internationale de la mesure et des normes de fonds propres (1988 treaty)
- ♦ Convergences (internationally oriented national body)
- ♦ Convoy of Hope (internationally oriented national body)
- ♦ CONy – World Congress on Controversies in Neurology (meeting series)
- ♦ **COODTUR** International Network of Research into Tourism, Cooperation and Development (#14318)
- ♦ Cook Communications Ministries International / see Cook International

♦ Cook & Health Network 04789

Address not obtained.

URL: http://www.cookandhealth.org/

Aims Research the impact of home cooking and its replacement by away-from-home food preparation on individuals' nutrition, health, economic and psychosocial status. **Structure** An informal network. **Activities** Events/meetings. **Events** *Symposium* Lisbon (Portugal) 2019, *Symposium* London (UK) 2017, *Symposium* San Sebastian (Spain) 2015. [2020/AA0323/v/F]

- Cook International (internationally oriented national body)
- **COOLA** Conference on Oceanian Linguistic Anthropology (#04636)
- Cool Farm Alliance (unconfirmed)
- **COOMET** Euro-Asian Cooperation of National Metrological Institutions (#05638)
- Cooperacció, Spain (internationally oriented national body)
- Cooperación Andina en Salud (no recent information)
- Cooperación al Desarrollo y Promoción de Actividades Asistenciales / see Fundación CODESPA
- Cooperación Internacional (internationally oriented national body)
- Cooperación Internacional para el Desarrollo Socio-Económico / see CIDSE (#03926)
- Cooperación Internacional para el Desarrollo y la Solidaridad / see CIDSE (#03926)

♦ Cooperación Latino Americana de Redes Avanzadas (RedCLARA) .. 04790

Latin American Cooperation of Advanced Networks

Exec Dir Avda El Parque 4680-A, Oficina 108, Santiago, Santiago Metropolitan, Chile. T. +56225848618ext502. E-mail: direccion.ejecutiva@redclara.net.
Registered Address Rambla República de México 6125, 11400 Montevideo, Uruguay.
URL: http://www.redclara.net/

History Founded 23 Dec 2003, as *CLARA*, during meeting in Mexico and statutes signed. Initial idea arose in Jun 2002, Toledo (Spain) during a meeting organized within the framework of the CEASAR Project, financed by European Commission DG IST Programme. Subsequent meetings followed in: Rio de Janeiro (Brazil); Buenos Aires (Argentina); Santiago (Chile); Mexico. Current title adopted Mar 2011. **Aims** Serve as a Latin American collaboration system by means of *telecommunications* advanced networks for research, innovation and education. **Structure** Assembly; Directing Council; Executive Secretariat; Technical Commission. **Languages** English, Portuguese, Spanish. **Staff** 15.00 FTE, paid. **Events** *TICAL Conference* Cancún (Mexico) 2014, *TICAL Conference* Cartagena de Indias (Colombia) 2013, *TICAL Conference* Lima (Peru) 2012, *TICAL Conference* Panama (Panama) 2011. **Publications** *DeCLARA al Dia* – newsletter; *DeCLARA Bulletin*.
Members Full Associates in 12 countries:
Argentina, Brazil, Chile, Colombia, Costa Rica, Ecuador, El Salvador, Guatemala, Mexico, Nicaragua, Paraguay, Uruguay.
[2018.06.01/XJ7073/**D**]

♦ Cooperación Misionera Iberoamericana (COMIBAM) 04791

Ibero-American Mission Alliance

Exec Dir Avda Ponce de Leon 613, Centro Benet, Oficina 210, San Juan PR 00917, USA. E-mail: correo@comibam.org.
URL: http://www.comibam.org/

History 1987, Sao Paulo (Brazil). Founded at the first Iberoamerican Missionary Congress. Former names and other names: *COMIBAM Internacional* – alias. **Aims** Transform the church of Iberoamerica into a missionary people capable of taking the gospel of Jesus Christ to all nations. **Structure** Board of Directors; Executive Committee; Departments; Networks; Programs; National Missions Movements. **Activities** Networking/liaising; capacity building; training/education; events/meetings. **Events** *Congress* Bogota (Colombia) 2017, *Congress* Spain 2006, *Congreso de misiones nacionales y mundiales* Mexico City (Mexico) 2003, *Indolatin congress* San Salvador (El Salvador) 2003, *International assembly* San Salvador (El Salvador) 2003.
Members National Missions Movements in 25 countries and territories:
Argentina, Belize, Bolivia, Brazil, Canada, Chile, Colombia, Costa Rica, Cuba, Dominican Rep, Ecuador, El Salvador, Guatemala, Honduras, Mexico, Nicaragua, Panama, Paraguay, Peru, Portugal, Puerto Rico, Spain, Uruguay, USA, Venezuela.
NGO Relations Associate member of: *World Evangelical Alliance (WEA, #21393)*. [2022/XF6911/**F**]

- Cooperadores Paroquiales de Cristo Rey (religious order)
- Coopérateurs Paroissiaux du Christ Roi (religious order)
- Cooperation for the Advancement of Developing Countries (internationally oriented national body)
- Cooperation Agreement on the Forecast, Prevention and Mitigation of Natural and Technological Disasters (1992 treaty)
- Cooperation Agreement for the Protection of North-East Atlantic Coasts and Waters Against Pollution (1990 treaty)
- Coopération pour l'aide aux pays de développement (internationally oriented national body)
- Coopération bancaire pour l'Europe (internationally oriented national body)
- Cooperation Canada (internationally oriented national body)
- Cooperation Centre for Scientific Research Relative to Tobacco (#03735)
- Cooperation Committee for Cambodia (internationally oriented national body)

♦ Cooperation for the Continuing Development of Urban and Suburban Transportation 04792

Coopération pour le développement et l'amélioration des transports urbains et périurbains (CODATU)

Main Office 44 avenue Paul Kruger, 69100 Villeurbanne, France. E-mail: contact@codatu.org.
URL: http://www.codatu.org/

History 1980. Former names and other names: *Conferences on the Development and the Planning of Urban Transport in Developing Countries* – former (1980); *Conférences sur le développement et l'aménagement des transports urbains dans les pays en développement* – former (1980). Registration: France. **Aims** Promote research and encourage an exchange of know-how and experience on matters relating to urban transportation systems in *developing countries*. **Structure** General Assembly. General Council, including President, 3 Vice-Presidents, General Secretary, Adviser near the President, Executive Director, Assistant and a member. Board of Administration, comprising UTO and international research bodies working in the field. An international network of specialized study and research centres. **Languages** English, French. **Finance** Members' dues. **Activities** Priority concerns are: reappraisal of ready-made models; conditions for transfer of know-how; responsibility and contribution of industrialized countries in the field. **Events** *Conference* 2021, *Conference* Dakar (Senegal) 2020, *Conference* Hyderabad (India) 2017, *Energy, climate and air quality challenges – the role of urban transport policies in developing countries and emerging economies* Istanbul (Turkey) 2015, *Conference / World Congress* Addis Ababa (Ethiopia) 2012.
Members Bodies (81) in 31 countries:
Algeria, Argentina, Belgium, Benin, Brazil, Burkina Faso, Cameroon, Canada, Chile, China, Congo Brazzaville, Côte d'Ivoire, Egypt, France, Gabon, India, Indonesia, Italy, Japan, Mexico, Niger, Nigeria, Romania, Senegal, South Africa, Switzerland, Togo, Tunisia, UK, USA, Zimbabwe.
IGO Relations Close collaboration with United Nations Specialized agencies and: *International Bank for Reconstruction and Development (IBRD, #12317)*. **NGO Relations** Partner of: *Partnership on Sustainable, Low Carbon Transport Foundation (SLoCaT Foundation, #18244)*. [2021/XE0208/**F**]

- Cooperation Council for the Arab States of the Gulf / see Gulf Cooperation Council (#10826)

♦ Cooperation Council of Turkic Speaking States (Turkic Council) ... 04793

Türk Dili Konusan Ülkeler Isbirligi Koseyi (Türk Donseyi – TDIK)

Secretariat Binbirdirek, Piyer Loti Cd No 2, Fatih, 34122 Istanbul/Istanbul, Türkiye. T. +902122831644. Fax +902122831686. E-mail: info@turkkon.org.
URL: http://www.turkkon.org/

History Founded following summits organized since 1992. *Nakhchivan Agreement on Establishment of the Cooperation Council of Turkic Speaking States* signed 2009; entered into force Nov 2010. Activities started at Istanbul Summit, 2010. **Aims** Promote comprehensive cooperation among Turkic speaking states. **Structure** Council of Heads of State; Council of Foreign Ministers; Senior Officials Committee; Council of Elders; Secretariat. **Activities** Politics/policy/regulatory. **Events** *Summit* Astana (Kazakhstan) 2015, *Summit* Bodrum (Turkey) 2014, *Summit* Gabala (Azerbaijan) 2013, *Summit* Bishkek (Kyrgyzstan) 2012, *Summit* Almaty (Kazakhstan) 2011.
Members Founding member States (4):
Azerbaijan, Kazakhstan, Kyrgyzstan, Türkiye.
IGO Relations Affiliated organizations: *International Organization of Turkic Culture (TURKSOY, #14482)*; *Parliamentary Assembly of Turkic Speaking Countries (TURKPA, #18215)*; Turkic Academy; Turkic Business Council; Turkic Culture and Heritage Foundation. Cooperates with: *Economic Cooperation Organization (ECO, #05313)*; *Organization of Black Sea Economic Cooperation (BSEC, #17857)*; *Organisation of Islamic Cooperation (OIC, #17813)*; *Organization for Security and Cooperation in Europe (OSCE, #17887)*; United Nations. [2021/XM5943/**D***]

- Coopération culturelle nordique (1971 treaty)
- Cooperation for the Development of the Craft Industry (internationally oriented national body)
- Cooperation and Development Network Eastern Europe / see Cooperation and Development Network Eastern Europe (#04794)

♦ Cooperation and Development Network Eastern Europe (CDN) 04794

Network Coordinator Green House, Dr Dragoslava Popovica 24, Belgrade, 11000, Serbia. T. +381641731725. E-mail: office@cdnee.org.
Registered Address Rue du Taciturne 34, 1000 Brussels, Belgium.
URL: http://www.cdnee.org/

History Dec 2002. Former names and other names: *Cooperation and Development Network Eastern Europe (CDNEE)* – former. Registration: Banque-Carrefour des Entreprises, Belgium. **Aims** Develop and implement *green* ideas in Eastern Europe. **Structure** General Assembly; Executive Committee; Working Groups; Secretariat. **Languages** English. **Staff** 3.00 FTE, paid. **Finance** Supported by: *European Commission (EC, #06633)*; *European Youth Foundation (EYF, #09141)*; Green Forum (Sweden). **Activities** Capacity building; events/meetings; networking/liaising; training/education. **Events** *Annual Meeting* Chisinau (Moldova) 2015, *Annual Meeting* Belgrade (Serbia) 2014, *Annual Meeting* Bucharest (Romania) 2006, *Annual Meeting* Ohrid (Macedonia) 2005, *Annual Meeting* Belgrade (Serbia-Montenegro) 2003.
Members National organizations in 18 countries:
Albania, Armenia, Azerbaijan, Belarus, Bosnia-Herzegovina, Bulgaria, Croatia, Cyprus, Georgia, Germany, Hungary, Latvia, Moldova, North Macedonia, Poland, Serbia, Türkiye, Ukraine.
IGO Relations Member of (1): *European Youth Centres (EYCs, #09138)*. [2021.09.01/XM2864/**F**]

- Coopération pour le développement et l'amélioration des transports urbains et périurbains (#04792)
- Coopération au développement de l'artisanat (internationally oriented national body)
- Coopération économique de la Mer Noire / see Organization of Black Sea Economic Cooperation (#17857)
- Coopération par l'éducation et la culture (internationally oriented national body)
- Coopération euro-méditerranéenne en métrologie légale (no recent information)
- Coopération européenne dans le domaine de l'information et de la documentation en sciences sociales (inactive)
- Coopération européenne dans le domaine de la recherche scientifique et technique (#06784)
- Coopération européenne pour l'informatique (inactive)
- Coopération européenne pour la pédagogie curative et la sociothérapie anthroposophiques (#06783)

♦ Coopération européenne des sites majeurs d'accueil (COESIMA) .. 04795

Coordinator Lourdes développement, Place Peyramale BP 135, 65104 Lourdes CEDEX, France.
URL: http://www.coesima.eu/

Aims Build a perpetual network of shrine-towns living the same reality, the *pilgrimages*, and that also share the will and the motivation necessary to better and more rationally manage this activity for the benefit of the economic and social development of its territories. **Activities** Studies visits so as to identify visitors' needs; defines a public working programme for the adaptation to the new public (adaptation of the infrastructures); values the cultural heritage and promotes these places in the international market (development of the economy and of employment based on diversification); organizes thematic working meetings.
Members Pilgrimage sites in 7 countries:
France (Lourdes), Germany (Altötting), Greece (Patmos), Italy (Loreto), Poland (Czestochowa), Portugal (Fatima), Spain (Santiago de Compostela). [2010/XJ1024/**F**]

- Cooperation for Fair Trade in Africa / see World Fair Trade Organization – Africa (#21397)
- Cooperation in the Field of Justice and Home Affairs / see European Commission (#06633)
- Coopération et Formation au Développement (internationally oriented national body)
- Coopération francophone des associations de scoutisme laïque (inactive)

♦ Co-operation Group to Combat Drug Abuse and Illicit Trafficking in Drugs (Pompidou Group) 04796

Groupe de coopération en matière de lutte contre l'abus et le trafic illicite des stupéfiants (Groupe Pompidou)

Exec Sec c/o Council of Europe, 67075 Strasbourg CEDEX, France. T. +33388412000. E-mail: pompidougroup@coe.int.
URL: http://www.coe.int/pompidou/

History 1971, following a proposal made by French President Georges Pompidou, to combat both drug abuse and illicit trafficking. Became a Cooperation Group under the aegis of *Council of Europe (CE, #04881)* in 1980, pursuant to Resolution (80) 2 of *Committee of Ministers of the Council of Europe (#04273)*. **Aims** Contribute to the development of multidisciplinary, innovative, effective and evidence-based drug policies in Member States. **Structure** Ministerial Conference (every 4 years); Permanent Correspondents; Bureau of Permanent Correspondents; Ad hoc expert groups. Secretariat. Meets at ministerial level every 3-4 years, but circumstances and urgency may justify additional special meetings. Permanent Correspondents, appointed for each state, meet about every 6 months between ministerial meetings. **Languages** English, French. **Staff** 10.00 FTE, paid. **Finance** Member states' contributions. Ordinary Budget (2017): euro 1,533,000, plus extra-budgetary resources depending on voluntary contributions received. **Activities** Knowledge management/information dissemination; networking/liaising; research/documentation; monitoring/evaluation; training/education; awards/prizes/competitions. **Events** *European Conference on Addictive Behaviours and Dependencies* Lisbon (Portugal) 2015, *Meeting* Oslo (Norway) 2015, *Symposium on Experience with New Evolutions in Drug Policy* Oslo (Norway) 2015, *Meeting* Paris (France) 2015, *Meeting* Strasbourg (France) 2015. **Publications** Pilot studies; reports; symposium and seminar proceedings; handbooks on training, prevention and outreach work.
Members Member states (39):
Austria, Azerbaijan, Belgium, Bosnia-Herzegovina, Bulgaria, Croatia, Cyprus, Czechia, Estonia, Finland, France, Greece, Hungary, Iceland, Ireland, Israel, Italy, Liechtenstein, Lithuania, Luxembourg, Malta, Mexico, Moldova, Monaco, Montenegro, Morocco, North Macedonia, Norway, Poland, Portugal, Romania, Russia, San Marino, Serbia, Slovakia, Slovenia, Sweden, Switzerland, Türkiye.
Regional entity:
European Commission (EC, #06633).
IGO Relations *European Commission (EC, #06633)* participates in the work of the Group. Treaties involved: *Convention on Laundering, Search, Seizure and Confiscation of the Proceeds from Crime (1990)*; *United Nations Convention against Illicit Traffic in Narcotic Drugs and Psychotropic Substances (1988)*. Close but informal relations maintained with: *International Criminal Police Organization – INTERPOL (ICPO-INTERPOL, #13110)*; *International Narcotics Control Board (INCB, #14212)*; *UNESCO (#20322)*; *United Nations (UN, #20515)*; *United Nations Commission on Narcotic Drugs (CND, #20532)*; *WHO (#20950)*; *World Customs Organization (WCO, #21350)*; *United Nations Interregional Crime and Justice Research Institute (UNICRI, #20580)*. **NGO Relations** Supports: *European Society for Social Drug Research (ESSD, #08736)*.
[2018/XE2000/**E***]

- Coopération internationale pour le développement et la solidarité / see CIDSE (#03926)
- Coopération internationale, Milan / see Cooperazione Internazionale
- Coopération internationale de promotion et aides au développement (internationally oriented national body)
- Coopération internationale des risques aggravés (meeting series)

♦ Cooperation on International Traceability in Analytical Chemistry (CITAC) 04797

Sec Fac of Sciences of the Univ of Lisbon – edificio C8, Campo Grande, 1749-016 Lisbon, Portugal. T. +351217500659. E-mail: rjsilva@fc.ul.pt.
URL: http://www.citac.cc/

History Mar 1993, Atlanta GA (USA). Aims Foster collaboration between existing organizations to improve international comparability of chemical measurement. Structure Members' Meeting (annual, in Paris, France). Officers: Chair; Vice-Chair; Secretary; Treasurer. Languages English. Staff None. Finance Members' dues. Activities Networking/liaising; knowledge management/information dissemination; standards/guidelines; events/meetings; awards/prizes/competitions. Events *Members Meeting* Sèvres (France) 2015, *Members Meeting* Sèvres (France) 2014, *Members meeting* Berlin (Germany) 2003, *International conference on metrology* Eilat (Israel) 2003, *Members Meeting* New Orleans, LA (USA) 2002. Publications *CITAC Newsletter* (annual). *Traceability in Chemical Measurement: A Guide to Achieving Comparable Results in Chemical Measurement* (2003); *Quantifying Uncertainty in Analytical Measurement* (2nd ed 2000); *Quality Assurance for Research and Development and Non-routine Analysis* (1998); *Guide to Quality in Analytical Chemistry*. Guides; discussion papers; scientific papers.
Members Full; Corresponding; Corporate. Organizations (21) and individuals (35) in 28 countries:
Argentina, Australia, Austria, Belgium, Brazil, China, Finland, Germany, Greece, Hong Kong, India, Ireland, Israel, Italy, Japan, Korea Rep, Malaysia, Mexico, Netherlands, New Zealand, Russia, Singapore, South Africa, Sweden, Switzerland, Thailand, UK, USA.
Included in the above, 3 organizations listed in this Yearbook:
AOAC INTERNATIONAL (#00863); International Atomic Energy Agency (IAEA, #12294); Joint Research Centre (JRC, #16147) (Geel (Belgium)).
IGO Relations Comité Consultatif pour la Quantité de Matière of *Bureau international des poids et mesures (BIPM, #03367); International Atomic Energy Agency (IAEA, #12294)*. NGO Relations In liaison with technical committees of: *International Organization for Standardization (ISO, #14473)*. Observer to: *EURACHEM (#05595)*. [2017/XF4389/v/**F**]

♦ Coopération liant les universités en science et technologie pour l'enseignement et la recherche (#04751)
♦ Coopération médicale internationale / see Artsen Zonder Vakantie
♦ Coopération médicale internationale – Afrique / see Artsen Zonder Vakantie
♦ Coopération nordique en matière d'éducation des adultes (#17504)
♦ Coopération nordique des télévisions (#17446)
♦ Cooperation for Peace / see Peace Quest International (#18282)

♦ Cooperation Process in the Western Mediterranean (Five plus Five Group) 04798
Address not obtained.
History 10 Oct 1990, Rome (Italy), as *Four plus Five Group*, by 9 countries on both sides of the Western Mediterranean (Malta joined later), following proposal, Marrakech (Morocco), by President Mitterand of France. Previously also referred to as *4 plus 5 Group*. Also known as *Dialogue 5 plus 5*. Events *Foreign ministers conference / Summit* Rabat (Morocco) 2008, *Ministerial conference* Algeria 2004, *Foreign ministers conference* Sainte-Maxime (France) 2003, *Ministerial Conference* Sainte-Maxime (France) 2003, *Summit of the heads of state and government / Summit* Tunis (Tunisia) 2003.
Members Governments of 10 countries:
Algeria, France, Italy, Libya, Malta, Mauritania, Morocco, Portugal, Spain, Tunisia. [2008/XF1505/**F***]

♦ Cooperation for the Promotion and Development of Welfare Activities / see Fundación CODESPA
♦ Coopération régionale de développement (inactive)
♦ Coopération technique belge / see Enabel
♦ Coopération technique internationale – Centre de formation pour le développement / see ITECO – Centre de formation pour le développement
♦ Cooperativas de la Vivienda de la ACI / see Co-operative Housing International (#04799)
♦ Cooperative Agreement for Arab States in Asia for Research, Development and Training Related to Nuclear Science and Technology (2002 treaty)
♦ Cooperative for American Relief Everywhere / see CARE International (#03429)
♦ Cooperative for American Remittances to Europe / see CARE International (#03429)
♦ Cooperative for Assistance and Relief Everywhere / see CARE International (#03429)
♦ Cooperative Club International / see Sertoma International
♦ Co-operative College (internationally oriented national body)
♦ Cooperative College Trust / see Co-operative College
♦ Coopérative européenne Longo Maï (#06786)
♦ Cooperative Housing Foundation / see Global Communities

♦ Co-operative Housing International (CHI) 04799
Program Director c/o 225 Metcalfe St, Ste 311, Ottawa ON K2P 1P9, Canada. T. +16132302201. Fax +16132302231.
ICA – Brussels Av Milcamps 105, 1030 Brussels, Belgium. T. +3227431030. Fax +3227431039. E-mail: info@chi.coop.
URL: http://www.housinginternational.coop/
History 1952. One of 8 sectorial organizations of *International Co-operative Alliance (ICA, #12944)*. Former names and other names: *International Cooperative Housing Committee* – former (1952); *ICA Housing Cooperatives* – former; *Coopératives d'habitation de l'ACI* – former; *Cooperativas de la Vivienda de la ACI* – former; *International Co-operative Housing Organization* – former; *ICA Housing* – former. Aims Unite, represent and lead the international movement for cooperative and mutual self-help housing. Structure General Assembly (every 2 years); Board; Executive. Languages English, French, German, Spanish. Staff 0.50 FTE, paid. Finance Sources: members' dues. Activities Capacity building; events/meetings; guidance/assistance/consulting; knowledge management/information dissemination; networking/liaising; projects/programmes; research/documentation; training/education. Events *Symposium on Securing Reliable Cooperative Capital* Antalya (Turkey) 2015, *Seminar* Cape Town (South Africa) 2013, *Seminar* Brussels (Belgium) 2012, *Conference* Cancún (Mexico) 2011, *Conference* Istanbul (Turkey) 2011. Publications *The Blueprint for a Co-operative Decade: A Co-operative Housing Perspective* (2016); *Profiles of a Movement: Co-operative Housing Around the World* (2012); *ICA Housing/CECODHAS: Application of Co-operative Principles in Practice – 21 Cases of Housing Co-operatives from 12 Countries* (2008); *Housing and Special Services for Families, Women and Children* (2004); *Housing Practitioner's Handbook: A Guide to Practical Approaches to Housing Sector Development in Transition Countries* (2004); *Housing and Services for People with Special Needs* (2003); *HABITAT II plus Innovative Approaches to Cooperative Solutions of Housing Problems of the Poor* (2001) – includes 5 best practices; *Organized Self-help Solve Housing Problems* (1999). Position papers; address lists.
Members National organizations in 66 countries and territories:
Algeria, Argentina, Australia, Austria, Belgium, Bosnia-Herzegovina, Brazil, Canada, Chile, China, Colombia, Costa Rica, Croatia, Czechia, Denmark, Dominican Rep, Egypt, El Salvador, Estonia, Ethiopia, Finland, France, Germany, Honduras, Hungary, India, Indonesia, Iran Islamic Rep, Ireland, Israel, Italy, Jamaica, Japan, Kenya, Mali, Mexico, Netherlands, New Zealand, Norway, Pakistan, Panama, Paraguay, Philippines, Poland, Portugal, Romania, Russia, Senegal, Slovakia, South Africa, Spain, Sweden, Switzerland, Syrian AR, Taiwan, Tanzania UR, Thailand, Türkiye, Uganda, UK, Uruguay, USA, Venezuela, Vietnam, Zambia, Zimbabwe. [2020/XE2317/**E**]

♦ Cooperative Insurance Development Bureau (inactive)
♦ Cooperative International Neuromuscular Research Group (internationally oriented national body)
♦ Cooperative Investigations of the Caribbean and Adjacent Areas (inactive)
♦ Cooperative League / see The Century Foundation
♦ Cooperative Link Between Universities in Science and Technology for Education and Research / see Consortium Linking Universities in Science and Technology for Education and Research (#04751)
♦ Coopérative nordique des associations de briquetage et de tuilerie (inactive)
♦ Cooperative Program for the Agri-Food and Agro-Industrial Technological Development of the Southern Cone / see *Programa Cooperativo para el Desarrollo Tecnológico Agroalimentario y Agroindustrial del Cono Sur* (#18522)
♦ Cooperative Program for the Development of Agricultural Technology in the Southern Cone (#18522)
♦ Cooperative Programme in Europe for Research on Nature and Industry through Coordinated University Studies / see COPERNICUS Alliance – European Network on Higher Education for Sustainable Development (#04830)

♦ Cooperative Programme for Monitoring and Evaluation of the Long-range Transmission of Air Pollutants in Europe (EMEP) 04800
Programme concerté de surveillance continue et d'évaluation du transport à longue distance des polluants atmosphériques en Europe
Contact c/o UNECE, Environment Div, Palais des Nations, Avenue de la Paix 8-14, 1211 Geneva, Switzerland. Fax +41229070107 – +41229070621. E-mail: air.env@unece.org.
Chair c/o INERIS, Parc Technologique Alata BPno2, 60550 Verneuil-en-Halatte, France. T. +33344556113. Fax +33344556899.
URL: http://www.emep.int/
History 1979, under the auspices of the *United Nations Economic Commission for Europe (UNECE, #20555)*, in cooperation with *World Meteorological Organization (WMO, #21649)*. Implemented under *Convention on Long-range Transboundary Air Pollution (#04787)*. Protocol on long-term financing of EMEP adopted 28 Sep 1984, Geneva (Switzerland). Aims Provide sound scientific support for the Convention on Long-Range Transboundary Air Pollution, in particular: *atmospheric* monitoring and modelling; *emission* inventories and projections; integrated assessment. Structure Executive Body for the Convention on Long-Range Transboundary Air Pollution. Steering Body (meets annually). Bureau. Centers (5): Emission Inventories and Projections (CEIP); Chemical Coordinating (CCC); Meteorological Synthesizing – West (MSC-W); Meteorological Synthesizing – East (MSC-E); Integrated Assessment Modelling (CIAM), at *International Institute for Applied Systems Analysis (IIASA, #13861)*. Task Forces (currently 4). Secretariat. Languages English, French, Russian. Staff 3 members of UNECE staff provide Secretariat, part-time. Finance International Centres funded by mandatory contributions. Other sources: voluntary contributions; contributions in kind. Budget (annual): US$ 2,152,700. Activities Knowledge management/information dissemination. Management of treaties and agreements: *Protocol to the 1979 Convention on Long Range Transboundary Air Pollution Concerning the Control of Nitrogen Oxides Emissions or Their Transboundary Fluxes (1988 NOx protocol, 1988); Protocol to the 1979 Convention on Long Range Transboundary Air Pollution Concerning the Control of Emissions of Volatile Organic Compounds on Their Transboundary Fluxes (1991 VOC protocol, 1991); Protocol to the 1979 Convention on Long Range Transboundary Air Pollution on the Reduction of Sulphur Emissions or Their Transboundary Fluxes by at Least 30 per Cent (1985 Sulphur protocol, 1985); Protocol to the 1979 Convention on Long Range Transboundary Air Pollution on Further Reduction of Sulphur Emissions (1994); Protocol to the Convention on Long-range Transboundary Air Pollution on Heavy Metals (1998); Protocol to the Convention on Long Range Transboundary Air Pollution on Persistent Organic Pollutants (POP protocol, 1998); Protocol to the 1979 Convention on Long-range Transboundary Air Pollution to Abate Acidification, Eutrophication and Ground-level Ozone (1999)*. Events *Annual Session* Geneva (Switzerland) 2009, *Annual Session* Geneva (Switzerland) 2008, *Annual Session* Geneva (Switzerland) 2007, *Annual Session* Geneva (Switzerland) 2006, *Workshop on enterprise self-monitoring and reporting* Warsaw (Poland) 2006.
Members Parties to the EMEP Protocol. Governments of 41 countries:
Austria, Belarus, Belgium, Bosnia-Herzegovina, Bulgaria, Canada, Croatia, Cyprus, Czechia, Denmark, Estonia, Finland, France, Germany, Greece, Hungary, Ireland, Italy, Latvia, Liechtenstein, Lithuania, Luxembourg, Malta, Monaco, Montenegro, Netherlands, Norway, Poland, Portugal, Romania, Russia, Serbia, Slovakia, Slovenia, Spain, Sweden, Switzerland, Türkiye, UK, Ukraine, USA.
Intergovernmental contracting party (1), listed in this Yearbook:
European Union (EU, #08967).
IGO Relations *Baltic Marine Environment Protection Commission – Helsinki Commission (HELCOM, #03126); OSPAR Commission for the Protection of the Marine Environment of the North-East Atlantic (OSPAR Commission, #17905)*. Cooperates with: *Arctic Monitoring and Assessment Programme (AMAP, #01100); European Environment Agency (EEA, #06995); UNEP (#20299)*; WMO. NGO Relations Cooperates with: *International Union for Conservation of Nature and Natural Resources (IUCN, #15766)*. [2017.03.09/XF0831/**F***]

♦ Cooperative Program on Research and Technology Transfer for the South American Tropics / see Programa Cooperative de Investigación, Desarrollo e Innovación Agricolo para los Trópicos Suramericanos (#18521)

♦ Cooperatives Europe 04801
Main Office Av Milcamps 105, 1030 Brussels, Belgium. T. +3227431033. E-mail: info@coopseurope.coop.
URL: http://www.coopseurope.coop/
History 2005. European region of *International Co-operative Alliance (ICA, #12944)*. Registration: Belgium. Aims Promote the cooperative business model in Europe. Structure General Assembly (annual); Board of Directors; EU Coordination Committee. Working Groups. Languages English, French, Russian. Staff 7.00 FTE, paid. Finance Members' dues. Activities Research and development. Events *General Assembly* Brussels (Belgium) 2022, *Young People and the Future of Cooperation in Europe* Cardiff (UK) 2022, *Cooperatives and innovation, building the future of care in Europe* Brussels (Belgium) 2017, *General Assembly* Paris (France) 2015, *General Assembly* Warsaw (Poland) 2014.
Members Category A members Organizations (83) in 33 countries:
Austria, Belarus, Belgium, Bulgaria, Croatia, Cyprus, Czechia, Denmark, Finland, France, Georgia, Germany, Hungary, Italy, Latvia, Lithuania, Malta, Moldova, Netherlands, Norway, Poland, Portugal, Romania, Russia, Serbia, Slovakia, Slovenia, Spain, Sweden, Switzerland, Türkiye, UK, Ukraine.
Category B members European Sector Organizations (6):
Confédération européenne des coopératives de travail associé, des coopératives sociales et des entreprises sociales et participatives (CECOP, #04541); Cooperative Section of ; European Association of Co-operative Banks (EACB, #05990); European Community of Consumer Cooperatives (EURO COOP, #06678); General Confederation of Agricultural Cooperatives in the European Union (#10107); Union européenne des Pharmacies sociales (UEPS, #20401).
IGO Relations Member of: *European Economic and Social Committee (EESC, #06963)* Liaison Group. NGO Relations Member of: *SDG Watch Europe (#19162)*. Instrumental in setting up: *European Research Institute on Cooperative and Social Enterprises (EURICSE)*. [2022/XM1267/y/**E**]

♦ Coopératives d'habitation de l'ACI / see Co-operative Housing International (#04799)
♦ Cooperative Society for Staff Members of Intergovernmental Organizations Having their Headquarters or Permanent Offices in Europe / see Association coopérative financière des fonctionnaires internationaux (#02455)

♦ Co-operative Studies on Brain Injury Depolarizations (COSBID) 04802
Contact address not obtained. E-mail: contact@cosbid.org.
URL: http://www.cosbid.org
History 2002. Aims Promote research and education in the new clinical science of spreading depolarizations; encourage collaborative efforts between clinicians and experimentalists; advance basic science understanding of spreading depolarizations and related disease phenomena. Structure Steering Committee. Activities Events/meetings; research/documentation. Events *International Conference on Spreading Depolarization* Lyon (France) 2021, *International Conference on Spreading Depolarization* Lyon (France) 2020.
Members Participating centres in 5 countries:
Denmark, Germany, Spain, UK, USA. [2021/AA1603/j/**D**]

♦ Cooperatori Salesiani (religious order)
♦ Cooperazione Internazionale (internationally oriented national body)
♦ Cooperazione Internazionale Sud-Sud (internationally oriented national body)
♦ Cooperazione Italiana Nord-Sud (internationally oriented national body)
♦ Cooperazione Paesi Emergenti (internationally oriented national body)
♦ Cooperazione e Sviluppo / see CESVI Fondazione
♦ Cooperazione per lo Sviluppo dei Paesi Emergenti (internationally oriented national body)
♦ COOPERMONDO – Associazione per la Cooperazione Internazionale allo Sviluppo (internationally oriented national body)
♦ COOPI – Cooperazione Internazionale (internationally oriented national body)
♦ COORDCOM – Coordinating Committee of South-East Asian Senior Officials on Transport and Communications (inactive)
♦ Coordenação Europeia para o Direito dos Estrangeiros a Viverem em Familila (#06794)
♦ Coordenadora Agricola Européia / see European Coordination Via Campesina (#06795)
♦ Coordenadora Europea Via Campesina (#06795)

Coordenadora Européia Via
04802

alphabetic sequence excludes
For the complete listing, see Yearbook Online at

- ♦ Coordenadora Européia Via Campesina (#06795)
- ♦ Coordenadora Galega de ONG's para o Desenvolvemento (internationally oriented national body)
- ♦ Coordenadora Labrega Europea / see European Coordination Via Campesina (#06795)
- ♦ Coordenadora das Organizações Indigenas da Bacia Amazônica (#04811)
- ♦ Coordenadoria Latinoamericana de Estudantes de Arquitetura e Urbanismo do Cono Sul / see Coordinadora Latinoamericana de Estudiantes de Arquitectura (#04807)
- ♦ **COORDEUROP** European Coordination for Foreigners' Right to Family Life (#06794)
- ♦ Coordinación Centroamericana de Organizaciones de Derechos Humanos (inactive)
- ♦ Coordinación Educativa Centroamericana / see Coordinación Educativa y Cultural Centroamericana (#04803)

♦ Coordinación Educativa y Cultural Centroamericana (CECC) 04803

Central American Educational and Cultural Coordination

Contact Barrio Escalante 25m sur del Parque Francia, San José, San José, San José, Costa Rica. T. +50622480542. E-mail: sececc@ceccsica.com.
URL: http://www.ceccsica.info/

History 13 Nov 1982. Comes within the framework of *Central American Integration System (#03671)*. Former names and other names: *Coordinación Educativa Centroamericana (CEC)* – former; *Central American Education Coordination System* – former. **Aims** Promote and advance Central American regional integration in the areas of education and culture, as core axes for sustainable human development in the framework of respect for socio-cultural and natural diversity of its member countries. **Structure** Council of Ministers; General Secretariat headed by General Secretary. **Languages** English, Spanish. **Staff** 7.00 FTE, paid. **Finance** Sources: members' dues; revenue from activities/projects. Projects funded through support of international cooperation. **Activities** Events/meetings; research and development; training/education. **Publications** *Encuentro Regional de Intercambio de Políticas y Experiencias en Educación Secundaria*; *II Encuentro Regional sobre Políticas y Experiencias en Educación Secundaria*; *Políticas Educativas relacionadas con la Violencia en los Centros Educativos*.
Members Full in 8 countries:
Belize, Costa Rica, Dominican Rep, El Salvador, Guatemala, Honduras, Nicaragua, Panama.
IGO Relations Formal agreement with: *UNESCO (#20322)*. **NGO Relations** Cooperation agreement with: *Campaña Latinoamericana por el Derecho a la Educación (CLADE, #03407)*. [2023.02.13/XD8945/**E***]

- ♦ Coordinación Europea por el Derecho de los Extranjeros de Vivir en Familia (#06794)
- ♦ Coordinación Indígena Campesina de Agroforesteria Comunitaria / see Asociación Coordinadora Indigena y Campesina de Agroforesteria Comunitaria (#02120)
- ♦ Coordinación Internacional de la Juventud Obrera Cristiana (#12960)
- ♦ Coordinación Latinoamericana de Trabajadores Minero-Metalúrgicos (inactive)

♦ Coordinadora Andina de Organizaciones Indígenas (CAOI) 04804

Contact Jr Carlos Arrieta No 1049 Santa Beatriz, Lima, Peru. T. +5112656250. Fax +5112656250. E-mail: carlosperezunagua@gmail.com.
Facebook: https://www.facebook.com/caoi.andina

History Founded 17 Jul 2006, Cusco (Peru), at Founding Congress. **Aims** Represent indigenous peoples of the Andes region by proposing alternatives for well-being according to the principles of the Andean world; exercise collective rights in territorial, political, cultural and spirtual areas; promote integration of the indigenous mouvement Abya Yala; develop partnerships with social sectors; advocate for the rights of indigenous peoples in international fora. **Structure** Board of Directors. **Activities** Research/documentation; advocacy/lobbying/activism. **Events** *Congress* Quito (Ecuador) 2010.
Members Organizations in 4 countries:
Bolivia, Colombia, Ecuador, Peru.
Consultative Status Consultative status granted from: *ECOSOC (#05331)* (Special). **NGO Relations** Member of: *Alianza Social Continental (ASC, #00635)*; *OECD Watch (#17694)*. [2017/XJ2847/**D**]

- ♦ Coordinadora Campesina Europea / see European Coordination Via Campesina (#06795)

♦ Coordinadora de Centrales Sindicales del Cono Sur (CCSCS) 04805

Southern Cone Trade Union Coordinating Body

Secretariat Virrey Cevallos 520, 1077 Buenos Aires, Argentina.
Contact Juan D Jackson 1283, 11200 Montevideo, Uruguay.
Twitter: https://twitter.com/ccscs_org

History 1986, Buenos Aires (Argentina). Founded with help from ORIT, as a regional umbrella organization of trade unions. **Aims** Serve as the voice and coordinating body of central *trade unions* in countries of the Southern Cone. **Structure** Plenary. General Secretary; Technical Secretary. **Languages** Guarani, Portuguese, Spanish. **Finance** Members' dues. Support for specific events. **Events** *Meeting* Montevideo (Uruguay) 2013, *Meeting* Montevideo (Uruguay) 2002, *Meeting* Florianópolis (Brazil) 2000. **Publications** Journals.
Members Trade unions (13) in 6 countries:
Argentina, Brazil, Chile, Paraguay, Uruguay, Venezuela.
NGO Relations Member of: *Alianza Social Continental (ASC, #00635)*. Close links with: *International Trade Union Confederation (ITUC, #15708)*; *Confederación Sindical de Trabajadores y Trabajadoras de las Américas (CSA, #04480)*. [2019/XD9455/t/**D**]

- ♦ Coordinadora Centroamericana de Trabajadores (no recent information)
- ♦ Coordinadora de la Conferencia Episcopal de Austria para el Desarrollo Internacional y la Misión (internationally oriented national body)
- ♦ Coordinadora Europea de Familias Numerosas / see European Large Families Confederation (#07651)
- ♦ Coordinadora Europea Via Campesina (#06795)
- ♦ Coordinadora Latinoamericana y del Caribe de Pequeños Productores de Comercio Justo (#16282)

♦ Coordinadora Latinoamericana de Cine et de Comunicación de los Pueblos Indigenas (CLACPI) 04806

Coordinator of Latin American Cinema and Communication Indigenous Peoples

Coordinator address not obtained. T. +56229804591. E-mail: festivalindigena@yahoo.es – difusion@clacpi.org.
Contact c/o Otero de la Vega 812, 2do Piso, zona San Pedro, La Paz, Bolivia.
URL: http://www.clacpi.org/

History 8 Sep 1985, Mexico City (Mexico), as *Latin American Committee on Films on Indian Peoples – Comité Latinoamericano de Cine de Pueblos Indígenas*, at 1st Latin American Film Festival of Indigenous Peoples. Subsequently referred to as *Latin American Council of Indigenous Film and Communication – Consejo Latinoamericano de Cine et de Comunicación de los Pueblos Indigenas*. **Aims** Promote, stimulate and publicize film and *video* production on the *indigenous* and *peasant* world in the Americas; provide and exchange information and knowledge through video and film among the different countries, areas and groups of indigenous peoples of the continent. **Structure** General Assembly; Board of Directors; Directive Committee. Special Commissions. Regional and national delegates. **Languages** English, French, Portuguese, Spanish. **Staff** 12.00 FTE, paid. **Finance** Contributions from institutions in various countries and from international bodies for the execution of projects. **Activities** Organizes film and video festivals. Ongoing projects: Videomaking Workshops for Latin American Indians and Peasants; Network for Circulation of Audiovisual Messages for Indigenous Peoples Grassroots. **Events** *Inter-American Film Festival of Indigenous Peoples* La Paz (Bolivia) 2008, *Inter-American Film Festival of Indigenous Peoples* Oaxaca (Mexico) 2006, *Inter-American Film Festival of Indigenous Peoples* Santiago (Chile) 2004, *Colloquium of visual anthropology / Inter-American Film Festival of Indigenous Peoples* Lima (Peru) / Cusco (Peru) 1992, *Inter-American Film Festival of Indigenous Peoples* Caracas (Venezuela) 1989. **Publications** *CLACPI Newsletter* (occasional).
Members Organizations in 8 countries:
Bolivia, Brazil, Chile, Colombia, Cuba, Guatemala, Mexico, Peru.
NGO Relations Affiliated to the Commission on Visual Anthropology of: *International Union of Anthropological and Ethnological Sciences (IUAES, #15755)*. [2014/XE0543/**E**]

♦ Coordinadora Latinoamericana de Estudiantes de Arquitectura (CLEA) 04807

Pres address not obtained. T. +5492616336994. E-mail: contacto@arquitecturamendoza.com.
URL: http://arquitecturamendoza.com/clea.php/

History 1983, as *Coordinadora Latinoamericana de Estudiantes de Arquitectura y Urbanismo del Cono Sur (COLEA)* – *Coordenadoria Latinoamericana de Estudantes de Arquitetura e Urbanismo do Cono Sul*. **Structure** General Assembly; Executive Committee. **Activities** Events/meetings. **Events** *Encuentro Latinoamericano de Estudiantes de Arquitectura – ELEA* Santa Cruz (Bolivia) 2018, *Encuentro Latinoamericano de Estudiantes de Arquitectura – ELEA* Santo Domingo (Dominican Rep) 2017, *Encuentro Latinoamericano de Estudiantes de Arquitectura – ELEA* Zacatecas (Mexico) 2016, *Encuentro Latinoamericano de Estudiantes de Arquitectura – ELEA* Arequipa (Peru) 2015, *Forum* Puebla (Mexico) 2014.
Members National organizations in 15 countries:
Bolivia, Colombia, Costa Rica, Cuba, Dominican Rep, Ecuador, El Salvador, Guatemala, Honduras, Mexico, Nicaragua, Panama, Peru, Puerto Rico, Venezuela. [2020/XJ4474/**D**]

- ♦ Coordinadora Latinoamericana de Estudiantes de Arquitectura y Urbanismo del Cono Sur / see Coordinadora Latinoamericana de Estudiantes de Arquitectura (#04807)

♦ Coordinadora Latinoamericana de Organizaciones del Campo (CLOC) 04808

Latin American Coordination of Rural Organizations

Contact Rotonda Ruben Dario, 100 mts Oeste, 100 mts Norte, contiguo a oficina de ATC, Managua, Nicaragua.
URL: http://www.cloc-viacampesina.net/

Events *Congress* Iximulew (Guatemala) 2005, *Congress* Tlalpan (Mexico) 2001, *Congress* Brasilia (Brazil) 1997, *Congress* Lima (Peru) 1994. **Publications** *Boletín de Intercambio*.
Members National organizations in 16 countries:
Argentina, Belize, Bolivia, Brazil, Chile, Colombia, Costa Rica, Cuba, Dominican Rep, Ecuador, Guatemala, Honduras, Mexico, Nicaragua, Paraguay, Peru.
NGO Relations Member of: *Alianza Social Continental (ASC, #00635)*; *La Via Campesina (#20765)*. [2012/XF6348/**F**]

- ♦ Coordinadora Latinoamericana de Servidores Públicos / see Coordinadora Latinoamericana de Trabajadores de los Servicios Públicos (#04809)

♦ Coordinadora Latinoamericana de Trabajadores de los Servicios Públicos (CLATSEP) 04809

Latin American Coordinator of Public Service Workers

SG c/o CGTD, Calle 39, A No 14-48, Bogota, Bogota DC, Colombia. T. +5712881560. Fax +5715734021.

History Founded 1968, as regional organization of *International Federation of Employees in Public Services (INFEDOP, #13410)*, acting in this capacity under the acronym *AMLATFEDOP*. Previously known as *Latin American Committee for Civil Servants – Commission latinoaméricaine des fonctionnaires des services publics – Comisión Latinoamericana de Servidores Públicos (CLASEP)* when it was also referred to as *Coordinadora Latinoamericana de Servidores Públicos*. Present name adopted, 2001. **Events** *Conference* Mexico 2001. **Members** Membership countries not specified. [2016/XD4515/**D**]

- ♦ Coordinadora Latinoamericano de Sindicatos Bananeros / see Coordinadora Latinoamericano de Sindicatos Bananeros en Agroindustriales (#04810)

♦ Coordinadora Latinoamericano de Sindicatos Bananeros en Agroindustriales (COLSIBA) 04810

Latin American Banana and Agroindustrial Workers' Union Coordination

Coordinator Apdo Postal 4128, La Lima, Cortés, Honduras. E-mail: colsiba@colsiba.org.
URL: http://colsiba.org/

History 1993, San José (Costa Rica). Former names and other names: *Coordinadora Latinoamericano de Sindicatos Bananeros (COLSIBA)* – former (1993); *Latin American Banana Workers' Union Coordination* – former (1993). **Structure** Executive Committee. **Events** *International banana conference* Brussels (Belgium) 2005, *Conference* Guayaquil (Ecuador) 2003.
Members Banana workers unions in 8 countries:
Colombia, Costa Rica, Ecuador, Guatemala, Honduras, Nicaragua, Panama, Peru.
NGO Relations *European Banana Action Network (EUROBAN, #06310)*. [2021/XD7433/t/**D**]

- ♦ Coordinadora de ONG para el Desarrollo, España / see Coordinadora de Organizaciones No Gubernamentales para el Desarrollo, España
- ♦ Coordinadora de ONGD España / see Coordinadora de Organizaciones No Gubernamentales para el Desarrollo, España

♦ Coordinadora de las Organizaciones Indígenas de la Cuenca Amazónica (COICA) 04811

Coordenadora das Organizações Indigenas da Bacia Amazônica – Coordinating Body for the Indigenous Organizations of the Amazon Basin

Main Office Calle Sevilla N24-358 y Guipuzcoa, 170525 Quito, Ecuador. T. +59323226744. Fax +59323226744. E-mail: coica@coicamazonia.org – coica@coica.org.ec.
URL: https://coicamazonia.org/

History 26 Mar 1984, Lima (Peru). **Aims** Gain international recognition for the collective *rights* of indigenous peoples; promote, develop and implement means for members to interact; defend *territorial* claims and *self-determination* of indigenous peoples, respect for their human and other rights and their interests; strengthen unity and mutual collaboration among indigenous peoples; develop Indian alternatives for the future of Amazonia. **Structure** Congress (every 4 years); Coordinating Council; Management Board. **Languages** English, Portuguese, Spanish. **Events** *Continental summit of the indigenous peoples and nationalities of Abya Yala* Quito (Ecuador) 2004, *Meeting on biological diversity and indigenous people* Guiana Fr 2000, *Quadrennial Congress* Georgetown (Guyana) 1997, *Quadrennial Congress* Valencia (Spain) 1997, *Workshop* Quito (Ecuador) 1995. **Publications** *Nuestra Amazonia* (4 a year). *Ambiente y Derechos Indígenas en la Agenda Política* (1999); *Biodiversidad Derechos Colectivos, y Regimen Sui Generis de Propiedad Intelectual* (1999); *Entro lo Propio y lo Ajeno* (1997).
Members National Indian organizations (9) in 9 Amazon countries and territories:
Bolivia, Brazil, Colombia, Ecuador, Guiana Fr, Guyana, Peru, Suriname, Venezuela.
Consultative Status Consultative status granted from: *UNEP (#20299)*. **IGO Relations** Accredited by: *Green Climate Fund (GCF, #10714)*; *United Nations Framework Convention on Climate Change – Secretariat (UNFCCC, #20564)*. **NGO Relations** Member of (2): *EarthAction (EA, #05159)*; *International Union for Conservation of Nature and Natural Resources (IUCN, #15766)*. Partner of (1): *Re:wild*. President is Chairman of: *Climate Alliance (#04005)*. [2020/XF1642/**F**]

- ♦ Coordinadora de Organizaciones No Gubernamentales para el Desarrollo, España (internationally oriented national body)
- ♦ Coordinador del Area Maritima del Atlantico Sur / see South Atlantic Maritime Area (#19750)

♦ Coordinadora Regional de Investigaciones Económicas y Sociales (CRIES) 04812

Regional Coordination of Economic and Social Research – Coordination régionale de recherches économiques et sociales

Admin Coordinator Lavalle 1619, Piso 9 / Ofic A, 1048 Buenos Aires, Argentina. T. +541143728351. E-mail: info@cries.org.
URL: http://www.cries.org/

History Jun 1982, Managua (Nicaragua). Former names and other names: *Regional Coordination of Economic and Social Research on Central America and Caribbean* – former. **Aims** Promote civil society participation in regional integration processes and in public debate on issues related to regional and global agendas; empower networks and civil society organizations in formulation, implementation and monitoring of public policies related to thematic foci. **Structure** General Assembly; Board of Directors; Executive Presidency; Executive Committee; Secretariat. **Languages** English, Portuguese, Spanish. **Staff** 5.00 FTE, paid. **Finance** Past and current financial assistance from various organizations, foundations and governments, including: *Agencia Española de Cooperación Internacional para el Desarrollo (AECID)*; *Arca Foundation*; *Canadian International Development Agency (CIDA, inactive)*; *Catholic Organization for Relief and Development (Cordaid)*; *Ford Foundation (#09858)*; *Global Partnership for the Prevention of Armed Conflict Foundation (GPPAC Foundation)*; *Heinrich Böll Foundation*; *ICCO – Interchurch Organization for Development Cooperation*; *Instituto de Estudios Politicos para América Latina y Africa (IEPALA)*; *International Development Research Centre (IDRC, #13162)*; *The Lutheran World Federation (LWF, #16532)*; Norwegian government; *Oxfam Novib*; *Swiss Agency for Development and Cooperation (SDC)*. **Activities** Research and development; networking/liaising; advocacy/lobbying/activism; awareness raising; training/education; conflict resolution; publishing activities; projects/programmes. **Events** *Civil society regional forum* Mexico City (Mexico) 2003, *Forum on debt and development* Santo Domingo (Dominican Rep) 1990, *Academic conference* Washington, DC (USA) 1990. **Publications** *Anuario de América Latina y el Caribe*; *Pensamiento Propio* – journal. Special Dossiers.

Members Research centres; think tanks; NGOs; foundations; professional associations; thematic experts; academic institutions. Network members (over 70) in 22 countries:
Argentina, Barbados, Bolivia, Brazil, Chile, Colombia, Costa Rica, Cuba, Dominican Rep, Ecuador, El Salvador, Guatemala, Haiti, Honduras, Jamaica, Mexico, Nicaragua, Panama, Paraguay, Peru, Trinidad-Tobago, Venezuela.

IGO Relations Observer at: *OAS (#17629)*. Member of: Civil Society Council of *Southern Common Market (#19868)*. Recognized as social actor by *Association of Caribbean States (ACS, #02411)*. Memorandum of Understanding with: *UNDP (#20292)* – Regional Office for Latin America and the Caribbean. Cooperates with: *Latin American Faculty of Social Sciences (#16316)*.

NGO Relations Regional secretariat and member of International Steering Group of: *Global Partnership for the Prevention of Armed Conflict (GPPAC, #10538)*. Founding member of: *'International Coalition for the Responsibility to Protect (ICRtoP, #12620)*. Cooperates wit civil society networks, research centres and academic institutions, including:
- *Argentine Council for International Relations (CARI)*;
- *Arias Foundation for Peace and Human Progress*;
- *Center for International Development and Conflict Management (CIDCM)*;
- *Centre for Peace Research, Madrid (CIP-FUHEM)*;
- *Centro de Estudios de Centroamérica y Relaciones Internacionales, Mexico (CECARI, no recent information)*;
- *Centro de Investigaciones de la Economia Mundial, Habana (CIEM)*;
- *Friedrich-Ebert-Stiftung (FES)*;
- *Instituto de Estudios Politicos para América Latina y Africa (IEPALA)*;
- *International Union for Conservation of Nature and Natural Resources (IUCN, #15766)* – Central America;
- *The Lutheran World Federation (LWF, #16532)*;
- *North-South Institute (NSI)*;
- *Stanley Center for Peace and Security*;
- *Washington Office on Latin America (WOLA)*;
- *World Federalist Movement – Movement for a Just World Order through a Strengthened United Nations (WFM, #21404)*.

[2021/XF0025/**F**]

♦ Coordinamento Europeo per il Diritto degli Stranieri a Vivere in Famiglia (#06794)
♦ Coordinamento di Iniziative Popolari di Solidarietà Internazionale (internationally oriented national body)
♦ Coordinamento Internazionale della Gioventù Operaia Cristiana (#12960)
♦ Coordinamento delle Organizzazioni Non Governative per la Cooperazione Internazionale allo Sviluppo (internationally oriented national body)
♦ Coordinated African Programme of Assistance on Services (no recent information)
♦ Coördinatiecentrum Mensenhandel (internationally oriented national body)
♦ Coördinatie Comité voor de Samenwerking der Fabrikanten van Schakelapparatuur in de EG / see European Coordinating Committee of Manufacturers of Electrical Switchgear and Controlgear (#06790)
♦ Coördinatie Comité voor de Samenwerking der Fabrikanten van Schakelapparatuur in de Europese Unie / see European Coordinating Committee of Manufacturers of Electrical Switchgear and Controlgear (#06790)
♦ Coördinatie-orgaan voor Internationale Jongerenwerking (internationally oriented national body)

♦ Coordinating Board of Jewish Organizations (CBJO) 04813

Comité de coordination d'organisations juives – Comité de Coordinación de Organizaciones Judias – Koordinierungs-Ausschuss Jüdischer Organisationen

Contact address not obtained. E-mail: hoschoenberg@aol.com.

History 1947, New York NY (USA). **Aims** Coordinate the work at the United Nations of the 3 constituent organizations primarily in promoting *human rights*, with special attention to combating *persecution* or *discrimination* on grounds of race, religion or origin. **Structure** Governing Body (meets every 2 years). Membership and meetings closed. **Languages** English. **Staff** 8.00 FTE, paid; 16.00 FTE, voluntary. **Finance** Contributions by constituent bodies. Budget (annual): US$ 16 million. **Activities** Serves as liaison and documentation centre for constituent bodies. Runs social, humanitarian and environmental programmes. **Publications** Reports.

Members Combined membership of constituent bodies is 1,129,000 individual members in 47 countries. Membership countries not specified. National constituent bodies in 2 countries:
South Africa, UK.
Included in the above, 1 international organization listed in this Yearbook:
B'nai B'rith International (BBI, #03290).

Consultative Status Consultative status granted from: *ECOSOC (#05331)* (Special); *ILO (#11123)* (Special List); *UNICEF (#20332)*; *UNEP (#20299)*. **IGO Relations** Accredited by: *United Nations Office at Vienna (UNOV, #20604)*. Associated with Department of Global Communications of the United Nations. **NGO Relations** Board member of: *Conference of Non-Governmental Organizations in Consultative Relationship with the United Nations (CONGO, #04635)*. Member of: *NGO Committee on Freedom of Religion or Belief, New York NY (#17109)*. [2011/XE0420/y/**E**]

♦ Coordinating Body for the Indigenous Organizations of the Amazon Basin (#04811)

♦ Coordinating Body on the Seas of East Asia (COBSEA) 04814

Sec c/o UNEP/ROAP, UN Bldg 2nd Floor, Block B, Rajadamnern-Nok Avenue, Bangkok, 10200, Thailand. T. +6622881860 – +6622881889.
Officer-in-Charge address not obtained.
URL: http://www.cobsea.org/

History 1981, as the policy coordination and decision-making body for the *Action Plan for the Protection and Development of the Marine Environment and Coastal Areas of the East Asian Region (EAS, #00093)*. **Aims** Determine the content of the action plan, review its progress and approve its programme of implementation. **Structure** Intergovernmental Meeting of Governments (IGM). Secretariat. **Languages** English. **Staff** 3.00 FTE, paid. **Finance** Funded by East Asian Seas Trust Fund. **Activities** Politics/policy/regulatory. **Events** *Workshop on Protecting Marine Ecosystems in MFF Countries using the Green Fins Approach* Bangkok (Thailand) 2014, *Workshop on Strengthening the Resilience of Coastal Communities, Ecosystems and Economies to Sea-Level Rise and Coastal Erosion* Thailand 2014, *Meeting* Siem Reap (Cambodia) 2008, *Meeting* Bandar Seri Begawan (Brunei Darussalam) 1989. **Publications** *Regional Programme of Action for the Protection of the Marine Environment of the East Asian Seas from the Effects of Land-based Activities* (2000); *Action Plan for the Protection and Sustainable Development of the Marine and Coastal Areas of the East Asian Seas Region* (1994); *Action Plan for the Protection and Development of the Marine and Coastal Areas of the East Asian Region* (1993). Meeting reports.

Members Full in 9 countries:
Cambodia, China, Indonesia, Korea Rep, Malaysia, Philippines, Singapore, Thailand, Vietnam.

IGO Relations *UNEP (#20299)*. [2014.11.17/XE6107/**E***]

♦ Coordinating Bureau of the Non-Aligned Countries 04815

Bureau de coordination des pays non alignés

Contact United Nations Headquarters, New York NY 10017, USA. T. +12129631234. Fax +12127582718.

History 5 Sep 1973, Algiers (Algeria). Established 5-9 Sep 1973, Algiers (Algeria), at 4th *Conference of Heads of State or Government of Non-Aligned Countries*, also referred to as *Conference of Non-Aligned Countries*, following a resolution of *Conference of Foreign Ministers of Non-Aligned Countries*, 8-12 Aug 1972, Georgetown (Guyana), and meeting of Preparatory Committee, 13-15 May 1973, Kabul (Afghanistan). 1st meeting: 19-21 Mar 1974, Algiers. Also known as Coordinating Bureau of the *Non-Aligned Movement (NAM, #17146)*, the latter having existed since 1961, Belgrade (Yugoslavia), and sometimes referred to as *'Movement of Non-Aligned Countries'*. **Aims** Work towards establishment of a *new international economic order*, elaborate an *economic* strategy for non-aligned countries.

Structure Coordinating Bureau (currently 69 countries) meets at Ministerial and Senior Official levels. The Chairman of the Non-Aligned Movement is assisted by: an Advisory Council; a team of economic experts; Ambassadors-at-Large (4) for 4 regions (Africa, America, Europe, Asia and Middle East); an Office of the Executive Assistant to the NAM Chairman; a Technical Committee attached to the latter Office. The Bureau has no secretariat but normally meets at United Nations Headquarters, New York NY (USA).
Ministerial meetings include: *Ministerial Meeting of the Mediterranean Non-Aligned Countries*; *Non-Aligned Movement Committee of Ministers on Imposition of Sanctions (no recent information)*; *Non-Aligned Movement Ministerial Committee on Methodology (no recent information)*, unofficially known as *'Committee for the Movement's Functioning'*; *Standing Ministerial Committee for Economic Cooperation of the Non-Aligned Movement (SMC, no recent information)*.
Organizations within the Non-Aligned Movement include: *Non-Aligned Committee of Nine on Palestine (no recent information)*; *Non-aligned Countries Ad Hoc Group for the Solidarity Fund for Economic and Social Development (no recent information)*; *Broadcasting Organizations of the Non-aligned Countries (BONAC, no recent information)*; *Non-Aligned News Agency Pool (NANAP, inactive)*; *Research and Information System for Developing Countries, India (RIS, India)*; *Group for South-South Consultation and Cooperation (no recent information)*; Intergovernmental Council for Coordination of Cooperation of Non-Aligned Countries in the Field of Information and Communication; *Centre for Science and Technology of the Non-Aligned and Other Developing Countries (NAM S and T Centre, #03784)*.

Languages Arabic, English, French, Spanish. **Staff** Personnel of and paid by the Government of Indonesia. **Events** *Ministerial Meeting of Coordinating Bureau* Algiers (Algeria) 2014, *Ministerial Meeting of Coordinating Bureau* Bali (Indonesia) 2011, *Ministerial Meeting of Coordinating Bureau* Havana (Cuba) 2009, *Ministerial Meeting of Coordinating Bureau* Teheran (Iran Islamic Rep) 2008, *Ministerial Meeting of Coordinating Bureau* Teheran (Iran Islamic Rep) 2007. **Publications** *Twenty Five Years of the Nonaligned Movement* – Vol 1 1961-1982, Vol 2 1983-1986.

Members 113 countries are members of the non-aligned movement:
Afghanistan, Algeria, Angola, Bahamas, Bahrain, Bangladesh, Barbados, Belize, Benin, Bhutan, Bolivia, Botswana, Brunei Darussalam, Burkina Faso, Burundi, Cambodia, Cameroon, Cape Verde, Central African Rep, Chad, Chile, Colombia, Comoros, Congo Brazzaville, Congo DR, Côte d'Ivoire, Cuba, Cyprus, Djibouti, Ecuador, Egypt, Equatorial Guinea, Eritrea, Eswatini, Ethiopia, Gabon, Gambia, Ghana, Grenada, Guatemala, Guinea, Guinea-Bissau, Guyana, Honduras, India, Indonesia, Iran Islamic Rep, Iraq, Jamaica, Jordan, Kenya, Korea DPR, Kuwait, Laos, Lebanon, Lesotho, Liberia, Libya, Madagascar, Malawi, Malaysia, Maldives, Mali, Malta, Mauritania, Mauritius, Mongolia, Morocco, Mozambique, Myanmar, Namibia, Nepal, Nicaragua, Niger, Nigeria, Oman, Pakistan, Palestine, Panama, Papua New Guinea, Peru, Philippines, Qatar, Rwanda, Sao Tomé-Principe, Saudi Arabia, Senegal, Serbia, Seychelles, Sierra Leone, Singapore, Somalia, South Africa, Sri Lanka, St Lucia, Sudan, Suriname, Syrian AR, Tanzania UR, Thailand, Togo, Trinidad-Tobago, Tunisia, Turkmenistan, Uganda, United Arab Emirates, Uzbekistan, Vanuatu, Venezuela, Vietnam, Yemen, Zambia, Zimbabwe.
Countries with Observer Status (12):
Antigua-Barbuda, Armenia, Azerbaijan, Brazil, China, Costa Rica, Croatia, Dominica, El Salvador, Kyrgyzstan, Mexico, Uruguay.
Countries with Guest Status (26):
Australia, Austria, Bosnia-Herzegovina, Bulgaria, Canada, Czechia, Dominican Rep, Finland, Germany, Greece, Holy See, Hungary, Italy, Netherlands, New Zealand, Norway, Poland, Romania, Russia, San Marino, Slovakia, Slovenia, Spain, Sweden, Switzerland, Ukraine.
Member countries of the Coordinating Bureau are not specified. [2016/XC2507/**E***]

♦ Coordinating Committee of Asia-Pacific National Safety Councils / see Asia Pacific Occupational Safety and Health Organization (#01981)
♦ Coordinating Committee for the Associations of Manufacturers of Industrial Electrical Switchgear and Controlgear in the European Union / see European Coordinating Committee of Manufacturers of Electrical Switchgear and Controlgear (#06790)
♦ Coordinating Committee for Coastal and Offshore Geoscience Programmes in East and Southeast Asia / see Coordinating Committee for Geoscience Programmes in East and Southeast Asia (#04816)
♦ Coordinating Committee for Common Market Associations of Manufacturers of Industrial Electrical Switchgear and Controlgear / see European Coordinating Committee of Manufacturers of Electrical Switchgear and Controlgear (#06790)

♦ Coordinating Committee for Geoscience Programmes in East and Southeast Asia (CCOP) 04816

Dir CCOP Building, 75/10 Rama VI Road, Phayathai – Ratchathewi, Bangkok, 10400, Thailand. T. +666445468. Fax +666445429. E-mail: ccopts@ccop.or.th.
URL: https://ccop.asia/

History 1966, Bangkok (Thailand). Founded by 4 countries. A special regional body, originally under the aegis of the then United Nations Economic Commission for Asia and the Far East (ECAFE), currently *United Nations Economic and Social Commission for Asia and the Pacific (ESCAP, #20557)*. Became an independent intergovernmental organization in 1987 with 11 East and Southeast Asian member countries. Former names and other names: *Committee for Coordination of Joint Prospecting for Mineral Resources in Asian Offshore Areas* – former (1966 to 1994); *Comité pour la coordination de la prospection commune des ressources minérales au large des côtes de l'Asie* – former (1966 to 1994); *Coordinating Committee for Coastal and Offshore Geoscience Programmes in East and Southeast Asia* – former (1994 to 2002). **Aims** Facilitate and coordinate implementation of applied geoscience programmes in East and Southeast Asia in order to contribute to economic development and improvement of quality of life in the region. **Structure** Steering Committee; Advisory Group; Technical Secretariat. **Languages** English. **Finance** Contributions by member countries. **Activities** Networking/liaising; awareness raising; projects/programmes; capacity building; knowledge management/information dissemination; events/meetings; monitoring/evaluation; standards/guidelines. **Events** *Annual Session* Chiang Mai (Thailand) 2019, *Annual Session* Busan (Korea Rep) 2018, *Annual Session* Cebu City (Philippines) 2017, *Annual Session* Bangkok (Thailand) 2016, *International Workshop on Electromagnetic Induction* Chiang Mai (Thailand) 2016. **Publications** *CCOP E-News*. Annual Report; technical publications; proceedings of annual and thematic sessions.

Members Governments of 14 countries:
Cambodia, China, Indonesia, Japan, Korea Rep, Laos, Malaysia, Myanmar, Papua New Guinea, Philippines, Singapore, Thailand, Timor-Leste, Vietnam.
Cooperating countries (14):
Australia, Belgium, Canada, Denmark, Finland, France, Germany, Netherlands, Norway, Poland, Russia, Sweden, UK, USA.

[2017.06.01/XE6119/**E***]

♦ Coordinating Committee for Intercontinental Research Networking (CCIRN) 04817

Co-Chair address not obtained.
URL: http://ccirn.net/

History Nov 1987, Washington DC (USA). **Aims** Stimulate cooperative intercontinental research through enhanced interoperable networking services; achieve *interoperable* networking services between participating entities in support of open research and scholarly pursuit; coordinate development of international network management techniques; optimize use of resources and coordinate intercontinental connections; exchange results of networking research and development. **Activities** Research/documentation. **Events** *Annual Meeting* Reykjavik (Iceland) 2011, *Annual Meeting* Sydney, NSW (Australia) 2010, *Annual Meeting* Arlington, VA (USA) 2009, *Annual Meeting* Bruges (Belgium) 2008, *Annual meeting* Xian (China) 2007.

Members Membership countries not specified. Appropriate members in the relevant regions assembled by 4 regional bodies:
Asia-Pacific Advanced Network (APAN, #01819); Canadian Network for the Advancement of Research, Industry and Education (CANARIE); Cooperación Latino Americana de Redes Avanzadas (CLARA); Internet2.
NGO Relations Liaises with: *Internet Society (ISOC, #15952)*. [2012/XF1495/y/F]

♦ Coordinating Committee for International Staff Unions and Associations of the United Nations System (CCISUA) 04818

Comité de coordination des associations et syndicats internationaux du personnel du système des Nations Unies (CCASIP)

Gen Sec c/o ILO Staff Union, Route des Morillons 4, 1211 Geneva 22, Switzerland. E-mail: contact@ccisua.org.
URL: http://www.ccisua.org/

History 1982. Founded when staff unions of the United Nations Secretariats in New York NY (USA) and Geneva (Switzerland) withdrew from *Federation of International Civil Servants' Associations (FICSA, #09603)*. **Aims** Provide equitable and effective representation of staff at all levels. **Structure** General Assembly (annual); Bureau. **Languages** English. **Finance** Voluntary members' contributions. **Events** *General Assembly* Bangkok (Thailand) 2015, *General Assembly* Rome (Italy) 2014, *General Assembly* Rome (Italy) 2014, *General Assembly* Oropesa del Mar (Spain) 2013, *General Assembly* Paris (France) 2001.
Members UN common system staff unions and associations (17), representing over 60000 international civil servants worldwide:
ECLAC Staff Association (#05285); *ESCAP Staff Council (no recent information)*; *International Court of Justice (ICJ, #13098)* (Staff Committee); *International Criminal Court (ICC, #13108)* (Staff Union); *ITU Staff Union (#16077)*; *Nairobi Staff Union (#16930)*; *Special Tribunal for Lebanon (STL, #19911)* (Staff Union); *Staff Union of the International Labour Office (#19945)*; *Staff Union of the United Nations Economic and Social Commission for Western Asia (Staff Union-ESCWA, #19946)*; *UNHCR Global Staff Council (#20326)*; *UNICEF Global Staff Association (GSA, #20330)*; *United Nations Criminal Tribunals Staff Union (UN-CTSU, #20550)*; *United Nations Staff Union (#20630)*; *United Nations Staff Union, Vienna (#20631)*; *UNOG Staff Coordinating Council (#20712)*; *UNU Staff Council (#20721)*; WFP Professional Staff Association.
Observer members (2):
Secretariat of the Convention on Biological Diversity (SCBD, #19197) (Staff Assocation); *United Nations Institute for Training and Research (UNITAR, #20576)* (Staff Association). [2022/XE0236/y/E]

♦ Coordinating Committee of International Trading Houses Associations / see European Confederation of International Trading Houses Associations (#06708)

♦ Coordinating Committee for International Voluntary Service (CCIVS) 04819

Comité de coordination du service volontaire international (CCSVI) – Comité Coordinador del Servicio Voluntario Internacional (CCSVI)

Dir UNESCO House, 1 rue Miollis, 75732 Paris CEDEX 15, France. T. +33145684936. E-mail: secretariat@ccivs.org.
URL: http://ccivs.org/

History 22 Apr 1948, Paris (France). Founded during 1st Conference of Organizers of International Voluntary Work Camps, and under the auspices of *UNESCO (#20322)*. Former names and other names: *Coordinating Committee for International Voluntary Work Camps (CCIVW)* – former; *Comité de coordination des chantiers internationaux de volontaires (CCCIV)* – former. **Aims** Promote and develop the voluntary service movement on a global level. **Structure** General Assembly of delegates from member organizations (every 2 years). Executive Committee (meets twice a year), comprising representatives from member organizations and including President, General Secretary and Treasurer. Ad hoc and permanent working groups; Secretariat. **Languages** English. **Staff** 3.00 FTE, paid; 4.00 FTE, voluntary. **Finance** Sources: contributions; donations; grants; members' dues; revenue from activities/projects. Contracts with UNESCO and other Specialized Agencies. **Activities** Advocacy/lobbying/activism; capacity building; networking/liaising; training/education. **Events** *Conference* 2021, *General Assembly* 2021, *Stronger Together – Building partnerships for successful volunteering projects* 2021, *General Assembly* Kundapura (India) 2018, *General Assembly* Bouznika (Morocco) 2016. **Publications** *CCIVS Newsletter* in English.
Members Full; Associate. International organizations and branches (2):
International Cultural Youth Exchange (ICYE Federation, #13122); *Service Civil International (SCI, #19238)*.
Regional structures and partners (9):
Alliance of European Voluntary Service Organizations (ALLIANCE, #00677); *Association of Voluntary Service Organisations (AVSO, no recent information)*; ICYE African Region; ICYE Asia Pacific Region; ICYE Panamerican Region (APIC); *Network for Voluntary Development in Asia (NVDA, #17063)*; Southern Africa Workcamp Coordination (SAWAC); Union Marocaine des Associations de Chantiers (UMAC); West Africa Voluntary Association Network (WAVAN).
National organizations and branches of international organizations in 78 countries and territories:
Argentina, Armenia, Australia, Austria, Bangladesh, Belarus, Belgium, Bolivia, Botswana, Brazil, Bulgaria, Burundi, Cambodia, Canada, China, Colombia, Congo Brazzaville, Congo DR, Costa Rica, Croatia, Czechia, Denmark, Ecuador, Estonia, Finland, France, Germany, Ghana, Greece, Guatemala, Honduras, Hungary, India, Indonesia, Ireland, Italy, Japan, Kenya, Korea Rep, Kyrgyzstan, Lesotho, Malawi, Malaysia, Mexico, Morocco, Mozambique, Nepal, Netherlands, New Zealand, Nigeria, Pakistan, Palestine, Peru, Philippines, Poland, Portugal, Romania, Russia, Serbia, Slovakia, Slovenia, South Africa, Spain, Sri Lanka, Sweden, Switzerland, Taiwan, Thailand, Togo, Tunisia, Türkiye, Uganda, UK, Ukraine, USA, Vietnam, Zambia, Zimbabwe.
Consultative Status Consultative status granted from: *ECOSOC (#05331)* (Special); *UNESCO (#20322)* (Associate Status); *FAO (#09260)* (Liaison Status). **IGO Relations** Accredited by (1): *United Nations Office at Vienna (UNOV, #20604)*. Member of (1): *European Youth Centres (EYCs, #09138)*. **NGO Relations** Member of (2): *International Conference of NGOs (#12883)*; *NGO-UNESCO Liaison Committee (#17127)*. [2021.10.29/XC0424/y/B]

♦ Coordinating Committee for International Voluntary Work Camps / see Coordinating Committee for International Voluntary Service (#04819)
♦ Coordinating Committee of the Lagos-Tangier Axis (inactive)
♦ Coordinating Committee of Nordic Associations of Social Workers (#17495)
♦ Coordinating Committee of the Organization for Voluntary Service (internationally oriented national body)
♦ Coordinating Committee of South-East Asian Senior Officials on Transport and Communications (inactive)
♦ Coordinating Council of Agricultural Worker and Peasant Organizations in Latin America (inactive)

♦ Co-ordinating Council of Audiovisual Archives Associations (CCAAA) 04820

Rapporteur SWR, Neckarstrasse 230, 70190 Stuttgart, Germany.
URL: http://www.ccaaa.org/

History as *International Round Table of Audiovisual Records*. Present name adopted 1999. **Aims** Provide a platform for members wishing to cooperate on influencing development of public policy on issues of importance to professional audiovisual archivists. **Structure** Informal forum of executive officers of international organizations in the field, meets at least annually. **Languages** English. **Activities** Events/meetings; politics/policy/regulatory. **Events** *Joint Technical Symposium* Singapore (Singapore) 2016, *Meeting* Paris (France) 2014, *Meeting* Paris (France) 2013, *Meeting* Paris (France) 2012, *Meeting* Kuala Lumpur (Malaysia) 2011.
Members Executive officers of 9 organizations:
Association for Recorded Sound Collections (ARSC); Association of Moving Image Archivists (AMIA); *Federation of Commercial Audiovisual Libraries International (FOCAL International)*; *International Association of Sound and Audiovisual Archives (IASA, #12172)*; *International Council on Archives (ICA, #12996)*; *International Federation of Film Archives (#13427)*; *International Federation of Library Associations and Institutions (IFLA, #13470)*; *International Federation of Television Archives (IFTA, #13568)*; *Southeast Asia-Pacific Audiovisual Archive Association (SEAPAVAA, #19790)*.
Consultative Status Consultative status granted from: *World Intellectual Property Organization (WIPO, #21593)* (Permanent Observer Status). **IGO Relations** *UNESCO (#20322)* Information for all Programme. [2014.10.28/XE3910/y/E]

♦ Coordinating Council on Trans-Siberian Transportation (CCTT) 04821

Officer Weltpoststrasse 20, 3015 Bern, Switzerland.
URL: http://www.icctt.com/

History Established 23 Nov 1993, Moscow (Russia), by the Russian Ministry of Railway Transport and regional organizations. Former title: *International Cooperation Coordinating Council on Transsiberian Transportation (CCTT)*. Previously also known under the acronym *CCTST*. Registered in accordance with Swiss Civil Code, 23 Nov 1993; re-registered, 21 Feb 1997, reg no: CH-32060421485. Relocated to Bern (Switzerland) 2019 and re-registered, reg no: CHE-108.607.583. **Aims** Unite overland and sea forwarders within the Asia-Europe route. **Structure** Plenary Meeting; CCTT Chairman; Secretariat. **Languages** English, Russian. **Finance** Members' dues. **Activities** Networking/liaising; events/meetings. **Events** *Annual Meeting* Moscow (Russia) 2021, *Annual Meeting* Moscow (Russia) 2020, *Annual Meeting* Nur-Sultan (Kazakhstan) 2019, *Annual Meeting* Sochi (Russia) 2018, *Annual Meeting* Beijing (China) 2017. **Publications** *Annual TSR Digest*. *TSR Atlas*.
Members Railways; shipping companies; ports and stevedoring companies; state organizations, administrations and municipalities; associations of operators and forwarders; operators and forwarders; cargo owners; Telecommunication and IT companies; insurance companies; service and transport engineering. Standing and associate members (105) in 23 countries:
Austria, Belarus, Bulgaria, China, Czechia, Estonia, Finland, France, Germany, Hungary, Japan, Kazakhstan, Korea Rep, Latvia, Lithuania, Mongolia, Norway, Poland, Russia, Slovakia, Sweden, Switzerland, Ukraine.
IGO Relations *Committee on Inland Transport (#04262)*; *Organisation intergouvernementale pour les transports internationaux ferroviaires (OTIF, #17807)*; *Organisation for Cooperation between Railways (OSJD, #17803)*; *United Nations Economic and Social Commission for Asia and the Pacific (ESCAP, #20557)*; *Universal Postal Union (UPU, #20682)*; *World Customs Organization (WCO, #21350)*. **NGO Relations** *Bureau international des containers et du transport intermodal (BIC, #03364)*; *Comité international des transports ferroviaires (CIT, #04188)*; *Community of European Railway and Infrastructure Companies (CER, #04396)*; *FERRMED*; *Fédération internationale des associations de transitaires et assimilés (FIATA, #09610)*; *Gemeinschaft der Europäischen Transsibirien Operateure (GETO, #10091)*; *International Rail Freight Business Association (IBS)*; *International Union of Railways (#15813)*; *International Union for Combined Road – Rail Transport (UIRR, #15765)*; national associations. [2019.06.20/XE3939/E*]

♦ Coordinating European Council for the Development of Performance Tests for Lubricants and Engine Fuels / see Coordinating European Council for the Development of Performance Tests for Transportation Fuels, Lubricants and Other Fluids (#04822)

♦ Coordinating European Council for the Development of Performance Tests for Transportation Fuels, Lubricants and Other Fluids (CEC) 04822

Conseil européen de coordination pour le développement des essais de performance des combustibles, lubrifiants et autres fluides utilisés dans les transports

Secretariat c/o Kellen Europe, Av de Tervuren 188-A, Box 4, 1150 Brussels, Belgium. T. +3227611684. E-mail: info@cectests.org.
URL: http://www.cectests.org/

History 5 Nov 1963, Turin (Italy). Founded as *Coordinating European Council for the Development of Performance Tests for Lubricants and Engine Fuels – Conseil européen de coordination pour le développement des essais de performance des lubrifiants et des combustibles pour moteurs*. Articles and Guidelines adopted Jul 2001; most recent Articles and Guidelines adopted 2013. Registration: Banque-Carrefour des Entreprises, No/ID: 0453.782.034, Start date: 18 Oct 1994, Belgium. **Aims** Promote a joint industry approach to developing test methods and procedures for performance evaluation of fuels, lubricants and other fluids used in combustion engines and transport equipment. **Structure** Management Board; Secretariat provided by professional administration company; Groups (38); Special Project and Liaison Groups. **Languages** English. **Staff** None. **Finance** Supported by European automotive, engine, petroleum and additive industries. **Activities** Networking/liaising; knowledge management/information dissemination; research and development. **Events** *Symposium* Paris (France) 2000, *Quadrennial Symposium* Gothenburg (Sweden) 1997, *Quadrennial Symposium* Birmingham (UK) 1993, *Quadrennial symposium* Paris (France) 1989. **Publications** Newsletters. Test methods; codes of practice; technical publications; presentations.
Members International organizations (4):
Association technique de l'industrie européenne des lubrifiants (ATIEL, #02950); *European Automobile Manufacturers' Association (ACEA, #06300)*; *Oil Companies' European Association for Environment, Health and Safety in Refining and Distribution (CONCAWE, #17708)*; *Technical Committee of Petroleum Additive Manufacturers in Europe (ATC, #20115)*. [2022/XD9876/y/D]

♦ Coordinating Group for Religion in Education (CoGREE) 04823

Moderator Comenius-Institut, Schreiberstr 12, 48149 Münster, Germany. T. +492519810125. Fax +492519810150. E-mail: cogree@comenius.de – info@cogree.org.
URL: https://cogree.org/

History Founded 1998, as *Coordinating Group for Religious Education in Europe (CoGREE)*. **Aims** Facilitate cooperation between networks and organizations concerned with religion in education and religious education. **Structure** Steering Group (meets twice a year). **Languages** English. **Staff** 1.00 FTE, paid. **Finance** Members' dues. Support from: Comenius-Institut, Germany; VERUS, Netherlands. **Events** *Conference* Dublin (Ireland) 2019, *Conference* Klingenthal (France) 2016, *Conference* Klingenthal (Germany) 2016, *Conference* Vienna (Austria) 2016, *Conference* Klingenthal (France) 2014. **Publications** Declaration; discussion paper; statements.
Members International organizations (5), listed in this Yearbook:
European Association for World Religions in Education (EAWRE, #06279); *European Forum for Religious Education in Schools (EUFRES)*; *European Forum for Teachers of Religious Education (EFTRE, #07337)*; *Intereuropean Commission on Church and School (ICCS, #11469)*; *International Association for Christian Education (#11770)*.
IGO Relations *Council of Europe (CE, #04881)*. **NGO Relations** *Community of Protestant Churches in Europe (CPCE, #04405)*; *Conference of European Churches (CEC, #04593)*; *World Council of Churches (WCC, #21320)*. [2017.11.28/XF6046/y/F]

♦ Coordinating Group for Religious Education in Europe / see Coordinating Group for Religion in Education (#04823)
♦ Coordinating Secretariat of National Unions of Students (inactive)
♦ Coordination of Action Research on AIDS and Mobility – Asia (internationally oriented national body)
♦ Coordination pour l'Afrique de demain (#04828)
♦ Coordination des Associations and Particuliers pour la Liberté de Conscience (internationally oriented national body)

♦ Coordination des comités européens de soutien au peuple sahraoui (EUCOCO Sahara) 04824

European Coordination of Support for the Sahrawi People

President Forum NS, 115 rue Stévin, 1000 Brussels, Belgium.

History 1975. Also referred to as *European Conference of Support and Solidarity with the Saharawi People – Conférence européenne de soutien et de solidarité avec le peuple sahraoui*. **Events** *For the independence of Western Sahara – the respondibility of Spain and Europe in the solution* Madrid (Spain) 2018, *Conference* Madrid (Spain) 2015, *European Conference* Madrid (Spain) 2014, *Conference* Las Palmas de Gran Canaria (Spain) 1999. [2014/XE2206/E]

♦ Coordination Committee of the East Asian National Olympic Committees / see East Asian Olympic Committee (#05206)
♦ Coordination Committee on Multilateral Payments Arrangements and Monetary Cooperation among Developing Countries (no recent information)
♦ Coordination Committee between National and Regional Arab Development Institutions / see Coordination Group of Arab National and Regional Development Institutions (#04826)
♦ Coordination Committee of Northwestern Mediterranean Ports (inactive)
♦ Coordination and Cooperation Organization for the Control of the Major Endemic Diseases (inactive)

- Coordination of European Independent Producers / see European Audiovisual Production (#06295)
- Coordination of European Picture Agencies / see Coordination of European Picture Agencies, Press Stock Heritage (#04825)
- Coordination of European Picture Agencies, Press and Stock / see Coordination of European Picture Agencies, Press Stock Heritage (#04825)

♦ Coordination of European Picture Agencies, Press Stock Heritage (CEPIC) 04825

Main Office Postfach 12 07 18, 10597 Berlin, Germany. E-mail: cepic@cepic.org.
Registered Office 46 rue de la Mare, 75020 Paris, France.
URL: https://cepic.org/

History 1993. Founded under the name *Coordination of European Picture Agencies*, as a grouping of the type *European Economic Interest Grouping (EEIG, #06960)*. Subsequently changed title to *Coordination of European Picture Agencies, Press and Stock*. Registration: Start date: 1999, France. **Aims** Preserve *copyright* protection for *photography*; represent the interests of European picture agencies at international level; promote uniformity of regulations pertaining to photographers, picture agencies and users; develop ethical standards. **Structure** Steering Committee; Board; Administration, headed by Executive Director. **Languages** English. **Staff** 2.00 FTE, paid. **Finance** Members' dues. Sale of publications; congress proceeds. **Activities** Advocacy/lobbying/activism; standards/guidelines; events/meetings. **Events** *Congress* Juan-les-Pins (France) 2023, *Congress* Paris (France) 2019, *Congress* Berlin (Germany) 2018, *Congress* Berlin (Germany) 2017, *Congress* Zagreb (Croatia) 2016. **Publications** *CEPIC Newsletter*. Guidelines.
Members Full National organizations in 7 countries:
France, Germany, Netherlands, Spain, Sweden, Switzerland, UK.
Associate Affiliates in 27 countries:
Austria, Canada, Czechia, Denmark, Finland, France, Germany, Greece, Hungary, India, Ireland, Israel, Italy, Korea Rep, Norway, Poland, Portugal, Romania, Russia, Slovakia, Slovenia, Spain, Türkiye, UK, Ukraine, USA.
Consultative Status Consultative status granted from: *World Intellectual Property Organization (WIPO, #21593)* (Permanent Observer Status). **NGO Relations** Member of: *Initiative for a Competitive Online Marketplace (ICOMP, #11209)*; *International Press Telecommunications Council (IPTC, #14637)*; *Linked Content Coalition (LCC)*. [2022/XF4524/**F**]

- Coordination européenne des Amis de la terre / see Friends of the Earth Europe (#10001)
- Coordination européenne des Amis de la Terre Europe (#10001)
- Coordination européenne pour le droit des étrangers à vivre en famille (#06794)
- Coordination européenne des immigrés (inactive)
- Coordination européenne JECI-MIEC – Coordination européenne Jeunesse étudiante catholique internationale – Mouvement international d'étudiants catholiques (inactive)
- Coordination européenne Jeunesse étudiante catholique internationale – Mouvement international d'étudiants catholiques (inactive)
- Coordination européenne des maisons de jeunes et de la culture 'Youthclubs and Youth Associations / see Contact-2103 (#04775)
- Coordination européenne de MJC, Youthclubs and Youth Associations / see Contact-2103 (#04775)
- Coordination européenne des producteurs indépendants / see European Audiovisual Production (#06295)
- Coordination Européenne Via Campesina (#06795)

♦ Coordination Group of Arab National and Regional Development Institutions 04826

Secretariat c/o Arab Fund for Economic and Social Development, PO Box 21923, 13080 Safat, Kuwait. T. +96524959000. Fax +96524815750 – +96524815760. E-mail: hq@arabfund.org.

History Founded 1975, the original idea having been adopted in 1974. Previously also referred to as *Coordination Committee between National and Regional Arab Development Institutions*. **Aims** Coordinate Arab funds' activities; optimize the use of available resources and competence; synchronize funding policies and operating procedures; increase the efficiency of Arab aid; help beneficiary countries obtain the required funding for their high priority projects; avoid overlapping and duplication of donors efforts; increase the efficiency of utilization of resources; coordinate project evaluation activities; apply unified rules and procedures at the project implementation stage; exchange information and data relating to projects and development plans; coordinate interventions with international and regional financing institutions; arrange meetings; follow up recommendations. **Structure** AFESD provides secretariat. **Languages** Arabic, English, French. **Activities** Events/meetings; projects/programmes. **Events** *Meeting of the Heads of Institutions* Vienna (Austria) 2016, *Meeting* Riyadh (Saudi Arabia) 2005. **Publications** Reports.
Members (9):
Abu Dhabi Fund for Development (Abu Dhabi Fund); *Arab Bank for Economic Development in Africa (#00904)*; *Arab Fund for Economic and Social Development (AFESD, #00965)*; *Arab Gulf Programme for United Nations Development Organizations (AGFUND, #00971)*; *Arab Monetary Fund (AMF, #01009)*; *Islamic Development Bank (IsDB, #16044)*; *Kuwait Fund for Arab Economic Development (KFAED)*; *OPEC Fund for International Development (OFID, #17745)*; Qatar Development fund (QDF); *Saudi Fund for Development (SFD)*.
[2017.12.11/XE3164/y/**E**]

♦ Coordination Group for Meteorological Satellites (CGMS) 04827

Secretariat c/o EUMETSAT, Eumetsat-Allee 1, 64295 Darmstadt, Germany. T. +4961518074190. Fax +4961518076150. E-mail: cgmssec@eumetsat.int.
URL: http://www.cgms-info.org/

History 19 Sep 1972, Washington DC (USA), when representatives of European Space Research Organisation – since 1975 *European Space Agency (ESA, #08798)*, Japan, USA, Observers from *World Meteorological Organization (WMO, #21649)* and Joint Planning Staff for the Global Atmosphere Research Programme met. **Aims** Coordinate operational meteorological satellite systems, including protection of in orbit assets, contingency planning, improvement of quality of data, support to users, facilitation of shared data access and development of the use of satellite products in key application areas. **Structure** CGMS Plenary (annual); Working Groups; Task Team; Secretariat, hosted by: *European Organisation for the Exploitation of Meteorological Satellites (EUMETSAT, #08096)*. **Languages** English. **Staff** None. **Finance** Members contribute staff and working time. Costs of rotating plenary provided by hosting members. **Events** *International Winds Workshop* Jeju (Korea Rep) 2018, *Meeting* Jeju (Korea Rep) 2017.
Members Agencies in 7 countries:
China, France, India, Japan, Korea Rep, Russia, USA.
Regional agencies (4):
European Organisation for the Exploitation of Meteorological Satellites (EUMETSAT, #08096); *European Space Agency (ESA, #08798)*; *Intergovernmental Oceanographic Commission (IOC, #11496)*; *World Meteorological Organization (WMO, #21649)*. [2019.12.18/XJ7741/y/**E***]

- Coordination des initiatives populaires de solidarité internationale (internationally oriented national body)
- Coordination et initiatives pour réfugiés et étrangers (internationally oriented national body)
- Coordination internationale pour une culture de non-violence et de paix (#14247)
- Coordination Internationale de la Jeunesse Ouvrière Chrétienne (#12960)
- Coordination nationale des ONG de Solidarité, Urgence et Développement / see Coordination SUD
- Coordination of Nongovernmental Organizations for International Development Cooperation (internationally oriented national body)
- Coordination Office for International Development and Mission of the Austrian Bishops' Conference (internationally oriented national body)
- Coordination des ONG de coopération pour le développement (internationally oriented national body)
- Coordination des organisations des droits de l'homme d'Amérique centrale (inactive)
- Coordination des organisations familiales catholiques en Europe / see Federation of Catholic Family Associations in Europe (#09468)
- Coordination paysanne européenne / see European Coordination Via Campesina (#06795)
- Coordination Platform of Youth Organizations in Latin America / see Foro Latinoamericano de Juventud (#09881)
- Coordination régionale de recherches économiques et sociales (#04812)
- Coordination for Southern Africa (internationally oriented national body)
- Coordination SUD (internationally oriented national body)

♦ Coordination for Tomorrow's Africa 04828

Coordination pour l'Afrique de demain (CADE)
Main Office 33 ave Philippe Auguste, 75011 Paris, France.
URL: http://www.afrique-demain.org/

History 1995. Registered in accordance with French law. **Aims** Campaign against Afro-*pessimism*. **Structure** Executive Committee. **Publications** *La lettre de la CADE* (10 a year). [2021/XE4224/**E**]

- Coordination verte des verts européens / see European Green Party (#07409)
- Coordinator of Galician Development NGOs (internationally oriented national body)
- Coordinator of Latin American Cinema and Communication Indigenous Peoples (#04806)
- Coordinator of Spanish Nongovernmental Development Organizations (internationally oriented national body)
- COPABA / see FIBA Americas (#09745)
- **COPABE** Confederación Panamericana de Béisbol (#04468)
- **COPAC** Committee for the Promotion and Advancement of Cooperatives (#04279)
- **COPAC** Confederación Panamericana de Canoas (#04471)
- **COPACE** Comité des pêches pour l'Atlantique centre-Est (#09784)
- **COPACI** Confederación Panamericana de Ciclismo (#18092)
- **COPA** Coalition for Peace in Africa (#04064)
- **COPACO** Comisión de Pesca para el Atlantico Centro-Occidental (#20911)
- **COPACO** Commission des pêches pour l'Atlantique centre-Ouest (#20911)
- COPA / see Confederación Parlamentaria de las Américas (#04479)
- **COPA** Confederación Parlamentaria de las Américas (#04479)
- COPA / see COPA – european farmers (#04829)
- **COPA** COPA – european farmers (#04829)
- COPACS / see Central American Federation of Pharmaceutical Industries (#03669)
- **COPADET** Confederación Panamericana del Deporte de los Trabajadores (#04473)

♦ COPA – european farmers (COPA) 04829

SG Rue de Trèves 61, 1040 Brussels, Belgium. T. +3222872711. Fax +3222872700. E-mail: communication.consultant@copa-cogeca.eu – mail@copa-cogeca.eu.
URL: http://www.copa-cogeca.eu/

History 6 Sep 1958, Brussels (Belgium). Secretariat set up, 1 Apr 1959, Brussels; merged, 1 Dec 1962, with that of *General Confederation of Agricultural Cooperatives in the European Union (#10107)*. Currently known under its acronym. Integrated activities of *European Confederation of Agriculture (CEA, inactive)* with COGECA, Jul 2006. Former names and other names: *Committee of Agricultural Organizations in the EC* – former (6 Sep 1958); *Comité des organisations professionnelles agricoles de la CE* – former (6 Sep 1958); *Ausschuss der Berufsständischen Landwirtschaftlichen Organisationen der EG* – former (6 Sep 1958); *Comitato delle Organizzazioni Professionali Agricole della CE* – former (6 Sep 1958); *Committee of Agricultural Organizations in the EU* – former; *Comité des organisations professionnelles agricoles de l'UE (COPA)* – former; *Committee of Professional Agricultural Organizations in the EU* – former; *Comité des Organizaciones Profesionales Agrarias de la Unión Europea* – former; *Ausschuss der Berufsständischen Landwirtschaftlichen Organisationen der Europäischen Union* – former; *Comitato delle Organizzazioni Professionali Agricole dell'Unione Europea* – former. Registration: EU Transparency Register, No/ID: 44856881231-49. **Aims** Represent general and specific interests of *farmers* in discussions with the EU institutions and other EU bodies; coordinate proposals in order to define common attitudes to be submitted to *European Union* institutions; defend the interests of agriculture as a whole; examine any matters related to the development of the Common Agricultural Policy (CAP), in coordination with COGECA; maintain and develop relations with Comunity authorities and with any other representative organizations or social partners established at the European level. **Structure** Praesidium; Conference (every 2 years); Presidency; Policy Coordination Committee (POCC); Secretariat, headed by Secretary General. Liaison with COGECA: Coordination Committee; Secretariat; Finance and Management Committee; Joint Working Parties. **Languages** English, French, German, Italian, Polish, Spanish. **Staff** Permanent staff of the joint COPA/COGECA Secretariat: about 50. **Finance** Members' dues. **Activities** Events/meetings; advocacy/lobbying/activism. **Events** *Congress of European Farmers* Sibenik (Croatia) 2022, *Congress of European Farmers* 2020, *Congress of European Farmers* Linz (Austria) 2018, *Conference on Availability of Animal Health Solutions for the Future of Livestock in Europe* Brussels (Belgium) 2017, *Workshop on Farmers, Forest Owners and their Cooperatives* Brussels (Belgium) 2017. **Publications** Fact sheets; position papers; press releases; congress brochures.
Members National associations (60) in 26 EU countries:
Austria, Belgium, Cyprus, Czechia, Denmark, Estonia, Finland, France, Germany, Greece, Hungary, Ireland, Italy, Latvia, Lithuania, Luxembourg, Malta, Netherlands, Poland, Portugal, Romania, Slovakia, Slovenia, Spain, Sweden, UK.
Consultative Status Consultative status granted from: *ECOSOC (#05331)* (Ros C); *FAO (#09260)* (Liaison Status). **IGO Relations** Liaises with: *European Parliament (EP, #08146)*. Recognized by: *European Commission (EC, #06633)*. Member of Agricultural Advisory Group. Member of: *European Economic and Social Committee (EESC, #06963)*. Observer status with: *Intergovernmental Negotiating Committee for a Legally Binding Agreement on Forests in Europe (INC-Forests, inactive)*; *Union internationale pour la protection des obtentions végétales (UPOV, #20436)*. **NGO Relations** Member of (8): *Agri-Food Chain Coalition (AFCC, #00577)*; *Alliance for Internet of Things Innovation (AIOTI, #00697)*; *Circular Plastics Alliance (#03936)*; *European Aquaculture Technology and Innovation Platform (EATIP, #05910)*; *European Bioeconomy Alliance (EUBA, #06334)*; *European Technology Platform 'Plants for the Future' (Plant ETP, #08890)*; *TP Organics – European Technology Platform (TP Organics, #20180)*; *Water Europe (WE, #20828)*. Founding Member of: *European Food Sustainable Consumption and Production Round Table (European Food SCP Roundtable, #07289)*. Associate member of: *European Network of Agricultural Journalists (ENAJ, #07864)*. Close cooperation with: COGECA. Liaison Committee with: *International Confederation of European Beet Growers (CIBE, #12860)*.
[2019/XE0297/**E**]

- COPAFE – Comité protestant des amitiés françaises à l'étranger (internationally oriented national body)
- **COPAGEN** Coalition pour la Protection du Patrimoine Génétique Africain (#04065)
- COPAJE-AF – Conseil promotionnel pour l'action des jeunes en Afrique (unconfirmed)
- COPAL – Alliance of Cocoa Producing Countries (no recent information)
- COPAL / see Federación Psicoanalitica de América Latina (#09386)
- COPAMEDE – Confederación Pan Americana de Medicina del Deporte (no recent information)
- COPANARCO / see World Archery Americas (#21106)
- **COPANT** Comisión Panamericana de Normas Técnicas (#18133)
- **COPAPROSE** Confederación Panamericana de Productores de Seguros (#18088)
- **COPARCO** World Archery Americas (#21106)
- **COPARE** Confederación Panamericana de Remo (#04478)
- COPA – Symposium on Conformal and Probabilistic Prediction with Applications (meeting series)
- COPATI – Comité Panamericano de Transporte Integral (unconfirmed)
- **COPAX** Council for Peace and Security in Central Africa (#04913)
- CoP – Community of Practice for Caribbean Immigrant Entrepreneurs (unconfirmed)
- COp – Congregatio pro Operariis Christianis a Sancto Iosepho Calasanctio (religious order)
- **COPEAM** Conférence permanente de l'audiovisuel méditerranéen (#18320)
- **COPEAM** Permanent Conference of Mediterranean Audiovisual Operators (#18320)
- **COPE** Children of Prisoners Europe (#03875)
- **COPE** Committee on Publication Ethics (#04281)
- **COPE** Congress of Political Economists, International (#04678)
- COPE – Cooperazione Paesi Emergenti (internationally oriented national body)
- COPE – Council of Pacific Education (unconfirmed)
- **COPECSA** College of Pathologists of East Central and Southern Africa (#04109)
- COPEDEC – International Conference on Coastal and Port Engineering in Developing Countries (meeting series)

- ♦ COPED Europe – Conseil pour l'éducation et le développement Europe (internationally oriented national body)
- ♦ COPE International / see Congress of Political Economists, International (#04678)
- ♦ Copenhagen Agreement (1972 treaty)
- ♦ Copenhagen amendment – Amendment to the Montreal Protocol on Substances That Deplete the Ozone Layer, 1992 (1992 treaty)
- ♦ Copenhagen Institute for Futures Studies (internationally oriented national body)
- ♦ Copenhagen International Theatre (internationally oriented national body)

♦ COPERNICUS Alliance – European Network on Higher Education for Sustainable Development (CA) 04830

Communications Manager address not obtained. E-mail: office@copernicus-alliance.org.
URL: http://www.copernicus-alliance.org/

History Founded 1988 as a special project of the *Association of European Universities (CRE, inactive)*. COPERNICUS Campus was launched and CRE COPERNICUS Charta published in 1993. Activities reframed and network strengthened in 2007. Official constitution 2010, Graz (Austria). Updated version of the COPERNICUS Charta in 2011. Former names and other names: *Cooperative Programme in Europe for Research on Nature and Industry through Coordinated University Studies (COPERNICUS CAMPUS)* – former (1988 to 2007); *CRE – Copernicus Programme* – former. Registration: No/ID: VR200489, Germany. **Aims** Enable European higher education institutions and their partners to jointly identify challenges in higher education for sustainable development (HESD) and spearhead development of processes, tools and knowledge to address these challenges. **Structure** Leadership Team; Advisory Board. **Languages** English. **Finance** Sources: members' dues. **Activities** Capacity building; events/meetings; knowledge management/information dissemination; publishing activities; research/documentation. **Events** *Higher Education Summit* Hasselt (Belgium) 2022, *Higher Education Summit* Hasselt (Belgium) 2021, *Higher Education Summit* Bern (Switzerland) 2020, *Conference* Bern (Switzerland) 2019, *Future Forward Summit* Brussels (Belgium) 2018. **Publications** *Do European quality assurance frameworks support integration of transformative learning for sustainable development in higher education?* (2022) in English; *Guidelines for Virtual Conferencing – inspired by the COPERNICUS Alliance Online Conference 2019* – Diethart M. , Zimmermann A.B. , Mulà I. 2020. Bern, Switzerland: CDE and COPERNICUS Alliance. DOI: 10.7892/boris.139254; *Virtual conferences in higher education: Teasing out their transformative potential for sustainable development* – Mader C, Zimmermann AB, Diethart M, Mulà I. in GAIA – Ecological Perspectives for Science and Society, Volume 29, Number 1, 2020, pp. 57-59(3).
Members Higher education institutions (over 20) in 13 countries:
Andorra, Austria, Belgium, Czechia, Germany, Greece, Lithuania, Netherlands, Poland, Slovenia, Spain, Sweden, Switzerland.
[2022.05.04/XE2255/**E**]

- ♦ COPERNICUS CAMPUS / see COPERNICUS Alliance – European Network on Higher Education for Sustainable Development (#04830)
- ♦ **COPESCAALC** Comisión de Pesca Continental y Acuicultura para América Latina y el Caribe (#04142)
- ♦ COPESCAL / see Comisión de Pesca Continental y Acuicultura para América Latina y el Caribe (#04142)
- ♦ **COPEVET** Consejo Panamericano de Educación en las Ciencias Veterinarias (#18091)
- ♦ COPHy EU – Annual Congress on Controversies in Ophthalmology: Europe (meeting series)
- ♦ **COPIMERA** Confederación Panamericana de Ingenieria Mecanica, Eléctrica y Ramas Afines (#18089)
- ♦ Coping International / see Children of Priests International
- ♦ COPING INTERNATIONAL – Children of Priests International (internationally oriented national body)
- ♦ **COPPEM** Comitato Permanente per il Partenariato Euromediterraneo dei Poteri Locali e Regionali (#19954)
- ♦ Copper Alliance / see International Copper Association (#12962)
- ♦ Copper Development Association (internationally oriented national body)
- ♦ Copper Development Association Africa (internationally oriented national body)
- ♦ Copper Development Centre of South East Asia / see International Copper Association Southeast Asia

♦ Coppieters Foundation 04831

Headquarters Boomkwekerijstraat 1, 1000 Brussels, Belgium. T. +3225137224. E-mail: info@ideasforeurope.eu.
URL: https://ideasforeurope.eu/

History 2007. A European Political Foundation, founded and recognized by *European Parliament (EP, #08146)*. Former names and other names: *Centre Maurits Coppieters (CMC)* – former. Registration: Moniteur belge, No/ID: 892.342.491, Belgium. **Aims** Develop new ideas and produce knowledge on the management of cultural and linguistic *diversity*, collective and minority *rights*, multi-level *governance*, decentralization, state and constitutional *reform*, statehood processes, self-determination, migration, peace studies and the protection of human rights in *Europe*. **Structure** General Assembly; Bureau; Advisory Scientific Council. **Languages** English. **Staff** 2.50 FTE, paid. **Finance** Supported by: *European Parliament (EP, #08146)* (and its members). Annual budget: 671,224 EUR (2021). **Activities** Capacity building; events/meetings; research/documentation; training/education. Europe. **Events** *Feminisms from the Peripheries* Brussels (Belgium) 2022, *European Workshop on Geopolitics* Santiago de Compostela (Spain) 2022, *Round Table* Ajaccio (France) 2020. **Publications** *Facing the New Far Right in Southern Europe – Encarant la nova dreta radical del sud d'Europa* (1st ed 2021) in Catalan, English; *Post-Covid Europe* (1st 2021) by Serafin Pazos-Vidal and Andreia Silva et al in English; *Self-Determination in a Context of Shared Sovereignty* (2020) by Montserrat Guibernau and Maggie Lennon et al in English; *The New Audiovisual Paradigm and Non-Hegemonic Languages* (1st ed 2020) by Josu Amezaga Albizu and Carlos Ares et al in English. *Challenges and solutions to International Peace and Security* (2022) in English; *Contribution to the Conference on the Future of Europe* (2022) in English.
Members Full in 8 countries:
Belgium, Croatia, France, Greece, Hungary, Italy, Spain, UK.
NGO Relations Cooperates with (5): *European Association of Daily Newspapers in Minority and Regional Languages (Midas, #06002)*; *European Centre for Minority Issues (ECMI)*; *European Language Equality Network (ELEN, #07647)*; *Network to Promote Linguistic Diversity (NPLD, #17052)*; *Unrepresented Nations and Peoples Organization (UNPO, #20714)*. [2022.10.19/XM8424/f/**F**]

- ♦ **COPPPAL** Conferencia Permanente de Partidos Políticos de América Latina y el Caribe (#04657)
- ♦ **COPROFAM** Confederação das Organizações de Produtores Familiares do Mercosul Ampliado (#04437)
- ♦ Coprogram / see Vlaamse Federatie van NGO's voor Ontwikkelingssamenwerking
- ♦ CoPS – Conference of Philosophical Societies (internationally oriented national body)
- ♦ **COPTAC** Conférence des postes et télécommunications de l'Afrique centrale (#04642)
- ♦ COPTAC / see Conference of Posts and Telecommunications of Central Africa (#04642)
- ♦ **COPUOS** Committee on the Peaceful Uses of Outer Space (#04277)

♦ Copyright for Creativity (C4C) 04832

Coordinator address not obtained. T. +32474840515. E-mail: cdc@n-square.eu.
URL: http://copyright4creativity.eu/

History Set up 2010. Full title: *Copyright for Creativity – A Declaration for Europe*. Also referred to as *Copyright for Creativity Coalition*. EU Transparency Register: 342464912839-08. **Aims** Seek an informed debate on how copyright can more effectively promote innovation, access and creativity. **Structure** General Assembly.
Members Signatories (42) in 11 countries:
Belgium, Bulgaria, Germany, Italy, Lithuania, Netherlands, Poland, Spain, Switzerland, UK, USA.
Included in the above, 19 organizations listed in this Yearbook:
Association of European Research Libraries (#02540); *Bureau Européen des Unions de Consommateurs (BEUC, #03360)*; *Computer and Communications Industry Association (CCIA)*; *Creative Commons International (CCI)*; *Electronic Frontier Foundation (EFF)*; *Electronic Information for Libraries (EIFL, #05425)*; *European Bureau of Library, Information and Documentation Associations (EBLIDA, #06413)*; *European Digital Rights (EDRi, #06924)*; *European Internet Services Providers Association (EuroISPA, #07592)*; *European Network for Copyright in support of Education and Science (ENCES, #07885)*; *Free Software Foundation Europe (FSFE)*; *International Federation of Library Associations and Institutions (IFLA, #13470)*; *International Music Managers' Forum (IMMF, #14200)*; *IP Justice*; *Knowledge Ecology International (KEI, #16200)*; *Network of European Museum Organizations (NEMO, #17024)*; *OpenForum Europe (OFE)*; *Open Knowledge International*; *Special Libraries Association (SLA)*. [2017/XM6129/y/**F**]

- ♦ Copyright for Creativity Coalition / see Copyright for Creativity (#04832)
- ♦ Copyright for Creativity – A Declaration for Europe / see Copyright for Creativity (#04832)
- ♦ CORA – Confederación Odontológica Regional Andina (inactive)
- ♦ **CORAF** Conseil Ouest et Centre Africain pour la Recherche et le Développement Agricoles (#20907)
- ♦ CORAF / see West and Central African Council for Agricultural Research and Development (#20907)
- ♦ CORA – International Congress on Controversies in Rheumatology and Autoimmunity (meeting series)
- ♦ **CORAL** Consejo Regional de Ingeniería Biomédica para América Latina (#04724)
- ♦ CORAL – The Coral Reef Alliance (internationally oriented national body)
- ♦ Coral Guardian (internationally oriented national body)
- ♦ The Coral Reef Alliance (internationally oriented national body)
- ♦ Coral Restoration Foundation (internationally oriented national body)

♦ Coral Triangle Initiative on Coral Reefs, Fisheries and Food Security (CTI-CFF) 04833

Regional Secretariat CTI Center Bldg, Jl A A Maramis Kayuwatu, Kairagi II, Manado 95254, Indonesia. T. +624317241927. E-mail: regional.secretariat@cticff.org.
URL: http://coraltriangleinitiative.org/

History Aug 2007. Formally endorsed in *Asia-Pacific Economic Cooperation (APEC, #01887)* Leaders Declaration on Climate Change, Energy Security and Clean Development, Sep 2007; and further endorsed by *Brunei Darussalam-Indonesia-Malaysia-Philippine – East ASEAN Growth Area (BIMP-EAGA, #03340)* and *ASEAN (#01141)*. Regional Plan of Action (CTI RPOA) adopted, 2009. **Aims** Preserve and manage the marine, coastal and small islands ecosystems and unique biodiversity of the Coral Triangle region of the Indo Pacific. **Structure** Council of Ministries (CTI COM); Committee of Senior Officials (CTI CSO); National Coordinating Committees (NCCs); Regional Secretariat. **Languages** English. **Staff** 10.00 FTE, paid. **Finance** Member States' contributions. Funding for projects/activities from development partners and interested parties. Annual budget (2018): US$ 948,735. **Activities** Awards/prizes/competitions; capacity building; events/meetings; knowledge management/information dissemination; networking/liaising; projects/programmes; standards/guidelines; training/education. **Events** *Senior Officials Meeting* Dili (Timor-Leste) 2014, *Senior Officials Meeting* Manila (Philippines) 2013, *Senior Officials Meeting* Kuala Lumpur (Malaysia) 2012, *Senior official meeting / Summit* Manado (Indonesia) 2009, *Summit* Manado (Indonesia) 2009. **Publications** *CTI-CFF Newsletter*. Action plans; guidelines; toolkits; brochures; technical reports.
Members Governments (6):
Indonesia, Malaysia, Papua New Guinea, Philippines, Solomon Is, Timor-Leste.
IGO Relations Partners include: *Asian Development Bank (ADB, #01422)*; Australian Government – Department of Energy and Environment; *Deutsche Gesellschaft für Internationale Zusammenarbeit (GIZ)*; *Secretariat of the Pacific Regional Environment Programme (SPREP, #19205)*; *Southeast Asian Fisheries Development Center (SEAFDEC, #19767)*; *United States Agency for International Development (USAID)*. **NGO Relations** Partners include: *Conservation International (CI)*; Coral Triangle Center; *The Nature Conservancy (TNC)*; *Wildlife Conservation Society (WCS)*; *World Wide Fund for Nature (WWF, #21922)*; universities. [2020/XJ0377/**E***]

- ♦ Cor Ardens, International Society of Artists (inactive)
- ♦ Cor Ardens, Société internationale des artistes (inactive)
- ♦ **CORAT Africa** Christian Organization Research and Advisory Trust of Africa (#03906)
- ♦ CORC / see Caritas Australia
- ♦ **COR** Club of Rome (#04038)
- ♦ Cordaid – Catholic Organization for Relief and Development (internationally oriented national body)
- ♦ CORD – Christian Outreach – Relief and Development (internationally oriented national body)
- ♦ CORD – Collegium Orbis Radiologiae Docentium (inactive)
- ♦ CORDE – Caribbean Organization for Rural Development and Education (inactive)
- ♦ Cordell Hull Foundation / see Cordell Hull Foundation for International Education
- ♦ Cordell Hull Foundation for International Education (internationally oriented national body)
- ♦ Cordimarian Filiation (religious order)
- ♦ CORD International (internationally oriented national body)
- ♦ CORDIO / see Coastal Oceans Research and Development – Indian Ocean (#04073)
- ♦ CORDIO East Africa / see Coastal Oceans Research and Development – Indian Ocean (#04073)
- ♦ **CORDIO East Africa** Coastal Oceans Research and Development – Indian Ocean (#04073)
- ♦ Cordis Mariae Filius – Congregatio Missionariorum Filiorum Immaculati Cordis Beatae Virginis Mariae (religious order)
- ♦ CORE – Center for Operations Research and Econometrics (internationally oriented national body)
- ♦ CORE – Centre for OSCE Research (internationally oriented national body)
- ♦ CORE – Community Organized Relief Effort (internationally oriented national body)
- ♦ CORE – Congress of Racial Equality (internationally oriented national body)
- ♦ CORE Group (internationally oriented national body)
- ♦ Core Humanitarian Standard on Quality and Accountability – CHS- Alliance / see CHS Alliance (#03911)

♦ CORE Internet Council of Registrars 04834

Chair 2 Cours de Rive, 1204 Geneva, Switzerland. T. +41223125610. Fax +41223125612. E-mail: secretariat@corenic.org.
URL: http://www.corenic.org/

History 1997. Registered in accordance with Swiss law. **Aims** Operate a shared registration system for Internet domain names. **Structure** Executive Committee, including Chairman and Deputy Chairman.
Members Registrars in 14 countries:
Australia, Austria, Canada, Croatia, Czechia, France, Germany, Italy, Monaco, Netherlands, Portugal, Spain, Switzerland, USA.
NGO Relations Accredited by: *Internet Corporation for Assigned Names and Numbers (ICANN, #15949)*.
[2015/XM0917/**F**]

- ♦ **CORENET Global** Global Corporate Real Estate Network (#10308)
- ♦ **COREP** Comité régional des pêches du Golfe de Guinée (#18785)
- ♦ **COREPER** Comité des représentants permanents de l'Union européenne (#04278)
- ♦ CORE Response / see Community Organized Relief Effort
- ♦ CORESA – Comité Regional de Salud Animal (no recent information)
- ♦ **CORESTA** Centre de coopération pour les recherches scientifiques relatives au tabac (#03735)

♦ Core Technologies for Life Sciences (CTLS) 04835

Contact 25-28 rue du Docteur Roux, 75015 Paris, France. E-mail: contact@ctls-org.eu.
URL: http://www.ctls-org.eu/

Aims Bring together scientists, technical and administrative staff working in or in close association with shared resource laboratories, such as core facilities (CFs), and research infrastructures. **Structure** Executive Council; Board of Directors. Working Groups (5): Communication; Funding; Membership; Networking and Outreach; Training. **Languages** English. **Activities** Events/meetings; guidance/assistance/consulting; certification/accreditation; training/education; networking/liaising. **Events** *Biennial Conference* Lisbon (Portugal) 2021, *Biennial Conference* Lisbon (Portugal) 2020, *Biennial Conference* Ghent (Belgium) 2018, *Biennial Conference* Heidelberg (Germany) 2016, *Biennial Conference* Paris (France) 2014. **Members** Full in 22 countries. Membership countries not specified. [2020.02.06/XM7890/**D**]

- ♦ **CoR** European Committee of the Regions (#06665)
- ♦ COREVIP – Conference of Vice-Chancellors, Presidents and Rectors of Institutions of Higher Learning in Africa (meeting series)
- ♦ Córki Bozje Milósci (religious order)
- ♦ **CORLAS** Collegium Oto-Rhino-Laryngologicum Amicitiae Sacrum (#04117)
- ♦ **CORLEAP** Conference of the Regional and Local Authorities for the Eastern Partnership (#04645)
- ♦ CORMOSEA – Committee on Research Materials on Southeast Asia (internationally oriented national body)
- ♦ Cornea Society (internationally oriented national body)
- ♦ COR-NTD – Coalition for Operational Research on Neglected Tropical Diseases (internationally oriented national body)

♦ Coro das Comunidades Européias / see European Union Choir (#08980)
♦ Coro delle Comunità Europee / see European Union Choir (#08980)
♦ Coro Juvenil Mundial (#21955)

♦ Corona Worldwide 04836

Chairman Room 148 China Works, 100 Black Prince Road, London, SE1 7SJ, UK. T. +442077934020. E-mail: corona@coronaworldwide.org.
URL: http://www.coronaworldwide.org/

History 1950. Established, at behest of Colonial Office, to assist families and women going overseas to work, providing information on local schools, medical facilities and the like. Merged, 1970, with *Women Speakers of the Commonwealth*, which became part of the Society. Current title adopted when membership opened to men. Former names and other names: *Women's Corona Club* – former; *Women's Corona Society* – former. Registration: Charity Commission for England and Wales, No/ID: 240802, Start date: 1962, England and Wales. **Aims** Promote and advance education in, and knowledge of, the peoples and culture of the countries of the world, with special reference to the Commonwealth, offering friendship, understanding and support to prepare those from all walks of life to adapt to new and different environment; offer practical aid locally, particularly to women and children. **Structure** General Meeting (annual); Board of Trustees; Executive Committee. **Languages** English. **Staff** None. **Finance** Sources: fundraising; members' dues. Annual budget: 12,000 GBP. **Activities** Networking/liaising; training/education. **Events** *Annual General Meeting* London (UK) 2021, *Annual General Meeting* London (UK) 2020, *Annual General Meeting* London (UK) 1998, *Annual General Meeting* London (UK) 1997, *Annual General Meeting* London (UK) 1996. **Publications** *Corona News* (2 a year). *Culture Shock, Forty Years of Service: The Women's Corona Society 1950-1990* (1992) by Cecillie Swaisland; *Living in a Muslim Country*.
Members Branches and individuals in 24 countries and territories:
Bahamas, Denmark, Fiji, France, Gibraltar, Greece, Hong Kong, India, Indonesia, Jamaica, Kuwait, Luxembourg, Malawi, Mauritius, New Zealand, Oman, Pakistan, Saudi Arabia, South Africa, St Helena, UK, USA, Zambia, Zimbabwe.
NGO Relations Member of (2): *Council of Commonwealth Societies (CCS, #04878)*; *Federation of International Women's Associations in London (FIWAL)*. Also links with British and Commonwealth women's organizations in European Union countries. [2021.06.09/XD2589/**F**]

♦ Coronelli World League of Friends of the Globe / see International Coronelli Society for the Study of Globes (#12967)
♦ Coros de las Comunidades Europeas / see European Union Choir (#08980)
♦ Coros de la Unión Europea / see European Union Choir (#08980)
♦ Coro da União Européia / see European Union Choir (#08980)
♦ Coro dell'Unione Europea / see European Union Choir (#08980)
♦ Corporação Iberoamericana de Loterias e Apostas de Estado (#04838)
♦ Corporação Interamericana de Investimentos (#11438)
♦ Corporación Africana de Reaseguros (#00438)
♦ Corporación Andina de Fomento / see Development Bank of Latin America (#05055)
♦ Corporación Asiatica de Reaseguros (#01685)
♦ Corporación de Bibliotecarios, Archiveros y Conservadores de Museos del Caribe (inactive)

♦ Corporación Centroamericana de Servicios de Navegación Aérea (COCESNA) 04837

Corporation des services de navigation aérienne d'Amérique centrale – Central American Corporation for Air Navigation Services

Exec Pres Apartado Postal No 660, Tegucigalpa, Francisco Morazán, Honduras. T. +50422757090. Fax +5042342550. E-mail: relacionespublicas@cocesna.org.
Street Address 150 Mts al Sur Aeropuerto Toncontin, Tegucigalpa, Francisco Morazán, Honduras.
URL: http://www.cocesna.org/

History 26 Feb 1960, Tegucigalpa (Honduras), as *Central American Air Safety Services Corporation*, on signature of agreement by 5 Central American governments. The Convention was subsequently ratified by the governments of Honduras (17 May 1960), Nicaragua (30 Jun 1960), Guatemala (Guatemala) (8 Jun 1961), El Salvador (14 Sep 1961), Costa Rica (20 Nov 1963). Statutes registered in *'UNTS 1/6022'* and *ICAO 1597*. Belize (Belize) subscribed the document, 1 Oct 1996. **Aims** Protect human life in the air space of Central America by putting into operation speedy, safe and efficient installations and services for aerial navigation and *telecommunications*. **Structure** Board of Directors; Officers: President and Vice-President. Area Services: *Agencia Centroamericana de Navegación Aérea (ACNA, see: #04837)*; *Agencia Centroamericana de Seguridad Aeronautica (ACSA, see: #04837)*; *Instituto Centroamericano de Capacitación Aeronautica (ICCAE, see: #04837)*. **Languages** English, Spanish. **Finance** 'Flight protection charge' on aircraft using Central American airspace; renting of frequency channels and communications services; support also from fees for services of ICCAE. **Activities** Training/education; events/meetings. **Events** *Anniversary meeting* Honduras 2010, *Anniversary meeting* Tegucigalpa (Honduras) 1990, *Meeting* 1986, *Meeting* 1986, *Meeting* 1986.
Members Governments of 6 countries:
Belize, Costa Rica, El Salvador, Guatemala, Honduras, Nicaragua.
IGO Relations Specialized Institution of: *Central American Integration System (#03671)*. **NGO Relations** Member of: *International Federation of Air Traffic Controllers' Associations (IFATCA, #13350)*.
[2017/XF0228/e/**F***]

♦ Corporación Pro-Cruzada Mundial (#20850)
♦ Corporación Financiera Internacional (#13597)

♦ Corporación Iberoamericana de Loterias y Apuestas de Estado (CIBELAE) 04838

Iberoamerican Corporation of State Lotteries and Betting – Corporation Ibéroaméricaine de Loteries et de Paris d'État – Corporação Iberoamericana de Loterias e Apostas de Estado

Exec Dir Av Congreso 2157 ° A, C1428BVE Buenos Aires, Argentina.
URL: https://cibelae.net/

History Oct 1988, Madrid (Spain). **Structure** Executive Committee. **Languages** Portuguese, Spanish. **Staff** 6.00 FTE, voluntary. **Finance** Sources: members' dues. **Events** *Congress* Brazil 2011, *Security seminar* Acapulco (Mexico) 2010, *Congress* Chile 2009, *Seminar on responsible gaming and marketing* Lima (Peru) 2008, *Responsible gaming and marketing* Mexico 2008.
Members Regular; Associate. Regular members in 20 countries:
Argentina, Bolivia, Brazil, Chile, Colombia, Costa Rica, Dominican Rep, Ecuador, El Salvador, France, Honduras, Mexico, Nicaragua, Panama, Paraguay, Portugal, Puerto Rico, Spain, Uruguay, Venezuela.
Associate members in 9 countries:
Argentina, Austria, Brazil, Canada, Chile, France, Germany, Spain, USA.
Observer in 5 countries:
Colombia, Dominican Rep, Guatemala, Honduras, Uruguay.
NGO Relations Regional association of: *World Lottery Association (WLA, #21628)*. [2021/XD7714/**D**]

♦ Corporación Interamericana de Inversiones (#11438)
♦ Corporación de Inversiones del Caribe (inactive)
♦ Corporación de Solución de Controversias sobre Frutas y Hortalizas (#10009)
♦ Corpora for Language and Aging Research (meeting series)
♦ Corporate Accountability International (internationally oriented national body)
♦ Corporate Council on Africa (internationally oriented national body)

♦ Corporate Europe Observatory (CEO) 04839

Main Office Rue d'Edimbourg 26, 1050 Brussels, Belgium. T. +3228930930. E-mail: ceo@corporateeurope.org.
Registered Office Vismarkt 15, 6511 VJ Nijmegen, Netherlands.
URL: http://corporateeurope.org/

History Founded 1997, Amsterdam (Netherlands). A research and campaign group. Registered in accordance with Dutch law. **Aims** Target threats to democracy, equity, social justice and the environment posed by the economic and political power of *corporations* and their *lobby* groups. **Structure** International Advisory Board. **Languages** Dutch, English, French, German, Spanish. **Finance** Donations from individual supporters; grants from trusts and grant-making foundations. **Activities** Research/documentation; events/meetings; training/education; advocacy/lobbying/activism. **Publications** Online publications. **Members** Not a membership organization. **NGO Relations** Member of: *EDC Free Europe (#05355)*; [2019.12.12/XG8784/**F**]

♦ Corporate Funding Programme (internationally oriented national body)

♦ Corporate Leaders Network for Climate Action (CLN) 04840

Main Office CISL, 1 Trumpington Str, Cambridge, CB2 1QA, UK. T. +441223768840. Fax +441223768831. E-mail: clg@cisl.cam.ac.uk.
URL: http://www.corporateleadersgroup.com/

History 2010. Founded by *CLG Europe*. Convened by the University of Cambridge Institute for Sustainability Leadership (CISL). After a period of dormancy, relaunched at COP27, 2022. **Aims** Create political space for government action in support of low carbon societies.
Members Full in 11 countries and territories:
Brazil, Chile, Germany, Hong Kong, Ireland, Japan, Korea Rep, Spain, Türkiye, UK, USA.
Regional entity:
CLG Europe. [2022/XJ5128/**E**]

♦ Corporate and Marketing Communication Association (unconfirmed)

♦ Corporate Registers Forum (CRF) 04841

Registry Services Manager Operations Manager Registries, New Zealand Companies Office, Ministry of Business Development and Employment, Companies Office, Private Bag 92061, Auckland 1142, New Zealand. T. +6499164541. Fax +6499164559. E-mail: corporateregistersforum@gmail.com.
URL: http://www.corporateregistersforum.org/

History Inaugurated Feb 2003, Auckland (New Zealand), as *Asia Pacific Corporate Registers Forum (APCRF)*. Constitution adopted 11 Mar 2005, Melbourne (Australia), when current title was adopted. Constitution amended 3 Apr 2008, Vancouver BC (Canada) and 14 Mar 2013, Auckland (New Zealand). Registered under the Hong Kong Business Ordinance as an unincorporated entity, 2006. **Aims** Provide delegates with the opportunity to review the latest developments in corporate business registers internationally and exchange experiences and information on the present and future operation of corporate business registration systems. **Structure** General Meeting (annual); Executive Committee. **Languages** English. **Staff** Voluntary. **Finance** Members' dues. **Activities** Networking/liaising; events/meetings. **Events** *Annual Conference* Gaborone (Botswana) 2018, *Annual Conference* Hong Kong (Hong Kong) 2017, *Annual Conference* Cardiff (UK) 2016, *Annual Conference* Abu Dhabi (United Arab Emirates) 2015, *Annual Conference* Rio de Janeiro (Brazil) 2014. **Publications** *CRF Newsletter* (4 a year).
Members Jurisdictions (60) in 57 countries and territories:
Anguilla, Australia, Azerbaijan, Bangladesh, Bermuda, Botswana, Cambodia, Canada, Colombia, Cook Is, Germany, Ghana, Gibraltar, Guernsey, Hong Kong, Ireland, Israel, Jersey, Kenya, Kiribati, Kuwait, Labuan, Lesotho, Malaysia, Maldives, Mauritius, Mongolia, Myanmar, Namibia, Netherlands, New Zealand, Nigeria, North Macedonia, Pakistan, Philippines, Qatar, Romania, Russia, Samoa, Sierra Leone, Singapore, South Africa, Spain, Sri Lanka, Suriname, Thailand, Timor-Leste, Tonga, Tunisia, Türkiye, Uganda, UK, United Arab Emirates, Vanuatu, Vietnam, Virgin Is UK, Zambia. [2022/XJ7777/c/**F**]

♦ Corporate Responsibility Research Conference (meeting series)

♦ Corporate Secretaries International Association (CSIA) 04842

CEO 3F HK Diamond Exchange, 8 Duddell St, Hong Kong, Central and Western, Hong Kong.
URL: http://www.csiaorg.com/

History Dec 2009, Geneva (Switzerland). Launched 22 Mar 2010, Paris (France). Registration: Switzerland. **Aims** Be the global voice of corporate secretaries and governance professionals; develop and grow the study and practice of secretaryship to improve professional standards, the quality of governance practice and to improve organizational performance. **Structure** Council; Executive Committee. **Activities** Advocacy/lobbying/activism; events/meetings. **Events** *Council Meeting* Hong Kong (Hong Kong) 2018, *Annual General Meeting* Bangkok (Thailand) 2016, *International Corporate Governance Conference* Delhi (India) 2013, *Round Table* Kuala Lumpur (Malaysia) 2013, *Round Table* New York, NY (USA) 2012. **Publications** *CSIA Corporate Secretaries Toolkit* (2014); *Governance Principles for Corporate Secretaries* (2013); *Twenty Practical steps to Better Corporate Governance* (2010).
Members National institutes and associations in 18 countries and territories:
Australia, Bangladesh, Canada, Hong Kong, India, Indonesia, Kenya, Malaysia, Mongolia, New Zealand, Nigeria, Singapore, South Africa, Sri Lanka, Thailand, UK, USA, Zimbabwe. [2022/XM3939/**C**]

♦ Corporate Social Responsibility in Asia (CSR Asia) 04843

Hong Kong Office 20/F Leighton Centre, 77 Leighton Road, Causeway Bay, Hong Kong. E-mail: info@csr-asia.com.
URL: http://www.csr-asia.com/

History 2004, Hong Kong. Provide information, research, training and analysis of *corporate social responsibility* issues in the Asia Pacific region. 2017, acquired by ELEVATE. **Structure** Offices (5): Australia; Hong Kong; Japan; Singapore; Thailand. **Activities** Organizes conferences and training courses. **Events** *Community Investment Forum* Singapore (Singapore) 2015, *Annual Summit* Bangkok (Thailand) 2013, *Annual Summit* Beijing (China) 2012, *Annual Summit* Beijing (China) 2012, *International Conference on Governance and Accountability (ICGA)* Kuching (Malaysia) 2012. **Publications** *CSR Asia Weekly*. **Members** Not a membership organization. [2019/XM1297/e/**F**]

♦ Corporation des bibliothécaires, archivistes et conservateurs de musée des Caraïbes (inactive)
♦ Corporation of Caribbean Librarians, Archivists, and Curators of Museums (inactive)
♦ Corporation européenne des ébénistes restaurateurs (internationally oriented national body)
♦ Corporation Ibéroaméricaine de Loteries et de Paris d'État (#04838)
♦ Corporation de règlement des différends dans les fruits et légumes (#10009)
♦ Corporation des services de navigation aérienne d'Amérique centrale (#04837)
♦ Corps commun d'inspection des Nations Unies (#16133)
♦ Corps diplomatique (#05089)
♦ Corps européen (#05671)

♦ Corps of Imperial Frontiersmen of the Commonwealth 04844

Contact address not obtained.
URL: http://www.frontiersmenhistorian.info/

History 1904, London (UK), as *Legion of Frontiersmen*. UK Registered Charity: 284541. **Aims** Function as a voluntary self-governing *military* organization. **Publications** *The Call*. **Members** Membership countries not specified. [2009/XF6979/**F**]

♦ Corps mondial de secours (CMS) 04845

Search and Rescue (SAR)

Pres Villaroche Nord, Chemin de Viercy, 77550 Limoges-Fourches, France. E-mail: contact@corpsmondialdesecours.fr.
URL: http://corpsmondialdesecours.fr/WordPress3/

History 2 Mar 1972, Paris (France), by Constituent General Assembly, a Provisional Committee having been set up in 1970. Registered in accordance with Swiss law. Previous subsidiary title: *Pour le sauvetage des victimes de catastrophes naturelles*. Previously referred to as *Corps volontaire mondial de secours en cas de catastrophes naturelles* and in English as *World Assistance Corps*. **Aims** Promote an international convention allowing for the establishment and operation of a World Assistance Corps of *volunteers*, with freedom to cross frontiers, in cases of *natural disaster*. **Structure** General Assembly (annual) elects Managing Committee for 3-year term; Bureau. **Languages** French. **Staff** 17.00 FTE, voluntary. **Finance** Members' dues. Donations. **Activities** Rescue training and missions; aid for victims of disasters. **Events** *Annual meeting* France 1986.
Members Associations; Individuals. Associations in 2 countries:
Greece, Tunisia.
Individuals in 6 countries and territories:

Andorra, France, French Antilles, Germany, Réunion, Switzerland.
Associated international bodies (3):
European Council of Liberal Professions (#06828); International Movement for Universal Peace (IMUP, inactive); World Federalist Movement – Movement for a Just World Order through a Strengthened United Nations (WFM, #21404).
IGO Relations Partner of: *United Nations Office for the Coordination of Humanitarian Affairs (OCHA, #20593).*
[2017/XF4441/y/**F**]

- ♦ Corps mondial de secours en cas de catastrophe naturelle / see International Emergency Action (#13258)
- ♦ Corps de la Paix (internationally oriented national body)
- ♦ Corps volontaire mondial de secours en cas de catastrophes naturelles / see Corps mondial de secours (#04845)

♦ Corpus Christi 04846

Chairman Kalevankatu 53, FI-00180 Helsinki, Finland.
URL: http://www.corpuschristi.eu/
History Founded 2009, Sweden. **Aims** Lead young adults into an Evangelical-Lutheran church life. **Structure** Board. **Activities** Events/meetings. **Events** *Shaping our expectations for our life, the church, and the world* Prague (Czechia) 2018. [2020/XM7949/c/**F**]

- ♦ Corpus Christi Carmelite Sisters (religious order)
- ♦ Corpus Christi Watershed (unconfirmed)
- ♦ Corpus of Medieval Stained Glass / see Corpus Vitrearum (#04847)
- ♦ Corpus of Postmedieval Stained Glass / see Corpus Vitrearum (#04847)
- ♦ Corpus of Stained Glass (#04847)

♦ Corpus Vitrearum (CV) 04847

Corpus of Stained Glass
Pres Centre of Medieval Studies, University of York, The King's Manor, York, YO1 7EP, UK.
Sec c/o Institut of Art History, Jagiellonian University, ul Grodzka 53, 31-001 Krakow, Poland.
URL: http://www.corpusvitrearum.org/
History 1952, Amsterdam (Netherlands). Founded as an international research project. Former names and other names: *Corpus Vitrearum Medii Aevi (CVMA)* – former; *Corpus of Medieval Stained Glass* – former; *Corpus Vitrearum International* – former; *Corpus of Postmedieval Stained Glass* – former. **Aims** Research stained glass from the middle ages to the present, with a view to disseminating the results, principally through their full publication. **Structure** International Board; National Committees. **Languages** English, French, German. **Activities** Events/meetings. **Events** *International Colloquium of the Corpus Vitrearum* Barcelona (Spain) 2022, *International Colloquium of the Corpus Vitrearum* Barcelona (Spain) 2021, *International Colloquium of the Corpus Vitrearum* Barcelona (Spain) 2020, *International Colloquium of the Corpus Vitrearum* Antwerp (Belgium) 2018, *Colloquium* York (UK) 2014. **Publications** *Corpus Vitrearum/Corpus Vitrearum Medii Aevi.*
Members in 15 countries and territories:
Austria, Belgium, Canada, France, Germany, Italy, Luxembourg, Netherlands, Poland, Portugal, Russia, Spain, Switzerland, UK, USA.
NGO Relations Cooperates with (1): *Union académique internationale (UAI, #20345).*
[2022.06.18/XF6675/**F**]

- ♦ Corpus Vitrearum International / see Corpus Vitrearum (#04847)
- ♦ Corpus Vitrearum Medii Aevi / see Corpus Vitrearum (#04847)
- ♦ CorpWatch (internationally oriented national body)

♦ Correlation – European Harm Reduction Network (C-EHRN) 04848

Coordination c/o Foundation De Regenboog, Droogbak 1d, 1013 GE Amsterdam, Netherlands. T. +31205707829. Fax +31204203528.
Coordination address not obtained.
URL: http://www.correlation-net.org/
History 2004, Netherlands. Set up as a project, as a restructuring of *European Network Male Prostitution (ENMP)*, set up 1997, on combining with *AC Company Network on Mobile Drug Users.* Project periods: 2005-2008; 2009-2012. Since 2012 an independent network. Former names and other names: *Correlation Network – European Network Social Inclusion and Health* – former; *Correlation – European Harm Reduction Network (Correlation Network)* – former. **Aims** Improve access to, and quality of, harm reduction services for PWUD including other related vulnerable and marginalised people; enhance policies and practices that increase social inclusion. **Structure** Steering Committee; Office, based in Amsterdam (Netherlands). **Languages** English. **Staff** 5.00 FTE, paid. **Finance** Supported by: *European Commission (EC, #06633).* **Activities** Advocacy/lobbying/activism; capacity building; politics/policy/regulatory. **Events** *FENIQS-EU – Further enhancing the implementation of quality standards in DDR across Europe* Palma (Spain) 2022, *European Harm Reduction Conference* Prague (Czechia) 2021, *European Harm Reduction Conference* Bucharest (Romania) 2018, *HEP-C Community Summit* Lisbon (Portugal) 2018, *Central and Eastern European Meeting on Viral Hepatitis and HIV* Prague (Czechia) 2018. **Publications** *Correlation Newsletter* (2 a year). Reports; manuals; booklets; CD-ROM.
Members Organizations (180) in 40 countries:
Albania, Armenia, Austria, Belgium, Bulgaria, Canada, Croatia, Czechia, Denmark, Estonia, Finland, France, Germany, Greece, Hungary, Ireland, Italy, Kosovo, Latvia, Lithuania, Luxembourg, Moldova, Montenegro, Netherlands, North Macedonia, Norway, Poland, Portugal, Romania, Russia, Serbia, Slovakia, Slovenia, Spain, Sweden, Switzerland, Tanzania UR, UK, Ukraine, USA.
NGO Relations Member of (3): *ACHIEVE (#00068); Civil Society Forum on Drugs (CSFD, #03968);* Civil Society Forum on HIV, Hepatitis and Tuberculosis. Cooperates with (1): *Liver Patients International (LPI, #16498).* Links with several organizations, including: *Drug Policy Network South East Europe (DPNSEE, #05136); European AIDS Treatment Group (EATG, #05850). Harm Reduction International (HRI, #10861).* [2022.05.10/XF6309/**F**]

- ♦ Correlation – European Harm Reduction Network (Correlation Network) / see Correlation – European Harm Reduction Network (#04848)
- ♦ Correlation Network – European Network Social Inclusion and Health / see Correlation – European Harm Reduction Network (#04848)
- ♦ Corrente Comunista Internacional (#12818)
- ♦ Corrente Comunista Internazionale (#12818)
- ♦ Correspondance internationale (#14554)
- ♦ Correspondance internationale en faveur de la paix (inactive)
- ♦ Correspondants internationaux / see International Pen Friends (#14554)

♦ Correspondence Service in Esperanto 04849

Service de correspondance en espéranto – Koresponda Servo Mondskala (KSM)
Contact 33 rue Louvière, 55190 Void Vacon, France. E-mail: ksmesperanto@wanadoo.fr.
URL: http://membres.lycos.fr/kosomo/
History 1957, by *Universal Esperanto Association (UEA, #20676).* **Aims** Establish relations among Esperantists by correspondence in Esperanto (addresses selected by computer). **Structure** A service of UEA. **Languages** Esperanto. **Finance** Members' dues. Budget (annual): euro 2,000. **Activities** Correspondence Service. **Events** *Congress* Reykjavik (Iceland) 2013, *Congress* Hanoi (Vietnam) 2012, *Annual Congress* Australia 1988, *Annual Congress* Warsaw (Poland) 1987, *Annual Congress* Beijing (China) 1986. **Publications** List of correspondents by topic.
Members Correspondents (about 9,200) in 97 countries and territories:
Albania, Algeria, Andorra, Angola, Argentina, Australia, Austria, Belarus, Belgium, Benin, Bermuda, Bolivia, Brazil, Bulgaria, Burkina Faso, Burundi, Cameroon, Canada, Central African Rep, Chile, China, Colombia, Congo Brazzaville, Congo DR, Costa Rica, Côte d'Ivoire, Cuba, Czechia, Denmark, Ecuador, Egypt, El Salvador, Estonia, Finland, France, Germany, Ghana, Greece, Guatemala, Haiti, Holy See, Hong Kong, Hungary, Iceland, India, Indonesia, Iran Islamic Rep, Ireland, Israel, Italy, Japan, Kenya, Korea Rep, Latvia, Lithuania, Luxembourg, Madagascar, Mali, Malta, Mexico, Monaco, Mongolia, Nepal, Netherlands, New Zealand, Nicaragua, Niger, Nigeria, Norway, Pakistan, Panama, Peru, Poland, Portugal, Romania, Russia, San Marino, Senegal, Serbia, Singapore, Slovakia, South Africa, Spain, Sri Lanka, Sweden, Switzerland, Tanzania UR, Thailand, Togo, Türkiye, UK, Ukraine, Uruguay, USA, Venezuela, Vietnam. [2012.06.29/XE8750/v/**E**]

- ♦ Corriente Comunista Internacional (#12818)
- ♦ Corrosion Institute of Southern Africa (internationally oriented national body)
- ♦ Corte Arbitrale Europea (#06853)

♦ Corte Centroamericana de Justicia (CCJ) 04850

Cour de justice centroaméricaine – Central American Court of Justice
SG Apartado Postal 907, Del portón del Hospital El Retiro 1 1/2 c al Lago, Casa 1804, Bolognia, Managua, Nicaragua. T. +5052666273 – +5052666274 – +5052664604. Fax +5052668486.
URL: http://portal.ccj.org.ni/
History 20 Dec 1907, Washington DC (USA), on the signing of then 'Treaty of Washington'. Official rules of the court adopted 2 Dec 1911. Ordinance of Procedure adopted 6 Nov 1912. Operated from 1908 to 1918 in Cartago (Costa Rica) and San José (Costa Rica). Ceased operations Apr 1918. Re-established, 13 Dec 1991, by *Protocol of Tegucigalpa (1991)*, which replaced *Organization of Central American States (ODECA, inactive)* by *Central American Integration System (#03671).* Became operational 12 Oct 1994. Also referred to as *Corte de Managua* and *Tribunal Centroamericano.* **Aims** Based on the honour of member states, and within the limits of the powers which they granted, guarantee the rights of each of them in their reciprocal relations and maintain peace and harmony among them; both by its attributions and by the character of its jurisdiction, act as a Permanent Court of International Justice with power to adjudge and decide, upon petition, all cases included in its constitutive law. **Languages** Spanish. **Activities** As of end 2001, the Court had heard 29 cases of contention and 19 advisory cases. Organizes seminars and conferences. *Centro de Altos Estudios de Derecho de Integración Dr Roberto Ramirez* established 16 Mar 1997. **Publications** *El Boletín*; *Gaceta Oficial.* Books.
Members Signatories to the Protocol of Tegucigalpa (6):
Costa Rica, El Salvador, Guatemala, Honduras, Nicaragua, Panama.
IGO Relations *United Nations Commission on International Trade Law (UNCITRAL, #20531).*
[2010/XF4225/**F***]

- ♦ **CORTE** Confederation of Organizations in Road Transport Enforcement (#04574)
- ♦ Corte dei Conti delle Comunità Europee / see European Court of Auditors (#06854)
- ♦ Corte dei conti europea (#06854)
- ♦ Corte Europea de Arbitraje (#06853)
- ♦ Corte di Giustizia delle Comunità Europee / see Court of Justice of the European Union (#04938)
- ♦ Corte di Giustizia dell'Unione Europea (#04938)
- ♦ **Corte IDH** Corte Interamericana de Derechos Humanos (#04851)

♦ Corte Interamericana de Derechos Humanos (Corte IDH) 04851

Inter-American Court of Human Rights – Cour interaméricaine des droits de l'homme – Corte Interamericana dos Direitos Humanos
Sec Apdo 6906, San José, San José, San José, 1000, Costa Rica. T. +50625271600. Fax +50622340584. E-mail: corteidh@corteidh.or.cr.
URL: http://www.corteidh.or.cr/
History Established 18 Jul 1978, Washington DC (USA), on entry into force of the *Inter-American Convention on Human Rights (Pact of San José de Costa Rica, 1969) – Pact of San José, Costa Rica – Pacto de San José de Costa Rica* – signed 22 Nov 1969. An autonomous judicial institution of the *OAS (#17629).* Previously also known under the acronym *CIDH.* **Aims** Apply and interpret the American Convention on Human Rights. **Structure** Composed of 7 judges from OAS member countries, including President and Vice-President elected from among its own members (2-year terms, renewable) and 5 judges of the Tribunal. Judges are elected for 6-year terms by States Party at the General Assembly of OAS and meeting regularly 4 times a year. Secretariat. **Languages** English, French, Portuguese, Spanish. **Staff** 65.00 FTE, paid. **Finance** Source: The Court draws up its own annual budget and submits it for approval to the General Assembly of OAS through its General Secretariat, which may not introduce changes on it. The Court administers its own budget. **Activities** Conflict resolution; guidance/assistance/consulting; training/education; knowledge management/information dissemination. **Events** *Regular session* San José (Costa Rica) 2000, *Regular session* San José (Costa Rica) 1993, *Regular session* San José (Costa Rica) 1992, *Regular session* San José (Costa Rica) 1990, *Session* San José (Costa Rica) 1988. **Publications** *Jurisprudence Bulletin* in English, Spanish. Booklets.
Members Parties to the American Convention on Human Rights (25):
Argentina, Barbados, Bolivia, Brazil, Chile, Colombia, Costa Rica, Dominica, Dominican Rep, Ecuador, El Salvador, Grenada, Guatemala, Haiti, Honduras, Jamaica, Mexico, Nicaragua, Panama, Paraguay, Peru, Suriname, Trinidad-Tobago, Uruguay, Venezuela. [2017.10.30/XF8702/**F***]

- ♦ Corte Interamericana dos Direitos Humanos (#04851)
- ♦ Corte Internacional de Arbitraje y Conciliación Ambiental (#13096)
- ♦ Corte Internacional de Justicia (#13098)
- ♦ Corte de justicia del Mercado Común para Africa Orientale e Austral (#04937)
- ♦ Corte de Managua / see Corte Centroamericana de Justicia (#04850)
- ♦ Corte Penal Internacional (#13108)
- ♦ COS / see COS West and Midden Brabant Centrum voor Internationale Samenwerking
- ♦ **COSAC** Conférence des Organes Parlementaires Spécialisés dans les Affaires de l'Union des Parlements de l'Union Européenne (#04637)
- ♦ COSA CMF – Collège d'odonto-stomatologie africain et de chirurgie maxillo-faciale (no recent information)
- ♦ **COSAFA** Council of Southern Africa Football Associations (#04920)
- ♦ COSAFCO – Confederación Sudamericana de Fútbol Corporativo (unconfirmed)
- ♦ **COSALFA** Comisión Sudamericana para la Lucha contra la Fiebre Aftosa (#04143)
- ♦ Cosa Nostra / see Mafia (#16541)
- ♦ **COSAT** Confederación Sudamericana de Tenis (#19709)
- ♦ COSATT – Consortium of South Asian Think Tanks (unconfirmed)
- ♦ **COSAVE** Comité Regional de Sanidad Vegetal del Cono Sur (#04197)
- ♦ **COSBID** Co-operative Studies on Brain Injury Depolarizations (#04802)
- ♦ **Coscabal** Confederación de Sur y Centro America de Balonmano (#04443)
- ♦ COSEC – Coordinating Secretariat of National Unions of Students (inactive)
- ♦ **CoSE** Communities of Sustainable Europe (#04389)
- ♦ **COSECSA** College of Surgeons of East, Central and Southern Africa (#04110)
- ♦ COSERV / see Global Ties US
- ♦ **COSMAM** Conférence continentale des supérieurs-es majeurs-es pour l'Afrique et Madagascar (#04627)
- ♦ Cosmetic Physicians Society of Australasia (internationally oriented national body)
- ♦ Cosmetics Clusters – International Network / see Global Cosmetics Cluster (#10309)

♦ Cosmetics Europe – The Personal Care Association 04852

Dir-Gen Ave Herrmann Debroux 40, 1160 Brussels, Belgium. T. +3222276610. Fax +3222276627.
URL: https://cosmeticseurope.eu/
History 1962, Brussels (Belgium). Former names and other names: *Comité de liaison des associations européennes de l'industrie de la parfumerie, des produits cosmétiques et de toilette* – former (1962); *Dachverband der Europäischen Verbände der Parfümerie- und Kosmetik-Industrie* – former (1962); *European Cosmetic, Toiletry and Perfumery Association* – former (2012); *Association européenne de la parfumerie, des produits cosmétiques et de toilette (COLIPA)* – former (2012); *Dachverband der Europäischen Parfümerie-, Kosmetik- und Körperpflege-Industrie* – former (2012). Registration: EU Transparency Register, No/ID: 83575061669-96; Banque-Carrefour des Entreprises, No/ID: 0538.183.318, Start date: 1 Jan 1974, Belgium. **Aims** Act as an *industry* voice with international authorities and organizations; serve as a communication and information centre for the European cosmetic industry, systematically promoting sound scientific approaches; foster and promote an enhanced global trade environment for cosmetic products through the principles of regulatory harmonization and the removal of barriers to trade. **Structure** General Assembly; Board of Directors; Association Officers' Council; International Companies Council; General Secretariat. Committees, Sub-Committees and Task Forces (41). **Languages** English. **Staff** 19.00 FTE, paid. **Finance** Sources: members' dues. **Events** *Annual Conference (CEAC)* Brussels (Belgium) 2023, *Annual Conference* Brussels (Belgium) 2022, *Annual Conference* Brussels (Belgium) 2021, *Annual Conference* Brussels (Belgium) 2020, *Meeting* Brussels (Belgium) 2019. **Publications** *Colipa Statistics* (annual). *International Sun Protection Factor Test Method* (2003); *Alternatives to Animal Testing – The Fact* (1999). Guidelines; conference proceedings; directives; brochures; statistics. **Information Services** *COLIPA Database EU Inventory of Cosmetic Ingredients.*

Members Full 24 national associations (Belgium and Luxembourg being represented by the same association) in 25 EU Member States:
Austria, Belgium, Cyprus, Czechia, Denmark, Estonia, Finland, France, Germany, Greece, Hungary, Ireland, Italy, Latvia, Lithuania, Luxembourg, Malta, Netherlands, Poland, Portugal, Slovakia, Slovenia, Spain, Sweden, UK.
Associate or Corresponding members in 7 countries:
Australia, Brazil, Bulgaria, Romania, Russia, South Africa, Türkiye.
International Companies Council comprises 23 major international companies.
IGO Relations Accredited by (2): *European Commission (EC, #06633)*; *European Parliament (EP, #08146)*. Involved in the work of: *United Nations Committee of Experts on the Transport of Dangerous Goods and on the Globally Harmonized System of Classification and Labelling of Chemicals (Committee of Experts on TDG and GHS, #20543)*. **NGO Relations** Member of (4): *Downstream Users of Chemicals Co-ordination group (DUCC, #05127)*; *European Policy Centre (EPC, #08240)*; *Federation of European and International Associations Established in Belgium (FAIB, #09508)*; *Industry4Europe (#11181)*. Partner of (1): *European Partnership for Alternative Approaches to Animal Testing (EPAA, #08155)*. In liaison with technical committees of: *Comité européen de normalisation (CEN, #04162)*. Associate Expert Group of: *Business and Industry Advisory Committee to the OECD (BIAC, #03385)*. [2023/XD7480/**D**]

♦ Cosmobilities Network 04853

Contact Arcisstrasse 21, 80333 Munich, Germany. T. +498928928598. Fax +498928922333.
Contact Dept of Development and Planning, Aalborg Univ, Skibrogade 5, Room B1-08, 9000 Aalborg, Denmark.
URL: http://www.cosmobilities.net/

History 2004. Full title *Cosmobilities Network – The European Network of Mobility Research*. **Aims** Promote *mobility* research based on *social science*. **Activities** Research/documentation; events/meetings; publishing activities. **Events** *Future of Mobilities Conference* Caserta (Italy) 2015, *Cosmobilities Network Conference* Montréal, QC (Canada) 2013. **NGO Relations** *International Association for the History of Transport, Traffic and Mobility (T2M Association, #11937)*. [2018/XJ9130/**F**]

- ♦ Cosmobilities Network – The European Network of Mobility Research / see Cosmobilities Network (#04853)

♦ COSMOS-standard 04854

Main Office Rue du Commerce 124, 1000 Brussels, Belgium. E-mail: info@cosmos-standard.org.
URL: http://cosmos-standard.org/

History Founded Jun 2010, Belgium, by the five main European (and international) organizations involved with organic and natural cosmetics standards: BDIH (Germany); Cosmebio and Ecocert (France); ICEA (Italy); Soil Association (UK). Registered in accordance with Belgian law. **Aims** Own, manage and develop the SOCMOS-standard as and international (and internationally accepted) standard for organic and natural *cosmetics*. Define common requirements and definitions for organic and/or *natural cosmetics*. **Structure** General Assembly (annual), elects Board of Directors. **Languages** English, French, German, Italian, Spanish. **Staff** 1.00 FTE, paid. **Finance** Members' dues. Other sources: certifier fees; licence fees. **Activities** Awareness raising; certification/accreditation; knowledge management/information dissemination; monitoring/evaluation; standards/guidelines. **Publications** *COSMOS-standard*.
Members Categories: Full – national, European or international associations (voting rights); Associate – companies or individuals (no voting rights). Members in 4 countries:
France, Germany, Italy, UK.
NGO Relations Member of: *IFOAM – Organics International (IFOAM, #11105)*. Cooperates with: *IOAS (#16001)*. [2018/XJ5622/**D**]

- ♦ **COSPAR** Committee on Space Research (#04287)
- ♦ Cospas-Sarsat / see International Cospas-Sarsat Programme (#12975)
- ♦ COSPE – Cooperazione per lo Sviluppo dei Paesi Emergenti (internationally oriented national body)
- ♦ **COSRA** Conselho de Reguladores de Valores Mobiliarios das Américas (#04918)
- ♦ **CoSSE** Committee of SADC Stock Exchanges (#04285)
- ♦ COSTASALVAJE (internationally oriented national body)
- ♦ Costas Grammenos Centre for Shipping, Trade and Finance, The (internationally oriented national body)
- ♦ CoST / see CoST – the Infrastructure Transparency Initiative (#04855)
- ♦ **CoST** CoST – the Infrastructure Transparency Initiative (#04855)
- ♦ COSTEFF (internationally oriented national body)
- ♦ COSTEFF – alliance for cost-efficiency in healthcare / see COSTEFF
- ♦ Cost Engineering Association of Southern Africa / see Southern African Project Controls Institute
- ♦ COST / see European Cooperation in Science and Technology (#06784)
- ♦ **COST** European Cooperation in Science and Technology (#06784)

♦ CoST – the Infrastructure Transparency Initiative (CoST) 04855

Dir 6th Floor Alliance House, 29-30 High Holborn, London, WC1V 6AZ, UK. T. +442080573052. E-mail: cost@infrastructuretransparency.org.
URL: http://infrastructuretransparency.org/

History Established by: *Department for International Development (DFID, inactive)* and *International Bank for Reconstruction and Development (IBRD, #12317)* (World Bank). Pilot launch, 2008, Dar es Salaam (Tanzania UR). Former names and other names: *Construction Sector Transparency Initiative (CoST)* – former. **Aims** Work with government, industry and civil society to promote disclosure, validation and interpretation of data from infrastructure projects to inform and empower citizens and enable them to hold decision-makers to account. **Structure** Board; Regional Managers; Country Teams; Secretariat hosted in London (UK). **Finance** Supported by: *Deutsche Gesellschaft für Internationale Zusammenarbeit (GIZ)*; *Inter-American Defense Board (IADB, #11425)*; *The World Bank Group (#21218)*; UK Cross-Government Prosperity Fund; UK Foreign, Commonwealth and Development Office.
Members Member countries (18):
Argentina, Colombia, Costa Rica, Ecuador, El Salvador, Ethiopia, Ghana, Guatemala, Honduras, Indonesia, Malawi, Mexico, Mozambique, Panama, Thailand, Timor-Leste, Uganda, Ukraine.
NGO Relations Also links with national organizations. [2023.02.15/XJ0754/**E***]

- ♦ **COSUBA** Confederación Sudamericana de Badminton (#04481)
- ♦ **COSUD** Confederación Sudamericana Universitaria de Deportes (#19711)
- ♦ COSUDE – Agencia Suiza para el Desarrollo y la Cooperación (internationally oriented national body)
- ♦ **COSUTRI** Confederación Sudamericana de Triatlón (#19710)
- ♦ COSV – Comitato di Coordinamento delle Organizzazioni per il Servizio Volontario (internationally oriented national body)
- ♦ **COSW** Commonwealth Organisation for Social Work (#04354)
- ♦ COS West and Midden Brabant Centrum voor Internationale Samenwerking (internationally oriented national body)
- ♦ **COTA** Caribbean Organization of Tax Administrators (#03537)
- ♦ COTA – Collectif d'échanges pour la technologie appropriée (internationally oriented national body)
- ♦ **COTAL** Confederação de Organizações Turisticas da América Latina (#04466)
- ♦ **COTAL** Confederación de Organizaciones Turisticas de la América Latina (#04466)
- ♦ **COTANCE** Confédération des associations nationales de tanneurs et mégissiers de la Communauté européenne (#04515)
- ♦ COTAP – Carbon Offsets To Alleviate Poverty (internationally oriented national body)
- ♦ **COTECC** Confederación de Tenis de Centroamérica y el Caribe (#04496)
- ♦ **COTEC** Council of Occupational Therapists for the European Countries (#04912)
- ♦ COTIF – Convention relative aux transports internationaux ferroviaires, 1980 (1980 treaty)
- ♦ COTIF – Convention relative aux transports internationaux ferroviaires, 1999 (1999 treaty)
- ♦ COTMEC – Commission Tiers-Monde de l'Eglise catholique, Genève (internationally oriented national body)
- ♦ Cotonou agreement – ACP-EU Partnership Agreement (2000 treaty)
- ♦ **COTSOES** Conference of Translation Services of European States (#04650)
- ♦ Cottolenghini – Fratelli di San Giuseppe Benedetto Cottolengo (religious order)
- ♦ Cottolenghini – Società dei Sacerdoti di San Giuseppe Benedetto Cottolengo (religious order)
- ♦ Cotton Council International (inactive)
- ♦ Cotton Expert House Africa / see Cotton House Africa
- ♦ Cotton House Africa (internationally oriented national body)
- ♦ Coudenhove-Kalergi Foundation / see European Society Coudenhove-Kalergi (#08573)
- ♦ COUNCARID – Council of Caribbean Institutions for Development (inactive)
- ♦ The Council / see Council of Insurance Agents & Brokers
- ♦ Council of Academies of Engineering and Technological Sciences / see International Council of Academies of Engineering and Technological Sciences (#12982)
- ♦ Council for the Advancement of Arab-British Understanding (internationally oriented national body)
- ♦ Council for Advancement and Support of Education (internationally oriented national body)
- ♦ Council of African Instituted Churches (no recent information)

♦ Council of Africa Political Parties (CAPP) 04856

SG Natl Congress – Khartoum, PO Box 6892, Riyadh 11452, Khartoum, Sudan. T. +24914802697 ext123. Fax +24914808712.
URL: http://africappc.org/

History Apr 2013. Official inauguration of Secretariat, 10 Mar 2014. **Structure** General Assembly; Executive Committee; Secretariat. **Events** *Conference* Khartoum (Sudan) 2013. **IGO Relations** Memorandum of Understanding with: *African Union (AU, #00488)*. **NGO Relations** *Conferencia Permanente de Partidos Políticos de América Latina y el Caribe (COPPPAL, #04657)*. [2015/XJ9487/**D**]

- ♦ Council of American Chambers of Commerce in Europe / see European Council of American Chambers of Commerce (#06803)
- ♦ Council of American Chambers of Commerce Europe and Mediterranean / see European Council of American Chambers of Commerce (#06803)
- ♦ Council of American Overseas Research Centers (internationally oriented national body)
- ♦ Council of the Americas (internationally oriented national body)

♦ Council of Anglican Provinces of Africa (CAPA) 04857

Secretariat PO Box 10329-00100, Nairobi, Kenya. T. +254202632640. Fax +254202692327. E-mail: info@capa-hq.org.
URL: http://capa-hq.org/

History 1979, Chilema (Malawi). **Aims** Unite the Anglican community in Africa; articulate issues affecting the Church. **NGO Relations** Member of: *Christian Connections for International Health (CCIH)*. *Anglican Church of the Province of the Indian Ocean (#00824)* and *Anglican Church of Southern Africa (ACSA, #00826)* are members. [2019/XU8245/**D**]

♦ Council of Arab Central Banks and Monetary Agencies' Governors (CGACB) 04858

Contact c/o AMF, PO Box 2818, Abu Dhabi, United Arab Emirates. T. +9712215000. Fax +9712326454.

History Previously referred to as *Arab Central Bank Governors Council (ACB)*; *Board of Governors of Central Banks and Heads of Arab Monetary Agencies*; *Board of Governors of Arab Central Banks and Monetary Agencies*; *Council of Governors of Arab Central Banks and Monetary Agencies (CGACB)*. **Structure** Secretariat provided by *Arab Monetary Fund (AMF, #01009)*. **Activities** Set up *Arab Committee on Banking Supervision (ACBS, #00925)*, Aug 1991. [2015/XE2603/**E***]

♦ Council of Arab Economic Unity (CAEU) 04859

Conseil de l'unité économique arabe (CUEA)

SG 14 Haron Street, Dokki, Giza, Egypt.
Contact PO Box 1, Cairo, Egypt. T. +20237602459 – +20237602432. Fax +20237602698.
Facebook: https://www.facebook.com/caeu2018/

History 3 Jun 1957, Cairo (Egypt), when Convention on establishment was adopted, under Economic Unity Agreement between States of *League of Arab States (LAS, #16420)*. Agreement entered into force 30 May 1964, representing a multilateral framework for economic development on a regional basis. Agreement was ratified by 11 countries: Egypt; Jordan; Kuwait; Libyan AJ; Mauritania; Palestine; Somalia; Sudan; Syria AR; Yemen Democratic Republic; Republic of Yemen. **Aims** Promote *trade* among Arab countries; work to achieve full economic unity among member countries; ensure equal rights to member states and their citizens, according to founding agreement, of freedom of movement of individuals and capital, of exchange of domestic and foreign goods, of residence, work, employment and economic activities, of transport, transit and civil airports facilities and of ownership and inheritance. **Structure** Council and subsidiaries constitute one entity with an independent jurisdictional, financial and administrative status. Council (meets twice a year); Chairmanship (rotates annually); General Secretariat, includes Secretary-General and Assistant Secretary-General. **Languages** Arabic. **Staff** 35.00 FTE, paid. **Finance** Member states' contributions.
Activities *Arab Common Market (ACM, no recent information)*, established 13 Aug 1964. The *'Common Market Accord'*, to which Egypt, Iraq, Jordan, Libyan AJ, Mauritania, Syrian AR and Yemen are parties, provides for increasing free mouvement of capital, goods and people among members and reduction of duties on goods and commodities. Although in practice all trade restrictions have not been abolished, customs duties, etc have been diminished. The following measures have been undertaken: flexible membership conditions for least developed countries and funds to compensate for losses on joining; approval of legal, technical and administrative procedures for common tariffs for goods imported from non-member countries; formation of a committee to deal with market rulings and promote activities. Five agreements have been established in the field of investment and mouvement of capital and an *Arab Monetary Fund (AMF, #01009)* was set up on 27 Apr 1976, Rabat (Morocco). Multilateral agreements have been initiated on: basic levels of social insurance; reciprocity in social insurance systems; labour mobility; organization of transit trade; avoidance of double taxation and elimination of tax evasion; cooperation in collection of taxes; capital investment and mobility; settlement of investment disputes. A number of Arab joint ventures and specialized unions in different fields of economic activity and a programme for the coordination of Arab Development Plans have been established. Joint companies and unions and federations coordinate efforts on international markets and encourage closer cooperation in production and marketing of agricultural, fishing, and industrial products and of transport and natural resources. Instrumental in setting up:

- *Arab Academy for Electronic Fields*;
- *Arab Cooperative Union (UCA, inactive)*;
- *Arab Distributors' Union (inactive)*;
- *Arab Federation of Accountants and Auditor*;
- *Arab Federation of Chambers of Shipping (#00940)*;
- *Arab Federation of Chemical and Petrochemical Industries (AFCPI, no recent information)*;
- *Arab Federation for the Consumer (AFC, #00942)*;
- *Arab Federation for Engineering Industries (AFEI, #00943)*;
- *Arab Federation of Fish Producers (AFFP, #00945)*;
- *Arab Federation for Food Industries (AFFI, #00946)*;
- *Arab Federation of Leather Industries (inactive)*;
- *Arab Federation for Paper, Printing and Packaging Industries (AFPPPI, #00950)*;
- *Arab Federation of Shipping (AFS, #00953)*;
- *Arab Federation for Textile Industries (AFTI, inactive)*;
- *Arab Federation of Tire and Rubber Industries (#00956)*;
- *Arab Federation for Wildlife Protection*;
- *Arab Fertilizer Association (AFA, #00958)*;
- *Arab Importers and Experters Association*;
- *Arab Investors Union (AIU, no recent information)*;
- *Arab Iron and Steel Union (AISU, #00998)*;
- *Arab Paint and Coating Producers Association*;
- *Arab Private Equity Association (APEA)*;
- *Arab Sea Ports Federation (ASPF, #01040)*;
- *Arab Society for Intellectual Property (ASIP, #01046)*;
- *Arab Tour Guides Federation (no recent information)*;
- *Arab Union for Astronomy and Space Sciences (AUASS, #01063)*;
- *Arab Union for Cement and Building Materials (AUCBM, #01065)*;
- *Arab Union for Dealers in the Financial Markets*;
- *Arab Union for Economy and Business Forum*;

– *Arab Union of Information Technology (#01067)*;
– *Arab Union for International Exhibitions and Conferences (no recent information)*;
– *Arab Union of Land Transport (AULT, #01069)*;
– *Arab Union of Manufacturers of Pharmaceuticals and Medical Appliances (AUPAM, #01070)*;
– *Arab Union for Providers of Internet and Communication Services*;
– *Arab Union for Small Enterprises (AUSE, inactive)*;
– *Arab Women Investors Union (AWIU, #01077)*;
– *Federation of Arab Businessmen (#09418)*;
– *Federation of Arab Contractors (FAC, #09419)*;
– *General Arab Insurance Federation (GAIF, #10104)*;
– *General Federation for Plastic Producers and Manufacturers in the Arab World (no recent information)*;
– *General Union of Arab Peasants and Agricultural Cooperatives (GUAAPC, no recent information)*;
– *Inter-Arab Union of Hotels and Tourism (inactive)*.

Set up a 'WTO Unit', 2006, to enhance awareness in Arab countries about WTO agreements and their effects on their economies, assist Arab negotiators to participate effectively in the ongoing WTO negotiations and provide assistance to Arab countries acceding to WTO. Training and Research Centre, set up 2006, to assist member countries to understand and cope with increasing and speedy international economic developments through training programmes and facilities for research.
Events *Conference for construction and building products* Dakar (Senegal) 2003. **Publications** *WTO News* (4 a year); *Arab Economic Unity Bulletin* (2 a year); *Annual Bulletin for Arab Countries' Foreign Trade Statistics*; *Annual Bulletin for Official Exchange Rates of Arab Countries*; *Demographic Yearbook for Arab Countries*; *Economic Indicators for Arab Countries (annual)*; *Statistical Yearbook for Arab Countries*; *Yearbook for Intra-Arab Trade Statistics*; *Yearbook of National Accounts for Arab Countries*. Reports; guides; list of publications. Information Services: *Arab Central Bureau of Statistics and Documentation (see: #04859)*, created in 1975, provides technical assistance to member states. Library; trade documentation.
Members Governments of 9 countries and territories:
Egypt, Iraq, Jordan, Mauritania, Palestine, Somalia, Sudan, Syrian AR, Yemen.
IGO Relations Relationship agreement signed with: *FAO (#09260)*; *UNIDO (#20336)*. Participates in the activities of: *UNCTAD (#20285)*. **NGO Relations** Related to: *Arab Federation of Petro-chemical Producers (no recent information)*; *Federation of GCC Chambers (FGCCC, #09590)*. [2018/XD0433/**D***]

♦ Council of Arab Environmental Affairs Ministers / see Council of Arab Ministers Responsible for the Environment (#04863)

♦ Council of Arab Ministers of Finance 04860

Secretariat c/o Arab Monetary Fund, PO Box 2818, Abu Dhabi, United Arab Emirates. T. +97126171574 – +97126171572.
URL: http://www.amf.org.ae/en/page/background/
History Established considering decision of Arab League Summit, 2009, Kuwait, which called for increased coordination between Finance Ministers of the Arab countries. **Aims** Enhance cooperation and exchange in the field of fiscal policies. **Structure** Technical Secretariat provided by *Arab Monetary Fund (AMF, #01009)*. **Activities** Events/meetings; politics/policy/regulatory. **Events** *Annual Meeting* Amman (Jordan) 2018, *Annual Meeting* Rabat (Morocco) 2017, *Annual Meeting* Manama (Bahrain) 2016.
Members Governments of 22 countries:
Algeria, Bahrain, Comoros, Djibouti, Egypt, Iraq, Jordan, Kuwait, Lebanon, Libya, Mauritania, Morocco, Oman, Palestine, Qatar, Saudi Arabia, Somalia, Sudan, Syrian AR, Tunisia, United Arab Emirates, Yemen. [2018/XM6554/c/**E***]

♦ Council of Arab Ministers of Health 04861

Conseil des ministres arabes de la santé

Head of Technical Secretariat c/o LAS, Tahrir Square, PO Box 11642, Cairo, Egypt. T. +202750511.
History 1975, Cairo (Egypt), within the framework of *League of Arab States (LAS, #16420)*. **Aims** Coordinate among the Arab ministers of health the improvement of basic health services in the Arab world; carry out studies and research on health problems in the Arab world and their solution. **Structure** Council, comprising all member countries. Executive Board, consisting of 5 countries. Secretariat, called *'Technical Secretariat of the Council of Ministers of Health'*. **Finance** Contributions of member countries. **Activities** Maintains: *Arab Centre for Medical Literature (ACML, no recent information)*; *Arab Council for Medical Specializations (no recent information)*; *Arab Fund for Health Services Development (no recent information)*; *Arab Scientific Advisory Committee for Blood Transfer (no recent information)*; *Arab Technical Committee for Endemic Diseases (no recent information)*; *Arab Training Centre for Maintenance and Repair of Medical Equipment (inactive)*.
Members Ministers of Health of 21 Arab countries:
Algeria, Bahrain, Djibouti, Egypt, Iraq, Jordan, Kuwait, Lebanon, Libya, Mauritania, Morocco, Oman, Palestine, Qatar, Saudi Arabia, Somalia, Sudan, Syrian AR, Tunisia, United Arab Emirates, Yemen. [2010/XE8080/**E***]

♦ Council of Arab Ministers of Housing / see Council of Arab Ministers for Housing and Reconstruction (#04862)
♦ Council of Arab Ministers for Housing and Construction / see Council of Arab Ministers for Housing and Reconstruction (#04862)

♦ Council of Arab Ministers for Housing and Reconstruction (CAMHR) 04862

Contact UNCHS Regional Information Office, PO Box 35286, Amman, Jordan. T. +9626668171 – +9626668172 – +9626668176. Fax +9626676582.
History within the framework of *League of Arab States (LAS, #16420)*. Previously referred to as *Council of Arab Ministers of Housing – Conseil des Ministres arabes de l'habitat*. **Activities** Arab Ministerial Forum for Housing and Urban Development (AMFUD). **Events** *Session* Cairo (Egypt) 1995, *Regional seminar for Arab states on HABITAT II issues* Amman (Jordan) 1994, *Regional seminar for Arab states on HABITAT II issues* Cairo (Egypt) 1994. **IGO Relations** *United Nations Human Settlements Programme (UN-Habitat, #20572)*. [1996/XE5265/**E***]

♦ Council of Arab Ministers for Information and Communication Technology (inactive)
♦ Council of Arab Ministers of the Interior / see Arab Interior Ministers' Council (#00990)
♦ Council of Arab Ministers of Justice (no recent information)

♦ Council of Arab Ministers Responsible for the Environment (CAMRE) 04863

Chairman c/o LAS, Tahrir Square, PO Box 11642, Cairo, Egypt. T. +202750511. Fax +202740331.
History within the framework of *League of Arab States (LAS, #16420)*. Also referred to as *Council of Arab Ministers Responsible for Environment Affairs* and as *Council of Arab Environmental Affairs Ministers*. **Structure** Executive Bureau, headed by Chairman. **Events** *Meeting* Jeddah (Saudi Arabia) 2014, *Session* Cairo (Egypt) 2010, *Meeting* Cairo (Egypt) 2005, *Session* Cairo (Egypt) 1997, *Session* Cairo (Egypt) 1996. **IGO Relations** *Organization of Arab Petroleum Exporting Countries (OAPEC, #17854)* is an Observer. **NGO Relations** *Arab NGO Network for Environment and Development (RAED, #01017)*. [2014/XE2354/**E***]

♦ Council of Arab Ministers Responsible for Environment Affairs / see Council of Arab Ministers Responsible for the Environment (#04863)
♦ Council of Arab Ministers for Social Affairs / see Council of Arab Ministers for Social and Economic Affairs (#04864)
♦ Council of Arab Ministers for Social Affairs and Labour / see Council of Arab Ministers for Social and Economic Affairs (#04864)

♦ Council of Arab Ministers for Social and Economic Affairs 04864

Contact c/o Social Affairs Dept, League of Arab States, Tahrir Square, PO Box 11642, Cairo, Egypt. T. +202750511. Fax +202740331.
History 26 Mar 1980, by Resolution 3927 of the *League of Arab States (LAS, #16420)* Council, as *Council of Arab Ministers for Social Affairs*. Also referred to as *Council of Arab Ministers for Social Affairs and Labour*. **Aims** Promote Arab cooperation in the fields of social development and social work and realization of the aims of the Arab Charter for Social Work. **Structure** The Council meets once a year (beginning of Dec). Executive Bureau (meets twice a year), consisting of 7 Arab Ministers. **Finance** Has a US$ 1 million fund, entitled *Arab Fund for Social Work*. **Activities** Current major programmes: training in the field of social work (sub-regional); documentary (film) on the productive family in Tunisia. Instrumental in setting up *Pan Arab Project for Child Development (PAPCHILD, no recent information)*. **Events** *Annual meeting* Cairo (Egypt) 1990, *Annual ministerial meeting* Tunis (Tunisia) 1989, *Annual meeting* Khartoum (Sudan) 1988. **Publications** *Evaluating Social Projects in Developing Countries* in Arabic; *Juvenile Delinquency* in Arabic; *Management of Social Institutions* in Arabic; *Rural and Local Community Development* in Arabic.
Members Governments of 21 countries:
Algeria, Bahrain, Djibouti, Egypt, Iraq, Jordan, Kuwait, Lebanon, Libya, Mauritania, Morocco, Oman, Palestine, Qatar, Saudi Arabia, Somalia, Sudan, Syrian AR, Tunisia, United Arab Emirates, Yemen.
IGO Relations *ILO (#11123)*; *UNDP (#20292)*; *UNICEF (#20332)*; *United Nations Office at Vienna (UNOV, #20604)*; *United Nations Population Fund (UNFPA, #20612)*; *Arab Gulf Programme for United Nations Development Organizations (AGFUND, #00971)*; *Arab Labour Organization (ALO, #01001)*; *Arab League Educational, Cultural and Scientific Organization (ALECSO, #01003)*; *Gulf Cooperation Council (GCC, #10826)*. **NGO Relations** Cooperates with: *International Federation of Social Workers (IFSW, #13544)*. [2010/XE5264/**E***]

♦ Council of Arab Ministers of Tourism 04865

Chairman Cabinet of the Minister, Ministry of Tourism, Misr Travel Tower, Abbasya Square, Cairo, 11381, Egypt. T. +2026837665. Fax +2026837665.
History 1998, Cairo (Egypt), by *Arab Economic and Social Council (AESC, #00937)*, within the framework of *League of Arab States (LAS, #16420)*. **Events** *Meeting* Dubai (United Arab Emirates) 2004, *Conference* Algeria 2000. [2020/XE3929/**E***]

♦ Council of Arab Ministers of Transport (no recent information)
♦ Council of Arab Ministers for Youth / see Council of Arab Ministers for Youth and Sports (#04866)

♦ Council of Arab Ministers for Youth and Sports 04866

Contact c/o LAS, Department of Youth and Sports, Tahrir Square, PO Box 11642, Cairo, Egypt. T. +2025750511 – +2025752966. Fax +2025740331 – +202761017.
History Comes within the framework of *League of Arab States (LAS, #16420)*. Also referred to as: *Council of Arab Ministers for Youth*; *Bureau of Arab Sports Ministers for the Arab League*. **Events** *Session* Dubai (United Arab Emirates) 2015, *Regional meeting of government ministers responsible for youth* Cairo (Egypt) 1997.
Members All Arab countries, members of LAS. Governments of 21 countries and territories:
Algeria, Bahrain, Djibouti, Egypt, Iraq, Jordan, Kuwait, Lebanon, Libya, Mauritania, Morocco, Oman, Palestine, Qatar, Saudi Arabia, Somalia, Sudan, Syrian AR, Tunisia, United Arab Emirates, Yemen. [2015/XE5278/**E***]

♦ Council of Arab Telecom Ministers / see Arab Telecommunication and Information Council of Ministers (#01054)
♦ Council for Asia Europe Cooperation (no recent information)

♦ Council of Asian Liberals and Democrats (CALD) 04867

Exec Dir Unit 410, 4/F La Fuerza Plaza 2, 2241 Don Chino Roces Ave, 1231 Makati, Philippines. T. +6328196071. Fax +6328101431. E-mail: info@cald.org.
SG address not obtained.
URL: http://www.cald.org/
History 12 Dec 1993, Bangkok (Thailand). **Aims** Foster growth of society based on personal liberty, personal responsibility, social justice, the rule of law and free market economy; provide the means of cooperation, exchange of ideas, interchange of information and network-building among and between liberal parties and organizations with a liberal orientation and vision; discuss and analyse current as well as future political, social and economic concepts and developments in Asia. **Structure** General Assembly (every 2 years). Executive Committee, comprising 1 representative of each member party. Secretariat. **Languages** English. **Staff** 4.00 FTE, paid. **Finance** Members' dues. Grants. **Activities** Organizes: conferences; symposia; workshops; visits; missions. Publishes books. **Events** *Conference* Siem Reap (Cambodia) 2006, *Conference* Taipei (Taiwan) 2005, *Conference* Bangkok (Thailand) 2003, *Conference* Colombo (Sri Lanka) 2003, *Conference* Manila (Philippines) 2001. **Publications** *Liberal News Asia* (6 a year). *September 11 and Political Freedom: Asian Perspectives* (2002); *Democratic Transitions in Asia: Agenda for Action* (2001); *Political Dimensions of the Asian Crisis* (2000). Annual Report.
Members Political parties in 8 countries:
Cambodia, Malaysia, Myanmar, Philippines, Singapore, Sri Lanka, Taiwan, Thailand.
Associate members in 2 countries:
Pakistan, Philippines.
Included in the above, 1 associate member listed in this Yearbook:
Young Liberals and Democrats of Asia (YLDA, #21994).
Individual members (2) in 1 territory:
Hong Kong.
NGO Relations Partner of: *Friedrich Naumann Foundation for Freedom*; *Liberal International (LI, #16454)*. [2010/XD7932/**D**]

♦ Council of Asian Press Institutes (no recent information)

♦ Council of Asian Science Editors (CASE) 04868

SG Korea Science and Technology Ctr, 2nd Floor – 22 Buk-7-gil, Teheran-ro, Gangnam-gu, Seoul 06130, Korea Rep. T. +82328626808. Fax +82328625546. E-mail: case@asianeditor.org.
Pres address not obtained.
URL: http://www.asianeditor.org/
History Officially set up 2 Jul 2014, Seoul (Korea Rep). **Aims** Improve the quality of science journals published in Asia. **Structure** Executive Board. Committees (5): Education and Training; Publication Ethics; Information and Publication; External Affairs; Advisory. **Languages** English, Korean. **Staff** 2.00 FTE, paid. **Finance** Event registration fees; public subsidies; contract fees; subsidies from other organizations; donations. Budget (annual): US$ 25,000. **Activities** Capacity building; guidance/assistance/consulting; knowledge management/information dissemination; events/meetings; networking/liaising; publishing activities; research/documentation; training/education. **Events** *Conference* Seoul (Korea Rep) 2022, *Conference* Seoul (Korea Rep) 2020, *Conference* Bogor (Indonesia) 2018, *Conference* Ho Chi Minh City (Vietnam) 2017, *Conference* Seoul (Korea Rep) 2016. **Publications** *CASE Newsletter*.
Members Full in 23 countries and territories:
Austria, Bangladesh, Canada, China, Greece, India, Indonesia, Iran Islamic Rep, Italy, Japan, Korea Rep, Malaysia, Nepal, Pakistan, Philippines, Russia, Singapore, Taiwan, Thailand, Türkiye, UK, USA, Vietnam. [2022/XM4378/**D**]

♦ Council of Associations of Long Cycle Engineers of a University or Higher School of Engineering of the European Union (CLAIUEU) 04869

Conseil des associations d'ingénieurs de cycle long d'université ou d'école d'ingénieurs de l'union européenne

SG Rue Hobbema 2, 1000 Brussels, Belgium. T. +3227347510. Fax +3227345315.
URL: http://www.claiu.org/
History 1988. Current by-laws adopted, 29 Mar 1990, Brussels (Belgium). Former names and other names: *Comité de liaison d'associations d'ingénieurs universitaires de la Communauté européenne (CLAIU)* – former (1988); *Liaison Committee of the Associations of University Graduate Engineers of the European Union* – former (1988). **Aims** Promote engineering science and technology by fundamental and applied research; maintain the level of university education and of continuous *professional* training in engineering, in close conjunction with scientific research; guarantee quality and ethics of professional practice of the university graduate engineer; remove limitations to free movement and of obstacles to professional practice of different types of equivalent education; defend professional interests and the highest level engineering worldwide. **Structure** General Assembly (at least twice a year). Executive Board comprising 6 members. Presidency (rotating following the order of nationalities). Administrative Secretariat. **Languages** English, French. **Finance** Members' dues. **Events** *Conference* Madrid (Spain) 2012, *The formation of the engineer – international models* Rome (Italy) 2011, *Seminar on engineering master degrees in Europe* Brussels (Belgium) 2010, *The engineer in the European Union of knowledge* 2006, *Annual General Assembly* Madrid (Spain) 2005. [2014/XE3279/**E**]

♦ Council of Australasian Weed Societies (internationally oriented national body)
♦ Council of the Baltic Islands / see Islands of the Baltic Sea (#16060)

◆ **Council of the Baltic Sea States (CBSS)** 04870
Dir Gen Momma Reenstiernas Palats, Wollmar Yxkullsgatan 23, SE-118 50 Stockholm, Sweden. T. +4684401920. Fax +4684401944. E-mail: cbss@cbss.org.
URL: http://www.cbss.org/
History 6 Mar 1992, Copenhagen (Denmark). Established at a conference of the Ministers of Foreign Affairs of the 10 riparian countries. Iceland joined, 1995. International permanent secretariat officially inaugurated 20 Oct 1998, Stockholm (Sweden). Former names and other names: *Conseil des Etats de la Mer baltique (CEB)* – alias. Registration: EU Transparency Register, No/ID: 448161944093-19, Start date: 17 Sep 2021. **Aims** Serve as an overall political forum for regional intergovernmental cooperation among the Baltic Sea States promoting regional identity, ensuring a safe and secure region and creating a sustainable and prosperous region. **Structure** Council (meets every 2 years), headed by Chairman (rotating among member states on an annual basis) and comprising Ministers for Foreign Affairs of each member state and a representative of the European Commission. Foreign minister of the presiding country is responsible for coordinating activities, assisted by Committee of Senior Officials (CSO), comprising high-ranking representatives of the Ministry of Foreign Affairs of each member state and of the European Commission. CSO serves as main discussion forum and decision making body for matters related to the Council's work between ministerial sessions. Expert Groups operate under CSO. Permanent International Secretariat in Stockholm (Sweden) includes 3 specialized units: Task Force against Trafficking in Human Beings TF-THB; Expert Group on Sustainable Development; Expert Group for Cooperation on Children at Risk. Other working bodies include: *Baltic Sea Region Energy Cooperation (BASREC, #03148); Task Force on Organized Crime in the Baltic Sea Region (#20099)* (1996). **Languages** English. **Staff** 24.00 FTE, paid. **Finance** Sources: members' dues. Project facilitation line added to the budget; secretariat units increasingly use external funding opportunities; members are responsible for funding of agreed common activities and/or for seeking and coordinating financing from other sources. Since 1998, member states jointly finance Secretariat; specialized units of the Secretariat are funded in accordance with separate agreements made by member states, channelled through the Secretariat. **Activities** Events/meetings; monitoring/evaluation; networking/liaising; politics/policy/regulatory; research and development. **Events** *Soft Security Conference* Helsinki (Finland) 2017, *Energy Efficiency Seminar* Helsinki (Finland) 2014, *How to enhance assistance to victims of human trafficking in the Baltic Sea region* Helsinki (Finland) 2014, *Seminar on EU Strategy in the Sphere of Education for the Baltic Sea region* St Petersburg (Russia) 2014, *Joint Seminar on Creativity and Cooperation in the South Eastern Baltic Area* Kaliningrad (Russia) 2013. **Publications** *Balticness* (2 a year) – official journal; *Balticness Light* – bulletin.
Members Member governments (11):
Denmark, Estonia, Finland, Germany, Iceland, Latvia, Lithuania, Norway, Poland, Sweden.
European Union (EU, #08967).
Observer states (11):
Belarus, France, Hungary, Italy, Netherlands, Romania, Slovakia, Spain, UK, Ukraine, USA.
Strategic Partners (7), listed in this Yearbook:
Baltic Sea Parliamentary Conference (BSPC, #03146); Baltic Sea States Subregional Cooperation (BSSSC, #03150); Conference of Peripheral Maritime Regions of Europe (CPMR, #04638); International Organization for Migration (IOM, #14454); Islands of the Baltic Sea (B7, #16060); OECD (#17693); Union of the Baltic Cities (UBC, #20366).
IGO Relations Observer status with: *Baltic Marine Environment Protection Commission – Helsinki Commission (HELCOM, #03126).* **NGO Relations** Instrumental in setting up: *Business Advisory Council (BAC, #03376).*
[2022/XD4344/y/**D***]

◆ Council of the Barents Arctic Region / see Barents Euro-Arctic Council (#03177)
◆ Council of the Barents Region / see Barents Euro-Arctic Council (#03177)
◆ Council of the Bars of the European Community / see Council of Bars and Law Societies of Europe (#04871)
◆ Council of Bars and Law Societies of Europe / see Council of Bars and Law Societies of Europe (#04871)

◆ **Council of Bars and Law Societies of Europe (CCBE)** 04871
Conseil des barreaux européens
Permanent SG Rue Joseph II 40/8, 1000 Brussels, Belgium. T. +3222346510. E-mail: ccbe@ccbe.eu.
URL: http://www.ccbe.eu/
History 1960, Brussels (Belgium). Established following congress of the Union Internationale des Avocats (UIA), Sep 1960, where participants discussed the need for a representative body that would act in the interests of lawyers before the *European Community (inactive)*, whose construction was perceived as a threat to the independence of their profession. Given this perception, an "agreement-in-principle" was obtained to establish a body of representatives from the then-six *European Community (inactive)* Member States. Today, the CCBE has grown to include the bars and law societies of 46 countries that represent the *European Union (EU, #08967)* and the *European Economic Area (EEA, #06957)* and a wider Europe. Former names and other names: *Consultative Committee of Bars and National Associations of the Six States of the EEC* – former (1960); *Council of Bars and Law Societies of Europe* – former (1960); *Consultative Committee of the Bars and Law Societies of the European Community* – former; *Commission consultative des barreaux de la Communauté européenne* – former; *Council of the Bars of the European Community* – former; *Conseil des barreaux de la Communauté européenne* – former. Registration: Banque-Carrefour des Entreprises, No/ID: 0467.250.186, Start date: 15 Jun 1999; EU Transparency Register, No/ID: 4760969620-65, Start date: 6 Nov 2008. **Aims** Study questions affecting the *legal profession* in member states of the *European Union* and formulate solutions designed to coordinate and harmonize professional practice. **Structure** Plenary Session; Standing Committee; Presidency; Secretariat. **Languages** English, French. **Staff** 11.50 FTE, paid. **Finance** Sources: members' dues. **Activities** Conflict resolution; events/meetings. **Events** *Meeting* Vienna (Austria) 2020, *Conference on the Modernisation of European Company Law* Brussels (Belgium) 2019, *Plenary Session* Porto (Portugal) 2019, *Meeting* Vienna (Austria) 2019, *Conference on Artificial Intelligence and Human Justice* Lille (France) 2018. **Publications** *CCBE INFO* – newsletter. *CCBE Code of Conduct*. Position papers; press releases; charter of core principles of the European legal profession; practical guides for lawyers.
Members Full: bars and law societies in 31 countries:
Austria, Belgium, Bulgaria, Croatia, Cyprus, Czechia, Denmark, Estonia, Finland, France, Germany, Greece, Hungary, Iceland, Ireland, Italy, Latvia, Liechtenstein, Lithuania, Luxembourg, Malta, Netherlands, Norway, Poland, Portugal, Romania, Slovakia, Slovenia, Spain, Sweden, Switzerland.
Associate in 5 countries:
Albania, Montenegro, North Macedonia, Serbia, Türkiye.
Observers in 9 countries:
Andorra, Armenia, Azerbaijan, Bosnia-Herzegovina, Georgia, Moldova, Russia, San Marino, Ukraine.
Affiliate in 1 country:
UK.
Consultative Status Consultative status granted from: *Council of Europe (CE, #04881)* (Participatory Status). **IGO Relations** Observer status with (2): *Commission européenne pour l'efficacité de la justice (CEPEJ, #04213); Consultative Council of European Judges (CCJE, #04767).* **NGO Relations** Member of (2): *European Services Forum (ESF, #08469); Federation of European and International Associations Established in Belgium (FAIB, #09508).*
[2022.10.19/XE0412/**E**]

◆ Council of Biology Editors / see Council of Science Editors (#04917)
◆ Council of British Independent Schools in the European Communities / see Council of British International Schools (#04872)

◆ **Council of British International Schools (COBIS)** 04872
CEO 55-56 Russell Square, London, WC1B 4HP, UK. T. +442038267190. E-mail: ceo@cobis.org.uk – comms@cobis.org.uk.
Executive Assistant to the CEO address not obtained. E-mail: pa@cobis.org.uk.
URL: http://www.cobis.org.uk/
History 1981, Netherlands. Former names and other names: *Council of British Independent Schools in the European Communities (COBISEC)* – former (1981). Registration: Netherlands. **Aims** Support members and represent their interests in Britain and overseas, particularly with Government, education authorities and educational associations in order to advance the interests of British schools outside the UK. **Structure** General Meeting (annual); Board. **Languages** English. **Staff** 19.00 FTE, paid. **Finance** Sources: meeting proceeds; subscriptions. **Activities** Capacity building; certification/accreditation; events/meetings; guidance/assistance/consulting; training/education. **Events** *Annual Conference* London (UK) 2022, *Annual Conference* London (UK) 2016, *Annual Conference* London (UK) 2015, *Professional Development Meeting* Madrid (Spain) 2015, *Student Leadership Conference* Madrid (Spain) 2015. **Publications** *The Source* (annual). **Members** British Schools (over 260) in 78 countries. Membership countries not specified. **NGO Relations** *British Council*; UK Department for Education; UK Department for International Trade.
[2023.02.14/XE4746/**E**]

◆ **Council of Bureaux (CoB)** 04873
Conseil des bureaux
Main Office Av Louise 166 – bte 1E, 1050 Brussels, Belgium. T. +3226270920. E-mail: secretariat@cobx.org.
URL: http://www.cobx.org/
History 1949. Also referred to as *Council of Insurers' Bureaux – Conseil des bureaux d'assureurs* and *International Association of National Motor Insurers' Bureaux*. Registered in accordance with Belgian law. **Aims** Act for the protection of cross-border *road traffic* victims by coordinating the activities of: national motor insurers' Bureaux in the framework of the Green Card system; Compensation Bodies, Guarantee Funds and information Centres in the framework of the European Motor Insurance Directives. **Structure** General Assembly; Management Committee; Secretariat based in Brussels (Belgium). **Languages** English. **Activities** Monitoring/evaluation; knowledge management/information dissemination. **Events** *General Assembly* Marrakech (Morocco) 2019, *General Assembly* Madrid (Spain) 2018, *General Assembly* Helsinki (Finland) 2017, *General Assembly* Stockholm (Sweden) 2010.
Members Bureaux (48) in 48 countries:
Albania, Andorra, Austria, Azerbaijan, Belarus, Belgium, Bosnia-Herzegovina, Bulgaria, Croatia, Cyprus, Czechia, Denmark, Estonia, Finland, France, Germany, Greece, Hungary, Iceland, Iran Islamic Rep, Ireland, Israel, Italy, Latvia, Liechtenstein, Lithuania, Luxembourg, Malta, Moldova, Montenegro, Morocco, Netherlands, North Macedonia, Norway, Poland, Portugal, Romania, Russia, Serbia, Slovakia, Slovenia, Spain, Sweden, Switzerland, Tunisia, Türkiye, UK, Ukraine.
Consultative Status Consultative status granted from: *ECOSOC (#05331)* (Ros A). **IGO Relations** Participates in the work of: *United Nations Economic Commission for Europe (UNECE, #20555).*
[2020.01.27/XN4059/**D**]

◆ **Council of Caribbean Engineering Organizations (CCEO)** 04874
SG PO Box 715, Bridgetown, St Michael BB11000, Bridgetown ST MICHAEL BB11000, Barbados.
Street address c/o Concept, Dayrells Road, Bridgetown, St Michael BB14030, Bridgetown ST MICHAEL BB14030, Barbados.
History Previously referred to as *Caribbean Council of Engineering Organizations.* **Aims** Coordinate activities of national engineering associations and institutions in the Commonwealth Caribbean. **Languages** English. **Activities** Events/meetings.
Members Engineering organizations in 12 countries:
Antigua-Barbuda, Bahamas, Barbados, Belize, Dominica, Grenada, Guyana, Jamaica, St Kitts-Nevis, St Lucia, St Vincent-Grenadines, Trinidad-Tobago.
[2018.06.01/XE0252/**E**]

◆ Council of Caribbean Institutions for Development (inactive)
◆ Council of Caribbean Workers (no recent information)

◆ **Council of Catholic Patriarchs of the Orient (CCPO)** 04875
Conseil des Patriarches catholiques d'Orient (CPCO)
Gen Sec Sanctuary Our Lady of Lebanon, Harissa, Lebanon. T. +9613871118 – +9613(9619261330.
URL: http://www.cpco.me/
History 1990. Former names and other names: *Conseil permanent des sept Patriarches catholiques de l'Orient* – former; *Conseil des sept Patriarches catholiques de l'Orient* – former; *Conseil permanent des sept Patriarches catholiques de l'Orient; Conseil des sept Patriarches catholiques de l'Orient.* – alias. **Aims** Reflect on the situation of Catholics of the Orient to promote Christian life; coordinate pastoral activity of Catholic Churches of the Orient; give Catholic Churches of the Orient the possibility to express their point of view and to study questions that concern their congregations and countries; strengthen the future of *Christianity* in the Orient as a priority, in the conscience of the Churches of the Orient themselves in the care of the Universal Church, and close to the national and international requests; consolidate ties between the faithful of the Diaspora and their Churches in the Orient; favour ecumenical and *inter-religious* dialogue; secure an active involvement of the Catholic family in the works of the *'Middle East Council of Churches (MECCE)'*; promote justice, peace, development, respect of human rights especially of the woman and the family in our countries and in the relations between people. **Structure** General Secretariat composed of Secretary-General and one Delegate and one Assistant of each Patriarchy. **Languages** Arabic, French. **Staff** 1.00 FTE, paid. Voluntary. **Finance** Members' dues. Donations. **Activities** Events/meetings; research/documentation; networking/liaising. **Events** *Congress* Cairo (Egypt) 2019, *Annual Session* Baghdad (Iraq) 2018, *Annual Session* Dimane (Lebanon) 2017, *Annual Session* Rome (Italy) 2015, *Annual Session* Rome (Italy) 2014. **Publications** *Pastoral Letters of the Council of Catholic Patriarchs of the Orient – Lettres pastorales du Conseil des Patriarches catholiques d'Orient.*
Members Patriarchs in 10 countries:
Armenia, Egypt, Iran Islamic Rep, Iraq, Jordan, Lebanon, Palestine, South Africa, Syrian AR, Türkiye.
IGO Relations Contact with: Secretariat of Sate of Vatican; Governments of Middle East nations.
[2019.03.22/XF5733/v/**F**]

◆ Council of Central American Humanities Faculties (#04711)
◆ Council on Chiropractic Education Australasia (internationally oriented national body)

◆ **Council of Christian Churches in the Barents Region (SKKB/CCCBR)** 04876
Chairman Church of Norway, PO Box 799 Sentrum, 0106 Oslo, Norway. E-mail: post.kirkeradet@kirken.no.
History 1996, Norway. **Aims** Promote the understanding of inter-church cooperation in the Barents region; foster contacts and relations between the Churches on different levels in the region; be a platform for the Churches of the region for information and discussions on topics of mutual interests; be a forum for cooperation with other development agencies in the region in matters of common interest. **Events** *Session* Petrozavodsk (Russia) 2013, *Seminar on environmental, social and diaconal responsibility* Oulu (Finland) 2008.
Members Dioceses in 4 countries:
Finland, Norway, Russia, Sweden.
[2013/XJ0342/**D**]

◆ Council for Christian Colleges and Universities (internationally oriented national body)

◆ **Council of Churches of East Asia (CCEA)** 04877
Contact address not obtained.
History Proposed at 1st meeting of Central Anglican Council of Missionary Strategy, 1954, Minneapolis MN. Functions as an autonomous member Church of *Anglican Communion (#00827).* **Structure** General Assembly (every 4 years); Council. **Activities** Events/meetings. **Events** *Quinquennial General Assembly* Seoul (Korea Rep) 2003, *House of bishops meeting* 2001, *House of bishops meeting* 2000, *House of bishops meeting* Melaka (Malaysia) 1999, *Quinquennial General Assembly* Melaka (Malaysia) 1999.
Members Membership registered on individual Diocese basis in 9 countries and territories:
Australia, Hong Kong, Japan, Korea Rep, Malaysia, Myanmar, Philippines, Singapore, Taiwan.
[2022.05.17/XE2132/v/**E**]

◆ Council Circumpolar Inuit (#15995)
◆ Council of Cities and Regions in Africa / see United Cities and Local Governments of Africa (#20500)
◆ Council of Commonwealth Municipalities (inactive)

◆ **Council of Commonwealth Societies (CCS)** 04878
Contact c/o The Royal Commonwealth Society, Commonwealth House, 55-58 Pall Mall, London, SW1Y 5JH, UK. E-mail: info@thercs.org.
History Founded 1938, as *Joint Commonwealth Societies' Council (JCSC)* at Joint Commonwealth Societies Conference. **Aims** Promote understanding of the peoples and cultures of the Commonwealth through annual celebration of Commonwealth Day. **Structure** Secretariat administered by *Royal Commonwealth Society (RCS, #18990).* **Languages** English. **Staff** 0.50 FTE, paid. **Finance** Members' dues. Other sources: donations; British government. **Activities** Events/meetings; awareness raising. **Events** *Annual Congress* Milan (Italy) 2008.
Members Organizations (16):

Council Community Democracies
04878

alphabetic sequence excludes
For the complete listing, see Yearbook Online at

Association of Commonwealth Universities, The (ACU, #02440); *Commonwealth Countries League (CCL, #04320)*; *Commonwealth Foundation (CF, #04330)*; *Commonwealth Games Federation (CGF, #04332)*; *Commonwealth Local Government Forum (CLGF, #04348)*; *Commonwealth Parliamentary Association (CPA, #04355)*; Commonwealth Parliamentary Association – UK; *Commonwealth Secretariat (#04362)*; *Corona Worldwide (#04836)*; *English-Speaking Union (ESU, #05482)*; Foreign and Commonwealth Office; Goodenough College; *Pacific Islands Society of the United Kingdom and Ireland (PISUKI)*; *Royal Commonwealth Society (RCS, #18990)*; *Royal Over-Seas League (ROSL)*. [2017.10.26/XD0983/y/**E**]

- ♦ Council for a Community of Democracies (internationally oriented national body)
- ♦ Council on the Continuing Education Unit / see International Association for Continuing Education and Training
- ♦ Council for the Coordination of International Congresses of Medical Sciences / see Council for International Organizations of Medical Sciences (#04905)
- ♦ Council for Creative Education (unconfirmed)
- ♦ Council for the Development of Economic and Social Research in Africa / see Council for the Development of Social Science Research in Africa (#04879)

♦ Council for the Development of Social Science Research in Africa (CODESRIA) 04879

Conseil pour le développement de la recherche en sciences sociales en Afrique – Conselho para o Desenvolvimento da Pequina em Ciências Sociais na Africa

Exec Sec Avenue Cheikh Anta Diop x Canal IV, BP 3304, CP 18524, Dakar, Senegal. T. +221338240374. Fax +221338245795.

Pres Eduardo Mondlane Univ, Av Julius Nyerere 3453, Maputo, Cidade de Maputo, Mozambique.

URL: http://www.codesria.org/

History 1 Feb 1973, Dakar (Senegal), at a meeting of representatives of African universities and research institutes, when charter and work programme were approved and Executive Committee elected. Charter revised 1982. Registered in accordance with the law of Senegal. Previously also referred to as *Council for the Development of Economic and Social Research in Africa – Conseil pour le développement de la recherche économique et sociale en Afrique – Consejo para el Desarrollo de la Investigación Económica y Social de Africa*. **Aims** Facilitate research, promote research-based publishing and create multiple fora for exchange of views and information among African researchers; challenge existing orthodox development theories by activating concerned African social scientists and research institutes to undertake fundamental and problem-oriented research in the field of development from a perspective relevant to the needs of the African people, thus counteracting stagnation and underdevelopment; break down linguistic and geographical barriers between African social scientists, define priorities and organize collaborative research teams. **Structure** General Assembly (every 3 years), comprising representatives of full member African social science research institutions. Executive Committee of 10 social scientists (meets twice a year). Scientific Committee. **Languages** Arabic, English, French, Portuguese. **Staff** 46.00 FTE, paid.

Finance Members' dues. Other sources: grants from African governments; funding organizations (not specified); revenue from publications and other activities. Research programmes co-financed, including by:
- *The African Capacity Building Foundation (ACBF, #00233)*;
- *Carnegie Corporation of New York*;
- City of Dakar;
- *DANIDA*;
- *Ford Foundation (#09858)*;
- Government of Senegal;
- *International Development Research Centre (IDRC, #13162)*;
- *Norwegian Agency for Development Cooperation (Norad)*;
- *Open Society Foundations (OSF, #17763)*;
- *The Rockefeller Foundation (#18966)*;
- *Swedish International Development Cooperation Agency (Sida)*;
- *TrustAfrica (#20251)*;
- *UN Women (#20724)*;
- *UNDP (#20292)*;
- *UNESCO (#20322)*.

Activities Research and development; projects/programmes; training/education. **Events** *Conference on Electronic Publishing* Dakar (Senegal) 2016, *Triennial General Assembly* Dakar (Senegal) 2015, *International Conference on Academic Freedom in Africa* Kampala (Uganda) 2015, *International Conference on Public Health Governance* Windhoek (Namibia) 2015, *Triennial General Assembly* Dakar (Senegal) 2014. **Publications** *CODRESIA Bulletin*. Journal; books; monographs. **Information Services** *CODESRIA Information and Documentation Centre (CODICE)*.

Members Full individual (African social scientists); Full institutional (universities, social science faculties, research institutes, centres and NGOs on the African continent); Associate individual (non-African social scientists, whose research interests include Africa); Associate institutional (non-African institutions and research centres). Members in 87 countries:
Algeria, Angola, Argentina, Australia, Austria, Bahamas, Barbados, Belgium, Benin, Botswana, Brazil, Burkina Faso, Burundi, Cameroon, Canada, Cape Verde, Central African Rep, Chad, China, Colombia, Comoros, Congo Brazzaville, Congo DR, Côte d'Ivoire, Cuba, Denmark, Djibouti, Egypt, Equatorial Guinea, Eritrea, Eswatini, Ethiopia, Finland, France, Gabon, Gambia, Germany, Ghana, Guinea, Guinea-Bissau, Haiti, India, Indonesia, Ireland, Italy, Jamaica, Kenya, Lesotho, Liberia, Libya, Madagascar, Malawi, Malaysia, Mali, Mauritania, Mauritius, Mexico, Morocco, Mozambique, Namibia, Netherlands, Niger, Nigeria, Norway, Pakistan, Portugal, Russia, Rwanda, Sao Tomé-Principe, Senegal, Seychelles, Sierra Leone, Somalia, South Africa, South Sudan, Spain, Sudan, Sweden, Switzerland, Tanzania UR, Togo, Trinidad-Tobago, Tunisia, Uganda, USA, Zambia, Zimbabwe.

Consultative Status Consultative status granted from: *African Commission on Human and Peoples' Rights (ACHPR, #00255)* (Observer); *ECOSOC (#05331)* (Ros B). **IGO Relations** Observer to: *African Union (AU, #00488)*. Regular contacts with: *OECD Development Centre (#17692)*. Working relationships with: *FAO (#09260)*; *UNEP (#20299)*; *UNCTAD (#20285)*; *UNDP (#20292)*; *UNIDO (#20336)*; *United Nations Economic Commission for Africa (ECA, #20554)*; *United Nations Institute for Training and Research (UNITAR, #20576)*; *United Nations University (UNU, #20642)*. Cooperates with: *African Centre for Applied Research and Training in Social Development (ACARTSOD, #00237)*; *African Development Bank (ADB, #00283)*; *African Regional Centre of Technology (ARCT, #00432)*; *African Training and Research Centre in Administration for Development (CAFRAD, #00486)*; *Centre for the Coordination of Research and Documentation in Social Science for Sub-Saharan Africa (no recent information)*; *United Nations African Institute for Economic Development and Planning (#20518)*. **NGO Relations** Participated in the formation of: *Southern African Universities Social Science Conference (SAUSSC, inactive)*. Collaboration agreement with: *African Association of Political Science (AAPS)*; *Association of African Women for Research and Development (AAWORD, #02362)* (providing secretarial facilities for the latter). Member of: *Childwatch International Research Network (#03887)*; *International Center for Economic Growth (ICEG, inactive)*; *International Federation of Social Science Organizations (IFSSO, #13543)*; *International Science Council (ISC, #14796)*. Informal collaboration with African regional offices of: *Association des universités partiellement ou entièrement de langue française (AUPELF, inactive)*. Joint publications with: *International Centre for Ethnic Studies (ICES, #12490)*. [2019/XD0006/**D**]

- ♦ Council of Directors of Highways of Iberia and Ibero-America (#04706)
- ♦ Council of Directors of Institutes of Tropical Medicine in Europe (inactive)
- ♦ Council on East Asian Community (internationally oriented national body)
- ♦ Council on East Asian Libraries (internationally oriented national body)
- ♦ Council for East and Central Africa Football Associations (unconfirmed)
- ♦ Council on Economic Priorities Accreditation Agency / see Social Accountability International
- ♦ Council of Educational Facility Planners International / see Association for Learning Environments
- ♦ Council for Education in the Commonwealth (internationally oriented national body)
- ♦ Council of Engineering and Scientific Society Executives (internationally oriented national body)
- ♦ Council of the Entente / see Entente Council (#05491)
- ♦ Council of the Entente States / see Entente Council (#05491)

♦ Council for Environmentally Friendly Aviation (CEFA) 04880

Contact c/o ERA, Park House, 127 Guildford Road, Lightwater, GU18 5RA, UK. T. +441276856495. Fax +441276857038. E-mail: info@eraa.org.

History on the initiative of Mike Ambrose, under the aegis of *European Regions Airline Association (ERA, #08347)*. **Aims** Coordinate industry policy; promote aviation's activities in the area of the *environment*.

Members Industry associations (7):
Aerospace and Defence Industries Association of Europe (ASD, #00146); *Airlines International Representation in Europe (AIRE, #00608)*; *European Business Aviation Association (EBAA, #06415)*; *European Express Association (EEA, #07017)*; *European Low Fares Airline Association (ELFAA, #07713)*; *European Regions Airline Association (ERA, #08347)*; *General Aviation Manufacturers Association (GAMA)*. [2018/XM2999/y/**E**]

- ♦ Council of the Euro Arctic Region / see Barents Euro-Arctic Council (#03177)

♦ Council of Europe (CE) 04881

Conseil de l'Europe (CE) – Consejo de Europa – Europarat

SG Av de l'Europe, 67075 Strasbourg CEDEX, France. T. +33388412000.

General: http://www.coe.int/

History 5 May 1949, London (UK). Established on signature of Statute of the Council of Europe by government representatives of Belgium, Denmark, France, Ireland, Italy, Luxembourg, Netherlands, Norway, Sweden and the United Kingdom. Initiative was taken by the 5 governments signatory, 17 Mar 1948, to the *Brussels Treaty Organization – Organisation du Traité de Bruxelles*, chiefly as a result of a *Congress of Europe – Congrès de l'Europe*, May 1948, The Hague (Netherlands), and following the proposals developed by a non-governmental organization, the European Movement. The Statute lays down that every member of the Council of Europe must accept the principles of the rule of law and of the enjoyment by all persons within its jurisdiction of human rights and fundamental freedoms. Since the events of 1989 the Council of Europe has been the pre-eminent European organization for the intergovernmental and parliamentary cooperation, capable of welcoming on an equal footing and in permanent structures the new democracies of Europe. Currently, membership of the Council of Europe has expanded to 47 states. The latest accessions are Hungary on 6 Nov 1990, Poland on 26 Nov 1991, Bulgaria on 7 May 1992, Estonia, Lithuania and Slovenia on 14 May 1993, the Czech Republic and the Slovak Republic on 30 Jun 1993, Romania on 7 Oct 1993, Andorra on 10 Nov 1994, Latvia on 10 Feb 1995, Albania and Moldova on 13 Jul 1995, Ukraine and the Former Yugoslav Republic of Macedonia on 9 Nov 1995, Russian Federation on 28 Feb 1996, Croatia on 6 Nov 1996, Georgia on 27 Apr 1999, Armenia and Azerbaijan on 25 Jan 2001, Bosnia-Herzegovina on 24 Apr 2002, Serbia-Montenegro on 3 Apr 2003 (currently only Serbia), Monaco on 5 Oct 2004, Montenegro on 11 May 2007. Russian Federation ceased to be a member, 16 Mar 2022, following invasion of Ukraine, Feb 2022. Action Plan adopted by 3rd Summit of Heads of State and Government of Member States, 16-17 May 2005, Warsaw (Poland), sets-up strategic priorities of the organization. **Aims** Strengthen human rights, democracy and the rule of law throughout the continent and beyond; advocate freedom of expression and of the media, freedom of assembly, equality, and the protection of minorities; help member states fight corruption and terrorism and undertake necessary judicial reforms. **Structure** Based at the 'Palais de l'Europe' in Strasbourg (France).

– *Committee of Ministers of the Council of Europe (#04273)* is the decision-making body and is made up of Ministers of Foreign Affairs of each Member State or their permanent diplomatic representatives. It decides CE policy and approves budget and programme of activities.

– *Parliamentary Assembly of the Council of Europe (PACE, #18211)* consists of 318 members of parliament from all Member States. It elects Secretary General, Human Righs Commissioner and judges to European Court of Human Rights. It provides a democratic forum for debate and monitors elections with its committees playing an important role in examining current issues.

– *Congress of Local and Regional Authorities of the Council of Europe (#04677)* is composed of 2 chambers – Chamber of Local Authorities and Chamber of Regions – and 3 Committees. It comprises 636 elected representatives representing over 200,000 local and regional authorities. It is responsible for strengthening local and regional democracy.

– *European Court of Human Rights (#06855)*, set up 1959, is the permanent judicial body which guarantees for all Europeans the rights safeguarded by *Convention for the Protection of Human Rights and Fundamental Freedoms (1950)*. Current structure brought into being by *Protocol no 11 to the Convention for the Protection of Human Rights and Fundamental Freedoms (1994)*. Court is open to states as well as to individuals regardless of nationality.

– The Human Rights Commissioner, elected by the Parliamentary Assembly, is an independent and impartial non-judicial institution aiming to promote awareness of and respect for human rights in Member States.

– International Secretariat, serves various bodies and directorates and headed by Secretary General (5-year term), who is responsible for strategic planning and direction of the Council's work programme and budget, and leads and represents the Organization. Directorates (8): Directorate General Human Rights and Rule of Law; Directorate General Democracy; Directorate of External Relations; Directorate of Policy Planning; Directorate of Legal Advice and Public International Law; Treaty Office; Directorate of Internal Oversight; Office of the Directorate General of Programmes.

– Offices and Programme Offices in: Ankara (Turkey); Baku (Azerbaijan); Belgrade (Serbia); Bucharest (Romania); Chisinau (Moldova); Kiev (Ukraine); Moscow (Russia); Podgorica (Montenegro); Sarajevo (Bosnia-Herzegovina); Skopje (North Macedonia); Tbilisi (Georgia); Tirana (Albania); Venice (Italy); Yerevan (Armenia). Offices outside Member States: Pristina (Kosovo); Rabat (Morocco); Tunis (Tunisia). Liaison Offices: Brussels (Belgium) – in charge of liaison with the European Union; Geneva (Switzerland) – Permanent Delegation to the UN Office and other international organizations in Geneva; Vienna (Austria) – in charge of liaison with the OSCE, UN Office and other international organizations in Vienna; Warsaw (Poland) – in charge of liaison with other international organizations or institutions in Warsaw, particularly OSCE/ODIHR. Office in Paris (France).

– Partial Agreements:

- *'Partial Agreements'*: *Council of Europe Development Bank (CEB, #04897)*; *European Pharmacopoeia Commission (#08198)*; *European Card for Substantially Handicapped Persons* – not instituted; *Open Partial Agreement on the Prevention of, Protection against and Organization of Relief in Major Natural and Technological Disasters (EUR-OPA Major Hazards Agreement, #17762)*; *European Support Fund for the Co-Production and Distribution of Creative Cinematographic and Audiovisual Works (EURIMAGES, #08859)*.
- *'Enlarged Partial Agreements'*: *Co-operation Group to Combat Drug Abuse and Illicit Trafficking in Drugs (Pompidou Group, #04796)*; *European Centre for Global Interdependence and Solidarity (North-South Centre, #06483)*; *Partial Agreement on Youth Mobility Through the Youth Card (#18224)*; *European Audiovisual Observatory (#06294)*; *European Centre for Modern Languages (ECML, #06491)*; *Enlarged Partial Agreement on Sport (EPAS, #05487)*; *Enlarged Partial Agreement on Cultural Routes (#05486)*.
- *'Enlarged Agreements'*: *European Commission for Democracy through Law (Venice Commission, #06636)*; *Group of States Against Corruption (#10789)*.

Instrumental in setting up: *Pan-European Ecological Network (PEEN, see: #04881)*.

Languages English, French, German, Italian, Russian. **Staff** 2200.00 FTE, paid. Staff Committee elected every 2 years. **Finance** Each member state bears expenses for its own representation in the Committee of Ministers and the Parliamentary Assembly. Other expenses are shared between member states in proportion to population and GNP. Annual budget (2019): euro 437,180,100.

Activities Develops standards on civil and political rights, social rights, minority rights, treatment of persons deprived of their liberty, the fight against racism and the fight against corruption and money laundering. Activities are centred around 3 themes, with several bodies working on these fields: Human Rights; Democracy; Rule of Law.

Bodies working in the field of Human Rights, include:
- *European Court of Human Rights (#06855)*;
- *Comité européen pour la prévention de la torture et des peines ou traitements inhumains ou dégradants (CPT, #04164)*;
- *European Committee on Social Cohesion, Human Dignity and Equality (CDDECS, #06667)*;
- *European Commission Against Racism and Intolerance (ECRI, see: #04881)*;
- *European Pharmacopoeia Commission (#08198)*;
- *European Committee of Social Rights (ECSR, #06668)*.

Bodies working in the field of Democracy, include:
- *Parliamentary Assembly of the Council of Europe (PACE, #18211)*;
- *Congress of Local and Regional Authorities of the Council of Europe (#04677)*;
- *Council of Europe Development Bank (CEB, #04897)*;
- *Open Partial Agreement on the Prevention of, Protection against and Organization of Relief in Major Natural and Technological Disasters (EUR-OPA Major Hazards Agreement, #17762)*;
- *Enlarged Partial Agreement on Cultural Routes (#05486)*;
- *European Support Fund for the Co-Production and Distribution of Creative Cinematographic and Audiovisual Works (EURIMAGES, #08859)*;

- *European Centre for Global Interdependence and Solidarity (North-South Centre, #06483)*;
- *European Centre for Modern Languages (ECML, #06491)*;
- *European Youth Centres (EYCs, #09138)*;
- *European Youth Foundation (EYF, #09141)*;
- *Partial Agreement on Youth Mobility Through the Youth Card (#18224)*;
- *Enlarged Partial Agreement on Sport (EPAS, #05487)*.

Bodies working in the field of Rule of Law, include:
- *Commission européenne pour l'efficacité de la justice (CEPEJ, #04213)*;
- *Consultative Council of European Judges (CCJE, #04767)*;
- *Conseil consultatif de procureurs européens (CCPE, #04685)*;
- *European Commission for Democracy through Law (Venice Commission, #06636)*;
- *European Committee on Crime Problems (CDPC, #06645)*;
- *European Committee on Legal Cooperation (#06655)*;
- *Committee of Legal Advisers on Public International Law (CAHDI, #04267)*;
- *European Audiovisual Observatory (#06294)*;
- *Group of States Against Corruption (#10789)*;
- *Committee of Experts on the Evaluation of Anti-Money Laundering Measures and the Financing of Terrorism (MONEYVAL, #04257)*;
- *Co-operation Group to Combat Drug Abuse and Illicit Trafficking in Drugs (Pompidou Group, #04796)*.

Other initiatives include: *European Network of National Information Centres on Academic Recognition and Mobility (ENIC, #07950)*; *European Information Network on Cultural Heritage Policies (HEREIN Project, #07533)*.

Management of treaties and agreements (status end Nov 2015):
- 001-Statute of the Council of Europe, signed and in force 1949;
- 002- *General Agreement on Privileges and Immunities of the Council of Europe (1949)*, signed 1949, in force 1952;
- 005- *Convention for the Protection of Human Rights and Fundamental Freedoms (1950)*, signed 1950, in force 1953;
- 009- *Protocol to the Convention for the Protection of Human Rights and Fundamental Freedoms (1952)*, signed 1952, in force 1954;
- 010- *Protocol to the General Agreement on Privileges and Immunities of the Council of Europe (1952)*, signed 1952, in force 1956;
- 012- *European Interim Agreement on Social Security Schemes Relating to Old Age, Invalidity and Survivors (1953)*, signed 1953, in force 1954; denounced and ceased to be in force 1999;
- 012A- *Protocol to the European Agreement on Social Security Schemes Relating to Old Age, Invalidity and Survivors (1953)*, signed 1953, in force 1954;
- 013- *European Interim Agreement on Social Security other Than Schemes for Old Age, Invalidity and Survivors (1953)*, signed 1953, in force 1954;
- 013A- *Protocol to the European Interim Agreement on Social Security other Than Schemes for Old Age, Invalidity and Survivors (1953)*, signed 1953, in force 1954;
- 014- *European Convention on Social and Medical Assistance (1953)*, signed 1953, in force 1954;
- 014A- *Protocol to the European Convention on Social and Medical Assistance (1953)*, signed 1953, in force 1954;
- 015- *European Convention on the Equivalence of Diplomas Leading to Admission to Universities (1953)*, signed 1953, in force 1954;
- 016- *European Convention Relating to the Formalities Required for Patent Applications (1953)*, signed 1953, in force 1955;
- 017- *European Convention on the International Classification of Patents for Inventions (inactive)*, signed 1954, in force 1955;
- 018- *European Cultural Convention (1954)*, signed 1954, in force 1955;
- 019- *European Convention on Establishment (1955)*, signed 1955, in force 1965;
- 020- *Agreement on the Exchange of War Cripples between Member Countries of the Council of Europe with a View to Medical Treatment (1955)*, signed 1955, in force 1956;
- 021- *European Convention on the Equivalence of Periods of University Study (1956)*, signed 1956, in force 1957;
- 022- *Second Protocol to the General Agreement on Privileges and Immunities of the Council of Europe (1956)*, signed 1956, in force 1956;
- 023- *European Convention for the Peaceful Settlement of Disputes (1957)*, signed 1957, in force 1958;
- 024- *European Convention on Extradition (1957)*, signed 1957, in force 1960;
- 025- *European Agreement on Regulations Governing the Movement of Persons between Member States of the Council of Europe (1957)*, signed 1957, in force 1958;
- 026- *European Agreement on the Exchange of Therapeutic Substances of Human Origin (1958)*, signed 1958, in force 1959;
- 027- *European Agreement Concerning Programme Exchanges by Means of Television Films (1958)*, signed 1958, in force 1961;
- 028- *Third Protocol to the General Agreement on Privileges and Immunities of the Council of Europe (1959)*, signed 1959, in force 1963;
- 029- *European Convention on Compulsory Insurance Against Civil Liability in Respect of Motor Vehicles (1959)*, signed 1959, in force 1969;
- 030- *European Convention on Mutual Assistance in Criminal Matters (1959)*, signed 1959, in force 1962;
- 031- *European Agreement on the Abolition of Visas for Refugees (1959)*, signed 1959, in force 1960;
- 032- *European Convention on the Academic Recognition of University Qualifications (1959)*, signed 1959, in force 1961;
- >0233- *Agreement on the Temporary Importation, Free of Duty, of Medical, Surgical and Laboratory Equipment for Use on Free Loan in Hospitals and other Medical Institutions for Purposes of Diagnosis or Treatment (1960)*, signed 1960, in force 1960;
- 034- *European Agreement on the Protection of Television Broadcasts (1960)*, signed 1960, in force 1961;
- 035- *European Social Charter (1961)*, signed 1961, in force 1965;
- 036- *Fourth Protocol to the General Agreement on Privileges and Immunities of the Council of Europe (1961)*, signed 1961, in force 1961;
- 037- *European Agreement on Travel by Young Persons on Collective Passports between the Member Countries of the Council of Europe (1961)*, signed 1961, in force 1962;
- 028- *European Agreement on Mutual Assistance in the Matter of Special Medical Treatments and Climatic Facilities (1962)*, signed 1962, in force 1962;
- 039- *European Agreement on the Exchanges of Blood-grouping Reagents (1962)*, signed 1962, in force 1962;
- 040- *Agreement between the Member States of the Council of Europe on the Issue to Military and Civilian War-disabled of an International Book of Vouchers for the Repair of Prosthetic and Orthopaedic Appliances (1962)*, signed 1962, in force 1963;
- 041- *Convention on the Liability of Hotel-keepers Concerning the Property of Their Guests (1962)*, signed 1962, in force 1967;
- 042- *Agreement Relating to Application of the European Convention on International Commercial Arbitration (1962)*, signed 1962, in force 1965;
- 043- *Convention on Reduction of Cases of Multiple Nationality and Military Obligations in Cases of Multiple Nationality (1963)*, signed 1963, in force 1968;
- 044- *Protocol no 2 to the Convention for the Protection of Human Rights and Fundamental Freedoms, conferring upon the European Court of Human Rights competence to give advisory opinions (1963)*, signed 1963, in force 1970;
- 045- *Protocol no 3 to the Convention for the Protection of Human Rights and Fundamental Freedoms, amending Articles 29, 30 and 34 of the Convention (1963)*, signed 1963, in force 1970;
- 046- *Protocol no 4 to the Convention for Protection of Human Rights and Fundamental Freedoms, securing certain rights and freedoms other than those already included in the Convention and in the first Protocol thereto (1963)*, signed 1963, in force 1968;
- 047- *Convention on the Unification of Certain Points of Substantive Law on Patents for Invention (1963)*, signed 1963, in force 1980;
- 048- *European Code of Social Security (1964)*, signed 1964, in force 1968;
- 048A- *Protocol to the European Code of Social Security (1964)*, signed 1964, in force 1968;
- 049- *Protocol to the European Convention on the Equivalence of Diplomas Leading to Admission to Universities (1964)*, signed 1964, in force 1964;
- 050- *Convention on the Elaboration of a European Pharmacopoeia (1964)*, signed 1964, in force 1974;
- 051- *European Convention on the Supervision of Conditionally Sentenced or Conditionally Released Offenders (1964)*, signed 1964, in force 1975;
- 052- *European Convention on the Punishment of Road Traffic Offences (1964)*, signed 1964, in force 1972;
- 053- *European Agreement for the Prevention of Broadcasts Transmitted from Stations Outside National Territories (1965)*, signed 1965, in force 1967;
- 054- *Protocol to the European Agreement on the Protection of Television Broadcasts (1965)*, signed 1965, in force 1965;
- 055- *Protocol No. 5 to the Convention for the Protection of Human Rights and Fundamental Freedoms, amending Articles 22 and 40 of the Convention (1966)*, signed 1966, in force 1971;
- 056- *European Convention Providing a Uniform Law on Arbitration (1966)*, signed 1966, not yet in force;
- 057- *European Convention on Establishment of Companies (1966)*, signed 1966, not yet in force;
- 058- *European Convention on the Adoption of Children (1967)*, signed 1967, in force 1968;
- 059- *European Agreement on the Instruction and Education of Nurses (1967)*, signed 1967, in force 1969;
- 060- *European Convention on Foreign Money Liabilities (1967)*, signed 1967, not yet in force;
- 061- *European Convention on Consular Functions (1967)*, signed 1967, in force 2011;
- 061A- *Protocol to the European Convention on Consular Functions Concerning the Protection of Refugees (1967)*, signed 1967, not yet in force;
- 061B- *Protocol to the European Convention on Consular Functions Relating to Consular Functions in Respect of Civil Aircraft (1967)*, signed 1967, net yet in force;
- 062- *European Convention on Information on Foreign Law (1968)*, signed 1968, in force 1969;
- 063- *European Convention on the Abolition of Legalisation of Documents Executed by Diplomatic Agents or Consular Officers (1968)*, signed 1968, in force 1970;
- 064- *European Agreement on the Restriction of the Use of Certain Detergents in Washing and Cleaning Products (1968)*, signed 1968, in force 1971;
- 065- *European Convention for the Protection of Animals During International Transport (1968)*, signed 1968, in force 1971;
- 066- *European Convention on the Protection of the Archaeological Heritage (1969)*, signed 1969, in force 1970;
- 067- *European Agreement Relating to Persons Participating in Proceedings of the European Commission and Court of Human Rights (1969)*, signed 1969, in force 1971;
- 068- *European Agreement on 'au Pair' Placement (1969)*, signed 1969, in force 1971;
- 069- *European Agreement on Continued Payment of Scholarships to Students Studying Abroad (1969)*, signed 1969, in force 1971;
- 070- *European Convention on the International Validity of Criminal Judgments (1970)*, signed 1970, in force 1974;
- 071- *European Convention on the Repatriation of Minors (1970)*, signed 1970, in force 2015;
- 072- *Convention Relating to Stops on Bearer Securities in International Circulation (1970)*, signed 1970, in force 1979;
- 073- *European Convention on the Transfer of Proceedings in Criminal Matters (1972)*, signed 1972, in force 1978;
- 074- *European Convention on State Immunity (1972)*, signed 1972, in force 1976;
- 074A- *Additional Protocol to the European Convention on State Immunity (1972)*, signed 1972, in force 1985;
- 075- *European Convention on the Place of Payment of Money Liabilities (1972)*, signed 1972, not yet in force;
- 076- *European Convention on the Calculation of Time-limits (1974)*, signed 1972, in force 1983;
- 077- *Convention on the Establishment of a Scheme of Registration of Wills (1972)*, signed 1972, in force 1976;
- 078- *European Convention on Social Security (1972)*, signed 1972, in force 1977;
- 078A- *Supplementary Agreement to the Application of the European Convention on Social Security (1972)*, signed 1972, in force 1977;
- 079- *European Convention on Civil Liability for Damage Caused by Motor Vehicles (1973)*, signed 1973, not yet in force;
- 080- *Agreement on the Transfer of Corpses (1973)*, signed 1973, in force 1975;
- 081- *Additional Protocol to the Protocol to the European Agreement on the Protection of Television Broadcasts, 1974 (1974)*, signed 1974, in force 1974;
- 082- *European Convention on the Non-applicability of Statutory Limitation to Crimes Against Humanity and War Crimes (1974)*, signed 1974, in force 2003;
- 083- *European Convention on the Social Protection of Farmers (1974)*, signed 1974, in force 1977;
- 084- *European Agreement on the Exchange of Tissue-typing Reagents (1974)*, signed 1974, in force 1977;
- 085- *European Convention on the Legal Status of Children Born out of Wedlock (1975)*, signed 1975, in force 1978;
- 086- *Additional Protocol to the European Convention on Extradition (1975)*, signed 1975, in force 1979;
- 087- *European Convention for the Protection of Animals Kept for Farming Purposes (1976)*, signed 1976, in force 1979;
- 088- *European Convention on the International Effects of Deprivation of the Right to Drive a Motor Vehicle (1976)*, signed 1976, in force 1983;
- 089- *Additional Protocol to the European Agreement on the Exchange of Tissue-typing Reagents (1976)*, signed 1976, in force 1977;
- 090- *European Convention on the Suppression of Terrorism (1977)*, signed 1977, in force 1978;
- 091- *European Convention on Products Liability in Regard to Personal Injury and Death (1977)*, signed 1977, not yet in force;
- 092- *European Agreement on the Transmission of Applications for Legal Aid (1977)*, signed 1977, in force 1977;
- 093- *European Convention on the Legal Status of Migrant Workers (1977)*, signed 1977, in force 1983;
- 094- *European Convention on the Service Abroad of Documents Relating to Administrative Matters (1977)*, signed 1977, in force 1982;
- 095- *Protocol Amending the Convention on the Reduction of Cases of Multiple Nationality and Military Obligations in Cases of Multiples Nationality (1977)*, signed 1977, in force 1978;
- 096- *Additional Protocol to the Convention on the Reduction of Cases of Multiple Nationality and Military Obligations in Cases of Multiple Nationality (1977)*, signed 1977, in force 1983;
- 097- *Additional Protocol to the European Convention on Information on Foreign Law (1978)*, signed 1978, in force 1979;
- 098- *Second Additional Protocol to the European Convention on Extradition (1978)*, signed 1978, in force 1983;
- 099- *Additional Protocol to the European Convention on Mutual Assistance in Criminal Matters (1978)*, signed 1978, in force 1982;
- 100- *European Convention on the Obtaining Abroad of Information and Evidence in Administrative Matters (1978)*, signed 1978, in force 1983;
- 101- *European Convention on the Control of the Acquisition and Possession of Firearms by Individuals (1978)*, signed 1978, in force 1982;
- 102- *European Convention for the Protection of Animals for Slaughter (1979)*, signed 1979, in force 1982;
- 103- *Additional Protocol to the European Convention for the Protection of Animals During International Transport (1979)*, signed 1979, in force 1989;
- 104- *Convention on the Conservation of European Wildlife and Natural Habitats (Bern convention, 1979)*, signed 1979, in force 1982;
- 105- *European Convention on Recognition and Enforcement of Decisions Concerning Custody of Children and on Restoration of Custody of Children (1980)*, signed 1980, in force 1983;
- 106- *European Outline Convention on Transfrontier Cooperation between Territorial Communities or Authorities (1980)*, signed 1980, in force 1981;
- 107- *European Agreement on Transfer of Responsibility for Refugees (1980)*, signed 1980, in force 1980;
- 108- *Convention for the Protection of Individuals with Regard to Automatic Processing of Personal Data (1981)*, signed 1981, in force 1985;
- 109- *Additional Protocol to the European Agreement on the Exchange of Therapeutic Substances of Human Origin (1983)*, signed 1983, in force 1985;
- 110- *Additional Protocol to the Agreement on the Temporary Importation, Free of Duty, of Medical, Surgical and Laboratory Equipment for Use on Free Loan in Hospitals and other Medical Institutions for Purposes of Diagnosis or Treatment (1983)*, signed 1983, in force 1985;
- 111- *Additional Protocol to the European Agreement on the Exchanges of Blood-grouping Reagents (1983)*, signed 1983, in force 1985;
- 112- *Convention on the Transfer of Sentenced Persons (1983)*, signed 1983, in force 1985;
- 113- *Additional Protocol to the Protocol to the European Agreement on the Protection of Television Broadcasts (1983)*, signed 1983, in force 1985;
- 114- *Protocol no 6 to the Convention for the Protection of Human Rights and Fundamental Freedoms Concerning the Abolition of the Death Penalty (1983)*, signed 1983, in force 1985;
- 115- *Protocol Amending the European Agreement on the Restriction of the Use of Certain Detergents in Washing and Cleaning Products (1983)*, signed 1983, in force 1984;
- 116- *European Convention on the Compensation of Victims of Violent Crimes (1983)*, signed 1983, in force 1988;
- 117- *Protocol no 7 to the Convention for the Protection of Human Rights and Fundamental Freedoms (1984)*, signed 1984, in force 1988;
- 118- *Protocol no 8 to the Convention for the Protection of Human Rights and Fundamental Freedoms (1985)*, signed 1985, in force 1990;
- 119- *European Convention on Offences Relating to Cultural Property (1985)*, signed 1985, not yet in force;
- 120- *European Convention on Spectator Violence and Misbehaviour at Sports Events and in Particular at Football Matches (1985)*, signed 1985, in force 1985;
- 121- *Convention for the Protection of the Architectural Heritage of Europe (1985)*, signed 1985, in force 1987;
- 122- *European Charter of Local Self-government (1985)*, signed 1985, in force 1988;
- 123- *European Convention for the Protection of Vertebrate Animals Used for Experimental and other Scientific Purposes (1986)*, signed 1986, in force 1991;
- 124- *European Convention on the Recognition of the Legal Personality of International Non-Governmental Organisations (1986)*, signed 1986, in force 1991;
- 125- *European Convention for the Protection of Pet Animals (1987)*, signed 1987, in force 1992;
- 126- *European Convention for the Prevention of Torture and Inhuman or Degrading Treatment or Punishment (1987)*, signed 1987, in force 1989;
- 127- *Multilateral Convention on Mutual Administrative Assistance in Tax Matters (1988)*, signed 1988, in force 1995;
- 128- *Additional Protocol to the European Social Charter, 1988 (1988)*, signed 1988, in force 1992;
- 129- *Arrangement for the Application of the European Agreement of 17 October 1980 Concerning the Provision of Medical Care to Persons During Temporary Residence (1988)*, signed 1988, not yet in force;
- 130- *Convention on Insider Trading (1989)*, signed 1989, in force 1991;
- 131- *Third Additional Protocol to the Protocol to the European Agreement on the Protection of Television Broadcasts (1989)*, signed 1989, not yet in force;
- 132- *European Convention on Transfrontier Television (1989)*, signed 1989, in force 1993;
- 133- *Protocol to the Convention on Insider Trading (1989)*, signed 1989, in force 1991;
- 134- *Protocol to the Convention on the Elaboration of a European Pharmacopoeia (1989)*, signed 1989, in force 1992;
- 135- *Anti-doping Convention (1989)*, signed 1989, in force 1990;
- 136- *European Convention on Certain International Aspects of Bankruptcy (1990)*, signed 1990, not yet in force;
- 137- *Fifth Protocol to the General Agreement on Privileges and Immunities of the Council of Europe (1990)*, signed 1990, in force 1991;
- 138- *European Convention on the General Equivalence of Periods of University Study (1990)*, signed 1990, in force 1991;
- 139- *European Code of Social Security, Revised (1990)*, signed 1990, not yet in force;
- 140- *Protocol no 9 to the Convention for the Protection of Human Rights and Fundamental Freedoms (1990)*, signed 1990, in force 1994;
- 141- *Convention on Laundering, Search, Seizure and Confiscation of the Proceeds from Crime (1990)*, signed 1990, in force 1993;
- 142- *Protocol Amending the European Social Charter (1991)*, signed 1991, not yet in force;
- 143- *European Convention on the Protection of the Archaeological Heritage, Revised (1992)*, signed 1992, in force 1995;
- 144- *Convention on the Participation of Foreigners in Public Life at Local Level (1992)*, signed 1992, in force 1997;

– 145- *Protocol of Amendment to the European Convention for the Protection of Animals Kept for Farming Purposes (1992)*, signed 1992, not yet in force;
– 146- *Protocol no 10 to the Convention for the Protection of Human Rights and Fundamental Freedoms (1992)*, signed 1992, not yet in force;
– 147- *European Convention on Cinematographic Co-production (1992)*, signed 1992, in force 1994;
– 148- *European Charter for Regional or Minority Languages (ECRML, 1992)*, signed 1992, in force 1998;
– 149- *Second Protocol Amending the Convention on the Reduction of Cases of Multiple Nationality and Military Obligations in Cases of Multiple Nationality (1993)*, signed 1993, in force 1995;
– 150- *Convention on Civil Liability for Damage Resulting from Activities Dangerous to the Environment (1993)*, signed 1993, not yet in force;
– 151- *Protocol no 1 to the European Convention for the Prevention of Torture and Inhuman or Degrading Treatment or Punishment (1993)*, signed 1993, in force 2002;
– 152- *Protocol no 2 to the European Convention for the Prevention of Torture and Inhuman or Degrading Treatment or Punishment (1993)*, signed 1993, in force 2002;
– 153- *European Convention Relating to Questions on Copyright Law and Neighbouring Rights in the Framework of Transfrontier Broadcasting by Satellite (1994)*, signed 1994, not yet in force;
– 154- *Protocol to the European Convention on Social Security (1994)*, signed 1994, not yet in force;
– 155- *Protocol no 11 to the Convention for the Protection of Human Rights and Fundamental Freedoms (1994)*, signed 1994, in force 1998;
– 156- *Agreement on Illicit Traffic by Sea, Implementing Article 17 of the United Nations Convention Against Illicit Traffic in Narcotic Drugs and Psychotropic Substances (1995)*, signed 1995, in force 2000;
– 157- *Framework Convention for the Protection of National Minorities (1995)*, signed 1995, in force 1998;
– 158- *Additional Protocol to the European Social Charter Providing for a System of Collective Complaints (1995)*, signed 1995, in force 1998;
– 159- *Additional Protocol to the European Outline Convention on Transfrontier Cooperation between Territorial Communities or Authorities (1995)*, signed 1995, in force 1998;
– 160- *European Convention on the Exercise of Children's Rights (1996)*, signed 1996, in force 2000;
– 161- *European Agreement Relating to Persons Participating in Proceedings of the European Court of Human Rights (1996)*, signed 1996, in force 1999;
– 162- *Sixth Protocol to the General Agreement on Privileges and Immunities of the Council of Europe (1996)*, signed 1996, in force 1998;
– 163- *European Social Charter – Revised (1996)*, signed 1996, in force 1999;
– 164- *Convention for the Protection of Human Rights and Dignity of the Human Being with regard to the Application of Biology and Medicine: Convention on Human Rights and Biomedicine (1997)*, signed 1997, in force 1999;
– 165- *Convention on the Recognition of Qualifications Concerning Higher Education in the European Region (1997)*, signed 1997, in force 1999;
– 166- *European Convention on Nationality (1997)*, signed 1997, in force 2000;
– 167- *Additional Protocol to the Convention on the Transfer of Sentenced Persons (1997)*, signed 1977, in force 2000;
– 168- *Additional Protocol to the Convention for the Protection of Human Rights and Dignity of the Human Being with Regard to the Application of Biology and Medicine, on the Prohibition of Cloning Human Beings (1998)*, signed 1998, in force 2001;
– 169- *Protocol no 2 to the European Outline Convention on Transfrontier Cooperation between Territorial Communities or Authorities Concerning Interterritorial Cooperation (1998)*, signed 1998, in force 2001;
– 170- *Protocol of Amendment to the European Convention for the Protection of Vertebrate Animals Used for Experimental and other Scientific Purposes (1998)*, signed 1998, in force 2005;
– 171- *Protocol Amending the European Convention on Transfrontier Television (1998)*, signed 1998, in force 2002;
– 172- *Convention on Protection of the Environment through Criminal Law (1998)*, signed 1998, not yet in force;
– 173- *Criminal Law Convention on Corruption (1999)*, signed 1999, in force 2002;
– 174- *Civil Law Convention on Corruption (1999)*, signed 1999, in force 2003;
– 175- *European Convention on the Promotion of a Transnational Long-term Voluntary Service for Young People (2000)*, signed 2000, not yet in force;
– 176- *European Landscape Convention (2000)*, signed 2000, in force 2004;
– 177- *Protocol no 12 to the Convention for the Protection of Human Rights and Fundamental Freedoms (2000)*, signed 2000, in force 2005;
– 178- *European Convention on the Legal Protection of Services Based On, or Consisting Of, Conditional Access (2001)*, signed 2001, in force 2003;
– 179- *Additional Protocol to the European Agreement on the Transmission of Applications for Legal Aid (2001)*, signed 2001, in force 2002;
– 180- *Convention on Information and Legal Cooperation Concerning "Information Society Services" (2001)*; signed 2001, not yet in force;
– 181- *Additional Protocol to the Convention for the Protection of Individuals with Regard to Automatic Processing of Personal Data, Regarding Supervisory Authorities and Transborder Data Flows (2001)*, signed 2001, in force 2004;
– 182- *Second Additional Protocol to the European Convention on Mutual Assistance in Criminal Matters (2001)*, signed 2001, in force 2004;
– 183- *European Convention on the Protection of the Audiovisual Heritage (2001)*, signed 2001, in force 2008;
– 184- *Protocol to the European Convention on the Protection of the Audiovisual Heritage, on the Protection of Television Productions (2001)*, signed 2001, in force 2014;
– 185- *Convention on Cybercrime (Budapest Convention, 2001)*, signed 2001, in force 2004;
– 186- *Additional Protocol to the Convention on Human Rights and Biomedicine Concerning Transplantation of Organs and Tissues of Human Origin (2002)*, signed 2002, in force 2006;
– 187- *Protocol no 13 to the Convention for the Protection of Human Rights and Fundamental Freedoms, Concerning the Abolition of the Death Penalty in all Circumstances (2002)*, signed 2002, in force 2003;
– 188- *Additional Protocol to the Anti-doping Convention (2002)*, signed 2002, in force 2004;
– 189- *Additional Protocol to the Convention on Cybercrime, Concerning the Criminalisation of Acts of a Racist and Xenophobic Nature Committed through Computer Systems (2003)*, signed 2003, in force 2006;
– 190- *Protocol Amending the European Convention on the Suppression of Terrorism (2003)*, signed 2003, not yet in force;
– 191- *Additional Protocol to the Criminal Law Convention on Corruption (2003)*, signed 2003, in force 2005;
– 192- *Convention on Contact Concerning Children (2003)*, signed 2003, in force 2005;
– 193- *European Convention for the Protection of Animals During International Transport – Revised (2003)*, signed 2003, in force 2006;
– 194- *Protocol no 14 to the Convention for the Protection of Human Rights and Fundamental Freedoms, Amending the Control System of the Convention (2004)*, signed 2004, in force 2010;
– 195- *Additional Protocol to the Convention on Human Rights and Biomedicine, Concerning Biomedical Research (2005)*, signed 2005, in force 2007;
– 196- *Council of Europe Convention on the Prevention of Terrorism (2005)*, signed 2005, in force 2007;
– 197- *Council of Europe Convention on Action Against Trafficking in Human Beings (2005)*, signed 2005, in force 2008;
– 198- *Council of Europe Convention on Laundering, Search, Seizure and Confiscation of the Proceeds from Crime and on the Financing of Terrorism (2005)*, signed 2005, in force 2008;
– 199- *Council of Europe Framework Convention on the Value of Cultural Heritage for Society (2005)*, signed 2005, in force 2011;
– 200- *Council of Europe Convention on the Avoidance of Statelessness in Relations to State Succession (2006)*, signed 2006, in force 2009;
– 201- *Council of Europe Convention on the Protection of Children against Sexual Exploitation and Sexual Abuse (2007)*, signed 2007, in force 2010;
– 202- *European Convention on the Adoption of Children – Revised (2008)*, signed 2008, in force 2011;
– 203- *Additional Protocol to the Convention on Human Rights and Biomedicine concerning Genetic Testing for Health Purposes (2008)*, signed 2008, not yet in force;
– 204- *Protocol No 14bis to the Convention for the Protection of Human Rights and Fundamental Freedoms (inactive)*, signed 2009, in force 2009;
– 205- *Council of Europe Convention on Access to Official Documents (2009)*, signed 2009, not yet in force;
– 206- *Protocol No 3 to the European Outline Convention on Transfrontier Co-operation between Territorial Communities or Authorities concerning Euroregional Co-operation Groupings – ECGs (2009)*, signed 2009, in force 2013;
– 207- *Additional Protocol to the European Charter of Local Self-Government on the right to participate in the affairs of a local authority (2009)*, signed 2009, in force 2012;
– 208- *Protocol amending the Convention on Mutual Administrative Assistance in Tax Matters (2010)*, signed 2010, in force 2011;
– 209- *Third Additional Protocol to the European Convention on Extradition (2010)*, signed 2010, in force 2012;
– 210- *Council of Europe Convention on Preventing and Combating Violence against Women and Domestic Violence (2011)*, signed 2011, in force 2014;
– 211- *Council of Europe Convention on the Counterfeiting of Medical Products and Similar Crimes involving Threats to Public Health (Medicrime Covention, 2011)*, signed 2011, in force 2016;
– 212- *Fourth Additional Protocol to the European Convention on Extradition (2012)*, signed 2012, in force 2014;
– 213- *Protocol No 15 amending the Convention for the Protection of Human Rights and Fundamental Freedoms (2013)*, signed 2013, not yet in force;
– 214- *Protocol No 16 to the Convention for the Protection of Human Rights and Fundamental Freedoms (2013)*, signed 2013, not yet in force;
– 215- *Council of Europe Convention on the Manipulation of Sports Competitions (2014)*, signed 2014, not yet in force;
– 216- *Council of Europe Convention against Trafficking in Human Organs (2015)*, signed 2015, not yet in force;
– 217- *Additional Protocol to the Council of Europe Convention on the Prevention of Terrorism (2015)*, signed 2015, not yet in force;
– 218 – *Council of Europe Convention on an Integrated Safety, Security and Service Approach at Football Matches and Other Sports Events (2016)*, signed 2016, not yet in force.

Cooperation with: *Eurolib (#05703)*; *European Information Network on International Relations and Area Studies (EINIRAS, #07534)*; *European Centre for Parliamentary Research and Documentation (ECPRD, #06495)*. The anniversary of the founding of the Council of Europe, 5th May, is celebrated as *'Europe Day – Journée de l'Europe'*.

Events *International Conference of Ministers and Senior Officials Responsible for Physical Education and Sport (MINEPS)* Baku (Azerbaijan) 2023, *Study Session* Budapest (Hungary) 2022, *Europakonferansen for demokrati og menneskerettigheter / European Conference on Democracy and Human Rights* Kristiansand (Norway) 2022, *Conference on the Future of Europe Plenary Session* Strasbourg (France) 2022, *Conference on the Future of Europe Plenary Session* Strasbourg (France) 2022. **Publications** *Council of Europe Programme and Budget* (annual); *Council of Europe Highlights – Annual Activity Report*; *State of Democracy, Human Rights and the Rule of Law in Europe – Annual Report*. **Information Services** *Council of Europe Archives* – comprising thematic historical files (1948-1980), referenced documents (1949-) and intermediate archives of the Council of Europe instances and services; *Council of Europe Documents Collection* – documents of general interest, conventions and adopted texts; *Council of Europe Retrieval System* – bibliographic database of Council of Europe libraries and documentation centres, comprising both paper and electronic documentary resources; *Giuseppe Vedovato Library* – reference, international organizations' documentation, diplomacy, international relations, subjects covering activities of the Council of Europe; *HUDOC* – web-based system for searching case law on control bodies established under European Convention on Human Rights; *Information and Documentation Centres in Central and Eastern Europe* – network of 22 centres in 18 countries; *Production and Retrieval of Information and Documents through Electronics (PRIDE)* – project, with 3 service areas: on-demand real time printing of documents to institutional authors (WWW service), digital library, advance distribution services.

Members Governments of 46 countries:
Albania, Andorra, Armenia, Austria, Azerbaijan, Belgium, Bosnia-Herzegovina, Bulgaria, Croatia, Cyprus, Czechia, Denmark, Estonia, Finland, France, Georgia, Germany, Greece, Hungary, Iceland, Ireland, Italy, Latvia, Liechtenstein, Lithuania, Luxembourg, Malta, Moldova, Monaco, Montenegro, Netherlands, North Macedonia, Norway, Poland, Portugal, Romania, San Marino, Serbia, Slovakia, Slovenia, Spain, Sweden, Switzerland, Türkiye, UK, Ukraine.
Observer status granted to 5 countries:
Canada, Holy See, Japan, Mexico, USA.
Observer to the Parliamentary Assembly – 1 country:
Israel.

Consultative Status *Conference of INGOs of the Council of Europe* ensures liaison with civil society. Introduction of Participatory Status in 2003 enabled INGOs to increase active participation in policies and work programme of Council of Europe, and reinforce cooperation. As of 2021, participatory status is granted to 326 organizations:
Organizations granted consultative status:
Participatory Status (326):
– *Advice on Individual Rights in Europe Centre (AIRE Centre)*;
– *AGE Platform Europe (#00557)*;
– *AIESEC (#00593)*;
– *Alzheimer Europe (AE, #00761)*;
– *Amnesty International (AI, #00801)*;
– *Anti-Slavery International (#00860)*;
– *Association Catholique Internationale de Services pour la Jeunesse Féminine (ACISJF/In Via, #02417)*;
– *Association des femmes de l'Europe méridionale (AFEM, #02594)*;
– *Association des états généraux des étudiants de l'Europe (AEGEE-Europe, #02495)*;
– *Association Europa*;
– *Association européenne des cheminots (AEC, #02558)*;
– *Association européenne des enseignants (AEDE, #02565)*;
– *Association for the Prevention of Torture (APT, #02869)*;
– *Association Internationale des Charités (AIC, #02675)*;
– *Association internationale pour la défense de la liberté religieuse (AIDLR, #02681)*;
– *Association Mondiale des Amis de l'Enfance (AMADE, #02808)*;
– *Association of European Border Regions (AEBR, #02499)*;
– *Association of European Election Officials (ACEEEO, #02508)*;
– *Association of European Journalists (AEJ, #02516)*;
– *Association of Language Testers in Europe (ALTE, #02779)*;
– *Association of Non-Governmental Organizations of Southeast Europe (CIVIS, #02825)*;
– *Association of Schools of Political Studies of the Council of Europe (#02902)*;
– *Association of the European Self-Care Industry (#02543)*;
– *Association of Working Communities of the Alpine Regions (AWCAR, #02981)*;
– *Association pour le volontariat en Europe (AVE, #02978)*;
– *Atheist Alliance International (AAI, #03003)*;
– *Autism-Europe (AE, #03040)*;
– *Balkan Civil Society Development Network (BCSDN, #03070)*;
– *BirdLife Europe (#03265)*;
– *B'nai B'rith International (BBI, #03290)*;
– *Caritas Europa (#03579)*;
– *Catholic International Education Office (#03604)*;
– *CEJI (#03628)*;
– *Center for Reproductive Rights*;
– *Centre d'étude et de prospective stratégique (CEPS, #03739)*;
– *Centre for European Volunteering (CEV, #03743)*;
– *Child Helpline International (CHI, #03870)*;
– *ChildPact (#03874)*;
– *Children of Prisoners Europe (COPE, #03875)*;
– *Child Rights International Network (CRIN, #03885)*;
– *Churches' Commission for Migrants in Europe (CCME, #03912)*;
– *CISV International (#03949)*;
– *CIVICUS: World Alliance for Citizen Participation (#03962)*;
– *Civil Rights Defenders*;
– *Civilscape (#03966)*;
– *COJEP International – Conseil pour la Justice, l'Egalité et la Paix (COJEP International, #04090)*;
– *Colloquy of European Parishes (#04119)*;
– *Comité européen d'action spécialisée pour l'enfant et la famille dans leur milieu de vie (EUROCEF, #04150)*;
– *Community Media Forum Europe (CMFE, #04402)*;
– *Confederation of European Companions (#04522)*;
– *Confederation of European Probation (CEP, #04530)*;
– *Conference of European Churches (CEC, #04593)*;
– *Conference of European Justice and Peace Commissions (#04596)*;
– *Conference of European Rabbis (CER, #04598)*;
– *Confédération internationale des travailleurs intellectuels (CITI, #04564)*;
– *Council of Bars and Law Societies of Europe (CCBE, #04871)*;
– *Council of European Professional Informatics Societies (CEPIS, #04893)*;
– *Crans Montana Forum (#04944)*;
– *Danish Refugee Council (DRC)*;
– *Defence for Children International (DCI, #05025)*;
– *Disabled Peoples' International (DPI, #05097)* (European Region);
– *Dynamo International – Street Workers Network*;
– *Eastern Partnership Civil Society Forum (EaP CSF, #05247)*;
– *Ecumenical Forum of European Christian Women (EFECW, #05347)*;
– *Education International (EI, #05371)*;
– *Equal Rights Trust (#05520)*;
– *Erasmus Student Network (ESN, #05529)*;
– *euroart – the European Federation of Artists' Colonies (euroart, #05632)*;
– *Eurochild (#05657)*;
– *Eurodesk Network (#05675)* (Eurodesk Brussels Link);
– *Eurogroup for Animals (#05690)*;
– *EuroMed Rights (#05733)*;
– *Europa Nostra (#05767)*;
– *EUROPARC Federation (#05768)*;
– *European Action of the Disabled (#05825)*;
– *European Alliance of Catholic Women's Organisations (ANDANTE, #05864)*;
– *European Anti-Poverty Network (EAPN, #05908)*;
– *European Association for Audiovisual Media Education (EAAME, #05946)*;

- European Association for Language Testing and Assessment (EALTA, #06103);
- European Association for Local Democracy (ALDA, #06110);
- European Association for Palliative Care (EAPC, #06141);
- European Association for Psychotherapy (EAP, #06176);
- European Association for the Defence of Human Rights (AEDH, no recent information);
- European Association for the Education of Adults (EAEA, #06018);
- European Association of Archaeologists (EAA, #05940);
- European Association of Elected Representatives from Mountain Regions (#06021);
- European Association of Geographers (EUROGEO, #06054);
- European Association of History Educators (EUROCLIO, #06069);
- European Association of Régies de quartier (AERDO);
- European Association of Schools of Social Work (EASSW, #06200);
- European Association of Service Providers for Persons with Disabilities (EASPD, #06204);
- European Bars Federation (#06320);
- European Blind Union (EBU, #06350);
- European Broadcasting Union (EBU, #06404);
- European Buddhist Union (EBU, #06407);
- European Bureau for Conscientious Objection (EBCO, #06411);
- European Centre of the International Council of Women (ECICW, #06485);
- European Civic Forum (ECF, #06563);
- European Committee Promoting the Education of Gifted and Talented Young People (EUROTALENT, #06664);
- European Confederation of Independent Trade Unions (CESI, #06705);
- European Confederation of Police (EuroCOP, #06719);
- European Confederation of Youth Clubs (ECYC, #06727);
- European Council of Doctoral Candidates and Junior Researchers (EURODOC, #06815);
- European Council of Police Unions (ECPU, #06837);
- European Council of Spatial Planners (ECTP-CEU, #06843);
- European Council of WIZO Federations (ECWF, #06850);
- European Council on Refugees and Exiles (ECRE, #06839);
- European Democrat Students (EDS, #06901);
- European Disability Forum (EDF, #06929);
- European Drama Encounters (EDERED);
- European Educational Exchanges – Youth for Understanding (EEE-YFU, #06965);
- European Environmental Bureau (EEB, #06996);
- European Federation for Intercultural Learning (EFIL, #07146);
- European Federation of Centres of Research and Information on Cults and Sects (#07072);
- European Federation of Christian Student Associations (#07076);
- European Federation of Employees in Public Services (EUROFEDOP, #07106);
- European Federation of National Organisations Working with the Homeless (#07174);
- European Forum for Urban Security (Efus, #07340);
- European Forum of Lesbian, Gay, Bisexual and Transgender Christian Groups (Forum LGBT, #07318);
- European Gay and Lesbian Sport Federation (EGLSF, #07382);
- European Grassroots Antiracist Movement (EGAM, #07407);
- European Humanist Federation (EHF, #07507);
- European Human Rights Association (EHRA);
- European Implementation Network (EIN, #07521);
- European Jewish Congress (EJC, #07609);
- European Local Inclusion and Social Action Network (ELISAN, #07707);
- European Movement International (EMI, #07825);
- European Muslim Initiative for Social Cohesion (EMISCO, #07839);
- European Network against Racism (ENAR, #07862);
- European Network Church-on-the-Move (#07878);
- European Network for Education and Training (EUNET, #07899);
- European Network of Ombudspersons for Children (ENOC, #07959);
- European Network of Universities for the Implementation of the European Landscape Convention (UNISCAPE, #08030);
- European Network on Independent Living (ENIL, #07929);
- European Network on Statelessness (ENS, #08013);
- European Ombudsman Institute (#08085);
- European Organisation of Military Associations and Trade Unions (EUROMIL, #08099);
- European Paralympic Committee (EPC, #08140);
- European Parents' Association (EPA, #08142);
- European Parliamentary Forum for Sexual & Reproductive Rights (EPF, #08149);
- European Platform for Rehabilitation (EPR, #08230);
- European Prison Education Association (EPEA, #08276);
- European Prison Litigation Network (EPLN, #08277);
- European Psychiatric Association (EPA, #08290);
- European Roma and Travellers Forum (ERTF, #08402);
- European Roma Rights Centre (ERRC, #08401);
- European Sex Workers' Rights Alliance (ESWA, #08472);
- European Social Action Network (ESAN, #08499);
- European Social Network (ESN, #08505);
- European String Teachers Association (ESTA, #08842);
- European Students' Union (ESU, #08848);
- European Trade Union Confederation (ETUC, #08927);
- European Union of Deaf Youth (EUDY, #08986);
- European Union of Former Pupils of Catholic Education (#08992);
- European Union of Jewish Students (EUJS, #08997);
- European Union of Judges in Commercial Matters (EUJC, #08998);
- European Union of Rechtspfleger (#09012);
- European Union of the Deaf (EUD, #08985);
- European Union of Women (EUW, #09022);
- European University Sports Association (EUSA, #09036);
- European Women's Lobby (EWL, #09102);
- European Young Bar Association (EYBA, #09132);
- European Youth Card Association (EYCA, #09137);
- European Youth Forum (#09140);
- European Youth Information and Counselling Agency (ERYICA, #09142);
- Europäisches Forum für angewandte Kriminalpolitik (EFK);
- EU-Russia Civil Society Forum (CSF, #09199);
- Evaluation and Accreditation of Quality in Language Services (Eaquals, #09209);
- Federal Union of European Nationalities (FUEN, #09396);
- Federatie voor Mondiale Democratische Organisaties (FMDO);
- Federation for EDucation in Europe (FEDE, #09479);
- Federation of Catholic Family Associations in Europe (#09468);
- Femmes chefs d'entreprises mondiales (FCEM, #09733);
- Fondation pour l'économie et le développement durable des régions d'Europe (FEDRE, #09817);
- Formation d'éducateurs sociaux européens (FESET, #09873);
- Forum of European Muslim Youth and Student Organisations (FEMYSO, #09909);
- Foundation for Language and Educational Centres (EUROCENTRES, #09964);
- Friedrich-Ebert-Stiftung (FES);
- Fédération européenne de psychanalyse et Ecole psychanalytique de Strasbourg (FEDEPSY);
- Fédération internationale des associations de personnes âgées (FIAPA, #09609);
- Fédération internationale des Jardins Familiaux (#09641);
- Fédération internationale des professeurs de français (FIPF, #09652);
- Fédération internationale des thérapies et relations d'aide par la médiation (FITRAM, #09664);
- Global Organization of Parliamentarians Against Corruption (GOPAC, #10518);
- Greenpeace International (#10727);
- Groupement Européen pour la Recherche et la Formation des Enseignants Chrétiens, Croyants et de toutes Convictions (GERFEC, #10759);
- Helsinki Citizens' Assembly (hCa, #10905);
- Hope and Homes for Children;
- "Hope for Children" CRC Policy Center (HFC, #10943);
- Howard League for Penal Reform;
- Humanists International (#10972);
- Human Rights Education Youth Network (HREYN, #10982);
- Human Rights House Foundation (#10984);
- Human Rights Watch (HRW, #10990);
- IFEX (#11100);
- IFLA Europe (#11103);
- ILGA-Europe (#11118);
- Inclusion Europe – European Association of Societies of Persons with Intellectual Disability and their Families (Inclusion Europe, #11144);
- Initiatives of Change International – Caux (IofC, #11213);
- Institute for Reporters' Freedom and Safety;
- Intereuropean Commission on Church and School (ICCS, #11469);
- International Alliance of Women (IAW, #11639);
- International Antiterrorism Unity (IAU);
- International Association for Research in Hospital Hygiene (IARHH, no recent information);
- International Association of Judges (IAJ, #11978);
- International Association of Penal Law (IAPL, #12074);
- International Association of Refugee and Migration Judges (IARMJ, #12126);
- International Association of Social Educators (#12167);
- International Association of the European Heritage Network (HEREIN Association, #11881);
- International Association of Universities (IAU, #12246);
- International Association of Youth and Family Judges and Magistrates (IAYFJM, #12283);
- International Bar Association (IBA, #12320);
- International Catholic Child Bureau (#12450);
- International Catholic Migration Commission (ICMC, #12459);
- International Chamber of Commerce (ICC, #12534);
- International Commission of Jurists (ICJ, #12695);
- International Council of Jewish Women (ICJW, #13036);
- International Council on Shared Parenting (ICSP, #13072);
- International Council on Social Welfare (ICSW, #13076) (Europe);
- International Detention Coalition (IDC, #13154);
- International Diabetes Federation Europe (IDF Europe, #13165);
- Internationales Institut für Nationalitätenrecht und Regionalismus (INTEREG, #13300);
- International Falcon Movement – Socialist Educational International (IFM-SEI, #13327);
- International Federation for Housing and Planning (IFHP, #13450);
- International Federation for Human Rights (#13452);
- International Federation for Parent Education (IFPE, #13499);
- International Federation for Peace and Conciliation (IFPC, #13501);
- International Federation of ACATs – Action by Christians for the Abolition of Torture (#13334);
- International Federation of Actors (#13337);
- International Federation of Business and Professional Women (BPW International, #13376);
- International Federation of Catholic Universities (IFCU, #13381);
- International Federation of Journalists (IFJ, #13462);
- International Federation of Language Teacher Associations (#13468);
- International Federation of Liberal Youth (IFLRY, #13469);
- International Federation of Medical Students' Associations (IFMSA, #13478);
- International Federation of Social Workers (IFSW, #13544);
- International Federation of Training Centres for the Promotion of Progressive Education (#13572);
- International Institute of Humanitarian Law (IIHL, #13885);
- International League Against Racism and Antisemitism (#14014);
- International League for Teaching, Education and Popular Culture (ILFCAAE, #14023);
- International Media Support (IMS, #14128);
- International Movement ATD Fourth World (#14193);
- International Network of Civil Liberties Organizations (INCLO, #14242);
- International Organization for the Right to Education and Freedom of Education (#14468);
- International Partnership for Human Rights (IPHR);
- International Planned Parenthood Federation (IPPF, #14589) (European Network);
- International Press Institute (IPI, #14636);
- International Scientific Conference Minorities for Europe of Tomorrow (ISCOMET, #14808);
- International Society of City and Regional Planners (ISOCARP, #15012);
- International Union of Judicial Officers (#15785);
- International Union of Socialist Youth (IUSY, #15815);
- International Union of Tenants (IUT, #15822);
- International Young Catholic Students (IYCS, #15926) (International Movement of Catholic Students, European Coordination);
- International Youth Human Rights Movement (YHRM, #15934);
- KOLPING INTERNATIONAL (#16203);
- La Strada International (LSI, #20002);
- Liberal International (LI, #16454);
- Lifelong Learning Platform – European Civil Society for Education (LLLP, #16466);
- Lions International – European Districts (no recent information);
- Magistrats européens pour la démocratie et les libertés (MEDEL, #16546);
- Marangopoulos Foundation for Human Rights (MFHR);
- Mental Health Europe (MHE, #16715);
- Mouvement international d'apostolat des milieux sociaux indépendants (MIAMSI, #16864);
- Mouvement international de la jeunesse agricole et rurale catholique (MIJARC, #16865);
- Médecins du Monde – International (MDM, #16613);
- Network of European LGBTIQ Families Associations (NELFA, #17021);
- Observatoire Européen de la Non-Discrimination et des Droits Fondamentaux (OENDDF);
- Oiseaux migrateurs du paléarctique occidental (OMPO, #17712);
- Open Society Foundations (OSF, #17763) (European Policy Institute);
- Parents International (IPA, #18198);
- Pax Christi – International Catholic Peace Movement (#18266);
- Pax Romana, International Catholic Movement for Intellectual and Cultural Affairs (ICMICA, #18267);
- Penal Reform International (PRI, #18290);
- Platform for International Cooperation on Undocumented Migrants (PICUM, #18401);
- Quaker Council for European Affairs (QCEA, #18587);
- Religious in Europe Networking Against Trafficking and Exploitation (RENATE, #18833);
- Reporters sans frontières (RSF, #18846);
- Right to Die Europe (RtDE, #18941);
- RI Global (#18948);
- Robert Schuman Institute for Europe (IRSE, #18959);
- Rotary International (RI, #18975);
- Rurality – Environment – Development (RED, #19003);
- Russian Peace Foundation (RPF);
- Réseau européen d'instituts de formation d'enseignants (Assocation Comenius, #18875);
- Service Civil International (SCI, #19238);
- Simon Wiesenthal Centre-Europe (CSWE);
- Social Platform (#19344);
- Society for Threatened Peoples International (STP International, #19654);
- Soroptimist International of Europe (SI/E, #19689);
- SOS-Kinderdorf International (#19693);
- Special Olympics International (SOI, #19910);
- Standing Committee of European Doctors (#19955);
- Stichting Justice Initiative (SJI, #19985);
- Terre des Hommes International Federation (TDHIF, #20133);
- TGEU (#20138);
- Thalassaemia International Federation (#20139);
- The European Law Students' Association (ELSA, #07660);
- Transparency International (TI, #20223);
- Union des avocats européens (UAE, #20365);
- Union for the Cultural and Professional Future in Europe (#20373);
- Union internationale des architectes (UIA, #20419);
- Union Internationale des Avocats (UIA, #20422);
- Union Internationale des Guides et Scouts d'Europe – Fédération du Scoutisme Européen (UIGSE-FSE, #20426);
- Union professionnelle internationale des gynécologues et obstétriciens (UPIGO, #20473);
- UNITED for Intercultural Action – European Network Against Nationalism, Racism, Fascism and in Support of Migrants and Refugees (UNITED, #20511);
- University Women of Europe (UWE, #20707);
- Validity Foundation (#20743);
- Victim Support Europe (VSE, #20767);
- Volonteurope (#20807);
- World Association of Girl Guides and Girl Scouts (WAGGGS, #21142);
- World Association of Newspapers and News Publishers (WAN-IFRA, #21166);
- World Catholic Association for Communication (SIGNIS, #21264);
- World Congress of Free Ukrainians (WCFU, #21305);
- World Federalist Movement – Movement for a Just World Order through a Strengthened United Nations (WFM, #21404) (Institute for Global Policy);

- *World Federation of the Deaf (WFD, #21425)*;
- *World Organisation Against Torture (OMCT, #21685)*;
- *World Organization of the Scout Movement (WOSM, #21693)*;
- *World ORT (WO, #21698)*;
- *World Student Christian Federation (WSCF, #21833)* (Europe);
- *World Union of Ahiska Turks (DATÜB)*;
- *World Union of Catholic Women's Organisations (WUCWO, #21876)*;
- *World Vision International (WVI, #21904)* (Middle East and Eastern Europe Regional Office);
- *Young European Federalists (#21984)*;
- *Youth Express Network (Y-E-N, #22017)*;
- *Youth of the European People's Party (YEPP, #22014)*;
- *Zonta International (#22038)*.

IGO Relations *European Union (EU, #08967)* is most important institutional partner at both political and technical levels; cooperation currently governed by 2007 Memorandum of Understanding. Major partner and Observer to General Assembly of: *United Nations (UN, #20515)*. Institutionalized relations/agreements with:
- *Anna Lindh Euro-Mediterranean Foundation for the Dialogue between Cultures (Anna Lindh Foundation, #00847)*;
- *Arab League Educational, Cultural and Scientific Organization (ALECSO, #01003)*;
- *Benelux Inter-Parliamentary Consultative Council (Benelux Parliament, #03201)*;
- *CIHEAM – International Centre for Advanced Mediterranean Agronomic Studies (CIHEAM, #03927)*;
- *Commonwealth of Independent States (CIS, #04341)*;
- *Conférence des assemblées législatives régionales d'Europe (CALRE, #04582)*;
- *Convention on Biological Diversity (Biodiversity convention, 1992)*;
- *European Agency for Reconstruction (inactive)*;
- *European Bank for Reconstruction and Development (EBRD, #06315)*;
- *European Civil Aviation Conference (ECAC, #06564)*;
- *European Foundation for the Improvement of Living and Working Conditions (Eurofound, #07348)*;
- *European Investment Bank (EIB, #07599)*;
- *European Monitoring Centre for Drugs and Drug Addiction (EMCDDA, #07820)*;
- *European Wergeland Centre (EWC, #09092)*;
- *FAO (#09260)*;
- *General Agreement on Tariffs and Trade, 1994 (GATT 1994, 1994)*;
- *The Hague Conference on Private International Law (HCCH, #10850)*;
- *ILO (#11123)*;
- *International Bank for Reconstruction and Development (IBRD, #12317)*;
- *International Centre for the Study of the Preservation and Restoration of Cultural Property (ICCROM, #12521)*;
- *International Commission on Civil Status (ICCS, #12671)*;
- *International Criminal Police Organization – INTERPOL (ICPO-INTERPOL, #13110)*;
- *International Criminal Tribunal for the former Yugoslavia (ICTY, inactive)*;
- *International Development Association (IDA, #13155)*;
- *International Institute for the Unification of Private Law (UNIDROIT, #13934)*;
- *International Organization for Migration (IOM, #14454)*;
- *International Telecommunication Union (ITU, #15673)*;
- *International Transport Forum (ITF, #15725)*;
- *NATO (#16945)*;
- *Nordic Council (NC, #17256)*;
- *OAS (#17629)*;
- *OECD (#17693)*;
- *Office of the United Nations High Commissioner for Human Rights (OHCHR, #17697)*;
- *Organisation internationale de la Francophonie (OIF, #17809)*;
- *Organization of Ibero-American States for Education, Science and Culture (#17871)*;
- *Organization for Security and Cooperation in Europe (OSCE, #17887)*;
- *Pan-African Parliament (PAP, #18058)*;
- *Parlamento Latinoamericano (PARLATINO, #18203)*;
- *REGLEG (#18823)*;
- *Treaty for Collaboration in Economic, Social and Cultural Matters and for Collective Self-defence (Brussels Treaty, 1948)*;
- *UNEP (#20299)*;
- *UN Interim Administration Mission in Kosovo (UNMIK, #20343)*;
- *UN Women (#20724)*;
- *UNDP (#20292)*;
- *UNESCO (#20322)*;
- *UNHCR (#20327)*;
- *UNICEF (#20332)*;
- *United Nations Alliance of Civilizations (UNAOC, #20520)*;
- *United Nations Office for Disaster Risk Reduction (UNDRR, #20595)*;
- *United Nations Office for Disaster Risk Reduction (UNDRR, #20595)*;
- *Western European Union (WEU, inactive)*;
- *WHO (#20950)*;
- *World Intellectual Property Organization (WIPO, #21593)*;
- *World Tourism Organization (UNWTO, #21861)*.

NGO Relations Additional agreements with: *Africa Institute of South Africa (AISA)*; *Association des cours constitutionnelles Francophone (ACCF, #02459)*; *Committee to Protect Journalists (CPJ, #04280)*; *European Cultural Foundation (ECF, #06868)*; *Global Campus of Human Rights (#10269)*; *Index on Censorship (Index)*; *Inter-Parliamentary Union (IPU, #15961)*; *International Association of Amusement Parks and Attractions (IAAPA, #11699)*; *International Union of Railways (#15813)*; *Yad Vashem, the Holocaust Martyrs' and Heroes' Remembrance Authority*. [2022/XD0435/**D***]

♦ Council of European Aerospace Societies (CEAS) 04882

Head Office c/o DLR, Rue du Trône 98, 1050 Brussels, Belgium. E-mail: info@ceas.org.
URL: http://www.ceas.org/

History 1992, Farnborough (UK). Founded at inaugural meeting. Constitution signed Jun 1993, Paris (France). Former names and other names: *Confederation of European Aerospace Societies (CEAS)* – former (1992 to 2006). Registration: Belgium. **Aims** Support the European aerospace community by promoting the highest standard of professional expertise and facilitating resolution of key issues which extend beyond the constraints of competitive commercial scenarios. **Structure** Board of Trustees (meets 3 times a year); Board of Officers; Branches (2). **Languages** English. **Events** *EuroGNC : European Specialist Conference on Guidance, Navigation and Control* Berlin (Germany) 2022, *HiSST – International Conference on High-Speed Vehicle Science and Technology* Bruges (Belgium) 2022, *International Conference on High-Speed Vehicle Science and Technology* Bruges (Belgium) 2021, *Women in Aerospace Conference* Madrid (Spain) 2021, *Aerospace Europe Conference* Warsaw (Poland) 2021. **Publications** *CEAS Aeronautical Journal*; *CEAS Quarterly Bulletin*; *CEAS Space Journal*.
Members National organizations. Full corporate (12) in 12 countries:
Czechia, France, Germany, Italy, Netherlands, Poland, Romania, Russia, Spain, Sweden, Switzerland, UK.
Corporate Members (4):
EUROCONTROL (#05667); *European Association of Aerospace Students (EUROAVIA, #05930)*; *European Space Agency (ESA, #08798)*; *European Union Aviation Safety Agency (EASA, #08978)*. [2022.05.11/XD4639/**D**]

♦ Council of European BioRegions (CEBR) 04883

Pres Square de Meeus, 1005 Brussels, Belgium.
URL: http://www.cebr.net/

Aims Strengthen transfer of knowledge and collaboration with life science clusters/*ecosystems* in Europe; support *sustainable* growth for *SMEs*, creating a competitive Europe in the global economy. **Structure** Board.
Members Full in 14 countries:
Austria, Belgium, Denmark, Finland, France, Germany, Greece, Italy, Luxembourg, Portugal, Spain, Sweden, Türkiye, UK.
[2019/XM7318/**D**]

♦ Council of European Bishops' Conferences 04884

Conseil des conférences épiscopales d'Europe – Rat der Europäischen Bischofskonferenzen – Consiglio delle Conferenze Episcopali d'Europa – Consilium Conferentiarum Episcoporum Europae (CCEE)

Secretariat Gallusstrasse 24, 9000 St Gallen, Switzerland. T. +41712276040. Fax +41712276041. E-mail: ccee@ccee.eu.
URL: http://www.ccee.eu/

History 24 Mar 1971, Rome (Italy). Structure amended: 23 Oct 1971, Rome; 20 Oct 1973, Rome; 10 Jan 1977, Rome; 2 Dec 1995, Rome. Recognized by the Holy See. Former names and other names: *Council of European Episcopal Conferences* – alias. **Aims** Promote cooperation between the individual episcopal conferences in Europe. **Structure** General Assembly (annual); Praesidium; Secretariat. Commissions (4): Family & Life; Evangelisation & Culture; Pastroal Social Work; Youth. Bishops (4) appointed for special themes: Catechesis; Vocations; Migrations; Media. **Languages** English, French, German, Italian, Latin. **Staff** 5.50 FTE, paid. **Finance** Sources: meeting proceeds. **Activities** Events/meetings. **Events** *Meeting of the Media Officers and Spokespersons* Glasgow (UK) 2016, *Catholic Social Days for Europe* Madrid (Spain) 2014, *Annual Plenary Assembly* Rome (Italy) 2014, *Annual Plenary Assembly* Bratislava (Slovakia) 2013, *Annual Plenary Assembly* St Gallen (Switzerland) 2012. **Publications** *Litterae Communionis* (3 a year). *Conspectus Conferentiarum Episcopalium Europae*. Conference reports.
Members President (39) of each European Episcopal Conference. Bishops' conferences in 43 countries and territories:
Albania, Austria, Belarus, Belgium, Bosnia-Herzegovina, Bulgaria, Croatia, Czechia, Denmark, England and Wales, Estonia, Finland, France, Germany, Greece, Hungary, Iceland, Ireland, Italy, Kosovo, Latvia, Lithuania, Luxembourg, Malta, Moldova, Monaco, Montenegro, Netherlands, North Macedonia, Norway, Poland, Portugal, Romania, Russia, Scotland, Serbia, Slovakia, Slovenia, Spain, Sweden, Switzerland, Türkiye, Ukraine (3).
President of Scandinavian Conference:
Nordisk Bispekonferance (NBK, #17498). [2020/XD4492/y/**D**]

♦ Council of European Chief Dental Officers (CECDO) 04885

Sec GÖG, Stubenring 6, 1010 Vienna, Austria.
Pres Univ of Brescia – Dental Clinic, Piazzale Spedali Civil 5, 25123 Brescia BS, Italy. T. +3930383424.
URL: http://www.cecdo.org/

History Founded Jul 1992. Current constitution adopted 27 Jun 1995. Registered in accordance with Dutch law. **Aims** Advance public oral health across Europe through creation and maintenance of a network of European chief dental officers. **Structure** General Assembly (twice a year); Executive Board. **Languages** English. **Staff** 3.00 FTE, voluntary. **Finance** Members' dues. Meetings supported by EU country holding the Presidency. Other sources: grants from funding agencies. **Activities** Guidance/assistance/consulting; events/meetings; knowledge management/information dissemination. **Events** *Half-Yearly Meeting* Bern (Switzerland) 2015, *Half-yearly Scientific Meeting* Latvia 2015, *Half-Yearly Meeting* Riga (Latvia) 2015, *Half-yearly Scientific Meeting* Switzerland 2015, *Half-Yearly Meeting* Athens (Greece) 2014. **Publications** Reports; article. Information Services: Databank on European oral health, dental care, dental workforce and education.
Members Full; Associate. Members in 30 countries:
Albania, Austria, Belgium, Croatia, Czechia, Denmark, Estonia, Finland, France, Germany, Greece, Hungary, Iceland, Ireland, Israel, Italy, Latvia, Lithuania, Malta, Netherlands, Norway, Poland, Portugal, Romania, Slovakia, Slovenia, Spain, Sweden, Switzerland, UK.
NGO Relations Member of: *Platform for Better Oral Health in Europe (#18399)*. [2018.03.08/XD6019/**D**]

♦ Council of the European Coal and Steel Community / see Council of the European Union (#04895)
♦ Council of European Commercial Federations (inactive)
♦ Council of the European Communities / see Council of the European Union (#04895)

♦ Council of European Dentists (CED) 04886

Conseil des chirurgiens-dentistes Européens – Rat der Europäischen Zahnärzte

SG Av Cortenbergh 89/6, 1000 Brussels, Belgium. T. +3227363429. E-mail: ced@cedentists.eu.
Office Manager address not obtained.
URL: https://cedentists.eu/

History 1961, Brussels (Belgium). Former names and other names: *Dental Liaison Committee for the EEC* – former; *Comité de liaison des praticiens de l'art dentaire des pays de la CEE* – former; *Zahnärztlicher Verbindungs-Ausschuss der EWG* – former; *Dental Liaison Committee in the European Union (DLC in the EU)* – former; *Comité de liaison des praticiens de l'art dentaire des pays de l'Union européenne* – former; *Zahnärztlicher Verbindungs-Ausschuss zur EU* – former; *EU – Dental Liaison Committee (EU-DLC)* – former; *UE – Comité de liaison des praticiens de l'art dentaire* – former; *EU – Zahnärztlicher Verbindungs-Ausschuss* – former; *Conseil des dentistes Européens* – former. Registration: Banque-Carrefour des Entreprises, No/ID: 0480.222.749, Start date: 19 Nov 2002, Belgium; EU Transparency Register, No/ID: 4885579968-84, Start date: 15 Jan 2009. **Aims** Represent the dental *profession* in the EU; promote a high level of oral health and high-quality dental care; shape EU policy in areas affecting the dental profession; better guarantee patient safety; ensure appropriate regulation of medical devices; seek to tackle the causes of oral diseases and reduce health inequalities. **Structure** General Meeting (twice a year); Board of Directors; Working Groups; Permanent Secretariat in Brussels (Belgium). **Languages** English, French, German. **Staff** 4.00 FTE, paid. **Finance** Sources: members' dues. **Activities** Advocacy/lobbying/activism; politics/policy/regulatory. **Events** *Half-Yearly Meeting* Stockholm (Sweden) 2023, *Half-Yearly Meeting* Brussels (Belgium) 2022, *Half-Yearly Meeting* Porto (Portugal) 2022, *Half-Yearly Meeting* Brussels (Belgium) 2021, *Half-Yearly Meeting* Brussels (Belgium) 2021. **Publications** *EU Manual of Dental Practice*. Annual Report.
Members Full in 26 countries:
Austria, Belgium, Bulgaria, Croatia, Cyprus, Czechia, Denmark, Estonia, Finland, France, Germany, Greece, Hungary, Ireland, Italy, Latvia, Lithuania, Luxembourg, Malta, Netherlands, Poland, Portugal, Slovakia, Slovenia, Spain, Sweden.
Affiliate in 4 countries:
Iceland, Norway, Switzerland, UK.
Observer:
Albania.
NGO Relations Member of (2): *European Movement International (EMI, #07825)*; *Federation of European and International Associations Established in Belgium (FAIB, #09508)*. [2022.10.21/XE0466/**E**]

♦ Council of European Employers of the Metal, Engineering and Technology-Based Industries (CEEMET) 04887

Dir-Gen Rue Belliard 40, 1040 Brussels, Belgium. T. +3227863045. E-mail: secretariat@ceemet.org.
Office Manager address not obtained.
URL: https://www.ceemet.org/

History 1962, London (UK). Founded as ad hoc forum for information exchange amongst representatives of national metal trades employers' associations. Formalized in 1970. Statutes adopted 1984; revised 1998. Former names and other names: *Western European Metal Trades Employers' Organization* – former; *Employers' Organization of the Metal Trades in Europe (WEM)* – former. Registration: Banque-Carrefour des Entreprises, No/ID: 0466.159.531, Start date: 17 Jun 1999, Belgium; EU Transparency Register, No/ID: 61370904700-45. **Aims** Represent, promote and defend the social policy-related interests of employers in metal, engineering and technology-based industries at European level. **Structure** General Assembly; Board of Directors; Committees; Secretariat. **Languages** English. **Staff** 6.00 FTE, paid. **Events** *Conference* Brussels (Belgium) 2012, *Conference* Brussels (Belgium) 2012, *Conference* Brussels (Belgium) 2010, *General Assembly* Rome (Italy) 2010, *Meeting* Cologne (Germany FR) 1990. **Publications** Reports; studies; position papers.
Members Associations and federations in 20 countries:
Australia, Austria, Belgium, Bulgaria, Croatia, Denmark, Finland, France, Germany, Hungary, Italy, Netherlands, Norway, Portugal, Slovenia, Spain, Sweden, Switzerland, Türkiye, UK.
IGO Relations *European Union (EU, #08967)*. **NGO Relations** Member of (1): *European Network on Silica (NEPSI, #08001)*. Associate Expert Group of *Business and Industry Advisory Committee to the OECD (BIAC, #03385)*. [2023.02.15/XD2343/t/**D**]

♦ Council of European Energy Regulators (CEER) 04888

SG Cours Saint-Michel 30A, Box F, 1040 Brussels, Belgium. T. +3227887330. Fax +3227887350. E-mail: brussels@ceer.eu.
URL: https://www.ceer.eu/

History 7 Mar 2000, Brussels (Belgium). Statutes adopted, 21 Oct 2003. Registration: Banque-Carrefour des Entreprises, No/ID: 0861.035.445, Start date: 14 Oct 2003, Belgium; EU Transparency Register, No/ID: 65470797015-89, Start date: 25 Oct 2011. **Aims** Promote development of *electricity* and *gas markets* in Europe; increase cooperation between national energy regulators in Europe, and between regulators and the European Commission; improve and share regulatory best practice worldwide. **Structure** General Assembly; Board of Directors; Secretariat; Technical Working Groups (6). **Languages** English, French. **Finance** Sources: members' dues. **Activities** Advocacy/lobbying/activism; monitoring/evaluation; politics/policy/regulatory.

Events *World Forum on Energy Regulation (WFER)* Lima (Peru) 2023, *Annual Conference* Brussels (Belgium) 2021, *Annual Conference* Brussels (Belgium) 2020, *Customer Conference* Brussels (Belgium) 2019, *Workshop on Bundled Products : Dispute Resolution and Consumer Rights Enforcement* Brussels (Belgium) 2019. **Publications** *CEER Benchmarking Report on the Quality of Electricity Supply* (every 3 years). Annual Activity Report; Work Programme; technical papers.
Members National energy regulators in 30 countries:
Austria, Belgium, Bulgaria, Croatia, Cyprus, Czechia, Denmark, Estonia, Finland, France, Germany, Greece, Hungary, Iceland, Ireland, Italy, Latvia, Lithuania, Luxembourg, Malta, Netherlands, Norway, Poland, Portugal, Romania, Slovakia, Slovenia, Spain, Sweden, UK.
Observers in 9 countries:
Albania, Bosnia-Herzegovina, Georgia, Kosovo, Moldova, Montenegro, North Macedonia, Serbia, Switzerland.
IGO Relations Cooperates with (1): *European Commission (EC, #06633).* **NGO Relations** Member of (1): *International Confederation of Energy Regulators (ICER, #12859).* Also links with national organizations.
[2023.02.14/XE4505/**E**]

♦ Council of European Episcopal Conferences / see Council of European Bishops' Conferences (#04884)

♦ Council of European Foresters (CEF) 04889

Pres B-dul Magheru nu 31, Sector 1, Bucharest, Romania.
URL: http://www.ceforg.eu/
History Set up 25 Aug 2011, Sibiu (Romania). EU Transparence Register: 37914257766-19. **Aims** Promote the performance, activity and professionalism of the foresters, the interest and performance of the students and graduates of forest schools and faculties, as well as the performance level of the forest faculties and research. **Structure** Council; President.
Members Full in 12 countries:
Bosnia-Herzegovina, Croatia, Finland, Germany, Hungary, Italy, Moldova, Romania, Russia, Serbia, Türkiye, Ukraine.
IGO Relations Accredited to the Conference of the Parties of: *Secretariat of the United Nations Convention to Combat Desertification (Secretariat of the UNCCD, #19208).* [2019/XM5733/**D**]

♦ Council of European Geodetic Surveyors 04890

Comité de liaison des géomètres européens (CLGE)
SG Rue du Nord 76, 1000 Brussels, Belgium.
Pres address not obtained. T. +32475453990.
URL: http://www.clge.eu/
History 1972, Germany FR. 1972, Wiesbaden (Germany FR), as *Comité de liaison des géomètres de la CEE.* Subsequently referred to as *European Surveyors' Liaison Committee – Comité de liaison des géomètres-experts européens.* **Aims** Represent the interests of the *profession* in Europe with institutions of the European Union by active participation in the legislative processes at European level; cooperate with and assist the Commission in recognition of *qualifications* for academic and professional purposes; facilitate mutual recognition and stimulate and facilitate harmonization of *standards* of academic and professional qualifications; promote geodetic surveying activity; aid administrative and scientific development of the profession; assist in dealing with national problems arising from activities in members' countries. **Structure** General Assembly (2 a year). Standing Committee (meets 4 times a year), consisting of Executive Board – President, Vice-President, Secretary-General and Treasurer – and 6 further members. Meetings closed. **Languages** English. **Finance** Members' dues. **Activities** Principal areas of expertise: Land and geodetic surveying; Hydrography; Photogrammetry and remote sensing; Cadastral and boundary surveying; Land and geographical information systems; Minerals and mining surveying; Engineering surveying and metrology; Cartography. **Events** *Seminar on 3D Cadastral Systems, Urban Dimensions into Surveying* Helsinki (Finland) 2016, *Half-Yearly General Assembly* Tirana (Albania) 2016, *Half-yearly General Assembly* Budapest (Hungary) 2013, *Half-Yearly General Assembly* Edinburgh (UK) 2012, *Half-Yearly General Assembly* Hannover (Germany) 2012.
Members Principal members: national organizations and liaison groups in 36 countries:
Albania, Austria, Belgium, Bulgaria, Croatia, Cyprus, Czechia, Denmark, Estonia, Finland, France, Germany, Greece, Hungary, Iceland, Ireland, Italy, Latvia, Lithuania, Luxembourg, Malta, Moldova, Netherlands, North Macedonia, Norway, Poland, Portugal, Romania, Russia, Serbia, Slovakia, Slovenia, Spain, Sweden, Switzerland, UK.
IGO Relations Recognized by: *European Commission (EC, #06633).* Cooperates with: *European Position Determination System (EUPOS, #08256).* **NGO Relations** Member of: *European Council of Liberal Professions (#06828); International Ethics Standards Coalition (IES Coalition, #13307); International Property Measurement Standards Coalition (IPMSC, #14656).* [2015/XD2381/**E**]

♦ Council of European and Japanese National Shipowners' Associations (inactive)
♦ Council of European Municipalities / see Council of European Municipalities and Regions (#04891)

♦ Council of European Municipalities and Regions (CEMR) 04891

Conseil des communes et régions d'Europe (CCRE) – Consejo de Municipios y Regiones de Europa (CMRE) – Rat der Gemeinden und Regionen Europas (RGRE) – Conselho dos Municipios e Regiões da Europa – Consiglio dei Comuni e delle Regioni d'Europa – Raad der Europese Gemeenten en Regios – Rådet för Europas Kommuner och Regioner – Europaeiske Kommuners og Regioners Råd – Euroopan Kuntien ja Alueiden Neuvosto
Assistant to SG Square de Meeûs 1, 1000 Brussels, Belgium. T. +3225117477. Fax +3225110949. E-mail: info@ccre-cemr.org.
Paris Office 15 rue de Richelieu, 75001 Paris, France. T. +33144505959. Fax +33144505960. E-mail: info@ccre-cemr.org.
URL: http://www.ccre.org/
History 29 Jan 1951, Geneva (Switzerland). As from 1 Jan 1991, following agreement signed 3 Oct 1990, Lisbon (Portugal), European regional section of *World Organization of United Cities and Local Governments (UCLG, #21695).* Most recent statutes adopted 11 Oct 2001. Former names and other names: *Council of European Municipalities (CEM)* – former; *Conseil des communes d'Europe (CCE)* – former; *Consejo de Municipios de Europa* – former; *Rat der Gemeinden Europas (RGE)* – former; *Consiglio dei Comuni d'Europa* – former; *Raad der Europese Gemeenten* – former; *Association of Local and Regional Authorities of Europe* – former; *Conseil européen des pouvoirs municipaux et régionaux (REG)* – former. Registration: Banque-Carrefour des Entreprises, No/ID: 0544.372.611, Start date: 14 Jan 2014, Belgium; RNA, No/ID: W751083208, End date: Mar 2015, France; EU Transparency Register, No/ID: 81142561702-61, Start date: 15 May 2009. **Aims** Secure, strengthen and protect *autonomy* of local and regional authorities; facilitate operations of local and regional *authorities,* safeguard their liberties and contribute to their prosperity, in particular through development of inter-authority arrangements and undertakings; develop the European spirit amongst local and regional authorities with a view to promoting a federation of the European States founded on the autonomy of these communities; provide for the participation and representation of local and regional authorities in European and international institutions; achieve establishment amongst existing and future European institutions of an assembly representing local and regional authorities. **Structure** *'Assembly of Delegates'* (every 3 years) consists of delegates of national associations and of direct members, representation depending on number of inhabitants of the country concerned: one for up to 100,000 inhabitants; 2 for 100,000-1 million; 3 for 1-5 million; 4 for 5-10 million; 5 for 10-20 million; 6 for 20-30 million; 7 for 30-40 million; 8 for 40-50 million; 9 for 50-60 million; 10 for over 60 million. *'Policy Committee'* (meets twice a year), also with representation depending on number of inhabitants: one for up to 100,000 inhabitants; 2 for 100,000 to 5 million; 3 for 5-10 million; 4 for 10-30 million; 5 for 30-60 million; 6 for over 60 million. Policy Committee; *'Executive Bureau'*; Financial Management Committee. International leadership. **Languages** English, French. **Staff** 30.00 FTE, paid. **Finance** Sources: grants; members' dues. Supported by: *European Union (EU, #08967).* **Activities** Knowledge management/information dissemination; management of treaties and agreements; politics/policy/regulatory. Manages the following treaties/agreements: *European Charter of Local Self-government (1985).* **Events** *Congress* Innsbruck (Austria) 2020, *Meeting* Orléans (France) 2020, *Workshop on Delivering Sustainable Development Goals at Regional and Local Levels* Brussels (Belgium) 2018, *Meeting* Maastricht (Netherlands) 2016, *Steering Committee Meeting* Brussels (Belgium) 2012. **Publications** *CEMR Newsletter.* Books; reports; brochures; fact sheets.
Members National associations of local and regional government, whose own members are local and regional authorities in their country. Associations (61) in 39 countries:
Albania, Austria, Belgium, Bosnia-Herzegovina, Bulgaria, Croatia, Cyprus, Czechia, Denmark, Estonia, Finland, France, Georgia, Germany, Greece, Hungary, Iceland, Israel, Italy, Latvia, Lithuania, Luxembourg, Malta, Moldova, Montenegro, Netherlands, North Macedonia, Norway, Poland, Portugal, Romania, Serbia, Slovakia, Slovenia, Spain, Sweden, Türkiye, UK, Ukraine.

IGO Relations Observer status with (1): *Congress of Local and Regional Authorities of the Council of Europe (#04677).* **NGO Relations** Observer status with (1): *European Umbrella Organization for Geographical Information (EUROGI, #08964).* [2022/XD0448/y/**D**]

♦ Council of European National Top-Level Domain Registries (CENTR) 04892

Secretariat Rue Belliard 20, 6th Floor, 1040 Brussels, Belgium. T. +3226275550. Fax +3226275559. E-mail: secretariat@centr.org.
URL: http://www.centr.org/
History 1999. Registration: Start date: 2006, Belgium; Start date: 1999, End date: 2006, England and Wales. **Aims** Promote the interests of not-for-profit ccTLDs; provide a forum to discuss policy matters affecting ccTLD registries. **Structure** General Assembly; Board of Directors; Secretariat, based in Brussels (Belgium). **Languages** English. **Staff** 2.50 FTE, paid. **Finance** Members' dues. **Activities** Sponsors and facilitates collaborative projects on technical, managerial and legal issues affecting ccTLDs. **Events** *General Assembly* Bordeaux (France) 2019, *General Assembly* Brussels (Belgium) 2018, *General Assembly* Zurich (Switzerland) 2018, *General Assembly* Brussels (Belgium) 2017, *General Assembly* Jurmala (Latvia) 2017. **Publications** *Domain Wire.* Monthly Roundups; Issue Papers; reports.
Members Full organizations managing an ISO 3166-1 country-code top level domain in 49 countries and territories:
Afghanistan, Albania, Andorra, Armenia, Austria, Belarus, Belgium, Bulgaria, Canada, Croatia, Cyprus, Czechia, Denmark, Estonia, Faeroe Is, Finland, France, Germany, Gibraltar, Greece, Holy See, Hungary, Iceland, Iran Islamic Rep, Ireland, Isle of Man, Israel, Italy, Latvia, Lithuania, Luxembourg, Malta, Montenegro, Netherlands, Norway, Palestine, Poland, Portugal, Romania, Russia, Serbia, Slovakia, Slovenia, Spain, Sweden, Switzerland, Türkiye, UK, Ukraine.
Included in the above, one organizations listed in this Yearbook:
European Registry of Internet Domain Names (EURid, #08351).
Associate in 6 countries:
China, Ireland, Japan, New Zealand, Spain, USA.
Observers in 7 countries and territories:
Belgium, Hong Kong, Netherlands, Sweden, Switzerland, Uruguay, USA.
NGO Relations Observer status with: *RIPE Network Coordination Centre (RIPE NCC, #18951).* Member of: *European Internet Forum (EIF, #07591).* [2021/XD7214/**D**]

♦ Council of European National Youth Committees (inactive)
♦ Council of European Producers of Materials for Construction / see Construction Products Europe AISBL (#04761)

♦ Council of European Professional Informatics Societies (CEPIS) . . . 04893

SG Av Roger Vandendriessche 18, 1150 Brussels, Belgium. T. +3227721836. Fax +3226463032. E-mail: info@cepis.org.
URL: http://www.cepis.org/
History 1988, London (UK). Registration: Netherlands. **Aims** Recognizing the impact of informatics on employment, business, education and society: improve and promote high standards among informatics professionals; promote development of the *Information Society* through digital literacy, skills, education, research and professionalism; raise the profile and promote the views of European informatics societies and informatics professionals to the European Commission and other European institutions. **Structure** Council (meets twice a year). Executive Committee, including President, Past-President or President-Elect, 3 Vice-Presidents, Honorary Secretary and Honorary Treasurer. Task forces (4): IT Professionalism; Women in ICT; Green ICT; Research. Special Interest Networks (SINs): Legal and Security Issues (CEPIS LSI SIN); Software Quality Group (CEPIS SQ SIN). Secretariat in Brussels (Belgium). **Languages** English. **Staff** 4.00 FTE, paid. **Finance** Members' dues. **Activities** Areas: Skills; Professionalism; Education and Research; Legal and Security Issues; Women in ICT; Green ICT; Software Quality. Developed: *'European Computer Driving Licence (ECDL)',* 1996, licensed by *ICDL Europe (#11052); 'European Certificate for Informatics Professionals (EUCIP)'.* Projects: Euro-Inf Spread; E-Skills Foresights; Harmonise. Organizes workshops. Conducts projects for the European Commission. **Events** *International symposium on advances in artificial intelligence and applications* Wisla (Poland) 2010, *European software engineering conference* Dubrovnik (Croatia) 2007, *European software engineering conference* Lisbon (Portugal) 2005, *International Conference on Computers Helping People with Special Needs* Paris (France) 2004, *European software engineering conference* Helsinki (Finland) 2003. **Publications** *CEPIS Newsletter* (11 a year). Internal publications; papers; statements; research reports.
Members represent individual informatics professional associations. Members (35) in 32 countries:
Austria, Belgium, Bosnia-Herzegovina, Bulgaria, Croatia, Cyprus, Czechia, Denmark, Finland, Germany, Greece, Hungary, Iceland, Ireland, Italy, Latvia, Lithuania, Luxembourg, Malta, Montenegro, Netherlands, Norway, Poland, Portugal, Romania, Serbia, Slovakia, Slovenia, Spain, Sweden, Switzerland, Türkiye, UK.
Consultative Status Consultative status granted from: *Council of Europe (CE, #04881)* (Participatory Status). **NGO Relations** Member of: *European e-Skills Association (EeSA, #08489); European Registry of Internet Domain Names (EURid, #08351).* Associate Member of: *European Internet Forum (EIF, #07591).* Affiliate member of: *International Federation for Information Processing (IFIP, #13458).* Liaison Organization of: *Comité européen de normalisation (CEN, #04162).* [2019/XD4181/t/**D**]

♦ Council of European Regions / see Assembly of European Regions (#02316)
♦ Council of European Social Science Data Archives / see Consortium of European Social Science Data Archives (#04743)

♦ Council for European Studies (CES) 04894

Dir Columbia Univ, 475 Riverside Drive, Room 3081, New York NY 10115, USA. T. +16467458550.
European Office Inst Barcelona d'Estudis Internacionals, Ramon Trias Fargas 25-27, 08005 Barcelona, Spain. E-mail: info@ces-europe.org.
URL: http://councilforeuropeanstudies.org/
History 1970, New York, NY (USA). **Aims** Promote and recognize outstanding, multidisciplinary research in European Studies through a range of programmes. **Structure** Executive Committee. European Office: *Fundació Institut Barcelona d'Estudis Internacionals (IBEI).* **Languages** English, French, German. **Finance** Sources: members' dues. Supported by: *Andrew W Mellon Foundation; Ford Foundation (#09858); German Marshall Fund of the United States (GMF).* **Activities** Awards/prizes/competitions; events/meetings. **Events** *International Conference of Europeanists* Reykjavik (Iceland) 2023, *Conference* Lisbon (Portugal) 2022, *Conference* New York, NY (USA) 2021, *Conference* Reykjavik (Iceland) 2020, *International Conference of Europeanists* Madrid (Spain) 2019. **Publications** *CES Newsletter, EuropeNow.* **Members** Individual; Institutional (universities). Membership countries not specified. [2023.02.13/XG7110/**E**]

♦ Council for European Studies, Pittsburgh / see European Studies Center, Pittsburgh PA

♦ Council of the European Union 04895

Conseil de l'Union européenne – Consejo le la Unión Europea – Rat der Europäischen Union – Conselho da União Europeia – Consiglio dell'Unione Europea – Raad van de Europese Unie – Europeiska Unionens Råd – Rådet for Den Europaeske Union – Euroopan Unionin Neuvosto – Comhairle an Aontais Eorpaigh – Rada Evropské Unie – Rada Európskej Unie – Az Európai Unió Tanacsa – Rada Unii Europejskiej – Svet Evropske Unije – Euroopa Liidu Nõukogu – Eiropas Savienibas Padome – Europos Sajungos Taryba – Kunsill ta' l-Unjoni Ewropea – Vijece Europske Unije – Consiliul Uniunii Europene
Address not obtained.
URL: http://www.consilium.europa.eu/
History Sep 1952, as *Council of the European Coal and Steel Community,* the *European Coal and Steel Community (ECSC, inactive)* having been created by the *Treaty Establishing the European Coal and Steel Community (Treaty of Paris, 1951). Council of the European Economic Community* and *Council of the European Atomic Energy Community* were created, Jan 1958, under twin Treaties, *Treaty Establishing the European Economic Community (Treaty of Rome)* and *Treaty Establishing the European Atomic Energy Community (Treaty of Rome, 1957),* establishing *'European Economic Community (EEC)'* – subsequently called *European Community (inactive)* – and *European Atomic Energy Community (Euratom, inactive).* Since Jul 1967, when the 'Merger' Treaty of 8 Apr 1965 came into force, Council functions as a single entity, originally referred to as *Council of the European Communities – Conseil des Communautés européennes – Consejo de las Comunidades Europeas – Rat der Europäischen Gemeinschaften – Conselho das Comunidades Européias – Consiglio delle Comunità Europee – Raad van de Europese Gemeenschappen – Rådet for de Europaeiske*

Faellesskaber – Simvulio ton Evropaikon Kinotiton, an organ common to the three European Communities: ECSC, EEC and Euratom. Council formerly also known as *Council of Ministers of the European Communities – Conseil des ministres des Communautés européennes*. No formal merger of the 3 European Communities ever took place, but there were good reasons for regarding them as one unit so far as their political and legal structure was concerned. Not only were they managed by common institutions, but in common usage they were frequently referred to collectively as *'European Community'*, an approach adopted by the European Parliament in a resolution of 16 Feb 1978. The ECSC ceased to exist in Jul 2002, following expiration of the Paris Treaty; the European Community then became responsible for the steel sector.
The *Single European Act (SEA, 1986)*, signed Feb 1986, ratified by national parliaments by 31 Mar 1987 and came into force 1 Jul 1987, strengthened Community decision-making by expanding majority voting, in particular with respect to completion of the European internal market, research and technology, regional policy, and improvement of the working environment. The *Treaty on European Union (Maastricht Treaty, 1992)* of 7 Feb 1992 culminated efforts towards closer union with the establishment of *European Union (EU, #08967)*, expanding the concept of the European Communities – which became the Union's first "pillar", and confirmed the activities of the Council as set out in this and previous acts and treaties. The Council's current title was formally adopted on 9 Nov 1993; also known as *Council of Ministers of the European Union – Conseil des ministres de l'Union européenne*, or simply *'Council of Ministers – Conseil des ministres'*. The Maastricht Treaty also officially replaced the term *'European Economic Community'* by *'European Community'* in the treaties setting up the EEC and makes the Council responsible, with the *European Commission (EC, #06633)*, for ensuring consistency and implementation of policies. *Treaty of Amsterdam (1997)*, signed 2 Oct 1997 following agreement among the Heads of State and Government meeting as the European Council, 16-17 Jun 1997, Amsterdam (Netherlands), gives the European Union full legal personality and allows it to negotiate as one entity. The Laeken Declaration, signed by members of the European Council 15 Dec 2001, Brussels (Belgium), and the associated *Convention on the Future of Europe (inactive)*, looked forward to the creation of an Area of Freedom, Security and Justice (AFSJ). The Convention completed its work 10 Jul 2003. *Treaty of Lisbon (2007)* gave further power to the European Union, abolished the European Community, redesigned part of the Council's structure, and renamed original Treaty of Rome to the *Treaty on the Functioning of the European Union (TFEU, 1957)*. Together with *European Parliament (EP, #08146)*, serves as the Eu's main decision-making body.
Aims Negotiate and adopt EU laws; coordinate member states' policies; develop the EU's common foreign and *security policy*; conclude international *agreements*; adopt the EU budget. **Structure** Comprises government ministers from each EU country, according to the policy area to be discussed. As a single legal entity, it can meet in 10 different configurations, depending on the subject being discussed: Agriculture and fisheries; Competitiveness; Economic and financial affairs (Ecofin); Education, youth, culture and sport; Employment, social policy, health and consumer affairs; Environment; Foreign affairs; General Affairs; Justice and home affairs; Transport, telecommunications and energy. No hierarchy among Council configurations, although General Affairs has special coordination role, with Foreign Affairs Council also having special remit. Council meetings attended by representatives from each member state at ministerial level, with European Commissioners responsible for the areas concerned also invited. *European Central Bank (ECB, #06466)* is invited when they launched the legislative procedure. Meetings chaired by minister of member state holding the 6-month Council presidency. Foreign Affairs Council is usually chaired by *High Representative of the Union for Foreign Affairs and Security Policy*. Decisions taken by simple majority, qualified majority or unanimous vote, depending on decision. Member states holding the current and next 2 Presidencies make up the 'trio'. *Eurogroup (#05689)* usually meets on eve of Ecofin meeting. The Council is supported by *Committee of Permanent Representatives to the European Union (#04278)* and over 150 highly specialized working parties and committees, known as the 'Council preparatory bodies'. General Secretariat of the Council – shared with *European Council (#06801)* – assists the Council. **Languages** EU languages. **Staff** 3048.00 FTE, paid. **Finance** On the budget of the European Union.
Activities Politics/policy/regulatory. EU organizations within its remit or with which it cooperates: *European Union Agency for Law Enforcement Training (CEPOL, #08970)*; *European Committee of the Regions (CoR, #06665)*; *European Central Bank (ECB, #06466)*; *European Economic and Monetary Union (EMU, #06961)*; *European Economic and Social Committee (EESC, #06963)*; *European Environment Agency (EEA, #06995)*; *Euratom Supply Agency (ESA, #05617)*.
Concludes international agreements, including:
- *Schengen Convention (1990)*;
- *Community Charter of Fundamental Social Rights for Workers (European Social Charter, 1989)*;
- *Energy Charter Treaty (ECT, 1994)*;
- *Convention on Mutual Legal Assistance in Criminal Matters between the Member States of the European Union (2000)*;
- *ACP-EEC Convention (Lomé convention, 1975)*;
- *Second ACP-EEC Convention (Lomé II, 1979)*;
- *Third ACP-EEC Convention (Lomé III, 1984)*;
- *Fourth ACP-EEC Convention (Lomé IV, 1989)*;
- *ACP-EU Partnership Agreement (Cotonou agreement, 2000)*;
- *European Declaration Against Racism and Xenophobia (1986)*.

Events *Brussels Seminar* Brussels (Belgium) 2022, *EU-GCC Business Forum* Brussels (Belgium) 2022, *Summit* Brussels (Belgium) 2022, *Military Mobility Symposium* Brussels (Belgium) 2021, *Summit* Brussels (Belgium) 2020. **Publications** All publication go through *Publications Office of the European Union (Publications Office, #18562)*.
Members Government ministers, representatives of the 27 EU states:
Austria, Belgium, Bulgaria, Croatia, Cyprus, Czechia, Denmark, Estonia, Finland, France, Germany, Greece, Hungary, Ireland, Italy, Latvia, Lithuania, Luxembourg, Malta, Netherlands, Poland, Portugal, Romania, Slovakia, Slovenia, Spain, Sweden.
IGO Relations Liaises with: *EEA Council (#05379)*, within *European Economic Area (EEA, #06957)*. Cooperates with: *European Defence Agency (EDA, #06895)*; *European Union Institute for Security Studies (EUISS, #08994)*; *European Union Satellite Centre (SatCen, #09015)*. Through Secretariat of *ACP-EU Council of Ministers (#00076)*, cooperates with *Organisation of African, Caribbean and Pacific States (OACPS, #17796)*.
[2016/XE3068/**E***]

♦ Council for European Urbanism (CEU) 04896
Conseil pour l'urbanisme européen
Board Sec address not obtained.
Board Sec address not obtained.
URL: http://www.ceunet.org/
History 2003, Bruges (Belgium). **Aims** Promote the well being of present and future generations through the advancement of humane cities, towns, villages and countryside in Europe. **Structure** Officers include: Chair; 2 Deputy Chairs; Secretary; Technical Advisor. **Finance** Finance from Swedish Foundation. **Activities** Organizes: regular meetings; conferences; country-based events. **Events** *International congress on climate change and urban design* Oslo (Norway) 2008, *Congress* Leeds (UK) 2006, *Congress* Berlin (Germany) 2005, *Congress* Viseu (Portugal) 2004. [2019/XM0373/**D**]

- ♦ Council of Europe Convention on Access to Official Documents (2009 treaty)
- ♦ Council of Europe Convention on Action Against Trafficking in Human Beings (2005 treaty)
- ♦ Council of Europe Convention against Trafficking in Human Organs (2015 treaty)
- ♦ Council of Europe Convention on the Avoidance of Statelessness in Relations to State Succession (2006 treaty)
- ♦ Council of Europe Convention on Cinematographic Co-Production (revised) (2017 treaty)
- ♦ Council of Europe Convention on the Counterfeiting of Medical Products and Similar Crimes involving Threats to Public Health (2011 treaty)
- ♦ Council of Europe Convention on an Integrated Safety, Security and Service Approach at Football Matches and Other Sports Events (2016 treaty)
- ♦ Council of Europe Convention on Laundering, Search, Seizure and Confiscation of the Proceeds from Crime and on the Financing of Terrorism (2005 treaty)
- ♦ Council of Europe Convention on the Manipulation of Sports Competitions (2014 treaty)
- ♦ Council of Europe Convention on Offences relating to Cultural Property (2017 treaty)
- ♦ Council of Europe Convention on Preventing and Combating Violence against Women and Domestic Violence (2011 treaty)
- ♦ Council of Europe Convention on the Prevention of Terrorism (2005 treaty)
- ♦ Council of Europe Convention on the Protection of Children against Sexual Exploitation and Sexual Abuse (2007 treaty)

♦ Council of Europe Development Bank (CEB) 04897
Banque de développement du Conseil de l'Europe (CEB)
Governor 55 av Kléber, 75116 Paris, France. T. +33147555500. Fax +33147550338.
URL: http://www.coebank.org/
History 16 Apr 1956, Strasbourg (France), by *Council of Europe (CE, #04881)*, on adoption by 8 countries of Resolution (55) 34 of 13 Dec 1955, as *Resettlement Fund for National Refugees and Over-Population in Europe*. Subsequently referred to as *Council of Europe Resettlement Fund – Fonds de rétablissement du Conseil de l'Europe*. In 1996, became *Council of Europe Social Development Fund (CEF) – Fonds de développement social du Conseil de l'Europe*. Present name adopted 1999. Also referred to by initials *CEB*. **Aims** Promote *social* cohesion and strengthen social integration in Europe through provision of financial and technical expertise for projects with a high social impact in Member States. **Structure** Governing Board; Administrative Council. **Languages** English, French. **Staff** 200.00 FTE, paid. **Finance** Total assets (end 2017): euro 23,798,000. Subscribed capital (2017): euro 5,472,219. In 2017, loans disbursed amounted to euro 2,302,000; loans outstanding amounted to euro 13,792,000. **Activities** Financial and/or material support. **Events** *Meeting* Berlin (Germany) 2015, *Meeting* Vatican City (Vatican) 2010, *Meeting* Paris (France) 2001, *Meeting* Portoroz (Slovenia) 1999, *Meeting* Malta 1995. **Publications** *CEB Info* (4 a year) in English, French – magazine; *Financial Report* (annual) in English, French; *Half-Year Report* (annual) in English, French; *Report of the Governor* (annual) in English, French. *Corporate Social Responsibility Report* in English, French. Economic studies.
Members Governments of 41 countries and territories:
Albania, Belgium, Bosnia-Herzegovina, Bulgaria, Croatia, Cyprus, Czechia, Denmark, Estonia, Finland, France, Georgia, Germany, Greece, Holy See, Hungary, Iceland, Ireland, Italy, Kosovo, Latvia, Liechtenstein, Lithuania, Luxembourg, Malta, Moldova, Montenegro, Netherlands, North Macedonia, Norway, Poland, Portugal, Romania, San Marino, Serbia, Slovakia, Slovenia, Spain, Sweden, Switzerland, Türkiye.
IGO Relations Member of: *Regional Cooperation Council (RCC, #18773)*. Supports: *UNDP (#20292)* – and a Memorandum of Understanding; *UNHCR (#20327)*. Cooperation agreement signed with: *European Bank for Reconstruction and Development (EBRD, #06315)* (1999 and 2000); *European Commission (EC, #06633)* (2000); *European Stability Mechanism (ESM, #08829)* (2014); *International Bank for Reconstruction and Development (IBRD, #12317)* (2000); *International Development Association (IDA, #13155)* (2000); *International Finance Corporation (IFC, #13597)* (2000); *Nordic Environment Finance Corporation (NEFCO, #17281)* (2000); *Nordic Investment Bank (NIB, #17327)* (2000) – and a Memorandum of Understanding. **NGO Relations** Member of: *European Association of Long-Term Investors (ELTI, #06112)*. Partner of: 100 Resilient Cities (100RC). [2018.09.19/XF0445/**F***]

- ♦ Council of Europe Framework Convention on the Value of Cultural Heritage for Society (2005 treaty)
- ♦ Council of Europe Resettlement Fund / see Council of Europe Development Bank (#04897)
- ♦ Council of Europe Social Development Fund / see Council of Europe Development Bank (#04897)
- ♦ Council of Europe Staff Trade Union (#20079)
- ♦ Council of Europe Steering Committee on Crime Problems / see European Committee on Crime Problems (#06645)
- ♦ Council of Evangelical Methodist Churches of Latin America and the Caribbean (#04714)
- ♦ Council for Exceptional Children (internationally oriented national body)
- ♦ Council of Foreign Ministers (see: #17813)
- ♦ Council of Foreign Ministers (inactive)
- ♦ Council on Foreign Relations (internationally oriented national body)
- ♦ Council on Forest Engineering (internationally oriented national body)
- ♦ Council on Foundations (internationally oriented national body)
- ♦ Council for Global Equality (internationally oriented national body)

♦ Council for Global Problem-Solving (CGP) 04898
Acting Managing Dir c/o Global Solutions Initiatve Foundation, Friedrichstr 194-199, 10117 Berlin, Germany. E-mail: contact@global-solutions.international.
URL: https://www.cgp-council.org/
History Founded as the research base and intellectual core of *Global Solutions Initiative Foundation (#10611)* to provide policy advice to the *Group of Twenty (G20, #10793)*. **Aims** Provide long-term policy advice and support to the G20 and associated international organizations and think tanks. **Structure** Membership Structure, The Global Solutions Initiative Foundation gemeinnützige GmbH. **Languages** English, German. **Activities** Events/meetings; guidance/assistance/consulting. **Publications** Policy Briefs; articles; policy papers.
Members Research institutions from the G20 member states, including 17 institutions listed in the Yearbook: *Argentine Council for International Relations (CARI)*; *Asian Development Bank Institute (ADB Institute, #01423)*; *Bertelsmann Foundation*; *Brookings Institution (BI)*; *Bruegel*; *Centre for International Governance Innovation (CIGI)*; *Centre for Strategic and International Studies, Jakarta (CSIS)*; *Economic Research Institute for ASEAN and East Asia (ERIA, #05319)*; *Institut français des relations internationales (IFRI)*; *International Institute for Applied Systems Analysis (IIASA, #13861)*; *International Panel on Social Progress (IPSP, #14508)*; *Italian Institute for International Political Studies (ISPI)*; *Kiel Institute for the World Economy (IfW)*; *OECD (#17693)* (Policy Studies Branch); *Real Instituto Elcano de Estudios Internacionales y Estratégicos*; *South African Institute of International Affairs (SAIIA)*; *Stiftung Mercator*. [2020.05.07/XM8585/y/**E**]

- ♦ Council of Governors of Arab Central Banks and Monetary Agencies / see Council of Arab Central Banks and Monetary Agencies' Governors (#04858)
- ♦ Council for Harmonization of Electrotechnical Standards of the Nations in the Americas (#04700)
- ♦ Council for Health Service Accreditation in Southern Africa (internationally oriented national body)
- ♦ Council of Hellenes Abroad / see World Council of Hellenes Abroad (#21329)
- ♦ Council on Hotel, Restaurant and Institutional Education / see International Council on Hotel, Restaurant and Institutional Education
- ♦ Council of Insurance Agents & Brokers (internationally oriented national body)
- ♦ Council of Insurers' Bureaux / see Council of Bureaux (#04873)
- ♦ Council of the Inter-American Conference on Physics Education / see Inter-American Council on Physics Education (#11424)

♦ Council for International Congresses of Dipterology (CICD) 04899
Sec-Treas African Natural History Research Trust, Natural History Museum, Street Court, Kingsland, London, HR6 9QA, UK.
Chairman Leibniz Institute for Evolution and Biodiversity Science, Museum für Naturkunde, Invalidenstrasse 43, 10115 Berlin, Germany.
URL: http://www.nadsdiptera.org/ICD/ICDhome.htm
History 1986. Constitution adopted Sep 1988. **Aims** Provide continuity and direction for International Congresses of Dipterology. **Structure** Congress (held every 4 years); Council (meets at least twice during Congresses and once between Congresses). **Languages** English. **Staff** None. **Finance** Financed by Congress Organizing Committee. **Activities** Events/meetings. **Events** *Afrotropical dipterology* Windhoek (Namibia) 2018, *Quadrennial Congress / Congress* Potsdam (Germany) 2014, *Quadrennial congress / Congress* San José (Costa Rica) 2010, *Quadrennial congress / Congress* Fukuoka (Japan) 2006, *Quadrennial congress / Congress* Brisbane, QLD (Australia) 2002.
Members Individuals in 13 countries:
Australia, Belgium, Brazil, Canada, Costa Rica, Denmark, Japan, Singapore, South Africa, Spain, UK, Ukraine, USA.
NGO Relations Member of (1): *International Union of Biological Sciences (IUBS, #15760)* (as Scientific member of). [2022/XD2174/v/**F**]

♦ Council for International Congresses of Entomology (ICE Council) . 04900
Conseil pour les congrès internationaux d'entomologie
SG / Treas address not obtained.
Chair address not obtained.
URL: https://www.icecouncil.org/

History 1910, Brussels (Belgium). Founded at 1st International Congress of Entomology. Functions as a section of *International Union of Biological Sciences (IUBS, #15760)*. Former names and other names: *Permanent Committee of the International Congresses of Entomology* – former (1910). **Aims** Provide continuity and direction for the International Congresses of Entomology; serve as entomology section of the IUBS. **Structure** Congress (every 4 years); Council. **Languages** English. **Staff** None. **Finance** Sources: grants; donations; congresses. **Events** *International Congress of Entomology* Kyoto (Japan) 2024, *International Congress of Entomology* Helsinki (Finland) 2022, *International Congress of Entomology* Helsinki (Finland) 2020, *International Congress of Entomology* Orlando, FL (USA) 2016, *International Congress of Entomology* Daegu (Korea Rep) 2012. **Publications** Congress proceedings.
Members Individuals (23) in 20 countries and territories:
Argentina, Australia, Brazil, Canada, China, Czechia, Germany, Ghana, India, Israel, Italy, Japan, Kenya, Korea Rep, Netherlands, Peru, Russia, Taiwan, UK, USA. [2022/XF3097/v/F]

♦ Council for International Development (internationally oriented national body)
♦ Council for International Education / see UK Council for International Student Affairs

♦ Council on International Educational Exchange (CIEE) 04901

Main Office 600 Southborough Dr, Ste 104, Portland ME 04106, USA.
URL: http://www.ciee.org/

History 1947, USA. Former names and other names: *Council on Student Travel (CST)* – former (1947 to 1967). **Aims** Develop, serve and support international educational exchange as a means to build understanding and peaceful cooperation between nations; foster academic excellence in international educational exchange and offer personal and professional development opportunities to participants in exchange programmes; contribute to formation of public policy and distribution of information concerning international educational exchange; encourage research to foster support and attract public investment to the field; facilitate international student, youth and budget travel opportunities worldwide. **Structure** Board of Directors; Academic Consortium Board; Officers of Council. Regional Administrative Centers (3): North America (Portland ME – USA); Europe (Paris – France); Asia (Tokyo – Japan). Administrative Offices (2): Portland ME (USA); Tokyo (Japan). **Activities** Training/education; knowledge management/information dissemination; guidance/assistance/consulting; research/documentation; events/meetings. **Events** *Annual Conference* Portland, ME (USA) 2020, *Annual Conference* Brooklyn, NY (USA) 2019, *Annual Conference* Barcelona (Spain) 2018, *Annual Conference* Austin, TX (USA) 2017, *Annual Conference* Los Angeles, CA (USA) 2016. **Members** Universities, colleges, schools, institutes, associations (over 350, mostly in USA) but in a total of 22 countries (not specified). **NGO Relations** Instrumental in setting up: *International Committee for the Study of Educational Exchange (ICSEE, inactive)*. Member of: *Alliance for International Exchange*; *Association for Studies in International Education (ASIE, #02934)*; *EFMD – The Management Development Network (#05387)*; *World Youth Student and Educational Travel Confederation (WYSE Travel Confederation, #21959)*. [2019/XF0294/F]

♦ Council of International Fellowship (CIF) 04902

Pres 43 rue Paul Langevin, 18400 Saint-Florent-sur-Cher, France. T. +33607378617 – +33633248556645. E-mail: president@cifinternational.com.
URL: http://www.cifinternational.com/

History 1960, as *Cleveland International Fellowship (CIF)*, by Dr Henry B Ollendorff (1907-1979). Registered in accordance with German law, 1964. **Aims** Promote international understanding and world *peace* through exchange of experience for social workers, special educators, youth leaders and others in closely related fields. **Structure** Board of Directors; Executive Committee. **Languages** English. **Finance** Members' dues. Donations. Budget (biennial): US$ 26,000. **Activities** Networking/liaising. **Events** *Conference* Hannover (Germany) 2023, *Biennial Conference* Sigtuna (Sweden) 2015, *Biennial Conference* Ankara (Turkey) 2013, *Biennial conference* Larnaca (Cyprus) 2011, *Biennial Conference* Kiljava (Finland) 2009. **Publications** *CIF World News* (2 a year).
Members National branches in 32 countries:
Argentina, Australia, Austria, Cameroon, Cyprus, Czechia, Estonia, Finland, France, Germany, Greece, India, Israel, Italy, Japan, Kenya, Kyrgyzstan, Latvia, Lithuania, Nepal, Netherlands, New Zealand, Norway, Russia, Slovenia, Spain, Sweden, Switzerland, Thailand, Türkiye, UK, USA.
NGO Relations Joint conferences with: *Council of International Programs USA (CIPUSA)*. [2022/XF7203/F]

♦ Council of International Investigators (internationally oriented national body)

♦ Council of International Lawn Tennis Clubs (IC Council) 04903

Contact PO Box 400, Wimbledon, London, SW20 0QU, UK. T. +442089469374.
URL: http://www.ictennis.net/

History 22 Jul 1947, London (UK). **Aims** Maintain, protect and foster the ideals of international clubs worldwide; promote good fellowship among players; develop, encourage and maintain the highest standard of sportsmanship and understanding amongst players and junior players in particular. **Structure** General Meeting (annual). Executive Committee, comprising President, Chairman, Honorary Secretary, Honorary Treasurer and 3 permanent members representing France, UK and USA. Committee meets 3 times a year, 1 meeting always in Paris (France) during the Roland-Garros match. **Finance** Subscriptions. **Activities** Competitions supervised by the Council: Week Competitions; Potter Cup; Columbus Trophy; IC World Junior Challenge. Works closely with national federations to expand development of the game in IC countries and on a worldwide basis; fosters international competition and friendship; encourages talented young players; networks with the wider world of tennis.
Members Clubs, representing 4,000 tennis players worldwide who play or have played international representative tennis overseas, in 33 countries and territories:
Argentina, Australia, Austria, Bahamas, Belgium, Brazil, Canada, Czechia, Denmark, France, Germany, Hong Kong, India, Ireland, Israel, Italy, Japan, Luxembourg, Mexico, Monaco, Netherlands, New Zealand, Norway, Pakistan, Russia, South Africa, Spain, Sweden, Switzerland, UK, Uruguay, USA, Zimbabwe.
NGO Relations Associate member of: *International Tennis Federation (ITF, #15676)*. [2014/XE4689/E]

♦ Council of International Needs / see International Needs (#14222)
♦ Council of Inter-National Needs Network / see International Needs (#14222)

♦ Council of International Neonatal Nurses (COINN) 04904

Pres 2110 Yardley Rd, Yardley PA 19067, USA. E-mail: president@coinnurses.org.
URL: http://www.coinnurses.org/

History 2005. Registration: 501(c)(3) organization, No/ID: EIN: 20-2634091, Start date: 2008, USA, Pennsylvania. **Aims** Promote excellence in neonatal nursing and health outcomes for infants and families; act as an international leader in development of professional standards of neonatal nursing. **Structure** Board of Directors. **Languages** English. **Activities** Advocacy/lobbying/activism; networking/liaising; standards/guidelines. **Events** *International Neonatal Nursing Conference* Auckland (New Zealand) 2019, *International Neonatal Nursing Conference* Vancouver, BC (Canada) 2016, *International Neonatal Nursing Conference / Conference* Belfast (UK) 2013.
Members Full in 12 countries and in Southern Africa:
Australia, Canada, Denmark, Finland, India, Japan, Netherlands, New Zealand, Rwanda, UK, USA, Zambia.
Affiliate in 3 countries:
Singapore, Sweden, USA.
NGO Relations Member of (2): *Alliance of Global Neonatal Nursing (ALIGNN)*; *International Childbirth Initiative (ICI, #12547)*. Cooperates with (6): *European Foundation for the Care of Newborn Infants (EFCNI, #07344)*; *Healthy Newborn Network (HNN, #10894)*; *International Council of Nurses (ICN, #13054)*; *International Neonatal Consortium (INC, #14223)*; *PMNCH (#18410)*; *White Ribbon Alliance for Safe Motherhood (WRA, #20934)*. *Neonatal Nursing Association of Southern Africa (NNASA)* is member. [2023/XJ4553/C]

♦ Council of International Organizations Directly Interested in Children and Youth (inactive)

♦ Council for International Organizations of Medical Sciences (CIOMS) 04905

Conseil des organisations internationales des sciences médicales – Consejo de Organizaciones Internacionales de las Ciencias Médicas

SG Case Postale 2100, 1211 Geneva, Switzerland. T. +41227916497. E-mail: info@cioms.ch.
Street Address 1 Route des Morillons, 1202 Geneva, Switzerland.
URL: http://cioms.ch/

History 4 Apr 1949, Brussels (Belgium). Founded under the auspices of WHO and UNESCO. Statutes amended: 1961; 1967; 1979; 2016. Former names and other names: *Council for the Coordination of International Congresses of Medical Sciences (CCICMS)* – former; *Conseil pour la coordination des congrès internationaux des sciences médicalesi* – former. Registration: Start date: 20 Mar 1964, Belgium; Swiss Civil Code, Start date: 24 Apr 2019, Switzerland. **Aims** Advance *public health* through guidance on health research including ethics, medical product development and safety. **Structure** General Assembly (every 2 years); Executive Committee; Permanent Secretariat. **Languages** English, French. **Staff** 4.00 FTE, paid. **Finance** Sources: meeting proceeds; members' dues; revenue from activities/projects; sale of publications. **Activities** Healthcare; publishing activities; standards/guidelines. **Events** *Executive Committee Meeting* Geneva (Switzerland) 2021, *Executive Committee Meeting* Geneva (Switzerland) 2020, *General Assembly* Geneva (Switzerland) 2019, *Meeting* Geneva (Switzerland) 2019, *Meeting* Geneva (Switzerland) 2018. **Publications** *CIOMS Newsletter*. Books; working group reports; guidelines.
Members National members in 10 countries:
Bangladesh, Belgium, Czechia, Georgia, Germany, India, Israel, Korea Rep, South Africa, Switzerland.
International members: specialized international non-governmental medical organizations (12):
International College of Angiology (ICA, #12640); *International Federation of Associations of Pharmaceutical Physicians (IFAPP, #13363)*; *International Federation of Oto-Rhino-Laryngological Societies (IFOS, #13496)*; *International Rhinologic Society (IRS, #14753)*; *International Society for Pharmacoepidemiology (ISPE, #15355)*; *International Society of Internal Medicine (ISIM, #15212)*; *International Society of Pharmacovigilance (ISoP, #15356)*; *International Union of Basic and Clinical Pharmacology (IUPHAR, #15758)*; *Medical Women's International Association (MWIA, #16630)*; *World Allergy Organization – IAACI (WAO, #21077)*; *World Association of Societies of Pathology and Laboratory Medicine (WASPaLM, #21191)*; *World Medical Association (WMA, #21646)*.
Associate members (19):
American Society for Bioethics and Humanities; *Asia-Pacific Academy of Ophthalmology (APAO, #01814)*; Consulta di Bioetica; *European Association of Hospital Pharmacists (EAHP, #06074)*; Federation of Polish Medical Organizations Abroad; Good Clinical Practice Alliance; *International Council for Laboratory Animal Science (ICLAS, #13039)*; *International Federation of Clinical Chemistry and Laboratory Medicine (IFCC, #13392)*; *International Federation of Medical Students' Associations (IFMSA, #13478)*; *International Medical Sciences Academy (IMSA)*; *International Society for Hepatic Encephalopathy and Nitrogen Metabolism (ISHEN, #15161)*; *International Union of Microbiological Societies (IUMS, #15794)*; *International Union of Physiological Sciences (IUPS, #15800)*; Medical Sciences Society (MSS-UQ); National Fund for Scientific Research (NSFR); Saudi Neonatology Society; *World Association for Medical Law (WAML, #21164)*; *World Federation of Chiropractic (WFC, #21420)*; *World Organization of Family Doctors (WONCA, #21690)*.
Consultative Status Consultative status granted from: *ECOSOC (#05331)* (Ros C); *UNESCO (#20322)* (Associate Status); *WHO (#20950)* (Official Relations). **IGO Relations** Accredited by (1): *United Nations Office at Vienna (UNOV, #20604)*. **NGO Relations** Observer status with (1): *International Council on Harmonisation of Technical Requirements for Registration of Pharmaceuticals for Human Use (ICH, #13027)*. [2021.10.27/XA0431/y/A]

♦ Council of International Plastics Associations Directors (CIPAD) 04906

Dir Gen c/o SPI, 1425 K St NW, Ste 500, Washington DC 20005, USA.

Aims Service and advocate the plastics industry's interests worldwide; share information among international plastics associations. **Structure** General Assembly. **Events** *Meeting* Düsseldorf (Germany) 2004, *Annual General Assembly* Shanghai (China) 2004, *Annual General Assembly* Richmond (UK) 2003, *Annual General Assembly* Vienna (Austria) 2001.
Members Associations (63) in 49 countries and territories:
Argentina, Australia, Austria, Belgium, Bolivia, Brazil, Canada, Chile, China, Colombia, Cyprus, Denmark, Ecuador, El Salvador, Finland, France, Germany, Hong Kong, Hungary, India, Iran Islamic Rep, Ireland, Israel, Italy, Japan, Korea Rep, Malaysia, Mexico, Netherlands, New Zealand, Norway, Paraguay, Peru, Philippines, Portugal, Romania, Singapore, South Africa, Spain, Sweden, Switzerland, Taiwan, Thailand, Türkiye, UK, Uruguay, USA, Venezuela, Vietnam. [2015.11.30/XE4693/E]

♦ Council of International Programs USA (internationally oriented national body)
♦ Council of International Programs for Youth Leaders and Social Workers / see Council of International Programs USA
♦ Council on International and Public Affairs (internationally oriented national body)

♦ Council of International Schools (CIS) 04907

Administration Schipolweg 113, 2316 XC Leiden, Netherlands. T. +31715243300. E-mail: info@cois.org.
Chair c/o The American School of the Hague, Rijkstraatweg 200, 2241 BX Wassenaar, Netherlands.
URL: http://www.cois.org/

History Jul 2003. Registration: England and Wales; USA. **Aims** Provide services to schools, higher education institutions and individuals focused on international *education*. **Events** *Global Forum on International Admission and Guidance* Madrid (Spain) 2022, *Global Forum on International Admission and Guidance* 2020, *Forum on International Admission and Guidance* Vienna (Austria) 2018, *Forum on International Admission and Guidance* Barcelona (Spain) 2016, *Forum on International Admission and Guidance* Amsterdam (Netherlands) 2014. **Members** International schools and post-secondary institutions worldwide. Membership countries not specified. **NGO Relations** Founding member of: *International Alliance for School Accreditation*. [2022/XE4683/E]

♦ Council of International String Teachers Associations (inactive)
♦ Council of Islamic Banks and Financial Institutions / see General Council for Islamic Banks and Financial Institutions (#10111)
♦ Councilium on International and Area Studies / see MacMillan Center for International and Area Studies
♦ Council for Latin America / see Council of the Americas

♦ Council of Legal Education (CLE) 04908

Conseil de l'enseignement du droit

Chairman CARICOM, Turkeyen, Greater Georgetown, PO Box 10827, Georgetown, Guyana. T. +5922220001 – +5922220002 – +5922220075. Fax +5922220173 – +5922220170.
URL: http://www.caricom.org

History 17 Mar 1971, on coming into force of an agreement among contracting parties. Became an Associate Institution of *Caribbean Community (CARICOM, #03476)* following signature of *Treaty of Chaguaramas (1973)*, 4 Jul 1973. Has also been referred to as *Caribbean Council of Legal Education*. **Aims** Undertake and discharge general responsibility in the Caribbean region for practical professional training of persons seeking to become members of the legal profession; establish, equip and maintain law schools; make proper provision for courses of study and practical instructions for the award of prizes and for holding examinations and granting the Legal Education Certificate; evaluate courses of study provided at other institutions and accord appropriate recognition of legal qualifications. **Structure** Council, consisting of: Dean of the Faculty of Law of The University of the West Indies and another member of the Faculty nominated by him; Principals of the 3 Law Schools; Head of the Judiciary of each participating territory; Attorney-General of each participating territory; 2 members of the profession nominated by the appropriate body, from each of 4 participating territories (Jamaica, Barbados, Trinidad and Tobago, Guyana); one member of the profession nominated by the appropriate professional body from each of the other participating territories. **Languages** English. **Staff** 60.50 FTE, paid. **Finance** Contributions of participating territories. **Activities** Alternative Dispute Resolution and Mediation Clinic; Family Law Clinic; Criminal Law Clinic; Human Rights Clinic; Corporate Law Clinic; General Clinic; Moots. **Publications** *West Indian Law Journal* (2 a year).
Members Governments of countries and territories signatory to original agreement (9):
Antigua-Barbuda, Bahamas, Barbados, Dominica, Grenada, Guyana, Jamaica, St Kitts-Nevis, Trinidad-Tobago.
Other participating countries and territories (4):
Belize, Montserrat, St Lucia, St Vincent-Grenadines.
Organizations signatory to original agreement (2), including 1 organization listed in this Yearbook:
University of the West Indies (UWI, #20705). [2018/XD5213/D*]

♦ **Council for the Lindau Nobel Laureate Meetings** **04909**
Kuratorium für die Tagungen der Nobelpreisträger in Lindau
Dir Lennart-Bernadotte-Haus, Alfred-Nobel-Platz 1, 88131 Lindau, Germany. T. +498382277310. Fax +4983822773113. E-mail: info@lindau-nobel.org.
URL: http://www.lindau-nobel.org
History 1951. Former names and other names: *Standing Committee for Nobel Prize Winners' Congresses in Lindau* – former; *Ständiger Arbeitsausschuss für die Tagungen der Nobelpreisträger in Lindau* – former; *Executive Secretary of the Committee for the Meetings of Nobel Laureates in Lindau* – former; *Geschäftsführendes Sekretariat des Kuratoriums für die Tagungen der Nobelpreisträger in Lindau* – former. **Aims** Bring together Nobel Laureates and top Young Scientists from around the world; foster cross-cultural and inter-generational exchange of knowledge and ideas as well as establishment of networks. **Languages** English, German. **Activities** Events/meetings; networking/liaising. **Events** *Meeting* Lindau (Germany) 2023, *Lindau Meeting on Economic Sciences* Lindau (Germany) 2022, *Meeting* Lindau (Germany) 2022, *Meeting* Lindau (Germany) 2019, *Meeting* Lindau (Germany) 2018. **Publications** Annual Report. [2022.10.20/XE3275/**E**]

♦ Council for a Livable World (internationally oriented national body)
♦ Council of Local Authorities for International Relations (internationally oriented national body)
♦ Council of Logistics Management / see Council of Supply Chain Management Professionals
♦ Council for the Lutheran Churches in Central America and Panama (inactive)

♦ **Council of Managers of National Antarctic Programs (COMNAP)** ... **04910**
Exec Sec Private Bag 4800, Christchurch 8041, New Zealand. T. +6433692169. Fax +6433642197. E-mail: sec@comnap.aq.
Street Address COMNAP Secretariat, Univ of Canterbury, 20 Kirkwood Ave, Upper Riccarton, Christchurch 8041, New Zealand.
URL: http://www.comnap.aq/
History 1988. **Aims** Develop and promote best practice in managing the support of scientific research in Antarctica by: serving as a forum to develop practices that improve effectiveness of activities in an environmentally responsible manner; facilitating and promoting international partnerships; providing opportunities and systems for information exchange; providing the Antarctic Treaty System with objective and practical, technical and non-political advice drawn from the National Antarctic Programs' pool of expertise. **Structure** Council (meets annually); Executive Committee; Secretariat. **Languages** English. **Finance** Sources: members' dues. **Activities** Events/meetings; publishing activities; standards/guidelines; training/education. **Events** *Annual General Meetingn* Christchurch (New Zealand) 2021, *Annual General Meeting* 2020, *Annual General Meeting* Plovdiv (Bulgaria) 2019, *Annual General Meeting* Garmisch-Partenkirchen (Germany) 2018, *Annual General Meeting* Brno (Czechia) 2017. **Publications** *Antarctic Flight Information Manual.* Brochures; maps.
Members Full in 31 countries:
Argentina, Australia, Belarus, Belgium, Brazil, Bulgaria, Chile, China, Czechia, Ecuador, Finland, France, Germany, India, Italy, Japan, Korea Rep, Netherlands, New Zealand, Norway, Peru, Poland, Russia, South Africa, Spain, Sweden, Türkiye, UK, Ukraine, Uruguay, USA.
IGO Relations Observer status with (2): *Antarctic Treaty (AT, #00850)* (Consultative Meeting); Committee for Environmental Protection of the Antarctic Treaty. **NGO Relations** Cooperates with (1): *International Association of Antarctica Tour Operators (IAATO, #11702).* [2021.09.01/XE4324/**E**]

♦ Council for MENA Affairs (unconfirmed)
♦ Council of the Methodist Central Conferences in Europe (inactive)
♦ Council of Microfinance Equity Funds / see Financial Inclusion Equity Council (#09766)
♦ Council of Ministers / see Council of the European Union (#04895)
♦ Council of Ministers for Asian Economic Cooperation (inactive)
♦ Council of Ministers of the European Communities / see Council of the European Union (#04895)
♦ Council of Ministers of the European Union / see Council of the European Union (#04895)
♦ Council of Ministers of Health for GCC States / see Gulf Health Council (#10830)
♦ Council of Ministers of Interior of Arab Countries / see Arab Interior Ministers' Council (#00990)
♦ Council of Muslim Cooperation in Europe (no recent information)
♦ Council for Mutual Economic Assistance (inactive)
♦ Council for National and International Relations of Organizations of Youth and Popular Education (internationally oriented national body)

♦ **Council of Non-Governmental Organizations for Development Support** **04911**
Conseil des organisations non-gouvernementales d'appui au développement (CONGAD)
Exec Dir 2 Voies Liberté Extension, Cité Aliou SOW en Face Magasin Uno, BP 4109, 10200 Dakar, Senegal. T. +221778275494. Fax +221778275494. E-mail: congad@orange.sn.
URL: https://www.congad.org/
History Feb 1982, Dakar (Senegal). Current Statutes adopted by General Assembly, 12 May 1984, Dakar. **Aims** Coordinate work of non-governmental organizations which contribute to the economic and social development of Senegalese populations; develop exchange of experience and information among them; coordinate their activities and provide them with administrative support; serve as a forum to consolidate *North/South* cooperation; improve *living conditions* of both urban and rural communities. **Structure** General Assembly (annual); Board of Directors; Executive Management; Regional units. **Languages** French. **Finance** Members' dues. Other sources: grants; donations. **Publications** *CONGAD/LIANE* (12 a year); *CONGAD Infos* (4 a year); *Cahier du CONGAD* (2 a year). *Répertoire des ONG.*
Members Non-governmental organizations (178), of which 34 listed in this Yearbook:
- *African Network for Integrated Development (ANID, #00390)*;
- *African Office for Development and Cooperation (OFADEC)*;
- *Alternative Action for African Development (AGADA)*;
- *Association culturelle d'aide à la promotion éducative et sociale (ACAPES)*;
- *Association des professionnelles africaines de la communication (APAC, no recent information)*;
- *Association entr'aide franco-arabe (AEFAR, no recent information)*;
- *Association of African Women for Research and Development (AAWORD, #02362)*;
- *Association pour le développement des activités rurales au Sénégal et au Sahel (no recent information)*;
- *Association pour le développement naturel d'une architecture et d'un urbanisme africain (ADAUA, no recent information)*;
- *Canadian Centre for International Studies and Cooperation (CECI)*;
- *Catholic Relief Services (CRS, #03608)*;
- *ChildFund International (#03869)*;
- *Church World Service (CWS)*;
- *Développement solidaire (DEVSOL, no recent information)*;
- *Evangelical Lutheran Church in America (ELCA)*;
- *Fédération des associations du fouta pour le développement (no recent information)*;
- *Femmes, développement et entreprise en Afrique (FDEA, inactive)*;
- *Fondation internationale pour le développement (FID, no recent information)*;
- *France Volontaires*;
- *Groupe africain des volontaires pour le développement (GAVD, no recent information)*;
- *Groupe de recherche et de réalisations pour le développement rural dans le Tiers-monde (GRDR)*;
- *Groupe de recherches et de réalisations pour l'éco-développement (GRED, no recent information)*;
- *International Movement ATD Fourth World (#14193)*;
- *International Relief Friendship Foundation (IRFF, #14713)*;
- *Lay Volunteers International Association (LVIA)*;
- *Oxfam GB*;
- *Oxfam International (#17922)* (American Section);
- *Pan African Association for Community Development (PADEC, no recent information)*;
- *Plan International (#18386)*;
- *Rikolto*;
- *SOS SAHEL (#19695)*;
- *Vétérinaires Sans Frontières International (VSF International, #20760)*;
- *Winrock International*;
- *World Vision International (WVI, #21904).*

Non-African NGOs in 8 countries:
Belgium, Canada, France, Germany, Italy, Switzerland, UK, USA.
IGO Relations Invited to Governing Council sessions of: *International Fund for Agricultural Development (IFAD, #13692).* **NGO Relations** Member of: *International Council of Voluntary Agencies (ICVA, #13092).* Partner of: *Development Innovations and Networks (#05057).* Participates in: *FIM-Forum for Democratic Global Governance (FIM, #09761).* [2020/XE3790/y/**E**]

♦ Council of Nordic Dental Students (inactive)
♦ Council of Nordic Medical Associations (no recent information)
♦ Council of Nordic Patent Agents / see Committee of Nordic Intellectual Property Attorneys (#04276)
♦ Council of Nordic Teachers' Associations / see Nordic Teachers' Council (#17444)
♦ Council of Nordic Trade Unions (#17158)
♦ Council of the Notariats of the European Union / see Notaries of Europe (#17609)

♦ **Council of Occupational Therapists for the European Countries (COTEC)** **04912**
Contact Becker-Göringstrasse 26/1, 76303 Karlsbad, Germany. E-mail: info@coteceurope.eu.
URL: http://www.coteceurope.eu/
History 1986. Former names and other names: *Committee of Occupational Therapists for the European Communities* – former (1986 to May 2001). Registration: German Register of Associations, Start date: 2011, Germany; European Transparency Register, No/ID: 354869713074-35, Start date: 10 Mar 2014. **Aims** Enable national associations of occupational therapists to work together to develop, harmonize and improve *standards* of professional practice and advance the theory of occupational therapy throughout Europe. **Structure** General Assembly; Executive Committee. **Languages** English. **Staff** 0.20 FTE, paid. **Finance** Sources: members' dues. **Activities** Events/meetings; knowledge management/information dissemination; networking/liaising; research and development; standards/guidelines. **Events** *Occupational Therapy Europe Congress* Krakow (Poland) 2024, *Joint Congress* Prague (Czechia) 2021, *Joint Congress* Prague (Czechia) 2020, *Joint Congress* Galway (Ireland) 2016, *Meeting* Bugibba (Malta) 2013. **Publications** *Summary of the Profession in Europe* (annual). Online news updates.
Members Full Membership: organisations in 32 countries
Austria, Belgium, Bosnia-Herzegovina, Bulgaria, Croatia, Cyprus, Czechia, Denmark, Estonia, Finland, France, Georgia, Germany, Greece, Iceland, Ireland, Italy, Latvia, Lithuania, Luxembourg, Malta, Netherlands, Norway, Poland, Portugal, Romania, Serbia, Slovenia, Spain, Sweden, Switzerland, UK.
Associate Member: organisations in 1 country
Russia.
NGO Relations Member of (2): *European Forum for Primary Care (EFPC, #07326)* (associated); *Occupational Therapy Europe (OT-Europe, #17647)* (Founding). Instrumental in setting up (1): *European Network of Occupational Therapy in Higher Education (ENOTHE, #07956).* [2022.10.23/XE3926/**E**]

♦ Council of Pacific Arts / see Pacific Cultural Council (#17944)
♦ Council of Pacific Education (unconfirmed)
♦ Council of Pacific Teachers Organizations (inactive)
♦ Council for the Pan-European Biological and Landscape Diversity Strategy (inactive)
♦ Council for a Parliament of the World's Religions / see Parliament of the World's Religions (#18222)
♦ Council on Peace Research in History / see Peace History Society

♦ **Council for Peace and Security in Central Africa (COPAX)** **04913**
Pres c/o CEEAC, Mairie de Haut de Gue gue, BP 2112, Libreville, Gabon. T. +241444731. Fax +241444732.
URL: http://www.ceeac-eccas.org/
History 25 Feb 1999, Yaoundé (Cameroon), by member countries of *Economic Community of Central African States (ECCAS, #05311).* Became operational in 2003, when 8 ECCAS Member States out of 11 ratified its instruments. **Events** *Meeting* Ndjamena (Chad) 2010, *Meeting* Libreville (Gabon) 2008. [2009/XE4464/**E***]

♦ Council of the Professional Photographers of Europe (inactive)

♦ **Council of Regional Organisations of the Pacific (CROP)** **04914**
Main Office Forum Secretariat, Private Mail Bag, Suva, Fiji. T. +679312600. Fax +6793316151. E-mail: info@forumsec.org.
URL: https://www.forumsec.org/council-of-regional-organisations-of-the-pacific/
History Set up 1988, as *South Pacific Organizations Coordinating Committee (SPOCC)*, by *Pacific Islands Forum (#17968).* New name adopted, 1999. **Aims** Ensure coordination between the heads of the regional organizations in the Pacific; provide policy advice and falicitate policy formulation at national, regional and international level; provide a forum to enable CROP heads to collectively review progress with their respective organisations' contributions on the Framework for Pacific Regionalism. **Structure** Permanent Chair of CROP is the Secretary General of the *Pacific Islands Forum Secretariat (#17970).* Council; Working Groups; Agencies (8). **Languages** English. **Activities** Events/meetings; politics/policy/regulatory. **Publications** Annual Reports.
Members Representatives of participating regional organizations and institutions (8):
Pacific Community (SPC, #17942); Pacific Islands Forum Fisheries Agency (FFA, #17969); Pacific Islands Forum Secretariat (#17970); Pacific Power Association (PPA, #17991); Pacific Tourism Organization (SPTO, #18008); Secretariat of the Pacific Regional Environment Programme (SPREP, #19205); University of the South Pacific (USP, #20703). [2019.11.27/XE3221/y/**E***]

♦ Council on Religion and International Affairs / see Carnegie Council for Ethics in International Affairs

♦ **Council for Research in Values and Philosophy (RVP)** **04915**
Exec Dir Gibbons Hall B-20, 620 Michigan Ave NE, Washington DC 20064, USA. T. +12023196089. E-mail: cua-rvp@cua.edu.
URL: http://www.crvp.org/
History 1983, Washington, DC (USA). **Aims** Identify areas related to values and social life which are in need of research, bring together the professional competencies in philosophy and related human sciences needed for this research, and publish the resulting studies. **Structure** Board of Directors; Council; Secretariat. **Languages** English. **Staff** None. **Activities** Events/meetings; publishing activities; research/documentation. **Events** *Conference* Jinan (China) 2018, *General Meeting* Athens (Greece) 2013, *General Meeting* Seoul (Korea Rep) 2008, *Conference / General Meeting* Istanbul (Turkey) 2003, *Eastern European countries and the challenges of globalizations* Poznań (Poland) 2003. **Publications** *Cultural Heritage and Contemporary Change* – series. Research results (over 300 vols to date).
Members Individuals in academies and universities in 59 countries:
Argentina, Austria, Belgium, Brazil, Bulgaria, Cameroon, Canada, China, Colombia, Congo DR, Costa Rica, Côte d'Ivoire, Croatia, Czechia, Ecuador, Egypt, France, Georgia, Germany, Ghana, Guatemala, Hungary, India, Indonesia, Iran Islamic Rep, Israel, Italy, Japan, Kazakhstan, Kenya, Korea Rep, Kyrgyzstan, Lesotho, Lithuania, Nigeria, Pakistan, Paraguay, Peru, Philippines, Poland, Russia, Senegal, Serbia, Singapore, Slovakia, South Africa, Spain, Tajikistan, Tanzania UR, Tunisia, Türkiye, Turkmenistan, Uganda, UK, Ukraine, USA, Uzbekistan, Venezuela, Vietnam.
NGO Relations Member of (1): *International Federation of Philosophical Societies (FISP, #13507).* [2023.02.13/XF2247/v/**F**]

♦ Council Resolution on a Community Policy on Tourism (1984 treaty)
♦ Council for Responsible Jewellery Practices / see Responsible Jewellery Council (#18920)
♦ Council of Sales Promotion Agencies / see Marketing Agencies Association Worldwide (#16585)

♦ **Councils on Chiropractic Education International (CCEI)** **04916**
Exec Dir PO Box 4943, Pocatello ID 83205, USA. T. +12082414855. E-mail: secretariat@cceintl.org.
URL: http://www.cceintl.org/
History Founded Jul 2001, Brussels (Belgium). **Aims** Improve worldwide standards of chiropractic education. **Structure** Board of Directors. Officers: President; Vice-President; Executive Director. **Languages** English. **Staff** 1.00 FTE, paid. **Finance** Members' dues. **Activities** Provides consulting services.
Members National (2) and international (2) organizations in 4 countries:
Australia, Canada, UK, USA.
Included in the above, 1 organization listed in this Yearbook:
European Council on Chiropractic Education (ECCE, #06809). [2018/XE4319/y/**E**]

♦ Council of Science Editors (CSE) 04917

Main Office 355 Lexington Ave, 15th Floor, New York NY 10017, USA. E-mail: csecouncilofscience-editors@gmail.com.
URL: http://www.councilscienceeditors.org/

History Apr 1957, New Orleans LA (USA), as *Conference of Biological Editors*. Incorporated in the District of Columbia (USA) and name changed to *Council of Biology Editors (CBE)*, 7 Jul 1965. Constitution and bylaws adopted 1957; latest constitution and bylaws combined 1982; amended: 1983, 1987, 1992. Present name adopted 1 Jan 2000. **Aims** Improve communication in the *life sciences* by educating *authors*, editors and *publishers*; by providing efficient means of cooperation among persons interested in publishing in the life sciences and by promoting effective communication practices in primary and secondary publishing in any form. **Structure** Board of Directors, consisting of President of CBE (who serves as Chairman of the Board), immediate Past President, Vice President, Secretary (who serves as Secretary of the Board), Treasurer, 3 at-large Directors and an appointed non-voting Executive Director. Standing Committees; ad hoc Committees. **Languages** English. **Finance** Members' annual dues. Book sales; annual meeting registration. Budget (annual): US$ 250,000. **Activities** Annual Meeting. Committees meet throughout the year to work on topics of special interest and to achieve particular goals. **Events** *Annual Meeting* Portland, OR (USA) 2024, *Annual Meeting* Toronto, ON (Canada) 2023, *Annual Meeting* Phoenix, AZ (USA) 2022, *Annual Meeting* Minneapolis, MN (USA) 2021, *Annual Meeting* Portland, OR (USA) 2020. **Publications** *CBE Views* (6 a year). *CBE Style Manual* (1995); *Latin American Research Libraries in Natural History* (1994); *Peer Review in Scientific Publishing* (1991); *Ethics and Policy in Scientific Publication* (1990); *Financial Management of Scientific Journals* (1989); *Scientific Writing for Graduate Students* (1989) – latest vol; *Illustrating Science: Standards for Publication* (1988); *Editorial Forms: A Guide to Journal Management* (1987); *Economics of Scientific Journals* (1982).

Members Regular; Emeritus; Sustaining. Individuals (1,100) in 33 countries and territories:
Argentina, Australia, Belgium, Brazil, Canada, China, Denmark, Egypt, Ethiopia, Finland, France, Germany, Guyana, India, Indonesia, Israel, Italy, Japan, Kenya, Mexico, Netherlands, Nigeria, Norway, Papua New Guinea, Peru, South Africa, Spain, Sweden, Switzerland, Taiwan, UK, United Arab Emirates, USA. [2022/XF0232/v/F]

♦ Council for Secular Humanism (internationally oriented national body)

♦ Council of Securities Regulators of the Americas 04918

Consejo Interamericano de las Autoridades Regulatorias de Valores – Conselho de Reguladores de Valores Mobiliarios das Américas (COSRA)

No fixed address address not obtained.

History Founded 1992, Cancún (Mexico). Also referred to in English as *Council of Stock Market Regulatory Authorities of the Americas*. **Aims** Serve as a forum for high level discussions on regulatory and supervisory key issues related to the securities markets in the Americas. **Structure** Meets twice a year. Chairman; Working Groups (3): IARC-COSRA Relationship; Corporate Governance; SROs Conflict of Interest. **Languages** English, Spanish. **Staff** Secretariat supported by staff from the authority to which the Chairman belongs. **Finance** No financing. Meetings and conference financed by organizing member. **Activities** Networking/liaising. **Events** *Meeting* Paradise Is (Bahamas) 2016, *Meeting* Kingston (Jamaica) 2015.

Members Authorities responsible for securities regulation and supervision in the America; SROs in the Americas. Organizations (2):
Instituto Iberoamericano de Mercados de Valores (IIMV, #11333); *North American Securities Administrators Association (NASAA)*.

NGO Relations Meets in conjunction with Inter-American Regional Committee (IARC) of *International Organization of Securities Commissions (IOSCO, #14470)*. [2019/XD6772/E]

♦ Council for Security Cooperation in the Asia Pacific (CSCAP) 04919

Secretariat c/o ISIS Malaysia, 1 Pesiaran Sultan Salahuddin, PO Box 12424, 50778 Kuala Lumpur, Malaysia. T. +60326939366. Fax +60326939375. E-mail: cscap@isis.org.my.
Communications CSCAP New Zealand Office, Centre for Strategic Studies, School of Government, Victoria Univ of Wellington, PO Box 600, Wellington, New Zealand. T. +6444635434. Fax +6444635437. E-mail: css@vuw.ac.nz.
URL: http://www.cscap.org/

History 8 Jun 1993, Kuala Lumpur (Malaysia). Founded at meeting of the 10 founding research institutes, following a series of conferences held as *Conference on Security Cooperation in the Asia Pacific (SCAP)*. Charter adopted 16 Dec 1993, Lombok (Indonesia); amended Aug 1995, 14 Dec 1998, Manila (Philippines); 2 Jun 2011, Kuala Lumpur (Malaysia). **Aims** Provide a more structured regional process in contributing to regional *confidence building* and enhancing regional security through dialogue, consultation and cooperation. **Structure** Steering Committee (meets twice a year); Sub-Committees (4); Study Groups (6). **Finance** Members' dues. **Activities** Events/meetings; research/documentation; training/education. **Events** *Nuclear Energy Experts Group Meeting* Singapore (Singapore) 2021, *Nuclear Energy Experts Group Meeting* Singapore (Singapore) 2020, *CSAP Study Group Meeting* Singapore (Singapore) 2019, *Nuclear Energy Experts Group Meeting* Singapore (Singapore) 2019, *Seminar on Developing Macrosecuritisation Theory* Singapore (Singapore) 2019. **Publications** *CSCAP Regional Security Outlook (CRSO)* (annual). Memoranda; books; conference report.

Members Research institutes (21):
Brunei Darussalam Institute of Policy and Strategic Studies; *Cambodian Institute for Cooperation and Peace (CICP)*; *Centre for International Governance Innovation (CIGI)* (Canada); *Centre for Strategic and International Studies, Jakarta (CSIS)*; *Centre for Strategic Studies, New Zealand (CSS-NZ)*; *China Institute of International Studies (CIIS)*; *Diplomatic Academy of Vietnam (DAV)*; *European Union Institute for Security Studies (EUISS, #08994)*; *Ilmin International Relations Institute (IIRI)* (Korea Rep); *Indian Council of World Affairs (ICWA)*; *Institute for Strategic and Development Studies, Quezon City (ISDS)*; *Institute for Strategic Studies, Ulaanbaatar (ISS)*; *Institute of Disarmament and Peace, Pyongyang (no recent information)*; *Institute of Security and International Studies, Bangkok (ISIS)*; *Institute of Strategic and International Studies, Malaysia (ISIS)*; *Japan Institute of International Affairs (JIIA)*; *Pacific Forum Center for Security and International Studies (Pacific Forum CSIS)* (USA); *S Rajaratnam School of International Studies (RSIS)* (Singapore); *Strategic and Defence Studies Centre (SDSC)* (Australia).
Associate member:
Pacific Islands Forum Secretariat (#17970).

NGO Relations Based at: *Institute of Strategic and International Studies, Malaysia (ISIS)*. [2020/XE1817/y/E]

♦ Council of Societies for the Study of Religion (internationally oriented national body)

♦ Council of Southern Africa Football Associations (COSAFA) 04920

Administrative Office address not obtained. T. +27114471669.
URL: http://www.cosafa.com/

History Set up by *Supreme Council for Sport in Africa (SCSA, inactive)* – Zone 6. Administrative Office opened 2008, Johannesburg (South Africa). **Structure** Secretariat; Administrative Office headed by Chief Operations Officer.

Members Full in 14 countries:
Angola, Botswana, Comoros, Eswatini, Lesotho, Madagascar, Malawi, Mauritius, Mozambique, Namibia, Seychelles, South Africa, Zambia, Zimbabwe.
Associate in 1 territory:
Réunion. [2014/XJ8861/D]

♦ Council on Standards for International Educational Travel (internationally oriented national body)
♦ Council of Stock Market Regulatory Authorities of the Americas / see Council of Securities Regulators of the Americas (#04918)
♦ Council on Student Travel / see Council on International Educational Exchange (#04901)
♦ Council of Supply Chain Management Professionals (internationally oriented national body)
♦ Council for Sustainable Development of Central Asia (inactive)
♦ Council of Sustainable Settlements in Latin America (unconfirmed)

♦ Council on Tall Buildings and Urban Habitat (CTBUH) 04921

Conseil des bâtiments élevés et de l'habitat urbain

Global Headquarters The Monroe Bldg, 104 South Michigan Ave, Ste 620, Chicago IL 60603, USA. T. +13122835599. Fax +18448239392. E-mail: info@ctbuh.org.
URL: http://www.ctbuh.org/

History 1969. Founded as a group formed by American Society of Civil Engineers (ASCE) and *International Association for Bridge and Structural Engineering (IABSE, #11737)*. Since 1973, as a result of increased emphasis on planning and environmental criteria, 7 other organizations were invited to join the forming bodies as equal participants. Former names and other names: *Joint Committee on Tall Buildings* – former (1969 to 1976). **Aims** Facilitate exchange of the latest knowledge available on tall buildings around the world. **Structure** Board of Trustees; Executive Committee; Advisory Group; Regional Representatives. Asia Headquarters in Shanghai (China); Research Office in Venice (Italy); Academic Office in Chicago IL (USA). **Languages** English. **Staff** 31.00 FTE, paid. **Finance** Members' dues. **Activities** Events/meetings; knowledge management/information dissemination; awards/prizes/competitions; research and development; networking/liaising; publishing activities. **Events** *International Conference* Chicago, IL (USA) 2022, *The Post-Crisis City – Rethinking Sustainable Vertical Urbanism* Singapore (Singapore) / London (UK) / Chicago, IL (USA) 2020, *World Congress* Chicago, IL (USA) 2019, *China-Japan-Korea Tall Building Forum* Nara (Japan) 2019, *Tall and Urban Innovation Conference* Shenzhen (China) 2019. **Publications** *CTBUH Journal* (4 a year); *CTBUH Best Tall Buildings Awards Book* (annual). Books; monographs; conference proceedings; special reports; research reports; technical guides. **Information Services** *The Skyscraper Center* – database.

Members Individual; Organizational. Members in 45 countries and territories:
Australia, Austria, Belgium, Brazil, Canada, Chile, China, Costa Rica, Czechia, Denmark, Egypt, Finland, France, Germany, India, Indonesia, Ireland, Israel, Italy, Japan, Korea Rep, Kuwait, Lebanon, Malaysia, Mexico, Netherlands, New Zealand, Nigeria, Peru, Philippines, Qatar, Russia, Saudi Arabia, Singapore, South Africa, Spain, Sweden, Switzerland, Taiwan, Thailand, Türkiye, UK, United Arab Emirates, USA, Vietnam. [2022/XF0776/F]

♦ Council for Tropical and Subtropical Agricultural Research (internationally oriented national body)
♦ Council of University Institutes for Urban Affairs / see Urban Affairs Association (#20728)
♦ Council of Valuers Associations of the CIS / see Council of Valuers' Associations of Eurasia (#04922)

♦ Council of Valuers' Associations of Eurasia 04922

Contact PO Box 11, 220029 Minsk, Belarus. T. +375296776776. Fax +375293242839. E-mail: guild@unibel.by.

History Current title adopted 2011. Former names and other names: *Council of Valuers Associations of the CIS* – former. **Languages** Russian. **Staff** 1.00 FTE, paid. **Events** *International Congress of Valuers of Eurasia* Tashkent (Uzbekistan) 2021, *International Congress of Valuers of Eurasia* Baku (Azerbaijan) 2019. **Publications** *Eurasian Valuation Standards 2014* (2014).

Members National societies (9) in 8 countries:
Azerbaijan, Belarus, Georgia, Kyrgyzstan, Moldova, Russia, Turkmenistan, Uzbekistan.

NGO Relations Member of (1): *International Valuation Standards Council (IVSC, #15840)*. [2020.03.26/XM8202/D]

♦ Council of the Wholesale Merchants Federations in the Northern Countries (inactive)

♦ Council of Women World Leaders (CWWL) 04923

SG c/o WWISC – Reagan Bldg, One Woodrow Wilson Plaza, 1300 Pennsylvania Ave NW, Washington DC 20004-3027, USA.
URL: http://www.wilsoncenter.org/program/council-women-world-leaders

History 1997, on the initiative of Laura Liswood and Vigdis Finnbogadóttir. **Aims** Promote good governance; enhance the experience of democracy globally by increasing the number, effectiveness and visibility of women who lead at the highest levels in their countries. **Events** *Meeting* Geneva (Switzerland) 2005, *Meeting* Reykjavik (Iceland) 2005, *Meeting* Geneva (Switzerland) 2004, *Meeting* Dubai (United Arab Emirates) 2003, *Meeting* Washington, DC (USA) 2003.

Members Individuals (29) in 22 countries:
Bangladesh, Bermuda, Canada, Dominica, Finland, France, Guyana, Iceland, Ireland, Latvia, Lithuania, Neth Antilles, New Zealand, Nicaragua, Norway, Pakistan, Philippines, Poland, Portugal, Sri Lanka, Switzerland, Türkiye.

NGO Relations Support from: *Arca Foundation*. [2012/XD7536/v/D]

♦ Council of Working Women / see NA'AMAT Movement of Working Women and Volunteers

♦ Council of the World Communion of Reformed Churches in Europe (WCRC Europe) 04924

Sec address not obtained.
URL: http://www.wcrc-europe.eu/

History Set up as *WARC European Area Council*, within *World Alliance of Reformed Churches (WARC, inactive)*, currently *World Communion of Reformed Churches (WCRC, #21289)*. Re-structured 2006-2007, when referred to as *WCRC European Area Council*. **Aims** Strengthen cooperation and fellowship among WCRC member churches in Europe; strengthen involvement of European WCRC member churches within WCRC worldwide; strengthen involvement of WCRC member churches in the Community of Protestant Churches in Europe (CPCE); foster studies in reformed theology. **Structure** Steering Committee. **Languages** English. **Activities** Events/meetings. **Events** *Meeting* Zurich (Switzerland) 2016, *Meeting* Belfast (UK) 2015, *Meeting* Warsaw (Poland) 2014, *Meeting* Athens (Greece) 2013, *Meeting* Vienna (Austria) 2012. **Publications** *Europe Covenanting for Justice*.

Members Churches (40) in 28 countries:
Austria, Belgium, Bulgaria, Croatia, Czechia, Denmark, France, Germany, Greece, Hungary, Ireland, Italy, Latvia, Lithuania, Luxembourg, Montenegro, Netherlands, Poland, Portugal, Romania, Serbia, Slovakia, Slovenia, Spain, Sweden, Switzerland, UK, Ukraine. [2019.12.11/XK0529/E]

♦ Council for World Mission (CWM) 04925

Gen Sec 114 Lavender Street, Ste 12-01 CT Hub 2, Singapore 338729, Singapore. T. +6568873400. Fax +6562357760. E-mail: council@cwmission.org.
URL: http://www.cwmission.org/

History 18 Jul 1977, London (UK). Founded as an international council; formerly called *Congregational Council for World Mission*. Known also as *Council for World Mission – Congregational and Presbyterian*. The Council continues the work of: *London Missionary Society*, set up 1795, *Commonwealth Missionary Society* which came into being 1836, and *Presbyterian Church of England Overseas Mission Committee*, formed in 1847. **Aims** Spread knowledge of *Christ* throughout the world by sharing resource such as mission ideas, people, financial resources and power among member *Churches*. **Structure** Assembly (every 4 years). Trustee Body (meets at least annually) of one representative per member body. Executive Staff. Headquarters, based in Singapore. **Staff** 6.00 FTE, paid. **Finance** Sources: contributions from constituent bodies; legacies; property and investment income; direct contributions. Budget (annual): pounds5 million. **Activities** Programmes (3): Mission Education Unit; Mission Programme Unit; Personnel and Training Unit. Sharing ideas about mission; sharing people in mission (exchanges of full time mission partners, long and short term workers); finance and stewardship. Training in mission (international groups of young people). **Events** *Annual Members Meeting* London (UK) 2022, *Annual Members Meeting* Apia (Samoa) 2019, *Annual Members Meeting* Singapore (Singapore) 2017, *Council Meeting* Montego Bay (Jamaica) 2015, *Council Meeting* Shillong (India) 2014. **Publications** Reports of consultations and programmes; materials on such topics as women, youth, children, Bible studies and environmental research.

Members Constituent member Churches in 30 countries and territories:
Bangladesh, Botswana (*), Cayman Is, Guyana, Hong Kong, India, Jamaica, Kiribati, Korea Rep, Madagascar, Malawi, Malaysia, Mozambique (*), Myanmar, Namibia (*), Nauru, Netherlands, New Zealand, Papua New Guinea, Samoa, Samoa USA, Singapore, Solomon Is, South Africa (*), Sri Lanka, Taiwan, Tuvalu, UK, Zambia, Zimbabwe (*).
Regional members (UCCSA constituent churches are marked " above) (2):
United Congregational Church of Southern Africa (UCCSA, #20503); *Uniting Presbyterian Church in Southern Africa (UPCSA, #20668)*.

NGO Relations Member of: *African Network for Basin Organizations (ANBO, #00381)*; *Ecumenical Advocacy Alliance (EAA, inactive)*. [2022/XF0241/y/F]

♦ Council for World Mission – Congregational and Presbyterian / see Council for World Mission (#04925)
♦ Council on World Tensions (inactive)

♦ COUNTER 04926

Contact 25 Egbert road, Winchester, SO23 7EB, UK. T. +441962866843.
URL: http://www.projectcounter.org/

History 2002, resulting from a collaborative effort of scholarly publishers and librarians. Full title: *Counting Online Usage of NeTworked Electronic Resources (COUNTER).* **Aims** Provide the Code of Practice enabling publishers and vendors to report usage of their *electronic* resources in a consistent way. **Structure** Board of Directors; Executive Committee. **Languages** English. **Staff** 0.50 FTE, paid. Other voluntary. **Finance** Members' dues. **Activities** Standards/guidelines; training/education. **Publications** Guides. **Members** Industry Organizations; Library Consortia; Libraries; Small Publishers; Large Vendors; Medium Vendors; Affiliate. Membership countries not specified. [2017.12.07/XM5386/**F**]

♦ Counterpart Europe / see Counterpart Global Network (#04927)
♦ Counterpart Foundation / see Counterpart International

♦ Counterpart Global Network 04927

Sec Rue Dupré 15, 1090 Brussels, Belgium. T. +3225357272. Fax +3225357275.
URL: http://www.counterpart.org/

History Originally founded as an affiliate of *Counterpart International (FSP).* Former names and other names: *Counterpart Europe (CE)* – former. Registration: Banque Carrefour des Entreprises, No/ID: 0472.146.510, Start date: 29 Jun 2000, Belgium. **Structure** General Assembly. Executive Committee. **NGO Relations** *Foundation of the Peoples of the South Pacific International (FSPI, #09968); Just World Partners.* [2007/XK2087/**F**]

♦ Counterpart International (internationally oriented national body)

♦ Counter-Terrorism Committee (CTC) 04928

Comité contre le terrorisme – Comité contra el Terrorismo

Executive Directorate CH Room 5144, 405 East 42 St, New York NY 10017-3599, USA.
URL: http://www.un.org/en/sc/ctc/

History 28 Sep 2001. Established by *United Nations Security Council (UNSC, #20625)* Resolution 1373, within *United Nations (UN, #20515),* following the terrorist attacks 11 Sep 2001, USA. Former names and other names: *United Nations Security Council Counter-Terrorism Committee* – alias. **Aims** Monitor implementation of Security Council Resolutions 1373 and 1624; increase capability to fight terrorism. **Structure** Counter-Terrorism Committee Executive Directorate (CTED). Committee, comprises all 15 members of the Security Council, including Chairman and 3 Vice-Chairmen. Subcommittees (3).
Activities Guidance/assistance/consulting; knowledge management/information dissemination.
Conventions and protocols (13) play an integral part in the global fight against terrorism:
- *Convention on Offences and Certain other Acts Committed on Board Aircraft (Tokyo convention, 1963);*
- *Convention for the Suppression of Unlawful Seizure of Aircraft (1970);*
- *Convention for the Suppression of Unlawful Acts Against the Safety of Civil Aviation (1971);*
- *Convention on the Prevention and Punishment of Crimes Against Internationally Protected Persons, Including Diplomatic Agents (1973);*
- *International Convention Against the Taking of Hostages (1979);*
- *Convention on the Physical Protection of Nuclear Material (1979);*
- *Protocol for the Suppression of Unlawful Acts of Violence at Airports Serving International Civil Aviation (1988);*
- *Convention for the Suppression of Unlawful Acts Against the Safety of Maritime Navigation (SUA, 1988);*
- *Protocol for the Suppression of Unlawful Acts Against the Safety of Fixed Platforms Located on the Continental Shelf (SUA PROT, 1988);*
- *Convention on the Marking of Plastic Explosives for the Purpose of Identification (1991);*
- *International Convention for the Suppression of Terrorist Bombings (1997);*
- *International Convention for the Suppression of the Financing of Terrorism (1999);*
- *International Convention for the Suppression of Acts of Nuclear Terrorism.*

Members Member governments of the Security Council 2011 (15):
Bosnia-Herzegovina, Brazil, China, Colombia, France, Gabon, Germany, India, Lebanon, Nigeria, Portugal, Russia, Tanzania UR, UK, USA.
IGO Relations Observer status with: *Financial Action Task Force (FATF, #09765).* Participates in: *Committee of Experts on the Evaluation of Anti-Money Laundering Measures and the Financing of Terrorism (MONEYVAL, #04257).* [2017/XM0409/**E***]

♦ Counting Online Usage of NeTworked Electronic Resources / see COUNTER (#04926)
♦ Countries of Visegrad / see Visegrad Group (#20794)

♦ Coupe de la jeunesse 04929

SG c/o FFA, 17 Boulevard de la Marne, 94736 Nogent-sur-Marne CEDEX, France. T. +33145142640.
URL: http://www.couperowing.org/

Structure Executive Committee, including President, Honorary President and Secretary-General. **Activities** Organizes matches.
Members National federations in 12 countries:
Austria, Belgium, France, Hungary, Ireland, Italy, Netherlands, Portugal, Slovenia, Spain, Switzerland, UK.
NGO Relations *World Rowing (#21756).* [2014/XJ4092/**F**]

♦ Cour de l'AELE (#05390)
♦ Cour Africaine de justice et des droits de l'homme (unconfirmed)
♦ Courage / see Courage International (#04930)

♦ Courage International 04930

Address not obtained.
URL: http://couragerc.org/

History Founded Sep 1980, New York NY (USA), as *Courage.* **Aims** Encourage and provide spiritual support for men and women with *same-sex* attractions who strive to live chaste lives in accordance with the Roman *Catholic* Church's pastoral teaching on *homosexuality,* as well as support to parents, spouses, relatives and friends of persons with same-sex attraction. **Structure** Episcopal Board; Board of Directors. **Languages** English. **Staff** 6.00 FTE, paid. **Finance** Grants; contributions. **Activities** Events/meetings; networking/liaising. **Events** *Annual International Courage/Encourage Conference* Mundelein, IL (USA) 2019, *Annual International Courage/Encourage Conference* Philadelphia, PA (USA) 2018, *Annual International Courage/Encourage Conference* Mundelein, IL (USA) 2017, *Annual international courage/encourage conference* Washington, DC (USA) 2016, *Annual international courage/encourage conference* Mundelein, IL (USA) 2015. **Publications** Handbook; documentary; 5-part catechetical series.
Members Chapters contacts (over 100) in 14 countries and territories:
Australia, Brazil, Canada, Costa Rica, Ecuador, El Salvador, France, Ireland, Italy, Mexico, New Zealand, Philippines, UK, USA. [2017/XF5940/**F**]

♦ Courant communiste international (#12818)
♦ Cour d'appel de l'Afrique orientale (inactive)
♦ Cour des comptes des Communautés européennes / see European Court of Auditors (#06854)
♦ Cour des comptes européenne (#06854)
♦ Cour des comptes de l'UEMOA (see: #20377)
♦ Cour de conciliation et d'arbitrage au sein de l'OSCE (#04934)
♦ Cour criminelle internationale / see International Criminal Court (#13108)
♦ Cour européenne d'arbitrage (#06853)
♦ Cour européenne de conciliation et d'arbitrage / see Court of Conciliation and Arbitration within the OSCE (#04934)
♦ Cour européenne des droits de l'homme (#06855)
♦ Coureurs du monde (#21758)
♦ Cour interaméricaine des droits de l'homme (#04851)
♦ Cour internationale d'arbitrage de la CCI / see ICC International Court of Arbitration (#11049)
♦ Cour internationale d'arbitrage de la Chambre de commerce internationale (#11049)
♦ Cour internationale d'honneur (inactive)
♦ Cour internationale de Justice (#13098)
♦ Cour internationale de justice des droits de l'animal (#13099)
♦ Cour internationale des prix (inactive)
♦ Cour de justice andine / see Court of Justice of the Andean Community (#04936)
♦ Cour de justice Benelux (#03200)
♦ Cour de justice de la CECA / see Court of Justice of the European Union (#04938)
♦ Cour de justice centroaméricaine (#04850)

♦ Cour de justice communautaire de la CEMAC (CJ-CEMAC) 04931

CEMAC Community Court of Justice

Fist Pres BP 5780, Ndjamena, Chad. T. +235520827 – +235520474. Fax +235520592.
URL: https://www.cemac.int/cour_justice/

History within the framework of *Communauté économique et monétaire d'Afrique centrale (CEMAC, #04374),* with composition, function and field of competence being contained in the convention setting up *Union économique de l'Afrique centrale (UEAC, #20376).* **Aims** Ensure respect for *law* in the interpretation and application of current and subsequent *treaties* and conventions. **Structure** Comprises 2 chambers appointed by CEMAC Conference of Heads of State and each including a registry: *'Judicial Chamber – Chambre judiciaire',* consisting of 6 judges; *'Chamber of Auditors – Chambre des comptes',* comprising 6 individuals. [2018/XF5822/**F***]

♦ Cour de justice de la communauté (#04393)
♦ Cour de justice de la Communauté andine (#04936)
♦ Cour de justice des Communautés européennes / see Court of Justice of the European Union (#04938)
♦ Cour de justice du Marché commun de l'Afrique de l'est et de l'Afrique australe (#04937)

♦ Cour de justice de l'UEMOA 04932

UEMOA Court of Justice

Contact Place du Mémorial aux Héros Nationaux, Ouagadougou 01, Burkina Faso. T. +22625318873. Fax +22625300637. E-mail: cdj@uemoa.int – greffecdj@uemoa.int.
URL: http://www.uemoa.int/

History as the judicial organ of *Union économique et monétaire Ouest africaine (UEMOA, #20377).* **Aims** Ensure adherence to the law regarding interpretation and application of UEMOA founding Treaty. **Structure** Court comprises 8 members. **Languages** French.
Members Full (8) in 8 countries:
Benin, Burkina Faso, Côte d'Ivoire, Guinea-Bissau, Mali, Niger, Senegal, Togo. [2020/XF3675/**F***]

♦ Cour de justice de l'Union européenne (#04938)
♦ **Cour OSCE** Cour de conciliation et d'arbitrage au sein de l'OSCE (#04934)
♦ Cour pénale internationale (#13108)
♦ Cour permanente d'arbitrage (#18321)
♦ Cour permanente de justice internationale (inactive)
♦ Courrier sud – Association francophone des professionnels de l'aéronautique (internationally oriented national body)

♦ Court of Arbitration for Sport (CAS) 04933

Tribunal arbitral du sport (TAS) – Tribunal Arbitral del Deporte (TAS)

Dir-Gen Palais de Beaulieu, Bergières 10, 1004 Lausanne VD, Switzerland. T. +41216135000. Fax +41216135001. E-mail: info@tas-cas.org.
URL: http://www.tas-cas.org/

History Mar 1983. Founded by *International Olympic Committee (IOC, #14408),* the members of CAS being completely independent from IOC in the exercise of their duties. Statute entered into force and Regulation adopted 30 Jun 1984. Statute amended 20 Sep 1990. Recognized as an independent arbitration institution, 15 Mar 1993, by Swiss Federal Tribunal. Code of sports-related arbitration adopted 22 Nov 1994. Former names and other names: *Tribunal de Arbitraje Deportivo* – former. **Aims** Enable sports organizations, *athletes* and their partners to settle *disputes* of a private nature arising out of the practice or development of sport, and, in a general way, all activities pertaining to sport, without intervention by ordinary courts. **Structure** President, elected by *International Council of Arbitration for Sport (ICAS, #12994).* ICAS ensures total autonomy of the Court, independent from IOC. The Court comprises 2 Divisions: Ordinary Arbitration Division; Appeals Arbitration Division. It is assisted by a Court Office, managed by Director General under the authority of the ICAS. **Languages** English, French, Spanish. **Staff** 27.00 FTE, paid. **Finance** The operating costs of CAS are borne by *International Council of Arbitration for Sport (ICAS, #12994).* **Activities** Dispute resolution services – arbitration / mediation **Events** *International congress on law and sport* Barcelona (Spain) 1992. **Publications** *Bulletin TAS – CAS Bulletin* (2 a year). **Members** Arbitrators (390) from 81 countries with legal training and acknowledged competences in sport issues, appointed by ICAS for 4 years. Membership countries not specified. [2022.10.20/XF0590/v/**F**]

♦ Court of Auditors of the European Communities / see European Court of Auditors (#06854)
♦ Court of Conciliation and Arbitration in the Framework of the OSCE / see Court of Conciliation and Arbitration within the OSCE (#04934)

♦ Court of Conciliation and Arbitration within the OSCE (OSCE Court) 04934

Cour de conciliation et d'arbitrage au sein de l'OSCE (Cour OSCE)

Pres Av de France 23, 1202 Geneva, Switzerland. T. +41227580025. Fax +41227582510. E-mail: info@oscecourt.org.
URL: http://www.osce.org/cca/

History May 1995, Geneva (Switzerland). Established persuant to the signature, 15 Dec 1992, Stockholm (Sweden), of the *Convention on Conciliation and Arbitration within the CSCE (1992)* by Ministers of Foreign Affairs of *Organization for Security and Cooperation in Europe (OSCE, #17887).* The Convention, which is open for accession by all participating states, entered into force on 5 Dec 1994 by the deposition of the twelfth instrument of ratification. As of Jun 2005, 34 participating states had ratified / acceded to the Convention. Sweden is the depositary. Rules of procedure of the Court adopted 1 Feb 1997. Former names and other names: *Cour européenne de conciliation et d'arbitrage* – alias; *Court of Conciliation and Arbitration in the Framework of the OSCE* – former. **Aims** Settle, by means of conciliation and/or arbitration, the disputes involving States Parties to the Convention and/or OSCE participating States on a special agreement. that are submitted to it, including conflicts in respect of territorial integrity, maritime delimitation, environmental and economic issues. **Structure** Court, comprising 34 States Parties, each represented by 2 conciliators, an arbitrator and an alternate; Bureau, consisting of President, Vice-President, 3 additional members and 4 alternate members; Court Registrar. **Languages** English. **Finance** Financed by states party to the Convention.
Activities The OSCE framework provides the following means for peaceful settlement of disputes:
Two mutually supporting forms of action: *'Joint Political Decisions'* and *'Direct Action through Agreed Mechanisms'.* OCSE decisions are normally based on consensus while direct action through agreed mechanisms may be activated by the initiative of a limited number of participating states. Current mechanisms relate to: (i) Military developments – "Vienna mechanisms on unusual military activities"; (ii) Human dimension – "Moscow mechanism"; (iii) Serious emergency situations – "Berlin mechanism". They provide for a phased approach, starting with clarification of the situation through consultations between the states directly involved and extending to all-OSCE meetings with the possibility of fact-finding procedures being initiated.
'Independent Action by the Officers' – the complementary procedure implemented through operational initiative of the Chairman-in-Office and the officers and institutions authorized by him.
'Ad Hoc Conciliatory Commissions' established by the Court. These may hear cases brought before them even by a single state and their deliberations are designed to bring the parties together. On conclusion of its hearings, a commission presents a report to the parties, after which time the parties have 30 days to decide whether they are willing to accept its conclusions. If no agreement is reached within that period and if the parties have agreed to arbitration, then the Court may establish an *'Ad Hoc Arbitral Tribunal',* whose ruling is legally binding on the parties. Conciliatory commissions and the arbitral tribunals take decisions by majority voting. In the absence of a simple majority, the president of the commission or tribunal has the decisive vote.
Publications *Flexibility in International Dispute Settlement – Conciliation Revisited* (1st ed 2020) by Prof Christian Tomuschat and Prof Marcelo Kohen; *Conciliation in International Law – The OSCE Court of Conciliation and Arbitration; Peaceful Settlement of Disputes between States: Universal and European Perspectives* – published jointly with Kluwer Law International. Articles.
Members Participating states having ratified/acceded to the Convention as of Dec 2019 (34):

Albania, Armenia, Austria, Belarus, Bosnia-Herzegovina, Croatia, Cyprus, Denmark, Finland, France, Germany, Greece, Hungary, Italy, Latvia, Liechtenstein, Lithuania, Luxembourg, Malta, Moldova, Monaco, Montenegro, North Macedonia, Norway, Poland, Portugal, Romania, San Marino, Slovenia, Sweden, Switzerland, Tajikistan, Ukraine, Uzbekistan.
States party not having ratified/acceded to the Convention (6):
Belgium, Bulgaria, Canada, Russia, Slovakia. [2021.09.01/XF3997/**F***]

♦ Court of Justice of the African Union 04935

Contact c/o African Union, PO Box 3243, Addis Ababa, Ethiopia. T. +2511517700. Fax +2511517844.
URL: http://www.africa-union.org/

History Established within the framework of *African Union (AU, #00488)*. Protocol adopted 11 Jul 2003, Maputo (Mozambique); entered into force 30 days after deposit of the instruments of ratification by 15 member states, 11 Feb 2009. Will merge with *African Court on Human and Peoples' Rights (AfCHPR, #00278)*, when Protocol on the Statute of *African Court of Justice and Human Rights* enters into force, merging both courts into a single court. **Structure** Court consisting of 11 judges, elected for 6 years (may be re-elected once). Officers: President; Vice-President. **Languages** Arabic, English, French, Portuguese.
Members Member states of AU (55):
Algeria, Angola, Benin, Botswana, Burkina Faso, Burundi, Cameroon, Cape Verde, Central African Rep, Chad, Comoros, Congo Brazzaville, Congo DR, Côte d'Ivoire, Djibouti, Egypt, Equatorial Guinea, Eritrea, Eswatini, Ethiopia, Gabon, Gambia, Ghana, Guinea, Guinea-Bissau, Kenya, Lesotho, Liberia, Libya, Madagascar, Malawi, Mali, Mauritania, Mauritius, Morocco, Mozambique, Namibia, Niger, Nigeria, Rwanda, Sahara West, Sao Tomé-Principe, Senegal, Seychelles, Sierra Leone, Somalia, South Africa, South Sudan, Sudan, Tanzania UR, Togo, Tunisia, Uganda, Zambia, Zimbabwe.
NGO Relations Establishment supported by: *African Unification Front (AUF, no recent information)*.
[2009/XJ0151/**F***]

♦ Court of Justice of the Andean Community 04936

Cour de justice de la Communauté andine – Tribunal de Justicia de la Comunidad Andina
SG Calle Portete N11-27 y Gregorio Munga, 170504 Quito, Ecuador. T. +59323801980 – +59323801980. E-mail: secretaria@tribunalandino.org.
URL: http://www.tribunalandino.org.ec/

History 28 May 1979, Cartagena de Indias (Colombia). Founded on signature of a Treaty by representatives of Bolivia, Colombia, Ecuador, Peru and Venezuela, member countries of the *Andean Community (#00817)*, as a principal organ of *Andean Subregional Integration Agreement (Cartagena Agreement, 1969)* (Article 6 of the Treaty), by *'Tratado de Creación del Tribunal de Justicia de la Comunidad Andina'*. The Court is currently the judicial organ of *Sistema Andino de Integración (SAI, #19292)*. Under *'Protocol Modifying the Charter the Court of Justice of the Andean Community'*, approved 28 May 1996, Trujillo (Peru), entered into force 25 Aug 1999, it took on new functions, including: hearing of actions with regard to an omission or failure to act; acting as arbitrator; jurisdiction in labour actions. Former names and other names: *Andean Tribunal of Justice* – former; *Cour de justice andine* – former; *Tribunal Andino de Justicia* – former; *Tribunal de Justicia del Acuerdo de Cartagena* – former. **Aims** Interpret Andean Community law to ensure that it is applied uniformly in the territories of member countries; settle *disputes* arising from implementation of the rules which form the *legal system* of the Cartagena Agreement. **Structure** Tribunal comprises 4 judges, one of each country, but representing the Community as a whole and not their countries of origin, and each assuming the Presidency in rotation. Permanent headquarters in Quito (Ecuador). **Languages** Spanish. **Finance** Sources: contributions of member/participating states. **Activities** the Court is empowered to establish community law, settle differences and interpret the rules of the legal system of the Cartagena Agreement in a uniform manner. It has territorial jurisdiction in the 4 countries, covering cases of voiding of decisions, non-compliance and interpretation. Matters may be brought before the Court by any member country, by the Commission of the Andean Community, by the Andean Presidential Council or, in some cases, by any natural or legal person in the Andean subregion. **Events** *Seminar* Quito (Ecuador) 1987. **Publications** *Apuntes de Derecho Comunitario Andino* (2019) – A propósito de los 50 años de la Comunidad Andina y los 40 años de creación de su Tribunal de Justicia; *Testimonio Comunitario* (2004).
Members Judges () appointed by common accord of governments of the 4 member countries of the Andean Community:
Bolivia, Colombia, Ecuador, Peru.
IGO Relations Observer to: *Sistema Económico Latinoamericano (SELA, #19294)*. Agreement with: *Andean Parliament (#00820)*. Cooperates with: *UNCTAD (#20285)*. [2020.08.27/XF8363/**F***]

♦ Court of Justice of the Common Market for Eastern and Southern Africa (COMESA Court of Justice) 04937

Cour de justice du Marché commun de l'Afrique de l'est et de l'Afrique australe – Corte de justicia del Mercado Común para Africa Orientale e Austral
Registrar AL Tijani Almahi Street, 12222, Khartoum, Sudan. E-mail: info@comesacourt.org.
URL: https://comesacourt.org/

History 29 Jun 1998. Established with the appointment of 7 Judges by 3rd Summit of the Authority of Heads of State and Government, under Article 19 of the Treaty establishing *Common Market for Eastern and Southern Africa (COMESA, #04296)*. First proposed, 5 Nov 1993, Kampala (Uganda), by Heads of State and Government and plenipotentiaries of *Preferential Trade Area for Eastern and Southern African States (PTA, inactive)*, to replace *PTA Tribunal (inactive)* and *PTA Administrative Appeals Board*. Registry of the Court is temporarily located at COMESA Headquarters, Lusaka (Zambia). **Aims** Ensure adherence to *law* in the interpretation and application of the Treaty and adjudicate any disputes that may arise among member states regarding the interpretation and application of its provisions. **Structure** Two-tier judicial system: First Instance Division of 7 Judges, including Principal Judge; Appellate Division of 5 Judges, including President of the Court. **Finance** Sources: members' dues. **Activities** Politics/policy/regulatory. **Members** All COMESA member states.
[2020/XF3766/**F***]

♦ Court of Justice of the ECSC / see Court of Justice of the European Union (#04938)
♦ Court of Justice of the European Communities / see Court of Justice of the European Union (#04938)

♦ Court of Justice of the European Union (CJEU) 04938

Cour de justice de l'Union européenne – Tribunal de Justicia de la Unión Europea – Gerichtshofs der Europäischen Union – Tribunal de Justica da União Europeia – Corte di Giustizia dell'Unione Europea – Hof van Justitie van de Europese Unie – Europeiska Unionens Domstol – Europaeiske Unions Domstol – Euroopan Unionin Tuomioistuimen – Soudniho dvora Evropské Unie – Súdneho dvora Európskej Unie – as Európai Unió Bírósaganak – Trybunau Sprawiedliwos'ci Unii Europejskiej – Sodisse Evropske Unije – Euroopa Liidu Kohus – Eiropas Savieni-bas Tiesas – Europos Sajungos Teisingumo Teismas – Curtea de Justitie a Uniunii Europene
Registrar Bd Konrad Adenauer, L-2925 Luxembourg, Luxembourg. T. +35243032600. Fax +352433766. E-mail: ecj.registry@curia.europa.eu.
URL: http://www.curia.europa.eu/

History Set up 1952, Luxembourg, as *Court of Justice of the ECSC – Cour de justice de la CECA*, by *Treaty Establishing the European Coal and Steel Community (Treaty of Paris, 1951)* Article 4 (1) of the Convention, establishing *European Coal and Steel Community (ECSC, inactive)*, Article 4 (1) of the Convention. By virtue of Articles 4 (1) and 3 (1) respectively of the two Treaties of Rome (Italy) – *Treaty Establishing the European Economic Community (Treaty of Rome)* – and *Treaty Establishing the European Atomic Energy Community (Treaty of Rome, 1957)*, transformed into *Court of Justice of the European Communities (CJEC) – Cour de justice des Communautés européennes – Tribunal de Justicia de las Comunidades Europeas – Gerichtshof der Europäischen Gemeinschaften – Tribunal de Justiça das Comunidades Europeias – Corte di Giustizia delle Comunità Europee – Hof van Justitie van de Europese Gemeenschappen – Europaeiska Gemenskapernas Domstol – Europaeiske Faellesskabers Domstol – Euroopan Yhteisöjen Tuomioistuin – Dikastirio ton Evropaikon Kinotiton – Soudni dvur Evropskych Spolecenstvi – Súdney dvor Európskych Spolocenstiev – Európai Közösségek Birósaga – Trybunal Sprawiedliwosci Wspólnot Europejskich – Sodisse Europskih Skupnosti – Euroopa Ühenduste Kohus – Eiropas Kopienu Tiesa – Europos Bendriju Teisingumo Teismas – Il-Qorti tal-Gustizzja tal-Komunitajiet Ewropej – Cúirt Bhreithiúnais na gComhphobal Eorpach – Curtea de Justitie a Comunitatila Europene – Curtea de Justitie a Uniunii Europene*, 25 Mar 1957, when it became an institute of the *'European Economic Community (EEC)'*, and later called *European Community (inactive)*. Subsequent treaties amended its function: *Single European Act (SEA, 1986)*, signed Feb 1986, and into force 1 Jul 1987; *Treaty on European Union (Maastricht Treaty, 1992)*, signed 7 Feb 1992, and into force 1 Nov 1993; *Treaty of Amsterdam (1997)*, signed 2 Oct 1997, and into force 1999; *Nice Treaty (2001)*, signed 26 Feb 2001, Nice, and into force 1 Feb 2003; Current name adopted following the entry into force of the *Treaty of Lisbon (2007)*, 1 Dec 2009, when the *European Union (EU, #08967)* was recognized as a legal personality, acquired the competences previously conferred on the European Community, and Community law therefore became European Union law. The Court acquired its new function through Under the Treaty of Lisbon, which also altered the original Treaty of Rome to *Treaty on the Functioning of the European Union (TFEU, 1957)*, the court acquired its current function. **Aims** Ensure that the *law* is observed in the interpretation and application of relevant Treaties; review the legality of the acts of the institutions of the European Union; ensure that Member States comply with their obligations under Community law; interpret Community law at the request of the national courts and tribunals. **Structure** Consists of 2 courts: *'Court of Justice'*, comprising 28 Judges (one from each Member State), 11 Advocates General and 1 Registrar, including President and Vice-President. The Court may sit as a full court, in a Grand Chamber of 15 Judges, or in a chamber of 3 or 5 Judges. *'General Court'*, created in 1988, currently comprising 47 Judges (as part of a reform of the General Court which is taking place in 3 phases. By 2019 the General Court will have 2 judges per Member State) and 1 Registrar, including President. The Court meets in chambers of 3 or 5 Judges, and occasionally by a single Judge, and it may also sit as a Grand Chamber of 15 Judges. As of 1 Sep 2016 the jurisdiction of the separate *'Civil Service Tribunal'*, created in 2004, became part of the General Court. The Civil Service Tribunal no longer exists as a separate court within the CJEU. Registrar of the Court of Justice, under the authority of the President of the Court, is responsible for all departments, except Internal Audit, which is attached to the President: Directorate-General for Personnel and Finance; Directorate-General for Library, Research and Documentation; Directorate-General for Infrastructures; Directorate-General for Translation; Interpretation Directorate; Directorate for Protocol and Visits; Communication Directorate; Legal Advisor on Administrative Matters. **Languages** EU languages. **Staff** Staff negotiations through *Union syndicale du service public européen (#20486)* Luxembourg. **Finance** Annual budget (2016): euro 410,030,000. **Activities** As the judicial authority of the European Union and, in cooperation with the courts and tribunals of the Member States, the Court ensures the uniform application and interpretation of European Union law. Between 1952-2017, the Court delivered 35,382 judgements and orders: Court of Justice, about 20,967; General Court – about 12,866 (since 1989); Civil Service Tribunal – about 1,549 (between 2005 and 2016). **Events** *Seminar on the European court of justice for journalists* Luxembourg (Luxembourg) / Trier (Germany) 2010, *European seminar on the reform of the Brussels convention* Paris (France) 2002. **Publications** All publications go through *Publications Office of the European Union (Publications Office, #18562)*.
Members Judges (28) assisted by Advocates-General (11) and 1 Registrar for the Court of Justice and Judges (47) and 1 Registrar for the General Court, appointed by the governments of the 27 member states:
Austria, Belgium, Bulgaria, Croatia, Cyprus, Czechia, Denmark, Estonia, Finland, France, Germany, Greece, Hungary, Ireland, Italy, Latvia, Lithuania, Luxembourg, Malta, Netherlands, Poland, Portugal, Romania, Slovakia, Slovenia, Spain, Sweden.
IGO Relations EU institutions: *Council of the European Union (#04895)*; *European Central Bank (ECB, #06466)*; *European Commission (EC, #06633)*; *European Council (#06801)*; *European Court of Auditors (#06854)*; *European Parliament (EP, #08146)*. Member of: *Association of the Councils of State and Supreme Administrative Jurisdictions of the European Union (ACA-Europe, #02458)*. [2018.09.11/XF0668/**F***]

♦ Court of Master Sommeliers (internationally oriented national body)
♦ Court of Master Sommeliers Americas / see Court of Master Sommeliers
♦ Courtoisie internationale (#04200)
♦ Cousteau Society (internationally oriented national body)
♦ COV – Centrum Ontmoeting der Volkeren (internationally oriented national body)
♦ Covenant House (internationally oriented national body)
♦ Covenant House International / see Covenant House
♦ Covenant of Mayors / see Covenant of Mayors for Climate and Energy (#04939)

♦ Covenant of Mayors for Climate and Energy 04939

Head of Office Mundo Madou, Avenue des Arts 7-8, 1210 Brussels, Belgium. E-mail: info@eumayors.eu.
URL: http://www.eumayors.eu/

History 2008. Launched by *European Commission (EC, #06633)*, after adoption of the EU Climate and Energy Package. Former names and other names: *Covenant of Mayors* – alias; *EU Covenant of Mayors for Climate and Energy* – alias; *Covenant of Mayors for Climate and Energy – Europe* – alias. **Aims** Accelerate decarbonisation of territories, strengthening capacity to adapt to unavoidable climate change impacts and allowing citizens to access secure, sustainable and affordable energy. **Structure** Political Board; Office. *Joint Research Centre (JRC, #16147)* provides scientific and technical support. **Languages** English. **Staff** 14.00 FTE, paid. **Finance** Supported by: *European Commission (EC, #06633)*. **Activities** Awareness raising; capacity building; events/meetings. **Events** *Investment Forum* Brussels (Belgium) 2022, *Investment Forum* Brussels (Belgium) 2019, *Seminar on Decarbonising Cities with Geothermal District Heating : How to Finance It ?* Brussels (Belgium) 2019, *Investment Forum* Brussels (Belgium) 2018. **Publications** Core documents; technical materials; brochures; reports.
Members Local authorities in 20 countries:
Austria, Croatia, Cyprus, Estonia, Finland, France, Germany, Hungary, Ireland, Italy, Latvia, Lithuania, Malta, Norway, Poland, Portugal, Spain, Sweden, Switzerland, UK.
IGO Relations Accredited by (4): *European Commission (EC, #06633)*; *European Committee of the Regions (CoR, #06665)*; *European Investment Bank (EIB, #07599)*; *European Parliament (EP, #08146)*. **NGO Relations** Cooperates with (2): *Global Covenant of Mayors for Climate and Energy (GCoM, #10312)*; *World Alliance for Efficient Solutions*. [2021.05.26/XJ7598/**E**]

♦ Covenant of Mayors for Climate and Energy – Europe / see Covenant of Mayors for Climate and Energy (#04939)

♦ Covered Bond and Mortgage Council (CBMC) 04940

SG EMF-ECBC, Rue de la Science 14A, 1040 Brussels, Belgium. T. +3222854030. E-mail: info@hypo.org.
URL: http://www.hypo.org/

History 1967, Brussels (Belgium). Founded on the initiative of Belgian and Dutch associations. Current title adopted on merger with *European Covered Bond Council (ECBC, #06856)*, Jun 2014, which replaced EMF and ECBC as the legal name under which both entities operate, but in practice both brands are maintained and used for identification. Former names and other names: *Fédération hypothécaire auprès de la Communauté économique européenne* – former (1967); *European Mortgage Federation (EMF)* – former; *Fédération hypothécaire européenne* – former; *Europäischer Hypothekenverband* – former; *European Mortgage Federation – European Covered Bond Council (EMF-ECBC)* – alias. Registration: Banque-Carrefour des Entreprises, No/ID: 0411.583.173, Start date: 5 Nov 1971, Belgium. **Aims** Represent interests of mortgage lenders and covered bond issuers at European level; bring together covered bond issuers, analysts, investment bankers, rating agencies and a wide range of interested stakeholders. **Structure** EMF bodies: Executive Committee; 4 Committees: Economic Affairs; Legal Affairs; Statistics; Valuation. ECBC bodies: Plenary Meetings; Steering Committee; Working Groups; Task Forces; *Covered Bond Label Foundation* & *Energy Efficient Mortgage Label*; Secretariat. **Languages** English. **Staff** 10.00 FTE, paid. **Finance** Sources: members' dues. **Activities** Events/meetings; knowledge management/information dissemination; research/documentation. **Events** *Annual meeting* Brussels (Belgium) 2000, *Annual meeting* Brussels (Belgium) 1999, *Annual meeting* Brussels (Belgium) 1998, *Annual meeting* Brussels (Belgium) 1997, *Annual meeting* Brussels (Belgium) 1996. **Publications** *EMF Quarterly Review* (4 a year) in English; *ECBC Fact Book* (annual) in English; *EMF Hypostat* (annual) in English.
Members EMF: full (14) in 12 EU Member States, and several observer members. Membership countries not specified.
ECBC: full (123) across 30 active covered bond jurisdictions and several market segments.
NGO Relations Instrumental in setting up (1): *European Banking Industry Committee (EBIC, #06314)*.
[2021.06.22/XE2961/**D**]

♦ **COVESA** Connected Vehicle Systems Alliance (#04681)
♦ **COWAP** Coalition of Women in Africa for Peace and Development (#04070)
♦ Coworking Europe conference (meeting series)

Cox Centre
04940

alphabetic sequence excludes
For the complete listing, see Yearbook Online at

- ♦ Cox Centre – James M Cox Jr Center for International Mass Communication Training and Research (internationally oriented national body)
- ♦ CPA – Canadian Peace Alliance (internationally oriented national body)
- ♦ CPA – Caribbean Philosophical Association (internationally oriented national body)
- ♦ **CPA** Caribbean Poultry Association (#03542)
- ♦ CPA – Center for Preventive Action (internationally oriented national body)
- ♦ CPA – Christian Partners in Africa (internationally oriented national body)
- ♦ **CPA** Commonwealth Parliamentary Association (#04355)
- ♦ **CPA** Commonwealth Pharmacists Association (#04357)
- ♦ CPA – Commonwealth Police Association (unconfirmed)
- ♦ **CPA** Cour permanente d'arbitrage (#18321)
- ♦ **CPA** Cyclistes professionnels associés (#04989)
- ♦ CPA / see Industrial Fabrics Association International (#11174)
- ♦ CPAIOR – International Conference on the Integration of Constraint Programming, Artificial Intelligence, and Operations Research (meeting series)
- ♦ **CPAL** Conferencia de Provinciales Jesuitas de América Latina y El Caribe (#04658)
- ♦ **CPANE** Commission des pêches de l'Atlantique Nord-Est (#17581)
- ♦ CPANT / see Pan American Standards Commission (#18133)
- ♦ **CPAP** Comisión de Pesca para Asia-Pacifico (#01907)
- ♦ CPAPD – Chinese People's Association for Peace and Disarmament (internationally oriented national body)
- ♦ CPAR – Canadian Physicians for Aid and Relief (internationally oriented national body)
- ♦ CPAS – Center for Pacific and American Studies (internationally oriented national body)
- ♦ CPBA – Caribbean Publishing and Broadcasting Association (inactive)
- ♦ **CPB** Confederación Panamericana de Billar (#04469)
- ♦ **CPB** Confederación Panamericana de Bochas (#04470)
- ♦ CPC / see Center for Applied Conflict Management
- ♦ CPCAT / see African Regional Labour Administration Centre, Yaoundé (#00436)
- ♦ **CPCCAF** Conférence Permanente des Chambres Consulaires Africaines et Francophones (#04639)
- ♦ CPC – Caribbean Press Council (inactive)
- ♦ CPCC – Canadian Peacebuilding Coordinating Committee (internationally oriented national body)
- ♦ CPC – Christian Peace Conference (inactive)
- ♦ CPCCI / see Association des chambres de commerce et d'industrie européennes (#02423)
- ♦ **CPC** Circum-Pacific Council (#03939)
- ♦ CPCCN / see International Federation of Social Science Organizations (#13543)
- ♦ CPC – Conflict Prevention Centre, Vienna (see: #17887)
- ♦ CPCD / see Amsterdam Institute for Global Health and Development
- ♦ **CPCE** Community of Protestant Churches in Europe (#04405)
- ♦ CPCEMR / see Circum-Pacific Council (#03939)
- ♦ CPCFPU – Center for Peace, Conversion and Foreign Policy of Ukraine (internationally oriented national body)
- ♦ CPC-I / see PCI Media
- ♦ **CP** Citizens' Pact for South Eastern Europe (#03957)
- ♦ CPCIZ / see International Society of Zoological Sciences (#15552)
- ♦ CPC Learning Network (internationally oriented national body)
- ♦ CPCM – Comité permanent consultatif du Maghreb (inactive)
- ♦ **CPCO** Conseil des Patriarches catholiques d'Orient (#04875)
- ♦ CP – Congregatio Passionis Jesu Christi (religious order)
- ♦ CP – Contemplatives Passionistes (religious order)
- ♦ CPCR – Coopérateurs Paroissiaux du Christ Roi (religious order)
- ♦ CPCS – Center for Peace and Conflict Studies, Detroit (internationally oriented national body)
- ♦ **CPCS** Centre for Peace and Conflict Studies (#03774)
- ♦ **CPC** United Nations Committee for Programme and Coordination (#20546)
- ♦ **CPDC** Caribbean Policy Development Centre (#03540)
- ♦ **CPDE** CSO Partnership for Development Effectiveness (#04976)
- ♦ CPDH – Comité Protestant évangélique pour la Dignité Humaine (internationally oriented national body)
- ♦ **CPDP** Computers, Privacy and Data Protection (#04428)
- ♦ **CPD** United Nations Commission on Population and Development (#20533)
- ♦ CPeace – Center for Conservation Peacebuilding (internationally oriented national body)
- ♦ **CPEA** Climate Positive Europe Alliance (#04021)
- ♦ **CPEA** Conseil de partenariat euro-atlantique (#05646)
- ♦ CPEACT / see Initiative de mobilisation panafricaine de controle de tabac (#11211)
- ♦ **CPEAO** Conférence des Postes des Etats de l'Afrique de l'Ouest (#20893)
- ♦ CPE / see Business Africa (#03377)
- ♦ **CP-ECA** Cerebral Palsy – European Community Association (#03832)
- ♦ CPE – Capital Policing Europe (meeting series)
- ♦ **CPE** Confederación Panamericana de Esgrima (#04475)
- ♦ CPE / see European Coordination Via Campesina (#06795)
- ♦ CPEF – Congreso Panamericano de Educación Fisica (meeting series)
- ♦ CPESE – International Conference on Power and Energy Systems Engineering (meeting series)
- ♦ CPFC / see African University for Cooperative Development (#00494)
- ♦ CPFC – Comisión de Protección Fitosanitaria para el Caribe (inactive)
- ♦ **CPF** Cetinje Parliamentary Forum (#03839)
- ♦ **CPF** Cetinjski parlamentarni forum (#03839)
- ♦ **CPF** Collaborative Partnership on Forests (#04100)
- ♦ **CPF** Commonwealth Powerlifting Federation (#04358)
- ♦ **CPF** Conseil permanent de la Francophonie (#04697)
- ♦ CPFI / see Cummings Foundation
- ♦ CPFS / see Pan American Indoor Football Confederation (#18112)
- ♦ CPGIS – International Association of Chinese Professionals in Geographic Information Sciences (internationally oriented national body)
- ♦ **CPGPS** International Association of Chinese Professionals in Global Positioning Systems (#11769)
- ♦ CPGRFA / see Commission on Genetic Resources for Food and Agriculture (#04215)
- ♦ **CPHD Forum** Caribbean Plant Health Directors Forum (#03539)
- ♦ CPIA – Comité permanent international des architectes (inactive)
- ♦ CPI – Clear Path International (internationally oriented national body)
- ♦ **CPI** Climate Policy Initiative (#04020)
- ♦ CPI – Community Partners International (internationally oriented national body)
- ♦ **CPI** Conseil parlementaire interrégional (#04696)
- ♦ **CPI** Conseil phytosanitaire interafricain (#11386)
- ♦ **CPI** Cour pénale internationale (#13108)
- ♦ CPI – Culture of Peace Initiative (unconfirmed)
- ♦ CPI – Cyber Policy Institute (internationally oriented national body)
- ♦ CP-IDEA / see Regional Committee of the UN on Global Geospatial Information Management for the Americas (#18765)
- ♦ CPI / see European Industrial Gases Association (#07525)
- ♦ **CPII** Commonwealth Private Investment Initiative (#04359)
- ♦ CPIRS – Centre for Peace and International Relations Studies (internationally oriented national body)
- ♦ CPIS – Center for Political and International Studies, Moscow (internationally oriented national body)
- ♦ CPIS – Colombo Plan International Society (internationally oriented national body)
- ♦ **CPISRA** Cerebral Palsy International Sports and Recreation Association (#03833)
- ♦ CPISS – Comité Permanente Interamericano de Seguridad Social (see: #11419)
- ♦ CPIV / see Glass Alliance Europe (#10156)
- ♦ **CPJ** Committee to Protect Journalists (#04280)
- ♦ **CPJ** Confederación Panamericana de Judo (#04476)
- ♦ **CPLF** Conférence des peuples de langue française (#04640)
- ♦ CPLF – Congrès des psychanalystes de langue française (meeting series)
- ♦ CPLOL / see European Speech and Language Therapy Association (#08812)
- ♦ **CPLP** Comunidade dos Paises de Lingua Portuguesa (#04430)
- ♦ CPLRE / see Congress of Local and Regional Authorities of the Council of Europe (#04677)
- ♦ CPM – Annual Symposium on Combinatorial Pattern Matching (meeting series)
- ♦ CPM – Center for Peace Mediation (internationally oriented national body)
- ♦ **CPM** Confederación Panamericana de Minifutbol (#04477)
- ♦ **CPM** Corporación Pro-Cruzada Mundial (#20850)
- ♦ **CPME** Comité permanent des médecins européens (#19955)
- ♦ CPME / see PET EUROPE – Producers' Association (#18340)
- ♦ CPMR – Balkan and Black Sea Regional Commission / see Balkan and Black Sea Regional Commission (#03068)
- ♦ **CPMR** Conference of Peripheral Maritime Regions of Europe (#04638)
- ♦ **CPN** Caribbean Philanthropy Network (#03538)
- ♦ CPN – Catholic Peacebuilding Network (internationally oriented national body)
- ♦ CPNCP / see Notaries of Europe (#17609)
- ♦ **CPNLF** Congrès de psychiatrie et de neurologie de langue française (#04675)
- ♦ CPP / see Asian Center for the Progress of Peoples
- ♦ CPPC – Caribbean Plant Protection Commission (inactive)
- ♦ CPPC – Commission de la protection des plantes des Caraïbes (inactive)
- ♦ CPPC – Consejo Panamericano Pro-Ciegos (inactive)
- ♦ CPP – Concerned Philosophers for Peace (internationally oriented national body)
- ♦ CPPED – Conseil panafricain pour la protection de l'environnement et le développement (inactive)
- ♦ **CPPS** Comisión Permanente del Pacifico Sur (#04141)
- ♦ CPPS – Congregatio Missionariorum Pretiosissimi Sanguinis (religious order)
- ♦ CPPS – Sisters of the Most Precious Blood of O'Fallon, Missouri (religious order)
- ♦ CPPV – Confederación Panamericana de Pelota Vasca (unconfirmed)
- ♦ CP/RAC / see Regional Activity Centre for Sustainable Consumption and Production (#18747)
- ♦ CPR – Conselho Português para os Refugiados (internationally oriented national body)
- ♦ CPREA – Canadian Peace Research and Education Association (internationally oriented national body)
- ♦ CPRH / see Peace History Society
- ♦ CPR Institute for Dispute Resolution / see International Institute for Conflict Prevention and Resolution
- ♦ CPR Institute – International Institute for Conflict Prevention and Resolution (internationally oriented national body)
- ♦ CPRLatam / see Communication Policy Research Latin America (#04382)
- ♦ **CPRLATAM** Communication Policy Research Latin America (#04382)
- ♦ CPRL / see Project Counselling Service (#18532)
- ♦ CPRS / see Centre for Research on Peace and Development
- ♦ CPSA / see Anglican Church of Southern Africa (#00826)
- ♦ **CPSA** Caribbean Public Services Association (#03545)
- ♦ CPSA – Cosmetic Physicians Society of Australasia (internationally oriented national body)
- ♦ CPSC / see Colombo Plan Staff College (#04121)
- ♦ **CPSC** Colombo Plan Staff College (#04121)
- ♦ CPS – Centre for Peace Studies, Tromsí (internationally oriented national body)
- ♦ CPS – Civil Peace Service (internationally oriented national body)
- ♦ **CPS** Collegium Palynologicum Scandinavicum (#04118)
- ♦ **CPS** Colombo Plan for Cooperative Economic and Social Development in Asia and the Pacific (#04120)
- ♦ **CPS** Communauté du Pacifique (#17942)
- ♦ CPS – Comunità Promozione e Sviluppo (internationally oriented national body)
- ♦ CPSDSAP – Centre de protection sociale et de développement social pour l'Asie et le Pacifique (inactive)
- ♦ CPSEES / see Center for Russian, East European and Eurasian Studies, Austin TX
- ♦ **CPSOOI** Commission des pêches pour le sud-ouest de l'océan indien (#19894)
- ♦ CPSS / see Al Ahram Centre for Political and Strategic Studies
- ♦ CPSU – Commonwealth Policy Studies Unit (internationally oriented national body)
- ♦ CPT – Christian Peacemaker Teams (internationally oriented national body)
- ♦ **CPT** Comité européen pour la prévention de la torture et des peines ou traitements inhumains ou dégradants (#04164)
- ♦ **CPTI** Conscience and Peace Tax International (#04683)
- ♦ **CPTM** Commonwealth Partnership for Technology Management (#04356)
- ♦ CPTO – Council of Pacific Teachers Organizations (inactive)
- ♦ CPTPP – Comprehensive and Progressive Agreement for Trans-Pacific Partnership (2018 treaty)
- ♦ **CPU** Caribbean Postal Union (#03541)
- ♦ CPU / see CPU Media Trust (#04941)

♦ CPU Media Trust 04941

Contact c/o University Centre, Granta Place, Mill Lane, Cambridge, CB2 1RU, UK. E-mail: office@cpu.org.uk.
URL: http://www.cpu.org.uk/

History Founded 29 Dec 1909, London (UK), as *Empire Press Union. Commonwealth Press Union (CPU) – Union de la presse du Commonwealth* adopted 1950. Previously also referred to as *Association of Commonwealth Newspapers, News Agencies and Periodicals.* Terminated 31 Dec 2008, and restarted under current provisional title, Jan 2009. Registered in accordance with UK Companies (Consolidated) Act 1908. **Aims** Defend the freedom of the Commonwealth media. **Structure** General Meeting (annual); Council; Executive Committee; Standing Committees; Secretariat; Chairman; 7 Trustees. **Languages** English. **Staff** Part-time, paid. **Finance** Sources: members' dues. Other sources: Donations to Training Fund. **Activities** Events/meetings. **Events** *Biennial Conference* Sydney, NSW (Australia) 2005, *Editors forum* Sydney, NSW (Australia) 2005, *Biennial Conference* Colombo (Sri Lanka) 2003, *Workshop for cartoonists* Dar es Salaam (Tanzania UR) 2002, *Biennial Conference* Bridgetown (Barbados) 2000.

Members Proprietors and publishers of newspapers, journalists, news agencies and periodicals. Corporate full (over 500) and individual associate (over 50) members in 35 Commonwealth countries. Members in a total of 47 countries and territories:

Austria, Bahamas, Bangladesh, Belize, Botswana, Cameroon, Canada, Cyprus, Eswatini, France, Gambia, Ghana, Guyana, Hong Kong, India, Kenya, Kiribati, Lesotho, Malawi, Malaysia, Malta, Mauritius, Mozambique, Namibia, Nauru, New Zealand, Nigeria, Pakistan, Papua New Guinea, Samoa, Seychelles, Sierra Leone, Singapore, South Africa, Sri Lanka, St Kitts-Nevis, St Lucia, Tanzania UR, Tonga, Trinidad-Tobago, Tuvalu, Uganda, UK, USA, Vanuatu, Zambia, Zimbabwe.

IGO Relations Invited to sessions of Intergovernmental Council of: *International Programme for the Development of Communication (IPDC, #14651).* **NGO Relations** Instrumental in setting up: *International Press Telecommunications Council (IPTC, #14637).* [2020/XC0373/**C**]

- ♦ CPUSTAL – Congreso Permanente de Unidad Sindical de los Trabajadores de América Latina (inactive)
- ♦ **CPVO** Community Plant Variety Office (#04404)
- ♦ **CPWA** Church of the Province of West Africa (#03920)
- ♦ **CPWI** Church in the Province of the West Indies (#03921)
- ♦ CPWR / see Parliament of the World's Religions (#18222)
- ♦ CQRI / see École supérieure d'études internationales
- ♦ CRA – Caribbean Rice Association (no recent information)
- ♦ CRACFT – Centre régional africain de conception et de fabrication techniques (no recent information)
- ♦ **CRA** Christian Research Association (#03907)
- ♦ CRAC / see Institut Régional d'Enseignement Supérieur et de Recherche en Développement Culturel (#11355)

♦ Cracking the Language Barrier 04942

Contact address not obtained. E-mail: contact@cracking-the-language-barrier.eu.
URL: http://www.cracking-the-language-barrier.eu/
Aims Overcome any kind of language or communication barrier with the help of sophisticated language *technologies*.
Members Projects and projects, including 10 organizations listed in this Yearbook:
Common Language Resources and Technology Infrastructure (CLARIN, #04295); European Civil Society Platform for Multilingualism (ECSPM, #06569); European Federation of National Institutions for Language (EFNIL, #07172); European Language Equality Network (ELEN, #07647); European Language Resources Association (ELRA, #07650); Language Technology Industry Association (LT-Innovate, #16231); Multilingual Europe Technology Alliance (META, #16892) (Net); *Translation Automation User Society (TAUS, #20214); World Wide Web Consortium (W3C, #21935).* [2018/XM7347/y/**F**]

- ♦ CRA – Commonwealth Rowing Association (internationally oriented national body)
- ♦ **CRADAT** Centre régional africain d'administration du travail, Yaoundé (#00436)

♦ Cradle to Cradle Products Innovation Institute 04943

CEO 475 14th Street Suite 290, Oakland CA 94612, USA. E-mail: info@c2ccertified.org.
Contact Piet Heinkade 55, 1019 GM Amsterdam, Netherlands.
URL: https://www.c2ccertified.org/
History 2010. **Aims** Lead, inspire and empower all stakeholders in a global ecosystem in the making of positive products and materials through the Cradle to Cradle® methodology. **Structure** Board of Directors. Certification Standards Board; Stakeholder Advisory Council; Technical Advisory Groups; User & Working Groups. **Activities** Events/meetings; standards/guidelines. **Events** *Cradle to Cradle Design & Innovation Forum* Stockholm (Sweden) 2019. [2020/AA0759/**E**]

- ♦ CRAES – Centre régional africain pour l'énergie solaire (no recent information)
- ♦ CRAF – ESF Committee on Radio Astronomy Frequencies (see: #08441)
- ♦ Crafts Center (internationally oriented national body)
- ♦ Craftsmen of the World Federation (internationally oriented national body)
- ♦ CRAM / see Centre for Asian Studies
- ♦ CRAMRA – Convention on the Regulation of Antarctic Mineral Resource Activities (1988 treaty)

♦ Crans Montana Forum 04944

Forum de Crans Montana
Contact Le Patio Palace, 41 avenue Hector Otto, 98000 Monte Carlo, Monaco. T. +37797707000. Fax +37797707040. E-mail: info@montana30.org.
URL: http://www.cmf.ch/
History Set up 1986 as a joint venture of *Fondation du forum universale* and the Government of Malta. First Forum 1990. **Aims** Committed to a more humane and impartial world: promote international *cooperation*; contribute to global growth; ensure high levels of *stability*, equity and *security*; provide the opportunity for *business* and *government* officials to implement strategies, strengthen relations with current partners and meet potential new ones, and build new cooperation opportunities. **Activities** Events/meetings; awards/prizes/competitions. **Events** *Annual Session* Brussels (Belgium) 2018, *Annual Session* Barcelona (Spain) 2017, *Forum on Central to Far-Eastern Europe* Vienna (Austria) 2016, *Forum on Africa and South-South Cooperation* Brussels (Belgium) 2013, *Annual Session* Brussels (Belgium) 2009. **Consultative Status** Consultative status granted from: *Council of Europe (CE, #04881)* (Participatory Status). **IGO Relations** Close cooperation with: *United Nations (UN, #20515); UNESCO (#20322); UNIDO (#20336); Council of Europe (CE, #04881); European Union (EU, #08967); Islamic World Educational, Scientific and Cultural Organization (ICESCO, #16058); NATO (#16945); OPEC Fund for International Development (OFID, #17745).* **NGO Relations** Supports: *Academy of Peace.* [2016/XG5553/c/**F**]

- ♦ **CRASA** Communications Regulators' Association of Southern Africa (#04384)
- ♦ CRAS – Joint Workshop on New Technologies for Computer/Robot Assisted Surgery (meeting series)
- ♦ CRASTE-LF – Centre régional africain des sciences et technologies de l'espace en langue française / Affilié à l'Organisation des nations unies/ (see: #04277)
- ♦ **CRAT** Centre régional africain de technologie (#00432)
- ♦ **CRATerre-ENSAG** Centre international de la construction en terre (#12485)
- ♦ CRATerre-ENSAG / see International Centre for Earth Construction (#12485)
- ♦ Crawford Fund for International Agricultural Research (internationally oriented national body)
- ♦ Crawford School of Economics and Government (internationally oriented national body)

♦ Cray User Group (CUG) 04945

Contact Oak Ridge National Laboratory, 1 Bethel Valley Rd, PO Box 2008, Oak Ridge TN 37831-6008, USA. E-mail: office@cug.org.
URL: http://www.cug.org/
History 1978. **Aims** Provide the high performance computing community with leadership and information exchange to enable the development and effective use of Cray and SGI *computational* tools. **Structure** General Meeting. Board of Directors, including President, Vice-President, Secretary and Treasurer. Standing Committees (2): Finance; Membership. **Activities** Organizes annual conference, summits and workshops. **Events** *Annual technical conference* Auckland (New Zealand) 2020, *Annual technical conference* Montréal, QC (Canada) 2019, *Annual technical conference* Stockholm (Sweden) 2018, *Annual technical conference* Edinburgh (UK) 2010, *Annual technical conference / Annual Conference* Atlanta, GA (USA) 2009. [2020/XF6688/**E**]

- ♦ CRBP / see Centre Africain de Recherches sur Bananiers et Plantains (#03725)
- ♦ CRCA – Commission régionale de contrôle des assurances dans les Etats africains (see: #11385)
- ♦ **CRC Asia** Child Rights Coalition Asia (#03883)
- ♦ **CRC** Commission for Controlling the Desert Locust in the Central Region (#04208)
- ♦ CRC – Conflict Research Consortium (internationally oriented national body)
- ♦ CRCEES – Centre for Russian, Central and East European Studies (internationally oriented national body)
- ♦ **CRCICA** Cairo Regional Centre for International Commercial Arbitration (#03398)
- ♦ CR – Conciliation Resources (internationally oriented national body)
- ♦ CR – Congregation of Regular Clerics (religious order)
- ♦ CR – Congregatio a Resurrectione Domini Nostri Jesu Christi (religious order)
- ♦ CRC-OP-AC – Optional Protocol to the Convention on the Rights of the Child on the Involvement of Children in Armed Conflict (2000 treaty)
- ♦ CRC-OP-SC – Optional Protocol to the Convention on the Rights of the Child on the Sale of Children, Child Prostitution and Child Pornography (2000 treaty)
- ♦ **CR** Creation Research (#04946)
- ♦ CRC – United Nations Convention on the Rights of the Child (1989 treaty)
- ♦ CRDA / see Consortium of Christian Relief and Development Association
- ♦ CRD / see Centre for Research and Documentation on World Language Problems (#03780)
- ♦ CRD – Coopération régionale de développement (inactive)
- ♦ CRDF / see CRDF Global
- ♦ CRDF Global (internationally oriented national body)
- ♦ **CRDI** Centre de recherches pour le développement international (#13162)
- ♦ CRDT / see Centre for International Development and Training
- ♦ CRDTL – CARPHA Drug Testing Laboratory (inactive)
- ♦ CRDTO / see Centre for Linguistic and Historical Studies by Oral Tradition (#03771)
- ♦ CREAA – Conseil régional pour l'éducation et l'alphabétisation des adultes en Afrique (no recent information)
- ♦ **CREA** Consortium pour la recherche économique en Afrique (#00292)
- ♦ CREAD – Centre de recherche en économie appliquée pour le développement (internationally oriented national body)
- ♦ **CREAD** Consorcio-Red de Educación a Distancia (#11428)
- ♦ **CREAN** Children's Rights European Academic Network (#03878)
- ♦ CRE / see Assembly of European Regions (#02316)
- ♦ CRE – Association des universités européennes (inactive)
- ♦ CREATE-NET – Center for Research and Telecommunication Experimentation for Networked Communities (internationally oriented national body)
- ♦ Creating Hope International (internationally oriented national body)
- ♦ Creating Knowledge (meeting series)

♦ Creation Research (CR) 04946

International Dir PO Box 260, Capalaba, Redland City QLD 4157, Australia. T. +61732064467. E-mail: info@creationresearch.net.
URL: http://www.creationresearch.net/
Aims Outreach to those who have been indoctrinated into the theory of *evolution* so as to reject the *Bible* as false, creation as myth and Christ as irrelevant; challenge evolutionists by presenting scientific and historical evidence for Christ, for creation and for the *accuracy* of the Biblical record. **Activities** Organizes seminars and field trips. **Publications** Books; DVDs.
Members Offices in 4 countries (" indicates HQ):
Australia (*), Canada, New Zealand, UK, USA. [2017/XF6887/**F**]

- ♦ Creative Associates International (internationally oriented national body)
- ♦ Creative Commons International (internationally oriented national body)
- ♦ Creative – Creative Associates International (internationally oriented national body)
- ♦ Creative Initiative Foundation / see Foundation for Global Community – Global Initiatives Team for the CSCE
- ♦ Creative Learning (internationally oriented national body)

♦ Creative Media Business Alliance (CMBA) 04947

No fixed address address not obtained. E-mail: secretariat@cmba-alliance.eu.
URL: http://cmba-alliance.eu/
History Founded Nov 2004. **Aims** Give the creative media sector a strong and united voice at the European Union level; call upon the European Commission, European Parliament and EU member states to focus on creative and media businesses in their joint efforts to foster innovation, growth and employment in information society. **Structure** Informal structure. Secretariat voluntarily hosted by members on a 6-month rotating basis. **Languages** English. **Publications** *Create, Engage, Inspire.* Position Papers.
Members Media and creative businesses and industry associations, including the following 9 organizations listed in this Yearbook:
Association of Commercial Television in Europe (ACT, #02436); European Association of Communications Agencies (EACA, #05983); European Magazine Media Association (EMMA, #07723); European Newspaper Publishers' Association (ENPA, #08048); European Publishers Council (EPC, #08304); Federation of European Publishers (FEP, #09536); International Federation of the Phonographic Industry (IFPI, #13508); International Video Federation (IVF, #15852); Motion Picture Association (MPA). [2014.06.01/XJ0389/y/**F**]

♦ Creators Union of Arab (CUA) 04948

Contact Seventh area – square no 58, villa no 12, Obour City, Cairo, 12411, Egypt. T. +201001948386 – +201011709020 – +971547748386. Fax +971557726305. E-mail: info@arabcreators.org – almobdien22@yahoo.com.
URL: http://www.arabcreators.org/
History 2001. **Aims** Upgrade all fields of culture, education, creativity, and media and sports. **Structure** Board. **Languages** Arabic, English. **Finance** Sources: fees for services; members' dues; revenue from activities/projects. **Activities** Awareness raising; knowledge management/information dissemination; training/education. Establishing a database for audiovisual teaching materials. **Publications** *Creators Magazine* (2 a year).
Members Full (900) in 9 countries:
Egypt, Kuwait, Lebanon, Libya, Palestine, Saudi Arabia, Sudan, United Arab Emirates, Yemen.
Consultative Status Consultative status granted from: *ECOSOC (#05331)* (Special). **NGO Relations** *Arab Media Union*; Federation of Arab Women Leaders. [2023.02.14/XM7169/**D**]

- ♦ CRE – Cercle des Réseaux Européens (unconfirmed)
- ♦ CRE – Copernicus Programme / see COPERNICUS Alliance – European Network on Higher Education for Sustainable Development (#04830)
- ♦ CRECTEALC – Centro Regional de Enseñanza en Ciencia y Tecnologia Espacial para América Latina y el Caribe (see: #04277)
- ♦ CRE – Current Research in Egyptology (meeting series)
- ♦ **CREDAF** Centre de rencontres et d'études des dirigeants des administrations fiscales (#03779)
- ♦ CREDAL – Centre de recherche et de documentation sur l'Amérique Latine (internationally oriented national body)
- ♦ **CRED** Centre for Research on the Epidemiology of Disasters (#03781)
- ♦ CREDIL – Comité régional d'éducation pour le développement international de Lanaudière (internationally oriented national body)
- ♦ CREDIT – Centre for Research in Economic Development and International Trade (internationally oriented national body)
- ♦ Credit Union Foundation Australia (internationally oriented national body)
- ♦ CREDU / see Institut français de recherche en Afrique
- ♦ CREECA – Center for Russia, East Europe and Central Asia, Madison WI (internationally oriented national body)
- ♦ **CREE** Centre for Registration of European Ergonomists (#03776)
- ♦ CREEES – Center for Russian, East European and Eurasian Studies, Austin TX (internationally oriented national body)
- ♦ CREES / see Centre for European, Russian, and Eurasian Studies, Toronto
- ♦ CREES – Centre for Russian and East European Studies, Birmingham (internationally oriented national body)
- ♦ **CREFAL** Centro de Cooperación Regional para la Educación de Adultos en América Latina y el Caribe (#03794)
- ♦ CREFAP – Centre régional francophone pour l'Asie-Pacifique (internationally oriented national body)
- ♦ CREF – Cerebrovascular Research and Education Foundation (unconfirmed)
- ♦ CREFC Europe (internationally oriented national body)
- ♦ **CREFECO** Centre régional francophone pour l'Europe centrale et orientale, Sofia (#03775)
- ♦ **CREFIAF** Conseil Régional de Formation des Institutions Supérieures de Contrôle des Finances Publiques de l'Afrique Francophone Subsaharienne (#04699)
- ♦ CRE-FMSM / see Mental Health Europe (#16715)
- ♦ CREFOB – Association européenne des centres de rééducation fonctionnelle et de formation professionnelle d'orthopédie de précision et de haute botterie pour jeunes handicapés physiques (inactive)
- ♦ CREI – Centre de Recerca en Economia Internacional, Barcelona (internationally oriented national body)
- ♦ **CREID** Coalition for Religious Equality and Inclusive Development (#04067)
- ♦ **CREIPAC** Centre de rencontres et d'échanges internationaux du Pacifique (#03778)
- ♦ CREM – Centre for Economic Research on Mediterranean Countries (internationally oriented national body)
- ♦ **CREMO** Centre de recherche et d'études sur la Méditerranée orientale (#03782)
- ♦ CRENO – Conférence des régions de l'Europe du Nord-Ouest (inactive)
- ♦ CRENWE – Conference of Regions of North-West Europe (inactive)
- ♦ CREOi – Conservation, Research and Education Opportunities International (internationally oriented national body)
- ♦ CREON / see CREON Network (#04949)
- ♦ **CREON** CREON Network (#04949)

♦ **CREON Network (CREON)** **04949**

Treas c/o Danish Building Research Inst, Aalborg Univ, A C Meyers Vaenge 15, 2450 Copenhagen, Denmark.
URL: https://creon-net.org/

History 15 Apr 2011. Current constitution adopted June 2013. Former names and other names: *CREON Network – Construction Researchers on Economics and Organisation in the Nordic region (CREON)* – full title. Registration: Central Business Register, No/ID: 33806094, Denmark. **Aims** Promote education, dissemination and research connected with management in and of construction by any means available. **Structure** General Assembly; Board; Secretariat. **Finance** Sources: members' dues. **Activities** Advocacy/lobbying/activism; events/meetings; research/documentation. **Events** *Nordic Conference on Construction Economics and Organisation* Copenhagen (Denmark) / Malmö (Sweden) 2022, *Nordic Conference on Construction Economics and Organisation* Copenhagen (Denmark) 2021, *Nordic Conference on Construction Economics and Organisation* Tallinn (Estonia) 2019, *Nordic Conference on Construction Economics and Organisation* Gothenburg (Sweden) 2017, *Nordic Conference on Construction Economics and Organisation* Tampere (Finland) 2015.
Members Individidual; Institutional. Members in 4 countries:
Denmark, Finland, Norway, Sweden. [2021/AA1402/**F**]

♦ CREON Network – Construction Researchers on Economics and Organisation in the Nordic region / see CREON Network (#04949)
♦ CREPA / see Water and Sanitation for Africa (#20836)
♦ **CREPMF** Conseil régional de l'épargne publique et des marchés financiers (#04698)
♦ CRE – RAND Center for Russia and Eurasia (internationally oriented national body)
♦ **CRESA** Centres régionaux d'enseignement spécialisé en agriculture (#03787)
♦ CRESALC / see UNESCO International Institute for Higher Education in Latin America and the Caribbean (#20309)
♦ CRESCENDO / see Crescendo Worldwide Network (#04950)

♦ **Crescendo Worldwide Network** **04950**

Réseau mondial Crescendo – Red Mundial Crescendo

SG c/o CCIG, 1 rue de Varembé, 1202 Geneva 20, Switzerland. E-mail: rcrescendo@bluewin.ch.
URL: https://www.reseaucrescendo.org/

History Founded 9 Jul 2001, Paris (France). Also referred to as *CRESCENDO*. Previously registered in accordance with Belgian law when statutes adopted 9 Oct 2005. Registered in accordance with Swiss Civil Code. **Aims** Serve as a network to facilitate sharing of information and common activities for members; promote at international and local levels a positive image of *ageing* through respect for the dignity and *rights* of *retired* and older persons, thus contributing to their development and individual missions. **Structure** General Assembly (every 2 years); Executive Committee. **Languages** English, French. **Staff** All voluntary. **Finance** Contributions of member organizations; gifts and subsidies from various institutions. **Activities** Networking/liaising; training/education; knowledge management/information dissemination. **Publications** *Bulletin* (3 a year) in English, French, Spanish.
Members International Catholic organizations (14):
Apostolat Militaire International (AMI); Association Internationale des Charités (AIC, #02675); Congregation of the Oblates of St Joseph (OSJ); Daughters of Wisdom (DW); FONDACIO (#09812); Forum international d'action catholique (FIAC, #09919); International Catholic Committee of Nurses and Medico-social Assistants (#12451); International Federation of Catholic Medical Associations (#13378); International Federation of Catholic Pharmacists (#13380); International Federation of Catholic Universities (IFCU, #13381); Little Sisters of the Poor (LSP); Mouvement international d'apostolat des milieux sociaux indépendants (MIAMSI, #16864); Vie montante internationale (VMI, #20769); World Catholic Association for Communication (SIGNIS, #21264).
NGO Relations Member of: *Forum of Catholic Inspired NGOs (#09905); International Catholic Centre of Geneva (ICCG, #12449).* [2019/XF6780/y/**F**]

♦ CRESOI – Centre de Recherche sur les sociétés de l'océan Indien (internationally oriented national body)
♦ **CRESPIAL** Centro Regional para la Salvaguardia del Patrimonio Cultural Inmaterial de América Latina (#03817)

♦ **CREST International** **04951**

CEO Seven Stars House, 1 Wheler Road, Coventry, CV3 4LB, UK. T. +442030583122. E-mail: admin@crest-approved.org.
URL: https://www.crest-approved.org/

History 2015. CREST (UK) set up 2006. CREST International set up to act as an umbrella organization for CREST's regional operations. Registration: Companies House, No/ID: 09805375, Start date: 2 Oct 2015, England and Wales. **Aims** Build capability, capacity, consistency and community in the global cyber security industry. **Structure** International Council; Regional Councils (5): Americas; Asia; Australasia; European Union; UK. **Activities** Certification/accreditation; events/meetings. **Events** *Asia Conference* Singapore (Singapore) 2021, *Asia Conference* Singapore (Singapore) 2019. **Publications** *Script Bulletin* (4 a year). [2022.10.12/AA0200/**C**]

♦ CRF – Christian Relief Fund (internationally oriented national body)
♦ CRF – Coral Restoration Foundation (internationally oriented national body)
♦ **CRF** Corporate Registers Forum (#04841)
♦ CRFEA – Christian Rural Fellowship of East Africa (inactive)
♦ **CRFM** Caribbean Regional Fisheries Mechanism (#03547)
♦ CRG – Centre for Research on Globalization (internationally oriented national body)
♦ CRHC / see East, Central and Southern African Health Community (#05216)
♦ CRHCS / see East, Central and Southern African Health Community (#05216)
♦ CRIA / see Carnegie Council for Ethics in International Affairs
♦ CRIAA – Centre de recherche – information – action pour le développement en Afrique (internationally oriented national body)
♦ **CRIABD** Centre international chrétien de recherche, d'information et d'analyse de la bande dessinée (#12557)
♦ CRIB / see EFRAT – International Organization for Saving Jewish Babies (#05389)
♦ CRIC – Centro Regionale d'Intervento per la Cooperazione (internationally oriented national body)
♦ CRI – Children's Resources International (internationally oriented national body)
♦ **CRI** Children's Rights International (#03879)

♦ **Cricket Council of the Americas (ICC Americas)** **04952**

Contact 1 Blue Jays Way, Ste 4000, Toronto ON M5V 1J3, Canada. T. +14164267312. Fax +14164267172. E-mail: feedback@iccamericas.ca – rpo@iccamericas.ca.
URL: http://www.icc-cricket.com/the-icc/icc_members/americas/index.php

History 12 Apr 2001, Antigua-Barbuda. Regional council of *International Cricket Council (ICC, #13105).* **Activities** Organizes seminars.
Members National organizations in 14 countries and territories:
Argentina, Bahamas, Belize, Bermuda, Brazil, Canada, Cayman Is, Chile, Costa Rica, Cuba, Panama, Paraguay, Turks-Caicos, USA.
Regional organization (1):
Cricket West Indies (CWI, #04953). [2017/XE4615/**E**]

♦ **Cricket West Indies (CWI)** **04953**

Mailing Address PO Box 616 W, Factory Road, St John's, St John, Antigua-Barbuda. T. +12684812450. Fax +12684812498. E-mail: cwi@cricketwestindies.org.
URL: http://cricketwestindies.org/

History under the name *West Indies Cricket Board of Control*, as a regional body of *International Cricket Council (ICC, #13105).* Subsequently known as *West Indies Cricket Board*. Present name adopted 2017. **Aims** Lead, inspire and unite cricket in the West Indies, from thriving grassroots to exciting WINDIES teams, ensuring sustainable success.
Members Cricket associations of 6 countries:
Barbados, Guyana, Jamaica, Leeward Is, Trinidad-Tobago, Windward Is.
NGO Relations Member of: *Cricket Council of the Americas (ICC Americas, #04952).* [2021/XD9080/**F**]

♦ CRID – Centre de recherche et d'information pour le développement, Paris (internationally oriented national body)
♦ **CRID** Centro Regional de Información sobre Desastres para América Latina y el Caribe (#18778)
♦ CRIDES – LES TROIS MONDES – Centre de recherche et d'information pour un développement solidaire (internationally oriented national body)
♦ CRIDEV – Centre rennais d'information pour le développement et la libération des peuples (internationally oriented national body)
♦ CRIDNET – Caribbean Rice Industry Development Network (no recent information)
♦ CRIE / see Centro de Estudios Ecuménicos, México
♦ CRIED – Centro Ricerche Istituto Europeo di Design (internationally oriented national body)
♦ **CRIES** Coordinadora Regional de Investigaciones Económicas y Sociales (#04812)
♦ CRIET (no recent information)
♦ **CRIHAP** International Training Center for Intangible Cultural Heritage in the Asia-Pacific Region under the auspices of UNESCO (#15716)
♦ CRI / see International Red Cross and Red Crescent Movement (#14707)

♦ **Crime Stoppers International (CSI)** **04954**

Pres Postbus 988, 3800 AZ Amersfoort, Netherlands. E-mail: csi@csiworld.org.
URL: https://csiworld.org/

History 1976. Registration: No/ID: KVK 67053459, Netherlands; EU Transparency Register, No/ID: 790405735996-24, Start date: 24 Sep 2019. **Aims** Mobilize the world to provide information on crime anonymously. **Structure** Board of Directors; Management Team **Languages** English. **Staff** 6.00 FTE, voluntary. **Finance** Sources: grants; in-kind support; international organizations; private foundations; sponsorship. **Activities** Awards/prizes/competitions; events/meetings; training/education. **Events** *Annual Conference* Singapore (Singapore) 2019, *Annual Conference* The Hague (Netherlands) 2018.
Members National organizations in 28 countries and territories:
Antigua-Barbuda, Argentina, Australia, Bahamas, Barbados, Belize, Bermuda, Canada, Cayman Is, Dominica, El Salvador, Guatemala, Honduras, Jamaica, Netherlands, New Zealand, Northern Mariana Is, Panama, Paraguay, South Africa, St Kitts-Nevis, St Lucia, Trinidad-Tobago, Turks-Caicos, UK, Ukraine, USA, Virgin Is UK.
IGO Relations Memorandum of Understanding with (1): *United Nations Office on Drugs and Crime (UNODC, #20596).* Cooperation Agreement with: *International Criminal Police Organization – INTERPOL (ICPO-INTERPOL, #13110).* **NGO Relations** Memorandum of Understanding with (8): *Airline Ambassadors International (AAI)*; Crystal Blockchain BV; Entreprise et Diplomatie; International Cyber Threat Task Force; *International Police Training Institute (IPTI)*; Organized Crime and Corruption Reporting Project; RisikoTek Pte; *World Free Zones Organization (World FZO, #21530).* Member of (1): Global Coalition to Fight Financial Crime. [2022.05.04/XN0076/**F**]

♦ **Crime Writers of Scandinavia (CWS)** **04955**

Skandinaviska Kriminalsällskapet (SKS) – Skandinavisk Kriminalselskap

Address not obtained.
Vice Pres Evagatan 26, SE-214 59 Malmö, Sweden.
URL: http://krimi.blogspot.com/

History 1991, Krogerup (Denmark), as a part of *International Association of Crime Writers (IACW, #11825).* **Aims** Spread knowledge about crime *fiction* in order to strengthen its position in *Nordic* countries and the position of Scandinavian writers abroad. **Finance** Members' dues. Sales of publications. Budget (annual): Danish Kr 100,000. **Activities** Annual international seminar; annual 'Glasnyckeln' award. **Events** *Annual seminar / Seminar* Uppsala (Sweden) 1998, *Annual seminar* Aalborg (Denmark) 1997, *Seminar* Aalborg (Denmark) 1997, *Annual seminar / Seminar* Bergen (Norway) 1996, *Crime fiction* Nesjavellir (Iceland) 1995. **Publications** *Gränsfallet* (irregular) in Danish, Norwegian, Swedish – newsletter. Guides; books. [2011/XF2558/**F**]

♦ Criminal Law Convention on Corruption (1999 treaty)
♦ Criminological Society of the German Speaking Countries (#16209)
♦ Criminologists without Borders (internationally oriented national body)

♦ **Crimmigration Control – International Net of Studies (CINETS)** **04956**

Contact address not obtained. T. +351962371675. E-mail: maria.joao.guia@ij.uc.pt – marie.provine@gmail.com – jstumpf@lclark.edu.
URL: http://www.crimmigrationcontrol.com/

History Created Sep 2011. **Aims** Bring together scholar who intend to develop comparative studies and issues on the central subject of "crimmigration" and parallel subjects; build knowledge on crimmigration and help decisors to have inforamtion on how to improve public policies over *migration* and related topics. **Languages** English. **Staff** 6.00 FTE, paid. **Activities** Research/documentation; events/meetings. **Events** *Conference* Portland, OR (USA) 2020, *Conference* London (UK) 2018, *Conference* College Park, MD (USA) 2016, *Conference* Leiden (Netherlands) 2014, *Conference* Coimbra (Portugal) 2012. **Publications** Books. **Members** Full (about 80) in about 15 countries. Membership countries not specified. [2020.03.12/XM7980/**F**]

♦ **CrimS** Criminological Society of the German Speaking Countries (#16209)
♦ CRIN / see Child Rights International Network (#03885)
♦ **CRIN** Child Rights International Network (#03885)
♦ CRIOLA – Rede Latino-Americana e Caribenha de Mulheres Negras (internationally oriented national body)
♦ **CRIRSCO** Committee for Mineral Reserves International Reporting Standards (#04272)
♦ CRISA – Centre for Research and Information on Substance (internationally oriented national body)

♦ **Crisis Action** **04957**

Main Office Audrey House, 16-20 Ely Place, London, EC1N 6SN, UK. T. +442072699450.
EU Office Rue de Trèves 45, 1040 Brussels, Belgium. E-mail: brussels1@crisisaction.org.
USA Office 405 Lexington Ave, Floors 1 & 7-9, New York NY 10174, USA.
URL: http://crisisaction.org/

History 2003, UK. Founded on the initiative of Guy Hughes (1974-2006). Registration: Companies House, No/ID: 04932380, England and Wales; 501(c)3, USA. **Aims** Work with individuals and organizations from global civil society to protect civilians from armed conflict. **Structure** Offices in: Addis Ababa (Ethiopia); Beirut (Lebanon); Brussels (Belgium); Johannesburg (South Africa); London (UK); Nairobi (Kenya); New York NY (USA); Paris (France); Washington DC (USA). **Languages** English. **Staff** 34.00 FTE, paid. **Finance** Sources: voluntary contributions; support from foundations, governments and private individuals. **Activities** Conflict resolution. **Publications** Annual Report.
Members include the following 21 organizations listed in this Yearbook:
- *Anti-Slavery International (#00860);*
- *Chatham House Foundation (CHF);*
- *Council for the Advancement of Arab-British Understanding (CAABU);*
- *CSW;*
- *Foreign Policy Centre, London (FPC);*
- *Friends of the Earth International (FoEI, #10002);*
- *Greenpeace International (#10727);*
- *Humanitarian Crisis Hub;*
- *International Action Network on Small Arms (IANSA, #11585);*
- *New Israel Fund (NIF);*
- *Peace Direct;*
- *People and Planet;*
- *Quaker Peace and Social Witness (QPSW, see: #10004);*
- *Refugee Council (#18739);*
- *René Cassin;*
- *Royal Institute of International Affairs (RIIA);*
- *The Mothers' Union (#16860);*
- *The United Methodist Church (UMC, #20514);*
- *Verification Research, Training and Information Centre (VERTIC);*
- *Vishva Hindu Parishad (VHP);*
- *War on Want.*

IGO Relations Partners: *European Union Institute for Security Studies (EUISS, #08994).*

NGO Relations Member of: *NGO Working Group on the Security Council (#17128).* Partners:
- *ACORD – Agency for Cooperation and Research in Development (#00073)*;
- *Action Against Hunger (#00086)*;
- *AEGIS Trust*;
- *Africa Peace Forum (APFO)*;
- African Centre for Justice and Peace Studies;
- *Amnesty International (AI, #00801)* (UK);
- *Arab Programme for Human Rights Activists (APHRA)*;
- *Arabic Network for Human Rights Information (ANHRI, #00979)*;
- *Bonn International Center for Conversion (BICC, #03300)*;
- *Cairo Institute for Human Rights Studies (CIHRS, #03397)*;
- *CARE International (CI, #03429)*;
- *Catholic Agency for Overseas Development (CAFOD)*;
- *Catholic Organization for Relief and Development (Cordaid)*;
- Center for Civilians in Conflict;
- *Christian Aid*;
- *Concordis International*;
- *Diakonia*;
- *The Elders Foundation (#05413)*;
- *Finn Church Aid (FCA)*;
- *Global Centre for the Responsibility to Protect (GCR2P, #10277)*;
- *Human Rights Watch (HRW, #10990)*;
- *Humanitarian Aid Relief Trust (HART)*;
- *ICCO – Interchurch Organization for Development Cooperation*;
- *International Alert (#11615)*;
- *International Center for Policy and Conflict (ICPC)*;
- *International Crisis Group (Crisis Group, #13111)*;
- *International Federation for Human Rights (#13452)*;
- *International Refugee Rights Initiative (IRRI, #14708)*;
- *International Rescue Committee (IRC, #14717)*;
- *Islamic Relief Worldwide (IRWW, #16048)*;
- *Media in Cooperation and Transition (MiCT)*;
- *Medica Mondiale*;
- *Medico International*;
- Mensen met een missie;
- *Mercy Corps International (MCI)*;
- *Netherlands Refugee Foundation*;
- *Nobel Women's Initiative (#17144)*;
- *Norwegian Refugee Council (NRC)*;
- Nuba Relief, Rehabilitation and Development Organization (NRRDO);
- *Oxfam International (#17922)*;
- *PAX*;
- *Permanent Peace Movement (PPM)*;
- *Refugees International (RI)*;
- *Saferworld*;
- *Save the Children International (#19058)*;
- *Tearfund, UK*;
- *Trocaire – Catholic Agency for World Development*;
- *War Child International (#20817)*;
- *World Vision International (WVI, #21904).* [2021/XJ0689/y/**F**]

♦ **Crisis Group** International Crisis Group (#13111)
♦ Crisis Management Initiative (internationally oriented national body)
♦ CRISTAL (inactive)
♦ Cristo Re (religious order)

♦ Critical Ecosystem Partnership Fund (CEPF) 04958

Exec Dir c/o Conservation Intl, 2011 Crystal Dr, Suite 600, Arlington VA 22202, USA. T. +17033412400. E-mail: cepf@cepf.net.
URL: http://www.cepf.net/

History 2000. A joint initiative of l'Agence Française de Développement (AFD), *Conservation International (CI)*, European Union, *Global Environment Facility (GEF, #10346)*, Government of Japan, *MacArthur Foundation* and *International Bank for Reconstruction and Development (IBRD, #12317)* (World Bank). **Aims** Protect biodiversity, build local conservation leadership and nurture sustainable development. **Languages** English, French, Japanese, Portuguese, Spanish. **Staff** 21.00 FTE, paid. **Finance** Has committed US$ 259,000,000 in grants to over 2,552 organizations and individuals for projects in 905 countries and territories. **Activities** Awareness raising; capacity building; financial and/or material support; monitoring/evaluation; networking/liaising; projects/programmes; training/education. **Publications** *CEPF Newsletter*. Annual Report; annual impact report; ecosystem profiles. **NGO Relations** Member of (2): *International Partnership for the Satoyama Initiative (IPSI, #14525)*; Key Biodiversity Areas Partnership. Partner of (1): *Re:wild.* [2021.11.23/XM2987/f/**E**]

♦ Critical Path Institute / see International Neonatal Consortium (#14223)

♦ Critical Raw Materials Alliance (CRM Alliance) 04959

SG c/o Ridens Public Affairs, Rue Belliard 205, 1040 Brussels, Belgium. T. +327863104. E-mail: info@crmalliance.eu.
URL: https://www.crmalliance.eu/

Aims Advocate the importance of CRMs for the European economy; promote a strong European CRM policy. **Structure** Board; Secretariat. **Publications** *CRM Alliance Newsletter* (4 a year).
Members Full; Associate. Full include 6 organizations listed in this Yearbook:
Barytes Association, The (#03180); *Beryllium Science and Technology Association (BeST, #03214)*; *International Antimony Association (i2a, #11657)*; *International Magnesium Association (IMA, #14073)*; *International Precious Metals Institute (IPMI)*; *Tantalum-Niobium International Study Center (T.I.C., #20095).*
Associate include 2 members listed in this Yearbook:
Bureau international pour la standardisation de la rayonne et des fibres synthétiques (BISFA, #03369); *MedTech Europe (#16692).*
NGO Relations Member of: *Minor Metals Trade Association (MMTA, #16821).* [2023/XM6905/y/**D**]

♦ Critical Research on Men in Europe (CROME) 04960

Contact address not obtained. T. +441915153238. Fax +441915152229.
URL: http://www.cromenet.org/

History Also referred to as *European Research Network on Men in Europe.* **Aims** Develop empirical, theoretical and policy outcomes on the *gender* of men and *masculinity.* **Finance** Supported by: *European Commission (EC, #06633).* **Activities** Main project: 'The Social Problem of Men'. Includes European documentation centre and data base on men and men's practices. **Events** *EU conference on research, policy and practice* Helsinki (Finland) 2003.
Members Individuals in 10 countries:
Estonia, Finland, Germany, Ireland, Italy, Latvia, Norway, Poland, Russia, UK. [2008/XJ3331/**F**]

♦ Critical Tourism Studies (CTS) 04961

Contact address not obtained.
Contact address not obtained.
URL: https://www.criticaltourismstudies.info/

Aims Produce and promote social change in and through tourism practice, research and education. **Activities** Events/meetings. **Events** *Conference* Mahón (Spain) 2022, *Conference* Ibiza (Spain) 2019, *Conference* Palma (Spain) 2017, *Conference* Opatija (Croatia) 2015, *Conference* Sarajevo (Bosnia-Herzegovina) 2013. [2019/AA1519/c/**F**]

♦ Critical Tourism Studies – Asia Pacific (CTS-AP) 04962

Contact address not obtained. E-mail: criticaltourismstudies@gmail.com.
URL: https://www.criticaltourismstudies.com/

Aims Facilitate networking opportunities, exchange of ideas, research collaboration as well as conversations thta critically address contemporary issues in tourism studies. **Activities** Events/meetings. **Events** *Conference* Hanoi (Vietnam) 2022, *Conference* Wakayama (Japan) 2020, *Conference* Yogyakarta (Indonesia) 2018. **Members** Individuals. Membership countries not specified. [2021/AA1520/v/**F**]

♦ **CRITI** Caribbean Regional Information and Translation Institute (#03548)
♦ CRIWG – Collaboration Researchers International Working Group (unconfirmed)
♦ **CRIWG** Collaboration Researchers International Working Group (#04095)
♦ CRLP / see Center for Reproductive Rights
♦ **CRLRD** International Association for Comparative Research on Leukemia and Related Diseases (#11799)
♦ **CRM Alliance** Critical Raw Materials Alliance (#04959)
♦ **CRM** Conferencia Regional sobre Migración (#18769)
♦ CRMD – Chierici Regolari della Madre di Dio (religious order)
♦ CRMP – Centre de recherche en matière pénale – Fernand Boulan (internationally oriented national body)
♦ **CRM Society** Charles Rennie Mackintosh Society (#03853)
♦ **CRN+** Caribbean Regional Network of People Living with HIV/AIDS (#03549)
♦ CRN – Conflict Resolution Network (internationally oriented national body)
♦ **CRNGOs** Committee of Religious NGOs at the United Nations (#04282)
♦ **CRN International** Cartoonists Rights Network International (#03594)
♦ CRNSA – Child Rights Network for Southern Africa (unconfirmed)
♦ CROA – Centre de recherche Ouest Africain (internationally oriented national body)
♦ CROASE – Caribbean Regional Organization of Associations for Science Education (inactive)
♦ Crociata Evangelica (religious order)
♦ Crocigeri – Ordine della Santa Croce (religious order)
♦ CRO – Cyber Rights Organization (unconfirmed)
♦ CRO Forum (unconfirmed)
♦ Croisiers – Ordre de la Sainte Croix (religious order)
♦ Croix-Rouge internationale / see International Red Cross and Red Crescent Movement (#14707)
♦ Croix verte internationale (#10715)
♦ **CROME** Critical Research on Men in Europe (#04960)
♦ CRONWE – Conferentie voor Regionale Ontwikkeling in Noord-West Europa (inactive)
♦ CROP 1100053199
♦ **CROP** Comparative Research Programme on Poverty 1100053199
♦ **CROP** Council of Regional Organisations of the Pacific (#04914)

♦ CropLife Africa Middle East (CLAME) 04963

Coordinator West and Central Africa Cocody Angré Bv Latrille, Rés Caféiers 3 Villa 308, Abidjan 28, Côte d'Ivoire. T. +22522507783. Fax +22522507782. E-mail: bama@croplifeafrica.org.
Coordinator East and South Africa PO Box 72127, Parkview, 2122, South Africa. T. +27116468682.
URL: http://www.croplifeafrica.org/

History Founded 1980, as a regional body of *CropLife International (#04966).* Previously referred to as *Africa-Middle East Working Group (AMEWG).* Incorporated as an international association 10 Nov 2002, when registered in accordance with Belgian law. **Aims** Represent the *plant science* industry in Africa and the Middle East, so as to work for sustainable *agriculture.* **Structure** General Assembly; Executive Committee of 9 members. Executive Secretaries (4): 3 serve as coordinators for their respective regions (Africa and the Middle East; West and Central Africa; East and Southern Africa; Africa and Middle East). **Finance** Members' dues. Central funding from *CropLife International (#04966).* **Activities** Projects/programmes. **Events** *General Assembly* Brussels (Belgium) 2016. **Publications** *CropLife Africa Middle East Newsletter* (12 a year). Guidelines; specialized brochures; training manuals; posters; pictograms.
Members Full (companies; associations); Associate (companies; associations). Full member associations in 5 countries:
Côte d'Ivoire, Egypt, Kenya, Morocco, South Africa.
Associate members in 24 countries:
Algeria, Cameroon, Ethiopia, Ghana, Jordan, Kuwait, Lebanon, Madagascar, Malawi, Mali, Mauritius, Namibia, Nigeria, Saudi Arabia, Senegal, Sudan, Syrian AR, Tanzania UR, Tunisia, Uganda, United Arab Emirates, Yemen, Zambia, Zimbabwe.
IGO Relations Cooperates with: *African Union (AU, #00488)*; *FAO (#09260)*; *International Bank for Reconstruction and Development (IBRD, #12317)* (World Bank); *New Partnership for Africa's Development (NEPAD, #17091).* **NGO Relations** Cooperates with: *COLEACP (#04091)*; *Food, Agriculture and Natural Resources Policy Analysis Network (FANRPAN, #09839)*; *International Fertilizer Development Center (IFDC, #13590)*; *World Wide Fund for Nature (WWF, #21922).* [2016/XE3559/**E**]

♦ CropLife Asia 04964

Exec Dir 20 Malacca Street, 06-00 Malacca Center, Singapore 048979, Singapore. T. +6562211615. Fax +6562221615.
URL: http://www.croplifeasia.org/

History 1991. Initially launched as a project by *CropLife International (#04966)*; developed into an association when set up by 12 member companies. Former names and other names: *Safe-Use Pilot Project* – former (1991 to 1996); *Asia-Pacific Crop Protection Association* – former (15 Apr 1996 to 2002). **Aims** Help farmers grow sufficient amounts of food for a growing population through access to innovative technologies. **Structure** Annual General Meeting; Committees; Secretariat, headed by Executive Director. **Languages** English. **Staff** 6.00 FTE, paid. **Finance** Funded by some member companies. **Activities** Research and development; advocacy/lobbying/activism; projects/programmes; events/meetings. **Events** *Annual General Meeting* Singapore (Singapore) 2021, *Annual General Meeting* Singapore (Singapore) 2018, *Annual General Meeting* Singapore (Singapore) 2017, *Crop functional genomics conference* Jeju (Korea Rep) 2010, *Conference on sustainable agriculture* Bangkok (Thailand) 1999. **Publications** *Agrolinks* (2 a year). *Biotech Farmer Case Stuies*; *Biotech Fact Sheets*; *Crop Protection Farmer Case Studies.* Annual Report. Brochure.
Members National associations in 14 countries and territories:
Australia, Bangladesh, China, India, Indonesia, Japan, Korea Rep, Malaysia, New Zealand, Pakistan, Philippines, Sri Lanka, Taiwan, Thailand.
NGO Relations Member of: *CropLife International (#04966).* [2021/XD5748/**D**]

♦ CropLife Europe 04965

Dir Gen Rue Guimard 9, 1040 Brussels, Belgium. T. +3226631550. Fax +3226631560.
URL: https://croplifeeurope.eu/

History Jun 1992. Expanded scope of mandate, 1 Jan 2021. Former names and other names: *European Crop Protection Association (ECPA)* – former (Jan 2021). Registration: Banque-Carrefour des Entreprises, No/ID: 0447.618.871, Start date: 7 Apr 1992, Belgium; EU Transparency Register, No/ID: 0711626572-26, Start date: 29 Oct 2008. **Aims** Develop innovative and science-based solutions that keep crops healthy and contribute to provide Europeans a safe, affordable, healthy and *sustainable food supply.* **Structure** General Assembly (annual); Executive Committee; Secretariat. **Languages** English. **Staff** 13.00 FTE, paid. **Finance** Sources: members' dues. **Activities** Projects/programmes. **Events** *Annual Conference* Brussels (Belgium) 2023, *Annual Conference* Brussels (Belgium) 2022, *Conference* Brussels (Belgium) 2021, *Regulatory Conference* Ghent (Belgium) 2019, *Regulatory Conference* Brussels (Belgium) 2018. **Publications** *CEE Voice*; *Perspectives.* Annual Report; studies; statistics; booklets.
Members Full: Corporate; Associations. Associations in 24 countries:
Austria, Belgium, Bulgaria, Croatia, Cyprus, Czechia, Denmark, Finland, France, Germany, Greece, Hungary, Ireland, Italy, Latvia, Lithuania, Netherlands, Poland, Portugal, Romania, Slovakia, Slovenia, Spain, Sweden.
Associate in 8 countries:
Kazakhstan, Norway, Russia, Serbia, Switzerland, Türkiye, UK, Ukraine.
Consultative Status Consultative status granted from: *World Intellectual Property Organization (WIPO, #21593)* (Permanent Observer Status). **NGO Relations** Member of (12): *Agri-Food Chain Coalition (AFCC, #00577)*; *Circular Plastics Alliance (#03936)*; *Conseil européen de l'industrie chimique (CEFIC, #04687)* (Affiliate); *CropLife International (#04966)* ((also acts as its European regional body)); *Downstream Users of Chemicals Co-ordination group (DUCC, #05127)*; *European Food Sustainable Consumption and Production Round Table (European Food SCP Roundtable, #07289)*; *European Network of Agricultural Journalists (ENAJ, #07864)* (Associate); *European Policy Centre (EPC, #08240)*; *Federation of European and International Associations Established in Belgium (FAIB, #09508)*; *GLOBALG.A.P (#10386)* (Associate); *Industry4Europe (#11181)*; *Knowledge4Innovation (K4I, #16198).* Partner of (1): *European Partnership for Alternative Approaches to Animal Testing (EPAA, #08155).* In liaison with technical committees of: *International Organization for Standardization (ISO, #14473).* [2022/XD3375/**D**]

♦ **CropLife International** **04966**
Interim Pres & CEO Av Louise 326 – Bte 35, 1050 Brussels, Belgium. T. +3225420410. Fax +3225420419. E-mail: croplife@croplife.org.
Communications Dir address not obtained.
URL: http://www.croplife.org/

History 29 Sep 1967, Brussels (Belgium). Derives from *Groupement européen des associations nationales de fabricants de pesticides (GEFAP, inactive)*, set up Jan 1960. Legally registered 2002 under current title. Statutes most recently registered 16 Jun 2006. Former names and other names: *International Group of National Pesticide Manufacturers' Associations* – former (1967 to 1980); *Groupement international des associations nationales de fabricants de pesticides* – former (1967 to 1980); *International Group of National Associations of Manufacturers of Agrochemical Products* – former (Nov 1980 to 1996); *Groupement international des associations nationales de fabricants de produits agrochimiques (GIFAP)* – former (Nov 1980 to 1996); *Global Crop Protection Federation (GCPF)* – former (1996 to 2001). Registration: No/ID: 0407.599.740, Start date: 4 Apr 1968, Belgium; EU Transparency Register, No/ID: 830666939110-20, Start date: 30 Jul 2020. **Aims** Act as ambassador for the *plant science* industry, encouraging understanding and dialogue while promoting sound science and agricultural *technology* in the context of *sustainable development*. **Structure** General Assembly (annual); Board of Directors; Strategy Councils (2); Secretariat based in Brussels (Belgium). **Languages** English, French. **Staff** 20.00 FTE, paid. **Finance** Sources: contributions of member/participating states; members' dues. **Activities** Events/meetings; knowledge management/information dissemination; politics/policy/regulatory; research/documentation. **Events** *Annual conference* Geneva (Switzerland) 2006, *Annual Conference* Brussels (Belgium) 2005, *Annual Conference* Brussels (Belgium) 2004, *Annual Conference* Brussels (Belgium) 2003, *Annual Conference* Brussels (Belgium) 2002. **Publications** *Guidelines*; *Plant Science and Sustainability*. *Integrated Pest Management* – case studies. Technical monographs; position papers; brochures; code of conduct; training manuals; videos. Information Services: Disseminates scientific studies, documentation and publications of common interest.
Members Associations (15), including the following 6 organizations listed in this Yearbook:
AfricaBio (#00159); *CropLife Africa Middle East (CLAME, #04963)*; *CropLife Asia (#04964)*; *CropLife Europe (#04965)*; *CropLife Latin America (#04967)*; *European Association of Bioindustries (EuropaBio, #05956)*.
International companies (8). Membership countries not specified.
Consultative Status Consultative status granted from: *ECOSOC (#05331)* (Ros A); *FAO (#09260)* (Special Status); *WHO (#20950)* (Official Relations); *World Intellectual Property Organization (WIPO, #21593)* (Permanent Observer Status); *UNEP (#20299)*. **IGO Relations** Observer status with (1): *Union internationale pour la protection des obtentions végétales (UPOV, #20436)*. Represents members interests with, among others: FAO; *ILO (#11123)*; *International Bank for Reconstruction and Development (IBRD, #12317)*; *UNIDO (#20336)*; WHO; *OECD (#17693)*; *UNESCO (#20322)*. Participates as observer in the activities of: *Codex Alimentarius Commission (CAC, #04081)*. Participates in the work of: *United Nations Economic Commission for Europe (UNECE, #20555)*. **NGO Relations** Member of (3): *Federation of European and International Associations Established in Belgium (FAIB, #09508)*; *GLOBALG.A.P (#10386)*; *International Agri-Food Network (IAFN, #11599)*. Supports (2): *Farming First*; *International Institute of Tropical Agriculture (IITA, #13933)*. Formal contacts with: *Collaborative International Pesticides Analytical Council (CIPAC, #04099)*. In liaison with technical committees of: *International Organization for Standardization (ISO, #14473)*. Associate expert of: *Business and Industry Advisory Committee to the OECD (BIAC, #03385)*. [2022/XC2090/y/**C**]

♦ **CropLife Latin America** **04967**
Pres Carretera a Santa Ana, Frente a Price Smart de Escazú, Condominio Trilogia, Edificio 1 – Of 112, San José, San José, San José, Costa Rica. T. +50622886772 – +506(13053733713.
URL: http://www.croplifela.org/

History Founded 12 May 1977, Montevideo (Uruguay), as *Latin American Crop Protection Association (LACPA) – Asociación Latinoamericana para la Protección de los Cultivos*. Has taken over activities of *FECCOPIA (inactive)*. Current title adopted 4 Mar 2003. One of 8 regional associations of *CropLife International (#04966)*. **Aims** Promote responsibly science based legal and regulatory frameworks; communicate effectively the industry's contributions to innovation and productivity in support of *sustainable agriculture* in Latin America. **Structure** General Assembly; Board of Directors; Regional Councils. **Languages** English, Portuguese, Spanish. **Staff** 11.00 FTE, paid. **Finance** Members' dues. Other sources: companies. **Events** *Forum* Punta del Este (Uruguay) 2012, *Forum* Bogota (Colombia) 2011, *Forum* Lima (Peru) 2010, *Forum* San José (Costa Rica) 2009, *Forum* Antigua (Guatemala) 2008. **Publications** *Notas de Interés* – newsletter; *Tierra Fertil* – magazine. Annual Report.
Members Associated multinational companies (9). National associations in 18 countries:
Argentina, Bolivia, Brazil, Chile, Colombia, Costa Rica, Dominican Rep, Ecuador, El Salvador, Guatemala, Honduras, Mexico, Nicaragua, Panama, Paraguay, Peru, Uruguay, Venezuela.
NGO Relations Member of: *GLOBALG.A.P (#10386)*. [2016/XD5616/y/**D**]

♦ **Crops For the Future (CFF)** **04968**
Dir c/o NIAB, 93 Lawrence Weaver Road, Cambridge, CB3 OLE, UK. T. +441245492777. E-mail: sean.mayes@cropsforthefutureuk.org.
URL: http://cropsforthefutureuk.org

History 1 Dec 2008, as a merger between *International Centre for Underutilized Crops (ICUC, inactive)* and *Global Facilitation Unit for Underutilized Species (GFU, inactive)*. Operational activities started in Apr 2009. *Crops For the Future Research Centre (CFFRC)*, set up 2011, merged into CFF, 2014. Registered in accordance with UK law. **Aims** Develop solutions that diversify agriculture using underutilized crops. **Structure** Executive Committee; Senior Management. **Languages** English. **Staff** 4 regular; 3 temporary. **Finance** Supported by several bilateral donor agencies. Budget (annual): about US$ 1 million. **Activities** Research/documentation; advocacy/lobbying/activism; training/education. **Events** *International conference on horticulture* Bangalore (India) 2009. **Publications** Electronic newsletter. Annual Report. Monographs; manuals; research reports; position papers. Information Services: Develops, updates and maintains databases. **IGO Relations** Secretariat hosted by: *Bioversity International (#03262)*. **NGO Relations** Member of: *Association of International Research and Development Centers for Agriculture (AIRCA, #02760)*. Cooperates with: *Global Forum on Agricultural Research (GFAR, #10370)*. [2021/XM2982/**F**]

♦ **Crop Trust** Global Crop Diversity Trust (#10313)
♦ Crosiers – Order of the Holy Cross (religious order)
♦ **CROSQ** CARICOM Regional Organization for Standards and Quality (#03574)

♦ **Cross Border Benefits Alliance-Europe (CBBA-Europe)** **04969**
General Manager Square de Meeûs 38-40, 1000 Brussels, Belgium. T. +3224018792. Fax +3224016868. E-mail: info@cbba-europe.eu.
URL: http://www.cbba-europe.eu/

History Launched Dec 2017. **Aims** Promote the creation and development of cross-border/pan-European employee benefit plans in Europe, including – but not limited to – pensions, healthcare, disability, long-term care, or programmes for the well-being/wellness of people in the workplace and private life. **Structure** Scientific Council. **Events** *Annual Conference* Brussels (Belgium) 2019, *Annual Conference* Brussels (Belgium) 2018.
Members Companies and institutions. Membership countries not specified. Included in the above, 1 organization listed in this Yearbook:
European Public Real Estate Association (EPRA, #08301). [2019/XM7851/**D**]

♦ Cross-Cultural Solutions (internationally oriented national body)

♦ **Crossing Borders (CB)** **04970**
CEO Kobmagergade 43, 1150 Copenhagen, Denmark. T. +4521639432. E-mail: cb@crossingborders.dk.
URL: http://crossingborders.dk/

History Oct 1999, Denmark, following the activities of the 'Learning to Live Together in the Middle East' project initiated in 1994. Registered in accordance with Danish law, 2004. **Aims** Educate and empower young people to become active global citizens. **Structure** Advisory Council; Executive Board; Secretariat, headed by Executive Director. **Languages** Danish, English. **Staff** 6.00 FTE, paid; 15.00 FTE, voluntary. **Finance** Members' dues. Other sources: grants from *European Commission (EC, #06633)*, Danish Ministry of Foreign Affairs and private foundations. Annual budget: about euro 400,000. **Activities** Training/education; projects/programmes; capacity building; awareness raising; events/meetings. **Publications** *Crossing Borders* (20 a year).
Members Not a membership organization. Partners in 17 countries and territories:
Austria, Bulgaria, Egypt, Ethiopia, Finland, France, Germany, Hungary, Israel, Italy, Jordan, Latvia, Netherlands, Palestine, Somalia, Sudan, Yemen.
IGO Relations Contacts with: *Anna Lindh Euro-Mediterranean Foundation for the Dialogue between Cultures (Anna Lindh Foundation, #00847)*; *UNESCO (#20322)*. [2020/XJ8144/**F**]

♦ Cross International (internationally oriented national body)
♦ CrossLink International (internationally oriented national body)
♦ Crosslinks (internationally oriented national body)
♦ CrossRoads (internationally oriented national body)
♦ Crossroads International Centre (internationally oriented national body)
♦ Crossroads Movement / see International Churches of Christ
♦ Crossworld (internationally oriented national body)
♦ Crown Agents for the Colonies / see Crown Agents for Overseas Governments and Administrations
♦ Crown Agents for Overseas Governments and Administrations (internationally oriented national body)
♦ CRP – Canonici Regolari Premostratensi (religious order)
♦ **CRP** Consejo Regional de Planificación (#04725)
♦ CRPD – Centre for Research on Peace and Development (internationally oriented national body)
♦ **CRPD** Committee on the Rights of Persons with Disabilities (#04284)
♦ CRPD – Convention on the Rights of Persons with Disabilities (2006 treaty)
♦ CRPE – Centrul Roman de Politici Europene (internationally oriented national body)
♦ **CRPM** Conférence des régions périphériques maritimes d'Europe (#04638)
♦ **CRPM** Conferência das Regiões Periféricas Marítimas da Europa (#04638)
♦ **CRPM** Conferencia de las Regiones Periféricas Marítimas de Europa (#04638)
♦ **CRPM** Conferenza delle Regioni Periferiche Marittime d'Europa (#04638)
♦ **CRPT** Communauté régionale des postes et télécommunications (#18767)
♦ CRRC – Corporate Responsibility Research Conference (meeting series)
♦ **CRRH** Comité Regional de Recursos Hidraulicos del Istmo Centroamericano (#04196)
♦ **CRSA** Clinical Robotic Surgery Association (#04025)
♦ CRSA – Sacer et Apostolicus Ordo Canonicorum Regularium Sancti Augustini (religious order)
♦ **CRS** Catholic Relief Services (#03608)
♦ **CRS** Controlled Release Society (#04784)
♦ CRSD – Dominicaines de la Congrégation Romaine de Saint-Dominique (religious order)
♦ **CRSEA** Confederation of Rightholders' Societies of Europe and Asia (#04576)
♦ CRSESFPI / see Statistical, Economic and Social Research and Training Centre for Islamic Countries (#19971)
♦ CRSG – Centrul Român de Studii Globale (internationally oriented national body)
♦ **CRSI** Concrete Reinforcing Steel Institute (#04434)
♦ CRS – Ordo Clericorum Regularium a Somascha (religious order)
♦ CRSP – Congregatio Clericorum Regularium Sancti Pauli (religious order)
♦ CRST / see African Union Scientific Technical Research Commission (#00493)
♦ CRSTRA – Euro-Mediterranean Centre for Research on Arid Areas (internationally oriented national body)
♦ CRS-USCC / see Catholic Relief Services (#03608)
♦ CRSVI / see International Forum for Volunteering in Development (#13659)
♦ **CRT** Caux Round Table, The (#03614)
♦ CRT – Conférence rail tourisme (inactive)
♦ CRTD – Convention on Civil Liability for Damage Caused During Carriage of Dangerous Goods by Road, Rail and Inland Navigation Vessels (1989 treaty)
♦ **CRTEAN** Centre Régional de Télédétection des Etats de l'Afrique du nord (#18807)
♦ CRTO – Centre régional de télédétection, Ouagadougou (inactive)
♦ CRUA – Conférence de recteurs d'universités africaines (meeting series)
♦ Crucigeri – Ordo Sanctae Crucis (religious order)

♦ **Cruelty Free Europe** **04971**
Registered Address Drève du Pressoir 38, 1190 Brussels, Belgium. E-mail: info@crueltyfreeeurope.org.
URL: https://crueltyfreeeurope.org/

History Registration: Banque-Carrefour des Entreprises, No/ID: 0721.976.146, Start date: 7 Mar 2019, Belgium; EU Transparency Register, No/ID: 842315534764-63, Start date: 29 May 2019. **Aims** Bring animal testing to an end across Europe. **Structure** Board. **Activities** Advocacy/lobbying/activism.
Members Associate in 21 countries:
Belgium, Bosnia-Herzegovina, Bulgaria, Croatia, Czechia, Denmark, Estonia, Finland, France, Germany, Hungary, Ireland, Italy, Malta, Netherlands, Norway, Poland, Portugal, Serbia, Slovakia, Spain, UK.
Cruelty Free International. [2022/AA2934/**F**]

♦ Cruelty Free International (internationally oriented national body)
♦ Cruelty Free International Trust / see Cruelty Free International
♦ CRUFA / see Conférence des recteurs des universités francophones d'Afrique et de l'Océan indien (#04644)
♦ **CRUFAOCI** Conférence des recteurs des universités francophones d'Afrique et de l'Océan indien (#04644)

♦ **Cruise Europe (CE)** **04972**
Acting Managing Dir Tinggata 3, 6783 Stryn, Norway. T. +4791781441.
URL: https://www.cruiseeurope.com/

History 1991. **Aims** Promote and develop a thriving and "must see" North and Atlantic European destination while working constructively with the Cruise Lines. **Structure** Annual General Meeting; Council. **Finance** Sources: members' dues. **Events** *Conference and Annual General Meeting* Bruges (Belgium) 2019. **Members** Cruise ports and destinations (about 140). Membership countries not specified. [2020/AA0084/**D**]

♦ **Cruise Lines International Association (CLIA)** **04973**
CEO 1201 F St NW, Ste 250, Washington DC 20004, USA. T. +12027599370. Fax +12027599344. E-mail: mrivera@cruising.org – info@cruising.org.
URL: http://www.cruising.org/

History Set up 1975, with primarily North American membership. Merged activities of *International Council of Cruise Lines (ICCL, inactive)*, 2006. Became an international organization, Dec 2012, on merger of CLIA with European Cruise Council (ECC), Asia Cruise Association (ACA), Passenger Shipping Association (PSA/ACE), France's AFCC, Brazil's ABREMAR, Northwest and Canada Cruise Association (NWCCA), Alaska Cruise Association (ACA), and International Cruise Council Australasia (ICCA). **Aims** Provide increased benefits and a globally unified voice for cruise lines, travel agents and business partners. **Structure** Global Executive Committee. Offices worldwide (15), including: *CLIA Europe (#03995)*; *CLIA Australasia*. **Events** *Cruise360 Conference* Vancouver, BC (Canada) 2020, *River Cruise Conference* Amsterdam (Netherlands) 2019, *International Cruise Summit* Madrid (Spain) 2019, *Executive Partner Summit* Miami, FL (USA) 2019, *Cruise in Asia Forum* Singapore (Singapore) 2019. **Consultative Status** Consultative status granted from: *ECOSOC (#05331)* (Ros C); *International Maritime Organization (IMO, #14102)*. **IGO Relations** *ILO (#11123)*. Accredited by: *International Hydrographic Organization (IHO, #13825)*. **NGO Relations** Associate member of: *International Chamber of Shipping (ICS, #12535)*. [2020/XG0122/**C**]

♦ Crusaders International / see Urban Saints

♦ The Crustacean Society (TCS) 04974

Exec Dir 1320 Winding Way, New Braunfels TX 78132, USA. T. +12108429152. E-mail: tcs1921@hotmail.com.
URL: http://www.crustaceansociety.org/

History Dec 1979, Tampa, FL (USA). Interest in forming a scientific society began to develop late 1975, and the idea was first formally brought up in 1977, New Orleans LA (USA), during a meeting of the Crustacean Club, but had no support. The idea was discussed again, Oct 1978, Beaufort NC (USA), by individuals attending a joint USA/USSR Conference on Cold-Water Crustaceans. Formation of the Society proposed, Dec 1978, Richmond VA (USA), during a meeting of the Crustacean Club. **Aims** Advance the study of all aspects of crustacean *biology*; enhance information exchange. **Structure** Meeting (twice a year, once jointly with Society of Integrative and Comparative Biology); Board of Governors; International Crustacean Council coordinates planning and scheduling of the International Crustacean Congress. **Languages** English. **Staff** 0.50 FTE, paid. **Finance** Sources: members' dues; sale of publications. **Activities** Awards/prizes/competitions; events/meetings. **Events** *Annual Summer Meeting* Paris (France) 2021, *Annual Summer Meeting* Santos (Brazil) 2020, *Annual Summer Meeting* Hong Kong (Hong Kong) 2019, *International Congress* Washington, DC (USA) 2018, *Annual Summer Meeting* Barcelona (Spain) 2017. **Publications** *Ecdysiast*; *Journal of Crustacean Biology*.
Members Individuals (429) in 67 countries and territories:
Argentina, Australia, Bahrain, Belarus, Belgium, Brazil, Bulgaria, Canada, Chile, China, Colombia, Costa Rica, Croatia, Czechia, Denmark, Egypt, Estonia, Finland, France, Georgia, Germany, Greece, Hong Kong, Hungary, Iceland, India, Indonesia, Ireland, Israel, Italy, Jamaica, Japan, Kenya, Korea Rep, Latvia, Lithuania, Luxembourg, Malaysia, Malta, Mexico, Mozambique, Netherlands, New Zealand, Norway, Pakistan, Panama, Papua New Guinea, Peru, Poland, Portugal, Puerto Rico, Romania, Russia, Saudi Arabia, Singapore, Slovenia, South Africa, Spain, Sweden, Switzerland, Taiwan, Thailand, Türkiye, UK, Ukraine, USA, Venezuela.
NGO Relations Also links with other groups and national organizations. [2021/XF5753/v/**F**]

- ♦ Crux, Fédération internationale catholique d'abstinence totale (inactive)
- ♦ Crux, International Catholic Federation of Total Abstainers (inactive)
- ♦ Cruzada Evangélica (religious order)
- ♦ Cruz Roja Internacional / see International Red Cross and Red Crescent Movement (#14707)
- ♦ CRWRC / see World Renew
- ♦ CRY – Care and Relief for the Young (internationally oriented national body)
- ♦ **CRYC** Caribbean Regional Youth Council (#03551)

♦ Cryogenics Society of Europe (CSE) 04975

Chairman Postbus 217, 7500 AE Enschede, Netherlands. E-mail: info@cryoeurope.org.
URL: https://www.cryoeurope.org/

History 22 Apr 2015. Registration: No/ID: KVK 63168790, Netherlands, Twente; RSIN, No/ID: 855121695, Netherlands, Twente. **Aims** Strengthen the European position of cryogenic technologies; represent European activities in cryogenic technologies in social, scientific, industrial and political forums; promote communication and information exchange in the area of cryogenic technologies; foster training of young researchers in the field; bring together those active in cryogenic technologies and potential user communities so as to stimulate applications of these technologies. **Structure** General Meeting; Board. **Finance** Members' dues. **Events** *European Cryogenic Days* Darmstadt (Germany) 2023, *European Cryogenic Days* 2021, *General Meeting* 2020, *European Cryogenic Days* Lund (Sweden) 2019, *General Meeting* Lund (Sweden) 2019. **Publications** *CSE Newsletter*.
Members Individual; Corporate. Membership countries not specified. Included as member European Organization for Nuclear Research.
Included as member:
European Organization for Nuclear Research (CERN, #08108). [2023/XM4932/**D**]

- ♦ CS / see Commonwealth Secretariat (#04362)
- ♦ (CS)²AI – Control System Cyber Security Association International (internationally oriented national body)
- ♦ **CSA APAC** Cloud Security Alliance Asia Pacific (#04028)
- ♦ **CSA** Caribbean Shipping Association (#03554)
- ♦ **CSA** Caribbean Studies Association (#03559)
- ♦ **CSA** Carsharing Association (#03588)
- ♦ CSAC – Center for Sustainable Asian Cities (internationally oriented national body)
- ♦ **CSA** Channel Swimming Association (#03851)
- ♦ CSA – Clean Shipping Alliance (unconfirmed)
- ♦ CSA – Cloud Security Alliance (internationally oriented national body)
- ♦ CSA – Collectif Stratégies Alimentaires (internationally oriented national body)
- ♦ CSA – Comité de Seguridad Alimentaria Mundial (see: #09260)
- ♦ **CSA** Commonwealth Students' Association (#04363)
- ♦ **CSA** Confederación Sindical de Trabajadores y Trabajadoras de las Américas (#04480)
- ♦ CSA – Confédération syndicale africaine (inactive)
- ♦ CSA – Congregation of Sisters of St Agnes (religious order)
- ♦ CSA – Conseil scientifique pour l'Afrique au Sud du Sahara (inactive)
- ♦ CSAC – Sisters of the Catholic Apostolate Pallottine (religious order)
- ♦ CSAE – Centre for the Study of African Economies, Oxford (internationally oriented national body)
- ♦ CSAfrica – Coalition for a Sustainable Africa (unconfirmed)
- ♦ CSAI – Comité acteurs interprètes (no recent information)
- ♦ CSA International – Canadian Standards Association (internationally oriented national body)
- ♦ **CSAM** Centre for Sustainable Agricultural Mechanization (#03789)
- ♦ **CSAO** Club de Sahel et de l'Afrique de l'Ouest (#19034)
- ♦ CSAR / see Confederación Panamericana de Remo (#04478)
- ♦ CSAS / see National Centre for South Asian Studies, Clayton
- ♦ CSAS – Center for South Asian Studies, Charlottesville VA (internationally oriented national body)
- ♦ CSAS – Centre for South Asian Studies, Lahore (internationally oriented national body)
- ♦ CSA – UNWTO Commission for South Asia (see: #21861)
- ♦ CSAW – CTNNB1 Syndrome Awareness Worldwide (internationally oriented national body)
- ♦ CSBAOC – Comité des Superviseurs de Banque de l'Afrique de l'Ouest et du Centre (unconfirmed)
- ♦ **CSB** Confederación Sudamericana de Bridge (#04484)
- ♦ CSB – Confédération sudaméricaine de billard (inactive)
- ♦ **CSBR** Coalition for Sexual and Bodily Rights in Muslim Societies (#04068)
- ♦ CSB – Sisters of Saint Brigid (religious order)
- ♦ **CSCAP** Council for Security Cooperation in the Asia Pacific (#04919)
- ♦ **CSCCC** Civil Society Coalition on Climate Change (#03967)
- ♦ **CSCC** Centre for the Study of Communication and Culture (#03788)
- ♦ CSCC – International Conference on Circuits, Systems, Communications and Computers (meeting series)
- ♦ **CSC** Clean Shipping Coalition (#03989)
- ♦ **CSC** Commission syndicale consultative auprès de l'OCDE (#20186)
- ♦ **CSC** Commonwealth Scholarship Commission in the United Kingdom (#04360)
- ♦ **CSC** Commonwealth Science Council (#04361)
- ♦ CSC – Congrégation de Sainte-Croix (religious order)
- ♦ CSC – Congregatio a Sancta Cruce (religious order)
- ♦ CSC – Consortium for Street Children (internationally oriented national body)
- ♦ CSCE – Commission on Security and Cooperation in Europe (internationally oriented national body)
- ♦ CSCE ODIHR / see OSCE – Office for Democratic Institutions and Human Rights (#17902)
- ♦ CSCE – Office for Democratic Institutions and Human Rights / see OSCE – Office for Democratic Institutions and Human Rights (#17902)
- ♦ CSCE / see Organization for Security and Cooperation in Europe (#17887)
- ♦ **CSCG** EU Civil Society Contact Group (#05572)
- ♦ CSC – International Convention for Safe Containers (1972 treaty)
- ♦ CSCM / see Catholic Radio and Television Network (#03607)
- ♦ CSCMP – Council of Supply Chain Management Professionals (internationally oriented national body)
- ♦ CSC-OCDE / see Trade Union Advisory Committee to the OECD (#20186)
- ♦ CS – Columbian Squires (religious order)
- ♦ CS – Congregatio Missionariorum a Sancto Carolo (religious order)
- ♦ CSCSASPS – Centre for South, Central South East-Asian and South-West Pacific Studies, Delhi (internationally oriented national body)
- ♦ CSC – Sisters of Holy Cross (religious order)
- ♦ CSCT / see Association for the Prevention of Torture (#02869)
- ♦ **CS/CWC** Conference of Secretaries of Christian World Communions (#04647)
- ♦ CSDA – Center for Sustainable Development in the Americas (internationally oriented national body)
- ♦ CSD – Centre for Safety and Development (internationally oriented national body)
- ♦ CSD – Chartered Society of Designers (internationally oriented national body)
- ♦ CSDEA – Centre for Sustainable Development and Education in Africa (unconfirmed)
- ♦ CSDILE – Centre for Studies in Diplomacy, International Law and Economics, Delhi (internationally oriented national body)
- ♦ **CSDS** Cardiovascular System Dynamics Society (#03428)
- ♦ CSDS – Center for Strategic and Defense Studies, Budapest (internationally oriented national body)
- ♦ CSDS – Centre for Strategic and Defence Studies, Africa (internationally oriented national body)
- ♦ CSD – United Nations Commission on Sustainable Development (inactive)
- ♦ **CSEAR** Centre for Social and Environmental Accounting Research (#03786)
- ♦ CSEAS – Centre for Southeast Asian Studies, Kyoto (internationally oriented national body)
- ♦ CSEASI / see Center for Southeast Asian Studies-Indonesia
- ♦ CSEAS-Indonesia – Center for Southeast Asian Studies-Indonesia (internationally oriented national body)
- ♦ CSECD / see KIBANDA – European Spiritan Centre for Cooperation and Development (#16188)
- ♦ CSE – Centre de sociologie européenne (internationally oriented national body)
- ♦ **CSE** Commission Séismologique Européenne (#08461)
- ♦ CSE – Confédération syndicale européenne (no recent information)
- ♦ **CSE** Council of Science Editors (#04917)
- ♦ **CSE** Cryogenics Society of Europe (#04975)
- ♦ **CSEE** Comité syndical européen de l'éducation (#08926)
- ♦ CS-EF – Committee of Experts on Children and Families (inactive)
- ♦ CSEF – Common Sense Environmental Fund (unconfirmed)
- ♦ **CSEM** Centre sismologique euro-méditerranéen (#07774)
- ♦ CSEPE – Comité syndical européen des personnels enseignants (inactive)
- ♦ CSER – Centro Studi Emigrazione, Roma (internationally oriented national body)
- ♦ CSERGE – Centre for Social and Economic Research on the Global Environment (internationally oriented national body)
- ♦ **CSES** Caribbean Solar Energy Society (#03557)
- ♦ CSESP / see European Federation of Public Service Unions (#07202)
- ♦ CS-Europe – Christianson Syndrome Europe (unconfirmed)
- ♦ CSF / see Confederación Sudamericana de Fútbol (#04487)
- ♦ CSF – Congregatio a Sacra Familia (religious order)
- ♦ **CSFD** Civil Society Forum on Drugs (#03968)
- ♦ **CSFEF** Comité syndical francophone de l'éducation et de la formation (#04198)
- ♦ **CSF** European Civil Society Forum on HIV/AIDS (#06568)
- ♦ **CSF** EU-Russia Civil Society Forum (#09199)
- ♦ CSFM – Centre for the Study of Forced Migration (internationally oriented national body)
- ♦ CSFN – Sisters of the Holy Family of Nazareth (religious order)
- ♦ CSFPE – Commission des services financiers postaux européens (inactive)
- ♦ CSFS – Confederación Sudamericana de Futsal (no recent information)
- ♦ CSG / see Centre for the Study of Globalization, Athens
- ♦ CSGC – Center for the Study of Global Christianity (internationally oriented national body)
- ♦ CSG – Centre for the Study of Globalization, Aberdeen (internationally oriented national body)
- ♦ CSG – Centre for the Study of Globalization, Athens (internationally oriented national body)
- ♦ CSGH / see Dorcas (#05123)
- ♦ CSGR – Centre for the Study of Globalization and Regionalization (internationally oriented national body)
- ♦ **CSHAE** Caribbean Society of Hotel Association Executives (#03555)
- ♦ CSHR / see Institute for the Study of Human Rights, Columbia University
- ♦ **CSIA** Corporate Secretaries International Association (#04842)
- ♦ CSIBP – Congregation of Saint John the Baptist Precursor (religious order)
- ♦ CSI – Caritas international (internationally oriented national body)
- ♦ CSI – Carrefour de solidarité internationale (internationally oriented national body)
- ♦ CSI – Centrale sanitaire internationale (inactive)
- ♦ CSI – Centre de solidarité internationale du Saguenay Lac-Saint-Jean (internationally oriented national body)
- ♦ CSI – Cetacean Society International (internationally oriented national body)
- ♦ CSI – Childbirth Survival International (internationally oriented national body)
- ♦ CSI – Children's Surgery International (internationally oriented national body)
- ♦ CSI – ChildSafe International (internationally oriented national body)
- ♦ CSI – Christian Schools International (internationally oriented national body)
- ♦ **CSI** Christian Solidarity International (#03909)
- ♦ **CSI** Church of Scientology International (#03922)
- ♦ **CSI** Coatings Societies International (#04075)
- ♦ CSI – Collaboration santé internationale (internationally oriented national body)
- ♦ CSI – Colloquium Spectroscopicum International (meeting series)
- ♦ **CSI** Comisión Sericicola Internacional (#14837)
- ♦ **CSI** Comité Scout Interamericano (#11445)
- ♦ **CSI** Commission séricicole internationale (#14837)
- ♦ CSI – Committee for Skeptical Inquiry (internationally oriented national body)
- ♦ **CSI** Confédération syndicale internationale (#15708)
- ♦ CSI – Congregatio Sancti Ioseph (religious order)
- ♦ CSICOP / see Committee for Skeptical Inquiry
- ♦ **CSI** Crime Stoppers International (#04954)
- ♦ CSID – Centre for the Study of Islam and Democracy (internationally oriented national body)
- ♦ CSIET – Council on Standards for International Educational Travel (internationally oriented national body)
- ♦ CSIH / see Canadian Association Global Health
- ♦ **CSIRA** Comprehensive System International Rorschach Association (#04421)
- ♦ CSIRO – Commonwealth Scientific and Industrial Research Organization (internationally oriented national body)
- ♦ CSIRS / see Centre européen de recherche internationales et stratégiques
- ♦ CSIS – Center for Strategic and International Studies, Washington DC (internationally oriented national body)
- ♦ CSIS – Centre for Strategic and International Studies, Jakarta (internationally oriented national body)
- ♦ **CSIT** Confédération Sportive Internationale Travailliste et Amateur (#15905)
- ♦ CSIT / see International Workers and Amateurs in Sports Confederation (#15905)
- ♦ CSJB – Congregation of the Sisters of St John the Baptist (religious order)
- ♦ **CSJ** Confederación Sudamericana de Judo (#19704)
- ♦ **CSJs** Congregations of St Joseph (#04673)
- ♦ **CSK** Confederación Sudamericana de Karate (#04489)
- ♦ **CSLF** Carbon Sequestration Leadership Forum (#03425)
- ♦ CSLI / see Lazarus Union (#16411)

- ♦ CSLP – Confederación Sudamericana de Levantamiento de Pesas (inactive)
- ♦ CSMA – Congregatio Sancti Michaelis Archangeli (religious order)
- ♦ CSMA / see Consumer Specialty Products Association (#04774)
- ♦ CSM – Centre for Social Markets (internationally oriented national body)
- ♦ CSM / see Civil Society and Indigenous Peoples' Mechanism for Relations with the UN Committee on World Food Security (#03969)
- ♦ **CSM** Civil Society and Indigenous Peoples' Mechanism for Relations with the UN Committee on World Food Security (#03969)
- ♦ **CSME** CARICOM Single Market and Economy (#03575)
- ♦ CSME – Confederación Sindical Mundial de la Enseñanza (inactive)
- ♦ CSME – Confédération syndicale mondiale de l'enseignement (inactive)
- ♦ CSMN / see Duke Islamic Studies Center
- ♦ CSN – Congregation of the Sisters of Nazareth (religious order)
- ♦ CSNEA – Centro Studi Nord Est e Adriatico (internationally oriented national body)
- ♦ CSN – International Symposium on Concrete and Structures for Next Generation (meeting series)
- ♦ CSN / see Union of South American Nations (#20481)
- ♦ **CSocD** United Nations Commission for Social Development (#20535)
- ♦ **CSO-NB8-Food** Committee of Senior Officials of the Nordic Countries, Estonia, Latvia and Lithuania in the Field of Food Issues (#04286)
- ♦ CSoNet – International Conference on Computational Data and Social Networks (meeting series)

♦ CSO Partnership for Development Effectiveness (CPDE) 04976

Partenariat des OSC pour l'efficacité du développement (POED)

Global Coordinator c/o IBON Intl, 3rd Fl- IBON Ctr, 114 Timog Ave, 1103 Quezon City, Philippines. T. +6329277060 – +6329277061 – +6329277062. Fax +6329276981. E-mail: secretariat@csopartnership.org – info@csopartnership.org.
URL: http://www.csopartnership.org/

History Dec 2012, Nairobi (Kenya). **Aims** Promote development effectiveness where respect for human rights, participatory democracy, social and environmental justice and sustainability, gender equality, decent work, sustainable change, and peace and security are achieved. **Structure** Global Council; Coordination Committee; Global Secretariat; Independent Accountability Committee; Regional, Sub-regional, and National Coordination Bodies. **Languages** English, French, Spanish. **Staff** 5.00 FTE, paid. **Finance** Donations from: Canadian Government; *Irish Aid*; *Swedish International Development Cooperation Agency (Sida)*. Budget (annual): US$ 2 million.
Members Organizations (about 2000). Membership countries not specified. Included in the above, 3 organizations listed in this Yearbook:
Included in the above, 3 organizations listed in this Yearbook:
IBON International (#11037); *Pacific Islands Association of Non-Governmental Organizations (PIANGO, #17961)*; *People's Coalition on Food Sovereignty (PCFS, #18303)*.
NGO Relations Member of: *Effective Institutions Platform (EIP, #05384)*. Supports: *Pacific Islands Association of Non-Governmental Organizations (PIANGO, #17961)*. [2020/XJ7758/y/**F**]

- ♦ **CSPA** Consumer Specialty Products Association (#04774)
- ♦ CSPA / see Marketing Agencies Association Worldwide (#16585)
- ♦ CSPEC / see Party of European Socialists (#18249)
- ♦ CSPI – Center for Science in the Public Interest (internationally oriented national body)
- ♦ CSPI – Convention Sales Professionals International (internationally oriented national body)
- ♦ **CSPLP** Comunidade Sindical dos Paises de Lingua Portuguesa (#04431)
- ♦ **CSPM** Confederación Sudamericana de Pentatlon Moderno (#04492)
- ♦ CSPOC / see Consensus for Sustainable People, Organisations and Communities
- ♦ **CSPOC** Conference of Speakers and Presiding Officers of the Commonwealth (#04649)
- ♦ CSPOC – Consensus for Sustainable People, Organisations and Communities (internationally oriented national body)
- ♦ **CSPPS** Civil Society Platform for Peacebuilding and Statebuilding (#03970)
- ♦ CSPS – Centre for Security and Peace Studies (internationally oriented national body)
- ♦ CSP – Societas Sacerdotum Missionariorum a Sancto Paulo Apostolo (religious order)
- ♦ CSP / see World Skate America (#21788)
- ♦ **CSR Asia** Corporate Social Responsibility in Asia (#04843)
- ♦ CSRCAE / see International Society for Comparative Adult Education (#15022)
- ♦ **CSR** Caribbean Society of Radiologists (#03556)
- ♦ CSR Conflict Management Center / see ACCESS Facility (#00048)
- ♦ **CSR** Convenio Simón Rodriguez (#19284)

♦ CSR Europe 04977

Exec Dir Rue Victor Oudart 7, 1030 Brussels, Belgium. T. +3225411610. Fax +3225028458. E-mail: info@csreurope.org.
URL: http://www.csreurope.org/

History Founded 1995, as *European Business Network for Social Cohesion (EBNSC)*, following the signing of the 'the European Declaration of Businesses against Social Exclusion'. Current title adopted, Nov 2000. Full title: *CSR Europe: Business Network for Corporate Social Responsibility*. Launched joint Enterprise 2020 initiative, 2010. EU Transparency Register: 56502415122-32. **Aims** Allow companies to share best practices on Corporate Social Responsibility (CSR) and innovate with peers, thus shaping the business and political agenda on sustainability and competitiveness. **Structure** General Assembly; Advisory Board; Board of Directors; Executive Office. **Languages** English. **Staff** 20.00 FTE, paid. **Finance** Members' dues. Paid services for members. **Activities** Awareness raising; guidance/assistance/consulting; training/education; events/meetings. **Events** *European SDG Summit* Brussels (Belgium) 2021, *European SDG Summit* Brussels (Belgium) 2020, *Brussels SDG Summit* Brussels (Belgium) 2019, *Workshop on Circular Economy : Business and Policy* Brussels (Belgium) 2019, *Workshop on Circular Use of Materials in Renewable Energy* Brussels (Belgium) 2019. **Publications** Guides; books; toolkits.
Members National partner organizations (44) in 31 countries:
Austria, Belgium, Bulgaria, Croatia, Czechia, Denmark, Estonia, Finland, France, Germany, Greece, Hungary, Ireland, Italy, Kosovo, Latvia, Lithuania, Luxembourg, Netherlands, Norway, Poland, Portugal, Romania, Serbia, Slovakia, Slovenia, Spain, Sweden, Türkiye, UK, Ukraine.
Multinational companies (about 54). Membership countries not specified.
IGO Relations *European Commission (EC, #06633)* European Alliance for Apprenticeships (EAfA); *European Schoolnet (EUN, #08433)*. **NGO Relations** Partners include: *Association des chambres de commerce et d'industrie européennes (EUROCHAMBRES, #02423)*; *JA Europe (#16085)*; national organizations. [2020/XF4895/**F**]

- ♦ CSR Europe: Business Network for Corporate Social Responsibility / see CSR Europe (#04977)
- ♦ CSRMESS – Centre for Scientific Research and Middle East Strategic Studies (internationally oriented national body)
- ♦ **CSRP** Commission sous-régionale des pêches (#20026)
- ♦ CSRS – Cervical Spine Research Society (internationally oriented national body)
- ♦ **CSRS-Europe** Cervical Spine Research Society – Europe (#03837)
- ♦ CSS / see Institute for Strategic Studies, Ulaanbaatar
- ♦ CSSA – Concrete Society of Southern Africa (internationally oriented national body)
- ♦ CSSA – Conseil supérieur du sport en Afrique (inactive)
- ♦ CSSC – Centre for Science, Society and Citizenship (internationally oriented national body)
- ♦ CSS – Center for Security Studies (internationally oriented national body)
- ♦ CSS – Centre for Strategic Studies, Amman (internationally oriented national body)
- ♦ CSSC – International Workshop on Crystalline Silicon for Solar Cells (meeting series)
- ♦ **CSS** Cognitive Science Society (#04086)
- ♦ **CSS** Complex Systems Society (#04418)
- ♦ CSS – Congregatio a SS Stigmatibus Domini Nostri Jesu Christi (religious order)
- ♦ CSSCR – International Symposium on Cutting Edge of Computer Simulation of Solidification, Casting and Refining (meeting series)
- ♦ CSSDCA – Conference on Security, Stability, Development and Cooperation in Africa (inactive)
- ♦ **CSSI** Cell Stress Society International (#03629)
- ♦ CSSI Community (unconfirmed)
- ♦ CSS-NZ – Centre for Strategic Studies, New Zealand (internationally oriented national body)
- ♦ **CSSP** Chemical Society of the South Pacific (#03862)
- ♦ CSSp – Congregatio Sancti Spiritus sub Tutela Immaculati Cordis Beatissimae Virginis Mariae (religious order)
- ♦ CSSR – Centre for Strategic Studies and Research (internationally oriented national body)
- ♦ **CSSR** Confederación Sudamericana de Squash Racket (#19702)
- ♦ CSSR – Congregatio Sanctissimi Redemptoris (religious order)
- ♦ CSSR – Council of Societies for the Study of Religion (internationally oriented national body)
- ♦ CSSS – Institute of International Affairs – Centre for Small State Studies (internationally oriented national body)
- ♦ CSSTC / see Non-Aligned Movement Centre for South-South Technical Cooperation (#17147)
- ♦ CSSTE-AF – Centre for Space Science and Technology in Africa, Morocco /Affiliated to the United Nations/ (see: #04277)
- ♦ CSSTEAP – Centre for Space Science and Technology Education in Asia and the Pacific /Affiliated to the United Nations/ (see: #04277)
- ♦ CSSTE-LAC – Centre for Space Science and Technology Education in Latin America and the Caribbean /Affiliated to the United Nations/ (see: #04277)
- ♦ CSTA – Consejo Sindical de Trabajadores Andinos (inactive)
- ♦ CSTAL – Confederación Sindical de los Trabajadores de América Latina (inactive)
- ♦ CSTCE / see European Transport Workers' Federation (#08941)
- ♦ CST – Commonwealth of Independent States' Collective Security Treaty (1992 treaty)
- ♦ **CST** Confederación Sudamericana de Tiro (#04494)
- ♦ **CST** Conférence des services de traduction des états européens (#04650)
- ♦ CST / see Council on International Educational Exchange (#04901)
- ♦ **CSTD** United Nations Commission on Science and Technology for Development (#20534)
- ♦ CSTE – Consortium for the Study of European Transition (no recent information)
- ♦ CSTM – Centro Studi Terzo Mondo (internationally oriented national body)
- ♦ CSTM / see Confederación Sudamericana de Tenis de Mesa (#04493)
- ♦ **CSTO** Collective Security Treaty Organization (#04103)
- ♦ CSUA – Conseil du sport de l'Union Africaine (unconfirmed)
- ♦ CSUCA / see Confederación Universitaria Centroamericana (#04497)
- ♦ **CSUCA** Confederación Universitaria Centroamericana (#04497)
- ♦ CSUN – Coalition for a Strong United Nations (internationally oriented national body)
- ♦ CSV / see Volunteering Matters
- ♦ CSVBD / see Village Earth
- ♦ **CSV** Confederación Sudamericana de Voleibol (#04495)
- ♦ CSV – Congregatio Clericorum Parochialium seu Catechistarum Sancti Viatoris (religious order)
- ♦ **CSVGC** NGO Committee on Spirituality, Values and Global Concerns (#17116)
- ♦ **CSVPA** IUCN WCPA Specialist Group on Cultural and Spiritual Values of Protected Areas (#16080)
- ♦ CSVR – Centre for the Study of Violence and Reconciliation (internationally oriented national body)
- ♦ CSW (internationally oriented national body)
- ♦ **CSWA** Caribbean Spa and Wellness Association (#03558)
- ♦ CSWE – Simon Wiesenthal Centre-Europe (internationally oriented national body)
- ♦ **CSW** United Nations Commission on the Status of Women (#20536)
- ♦ CTA – Caribbean Tourism Association (inactive)
- ♦ CTA – Centre technique de coopération agricole et rurale (inactive)
- ♦ CTA – Communicating the Arts (meeting series)
- ♦ CTAD – Clinical Trials on Alzheimer's Disease (meeting series)
- ♦ CTAL – Confederación de Trabajadores de América Latina (inactive)

♦ CTAM Europe 04978

Main Office 41 Av des Arts, 1040 Brussels, Belgium. E-mail: info@ctameurope.com.
URL: http://www.ctameurope.com/

History Set up by US CTAM. CTAM stands for *Cable and Telecommunications Association for Marketing*. Since Aug 2015, integrated into *GIGAEurope AISBL (#10151)*. **Aims** Be a resource of marketing education, information and networking opportunities for individuals who work for *European* cable companies, and for programmers and broadband companies seeking to distribute products and services via cable's broadband pipe throughout Europe. **Structure** Board of Directors, comprising Chairman, Secretary/Treasurer and 20 members. **Events** *Annual EuroSummit* Amsterdam (Netherlands) 2015, *Annual EuroSummit* Barcelona (Spain) 2013, *Annual EuroSummit* Budapest (Hungary) 2010, *Annual EuroSummit* Lisbon (Portugal) 2009. **Members** Full (about 300). [2020/XJ0713/**E**]

- ♦ CTB / see Enabel
- ♦ CTBT – Comprehensive Nuclear-Test-Ban Treaty (1996 treaty)
- ♦ **CTBTO** Comprehensive Nuclear-Test-Ban Treaty Organization (#04420)
- ♦ **CTBTO** Preparatory Commission for the Comprehensive Nuclear-Test-Ban Treaty Organization (#18482)
- ♦ **CTBUH** Council on Tall Buildings and Urban Habitat (#04921)
- ♦ CTCA – Commission for Technical Cooperation in Africa South of the Sahara (inactive)
- ♦ **CTCAP** Comisión para el Desarrollo Cientifico y Tecnológico de Centro América y Panama (#04132)
- ♦ CTC – Caribbean Telecommunications Council (no recent information)
- ♦ CTC – Combating Terrorism Center (internationally oriented national body)
- ♦ CTC – Commonwealth Tourism Centre (internationally oriented national body)
- ♦ CTC – Consejo de Trabajadores del Caribe (no recent information)
- ♦ **CTC** Counter-Terrorism Committee (#04928)
- ♦ CTC International – Comfort the Children International (internationally oriented national body)
- ♦ **CTCN** Climate Technology Centre and Network (#04023)
- ♦ CTCP – Centre for Transnational Crime Prevention, University of Wollongong (internationally oriented national body)
- ♦ CTCS Network – Caribbean Technological Consultancy Services Network (see: #03492)
- ♦ **CTCS** Steering Committee on Trade Capacity and Standards (#19979)
- ♦ CTEF / see EUROFLUOR (#05681)
- ♦ **CTeurope** Communication Technique en Europe (#20116)
- ♦ CTF – Communauté des télévisions francophones (inactive)
- ♦ **CTF Europe** Children's Tumor Foundation Europe (#03880)
- ♦ **CTFM** Comité des transports ferroviaires du Maghreb (#18609)
- ♦ **CTGA** Comité transnational des géotechniciens d'Afrique (#04199)
- ♦ CTI / see Bountifield International
- ♦ **Cti** Castings Technology International (#03598)
- ♦ **CTIC** Central American Table Tennis Confederation (#03673)
- ♦ **CTI-CFF** Coral Triangle Initiative on Coral Reefs, Fisheries and Food Security (#04833)
- ♦ CTI – Climate Technology Initiative (inactive)
- ♦ **CTI** Convention against Torture Initiative (#04786)
- ♦ CTIF / see CTIF International Association of Fire and Rescue Services (#04979)

♦ CTIF International Association of Fire and Rescue Services 04979

Association internationale des services d'incendie et de secours CTIF – Internationale Vereinigung des Feuerwehr- und Rettungswesen CTIF

Gen Sec c/o Fire Association Slovenia, Trzaska 221, 1000 Ljubljana, Slovenia. T. +38612419754. E-mail: contact@ctif.org.
Pres address not obtained.
URL: http://www.ctif.org/

History 12 Aug 1900, Paris (France), as *Comité international des sapeurs-pompiers.* Reconstituted 1929, Paris. Statutes adopted 1930, Liège (Belgium). Reconstituted under the following title: *International Technical Committee for the Prevention and Extinction of Fire – Comité technique international de prévention et d'extinction du feu (CTIF) – Internationales Technisches Komitee für Vorbeugenden Brandschutz und Feuerlöschwesen – Mezdunarodnyj Tehniceskij Komitet po Predotvrasceniju i Tuseniju Pozarov – Comitato Tecnico Internazionale di Prevenzione ed Estinzione Incendi*, 17 Jul 1946, Paris, when new statutes were adopted; these latter statutes replaced 30 Apr 1966, Titisee (Germany FR), and further modified: 1 Jul 1969, Vienna (Austria); 26 Sep 1974, Luxembourg; 22 Jul 1981, Böblingen (Germany FR). Present statutes adopted 28 Jul 2001, Kuopio (Finland). Sometimes referred to as *Association internationale des pompiers.* Previously also referred to in French and German as: *CTIF Organisation internationale des sapeurs-pompiers – CTIF Internationaler Feuerwehrverband.* **Aims** Develop theories and practice relating to preventive fire protection and *firefighting*; stimulate research into the organization and techniques of firefighting, and publish resulting inventions and research in this field; initiate and promote friendly relationships among active members in all countries, both from fire brigades and from the fire protection industry; coordinate and organize symposia and fire brigade competitions. **Structure** Delegates' Conference (annual), consisting of President and up to 3 delegates from each member nation. Executive Committee, consisting of President, General Secretary, Treasurer and 7 Vice-Presidents. General Secretariat, headed by Secretary-General. Commissions (9): Europe; History of Fire Services and CTIF, Museums and Fires; Hazardous Materials; Youth Leaders; Fire Prevention; Fire Brigade Health Services; Rescue and Fire Services at Airports. **Languages** English, French, German. **Staff** 0.50 FTE, voluntary. **Finance** Sources: members' dues. **Activities** Draws up working programmes; gathers data on technical and scientific experiments and achievements in the field of fire protection and rescue. Studies and disseminates scientific, technical and practical knowledge and experience in the field, and draws up appropriate recommendations. Sessions, meetings, international symposia, exhibitions devoted to fire protection techniques, drill contests for firemen and junior firemen. **Events** *Delegates Assembly* Ljubljana (Slovenia) 2020, *Delegates Assembly* Martigny (Switzerland) 2019, *Delegates Assembly* Helsinki (Finland) 2016, *Meeting* Kongsberg (Norway) 2016, *Delegates Conference* Bratislava (Slovakia) 2012. **Publications** *CTIF Hotnews* – bulletin. *Fire Fighter Safety Survey*; *First Response Manual for Radioactive Emergencies.*
Members National associations in 51 countries:
Albania, Angola, Austria, Belarus, Belgium, Belize, Bosnia-Herzegovina, Bulgaria, Costa Rica, Croatia, Czechia, Denmark, El Salvador, Estonia, Finland, France, Georgia, Germany, Greece, Guatemala, Holy See, Honduras, Hungary, Ireland, Israel, Italy, Latvia, Liechtenstein, Lithuania, Luxembourg, Montenegro, Netherlands, New Zealand, Nicaragua, North Macedonia, Norway, Panama, Poland, Portugal, Romania, Russia, Serbia, Slovakia, Slovenia, Spain, Sweden, Switzerland, Türkiye, UK, Ukraine, USA.
Associate members in 9 countries:
Austria, Bulgaria, France, Germany, Russia, Spain, Sweden, Switzerland, USA.
Included in the above, 1 international association:
European Committee of the Manufacturers of Fire Protection Equipment and Fire Fighting Vehicles (#06659).
IGO Relations *United Nations Committee of Experts on the Transport of Dangerous Goods and on the Globally Harmonized System of Classification and Labelling of Chemicals (Committee of Experts on TDG and GHS, #20543).* **NGO Relations** In liaison with technical committees of: *International Organization for Standardization (ISO, #14473).* [2020/XC2617/**C**]

- ♦ CTIF Internationaler Feuerwehrverband / see CTIF International Association of Fire and Rescue Services (#04979)
- ♦ CTIF Organisation internationale des sapeurs-pompiers / see CTIF International Association of Fire and Rescue Services (#04979)
- ♦ CTI Music Ministries (internationally oriented national body)
- ♦ CTIO – Cerro Tololo Inter-American Observatory (internationally oriented national body)
- ♦ CTIR – Center for Teaching International Relations (internationally oriented national body)
- ♦ CTJ / see Conférence TransJurassienne
- ♦ CTJ – Conférence TransJurassienne (internationally oriented national body)
- ♦ **CTLS** Core Technologies for Life Sciences (#04835)
- ♦ CTM / see Carrefour d'éducation à la solidarité internationale – Québec
- ♦ CTM-SIV – Controinformazione Terzo Mondo – Servizio Internazionale Volontario (internationally oriented national body)
- ♦ **CTN** Coalition Theory Network (#04069)
- ♦ CTNNB1 Syndrome Awareness Worldwide (internationally oriented national body)
- ♦ **CTO** Caribbean Tourism Organization (#03561)
- ♦ **CTO** Commonwealth Telecommunications Organisation (#04365)
- ♦ CTOD – IAGOD Commission on Tectonics of Ore Deposits (see: #11910)
- ♦ **CTOS** Connective Tissue Oncology Society (#04682)
- ♦ CTPA – Continental Tournaments Players Association (inactive)
- ♦ CTP – Caribbean Telecommunications Partnership (unconfirmed)
- ♦ **CTP** Communauté de travail des Pyrénées (#21057)
- ♦ CTPH – Conservation Through Public Health (unconfirmed)
- ♦ CT/RAC / see Regional Activity Centre for Sustainable Consumption and Production (#18747)
- ♦ CTRC – Caribbean Tourism Research and Development Centre (inactive)
- ♦ **CTRMS** Cell Transplant and Regenerative Medicine Society (#03630)
- ♦ **CTS-AP** Critical Tourism Studies – Asia Pacific (#04962)
- ♦ CTS / see Cell Transplant and Regenerative Medicine Society (#03630)
- ♦ CTSC International – International Association of Community TeleService Centres (no recent information)
- ♦ **CTS** Critical Tourism Studies (#04961)
- ♦ CTSSA – Catholic Theological Society of Southern Africa (internationally oriented national body)
- ♦ CT / see Steering Committee on Trade Capacity and Standards (#19979)
- ♦ CTTA / see Commonwealth Table Tennis Federation (#04364)
- ♦ CTTE (meeting series)
- ♦ CTTF – Caribbean Table Tennis Federation (no recent information)
- ♦ **CTU** Caribbean Telecommunications Union (#03560)
- ♦ CTUC – Commonwealth Trade Union Council (inactive)
- ♦ CTVM – Centre for Tropical Veterinary Medicine, Edinburgh (internationally oriented national body)
- ♦ CTWO – Center for Third World Organizing (internationally oriented national body)
- ♦ CTWU / see European Transport Workers' Federation (#08941)
- ♦ CUA – Circumpolar Universities Association (inactive)
- ♦ **CUA** Creators Union of Arab (#04948)
- ♦ CUAHA – Churches United Against HIV and AIDS (inactive)
- ♦ CUAMM – Medici con l'Africa (internationally oriented national body)
- ♦ CUA / see Red de Ciclovias Recreativas de las Américas (#18640)
- ♦ **CUCSA** Confederation of University and College Sports Associations (#04578)
- ♦ CUE / see International Education Centre of Svendborg
- ♦ **CUEA** Catholic University of Eastern Africa, The (#03610)
- ♦ **CUEA** Conseil de l'unité économique arabe (#04859)
- ♦ CUEBC – Centro Universitario Europeo per i Beni Culturali, Ravello (internationally oriented national body)
- ♦ CUE – Citizens for a United Earth (internationally oriented national body)
- ♦ CUFA – Credit Union Foundation Australia (internationally oriented national body)
- ♦ CUFDES – Comité universitaire francophone pour le développement des échanges scientifiques (internationally oriented national body)
- ♦ **CUG** Cray User Group (#04945)
- ♦ CUGH – Consortium of Universities for Global Health (internationally oriented national body)
- ♦ **CUHD** Colegio Universitario Henry Dunant (#04111)
- ♦ **CUHD** Collège universitaire Henry Dunant (#04111)
- ♦ **CUIB** Consejo Universitario Iberoamericano (#04727)
- ♦ CUIC – Churches United In Christ (internationally oriented national body)
- ♦ CUIDES – Consejo Universitario Interamericano para el Desarrollo Económico y Social (no recent information)
- ♦ CUIROP – Confédération européenne du commerce de cuir en gros (inactive)
- ♦ Cúirt Bhreithiúnais na gCómhphobal Eorpach / see Court of Justice of the European Union (#04938)
- ♦ Cúirt Chéadchéime na gCómhphobal Eorpach (inactive)
- ♦ Cúirt Iniúchóiri na Heorpa (#06854)

♦ CULINARIA EUROPE 04980

SG Reuterstr 151, 53113 Bonn, Germany. E-mail: info@culinaria-europe.eu.
URL: http://www.culinaria-europe.eu/

History 2010, by restructuring and merging *Association internationale de l'industrie des bouillons et potages (AIIBP, inactive), Fédération des associations de l'industrie des bouillons et potages de la CEE (FAIBP, inactive)* and *Federation of the Condiment Sauce Industries, Mustard and Fruit and Vegetables Prepared in Oil and Vinegar of the European Union (FIC EUROPE, inactive).* Full title: *Federation of Association and Enterprises of Industrial Culinary Product Producers in Europe – Vereinigung der Verbände und Hersteller Kulinarischer Lebensmittel in Europa.* **Aims** Promote and protect members' interests vis à vis authorities and other administrative offices; give advice and submit proposals to authorities and other administrative offices; cultivate cooperation with other organizations particularly of the food industry; act as a central medium of communication with the European Commission, European Parliament and FoodDrinkEurope. **Structure** General Assembly. Board; Technical Commission; Vinegar Committee. **Languages** English. **Staff** 4.00 FTE, paid. **Finance** Members' dues.
Members National associations of produces of culinary products; individual companies involved in the industrial production of culinary products. Members in 13 countries:
Austria, Belgium, Denmark, France, Germany, Greece, Italy, Netherlands, Norway, Poland, Spain, Switzerland, UK.
IGO Relations Participates as observer in the activities of: *Codex Alimentarius Commission (CAC, #04081).*
NGO Relations Member of: *FoodDrinkEurope (#09841).* [2013.07.02/XJ4598/**D**]

- ♦ Cultivating New Frontiers in Agriculture (internationally oriented national body)
- ♦ Cultural Council of the Nordkallot Committee (inactive)
- ♦ Cultural Creative Industry Association / see Asia-Pacific Cultural Creative Industry Association
- ♦ Cultural Exchanges in the Mediterranean (#05281)
- ♦ Cultural Foundation of the Americas (internationally oriented national body)
- ♦ Cultural Heritage Asia Pacific Network (internationally oriented national body)
- ♦ Cultural Heritage without Borders (internationally oriented national body)
- ♦ Cultural Heritage without Borders (internationally oriented national body)
- ♦ Cultural Heritage Centre for Asia and the Pacific / see Cultural Heritage Asia Pacific Network
- ♦ Cultural Homestay International (internationally oriented national body)
- ♦ Cultural Integration Fellowship (internationally oriented national body)
- ♦ Cultural Survival (internationally oriented national body)
- ♦ Cultural Treaty (1945 treaty)
- ♦ Cultural Vistas (internationally oriented national body)

♦ Culture Action Europe (CAE) 04981

Main Office Rue Baron Horta 13, 1st Floor, 1000 Brussels, Belgium. T. +3225344002. Fax +3225341150. E-mail: contact@cultureactioneurope.org.
Registered Address Rue Ravenstein 23, 1000 Brussels, Belgium.
URL: http://cultureactioneurope.org/

History 1992, Brussels (Belgium). Former names and other names: *European Forum for the Arts and Heritage (EFAH)* – former (1922 to 24 Apr 2008); *Forum européen pour les arts et le patrimoine (FEAP)* – former (1922 to 24 Apr 2008). Registration: Banque Carrefour des Entreprises, No/ID: 0453.404.526, Start date: 1 Sep 1994, Belgium, Bruxelles; EU Transparency Register, No/ID: 237149421566-71, Start date: 3 May 2016. **Aims** Be the first port of call for informed opinion and debate about arts and cultural policy in the EU. **Structure** General Assembly (annual); Executive Committee; Secretariat, based in Brussels (Belgium). **Languages** English, French. **Staff** 4.00 FTE, paid. **Finance** Sources: members' dues. Supported by: *European Commission (EC, #06633); European Cultural Foundation (ECF, #06868).* **Activities** Advocacy/lobbying/activism; events/meetings; networking/liaising; research/documentation. **Events** *Annual General Assembly* Brussels (Belgium) 2021, *Members Forum* Brussels (Belgium) 2021, *Annual General Assembly and Members Meeting* Brussels (Belgium) 2020, *Members Forum* Brussels (Belgium) 2019, *General Assembly* Timisoara (Romania) 2018. **Publications** *CAE Dispatches* in English, French; *CAE Reflection Papers.* Policy positions; ad-hoc publications; working papers; reports; minutes of meetings.
Members Full: organizations working in the arts and heritage world and which have members of their own, such as artists' organizations, networks, umbrella associations and federations. Associate: individual organizations (eg venues, theatre companies, galleries, orchestras). Honorary. Members (over 110) in 17 countries:
Albania, Austria, Belgium, Cyprus, Finland, France, Germany, Ireland, Italy, Netherlands, Norway, Portugal, Romania, Slovakia, Sweden, Switzerland, UK.
Included in the above, 33 organizations listed in this Yearbook:
- *Amateo (#00765);*
- *Association Européenne des Conservatoires, Académies de Musique et Musikhochschulen (AEC, #02560);*
- *Baltic Sea Culture Centre, Gdansk;*
- *Conseil européen des associations de traducteurs littéraires (CEATL, #04686);*
- *Culture and Media Agency Europe (CUMEDIAE, #04983);*
- *Dutch Centre for International Cooperation (DutchCulture);*
- *European Association for Heritage Interpretation (Interpret Europe, #06067);*
- *European Choral Association – Europa Cantat (#06541);*
- *European Concert Hall Organisation (ECHO, #06696);*
- *European Federation of National Youth Orchestras (EFNYO, #07176);*
- *European Festivals Association (EFA, #07242);*
- *European League of Institutes of the Arts (ELIA, #07670);*
- *European Museum Forum (EMF, #07836);*
- *European Music Council (EMC, #07837);*
- *European Network of Cultural Centres (ENCC, #07888);*
- *European Network of Cultural Centres in Historic Monuments (ACCR);*
- *European Theatre Convention (ETC, #08905);*
- *Europe Jazz Network (EJN, #09160);*
- *Fonds Roberto Cimetta (FRC, #09837);*
- *IETM – International Network for Contemporary Performing Arts (#11098);*
- *International Association for the Biennial of Young Artists from Europe and the Mediterranean (#11724);*
- *International Association of Music Information Centres (IAMIC, #12041);*
- *Internationale Gesellschaft der Bildende Künste (IGBK);*
- *Jeunesses Musicales International (JMI, #16110);*
- *Literature Across Frontiers (LAF, #16492);*
- *Network of European Museum Organizations (NEMO, #17024);*
- *Nordic Centre of Heritage Learning and Creativity (#17230);*
- *Opera Europa (#17771);*
- *Pearle – Live Performance Europe (#18284);*
- *Regional Observatory on Financing Culture in East-Central Europe (The Budapest Observatory);*
- *Réseau européen pour la sensibilisation à l'opéra et à la danse (RESEO, #18878);*
- *Trans Europe Halles – A Network of Independent Cultural Centres (TEH, #20211);*
- *Worldwide Network of Artists Residencies (Res Artis, #21928).*

Contributing Partners (6):
Council of Europe (CE, #04881); EUROCITIES (#05662); European Commission (EC, #06633); European Cultural Foundation (ECF, #06868); European Parliament (EP, #08146); INTERARTS Foundation.
NGO Relations Member of (2): *EU Civil Society Contact Group (CSCG, #05572); SDG Watch Europe (#19162).* [2022/XF2692/y/**F**]

- ♦ Culture et Liberté (internationally oriented national body)

♦ Culturelink – the Network of Networks for Research and Cooperation in Cultural Development 04982

Culturelink – Réseau des Réseaux our la Recherche et la Cooperation dans le Développement Culturel – Culturelink – la Red de las Redes para la Investigación y Cooperación en el Desarrollo Cultural

Contact c/o IRMO, Vukotinoviceva 2, PO Box 303, HR-10000 Zagreb, Croatia. T. +38514877460. Fax +38514828361. E-mail: clink@irmo.hr.
URL: http://www.culturelink.org/

History Jun 1989, Paris (France). Founded by *UNESCO (#20322)* and *Council of Europe (CE, #04881)*, at 'Consultation of Representatives of Regional and Subregional Networks for Cultural Development Research and Cooperation'. Focal point: *Institute for Development and International Relations (IRMO)*. **Aims** Serve as a collaboration platform for cultural researchers, policy makers and practitioners. **Structure** Team; Editorial Board. **Languages** English, French, Spanish. **Staff** 5.00 FTE, paid. **Finance** Sources: contributions; government support; grants; sponsorship. Supported by: *Council of Europe (CE, #04881); UNESCO (#20322)*. **Activities** Events/meetings; knowledge management/information dissemination; publishing activities; research and development. **Events** *International Conference on International Cultural Relations of the European Union and the role of Croatia* Rijeka (Croatia) 2019, *World Conference* Zagreb (Croatia) 2009, *World Conference* Zagreb (Croatia) 2005, *World conference* South Africa 2003, *Joint seminar / Round Table* Zagreb (Croatia) 2003. **Publications** *C-News* (12 a year) – newsletter. *Cultures in Cooperation: Realities and Tendencies – Culturelink Joint Publications Series* (2021); *Networks: The Evolving Aspects of Culture in the 21st Century – Culturelink Joint Publications Series* (2011); *Digital Cultures: The Changing Dynamics – Culturelink Joint Publications Series* (2008); *Dynamics of Communication: New Ways and New Actors – Culturelink Joint Publications Series* (2006). **Information Services** *Culturelink Members and Partners Database*; *WWW Resource Centre*.
Members Networks, associations, foundations, institutions and individuals (about 1,000) in 102 countries:
Albania, Algeria, Andorra, Angola, Argentina, Armenia, Australia, Austria, Azerbaijan, Bangladesh, Belarus, Belgium, Bolivia, Bosnia-Herzegovina, Botswana, Brazil, Bulgaria, Burkina Faso, Cameroon, Canada, Chile, China, Colombia, Congo Brazzaville, Congo DR, Costa Rica, Côte d'Ivoire, Croatia, Cuba, Cyprus, Czechia, Denmark, Ecuador, El Salvador, Estonia, Ethiopia, Finland, France, Gabon, Gambia, Germany, Ghana, Greece, Guinea, Holy See, Hungary, India, Indonesia, Iran Islamic Rep, Ireland, Italy, Jamaica, Japan, Kenya, Korea Rep, Latvia, Lithuania, Luxembourg, Macau, Malaysia, Mali, Malta, Mexico, Moldova, Mongolia, Morocco, Mozambique, Netherlands, New Zealand, Nicaragua, Nigeria, Norway, Pakistan, Panama, Paraguay, Peru, Philippines, Poland, Portugal, Romania, Russia, Samoa, Senegal, Serbia, Singapore, Slovakia, Slovenia, South Africa, Spain, Sweden, Switzerland, Tanzania UR, Thailand, Togo, Tunisia, Türkiye, Uganda, UK, Ukraine, USA, Venezuela, Zimbabwe.
IGO Relations Support from: *Council of Europe (CE, #04881); UNESCO (#20322)*. [2022.03.04/XF4213/**F**]

- ♦ Culturelink – la Red de las Redes para la Investigación y Cooperación en el Desarrollo Cultural (#04982)
- ♦ Culturelink – Réseau des Réseaux our la Recherche et la Cooperation dans le Développement Culturel (#04982)

♦ Culture and Media Agency Europe (CUMEDIAE) 04983

CEO Chaussée de Wavre 220, 1050 Brussels, Belgium. T. +3222580877. E-mail: info@culture-media.eu.
URL: http://culture-media.eu/

History 2012. Registration: Royaume de Belgique Service public fédéral justice, No/ID: WL22/16.124, Start date: 15 Feb 2012, Belgium; Banque-Carrefour des Entreprises, No/ID: 0844.076.380, Start date: 1 Mar 2012, Belgium; EU Transparency Register, No/ID: 373648915745-30. **Aims** Support the international dimension of projects and activities linked to the arts and the creative economy, and their access to funding. **Languages** English. **Staff** 3.00 FTE, paid; 3.00 FTE, voluntary. **Finance** Sources: private foundations; revenue from activities/projects. **Activities** Advocacy/lobbying/activism; capacity building; events/meetings; guidance/assistance/consulting; research/documentation. **Publications** *CUMEDIAE Newsletter* (12 a year).
Members Full in 9 countries:
Austria, Belgium, China, France, Germany, Italy, Netherlands, Slovenia, Spain.
IGO Relations *Convention on the Protection and Promotion of the Diversity of Cultural Expressions (2005)*.
NGO Relations Member of: *Culture Action Europe (CAE, #04981)*. [2022/XM6909/**F**]

- ♦ Culture of Peace Initiative (unconfirmed)

♦ Culture Resource 04984

Al Mawred Al Thaqafy

Main Office Square Sainctelette 19, 1000 Brussels, Belgium.
Regional Office Ghazzawi Bld, Ground Flr, Bliss St, Beirut, Lebanon. T. +96111360415 – +961181776797.
URL: http://www.mawred.org/

History 2003. **Aims** Seek to support *artistic creativity* in the *Arab* region; encourage *cultural exchange* within the region and beyond. **Structure** General Assembly; Artistic Board. **Languages** Arabic, English, French. **Activities** Projects/programmes; capacity building; training/education; publishing activities. [2019.10.17/XJ6167/**F**]

- ♦ Between Cultures (internationally oriented national body)
- ♦ Cumann Eorpach na Muinteoiri (#02565)
- ♦ Cumann Scriobhnoiri Eorpach (#02516)
- ♦ Cumbre de las Américas (meeting series)
- ♦ Cumbre Mundial de Comunicación Política (meeting series)
- ♦ CUM – Centro Unitario per la Cooperazione Missionaria tra le Chiese (internationally oriented national body)
- ♦ **CUM** Communauté des universités méditerranéennes (#04403)
- ♦ **CUM** Comunità delle Università Mediterranee (#04403)
- ♦ **CUMEDIAE** Culture and Media Agency Europe (#04983)
- ♦ Cummings Center for Russian and East European Studies (internationally oriented national body)
- ♦ Cummings Foundation (internationally oriented national body)
- ♦ Gummings Institute for World Justice (internationally oriented national body)
- ♦ Cummings Properties Foundation / see Cummings Foundation
- ♦ Cumulus / see The Global Association of Art and Design Education and Research (#10241)
- ♦ **Cumulus Association** The Global Association of Art and Design Education and Research (#10241)
- ♦ CUNA International / see World Council of Credit Unions (#21324)
- ♦ **CUNCR** Center for United Nations Constitutional Research (#03653)
- ♦ CUNR / see Citizens for Global Solutions
- ♦ Cuntelles Keltek (#03632)
- ♦ CUPUM – International Conference on Computers in Urban Planning and Urban Management (meeting series)
- ♦ **CURA** Caribbean Urological Association (#03563)
- ♦ Curamericas (internationally oriented national body)
- ♦ Curatio International Foundation (internationally oriented national body)
- ♦ CURE – Center for UN Reform Education (internationally oriented national body)
- ♦ Cure International (internationally oriented national body)
- ♦ Currency Snake System (inactive)
- ♦ Current Research in Egyptology (meeting series)
- ♦ Curtea de Conturi Europeana (#06854)
- ♦ Curtea de Justitie a Comunitatila Europene / see Court of Justice of the European Union (#04938)
- ♦ Curtea de Justitie a Uniunii Europene (#04938)
- ♦ Cuso / see Cuso International
- ♦ Cuso International (internationally oriented national body)
- ♦ Custodia Terrae Sanctae (#04985)
- ♦ Custodia di Terra Santa (#04985)
- ♦ Custodie de Terre Sainte (#04985)

♦ Custody of the Holy Land 04985

Custodie de Terre Sainte – Custodia di Terra Santa – Custodia Terrae Sanctae

Custos Custodia di Terra Santa, St Saviour Monastery, PO Box 186, 9100101 Jerusalem, Israel. T. +97226266561. E-mail: custodia@custodia.org.
URL: http://www.custodia.org/

History Founded 1217, by Saint Francis of Assisi, and present since that time in the Middle East. A Religious Province of the *Order of Friars Minor (OFM)*. **Aims** Maintain Holy Places; render assistance to the *spiritual* and physical needs of local people; assist pilgrim groups from around the world. **Structure** Headed by Custos and Discretorium (Board of Counsellors). **Languages** Arabic, English, Hebrew, Italian. **Staff** Franciscan friars (about 300) from 32 countries, with the collaboration of about 130 sisters from various women's Congregations. **Finance** Sources: part of the annual Good Friday Collection collected from Catholic parishes worldwide; OFM (Friars Minor). **Activities** Financial and/or material support; training/education; knowledge management/information dissemination. **Publications** *The Holy Land Review* (6 a year) in Arabic, English, French, Italian, Spanish. *Analecta* – series; *Collectanea of Studia Orientalia Christiana (SOC)* – series; *Collectio Maior* – series; *Collectio Minor* – series; *Ex Archivis Custodiae Terrae Sanctae* – series; *Liber Annus* – series. *Holy Land Sketchbooks* – collection; *Holy Places of Palestine* – collection. Religious, illustrative and tourist publications on the life of the Custody and of the Holy Land in general.
Members Works in 12 countries and territories:
Argentina, Cyprus, Egypt, Greece, Israel, Italy, Jordan, Lebanon, Palestine, Spain, Syrian AR, USA.
Commissariats (82) in 45 countries and territories:
Argentina, Australia, Austria, Belgium, Bolivia, Bosnia-Herzegovina, Brazil, Canada, Chile, Colombia, Costa Rica, Croatia, Cyprus, Czechia, Ecuador, El Salvador, France, Germany, Greece, Guatemala, Ireland, Italy, Malaysia, Malta, Mexico, Montenegro, Netherlands, New Zealand, Nicaragua, Panama, Papua New Guinea, Peru, Philippines, Poland, Portugal, Puerto Rico, Serbia, Singapore, South Africa, Spain, Switzerland, Taiwan, UK, USA, Venezuela. [2016.12.15/XF0778/**F**]

- ♦ Custom Electronic Design and Installation Association (internationally oriented national body)
- ♦ Customs Convention on the ATA Carnet for the Temporary Admission of Goods (1961 treaty)
- ♦ Customs Convention Concerning Facilities for the Importation of Goods for Display or Use at Exhibitions, Fairs, Meetings or Similar Events (1961 treaty)
- ♦ Customs Convention Concerning Spare Parts Used for Repairing EUROP Wagons (1958 treaty)
- ♦ Customs Convention Concerning Welfare Material for Seafarers (1964 treaty)
- ♦ Customs Convention on Containers, 1956 (1956 treaty)
- ♦ Customs Convention on Containers, 1972 (1972 treaty)
- ♦ Customs Convention on the International Transit of Goods (1971 treaty)
- ♦ Customs Convention on the International Transport of Goods under Cover of TIR Carnets, 1959 (1959 treaty)
- ♦ Customs Convention on the International Transport of Goods under Cover of TIR Carnets, 1975 (1975 treaty)
- ♦ Customs Convention Regarding ECS Carnets for Commercial Samples (1956 treaty)
- ♦ Customs Convention on the Temporary Importation of Commercial Road Vehicles (1956 treaty)
- ♦ Customs Convention on the Temporary Importation of Packings (1960 treaty)
- ♦ Customs Convention on the Temporary Importation of Pedagogic Material (1970 treaty)
- ♦ Customs Convention on the Temporary Importation of Private Road Vehicles (1954 treaty)
- ♦ Customs Convention on the Temporary Importation for Private Use of Aircraft and Pleasure Boats (1956 treaty)
- ♦ Customs Convention on the Temporary Importation of Professional Equipment (1961 treaty)
- ♦ Customs Convention on the Temporary Importation of Scientific Equipment (1968 treaty)
- ♦ Customs Co-operation Council / see World Customs Organization (#21350)
- ♦ Customs Heads of Administration Regional Meeting / see Oceania Customs Organisation (#17658)
- ♦ Customs and International Trade Bar Association (internationally oriented national body)

♦ Customs Laboratories European Network (CLEN) 04986

Address not obtained.
URL: https://ec.europa.eu/taxation_customs/business/customs-controls/customs-laboratories_en

History Set up to promote coordination among European Customs Laboratories of the *European Union (EU, #08967)*. Former names and other names: *Group of European Customs Laboratories (GCL)* – former (1999 to 2014). **Aims** Rationalize, coordinate and optimize the use of human and technical resources among the European Customs Laboratories. **Structure** Steering Group. **Activities** Networking/liaising. **Events** *Conference of the European customs chemists* Helsinki (Finland) 2010, *Conference of the European customs chemists* Athens (Greece) 2007, *Conference of the European customs chemists* Prague (Czech Rep) 2003, *Conference of the European customs chemists* Fiuggi Fonte (Italy) 2000. **Members** Laboratories and mobile laboratories (89) in all European Union countries. [AA2308/**F***]

- ♦ Customs Union Agreement between the Governments of South Africa, Botswana, Lesotho and Swaziland (1910 treaty)
- ♦ **CUT** Caribbean Union of Teachers (#03562)
- ♦ Cutis Laxa Internationale (internationally oriented national body)
- ♦ Cutis Marmorata Telangiectatica Congenita and Other Vascular Malformations / see CMTC-OVM
- ♦ CUTS – Consumer Unity and Trust Society (internationally oriented national body)
- ♦ **CUW** Clean Up the World (#03992)
- ♦ CVAA / see Atlantic Cities (#03008)
- ♦ **CVA** Commonwealth Veterinary Association (#04366)
- ♦ **CVC** Caribbean Vulnerable Communities Coalition (#03565)
- ♦ CV – Congregatio Vincentiana (religious order)
- ♦ **CV** Corpus Vitrearum (#04847)
- ♦ CVCS – Centro Volontari Cooperazione allo Sviluppo (internationally oriented national body)
- ♦ **CVE** CO2 Value Europe (#04042)
- ♦ CVG / see ELIX – Conservation Volunteers Greece
- ♦ **CVHH** Cirujanos Vasculares de Habla Hispana (#03947)
- ♦ CVJM-Komitee für den Nahen Osten (#16755)
- ♦ **CVJM** Weltbund der Christlichen Vereine Junger Männer (#21090)
- ♦ CVM / see Comunità Volontari per il Mondo
- ♦ **CVMA** Caribbean Veterinary Medical Association (#03564)
- ♦ CVMA / see Corpus Vitrearum (#04847)
- ♦ CVM – Christian Veterinary Mission (internationally oriented national body)
- ♦ CVM – Comunità Volontari per il Mondo (internationally oriented national body)
- ♦ CVN – Convention on the Contract for the International Carriage of Passengers and Luggage by Inland Waterway (1976 treaty)
- ♦ CVN – Protocol to the Convention on the Contract for the International Carriage of Passengers and Luggage by Inland Waterways (1978 treaty)
- ♦ CVO / see Centre for Research on Peace and Development
- ♦ CVR – Convention on the Contract for the International Carriage of Passengers and Luggage by Road (1973 treaty)
- ♦ CVR – Protocol to the Convention on the Contract for the International Carriage of Passengers and Luggage by Road (1978 treaty)
- ♦ **CVRS** Child Vision Research Society (#03886)
- ♦ CVSA – Commission on Voluntary Service and Action (internationally oriented national body)
- ♦ CVT – Center for Victims of Torture (internationally oriented national body)
- ♦ **CVX** Communauté de vie chrétienne (#03905)
- ♦ **CVX** Comunidad de Vida Cristiana (#03905)
- ♦ CWAAS – Centre for West Asian and African Studies, Delhi (internationally oriented national body)
- ♦ CWAS – Centre of West African Studies, Birmingham (internationally oriented national body)
- ♦ CWBCI – Conseil Wallonie Bruxelles de la coopération internationale (internationally oriented national body)
- ♦ **CWBI** Clowns Without Borders International (#04029)
- ♦ CWCC – Chemical Weapons Convention Coalition (unconfirmed)
- ♦ CWC – Convention on the Prohibition of the Development, Production, Stockpiling and Use of Chemical Weapons and on Their Destruction (1992 treaty)
- ♦ **CWC** Global Unions Committee on Workers' Capital (#10639)
- ♦ CWCSG – George Washington Center for the Study of Globalization (internationally oriented national body)

- ♦ CWDS – Centre for Women's Development Studies (internationally oriented national body)
- ♦ CWE – Coastwatch Europe (internationally oriented national body)
- ♦ **CWEIC** Commonwealth Enterprise and Investment Council (#04325)
- ♦ CWES / see European Studies Center, Pittsburgh PA
- ♦ CWES – Center for West European Studies, Seattle WA (internationally oriented national body)
- ♦ CWES – European Studies Center, Pittsburgh PA (internationally oriented national body)
- ♦ CWEurope – Coworking Europe conference (meeting series)
- ♦ **CWF** Commonwealth Weightlifting Federation (#04368)
- ♦ **CWGC** Commonwealth War Graves Commission (#04367)
- ♦ **CWG** Collaborative Working Group on Solid Waste Management in Low- and Middle-income Countries (#04101)
- ♦ CWGL / see Center for Women's Global Leadership
- ♦ CWGL – Center for Women's Global Leadership (internationally oriented national body)
- ♦ CWI – Coastal Watershed Institute (internationally oriented national body)
- ♦ **CWI** Committee for a Workers' International (#04290)
- ♦ **CWI** Cricket West Indies (#04953)
- ♦ **CWIG** Chest Wall International Group (#03864)
- ♦ CWIS – Center for World Indigenous Studies (internationally oriented national body)
- ♦ **CWM** Council for World Mission (#04925)
- ♦ **CWN** NGO Commonwealth Women's Network (#17122)
- ♦ CWP – Common Wagon Pool (inactive)
- ♦ **CWP** Commonwealth Women Parliamentarians (#04369)
- ♦ CW/PS – Center for War Peace Studies (internationally oriented national body)
- ♦ CWS – Centre for World Solidarity (internationally oriented national body)
- ♦ CWS – Christian World Service (internationally oriented national body)
- ♦ CWS – Church World Service (internationally oriented national body)
- ♦ **CWS** Crime Writers of Scandinavia (#04955)
- ♦ **CWSS** Common Wadden Sea Secretariat (#04297)
- ♦ CWU – Church Women United (internationally oriented national body)
- ♦ CwVA / see Commonwealth Veterinary Association (#04366)
- ♦ **CWWA** Caribbean Water and Wastewater Association (#03568)
- ♦ **CWW** Children Without Worms (#03881)
- ♦ CWW – Conference on Wind energy and Wildlife impacts (meeting series)
- ♦ **CWWL** Council of Women World Leaders (#04923)
- ♦ **CXC** Caribbean Examinations Council (#03500)
- ♦ Cyan International (internationally oriented national body)
- ♦ Cyber Policy Institute (internationally oriented national body)
- ♦ **CYBERPOL** INTERNATIONAL CYBER POLICING ORGANIZATION (#13125)
- ♦ Cyber Rights Organization (unconfirmed)

♦ Cybersecurity Alliance for Mutual Progress (CAMP) 04987

Secretariat IT Venture Tower, 135 Jungdaero, Songpagu, Seoul 05717, Korea Rep. E-mail: camp-sec@cybersec-alliance.org.
URL: https://www.cybersec-alliance.org/

History 11 Jul 2016, Korea Rep. Initiated by the Korean govenment, with preparatory meeting held 8 July 2015, Korea Rep. **Aims** Serve as a network platform to lift up the overall level of cybersecurity of members. **Structure** Annual Meeting; Secretariat. **Activities** Events/meetings; knowledge management/information dissemination. **Events** *Annual Meeting* Sejong (Korea Rep) 2021, *Annual Meeting* Seoul (Korea Rep) 2019. **Members** Government bodies; public organizations; non-profit organizations in 46 countries and territories:
Azerbaijan, Bangladesh, Brazil, Cambodia, Costa Rica, Côte d'Ivoire, Ecuador, El Salvador, Estonia, Ethiopia, Fiji, Gabon, Ghana, Guatemala, Haiti, Indonesia, Iran Islamic Rep, Kazakhstan, Kenya, Korea Rep, Kosovo, Laos, Malaysia, Mauritius, Moldova, Mongolia, Montenegro, Morocco, Nepal, Nicaragua, Nigeria, Oman, Paraguay, Peru, Philippines, Rwanda, Senegal, Sierra Leone, Sri Lanka, Taiwan, Tanzania UR, Thailand, Türkiye, Uganda, Uzbekistan, Vietnam.
Arab Information and Communication Technologies Organization (AICTO, #00982); *Centro de Estudios Avanzados en Banda Ancha para el Desarrollo (CEABAD, #03797)*; *Economic Community of West African States (ECOWAS, #05312)*. [2020/AA0211/y/**C**]

- ♦ **CYC** Commonwealth Youth Council (#04371)
- ♦ Cycle North-South (internationally oriented national body)

♦ Cycling Industries Europe (CIE) 04988

CEO c/o Tribes European Quarter, Av Marnix 17, 1000 Brussels, Belgium. T. +3226694298. E-mail: info@cyclingindustries.com.
URL: https://cyclingindustries.com/

History 11 Oct 2018, Brussels (Belgium). Launched by the Cycling Industry Club of *European Cyclists' Federation (ECF, #06877)*. Registration: EU Transparency Register, No/ID: 762247734758-18, Start date: 6 May 2019. **Aims** Support the EU Cycling Strategy and extend them to the whole of Europe. **Structure** Board of Directors. **Finance** Members' dues. **Activities** Advocacy/lobbying/activism. **Events** *CIE Summit* Brussels (Belgium) 2022. **Members** Companies (around 50). Membership countries not specified. **NGO Relations** Cooperates with (4): *Confederation of the European Bicycle Industry (CONEBI, #04519)*; *European Cycle Logistics Federation (ECLF, #06875)*; *European Cyclists' Federation (ECF, #06877)*; *International Mountain Bicycling Association Europe (IMBA Europe, #14189)*. [2021/XM7355/t/**E**]

♦ Cyclistes professionnels associés (CPA) 04989

Gen Sec c/o Ctre Mondial du Cyclisme, Route Industrielle, La Mélée, 1860 Aigle VD, Switzerland. E-mail: info@cpacycling.com.
URL: http://www.cpacycling.com/

History Founded 15 May 1999, Agrigento (Italy). Replaces *International Association of Professional Cyclists (AICPRO, inactive)*. Registered in accordance with Swiss law. **Aims** Defend and improve the status of professional riders. **Languages** English, French. **Staff** Voluntary. **Finance** Course fees; contributions from: *Union Cycliste Internationale (UCI, #20375)*.
Members National associations in 13 countries:
Belgium, Czechia, France, Germany, Italy, Netherlands, Poland, Portugal, Slovakia, Spain, Switzerland, UK, USA.
Members also in Scandinavia. Membership countries not specified. [2021/XM0492/**D**]

♦ The Cyclists' Alliance (TCA) 04990

Exec Dir address not obtained. E-mail: info@cyclistsalliance.org.
URL: https://cyclistsalliance.org/

History 2007, Rotterdam (Netherlands). **Aims** Provide holistic support to female cyclists during and after their careers. **Structure** Elected Board; Elected Riders Council; Advisory Board. **Staff** 7.00 FTE, voluntary. **Finance** Sources: donations; sponsorship; subscriptions. **Activities** Guidance/assistance/consulting. **Members** Individual riders (about 200) in 19 countries. Membership countries not specified. **NGO Relations** Member of (1): *European Elite Athletes Association (EU Athletes, #06977)*. [2023.03.06/AA1284/v/**C**]

- ♦ Cyclo nord-sud (internationally oriented national body)
- ♦ CYCN / see Commonwealth Youth Climate Initiative (#04370)
- ♦ CYC-Net – International Child and Youth Care Network (unconfirmed)
- ♦ CYDU – Caribbean Young Democrat Union (unconfirmed)
- ♦ CYEC – Commonwealth Youth Exchange Council (internationally oriented national body)
- ♦ **CYEN** Caribbean Youth Environment Network (#03570)
- ♦ **CYI** Children and Youth International (#03882)
- ♦ CYI – Communist Youth International (inactive)
- ♦ Cymanfa Gyffredinol Eglwysi Undodaidd a Christnogion Rhydd (#10105)
- ♦ CYMM – Commonwealth Youth Ministers Meeting (meeting series)
- ♦ **CYNESA** Catholic Youth Network for Environmental Sustainability in Africa (#03611)
- ♦ Cynllun Mercator (#16718)
- ♦ CYPAN – Commonwealth Youth Peace Ambassadors Network (unconfirmed)
- ♦ CYP Asia Centre – Asia Centre of the Commonwealth Youth Programme (see: #04362)
- ♦ CYPCC – Commonwealth Youth Programme – Caribbean Centre (see: #04362)
- ♦ **CYP** Commonwealth Youth Programme (#04372)
- ♦ Cyprus Centre for European and International Affairs (internationally oriented national body)
- ♦ Cyprus International Institute of Management (internationally oriented national body)
- ♦ Cyprus International School of Management / see Cyprus International Institute of Management
- ♦ CYP-SPRC – Commonwealth Youth Programme South Pacific Regional Centre (see: #04362)
- ♦ Cyrus R Vance Center for International Justice (internationally oriented national body)

♦ Cystic Fibrosis Europe (CF Europe) 04991

Address not obtained.
URL: https://www.cf-europe.eu/

History 2003, Belfast (UK), at European CF Conference, as the European Division of *Cystic Fibrosis Worldwide (CFW, #04992)*. **Aims** Improve the quality of life of Cystic Fibrosis patients and their families in Europe; represent and defend the interests of CF patients and their families in all walks of life; raise public awareness and understanding of the concerns of the CF patients and their families; promote appropriate medical care for Cystic Fibrosis patients everywhere in Europe. **Structure** Board, comprising President, Vice-President, Secretary and 3 members. **Events** *European CF Young Investigator Meeting* Paris (France) 2019. **Publications** *EuroCareCF Newsletter*.
Members Organizations in 24 countries:
Albania, Belgium, Croatia, Czechia, Estonia, France, Germany, Greece, Ireland, Israel, Italy, Latvia, Lithuania, Netherlands, North Macedonia, Norway, Poland, Romania, Slovakia, Spain, Sweden, Switzerland, UK, Ukraine.
NGO Relations Member of (2): *European Patients' Forum (EPF, #08172)*; *EURORDIS – Rare Diseases Europe (#09175)*. [2020/XM1561/**E**]

♦ Cystic Fibrosis Worldwide (CFW) 04992

CEO c/o Cystic Fibrosis Australia, PO Box 268, North Ryde NSW 1670, Australia. T. +61298895171. E-mail: general@cfa.org.au.
USA Office 474 Howe St, Brookfield MA 01515, USA.
URL: http://www.cfww.org/

History Jan 2003. Founded by merger of *International Association of Cystic Fibrosis Adults (IACFA, inactive)* and *International Cystic Fibrosis / Mucoviscidosis / Association (ICFMA, inactive)*. **Aims** Promote access to knowledge and appropriate care for all people living with cystic fibrosis and among medical, health professionals and governments worldwide. **Structure** Board; Executive Director. European division: *Cystic Fibrosis Europe (CF Europe, #04991)*. **Languages** English. **Staff** 1.00 FTE, paid; 70.00 FTE, voluntary. **Finance** Sources: donations; members' dues; sponsorship. **Events** *Annual Meeting* Lisbon (Portugal) 2013, *Annual meeting* Brisbane, QLD (Australia) 2009, *Annual meeting* Prague (Czech Rep) 2008, *Annual meeting* Belek (Turkey) 2007, *Annual meeting* Birmingham (UK) 2004. **Publications** *CFW Newsletter* (4 a year) in Dutch, English, French, German, Hindi, Hungarian, Italian, Persian, Portuguese, Romanian, Spanish, Turkish – paper and online. Annual report; booklets.
Members Full: national organizations in 43 countries:
Argentina, Australia, Austria, Belgium, Brazil, Bulgaria, Canada, Chile, Colombia, Costa Rica, Cuba, Czechia, Denmark, Ecuador, El Salvador, France, Germany, Greece, Hungary, Iceland, Ireland, Israel, Italy, Latvia, Lithuania, Mexico, Netherlands, New Zealand, Norway, Panama, Poland, Portugal, Romania, Slovakia, South Africa, Spain, Sweden, Switzerland, Türkiye, UK, Uruguay, USA, Venezuela.
Associate: national organizations in 16 countries:
Azerbaijan, Bahrain, Dominican Rep, Egypt, Estonia, Finland, Georgia, Guatemala, India, Jordan, Luxembourg, North Macedonia, Paraguay, Qatar, Russia, Saudi Arabia.
Consultative Status Consultative status granted from: *ECOSOC (#05331)* (Ros C). **IGO Relations** Accredited by (1): *United Nations Office at Vienna (UNOV, #20604)*. Associated with Department of Global Communications of the United Nations. **NGO Relations** Affiliated with (1): *International Pediatric Association (IPA, #14541)*. [2023.02.15/XC0133/**C**]

- ♦ Cystinosis Foundation (internationally oriented national body)

♦ Cystinosis Network Europe (CNE) 04993

Contact c/o Cystinosis Ireland, 1-2 Cavendish Row, Dublin, CO. DUBLIN, D01 K883, Ireland. T. +35316875758.
URL: https://cystinosis-europe.eu/

Structure Community Advisory Board. **Events** *International Cystinosis Conference* Leuven (Belgium) 2022, *European Cystinosis Conference* Dublin (Ireland) 2020, *European Cystinosis Conference* Berlin (Germany) 2018.
Members Organizations (members and partners) in 12 countries:
Belgium, France, Germany, Ireland, Italy, Mexico, Netherlands, Russia, Spain, Türkiye, UK, USA.
NGO Relations Partner of (2): *EURORDIS – Rare Diseases Europe (#09175)*; *Federation of European Patient Groups Affected by Renal Genetic Diseases (FEDERG, #09526)*. [2021/AA2004/**F**]

- ♦ **CYTED** Programa Iberoamericano de Ciencia y Tecnologia para el Desarrollo (#18524)
- ♦ **CZAPA** Coastal Zone Asia-Pacific Association (#04074)
- ♦ CzDA – Czech Development Agency (internationally oriented national body)
- ♦ CzechAid / see Czech Development Agency
- ♦ Czech Development Agency (internationally oriented national body)
- ♦ Czech Forum for Development Cooperation (internationally oriented national body)
- ♦ D-8 / see D-8 Organization for Economic Cooperation (#04994)
- ♦ **D-8** D-8 Organization for Economic Cooperation (#04994)

♦ D-8 Organization for Economic Cooperation (D-8) 04994

SG Darüşşafaka Caddesi Seba Ctr, No 45, Kat: 3, Istinye, Sariyer, 34460 Istanbul/Istanbul, Türkiye. T. +902123561823 – +902123561824. Fax +902123561829. E-mail: secretariat@developing8.org – info@developing8.org.
URL: http://developing8.org/

History 15 Jun 1997, Istanbul (Türkiye). Officially announced through Istanbul Declaration of Summit of Heads of State/Government. Former names and other names: *Developing-8* – alias; *Developing Eight Economic Cooperation Group (D-8)* – former. **Aims** Improve developing countries' positions in the world economy; diversify and create new opportunities in trade relations; enhance participation in decision-making at the international level; provide better standard of living. **Structure** Summit (every 2 years); Council (annual); Commission (twice a year); Secretariat, located in Istanbul (Turkey) and headed by Secretary General. **Activities** Events/meetings; knowledge management/information dissemination; networking/liaising. **Events** *Summit* Dhaka (Bangladesh) 2021, *Summit* Istanbul (Turkey) 2017, *Summit* Islamabad (Pakistan) 2012, *Summit* Abu Dhabi (United Arab Emirates) 2010, *Summit* Kuala Lumpur (Malaysia) 2008. **Publications** *D-8 Journal*; *D-8 Media Report*; *D-8 Newsletter*.
Members Governments of 8 countries:
Bangladesh, Egypt, Indonesia, Iran Islamic Rep, Malaysia, Nigeria, Pakistan, Türkiye.
IGO Relations Observer status with (1): *United Nations (UN, #20515)* (General Assembly). Memorandum of Understanding with (7): *African-Asian Rural Development Organization (AARDO, #00203)*; *Economic Community of West African States (ECOWAS, #05312)*; *Economic Cooperation Organization (ECO, #05313)*; *Islamic Development Bank (IsDB, #16044)*; *Organisation of Islamic Cooperation (OIC, #17813)*; *Organization of Black Sea Economic Cooperation (BSEC, #17857)*; *UNIDO (#20336)*. **NGO Relations** Memorandum of Understanding with (2): *International Youth Foundation (IYF)*; *United Cities and Local Governments Middle East and West Asia (UCLG-MEWA, #20502)*. [2021.03.11/XF6094/**D***]

- ♦ **DAAAM International** Danube Adria Association for Automation and Manufacturing (#05002)
- ♦ DAAD – Deutscher Akademischer Austauschdienst (internationally oriented national body)
- ♦ DAB – Directors Across Borders (internationally oriented national body)
- ♦ DAC EMEA / see Partner Community Council (#18228)
- ♦ **DACHELA** Deutschsprachige Ex-Libris-Anwendergruppe (#05050)
- ♦ D-A-CH FIB Arbeitskreis / see European Focused Ion Beam Network (#07276)
- ♦ Dachverband der Europäischen Parfümerie-, Kosmetik- und Körperpflege-Industrie / see Cosmetics Europe – The Personal Care Association (#04852)

♦ Dachverband der Europäischen Verbände der Parfümerie- und Kosmetik-Industrie / see Cosmetics Europe – The Personal Care Association (#04852)
♦ Dachverband des internationalen Strassentransports temperaturgeführter Güter / see Transfrigoroute International (#20213)
♦ Dachverband Schwuler und Lesbischer Chöre in Europa / see LEGATO (#16441)
♦ Dacia Revival International Society (internationally oriented national body)
♦ **daCi** Dance and the Child International (#04999)
♦ DAC – International Deaf Academics and Researchers Conference (meeting series)
♦ DAC – OECD Development Assistance Committee (see: #17693)
♦ DA – Design for All Foundation (internationally oriented national body)
♦ DA – Diplomatic Academy of Vienna (internationally oriented national body)
♦ DAE / see Association for the Development of Education in Africa (#02471)
♦ DAE – Dialogue Afrique-Europe (internationally oriented national body)
♦ DAFOH – Doctors Against Forced Organ Harvesting (unconfirmed)
♦ DAFX – International Conference on Digital Audio Effects (meeting series)
♦ DAGA – Documentation for Action Groups in Asia (internationally oriented national body)
♦ DAG – Dialogue Advisory Group (internationally oriented national body)
♦ DAGENE / see Dunamenti Állatfajták Génmegőrző Nemzetközi Egyesülete (#05146)
♦ **DAGENE** Dunamenti Állatfajták Génmegőrző Nemzetközi Egyesülete (#05146)

♦ Dag Hammarskjöld Foundation (DHF) 04995

Fondation Dag Hammarskjöld – Fundación Dag Hammarskjöld – Dag Hammarskjölds Minnesfond

Exec Dir Övre Slottsgatan 2, SE-753 10 Uppsala, Sweden. T. +46184101000. E-mail: secretariat@daghammarskjold.se.
Communications Manager address not obtained.
URL: http://www.daghammarskjold.se/

History Mar 1962, Uppsala (Sweden). Founded following the sudden death of Dag Hammarskjöld. **Aims** Promote principles outlined in UN Charter; encourage dialogue and policy for sustainable development and peace. **Structure** Board of Trustees; International Honorary Committee; extensive international network of individuals and organisations. **Languages** English. **Staff** 13.00 FTE, paid. **Finance** Swedish government support; foundations; own resources. **Activities** Events/meetings; training/education. **Events** *Can citizen action save the world meeting* New York, NY (USA) 2010, *Meeting on COP 15 and climate justice* New York, NY (USA) 2010, *People's health assembly* Dhaka (Bangladesh) 2000, *International workshop on the problematization of the biotechnology discourse* Luleå (Sweden) 1999, *Seminar on equity in health* Kasane (Botswana) 1997. **Publications** *Development Dialogue* – series. Monographs; volumes; booklets; reports; proceedings; papers. **Members** Not a membership body. **Consultative Status** Consultative status granted from: *ECOSOC (#05331)* (Special). **NGO Relations** Member of: *Academic Council on the United Nations System (ACUNS, #00020)*. Links with UN agencies and international NGOs, not specified. [2021/XF0117/f/**F**]

♦ Dag Hammarskjölds Minnesfond (#04995)
♦ Dahlia – Development and Humanitarian Learning in Action (unconfirmed)
♦ **DAI** Dementia Alliance International (#05028)
♦ DAI – Development Associates International (internationally oriented national body)
♦ DAI / see Dorcas (#05123)

♦ DAISY Consortium 04996

CEO Richard Orme, c/o SBS, Grubenstrasse 12, 8045 Zurich ZH, Switzerland. T. +41433333232. Fax +41433333233.
URL: http://www.daisy.org/

History May 1996, Stockholm (Sweden), by talking book libraries to lead the worldwide transition from analog to Digital Talking Books. Registered in accordance with Swiss Civil Code. Registration: Switzerland. **Aims** Develop and promote international standards and technologies which enable equal access to information and knowledge by all people with print disabilities and which also benefit the wider community. **Structure** General Meeting (annual); Board of Directors. **Languages** English. **Staff** 15.00 FTE, paid. **Activities** Research and development; standards/guidelines; training/education. **Events** *Board Meeting* Italy 2021, *Board Meeting* Zurich (Switzerland) 2021, *General Meeting* Zurich (Switzerland) 2021, *General Meeting* Madrid (Spain) 2020, *Meeting* Sao Paulo (Brazil) 2020. **Publications** *DAISY Planet* in English, French, Spanish. Annual Report; bulletins; other publications.
Members Full and Associate; Friends and various Supporters. Full members (18) in 16 countries:
Australia, Canada, Denmark, Finland, France, Germany, Japan, Korea Rep, Netherlands, New Zealand, Norway, Spain, Sweden, Switzerland, UK, USA.
Associate members (over 25) in 12 countries and territories:
Belgium, Canada, China, Egypt, Iceland, Italy, Russia, South Africa, Taiwan, Thailand, UK, USA.
Friends and Developers (16) in 10 countries:
Belgium, Canada, Denmark, Finland, Japan, Netherlands, Sweden, Switzerland, UK, USA.
Publishers, Educators and Advocates (5) in 4 countries:
Brazil, Canada, Ireland, USA.
Individual Supporters (7) in 6 countries:
Australia, Canada, Finland, Switzerland, UK, USA.
Focal Points in 12 countries:
Bangladesh, India, Indonesia, Kazakhstan, Malaysia, Nepal, Pakistan, Philippines, South Africa, Sri Lanka, Thailand, Vietnam.
NGO Relations Member of (2): *World Blind Union (WBU, #21234)*; *World Wide Web Consortium (W3C, #21935)*. [2023/XJ1979/**C**]

♦ Dakar Union – Association of Export Credit Insurers and of Export Promotion Organizations (inactive)
♦ Dallas Peace Center (internationally oriented national body)
♦ **DAMA International** Data Administration Management Association International (#05010)
♦ Damascus Declaration (1991 treaty)
♦ DAM – Deaf Africa Mission (internationally oriented national body)
♦ **DAM** Deutschsprachige Arbeitsgemeinschaft für Mikrochirurgie der peripheren Nerven und Gefässe (#05049)
♦ DAM – Dhaka Ahsania Mission (internationally oriented national body)
♦ Dame Inglesi – Istituto della Beata Vergine Maria (religious order)
♦ Dame dell'Istruzione Cristiana (religious order)
♦ The Dame Jane Foundation (internationally oriented national body)
♦ Dames Anglaises – Institut de la Bienheureuse Vierge Marie (religious order)
♦ DAMES – Data Analysis and Modeling in Earth Sciences (meeting series)
♦ Dames de l'Instruction Chrétienne de Flône-lez-Amay (religious order)
♦ Damiaanactie – Vereniging ter Bestrijding van de Melaatsheid (internationally oriented national body)
♦ Damian Stiftung – Aussätzigen Hilfswerk (internationally oriented national body)
♦ Damien Foundation – Voluntary Organization for Leprosy and TB Control (internationally oriented national body)
♦ Dana Center for Preventive Ophthalmology / see Dana Center for Preventive Ophthalmology (#04997)

♦ Dana Center for Preventive Ophthalmology (DCPO) 04997

Dir Ste 122, 600 N Wolfe St, Baltimore MD 21287-9019, USA. T. +13019552777. Fax +13019552542.
URL: http://www.hopkinsmedicine.org/wilmer/danacenter/

History 1979, as *International Center for Epidemiologic and Preventive Ophthalmology (ICEPO)*. Part of Wilmer Eye Institute and a joint undertaking of The Johns Hopkins University Schools of Medicine and Public Health. Referred to as *Dana Center for Preventive Ophthalmology*. **Aims** Prevent *blinding ocular disease* and alleviate *visual impairment* worldwide through the innovative application of *public health* techniques and appropriate technology. **Finance** Financed by grants from national institutes of health (ageing, eye), *Agency for Health Care Policy and Research*, private foundations and private donors. **Activities** Carries out an integrated program of; research, generating knowledge needed to design effective intervention strategies; technical assistance, providing colleagues access to these formulations and help in implementing sound and effective prevention programs; training, preparing future leaders for the fight against blindness. **IGO Relations** Official Collaborating Center for the Prevention of Blindness, Cataract, Glaucoma, Xerophthalmia, Trachoma and Onchocerciasis of: *WHO (#20950)*. **NGO Relations** Works closely with: *Light for the World (#16474)*; *Helen Keller International (HKI, #10902)*; *International Agency for the Prevention of Blindness (IAPB, #11597)*; *International Organization Against Trachoma (IOAT, #14436)*. [2014/XE6118/**E**]

♦ DAN Asia-Pacific – Divers Alert Network Asia-Pacific (see: #13181)

♦ DANASWAC Group 04998

Contact Durham Univ Wolfson Research Inst, Queen's Campus, Stockton-on-Tees, TS17 6BH, UK.
Contact Prof Kirsi Juhila, Social Work Research Dept, Univ of Tampere, FI-33014 Tampere, Finland. E-mail: kirsi.juhila@uta.fi.
URL: http://www.uta.fi/laitokset/sostyo/danaswac/

History DANASWAC stands for: Discourse and Narrative Approaches to Social Work and Counselling. **Aims** Study practices of *social work* and *counselling* by using discourse, narrative and ethnographic approaches. **Events** *Meeting* Ljubljana (Slovenia) 2012, *Meeting* Utrecht (Netherlands) 2011, *Meeting* Basel (Switzerland) 2010, *Meeting* Ghent (Belgium) 2009, *Meeting* Aarhus (Denmark) 2008.
Members Individuals in 10 countries:
Belgium, Denmark, Finland, Germany, Netherlands, Norway, Slovenia, Spain, Sweden, UK. [2012.07.10/XM2898/**F**]

♦ DANAYA (internationally oriented national body)

♦ Dance and the Child International (daCi) 04999

Danse et l'enfant international

Chair York Univ, Dept of Dance, 301 Accolade East Bldg, 4700 Keele St, Toronto ON M3J 1P3, Canada. E-mail: chair@daci.international.
Sec address not obtained. E-mail: secretary@daci.international.
URL: https://daci.international/

History Set up 1978, Edmonton AB (Canada), as *International Dance Educators / Education Association (IDEA)*, at Dance and the Child Conference. **Aims** Promote all that can benefit dance and the child and young people, irrespective of race, colour, sex, religion, national or social origin. **Structure** Advisory Board; Executive Committee. **Languages** English. **Staff** All voluntary. **Finance** Sources: members' dues. **Events** *Conference* Toronto, ON (Canada) 2021, *Conference* Adelaide, SA (Australia) 2018, *Conference* Copenhagen (Denmark) 2015, *Conference* Taipei (Taiwan) 2012, *Conference* Kingston (Jamaica) 2009. **Publications** *daCi Newsletter* (2 a year).
Members National representatives from 23 countries and territories:
Argentina, Australia, Brazil, Canada, Colombia, Croatia, Denmark, Estonia, Finland, Germany, Jamaica, Japan, Mexico, Netherlands, New Zealand, Portugal, Russia, Slovenia, Suriname, Sweden, Switzerland, Taiwan, USA.
NGO Relations Branch of: *International Dance Council (#13130)*. [2019/XG1235/**C**]

♦ Dance Roads (#03160)

♦ Dances of Universal Peace International 05000

Contact PO Box 55994, Seattle WA 98155-0994, USA. T. +12063670389. E-mail: inoffice@dancesofuniversalpeace.org.
URL: http://www.dancesofuniversalpeace.org/

History Founded 1982, as *International Network for the Dances of Universal Peace (INDUP)*. **Structure** Board of Directors, comprising President, Vice-President, Treasurer and Secretary. **Activities** Organizes Dances of Universal Peace around the world. [2012.06.01/XF6284/**F**]

♦ DanChurchAid (internationally oriented national body)
♦ DAN Europe – Divers Alert Network Europe (see: #13181)
♦ DANFUNDS / see Danish International Investment Funds

♦ Dangerous Goods Advisory Council (DGAC) 05001

Office Manager 7501 Greenway Center Dr, Ste 760, Greenbelt MD 20770, USA. T. +12022894550. Fax +12022894074. E-mail: info@dgac.org.
URL: http://www.dgac.org/

History Founded 1978. Also known as *Hazardous Materials Advisory Council (HMAC)*. **Aims** Promote safety and regulatory compliance in the *transportation* and handling of hazardous materials, substances and wastes. **Structure** Board of Directors. Departments (4): Communications and Public Relations; Education and Training; Administrative and Member Services; Technical Support. **Finance** Members' dues. Other sources: conferences; training programs. Budget (annual) over US$ 1 million. **Activities** Organizes: Annual Meeting (May each year, mostly in Washington DC); Semi-annual Conference (November each year, in varying locations); training programmes; conferences; seminars. **Events** *International dangerous goods conference / Annual Conference* Prague (Czech Rep) 2007, *Annual Conference* Arlington, VA (USA) 2006, *Annual Conference* Tempe, AZ (USA) 2002, *Semi-annual conference* St Louis, MO (USA) 1999, *Annual Conference* Washington, DC (USA) 1999. **Publications** *HMAC Courier* (11 a year). Special issue bulletins; in-depth reports. **Information Services** *Federal Register Extract Service*.
Members Shippers of varying size, carriers of all modes, container manufacturers and reconditioners, emergency response and waste management firms. Companies (300, mainly in USA) in 16 countries and territories:
Argentina, Australia, Brazil, Canada, France, Germany, Hong Kong, Japan, Mexico, Pakistan, Panama, Puerto Rico, Switzerland, UK, United Arab Emirates, USA.
Consultative Status Consultative status granted from: *ECOSOC (#05331)* (Ros C); *International Maritime Organization (IMO, #14102)*. **IGO Relations** Advisor to: *International Civil Aviation Organization (ICAO, #12581)*. Observer status: *United Nations Committee of Experts on the Transport of Dangerous Goods and on the Globally Harmonized System of Classification and Labelling of Chemicals (Committee of Experts on TDG and GHS, #20543)*. Participates in the activities of: *FAO (#09260)*; *ILO (#11123)*; *OECD (#17693)*; *UNIDO (#20336)*; *United Nations Economic Commission for Europe (UNECE, #20555)*; *WHO (#20950)*. [2018/XF1443/**F**]

♦ DANIDA (internationally oriented national body)
♦ S Daniel Abraham Center for Middle East Peace (internationally oriented national body)
♦ Danijas Kulturas Instituts (internationally oriented national body)
♦ Danijos Kulturos Institutas (internationally oriented national body)
♦ DAN / see Include Network (#11143)
♦ Dänisches Kulturininstitut (internationally oriented national body)
♦ Danish Association for International Cooperation (internationally oriented national body)
♦ Danish Association for International Cooperation in Environment and Development / see Mellemfolkeligt Samvirke
♦ Danish Association for Nordic Collaboration (internationally oriented national body)
♦ Danish Atlantic Treaty Association (internationally oriented national body)
♦ Danish Center for Conflict Resolution (internationally oriented national body)
♦ Danish Centre for Gender, Equality and Diversity (internationally oriented national body)
♦ Danish Coalition for North/South Cooperation (internationally oriented national body)
♦ Danish Cultural Institute (internationally oriented national body)
♦ Danish European Mission (internationally oriented national body)
♦ Danish Foreign Policy Society (internationally oriented national body)
♦ Danish Government Institute of Seed Pathology for Developing Countries / see Danish Seed Health Centre for Developing Countries
♦ Danish Institute for Human Rights (internationally oriented national body)
♦ Danish Institute for Information about Denmark and Cultural Cooperation with other Countries / see Danish Cultural Institute
♦ Danish Institute for International Studies (internationally oriented national body)
♦ Danish International Development Assistance / see DANIDA
♦ Danish International Human Settlement Service (internationally oriented national body)
♦ Danish International Investment Funds (internationally oriented national body)
♦ Danish Mission Council (internationally oriented national body)
♦ Danish National Church's Relief Aid / see Folkekirkens Nødhjaelp

- Danish National Evangelical Lutheran Church's Relief Aid for the Evangelical Churches of Europe / see Folkekirkens Nødhjaelp
- Danish Peace Foundation (internationally oriented national body)
- Danish Refugee Council (internationally oriented national body)
- Danish Seed Health Centre for Developing Countries (internationally oriented national body)
- Danish Society for Central Asia (internationally oriented national body)
- Danish Society for European Studies (internationally oriented national body)
- Danish Trade Union Council for International Development Cooperation (internationally oriented national body)
- Dan Kulturalis Intezét (internationally oriented national body)
- Danmission (internationally oriented national body)
- Danse et l'enfant international (#04999)
- Danses macabres d'Europe (internationally oriented national body)
- Det Danske Kulturinstitut (internationally oriented national body)
- Danske Selskab for Oplysning om Danmark og Kulturelt Samvirke met andre Nationer / see Danish Cultural Institute
- Dansk Europamission (internationally oriented national body)
- Dansk European Community Studies Association / see Danish Society for European Studies
- Dansk Flygtningehjaelp (internationally oriented national body)
- Dansk Institut for Menneskerettigheder / see Danish Institute for Human Rights
- Dansk International Bosaetningsservice (internationally oriented national body)
- Dansk Missionsråd (internationally oriented national body)
- Dansk Selskab for Europaforskning (internationally oriented national body)
- Dansk Ungdoms Faellesraad (internationally oriented national body)
- DAN Southern Africa – Divers Alert Network Southern Africa (see: #13181)

♦ Danube Adria Association for Automation and Manufacturing (DAAAM International) 05002

Pres TU Vienna, Karlsplatz 13, 1040 Vienna, Austria. T. +4315880131121. Fax +4315880131199. E-mail: president@daaam.com.
SG address not obtained. E-mail: secretary@daaam.info.
URL: http://daaam.info/

History 5 Nov 1990, Vienna (Austria). **Aims** Provide a forum to present and discuss the status and impact of advanced manufacturing and automation. **Structure** Officers: President, 3 Vice-Presidents, 2 Associated Vice-Presidents, Secretary-General, Administrator, Designer and 2 Organizers. **Activities** Training/education; events/meetings. **Events** *International Symposium / Annual Symposium* Vienna (Austria) 2014, *International Symposium* Vienna (Austria) 2011, *International symposium* Zadar (Croatia) 2010, *International symposium* Vienna (Austria) 2009, *International Symposium / Annual Symposium* Trnava (Slovakia) 2008. **Publications** *International Journal of Simulation Modelling. Manufacturing Technology* – series. Books. [2014/XD7851/**D**]

- Danube, Le – Association de promotion touristique internationale (#05005)

♦ Danube Civil Society Forum (DCSF) 05003

Contact Schloss Esterhazy, 7000 Eisenstadt, Austria. T. +4328626342620. E-mail: luetgenau@foster-europe.org – office@foster-europe.org.
URL: http://www.danubestrategy.eu/

History 30 Jun 2011, Eisenstadt (Austria). Founding General Assembly 30 Jun – 1 Jul 2011, Eisenstadt (Austria). Set up to be the platform for civil society dialogue and networking in the Danube basin under the EU Strategy for the Danube Region (EUSDR). **Aims** Support civil society organizations in the Danube basin; promote and enhance civil society participation and networking in the framework of the European Union Strategy for the Danube Region. **Structure** General Assembly; Executive Committee; Working Groups (4). **Languages** English. **Activities** Events/meetings. **Events** *Danube Participation Day in the EU Danube Strategy* Budapest (Hungary) 2017, *Danube Participation Days in the EU Danube Strategy* Bratislava (Slovakia) 2016, *Danube Participation Day in the EU Danube Strategy* Ulm (Germany) 2015, *General Assembly* Ulm (Germany) 2015, *Danube Participation Day in the EU Danube Strategy* Eisenstadt (Austria) 2014. **Publications** Resolutions; position papers. **Members** in the Danube Region. Membership countries not specified. **NGO Relations** Member of: *Eastern Partnership Civil Society Forum (EaP CSF, #05247).* [2016.12.15/XJ2842/**F**]

- Danube Commission (#04210)
- Danube Delta National Institute for Research and Development (internationally oriented national body)
- Danube Delta Research and Design Institute / see Danube Delta National Institute for Research and Development
- Danube Rectors' Association / see Danube Rectors' Conference (#05004)

♦ Danube Rectors' Conference (DRC) 05004

SG c/o IDM, Hahngasse 6/24, 1090 Vienna, Austria. T. +4313197258. E-mail: info@drc-danube.org.
Pres Univ of Maribor, Slomškov trg 15, 2000 Maribor, Slovenia. E-mail: rektor@um.si – mladen.kraljic@um.si.
URL: http://www.drc-danube.org/

History 1983, Vienna (Austria). Former names and other names: *Danube Rectors' Association (DRC)* – former. **Aims** Raise academic performance; promote mobility; reduce drop-out rates; lower the cost of tertiary *education* in the Danube region. **Structure** General Assembly (annual); Permanent Committee. **Languages** English. **Staff** 2.00 FTE, paid. **Finance** Sources: members' dues. **Activities** Networking/liaising; training/education. **Events** *General Assembly* Bucharest (Romania) 2019, *General Assembly* Bratislava (Slovakia) 2018, *General Assembly* Zagreb (Croatia) 2017, *General Assembly* Krems (Austria) 2016, *General Assembly* Maribor (Slovenia) 2015. **Publications** *DRC Newsletter* (10 a year).
Members Universities (64) in 15 countries:
Austria, Bosnia-Herzegovina, Bulgaria, Croatia, Czechia, Germany, Hungary, Italy, Kosovo, Moldova, Romania, Serbia, Slovakia, Slovenia, Ukraine. [2022/XD7114/**D**]

- Danube Soya / see Donau Soja (#05116)
- Danube Summit (meeting series)
- Danube Symposium on Chromatography (meeting series)

♦ Danube Tourist Commission 05005

Danube, Le – Association de promotion touristique internationale – Internationale Touristische Werbegemeinschaft – Die Donau

Pres Schifffahrtszentrum, Handelskai 265, 1020 Vienna, Austria. T. +4319229394. Fax +43125330331475. E-mail: office@danube-river.org.
URL: http://www.danube-river.org/

History 1972, as *Groupe de travail sur la promotion touristique de la région danubienne.* **Aims** Enhance awareness of the Danube Region; promote tourism in the area. **Structure** General Meeting (annual). Marketing Committee, comprising delegates of member countries and supporting members. Managing Board, comprising President and 2 deputies. Secretariat headed by Secretary General, located in Vienna (Austria). **Languages** English, German. **Staff** 4.50 FTE, paid. **Finance** Members' dues. Sponsors. **Activities** range from creation of a uniform corporate identity to production of brochures and media work. Organizes: annual Danube Salon – specialized tourism trade fair; Danube Bicycle Conference; Danube Shipping Conference; joint promotional campaigns to create a touristic identity for the Danube region; familiarization trips for journalists; press conferences at major tourist trade fairs; symposia; 'Danube Day'; 'Danube Navigation Day'. Collaborates with: EU Corridor VII (Danube) / Tina Vienna Transport Strategies; *'The Route of Emperors and Kings – Regensburg to Budapest'.* **Events** *International Danube Marine and Tourism Conference* Vienna (Austria) 2017, *Danube shipping conference* Linz (Austria) 2006, *Biennial Danube Travel Mart* Vienna (Austria) 2006, *Biennial Danube Travel Mart* Vienna (Austria) 2004, *Danube shipping conference* Passau (Germany) 2002. **Publications** *Danube Press Service* (12 a year) in English, German – online. *Danube Sales Manual* – online guide; *The Musical Danube* – compendium of musical events. Brochures; posters; video films; excursion and cruise ship schedules; yacht guide.
Members National tourist organizations in 8 countries:
Austria, Croatia, Germany, Hungary, Moldova, Romania, Serbia, Slovakia.
Supporting member Casinos Austria. Sponsoring member Bonaventura River Cruises.
IGO Relations Member of: *International Commission for the Protection of the Danube River (ICPDR, #12720); UNESCO (#20322)* Working Group Vienna. Cooperates with: *Working Community of the Danube Regions (#21056).* [2019/XD5579/**D**]

- Danubian Alliance for the Preservation of Animal Breeds / see Dunamenti Állatfajták Génmegőrző Nemzetközi Egyesülete (#05146)

♦ Danubiana Network 05006

Coordinator c/o European House, Pf 113, Budapest 1389, Hungary. T. +3613568440. E-mail: danubiananetwork@gmail.com.
URL: https://danubiananetwork.eu/

History Set up as a result of the "Building Bridges of Democracy" project, an international initiative in 2011 which contributed to the elaboration of the EU Strategy for the Danube Region (EUSDR). **Aims** Enhance intra- and cross sectoral cooperation among the stakeholders of the EUSDR on a partnership basis; find synergies with other macro-regional strategies of the European Union including the Baltic Sea and the Adriatic-Ionian strategies. **Activities** Monitoring/evaluation; networking/liaising; training/education; research/documentation.
Members Full in 14 countries:
Austria, Bosnia-Herzegovina, Bulgaria, Croatia, Czechia, Germany, Hungary, Moldova, Montenegro, Romania, Serbia, Slovakia, Slovenia, Ukraine.
Included in the above, 1 organization listed in this Yearbook:
World of NGOs, The. [2022/XJ9309/**F**]

- Danubian Congress of Gynecologists and Obstetricians (meeting series)
- Danubian Countries Alliance for Conservation of Genes in Animal Species / see Dunamenti Állatfajták Génmegőrző Nemzetközi Egyesülete (#05146)

♦ Danubian League Against Thrombosis and Haemorrhagic Disorders 05007

Ligue danubienne contre la thrombose et les troubles hémorragiques

SG Hemostasis Dept and Hemophilia Center, Svetog Save 39, Belgrade, PAK 11000, Serbia.
URL: http://www.dlth.org/

History Founded 23 Nov 1983, Linz (Austria). **Aims** Intensify the scientific contact of the former communistic countries with western countries along the Danubian river. **Structure** Scientific Council; National Scientific Committees. **Languages** English. **Activities** Research/documentation; awareness raising. Active in Europe. **Events** *Congress* Istanbul (Turkey) 2019, *Congress* Skopje (Macedonia) 2017, *Congress* Sarajevo (Bosnia-Herzegovina) 2015, *Congress* Hradec Kralové (Czech Rep) 2013, *Congress* Timisoara (Romania) 2011.
Members in 28 countries:
Austria, Belgium, Bosnia-Herzegovina, Bulgaria, Croatia, Cyprus, Czechia, Estonia, Finland, France, Georgia, Germany, Hungary, Italy, Latvia, Lithuania, Moldova, Montenegro, North Macedonia, Poland, Romania, Russia, Serbia, Slovakia, Slovenia, Spain, Switzerland, Ukraine.
NGO Relations Member of: *European Thrombosis and Haemostasis Alliance (ETHA, #08911).* [2015.06.01/XE0756/**F**]

♦ Danubian Psychiatric Association 05008

Donauländischer Verein für Psychiatrie und ihre Grenzgebiete – Dunajské psychiatrické asociaci

Contact Isidora Kršnjavoga 25, HR-10105 Zagreb, Croatia. T. +38514553290. E-mail: danubepsychiatry@danubepsychiatry.com.
URL: http://www.danubepsychiatry.com/

History 1964. Founded as a 'Kuratorium', a working group for the organization of Danube Symposia. Transformed into current association, 1994. Former names and other names: *Kuratorium of the Danube Symposium for Psychiatry* – former. **Aims** Promote collaboration among experts, scientific and professional organizations and institutions in the field of psychiatry and neighbouring disciplines in matters concerning science, research, education and planning and development of services for in-patient and outpatient treatment of psychiatric patients. **Structure** General Assembly (every 2 years); Executive Committee; Advisory Board; Board of Appeal. **Languages** English, German. **Staff** 2.00 FTE, voluntary. **Finance** Sources: members' dues. **Activities** Research groups (3): Development of psychiatric care; Suicidology; Census of psychiatric hospital care in the region. Organizes symposia and seminars. **Events** *Danubian Psychiatric Symposium* Tuzla (Bosnia-Herzegovina) 2022, *Danube Symposium of Psychiatry / Symposium* Munich (Germany) 2015, *Symposium* Timisoara (Romania) 2012, *Danube symposium of psychiatry / Symposium* Zagreb (Croatia) 2010, *Danube symposium of psychiatry* Portoroz (Slovenia) 2004. **Publications** *Psychiatria Danubina* (4 a year) – journal.
Members National associations in 17 countries:
Armenia, Austria, Bosnia-Herzegovina, Bulgaria, Croatia, Czechia, Germany, Hungary, Moldova, Poland, Romania, Russia, Serbia, Slovakia, Slovenia, Switzerland, Ukraine.
NGO Relations Affiliated member of: *World Psychiatric Association (WPA, #21741).* [2022/XD6771/c/**D**]

- **DAP** DIAKONIA of Asia-Pacific (#05064)

♦ DARA 05009

Vice-Chair/Founder/Dir Calle Felipe IV 9, 28014 Madrid, Spain. T. +34915310372. Fax +34915220039. E-mail: info@daraint.org.
URL: http://www.daraint.org/

History 2003. Registered in accordance with Spanish and US laws. Also recognized as an international organization in Switzerland. **Aims** Improve quality and effectiveness of *humanitarian* action for *vulnerable* populations affected by armed conflict and natural disasters. **Structure** Board of Trustees; National Boards. **Languages** English, French, Italian, Portuguese, Spanish. **Staff** 8.00 FTE, paid. **Finance** Funded by: governments; several organizations including: *DANIDA; Department for International Development (DFID, inactive); ECHO (inactive); European Cadmium Stabilisers Association (ECADSA, inactive); European Commission (EC, #06633); Inter-Agency Standing Committee (IASC, #11393); International Committee of the Red Cross (ICRC, #12799); Norwegian Agency for Development Cooperation (Norad); Swedish International Development Cooperation Agency (Sida); UNDP (#20292); UNHCR (#20327); UNICEF (#20332); United Nations Office for the Coordination of Humanitarian Affairs (OCHA, #20593).* **Activities** Monitoring/evaluation; guidance/assistance/consulting; humanitarian/emergency aid. **Publications** *Risk Reduction Index* (2013); *Climate Vulnerability Monitor* (2012); *Humanitarian Response Index* (2011). Evaluation reports.
Members Humanitarian aid organizations (5):
Active Learning Network for Accountability and Performance in Humanitarian Action (ALNAP, #00101); American Evaluation Association (AEA); *European Evaluation Society (EES, #07009); European Policy Centre (EPC, #08240); International Initiative for Impact Evaluation (3ie, #13851).*
IGO Relations Partner of: *United Nations Office for Disaster Risk Reduction (UNDRR, #20595).* **NGO Relations** Partner: *African Leadership Centre (ALC, #00358); Centro Internacional de Toledo para la Paz (CITpax); World Leadership Alliance – Club de Madrid (WLA-CdM, #21619); European Council on Foreign Relations (ECFR, #06821); Global Call for Climate Action (GCCA, inactive).* Refugee Response Index Partners: *Asylum Access; CARE International (CI, #03429); Danish Refugee Council (DRC); International Council of Voluntary Agencies (ICVA, #13092).* [2019.02.13/XJ5541/**F**]

- **DARE Network** Democracy and Human Rights Education in Europe (#05031)
- Darfur Consortium / see Sudan Consortium (#20031)
- Darfur Relief Collaboration / see Global Relief Alliance
- **DARIAH-EU** Digital Research Infrastructure for the Arts and Humanities (#05083)
- DaR International Alliance – Diabetes and Ramadan International Alliance (unconfirmed)
- Darkawa (religious order)
- Dart Centre Europe (internationally oriented national body)
- Dart Centre Europe for Journalism and Trauma / see Dart Centre Europe
- Darwin Initiative (internationally oriented national body)
- DASFAA – Database Systems for Advanced Applications (meeting series)
- DASIL / see Dermatology, Aesthetics, and Surgery International League (#05040)
- **DASIL** Dermatology, Aesthetics, and Surgery International League (#05040)
- **Data4SDGS** Global Partnership for Sustainable Development Data (#10542)

♦ Data Administration Management Association International (DAMA International) 05010

Contact Dama International, 2512 East Evergreen Blvd, Ste 1023, Vancouver WA 98661-4323, USA. E-mail: info@dama.org.
Pres address not obtained. E-mail: president@dama.org.
URL: https://www.dama.org/

History 1988. **Aims** Promote the understanding, development and practice of managing data and information as key enterprise assets to support the organization. **Structure** Executive Board; Advisory Board. **Activities** Certification/accreditation; events/meetings. **Events** *Data Governance and Information Quality Conference* San Diego, CA (USA) 2022, *Data governance European conference* London (UK) 2011, *Master data management European summit* London (UK) 2011, *Data quality Asia Pacific congress* Sydney, NSW (Australia) 2011, *Data quality Asia Pacific congress* Sydney, NSW (Australia) 2010. **Publications** *DAMA International Newsletter* (4 a year). *Model for Data Resource Management Standards Manual.* Directory; conference planning handbook; brochure; new chapter kit; video tapes.
Members Affiliated chapters and officers in 9 countries:
Australia, Canada, Denmark, India, Italy, Norway, Sweden, USA, Venezuela. [2022/XF5844/**C**]

- ♦ Data Analysis and Modeling in Earth Sciences (meeting series)
- ♦ Database Systems for Advanced Applications (meeting series)

♦ DataCite 05011

Exec Dir Welfengarten 1B, 30167 Hannover, Germany. T. +4915120417763. E-mail: info@datacite.org.
URL: http://www.datacite.org/

History 2009, Germany. Registration: EU Transparency Register, No/ID: 026192614550-66, Start date: 30 Sep 2014. **Aims** Be a world leading provider of persistent identifier services to help make research outputs and resources findable, citable, connected and reused globally; create value for members through community-driven, innovative, open, integrated, usable and sustainable services for research. **Structure** General Assembly; Executive Board; Steering Groups (2); Metadata Working Group. **Languages** English. **Staff** 17.00 FTE, paid. **Activities** Advocacy/lobbying/activism; guidance/assistance/consulting.
Members Full in 24 countries:
Australia, Canada, China, Denmark, Estonia, Finland, France, Germany, Hungary, Italy, Japan, Korea Rep, Latvia, Netherlands, Norway, Russia, Singapore, South Africa, Spain, Sweden, Switzerland, Thailand, UK, USA.
Included in the above, 7 organizations listed in this Yearbook:
Dryad (#05139); European Organization for Nuclear Research (CERN, #08108); Global Campus of Human Rights (#10269); Institute of Electrical and Electronics Engineers (IEEE, #11259); International Treaty on Plant Genetic Resources for Food and Agriculture (2001); Inter-University Consortium for Political and Social Research (ICPSR); ORCID (#17790). [2022.02.02/XM6855/y/**C**]

- ♦ DATA – Danish Atlantic Treaty Association (internationally oriented national body)
- ♦ Data for Development International Association (inactive)

♦ Data Documentation Initiative Alliance (DDI Alliance) 05012

Address not obtained.
URL: https://ddialliance.org/

Aims Establish metadata standards and semantic products for describing social science data, data covering human activity, and other data based on observational methods. **Structure** Executive Board; Scientific Board; Technical Committee. Working Groups. **Activities** Events/meetings; networking/liaising; standards/guidelines; training/education. **Events** *Annual European DDI User Conference* Paris (France) 2020, *Annual European DDI User Conference* Tampere (Finland) 2019, *Annual European DDI User Conference* Berlin (Germany) 2018, *Annual European DDI User Conference* Lausanne (Switzerland) 2017, *Annual European DDI User Conference* Cologne (Germany) 2016. [2020/AA0440/**E**]

- ♦ DATE – Design, Automation and Test in Europe Conference (meeting series)

♦ Date Palm Global Network (DPGN) 05013

Coordinator Date Palm Research and Development Programme/UAE Univ, PO Box 81908, Al Ain, United Arab Emirates. T. +97137832334. Fax +97137832472.

History Apr 2002, Al Ain (United Arab Emirates). *AARINENA Regional Date Palm Network* absorbed through merger into DPGN. **Aims** Promote development and improvement of the date palm industry; work towards self-sufficiency, enhancement of the quality of life and conservation of the eco-system in date producing countries. **Structure** Board (meets once a year), including Coordinator. Technical Secretariat, comprising 1 officer of *FAO (#09260)* headquarters and 1 officer from *FAO Regional Office for the Near East and North Africa (#09269).* Working Groups (4). Regional Coordinators (6): Asia; Middle East; North Africa; Sahel; Southern Africa; Southern America. **Activities** Technical Working Groups (4): Germplasm/Propagation; Production; Pests and Disease Management; Post Harvest Technologies and Marketing. **Events** *Conference* Abu Dhabi (United Arab Emirates) 2010, *International conference on date palm* Abu Dhabi (United Arab Emirates) 2005, *Conference* Cairo (Egypt) 2003, *Conference* Abu Dhabi (United Arab Emirates) 2002.
Members Individuals and organizations in 32 countries:
Algeria, Australia, Chile, Egypt, Eritrea, Eswatini, France, Holy See, Iran Islamic Rep, Iraq, Italy, Jordan, Libya, Mali, Morocco, Namibia, Niger, Nigeria, Palestine, Peru, Qatar, Saudi Arabia, Senegal, South Africa, Sudan, Syrian AR, Tunisia, Türkiye, UK, United Arab Emirates, USA, Yemen.
Included in the above, 1 organization listed in this Yearbook:
Arab Centre for the Studies of Arid Zones and Dry Lands (ACSAD, #00918).
IGO Relations *FAO (#09260); United Nations Office for Project Services (UNOPS, #20602);* national associations. **NGO Relations** *Association of Agricultural Research Institutions in the Near East and North Africa (AARINENA, #02364).* [2010.06.01/XM0497/**F**]

- ♦ DATEX II (unconfirmed)
- ♦ DATF – Benelux Deployable Air Task Force (1996 treaty)
- ♦ Datskij Institut Kultury (internationally oriented national body)
- ♦ DATÜB – Dünya Ahiska Türkleri Birligi (internationally oriented national body)
- ♦ Daughters of Charity of the Sacred Heart of Jesus (religious order)
- ♦ Daughters of the Cross of Liège (religious order)
- ♦ Daughters of Divine Charity (religious order)
- ♦ Daughters of the Heart of Mary (religious order)
- ♦ Daughters of the Holy Spirit (religious order)
- ♦ Daughters of Mary (religious order)
- ♦ Daughters of Mary – Congregation of the Daughters of Mary Immaculate (religious order)
- ♦ Daughters of Mary Help of Christians (religious order)
- ♦ Daughters of Mary and Joseph (religious order)
- ♦ Daughters of Our Lady of Mercy (religious order)
- ♦ Daughters of Our Lady of the Sacred Heart (religious order)
- ♦ Daughters of the Passion of Jesus Christ and the Sorrows of Mary (religious order)
- ♦ Daughters of Penelope (internationally oriented national body)
- ♦ Daughters of St Anne (religious order)
- ♦ Daughters of St Mary of the Presentation (religious order)
- ♦ Daughters of St Mary of Providence (religious order)
- ♦ Daughters of St Paul – Pious Society of the Daughters of St Paul (religious order)
- ♦ Daughters of Wisdom (religious order)
- ♦ Daughters of Zion / see Hadassah
- ♦ DAV – Deutschsprachige Arbeitsgemeinschaft für Verbrennungsbehandlung (internationally oriented national body)
- ♦ DAV – Diplomatic Academy of Vietnam (internationally oriented national body)
- ♦ DAVIC – Digital Audio-Visual Council (inactive)
- ♦ David Davies Memorial Institute of International Studies (internationally oriented national body)
- ♦ David and Elaine Potter Charitable Foundation (unconfirmed)
- ♦ David Horowitz Institute for the Research of Developing Countries (internationally oriented national body)
- ♦ David Horowitz Research Institute on Society and Economy / see David Horowitz Institute for the Research of Developing Countries
- ♦ David and Lucile Packard Foundation (internationally oriented national body)
- ♦ David Lynch Foundation (internationally oriented national body)
- ♦ David Lynch Foundation for Consciousness-Based Education and World Peace / see David Lynch Foundation
- ♦ David McAntony Gibson Foundation / see GlobalMedic
- ♦ David M Kennedy Center for International Studies (internationally oriented national body)
- ♦ David Rockefeller Center for Latin American Studies (internationally oriented national body)
- ♦ David Rockefeller Center for Latin American Studies, Harvard University / see David Rockefeller Center for Latin American Studies
- ♦ David Sheldrick Wildlife Trust / see Sheldrick Wildlife Trust
- ♦ David Shepherd Wildlife Foundation (internationally oriented national body)
- ♦ DAVO – Deutsche Arbeitsgemeinschaft Vorderer Orient für Gegenwartsbezogene Forschung und Dokumentation (internationally oriented national body)
- ♦ Davviriikkaid Samiraddi / see Saami Council (#19012)
- ♦ Davviriikkalas Nisson- ja Sohkabealedutkama Instituhtta / see Nordic Information for Gender Knowledge (#17317)
- ♦ **DAWN** Development Alternatives with Women for a New Era (#05054)
- ♦ DAWN Group / see Development Alternatives with Women for a New Era (#05054)
- ♦ Dayemi Complex / see Dayemi Complex Bangladesh
- ♦ Dayemi Complex Bangladesh (internationally oriented national body)
- ♦ Days for Girls International (internationally oriented national body)
- ♦ DÄZ – Deutsche Ärztegemeinschaft für Humanitäre Zusammenarbeit (internationally oriented national body)
- ♦ DBA – Défi Belgique-Afrique (internationally oriented national body)
- ♦ dba YEM FOUNDATION / see YEM Foundation (#21974)
- ♦ DBEI – Digital Built Environment Institute (unconfirmed)
- ♦ **DbI** Deafblind International (#05014)
- ♦ **DBI** Don Bosco International (#05117)
- ♦ DBLP – International Symposium on Principles and Practice of Declarative Programming (meeting series)
- ♦ **DBN** Don Bosco Network (#05118)
- ♦ DBSA – Development Bank of Southern Africa (internationally oriented national body)
- ♦ **DBTG** International Dry Bulk Terminals Group (#13206)
- ♦ **DBYN** Don Bosco Youth-Net (#05119)
- ♦ DCA – DanChurchAid (internationally oriented national body)
- ♦ DCA / see Eastern Caribbean Civil Aviation Authority (#05232)
- ♦ **DCA Europe** Drilling Contractors Association (#05133)
- ♦ DCAF / see Geneva Centre for Security Sector Governance (#10121)
- ♦ **DCAF** Geneva Centre for Security Sector Governance (#10121)
- ♦ DCB – Dayemi Complex Bangladesh (internationally oriented national body)
- ♦ DCC – Délégation catholique pour la coopération (internationally oriented national body)
- ♦ DC – Company of the Daughters of Charity of St Vincent de Paul (religious order)
- ♦ DC – Congregatio Patrum Doctrinae Christianae (religious order)
- ♦ DCCR – Danish Center for Conflict Resolution (internationally oriented national body)
- ♦ DC – Diplomatic Council (unconfirmed)
- ♦ **DCED** Donor Committee for Enterprise Development (#05122)
- ♦ Dcery Bozské Lasky (religious order)
- ♦ DCFRN / see Farm Radio International (#09274)
- ♦ DCI / see Irish Aid
- ♦ DCID – Duke Center for International Development (internationally oriented national body)
- ♦ **DCI** Defence for Children International (#05025)
- ♦ DCI – Development Center International, Dhaka (internationally oriented national body)
- ♦ **DCL** Deaf Champions League (#05015)
- ♦ DCLI / see Centre international LEBRET-IRFED
- ♦ **DCO** Digital Cooperation Organization (#05072)
- ♦ **DCPO** Dana Center for Preventive Ophthalmology (#04997)
- ♦ **DCSA** Digital Container Shipping Association (#05071)
- ♦ **DCSF** Danube Civil Society Forum (#05003)
- ♦ DCSHJ – Daughters of Charity of the Sacred Heart of Jesus (religious order)
- ♦ **DCVMN** Developing Countries Vaccine Manufacturers Network (#05052)
- ♦ DDC – Direction du développement et de la coopération (internationally oriented national body)
- ♦ DDF / see International Downtown Association
- ♦ **DDI Alliance** Data Documentation Initiative Alliance (#05012)
- ♦ DDI – International Conference on Driver Distraction and Inattention (meeting series)
- ♦ DDI International – Deep Democracy Institute International (unconfirmed)
- ♦ DDMI – David Davies Memorial Institute of International Studies (internationally oriented national body)
- ♦ DDNI – Danube Delta National Institute for Research and Development (internationally oriented national body)
- ♦ DDP – Digital Defenders Partnership (internationally oriented national body)
- ♦ DDW – Discovering Deaf Worlds (internationally oriented national body)
- ♦ DEA / see Diakonie Katastrophenhilfe
- ♦ DEA Club – Dissociative Electron Attachment Club (unconfirmed)
- ♦ Deadong Institute for Korean Studies (internationally oriented national body)
- ♦ DEA – Drilling Engineering Association (internationally oriented national body)
- ♦ **DEA Europe** Drilling Engineering Association Europe (#05134)
- ♦ Deaf Africa Mission (internationally oriented national body)
- ♦ Deaf-Blind International / see Deafblind International (#05014)

♦ Deafblind International (DbI) 05014

Secretariat 50 Main Street, Paris ON N3L 2E2, Canada. E-mail: dbi-secretariat@sensity.ca.
URL: http://www.deafblindinternational.org/

History Prior to 1960, as *International Association for Education of the Deaf-Blind – Association internationale pour l'éducation des sourds-muets.* Current constitution ratified 2009, when organization changed into an International Association. **Aims** Promote awareness and knowledge of deafblindness as a unique disability; influence for appropriate services for people who are deafblind around the world. **Structure** General Meeting (annual); Board; Management Committee. **Languages** English. **Staff** Voluntary. **Finance** Sources: members' dues. **Activities** Advocacy/lobbying/activism; events/meetings. **Events** *Annual Conference* Ottawa, ON (Canada) 2023, *African Conference* Nairobi (Kenya) 2022, *African Conference* Nairobi (Kenya) 2021, *Quadrennial International Conference* Gold Coast, QLD (Australia) 2019, *Quadrennial European Conference* Aalborg (Denmark) 2017. **Publications** *DbI Review* (2 a year) in English, Spanish.
Members Networks (16). Corporate members (62) in 28 countries and territories:
Argentina, Australia, Austria, Canada, Croatia, Cyprus, Denmark, Ethiopia, Finland, France, Germany, Greece, Hong Kong, Iceland, India, Ireland, Italy, Malawi, Netherlands, New Zealand, Norway, Russia, Singapore, Spain, Sweden, Switzerland, UK, USA.
Included in the above, 2 organizations listed in this Yearbook:
European Deafblind Network (EDbN, #06890); Usher Study Group.
Individuals in 36 countries and territories:
Argentina, Australia, Austria, Belgium, Brazil, Canada, Czechia, Denmark, Ethiopia, Finland, France, Germany, Guatemala, Hong Kong, Hungary, Iceland, India, Ireland, Israel, Italy, Japan, Malta, Netherlands, New Zealand, Norway, Poland, Portugal, Romania, Russia, Singapore, South Africa, Spain, Sweden, Switzerland, UK, USA.
NGO Relations Member of (1): *International Council for Education of People with Visual Impairment (ICEVI, #13015). Sense International* is Full Member. [2022.12.05/XD2223/**B**]

♦ Deaf Champions League (DCL) 05015
SG Avda Mar Mediterraneo 792oB, Valdemoro, 28341 Madrid, Spain. E-mail: deafchampionsleague@gmail.com.
Pres address not obtained.
URL: http://www.deafchampionsleague.eu/
History Also referred to as *European Deaf Champions League*. Current constitution adopted 14 Mar 2014. **Aims** Encourage elite club level competition of *football*; allow elite clubs to compete against other elite clubs within Europe; foster and promote friendships, sportmanship and unity across countries and clubs within Europe; encourage and promote fair play. **Structure** Annual General Meeting; Executive Committee; Management Committee. **Languages** English. **Staff** 19.00 FTE, voluntary. **Activities** Sporting activities; events/meetings. **Publications** None. **NGO Relations** *European Deaf Sport Organization (EDSO, #06892)*.
[2017/XM4376/**D**]

♦ Deaf Child Worldwide (internationally oriented national body)

♦ Deaf History International (DHI) 05016
Sec-Treas address not obtained.
URL: http://www.deafhistoryinternational.com/
History 1989. 1994, formally established. **Aims** Study, preserve and disseminate deaf people's history. **Structure** Bureau, comprising President, Vice-President, Secretary-Treasurer and 4 members at large. **Languages** English, International Sign Language. **Staff** None. **Finance** Members' dues. **Events** *Conference* Chiba (Japan) 2027, *Conference* Montpellier (France) 2024, *Conference* Ljubljana (Slovenia) / Zagreb (Croatia) 2022, *Conference* Sydney, NSW (Australia) 2018, *Conference* Edinburgh (UK) 2015. **Publications** *DHI Newsletter* (3 a year).
Members Full in 24 countries:
Australia, Belgium, Canada, Croatia, Denmark, Finland, France, Germany, Ireland, Italy, Japan, Korea Rep, Lithuania, Netherlands, New Zealand, Norway, Russia, Slovakia, Slovenia, Spain, Sweden, Switzerland, UK, USA.
[2014/XF2993/**F**]

♦ Deaf International Basketball Federation (DIBF) 05017
Gen Sec Maasstrasse 26, 69123 Heidelberg, Germany. Fax +4932121449162. E-mail: info@dibf.org – secretary.general@dibf.org.
URL: http://www.dibf.org/
History 2 May 1998, Turku (Finland). Officially founded at first world congress, 20 July 2002, Athens (Greece). Former names and other names: *International Deaf Basketball Association (IDBA)* – former (1998 to 2002). **Aims** Organize all official events of world and regional deaf basketball and 3x3; encourage growth and development of deaf basketball and 3x3 worldwide. **Structure** Central Board, comprising President, Vice President, Secretary General, Treasurer, 2 Board Members and 4 Zone Presidents. **Languages** English, International Sign Language. **Staff** 0.00 FTE, paid; 40.00 FTE, voluntary. Administration: media staff; members of commissions; etc. **Finance** Sources: fees for services; fundraising; members' dues. Supported by: *Fédération internationale de basketball (FIBA, #09614)*. Annual budget: 20,000 USD. **Activities** Awards/prizes/competitions; certification/accreditation; events/meetings; financial and/or material support; guidance/assistance/consulting; monitoring/evaluation; politics/policy/regulatory; projects/programmes; research and development; sporting activities; standards/guidelines; training/education. **Members** National Deaf Sports Federations; National Deaf Basketball Associations. Membership countries not specified. **NGO Relations** Affiliated with (2): *Fédération internationale de basketball (FIBA, #09614)*; *International Committee of Sports for the Deaf (ICSD, #12805)*.
[2021.08.31/XD9423/**D**]

♦ Deaf International Football Association (DIFA) 05018
Pres 72/2-62 Nizhegorodskaya Str, Moscow MOSKVA, Russia. Fax +74956712283. E-mail: jakov.difa@gmail.com.
URL: http://www.difa.org/
History 2011. Registration: Swiss Civil Code, No/ID: CH-660-0477010-8, Switzerland. **Aims** Offer know-how and managing experience; safeguard and promote the interests of deaf football and development. **Structure** Executive Board. **Events** *Congress* Salerno (Italy) 2016.
[2020.08.26/XM4756/**C**]

♦ DeafKidz International (unconfirmed)

♦ Deaf Ministries International (DMI) 05019
Contact PO Box 395, Beaconsfield VIC 3807, Australia. T. +61359405431. Fax +61359405432.
URL: http://www.deafmin.org/
History 1979, Korea Rep. Originally under *World Opportunities International – Help the Children (WOI, no recent information)*. Became independent 2000. **Aims** Establish resources and facilities to bring the message of Christ and aid to deaf people. **Events** *International Conference / Conference* Seoul (Korea Rep) 2014, *Conference* Stanwell Tops, NSW (Australia) 2011, *International conference* Sydney, NSW (Australia) 2011, *International conference / Conference* Alexandria (Egypt) 2008. **Publications** *Deaf Ministries Update*.
[2018/XJ4658/**F**]

♦ DeafNET Centre for Knowledge (internationally oriented national body)
♦ DeafNET – DeafNET Centre for Knowledge (internationally oriented national body)
♦ **DEAfrica** Distance Education for Africa (#05103)
♦ **DEASA** Distance Education Association of Southern Africa (#05104)
♦ DEA – Think Global – Development Education Association (internationally oriented national body)
♦ Death Online Research Network (unconfirmed)
♦ Death Penalty Project (internationally oriented national body)
♦ Death Watch International (internationally oriented national body)

♦ Deauville Partnership 05020
Address not obtained.
History Launched May 2011, Deauville (France), by *Group of Eight (G-8, #10745)*. Also referred to as *Deauville Partnership with Arab Countries in Transition*. **Aims** Support countries in the *Arab* world engaged in *transitions* toward 'free, democratic and tolerant societies'. **Structure** Rotating Chairmanship. **Events** *G7 Senior Officials' Meeting* Paris (France) 2017, *Invesment Conference* London (UK) 2013, *Women in Business Conference on the Role of Arab Women in Supporting Open Economies and Inclusive Growth* London (UK) 2013.
Members Governments (18):
Canada, Egypt, France, Germany, Italy, Japan, Jordan, Kuwait, Libya, Morocco, Qatar, Russia, Saudi Arabia, Tunisia, Türkiye, UK, United Arab Emirates, USA.
Regional entity:
European Union (EU, #08967).
Financial institutions:
African Development Bank (ADB, #00283); *Arab Fund for Economic and Social Development (AFESD, #00965)*; *Arab Monetary Fund (AMF, #01009)*; *European Bank for Reconstruction and Development (EBRD, #06315)*; *European Investment Bank (EIB, #07599)*; *International Bank for Reconstruction and Development (IBRD, #12317)* (World Bank); *International Finance Corporation (IFC, #13597)*; *International Monetary Fund (IMF, #14180)*; *Islamic Development Bank (IsDB, #16044)*; *OPEC Fund for International Development (OFID, #17745)*.
IGO Relations *OECD (#17693)*; *League of Arab States (LAS, #16420)*; UN organizations. Instrumental in setting up: *Middle East and North Africa Transition Fund (MENA Transition Fund, #16785)*.
[2017/XM6833/**E***]

♦ Deauville Partnership with Arab Countries in Transition / see Deauville Partnership (#05020)
♦ DEBELUX / see Chambre de commerce belgo-luxembourgeoise-allemande

♦ DEBRA International 05021
Registered Address Am Heumarkt 27/1, 1030 Vienna, Austria. E-mail: office@debra-international.org.
URL: http://www.debra-international.org/

History Oct 1995, Marbella (Spain). Founded at a meeting of national EB support groups, arising from *DEBRA-Europe (inactive)* which it superseded in 2009. Registration: State Police Directorate Vienna, No/ID: ZVR932762489, Austria. **Aims** Coordinate, in collaboration with its members, activities that are for the benefit of everyone affected by EB globally: the international patient community, patient support and advocacy groups, healthcare professionals, researchers and industry. **Structure** Executive Committee. **Languages** English. **Staff** 2.10 FTE, paid. **Finance** Sources: donations; members' dues; sponsorship. **Activities** Events/meetings; guidance/assistance/consulting; research and development. **Events** *Annual Conference* Moscow (Russia) 2021, *Global Congress on Epidermolysis Bullosa* London (UK) 2020, *Annual Conference* Zermatt (Switzerland) 2018, *Epidermolysis Bullosa Research Conference* Salzburg (Austria) 2017, *Annual Conference* Wellington (New Zealand) 2017.
Members National organizations in 46 countries and territories:
Argentina, Australia, Austria, Belarus, Belgium, Bosnia-Herzegovina, Brazil, Canada, Chile, China, Colombia, Costa Rica, Croatia, Cuba, Czechia, Egypt, Finland, France, Germany, Hungary, India, Indonesia, Ireland, Italy, Japan, Libya, Malaysia, Mexico, Netherlands, New Zealand, Norway, Pakistan, Poland, Romania, Russia, Serbia, Singapore, Slovakia, Slovenia, Spain, Sweden, Switzerland, Taiwan, UK, Ukraine, USA.
NGO Relations Member of (5): *EGAN – Patients Network for Medical Research and Health (EGAN, #05394)*; *European Disability Forum (EDF, #06929)*; *European Patients' Forum (EPF, #08172)*; *EURORDIS – Rare Diseases Europe (#09175)*; *Rare Diseases International (RDI, #18621)*.
[2021.09.03/XC0037/**C**]

♦ Debt Relief International (internationally oriented national body)
♦ DECA – International Study Group for the Detection and Prevention of Cancer (inactive)
♦ **DECC** Disciples Ecumenical Consultative Council (#05100)
♦ DEC – Disasters Emergency Committee (internationally oriented national body)
♦ December 18 – International Advocacy and Resource Centre on the Human Rights of Migrant Workers (internationally oriented national body)
♦ December Twelfth Movement International Secretariat (internationally oriented national body)
♦ Decentralisation and Local Governance / see Development Partners Network on Decentralisation and Local Governance (#05058)
♦ Decent Work City Network (unconfirmed)
♦ DECEP – European Perspective (internationally oriented national body)
♦ DECERE – Démocratie, construction européenne et religions (internationally oriented national body)
♦ **DECET** Diversity, Early Childhood Education and Training (#05106)
♦ Decision Sciences Institute (internationally oriented national body)
♦ Declaração sobre a personalidade jurídica das companhias estrangeiras (1936 treaty)
♦ Declaração universal dos direitos humanos (1948 treaty)
♦ Declaración de Bogota / see Comisión Permanente del Pacífico Sur (#04141)
♦ Declaración de Cali / see Comisión Permanente del Pacífico Sur (#04141)
♦ Declaración de compromiso en la lucha contra el VIH/SIDA (2001 treaty)
♦ Declaración de Damasco (1991 treaty)
♦ Declaración internacional sobre los datos genéticos humanos (2003 treaty)
♦ Declaración de Lima / see Comisión Permanente del Pacífico Sur (#04141)
♦ Declaración sobre la personalidad jurídica de las compañías extranjeras (1936 treaty)
♦ Declaración sobre el principio tripartita en empresas multinacionales y política social (1977 treaty)
♦ Declaración de Quito / see Comisión Permanente del Pacífico Sur (#04141)
♦ Declaración de Santiago / see Comisión Permanente del Pacífico Sur (#04141)
♦ Declaración universal de derechos humanos (1948 treaty)
♦ Declaración de Viña del Mar / see Comisión Permanente del Pacífico Sur (#04141)
♦ Declaración sobre la Zona Marítima / see Comisión Permanente del Pacífico Sur (#04141)
♦ Declaration of Amnesty (1923 treaty)
♦ Declaration of Bern / see Public Eye
♦ Declaration of Bern Association / see Public Eye
♦ Déclaration de Berne / see Public Eye
♦ Déclaration de Berne, Association suisse pour un développement solidaire / see Public Eye
♦ Declaration of Bogota / see Comisión Permanente del Pacífico Sur (#04141)
♦ Declaration of Cali / see Comisión Permanente del Pacífico Sur (#04141)
♦ Declaration of Commitment on HIV/AIDS (2001 treaty)
♦ Déclaration concernant l'enseignement de l'histoire (1937 treaty)
♦ Déclaration conjointe relative aux problèmes de la pêche dans le Pacifique Sud (1952 treaty)
♦ Déclaration sur la construction de grandes routes de trafic international (1950 treaty)
♦ Declaration on the Construction of Main International Traffic Arteries (1950 treaty)
♦ Déclaration des droits des personnes appartenant à des minorités nationales ou ethniques, religieuses et linguistiques (1992 treaty)
♦ Déclaration d'engagement sur le VIH/sida (2001 treaty)
♦ Déclaration finale de la Conférence internationale de Tanger (1956 treaty)
♦ Declaration on Fundamental Principles Concerning the Contribution of the Mass Media to Strengthening Peace and International Understanding, to the Promotion of Human Rights and to Countering Racialism, Apartheid and Incitement to War (1978 treaty)
♦ Déclaration des gouvernements signataires de l'Arrangement du 28 mai 1937 pour le développement des échanges commerciaux (1938 treaty)
♦ Declaration by the Governments Signatories of the Agreement of May 28th 1937, for the Promotion of Commercial Exchanges (1938 treaty)
♦ Declaration of Guiding Principles on the Use of Satellite Broadcasting for the Free Flow of Information, the Spread of Education and Greater Cultural Exchange (1972 treaty)
♦ Declaration on International Cooperation in the Exploration and Use of Outer Space for the Benefit and in the Interest of all States, Taking into Particular Account the Needs of Developing Countries (1996 treaty)
♦ Déclaration internationale sur les données génétiques humaines (2003 treaty)
♦ Declaration on the Juridical Personality of Foreign Companies (1936 treaty)
♦ Declaration of Legal Principles Governing the Activities of States in the Exploration and Use of Outer Space (1963 treaty)
♦ Declaration of Lima / see Comisión Permanente del Pacífico Sur (#04141)
♦ Declaration for the Maintenance of the Status Quo in the Baltic (1908 treaty)
♦ Declaration on the Maritime Zone / see Comisión Permanente del Pacífico Sur (#04141)
♦ Déclaration sur la personnalité juridique des sociétés étrangères (1936 treaty)
♦ Déclaration portant reconnaissance du droit au pavillon des Etats dépourvus de littoral maritime (1921 treaty)
♦ Déclaration des Principes de la Coopération Culturelle Internationale (1966 treaty)
♦ Déclaration des Principes Directeurs de L'utilisation de la Radiodiffusion par Satellites pour la Libre Circulation de L'information, L'extension de L'éducation et le Développement des échanges Culturels (1972 treaty)
♦ Déclaration sur les Principes Fondamentaux Concernant la Contribution des Organes D'information au Renforcement de la Paix et de la Compréhension Internationale, à la Promotion des Droits de L'homme et à la Lutte Contre le Racisme et L'apartheid et L'incitation à la Guerre (1978 treaty)
♦ Déclaration de principes tripartite sur les entreprises multinationales et la politique sociale (1977 treaty)
♦ Declaration of principles of international cultural cooperation (1966 treaty)
♦ Declaration for the Purpose of Establishing Similar Rules of Neutrality (1938 treaty)
♦ Declaration of Quito / see Comisión Permanente del Pacífico Sur (#04141)
♦ Déclaration sur la Race et les Préjugés Raciaux (1978 treaty)
♦ Declaration on Race and Racial Prejudice (1978 treaty)
♦ Declaration Recognising the Right to a Flag of States Having no Sea-coast (1921 treaty)
♦ Declaration Regarding Article 14 of the 1965 Convention on the Elimination of all Forms of Racial Discrimination (treaty)
♦ Declaration Regarding Article 25 of the 1950 Convention for the Protection of Human Rights and Fundamental Freedoms (treaty)

- ♦ Declaration Regarding Article 41 of the 1966 Covenant on Civil and Political Rights (treaty)
- ♦ Declaration Regarding Article 46 of the 1950 Convention for the Protection of Human Rights and Fundamental Freedoms (treaty)
- ♦ Declaration Regarding the Teaching of History (1937 treaty)
- ♦ Déclaration relative à l'amnistie (1923 treaty)
- ♦ Déclaration relative à l' énergie atomique (1945 treaty)
- ♦ Declaration Relative to the Maintenance of the Status Quo in the North Sea (1908 treaty)
- ♦ Déclaration relative au Pacte de Bagdad (1958 treaty)
- ♦ Declaration Respecting the Baghdad Pact (1958 treaty)
- ♦ Declaration Respecting Maritime Law (1856 treaty)
- ♦ Declaration Respecting the Monetary Convention of 6 Nov 1885 and the Additional Convention of 4 Nov 1908 (1909 treaty)
- ♦ Declaration on the Responsibilities of Present Generations Towards Future Generations (1997 treaty)
- ♦ Declaration on the Rights of Persons Belonging to National or Ethnic, Religious and Linguistic Minorities (1992 treaty)
- ♦ Declaration of Santiago / see Comisión Permanente del Pacifico Sur (#04141)
- ♦ Declaration of Santiago on the Maritime Zone (1952 treaty)
- ♦ Déclaration de Santiago sur la zone maritime (1952 treaty)
- ♦ Declarations Relative to the Open Door in China Policy (1900 treaty)
- ♦ Déclaration Trilatérale des Présidents des Etats-Unis, de la Russie et de L'Ukraine (1994 treaty)
- ♦ Déclaration universelle sur la bioéthique et les droits de l'homme (2005 treaty)
- ♦ Déclaration universelle des droits de l'homme (1948 treaty)
- ♦ Declaration of Viña del Mar / see Comisión Permanente del Pacifico Sur (#04141)
- ♦ Déclaration en vue de fixer des règles similaires de neutralité (1938 treaty)
- ♦ Declarative AI (meeting series)
- ♦ Decom North Sea (internationally oriented national body)

♦ DECT Forum 05022

Secretariat Wabernstr 40, 3007 Bern, Switzerland. T. +498951662456. E-mail: secretariat@dect.org.
URL: http://www.dect.org/

History Set up 1997, Paris (France), as an industry association. DECT stands for *Digital Enhanced Cordless Telecommunications*. **Aims** Create and maintain a collaborative environment of the CAT-iq/DECT industry; drive programmes to develop and improve CAT-iq/DECT *wireless technology* so as to exceed wireless communications expectations and meet the needs of a technology-shifting world. **Structure** General Assembly. Board. Working Groups. **Languages** English. **Staff** 1.00 FTE, paid. **Finance** Members' dues. **Activities** Certification programmes; meeting activities. **Events** *Annual Forum* Barcelona (Spain) 2014, *Annual DECT (Digital Enhanced Cordless Telecommunications) and CAT-IQ (Cordless Advanced Technology – Internet and Quality) Conference* Amsterdam (Netherlands) 2011. **Publications** *DECT Forum Newsletter* (4 a year); *DECT Magazine*. Whitepapers; press releases. **Members** Companies. Membership countries not specified. **IGO Relations** *Electronic Communications Committee (ECC, see: #04602)*. **NGO Relations** *European Telecommunications Standards Institute (ETSI, #08897); GSM Association (GSMA, #10813).* [2014.02.25/XJ7881/F]

- ♦ Deens Cultureel Instituut (internationally oriented national body)
- ♦ Deep Democracy Institute International (unconfirmed)

♦ Deep-Ocean Stewardship Initiative (DOSI) 05023

Contact address not obtained.
Contact address not obtained.
URL: https://www.dosi-project.org/

History 2013. **Aims** Utilise independent scientific findings about the deep ocean to support its ecosystem-based management and integrate other fields of expertise in the development of deep-ocean strategies and solutions. **Structure** Executive Team; Advisory Board; Working Group Leads; Working Group Members. **Activities** Knowledge management/information dissemination; networking/liaising; politics/policy/regulatory. **Publications** *Deep-Sea Round-Up* (weekly) in English – A weekly newsletter sharing the latest research and news from the deep ocean community.; *Deep Sea Life* (2 a year) in English – A twice-yearly update on deep-ocean research and events, featuring articles by members of the scientific community. Co-published with the Deep Sea Biology Society.. **Information Services** *DOSI Policy Briefs* – DOSI releases policy briefs and information sheets on key deep-ocean topics to help bring science to decision-making.. **Members** Individuals. Membership countries not specified. **IGO Relations** Observer status with (1): *International Seabed Authority (ISBA, #14813).* [2022.11.11/AA1942/v/F]

- ♦ Deep Ocean Water Applications Society (unconfirmed)

♦ Deep Sea Conservation Coalition (DSCC) 05024

Sec Postbus 59681, 1040 LD Amsterdam, Netherlands. T. +31646168899. E-mail: info@savethehighseas.org.
URL: http://www.savethehighseas.org/

History Founded 2004. Registered in accordance with Dutch law: 59473460. EU Transparency Register: 451986010410-20. **Aims** Protect marine life in the world's deep oceans. **Structure** Steering Group. **Publications** *DSCC Newsletter.*

Members Organizations (over 70) in 19 countries:
Argentina, Australia, Canada, Chile, Costa Rica, Ecuador, France, Germany, Iceland, Malaysia, Malta, Mexico, New Zealand, Peru, Spain, Sweden, UK, Uruguay, USA.
Included in the above, 23 listed in this Yearbook:
- *Antarctic and Southern Ocean Coalition (ASOC, #00849);*
- *BirdLife International (#03266);*
- *Center for International Environmental Law (CIEL);*
- *Centro Desarrollo y Pesca Sustenable (CeDePesca, #03796);*
- *Coalition Clean Baltic (CCB, #04053);*
- *Conservation International (CI);*
- *Earthworks;*
- *European Community on Protection of Marine Life (ECOP Marine);*
- *Friends of the Earth International (FoEI, #10002);*
- *Global Ocean Trust (GOT);*
- *Greenpeace International (#10727);*
- *International Collective in Support of Fishworkers (ICSF, #12639);*
- *International Fund for Animal Welfare (IFAW, #13693);*
- *International Ocean Institute (IOI, #14394);*
- *Marine Conservation Institute;*
- *Marine Conservation Society (MCS);*
- *Oceana;*
- *Ocean Futures Society;*
- *Pew Charitable Trusts;*
- *Save our Seas Foundation (SOSF);*
- *Seas at Risk (SAR, #19189);*
- *World Forum of Fisher Peoples (WFFP, #21517);*
- *World Wide Fund for Nature (WWF, #21922).*

NGO Relations Member of: *High Level Panel for a Sustainable Ocean Economy (Panel, #10917)* – Advisory Network. [2018/XM0881/y/F]

- ♦ Deep Water Circulation Research Conference (meeting series)
- ♦ Defence Agreement (1960 treaty)
- ♦ Defence for Children / see Defence for Children International (#05025)

♦ Defence for Children International (DCI) 05025

Défense des Enfants International (DEI) – Defensa de Niñas y Niños Internacional (DNI)

Exec Dir Intl Secretariat, Rue de Varembé 1, Case Postale 88, 1211 Geneva 20, Switzerland. T. +41227340558. E-mail: info@defenceforchildren.org.
URL: http://www.defenceforchildren.org/

History Founded 5 Jul 1979, Geneva (Switzerland), as *Defence for Children*, by Nigel Cantwell and Canon Moerman, Chair of the *'International Year of the Child'* (1979). Subsequently also referred to as *Defence for Children International Movement*. Present name adopted 1982. Previously also referred to in Spanish as *Defensa de los Niños Internacional*. Statutes adopted by International General Assembly, 5 Apr 1986, Xalapa (Mexico); amended 2014. **Aims** Work towards a world where children enjoy and exercise their rights in a just and responsible society; ensure on-going practical, systematic and concerted international action directed towards promoting and protecting the rights of the child, as articulated in the UN Convention on the Rights of the Child, its optional protocols and other human rights instruments. **Structure** International General Assembly (every 4 years); International Executive Council; International Secretariat, based in Geneva (Switzerland); World Service Foundation, based in Brussels (Belgium). **Languages** English, French, Spanish. **Staff** At international secretariat: 4.5 FTE; worldwide: about 200. **Finance** Members' dues. Other sources: grants from governments, foundations, international and national bodies; individual donations. **Activities** Advocacy/lobbying/activism; research/documentation; guidance/assistance/consulting; networking/liaising; events/meetings. **Events** *Latin American Regional Conference* Buenos Aires (Argentina) 2019, *World Congress on Justice for Children* Paris (France) 2018, *Tribunal d'opinion sur la détention d'enfants innocents en centres fermés pour étrangers* Brussels (Belgium) 2008, *International conference on child labour and child exploitation* Cairns, QLD (Australia) 2008, *International conference on kids behind bars – a child rights perspective* Bethlehem (Palestine) 2005. **Publications** Books; manuals. Maintains a Documentation Centre.

Members Full: national sections in 34 countries and territories:
Argentina, Australia, Belgium, Bolivia, Brazil, Burkina Faso, Cameroon, Canada, Central African Rep, Colombia, Costa Rica, Czechia, Egypt, France, Ghana, Greece, Guinea, Iraq, Italy, Lebanon, Liberia, Mauritania, Mauritius, Morocco, Netherlands, Palestine, Sierra Leone, Somalia, Spain, Switzerland, Tunisia, Uganda, Uruguay, Yemen.
Associate in 2 countries:
Jordan, Pakistan.

Consultative Status Consultative status granted from: *ECOSOC (#05331)* (Special); *UNESCO (#20322)* (Consultative Status); *ILO (#11123)* (Special List); *UNICEF (#20332); Council of Europe (CE, #04881)* (Participatory Status); *African Committee of Experts on the Rights and Welfare of the Child (ACERWC, #00257)* (Observer Status). **IGO Relations** Panel member of: *Interagency Panel on Juvenile Justice (IPJJ, #11390).* Associated with Department of Global Communications of the United Nations. **NGO Relations** Member of: *Eurochild (#05657); Global Partnership to End Violence Against Children (End Violence Against Children, #10533); Movimiento Mundial por la Infancia de Latinoamérica y El Caribe (MMI-LAC, #16873).* Stakeholder in: *Child and Youth Finance International (CYFI, inactive).* Netherlands section supports: *End Child Prostitution, Child Pornography and Trafficking of Children for Sexual Purposes (ECPAT, #05456).* [2019.02.13/XF0050/F]

- ♦ Defence for Children International Movement / see Defence for Children International (#05025)
- ♦ In Defence of Christians (internationally oriented national body)
- ♦ Defence Council for Equatorial Africa (inactive)

♦ DefendDefenders 05026

Exec Dir Human Rights House, Plot 1853, John Kiyingi Road, Nsambya PO Box 70356, Kampala, Uganda. T. +256414510263. E-mail: info@defenddefenders.org.
Geneva Office Rue de Varembé 1, 5th floor, 1202 Geneva, Switzerland. E-mail: geneva@defenddefenders.org.
URL: https://defenddefenders.org/

History 2005. Former names and other names: *East and Horn of Africa Human Rights Defenders Project* – former. Registration: No/ID: S.5914/5983, Uganda. **Aims** Maximize the protection of Human Rights Defenders working in the sub-region; enhance the awareness of human rights work through linkages with national, regional and international like-minded entities.. **Structure** Board. **NGO Relations** Member of (1): *ProtectDefenders.eu (#18546).* [2022/AA2845/D]

- ♦ Defend Democracy (internationally oriented national body)
- ♦ Defending Democracy / see Defend Democracy

♦ Defend International (DI) 05027

Pres Postboks 196, 1411 Kolbotn, Norway. T. +4767410415. E-mail: post@defendinternational.org.
URL: http://www.defendinternational.org/

History Founded 2007. **Aims** Respond to grave *violations* of human *rights* and of International *Humanitarian* Law; monitor the implementation of preventive measures that are designed to end *impunity* for the perpetrators of these crimes; conduct medical research that may either directly or indirectly improve the health standard of communities; promote peace and democracy through cultural relations and diplomacy. **Structure** Committees (13). **Languages** English. **Staff** 41.00 FTE, paid. **Activities** Awareness raising; research/documentation; knowledge management/information dissemination; advocacy/lobbying/activism; capacity building; monitoring/evaluation; events/meetings.

Members Organizations in 23 countries and territories:
Algeria, Bahrain, Djibouti, Egypt, Germany, Ghana, India, Iran Islamic Rep, Iraq, Japan, Lebanon, Morocco, Nepal, Netherlands, Norway, Palestine, Russia, Saudi Arabia, South Africa, Sweden, Syrian AR, Tunisia, Yemen. [2019.06.21/XJ5709/F]

- ♦ Defensa de Niñas y Niños Internacional (#05025)
- ♦ Defensa de los Niños Internacional / see Defence for Children International (#05025)
- ♦ Défense aérienne de l'Amérique du Nord (internationally oriented national body)
- ♦ Défense des Enfants International (#05025)
- ♦ Defensores do Planeta (internationally oriented national body)
- ♦ Defensor del Pueblo Europeo (#08084)
- ♦ Défi Belgique-Afrique (internationally oriented national body)
- ♦ **DEFI** Europeiske Fagforeningsinstitut (#08928)
- ♦ **DEFNET** EU Defence Environmental Network (#05581)
- ♦ **DEFS** Den Europeiske Faglige Samorganisasjon (#08927)
- ♦ DEG / see DEG – Deutsche Investitions- und Entwicklungsgesellschaft
- ♦ DEG – Deutsche Investitions- und Entwicklungsgesellschaft (internationally oriented national body)
- ♦ DeGPT – Deutschsprachige Gesellschaft für Psychotraumatologie (internationally oriented national body)
- ♦ **DEI** Défense des Enfants International (#05025)
- ♦ DEI – Dublin European Institute (internationally oriented national body)
- ♦ Delegation for the Adoption of an International Language (inactive)
- ♦ Délégation pour l'adoption d'une langue universelle internationale (inactive)
- ♦ Délégation catholique pour la coopération (internationally oriented national body)
- ♦ Délégation générale à la langue française / see Délégation générale à la langue française et aux langues de France
- ♦ Délégation générale à la langue française et aux langues de France (internationally oriented national body)
- ♦ Délégation internationale permanente de technique sanitaire et d'hygiène communale (inactive)
- ♦ Deleuze and Guattari Conference (meeting series)
- ♦ Delian League (inactive)
- ♦ Délice Network (unconfirmed)
- ♦ DELIPRO / see Centre d'aide au développement dans la liberté et le progrès
- ♦ Délipro – Centre d'aide au développement dans la liberté et le progrès (internationally oriented national body)
- ♦ **DeLoG** Development Partners Network on Decentralisation and Local Governance (#05058)
- ♦ Delovna Skupnost Alpe-Jadran / see Alps-Adriatic-Alliance (#00747)
- ♦ Delovna Skupnost Dezel, Zupanij, Regij in Republik Vzhodnoalpskega Obmocja / see Alps-Adriatic-Alliance (#00747)
- ♦ DELPHIS / see Oceanomare-Delphis
- ♦ Delta Kappa Gamma Society International (internationally oriented national body)
- ♦ Delta Organization / see Ocean Conservancy
- ♦ DEMAC – Diaspora Emergency Action & Coordination (unconfirmed)
- ♦ DEMAS – Asociace pro Podporu Demokracie a Lidskych Prav (internationally oriented national body)
- ♦ DEMAS – Association for Democracy Assistance and Human Rights (internationally oriented national body)

♦ Dementia Alliance International (DAI) 05028

Chair C/- Patrick with Durio & Korpal PC, 6575 West Loop S, Suite 400, Bellaire TX 77401-3512, USA. T. +159913964. E-mail: info@infodai.org – chair@infodai.org.
Co-founder address not obtained.
URL: http://www.dementiaallianceinternational.org/

History 1 Jan 2014, Texas (USA). Bylaws updated and adopted: Aug 2017; Feb 2022. Registration: Office of the Secretary of State, Texas, No/ID: 801312800, Start date: 6 Jul 2014, USA, Texas; Section 501(c)(3), No/ID: EIN 27-3538654, USA, Texas. **Aims** Provide advocacy and support for people diagnosed with dementia; promote education and awareness about dementia to help reduce the myths and eradicate stigma and discrimination; improve the quality of the lives of people with dementia and their families and care partners; advocate for human and legal rights for all people with dementia and for dementia as a disability. **Structure** Board of Directors; Internal, External and Governance Committees; Finance Committee; Work Health and Safety Officer; Board Secretariat; Finance Officer; Marketing. **Languages** English. **Staff** Voluntary. **Finance** Sources: fundraising; sponsorship. Supported by: *Alzheimer's Disease International (ADI, #00762)*; Dementia Australia. Annual budget: 50,000 USD (2019). **Activities** Advocacy/lobbying/activism; capacity building; events/meetings; guidance/assistance/consulting; networking/liaising; projects/programmes; training/education. **Events** *Meeting of The Minds* 2021, *Meeting of the Minds Seminar* Adelaide, SA (Australia) 2020. **Publications** *The Advocate. DAI Sponsor Donor and Guest Charter* (2nd ed 2018); *Opportunities for Researchers Partners Sponsors and Associates* (2nd ed 2018); *Value To A Sponsor Partner or Donor* (2nd ed 2018); *DAI Response to the WHO Draft Zero Global Action Plan on Dementia* (2016); *Human Rights for People with Dementia: From Rhetoric to Reality* (2nd ed 2016); *Supporting and Accommodating People with Dementia at Conferences and Other Events* (2016). Blogs; position papers; guidelines. **Members** Members in 49 countries. Membership countries not specified. **Consultative Status** Consultative status granted from: *ECOSOC (#05331)* (Special). **IGO Relations** Convention of State Parties (COSP) on: *Convention on the Rights of Persons with Disabilities (CRPD, 2006)*. **NGO Relations** Member of (4): Community of Practice (CoP) for the Meaningful Involvement of People Living with NCDs (as Steering Committee Member of); *Global Rehabilitation Alliance (#10565)* (as Founding member of); *International Disability Alliance (IDA, #13176)* (as Observer member of); *Worldwide Hospice Palliative Care Alliance (WHPCA, #21924)* (as Committee member of). Partner of (2): *Alzheimer's Disease International (ADI, #00762)* (Strategic partnership); Dementia Australia (Strategic partnership).
[2022.06.16/XM6627/**C**]

♦ Demeter International 05029

Brussels Office Rue du Trône 194, 1050 Brussels, Belgium. T. +3226462117.
Communication Officer Brandschneise 1, 64295 Darmstadt, Germany. T. +496155846981. Fax +496155846911.
URL: http://www.demeter.net/

History 1997. **Aims** Promote biodynamic agriculture and Demeter food in the EU; protect organizational interests with regard to EU legislation in the field of *agriculture*, *food safety* and *consumer* protection; lobby for organic and biodynamic farming in the CAP. **Structure** Board, including President, Vice-President, General Secretary Treasurer. **Languages** English, French, German, Irish Gaelic. **Staff** 4.00 FTE, paid. **Finance** Foundation grants for projects. **Activities** Advocacy/lobbying/activism; projects/programmes; events/meetings. **Events** *Conference on Organic Plant Breeding* Brussels (Belgium) 2018. **Publications** Conference and workshop reports.
Members National Demeter and biodynamic associations in 18 countries:
Austria, Brazil, Denmark, Egypt, Finland, France, Germany, Italy, Luxembourg, Netherlands, New Zealand, Norway, Slovenia, Spain, Sweden, Switzerland, UK, USA.
[2017.03.17/XM8290/**E**]

- ♦ **DEMHIST** ICOM International Committee for Historic House Museums (#11057)
- ♦ Democracia Global (internationally oriented national body)
- ♦ Democracy Without Borders (internationally oriented national body)

♦ Democracy in Europe Movement 2025 (DiEM25) 05030

Registered Office Rue Washington 40, 1050 Brussels, Belgium. E-mail: info@diem25.org.
URL: https://diem25.org/

History Registration: No/ID: 0662.528.113, Start date: 2016, Belgium. **Aims** Democratize Europe. **Structure** General Assembly; Coordinating Collective; Advisory Panel; Validating Council. **Finance** Sources: members' dues. **Activities** Advocacy/lobbying/activism; events/meetings. **Members** Individuals (over 132000) worldwide.
[2020/AA0078/v/**E**]

♦ Democracy and Human Rights Education in Europe (DARE Network) 05031

Sec Arbeitskreis Deutscher Bildungsstätten, Mühlendamm 3, 10178 Berlin, Germany. E-mail: office@dare-network.eu.
Registered Address c/o Lifelong Learning Platform, Rue de l'Industrie 10, 1000 Brussels, Belgium.
URL: https://www.dare-network.eu/

History 28 Jun 2003, Antwerp (Belgium). Registration: Banque-Carrefour des Entreprises, No/ID: 0480.114.168, Start date: 10 Feb 2003, Belgium. **Aims** As an Europe-wide network of primarily NGOs, academic institutions and training providers, promote active democratic citizenship and human rights through formal education, non-formal and informal education, and life-long learning. **Structure** General Assembly; Board of Directors, Secretariate, Projects. **Languages** English. **Activities** Advocacy/lobbying/activism; events/meetings; guidance/assistance/consulting; projects/programmes. **Events** *Conference* Berlin (Germany) 2009, *NECE : networking European citizenship education conference* Berlin (Germany) 2005, *Founding conference* St Andreasberg (Germany) 2002. **Publications** *DARE Blue Lines* in English – The publications of the DARE network on aspects of Education for Active Citizenship/Human Rights Education.
Members Full in 20 countries:
Austria, Belgium, Bulgaria, Croatia, Cyprus, Czechia, Estonia, Germany, Greece, Italy, Latvia, Moldova, Netherlands, Norway, Portugal, Romania, Russia, Spain, Switzerland, UK.
European Association of History Educators (EUROCLIO, #06069).
IGO Relations Participant in Fundamental Rights Platform of: *European Union Agency for Fundamental Rights (FRA, #08969)*. **NGO Relations** Member of (1): *Lifelong Learning Platform – European Civil Society for Education (LLLP, #16466)*.
[2021.05.21/XJ0121/**F**]

- ♦ Democracy International (internationally oriented national body)

♦ Democracy International (TDI) 05033

Internationale democratique

Address not obtained.
URL: http://www.thedemocracyinternational.org/

History 19 Mar 1979, New York NY (USA), at founding meeting following work of *'Democratic International Organizing Committee'*, as a working group of exiles and dissidents from repressive governments (of both left and right) and from European and American democracies. Reorganized, Dec 1980, on transfer of headquarters to Washington DC (USA). **Aims** Strengthen democracy where it exists; revive democracy where it has been destroyed; inspire democracy where it is a distant dream; unite efforts of individuals seeking *freedom* from *unrepresentative government*. **Structure** Members meet annually, elect Executive Board (3-year term, one third elected each year), which elects the Officers (1-year term); Board of Directors; Working Committee. **Languages** English, French, German, Pashto, Russian, Spanish. **Publications** *The Pluralist* (periodical); *World Democracy News* – booklet.
Members Individuals (600) in 6 countries:
Afghanistan, Canada, Germany, Russia, Serbia, USA.
[2014/XF9741/v/**F**]

♦ Democracy International 05032

Main Office Gürzenichstr 21 a-c, 50667 Cologne, Germany. T. +492216696650. Fax +4922166966599. E-mail: contact@democracy-international.org.
URL: http://www.democracy-international.org/

History Jun 2011, Brussels (Belgium). Registration: No/ID: 17139, Germany; EU Transparency Register, No/ID: 014120028084-09, Start date: 23 Aug 2017. **Aims** Support and promote the development of democracy worldwide, in particular through the enhancement of direct and participatory democracy. **Structure** General Assembly (at least every 3 years); Executive Board; Initiative Council; Board of Trustees. **Finance** Sources: members' dues. **Events** *Global Forum on Modern Direct Democracy* Mexico City (Mexico) 2021, *Global Forum on Modern Direct Democracy* Bern (Switzerland) 2020, *Global Forum on Modern Direct Democracy* Taichung (Taiwan) 2019, *Global Forum on Modern Direct Democracy* Rome (Italy) 2018, *Global Forum on Modern Direct Democracy* San Sebastian (Spain) 2016. **NGO Relations** Member of (1): *European Movement International (EMI, #07825)*.
[2021/XJ5111/**F**]

♦ Democracy Reporting International (DRI) 05034

Exec Dir Prinzessinnenstr 30, D-10969, Berlin, Germany. T. +4930278773000. Fax +49302787730010. E-mail: m.meyer@democracy-reporting.org – info@democracy-reporting.org.
URL: http://www.democracy-reporting.org/

History Registered in accordance with German law. **Aims** Promote political participation of citizens, accountability of state bodies and the development of democratic institutions worldwide. **Structure** Supervisory Board; Executive Director. **Languages** English. **Staff** 60.00 FTE, paid. **Finance** Project funding. **Publications** *DRI Newsletter*. Annual Report; country reports; opinion pieces.
[2019/XJ5079/**F**]

- ♦ Democracy Resource Center (internationally oriented national body)
- ♦ Démocrates chrétiens nordiques (#17237)
- ♦ Democratic Organization of African Workers' Trade Unions (inactive)

♦ Democratic Pacific Union (DPU) 05035

Unión del Pacifico Democratico

Contact address not obtained. T. +886227786520. Fax +886227786530.

History 14 Aug 2005, Taipei (Taiwan), when Charter was ratified by members during inaugural meeting, preparatory meetings having been held since 2002. **Aims** Safeguard *human rights*, democracy and the rule of law in the Pacific; ensure *peaceful resolution* of regional disputes and the protection of human *security*; promote maritime culture and sustainable development in the Pacific region; encourage development of *cooperation* in industry, trade and technology. **Structure** General Assembly; Board of Directors. Officers: Chair; Regional Vice-Chairs (Asia; Americas; South Pacific). Local (national) Chapters or, where no Local Chapter, 'Friends of DPU'. Board of Advisors. Financial Committee. Advisory Committee. International Secretariat, headed by Secretary-General and including Deputy Secretaries-General and 2 Departments: Department of Cooperation and Development, including 6 commissions – Law and Political Affairs; Human and Social Affairs; Peace and Security; Science and Technology; Industries and Economics. Department of General Affairs, including 6 Divisions – Membership Services; International Liaison; Publications; General Affairs; Information; Secretarial. **Languages** Chinese, English, Spanish. **Staff** 3.00 FTE, paid. **Publications** *DPU Quarterly*.
Members in 25 countries:
Australia, Canada, Chile, Costa Rica, El Salvador, Guatemala, Indonesia, Japan, Kiribati, Korea Rep, Malaysia, Marshall Is, Mexico, New Zealand, Nicaragua, Palau, Panama, Peru, Philippines, Russia, Solomon Is, Taiwan, Timor-Leste, Tuvalu, USA.
[2012.07.23/XM2320/**D**]

- ♦ Democratic Party of the Peoples of Europe – European Free Alliance / see European Free Alliance (#07356)
- ♦ Democratic Progress Institute (internationally oriented national body)
- ♦ Democratic World Federalists (internationally oriented national body)
- ♦ Démocratie, construction européenne et religions (internationally oriented national body)

♦ Democrat Union of Africa (DUA) 05036

Address not obtained.
URL: http://www.idu.org/

History 1992, as *African Dialogue Group (ADG)*. Present name adopted 10 Mar 1999, Cape Town (South Africa). Regional union of: *International Democrat Union (IDU, #13147)*. Re-established, 2019. **Aims** Serve as a forum for dialogue between member organizations and policy makers on issues of democracy, good government, economic policy, human rights and human development. **Activities** Events/meetings.
Members Political parties in 11 countries:
Côte d'Ivoire, Ghana, Kenya, Lesotho, Liberia, Malawi, Namibia, Seychelles, Sierra Leone, Tanzania UR, Uganda.
[2019/XD7916/**E**]

♦ Democrat Youth Community of Europe (DEMYC) 05037

Union des jeunes démocrates européens – Unión de Juventudes Demócratas Europeas – Demokratischer Jugendverband Europas

Main Office 22 Rue de Pascale, 1040 Brussels, Belgium.
Facebook: https://www.facebook.com/demyc.org/

History 3 May 1964, Hamburg (Germany). Founded by Conservative and Christian Democrat youth organizations of Scandinavian countries, Federal Republic of Germany, Austria, Luxembourg and the United Kingdom. Former names and other names: *Conservative and Christian Democrat Youth Community (COCDYC)* – former; *Communauté des jeunes chrétiens populaires* – former; *Communauté de la jeunesse démocrate de l'Europe* – alias. **Aims** Emphasize the freedom of the individual, the social market economy, a decentralized society and worldwide cooperation; further contacts and strengthen cooperation between member organizations from different European countries and thereby contribute to a united Europe; serve as a platform for dialogue and exchange of opinions, ideas and experience on political issues, which often leads to adopting common standpoints, working papers, policy papers and resolutions. **Structure** Congress (every 2 years); Executive Committee; Bureau. **Languages** English, French, German. **Staff** 1.00 FTE, paid. **Finance** Sources: members' dues. **Activities** Advocacy/lobbying/activism; events/meetings; networking/liaising; training/education. *DEMYC Contact Group of Members of the European Parliament* set up 1985. *Youth of the European People's Party (YEPP, #22014)*, set up 30 Jan – 2 Feb 1997, Brussels (Belgium). **Events** *Biennial Congress* Larnaca (Cyprus) 2010, *Biennial Congress* Athens (Greece) 2008, *Biennial Congress* Vienna (Austria) 2006, *EU prospects – the constitution and the alternatives* Prague (Czech Rep) 2005, *Youth promoting human rights and social cohesion* Tbilisi (Georgia) 2004. **Publications** *DEMYC Newsletter*.
Members Full in 30 countries:
Albania, Armenia, Austria, Belarus, Bosnia-Herzegovina, Bulgaria, Croatia, Cyprus, Czechia, Denmark, Estonia, Finland, France, Georgia, Greece, Hungary, Iceland, Israel, Italy, Latvia, Lithuania, Montenegro, Poland, Portugal, Romania, Serbia, Slovakia, Slovenia, Spain, Ukraine.
Observer organizations in 6 countries:
Belarus, Estonia, Georgia, Hungary, Latvia, North Macedonia.
NGO Relations Member of (1): *European Youth Forum (#09140)*. Regional member association of: *International Young Democrat Union (IYDU, #15928)*. Other links include: *European Democrat Students (EDS, #06901)*; *European Young Conservatives (EYC, no recent information)*; *Unión de Juventudes Democraticas Hispanoamericanas (UJDH, no recent information)*; *Tutmonda Esperantista Junulara Organizo (TEJO, #20268)*.
[2020/XD3881/**D**]

- ♦ Demographic Training and Research Centre / see International Institute for Population Sciences (#13911)
- ♦ Demokratie ohne Grenzen / see Democracy Without Borders
- ♦ Demokratischer Jugendverband Europas (#05037)
- ♦ DeMolay International (internationally oriented national body)
- ♦ Demos (internationally oriented national body)
- ♦ demosEuropa – Centre for European Strategy / see WiseEuropa
- ♦ **DEMYC** Democrat Youth Community of Europe (#05037)
- ♦ Denå Committee (inactive)
- ♦ Denå-Komitteen (inactive)
- ♦ Den Europaeiske revisionsret (#06854)
- ♦ Den Europeiske Faglige Samorganisasjon (#08927)
- ♦ Den Europ'iske Unions Publikationskontor (#18562)

♦ Dengue Vaccine Initiative (DVI) 05038

Dir c/o Sabin Vaccine Inst, 2000 Pennsylvania Ave NW, Ste 7100, Washington DC 20006, USA. T. +12028425025. E-mail: rebecca.vanroy@sabin.org – denguevaccines@gmail.com.
URL: http://www.denguevaccines.org/

History Founded 2010, as a consortium of organizations, building on the 'Pediatric Dengue Vaccine Initiative (PDVI)' of *International Vaccine Institute (IVI, #15839)*. Launched Jan 2011. **Aims** Lay the groundwork for dengue vaccine introduction in endemic areas so that, once licensed, vaccines to prevent dengue will be swiftly adopted by countries most in need. **Structure** Boards (2): Asia-Pacific; Americas. **Events** *Regional Dengue Symposium* Rio de Janeiro (Brazil) 2015. **Publications** *Dengue News*.

Members Organizations (4):
International Vaccine Access Center (IVAC); International Vaccine Institute (IVI, #15839); SABIN Vaccine Institute; *WHO (#20950).*
NGO Relations *Partnership for Dengue Control (PDC, #18232).* [2015/XJ3022/y/**E**]

- ♦ Denis de Rougemont Foundation for Europe (internationally oriented national body)
- ♦ Den Nordiske Investeringsbank (#17327)
- ♦ Den Norske Israelmisjon (internationally oriented national body)
- ♦ Dentaid (internationally oriented national body)
- ♦ Dental Liaison Committee for the EEC / see Council of European Dentists (#04886)
- ♦ Dental Liaison Committee in the European Union / see Council of European Dentists (#04886)
- ♦ DentEd / see Association for Dental Education in Europe (#02467)
- ♦ Pro Deo – International Association for the Promotion of Democracy under God (inactive)
- ♦ **DEON** Society of Deontic Logic and Normative Systems (#19541)
- ♦ Departamento de Emergencias en Salud de la OPS/OMS (#18023)
- ♦ Département météorologique d'Afrique orientale (inactive)
- ♦ Département des urgences sanitaires OPS/OMS (#18023)
- ♦ Department of Culture Studies and Oriental Languages (internationally oriented national body)
- ♦ Department for International Development Cooperation (internationally oriented national body)
- ♦ Department of Peace and Development Research, Gothenburg University (internationally oriented national body)
- ♦ Department of Political Science, Innsbruck (internationally oriented national body)
- ♦ Department for Timber Utilisation (inactive)
- ♦ Department of Tropical Hygiene and Public Health, Heidelberg / see Heidelberg Institute of Global Health
- ♦ Department of World Agriculture and Forestry / see Institute of Tropics and Subtropics, Prague
- ♦ Depaul Foundation / see Depaul International
- ♦ Depaul International (internationally oriented national body)
- ♦ Dependencia Común de Inspección de las Naciones Unidas (#16133)
- ♦ Depling – International Conference on Dependency Linguistics (meeting series)
- ♦ **DERA** Drawdown Europe Research Association (#05131)
- ♦ DERA International – Disaster Preparedness and Emergency Response Association, International (internationally oriented national body)
- ♦ Derde Wereld Centrum, Nijmegen / see Centre for International Development Issues, Nijmegen
- ♦ **Derechos-hr** Derechos Human Rights (#05039)

♦ Derechos Human Rights (Derechos-hr) 05039

Contact US Office, 46 Estabrook St, San Leandro CA 94577, USA. T. +15104834005. E-mail: hr@derechos.org.
European Office BP 10003, Rue d'Orleans 1, 6000 Charleroi, Belgium. T. +3271798634.
URL: http://www.derechos.org/

Aims As an internet-based human rights organization, work: for promotion and respect of human rights worldwide; for the right to privacy; against impunity for human rights violators; on preserving the memory of and justice for the disappeared; with other human rights organizations in Latin America and elsewhere to provide accurate and up-to-date information on the human rights situation in their countries and on opportunities to help. **Languages** English, Spanish. **Activities** Coordinates human rights mailing lists, using the internet as the primary information and communication tool and collating information provided by sister organization 'Equipo Nizkor'. Encourages letter campaigns against human rights violations and provides sample letters. Campaigns: Boycott Nike; Clean Clothes – for improving working conditions in the garment industry. **Publications** *What's New at Derechos* (weekly) – update on English and Spanish documents and pages added to Derechos website; *Without Impunity* – internet journal. Information Services: Website of over 4,000 documents and web pages, added to daily and categorized by subject: Death Penalty; The Disappeared; Freedom of Speech. **Information Services** *Freedom of Speech; Human Rights Action Network; Human Rights Actions Network* – disseminates information to members by e-mail; *Human Rights Discussion List (hrights); Human Rights Law Students (hr-law); Human Rights News List; Human Rights NGOs Mailing List; The Disappeared.* **NGO Relations** Numerous national organizations and the following international or regional bodies: *Amnesty International (AI, #00801); Asociación de Familiares de Presos y Desaparecidos Saharauis (AFAPREDESA, no recent information)* (Spain Office); *Center for Justice and International Law (CEJIL, #03647); Christian Task Force on Central America (CTFCA, no recent information); Equipo Nizkor; Latin American and Caribbean Committee for the Defense of Women's Rights (#16268); Federación Latinoamericana de Asociaciones de Familiares de Detenidos-Desaparecidos (FEDEFAM, #09344); Servicio Paz y Justicia en América Latina (SERPAJ-AL, #19247); School of the Americas Watch (SOA Watch); World Organisation Against Torture (OMCT, #21685).* [2008/XF4832/**F**]

- ♦ **DERlab** European Distributed Energy Resources Laboratories (#06930)
- ♦ Dermatologic & Aesthetic Surgery International League / see Dermatology, Aesthetics, and Surgery International League (#05040)

♦ Dermatology, Aesthetics, and Surgery International League (DASIL) 05040

Exec Dir 3322 N 92nd Street, Milwaukee WI 53222, USA. T. +14147504404. E-mail: info@thedasil.org.
URL: https://www.thedasil.org/

History Former names and other names: *Dermatologic & Aesthetic Surgery International League (DASIL)* – former. **Aims** Create a global community for the open exchange of knowledge and innovation by physicians specializing in Dermatologic and Aesthetic Surgery. **Structure** Board of Directors. **Activities** Awards/prizes/competitions; events/meetings; standards/guidelines; training/education. **Events** *World Congress* Bangkok (Thailand) 2023, *World Congress* Mexico City (Mexico) 2022, *World Congress* Mexico City (Mexico) 2021.
Members National Affiliated Societies in 21 countries and territories:
Argentina, Australia, Canada, Colombia, Ecuador, France, Georgia, Greece, India, Iran Islamic Rep, Israel, Italy, Philippines, Poland, Romania, South Africa, Spain, Taiwan, Türkiye, UK, United Arab Emirates.
Afro-Asian Society for Cosmetic Dermatology and Laser (ASCDL, no recent information).
NGO Relations Member of (1): *International League of Dermatological Societies (ILDS, #14018).* [2023.02.16/AA2127/y/**C**]

- ♦ Désarmement et développement (internationally oriented national body)
- ♦ Désarmement nucléaire en Europe (inactive)
- ♦ Desarrollo Juvenil Comunitario (internationally oriented national body)

♦ Descartes Cancer Consortium 05041

Contact Karolinska Inst, SE-171 77 Stockholm, Sweden. E-mail: mats.hellstrom@karolinska.se.
URL: http://www.dcconsortium.eu/

History 5 Sep 2008, as *European Comprehensive Cancer Centre Alliance (ECCCA)*, by 3 cancer centres in Paris (France), Amsterdam (Netherlands) and Stockholm (Sweden). **Aims** Develop and implement innovative strategies to improve cancer cure and reduce treatment related side effects. [2010/XJ1366/**E**]

- ♦ DESCO – Centro de Estudios y Promoción del Desarrollo (internationally oriented national body)
- ♦ DesdelChaco – Fundación para el Desarrollo Sustentable del Chaco Sudamericano (internationally oriented national body)
- ♦ DES – Diobass, écologie et société (internationally oriented national body)
- ♦ DESERTEC Foundation (unconfirmed)

♦ Desert Locust Control Organization for Eastern Africa (DLCO-EA) . . 05042

Organisation de lutte contre le criquet pèlerin dans l'Est africain (OLCP-EA)
Dir PO Box 4255, Addis Ababa, Ethiopia. T. +251116461477 – +251116460284. E-mail: dlc@ethionet.et.
Regional Office Kenya PO Box 30023, Nairobi, Kenya. T. +254206002305. Fax +254206001576. E-mail: operations@dlcoea.org.
URL: http://www.dlco-ea.org/

History 20 Aug 1962, Addis Ababa (Ethiopia), on signature of Convention by representatives of the Governments of Ethiopia, Somalia, Kenya, Tanganyika (Tanzania UR) and Uganda, acting with the authority and consent of the Government of the United Kingdom. France became party signing the Convention on 9 Oct 1962, Ethiopia; Sudan became a full member in 1968, Eritrea in Jul 1993 and South Sudan in 2012. Agreement with *FAO (#09260)* came into force Jun 1965. Convention amended Jun 1973, renewed every 5 years. **Aims** Promote control operations and forecast techniques against upsurges and *plagues* of the Desert Locust and other migratory *pests* such as the larvae of the African Armyworm moth, the Quelea Bird and the Tsetse fly. **Structure** Ministerial Council (annual) of one delegate from each Contracting Government, appoints Executive Committee and Director, who is also Chief Executive Officer. Divisions (4): Administration; Finance; Operations/Air Unit; Scientific Research; Information and Forecasting Systems. Headquarters in Addis Ababa (Ethiopia). Country Liaison Offices or Control Reserve Bases in Member Countries (9). **Languages** English, French. **Staff** 112 paid, of which 28 are regional/professional staff. Negotiations through *Staff Association for the Desert Locust Control Organization for Eastern Africa (no recent information).* **Finance** Core finances from annual contributions paid by member countries based on agreed percentages: Djibouti (Djibouti) 6%; Eritrea 6%; Ethiopia 19%; Kenya 19%; Sudan 18%; Tanzania UR 20%; Uganda 6%, provided that the cost in any financial year is less that US$ 2.5 million. Contributions in money, supplies or services may be received from governments not party to the Convention or from organizations and other sources. During severe locust outbreaks, liaises with FAO and international donor agencies for support. Revenue generation through DLCO-EA/UNHCR-WFP contracts (1994-2013) in the Great Lakes Region. **Activities** Migrant pest surveys, monitoring and forecasting; Migrant pest control; Training/Manpower Development; Scientific/Applied Research. Air Unit (Nairobi) has a fleet of 8 operational aircraft. **Publications** *Desert Locust Situation Report* (12 a year). *Desert Locust Control Organization for Eastern Africa: Celebrating 50 Years of Service to Member Countries 1962-2012.* Annual Report; technical reports.
Members Governments of 9 countries:
Djibouti, Eritrea, Ethiopia, Kenya, Somalia, South Sudan, Sudan, Tanzania UR, Uganda.
IGO Relations Cooperation agreement with: FAO. Formal contact with: *African Development Bank (ADB, #00283).* **NGO Relations** Universities and relevant organizations, including: *International Centre of Insect Physiology and Ecology (ICIPE, #12499).* [2020.03.10/XD0467/**D***]

- ♦ **DesertNet International** Association of the Network for International Research on Desertification (#02823)
- ♦ Design for All Foundation (internationally oriented national body)

♦ the Design Alliance Asia (tDA Asia) 05043

Secretariat 3-4-5 – Level 4, Wisma Prima Peninsula, Jalan Setiawangsa 11, 54200 Kuala Lumpur, Malaysia. E-mail: info@tdaasia.com.
Contact Room 416, Innocentre, 72 Tat Chee Avenue, Kowloon, Hong Kong.
URL: http://www.tdaasia.com/

History Founded 1999. **Aims** Promote the original *creativity* of Asian designers. **Structure** Executive Committee; Secretariat. **Languages** English, Mandarin Chinese. **Staff** Voluntary. **Finance** Supported by government organizations and sponsoring bodies. **Activities** Networking/liaising; events/meetings. **Publications** *Colours of Asia.*
Members Full in 14 countries and territories:
Bangladesh, China, Hong Kong, India, Indonesia, Korea Rep, Laos, Lebanon, Malaysia, Philippines, Singapore, Taiwan, Thailand, Vietnam.
NGO Relations *Global Design Network (GDN); International Council of Design (ICoD, #13013);* national organizations. [2019.03.01/XM7416/**D**]

- ♦ Design, Automation and Test in Europe Conference (meeting series)
- ♦ Design Management Institute (internationally oriented national body)
- ♦ Design Principles and Practices Research Network (unconfirmed)

♦ Design Research Society (DRS) 05044

Communications Sec School of Engineering and Innovation, The Open University, Milton Keynes, MK7 6AA, UK.
Pres address not obtained.
URL: http://www.designresearchsociety.org/

History 1966, UK. **Aims** Promote the study of and research into the process of designing in all its many fields, and of furthering education and the application of design knowledge. **Structure** Council, including President, Chair, Vice-Chair, Honorary Secretary, Honorary Treasurer and 3 Secretaries (Membership, Events, Communications). **Languages** English. **Finance** Members' dues. **Activities** Events/meetings. **Events** *Biennial International Conference* Brisbane, QLD (Australia) 2020, *Research through Design Conference* Rotterdam (Netherlands) 2019, *Biennial International Conference* Limerick (Ireland) 2018, *Biennial International Conference* Brighton (UK) 2016, *Biennial International Conference* Umeå (Sweden) 2014. **Publications** *Design Studies Journal.* **Members** Members (1000). Membership countries not specified. **NGO Relations** Founding member of: *International Association of Societies of Design Research (IASDR, #12170).* [2017.03.07/XM3721/**D**]

♦ Design Society, the 05045

Main Office 109 Dundee Drive, Glasgow, G52 3HL, UK. T. +447767165026. E-mail: admin@designsociety.org.
Registered Office DMEM, University Of Strathclyde, 75 Montrose Street, Glasgow, G1 1XJ, UK.
URL: http://www.designsociety.org/

History Mar 2000, Switzerland. Built on foundation laid by *International Society for the Science of Engineering Design (inactive)*, which activities it took over. Registration: Charity Commission, No/ID: SC 031694, Scotland; Companies House, No/ID: SC401016, Scotland. **Aims** Contribute to a broad and established understanding of development and design; promote the use of results and knowledge for the good of humanity. **Structure** General Meeting (every 2 years). Board, comprising President, Secretary and 3 members. Advisory Board, consisting of Chair and up to 26 members. Special Interest Groups (SIGs). Branches. Management Committees. **Languages** English. **Finance** Sources: gifts, legacies; grants; members' dues; revenue from activities/projects. **Activities** Events/meetings; knowledge management/information dissemination; networking/liaising; publishing activities; research/documentation. **Events** *International Design Conference* Cavtat (Croatia) 2022, *NordDesign Conference* Copenhagen (Denmark) 2022, *International Conference on Engineering and Product Design Education* London (UK) 2022, *ICED : International Conference on Engineering Design* Gothenburg (Sweden) 2021, *ICDC : International Conference on Design Creativity* Oulu (Finland) 2020. **Publications** *Artificial Intelligence for Engineering Design* – journal; *Co-Design* – journal; *Design Studies* – journal; *Journal of Design Research; Journal of Engineering Design; Research in Engineering Design* – journal; *The Design Science Journal; The Design Society Newsletter. WDK Series. Design Science: Introduction to the Needs, Scope and Organization of Engineering Design Knowledge* (1996) by V Hubka and E Eder; *Engineering Design and Creativity* (1996) by W E Eder; *Engineering Design* (1992) by V Hubka and E Eder; *Engineering Design Education* (1992) by W E Eder et al; *Practical Studies in Systematic Design* (1988) by V Hubka et al; *Theory of Technical Systems* (1988) by V Hubka and E Eder.
Members Full; Associate; Fellow; Honorary Fellow individuals with recognized design qualifications and/or experience in the fields of design research, practice, management and education. Members in 35 countries and territories:
Australia, Austria, Belarus, Belgium, Brazil, Canada, China, Croatia, Czechia, Denmark, Finland, France, Germany, Greece, Guinea-Bissau, India, Israel, Italy, Japan, Korea Rep, Luxembourg, Malaysia, Malta, Mexico, Netherlands, Norway, Portugal, Singapore, Slovenia, Spain, Sweden, Switzerland, Taiwan, UK, USA.
NGO Relations Member of (1): *International Association of Societies of Design Research (IASDR, #12170).* [2022/XD9156/v/**D**]

- ♦ Design, Technology and Management Society International
- ♦ desiguALdades.net – International Research Network on Interdependent Inequalities in Latin America (internationally oriented national body)
- ♦ **DESMOS** International Link of Orthodox Christian Scouts (#14054)
- ♦ DESRIST – International Conference on Design Science Research in Information Systems and Technology (meeting series)
- ♦ DESSI International (internationally oriented national body)

♦ Dessins pour la Paix (#03593)
♦ Destination Marketing Association International / see Destinations International (#05046)

♦ Destinations International 05046

CEO 2025 M St NW, Ste 500, Washington DC 20036, USA. T. +12022967888 – +12028354211. Fax +12022967889. E-mail: info@destinationsinternational.org.
URL: https://destinationsinternational.org/

History 1914, USA, as *International Association of Convention Bureaus*. 1974, Miami FL (USA), name changed to *International Association of Convention and Visitor Bureaus (IACVB) – Association internationale des bureaux de congrès et de tourisme*. Aug 2005, San Diego CA (USA), changed title to *Destination Marketing Association International (DMAI)*. Current title adopted 2017. **Aims** Provide a forum for the exchange of information; promote sound *professional* practices in *travel* marketing and in solicitation and servicing of meetings, conventions and visitors. **Structure** Board of Directors; Executive Committee. Committees (10): Advocacy; Audit; Finance; Global Leadership; Governance; Awards; Nominating Organization Accreditation Program; Professional Accreditation Program; Professional Development; Sales and Marketing. Advisory Councils and Task Forces. Includes: *Destinations International Foundation*. **Languages** English. **Staff** 17.00 FTE, paid. **Finance** Budget (annual): US$ 3.5 million. **Activities** Advocacy/lobbying/activism; research/documentation; training/education; events/meetings; awards/prizes/competitions. **Events** *Annual Convention* Montréal, QC (Canada) 2017, *Annual Convention* Seattle, WA (USA) 2012, *EMIF : European meetings industry fair meeting* Brussels (Belgium) 2011, *Annual Convention* New Orleans, LA (USA) 2011, *Annual Convention* Hollywood, FL (USA) 2010. **Publications** *Destination Marketing News* (52 a year) – electronic.
Members City convention bureaux (600) mainly in North America, but in a total of 23 countries and territories:
Aruba, Australia, Austria, Brazil, Canada, Croatia, Cuba, Denmark, France, Greece, Guatemala, Hungary, Korea Rep, Mexico, Peru, Philippines, Portugal, South Africa, Taiwan, Türkiye, UK, USA, Venezuela.
Also members in the West Indies. Membership countries not specified.
NGO Relations Instrumental in setting up: *Data on Meetings and Events (DOME, inactive)*. Member of: *Events Industry Council (EIC, #09212)*. Partner of: *International Institute for Peace through Tourism (IIPT)*.
[2022/XD0102/**F**]

♦ Destination Unknown 05047

Office Rue de la Pépinière 10, 1000 Brussels, Belgium. T. +3225036488. E-mail: info@destination-unknown.org.
URL: https://destination-unknown.org/

History Full title: *Destination Unknown – Championing the rights of children on the move*. **Aims** Ensure that the rights of children and young people on the move are respected and protected. **Structure** Steering Committee; Regional Coordinators; Global Team. **Activities** Advocacy/lobbying/activism; awareness raising; training/education.
Members Organizations. Membership countries not specified. Members include 2 organizations listed in this Yearbook:
Members include 2 organizations listed in this Yearbook:
"Hope for Children" CRC Policy Center (HFC, #10943); *Terre des Hommes International Federation (TDHIF, #20133)*. [2020/XM8808/y/**F**]

♦ Destination Unknown – Championing the rights of children on the move / see Destination Unknown (#05047)
♦ Destrée Institute (internationally oriented national body)
♦ DESWOS – Deutsche Entwicklungshilfe für Soziales Wohnungs- und Siedlungswesen (internationally oriented national body)
♦ DEULA / see DEULA-Nienburg
♦ DEULA-Nienburg (internationally oriented national body)
♦ Deutsch-Belgisch-Luxemburgische Handelskammer (internationally oriented national body)
♦ Deutsche Arbeitsgemeinschaft Vorderer Orient für Gegenwartsbezogene Forschung und Dokumentation (internationally oriented national body)
♦ Deutsche Ärztegemeinschaft für Humanitäre Zusammenarbeit (internationally oriented national body)
♦ Deutsche Atlantische Gesellschaft (internationally oriented national body)
♦ Deutsche Entwicklungshilfe für Soziales Wohnungs- und Siedlungswesen (internationally oriented national body)
♦ Deutsche Finanzierungsgesellschaft für Beteiligungen in Entwicklungsländern / see DEG – Deutsche Investitions- und Entwicklungsgesellschaft
♦ Deutsche Friedensgesellschaft-Vereinigte Kriegsdienstgegnerinnen (internationally oriented national body)
♦ Deutsche Gesellschaft für Amerikastudien (internationally oriented national body)
♦ Deutsche Gesellschaft für Asienkunde (internationally oriented national body)
♦ Deutsche Gesellschaft für Auswärtige Politik (internationally oriented national body)
♦ Deutsche Gesellschaft für Globale- und Tropenchirurgie (internationally oriented national body)
♦ Deutsche Gesellschaft für Internationale Zusammenarbeit (internationally oriented national body)
♦ Deutsche Gesellschaft für Kinder- und Jugendmedizin / see Gesellschaft für Tropenpädiatrie und Internationale Kindergesundheit
♦ Deutsche Gesellschaft für Osteuropakunde (internationally oriented national body)
♦ Deutsche Gesellschaft für Tropenchirurgie / see Deutsche Gesellschaft für Globale- und Tropenchirurgie
♦ Deutsche Gesellschaft für Tropenmedizin und Internationale Gesundheit (internationally oriented national body)
♦ Deutsche Hegel-Gesellschaft / see International Hegel Society (#13788)
♦ Deutsche Humanitäre Stiftung (internationally oriented national body)
♦ Deutsche Lehranstalt für Agrartechnik, Nienburg / see DEULA-Nienburg
♦ Deutsche Missionsgemeinschaft (internationally oriented national body)
♦ Deutsche Morgenländische Gesellschaft (internationally oriented national body)
♦ Deutscher Akademischer Austauschdienst (internationally oriented national body)
♦ Deutscher Friedensrat (internationally oriented national body)
♦ Deutscher Orden – Deutsch-Ordens-Priester (religious order)
♦ Deutsches Handelsinstitut / see EHI Retail Institute
♦ Deutsches Institut für Afrika-Forschung / see Institute of African Affairs, Hamburg
♦ Deutsches Institut für Ärztliche Mission (internationally oriented national body)
♦ Deutsches Institut für Entwicklungspolitik (internationally oriented national body)
♦ Deutsches Medikamenten-Hilfswerk – action medeor (internationally oriented national body)
♦ Deutsches Orient-Institut (internationally oriented national body)
♦ Deutsche Stiftung Friedensforschung (internationally oriented national body)
♦ Deutsche Stiftung für Internationale Rechtliche Zusammenarbeit (internationally oriented national body)
♦ Deutsche Stiftung Weltbevölkerung (internationally oriented national body)
♦ Deutsche Tropenmedizinische Gesellschaft / see German Society of Tropical Medicine and International Health
♦ Deutsche Vereinigung für Internationales Recht (internationally oriented national body)
♦ Deutsche Welthungerhilfe / see Welthungerhilfe
♦ Deutsch-Ordens-Priester (religious order)

♦ Deutschsprachige Arbeitsgemeinschaft für Handchirurgie 05048

German-Speaking Society for Hand Surgery – Société germanophone de la chirurgie de la main
Contact c/o AMACI GmbH, Landstrasser Hauptstrasse 9a/20, 1030 Vienna, Austria. T. +4318903513. Fax +4318907831. E-mail: office@dah.at.
URL: http://www.dah.at/

History 1960, Hamburg (Germany FR). **Aims** Organize scientific meetings on the surgery of the hand. **Structure** Members Assembly; Executive Committee; Secretary General. **Languages** German. **Finance** Annual budget: about euro 50,000. **Activities** Events/meetings. **Events** *Annual Symposium* Bad Homburg (Germany) 2023, *Annual Symposium* Bolzano (Italy) 2022, *Annual Symposium* Frankfurt-Main (Germany) 2021, *Virtual Symposium* Vienna (Austria) 2021, *Annual Symposium* Bolzano (Italy) 2020. **Publications** *Handchirurgie-Mikrochirurgie-Plastische Chirurgie*.
Members Individuals (about 540) in 13 countries:
Austria, Czechia, France, Germany, Hungary, Italy, Poland, Slovakia, Slovenia, Spain, Sweden, Switzerland, Türkiye.
[2018.07.04/XE0085/v/**E**]

♦ Deutschsprachige Arbeitsgemeinschaft für Mikrochirurgie der peripheren Nerven und Gefässe (DAM) 05049

Secretariat address not obtained. T. +491783172537. E-mail: info@dam-mikrochirurgie.org.
Registered Address Spitalstrasse 21, 4031 Basel BS, Switzerland.
URL: https://dam-mikrochirurgie.org

History 18 Oct 1977. Registration: Switzerland, Basel. **Events** *Conference* Graz (Austria) 2021, *Meeting* Linz (Austria) 2016, *Meeting* Zurich (Switzerland) 2014, *Meeting* Deidesheim (Germany) 2013, *Joint meeting* Innsbruck (Austria) 1995. [2020/XJ0716/**D**]

♦ Deutschsprachige Arbeitsgemeinschaft für Verbrennungsbehandlung (internationally oriented national body)
♦ Deutschsprachige Diatomologen mit Internationaler Beteiligung / see Central European Diatomists (#03707)

♦ Deutschsprachige Ex-Libris-Anwendergruppe (DACHELA) 05050

Contact address not obtained.
URL: http://www.dachela.org/

History Current statutes adopted 12 May 2009; amended 6 Jun 2012. **Structure** General Assembly; Executive Committee. **Finance** Sources: members' dues. **Events** *Annual Meeting* Vienna (Austria) 2022, *Annual Online Meeting* 2021, *Annual Meeting* Mannheim (Germany) 2019, *Annual Meeting* Berlin (Germany) 2018.
Members Full in 4 countries:
Austria, Germany, Liechtenstein, Switzerland.
NGO Relations *International Group of Ex Libris Users (IGeLU, #13745)*. [2022.05.11/XM8374/**D**]

♦ Deutschsprachige Gesellschaft für Arthroskopie / see Gesellschaft für Arthroskopie und Gelenkchirurgie (#10141)
♦ Deutschsprachige Gesellschaft für Psychotraumatologie (internationally oriented national body)
♦ Deutschsprachige Medizinische Gesellschaft für Paraplegie (internationally oriented national body)

♦ Deutschsprachige Mykologische Gesellschaft (DMykG) 05051

German-Speaking Mycology Society – Société de mycologie de langue allemande
Main Office c/o Conventus, Carl-Pulfrich-Str 1, 07745 Jena, Germany. E-mail: dmykg-geschaeftsstelle@conventus.de – info@dmykg.de.
URL: http://www.dmykg.de/

History 1961, as a section of *International Society for Human and Animal Mycology (ISHAM, #15181)*. **Aims** Promote the study of mycoses. **Staff** Voluntary. **Finance** Members' dues. **Events** *Annual Meeting* Würzburg (Germany) 2020, *Annual Meeting* Mannheim (Germany) 2019, *Annual Meeting* Innsbruck (Austria) 2018, *Annual Meeting* Salzburg (Austria) 2014, *Annual Meeting / Annual Scientific Meeting* Kiel (Germany) 2011. **Publications** *Mykologie Forum* (4 a year); *Mycoses* (periodical).
Members Individuals in 11 countries:
Austria, Czechia, Germany, Luxembourg, Netherlands, Norway, Poland, Serbia, Sweden, Switzerland, Türkiye.
[2018/XE3206/v/**E**]

♦ Deuxième convention ACP-CEE (1979 treaty)
♦ Deuxième internationale (inactive)
♦ Deuxième protocole additionnel à l'Accord général sur les privilèges et immunités du Conseil de l'Europe (1956 treaty)
♦ Deuxième protocole additionnel à la Convention européenne d'entraide judiciaire en matière pénale (2001 treaty)
♦ Deuxième protocole additionnel à la Convention européenne d'extradition (1978 treaty)
♦ Deuxième protocole portant amendement à la convention au sujet de la canalisation de la Moselle (1983 treaty)
♦ Deuxième protocole portant modification à la Convention sur la réduction des cas de pluralité de nationalités et sur les obligations militaires en cas de pluralité de nationalités (1993 treaty)
♦ Deuxième protocole relatif à la Convention de La Hay de 1954 pour la protection des biens culturels en cas de conflit armé (1999 treaty)
♦ Developing-8 / see D-8 Organization for Economic Cooperation (#04994)
♦ Developing Countries Farm Radio Network / see Farm Radio International (#09274)

♦ Developing Countries Vaccine Manufacturers Network (DCVMN) .. 05052

Exec Sec Route de Crassier 7, 1262 Nyon VD, Switzerland. T. +41225951393. Fax +41225956700. E-mail: info@dcvmn.net.
Admin 4th Floor, Gumidelli Commercial Complex 1-10-39 to 44, Old Airport road, Begumpet, Hyderabad, Telangana 500016, Hyderabad TELANGANA 500016, India. T. +914067043947. Fax +914067043999. E-mail: admin@dcvmn.org.
URL: http://www.dcvmn.org/

History 2000. **Aims** Make a consistent supply of quality vaccines that are accessible to developing countries. **Structure** Executive Committee. **Events** *Annual General Meeting* Pune (India) 2022, *Annual General Meeting* Cape Town (South Africa) 2021, *Annual General Meeting* Switzerland 2020, *Annual General Meeting* Rio de Janeiro (Brazil) 2019, *Annual General Meeting* Seoul (Korea Rep) 2017.
Members Full in 16 countries and territories:
Argentina, Bangladesh, Brazil, China, Cuba, Egypt, India, Indonesia, Iran Islamic Rep, Korea Rep, Mexico, Pakistan, South Africa, Taiwan, Thailand, Vietnam.
Resource members (16) include 10 organizations listed in this Yearbook:
Aeras Global TB Vaccine Foundation; *Asia-Pacific Alliance for the Control of Influenza (APACI, #01822)*; *Coalition against Typhoid (CaT, #04049)*; *European Vaccine Initiative (EVI, #09043)*; *International Alliance for Biological Standardization (IABS, #11622)*; *International Vaccine Access Center (IVAC)*; *International Vaccine Institute (IVI, #15839)*; *Sabin Vaccine Institute (Sabin)*; *TuBerculosis Vaccine Initiative (TBVI, #20257)*; *United States Agency for International Development (USAID)*; *WHO (#20950)*. [2023/XJ8379/y/**F**]

♦ Developing Eight Economic Cooperation Group / see D-8 Organization for Economic Cooperation (#04994)

♦ Developmental Leadership Program (DLP) 05053

Dir c/o International Development Dept, Univ of Birmingham, Edgbaston, Birmingham, B15 2TT, UK. E-mail: dlp@contacts.bham.ac.uk.
URL: http://www.dlprog.org/

History Jul 2009, as *The Leadership Program: Developmental Leaders, Elites and Coalitions* with funding from Australian government. **Aims** Identify and communicate the strategic, policy and operational implications of emerging research evidence about the critical role of developmental leadership and coalitions in the formation of institutions which promote inclusive development. **Structure** Steering Committee, comprising Chair and 6 members. Management Team of 2. **Finance** Mainly through Australian government. **Activities** Research and Analysis; Policy and Operational Implications; Communication and Dissemination. **IGO Relations** Cooperates with: *Australian Aid (inactive)*; *Deutsche Gesellschaft für Internationale Zusammenarbeit (GIZ)*; *New Zealand Ministry of Foreign Affairs and Trade – New Zealand Aid Programme*. **NGO Relations** Cooperates with: *Asia Foundation*; *Oxfam Australia*; *Leadership for Environment and Development (LEAD International, #16416)*; *Lowy Institute for International Policy*; *Overseas Development Institute (ODI)*; *Transparency International (TI, #20223)*. [2020/XJ5916/**F**]

♦ Development Alternatives / see Society for Development Alternatives

♦ Development Alternatives with Women for a New Era (DAWN) 05054

Secretariat Private Mail Bag, Suva, Fiji. T. +6793311330. Fax +6793311328. E-mail: info@dawnnet.org.
URL: http://www.dawnnet.org/

History 1984, Bangalore (India). Former names and other names: *DAWN Group* – alias. **Aims** Develop *feminist* frameworks for: understanding the economic, social, cultural and political processes which cause and perpetuate social *inequalities*; advocating change. Through a *gender* perspective, analyse development strategies and policies applied to countries in the *economic South* and their impact on women and other subordinated groups, so as to articulate a critique of development processes and promote alternatives. **Structure** Board; Executive Committee. **Staff** 3.00 FTE, paid. **Finance** Grants from: private foundations; governmental funding agencies; intergovernmental organizations. **Activities** Advocacy/lobbying/activism; healthcare; knowledge management/information dissemination; networking/liaising; research/documentation; training/education. **Events** *International conference for the reform of international institutions* Geneva (Switzerland) 2006, *Interregional meeting* Niterói (Brazil) 1989. **Publications** *DAWN Informs* (2 a year) in English, French, Spanish – newsletter; *DAWN Supplements* – to newsletter. Books. **Members** Not a membership organization. **Consultative Status** Consultative status granted from: *ECOSOC (#05331)* (Special). **IGO Relations** Contacts with: *Asian and Pacific Development Centre (APDC, #01608)*; *International Bank for Reconstruction and Development (IBRD, #12317)*; *UNDP (#20292)*. Participates in activities of: *World Trade Organization (WTO, #21864)*.

NGO Relations Member of: *Coalition for an Effective African Court on Human and Peoples' Rights (African Court Coalition, #04055)*; *Conference of Non-Governmental Organizations in Consultative Relationship with the United Nations (CONGO, #04635)*; *Just Net Coalition (JNC, #16173)*; *NGO Forum on ADB (#17123)*. Contacts with:
- *African Women's Development and Communication Network (FEMNET, #00503)*;
- *Asian-Pacific Resource and Research Centre for Women (ARROW, #01629)*;
- *Association of African Women for Research and Development (AAWORD, #02362)*;
- *Association for Women's Rights in Development (AWID, #02980)*;
- *Caribbean Association for Feminist Research and Action (CAFRA, #03445)*;
- *Center for Women's Global Leadership (CWGL)*;
- *Focus on the Global South (Focus, #09807)*;
- *Global Call for Action Against Poverty (GCAP, #10263)*;
- *International Gender and Trade Network (IGTN, #13707)*;
- *International Women's Health Coalition (IWHC)*;
- *IO – Facilitating Space for Feminist Conversations (Io, #16005)*;
- *Society for International Development (SID, #19581)*;
- *Women's Environment and Development Organization (WEDO, #21016)*. [2020/XF0751/v/**F**]

♦ Development Associates International (internationally oriented national body)
♦ Development Bank of the Great Lakes States (inactive)

♦ Development Bank of Latin America (CAF) 05055

Banco de Desarrollo de América Latina – Banco de Desenvolvimento de América Latina

Exec Pres – CEO CAF Headquarters, Av Luis Roche, Torre CAF – Altamira, Caracas DF, Venezuela. T. +582122092111. Fax +582122092444. E-mail: infocaf@caf.com.
URL: http://www.caf.com/

History 7 Feb 1968, Bogota (Colombia), as a development institution responsible for cooperation in carrying out projects of common interest in accordance with agreements mentioned in the Declaration of Bogota, following approval of Annex to the Declaration, Aug 1966, by Presidents of Chile, Colombia and Venezuela and representatives of Presidents of Ecuador and Peru. Set up on signature of Agreement by representatives of these 5 countries, which subsequently formed the Andean Group, following approval of draft agreement by 5th Session of Joint Commission of Representatives of Signatory States of the Bogota Declaration. Government of Bolivia joined 1967. Declaration of Bogota, considered as cornerstone of CAF and Andean Group, approved immediate action programme for Andean countries and Chile, for the application of economic integration measures and policy coordination among participating countries in trade, industry, finance and technical cooperation areas. A Joint Commission was formed to address these issues, and a proposal was made to set up a Development Corporation. In 1967, the Joint Commission mapped out CAF basic principles, and on 7 Feb 1968, member countries signed its Establishing Agreement, Bogota. Corporation was conceived as a multi-purpose bank and agency for promoting Andean development and integration. Agreement entered in force 30 Jan 1970; formal commencement of operations, 8 Jun 1970. Original title: *Corporación Andina de Fomento (CAF) – Société andine de développement – Andean Development Corporation*.
Andean Subregional Integration Agreement (Cartagena Agreement, 1969), signed May 1969, created political framework for the Andean sub-regional group and proposed the adoption of a joint economic, social and trade development model for countries with similar characteristics and willing to obtain the benefits which, according to the regional integration scheme at the time (LAFTA – Latin American Free Trade Association), tended to be reserved for the larger nations. The agreement adopted common strategies for industrial, energy and agricultural development, as well as research, technology transfer, capital investment, construction of physical infrastructure and mouvement of persons, among others. Under the Cartagena Agreement and subsequent agreements, the Corporation is an Andean integration organ of the *Sistema Andino de Integración (SAI, #19292)* within the *Andean Community (#00817)*. Since all matters relating to the establishment of CAF were kept separate from the agreement on economic integration, Venezuela was able to sign the agreement establishing CAF, even though it did not sign the Cartagena Agreement as an original contracting party. Chile withdrew from participation as a shareholder in Oct 1977. CAF is sometimes referred to by English initials *ADC*. Statutes registered in UNTS 1/110917.
Aims 'Mission': promote sustainable development and regional integration by efficiently attracting capital resources to provide a wide range of financial services, with high value added, to the public and private sectors of shareholders' countries. **Structure** A financial institution with Latin American and Caribbean shareholders. Shareholders' Assembly (annual), consisting of holders of ordinary shares or their representatives or agents. Board of Directors, comprising 12 members. Executive Committee, comprising 6 Directors. Executive President. Headquarters in Caracas (Venezuela); regional offices in the other 4 Andean capitals. **Languages** Spanish. **Finance** Authorized capital: US$ 10,000 million, formed by the shares of the A, B and C Series. **Activities** Services are targeted at the governments of the shareholder countries and the public institutions and private or mixed companies which operate in these nations, and are aimed at: strengthening the Corporation's competitive advantages in the areas of infrastructure, industry and financial systems; promoting integration of public and private action in shareholder countries; strengthening the catalytic, innovative and integrationist role in the region. Products and services offered are: Loans (short, medium and long term); Structured Finance, without recourse or limited guaranties; Loans, with multilateral institutions and international banks; Financial Advisory Services; Bonds and Guaranties; Partial Guaranties; Equity; Treasury Services; Technical Cooperation; Credit Lines. Strategic programmes include: *Programa Latinoamericano del Carbono (PLAC, see: #05055)*. **Events** *Economic Studies Conference* Cartagena de Indias (Colombia) 2018, *Latin American Carbon Forum* Montevideo (Uruguay) 2018, *Latin American Climate Week* Montevideo (Uruguay) 2018, *Financial Department Conference* Bogota (Colombia) 2017, *Economic Studies Conference* Cartagena de Indias (Colombia) 2017. **Publications** *Sinergia Magazine*. Annual Report; e-books; agreements; brochures.
Members Main shareholders – Series A governments of 10 countries:
Argentina, Bolivia, Brazil, Colombia, Ecuador, Panama, Paraguay, Peru, Uruguay, Venezuela.
Private banks (15) from the Andean region – Series B (partners).
Associate countries – Series C governments of 18 countries:
Argentina, Bolivia, Brazil, Chile, Colombia, Costa Rica, Dominican Rep, Ecuador, Jamaica, Mexico, Panama, Paraguay, Peru, Portugal, Spain, Trinidad-Tobago, Uruguay, Venezuela.
IGO Relations Member of: *Andean Foreign Trade Company (no recent information)*. Participates in the activities of: *UNCTAD (#20285)*. Accredited by: *United Nations Framework Convention on Climate Change – Secretariat (UNFCCC, #20564)*. Cooperation agreement with: *Caribbean Community (CARICOM, #03476)*; *Sistema Económico Latinoamericano (SELA, #19294)*; *Latin American Energy Organization (#16313)*. Cooperation Agreement with: *International Fund for Agricultural Development (IFAD, #13692)*. Implementing agency of: *Global Environment Facility (GEF, #10346)*. **NGO Relations** Adhering member of: *Latin American Banking Association (#16254)*. Participates in: *Scudder Latin American Trust for Independent Power (SLATIP, no recent information)*. Supports: *International Centre for Trade and Sustainable Development, Geneva (ICTSD, #12524)*. [2020/XF0409/e/**F***]

♦ Development Bank of Southern Africa (internationally oriented national body)
♦ Development Center International, Dhaka (internationally oriented national body)
♦ **Development Committee** Joint Ministerial Committee of the Boards of Governors of the Bank and the Fund on the Transfer of Real Resources to Developing Countries (#16141)
♦ Development Cooperation Ireland / see Irish Aid
♦ Development Cooperation with the Third World (internationally oriented national body)
♦ Development, Empowerment and Sustainability Solutions Initiatives / see DESSI International
♦ Development Ethics Working Group / see International Development Ethics Association (#13157)
♦ Development Finance International Group (internationally oriented national body)
♦ Development Fund (internationally oriented national body)
♦ Development GAP / The (internationally oriented national body)

♦ Development Gateway 05056

CEO 1110 Vermont Ave NW, Ste 500, Washington DC 20005, USA. T. +12025729200. Fax +12025729290. E-mail: info@developmentgateway.org.
Brussels Office Rue de Trèves 49, 1040 Brussels, Belgium. T. +3222850611.
URL: http://www.developmentgateway.org/

History as a programme of *International Bank for Reconstruction and Development (IBRD, #12317)* (World Bank). Became independent, 2001. Original title: *Development Gateway Foundation*. **Aims** Increase the impact of international development activities through innovative, sustainable information management solutions and services. **Structure** Board of Directors. **Languages** English. **Staff** 25.00 FTE, paid. **Finance** Donors; service revenue; sponsorship. Budget (annual): about US$ 8 million. **Activities** Services include aid coordination and management tools, online government tendering systems, and online knowledge-sharing platforms at global and local levels. **Events** *AIDF Washington Summit* Washington, DC (USA) 2010. **IGO Relations** *International Bank for Reconstruction and Development (IBRD, #12317)* (World Bank); *OECD (#17693)*; *OECD Development Assistance Committee (DAC, see: #17693)*; *UNDP (#20292)*. Adheres to: *Global Partnership for Effective Development Co-operation (GPEDC, #10532)*. **NGO Relations** Member of: *American Council for Voluntary International Action (InterAction)*; *Global Innovation Exchange (The Exchange, inactive)*. Steering Committee member of: *International Aid Transparency Initiative (IATI, #11604)*. [2015/XD8352/f/**F**]

♦ Development Gateway Foundation / see Development Gateway (#05056)
♦ Development Generation Africa International (internationally oriented national body)
♦ Development Group for Alternative Policies / see Development GAP / The
♦ Development and Humanitarian Learning in Action (unconfirmed)

♦ Development Innovations and Networks 05057

Innovations et réseaux pour le développement (IRED) – Innovaciones y Redes para el Desarrollo

Pres Rue Varembé 3, Case postale 116, 1211 Geneva 20, Switzerland. T. +41227341716. Fax +41227400011. E-mail: info@ired.org.
URL: http://www.ired.org/

History 8 Sep 1980, Geneva (Switzerland). Founded 1980 when Articles were adopted; Articles modified on 3 Oct 1988, Harare (Zimbabwe). Rules of Procedure adopted 4 Oct 1988, Harare. Articles and Rules of Procedure modified on 21 Oct 1994, Mexico. Former names and other names: *Association of Development Innovations and Networks* – former. **Aims** Find out or instigate anywhere in the world innovating initiatives likely to contribute to self-reliant development at local, regional and national levels. **Structure** Community of Members; General Assembly of Delegates (annual); Executive Committee; Secretariat General. **Languages** English, French. **Staff** 2.00 FTE, voluntary. **Finance** Sources: members' dues. Grants from national governmental and non-governmental organizations and foundations in Switzerland, Germany, Belgium and USA. **Activities** Capacity building; events/meetings; financial and/or material support; knowledge management/information dissemination; networking/liaising. Active in: Burkina Faso, Burundi, Senegal, Switzerland. **Events** *General Assembly* Geneva (Switzerland) 2012, *General Assembly* Geneva (Switzerland) 2010, *Forum on higher education in the Europe region* Bucharest (Romania) 2009, *General Assembly* Geneva (Switzerland) 2006, *General Assembly* Geneva (Switzerland) 2000. **Publications** *IRED online Forum* (4 a year) in English, French, Spanish; *IRED Newsletter*. *Towards Greater Financial Autonomy of Development NGOs and Community Organizations* by Fernand Vincent and Piers Campbell. Studies; reports on exchanges and seminars; management and alternative financing manuals.
Members Regional networks covering Africa, the Americas, Europe, the Pacific; individual members and partners in 53 countries:
Angola, Bangladesh, Belgium, Benin, Bolivia, Botswana, Brazil, Burkina Faso, Burundi, Cameroon, Canada, Central African Rep, Chile, China, Colombia, Congo DR, Costa Rica, Côte d'Ivoire, El Salvador, Eswatini, Ethiopia, France, Ghana, Greece, Guinea, India, Indonesia, Italy, Kenya, Lesotho, Madagascar, Malaysia, Mali, Mauritius, Mozambique, Namibia, Nepal, Niger, Nigeria, Pakistan, Philippines, Rwanda, Senegal, South Africa, Sri Lanka, Switzerland, Tanzania UR, Thailand, Togo, Uganda, USA, Zambia, Zimbabwe.
Included in the partners, 43 bodies listed in this Yearbook:
- *ACORD – Agency for Cooperation and Research in Development (#00073)*;
- *African Association for Literacy and Adult Education (AALAE, inactive)*;
- *ASEAN Handicraft Promotion and Development Association (AHPADA, #01194)*;
- *Asian and Pacific Development Centre (APDC, #01608)*;
- *Asian Cultural Forum on Development Foundation (ACFOD, no recent information)*;
- *Asian Institute for Rural Development (AIRD, inactive)*;
- *Asian Network for Industrial Technology Information and Extension (TECHNONET ASIA, no recent information)*;
- *Asian NGO Coalition for Agrarian Reform and Rural Development (ANGOC, #01566)*;
- *Asian Recycling Association (ARA, inactive)*;
- *Asian Regional Exchange for New Alternatives (ARENA, #01684)*;
- *Asian Social Institute (ASI)*;
- *Asia-Pacific People's Environment Network (APPEN, no recent information)*;
- *Asia South Pacific Association for Basic and Adult Education (ASPBAE, #02098)*;
- *Asociación Latinoamericana de Organizaciones de Promoción (ALOP, inactive)*;
- *Association for the Promotion of African Community Initiatives (#02874)*;
- *Association of Development Research and Training Institutes of Asia and the Pacific (ADIPA, inactive)*;
- *Centro de Información y Desarrollo Integral de Autogestión (CIDIAG, no recent information)*;
- *Centro de Investigación y Promoción Amazónica (CIPA, no recent information)*;
- *Consejo de Educación de Adultos de América Latina (CEAAL, #04707)*;
- *Consumers International (CI, #04773)*;
- *Corporation for Cultural and Social Development (no recent information)*;
- *Council for the Development of Social Science Research in Africa (CODESRIA, #04879)*;
- *Council of Non-Governmental Organizations for Development Support (#04911)*;
- *Environnement et développement du Tiers-monde (enda, #05510)*;
- *Federation of Asian Bishops' Conferences (FABC, #09430)*;
- *ILAW International Centre, Bohol (no recent information)*;
- *Institut Africain pour le Développement Economique et Social – Centre Africain de Formation (INADES-Formation, #11233)*;
- *International Co-operative Alliance (ICA, #12944)*;
- *International Development Research Centre (IDRC, #13162)*;
- *International Institute of Rural Reconstruction (IIRR, #13921)*;
- *Latin American Institute of Transnational Studies (LAITS, no recent information)*;
- *Marga Institute*;
- *Organisation internationale et communautaire pour le développement du Zaïre (no recent information)*;
- *Pan African Institute for Development (PAID, #18053)*;
- *Programme régional de formation et d'échanges pour le développement (PREFED, no recent information)*;
- *Sahel Solidarity (no recent information)*;
- *Sarvodaya Shramadana Movement (SSM)*;
- *Society for Participatory Research in Asia (PRIA)*;
- *SOLIDAMI – Cooperação Internacional (no recent information)*;
- *Southeast Asia Regional Initiatives for Community Empowerment (SEARICE, #19795)*;
- *Southeast Asia Rural Social Leadership Institute (SEARSOLIN, #19797)*;
- *South-South Solidarity (3S, no recent information)*;
- *The Lutheran World Federation (LWF, #16532)*.

Consultative Status Consultative status granted from: *ECOSOC (#05331)* (Special); *UNESCO (#20322)* (Consultative Status); *UNCTAD (#20285)* (General Category). **IGO Relations** Cooperates with: *International Atomic Energy Agency (IAEA, #12294)*. **NGO Relations** Member of: *Asia Civil Society Forum (ACSF, no recent information)*; *EarthAction (EA, #05159)*; *Fédération des Institutions Internationales établies à Genève (FIIG, #09599)*; *Global Forum on Sustainable Food and Nutritional Security (no recent information)*; *Settlements Information Network Africa (SINA, #19250)*. [2020.05.05/XD0066/y/**F**]

♦ Development of Islamic Countries Transport Organization (inactive)

♦ Development Media International (internationally oriented national body)

♦ Development Partners Network on Decentralisation and Local Governance (DeLoG) 05058

Secretariat c/o GIZ, Friedrich-Ebert-Allee 36, 53113 Bonn, Germany. T. +492284460803586. E-mail: info@delog.org.
URL: http://www.delog.org/

History 2006. Founded as an informal network of bi- and multilateral development partners. Former names and other names: *Development Partners Working Group on Decentralisation and Local Governance* – former; *Decentralisation and Local Governance* – former. **Aims** Promote effective and coordinated decentralization and local governance (DLG) approaches among members; develop exchange in the field of DLG support. **Languages** English, German. **Staff** 4.00 FTE, paid. **Activities** Capacity building; knowledge management/information dissemination; politics/policy/regulatory; training/education. **Events** *Annual Meeting* 2021, *Annual Meeting* 2020, *Annual Meeting* Bern (Switzerland) 2019, *Annual Meeting* The Hague (Netherlands) 2018, *Annual Meeting* Brussels (Belgium) 2017. **Publications** *DeLoG Newsletter. Building Country Monitoring and Evaluation Systems to Support Decentralisation Reforms* (2015). Reports; books. **Information Services** *Social Media, Website, LinkedIn.*

Members Bilateral and multilateral development partners (34). Multilateral organizations (9):
African Development Bank (ADB, #00283); Asian Development Bank (ADB, #01422); European Commission (EC, #06633) (Europe Aid); *Inter-American Development Bank (IDB, #11427); International Bank for Reconstruction and Development (IBRD, #12317)* (World Bank); *UNDP (#20292); UNICEF (#20332); United Nations Capital Development Fund (UNCDF, #20524); United Nations Human Settlements Programme (UN-Habitat, #20572).*
Bilateral organizations in 16 countries:
Austria, Belgium, Canada, Denmark, Finland, France, Germany, Ireland, Luxembourg, Netherlands, Norway, Spain, Sweden, Switzerland, UK, USA.
Included in the above, 16 organizations listed in this Yearbook:
Agence française de développement (AFD); Austrian Development Agency (ADA); Department for International Development (DFID, inactive); Deutsche Gesellschaft für Internationale Zusammenarbeit (GIZ); Enabel; Irish Aid; Kreditanstalt für Wiederaufbau (KfW); Luxembourg Agency for Development Cooperation (LUXDEV); Network of Associations of Local Authorities of South-East Europe (NALAS, #16997); Norwegian Agency for Development Cooperation (Norad); ROAID; *Swedish International Development Cooperation Agency (Sida); Swiss Agency for Development and Cooperation (SDC); United Cities and Local Governments of Africa (UCLG Africa, #20500); United States Agency for International Development (USAID); World Organization of United Cities and Local Governments (UCLG, #21695).*
NGO Relations Member of (1): *Effective Institutions Platform (EIP, #05384).* [2021.08.23/XJ9645/**F***]

♦ Development Partners Working Group on Decentralisation and Local Governance / see Development Partners Network on Decentralisation and Local Governance (#05058)
♦ Development and Peace (internationally oriented national body)
♦ Development and Peace Foundation (internationally oriented national body)
♦ Development and Peace Movement (internationally oriented national body)
♦ Development Perspectives (internationally oriented national body)
♦ Development Planning Unit (internationally oriented national body)
♦ Development Policy Association of German Non-Governmental Organizations / see Verband Entwicklungspolitik und Humanitäre Hilfe e.V.
♦ Development Policy and Practice (internationally oriented national body)
♦ Development and Project Planning Centre / see Bradford Centre for International Development
♦ Development – Relief – Advocacy / see Anglican Alliance (#00822)
♦ Development Studies Association (internationally oriented national body)
♦ Development Studies Association of Britain and Ireland / see Development Studies Association
♦ Development Studies Group, Milton Keynes / see Development Policy and Practice
♦ Development Study Centre / see Weitz Center for Development Studies
♦ Development Training Centre, Strasbourg / see Coopération et Formation au Développement
♦ Development Training International (internationally oriented national body)
♦ Development Workshop / see Development Workshop France
♦ Development Workshop Austria (internationally oriented national body)
♦ Development Workshop France (internationally oriented national body)
♦ Développement international Desjardins (internationally oriented national body)
♦ Développement et paix (internationally oriented national body)
♦ Développement social international (internationally oriented national body)
♦ Device Language Message Specification / see DLMS User Association (#05109)
♦ DEVNET – Aotearoa New Zealand International Development Studies Network (internationally oriented national body)
♦ DEVNET – Development Information Network / see DEVNET International (#05059)

♦ DEVNET International 05059

Chairman and CEO Viale Gorizia 20, 00198 Rome RM, Italy. E-mail: info@devnetinternational.org.
Sec address not obtained. E-mail: lydiap@devnetinternational.org.
URL: http://www.devnetinternational.org/

History Founded 1989, Italy, as *DEVNET – Development Information Network*, with the support of *UNDP (#20292)*. Originally set up to implement *Technological Trade and Information Promotion System (TIPS, #20119)*. **Aims** Strengthen technical economic cooperation among developing countries, in accordance with the principles laid down by the competent bodies of the United Nations. **Structure** Board of Directors of 2 officers and 3 members. **Languages** Chinese, English, Italian, Spanish. **Consultative Status** Consultative status granted from: *ECOSOC (#05331)* (General). **NGO Relations** Member of: *Conference of Non-Governmental Organizations in Consultative Relationship with the United Nations (CONGO, #04635).* Participant of: *United Nations Global Compact (#20567).* [2016.06.01/XG4785/**E**]

♦ DEV – School of Development Studies (internationally oriented national body)
♦ DevWorks International (internationally oriented national body)

♦ DEXA Society 05060

Contact Biesenfeldweg 12, 4040 Linz, Austria. E-mail: dexa@iiwas.org – hesti@iiwas.org.
URL: http://www.dexa.org/

Events *International Conference on Database and Expert Systems Applications* Vienna (Austria) 2022, *International Conference on Database and Expert Systems Applications* Linz (Austria) 2020, *International Conference on Database and Expert Systems Applications* Linz (Austria) 2019, *International Conference on Database and Expert Systems Applications* Regensburg (Germany) 2018, *International Conference on Database and Expert Systems Applications* Lyon (France) 2017. **Members** Membership countries not specified. [2021/XJ0620/c/**E**]

♦ DEZA – Direktion für Entwicklung und Zusammenarbeit (internationally oriented national body)
♦ DF / see Danish Refugee Council
♦ DFD – Data for Development International Association (inactive)
♦ **DFE** Dolphinaria-Free Europe (#05112)
♦ **DFF** Digital Freedom Fund (#05075)
♦ DfGI – Days for Girls International (internationally oriented national body)
♦ DFG-VK – Deutsche Friedensgesellschaft-Vereinigte Kriegsdienstgegnerinnen (internationally oriented national body)
♦ DFH – Dansk Flygtningehjaelp (internationally oriented national body)
♦ DFI – Development Finance International Group (internationally oriented national body)
♦ DFLM / see Association internationale pour la recherche en didactique du français (#02736)
♦ DFMS – Domestic and Foreign Missionary Society of the Protestant Episcopal Church (internationally oriented national body)
♦ DFN – Digital Freedom Network (internationally oriented national body)

♦ D-Foot International 05061

CEO Prins Boudewijnlaan 159, 2650 Edegem, Belgium. T. +32485805588. E-mail: contact@d-foot.org – secretariat@d-foot.org.
URL: http://www.d-foot.org/

History 1996. Initially set up to establish an internationally accepted consensus on the diabetic foot. Former names and other names: *International Working Group on the Diabetic Foot (IWGDF)* – former (1996 to 2013); *International Working Group on the Diabetic Foot – Implementation* – former (2013 to 4 Apr 2017). Registration: No/ID: 0677.800.861, Start date: 5 Apr 2017, Belgium, Flanders. **Aims** End avoidable lower-limb amputations from diabetes worldwide. **Structure** General Assembly; Board. Standing Committees. **Languages** Dutch, English. **Staff** None paid. **Finance** Sources: donations; members' dues; revenue from activities/projects. Annual budget: 500,000 EUR (2020). **Activities** Awareness raising; events/meetings; guidance/assistance/consulting; research/documentation; training/education. **Events** *Quadrennial International Symposium on the Diabetic Foot* The Hague (Netherlands) 2023, *Quadrennial International Symposium on the Diabetic Foot* The Hague (Netherlands) 2019, *Implementation Summit* Dubai (United Arab Emirates) 2018, *Implementation Summit* Madrid (Spain) 2018, *Quadrennial International Symposium on the Diabetic Foot* The Hague (Netherlands) 2015. **Publications** *Footnote.* **Members** Full (185) in 150 countries. Membership countries not specified. [2020.08.18/XM2266/**C**]

♦ DFR – Deutscher Friedensrat (internationally oriented national body)
♦ **DFRWS** Digital Forensic Research Workshop (#05074)
♦ **DGAC** Dangerous Goods Advisory Council (#05001)
♦ DGA – Deutsche Gesellschaft für Asienkunde (internationally oriented national body)
♦ DGAi – Development Generation Africa International (internationally oriented national body)
♦ DGAP / see Development GAP / The
♦ DGAP – Deutsche Gesellschaft für Auswärtige Politik (internationally oriented national body)
♦ DGCD – Direction-générale de la coopération au développement (internationally oriented national body)
♦ DGDC – Directorate-General for Development Cooperation (internationally oriented national body)
♦ DGfA – Deutsche Gesellschaft für Amerikastudien (internationally oriented national body)
♦ DGH – Doctors for Global Health (internationally oriented national body)
♦ DGISP / see Danish Seed Health Centre for Developing Countries
♦ DGLF / see Délégation générale à la langue française et aux langues de France
♦ DGLFLF – Délégation générale à la langue française et aux langues de France (internationally oriented national body)
♦ DGO – Deutsche Gesellschaft für Osteuropakunde (internationally oriented national body)
♦ DGOS – Directie-Generaal voor Ontwikkelings-Samenwerking (internationally oriented national body)
♦ **DGS** Digital Government Society (#05077)
♦ DHA – Dyes in History and Archaeology (unconfirmed)
♦ Dhaka Ahsania Mission (internationally oriented national body)
♦ Dhaka Centre / see Islamic University of Technology (#16055)
♦ **DHAMAN** Arab Investment and Export Credit Guarantee Corporation (#00997)
♦ **DHAT** Disability HIV and AIDS Trust (#05094)
♦ DHA / see United Nations Office for the Coordination of Humanitarian Affairs (#20593)
♦ DHD / see Digital Humanities im deutschsprachigen Raum (#05079)
♦ **DHd** Digital Humanities im deutschsprachigen Raum (#05079)
♦ **DHE** DigitalHealthEurope (#05078)
♦ DHE-EPPOSI / see DigitalHealthEurope (#05078)
♦ **DHF** Dag Hammarskjöld Foundation (#04995)
♦ DHI – David Horowitz Institute for the Research of Developing Countries (internationally oriented national body)
♦ **DHI** Deaf History International (#05016)
♦ DHI / see Dorcas (#05123)
♦ DHM – Daughters of the Heart of Mary (religious order)
♦ **DHNB** Digital Humanities in the Nordic and Baltic Countries (#05080)
♦ DHN / see Digital Humanities in the Nordic and Baltic Countries (#05080)
♦ DHRE / see People's Movement for Human Rights Learning (#18307)
♦ DHS – Digital Health Society (unconfirmed)
♦ Diabetes and Ramadan International Alliance (unconfirmed)
♦ Diabetes Self-Management Alliance (unconfirmed)
♦ **DIA** Drug Information Association (#05135)

♦ Diagnostics For Animals 05062

Contact 50 rue de Paradis, 75010 Paris, France. T. +33153344345. E-mail: contact@diagnosticsforanimals.com.
URL: https://diagnosticsforanimals.com/

History 2006. Former names and other names: *Association Européenne des Fabricants de Réactifs Vétérinaires (AEFRV)* – former. Registration: Start date: 16 Oct 1999, France. **Aims** Federate and represent manufacturers of animal health diagnostics at large; explain the benefit of a harmonized, efficient and transparent regulatory framework to ensure the future veterinary health industry; promote initiatives for development of animal health diagnostics. **Structure** General Assembly (annual). Board; Executive Committee. **Languages** English. **Staff** 0.50 FTE, paid. **Finance** Sources: members' dues. **Events** *General Assembly* Madrid (Spain) 2016, *General Assembly* Paris (France) 2014.
Members Full in 10 countries:
Austria, Belgium, France, Germany, Ireland, Italy, Netherlands, Spain, Sweden, Switzerland.
IGO Relations *European Commission (EC, #06633).* **NGO Relations** Member of: *European Platform for the Responsible Use of Medicines in Animals (EPRUMA, #08231).* [2020/XJ8486/**D**]

♦ Dia internacional de la Criancia Africana / see International Day of the African Child and Youth (#13140)
♦ Dia internacional del Infante y Yuventud Africanas / see International Day of the African Child and Youth (#13140)
♦ Diakonia (internationally oriented national body)
♦ Diakonia of the Americas / see DIAKONIA of the Americas and the Caribbean (#05063)

♦ DIAKONIA of the Americas and the Caribbean (DOTAC) 05063

Pres 162 West Gate, Winnipeg MB R3C 2E1, Canada.
Treas address not obtained.
URL: http://diakonia-world.org/

History Jul 1968, Racine, WI (USA). Founded within the framework of *World Federation of Diaconal Associations and Diaconal Communities (DIAKONIA, #21429)*, during a meeting of representatives of 9 existing North American organizations. Former names and other names: *North American Diakonia* – former (1971); *Diakonia of the Americas (DOTA)* – former (1978). **Aims** Encourage *ecumenical* relationships between *diaconal* associations in various countries; reflect on the nature and task of DIAKONIA in the New Testament sense and further the understanding of it; strengthen a sense of community among the associations; render mutual aid; undertake common tasks. **Structure** Regional Conference (every 4 years); Central Committee. **Finance** Sources: members' dues. **Activities** Events/meetings; networking/liaising; religious activities. **Events** *Quadrennial Regional Conference* Vancouver, BC (Canada) 2019, *Quadrennial Conference* Porto Alegre (Brazil) 2015, *Quadrennial Regional Conference* Oklahoma City, OK (USA) 2011, *Quadrennial regional conference* Trinidad-Tobago 2006, *Quadrennial regional conference* Canada 2002.
Members Diaconal associations and communities in 9 countries:
Barbados, Brazil, Canada, El Salvador, Guyana, Haiti, Jamaica, St Kitts-Nevis, USA. [2020.05.07/XE2853/**E**]

♦ DIAKONIA of Asia-Pacific (DAP) 05064

Contact Pilgrim Uniting Church in the City, 12 Flinders Street, Adelaide SA 5000, Australia. E-mail: office@pilgrim.org.au.
URL: http://diakonia-asiapacific.org/

History within the framework of *World Federation of Diaconal Associations and Diaconal Communities (DIAKONIA, #21429).*
Members Associations and communities of deaconesses, diaconal sisterhoods and brotherhoods, organizations of diaconal ministers and church workers in 8 countries:
Australia, Fiji, India, Indonesia, Japan, Korea Rep, New Zealand, Philippines.
NGO Relations Supports: *NGO Forum on Cambodia (#17124).* [2013/XE3567/**E**]

♦ DIAKONIA – Protestant Refugee Service (internationally oriented national body)
♦ DIAKONIA Region Africa/Europe (see: #21429)
♦ DIAKONIA Region Afrika/Europa (see: #21429)
♦ DIAKONIA World Federation / see World Federation of Diaconal Associations and Diaconal Communities (#21429)
♦ **DIAKONIA** World Federation of Diaconal Associations and Diaconal Communities (#21429)
♦ Diakonie Emergency Aid / see Diakonie Katastrophenhilfe
♦ DIAKONIE – Evangelischer Flüchtlingsdienst (internationally oriented national body)
♦ Diakonie Katastrophenhilfe (internationally oriented national body)
♦ DIAL – Centre européen de recherche en économie du développement (internationally oriented national body)
♦ Dialog International (internationally oriented national body)
♦ Dialog International – Association pour la promotion de la paix et du développement (internationally oriented national body)
♦ Dialog International – Fördergemeinschaft für demokratische Friedens-Entwicklung (internationally oriented national body)
♦ Dialogo y Cooperación (#05066)
♦ Dialogo Europeo (internationally oriented national body)
♦ Dialogo Regional sobre la Sociedad de la Información (#18777)
♦ Dialogos para el progreso de la humanidad / see Dialogues, propositions, histoires pour une citoyenneté mondiale (#05067)
♦ Dialogos, Propostas, Histórias para uma Cidadania Mundial (#05067)
♦ Dialogos, Propuestas, Histórias para una Ciudadania Mundial (#05067)
♦ Dialogue 5 plus 5 / see Cooperation Process in the Western Mediterranean (#04798)
♦ Dialogue Advisory Group (internationally oriented national body)
♦ Dialogue Afrique-Europe (internationally oriented national body)

♦ Dialogue of Civilizations Research Institute (DOC Research Institute) 05065

CEO Französische Str 23, 10117 Berlin, Germany. T. +4930209677900. E-mail: info@doc-research.org.
URL: https://doc-research.org/
History Launched 1 Jul 2016. Successor to *World Public Forum – Dialogue of Civilizations (WPF-DoC, inactive).* **Aims** Forge shared world views through dialogue; contribute to a fair, sustainable and peaceful world order. **Structure** Supervisory Board; Programme Council; Executive Board. **Activities** Research/documentation; events/meetings; guidance/assistance/consulting. Events/meetings; research/documentation. **Events** *World forum* Rhodes Is (Greece) 2019, *World Forum* Rhodes Is (Greece) 2018, *World Forum* Rhodes Is (Greece) 2017, *World Forum* Rhodes Is (Greece) 2016. **IGO Relations** *FAO (#09260); United Nations Economic and Social Commission for Asia and the Pacific (ESCAP, #20557); UNESCO (#20322).* **NGO Relations** Partners include: *Institute for Political and International Studies, Teheran (IPIS).* [2019.03.15/XM6967/j/**F**]

♦ Dialogue et coopération (#05066)

♦ Dialogue and Cooperation 05066

Dialogue et coopération – Dialogo y Cooperación
Pres 140 avenue Daumesnil, 75012 Paris, France. T. +33143440506. Fax +33143440506. E-mail: dialogue.cooperation@wanadoo.fr.
History 1965, Paris (France). **Aims** Facilitate dialogue between *Christian teachers* in public *schools.* **Structure** One Delegate per continent. **Languages** English, French, Spanish. **Finance** Members' dues. Grants. Budget (annual): about euro 22,870. **Events** *Meeting* Kara (Togo) 2012, *Meeting* Guayaquil (Ecuador) 2011, *Meeting* Chittagong (Bangladesh) 2010, *Meeting* Abidjan (Côte d'Ivoire) 2008, *Meeting* Bangalore (India) 2006. **Publications** *Entre nous – Entre Nosotros – Among Us* (2 a year) in English, French, Spanish.
Members Teachers in 15 countries and territories:
Cameroon, Canada, Chad, Costa Rica, Germany, Ghana, Hong Kong, Myanmar, Nicaragua, Portugal, Singapore, South Africa, Spain, Taiwan, Tanzania UR.
Organizations in 39 countries:
Argentina, Bangladesh, Benin, Bolivia, Burkina Faso, Burundi, Central African Rep, Chile, Colombia, Congo Brazzaville, Côte d'Ivoire, Cuba, Dominican Rep, Ecuador, El Salvador, France, Gambia, Guinea, Haiti, Honduras, India, Indonesia, Korea Rep, Malaysia, Mali, Mexico, Pakistan, Paraguay, Peru, Philippines, Romania, Rwanda, Senegal, Sri Lanka, Thailand, Togo, Uruguay, Venezuela, Vietnam.
NGO Relations Member of: *EarthAction (EA, #05159); Union des organisations internationales non-gouvernementales établies en France (UOIF, inactive).* [2014.07.08/XF1886/v/**F**]

♦ Dialogue of Cultures – United World – International Public Charity Fund / see Dialogue of Culture – United World
♦ Dialogue of Culture – United World (internationally oriented national body)
♦ Dialogue Institute (internationally oriented national body)
♦ Dialogue Interreligieux Monastique (#16849)
♦ Dialogues et documents pour le progrès de l'humanité / see Dialogues, propositions, histoires pour une citoyenneté mondiale (#05067)
♦ Dialogues and Documents for the Progress of Humanity / see Dialogues, propositions, histoires pour une citoyenneté mondiale (#05067)
♦ Dialogues for Human Progress / see Dialogues, propositions, histoires pour une citoyenneté mondiale (#05067)
♦ Dialogues pour le progrès de l'humanité / see Dialogues, propositions, histoires pour une citoyenneté mondiale (#05067)
♦ Dialogues, Proposals, Stories for Global Citizenship (#05067)

♦ Dialogues, propositions, histoires pour une citoyenneté mondiale (DPH) 05067

Dialogues, Proposals, Stories for Global Citizenship – Dialogos, Propuestas, Histórias para una Ciudadania Mundial – Dialogos, Propostas, Histórias para uma Cidadania Mundial
Contact RITIMO, 21 ter rue Voltaire, 75011 Paris, France. T. +33144647416. E-mail: c.makhloufi@ritimo.org.
URL: http://www.d-p-h.info/
History 1986, by *Réseau d'information Tiers-Monde des centres de documentation pour le développement (RITIMO)* and *Fondation Charles Léopold Mayer pour le progrès de l'homme (FPH, #09815),* as *Dialogues et documents pour le progrès de l'humanité – Dialogues for Human Progress – Dialogos para el progreso de la humanidad.* Previously also referred to in English as *Dialogues and Documents for the Progress of Humanity.* Also referred to as: *International Network for the Exchange of Experiences and Reflections Useful for Action – Réseau dialogues pour le progrès de l'humanité (Réseau DPH); Dialogues pour le progrès de l'humanité.* **Aims** Help the global community to come together, structure their information, exchange experience, jointly build their knowledge, develop citizens' alliances, elaborate alternative proposals and organize a democratic citizen's approach. **Languages** English, French, Portuguese, Spanish. **Finance** Funded by the Charles-Léopold Mayer Foundation for Human Progress. **Events** *Journées annuelles* Paris (France) 1994. **Publications** *Thematic Dossiers* – online. Information Services: Animates a website, based on DPH data. Resource site holds a database, representing 7,000 sheets. [2012/XF2833/y/**F**]

♦ Dialogue transatlantique des consommateurs (#20203)
♦ Dialysis Society of Australasia / see Renal Society of Australasia
♦ Diamond Way Buddhism Network / see Karma Kagyu Buddhist Network (#16181)
♦ DIANA Ontwikkelings Vereniging (internationally oriented national body)
♦ DIANA Users Association (internationally oriented national body)
♦ Dian Fossey Gorilla Fund International (internationally oriented national body)

♦ DIANOVA International 05068

Gen Dir Pasaje Pintor Serrasanta 15A 1o-3a, 08860 Castelldefels, Barcelona, Spain. T. +34936365730. E-mail: dianova@dianova.org.
Headquarters 27 chemin des Crêtes-de-Pregny, 1218 Le Grand-Saconnex GE, Switzerland. T. +41225087021. E-mail: switzerland@dianova.org.
URL: http://www.dianova.org/
History 1996. Registration: Swiss Civil Code, Switzerland. **Aims** Contribute to development of individuals, communities and organizations through programmes and interventions in social, health and humanitarian sectors. **Structure** Assembly of Delegates; Assembly Council. **Languages** English, French, Spanish. **Staff** 396.00 FTE, paid; 549.00 FTE, voluntary. **Finance** Sources: donations; investments; members' dues. Annual budget: 700,000 EUR (2020). **Activities** Advocacy/lobbying/activism; awareness raising; healthcare; knowledge management/information dissemination; publishing activities. **Events** *Learning network – Trends and Challenges for 21st century NGOs* Lisbon (Portugal) 2018, *Conference* Portugal 2018, *Conference* Santiago (Chile) 2009, *Conference* Madrid (Spain) 2008, *Conference* Lisbon (Portugal) 2007. **Publications** *The Dianova Network NewsBriefs.*
Members Ordinary (6); Affiliate (6); Associate (11). Members in 17 countries and territories:
Bangladesh, Canada, Chile, Congo DR, India, Italy, Izmir, Kenya, Nicaragua, Norway, Pakistan, Portugal, Sweden, Switzerland, Togo, Uruguay, USA.
Consultative Status Consultative status granted from: *OAS (#17629)* (Registry); *ECOSOC (#05331)* (Special); *UNESCO (#20322)* (Consultative Status). [2022.05.05/XF6959/s/**F**]

♦ Diaskepsi ton Periferiakon Paraktion Periohon tis EK / see Conference of Peripheral Maritime Regions of Europe (#04638)
♦ Diaskepsi ton Periferiakon Paraktion Periohon tis Evropis (#04638)
♦ Diaspora Emergency Action & Coordination (unconfirmed)
♦ DIB – Dansk International Bosaetningsservice (internationally oriented national body)
♦ **DIBF** Deaf International Basketball Federation (#05017)
♦ **DiCE** Digestive Cancers Europe (#05070)
♦ Dichiarazione universale dei diritti umani (1948 treaty)

♦ Dickens Fellowship 05069

Contact Charles Dickens Museum, 48 Doughty Street, London, WC1N 2LX, UK. T. +442074052127. Fax +442078315175. E-mail: postbox@dickensfellowship.org.
URL: http://www.dickensfellowship.org/
History 1902, London (UK). **Aims** Create and maintain a common bond of friendship among admirers of the *literary* works of Charles Dickens (1812-1870); promote knowledge and appreciation of his works; disseminate love of *humanity* as embodied in his works; initiate and support measures to remedy social evils and favour the *poor* and *oppressed*; assist in the preservation and purchase of buildings and objects associated with his name or mentioned in his works. **Structure** Annual Conference; Council; Management Committee. **Languages** English. **Staff** 10.00 FTE, voluntary. **Finance** Sources: donations; gifts, legacies; members' dues. **Activities** Events/meetings. **Events** *Annual Conference* London (UK) 2023, *Mini Conference* 2022, *Annual Conference* 2021, *Annual Conference* London (UK) 2020, *Annual Conference* Eastbourne (UK) 2019. **Publications** *The Dickensian* (3 a year).
Members Branches (54) and affiliated societies (5) in 10 countries:
Australia, Canada, Denmark, France, Italy, Japan, Netherlands, New Zealand, UK, USA.
Individuals in over 20 countries. Membership countries not specified. [2023.02.22/XE2862/**E**]

♦ Dickey Endowment for International Understanding / see John Sloan Dickey Center for International Understanding
♦ Dictionary Society of North America (internationally oriented national body)
♦ DICTO – Development of Islamic Countries Transport Organization (inactive)
♦ DID – Développement international Desjardins (internationally oriented national body)
♦ **DI** Defend International (#05027)
♦ DI – Democracy International (internationally oriented national body)
♦ Die Brücke, Institut international pour l'organisation du travail intellectuel (inactive)
♦ Die Brücke, Internationales Institut für Organisierung der Geistigen Arbeit (inactive)
♦ DIE – Deutsches Institut für Entwicklungspolitik (internationally oriented national body)
♦ Die Europäischen Brauer / see The Brewers of Europe (#03324)
♦ Die Europeer in der Welt (#08839)
♦ DIE – German Development Institute (internationally oriented national body)
♦ **DiEM25** Democracy in Europe Movement 2025 (#05030)
♦ Dienerinnen des Heiligen Geistes von der Ewigen Anbetung (religious order)
♦ Dienst en Aktie voor de Europese Burgers / see European Citizen Action Service (#06555)
♦ Dienste in Übersee / see Brot für die Welt
♦ Dienst van de Europese Kerken voor Internationale Studenten (#19242)
♦ Dienst voor Internationale Samenwerking aan Ontwikkelingsprojecten (internationally oriented national body)
♦ Dienst Missie en Ontwikkelingssamenwerking / see VIA Don Bosco (#20766)
♦ Dierenartsen zonder Grenzen Europa / see Vétérinaires Sans Frontières International (#20760)
♦ Dieren zonder Grenzen – Internationaal (internationally oriented national body)
♦ Dierkundige Vereniging van Suidelike Africa (#22040)
♦ **DIESIS** European Research and Development Service for the Social Economy (#08365)
♦ **DIFA** Deaf International Football Association (#05018)
♦ DIFÄM – Deutsches Institut für Ärztliche Mission (internationally oriented national body)
♦ **DIFI** Doha International Family Institute (#05111)

♦ Digestive Cancers Europe (DiCE) 05070

CEO Rue de la Loi 235/27, 1040 Brussels, Belgium. E-mail: info@digestivecancers.eu.
URL: http://digestivecancers.eu/
History 2004. Former names and other names: *EuropaColon* – former. Registration: Banque Carrefour des Entreprises, No/ID: 0717.836.325, Start date: 9 Jan 2019, Belgium; EU Transparency Register, No/ID: 473945434136-05, Start date: 1 Mar 2019. **Aims** Contribute to early diagnosis and decreased mortality from digestive cancers and to an increase of overall survival and quality of life. **Structure** Board of Directors; Management Team. **Staff** 8.50 FTE, paid. **Activities** Awareness raising; events/meetings; training/education. **Events** *European Colorectal Cancer Awareness Month (ECCAM 2023)* Brussels (Belgium) 2023, *Colorectal Patient Conference* Barcelona (Spain) 2013, *Colorectal Patient Conference* Barcelona (Spain) 2011. **Publications** *The Impact of Nutrition on the Lives of Patients with Digestive Cancers: A Position Paper.*
Members Patient organizations. Full in 24 countries:
Belarus, Belgium, Bosnia-Herzegovina, Cyprus, Czechia, Finland, France, Greece, Hungary, Italy, Lithuania, Malta, Netherlands, North Macedonia, Poland, Portugal, Romania, Russia, Serbia, Slovakia, Slovenia, Spain, Türkiye, UK.
Associate in 6 countries:
Germany, Greece, Israel, Lebanon, Malta, Ukraine.
IGO Relations Partnership with: *WHO (#20950).* Policy partner: *European Commission (EC, #06633).* **NGO Relations** Member of (7): *Alliance for Safe Online Pharmacy – EU (ASOP EU, #00720); EU Health Coalition; European Cancer Organisation (ECO, #06432)* (Patient Advisory Committee); *European Patients' Forum (EPF, #08172); Global Colon Cancer Association (GCCA, #10300); Workgroup of European Cancer Patient Advocacy Networks (WECAN, #21054); World Pancreatic Cancer Coalition (WPCC, #21708).* Policy partners: *Central European Cooperative Oncology Group (CECOG, #03706); European Cancer Patient Coalition (ECPC, #06433); European Oncology Nursing Society (EONS, #08086); European Organisation for Research and Treatment of Cancer (EORTC, #08101); European School of Oncology (ESO, #08434); European Society of Coloproctology (ESCP, #08556); European Society of Digestive Oncology (ESDO, #08582); European Society for Medical Oncology (ESMO, #08648); European Society of Surgical Oncology (ESSO, #08753); EURORDIS – Rare Diseases Europe (#09175); MEPs against Cancer (MAC, #16717); Pancreatic Cancer Europe (PCE, #18172); Rare Cancers Europe (RCE, #18620); United European Gastroenterology (UEG, #20506).* [2023.03.06/XJ5993/**D**]

♦ DigiTAG Digital Television Action Group (#05084)
♦ Digital Audio-Visual Council (inactive)
♦ Digital Built Environment Institute (unconfirmed)

♦ Digital Container Shipping Association (DCSA) 05071

CEO Strawinskylaan 4117, 1077 ZX Amsterdam, Netherlands.
URL: https://dcsa.org/

History 2019. Registration: Handelsregister, No/ID: KVK 74567837, Netherlands. **Aims** Shape the digital future of container shipping, by being the industry's collective voice, working towards alignment and standardization. [2021/AA2029/**C**]

♦ Digital Cooperation Organization (DCO) 05072

SG address not obtained. E-mail: media@dco.org.
URL: https://www.dco.org/

History 2020. Established by governments of Bahrain, Jordan, Kuwait, Nigeria, Oman, Pakistan and Saudi Arabia. **Aims** Increase social prosperity by accelerating the growth of the digital economy. **Structure** Council; General Secretariat; temporary Committees. **Activities** Projects/programmes.
Members Member nations (9):
Bahrain, Jordan, Kuwait, Morocco, Nigeria, Oman, Pakistan, Rwanda, Saudi Arabia. [2022/AA2783/**D***]

♦ Digital Council Africa (internationally oriented national body)
♦ Digital Defenders Partnership (internationally oriented national body)

♦ DIGITALEUROPE 05073

Dir Gen Rue de la Science 14, 1040 Brussels, Belgium. T. +3226095310. E-mail: info@digitaleurope.org.
Executive Coordination address not obtained.
URL: http://www.digitaleurope.org/

History 16 Nov 1999. Founded by merger of *ECTEL-European Telecommunications and Professional Electronics Industry (inactive)* and *European Association of Manufacturers of Business Machines and Information Technology Industry (EUROBIT, inactive)*. Became operational 1 Jan 2000. Has taken over activities of *European Association of Consumer Electronics Manufacturers (EACEM, inactive)*, Oct 2001. Former names and other names: *European Information and Communications Technology Industry Association* – former; *European ICT/CE Industry Association* – former; *European Information Communications and Consumer Electronics Technology Industry Association (EICTA)* – former; *Association européenne des industries de l'informatique et des télécommunications* – former. Registration: Banque-Carrefour des Entreprises, Belgium; EU Transparency Register, No/ID: 64270747023-20. **Aims** Represent the digital technology industry in Europe; assist European businesses and citizens to benefit fully from digital technologies and for Europe to grow, attract and sustain the world's best digital technology companies; ensure industry participation in development and implementation of EU policies. **Structure** General Assembly (annual); Executive Board; Secretariat, headed by Director General. **Languages** English, French. **Staff** 32.00 FTE, paid. **Finance** Sources: members' dues. **Activities** Events/meetings; politics/policy/regulatory. **Events** *General Assembly & Conference* Brussels (Belgium) 2022, *Annual General Assembly* Brussels (Belgium) 2021, *Annual Summit* Brussels (Belgium) 2021, *Annual General Assembly* Brussels (Belgium) 2020, *How to Spend It – A Digital Investment Plan for Europe* Brussels (Belgium) 2020. **Publications** *A STRONGER DIGITAL EUROPE – our call to action towards 2025* in English; *A stronger digital industrial Europe – Digital Transformation as its FOCUS* in English; *How to spend it: A digital investment plan for Europe* in English; *Scaling in Europe* in English; *Schrems II Impact Survey Report* in English.
Members Corporate (76) and National Trade Associations (39) representing 36,000 digital and digitally-transforming companies from 28 European countries. Membership countries not specified. **Consultative Status** Consultative status granted from: *World Intellectual Property Organization (WIPO, #21593)* (Permanent Observer Status). [2022/XD7776/**D**]

♦ Digital Forensic Research Workshop (DFRWS) 05074

CEO/COO PO Box 422, Trumansburg NY 14886, USA. T. +15044071740. E-mail: dfrws@dfrws.org.
URL: https://dfrws.org/

History Aug 2001. Originally a workshop series; but institutionalized 2005. Registration: 501(c)(3) non-profit organization, Start date: 2005, USA. **Aims** Bring together everyone with a legitimate interest in digital forensics to address the emerging challenges of the field. **Structure** Board of Directors. **Events** *Annual Digital Forensics Research European Conference* Bonn (Germany) 2023, *DFRWS APAC Conference* Adelaide, SA (Australia) 2022, *Annual Digital Forensics Research European Conference* Oxford (UK) 2022, *Annual Digital Forensics Research European Conference* 2021, *Annual Digital Forensics Research European Conference* Oslo (Norway) 2019. [2023/AA0689/c/**F**]

♦ Digital Freedom Fund (DFF) 05075

Dir Nieuwezijds Voorburgwal 104-108, 1012 SG Amsterdam, Netherlands. E-mail: info@digitalfreedomfund.org.
URL: https://digitalfreedomfund.org/

History 1 Sep 2017, Berlin (Germany). **Aims** Support strategic litigation to advance digital rights in Europe; lead processes to decolonise the digital rights field in Europe. **Staff** 11.00 FTE, paid; 2.00 FTE, voluntary. **Finance** Supported by: *Adessium Foundation*; Fondation Nicolas Puech; *Ford Foundation (#09858)*; Limelight; Luminate; *Open Society Foundations (OSF, #17763)*; *Robert Bosch Foundation*; *Sigrid Rausing Trust*; *Stiftung Mercator*. **Activities** Capacity building; events/meetings; financial and/or material support; guidance/assistance/consulting; projects/programmes. **Publications** Annual Reports. [2022.10.19/AA1320/f/**F**]

♦ Digital Freedom Network (internationally oriented national body)

♦ Digital Games Research Association (DiGRA) 05076

Pres address not obtained. E-mail: coordinator@digra.org – admin@digra.org.
URL: http://www.digra.org/

History 2003, Finland. **Aims** Encourage research on digital games and associated phenomena; promote collaboration and dissemination of work by its members. **Structure** Board; Chapters (3). **Languages** English. **Staff** 2.00 FTE, paid. **Finance** Sources: members' dues. **Activities** Events/meetings. **Events** *International Conference* Krakow (Poland) 2022, *International Conference* Tampere (Finland) 2020, *International Conference* Kyoto (Japan) 2019, *Nordic Conference* Bergen (Norway) 2018, *International Conference* Singapore (Singapore) 2013. **Publications** *Transactions of the Digital Games Research Association (ToDIGRA)* – journal. [2021.06.08/XM0552/**D**]

♦ Digital Government Society (DGS) 05077

Address not obtained.
URL: http://www.gdsociety.org/

History 2006, as *Digital Government Society of North America*. Current title adopted Oct 2013. Registered in the State of California (USA), as a Charitable Organization: 2925410. **Aims** Study the development and impacts of digital government. **Structure** Board; Committees. **Activities** Awards/prizes/competitions; events/meetings. **Events** *Annual International Conference on Digital Government Research* Seoul (Korea Rep) 2020, *Annual International Conference on Digital Government Research* Dubai (United Arab Emirates) 2019, *Annual International Conference on Digital Government Research* Shanghai (China) 2016, *Annual International Conference on Digital Government Research* Phoenix, AZ (USA) 2015, *Annual International Conference on Digital Government Research* Aguascalientes (Mexico) 2014. [2016/XM4828/**C**]

♦ Digital Government Society of North America / see Digital Government Society (#05077)
♦ Digital Green (internationally oriented national body)
♦ Digital Health Europe / see DigitalHealthEurope (#05078)

♦ DigitalHealthEurope (DHE) 05078

Secretariat Visverkopersstraat 8, bus 7, 1000 Brussels, Belgium.
URL: https://digitalhealtheurope.eu/

History 1994. Founded as a human health and care innovation think-tank that evolved to a partisan multi-stakeholder platform. Restructured in 2017. Former names and other names: *European Platform for Patients' Organizations, Science and Industry (Epposi)* – former; *Digital Health Europe (DHE-EPPOSI)* – former (2017). **Aims** Provide a consensus-driven multi-stakeholder perspective from European patient organizations, science and industry to improve European public health outcomes. **Structure** General Assembly; Board; Executive Committee; Director; Working Groups (4); Organizing Committees. **Languages** English. **Staff** 4.00 FTE, paid. **Finance** Sources: meeting proceeds; members' dues; revenue from activities/projects. **Events** *AIP-CCM Meeting* Brussels (Belgium) 2013, *Annual General Assembly* Brussels (Belgium) 2013, *Workshop on Building a Framework for Social Benefits approch to Health Technology Assessment* Brussels (Belgium) 2013, *Meeting* Brussels (Belgium) 2011, *Workshop on partnering for rare disease therapy development* Prague (Czech Rep) 2010. **Publications** Reports; white papers.
Members Consortium comprises 17 partners from 10 countries. Membership countries not specified. Includes 11 organizations listed in this Yearbook:
AGE Platform Europe (#00557); *Central European Initiative (CEI, #03708)*; *European Alliance for Personalised Medicine (EAPM, #05878)*; *European Connected Health Alliance (ECHAlliance, #06741)*; *European Coordination Committee of the Radiological, Electromedical Healthcare IT Industry (COCIR, #06792)*; *European Health Telematics Association (EHTEL, #07463)*; *European Institute for Health Records (EuroRec Institute, #07560)*; *European Patients' Forum (EPF, #08172)*; *European Regions Research and Innovation Network (ERRIN, #08349)*; *International Foundation for Integrated Care (IFIC, #13672)*; *Lisbon Council for Economic Competitiveness and Social Renewal (Lisbon Council, #16491)*. [2022/XF4953/y/**F**]

♦ Digital Health Society (unconfirmed)
♦ Digital Humaniora i Norden / see Digital Humanities in the Nordic and Baltic Countries (#05080)
♦ Digital Humanities Deutschland / see Digital Humanities im deutschsprachigen Raum (#05079)

♦ Digital Humanities im deutschsprachigen Raum (DHd) 05079

Chairman Uni Trier – Fachbereich II, DM321, 54286 Trier, Germany. E-mail: info@dig-hum.de.
URL: https://dig-hum.de/

History 17 Jul 2012, Hamburg (Germany). Former names and other names: *Digital Humanities Deutschland (DHD)* – former. Registration: Hamburg District court, No/ID: VR 21873, Start date: 19 Aug 2013, Germany, Hamburg. **Aims** Promote the digital humanities and cultural studies in Germany and German-speaking countries and regions. **Structure** Board. **Activities** Events/meetings; knowledge management/information dissemination; research/documentation. **Events** *Annual Meeting* Potsdam (Germany) 2022, *Annual Meeting* 2021. **NGO Relations** Member of (1): *Alliance of Digital Humanities Organizations (ADHO, #00671)*. [2022/AA2538/**D**]

♦ Digital Humanities in the Nordic and Baltic Countries (DHNB) 05080

Chair c/o Dept Digital Humanities, PO Box 24, University of Helsinki, FI-00014 Helsinki, Finland.
URL: https://dhnb.eu/

History 23 Apr 2015, Oslo (Norway). Former names and other names: *Digital Humaniora i Norden (DHN)* – former (Apr 2015 to Oct 2020); *Digital Humanities in the Nordic Countries* – former (Apr 2015 to Oct 2020). **Aims** Strengthen research, education and mediation in the digital humanities in the Nordic countries. **Structure** Board. **Staff** None paid. **Finance** Members' dues. Funding from Gothenburg University (Sweden). **Activities** Events/meetings; training/education; research/documentation; networking/liaising. **Events** *Conference* Uppsala (Sweden) 2022, *Conference* Riga (Latvia) 2020, *Annual Meeting* Copenhagen (Denmark) 2019, *Annual Meeting* Helsinki (Finland) 2018, *Conference* Gothenburg (Sweden) 2017. **NGO Relations** *European Association for Digital Humanities (EADH, #06014)*. [2022/XJ9992/**F**]

♦ Digital Humanities in the Nordic Countries / see Digital Humanities in the Nordic and Baltic Countries (#05080)
♦ Digital Media Association (internationally oriented national body)
♦ Digital Network of the Church in Latin America (#18689)

♦ Digital Olfaction Society (DOS) 05081

Contact Kanaya Bldg 4F,, 4-11-3, Hatchobori Chuo-ku, Tokyo, 104-0032 Japan. E-mail: olfaction@digital-olfaction.com.
URL: https://digital-olfaction.com/

History Mar 2012. **Aims** Exploit the advances of digital olfaction research and development; consider the practical applications of digital olfaction; project these applications to daily life to measure their impact on today's lifestyle. **Structure** Committee. **Activities** Events/meetings. **Events** *World Congress* Tokyo (Japan) 2022, *World Congress* Tokyo (Japan) 2021, *World Congress* Tokyo (Japan) 2018, *World Congress on Digital Olfaction and Issues* Milan (Italy) 2016, *World Congress* Tokyo (Japan) 2016. **Members** Individuals. Membership countries not specified. [2021/AA2041/cv/**C**]

♦ Digital Opportunity Task Force (no recent information)

♦ Digital Radio Mondiale Consortium (DRM) 05082

Chair 610 Chiswick High Road, London, W4 5RU, UK. T. +447718175879. E-mail: projectoffice@drm.org – pressoffice@drm.org.
Registered Office Postal Box 360, Grand Saconex, 1218 Geneva, Switzerland.
URL: https://www.drm.org/

History 1998, Guangzhou (China). **Aims** Make the DRM standard accepted and widely known with all its features and adopted at regional, national and international level. **Structure** General Assembly; Steering Board; Executive Board; Technical and ad-hoc Committees; National Platforms. **Languages** English, French, German. **Finance** Sources: members' dues. **Activities** Research and development; standards/guidelines. **Events** *Symposium* Dallas, TX (USA) 2004, *Annual General Assembly* Hangzhou (China) 2004, *Symposium* Hangzhou (China) 2004, *Consortium meeting* Moscow (Russia) 2004, *Consortium meeting* Lisbon (Portugal) 2003. **Publications** *DRM Handbook* (5th ed 2019).
Members Full; Associate: Supporters. Full in 14 countries:
Brazil, Canada, Croatia, France, Germany, India, Indonesia, Japan, Netherlands, Russia, South Africa, Switzerland, UK, USA.
Included in the above, 1 organization listed in this Yearbook:
International Broadcasting Bureau (IBB).
Associate in 22 countries:
Australia, Belgium, Canada, China, Czechia, Denmark, Ecuador, Finland, France, Germany, Hungary, India, Iran Islamic Rep, Japan, Korea Rep, Malaysia, Mongolia, Netherlands, Nigeria, Norway, Switzerland, Tunisia.
Included in the above, 6 organizations listed in this Yearbook:
Arab States Broadcasting Union (ASBU, #01050); *Asia-Pacific Broadcasting Union (ABU, #01863)*; *Community Media Forum Europe (CMFE, #04402)*; *European Broadcasting Union (EBU, #06404)*; *International Committee of the Red Cross (ICRC, #12799)*; *International Telecommunication Union (ITU, #15673)*.
Supporters in 25 countries and territories:
Australia, Austria, Brazil, Bulgaria, China, Denmark, France, Germany, Hong Kong, India, Ireland, Italy, Japan, Mexico, New Zealand, North Macedonia, Romania, Russia, Singapore, South Africa, Spain, Switzerland, Taiwan, UK, USA.
Included in the above, 1 organization listed in this Yearbook:
World Family of Radio Maria (WF, #21400). [2021.09.07/XF6980/y/**F**]

♦ Digital Research Infrastructure for the Arts and Humanities (DARIAH-EU) 05083

SG DARIAH-EU Coordination Office, Centre Marc Bloch, Friedrichstrasse 191, 10117 Berlin, Germany. T. +4930209370732. E-mail: info@dariah.eu.
Host Country c/o TGIR Huma-Num, CNRS UMS 3598, 190-198 av de France, CS no 71345, 75648 Paris CEDEX 13, France. T. +33149542194. Fax +33149542641.
URL: https://www.dariah.eu/

History Set up as a *European Research Infrastructure Consortium (ERIC)* 2014. Registration: EU Transparency Register, No/ID: 714943922947-18, Start date: 9 Aug 2016. **Aims** Enhance and support digitally-enabled research and teaching across the humanities and arts by: developing, maintaining and operating infrastructure in support of ICT-based research practices, and by sustaining researchers in using them to build, analyse and interpret digital resources; bring together individual state-of-the-art digital arts and humanities activities and scales their results to a European level. **Structure** General Assembly; Board of Directors; Scientific

Board; Coordination Office. **Languages** English, French, German. **Staff** 9.50 FTE, paid. **Activities** Research and development; training/education; financial and/or material support; projects/programmes; advocacy/lobbying/activism; awards/prizes/competitions; events/meetings; knowledge management/information dissemination; networking/liaising; publishing activities. **Events** *Annual Event* 2021, *Annual Event* 2020, *Annual Meeting* Zagreb (Croatia) 2020, *Annual Meeting* Warsaw (Poland) 2019, *Annual Meeting* Paris (France) 2018. **Publications** *The DARIAH ERIC: Redefining Research Infrastructure for the Arts and Humanities in the Digital Age* (2017) by Jennifer Edmond et al; *Data fluidity in DARIAH – pushing the agenda forward* (2016) by Laurent Romary et al. Articles; conference papers.
Members Partners in 17 countries:
Austria, Belgium, Croatia, Cyprus, Denmark, France, Germany, Greece, Ireland, Italy, Luxembourg, Malta, Netherlands, Poland, Portugal, Serbia, Slovenia.
NGO Relations Memorandum of Understanding with (1): *Association of European Research Libraries (#02540)*. *European Alliance for the Social Sciences and Humanities (EASSH, #05885)*; *Europeana Foundation (#05839)*. [2021/XM4260/**F**]

- ♦ Digital Society Foundation (internationally oriented national body)
- ♦ Digital Solutions Cooperative / see Dscoop (#05141)

♦ Digital Television Action Group (DigiTAG) 05084

Project Office L'Ancienne-Route 17A, Le Grand-Saconnex, 1218 Geneva, Switzerland. T. +41227172735. Fax +41227474735. E-mail: projectoffice@digitag.org.
URL: http://www.digitag.org/

Aims Defend and promote digital terrestrial television (DTT) on a worldwide basis bringing together industrial players to protect spectrum for broadcasting, regardless of the technical standard used on the DTT platform. **Structure** Steering Board; Presidency. Working Groups.
Members Full in 16 countries:
Andorra, Belgium, Denmark, France, Germany, Italy, Korea Rep, Netherlands, Norway, Poland, Portugal, Spain, Sweden, Switzerland, UK, Ukraine.
Included in the above, 3 organizations listed in this Yearbook:
Broadcast Network Europe (BNE, #03335); *DIGITALEUROPE (#05073)*; *European Broadcasting Union (EBU, #06404)*. [2015/XJ9186/y/**D**]

♦ Digital Trusts and Compliance Europe (DTCE) 05085

Secretariat Tiensestraat 12, 3320 Hoegaarden, Belgium. E-mail: info@dtce.eu.
URL: http://www.dtce.eu/

History Registered in accordance with Belgian law. **Aims** Represent interests of ICT trust and compliance vendors and practitioners in Europe. **Structure** Board. **Activities** Events/meetings. **NGO Relations** Liaison Organization of: *Comité européen de normalisation (CEN, #04162)*. [2016/XM4797/**F**]

- ♦ Digit Fund / see Dian Fossey Gorilla Fund International
- ♦ Digni (internationally oriented national body)
- ♦ Dignitas International (internationally oriented national body)
- ♦ DIGNITY – Danish Institute Against Torture (internationally oriented national body)
- ♦ DIGNITY – Dansk Institut Mod Tortur (internationally oriented national body)

♦ Dignity International 05086

Admin Officer A-2-7 Pusat Perdagangan Seksyen 8, Jalan SG Jernih 8/1, 46050 Petaling Jaya, Selangor, Malaysia. T. +6060379310741.
URL: http://www.dignityinternational.org/

History Oct 1999, at the Global Forum for Poverty Eradication, organized by *Council of Europe (CE, #04881)*. Registered in accordance with Dutch law, Oct 2001. Became operational as an independent organization, Jan 2003. **Aims** Promote and defend human rights for all, including social, economic and cultural rights. **Structure** Board of Directors; International Secretariat. **Languages** English, French, Spanish. **Finance** Core donors: *Oxfam Novib*; *Ford Foundation (#09858)*; *Mertz Gilmore Foundation*. Also project donors. **Activities** Human Rights Based Development; Activities on human rights and community organizers. **Publications** *Dignity Online* – newsletter. *From Poverty to Dignity: Learning Manual on Human Rights Based Development*. **Consultative Status** Consultative status granted from: *African Commission on Human and Peoples' Rights (ACHPR, #00255)* (Observer); *ECOSOC (#05331)* (Special). **NGO Relations** Member of: *International Network for Economic, Social and Cultural Rights (ESCR-Net, #14255)*. (Past) Projects with: *Asia Pacific Forum on Women, Law and Development (APWLD, #01912)*; *Asian Forum for Human Rights and Development (FORUM-ASIA, #01491)*; *Asian Regional Resource Centre for Human Rights Education (ARRC)*; *IPS – Inter Press Service International Association (#16013)*; *People's Movement for Human Rights Learning (PDHRE, #18307)*; *Social Watch (#19350)*. [2017/XM0627/**F**]

- ♦ **DiGRA** Digital Games Research Association (#05076)
- ♦ **DIGSA** Committee of Directors of Geographic Institutes of South American Countries, Spain and Portugal (#04248)
- ♦ DIHR – Danish Institute for Human Rights (internationally oriented national body)
- ♦ DIIFSD / see Doha International Family Institute (#05111)
- ♦ DIIS – Danish Institute for International Studies (internationally oriented national body)
- ♦ Dikastirio ton Evropaikon Kinotiton / see Court of Justice of the European Union (#04938)
- ♦ DIKS – Deadong Institute for Korean Studies (internationally oriented national body)
- ♦ **DILA** Foundation for the Development of International Law in Asia (#09945)
- ♦ DiMA – Digital Media Association (internationally oriented national body)
- ♦ Dimension humaine mondiale (internationally oriented national body)
- ♦ DIML – Dokumentations- und Informationszentrum Menschenrechte in Lateinamerika (internationally oriented national body)
- ♦ **DIMMID** Dialogue Interreligieux Monastique (#16849)
- ♦ DIMVA – Conference on Detection of Intrusions and Malware and Vulnerability Assessment (meeting series)
- ♦ DINAMO – Discussions on Nano & Mesoscopic Optics (meeting series)
- ♦ Dining for Women / see Together Women Rise
- ♦ Diobass, écologie et société (internationally oriented national body)
- ♦ Diocesan Labourer Priests (religious order)

♦ Dioxin20XX 05087

Co-Sec address not obtained.
Co-Sec address not obtained.
URL: http://dioxin20xx.org/

History Founded by the International Advisory Board of the International Symposium on Halogenated Persistent Organic Pollutants (POPs). **Aims** Promote scientific education and research on POPs. **Structure** International Advisory Board. **Activities** Awards/prizes/competitions; events/meetings. **Events** *International Symposium on Halogenated Persistent Organic Pollutants* 2019. **Publications** *Organohalogen Compounds*. [2021.08.31/AA0133/c/**E**]

- ♦ DIP – International Symposium on Diabetes, Hypertension, Metabolic Syndrome and Pregnancy (meeting series)
- ♦ Diplo Foundation (internationally oriented national body)

♦ Diplomaten International (DMW) 05088

DIPLOMATS INTERNATIONAL
Chair Genève Nations, Rue Du Pré-de-la-Bichette 1, 1201 Geneva, Switzerland. T. +41225480888. Fax +4922165078450. E-mail: info@diplomaten.eu – europabuero@diplomaten.eu.
Head Office DMW – Diplomaten International, Schloss Knonau, Knonau, 8934 Affoltern am Albis ZH, Switzerland.
URL: http://www.diplomaten.eu/

History Former names and other names: *INGO DMW* – alias. **Aims** Bring about European integration and EU enlargement through the involvement and participation of people; promote peace negotiations, comity of nations and the teaching and implementation of diplomacy. **Structure** Annual General Meeting; Board of Directors. **Activities** Advocacy/lobbying/activism; awards/prizes/competitions; conflict resolution; projects/programmes; training/education. Active in: Austria, Belgium/Brussels Capital Region, Budapest, Cyprus, Germany, Istanbul, Moskva, Netherlands, Oslo, Prague, Switzerland. **Publications** *Die DMW Zeitung*. **Members** As of 2022, 366 members. Membership countries not specified. **Consultative Status** Consultative status granted from: *ECOSOC (#05331)* (Special). [2022.07.16/XJ9903/**F**]

- ♦ Diplomatic Academy of Vienna (internationally oriented national body)
- ♦ Diplomatic Academy of Vienna/Vienna School of International Studies / see Diplomatic Academy of Vienna
- ♦ Diplomatic Academy of Vietnam (internationally oriented national body)
- ♦ Diplomatic Conference of International Maritime Law (inactive)

♦ Diplomatic Corps 05089

Corps diplomatique (CD)
Address not obtained.

Structure Recognized, especially through the privileges and immunities conferred by international customary law and by *Vienna Convention on Diplomatic Relations (1961)* of 18 Apr 1961 (in force since 24 Apr 1964), as the body of diplomatic officers accredited to governments, to intergovernmental organizations, or to quasi-governmental institutions such as the Holy See or the Sovereign Military Order of Malta. Not a formal organization with elected officers and decision-making structures, despite acceptance of the role of Dean or Doyen and the meetings of its members. One interpretation limits the term to all diplomats accredited to one ('receiving') government, another applies it to all diplomats accredited by one ('sending') government. [2008/XF5202/**F**]

- ♦ Diplomatic Council (unconfirmed)
- ♦ Diplomatic Order of the Knights of Saint Gabriel / see Diplomatic Society of St Gabriel
- ♦ Diplomatic Quartet / see Quartet Group (#18593)

♦ Diplomatic Research and Policy Foundation (DRPF) 05090

SG Mito Hadzivasilev Jasmin bb, 1000 Skopje, North Macedonia. T. +38970256135.
URL: https://drpf.edu.mk/

History 2017, Skopje (North Macedonia). **Aims** Define the future of education and politics. **Structure** Administrative Council; Executive Committee; Academic Council; Rector. **Languages** English, French. **Staff** 3.00 FTE, paid; 10.00 FTE, voluntary. **Activities** Advocacy/lobbying/activism; capacity building; certification/accreditation; knowledge management/information dissemination; publishing activities; research/documentation; training/education. Active in all member countries.
Members Full in 3 countries:
Albania, Kosovo, North Macedonia. [2020.12.08/AA1236/f/**F**]

- ♦ Diplomatic Society of St Gabriel (internationally oriented national body)
- ♦ Diplomatische Akademie Wien (internationally oriented national body)
- ♦ DIPLOMATS INTERNATIONAL (#05088)
- ♦ DIPNET – Diphtheria Surveillance Network / see European Diphtheria Surveillance Network (#06927)
- ♦ **DiPVaC** Discourse-Pragmatic Variation and Change Research Network (#05101)
- ♦ **DIRCAIBEA** Consejo de Directores de Carreteras de Iberia e Iberoamérica (#04706)
- ♦ Dirección General de Cooperación con Africa, Asia y Europa Oriental (internationally oriented national body)
- ♦ Dirección General de Cooperación con América Latina / see Dirección General de Cooperación con Iberoamérica
- ♦ Dirección General de Cooperación con Iberoamérica (internationally oriented national body)

♦ Direct Aid International 05091

Jami-ayyat al-'Awn al-Mubahsir
Contact Third ring way in front of Al Dadissiya Area, Block 212 St Mosa Ibin Nosier, Beside Al Wzan Mosque, Kuwait, Kuwait.
URL: http://www.direct-aid.org/

History 1981, Kuwait, as Malawi Muslim Agency. Subsequently changed title to *Africa Muslims Agency*. Current titled adopted, 1999, although some branches still function under previous title. **Aims** Give *humanitarian*, social and educational *assistance* to the various countries and peoples of Africa. **Structure** Board of Directors. **Languages** Arabic, English, French. **Staff** 43.50 FTE, paid. **Finance** Source: individual voluntary donors. Budget (annual): US$ 3 million. **Activities** Attention mainly focused on educational and social projects in Africa, the programme covering the running of schools (both primary and secondary), orphanages and clinics and the digging of wells. Helps students financially to complete secondary and higher education abroad, especially in the field of science engineering and medicine. Organizes seminars and workshops. The Agency comprises mainly volunteers from Kuwait, Bahrain, Saudi Arabia, United Arab Emirates and most of the African countries. **Publications** Newsletter (12 a year). **Members** Not a membership organization. The Agency is involved, through local officers, in 37 countries across Africa. **IGO Relations** *UNHCR (#20327)*. [2011/XF5013/f/**F**]

- ♦ Directie-Generaal voor Ontwikkelings-Samenwerking (internationally oriented national body)
- ♦ Directing Council of Pan American Congresses of Veterinary Medicine / see Asociación Panamericana de Ciencias Veterinarias (#02287)
- ♦ Direction du développement et de la coopération (internationally oriented national body)
- ♦ Direction-générale de la coopération au développement (internationally oriented national body)
- ♦ Direction générale de la coopération internationale pour le développement (internationally oriented national body)
- ♦ Direct Marketing Association (internationally oriented national body)
- ♦ Directorate-General for Development Cooperation (internationally oriented national body)
- ♦ Directors Across Borders (internationally oriented national body)
- ♦ Direct Relief (internationally oriented national body)
- ♦ Direct Relief Foundation / see Direct Relief
- ♦ Direct Relief International / see Direct Relief

♦ Direct Selling Europe (DSE) 05092

Managing Dir Av de la Toison d'Or 51, 1060 Brussels, Belgium. T. +3225031856. Fax +3225131435. E-mail: info@directsellingeurope.eu.
URL: http://www.directsellingeurope.eu/

History Jan 2007. Registration: EU Transparency Register, No/ID: 9435658947-27; No/ID: 0890.404.471, Belgium. **Aims** Represent companies and associations with an irreproachable reputation and implement sustainable and ethical business practices towards both consumers and sales consultants. **Structure** General Assembly (annual); Board of Directors; CEO Council; Working Groups; Managing Director. **Languages** English, French, German. **Staff** 3.00 FTE, paid. **Finance** Sources: members' dues. Annual budget: 350,000 EUR. **Events** *Meeting* Brussels (Belgium) 2018.
Members Associations (5); companies (14). Associations in 11 countries:
Austria, Belgium, Czechia, France, Germany, Greece, Italy, Poland, Slovakia, Spain, Switzerland.
NGO Relations Member of (1): *EuroCommerce (EC, #05665)*. [2022/XJ5877/**D**]

- ♦ Direktion für Entwicklung und Zusammenarbeit (internationally oriented national body)
- ♦ Direktoratet for utviklingssamarbeid (internationally oriented national body)
- ♦ Direzione dello sviluppo e della cooperazione (internationally oriented national body)
- ♦ DIR – Research Centre on Development and International Relations (internationally oriented national body)
- ♦ **DIRSI** Dialogo Regional sobre la Sociedad de la Información (#18777)
- ♦ **DisabCouncil** Disability Council International (#05093)

♦ **Disability Council International (DisabCouncil)** **05093**

Chairperson PO Box 45, Collex, 1239 Geneva, Switzerland. T. +41774032345. Fax +41225802781. E-mail: info@disabilitycouncilinternational.org.
URL: http://disabilitycouncilinternational.org/

Aims Work for inclusive and accessible societies for persons with disabilities all over the world. **Structure** Executive Board of 9. **IGO Relations** *Committee on the Rights of Persons with Disabilities (CRPD, #04284).* **NGO Relations** Supporter of: *End Corporal Punishment (#05457).* [2022/XJ7690/C]

♦ **Disability HIV and AIDS Trust (DHAT)** **05094**

Exec Dir PO Box CY1515, Causeway, Causeway, Zimbabwe. T. +2634778565. E-mail: info@dhatregional.org.
Street Address 9 St Quinton Avenue Eastlea, Harare, HARARE, Zimbabwe.
URL: http://www.dhatregional.org/

History Registered in accordance with the laws of Zimbabwe, 2007. **Aims** Create an environment of involvement and support for disability inclusive legislation, policy and practice in SRH, HIV and AIDS service delivery using a rights-based approach. **Structure** Board of Trustees, including Chairperson, Vice-Chairperson, Secretary, Treasurer and Executive Director. **Languages** English. **Staff** 12.00 FTE, paid; 20.00 FTE, voluntary. **Finance** Donations; donor funding. Annual budget: US$ 1,000,000.
Members Country programmes in 4 countries:
Botswana, Malawi, Zambia, Zimbabwe.
IGO Relations Partners include: *UNDP (#20292).* **NGO Relations** Member of: *Regional Inter-Agency Task Team on Children and AIDS in Eastern and Southern Africa (RIATT-ESA, #18791).* Partners include: *Humanity and Inclusion (HI, #10975); Oxfam International (#17922); Progressio (inactive); SRHR Africa Trust (SAT, #19934); Southern Africa HIV/AIDS Information Dissemination Service (SAfAIDS, #19831).* [2018/XJ7272/F]

♦ **Disability Rights Advocacy Fund (DRAF)** **05095**

Exec Dir 89 South St, Ste 203-B, Boston MA 02111-2670, USA. T. +16172614593. Fax +16172611977. E-mail: info@drafund.org.
URL: http://drafund.org/

History Incorporated in the State of Massachusetts (USA), 2012. **Aims** Support persons with disabilities in the developing world to advance legal frameworks to realize their rights. **Structure** Board of Directors. **Staff** 12.00 FTE, paid. **Activities** Financial and/or material support. **NGO Relations** Sister Organization: *Disability Rights Fund (DRF, #05096).* [2017/XM5529/f/F]

♦ **Disability Rights Fund (DRF)** **05096**

Exec Dir 89 South St, Ste 203, Boston MA 02111-2670, USA. T. +16172614593. Fax +16172611977. E-mail: info@disabilityrightsfund.org.
URL: http://www.disabilityrightsfund.org/

History 2008. Incorporated in the State of Massachusetts (USA), 2012. **Aims** Support persons with disabilities around the world to build diverse movements, ensure inclusive developments agendas, and archive equal rights and opportunity for all. **Structure** Board of Directors; Global Advisory Panel. **Staff** 12.00 FTE, paid. **Activities** Financial and/or material support. **Consultative Status** Consultative status granted from: *ECOSOC (#05331)* (Special). **NGO Relations** Sister Organization: *Disability Rights Advocacy Fund (DRAF, #05095).* Supports: *International Disability Alliance (IDA, #13176).* Member of: *Global Action on Disability Network (GLAD, #10165).* [2017/XM5528/f/F]

♦ Disability Rights International (internationally oriented national body)
♦ Disability Studies in Art Education (unconfirmed)

♦ **Disabled Peoples' International (DPI)** **05097**

Organisation internationale des personnes handicapées (OMPH) – Organización Mundial de Personas con Discapacidad (OMPD) – Mezdunarodnoe Obscestvo Invalidov

Sec 160 Elgin St, Place Bell R PO, PO Box 70073, Ottawa ON K2P 2M3, Canada. E-mail: secretariat.dpi@gmail.com.
URL: http://www.dpi.org/

History 4 Dec 1981, Singapore (Singapore). Founded during 1st World Congress, replacing the first working name of *World Coalition of Disabled* set up 1980, Winnipeg MB (Canada). **Aims** Promote the *human rights* of people with disabilities and their economic and *social integration*; develop and support organizations of people with disabilities. **Structure** World Congress. World Council of 35 members. Executive Officers: Chairperson; 2 Deputy Chairpersons; Honorary Secretary; Treasurer; Info Officer. Regional Councils with Regional Chairpersons for 5 Regions: Europe; Latin America; North America/Caribbean; Africa; Asia/Pacific. National Assemblies (135). Head Office in Canada. Committees (5): Human Rights; Women; Under-Represented Groups; Governance; Fundraising. **Languages** English, French, Spanish. **Staff** 8.00 FTE, paid. 3 contractual. **Finance** Sources: members' dues. Grants from: *Canadian International Development Agency (CIDA, inactive); Swedish International Development Cooperation Agency (Sida)*; UN Agencies. **Activities** Advocacy/lobbying/activism; events/meetings; knowledge management/information dissemination; research/documentation; training/education. Human Rights Programme - *Convention on the Rights of Persons with Disabilities (CRPD, 2006).* **Events** *World Assembly* Cairo (Egypt) 2016, *World assembly* Durban (South Africa) 2011, *International conference on accessible tourism* Singapore (Singapore) 2009, *World congress / World Assembly* Seoul (Korea Rep) 2007, *World summit* Winnipeg, MB (Canada) 2004. **Publications** *E-update* (weekly); *DPI Happenings* (6 a year); *Disability International* (2 a year) – journal. Congress and seminar proceedings; reports; information package.
Members Approved member countries and territories (131):
Albania, Algeria, Angola, Antigua-Barbuda, Argentina, Australia, Azerbaijan, Bahamas, Bangladesh, Barbados, Belarus, Belgium, Belize, Benin, Bolivia, Botswana, Brazil, Bulgaria, Burkina Faso, Cambodia, Cameroon, Canada, Cape Verde, Chad, Chile, China, Colombia, Congo Brazzaville, Cook Is, Costa Rica, Côte d'Ivoire, Croatia, Cuba, Czechia, Dominica, Dominican Rep, Ecuador, El Salvador, Estonia, Eswatini, Ethiopia, Fiji, Finland, France, Gabon, Gambia, Germany, Ghana, Greece, Grenada, Guatemala, Guinea, Guyana, Honduras, Hungary, Iceland, India, Indonesia, Ireland, Italy, Jamaica, Japan, Kenya, Korea Rep, Laos, Latvia, Lebanon, Lesotho, Liberia, Libya, Madagascar, Malawi, Malaysia, Maldives, Mali, Mauritania, Mauritius, Mexico, Mongolia, Morocco, Mozambique, Namibia, Nepal, New Zealand, Nicaragua, Niger, Nigeria, North Macedonia, Norway, Pakistan, Panama, Papua New Guinea, Paraguay, Peru, Philippines, Portugal, Romania, Russia, Rwanda, Samoa, Senegal, Serbia, Seychelles, Sierra Leone, Singapore, Slovakia, Slovenia, Solomon Is, Somalia, South Africa, Spain, Sri Lanka, St Kitts-Nevis, St Lucia, St Vincent-Grenadines, Sweden, Switzerland, Tanzania UR, Thailand, Togo, Trinidad-Tobago, Tunisia, Türkiye, Uganda, UK, Ukraine, Uruguay, USA, Vanuatu, Zambia, Zimbabwe.
Consultative Status Consultative status granted from: *ECOSOC (#05331)* (Special); *UNESCO (#20322)* (Consultative Status); *ILO (#11123)* (Special List); *Council of Europe (CE, #04881)* (Participatory Status). **IGO Relations** Accredited by: *United Nations Office at Vienna (UNOV, #20604).* **NGO Relations** Member of (3): *CIVICUS: World Alliance for Citizen Participation (#03962); End Corporal Punishment (#05457); World Vision International (WVI, #21904).* Participates in: *Global Partnership on Children with Disabilities (GPcwd, #10529). Southern Africa Federation of the Disabled (SAFOD, #19829)* is a member. Coordinator for the sector within: *European Disability Forum (EDF, #06929).* Cooperates with: *International Council for Adult Education (ICAE, #12983).* [2021/XD1612/B]

♦ Disarm / see Global Health Partners
♦ Disarmament Committee of the Student International Organizations (inactive)
♦ Disarmament and Security Centre (internationally oriented national body)
♦ Disarm Education Fund / see Global Health Partners
♦ DISARM/GHP / see Global Health Partners
♦ DISARM / Global Health Partners / see Global Health Partners
♦ Disaster Preparedness and Emergency Response Association, International (internationally oriented national body)

♦ **Disaster Preparedness and Prevention Initiative for South-Eastern Europe (DPPI SEE)** **05098**

Head Secretariat Branilaca Sarajeva 34, 71000 Sarajevo, Bosnia-Herzegovina. T. +38733218558. E-mail: ivana.ljubojevic@dppi.info – vildana.bijedic@dppi.info.
URL: http://www.dppi.info/

History Nov 2000, by *Stability Pact for South Eastern Europe (inactive)*, currently taken over by *Regional Cooperation Council (RCC, #18773).* **Aims** Foster regional cooperation and coordination in disaster preparedness and prevention for natural and man-made disasters in South Eastern Europe, without creating new structures or layers of bureaucracy. [2017/XJ2478/E*]

♦ Disaster Recovery Institute International / see DRI International (#05132)
♦ Disaster Resource Network / see Disaster Resource Partnership (#05099)

♦ **Disaster Resource Partnership (DRP)** **05099**

Address not obtained.
URL: https://www.weforum.org/projects/disaster-resource-partnership-drp/

History Set up by *World Economic Forum (WEF, #21367)*, as *Disaster Resource Network (DRN).* Registered in accordance with Swiss law. **Aims** Develop a cross-sector, professional, scalable and accountable humanitarian response to disasters that has the ability to meet growing demands to reduce suffering and save lives. **Structure** Board of Directors. Steering Board includes: *International Federation of Red Cross and Red Crescent Societies (#13526); United Nations Office for the Coordination of Humanitarian Affairs (OCHA, #20593).* **Activities** Support existing networks and catalyzes new ones; establishes partnerships and framework agreements; captures and shares best practice/institutional knowledge; provides a focal point for the EandC sector in global humanitarian coordination. **Members** Not a membership organization. **NGO Relations** Numerous relationships with humanitarian agencies. [2016/XM1073/F]

♦ Disasters Emergency Committee (internationally oriented national body)
♦ Discalced Carmelite Fathers – Order of Discalced Brothers of the Blessed Virgin Mary of Mount Carmel (religious order)
♦ Discalced Carmelite Nuns (religious order)
♦ DISC – Duke Islamic Studies Center (internationally oriented national body)
♦ Disciples of Christ – Christian Church (internationally oriented national body)

♦ **Disciples Ecumenical Consultative Council (DECC)** **05100**

Gen Sec 130 E Washington St, PO Box 1986, Indianapolis IN 46206, USA. Fax +13177132588.
URL: http://councilonchristianunity.org/

History 1975. **Aims** Deepen the *fellowship* of Disciples of *Christ* with each other and with other *churches* on their way to the visible unity *God* wills for all *Christians.* **Structure** Council; Reference Committee; Advisory Committee; General Secretary. **Finance** Sharing of central costs among all of the member Churches. Representatives appointed to represent DECC at international meetings are paid by the Churches from which they come. **Activities** Events/meetings; networking/liaising. **Events** *Meeting* Canberra, ACT (Australia) 1991.
Members Member Churches in 16 countries and territories:
Argentina, Australia, Canada, Congo DR, Ghana, India, Jamaica, Mexico, New Zealand, Paraguay, Puerto Rico, South Africa, UK, USA, Vanuatu, Zimbabwe.
NGO Relations *Christian Church (Disciples of Christ).* Regional member: *United Congregational Church of Southern Africa (UCCSA, #20503).* International dialogues with: Roman Catholic Church. [2016/XE4004/E]

♦ Disciples Peace Fellowship (internationally oriented national body)
♦ Discipling for Development (internationally oriented national body)
♦ DiscourseNet / see International Association for Discourse Studies (#11850)
♦ **DiscourseNet** International Association for Discourse Studies (#11850)

♦ **Discourse-Pragmatic Variation and Change Research Network (DiPVaC)** **05101**

Contact School of Languages and Linguistics, Babel Bldg, Univ of Melbourne, Parkville VIC 3010, Australia. T. +61383443676. E-mail: dipvac.network@gmail.com.
URL: http://www.dipvac.org/

History Conference series launched 2012. **Aims** Provide a platform for the dissemination and discussion of new research findings, formation of new research collaborations, and promotion of the field within and beyond linguistics. **Structure** Steering Committee. **Activities** Events/meetings; research and development. **Events** *Biennial Conference* Melbourne, VIC (Australia) 2020, *Biennial Conference* Helsinki (Finland) 2018, *Biennial Conference* Ottawa, ON (Canada) 2016, *Biennial Conference* Newcastle upon Tyne (UK) 2014, *Biennial Conference* Salford (UK) 2012.
Members Individuals in 25 countries:
Australia, Austria, Belgium, Canada, China, Denmark, Finland, Germany, Hungary, Ireland, Italy, Japan, Lithuania, Mexico, Netherlands, New Zealand, North Macedonia, Norway, Spain, Sweden, Switzerland, Trinidad-Tobago, Türkiye, UK, USA. [2020.01.23/XM7926/c/F]

♦ Discovering Deaf Worlds (internationally oriented national body)
♦ DISCRETE – Symposium on Prospects in the Physics of Discrete Symmetries (meeting series)
♦ Discussions on Nano & Mesoscopic Optics (meeting series)
♦ DISOP – Dienst voor Internationale Samenwerking aan Ontwikkelingsprojecten (internationally oriented national body)
♦ Dis Politika Enstitüsü (internationally oriented national body)
♦ Disposiciones relativas a una unidad de cuenta (1982 treaty)
♦ Dispositions relatives à une unité de compte (1982 treaty)

♦ **Dispute Resolution Board Foundation (DRBF)** **05102**

Exec Dir 3440 Toringdon Way, Ste 205, Charlotte NC 28277, USA. T. +19802652367. E-mail: info@drb.org.
URL: http://www.drb.org/

History 1996. **Aims** Promote the avoidance and resolution of disputes worldwide using the unique and proven Dispute Resolution Board (DRB) method. **Structure** Executive Board of Directors; Region Boards of Directors (US and Canada; All other countries; Australia and New Zealand). **Activities** Events/meetings; training/education. **Events** *Annual International Conference* Sao Paulo (Brazil) 2023, *Central and Eastern European Regional Conference* Vienna (Austria) 2023, *Annual Connections Conference* Austin, TX (USA) 2022, *Annual International Conference* London (UK) 2022, *Annual International Conference* Lisbon (Portugal) 2021. [2023.02.13/XJ9833/f/F]

♦ Dissociative Electron Attachment Club (unconfirmed)

♦ **Distance Education for Africa (DEAfrica)** **05103**

Enseignement à Distance pour l'Afrique

Contact 5202 Dartmoor Ct, Lanham MD 20706, USA.
Founder/Pres PO Box 58161, Nairobi, 00200, Kenya. T. +254202483842.
URL: http://deafrica.org/

History Registration: USA. **Aims** Relieve *poverty*; promote ICT; improve access to efficient and effective world-class training and education courses to poor communities in Africa. **Structure** Board. **Consultative Status** Consultative status granted from: *ECOSOC (#05331)* (Special). [2021/XM7172/D]

♦ **Distance Education Association of Southern Africa (DEASA)** **05104**

Exec Sec SADC-CDE, c/o BOCODOL, Private Bag BO 187, Bontleng, Gaborone, Botswana. T. +2673180094. Fax +2673191089.
URL: http://www.deasa.org.za/

Events *Conference and Annual General Meeting* Maputo (Mozambique) 2020, *Conference and Annual General Meeting* Swaziland 2015, *Conference and Annual General Meeting* Mauritius 2014, *Conference and Annual General Meeting* Quatre-Bornes (Mauritius) 2014, *Conference and Annual General Meeting* Gaborone (Botswana) 2013. **Publications** *DEASE Journal.* [2020/XD5817/D]

♦ Distance Learning Center (see: #11434)
♦ Distributor Alliance Council EMEA / see Partner Community Council (#18228)
♦ **DISTRIPRESS** Association for the Promotion of the International Circulation of the Press (#02876)
♦ DISTRIPRESS – Bringing the world of press distribution together / see Association for the Promotion of the International Circulation of the Press (#02876)
♦ DISVI – Associazione Internazionale Disarmo e Sviluppo (internationally oriented national body)
♦ **DITTA** Global Diagnostic Imaging, Healthcare IT, and Radiation Therapy Trade Association (#10319)
♦ Divers Alert Network Asia-Pacific (see: #13181)
♦ Divers Alert Network Europe (see: #13181)
♦ Divers Alert Network Southern Africa (see: #13181)
♦ Diverse Network (meeting series)

♦ **DIVERSITAS in Western Pacific and Asia (DIWPA Network)** **05105**

SG Ctr for Ecological Research, Kyoto Univ, 509-3, 2-chome – Hirano, Otsu SHIGA, 520-2113 Japan. T. +81775498233. Fax +81775498201. E-mail: diwpa@ecology.kyoto-u.ac.jp.
Chair address not obtained. T. +81775498239.
URL: http://diwpa.ecology.kyoto-u.ac.jp/

History Founded 1993, Japan, as an international network developing from a biodiversity project in Kyoto (Japan), part of *DIVERSITAS – International Programme of Biodiversity Science (inactive)*, previously within the framework of *Programme on Man and the Biosphere (MAB, #18526)*. Originally covered wet climate terrestrial regions and surrounding oceanic regions but expanded to cover whole region. **Aims** Connect existing networks of people working on *biodiversity* and research projects in Asia and the Western Pacific. **Structure** Steering Committee. **Languages** English. **Staff** 0.50 FTE, paid; 2.00 FTE, voluntary. **Finance** Steering grant. **Activities** Research; information dissemination; capacity building. **Events** *Workshop* Nagano (Japan) 2014, *Workshop* Tokyo (Japan) 2014, *Workshop* Tokyo (Japan) 2013, *Workshop* Fukuoka (Japan) 2012, *Workshop* Nagano (Japan) 2012. **Publications** *DIWPA Newsletter. Biodiversity Research Methods – IBOY in Western Pacific and Asia.* AP-BON book series – Asia-Pacific Biodiversity Observation Network. Other occasional publications.
Members Individuals (440) in 39 countries and territories:
Australia, Bangladesh, Brunei Darussalam, Cambodia, Canada, China, Cook Is, Fiji, Finland, France, Germany, Guam, Hungary, India, Indonesia, Ireland, Japan, Korea Rep, Laos, Malaysia, Mongolia, Myanmar, Nepal, Netherlands, New Zealand, Palau, Papua New Guinea, Philippines, Russia, Samoa, Singapore, Sri Lanka, Switzerland, Taiwan, Thailand, UK, USA, Vietnam, Zambia. [2016.10.19/XF3748/v/**E**]

♦ **Diversity, Early Childhood Education and Training (DECET)** **05106**

Secretariat Hallepoortlaan 27, 1060 Brussels, Belgium. T. +3225393228. E-mail: decet.org@gmail.com.
Vice-Chair/Treas RIEPP, Av de l'Espinette 16, 1348 Louvain-la-Neuve, Belgium. T. +3210861800. Fax +3210861800.
URL: http://decet.org/

History As a network of projects and centres. **Aims** Empower knowledge, skills and attitudes to enable children and adults to construct together early childhood education services and communities where everyone: feels they belong; has all aspects of their identity confirmed; can learn from each other across cultural and other boundaries; can participate as active citizens; actively addresses bias through open communication and willingness to grow; works together to challenge institutional forms of prejudice and discrimination. **Structure** General Assembly; Bureau. **Finance** Financed by *Bernard van Leer Foundation (BvLF)*. **Activities** Events/meetings; training/education. **Events** *Conference* Birmingham (UK) 2015. **Publications** Newsletter. Training manual.
Members Organizations in 11 countries:
Belgium, Denmark, France, Germany, Greece, Ireland, Italy, Netherlands, Spain, Sweden, UK.
NGO Relations Member of: *Eurochild (#05657)*; *Global Learning Initiative on Children and Ethnic Diversity (Una, #10455)*. [2018/XF4858/**F**]

♦ **Divine Life Society** **05107**

Headquarters PO Shivanandanagar – 249 192, District Tehri-Garhwal, Rishikesh, Uttarakhand, Rishikesh UTTARAKHAND, India. T. +911352430040. E-mail: generalsecretary@sivanandaonline.org.
URL: http://www.sivanandaonline.org/

History Founded in 1936, by Sri Swami Sivananda. **Aims** Propagate the best and most precious elements of *Hindu* culture – asceticism, knowledge of *Yoga*, Vedantic system, Dharma – in order to establish *universal brotherhood*; revive worldwide *spirituality* and bring about transformation in man, gradually eradicating the animal and unfolding the divinity within; deal scientifically with all aspects of Yoga and *Vedanta*, universal *religion* and *philosophy* and ancient medicine. **Finance** Donations. **Activities** Events/meetings; training/education; publishing activities. **Events** *International conference* Montréal, QC (Canada) 2005, *International conference* Cuttack (India) 2001, *International conference* Mumbai (India) 1999. **Publications** *Divya Jeevan* (12 a year) in Hindi – periodical; *The Divine Life* (12 a year) in English – periodical. Books; pamphlets; magazines.
Members Members accept the practice of 'Ahimsa' non-violence, 'Satyam' truth, 'Brahmacharya' continence. Centres in 16 countries:
Australia, Austria, Belgium, Brazil, France, Germany, India, Italy, Malaysia, Mauritius, Netherlands, South Africa, Spain, UK, USA, Venezuela.
Also members in the West Indies. Membership countries not specified. [2019.10.24/XF0472/**F**]

♦ Division bactériologie et microbiologie appliquée de l'UISM (see: #15794)
♦ Division mycologie de l'UISM (see: #15794)
♦ Division virologie de l'UISM (see: #15794)
♦ DIVO – Doctors International Volunteer Organization (internationally oriented national body)
♦ **DIWPA Network** DIVERSITAS in Western Pacific and Asia (#05105)
♦ Djibouti Code of Conduct – Code of Conduct concerning the Repression of Piracy and Armed Robbery against Ships in the Western Indian Ocean and the Gulf of Aden (2009 treaty)
♦ DKA Austria – Three Kings Action (internationally oriented national body)
♦ DKA – Dreikönigsaktion (internationally oriented national body)
♦ **DK** Donaukommission (#04210)
♦ **DK** Dunajskaja Komissija (#04210)
♦ DKG – Delta Kappa Gamma Society International (internationally oriented national body)
♦ DKT International (internationally oriented national body)
♦ DLC in the EU / see Council of European Dentists (#04886)
♦ **DLCO-EA** Desert Locust Control Organization for Eastern Africa (#05042)
♦ **DLEARN** European Digital Learning Network (#06922)
♦ DLF – David Lynch Foundation (internationally oriented national body)

♦ **DLM Forum** **05108**

Registered Office Nooruse tn 3, 5041 Tartu, Estonia. E-mail: secretariat@dlmforum.eu.
URL: http://www.dlmforum.eu/

History Created following resolution adopted, 4 Nov 1999, by *Council of the European Union (#04895)* – then Council of the European Communities- and the Ministers of Culture, concerning archives. Subsequently established by *European Commission (EC, #06633)*. Since 2002, DLM stands for *Document Lifecycle Management*. Registration: Estonia. **Structure** Executive Committee. **Activities** Events/meetings; research/documentation. **Events** *Triennial Conference* Berlin (Germany) 2021, *DLM Members Meeting* Tallinn (Estonia) 2021, *Triennial Conference* Berlin (Germany) 2020, *Annual General Meeting* Tartu (Estonia) 2020, *Annual General Meeting* Zagreb (Croatia) 2020.
Members Full in 22 countries:
Austria, Czechia, Denmark, Estonia, Finland, Germany, Hungary, Ireland, Latvia, Lithuania, Luxembourg, Malta, Netherlands, Norway, Oman, Poland, Portugal, Slovenia, Spain, Sweden, Switzerland, UK.
Included in the above, 1 organization listed in this Yearbook:
European Central Bank (ECB, #06466). [2021/XM8002/**F**]

♦ **DLMS User Association** **05109**

Main Office Industriestr 53, 6312 Steinhausen ZG, Switzerland. E-mail: dlms@dlms.com.
URL: http://www.dlms.com/

History "DLMS" is an abbreviation of *Device Language Message Specification*. Statutes adopted 31 Mar 1997; replaced 6 Sep 2000 and 3 Oct 2011. Registration: No/ID: CHE-440.972.101, Switzerland. **Aims** Create generic and compatible *communication* objects, thereby enabling the integration of diverse systems and simplifying operational and commercial processes. **Structure** General Meeting (annual). Management Committee of 3 up to 11 members, including President. General Secretary. Working Groups. **Languages** English. **Finance** Sources: members' dues.
Members Companies in 41 countries:
Australia, Belgium, Bosnia-Herzegovina, Bulgaria, Canada, China, Colombia, Czechia, Denmark, Egypt, France, Germany, Hungary, India, Iran Islamic Rep, Italy, Japan, Korea Rep, Mexico, Moldova, Netherlands, Nigeria, Pakistan, Poland, Portugal, Romania, Russia, Saudi Arabia, Serbia, Singapore, Slovenia, South Africa, Spain, Sweden, Switzerland, Taiwan, Türkiye, UK, Ukraine, United Arab Emirates, USA.
Included in the above, 2 organizations listed in this Yearbook:
ESMIG (#05539); *ZigBee Alliance*.
NGO Relations In liaison with technical committees of: *European Committee for Electrotechnical Standardization (CENELEC, #06647)*. [2021/XJ4942/y/**C**]

♦ **DLP** Developmental Leadership Program (#05053)
♦ DMA – Direct Marketing Association (internationally oriented national body)
♦ DMAI / see Destinations International (#05046)
♦ DM – Daughters of Our Lady of Mercy (religious order)
♦ DMG – Deutsche Missionsgemeinschaft (internationally oriented national body)
♦ DMG – Deutsche Morgenländische Gesellschaft (internationally oriented national body)
♦ DMGF / see GlobalMedic
♦ DMGP – Deutschsprachige Medizinische Gesellschaft für Paraplegie (internationally oriented national body)
♦ **DMI** Deaf Ministries International (#05019)
♦ DMI – Design Management Institute (internationally oriented national body)
♦ DMI – Development Media International (internationally oriented national body)
♦ DMJ – Daughters of Mary and Joseph (religious order)
♦ DMOS / see VIA Don Bosco (#20766)
♦ DMS International Research Centre / see International Centre for Research on Delinquency, Marginality and Social Relationships (#12510)
♦ **DMW** Diplomaten International (#05088)
♦ **DMykG** Deutschsprachige Mykologische Gesellschaft (#05051)
♦ DMZ Forum (internationally oriented national body)
♦ The DMZ Forum – For Peace and Nature Conservation / see DMZ Forum
♦ DNAK – Norske Atlanterhavskomité (internationally oriented national body)
♦ **DNDi** Drugs for Neglected Diseases initiative (#05137)
♦ DNF / see Service- og Tjenestebranchens Union i Norden (#19244)
♦ DNHFU – Nordiska Handikappförbundens Ungdom (inactive)
♦ DNI / see Association of the Network for International Research on Desertification (#02823)
♦ **DNI** Defensa de Niñas y Niños Internacional (#05025)
♦ DNI – Den Norske Israelmisjon (internationally oriented national body)
♦ DN / see International Association for Discourse Studies (#11850)
♦ **DNPN** D'abord ne pas nuire (#10875)
♦ **DNR** Dövas Nordiska Råd (#05126)
♦ DOAWTU – Democratic Organization of African Workers' Trade Unions (inactive)
♦ Dóchas – Irish Association of Non-Governmental Development Organisations (internationally oriented national body)
♦ Dochters van Maria en Josef (religious order)
♦ Dochters van Onze Lieve Vrouw van het Heilig Hart (religious order)
♦ DOCIP – Indigenous Peoples' Center for Documentation, Research and Information (internationally oriented national body)
♦ **DOCOMOMO International** Documentation and Conservation of the Modern Movement (#05110)
♦ **DOC Research Institute** Dialogue of Civilizations Research Institute (#05065)
♦ Doc Society (internationally oriented national body)
♦ Doctor To Doctor (internationally oriented national body)
♦ Doctores para la Salud Global (internationally oriented national body)
♦ Doctors with Africa CUAMM (internationally oriented national body)
♦ Doctors Against Forced Organ Harvesting (unconfirmed)
♦ Doctors Without Borders (#03366)
♦ Doctors for Developing Countries / see Comitato Collaboriazione Medica
♦ Doctors for Global Health (internationally oriented national body)
♦ Doctors' International Professional Association (inactive)
♦ Doctors International Volunteer Organization (internationally oriented national body)
♦ Doctors of the World – International (#16613)
♦ Doctors Worldwide (internationally oriented national body)
♦ Doctrinaires – Prêtres de la Doctrine Chrétienne (religious order)
♦ Documentation for Action Groups in Asia (internationally oriented national body)
♦ Documentation Center for Asian Studies / see Research and Information Center for Asian Studies
♦ Documentation Centre on Aerochemical War (inactive)

♦ **Documentation and Conservation of the Modern Movement (DOCOMOMO International)** **05110**

SG PO Box 5043, Faculty of Architecture – Heritage, TU Delft, 2600 GA Delft, Netherlands. E-mail: docomomo@tudelft.nl.
URL: http://www.docomomo.com/

History 1988. Founded by Hubert-Jan Henket, architect and professor, and Wessel de Jonge, architect and research fellow, at the School of Architecture at the Technical University, Eindhoven (Netherlands). Former names and other names: *International Working Party for the Documentation and Conservation of Buildings, Sites and Neighbourhoods of the Modern Movement* – alias. **Aims** Act as watchdog when important modern movement *buildings* anywhere are under threat; exchange ideas relating to conservation technology, history and education; foster interest in the ideas and *heritage* of the modern movement; elicit responsibility towards this recent *architectural* inheritance. **Structure** General Council; Executive Committee; Advisory Board. Specialist Committees (6); Working Parties (67). **Languages** English, French, Portuguese, Spanish. **Staff** 3.00 FTE, paid. **Finance** Sources: members' dues; sale of publications. Other sources: subsidy from Lisbon City Council. **Activities** Events/meetings; publishing activities. **Events** *International DOCOMOMO Conference* Santiago (Chile) 2024, *International Docomomo Conference* Valencia (Spain) 2022, *International Docomomo Conference* Tokyo (Japan) 2021, *Biennial Conference* Tokyo (Japan) 2020, *Modern Asean Architecture International Conference* Singapore (Singapore) 2019. **Publications** *DOCOMOMO Journal* (2 a year). Conference proceedings; books; preservation technology dossiers.
Members Full in 65 countries and territories:
Angola, Argentina, Australia, Austria, Belgium, Brazil, Canada, Chile, China, Colombia, Cuba, Curaçao, Cyprus, Czechia, Denmark, Dominican Rep, Ecuador, Egypt, Estonia, Finland, France, Georgia, Germany, Ghana, Greece, Guatemala, Hong Kong, Hungary, Iran Islamic Rep, Iraq, Ireland, Israel, Italy, Japan, Korea Rep, Kosovo, Kuwait, Latvia, Lebanon, Macau, Mexico, Morocco, Netherlands, New Zealand, Norway, Panama, Peru, Poland, Portugal, Puerto Rico, Russia, Scotland, Serbia, Slovakia, Slovenia, South Africa, Spain, Switzerland, Taiwan, Thailand, Türkiye, UK, Ukraine, USA, Venezuela.
Consultative Status Consultative status granted from: *UNESCO (#20322)* (Consultative Status). [2023/XF6347/**F**]

♦ Documentation and Research Centre / see Service of Documentation and Studies on Global Mission (#19241)
♦ Document Lifecycle Management / see DLM Forum (#05108)
♦ Document Lifecycle Management Forum / see DLM Forum (#05108)
♦ DOD – International Conference on Dynamics of Disasters (meeting series)
♦ DOEN Foundation (internationally oriented national body)
♦ Dogs Trust Worldwide (internationally oriented national body)
♦ Doha Amendment to the Kyoto Protocol (2012 treaty)
♦ **DOHaD** International Society for Developmental Origins of Health and Disease (#15055)

♦ **Doha International Family Institute (DIFI)** **05111**

Mailing Address PO Box 34080, Doha, Qatar. T. +97444548200. Fax +97444548249. E-mail: difi@qf.org.qa.
URL: http://www.difi.org.qa/

History Set up 2006, as *Doha International Institute for Family Studies and Development (DIIFSD)*. Mandate based upon Doha Declaration on the Family, as noted by UN General Assembly (A/RES/59/111), 6 Dec 2004. Operates within framework of Qatar Foundation. **Aims** Foster knowledge on Arab families and advance family policies through research; promote development of policies to strengthen and support families at national, regional and international levels; build networks and facilitate transfer of knowledge and best practices to strengthen Arab families. **Structure** Management Departments (4). **Languages** Arabic, English. **Staff** 25.00 FTE, paid. **Finance** Financed by: Qatar Foundation for Education, Science and Community Development

(QF). **Activities** Research and development; research/documentation; advocacy/lobbying/activism; events/meetings; financial and/or material support; knowledge management/information dissemination; politics/policy/regulatory; projects/programmes; publishing activities. **Events** *Annual Family Policy Forum* Doha (Qatar) 2017, *Annual Conference on Family Research and Policy* Doha (Qatar) 2016, *Annual Family Policy Forum* Doha (Qatar) 2016, *Regional Seminar on Protecting the Best Interests of the Child in Cross-Border Family Disputes* Doha (Qatar) 2016, *Seminar on the Experiences of Home Caregivers for Elderly People in Qatar* Doha (Qatar) 2016. **Publications** *Special Series.* Books; reports; conference proceedings; articles. **Information Services** *Global Family Matters Information System (FAMIS); World Family News Service (WFNS); World Family Scholars Database (WFSD).* **Consultative Status** Consultative status granted from: *ECOSOC (#05331)* (Special). [2020/XJ1088/j/**E**]

♦ Doha International Institute for Family Studies and Development / see Doha International Family Institute (#05111)
♦ DOI – Deutsches Orient-Institut (internationally oriented national body)
♦ Dokters van de Wereld – International (#16613)
♦ Dokumentations- und Informationszentrum Menschenrechte in Lateinamerika (internationally oriented national body)
♦ Dokumentations- und Kooperationszentrum Südliches Afrika (internationally oriented national body)
♦ Doloristes – Fils de la Mère de Dieu Douloureuse (religious order)
♦ Doloristi – Figli della Madre di Dio Addolorata (religious order)
♦ Dolorysci – Synowie Matki Bozej Bolesnej (religious order)

♦ Dolphinaria-Free Europe (DFE) 05112

Chair address not obtained. E-mail: info@dfe.ngo.
URL: http://dfe.ngo/

Aims Phase out the keeping of *dolphins* and whales in captivity in Europe, whilst striving towards greater protection for those cetaceans still held captive. **Activities** Research/documentation; awareness raising; advocacy/lobbying/activism.
Members Animal welfare organizations in 13 countries:
Finland, France, Germany, Ireland, Italy, Lithuania, Netherlands, Poland, Portugal, Spain, Sweden, Switzerland, UK.
Included in the above, 5 organizations listed in this Yearbook:
Marine Connection; OceanCare; Sea First Foundation (SFF); Whale and Dolphin Conservation (WDC); World Cetacean Alliance (WCA, #21268). [2019.02.26/XM6885/y/**F**]

♦ Domenicane di S Caterina da Siena (religious order)
♦ Domenicani – Fratri Predicatori (religious order)
♦ Domenicani della Presentazione (religious order)
♦ Domestic and Foreign Missionary Society of the Protestant Episcopal Church (internationally oriented national body)
♦ Domestic Workers Convention, 2011 (2011 treaty)
♦ Dominicaines de Béthanie (religious order)
♦ Dominicaines de la Congrégation Romaine de Saint-Dominique (religious order)
♦ Dominicaines Missionnaires des Campagnes (religious order)
♦ Dominicaines de Notre-Dame-de-Grâce (religious order)
♦ Dominicaines de la Présentation de Tours – Soeurs de la Charité, Dominicaines de la Présentation de la Sainte Vierge (religious order)
♦ Dominicaines de Sainte-Marie des Tourelles (religious order)
♦ Dominicaines du Verbe Incarné (religious order)
♦ Dominicains – Ordre des Frères Prêcheurs (religious order)
♦ Dominican Congregation of St Catherine of Siena (religious order)
♦ Dominicanessen Congregatie van de Heilige Catherina van Siena (religious order)
♦ Dominican Nuns of the Second Order of Perpetual Adoration (religious order)
♦ Dominican Sisters (religious order)
♦ Dominican Sisters of the Congregation of the Most Holy Rosary (religious order)
♦ Dominican Sisters of the Congregation of St Catherine of Siena (religious order)

♦ Dominicans for Justice and Peace (OP) 05113

Dir 37/39 rue de Vermont, CP 104, 1211 Geneva 20, Switzerland. T. +41227794010. E-mail: contact@un.op.org.
URL: http://un.op.org/

History 1998. Founded following approval, 1997, of General Council of *Order of Preachers (Dominicans)*, to function as a permanent presence at *United Nations Commission on Human Rights (inactive)*, currently *United Nations Human Rights Council (HRC, #20571).* **Aims** Witness to the *Gospel* message, especially focusing on the challenge of justice and peace; contribute to the ongoing discourse on *social justice* and *human rights violations* worldwide; provide an international forum for members of the Dominican family in these fields to advocate on behalf of *victims* of human rights violations; work with NGOs working within the *United Nations.* **Languages** English, French, Spanish. **Activities** Advocacy/lobbying/activism; training/education. **Consultative Status** Consultative status granted from: *ECOSOC (#05331)* (Special); *UNEP (#20299).* **NGO Relations** Member of (3): *Forum of Catholic Inspired NGOs (#09905); International Catholic Centre of Geneva (ICCG, #12449); Vienna NGO Committee on the Status of Women (#20775).* Collaborates with: office of the Dominican Leadership Conference at the United Nations, New York NY (USA). [2020.05.06/XM7203/**E**]

♦ Dominicans – Order of Preachers (religious order)
♦ Dominicans of the Presentation (religious order)
♦ Dominikanerinnen von der Heilige Katharina von Siena (religious order)
♦ Domitor – Association internationale pour le développement de la recherche sur le cinéma des premiers temps / see Domitor – International Association for the Study of Early Cinema (#05114)
♦ Domitor – Association internationale pour la recherche sur le cinéma des premiers temps (#05114)
♦ Domitor – Associazione Internazionale di Promozione delle Ricerche sul Cinema dei Primi Tempi / see Domitor – International Association for the Study of Early Cinema (#05114)
♦ Domitor – Associazione Internazionale di Ricerche sul Cinema dei Primi Tempi (#05114)
♦ Domitor – International Association to Promote the Study of Early Cinema / see Domitor – International Association for the Study of Early Cinema (#05114)

♦ Domitor – International Association for the Study of Early Cinema . 05114

Domitor – Association internationale pour la recherche sur le cinéma des premiers temps –
Domitor – Associazione Internazionale di Ricerche sul Cinema dei Primi Tempi

Sec Univ of Wisconsin Milwaukee, PO Box 413, Milwaukee WI 53201, USA.
Sec address not obtained.
URL: http://www.domitor.org/

History Oct 1985, Pordenone (Italy), as *Domitor – International Association to Promote the Study of Early Cinema – Domitor – Association internationale pour le développement de la recherche sur le cinéma des premiers temps – Domitor – Associazione Internazionale di Promozione delle Ricerche sul Cinema dei Primi Tempi.* **Aims** Explore new methods of historical research and understanding, promoting the international exchange of information, documents and ideas; promote close relationships between scholars and archivists. **Structure** Executive Committee of 9. **Languages** English, French. **Staff** 0.50 FTE, paid; 3.00 FTE, voluntary. **Finance** Members' dues. **Events** *Conference* Culpeper, VA (USA) 2022, *Conference* Paris (France) 2020, *Conference* Rochester, NY (USA) 2018, *Conference* Stockholm (Sweden) 2016, *Conference* Chicago, IL (USA) / Evanston, IL (USA) 2014. **Publications** *Bibliographie internationale du cinéma des premiers temps* (1987) – revised 1995. Conference proceedings.
Members Individuals in 32 countries:
Argentina, Australia, Austria, Belgium, Bosnia-Herzegovina, Canada, Czechia, Denmark, Finland, France, Germany, Hungary, Ireland, Israel, Italy, Japan, Latvia, Luxembourg, Mexico, Netherlands, New Zealand, Norway, Peru, Philippines, Poland, Portugal, Russia, Slovenia, Spain, Sweden, Switzerland, UK. [2012.07.17/XD2770/v/**D**]

♦ Domus Charitatis (inactive)

♦ DONA International 05115

Exec Dir 35 E Wacker Dr, Str 850, Chicago IL 60601-2106, USA. T. +13122242595. Fax +13126448557. E-mail: dona@dona.org.
URL: http://www.dona.org/

History 1992. **Aims** Promote high quality *birth* and *postpartum* support by setting the standard for the *doula profession* through evidence-based training and certification for doulas of diverse backgrounds. **Structure** Board of Directors. **Events** *DONA Summit* 2021, *DONA Summit* 2020, *DONA Summit* Houston, TX (USA) 2019, *DONA Summit* Fort Lauderdale, FL (USA) 2018, *DONA Summit* Chicago, IL (USA) 2017.
Members Individuals (over 6,000) in 46 countries and territories:
Argentina, Australia, Belgium, Bermuda, Canada, Cayman Is, Chile, Costa Rica, Czechia, Denmark, Egypt, France, Germany, Greece, Guatemala, Haiti, Hungary, Indonesia, Ireland, Israel, Italy, Japan, Kenya, Korea Rep, Mexico, Netherlands, New Zealand, Nicaragua, Norway, Puerto Rico, Russia, Singapore, Slovenia, South Africa, Spain, Sweden, Switzerland, Taiwan, Tanzania UR, Thailand, Trinidad-Tobago, UK, United Arab Emirates, Uruguay, USA, Zambia.
Also members in the West Indies. Membership countries not specified.
NGO Relations Member of (1): *International Childbirth Initiative (ICI, #12547).* [2021/XM4187/**F**]

♦ Doñana Foundation / see Fundación Monte Mediterraneo
♦ Donaueuropäisches Institut / see Organization for International Economic Relations (#17873)
♦ Donaukommission (#04210)
♦ Donauländischer Verein für Psychiatrie und ihre Grenzgebiete (#05008)

♦ Donau Soja 05116

Head of Communications Wiesingerstr 6/14, 1010 Vienna, Austria. T. +431512174410. Fax +43151217443. E-mail: office@donausoja.org.
Pres address not obtained.
URL: http://www.donausoja.org/

History 2012. Current statutes adopted Mar 2017. Former names and other names: *Association for Promoting European Soya Production – Danube Soya* – full title; *Verein zur Förderung der europäischen Sojaproduktion – Donau Soja* – full title; *Danube Soya* – former; *Europe Soya* – former. Registration: Austria; EU Transparency Register, No/ID: 022735321330-86, Start date: 28 Apr 2016. **Aims** Maintain a sustainable, safe and European protein supply. **Structure** General Meeting; Board; President; Steering Committee; Advisory Board; Scientific Advisory Board; Headquarters: Vienna; Field Offices (4): Moldova, Romania, Serbia, Ukraine. **Languages** English, German. **Staff** 45.00 FTE, paid. **Finance** Sources: grants; members' dues; revenue from activities/projects. Other sources: license fees; partnerships. Supported by: *Austrian Development Agency (ADA).* Annual budget: 5,000,000 EUR (2022). **Activities** Advocacy/lobbying/activism; certification/accreditation; events/meetings; knowledge management/information dissemination; networking/liaising; research and development; standards/guidelines. **Events** *Donau Soja 10 Years Anniversary Event Meeting* Vienna (Austria) 2022, *General Assembly and Networking Event* Vienna (Austria) 2021, *International Donau Soja Congress* Novi Sad (Serbia) 2020, *International Donau Soja Congress* Schwäbisch Gmünd (Germany) 2018, *International Donau Soja Congress* Budapest (Hungary) 2016. **Publications** *Donau Soja Market Report* (12 a year); *Donau Soja Newsletter.* **Members** Full; Associate. Partners (900) in 25 countries. Members (over 300) in 28 countries Membership countries not specified. **NGO Relations** Member of (1): *TP Organics – European Technology Platform (TP Organics, #20180).* [2022.10.19/XM6456/**D**]

♦ Don Bosco-Comide International / see VIA Don Bosco (#20766)

♦ Don Bosco International (DBI) 05117

Contact Clos André Rappe 8 B, 1200 Brussels, Belgium. T. +32494549698. E-mail: dbi@sdb.org.
URL: http://www.donboscointernational.eu/

History 1995. Former names and other names: *Don Bosco International – Salesians of Don Bosco in the European Institutions* – full title. Registration: Belgium; EU Transparency Register, No/ID: 874082316357-71. **Aims** Represent the Congregation of the Salesians of Don Bosco in several European institutions and international bodies. advocate for young people in the field of poverty and social inclusion, migration and refugees, integral human development, including youth participation and integral ecology. **Structure** General Assembly; General Council; General Directorate. Departments (5): Formation; Youth Ministry; Social Communication; Missions; Finance/Administration. **Publications** Advocacy from a Salesian Perspective (2020); Next Generation Edu – Education for the Future of Europe (2021); Don Bosco Web for a more Accessible and inclusive VET in Europe (2022); Job Services Offices in VET – Guidelines (2022); Towards a DB Tech Europe (2022); Is 2022 the European Year of Youth for real? (2022); No Hate Speech: Building Together a Culture of Human Rights (2022); From malaise to rebirth. Research by Caritas Europa and Don Bosco International on the social and professional future of young people in post-Covid Europe (2023). **IGO Relations** Recognized by (1): *European Union Agency for Asylum (EUAA, #08968).* Participant in Fundamental Rights Platform of *European Union Agency for Fundamental Rights (FRA, #08969).* **NGO Relations** Member of (14): *Caritas Europa (#03579); Centre for European Volunteering (CEV, #03743); COFACE Families Europe (#04084); Commission of the Bishops' Conferences of the European Union (COMECE, #04205); Don Bosco Network (DBN, #05118); Don Bosco Youth-Net (DBYN, #05119);* EU Alliance for Investing in Children; *Eurochild (#05657); European Sunday Alliance (#08856); Federation of Catholic Family Associations in Europe (#09468); Forum of Catholic Inspired NGOs (#09905); Lifelong Learning Platform – European Civil Society for Education (LLLP, #16466); SDG Watch Europe (#19162); SIRIUS – Policy Network on Migrant Education (SIRIUS, #19291).* [2023.02.13/XN9625/**E**]

♦ Don Bosco International – Salesians of Don Bosco in the European Institutions / see Don Bosco International (#05117)

♦ Don Bosco Network (DBN) 05118

Coordinator Via Appia Antica 126, 00179 Rome RM, Italy. E-mail: info@donbosconetwork.org – coordinator@donbosconetwork.org.
Pres address not obtained.
URL: http://donbosconetwork.org/

History Registration: Start date: 2010, Italy; EU Transparency Register, No/ID: 09370344390-06, Start date: 22 Oct 2010. **Aims** Promote fundamental values of social justice, fraternity and solidarity with the most *vulnerable* people, especially youth, in the world. **Structure** Executive Board. **Languages** English, French, Italian, Spanish. **Staff** 1.00 FTE, paid. **Activities** Advocacy/lobbying/activism; awareness raising; capacity building; humanitarian/emergency aid; networking/liaising; training/education. Active in all member countries.
Members Organizations in 9 countries:
Belgium, Germany, India, Ireland, Italy, Slovakia, Spain, Switzerland, USA.
Included in the above, 2 organizations listed in this Yearbook:
VIA Don Bosco (#20766); Volontariato Internazionale per lo Sviluppo (VIS). [2022.10.19/XM5490/y/**F**]

♦ Don Bosco Volunteers (religious order)

♦ Don Bosco Youth-Net (DBYN) 05119

Gen Sec Naamsesteenweg 37, 3001 Leuven, Belgium. T. +3216487880. E-mail: info@donboscoyouth.net.
URL: http://www.donboscoyouth.net/

History 2000. Registration: Banque-Carrefour des Entreprises, No/ID: 0871.319.722, Start date: 10 Jan 2005, Belgium. **Aims** Create international projects for and by young people in the style of Don Bosco; exchange information, experiences and ideas between members; represent the voice of Don Bosco young people at international level. **Structure** General Executive Body; Administrative Body; Secretariat. **Languages** English. **Staff** 2.00 FTE, paid. **Finance** Sources: grants; members' dues. Supported by: *European Commission (EC, #06633); European Youth Foundation (EYF, #09141).* Annual budget: 100,000 EUR. **Activities** Events/meetings; networking/liaising; training/education. **Publications** *Act Now! – Workbook on Sustainable Management* (2021) by Sarah Kusché in English; *dignity* – e-book; *Jabbertalk* – e-book. *GamesApp* in English.
Members Full in 16 countries:
Austria, Belgium, Czechia, France, Germany, Ireland, Italy, Malta, Montenegro, Netherlands, Poland, Slovakia, Slovenia, Spain, UK, Ukraine.
IGO Relations Executive Agency of *European Commission (EC, #06633).* **NGO Relations** Member of (1): *European Youth Forum (#09140)* (as Observer member). [2022.08.10/XM2701/**E**]

♦ Don Calabria – Pauvres Serviteurs de la Divine Providence (religious order)

♦ Donkey Sanctuary, The 05120

Founder Slade House Farm, Sidmouth, EX10 0NU, UK. T. +441395578222. Fax +441395579266. E-mail: enquiries@thedonkeysanctuary.org.uk.
URL: http://www.thedonkeysanctuary.org.uk/

History 1969, by Dr Elisabeth Svendsen MBE. Became a registered charity, 1973. Incorporates the *International Donkey Protection Trust (IDPT).* UK Registered Charity: 264818. **Aims** Protect donkeys and mules and promote their welfare worldwide. **Staff** 541.00 FTE, paid. **Activities** Provides: permanent refuge to neglected and unwanted donkeys in the UK, Ireland and other parts of Europe; veterinary assistance and educational support in Africa, Asia and South America to working donkeys and their owners through mobile teams; professional advice, training and support on donkey welfare; donkey-assisted therapy for children with additional needs and therapeutic visits for elderly people (UK only). **Events** *World symposium on donkeys and mules* Exeter (UK) 1993. **Publications** *The Donkey Sanctuary* – newsletter. *A Guide to Caring for Your Donkey*; *Professional Handbook of the Donkey*; *The Complete Book of the Donkey.*
Members Individuals in 9 countries:
Cyprus, France, Greece, Ireland, Italy, Portugal, Romania, Spain, UK.
Consultative Status Consultative status granted from: *UNEP (#20299).* [2012.07.12/XF2116/**F**]

- ♦ Donne d'Europa / see Association femmes d'Europe
- ♦ Donne di Pace nel Mondo (#18283)
- ♦ Donne per la Pace, Svizzera (internationally oriented national body)
- ♦ Donne nella scienza, tecnologia, ingegneria (#06276)

♦ Donor Action Foundation 05121

Managing Dir Prinsendreef 10, 3210 Linden, Belgium. T. +3216621469. Fax +3216623443.

History 1994. Founded by *Eurotransplant International Foundation (#09192)*, Organización Nacional de Trasplantes (Spain) and the former *'Partnership for Organ Donation'* (USA). A foundation since 1998. Former names and other names: *Donor Action Working Group* – former (1994). **Aims** Increase organ and *tissue* donation rates; provide leadership in *hospital* organ donation processes and protocols; bring quality to the organ donation process within hospital critical care units through the Donor Action Programme; ensure that every hospital implementing the Programme realizes quantifiable, sustainable improvements in their donation process; collaborate with public and private organizations to implement the Programme as widely as possible; facilitate hospitals' internal review of donation practices and enable quality improvements in their organ donation processes; ensure that families of potential donors are treated in a professional, supportive and caring manner. **Structure** Board of Directors, comprising Chairman, Secretary-Treasurer and 3 members. Advisory Council; Programme Manager. **Languages** Dutch, English, French. **Staff** 3.00 FTE, paid. **Finance** Sources: educational grants; license fees; industry sponsorship; EU project grants. **Activities** Offers training courses. Cooperates in EC projects. **Publications** *DA News.* Annual Report; articles. **Information Services** *DA System Database.*
Members Implemented in over 500 critical care units in 30 countries.
Austria, Belgium, Brazil, Canada, Colombia, Croatia, Czechia, Denmark, Finland, France, Germany, Greece, Hungary, Israel, Italy, Japan, Korea Rep, Kuwait, Luxembourg, Netherlands, New Zealand, Norway, Poland, Slovakia, Slovenia, Sweden, Switzerland, Türkiye, UK, Venezuela. [2013.06.20/XF7028/f/**F**]

- ♦ Donor Action Working Group / see Donor Action Foundation (#05121)

♦ Donor Committee for Enterprise Development (DCED) 05122

Comité des donateurs pour la développement de l'enterprise

Coordinator 8B Kings Parade, Cambridge, CB2 1SJ, UK. T. +441223362211. E-mail: coordinator@enterprise-development.org – admin@enterprise-development.org.
URL: http://www.enterprise-development.org/

History 1979. Former names and other names: *Committee of Donor Agencies for Small Enterprise Development* – former (2005). **Aims** Provide the 'institutional memory' for those working in private sector development (PSD). **Structure** Executive Committee; Secretariat. **Activities** Events/meetings. **Events** *Annual Meeting* Geneva (Switzerland) 2023, *Annual Meeting* Cambridge (UK) 2022, *Annual Meeting* Cambridge (UK) 2021, *Annual Meeting* Cambridge (UK) 2020, *Annual Meeting* Vienna (Austria) 2019. **Publications** *DCED Newsletter.*
Members (Governmental) Agencies (24):
Australia, Canada, Denmark, Finland, Germany, Luxembourg, Netherlands, Switzerland, UK.
Austrian Development Agency (ADA); European Commission (EC, #06633); FAO (#09260); ILO (#11123); International Finance Corporation (IFC, #13597); International Trade Centre (ITC, #15703); Irish Aid; Japan International Cooperation Agency (JICA); Mastercard Foundation; Norwegian Agency for Development Cooperation (Norad); OECD (#17693); Swedish International Development Cooperation Agency (Sida); Swiss Agency for Development and Cooperation (SDC); UNIDO (#20336); United States Agency for International Development (USAID). [2022/XJ3867/y/**E**]

- ♦ Don Orione – Piccola Opera della Divina Provvidenza (religious order)
- ♦ Donornet / see Bellanet Alliance of Social Entrepreneurs (#03196)
- ♦ Donors to African Education / see Association for the Development of Education in Africa (#02471)
- ♦ Dooley Foundation / see Dooley Foundation Intermed International
- ♦ Dooley Foundation Intermed International (internationally oriented national body)
- ♦ Dopamine Society (unconfirmed)
- ♦ DOP – Daughters of Penelope (internationally oriented national body)
- ♦ Doppler Orbit determination and Radiopositioning Integrated on Satellite / see International DORIS Service (#13192)
- ♦ Dora et Kommandos / see International Committee Buchenwald Dora and Commandos (#12749)

♦ Dorcas 05123

CEO Postbus 1500, 1300 BM Almere, Netherlands. T. +31880502800. E-mail: info@dorcas.nl.
Street address Radioweg 1, 1324 KW Almere, Netherlands.
URL: http://www.dorcas.org/

History Founded 1980, as *Christian Foundation for Aid to the Persecuted for Cause of Conscience (CSGH).* Following fall of Berlin Wall, 1989, *Foundation Dorcas Aid International – Dorcas Hulp Internationaal (DHI)* set up. Boards of Dorcas Aid Netherlands and Dorcas Aid International merged, 2013, as of when organization trades under brand name *Dorcas.* **Aims** Strive for lasting change for those who live in *poverty*, are excluded, or are caught in a crisis. **Structure** Supervisory Board; Executive Board; International Office; Field Offices (132). **Languages** Dutch, English. **Staff** International Office: 66; Field Offices: 254. **Finance** Donations; grants; subsidies; thrift shops. Annual budget (2018): euro 25,000,000. **Activities** Humanitarian/emergency aid; capacity building. **Publications** Annual Report; website publications. **Information Services** *Dorcas Knowledge Centre.* **IGO Relations** Partner relations with a variety of IGOs, including: *UNHCR (#20327).* **NGO Relations** Member of: *European Christian Organisations in Relief and Development (EU-CORD, #06545); Prisma; Start Network (#19969);* national associations. [2022/XF3233/**F**]

- ♦ Dorcas Aid International / see Dorcas (#05123)
- ♦ Dorcas Hulp Internationaal / see Dorcas (#05123)
- ♦ DORIS Pilot Experiment / see International DORIS Service (#13192)
- ♦ DORN – Death Online Research Network (unconfirmed)
- ♦ **DOS** Digital Olfaction Society (#05081)
- ♦ **DOSI** Deep-Ocean Stewardship Initiative (#05023)
- ♦ **DOTAC** DIAKONIA of the Americas and the Caribbean (#05063)
- ♦ Dotación de Carnegie para la Paz International (internationally oriented national body)
- ♦ DOTA / see DIAKONIA of the Americas and the Caribbean (#05063)
- ♦ **DotAsia** DotAsia Organisation (#05124)

♦ DotAsia Organisation (DotAsia) 05124

CEO 12/F Daily House, 35-37 Haiphong Road, Tsim Sha Tsui, Kowloon, Hong Kong. T. +85222447900. E-mail: info@dot.asia.
URL: http://www.dot.asia/

History DotAsia proposal approved by *Internet Corporation for Assigned Names and Numbers (ICANN, #15949)* board, Dec 2005; agreement signed Dec 2006. Incorporated in Hong Kong. **Aims** Promote *Internet* development and adoption in Asia. **Structure** Board of Directors; Advisory Council. **Activities** Advocacy/lobbying/activism; research/documentation; training/education.
Members Sponsor; Co-Sponsor. Sponsor members in 20 countries and territories:
Armenia, Bhutan, Cambodia, China, Hong Kong, India, Indonesia, Japan, Korea Rep, Macau, Mongolia, New Zealand, Niue, Philippines, Singapore, Taiwan, Tajikistan, Thailand, Uzbekistan, Vietnam.
Co-Sponsor members (7):
Asia and Pacific Internet Association (APIA, #01936); Asian-Pacific Network Information Centre (APNIC); Asia Pacific Computer Emergency Response Team (APCERT, #01874); Asia-Pacific Networking Group (APNG, #01968); Asia Pacific Regional At-Large Organisation (APRALO); Pan Asia Networking (PAN); *South Asian Network Operators Group (SANOG, #19737).*
NGO Relations *Internet Corporation for Assigned Names and Numbers (ICANN, #15949).* Member of: *Internet Society (ISOC, #15952).* [2018/XM6973/y/**D**]

- ♦ Dotation Carnegie pour la paix internationale (internationally oriented national body)

♦ DOT Europe 05125

Dir Gen Rue du Trône 60, 1050 Brussels, Belgium. T. +32472268302. E-mail: info@doteurope.eu.
URL: https://doteurope.eu/

History Mar 2000, Belgium. Relaunched 2020. Former names and other names: *European Digital Media Association (EDiMA)* – former; *Association européenne des média numériques* – former; *EDiMA* – former. Registration: Belgium; EU Transparency Register, No/ID: 53905947933-43. **Aims** Develop ideas and support policy initiatives that foster an innovative, open and safe internet for Europe's citizens and businesses. **Structure** General Assembly (annual); Board of Directors. **Languages** English, French. **Staff** 4.00 FTE, paid. **Activities** Politics/policy/regulatory; research and development. **Events** *Annual European e-Commerce Conference* Brussels (Belgium) 2013, *Annual European e-Commerce Conference* Brussels (Belgium) 2012, *Annual European e-commerce conference* Brussels (Belgium) 2010.
Members New media companies (18) in 10 countries:
Belgium, France, Germany, Ireland, Italy, Netherlands, Poland, Sweden, UK, USA.
Consultative Status Consultative status granted from: *World Intellectual Property Organization (WIPO, #21593)* (Permanent Observer Status). **NGO Relations** Associate member of: *European Internet Forum (EIF, #07591).* [2022.11.15/XD4185/**D**]

- ♦ DOT Force – Digital Opportunity Task Force (no recent information)
- ♦ Dottrinari (religious order)
- ♦ Dövas Afrika Mission (internationally oriented national body)

♦ Dövas Nordiska Råd (DNR) 05126

Conseil nordique pour les sourds – Nordic Council of the Deaf

Contact Norwegian Assn of the Deaf, Grensen 9, 0159 Oslo, Norway.
URL: http://www.dnr.fi/

History 1907, Copenhagen (Denmark), as *Nordic Cooperation Organization.* Present name adopted 1972. Previously also referred to as *Northern Council of the Deaf.* **Aims** Promote *sign language* as the first language of the deaf and acceptance of sign language by the community; promote cooperative action for the deaf in Nordic countries; work to provide the deaf with the same rights, living conditions and opportunities as other citizens in Scandinavia; maintain contact with authorities and Nordic organizations; act as a channel towards international organizations; intensify efforts to support and develop deaf movements in developing countries. **Structure** Council; Chairmanship/Secretariat rotates every 4 years. **Languages** English, International Sign Language, International Sign Language, Norwegian. **Staff** 0.00 FTE, paid. **Finance** Support from Nordic Welfare Centre. Annual budget: Swedish Kr 50,000. **Activities** Knowledge management/information dissemination; events/meetings. **Events** *Nordic pensioners meeting / Meeting* Copenhagen (Denmark) 1996, *Nordic seminar on deaf history / Meeting* Norway 1996, *The unemployment situation of the deaf in the Nordic countries* Helsinki (Finland) 1994.
Members Organizations in 5 countries:
Denmark, Finland, Iceland, Norway, Sweden.
IGO Relations *Nordic Council of Ministers (NCM, #17260).* **NGO Relations** *Handikapporganisationernes Nordiska Råd (HNR, no recent information).* [2019.07.01/XD0282/**D**]

- ♦ DOV – DIANA Ontwikkelings Vereniging (internationally oriented national body)
- ♦ DOWAS – Deep Ocean Water Applications Society (unconfirmed)
- ♦ **DOW** Doctors of the World – International (#16613)

♦ Downstream Users of Chemicals Co-ordination group (DUCC) 05127

Contact c/o CEPE, Blvd du Triomphe 172, 4th fl, 1160 Brussels, Belgium. T. +3226767487. Fax +3226767490.
URL: http://www.ducc.eu/

History 2001. **Aims** Contribute, with a common voice, to the successful implementation of the requirements of the REACH and CLP Regulations. **Activities** Guidance/assistance/consulting; knowledge management/information dissemination; research/documentation.
Members Organizations (10):
Conseil européen de l'industrie des peintures, des encres d'imprimerie et des couleurs d'art (CEPE, #04688); Cosmetics Europe – The Personal Care Association (#04852); CropLife Europe (#04965); European Federation for Construction Chemicals (EFCC, #07088); Fédération Européenne des Aérosols (FEA, #09557); Fédération européenne des industries de colles et adhésifs (FEICA, #09572); Fédération européenne du commerce chimique (Fecc, #09563); I and P Europe Imaging and Printing Association (I and P Europe); International Association for Soaps, Detergents and Maintenance Products (#12166); International Fragrance Association (IFRA, #13680). [2019/XM5111/**F**]

- ♦ Down Syndrome Education International (internationally oriented national body)

♦ Down Syndrome International (DSi) 05128

Exec Dir 7-9 Chapel St, Exmouth, EX8 1HR, UK. E-mail: contact@ds-int.org.
Registered Office Langdon Down Ctr, 2A Langdon Park, Teddington, TW11 9PS, UK. T. +441395493108.
URL: http://www.ds-int.org/

History 1993. Founded following a series of congresses since 1981. Former names and other names: *International Down Syndrome Federation* – former (1993 to 2001). Registration: Charity Commission, No/ID: 1091843, England and Wales. **Aims** Improve quality of life for people with Down syndrome worldwide and promote their inherent right to be included and accepted as equal members of society. **Structure** Board. **Languages** English. **Staff** 7.00 FTE, paid. **Finance** Sources: donations. Annual budget: 231,000 GBP. **Activities** Advocacy/lobbying/activism; guidance/assistance/consulting; knowledge management/information dissemination; networking/liaising; politics/policy/regulatory; training/education. **Events** *World Down Syndrome Congress* Brisbane, QLD (Australia) 2024, *World Down Syndrome Congress* Dubai (United Arab Emirates) 2021, *World Congress* Dubai (United Arab Emirates) 2020, *World Congress* Glasgow (UK) 2018, *World Congress* Chennai (India) 2015. **Publications** *DSi News*; *International Journal of Down Syndrome.*
Members Representative organizations in 12 countries:
Albania, Australia, India, Ireland, New Zealand, Pakistan, Singapore, South Africa, Tajikistan, Uganda, UK, United Arab Emirates.
Affiliate organizations in 58 countries and territories:
Australia, Belgium, Bolivia, Brazil, Canada, Chile, Costa Rica, Dominica, El Salvador, Georgia, Germany, Ghana, Gibraltar, Guatemala, Honduras, Hong Kong, Hungary, India, Indonesia, Iraq, Jamaica, Japan, Jordan, Kosovo, Lebanon, Malaysia, Maldives, Malta, Mauritius, Mexico, Nepal, Netherlands, Nicaragua, Nigeria, North Macedonia, Norway, Panama, Paraguay, Peru, Philippines, Poland, Romania, Russia, Saudi Arabia, Spain, Sri Lanka, Sudan, Sweden, Switzerland, Tanzania UR, Togo, Trinidad-Tobago, Türkiye, Uganda, UK, Ukraine, USA, Venezuela.
Included in the above, 3 organizations listed in this Yearbook:
Down Syndrome International Swimming Organisation (DSISO, #05129); European Centre for the Rights of Children with Disabilities (ECRCD); European Down Syndrome Association (EDSA, #06942).
Consultative Status Consultative status granted from: *ECOSOC (#05331)* (Special). **NGO Relations** Member of (1): *International Disability Alliance (IDA, #13176).* [2023.02.15/XE4399/y/**E**]

- ♦ Down Syndrome International Gymnastic Organization (unconfirmed)

♦ Down Syndrome International Swimming Organisation (DSISO) . . . 05129
Pres address not obtained.
URL: http://www.dsiso.org/
Aims Give swimmers with Down Syndrome a fair and equal opportunity to be successful in swimming. **Structure** Executive Committee, including President and Treasurer. **Activities** Organizes World Championships.
Members Full in 28 countries and territories:
Australia, Brazil, Canada, Costa Rica, Croatia, Denmark, Estonia, France, Gibraltar, Great Britain, Hong Kong, India, Ireland, Italy, Japan, Macau, Mexico, New Zealand, Norway, Portugal, Puerto Rico, South Africa, Spain, Sweden, Taiwan, Türkiye, USA, Venezuela.
NGO Relations Member of: *Down Syndrome International (DSi, #05128)*; *Sports Union for athletes with Down Syndrome (SU-DS, #19930)*. [2013.09.04/XJ6947/**C**]

♦ Downtown Development Foundation / see International Downtown Association
♦ DPC – International Conference on Dynamical Processes in Excited States of Solids (meeting series)
♦ DPD – Association internationale Données pour le développement (inactive)
♦ DP – Development Perspectives (internationally oriented national body)
♦ DPE – Dis Politika Enstitüsü (internationally oriented national body)
♦ DPF – Disciples Peace Fellowship (internationally oriented national body)
♦ **DPGN** Date Palm Global Network (#05013)
♦ **DPH** Dialogues, propositions, histoires pour une citoyenneté mondiale (#05067)
♦ DPI – Democratic Progress Institute (internationally oriented national body)
♦ **DPI** Disabled Peoples' International (#05097)
♦ **DPLF** Due Process of Law Foundation (#05144)
♦ **DPNSEE** Drug Policy Network South East Europe (#05136)
♦ DPPC / see Bradford Centre for International Development
♦ DPP – Death Penalty Project (internationally oriented national body)
♦ DPPE-EFA / see European Free Alliance (#07356)
♦ DPP – International Symposium on Digestive Physiology of Pigs (meeting series)
♦ **DPPI SEE** Disaster Preparedness and Prevention Initiative for South-Eastern Europe (#05098)
♦ **DPPP** Diaskepsi ton Periferiakon Paraktion Periohon tis Evropis (#04638)
♦ DPS – International Symposium on Dry Process (meeting series)
♦ **DPU** Democratic Pacific Union (#05035)
♦ DPU – Development Planning Unit (internationally oriented national body)
♦ DRAE – DIAKONIA Region Africa/Europe (see: #21429)
♦ **DRAF** Disability Rights Advocacy Fund (#05095)

♦ Dravet Syndrome European Foundation (DSEF) 05130
Sec Don Rafela Radice 11, Žrnovnica, HR-21251 Split, Croatia. E-mail: info@dravet.eu.
URL: http://www.dravet.eu/
History 2014. Registration: EU Transparency Register, No/ID: 054930843709-52, Start date: 26 Jul 2021. **Aims** Improve the lives of affected people through collaboration, education, awareness and facilitating research. **Structure** General Assembly; Board of Directors; Scientific Advisory Board. **Activities** Advocacy/lobbying/activism; awareness raising; guidance/assistance/consulting.
Members Full in 16 countries:
Austria, Belgium, Croatia, France, Germany, Italy, Netherlands, Norway, Poland, Portugal, Romania, Serbia, Spain, Sweden, Switzerland, UK.
NGO Relations Member of (1): *EURORDIS – Rare Diseases Europe (#09175)*. Cooperates with (1): *Orphanet (#17898)*. [2021/XM7442/f/**F**]

♦ Drawdown Europe Research Association (DERA) 05131
Registered Address Tolhuisweg 2, 1031 CL Amsterdam, Netherlands.
URL: https://www.drawdowneurope.org/
History Founded as an initiative of Project Drawdown and EIT-Climate_KIC. Registration: No/ID: KVK 74687107; EU Transparency Register, No/ID: 415506540473-56, Start date: 26 Nov 2020. **Structure** Board.
NGO Relations Partner of (1): *Climate Cleanup Foundation (CC)*. [2020/AA1253/**D**]

♦ **DRBF** Dispute Resolution Board Foundation (#05102)
♦ Dr Bruno Kreisky Foundation for Human Rights / see Bruno Kreisky Foundation for Outstanding Achievements in the Area of Human Rights
♦ DRC – Danish Refugee Council (internationally oriented national body)
♦ DRC / see Danube Rectors' Conference (#05004)
♦ **DRC** Danube Rectors' Conference (#05004)
♦ DRC – Democracy Resource Center (internationally oriented national body)
♦ **DRC** Fruit and Vegetable Dispute Resolution Corporation (#10009)
♦ DRCLAS – David Rockefeller Center for Latin American Studies (internationally oriented national body)
♦ DR – Direct Relief (internationally oriented national body)
♦ DREB – International Conference on Direct Reactions with Exotic Beams (meeting series)
♦ Dreikönigsaktion (internationally oriented national body)
♦ Dreiländerpark – Offener Raum ohne Grenzen (#18195)
♦ DRF / see Direct Relief
♦ **DRF** Disability Rights Fund (#05096)
♦ DRI / see Direct Relief
♦ DRI – Debt Relief International (internationally oriented national body)
♦ **DRI** Democracy Reporting International (#05034)
♦ DRI – Disability Rights International (internationally oriented national body)
♦ Drielandenpark – Open Ruimte zonder Grenzen (#18195)
♦ **DRII** DRI International (#05132)

♦ DRI International (DRII) 05132
CEO 119 W 23rd St, Ste 704, New York NY 10011, USA. T. +12126279796.
URL: http://www.drii.org/
History 1988, USA, as *Disaster Recovery Institute International*. **Aims** Help organizations worldwide prepare for and recover from *disasters* by providing education, accreditation, and thought leadership in business continuity and related fields. **Structure** Board of Directors; Committees (5). *Disaster Recovery International Foundation (DRI Foundation)* acts as charitable arm. **Languages** Arabic, English, French, Hebrew, Italian, Japanese, Mandarin Chinese, Portuguese, Russian, Spanish, Turkish. **Staff** 40.00 FTE, paid; 60.00 FTE, voluntary. **Finance** Fees for courses, event registration, exams, certification application; certification renewal; sponsorship. Annual budget: 4,000,000 USD. **Activities** Awards/prizes/competitions; certification/accreditation; events/meetings; guidance/assistance/consulting; training/education. **Events** *Annual Conference* Savannah, GA (USA) 2020, *Annual Conference* Savannah, GA (USA) 2020, *Annual Conference* Las Vegas, NV (USA) 2019, *Annual Conference* Nashville, TN (USA) 2018, *Annual Conference* Las Vegas, NV (USA) 2017. **Publications** *International Glossary for Resilience*; *The Professional Practices for Business Continuity Management*. Information Services: Resource library.
Members Certified professionals in over 100 countries. Membership countries not specified. Partners in 33 countries:
Partners in 33 countries:
Argentina, Australia, Belgium, Brazil, Canada, Chile, China, Colombia, Costa Rica, Côte d'Ivoire, Denmark, Finland, France, Ghana, Greece, India, Italy, Japan, Luxembourg, Malaysia, Mexico, Morocco, Netherlands, New Zealand, Nigeria, Norway, Singapore, Spain, Sweden, Türkiye, UK, Uruguay, USA.
Also partners in the Caribbean and the Middle East. Membership countries not specified.
IGO Relations Member of: *United Nations Office for Disaster Risk Reduction (UNDRR, #20595)* – ARISE Initiative. **NGO Relations** Observer to: *International Organization for Standardization (ISO, #14473)* – Technical Committee 292 for Societal Security and Resilience. [2018.10.02/XJ8852/**C**]

♦ Drilling Contractors Association (DCA Europe) 05133
Association des entrepreneurs de forage dirigé – Verband Güteschutz Horizontalbohrungen
Exec Sec Charlottenburger Allee 39, 52068 Aachen, Germany. T. +492419019290. Fax +492419019299. E-mail: dca@dca-europe.org.
URL: http://www.dca-europa.de/
Structure Board, comprising President, Vice-President, Treasurer, Protocol Secretary and 4 members. **Events** *Annual Congress* Düsseldorf (Germany) 2014, *Annual Congress* Berlin (Germany) 2013, *Annual Congress* Cambridge (UK) 2012, *Annual Congress* The Hague (Netherlands) 2010, *Annual Congress* Strasbourg (France) 2009. **Publications** *DCA Newsletter* (2 a year). **IGO Relations** *Arab Drilling and Workover Company (ADWOC, see: #17854)* is member. [2014/XD9003/**D**]

♦ Drilling Engineering Association (internationally oriented national body)

♦ Drilling Engineering Association Europe (DEA Europe) 05134
Contact c/o OTM Consulting, Great Burgh, Yew Tree Bottom Rd, Epsom, KT18 5XT, UK. T. +441372631950. E-mail: networks@otmconsulting.com.
Contact address not obtained.
URL: http://www.dea-europe.com/
Aims Share knowledge and experience of drilling engineering and technology. **Structure** Steering Committee including Chairman. **Finance** Sources: members' dues. **Activities** Events/meetings. **Events** *Meeting* UK 2022.
Members Operators; contractors; service companies. Members in 9 countries:
Austria, Denmark, France, Germany, Italy, Norway, Spain, Switzerland, UK.
NGO Relations Sister organization: *Drilling Engineering Association (DEA)*. [2022/XD9195/**D**]

♦ Drinkable Rivers (internationally oriented national body)
♦ DRIP – International Conference on Defects-Recognition, Imaging and Physics in Semiconductors (meeting series)
♦ Drittes Orden vom Karmel (religious order)
♦ Drittes protokoll zum Allgemeinen abkommen über die vorrechte und befreiungen des Europarats (1959 treaty)
♦ Drittes zusatzprotokoll zu dem Protokoll zu dem Europäischen abkommen zum schutz von fernsehsendungen (1989 treaty)
♦ Dritte Welt Haus Bielefeld / see World House, Bielefeld
♦ Dritte-Welt-Laden (internationally oriented national body)
♦ Dritte-Welt Partner / see WeltPartner
♦ Dr Kiran C Patel Center for Global Solutions (internationally oriented national body)
♦ **DRM** Digital Radio Mondiale Consortium (#05082)
♦ DRM – World Institute for Disaster Risk Management (internationally oriented national body)
♦ DRN / see Disaster Resource Partnership (#05099)
♦ Droit à l'énergie – SOS futur (internationally oriented national body)
♦ Droits égaux – responsabilités égales / see International Alliance of Women (#11639)
♦ Droits de l'homme sans frontières (#10983)
♦ **DRP** Disaster Resource Partnership (#05099)
♦ **DRPF** Diplomatic Research and Policy Foundation (#05090)
♦ DRR – WMO Disaster Risk Reduction Programme (see: #21649)
♦ **DRS** Design Research Society (#05044)

♦ Drug Information Association (DIA) 05135
Global Chief Exec 21 Dupont Circle, Ste 300, Washington DC 20036, USA. T. +12154426138. Fax +12154426199. E-mail: dia@diahome.org – americas@diaglobal.org.
URL: http://www.diahome.org/
History 1964. Registration: USA, Maryland. **Aims** Facilitate communications and foster cooperative efforts among professionals working in *health care* industries primarily engaged in *drug* development, medical communications and health information. **Structure** Board of Directors; Executive Committee; Committees (5); Regional Advisory Councils. Executive Director. Global Center: Washington DC (USA). Regional offices: Horsham PA (USA); Basel (Switzerland); Beijing (China); Mumbai (India); Tokyo (Japan). **Staff** 100.00 FTE, paid. **Finance** Members' dues (annual): US$ 175. **Activities** Events/meetings; publishing activities; training/education. **Events** *DIA Europe Meeting* Basel (Switzerland) 2023, *DIA Europe Meeting* Brussels (Belgium) 2022, *Global Annual Meeting* Chicago, IL (USA) 2022, *NIFDS-DIA Conference* Seoul (Korea Rep) 2022, *Japan Annual Meeting* Tokyo (Japan) 2022. **Publications** *Global Forum* (6 a year); *Therapeutic Innovation and Regulatory Science (TIRS)* (6 a year). Annual Report. **IGO Relations** *European Medicines Agency (EMA, #07767)*; US Food and Drug Administration (FDA). [2021/XD4785/**C**]

♦ Drug Policy Network South East Europe (DPNSEE) 05136
Contact Pregrevica 35, Zemun, 11080, Serbia. T. +381112198344. E-mail: office@dpnsee.org.
Main Website: http://dpnsee.org/
History 2015, Serbia. Founded as an umbrella organization, initiated by *Association DIOGENIS – Initiative for Drug Policy Dialogue in South East Europe (Association DIOGENIS)*. Registration: Serbia. **Aims** Create close and constructive relationships through open and objective dialogue with experts, key policy makers in national governments, regional bodies and international organisations in order to promote humane and effective drug policies. **Structure** General Assembly; Board. **Languages** English. **Staff** 2.00 FTE, paid. **Finance** Annual budget: 80,000 EUR (2021). **Activities** Advocacy/lobbying/activism; awareness raising; capacity building; events/meetings; healthcare; knowledge management/information dissemination; monitoring/evaluation; networking/liaising; publishing activities; training/education.
Members Full in 11 countries:
Albania, Bosnia-Herzegovina, Bulgaria, Croatia, Greece, Kosovo, Montenegro, North Macedonia, Romania, Serbia, Slovenia.
NGO Relations Member of (2): *Correlation – European Harm Reduction Network (C-EHRN, #04848)*; *International Drug Policy Consortium (IDPC, #13205)*. [2022.02.09/XM4712/y/**F**]

♦ Drugs for Neglected Diseases initiative (DNDi) 05137
Exec Dir Chemin Camille-Vidart 15, 1202 Geneva, Switzerland. T. +41229069230. Fax +41229069231. E-mail: dndi@dndi.org.
URL: https://dndi.org/
History 2003, Geneva (Switzerland). Founded by *WHO (#20950)* and five international research institutions. **Aims** Develop new treatments for neglected patients. **Structure** Board of Directors. **Languages** English, French, Japanese, Portuguese, Spanish. **Staff** 238.00 FTE, paid. **Finance** Sources: donations. **Publications** *Publications*; *Scientific articles*.
Members Regional offices in 9 countries:
Brazil, Congo DR, India, Japan, Kenya, Malaysia, South Africa, Switzerland, USA.
Founding members include the following 2 organizations listed in this Yearbook:
Bureau international des Médecins sans frontières (MSF International, #03366); *Pasteur Institute*.
Consultative Status Consultative status granted from: *WHO (#20950)* (Official); *World Intellectual Property Organization (WIPO, #21593)* (Observer Status). **NGO Relations** Member of (2): COVID-19 clinical research coalition; *Global Health Technologies Coalition (GHTC)*. Instrumental in setting up (3): GARDP; *Leishmania East Africa Platform (LEAP, inactive)*; national networks and platforms. [2023.02.14/XF7136/**F**]

♦ DRUID (meeting series)

♦ Drupal Association 05138
Pres Engelse Wandeling 76, 8510 Kortrijk, Belgium.
URL: http://association.drupal.org/
History 4 Dec 2006. Registered in accordance with Belgian law. **Aims** Provide support in developing, communicating, promoting and distributing the Drupal project; support deployment of an infrastructure for the project. **Structure** General Assembly (annual). Board of Directors, including President, Treasurer and Secretary. **Events** *DRUPALCON Barcelona Conference* Barcelona (Spain) 2020, *Drupal Developer Days* Ghent (Belgium) 2020, *Drupalcon Fall Conference* Amsterdam (Netherlands) 2019, *Drupalcon Fall Conference* Vienna (Austria) 2017, *DRUPALCON Barcelona Conference* Barcelona (Spain) 2015. **Members** Permanent; admitted. Membership countries not specified. [2011/XM3300/**E**]

♦ Društvo Alpsko mesto leta (#20753)

Dryad
05139

alphabetic sequence excludes
For the complete listing, see Yearbook Online at

♦ **Dryad** **05139**
Operations Manager PO Box 585, Durham NC 27702-0585, USA. E-mail: director@datadryad.org.
Exec Dir address not obtained.
URL: http://datadryad.org/
History A US organization of the type 501(c)3. **Aims** Provide the infrastructure for, and promote the re-use of, *data* underlying the scholarly *literature*. **Structure** Board of Directors. **Languages** English. **Staff** 5.00 FTE, paid. **Activities** Knowledge management/information dissemination.
Members Full in 4 countries:
Germany, Switzerland, UK, USA.
Included in the above, 2 organizations listed in this Yearbook:
Association for Tropical Biology and Conservation (ATBC, #02963); European Society for Evolutionary Biology (ESEB, #08600).
NGO Relations Member of: *DataCite (#05011).* [2018.10.03/XM6856/y/**F**]

♦ **Drynet** **05140**
Administrator c/o Environmental Monitoring Group, PO Box 13378, Mowbray, 7705, South Africa. T. +27214482881. Fax +27214482922. E-mail: dryland@global.co.za.
Street address 10 Nuttal Road, Observatory 7925, Cape Town, South Africa.
URL: http://dry-net.org/
History 2007. Set up by 14 Civil Society Organizations. Former names and other names: *Drynet Network* – alias. **Aims** Links Civil Society Organizations (CSOs) that address the situation of vulnerable people and *ecosystems* in the global *drylands* that are threatened by *climate change* and inappropriate land and water use. **Structure** General Assembly; Board; Secretariat, headed by Coordinator. **Languages** English. **Staff** 2.00 FTE, paid. **Finance** Sources: members' dues. **Publications** *Drynet Newsletter.*
Members Organizations: Associate; Organizational. CSOs in 21 countries:
Bolivia, Brazil, Chad, Chile, France, India, Iran Islamic Rep, Kazakhstan, Kyrgyzstan, Mali, Mauritania, Netherlands, Norway, Pakistan, Peru, Senegal, South Africa, Tajikistan, Türkiye, Turkmenistan, Uzbekistan.
Included in the above, 7 organizations listed in this Yearbook:
Both ENDS (#03307); Centre d'actions et de réalisations internationales (CARI); Environnement et développement du Tiers-monde (enda, #05510); La Route du Sel et de l'Espoir (La ROSE); Observatorio Latinoamericano de Conflictos Ambientales, Chile (OLCA); Regional Environmental Centre for Central Asia (CAREC); Society for Conservation and Protection of Environment (SCOPE). [2022.02.09/XM5971/y/**F**]

♦ Drynet Network / see Drynet (#05140)
♦ DSA – Development Studies Association (internationally oriented national body)
♦ DSAE – Disability Studies in Art Education (unconfirmed)
♦ **DSA** World Digital Solidarity Agency (#21362)
♦ DSC / see Weitz Center for Development Studies
♦ DSCA – Danish Society for Central Asia (internationally oriented national body)
♦ **DSCC** Deep Sea Conservation Coalition (#05024)
♦ DSC – Direzione dello sviluppo e della cooperazione (internationally oriented national body)
♦ DSC – Disarmament and Security Centre (internationally oriented national body)

♦ **Dscoop** **05141**
CEO address not obtained. T. +13125276707. E-mail: hello@dscoop.org.
URL: http://dscoop.com
History Dscoop stands for *Digital Solutions Cooperative.* **Aims** Bring together HP *Graphics* Solutions technology owners and technical professionals. **Structure** Board of Directors. **Activities** Events/meetings; networking/liaising. **Events** *EMEA Conference* Tarragona (Spain) 2019, *EMEA Conference* Vienna (Austria) 2018. [2020/XM6391/**C**]

♦ DSDM Consortium / see Agile Business Consortium
♦ DSE – Dansk Selskab for Europaforskning (internationally oriented national body)
♦ **DSE** Direct Selling Europe (#05092)
♦ DSE – Down Syndrome Education International (internationally oriented national body)
♦ **DSEF** Dravet Syndrome European Foundation (#05130)
♦ DSF – Deutsche Stiftung Friedensforschung (internationally oriented national body)
♦ DSHC – Danish Seed Health Centre for Developing Countries (internationally oriented national body)
♦ DSI – Decision Sciences Institute (internationally oriented national body)
♦ DSI – Développement social international (internationally oriented national body)
♦ **DSi** Down Syndrome International (#05128)
♦ DSIGO – Down Syndrome International Gymnastic Organization (unconfirmed)
♦ **DSISO** Down Syndrome International Swimming Organisation (#05129)
♦ DSL – International Conference on Diffusion in Solids and Liquids (meeting series)
♦ DSMA – Diabetes Self-Management Alliance (unconfirmed)
♦ DSMP – Daughters of St Mary of Providence (religious order)
♦ DSNA – Dictionary Society of North America (internationally oriented national body)
♦ DSSG – Diplomatic Society of St Gabriel (internationally oriented national body)
♦ DSW – Deutsche Stiftung Weltbevölkerung (internationally oriented national body)
♦ DSWT / see Sheldrick Wildlife Trust
♦ DTC / see Deutsche Gesellschaft für Globale- und Tropenchirurgie
♦ DTC – Deutsche Gesellschaft für Globale- und Tropenchirurgie (internationally oriented national body)
♦ **DTCE** Digital Trusts and Compliance Europe (#05085)
♦ DTG – Deutsche Gesellschaft für Tropenmedizin und Internationale Gesundheit (internationally oriented national body)
♦ DTI – Development Training International (internationally oriented national body)
♦ DTMSI – Design, Technology and Management Society International
♦ DTRC / see International Institute for Population Sciences (#13911)
♦ D-tree International (internationally oriented national body)
♦ DTU – Department for Timber Utilisation (inactive)
♦ DÜ / see Brot für die Welt
♦ **DUA** Democrat Union of Africa (#05036)
♦ Duais Mhna na hEorpa (#20993)
♦ Dubai Cares (internationally oriented national body)
♦ Dubbelbeskattning beträffande skatter på arv och på gåva (1989 treaty)
♦ Dubbeltskatning med hensyn til skatter av arv og gaver (1989 treaty)
♦ Dublin Convention on Asylum (1990 treaty)
♦ Dublin European Institute (internationally oriented national body)

♦ **Dublin Group** **05142**
Secretariat c/o Council of the European Union, Bât Justus Lipsius, Rue de la Loi 175, 1048 Brussels, Belgium.
History 1990, Ireland. Founded as an informal coordination group. **Structure** Secretariat hosted at *Council of the European Union (#04895).* **Activities** Events/meetings; politics/policy/regulatory.
Members Members:
Australia, Austria, Belgium, Bulgaria, Canada, Croatia, Cyprus, Czechia, Denmark, Estonia, Finland, France, Germany, Greece, Hungary, Ireland, Italy, Japan, Latvia, Luxembourg, Malta, Netherlands, Norway, Poland, Portugal, Romania, Slovakia, Slovenia, Spain, Sweden, Türkiye, UK, USA.
European Commission (EC, #06633).
Participant:
United Nations Office on Drugs and Crime (UNODC, #20596). [2019/AA0618/**E***]

♦ Dubna / see Joint Institute for Nuclear Research.(#16134)
♦ **DUCC** Downstream Users of Chemicals Co-ordination group (#05127)
♦ DUCIGS – Duke University Center for International and Global Studies (internationally oriented national body)
♦ DUCIS / see Duke University Center for International and Global Studies

♦ **Ducks Unlimited (DU)** **05143**
Contact One Waterfowl Way, Memphis TN 38120, USA. T. +19017583825.
URL: http://www.ducks.org/
History 1937, USA, by Joseph Knapp. **Aims** Support the habitat needs of North America's *waterfowl* and other other *wildlife* by protecting, enhancing, restoring and managing important *wetlands* and associated wetlands. **Structure** Board of Directors. Council of State Trustees and National Delegates. Officers: President, Chairman of the Board, Executive Vice President, Treasurer, Secretary, 9 Flyway Senior Vice Presidents, 8 Senior Vice Presidents, Executive Secretary, Secretary Emeritus, 6 Assistant Treasurers, 21 Regional Vice Presidents. **Finance** Members' dues. Other sources: donations; fundraising. **Events** *Annual Convention* Anchorage, AK (USA) 2007, *Annual Convention* Phoenix, AZ (USA) 2006, *Annual convention / Annual Meeting* Honolulu, HI (USA) 2000, *Annual convention / Annual Meeting* San Francisco, CA (USA) 1999, *Annual convention / Annual Meeting* Québec, QC (Canada) 1998. **Publications** Annual Report.
Members Individuals and groups in 3 countries:
Canada, Mexico, USA.
IGO Relations *Secretariat of the Convention of Wetlands (#19200).* [2019/XF5058/**F**]

♦ **DU** Ducks Unlimited (#05143)

♦ **Due Process of Law Foundation (DPLF)** **05144**
Fundación para el Debido Proceso
Exec Dir 1800 Massachusetts Ave NW, Ste 401, Washington DC 20036, USA. T. +12024627701. E-mail: info@dplf.org.
URL: https://www.dplf.org/
History 1996. Registration: USA, Washington. **Aims** Promote the rule of law and respect for human rights in Latin America. **Structure** Board of Directors. **Languages** English, Spanish. **Staff** 14.00 FTE, paid. **Finance** Private foundations; US Department of State; international development agencies, including: *Southern Common Market (#19868); United States Agency for International Development (USAID).* **Activities** Advocacy/lobbying/activism; events/meetings; networking/liaising; projects/programmes; research/documentation. **Publications** *AportesDPLF* – magazine. **IGO Relations** Consultative Status with: *OAS (#17629).* **NGO Relations** Member of (3): *Freedom of Information Advocates Network (FOIAnet, #09985); Global Initiative for Justice, Truth and Reconciliation (GIJTR); International Corporate Accountability Roundtable (ICAR, #12968).* Also member of regional and national networks in Latin America. [2022/XJ9314/f/**F**]

♦ DUF – Dansk Ungdoms Faellesraad (internationally oriented national body)
♦ DÜI / see GIGA – German Institute of Global and Area Studies
♦ Duke Center for International Development (internationally oriented national body)
♦ Duke Center for International Development, Durham NC / see Duke Center for International Development
♦ The Duke of Edinburgh's Award / see The Duke of Edinburgh's International Award Foundation (#05145)
♦ The Duke of Edinburgh's Award International Association / see The Duke of Edinburgh's International Award Foundation (#05145)

♦ **The Duke of Edinburgh's International Award Foundation** **05145**
SG Award House, 7-11 St Matthew St, London, SW1P 2JT, UK. T. +442072224242. Fax +442072224141. E-mail: info@intaward.org.
URL: http://www.intaward.org/
History 1956, UK. Present international association formed in 1988, linking all National Award Programmes. Former names and other names: *The Duke of Edinburgh's Award* – former; *The Duke of Edinburgh's Award International Association* – former. Registration: Charity Commission, No/ID: 1072453, England and Wales; Companies House, No/ID: 3666389, England and Wales. **Aims** Help young people to become world ready and find their purpose, passion and place in the world through developing transferable skills, increasing fitness levels, cultivating a sense of adventure and volunteering in their communities. **Structure** International Award Forum (every 3 years); International Council; International Award Foundation. **Languages** English. **Staff** 15.50 FTE, paid. **Finance** Sources: private and corporate revenue; capital endowment income; World Fellowship donor group; Young Fellowship donor group. **Activities** Awards/prizes/competitions; events/meetings. **Events** *Triennial Forum* Cluj-Napoca (Romania) 2022, *Triennial International Award Forum* Toronto, ON (Canada) 2015, *Triennial International Award Forum* Toronto, ON (Canada) 2015, *Triennial International Award Forum* Valletta (Malta) 2012, *Triennial international award forum* Sydney, NSW (Australia) 2009. **Publications** Newsletters (4 a year); Annual Review; training and support manuals; partnership leaflets; flyers; overviews; postcards; infographics.
Members Not a membership organization. Active in 128 countries and territories:
Angola, Antigua-Barbuda, Argentina, Ascension Is, Australia, Bahamas, Bahrain, Bangladesh, Barbados, Belgium, Belize, Benin, Bermuda, Botswana, Brazil, Brunei Darussalam, Bulgaria, Burundi, Cambodia, Cameroon, Canada, Cayman Is, China, Colombia, Congo DR, Cook Is, Costa Rica, Côte d'Ivoire, Curaçao, Cyprus, Czechia, Denmark, Dominica, Ecuador, Egypt, Eswatini, Ethiopia, Falklands/Malvinas, Fiji, Finland, France, Gambia, Germany, Ghana, Gibraltar, Greece, Grenada, Guinea, Guinea-Bissau, Guyana, Hong Kong, Hungary, India, Indonesia, Ireland, Israel, Italy, Jamaica, Japan, Jordan, Kazakhstan, Kenya, Korea Rep, Kuwait, Latvia, Lesotho, Liberia, Lithuania, Luxembourg, Macau, Madagascar, Malawi, Malaysia, Maldives, Malta, Mauritius, Monaco, Namibia, Nepal, Netherlands, New Zealand, Nigeria, Norfolk Is, Norway, Oman, Pakistan, Peru, Philippines, Poland, Portugal, Qatar, Réunion, Romania, Russia, Rwanda, Saudi Arabia, Senegal, Serbia, Seychelles, Sierra Leone, Singapore, Slovakia, Slovenia, Solomon Is, Somalia, South Africa, Spain, Sri Lanka, St Helena, St Lucia, St Vincent-Grenadines, Sudan, Switzerland, Taiwan, Tanzania UR, Thailand, Togo, Tonga, Trinidad-Tobago, Türkiye, Turks-Caicos, Uganda, UK, USA, Vanuatu, Vietnam, Zambia, Zimbabwe.
IGO Relations Accredited by: *United Nations Office at Vienna (UNOV, #20604).* Associated with Department of Global Communications of the United Nations. **NGO Relations** Member of: *Commonwealth Youth Exchange Council (CYEC); CIVICUS: World Alliance for Citizen Participation (#03962); European Youth Forum (#09140).* Links with a large number of youth organizations, including: *Girls' Brigade International (GB, #10152); International Corrections and Prisons Association for the Advancement of Professional Corrections (ICPA, #12970); International Federation of Red Cross and Red Crescent Societies (#13526); World Alliance of Young Men's Christian Associations (YMCA, #21090); World Association of Girl Guides and Girl Scouts (WAGGGS, #21142); World Organization of the Scout Movement (WOSM, #21693); World Young Women's Christian Association (World YWCA, #21947).* [2021/XF5053/f/**F**]

♦ Duke Islamic Studies Center (internationally oriented national body)
♦ Duke University Center for International and Global Studies (internationally oriented national body)
♦ Duke University Center for International Studies / see Duke University Center for International and Global Studies
♦ Dumping Protocol – Protocol for the Prevention of Pollution of the Mediterranean Sea by Dumping from Ships and Aircraft (1976 treaty)
♦ Dunajskaja Komissija (#04210)
♦ Dunajské psychiatrické asociaci (#05008)

♦ **Dunamenti Állatfajták Génmegőrző Nemzetközi Egyesülete (DAGENE)** **05146**
Pres Istvan utca 2, Budapest 1078, Hungary.
Exec Sec Böszörményi utca 138, Debrecen 4032, Hungary.
URL: http://www.dagene.eu/
History 1989, Bugacpuszta (Hungary). Established upon General Assembly approval of first Constitution by resolution No 1/1998. Former names and other names: *Danubian Countries Alliance for Conservation of Genes in Animal Species* – former; *Danubian Alliance for the Preservation of Animal Breeds (DAGENE)* – former; *International Association for the Conservation of Animal Breeds in the Danubian Region* – alias. Registration: Metropolitan Court, No/ID: 8.361, Start date: 1998, Hungary, Budapest. **Aims** Promote cooperation among breeders in neighbouring countries, giving prominence to conservation of genetic resources of domestic animals. **Structure** Praesidium. **Languages** English, German, Hungarian. **Staff** 0.25 FTE, paid. **Finance** Sources: grants; in-kind support; members' dues. Annual budget: 6,500 EUR. **Activities** Events/meetings. **Events** *Annual Conference & Joint International Congress on Farm Animal Diversity* Osijek (Croatia) 2022. **Publications** *Danubian Animal Genetic Resources (DAGR)* – in 5 vols; 2 issues (2020). *25 Years with DAGENE* – Jubilee proceedings.

Members Full in:
Austria, Bulgaria, Croatia, Czechia, Germany, Hungary, Romania, Serbia, Slovakia, Slovenia, Switzerland.
NGO Relations Accredited by (2): *European Regional Focal Point for Animal Genetic Resources (ERFP, #08343); Safeguard for Agricultural Varieties in Europe (SAVE Foundation, #19027).* Also links with national associations. [2022.02.18/XM6304/**D**]

♦ Dunamenti Tartomanyok Munkaközössége (#21056)
♦ Dunski Instytut Kultury (internationally oriented national body)
♦ Dünya Ahiska Türkleri Birligi (internationally oriented national body)
♦ Dünya Engelliler Birligi (unconfirmed)
♦ Dünya Türkçe Konusan Kibrislilar Birligi / see Union of Cypriots
♦ Dünya Uygur Kurultayi (#21896)
♦ Durrell Wildlife Conservation Trust (internationally oriented national body)
♦ **Duryog Nivaran** South Asian Initiative on Disaster Migration (#19734)
♦ DUST – International Conference on Atmospheric Dust (meeting series)
♦ Dutch Association for Tropical Forests (internationally oriented national body)
♦ Dutch Centre for International Cooperation (internationally oriented national body)
♦ Dutch Coordination Center Against Human Trafficking (internationally oriented national body)
♦ Dutch Council for Refugees / see Dutch Refugee Council
♦ DutchCulture – Dutch Centre for International Cooperation (internationally oriented national body)
♦ Dutch-German Connection / see European Federation for Living (#07155)
♦ Dutch Language Union (internationally oriented national body)
♦ Dutch Organization for International Cooperation in Higher Education / see Netherlands Organization for International Cooperation in Higher Education
♦ Dutch Refugee Council (internationally oriented national body)
♦ Dutch-Speaking Society of Comparative Education (internationally oriented national body)
♦ Duty Free and Travel Retail World Council / see Duty Free World Council
♦ Duty Free World Council (internationally oriented national body)
♦ DVB – Digital Video Broadcasting Project / see DVB Project (#05147)
♦ DVB / see DVB Project (#05147)

♦ DVB Project 05147

Project Office Ancienne Route 17a, Grand Saconnex, 1218 Geneva, Switzerland. T. +41227172719. E-mail: dvb@dvb.org.
URL: https://dvb.org/

History 10 Sep 1993, Bonn (Germany). Founded on signature of *'Memorandum of Understanding for the Development of Harmonized Digital Video Broadcasting (DVB) Services in Europe'* by members of *'European Launching Group (ELG)'*, set up in 1991 to oversee development of digital television in Europe and which formed the basis of the Project. Second phase commenced 1997. Former names and other names: *Group DVB – Digital Video Broadcasting* – former; *Groupe européen sur la radiodiffusion télévisuelle numérique (GERTN)* – former; *European Digital Video Broadcasting Project* – former; *European Project for Digital Video Broadcasting (DVB)* – former; *DVB – Digital Video Broadcasting Project* – former; *Projet sur la radiodiffusion télévisuelle numérique* – former. **Aims** Design open interoperable standards for the global delivery of digital *media* services, including broadcasting. **Structure** General Assembly (annual). Steering Board. Modules: Technical (TM); Commercial (CM); Promotion and Communications (PCM); Intellectual Property Rights (IPRM). Project Office in Geneva (Switzerland). **Languages** English. **Staff** 4.00 FTE, paid. **Finance** Sources: members' dues. **Activities** Knowledge management/information dissemination; standards/guidelines. **Events** *Digital Video Broadcasting Conference / DVB World Conference* Copenhagen (Denmark) 2015, *DVB World Conference* Prague (Czech Rep) 2014, *DVB World Conference* Madrid (Spain) 2013, *DVB World Conference* Rome (Italy) 2012, *DVB World Conference* Nice (France) 2011. **Publications** *DVB Scene* (2 a year). *DVB Identifiers Directory* – online listing of broadcasts compliant to DVB-Service Information standard.
Members Categories (4) Content providers/broadcasters; Infrastructure providers; Manufacturers/software suppliers; Governments/national regulatory bodies. Academic institutions also welcome to apply. Membership countries not specified but including one regional/international organization listed in this Yearbook:
European Space Agency (ESA, #08798).
Consultative Status Consultative status granted from: *World Intellectual Property Organization (WIPO, #21593)* (Permanent Observer Status). **NGO Relations** Located at: *European Broadcasting Union (EBU, #06404).* [2022.02.17/XE2108/y/**E**]

♦ **DVI** Dengue Vaccine Initiative (#05038)
♦ DVLP – Institut d'études du développement, Louvain-la-Neuve (internationally oriented national body)
♦ DVV-International – Institut für Internationale Zusammenarbeit des Deutschen Volkshochschul-Verbandes (internationally oriented national body)
♦ DW / see Development Workshop France
♦ DWB – Democracy Without Borders (internationally oriented national body)
♦ DWBN / see Karma Kagyu Buddhist Network (#16181)
♦ DWC – Deep Water Circulation Research Conference (meeting series)
♦ DWCN – Decent Work City Network (unconfirmed)
♦ DW – Daughters of Wisdom (religious order)
♦ DWF – Development Workshop France (internationally oriented national body)
♦ DWH / see World House, Bielefeld
♦ DWP / see WeltPartner
♦ DWW – Doctors Worldwide (internationally oriented national body)
♦ Dyes in History and Archaeology (unconfirmed)

♦ DYMAT Association 05148

Contact CEA Centre de Gramat, BP 80200, 46500 Gramat, France.
URL: http://www.dymat.org/

History Full title: *European Association for the Promotion of Research into the Dynamic Behaviour of Materials and its Applications – Association européenne pour la promotion des études du comportement dynamique des matériaux et applications.* Current Statutes adopted, 6 Sep 2007, Cambridge (UK). Registered in accordance with French law. **Aims** Bring together engineers and scientists working in the general field, focusing on the study of mechanical properties of materials at high rates of strain, their modelling and associated numerical simulations, and on applications of this work. **Structure** General Assembly; Governing Board; Board Committee. **Languages** English. **Activities** Events/meetings. **Events** *Technical Meeting on Dynamic Fracture of Ductile Materials* Trondheim (Norway) 2017, *International Conference* Lugano (Switzerland) 2015, *Hopkinson Centenary Conference / General Assembly* Cambridge (UK) 2014, *General Assembly* London (UK) 2013, *International Conference / General Assembly* Freiburg (Germany) 2012. **Publications** Proceedings. [2015.01.05/XJ1394/**D**]

♦ Dynamo International – Street Workers Network (internationally oriented national body)
♦ Dysautonomia International (internationally oriented national body)

♦ The Dysmelia Network (DysNet) 05149

Contact Axelstorpsvägen 2, SE-269 42 Båstad, Sweden. E-mail: info@dysnet.org.
URL: http://www.dysnet.org/

History 2009. Set up by a Swedish and UK organization. Registration: Stockholm, No/ID: 802444-3015, Start date: 7 Jan 2009, Sweden; EU Transparency Register, No/ID: 047603512537-13, Start date: 4 Jan 2014. **Aims** Reduce health inequalities experienced by people with *congenital limb* and internal damage that is generically described as dysmelia; build an online network architecture on the principal of patient centricity suitable to resolve health inequalities for people with rare limb difference conditions, including a Rare Disease European Reference Network in accordance with European recommendations. **Structure** Board of Directors. **Languages** English, French, German, Italian, Spanish. **Staff** 10.00 FTE, paid. **Finance** Members' dues. Other sources: donations; revenue from advertising and other activities; grants. **Events** *Dysmelia Experts Forum / Dysmelia Expert Forum* Stockholm (Sweden) 2014. **Information Services** *DysNet* – an online tool including several databases. **Members** Organizations (23) representing individuals (about 3,000) in 19 mainly European countries. Membership countries not specified. **NGO Relations** Member of: *European Disability Forum (EDF, #06929); EURORDIS – Rare Diseases Europe (#09175).* [2020/XJ2038/**D**]

♦ **DysNet** The Dysmelia Network (#05149)

♦ Dyspnea Society 05150

Address not obtained.
URL: http://dyspneasociety.com/

History Founded 2013, resulting from meetings organized since 2005. **Aims** Advance scientific knowledge of dyspnea and its translation to *clinical* practice. **Finance** Members' dues. **Activities** Events/meetings. **Events** *Conference* Montréal, QC (Canada) 2018. [2018/XM7912/c/**E**]

♦ Dystonia Europe 05151

Exec Dir Square de Meeus 37, 4th Floor, 1000 Brussels, Belgium. T. +447736625450 – +44773(46739984961. E-mail: sec@dystonia-europe.org.
URL: http://www.dystonia-europe.org/

History Jun 1993, Spoleto (Italy), as *European Dystonia Federation (EDF).* Current title adopted, 2012. Registered in accordance with Belgian law. **Aims** Establish a pan-European platform which will allow members to add value to their own activities and services to improve the lives of people living with dystonia; stimulate research for more effective treatments and, in the longer term, to find a cure for dystonia. **Structure** Annual General Assembly; Board; Secretariat. **Languages** English. **Staff** 1.00 FTE, paid. **Finance** Donations. Specific projects are funded by individual applications for grants to appropriate bodies. **Activities** Events/meetings; research/documetntation; networking/liaising; awards/prizes/competitions. **Events** *General Assembly* London (UK) 2019, *General Assembly* Brussels (Belgium) 2018, *General Assembly* Oslo (Norway) 2016, *General Assembly* Rotterdam (Netherlands) 2015, *General Assembly* Paris (France) 2014.
Members National dystonia patient support groups (21) in 18 countries:
Austria, Belgium, Croatia, Czechia, Denmark, Finland, France, Germany, Ireland, Italy, Norway, Poland, Portugal, Romania, Spain, Sweden, Switzerland, UK.
NGO Relations Full member of: *European Patients' Forum (EPF, #08172).* Member of: *EGAN – Patients Network for Medical Research and Health (EGAN, #05394).* [2019/XD4694/**D**]

♦ Dzeno Association (internationally oriented national body)
♦ DZG-Internationaal – Dieren zonder Grenzen – Internationaal (internationally oriented national body)
♦ E3 European Agency Network / see E3 International Agency Network (#05152)
♦ E3G – Third Generation Environmentalism (internationally oriented national body)

♦ E3 International Agency Network 05152

Admin Office Anton Loos, E3 Network, Stationsstraat 60, 2800 Mechelen, Belgium. T. +3215642512. E-mail: loos@bbc.be – veerle@e3network.com.
URL: http://www.e3network.com/

History Founded 1978, as *E3 European Agency Network*, on the initiative of Otto Pril, by marketing communications agencies. Current name adopted 2011. **Aims** Assist clients to exploit global opportunities through planning, supporting and executing international *marketing* activities. **Structure** General Meeting (twice a year). **Languages** English. **Staff** 0.50 FTE, paid. **Finance** Members' dues. Annual budget: about euro 85,000. **Activities** Networking/liaising; knowledge management/information dissemination; events/ meetings. **Events** *Annual General Meeting* Linz (Austria) 2015, *Annual General Meeting* Milan (Italy) 2014, *Annual General Meeting* Lisbon (Portugal) 2013, *Annual General Meeting* Prague (Czech Rep) 2012, *Annual General Meeting* Budapest (Hungary) 2011.
Members Full in 30 countries:
Australia, Belgium, China, Czechia, Denmark, Egypt, Finland, France, Germany, Ghana, Hungary, Israel, Italy, Kenya, Liberia, Myanmar, Netherlands, Nigeria, Norway, Poland, Romania, Sierra Leone, Singapore, Spain, Sweden, Switzerland, Thailand, UK, USA, Vietnam. [2019.12.13/XJ0203/**F**]

♦ **E3PO** European PPP Operating Companies in Infrastructure and Services (#08266)
♦ **E3S** European Sensory Science Society (#08468)
♦ **e5** European Business Council for a Sustainable Energy Future (#06417)
♦ e7 / see Global Sustainable Electricity Partnership (#10617)
♦ e8 / see Global Sustainable Electricity Partnership (#10617)
♦ EAA / see ACORD – Agency for Cooperation and Research in Development (#00073)
♦ **EAAA** East Asia Airports Alliance (#05194)
♦ **EAAA** East Asian Anthropological Association (#05195)
♦ **EAAAE** Euro-Asian Association of Agricultural Engineers (#05636)
♦ **EAAA** Euro-Asian Accrediting Association of Evangelical Seminaries (#05635)
♦ **EAAA** European Association for Asian Art and Archaeology (#05944)
♦ EAAA / see European Association of Communications Agencies (#05983)
♦ EAAA – European Atomized Aluminium Association (inactive)
♦ EAA Aviation Foundation / see Experimental Aircraft Association
♦ EAAB – European Accreditation Advisory Board (see: #06782)
♦ **EAACA** European Autoclaved Aerated Concrete Association (#06297)
♦ EAACC – European Association of Agrochemical Companies (unconfirmed)
♦ **EAACI** European Academy of Allergy and Clinical Immunology (#05779)
♦ EAAD – Euro-Asian Association of Dermatovenereologists (unconfirmed)
♦ **EAAD** European Alliance Against Depression e.V (#05860)
♦ EAA – East African Airways Corporation (inactive)
♦ **EAA** Eastern Africa Association (#05218)
♦ **EAA** Eau et Assainissement pour l'Afrique (#20836)
♦ EAAED / see Euro-American Association of Economic Development Studies
♦ EAAEDs – Euro-American Association of Economic Development Studies (internationally oriented national body)
♦ EAA – Education Above All (internationally oriented national body)
♦ **EAAE** European Association of Agricultural Economists (#05932)
♦ **EAAE** European Association for Architectural Education (#05941)
♦ **EAAE** European Association for Astronomy Education (#05945)
♦ **EAAEP Foundation** European Agricultural and Applied Economics Publications Foundation (#05845)
♦ EAAERE / see Asian Association of Environmental and Resource Economics (#01322)
♦ EAA – European Academy of Anaesthesiology (inactive)
♦ **EAA** European Academy of Andrology (#05780)
♦ EAA – European Academy of Architecture (internationally oriented national body)
♦ **EAA** European Accounting Association (#05820)
♦ **EAA** European Acoustics Association (#05824)
♦ EAA – European Actuarial Academy (unconfirmed)
♦ **EAA** European Advertising Academy (#05828)
♦ **EAA** European Aerosol Assembly (#05836)
♦ EAA / see European Aluminium (#05893)
♦ **EAA** European Anglers Alliance (#05900)
♦ **EAA** European Anthropological Association (#05904)
♦ **EAA** European Arenas Association (#05914)
♦ **EAA** European Association of Archaeologists (#05940)
♦ EAA / see European Athletics (#06291)
♦ **EAA** European AVM Alliance (#06305)
♦ EAA – European Enamel Association (unconfirmed)
♦ EAA – Experimental Aircraft Association (internationally oriented national body)
♦ **EAAF** CARTOON – European Association of Animation Film (#03592)
♦ EAAF Partnership / see East Asian – Australasian Flyway Partnership (#05198)
♦ **EAAFP** East Asian – Australasian Flyway Partnership (#05198)
♦ EAAFRO – East African Agriculture and Forestry Research Organization (inactive)
♦ EAAG / see East Africa Philanthropy Network (#05192)
♦ EAAIA – Eastern Africa Association for Impact Assessment (inactive)
♦ EAALCE / see Oikosnet Europe – Ecumenical Association of Academies and Laity Centres in Europe (#17706)

- ♦ **EAALCE** Oikosnet Europe – Ecumenical Association of Academies and Laity Centres in Europe (#17706)
- ♦ **EAALS** European Accreditation Agency for the Life Sciences (#05821)
- ♦ EAAME – European Association of Air Medical Escorts (unconfirmed)
- ♦ **EAAME** European Association for Audiovisual Media Education (#05946)
- ♦ **EAAM** European Association for Aquatic Mammals (#05938)
- ♦ EAANetwork / see Society for East Asian Archaeology (#19544)
- ♦ **EAANSA** Eastern Africa Action Network on Small Arms (#05217)
- ♦ EAAN / see Society for East Asian Archaeology (#19544)
- ♦ EAAO – European Association of Amateur Orchestras (inactive)
- ♦ **EAAOMS** Eastern Africa Association of Oral Maxillofacial Surgeons (#05219)
- ♦ **EAAP** European Association for Aviation Psychology (#05950)
- ♦ EAAP / see European Federation of Animal Science (#07046)
- ♦ **EAAP** European Federation of Animal Science (#07046)
- ♦ **EAAPP** East African Association for Paleoanthropology and Paleontology (#05175)
- ♦ EAAPS / see International Association of Aviation Personnel Schools (#11721)
- ♦ **EAAR** European Association of Authorised Representatives (#05947)
- ♦ EAARM / see European Marketing Academy (#07745)
- ♦ EAARP – Eastern Africa Association for Radiation Protection (internationally oriented national body)
- ♦ **EAAS** Euro-Asian Astronomical Society (#05637)
- ♦ **EAAS** European Association for American Studies (#05935)
- ♦ **EAASH** European Academy of Arts, Sciences and Humanities (#05781)
- ♦ **EAASI** European Association of Aerial Surveying Industries (#05929)
- ♦ **EAASI** European Association of Amusement Suppliers Industry (#05936)
- ♦ **EAASM** European Alliance for Access to Safe Medicines (#05859)
- ♦ **EAASP** European Association of Airport and Seaport Police (#05934)
- ♦ EAASR – Eastern African Association for the Study of Religions (no recent information)
- ♦ EAATCA – East African Air Traffic Controllers Association (inactive)
- ♦ EAATEE – Eastern Africa Association for Theological Education by Extension (no recent information)
- ♦ EAAT – European Association of Addiction Therapy (no recent information)
- ♦ **EAAV** European Association of Avian Veterinarians (#05949)
- ♦ EAAW – Education for Africa Animal Welfare (internationally oriented national body)
- ♦ EAB / see European Association for Bronchology and Interventional Pulmonology (#05959)
- ♦ **EABA** European Algae Biomass Association (#05857)
- ♦ **EABA** European Association for Behaviour Analysis (#05954)
- ♦ EABA / see European Boxing Confederation (#06387)
- ♦ **EABC** East African Business Council (#05177)
- ♦ **EABCN** Euro Area Business Cycle Network (#05631)
- ♦ **EABCT** European Association for Behavioural and Cognitive Therapies (#05953)
- ♦ **EABDA** East African Book Development Association (#05176)
- ♦ EAB – Europäische Akademie Bayern (internationally oriented national body)
- ♦ **EAB** European Association for Biometrics (#05957)
- ♦ **EABF** East Asian Bipolar Forum (#05200)
- ♦ EABH / see European Association for Banking and Financial History (#05951)
- ♦ **EABIP** European Association for Bronchology and Interventional Pulmonology (#05959)
- ♦ EABIS / see Academy of Business in Society (#00032)
- ♦ **EABP** European Association for Body Psychotherapy (#05958)
- ♦ **EABRN** East Asian Biosphere Reserve Network (#05199)
- ♦ EABS / see Asian Biophysics Association (#01358)
- ♦ **EABS** European Association for Biblical Studies (#05955)
- ♦ EABS – European Association for Bioeconomic Studies (inactive)
- ♦ EABT / see European Association for Behavioural and Cognitive Therapies (#05953)
- ♦ **EACA** European Association of Clinical Anatomy (#05976)
- ♦ **EACA** European Association of Communications Agencies (#05983)
- ♦ **EACA** European Athletics Coaches Association (#06292)
- ♦ **EAC** African Elephant Coalition (#00296)
- ♦ **EACAS** European Association for Critical Animal Studies (#05999)
- ♦ **EACB** European Association of Co-operative Banks (#05990)
- ♦ EACC / see Christian Conference of Asia (#03898)
- ♦ **EACCME** European Accreditation Council for Continuing Medical Education (#05823)
- ♦ **EACCU** East African Community Customs Union (#05182)
- ♦ EACDCPPE / see Asian Conference on Clinical Pharmacy (#01399)
- ♦ **EACD** European Academy of Childhood Disability (#05783)
- ♦ **EACD** European Academy of Craniomandibular Disorders (#05785)
- ♦ **EACD** European Association of Communication Directors (#05982)
- ♦ EACDLA – European Association of Christian Democratic Local Administrators (no recent information)
- ♦ **EAC** East African Community (#05181)
- ♦ EAC – East African Community – 1967 (inactive)
- ♦ **EACE** European Association for Cancer Education (#05961)
- ♦ **EACE** European Association for Cognitive Ergonomics (#05980)
- ♦ **EACEF** Euro Asia Civil Engineering Forum (#05633)
- ♦ EACEM – European Association of Consumer Electronics Manufacturers (inactive)
- ♦ **EACES** European Association for Comparative Economic Studies (#05984)
- ♦ **EAC** EU-ASIA Centre (#05567)
- ♦ **EAC** Europae Archaeologiae Consilium (#05746)
- ♦ EAC – European Academy of Chiropractic (see: #06538)
- ♦ EAC – European Accreditation of Certification (inactive)
- ♦ **EAC** European Advisory Council for Women's Health (#05831)
- ♦ **EAC** European Arboricultural Council (#05911)
- ♦ **EAC** European Assembly of Citizens (#05922)
- ♦ EAC – European Association for Cooperation (inactive)
- ♦ **EAC** European Association for Counselling (#05993)
- ♦ **EAC** European Astronaut Centre (#06287)
- ♦ EAC – European Automobile Clubs (unconfirmed)
- ♦ **EAC** Evangelical Association of the Caribbean (#09210)
- ♦ EACFP-Moldova / see European Centre for Mitigation of Natural Risks
- ♦ **EACG** European Association of Career Guidance (#05965)
- ♦ EACGI – European Association of the Chewing Gum Industry (inactive)
- ♦ EACGT – East Asian Conference on Geometric Topology (meeting series)
- ♦ **EACHA** European Automated Clearing House Association (#06298)
- ♦ **EACH** European Alliance for Cardiovascular Health (#05863)
- ♦ **EACH** European Association of Central Counterparty Clearing Houses (#05967)
- ♦ **EACH** European Association for Children in Hospital (#05970)
- ♦ EACHH – European Association of Care and Help at Home (inactive)
- ♦ EACH / see International Association for Communication in Healthcare (#11792)
- ♦ **EACH** International Association for Communication in Healthcare (#11792)
- ♦ EACHRights – East African Centre for Human Rights (internationally oriented national body)
- ♦ EACIC – East Asian Conference on Infection Control and Prevention (meeting series)
- ♦ **EACIC** European Accreditation Committee in the Central Nervous System (#05822)
- ♦ EACI – East Africa Consortium International (internationally oriented national body)
- ♦ **EACI** European Association for Creativity and Innovation (#05997)
- ♦ EACJS – East Asian Consortium of Japanese Studies (unconfirmed)
- ♦ **EACLALS** European Association for Commonwealth Literature and Language Studies (#05981)
- ♦ **EACLE** European-American Consortium for Legal Education (#05897)
- ♦ **EACL** European Association for Chinese Law (#05971)
- ♦ EACL – European Chapter of the Association for Computational Linguistics (see: #02445)
- ♦ EACLPP – European Association for Consultation Liaison Psychiatry and Psychosomatics (inactive)
- ♦ **EACME** European Association of Centres of Medical Ethics (#05968)
- ♦ **EACMFS** European Association for Cranio-Maxillo-Facial Surgery (#05995)
- ♦ EACMI / see Eastern and Southern African Management Institute (#05254)
- ♦ EACN – European Alliance for Community Networking (inactive)
- ♦ **EACN** European Contact-point Network against Corruption (#06776)
- ♦ **EACOA** East Asian Core Observatories Association (#05201)
- ♦ **EACO** East African Communications Organisation (#05180)
- ♦ EACO – Eastern Africa College of Ophthalmologists (inactive)
- ♦ EACoN – East Asian Conference of Neurointervention (meeting series)
- ♦ EACOR – Eastern Africa Coalition on Economic, Social and Cultural Rights (internationally oriented national body)
- ♦ **EA-CoR** European Alliance Group at the Committee of the Regions (#05871)
- ♦ EACP – East Asian Conference on Phonosurgery (meeting series)
- ♦ **EACP** European Aerospace Cluster Partnership (#05837)
- ♦ **EACP** European Association for Chinese Philosophy (#05972)
- ♦ EACP – European Association of Coloproctology (inactive)
- ♦ **EACP** European Association of Counselling Psychology (#05994)
- ♦ EACPR / see European Association of Preventive Cardiology (#06164)
- ♦ **EACPT** European Association for Clinical Pharmacology and Therapeutics (#05977)
- ♦ EACRACT – East African Centre for Rural and Agricultural Credit Training (meeting series)
- ♦ **EACRA** European Association of Credit Rating Agencies (#05998)
- ♦ EAC-RAND / see RAND Europe
- ♦ **EACRB** Eurasian Association of Contitutional Review Bodies (#05602)
- ♦ **EACREEE** East African Centre of Excellence for Renewable Energy and Efficiency (#05178)
- ♦ **EACR** European Association for Cancer Research (#05962)
- ♦ EACRO – European Association of Contract Research Organizations (inactive)
- ♦ EACROTANAL – Eastern African Centre for Research on Oral Traditions and African National Languages (inactive)
- ♦ EACRT – East Asia Conference of Radiological Technologists (meeting series)
- ♦ EAC Secretariat / see East African Community (#05181)
- ♦ **EACS** European Academy of Caring Science (#05782)
- ♦ **EACS** European Academy of Cosmetic Surgery (#05784)
- ♦ **EACS** European AIDS Clinical Society (#05849)
- ♦ EACS – European Association of Campus Security (inactive)
- ♦ **EACS** European Association for Chinese Studies (#05973)
- ♦ EACS – European Association for the Control of Structures (no recent information)
- ♦ **EACSL** European Association for Computer Science Logic (#05987)
- ♦ EACSO – East African Common Services Organization (inactive)
- ♦ **EACSOF** East African Civil Society Organizations' Forum (#05179)
- ♦ EACTA / see European Association of Cardiothoracic Anaesthesiology and Intensive Care (#05963)
- ♦ **EACTAIC** European Association of Cardiothoracic Anaesthesiology and Intensive Care (#05963)
- ♦ EACT / see EURO-CHINA (#05658)
- ♦ **EACT** European Association of Corporate Treasurers (#05992)
- ♦ **EACTP** European Association of Certified Turnaround Professionals (#05969)
- ♦ **EACTS** European Association for Cardio-Thoracic Surgery (#05964)
- ♦ EACVA – European Association of Certified Valuators and Analysts (unconfirmed)
- ♦ EACVI – European Association of Cardiovascular Imaging (see: #08536)
- ♦ **EACWP** European Association of Creative Writing Programmes (#05996)
- ♦ EADA – East African Dental Association (inactive)
- ♦ **EADA** Eastern Dredging Association (#05238)
- ♦ EADA – European-African Development Association (internationally oriented national body)
- ♦ **EADB** East African Development Bank (#05183)
- ♦ **EADCare** European Association for Developmental Care (#06009)
- ♦ **EADC** European Alzheimer's Disease Consortium (#05895)
- ♦ **EAD** European Academy of Design (#05789)
- ♦ EAD – European Academy of Diplomacy (internationally oriented national body)
- ♦ EADH / see European Association for Dance History (#06004)
- ♦ **EADH** European Association for Dance History (#06004)
- ♦ **EADH** European Association for Digital Humanities (#06014)
- ♦ EADI / see African Development Institute (#00286)
- ♦ **EADI** European Association of Development Research and Training Institutes (#06012)
- ♦ **EADK** Europäische Autorenvereinigung "DIE KOGGE" (#05749)
- ♦ **EADL** European Association for Distance Learning (#06015)
- ♦ **EADM** European Association for Decision Making (#06006)
- ♦ **EADMFR** European Academy of Dento Maxillo Facial Radiology (#05787)
- ♦ **EADN** East Asian Development Network (#05202)
- ♦ **EADO** European Association of Dermato-Oncology (#06008)
- ♦ **EADP** European Association of Developmental Psychology (#06010)
- ♦ **EADPH** European Association of Dental Public Health (#06007)
- ♦ EADPP – European Association of Data Protection Professionals (unconfirmed)
- ♦ EADRCC / see Euro-Atlantic Disaster Response Coordination Centre (#05644)
- ♦ **EADRCC** Euro-Atlantic Disaster Response Coordination Centre (#05644)
- ♦ **EADRU** Euro-Atlantic Disaster Response Unit (#05645)
- ♦ **EADSM** European Academy of Dental Sleep Medicine (#05786)
- ♦ **EAD Society** Euro Atlantic Diplomacy Society (#05643)
- ♦ EADT – European Association for Digital Transition (unconfirmed)
- ♦ **EADTU** European Association of Distance Teaching Universities (#06016)
- ♦ **EADV** European Academy of Dermatology and Venereology (#05788)
- ♦ **EAEA** East Asian Economic Association (#05203)
- ♦ **EAEA** European Architectural Endoscopy Association (#05912)
- ♦ **EAEA** European Arts and Entertainment Alliance (#05918)
- ♦ **EAEA** European Association for the Education of Adults (#06018)
- ♦ **EA** EarthAction (#05159)
- ♦ EAEC – East African Examinations Council (inactive)
- ♦ **EAEC** European Association of ERASMUS Coordinators (#06030)
- ♦ **EAEC** European Automobile Engineers Cooperation (#06299)
- ♦ **EAED** European Academy of Esthetic Dentistry (#05791)
- ♦ **EAEE** European Association for Earthquake Engineering (#06017)
- ♦ EAEE – Evangelische Arbeitsgemeinschaft für Erwachsenenbildung in Europa (inactive)
- ♦ **EAEEIE** European Association for Education in Electrical and Information Engineering (#06019)
- ♦ EAE – Energy Academy Europe (internationally oriented national body)
- ♦ **EAE** Epilepsy Alliance Europe (#05512)
- ♦ **EAE** European Association for External Thermal Insulation Composite Systems (#06035)
- ♦ **EAEF** Employee Assistance European Forum (#05446)
- ♦ EAEG – European Association of Exploration Geophysicists (inactive)
- ♦ EAEI / see Eurlyaid – European Association on Early Childhood Intervention (#05626)
- ♦ EAEME – European Association for Environmental Management Education (inactive)
- ♦ **EAEN** Eastern Africa Environmental Network (#05221)
- ♦ EA – Environment Africa (internationally oriented national body)
- ♦ **EAEPE** European Association for Evolutionary Political Economy (#06033)
- ♦ **EAEP** European Association of E-Pharmacies (#06029)

- ♦ **EAERCD** European Association for Education and Research in Commercial Distribution (#06020)
- ♦ **EAERE** European Association of Environmental and Resource Economists (#06028)
- ♦ **EAES** European Association for Endoscopic Surgery and Other Interventional Techniques (#06026)
- ♦ **EAES** European Atomic Energy Society (#06293)
- ♦ EAESP / see European Association of Social Psychology (#06210)
- ♦ **EAEU** Eurasian Economic Union (#05607)
- ♦ **EA** European Alternatives (#05891)
- ♦ **EA** European Association for the Advancement of Social Sciences (#05928)
- ♦ **EA** European Cooperation for Accreditation (#06782)
- ♦ **EAEVE** European Association of Establishments for Veterinary Education (#06031)
- ♦ **EAFA** European Aluminium Foil Association (#05894)
- ♦ EAFAIPA – East African Association of Investment Promotion Agencies (see: #05181)
- ♦ EAFAS – European Academy for Aviation Safety (inactive)
- ♦ EAFCA / see African Fine Coffees Association (#00316)
- ♦ **EAF** EECONET Action Fund (#05383)
- ♦ **EAFE** European Academy of Food Engineering (#05793)
- ♦ **EAFE** European Association of Fisheries Economists (#06039)
- ♦ **EAFE** European Association for Forensic Entomology (#06046)
- ♦ EAFES – East Asian Federation of Ecological Societies (internationally oriented national body)
- ♦ **EAF** European Anglers Federation (#05901)
- ♦ **EAF** European Armwrestling Federation (#05915)
- ♦ **EAFF** East Asian Football Federation (#05204)
- ♦ **EAFF** Eastern African Farmers Federation (#05223)
- ♦ **EAFF** European Amputee Football Federation (#05898)
- ♦ **EAFF** European Association of Folklore Festivals (#06043)
- ♦ EAFFRO – East African Freshwater Fisheries Research Organization (inactive)
- ♦ EAFG – European Association for Flower Growers (unconfirmed)
- ♦ EAFGS – European association for gender surgery (unconfirmed)
- ♦ EAFJD – European Armenian Federation for Justice and Democracy (internationally oriented national body)
- ♦ EAFOD – Eastern Africa Federation of the Disabled (unconfirmed)
- ♦ EAFO / see Lake Victoria Fisheries Organization (#16222)
- ♦ **EAFONS** East Asian Forum of Nursing Scholars (#05205)
- ♦ **EAFORD** International Organization for the Elimination of All Forms of Racial Discrimination (#14445)
- ♦ EAFORM – East Asia Forum on Radwaste Management Conference (meeting series)
- ♦ EAFPA – European Association of Fishing Ports and Auctions (inactive)
- ♦ EAFP – European Association Against Fibre Pollution (inactive)
- ♦ **EAFP** European Association of Faculties of Pharmacy (#06036)
- ♦ **EAFP** European Association of Fish Pathologists (#06040)
- ♦ **EAFPS** European Academy of Facial Plastic Surgery (#05792)
- ♦ EAFS / see European Network of Forensic Science Institutes (#07910)
- ♦ **EAFT** European Association of the Free Thought (#06048)
- ♦ **EAFT** European Association for Terminology (#06252)
- ♦ EAfV – European Alliance for Volunteering (inactive)
- ♦ EAGA / see East Asian Olympic Committee (#05206)
- ♦ **EAGC** Eastern Africa Grain Council (#05222)
- ♦ **EAGC** European Academy of Gynaecological Cancer (#05794)
- ♦ EAGE / see European Academy of Gynaecological Surgery (#05795)
- ♦ EAGE / see European Association for Gastroenterology, Endoscopy and Nutrition (#06051)
- ♦ **EAGE** European Association of Geoscientists and Engineers (#06055)
- ♦ EAGEM – European Association for Gastrointestinal Emergencies and Intensive Care (inactive)
- ♦ **EAGEN** European Association for Gastroenterology, Endoscopy and Nutrition (#06051)
- ♦ **EAG** Eurasian Group on Combating Money Laundering and Financing of Terrorism (#05608)
- ♦ **EAG** European Association of Geochemistry (#06053)
- ♦ **EAGHC** European Association of Golf Historians and Collectors (#06059)
- ♦ **EAGM** European Association of Geosynthetic product Manufacturers (#06056)
- ♦ EAGO – EurAsian Geophysical Society (internationally oriented national body)
- ♦ EAGO – European Association of Gynaecologists and Obstetricians (inactive)
- ♦ EAGOR – East Asia Group of Rheumatology (unconfirmed)
- ♦ **EAGP** European Association of Geriatric Psychiatry (#06057)
- ♦ Eagriochtna Dtionscal um Leasú Glasnai (inactive)
- ♦ EAGS / see EGAN – Patients Network for Medical Research and Health (#05394)
- ♦ **EAGS** European Academy of Gynaecological Surgery (#05795)
- ♦ **EAGT** European Association for Gestalt Therapy (#06058)
- ♦ **EAHAD** European Association for Haemophilia and Allied Disorders (#06063)
- ♦ EAHAE / see International Association for Horse Assisted Education (#11939)
- ♦ **EAHAE** International Association for Horse Assisted Education (#11939)
- ♦ EAHC – East African High Commission (inactive)
- ♦ EAHC – East Asia Hydrographic Commission (see: #13825)
- ♦ **EAHE** European Association for Home Economics (#06072)
- ♦ EAHE – European Association of Human Ecology (inactive)
- ♦ EAH – Europäische Akademie Hessen (internationally oriented national body)
- ♦ EAHHSSW – European Association of Hospital and Health Services Social Workers (inactive)
- ♦ **EAHIL** European Association for Health Information and Libraries (#06064)
- ♦ **EAHL** European Association of Health Law (#06065)
- ♦ EAHMA – European Aluminium Holloware Manufacturer's Association (inactive)
- ♦ **EAHM** European Association of Hospital Managers (#06073)
- ♦ **EAHMH** European Association for the History of Medicine and Health (#06070)
- ♦ **EAHN** European Architectural History Network (#05913)
- ♦ **E-AHPBA** European-African Hepato-Pancreato-Biliary Association (#05840)
- ♦ **EAHP** European Association for Haematopathology (#06062)
- ♦ EAHP – European Association for the History of Psychiatry (inactive)
- ♦ **EAHP** European Association of Hospital Pharmacists (#06074)
- ♦ EAHP – European Association for Humanistic Psychology (inactive)
- ♦ EAHP – European Association for Hypno Psychotherapy (internationally oriented national body)
- ♦ EAHP / see Hospital Organization of Pedagogues in Europe (#10949)
- ♦ EAHSA – European Association of Homes and Services for the Ageing (inactive)
- ♦ EAHT / see Hospital Organization of Pedagogues in Europe (#10949)
- ♦ EAHTR / see European Association of Historic Towns and Regions (#06068)
- ♦ EAI / see East Asian Institute, National University of Singapore
- ♦ EAI / see Enterprise for the Americas Initiative and Tropical Forest Conservation Act
- ♦ EAIC – East Asian Insurance Congress (meeting series)
- ♦ **EAIC** European Association of Innovation Consultants (#06084)
- ♦ EAICY / see European Association of Institutions of Non-formal Education of Children and Youth (#06087)
- ♦ **EAICY** European Association of Institutions of Non-formal Education of Children and Youth (#06087)
- ♦ **EAIDSNet** East African Integrated Disease Surveillance Network (#05184)
- ♦ EAI – East Asia Institute, Cambridge (internationally oriented national body)
- ♦ EAI – East Asia Institute, Seoul (internationally oriented national body)
- ♦ EAI – East Asian Institute, National University of Singapore (internationally oriented national body)
- ♦ **EAIE** European Association for International Education (#06092)
- ♦ EAI – Equal Access International (internationally oriented national body)
- ♦ **EAI** European Alliance for Innovation (#05872)
- ♦ EAI – European Association of Individual Investors (inactive)
- ♦ **EAI** European Astrobiology Institute (#06285)
- ♦ **EAIPA** European Association of Independent Performing Arts (#06078)
- ♦ **EAIP** European Association for Integrative Psychotherapy (#06088)
- ♦ EAIR / see EAIR, The European Higher Education Society (#05153)

♦ EAIR, The European Higher Education Society 05153

Contact Berkenkade 24, 2351 NC Leiderdorp, Netherlands. E-mail: eair@eairweb.org.
URL: http://www.eairweb.org/

History 1979. Founded as a European branch of the US-based *Association for International Research (AIR)*, currently *Association for Institutional Research (AIR)*. Became an independent organization at EAIR 11th Forum, Sep 1989, Trier (Germany FR). Current constitution adopted 2003. Former names and other names: *European Association for Institutional Research (EAIR)* – former; *Europese Hoger Onderwijs Samenleving* – former. Registration: Handelsregister, Netherlands. **Aims** Support research and development in higher education research, policy and practice, to the general benefit of higher education. Referring to institutional, national and international contexts, as appropriate: encourage research in higher education; promote development of institutional management, planning and policy implementation; disseminate information that supports policy-making, policy implementation and good practice in higher education; support membership by providing opportunities for networking and profesional development in the field of education. **Structure** Executive Committee; Steering Committee. **Languages** English. **Staff** 0.30 FTE, paid; 1.00 FTE, voluntary. **Finance** Sources: members' dues. **Activities** Events/meetings; knowledge management/information dissemination. **Events** *Annual EAIR Forum* Linz (Austria) 2023, *Annual EAIR Forum* Paola (Malta) 2022, *Annual EAIR Forum* Berlin (Germany) 2021, *Annual International Forum on Higher Education* Cork (Ireland) 2020, *Annual International Forum on Higher Education* Leiden (Netherlands) 2019. **Publications** *Tertiary Education and Management (TEAM)* (4 a year) – journal.

Members Regular; Student; Emeritus; Distinguished individuals involved in higher education research and management and policy making; teaching and research institutions; professional, industrial and governmental bodies. Members (nearly 400) in 40 countries and territories:
Argentina, Australia, Austria, Belgium, Brazil, Bulgaria, Canada, Croatia, Cyprus, Czechia, Denmark, Estonia, Finland, France, Georgia, Germany, Greece, Hungary, Ireland, Italy, Japan, Kosovo, Latvia, Lithuania, Netherlands, New Zealand, Norway, Poland, Portugal, Russia, Singapore, Slovakia, Slovenia, South Africa, Spain, Sweden, Switzerland, Türkiye, UK, USA.

[2022.02.16/XD3495/v/**D**]

- ♦ **EAIS** European Association of Israel Studies (#06094)
- ♦ EAIT – European Academy for International Training (internationally oriented national body)
- ♦ EAI/TFCA – Enterprise for the Americas Initiative and Tropical Forest Conservation Act (internationally oriented national body)
- ♦ **EAIVT** European Association of Independent Vehicle Traders (#06081)
- ♦ EAJA – Eastern Africa Journalists Association (unconfirmed)
- ♦ **EAJCC** European Association of Jewish Community Centres (#06097)
- ♦ **EAJC** Euro-Asian Jewish Congress (#05640)
- ♦ EAJC – European Association for Jewish Culture (no recent information)
- ♦ **EAJ** European Association of Judges (#06100)
- ♦ EAJK – Europäisches Amt für Jugend und Kinder (inactive)
- ♦ EAJP / see European Association for the Trade in Jute and Related Products (#06256)
- ♦ **EAJRS** European Association of Japanese Resource Specialists (#06095)
- ♦ **EAJS** European Association for Japanese Studies (#06096)
- ♦ **EAJS** European Association for Jewish Studies (#06098)
- ♦ **EAKBT** Europäischer Arbeitskreis für Konzentrative Bewegungstherapie (#05757)
- ♦ EAKLE – European Association for Korean Language Education (unconfirmed)
- ♦ **EALA** East African Legislative Assembly (#05185)
- ♦ EALA – East African Library Association (inactive)
- ♦ **EALA** European Air Law Association (#05851)
- ♦ EALAF / see Forum for East Asia-Latin America Cooperation (#09907)
- ♦ EALA / see Global Advertising Lawyers Alliance (#10171)
- ♦ **EALD** European Academy of Land Use and Development (#05797)
- ♦ EALEA – European Association of Logotherapy and Existential Analysis (no recent information)
- ♦ EAL / see Earth League International (#05166)
- ♦ **EALE** European Association of Labour Economists (#06102)
- ♦ **EALE** European Association of Law and Economics (#06104)
- ♦ **EALGA** East African Local Governments Association (#05186)
- ♦ EAL / see International Association of Legislation (#11998)
- ♦ **EALIZ** Europäische Akademie für Lebensforschung, Integration und Zivilgesellschaft (#05799)
- ♦ EALLT – European Association of Linguists and Language Teachers (no recent information)
- ♦ EALSC / see European Network for the Cure of ALS (#07889)
- ♦ **EALS** East Africa Law Society (#05173)
- ♦ **EALTA** European Association for Language Testing and Assessment (#06103)
- ♦ **EALT** European Academy of Legal Theory (#05798)
- ♦ **EALTH** European Association for Logistics and Transportation in Healthcare (#06111)
- ♦ EAMA – Association entre la Communauté européenne et les Etats africains et malgache associés (inactive)
- ♦ **EAMAC** Ecole africaine de la méteorologie et de l'aviation civile (#05295)
- ♦ **EAMA** European Academy for Medicine of Ageing (#05802)
- ♦ EAMA – European Asset Management Association (inactive)
- ♦ E-AMARC – Euro-African Management Research Centre (internationally oriented national body)
- ♦ **EAMAU** Ecole africaine des métiers d'architecture et d'urbanisme (#00450)
- ♦ **EAMBES** European Alliance for Medical and Biological Engineering and Science (#05873)
- ♦ **EAMC** Engineering Association of Mediterranean Countries (#05480)
- ♦ EAMC – European Alliance for Medicinal Cannabis (unconfirmed)
- ♦ EAMC – European Association for Mediated Learning and Cognitive Modifiability (no recent information)
- ♦ **EAMDA** European Alliance of Neuromuscular Disorders Associations (#05876)
- ♦ EAMD – East African Meteorological Department (inactive)
- ♦ EAME – Express Association of the Middle East (no recent information)
- ♦ **EAM** European Association of Methodology (#06119)
- ♦ **EAM** European Network for Avant-Garde and Modernism Studies (#07867)
- ♦ **EAMF** Eurasian Media Forum Foundation (#05611)
- ♦ EAMF / see European Festivals Association (#07242)
- ♦ EAMFRO – East African Marine Fisheries Research Organization (inactive)
- ♦ EAMFS / see European Association for Cranio-Maxillo-Facial Surgery (#05995)
- ♦ **EAMHID** European Association for Mental Health in Intellectual Disability (#06118)
- ♦ **EAMHMS** European Association of Museums of the History of Medical Sciences (#06125)
- ♦ EAMIC – Eastern African Mining Industry Convention (meeting series)
- ♦ EAMI / see Eastern and Southern African Management Institute (#05254)
- ♦ **EAMI** European Association of Music and Imagery (#06126)
- ♦ EAMM – European Association of Mozzarella Manufacturers (inactive)
- ♦ **EAMN** European Age Management Network (#05842)
- ♦ EAMPCS – European Association of Manufacturers of Polycarbonate Sheet (inactive)
- ♦ EAMP / see European Mollusc Producers' Association (#07818)
- ♦ EAMRC – East Africa Medical Research Council (inactive)
- ♦ EAMRDC / see African Minerals and Geosciences Centre (#00373)
- ♦ **EAMSA** Euro-Asia Management Studies Association (#05634)
- ♦ **EAMS** East African Meteorological Society (#05187)
- ♦ **EAMS** European Airway Management Society (#05854)
- ♦ EAMSP / see European Association of E-Pharmacies (#06029)
- ♦ EAMST – European Association of Musculo-Skeletal Transplantation (inactive)

♦ EAMTC – European Association of Management Training Centres (inactive)
♦ **EAMTC** European Aviation Maintenance Training Committee (#06303)
♦ **EAMT** European Association for Machine Translation (#06115)
♦ **EAMTM** European Association of Machine Tool Merchants (#06114)
♦ EANAC – European Association of Nurses in HIV/AIDS Care (inactive)
♦ **EANA** Europäische Arbeitsgemeinschaft der Niedergelassenen Ärzte (#05154)
♦ **EANA** European Alliance of News Agencies (#05877)
♦ **EANA** European Astrobiology Network Association (#06286)

♦ EANA – European Working Group of Physicians in Private Practice . 05154

Groupement européen des médecins en pratique libre – Europäische Arbeitsgemeinschaft der Niedergelassenen Ärzte (EANA)

Pres EANA Secretariat, c/o AMMD, Rue de Vianden, L-2680 Luxembourg, Luxembourg. E-mail: secretariat@ammd.lu.
URL: http://www.eana.at/

History 1974, as *European Working Group of Practitioners and Specialists in Free Practice.* **Aims** Promote exchange of experience and information on health care structures and social security systems within Europe and information on the current political evolution in health care and social security; develop and examine new concepts of ambulatory care with priority to interdisciplinary basic health care; improve cooperation between doctors in private practice and other health and social professionals; promote: self-help groups, home care and social services; prevention and health education; continuous training, postgraduate and basic training; outpatient care structures. **Structure** Officers: President; Vice-President; Treasurer; General Secretary. Secretariat. **Languages** English, French, German. **Finance** Members' dues: euro 1,000-2,000 per nation. **Activities** Research and development; training/education. **Events** *Meeting* Bratislava (Slovakia) 2012, *Meeting* Paris (France) 2012, *Spring meeting* Gibraltar 2011, *Autumn meeting* Halle (Saale) (Germany) 2011, *Meeting* Luxembourg (Luxembourg) 2010.
Members Individuals in 9 countries:
Austria, Belgium, Czechia, Germany, Hungary, Luxembourg, Slovakia, Spain, Switzerland.
NGO Relations Member of: *Standing Committee of European Doctors (#19955).* [2015.01.20/XE0415/v/**E**]

♦ EANAM – European Association for Negotiation and Mediation (unconfirmed)
♦ **EANET** Acid Deposition Monitoring Network in East Asia (#00070)
♦ **EAN** European Academy of Neurology (#05803)
♦ **EAN** European Access Network (#05819)
♦ **EAN** European Aeroallergen Network (#05832)
♦ **EAN** European Ageing Network (#05841)
♦ **EAN** European ALARA Network (#05855)
♦ **EAN** European Antibullying Network (#05905)
♦ EAN / see GS1 (#10809)
♦ EANGTI – European Association of Next Generation Telecommunications Innovators (unconfirmed)
♦ EAN International / see GS1 (#10809)
♦ EANLP – European Association of Neuro-Linguistic Programming (unconfirmed)
♦ **EANLPt** European Association for Neuro-Linguistic Psychotherapy (#06131)
♦ **EANM** European Association of Nuclear Medicine (#06136)
♦ EANM – European Association of Producers and Distributors of Natural Medicines (no recent information)
♦ EANNASO – Eastern African Network of AIDS Service Organizations (see: #00272)
♦ **EANN** European Association of Neuroscience Nurses (#06133)
♦ EANOC / see East Asian Olympic Committee (#05206)
♦ **EANO** European Association for Neuro-Oncology (#06132)
♦ **EANPC** European Association of National Productivity Centres (#06130)
♦ **EANS** European Academy of Nursing Science (#05804)
♦ **EANS** European Academy of Nutritional Sciences (#00045)
♦ **EANS** European Association of Neurosurgical Societies (#06134)
♦ EAO – Europäische Akademie Otzenhausen (internationally oriented national body)
♦ **EAO** European Academy of Ophthalmology (#05806)
♦ EAO – European Association of Organizations for Home Care and Help at Home (inactive)
♦ **EAO** European Association for Osseointegration (#06139)
♦ **EAOG** European Association of Organic Geochemists (#06138)
♦ **EA-OHP** European Academy of Occupational Health Psychology (#05805)
♦ **EAOM** European Association for Oral Medicine (#06137)
♦ **EAONO** European Academy of Otology and Neuro-Otology (#05809)
♦ **EAOO** European Academy of Optometry and Optics (#05807)
♦ **EAOPD** European Academy of Orofacial Pain and Dysfunction (#05808)
♦ EAOSEF / see Asian and Oceanian Stock Exchanges Federation (#01585)
♦ **EAPAA** European Association for Public Administration Accreditation (#06177)
♦ EAPA / see European Alliance of News Agencies (#05877)
♦ **EAPA** European Animal Protein Association (#05902)
♦ **EAPA** European Asphalt Pavement Association (#05920)
♦ **EAPA** European Association of Psychological Assessment (#06172)
♦ EAPA / see International Employee Assistance Professionals Association (#13264)
♦ **EAPA** International Employee Assistance Professionals Association (#13264)
♦ EAPAP – European Association of Parental Alienation Practitioners (inactive)
♦ **EAPB** European Association of Pharma Biotechnology (#06150)
♦ EAPB / see European Association of Public Banks (#06178)
♦ **EAPB** European Association of Public Banks (#06178)
♦ EAPCA – European Audio Phonological Centres Association (inactive)
♦ EAPCCO – Eastern Africa Police Chiefs Cooperation Organization (unconfirmed)
♦ **EAPCCT** European Association of Poisons Centres and Clinical Toxicologists (#06155)
♦ **EAPC** Euro Atlantic Partnership Council (#05646)
♦ **EAPC** European Association for Palliative Care (#06141)
♦ **EAPC** European Association of Political Consultants (#06156)
♦ **EAPC** European Association of Preventive Cardiology (#06164)
♦ **EAPCI** European Association of Percutaneous Cardiovascular Interventions (#06147)
♦ EAPC Onlus / see European Association for Palliative Care (#06141)
♦ **EaP CSF** Eastern Partnership Civil Society Forum (#05247)
♦ **EAPD** European Academy of Paediatric Dentistry (#05810)
♦ EAPE / see Association for Paediatric Education in Europe (#02847)
♦ EAP – Engineers Against Poverty (internationally oriented national body)
♦ EAP – Environmental Action Programme for Central and Eastern Europe (inactive)
♦ EAP – Escuela Agricola Panamericana del Zamorano (internationally oriented national body)
♦ EAPETEA – East Asia Joint Symposium on Plasma and Electrostatics Technologies for Environmental Applications (meeting series)
♦ **EAP** European Academy of Paediatrics (#05811)
♦ **EAP** European Association for Psychotherapy (#06176)
♦ EAPF – European Alliance for Plant-based Foods (unconfirmed)
♦ **EAPFP** European Association for Passive Fire Protection (#06143)
♦ EAPG – European Association of Petroleum Geoscientists and Engineers (inactive)
♦ EAPG – European Association for Planned Giving (internationally oriented national body)
♦ **EAPH** European Association for Physician Health (#06151)
♦ EAPH – European Association for the Promotion of Hand Hygiene (inactive)
♦ EAPH / see European network for health promotion and economic development (#07920)
♦ **EAPHM** European Association of Porcine Health Management (#06159)
♦ EAPHSS / see European Health Management Association (#07458)
♦ EAPIC – Eastern African Power Industry Convention (meeting series)
♦ **EAPI** East Asian Pastoral Institute (#05207)
♦ **EAPIL** European Association of Private International Law (#06165)
♦ **EAPIRF** East Asia and Pacific Infrastructure Regulatory Forum (#05212)
♦ **EAPL** European Association of Psychology and Law (#06174)
♦ **EA-PLF** European Association for Precision Livestock Farming (#06162)
♦ **EAPLS** European Association for Programming Languages and Systems (#06171)
♦ **EAPM** European Alliance for Personalised Medicine (#05878)
♦ EAPM / see European Association for People Management (#06146)
♦ **EAPM** European Association for People Management (#06146)
♦ **EAPM** European Association of Perinatal Medicine (#06148)
♦ **EAPM** European Association of Psychosomatic Medicine (#06175)
♦ **EAPN** East Africa Philanthropy Network (#05192)
♦ **EAPN** European Anti-Poverty Network (#05908)
♦ **EAPO** Eurasian Patent Office (#05612)
♦ **EAPO** Eurasian Patent Organization (#05613)
♦ **EAPO** European Association of Fish Producers Organizations (#06041)
♦ **EAP** Oil and Gas Industry Energy Access Platform (#17710)
♦ **EAPP** Eastern Africa Power Pool (#05226)
♦ **EAPP** European Association of Personality Psychology (#06149)
♦ **EAPPM** European Association for Product and Process Modelling in the Building Industry (#06168)
♦ **EAPR** European Association for Potato Research (#06160)
♦ EAPRIL / see European Association for Practitioner Research on Improving Learning (#06161)
♦ **EAPRIL** European Association for Practitioner Research on Improving Learning (#06161)
♦ EAPS – European Academy of Paediatrics Societies (meeting series)
♦ **EAPS** European Association for Population Studies (#06158)
♦ EAPS / see International Management Assistants (#14081)
♦ **EAPSPI** European Association of Public Sector Pension Institutions (#06180)
♦ **EAPT** European Association for Psychological Type (#06173)
♦ EAPU – European Academy of Paediatric Urology (see: #16883)
♦ **EAPV** Evraziiskoe patentnoe vedomstvo (#05612)
♦ **EAPVP Forum** East Asia Plant Variety Protection Forum (#05213)
♦ **EAQG** European Aerospace Quality Group (#05838)
♦ EAQOM / see European Association of Quality Organisations in Mobility (#06185)
♦ **EAQOM** European Association of Quality Organisations in Mobility (#06185)
♦ **EAQUA** Eastern African Quaternary Research Association (#05224)
♦ **Eaquals** Evaluation and Accreditation of Quality in Language Services (#09209)
♦ **EARA** European Animal Research Association (#05903)
♦ **EARA** European Asbestos Removal Association (#05919)
♦ **EARA** European Association for Research on Adolescence (#06192)
♦ EARAPA / see European Federation of Adapted Physical Activity (#07038)
♦ EARARA – East African Rock Art Research Association (no recent information)
♦ **EARAZA** Eurasian Regional Association of Zoos and Aquariums (#05614)
♦ EARCAG – East Asian Regional Conference in Alternative Geography (meeting series)
♦ **EARCOS** East Asia Regional Council of Overseas Schools (#05214)
♦ EARDHE – European Association for Research and Development in Higher Education (inactive)
♦ EARE – European Alliance for Research Excellence (unconfirmed)
♦ EAR – European Association of Radiology (inactive)
♦ **EARIE** European Association for Research in Industrial Economics (#06193)
♦ **EARLALL** European Association of Regional and Local Authorities for Lifelong Learning (#06188)
♦ EARL – European Association of Reference Laboratories (no recent information)
♦ **EARLI** European Association for Research on Learning and Instruction (#06194)
♦ **EARLS** European Alliance for Restless Legs Syndrome (#05881)
♦ Early Book Society (internationally oriented national body)
♦ Early Book Society for the Study of Manuscripts and Printing History / see Early Book Society

♦ Early Childhood Development Action Network (ECDAN) 05155

Exec Dir 700 12th St NW, Suite 700, PMB 91319, Washington DC 20005, USA. T. +13018441992. E-mail: info@ecdan.org.
URL: https://www.ecdan.org/

History Launched Apr 2016, by *UNICEF (#20332)* and *The World Bank Group (#21218).* **Aims** Catalyze collective action on behalf of young children and their families around the world by connecting with global and regional partners, facilitating knowledge exchange and learning and coordinating advocacy for increased investment for quality services. **Structure** Executive Group; Secretariat. **Activities** Knowledge management/information dissemination; networking/liaising; advocacy/lobbying/activism. **Publications** *ECDAN Newsletter.*
Members Organizations and networks (over 100), including 22 organizations listed in this Yearbook:
- *Africa Early Childhood Network (AfECN, #00166);*
- *Aga Khan Development Network (AKDN, #00544);*
- *Asia-Pacific Regional Network for Early Childhood (ARNEC, #02009);*
- *Catholic Relief Services (CRS, #03608);*
- *ChildFund International (#03869);*
- *Childhood Education International (CE International);*
- *Children's Investment Fund Foundation (CIFF);*
- *CPC Learning Network;*
- *Global Partnership for Education (GPE, #10531);*
- *Inter-American Development Bank (IDB, #11427);*
- *International Rescue Committee (IRC, #14717);*
- *International Step by Step Association (ISSA, #15605);*
- *Jacobs Foundation (JF, #16084);*
- *LEGO Foundation;*
- *Mother Child Education Foundation (ACEV);*
- *Plan International (#18386);*
- *Results for Development (R4D, #18923);*
- *Save the Children International (#19058);*
- *The World Bank Group (#21218);*
- *UNESCO (#20322);*
- *UNICEF (#20332);*
- *WHO (#20950).*

NGO Relations *Early Childhood Peace Consortium (ECPC, #05156).* [2020/XM8789/y/**F**]

♦ Early Childhood Peace Consortium (ECPC) 05156

Address not obtained.
URL: https://ecdpeace.org/

History Inception 2012; launched 2013. **Aims** Create an inclusive movement for peace, social cohesion, social justice, and the prevention of violence through using early childhood development strategies to enable the world community to advance peace, security and development. **Structure** Steering Committee; Executive Board; Advisory Group. **Publications** *ECPC Newsletter.* **IGO Relations** *UNICEF (#20332).* **NGO Relations** Partners include: *Arab Resource Collective (ARC); Early Childhood Development Action Network (ECDAN, #05155); International Center for Education and Human Development (CINDE); International Step by Step Association (ISSA, #15605); Mother Child Education Foundation (ACEV); Sesame Workshop; World Childhood Foundation (#21272); World Organization for Early Childhood Education (OMEP, #21689); World Vision International (WVI, #21904).* [2020/XM8788/**C**]

♦ Early English Text Society (EETS) 05157

Exec Sec Univ of Oxford, Fac of English, St Cross Building, Manor Road, Oxford, OX1 3UL, UK. T. +441865271933.
URL: http://www.eets.org.uk/

History Founded 1864, Oxford (UK), by Frederick James Furnivall, with the help of Richard Morris, Walter Skeat and others. **Aims** Study and publish pre-1550 English texts. **Structure** Council. **Languages** English. **Finance** Members' dues. **Publications** *EETS Supplementary Series* (1970-); *EETS Extra Series* (1867-1920); *EETS Original Series* (1864-).
Members Individuals university teachers and scholars; Institutional membership public libraries, universities and specialized bodies. Members in 31 countries:
Australia, Austria, Belgium, Brazil, Bulgaria, Canada, Czechia, Denmark, Egypt, Finland, France, Germany, Iceland, Ireland, Italy, Japan, Korea Rep, Luxembourg, Malaysia, Malta, Netherlands, New Zealand, Norway, Poland, Romania, South Africa, Spain, Sweden, Switzerland, UK, USA. [2019.04.25/XE3998/E]

♦ **EARMA** European Association of Research Managers and Administrators (#06195)
♦ **EARNet** European Auditing Research Network (#06296)
♦ **EARN** European Advanced Recycling Network (#05827)
♦ **EAROC** European Association for Research on Obesity in Childhood (#06196)
♦ EAROPH / see Eastern Regional Organization for Planning and Human Settlements (#05248)
♦ **EAROPH** Eastern Regional Organization for Planning and Human Settlements (#05248)
♦ **EARPA** European Automotive Research Partners Association (#06301)
♦ **EARPTO** East Africa Regulatory Postal and Telecommunications Organization (#05193)
♦ **EARSC** European Association of Remote Sensing Companies (#06190)
♦ **EARSeL** European Association of Remote Sensing Laboratories (#06191)
♦ **EARS-Net** European Antimicrobial Resistance Surveillance Network (#05907)
♦ EARS / see Rett Syndrome Europe (#18928)
♦ EARSS / see European Antimicrobial Resistance Surveillance Network (#05907)
♦ EART – European Association for Reality Therapy (internationally oriented national body)

♦ Earth5R 05158

Contact Raheja Vihar, Chandivali, Mumbai, Maharashtra 400072, Mumbai MAHARASHTRA 400072, India. E-mail: community@earth5r.org.
URL: https://earth5r.org/

History 1 Nov 2014, Mumbai (India). Registration: Registrar of Companies, Mumbai, No/ID: U74900MH2015OPC268255, Start date: 9 Sep 2015, India, Maharashtra. **Aims** Create global circular economy projects, thereby also creating livelihood by restoring local ecosystems worldwide. **Languages** Afrikaans, Arabic, English, Finnish, French, German, Hebrew, Hindi, Indonesian, Italian, Spanish, Thai. **Staff** Voluntary. **Activities** Advocacy/lobbying/activism; awareness raising; projects/programmes. Active in all member countries. [2021.12.02/XM8633/F]

♦ EarthAction (EA) 05159

Exec Dir PO Box 63, Amherst MA 01004, USA. T. +14135498118. Fax +14132568871. E-mail: contact@earthaction.org.
Street Address 44 N Prospect Street, Amherst MA 01002, USA.
Latin American Coordinator c/o Casa de la Paz, Antonia López de Bello 80, Recoleta, Santiago, Santiago Metropolitan, Chile. T. +5626659213. Fax +5626659896.
URL: http://www.earthaction.org/

History Jun 1992, Rio de Janeiro (Brazil). Founded at *United Nations Conference on Environment and Development (UNCED)*, deriving from *EarthAction International (inactive)*. Former names and other names: *EarthAction Network* – alias. Registration: Companies House, No/ID: 02919215, Start date: 14 Apr 1994, End date: 7 Jun 2016, England and Wales; USA; Chile. **Aims** Emphasize issues of global survival in national elections; make government leaders more accountable to world *public opinion* for their decisions on global issues; create pressure for fundamental changes in the international system; empower ordinary voters and global citizens' groups to work on global change. Working through existing organizations, create a global citizens' action network of citizen groups working on environment, development, peace and human rights issues so as to: link citizens and groups in global action; alert concerned members of parliament. As a global network of voters, persuade politicians to work to protect the Earth through: protection of the global environment; combating hunger and poverty; ending militarization and the production of nuclear, chemical and biological weapons; strengthening the capacity of the United Nations to keep the peace, defend human rights and safeguard the atmosphere and oceans. **Structure** Global Steering Committee; International Coordinators; Regional Coordinator in Latin America. **Languages** English, French, Spanish. **Staff** 3.50 FTE, paid; 5.00 FTE, voluntary. **Finance** Sources: members' dues; private foundations. Other Sources: UN agencies, individuals, development agencies. **Activities** Advocacy/lobbying/activism; networking/liaising. **Publications** *Action of the Month* (12 a year) – postcards. *Parliamentary Alert* – recommended questions for members to put to ministers. Action Kit; Editorial Advisory – media briefing package. **Information Services** *Action Alerts* – distributed at least 4 times a year, result in individual activists spending 20 minutes communicating on a global survival issue with a key decision-maker – a national politician, an election candidate, the head of a multinational organization, or a single world leader; *EarthAction Tool Kit* – (4 a year) – focuses on one concrete issue that is or should be on the international agenda and is sent to citizen groups interested in the issue.
Members Civil Society Organizations (over 2,500) in 159 countries and territories:
Albania, Algeria, Angola, Antigua-Barbuda, Argentina, Armenia, Australia, Austria, Azerbaijan, Bahrain, Bangladesh, Barbados, Belarus, Belgium, Belize, Benin, Bermuda, Bolivia, Bosnia-Herzegovina, Botswana, Brazil, Bulgaria, Burkina Faso, Burundi, Cambodia, Cameroon, Canada, Cayman Is, Central African Rep, Chad, Chile, China, Colombia, Comoros, Congo Brazzaville, Congo DR, Costa Rica, Côte d'Ivoire, Croatia, Cuba, Cyprus, Czechia, Denmark, Dominican Rep, Ecuador, Egypt, El Salvador, Estonia, Eswatini, Ethiopia, Fiji, Finland, France, Gabon, Gambia, Georgia, Ghana, Gibraltar, Greece, Grenada, Guatemala, Guinea, Haiti, Honduras, Hong Kong, Hungary, Iceland, India, Indonesia, Iraq, Ireland, Israel, Italy, Jamaica, Japan, Jordan, Kazakhstan, Kenya, Korea Rep, Kyrgyzstan, Laos, Latvia, Lebanon, Liberia, Lithuania, Madagascar, Malawi, Malaysia, Maldives, Mali, Mauritania, Mauritius, Mexico, Morocco, Mozambique, Namibia, Nauru, Nepal, Netherlands, New Caledonia, New Zealand, Nicaragua, Niger, Nigeria, North Macedonia, Northern Ireland, Norway, Oman, Pakistan, Palestine, Panama, Papua New Guinea, Paraguay, Peru, Philippines, Poland, Portugal, Romania, Russia, Rwanda, Senegal, Serbia, Seychelles, Sierra Leone, Singapore, Slovakia, Solomon Is, Somalia, South Africa, Spain, Sri Lanka, St Kitts-Nevis, St Lucia, St Vincent-Grenadines, Sudan, Suriname, Sweden, Switzerland, Taiwan, Tajikistan, Tanzania UR, Thailand, Togo, Trinidad-Tobago, Tunisia, Türkiye, Uganda, UK, Ukraine, United Arab Emirates, Uruguay, USA, Uzbekistan, Vanuatu, Venezuela, Vietnam, Virgin Is USA, Zambia, Zimbabwe.
Included in the above, the following 328 organizations listed in this Yearbook:
- *ABANTU for Development (#00003)*;
- *Abolition 2000 – Global Network to Eliminate Nuclear Weapons (Abolition 2000, #00006)*;
- *ActionAid (#00087)* (Ireland);
- *Action contre le désert (no recent information)*;
- *Action for Solidarity, Equality, Environment and Diversity (A SEED, #00098)*;
- *Action pour le développement – SOS Faim (SOS Faim)*;
- *Advisory Committee on Protection of the Sea (ACOPS, #00139)*;
- *Advocates for Human Rights*;
- *AFREPREN/FWD (#00153)*;
- *African Centre for Environmental Studies (ACES, no recent information)*;
- *African Child Association (ACA, no recent information)*;
- *African Development Fund (ADF, #00285)*;
- *African Forum for Mathematical Ecology (AFME, no recent information)*;
- *African Network for Prevention and Protection Against Child Abuse and Neglect (ANPPCAN, #00393)*;
- *African Office for Development and Cooperation (OFADEC)*;
- *African Peace Network (APNET)*;
- *African Timber Organization (ATO, no recent information)*;
- *African Water Network (AWN, no recent information)*;
- *Agape International Spiritual Center*;
- *AID/WATCH*;
- *AIESEC (#00593)*;
- *All-Africa Students Union (AASU, #00644)*;
- *Alliance Sud, Swiss Alliance of Development Organisations Swissaid – Catholic Lenten Fund – Bread for All – Helvetas – Caritas – Interchurch Aid*;
- *Alternative Action for African Development (AGADA)*;
- *American Friends Service Committee (AFSC)*;
- *AME World Ecology Foundation*;
- *Amnesty International (AI, #00801)*;
- *Andean Institute of Ecology and Development*;
- *Anti-Slavery International (#00860)*;
- *Anuvrat Global Organization (ANUVIBHA)*;
- *APECO Peace and Energy Council (no recent information)*;
- *Arab Office for Youth and Environment (AOYE)*;
- *Arab Organization for Human Rights (AOHR, #01020)*;
- *Arab Society of Environmental Health and Safety (no recent information)*;
- *ARKADAS (no recent information)*;
- *Asian Federation Against Involuntary Disappearances (AFAD, #01453)*;
- *Asociación Andar, Costa Rica (no recent information)*;
- *Associação para a Cooperação e Desenvolvimento (SUL)*;
- *Associação SOS Amazonia*;
- *Association of African Women for Research and Development (AAWORD, #02362)*;
- *Association pour la coopération des Eglises, l'environnement et le développement de l'Afrique centrale (ACEEDAC, no recent information)*;
- *AWARE International*;
- *Baha'i International Community (#03062)*;
- *Biomass Users' Network (BUN, no recent information)*;
- *Campaign for Nuclear Disarmament (CND)*;
- *Canadian Ecumenical Justice Initiatives (KAIROS)*;
- *Care and Relief for the Young (CRY)*;
- *CARE International (CI, #03429)*;
- *Caribbean Association for Feminist Research and Action (CAFRA, #03445)*;
- *Caritas Internationalis (CI, #03580)*;
- *Casa de la Paz, Santiago de Chile*;
- *Center for Action-Oriented Research on African Development (CARAD, no recent information)*;
- *Center for Global Citizens (no recent information)*;
- *Center for Global Environmental Education (CGEE, no recent information)*;
- *Center for International Environmental Law (CIEL)*;
- *Center for UN Reform Education (CURE)*;
- *Centre for Environment and Development in Africa (CEDA, no recent information)*;
- *Centre for International Cooperation (no recent information)*;
- *Centre for International Studies, Nova Scotia (no recent information)*;
- *Centre for International Trade, Economics and Environment (CITEE)*;
- *Centre for Peace and Development, Bangalore*;
- *Centre of People's Aid Blagovest – International Public Charity Organization (CPA Blagovest, no recent information)*;
- *Centre rennais d'information pour le développement et la libération des peuples (CRIDEV)*;
- *Centro Andino de Educación y Promoción 'José Maria Arguedas', Cusco (CADEP-JMA, no recent information)*;
- *Centro de Cooperación Regional para la Educación de Adultos en América Latina y el Caribe (CREFAL, #03794)*;
- *Centro de Estudios Latinoamericanos, México (CELA, no recent information)*;
- *Centro de Estudios para el Desarrollo Andino, Peru (no recent information)*;
- *Centro de Estudios para el Desarrollo de los Pueblos Andinos (CEDPAN, no recent information)*;
- *Centro de Investigación y Promoción Amazónica (CIPA, no recent information)*;
- *Centro Educazione alla Mondialità (CEM)*;
- *Centro Internacional de Información sobre Cultivos de Cobertura (CIDICCO)*;
- *Centro para la Investigación y el Desarrollo Económico y Social de Amazonas (CIDESAM, no recent information)*;
- *Centro Popular para América Latina de Comunicación (CEPALC)*;
- *Children of the Earth (COE)*;
- *Children's Alliance for the Protection of the Environment (CAPE, no recent information)*;
- *Children's Campaign for Nuclear Disarmament (CCND, no recent information)*;
- *Christian Mission Aid (CMA)*;
- *Church of the Brethren*;
- *Citizens for a United Earth (CUE)*;
- *Citizens for Global Solutions*;
- *Climate Action Network (CAN, #03999)*;
- *Coalition for Peace and Reconciliation (CPR, no recent information)*;
- *Commission for Justice and Peace (no recent information)*;
- *Committee for International Self-Reliance (CIS, no recent information)*;
- *Commonweal*;
- *Concern for Development Initiatives in Africa (ForDIA)*;
- *Concern Worldwide*;
- *Concordia*;
- *Confédération des ONG d'environnement et de développement de l'Afrique centrale (CONGAC, #04572)*;
- *Conservation International (CI)*;
- *Consumers International (CI, #04773)*;
- *Consumer Unity and Trust Society (CUTS)*;
- *Coordinadora de las Organizaciones Indígenas de la Cuenca Amazónica (COICA, #04811)*;
- *Coordination et initiatives pour réfugiés et étrangers (CIRE)*;
- *CORSO (no recent information)*;
- *Council for a Livable World Education Fund (CLWEF, no recent information)*;
- *Council for Economic Empowerment of Women in Africa (CEEWA, no recent information)*;
- *Dallas Peace Center*;
- *Danube Delta Friends – Foundation Sulina (no recent information)*;
- *Deutsche Stiftung Weltbevölkerung (DSW)*;
- *Development Innovations and Networks (#05057)*;
- *Dialogue and Cooperation (#05066)*;
- *Dialogue Institute*;
- *EarthCare Africa (ECAF)*;
- *Earth Day Network (EDN, #05164)*;
- *Earthlands International (no recent information)*;
- *Earthlife Africa (ELA)*;
- *EarthVoice*;
- *Earthways Foundation* (Atomic Mirror Project);
- *East African Communities' Organization for Management of Lake Victoria (ECOVic, no recent information)*;
- *Eastern Africa Association of ARI Graduates (EAAG, no recent information)*;
- *Eastern Africa Environmental Network (EAEN, #05221)*;
- *Ecumenical Movement for Justice and Peace (no recent information)*;
- *Energy and Environment Group (see: #20292)*;
- *Environment Liaison Centre International (ELCI, no recent information)*;
- *Environnement et développement du Tiers-monde (enda, #05510)*;
- *European Commission (EC, #06633)*;
- *European Coordination, International Young Catholic Students – International Movement of Catholic Students (European Coordination IYCS-IMCS, inactive)*;
- *European ECO Forum (#06955)*;
- *European Environmental Bureau (EEB, #06996)*;
- *European Environmental Centre, Warsaw*;
- *Evangelical Lutheran Church in America (ELCA)*;
- *Findhorn Foundation (#09774)* (Ecology Building Programme);
- *Fondation internationale pour le développement économique et social, Paris (FINDES)*;
- *Fondation internationale pour le développement (FID, no recent information)*;
- *Forum maghrébin pour l'environnement et le développement*;
- *Forum of African Voluntary Development Organizations (FAVDO, inactive)*;
- *Foundation for African Women's Advancement (FAWA, no recent information)*;
- *Foundation for Peace Studies Aotearoa/New Zealand*;
- *Foundation for Sustainable Development, Padasjoki (no recent information)*;
- *Foundation of the Peoples of the South Pacific International (FSPI, #09968)*;
- *France Volontaires*;
- *Friends of the Earth International (FoEI, #10002)*;
- *Friends of the Third World*;
- *Friends of the United Nations (FUN)*;
- *Fundación Ecológica Universal (FEU, no recent information)*;
- *Future in Our Hands (FIOH, #10050)*;
- *Gaia Network (no recent information)*;
- *General Arab Women Federation (GAWF, no recent information)*;
- *Global Justice Now*;
- *Global Ministries of The United Methodist Church (GM-UMC)*;
- *Global Resource Action Center for the Environment (GRACE)*;
- *Global Resource Bank (GRB)*;
- *GLOBE International (#10668)*;
- *Green Cross International (GCI, #10715)*;
- *Green Earth Foundation*;
- *Green Earth Organization (GEO, inactive)*;
- *Green Help International, Kiev (no recent information)*;
- *Greenpeace International (#10727)*;

EarthAction
05159

alphabetic sequence excludes
For the complete listing, see Yearbook Online at

- *Habitat International Coalition (HIC, #10845)*;
- *Human Rights Watch (HRW, #10990)*;
- *Human Rights without Frontiers International (HRWF, #10983)*;
- *Indian Institute for Peace, Disarmament and Environmental Protection (IIPDEP)*;
- *Information Bureau for Peace Work*;
- *Institute for Development, Environment and Peace (Vitae Civilis)*;
- *Institute for Sustainable Rural Development Foundation (ISSRI)*;
- *Institute of Development Studies, Jaipur*;
- *Institute of Global Education*;
- *Instituto Centroamericano de Educación, Nicaragua (no recent information)*;
- *Instituto del Tercer Mundo, Montevideo (ITEM)*;
- *Inter-American Legal Services Association (ILSA, #11439)*;
- *Interfaith Center for Peace and Justice, Gettysburg PA*;
- *International Alert (#11615)*;
- *International Association for Democracy in Africa (#11836)*;
- *International Association for Religious Freedom (IARF, #12130)*;
- *International Association of Democratic Lawyers (IADL, #11837)*;
- *International Association of Educators for World Peace (IAEWP)*;
- *International Center for Law in Development (ICLD)*;
- *International Centre for Environmental Social and Policy Studies (ICESPS)*;
- *International Centre for Study and Development, Kerala (ICSD, no recent information)*;
- *International Centre for Tropical Agriculture (#12527)*;
- *International Circle for the Promotion of the Creation (#12575)*;
- *International Commission of Jurists (ICJ, #12695)*;
- *International Development, UEA*;
- *International Doctors – ILDAV (#13186)*;
- *International Federation of Red Cross and Red Crescent Societies (#13526)*;
- *International Federation of Women Lawyers (FIDA, #13578)*;
- *International Fellowship of Reconciliation (IFOR, #13586)*;
- *International Institute for Human Rights, Environment and Development (INHURED International, #13886)*;
- *International Institute for Sustainable Development (IISD, #13930)*;
- *International Institute for Sustainable Future, Mumbai (IISFB, no recent information)*;
- *International Institute for the Urban Environment (IIUE)*;
- *International Juridical Organization for Environment and Development (IJO, no recent information)*;
- *International Peace Bureau (IPB, #14535)*;
- *International Rivers*;
- *Internationals amis de la nature (IAN, #14780)*;
- *International Service Society (no recent information)*;
- *International Society for Human Rights (ISHR, #15183)*;
- *International Society for Preservation of the Tropical Rainforest (ISPTR, #15384)*;
- *International Society of Doctors for the Environment (ISDE, #15065)*;
- *International Task Force for the Rural Poor (INTAF, #15656)*;
- *International Union for Conservation of Nature and Natural Resources (IUCN, #15766)*;
- *International Voluntary Service, UK (IVS)*;
- *International Waterlogging and Salinity Research Institute (IWASRI)*;
- *International Wildlife Coalition (IWC, inactive)*;
- *International Youth Civic Association*;
- *Islamic Society for International Unity and Peace (ISIUP, no recent information)*;
- *John E Mack Institute*;
- *La main tendue*;
- *Latin American Center of Social Ecology (#16292)*;
- *Latin American Centre for Development Administration (#16294)*;
- *Lawyers Committee on Nuclear Policy (LCNP)*;
- *Learning for Life (LFL)*;
- *Life-Link Friendship-Schools*;
- *Limbless Swimmers International (no recent information)*;
- *Lutheran Office for World Community*;
- *Lutheran World Relief (LWR)*;
- *Maryknoll Sisters of Saint Dominic* (Office for Global Concerns);
- *Maryland United for Peace and Justice (MUPJ)*;
- *Meadows International (no recent information)*;
- *Missionary Sisters of the Immaculate Conception (MIC)*;
- *Near East Foundation (NEF)*;
- *New Global Freedom Movement (no recent information)*;
- *NOAH International*;
- *Nonviolence International (NI, #17152)*;
- *Nordic Folkecenter for Renewable Energy*;
- *Norwegian Peace Council*;
- *Nuclear Age Peace Foundation*;
- *Ohdake Foundation*;
- *OneWorld International Foundation (OWIF, #17738)*;
- *Oxfam Australia*;
- *Oxfam International (#17922)*;
- *Oxfam Novib*;
- *Pace Peace Center (PPC, no recent information)*;
- *Pacific Concerns Resource Centre (PCRC)*;
- *Pacific Institute for Women's Health (PIWH)*;
- *PAI (#18025)*;
- *Pakistan Futuristics Foundation and Institute (PFI)*;
- *Pan African Association for Community Development (PADEC, no recent information)*;
- *Pan-African Reconciliation Council (PARC, #18063)*;
- *Pan African Women's Organization (PAWO, #18074)*;
- *Panos Network (#18183)*;
- *Parliamentarians for Global Action (PGA, #18208)*;
- *Partners for Development (PFD)*;
- *Partners for Peace and the Protection of the Environment (no recent information)*;
- *PAX*;
- *Pax Christi – International Catholic Peace Movement (#18266)*;
- *Paz y Cooperación*;
- *Peace Action Education Fund (PAEF)*;
- *Peace Action Network (PAN)*;
- *Peace and Disarmament Society of Kerala*;
- *Peace and Justice Studies Association (PJSA)*;
- *Peace Child International (PCI, #18278)*;
- *Peace Committee of Lapland*;
- *Peace Corps*;
- *Peace Corps Service (no recent information)*;
- *Peace Farm*;
- *Peace House*;
- *Peace Resource Center of San Diego*;
- *Peace Roundtable*;
- *Peace Trust*;
- *Peaceworks*;
- *Perhaps Kids Meeting Kids can make a Difference (KMK)*;
- *Pesticide Action Network (PAN, #18336)*;
- *Planetary Citizens' Council for Peace, Development and the Environment (no recent information)*;
- *Population Institute (PI)*;
- *Pro-Natura International (#16951)*;
- *PROTERRA (no recent information)*;
- *Rainforest Action Network (RAN, #18614)*;
- *Rainforest Foundation International (RFI, #18615)*;
- *Refugees International (RI)*;
- *Registre des Citoyens du Monde (RICM, #18822)*;
- *Rencontre africaine pour la défense des droits de l'homme (RADDHO)*;
- *Resource Africa*;
- *Rettet den Regenwald (RdR)*;
- *Rodale Institute (RI)*;
- *Ryan Foundation International*;
- *Sahel défis – développement et environnement, formation et insertion sociale (inactive)*;
- *Sahel Solidarity (no recent information)*;
- *Samburu Aid in Africa (SAIDIA, no recent information)*;
- *Sarvodaya Shramadana Movement (SSM)*;
- *Save the Children Federation (SCF)*;
- *School for International Training (SIT)*;
- *Secours catholique – Caritas France*;
- *Service Civil International (SCI, #19238)*;
- *Seva Foundation (SF)*;
- *Sierra Club International Program (#19266)*;
- *Sisters of St Francis of Philadelphia*;
- *SNV Netherlands Development Organisation (SNV)*;
- *Society for Development Alternatives*;
- *Solidaridad Internacional (SI)*;
- *Solidarité*;
- *Soroptimist International (SI, #19686)*;
- *South Asian Institute for Peace Studies (SAIPS, no recent information)*;
- *The United Methodist Church (UMC, #20514)*;
- *Topeka Center for Peace and Justice*;
- *TRANSCEND-A Peace Development Environment Network (#20206)*;
- *Transnational Perspectives (TP, no recent information)*;
- *Traprock Peace Center*;
- *Tropical Botanic Garden and Research Institute*;
- *TVE International*;
- *United Nations Information Centres (UNICs, #20574)*;
- *Universal Alliance (UA, #20671)*;
- *US Overseas Cooperative Development Council (OCDC)*;
- *Veterans for Peace (VFP)*;
- *Vineyard International Consortium (VIC, #20778)*;
- *Vivekananda International Health Centre (no recent information)*;
- *War and Peace Foundation*;
- *West and Central African Association of Soil Science (WCAASS, no recent information)*;
- *Women and Children International (WCI, no recent information)*;
- *Women for a Meaningful Summit (no recent information)*;
- *Women International Association for Communication – Mediterranean Media*;
- *Women's Environment and Development Organization (WEDO, #21016)*;
- *Women's Federation for World Peace International (WFWPI)*;
- *Women's International League for Peace and Freedom (WILPF, #21024)*;
- *World Alliance of Young Men's Christian Associations (YMCA, #21090)* (Canada);
- *World Assembly of Youth (WAY, #21113)*;
- *World Association for Christian Communication (WACC, #21126)*;
- *World Association of Girl Guides and Girl Scouts (WAGGGS, #21142)*;
- *World Civil Society Forum (WCSF, #21278)*;
- *World Constitution and Parliament Association (WCPA, #21313)*;
- *World Energy Council (WEC, #21381)*;
- *World Federalist Movement – Movement for a Just World Order through a Strengthened United Nations (WFM, #21404)*;
- *World Federation of Democratic Youth (WFDY, #21427)*;
- *World Federation of UNESCO Clubs, Centres and Associations (WFUCA, #21498)*;
- *World Future Society (WFS, #21534)*;
- *World Game Institute (WGI, inactive)*;
- *World Neighbors (WN)*;
- *World Party Association (no recent information)*;
- *World Renew*;
- *World Society for Ekistics (WSE, #21801)*;
- *Worldview International Foundation (WIF, #21903)*;
- *WorldViews (inactive)*;
- *World Vision International (WVI, #21904)*;
- *World Wide Fund for Nature (WWF, #21922)*;
- *World Young Women's Christian Association (World YWCA, #21947)*;
- *WSM*;
- *Youth for Unity and Voluntary Action (YUVA)*.

Consultative Status Consultative status granted from: *UNEP (#20299)*; *United Nations Population Fund (UNFPA, #20612)*. **IGO Relations** Accredited by (1): *United Nations Framework Convention on Climate Change – Secretariat (UNFCCC, #20564)*. Accredited to the Conference of the Parties of: *Secretariat of the United Nations Convention to Combat Desertification (Secretariat of the UNCCD, #19208)*. Associated with Department of Global Communications of the United Nations. **NGO Relations** Represented on the Organizing Committee of: *Hague Appeal for Peace (HAP, #10848)*. [2023.02.20/XF1672/y/**F**]

♦ EarthAction Network / see EarthAction (#05159)

♦ Earth Association for Regression Therapy (EARTh) 05160

Exec Sec Lanterdweg 15, 5995 SC Kessel-Eik, Netherlands.
URL: http://www.earth-association.org/

History 23 Aug 2006, Frankfurt-Main (Germany), as *European Association for Regression Therapy*. **Events** *Annual Convention* Kleve (Germany) 2010, *Annual convention / Convention* Kleve (Germany) 2010, *Annual Convention* Kleve (Germany) 2009, *Annual convention / Convention* Istanbul (Turkey) 2007, *Annual convention / Convention* Frankfurt-Main (Germany) 2006. **Members** Individuals (150) in 15 countries. Membership countries not specified. [2019/XJ8155/**D**]

♦ EarthCare Africa (internationally oriented national body)
♦ Earthcare Africa Monitoring Institute / see EarthCare Africa
♦ Earth Champions Foundation (unconfirmed)
♦ Earth Charter Associates Ltd / see Earth Charter International (#05161)

♦ Earth Charter International (ECI) 05161

Exec Dir c/o University for Peace, PO Box 138-6100, San José, San José, San José, 10701, Costa Rica. T. +50622059060. Fax +50622491929. E-mail: info@earthcharter.org.
URL: http://www.earthcharter.org/

History Originated in the 1987 call of *World Commission on Environment and Development (WCED, inactive)* – Brundtland Commission, for a "new charter". Initiative to develop an *Earth Charter* launched 1994, by Maurice Strong and Mikhail Gorbachev, working through their respective organizations: *Earth Council Alliance (ECA, inactive)* – then Earth Council; *Green Cross International (GCI, #10715)*. Independent *Earth Charter Commission* set up 1997 to oversee development. First Benchmark Draft of Earth Charter released, Mar 1997; Benchmark Draft II released, Apr 1999; consensus on Earth Charter reached, Mar 2000, Paris (France), following which Earth Charter was formally launched, The Hague (Netherlands). Former names and other names: *Earth Charter Associates Ltd* – legal name. Registration: USA, New York. **Aims** Contribute to the transition to sustainable ways of living by offering learning opportunities for young leaders, educators, business executives and others to enhance their capacity to influence change towards a more just, sustainable, and peaceful world. **Structure** Council; Board; Earth Charter Education Center; Secretariat; Network of Affiliates and Action Groups; Youth Network; Commission; Advisors. **Languages** English, French, Portuguese, Spanish. **Staff** 4.00 FTE, paid; 3.00 FTE, voluntary. **Finance** Sources: contributions; donations; grants; in-kind support; revenue from activities/projects. Annual budget: 308,033 USD. **Activities** Advocacy/lobbying/activism; awareness raising; events/meetings; publishing activities; training/education. **Events** *Conference* The Hague (Netherlands) 2010. **Publications** *Newsflash* (6-12 a year). Annual Report; handbooks; guides. Information Services: Virtual library and bibliography.

Members Individuals and organizations in 73 countries and territories:
Argentina, Armenia, Australia, Austria, Bahrain, Belarus, Bolivia, Brazil, Bulgaria, Burkina Faso, Burundi, Cameroon, Canada, Chile, China, Colombia, Congo Brazzaville, Congo DR, Costa Rica, Denmark, Dominican Rep, Ecuador, Egypt, Ethiopia, Finland, France, Gambia, Germany, Ghana, Greece, Greenland, Guatemala, Honduras, Hungary, India, Italy, Japan, Jordan, Kazakhstan, Kenya, Korea Rep, Kyrgyzstan, Latvia, Malaysia, Mauritius, Mexico, Nepal, Netherlands, New Zealand, Nigeria, Norway, Panama, Peru, Philippines, Portugal, Romania, Russia, Saudi Arabia, Seychelles, Sierra Leone, South Africa, Spain, Sweden, Tajikistan, Tatarstan, Thailand, Uganda, UK, United Arab Emirates, USA, Uzbekistan, Venezuela, Zambia.

Consultative Status Consultative status granted from: *UNEP (#20299)* (Observer – Accredited as an observer); *ECOSOC (#05331)* (Special). **IGO Relations** Partner of (4): *ECOSOC (#05331)*; *UNEP (#20299)*; *UNESCO (#20322)*; *University for Peace (UPEACE, #20702)*. **NGO Relations** Member of (2): *Global Methane Initiative (GMI, #10471)* (Project Network); *Wellbeing Economy Alliance (WEAll, #20856)*. Cooperates with (4): *Economy for the Common Good (ECG, #05323)*; *Global Reporting Initiative (GRI, #10567)*; *Social Development International (SDI)*; *Soka Gakkai International (SGI, #19672)*. [2021.05.19/XF7087/**F**]

♦ **Earth Child Institute (ECI)** **05162**
Dir address not obtained. E-mail: info@earthchildinstitute.org.
URL: http://www.earthchildinstitute.org/
History Registered in accordance with US law: 20-0419094. **Aims** Engage with and empower children and *young people* to combat *climate change*, *deforestation* and *water* scarcity. **Structure** Board; Advisory Board. **Languages** English, Japanese, Portuguese. **Finance** Grants and donations from private citizens and foundations; corporate sponsorship. **Consultative Status** Consultative status granted from: *ECOSOC (#05331)* (Special). **IGO Relations** Partners and affiliates include: *UNICEF (#20332)*; *United Nations (UN, #20515)*; *United Nations Framework Convention on Climate Change (UNFCCC, 1992)*. Associated with the Department of Global Communications of the United Nations. **NGO Relations** Member of: *United Nations Global Compact (#20567)*. Partner of: *British Council*; *Global Call for Climate Action (GCCA, inactive)*; *World Association of Girl Guides and Girl Scouts (WAGGGS, #21142)*. [2019/XJ5542/j/F]

♦ **Earth Commission** **05163**
Secretariat Future Earth, Global Hub Sweden, c/o Royal Swedish Academy, Box 50005, SE-104 05 Stockholm, Sweden.
URL: https://earthcommission.org/
History Founded Sep 2019, as an initiative of *Future Earth (#10048)* and part of *Global Commons Alliance*. **Aims** Provide a scientific synthesis to identify thresholds for, and pathways to preserve, the stability and resilience of the Global Commons – shared land, water, atmosphere and biodiversity that are critical to supporting life on Earth. **Structure** Core Group; Working Groups. **Languages** English. **Staff** 10.00 FTE, paid. **Finance** Funding from: *Global Environment Facility (GEF, #10346)*; *Porticus*; *Oak Foundation*; *MAVA Foundation*; Gordon and Betty Moore Foundation. **Activities** Research/documentation; knowledge management/information dissemination. **Events** *Meeting* Washington, DC (USA) 2019.
Members Scientists from 12 countries:
Argentina, Australia, Austria, China, France, Germany, Ghana, India, Japan, Kenya, Netherlands, USA.
NGO Relations *Science Based Targets Network*. [2020.03.11/XM8563/E]

♦ Earth Community Organization / see Global Community Earth Government
♦ Earthcorps (internationally oriented national body)
♦ Earth Council (internationally oriented national body)

♦ **Earth Day Network (EDN)** **05164**
Office 1616 P St NW, Ste 340, Washington DC 20036, USA. T. +12025180044. Fax +12025188794. E-mail: communications@earthday.org.
URL: http://www.earthday.org/
History as an international committee for celebrating the Earth day. Registered in the State of New York. **Structure** International Council of 28 members. **Members** Groups (about 3,200) in 166 countries. Membership countries not specified. **Consultative Status** Consultative status granted from: *ECOSOC (#05331)* (Special); *UNEP (#20299)*. **NGO Relations** Member of: *Environmental Paper Network (EPN, #05507)*; *EarthAction (EA, #05159)*; *Freshwater Action Network (FAN, inactive)*; *GEF CSO Network (GCN, #10087)*; *International Union for Conservation of Nature and Natural Resources (IUCN, #15766)*. Support from: *Arca Foundation*. Cooperates with: *Global Call for Climate Action (GCCA, inactive)*; *1% for the Planet*. [2014/XF5551/F]

♦ Earth Defenders / see Defensores do Planeta
♦ **EARTh** Earth Association for Regression Therapy (#05160)
♦ EarthEcho International (internationally oriented national body)
♦ Earth Economics (internationally oriented national body)
♦ Earth Energy – Europäische Plattform für die Gewinnung unterirdischer Energie "Earth Energy" (unconfirmed)
♦ **EARTH** European Alliance of Responsible Tourism and Hospitality (#05880)
♦ Earth Federation Movement (see: #21313)
♦ Earth First (internationally oriented national body)
♦ Earth Focus Foundation (internationally oriented national body)
♦ Earth Force Society / see Sea Shepherd International
♦ Earth-Friendly Schools Hawaii-International (see: #18312)

♦ **Earth Innovation Institute** **05165**
Exec Dir 98 Battery Str, Suite 250, San Francisco CA 94111, USA. T. +14154499900.
URL: https://earthinnovation.org/
History Founded 2010, as a US 501 (c)3 non-profit, registered in the State of California (USA). Originally an International Program of *Instituto de Pesquisa Ambiental da Amazônia (IPAM)*. Became independent, 2013. **Aims** Advance climate-friendly rural development through innovative approaches to sustainable farming, forestry and fisheries in tropical regions around the world. **Structure** Board of Directors. **Activities** Networking/liaising; events/meetings; projects/programmes. **NGO Relations** Partner of: *Tropical Forest Alliance (TFA, #20249)*. Member of: *Global Roundtable for Sustainable Beef (GRSB, #10583)*. [2019/XM8964/E]

♦ Earth Institute at Columbia University (internationally oriented national body)
♦ Earth Island Institute (internationally oriented national body)
♦ Earthjustice (internationally oriented national body)
♦ Earthjustice Legal Defense Fund / see Earthjustice
♦ Earth Law Alliance (unconfirmed)
♦ Earth Law Center (internationally oriented national body)

♦ **Earth League International** **05166**
Exec Dir PO Box 661623, Los Angeles CA 90066, USA. E-mail: info@earthleagueinternational.org.
URL: https://earthleagueinternational.org/
History 2013, Los Angeles, CA (USA). Former names and other names: *Elephant Action League (EAL)* – former (2013 to 2019). Registration: 501(c)(3), USA. **Aims** Protect wildlife, forests, and oceans through effective intelligence collection and investigative actions, and cooperation with key governmental agencies. **Structure** Board. **Languages** English. **Activities** Advocacy/lobbying/activism; awareness raising; capacity building; knowledge management/information dissemination; monitoring/evaluation; research/documentation; training/education. Active in all member countries. **Publications** Reports; case studies. **IGO Relations** Key national and international government agencies. **NGO Relations** Like-minded NGOs. [2020.05.09/XJ8376/F]

♦ Earth Liberation Front (internationally oriented national body)
♦ Earthlife Africa (internationally oriented national body)
♦ Earth Link (internationally oriented national body)
♦ Earthmind (internationally oriented national body)
♦ Earth Observing System (internationally oriented national body)
♦ Earth Partners / see Earth Partners Foundation
♦ Earth Partners Foundation (internationally oriented national body)
♦ Earth Partners Trust / see Earth Partners Foundation
♦ EarthPercent (unconfirmed)

♦ **Earthquakes and Megacities Initiative (EMI)** **05167**
Exec Dir 3F Puno Annex Bldg, 47 Kalayaan Avenue, Diliman, 1101 Quezon City, Philippines. T. +63289279643. E-mail: info@emi-megacities.org.
URL: https://emi-megacities.org/
History 1998. Set up as a non-profit 2003, Philippines. Registration: Securities and Exchange Commission, No/ID: CN200324851, Start date: 23 Dec 2022, Philippines, Metro Manila. **Aims** Advance knowledge, policy, and practice of urban disaster risk reduction, particularly focusing on megacities and fast-growing metropolises. **Structure** Board of Trustees; Secretariat. **Languages** English. **Staff** 7.00 FTE, paid. Also Associated Experts. **Finance** Sources: fees for services; international organizations. **Activities** Active in: Bangladesh, India, Jordan, Myanmar, Nepal, Philippines, Türkiye. **Consultative Status** Consultative status granted from: *ECOSOC (#05331)* (Special). [2023.03.01/XJ9766/F]

♦ Earthrace Charitable Trust / see Earthrace Conservation (#05168)

♦ **Earthrace Conservation** **05168**
Founder 237 Te Rongo Rd, RD4 Parua Bay, Whangarei 0174, New Zealand.
USA Office 23661 Summit Dr, Calabasas CA 91302-2033, USA.
URL: https://www.earthrace.net/
History Founded by Peter James Bethune (1965-). Former names and other names: *Earthrace Charitable Trust* – legal name; *Earthrace Conservation Organization* – legal name. Registration: Charity, No/ID: EAR53359, New Zealand; Incorporated Society, No/ID: 1290805, New Zealand; 501(c)3, No/ID: 46-1361707, USA. **Aims** Identify *marine conservation* issues, and intervene where and when necessary to protect and defend threatened marine *ecosystems* world-wide. **Structure** Executive Board. Virtual office.
Members Chapters in 7 countries:
Argentina, Australia, Denmark, New Zealand, Sweden, UK, USA.
NGO Relations Member of: *World Cetacean Alliance (WCA, #21268)*. [2020/XJ6575/F]

♦ Earthrace Conservation Organization / see Earthrace Conservation (#05168)
♦ Earth Restoration Service (internationally oriented national body)
♦ Earth Rights Institute (internationally oriented national body)
♦ EarthRights International (internationally oriented national body)
♦ Earthsave International (internationally oriented national body)

♦ **Earth Science Matters Foundation (ESM)** **05169**
Deputy Dir address not obtained. E-mail: director@earthsciencematters.org – secretariat@earthsciencematters.org.
URL: http://www.earthsciencematters.org/
History 17 Dec 2010, Wageningen (Netherlands), as *The Planet Earth Institute*, as an outcome of the International Year of Planet Earth (IYPE). Registered in accordance with Dutch law. **Aims** Make the lives of future generations around the world healthier, safer and more prosperous by promoting smart, earth science-based solutions. **Structure** Board, including Chair. Secretariat. **Activities** Meeting activities. **NGO Relations** Partners include: *Geological Society of Africa (GSAf, #10135)*; *International Lithosphere Program (ILP, #14059)*; *International Association for Mathematical Geosciences (IAMG, #12017)*; *ISRIC – World Soil Information (#16068)*; *Promoting Earth Science for Society (YES Network, #18541)*. Member of: *International Union of Geological Sciences (IUGS, #15777)*. [2016/XJ7372/t/F]

♦ Earth Security Group / see Earth Security Initiative
♦ Earth Security Initiative (internationally oriented national body)
♦ Earth Share (internationally oriented national body)
♦ Earth Society Foundation (internationally oriented national body)
♦ EarthSpark International (internationally oriented national body)
♦ Earthstewards Network (internationally oriented national body)
♦ Earth Train Foundation (internationally oriented national body)
♦ Earthtrust (internationally oriented national body)

♦ **EARTH University** **05170**
Contact Apartado 4442-1000, San José, San José, San José, Costa Rica. T. +50627130000. Fax +50627130001.
URL: http://www.earth.ac.cr/
History 1986. Registered in accordance with Costa Rican law. **Aims** Prepare *leaders* with *ethical* values to contribute to the *sustainable* development of the humid *tropics* and construct a prosperous and just society. **Structure** Board of Directors, comprising President, Vice-President and 8 members. Board of Trustees; Foundation Board of Trustees; President's Advisory Board; President's Young Advisory Board. **Finance** Support from: Costa Rican government; *United States Agency for International Development (USAID)*; *W K Kellogg Foundation (WKKF)*. **Consultative Status** Consultative status granted from: *UNEP (#20299)*. **NGO Relations** Member of: *Global Confederation of Higher Education Associations for Agriculture and Life Sciences (GCHERA, #10304)*. [2012/XJ6113/F]

♦ EarthVoice (internationally oriented national body)
♦ Earthwatch (inactive)
♦ Earthwatch Europe (internationally oriented national body)
♦ Earth Watch Europe, Oxford / see Earthwatch Europe

♦ **Earthwatch Institute** **05171**
Earthwatch USA 114 Western Ave, Boston MA 02134, USA. T. +19784610081. Fax +19784612332. E-mail: info@earthwatch.org.
URL: http://www.earthwatch.org/
History 1972, Belmont MA (USA), as *Educational Expeditions International (EEI)*. Subsequently referred to as *Earthwatch, USA*. **Aims** Engage people worldwide in scientific field research and education to promote understanding and action necessary for a sustainable environment. **Structure** Regional offices (4): *Earthwatch Europe*; Boston MA (USA); Melbourne (Australia); Tokyo (Japan). **Finance** Participants' project fees (including contribution to research costs); foundations; trusts; donations; corporate partnerships. **Activities** Projects/programmes; training/education. **Events** *International Conference* Boston, MA (USA) 1998, *Annual Conference* USA 1987, *Annual Conference* USA 1986. **Publications** *Earthwatch Newsletter*. **Members** Mainly in USA and UK. Membership countries not specified. **NGO Relations** Member of: *InsideNGO (inactive)*; *Natural Capital Coalition (NCC, #16952)*. [2018.07.05/XE3332/j/F]

♦ Earthwatch, USA / see Earthwatch Institute (#05171)
♦ Earthways Foundation (internationally oriented national body)
♦ Earthworks (internationally oriented national body)

♦ **Earthworm Foundation** **05172**
CEO Chemin de Chantavril 2, 1260 Nyon VD, Switzerland. T. +41223679440. E-mail: info@earthworm.org.
URL: http://www.earthworm.org/
History 1999, as *Tropical Forest Trust*. Subsequently also referred to as *The Forest Trust*. Current title adopted 2019. **Aims** Bring transformation in commodity *supply* chains to benefit people and the planet. **Structure** Board; Executive Team. **Languages** English. **Staff** 220 full-time and part-time. **Finance** Members' dues. Donations. **Activities** Guidance/assistance/consulting; knowledge management/information dissemination; advocacy/lobbying/activism. **Publications** *Earthworm Foundation newsletter*. Guides; reports. **Members** Companies. Membership countries not specified. **NGO Relations** *Synchronicity Earth*; *Tropical Forest Alliance (TFA, #20249)*. [2020.03.10/XM6806/f/F]

♦ **EARTO** European Association of Research and Technology Organizations (#06197)
♦ **EAS** / see European Academy of Sciences (#05813)
♦ **EASAA** European Association for South Asian Archaeology and Art (#06214)
♦ EASAAP – European Association on the Study of Acute Abdominal Pain (inactive)
♦ EASA – Assemblée européenne des étudiants en architecture (meeting series)
♦ **EASAC** European Academies' Science Advisory Council (#05778)
♦ **EAS** Action Plan for the Protection and Development of the Marine Environment and Coastal Areas of the East Asian Region (#00093)
♦ **EASA** European Academy of Sciences and Arts (#05814)
♦ **EASA** European Advertising Standards Alliance (#05829)
♦ **EASA** European Association of Social Anthropologists (#06209)
♦ **EASA** European Association for Studies of Australia (#06226)
♦ **EASA** European Union Aviation Safety Agency (#08978)
♦ **EASAPS** European Association of Societies of Aesthetic Plastic Surgery (#06211)
♦ **EASAR** European Association for Substance Abuse Research (#06238)
♦ **EASAS** European Association for South Asian Studies (#06215)
♦ EASA – South-East Asia Shariah Association (inactive)
♦ EASBH – East Asian Society of British History (unconfirmed)
♦ EASBRIG / see Eastern Africa Standby Force (#05227)
♦ EASC – East Asian Studies Center, Bloomington (internationally oriented national body)

- ♦ **EASC** EuroAsian Interstate Council for Standardization, Metrology and Certification (#05639)
- ♦ EASC – European Air Shippers' Council (inactive)
- ♦ **EASC** European Association for Supervision and Coaching (#06240)
- ♦ EASD / see Environmental Ambassadors for Sustainable Development
- ♦ **EASDEC** European Association for the Study of Diabetic Eye Complications (#06229)
- ♦ EASD – European Association of Securities Dealers (inactive)
- ♦ **EASD** European Association for Structural Dynamics (#06225)
- ♦ **EASD** European Association for the Study of Diabetes (#06228)
- ♦ **EASD** European Association for the Study of Dreams (#06230)
- ♦ EASDP – European Association of Search and Database Publishing (inactive)
- ♦ EAS – The Dual Career Network / see European Athlete Student Network (#06290)
- ♦ **EASEA** European Alliance for the Statute of the European Association (#05886)
- ♦ E-ASEAN Framework Agreement (2000 treaty)
- ♦ EASEC / see Asian and Oceanian Stock Exchanges Federation (#01585)
- ♦ EASEC – East Asian Stock Exchange Conference (meeting series)
- ♦ EASEC – East Asia-Pacific Conference on Structural Engineering and Construction (meeting series)
- ♦ **EASE** East-Asian Association for Science Education (#05197)
- ♦ **EASE** East Asian Society of Endourology (#05208)
- ♦ **EASEE-gas** European Association for the Streamlining of Energy Exchange-gas (#06224)
- ♦ **EASE** European Association of Science Editors (#06201)
- ♦ EASE – European Association for Special Education (no recent information)
- ♦ **EASE** European Association of Sport Employers (#06218)
- ♦ **EASE** European Association for Storage of Energy (#06223)
- ♦ EASE – European Association for the Support of TV Programmes Exports (no recent information)
- ♦ EASE – International Conference on Evaluation and Assessment in Software Engineering (meeting series)
- ♦ **EAS** Europe Air Sports (#05776)
- ♦ **EAS** European Aerobiology Society (#05833)
- ♦ **EAS** European Aligner Society (#05858)
- ♦ EAS – European Allelopathy Society (no recent information)
- ♦ **EAS** European Aquaculture Society (#05909)
- ♦ **EAS** European Association for Music in Schools (#06127)
- ♦ EAS – European Association SIBIU2020 for Education and Culture (unconfirmed)
- ♦ EAS / see European Association for Supervision and Coaching (#06240)
- ♦ **EAS** European Astronomical Society (#06288)
- ♦ **EAS** European Atherosclerosis Society (#06289)
- ♦ **EAS** European Athlete Student Network (#06290)
- ♦ EAS / see European School of Administration (#08427)
- ♦ EAS – Europese Associatie voor Samenwerking (inactive)
- ♦ **EASF** East Asian Squash Federation (#05210)
- ♦ **EASF** Eastern Africa Standby Force (#05227)
- ♦ EASFP / see European Association for Passive Fire Protection (#06143)
- ♦ **EASG** European Association for the Study of Gambling (#06231)
- ♦ EASH – Europäische Akademie, Schleswig Holstein (internationally oriented national body)
- ♦ EASHW / see European Agency for Safety and Health at Work (#05843)
- ♦ EASI – European Association for Shipping Informatics (inactive)
- ♦ EASIM / see International Association for Spectral Imaging (#12176)
- ♦ EASIU – East Asian Spa Industry Union (unconfirmed)
- ♦ EASK – European Association for Skills and Knowledge (inactive)
- ♦ **EASLCE** European Association for the Study of Literature, Culture and Environment (#06232)
- ♦ EASL – Ecole de bibliothécaires d'Afrique de l'Est / see East African School of Library and Information Science (#05188)
- ♦ **EASL** European Association of Sinological Librarians (#06206)
- ♦ **EASL** European Association for the Study of the Liver (#06233)
- ♦ **EASLHE** European Association of Service-Learning in Higher Education (#06203)
- ♦ **EASLIS** East African School of Library and Information Science (#05188)
- ♦ EASMA / see SMA Europe (#19310)
- ♦ **EASM** European Association for Sport Management (#06219)
- ♦ EASM – European Association of Syrups Producers (inactive)
- ♦ **EASN** European Aeronautics Science Network (#05835)
- ♦ EASOB – European Association for the Study of Bioprostheses (inactive)
- ♦ **EASO** European Association for the Study of Obesity (#06234)
- ♦ EASO / see European Union Agency for Asylum (#08968)
- ♦ **EASOM** European Association of Schools of Occupational Medicine (#06199)
- ♦ EAS – Oxford University European Affairs Society (internationally oriented national body)
- ♦ **EASPA** European Alliance of Subject-Specific and Professional Accreditation and Quality Assurance (#05887)
- ♦ **EASPD** European Association of Service Providers for Persons with Disabilities (#06204)
- ♦ **EASP** European Association of Social Psychology (#06210)
- ♦ EASP – European Association of Sustainability Professionals (unconfirmed)
- ♦ EASPS / see Association of Schools of Political Studies of the Council of Europe (#02902)
- ♦ EASRA – East African Securities Regulatory Authorities (see: #05181)
- ♦ EASRA – European Automotive Services and Repairers Association (unconfirmed)
- ♦ EA/SRDC Kigali / see ECA Sub-Regional Office for Eastern Africa (#05275)
- ♦ **EASR** European Association for the Study of Religions (#06235)
- ♦ EASR / see European Survey Research Association (#08862)
- ♦ EASRHA – East African School on Refugee and Humanitarian Affairs (internationally oriented national body)
- ♦ **EASS** European Association for Sociology of Sport (#06212)
- ♦ EASS – European Association of Surgical Sciences (no recent information)
- ♦ **EASSH** European Alliance for the Social Sciences and Humanities (#05885)
- ♦ **EASSI** The Eastern African Sub-Regional Support Initiative for the Advancement of Women (#05225)
- ♦ **EASSI** European Association of the Surgical Suture Industry (#06243)
- ♦ EASSP – European Association for Study of Safety Problems in Production and Use of Propellant Powders (inactive)
- ♦ **EASSSR** East Asian Society for the Scientific Study of Religion (#05209)
- ♦ **EASST** European Association of Software Science and Technology (#06213)
- ♦ **EASST** European Association for the Study of Science and Technology (#06236)
- ♦ **EASSW** European Association of Schools of Social Work (#06200)
- ♦ East Africa Association / see Eastern Africa Association (#05218)
- ♦ East Africa Association of Grantmakers / see East Africa Philanthropy Network (#05192)
- ♦ East Africa Consortium International (internationally oriented national body)

♦ East Africa Law Society (EALS) 05173

Main Office No 6 Corridor Area, Off Jandu Road, PO Box 6240, Arusha, Tanzania UR. T. +255272543227 – +255272543226 – +25527(255786821010. E-mail: info@ealawsociety.org.
URL: http://www.ealawsociety.org/

History 1995, within the framework of *East African Community (EAC, #05181)*. **Structure** General Meeting (annual). **Events** *Annual Conference* Mombasa (Kenya) 2018, *Annual Conference* Entebbe (Uganda) 2017, *Annual Conference* Zanzibar (Tanzania UR) 2015, *Conference and AGM* Kigali (Rwanda) 2014. **Publications** *EALS Newsletter*.
Members Individuals (6,000) and national law societies in six countries:
Burundi, Kenya, Rwanda, Tanzania UR, Uganda.

NGO Relations Founding member of: *International Coalition for the Responsibility to Protect (ICRtoP, #12620)*. Instrumental in setting up: *East African Civil Society Organizations' Forum (EACSOF, #05179)*. Member of: *Coalition for an Effective African Court on Human and Peoples' Rights (African Court Coalition, #04055)*; *Sudan Consortium (#20031)*. Cooperates with: *Southern African Development Community Lawyers Association (#19845)*. [2015.01.13/XD8584/**D**]

- ♦ East Africa Medical Research Council (inactive)
- ♦ East African Academy (inactive)
- ♦ East African Agricultural Research Institute (inactive)
- ♦ East African Agricultural Research Station (inactive)
- ♦ East African Agriculture and Forestry Research Organization (inactive)
- ♦ East African Air Traffic Controllers Association (inactive)
- ♦ East African Airways Corporation (inactive)
- ♦ East African Association of Investment Promotion Agencies (see: #05181)

♦ East African Association of Neurological Surgeons 05174

Contact Dept of Surgery, Kenyatta Natl Hosp Campus, Univ of Nairobi, PO Box 671 00621, Nairobi, Kenya. E-mail: nim.juniahs@gmail.com.

History Founded 20 Dec 2010, Nairobi (Kenya). **Aims** Promote public good through the advancement of neurological surgery and the dissemination of scientific knowledge; elevate and sustain education of physicians in formal institutions of learning; operate exclusively for charitable, educational and scientific purposes. **Structure** Officers. **Languages** English. **Staff** 7.00 FTE, voluntary. **Finance** Donations. **Activities** Advocacy/lobbying/activism; research/documentation; events/meetings. **Events** *Congress* Mombasa (Kenya) 2022.
Members Full in 5 countries:
Burundi, Kenya, Rwanda, Tanzania UR, Uganda. [2019.03.11/XJ5495/**D**]

♦ East African Association for Paleoanthropology and Paleontology (EAAPP) 05175

Sec address not obtained. E-mail: eaapp.committee@gmail.com.
URL: https://eaappinfo.wordpress.com/

History 18 Jul 2005. **Aims** Strengthen prehistory research in eastern Africa through uniting palaeoanthropologists and palaeontologists and other relevant scholars in prehistory studies within the region. **Finance** Sources: grants; members' dues. Supported by: *Wenner-Gren Foundation for Anthropological Research (Wenner-Gren Foundation)*. **Activities** Events/meetings. **Events** *Biennial Conference* Arusha (Tanzania UR) 2022, *Biennial Conference* Arusha (Tanzania UR) 2021, *Biennial Conference* Nairobi (Kenya) 2019, *Biennial Conference* Addis Ababa (Ethiopia) 2017, *Biennial Conference* Dar es Salaam (Tanzania UR) 2015. **Members** Individuals. Membership countries not specified. [2022.06.14/XM4389/v/**C**]

♦ East African Book Development Association (EABDA) 05176

Secretariat PO Box 6618, Kampala, Uganda.
Exec Sec PO Box 13422, Nairobi, 00800, Kenya. T. +254204447815. Fax +254204447815.
URL: http://eabda.or.ke/

History Jun 1998. **Aims** Promote *literacy* in order to fight poverty.
Members Organizations in 3 countries:
Kenya, Tanzania UR, Uganda.
IGO Relations *Swedish International Development Cooperation Agency (Sida)*. [2011/XD8826/**D**]

♦ East African Business Council (EABC) 05177

Exec Dir PO Box 2617, Arusha, Tanzania UR. T. +255272520162 – +255272520163. E-mail: info@eabc-online.com – director@eabc-online.com.
Street Address Mafao House – 9th floor, Old Moshi Rd, Arusha, Tanzania UR.
URL: http://eabc-online.com/

History 1997, by chambers of commerce and industry, associations of manufacturers and employers' organizations in East African countries. **Aims** Represent and promote interests of the EAC business community; provide value added services that create new business opportunities, enhance global competitiveness of EAC businesses, and actively influence government policies to improve enabling of the business environment. **Structure** Annual General Meeting; Executive Committee; National Focal Points; Secretariat. **Languages** English, Swahili. **Events** *East African Business and Investment Summit* Arusha (Tanzania UR) 2019, *Regional public-private dialogue on tax East African community harmonization* Arusha (Tanzania UR) 2009, *East African media summit* Kampala (Uganda) 2009, *Regional conference on Northern corridor trade logistics* Mombasa (Kenya) 2009, *Annual EAC investment conference* Nairobi (Kenya) 2009.
Members Organizations in 5 countries:
Burundi, Kenya, Rwanda, Tanzania UR, Uganda.
IGO Relations *East African Community (EAC, #05181)*; *Deutsche Gesellschaft für Internationale Zusammenarbeit (GIZ)*; The Federation of German Industries. [2019/XD8589/**D**]

♦ East African Centre of Excellence for Renewable Energy and Efficiency (EACREEE) 05178

Exec Dir Makerere Univ, College of Engineering/Design/Art/Technology, Third Fl – New Bldg, PO Box 16775, Kampala, Uganda. T. +256752738990. E-mail: info@eacreee.org.
URL: http://www.eacreee.org/

History 11 Jun 2016, Kampala (Uganda). Proposed by Sectoral Council on Energy *East African Community (EAC, #05181)*, Oct 2011. At a request from EAC Secretariat, *UNIDO (#20336)* launched a 4-year project: 'Establishment and First Operational Phase of the East African Centre for Renewable Energy and Energy Efficiency (EACREEE)', 2014, sponsored by UNIDO, *Austrian Development Agency (ADA)* and EAC. Interim entity 'Centre of Excellence for the East African Centre for Renewable Energy and Energy Efficiency ' launched Jun 2016, Kampala (Uganda), at Makere University College of Engineering, Design, Art and Technology (CEDAT). Registered Mar 2018 as a not-for-profit organization limited by guarantee. Registration: Uganda Registration Services Bureau, Start date: 7 Mar 2018, Uganda. **Aims** Create an enabling environment for renewable energy and energy efficiency markets and investments, so as to contribute to: increased access of modern, affordable and reliable energy services; energy security; mitigation of negative effect. **Structure** Board of Directors; Technical Committee; Secretariat, headed by Executive Director. **Languages** English. **Staff** 10.00 FTE, paid. **Finance** Sources: contributions; in-kind support. **Activities** Events/meetings. **Events** *Sustainable Energy Forum* Kigali (Rwanda) 2018.
Members Partner States (6):
Burundi, Kenya, Rwanda, South Sudan, Tanzania UR, Uganda.
IGO Relations Core partners: *Austrian Development Agency (ADA)*; *East African Community (EAC, #05181)*; *UNIDO (#20336)*. [2020.08.27/XM6105/**D***]

- ♦ East African Centre for Human Rights (internationally oriented national body)
- ♦ East African Centre for Renewable Energy and Energy Efficiency / see East African Centre of Excellence for Renewable Energy and Efficiency (#05178)
- ♦ East African Centre for Rural and Agricultural Credit Training (meeting series)

♦ East African Civil Society Organizations' Forum (EACSOF) 05179

CEO Njiro Nane Nane Plot No Taso 155 286, PO Box 12583, Arusha, Tanzania UR. T. +255272549029. E-mail: eacsof@gmail.com – info@eacsof.net.
URL: http://www.eacsof.net/

History 2007. Founded under the instigation of *East Africa Law Society (EALS, #05173)*. Current constitution adopted 2017. Registration: Tanzania UR. **Aims** Build a critical mass of knowledgeable and empowered civil society in the region, so as to their confidence and capacity in articulating grassroots needs and interests to the EAC, and its various organs, institutions and agencies. **Structure** General Assembly; Governing Council; Secretariat. **Publications** *EACSOF Newsletter*. **IGO Relations** *East African Community (EAC, #05181)*. **NGO Relations** *West Africa Civil Society Forum (WACSOF, #20864)*. [2020/XM8682/**F**]

- ♦ East African Common Services Organization (inactive)

♦ **East African Communications Organisation (EACO)** **05180**

Exec Sec RURA Bldg (Ex-Fair House), KN6 AV 11, PO Box 6309, Kigali, Rwanda. T. +250788155100. E-mail: info@eaco.int.

URL: http://www.eaco.int/

History Registered in accordance with the law of Rwanda. **Aims** Coordinate development of the communications sector through harmonization of policy and regulatory frameworks in the East African Community. **Structure** Congress (annual); Executive Committee; Assemblies (4); Executive Secretariat, headed by Executive Secretary. **Languages** English. **Staff** 7.00 FTE, paid. **Finance** Members' dues. **Activities** Projects/programmes; events/meetings; awards/prizes/competitions. **Events** *Making broadband work for socio-economic growth in Africa* Nairobi (Kenya) 2013, *Congress* Kigali (Rwanda) 2011, *Congress* Kampala (Uganda) 2010. **Publications** *EACO Newsletter*.

Members Full; Associate. Full in 6 countries:
Burundi, Kenya, Rwanda, South Sudan, Tanzania UR, Uganda.

IGO Relations Affiliated with (10): *African Telecommunications Union (ATU, #00482); Common Market for Eastern and Southern Africa (COMESA, #04296); Commonwealth Telecommunications Organisation (CTO, #04365); East African Community (EAC, #05181); Economic Community of West African States (ECOWAS, #05312); International Telecommunications Satellite Organization (ITSO, #15670); International Telecommunication Union (ITU, #15673); Pan African Postal Union (PAPU, #18060); Southern Africa Postal Operators Association (SAPOA, #19866); Universal Postal Union (UPU, #20682).* **NGO Relations** Affiliated with (9): *African Advanced Level Telecommunications Institute (AFRALTI, #00197); AFRINIC (#00533); Association for Progressive Communications (APC, #02873); Association of Regulators of Information and Communications for Eastern and Southern Africa (ARICEA, no recent information); Communications Regulators' Association of Southern Africa (CRASA, #04384); GSM Association (GSMA, #10813); Internet Society (ISOC, #15952); Southern Africa Telecommunications Association (SATA, #19867); West Africa Telecommunications Regulators Association (WATRA, #20903).* [2020.03.05/XJ6945/**D**]

- East African Communications Regulators, Postal and Telecommunications Companies Organization / see East Africa Regulatory Postal and Telecommunications Organization (#05193)
- East African Communities' Organization for Management of Lake Victoria (no recent information)

♦ **East African Community (EAC)** **05181**

SG Arusha International Conference Centre Bldg, Kilimanjaro Wing – 5th Fl, PO Box 1096, Arusha, Tanzania UR. T. +255272504253 – +255272504254 – +255272504258. Fax +255272504255. E-mail: eac@eachq.org.

Office EAC Close, off Afrika Mashariki Road, PO Box 1096, Arusha, Tanzania UR. T. +255272162100. Fax +255272162190. E-mail: eac@eachq.org.

URL: http://www.eac.int/

History 7 Jul 2000, on entry into force of *East African Cooperation Treaty (1999)* – the *'Treaty for the establishment of the East African Community'* – signed 30 Nov 1999, Arusha (Tanzania UR). Formally launched 15 Jan 2001. Establishment followed the work of the *Commission for East African Cooperation (CEAC)*, set up 14 Mar 1996, Arusha (Tanzania UR), on signature of a cooperation agreement by Presidents of Kenya, Tanzania UR and Uganda, following preparatory work begun after signature of a Treaty, Nov 1993, by the countries involved. The Commission was also referred to as: *Permanent Tripartite Commission Secretariat on East African Cooperation; Secretariat of the Commission for East African Cooperation (EAC Secretariat).* The preparatory *East African Cooperation*, 1993-2000, revitalized previous formal cooperation among the 3 countries, which was suspended in 1977 with the disintegration of *East African Community – 1967 (EAC, inactive)*; this had been set up, 1 Dec 1967, to replace *East African Common Services Organization (EACSO, inactive)*, formed 9 Dec 1961, which in its turn took over the activities of *East African High Commission (EAHC, inactive)*, set up 1 Jan 1948. During the period 1977-1993, member states signed a *'Mediation Agreement for the Division of Assets and Liabilities'*, 1984, which paved the way for future cooperation. The Community aims ultimately to achieve a *Political Federation of East African States*. In this regard, the Protocol on the Establishment of *East African Community Customs Union (EACCU, #05182)* was signed Mar 2004. **Aims** Widen and deepen cooperation among partner states in political, economic, social, cultural, health, education, science and technology, defence, security, legal and judicial areas, for their mutual benefit; to this end, establish a *customs union* as entry point, a common market, subsequently a *monetary* union and ultimately a *political* federation. Achieve these goals by: promoting sustainable growth and equitable development of partner states, including rational utilization of the region's natural resources and protection of the environment; strengthening and consolidating longstanding political, economic, social, cultural and traditional ties among the peoples of the region, promoting a people-centred development; enhancing and strengthening participation of the private sector and civil society; mainstreaming gender in all programmes and enhancing the role of women in development; promoting good governance, including adherence to the principles of democracy, rule of law, accountability, transparency, social justice, equal opportunities and gender equality; promoting peace, security and stability in the region and good neighbourliness among partner states. **Structure** Summit of Heads of State and or Government of the Partner States (at least once a year). Council of Ministers (meeting twice a year, one meeting being immediately prior to Summit), comprises Ministers responsible for regional cooperation of each partner state together with further Ministers as each partner state determines. Coordination Committee consists of Permanent Secretaries responsible for regional cooperation in each partner state together with further Permanent Secretaries as each partner state determines. Sectoral Committees report to the Coordination Committee; they prepare programmes, set out priorities with respect to various sectors and monitor their implementation. *East African Court of Justice (see: #05181)* initially has jurisdiction over interpretation and application of the Treaty on Common Market Matters; the Court's appellate, human rights and other jurisdiction will be determined by the Council of Ministers in a protocol to be concluded at a suitable future date. *East African Legislative Assembly (EALA, #05185)* comprises 27 elected members, 9 from each partner state, plus (ex officio) the 3 Ministers responsible for regional cooperation, the Secretary-General and the Counsel to the Community. Secretariat, headed by Secretary-General. *EAC Defence Liaison Office* set up at the Secretariat in 1998. Autonomous institutions: *East African Development Bank (EADB, #05183); Inter-University Council for East Africa (IUCEA, #15987); Lake Victoria Fisheries Organization (LVFO, #16222).* Also includes: *East African Association of Investment Promotion Agencies (EAFAIPA, see: #05181); East African Securities Regulatory Authorities (EASRA, see: #05181).* **Finance** Core budget: equal contributions of partner states. Regional projects and programmes funded through resources mobilized from inside and outside of the region.

Activities *'Second East African Community Development Strategy'* launched by Heads of State, 24 Apr 2001. Areas of cooperation include: trade, investment and industrial development; monetary and fiscal affairs; infrastructure and services; human resources, science and technology; free movement of factors of production; agriculture and food security; environment and natural resources management; tourism and wildlife management; health, social and cultural activities; the role of women, in socio-economic development; participation of the private sector and civil society; cooperation on political matters, including defence, security, foreign affairs and legal and judicial affairs. Together with: *Southern African Development Community (SADC, #19843)* and *Common Market for Eastern and Southern Africa (COMESA, #04296)*, announced setting up of *African Continental Free Trade Area (AfCFTA, #00267)*, Oct 2008.

Ongoing activities include: tariff reductions; removal of non-tariff barriers; harmonization of standards and specifications for goods and services, of investment incentives and codes, of customs classification codes, of banking rules and regulations, of VAT rates, of pre-shipment requirements threshold, of policies and trading practices and regulations of partner states' stock exchanges, of road transit charges, of environmental regulations and of regional judicial training syllabi and activities. Central banks of member countries agreed in 1996 to make the three currencies convertible. Committees include: *'Capital Markets Development Committee'*. Current projects and programmes: East African Road Network Project; projects on the state of railways in East Africa; construction of the Tanga-Arusha-Musoma-Port Bell/Jinja Railway; East African Digital Transmission Project; Cross-Border Telecommunication Connectivity Project; East African Postal Automation Project; East African Civil Aviation Project; Project on Safety of Navigation on Lake Victoria; projects on East African Energy Master Plan, including fossil fuels, new and renewable source of energy and power; Power Interconnectivity Project; On-going studies: on establishment of an East African Trade Regime; *Regional Programme for the Control of Cholera and Yellow Fever, Regional Programme on HIV/AIDS Control, Regional Gender and Community Development Programme*; Project on Approximation/Harmonization on Municipal Laws; formulation of an *'East African Private Sector Development Strategy'*; development of a comprehensive East African Agricultural and Rural Development Strategy; development of regional tourism in East Africa; standardization of hotels; economic potential and constraints to development of Lake Victoria and its basin as an economic growth zone; Memoranda of Understanding: on cooperation on environment management, signed 22 Oct 1998; on cooperation in defence, signed Apr 1998, revised 2001. Treaties: *Tripartite Inland Waterways Agreement (1998)* and *Tripartite Agreement on Road Transport (1998)*, signed 29 Apr 1998.

Events *East African Business and Investment Summit* Arusha (Tanzania UR) 2019, *Meeting of senior officials of the EAC Forum of National Electoral Commissions* Nairobi (Kenya) 2019, *Japan-EAC Investment Seminar* Tokyo (Japan) 2014, *Meeting on operationalizing the Ouagadougou Action Plan to Combat Trafficking In Human Beings Especially Women and Children* Arusha (Tanzania UR) 2011, *Workshop on rule of law, democray and human rights in the EAC integration* Nairobi (Kenya) 2009. **Publications** *EAC News* (4 a year). *Dialogue on East African Competition Policies* (2001); *Science and Technology Policy in East Africa* (2000); *Investors Guide to East Africa: Emerging Investment Location and Single Market Area* (1999); *East African Cooperation Development Strategy 1997-2000* (1997); *East African Community: Challenges and Opportunities.* Brochures; seminar proceedings; treaties; reports. **Information Services** *EAC Statistical Database.*

Members Partner states – 3 countries:
Kenya, Tanzania UR, Uganda.

IGO Relations Cooperates with other African organizations in the spirit of: *Treaty Establishing the African Economic Community (Abuja treaty, 1991).* These include: *Common Market for Eastern and Southern Africa (COMESA, #04296); Intergovernmental Authority on Development (IGAD, #11472); Southern African Development Community (SADC, #19843).* Memoranda of Understanding or cooperation agreements with: *African Development Bank (ADB, #00283); Agence française de développement (AFD);* COMESA; *Deutsche Gesellschaft für Technische Zusammenarbeit (GTZ, inactive); European Union (EU, #08967); ILO (#11123); Swedish International Development Cooperation Agency (Sida).* Regional Economic Community of: *African Union (AU, #00488).* Permanent Observer to: *ECOSOC (#05331).* Observer to: *Codex Alimentarius Commission (CAC, #04081);* General Assembly of *United Nations (UN, #20515).* **NGO Relations** Set up under EAC auspices: *East Africa Law Society (EALS, #05173); East African Business Council (EABC, #05177); East Africa Regulatory Postal and Telecommunications Organization (EARPTO, #05193); East African Investment Promotion Authority Organization (no recent information); East African Resource Facility (EARF, no recent information); East African Tourism Coordinating Agency (EATCA, no recent information); East African Trade Union Coordinating Council (EATUC, no recent information); East African Youth Council (EAYCO, #05191); Joint Research Council for East Africa (no recent information).* Participates in: *Global Island Partnership (GLISPA, #10436).* Member of: *Reproductive Health Supplies Coalition (RHSC, #18847).* Library is member of: *International Federation of Library Associations and Institutions (IFLA, #13470).* Cooperates with: *International Fertilizer Development Center (IFDC, #13590); Rainwater Partnership (no recent information).* [2014/XD6196/**F***]

- East African Community – 1967 (inactive)

♦ **East African Community Customs Union (EACCU)** **05182**

Dir Gen EAC Directorate of Customs and Trade, PO Box 1096, Arusha, Tanzania UR. T. +255272504253 – +255272504254 – +255272504258. Fax +255272504255 – +255272504481. E-mail: eac@eachq.org.

URL: http://www.eac.int/

History 31 Jan 2004, Uganda. 31 Jan 2004, Dar es Salaam and Kampala (Uganda) (simultaneously), within *East African Community (EAC, #05181)*, following a Protocol signed Mar 2004. **Aims** Create a single market by: liberalizing intra-regional *trade* in goods on the basis of mutually beneficial trade arrangements; promoting efficiency in production; enhancing domestic, cross border trade and foreign investment; promoting economic development, diversification and industrialization. Create a Common External Tariff (CET) regime for goods originating from outside East Africa; establish common customs laws and regulations; harmonize and simplify customs procedures and documentation.

Members Governments of 3 countries:
Kenya, Tanzania UR, Uganda. [2018/XJ4397/**D***]

- East African Community Management Institute / see Eastern and Southern African Management Institute (#05254)
- East African Consortium International / see East Africa Consortium International
- East African Cooperation Treaty (1999 treaty)
- East African Court of Appeal (inactive)
- East African Court of Justice (see: #05181)
- East African Currency Area (inactive)
- East African Dental Association (inactive)

♦ **East African Development Bank (EADB)** **05183**

Banque de développement de l'Afrique de l'Est

Directorate 4 Nile Avenue, PO Box 7128, Kampala, Uganda. T. +256417112900 – +256417112901. Fax +256414253585. E-mail: dg@eadb.org – admin@eadb.org.

URL: http://www.eadb.org/

History 6 Jun 1967, Kampala (Uganda), on signature of the Treaty for East African Cooperation creating *East African Community – 1967 (EAC, inactive)*, which entered into force 1 Dec 1967. Following break-up of East African Cooperation, 1977, re-established under its own charter, 23 Sep 1980, when role and mandate were reviewed and operational scope expanded. **Aims** Provide financial and related assistance to enterprises in member states which, by their activities, are expected to make a positive contribution to socio-economic development in the region. **Structure** Governing Council; Board of Directors; Advisory Panel; Directorate headed by Director General. Country Offices (4). **Languages** English. **Staff** 82.00 FTE, paid. **Finance** Class A shareholders: Governments of Kenya, Tanzania UR, Uganda and Rwanda. Class B shareholders include the following organizations listed in this Yearbook: *African Development Bank (ADB, #00283); Nederlandse Financierings-Maatschappij voor Ontwikkelingslanden (FMO).* **Activities** Financial and/or material support. **Publications** Annual Report.

Members Governments of 4 countries:
Kenya, Rwanda, Tanzania UR, Uganda.

IGO Relations Member of: *Eastern and Southern African Anti-Money Laundering Group (ESAAMLG, #05252).* **NGO Relations** Special member of: *Association of African Development Finance Institutions (AADFI, #02353).* [2014.05.28/XF4208/**F***]

- East African Examinations Council (inactive)
- East African External Telecommunications Company (inactive)
- East African Fisheries Organization / see Lake Victoria Fisheries Organization (#16222)
- East African Flying Doctor Services / see Flying Doctors' Society of Africa
- East African Freshwater Fisheries Research Organization (inactive)
- East African High Commission (inactive)
- East African Industrial Licensing Council (inactive)
- East African Institute of Malaria and Vector-Borne Diseases (inactive)
- East African Institute for Medical Research (inactive)

♦ **East African Integrated Disease Surveillance Network (EAIDSNet)** . **05184**

Contact EAC Close, Afrika Mashariki Road, PO Box 1096, 23100 Arusha, Tanzania UR. T. +255272162100. E-mail: eac@eachq.org.

URL: https://www.eac.int/health/disease-prevention/east-african-integrated-disease-surveillance-network

History 2000. A collaborate effort of the Ministries of Health of Kenya, Tanzania and Uganda, as well as national health research, and academic institutions. Phase II (2003) set up under the auspices of *East African Community (EAC, #05181).* **Aims** Improve the quality of data on communicable diseases and the flow and sharing of information to improve the health of the East African population. **Finance** Financial assistance from *The Rockefeller Foundation (#18966).* [2020/XJ8949/**F***]

♦ **East African Legislative Assembly (EALA)** **05185**

Assemblée législative de l'Afrique orientale

Mailing Address c/o EAC – EALA Wing, Afrika Mashariki Road / EAC Close, PO Box 1096, Arusha, Tanzania UR. T. +255272162126. Fax +255272162179. E-mail: eala@eachq.org.

URL: http://www.eala.org/

East African Library
05185

alphabetic sequence excludes
For the complete listing, see Yearbook Online at

History Established within the framework of *East African Community (EAC, #05181)*, through Article 49 of the EAC Treaty. **Aims** Legislate, do oversight and represent the people of East Africa in a bid to foster economic, social, cultural and political integration. **Structure** Comprises 27 elected members, 9 from each EAC partner state, plus (ex officio) the 3 Ministers responsible for regional cooperation, EAC Secretary-General and the Counsel to the Community. Commission. Committees (6). **Events** *Fourth meeting* Arusha (Tanzania UR) 2009, *Second meeting* Arusha (Tanzania UR) 2009, *Sixth meeting* Bujumbura (Burundi) 2009, *First meeting* Dar es Salaam (Tanzania UR) 2009, *First meeting* Arusha (Tanzania UR) 2001.
Members Indvididuals from governments (6):
Burundi, Kenya, Rwanda, South Sudan, Tanzania UR, Uganda.
IGO Relations *Eastern and Southern African Management Institute (ESAMI, #05254).* **NGO Relations** Member of (3): *Association of Secretaries General of Parliaments (ASGP, #02911); Inter-Parliamentary Union (IPU, #15961); Parliamentary Forum on Small Arms and Light Weapons (Parliamentary Forum on SALW, #18218).* [2021/XK2203/**E***]

♦ East African Library Association (inactive)

♦ East African Local Governments Association (EALGA) 05186

SG PO Box 1899, Arusha, Tanzania UR. T. +255272504703. Fax +255272504703. E-mail: ealga@tz2000.com – info@ealga.org.
URL: http://www.ealga.org/
History 10 May 2005. **Structure** Governing Council; Executive Committee; Secretariat.
Members National associations in 4 countries:
Kenya, Rwanda, Tanzania UR, Uganda. [2013/XM2986/**D**]

♦ East African Management Institute / see Eastern and Southern African Management Institute (#05254)
♦ East African Marine Fisheries Research Organization (inactive)
♦ East African Meteorological Department (inactive)

♦ East African Meteorological Society (EAMS) 05187

Contact c/o EAC, Arusha Intl Conference Ctr, 5th Floor Kilimanjaro Wing, PO Box 1096, Arusha, Tanzania UR. T. +255272504253 – +255272504258. Fax +255272504255. E-mail: eac@eachq.org.
IGO Relations *East African Community (EAC, #05181).* **NGO Relations** Member of: *International Forum of Meteorological Societies (IFMS, #13644).* [2011/XJ5013/**D**]

♦ East African Mineral Resources Development Centre / see African Minerals and Geosciences Centre (#00373)
♦ East African Natural Resources Research Council (inactive)
♦ East African Posts and Telecommunications Administration (inactive)
♦ East African Professional Hunters Association (inactive)
♦ East African Rock Art Research Association (no recent information)
♦ East African School of Librarianship / see East African School of Library and Information Science (#05188)

♦ East African School of Library and Information Science (EASLIS) . . 05188

Dir Makerere Univ, Box 7062, Kampala, Uganda. T. +256414540628.
URL: http://easlis.mak.ac.ug/
History Founded 1963, with initial assistance from *UNESCO (#20322).* Previously referred to as *East African School of Librarianship (EASL) – Ecole de bibliothécaires d'Afrique de l'Est.* **Aims** Provide education and training in information science; conduct research in information science; disseminate research information; conduct research; produce high quality information professionals capable of responding to present and future needs. **Structure** Director; Vice-Chancellor; Deputy-Director; Heads of Departments; Lecturers. Departments (3): Information Science; Library Science; Records and Archives Management. **Languages** English. **Staff** 21.00 FTE, paid. **Finance** Funded by Government of Uganda through Makerere University. **Activities** Training/education; events/meetings. **Publications** *Library and Information Science Training Voice* (2 a year) – newsletter. Books.
Members Covers 3 countries:
Kenya, Tanzania UR, Uganda.
IGO Relations Sponsored by: *UNESCO (#20322).* Joint courses with: *Deutsche Stiftung für Internationale Entwicklung (DSE, inactive); FAO (#09260); Organization for the Management and Development of the Kagera River Basin (KBO, no recent information).* [2016/XF0258/**F**]

♦ East African School on Refugee and Humanitarian Affairs (internationally oriented national body)
♦ East African Securities Regulatory Authorities (see: #05181)
♦ East African Society for Parasitology (unconfirmed)
♦ East African Staff College (inactive)
♦ East African Statistical Training Centre / see Eastern Africa Statistical Training Centre (#05228)

♦ East African Tea Trade Association (EATTA) 05189

Association de l'Afrique de l'Est pour le commerce du thé

Managing Dir Nyerere Avenue, PO Box 85174-80100, Mombasa, Kenya. T. +254412220093 – +254412228460. Fax +254412225823. E-mail: info@eatta.co.ke.
Street address Tea Trade Centre, Nyerere Avenue, Mombasa, Kenya.
URL: http://www.eatta.com/
History 1957, when Constitution Rules and Regulations were adopted. **Aims** Promote the best interests of tea trade in Africa by fostering closer working relations among members of the tea industry; establish facilities for the orderly sale of teas of African origin in a centralized format in the international auctions in Mombasa; facilitate the settlement of disputes within the trade; collect and circulate statistics and trade information, and maintain such records as may be of assistance to members; act as a link between the trade and governmental and related bodies. **Structure** General Meeting (annual); Management Committee; Sub-Committees. Branches have their own Association, managed by Office holders. **Languages** English. **Staff** 5.00 FTE, paid. **Finance** Members' dues. Annual budget: Kenyan Shillings 12,000,000. **Activities** International Tea Convention (every 5 years); biennial seminar; annual tea trade dinner; annual sports day; annual social weekend; annual sports/fun day. **Events** *African Tea Convention* Kampala (Uganda) 2019, *African Tea Convention* Kigali (Rwanda) 2013, *African tea convention* Mombasa (Kenya) 2011, *Convention* Nairobi (Kenya) / Mombasa (Kenya) 2006, *Convention* Kenya 2001. **Publications** None.
Members Buyer; Producer; Warehouse; Associate; Packer. Members in 11 countries:
Burundi, Congo DR, Ethiopia, Kenya, Madagascar, Malawi, Mozambique, Rwanda, Tanzania UR, Uganda, Zambia. [2018/XD4345/t/**D**]

♦ East African Trade Union Coordinating Council (no recent information)
♦ East African Trypanosomiasis Research Organization (inactive)
♦ East African Wattle Manufacturers Association (inactive)

♦ East African Wild Life Society (EAWLS) 05190

Contact EAWLS Bdg, Riara Road, Kilimani, PO Box 20110, Nairobi, 00200, Kenya. T. +254203870335. E-mail: info@eawildlife.org.
URL: http://www.eawildlife.org/
History 1961, on the amalgamation of Kenya and Tanzania Wildlife Societies (both formed in 1956) and Ugandan conservationists. **Aims** Enhance conservation and wise use of the environment and natural resources in East Africa for the benefit of current and future generations. **Structure** Board. **Languages** English, Swahili. **Staff** 40.00 FTE, paid; 10.00 FTE, voluntary. **Finance** Members' dues. Other sources: donations; sale of publications. **Activities** Advocacy/lobbying/activism; knowledge management/information disssemination; projects/programmes; publishing activities; financial and/or material support. **Events** *Coastal ecology conference* Mombasa (Kenya) 2006. **Publications** *EAWLS Newsletter* (12 a year); *African Journal of Ecology* (4 a year); *Swara Magazine* (4 a year) in English – also in Chinese (2 a year).
Members Ordinary; Corporate. Representatives or corporate members in 28 countries:
Argentina, Australia, Austria, Belgium, Canada, Denmark, Egypt, Finland, Germany, Greece, Ireland, Israel, Italy, Japan, Kenya, Mexico, Netherlands, Norway, South Africa, Spain, Sweden, Switzerland, Tanzania UR, Uganda, UK, United Arab Emirates, USA, Zimbabwe.
Included in the above, 4 organizations listed in this Yearbook:
African Wildlife Foundation (AWF, #00498); Africa Safari Club; CARE International (CI, #03429) (Uganda branch); *FAO (#09260).*
NGO Relations Member of: *Fauna & Flora International (FFI, #09277).* Works with: *Young Professionals for Agricultural Development (YPARD, #21996).* [2018/XD4296/y/**D**]

♦ East African Youth Council (EAYCO) 05191

Contact c/o EAC, PO Box 1096, Arusha, Tanzania UR. T. +255272504253 – +27272504254 – +27272504258. Fax +255272504255 – +255272504481. E-mail: eac@eachq.org.
History Comes within the framework of *East African Community (EAC, #05181).* [2009/XE4535/**E**]

♦ East Africa Philanthropy Network (EAPN) 05192

CEO PO Box 49626-00100 GPO, Nairobi, Kenya. T. +254202244470. Fax +254202244470. E-mail: info@eaphilanthropynetwork.org.
Street Address 4th Floor, Rattansi educational Trust Bldg, Koinange Str, Nairobi, Kenya.
URL: http://www.eaphilanthropynetwork.org/
History 27 Feb 2003, Nairobi (Kenya). Former names and other names: *East Africa Association of Grantmakers (EAAG)* – former (2003). **Aims** Promote local resourcing and effective grantmaking. **Structure** Board; Secretariat. **Languages** English. **Finance** Members' dues. **Events** *Conference* Mombasa (Kenya) 2013, *Annual East Africa Grantmakers Conference / Conference* Entebbe (Uganda) 2012.
Members in 5 countries:
Burundi, Kenya, Rwanda, Tanzania UR, Uganda.
NGO Relations Member of: *Worldwide Initiatives for Grantmaker Support (WINGS, #21926).* Supports: *SDG Philanthropy Platform (SDGfunders).* [2021/XD9108/**D**]

♦ East Africa Regulatory Postal and Telecommunications Organization (EARPTO) 05193

Contact c/o Communications Commission, Waiyaki Way, PO Box 14448, Westlands, Nairobi, 00800, Kenya.
History Comes within the framework of *East African Community (EAC, #05181).* Previously referred to as *East African Communications Regulators, Postal and Telecommunications Companies Organization.* **Aims** Harmonize and promote the development of postal and telecommunications services and regulatory matters; ensure provision of tariff structure and settlement of account; promote the development and application of information communications technologies; serve as a consultative organization for settlement of postal and telecommunications matters; harmonize policies and legislation in the communications sector. **Structure** Congress (every 2 years) Assembly of Regulators Assembly of Postal Operators Assembly of Telecommunications Operators. **Events** *Biennial Congress* Dar es Salaam (Tanzania UR) 2009, *Biennial Congress* Kenya 2007, *Biennial Congress* Uganda 2005.
Members Organizations and companies (19) in 3 countries:
Kenya, Tanzania UR, Uganda. [2009/XJ7445/**E**]

♦ East Africa Women's League (internationally oriented national body)
♦ East Africa Work Campers Association (no recent information)
♦ East Africa Yearly Meeting of Friends (internationally oriented national body)
♦ **EASTAP** European Association for the Study of Theatre and Performance (#06237)
♦ East ASEAN Growth Area / see Brunei Darussalam-Indonesia-Malaysia-Philippine – East ASEAN Growth Area (#03340)

♦ East Asia Airports Alliance (EAAA) 05194

Contact Macau Intl Airport, 4th Floor CAM Office Building, Av Wai Long, Taipa, Macau. E-mail: cam@macau-airport.com.
URL: http://www.camacau.com/en
History Dec 2001, Jeju (Korea Rep). **Aims** Improve air transport services and passenger service in the East Asia region through discussion of common problems associated with airport operations and management. **Events** *Annual Meeting* Tokyo (Japan) 2017, *Annual Meeting* Shanghai (China) 2016, *Annual Meeting* Tokyo (Japan) 2015, *Annual Meeting* Dalian (China) 2014, *Annual Meeting* Japan 2013.
Members Full in 3 countries:
China, Japan, Korea Rep. [2018/XJ1278/**D**]

♦ East Asia Christian Conference / see Christian Conference of Asia (#03898)
♦ East Asia Conference of Radiological Technologists (meeting series)
♦ East Asia Forum on Radwaste Management Conference (meeting series)
♦ East Asia Group of Rheumatology (unconfirmed)
♦ East Asia Hydrographic Commission (see: #13825)
♦ East Asia Institute, Cambridge (internationally oriented national body)
♦ East Asia Institute, Seoul (internationally oriented national body)
♦ East Asia Joint Symposium on Plasma and Electrostatics Technologies for Environmental Applications (meeting series)
♦ East Asia-Latin America Forum / see Forum for East Asia-Latin America Cooperation (#09907)

♦ East Asian Anthropological Association (EAAA) 05195

Contact CUHK – Anthropology, Room 407 Humanities Bldg, New Asia College, Shatin, Hong Kong.
History Formal inauguration at 4th Conference, Jul 2012, Hong Kong. **Aims** Facilitate information exchange and professional contacts among anthropologists in East Asia and the wider intellectual community. **Structure** Executive Board. **Events** *Conference* Jeonju (Korea Rep) 2019, *Cultural realms and boundaries crossing* Xiamen (China) 2013, *The world in East Asia/East Asia in the world* Hong Kong (Hong Kong) 2012, *Conference* Korea Rep 2010, *Conference* Taipei (Taiwan) 2009.
Members Full in 5 countries and territories:
China, Hong Kong, Japan, Korea Rep, Taiwan. [2012/XJ6518/**D**]

♦ East Asian Archaeology Network / see Society for East Asian Archaeology (#19544)
♦ East Asian Assistancy / see Jesuit Conference of Asia Pacific (#16099)
♦ East Asian Association for Bioethics / see Asian Bioethics Association (#01357)
♦ East Asian Association of Environmental and Resource Economics / see Asian Association of Environmental and Resource Economics (#01322)

♦ East Asian Association of Insolvency and Restructuring 05196

Secretariat c/o Business Planning Forum Co Ltd, Hirakawa-cho Bldg, 2-7-2 Hirakawa-cho, Chiyoda-ku, Tokyo, 102-0093 Japan. T. +81332656900. Fax +8133265014. E-mail: secretariat@eaa-ir.com.
URL: http://www.eaa-ir.com/
History Apr 2011, Tokyo (Japan). **Aims** Provide a forum for sharing information and exchanging views on insolvency law and practice in East Asian countries. **Structure** Board. **Languages** Japanese, Korean, Mandarin Chinese. **Staff** None. **Finance** Members' dues. **Activities** Events/meetings; research/documentation; knowledge management/information dissemination; networking/liaising. **Events** *Annual Symposium* Seoul (Korea Rep) 2018, *Annual Symposium* Tokyo (Japan) 2017, *Annual Symposium* Shanghai (China) 2016, *Annual Symposium* Seoul (Korea Rep) 2015, *Annual Symposium* Seoul (Korea Rep) 2009.
Members Chapters (3):
China, Japan, Korea Rep. [2019/XM4394/**D**]

♦ East-Asian Association for Science Education (EASE) 05197

Sec Science Ed Bldg 304, Gyeongin NU of Education, 62 Gyesan-ro, Incheon 21044, Korea Rep. E-mail: ease2022@gmail.com.
URL: http://www.theease.org/
History Seoul (Korea Rep). **Aims** Serve as a platform for science education in East Asia regions to exchange and share ideas and practices. **Structure** Executive Board. Officers: President; 2 Vice-Presidents; Secretary; Treasurer. **Events** *International Conference* Daegu (Korea Rep) 2022, *International Conference* 2021, *International Conference* Daegu (Korea Rep) 2020, *International Conference* Hualien (Taiwan) 2018, *International Conference* Tokyo (Japan) 2016. **Publications** *The Newsletter of the East-Asian Association for Science Education.* Annual Report. [2022/XJ5531/**D**]

♦ **East Asian – Australasian Flyway Partnership (EAAFP)** **05198**
Programme Officer 3F Bon-dong G-Tower, 175 Art center-daero, Yeonsu-gu, Incheon 406-840, Korea Rep. Fax +82324586508. E-mail: programme@eaaflyway.net.
URL: http://www.eaaflyway.net/
History Launched 6 Nov 2006, as an informal and voluntary initiative. Also referred to as *Partnership for the East Asian-Australasian Flyway (EAAF Partnership)*. **Aims** Protect *migratory waterbirds*, their habitat and the livelihoods of people dependent upon them. **Structure** Management Committee; Working Groups (6), include: *North East Asian Crane Site Network (NEACSN, #17579)*; Task Forces (8); Secretariat. **Languages** English. **Activities** Networking/liaising; events/meetings; training/education; awareness raising. **Events** *Meeting of Partners* Brisbane, QLD (Australia) 2021, *International Symposium for the Hwaseong Wetlands* Hwaseong (Korea Rep) 2021, *Black Faced Spoonbill Conservation Cooperation Forum* Incheon (Korea Rep) 2021, *Development of a Joint Inventory of the Status of Migratory Birds in the West/Yellow Sea* Incheon (Korea Rep) 2021, *International Symposium on the Hwaseong Wetlands* Hwaseong (Korea Rep) 2019. **Publications** *EAAFP Newsletter*. Information brochure; poster.
Members Governments; IGOs; NGOs. Governments (17):
Australia, Bangladesh, Cambodia, China, Indonesia, Japan, Korea Rep, Malaysia, Mongolia, Myanmar, New Zealand, Philippines, Russia, Singapore, Thailand, USA, Vietnam.
Organizations include the following listed in this Yearbook:
ASEAN Centre for Biodiversity (ACB, #01149); *Australasian Wader Studies Group (AWSG)* (BirdLife Australia); *BirdLife International (#03266)*; *Convention on Biological Diversity (Biodiversity convention, 1992)*; *Hanns Seidel Foundation*; *International Crane Foundation (ICF, #13102)*; *International Union for Conservation of Nature and Natural Resources (IUCN, #15766)*; *Secretariat of the Convention of Wetlands (#19200)*; *Secretariat of the Convention on the Conservation of Migratory Species of Wild Animals (UNEP/CMS, #19198)*; *Wetlands International (#20928)*; *Wildfowl and Wetlands Trust (WWT)*; *World Wide Fund for Nature (WWF, #21922)*.
IGO Relations Cooperates with: *Conservation of Arctic Flora and Fauna (CAFF, #04728)*. **NGO Relations** Partner of: *Wetland Link International (WLI, #20927)*. [2019/XJ1723/y/**E**]

♦ East Asian Biophysics Symposium / see Asian Biophysics Association (#01358)

♦ **East Asian Biosphere Reserve Network (EABRN)** **05199**
Réseau de réserves de biosphère d'Asie de l'Est
Contact 5-15-3 Jianguomenwai, Diplomatic Compound, Chaoyang District, 11 100800 Beijing, China. E-mail: beijing@unesco.org.
History Founded May 1995, Seoul (Korea Rep), within the framework of *Programme on Man and the Biosphere (MAB, #18526)*. Regional network of *UNESCO Office, Jakarta – Regional Bureau for Sciences in Asia and the Pacific (#20313)*. **Aims** Promote exchange of scientific research results and experience in management of biosphere reserves. **Events** *Meeting* Yamanouchi (Japan) 2015, *Meeting* Terelj Camp (Mongolia) 2007, *Meeting* Jeju (Korea Rep) 2005, *Meeting* Seoul (Korea Rep) 2005, *Meeting* Mongolia 2003.
Members Biosphere reserves in 6 countries:
China, Japan, Korea DPR, Korea Rep, Mongolia, Russia. [2015/XF4049/**F**]

♦ **East Asian Bipolar Forum (EABF)** **05200**
Secretariat c/o JTB Business Support Kyushu Inc, ICS Sales Div, 6F Shin-KBC Bldg, 1-1-35 Nagahama, Chuo-ku, Fukuoka, 810-0072 Japan. T. +81927513244. Fax +81927513250.
Events *Forum* Fukuoka (Japan) 2012, *Forum* Seoul (Korea Rep) 2010. **NGO Relations** Affiliated to: *International Society for Bipolar Disorders (ISBD, #14977)*. [2013/XJ6678/c/**F**]

♦ East Asian Conference on Geometric Topology (meeting series)
♦ East Asian Conference on Infection Control and Prevention (meeting series)
♦ East Asian Conference of Neurointervention (meeting series)
♦ East Asian Conference on Phonosurgery (meeting series)
♦ East Asian Consortium of Japanese Studies (unconfirmed)

♦ **East Asian Core Observatories Association (EACOA)** **05201**
Contact address not obtained. E-mail: web@asiaa.sinica.edu.tw.
URL: http://www.eacoa.net/
History Memorandum of Understanding signed 21 Sep 2005. **Aims** Foster and coordinate collaborations between the major astronomical observatories in the region. **Structure** Directors' Meeting; Office; Financial and Supporting Committee. Maintains *East Asian Observatory (EAO)*. **Events** *Users Meeting* Seoul (Korea Rep) 2018.
Members Core observatories in 4 countries and territories:
China, Japan, Korea Rep, Taiwan. [2020/XM8130/**D**]

♦ **East Asian Development Network (EADN)** **05202**
Regional Coordinator c/o Philippine Inst for Development Studies, 18F Three Cyberpod Centris-North Tower, EDSA corner Queaon Avenue, 1100 Quezon City, Philippines. T. +6328774000. Fax +6328774099.
URL: http://www.eadn.org/
History 1998, Singapore (Singapore). **Aims** As a network of research institutes, centres and think-tanks in *developing countries* of East Asia, build research capacity and research policy networking. **Structure** Steering Committee; Regional Coordinator; Secretariat. **Languages** English. **Staff** 1.50 FTE, paid. **Finance** Grants from: *Global Development Network (GDN, #10318)*. Annual budget (2016): US$ 126,000. **Activities** Financial and/or material support; events/meetings; projects/programmes; research and development. **Events** *Annual Forum* Pasig City (Philippines) 2016, *Annual Forum* Bangkok (Thailand) 2010, *Annual Forum* Bangkok (Thailand) 2009, *Annual Forum* Bangkok (Thailand) 2008, *Annual Forum* Beijing (China) 2007. **Publications** Working Papers.
Members Research institutes, centers and think tanks (38) in 12 countries and territories:
Cambodia, China, Hong Kong, Indonesia, Korea Rep, Laos, Malaysia, Myanmar, Philippines, Singapore, Thailand, Vietnam.
Included in the above, 13 organizations listed in this Yearbook:
Cambodian Institute for Cooperation and Peace (CICP); *Centre for Asia-Pacific Studies, Yogyakarta (no recent information)*; *Centre for Strategic and International Studies, Jakarta (CSIS)*; *Institute for Southeast Asian Studies, Hanoi*; *Institute for Strategic and Development Studies, Quezon City (ISDS)*; *Institute of Asia-Pacific Studies, Beijing*; *Institute of East Asian Studies, Bangkok*; *Institute of Malaysian and International Studies (IKMAS)*; *Institute of Strategic and International Studies, Malaysia (ISIS)*; *Institute of World Economics and Politics, Hanoi (IWEP)*; *ISEAS – Yusof Ishak Institute (ISEAS)* (Singapore); *Korea Institute for International Economic Policy (KIEP)*; *Singapore Institute of International Affairs (SIIA)*.
NGO Relations Partner of: *Global Development Network (GDN, #10318)*. [2017.08.15/XF5961/y/**F**]

♦ **East Asian Economic Association (EAEA)** **05203**
Contact Center for Southeast Asian Studies, Kyoto University, 46 Yoshida Shimo-Adachi-cho, Kyoto, 606-8501 Japan. Fax +81757537350. E-mail: eaea@nacos.com.
URL: http://www.eaeaweb.com/
History 1987. **Aims** Promote advancement of economic science with particular reference to Asian economic problems. **Structure** Board of Directors; Council of Fellows; Executive Committee. **Languages** English. **Staff** Voluntary. **Finance** Members'dues. Donations. **Events** *International Convention* Seoul (Korea Rep) 2023, *International Convention* Kuala Lumpur (Malaysia) 2022, *Biennial Convention* Bangkok (Thailand) 2014, *Biennial Convention* Singapore (Singapore) 2012, *Biennial Convention* Seoul (Korea Rep) 2010. **Publications** *Asian Economic Journal* (4 a year).
Members Regular; Supportive members in 14 countries and territories:
Australia, Brunei Darussalam, China, Hong Kong, Indonesia, Japan, Korea Rep, Malaysia, Philippines, Singapore, Sweden, Taiwan, Thailand, USA. [2023/XD6399/**D**]

♦ East Asian Entrepreneurs' Summit (meeting series)
♦ East Asian Federation of Ecological Societies (internationally oriented national body)

♦ **East Asian Football Federation (EAFF)** **05204**
Secretariat c/o KFA, Gyeonghuigung-gil, Jongno-Gu, Seoul 03175, Korea Rep.
URL: http://eaff.com/
History 28 May 2002. **Aims** Develop football in the region by promoting an active interchange within East Asia, strengthening unity and solidarity among its members, and making contributions to peace through football. **Structure** Congress; Executive Committee; Committees (5); Secretariat. **Activities** Sporting activities. **Events** *Congress* Busan (Korea Rep) 2018.
Members National associations in 10 countries and territories:
China, Guam, Hong Kong, Japan, Korea DPR, Korea Rep, Macau, Mongolia, Northern Mariana Is, Taiwan.
NGO Relations A regional zone of *Asian Football Confederation (AFC, #01487)*. [2021/XJ9408/**D**]

♦ **East Asian Forum of Nursing Scholars (EAFONS)** **05205**
Conference Manager c/o Alice Lee Ctr for Nursing Studies, Nat Univ Singapore – Level 2, Clinical Research Ctr – Block MD11, 10 Medical Drive, Singapore 117597, Singapore. T. +65163320. Fax +6567767135. E-mail: eafons_aprs@nuhs.edu.sg.
URL: http://eafons.org/
History 1997. **Aims** Strengthen and promote high quality doctoral education in nursing; create an academic environment and socialization for East Asian Scholars through international collaboration and cooperation. **Structure** Executive Committee. **Events** *East Asian Forum of Nursing Scholars* Manila (Philippines) 2021, *East Asian Forum of Nursing Scholars* Chiang Mai (Thailand) 2020, *Forum* Singapore (Singapore) 2019, *Forum* Seoul (Korea Rep) 2018, *East Asian Forum of Nursing Scholars* Hong Kong 2017. **NGO Relations** Founding member of: *World Academy of Nursing Science (WANS, #21069)*. [2021/XJ5529/**F**]

♦ East Asian Games Association / see East Asian Olympic Committee (#05206)
♦ East Asian Institute, National University of Singapore (internationally oriented national body)
♦ East Asian Institute, Singapore / see East Asian Institute, National University of Singapore
♦ East Asian Insurance Congress (meeting series)
♦ East Asian Joint Symposium on Biomedical Research (meeting series)
♦ East Asian and Oceanian Stock Exchanges Federation / see Asian and Oceanian Stock Exchanges Federation (#01585)

♦ **East Asian Olympic Committee** **05206**
Contact address not obtained. E-mail: eaga@olympic.cn.
URL: http://2009eagarchive.lcsd.gov.hk/
History 27 Jan 1992, Shanghai (China), as *Coordination Committee of the East Asian National Olympic Committees (EANOC)*. Subsequently changed title to *East Asian Games Association (EAGA)*, May 1993. **Aims** Promote the Olympic Movements and its ideal in East Asia; organize and hold the East Asian Games on a regular basis; coordinate and promote the *sports* exchange and cooperation in the region. **Events** *Meeting* Tianjin (China) 2013, *Meeting* Hong Kong (Hong Kong) 2009, *Meeting* Macau 2005, *Meeting* Osaka (Japan) 2001, *Busan congress* Busan (Korea Rep) 1997.
Members National Olympic Committees in the East Asian Zone (10, listed in accordance with the convention in this Yearbook with Chinese Taipei referred to as Taiwan):
China, Guam, Hong Kong, Japan, Kazakhstan, Korea DPR, Korea Rep, Macau, Mongolia, Taiwan. [2017/XE1995/**E**]

♦ **East Asian Pastoral Institute (EAPI)** **05207**
Institut pastoral de l'Asie orientale
Dir Ateneo de Manila Univ Campus, Katipunan Road, Loyola Heights, 1108 Quezon City, Philippines. T. +63284265901. E-mail: admission@eapi.org.ph.
URL: http://www.eapi.org.ph/
History Founded 1954; restructured 1965. A federated unit of Ateneo de Manila (Philippines) University, operated by *Society of Jesus (SJ)*. **Aims** Facilitate personal renewal, *theological* updating and pastoral training for pastoral leaders and workers for local *Catholic churches* of Asia and the *Pacific*. **Structure** Board of Directors, consisting of Major Superiors of East Asia and Pacific regions of the Society of Jesus. Board of Trustees; Director; Staff Committees. **Activities** Networking/liaising; training/education. **Events** *Conference on globalization* Manila (Philippines) 2002, *Workshop on science and religion* Manila (Philippines) 2002, *Seminar on comprehensive plan and action for refugees* Manila (Philippines) 1992, *Training of Roman catholic church workers* Manila (Philippines) 1991, *Planning in religious organizations* Manila (Philippines) 1990. **Publications** *Asia-Pacific Mission Studies (APMS)*.
Members Individuals in 80 countries and territories:
Argentina, Australia, Austria, Bangladesh, Belgium, Bolivia, Botswana, Brazil, Brunei Darussalam, Cambodia, Cameroon, Canada, Chad, China, Chuuk, Colombia, Congo Brazzaville, Congo DR, Egypt, Ethiopia, Falklands/Malvinas, Fiji, France, Germany, Ghana, Guatemala, Guinea, Hong Kong, India, Indonesia, Ireland, Israel, Italy, Jamaica, Japan, Kazakhstan, Kenya, Kiribati, Korea Rep, Laos, Malawi, Malaysia, Malta, Marshall Is, Mauritius, Mexico, Micronesia FS, Myanmar, Nepal, Netherlands, New Zealand, Nigeria, Northern Mariana Is, Pakistan, Palau, Papua New Guinea, Peru, Philippines, Poland, Russia, Samoa, Seychelles, Singapore, Slovakia, Solomon Is, Spain, Sri Lanka, Sudan, Sweden, Switzerland, Taiwan, Tanzania UR, Thailand, Timor-Leste, Tonga, UK, USA, Vanuatu, Vietnam, Zambia.
NGO Relations Member of (1): *Catholic Biblical Federation (CBF, #03600)*. [2021.09.01/XE3997/jv/**E**]

♦ East Asian Regional Branch of the ICA (see: #12996)
♦ East Asian Regional Conference in Alternative Geography (meeting series)
♦ East Asian Seas Action Plan / see Action Plan for the Protection and Development of the Marine Environment and Coastal Areas of the East Asian Region (#00093)
♦ East Asian Society of British History (unconfirmed)

♦ **East Asian Society of Endourology (EASE)** **05208**
Secretariat Dept of Urology, Tokai Univ School of Medicine, 143 Shimokasuya, Isehara KANAGAWA, 259-1193 Japan. T. +81463931121ext2340. Fax +81463938612. E-mail: urotokai@tokai-u.jp.
History 2003. **Events** *Annual Meeting* 2021, *Annual Meeting* Seoul (Korea Rep) 2019, *Annual Meeting* Osaka (Japan) 2016, *Annual Meeting* Hong Kong (Hong Kong) 2014, *Annual Meeting* Hefei (China) 2013. **NGO Relations** *Asia Pacific Association of Pediatric Urologists (APAPU, #01850)*. [2016/XM8283/**D**]

♦ **East Asian Society for the Scientific Study of Religion (EASSSR)** ... **05209**
Contact Room 308, Fac of Humanities and Human Sciences, Hokkaido University, Kita 10, Nishi 7, Kita-ku, Sapporo HOKKAIDO, 060-0810 Japan. E-mail: eassr2021@gmail.com.
URL: https://easssr.org/
Aims Provide an academic platform, in which all scholars of religion can extend the boundaries of social scientific understanding of religions by communicating and exchanging their ideas and knowledge about religious situations of East Asian societies. **Structure** Executive Council; Standing Committee. **Finance** Sources: members' dues. **Events** *Annual Meeting* Hanoi (Vietnam) 2023, *Annual Meeting* Taipei (Taiwan) 2022, *Annual Meeting* Jeju (Korea Rep) 2021. **Members** Regular; Student. Membership countries not specified. [2023.02.22/AA2759/**C**]

♦ East Asian Spa Industry Union (unconfirmed)

♦ **East Asian Squash Federation (EASF)** **05210**
Pres c/o Korea Squash Fed, 503 Olympic Hall, 88 Oryun-Dong, Songpa-Gu, Seoul 138-749, Korea Rep. T. +8224196454 – +8224196455. Fax +8224199479.
Events *Annual Meeting* Daegu (Korea Rep) 2018. **NGO Relations** Affiliate member of: *World Squash Federation (WSF, #21826)*. [2010/XJ2150/**D**]

♦ East Asian Stock Exchange Conference / see Asian and Oceanian Stock Exchanges Federation (#01585)
♦ East Asian Stock Exchange Conference (meeting series)
♦ East Asian Studies Center, Bloomington (internationally oriented national body)
♦ East Asian Tigers / see Four Dragons (#09977)

♦ **East Asian Union of Human Genetics Societies (EAUHGS)** **05211**
Sec 9284 – Guro Hosp, Korea Univ Medical Ctr, 97 Gurodong-gil, Guro-gu, Seoul 152-703, Korea Rep. T. +82226263139. Fax +8228381560. E-mail: jchoe@hamchoon.com – lateroman@naver.com.
History Launched 2001. **Structure** Executive Board, including President, Vice-President, Liaison Officer of IFHGS, Secretary and Treasurer. **Events** *Annual Meeting* Seoul (Korea Rep) 2012, *Annual Meeting* Chiba (Japan) 2011, *Annual Meeting* Sapporo (Japan) 2008, *Annual Meeting* Changsha (China) 2007, *Annual Meeting* Suwon (Korea Rep) 2006. **Publications** *Journal of Human Genetics*. **NGO Relations** Full member of: *International Federation of Human Genetics Societies (IFHGS, #13451)*. [2015/XM3787/**D**]

♦ East Asia and Oceania Assistancy / see Jesuit Conference of Asia Pacific (#16099)
♦ East Asia-Pacific Conference on Structural Engineering and Construction (meeting series)

♦ East Asia and Pacific Infrastructure Regulatory Forum (EAPIRF) . . . 05212

Coordinator CRISIL Risk and Infrastructure Solutions Ltd, The Mira – G 1 – 1st Floor, Plot No 1 and 2, Ishwar Nagar, Delhi 110065, DELHI 110065, India. T. +911142505106. Fax +911126842213. E-mail: trevor.w.bull@gmail.com.
History 2003. **Aims** Foster capacity building and knowledge exchange among infrastructure regulators in the East Asia and Pacific (EAP) region. **Structure** General Assembly; Executive Committee; Secretariat. **Finance** Sources: members' dues. Also Indian sources. Supported by: *International Bank for Reconstruction and Development (IBRD, #12317)* (World Bank). **Events** *World Forum on Energy Regulation (WFER)* Istanbul (Turkey) 2015, *Annual Event* Bangkok (Thailand) 2011. **Members** Core Regulators from East Asia and Pacific Region. Affiliate Regulators from other countries; NGOs; Universities/research institutions; donor organizations. **NGO Relations** Member of (1): *International Confederation of Energy Regulators (ICER, #12859).* [2015/XJ4637/**F**]

♦ East Asia Pacific Mountain Association (inactive)
♦ East Asia Paralympic Committee / see Asian Paralympic Committee (#01652)

♦ East Asia Plant Variety Protection Forum (EAPVP Forum) 05213

Office JATAFF, 7th floor – Sankaido Bldg, 1-9-13 Akasaka, Minato-ku, Tokyo, 107-0052 Japan. E-mail: st-pgr@jataff.or.jp – jpvp@maff.go.jp.
URL: http://eapvp.org/
History 2007. **Aims** Exchange ideas and information to establish effective PVP systems consistent with the UPOV Convention among members towards achieving membership of UPOV, as a basis of further PVP harmonization and cooperation in the region so as to contribute to developing sustainable agriculture and achieving food security. **Activities** Events/meetings; training/education. **Events** *Annual Meeting* Tokyo (Japan) 2021, *Annual Meeting* Hanoi (Vietnam) 2020, *Annual Meeting* Beijing (China) 2019, *Annual Meeting* Muntinlupa City (Philippines) 2018, *Annual Meeting* Nay Pyi Taw (Myanmar) 2017.
Members Governments (13):
Brunei Darussalam, Cambodia, China, Indonesia, Japan, Korea Rep, Laos, Malaysia, Myanmar, Philippines, Singapore, Thailand, Vietnam. [2021/AA2049/**F***]

♦ East Asia Regional Council of Overseas Schools / see East Asia Regional Council of Overseas Schools (#05214)

♦ East Asia Regional Council of Overseas Schools (EARCOS) 05214

Exec Dir Brentville Subdivision, Barangay Mamplasan, Biñan, Laguna, 4024 Santa Cruz, Manila, Philippines. T. +63495115993 – +63495115994. Fax +63495114694. E-mail: info@earcos.org.
URL: http://www.earcos.org/
History 1968. Constitution adopted Nov 1969, Hong Kong (Hong Kong). Former names and other names: *East Asia Regional Council of Overseas Schools* – former. **Aims** Develop collaborative educational partnerships within the region as well as worldwide to foster greater access to expertise. **Structure** Board of Trustees. **Activities** Awards/prizes/competitions; events/meetings; training/education. **Events** *Annual Teachers Conference* Kuala Lumpur (Malaysia) 2024, *Annual Teachers Conference* Kota Kinabalu (Malaysia) 2023, *Annual Leadership Conference* Bangkok (Thailand) 2022, *Annual Teachers Conference* Bangkok (Thailand) 2022, *Annual Teachers Conference* Bangkok (Thailand) 2021. **Publications** *EARCOS TriAnnual* (3 a year) – newsletter.
Members Schools (142) in East Asia. Schools in 20 countries and territories:
Brunei Darussalam, Cambodia, China, Fiji, Guam, Hong Kong, India, Indonesia, Japan, Kazakhstan, Korea Rep, Laos, Malaysia, Mongolia, Myanmar, Philippines, Singapore, Taiwan, Thailand, Vietnam.
Included in the above, 1 organization listed in this Yearbook:
United World College of South East Asia (UWCSEA).
NGO Relations Sponsors: *South East Asia Teachers and Counsellors Conference (SEATCCO).* [2022/XG4243/**E**]

♦ East Asia Research Association for Agricultural Heritage Systems (unconfirmed)
♦ East Asia School of Theology (internationally oriented national body)
♦ East Asia Science Parks Council / see Asian Science Park Association (#01693)
♦ East Asia Studies Institute, Bangkok / see Institute of East Asian Studies, Bangkok
♦ East Asia Urological Oncology Society (unconfirmed)
♦ East Asia/US/Puerto Rico Women's Network Against Militarism / see Women for Genuine Security
♦ East Asia/US Women's Network Against Militarism / see Women for Genuine Security
♦ East Asia Weather Research Association (unconfirmed)
♦ East Caribbean Common Market (inactive)
♦ East Caribbean Organization of Development Foundations (inactive)
♦ **EASTC** Eastern Africa Statistical Training Centre (#05228)
♦ East and Central African Association for Indigenous Rights (internationally oriented national body)
♦ East-Central European Institute, Lublin (internationally oriented national body)
♦ East Central Europe Center, New York NY (internationally oriented national body)
♦ East, Central and Southern Africa Association of Food Science and Technology (inactive)
♦ East, Central and Southern African College of Nursing / see East, Central and Southern African College of Nursing and Midwifery (#05215)

♦ East, Central and Southern African College of Nursing and Midwifery (ECSACONM) 05215

Senior Programme Officer c/o ECSA-HC, Plot No 157, Oloirien Njiro Road, PO Box 1009, Arusha, Tanzania UR. T. +255272549362 – +255272549363. Fax +255272549392. E-mail: info@ecsacon.org.
URL: http://ecsacon.org/
History 1988. Founded by 15th Advisory Committee of the *East, Central and Southern African Health Community (ECSA-HC, #05216).* Endorsed by 16th *Conference of Ministers of Health of East, Central and Southern Africa* and formally inaugurated in Aug 1990, Malawi. Former names and other names: *East, Central and Southern African College of Nursing (ECSACON)* – former. **Aims** Strengthen nursing and *midwifery* education, practice and management, including leadership and research, so as to effectively respond to health issues in the region. **Structure** General Assembly (every 4 years); Council of National Representatives (CNR); Secretariat. **Languages** English. **Staff** 4.00 FTE, paid. **Finance** Sources: donations; grants; members' dues. Other sources: contributions from ECSA-HC member states fund some activities. ECSA-HC Finance Department administers finances. **Activities** Advocacy/lobbying/activism; events/meetings; guidance/assistance/consulting; knowledge management/information dissemination; research/documentation; standards/guidelines; training/education. Active in all member countries. **Events** *Scientific Conference* Manzini (Eswatini) 2022, *Scientific Conference* Arusha (Tanzania UR) 2021, *Biennial Scientific Conference* Mbabane (Eswatini) 2020, *Biennial Scientific Conference* Nairobi (Kenya) 2018, *Biennial Scientific Conference* Nairobi (Kenya) 2016. **Publications** *ECSACON Newsletters. Essential Care for Newborn Baby; Professional Regulatory Framework.* Guidelines; articles.
Members National Nursing Councils, National Nursing Associations and individuals. Members in 16 countries:
Botswana, Eswatini, Kenya, Lesotho, Malawi, Mauritius, Mozambique, Namibia, Rwanda, Seychelles, South Africa, South Sudan, Tanzania UR, Uganda, Zambia, Zimbabwe. [2023.02.14/XE1367/**E**]

♦ East, Central and Southern African Employers' Conference (meeting series)

♦ East, Central and Southern African Health Community (ECSA-HC) . . 05216

Dir Gen Plot No 157 Oloirien, Njiro Road, PO Box 1009, Arusha, Tanzania UR. T. +255272549362 – +2552749365. E-mail: regsec@ecsa.or.tz – info@ecsa.or.tz.
URL: http://ecsahc.org/
History 1974. Established under the auspices of *Commonwealth Secretariat (#04362).* Authority transferred from ComSec to member countries, 1980. Former names and other names: *Commonwealth Regional Health Community Secretariat for East, Central and Southern Africa (CRHCS)* – former; *Commonwealth Regional Health Community (CRHC)* – alias; *ECSA Health Community* – alias. **Aims** Foster regional cooperation for better health in East, Central and Southern Africa; promote efficiency and relevance in the provision of health related services in the region. **Structure** Conference of Health Ministers; Advisory Committee; Directors' Joint Consultative Committee; Programme Experts' Committees; Secretariat. Includes: *College of Surgeons of East, Central and Southern Africa (COSECSA, #04110); East, Central and Southern African College of Nursing and Midwifery (ECSACONM, #05215).* **Languages** English. **Staff** 40.00 FTE, paid. **Finance** Contributions of member states; donors; collaborating organizations. **Activities** Capacity building; events/meetings; healthcare; knowledge management/information dissemination; monitoring/evaluation. **Events** *Health Ministers Conference* Maseru (Lesotho) 2023, *Annual meeting of the conference of regional health ministers* Mauritius 1996, *Annual meeting of the conference of regional health ministers* Seychelles 1995, *Annual meeting of the conference of regional health ministers* Lilongwe (Malawi) 1994, *Conference on nutrition* Nairobi (Kenya) 1993. **Publications** *ECSA Newsletter.* Documents.
Members Participating countries (9):
Eswatini, Kenya, Lesotho, Malawi, Mauritius, Tanzania UR, Uganda, Zambia, Zimbabwe.
IGO Relations Formal contact with: *European Commission (EC, #06633); Global Fund to Fight AIDS, Tuberculosis and Malaria (Global Fund, #10383); United States Agency for International Development (USAID); WHO (#20950).* **NGO Relations** Member of: *Global Health Workforce Alliance (GHWA, inactive).* [2023/XE4701/**E***]

♦ East, Central and Southern African Public Health Association (inactive)
♦ EAST – East Asia School of Theology (internationally oriented national body)
♦ EAST – Eau, agriculture et santé en milieu tropical (internationally oriented national body)

♦ Eastern Africa Action Network on Small Arms (EAANSA) 05217

Coordinator 20 Bukoto Street, PO Box 5460, Kampala, Uganda. T. +256312262134.
History within *International Action Network on Small Arms (IANSA, #11585).* **Aims** Serve as a forum for the exchange of information, experiences and strategies in combating the proliferation of small arms and light weapons in the Great Lakes region and Horn of Africa. **IGO Relations** *Regional Centre on Small Arms and Light Weapons in the Great Lakes Region, the Horn of Africa and Bordering States (RECSA, #18760).* **NGO Relations** Member of: *International Action Network on Small Arms (IANSA, #11585).* [2012/XM4533/**E**]

♦ Eastern Africa Amateur Boxing Union (inactive)

♦ Eastern Africa Association (EAA) 05218

Chief Exec Harlow Enterprise Hub, Kao Hockham Building, Edinburgh Way, Harlow, CM20 2NQ, UK. T. +441279312203. Fax +441279312204.
URL: http://www.eaa-lon.co.uk/
History Founded 1964, on the initiative of prominent companies with interests in East Africa who became founder members. From 1967, when activity extended to Mauritius, known as *East Africa and Mauritius Association.* Coverage subsequently extended to Seychelles (1977), Madagascar (1990), Ethiopia and Eritrea (1995). Incorporated in UK as a company limited by guarantee, 1 Jan 1992. Previously also known as *East Africa Association.* **Aims** Facilitate participation in the *economic development* of Eastern Africa and the Indian Ocean region by firms and *companies* from other countries, to the mutual economic advantage of members and countries concerned; represent and sustain existing foreign private *investment* in the countries covered; provide a forum for exchange of views on matters of common interest to foreign investors and businessmen and a channel of communication for representing these views to governments; cooperate with governments in promoting and encouraging new private investment. **Structure** General Meeting (annual); Executive Committee of 10 to 23 members; Sub-committees. Chief Executive liaises with governments, British government departments, European Business Council, Africa and the Mediterranean and with other bodies concerned with trade and investment in Africa. Resident representatives in: Nairobi (Kenya); Kampala (Uganda); Dar es Salaam (Tanzania UR); Kigali (Rwanda); Addis Ababa (Ethiopia). **Languages** English. **Staff** 2.00 FTE, paid. **Finance** Members' dues. Revenues (annual): about pounds150,000. **Activities** Knowledge management/information dissemination; politics/policy/ regulatory; advocacy/lobbying/activism; guidance/ assistance/consulting; networking/liaising; events/meetings. **Events** *Investment conference on Kenya* London (UK) 1994. **Publications** *Eastern Africa Association Newsletter* (6-8 a year).
Members Subscribing individuals and companies (420), resident or controlled outside the concerned countries, in the fields of banking, insurance, manufacturing, trading, mining and agriculture, transport and shipping, publishing, the petroleum industry and the professions, in 25 countries:
Belgium, Canada, Denmark, Ethiopia, France, Germany, Greece, India, Kenya, Malawi, Mauritius, Monaco, Netherlands, Nigeria, Rwanda, South Africa, Spain, Sweden, Switzerland, Tanzania UR, Uganda, UK, United Arab Emirates, USA, Zimbabwe.
Concerned countries (8):
Burundi, Eritrea, Ethiopia, Kenya, Rwanda, Seychelles, Tanzania UR, Uganda.
NGO Relations Member of: *European Business Council for Africa (EBCAM, #06416).* [2015.09.01/XD6700/**F**]

♦ Eastern Africa Association for Impact Assessment (inactive)

♦ Eastern Africa Association of Oral Maxillofacial Surgeons (EAAOMS) 05219

Pres Nairobi Hosp, Uhmc, Fifth Floor, PO Box 76, Ralph Bunche Rd, Nairobi, Kenya.
URL: http://eaaoms.org/
History Nov 1998. Launched 5 Jul 2002, Nairobi (Kenya). **Aims** Advance the science and art of oral and maxillofacial surgery in the region through training, research, international collaboration and providing community service. **Structure** Board, comprising President, Immediate Past President, Secretary General, Treasurer and 5 country representatives. **Events** *Role and challenges of evidence-based practice of oral and maxillofacial surgery in Africa* Kenya 2009.
Members Full in 11 countries:
Botswana, Burundi, Ethiopia, Kenya, Malawi, Rwanda, Somalia, Sudan, Tanzania UR, Uganda, Zambia.
NGO Relations Member of: *International Association of Oral and Maxillofacial Surgeons (IAOMS, #12057).* [2013/XJ0424/**D**]

♦ Eastern Africa Association for Radiation Protection (internationally oriented national body)
♦ Eastern Africa Association for Theological Education by Extension (no recent information)

♦ Eastern Africa Centre for Constitutional Development (Kituo Cha Katiba) 05220

Exec Dir PO Box 3277, Plot 7 – Estate Link Road, Bukoto (Off Lugogo By-pass), Kampala, Uganda. T. +256414533295. E-mail: kituo@kituochakatiba.org.
URL: http://www.kituochakatiba.org/
History 1997. **Aims** Promote multi-disciplinary debate, dialogue and action on constitutionalism, good governance and democratic development in Eastern Africa through research, information dissemination, networking, advocacy and activism. **Structure** Board, comprising Chairperson and 10 members; Secretariat. **Activities** Active in: Burundi, Kenya, Rwanda, Tanzania UR, Uganda. **Publications** Reports; books; study series. **Consultative Status** Consultative status granted from: *African Commission on Human and Peoples' Rights (ACHPR, #00255)* (Observer). **IGO Relations** Non-accredited organization of: *Commonwealth Secretariat (#04362).* [2023.02.15/XJ1015/**F**]

♦ Eastern Africa Coalition on Economic, Social and Cultural Rights (internationally oriented national body)
♦ Eastern Africa College of Ophthalmologists (inactive)

♦ Eastern Africa Environmental Network (EAEN) 05221

Dir PO Box 555, Uhuru Gardens 00517, Nairobi, Kenya. T. +25420601064. Fax +25420601263.
URL: http://eaen.kbo.co.ke/

History Sep 1990, Nairobi (Kenya), at an international workshop organized by Eastern Africa Regional Committee of the Commission on Education and Communication of the *International Union for Conservation of Nature and Natural Resources (IUCN, #15766)*. **Aims** Raise public awareness on environmental issues and problems in the Eastern Africa Region. **Structure** Board of Directors, consisting of Chairperson, Vice Chairperson, Treasurer, Secretary and 3 members. Secretariat based in Nairobi (Kenya) in the office premises of *East African Wild Life Society (EAWLS, #05190)*. **Staff** 4.00 FTE, paid. **Finance** Financed by: Global Environment Project Institute. **Activities** Stimulates regional communication on issues of environmental concern. Facilitates the access to and exchange of information expertise on environmental and development issues in the region. Creates fora for discussions on environment and development with the view to finding practicable and lasting solutions to the existing and emerging environmental issues in Eastern Africa. Supports Eastern Africa conservation initiatives. Holds: Annual Network Conference (always in Nairobi); annual Environmental Education Training for teachers from member countries. **Events** *Annual Conference* Nairobi (Kenya) 1998, *Annual Conference* Nairobi (Kenya) 1997, *Annual Conference* Nairobi (Kenya) 1996, *Annual conference* Nairobi (Kenya) 1995, *Annual Conference* Nairobi (Kenya) 1994. **Publications** *Njiwa* (4 a year) – magazine; *EAEN Directory* (every 2 years). Conference Proceedings (annual); Conference Programmes (annual).
Members Governmental and non-governmental organizations (over 200) in 11 countries:
Burundi, Djibouti, Eritrea, Ethiopia, Kenya, Mauritius, Rwanda, Somalia, Sudan, Tanzania UR, Uganda.
Overseas members in 3 countries:
Spain, UK, USA.
Consultative Status Consultative status granted from: *UNEP (#20299)*. **NGO Relations** Member of: *Earth-Action (EA, #05159)*. [2010/XF2438/**F**]

♦ Eastern Africa Federation of the Disabled (unconfirmed)

♦ Eastern Africa Grain Council (EAGC) 05222

Exec Dir Maple Court, Westlands Close, off Westlands Rd, PO Box 218, Sarit Ctr, Nairobi, 00606, Kenya. T. +254203745840 – +254202437533. Fax +254203745841. E-mail: grains@eagc.org.
URL: http://www.eagc.org/

History 2006, Kenya, as a Company Limited by Guarantee. **Aims** Improve the policy and trade environment for the betterment of the grain sector from producer to consumer. **Structure** General Meeting Board of Directors, comprising Chairman, Vice-Chairperson and Treasurer. **Events** *All Africa Postharvest Congress* Addis Ababa (Ethiopia) 2019, *Dialogue Meeting on Agricultural Trade Policy and Sustainable Development in East Africa* Nairobi (Kenya) 2015, *African grain trade summit* Dar es Salaam (Tanzania UR) 2009, *African grain trade summit* Nairobi (Kenya) 2007, *African grain trade summit* Nairobi (Kenya) 2005.
Members Active; Affiliated; Associate. Members (67) in 7 countries:
Kenya, Senegal, South Africa, Tanzania UR, Uganda, USA, Zambia.
Included in the above, 2 organizations listed in this Yearbook:
International Fertilizer Development Center (IFDC, #13590); *Partnership to Cut Hunger and Poverty in Africa*.
IGO Relations *Swedish International Development Cooperation Agency (Sida)*; *United States Agency for International Development (USAID)*. **NGO Relations** Member of: *International Grain Trade Coalition (IGTC, #13732)*. [2010/XJ1121/**D**]

♦ Eastern Africa Journalists Association (unconfirmed)
♦ Eastern African Association for the Study of Religions (no recent information)
♦ Eastern African Centre for Research on Oral Traditions and African National Languages (inactive)

♦ Eastern African Farmers Federation (EAFF) 05223

CEO Nelleon Place, Rhapta Road, Westlands, Nairobi, 254, Kenya. T. +254204451691. E-mail: info@eaffu.org.
URL: http://eaffu.org/

History 2001. **Aims** Represent, lobby and advocate for Eastern Africa farmers' interests and build their capacities. **Structure** Council. Board, comprising Regional President, 2 Vice-Presidents, Regional Secretary, Regional Treasurer, Regional Women Representative, Regional Youth Affairs Representative and 4 members.
Members Full in 7 countries:
Burundi, Congo DR, Eritrea, Ethiopia, Kenya, Tanzania UR, Uganda.
NGO Relations *Southern African Confederation of Agricultural Unions (SACAU, #19840)*; *TradeMark East Africa (TMEA, #20183)*. Member of: *PanAfrican Farmers' Organization (PAFO, #18049)*. [2014/XJ3018/**D**]

♦ Eastern African Fine Coffees Association / see African Fine Coffees Association (#00316)
♦ Eastern African Mining Industry Convention (meeting series)
♦ Eastern African Network of AIDS Service Organizations (see: #00272)
♦ Eastern African Power Industry Convention (meeting series)
♦ Eastern African Power, Mining and Telecoms Industry Convention (meeting series)

♦ Eastern African Quaternary Research Association (EAQUA) 05224

Contact Inst of Marine Sciences, Univ of Dar es Salaam, PO Box 668, Dar es Salaam, Tanzania UR.

History 7 Jun 2007, Kampala (Uganda). **Aims** Enhance the growth of quaternary science community in the eastern and central African region through training, promotion of collaborative research and information exchange. **Events** *Workshop* Dar es Salaam (Tanzania UR) 2011, *Workshop* Addis Ababa (Ethiopia) 2009, *Workshop* Kampala (Uganda) 2007. [2017/XJ1755/**D**]

♦ Eastern African Students and Youth Organization (internationally oriented national body)

♦ The Eastern African Sub-Regional Support Initiative for the Advancement of Women (EASSI) 05225

Exec Dir PO Box 24965, Kampala, Uganda. T. +256393266451. E-mail: eassi@eassi.org – eassi.eassi@gmail.com.
URL: https://www.eassi.org/

History 1996. **Aims** Advance the rights of women and promote gender equality and equity. **Structure** General Assembly (meets every 2 years); Board of Directors. **Languages** English, French. **Staff** 15.00 FTE, paid; 2.00 FTE, voluntary. **Finance** Sources: donations; grants. **Activities** Advocacy/lobbying/activism; events/meetings; knowledge management/information dissemination; networking/liaising; training/education. **Publications** *Women's Lexis* (6 a year) – newsletter; *EASSI Annual Report 2020* (annual) in English. *Gender Perspectives in the Karamoja Cluster – Invisible Women* (1st ed 2020) in English; *The Escalation of Non-Tariff Barriers in the East African Community and the Impact on Women Traders during the COVID-19 Pandemic* (1st ed 2020) in English. *Strategic Plan 2019-2023*. Annual Report.
Members Covers 9 countries:
Burundi, Eritrea, Ethiopia, Kenya, Rwanda, Somalia, South Sudan, Tanzania UR, Uganda.
Consultative Status Consultative status granted from: *ECOSOC (#05331)* (Special). **NGO Relations** Member of (3): *Association for Women's Rights in Development (AWID, #02980)*; *Control Arms (#04782)*; *International Action Network on Small Arms (IANSA, #11585)*. [2021.05.20/XF7038/**F**]

♦ Eastern African Support Unit for NGOs (internationally oriented national body)
♦ Eastern African Telecommunications Industry Convention (meeting series)
♦ Eastern Africa Police Chiefs Cooperation Organization (unconfirmed)

♦ Eastern Africa Power Pool (EAPP) 05226

SG Wereda 02, House 059, Bole Sub City, Addis Ababa, Ethiopia. T. +251116671669. E-mail: eapp@eappool.org.
URL: http://eappool.org/

History Memorandum of Understanding signed 24 Feb 2005. **Aims** Optimize use of clean energy resources in the region to benefit society with reduced cost of electricity production and increased rate of access. **Structure** Council of Ministers (COM); Independent Regulatory Board (IRB); Steering Committee; Technical Committees (4); General Secretariat headed by Secretary General. **Languages** English, French. **Staff** 15.00 FTE, paid. **Finance** Members' contributions. Development partners support: *African Development Bank (ADB, #00283)*; *Association of Power Utilities in Africa (APUA, #02867)*; *International Bank for Reconstruction and Development (IBRD, #12317)* (World Bank); *United States Agency for International Development (USAID)*. **Activities** Politics/policy/regulatory; research and development; projects/programmes; knowledge management/information dissemination. **Publications** *Eastern Africa Power Pool Strategic Plan (2018-2027)*.
Members Governments of 11 countries:
Burundi, Congo DR, Djibouti, Egypt, Ethiopia, Kenya, Libya, Rwanda, Sudan, Tanzania UR, Uganda.
NGO Relations Member of: *Global Energy Interconnection Development and Cooperation Organization (GEIDCO, #10342)*. Affiliate member of: *African Electrotechnical Standardization Commission (AFSEC, #00295)*. [2019.12.20/XJ1502/**E***]

♦ Eastern Africa Standby Brigade / see Eastern Africa Standby Force (#05227)

♦ Eastern Africa Standby Force (EASF) 05227

Contact PO Box 1444-00502, Westwood park Road, Karen, Nairobi, Kenya. T. +254203884720. Fax +254203884633. E-mail: easfcom@easbrig.org.
URL: http://www.easfcom.org/

History Set up following decision of Summit of *African Union (AU, #00488)*, Jul 2004, Addis Ababa (Ethiopia), to create *Eastern Africa Standby Brigade (EASBRIG)*. Memorandum of Understanding signed Apr 2005 expressly establishes EASF as constituent organization of *African Standby Force (ASF)*; MOU amended Jan 2011. **Aims** Contribute to regional and continental peace, security, stability and enhance regional integration. **Structure** Assembly (annual); Council of Ministers of Defence and Security; Committee of Chiefs of Defence Staff (EACDS). Eastern Africa Standby Force Coordination Mechanism (EASFCOM); Planning Element (PLANELM); Eastern Africa Standby Brigade (EASBRIG) Headquarters; Logistics Base (LOGBASE). **Events** *High-Level Regional Workshop on Mechanisms for Promoting Maritime Domain Awareness in the West Indian Ocean* Dar es Salaam (Tanzania UR) 2015, *EACDS Ordinary Meeting* Djibouti 2015, *EACDS Ordinary Meeting* Nairobi (Kenya) 2014. **Publications** *EASF Bulletin*.
Members States (10):
Burundi, Comoros, Djibouti, Ethiopia, Kenya, Rwanda, Seychelles, Somalia, Sudan, Uganda. [2015/XM4261/**E***]

♦ Eastern Africa Statistical Training Centre (EASTC) 05228

Centre de formation statistique de l'Afrique de l'Est

Contact PO Box 351053, Dar es Salaam, Tanzania UR. T. +255784784106. E-mail: info@eastc.ac.tz.
URL: http://www.eastc.ac.tz/

History Jul 1965, by *East African Common Services Organization (EACSO, inactive)* and *UNDP (#20292)*, as *East African Statistical Training Centre*. Proposed Jul 1961, Tunis (Tunisia), during Second Conference of African Statisticians. UNDP ended support, and *East African Community (EAC, #05181)* – successor to EACSO – took full control of the Centre until 1977. Statistical Training Programme for Africa (STPA) took over 1979-1993. *United Nations Economic Commission for Africa (ECA, #20554)* requested Tanzanian government to take care of Centre, before being handed back to UNECA. Re-established in accordance with No 28 of Tanzania UR, 18 Nov 1994, taking effect on 1 Oct 1995. A protocol (memorandum of understanding) signed by member countries opens EASTC for use to user countries. **Aims** Be a centre of excellence in training official statistics in Africa; promote production and use of high quality statistics through training, research and consultancy for evidence-based decision making. **Structure** Ministerial Advisory Board; Regional Advisory Board. **Languages** English. **Staff** Teaching: 45; Administrative: 27. **Finance** Sources: Tanzanian government subsidy; fees; conference; training; grants. **Activities** Training/education; research/documentation; knowledge management/information dissemination; guidance/assistance/consulting. **Publications** Articles.
Members User countries (19):
Botswana, Eritrea, Eswatini, Ethiopia, Gambia, Kenya, Lesotho, Malawi, Mauritius, Namibia, Seychelles, Somalia, South Africa, South Sudan, Sudan, Tanzania UR, Uganda, Zambia, Zimbabwe.
IGO Relations *African Development Bank (ADB, #00283)*; *Commonwealth Fund for Technical Cooperation (CFTC, #04331)*; *International Bank for Reconstruction and Development (IBRD, #12317)*; *Southern African Development Community (SADC, #19843)*; *UNICEF (#20332)*; *United Nations Economic Commission for Africa (ECA, #20554)*; *United Nations Population Fund (UNFPA, #20612)*; *United States Agency for International Development (USAID)*; *The World Bank Group (#21218)*; National Statistical Offices of member countries. **NGO Relations** *International Statistical Institute (ISI, #15603)*; national institutes and universities. [2019.02.27/XE0190/**E***]

♦ Eastern Asia Society for Transportation Studies (EASTS) 05229

SG c/o JTTRI, 3-18-19 Toranomon, Minato-ku, Tokyo, 105-0001 Japan. E-mail: easts@easts.info.
Pres Tokyo Inst of Technology, 2 Chone-12-1 Ookayama, Meguro, Tokyo, 152-8550 Japan.
URL: http://www.easts.info/

History 28 Nov 1994, Japan. **Aims** Foster and support excellence in transportation research and practice; stimulate professional interchange in all aspects and modes of transportation. **Structure** Board of Directors. **Languages** English. **Staff** 1.50 FTE, paid. **Finance** Members' dues. **Activities** Events/meetings; training/education; financial and/or material support. **Events** *International Conference* Kuala Lumpur (Malaysia) 2023, *International Conference* Hiroshima (Japan) 2021, *Conference* Colombo (Sri Lanka) 2019, *Seminar on the Future of Transportation in Eastern Asia at the Era of Mass and big Data* Tokyo (Japan) 2019, *Conference* Ho Chi Minh City (Vietnam) 2017. **Publications** *Asian Transport Studies (ATS)* (4 a year); *Journal of the Eastern Asia Society for Transportation Studies* (every 2 years). Conference proceedings.
Members Full in 19 countries and territories:
Australia, Cambodia, China, Hong Kong, Indonesia, Japan, Korea Rep, Laos, Malaysia, Mongolia, Myanmar, Nepal, New Zealand, Philippines, Singapore, Sri Lanka, Taiwan, Thailand, Vietnam. [2021/XD7553/**D**]

♦ Eastern Association for Computing Machinery / see Association for Computing Machinery (#02447)
♦ Eastern Atlantic Hydrographic Commission (see: #13825)

♦ Eastern Caribbean Alliance for Diversity and Equality (ECADE) 05230

Exec Dir Post Office Box 772, LC04 101, Castries, St Lucia. T. +17584509498. E-mail: info@ecequality.org – info4ecade@gmail.com.
Communications Dir address not obtained.
URL: http://www.ecequality.org/

History 2015, Grenada. Officially launched Dec 2016. Registration: Start date: 21 Jun 2016, St Lucia, Caribbean. **Aims** Strengthen regional capacity for the defence and full recognition of human *rights* of the *LGBTQI* community in the eastern Caribbean. **Structure** Board of Directors. **Languages** English, Saint Lucian Creole French. **Staff** 6.00 FTE, paid; 5.00 FTE, voluntary. **Finance** Annual budget: 495,000 USD (2020). **Activities** Events/meetings. **Events** *Annual Caribbean Women and Sexual Diversity Conference* Kingston (Jamaica) 2019, *Annual Caribbean Women and Sexual Diversity Conference* San Jose Succotz (Belize) 2018, *Annual Caribbean Women and Sexual Diversity Conference* Castries (St Lucia) 2017, *Annual Caribbean Women and Sexual Diversity Conference* St Croix (Virgin Is USA) 2016, *Annual Caribbean Women and Sexual Diversity Conference* Port-of-Spain (Trinidad-Tobago) 2015.
Members Full in 9 countries and territories:
Antigua-Barbuda, Barbados, Dominica, Grenada, St Croix Is, St Kitts-Nevis, St Lucia, St Maarten, St Vincent-Grenadines.
NGO Relations Member of (1): *The Commonwealth Equality Network (TCEN, #04327)*. [2022.04.04/XM8661/**D**]

♦ Eastern Caribbean Central Bank (ECCB) 05231

Banque centrale des Caraïbes orientales

Governor PO Box 89, Basseterre, ST KITTS, St Kitts-Nevis. T. +18694652537. Fax +18694651051. E-mail: governor@eccb-centralbank.org – info@eccb-central.org – eccbinfo@eccb-centralbank.org.
URL: http://www.eccb-centralbank.org/

History 1 Oct 1983, on the signing of the Eastern Caribbean Central Bank Agreement by representatives of the Governments of Antigua and Barbuda, Dominica, Grenada, Montserrat, St Kitts-Nevis, St Lucia and St Vincent-Grenadines, 5 Jul 1983. Took over activities of *East Caribbean Currency Authority (ECCA) – Autorité monétaire des Caraïbes orientales*, set up 18 Jan 1965, on signing of *East Caribbean Currency Agreement*, by representatives of the Governments of Antigua, Barbados, Dominica, Montserrat, St Kitts-Nevis, Anguilla, St Lucia and St Vincent. An Amendment was signed, Nov 1973, permitting the withdrawal of Barbados, effective 31 Mar 1974. This Authority succeeded *British Caribbean Currency Board (BCCB)*, formed in 1950; and was also referred to as *East Caribbean Monetary Authority*. **Aims** Maintain stability the Eastern Caribbean currency and the integrity of the banking system. **Structure** Monetary Council, comprising 8 ministers (one from each participating government) Chairmanship (rotates annually); Board of Directors. **Languages** English. **Staff** 236.00 FTE, paid. **Activities** Functions: note issuing powers; services to Governments; services to commercial banks; services to the community at large. Policy areas: monetary stability; financial stability;

money and credit; money and capital market development; economic development. Area covered by ECCB is the *East Caribbean Currency Union (ECCU, no recent information)*. **Events** *Half-yearly meeting* Dominica 1993, *Economic conference* St Kitts-Nevis 1993. **Publications** *Economic and Financial Review* (quarterly and annual); *ECCB Monthly Unaudited Balance Sheet*. *Strategic Plan 2017-2021*. Reports; communiqués; surveys; research papers; presentations; newsletters.
Members Governments of 8 countries and territories:
Anguilla, Antigua-Barbuda, Dominica, Grenada, Montserrat, St Kitts-Nevis, St Lucia, St Vincent-Grenadines.
IGO Relations *Caribbean Group of Banking Supervisors (CGBS, #03512)*. Payments agent for pharmaceuticals and medical supplies purchased through: *Pharmaceutical Procurement Service (PSS, #18354)* (Pharmaceuticals Procurement Services). Cooperates in related fields of interest with: *United Nations Economic Commission for Latin America and the Caribbean (ECLAC, #20556)*; *Caribbean Community (CARICOM, #03476)*; *Caribbean Development Bank (CDB, #03492)*. **NGO Relations** Founding member of: *Caribbean Digital Library Consortium (no recent information)*. Member of: Supports: *Caribbean Centre for Money and Finance (#03469)*. [2018.07.26/XF0488/**F***]

♦ Eastern Caribbean Civil Aviation Authority (ECCAA) 05232

Dir Gen PO Box 1130, Factory Road, St John's, St John, Antigua-Barbuda. T. +12684620000 – +12684620907. Fax +12684620082. E-mail: contact@eccaa.aero.
URL: http://www.eccaa.aero/
History 1986. Established when became formally a subsidiary institution of *Organisation of Eastern Caribbean States (OECS, #17804)*. Evolved into a fully autonomous authority, following Agreement establishing ECCAA, Oct 2003, St Georges (Grenada). Officially set up, Oct 2004, when 5 Member States had passed the Eastern Caribbean Civil Aviation Authority Agreement Act. Former names and other names: *OECS Directorate of Civil Aviation (DCA)* – former (1986). **Aims** Strive to ensure safe, orderly and efficient *air transportation* in the islands of the Organization of Eastern *Caribbean* States. **Structure** Council of Ministers; Board of Directors, headed by Director General. **Activities** Monitoring/evaluation. **Events** *Meeting* St John's (Antigua-Barbuda) 1990.
Members Serves airports in 9 countries and territories:
Anguilla, Antigua-Barbuda, Dominica, Grenada, Montserrat, St Kitts-Nevis, St Lucia, St Vincent-Grenadines, Virgin Is UK.
[2022.11.29/XF1296/**E***]

♦ Eastern Caribbean Coalition for Environmental Awareness (ECCEA) . 05233

Regional Coordinator 1 Place José Marti, Galeries de Géologie et de Botanique, 97254 Fort de France Martinique, France.
URL: http://www.eccea.com/
History 1995. **Aims** Coordinate and implement regional *conservation* programmes; develop and prepare project proposals for national environmental and nongovernmental organizations, grass roots movements and communities. **Structure** Board, including President, Honorary Chairman and Vice-President. **Finance** Private financing: 26%; EU financing: 76%. Other sources: donations, including from *International Union for Conservation of Nature and Natural Resources (IUCN, #15766)* Species Survival Commission (SSC). **Activities** Monitors and evaluates the effects of deforestation, coastal development, coastal and distant water fishing fleets activities in the Caribbean. Conducts research. Organizes conferences, seminars and training. **IGO Relations** Observer at: *Convention on Biological Diversity (Biodiversity convention, 1992)*; *Convention for the Protection and Development of the Marine Environment of the Wider Caribbean Region (Cartagena Convention, 1983)* and its *Protocol Concerning Specially Protected Areas and Wildlife to the Convention for the Protection and Development of the Marine Environment of the Wider Caribbean Region (1990)*; *Convention on International Trade in Endangered Species of Wild Fauna and Flora (CITES, 1973)*. Accredited by: *International Whaling Commission (IWC, #15879)*. Formal contacts with: *European Commission (EC, #06633)*. **NGO Relations** Observer at: *International Association for Caribbean Archaeology (IACA, #11756)*; *Museums Association of the Caribbean (MAC, #16909)*; *World Archaeological Congress (WAC, #21103)*. Member of: *Species Survival Network (SSN, #19916)*. [2017/XF6278/**F**]

- ♦ Eastern Caribbean Commission (inactive)
- ♦ Eastern Caribbean Consultative Committee (inactive)
- ♦ Eastern Caribbean Council of Credit Unions / see Caribbean Confederation of Credit Unions (#03478)
- ♦ Eastern Caribbean Drug Service / see Pharmaceutical Procurement Service (#18354)
- ♦ Eastern Caribbean Farm and Forestry Institute / see Eastern Caribbean Institute of Agriculture and Forestry (#05234)
- ♦ Eastern Caribbean Farm Institute / see Eastern Caribbean Institute of Agriculture and Forestry (#05234)

♦ Eastern Caribbean Institute of Agriculture and Forestry (ECIAF) . . . 05234

Contact Univ of Trinidad and Tobago, Caroni North Bank Road, Centeno Via Arima, Mausica, Arima, Trinidad-Tobago. T. +18686428888. E-mail: callcentre@utt.edu.tt – utt.marketing@utt.edu.tt.
History 1954, as *Eastern Caribbean Farm Institute*, under the Colonial Development and Welfare Scheme to provide training in agriculture. Subsequently changed name to *Eastern Caribbean Farm and Forestry Institute*, when the Forestry School was technically set up in 1966 (with limited physical facilities). The facilities of the Forestry School were bolstered as a result of a project undertaken in 1968 by the Government of Trinidad and Tobago with assistance from *UNDP (#20292)* and *FAO (#09260)*. Present name adopted 1969. In 1983, with the assistance from a World Bank Loan, a third school, the Agriculture Teacher Education Centre, was established, as a joint programme between the Ministry of Education and the Ministry of Agriculture of the Trinidad and Tobago Government. This programme was discontinued in 2001. In 2002, became a campus of the 'College of Science, Technology and Tertiary Education (COSTAATT), a multi-campus college legally authorized to offer the associate degree programme, and offered the Associate of Applied Science Degrees in Agriculture and Forestry in 2007. **Aims** Offer the best possible residential training in agriculture, forestry and ornamental horticulture at the para-professional level; provide specialized training for a diploma in animal health for para-professionals and professionals. **Structure** Board. President; Provost; Director. Located at the campus of the University of Trinidad and Tobago (UTT). **Languages** English. **Staff** 10 full-time faculty; 18 part-time lecturers; 70 other support staff; farm manager; 63 subordinate staff. **Finance** Funded by the Government of Trinidad and Tobago, through the Ministry of Science, Technology and Tertiary Education (MSTTE). **Activities** Training programmes offer a mix theory and practice for acquisition of skills, specific techniques, understanding and appreciation of methods and techniques. Offers diplomas in: Agriculture; Forestry; Ornamental Horticulture; Animal Health; Veterinary Public Health. **Publications** Annual report.
Members Students from 11 countries and territories:
Antigua-Barbuda, Barbados, Belize, Dominica, Grenada, Guyana, Jamaica, St Kitts-Nevis, St Lucia, St Vincent-Grenadines, Virgin Is UK.
NGO Relations Member of: *Association of Caribbean Higher Education Administrators (ACHEA, #02406)*; *Caribbean Area Network for Quality Assurance in Tertiary Education (CANQATE, #03441)* *Caribbean Council of Higher Education in Agriculture (CACHE, #03484)*; *Caribbean Food Crops Society (CFCS, #03509)*. [2016/XE0990/jv/**E***]

- ♦ Eastern Caribbean Islands Regional Security System (inactive)
- ♦ Eastern Caribbean Natural Area Management Programme / see Caribbean Natural Resources Institute (#03525)
- ♦ Eastern Caribbean Popular Theatre Organization (no recent information)

♦ Eastern Caribbean-Southeast Asia Economic and Cultural Chamber (EC-SEA Chamber) 05235

Eastern Carribean No 3 Victoria Street, Roseau, Dominica. E-mail: inquiry@ecseachamber.org.
Southeast Asia Suite B – 7th floor, Strata 2000 Bldg, F Ortigas Jr Road, Ortigal Cntr Business District, Pasic City, METRO 1605 Manila, Philippines.
URL: http://www.ecseachamber.org/
History Registration: Companies House, No/ID: 10555443, Start date: 10 Jan 2017, England and Wales; EU Transparency Register, No/ID: 038414027932-81, Start date: 3 Aug 2017. **Aims** Promote and develop economic and cultural exchange between the leading Eastern Caribbean States and the Southeast Asian region.
Members Full in 6 countries:
Antigua-Barbuda, Dominica, Grenada, St Kitts-Nevis, St Lucia, St Vincent-Grenadines.
NGO Relations Administers *Caribbean ASEAN Voluntary Council for Sustainable Development Goals (Caribbean ASEAN Council)*. [2022/XM8683/**F**]

- ♦ Eastern Caribbean Standing Conference on Teacher Education (meeting series)

♦ Eastern Caribbean Supreme Court (ECSC) 05236

Court Administrator PO Box 1093, Castries, St Lucia. T. +17584573600. Fax +17584573601. E-mail: offices@eccourts.org.
Chief Justice Chief Justice's Chambers, Heraldine Rock Building, 2nd Floor Block B, The Waterfront, Castries, St Lucia.
URL: http://www.eccourts.org/
History Established 27 Feb 1967, as *West Indies Associated States Supreme Court*, by the West Indies Associated States Supreme Court Order (1967 No 223), which has been incorporated into and forms part of the Constitution of all Independent States of *Organisation of Eastern Caribbean States (OECS, #17804)*, and has also been given jurisdiction in the Overseas Territories by the Supreme Court Acts and the Constitutions, in some cases, of those Territories. **Aims** Provide access to a system of *justice* that is accountable and independent, and administered by officers in a prompt, fair, efficient and effective manner. **Structure** Levels (2): *'High Court'*, currently comprising 23 judges and 4 Masters, operating in 3 Divisions (Criminal; Civil; Family); *'Court of Appeal'*, functioning as an itinerant Court sitting in various territories on a regular basis and comprising President and 7 Justices of Appeal. Chief Justice is Head of Court and President of Court of Appeal. Jurisdiction runs through all territories. Commercial Division set up and based at Virgin Is UK. **Languages** English. **Finance** Members' contributions. **Activities** Projects/programmes, including: court restructuring to include implementation of Trial Court structure and integration of the Magistracy; improvement of physical facilities through the development of the 'Halls of Justice'. **Publications** *E-Newsletter* (4 a year). *Eastern Caribbean Supreme Court: Model Regional Court* (2008); *40th Anniversary Magazine* (2007); *Eastern Caribbean Law Reports* (1996-1999); *Civil Procedure Rules 2000*. *Eastern Caribbean Supreme Court: An Evolving Court* (2008) – CD. Annual Report.
Members Jurisdiction covers 9 countries and territories:
Anguilla, Antigua-Barbuda, Dominica, Grenada, Montserrat, St Kitts-Nevis, St Lucia, St Vincent-Grenadines, Virgin Is UK.
NGO Relations Member of (1): *Standing International Forum of Commercial Courts (SIFoCC, #19964)*. Instrumental in setting up (1): *Organization of Eastern Caribbean Bar Associations (OECS Bar Association, #17863)*. [2021/XF1297/**F***]

♦ Eastern Caribbean Telecommunications Authority (ECTEL) 05237

Managing Dir PO Box 1886, Castries, St Lucia. T. +17584581701 – +17581702. Fax +17584581698. E-mail: ectel@ectel.int.
URL: http://www.ectel.int/
History St George's (Grenada), upon signing of the *Treaty of St Georges*, 4 May 2000. Establishment followed a decision by participating states to work together for the liberalization and development of the telecommunications sector. Also known as *Eastern Caribbean Telecommunications Regulatory Authority*. **Aims** Promote open entry, *market* liberalization and *competition* in telecommunications in member countries. **Structure** Council of Ministers, comprising Ministers of the contracting states responsible for telecommunications and Director General of *Organisation of Eastern Caribbean States (OECS, #17804)* (ex officio). Board of Directors; Secretariat headed by Managing Director. **Finance** Fees. Budget (annual): about US$ 3.12 million.
Members Governments of 5 countries:
Dominica, Grenada, St Kitts-Nevis, St Lucia, St Vincent-Grenadines.
IGO Relations Member of: *Organisation of Caribbean Utility Regulators (OOCUR, #17800)*. Formal contacts with: *Caribbean Development Bank (CDB, #03492)*; *African University for Cooperative Development (AUCD, #00494)*; *International Bank for Reconstruction and Development (IBRD, #12317)* (World Bank); *International Telecommunication Union (ITU, #15673)*. **NGO Relations** Member of: *Internet Society (ISOC, #15952)*. [2011.11.30/XF6736/**F***]

- ♦ Eastern Caribbean Telecommunications Regulatory Authority / see Eastern Caribbean Telecommunications Authority (#05237)
- ♦ Eastern Caribbean Tourist Association (inactive)
- ♦ Eastern Central and Southern African Federation of Accountants (inactive)
- ♦ Eastern Churches Association / see Anglican and Eastern Churches Association (#00829)
- ♦ Eastern Council for Travel Research / see Travel and Tourism Research Association

♦ Eastern Dredging Association (EADA) 05238

Association orientale de dragage
Secretariat c/o Port Klang Authority, Mail Bag Service 202, 42005 Port Klang, Selangor, Malaysia. E-mail: subra@pka.gov.my.
URL: http://www.eada.asia/
History 1982, as one of the regional groupings associated with *World Organization of Dredging Associations (WODA, #21688)*. **Aims** Promote exchange of knowledge in the fields concerned with dredging in the widest sense of the term, in Asia and Australasia; further contacts between the various groups from which members are drawn and between the dredging fraternity and the rest of the world; strengthen the image of dredging from both the academic as well as practical sides. **Finance** Members' dues (annual): Corporate – US$ 250; Ordinary – US$ 30. **Activities** Promotes and assists with congresses, seminars and courses; assists and promotes reports on special studies or workshops (ie, measurement of dredged quantities, environmental aspects, etc); supplies assistance or information on dredging subjects to members and others. **Events** *World Dredging Congress* Shanghai (China) 2019, *World Dredging Congress* Miami, FL (USA) 2016, *World Dredging Congress* Beijing (China) 2010, *Triennial World Congress* Orlando, FL (USA) 2007, *World Dredging Congress* Hamburg (Germany) 2004. **Publications** *EADA Newsletter*.
Members Categories Corporate – authorities, organizations, companies and institutions; Ordinary – individual non-transferable membership. Executives and engineers in the Far East and Pacific region, in 15 countries and territories:
Australia, Bangladesh, China, Hong Kong, India, Indonesia, Japan, Malaysia, New Zealand, Pakistan, Philippines, Singapore, Sri Lanka, Taiwan, Thailand. [2019/XE1215/**E**]

- ♦ Eastern European Industrial Development Organization (unconfirmed)
- ♦ Eastern European Network / see Central and Eastern European Regional Network
- ♦ Eastern European University Association (internationally oriented national body)

♦ Eastern European Volleyball Zonal Association (EEVZA) 05239

SG Gostonas Str 6b, Riga LV-1013, Latvia. T. +37167876317. Fax +37167334359. E-mail: lvf@volejbols.lv.
Pres Luzhnetskaia nab 8, Moscow MOSKVA, Russia, 119992. T. +74956370971. Fax +74956370971. E-mail: rus@volley.ru.
URL: http://www.eevza.eu/
History 20 Aug 2005. **Structure** Executive Committee. Commissions. **Activities** Events/meetings.
Members Federations in 10 countries:
Armenia, Azerbaijan, Belarus, Estonia, Georgia, Latvia, Lithuania, Poland, Russia, Ukraine.
NGO Relations Affiliated to: *European Volleyball Confederation (#09078)*; *Fédération internationale de volleyball (FIVB, #09670)*. [2014/XJ8513/**D**]

- ♦ Eastern Europe Studies Centre (internationally oriented national body)

♦ Eastern Mediterranean Association for Child and Adolescent Psychiatry and Allied Professions (EMACAPAP) 05240

Contact Dept of Psychiatry and Psychology, St George Univ Hospital, PO Box 166378, Beirut, Lebanon. T. +9611587190 – +9611748000.
History Feb 2000, Sharm el Sheikh (Egypt). **Aims** Promote mental health, development and welfare of children and adolescents and support their families. **Activities** Research methodology training courses/seminars. **Events** *Conference on Systems of Care for Autism Spectrum Disorder* Dubai (United Arab Emirates) 2017, *Research methodology seminar* Alexandria (Egypt) 2007, *Research methodology seminar* Djerba (Tunisia) 2006, *Research methodology seminar* Sharm el Sheikh (Egypt) 2005, *Research methodology seminar* Sharm el Sheikh (Egypt) 2004.
Members Full in 16 countries and territories:
Algeria, Egypt, Iraq, Jordan, Kuwait, Lebanon, Morocco, Oman, Palestine, Qatar, Saudi Arabia, Sudan, Syrian AR, Tunisia, United Arab Emirates, Yemen. [2011/XM1279/**D**]

♦ Eastern Mediterranean Association of Medical Editors (ENAME) . . . 05241

Contact c/o EMRO, Monazamet El Seha El Alamia Str, Extension of Abdel Razak El Sanhouri Str, PO Box 7608, Nasr City, Cairo, 11371, Egypt.
URL: http://www.emro.who.int/entity/emame/

History Set up following conferences held 2003, Cairo (Egypt) and 2004, Riyadh (Saudi Arabia). **Aims** Support and promote medical journalism in the Eastern Mediterranean region by fostering networking, education, discussion, and exchange of information and knowledge. **Structure** Executive Council. Committees. **Events** *Regional Conference on Medical Journals in the Eastern Mediterranean Region* Shiraz (Iran Islamic Rep) 2015, *Joint Conference* Brussels (Belgium) 2014, *Regional Conference on Medical Journals in the Eastern Mediterranean Region (EMMJ6)* Cairo (Egypt) 2013, *Regional Conference on Medical Journals in the Eastern Mediterranean Region* Karachi (Pakistan) 2010, *Fourth Regional Conference on Medical Journals in the Eastern Mediterranean* Manama (Bahrain) 2008. **IGO Relations** *WHO Regional Office for the Eastern Mediterranean (EMRO, #20944).* **NGO Relations** *Asia Pacific Association of Medical Journal Editors (APAME, #01846).* Cooperates with: *World Association of Medical Editors (WAME, #21162).* [2014/XJ7781/**D**]

♦ Eastern Mediterranean Blood and Marrow Transplantation Group (EMBMT) 05242

Secretariat King Faisal Specialist Hosp and Research Centre, PO Box 3354, MBC 64, Riyadh 11211, Saudi Arabia. E-mail: fhussain@kfshrc.edu.sa.
Main: http://www.embmt.org/

History Founded 2008. **Aims** Share experience, initiate cooperative trials and establish common strategy to achieve optimization in the field of *hematopoietic* stem cell transplantation (HSCT); promote all aspects of patient care, academic and research activities associated with the field of HSCT in the region; standardize quality control and accreditation. **Structure** Board of Directors; Working Committees. **Activities** Events/meetings; training/education; knowledge management/information dissemination. **Events** *Business Meeting* Milan (Italy) 2014, *Business Meeting* London (UK) 2013, *Business Meeting / Scientific Meeting* Muscat (Oman) 2013, *Business Meeting* Dubai (United Arab Emirates) 2012, *Business Meeting* Geneva (Switzerland) 2012. **Publications** *Hematology/Oncology and Stem Cell Therapy Journal.* Newsletter; reports; articles.
Members Open to individuals, institutions and corporations in Eastern Mediterranean region as defined by WHO. Current membership countries not specified but members of the Board of Directors in 15 countries:
Algeria, Bahrain, Egypt, Iran Islamic Rep, Iraq, Jordan, Lebanon, Morocco, Oman, Pakistan, Qatar, Saudi Arabia, Syrian AR, Tunisia, United Arab Emirates.
NGO Relations Member of: *Alliance for Harmonisation of Cellular Therapy Accreditation (AHCTA, #00686).* [2019.06.30/XJ8077/**E**]

♦ Eastern Mediterranean Council of Optometry (EMCO) 05243

Exec Dir Hamra, Kahira Street, Serhal Bldg, Beirut, Lebanon. E-mail: executivedirector@emco-opt.org – president@emco-opt.org.
Pres address not obtained.
URL: http://emco-opt.org/En/

History . Former names and other names: *Middle East Optical and Optometric Association* – former. **Aims** Provide a forum for the optometric profession in the region to exchange information and views and present those views to national authorities and inform the public; represent the profession to institutions of member nations and assist in relations with the World Council of Optometry; promote education and research and adopt common standards for public benefit; encourage expansion of scope of practice and development of optometry; gain national recognition and secure best legislative framework for the profession; establish special commissions or working parties to carry out studies; participate with other bodies for the benefit of optometry, and eye and vision care in general; achieve the goals of Vision 2020: Right to Sight through interprofessional collaboration. **Structure** Executive Management Board. Officers include: President; Vice-President; Finance Secretary; General Secretary; Joint Secretary. **Languages** Arabic, English. **Staff** 2.00 FTE, paid. **Events** *International Congress of Optometry* Marrakech (Morocco) 2018, *Meeting* Iran Islamic Rep 2015, *Meeting* Lebanon 2014, *Meeting* Dubai (United Arab Emirates) 2013, *Meeting* Ajman (United Arab Emirates) 2011.
Members Optometric Associations in 22 countries and territories:
Afghanistan, Algeria, Bahrain, Djibouti, Egypt, Iran Islamic Rep, Iraq, Jordan, Kuwait, Lebanon, Libya, Morocco, Oman, Pakistan, Palestine, Qatar, Saudi Arabia, Somalia, Sudan, Syrian AR, Tunisia, United Arab Emirates, Yemen.
NGO Relations Regional member of: *World Council of Optometry (WCO, #21335).* [2021.09.03/XD1181/**D**]

♦ Eastern Mediterranean Gas Forum (EMGF) 05244

Mailing Address 1A Ahmed El Zomor St, Nasr City, next to Enppi, Cairo, Egypt.
URL: https://emgf.org/

History 2019. Inaugurated 14 Jan, Cairo (Egypt), by energy ministers of Egypt, Cyprus, Greece, Israel, Italy, Jordan and Palestine. Former names and other names: *EastMed Gas Forum* – alias; *East-Med Gas Forum* – alias. **Aims** Create a regional gas market that serves member interests by ensuring supply and demand, optimizing resource development, rationalizing the cost of infrastructure, offering competitive prices, and improving trade relations. **Structure** Includes the *Gas Industry Advisory Committee (GIAC).*
Members Governments of 7 countries:
Cyprus, Egypt, Greece, Israel, Italy, Jordan, Palestine. [2022/XM8864/**F***]

♦ Eastern Mediterranean and Middle East Chiropractic Federation (no recent information)

♦ Eastern Mediterranean Public Health Network (EMPHNET) 05245

Exec Dir Abdallah Ben Abbas St, Bldg No 42, Amman, Jordan. T. +96265519962. Fax +96265519963. E-mail: comm@emphnet.net.
URL: http://emphnet.net/

History Proposed 2008, Kuala Lumpur (Malaysia), during a bilateral meeting of *Training Programs in Epidemiology and Public Health Interventions NETwork (TEPHINET, #20198).* Officially announced and registered May 2009, Jordan. **Aims** Assist countries in the region in achieving better population health outcomes. **Structure** Board of Directors. **Languages** Arabic, English, French. **Staff** 43.50 FTE, paid. **Finance** Funds from agreements. Annual budget: US$ 2,000,000 – 4,000,000. **Activities** Capacity building; research/documentation; networking/liaising; healthcare; training/education; events/meetings. **Events** *International Conference on Emergency Medicine and Public Health* Doha (Qatar) 2016, *Regional Conference* Aqaba (Jordan) 2015, *Regional Conference* Marrakech (Morocco) 2013, *Regional Conference* Sharm el Sheikh (Egypt) 2011. **Publications** *Newsletter* (4 a year). Annual Report; 5 Year Report; capability statements; reports.
Members Full in 10 countries:
Afghanistan, Egypt, Iraq, Jordan, Morocco, Pakistan, Saudi Arabia, Sudan, Tunisia, Yemen.
IGO Relations *UNICEF (#20332); WHO (#20950); WHO Regional Office for the Eastern Mediterranean (EMRO, #20944);* Ministries of Health; Centers for Disease Control and Prevention. **NGO Relations** Partner of: *Global Outbreak Alert and Response Network (GOARN, #10521).* [2019/XM4315/**F**]

♦ Eastern Mediterranean University (internationally oriented national body)
♦ Eastern and Middle European Confederation of National Societies of Plastic Aesthetic Restorative Surgery and Aesthetic Medicine (no recent information)
♦ Eastern Pacific Ocean Tuna Fishing Agreement (1983 treaty)

♦ Eastern Partnership 05246

No fixed address address not obtained.
URL: http://www.easternpartnership.org/

History Launched 7 May 2009, Prague (Czech Rep), by the then 27 Member States of *European Union (EU, #08967)* and 6 partner countries of the former Soviet Union. **Aims** Tighten the relationship between the *EU* and the Eastern partners by deepening their *political co-operation* and *economic integration.* **Structure** Summit of Heads of States and Governments. Ministerial Meeting. Thematic Platforms (4). *Eastern Partnership Civil Society Forum (EaP CSF, #05247).* **Events** *Summit* Vilnius (Lithuania) 2013, *Summit* Warsaw (Poland) 2011.
Members Partner States (6):
Armenia, Azerbaijan, Belarus, Georgia, Moldova, Ukraine.
Regional Entity:
European Union (EU, #08967).
IGO Relations *Regional Environmental Centre for the Caucasus (REC Caucasus, #18781).* **NGO Relations** *Centre for European Transformation (CET).* [2013/XJ7635/**E***]

♦ Eastern Partnership Civil Society Forum (EaP CSF) 05247

Dir Rue de l'Industrie 10, 1000 Brussels, Belgium. T. +328932585. E-mail: communications@eap-csf.eu.
URL: http://eap-csf.eu/

History 2009. Set up as part of *Eastern Partnership (#05246).* Articles adopted 2012. Former names and other names: *Secretariat of the Steering Committee of the Eastern Partnership Civil Society Forum* – legal name; *Secrétariat du Comité de Pilotage du Forum de la Société Civile du Partenariat Oriental* – legal name. Registration: Banque-Carrefour des Entreprises, No/ID: 0848.169.582, Start date: 23 Aug 2012, Belgium; EU Transparency Register, No/ID: 112703312593-49, Start date: 10 Jan 2014. **Aims** Promote European integration and facilitate reforms and democratic transformation in the Eastern Partnership countries. **Structure** General Assembly; Steering Committee; Secretariat. Working Groups; National Platforms; Compliance Committee. **Languages** English, Russian. **Staff** 7.00 FTE, paid. **Activities** Advocacy/lobbying/activism; monitoring/evaluation. **Events** *Annual Assembly* Brussels (Belgium) 2021, *Annual Assembly* Brussels (Belgium) 2020, *Annual Assembly* Brussels (Belgium) 2019, *Annual Assembly* Brussels (Belgium) 2016, *Assembly* Stockholm (Sweden) 2012. **Publications** *Eastern Partnership Index.*
Members Organizations in 27 countries:
Armenia, Austria, Azerbaijan, Belarus, Belgium, Bulgaria, Cyprus, Czechia, Estonia, Finland, France, Georgia, Germany, Greece, Hungary, Italy, Latvia, Lithuania, Moldova, Netherlands, Poland, Romania, Slovakia, Slovenia, Spain, Sweden, Ukraine.
Included in the above, 35 organizations listed in this Yearbook:
- *Association des états généraux des étudiants de l'Europe (AEGEE-Europe, #02495);*
- *Caucasian Institute for Peace, Democracy and Development (CIPDD);*
- *Caucasus Environmental NGO Network (CENN, #03613);*
- *Centre for European Transformation (CET);*
- *Climate Action Network Europe (CAN Europe, #04001);*
- *Council of Europe (CE, #04881);*
- *Danube Civil Society Forum (DCSF, #05003);*
- *Erasmus Mundus Students and Alumni Association (EMA, #05527);*
- *European Alternatives (EA, #05891);*
- *European Association for Local Democracy (ALDA, #06110);*
- *European Association for the Education of Adults (EAEA, #06018);*
- *European Association of History Educators (EUROCLIO, #06069);*
- *European Center for Not-for-Profit Law (ECNL, #06463);*
- *European Centre for Minority Issues (ECMI);*
- *European Cultural Foundation (ECF, #06868);*
- *European Economic and Social Committee (EESC, #06963);*
- *European Movement International (EMI, #07825);*
- *European Trade Union Confederation (ETUC, #08927);*
- *Europe Foundation (EPF, #09158);*
- *Europe Without Barriers (EWB);*
- *Forus (#09934);*
- *HealthProm;*
- *Institute for Regional and International Studies, Sofia (IRIS);*
- *Institut für Europäische Politik, Berlin (IEP);*
- *Institutul pentru Politici si Reforme Europene (IPRE);*
- *International Business and Economic Development Center (IBEDC);*
- *International Centre for Policy Studies, Kiev (ICPS);*
- *International Renaissance Foundation (IRF);*
- *International Society for Fair Elections and Democracy (ISFED);*
- *IREX Europe (#16019);*
- *Pan-European Regional Council (PERC, #18180);*
- *People in Need (PIN);*
- *Policy Association for an Open Society (PASOS, #18416);*
- *SMEunited (#19327);*
- *West-East Bridges Foundation (#20909).*

Consultative Status Consultative status granted from: *Council of Europe (CE, #04881)* (Participatory Status). **IGO Relations** *Conference of the Regional and Local Authorities for the Eastern Partnership (CORLEAP, #04645).* **NGO Relations** *Centre for International Security and Strategic Studies, Kiev (CISSS).* [2022.10.31/XM5652/y/**F**]

♦ Eastern Regional Organization for Planning and Housing / see Eastern Regional Organization for Planning and Human Settlements (#05248)

♦ Eastern Regional Organization for Planning and Human Settlements (EAROPH) 05248

Organisation régionale orientale pour l'habitation et l'urbanisme

SG Level 20, Ministry of Urban Wellbing/Housing/Local Government, No 51 Persian Perdana, presint 4, 62100 Putrajaya, Malaysia. E-mail: earophsecretariat@gmail.com.
URL: https://earoph.org/

History Feb 1958, Delhi (India). Original English title: *Eastern Regional Organization for Planning and Housing (EAROPH).* Formally constituted and Officers elected Aug 1958. A Regional Chapter of *International Federation for Housing and Planning (IFHP, #13450).* Originally based in Delhi, when registered in accordance with Indian law; transferred to Kuala Lumpur (Malaysia), 1978, and currently registered under Malaysian law. **Aims** With special application to potentialities and needs of the countries in the region, study and promote for the purpose of attaining a better quality of life: improvement of housing; theory, practice and implementation of urban housing and rural planning, including creation of new agglomerations, at local, regional, national and international levels. **Structure** Council. National Chapters (4): Australia; Korea Rep; Japan; Indonesia. Setting up: *Asia Pacific Institute of Good Asset Management (APIGAM).* **Languages** English. **Staff** 2.00 FTE, paid. **Finance** Members' dues. Sale of publications; grants from governments. **Activities** Events/meetings; training/education. **Events** *Biennial Congress* Surabaya (Indonesia) 2022, *Smart Living 2030: Sustainable Cities and Communities* Manila (Philippines) 2020, *Biennial Congress* Newcastle, NSW (Australia) 2018, *Regional Conference* Quezon City (Philippines) 2017, *International Housing Forum* Singapore (Singapore) 2017. **Publications** *EAROPH Bulletin* (4 a year). Congress reports.
Members Individuals (315); Organizations (77), in 14 countries and territories:
Australia, Hong Kong, India, Indonesia, Japan, Korea Rep, Malaysia, Pakistan, Papua New Guinea, Philippines, Singapore, Sri Lanka, Taiwan, Thailand. [2023/XD0479/**D**]

♦ Eastern Regional Organization for Public Administration (EROPA) . . 05249

Organisation régionale de l'Orient pour l'administration publique – Organización Regional del Oriente para la Administración Pública

Secretary General NCPAG Bldg, RP de Guzman St, Univ of the Philippines, Diliman, 1101 Quezon City, Philippines. T. +639706707251. Fax +63289297789. E-mail: secretariat@eropa.co – publications@eropa.co.
URL: https://www.eropa.co/

History Founded at a region-wide conference on public administration, 7-20 Jun 1958, Manila and Baguio (Philippines). Constitution, adopted by 1st General Assembly, 4-10 Dec 1960, Manila, came into force 5 Dec 1960. Amended: 9 Oct 1962, Bangkok (Thailand); 27 Jun 1968, Kuala Lumpur (Malaysia); 9 May 1971, Manila; 31 Oct 1973, Tokyo (Japan); 21 Oct 1983, Seoul (Korea Rep); 10 Dec 1989, Kathmandu (Nepal); May/Jun 1999, Manila (Philippines). Registration: Securities and Exchange Commission, No/ID: CN201402211, Philippines, Asia-Pacific. **Aims** Promote good practice and conduct in public administration and management within the region so as to achieve a high standard of service to the governments and their publics; appreciate the value and importance of effective and efficient public administration; develop and promote the study of public administration; foster cooperation, communication and understanding amongst interested organizations and individuals; develop leadership qualities and management expertise, especially at executive and middle management levels. **Structure** General Assembly (every 2 years); Executive Council (meets annually); Secretariat-General. **Languages** English. **Staff** 6.50 FTE, paid. **Finance** Sources: donations; investments; members' dues; sale of publications; sponsorship. Annual budget: 78,406 USD (2021). **Activities** Events/meetings; publishing activities; research/documentation; training/education. **Events** *EROPA Conference* Hanoi (Vietnam) 2023, *International Conference* Bangkok (Thailand) 2022, *EROPA Conference* Kathmandu (Nepal) 2022, *Joint Seminar* Quezon City (Philippines) 2022, *EROPA and CAPS International Seminar* Shanghai (China) 2021. **Publications** *EROPA Bulletin* (4 a year); *Asian Review of Public Administration (ARPA)* (2 a year). Books; conference proceedings. **Information Services** *EROPA Featured Public Administration News; Online Resource Center of the United Nations Public Administration Network (UNPAN).*

Members State; Group: institutions such as institutes and schools of public administration, universities, government agencies and cities within the region; Individual: persons whose work and professional activities have served to promote the interests of the Organization. States members (10):
China, India, Indonesia, Iran Islamic Rep, Japan, Korea Rep, Nepal, Philippines, Thailand, Vietnam.
Group members in 22 countries and territories:
Australia, Bangladesh, Brunei Darussalam, China, Fiji, Hong Kong, India, Indonesia, Iran Islamic Rep, Japan, Korea Rep, Macau, Maldives, Nepal, Pakistan, Philippines, Russia, Samoa, Sierra Leone, Thailand, USA, Vietnam.
Individuals in 27 countries and territories:
Albania, Australia, Bangladesh, China, Czechia, Fiji, Hong Kong, India, Indonesia, Iran Islamic Rep, Japan, Korea Rep, Macau, Nepal, Netherlands, New Zealand, Nigeria, Papua New Guinea, Philippines, Poland, Samoa, Singapore, Sri Lanka, Thailand, Timor-Leste, USA, Vietnam.
Consultative Status Consultative status granted from: *ECOSOC (#05331)* (General). **IGO Relations** Associated with: Department of Global Communications of the United Nations. [2022.05.11/XD0480/**D**]

♦ Eastern and Southern Africa Association of Agricultural Economists (inactive)

♦ Eastern and Southern Africa Centre of International Parasite Control (ESACIPAC) 05250

Contact Kenya Medical Research Inst, Mbagathi Road, PO Box 54840, Nairobi, Kenya. T. +254202722541. Fax +254202720030. E-mail: director@kemri.org – cmwandawiro@kemri.org – esacipac@kemri.org.
URL: http://www.kemri.org/index.php/centres-a-departments/esacipac

History 2002, Nairobi (Kenya). A regional centre of *Collaborative International Pesticides Analytical Council (CIPAC, #04099)* under Global Parasite Control Initiative, also referred to as Hashimoto Initiative. **Aims** Promote parasite control in the Eastern and Southern Africa region. **Activities** Organizes courses. **Publications** *ESACIPAC Quarterly*.
Members in 8 countries and territories:
Botswana, Kenya, Malawi, Tanzania UR, Uganda, Zambia, Zimbabwe. [2016/XM0680/**E**]

♦ Eastern and Southern Africa Laboratory Managers Association (E-SALAMA) 05251

Exec Sec Univ of Nairobi, College of Chemistry, PO Box 30197, Nairobi, GPO 00100, Kenya.
URL: http://www.e-salama.com/

History 2001. Officially launched Nov 2002, Dar es Salaam (Tanzania UR). **Aims** Interlink laboratory managers in the region and the world at large; establish and manage proficiency testing schemes, quality audit and quality assurance; establish proper procedures for procurement and disposal of chemicals, equipment and their wastes; build capacity in acquisition of laboratory related technical skills; offer consultancy; develop mechanisms aimed at establishing of an accreditation body in the region; act as an advisory body. **Structure** International Organizing Committee, including Chairman, Treasurer and 2 Secretaries. **Activities** Testing schemes; quality audits and assurance; development; training; information dissemination; consultancy.
Members Full in 9 countries:
Botswana, Ethiopia, Kenya, Lesotho, Rwanda, Sudan, Tanzania UR, Uganda, Zimbabwe. [2013.10.11/XJ6111/**D**]

♦ Eastern and Southern Africa Leather Industries Association (no recent information)

♦ Eastern and Southern African Anti-Money Laundering Group (ESAAMLG) 05252

Groupe anti-blanchiment d'Afrique orientale et australe (GABAOA)

Exec Sec Msese Road Plot 96 Kinondoni, PO Box 9923, Dar es Salaam, Tanzania UR. T. +255222667895. Fax +255222668745. E-mail: flkweka@esaamlg.or.tz.
URL: http://www.esaamlg.org/

History 27 Aug 1999, Arusha (Tanzania UR), by members of *Financial Action Task Force (FATF, #09765)*. **Aims** Combat laundering of the proceeds of all serious crimes. **Structure** Ministerial Council (meets annually), comprising at least one ministerial representative or duly authorized alternate from each member country. Task Force of Senior Officials. Secretariat. **Languages** English. **Finance** Members' dues. Other sources: contributions from cooperating supporting nations. **Activities** Organizes workshops. **Events** *Meeting* Arusha (Tanzania UR) 2018, *Plenary Meeting* Arusha (Tanzania UR) 2017, *Meeting* Zanzibar (Tanzania UR) 2017, *Meeting* Zanzibar (Tanzania UR) 2017, *Meeting* Victoria Falls (Zimbabwe) 2016. **Publications** *ESAAMLG Newsletter* (4 a year). Annual Report.
Members Governments of 14 countries:
Botswana, Eswatini, Kenya, Lesotho, Malawi, Mauritius, Mozambique, Namibia, Seychelles, South Africa, Tanzania UR, Uganda, Zambia, Zimbabwe.
IGO Relations Observers:
- *African Development Bank (ADB, #00283)*;
- *Common Market for Eastern and Southern Africa (COMESA, #04296)*;
- *Commonwealth Secretariat (#04362)*;
- *East African Community (EAC, #05181)*;
- *East African Development Bank (EADB, #05183)*;
- FATF;
- *International Bank for Reconstruction and Development (IBRD, #12317)* (World Bank);
- *International Criminal Police Organization – INTERPOL (ICPO-INTERPOL, #13110)*;
- *International Monetary Fund (IMF, #14180)*;
- *Southern African Development Community (SADC, #19843)*;
- *Trade and Development Bank (TDB, #20181)*;
- *United Nations Global Programme Against Money Laundering, Proceeds of Crime and the Financing of Terrorism (GPML, #20568)*;
- *World Customs Organization (WCO, #21350)*.

Observer to: *Asia/Pacific Group on Money Laundering (APG, #01921)*. [2016/XE4156/**E***]

♦ Eastern and Southern African Business Organization (no recent information)

♦ Eastern and Southern African Dairy Association (ESADA) 05253

Exec Dir Liberty Plaza, 4th Floor, Suite 4, Mombasa Rd, Nairobi, 00100, Kenya. T. +254721266481. Fax +254703501532. E-mail: secretariat@dairyafrica.com.
URL: http://www.dairyafrica.com/

History Founded 2004. **Aims** Promote and increase trade of high quality dairy products within and outside the region. **Structure** Board of Directors; Secretariat. **Languages** English. **Staff** 3.00 FTE, paid. **Finance** Members' dues. Other sources: grants; income from conferences. **Activities** Knowledge management/ information dissemination; networking/liaising; awareness raising; capacity building. **Events** *Annual African Dairy Conference* Kampala (Uganda) 2021, *Annual African Dairy Conference* Kampala (Uganda) 2020, *Annual African Dairy Conference* Nairobi (Kenya) 2019, *Annual African Dairy Conference* Nairobi (Kenya) 2018, *Annual African Dairy Conference* Nairobi (Kenya) 2017. **Publications** *Dairy Mail Africa*.
Members Chapters in 10 countries:
Kenya, Malawi, Mauritius, Rwanda, South Africa, Sudan, Tanzania UR, Uganda, Zambia, Zimbabwe. [2019/XM0403/**D**]

♦ Eastern and Southern African Initiative on Debt and Reserves Management / see Macroeconomic and Financial Management Institute of Eastern and Southern Africa (#16539)

♦ Eastern and Southern African Management Institute (ESAMI) 05254

Institut de gestion pour l'Afrique orientale et l'Afrique australe

Main Office PO Box 3030, Arusha, Tanzania UR. T. +255578383 – +255578388. Fax +255578285.
URL: http://www.esami-africa.org/

History 28 Feb 1980, following recommendations, 4 Nov 1977, Lusaka (Zambia), of 3rd Conference of the Council of Ministers of MULPOC for Eastern and Southern Africa, currently *ECA Sub-Regional Office for Eastern Africa (SRO-EA Kigali, #05275)*. Constitution drafted 2 Feb 1979, Nairobi (Kenya), at 4th Conference, and at meeting of experts 24-26 Oct 1979. Previously functioned from 1974 as *East African Community Management Institute (EACMI)* or *East African Management Institute (EAMI)*, set up by *East African Legislative Assembly (EALA, #05185)*. **Aims** Develop and provide effective advice for management and governance of private, civic and public sector organizations in Africa. **Structure** Governing Board, consisting of representatives of full member countries. Academic Board. Director General, assisted by Deputy Director General, heads Management Team, composed of Directors of Sectors and Departments. Management Development Committee (MDC) provides inputs in professional activities. Regional offices (9) in: Dar es Salaam; Harare (Zimbabwe); Kampala (Uganda); Lilongwe (Malawi); Lusaka (Zambia); Maputo (Mozambique); Mbabane (Eswatini); Nairobi (Kenya). **Finance** Sources: self financing (85%); donor grants (5%); government Windhoek (Namibia), s (10%). **Activities** Promotes and organizes training courses, workshops, seminars and symposia, serving as specialized regional centre and focusing in particular on the management of public enterprises in such strategic sectors as: finance and banking; information technology (MIS); women in development/ management (WID/WIM); management of small scale enterprises; transport and communications; materials; natural resources, science and technology; health administration and hospitals; industrial and agro-industrial planning; municipal and local authorities; human resources. Offers Executive MBA course. Organizes: *Commonwealth Advanced Management Programme*; consultancy service; action oriented research. **Events** *Seminar for information professionals in East Africa* Arusha (Tanzania UR) 1992, *Annual seminar for heads of civil/public services* Windhoek (Namibia) 1991, *Case writing workshop* Arusha (Tanzania UR) 1989, *Seminar on productivity improvement of parastatals* Harare (Zimbabwe) 1989, *Top level seminar on computer policy* Swaziland 1989. **Publications** *ESAMI Newsletter* (4 a year); *Africa Management Development Forum (AMDF)* (2 a year); *ESAMI Management Training Programmes Prospectus* (annual). Information Services: Library and documentation centre (15,000 vols and 70 core professional journals); computer database.
Members Full: governments of 12 countries:
Comoros, Djibouti, Eswatini, Kenya, Malawi, Mozambique, Namibia, Seychelles, Tanzania UR, Uganda, Zambia, Zimbabwe.
Other countries using ESAMI services (8):
Algeria, Botswana, Eswatini, Ethiopia, Lesotho, Madagascar, Mauritius, Somalia.
IGO Relations Under Lom Conventions, links with: *European Commission (EC, #06633)*. Cooperates with:
- *African Centre for Gender (ACG)*;
- *African Training and Research Centre in Administration for Development (CAFRAD, #00486)*;
- *Asian Development Bank (ADB, #01422)*;
- *Canadian International Development Agency (CIDA, inactive)*;
- *Centre on Integrated Rural Development for Africa (CIRDAFRICA, no recent information)*;
- *Common Market for Eastern and Southern Africa (COMESA, #04296)*;
- *Commonwealth Fund for Technical Cooperation (CFTC, #04331)*;
- *Commonwealth Secretariat (#04362)*;
- *ILO (#11123)*;
- *International Bank for Reconstruction and Development (IBRD, #12317)*;
- *International Civil Aviation Organization (ICAO, #12581)*;
- *International Development Research Centre (IDRC, #13162)*;
- *Regional Centre for Mapping of Resources for Development (RCMRD, #18757)*;
- *UNDP (#20292)*;
- *UNIDO (#20336)*;
- *United Nations Economic Commission for Africa (ECA, #20554)*;
- *United States Agency for International Development (USAID)*;
- *WHO (#20950)*.

NGO Relations Member of: *African Association for Public Administration and Management (AAPAM, #00215)*; *Association of Management Training Institutions of Eastern and Southern Africa (AMTIESA, no recent information)*; *Africa Capacity Alliance (ACA, #00160)*. Cooperates with: *African Airlines Association (AFRAA, #00200)*; *Commonwealth Association of Polytechnics in Africa (CAPA, #04308)*; *Eastern and Southern African Universities Research Programme (ESAURP, #05255)*; *International Council on the Management of Population Programs (ICOMP, #13043)*. [2016/XF0363/j/**E***]

♦ Eastern and Southern African Mineral Resources Development Centre / see African Minerals and Geosciences Centre (#00373)

♦ Eastern and Southern African Trade and Development Bank / see Trade and Development Bank (#20181)

♦ Eastern and Southern African Universities Research Programme (ESAURP) 05255

Exec Dir PO Box 35048, Dar es Salaam, Tanzania UR. T. +255222115608.
URL: http://esaurp.org/

History 1977, as *Eastern and Southern African Universities Research Project*. **Aims** Carry out research in *human resources* development and usage within the 15 countries in the Eastern and Southern African region. **Structure** Secretariat; Advisory Committee. **Staff** 19, including Executive Director, 11 professional staff and 7 supporting staff. **Finance** Funded by research and training projects, Tanzania government and participating universities. **Activities** Research/documentation; events/meetings. **Events** *Technical and labour market conference* Dar es Salaam (Tanzania UR) 1991, *Session* Geneva (Switzerland) 1991. **Publications** *The Cost of Peace* (1994); *Fisheries Development in Tanzania* (1994); *Technical Education and Labour Market in Eastern and Southern African Countries* (1993); *Research Undertaken Recently in Eastern and Southern Africa* (1990) – published by EUSARIP/ECA-PADIS; *University Capacity in Eastern and Southern African Countries* (1987); *Development of Higher Education in Eastern and Southern Africa* (1985) by L Tembo et al; *Inventory of Universities and Selected Tertiary Institutions in Eastern and Southern African Countries* (1983); *Higher Education and Development in Eastern Africa* (1982) by T L Maliyamkono et al; *Training and Productivity in Eastern Africa* (1982) by T L Maliyamkono et al; *Policy Development in Overseas Training* (1980) by T L Maliyamkono; *Overseas Training: Its Impact on Development* (1979) by T L Maliyamkono. Monographs; pamphlets.
Members Participating countries (15):
Angola, Botswana, Eswatini, Ethiopia, Kenya, Lesotho, Malawi, Mauritius, Mozambique, Somalia, Sudan, Tanzania UR, Uganda, Zambia, Zimbabwe.
IGO Relations *Eastern and Southern African Management Institute (ESAMI, #05254)*; *Southern African Development Community (SADC, #19843)*. **NGO Relations** *African Association for Public Administration and Management (AAPAM, #00215)*; *Association of African Universities (AAU, #02361)*; *Council for the Development of Social Science Research in Africa (CODESRIA, #04879)*; *Regional Council for Democracy (no recent information)*. [2004/XF0429/**F**]

♦ Eastern and Southern African Universities Research Project / see Eastern and Southern African Universities Research Programme (#05255)

♦ Eastern and Southern Africa Regional Branch of the International Council on Archives (see: #12996)

♦ Eastern and Southern Africa Regional Inter Agency Task Team on Children and AIDS / see Regional Inter-Agency Task Team on Children and AIDS in Eastern and Southern Africa (#18791)

♦ Eastern and Southern Africa small scale Farmers' Forum (ESAFF) 05256

Chairman PO Box 1782, Old Dar es Salaam Road, Morogoro, Tanzania UR. E-mail: coordinator@esaff.org.
Gen Sec address not obtained. E-mail: mariamphakmal@gmail.com – esaff@esaff.org.
URL: http://www.esaff.org/

History 2002, resulting from Small Scale Farmers' Convergence (SFC), at World Summit on Sustainable Development (WSSD), Johannesburg (South Africa). Registered in Tanzania. **Aims** Empower small scale farmers in Eastern and Southern Africa to influence development policies and promote ecological agriculture through capacity strengthening, research and networking. **Structure** General Summit (every 3 years); General Meeting (annual); Regional Board; Secretariat, headed by Regional Coordinator. **Languages** English, French. **Staff** 6.00 FTE, paid. **Finance** Funding from: *Brot für die Welt*; *European Union (EU, #08967)*; *Oxfam Novib*; *TrustAfrica (#20251)*. **Events** *AU Year of Agriculture Conference* Addis Ababa (Ethiopia) 2014, *Regional Workshop on Agriculture Policy Advocacy, Communications and Public Expenditure Tracking* Dar es Salaam (Tanzania UR) 2014, *Women's Smallholder Farmers Conference on the SADC Regional Agriculture Policy* Johannesburg (South Africa) 2014, *Regional Workshop on Public Expenditure Tracking* Nairobi (Kenya) 2014, *Annual General Meeting* Nairobi (Kenya) 2012. **Publications** *ESAFF Newsletter*.
Members Full in 11 countries:
Burundi, Kenya, Lesotho, Madagascar, Malawi, Seychelles, South Africa, Tanzania UR, Uganda, Zambia, Zimbabwe. [2014.11.21/XJ6325/**F**]

♦ Eastern and Western Association for Liver Tumors (unconfirmed)

♦ **EAST** European Academy of Surface Technology (#05816)

♦ East European Acoustical Association (internationally oriented national body)

♦ **EAST** European Association for Secure Transactions (#06202)

♦ **East European and Central Asian Union of PLWH (ECUO)** **05257**
Secretariat 87a Mezhygirska St, Kiev, 04080, Ukraine. T. +380444677565 – +380444677582. Fax +380444677593. E-mail: secretariat@ecuo.org.
URL: http://ecuo.org/en/
History 2005. Officially registered Oct 2007. PLWH stands for *People Living with HIV*. **Aims** Improve access to timely, comprehensive, high-quality treatment, care and support services for adults and children with *HIV*. **Structure** General Assembly. Supervisory Committee. President; Secretariat. **Languages** English, Russian. **Finance** Support from: Aids Fonds; *European Commission (EC, #06633)*; *Joint United Nations Programme on HIV/AIDS (UNAIDS, #16149)*; *Oxfam Novib*; Robert Carr Fund; *UNICEF (#20332)*; ViiV Healthcare Ltd. **Events** *International AIDS conference* Vienna (Austria) 2010, *Regional cooperation – joint the efforts for universal access* Moscow (Russia) 2009, *Conference* Moscow (Russia) 2008, *Conference* Moscow (Russia) 2006. **Publications** *In Focus: PLWH* – newsletter. Country profiles; reports.
Members Full in 15 countries:
Armenia, Azerbaijan, Belarus, Estonia, Georgia, Kazakhstan, Kyrgyzstan, Latvia, Lithuania, Moldova, Poland, Russia, Tajikistan, Ukraine, Uzbekistan.
NGO Relations Member of: *European Alliance for Responsible R and D and Affordable Medicines (#05879)*.
[2016.12.15/XJ0592/**D**]

♦ **East European Dance Sport Federation (EEDSF)** **05258**
Pres Valchenko Str 9, ap 249, Rîbnita, Moldova. T. +38512552237. Fax +38512463714. E-mail: vl-konstantinov@mail.ru.
URL: http://idsa.com.ua/eedsf/
Members Federations in 3 countries:
Moldova, Russia, Ukraine.
NGO Relations Member of: *International Dance Sport Association (IDSA, #13132)*. [2013/XJ6349/**D**]

♦ East European Engineering Organizations (no recent information)
♦ East European Family History Association / see Foundation for East European Family History Societies
♦ East European Psychoanalytic Institute (see: #14662)
♦ East European Schools Association / see Central and Eastern European Schools Association (#03697)
♦ East European Socialist Women's Committee (inactive)
♦ East-European Solidarity Committee (internationally oriented national body)
♦ East and Horn of Africa Election Observers Network (unconfirmed)

♦ **East and Horn of Africa Human Rights Defenders Network (EHAHRD-Net)** **05259**
Exec Dir Human Rights House, Plot 1853 Lulume Road, Nsambya, PO Box 70356, Kampala, Uganda. T. +256393265820 – +256312265821. E-mail: executive@defenddefenders.org.
URL: http://www.defenddefenders.org/
History 2005. **Aims** Strengthen the work of human rights defenders (HRDs) throughout the region by reducing their vulnerability to the risk of persecution and by enhancing their capacity to effectively defend human rights. **Structure** General Assembly; Advisory Council; Secretariat, provided by *DefendDefenders*. **Activities** Advocacy/lobbying/activism. Active in: Burundi, Djibouti, Eritrea, Ethiopia, Kenya, Rwanda, Somalia, South Sudan, Sudan, Tanzania UR, Uganda. **NGO Relations** Sub-regional member of: *Pan-African Human Rights Defenders Network (AfricanDefenders, #18052)*. [2018.02.06/XM5773/**F**]

♦ East and Horn of Africa Human Rights Defenders Project / see DefendDefenders (#05026)
♦ EASTICA – East Asian Regional Branch of the ICA (see: #12996)
♦ **EASTI** European Aviation Security Training Institute (#06304)
♦ **EASTIN Association** Global Assistive Technology Information Network (#10240)
♦ EASTIN / see Global Assistive Technology Information Network (#10240)
♦ EastMed Gas Forum / see Eastern Mediterranean Gas Forum (#05244)
♦ East-Med Gas Forum / see Eastern Mediterranean Gas Forum (#05244)
♦ East Meets West / see Thrive Networks

♦ **East meets West (EMW)** **05260**
Contact Belvederegasse 11/5, 1040 Vienna, Austria. E-mail: info@eastmeetswest.eu.
URL: http://www.eastmeetswest.eu/
History 2013, Vienna (Austria). Former names and other names: *East meets West Forum (EMW)* – legal name; *Gemeinnütziger Verein zur Förderung von Micro LGBT Geschäftsinitiativen in Österreich und Zentral- und Osteuropa* – legal name. Registration: No/ID: ZVR 231608652, Austria. **Aims** As a network of *LGBTIQ* professionals from Western and mainly *Eastern Europe* , facilitate exchange of ideas and sharing of best practices; generate mutual inspiration to improve social acceptance of *LGBTIQ* people in different countries. **Structure** Run by 2 Co-Founders. **Languages** Czech, Dutch, English, French, German, Slovakian. **Staff** None paid. **Finance** Private funding. **Activities** Advocacy/lobbying/activism; capacity building; events/meetings; knowledge management/information dissemination; networking/liaising. **Events** *Conference* Bratislava (Slovakia) 2022, *Conference* Vienna (Austria) 2020, *Conference* Vienna (Austria) 2019, *Conference* Vienna (Austria) 2018.
Members Professionals (about 1,300) in 22 countries:
Albania, Armenia, Austria, Belarus, Belgium, Bosnia-Herzegovina, Bulgaria, Croatia, Czechia, Hungary, Kosovo, Latvia, Lithuania, Montenegro, North Macedonia, Poland, Romania, Russia, Serbia, Slovakia, Slovenia, Ukraine.
[2020.10.14/XM7991/**F**]

♦ East meets West Forum / see East meets West (#05260)
♦ **EASTR** European Association of State Territorial Representatives (#06220)
♦ **EASTS** Eastern Asia Society for Transportation Studies (#05229)

♦ **East and Southeast Asia Federation of Soil Science Societies (ESAFS)** **05261**
Support Office c/o JSSSPN, Tamura Bldg- 10F, 5-23-13 Hongou, Bunkyo-ku, Tokyo, 113-0033 Japan. T. +81338152085. Fax +81338156018.
URL: https://www.esafs-support.com/
History Aug 1990, Kyoto (Japan). Founded at 14th International Congress of Soil Science. **Aims** Promote research in soil and related sciences and disseminate the acquired knowledge and technology for the benefit of member societies in the region; contribute to the sustainable development of the region through harmonization of agricultural production and environmental protection. **Structure** Officers: President, Vice-President, Secretary General and Society Representative. Office of the Federation rotates every 2 years. **Languages** English. **Staff** 1.50 FTE, voluntary. **Finance** National society holding Office of the Federation finances publication and distribution of newsletter. **Activities** Awards/prizes/competitions; events/meetings; knowledge management/information dissemination; research/documentation. **Events** *International Conference* Vietnam 2024, *International Conference* Kuala Lumpur (Malaysia) 2022, *International Conference* Kuala Lumpur (Malaysia) 2021, *International Conference* Taipei (Taiwan) 2019, *International Conference* Pattaya (Thailand) 2017. **Publications** *ESAFS Newsletter* (every 2 years). Conference proceedings.
Members National societies in 15 countries and territories:
Bangladesh, China, India, Indonesia, Japan, Korea DPR, Korea Rep, Malaysia, Mongolia, Nepal, Philippines, Sri Lanka, Taiwan, Thailand, Vietnam.
NGO Relations Proposed to set up: *Asian Soils and Environment Research Information Center (ASERIC)*.
[2022/XD2849/**D**]

♦ East and Southeast Asia Network for Better Local Governments (internationally oriented national body)
♦ East and Southern Africa Centre on International ICT Policy / see Collaboration on International ICT Policy-Making for East and Southern Africa

♦ **East and Southern African Association of Accountants-General (ESAAG)** **05262**
CEO 19th Floor, 240 Madiba Street, Pretoria, South Africa. T. +27123155630. E-mail: esaag@treasury.gov.za.
URL: http://esaag.co.za/
History Founded 1995, Arusha (Tanzania UR). **Aims** Establish cooperation between countries in the region in the area of government accounting; provide a forum for participants to review and discuss comparative experiences; encourage the development of government accounting personnel and trainers. **Structure** Governing Body; Committees; Secretariat. **Activities** Events/meetings; training/education. **Events** *Annual Conference* Livingstone (Zambia) 2019, *Annual Conference* Entebbe (Uganda) 2018, *Annual Conference* Boksburg (South Africa) 2017, *Annual Conference* Nairobi (Kenya) 2016, *Annual Conference* Dar es Salaam (Tanzania UR) 2015.
Members Full in 14 countries:
Botswana, Eswatini, Kenya, Lesotho, Malawi, Mauritius, Mozambique, Namibia, Rwanda, South Africa, Tanzania UR, Uganda, Zambia, Zimbabwe.
NGO Relations *Pan African Federation of Accountants (PAFA, #18050)*. [2018/XM7260/**D**]

♦ East and Southern African Society for Teacher Education (inactive)
♦ East Timor Action Network / see East Timor and Indonesia Action Network
♦ East Timor and Indonesia Action Network (internationally oriented national body)

♦ **East-West Center (EWC)** **05263**
Centre Orient-Occident
Communications Dir 1601 East-West Rd, J A Burns Hall, Honolulu HI 96848-1601, USA. T. +18089447111. Fax +18089447376. E-mail: ewcinfo@eastwestcenter.org – ewccontact@eastwestcenter.org.
URL: http://www.eastwestcenter.org/
History 14 May 1960, Honolulu HI (USA), as *Center for Cultural and Technical Interchange between East and West*, by US Congressional legislation. **Aims** Promote better relations and understanding among the peoples of *Asia*, the *Pacific* and the *United States* through cooperative study, training and research. **Structure** Board of Governors; Alumni Association: *East-West Center Association (EWCA, see: #05263)*; Finance: *East-West Center Foundation (see: #05263)*. Includes: *Pacific Islands Development Program (PIDP, see: #05263)*, which also serves as Secretariat for the *'Pacific Island Conference'* and its *Standing Committee of the Pacific Islands Conference of Leaders (#19957)*. Serves as secretariat to *United States/Pacific Island Nations Joint Commercial Commission (JCC)*, whose *Pacific Islands Business Network (PIBN)* is administered by PIDP. **Languages** English. **Staff** 33.00 FTE, paid. **Finance** Main source: annual appropriation by US Congress. Other sources: Asian and Pacific governments; private foundations, public agencies and corporations; individuals. **Activities** Projects/programmes; training/education; research and development; networking/liaising; financial and/or material support. **Events** *International Media conference* Honolulu, HI (USA) 2022, *International conference* Honolulu, HI (USA) 2022, *International Graduate Student Conference* Honolulu, HI (USA) 2019, *Joint Conference on Inclusive Growth and Fiscal Policy* Honolulu, HI (USA) 2019, *Indo-Pacific Regional Security Dialogue* Honolulu, HI (USA) 2018. **Publications** *Asia Pacific Bulletin*. *Asia Pacific Briefing Paper* – series; *Asia Policy* – series. Annual Report; books; monographs; studies; pamphlets. **NGO Relations** Institutional member of: *Regional Energy Resources Information Center (RERIC, #18780)*. Provides secretariat for: *US Consortium of APEC Study Centers*. Cooperative projects with: *Ford Foundation (#09858)*; *Pacific Basin Consortium for Environment and Health (PBC, #17937)*; *WorldFish (#21507)*. Member of: *APEC International Assessment Network (APIAN, no recent information)*; *Clean Air Asia (#03983)*; *Environment Liaison Centre International (ELCI, no recent information)*; *South Asian Humanist Network (see: #10972)*. [2020/XE3964/**E**]

♦ East-West Center Association (see: #05263)
♦ East-West Center Foundation (see: #05263)
♦ East-West Cultural Center (internationally oriented national body)
♦ Eastwest European Institute (internationally oriented national body)
♦ East-West European Institute (internationally oriented national body)
♦ East-West-European Women's Network / see OWEN – Mobile Academy for Gender Democracy and Promotion of Peace (#17920)

♦ **EastWest Institute (EWI)** **05264**
Pres/CEO 11 East 26th St, 20th Floor, New York NY 10010, USA. T. +12128244100. Fax +12128244149. E-mail: newyork@eastwest.ngo.
Brussels Office 59-61 Rue de Trèves, 1040 Brussels, Belgium. T. +3227434610. Fax +3227434639.
Moscow Office 7/5 Bolshaya Dmitrovka Str, Bldg 1 6th Floor, Moscow MOSKVA, Russia. T. +74952347797. Fax +74952347798. E-mail: vivanov@stimson.org.
URL: http://www.ewi.info/
History 1981, as *Institute for East West Security Studies* by John Edwin Mroz and Ira Wallach. Subsequently changed title to *Institute for East-West Studies (IEWS)*. **Aims** Through a transatlantic multinational *public policy* network and think tank, assist policymakers in Europe, Russia and the *newly independent* states and in the USA to: build a secure, democratic, prosperous and integrated *Europe*; overcome the divisive legacies of the 20th century while creating a *new order* in Europe in which governments, the private sector and nongovernmental organizations work together effectively. **Structure** Board of Directors, including Chairmen and Honorary Chairmen. Executive Office in New York NY (USA) includes President and Senior Vice Presidents. Network of affiliated centres (7): Brussels (Belgium); Belgrade (Serbia-Montenegro); Prague (Czech Rep); Kiev (Ukraine); New York; Helsinki (Finland); Moscow (Russia). **Finance** Supported by the following organizations listed in this Yearbook: *Carnegie Corporation of New York*; *Charles Stewart Mott Foundation*; *European Union (EU, #08967)*; *Ford Foundation (#09858)*; *The William and Flora Hewlett Foundation*; *MacArthur Foundation*; *OECD (#17693)*; *Rockefeller Brothers Fund (RBF)*; *Sasakawa Peace Foundation (SPF)*. **Activities** Projects/programmes; events/meetings; awards/prizes/competitions. Instrumental in setting up: *Carpathian Foundation International (CF, see: #05264)*; *Transatlantic Partners Against AIDS (TPAA)*. **Events** *Annual Worldwide Security Conference* Brussels (Belgium) 2012, *Annual worldwide security conference* Brussels (Belgium) 2010, *Annual worldwide security conference* Brussels (Belgium) 2009, *Annual worldwide security conference* Brussels (Belgium) 2008, *Annual worldwide security conference* Brussels (Belgium) 2006. **Publications** *Eurasia in the 21st Century: The Total Security Environment* – series; *Subregionalism in the New Europe* – series. *The Federal Budget and the Regions: Analyzing Fiscal Flows* (2001); *Regional Policy in Countries of Europe: Lessons for Ukraine* (2000); *Towards Europe: Ukrainian Experience of EuroRegions* (2000); *Regional Policy Goes East: Essays and Lessons Learned for Regional Development Policy in Central and Eastern Europe* (1999). Annual Report; regional publications; books; policy briefs; conference reports; booklets. Reference library (New York NY and Prague). **Members** Not a membership organization. **Consultative Status** Consultative status granted from: *ECOSOC (#05331)* (Special). [2022/XE2919/j/**E**]

♦ East-West Management Institute (internationally oriented national body)

♦ **East-West-Network Europe (EWNE)** **05265**
Contact Eichenallee 5, DINKER, 59514 Welver, Germany. T. +491732583770. Fax +492384941458.
History Registered in accordance with German law, 2009. **Aims** Promote East-West European *cooperation* among different networks and groups of organization so as to increase economic, institutional, cultural and social *development* in Europe. **Structure** General Assembly (annual); Executive Committee. **Languages** English, German, Spanish. **Staff** All voluntary. **Finance** Members' dues. [2015.01.05/XJ7250/**F**]

♦ **East-West Transport Corridor Association (EWTCA)** **05266**
Contact Plytines 27, LT-10105 Vilnius, Lithuania. T. +37052745075. E-mail: secretariat@ewtcassociation.net.
URL: http://www.ewtcassociation.net/
History Founded 29 Jun 2010, Vilnius (Lithuania). **Aims** Develop cooperation between transport and logistics companies, intermodal transport operators, consignors and consignees, authorities and academic institutions in relation to the establishment of multifaceted East West Transport corridor, capable of handling global *Asian-European trade* flows. **Structure** Council.
Members Companies and institutions in 11 countries:
Belgium, China, Denmark, France, Germany, Kazakhstan, Lithuania, Mongolia, Russia, Sweden, Ukraine.
[2018/XM7471/**D**]

♦ EASUN – Eastern African Support Unit for NGOs (internationally oriented national body)
♦ **EASVO** European Association of State Veterinary Officers (#06221)
♦ EASYEO – Eastern African Students and Youth Organization (internationally oriented national body)
♦ **EASyM** European Association of Systems Medicine (#06244)

- **EASY Net** Ecumenical Asia-Pacific Students and Youth Network (#05343)
- EAT / see Association européenne des enseignants (#02565)

♦ EAT ... 05267

Contact Kongens gate 11, 0153 Oslo, Norway. E-mail: info@eatforum.org.
URL: https://eatforum.org/

History Founded by Stordalen Foundation, *Stockholm Resilience Centre (#19995)* and *Wellcome Trust*. Former names and other names: *EAT Forum* – former. **Aims** Catalyze a *food* system transformation. **Structure** Board of Trustees; Advisory Board. **Activities** Events/meetings; networking/liaising; projects/programmes; research/documentation. **Events** *Eat Forum* Stockholm (Sweden) 2019. **IGO Relations** Partners include: *CGIAR System Organization (CGIAR, #03843)*; *Global Crop Diversity Trust (Crop Trust, #10313)*. **NGO Relations** Member of: *High Level Panel for a Sustainable Ocean Economy (Panel, #10917)*; *Science Based Targets Network*; *World Benchmarking Alliance (WBA, #21228)*. Partners include: *Stockholm Resilience Centre (#19995)*; *World Resources Institute (WRI, #21753)*. Core partner of: *Food and Land Use Coalition (FOLU)*. [2020/XM8565/**F**]

- EATA – European Aquarium and Terrarium Association (unconfirmed)
- **EATA** European Asphalt Technology Association (#05921)
- EATA – European Association for Telematic Applications (inactive)
- **EATA** European Association for Transactional Analysis (#06257)
- EATA – European Association of Turkish Academics (inactive)
- **EATA** European Automotive and Telecoms Alliance (#06302)
- **EATAG** European Association of Teachers of Ancient Greek (#06248)
- **EATAW** European Association for the Teaching of Academic Writing (#06249)
- **EATB** European Association of Tissue Banks (#06255)
- EATCB / see European Association of Tissue Banks (#06255)
- **EATC** European Air Transport Command (#05853)
- **EATC** European Alliance for Television and Culture (#05888)
- EATCI – European Association Trade-Crafts-Industry (internationally oriented national body)
- EATCM – European Association of Traditional Chinese Medicine (inactive)
- EATCSECW / see Formation d'éducateurs sociaux européens (#09873)
- **EATCS** European Association for Theoretical Computer Science (#06253)
- EATES – European Association for Trauma and Emergency Surgery (inactive)
- EAT / see Esophageal ATresia Global Support Groups (#05540)
- **EAT** Esophageal ATresia Global Support Groups (#05540)
- EAT – Europäische Vereinigung für Thermographie (inactive)
- **EAT** European Association of Thermology (#06254)
- EAT Forum / see EAT (#05267)
- **EATGA** European Association for Transcultural Group Analysis (#06258)
- **EATG** European AIDS Treatment Group (#05850)
- EAtHC – Eastern Atlantic Hydrographic Commission (see: #13825)
- EATIC – Eastern African Power, Mining and Telecoms Industry Convention (meeting series)
- EATI – European Academy of Tumor Immunology (internationally oriented national body)

♦ Eating Disorders Research Society (EDRS) ... 05268

Main Office 2111 Chestnut Ave, Ste 145, Glenview IL 60025, USA. T. +18479833519. E-mail: info@edresearchsociety.org.
URL: http://www.edresearchsociety.org/

History Registration: USA, North Dakota. **Structure** Board of Directors, comprising President, President-Elect, Immediate Past President, 2 Past Presidents, Secretary-Treasurer and Membership Chairperson. **Events** *Annual Meeting* Philadelphia, PA (USA) 2022, *Annual Meeting* Boston, MA (USA) 2021, *Annual Meeting* 2020, *Annual Meeting* Chicago, IL (USA) 2019, *Annual Meeting* Sydney, NSW (Australia) 2018. [2021/XM0619/**D**]

- **EATiP** European Aquaculture Technology and Innovation Platform (#05910)
- **EATIS** Euro American Association on Telematics and Information Systems (#05630)
- EATIS.org / see Euro American Association on Telematics and Information Systems (#05630)
- EATJP / see European Association for the Trade in Jute and Related Products (#06256)
- **EATLP** European Association of Tax Law Professors (#06247)
- **EATLT** European Association for the Teaching of Legal Theory (#06250)
- EATP – European Association for Textile Polyolefins (inactive)
- EATRIS ERIC / see European Infrastructure for Translational Medicine (#07536)
- **EATRIS** European Infrastructure for Translational Medicine (#07536)
- EATRO – East African Trypanosomiasis Research Organization (inactive)
- **EATSA** Euro-Asia Tourism Studies Association (#05642)
- **EATS** European Association of Taiwan Studies (#06245)
- EATS – European Automotive Trim Suppliers (inactive)
- **EATTA** East African Tea Trade Association (#05189)
- EATUC – East African Trade Union Coordinating Council (no recent information)
- **EATWOT** Ecumenical Association of Third World Theologians (#05344)
- Eau, agriculture et santé en milieu tropical (internationally oriented national body)
- Eau et Assainissement pour l'Afrique (#20836)
- EA-UE – European Academy of the Urban Environment, Berlin (internationally oriented national body)
- **EAU** European Association of Urology (#06264)
- **EAUH** European Association for Urban History (#06262)
- **EAUHGS** East Asian Union of Human Genetics Societies (#05211)
- Eau – Lait – Vaches, Structures laitières / see Enfance Tiers Monde
- **EAUM** European Association of Urban Missions (#06263)
- EAUN / see European Association of Urology Nurses (#06265)
- **EAUN** European Association of Urology Nurses (#06265)
- EAUOS – East Asia Urological Oncology Society (unconfirmed)
- Eau Sans Frontières Internationale (internationally oriented national body)
- De l'eau pour tous (internationally oriented national body)
- Eauvive (internationally oriented national body)
- Eau vive (internationally oriented national body)
- Eau Vive – Famiglia Missionaria Donum Dei (religious order)
- **EAVA** Euro-Arab Veterinary Association (#02975)
- **EAVA** European Association of Veterinary Anatomists (#06268)
- EAVA – European Audio Video Association (inactive)
- **EAVDI** European Association of Veterinary Diagnostic Imaging (#06269)
- **EAVE** Entrepreneurs de l'audiovisuel européen (#05495)
- **EAVI** European Association for Viewers Interests (#06272)
- **EAVLD** European Association of Veterinary Laboratory Diagnosticians (#06270)
- **EAV** Medizinische Gesellschaft für System- und Regulationsdiagnostik (#16689)
- **EAVP** European Association of Vertebrate Palaeontologists (#06266)
- **EAVPT** European Association for Veterinary Pharmacology and Toxicology (#06271)
- EAVS – European Association for Veterinary Specialization (no recent information)
- EAVSoM – European Association for the Visual Studies of Man (inactive)
- EAWA – East Africa Work Campers Association (no recent information)
- **EAWE** European Academy of Wind Energy (#05818)
- EAWHR – European Association for Women and Health Research (no recent information)
- EAWL – East Africa Women's League (internationally oriented national body)
- **EAWLS** East African Wild Life Society (#05190)
- **EAWOP** European Association of Work and Organizational Psychology (#06278)
- EAWRA – East Asia Weather Research Association (unconfirmed)
- **EAWRE** European Association for World Religions in Education (#06279)
- **EAYCO** East African Youth Council (#05191)
- **EAYE** European Association of Young Economists (#06280)
- EAYMF – East Africa Yearly Meeting of Friends (internationally oriented national body)
- EAYO – European Association of Youth Orchestras (inactive)
- EAY / see YMCA Europe (#21977)
- **EAZA** European Association of Zoos and Aquaria (#06283)
- EAZN – European Association for Zoological Nomenclature (inactive)
- **EAZWV** European Association of Zoo and Wildlife Veterinarians (#06284)
- **EBAA** European Business Aviation Association (#06415)
- **EBAC** European Board for Accreditation in Cardiology (#06353)
- **EBAD** Ecole de bibliothécaires, archivistes et documentalistes (#05296)
- EBAE / see European Association for the Education of Adults (#06018)
- EBA / see Energy Technologies Europe (#05477)
- **EBA** Euro Banking Association (#05647)
- **EBA** European Banking Authority (#06311)
- **EBA** European Biogas Association (#06336)
- **EBA** European Blood Alliance (#06351)
- **EBA** European Board of Anaesthesiology (#06354)
- EBA – European Boardsailing Association (inactive)
- **EBA** European Boating Association (#06376)
- **EBA** European Boatmen's Association (#06378)
- **EBA** European Bonsai Association (#06381)
- **EBA** European Borates Association (#06382)
- **EBA** European Bowhunting Association (#06385)
- **EBA** European Burns Association (#06414)
- EBA / see European Gaming and Betting Association (#07375)
- EBA – European Heating Boilers Association (inactive)
- EBAG / see Europäische Akademie Nordrhein-Westfalen
- **EBAN** European Trade Association for Business Angels, Seed Funds, and other Early Stage Market Players (#08923)
- EBANGS / see International Behavioural and Neural Genetics Society (#12332)
- **EBAss** European Baromedical Association for nurses, operators and technicians (#06319)
- **EBBA** European Brass Band Association (#06398)
- **EBB** European Biodiesel Board (#06333)
- EBBF / see ebbf – ethical business building the future (#05269)
- **ebbf** ebbf – ethical business building the future (#05269)

♦ ebbf – ethical business building the future (ebbf) ... 05269

Dir Gen Calle Urca 4 – Bajo C, Majadahonda, 28220 Madrid, Spain. T. +34661661563.
EU Office 39/1 Karel Janssenslaan, 8400 Ostend, Belgium. T. +32478872929.
URL: http://ebbf.org/

History Aug 1990, France. Former names and other names: *European Baha'i Business Forum (EBBF)* – former; *Association européenne baha'ie de management* – former; *ebbf – mindful people, meaningful work (ebbf)* – former. Registration: France. **Aims** Accompany mindful individuals and groups through daily work and discourse to transform business and the economy, thereby contributing to a prosperous, just and sustainable civilization. **Structure** General Assembly; Governing Board; National Chapters; Director-General. **Staff** 1.00 FTE, paid. **Finance** Sources: members' dues. Annual budget: 25,000 EUR. **Activities** Events/meetings; training/education. **Events** *Annual Conference* Geneva (Switzerland) 2019, *Annual Conference* Geneva (Switzerland) 2018, *Conference on transitioning towards the spiritual enterprise* Bucharest (Romania) 2017, *Annual Conference* Geneva (Switzerland) 2017, *Conference on Building Capacity* Bucharest (Romania) 2016. **Publications** Articles; presentations; statements. **Members** Organizations and individuals in over 50 countries. Membership countries not specified. **NGO Relations** Collaborates with: *AIESEC (#00593)*; *Junior Enterprises Europe (JE Europe, #16169)*. [2020/XF5297/**F**]

- EBBF – European Bioenergy Business Forum (internationally oriented national body)
- ebbf – mindful people, meaningful work / see ebbf – ethical business building the future (#05269)
- EBBH / see European Federation of Building and Woodworkers (#07065)
- **EBBS** European Brain and Behaviour Society (#06390)
- **EBCA** Europäische Bewegung Christlicher Arbeiter (#06546)
- **EBCA** European Branded Clothing Alliance (#06395)
- EBCA – European Business Club Association (unconfirmed)
- EBCAM / see European Business Council for Africa (#06416)
- **EBCAM** European Business Council for Africa (#06416)
- **EBCC** European Bird Census Council (#06347)
- **EBCC** European Breast Cancer Council (#06400)
- EBC Council / see European Breast Cancer Council (#06400)
- **EBCD** European Bureau for Conservation and Development (#06412)
- EBC / see European Balloon and Party Council (#06308)
- **EBC** European Bifurcation Club (#06329)
- **EBC** European Brain Council (#06391)
- **EBC** European Brewery Convention (#06401)
- **EBC** European Builders Confederation (#06408)
- EBC / see International Baptist Convention (#12318)
- EBC / see International Business Congress (#12419)
- EBCL – European Biological Control Laboratory (internationally oriented national body)
- **EBCO** European Bureau for Conscientious Objection (#06411)
- **EBCOG** European Board and College of Obstetrics and Gynaecology (#06357)
- **EBCP** European Board of Cardiovascular Perfusion (#06356)
- **EBCTS** European Board of Cardiothoracic Surgery (#06355)
- **EBCU** European Beer Consumers Union (#06325)
- EBDD / see European Monitoring Centre for Drugs and Drug Addiction (#07820)
- EBDO – European Developmental Biology Organization (inactive)
- **EBDV** European Board of Dermatology and Venereology (#06358)
- **EBEA** European BioElectromagnetics Association (#06335)
- EBEEC – International Conference Economies of the Balkan and Eastern European Countries (meeting series)
- EBEF – European Business Ethics Forum (meeting series)
- EBEMA – European Bakery Equipment Manufacturers Association (inactive)
- **EBEN** European Business Ethics Network (#06418)
- **EBES** Eurasia Business and Economics Society (#05599)
- EBFA – European Bottom Fisheries Alliance (unconfirmed)
- **EBF** Europäische BürgerInnen Forum (#06562)
- EBF – Europäisches Bioobst Forum (unconfirmed)
- **EBF** European Banking Federation (#06312)
- **EBF** European Baptist Federation (#06316)
- **EBF** European Bioanalysis Forum (#06331)
- **EBF** European Brain Foundation (#06392)
- EBF / see European and International Booksellers Federation (#07584)
- **EBGC** European Botanic Gardens Consortium (#06384)
- **EBG** Electronic Business Group (#05423)
- EBG / see European Board of Gastroenterology and Hepatology (#06359)
- **EBGH** European Board of Gastroenterology and Hepatology (#06359)
- **EBHA** European Business History Association (#06419)
- EBHL / see European Botanical and Horticultural Libraries Group (#06383)
- **EBHL** European Botanical and Horticultural Libraries Group (#06383)
- **EBIA** European Bedding Industries' Association (#06324)
- **EBIC** European Banking Industry Committee (#06314)

- **EBIC** European Biostimulants Industry Council (#06344)
- **EBIC** European Brain Injury Consortium (#06393)
- **EBID** ECOWAS Bank for Investment and Development (#05334)
- **EBI** – European Biochar Industry Consortium (unconfirmed)
- **EBI** European Boating Industry (#06377)
- **EBIF** – European Button Industries Federation (inactive)
- **EBIN** Europe and the Balkans International Network (#09150)
- **eBIO** – European Bioethanol Fuel Association (inactive)
- **EBIS** – ESCAP Bibliographic Information Systems (no recent information)
- **EBIS** European Brain Injury Society (#06394)
- **EBIT** – European Business Initiative on Taxation (unconfirmed)
- **EBJA** – European Bearing and Joint Manufacture Association (no recent information)
- **EBJIS** European Bone and Joint Infection Society (#06380)
- **EBLC** European Business Leaders' Convention (#06421)
- **EBL** – European Boxing League (unconfirmed)
- **EBL** European Bridge League (#06402)
- **EBLIDA** European Bureau of Library, Information and Documentation Associations (#06413)
- **EBMA** – European Bicycle Manufacturers Association (unconfirmed)
- **EBMA** European Bluegrass Music Association (#06352)
- **EBMA** European Board of Medical Assessors (#06360)
- **EBM** / see EBM International (#05270)
- **EBM** – European Association of Business and Management Teachers (inactive)
- **EBMG** European Board of Medical Genetics (#06361)

◆ EBM International 05270
SG Gottfried-Wilhelm-Lehmann-Str 4, 14641 Wustermark, Germany. T. +493323474150. Fax +493323474145. E-mail: info@ebm-international.org.
Pres address not obtained.
URL: http://www.ebm-international.org/
History 17 Sep 1954, Zurich (Switzerland). In 1979 absorbed *Missionarische Aktionen in Südamerika* and in 2009 absorbed *Hans-Herter-INDIENHILFE*. Former names and other names: *European Baptist Mission (EBM)* – former (1954 to 2009); *Mission baptiste européenne* – former (1954 to 2009); *Europäische Baptistische Mission (EBM)* – former (1954 to 2009). **Aims** Partnering with *Baptist churches* globally, share *Christ* to bring justice, restoration and hope to communities. **Structure** Executive Committee; Head Office in Wustermark (Germany). **Languages** English, French, German, Portuguese, Spanish. **Staff** 9.00 FTE, paid. **Finance** Donations from local churches, member unions and individuals. **Activities** Religious activities; capacity building; humanitarian/emergency aid. **Events** *Annual Mission Council* Arnhem (Netherlands) 2016, *Annual Mission Council* Dorfweil (Germany) 2015, *Annual Mission Council* Paris (France) 2014, *Annual Mission Council* Skien (Norway) 2013, *Annual Mission Council* Gandia (Spain) 2012. **Publications** *EBM Magazine* (3 a year).
Members Baptist unions in 27 countries:
Argentina, Austria, Bolivia, Brazil, Cameroon, Central African Rep, Croatia, Cuba, Czechia, Equatorial Guinea, Finland, France, Germany, Hungary, India, Italy, Malawi, Mozambique, Netherlands, Norway, Peru, Portugal, Sierra Leone, South Africa, Spain, Switzerland, Türkiye.
Included in the above, one organization listed in this Yearbook:
International Baptist Convention (IBC, #12318).
NGO Relations Member of: *Arbeitsgemeinschaft Evangelikaler Missionen (AEM)*. [2021/XD0592/F]

- **EBMT** European Society for Blood and Marrow Transplantation (#08533)
- **EBNA** European Board of National Archivists (#06362)
- **EBN** European Board of Neonatology (#06363)
- **EBN** European Board of Neurology (#06364)
- **EBN** European Business and Innovation Centre Network (#06420)
- **EBNLP** – European Board of NLP (unconfirmed)
- **EBNR** / see European Board of Neuroradiology (#06365)
- **EBNR** European Board of Neuroradiology (#06365)
- **EBNSC** / see CSR Europe (#04977)
- **EBO** European Board of Ophthalmology (#06366)
- **EBOMFS** European Board of Oro-Maxillo-Facial Surgery (#06367)
- **EBOPRAS** European Board of Plastic, Reconstructive and Aesthetic Surgery (#06372)
- **EBOR** – Economics, Business & Organization Research (meeting series)
- **EBOTA** European Bulk Oil Traders' Association (#06410)
- **EBO** Worldwide Network / see European Business Organisation Worldwide Network (#06422)
- **EBOWWN** / see European Business Organisation Worldwide Network (#06422)
- **EBO WWN** European Business Organisation Worldwide Network (#06422)
- **EBPA** European Bowling Proprietors Association (#06386)
- **EBPC** European Balloon and Party Council (#06308)
- **EBP** European Board of Paediatrics (#06368)
- **EBP** European Board of Pathology (#06370)
- **EBP** European Business Press (#06423)
- **EBPF** European Biocidal Product Forum (#06332)
- **EBPS** European Behavioural Pharmacology Society (#06327)
- **EBPS** European Board of Paediatric Surgery (#06369)
- **EBRA** European Battery Recycling Association (#06322)
- **EBRA** – European Biological Research Association (no recent information)
- **EBRA** – European Biomedical Research Association (inactive)
- **EBRA** European Business Registry Association (#06424)

◆ EBRAINS 05271
CEO Chaussée de La Hulpe 166, 1000 Brussels, Belgium. E-mail: info@ebrains.eu.
Swiss Office Chemin des Mines 9, 1202 Geneva, Switzerland.
URL: https://ebrains.eu/
History Registration: Banque-Carrefour des Entreprises, No/ID: 0740.908.863, Start date: 8 Jan 2020, Belgium. **Aims** Accelerate the effort to understand human brain function and disease; coordinate the Human Brain Project (HBP); build the future of the EBRAINS Research Infrastructure. **Structure** General Assembly; Board of Directors; Management Board.
Members Full in 8 countries:
Belgium, France, Germany, Italy, Jordan, Spain, Sweden, Switzerland.
Associate in 5 countries:
Belgium, France, Germany, Spain, Sweden. [2022/AA2936/D]

- **EBRD** European Bank for Reconstruction and Development (#06315)
- **EBR** European Board of Radiology (#06373)
- **EBRS** – European Bat Research Symposium (meeting series)
- **EBRS** European Biological Rhythms Society (#06337)
- **EBSA** European Billiards and Snooker Association (#06330)
- **EBSA** European Biophysical Societies' Association (#06341)
- **EBSA** European Biosafety Association (#06343)
- **EBSA** – European Building and Services Association (no recent information)
- **EBSA** European Business Services Alliance (#06426)
- **EBS** – Early Book Society (internationally oriented national body)
- **EBS** European Bamboo Society (#06309)
- **EBS** – European Business School, Dublin (internationally oriented national body)
- **EBS** European Business Summit (#06427)
- **EBSLG** European Business Schools Librarians's Group (#06425)
- **EBSN** European Basic Skills Network (#06321)
- **EBSN** European Beat Studies Network (#06323)
- **EBSO** European Begg Society of Orthodontics (#06326)
- **EBSO** – European Bitumen Shingle Organization (inactive)
- **EBTA** European Bobath Tutors Association (#06379)
- **EBTA** – European Brass Teachers Association (inactive)
- **EBTA** European Brief Therapy Association (#06403)
- **EBTA** – European Business Travel Association (inactive)
- **EBTCS** / see European Board of Cardiothoracic Surgery (#06355)
- **EBTNA** European Biotechnology Thematic Network Association (#06346)
- **EBTN** European Banking and Financial Services Training Association (#06313)
- **EBTP** / see European Technology and Innovation Platform Bioenergy (#08881)
- **EBTS** European Boxwood and Topiary Society (#06389)
- **EBU** / see Badminton Europe (#03058)
- **EBU** – Europäische Bestatter-Union (inactive)
- **EBU** Europäische Binnenschiffahrts Union (#06318)
- **EBU** Europäische Buddhistische Union (#06407)
- **EBU** European Barge Union (#06318)
- **EBU** European Blind Union (#06350)
- **EBU** European Board of Urology (#06374)
- **EBU** European Boxing Union (#06388)
- **EBU** European Broadcasting Union (#06404)
- **EBU** European Buddhist Union (#06407)
- **EBU** Europese Binnenvaart Unie (#06318)
- **EBUT** / see European Society of Residents in Urology (#08729)
- **EBV Association** International Association for Research on Epstein-Barr Virus and Associated Diseases (#12133)
- **EBV** – Europäischer Bergarbeiterverband (inactive)
- **EBVG** Europäischen Beratenden Verbrauchergruppe (#06771)
- **EBVS** European Board of Veterinary Specialisation (#06375)
- **EBWA** / see Watercoolers Europe (#20825)
- **EBWE** Europäische Bank für Wiederaufbau und Entwicklung (#06315)
- **EBWU** – see European Baptist Women United (#06317)
- **EBWU** European Baptist Women United (#06317)
- **EBYC** – European Bureau for Youth and Childhood (inactive)
- **EBY** – European Blue Cross Youth Association (inactive)
- **EBZ** Europäische Bildungs-und Begegnungszentren (#05750)
- **EBZ** – Europäisches Bildungszentrum der Wohnungs- und Immobilienwirtschaft (internationally oriented national body)
- **ECA** / see European Clusters Alliance (#06584)
- **ECA** / see European Concept for Accessibility Network (#06695)
- **ECAADE** / see Education and research in Computer Aided Architectural Design in Europe (#05373)
- **eCAADe** Education and research in Computer Aided Architectural Design in Europe (#05373)
- **ECAAH** European College of Aquatic Animal Health (#06607)
- **ECAAIR** – East and Central African Association for Indigenous Rights (internationally oriented national body)
- **ECAAR** / see Economists for Peace and Security (#05322)
- **ECAAT** European Committee for the Analytically Oriented Advanced Autogenic Training (#06641)
- **ECACC** European Collection of Authenticated Cell Cultures (#06604)
- **ECACC** European Council of American Chambers of Commerce (#06803)
- **ECAC** European Civil Aviation Conference (#06564)
- **ECADE** Eastern Caribbean Alliance for Diversity and Equality (#05230)
- **ECAD** European Cities Against Drugs (#06553)
- **ECA** – Educate a Child in Africa (unconfirmed)
- **ECA** Ending Clergy Abuse (#05460)
- **ECA** Ending Clerical Abuse (#05461)
- **ECA** eu can aid (#05570)
- **ECA** Europäische Cheerleading Assoziation (#06520)
- **ECA** – European Camac Association (no recent information)
- **ECA** – European Candle Association (inactive)
- **ECA** European Canoe Association (#06438)
- **ECA** European Carbon Association (#06445)
- **ECA** / see European Carpet and Rug Association (#06452)
- **ECA** European Casino Association (#06455)
- **ECA** European Cheerleading Association (#06520)
- **ECA** European Chimneys Association (#06536)
- **ECA** European Circus Association (#06552)
- **ECA** – European Claimants Association (inactive)
- **ECA** – European Cloud Alliance (unconfirmed)
- **ECA** European Club Association (#06579)
- **ECA** – European Coaching Association (internationally oriented national body)
- **ECA** European Cockpit Association (#06598)
- **ECA** European Cocoa Association (#06599)
- **ECA** European Commission on Agriculture (#06634)
- **ECA** – European Communication Association (inactive)
- **ECA** – European Conference on Argumentation (meeting series)
- **ECA** European Consortium for Accreditation in Higher Education (#06748)
- **ECA** – European Co-Production Association (no recent information)
- **ECA** European Council of Artists (#06805)
- **ECA** European Crystallographic Association (#06867)
- **ECA** European Cytogeneticists Association (#06880)
- **ECA** / see FAO/CIHEAM International Network for the Research and Development of Pasture and Forage Crops (#09257)
- **ECAF** – EarthCare Africa (internationally oriented national body)
- **ECAFE** / see United Nations Economic and Social Commission for Asia and the Pacific (#20557)
- **ECAF** European Conservation Agriculture Federation (#06743)

◆ ECafrique 05272
Coodinator Population Council, One Dag Hammarkskjold Plaza, New York NY 10017, USA.
Aims Expand the availability of quality emergency contraception (EC) services in Africa. **NGO Relations** Cooperates with (2): *International Consortium for Emergency Contraception (ICEC, #12911)*; *Population Council (#18458)*. [2019/AA1193/F]

- **ECA** – Global Justice Project / see Ending Clerical Abuse (#05461)
- **ECAHO** European Conference of Arab Horse Organizations (#06730)
- **ECAICT** – European Centre for Architecture and Information and Communication Technologies (internationally oriented national body)
- **ECA** / see Inter-Regional Cooperative Research Network on Buffalo (#15967)
- **ECAMA** European Citric Acid Manufacturers Association (#06561)
- **ECAMS** / see European College of Zoological Medicine (#06631)
- **ecancer** / see ecancer Global Foundation
- **ecancer** Global Foundation (internationally oriented national body)

◆ ECA Office for North Africa 05273
Bureau de la CEA pour l'Afrique du Nord
Dir Secteur 3-A5, Rue Attine, Hay Ryad, BP 2062, Rabat, Morocco. T. +212537717829 – +212537715613. Fax +212537712702. E-mail: srdc-na@uneca.org.
URL: http://www.uneca.org/

ECAPD
05273

History 1963, within the framework of *United Nations Economic Commission for Africa (ECA, #20554)*, to cover the countries of North Africa. Set up as a *Multinational Programming and Operational Centre – Centre multinational de programmation et d'éxécution de projets (UNECA/MULPOC)*, one of 5 'MULPOCs', replacing the subregional offices and the 3 *United Nations Development Advisory Teams (UNDATS, inactive)* under Resolution 311 (XIII) of the 4th meeting of ECA Conference of Ministers. Together with the other 4 MULPOCs: *ECA Subregional Office for Southern Africa (SRO-SA Lusaka, #05276)* for Eastern and Southern Africa; *ECA Sub-Regional Office for Eastern Africa (SRO-EA Kigali, #05275)*, for the countries of the CEPGL; *ECA Sub-Regional Office for Central Africa (ECA/SRO-CA, #05274)*, for the other countries of Central Africa; *ECA Sub-Regional Office for West Africa (SRO-WA, #05277)*, for the countries of ECOWAS – constituted the operational field arm of UN/ECA. Changed title to *ECA Subregional Development Centre for Northern Africa (NA/SDRC Tangiers) – CEA Centre de développement sous-regional pour l'Afrique du Nord (CDSR/AN)*, 8 May 1997, Addis Ababa (Ethiopia), under Resolution 828 (XXXII) of the 32nd Session (23rd meeting) of the ECA Conference of Ministers, under which all MULPOCs were transformed into ECA Subregional Development Centres (UNECA/SRDCs) covering subregional economic communities as defined by *Treaty Establishing the African Economic Community (Abuja treaty, 1991)* and with the task of achieving the objectives of *African Economic Community (AEC, #00290)*. Subsequently referred to as *ECA Subregional Office for North Africa – Bureau sous-régional de la CEA pour l'Afrique du Nord*. Previously also referred to by the initials *UNECA/SDRC-NA – CEA/CDSR-AN*. **Aims** Assist the North African subregional economic community to promote and strengthen the subregional *economic integration* process and achieve the objectives of the African Economic Community; provide support strategies and programmes for the enhancement of *production and trade*; promote institutional economic cooperation and integration. **Structure** Intergovernmental Committee of Experts; Secretariat. **Languages** Arabic, English, French. **Finance** Financed by regular budget of ECA. **Activities** Guidance/assistance/consulting; events/meetings. **Events** *Symposium on human capital in North Africa* Algiers (Algeria) 2003, *Forum on investment in North Africa* Casablanca (Morocco) 2002, *Liberalization and financing of maghrebin exchanges* Tangiers (Morocco) 1996, *New UNO national accountancy system* Tangiers (Morocco) 1996, *Economic cooperation and integration* Tangiers (Morocco) 1993. **Publications** Reports; studies; proceedings.

Members Countries covered by NA/SRDC (7):
Algeria, Egypt, Libya, Mauritania, Morocco, Sudan, Tunisia.

[2017/XE5961/E*]

♦ ECAPD – European Conference on Applications of Polar Dielectrics (meeting series)
♦ ECAP – Equipos Cristianos de Acción por la Paz (internationally oriented national body)
♦ ECAP European Consortium of Anchors Producers (#06749)
♦ ECARDC European Conference on Agriculture and Rural Development in China (#06729)
♦ ECARE / see European Centre for Advanced Research in Economics and Statistics
♦ ECARES – European Centre for Advanced Research in Economics and Statistics (internationally oriented national body)
♦ ECAR European College of Animal Reproduction (#06605)
♦ ECARF – European Centre for Allergy Research Foundation (internationally oriented national body)
♦ ECArTE European Consortium for Arts Therapies Education (#06750)
♦ ECASBA European Community Association of Ship Brokers and Agents (#06677)
♦ EC-ASEAN COGEN Programme (inactive)
♦ ECAS European Cardiac Arrhythmia Society (#06448)
♦ ECAS European Citizen Action Service (#06555)
♦ ECAS – European Council on African Studies (no recent information)
♦ ECA/SRO-CA ECA Sub-Regional Office for Central Africa (#05274)
♦ ECA/SRO-CA Yaoundé / see ECA Sub-Regional Office for Central Africa (#05274)
♦ ECAST European Centre for Advanced Studies in Thermodynamics (#06469)
♦ ECA Subregional Development Centre for Central Africa / see ECA Sub-Regional Office for Central Africa (#05274)
♦ ECA Subregional Development Centre for Eastern Africa / see ECA Sub-Regional Office for Eastern Africa (#05275)
♦ ECA Subregional Development Centre for Northern Africa / see ECA Office for North Africa (#05273)
♦ ECA Subregional Development Centre for Southern Africa / see ECA Subregional Office for Southern Africa (#05276)
♦ ECA Subregional Development Centre for West Africa / see ECA Sub-Regional Office for West Africa (#05277)

♦ ECA Sub-Regional Office for Central Africa (ECA/SRO-CA) 05274
CEA bureau sous-régional pour l'Afrique centrale (CEA/BSR-AC)
Media Relations Contact UN ECA SRO-CA, PO Box 14935, Yaoundé, Cameroon. T. +237222504348 – +237222231461 – +237222220861. Fax +237222233185.
URL: http://www.uneca.org/sro-ca/
History 8 May 1997, Addis Ababa (Ethiopia), as *ECA Subregional Development Centre for Central Africa (AC/SDRC Yaoundé) – CEA Centre de développement sous-régional pour l'Afrique central (CDSR/AC)*, within the framework of *United Nations Economic Commission for Africa (ECA, #20554)*, under Resolution 828 (XXXII) of the 32nd Session (23rd meeting) of the ECA Conference of Ministers, as one of 5 subregional centres with the task of achieving the objectives of *African Economic Community (AEC, #00290)* as defined by *Treaty Establishing the African Economic Community (Abuja treaty, 1991)*. Derives from *Multinational Programming and Operational Centre, UNECA/MULPOC, Yaoundé (MULPOC, Yaoundé) – Centre multinational de programmation et d'éxécution de projets, Yaoundé*, set up 1 Mar 1977, Yaoundé, to cover the countries of Central Africa not part of CEPGL as one of 5 'MULPOCs', replacing the subregional offices and the 3 *United Nations Development Advisory Teams (UNDATS, inactive)* under Resolution 311 (XIII) of the 4th meeting of ECA Conference of Ministers. The 'MULPOCS' constituted the operational field arm of UN/ECA and were all transformed into ECA Subregional Development Centres (UNECA/SRDCs) under the same Resolution. Also referred to by the initials *UNECA/SDRC-CA – CEA/CDSR-AC* and *ECA/SRO-CA Yaoundé – CEA/BSR-AC Yaoundé*. The SRDCs became SROs from Jan 2002. **Aims** Assist the Central African subregional economic community to promote harmonization of national policies in various sectors in support of *integration* efforts towards the consolidation of sub-regional economic communities in the overall framework of the African Union. **Structure** Intergovernmental Committee of Experts; Central Africa Subregional Conference of Ministers of Planning; Secretariat. **Languages** English, French. **Staff** 19.00 FTE, paid. **Finance** Financed by the regular budget of the United Nations and Extra Budgetary Resources from external donors. **Activities** Advocacy/lobbying/activism; networking/liaising; guidance/assistance/consulting; projects/programmes; events/meetings. **Publications** *Highlight* (weekly) – magazine; *Echos d'Afrique Centrale* (4 a year) – magazine; *Report on Economic and Social Conditions in Central Africa* (annual). Reports; technical publications.
Members Member States (7):
Cameroon, Central African Rep, Chad, Congo Brazzaville, Equatorial Guinea, Gabon, Sao Tomé-Principe.
IGO Relations Partners: *Banque de développement des Etats de l'Afrique centrale (BDEAC, #03168)*; *Banque des Etats de l'Afrique centrale (BEAC, #03169)*; *Communauté économique et monétaire d'Afrique centrale (CEMAC, #04374)*; *Economic Community of Central African States (ECCAS, #05311)*. Member of: *Commission des forêts d'Afrique centrale (COMIFAC, #04214)*; *International Commission of the Congo-Ubangui-Sangha Basin (#12674)*. **NGO Relations** Member of: *Central African Power Pool (CAPP, #03655)*.

[2017/XE5962/E*]

♦ ECA Sub-Regional Office for Eastern Africa (SRO-EA Kigali) 05275
CEA bureau sous-régional pour l'Afrique de l'Est
Communication Officer PO Box 4654, Kigali, Rwanda. T. +250252586548. Fax +25025258646. E-mail: easrdc@uneca.org.
URL: http://www.uneca.org/sro-ea/
History 8 May 1997, Addis Ababa (Ethiopia), *ECA Subregional Development Centre for Eastern Africa (EA/SRDC Kigali) – CEA Centre de développement sous-régional pour l'Afrique de l'Est (CDSR/AE)*, within the framework of *United Nations Economic Commission for Africa (ECA, #20554)*, under Resolution 828 (XXXII) of the 32nd Session (23rd meeting) of the ECA Conference of Ministers, as one of 5 subregional centres with the task of achieving the objectives of *African Economic Community (AEC, #00290)* as defined by *Treaty Establishing the African Economic Community (Abuja treaty, 1991)*. Derives from *Multinational Programming and Operational Centre, UNECA/MULPOC, Gisenyi (MULPOC, Gisenyi) – Centre multinational de programmation et d'éxécution de projets, MULPOC/CEA, Gisenyi*, set up Oct 1977, to cover the countries of *Communauté économique des pays des Grands Lacs (CEPGL, #04375)* as one of 5 'MULPOCs', replacing the subregional offices and the 3 *United Nations Development Advisory Teams (UNDATS, inactive)* under Resolution 311 (XIII) of the 4th meeting of ECA Conference of Ministers. The 'MULPOCS' constituted the operational field arm of UN/ECA and were all transformed into ECA Subregional Development Centres (UNECA/SRDCs) under the same Resolution. Also referred to by the initials *UNECA/SDRC-EA – CEA/CDSR-AE*. **Aims** Assist the East African subregional economic community to promote and strengthen the subregional economic integration process and achieve the objectives of the African Economic Community; provide support strategies and programmes for the enhancement of economic development in areas of macro economic policy, trade, industry, agriculture, food security, population, transport and communications and gender; promote institutional economic cooperation and integration. **Structure** Intergovernmental Committee of Experts; Secretariat. **Languages** English, French. **Activities** Guidance/assistance/consulting; networking/liaising; events/meetings; knowledge management/information dissemination. **Events** *Meeting* Kigali (Rwanda) 2000. **Publications** *EA/SRDC Bulletin* (2 a year). Annual Report of economic and social conditions in Eastern Africa. Seminar reports; studies.
Members Governments of 14 countries:
Burundi, Comoros, Congo DR, Djibouti, Eritrea, Ethiopia, Kenya, Madagascar, Rwanda, Seychelles, Somalia, South Sudan, Tanzania UR, Uganda.
IGO Relations Cooperates with the other 4 subregional centres: *ECA Sub-Regional Office for West Africa (SRO-WA, #05277)*; *ECA Subregional Office for Southern Africa (SRO-SA Lusaka, #05276)*; *ECA Sub-Regional Office for Central Africa (ECA/SRO-CA, #05274)*; *ECA Office for North Africa (#05273)*. Serves: *Communauté économique des pays des Grands Lacs (CEPGL, #04375)*; *Commission de l'Océan Indien (COI, #04236)*; *Intergovernmental Authority on Development (IGAD, #11472)*; *International Conference on the Great Lakes Region (ICGLR, #12880)*; *United Nations Economic Commission for Africa (ECA, #20554)*.

[2016/XE5963/E*]

♦ ECA Subregional Office for North Africa / see ECA Office for North Africa (#05273)

♦ ECA Subregional Office for Southern Africa (SRO-SA Lusaka) 05276
CEA bureau sous-régional pour l'Afrique australe
Dir c/o UN Economic Commission for Africa, Southern Africa Office, PO Box 30647, Lusaka, Zambia. T. +2601228502 – +2601228505. Fax +2601236949 – +2601234757. E-mail: srdcsa.uneca@un.org – director@uneca.org.
URL: http://www.uneca.org/sa/home.htm
History 8 May 1997, Addis Ababa (Ethiopia), as *ECA Subregional Development Centre for Southern Africa (SA/SRDC Lusaka) – CEA Centre de développement sous-régional pour l'Afrique australe (CDSR/AA)*, within the framework of *United Nations Economic Commission for Africa (ECA, #20554)*, under Resolution 828 (XXXII) of the 32nd Session (23rd meeting) of the ECA Conference of Ministers, as one of 5 subregional centres with the task of achieving the objectives of *African Economic Community (AEC, #00290)* as defined by *Treaty Establishing the African Economic Community (Abuja treaty, 1991)*. Derives from *Multinational Programming and Operational Centre, UNECA/MULPOC, Lusaka (MULPOC, Lusaka) – Centre multinational de programmation et d'éxécution de projets, Lusaka*, set up Nov 1977, Lusaka, to cover Eastern and Southern Africa as one of 5 'MULPOCs', replacing the subregional offices and the 3 *United Nations Development Advisory Teams (UNDATS, inactive)* under Resolution 311 (XIII) of the 4th meeting of ECA Conference of Ministers. The 'MULPOCS' constituted the operational field arm of UN/ECA and were all transformed into ECA Subregional Development Centres (UNECA/SRDCs) under the same Resolution. Also referred to by initials *UNECA/SDRC-SA – CEA/CDSR-AA*. **Aims** Provide leverage on multidisciplinary analytical skills; convene power and consensus building strength to facilitate *harmonization* of policies and strategies for harnessing regional *resources* to meet *development* priorities of the Southern Africa subregion. **Structure** Intergovernmental Committee of Experts; Secretariat in Subregional Development Centre. **Languages** English, French. **Activities** Provides technical support and advisory services and assistance in formulation and implementation of economic policies. Organizes workshops, seminars and studies. **Events** *Meeting* Gaborone (Botswana) 1995, *Workshop on science and technology* Kampala (Uganda) 1995, *Workshop on skill deficiencies in mining in Eastern and Southern Africa* Maputo (Mozambique) 1995, *Symposium on food security* Pretoria (South Africa) 1995, *Workshop on gemstone development and marketing strategies in Eastern and Southern Africa* Windhoek (Namibia) 1995. **Publications** Reports; studies. Implements *Eastern and Southern Africa Development Information System (ESADIS, no recent information)*.
Members Member States (11):
Angola, Botswana, Eswatini, Lesotho, Malawi, Mauritius, Mozambique, Namibia, South Africa, Zambia, Zimbabwe.

[2016/XE6080/E*]

♦ ECA Sub-Regional Office for West Africa (SRO-WA) 05277
CEA bureau sous-régional pour l'Afrique de l'Ouest (BSR-AO)
Contact PO Box 744, Niamey, Niger. T. +22720722961. Fax +22720722894.
URL: https://www.uneca.org/sro-wa/
History 8 May 1997, Addis Ababa (Ethiopia), as *ECA Subregional Development Centre for West Africa (WA/SDRC Niamey) – CEA Centre de développement sous-régional pour l'Afrique de l'Ouest (CDSR/AO)*, within the framework of *United Nations Economic Commission for Africa (ECA, #20554)*, under Resolution 828 (XXXII) of the 32nd Session (23rd meeting) of the ECA Conference of Ministers, as one of 5 subregional centres with the task of achieving the objectives of *African Economic Community (AEC, #00290)* as defined by *Treaty Establishing the African Economic Community (Abuja treaty, 1991)*. Derives from *Multinational Programming and Operational Centre, UNECA/MULPOC, Niamey (MULPOC, Niamey) – Centre multinational de programmation et d'éxécution de projets, Niamey*, set up to cover the countries of *Economic Community of West African States (ECOWAS, #05312)* as one of 5 'MULPOCs', replacing the subregional offices and the 3 *United Nations Development Advisory Teams (UNDATS, inactive)* under Resolution 311 (XIII) of the 4th meeting of ECA Conference of Ministers. The 'MULPOCS' constituted the operational field arm of UN/ECA and were all transformed into ECA Subregional Development Centres (UNECA/SRDCs) under the same Resolution. Also referred to as *West African Subregional Development Centre* and by the initials *UNECA/SDRC-WA – CEA/CDSR-AO*. **Aims** Strengthen development cooperation and subregional integration within the framework of NEPAD and internationally agreed goals, including those set out in the Millennium Declaration. **Structure** Intergovernmental Committee of Experts; Secretariat. **Languages** English, French. **Staff** 20.00 FTE, paid. **Finance** Regular Budget (RB) and External Budget (XB) of UN Secretariat. **Activities** Research and development; capacity building; knowledge management/information dissemination; guidance/assistance/consulting.
Members Member States (15):
Benin, Burkina Faso, Cape Verde, Côte d'Ivoire, Gambia, Ghana, Guinea, Guinea-Bissau, Liberia, Mali, Niger, Nigeria, Senegal, Sierra Leone, Togo.
IGO Relations Cooperates with the other 4 subregional offices: *ECA Subregional Office for Southern Africa (SRO-SA Lusaka, #05276)*; *ECA Sub-Regional Office for Eastern Africa (SRO-EA Kigali, #05275)*; *ECA Office for North Africa (#05273)*; *ECA Sub-Regional Office for Central Africa (ECA/SRO-CA, #05274)*.

[2017.09.06/XE5960/E*]

♦ ECAT – International Symposium on Electrocatalysis (meeting series)
♦ ECATRA – European Car and Truck Rental Association (inactive)

♦ ECATS International Association 05278
Pres DLR Brussels Office, Rue du Trone 98, 1050 Brussels, Belgium. T. +441612471592.
URL: http://www.ecats-network.eu/
History Set up 2005, as a Network of Excellence on Aviation and Environment. Transformed into an international association, when officially registered in accordance with Belgian law, 2 Nov 2010. ECATS stands for: *Environmentally Compatible Air Transport System*. **Aims** Act as the link and professional liaison between the aviation sector and the expert members within the association; promote and support members' joint activities and interests in the field of *aviation* and *environmental* impact. **Structure** General Assembly; Executive Board; Secretariat. **Languages** Dutch, English, French, German, Romanian, Swedish. **Activities** Training/education; events/meetings; research and development; knowledge management/information dissemination. **Events** *Conference* Germany 2019, *Making aviation environmentally sustainable* Athens (Greece) 2016, *Technical challenges for aviation in a changing environment* Berlin (Germany) 2013.
Members Full; Associate. Full in 8 countries:
France, Germany, Greece, Netherlands, Norway, Romania, Sweden, UK.

[2018.11.19/XM6059/E]

♦ **ECA** United Nations Economic Commission for Africa (#20554)
♦ ECA Watch (unconfirmed)
♦ **ECAWBM** European College of Animal Welfare and Behavioural Medicine (#06606)
♦ ECAZA / see European Association of Zoos and Aquaria (#06283)
♦ **ECBA** European Countries Biologists Association (#06852)
♦ **ECBA** European Criminal Bar Association (#06859)
♦ **ECBC** European Covered Bond Council (#06856)
♦ **ECBE** European Council for Business Education (#06807)
♦ **ECB** European Central Bank (#06466)
♦ **ECB** European Conference of Binational/Bicultural Relationships (#06731)
♦ ECB – European Coordination Bureau of International Youth Organizations (inactive)
♦ ECBF / see European Citizen's Band Federation (#06556)
♦ **ECBF** European Citizen's Band Federation (#06556)
♦ **ECBHM** European College of Bovine Health Management (#06608)
♦ ECBL / see Europacable (#05743)
♦ ECBL – European Certification Board for Logistics (inactive)
♦ ECBO – European Cell Biology Organization (inactive)
♦ ECBP – European Council for Building Professionals (inactive)
♦ ECBR – European Centre for Rehabilitation of Buildings (internationally oriented national body)
♦ ECBTA – European Community Banana Trade Association (inactive)
♦ **ECCAA** Eastern Caribbean Civil Aviation Authority (#05232)
♦ ECCAEA / see European Network of Engineering for Agriculture and Environment (#07901)
♦ **ECCA** European Cervical Cancer Association (#06512)
♦ **ECCA** European Coil Coating Association (#06601)
♦ **ECCA** European Crop Care Association (#06865)
♦ ECCA / see GIGAEurope AISBL (#10151)
♦ ECCAI / see European Association for Artificial Intelligence (#05943)
♦ EC / see Caritas Europa (#03579)
♦ **ECCAS** Economic Community of Central African States (#05311)
♦ **ECCB** Eastern Caribbean Central Bank (#05231)
♦ **ECCB** Europan Committee for Conservation of Bryophytes (#05766)
♦ ECCCA / see Descartes Cancer Consortium (#05041)
♦ ECCC / see European Cartridge Research Association (#06454)
♦ ECCC – European Continuous Casting Conference (meeting series)
♦ ECCC Foundation / see European Digital Competence Certificate Foundation
♦ ECCC Foundation – European Digital Competence Certificate Foundation (internationally oriented national body)
♦ ECCCH / see European Society for Clinical Hemorheology and Microcirculation (#08546)
♦ ECC / see CLIA Europe (#03995)
♦ ECCCO / see European Culture Collections' Organization (#06872)
♦ ECCD – European Cultural Centre of Delphi (internationally oriented national body)
♦ ECCE / see European Center for Sustainable Finance
♦ **ECCEA** Eastern Caribbean Coalition for Environmental Awareness (#05233)
♦ ECCE – European Center for Sustainable Finance (internationally oriented national body)
♦ **ECCE** European Conference on Christian Education (#06732)
♦ **ECCE** European Cooperation in Anthroposophical Curative Education and Social Therapy (#06783)
♦ **ECCE** European Council on Chiropractic Education (#06809)
♦ **ECCE** European Council of Civil Engineers (#06810)
♦ ECC – Electronic Communications Committee (see: #04602)
♦ **ECC** European Centre for Culture (#06472)
♦ **ECC** European Christian Convention (#06542)
♦ **ECC** European Coke Committee (#06602)
♦ ECC – European Consultative Commission (inactive)
♦ **ECC** European Controllers Cup (#06778)
♦ ECC – European Cooperation Centre (unconfirmed)
♦ ECC – European COPD Coalition (inactive)
♦ ECC – Experimental Chaos and Complexity Conference (meeting series)
♦ **ECCF** European Council for the Conservation of Fungi (#06811)
♦ **ECCF** European Critical Care Foundation (#06862)
♦ ECC Football / see European Controllers Cup (#06778)
♦ **ECCG** European Consumer Consultative Group (#06771)
♦ ECCH / see European Central Council of Homeopaths (#06467)
♦ **ECCH** European Central Council of Homeopaths (#06467)
♦ EC CHM – European Community Biodiversity Clearing House Mechanism (inactive)
♦ **ECCHRD** European Coordination Committee on Human Rights Documentation (#06791)
♦ ECCHR – European Center for Constitutional and Human Rights (internationally oriented national body)
♦ ECC / see International Cricket Council Europe Region (#13106)
♦ **ECCJ** European Coalition for Corporate Justice (#06591)
♦ ECCLA – Exchange and Cooperation Centre for Latin America (internationally oriented national body)

♦ Ecclesiastic Archivistics Association 05279

Association des archivistes ecclésiastiques – Asociación de Archiveros Eclesiasticos – Verein der Kirchlichen Archivare – Associazione Archivistica Ecclesiastica (AAE)

Office Piazza S Calisto 16, 00153 Rome RM, Italy. E-mail: info@archivaecclesiae.org.
URL: http://www.archivaecclesiae.org/

History 1956. Statutes adopted 13 Jul 1956; modified 18 Oct 1990. **Aims** Contribute, taking into account the instructions of the Holy Sea, to the proper conservation and the study of archives that concern the *history* of the *Church*; promote all the means to improve the scientific and technical activity of members. **Structure** Assembly; Council. **Languages** Italian. **Finance** Members' dues. Other sources: magazine sales; grants. **Activities** Correspondence with members; publishing activity. **Events** *Meeting* Rome (Italy) 1996, *Meeting* Naples (Italy) 1993, *Meeting* Rome (Italy) 1990, *Meeting* Rome (Italy) 1987, *Meeting* Loreto (Italy) 1984. **Publications** *Archiva Ecclesiae* – bulletin. Monographs; guides. Meeting proceedings.
Members Full; Sustaining; Honorary. Individuals in 19 countries:
Argentina, Austria, Belgium, Croatia, France, Germany, Greece, Holy See, Israel, Italy, Korea Rep, Malta, Mexico, Poland, Portugal, Slovakia, Slovenia, Spain, Switzerland. [2018.07.13/XF4201/v/**F**]

♦ **ECCL** European Coalition for Community Living (#06590)
♦ ECCLM – European Council for Clinical Laboratories Medicine (no recent information)
♦ ECCLS – European Council for Clinical and Laboratory Standardization (inactive)
♦ **ECCMA** Electronic Commerce Code Management Association (#05424)
♦ ECCM – East Caribbean Common Market (inactive)
♦ **ECC-Net** European Consumer Centres Network (#06770)
♦ ECCO / see European Cancer Organisation (#06432)
♦ **ECCO** European Chapter on Combinatorial Optimization (#06517)
♦ **ECCO** European Club for Countertrade and Offset (#06580)
♦ **ECCO** European Confederation of Conservator-Restorers' Organisations (#06701)
♦ ECCO – European Council of Conscripts Organizations (inactive)
♦ **ECCO** European Crohn's and Colitis Organisation (#06864)
♦ **ECCO** European Culture Collections' Organization (#06872)
♦ **ECCOMAS** European Committee on Computational Methods in Applied Sciences (#06644)
♦ ECCP / see Global Partnership for the Prevention of Armed Conflict Foundation
♦ ECCP – European Council of Coloproctology (inactive)
♦ ECCP / see Global Partnership for the Prevention of Armed Conflict (#10538)
♦ **ECCREDI** European Council for Construction Research, Development and Innovation (#06813)
♦ ECCR / see European Communication Research and Education Association (#06675)
♦ ECCR / see European Council for Cardiovascular Research (#06808)
♦ **ECCR** European Council for Cardiovascular Research (#06808)
♦ **ECCRI** European Consortium on Chronic Respiratory Insufficiency (#06751)
♦ ECCRR / see European Centre for Restoration Techniques
♦ **ECCSEL** European Carbon Dioxide Capture and Storage Laboratory Infrastructure (#06446)
♦ **ECCS** European Convention for Constructional Steelwork (#06779)
♦ ECCS / see European Democrat Students (#06901)
♦ ECCTCM – European Chamber of Commerce for Traditional Chinese Medicine (no recent information)
♦ ECCTO – European Community Cocoa Trade Organisation (inactive)
♦ **ECCVAT** European Charities' Committee on Value-Added Tax (#06519)
♦ ECCV – European Conference on Computer Vision (meeting series)
♦ **ECCVT** European Coordination Committee for Veterinary Training (#06793)
♦ ECCW / see European Federation for Welding, Joining and Cutting (#07233)
♦ ECC – Workshop on Elliptic Curve Cryptography (meeting series)
♦ ECCWS – European Conference on Cyber Warfare and Security (meeting series)
♦ **ECDA** European Chronic Disease Alliance (#06548)
♦ **ECDAN** Early Childhood Development Action Network (#05155)
♦ ECDBS / see European Deafblind Network (#06890)
♦ **ECDC** European Centre for Disease Prevention and Control (#06476)
♦ ECDE – European Conference of Defence and the Environment (meeting series)
♦ **ECD** European Coalition for Diabetes (#06592)
♦ ECD – Executive Council on Diplomacy (internationally oriented national body)
♦ ECD Global Alliance – Erdheim-Chester Disease Global Alliance (internationally oriented national body)
♦ ECDHM – European Conference on Donor Health and Management (meeting series)
♦ ECDHR – European Centre for Democracy and Human Rights (unconfirmed)
♦ ECDL Foundation / see ICDL Europe (#11052)
♦ ECDL / see International Conference on Theory and Practice of Digital Libraries (#12887)
♦ **ECDN** European Consumer Debt Network (#06772)
♦ **ECDO** European Cell Death Organization (#06458)
♦ ECDP – European Cities on Drug Policy (inactive)
♦ **ECDPM** European Centre for Development Policy Management (#06473)
♦ **ECDRSL** European Council of Deaf Researchers of Sign Language (#06814)
♦ ECDV – European Conference on Domestic Violence (meeting series)
♦ ECE / see United Nations Economic Commission for Europe (#20555)
♦ **ECEAE** European Coalition to End Animal Experiments (#06594)
♦ ECEAT International – European Centre for Ecological and Agricultural Tourism (inactive)
♦ **ECEC** European Consortium for Emergency Contraception (#06754)
♦ **ECEC** European Council of Engineers Chambers (#06819)
♦ ECED – European Confederation of Equipment Distributors (no recent information)
♦ **ECED** European Council on Eating Disorders (#06817)
♦ **ECEEE** European Council for an Energy Efficient Economy (#06818)
♦ ECE – Electronic Commerce Europe (no recent information)
♦ **ECE** European Chamber of Engineers (#06514)
♦ ECE – European Congress of Entomology (meeting series)
♦ **ECEG** European Chemical Employers Group (#06521)
♦ **ECEG** European Coalition for Economic Growth (#06593)
♦ ECEH – WHO European Centre for Environment and Health (see: #20945)
♦ **ECEIM** European College of Equine Internal Medicine (#06609)
♦ ECEL – European Conference on e-Learning (meeting series)
♦ ECENA – Environmental Compliance and Enforcement Network for Accession (inactive)
♦ **ECEN** European Christian Environmental Network (#06543)
♦ ECEPAA – European Center for Economic and Policy Analysis and Affairs (unconfirmed)
♦ **ECER** European Congress of Ethnic Religions (#06740)
♦ ECERS – European Centre for Ethnic and Regional Studies – University of Maribor (internationally oriented national body)
♦ **ECerS** European Ceramic Society (#06507)
♦ **ECES** European Centre for Electoral Support (#06478)
♦ **ECET** European Council of Enterostomal Therapy (#06820)
♦ **ECETOC** European Centre for Ecotoxicology and Toxicology of Chemicals (#06477)
♦ **ECE/TRANS** Comité des transports intérieurs (#04262)
♦ ECE/TRANS / see Committee on Inland Transport (#04262)
♦ **EC** Euclid Consortium (#05573)
♦ ECEU – European Union Center of Excellence, Madison WI (internationally oriented national body)
♦ **EC** EuroCommerce (#05665)
♦ **EC** European Commission (#06633)
♦ EC – European Communities (inactive)
♦ **EC** European Conservatives Group (#06744)
♦ ECFA – Egyptian Council for Foreign Affairs (internationally oriented national body)
♦ **ECFA** European Children's Film Association (#06530)
♦ **ECFA** European Committee for Future Accelerators (#06650)
♦ ECFASA / see European Union Foreign Affairs Spouses' Associations (#08991)
♦ ECFCN / see European Network Child Friendly Cities (#07877)
♦ ECFD / see Executive Council on Diplomacy
♦ **ECFD** European Confederation of Fuel Distributors (#06703)
♦ ECFED / see European Union Federation of Youth Hostel Associations (#08988)
♦ **ECF** European Canicross and Bikejöring Federation (#06437)
♦ **ECF** European Caravan Federation (#06443)
♦ **ECF** European Charcot Foundation (#06518)
♦ **ECF** European Civic Forum (#06562)
♦ **ECF** European Civic Forum (#06563)
♦ **ECF** European Climate Foundation (#06574)
♦ **ECF** European Coffee Federation (#06600)
♦ ECF – European Composers' Forum (inactive)
♦ **ECF** European Construction Forum (#06765)
♦ **ECF** European Cultural Foundation (#06868)
♦ **ECF** European Cyclists' Federation (#06877)
♦ **ECF** European Cytoskeleton Forum (#06882)
♦ ECFF – European Centre on Forest Fires (internationally oriented national body)
♦ **ECFF** European Chilled Food Federation (#06535)
♦ ECFG – European Conference on Fungal Genetics (meeting series)
♦ ECF / see Global Climate Forum (#10287)

♦ ECFIA 05280

Contact 3 rue du Colonol Moll, 75017 Paris, France. T. +33631487426. E-mail: info@ecfia.eu.
URL: http://www.ecfia.eu/

History 1979. Former names and other names: *European Ceramic Fibre Industry Association* – former (1979); *ECFIA – Representing the High Temperature Insulation Wool Industry* – full title. Registration: RNA, No/ID: W751118931, Start date: 1995, France; EU Transparency Register, No/ID: 437067914645-34, Start date: 10 Oct 2014. **Aims** Promote the safe use of High Temperature Insulation Wool (HTIW) products. **Staff** No permanent staff [2022.10.13/XM8684/**D**]

♦ ECFIA – Representing the High Temperature Insulation Wool Industry / see ECFIA (#05280)
♦ **ECFI** European Community Foundation Initiative (#06680)
♦ ECFMG – Educational Commission for Foreign Medical Graduates (internationally oriented national body)

- ♦ ECF / see Network of European Foundations (#17019)
- ♦ ECFR – European Council for Fatwa and Research (see: #09682)
- ♦ **ECFR** European Council on Foreign Relations (#06821)
- ♦ **ECF-SADC** Electoral Commissions Forum of SADC Countries (#05414)
- ♦ **ECFS** European Cystic Fibrosis Society (#06879)
- ♦ ECFTU / see European Trade Union Confederation (#08927)
- ♦ ECGA / see Eurochurch.net (#05660)
- ♦ **ECGA** European Carbon and Graphite Association (#06447)
- ♦ **ECGA** European Clay Groups Association (#06570)
- ♦ **ECG** Association of European Vehicle Logistics (#02551)
- ♦ ECGBL – European Conference on Games Based Learning (meeting series)
- ♦ ECGDH / see European Centre on Geomorphological Hazards (#06482)
- ♦ **ECG** Economy for the Common Good (#05323)
- ♦ **ECG** European College of Gerodontology (#06610)
- ♦ ECG / see European Contact Group – Ecumenical Network for Economic and Social Action (#06773)
- ♦ **ECG** European Contact Group – Ecumenical Network for Economic and Social Action (#06773)
- ♦ **ECGFF** European Coast Guard Functions Forum (#06597)
- ♦ EC GHHD – European Centre on Geodynamic Hazards of High Dams (internationally oriented national body)
- ♦ **ECGI** European Corporate Governance Institute (#06799)
- ♦ **ECGP** European Coal Geology Group (#06589)
- ♦ **ECGS** European Centre for Geodynamics and Seismology (#06481)
- ♦ **ECHA** European Chemicals Agency (#06523)
- ♦ **ECHA** European Council for High Ability (#06822)
- ♦ **ECHAlliance** European Connected Health Alliance (#06741)
- ♦ **ECHAMP** European Coalition on Homeopathic and Anthroposophic Medicinal Products (#06595)
- ♦ Echange éducatif européen – Youth for Understanding (#06965)
- ♦ Echange international chrétien de jeunes / see International Cultural Youth Exchange (#13122)
- ♦ Echange international des données et de l'information océanographique (#14396)
- ♦ Echange de lettres constituant un accord concernant la circulation des réfugiés (1964 treaty)
- ♦ Echange de lettres constituant un accord concernant le droit de retour des réfugiés travailleurs (1964 treaty)
- ♦ Echange de lettres constituant un accord concernant l'utilisation du livret de marin comme document de voyage (1964 treaty)
- ♦ Echange de lettres constituant un accord de coopération Allemagne-France-Luxembourg (1980 treaty)
- ♦ Echange de lettres constituant un accord relatif à l'utilisation de livrets de marin comme documents de voyage (1964 treaty)
- ♦ Echange de notes constituant un accord concernant les échanges sur base commerciale de fleurs coupées (1955 treaty)
- ♦ Echange de notes constituant un accord concernant la libération des échanges entre les trois pays des produits de la pêche (1954 treaty)
- ♦ Echanges et consultations techniques internationaux / see ECTI – Professionnels Seniors Bénévoles

♦ Echanges culturels en Méditerranée (ECUME) 05281

Cultural Exchanges in the Mediterranean – Intercambios Culturales en el Mediterraneo

Pres 1 place Gabriel Péri, 13001 Marseille, France. T. +33491914141. Fax +33491914040.
Facebook: https://www.facebook.com/%C3%89CUME-%C3%89changes-culturels-en-M%C3%A9diterran%C3%A9e-1434365326813340/

History 28 Jul 1983. Former names and other names: *Association d'échanges culturels en Méditerranée* – alias. **Aims** Participate in development of Mediterranean culture and exchanges. **Structure** Board of Directors; Operational Team. **Staff** 3.00 FTE, paid. **Finance** Budget (annual): euro 200,000. **Activities** Events/meetings; networking/liaising. **Events** *Colloque international* Aix-en-Provence (France) 1999, *Rencontre des écoles de musique de la Méditerranée* Genoa (Italy) 1999, *Rencontre des écoles de musique de la Méditerranée* Thessaloniki (Greece) 1997, *Biennale méditerranéenne des arts* Tunis (Tunisia) 1997, *Rencontre des écoles de musique de la Méditerranée* France 1993. **Publications** Newsletter; catalogue of events.
Members Full; individual. Members in 19 countries:
Albania, Algeria, Croatia, Cyprus, Egypt, France, Greece, Italy, Jordan, Lebanon, Malta, Morocco, Palestine, Portugal, Spain, Syrian AR, Tunisia, Türkiye, UK. [2020/XF4562/**F**]

- ♦ Echanges internationaux (internationally oriented national body)
- ♦ Echanges de notes constituant un accord relatif à des recherches scientifiques concernant les phoques à fourrure dans le Pacifique Nord (1952 treaty)
- ♦ Échanges et Partenariats (internationally oriented national body)
- ♦ **ECHDO** European Congenital Heart Disease Organisation (#06738)

♦ ECHELON Network 05282

Address not obtained.

History 1971, operated by intelligence agencies in Australia, Canada, New Zealand, UK and USA. Also referred to as *Project ECHELON.* **Aims** As a global electronic *communications surveillance* system, protect national *security* of participating countries. **Activities** Designed for primarily non-military targets, the system is believed to intercept up to 3 billion communications every day, including phone calls, e-mail messages, Internet downloads and satellite transmissions. [2008/XM0108/**F***]

- ♦ ECHELON Watch (internationally oriented national body)

♦ ECHEMS 05283

Contact Dept of Chemistry, Univ of Aarhus, Langelandsgade 140, 8000 Aarhus C, Denmark. E-mail: kdaa@chem.au.dk.
URL: http://www.old.chem.au.dk/echems/index.html

History 2004, following the previous conference series EUCHEM of Electrochemistry and the Sandbjerg Meetings of Organic Electrochemistry. **Aims** Promote use and development of *electrochemistry* to study scientific problems. **Structure** Board. **Events** *Annual Conference* Lochow (Poland) 2013, *Annual Conference* Bertinoro (Italy) 2012, *Annual Conference* Paris (France) 2011, *Annual conference* Sandbjerg (Denmark) 2010, *Annual conference* Weingarten (Germany) 2009. [2013/XM0193/c/**F**]

- ♦ **ECH** European Committee for Homeopathy (#06651)
- ♦ **ECHIC** European Consortium for Humanities Institutes and Centres (#06755)
- ♦ **ECHM** European Committee for Hyperbaric Medicine (#06652)
- ♦ ECHO / see Educational Concerns for Hunger Organization
- ♦ ECHO (inactive)
- ♦ ECHO – Educational Concerns for Hunger Organization (internationally oriented national body)
- ♦ Echoes of Service (internationally oriented national body)
- ♦ Echoes of Women in Africa (internationally oriented national body)
- ♦ **ECHO** European Children's Hospitals Organisation (#06531)
- ♦ **ECHO** European Concert Hall Organisation (#06696)
- ♦ ECHO / see European Confederation of Care-Home Organizations (#06700)
- ♦ **ECHO** European Confederation of Care-Home Organizations (#06700)
- ♦ Echoing Green (internationally oriented national body)
- ♦ ECHO – International Health Services (internationally oriented national body)
- ♦ Echos communication (internationally oriented national body)
- ♦ ECHP – European Centre for Health Policy (see: #20945)
- ♦ ECHR – European Center for Human Rights (unconfirmed)
- ♦ **EChr** European Club for Human Resources (#06581)
- ♦ **ECHSA** European Congenital Heart Surgeons Association (#06739)
- ♦ ECHT – European Conference on Heat Treatment (meeting series)
- ♦ **ECIA** European Cellulose Insulation Association (#06460)
- ♦ ECIA – European Council of Information Associations (no recent information)
- ♦ **ECIA** European Council of Interior Architects (#06824)
- ♦ **ECIAF** Eastern Caribbean Institute of Agriculture and Forestry (#05234)
- ♦ ECIAIR – European Conference on the Impact of Artificial Intelligence and Robotics (meeting series)
- ♦ **ECI Campaign** European Citizens' Initiative Campaign (#06558)
- ♦ **ECIC** European Christian Internet Conference (#06544)
- ♦ **ECICW** European Centre of the International Council of Women (#06485)
- ♦ **ECI** Earth Charter International (#05161)
- ♦ **ECI** Earth Child Institute (#05162)
- ♦ **ECI** ECO Cultural Institute (#05292)
- ♦ ECIE – European Conference on Innovation and Entrepreneurship (meeting series)
- ♦ **ECI** European Candle Institute (#06435)
- ♦ ECI – European Coalition for Israel (internationally oriented national body)
- ♦ **ECI** European Construction Institute (#06767)
- ♦ ECI – European Cooperation for Informatics (inactive)
- ♦ **ECI** European Copper Institute (#06796)
- ♦ ECIFAU / see International Federation Amateur Unifight (#13353)
- ♦ **ECIIA** European Confederation of Institutes of Internal Auditing (#06707)
- ♦ ECIMS – European Colloquium of Indonesian and Malay Studies (meeting series)
- ♦ **ECINEQ** Society for the Study of Economic Inequality (#19645)
- ♦ ECIO – European Conference on Integrated Optics (meeting series)
- ♦ **ECIPE** European Centre for International Political Economy (#06486)
- ♦ ECIP – European Community Investment Partners (inactive)
- ♦ **ECIPS** EUROPEAN CENTRE FOR INFORMATION POLICY and SECURITY (#06480)
- ♦ **ECIROA** European Captive Insurance and Reinsurance Owners' Association (#06442)
- ♦ ECIS / see Educational Collaborative for International Schools (#05365)
- ♦ **ECIS** Educational Collaborative for International Schools (#05365)
- ♦ **ECIS** European Colloid and Interface Society (#06632)
- ♦ **ECIS** European Committee for Interoperable Systems (#06654)
- ♦ **ECIS** European Conference on Information Systems (#06733)
- ♦ **ECIT Foundation** Foundation on European Citizens' Rights, Involvement and Trust (#09950)
- ♦ ECITO – European Central Inland Transport Organization (inactive)
- ♦ **ECIU** European Consortium of Innovative Universities (#06756)
- ♦ ECIWA – European Committee of Importers' and Wholesale Grocers' Associations (inactive)
- ♦ **ECIW** European Confederation of Independent Winegrowers (#06706)
- ♦ **ECJA** European Confederation of Jesuit Alumni/ae (#04536)
- ♦ **ECJC** European Council of Jewish Communities (#06825)
- ♦ ECJCS / see European Council of Jewish Communities (#06825)
- ♦ **ECJS** European Centre for Jewish Students (#06487)

♦ Eckankar, The Path of Spiritual Freedom 05284

Vice-Pres PO Box 2000, Chanhassen MN 55317-2000, USA. T. +19523802200. Fax +19523802295. E-mail: clc@eckankar.org.
URL: http://www.eckankar.org/

History 1965, USA. Founded by Paul Twitchell, as a non-profit religious organization based on ancient teachings. Current Living ECK Master is Sri Harold Klemp. Former names and other names: *Eckankar, Religion of the Light and Sound of God (ECK)* – former. **Aims** Help people find God and grow spiritually. **Structure** Living ECK Master; Board of Trustees; Parent Church Administration; Regional ECK Spiritual Aides (RESAs); Regional Societies; Spiritual Center located in Chanhassen MN (USA). **Languages** English, French, German, Spanish. **Finance** Sources: donations; sale of products. **Activities** Events/meetings; publishing activities; religious activities. **Events** *ECK Soul Adventure Seminar* Minneapolis, MN (USA) 2021, *Seminar* Minneapolis, MN (USA) 2021, *Seminar* Minneapolis, MN (USA) 2020, *Annual Spring Seminar* Minneapolis, MN (USA) 2019, *Worldwide Seminar* Minneapolis, MN (USA) 2019. **Publications** *The Golden Leaf* (4 a year); *ECKANKAR Soul Adventure Magazine* (4 a year) in English; *The Mystic World* (4 a year); *Animals Are Soul Blog* (24 a year). *Autobiography of a Modern Prophet* by Harold Klemp in English; *ECKANKAR – Ancient Wisdom for Today* (2nd ed) in English; *Shariyat-Ki-Sugmad, Books One & Two* by Paul Twitchell in English; *Spiritual Lessons from Living, Mahanta Transcripts, Book 18* by Harold Klemp in English. Sacred writings; introductory materials; resource materials.
Members Members in over 120 countries. Membership countries not specified. [2023.02.14/XF3399/v/**F**]

- ♦ Eckankar, Religion of the Light and Sound of God / see Eckankar, The Path of Spiritual Freedom (#05284)
- ♦ ECK / see Eckankar, The Path of Spiritual Freedom (#05284)
- ♦ ECKM – European Conference on Knowledge Management (meeting series)
- ♦ ECKSF – European Chinese Kuo Shu Federation (inactive)

♦ ECLAC Staff Association 05285

Contact Edificio Naciones Unidas, Avenida Dag Hammarskjöld 3477, Casilla 179-D, Santiago, Santiago Metropolitan, Chile. T. +5622102608. Fax +5622080252. E-mail: consejo@cepal.org.
URL: http://www.eclac.org/

History to represent staff members of *United Nations Economic Commission for Latin America and the Caribbean (ECLAC, #20556).* **Aims** Look after the labour interests of ECLAC staff members. **Structure** Council. **Languages** English, Spanish. **Finance** Members' dues: individual contribution of 0.002% of individual staff salary. **NGO Relations** Member of: *Coordinating Committee for International Staff Unions and Associations of the United Nations System (CCISUA, #04818).* [2014.11.25/XE1765/v/**E**]

- ♦ ECLAC Statistical Conference of the Americas (see: #20556)
- ♦ **ECLAC** United Nations Economic Commission for Latin America and the Caribbean (#20556)
- ♦ ECLA – European Clothing Association (inactive)
- ♦ **ECLA** European Company Lawyers Association (#06686)
- ♦ **ECLA** European Competition Lawyers Association (#06688)
- ♦ **ECLAMC** Estudio Colaborativo Latino Americano de Malformaciones Congénitas (#05552)
- ♦ **ECLAM** European College of Laboratory Animal Medicine (#06611)
- ♦ **ECLAN** European Criminal Law Academic Network (#06860)
- ♦ **ECLAS** European Council of Landscape Architecture Schools (#06826)
- ♦ **ECL** Association of European Cancer Leagues (#02500)
- ♦ ECLAT – European Computer Leasing and Trading Association (inactive)
- ♦ ECLA / see United Nations Economic Commission for Latin America and the Caribbean (#20556)
- ♦ **ECLF** European Contact Lens Forum (#06774)
- ♦ **ECLF** European Cycle Logistics Federation (#06875)
- ♦ ECLIM – European Conference on Laser Interaction with Matter (meeting series)

♦ Eclipse Foundation 05286

Exec Dir Rond Point Schuman 11, 1040 Brussels, Belgium. E-mail: emo@eclipse.org.
Managing Dir Europe address not obtained.
URL: https://www.eclipse.org/

History Jan 2004. Preceeded by the Eclipse Project, created by IBM Nov 2001. Registration: Banque-Carrefour des Entreprises, No/ID: 0760.624.114, Start date: 13 Nov 2020, Belgium; EU Transparency Register, No/ID: 583649748541-53, Start date: 10 Jan 2023. **Aims** Provide the global community of individuals and organizations with a mature, scalable, and business-friendly environment for open source software collaboration and innovation. **Structure** Board of Directors. Working Groups. OSGi Working Group took over function of *Open Services Gateway Initiative Alliance (OSGI Alliance, inactive).* **Finance** Sources: members' dues. **Activities** Projects/programmes. **Events** *Security, AI, Architecture and Modelling for Next Generation Mobility Conference* Oulu (Finland) 2021.
Members Strategic; Contributing; Associate; Committer.
IOTA Foundation (#16009).
NGO Relations Member of (1): *International Association of Trusted Blockchain Applications (INATBA).* [2023/AA1485/f/**F**]

- ♦ ECLIPS – European Convention of Library Suppliers and Information Providers (meeting series)
- ♦ ECLJ – European Centre for Law and Justice (internationally oriented national body)
- ♦ ECLM European Council of Legal Medicine (#06827)
- ♦ ECLN European Civil Liberties Network (#06566)
- ♦ ECLN European Constitutional Law Network (#06764)
- ♦ ECLOF / see ECLOF International (#05287)

♦ ECLOF International 05287
Secretariat Route de Ferney 150, PO Box 2100, 1211 Geneva 2, Switzerland. T. +41227916312. E-mail: office@eclof.org.
URL: http://www.eclof.org/
History 1946, Geneva (Switzerland). Derived from *Association protestante internationale de prêt (APIDEP, inactive)*, as Ecumenical Church Loan Fund (ECLOF) – *Ökumenischer Darlehensfonds*. Act of Incorporation amended: 8 Oct 1957; 10 Nov 1967; 12 Nov 1979; 17 Jun 1992; 9 Oct 1998; 6 Apr 2009; 2 Jul 2010. **Aims** Provide financial and non-financial services to micro entrepreneurs and smallholder farmers, thereby promoting human dignity and enabling self-sustainability. **Structure** Board of Directors; Special Committees (2); National offices (12). **Languages** English, French, Spanish. **Staff** 1014.00 FTE, paid. **Finance** Sources: donations; fees for services; fundraising; gifts, legacies; grants; investments; members' dues; revenue from activities/projects. Partners include the following organizations: *Brot für die Welt*; Church of Sweden; Mercy Partnership Fund; United Church of Canada. **Activities** Capacity building; events/meetings; financial and/or material support; projects/programmes. **Events** *Asia-Pacific regional workshop* 2004, *Africa regional workshop* Harare (Zimbabwe) 2001, *Africa regional workshop* Nairobi (Kenya) 1997, *Latin America and Caribbean Consultation* Montevideo (Uruguay) 1988. **Publications** Annual Report; promotional materials.
Members National ECLOFs (NECs) in 12 countries:
Armenia, Brazil, Colombia, Dominican Rep, Ecuador, India, Jamaica, Kenya, Myanmar, Philippines, Sri Lanka, Uganda.

[2022.02.15/XF6462/f/**F**]

- ♦ Eclosio (internationally oriented national body)
- ♦ ECLS European China Law Studies Association (#06537)
- ♦ ECLSO European Contact Lens Society of Ophthalmologists (#06775)
- ♦ ECLT Foundation Eliminate Child Labour in Tobacco Foundation (#05430)
- ♦ ECMA / see Ecma International (#05288)
- ♦ ECMA European Candle Manufacturers Association (#06436)
- ♦ ECMA European Carton Makers Association (#06453)
- ♦ ECMA European Castor and Wheel Manufacturers Association (#06456)
- ♦ ECMA European Catalyst Manufacturers Association (#06457)
- ♦ ECMA European Chamber Music Academy (#06515)
- ♦ ECMA European Cigar Manufacturers Association (#06549)
- ♦ ECMA – European Collectors and Modellers Association (no recent information)
- ♦ ECMA European Crisis Management Academy (#06861)
- ♦ ECMA European Cylinder Makers Association (#06878)

♦ Ecma International 05288
Contact Rue du Rhône 114, 1204 Geneva, Switzerland. T. +41228496000. Fax +41228496001. E-mail: helpdesk@ecma-international.org.
URL: http://www.ecma-international.org/
History 17 Jun 1961, Geneva (Switzerland). Conceived on 27 April 1960, Brussels. Officially founded at the constituent assembly. Former names and other names: *European Computer Manufacturers Association (ECMA)* – former (1961 to 1994); *Association européenne de constructeurs d'ordinateurs* – former (1961 to 1994); *Asociación Europea de Fabricantes de Computadoras* – former (1961 to 1994); *Europäische Vereinigung der Computer Hersteller* – former (1961 to 1994); *Ecma International – International Europe-based Industry Association for Standardizing Information and Communication Systems* – full title (1994). Registration: Swiss Civil Code, Switzerland; EU Transparency Register, No/ID: 792734423448-47. **Aims** Study and develop standards and technical reports in cooperation with appropriate national, European and international organizations to facilitate use of information processing, consumer electronics and telecommunication systems; encourage correct use of standards by influencing the environment in which they are applied; promulgate various standards applicable to functional design and use of information processing and telecommunication systems. **Structure** General Assembly; Management; Secretariat; Executive Committee; Technical Committees; Task Groups. **Languages** English. **Staff** 3.00 FTE, paid. **Finance** Sources: members' dues. **Activities** Research and development; standards/guidelines. **Events** *Half-yearly general assembly* Divonne (France) 2011, *Half-yearly general assembly* San Francisco, CA (USA) 2011, *Half-Yearly General Assembly* Montreux (Switzerland) 2010, *Half-yearly general assembly* Tokyo (Japan) 2010, *Half-yearly general assembly* Winterthur (Switzerland) 2010. **Publications** *Memento* (annual). *Ecma Standards; Ecma Technical Reports.*
Members Ordinary companies active in the field of IT or telecommunications. Associate companies dealing in matters related to one or more Technical Committee; Small and Medium fixed Enterprises (SME); Small Private Companies (SPC). Other Not-For-Profit organizations. Members in 16 countries:
Belgium, Canada, China, Denmark, France, Germany, Japan, Korea Rep, Netherlands, New Zealand, Norway, Singapore, Sweden, Switzerland, UK, USA.
Consultative Status Consultative status granted from: *ECOSOC (#05331)* (Ros C); *World Intellectual Property Organization (WIPO, #21593)* (Permanent Observer Status). **NGO Relations** Cooperates with (1): *European Telecommunications Standards Institute (ETSI, #08897)*.

[2022.05.16/XD0684/**D**]

- ♦ Ecma International – International Europe-based Industry Association for Standardizing Information and Communication Systems / see Ecma International (#05288)
- ♦ ECMAR / see European Council for Maritime Applied R and D (#06829)
- ♦ ECMAR European Council for Maritime Applied R and D (#06829)
- ♦ ECMC / see New Wineskins Missionary Network
- ♦ ECMC – Congregatio Eremitarum Camaldulensium Montis Coronae (religious order)
- ♦ ECM / see City Destinations Alliance (#03960)
- ♦ ECMD – European Centre for Mobility Documentation (internationally oriented national body)
- ♦ ECMEC / see European Centre for Missing and Sexually Exploited Children
- ♦ ECME – European Conference on Molecular Electronics (meeting series)
- ♦ ECM / see European Cylinder Makers Association (#06878)
- ♦ ECMF European Citizens' Mobility Forum (#06559)
- ♦ ECMF – European Commercial Managers Federation (internationally oriented national body)
- ♦ ECMH – European Conference on Mental Health (meeting series)
- ♦ ECMHT – European Centre on Training and Formation of Local and Regional Authorities and Population in the Field of Natural and Technological Disasters (internationally oriented national body)
- ♦ ECMI / see European Christian Mission
- ♦ ECMIA Enlace Continental de Mujeres Indigenas de las Americas (#05485)
- ♦ ECMI European Capital Markets Institute (#06439)
- ♦ ECMI – European Centre for Minority Issues (internationally oriented national body)
- ♦ ECMI European Consortium for Mathematics in Industry (#06757)
- ♦ ECM International – European Christian Mission (internationally oriented national body)
- ♦ ECML European Centre for Modern Languages (#06491)
- ♦ ECMLG – European Conference on Management Leadership and Governance (meeting series)
- ♦ ECMM European Confederation of Medical Mycology (#06712)
- ♦ ECMNR – European Centre for Mitigation of Natural Risks (internationally oriented national body)
- ♦ ECMO European Council of Medical Orders (#06830)
- ♦ ECMP European Confederation of Modern Pentathlon (#06713)
- ♦ ECMRN – European Congress of Magnetic Resonance in Neuropediatrics (meeting series)
- ♦ ECMSA – European Chemical Marketing and Strategy Association (inactive)
- ♦ ECMS European Council for Modelling and Simulation (#06831)
- ♦ ECMTA European Chamber Music Teachers' Association (#06516)
- ♦ ECMTF European CMT Federation (#06586)

- ♦ ECMT / see International Transport Forum (#15725)
- ♦ ECMWF European Centre for Medium-Range Weather Forecasts (#06490)
- ♦ ECNA – European Cardionephrology Association (no recent information)
- ♦ ECNAIS European Council of National Associations of Independent Schools (#06833)
- ♦ ECNAMP / see Caribbean Natural Resources Institute (#03525)

♦ ECNC – European Centre for Nature Conservation 05289
Exec Dir PO Box 90154, 5000 LG Tilburg, Netherlands. T. +31135944944. Fax +31135944945.
Regional Office for the Mediterranean c/o Consorci El Far, Carrer Escar 6-8, modulo 10, 08039 Barcelona, Spain. T. +34931054020. Fax +34932213150.
URL: http://www.ecncgroup.eu/
History Founded 15 Nov 1993, Maastricht (Netherlands), in cooperation with the Dutch government, *UN Environment Programme World Conservation Monitoring Centre (UNEP-WCMC, #20295)*, *International Union for Conservation of Nature and Natural Resources (IUCN, #15766)* and Netherlands, Belgian and Spanish universities. Operational Jan 1994. Statutes modified: 23 May 1996; new Statutes adopted 2 Apr 1997 and Nov 2004; modified 2005. Registered in accordance with Dutch law. **Aims** Work towards a Europe based on a rich *biodiversity*, healthy ecosystems and sustainable development; promote an integrated approach for both land and sea; stimulate interaction between science, society and policy. **Structure** Board; Secretariat; Network Partners (59). **Languages** English. **Staff** 10.00 FTE, paid. **Finance** Supported by subsidies, programmes and project revenues. Project turnover (2016): euro 1,300,000. **Activities** Politics/policy/regulatory. **Events** *Conference on Nature Outlook* Brussels (Belgium) 2015, *Workshop* Brussels (Belgium) 2010, *Joint annual European nature conference* Apeldoorn (Netherlands) 2005, *COHAB : international conference on the importance of biodiversity to human health* Galway (Ireland) 2005, *Pan-European CHM workshop* Bonn (Germany) 2001. **Publications** *ECNC Update* (6 a year); *Journal for Nature Conservation* (6 a year). Annual Report; technical reports; seminar reports.
Members An international network of 59 partners in Europe in 29 countries:
Austria, Belgium, Croatia, Cyprus, Czechia, Denmark, Estonia, France, Georgia, Germany, Greece, Hungary, Ireland, Italy, Lithuania, Netherlands, North Macedonia, Norway, Poland, Romania, Russia, Serbia, Slovakia, Slovenia, Spain, Sweden, Türkiye, UK, Ukraine.
Included in the above, 5 organizations listed in this Yearbook:
Central European University (CEU, #03717); *Coastal and Marine Union – EUCC (#04072)*; *Institute of Biology of the Southern Seas (IBSS, no recent information)*; *Plant Research International (PRI)*; *UN Environment Programme World Conservation Monitoring Centre (UNEP-WCMC, #20295)*.
IGO Relations Cooperates with: *Council of Europe (CE, #04881)*; *European Bank for Reconstruction and Development (EBRD, #06315)*; *European Commission (EC, #06633)*; *European Environment Agency (EEA, #06995)*; *European Union (EU, #08967)*; *OECD (#17693)*; *UNEP (#20299)*. Observer to: EU Coordination Group for Biodiversity and Nature. Member of: Standing Committee to the Bern Convention on the Conservation of European Wildlife and Natural Habitats (#19949). **NGO Relations** Member of: *Alternet (#00756)*; *Dinaric Arc Initiative (DAI, no recent information)*; *European Forum on Nature Conservation and Pastoralism (EFNCP, #07323)*; *Eurosite (#09181)*. Together with: *Coastal and Marine Union – EUCC (#04072)* and *Eurosite (#09181)*, set up: *EECONET Action Fund (EAF, #05383)*; *NatureNet Europe (#16959)*. Also together with EUCC and the MedCentre, forms: *ECNC Group (no recent information)*. Partner of: *1% for the Planet*.

[2016.11.01/XE1757/y/**E**]

- ♦ ECNDT – European Council for Non-Destructive Testing (inactive)
- ♦ ECN Eurochurch.net (#05660)
- ♦ ECN EuroCollectNet (#05664)
- ♦ ECN European Complement Network (#06690)
- ♦ ECN European Compost Network (#06694)
- ♦ ECN European Crowdfunding Network (#06866)
- ♦ ECNI – European Confederation of Nautical Industries (inactive)
- ♦ ECNL European Center for Not-for-Profit Law (#06463)
- ♦ ECNM – European College of Naturopathic Medicine (internationally oriented national body)
- ♦ ECNM European Competence Network on Mastocytosis (#06687)
- ♦ ECNN / see European Monitoring Centre for Drugs and Drug Addiction (#07820)
- ♦ ECNP European Centre for Nanostructured Polymers (#06493)
- ♦ ECNP European College of Neuropsychopharmacology (#06612)
- ♦ ECNS / see Electroencephalography and Clinical Neuroscience Society (#05422)
- ♦ ECNS Electroencephalography and Clinical Neuroscience Society (#05422)
- ♦ ECNT / see European Centre of New Technologies for the Management of Natural and Technological Major Hazards (#06494)
- ♦ ECNTRM European Centre of New Technologies for the Management of Natural and Technological Major Hazards (#06494)
- ♦ ECO / see Bureau Européen des Unions de Consommateurs (#03360)
- ♦ ECO / see Global Community Earth Government
- ♦ ECO2TERRA International – Global Society for Ecology and Sound Economy (internationally oriented national body)
- ♦ Eco-AB European Consortium for Organic Animal Breeding (#06759)
- ♦ ECO-Accord Centre – Centre for Environment and Sustainable Development (internationally oriented national body)

♦ EcoAgriculture Partners 05290
Pres/CEO 2961 A Hunter Mill Road, Ste 647, Oakton VA 22124, USA. T. +12026435605. E-mail: info@ecoagriculture.org.
URL: http://www.ecoagriculture.org/
History 2002. Founded as a project of *Forest Trends (#09870)*; *International Union for Conservation of Nature and Natural Resources (IUCN, #15766)* and *World Agroforestry Centre (ICRAF, #21072)*. Became independent in 2005. **Aims** Facilitate *landscape* management approaches that simultaneously enhance *rural* livelihoods, conserve biodiversity and *sustainably* produce crops, livestock, fish and forest products; scale up successful *eco-agriculture* approaches by catalyzing strategic connections, dialogue and joint action among key actors at local, national and international levels. **Structure** Board of Directors. **Languages** English. **Staff** 12.50 FTE, paid. **Finance** Non-profit status necessitates that funding be sought from a wide array of sources. Key principles include: (a) A diversity of financial and in-kind contributions from inter-governmental and governmental organizations, public and private foundations, non-profit organizations, for-profit enterprises and representative associations; (b) Financial supporters remain distinct from the governance of the association; (c) The principles of the United Nations Global Compact are used as a point of reference when considering support from businesses, business associations and foundations. Supporters include the following organizations listed in this Yearbook: *Canadian International Development Agency (CIDA, inactive)*; *Forest Trends (#09870)*; *International Bank for Reconstruction and Development (IBRD, #12317)* (World Bank); *The Nature Conservancy (TNC)*. Budget (annual): about US$ 1 million. **Activities** Research and development; events/meetings. **Publications** *Farming with Nature: The Science and Practice of Ecoagriculture* (2007); *Ecoagriculture: Strategies to Feed the World and Save Wild Biodiversity* (2002). **Members** Not a membership organization. **IGO Relations** Partners include: *Bioversity International (#03262)*; *European Committee for Hyperbaric Medicine (ECHM, #06652)*; *FAO (#09260)*; *International Bank for Reconstruction and Development (IBRD, #12317)* (World Bank); *International Livestock Research Institute (ILRI, #14062)*; *UNDP (#20292)*; *UNEP (#20299)*.
NGO Relations Member of (2): *Global Alliance for Climate-Smart Agriculture (GACSA, #10189)*; *International Union for Conservation of Nature and Natural Resources (IUCN, #15766)*.
Charter member of: *Global Landscapes Forum (GLF, #10451)*. Partners include:
- *African Conservation Tillage Network (ACT, #00265)*;
- *African Wildlife Foundation (AWF, #00498)*;
- *Commonwealth Scientific and Industrial Research Organization (CSIRO)*;
- *Conservation International (CI)*;
- *Forest Trends (#09870)*;
- *International Water Management Institute (IWMI, #15867)*;
- *Landcare International (LI, #16226)*;
- *The Nature Conservancy (TNC)*;

ECO Air
05290

alphabetic sequence excludes
For the complete listing, see Yearbook Online at

- *Rainforest Alliance;*
- *Rights and Resources Initiative (RRI, #18947);*
- *TerrAfrica (#20127);*
- *Tropical Forest Alliance (TFA, #20249);*
- *World Agroforestry Centre (ICRAF, #21072);*
- *World Resources Institute (WRI, #21753);*
- *World Wide Fund for Nature (WWF, #21922).* [2021/XM3112/**F**]

♦ ECO Air (inactive)
♦ ECOAN – Asociación de Conservación de los Ecosistemas Andinos (internationally oriented national body)
♦ ECO ASIA – Environment Congress for Asia and the Pacific (meeting series)
♦ **ECOBA** European Coal Combustion Products Association (#06588)
♦ ECOBALTIC Foundation, Gdansk (internationally oriented national body)
♦ Ecobank Development Corporation (internationally oriented national body)
♦ Ecobank Foundation (unconfirmed)
♦ **ECO-CCI** ECO Chamber of Commerce and Industry (#05291)
♦ ecOceanica (internationally oriented national body)
♦ ecOceanica – Centro para la Conservación Integral de Los Ecosistemas Marinos del Pacifico Este / see ecOceanica
♦ ECO / see CEPI ContainerBoard (#03824)
♦ ECOC – European Conference on Optical Communication (meeting series)

♦ ECO Chamber of Commerce and Industry (ECO-CCI) 05291

Contact ECO Secretariat, No 1 Goulbou Alley, Kamranieh, 19519-33114, Teheran, Iran Islamic Rep. T. +98212831731 – +98212831733. Fax +98212831732.
URL: https://www.eco.int/web_directory/55708-ECO-CCI-National-Chambers.html

History 1989, Istanbul (Türkiye). Established on approval of statutes by heads of founding member national chambers of commerce, as a regional institution of *Economic Cooperation Organization (ECO, #05313)* for the private sector. Established in conformity with Article 30 of the Treaty of Izmir, originally signed 12 Mar 1977. Revives the activities of *RCD Chamber of Commerce and Industry (inactive)*, which existed from 1965 to 1984. New ECO members admitted Jun 1993. **Aims** Facilitate *trade* and *economic cooperation*; promote closer relations among *free enterprises*; realize joint *investment* in member countries. **Structure** General Assembly; Executive Council; National Committees. Headquarters rotate biennially among member countries. **Activities** Advocacy/lobbying/activism; events/meetings. **Events** *General Assembly* Ankara (Turkey) 2015. **Members** Full (" founding member) in 10 countries:
Afghanistan, Azerbaijan, Iran Islamic Rep (*), Kazakhstan, Kyrgyzstan, Pakistan (*), Tajikistan, Türkiye (*), Turkmenistan, Uzbekistan.
IGO Relations Memorandum of Understanding with (1): *Secretariat of the Convention on International Trade in Endangered Species of Wild Fauna and Flora (CITES Secretariat, #19199).* [2018/XE2094/t/**E***]

♦ **Ecocide Alliance** International Parliamentary Alliance for the Recognition of Ecocide (#14517)
♦ Ecocity Builders (internationally oriented national body)
♦ ECOCLUBES / see International Network of Ecoclubs (#14253)
♦ **Ecoclubes International** International Network of Ecoclubs (#14253)
♦ ECO College of Insurance (inactive)
♦ Eco-conseil Europe – Association européenne des éco-conseillers/ères (inactive)
♦ Eco-Counselling Europe – European Association of Eco-Counsellors (inactive)

♦ ECO Cultural Institute (ECI) 05292

Pres No 10, Naz Alley, Movahed-Danesh St, Teheran, 1957653643, Iran Islamic Rep. T. +982127673000. Fax +982126124996. E-mail: info@ecieco.org – registry@ecieco.org.
URL: https://www.ecieco.org/

History 14 Mar 1995, Islamabad (Pakistan). 14-15 Mar 1995, Islamabad (Pakistan), on signature of a Charter by 8 of the member states of *Economic Cooperation Organization (ECO, #05313)*, to revive the activities of *RCD Cultural Institute (inactive)*, which existed from Jun 1966 to 1984. **Aims** Recognizing that development of economic relations among member countries is closely linked to active cultural relations: foster and promote closer cultural association and cooperation, in particular among *mass media*, *intellectuals* and *artists* and especially in the fields of *history*, demography, anthropology, *archaeology* and preservation and restoration of the common *architectural heritage* of the region and its literature, *folklore*, *traditional* music and national customs; revive the region's *spiritual values*, *civilization* and historical status; safeguard and preserve its *heritage* of literature, art and philosophy; strengthen ties of friendship and affinity among its people and guard their common identity. **Structure** Board of Trustees (meets every 2 years). Executive Committee, comprising cultural experts. Institute is headed by President, assisted by Executive Director and staff. Headquarters in Iran; coordination units in each member state. **Languages** English. **Staff** Nationals of member states, resident and locally recruited in Iran. **Finance** Grants and contributions of member states; donations; endowments. **Activities** Research; awards; programmes; publishing activities. **Publications** *ECI Journal.* Books; monographs; periodicals; scholarly papers.
Members Governments of 8 countries:
Afghanistan, Azerbaijan, Iran Islamic Rep, Kazakhstan, Pakistan, Tajikistan, Türkiye, Turkmenistan.
IGO Relations *Research Centre for Islamic History, Art and Culture (IRCICA, #18852).* [2022/XE2846/j/**E***]

♦ **ECOCYCLES** European Ecocycles Society (#06954)
♦ **ecoDa** European Confederation of Directors' Associations (#06702)
♦ ECODEF – East Caribbean Organization of Development Foundations (inactive)
♦ ECODES – Fundación Ecologia y Desarrollo (internationally oriented national body)
♦ EcoDesign – International Symposium on Environmentally Conscious Design and Inverse Manufacturing (meeting series)
♦ **ECO** Economic Cooperation Organization (#05313)

♦ ECO Educational Institute (ECOEI) 05293

Headquarters Mustafa Kemal Mahallesi, Tepe Prime, C Blok, Kat 7, No 88, 06510 Ankara/Ankara, Türkiye. T. +903126661609 – +903126661610. E-mail: registry@eieco.org.
URL: http://eieco.org/

History 1998, Almaty (Kazakhstan). Founded within the framework of *Economic Cooperation Organization (ECO, #05313).* **Aims** Broaden cooperation among ECO countries in the field of education and training along the principles, aims and spirit of the Treaty of Izmir. **Structure** Board of Trustees; President. **Languages** English, Russian. **Activities** Certification/accreditation; events/meetings; projects/programmes; publishing activities; research and development; research/documentation; training/education. **Events** *Seminar on Teaching Excellence* Ankara (Turkey) 2020, *Triennial Meeting* Ankara (Turkey) 2020, *Workshop on Distance Education Experience Sharing between ECO Member Countries* Ankara (Turkey) 2020, *Workshop on How to Write and Publish Articles for International Journals* Ankara (Turkey) 2020. **Publications** *ECOEI Newsletter. ECOEI Report on Covid-19 Pandemic and Its Impact on Education.*
Members Member States (7):
Afghanistan, Azerbaijan, Iran Islamic Rep, Kazakhstan, Kyrgyzstan, Pakistan, Tajikistan, Türkiye, Turkmenistan, Uzbekistan.
Observer State:
Northern Cyprus. [2022/XJ6732/j/**E***]

♦ **EC-OE** European Confederation of Outdoor Employers (#06716)
♦ **ECOEI** ECO Educational Institute (#05293)
♦ Eco-Ethics International Union (inactive)
♦ **ECO** European Cancer Organisation (#06432)
♦ **ECO** European Carbohydrate Organization (#06444)
♦ ECO / see European Cetacean Society (#06513)
♦ **ECO** European Cleft Organisation (#06572)
♦ **ECO** European Communications Office (#06676)
♦ ECOF – European Conference on Organized Films (meeting series)
♦ **ECOFI** European Consortium of the Organic-Based Fertilizer Industry (#06760)
♦ Eco Forum Global (internationally oriented national body)
♦ **ECOG** European Childhood Obesity Group (#06529)
♦ EcoHealth Alliance (internationally oriented national body)
♦ EcoHealth / see Ecohealth International (#05294)

♦ Ecohealth International 05294

Pres c/o School of Nursing UKZN, College of Health Sciences, Private Bag 7, Congella, 4013, South Africa. E-mail: contact@ecohealthinternational.org.
URL: https://www.ecohealthinternational.org/

History 2006, Madison, WI (USA). Founded during the EcoHealth ONE Conference. Current name adopted following 7th conference. Former names and other names: *International Association for Ecology and Health (EcoHealth)* – former. **Aims** Strive for sustainable health of people, wildlife and ecosystems by promoting discovery, understanding and the engagement with knowledges that promote ways of living in the confines of planetary resources. **Structure** Board. Regional Chapters: Africa; Americas; Asia; Europe; Oceania. **Finance** Sources: members' dues. **Events** *Biennial Ecohealth Conference* Durban (South Africa) 2022, *Biennial Ecohealth Conference* Durban (South Africa) 2020, *Biennial Ecohealth Conference* Cali (Colombia) 2018, *Biennial Ecohealth Conference* Melbourne, VIC (Australia) 2016, *Biennial Ecohealth Conference* Montréal, QC (Canada) 2014. **Publications** *EcoHealth* (4 a year). **Members** Membership countries not specified. [2022/XJ8073/**C**]

♦ ECOHOST / see ECOHOST – The Centre for Health and Social Change
♦ ECOHOST – The Centre for Health and Social Change (internationally oriented national body)
♦ ECOHOST – ECOHOST – The Centre for Health and Social Change (internationally oriented national body)
♦ ECOI – ECO College of Insurance (inactive)
♦ Ecole des affaires publiques et internationales Woodrow Wilson / see Princeton School of Public and International Affairs
♦ Ecole africaine et mauricienne d'architecture et d'urbanisme / see African School of Architecture and Town Planning (#00450)

♦ Ecole africaine de la méteorologie et de l'aviation civile (EAMAC) . . 05295

African School of Meteorology and Civil Aviation

Contact BP 746, Niamey, Niger. T. +22720722236. Fax +22720722236. E-mail: eamacsec@asecna.org.
URL: http://www.eamac.ne/

History 1963. A training centre of *Agency for the Safety of Aerial Navigation in Africa and Madagascar (#00556).* **Aims** Train technicians in aerial navigation, meteorology and installation. [2016/XE1876/**E***]

♦ Ecole africaine des métiers d'architecture et d'urbanisme (#00450)

♦ Ecole de bibliothécaires, archivistes et documentalistes (EBAD) . . . 05296

School for Librarians, Archivists and Documentalists

Main Office Univ Cheikh A Diop, BP 3252, Dakar, Senegal. T. +2218257660 – +2218642122. Fax +2218240542. E-mail: ebad@ucad.edu.sn.
URL: http://www.ebad.ucad.sn/

History 1963, under the title *Centre régional de formation de bibliothécaires des pays d'Afrique d'expression française*, as an African regional centre, at the recommendation of *UNESCO (#20322)* and the Government of Senegal. Current name adopted 1967, when the School became an Institute of the University of Dakar (Senegal). **Activities** Offers 2-year courses at 2 levels: undergraduate, leading to a Diploma of assistant librarian, archivist, or documentalist; postgraduate, leading to a Master's degree in information science studies. **NGO Relations** Member of: *International Federation of Library Associations and Institutions (IFLA, #13470).* [2020/XF1259/**F**]

♦ Ecole d'études orientales et africaines (internationally oriented national body)
♦ Ecole européenne des affaires / see ESCP Europe Business School (#05536)
♦ Ecole européenne de Chimie, Polymères et Matériaux, Strasbourg (internationally oriented national body)
♦ Ecole européenne d'hématologie (#08430)
♦ Ecole européenne d'oncologie (#08434)
♦ Ecole européenne d'ostéopathie (internationally oriented national body)
♦ Ecole européenne de psychothérapie socio- et somato-analytique, Strasbourg (internationally oriented national body)
♦ Ecole européenne de sciences du sport (#06616)
♦ Ecole de formation internationale (internationally oriented national body)
♦ Ecole française d'ostéopathie / see European School of Osteopathy

♦ Ecole Inter-Etats des Douanes de la CEMAC (EIED) 05297

Inter-State Customs School of CAEMC

Contact Ave Docteur Conjugo, BP 991, Bangui, Central African Rep. T. +23621610449 – +23621619073. Fax +23621610449. E-mail: contact@eied-cemac.org – eied.cemac@gmail.com.
URL: http://www.eied-cemac.org/

History 22 Dec 1972, Brazzaville (Congo Brazzaville), as *Ecole inter-états des douanes de l'UDEAC – Inter-State Customs School of CACEU*, coming within the framework of *Union douanière et économique de l'Afrique centrale (UDEAC, inactive)*. Became independent in 1994, when current title adopted on setting up of *Communauté économique et monétaire d'Afrique centrale (CEMAC, #04374).* Agreement signed 18 Oct 1998 with national customs school in Tourcoing (France) and with the administration of the customs and Belgian excises, 9 Mar 2006. **Aims** Initial and continuing training of customs officials of nationals of Member States of CEMAC. **Structure** Administrative Council, comprising: Director General (Financial Control; Agency Accountant) Director of Training (Training Service; Service of Surveillance; Supervisory; Service of Documentation and ICT); (Service of Human Resources and Social Medicine, Department of Finance, Service Equipment and Supply). **Languages** French. **Staff** 42.00 FTE, paid. **Finance** Contributions of CEMAC member states. Annual budget (2013): CFA 1,491,338,437. **Activities** Provides initial and in-service training for customs agents. Organizes seminars on current topics. **Publications** *L'idéal* – magazine. **Members** CEMAC member states. **IGO Relations** *European Union (EU, #08967); World Customs Organization (WCO, #21350).* [2013.10.31/XK0420/**E***]

♦ Ecole inter-états des douanes de l'UDEAC / see Ecole Inter-Etats des Douanes de la CEMAC (#05297)
♦ Ecole inter-Etats des Sciences et Médecine Vétérinaires (#15982)
♦ Ecole inter-Etats des techniciens supérieurs de l'hydraulique et de l'équipement rural (#15981)
♦ Ecole inter-Etats des techniciens supérieurs de l'hydraulique et de l'équipement rural (inactive)
♦ Ecole internationale de langue et de civilisation françaises (see: #09814)
♦ Ecole internationale des Nations Unies (internationally oriented national body)
♦ Ecole internationale de la rose-croix d'or (religious order)
♦ Ecole internationale de solidarité / see International Institute of Journalism, Berlin – Brandenburg
♦ Ecole internationale supérieure hautes études (internationally oriented national body)
♦ Ecole latinoaméricaine de mathématique (meeting series)
♦ Ecole des mines et de la géologie de la Communauté économique de l'Afrique de l'Ouest / see School of Mining Industry and Geology (#19132)
♦ Ecole des mines, de l'industrie et de la géologie (#19132)
♦ Ecole multinationale supérieure des postes, Abidjan (no recent information)
♦ Ecole du patrimoine africain (internationally oriented national body)
♦ Ecole régionale de la navigation aérienne et du management (#18809)
♦ Ecole régionale de la navigation aérienne et de la météorologie / see Regional School for Aerial Navigation and Management (#18809)
♦ Ecole régionale post-universitaire d'aménagement et de gestion intégré des forêts tropicales / see Ecole régionale post-universitaire d'aménagement et de gestion intégrés des forêts et territoires tropicaux
♦ Ecole régionale post-universitaire d'aménagement et de gestion intégrés des forêts et territoires tropicaux (internationally oriented national body)

♦ Ecole des relations internationales, Los Angeles (internationally oriented national body)
♦ Ecole de Soufisme Islamique (#16556)
♦ École supérieure d'études internationales (internationally oriented national body)
♦ Ecole supérieure de folklore nordique à Genève (#19087)

♦ École supérieure de la francophonie pour l'administration et le management (ESFAM) 05298

Dir 1 rue Léopold Sédar Senghor, BL-1618 Sofia, Bulgaria. T. +35929559571. Fax +35929559585. E-mail: info-esfam@auf.org.
URL: http://esfam.auf.org/

History Founded by *Université des réseaux d'expression française (UREF, inactive)*, within the framework of *Agence universitaire de La Francophonie (AUF, #00548)*, on receiving a mandate from *Conférence au sommet des chefs d'Etat et de gouvernement des pays ayant le français en partage (Sommet de la Francophonie, #04648)*, following a proposal, Mar 1994, by *Association des universités partiellement ou entièrement de langue française (AUPELF, inactive)* and the Minister of Science and Education of Bulgaria. Originally known as *Institut de la Francophonie pour l'Administration et la Gestion (IFAG)*. Became operational in Sep 1995. Present name adopted, 2015. **Aims** Assist the transition of *Central European* countries to a market economy by providing French language *higher education* in *management* for managers, in particular entrepreneurs and managers of *SMEs*. **Structure** An international francophone training and research institute located in Sofia (Bulgaria). **Activities** Applicants must already possess a first degree or equivalent (at least 4 years of university studies). Studies lead to a: 'Master Administration des Entreprises', delivered by the Université de Nantes (France); 'Master Management Public'', delivered by the Université de Liège (Belgium); 'Master Entrepreneuriat en Economie Sociale et Solidaire', delivered by the University Lumière Lyon 2 (France). Students come mainly from Central and Eastern Europe, and from other continents. **Events** *Séminaire* Sofia (Bulgaria) 2003. [2018.06.19/XE1951/j/**E**]

♦ Ecole supérieure multinationale des télécommunications de Dakar (#16898)
♦ Ecole supérieure nordique de la santé publique (inactive)
♦ École Universitaire Internationale (internationally oriented national body)
♦ Ecoliers du monde (#00087)
♦ ECOLIFE (internationally oriented national body)
♦ ECOLIFE Foundation / see ECOLIFE
♦ **ECOLISE** European Network for Community-Led Initiatives on Climate Change and Sustainability (#07882)
♦ ECOLOGIA – Ecologists Linked for Organizing Grassroots Initiatives and Action (internationally oriented national body)

♦ Ecologica International Association 05299

Contact Via Tasso 169, 80127 Naples NA, Italy. T. +39817613830. Fax +39817612734.
URL: http://www.ecologica.mobi/

History 2007, to use and disseminate the results and the products of the international project 'Ecologica', promoted within the EU Programme *LEONARDO DA VINCI (inactive)* (HU/05/B/F/PP-170018). **Activities** Training/education; knowledge management/information dissemination.
Members European experts in organic farming, in 8 countries:
Czechia, Estonia, Greece, Hungary, Italy, Latvia, Slovakia, Slovenia.
NGO Relations Partner of: *IFOAM Organics Europe (#11104)*. Member of: *European Alliance for Innovation (EAI, #05872)*; *IFOAM – Organics International (IFOAM, #11105)*; *TP Organics – European Technology Platform (TP Organics, #20180)*. [2009/XJ0891/**D**]

♦ Ecological Sanitation for Latin America and the Caribbean (internationally oriented national body)

♦ Ecological Society for Eastern Africa (ESEA) 05300

Sec National Museums of Kenya, Mammalogy Section, PO Box 40658, Nairobi, 00100 GPO, Kenya. T. +254202504665. E-mail: ecsea.org@gmail.com – info@ecsea.org.
URL: http://www.ecsea.info/

History Founded 2007, Kenya, by ecologists in the eastern African region at the inaugural conference. **Aims** Coordinate the collation and dissemination of information relating to ecology in Eastern Africa for sustainable natural resource management and conservation of biodiversity; bridge the ecological information gaps between ecologists in the region. **Languages** English. **Staff** 1.00 FTE, paid; 2.00 FTE, voluntary. **Finance** Proposal writing; fund raising. **Events** *Scientific Conference* Nairobi (Kenya) 2013.
Members Institutional; Ordinary; Student. Members in 6 countries:
Burundi, Ethiopia, Kenya, Rwanda, Tanzania UR, Uganda.
NGO Relations Cooperates with: *Panafrican Climate Justice Alliance (PACJA, #18046)*; *Wetlands International (#20928)*. [2019.10.02/XJ2095/**D**]

♦ Ecological Society of Germany, Austria and Switzerland 05301

Gesellschaft für Ökologie (GfÖ)
Contact Rothenburgstr 12, 12165 Berlin, Germany. E-mail: info@gfoe.org.
URL: http://www.gfoe.org/

History 1970, Giessen (Germany FR). **Aims** Promote collaborative work of all ecological disciplines; represent ecological interests in public. **Structure** President; Vice-President; Secretary; Treasurer. **Languages** English, German. **Staff** 0.50 FTE, paid; 3.00 FTE, voluntary. **Finance** Members' dues. **Activities** Organizes: annual scientific conference; symposia; scientific field trips and inspections. Specialist groups (13): Agroecology; Ecological Theory; Ecology of Deserts; Ecosystem Research; Environmental Education; Experimental Ecology; Genetical Engineering and Ecology; Landscape Ecology; Macro-Ecology; Plant Population Biology; Restoration Ecology; Soil Ecology; Urban Ecology. **Events** *Annual Meeting* Braunschweig (Germany) 2021, *Annual Meeting* 2020, *Annual meeting* Vienna (Austria) 2018, *Annual meeting* Oldenburg (Germany) 2011, *Annual Conference* Oxford (UK) 2011. **Publications** *Nachrichten der Gesellschaft für Ökologie* (2 a year) – periodical; *Basic and Appplied Ecology (BAE)* (8 a year) – scientific periodical. *Verhandlungen der Gesellschaft für Ökologie* – series. Abstract volume (annual).
Members Individuals (about 1,300) in 19 countries:
Australia, Austria, Belgium, Denmark, France, Georgia, Germany, Italy, Laos, Liechtenstein, Luxembourg, Netherlands, Oman, Spain, Sweden, Switzerland, UK, USA, Venezuela.
NGO Relations Member of: *European Ecological Federation (EEF, #06956)*; *International Association for Ecology (INTECOL, #11856)*. [2020/XF6894/v/**F**]

♦ Ecological Tourism in Europe (internationally oriented national body)

♦ Ecological and Toxicological Association of Dyes and Organic Pigments Manufacturers (ETAD) 05302

Exec Dir Stadhausgasse 18, 4051 Basel BS, Switzerland. T. +41616909966. Fax +41616914278. E-mail: info@etad.com.
URL: https://etad.com/

History 1974. Interests extended, 1976, to include synthetic organic pigments. Merged, 1982, with Dyes Environmental and Toxicology Organization (DETO), USA; in USA, only dyestuff interests are represented as those of pigment manufacturers are already covered by Color Pigments Manufacturers Association (CPMA). By-laws amended: 6 May 1993; 21 May 1997; 13 May 2004; 19 May 2006; 27 May 2011. Former names and other names: *Ecological and Toxicological Association of the Dyestuffs Manufacturing Industry* – former. Registration: EU Transparency Register, No/ID: 351783047867-48, Start date: 11 Oct 2022. **Aims** Coordinate efforts of manufacturers to minimize possible impact of synthetic organic colourants on health and environment in the most economic fashion without reducing protection of health and environment; encourage harmonization of health and environmental regulations in key geographical areas; represent the position and interests of members towards authorities, public institutions and media; promote responsible environmental and health risk management during manufacture, transport, use and disposal; enhance recognition of the commitment of members to responsible behaviour; provide customers with advice and information to enable the safe use and application of dyes for the manufacture of many different products. **Structure** General Assembly (annual); Board of Directors; Executive Committee; Secretariats: Basel (Switzerland); Washington DC (USA). Operating Committees (6): Dyes; US; India; Japan; Pigments; Regulatory Affairs. **Languages** English. **Staff** 4.00 FTE, paid. **Finance** Activities mainly financed through member contributions to cover specific services provided and a share of the overhead expenses. Annual budget: 1,200,000 CHF. **Activities** Events/meetings; guidance/assistance/consulting; knowledge management/information dissemination; research/documentation. **Events** *Annual General Assembly* Goa (India) 2015, *Annual General Assembly* Barcelona (Spain) 2014, *Annual General Assembly* Istanbul (Turkey) 2013, *Annual General Assembly* Vienna (Austria) 2012, *Annual General Assembly* Amsterdam (Netherlands) 2011. **Publications** *ETAD Information Notes* – series; *ETAD Methods* – series. *Safe Handling of Pigments* – brochure, in several languages. Annual Report; scientific papers; position papers; guidelines; lectures. Operating Committees produce their own guidlines and other publications. Information Services: Computerized database on toxicological and eco-toxicological properties of organic colorants.
Members Companies (33) in 15 countries and territories:
Belgium, Canada, Czechia, Denmark, Germany, India, Japan, Korea Rep, Netherlands, Switzerland, Taiwan, Thailand, Türkiye, UK, USA.
IGO Relations Cooperates with (1): *European Commission (EC, #06633)*. **NGO Relations** Member of (1): *Conseil européen de l'industrie chimique (CEFIC, #04687)*. [2022/XD5168/**D**]

♦ Ecological and Toxicological Association of the Dyestuffs Manufacturing Industry / see Ecological and Toxicological Association of Dyes and Organic Pigments Manufacturers (#05302)
♦ Ecologic – Centre for International and European Environmental Research / see Ecologic Institut (#05303)
♦ EcoLogic Development Fund (internationally oriented national body)
♦ Ecologic – Gesellschaft für Internationale und Europäische Umweltforschung / see Ecologic Institut (#05303)

♦ Ecologic Institut 05303

Ecologic Institute
Dir Pfalzburger Strasse 43/44, 10717 Berlin, Germany. T. +4930868800. Fax +493086880100. E-mail: berlin@ecologic.eu – director@ecologic.eu.
Brussels Office Rue Joseph II 36-38, 1000 Brussels, Belgium.
URL: http://www.ecologic.eu/

History Aug 1995. Brussels (Belgium) office opened 2001; Vienna (Austria) office opened 2007; Washington DC (USA) office opened 2009. Former names and other names: *Ecologic – Gesellschaft für Internationale und Europäische Umweltforschung* – former (Aug 1995 to 2002); *Ecologic – Centre for International and European Environmental Research* – former (Aug 1995 to 2002); *Ecologic – Institut für Internationale und Europäische Umweltpolitik* – former (2002); *Ecologic – Institute for International and European Environmental Policy* – former (2002). Registration: EU Transparency Register, No/ID: 608135048474-80, Start date: 10 Jan 2023. **Aims** Promote integration of *environmental* aspects with other *policy* fields and the effective organization, monitoring and evaluation of respective processes and discussions; work for ecologically sustainable resource management; analyse and assess European environmental policy and law and their implementation in EU member states. **Finance** Solely project funded. **Activities** Events/meetings. **Events** *Conference* Brussels (Belgium) 2023, *Conference* Berlin (Germany) 2022, *Towards a stronger system of international environmental governance international conference* Berlin (Germany) 2005. **Publications** Newsletter (12 a year). Reports; papers; books; articles. **IGO Relations** Accredited by (1): *United Nations Framework Convention on Climate Change – Secretariat (UNFCCC, #20564)*. **NGO Relations** Member of (6): *Academic Council on the United Nations System (ACUNS, #00020)*; *Bellagio Forum for Sustainable Development (BFSD, no recent information)*; *Climate Action Network Europe (CAN Europe, #04001)*; *European Forum on Integrated Environmental Assessment (EFIEA, no recent information)*; *Institute for European Environmental Policy (IEEP, #11261)*; *International Union for Conservation of Nature and Natural Resources (IUCN, #15766)*. Partner of (2): *Green Economy Coalition (GEC, #10717)*; *International Institute for Sustainability Analysis and Strategy (#13929)*. Acts as secretariat for: *Foundation for European Environmental Policy (FEEP, see: #11261)*. [2023/XG8446/j/**F**]

♦ Ecologic Institute (#05303)
♦ Ecologic – Institute for International and European Environmental Policy / see Ecologic Institut (#05303)
♦ Ecologic – Institut für Internationale und Europäische Umweltpolitik / see Ecologic Institut (#05303)
♦ Ecologistas en Pro de la Energia Nuclear (internationally oriented national body)
♦ Ecologists Without Borders (internationally oriented national body)
♦ Ecologists Linked for Organizing Grassroots Initiatives and Action (internationally oriented national body)
♦ ECOMA – European Computer Measurement Association (inactive)
♦ EcoMed 21 (unconfirmed)
♦ **ecoMEDIA-europe** ecoMEDIA-europe – The European Educational Network (#05304)

♦ ecoMEDIA-europe – The European Educational Network (ecoMEDIA-europe) 05304

Coordinator St Jakoberstr 2, 9400 Wolfsberg, Austria. E-mail: office@ecomedia-europe.net.
URL: http://www.ecomedia-europe.net/

History 2005. **Aims** Build know-how about different European *ICT* strategies in education; stimulate digital learning, international know-how transfer and sharing of experience. **Structure** Steering Committee. **Languages** English, German. **Staff** 70.00 FTE, paid. **Finance** Budget (annual): euro 3 million. **Activities** Training/education; events/meetings. **Events** *Developing Europe's young workforce through innovative education* Glasgow (UK) 2017, *Conference* Iasi (Romania) 2016, *Metal Congress* Wolfsberg (Austria) 2016, *Education and ICT – where do teachers go?* Zagreb (Croatia) 2015, *International Conference / Conference* Hamar (Norway) 2014. **Publications** Books.
Members National partners in 26 countries:
Austria, Belgium, Bulgaria, Croatia, Czechia, Estonia, Finland, France, Germany, Greece, Hungary, Ireland, Italy, Latvia, Lithuania, Norway, Poland, Portugal, Romania, Slovakia, Slovenia, Spain, Sweden, Switzerland, Türkiye, UK.
Associate 5000 schools in 40 European countries. Membership countries not specified.
IGO Relations *European Commission (EC, #06633)*. **NGO Relations** *Global Learning Across Borders (Global LAB)*; national institutions. [2017/XJ9513/**F**]

♦ EcoMENA 05305

Contact Palm Tower, Block B 15th Floor, West Bay, PO Box 26600, Doha, Qatar. T. +97440342094. E-mail: mkhalil@ecomena.org – info@ecomena.org.
URL: http://www.ecomena.org/

History Set up 2012. Full title: *EcoMENA – Echoing Sustainability in MENA*. **Aims** Raise *environmental* awareness in the MENA region; provide a one-stop destination for high-quality and credible *information* on environment, energy, waste, water, renewables, sustainability and related areas. **Structure** A volunteer-driven organization. **Languages** Arabic, English. **Staff** 150.00 FTE, voluntary. **Finance** Self-financed. **Activities** Awareness raising; research/documentation; knowledge management/information dissemination; guidance/assistance/consulting; advocacy/lobbying/activism; training/education.
Members Full in 13 countries and territories:
Bahrain, Egypt, Iraq, Jordan, Kuwait, Lebanon, Morocco, Oman, Palestine, Qatar, Saudi Arabia, Tunisia, United Arab Emirates.
NGO Relations *Zero Waste MENA (ZW MENA)*; national organizations. [2019.12.12/XM6920/**F**]

♦ EcoMENA – Echoing Sustainability in MENA / see EcoMENA (#05305)

♦ Ecomet 05306

Contact c/o KMI, Ringlaan 3, 1180 Brussels, Belgium. T. +3223721330. Fax +3223754950. E-mail: wmcairns@meteo.be.
URL: http://www.ecomet.eu/

History Dec 1995, as a grouping of the type *European Economic Interest Grouping (EEIG, #06960)*. Registered in accordance with Belgian law. **Aims** Preserve the free exchange of *data sets* and products among members within the framework of WMO regulations; assist members to maintain and improve their infrastructure; expand availability of *meteorological* information within ECOMET territory; increase the use and improve the distribution of members' data, products and services while maintaining/improving their quality; create conditions for members to develop their economic activities.

Members National meteorological institutions in 23 countries:
Austria, Belgium, Croatia, Denmark, Finland, France, Germany, Greece, Hungary, Iceland, Ireland, Italy, Latvia, Luxembourg, Netherlands, Norway, Portugal, Romania, Spain, Sweden, Switzerland, Türkiye, UK. [2012.06.01/XF5405/**F**]

♦ **ECOM** Eurasian Coalition on Male Health (#05603)
♦ **ECOM-LAC** Federación de Latinoamérica y el Caribe para Internet y el Comercio Electrónico (#09341)

♦ Ecommerce Europe 05307

SG Rue d'Arlon 69-71, 1040 Brussels, Belgium. T. +3225023134. Fax +3225143722. E-mail: info@ecommerce-europe.eu.
URL: http://www.ecommerce-europe.eu/

History *European eCommerce and Omni-Channel Trade Association (EMOTA, inactive)* merged into Ecommerce Europe, 1 Jan 2020. Registration: No/ID: 0511.953.330, Start date: 21 Feb 2013, Belgium; EU Transparency Register, No/ID: 867433111414-11, Start date: 25 Jun 2013. **Aims** Advance interests and influence of *e-commerce* in Europe through advocacy, communication and networking. **Structure** Board of Directors; Executive Committee. **Activities** Events/meetings; awards/prizes/competitions; advocacy/lobbying/activism; networking/liaising. **Events** *Global e-Commerce Summit* Barcelona (Spain) 2016, *Global e-Commerce Summit* Barcelona (Spain) 2015, *Global e-Commerce Summit* Barcelona (Spain) 2014, *Global e-Commerce Summit* Barcelona (Spain) 2013, *Global e-Commerce Summit* Barcelona (Spain) 2012.
Members National associations in 20 countries:
Austria, Belgium, Bulgaria, Czechia, Denmark, Estonia, Finland, France, Germany, Greece, Ireland, Italy, Netherlands, Norway, Poland, Portugal, Romania, Spain, Sweden, Switzerland.
NGO Relations Member of (2): *EuroCommerce (EC, #05665)* (Affiliate); *European Registry of Internet Domain Names (EURid, #08351).* [2020/XJ8937/**D**]

♦ EcoMobility Alliance 05308

Officer Kaiser-Friedrich-Str. 7, 53113 Bonn, Germany. T. +4922897629900. Fax +4922897629901. E-mail: ecomobility@iclei.org.
URL: https://sustainablemobility.iclei.org/ecomobility-alliance/

History Dec 2007. Founded on the occasion of the UN Climate Change Conference, and established as an initiative of *Local Governments for Sustainability (ICLEI, #16507)* Transformed under current title for a period of 6 years, Changwon (Korea Rep). Former names and other names: *Global Alliance for EcoMobility* – former. **Aims** Give priority to walking, cycling, public transport, and shared light electric vehicles by promoting commutes through integrated, socially inclusive, and environmentally-friendly options without depending on privately-owned vehicles; represent cities that have achieved or aiming to achieve results in ecomobility. **Structure** Network of 23 Alliance Cities, one of which hosting the Chair Office at each phase; Secretariat based in Bonn, Germany; Alliance Partners. **Languages** English. **Staff** 1.00 FTE, paid. **Finance** Sources: grants. Funding from the Alliance Chair City. **Activities** Events/meetings; knowledge management/information dissemination; networking/liaising; projects/programmes; training/education. Active in all member countries. **Events** *Ecomobility Congress* Kaohsiung (Taiwan) 2017, *EcoMobility Congress* Suwon (Korea Rep) 2013, *Congress* Changwon (Korea Rep) 2011. **Publications** *EcoMobility Alliance Report* (2018) in English, Mandarin Chinese; *EcoMobility Alliance Report* (2016-2017) in English, Mandarin Chinese; *EcoMobility Alliance Report* (2012-2015) in English. Case studies; technical documents; podcasts.
Members Alliance Cities (23) in 13 countries and territories:
Argentina, Australia, Brazil, Bulgaria, Colombia, Germany, India, Korea Rep, Mexico, Mozambique, Portugal, Taiwan, USA.
IGO Relations Partner of (2): *Asian Development Bank (ADB, #01422)*; *Deutsche Gesellschaft für Internationale Zusammenarbeit (GIZ)*. **NGO Relations** Partner of (14): *Clean Air Asia (#03983)*; *European Cyclists' Federation (ECF, #06877)*; *FIA Foundation (#09742)*; *Institute for Transportation and Development Policy (ITDP)*; *International Council on Clean Transportation (ICCT, #13007)*; *International Human-Powered Vehicle Association (IHPVA, #13822)*; *International Road Transport Union (IRU, #14761)*; *International Society of City and Regional Planners (ISOCARP, #15012)*; *Partnership on Sustainable, Low Carbon Transport Foundation (SLoCaT Foundation, #18244)*; *The William and Flora Hewlett Foundation*; *Walk21 Foundation (Walk21, #20814)*; *World Resources Institute (WRI, #21753)*; *World Wide Fund for Nature (WWF, #21922)*; *Wuppertal Institute for Climate, Environment and Energy.* Partners include national and local organizations and initiatives. [2021.06.18/XJ0257/**C**]

♦ EcoMod Network 05309

Pres Bldg H – 4th Fl – H4-233, Dept of Applied Economics, ULB, Avenue F Roosevelt 50 CP 140, 1050 Brussels, Belgium. T. +3226504115. Fax +3226504137. E-mail: office@ecomod.net.
URL: http://www.ecomod.net/

Aims Promote advanced *modelling* and *statistical* techniques in economic policy and decision making. **Activities** Events/meetings. **Events** *EcoMod Conference* Lisbon (Portugal) 2016, *EcoMod Conference* Chestnut Hill, MA (USA) 2015, *EcoMod Conference* Bali (Indonesia) 2014, *EcoMod Conference* Prague (Czech Rep) 2013, *EcoMod Conference* Seville (Spain) 2012. [2016/XJ7005/**F**]

♦ **ECONDAD** ECOWAS Network on Debt and Development (#05336)
♦ ECONET / see European Union Network for the Implementation and Enforcement of Environmental Law (#09005)
♦ **ECON** European Community Organizing Network (#06681)
♦ EcoNews Africa (internationally oriented national body)

♦ Econometric Society (ES) 05310

Société d'économétrie

Gen Manager c/o Cowles Fdn – Yale, 30 Hillhouse Ave, POB 208281, New Haven CT 06511, USA.
URL: http://www.econometricsociety.org/

History 29 Dec 1930, Cleveland, OH (USA). Founded by a group of economists, mathematicians and statisticians of various countries. Registration: USA. **Aims** Advance *economic* theory in its relation to statistics and *mathematics.* **Structure** Fellows (highest authority); Council; Executive Committee; Regional Councils (5); Regional Standing Committees (6). Meetings open. **Languages** English. **Staff** 5.00 FTE, paid. **Finance** Sources: members' dues. Institutional subscriptions. **Activities** Awards/prizes/competitions; events/meetings. **Events** *European Summer Meeting* Barcelona (Spain) 2023, *Asia Meeting* Beijing (China) 2023, *European Winter Meeting (EWMES)* Manchester (UK) 2023, *Asia Meeting in East and Southeast Asia* Singapore (Singapore) 2023, *Australasian Meeting* Sydney, NSW (Australia) 2023. **Publications** *Econometrica* – journal; *Quantitative Economics* – journal; *Theoretical Economics* – journal. Monograph Series. **Members** Individual (about 7,000); Institutional. Membership countries not specified. **NGO Relations** Cooperates with (1): *International Organization for Standardization (ISO, #14473).* [2020.03.04/XB0481/**B**]

♦ Economic Agreement of Bogota (1948 treaty)
♦ Economic Association for the International Advancement of Industrial and Cultural Interests (inactive)

♦ Economic Community of Central African States (ECCAS) 05311

Communauté économique des Etats de l'Afrique centrale (CEEAC) – Comunidad Económica de los Estados del Africa Central (CEEAC) – Comunidade Economica dos Estados da Africa Central (CEEAC)

SG Haute de Guégué, BP 2112, Libreville, Gabon. T. +241444731. Fax +241444732. E-mail: stellairigo@yahoo.fr – contact@ceeac-eccas.org.
URL: https://ceeac-eccas.org/

History Dec 1981, Libreville (Gabon), during a conference of the Heads of State of *Communauté économique des pays des Grands Lacs (CEPGL, #04375)* and *Union douanière et économique de l'Afrique centrale (UDEAC, inactive)*, following recommendations adopted, 1981, Lagos (Nigeria), by *Organization of African Unity (OAU, inactive)*, within the framework of the Plan of Action and the Final Act of Lagos of 1980. Treaty adopted 18 Oct 1983, Libreville; entered into force 18 Dec 1984. Inactive 1992-1997, mainly due to internal conflicts. Relaunched Feb 1998, Libreville, during 2nd extra-ordinary Summit. **Aims** Promote and reinforce harmonious cooperation and balanced, self-maintained development in all areas of economic, social, cultural, scientific and technical activity in order to: realize collective autonomy; raise the standard of living of the people; increase and maintain economic stability; promote peace, security and stability in the sub-region; reinforce close and peaceful relations among member States; contribute to the development of the African continent. Specific objectives: eliminate customs duties and all other equivalent taxes on the import and export of merchandise among member States; abolish quantitative restrictions and other hindrances to trade; establish a commercial policy with respect to third countries; progressively eliminate obstacles to free circulation of persons, goods, services, capital and right of establishment; harmonize national policies so as to promote common activities, notably in the areas of industry, transport and communications, energy, agriculture, natural resources, trade, currency and finance, human resources, tourism, education and culture, and science and technology; create a cooperation and development fund; accelerate development of member States either land-locked, partially islands, semi-enclosed and/or in the category of least developed countries. **Structure** Conference of Heads of State and Government; Council of Ministers; Consultative Commission (Experts Meeting); Court of Justice (not yet in operation). Secretariat General, comprising Secretary-General, 3 Assistant Secretaries-General and Directors of Sections: General Affairs (documentation, information, conference, translation, protocol and security); Administration and Finance (including personnel services); Trade, Customs, Financial and Monetary Questions; Transport, Communications and Tourism; Agriculture and Industry. Advisory Committee; Special Technical Committees. **Languages** English, French, Portuguese, Spanish. **Staff** 100.00 FTE, paid. **Finance** Currencies (4): Sao Tomé-Principe – Dobra; Burundi – Burundi Franc; Cameroon, Central African Rep, Chad, Congo Brazzaville, Equatorial Guinea and Gabon – CFA Franc; Congo DR – Congolese Franc.
Activities Events/meetings; politics/policy/regulatory. In the initial phase, priority is accorded to mutual trade, payments (including establishment of a clearing arrangement for ECCAS as a whole) and transport. New non-tariff barriers in intra-community trade are prohibited and ECCAS clearing house was established in Feb 1989. Free Trade Area was established, 4 Jul 2005. A Compensation Fund provides compensation for losses due to the setting up of common external customs tariffs (not yet in operation). To facilitate financial transactions a *'Chamber of Compensation'* is expected to come into operation shortly. A Food Security Regional Programme was established. Legislation on road transport is being harmonized, as are flight schedules and air transport tariffs; interconnection of telecommunication networks within *Pan African Telecommunications Network (PANAFTEL, no recent information)* is being agreed. Set up: *Council for Peace and Security in Central Africa (COPAX, #04913)*; *Central African Power Pool (CAPP, #03655).* Implements *Central African Convention for the Control of Small Arms and Light Weapons, Their Ammunition, Parts and Components That Can be Used for Their Manufacture, Repair and Assembly (Kinshasa Convention, 2010).*
Activities currently focus on the following areas: Promotion of interregional trade; Peace, security and stability; Support to election processes in Member States; Implementation of NEPAD in Central Africa; Consensual Transport Master Plan in Central Africa (PDCT-AC); Electrical networks interconnection of Member States; Development of NICT sector; Food security promotion and agro-based industry development; Fight against HIV/AIDS; Free movement of persons; Institutional, financial and human building capacity; Promotion of gender; Structuring of a Community vision for integrated development and prosperity; Bilateral and multilateral cooperation development.
Events *Joint Summit of Heads of State and Government* Lomé (Togo) 2018, *Regional Conference on Promoting Financial Inclusion in Central Africa* Brazzaville (Congo Brazzaville) 2015, *Conference of heads of state and government* Ndjamena (Chad) 2011, *Atelier sur le mécanisme régional de coordination intégré pour la lutte contre les maladies animales transfrontalières et les zoonoses* Libreville (Gabon) 2010, *Séminaire sur le schéma de référence de l'étude sur l'interconnexion des réseaux électriques des pays membres de la CEEAC* Libreville (Gabon) 2008. **Publications** Manuals; bibliographies. Information Services: Database on information sources.
Members Governments of 11 countries:
Angola, Burundi, Cameroon, Central African Rep, Chad, Congo Brazzaville, Congo DR, Equatorial Guinea, Gabon, Rwanda, Sao Tomé-Principe.
IGO Relations An intergovernmental grouping within: *Organisation of African, Caribbean and Pacific States (OACPS, #17796)* and recognized by *European Commission (EC, #06633)* under the Lom Convention. Accredited to the Conference of the Parties of: *Secretariat of the United Nations Convention to Combat Desertification (Secretariat of the UNCCD, #19208).* Member of: *Africa Partnership Forum (APF, #00510).* Relations agreement with: *UNIDO (#20336).* Regional Economic Community of: *African Union (AU, #00488).* Permanent Observer to: *ECOSOC (#05331).* Observer to General Assembly of: *United Nations (UN, #20515).* Indirect relationship with: *UNICEF (#20332).* **NGO Relations** Formal relations with: *Association of Power Utilities in Africa (APUA, #02867).* [2018/XD4308/**D***]

♦ Economic Community of the Great Lakes Countries (#04375)

♦ Economic Community of West African States (ECOWAS) 05312

Communauté économique des Etats de l'Afrique de l'Ouest (CEDEAO) – Comunidad Economica de los Estados de Africa Occidental

Chairman 101 Yakubu Gowon Crescent, Asokoro District, PMB 401, Abuja, Federal Capital Territory, Nigeria. T. +23493147646 – +23493147427 – +23493147429. Fax +23493147646 – +23493143005.
URL: http://www.ecowas.int/

History Established 28 May 1975, Lagos (Nigeria), on signature of *Treaty of Lagos* by Heads of State of 15 West African countries; outstanding technical protocols signed Nov 1976. Cape Verde joined in 1977. Mauritania withdrew membership, 1 jan 2001. Protocol on Mutual Assistance in Defence Matters adopted 1981. May 1990, Banjul (Gambia), agreed to rationalize subregional institutions in West Africa within the framework of ECOWAS so that ECOWAS would eventually become the sole economic community of the West African region. Statutes registered in *'UNTS 1/14843'.* **Aims** Promote cooperation and integration among member States leading to the establishment of an economic union in West Africa in order to to raise the living standard of its peoples and maintain and enhance the economic stability, foster relations among member States and contribute to the progress and *development* of the African continent.
Structure Governance:
- Executive arm comprises: *'Authority of Heads and State and Government'* (meets annually); *'Council of Ministers'* (meets twice a year); ECOWAS Commission (formerly Executive Secretariat).
- Legislative arm: *Parliament of the Economic Community of West African States (ECOWAS Parliament, #18221)*, also referred to as *'Community Parliament'*;
- Judicial arm: *Community Court of Justice (#04393).*

Specialized Institutions:
- *ECOWAS Bank for Investment and Development (EBID, #05334)*;
- *Intergovernmental Action Group against Money Laundering in West Africa (#11471)*;
- *West African Health Organization (WAHO, #20881).*

Specialized Agencies:
- ECOWAS Brown Card Scheme;
- *ECOWAS Centre for Renewable Energy and Energy Efficiency (ECREEE, #05335)*;
- ECOWAS Gender Development Centre;
- ECOWAS Infrastructure Projects preparation and Development Unit (PPDU);
- *ECOWAS Regional Electricity Regulatory Authority (ERERA, #05337)*;
- ECOWAS Youth and Sports Development Centre;
- *Regional Agency for Agriculture and Food (RAAF)*;
- *West African Monetary Agency (WAMA, #20887)*;
- *West African Monetary Institute (WAMI, #20888)*;
- *West African Power Pool (WAPP, #20894).*

Specialized Technical Commissions.
A second monetary zone, the
West African Monetary Zone (WAMZ, #20889) for the non-UEMOA Member States was initiated in 2000 to accelerate and complement ECOWAS efforts in creating a single West Africa-wide currency.
Languages English, French, Portuguese. **Staff** Executive Secretariat employs about 260 people, including 66 professionals. **Finance** Contributions by member states. Levy is calculated as 0.5% of duty on all goods imported from third party countries. In addition, also receives grants from development partners. **Activities** Monitors trends and developments in the regional economy, evolution of the economic development and integration process. Coordinates and harmonizes the macroeconomic policies of Member States, including: implementation of the ECOWAS single currency programme; monitoring and evaluation of performance and macroeconomic convergence; cooperation with other regional and international institutions. ECOWAS Sectors: Energy; Civil Society; Infrastructure; ICT; Trade; Water; Agriculture; Health and Social Affairs; Telecommunications; Political Affairs. Management of treaties and agreements: *Convention sur les Armes Légères et de Petit Calibre, leurs Munitions et Autres Matériels Connexes (2006).* **Events** *ECOMOF : ECOWAS Mining and*

Petroleum Forum Abidjan (Côte d'Ivoire) 2018, *Ordinary Summit* Abuja (Nigeria) 2018, *Extraordinary Summit* Lomé (Togo) 2018, *Joint Summit of Heads of State and Government* Lomé (Togo) 2018, *Ordinary Summit* Lomé (Togo) 2018. **Publications** *West African Bulletin* (12 a year); *ECOWAS Handbook on International Trade* (annual). **Information Services** *ASYCUDA* – customs computerization system, operational in 12 Member States; *ECOWAS Macroeconomic Database and Multilateral Surveillance System (ECOMAC)*; *EUROTRACE* – trade statistics system, operational in 14 Member States; *SIGOA TOPS* – software, operational in 4 Member States.

Members Governments of 15 English, French and Portuguese-speaking countries:
Benin, Burkina Faso, Cape Verde, Côte d'Ivoire, Gambia, Ghana, Guinea, Guinea-Bissau, Liberia, Mali, Niger, Nigeria, Senegal, Sierra Leone, Togo.

IGO Relations Observer status with: *ECOSOC (#05331)*; *International Bank for Reconstruction and Development (IBRD, #12317)*; *International Monetary Fund (IMF, #14180)*; *Union of African Shippers' Councils (UASC, #20348)*; *United Nations (UN, #20515)*; *World Trade Organization (WTO, #21864)*. Member of: *Africa Partnership Forum (APF, #00510)*; *Global Bioenergy Partnership (GBEP, #10251)*. Formal agreement with: *Euclid University (EUCLID, #05575)*; *UNESCO (#20322)*. Regional Economic Community of: *African Union (AU, #00488)*.
Cooperates with:
- *African Development Bank (ADB, #00283)*;
- *Codex Alimentarius Commission (CAC, #04081)*;
- *Entente Council (#05491)*;
- *FAO (#09260)*;
- *Inter-African Conference on Insurance Markets (#11385)*;
- *International Institute for Democracy and Electoral Assistance (International IDEA, #13872)*;
- *International Telecommunication Union (ITU, #15673)*;
- *Niger Basin Authority (NBA, #17134)*;
- *Organisation pour l'Harmonisation en Afrique du Droit des Affaires (OHADA, #17806)*;
- *Organisation internationale de la Francophonie (OIF, #17809)*;
- *UNEP (#20299)*;
- *UNCTAD (#20285)*;
- *UNHCR (#20327)*;
- *World Meteorological Organization (WMO, #21649)*.

Supports: *Volta Basin Authority (VBA, #20808)*. Accredited to the Conference of the Parties of: *Secretariat of the United Nations Convention to Combat Desertification (Secretariat of the UNCCD, #19208)*. Instrumental in setting up: *African Economic Community (AEC, #00290)*; *ECOWAS Computer Centre (no recent information)*; *Regional Information Centre and Database on Renewable Energy, Dakar (no recent information)*; *West African Central Bank (WACB, #20871)*; *West African Peace-Keeping Forces of ECOWAS (ECOMOG, no recent information)*.

NGO Relations Member of: *Association of Secretaries General of Parliaments (ASGP, #02911)*. Parliament is observer member of: *Assemblée parlementaire de la Francophonie (APF, #02312)*. Supports: *Institut Africain pour le Développement Economique et Social – Centre Africain de Formation (INADES-Formation, #11233)*. Cooperates with: *International Fertilizer Development Center (IFDC, #13590)*. Instrumental in setting up: *Conference of Directors of the West African National Meteorological and Hydrological Services (AFRIMET, #04589)*; *West African Road Safety Organisation (WARSO, #20896)*; *West African Women's Association (WAWA, #20900)*. Has proposed set up of: *West African Association of Universities and Research Institutions (no recent information)*. [2016/XD3462/**F***]

♦ Economic Cooperation Committee of the Central American Isthmus / see Central American Economic Cooperation Committee (#03667)

♦ Economic Cooperation Organization (ECO) 05313

SG No 1 Goulbou Alley, Kamranieh, Teheran, 1951933114, Iran Islamic Rep. T. +982122831733 – +982122831734. Fax +982122831732. E-mail: registry@eco.int.
URL: https://www.eco.int/

History 27 Jan 1985, Teheran (Iran Islamic Rep). Established by Iran, Pakistan and Turkey, as successor organization to *Regional Cooperation for Development (RCD, inactive)*, which had been set up 21 Jul 1964, Ankara (Turkey), and existed until 1979. The Organization was subsequently restructured and reviewed under its present name. The basic Charter of the Organization, *Treaty of Izmir*, originally signed 12 Mar 1977 at Izmir (Turkey), was amended accordingly following Ministerial Conference, Jun 1990, Islamabad (Pakistan), becoming operational on 11 Jan 1991 and providing a legal basis to the new Organization. Expanded, Nov 1992, to include 7 new members: Afghanistan, Azerbaijan, Kazakhstan, Kyrgyzstan, Tajikistan, Turkmenistan and Uzbekistan. The 6th Meeting of ECO Council of Ministers, May 1996, Ashgabat (Turkmenistan), approved the new organizational set-up and functional methodology; and the Foreign Ministers of member countries signed the revised Treaty of Izmir on 14 Sep 1996, Izmir (Turkey), at an Extraordinary Meeting of ECO Council of Ministers. The Council of Ministers also approved an Implementation Plan on Reorganization and Restructuring for the Secretariat of ECO. **Aims** Stimulate: sustainable economic development of Member States; progressive removal of trade barriers and promotion of intra-regional trade; greater role of ECO region in the growth of world trade; gradual integration of Member States' economies in world economy; development of transport and communications infrastructure linking Member States with each other and with the outside world; economic liberalization and privatization; mobilization and utilization of ECO region's material resources; effective utilization of agricultural and industrial potentials of ECO region; regional cooperation for drug abuse control, ecological and environmental protection and strengthening of historical and cultural ties among the peoples of the ECO region; mutually beneficial cooperation with regional and international organizations. **Structure** Summit; Council of Ministers; Council of Permanent Representatives; Regional Planning Council; Sectoral ministerial meetings and other meetings; Secretariat. Specialized agencies and regional instititions (13): *Economic Cooperation Organization Trade and Development Bank (ETDB, #05314)*; *ECO Cultural Institute (ECI, #05292)*; *ECO Science Foundation (ECOSF, #05328)*; *ECO Educational Institute (ECOEI, #05293)*; *ECO Chamber of Commerce and Industry (ECO-CCI, #05291)*; ECO College of Insurance; ECO Regional Coordination Centre for Food Security; ECO Institute of Environmental Science and Technology; ECO Consultancy and Engineering Company (ECO-CEC); ECO Regional Center for Risk Management of Natural Disasters. ECO Postal Staff College; ECO Seed Association (ECOSA); ECO Reinsurance Company. **Languages** English. **Staff** 60.00 FTE, paid. **Finance** Central Budget: member states' contributions as decided by the Council of Ministers, taking into account capacity to pay and the prevailing scale of assessment of contributions of the United Nations. **Activities** Capacity building; events/meetings; management of treaties and agreements; politics/policy/regulatory; training/education. Manages the following treaties/agreements: *Agreement on Simplification of Visa Procedures for the Businessmen of ECO Countries (1995)*; *ECO Transit Trade Agreement (1995)*. **Events** *Meeting of Council of Ministers* Teheran (Iran Islamic Rep) 2013, *Summit* Teheran (Iran Islamic Rep) 2012, *Meeting of Council of Ministers* Istanbul (Turkey) 2010, *Summit* Istanbul (Turkey) 2010, *Meeting of Council of Ministers* Teheran (Iran Islamic Rep) 2009. **Publications** *ECO Annual Economic Report*; *ECO News Bulletin*. *ECO Energy Data Booklet*; *ECO Guidebook*; *ECO Handbook*.

Members Governments of 10 countries:
Afghanistan, Azerbaijan, Iran Islamic Rep, Kazakhstan, Kyrgyzstan, Pakistan, Tajikistan, Türkiye, Turkmenistan, Uzbekistan.

IGO Relations Observer status with: General Assembly of *Islamic Development Bank (IsDB, #16044)*; *Organisation of Islamic Cooperation (OIC, #17813)*; *United Nations (UN, #20515)*; *World Trade Organization (WTO, #21864)*. Biennial Resolution on UN-ECO cooperation with: *United Nations (UN, #20515)* General Assembly (UNGA). Accredited by: *Secretariat of the United Nations Convention to Combat Desertification (Secretariat of the UNCCD, #19208)*. Special links with: *ECOSOC (#05331)*. Represented at: *Parliamentary Assembly of the ECO Countries (PAECO)*.
Memorandum of Understanding with:
- *ASEAN (#01141)*;
- *Colombo Plan for Cooperative Economic and Social Development in Asia and the Pacific (CPS, #04120)*;
- *Conference on Interaction and Confidence-Building Measures in Asia (CICA, #04609)*;
- *European Commission (EC, #06633)*;
- *FAO (#09260)*;
- IDB;
- *Organisation intergouvernementale pour les transports internationaux ferroviaires (OTIF, #17807)*;
- *International Center for Agricultural Research in the Dry Areas (ICARDA, #12466)*;
- *International Organization for Migration (IOM, #14454)*;
- OIC;
- *Organisation for Cooperation between Railways (OSJD, #17803)*;
- *Pacific Islands Forum (#17968)*;
- *Shanghai Cooperation Organization (SCO, #19256)*;
- *Transport Corridor from Europe-Caucasus-Asia (TRACECA, #20225)*;
- *UNEP (#20299)*;
- *UNCTAD (#20285)*;
- *UNDP (#20292)*;
- *UNESCO (#20322)*;
- *UNICEF (#20332)*;
- *UNIDO (#20336)*;
- *United Nations Economic Commission for Europe (UNECE, #20555)*;
- *United Nations Economic and Social Commission for Asia and the Pacific (ESCAP, #20557)*;
- *United Nations Office for Disaster Risk Reduction (UNDRR, #20595)*;
- *United Nations Population Fund (UNFPA, #20612)*;
- *Universal Postal Union (UPU, #20682)*;
- *World Customs Organization (WCO, #21350)*;
- *World Meteorological Organization (WMO, #21649)*.

Trilateral Memoranda of Understanding with: IDB and ESCAP; IDB and UNECE.

NGO Relations Memorandum of Understanding with (3): *European Association for International Education (EAIE, #06092)*; *International Road Transport Union (IRU, #14761)*; *International Union of Railways (#15813)*. [2022/XD3153/**D***]

♦ Economic Cooperation Organization Trade and Development Bank (ETDB) 05314

Headquarters Silahşör Caddesi Yeniyol Sokak No 8, Kat 14-16, Bomonti, 34380 Istanbul/Istanbul, Türkiye. T. +902123936300. Fax +902123936301. E-mail: info@etdb.org.
URL: https://www.etdb.org/

History 15 Mar 1995. Articles of Agreement became effective 3 Aug 2005, amongst founding members, namely Iran Islamic Rep, Pakistan and Turkey; registered in the United Nations under the number 44939, 19 May 2008, acknowledging the international legal status of the Bank. Headquarters Agreement ratified by Turkey, Jul 2007, and the Bank started operations Dec 2008. Former names and other names: *ECO Trade and Development Bank (ECOTDB)* – alias. **Aims** Initiate, promote and provide financial facilities to expand intra-regional trade and accelerate economic development of ECO member states. **Structure** Board of Governors; Board of Directors; Management Committee. Headquarters: Türkiye. Representative offices (2): Iran Islamic Republic; Pakistan. **Languages** English. **Activities** Financial and/or material support; guidance/assistance/consulting. **Publications** *Doing Business with ETDB*. Annual Report; Country Partnership Strategy Reports.

Members Founding members (6):
Afghanistan, Azerbaijan, Iran Islamic Rep, Kyrgyzstan, Pakistan, Türkiye. [2022/XF4135/t/**F***]

♦ Economic Court of the Commonwealth of Independent States 05315

Ekonomicheskij Sud Sodruzhestva Neezavismyh Gosudarstv

Pres Kirov Street 17, 220030 Minsk, Belarus. T. +375173286108. Fax +375173286207. E-mail: info@sudsng.org.
URL: http://courtcis.org/

History Set up 6 Jul 1992, in accordance with the Agreement on the status of the Economic Court of the *Commonwealth of Independent States (CIS, #04341)*. **Aims** Provide for uniform fulfillment of CIS treaties; settle economic and other specified disputes within the CIS system; interpret provisions of CIS agreements and acts of CIS bodies. **Structure** Plenum of CIS Economic Court; Judges appointed by states-parties serve 10 year terms; President of the Court serves 5 years. **Languages** English, Russian. **Staff** Permanent supporting staff. **Finance** Financed by states-parties in equal shares based on annual budget approved by the Council of the Head of States of the CIS. **Activities** Management of treaties.

Members Governments of 6 countries:
Belarus, Kazakhstan, Kyrgyzstan, Russia, Tajikistan, Uzbekistan. [2016.09.13/XF2855/**F***]

♦ Economic Development Institute / see World Bank Institute (#21220)

♦ Economic Freedom Network Asia (EFN Asia) 05316

Contact Friedrich Naumann Foundation for Freedom, Southeast and East Asia Regional Office, 25th Floor – BBC Tower, 29 Soi 63 Sukhumvit Road, Bangkok, 10110, Thailand. T. +6623650570. Fax +6627148384.
URL: http://www.efnasia.org/

History 1998, by *Friedrich Naumann Foundation for Freedom*. **Aims** Provide a platform for political dialogue, public education and academic exchange, so as to appeal to the public, policy advisors and political decision-makers, broaden the public policy debate on the merits of free economics and limited governments. **Activities** Cooperates with Economic Freedom of the World index in Asia; organizes annual conferences and workshops. **Events** *Annual Conference* Hong Kong (Hong Kong) 2012, *International Conference* Hong Kong (Hong Kong) 2012, *International Conference / Annual Conference* Kuala Lumpur (Malaysia) 2011, *International Conference / Annual Conference* Jakarta (Indonesia) 2010, *International Conference / Annual Conference* Siem Reap (Cambodia) 2009.

Members Institutes (20) in 12 countries and territories:
Cambodia, China, Hong Kong, India, Indonesia, Korea Rep, Malaysia, Mongolia, Nepal, Pakistan, Philippines, Thailand.
Individuals in 7 countries:
China, India, Indonesia, Pakistan, Sri Lanka, Thailand, Vietnam.

NGO Relations Partners include: *Atlas Economic Research Foundation (Atlas Network)*; *Friedrich Naumann Foundation for Freedom*; Fraser Institute. [2013/XJ5071/**E**]

♦ Economic Growth Quadrangle (no recent information)

♦ Economic Justice Network for Churches in Eastern and Southern Africa (EJN) 05317

Dir PO Box 2296, Cape Town, 8000, South Africa. T. +27214249563. Fax +27214249564. E-mail: admin@ejn.org.za.
URL: http://www.ejn.org.za/

History 1997, by *Fellowship of Councils of Churches in Southern Africa (FOCCISA, no recent information)*. Based at *Ecumenical Documentation and Information Centre in Southern Africa (EDICISA, #05346)*. **Aims** Harness the resources of the southern African region for all of its people, so as to bring about economic justice through the transforming agency of Christians compelled by the gospel of Jesus Christ. **Structure** Regional Steering Committee, comprising 5 individuals. **Publications** *Economic Justice Bulletin*.

Members Participants in 12 countries:
Angola, Botswana, Denmark, Eswatini, Kenya, Lesotho, Mozambique, Namibia, South Africa, Tanzania UR, Zambia, Zimbabwe.

IGO Relations Monitors and reports on: *ACP-EEC Convention (Lomé convention, 1975)*; *East African Cooperation Treaty (1999)*; South Africa – European Union Free Trade Agreement; trade protocol of *Southern African Development Community (SADC, #19843)*. **NGO Relations** Member of: *Ecumenical Advocacy Alliance (EAA, inactive)*; *The Reality Of Aid (ROA, #18626)*; *Tax Justice Network-Africa (TJN-A, #20101)*. [2015/XF5723/**F**]

♦ Economic and Monetary Community of Central Africa Parliament (no recent information)
♦ Economic Research Centre for the Caribbean (internationally oriented national body)
♦ Economic Research Centre on Mediterranean Countries / see Centre for Economic Research on Mediterranean Countries
♦ Economic Research Committee of the Gas Industry / see Eurogas (#05682)

♦ Economic Research Forum (ERF) 05318

Main Office PO Box 12311, 21 Al-Sad Al-Aaly St, Dokki, Giza, Egypt. T. +20233318600. Fax +20233318604. E-mail: erf@erf.org.eg.
URL: http://www.erf.org.eg/

History Jun 1993. Former names and other names: *Economic Research Forum for the Arab Countries, Iran and Turkey* – alias. **Aims** Act as a research network, clearing house and facilitator; initiate and fund policy-relevant economic research; publish and disseminate results of research activity to *scholars*, *policy makers* and the *business* community; serve as resource base for researchers through ERF's data bank and document library; act as a regional hub for international and regional institutions. **Structure** Board of

Trustees of 13 members, with up to 4 donor institutions represented and 9 non-institutional members, 7 of the remaining 9 elected by ERF's community of Research Fellows. Advisory Committee. **Finance** Business community donations; overheads from projects; extraregional government agencies and endowment funds; donations from: *Arab Fund for Economic and Social Development (AFESD, #00965); European Commission (EC, #06633); Ford Foundation (#09858); International Development Research Centre (IDRC, #13162); United Nations Sustainable Development Group (UNSDG, #20634).* **Activities** Knowledge management/information dissemination; events/meetings; research/documentation. **Events** *Annual Conference* Kuwait 2006, *Annual Conference* Cairo (Egypt) 2005, *Annual Conference* Beirut (Lebanon) 2004, *Annual Conference* Marrakech (Morocco) 2003, *Annual Conference* Sharjah (United Arab Emirates) 2002. **Publications** *Forum newsletter* (4 a year) in Arabic, English – also online; *EFR e-Bulletin* – online; *ERF Journal*. Working papers; conference proceedings. Information Services: Online search of 'Library' and 'Research Index'.
Members Affiliates in 23 countries and territories:
Algeria, Bahrain, Djibouti, Egypt, Iran Islamic Rep, Iraq, Jordan, Kuwait, Lebanon, Libya, Mauritania, Morocco, Oman, Palestine, Qatar, Saudi Arabia, Somalia, Sudan, Syrian AR, Tunisia, Türkiye, United Arab Emirates, Yemen.
National organizations and individuals in 46 countries and territories:
Algeria, Austria, Bahrain, Belgium, Cyprus, Denmark, Djibouti, Egypt, France, Germany, Greece, Iran Islamic Rep, Iraq, Ireland, Italy, Japan, Jordan, Korea DPR, Korea Rep, Kuwait, Lebanon, Libya, Luxembourg, Malta, Mauritania, Monaco, Morocco, Netherlands, Norway, Oman, Palestine, Portugal, Qatar, Saudi Arabia, Somalia, South Africa, Spain, Sudan, Sweden, Switzerland, Syrian AR, Tunisia, Türkiye, UK, United Arab Emirates, Yemen.
IGO Relations *International Bank for Reconstruction and Development (IBRD, #12317); UNDP (#20292).* **NGO Relations** Accredited by (1): *Globalization Studies Network (GSN, #10440).* Together with: *Global Development Network (GDN, #10318); Université de la Méditerranée, Marseille* coordinates: *Femise Network (#09731).*
[2021/XF4751/**F**]

♦ Economic Research Forum for the Arab Countries, Iran and Turkey / see Economic Research Forum (#05318)

♦ Economic Research Institute for ASEAN and East Asia (ERIA) 05319

Pres Sentral Senayan II, 6th Floor, Jalan Asia Afrika No 8, Gelora Bung Karno, Senayan, Pusat, Jakarta 10270, Indonesia. T. +622157974460. Fax +622157974463. E-mail: contactus@eria.org.
URL: http://www.eria.org/
History Established 3 Jun 2008, as an independent research institute based on formal agreement by 16 Heads of East Asia Summit countries during 3rd East Asia Summit (EAS), 21 Nov 2007, Singapore (Singapore). Since 30 Dec 2008, status of international organization based in Jakarta (Indonesia), following formal agreement reached between government of Indonesia and ASEAN Secretariat. **Aims** Provide innovative and analytical research and policy recommendations on deepening economic integration, narrowing development gaps and achieving sustainable development in ASEAN and East Asia. **Structure** Governing Board; Leaders; Academic Advisory Council; ERIA's Research Institute Network (RIN); ERIA's Energy Research Institute Network (ERIN); Departments (4). **Languages** English. **Staff** 82.00 FTE, paid. **Finance** Contributions from governments of 16 East Asia Summit countries. **Activities** Research/documentation; knowledge management/information dissemination; capacity building; policy/politics/regulatory; events/meetings; awards/prizes/competitions. **Events** *Asian Regional Round Table on Macroeconomic and Structural Policy Challenges* 2022, *Asia CCUS Network Forum* Tokyo (Japan) 2022, *Asian Regional Round Table on Macroeconomic and Structural Policy Challenges* Singapore (Singapore) 2021, *ERIA Editors Round Table* Singapore (Singapore) 2021, *ERIA Editors Round Table* Jakarta (Indonesia) 2020. **Publications** *East Asia Updates* (12 a year); *ERIA newsletter* (12 a year). Annual Report; books; policy briefs; discussion papers; research project reports.
Members Governments of 16 countries:
Australia, Brunei Darussalam, Cambodia, China, India, Indonesia, Japan, Korea Rep, Laos, Malaysia, Myanmar, New Zealand, Philippines, Singapore, Thailand, Vietnam.
NGO Relations Member of: *Council for Global Problem-Solving (CGP, #04898).* [2021/XJ0303/j/**E***]

♦ Economics, Business & Organization Research (meeting series)

♦ Economic Science Association (ESA) 05320

Treas Southern Methodist Univ, Dept of Economics, 3300 Dyer St, Ste 301, Umphrey Lee Center, Dallas TX 75275-0496, USA.
URL: http://www.economicscience.org/
History Founded 1986, Tucson AZ (USA). **Aims** Advance, enhance and further economics as an observational science through use of laboratory and field methods of observation and data collection. **Structure** Officers: President; Past President; President-Elect; 3 Regional Vice-Presidents (Asia-Pacific; North American; European); Vice-President of Information; Treasurer. Directors. **Staff** None. **Finance** Members' dues. **Activities** Sponsors international regional conferences and the journal 'Experimental Economics'. **Events** *Asia Pacific Regional Meeting* Abu Dhabi (United Arab Emirates) 2019, *European Regional Meeting* Dijon (France) 2019, *North American Meeting* Los Angeles, CA (USA) 2019, *World Meeting* Vancouver, BC (Canada) 2019, *North American Meeting* Antigua (Guatemala) 2018. **Publications** *Experimental Economics.*
Members Individuals in 36 countries and territories:
Argentina, Australia, Austria, Belgium, Brazil, Canada, Chile, China, Denmark, Finland, France, Germany, Guatemala, Hungary, Ireland, Israel, Italy, Japan, Kenya, Korea Rep, Luxembourg, Malaysia, Mexico, Netherlands, New Zealand, Norway, Portugal, Russia, Singapore, Spain, Sweden, Switzerland, Taiwan, Türkiye, UK, USA. [2015/XD7496/v/**D**]

♦ Economic and Social Committee / see European Economic and Social Committee (#06963)
♦ Economic and Social Committee of the European Communities / see European Economic and Social Committee (#06963)
♦ Economic and Social Development Bank (internationally oriented national body)
♦ Economic and Social Development Institute (internationally oriented national body)
♦ Economics of Payments (meeting series)

♦ Economic and Statistical Observatory for Sub-Saharan Africa (AFRISTAT) 05321

Observatoire économique et statistique d'Afrique subsaharienne
Dir Gen BP E 1600, Bamako, Mali. T. +22320215500 – +22320215580. Fax +22320211140. E-mail: afristat@afristat.org.
Communication Officer address not obtained.
URL: http://www.afristat.org/
History 21 Sep 1993, Abidjan (Côte d'Ivoire). Founded on signature of a treaty by 14 governments of *Zone franc (#22037).* Commenced activities 2 Jan 1996. **Aims** Contribute to development of, and reinforce competence in, economic, social and *environmental* statistics in Member States; contribute to harmonization of statistical information necessary for African regional economic integration. **Structure** Council of Ministers (supreme authority); Board of Directors; Scientific Council; Head Office in Bamako (Mali). **Languages** English, French. **Staff** 17 experts; 15 support staff. **Finance** Sources: grants; members' dues. Supported by Government of France, in particular during 2-year installation phase. Supported by: *African Development Bank (ADB, #00283); Centre européen de recherche en économie du développement (DIAL); CESD – statisticiens pour le développement; European Commission (EC, #06633); International Bank for Reconstruction and Development (IBRD, #12317)* (World Bank); *International Society of Extension Education (INSEE); UNDP (#20292).* Annual budget: 2,200,000 EUR. **Activities** Events/meetings; knowledge management/information dissemination; research and development. **Publications** *La Lettre d'AFRISTAT* (4 a year). *Série Annuaire; Série Etudes; Série Méthodes; Série Résultats. Guide d'élaboration d'une matrice de comptabilité sociale* (2020); *Guide pratique de projections démographiques par la méthode des composantes* (2020); *Indice de prix de production de l'agriculture* (2020); *Pratique des sondages* (2013); *Etat du système statistique dans les états membres d'AFRISAT* (1999); *The Common Minimum Statistical Programme* in English, French – reference 2001 – 2005. Handbook; seminar proceedings; statistics.
Members 22 Franc Zone states who have been members since the creation of AFRISTAT, except where otherwise indicated (" non-Franc Zone states):
Benin, Burkina Faso, Burundi (* joined 2006), Cameroon, Cape Verde (joined 2002), Central African Rep, Chad, Comoros, Congo Brazzaville, Côte d'Ivoire, Djibouti (*joined 2012), Equatorial Guinea, Gabon, Guinea (* joined 2000), Guinea-Bissau (joined 1998), Madagascar (*joined 2013), Mali, Mauritania (joined 1998), Niger, Sao Tomé-Principe (joined 2008), Senegal, Togo.
IGO Relations Partner of (1): *Inter-African Conference on Insurance Markets (#11385).* Assists *Commission de l'UEMOA (see: #20377)* in implementing *'Programme d'appui régional statistique à la surveillance multilatérale dans les pays de l'UEMOA (PARSTAT)'.* **NGO Relations** Institutional member of: *International Association of Survey Statisticians (IASS, #12218).* [2021.08.31/XF4650/**F***]

♦ Economisch en Sociaal Comité / see European Economic and Social Committee (#06963)
♦ Economisch en Sociaal Comité van de Europese Gemeenschappen / see European Economic and Social Committee (#06963)
♦ Economist Conferences (meeting series)
♦ Economists Against the Arms Race / see Economists for Peace and Security (#05322)
♦ Economists Allied for Arms Reduction / see Economists for Peace and Security (#05322)

♦ Economists for Peace and Security (EPS) 05322

Exec Dir c/o the Levy Inst, Box 5000, Annandale on Hudson NY 12504, USA. T. +18457580917. E-mail: info@epsusa.org.
URL: http://www.epsusa.org/
History Dec 1988, New York, NY (USA). Former names and other names: *Economists Against the Arms Race* – former; *Economists Allied for Arms Reduction (ECAAR)* – former. Registration: Nonprofit 501(c)(3), No/ID: EIN: 13-3429488, Start date: 1988, USA. **Aims** Create and promote a better understanding and a more friendly relationship between races, nations, and classes of people; foster a desire for universal, perpetual peace on the part of the nations of the world; promote the movement for world disarmament, nuclear disarmament, and a reduction in the stockpiling of weapons by all countries; support efforts to create economic incentives for peaceful relations; promote collective approaches to conflict and security problems; encourage submission of international disputes to negotiation, arbitration, judicial settlement, the United Nations or other multi-national institutions for the settlement of controversies. **Structure** Board of Directors; Board of Trustees; Fellows; Members. **Languages** English. **Staff** 2.00 FTE, paid. **Finance** Supported by foundations and individual donations, including the following bodies listed in this Yearbook: *Ford Foundation (#09858).* **Activities** Events/meetings; networking/liaising; training/education. **Events** *Conference* Brussels (Belgium) / Paris (France) 2016, *Australasian conference on the economics and politics of war and peace* Sydney, NSW (Australia) 2009, *Australasian conference on economics and politics of war and peace* Sydney, NSW (Australia) 2008. **Publications** *News Notes* (12 a year) – e-mail newsletter; *EPS Quarterly* (4 a year) – print newsletter; *The Economics of Peace and Security Journal* (2 a year) – online peer-reviewed journal. *Conflict or Development* (2003); *The Full Costs of Ballistic Missile Defense* (2003); *After Kosovo* (1999); *Disarmament and Development* (1999).
Members Organizations () and individuals in 71 countries:
Afghanistan, Albania, Argentina, Australia (*), Austria, Bangladesh, Belgium, Bolivia, Cameroon, Canada (*), Chile (*), China, Colombia, Costa Rica, Croatia, Czechia, Denmark, Egypt, El Salvador, Ethiopia, France (*), Germany, Ghana, Greece, Guatemala, Hungary, India (*), Iran Islamic Rep, Ireland, Israel (*), Italy, Jamaica, Japan (*), Kenya, Korea Rep, Kuwait, Lebanon, Malawi, Malaysia, Mexico, Mozambique, Namibia, Netherlands (*), New Zealand, Nicaragua, Nigeria, North Macedonia, Norway, Pakistan, Peru, Philippines, Poland, Portugal, Russia, Slovenia, South Africa (*), Spain, Sri Lanka, Sweden, Switzerland, Tanzania UR, Thailand, Türkiye, Uganda, UK, Ukraine, USA (*), Uzbekistan, Venezuela, Zambia, Zimbabwe.
Consultative Status Consultative status granted from: *ECOSOC (#05331)* (Special). **IGO Relations** *United Nations Commission on Sustainable Development (CSD, inactive).* Associated with Department of Global Communications of the United Nations. **NGO Relations** Member of: *International Action Network on Small Arms (IANSA, #11585); International Confederation of Associations for Pluralism in Economics (ICAPE, #12849); CONGO Committee on Human Rights (#04663); NGO Committee on Disarmament, Peace and Security, New York NY (#17106); NGO Committee on Social Development (#17115); NGO Committee on Sustainable Development, New York (#17118).* Represented on the Organizing Committee of: *Hague Appeal for Peace (HAP, #10848).* [2022/XF4567/**F**]

♦ Economy for the Common Good (ECG) 05323

Managing Dir Stresemannstr 23, 22769 Hamburg, Germany. E-mail: international@ecogood.org – federation@ecogood.org.
Registered Address Kleiner Schäferkamp 30, 20357 Hamburg, Germany.
URL: https://www.ecogood.org/
History Former names and other names: *International Federation for the Economy for the Common Good* – full title. Registration: Hamburg District court, No/ID: VR 24207, Start date: 18 Nov 2019, Germany, Hamburg; EU Transparency Register, No/ID: 339093641078-19, Start date: 27 Jan 2021. **Aims** Contribute to a culture of good living in a peaceful and sustainable civilization. **Structure** Delegates Assembly; Local Chapters; Hubs; Management Team. **Publications** *ECG Newsletter.*
Members Local chapters (over 150) in 33 countries:
Argentina, Austria, Belgium, Brazil, Burundi, Chile, Colombia, Côte d'Ivoire, Croatia, Dominican Rep, France, Germany, Ghana, Greece, Guinea, Italy, Kenya, Luxembourg, Mexico, Morocco, Netherlands, North Macedonia, Peru, Philippines, Portugal, Romania, Senegal, Serbia, Spain, Sweden, Switzerland, Uruguay, USA.
Companies (over 300) in 6 countries (predominantly in Germany):
Austria, Belgium, Germany, Italy, Sweden, Switzerland.
NGO Relations Member of (1): *Wellbeing Economy Alliance (WEAll, #20856).* Cooperates with (9): *Association for the Taxation of Financial Transactions for the Aid of Citizens (#02947); Earth Charter International (ECI, #05161); Global Ecovillage Network (GEN, #10331); Global Marshall Plan Initiative (#10466); Intercontinental Network for the Promotion of the Social Solidarity Economy (INPSSE, #11463); New Economics Foundation (NEF, #17082); Transition Network; Transnational Institute (TNI, #20219); World Future Council Foundation (WFC, #21533).* [2023/AA1059/**C**]

♦ Economy and Environment Programme for Southeast Asia (EEPSEA) 05324

Communication Manager c/o WorldFish – Philippine Country Office, SEARCA Bldg, College, Laguna, 4031 Los Baños LAG, Philippines. Fax +63495017493. E-mail: admin@eepsea.net.
URL: http://www.eepsea.net/
History Founded May 1993, by *International Development Research Centre (IDRC, #13162),* with co-funding from *Swedish International Development Cooperation Agency (Sida)* and *Canadian International Development Agency (CIDA, inactive).* Since Nov 2012, housed at *WorldFish (#21507).* **Aims** Strengthen local capacity in economic analysis of environmental issues so researchers can provide sound advice to policymakers. **Structure** Sponsors Group; Advisory Committee. Secretariat. Administered by *WorldFish (#21507)* on behalf of *International Development Research Centre (IDRC, #13162)* and *Swedish International Development Cooperation Agency (Sida).* **Languages** English. **Staff** 5.00 FTE, paid. **Finance** Donors. Annual budget depends on funds from donors. **Activities** Capacity building; training/education; financial and/or material support; research/documentation; events/meetings. **Events** *Meeting on Transition to Green Economy in Southeast Asia* Ho Chi Minh City (Vietnam) 2015, *International Conference on Conservation Financing in Southeast Asia* Manila (Philippines) 2015, *Conference / Annual Conference* Phuket (Thailand) 2014, *Conference on Economics of Climate Change in Southeast Asia* Siem Reap (Cambodia) 2014, *Half-yearly meeting* Kota Kinabalu (Malaysia) 2010. **Publications** *EEPSEA Practitioners Series.* Research reports; books; briefs.
Members Full in 10 countries:
Cambodia, China, Indonesia, Laos, Malaysia, Myanmar, Papua New Guinea, Philippines, Thailand, Vietnam.
IGO Relations Cooperates with: *International Development Research Centre (IDRC, #13162); Swedish International Development Cooperation Agency (Sida); United States Agency for International Development (USAID)* Biodiversity and Watershed Improved for Stronger Economy and Ecosystem Resilience (B++WISER); *WorldFish (#21507).* **NGO Relations** Cooperates with: *ASEAN Centre for Biodiversity (ACB, #01149); Asian Association of Environmental and Resource Economics (AAERE, #01322);* Enhancing the Economics of Biodiversity and Ecosystem Services in Southeast Asia (ECO-BEST); *South Asian Network for Development and Environmental Economics (SANDEE, #19735); Stockholm Environment Institute (SEI, #19993); Sustainable Mekong Research Network (SUMERNET, #20062).* [2015.09.01/XK2383/**E**]

♦ **ECOO** European Council of Optometry and Optics (#06835)
♦ **ecopa** European Consensus-Platform for Alternatives (#06742)
♦ **ECO-PB** European Consortium for Organic Plant Breeding (#06761)
♦ Ecopeace Asia (internationally oriented national body)

♦ EcoPeace Middle East 05325

Pres PO Box 840252, Amman 11181, Jordan. T. +96265866602 – +96265866603. Fax +96265866604. E-mail: info@ecopeaceme.org.
Pres 90 Menachem Begin Road, 6713837 Tel Aviv, Israel. T. +972035605383. Fax +972035604693.
Pres Fuad Hijazi St., Al-Bireh, West Bank PALESTINE, Via Israel. T. +970022400832. Fax +970022400836.
URL: http://ecopeaceme.org/

History 7 Dec 1994, Taba (Egypt). Founded at a historic meeting which came about as environmental non-governmental organizations from the Middle East met with the common goal of furthering sustainable development and peace in their region, and to promote the integration of environmental considerations into the regional development agenda. Former names and other names: *Ecopeace – Middle East Environmental NGO Forum* – former (1994 to 1998); *Friends of the Earth Middle East (FoEME)* – former (1998 to 2014). **Aims** Bring together Jordanian, Palestinian And Israeli Environmentalists; promote cooperative efforts to protect our shared environmental heritage and by so doing, advance both sustainable regional development and the creation of necessary conditions for lasting peace in our region. **Structure** General Assembly (annual); Board; Secretariat. Offices in Amman (Jordan), Ramallah (Palestine), and Tel-Aviv (Israel). **Languages** Arabic, English, Hebrew. **Staff** 55.00 FTE, paid. **Finance** Sources: government support; international organizations. Supporting organizations also include: German Federal Ministry for Economic Cooperation and Development (BMZ); foundations. Supported by: *European Union (EU, #08967)*; *Rockefeller Brothers Fund (RBF)*; *Swedish International Development Cooperation Agency (Sida)*; *The International Osprey Foundation (TIOF)*; *United States Agency for International Development (USAID)*. **Activities** Advocacy/lobbying/activism; awareness raising; events/meetings. Active in: Israel, Jordan, West Bank-Gaza. **Events** *Annual Conference* Amman (Jordan) 2019, *Conference on Euro-Mediterranean free trade zone* Brussels (Belgium) 2000, *Conference on saving the Dead Sea basin* Amman (Jordan) 1998, *Conference on campaigning for our environment* Eilat (Israel) 1997. **Publications** Studies; reports.

Members National organizations (4) in 3 countries and territories:
Israel, Jordan, Palestine.

IGO Relations Accredited to the Conference of the Parties of: *Secretariat of the United Nations Convention to Combat Desertification (Secretariat of the UNCCD, #19208)*. **NGO Relations** Member of (6): *Alliance for Middle East Peace (ALLMEP)*; *Clean Up the World (CUW, #03992)*; *Environmental Peacebuilding Association (EnPAx, #05509)*; *Mediterranean Information Office for Environment, Culture and Sustainable Development (MIO-ECSDE, #16657)*; *Mediterranean NGO Network for Ecology and Sustainable Development (MED Forum, no recent information)*; *Mediterranean Social-Ecological Youth Network (MARE, no recent information)*.
[2022.10.19/XF4592/**E**]

♦ Ecopeace – Middle East Environmental NGO Forum / see EcoPeace Middle East (#05325)

♦ ECO Platform 05326

Managing Dir Consulting Donath, Girardetstr 2-38 – Eingang 7, 45131 Essen, Germany. T. +492013203172. E-mail: info@eco-platform.org – contact@eco-platform.org.
Registered Office c/o Construction Products Europe, Boulevard du Souverain 68, 1170 Brussels, Belgium.
URL: http://www.eco-platform.org/

History 23 Sep 2013, Brussels (Belgium). Registration: Banque-Carrefour des Entreprises, No/ID: 0538.575.177, Start date: 12 Sep 2013, Belgium; EU Transparency Register, No/ID: 493644943548-47, Start date: 14 Jul 2021. **Aims** Support provision of unbiased credible and scientifically sound information in form of a type III *Environmental* Product Declaration (EPD) for *construction products* in form of a *Europe*-wide accepted Core-EPD. **Structure** General Assembly; Board. Working Groups. **Finance** Sources: members' dues. **Activities** Advocacy/lobbying/activism; knowledge management/information dissemination. **NGO Relations** Liaison Organization of: *Comité européen de normalisation (CEN, #04162)*. [2021/XJ7596/**F**]

♦ ECOP Marine – European Community on Protection of Marine Life
♦ ECOPNET – European Cooperation and Partnership Network (unconfirmed)

♦ Ecopreneur.eu – European Sustainable Business Federation 05327

Exec Dir Rue Belliard 40, 1040 Brussels, Belgium. T. +3228083588. E-mail: info@ecopreneur.eu.
URL: https://ecopreneur.eu/

History 1 Jan 2016. Registration: Banque-Carrefour des Entreprises, Start date: 2016, Belgium; EU Transparency Register, No/ID: 495144126378-48. **Aims** Pursue advocacy activities with an influence on sustainable development and the green economy; advance interests of green SMEs and green economy projects across Europe; work towards improving *environmental* standards. **Structure** Board of Directors. **Languages** English. **Staff** 1.50 FTE, paid. **Finance** Sources: grants; revenue from activities/projects. Supported by: *Adessium Foundation*; C&A Foundation; *European Commission (EC, #06633)*; TNO. Annual budget: 90,000 EUR (2020). **Activities** Advocacy/lobbying/activism; projects/programmes. **Events** *Workshop on Economic Incentives for a Circular Economy* Belgium 2020. **Publications** *Circular Economy Update report 2019*; *Circular Fashion Advocacy (2019)*; *MEETING THE SUSTAINABLE DEVELOPMENT GOALS REQUIRES STRONG CIRCULAR ECONOMY POLICIES*.

Members Associations in 7 countries:
Austria, Belgium, Estonia, France, Germany, Netherlands, Sweden. [2021.09.07/XM8685/**D**]

♦ **ECORD** European Consortium for Ocean Research Drilling (#06758)
♦ ECOSA / see European Child Safety Alliance (#06534)
♦ **ECOSA** ECO Seed Association (#05329)
♦ ECOSA – European Consumer Safety Association (inactive)
♦ ECOSANLAC – Saneamiento Ecológico en Latinoamérica y el Caribe (internationally oriented national body)

♦ ECO Science Foundation (ECOSF) 05328

Pres 5th Floor MoST Bldg, 1-Constitution Ave, Sector G-5/2, Islamabad 44000, Pakistan. T. +92519216658. Fax +92519215497. E-mail: registry@ecosf.org.
URL: http://www.eco4science.org/

History 20 Dec 2011, Islamabad (Pakistan). Established within the framework of *Economic Cooperation Organization (ECO, #05313)*. Charter signed by all ECO member states, Mar 1995, Islamabad (Pakistan). Became operational, Dec 2011. **Aims** Promote scientific, technological and innovative research collaboration; popularize science at grass roots level with emphasis on IBSE methodology for STEM education and standardization of engineering qualification. **Structure** Board of Trustees; Executive Committee; Headquarters located in Islamabad (Pakistan). **Languages** English. **Staff** 18.00 FTE, paid. **Finance** Sources: contributions of member/participating states. **Activities** Capacity building; events/meetings; financial and/or material support; training/education. **Events** *Eurasia Conference on Chemical Sciences (EuAsC2S-14)* Karachi (Pakistan) 2016. **Publications** *ECOSF Newsletter* (6 a year). Annual Report; research papers.

Members Governments of 10 countries:
Afghanistan, Azerbaijan, Iran Islamic Rep, Kazakhstan, Kyrgyzstan, Pakistan, Tajikistan, Türkiye, Turkmenistan, Uzbekistan.

IGO Relations Memorandum of Understanding with (1): *Isfahan Regional Center for Technology Incubators and Science Park Development (IRIS, #16028)*. Member of (1): *Intergovernmental Science-Policy Platform on Biodiversity and Ecosystem Services (IPBES, #11500)*. **NGO Relations** Scientific Institutes and Organizations.
[2022/XE2847/f/**F***]

♦ ECO Seed Association (ECOSA) 05329

Gen Sec Ehlibeyt Mah Tekstilciler Cad Libra Kule No:21, Libra Kule No 21, Balgat – Çankaya, Ankara/Ankara, Türkiye. T. +903124333065. Fax +903124333006. E-mail: info@ecosaseed.org.
URL: http://www.ecosaseed.org/

History 18 Jul 2009, Istanbul (Turkey). **Events** *International seed trade conference / Annual Conference* Antalya (Turkey) 2009.

Members Full in 10 countries:
Afghanistan, Azerbaijan, Iran Islamic Rep, Kazakhstan, Kyrgyzstan, Pakistan, Tajikistan, Türkiye, Turkmenistan, Uzbekistan.
[2022/XJ1130/**E**]

♦ ECOSE – European Cultural Organization for Social Education (internationally oriented national body)
♦ ECOS / see Environmental Coalition on Standards (#05499)
♦ **ECOS** Environmental Coalition on Standards (#05499)
♦ **ECOSEP** European College of Sports Medicine and Exercise Physicians (#06617)
♦ **ECOSF** ECO Science Foundation (#05328)
♦ EcoSoc / see European Economic and Social Committee (#06963)

♦ Ecosocialist International Network (EIN) 05330

Contact address not obtained. E-mail: ecosocialist@gmail.com.
URL: http://www.ecosocialistnetwork.org/

History 7 Oct 2007, Montreuil (France), following 1st Ecosocialist, 2001. **Events** *Conference* Belém (Brazil) 2009, *Conference* Montreuil (France) 2007. **Members** Membership countries not specified.
[2013/XJ0157/**F**]

♦ ECOSOC – United Nations Economic and Social Council 05331

Conseil économique et social des Nations Unies – Consejo Económico y Social de las Naciones Unidas

Sec Office for ECOSOC Support, 1 UN Plaza Room DC1-1428, New York NY 10017, USA. T. +12129631811. Fax +12129631712. E-mail: ecosocinfo@un.org.
URL: http://www.un.org/ecosoc/

History 24 Oct 1945, New York, NY (USA). Established by the *Charter of the United Nations – Charte des Nations Unies*, as the principal organ of *United Nations (UN, #20515)* within *United Nations System (#20635)*, to coordinate the economic and social work of the United Nations and the specialized agencies and institutions, known as 'United Nations family' of organizations. Officially constituted, 13 Jan 1946. Originally consisting of 18 members; enlarged to 27 members as of Jan 1966, in accordance with an amendment to the Charter which came into force on 31 Aug 1965. By resolution 2847 (XXVI) of 20 Dec 1971, UN General Assembly decided to adopt an amendment to Article 61 of the Charter providing for the increase of the membership to 54 members. Pending ratification of the amendment, ECOSOC, by resolution 1621 (LI) decided to enlarge its sessional committees from 27 to 54 members, the additional members to be elected annually by the Council. The amendment to Article 61 came into force on 24 Sep 1973. **Aims** Serve as a principal body for coordination, policy review, policy dialogue and recommendations on issues of economic and social development, as well as for implementation of the international development goals agreed at the major United Nations summits and conferences, including the Millennium Development Goals.

Structure Council comprises 54 member states, elected by UN General Assembly for 3-year terms, 18 at each year end, seats being allotted by geographical region: African states – 14; Asian states – 11; Eastern European states – 6; Latin American and Caribbean states – 10; 13 to Western European and other states – 13. Council usually meets for one regular Substantive Session a year, alternately in Geneva (Switzerland) and New York NY (USA). Decisions are usually arrived at by consensus, otherwise by a majority of members present and voting. Representatives of UN specialized agencies participate in ECOSOC proceedings without the right to vote. President; Bureau. Annual High-Level Segment includes: High-Level Political Forum; Development Cooperation Forum. Other sessions encompass: Integration Segment; Humanitarian Affairs Segment; Operational Activities for Development Segment; Management Segment; Youth Forum; Partnership Forum; Special meetings.

Subsidiary Bodies of ECOSOC:

'Functional Commissions' (8):
- *United Nations Statistical Commission (#20633)*;
- *United Nations Commission on Population and Development (CPD, #20533)*;
- *United Nations Commission for Social Development (CSocD, #20535)*;
- *United Nations Commission on the Status of Women (CSW, #20536)*;
- *United Nations Commission on Narcotic Drugs (CND, #20532)*;
- *United Nations Commission on Crime Prevention and Criminal Justice (CCPCJ, #20530)*;
- *United Nations Commission on Science and Technology for Development (CSTD, #20534)*;
- *United Nations Forum on Forests (UNFF, #20562)*.

'Regional commissions' (5):
- *United Nations Economic Commission for Africa (ECA, #20554)*;
- *United Nations Economic and Social Commission for Asia and the Pacific (ESCAP, #20557)*;
- *United Nations Economic Commission for Europe (UNECE, #20555)*;
- *United Nations Economic Commission for Latin America and the Caribbean (ECLAC, #20556)*;
- *United Nations Economic and Social Commission for Western Asia (ESCWA, #20558)*.

'Standing committees' (3):
- *United Nations Committee for Programme and Coordination (CPC, #20546)*;
- *United Nations Committee on Non-governmental Organizations (#20545)*;
- *United Nations Committee on Negotiations with Intergovernmental Agencies (#20544)*.

'Expert bodies' (4) comprising governmental experts:
- *United Nations Committee of Experts on the Transport of Dangerous Goods and on the Globally Harmonized System of Classification and Labelling of Chemicals (Committee of Experts on TDG and GHS, #20543)*;
- *Intergovernmental Working Group of Experts on International Standards of Accounting and Reporting (ISAR, #11503)*;
- *United Nations Group of Experts on Geographical Names (UNGEGN, #20569)*;
- *United Nations Committee of Experts on Global Geospatial Information Management (UN-GGIM, #20540)*.

'Expert bodies' (5) comprising members serving in their personal capacity:
- *United Nations Committee for Development Policy (CDP, #20537)*;
- *United Nations Committee of Experts on Public Administration (CEPA, #20542)*;
- *United Nations Committee of Experts on International Cooperation in Tax Matters (#20541)*;
- *United Nations Committee on Economic, Social and Cultural Rights (CESCR, #20538)*;
- *United Nations Permanent Forum on Indigenous Issues (UNPFII, #20609)*.

'Related bodies' (4):
- Committee for the United Nations Population Award;
- *International Narcotics Control Board (INCB, #14212)*;
- Programme Coordinating Board of *Joint United Nations Programme on HIV/AIDS (UNAIDS, #16149)*;
- *United Nations System Standing Committee on Nutrition (UNSCN, inactive)*.

Office of Intergovernmental Support and Coordination for Sustainable Development in the Department of Economic and Social Affairs (DESA) provides support to the work of the UN General Assembly, ECOSOC and HLPF).

Other UN bodies within the ECOSOC system:

Programmes and Funds (6):
- *UNDP (#20292)*;
- *UNEP (#20299)*;
- *United Nations Population Fund (UNFPA, #20612)*;
- *United Nations Human Settlements Programme (UN-Habitat, #20572)*;
- *UNICEF (#20332)*;
- *World Food Programme (WFP, #21510)*.

Research and Training (5):
- *United Nations Interregional Crime and Justice Research Institute (UNICRI, #20580)*;
- *United Nations Institute for Disarmament Research (UNIDIR, #20575)*;
- *United Nations Institute for Training and Research (UNITAR, #20576)*;
- *United Nations System Staff College (UNSSC, #20637)*;
- *United Nations University (UNU, #20642)*.

Other Entities (9):
- *International Trade Centre (ITC, #15703)*;
- *Joint United Nations Programme on HIV/AIDS (UNAIDS, #16149)*;
- *UNHCR (#20327)*;
- *United Nations Office for Disaster Risk Reduction (UNDRR, #20595)*;
- *United Nations Office on Drugs and Crime (UNODC, #20596)*;
- *United Nations Office for Project Services (UNOPS, #20602)*;
- *United Nations Relief and Works Agency for Palestine Refugees in the Near East (UNRWA, #20622)*;
- *UN Women (#20724)*;
- *World Trade Organization (WTO, #21864)*.

Specialized Agencies (14):
- *FAO (#09260)*;
- *International Civil Aviation Organization (ICAO, #12581)*;
- *International Fund for Agricultural Development (IFAD, #13692)*;
- *ILO (#11123)*;
- *International Monetary Fund (IMF, #14180)*;
- *International Maritime Organization (IMO, #14102)*;
- *International Telecommunication Union (ITU, #15673)*;
- *UNESCO (#20322)*;
- *UNIDO (#20336)*;
- *World Tourism Organization (UNWTO, #21861)*;
- *Universal Postal Union (UPU, #20682)*;
- *WHO (#20950)*;
- *World Intellectual Property Organization (WIPO, #21593)*;
- *World Meteorological Organization (WMO, #21649)*.

World Bank Group (5):
- *International Bank for Reconstruction and Development (IBRD, #12317)*;
- *International Development Association (IDA, #13155)*;
- *International Finance Corporation (IFC, #13597)*;
- *Multilateral Investment Guarantee Agency (MIGA, #16888)*;

– *International Centre for Settlement of Investment Disputes (ICSID, #12515).*

Languages Arabic, Chinese, English, French, Russian, Spanish. **Finance** Financed by the Regular Budget of the United Nations. **Activities** Promoting Sustainable Development; Advancing policy integration; Development Cooperation Forum; Financing for sustainable development;Coordinating humanitarian action; Guiding operational activities for development; Providing coordination and oversight; Building partnerships; Engaging youth; Raising awareness on emerging issues; Advising on Haiti's long-term development; Promoting the peace-development nexus. **Events** *Annual Multi-stakeholder Forum on Science Technology and Innovation for the Sustainable Development Goals (STI Forum)* New York, NY (USA) 2021, *Forum on Financing for Development* New York, NY (USA) 2021, *High Level Political Forum for Sustainable Development (HLPF)* New York, NY (USA) 2021, *Youth Forum* New York, NY (USA) 2021, *High Level Political Forum for Sustainable Development (HLPF)* New York, NY (USA) 2020.

Members ECOSOC Council: Governments of 53 states (term expiry date, 31 Dec of the year in parentheses, with one outstanding vacancy amongst the Eastern European State), as of 2023:

Afghanistan (2024), Argentina (2023), Austria (2023), Belgium (2024), Belize (2024), Bolivia (2023), Botswana (2025), Brazil (2025), Bulgaria (2023), Cameroon (2025), Canada (2024), Cape Verde (2025), Chile (2024), China (2025), Colombia (2025), Costa Rica (2025), Côte d'Ivoire (2024), Croatia (2024), Czechia (2024), Denmark (2025), Equatorial Guinea (2025), Eswatini (2024), France (2023), Germany (2023), Greece (2025), Guatemala (2023), India (2024), Indonesia (2023), Italy (2024), Japan (2023), Kazakhstan (2024), Korea Rep (2025), Laos (2025), Liberia (2023), Libya (2023), Madagascar (2023), Mauritius (2024), Mexico (2023), New Zealand (2025), Nigeria (2023), Oman (2024), Peru (2024), Portugal (2023), Qatar (2025), Slovakia (2025), Slovenia (2025), Solomon Is (2023), Sweden (2025), Tanzania UR (2024), Tunisia (2024), UK (2023), USA (2024), Zimbabwe (2023).

Consultative Status Article 71 of the UN Charter offers arrangements for consultation with NGOs. Consultative relationship with ECOSOC is currently governed by ECOSOC resolution 1996/31, which outlines the eligibility requirements for consultative status, rights and obligations of NGOs in consultative status, the role and functions of the ECOSOC Committee on NGOs, and the responsibilities of the UN Secretariat in supporting the consultative relationship. Consultative status is granted upon recommendation of the ECOSOC Committee on NGOs, comprised of 19 member states, and consists of 3 categories: General, Special and Roster. General consultative status is reserved for large international NGOs whose area of work covers most of the issues on the agenda of ECOSOC and its subsidiary bodies. These tend to be fairly large, established international NGOs with a broad geographical reach. Special consultative status is granted to NGOs which have a special competence in, and are concerned specifically with, only a few of the fields of activity covered by the ECOSOC. These NGOs tend to be smaller and more recently established. Organizations that apply for consultative status but do not fit in any of the other categories are usually included in the Roster. These NGOs tend to have a rather narrow and/or technical focus. NGOs that have formal status with other UN bodies or specialized agencies (FAO, ILO, UNCTAD, UNESCO, UNIDO, WHO and others), can be included on the ECOSOC Roster. The roster lists NGOs that ECOSOC or the UN Secretary-General considers can make "occasional and useful contributions to the work of the Council or its subsidiary bodies." NGOs with consultative status that wish to attend relevant international conferences or meetings are as a rule accredited for participation. Other NGOs should apply to the secretariat of the conference.

As of 2022: 142 in General Consultative Status; 5,235 in Special Consultative Status; 966 on the Roster.

Organizations granted consultative status:

General (133):

– *AARP International*;
– *Academic Council on the United Nations System (ACUNS, #00020)*;
– *Adventist Development and Relief Agency International (ADRA, #00131)*;
– *American Council for Voluntary International Action (InterAction)*;
– *Asia Crime Prevention Foundation (ACPF, #01263)*;
– *Asian Forum of Parliamentarians on Population and Development (AFPPD, #01493)*;
– *Asian Legal Resource Centre (ALRC, #01529)*;
– *Association for Progressive Communications (APC, #02873)*;
– *Association for Women's Rights in Development (AWID, #02980)*;
– *Association of Medical Doctors of Asia (AMDA)*;
– *AVSI Foundation*;
– *Bochasanwasi Shri Akshar Purushottam Swaminarayan Sanstha*;
– *Brahma Kumaris World Spiritual University (BKWSU, #03311)*;
– *Bureau international des Médecins sans frontières (MSF International, #03366)*;
– *CARE International (CI, #03429)*;
– *Caritas Internationalis (CI, #03580)*;
– *Centre de recherches et de promotion pour la sauvegarde des sites et monuments historiques en Afrique*;
– *China NGO Network for International Exchanges (CNIE)*;
– *Chinese People's Association for Friendship with Foreign Countries (CPAFFC, no recent information)*;
– *CIDSE (CIDSE, #03926)*;
– *CIVICUS: World Alliance for Citizen Participation (#03962)*;
– *Conference of Non-Governmental Organizations in Consultative Relationship with the United Nations (CONGO, #04635)*;
– *Congregations of St Joseph (CSJs, #04673)*;
– *Consumers International (CI, #04773)*;
– *Convention of Independent Financial Advisors (CIFA)*;
– *Covenant House*;
– *DEVNET International (#05059)*;
– *Eastern Regional Organization for Public Administration (EROPA, #05249)*;
– *Environnement et développement du Tiers-monde (enda, #05510)*;
– *Europe – Third World Centre (CETIM)*;
– *Femmes Africa solidarité (FAS, #09732)*;
– *Foundation for the Support of the United Nations (FSUN, no recent information)*;
– *Franciscans International (FI, #09982)*;
– *Friends World Committee for Consultation (FWCC, #10004)*;
– *Fundación Global Democracia y Desarrollo (FUNGLODE)*;
– *Fundación Promoción Social*;
– *Fédération des Agences Internationales pour le Développement (AIDE Fédération, #09414)*;
– *Fédération internationale des associations de personnes âgées (FIAPA, #09609)*;
– *Global Economist Forum (GEF, #10329)*;
– *Good Neighbors International*;
– *Greek Orthodox Archdiocesan Council of America (GOAC, #10708)*;
– *Green Cross International (GCI, #10715)*;
– *Greenpeace International (#10727)*;
– *HelpAge International (#10904)*;
– *HOPE International*;
– *Imam Al-Khoei Benevolent Foundation*;
– *Institute of International Law (#11276)*;
– *International Alliance of Women (IAW, #11639)*;
– *International Association for Religious Freedom (IARF, #12130)*;
– *International Association for the Exchange of Students for Technical Experience (IAESTE, #11885)*;
– *International Association of Peace Foundations (IAPF, #12071)*;
– *International Association of University Professors and Lecturers (IAUPL, #12250)*;
– *International Center for Research on Women (ICRW)*;
– *International Co-operative Alliance (ICA, #12944)*;
– *International Council for Adult Education (ICAE, #12983)*;
– *International Council of Environmental Law (ICEL, #13018)*;
– *International Council of Voluntary Agencies (ICVA, #13092)*;
– *International Council of Women (ICW, #13093)*;
– *International Council on Social Welfare (ICSW, #13076)*;
– *International Council on the Management of Population Programs (ICOMP, #13043)*;
– *International Electrotechnical Commission (IEC, #13255)*;
– *International Eurasia-Press Fund (IEPF, #13309)*;
– *International Federation for Family Development (IFFD, #13423)*;
– *International Federation of Business and Professional Women (BPW International, #13376)*;
– *International Federation of Settlements and Neighbourhood Centres (IFS, #13538)*;
– *International Federation on Ageing (IFA, #13345)*;
– *International Health Awareness Network (IHAN, #13778)*;
– *International Human Rights and Anti-Corruption Society (IHRAS)*;
– *International Indian Treaty Council (IITC, #13836)*;
– *International Informatization Academy (#13850)*;
– *International Institute for Applied Systems Analysis (IIASA, #13861)*;
– *International Institute for Non-Aligned Studies (IINS, #13904)*;
– *International Institute of Administrative Sciences (IIAS, #13859)*;
– *International Movement ATD Fourth World (#14193)*;
– *International Organisation of Employers (IOE, #14428)*;
– *International Organization for Standardization (ISO, #14473)*;
– *International Planned Parenthood Federation (IPPF, #14589)*;
– *International Road Transport Union (IRU, #14761)*;
– *International Social Security Association (ISSA, #14885)*;
– *International Trade Union Confederation (ITUC, #15708)*;
– *International Transport Workers' Federation (ITF, #15726)*;
– *International Union of Economists (IUE, #15769)*;
– *International Youth and Student Movement for the United Nations (ISMUN, inactive)*;
– *IPS – Inter Press Service International Association (#16013)*;
– *Junior Chamber International (JCI, #16168)*;
– *Latin American Confederation of Credit Unions (#16302)*;
– *Lazarus Union (#16411)*;
– *Legion of Good Will (LGW)*;
– *Liberal International (LI, #16454)*;
– *Lions Clubs International (LCI, #16485)*;
– *Make Mothers Matter (#16554)*;
– *Muslim World League (MWL, #16917)*;
– *Médecins du Monde – International (MDM, #16613)*;
– *New Humanity (#17088)*;
– *Nonviolent Radical Party, Transnational and Transparty (PRNTT, #17154)*;
– *ONG HOPE International*;
– *Organization for Industrial, Spiritual and Cultural Advancement International (OISCA International, #17872)*;
– *Organization of Islamic Capitals and Cities (OICC, #17875)*;
– *Oxfam International (#17922)*;
– *Parliamentarians for Global Action (PGA, #18208)*;
– *Plan International (#18386)*;
– *Religions for Peace (RfP, #18831)*;
– *RESO-Femmes International*;
– *Rotary International (RI, #18975)*;
– *Russian Peace Foundation (RPF)*;
– *Save the Children International (#19058)*;
– *Socialist International (SI, #19340)*;
– *Society for International Development (SID, #19581)*;
– *Soldiers of Peace International Association (SPIA, #19678)*;
– *Soroptimist International (SI, #19686)*;
– *Stiftung für Ökologische Entwicklung (Biovision)*;
– *Sulabh International Social Service Organization*;
– *The World Veterans Federation (WVF, #21900)*;
– *Universal Peace Federation (UPF International, #20681)*;
– *Voluntary Service Overseas (VSO)*;
– *Women's Federation for World Peace International (WFWPI)*;
– *Women's International Democratic Federation (WIDF, #21022)*;
– *World Animal Protection (#21092)*;
– *World Association of Girl Guides and Girl Scouts (WAGGGS, #21142)*;
– *World Blind Union (WBU, #21234)*;
– *World Council of Churches (WCC, #21320)* (Commission of the Churches on International Affairs);
– *World Family Organization (WFO, #21399)*;
– *World Federation of Trade Unions (WFTU, #21493)*;
– *World Federation of United Nations Associations (WFUNA, #21499)*;
– *World Fellowship of Buddhists (WFB, #21501)*;
– *World Information Transfer (WIT, #21583)*;
– *World Muslim Congress (WMC, #21664)*;
– *World Organization of the Scout Movement (WOSM, #21693)*;
– *World Organization of United Cities and Local Governments (UCLG, #21695)*;
– *World Vision International (WVI, #21904)*;
– *World Wide Fund for Nature (WWF, #21922)*;
– *Youth for Unity and Voluntary Action (YUVA)*;
– *Zonta International (#22038).*

Special (1404):

– *3Strands Global Foundation (3SGF)*;
– *5 Gyres Institute (5GYRES)*;
– *ABANTU for Development (#00003)*;
– *Academy for Future Science (AFFS)*;
– *Academy of Criminal Justice Sciences (ACJS)*;
– *Academy of Dentistry International (ADI)*;
– *Access Now (#00052)*;
– *ACHE Internacional*;
– *ACORD – Agency for Cooperation and Research in Development (#00073)*;
– *ACT Alliance (#00081)*;
– *Action Against Hunger (#00086)*;
– *ActionAid (#00087)*;
– *Action for Peace through Prayer and Aid (APPA)*;
– *Action internationale pour la paix et le développement dans la région des Grands Lacs, Switzerland (AIPD-GL)*;
– *Advocates for Human Rights*;
– *Advocates for Youth, Washington DC*;
– *AEqualia*;
– *Africa Centre for Citizens Orientation (ACCO)*;
– *Africa Civil Society for the Information Society (ACSIS, #00163)*;
– *Africa Culture Internationale Human Rights (ACI Human Rights)*;
– *Africa Development Interchange Network (ADIN)*;
– *Africa Humanitarian Action (AHA)*;
– *African Action on AIDS (AAA)*;
– *African Agency For Integrated Development (AAID)*;
– *African Aid Organization (AFAID)*;
– *African Artists for Development (AAD)*;
– *African Association of Education for Development (ASAFED, no recent information)*;
– *African Business Roundtable (ABR, #00232)*;
– *African Centre for Advocacy and Human Development (ACAHD)*;
– *African Centre for Community and Development (AFCOD)*;
– *African Centre for the Constructive Resolution of Disputes (ACCORD)*;
– *African Child Policy Forum (ACPF, #00246)*;
– *African Citizens Development Foundation (ACDF)*;
– *African Commission of Health and Human Rights Promoters (ACHHRP)*;
– *African Computer and Technology Literacy Awareness Program Charity (ACTLAP Charity)*;
– *African Development Assistance Consult (ADAC)*;
– *African Development Solutions (Adeso, #00287)*;
– *Africa Network for Animal Welfare (ANAW, #00301)*;
– *African Foundation For Human Advancement (AFFAH)*;
– *African Green Foundation International (AGFI)*;
– *African Law Center (ALC)*;
– *African Network of Young Leaders for Peace and Sustainable Development (ANYL4PSD, #00399)*;
– *African Services Committee (ASC)*;
– *Africans Unite against Child Abuse (AFRUCA)*;
– *African Trade Center (ATC)*;
– *African Wildlife Foundation (AWF, #00498)*;
– *African Women Empowerment Guild (AWEG)*;
– *African Women's Development and Communication Network (FEMNET, #00503)*;
– *African Youth Movement (AYM, #00506)*;
– *African Youths Initiative on Crime Prevention (AYICRIP)*;
– *Africa Speaks (no recent information)*;
– *Africa Unite (AU)*;
– *Afrihealth Optonet Association*;
– *Afro Centre for Development Peace and Justice (AFRODEP)*;
– *Afro-European Medical and Research Network (AEMRN, #00538)*;
– *Afromedianet (no recent information)*;
– *AfroPresencia (#00540)*;
– *AFS Intercultural Programs (AFS, #00541)*;
– *Agencia Latinoamericana de Información (ALAI, #00551)*;

– Agency for Technical Cooperation and Development (ACTED);
– AGE Platform Europe (#00557);
– Agir ensemble pour les droits humains;
– Agricultural Missions;
– Aide et action International (#00588);
– Aide internationale pour l'enfance (AIPE);
– AID FOR AIDS International (AFA);
– AIDS Foundation East-West (AFEW);
– AIDS Healthcare Foundation (AHF);
– AIESEC (#00593);
– AIP Foundation (#00598);
– Airline Ambassadors International (AAI);
– Alliance for Arab Women (AAW, #00657);
– Alliance for Health Promotion (A4HP, #00687);
– Alliance Internationale pour la défense des Droits et des Libertés (AIDL);
– All India Women's Conference (AIWC, #00737);
– All Pakistan Women's Association (APWA);
– Amazon Conservation Team (ACT);
– AMERA International;
– American Society of International Law (ASIL);
– American Youth Understanding Diabetes Abroad (AYUDA);
– Amigos do Protocolo de Kyoto (APK);
– Amizade;
– Amnesty International (AI, #00801);
– Anglican Consultative Council (ACC, #00828);
– Anti-Slavery International (#00860);
– Arab Anti-Corruption Organization (AACO, no recent information);
– Arab Centre for the Independence of the Judiciary and the Legal Profession (ACIJLP);
– Arab Commission for Human Rights (ACHR, #00924);
– Arab Council for Supporting Fair Trial (ACSFT);
– Arab Forum for Environment and Development (AFED, #00960);
– Arab Group for the Protection of Nature (APN, #00970);
– Arab Institute for Human Rights (AIHR, #00983);
– Arab Lawyers' Union (ALU, #01002);
– Arab NGO Network for Environment and Development (RAED, #01017);
– Arab Organization for Human Rights (AOHR, #01020);
– Arab Penal Reform Organization (APRO);
– Arab Red Crescent and Red Cross Organization (ARCO, #01033);
– Arab Society for Academic Freedoms (ASAF, #01042);
– ARC International;
– Ariel Foundation International (AFI, #01106);
– Arigatou International;
– Art of Living Foundation;
– Asia Indigenous Peoples Pact (AIPP, #01282);
– Asia Japan Women's Resource Centre (AJWRC);
– Asian Association for Public Administration (AAPA, #01334);
– Asian Centre for Human Rights (ACHR);
– Asian Centre for Organisation Research and Development (ACORD, #01374);
– Asian Consultancy on Tobacco Control (ACTC);
– Asian Disaster Preparedness Center (ADPC, #01426);
– Asian-Eurasian Human Rights Forum;
– Asian Forum for Human Rights and Development (FORUM-ASIA, #01491);
– Asian Indigenous and Tribal Peoples Network (AITPN, no recent information);
– Asian Institute of Transport Development (AITD);
– Asian Marine Conservation Association (AMCA);
– Asian NGO Coalition for Agrarian Reform and Rural Development (ANGOC, #01566);
– Asian-Pacific Resource and Research Centre for Women (ARROW, #01629);
– Asian People's Disability Alliance (APDA);
– Asian Science Park Association (ASPA, #01693);
– Asia Pacific Alliance for Disaster Management (A-PAD, #01823);
– Asia Pacific Forum on Women, Law and Development (APWLD, #01912);
– Asia Pacific Human Rights Information Center (HURIGHTS Osaka);
– Asia Pacific Women's Watch (APWW, #02077);
– Asociación Americana de Juristas (AAJ, #02110);
– Asociación Española para el Derecho Internacional de los Derechos Humanos (AEDIDH);
– Asociación Habitat Pro (AHAPRO);
– ASPAFRIQUE-JICS-HFFUN;
– Associated Country Women of the World (ACWW, #02338);
– Association Africa 21 (Africa 21);
– Association Apprentissages Sans Frontières (ASF);
– Association culturelle d'aide à la promotion éducative et sociale (ACAPES);
– Association Defending Victims of Terrorism (ADVT);
– Association des Jeunes Volontaires au Service du Monde Environnemental (AJVSME);
– Association des états généraux des étudiants de l'Europe (AEGEE-Europe, #02495);
– Association DIOGENIS – Initiative for Drug Policy Dialogue in South East Europe (Association DIOGENIS);
– Association for Aid and Relief – Japan (AAR);
– Association for Emissions Control by Catalyst (AECC, #02486);
– Association for the Prevention of Torture (APT, #02869);
– Association internationale de lutte contre la pauvreté et pour le développement, Senegal (AIPED, no recent information);
– Association Internationale des Droits de l'Homme (AIDH);
– Association Internationale des Médecins pour la promotion de l'Education et de la Santé en Afrique (AIMES -AFRIQUE, #02718);
– Association internationale pour la défense de la liberté religieuse (AIDLR, #02681);
– Association Internationale pour l'égalité des femmes (AIEF);
– Association Internationale Soufie Alâwiyya (AISA);
– Association of African Women for Research and Development (AAWORD, #02362);
– Association of Asian Confederation of Credit Unions (ACCU, #02377);
– Association of European Manufacturers of Sporting Ammunition (#02522);
– Association of Former International Civil Servants for Development (Greycells);
– Association of Immigrants from the Southern Hemisphere (no recent information);
– Association of Organisations of Mediterranean Businesswomen (#02840);
– Association of Pacific Rim Universities (APRU, #02846);
– Association of World Reindeer Herders (WRH, #02985);
– Association Points-Coeur (#02863);
– Associazione Amici dei Bambini (AiBi);
– Associazione Comunità Papa Giovanni;
– Atheist Alliance International (AAI, #03003);
– Athletes United for Peace;
– Avocats Sans Frontières (ASF, #03050);
– Baha'i International Community (#03062);
– Baltic Sea Forum (#03142);
– Bancroft Global Development;
– Baptist World Alliance (BWA, #03176);
– Bar Association of International Governmental Organizations;
– Basic Health International (BHI);
– Batey Relief Alliance (BRA);
– BC Council for International Cooperation (BCCIC);
– Beth Chabad – International Jewish Educational and Cultural Network (no recent information);
– Books2Africa;
– Both ENDS (#03307);
– Bread for All;
– Bridges International;
– British Overseas NGO's for Development (BOND);
– Buddha's Light International Association (BLIA, #03346);
– Buddhist Tzu Chi Foundation (#03347);
– Build Africa;
– Building and Wood Workers' International (BWI, #03355);
– Cairo Institute for Human Rights Studies (CIHRS, #03397);
– Campagne Internationale de l'Ordre de Malte contre la lèpre (Fondation CIOMAL, #03403);
– Canadian Council for Refugees (CCR);
– Canadian Voice of Women for Peace (VOW);
– Caribbean Association for Feminist Research and Action (CAFRA, #03445);
– Caribbean Medical Association (CMA);
– Caribbean Policy Development Centre (CPDC, #03540);
– Caring and Living As Neighbours (CLAN);
– Carmelite NGO (#03583);
– Catholic Agency for Overseas Development (CAFOD);
– Catholic Foreign Missionary Society of America (Maryknoll Fathers);
– Catholic International Education Office (#03604);
– Catholic Lenten Fund;
– Catholic Medical Mission Board (CMMB);
– Catholic Organization for Relief and Development (Cordaid);
– Catholics for Choice (#03609);
– Catholic Youth Network for Environmental Sustainability in Africa (CYNESA, #03611);
– Católicas por el Derecho a Decidir (CDD, #03612);
– Caucasus Environmental NGO Network (CENN, #03613);
– CDP (#03621);
– Center for Civilians in Conflict (CIVIC);
– Center for Economic and Social Rights (CESR);
– Center for Family and Human Rights (C-Fam);
– Center for Health, Human Rights and Development (CEHURD);
– Center for International Earth Science Information Network (CIESIN);
– Center for International Humanitarian Cooperation (CIHC);
– Center for International Virtual Schooling (IVECA);
– Center for Justice and International Law (CEJIL, #03647);
– Center for Migration Studies, New York (CMS);
– Center for Oceans Law and Policy (COLP);
– Center for Reproductive Rights;
– Center for the Study of State and Society, Buenos Aires (CEDES);
– Center for Women's Global Leadership (CWGL);
– Centre de liaison et d'information des puissances maçonniques signataires de l'Appel de Strasbourg (CLIPSAS, #03770);
– Centre de Politique Internationale et d'Analyse des Conflits (CDPIAC);
– Centre for Humanitarian Dialogue (The HD Centre);
– Centre for International Sustainable Development Law (CISDL);
– Centre of People's Aid Blagovest – International Public Charity Organization (CPA Blagovest, no recent information);
– Centre UNESCO de Catalunya (UNESCOCAT);
– Centrist Democrat International (CDI, #03792);
– Centro Latinoamericano de Derechos Humanos (CLADH, #03812);
– CESVI Fondazione;
– Chamber of Computer Logistics People Worldwide (CCLP Worldwide, #03847);
– Cherie Blair Foundation for Women;
– Child Family Health International (CFHI);
– ChildFund Alliance (#03868);
– Child Helpline International (CHI, #03870);
– Childhood Cancer International (CCI, #03871);
– Children International;
– Children of the Caribbean Foundation;
– Children's Investment Fund Foundation (CIFF);
– Child Rights Connect (#03884);
– China Association for International Science and Technology Cooperation (CAISTC);
– China Education Association for International Exchange (CEAIE);
– China International Council for the Promotion of Multinational Corporations (CICPMC);
– China International Public Relations Association (CIPRA);
– Chinese Association for International Understanding (CAFIU);
– Chinese People's Association for Peace and Disarmament (CPAPD);
– CHOICE for Youth and Sexuality;
– Christian Aid;
– Christian Conference of Asia (CCA, #03898);
– Church World Service (CWS);
– CIBJO – The World Jewellery Confederation (CIBJO, #03923);
– City2000 Youth Action International;
– Climate Institute;
– Coalition Against Trafficking in Women (CATW, #04047);
– COFACE Families Europe (#04084);
– Cohesive Communities Development Initiative (COCODEV);
– COJEP International – Conseil pour la Justice, l'Egalité et la Paix (COJEP International, #04090);
– Comisión Jurídica para el Autodesarrollo de los Pueblos Originarios Andinos (CAPAJ, #04139);
– Commission on Voluntary Service and Action (CVSA);
– Committee to Protect Journalists (CPJ, #04280);
– Commonwealth Association of Surveying and Land Economy (CASLE, #04313);
– Commonwealth Human Ecology Council (CHEC, #04339);
– Commonwealth Human Rights Initiative (CHRI, #04340);
– Commonwealth Medical Trust (Commat, #04352);
– Community and Family Services International (CFSI);
– Community of Sant'Egidio;
– Company of the Daughters of Charity of St Vincent de Paul (DC);
– Compassion Africa Aged Foundation (CAAF);
– Concile Mondiale de Congrès Diplomatiques des Aumoniers pour la Paix Universelle des Droits Humains et Juridiques (CMOCDAPUNDHJ);
– Conectas Human Rights;
– Confederation of European Maritime Technology Societies (CEMT, #04526);
– Conference of European Churches (CEC, #04593);
– Congregation of the Mission (Vincentians);
– Conscience and Peace Tax International (CPTI, #04683);
– Conseil international du sport militaire (CISM, #04695);
– Conservation Force (#04729);
– Conservation International (CI);
– Conserve Africa Foundation;
– Consortium for Street Children (CSC);
– Consultative Council of Jewish Organizations (CCJO, no recent information);
– Cooperazione Internazionale (COOPI);
– Coordinadora Andina de Organizaciones Indígenas (CAOI, #04804);
– Coordinating Board of Jewish Organizations (CBJO, #04813);
– Coordinating Committee for International Voluntary Service (CCIVS, #04819);
– Coral Guardian;
– Corporate Accountability International;
– Council for International Development (CID);
– Council of American Overseas Research Centers (CAORC);
– Council of International Programs USA (CIPUSA);
– Creators Union of Arab (CUA, #04948);
– Criminologists without Borders;
– Cross-Cultural Solutions;
– CSW;
– Cultural Survival;
– Dag Hammarskjöld Foundation (DHF, #04995);
– David Lynch Foundation (DLF);
– David M Kennedy Center for International Studies;
– Dayemi Complex Bangladesh (DCB);
– Days for Girls International (DfGI);
– Death Penalty Project (DPP);
– December Twelfth Movement International Secretariat;
– Defence for Children International (DCI, #05025);
– Dementia Alliance International (DAI, #05028);
– DESSI International;
– Deutsche Stiftung Weltbevölkerung (DSW);
– Development Alternatives with Women for a New Era (DAWN, #05054);
– Development Innovations and Networks (#05057);
– Dhaka Ahsania Mission (DAM);
– Dialogue Afrique-Europe (DAE);
– DIANOVA International (#05068);

- DIGNITY – Danish Institute Against Torture;
- Dignity International (#05086);
- Diplo Foundation;
- Diplomaten International (DMW, #05088);
- Diplomatic Council (DC);
- Disability Rights Fund (DRF, #05096);
- Disability Rights International (DRI);
- Disabled Peoples' International (DPI, #05097);
- Distance Education for Africa (DEAfrica, #05103);
- Doha International Family Institute (DIFI, #05111);
- Dominicans for Justice and Peace (OP, #05113);
- Dominican Union of Journalists for Peace (no recent information);
- Down Syndrome International (DSi, #05128);
- Du pain pour chaque enfant (APPCE);
- Dutch Refugee Council;
- Earth Charter International (ECI, #05161);
- Earth Child Institute (ECI, #05162);
- Earth Day Network (EDN, #05164);
- Earth Island Institute (EII);
- Earthjustice;
- Earthquakes and Megacities Initiative (EMI, #05167);
- Earth Society Foundation (ESF);
- East Africa Consortium International (EACI);
- EastWest Institute (EWI, #05264);
- East-West Management Institute (EWMI);
- Eau vive;
- EcoHealth Alliance;
- Edmund Rice International (ERI, #05362);
- Educate a Child in Africa (ECA);
- Education Above All (EAA);
- Educational Foundation for African Women (EFAW);
- Education Globale et Développement (EGD);
- Education International (EI, #05371);
- Educators Without Borders (EWB);
- EDUCO;
- Egyptian Council for Foreign Affairs (ECFA);
- Egyptian Organization for Human Rights (EOHR);
- Election Network Society in the Arab Region (ENAR);
- Eliminate Child Labour in Tobacco Foundation (ECLT Foundation, #05430);
- Emergency Architects;
- Emmaus International (#05445);
- End Child Prostitution, Child Pornography and Trafficking of Children for Sexual Purposes (ECPAT, #05456);
- Engage Now Africa (ENA);
- Engineers Without Borders International (EWB International, #05481);
- English International Association of Lund;
- Environmental Ambassadors for Sustainable Development (Environmental Ambassadors);
- Environmental Justice Foundation (EJF);
- Environmental Law Institute (ELI);
- Equality Fund (EF);
- Equality Now (#05518);
- Equal Rights Trust (#05520);
- Equitas – International Centre for Human Rights Education;
- Espace Afrique international;
- Essl Foundation;
- Eurasia Reiyukai;
- Euro Atlantic Diplomacy Society (EAD Society, #05643);
- Eurochild (#05657);
- Euromed Feminist Initiative (EFI, #05715);
- Euromontana (#05737);
- Europe Against Drugs (EURAD, #05774);
- European Association of Geographers (EUROGEO, #06054);
- European Business Club Association (EBCA);
- European Center for Constitutional and Human Rights (ECCHR);
- European Center for Preventing Addictions (ECPA);
- European Centre for Law and Justice (ECLJ);
- European Coordination of Associations and Individuals for Freedom of Conscience (CAPLC);
- European Disability Forum (EDF, #06929);
- European Federation of Centres of Research and Information on Cults and Sects (#07072);
- European Federation of Older Students at Universities (EFOS, #07181);
- European Federation of Psychologists Associations (EFPA, #07199);
- European Forum of Muslim Women (EFOMW, #07321);
- European Health Psychology Society (EHPS, #07462);
- European Humanist Federation (EHF, #07507);
- European Jewish Call for Reason (JCall);
- European Language Equality Network (ELEN, #07647);
- European Materials Handling Federation (#07752);
- European Network of Policewomen (ENP, #07970);
- European Network on Debt and Development (EURODAD, #07891);
- European Network on Independent Living (ENIL, #07929);
- European Organisation of Military Associations and Trade Unions (EUROMIL, #08099);
- European Parliamentary Forum for Sexual & Reproductive Rights (EPF, #08149);
- European Radio Amateurs' Organization (EURAO, #08320);
- European Roma and Travellers Forum (ERTF, #08402);
- European Space Policy Institute (ESPI, #08801);
- European Transport Safety Council (ETSC, #08940);
- European Tyre and Rim Technical Organisation (ETRTO, #08962);
- European Union Association (EU Association);
- European Union of Jewish Students (EUJS, #08997);
- European Union of the Deaf (EUD, #08985);
- European Union of Women (EUW, #09022);
- European Women's Lobby (EWL, #09102);
- European Youth Forum (#09140);
- Europe External Programme with Africa (EEPA, #09155);
- Europäische Plattform für die Gewinnung unterirdischer Energie "Earth Energy" (Earth Energy);
- Europäischer Interessenverband Handel-Gewerbe-Industrie (EIVHGI);
- EURORDIS – Rare Diseases Europe (#09175);
- Exchange and Cooperation Centre for Latin America (ECCLA);
- Fairfood International (#09237);
- Fairtrade International (FLO, #09240);
- Families of the Missing (FOM);
- Family Africa (TFA);
- Federación Internacional de Asociaciones de Ayuda Social, Ecológica y Cultural (FIADASEC, #09335);
- Federación Latinoamericana de Asociaciones de Familiares de Detenidos-Desaparecidos (FEDEFAM, #09344);
- Federal Union of European Nationalities (FUEN, #09396);
- Federation of American Women's Clubs Overseas (FAWCO, #09416);
- Federation of Associations of Former International Civil Servants (FAFICS, #09457);
- Federation of European Motorcyclists' Associations (FEMA, #09518);
- Federation of Islamic Medical Associations (FIMA, #09681);
- Federation of West Thrace Turks in Europe (ABTTF);
- Federazione Organismi Cristiani Servizio Internazionale Volontario (Volontari nel Mondo – FOCSIV);
- Feed the Children;
- Finance Center for South-South Cooperation (FCSSC);
- Fondation humanus – Humanus International;
- Fondation pour les études et recherches sur le développement international (FERDI);
- Fondation pour l'économie et le développement durable des régions d'Europe (FEDRE, #09817);
- Fondazione Marista per la Solidarietà Internazionale Onlus (#09831);
- Ford Foundation (#09858);
- Forest Stewardship Council (FSC, #09869);
- Forum des Organisations de Solidarité Internationale issues des Migrations (FORIM);
- Forum for Kvinner og Utviklingssporsmål (FOKUS);
- Foundation for European Progressive Studies (FEPS, #09954);
- Foundation for Global Sports Development (GSD);
- Foundation of International Servant Leadership Exchange Association (ISEA Foundation);
- Fracarita International (#09979);
- Framework Convention Alliance (FCA, #09981);
- France Libertés – Fondation Danielle Mitterrand;
- France terre d'asile (FTDA);
- Fraternité Notre Dame (FND);
- Free Africa Foundation (FAF);
- Freedom House;
- Freedom Now;
- Freehearts Africa Reach out Foundation (FAROF);
- Freemuse (#09988);
- Free World Foundation (FWF);
- Fridtjof Nansen Institute (FNI);
- Friendasia;
- Friendship Ambassadors Foundation (FAF);
- Friends of Africa International (FOAI);
- Frontline AIDS (#10007);
- Front Line Defenders (FLD, #10008);
- Fundación América Solidaria (#10020);
- Fundación Ecologia y Desarrollo (ECODES);
- Fundación Latinoamericana por los Derechos Humanos y el Desarrollo Social (FUNDALATIN, #10036);
- Fundación Migrantes y Refugiados sin Fronteras;
- Fundación Pro Humanae Vitae (FPHV);
- Future Hope International (FHI);
- Fédération européenne des femmes actives en famille (FEFAF, #09568);
- Fédération Internationale de l'Automobile (FIA, #09613);
- Fédération internationale des professions immobilières (FIABCI, #09653);
- Gandhi Worldwide Education Institute (GWEI);
- GenderCC – Women for Climate Justice (GenderCC, #10095);
- General Confederation of Trade Unions (GCTU, #10108);
- General Conference of Seventh-Day Adventists (SDA, #10109);
- General Forum of the Arabic and African Nongovernmental Organizations (FONGAF);
- Geneva Centre for Human Rights Advancement and Global Dialogue (GCHRAGD, #10120);
- Geneva for Human Rights – Global Training (GHR, #10124);
- Geneva Infant Feeding Association (GIFA);
- Geneva International Model United Nations (GIMUN);
- Geneva International Peace Research Institute (GIPRI);
- German Catholic Bishops' Organisation for Development Cooperation (MISEREOR);
- Girls' Brigade International (GB, #10152);
- Girls Learn International (GLI);
- Global Academy Institute of Technology Foundation (GAITF);
- Global Action on Aging;
- Global Advocacy for HIV Prevention (AVAC, #10172);
- Global Alert for Defence of Youth and the Less Privileged (GADYLP);
- Global Alliance against Female Genital Mutilation (GA-FGM, #10183);
- Global Alliance Against Traffic in Women (GAATW, #10184);
- Global Alliance for Improved Nutrition (GAIN, #10202);
- Global Alliance for Women's Health (GAWH, #10233);
- Global Alliance on Accessible Technologies and Environments (GAATES, #10180);
- Global Autism Project;
- Global Bioethics Initiative (GBI);
- Global Campaign for Education (GCE, #10264);
- Global Civic Sharing (GCS);
- Global Dairy Platform (GDP, #10314);
- Global Earthquake Model Foundation (GEM Foundation, #10327);
- Global Ecovillage Network (GEN, #10331);
- Global Education Motivators (GEM, #10336);
- Global Empowerment Movement (GEM);
- Global Energy Initiative (#10341);
- Global Environmental Action (GEA);
- Global Exchange (GX);
- Global Family for Love and Peace (GFLP);
- Global Financial Integrity (GFI, #10358);
- Global First Ladies Alliance (GFLA);
- Global Forest Coalition (GFC, #10368);
- Global Forum for Media Development (GFMD, #10375);
- Global Forum on Human Settlements (GFHS, #10372);
- Global Foundation for Democracy and Development (GFDD);
- Global Fund for Widows;
- Global Health Awareness Research Foundation (GHARF);
- Global Health Foundation (GHF);
- Global Health Partners (GHP);
- Global Hope Network International (GHNI, #10411);
- Global Housing Foundation (GHF);
- Global Human Rights Defence (GHRD);
- Global Initiative for Economic, Social and Cultural Rights (GI-ESCR);
- Global Initiative for Inclusive Information and Communication Technologies (G3ict, #10425);
- Global Institute for Water, Environment and Health (GIWEH, #10429);
- Global Justice Center (GJC);
- Global LPG Partnership (GLPGP, #10461);
- Global Mayors' Forum (GMF, #10467);
- Global Medicare Foundation (GMF);
- Global Migration Policy Associates (GMPA, #10473);
- Global Millennium Development Foundation (GMDF, no recent information);
- Global Millennium International NGO;
- Global Ministries of The United Methodist Church (GM-UMC);
- Global Network of Civil Society Organizations for Disaster Reduction (GNDR, #10485);
- Global Network of People Living with HIV/AIDS (GNP+, #10494);
- Global Network of Sex Work Projects (NSWP, #10498);
- Global New Car Assessment Programme (Global NCAP, #10506);
- Global Organization of Parliamentarians Against Corruption (GOPAC, #10518);
- Global Partnership for Local Action (GP 4 LA);
- GlobalPartnersUnited (GPU);
- Global Peace Development Organization (GPDO);
- Global Policy Forum (GPF);
- Global Political Trends Center (GPoT);
- Global Reporting Initiative (GRI, #10567);
- Global Sourcing Council (GSC);
- Global Utmaning;
- Global Voices;
- Global Volunteers;
- Global Wind Energy Council (GWEC, #10656);
- Global Witness (GW);
- Global Youth Action Network (GYAN);
- Global Zero (GZ, #10666);
- Globe Aware;
- GLOBE International (#10668);
- Globethics.net Foundation (#10669);
- Globetree Foundation;
- Goi Peace Foundation;
- Good Helpers;
- Good People International (GPI);
- Graduate Women International (GWI, #10688);
- Grassroots Organizations Operating Together in Sisterhood (GROOTS);
- Great Africa Youth Empowerment and Development Initiative (GAYEDI);
- Greek Council for Refugees (GCR);
- Green Asia Network (GAN);
- GS1 (#10809);

- Guerrand-Hermès Foundation for Peace (#10815);
- Gulf Research Centre;
- Guttmacher Institute;
- Habitat for Humanity International (HFHI);
- Habitat International Coalition (HIC, #10845);
- Hadassah;
- Harm Reduction International (HRI, #10861);
- Healey International Relief Foundation (HealeyIRF);
- Health and Global Policy Institute (HGPI);
- Heal The Planet – Global Organisation (HTP);
- HealthNet TPO;
- Health of Mother Earth Foundation (HOMEF);
- Health On the Net Foundation (HON, #10887);
- Healthy Caribbean Coalition (HCC, #10893);
- Heavenly Culture, World Peace, Restoration of Light (HWPL);
- Help for Children in Need (KNH);
- Help for the Andes Foundation;
- Heritage Foundation;
- HIAS;
- Himalayan Research and Cultural Foundation (no recent information);
- Holt International;
- Hope for Africa (HFA);
- Hope Worldwide;
- Horn of Africa Aid and Rehabilitation Action Network (HAARAN);
- Horn of Africa Voluntary Youth Committee (HAVOYOCO);
- Hostelling International (#10950);
- House of Jacobs International;
- Howard Center for Family, Religion and Society;
- Howard League for Penal Reform;
- Huairou Commission (#10960);
- Human Appeal (#10961);
- Human Dignity (HD, #10965);
- Humanic Relief;
- Humanistisch Instituut voor Ontwikkelingssamenwerking (Hivos);
- Humanists International (#10972);
- Humanitarian Aid Network for Distribution (Global Hand);
- Humanity and Inclusion (HI, #10975);
- Human Life International (HLI, #10977);
- Human Relief Foundation (HRF);
- Human Rights Advocates (HRA);
- Human Rights Council of Australia;
- Human Rights First;
- Human Rights Information and Documentation Systems, International (HURIDOCS, #10985);
- Human Rights Now (HRN);
- Human Rights Watch (HRW, #10990);
- IBON International (#11037);
- IBREA Foundation;
- IDEAS Centre;
- Ihsan Foundation for West Africa;
- ILGA World (International Lesbian, Gay, Bisexual, Trans and Intersex Association, #11120);
- Imamia Medics International (IMI);
- IMPACT (#11136);
- IMPACT Initiatives;
- Inclusion International (#11145);
- Indigenous Peoples' International Centre for Policy Research and Education (Tebtebba Foundation);
- Indigenous Peoples of Africa Coordinating Committee (IPACC, #11163);
- Indigenous Peoples Survival Foundation (IPSF);
- Indigenous World Association (#11166);
- Indo-European Chamber of Commerce and Industry (IECCI);
- Ingénieurs du monde (IdM);
- Initiative: Eau;
- Initiative for Equality (IfE);
- Initiative for the Development of Africa (IDA);
- Initiatives of Change International – Caux (IofC, #11213);
- Initiatives, Researches, Experiences for a New Europe (Association IRENE);
- Institut Destrée;
- Institut du développement durable et des relations internationales (IDDRI);
- Institute for Agriculture and Trade Policy (IATP);
- Institute for Conscious Global Change (ICGC);
- Institute for Economics and Peace (IEP, #11257);
- Institute for Global Environmental Strategies (IGES, #11266);
- Institute for Human Rights and Business (IHRB);
- Institute for International Urban Development (I2UD);
- Institute for International Women's Rights – Manitoba (IIWR-MB);
- Institute for Policy Studies, Washington DC (IPS);
- Institute of Asian Culture and Development (IACD);
- Institute of Cultural Affairs International (ICAI, #11251);
- Institute of Global Education;
- Institute of International Social Development (IISD, no recent information);
- Institute of Social Studies Trust (no recent information);
- Institute of the Blessed Virgin Mary, Irish Branch (Loreto);
- Institute on Human Rights and the Holocaust;
- Institut International de l'Écologie Industrielle et de l'Économie Verte (2ie);
- Instituto del Tercer Mundo, Montevideo (ITEM);
- Inter-African Committee on Traditional Practices Affecting the Health of Women and Children (IAC, #11384);
- Interamerican Association for Environmental Defense (#11398);
- Inter-American Housing Union (#11433);
- Inter American Press Association (IAPA, #11444);
- Inter-American Statistical Institute (IASI, #11452);
- Intercontinental Network for the Promotion of the Social Solidarity Economy (INPSSE, #11463);
- International Academy of Architecture (IAA, #11535);
- International Academy of Ecology and Life Protection Sciences (IAELPS);
- International Academy of Environmental Sanitation and Public Health (IAES and PH);
- International Accountability Project (IAP);
- International Action Network on Small Arms (IANSA, #11585);
- International Administrative Science Association (IASA);
- International AIDS Society (IAS, #11601);
- International Alert (#11615);
- International Alliance for Responsible Drinking (IARD, #11638);
- International Alliance of Carer Organizations (IACO, #11623);
- International Alliance of Patients' Organizations (IAPO, #11633);
- International Architects, Designers, Planners for Social Responsibility (ARC-PEACE, #11666);
- International Art and Technology Cooperation Organization (ArTech, no recent information);
- International Association Against Painful Experiments on Animals (IAAPEA, #11694);
- International Association Against Torture (IAAT, no recent information);
- International Association for Democracy in Africa (#11836);
- International Association for Hospice and Palliative Care (IAHPC, #11941);
- International Association for Humanitarian Medicine Chisholm-Gunn (IAHM, #11946);
- International Association for Human Values (IAHV, #11947);
- International Association for Integration, Dignity and Economic Advancement (IDEA, #11967);
- International Association for Media and Communication Research (IAMCR, #12022);
- International Association for the Advancement of Innovative Approaches to Global Challenges (IAAI, #11687);
- International Association for the Advancement of Space Safety (IAASS, #11689);
- International Association for Volunteer Effort (IAVE, #12260);
- International Association for Water Law (#12263);
- International Association for Women's Mental Health (IAWMH, #12272);
- International Association IUS Primi Viri (IPV);
- International Association of Applied Psychology (IAAP, #11705);
- International Association of Democratic Lawyers (IADL, #11837);
- International Association of Free Thought (AIFT, #11906);

- International Association of Gerontology and Geriatrics (IAGG, #11920);
- International Association of Homes and Services for the Ageing (IAHSA, #11938);
- International Association of Independent Journalists (IAIJ);
- International Association of Jewish Lawyers and Jurists (IJL, #11977);
- International Association of Judges (IAJ, #11978);
- International Association of Lawyers Against Nuclear Arms (IALANA, #11994);
- International Association of Peace Messenger Cities (IAPMC, #12073);
- International Association of Penal Law (IAPL, #12074);
- International Association of Ports and Harbors (IAPH, #12096);
- International Association of Public Transport (#12118);
- International Association of Schools of Social Work (IASSW, #12149);
- International Association of Technical Survey and Classification Institutions (TSCI, #12223);
- International Association of University Presidents (IAUP, #12248);
- International Association of Women in Radio and Television (IAWRT, #12271);
- International Association of Women Judges (IAWJ, #12267);
- International Authors Forum (IAF, #12298);
- International Automotive Lighting and Light Signalling Expert Group (GTB, #12301);
- International Bar Association (IBA, #12320);
- International Black Sea Club (IBSC, #12358);
- International Black Women for Wages for Housework (no recent information);
- International Blue Crescent (IBC);
- International Blue Cross (IBC, #12364);
- International Breathwork Foundation (IBF, #12396);
- International Bridges to Justice;
- International Buddhist Relief Organization (IBRO);
- International Bureau for Epilepsy (IBE, #12414);
- International Cable Protection Committee (ICPC, #12423);
- International Campaign to Ban Landmines (ICBL, inactive);
- International Career Support Association (ICSA);
- International Catholic Child Bureau (#12450);
- International Catholic Migration Commission (ICMC, #12459);
- International Center for Advocates Against Discrimination (ICAAD);
- International Center for Ethnobotanical Education Research and Service (ICEERS, #12469);
- International Center for Ethno-Religious Mediation (ICERM);
- International Center for Not-for-Profit Law (ICNL, #12471);
- International Center for Work and Family (ICWF);
- International Centre for Development Initiatives (ICDI);
- International Centre for Environmental Education and Community Development (ICENECDEV);
- International Centre for Missing and Exploited Children (ICMEC, #12505);
- International Centre for Trade and Sustainable Development, Geneva (ICTSD, #12524);
- International Centre for Women and Child (ICWC);
- International Centre of the Roerichs (ICR);
- International Chamber of Shipping (ICS, #12535);
- International Christian Organisation of the Media (ICOM, #12563);
- International Civil Society Centre (#12589);
- International Civil Society Support (ICSS);
- International Coalition of Sites of Conscience (ICSC, #12621);
- International Coalition to Ban Uranium Weapons (ICBUW, #12609);
- International Coastal and Ocean Organization (ICO, #12625);
- International Commission of Catholic Prison Pastoral Care (ICCPPC, #12670);
- International Commission on Irrigation and Drainage (ICID, #12694);
- International Committee for the Indigenous Peoples of the Americas (Incomindios);
- International Confederation of Christian Family Movements (ICCFM, #12851);
- International Confederation of the Society of St Vincent-de-Paul (#12870);
- International Congo Aid-Smile African Children (ICASAC);
- International Coordination Council of Educational Institutions Alumni (INCORVUZ-XXI, #12959);
- International Corrections and Prisons Association for the Advancement of Professional Corrections (ICPA, #12970);
- International Council for Caring Communities (ICCC);
- International Council for Education of People with Visual Impairment (ICEVI, #13015);
- International Council for Game and Wildlife Conservation (#13024);
- International Council for Research and Innovation in Building and Construction (CIB, #13069);
- International Council for Russian Compatriots;
- International Council for the Day of VESAK (ICDV, #13012);
- International Council of Academies of Engineering and Technological Sciences (CAETS, #12982);
- International Council of Chemical Associations (ICCA, #13003);
- International Council of Jewish Women (ICJW, #13036);
- International Council of Psychologists (ICP, #13065);
- International Council on Alcohol and Addictions (ICAA, #12989);
- International Council on Clean Transportation (ICCT, #13007);
- International Council on Jewish Social and Welfare Services (INTERCO, #13035);
- International Council Supporting Fair Trial and Human Rights (ICSFT, #13081);
- International Detention Coalition (IDC, #13154);
- International Development Enterprises (IDE, #13156);
- International Dialogue for Environmental Action (IDEA);
- International Disability Alliance (IDA, #13176);
- International Doctors for Healthier Drug Policies (IDHDP);
- International Drug Policy Consortium (IDPC, #13205);
- International Ecological Safety Collaborative Organization (UN-IESCO, #13221);
- International Emergency and Development Aid (IEDA Relief);
- International Environmental Law Research Centre (IELRC);
- International Falcon Movement – Socialist Educational International (IFM-SEI, #13327);
- International Family Forestry Alliance (IFFA, #13329);
- International Family Therapy Association (IFTA, #13331);
- International Federation for Home Economics (IFHE, #13447);
- International Federation for Housing and Planning (IFHP, #13450);
- International Federation for Human Rights (#13452);
- International Federation for Peace and Sustainable Development (IFPSD);
- International Federation for Spina Bifida and Hydrocephalus (IF SBH, #13552);
- International Federation of ACATs – Action by Christians for the Abolition of Torture (#13334);
- International Federation of Anti-Leprosy Associations (ILEP, #13355);
- International Federation of Beekeepers' Associations (APIMONDIA, #13370);
- International Federation of Blood Donor Organizations (IFBDO, #13374);
- International Federation of Coalitions for Cultural Diversity (IFCCD, #13394);
- International Federation of Fe y Alegria (FIFyA, #13425);
- International Federation of Hard of Hearing People (IFHOH, #13435);
- International Federation of Inventors' Associations (IFIA, #13461);
- International Federation of Journalists (IFJ, #13462);
- International Federation of Liberal Youth (IFLRY, #13469);
- International Federation of Medical Students' Associations (IFMSA, #13478);
- International Federation of Multimedia Associations (IFMA, #13483);
- International Federation of Private Water Operators (AquaFed, #13517);
- International Federation of Psoriasis Associations (IFPA, #13520);
- International Federation of Social Workers (IFSW, #13544);
- International Federation of Training and Development Organizations (IFTDO, #13573);
- International Federation of Translators (#13574);
- International Federation of Women in Legal Careers (IFWLC, #13579);
- International Federation of Women Lawyers (FIDA, #13578);
- International Fellowship of Reconciliation (IFOR, #13586);
- International First Aid Society (IFAS, no recent information);
- International Food and Beverage Alliance (IFBA, #13620);
- International Forestry Students' Association (IFSA, #13628);
- International Forum for Child Welfare (IFCW, #13633);
- International Foundation for Electoral Systems (IFES, #13669);
- International Fund for Animal Welfare (IFAW, #13693);
- International Geothermal Association (IGA, #13717);
- International Health Council;
- International Higher Education Teaching and Learning Association (HETL, #13795);
- International Housing Coalition (IHC Global);
- International Human Rights Council;
- International Human Rights Observer (IHRO);

– *International Human Rights Protector's Group (IHRPG);*
– *International Initiative for Peace (IIP);*
– *International Institute for Human Rights, Environment and Development (INHURED International, #13886);*
– *International Institute for Middle East and Balkan Studies (IFIMES, #13901);*
– *International Institute for Rights and Development-Geneva (IRD-Geneva);*
– *International Institute for the Rights of the Child (IDE);*
– *International Institute of Humanitarian Law (IIHL, #13885);*
– *International Institute of Space Law (IISL, #13926);*
– *International Investment Centre (IIC);*
– *International Islamic Relief Organization (IIRO);*
– *International Jurist Organization (IJO, #13979);*
– *International Justice Resource Center (IJRC);*
– *International Juvenile Justice Observatory (IJJO);*
– *International Lactation Consultant Association (ILCA);*
– *International Law Association (ILA, #14003);*
– *International-Lawyers.Org (INTLawyers, #14008);*
– *International League Against Racism and Antisemitism (#14014);*
– *International Legal Foundation (ILF, #14026);*
– *International Longevity Centre Global Alliance (ILC Global Alliance, #14064);*
– *International Mahavira Jain Mission (IMJM);*
– *International Mediation Institute (IMI, #14129);*
– *International Motor Vehicle Inspection Committee (CITA, #14187);*
– *International Movement for Advancement of Education Culture Social and Economic Development (IMAECSED);*
– *International Multiracial Shared Cultural Organization (IMSCO);*
– *International Native Tradition Interchange, New York (INTI, no recent information);*
– *International Network for Small and Medium Sized Enterprises (INSME, #14325);*
– *International Network for Standardization of Higher Education Degrees (INSHED, #14329);*
– *International Network for Sustainable Energy (INFORSE, #14331);*
– *International Network for the Prevention of Elder Abuse (INPEA, #14307);*
– *International Network of Basin Organizations (INBO, #14235);*
– *International Network of Liberal Women (INLW, #14294);*
– *International Network of Museums for Peace (INMP, #14297);*
– *International Network of Women Engineers and Scientists (INWES, #14345);*
– *International NGO Forum on Indonesian Development (INFID, #14366);*
– *International Ocean Institute (IOI, #14394);*
– *International Organisation for Least Developed Countries (IOLDCs, #14430);*
– *International Organization for Educational Development (IOED);*
– *International Organization for Promoting Public Diplomacy, Science, Education and Youth Cooperation (Eurasian Commonwealth, #14464);*
– *International Organization for the Elimination of All Forms of Racial Discrimination (EAFORD, #14445);*
– *International Organization for the Right to Education and Freedom of Education (#14468);*
– *International Organization for Victim Assistance (IOVA);*
– *International Organization of Folk Art (IOV World, #14447);*
– *International Organization of Supreme Audit Institutions (INTOSAI, #14478);*
– *International Partnership for Human Rights (IPHR);*
– *International PEN (#14552);*
– *International Petroleum Industry Environmental Conservation Association (IPIECA, #14562);*
– *International Platform for Black, Migrant and Refugee Women's Organizations (TIYE International);*
– *International Police Association (IPA, #14612);*
– *International Police Executive Symposium (IPES, #14613);*
– *International Pollutants Elimination Network (IPEN, #14616);*
– *International Port Community Systems Association (IPCSA, #14623);*
– *International Presentation Association (IPA, #14635);*
– *International Press Institute (IPI, #14636);*
– *International Prison Chaplains' Association (IPCA, #14643);*
– *International Psychoanalytical Association (IPA, #14662);*
– *International Radio Emergency Support Coalition (IRESC, no recent information);*
– *International Rainwater Harvesting Alliance (IRHA, #14695);*
– *International Rehabilitation Council for Torture Victims (IRCT, #14712);*
– *International Religious Liberty Association (IRLA);*
– *International Rescue Committee (IRC, #14717);*
– *International Right of Way Association (IRWA);*
– *International Risk Governance Council (IRGC, #14756);*
– *International Road Assessment Programme (iRAP, #14757);*
– *International Road Federation (IRF, #14758);*
– *International Romani Union (IRU, #14765);*
– *International Science Council (ISC, #14796);*
– *International Seafood Sustainability Foundation (ISSF);*
– *International Service for Human Rights (ISHR, #14841);*
– *International Shinto Foundation (ISF);*
– *International Social Service (ISS, #14886);*
– *International Society for Augmentative and Alternative Communication (ISAAC, #14949);*
– *International Society for Krishna Consciousness (ISKCON);*
– *International Society for Prosthetics and Orthotics (ISPO, #15390);*
– *International Society for Small and Medium Enterprises (ISSME, #15446);*
– *International Society for the Study of Trauma and Dissociation (ISSTD, #15488);*
– *International Society of Doctors for the Environment (ISDE, #15065);*
– *International Sociological Association (ISA, #15553);*
– *International Solidarity and Human Rights Institute (ISHRI);*
– *International Statistical Institute (ISI, #15603);*
– *International Supporting Association for War Victims (ISAWV);*
– *International Telecommunication Academy (ITA, no recent information);*
– *International Trademark Association (INTA, #15706);*
– *International Tunnelling and Underground Space Association (ITA, #15744);*
– *International Union for Land Value Taxation and Free Trade (The IU, #15787);*
– *International Union for the Scientific Study of Population (IUSSP, #15814);*
– *International Union of Judicial Officers (#15785);*
– *International Union of Notaries (#15795);*
– *International Union of Psychological Science (IUPsyS, #15807);*
– *International Union of Railways (#15813);*
– *International Union of Socialist Youth (IUSY, #15815);*
– *International Veterinary Students' Association (IVSA, #15851);*
– *International Voice of Justice (IVOJ);*
– *International Women and Family Foundation (IWFF);*
– *International Women Bond (no recent information);*
– *International Women's Convocation (IWC, #15896);*
– *International Women's Democracy Center (IWDC);*
– *International Women's Forum (IWF, #15899);*
– *International Women's Health Coalition (IWHC);*
– *International Women's Peace Group (IWPG);*
– *International Women's Rights Action Watch Asia Pacific (IWRAW Asia Pacific, #15902);*
– *International Women's Writing Guild (IWWG);*
– *International Women's Year Liaison Group (no recent information);*
– *International Work Group for Indigenous Affairs (IWGIA, #15907);*
– *International Young Professionals Foundation (IYPF, #15930);*
– *International Youth Aid Council (Iyaco);*
– *Internet Society (ISOC, #15952);*
– *Interpeace (#15962);*
– *Interregional Union of Life Help for Mentally Handicapped Persons (Sail of Hope);*
– *Intersections International;*
– *INTERSOS;*
– *Inuit Circumpolar Council (ICC, #15995);*
– *IPAS (#16010);*
– *Isis Women's International Cross Cultural Exchange (ISIS-WICCE, #16031);*
– *Islamic Chamber Research and Information Center (ICRIC, #16037);*
– *Islamic Human Rights Commission (IHRC);*
– *Islamic Relief Worldwide (IRWW, #16048);*
– *Islamic Research and Information Center (IRIC);*
– *Istituto Internazionale Maria Ausiliatrice delle Salesiane di Don Bosco (IIMA);*
– *Istituto per la Cooperazione Economica Internazionale e i Problemi dello Sviluppo (ICEPS);*
– *Italian Association for Women in Development ONLUS (AIDOS);*
– *Italian Centre of Solidarity (CeIS);*
– *Japan Council against A and H Bombs;*
– *Japanese Association of International Women's Rights (JAIWR, no recent information);*
– *Japanese NGO Center for International Cooperation (JANIC);*
– *Japanese Organization for International Cooperation in Family Planning (JOICFP);*
– *Japan Overseas Cooperative Association (JOCA);*
– *Jesuit Refugee Service (JRS, #16106);*
– *Jewish Voice Ministries International (JMVI);*
– *Joan B Kroc Institute for Peace and Justice (IPJ);*
– *Jubilee Debt Campaign;*
– *Justice and Peace Netherlands;*
– *Justice in Motion;*
– *Kataliko Action for Africa (KAF);*
– *Keeping Children Safe;*
– *Keystone Human Services International (KHSI);*
– *KidsRights;*
– *Kitakyushu Forum on Asian Women (KFAW);*
– *Kiwanis International (#16195);*
– *KOLPING INTERNATIONAL (#16203);*
– *Konrad Adenauer Foundation (KAF);*
– *Korea Civil Society Forum on International Development Cooperation (KoFID);*
– *Korea International Volunteer Organization (KVO International);*
– *Korean Foundation for World Aid;*
– *Korea NGO Council for Overseas Development Cooperation (KCOC);*
– *Kvinna till Kvinna Foundation;*
– *La Brique;*
– *Lama Gangchen World Peace Foundation (LGWPF, #16223);*
– *La Strada International (LSI, #20002);*
– *Latin American Blind Union (#16256);*
– *LAWASIA – Law Association for Asia and the Pacific (#16406);*
– *Lawyers for Lawyers Foundation (L4L);*
– *Lawyers' Rights Watch Canada (LRWC);*
– *LDC Watch (#16412);*
– *Leadership for Environment and Development (LEAD International, #16416);*
– *Leadership Initiative for Transformation and Empowerment (LITE-Africa);*
– *League of European Research Universities (LERU, #16423);*
– *Leonard Cheshire Disability (#16443);*
– *Leprosy Mission International (TLMI, #16446);*
– *Life for Relief and Development;*
– *Local Governments for Sustainability (ICLEI, #16507);*
– *Lotus World;*
– *Ludwig Boltzmann Institut für Grund- und Menschenrechte (LBI);*
– *Lumos Foundation;*
– *Maat for Peace, Development, and Human Rights;*
– *MacArthur Foundation;*
– *MADRE;*
– *Major Groups Partnership on Forests (MGPoF, #16553);*
– *Malteser International;*
– *Management Sciences for Health (MSH);*
– *Mandat International;*
– *Marangopoulos Foundation for Human Rights (MFHR);*
– *Maryknoll Sisters of Saint Dominic;*
– *MaterCare International (MCI, #16597);*
– *Mayors for Peace (#16605);*
– *Mediators Beyond Borders International (MBB);*
– *Medical Aid for Palestinians (MAP);*
– *Medical Mission Sisters;*
– *Medical Women's International Association (MWIA, #16630);*
– *Medico International;*
– *Mediterranean Information Office for Environment, Culture and Sustainable Development (MIO-ECSDE, #16657);*
– *Mennonite Central Committee (MCC);*
– *Mentor International (MI, #16716);*
– *Mercy Corps International (MCI);*
– *Mercy-USA for Aid and Development (MUSA);*
– *Microclinic International (MCI);*
– *Migrant Forum in Asia (MFA, #16798);*
– *Migrants Rights International (MRI, #16799);*
– *Migratory Wildlife Network (Wild Migration);*
– *Millennium Institute;*
– *Millennium Promise Alliance (MPA, #16806);*
– *Minhaj-ul-Quran International (no recent information);*
– *Minority Rights Group International (MRG, #16820);*
– *Miracle Corners of the World (MCW);*
– *Mission International Rescue Foundation (MIR Foundation);*
– *Mobility International USA (MIUSA);*
– *Mont-Blanc Meetings (MBM, #16850);*
– *Mother Child Education Foundation (ACEV);*
– *Mothers Legacy Project;*
– *Mountain Institute, The (TMI);*
– *Mouvement international d'apostolat des milieux sociaux indépendants (MIAMSI, #16864);*
– *Movement for a Better World (MBW, #16869);*
– *Movendi International (#16871);*
– *Muslim Women Lawyers for Human Rights (KARAMAH);*
– *Naija Worldwide Charities (NWC);*
– *Narcotics Anonymous (NA, #16936);*
– *Netherlands Centre for Indigenous Peoples (NCIV);*
– *New Human Rights – International (#17089);*
– *New Reality International (NRI);*
– *New Vision International (NVI);*
– *NGO Health Committee;*
– *NGO Sustainability;*
– *Nightingale Initiative for Global Health (NIGH World, #17136);*
– *Nippon International Cooperation for Community Development (NICCO);*
– *Nobre Ordem Para Excelência Humana (NOHE INTERNACIONAL);*
– *Non-Aligned Students, Youth and Civil Societies Organization (NASYO, #17148);*
– *Nonviolence International (NI, #17152);*
– *Nonviolent Peaceforce (NP, #17153);*
– *North-South Economic and Cultural Development Agency (ADEC-NS);*
– *North-South XXI (inactive);*
– *Norwegian People's Aid (NPA);*
– *Novartis Foundation;*
– *Nutrition and Education International (NEI);*
– *Objectif Sciences International (OSI, #17632);*
– *Observatoire international pour la non violence;*
– *Observatory for Cultural and Audio-Visual Communication in the Mediterranean (OCCAM, #17643);*
– *OceanCare;*
– *Ocean Lifeline (OLL);*
– *Ocean Policy Research Institute (OPRI);*
– *Ocean Sanctuary Alliance (OSA, #17687);*
– *Oil Change International;*
– *OISTE Foundation;*
– *Open City International Foundation (FOCA International, #17748);*
– *Open Data Watch (ODW);*
– *Operation Mercy;*
– *Operation Smile;*
– *Operation Underground Railroad (O.U.R.);*
– *Order of St John;*
– *Organisation camerounaise de promotion de la coopération économique internationale (OCAPROCE internationale);*
– *Organisation internationale pour la protection des animaux (OIPA, #17810);*

- Organisation Internationale pour l'Avancement Politique des Africaines (OIAPA);
- Organisation mondiale des anciens élèves de l'enseignement catholique (OMAEC, #17816);
- Organisation mondiale des associations pour l'éducation prénatale (OMAEP, #17817);
- Organisation mondiale des experts-conseils-arbitres (OMECA);
- Organisation non Gouvernementale des Cercles Nationaux de Réflexion sur la Jeunesse (ONG CNRJ, #17821);
- Organización Continental Latinoamericana y Caribeña de Estudiantes (OCLAE, #17834);
- Organización de Entidades Mutuales de las Américas (ODEMA, #17836);
- Organización de Solidaridad de los Pueblos de Africa, Asia y América Latina (OSPAAAL, #17849);
- Organization Earth;
- Organization for Defending Victims of Violence (ODVV);
- Organization for International Economic Relations (OiER, #17873);
- Organization for Poverty Alleviation and Development (OPAD);
- Organization of the Families of Asia and the Pacific (OFAP, #17867);
- OutRight Action International;
- Overseas Development Institute (ODI);
- Oxfam GB;
- Oxfam Novib;
- P3 Foundation;
- Pacific Disability Forum (PDF, #17945);
- Pacific Rim Institute for Development and Education (PRIDE);
- Pacific Women's Watch – New Zealand (PWW-NZ);
- Pan African Institute for Entrepreneurship and Community Development (Pan African Institute);
- Panafrican Women Association (PAWA);
- Pan African Women's Organization (PAWO, #18074);
- Pan-American / Pan-African Association (PAPA, no recent information);
- Pan Pacific and South East Asia Women's Association (PPSEAWA, #18186);
- Parlement Africain de la Société Civile (PASOCI, #18207);
- Partnership for Change (PfC);
- Partnership for Global Justice;
- Partnership for Indigenous Peoples Environment (PIPE, no recent information);
- Passionists International (PI, #18254);
- PATH (#18260);
- Pathfinder International (#18261);
- PathFinders Justice Initiative (PJI);
- Pathways To Peace (PTP, #18262);
- Pax Christi – International Catholic Peace Movement (#18266);
- Pax Romana, International Catholic Movement for Intellectual and Cultural Affairs (ICMICA, #18267);
- Pax Romana, International Movement of Catholic Students (IMCS, #18268);
- Paz y Cooperación;
- Peace and Life Enhancement Initiative International (PLEII);
- Peace Boat;
- Peacebuilders International (PBI);
- Peace Child International (PCI, #18278);
- Peace Education Foundation (PEF);
- Peacemaker Corps Association;
- Peace Parks Foundation (#18281);
- Peace Worldwide;
- PEFC Council (#18288);
- Penal Reform International (PRI, #18290);
- People's Movement for Human Rights Learning (PDHRE, #18307);
- People to People International (PTPI, #18300);
- Perhaps Kids Meeting Kids can make a Difference (KMK);
- Permanent Assembly for Human Rights;
- Permanent Secretariat of the World Summit of Nobel Peace Laureates (#18332);
- Physicians for Human Rights, USA (PHR-USA);
- Pirate Parties International (PPI, #18374);
- Planetary Association for Clean Energy (PACE, #18381);
- Plateforme pour le Développement Durable des Caraïbes (PLAC 21, no recent information);
- Platform for International Cooperation on Undocumented Migrants (PICUM, #18401);
- Population Council (#18458);
- Positive Planet International (#18465);
- Prison Fellowship International (PFI, #18503);
- PROCLADE Internazionale Onlus (#18507);
- Profugo;
- Public Eye;
- Public International Law and Policy Group (PILPG);
- Public Services International (PSI, #18572);
- Pugwash Conferences on Science and World Affairs (#18574);
- Pure Earth (#18578);
- Rainforest Foundation International (RFI, #18615);
- Rainforest Fund (RFUND);
- Rare;
- Reach Out to Asia (ROTA);
- Red de Educación Popular entre Mujeres de América Latina y el Caribe (REPEM LAC, #18647);
- Red Iberoamericana de Organizaciones no Gubernamentales que Trabajan en Drogodependencias (RIOD, #18679);
- REDRESS;
- Refugee Council of Australia (RCOA);
- Regional Network of Local Authorities for the Management of Human Settlements (CITYNET, #18799);
- Relief International;
- Religious of the Sacred Heart of Mary (RSHM);
- Rencontre africaine pour la défense des droits de l'homme (RADDHO);
- Reporters sans frontières (RSF, #18846);
- Reprieve;
- Responding to Climate Change (RTCC);
- Restless Development;
- Restored;
- RET International (#18927);
- Right Livelihood Foundation (#18944);
- Right to Energy – SOS Future;
- Right to Play International (#18945);
- RI Global (#18948);
- RIPE Network Coordination Centre (RIPE NCC, #18951);
- Rissho Kosei-Kai (RKK);
- Robert F Kennedy Human Rights;
- ROKPA INTERNATIONAL (#18967);
- Rooftops Canada;
- Royal Academy of Science International Trust (RASIT);
- Royal Institution of Chartered Surveyors (RICS, #18991);
- Rural Development Foundation Global (RDF Global);
- Russian Association of Indigenous Peoples of the North (RAIPON);
- Rutgers (#19011);
- Réseau des Femmes Africaines pour la Gestion Communautaire des forêts (REFACOF);
- Réseau des Organisations Féminines d'Afrique Francophone (ROFAF, #18900);
- Réseau des Plate-formes nationales d'ONG d'Afrique de l'Ouest et du Centre (REPAOC, #18902);
- Réseau International des Droits Humains (RIDH, #18891);
- Sabin Vaccine Institute (Sabin);
- SAE International;
- Safari Club International (SCI);
- Saferworld;
- Sakyadhita International Association of Buddhist Women (#19037);
- Salvation Army (#19041);
- SAMARITAN INTERNATIONAL (#19046);
- Samdong International (SDI);
- Saratoga Foundation for Women Worldwide;
- Sasakawa Peace Foundation (SPF);
- Scalabrini International Migration Network (SIMN, #19063);
- Scholars at Risk (SAR);
- School Sisters of Notre Dame (SSND);
- Schools Without Borders (SWB);
- SEALOEarth;

- Search for Common Ground (SFCG);
- Secure World Foundation (SWF);
- Service and Research Institute on Family and Children (SERFAC, #19243);
- Share International (#19257);
- Silambam Asia (#19276);
- SIL International (#19278);
- SIMAVI;
- Simon Wiesenthal Center (SWC);
- Simply Help;
- Singapore Institute of International Affairs (SIIA);
- Siracusa International Institute for Criminal Justice and Human Rights (SII, #19289);
- Sisterhood Is Global Institute (SIGI, #19298);
- Sisters of Mercy of the Americas;
- Sisters of Our Lady of Charity of the Good Shepherd;
- Sister to Sister International (STSI);
- Social Accountability International (SAI);
- Social Development International (SDI);
- Socialist International Women (SIW, #19341);
- Society for Nutrition Education and Behavior (SNEB, #19612);
- Society for Psychological Study of Social Issues (SPSSI);
- Society for the Protection of Human and Environmental Rights International (SPHER International);
- Society for the Protection of Unborn Children (SPUC);
- Society for Threatened Peoples International (STP International, #19654);
- Society of Research Administrators International (SRA);
- Soeurs de Notre-Dame de Namur (SNDN);
- Solar Cookers International (SCI, #19673);
- Solar Electric Light Fund (SELF);
- Solidaritetsaksjon for utvikling (FORUT);
- Soroptimist International of Europe (SI/E, #19689);
- Soroptimist International of Great Britain and Ireland (SIGBI, #19690);
- Soroptimist International South East Asia Pacific (SISEAP, #19691);
- SOS-Kinderdorf International (#19693);
- South Asian Forum for Environment (SAFE);
- South Caucasus Office on Drugs and Crime (SCODC, #19751);
- Sovereign Military Order of the Temple of Jerusalem (SMOTJ);
- Sozopol Foundation;
- Special Olympics International (SOI, #19910);
- SpellAfrica Initiative;
- Standing Voice;
- Stiftung Wissenschaft und Politik (SWP);
- St Joan's International Alliance (SJIA, #19992);
- Stockholm International Water Institute (SIWI);
- streetfootballworld (#20009);
- STUF United Fund;
- Surfrider Foundation Europe (#20041);
- Susila Dharma International Association (SDIA, #20048);
- Swedish Foundation for Human Rights (SFHR);
- Swisscontact – Swiss Foundation for Technical Cooperation;
- Swisspeace;
- Synergie Développement et Partenariat International (SYDEPI);
- SÜDWIND – Verein für Entwicklungspolitische Bildungs- und Öffentlichkeitsarbeit;
- Task Force for Global Health (TFGH, #20098);
- TB Alliance (#20103);
- Tchad Agir Pour l'Environnement (TCHAPE);
- Temple of Understanding (ToU, #20124);
- Teresian Association;
- Terra Renaissance;
- Terre des Hommes International Federation (TDHIF, #20133);
- Thalassaemia International Federation (#20139);
- The Anglican Patriarchate;
- The Brooke (#03338);
- The Carter Center;
- The Children's Project International (TCPI);
- The Dame Jane Foundation;
- The Eastern African Sub-Regional Support Initiative for the Advancement of Women (EASSI, #05225);
- The European Law Students' Association (ELSA, #07660);
- The Grail – International Movement of Christian Women (#10689);
- The Heart Fund (THF, no recent information);
- The International Movement Against All Forms of Discrimination and Racism (IMADR, #14191);
- The Lutheran World Federation (LWF, #16532);
- The Mothers' Union (#16860);
- The Nature Conservancy (TNC);
- The Next Century Foundation (NCF);
- The Reality Of Aid (ROA, #18626);
- The Rockefeller Foundation (#18966);
- The World Justice Project (WJP, #21605);
- Third World Network-Africa (TWN Africa);
- To Love Children Educational Foundation International;
- Traditions for Tomorrow (#20195);
- Transatlantic Christian Council (TCC);
- Transparency International (TI, #20223);
- TRIAL International;
- Tribal Link Foundation;
- TrustAfrica (#20251);
- Umut Foundation;
- UNANIMA International (#20281);
- Under The Same Sun (UTSS);
- Union for International Cancer Control (UICC, #20415);
- Union internationale des architectes (UIA, #20419);
- Union Internationale des Avocats (UIA, #20422);
- Union internationale des voyageurs;
- Union of Arab Doctors in Europe (#20352);
- Union of Arab Jurists (UAJ, #20354);
- Union of Ibero-American Capital Cities (#20412);
- Union of International Associations (UIA, #20414);
- Unis pour l'Equite et la Fin du Racisme (UFER, #20490);
- Unitarian Universalist Association (UUA, #20494);
- Unitarian Universalist Service Committee (UUSC);
- United Families International (UFI, #20508);
- UNITED for Intercultural Action – European Network Against Nationalism, Racism, Fascism and in Support of Migrants and Refugees (UNITED, #20511);
- United Help for International Children;
- United Nations Watch (UN Watch);
- United Network of Young Peacebuilders (UNOY, #20653);
- United Religions Initiative (URI, #20658);
- United States International Council on Disabilities (USICD);
- United Towns Agency for North-South Cooperation (no recent information);
- Universal Esperanto Association (UEA, #20676);
- Universal Great Brotherhood (UGB, #20677);
- Universalis Matter (UNIMATTER);
- Universal Networking Digital Language Foundation (UNDL Foundation, #20680);
- Universal Peace and Violence Amelioration Centre (UPVAC);
- Universal Rights Group (URG, #20683);
- Universitas 21 (#20690);
- Universities Allied for Essential Medicines (UAEM, #20692);
- Unspoken Smiles Foundation;
- UN Women for Peace Association (UNWFPA);
- UPR Info (#20727);
- Validity Foundation (#20743);
- Victim Support Europe (VSE, #20767);

– *Vie montante internationale (VMI, #20769);*
– *Vienna Economic Forum (VEF, #20770);*
– *Vienna Institute for International Dialogue and Cooperation (VIDC);*
– *Vienna NGO Committee on Drugs (VNGOC, #20773);*
– *Vier Pfoten International (#20776);*
– *Vision GRAM-International;*
– *Vital Strategies;*
– *Vital Voices Global Partnership (VVGP);*
– *Vitiligo Research Foundation (VR Foundation, #20799);*
– *VIVAT International (#20801);*
– *Voices of African Mothers (VAM);*
– *Volontariato Internazionale Donna Educazione Sviluppo (VIDES, #20806);*
– *Volontariato Internazionale per lo Sviluppo (VIS);*
– *Washington Office on Latin America (WOLA);*
– *WASH United;*
– *WaterAid (#20822);*
– *Water Environment Federation (WEF);*
– *WEConnect International;*
– *Welthungerhilfe;*
– *West Africa Centre for Peace Foundation (WACPF);*
– *West Africa Network for Peacebuilding (WANEP, #20878);*
– *Widows Rights International (WRI);*
– *Wildlife Conservation Society (WCS);*
– *Womankind Worldwide (#20982);*
– *Women Against Violence Europe (WAVE, #20986);*
– *Women Deliver (#20989);*
– *Women Enabled International (WEI, #20991);*
– *Women Engage for a Common Future (WECF, #20992);*
– *Women First International Fund (#20996);*
– *Women for Water Partnership (WfWP, #21041);*
– *Women for Women International (WFWI);*
– *Women in Dialogue (WinD);*
– *Women in Informal Employment: Globalizing and Organizing (WIEGO, #21003);*
– *Women in Law and Development in Africa-Afrique de l'Ouest (WiLDAF-AO, #21005);*
– *Women's Global Network for Reproductive Rights (WGNRR, #21019);*
– *Women's Home and Overseas Missionary Society (WHOMS);*
– *Women's Human Rights International Association (WHRIA);*
– *Women's Intercultural Network (WIN);*
– *Women's International League for Peace and Freedom (WILPF, #21024);*
– *Women's International Zionist Organization (WIZO, #21030);*
– *Women's Learning Partnership for Rights, Development and Peace (WLP, #21031);*
– *Women's Missionary Society – African Methodist Episcopal Church (WMS);*
– *WomenSport International (WSI, #21033);*
– *Women's Voices Now (WVN);*
– *Women's World Banking (WWB, #21037);*
– *Women's World Summit Foundation (WWSF, #21038);*
– *Women@theTable (w@tt);*
– *Women Watch Afrika (WWA);*
– *Woodenfish Foundation;*
– *World Academy of Art and Science (WAAS, #21065);*
– *World Alliance for Breastfeeding Action (WABA, #21079);*
– *World Alliance of Young Men's Christian Associations (YMCA, #21090);*
– *World Assembly of Youth (WAY, #21113);*
– *World Association for Supported Employment (WASE, #21195);*
– *World Association of Former United Nations Internes and Fellows (WAFUNIF, #21141);*
– *World Association of Industrial and Technological Research Organizations (WAITRO, #21145);*
– *World Association of Psychoanalysis (WAP, #21177);*
– *World Childhood Foundation (#21272);*
– *World Coal Association (WCA, #21280);*
– *World Congress of Mountain Jews (WCMJ);*
– *World Council for Curriculum and Instruction (WCCI, #21325);*
– *World Council for Psychotherapy (WCP, #21337);*
– *World Council of Arameans – Syriacs (WCA, #21318);*
– *World Council of Independent Christian Churches (WCICC, #21330);*
– *World Design Organization (WDO, #21358);*
– *World Education Foundation (WE Foundation);*
– *World Evangelical Alliance (WEA, #21393);*
– *World Family of Radio Maria (WF, #21400);*
– *World Farmers' Organisation (WFO, #21401);*
– *World Federalist Movement – Movement for a Just World Order through a Strengthened United Nations (WFM, #21404);*
– *World Federation Against Drugs (WFAD, #21408);*
– *World Federation for Mental Health (WFMH, #21455);*
– *World Federation for the Treatment of Opioid Dependence (WFTOD, #21495);*
– *World Federation of Consuls (FICAC, #21422);*
– *World Federation of Khoja Shia Ithna-Asheri Muslim Communities (World Federation of KSIMC, #21449);*
– *World Federation of Methodist and Uniting Church Women (WFM and UCW, #21457);*
– *World Federation of the Deafblind (WFDB, #21426);*
– *World Federation of the Deaf (WFD, #21425);*
– *World Federation of Therapeutic Communities (WFTC, #21491);*
– *World Federation of Ukrainian Women's Organizations (WFUWO, #21496);*
– *World Forum for Ethics in Business (WFEB, #21516);*
– *World for World Organization (WFWO);*
– *World Fund for Development and Planning (WFDP, #21531);*
– *World Future Council Foundation (WFC, #21533);*
– *World Futures Studies Federation (WFSF, #21535);*
– *World Habitat;*
– *World Hepatitis Alliance (WHA, #21564);*
– *World Human Dimension (WHD);*
– *World Hunger Education Service (WHES);*
– *World Igbo Congress (WIC);*
– *World Jewish Congress (WJC, #21599);*
– *World Jewish Relief (WJR, #21600);*
– *World Jurist Association (WJA, #21604);*
– *World Kabaddi Federation (WKF, #21606);*
– *World Leadership Alliance – Club de Madrid (WLA-CdM, #21619);*
– *World Lebanese Cultural Union (WLCU, #21622);*
– *World Leisure Organization (WLO, #21624);*
– *World Martial Arts Union (WoMAU, #21638);*
– *World Mission Foundation;*
– *World Network of Users and Survivors of Psychiatry (WNUSP, #21672);*
– *World Ocean Network (WON, #21681);*
– *World Organisation Against Torture (OMCT, #21685);*
– *World Organization for Early Childhood Education (OMEP, #21689);*
– *World Organization of Building Officials (WOBO, #21687);*
– *World Organization – Ovulation Method – Billings (WOOMB-International, #21692);*
– *World ORT (WO, #21698);*
– *World Peace Volunteers (WPV);*
– *World Protection for Dogs and Cats in the Meat Trade (NoToDogMeat);*
– *World Rehabilitation Fund (WRF, #21749);*
– *World Resources Institute (WRI, #21753);*
– *World Road Association (PIARC, #21754);*
– *World Russian People's Council (WRPC);*
– *World Safety Organization (WSO, #21759);*
– *Worldshare;*
– *World Shelter Organization;*
– *World Society of Victimology (WSV, #21815);*
– *World Space Week Association (WSWA);*
– *World Stroke Organization (WSO, #21831);*
– *World Student Christian Federation (WSCF, #21833);*
– *World's Woman's Christian Temperance Union (WWCTU, #21840);*
– *World Toilet Organization (WTO, #21854);*
– *World Trade Centers Association (WTCA, #21862);*
– *World Union of Catholic Women's Organisations (WUCWO, #21876);*
– *World Union of Small and Medium Enterprises (WUSME, #21886);*
– *World Water Council (WWC, #21908);*
– *World Welfare Association (WWA);*
– *Worldwide Coalition for Peace;*
– *Worldwide Hospice Palliative Care Alliance (WHPCA, #21924);*
– *Worldwide Network of the Experiment in International Living (Federation EIL, #21930);*
– *Worldwide Organization for Women (WOW);*
– *World Wide Web Foundation (#21936);*
– *World Wind Energy Association (WWEA, #21937);*
– *World Young Women's Christian Association (World YWCA, #21947);*
– *World Youth Alliance (WYA, #21949);*
– *World Youth Foundation (WYF);*
– *Yachay Wasi (#21970);*
– *Young African Leaders Initiative (YALI);*
– *Young Global Leadership Foundation (YGLF);*
– *Young People We Care (YPWC);*
– *Youth Afrique Leadership Forum;*
– *Youth Alliance for Leadership and Development in Africa (YALDA, #22004);*
– *Youth Coalition (YCSRR, #22011);*
– *Youth for Transparency International (YTI);*
– *Youth of European Nationalities (YEN, #22013);*
– *Youth Organisations for Drug Action (YODA, #22023);*
– *Youth with a Mission (YWAM, #22020);*
– *Y's Men International (#19326);*
– *ZOA;*
– *Åland Islands Peace Institute.*

Roster (604):

– *3HO Foundation (#22046);*
– *Accademia Internazionale d'Arte Moderna (AIAM);*
– *Action Group on Erosion, Technology and Concentration (ETC Group, #00091);*
– *Aerospace Medical Association (ASMA);*
– *Africa Genetics Association (inactive);*
– *African-American Society for Humanitarian Aid and Development (ASHAD);*
– *African Rural and Agricultural Credit Association (AFRACA, #00446);*
– *Agence universitaire de La Francophonie (AUF, #00548);*
– *Agri-Energy Roundtable (AER);*
– *Alliance Toward Harnessing Global Opportunities Corporation (ATHGO International);*
– *All-Russia Market Research Institute (VNIKI);*
– *Altrusa International (AI, #00757);*
– *American Association for the Advancement of Science (AAAS);*
– *American Fisheries Society (AFS);*
– *American Foreign Insurance Association (AFIA, no recent information);*
– *American Foreign Law Association (AFLA);*
– *American Oil Chemists' Society (AOCS);*
– *American Society for Engineering Education (ASEE, #00790);*
– *Americas Society (AS);*
– *Amitiés sans frontières (no recent information);*
– *Amref Health Africa (#00806);*
– *AOAC INTERNATIONAL (#00863);*
– *Arab Federation for Engineering Industries (AFEI, #00943);*
– *Arab Federation for Food Industries (AFFI, #00946);*
– *Arab Fertilizer Association (AFA, #00958);*
– *Arab Iron and Steel Union (AISU, #00998);*
– *Arab NGO Network for Development (ANND, #01016);*
– *Arab Society for Intellectual Property (ASIP, #01046);*
– *Arab Urban Development Institute (AUDI, #01071);*
– *Armenian International Women's Association (AIWA);*
– *Armenian Relief Society (ARS, #01111);*
– *ARTICLE 19 (#01121);*
– *Asia Darshana;*
– *Asian Buddhist Conference for Peace (ABCP, no recent information);*
– *Asian Cultural Forum on Development Foundation (ACFOD, no recent information);*
– *Asian Environmental Society (AES, #01438);*
– *Asian Media Information and Communication Centre (AMIC, #01536);*
– *Asian Pacific Youth Forum (APYF, #01647);*
– *Asian Youth Council (AYC, #01788);*
– *Asia-Pacific Broadcasting Union (ABU, #01863);*
– *Asia Pacific Rural and Agricultural Credit Association (APRACA, #02019);*
– *Asia South Pacific Association for Basic and Adult Education (ASPBAE, #02098);*
– *Asociación Latinoamericana de Industrias Farmacéuticas (ALIFAR, #02232);*
– *Association Catholique Internationale de Services pour la Jeunesse Féminine (ACISJF/In Via, #02417);*
– *Association fonds d'aide internationale au développement;*
– *Association for the Promotion of the International Circulation of the Press (DISTRIPRESS, #02876);*
– *Association for World Education (AWE, #02983);*
– *Association internationale de la critique littéraire (AICL, #02679);*
– *Association internationale de linguistique appliquée (AILA, #02713);*
– *Association internationale des traducteurs de conférence (AITC, #02748);*
– *Association internationale des universités du troisième âge (AIUTA, #02749);*
– *Association mondiale des sciences de l'éducation (AMSE, #02811);*
– *Association of African Development Finance Institutions (AADFI, #02353);*
– *Association of African Universities (AAU, #02361);*
– *Association of Arab Universities (AARU, #02374);*
– *Association of Chartered Certified Accountants (ACCA);*
– *Association of Commonwealth Universities, The (ACU, #02440);*
– *Association of Geoscientists for International Development (AGID, #02623);*
– *Association of Power Utilities in Africa (APUA, #02867);*
– *Association of World Citizens (AWC, #02982);*
– *Austrian Senior Experts Pool (ASEP);*
– *Austrian Society for Environment and Technology (ÖGUT);*
– *Battelle Memorial Institute (BMI, #03187);*
– *BIMCO (#03236);*
– *BirdLife International (#03266);*
– *B'nai B'rith International (BBI, #03290);*
– *Build Europe (#03350);*
– *Bureau of International Recycling (BIR, #03368);*
– *BUSINESSEUROPE (#03381);*
– *Business Humanitarian Forum (BHF, #03383);*
– *Cairo Regional Centre for International Commercial Arbitration (CRCICA, #03398);*
– *Caribbean Conservation Association (CCA, #03481);*
– *Caribbean Food Crops Society (CFCS, #03509);*
– *Carnegie Council for Ethics in International Affairs (CCEIA);*
– *Catholic International Union for Social Service (CIUSS, inactive);*
– *Celtic League (CL, #03633);*
– *Center for Development of International Law, New York (CDIL);*
– *Center for Health and Gender Equity (CHANGE);*
– *Center for International Environmental Law (CIEL);*
– *Center for Latin American Monetary Studies (#03648);*
– *Centre de coopération pour les recherches scientifiques relatives au tabac (CORESTA, #03735);*
– *Centre de recherche et d'information pour le développement, Paris (CRID);*
– *Centre for Studies on Asia and Oceania, Havana (CEAO);*
– *Centro de Derechos Humanos Miguel Agustin Pro Juarez (Centro Prodh);*
– *Childhood Education International (CE International);*
– *Christian Blind Mission (CBM);*
– *Christian Life Community (CLC, #03905);*
– *Church Women United (CWU);*
– *CIRFS – European Man-made Fibres Association (#03944);*
– *Citizens' Alliance for Saving the Atmosphere and the Earth (CASA);*

- *Citizens Network for Sustainable Development (CitNet);*
- *Collaborative International Pesticides Analytical Council (CIPAC, #04099);*
- *Collegium Internationale Neuropsychopharmacologicum (CINP, #04115);*
- *Comité européen des fabricants de sucre (CEFS, #04159);*
- *Comité International des Plastiques en Agriculture (CIPA, #04185);*
- *Comité International Radio-Maritime (CIRM, #04186);*
- *Commission Internationale de l'Eclairage (CIE, #04219);*
- *Commission to Study the Organization of Peace (CSOP, no recent information);*
- *Committee for Economic Development (CED);*
- *Committee for European Construction Equipment (CECE, #04254);*
- *Committee on Space Research (COSPAR, #04287);*
- *Commonweal;*
- *Commonwealth Pharmacists Association (CPA, #04357);*
- *Communications Coordination Committee for the United Nations (CCC/UN);*
- *Confederación de Organizaciones Turísticas de la América Latina (COTAL, #04466);*
- *Confederation of Asia-Pacific Chambers of Commerce and Industry (CACCI, #04512);*
- *Confederation of European Forest Owners (CEPF, #04525);*
- *Confederation of European Paper Industries (CEPI, #04529);*
- *Confederation of Fire Protection Associations International (CFPA-I, #04553);*
- *Confédération européenne des industries du bois (CEI Bois, #04545);*
- *Confédération internationale du crédit agricole (CICA, #04560);*
- *Congress of Racial Equality (CORE);*
- *Conseil européen de l'industrie chimique (CEFIC, #04687);*
- *Consejo de Educación de Adultos de América Latina (CEAAL, #04707);*
- *Consejo Latinoamericano de Ciencias Sociales (CLACSO, #04718);*
- *Consensus for Sustainable People, Organisations and Communities (CSPOC);*
- *Cooperation Canada;*
- *COPA – european farmers (COPA, #04829);*
- *Council for International Organizations of Medical Sciences (CIOMS, #04905);*
- *Council for the Development of Social Science Research in Africa (CODESRIA, #04879);*
- *Council of Bureaux (CoB, #04873);*
- *Council on International and Public Affairs (CIPA);*
- *CropLife International (#04966);*
- *Dangerous Goods Advisory Council (DGAC, #05001);*
- *Delta Kappa Gamma Society International (DKG);*
- *DEULA-Nienburg;*
- *Dzeno Association;*
- *Ecma International (#05288);*
- *EngenderHealth;*
- *English-Speaking Union (ESU, #05482);*
- *Environmental Coalition for North America (ENCONA, no recent information);*
- *Environmental Investigation Agency (EIA);*
- *EUCARPIA (#05571);*
- *EURAG – European Federation of Older Persons (#05597);*
- *EURATEX – The European Apparel and Textile Confederation (EURATEX, #05616);*
- *EURO-CHINA (#05658);*
- *European Academy of Arts, Sciences and Humanities (EAASH, #05781);*
- *European Alliance of News Agencies (EANA, #05877);*
- *European Association for e-Identity and Security (EEMA, #06077);*
- *European Association of Agricultural Economists (EAAE, #05932);*
- *European Association of Automotive Suppliers (CLEPA, #05948);*
- *European Association of Internal Combustion Engine Manufacturers (EUROMOT, #06090);*
- *European Boating Association (EBA, #06376);*
- *European Broadcasting Union (EBU, #06404);*
- *European Chemical Society (EuChemS, #06524);*
- *European Confederation of International Trading Houses Associations (CITHA, #06708);*
- *European Cyclists' Federation (ECF, #06877);*
- *European Environmental Bureau (EEB, #06996);*
- *European Federation of Animal Science (EAAP, #07046);*
- *European Federation of Management Consultancies Associations (#07159);*
- *European Federation of National Maintenance Societies (EFNMS, #07173);*
- *European Federation of Road Traffic Victims (#07207);*
- *European Food Law Association (EFLA, #07286);*
- *European Garage Equipment Association (EGEA, #07377);*
- *European Industrial Gases Association (EIGA, #07525);*
- *European Landowners' Organization (ELO, #07639);*
- *European Liaison Committee for Pulp and Paper (EUCEPA, #07688);*
- *European Logistic Platforms Association (Europlatforms, #07709);*
- *European Mediterranean Commission on Water Planning (EMCWP, no recent information);*
- *European Organization for Quality (EOQ, #08112);*
- *European Tyre and Rubber Manufacturers' Association (ETRMA, #08963);*
- *European Union of Public Relations (EUPR, #09011);*
- *Ev-K2-CNR Committee (#16175);*
- *Ex-Volunteers International (EVI, no recent information);*
- *Fauna & Flora International (FFI, #09277);*
- *FDI – World Dental Federation (#09281);*
- *Federación Latinoamericana de Periodistas (FELAP, #09359);*
- *Federación Panamericana de Lechería (FEPALE, #09382);*
- *Federation of Afro-Asian Insurers and Reinsurers (FAIR, #09413);*
- *Federation of European Aquaculture Producers (FEAP, #09491);*
- *Federation of European Manufacturers of Friction Materials (FEMFM, #09512);*
- *Federation of Zoroastrian Associations of North America (FEZANA);*
- *Femmes chefs d'entreprises mondiales (FCEM, #09733);*
- *Fertilizers Europe (#09738);*
- *FIA Foundation (#09742);*
- *FIAN International (#09743);*
- *FIDI Global Alliance (#09753);*
- *FIPP (#09776);*
- *FoodDrinkEurope (#09841);*
- *Food for the Hungry (fh, #09845);*
- *Forum francophone des affaires (FFA, #09916);*
- *Forum maghrébin pour l'environnement et le développement;*
- *Foundation for Global Community – Global Initiatives Team for the CSCE;*
- *Friedrich-Ebert-Stiftung (FES);*
- *Friedrich Naumann Foundation for Freedom;*
- *Friends of the Earth International (FoEI, #10002);*
- *Fédération africaine des associations nationales de parents d'élèves et étudiants (FAPE, #09398);*
- *Fédération Européenne d'Associations Nationales d'Ingénieurs (FEANI, #09558);*
- *Fédération européenne des industries de corderie ficellerie et de filets (EUROCORD, #09573);*
- *Fédération Internationale de Gynécologie et d'Obstétrique (FIGO, #09638);*
- *Fédération internationale des associations de transitaires et assimilés (FIATA, #09610);*
- *Fédération internationale des communautés éducatives (FICE-International, #09622);*
- *Fédération internationale des grossistes importateurs et exportateurs en fournitures automobiles (FIGIEFA, #09635);*
- *Fédération internationale syndicale de l'enseignement (FISE, #09662);*
- *General Board of Church and Society of the United Methodist Church (GBCS);*
- *Global Express Association (GEA, #10351);*
- *Global Health Council (GHC, #10402);*
- *Global Justice Now;*
- *Global Partners in Care;*
- *Global Pulse Confederation (GPC, #10562);*
- *Global Self-Care Federation (GSCF, #10588);*
- *Globus et Locus;*
- *Grain and Feed Trade Association (GAFTA, #10692);*
- *Grand Council of the Crees – Eeyou Istchee (GCCEI);*
- *Gray Panthers Project Fund;*
- *Hawaii Association of International Buddhists (HAIB);*
- *Heifer International;*
- *Heinrich Böll Foundation;*
- *Helen Keller International (HKI, #10902);*
- *Hunger Project (#10994);*
- *ICASO (#11040);*
- *ICC – International Association for Cereal Science and Technology (#11048);*
- *ICSC – World Laboratory (#11088);*
- *IFOAM – Organics International (IFOAM, #11105);*
- *Indian Council of South America (#11158);*
- *Indian Law Resource Center;*
- *Indigenous Peoples' Center for Documentation, Research and Information (DOCIP);*
- *Institute for African Alternatives (IFAA, #11241);*
- *Institute for Planetary Synthesis (IPS, #11287);*
- *Institute for Transportation and Development Policy (ITDP);*
- *Institute of International Container Lessors (IICL, #11273);*
- *Institute of International Education (IIE);*
- *Institute of Marine Engineering, Science and Technology (IMarEST, #11280);*
- *Instituto Iberoamericano de Derecho Marítimo (IIDM);*
- *Instituto Mundo Libre;*
- *INTERFERRY (#11470);*
- *InterManager (#11520);*
- *International Academy of Aviation and Space Medicine (IAASM, #11537);*
- *International Academy of Pathology (IAP, #11567);*
- *International Academy of Technological Sciences (IATS, no recent information);*
- *International Advertising Association (IAA, #11590);*
- *International Agency for the Prevention of Blindness (IAPB, #11597);*
- *International Amateur Radio Union (IARU, #11646);*
- *International Arab Society of Certified Accountants (IASCA, #11665);*
- *International Association for Bridge and Structural Engineering (IABSE, #11737);*
- *International Association for Community Development (IACD, #11793);*
- *International Association for Continuing Engineering Education (IACEE, #11817);*
- *International Association for Counselling (IAC, #11821);*
- *International Association for Educational Assessment (IAEA, #11861);*
- *International Association for Housing Science (IAHS, #11943);*
- *International Association for Hydro-Environment Engineering and Research (IAHR, #11950);*
- *International Association for Hydrogen Energy (IAHE, #11951);*
- *International Association for Research in Income and Wealth (IARIW, #12134);*
- *International Association for Suicide Prevention and Crisis Intervention (IASP, #12213);*
- *International Association for the Physical Sciences of the Oceans (IAPSO, #12082);*
- *International Association for the Study of Pain (IASP, #12206);*
- *International Association of Agricultural Economists (IAAE, #11695);*
- *International Association of Art (IAA, #11710);*
- *International Association of Broadcasting (IAB, #11738);*
- *International Association of Cancer Registries (IACR, #11753);*
- *International Association of Chiefs of Police (IACP, #11765);*
- *International Association of Classification Societies (IACS, #11778);*
- *International Association of Conference Interpreters (#11807);*
- *International Association of Drilling Contractors (IADC);*
- *International Association of Dry Cargo Shipowners (INTERCARGO, #11853);*
- *International Association of Educators for World Peace (IAEWP);*
- *International Association of Horticultural Producers (#11940);*
- *International Association of Hydatidology (IAH, #11949);*
- *International Association of Hydrogeologists (IAH, #11953);*
- *International Association of Independent Tanker Owners (INTERTANKO, #11959);*
- *International Association of Institutes of Navigation (IAIN, #11965);*
- *International Association of Islamic Banks (IAIB, no recent information);*
- *International Association of Logopedics and Phoniatrics (IALP, #12005);*
- *International Association of Oil and Gas Producers (IOGP, #12053);*
- *International Association of Safety Professionals (IASP);*
- *International Association of Students in Agricultural and Related Sciences (IAAS, #12191);*
- *International Association of Universities (IAU, #12246);*
- *International Baccalaureate (IB, #12306);*
- *International Board on Books for Young People (IBBY, #12366);*
- *International Buddhist Foundation (IBF);*
- *International Business Aviation Council (IBAC, #12418);*
- *International Catholic Committee of Nurses and Medico-social Assistants (#12451);*
- *International Catholic Rural Association (ICRA, #12461);*
- *International Cell Research Organization (ICRO, #12463);*
- *International Centre for Earth Construction (#12485);*
- *International Centre for Sustainable Cities, Vancouver (ICSC);*
- *International Centre for Trade Union Rights (ICTUR, #12525);*
- *International Centre of Films for Children and Young People (#12493);*
- *International Centre on Small Hydro-Power (IC-SHP);*
- *International Chrysotile Association (ICA, #12570);*
- *International Civil Aviation English Association (ICAEA, #12580);*
- *International Collective in Support of Fishworkers (ICSF, #12639);*
- *International Commission of Agricultural and Biosystems Engineering (#12661);*
- *International Commission on Distance Education (#12677);*
- *International Commission on Occupational Health (ICOH, #12709);*
- *International Commission on Radiation Units and Measurements (ICRU, #12722);*
- *International Commission on Radiological Protection (ICRP, #12724);*
- *International Committee for Animal Recording (ICAR, #12746);*
- *International Community Corrections Association (ICCA, #12822);*
- *International Confederation of European Beet Growers (CIBE, #12860);*
- *International Confederation of Midwives (ICM, #12863);*
- *International Congress of Industrialists and Entrepreneurs (ICIE, #12895);*
- *International Coordinating Council of Aerospace Industry Associations (ICCAIA, #12956);*
- *International Cost Engineering Council (ICEC, #12976);*
- *International Council for Commercial Arbitration (ICCA, #13010);*
- *International Council for Open and Distance Education (ICDE, #13056);*
- *International Council for Philosophy and Human Sciences (CIPSH, #13061);*
- *International Council for Standardization in Haematology (ICSH, #13078);*
- *International Council of Aircraft Owner and Pilot Associations (IAOPA, #12988);*
- *International Council of Design (ICoD, #13013);*
- *International Council of Forest and Paper Associations (ICFPA, #13023);*
- *International Council of Hides, Skins and Leather Traders Associations (ICHSLTA, #13029);*
- *International Council of Marine Industry Associations (ICOMIA, #13044);*
- *International Council of Museums (ICOM, #13051);*
- *International Council of Nurses (ICN, #13054);*
- *International Council of Organizations for Folklore Festivals and Folk Art (#13058);*
- *International Council of Toy Industries (ICTI, #13086);*
- *International Council on Archives (ICA, #12996);*
- *International Council on Education for Teaching (ICET, #13016);*
- *International Court of the Environment Foundation (ICEF, #13097);*
- *International Cremation Federation (ICF, #13104);*
- *International Cultural Youth Exchange (ICYE Federation, #13122);*
- *International Dairy Federation (IDF, #13128);*
- *International Desalination Association (IDA, #13152);*
- *International Economic Association (IEA, #13222);*
- *International Educational Development – Humanitarian Law Project;*
- *International Egg Commission (IEC, #13245);*
- *International Electrical Research Exchange (IERE, #13254);*
- *International Emergency Action (IEA, #13258);*
- *International Epidemiological Association (IEA, #13287);*
- *Internationale Raiffeisen Union e.V. (IRU, #13291);*
- *International Ergonomics Association (IEA, #13294);*
- *Internationale Vereinigung Sport- und Freizeiteinrichtungen (IAKS, #13319);*
- *International Eye Foundation (IEF, #13324);*
- *International Federation for Heat Treatment and Surface Engineering (IFHTSE, #13443);*
- *International Federation for Information Processing (IFIP, #13458);*
- *International Federation for Medical and Biological Engineering (IFMBE, #13477);*
- *International Federation for Parent Education (IFPE, #13499);*
- *International Federation for Peace and Conciliation (IFPC, #13501);*
- *International Federation of Agricultural Journalists (IFAJ, #13346);*

- International Federation of Air Line Pilots' Associations (IFALPA, #13349);
- International Federation of Automatic Control (IFAC, #13367);
- International Federation of Biomedical Laboratory Science (IFBLS, #13372);
- International Federation of Catholic Universities (IFCU, #13381);
- International Federation of Clinical Chemistry and Laboratory Medicine (IFCC, #13392);
- International Federation of Consulting Engineers (#13399);
- International Federation of Film Archives (#13427);
- International Federation of Health Information Management Associations (IFHIMA, #13441);
- International Federation of Helicopter Associations (IFHA, #13444);
- International Federation of Language Teacher Associations (#13468);
- International Federation of Library Associations and Institutions (IFLA, #13470);
- International Federation of Musicians (#13486);
- International Federation of Operational Research Societies (IFORS, #13493);
- International Federation of Pedestrians (IFP, #13502);
- International Federation of Pharmaceutical Manufacturers and Associations (IFPMA, #13505);
- International Federation of Purchasing and Supply Management (IFPSM, #13525);
- International Federation of Robotics (IFR, #13532);
- International Federation of Rural Adult Catholic Movements (#13535);
- International Federation of Shipmasters Associations (IFSMA, #13539);
- International Federation of Surgical Colleges (IFSC, #13560);
- International Federation of Surveyors (FIG, #13561);
- International Federation of Workers' Education Associations (IFWEA, #13580);
- International Fertilizer Association (IFA, #13589);
- International Fiscal Association (IFA, #13608);
- International Food Policy Research Institute (IFPRI, #13622);
- International Forum (IF);
- International Foundation for Dharma Nature Time;
- International Foundation for Science (IFS, #13677);
- International Fruit and Vegetable Juice Association (IFU, #13687);
- International Game Fish Association (IGFA);
- International Geographical Union (IGU, #13713);
- International Group of P and I Clubs (#13751);
- International Hospital Federation (IHF, #13812);
- International Human Rights Association of American Minorities (IHRAAM);
- International Immigrants Foundation (IIF);
- International Information Centre for Terminology (INFOTERM, #13846);
- International Inner Wheel (IIW, #13855);
- International Institute for Environment and Development (IIED, #13877);
- International Institute for Peace (IIP, #13907);
- International Institute for Sustainable Development (IISD, #13930);
- International Institute of Public Finance (IIPF, #13915);
- International Institute of Rural Reconstruction (IIRR, #13921);
- International Institute of Sugar Beet Research (IIRB, #13928);
- International Institute of Welding (IIW, #13935);
- International Jacques Maritain Institute (#13967);
- International League of Associations for Rheumatology (ILAR, #14016);
- International Leprosy Association (ILA, #14029);
- International Life Sciences Institute (ILSI, #14044);
- International Maritime Pilots' Association (IMPA, #14103);
- International Measurement Confederation (IMEKO, #14124);
- International Meat Secretariat (IMS, #14125);
- International Motorcycle Manufacturers Association (IMMA, #14186);
- International Movement of Apostolate of Children (IMAC, #14192);
- International Music Council (IMC, #14199);
- International Narcotic Enforcement Officers Association (INEOA);
- International Network for Environmental Management (INEM, #14263);
- International Network of Street Papers (INSP, #14330);
- International Organisation for Biological Control (IOBC, #14424);
- International Organization Against Trachoma (IOAT, #14436);
- International Organization of Psychophysiology (IOP, #14466);
- International Osteoporosis Foundation (IOF, #14490);
- International Parcel Tankers Association (IPTA);
- International Peace Bureau (IPB, #14535);
- International Peace Institute (IPI, #14536);
- International Peace Research Association (IPRA, #14537);
- International Pediatric Association (IPA, #14541);
- International Pharmaceutical Federation (#14566);
- International Pharmaceutical Students' Federation (IPSF, #14568);
- International Physicians for the Prevention of Nuclear War (IPPNW, #14578);
- International Play Association (IPA, #14604);
- International Police Commission (IPC);
- International Political Science Association (IPSA, #14615);
- International Potash Institute (IPI, #14626);
- International Press Telecommunications Council (IPTC, #14637);
- International Progress Organization (IPO, #14653);
- International Public Policy Institute (IPPI);
- International Public Relations Association (IPRA, #14671);
- International Publishers Association (IPA, #14675);
- International Radiation Protection Association (IRPA, #14686);
- International Real Estate Institute (IREI);
- International Right to Life Federation (IRLF, #14755);
- International Salvage Union (ISU, #14779);
- International Schools Association (ISA, #14789);
- International Ship Suppliers and Services Association (ISSA, #14850);
- International Social Democratic Union for Education (ISDUE, #14881);
- International Social Tourism Organisation (ISTO, #14889);
- International Society for Burn Injuries (ISBI, #14986);
- International Society for Engineering Pedagogy (#15089);
- International Society for Horticultural Science (ISHS, #15180);
- International Society for Human and Animal Mycology (ISHAM, #15181);
- International Society for Human Rights (ISHR, #15183);
- International Society for Mangrove Ecosystems (ISME, #15245);
- International Society for Military Law and the Law of War (#15270);
- International Society for Nurses in Cancer Care (ISNCC, #15312);
- International Society for Photogrammetry and Remote Sensing (ISPRS, #15362);
- International Society for Plant Pathology (ISPP, #15371);
- International Society of Addiction Medicine (ISAM, #14896);
- International Society of Citriculture (ISC, #15011);
- International Society of City and Regional Planners (ISOCARP, #15012);
- International Society of Hematology (ISH, #15159);
- International Society of Radiographers and Radiological Technologists (ISRRT, #15410);
- International Solar Energy Society (ISES, #15564);
- International Solid Waste Association (ISWA, #15567);
- International Special Dietary Food Industries (ISDI, #15576);
- International Spinal Cord Society (ISCoS, #15581);
- International Studies Association (ISA, #15615);
- International Tea Committee (ITC, #15664);
- International Technical Tropical Timber Association (ITTTA, #15668);
- International Textile Manufacturers Federation (ITMF, #15679);
- International Theatre Institute (ITI, #15683);
- International Union against Sexually Transmitted Infections (IUSTI, #15751);
- International Union Against Tuberculosis and Lung Disease (The Union, #15752);
- International Union for Health Promotion and Education (IUHPE, #15778);
- International Union of Aerospace Insurers (IUAI, #15750);
- International Union of Biological Sciences (IUBS, #15760);
- International Union of Food, Agricultural, Hotel, Restaurant, Catering, Tobacco and Allied Workers Associations (IUF, #15772);
- International Union of Food Science and Technology (IUFoST, #15773);
- International Union of Forest Research Organizations (IUFRO, #15774);
- International Union of Geodesy and Geophysics (IUGG, #15776);
- International Union of Leather Technologists and Chemists Societies (IULTCS, #15788);
- International Union of Marine Insurance (IUMI, #15789);
- International Union of Microbiological Societies (IUMS, #15794);
- International Union of Nutritional Sciences (IUNS, #15796);
- International Union of Pure and Applied Chemistry (IUPAC, #15809);
- International Union of Soil Sciences (IUSS, #15817);
- International Union of Tenants (IUT, #15822);
- International Valuation Standards Council (IVSC, #15840);
- International Wages Due Lesbians;
- International Water Association (IWA, #15865);
- International Wood Products Association (IWPA);
- International Wool Textile Organisation (IWTO, #15904);
- InterPortPolice (#15963);
- Inter-University European Institute on Social Welfare (IEISW, #15988);
- Iodine Global Network (IGN, #16004);
- Islamic Chamber of Commerce, Industry and Agriculture (ICCIA, #16036);
- ITOPF Ltd (#16073);
- Japan Atomic Industrial Forum (JAIF);
- Jeunesses Musicales International (JMI, #16110);
- La Leche League International (LLLI, #16433);
- Landscape Institute (LI);
- Latin American Confederation of Public Sector Workers (#16304);
- Latin American Industrialists Association (#16341);
- Latin American Railways Association (#16365);
- Latin American Shipowners Association (LASA, #16369);
- Liberation;
- Licensing Executives Society International (LESI, #16461);
- Liquid Gas Europe (#16488);
- Lucis Trust (LT, #16519);
- Maison de sagesse (MdS);
- Margaret Sanger Center International (MSCI);
- Medical Care Development International (MCDI);
- Medicus Mundi International – Network Health for All (MMI, #16636);
- MindFreedom International (#16807);
- Mouvement international de la jeunesse agricole et rurale catholique (MIJARC, #16865);
- Movement Against Racism and for Friendship between Peoples (MRAP);
- Multiple Sclerosis International Federation (MSIF, #16899);
- NGO Committee on UNICEF (#17120);
- NGV Global (#17131);
- Nippon Foundation;
- Nuclear Age Peace Foundation;
- nucleareurope (#17616);
- Oikos – Cooperação e Desenvolvimento (Oikos);
- Oil Companies International Marine Forum (OCIMF, #17709);
- Open Door International: for the Economic Emancipation of the Woman Worker (ODI, no recent information);
- ORBIS International (#17786);
- Organisation internationale des experts (ORDINEX, #17808);
- Organización de Telecomunicaciones de Iberoamérica (OTI, #17851);
- Organization of the Islamic Shipowners' Association (OISA, #17876);
- Pacific Science Association (PSA, #18003);
- PAI (#18025);
- Pan American Development Foundation (PADF, #18094);
- Pan American Standards Commission (#18133);
- Parliamentary Association for Euro-Arab Cooperation (PAEAC, #18217);
- PCI Media;
- Peace Trust;
- Pearl S Buck International (PSBI);
- PIANC (#18371);
- Population Institute (PI);
- Practical Action (#18475);
- Quota International (QI, #18596);
- Rainforest Alliance;
- Refugees International (RI);
- Regional Council on Human Rights in Asia (#18776);
- Regional Studies Association (RSA);
- Saami Council (#19012);
- Scientific Committee on Frequency Allocations for Radio Astronomy and Space Science (IUCAF, #19148);
- Secrétariat international des ingénieurs, des agronomes et des cadres économiques catholiques (SIIAEC, #19203);
- SERVAS International (#19234);
- Share the World's Resources (STWR);
- Sierra Club International Program (#19266);
- Sightsavers International (#19270);
- Sirius Global Animal Organisation (Sirius GAO);
- SITA (#19299);
- Society for Conservation and Protection of Environment (SCOPE);
- Society for Development Alternatives;
- Society of Chemical Industry (SCI);
- Society of International Gas Tanker and Terminal Operators (SIGTTO, #19582);
- Soka Gakkai International (SGI, #19672);
- Space Generation Advisory Council in Support of the United Nations Programme on Space Applications (SGAC, #19898);
- Stakeholder Forum for a Sustainable Future (SF);
- Star Spirit International;
- Stockholm Environment Institute (SEI, #19993);
- Sulphur Institute, The (TSI, #20034);
- Surgical Eye Expeditions International (SEE International);
- Survival International (#20047);
- Tearfund, UK;
- The Hague International Model United Nations (THIMUN);
- The Marine Ingredients Organisation (IFFO, #16579);
- Third World Foundation for Social and Economic Studies (TWF, #20150);
- Third World Network (TWN, #20151);
- Tinker Institute on International Law and Organizations;
- Trade Unions International of Agriculture, Food, Commerce, Textile and Allied Industries (#20190);
- Transfrigoroute International (TI, #20213);
- Trilateral Commission (TC, #20237);
- Tropical Growers' Association (TGA, #20250);
- TWAS (#20270);
- UFI – The Global Association of the Exhibition Industry (#20276);
- Union internationale de la presse francophone (UPF, #20435);
- Union internationale des laboratoires indépendants (UILI, #20429);
- Union of Arab Chambers (UAC, #20350);
- United Nations Foundation (UNF, #20563);
- United Schools International (USI, #20660);
- United Seamen's Service (USS, #20661);
- United Way Worldwide (#20663);
- Unión de Silvicultores del Sur de Europa (USSE, #20478);
- UNUM OMNES International Council of Catholic Men (ICCM, #20720);
- Verification Research, Training and Information Centre (VERTIC);
- Viva Network (#20800);
- Wainwright House;
- War on Want;
- Women's Environment and Development Organization (WEDO, #21016);
- World Association for Animal Production (WAAP, #21117);
- World Association for Christian Communication (WACC, #21126);
- World Association for the School as an Instrument of Peace (#21184);
- World Association of Societies of Pathology and Laboratory Medicine (WASPaLM, #21191);
- World Business Council for Sustainable Development (WBCSD, #21254);
- World Catholic Association for Communication (SIGNIS, #21264);
- World Chlorine Council (WCC, #21274);
- World Coatings Council (#21283);
- World Confederation for Physical Therapy (WCPT, #21293);

- *World Council of Muslim Communities*;
- *World Crafts Council AISBL (WCC International, #21342)*;
- *World Economic Processing Zones Association (WEPZA, #21368)*;
- *World Economy, Ecology and Development (WEED)*;
- *World Education Fellowship (WEF, #21370)*;
- *World Education (WE)*;
- *World Federation for Medical Education (WFME, #21454)*;
- *World Federation of Development Financing Institutions (WFDFI, #21428)*;
- *World Federation of Engineering Organizations (WFEO, #21433)*;
- *World Federation of Neurosurgical Societies (WFNS, #21466)*;
- *World Federation of Nuclear Medicine and Biology (WFNMB, #21467)*;
- *World Federation of Occupational Therapists (WFOT, #21468)*;
- *World Federation of Parasitologists (WFP, #21471)*;
- *World Federation of Public Health Associations (WFPHA, #21476)*;
- *World Federation of Scientific Workers (WFSW, #21480)*;
- *World Federation of Societies of Anaesthesiologists (WFSA, #21482)*;
- *World Forum on Shooting Activities (WFSA, #21523)*;
- *World Heart Federation (WHF, #21562)*;
- *World Hypertension League (WHL, #21574)*;
- *World Medical Association (WMA, #21646)*;
- *World Mining Congress (WMC, #21654)*;
- *World Movement of Christian Workers (WMCW, #21660)*;
- *World Nuclear Association (WNA, #21674)*;
- *World Organization of Family Doctors (WONCA, #21690)*;
- *World Packaging Organisation (WPO, #21705)*;
- *World Peace Council (WPC, #21717)*;
- *World Phosphate Institute (#21728)*;
- *World Society for Ekistics (WSE, #21801)*;
- *World's Poultry Science Association (WPSA, #21825)*;
- *World Steel Association (worldsteel, #21829)*;
- *World Sugar Research Organization (WSRO, #21837)*;
- *World Trade Point Federation (WTPF, #21865)*;
- *World Union for Progressive Judaism (WUPJ, #21883)*;
- *World Winter Cities Association for Mayors (WWCAM, #21940)*.

IGO Relations *Relations with Specialized Agencies*:
Even before the establishment of the United Nations, several inter-governmental agencies were dealing with specific problems. Some had been in existence for many years, such as the International Labour Organisation, set up in 1919. Article 57 of the UN Charter provides that *'the various specialized agencies, established by inter-governmental agreement and having wide international responsibilities, as defined in their basic instruments, in economic, social, cultural, educational, health, and related fields, shall be brought into relationship with the United Nations'*. The specialized agencies carry out much of the work on achieving the UN aim of improved economic and social conditions for all peoples. An important task of ECOSOC is to bring these specialized agencies into relationship with the United Nations by negotiated agreements and coordinating their activities. The individual agreements between the UN and the specialized agencies are the instruments defining this relationship. They are submitted for approval to ECOSOC, and by ECOSOC to the General Assembly. Before coming into force each agreement must also be approved by the appropriate organs of the specialized agency concerned. The following are the specialized agencies (dates indicate coming into force of agreement with ECOSOC):
- *FAO (#09260)*, 14 Dec 1946;
- *ILO (#11123)*, 14 Dec 1946;
- *International Bank for Reconstruction and Development (IBRD, #12317)*, 15 Nov 1947;
- *International Civil Aviation Organization (ICAO, #12581)*, 13 May 1947;
- *International Development Association (IDA, #13155)*, 27 Mar 1961;
- *International Finance Corporation (IFC, #13597)*, 20 Feb 1957;
- *International Fund for Agricultural Development (IFAD, #13692)*, 15 Dec 1977;
- *International Maritime Organization (IMO, #14102)*, 13 Jan 1959;
- *International Monetary Fund (IMF, #14180)*, 15 Nov 1947;
- *International Telecommunication Union (ITU, #15673)*, 1 Jan 1949;
- *Multilateral Investment Guarantee Agency (MIGA, #16888)*;
- *UNESCO (#20322)*, 14 Dec 1946;
- *UNIDO (#20336)*, 17 Dec 1985;
- *Universal Postal Union (UPU, #20682)*, 1 Jul 1948;
- *WHO (#20950)*, 10 Jul 1948;
- *World Intellectual Property Organization (WIPO, #21593)*, 17 Dec 1974;
- *World Meteorological Organization (WMO, #21649)*, 20 Dec 1951.

Agencies comprising the *The World Bank Group (#21218)* – IBRD, IDA, IFC and MIGA – submit a common report.
Autonomous UN bodies:
- *International Atomic Energy Agency (IAEA, #12294)* – officially came into being 29 Jul 1957, established under the aegis of the United Nations, its relationship with the UN being approved by UN General Assembly on 14 Nov 1957.
- *World Trade Organization (WTO, #21864)* – set up 1 Jan 1995, to supervise and liberalize international trade, following successful conclusion of the *Uruguay Round*, 15 Dec 1993. Prior to this coordination arrangements were made by *General Agreement on Tariffs and Trade (GATT, inactive)*, which brought into operation a code of international trade and provided machinery for reducing and stabilizing tariffs and for regular consultations on trade problems. GATT in turn arose out of the Interim Commission for the International Trade Organization, set up by the United Nations.

Related United Nations Programmes, Research Institutes and Other Bodies:
- *United Nations Capital Development Fund (UNCDF, #20524)*;
- *United Nations Institute for Training and Research (UNITAR, #20576)*;
- *United Nations Interregional Crime and Justice Research Institute (UNICRI, #20580)*;
- *United Nations Research Institute for Social Development (UNRISD, #20623)*;
- *United Nations University (UNU, #20642)*;
- *United Nations Volunteers (UNV, #20650)*.

Other bodies created within and by the United Nations and having links with ECOSOC:
- *International Olive Council (IOC, #14405)*;
- *International Trade Centre (ITC, #15703)*;
- *University for Peace (UPEACE, #20702)*.

Relations of Intergovernmental Organizations with the United Nations:
The UN General Assembly invited OAS, LAS, OAU, *European Union (EU, #08967)*; and Organization of the Islamic Conference (OIC) to send observers to its sessions under resolutions 253 (III), 477 (V), 2011 (XX), 3208 (XXIX), 3209 (XXIX) and 3369 (XXX) respectively. ECOSOC revised its rules of procedure at its 58th session and adopted a new rule (rule 79) regarding the participation of other intergovernmental organizations whereby, *'inter alia'*, representatives of intergovernmental organizations accorded permanent observer status by UN General Assembly may, on the recommendation of the Bureau, participate in the deliberations of ECOSOC (without the right to vote) on questions within the scope of their activities. The organizations mentioned below, having permanent observer status with UN General Assembly, are therefore, under rule 79 of ECOSOC rules of procedure, entitled to participate in the work of the ECOSOC on a continuing basis.
'List of non-member states, entities and organizations having received a standing invitation to participate as observers in the sessions and the work of the General Assembly (A/INF/62/6)':
- *Organisation of African, Caribbean and Pacific States (OACPS, #17796)*;
- *African Development Bank (ADB, #00283)*;
- *African Union (AU, #00488)*;
- *Agency for the Prohibition of Nuclear Weapons in Latin America and the Caribbean (#00554)*;
- *Andean Community (#00817)*;
- *ASEAN (#01141)*;
- *Asian-African Legal Consultative Organization (AALCO, #01303)*;
- *Association of Caribbean States (ACS, #02411)*;
- *Caribbean Community (CARICOM, #03476)*;
- *Central American Integration System (#03671)*;
- *Collective Security Treaty Organization (CSTO, #04103)*;
- *Common Fund for Commodities (CFC, #04293)*;
- *Commonwealth of Independent States (CIS, #04341)*;
- *Commonwealth Secretariat (#04362)*;
- *Comunidade dos Países de Língua Portuguesa (CPLP, #04430)*;
- *Community of Sahel-Saharan States (CEN-SAD, #04406)*;
- *Conference on Interaction and Confidence-Building Measures in Asia (CICA, #04609)*;
- *Council of Europe (CE, #04881)*;
- Customs Cooperation Council;
- *East African Community (EAC, #05181)*;
- *Economic Community of Central African States (ECCAS, #05311)*;
- *Economic Community of West African States (ECOWAS, #05312)*;
- *Economic Cooperation Organization (ECO, #05313)*;
- *Energy Charter Conference (#05466)*;
- *Eurasian Development Bank (EDB, #05605)*;
- European Community;
- *Gulf Cooperation Council (GCC, #10826)*;
- *The Hague Conference on Private International Law (HCCH, #10850)*;
- Holy See;
- *Ibero-American General Secretariat (#11024)*;
- *Commission de l'Océan Indien (COI, #04236)*;
- *Inter-American Development Bank (IDB, #11427)*;
- *International Centre for Migration Policy Development (ICMPD, #12503)*;
- *International Criminal Court (ICC, #13108)*;
- *International Criminal Police Organization – INTERPOL (ICPO-INTERPOL, #13110)*;
- *International Development Law Organization (IDLO, #13161)*;
- International Hydrographic Organization;
- International Institute for Democracy and Electoral Assistance;
- *International Organization for Migration (IOM, #14454)*;
- *International Seabed Authority (ISBA, #14813)*;
- *International Tribunal for the Law of the Sea (ITLOS, #15731)*;
- *International Union for Conservation of Nature and Natural Resources (IUCN, #15766)*;
- *Islamic Development Bank (IsDB, #16044)*;
- *Italian-Latin American Institute (ILAI, #16071)*;
- *Latin American Integration Association (LAIA, #16343)*;
- *League of Arab States (LAS, #16420)*;
- *OAS (#17629)*;
- OECD;
- *OPEC Fund for International Development (OFID, #17745)*;
- *Organisation of Eastern Caribbean States (OECS, #17804)*;
- *Organisation internationale de la Francophonie (OIF, #17809)*, replacing *Agence intergouvernementale de La Francophonie (inactive)*;
- *Organisation of Islamic Cooperation (OIC, #17813)*;
- *Organization of Black Sea Economic Cooperation (BSEC, #17857)*;
- *Organization for Democracy and Economic Development (GUAM, #17861)*;
- *Organization for Security and Cooperation in Europe (OSCE, #17887)*;
- *Pacific Islands Forum (#17968)*;
- *Parlamento Latinoamericano (PARLATINO, #18203)*;
- *Partners in Population and Development (PPD, #18247)*;
- *Permanent Court of Arbitration (PCA, #18321)*;
- *Regional Centre on Small Arms and Light Weapons in the Great Lakes Region, the Horn of Africa and Bordering States (RECSA, #18760)*;
- *Shanghai Cooperation Organization (SCO, #19256)*;
- *Sistema Económico Latinoamericano (SELA, #19294)*;
- *South Asian Association for Regional Cooperation (SAARC, #19721)*;
- *Southern African Development Community (SADC, #19843)*.

Intergovernmental organizations designated by the Council under Rule 79 of the Rules of Procedure for participation in the deliberations of the Council on questions within the scope of their activities – *Participation on a continuing basis*
'Organizations designated under Council decision 109 (LIX)':
- *Council of Arab Economic Unity (CAEU, #04859)*;
- *Organization of the Petroleum Exporting Countries (OPEC, #17881)*.

'Organizations designated under Council decision 1980/114':
- *Asian Productivity Organization (APO, #01674)*;
- *International Centre for Promotion of Enterprises (ICPE, #12509)*;
- *Latin American Energy Organization (#16313)*.

'Organization designated under Council decision 1980/151':
- *African Regional Centre of Technology (ARCT, #00432)*.

'Organization designated under Council decision 1986/156':
- *Organization of Ibero-American States for Education, Science and Culture (#17871)*.

'Organization designated under Council decision 1992/265':
- *Regional Organization for the Protection of the Marine Environment (ROPME, #18805)*.

'Organization designated under Council decision 1997/215':
- *International Centre for Genetic Engineering and Biotechnology (ICGEB, #12494)*.

'Organization designated under Council decision 2000/213':
- *Asian and Pacific Development Centre (APDC, #01608)*.

'Organization designated under Council decision 2003/212':
- *Intergovernment Institution for the use of Micro-Algae Spirulina against Malnutrition (IIMSAM, #11504)*;
- *Islamic Development Bank (IsDB, #16044)*.

'Organization designated under Council decision 2003/221':
- *Islamic World Educational, Scientific and Cultural Organization (ICESCO, #16058)*.

'Organization designated under Council decision 2003/312':
- *Baltic Marine Environment Protection Commission – Helsinki Commission (HELCOM, #03126)*.

'Organization designated under Council decision 2005/233':
- *Union économique et monétaire Ouest africaine (UEMOA, #20377)*.

'Organization designated under Council decision 2006/244':
- *South Centre (#19753)*.

Participation on an ad hoc basis
'Organization designated under Council decision 109 (LIX)':
- *International Civil Defence Organization (ICDO, #12582)*.

'Organization designated under Council decision 239 (LXII)':
- *Latin American Faculty of Social Sciences (#16316)*.

'Organizations designated under Council decision 1987/161'
- *African Accounting Council (AAC, no recent information)*;
- *Arab Interior Ministers' Council (AIMC, #00990)*.

'Organizations designated under Council decision 1989/165':
- *Naif Arab University for Security Sciences (NAUSS, #16929)*;
- *World Customs Organization (WCO, #21350)*.

Organization having received a standing invitation to participate as observer in the sessions and the work of UN General Assembly and maintaining permanent observer missions at headquarters: Permanent Observer Mission of Palestine to the United Nations.

NGO Relations All nongovernmental organizations in consultative status are eligible for membership of the Conference of Non-Governmental Organizations in Consultative Relationship with the United Nations (CONGO) and of its committees:
- *Alliance of NGOs on Crime Prevention and Criminal Justice (#00709)*;
- *CONGO Committee on Human Rights (#04663)*;
- *New York NGO Committee on Drugs (NYNGOC, #17097)*;
- *NGO Committee on Ageing, Geneva (see: #04635)*;
- *NGO Committee on Ageing, New York (#17103)*;
- *NGO Committee on Ageing, Vienna (see: #04635)*;
- *'NGO Committees on Disarmament (NGOCD)' – NGO Committee on Disarmament, Peace and Security, New York NY (#17106)* and *NGO Committee for Disarmament, Geneva (#17105)*;
- *NGO Committee on the Family, New York NY (#17107)*;
- *NGO Committee on Freedom of Religion or Belief, New York NY (#17109)*;
- *NGO Committee on Human Settlements (#17110)*;
- *NGO Committee on the Rights of Indigenous Peoples (#17114)*;
- *NGO Committee on the Status of Women, New York NY (see: #04635)*;
- *NGO Committee on Sustainable Development, New York (#17118)*;
- *NGO Committee on Youth (#17121)*.

Organizations having received a standing invitation to participate as observers in the sessions and the work of the General Assembly and maintaining permanent offices at headquarters:
- *International Committee of the Red Cross (ICRC, #12799)*;
- International Federation of Red Cross and Red Crescent Societies (IFRC);

EcoSouth Network Network
05331

alphabetic sequence excludes
For the complete listing, see Yearbook Online at

– *Sovereign Military Hospitaller Order of St John of Jerusalem, of Rhodes and of Malta (SMOM).*
Participation on a continuing basis:
– *International Association of Economic and Social Councils and Similar Institutions (IAESCSI, #11858).* [2023/XE3377/E*]

♦ **EcoSouth Network** Network for an Economical and Ecological Habitat (#17007)

♦ Eco-Sys Action Foundation 05332

Contact 302 Honour Center, 6 Sun Yip Street Chaiwan, Hong Kong, Central and Western, Hong Kong. T. +85225135930. Fax +85228861651.
France Moulinage de Bellevue, Chemin de Presles, 07800 Charmes sur Rhône, France.
URL: http://www.ecosysaction.org/

History Hong Kong. **Aims** Cooperate with *communities* so they can understand the benefits of protecting their fauna and flora; assist communities to be *self-financing* in the medium to long term outside assistance or charity, but with self-respect and pride for the people concerned. **Structure** Team of 3. Committees (4): Scientific; Artistic; Education; Economic. Offices in: Hong Kong; Valence (France); Nairobi (Kenya). **Activities** Develops projects by combining environment, health and education issues. [2011/XJ2241/f/F]

♦ ECOSY / see Young European Socialists (#21989)
♦ ECOTAL – Equipo de Conferencias de Trabajadores de América Latina (inactive)
♦ ECOTDB / see Economic Cooperation Organization Trade and Development Bank (#05314)

♦ Ecotechnie 05333

Contact c/o Cousteau Society, 732 Eden Way North, Ste E707, Chesapeake VA 23320, USA. T. +17575239335. Fax +17575238785.
Contact Cousteau Society, 92 avenue Kleber, 75116 Paris, France. T. +33144340606. Fax +33144340607. E-mail: communication@cousteau.org.
URL: http://www.cousteau.org/education/ecotechnie

History as a joint programme of *Cousteau Society* and *Programme on Man and the Biosphere (MAB, #18526)* of *UNESCO (#20322).* Also referred to as *UNESCO-Cousteau Ecotechnie Programme (UCEP).* **Aims** Promote interdisciplinary education, research and policy-making in the field of the *environment* and *development.* **Structure** Includes *International Network of UNESCO-Cousteau Ecotechnie Chairs (no recent information).* **Languages** English, French. **Finance** Members' dues. **Activities** Includes 4 regional networks: *Arab Region Ecotechnie Network (AREN, see: #05333); Asian Ecotechnology Network (AEN, no recent information); European Network on Human Response to Environmental Stress (HRES, see: #05333);* Latin American Ecotechnie Network (in progress). [2010.06.01/XF6125/F]

♦ ECOTERRA / see Global Society for Ecology and Sound Economy
♦ Eco-TIRAS – International Environmental Association of River Keepers (internationally oriented national body)
♦ The Ecotourism Society / see The International Ecotourism Society (#13225)
♦ ECO Trade and Development Bank / see Economic Cooperation Organization Trade and Development Bank (#05314)
♦ **ECOTRANS** European Network for Sustainable Tourism Development (#08018)
♦ ECO Transit Trade Agreement (1995 treaty)
♦ Eco-union (internationally oriented national body)
♦ **ECOVAST** European Council for the Village and Small Town (#06848)
♦ ECOVic – East African Communities' Organization for Management of Lake Victoria (no recent information)
♦ EcoViva (internationally oriented national body)
♦ ECOWA – Echoes of Women in Africa (internationally oriented national body)
♦ ECOWARM / see European Water Resources Association (#09085)

♦ ECOWAS Bank for Investment and Development (EBID) 05334

Banque d'Investissement et de Développement de la CEDEAO (BIDC) – Banco de Investimento e de Desenvolvimento da CEDEAO

Pres 128 Boulevard du 13 janvier, BP 2704, Lomé, Togo. T. +228216864. Fax +228218684. E-mail: bidc@bidc-ebid.org.
URL: http://www.bidc-ebid.org/

History following a proposal Dec 1999, Lomé (Togo), during the Head of State Summit of *ECOWAS Fund for Cooperation, Compensation and Development (ECOWAS Fund, inactive),* to take over its activities. Comes within *Economic Community of West African States (ECOWAS, #05312).* Fully operational in 2003, with 2 subsidiary bodies: *ECOWAS Regional Development Fund (ERDF, inactive)* and *ECOWAS Regional Investment Bank (ERIB, inactive).* Reorganized into a single structure, 14 Jun 2006. **Aims** Contribute towards the economic development of West Africa through the financing of ECOWAS and NEPAD projects and programmes, notably programmes relating to transport, energy, telecommunications, industry, poverty alleviation, environment and natural resources. **Structure** Board of Governors Board of Directors. President; 2 Vice-Presidents. **Finance** Initial authorized capital: about US$ 750,000,000. Regional members control 67%; non-regional members can subscribe to 33%. **Activities** Politics/policy/regulatory. **Events** *Meeting* 2009, *Joint meeting* Abuja (Nigeria) 2008.
Members Governments of 15 countries:
Benin, Burkina Faso, Cape Verde, Côte d'Ivoire, Gambia, Ghana, Guinea, Guinea-Bissau, Liberia, Mali, Niger, Nigeria, Senegal, Sierra Leone, Togo.
IGO Relations Cooperation Agreement with: *Fonds de solidarité africain (FSA, #09838); International Fund for Agricultural Development (IFAD, #13692)* through former ECOWAS Fund; *African Development Bank Group (ADB Group, #00284); Banque ouest africaine de développement (BOAD, #03170); FAO (#09260); Mutual Aid and Loan Guaranty Fund of the Entente Council (EC-Fund, no recent information).* **NGO Relations** Member of: *Global Network of Export-Import Banks and Development Finance Institutions (G-NEXID, #10489).* Cooperates with: *International Fertilizer Development Center (IFDC, #13590).* [2016.09.26/XF6592/F*]

♦ ECOWAS Centre for Renewable Energy and Energy Efficiency (ECREEE) 05335

Secretariat Achada Santo Antonio, Electra Bldg – 2nd Floor, CP 288, Praia, Santiago, Cape Verde. T. +2382604630 – +2382624608. Fax +2382624614. E-mail: info@ecreee.org.
URL: http://www.ecreee.org/

History 2008, Burkina Faso. Proposed Nov 2007, Burkina Faso. Set up by *Economic Community of West African States (ECOWAS, #05312)* Regulation C/REG 23/11/08, 2008, at 61st Session of ECOWAS Council of Ministers. Secretariat set up 2010, Praia (Cape Verde). Formally inaugurated 6 Jul 2010, Praia (Cape Verde). **Aims** Contribute to the sustainable economic, social and environmental development of West Africa by improving access to modern, reliable and affordable energy services, energy security and reduction of negative environmental externalities of the energy system. **Structure** Executive Board; Technical Committee; National Focal Institutions. **Publications** *ECREEE Newsletter.* **IGO Relations** Core partners: *Agencia Española de Cooperación Internacional para el Desarrollo (AECID); Austrian Development Agency (ADA); Caribbean Centre for Renewable Energy and Energy Efficiency (CCREEE, #03470);* EU Partnership Dialogue Facility; *Global Environment Facility (GEF, #10346); Pacific Centre for Renewable Energy and Energy Efficiency (PCREEE, #17941); UNIDO (#20336); United States Agency for International Development (USAID).* **NGO Relations** Member of: *Climate Technology Centre and Network (CTCN, #04023); LEDS Global Partnership (LEDS GP, #16435).* [2016/XM4409/E*]

♦ **ECOWAS** Economic Community of West African States (#05312)

♦ ECOWAS Network on Debt and Development (ECONDAD) 05336

Réseau sur la dette et le développement d'ECOWAS

Contact 39 Oyaide Avenue, off Benoni Str, GRA, Benin City, Edo, Nigeria. T. +2348187674339. E-mail: info@aneej.org – aneej2000@yahoo.co.uk.

History 28 Aug 1998, Djregbe (Benin), during a conference organized by *African Network for Environment and Economic Justice (ANEEJ)* and *European Network on Debt and Development (EURODAD, #07891).* Represents organizations in *Economic Community of West African States (ECOWAS, #05312)* member countries. **Aims** Coordinate West African NGO and civil society organizations working on debt, structural adjustment policy and the monitoring of international financial institutions within and outside the region. **IGO Relations** *UNDP (#20292).* **NGO Relations** Member of: *The Reality Of Aid (ROA, #18626). Foundation for Grassroots Initiatives in Africa (GrassRootsAfrica)* is a member. [2014.11.20/XM1997/F]

♦ ECOWAS Parliament / see Parliament of the Economic Community of West African States (#18221)
♦ **ECOWAS Parliament** Parliament of the Economic Community of West African States (#18221)

♦ ECOWAS Regional Electricity Regulatory Authority (ERERA) 05337

Contact Energy Commission Bldg, Ghana Airways Avenue (behind Alliance Française), PMB 76, Ministries Post Office, Accra, Ghana. T. +2333028170479. Fax +233302817050. E-mail: info@erera.arrec.org.
URL: http://www.erera.arrec.org/

History 18 Jan 2008. Established by Supplementary Act A/sa 2/1/08 of *Economic Community of West African States (ECOWAS, #05312).* **Aims** Regulate cross-border power exchange among ECOWAS Member States; contribute to setting up a regulatory and economic environment for development of the regional market; provide technical assistance and maintain cooperation among national regulatory authorities of ECOWAS Member States. **Structure** Regulatory Council; Consultative Committees (2); Working Groups (8). **Languages** English, French, Portuguese. **Staff** 21.00 FTE, paid. **Finance** Support from ECOWAS and partners. **Activities** Capacity building; events/meetings; politics/policy/regulatory. **Events** *Regulatory Forum* Cotonou (Benin) 2018. **Publications** *Note on the Official Launch of the ECOWAS Electricity Market.* Annual Report.
Members Full in 15 countries:
Benin, Burkina Faso, Cape Verde, Côte d'Ivoire, Gambia, Ghana, Guinea, Guinea-Bissau, Liberia, Mali, Niger, Nigeria, Senegal, Sierra Leone, Togo.
IGO Relations Ministries of Energy in all ECOWAS Member States. **NGO Relations** Member of (1): *Energy Regulators Regional Association (ERRA, #05476).* Cooperates with (4): *African Forum for Utility Regulators (AFUR, #00324); Association of Mediterranean Energy Regulators (MEDREG, #02800);* Energy Regulatory Authority of the Islamic Republic of Mauritania (ARE); *Regional Electricity Regulators Association of Southern Africa (RERA, #18779).* [2021.03.17/XJ4542/E*]

♦ EcoWB – Ecologists Without Borders (internationally oriented national body)

♦ ECOWEEK 05338

Dir PO Box 100, 180 10 Plakakia, Greece. E-mail: ecoweek@ecoweek.org.
URL: http://www.ecoweek.org/

History 2005. Registration: Start date: 2007, Greece; Start date: 2008, Israel. **Aims** Raise environmental awareness and promote the principles of sustainability through public participation and design. **Structure** Administration. **Languages** English. **Staff** 10.00 FTE, paid. **Finance** Sources: revenue from activities/projects. **Activities** Events/meetings; guidance/assistance/consulting. **Events** *International Conference* Aegina Is (Greece) 2021, *International Conference* Holon (Israel) 2019, *International Conference* Holon (Israel) 2018, *International Conference* Jerusalem (Israel) / Tel Aviv (Israel) 2017, *International Conference* Tilburg (Netherlands) 2017. **Publications** *ECOWEEK Book#2: 15 Paths to Sustainability: from Innovation to Social Design* by Dr Elias Messinas and Despoina Kouinoglou in English; *ECOWEEK The Book 1: 50 Voices for Sustainability* by Dr Elias Messinas and Dr Dan Price in English. Workshop proceedings. **IGO Relations** Also links with other governmental and municipal bodies. **NGO Relations** Partner of (1): *Global Call for Climate Action (GCCA, inactive).* Also links with embassies around Europe and the Middle East; universities and institutes; other national and local organizations. [2022.02.09/XJ0267/F]

♦ **ECP4** European Composites, Plastics and Polymer Processing Platform (#06693)
♦ ECPA / see CropLife Europe (#04965)
♦ **ECPA** European Card Payment Association (#06451)
♦ ECPA – European Cast Polymer Association (inactive)
♦ ECPA – European Center for Preventing Addictions (internationally oriented national body)
♦ **ECPA** European Centre for Public Affairs (#06498)
♦ **ECPA** European Community Psychology Association (#06682)
♦ ECPA / see European Society of Clinical Pharmacy (#08551)
♦ **ECPAT** End Child Prostitution, Child Pornography and Trafficking of Children for Sexual Purposes (#05456)
♦ ECPAT International / see End Child Prostitution, Child Pornography and Trafficking of Children for Sexual Purposes (#05456)
♦ **ECPB** European Club for Paediatric Burns (#06582)
♦ **ECPCA** European Cleft Palate Craniofacial Association (#06573)
♦ **ECPCC** European Council for Pastoral Care and Counselling (#06836)
♦ **ECPC** Early Childhood Peace Consortium (#05156)
♦ **ECPC** European Cancer Patient Coalition (#06433)
♦ ECPCI / see European Rolling Paper Association (#08399)
♦ **ECPCM** European Conference for Protestant Church Music (#05753)
♦ ECP / see Concrete Europe (#04433)
♦ **ECPCP** European Confederation of Primary Care Paediatricians (#06721)
♦ ECPD / see ABET
♦ **ECPD** European Centre for Peace and Development (#06496)
♦ ECP – Escola de Cultura de Pau (internationally oriented national body)
♦ ECPE / see SGI Europe (#19253)
♦ **ECP** European Cultural Parliament (#06870)
♦ **ECPG** European Conference on Politics and Gender (#06735)
♦ ECP/GR / see European Cooperative Programme for Plant Genetic Resources (#06787)
♦ **ECPGR** European Cooperative Programme for Plant Genetic Resources (#06787)
♦ ECPHG – European Centre for Public Health Genomics (unconfirmed)
♦ **ECPHM** European College of Porcine Health Management (#06613)
♦ ECPIC / see European Society of Paediatric and Neonatal Intensive Care (#08683)
♦ ECPI / see European Plasticisers (#08214)
♦ ECPIT / see EURO-CHINA (#05658)
♦ ECPM (internationally oriented national body)
♦ ECPM – Ecole européenne de Chimie, Polymères et Matériaux, Strasbourg (internationally oriented national body)
♦ **ECPM** European Council of Doctors for Plurality in Medicine (#06816)
♦ **ECPMF** European Centre for Press and Media Freedom (#06497)
♦ **ECPNM** European Conference of Promoters of New Music (#06736)
♦ **ECPO** European Cancer Prevention Organization (#06434)
♦ **ECPP** European Confederation of Psychoanalytic Psychotherapies (#06722)
♦ **ECPRD** European Centre for Parliamentary Research and Documentation (#06495)
♦ **ECPR** European Consortium for Political Research (#06762)

♦ ECPR European Political Science Network (EpsNet) 05339

Réseau européen de science politique

SG c/o Central European University, Nador u 9, Budapest 1051, Hungary. T. +3613273000 – +3613272842. Fax +3613256168.
Pres c/o Center for Comparative European Survey Data, Kolkata House, Old Castle Street, London, E1 7NT, UK. T. +442073201140. Fax +442073201157.

History Jun 2001, Paris (France), as *European Political Science Network (EpsNet).* Registered in accordance with French law. Since 2009, integrated into *European Consortium for Political Research (ECPR, #06762),* when current title was adopted. **Aims** Promote discussion, exchange of information and cooperation in the field of *teaching* political science in Europe; contribute to advancement of the discipline in Europe. **Structure** General Assembly (every 3 years). Executive Council of 18 members, elects (for 3-year terms) President and Coordinating Committee. **Languages** English, French. **Finance** Members' dues (1-3 years): Collective, pounds500 – pounds1,000; Individual in EU and EFTA countries, pounds100 – pounds200; Individual in other European countries, pounds50 – pounds100; Doctoral, pounds15; Collective Associate on sliding scale based on size of membership, euro 150 – euro 750 (annually). **Activities** Organizes Annual Plenary Conference (in June). **Events** *Annual Conference* Paris (France) 2003, *Annual Conference* Krakow (Poland) 2002, *Launch meeting* Paris (France) 2001. **Publications** *EpsNet KIOSK* – electronic newsletter; *EpsNet KIOSK Plus: The NET Journal of Political Science* – printed and online. *EpsNet Reports* – series; *EpsNet Teaching Political Science* – series. **Information Services** *Virtual Learning Units* – teaching/learning aids to study the EU.

Members Collective – political science departments and research institutes; Individual; Doctoral; Associate – national political science associations. Members in 31 countries:
Austria, Belgium, Bulgaria, Cyprus, Czechia, Denmark, Estonia, Finland, France, Germany, Greece, Hungary, Ireland, Italy, Latvia, Lithuania, Netherlands, Norway, Poland, Portugal, Romania, Russia, Slovakia, Slovenia, Spain, Sweden, Switzerland, Türkiye, UK, Ukraine, USA.
NGO Relations *International Association for Political Science Students (IAPSS, #12095)* is Associate Member. [2009/XF6236/**E**]

- ♦ **ECPSA** European Confederation of Political Science Associations (#06720)
- ♦ ECPSA / see International Port Community Systems Association (#14623)
- ♦ **ECPS** European Cell Proliferation Society (#06459)
- ♦ ECPS – European Council for Payment Systems (inactive)
- ♦ ECPTO – Eastern Caribbean Popular Theatre Organization (no recent information)
- ♦ **ECPU** European Council of Police Unions (#06837)
- ♦ **ECPVS** European College of Poultry Veterinary Science (#06614)
- ♦ **ECQA** European Certification and Qualification Association (#06511)
- ♦ ECR2P – European Centre for the Responsibility to Protect (internationally oriented national body)
- ♦ ECRAAL – European Centre for Research in Asia, Africa and Latin America (no recent information)
- ♦ **ECRA** European Carpet and Rug Association (#06452)
- ♦ **ECRA** European Cartridge Research Association (#06454)
- ♦ **ECRA** European Cement Research Academy (#06461)
- ♦ **ECRA** European Climate Research Alliance (#06576)
- ♦ ECRA – European Cold Rolled Section Association (internationally oriented national body)
- ♦ ECRAF / see European Commission for Road Safety in Armed Forces (#06638)
- ♦ **ECRAF** European Commission for Road Safety in Armed Forces (#06638)
- ♦ **ECR Asia Pacific** Efficient Consumer Response Asia Pacific (#05385)
- ♦ ECR – Association européenne pour la compétitivité par les ressources humaines (inactive)
- ♦ ECR Australasia – Efficient Consumer Response Australasia (internationally oriented national body)
- ♦ ECRCD – European Centre for the Rights of Children with Disabilities (internationally oriented national body)
- ♦ **ECRC** European Cool Roofs Council (#06781)

♦ ECR Community 05340

Project & Communications Manager Blvd du Jubilie 71 – bte 3, 1080 Brussels, Belgium.
Co-Chair address not obtained.
Co-Chair address not obtained.
URL: https://www.ecr-community.org/

History 1994. Former names and other names: *Efficient Consumer Response – ECR Europe* – former; *Réponse Optimale au Consommateur* – former; *ECR Europe* – former. Registration: Banque-Carrefour des Entreprises, No/ID: 0465.043.833, Start date: 25 Sep 1998, Belgium. **Aims** Provide a neutral platform to develop and share best practices among a network of ECR Nationals and their members. **Structure** Board of Directors. **Languages** English. **Activities** Events/meetings; research and development; research/documentation. **Events** *Meeting* Vienna (Austria) 2015, *Annual Leaders Forum* Brussels (Belgium) 2014, *Annual Conference* Brussels (Belgium) 2013, *Annual Conference* Brussels (Belgium) 2012, *Annual Conference* Brussels (Belgium) 2011. **Publications** *Best Practice Blue Books*. Case studies; guides; reviews.
Members Manufacturers and retailers through national ECR organizations. Members in 21 countries:
Austria, China, Colombia, Cyprus, Czechia, Finland, France, Germany, Greece, Guatemala, Ireland, Italy, Kazakhstan, Mexico, Poland, Portugal, Russia, Slovakia, Spain, Switzerland, UK.
NGO Relations Partner of (4): *EuroCommerce (EC, #05665)*; *European Brands Association (#06397)*; *GS1 in Europe (#10810)*; *The Consumer Goods Forum (CGF, #04772)*. [2022.10.20/XD5834/**D**]

- ♦ **ECR-CoR** European Conservatives and Reformists Group – Committee of the Regions (#06746)
- ♦ **ECREA** European Communication Research and Education Association (#06675)
- ♦ **ECRE** Conseil européen sur les réfugiés et les exilés (#06839)
- ♦ ECREEA – European Conference of Radio and Electronic Equipment Associations (inactive)
- ♦ **ECREEE** ECOWAS Centre for Renewable Energy and Energy Efficiency (#05335)
- ♦ ECRE – European Committee on Romani Emancipation (unconfirmed)
- ♦ **ECRE** European Council on Refugees and Exiles (#06839)
- ♦ **ECR** Euro Contrôle Route (#05668)
- ♦ ECR Europe / see ECR Community (#05340)
- ♦ ECR – European Centre for the Regions, Barcelona (see: #07569)
- ♦ ECR – European Centre for Restoration Techniques (internationally oriented national body)
- ♦ **ECR** European Conservatives and Reformists Group (#06745)
- ♦ **ECR** European Conservatives and Reformists Party (#06747)
- ♦ ECR – Europees Centrum voor Restauratietechnieken (internationally oriented national body)
- ♦ ECRF – European Centre for Research on Federalism (internationally oriented national body)
- ♦ ECRI – Engineering & Construction Risk Institute (internationally oriented national body)
- ♦ ECRI – European Commission Against Racism and Intolerance (see: #04881)
- ♦ **ECRI** European Credit Research Institute (#06857)
- ♦ ECRIN-ERIC / see European Clinical Research Infrastructure Network (#06577)
- ♦ **ECRIN** European Clinical Research Infrastructure Network (#06577)
- ♦ ECRIN-IA / see European Clinical Research Infrastructure Network (#06577)
- ♦ ECRIN Integration Activity / see European Clinical Research Infrastructure Network (#06577)
- ♦ ECRIN-PPI / see European Clinical Research Infrastructure Network (#06577)
- ♦ ECRIN Preparation Phase for the Infrastructure / see European Clinical Research Infrastructure Network (#06577)
- ♦ ECRIN – Reciprocal Knowledge Programme / see European Clinical Research Infrastructure Network (#06577)
- ♦ ECRIN-RKP / see European Clinical Research Infrastructure Network (#06577)
- ♦ ECRIN – Transnational Working Group / see European Clinical Research Infrastructure Network (#06577)
- ♦ ECRIN-TWG / see European Clinical Research Infrastructure Network (#06577)
- ♦ **ECRL** European Council of Religious Leaders – Religions for Peace (#06840)
- ♦ ECRM – European Conference on Research Methodology for Business and Management Studies (meeting series)
- ♦ ECRM – European Interregional Scientific and Educational Centre on Major Risk Management (internationally oriented national body)
- ♦ ECRML – European Charter for Regional or Minority Languages (1992 treaty)
- ♦ **ECRN** European Chemical Regions Network (#06522)
- ♦ **ECRN** European Climate Realist Network (#06575)
- ♦ **ECRO** European Chemoreception Research Organization (#06527)
- ♦ **ECRR** European Centre for River Restoration (#06499)
- ♦ ECRS – European Cancer Rehabilitation and Survivorship Symposium (meeting series)
- ♦ ECRS / see European Union of the Deaf (#08985)
- ♦ ECRS / see European Union of Deaf Youth (#08986)
- ♦ ECRTA / see European Chemical Transport Association (#06525)
- ♦ ECRT / see European Confederation of Tobacco Retailers (#06725)
- ♦ ECSA / see European Union Studies Association
- ♦ ECSACON / see East, Central and Southern African College of Nursing and Midwifery (#05215)
- ♦ **ECSACONM** East, Central and Southern African College of Nursing and Midwifery (#05215)
- ♦ ECSA-DK / see Danish Society for European Studies
- ♦ **ECSA** Estuarine and Coastal Sciences Association (#05551)
- ♦ **ECSA** European Child Safety Alliance (#06534)
- ♦ **ECSA** European Chlorinated Solvent Association (#06540)
- ♦ **ECSA** European Citizen Science Association (#06557)
- ♦ **ECSA** European Community Shipowners' Associations (#06683)
- ♦ **ECSA** European Community Studies Association (#06684)
- ♦ **ECSA** European Composer and Songwriter Alliance (#06691)
- ♦ ECSA – European Computing Services Association (inactive)
- ♦ ECSA – European Conference on Software Architecture (meeting series)
- ♦ ECSA – European Corporate Security Association (internationally oriented national body)
- ♦ ECSA / see European Snacks Association (#08498)
- ♦ ECSAFA – Eastern Central and Southern African Federation of Accountants (inactive)
- ♦ ECSAFoST – East, Central and Southern Africa Association of Food Science and Technology (inactive)
- ♦ **ECSA-HC** East, Central and Southern African Health Community (#05216)
- ♦ ECSA Health Community / see East, Central and Southern African Health Community (#05216)
- ♦ ECSAPHA – East, Central and Southern African Public Health Association (inactive)
- ♦ **ECSB** European Council for Small Business and Entrepreneurship (#06842)
- ♦ ECSBM – European Conference on the Spectroscopy of Biological Molecules (meeting series)
- ♦ **ECSC** Eastern Caribbean Supreme Court (#05236)
- ♦ ECSC – European Coal and Steel Community (inactive)
- ♦ ECSCW – European Conference on Computer Supported Cooperative Work (meeting series)
- ♦ **ECSDA** European Central Securities Depositories Association (#06468)
- ♦ **ECSDEV** European Center of Sustainable Development (#06464)
- ♦ **EC-SEA Chamber** Eastern Caribbean-Southeast Asia Economic and Cultural Chamber (#05235)
- ♦ EC Seed Crushers' and Oil Processors' Federation / see FEDIOL – The EU Vegetable Oil and Proteinmeal Industry (#09718)
- ♦ **ECS** Electrochemical Society (#05421)
- ♦ **ECS** European Calcium Society (#06431)
- ♦ **ECS** European Cetacean Society (#06513)
- ♦ ECS – European Chemical Society (no recent information)
- ♦ **ECS** European Circuit Society (#06551)
- ♦ ECS – European College of Surgeons (inactive)
- ♦ **ECS** European Cytokine Society (#06881)
- ♦ ECS – European Engineered Construction Systems Association (inactive)
- ♦ **ECS** Europese Culturele Stichting (#06868)
- ♦ **ECSF** European Cardiology Section Foundation (#06449)
- ♦ **ECSF** European Civil Service Federation (#06567)
- ♦ **ECSI** European Electronic Chips and Systems Design Initiative (#06973)
- ♦ **ECSITE** European Network of Science Centres and Museums (#07998)
- ♦ **ECSLA** European Cold Storage and Logistics Association (#06603)
- ♦ **ECSL** European Centre for Space Law (#06501)
- ♦ ECSM – European Conference on Social Media (meeting series)
- ♦ **ECSN** European Concrete Societies Network (#06698)
- ♦ **ECSO** European Council of Skeptical Organizations (#06841)
- ♦ **ECSOL** European Commission on Sexual Orientation Law (#06639)
- ♦ **ECSPA** European Calcium Silicate Producers Association (#06430)
- ♦ ECSP – European Council of Shopping Places (unconfirmed)
- ♦ **ECSPM** European Civil Society Platform for Multilingualism (#06569)
- ♦ ECSQARU – European Conference on Symbolic and Quantitative Approaches to Reasoning with Uncertainty (meeting series)
- ♦ **ECSR** European Committee of Social Rights (#06668)
- ♦ **ECSR** European Consortium for Sociological Research (#06763)
- ♦ **ECSRHM** European College of Small Ruminant Health Management (#06615)
- ♦ **ECSSA** European Confederation of Search and Selection Associations (#06723)
- ♦ ECSS / see Complex Systems Society (#04418)
- ♦ **ECSS** European College of Sport Science (#06616)
- ♦ **ECSS** European Cooperation for Space Standardization (#06785)
- ♦ ECSS / see European Salt Producers Association (#08425)
- ♦ ECSSID – European Cooperation in Social Science Information and Documentation (inactive)
- ♦ ECSSR – Emirates Centre for Strategic Studies and Research (internationally oriented national body)
- ♦ **ECSSS** European Confederation of Soil Science Societies (#06724)
- ♦ **ECStA** European Council for Student Affairs (#06845)
- ♦ **ECSVD** European College for the Study of Vulval Diseases (#06618)
- ♦ **ECSWE** European Council for Steiner Waldorf Education (#06844)
- ♦ ECSWPR / see European Centre for Social Welfare Policy and Research (#06500)
- ♦ ECSWS / see European Council for Steiner Waldorf Education (#06844)
- ♦ ECSWTR / see European Centre for Social Welfare Policy and Research (#06500)

♦ ECTA 05341

Head of Admin Rue des Colonies 18/24, 8th Floor, Box 8, 1000 Brussels, Belgium. T. +3225135285. Fax +3225130914. E-mail: ecta@ecta.org.
Manager Legal Affairs address not obtained.
URL: http://www.ecta.org/

History 8 Oct 1980. Former names and other names: *European Communities Trade Mark Practitioners' Association* – former (8 Oct 1980 to Jan 1992); *Association des praticiens des Communautés européennes dans le domaine des marques* – former (8 Oct 1980 to Jan 1992); *European Communities Trade Mark Association (ECTA)* – former (Jan 1992 to 1 Jan 2020); *Association communautaire du droit des marques* – former (Jan 1992 to 1 Jan 2020). Registration: Banque-Carrefour des Entreprises, No/ID: 0738.648.961, Start date: 2 Dec 2019, Belgium; Companies House, No/ID: 1520996, Start date: 8 Oct 1980, End date: 30 Mar 2021, England; Banque-Carrefour des Entreprises, No/ID: 0851.518.062, Start date: 1 Apr 1996, End date: 2 Dec 2019, Belgium; EU Transparency Register, No/ID: 932781112187-50, Start date: 4 Nov 2013. **Aims** Promote the knowledge and professionalism of members in the fields of trade marks, designs, geographical indications, copyright, anti-counterfeiting, data, internet and related intellectual property rights within the European Union. **Structure** General Meeting (at Annual Conference); Board of Directors; Supervisory Board; Committees (16); Task Force. **Languages** English. **Staff** 5.00 FTE, paid. **Finance** Sources: members' dues. **Activities** Events/meetings; networking/liaising; politics/policy/regulatory; projects/programmes. **Events** *Annual Conference* Prague (Czechia) 2023, *Annual Conference* Copenhagen (Denmark) 2022, *Annual Conference* Vienna (Austria) 2021, *Annual Conference* Copenhagen (Denmark) 2020, *Annual Conference* Edinburgh (UK) 2019. **Publications** *ECTA e-Bulletin*.
Members Ordinary (815): EU-national practitioners in the 27 European Union countries:
Austria, Belgium, Bulgaria, Croatia, Cyprus, Czechia, Denmark, Estonia, Finland, France, Germany, Greece, Hungary, Ireland, Italy, Latvia, Lithuania, Luxembourg, Malta, Netherlands, Poland, Portugal, Romania, Slovakia, Slovenia, Spain, Sweden.
Associate (353): non-EU national practitioners in EU countries and practitioners outside EU, in 67 countries and territories:
Albania, Andorra, Argentina, Australia, Bangladesh, Belize, Bolivia, Bosnia-Herzegovina, Brazil, Cameroon, Canada, Chile, China, Colombia, Costa Rica, Dominican Rep, Ecuador, Egypt, Guernsey, Honduras, Hong Kong, Iceland, India, Indonesia, Iran Islamic Rep, Israel, Japan, Jersey, Jordan, Kazakhstan, Korea Rep, Kuwait, Lebanon, Liechtenstein, Macau, Malaysia, Mauritius, Mexico, Montenegro, Morocco, New Zealand, Nicaragua, North Macedonia, Norway, Pakistan, Panama, Paraguay, Peru, Philippines, Puerto Rico, Russia, Saudi Arabia, Senegal, Serbia, Singapore, South Africa, Switzerland, Taiwan, Thailand, Türkiye, UK, Ukraine, United Arab Emirates, Uruguay, USA, Venezuela, Vietnam.
Affiliate (32): non-practitioners in or outside EU. Membership countries not specified.
Corporate (19): corporate entities not providing legal advice, incorporated or having a presence in a Member State. Membership countries not specified.
Members in Education (8): undertaking a full-time undergraduate or postgraduate course. Membership countries not specified.
Consultative Status Consultative status granted from: *World Intellectual Property Organization (WIPO, #21593)* (Permanent Observer Status). **IGO Relations** Observer status with (1): *European Union Intellectual Property Office (EUIPO, #08996)*. Also links with national patent and trade mark offices. **NGO Relations** Also links with national associations. [2022.10.26/XE5386/v/**E**]

- ♦ ECTAA / see The European Travel Agents' and Tour Operators' Associations (#08942)

- ♦ **ECTAA** The European Travel Agents' and Tour Operators' Associations (#08942)
- ♦ ECTA – Eastern Caribbean Tourist Association (inactive)
- ♦ **ECTA** Eurasian Colorectal Technologies Association (#05604)
- ♦ **ECTA** European Chemical Transport Association (#06525)
- ♦ **ECTA** European Competitive Telecommunications Association (#06689)
- ♦ **ECTA** European Core and Tube Association (#06797)
- ♦ **ECTA** European Cutting Tools Association (#06873)
- ♦ **ECTARC** European Centre for Training and Regional Cooperation (#06503)
- ♦ ECTC / see European Folklore Institute
- ♦ ECTC / see European Counter Terrorism Centre (#06851)
- ♦ **ectc** European Counter Terrorism Centre (#06851)
- ♦ **ECTE** European Council for Theological Education (#06846)
- ♦ **ECTEG** European Cybercrime Training and Education Group (#06874)
- ♦ **ECTEL** Eastern Caribbean Telecommunications Authority (#05237)
- ♦ ECT – Energy Charter Treaty (1994 treaty)
- ♦ ECTI / see ECTI – Professionnels Seniors Bénévoles
- ♦ ECTI – French Senior Volunteers (internationally oriented national body)
- ♦ **ECTIL** European Centre of Tort and Insurance Law (#06502)
- ♦ ECTI – Professionnels Seniors Bénévoles (internationally oriented national body)
- ♦ ECTJ – European Center for Transitional Justice (unconfirmed)
- ♦ ECTM – European Council of Teachers of Mathematics (no recent information)
- ♦ ECTN Association / see European Chemistry Thematic Network (#06526)
- ♦ **ECTN** European Chemistry Thematic Network (#06526)
- ♦ **ECTN** European Cultural Tourism Network (#06871)
- ♦ ECTODerm – European Confederation of Telemedical Organizations in Dermatology (inactive)
- ♦ **ECTP-CEU** European Council of Spatial Planners (#06843)
- ♦ **ECTP** European Construction Technology Platform (#06768)
- ♦ ECTP / see European Council of Spatial Planners (#06843)
- ♦ **ECTP** International Organizing Committee for European Conferences on Thermophysical Properties (#14484)
- ♦ ECTR / see European Interregional Scientific and Educational Centre on Major Risk Management
- ♦ **ECTR** European Council on Tolerance and Reconciliation (#06847)
- ♦ **ECTRI** European Conference of Transport Research Institutes (#06737)
- ♦ **ECTRIMS** European Committee for Treatment and Research in Multiple Sclerosis (#06673)
- ♦ **ECTS** European Calcified Tissue Society (#06429)
- ♦ **ECTSIA** European Cardiovascular and Thoracic Surgery Institute of Accreditation (#06450)
- ♦ **ECTS MA** ECTS Medicine Association (#05342)

♦ ECTS Medicine Association (ECTS MA) 05342

Sec Medical Univ of Vienna, Spitalgasse 23, 1090 Vienna, Austria. T. +4314016021023. Fax +43140160921001.
URL: http://www.med-ects.org/

History 2004, Crete (Greece), when it continued the work of *ECTS Inner Circle Medicine Group (ECTS ICMG)*, set up 1996. Registered in accordance with Belgian law. **Aims** Optimize exchanges of medical students within Europe using European Credit Transfer System (ECTS). **Structure** Executive Board, comprising President, Treasurer, Secretary and 4 members. **Languages** English. **Finance** Members' dues: euro 200. **Events** *Annual meeting* Edinburgh (UK) 2010, *Annual meeting* Coimbra (Portugal) 2009, *Annual Meeting* Lisbon (Portugal) 2009, *Annual meeting* Naples (Italy) 2008, *Annual meeting* Oslo (Norway) 2007.
Members Institutions in 20 countries:
Austria, Belgium, Bulgaria, Czechia, Denmark, Finland, France, Germany, Greece, Hungary, Italy, Netherlands, Norway, Poland, Portugal, Slovenia, Spain, Sweden, Switzerland, UK. [2017/XM3733/**D**]

- ♦ ECTUA – European Council of Telecommunications Users' Associations (inactive)
- ♦ **ECTUN** European Capitals Trade Unions Network (#06441)
- ♦ ECUA – European Conference on Underwater Acoustics (meeting series)
- ♦ ECU Banking Association Association bancaire pour l'Ecu / see Euro Banking Association (#05647)
- ♦ **ECUC** European Cloud User Coalition (#06578)
- ♦ ECU-Europe / see European Consultants Unit (#06769)
- ♦ **ECU** European Chess Union (#06528)
- ♦ **ECU** European Chiropractors' Union (#06538)
- ♦ ECU – European Committee for Umami (unconfirmed)
- ♦ **ECU** European Consultants Unit (#06769)
- ♦ **ECUME** Echanges culturels en Méditerranée (#05281)

♦ Ecumenical Asia-Pacific Students and Youth Network (EASY Net) . . 05343

Contact IMCS Asia-Pacific Resource Center, 20 Avocado Road, Pilar Village, Almanza, MM 1750 Las Piñas, Philippines. T. +6328006473. Fax +6328006466.
URL: http://www.wscfap.org/regionalprogramme/easynet/index.html/

Aims Promote ecumenical dialogue and cooperation between students in the Asia Pacific region. **Activities** Organizes 'Asia Pacific Students and Youth Week (APSYW)' (annual). Organizes workshops. **Events** *Annual Meeting* Bangkok (Thailand) 2004. **Publications** *EASY Net News*. **NGO Relations** *Asia and Pacific Alliance of YMCAs (APAY, #01826).* [2013/XM1764/**F**]

- ♦ Ecumenical Association of Academies and Laity Centres in Europe / see Oikosnet Europe – Ecumenical Association of Academies and Laity Centres in Europe (#17706)
- ♦ Ecumenical Association for Adult Education in Europe (inactive)

♦ Ecumenical Association of Third World Theologians (EATWOT) 05344

Association oecuménique des théologiens du Tiers-monde – Asociación Ecuménica de Teólogos del Tercer Mundo – Ökumenische Vereinigung von Dritte-Welt-Theologen

Exec Sec-Treas Deans Road, Suite 271, Colombo, 00010, Sri Lanka. T. +94717707403. E-mail: eatwotgensec@gmail.com.
URL: https://eatwotglobal.com/history.html

History Aug 1976, Dar es Salaam (Tanzania UR). Founded during 1st meeting of an Ecumenical Dialogue of Christian Theologians. **Aims** Foster a forum of theologians from Asia, Africa and Latin-America and representatives of US minorities who are committed to theologize from the perspective of the poor and marginalized; organize conferences and consultations that deepen the commitment to the struggle of the poor. **Structure** General Assembly. Executive Committee, consisting of President, Vice-President and Treasurer, Executive Secretary, and 4 Regional Coordinators for: Asia, Africa; Latin America; Minorities in the USA (Hispanic). Working Commissions (2): Theological; Women. **Languages** English, French, Spanish. **Staff** Voluntary. **Finance** Financed by ecumenical agencies. **Activities** Events/meetings. **Events** *General Assembly* Yogyakarta (Indonesia) 2012, *General Assembly* Johannesburg (South Africa) 2006, *General Assembly* Quito (Ecuador) 2001, *Asian conference* Sri Lanka 2000, *Women's conference* Chennai (India) 1999. **Publications** *EATWOT's Newsletter* (4 a year); *Voices from the Third World* (2 a year). *Commonalities, Differences and Crossfertilization among Third World Theologies*; *Liberation and Theology (Latin American Region)* – up to 50 vols; *We Dare to Dream: Doing Theology as Asian Women* by V Fabella and Sun Ai Lee Park; *With Passion and Compassion* by V Fabella and M Oduyoye.
Members Individuals in 38 countries and territories:
Angola, Argentina, Bolivia, Botswana, Brazil, Cameroon, Chile, Colombia, Congo DR, Costa Rica, Cuba, Egypt, Ghana, Hong Kong, India, Indonesia, Jamaica, Japan, Kenya, Korea Rep, Madagascar, Malawi, Mexico, Namibia, Nicaragua, Nigeria, Pakistan, Peru, Philippines, Senegal, Sierra Leone, South Africa, Sri Lanka, Taiwan, Tanzania UR, Uruguay, USA, Zimbabwe.
NGO Relations Instrumental in setting up (2): *Association des historiens de l'Eglise d'Asie (no recent information)*; *Association oecuménique des théologiens africains (AOTA, no recent information).* [2021/XD5449/v/**C**]

- ♦ Ecumenical Church Loan Fund / see ECLOF International (#05287)
- ♦ Ecumenical Commission on European Cooperation (inactive)
- ♦ Ecumenical Councils (meeting series)
- ♦ Ecumenical Development Cooperative Society / see Oikocredit International (#17704)

♦ Ecumenical Diaconal Year Network (EDYN) 05345

Registered Address Rue Brogniez 44, 1070 Brussels, Belgium. E-mail: edyn@edyn.org.
URL: http://www.edyn.org/

History Registration: No/ID: 0659.770.145, Start date: 19 Jul 2016, Belgium; Start date: 2009, End date: 2016, Hungary; Start date: 2005, End date: 2009. **Aims** Function as a network of ecumenical Christian *voluntary* service programmes, organizing exchanges of volunteers and coordinating members' support programmes. **Structure** Board. **Languages** English.
Members Organizations in 14 countries:
Belgium, Czechia, France, Germany, Great Britain, Hungary, Italy, Korea Rep, Latvia, Norway, Poland, Slovakia, Ukraine, USA.
NGO Relations Partner of (3): *European Federation for Diaconia (Eurodiaconia, #07099)*; *Network of European Voluntary Service Organisations (NEVSO)*; *Phiren Amenca (#18362).* [2017/XG5588/**F**]

- ♦ Ecumenical Documentation and Information Centre for Eastern and Southern Africa / see Ecumenical Documentation and Information Centre in Southern Africa (#05346)

♦ Ecumenical Documentation and Information Centre in Southern Africa (EDICISA) 05346

Centre oecuménique de documentation et d'information pour l'Afrique du Sud – Centro Ecumênico de Documentação e Informação para Africa Austral

Contact address not obtained. T. +2634570311 – +2634570312. Fax +2634572979.

History Mar 1987, Harare (Zimbabwe), as *Ecumenical Documentation and Information Centre for Eastern and Southern Africa (EDICESA) – Centre oecuménique de documentation et d'information pour l'Afrique australe et du Sud – Centro Ecumênico de Documentação e Informação para Africa Austral e Oriental*. Present name adopted 1999. **Aims** Give an authentic voice to the *Churches* themselves, to their ecumenical partners and to the world about the Southern African region, particularly those countries in the region which still face serious problems. Through publications: facilitate research on topical issues relevant to church and society in Southern Africa; seek to be an instrument of transformation of society in line with gospel values; nurture *South-South* and South-North dialogue. **Structure** Acts as Secretariat of *Fellowship of Councils of Churches in Southern Africa (FOCCISA, no recent information)*, whose General Assembly (annual) comprises the Board of General Secretaries of member National Councils of Churches. Director is assisted by Management Board, comprising a theologian, a lawyer, a chartered accountant, a documentalist and a communications specialist. **Finance** Sponsoring National Councils of Churches; ecumenical partners in Europe and North America. **Activities** Organizes: courses; workshops; research. Monitors political situations – eg elections in Zimbabwe in Jun 2000. Instrumental in setting up: *African Research Utilization Network (ARUNET, no recent information)*; *Economic Justice Network for Churches in Eastern and Southern Africa (EJN, #05317)*. **Events** *Closer union of Christian communication centres* Nairobi (Kenya) 1997, *Seminar on the plight of ex-combatants in Namibia* Windhoek (Namibia) 1997, *Meeting of African and global communications networks* Nairobi (Kenya) 1993. **Publications** *EDICISA News* (12 a year); *Ecumenical Journal for Southern Africa* (4 a year). Occasional papers and other publications on current developments in Southern Africa. **Information Services** *EDICISA Database on Documentation on Theological Reflections*; *EDICISA Database on Economic Justice*; *EDICISA Database on Political and Economic Situations in the Region*; *EDICISA Database on Refugees and Human Rights*; *EDICISA Historical Database on Apartheid as it was in Namibia and South Africa*.
Members Sponsored by National Christian Councils in 11 countries:
Angola, Botswana, Eswatini, Lesotho, Malawi, Mozambique, Namibia, South Africa, Tanzania UR, Zambia, Zimbabwe.
IGO Relations *UNHCR (#20327).* [2009/XE5944/**E**]

♦ Ecumenical Forum of European Christian Women (EFECW) 05347

Forum oecuménique de femmes chrétiennes d'Europe – Ökumenisches Forum Christlicher Frauen in Europa

Co-Pres Grinzingerstrasse 87/5, 1190 Vienna, Austria.
Contact 174 rue Joseph II, 1000 Brussels, Belgium.
URL: http://www.efecw.net/

History Founded 1982. **Aims** Strengthen the ecumenical women's network; support women in their search for a common European identity; link women together in the liberating message of the *Bible*; call for practical action. **Structure** General Assembly (every 4 years); Coordinating Committee; Executive Team of Officers; National Coordinators. Based at: *European Contact Group – Ecumenical Network for Economic and Social Action (ECG, #06773)*. **Languages** English. **Finance** Members' dues. Other sources: donations; contributions from the Churches; fund-raising for particular projects. **Activities** Events/meetings; networking/liaising; training/education; capacity building. **Events** *General assembly / European Assembly* Tinos (Greece) 2014, *Seminar* Vienna (Austria) 2013, *Seminar* Great Malvern (UK) 2012, *Seminar* Druskininkai (Lithuania) 2011, *General assembly / European Assembly* Loccum (Germany) 2010. **Publications** *Forum News* (4 a year) in English, French, German; *EFECW Bulletin* (occasional). Reports to general assemblies.
Members National and regional organizations of European Christian women, individuals, groups. Full in 32 countries:
Armenia, Austria, Belarus, Bulgaria, Croatia, Cyprus, Czechia, Denmark, Estonia, Finland, France, Germany, Greece, Hungary, Ireland, Italy, Lithuania, Malta, Moldova, Netherlands, Norway, Poland, Portugal, Romania, Russia, Serbia, Slovakia, Spain, Sweden, Switzerland, UK, Ukraine.
NGO Relations Member of: *Side by Side (#19265)*. Cooperates with: *Conference of European Churches (CEC, #04593)*; *Ecumenical Youth Council in Europe (EYCE, #05352)*; *European Society of Women in Theological Research (ESWTR, #08789)*; *European Women's Synod*; *Fellowship of the Least Coin (FLC, #09728)*; *International Committee for World Day of Prayer (#12811)*; *Oikosnet Europe – Ecumenical Association of Academies and Laity Centres in Europe (EAALCE, #17706)*; *World Council of Churches (WCC, #21320)*; *World Student Christian Federation (WSCF, #21833).* [2015.02.18/XF1955/**F**]

- ♦ Ecumenical Foundation of Southern Africa (internationally oriented national body)
- ♦ Ecumenical Group of Dombes (#10765)

♦ Ecumenical Group of Women (KAIRE) 05348

Groupe oecuménique de femmes consacrées

Contact address not obtained. E-mail: kairegroup@gmail.com.

History Sep 1971, Bossey (Switzerland), as a living interconfessional cell of women engaged in monastic, diaconal or active call in their Church and the world, moved by the Spirit to a conversion to prayer, to one another, to Unity. **Aims** Be a focus of communion and search, where women who share a calling within Church discover once again, and in a vital way, that which is the very heart of their various vocations; encourage an ecumenical and spiritual experience where both dimensions of contemplation and service to mankind should be lived; be a ferment in society, so that unity in the Church can be discerned, and give hope to all human beings. **Structure** Steering Group, composed of 8 members from Anglican, Orthodox, Catholic and Protestant communities. **Languages** English, French, German. **Staff** 8.00 FTE, voluntary. **Finance** Proceeds of meetings. Donations. **Events** *International Meeting* Durham (UK) 2014, *International Meeting* UK 2014, *International Meeting* Bossey (Switzerland) 2011, *International meeting* Paris (France) 2010, *International meeting* Erfurt (Germany) 2008. **Publications** *Information – Kaïre* in English, French, German – informal bulletin. [2018.06.01/XF2620/**F**]

- ♦ Ecumenical Human Rights Committee (internationally oriented national body)
- ♦ Ecumenical Institute for Theological Research / see Tantur Ecumenical Institute (#20096)
- ♦ Ecumenical Methodist Conference / see World Methodist Council (#21650)

♦ Ecumenical Patriarchate of Constantinople 05349

Patriarcat oecuménique de Constantinople – Ikumenikon Patriarhion

Contact Dr Sadik Ahmet Cad No 19, Fatih, 34083 Istanbul/Istanbul, Türkiye. T. +902125255416. Fax +902125316533. E-mail: ecpatr.english@gmail.com.
URL: http://www.ec-patr.org/

History Circa 300, the Ecumenical Patriarchs tracing their origins, according to the sacred tradition, back to St Andrew, the first-called the Apostle, who arrived in Byzantium (subsequently Constantinople) in 36 AD and is considered as the Founder of that Church. Nevertheless, from written sources it is not possible to ascertain the exact year in which Christianity was preached in Byzantium. For the sake of convenience, the history of the Ecumenical Patriarchate of Constantinople may be divided into 5 broad periods: (1) From 300 to 843 – the founding of Constantinople, to the end of the Iconoclastic struggle, climaxing in the triumph of Orthodoxy in 843. (2) 843 to 1261 – the triumph of the Orthodoxy, to the fall of Constantinople to the Latins, during the Fourth Crusade of 1204, followed by the Latin occupation of Constantinople. (3) 1261 to 1453 – the recovery of Constantinople by the Byzantine Emperor Michael Paleologos, to the fall of Constantinople to the Ottoman Turks in 1453. (4) 1453 to 1833 – from the beginning of 'Turkokratia' (Turkish subjugation), to the beginning of the Greek War of Independence (1821) when the Church of Greece declared its autonomy from the Patriarchate and established the autocephalous Church of Greece (1833). (5) Following 1833, there is a new phase of the Ecumenical Patriarchate until the present day.
The early organization of the Church followed the concept of Apostolic ranking so that by the 5th century the great Christian centres were five: Rome in the West, Constantinople, Alexandria, Antioch and Jerusalem in the East. Because of the Arab conquest, by the 8th century, Alexandria, Antioch and Jerusalem diminished in importance. Primacy over the Orthodox East inevitably passed to the capital city, Constantinople. The presence of those other Patriarchates, however, continued to be represented in Constantinople by delegates who were part of the *'Synodos Endemousa'* or Synodical Council. This Council dealt with ecclesiastical questions which arose from the various centres of Christendom. The concept of *'Pentarchy'* (the five great centres of Christendom) was firmly established by the 8th century when the Byzantine Emperor Justinian drafted his law codes in civil-ecclesiastical matters, also known as *'Nomocanones'*. The Ecumenical Patriarch and his canonical jurisdiction extended not only over the entire Byzantine Empire, but even beyond, to the lands where he had sent missionaries in order to proclaim the Gospel of Christ. Because of its leading historical role, notably in the formation of Christian dogma and institutions, the Patriarchate of Constantinople, *'Primus Inter Pares'*, expanded its pastoral activities in other Patriarchates and Dioceses, settling local problems of administrative and disciplinary nature, always with the approval from the other sister Patriarchates. It is for this reason that the 4th Ecumenical Council of Chalcedon (451), giving a definite shape to the organization of the Church of Constantinople, not only confirmed the Patriarchal rank as second to that of Rome, but also granted him the right to consecrate the bishops of "barbaric" nations, by extension, to the present day, bishops of the *'Orthodox Diaspora'*, or loosely translated, "colonies" of the Orthodox Christians. In the 6th century, the Patriarchate of Constantinople was named 'Ecumenical Patriarchate'.
In the 9th century, Photios the Great (857-867), who was considered the greatest of all Patriarchs, was responsible for the codification of canon law, a new legal code, and for the conversion of Slavs. He dispatched two Greek missionaries, Cyril and Methodios, to preach among Slavs to convert them and to translate the Greek Liturgy into Slavonic. Photios became a great problem for Rome and therefore was declared a heretic by the Western Church since he argued that the Pope of Rome did not have any jurisdiction over the Patriarchs of the East. He was anathematized at the altar of St Peter's by Pope John VIII. In the 11th century, during the Norman conquest of Sicily, they attempted to impose the Pope's jurisdiction over the Byzantine Christians there. Patriarch Michael Cerularios protested the papal intervention in Sicily and this and a series of other events led to the anathema and schism of 1054. In the summer of 1054 a papal delegation deposited a Bull of Excommunication on the altar of St Sophia Church against 'Michael and his followers'. Thus began the great breach between Eastern and Western Christianity which continued to the present day.
One of the great chapters in the history of the Ecumenical Patriarchate during the 'Turkokratia' deals with the subject of how the Greek Orthodox faithful, led by the Patriarch of Constantinople and, by extension, by local parish priests, preserved the Greek (ethnos) and Church (ecclesia) during periods of subjugation and cultural stagnation. This could be achieved since a precedence had existed in the Byzantine period which always conceived the Ethos and Ecclesia as working together so that the cultural heritage along with the Liturgical and Ecclesiastical tradition would be kept intact. Following the Greek War of Independence, and, in particular, following 1833, because of tensions between the governments of Greece and of the Ottoman Empire, the Church of Greece declared itself autocephalous (independent) from the Ecumenical Patriarchate while still remaining as a Daughter Church (in a spiritual and traditional sense) of the Mother Church at the Phanar (Constantinople). This 'spiritual' affinity continues to exist with all the Orthodox Churches throughout the world.
It is for this reason that the Ecumenical Patriarchate also became a leader in the emerging world-wide ecumenical movement. In 1902 an encyclical emanating from the Ecumenical Patriarchate was addressed to the Patriarchs of Alexandria and Jerusalem and the Heads of the autocephalous Churches of Cyprus, Russia, Greece, Romania and Montenegro which dealt with the 'Matter concerning our present and future relations with the two great bodies of Christianity, ie Roman Catholic and that of the Protestant, and the desired union in the present and the future with them, including the Old Catholics'. Later in 1920, another encyclical was issued by the Patriarchate, which is considered the first official Church document proposing the creation of a League of Churches, such as the one which finally came into being through the formation of the World Council of Churches, 1948, Amsterdam (Netherlands). Also, between 1920 and 1945, the Mother Church of all Orthodoxy recognized the independence of the Serbian Orthodox and Romanian Orthodox Patriarchates. The recognition of the independent Albanian Orthodox Church followed and the schism of the Bulgarian Church was healed when it was recognized in 1945 as a Patriarchate. In 1922 the Greek Orthodox Archdiocese of North and South America was organized. Between 1960 and 1970, the Ecumenical Patriarchate initiated three important pan-Orthodox conferences (1960, 1963, 1964) preparing the ground for a world-wide Orthodox Synod. *Holy and Great Council (#10937)*, gathering most of the Orthodox churches, met for the first time, Jun 2016.
In 1964, Patriarch Athenagoras and Pope Paul VI met in Jerusalem for the first meeting of Pope and Patriarch for over half a millennium. The result was the mutual annulment in both Rome and Constantinople, 7 Dec 1965, of the historic, mutual excommunication of 1054. The steps taken by Athenagoras also brought together various Orthodox and Oriental Orthodox Churches, such as Copts of Egypt (termed as monophysites), the Jacobites, the Armenian, and others. During the tenure of Patriarch Demetrios I, elected in Jul 1972, in addition to many trips that he has taken to sister Churches, two events were of utmost importance. The first was the visit of Dimitrios and members of the Holy Synod in 1987 to Rome in order to continue the ecumenical encounter between the Greek Orthodox Church and the Roman Catholic Church, for the second time after 900 years of division. The Patriarch also visited the Archbishop of Canterbury following the Rome visit. The second was the consecration and dedication of the new Patriarchal building which had been burned down by fire in 1941. At this occasion, 17 Dec 1989, heads of international religious, cultural and civic organizations and denominations came together in order to give witness and testimony to the importance of the Ecumenical Patriarchate for the World Orthodoxy. The Patriarch Bartholomew was elected in Oct 1991 as the 270th Ecumenical Patriarch of Constantinople – and invested with the ecclesiastical title 'Archbishop of Constantinople, New Rome, and Ecumenical Patriarch, by the Grace of God' – by the Holy Synod of the Ecumenical Patriarchate.
After the fall of Constantinople many treaties have been formulated within the international community with a view to protect the Ecumenical Patriarchate. Some of these treaties were: *Treaty of Kutschuk-Kainardji, of Jul 16, 1774*; *Law of Hatt-I Humayun, of February 18, 1856*; *Treaty of Berlin, Jul 13, 1878*; *Treaty of Sèvres, August 10, 1920*; *Treaty of Lausanne, 1922*.
Aims Spread the Gospel of Jesus Christ. **Structure** The Ecumenical Patriarchate, or the Ecumenical Patriarchate of Constantinople, is also referred to as the Great Church of Christ. It is the spiritual centre of the great Orthodox Christian Church worldwide and the official headquarters of the Ecumenical Patriarch, the highest spiritual authority of Orthodoxy, first among equals, of all the other Orthodox Patriarchs. The mission of the Ecumenical Patriarchate is to bear witness to the mystery of Orthodox unity. Its primacy among the Orthodox is a "primacy of service" and never one of authority over the other Orthodox churches. The term *Eastern Orthodox Churches* relates to three main groups: (a) Orthodox, composed of the patriarchates and churches mentioned under 'Members' (see below), which recognize each other and are recognized by the Ecumenical Patriarch of Constantinople, who is considered the keeper of the 'canons' of Orthodoxy; (b) Churches which have authentic Orthodox roots and adhere to Orthodox doctrine but which are historically estranged; (c) Ancient Oriental Orthodox, commonly referred to in the past as Monophysite (Copts, Nestorians, etc). *Commission orthodoxe européenne (no recent information)* represents the Patriarchate with the institutions of the European Union and the Council of Europe. **Languages** English, Greek, Turkish. **Finance** Christian stewardship. **Activities** Events/meetings; religious activities. **Publications** *Analecta Vlatadon* – ed Patriarchal Institution of Patristic Studies, Thessaloniki, Greece; *Contacts* – ed Greek Orthodox Archdiocese of France; *Episkepsis* – ed Orthodox Centre of the Ecumenical Patriarchate, Chambésy/Geneva; *Kleronomia* – ed Patriarchal Institution of Patristic Studies, Thessaloniki, Greece; *Le messager orthodox* – ed Greek Orthodox Archdiocese in France; *Orthodox Herald* – ed Greek Orthodox Archdiocese of Thyateira and Great Britain; *Orthodox Parousia* – ed Greek Orthodox Archdiocese of Germany; *Stachys* – ed Greek Orthodox Archdiocese of Austria; *Theologia Dokimia* – ed Patriarchal Institution of Patristic Studies, Thessaloniki, Greece; *The Orthodox Observer* – ed Greek Orthodox Archdiocese of North and South America; *Voice of Orthodoxy* – ed Greek Orthodox Archdiocese of Australia. **Members** Eastern Orthodox Churches, consisting of the Patriarchates, Autocephalous and Autonomous Churches united by the same faith of the Ecumenical Patriarchate in Istanbul: Ancient Patriarchates of Alexandria, Antioch and Jerusalem; Autocephalous Churches of Russia, Georgia, Serbia, Romania, Bulgaria, Cyprus, Greece, Poland, Albania, Czech Rep, Slovakia and Ukraine. Autonomous Churches of Sinai, Finland and Estonia. Also: Mount Athos (Monastic Community in Northern Greece under the Jurisdiction of the Ecumenical Patriarchate). **NGO Relations** Member of (2): *Conference of European Churches (CEC, #04593)*; *European Network of Health Care Chaplaincy (ENHCC, #07919)*. Official Theological Dialogue with: the Roman Catholic Church; the Anglican Church; the Oriental Churches; the Lutheran Church through *Lutheran-Orthodox Joint Commission (#16530)*; and the Reformed Churches through *Orthodox-Reformed Joint Commission*. Represented at: *World Council of Churches (WCC, #21320)*. [2022/XF9300/**F**]

♦ Ecumenical Pharmaceutical Network (EPN) 05350

Réseau Pharmaceutique Oecuménique

Exec Dir Gatunda Villas House No 1, Gatunda Road, Kileleshwa, PO Box 749, Sarit Centre, Nairobi, 00606, Kenya. T. +25420572522702. Fax +254204343395.
URL: http://www.epnetwork.org/

History Originally a programme within the Christian Medical Commission of *World Council of Churches (WCC, #21320)*, now an independent network. Registered in accordance with Kenyan law, 2004. **Aims** Support churches and church health systems provide just and compassionate quality pharmaceutical services. **Structure** General Assembly (annual). Board, comprising Chairman and 6 members, plus one non-voting member. Secretariat, including Executive Director. **Languages** English, French. **Staff** 9.00 FTE, paid. **Finance** Funding from church-related agencies and development organizations; course fees; fundraising. Budget (annual): about US$ 700,000. **Activities** Research, advocacy, information sharing and capacity building, implemented through activities in various countries and a central support system. Priority areas (4): Access to and rational use of medicines; HIV and AIDS treatment; Professionalization of pharmaceutical services; Pharmaceutical information sharing. Organizes frequent workshops. **Events** *Forum* Addis Ababa (Ethiopia) 2012, *Biennial forum / Forum* Nairobi (Kenya) 2010, *Biennial forum / Forum* Yaoundé (Cameroon) 2008, *Biennial forum / Forum* Germany 2006, *Forum* Moshi (Tanzania UR) 2004. **Publications** *Contact Magazine* (annual); *Pharmalink* (2-3 a year) – newsletter; *e-Pharmalink* – electronic newsletter; *Netlink* – electronic newsletter. Annual Report. Forum report.
Members Full in 34 countries:
Australia, Austria, Belgium, Burkina Faso, Cameroon, Central African Rep, Chad, Congo DR, Egypt, Ethiopia, Germany, Ghana, India, Kenya, Lesotho, Liberia, Malawi, Moldova, Namibia, Niger, Nigeria, Papua New Guinea, Peru, Rwanda, Sierra Leone, South Africa, Sudan, Switzerland, Tanzania UR, Togo, Uganda, USA, Zambia, Zimbabwe.
IGO Relations *WHO (#20950)*. **NGO Relations** Member of: *Christian Connections for International Health (CCIH)*; *Ecumenical Advocacy Alliance (EAA, inactive)*; *International Pharmaceutical Federation (#14566)*. [2012.08.14/XM1472/**F**]

- ♦ Ecumenical Program on Central America and the Caribbean (internationally oriented national body)
- ♦ Ecumenical Program for Inter-American Communication and Action / see Ecumenical Program on Central America and the Caribbean
- ♦ Ecumenical Satellite Commission (inactive)
- ♦ Ecumenical Service for Human Dignity (internationally oriented national body)
- ♦ Ecumenical Society of the Blessed Virgin Mary (religious order)

♦ Ecumenical Women's Initiative (EWI) 05351

Ekumenska inicijativa zena (EIZ)

Managing Dir Cetvrt kralja Slavca 3, HR-21310 Omis, Croatia. T. +38521862599. Fax +38521757085. E-mail: carolyn@eiz.hr – eiz@eiz.hr.
URL: http://www.eiz.hr/

History Launched 2007, Croatia, developing out of the *World Council of Churches (WCC, #21320)* – Ecumenical Women's Solidarity Fund (EWSF) (1993-2007). Registered as a Croatian non-profit, 2007. **Aims** Support and empower women and girls as advocates for women's human rights and *gender* equality and facilitators of interfaith and civil dialogue for peace and reconciliation. **Structure** Governing Assembly. **Languages** Croatian, English. **Staff** 4.00 FTE, paid. **Finance** International donations. Annual budget: euro 400,000. **Activities** Awareness raising; advocacy/lobbying/activism; financial and/or material support; capacity building; networking/liaising. Active in: Bosnia-Herzegovina, Croatia, Kosovo, Montenegro, North Macedonia, Serbia. **NGO Relations** Member of: *Prospera – International Network of Women's Funds (INWF, #18545)*. [2022/XM6638/**E**]

♦ Ecumenical Youth Council in Europe (EYCE) 05352

Conseil oecuménique de la jeunesse en Europe (COJE) – Ökumenischer Jugendrat in Europa

Chairperson Rue Brogniez 44, 1070 Brussels, Belgium. E-mail: general.secretary@eyce.org.
URL: http://www.eyce.org/

History 4 Oct 1968, Switzerland. 4-6 Oct 1968, Switzerland, functioning as a regional body of *World Council of Churches (WCC, #21320)* Youth Team. Constitution, adopted by General Meeting, 1-8 Oct 1995, Mikolajki (Poland), is effective as of 11 Oct 1995. Former names and other names: *European Ecumenical Youth Council* – former; *Conseil de la jeunesse oecuménique d'Europe* – former. Registration: Banque-Carrefour des Entreprises, Belgium. **Aims** Initiate and further the commitment of young people to Jesus *Christ* and His desire for reconciliation, justice, the integrity of creation and a permanent peace in Europe and the world; stimulate, encourage and facilitate ecumenical contacts between young people by all possible means. **Structure** General Meeting; Executive Committee; National Correspondents in each member country. **Languages** English. **Staff** Voluntary. **Finance** Sources: donations; government support; members' dues; subsidies. Subsidies from churches, church councils, governments and other bodies. **Activities** Events/meetings; networking/liaising; projects/programmes. **Events** *General Meeting* Brussels (Belgium) 2021, *General Meeting* Berlin (Germany) 2019, *General Meeting* Malaga (Spain) 2017, *General Meeting* Frankfurt-Main (Germany) 2011, *General Meeting* Denmark 2009. **Publications** Circular letter; newsletter; seminar reports.
Members National ecumenical youth councils or denominational bodies of church youth work in 25 countries:
Austria, Belgium, Bulgaria, Czechia, Denmark, Estonia, Finland, France, Germany, Hungary, Iceland, Ireland, Italy, Latvia, Malta, Netherlands, Norway, Poland, Portugal, Romania, Russia, Slovakia, Spain, Sweden, Switzerland.
Contact members in 11 countries:
Belarus, Croatia, Cyprus, Greece, Lithuania, Moldova, Serbia, Slovenia, Sweden, Türkiye, Ukraine.
Included in the above, 1 organization listed in this Yearbook:
International Old Catholic Youth (IOCY, no recent information).
IGO Relations A cooperating INGYO of: *European Youth Centres (EYCs, #09138)*. **NGO Relations** Member of: *Conference of European Churches (CEC, #04593)*; *European Youth Forum (#09140)*; *UNITED for Intercultural Action – European Network Against Nationalism, Racism, Fascism and in Support of Migrants and Refugees (UNITED, #20511)*. [2022.02.24/XE0483/**E**]

- ♦ **ECUO** East European and Central Asian Union of PLWH (#05257)
- ♦ **ECURES** European Association of Cultural Researchers (#06000)
- ♦ ECUSAT – Ecumenical Satellite Commission (inactive)
- ♦ **ECVAA** European College of Veterinary Anaesthesia and Analgesia (#06619)
- ♦ ECVA / see European College of Veterinary Anaesthesia and Analgesia (#06619)
- ♦ ECVAM – European Centre for the Validation of Alternative Testing Methods (inactive)
- ♦ ECVBM-CA / see European College of Animal Welfare and Behavioural Medicine (#06606)
- ♦ **ECVC** European Coordination Via Campesina (#06795)
- ♦ **ECVCN** European College of Veterinary and Comparative Nutrition (#06621)
- ♦ **ECVCP** European College of Veterinary Clinical Pathology (#06620)
- ♦ **ECVD** European College of Veterinary Dermatology (#06622)
- ♦ **ECVDI** European College of Veterinary Diagnostic Imaging (#06623)

ECVECC
05352

alphabetic sequence excludes
For the complete listing, see Yearbook Online at

- ♦ ECVECC – European College of Veterinary Emergency and Critical Care (unconfirmed)
- ♦ ECV – European Coalition for Vision (unconfirmed)
- ♦ **ECVIM – CA** European College of Veterinary Internal Medicine – Companion Animals (#06624)
- ♦ **ECVM** European College of Veterinary Microbiology (#06625)
- ♦ **ECVM** European Council of Vinyl Manufacturers (#06849)
- ♦ **ECVN** European College of Veterinary Neurology (#06626)
- ♦ ECVO – European College of Veterinary Ophthalmologists (see: #08783)
- ♦ ECVPar / see European Veterinary Parasitology College (#09058)
- ♦ **ECVP** European College of Veterinary Pathologists (#06627)
- ♦ **ECVPH** European College for Veterinary Public Health (#06629)
- ♦ **ECVPT** European College of Veterinary Pharmacology and Toxicology (#06628)
- ♦ **ECVS** European College of Veterinary Surgeons (#06630)
- ♦ ECWA / see United Nations Economic and Social Commission for Western Asia (#20558)
- ♦ **ECW** Education Cannot Wait (#05369)
- ♦ **ECWF** European Council of WIZO Federations (#06850)
- ♦ ECWITA – European Community Wholesalers and International Traders Association (inactive)
- ♦ **ECWM** European Christian Workers Movement (#06546)
- ♦ ECWM – Europejskie Centrum Współpracy Mlodziezy (internationally oriented national body)
- ♦ **ECWS** European Confederation of Watercolour Societies (#06726)
- ♦ **ECWT** European Centre for Women and Technology (#06504)
- ♦ ECYC – European Centre of Youth Cooperation (internationally oriented national body)
- ♦ **ECYC** European Confederation of Youth Clubs (#06727)
- ♦ ECYCS – European Club of Young Cardiac Surgeons (no recent information)
- ♦ ECYF4HC / see Rural Youth Europe (#19007)
- ♦ ECYO / see European Union Youth Orchestra (#09024)
- ♦ **ECYON** European Cooperative Youth Network (#06789)
- ♦ ECYTO – European Confederation of Youth Travel Organizations (inactive)
- ♦ **ECZM** European College of Zoological Medicine (#06631)
- ♦ E and D / see Planète Enfants & Développement
- ♦ **EDAA** European Design and Automation Association (#06910)
- ♦ **EDAA** European Interactive Digital Advertising Alliance (#07582)
- ♦ **EDAB** European Dana Alliance for the Brain (#06885)
- ♦ EDADU / see Organisation of Eastern Caribbean States/Competitive Business Unit (#17805)
- ♦ **EDA** Europäische Demokratische Anwälte (#03049)
- ♦ **EDA** European Dairy Association (#06883)
- ♦ **EDA** European Defence Agency (#06895)
- ♦ **EDA** European Delirium Association (#06897)
- ♦ **EDA** European Demolition Association (#06902)
- ♦ **EDA** European Depression Association (#06905)
- ♦ EDA – European Desalination Association (inactive)
- ♦ EDA – European Diabolo Association (unconfirmed)
- ♦ **EDA** European Dyslexia Association – International Organisation for Specific Learning Disabilities (#06951)
- ♦ EDA / see Federation of European Defence Technology Associations (#09500)
- ♦ **EDAL** Equipos Docentes de Latinoamérica y el Caribe (#05524)
- ♦ **EDAMBA** European Doctoral Programmes Association in Management and Business Administration (#06935)
- ♦ EDANA / see EDANA, the voice of nonwovens (#05353)
- ♦ **EDANA** EDANA, the voice of nonwovens (#05353)
- ♦ EDANA – International Association Serving the Nonwovens and Related Industries / see EDANA, the voice of nonwovens (#05353)

♦ EDANA, the voice of nonwovens (EDANA) 05353

Gen Manager Av Herrmann Debroux 46, 1160 Brussels, Belgium. T. +3227349310. Fax +3227333518. E-mail: info@edana.org.
URL: http://www.edana.org/

History 14 May 1971, Brussels (Belgium). Former names and other names: *European Disposables and Nonwovens Association (EDANA)* – former; *EDANA – International Association Serving the Nonwovens and Related Industries* – former. Registration: Banque-Carrefour des Entreprises, No/ID: 0411.532.101, Start date: 27 Aug 1971, Belgium; EU Transparency Register, No/ID: 0120704687-67, Start date: 27 Nov 2008. **Aims** Provide for its members a comprehensive range of services with the information and data necessary to enhance the industry's goals and performance; create the foundation for sustainable growth of the nonwovens and related industries through active promotion, education and dialogue with stakeholders. **Structure** General Assembly (annual); Board of Governors; Professional staff is headed by General Manager. **Languages** Danish, Dutch, English, French, German, Italian, Spanish. **Staff** 16.00 FTE, paid. **Finance** Sources: members' dues. **Activities** Advocacy/lobbying/activism; events/meetings; knowledge management/information dissemination; monitoring/evaluation; networking/liaising; standards/guidelines; training/education. **Events** *FILTREX Conference* Berlin (Germany) 2022, *International Nonwovens Symposium* Lyon (France) 2022, *FILTREX Asia Conference* Shanghai (China) 2022, *IMPERVIUS Conference* Sitges (Spain) 2022, *Outlook Conference* St Julian's (Malta) 2022. **Publications** *Regulatory enews* (12 a year) – For EDANA members only; *Sustainability enews* (12 a year) – For EDANA members only; *EDANA Newsletter* (3 a year); *EDANA e-news* (24 a year) – For members only. Reports; statistics; event publications and papers. **Members** Full; Trade Associate; Non-Trade Associate. Members in over 30 countries. Membership countries not specified. **NGO Relations** Member of (6): *Circular Plastics Alliance (#03936); EURATEX – The European Apparel and Textile Confederation (EURATEX, #05616); European Platform for Chemicals Using Manufacturing Industries (CheMI, #08223); Federation of European and International Associations Established in Belgium (FAIB, #09508); Industry4Europe (#11181); MedTech Europe (#16692).* In liaison with technical committees of: *Comité européen de normalisation (CEN, #04162); International Organization for Standardization (ISO, #14473).* [2022.05.11/XD3964/t/**D**]

- ♦ **EDB** Eurasian Development Bank (#05605)
- ♦ **EDBF** European Dragon Boat Federation (#06943)
- ♦ **EDbN** European Deafblind Network (#06890)

♦ EDBT Association 05354

Pres School of Computer Science, Univ of Manchester, Oxford Road, Manchester, M13 9PL, UK.
URL: http://www.edbt.org/

History 1990. Founded initially to support continuity of the EDBT Conference Series. Legal status changed 1995. Registration: Start date: 1995, Italy. **Aims** Promote and favour in Europe the progress and study of technology and applications concerning Extending *Database Technology* (EDBT). **Structure** Executive Board. **Activities** Awards/prizes/competitions; events/meetings; training/education. **Events** *International Conference on Extending Database Technology* Edinburgh (UK) 2022, *International Conference on Extending Database Technology* Nicosia (Cyprus) 2021, *International Conference on Extending Database Technology* Copenhagen (Denmark) 2020, *International Conference on Extending Database Technology* Lisbon (Portugal) 2019, *International Conference on Extanding Database Technology* Vienna (Austria) 2018. **Publications** Conference proceedings. **NGO Relations** Cooperates with (1): *International Conference on Database Theory (ICDT).* [2021/XJ6725/**E**]

- ♦ **EDBU** European Deafblind Union (#06891)
- ♦ EDC – Ecobank Development Corporation (internationally oriented national body)
- ♦ EDC – Education Development Center (internationally oriented national body)
- ♦ **EDC** European Dance Council (#06886)
- ♦ EDC – European Defence Community (inactive)
- ♦ **EDC** European Draughts Confederation (#06945)
- ♦ **EDC** European Drought Centre (#06947)
- ♦ **EDCF** European Digital Cinema Forum (#06920)

♦ EDC Free Europe 05355

Coordinator address not obtained. T. +3222343640.
URL: https://www.edc-free-europe.org/

Aims Raise awareness and urge faster governmental action on *endocrine* disrupting *chemicals* (EDCs) that are toxic to our health. **Activities** Advocacy/lobbying/activism.
Members Organizations; individuals. Campaign partners include 21 organizations listed in this Yearbook:
- *Baltic Environmental Forum (BEF, #03116);*
- *Center for International Environmental Law (CIEL);*
- *Centre for Environment and Sustainable Development (ECO-Accord Centre);*
- *CHEM Trust;*
- *Child Rights International Network (CRIN, #03885);*
- *ClientEarth (#03996);*
- *Commonweal;*
- *Corporate Europe Observatory (CEO, #04839);*
- *European Academy for Environmental Medicine (EUROPAEM, #05790);*
- *European Environmental Bureau (EEB, #06996);*
- *Fundación Ecologia y Desarrollo (ECODES);*
- *GLOBAL 2000;*
- *Greenpeace International (#10727);*
- *Health and Environment Alliance (HEAL, #10879);*
- *Health Care Without Harm (HCWH, #10875);*
- *International Chemical Secretariat (ChemSec);*
- *Mediterranean Information Office for Environment, Culture and Sustainable Development (MIO-ECSDE, #16657);*
- *Pesticide Action Network Europe (#18338);*
- *SumOfUs;*
- *WEMOS;*
- *Women Engage for a Common Future (WECF, #20992).* [2019/XM8676/y/**E**]

- ♦ **EDC Network** European Documentation Centres (#06937)
- ♦ EDCS / see Oikocredit International (#17704)
- ♦ **EDCTP** European and Developing Countries Clinical Trials Partnership (#06912)
- ♦ EDDA – European Digital Dealers Association (no recent information)
- ♦ EdDev – Education for Development (internationally oriented national body)
- ♦ **EDeAN** European Design for All e-Accessibility Network (#06909)
- ♦ **EDE** Energy Drinks Europe (#05469)
- ♦ EDE – European Association for Directors and Providers of Long-Term Care Services for the Elderly (inactive)
- ♦ EDEFA – European Decorative and Stationery Plastics Foils Association (inactive)

♦ EDEN Digital Learning Europe (EDEN) 05356

Secretary General Roosikrantsi 2, 10119 Tallinn, Estonia. E-mail: secretariat@eden-europe.eu.
URL: http://www.eden-europe.eu/

History 2019, Tallinn (Estonia). Following departure of United Kingdom from *European Union (EU, #08967)* (Brexit), took over operations of *European Distance and E-Learning Network*, created May 1991, Prague (Czech Rep). Established as an international educational association and not-for-profit organisation. Instrumental in setting up *European Foundation for Quality in eLearning (EFQUEL, inactive).* Former names and other names: *European Distance Education Network (EDEN)* – former; *Réseau européen d'enseignement à distance* – former; *Europäisches Netzwerk für Fernlehre* – former; *Platform for Collaboration in Distance Education in Europe (Hungary Platform)* – former; *European Distance and E-Learning Network* – former; *Réseau européen d'enseignement à distance* – former; *Europäisches Netzwerk für Fernlehre* – former. Registration: No/ID: 80562628, Start date: 2019, Estonia. **Aims** As a network for the professional community and a professional community for smart learning, share knowledge and improve understanding amongst professionals in distance and e-learning; promote policy and practice across the whole of Europe and beyond; promote networking, international co-operation and professional development. **Structure** General meeting (annual); Executive Committee; EDEN Network of Academics and professionals (NAP) Steering Committee; Secretariat. Since Jan 2014, institutions of *EuroPACE (inactive)* integrated into EDEN. **Finance** Sources: meeting proceeds; members' dues. Other sources: European Union project funds. **Activities** Events/meetings; networking/liaising; research/documentation; training/education. **Events** *Annual Conference* Dublin (Ireland) 2023, *Research Workshop* Dubrovnik (Croatia) 2022, *Annual Conference* Tallinn (Estonia) 2022, *Annual Conference* Madrid (Spain) 2021, *Annual Conference* Timisoara (Romania) 2020. **Publications** *EDEN Newsletter* (12 a year). Conference proceedings.
Members Membership of EDEN is grouped in 2 Sections Institutions; Network of Academics and Professionals (NAP). Institutional in 44 countries:
Argentina, Australia, Austria, Belgium, Bolivia, Brazil, Bulgaria, Canada, Croatia, Cyprus, Czechia, Denmark, Ecuador, Estonia, Finland, France, Germany, Greece, Hungary, Iceland, Ireland, Israel, Italy, Japan, Kuwait, Lithuania, Netherlands, Norway, Peru, Poland, Portugal, Romania, Russia, Serbia, Slovakia, Slovenia, South Africa, Spain, Sweden, Switzerland, Türkiye, UK, United Arab Emirates, USA.
Included in the above, 6 institutions listed in this Yearbook:
European Association for Distance Learning (EADL, #06015); European Students' Union (ESU, #08848); International Association for Intercultural Education (IAIE, #11969); International Higher Education Teaching and Learning Association (HETL, #13795); ORION (inactive); Société européenne pour la formation des ingénieurs (SEFI, #19462).
NGO Relations Member of (2): *EFMD – The Management Development Network (#05387); Lifelong Learning Platform – European Civil Society for Education (LLLP, #16466).* Affiliated with (1): *SPACE Network (#19899).* [2022.10.20/XF2402/y/**F**]

- ♦ EDEN / see EDEN Digital Learning Europe (#05356)
- ♦ **EDEN** EDEN Digital Learning Europe (#05356)
- ♦ EDEN / see European Dermato-Epidemiology Network (#06906)
- ♦ **EDEN** European Dermato-Epidemiology Network (#06906)

♦ EDEN Network 05357

Contact Grand Rue 24, 6941 Barvaux, Belgium.
URL: http://youredenexperience.com/

History EDEN Network launched by *European Commission (EC, #06633)*, 2006. Association set up Jan 2012. EDEN stands for *European Destinations of Excellence*. Registered in accordance with Belgian law. Registration: Belgium. **Aims** Promote sustainable *tourism* by: drawing attention of tourists, tour operators, media and institutions to the value and diversity of emerging European tourist destinations; support members in adopting good policies and practices; persuade other destinations in Europe to adopt sustainable tourism development models. **Structure** General Assembly; Board of Administration. **Languages** English. **Staff** Voluntary. **Finance** Members' dues. **Activities** Events/meetings.
Members Full in 25 countries:
Austria, Belgium, Croatia, Cyprus, Czechia, Estonia, Finland, France, Germany, Greece, Hungary, Iceland, Ireland, Italy, Latvia, Lithuania, Luxembourg, Malta, Netherlands, Poland, Portugal, Romania, Slovenia, Spain, Türkiye.
NGO Relations Partners include: European Best Destination; *European Network for Sustainable Tourism Development (ECOTRANS, #08018); European Travel Commission (ETC, #08943).* [2020/XJ8992/**D**]

- ♦ EDERED – European Drama Encounters (internationally oriented national body)
- ♦ EdeSA / see European Academy of Dental Sleep Medicine (#05786)
- ♦ Edesia – Edesia Nutrition (internationally oriented national body)
- ♦ Edesia Nutrition (internationally oriented national body)
- ♦ EDEUCHEM – European Association of Editors of Periodicals in Chemistry and Physics (inactive)
- ♦ ED – European Dialogue (internationally oriented national body)
- ♦ **EDFA** European Digital Finance Association (#06921)
- ♦ **EDFA** European Down and Feather Association (#06941)
- ♦ EDF / see Dystonia Europe (#05151)
- ♦ EDF – Environmental Defense Fund (internationally oriented national body)
- ♦ EDF – European Democracy Forum (internationally oriented national body)
- ♦ **EDF** European Dermatology Forum (#06907)
- ♦ **EDF** European Development Fund (#06914)

♦ **EDF** European Disability Forum (#06929)
♦ **EDF** European Foundation for Democracy (#07347)
♦ **EDFI** European Development Finance Institutions (#06913)
♦ **Edgar Cayce's ARE** Association for Research and Enlightenment (#02893)

♦ EDGE Funders Alliance 05358

Contact 2021 Fillmore St, Ste 66, San Francisco CA 94115, USA. E-mail: contactus@edgefunders.org.
URL: http://edgefunders.org/

Aims Raise awareness and deepen understanding of the interconnected nature of the social, economic and ecological *crises* threatening earth's common *future.* **Structure** Board of Directors; Regional Advisory Steering Groups. **Activities** Advocacy/lobbying/activism; events/meetings; knowledge management/information dissemination; networking/liaising. **Events** *Annual Conference* 2021, *Conference* Berlin (Germany) 2020, *Conference* Rio de Janeiro (Brazil) 2019, *Conference* New Orleans, LA (USA) 2018. **Publications** *Leading EDGE Newsletter.* **Members** Donors; foundation officers; trustees and advisors in over 30 countries. Membership countries not specified. **NGO Relations** Member of (1): *Worldwide Initiatives for Grantmaker Support (WINGS, #21926).* [2022.06.15/XM6704/v/**C**]

♦ EDG / see European Conservatives Group (#06744)
♦ EDG / see European Domestic Glass (#06938)
♦ **EDG** European Domestic Glass (#06938)
♦ **EDHF** European Dental Hygienists Federation (#06903)
♦ EDIA – European Carbon Dioxide Association (inactive)
♦ EDIBCIC / see Asociación de Educación e Investigación en Ciencia de la Información de Iberoamérica y el Caribe (#02122)

♦ EDIBUILD 05359

Sec address not obtained.
URL: http://www.edibuildeurope.dataexchangestandards.info/

History 1991. Also referred to as *EdiBuild Europe.* **Aims** Function as as a *user group* for *EDI* in the *construction industry.* **Finance** Members' dues. Contracts. **Activities** Annual conference.
Members Organizations and individuals in 9 countries:
Belgium, Denmark, Finland, France, Germany, Netherlands, Sweden, Switzerland, UK.
IGO Relations *European Commission (EC, #06633)* (DG XIII). **NGO Relations** *Comité européen de normalisation (CEN, #04162).* [2010/XE2216/**E**]

♦ EdiBuild Europe / see EDIBUILD (#05359)
♦ EDICESA / see Ecumenical Documentation and Information Centre in Southern Africa (#05346)
♦ **EDICIC** Asociación de Educación e Investigación en Ciencia de la Información de Iberoamérica y el Caribe (#02122)
♦ **EDICISA** Ecumenical Documentation and Information Centre in Southern Africa (#05346)
♦ EDI – Energy Delta Institute (internationally oriented national body)
♦ EDI – Enterprise Development International (internationally oriented national body)
♦ **EDI** European Decontamination Institute (#06894)
♦ EDI – European Development Institute (unconfirmed)

♦ EDIFICAS Europe 05360

Contact Rue de Livourne 45, 1050 Brussels, Belgium.

History 1992. European grouping established on the initiative of *Accountancy Europe (#00061)* (then known as FEE). Registration: Start date: 19 Jan 1993, France; Belgium. **Aims** Identify common characteristics of *accounting* and *auditing* data flow between companies; carry out studies and make recommendations on the consequences of *electronic* business – *EDI* (Electronic Data Interchange) – in the field, particularly as it concerns the legal position, telecommunications, security and general requirements of internal control; promote utilization of e-business or EDI for all accountancy operations, using UN/EDIFACT standards as a means of managing data flow; promote appropriate auditing techniques in the EDI environment; verify whether already defined UNSMs or ebXML messages can satisfy identified functional requirements and propose to the UN/EDIFACT International Trade and Business Processes Group the creation of new messages or modification to existing messages; ensure effective communications with other groups in the sector and with national bodies. **Structure** General Assembly (annual). Executive Committee: President; Vice-President; Secretary-Treasurer; Responsible for documentation; Responsible for technical matters; Working Group rapporteurs. **Finance** Members' dues. **Activities** Working Groups: GT1 – Accountancy; GT2 – Fiscal teleprocedures; GT3 – Electronic archives; GT4 – XML/UML; GT6 – Certificates of conformity; GT7 – Banking teletransmissions; GT9 – Social notifications; GT10 – Personal fiscal teleprocedures; GT11 – IAS/IFRS; GT12 – Nomenclature. **Members** Active subscriber. Open to organizations in all member states of the European Union and EFTA and of other European organizations with a clear interest. Membership countries not specified. **IGO Relations** *United Nations Centre for Trade Facilitation and Electronic Business (UN/CEFACT, #20527).* Represented at General Assembly: *European Commission (EC, #06633).* [2015/XE2067/**E**]

♦ **EDIFICE** Global Network for B2B Integration in High Tech Industries (#10481)
♦ EDiLiC – Éducation et Diversité Linguistique et Culturelle (unconfirmed)
♦ EDiMA / see DOT Europe (#05125)
♦ Edinburgh Association for Sending Medical Aid to Foreign Countries / see EMMS International
♦ Edinburgh Europa Institute (internationally oriented national body)
♦ Edinburgh International Health Centre / see HealthLink360
♦ Edinburgh Medical Missionary Society / see EMMS International
♦ **EDiNEB Network** Educational Innovation in Economics and Business Network (#05367)
♦ EDiS / see European Society of Dirofilariosis and Angiostrongylosis (#08584)
♦ EDISON – International Conference on Electron Dynamics in Semiconductors, Optoelectronics and Nanostructures (meeting series)
♦ EDITEAST – Association of Editors in the South-East Asia, Australasia and Oceania (inactive)
♦ EDITERRA – European Association of Earth Science Editors (inactive)

♦ EDItEUR 05361

Contact United House, North Road, London, N7 9DP, UK. T. +442075036418. Fax +442075036418. E-mail: info@editeur.org.
URL: https://www.editeur.org/

History 1991. Incorporated 1994. Registration: Companies House, No/ID: 02994705, England and Wales. **Aims** Function as a trade body coordinating development, support and promotion of the standards infrastructure for electronic commerce for the global book, audiobook, e-book and serials supply chains. **Structure** Board; Special Interest Groups and International Steering Committees, including: *International Committee on EDI for Serials (ICEDIS, #12764)*, ONIX ISC, Thema ISC; National User Groups; Working Groups as necessary. **Staff** 3.50 FTE, paid. **Finance** Sources: fees for services; members' dues. **Activities** Monitoring/evaluation; networking/liaising; standards/guidelines; training/education. **Publications** *ONIX 3.0 Implementation and Best Practice Guidelines* (3.0.8 ed 2021); *ONIX for Books Product Information Format Specification* (v3.0.8 ed 2021); *Thema Subject Categories* (1.5 ed 2020).
Members Companies and organizations (over 100) in 27 countries:
Australia, Austria, Belgium, Brazil, Canada, China, Colombia, Denmark, Finland, France, Germany, Hungary, India, Ireland, Italy, Japan, Korea Rep, Netherlands, Norway, Poland, Russia, Spain, Sweden, Switzerland, Türkiye, UK, USA.
Included in the above, 6 organizations listed in this Yearbook:
International DOI Foundation (IDF, #13188); International Federation of Reproduction Rights Organizations (IFRRO, #13527); International ISBN Agency (#13955); International Publishers Association (IPA, #14675); ISNI International Agency (ISNI-IA); Regional Centre for the Promotion of Books in Latin America and the Caribbean (#18758).
NGO Relations Member of: Book Industry Communications (BIC); Book Industry Study Group (BISG). [2022.05.04/XE3329/y/**E**]

♦ **EDIW** Education in an Interdependent World (#05370)
♦ EDI / see World Bank Institute (#21220)
♦ EDMA – European Diagnostic Manufacturers Association (inactive)
♦ EDMA – European Direct Marketing Association (inactive)
♦ EdM – Enfants du Monde (internationally oriented national body)
♦ EDMJI – Eglise de Dieu Ministérielle de Jesus – Christ Internationale (religious order)
♦ EDMMA – European Dessert Mixes Manufacturers' Association (no recent information)
♦ Edmond J Safra Foundation (internationally oriented national body)
♦ Edmond J Safra Philanthropic Foundation / see Edmond J Safra Foundation
♦ Edmundites – Society of St Edmund (religious order)

♦ Edmund Rice International (ERI) 05362

Contact PO Box 104, Rue de Vermont 37-39, PO Box 104, 1211 Geneva 20, Switzerland.
URL: http://www.edmundriceinternational.org/

History Set up by 2 Roman Catholic religious congregations: *Congregatio Fratrum Christianorum (CFC)* and *Presentation Brothers (FPCP).* Named after founder of founding organizations: Blessed Edmund Rice. Registered as legal entity 2007. **Aims** Advocate for *human rights*, especially for *children* and *young people* who are marginalized because of poverty, lack of access to education, legal status, environmental degradation, or involvement in armed conflict. **Structure** Board of Directors; Members of Congregational Leadership; Teams of Christian Brothers and Presentation Brothers. **Languages** English. **Staff** Geneva (Switzerland): 3; New York NY (USA): 1. **Finance** Donations; funding agencies. Annual budget: euro 200,000. **Activities** Training/education; advocacy/lobbying/activism. Free online course in human rights and advocacy. Active in 30 countries. **Publications** *ERI Newsletter.* Information Services: Free online course in human rights and advocacy. **Consultative Status** Consultative status granted from: *ECOSOC (#05331)* (Special). **NGO Relations** Member of (3): *Child Rights Connect (#03884); Forum of Catholic Inspired NGOs (#09905); International Catholic Centre of Geneva (ICCG, #12449).* Partner of (1): *Franciscans International (FI, #09982).* Allied partner of: *Financial Transparency Coalition (FTC, #09772).* [2019.06.25/XJ6280/**E**]

♦ Edna McConnel Clark Foundation (internationally oriented national body)
♦ **EDNAP** European DNA Profiling Group (#06934)
♦ **EDN** Earth Day Network (#05164)
♦ **EDN** European Documentary Network (#06936)
♦ **E-DOCA** European Designing Out Crime Association (#06911)
♦ EDO – European Doctors Orchestra (internationally oriented national body)
♦ EDPA / see Experiential Designers and Producers Association
♦ EDPA – Experiential Designers and Producers Association (internationally oriented national body)
♦ **EDPB** European Data Protection Board (#06889)
♦ **EDP** European Democratic Party (#06900)
♦ EDP – European Development Platform (internationally oriented national body)
♦ EDRA – Environmental Design Research Association (internationally oriented national body)
♦ EDRA / see European DIY-Retail Association – Global Home Improvement Network (#06933)
♦ **EDRA-GHIN** European DIY-Retail Association – Global Home Improvement Network (#06933)
♦ EDRC / see Institute for European Studies, Malta
♦ EDRC – Environment and Development Resource Centre (internationally oriented national body)
♦ EdReNe – Educational Repository Network (unconfirmed)
♦ EDRES / see Centre for Resilience and Socio-Emotional Health (#03783)
♦ **EDRi** European Digital Rights (#06924)
♦ **EDRLab** European Digital Reading Lab (#06923)
♦ **EDRS** Eating Disorders Research Society (#05268)
♦ **EDSA** European Dental Students Association (#06904)
♦ **EDSA** European Down Syndrome Association (#06942)
♦ **EDS** European Democrat Students (#06901)
♦ EDS / see European Dental Students Association (#06904)
♦ **EDS** European Desalination Society (#06908)
♦ **EDS** European Digestive Surgery (#06919)
♦ **EDSF** European Dance Sport Federation (#06887)
♦ **EDSF** European Door and Shutter Federation (#06940)
♦ **EDSN** European Diphtheria Surveillance Network (#06927)
♦ **EDSO** European Deaf Sport Organization (#06892)
♦ **EDSO** European Distribution System Operators' Association for Smart Grids (#06931)
♦ **EDSU** European Deaf Students' Union (#06893)
♦ EdTA – Educational Theatre Association (internationally oriented national body)
♦ EDTA – Electric Drive Transportation Association (internationally oriented national body)
♦ EDTA-ERA / see European Renal Association – European Dialysis and Transplant Association (#08353)
♦ **EDTA** Federation of European Defence Technology Associations (#09500)
♦ **EDTC** European Diving Technology Committee (#06932)
♦ **EDTCO** European Donation and Transplant Coordination Organisation (#06939)
♦ EDT – Europe Deaf Tech (unconfirmed)
♦ **EDTNA/ERCA** European Dialysis and Transplant Nurses Association – European Renal Care Association (#06918)

♦ EDU 05363

SG Rue Faider 67, 1050 Brussels, Belgium. T. +3228081582. Fax +3228081586. E-mail: sg@edu.int.
URL: http://www.edu.int/

History Jun 2011. Established by International Treaty to promote Education. Former names and other names: *International Accreditation for Learning Institutions* – former; *Promotion of Global Education and Research* – alias; *EDU Intergovernmental Organization* – full title. Registration: EU Transparency Register, No/ID: 43795106384-55. **Aims** Carry out *education* and research; promote gender equality; carry out peace operations and *humanitarian* work. **Structure** Secretary General; Assessment Committee; Board of Commissioners. **Languages** English. **Finance** Sources: donations; in-kind support; private foundations; sponsorship. Private sources. Annual budget: 3,000,000 EUR (2020). **Activities** Certification/accreditation; events/meetings; humanitarian/emergency aid; training/education. Active in: Afghanistan, Brazil, Iraq, Somalia, South Sudan, Syrian AR. **NGO Relations** Member of (2): *End Corporal Punishment (#05457); United Nations Academic Impact (UNAI, #20516).* [2021.09.20/XJ2935/**B***]

♦ Eduardo Frei Foundation (internationally oriented national body)
♦ Eduardo Frei Stichting (internationally oriented national body)
♦ Educación Mundial (internationally oriented national body)
♦ Educación para un Mundo Interdependiente (#05370)
♦ Educación, Trabajo Inserción Social, América Latina / see redEtis (#18651)
♦ Educaid.be – Belgian Platform for Education and Development (internationally oriented national body)
♦ Educate a Child in Africa (unconfirmed)

♦ Educating Students in Engineering and Medicine (ESEM) 05364

SG Ostbayerische Technische Hochschule Regensburg, Mechanical Engineering, Galgenbergstrasse 30, 93053 Regensburg, Germany. T. +499419435171.
URL: https://esem.eu/

History Feb 1991, Nice (France). Dissolved 2015; restarted under current name in 2015 to focus purely on educational purposes. Former names and other names: *European Society for Engineering and Medicine (ESEM)* – former; *Association européenne pour l'ingénierie et la médecine* – former. **Aims** Provide a European approach in education in the field of biomedical engineering to prepare students for a European future; train students in all fields of BME, as well as knowledge of other cultures, languages, habits and training. **Structure** General Assembly (at Congress); Council; Advisory Boards (3). **Languages** English. **Staff** None. **Finance** Sources: members' dues. **Activities** Training/education. **Events** *Middle East Conference on Biomedical Engineering* Sharjah (United Arab Emirates) 2011, *International conference on biomedical engineering* Innsbruck (Austria) 2010, *Conference* Regensburg (Germany) 2007, *International EGFL workshop on high tech rehabilitation after laryngectomy* Groningen (Netherlands) 2005, *International congress on surgical and prosthetic rehabilitation after laryngectomy* Groningen (Netherlands) 2005. **Publications** *ESEM News* (6 a year) – newsletter; *Technology and Health Care* (6 a year) – official journal. **Members** Not a membership organization. **NGO Relations** Member of (1): *European Alliance for Medical and Biological Engineering and Science (EAMBES, #05873).* [2019/XD3388/**D**]

- ♦ Education Above All (internationally oriented national body)
- ♦ Education for Africa Animal Welfare (internationally oriented national body)

♦ Educational Collaborative for International Schools (ECIS) 05365

Exec Dir 24 Greville Street, London, EC1N 8SS, UK. T. +442078247040. E-mail: ecis@ecis.org.
URL: http://www.ecis.org/

History Mar 1965, Geneva (Switzerland). Founded after a series of meetings, commencing 1962, of Heads of International Schools in Europe. Full-time Secretariat set up in London (UK), 1974. Former names and other names: *European Council of International Schools (ECIS)* – former (1965 to 2016); *Conseil européen des écoles internationales* – former (1965 to 2016). Registration: Start date: 2012, UK; 501(c)(3), Start date: 10 Jun 1974, USA, State of Delaware; Swiss Civil Code. **Aims** Promote and support the ideals and best practices of international education. **Structure** Board of Directors. **Languages** English. **Staff** 7.00 FTE, paid. **Finance** Sources: fees for services; grants; meeting proceeds; members' dues. Annual budget: 1,100,000 GBP. **Activities** Awards/prizes/competitions; events/meetings; guidance/assistance/consulting. **Events** *Leadership Conference* Welwyn Garden City (UK) 2022, *Physical Education Conference* Barcelona (Spain) 2019, *Multilingual Learning Conference* London (UK) 2019, *Leadership Conference* Berlin (Germany) 2018, *Annual Conference* Luxembourg (Luxembourg) 2018. **Publications** *ECIS SmartBrief* (weekly).
Members Full and Provisional international schools worldwide; Affiliate other educational organizations such as school suppliers, educational publishers, etc; Individual those who support the aims of international education. Members in 107 countries and territories:
Argentina, Australia, Austria, Azerbaijan, Bahamas, Bahrain, Bangladesh, Belgium, Bolivia, Botswana, Brazil, Brunei Darussalam, Bulgaria, Cambodia, Cameroon, Canada, Chile, China, Colombia, Congo DR, Costa Rica, Côte d'Ivoire, Croatia, Cuba, Cyprus, Czechia, Denmark, Ecuador, Egypt, El Salvador, Estonia, Ethiopia, Finland, France, Germany, Ghana, Greece, Hong Kong, Hungary, India, Indonesia, Iraq, Ireland, Israel, Italy, Japan, Jordan, Kazakhstan, Kenya, Korea Rep, Kuwait, Kyrgyzstan, Laos, Latvia, Lebanon, Lesotho, Lithuania, Luxembourg, Malawi, Malaysia, Malta, Mexico, Monaco, Mongolia, Morocco, Namibia, Nepal, Netherlands, New Zealand, Nigeria, Norway, Oman, Panama, Papua New Guinea, Philippines, Poland, Portugal, Qatar, Romania, Russia, Saudi Arabia, Serbia, Seychelles, Singapore, Slovakia, Slovenia, South Africa, Spain, Sri Lanka, Sweden, Switzerland, Syrian AR, Taiwan, Tajikistan, Tanzania UR, Thailand, Togo, Türkiye, Uganda, UK, Ukraine, United Arab Emirates, Uzbekistan, Venezuela, Vietnam, Zambia, Zimbabwe. [2022.10.19/XD5199/**D**]

- ♦ Educational Commission for Foreign Medical Graduates (internationally oriented national body)
- ♦ Educational Concerns for Haiti Organization / see Educational Concerns for Hunger Organization
- ♦ Educational Concerns for Hunger Organization (internationally oriented national body)
- ♦ Educational Expeditions International / see Earthwatch Institute (#05171)
- ♦ Educational Foundation for African Women (internationally oriented national body)

♦ Educational Initiative for Central and Eastern Europe (EICEE) 05366

Address not obtained.
URL: http://www.eicee.org/

History Registered in accordance with US law. **Aims** Foster and strengthen free, just and democratic societies in the nations of Central and Eastern Europe. **Structure** Board of Advisors. Offices (7): Washington DC (USA); Vienna (Austria); Budapest (Hungary); Prague (Czech Rep); Tallinn (Estonia); Skopje (North Macedonia); Sofia (Bulgaria). **NGO Relations** Member of: *European Coalition for Economic Growth (ECEG, #06593).* [2011/XJ1335/**F**]

♦ Educational Innovation in Economics and Business Network (EDiNEB Network) 05367

Contact Univ Maastricht, Postbus 616, 6200 MD Maastricht, Netherlands. T. +31433883770. Fax +31433084801.
URL: http://www.edineb.org/

History 1993, Netherlands, by Wim Gijselaers and Rick Milter. Registered in accordance with Dutch law. **Aims** Provide mutual support to member institutions who wish to adapt their curriculum to highly innovative programmes. **Structure** Management Team of 4. *EDINEB Foundation.* **Events** *Conference* Utrecht (Netherlands) 2017, *Conference* London (UK) 2010, *Preparing business professionals for the changing global workplace* Vienna (Austria) 2007, *Conference / Annual Conference* Lisbon (Portugal) 2006, *Conference / Annual Conference* Antwerp (Belgium) 2005. **Publications** *EDINEB Newsletter* (2 a year).
Members in 15 countries and territories:
Australia, Canada, France, Germany, Hong Kong, Hungary, Netherlands, Norway, Peru, Portugal, Russia, Sweden, UK, Ukraine, USA. [2017/XF5642/**F**]

- ♦ Educational Innovation Programme for Development in the Arab States (inactive)
- ♦ Education for All Fast Track Initiative / see Global Partnership for Education (#10531)
- ♦ Educational Quality Accrediting Commission (internationally oriented national body)
- ♦ Educational Repository Network (unconfirmed)

♦ Educational Research Network for Western and Central Africa (ERNWACA) 05368

Réseau de recherche en éducation pour l'Afrique de l'Ouest et centrale (ROCARE)
Regional Office PO Box E-1854, Bamako, Mali. T. +2232211612. Fax +2232212115.
URL: https://www.ernwaca.com/

History 1989, Freetown (Sierra Leone). **Aims** Promote research, researchers and educational practitioners in Africa, so as to positively affect educational practice and policy. **Events** *Meeting* Saly (Senegal) 1992.
Members Organizations and individuals. Members in 15 countries:
Benin, Burkina Faso, Cameroon, Canada, Côte d'Ivoire, France, Gambia, Ghana, Guinea, Kenya, Mali, Nigeria, Senegal, Sierra Leone, Togo, USA. [2017.03.09/XF3649/**F**]

- ♦ Educational Theatre Association (internationally oriented national body)
- ♦ Educational Training Consultancy / see ETC
- ♦ Education Beyond Borders (internationally oriented national body)

♦ Education Cannot Wait (ECW) 05369

Dir address not obtained. E-mail: info@educationcannotwait.org.
URL: https://www.educationcannotwait.org/

History Set up 2016, as a fund hosted and administered by *UNICEF (#20332).* **Aims** Help reposition education as a priority on the *humanitarian* agenda; usher in a more collaborative approach among actors on the ground; foster additional funding to ensure that every *crisis*-affected *child* and young person is in school and learning. **Structure** High-Level Steering Group (HLSG); Executive Committee; Secretariat. Ad hoc Task Teams. **Finance** Donors include civil society organizations, *European Commission (EC, #06633)* and governments of: UK; Denmark; Canada; Germany; Sweden; Netherlands; Norway; USA; Australia, France; Bulgaria. [2019/XM8607/f/**F**]

- ♦ **Education Commission** International Commission on Financing Global Education Opportunity (#12682)
- ♦ Education in Computer Aided Architectural Design in Europe / see Education and research in Computer Aided Architectural Design in Europe (#05373)
- ♦ Education for Development (internationally oriented national body)
- ♦ Education for Development (internationally oriented national body)
- ♦ Education Development Center (internationally oriented national body)
- ♦ Education Development Trust (internationally oriented national body)
- ♦ Éducation et Diversité Linguistique et Culturelle (unconfirmed)
- ♦ Education Foundation of the Latin American Confederation of Credit Unions (see: #16302)
- ♦ Education Globale et Développement (internationally oriented national body)
- ♦ Education for Health (internationally oriented national body)

♦ Education in an Interdependent World (EDIW) 05370

Education pour un monde interdépendant – Educación para un Mundo Interdependiente
Dir Blvd Lambermont 262-B, 1030 Brussels, Belgium. E-mail: jmgonzalezf@gmail.com.
URL: http://www.ediw.net/

History 20 Dec 1996. Registered in accordance with Belgian law. **Aims** Empower young people in Higher Education to promote and foster actions and projects to build an inclusive society towards a better understanding of a multicultural and interdependent world. **Structure** General Assembly (annual); Council. **Finance** Members' dues. Funding from: *European Commission (EC, #06633).* **Activities** Training/education; events/meetings.
Members Institutional; individual. Founding members (12) in 6 countries:
Belgium, France, Italy, Luxembourg, Portugal, Spain. [2016/XF4632/**F**]

♦ Education International (EI) 05371

Internationale de l'éducation (IE) – Internacional de la Educación (IE) – Bildungsinternationale (BI)
Secretariat 8e étage, Bd du Roi Albert II 5, 1210 Brussels, Belgium. T. +3222240611. Fax +3222240606. E-mail: headoffice@ei-ie.org.
URL: http://www.ei-ie.org/

History 26 Jan 1993. Founded on merger of the former *World Confederation of Organizations of the Teaching Profession (WCOTP, inactive)* and the former *International Federation of Free Teachers' Unions (IFFTU, inactive).* Also incorporates activities of 3 former teachers' organizations: *Fédération internationale des professeurs de l'enseignement secondaire officiel (FIPESO, inactive)*, which agreed to cease operations on setting up of EI, *International Federation of Teachers' Associations (IFTA, inactive)*, which was dissolved on 1 Jul 1995 following gradual take-over of its activities; *World Confederation of Teachers (WCT, inactive)*, which was dissolved Mar 2007. Constitution and By-Laws last revised in 2011. **Aims** Further the cause of organizations of *teachers* and other education employees; promote status, interests and welfare of members and defend their trade union and professional rights; promote peace, democracy, social justice, equality and application of the Universal Declaration on Human Rights through development of education and collective strength of teachers and education employees; seek and maintain recognition of *trade union rights* of workers in general and of teachers and education employees in particular. **Structure** World Congress; Executive Board; Committee of Experts on Membership; Regional Structures (6); Cross-Regional Structure; Other Committees (3). Headquarters and Secretariat at *International Trade Union House, Brussels (ITUH).* Regional offices (4); Units (7). **Languages** English, French, German, Spanish. **Staff** 70.00 FTE, paid. **Finance** Members' dues (regular budget). Other sources: project funds (extra-budgetary); Solidarity Fund. **Activities** Advocacy/lobbying/activism; events/meetings; training/education. **Events** *World Congress* Bangkok (Thailand) 2019, *International Summit on the Teaching Profession* Berlin (Germany) 2016, *International Summit on the Teaching Profession* Banff, AB (Canada) 2015, *Triennial World Congress* Ottawa, ON (Canada) 2015, *Global Education Conference* Montréal, QC (Canada) 2014. **Publications** *In Focus* (12 a year) in English, French, Spanish – newsletter; *ETUCE Newsletter* (12 a year) in English, French; *TradEducation* (4 a year) in English, French, Spanish – bulletin; *Worlds of Education* (2 a year) in English, French, Spanish – magazine in; *Connect* (occasional) in English, French, Spanish – newsletter. Annual Report in English, French, Spanish. **Members** National trade union organizations (402), representing 30 million teachers and workers in education, in 172 countries and territories (not specified). **Consultative Status** Consultative status granted from: *ECOSOC (#05331)* (Special); *UNESCO (#20322)* (Associate Status); *FAO (#09260)* (Special Status); *UNICEF (#20332); Council of Europe (CE, #04881)* (Participatory Status); *World Intellectual Property Organization (WIPO, #21593)* (Permanent Observer Status). **IGO Relations** Instrumental in setting up: *Focusing Resources on Effective School Health (FRESH, #09809).* Member of: *International Task Force on Teachers for Education 2030 (#15657).* Consultative member of: *European Higher Education Area (EHEA, #07483).* Board member of: *Global Partnership for Education (GPE, #10531).* Partner in Sectoral Social Dialogue with: *European Commission (EC, #06633).* Contacts with: *International Bank for Reconstruction and Development (IBRD, #12317)* (World Bank); *International Programme on the Elimination of Child Labour and Forced Labour (IPEC+, #14652); International Monetary Fund (IMF, #14180); Joint United Nations Programme on HIV/AIDS (UNAIDS, #16149); OECD (#17693); WHO (#20950).* Associated with Department of Global Communications of the United Nations. **NGO Relations** Member of (9): *Committee of NGOs on Human Rights, Geneva (#04275); Conference of Non-Governmental Organizations in Consultative Relationship with the United Nations (CONGO, #04635); European Quality Assurance Register for Higher Education (EQAR, #08311); Global Labour University (GLU, #10448); Informal Working Group on Gender and Trade (IWGGT, no recent information); Inter-agency Network for Education in Emergencies (INEE, #11387); NGO Committee on the Status of Women, Geneva (#17117); NGO-UNESCO Liaison Committee (#17127); SDG Watch Europe (#19162).* Associated with: *International Trade Union Confederation (ITUC, #15708).* Works closely with *Global Union Federations (GUF, #10638)*, and participates in the Council of Global Unions, established Jan 2007 by ITUC, 10 GUFs and the Trade Union Advisory Committee at the OECD (TUAC), but with guaranteed autonomy. Affiliated to: *International Federation of Workers' Education Associations (IFWEA, #13580).* Board member of: *Global Campaign for Education (GCE, #10264).* Supports: *Global Call for Action Against Poverty (GCAP, #10263).* Cooperates with: *International Council for Adult Education (ICAE, #12983).* [2020/XB1111/**B**]

- ♦ Education pour un monde interdépendant (#05370)
- ♦ Education mondiale (internationally oriented national body)
- ♦ Education North / see Arctic Vocational Foundation (#01102)
- ♦ Education for Peace Institute of the Balkans (internationally oriented national body)

♦ Education Reform Initiative of South Eastern Europe (ERI SEE) 05372

Dir Ctr for Technolog Transfer, Fac of Mechanical Engineering and Ship Building, Univ of Zagreb, pp 407, Trg Marsala Tita 14, HR-10002 Zagreb, Croatia. T. +38516310678.
URL: http://www.erisee.org/

History through a Memorandum of Understanding signed by the Ministers of Education, Science and Research of the South Eastern Europe. Initiated by Task Force Education and Youth (TFEY) of *Stability Pact for South Eastern Europe (inactive)*, 2004. When *Regional Cooperation Council (RCC, #18773)* succeeded Stability Pact, 2007, TFEY was succeeded by Task Force 'Fostering and Building Human Capital' (TFBHC). Work of ERI SEE Secretariat institutionalized in governmental *ERI SEE Agency*, which opened Nov 2006. **Aims** Foster shared European standards in education and training for a rapid integration of its member countries into a wider European area of education, thus contributing to the success and sustainability of the EU integration process. **Structure** Governing Board, comprising signatory ministries of member countries and of Austria as Co-Chair of the Task Force Fostering and Building Human Capital (TFBHC) of *Regional Cooperation Council (RCC, #18773).* Consultative Body, including representatives of Institutional Partners and donor countries. Secretariat. **Finance** Donor countries: Austria; Netherlands; Norway; Switzerland.
Members Signatory countries (10):
Albania, Bosnia-Herzegovina, Bulgaria, Croatia, Kosovo, Moldova, Montenegro, North Macedonia, Romania, Serbia.
IGO Relations Institutional Partners: *Council of Europe (CE, #04881); OECD (#17693).* **NGO Relations** Institutional Partner: *European University Association (EUA, #09027).* [2011/XJ2482/**E***]

♦ Education and research in Computer Aided Architectural Design in Europe (eCAADe) 05373

Secretariat Dept of Architecture Sint-Lucas, Hogeschool voor Wetenschap and Kunst, Paleizenstraat 65, 1030 Brussels, Belgium. T. +3222420000. Fax +3222451404.
URL: http://www.ecaade.org/

History 1983. Former names and other names: *Education in Computer Aided Architectural Design in Europe (ECAADE)* – former. Registration: Banque-Carrefour des Entreprises, No/ID: 0430.043.758, Start date: 17 Dec 1986, Belgium. **Aims** Collate and disseminate information about Computer Aided Architectural Design (CAAD) among European *schools* of architecture; encourage exchange of software, courseware, experience and staff/students among schools; identify research and development needs specific to CAAD *education* and initiate collaboration to satisfy them. **Structure** Annual General Meeting (normally during annual Conference); Administrative Council. **Finance** Student exchanges funded through: Lifelong Learning Programme (LLP) of *European Commission (EC, #06633).* Collaborative research and development projects funded by amongst others: *ALFA Programme (inactive); TEMPUS IV (inactive).* **Activities** Events/meetings; research/documentation; training/education. **Events** *Annual Conference* Ghent (Belgium) 2022, *Annual Conference* Novi Sad (Serbia) 2021, *Annual Conference* Berlin (Germany) 2020, *Annual Conference* Porto (Portugal) 2019, *Annual Conference* Lódz (Poland) 2018. **Publications** Conference proceedings.
Members Individuals from schools of architecture (about 390) in 23 countries and territories:
Austria, Belgium, Croatia, Czechia, Denmark, Finland, Germany, Greece, Hong Kong, Hungary, Ireland, Italy, Netherlands, Norway, Poland, Portugal, Serbia, Spain, Sweden, Switzerland, Türkiye, UK, USA.

NGO Relations Close liaison with: *Association for Computer Aided Design in Architecture (ACADIA)*; *Computer Aided Architectural Design Research in Asia (CAADRIA, #04425)*; *Sociedad Iberoamericana de Grafica Digital (SIGraDI, #19370).* [2022/XF5484/v/F]

♦ Education and Solidarity Network 05374

Réseau Education et Solidarité – Red Educación y Sólidaridad

Head Office Bd du Roi Albert II 5, 1210 Brussels, Belgium. E-mail: thierry.weishaupt@groupe-vyv.fr.
URL: http://www.educationsolidarite.org/

History Set up 2009, by Mutuelle Générale de l'Education Nationale (MGEN) – France, *Education International (EI, #05371)* and *Association internationale de la mutualité (AIM, #02721)*. Registered in accordance with Belgian law, Sep 2009. **Aims** Build bridges between education actors and health and social protection actors, so as to work for the well-being of the educational community worldwide. **Structure** General Assembly; Executive Board. Based at: *Education International (EI, #05371)*. **Events** *General Assembly* Ottawa, ON (Canada) 2015.
Members Organizations in 27 countries:
Australia, Belgium, Burkina Faso, Cameroon, Canada, Colombia, Congo DR, Costa Rica, Côte d'Ivoire, France, Gabon, Gambia, Haiti, Luxembourg, Mexico, Morocco, Niger, Peru, Philippines, Russia, Sweden, Switzerland, Tunisia, Uganda, UK, USA, Zambia.
Included in the above, 4 organizations listed in this Yearbook:
Association internationale de la mutualité (AIM, #02721); *Centro Interamericano de Estudios de Seguridad Social (CIESS, #03803)*; *Education International (EI, #05371)*; *Social Enterprise International (SEi)*.
NGO Relations Partners include: *Association Européenne des Institutions Paritaires de la Protection Sociale (AEIP, #02575)*; *International Centre for Development and Research (CIDR)*; *SOLIDAR (#19680)*. [2019/XJ5848/y/F]

- ♦ Educators Without Borders (internationally oriented national body)
- ♦ EDUCAUSE – Transforming Education Through Information Technologies (internationally oriented national body)
- ♦ EDUCO (internationally oriented national body)
- ♦ EDU – Europäische Demokratische Union (inactive)
- ♦ EDU – European Democrat Union (inactive)

♦ Eduforest International Forestry Training Network 05375

Réseau international des formations aux métiers de la forêt

Chairman Ctr Forestier région Provence-Alpes-Côte d'Azur, Pié de Gâche, 84240 La Bastide des Jourdans, France. T. +33490778800.
URL: http://www.eduforest.eu/

Aims Promote long life training in forestry; increase careers in the forestry sector; promote exchange of information about training and employment in the forestry sector. **Languages** English, French. **Activities** Forestry training centres; international cooperation. **Events** *International Conference of Forestry Training Centres* Solsona (Spain) 2016, *International Conference of Forestry Training Centres* Nürburg (Germany) 2014, *International Conference of Forestry Training Centres* Ossiach (Austria) 2011, *International Conference of Forestry Training Centres* Lyss (Switzerland) 2008, *International Conference of Forestry Training Centres* La Bastide des Jourdans (France) 2005. [2019/XJ4182/F]

- ♦ EDU Intergovernmental Organization / see EDU (#05363)

♦ EduNet World Association 05376

Registered Address Flachsmarktstr 8, 32825 Blomberg, Germany. E-mail: info@edunet-wa.com.
URL: https://www.edunet-wa.com/

History Registration: North Rhine-Westphalia District court, No/ID: VR 1569, Start date: 14 Aug 2017, Germany, Lemgo. **Aims** Promote global engineering and "Vocational Education 4.0" in electrical engineering, automation technology and information technology. **Structure** General Meeting; Executive Committee; Board. **Events** *International EduNet World Conference* Antwerp (Belgium) 2021, *International EduNet World Conference* Antwerp (Belgium) 2020.
Members Founding members in 6 countries:
Belgium, China, Germany, Netherlands, Spain, Türkiye. [2020/AA1414/C]

♦ Edward Jenner Vaccine Society (EJVS) 05377

Administrative Contact 611C Guggenheim Bldg, Mayo Clinic, 200 First Str SW, Rochester MN 55905, USA. T. +15072844968.

History 2010. Founded in honour of Dr Edward Jenner (1749-1823). Former names and other names: *The Jenner Society* – alias. **Aims** Serve as a professional home for academic vaccinologists. **Structure** Executive Committee. **Languages** English. **Staff** 1.00 FTE, paid. **Finance** Members' dues. **Activities** Events/meetings; conferences are coordinated in conjunction with its journal and the publisher. **Publications** *Vaccine* – journal.
Members Full in 6 countries:
Australia, Canada, Ethiopia, Netherlands, UK, USA. [2015.09.01/XJ9135/E]

- ♦ EDWCA – European Drinking Water Cooler Association (internationally oriented national body)
- ♦ **EDXC** European DX Council (#06950)
- ♦ **EDYN** Ecumenical Diaconal Year Network (#05345)
- ♦ EEAA – East European Acoustical Association (internationally oriented national body)
- ♦ EE AA / see European Council for Theological Education (#06846)
- ♦ **EEA CC** EEA Consultative Committee (#05378)
- ♦ EEAC / see European Environment and Sustainable Development Advisory Councils (#07003)
- ♦ **EEAC** European Environment and Sustainable Development Advisory Councils (#07003)
- ♦ EEAC Network / see European Environment and Sustainable Development Advisory Councils (#07003)

♦ EEA Consultative Committee (EEA CC) 05378

Comité consultatif de l'EEE

Contact EFTA Secretariat, Rue Joseph II 12-16, 1000 Brussels, Belgium. T. +3222861711. Fax +3222861750.
URL: http://www.efta.int/eea/eea-institutions/eea-consultative-committee/

History 1994, having been proposed, 21 May 1991, Vienna (Austria), at a meeting of *European Economic and Social Committee (EESC, #06963)* and EFTA Consultative Committee (CC). Comprises members of these two bodies within the framework of *European Economic Area (EEA, #06957)*. Provided for under the EEA Agreement signed 2 May 1992, Porto (Portugal), which came into force 1 Jan 1994. EESC and CC agreed, 2 Dec 1992, London (UK), that they would in the future constitute the EEA Consultative Committee as the single advisory body. Rules of procedure revised: 26 Jun 2002, Egilsstadir (Iceland); 15 May 2008, Longyearbyen (Norway); 26 May 2009, Brussels (Belgium). **Aims** Work to strengthen contacts between *social partners* in the *European Union* and *EFTA* states; cooperate so as to enhance awareness of the *economic* and *social* aspects of the EEA; provide input into deliberations of other EEA bodies. **Structure** Committee (meets annually), composed of 9 EEA representatives each from EESC and CC. Bureau, consisting of 3 members and including one Co-Chairman each from EESC and CC. Observers from interested bodies. Secretariat provided by EESC or CC according to venue of meeting. **Languages** Czech, Danish, Dutch, English, Estonian, Finnish, French, German, Hungarian, Irish Gaelic, Italian, Latvian, Lithuanian, Maltese, Polish, Portuguese, Slovakian, Slovene, Spanish, Swedish. **Activities** Acts as a voice for workers, employers and other civil society organizations in the 30 EEA countries and as the main forum for cooperation between EFTA Consultative Committee and EESC. **Events** *Meeting* Brussels (Belgium) 2009, *Meeting* Longyearbyen (Norway) 2008, *Meeting* Gdansk (Poland) 2007, *Meeting* Höfn (Iceland) 2006, *Meeting* Tallinn (Estonia) 2005. **NGO Relations** Permanent observers: *European Trade Union Confederation (ETUC, #08927)*; *BUSINESSEUROPE (#03381)*. [2013/XE1715/E*]

♦ EEA Council 05379

Conseil de l'EEE

Head of Policy Coordination c/o EFTA Brussels Secretariat, Rue Joseph II 12-16, 1000 Brussels, Belgium. T. +3222861737.
URL: http://www.efta.int/eea/eea-institutions/eea-council.aspx

History Established 1 Jan 1994, as the highest authority of the *European Economic Area (EEA, #06957)*, on coming into effect of the EEA Agreement, signed 2 May 1992, Porto (Portugal). Based in Brussels (Belgium). **Aims** Give *political* impetus to, and guidance for, implementation and development of the EEA Agreement. **Structure** Consists of the members of the *Council of the European Union (#04895)*, members of the *European Commission (EC, #06633)*, and one member of the governments of each of the EEA EFTA States. Secretariat provided jointly by *EFTA (#05391)* Secretariat and the General Secretariat of the Council of the European Union. **Languages** English, French, German. **Finance** Budgetary costs covered by the respective budgets of *EFTA (#05391)* and *Council of the European Union (#04895)*. **Activities** Politics/policy/regulatory. **Events** *Meeting* Brussels (Belgium) 2019, *Meeting* Brussels (Belgium) 2018, *Meeting* Luxembourg (Luxembourg) 2005, *Meeting* Brussels (Belgium) 2004, *Meeting* Luxembourg (Luxembourg) 2004. **Publications** EEA Council conclusions, adopted at each meeting.
Members Representatives of the 31 EEA countries:
Austria, Belgium, Bulgaria, Croatia, Cyprus, Czechia, Denmark, Estonia, Finland, France, Germany, Greece, Hungary, Iceland, Ireland, Italy, Latvia, Liechtenstein, Lithuania, Luxembourg, Malta, Netherlands, Norway, Poland, Portugal, Romania, Slovakia, Slovenia, Spain, Sweden, UK.
And representative of one regional organization:
European Commission (EC, #06633). [2021/XE2034/E*]

- ♦ EEA – Enterprise Ethereum Alliance (unconfirmed)
- ♦ EEA / see European Arts and Entertainment Alliance (#05918)
- ♦ **EEA** European Economic Area (#06957)
- ♦ **EEA** European Economic Association (#06958)
- ♦ **EEA** European Elasmobranch Association (#06972)
- ♦ EEA – European Enamel Authority (unconfirmed)
- ♦ EEA / see European Energy Forum (#06986)
- ♦ **EEA** European Environment Agency (#06995)
- ♦ **EEA** European Evangelical Alliance (#07010)
- ♦ **EEA** European Express Association (#07017)

♦ EEA Grants 05380

Financial Mechanism Office Rue Joseph II 12-16, 1000 Brussels, Belgium. T. +3222861701. Fax +3222111889. E-mail: info-fmo@efta.int.
Visiting Address Boulevard du Régent 47-48, 1000 Brussels, Belgium.
URL: http://eeagrants.org/

History Organized since Agreement on the *European Economic Area (EEA, #06957)* entered into force 1 Jan 1994. Funding periods organized in cycles. Current cycle: period: 2014-2021. **Aims** Reduce economic and social disparities and strengthen bilateral relations with 15 EU countries in Central and Southern Europe and the Baltics. **Structure** Financial Mechanism Committee (FMC); Financial Mechanism Office (FMO). **Staff** 61.00 FTE, paid. **Activities** Financial and/or material support. Active in: Bulgaria, Croatia, Cyprus, Czechia, Estonia, Greece, Hungary, Latvia, Lithuania, Malta, Poland, Portugal, Romania, Slovakia, Slovenia.
Members Donor governments (3):
Iceland, Liechtenstein, Norway.
IGO Relations *EFTA (#05391)*. [2018/XM6290/E*]

♦ EEA Joint Committee 05381

Comité mixte EEE

Senior Officer, Policy Coordination EFTA Secretariat, Av des Arts 19H, 1000 Brussels, Belgium. T. +3222861708. Fax +3212345678.
EEA Desk Officer European Commission / Secretariat-General, Rue de la Loi 170, 1040 Brussels, Belgium. T. +3222963989. E-mail: sg-h3-eea@ec.europa.eu.
URL: http://secretariat.efta.int/Web/EuropeanEconomicArea/

History 1 Jan 1994. Established within the framework of *European Economic Area (EEA, #06957)*, on entry into force of the EEA Agreement. **Aims** Maintain homogeneity of the *European Economic Area* by incorporating relevant EEA legislation into the EEA Agreement. **Structure** Committee meets 7 to 8 times a year and comprises high officials from the European External Action Service, from the 3 EFTA EEA countries and from EU Member States. The Committee is assisted by 5 subcommittees: I. Free Movement of Goods; II. Free Movement of Capital and Services; III. Free Movement of Persons; IV. Flanking and Horizontal Policies; V. Legal and Institutional Matters. **Languages** English. **Finance** Budgetary costs covered by respective budgets of EFTA and European Commission. **Activities** Politics/policy/regulatory. **Publications** *EEA Joint Committee Annual Report*.
Members Individuals representing governments of 31 countries:
Austria, Belgium, Bulgaria, Croatia, Cyprus, Czechia, Denmark, Estonia, Finland, France, Germany, Greece, Hungary, Iceland, Ireland, Italy, Latvia, Liechtenstein, Lithuania, Luxembourg, Malta, Netherlands, Norway, Poland, Portugal, Romania, Slovakia, Slovenia, Spain, Sweden, UK.
Regional member:
European Commission (EC, #06633).
IGO Relations Recommendations and opinions submitted by: *EEA Consultative Committee (EEA CC, #05378)*; *EEA Joint Parliamentary Committee (EEA JPC, #05382)*. EFTA representatives also represent their countries within: *Standing Committee of the EFTA States (#19953)*. [2023.02.14/XE1724/E*]

♦ EEA Joint Parliamentary Committee (EEA JPC) 05382

Comité parlement mixte de l'EEE

Secretariat Rue Joseph II 16-16, 1000 Brussels, Belgium. T. +3222861711 – +3222861715. Fax +3222861750. E-mail: mail.bxl@efta.int.
URL: http://www.efta.int/eea/eea-institutions/eea-joint-parliamentary-committee

History 2 May 1992, Porto (Portugal), by Article 95 of the Agreement on *European Economic Area (EEA, #06957)*. Title also written *European Economic Area Joint Parliamentary Committee*. Constituent meeting 22-24 Jan 1994, Brussels (Belgium). **Aims** Ensure parliamentary cooperation, providing a link between parliamentarians in the EEA and a forum where they can discuss EEA matters; contribute, through dialogue and debate, to a better understanding between EU and EFTA states in fields covered by the EEA Agreement. **Structure** Committee (meeting twice a year) comprises 12 members each of EFTA national parliamentary delegations – *Committee of Members of Parliament of the EFTA States Party to the EEA (EFTA MPS, #04270)* – and of *European Parliament (EP, #08146)*. Agenda Committee. Secretariat in Brussels (Belgium) provided by *EFTA (#05391)*. **Activities** Draws up recommendations and opinions to *EEA Joint Committee (#05381)*. Serves as a link between national EFTA parliaments and the European Parliament. **Events** *Meeting* Brussels (Belgium) 2005, *Meeting* Reykjavik (Iceland) 2005, *Meeting* Brussels (Belgium) 2004, *Meeting* Vaduz (Liechtenstein) 2004, *Meeting* Brussels (Belgium) 2003. [2019.02.12/XE2033/E*]

- ♦ **EEA JPC** EEA Joint Parliamentary Committee (#05382)
- ♦ **EEASA** Environmental Education Association of Southern Africa (#05501)
- ♦ **EEAS** European External Action Service (#07018)
- ♦ **EEBA** European Eye Bank Association (#07020)
- ♦ **EEB** European Environmental Bureau (#06996)
- ♦ **EECA** European Electronic Component Manufacturers Association (#06974)
- ♦ EEC Association of the Processed Cheese Industry / see Association de l'industrie de la fonte de fromage de l'UE (#02642)
- ♦ EEC Committee for the Wine, Aromatized Wine, Sparkling Wine and Liqueur Wine Industries and Trade / see Comité européen des entreprises vins (#04157)
- ♦ EEC / see Communion of Evangelical Episcopal Churches (#04385)
- ♦ EEC Community of Associations of Newspaper Publishers / see European Newspaper Publishers' Association (#08048)
- ♦ EEC Convention on the Mutual Recognition of Companies and Bodies Corporate (1968 treaty)
- ♦ EEC Cork Confederation: Industry and Commerce / see European Cork Federation (#06798)
- ♦ **EECDRG** European Environmental and Contact Dermatitis Research Group (#06998)
- ♦ **EECERA** European Early Childhood Education Research Association (#06952)
- ♦ EEC – European Energy Centre (unconfirmed)
- ♦ EEC Fish Processors Association / see European Union Fish Processors Association (#08989)

EEC Group Producers
05382

alphabetic sequence excludes
For the complete listing, see Yearbook Online at

♦ EEC Group of Producers of Mineral Insulating Material for Electrotechnical Use / see European Technical Ceramics Federation (#08878)
♦ **EECI-Network** European Energy Crops Inter-Network (#06984)
♦ EEC Liaison Committee of Midwives / see European Midwives Association (#07800)
♦ **EECN** European Environmental Communication Networks (#06997)

♦ EECONET Action Fund (EAF) 05383

SG Coastal and Marine Union – EUCC – EAF, PO Box 11232, 2301 EE Leiden, Netherlands. T. +31715122900. Fax +31715124069.
URL: http://www.eeconet.org/

History Founded Sep 1995, as a joint venture of *EuroNatur – European Nature Heritage Fund (#05738), ECNC – European Centre for Nature Conservation (#05289), Coastal and Marine Union – EUCC (#04072)* and *Eurosite (#09181)*. Registered in accordance with Dutch law, Dec 1999. **Aims** Undertake and support emergency action for *conservation* of *natural* sites in *Europe*. **Structure** Board of Directors. **Finance** Sponsorship. **Activities** Financial and/or material support; advocacy/lobbying/activism; capacity building; training/education. **Publications** Annual Report. [2014.06.01/XK1325/f/**F**]

♦ EECONET Alliance / see NatureNet Europe (#16959)
♦ EE Conference – International Entertainment Education Conference (meeting series)
♦ EEC Research and European Studies Centre / see Centre for Europe, University of Warsaw
♦ EEC Steel Manufacturers Club / see European Steel Association (#08835)
♦ EEC Wine and Spirit Importers Group / see European Federation of Wine and Spirit Importers and Distributors (#07235)
♦ EED / see Brot für die Welt
♦ EEDDA – Greek Committee for International Democratic Solidarity (internationally oriented national body)
♦ **EED** European Endowment for Democracy (#06983)
♦ **EED** European Society for Evolutionary Developmental Biology (#08601)
♦ **EEDSF** East European Dance Sport Federation (#05258)
♦ EEDYE – Greek Committee for International Detente and Peace (internationally oriented national body)
♦ **EEE** Espace économique européen (#06957)
♦ **EEE** Espacio Económico Europeo (#06957)
♦ **eeef** European Energy Efficiency Fund (#06985)
♦ **EEEI** European Expertise and Expert Institute (#07015)
♦ **EE** ENDA Europe (#05454)
♦ **EE** Entente Européenne d'Aviculture et de Cuniculture (#05492)
♦ **EEEOA** Système d'échanges d'énergie électrique ouest africain (#20894)
♦ EE / see Europengineers (#09164)
♦ **EE** Evropaiki Enosi (#08967)
♦ **EEE-YFU** European Educational Exchanges – Youth for Understanding (#06965)
♦ **EEF** Europäische Entwicklungsfond (#06914)
♦ **EEF** European Ecological Federation (#06956)
♦ EEF / see European Energy Forum (#06986)
♦ **EEF** European Energy Forum (#06986)
♦ **EEF** European Equestrian Federation (#07005)
♦ **EEF** European Esports Federation (#07007)
♦ **EEF** IEA European Epidemiology Federation (#11094)
♦ **EEFS** European Economics and Finance Society (#06962)
♦ EEG and Clinical Neuroscience Society / see Electroencephalography and Clinical Neuroscience Society (#05422)
♦ **EEG** European Expert Group on the transition from institutional to community-based care (#07014)
♦ **EEHYC** European Environment and Health Youth Coalition (#07001)
♦ **EEIA** European Exhibition Industry Alliance (#07012)
♦ EEIDO – Eastern European Industrial Development Organization (unconfirmed)
♦ EEI / see Earthwatch Institute (#05171)
♦ EEIE – RFF-CMCC European Institute on Economics and the Environment (internationally oriented national body)
♦ **EEI** European Enterprise Institute (#06993)
♦ **EEIF** Energy Efficiency Industrial Forum (#05470)
♦ **EEIG** European Economic Interest Grouping (#06960)
♦ **EEIP** Energy Efficiency in Industrial Processes (#05471)
♦ **EE-ISAC** European Energy Information Sharing and Analysis Centre (#06987)
♦ EEIU – Eco-Ethics International Union (inactive)
♦ **EEK** Evropejskaja Ekonomiceskaja Komissija OON (#20555)
♦ EEKMA – European Elephant Keeper and Manager Association (inactive)
♦ **EELA** European Employment Lawyers Association (#06979)
♦ **EEL** European Endometriosis League (#06982)
♦ **EELF** European Environmental Law Forum (#06999)
♦ EELV – Europe Écologie – Les Verts (internationally oriented national body)
♦ EEMA / see European Association for e-Identity and Security (#06077)
♦ **EEMA** European Association for e-Identity and Security (#06077)
♦ EEMA – European Engineering and Management Association (inactive)
♦ EEMA – European Environmental Management Association (inactive)
♦ **EEMA** European Evangelical Mission Association (#07011)
♦ EEMA European Forum for Electronic Business / see European Association for e-Identity and Security (#06077)
♦ EEMG – European Energy Mediators Group (unconfirmed)
♦ **EEMGS** European Environmental Mutagenesis and Genomics Society (#07000)
♦ **EEMN** European Early Music Network (#06953)
♦ EEMS / see European Environmental Mutagenesis and Genomics Society (#07000)
♦ **EENA** European Emergency Number Association (#06978)
♦ **EEN** Enterprise Europe Network (#05493)
♦ **EEN** Environmental Evaluators Network (#05502)
♦ **EEN** Equestrian Educational Network (#05522)
♦ **EENET** Enabling Education Network (#05450)
♦ **EENeT** European Expert Network on Terrorism Issues (#07016)
♦ EEN / see The Federation of International Employers (#09644)
♦ EEN / see Health and Environment Alliance (#10879)
♦ EEO / see European School of Osteopathy
♦ EEO – Ecole européenne d'ostéopathie (internationally oriented national body)
♦ EEO – Escuela de Estudios Orientales (internationally oriented national body)
♦ EEO – European Esports Observatory (unconfirmed)
♦ **EEPA** European Egg Processors Association (#06970)
♦ **EEPA** Europe External Programme with Africa (#09155)
♦ EEPCA / see European Testing Inspection Certification System (#08901)
♦ **EEPC** European Ethylene Producers Committee (#07008)
♦ EEP / see European Egg Processors Association (#06970)
♦ **EEPF** European 8-Ball Pool Federation (#05777)
♦ **EEPG** European Educational Publishers Group (#06966)
♦ EEPI – East European Psychoanalytic Institute (see: #14662)
♦ **EEPSEA** Economy and Environment Programme for Southeast Asia (#05324)
♦ EEPSSA – Ecole européenne de psychothérapie socio- et somato-analytique, Strasbourg (internationally oriented national body)
♦ **EEPTA** European Egg Packers and Traders Association (#06969)
♦ **EERA** European Educational Research Association (#06967)
♦ **EERA** European Electronics Recyclers Association (#06975)
♦ **EERA** European Energy Research Alliance (#06989)
♦ EER / see European Energy Retailers (#06990)
♦ **EER** European Energy Retailers (#06990)
♦ EERO – European Environmental Research Organization (inactive)
♦ EESA / see Central and Eastern European Schools Association (#03697)
♦ **EeSA** European e-Skills Association (#08489)
♦ EESC – Eastern Europe Studies Centre (internationally oriented national body)
♦ **EESC** European Economic and Social Committee (#06963)
♦ EESDA – European Electrostatic Discharge Association (inactive)
♦ **EES** European Evaluation Society (#07009)
♦ **EESPA** European E-Invoicing Service Providers Association (#06971)
♦ **EESTEC** Electrical Engineering STudents' European assoCiation (#05416)
♦ Eesti Välispoliitika Instituut (internationally oriented national body)
♦ **EESV** Europese Economische Samenwerkingsverbanden (#06960)
♦ **EETS** Early English Text Society (#05157)
♦ EEUA – Eastern European University Association (internationally oriented national body)
♦ **EEU** Europa Esperanto-Unio (#07006)
♦ **EEUG** European EMTP-ATP Users Group (#06981)
♦ EEVC / see European Enhanced Vehicle-Safety Committee (#06992)
♦ **EEVC** European Enhanced Vehicle-Safety Committee (#06992)
♦ **EEVZA** Eastern European Volleyball Zonal Association (#05239)
♦ EEW – Erfassung der Europäischen Wirbellosen (inactive)
♦ **EFAAD** European Federation for the Advancement of Anaesthesia in Dentistry (#07040)
♦ **EFAA** European Federation of Accountants and Auditors for SMEs (#07037)
♦ EFAA / see European Federation of Auctioneers (#07057)
♦ EFA / see Asia Evangelical Alliance (#01275)
♦ **EFAC** European Factory Automation Committee (#07024)
♦ **EFAC** European Federation of Associations of Certification Bodies (#07049)
♦ **EFACIS** European Federation of Associations and Centres of Irish Studies (#07048)
♦ **EFAD** European Federation of the Associations of Dietitians (#07050)
♦ EFAD / see European Film Agency Directors Association (#07245)
♦ **EFAD** European Film Agency Directors Association (#07245)
♦ EFADs / see European Film Agency Directors Association (#07245)
♦ EFA – Environmental Foundation for Africa (internationally oriented national body)
♦ EFA – Europäische Feuerstätten Arbeitsgemeinschaft (internationally oriented national body)
♦ EFA – Europäische Friedens-Aktion (internationally oriented national body)
♦ **EFA** Europäisches Forum Alpbach (#07304)
♦ EFA – Europäisches Forum für Aussenwirtschaft, Verbrauchssteuern und Zoll (internationally oriented national body)
♦ **EFA** European Federation of Allergy and Airways Diseases Patients' Associations (#07045)
♦ EFA – European Federation of Anaesthesiologists (inactive)
♦ **EFA** European Federation of Auctioneers (#07057)
♦ **EFA** European Festivals Association (#07242)
♦ EFA / see European Film Academy (#07244)
♦ **EFA** European Finance Association (#07248)
♦ EFA – European FinTech Association (unconfirmed)
♦ EFA – European Fireplaces Association (internationally oriented national body)
♦ EFA / see European Food Safety Authority (#07287)
♦ EFA / see European Free Alliance (#07356)
♦ **EFA** European Free Alliance (#07356)
♦ EFA – European Full-Scale Modelling Association (no recent information)
♦ **EFA** European Fundraising Association (#07367)
♦ **EFA** European Futsal Association (#07371)
♦ **EFA** Fédération européenne des auto-écoles (#09560)
♦ EFA FTI / see Global Partnership for Education (#10531)
♦ EFAH / see Culture Action Europe (#04981)
♦ EFAH – European Federation Against Hunting (inactive)
♦ EFAHSS / see Fédération européenne pour la santé animale et la sécurité sanitaire (#09581)
♦ E-FAITH / see European Federation of Associations of Industrial and Technical Heritage (#07053)
♦ **EFAITH** European Federation of Associations of Industrial and Technical Heritage (#07053)
♦ EFALS – European Familial ALS Association (no recent information)
♦ **EFAMA** European Fund and Asset Management Association (#07365)
♦ **EFAMRO** European Federation of Associations of Market Research Organizations (#07055)
♦ EFAPCO – European Federation of the Associations of Professional Congress Organisers (inactive)
♦ **EFAP** European Forum for Architectural Policies (#07306)
♦ **EFAP** European Foundation for the Accreditation of Hotel School Programmes (#07341)
♦ EFAP – Fédération européenne des associations d'allergiques (inactive)
♦ **EFAPH** European Federation of Associations of Patients with Haemochromatosis (#07056)
♦ EFAPIT – European Federation of Animal Protein Importers and Traders (no recent information)
♦ **EFARD** European Forum on Agricultural Research for Development (#07302)
♦ EFAR – European Federation for Agricultural Recycling (unconfirmed)
♦ EFAR – European Federation of AIDS Research (inactive)
♦ **EFARN** European Film Agency Research Network (#07246)
♦ **EFARO** European Fisheries and Aquaculture Research Organization (#07265)
♦ **EFAS** European Federation of Audiology Societies (#07058)
♦ **EFAS** European Federation of Autonomic Societies (#07059)
♦ **EFAS** European Foot and Ankle Society (#07290)
♦ EFAT – European Federation of Animal Technologists (unconfirmed)
♦ **EFAT** European Federation of Art Therapy (#07047)
♦ EFAW – Educational Foundation for African Women (internationally oriented national body)
♦ **EFAY** European Free Alliance Youth (#07357)
♦ **EFBA** European Fertiliser Blenders Association (#07241)
♦ EFBA – European Fur Breeders Association (inactive)
♦ EFBA / see European Sales and Marketing Association (#08422)
♦ **EFBA-P** European Federation for Bioenergetic Analysis Psychotherapy (#07061)
♦ **EFBCC** European Federation of Bilateral Chambers of Commerce (#07060)
♦ **EFB** European Family Businesses (#07028)
♦ **EFB** European Federation of Biotechnology (#07062)
♦ **EFB** European Federation of Green Roof and Wall Associations (#07135)
♦ **EFB** European Fund for the Balkans (#07366)
♦ EFB-GEEF / see European Family Businesses (#07028)
♦ **EFBH** Europäische Föderation der Bau- und Holzarbeiter (#07065)
♦ **EFBH** Europese Federatie van Bouw- en Houtarbeiders (#07065)
♦ EFBP / see European Federation of Psychologists Associations (#07199)
♦ EFBPW / see BPW Europe – European Region of BPW International (#03309)
♦ **EFBQ** European Foundation for Business Qualification (#07343)
♦ **EFBS** European Federation of Building Societies (#07064)
♦ **EFBT** Europaeisk Federation af Bygnings- og Traeindustriarbejdere (#07065)
♦ EFBW / see Natural Mineral Waters Europe (#16955)
♦ EFBWWC / see European Federation of Building and Woodworkers (#07065)
♦ **EFBWW** European Federation of Building and Woodworkers (#07065)
♦ EFCA – Eurasia Foundation of Central Asia (internationally oriented national body)
♦ **EFCA** European Federation of Clean Air and Environmental Protection Associations (#07079)

♦ **EFCA** European Federation of Concrete Admixtures Associations (#07085)
♦ **EFCA** European Federation of Engineering Consultancy Associations (#07109)
♦ **EFCA** European Fisheries Control Agency (#07266)
♦ EFCA International Mission / see EFCA ReachGlobal
♦ EFCAM / see European Federation for Complementary and Alternative Medicine (#07084)
♦ **EFCAM** European Federation for Complementary and Alternative Medicine (#07084)
♦ **EFCAP** European Association for Forensic Child and Adolescent Psychiatry, Psychology and Other Involved Professions (#06045)
♦ EFCA ReachGlobal (internationally oriented national body)
♦ **EFCATS** European Federation of Catalysis Societies (#07067)
♦ EFCC / see European Federation of Clinical Chemistry and Laboratory Medicine (#07080)
♦ **EFCCA** European Federation of Crohn's and Ulcerative Colitis Associations (#07095)
♦ **EFCC** European Federation for Construction Chemicals (#07088)
♦ **EfCCNa** European Federation of Critical Care Nursing Associations (#07094)
♦ **EFCD** European Federation of Conservative Dentistry (#07087)
♦ **EFCE** European Federation of Chemical Engineering (#07074)
♦ **EFCEM** European Federation of Catering Equipment Manufacturers (#07068)
♦ **EFC** European Federation for Colposcopy and Pathology of the Lower Genital Tract (#07081)
♦ **EFC** European Federation of Corrosion (#07090)
♦ **EFC** European Fencing Confederation (#07239)
♦ EFC – European Film College (internationally oriented national body)
♦ **EFC** European Financial Coalition against Commercial Sexual Exploitation of Children Online (#07249)
♦ **EFC** European Forestry Commission (#07299)
♦ **EFCF** European Federation of City Farms (#07078)
♦ **EFCF** European Fuel Cell Forum (#07364)
♦ EFCG – Europäische Föderation der Chemiegewerkschaften (inactive)
♦ **EFCG** European Fine Chemicals Group (#07257)
♦ EFCGU – European Federation of Chemical General Workers Unions (inactive)
♦ EFCI / see European Cleaning and Facility Services Industry (#06571)
♦ **EFCI** European Cleaning and Facility Services Industry (#06571)
♦ **EFCLIN** European Federation of the Contact Lens and IOL Industries (#07089)
♦ EFCM / see EFCA ReachGlobal
♦ **EFCNI** European Foundation for the Care of Newborn Infants (#07344)
♦ EFCNS / see European Paediatric Neurology Society (#08126)
♦ EFCO / see European Federation of Campingsite Organisations and Holiday Park Assocations (#07066)
♦ **EFCO and HPA** European Federation of Campingsite Organisations and Holiday Park Assocations (#07066)
♦ **EFCPP** European Federation of Centres for Positive Psychotherapy (#07071)
♦ **EFCSE** European Federation of Cybersecurity Experts (#07096)
♦ **EFCS** European Federation for Company Sport (#07083)
♦ **EFCS** European Federation of Cytology Societies (#07097)
♦ **EFCSN** European Fact-checking Standards Network (#07022)
♦ **EFCTC** European Fluorocarbons Technical Committee (#07274)
♦ EFCTC / see European Matrix Biology (#07756)
♦ EFCT – European Federation of Chinese Tourism (unconfirmed)
♦ EFCT – European Federation of Conference Towns (inactive)
♦ EFCT / see Timber Construction Europe (#20164)
♦ **EFDA** European Fastener Distributor Association (#07034)
♦ EFDA – European Formula Drivers' Association (inactive)
♦ EFDA – European Fusion Development Agreement (inactive)
♦ EFDA JET (inactive)
♦ EFD – Education for Development (internationally oriented national body)
♦ **EFDF** European Flying Disc Federation (#07275)
♦ **EFDI** European Forum of Deposit Insurers (#07308)
♦ **EFDN** European Football for Development Network (#07291)
♦ EFDN Foundation / see European Football for Development Network (#07291)
♦ **EFDPO** European Federation of Data Protection Officers (#07098)
♦ EFDPS – European Trade Union Federation of Diamond and Precious Stone Workers (no recent information)
♦ **EFDS** European Forum for Democracy and Solidarity (#07307)
♦ **EFDV** Europäische Freidenkervereinigung (#06048)
♦ EFEC – European Federation for Education and Culture (inactive)
♦ EFECOT – European Federation for the Education of the Children of the Occupational Travellers (inactive)
♦ **EFeCT** European Federation of Conflict Management and Treatment in Education and Care (#07086)
♦ El Efecto Mariposa (#03389)
♦ **EFECW** Ecumenical Forum of European Christian Women (#05347)
♦ EFEDA – European Foodservice Equipment Distributors Association (no recent information)
♦ EFEDS – European Federation of Paediatric Research Societies (inactive)
♦ EF Educational Foundation for Foreign Study / see EF Foundation for Foreign Study
♦ EFEED – European Fund for Engineering Education Development (unconfirmed)
♦ **EFEE** European Federation of Education Employers (#07101)
♦ **EFEE** European Federation of Explosives Engineers (#07117)
♦ **EFELA** European Federation of Energy Law Associations (#07107)
♦ **EFEMA** European Food Emulsifier Manufacturers' Association (#07281)
♦ EFEM – European Federation of Energy Management Associations (inactive)
♦ **EFEM** European Federation for Experimental Morphology (#07115)
♦ **EFEO** European Federation of Essential Oils (#07112)
♦ EFEO – European Flight Engineers Organization (inactive)
♦ EFEP – European Federation of Environmental Professionals (no recent information)
♦ **EFEPR** European Federation of EPR Groups (#07110)
♦ EF – Equality Fund (internationally oriented national body)
♦ **EFER** European Federation of Electronic Retailers (#07103)
♦ **EFES** European Federation of Employee Share Ownership (#07105)
♦ EFES – European Federation of Endocrine Societies (inactive)
♦ **EFESME** European Federation for Elevator Small and Medium-sized Enterprises (#07104)
♦ **EFET** European Federation of Energy Traders (#07108)
♦ **EF** Eurasia Foundation (#05600)
♦ EF – Europaeiske Faellesskaber (inactive)
♦ EF / see European Fellowship of Christian Youth (#07238)
♦ **EF** European Fellowship of Christian Youth (#07238)
♦ EF – Evens Foundation (internationally oriented national body)
♦ **EFFAB** European Forum of Farm Animal Breeders (#07310)
♦ **EFFA** Europäisches Forum für die Menschenrechte und die Rechte der Familie (#07315)
♦ **EFFA** European Federation of Farriers Associations (#07119)
♦ EFFA / see European Flavour Association (#07269)
♦ **EFFA** European Flavour Association (#07269)
♦ **EFFA** European Forum for Human Rights and Family (#07315)
♦ **EFFA** European Freight Forwarders Association (#07358)
♦ **EFFAS** European Federation of Financial Analysts Societies (#07123)
♦ EFFAS – European Federation of National Foot and Ankle Societies (inactive)
♦ **EFFAT** European Federation of Food, Agriculture and Tourism Trade Unions (#07125)
♦ **EFFCA** European Food and Feed Cultures Association (#07282)
♦ **EFFC** European Federation of Foundation Contractors (#07129)
♦ **EFfCI** European Federation for Cosmetic Ingredients (#07092)
♦ **EFFCM** European Federation of Fibre-Cement Manufacturers (#07120)
♦ **EFFECT** European Forum for Electroconvulsive Therapy (#07309)

♦ Effective Institutions Platform (EIP) 05384

Co-Chair CABRI – c/o Natl Treasury, 240 Madiba Str, Private Bag X115, Pretoria, 0001, South Africa. T. +27123155229. Fax +27123155108. E-mail: effectiveinstitutions@oecd.org.
Co-Chair Valhallavägen 199, SE-105 25 Stockholm, Sweden.
Secretariat c/o OECD, 2 rue André Pascal, 75775 Paris CEDEX 16, France.
URL: http://www.effectiveinstitutions.org/

History 2012. **Aims** Support country-led and evidence-based policy dialogue, knowledge sharing and peer learning on *public sector management* and institutional reform. **Structure** Advisory Group. Co-Chairs (2). Joint Secretariat – *OECD (#17693)* and *UNDP (#20292)* Global Centre for Public Service Excellence. **Languages** English, French. **Finance** Funded by bilateral and multilateral donors. **Publications** *EIP Newsletter* (2-3 a year). *EIP Policy Briefs.*
Members Governments; Organizations. Governments (35):
Australia, Bangladesh, Belgium, Benin, Bhutan, Cambodia, Cameroon, Canada, Ethiopia, Finland, France, Germany, Ghana, Honduras, Indonesia, Ireland, Korea Rep, Malawi, Nepal, Netherlands, New Zealand, Peru, Philippines, Rwanda, Samoa, Senegal, South Africa, Sweden, Switzerland, Timor-Leste, Uganda, UK, USA, Vietnam, Zambia.
– *Africa Evidence Network (AEN, #00173)*;
– *African Development Bank (ADB, #00283)*;
– *African Tax Administration Forum (ATAF, #00479)*;
– *Asian Development Bank (ADB, #01422)*;
– *Collaborative Africa Budget Reform Initiative (CABRI, #04097)*;
– *CSO Partnership for Development Effectiveness (CPDE, #04976)*;
– *Development Partners Network on Decentralisation and Local Governance (DeLoG, #05058)*;
– *European Union (EU, #08967)*;
– *Inter-American Development Bank (IDB, #11427)*;
– *International Bank for Reconstruction and Development (IBRD, #12317)* (World Bank);
– *International Federation of Red Cross and Red Crescent Societies (#13526)*;
– *International Institute for Democracy and Electoral Assistance (International IDEA, #13872)*;
– *International Network for the Availability of Scientific Publications (INASP, #14233)*;
– *Inter-Parliamentary Union (IPU, #15961)*;
– *Learning Network on Capacity Development (LenCD)*;
– *New Partnership for Africa's Development (NEPAD, #17091)*;
– *OECD (#17693)*;
– *Pacific Association of Supreme Audit Institutions (PASAI, #17935)*;
– *Pacific Islands Forum Secretariat (#17970)*;
– *Publish What You Fund*;
– *The African Capacity Building Foundation (ACBF, #00233)*;
– *The Reality Of Aid (ROA, #18626)*;
– *Transparency International (TI, #20223)*;
– *UNDP (#20292)*. [2021/XJ9643/y/**F**]

♦ Effective Methods in Algebraic Geometry (meeting series)
♦ **EFFE** European Federation of Family Employment (#07118)
♦ **EFFE** European Forum for Freedom in Education (#07311)
♦ **EFFEI** European Federation of Financial Executives Institutes (#07124)
♦ EFF – Electronic Frontier Foundation (internationally oriented national body)
♦ L'Effet Papillon (#03389)
♦ EFF – European Federation for the Family (inactive)
♦ EFF – European Fisheries Fund (inactive)
♦ **EFF** European Food Forum (#07283)
♦ **EFF** European Franchise Federation (#07354)
♦ EFF – European Franchising Federation (inactive)
♦ EFF – European Future Forum (unconfirmed)

♦ Efficient Consumer Response Asia Pacific (ECR Asia Pacific) 05385

Acting Managing Dir 10 Anson Rd, 18-13, International Plaza, Beernegemstraat, 81, Singapore 079903, Singapore.

History 1999. Registration: Start date: 23 Dec 2010, Singapore. **Aims** Bring together leading-edge *retailers* and consumer goods *manufacturers* to promote best practice and enhance value and service to consumers. **Structure** Council. **Events** *Conference* Bangkok (Thailand) 2016, *Conference* Hong Kong 2015, *Asia Pacific Conference* Singapore (Singapore) 2012, *Conference* Singapore (Singapore) 2012, *Conference* Kuala Lumpur (Malaysia) 2010. **NGO Relations** *ECR Community (#05340).* [2015/XD9019/**D**]

♦ Efficient Consumer Response Australasia (internationally oriented national body)
♦ Efficient Consumer Response – ECR Europe / see ECR Community (#05340)
♦ **EFFO** European Federation and Forum for Osteopathy (#07128)
♦ EFFO / see International Osteoporosis Foundation (#14490)
♦ **EFFORTS** European Federation of Fortified Sites (#07127)
♦ **EFFoST** European Federation of Food Science and Technology (#07126)
♦ EF Foundation – EF Foundation for Foreign Study (internationally oriented national body)
♦ EF Foundation for Foreign Study (internationally oriented national body)
♦ **EFFPA** European Former Foodstuff Processors Association (#07301)
♦ **EFFRA** European Factories of the Future Research Association (#07023)
♦ **EFFR** European Forum for Research in Rehabilitation (#07331)
♦ EFFRO – European Federation of Food Retail (inactive)
♦ EFFSEP – European Federation of Fire Separating Element Producers (inactive)
♦ **EFFS** European Federation for Freshwater Sciences (#07130)
♦ **EFFS** European Federation of Funeral Services (#07131)
♦ EFFW – European Federation of Freelance Writers (no recent information)
♦ **EFGCP** European Forum for Good Clinical Practice (#07313)
♦ EFG – Eco Forum Global (internationally oriented national body)
♦ **EFG** European Federation of Geologists (#07133)
♦ **EFG** European Fermentation Group (#07240)
♦ EFGMMT – Europäische Föderation der Gesellschaften für Meeresforschung und Marine Technology (inactive)
♦ EFGO International / see Ekklesia Foundation for Gender Education
♦ EFGP / see European Green Party (#07409)
♦ **EFGS** European Forum for Geography and Statistics (#07312)
♦ **EFHA** European Fashion Heritage Association (#07033)
♦ EFHA – European Federation Historic Aviation (internationally oriented national body)
♦ **EFHCO** European Federation of Healthcare Clown Organizations (#07137)
♦ **EFHOH** European Federation of Hard of Hearing People (#07136)
♦ **EFHPA** European Federation of Homeopathic Patients' Associations (#07139)
♦ EFHSS / see World Federation for Hospital Sterilisation Sciences (#21438)
♦ EFIA – European Fertilizer Import Association (inactive)
♦ EFIA – European Flexographic Industry Association (internationally oriented national body)
♦ **EFIBCA** European Flexible Intermediate Bulk Container Association (#07270)
♦ **EFIB** Europäische Föderation für Ingenieurbiologie (#05751)
♦ EFIC – European Fuel Information Centre (inactive)
♦ **EFIC** European Furniture Industries Confederation (#07369)
♦ EFIC / see European Pain Federation (#08131)
♦ **EFIC** European Pain Federation (#08131)
♦ **EFIEES** European Federation of Intelligent Energy Efficiency Services (#07145)
♦ **EFI** Environic Foundation International (#05498)
♦ **EFI** Euromed Feminist Initiative (#05715)
♦ EFI – Európai Folklór Intézet (internationally oriented national body)
♦ **EFI** European Federation for Immunogenetics (#07141)

♦ **EFI** European Forest Institute (#07297)
♦ **EFILA** European Federation for Investment Law and Arbitration (#07149)
♦ **EFIL** European Federation for Intercultural Learning (#07146)
♦ **EFIMED** European Forest Institute Mediterranean Facility (#07298)
♦ **EFIM** European Federation of Internal Medicine (#07147)
♦ **EFIN** European Financial Inclusion Network (#07250)
♦ **EFIP** European Federation of Inland Ports (#07144)
♦ EFIP – European Federation of Interconnection and Packaging (inactive)
♦ **EFIP** European Feed Ingredients Platform (#07237)
♦ EFIP – European Forum of Independent Professionals (unconfirmed)
♦ EFISC / see European Feed and Food Ingredients Safety Certification (#07236)
♦ **EFISC-GTP** European Feed and Food Ingredients Safety Certification (#07236)
♦ **EFISDS** European Federation – International Society for Digestive Surgery (#07148)
♦ **EFIS** European Federation of Immunological Societies (#07142)
♦ EFIS – European Future Innovation System (unconfirmed)
♦ **EFITA** European Federation for Information Technology in Agriculture (#07143)
♦ **EFJCA** European Family Justice Center Alliance (#07029)
♦ EFJC / see European Choral Association – Europa Cantat (#06541)
♦ **EFJ** European Federation of Jewellery (#07150)
♦ **EFJ** European Federation of Journalists (#07152)
♦ EFK – Europäische Reisezugfahrplankonferenz (inactive)
♦ EFK – Europäisches Forum für angewandte Kriminalpolitik (internationally oriented national body)
♦ EFK / see WKF Europe (#20975)
♦ **EFLA** European Food Law Association (#07286)
♦ EFLA / see European Lift Association (#07695)
♦ EFLA / see IFLA Europe (#11103)
♦ **EF LAW** European Franchise Lawyers Association (#07355)
♦ EFLE / see European Association of Law and Economics (#06104)
♦ EFLE – European Forum of Logistics Education (unconfirmed)
♦ **EFL** European Federation for Living (#07155)
♦ **EFLEVA** European Federation of Light, Experimental and Vintage Aircraft (#07154)
♦ **EFLM** European Federation of Clinical Chemistry and Laboratory Medicine (#07080)
♦ EFLRY – European Federation of Liberal and Radical Youth (inactive)

♦ Efma 05386

CEO 10 bd Haussmann, 75009 Paris, France. T. +33147425272. Fax +33147425676. E-mail: celine@efma.com – info@efma.com.
URL: https://www.efma.com/

History Apr 1971, Paris (France). Currently only known under its acronym. Former names and other names: *European Financial Marketing Association* – former (1971); *Association européenne de marketing financier* – former (1971); *European Financial Management and Marketing Association* – former; *Association européenne de management et de marketing financiers* – former. **Aims** Provide community intelligence to optimize, innovate and transform financial management and marketing. **Structure** General Assembly; Board of Directors; Chairman; 2 Vice-Chairmen. **Languages** English. **Staff** 50.00 FTE, paid. **Finance** Member's dues. Others sources: revenue from international events, partnerships and other services. **Activities** Knowledge management/information dissemination; publishing activities; networking/liaising; events/meetings; awards/prizes/competitions. **Events** *World Retail Banking Summit* Dubai (United Arab Emirates) 2020, *Congress* Madrid (Spain) 2020, *Congress* Paris (France) 2019, *Innovation Summit* Paris (France) 2019, *Retail Banking Summit in Asia* Singapore (Singapore) 2019. **Publications** Reports; studies; articles. **Members** Institutions (over 3,300), including 1 out of 3 world leading banks, and 25% of 5 largest retail banks of each of the 40 largest countries in the Americas, Europe, Middle-East-Africa and Asia-Pacific. Members in 130 countries. Membership countries not specified. [2020.01.30/XD3469/**D**]

♦ **EFMA** European Financial Management Association (#07251)
♦ EFMA – European Fittings Manufacturers Association (inactive)
♦ **EFMA** European Forum of Medical Associations and WHO (#07320)
♦ EFMA / see Fertilizers Europe (#09738)
♦ **EFMC** European Federation for Medicinal Chemistry (#07165)
♦ EFMD / see EFMD – The Management Development Network (#05387)

♦ EFMD – The Management Development Network 05387

Pres Rue Gachard 88, Bte 3, 1050 Brussels, Belgium. T. +3226290810. Fax +3226290811. E-mail: info@efmdglobal.org.
Vice-Pres address not obtained.
EFMD Global Network Route de Suisse 135 A, 1290 Versoix GE, Switzerland.
URL: http://www.efmdglobal.org/

History Oct 1971, Brussels (Belgium). Incorporated on 1 Jan 1972, by merger of *International University Contact for Management Education (IUC, inactive)*, set up 1952, and *European Association of Management Training Centres (EAMTC, inactive)*, formed Jan 1959, Geneva (Switzerland). New statutes adopted 27 Nov 1997. Former names and other names: *European Foundation for Management Development (EFMD)* – former; *Fondation européenne pour le développement du management* – former; *Europese Stichting voor Management Development* – former. Registration: Banque-Carrefour des Entreprises, No/ID: 0411.610.491, Start date: 11 Oct 1971. **Aims** Act as a forum for information, high-quality networking and worldwide cooperation in management development; encourage the dissemination of innovative ideas and practices, identify current management challenges, promote international cooperation and provide relevant data and information on management education in Europe. **Structure** General Assembly (annual); Board; Membership Review Committee; Functional Departments; President. **Languages** English. **Staff** 60.00 FTE, paid. **Finance** Sources: government support; international organizations; members' dues; revenue from activities/projects. **Activities** Awards/prizes/competitions; certification/accreditation; events/meetings; knowledge management/information dissemination; projects/programmes; research/documentation. **Events** *Assessing the Impact of Research in Business Schools* Brussels (Belgium) 2022, *MBA Conference* Brussels (Belgium) 2022, *Annual Conference* Prague (Czechia) 2022, *Annual Conference* Brussels (Belgium) 2020, *Undergraduate Conference* Frankfurt-Main (Germany) 2020. **Publications** *Documentation on Books, Cases, Teaching Material in Management* (4 a year); *efmd Bulletin* (3 a year); *Annual Review of Progress in Entrepreneurship (ARPENT)*; *Corporate News'at'efmd* – online newsletter; *FORUM* – magazine. *Aide Mémoire* (1997) – use and impact of learning technologies; *Training the Fire Brigade – Preparing for the Unimaginable* (1996); *European Management Education Report* (1995); *Guide to European Business Schools and Management Centres. European Directory on Executive Education* (2003) – CD-ROM. Guides; directories; reports; conference proceedings; brochures. **Members** Full; Affiliate; Associate. Business schools and executive development centres, company training divisions, public service institutions, consultants, national organizations and foundations and individuals concerned with training for management and public administration. Over 860 in 87 countries and territories:
Algeria, Argentina, Armenia, Australia, Austria, Azerbaijan, Belarus, Belgium, Bosnia-Herzegovina, Brazil, Brunei Darussalam, Bulgaria, Canada, Chile, China, Colombia, Costa Rica, Côte d'Ivoire, Croatia, Cuba, Cyprus, Czechia, Denmark, Ecuador, Egypt, Estonia, Finland, France, Germany, Greece, Hungary, Iceland, India, Indonesia, Iran Islamic Rep, Ireland, Israel, Italy, Japan, Kazakhstan, Kenya, Kiribati, Korea Rep, Latvia, Lebanon, Liechtenstein, Lithuania, Luxembourg, Madagascar, Malaysia, Malta, Mexico, Monaco, Morocco, Netherlands, New Zealand, Nigeria, Norway, Oman, Pakistan, Peru, Philippines, Poland, Portugal, Romania, Russia, Saudi Arabia, Senegal, Singapore, Slovakia, Slovenia, South Africa, Spain, Sweden, Switzerland, Taiwan, Thailand, Trinidad-Tobago, Tunisia, Türkiye, UK, Ukraine, United Arab Emirates, Uruguay, USA, Venezuela, Vietnam.
Included in the above, 86 organizations listed in this Yearbook:
- *AACSB International – Association to Advance Collegiate Schools of Business*;
- *Academy of Business in Society (ABIS, #00032)*;
- *AIESEC (#00593)*;
- *Andes University (ULA)*;
- *Arab Administrative Development Organization (ARADO, #00893)*;
- *ASEAN-EC Management Centre*;
- *Asian Institute of Management (AIM, #01518)*;
- *Asian Institute of Technology (AIT, #01519)*;
- *Association des institutions de formation et de perfectionnement au management d'Afrique francophone (AIMAF, no recent information)*;
- *Association of African Business Schools (AABS, #02351)*;
- *Association of Asia-Pacific Business Schools (AAPBS, #02386)*;
- *Association of Deans of Southeast Asian Graduate Schools of Management (ADSGM, no recent information)*;
- *Association of Management Development Institutions in South Asia (AMDISA, #02792)*;
- *Association of Management Training Institutions of Eastern and Southern Africa (AMTIESA, no recent information)*;
- *Association of MBAs (AMBA, #02795)*;
- *Baltic Management Development Association (BMDA, #03123)*;
- *BMI Executive Institute (BMI, #03288)*;
- *Brookings Institution (BI)*;
- *Business Association of Latin American Studies (BALAS, #03378)*;
- *CEEMAN – International Association for Management Development in Dynamic Societies (CEEMAN, #03625)*;
- *CEMS – The Global Alliance in Management Education (#03635)*;
- *Central Asian Foundation for Management Development (CAMAN, #03682)*;
- *Centro de Investigación de la Universidad del Pacífico (CIUP)*;
- *CEU Business School*;
- *China-Europe International Business School (CEIBS, #03888)*;
- *Council for Advancement and Support of Education (CASE)*;
- *Council on International Educational Exchange (CIEE, #04901)*;
- *Cyprus International Institute of Management (CIIM)*;
- *Eastern Mediterranean University*;
- *EDEN Digital Learning Europe (EDEN, #05356)*;
- *EFQM – European Foundation for Quality Management (EFQM, #05388)*;
- *EMCC Global (EMCC, #05434)*;
- *ESCP Europe Business School (#05536)*;
- *Escuela Superior de Administración y Dirección de Empresas (ESADE)*;
- *ESMT Berlin*;
- *Europa-Institut at Saarland University*;
- *European Academy of Management (EURAM, #05800)*;
- *European Accounting Association (EAA, #05820)*;
- *European Association for International Education (EAIE, #06092)*;
- *European Association for Research in Industrial Economics (EARIE, #06193)*;
- *European Business Ethics Network (EBEN, #06418)*;
- *European Centre for Executive Development (CEDEP, #06479)*;
- *European Council for Small Business and Entrepreneurship (ECSB, #06842)*;
- *European Doctoral Programmes Association in Management and Business Administration (EDAMBA, #06935)*;
- *European Finance Association (EFA, #07248)*;
- *European Institute for Advanced Studies in Management (EIASM, #07544)*;
- *European Institute for Asian Studies (EIAS, #07545)*;
- *European Institute of Purchasing Management (EIPM)*;
- *European International Business Academy (EIBA, #07585)*;
- *European Learning Industry Group (ELIG, #07674)*;
- *European Marketing Academy (EMAC, #07745)*;
- *European Trade Association for Business Angels, Seed Funds, and other Early Stage Market Players (EBAN, #08923)*;
- *European University Association (EUA, #09027)*;
- *European Women's Management Development International Network (EWMD, #09103)*;
- *Finnish Institute for International Trade (FINTRA)*;
- *Florida International University (FIU)*;
- *Foundation for International Business Administration Accreditation (FIBAA, #09961)*;
- *Global Business School Network (GBSN, #10260)*;
- *Graduate Management Admission Council (GMAC, #10687)*;
- *Hernstein International Management Institute*;
- *IESE Business School, University of Navarra (IESE)*;
- *INCAE Business School (#11141)*;
- *INSEAD (#11228)*;
- *Institute of Directors (IoD, #11254)*;
- *Instituto Internacional San Telmo*;
- *International Academy of Management (IAM)*;
- *International Centre for Promotion of Enterprises (ICPE, #12509)*;
- *International Engineering Alliance (#13275)*;
- *International Institute of Business (IIB)*;
- *International Leadership Association (ILA, #14010)*;
- *International Management Development Network (INTERMAN, no recent information)*;
- *International Management Institute, Kiev (IMI-Kiev)*;
- *International Management Institute, St Petersburg (IMISP)*;
- *International University of Monaco*;
- *Latin American Council of Business Schools (#16308)*;
- *Management Centre Europe (MCE, #16561)*;
- *MBA Roundtable (#16606)*;
- *Moscow International Higher Business School (MIRBIS)*;
- *Project Management Institute (PMI, #18534)*;
- *Riga International School of Economics and Business Administration (RISEBA)*;
- *Société européenne pour la formation des ingénieurs (SEFI, #19462)*;
- *Thunderbird – The Garvin School of International Management*;
- *Triple Helix Association (THA, #20242)*;
- *Universidad de las Américas (UDLA)*;
- *University Industry Innovation Network (UIIN, #20699)*;
- *West African Management Development Institutes Network (WAMDEVIN, #20886)*.

IGO Relations Maintains close contacts with: *European Commission (EC, #06633)*; *ILO (#11123)*; *OECD (#17693)*. **NGO Relations** Member of: *Baltic Management Development Association (BMDA, #03123)*; *European Policy Centre (EPC, #08240)*; *Federation of European and International Associations Established in Belgium (FAIB, #09508)*. Administers: *China-Europe International Business School (CEIBS, #03888)*; *European Quality Link (EQUAL, #08314)*. Co-convenor of: *Principles for Responsible Management Education (PRME, #18500)*. Associate member of: *European Association for Quality Assurance in Higher Education (ENQA, #06183)*. Affiliate member of: *SPACE Network (#19899)*. Cooperates with: *AACSB International – Association to Advance Collegiate Schools of Business*; *European Association of National Productivity Centres (EANPC, #06130)*. [2021.09.01/XF0570/y/**F**]

♦ EFM – Earth Federation Movement (see: #21313)
♦ **EFM** European Forum for Manufacturing (#07319)
♦ **EFMF** European Financial Markets Federation (#07252)
♦ **EFMI** European Federation for Medical Informatics (#07164)
♦ **EFML** European Federation of Lighter Manufacturers (#07153)
♦ **EFMN** European Foresight Monitoring Network (#07295)
♦ EFMS – European Federation of Marine Science and Technology Societies (inactive)
♦ **EFNA** European Federation of Neurological Associations (#07177)
♦ **EFNARC** Experts for Specialised Construction and Concrete Systems (#09226)
♦ **EFN Asia** Economic Freedom Network Asia (#05316)
♦ **EFNCP** European Forum on Nature Conservation and Pastoralism (#07323)
♦ **EFNDT** European Federation for Non-Destructive Testing (#07179)
♦ EFN – Environmentalists for Nuclear Energy (internationally oriented national body)
♦ EFN – European Federation for Naturopathy (inactive)
♦ **EFN** European Federation of Nurses Associations (#07180)
♦ **EFN** European Forecasting Network (#07293)
♦ **EFNIL** European Federation of National Institutions for Language (#07172)
♦ **EFNMS** European Federation of National Maintenance Societies (#07173)
♦ EFNMU – European Federation of Natural Medicine Users (no recent information)
♦ EFNNMA / see European Forum of Nursing and Midwifery Associations (#07324)
♦ EFNP – European Federation of NeuroPsychiatry (no recent information)
♦ **EFNR** European Federation for NeuroRehabilitation Societies (#07178)
♦ EFNS – European Federation of Neurological Societies (inactive)
♦ **EFNYO** European Federation of National Youth Orchestras (#07176)
♦ EFOA / see Sustainable Fuels (#20060)
♦ EFODL – European Federation of Open and Digital Learning (no recent information)

- ♦ EFO / see European Federation and Forum for Osteopathy (#07128)
- ♦ EFOGE – Ekklesia Foundation for Gender Education (internationally oriented national body)
- ♦ **EFOMP** European Federation of Organisations for Medical Physics (#07183)
- ♦ **EFOMW** European Forum of Muslim Women (#07321)
- ♦ **EFORT** European Federation of National Associations of Orthopaedics and Traumatology (#07169)
- ♦ **e-Forum** Forum for European e-Public Services (#09911)
- ♦ **EFOSA** European Federation of Orthodontic Specialists Associations (#07185)
- ♦ **EFOS** European Federation of Older Students at Universities (#07181)
- ♦ **EFOSS** European Federation of Oral Surgery Societies (#07182)
- ♦ EFOST – European Federation of National Associations of Orthopaedic Sports Traumatology (inactive)
- ♦ **EFOW** European Federation of Origin Wines (#07184)
- ♦ **EFPA** European Federation of Psychologists Associations (#07199)
- ♦ **EFPA** European Financial Planning Association (#07253)
- ♦ **EFPAM** European Federation of Patients' Associations for Anthroposophic Medicine (#07189)
- ♦ EFPA / see Pack2Go Europe (#18014)
- ♦ EFP Balkans – Education for Peace Institute of the Balkans (internationally oriented national body)
- ♦ **EFPC** European Federation of Press Clubs (#07194)
- ♦ **EFPC** European Forum for Primary Care (#07326)
- ♦ EFP – EuroFédération de psychanalyse (unconfirmed)
- ♦ **EFP** Europäische Föderation der Psychologenverbände (#07199)
- ♦ **EFP** European Federation of Parasitologists (#07186)
- ♦ **EFP** European Federation of Periodontology (#07190)
- ♦ **EFP** European Federation for Primatology (#07195)
- ♦ EFP – European Federation of Purchasing (inactive)
- ♦ **EFP** European Film Promotion (#07247)
- ♦ EFP / see Federation of European Pharmacological Societies (#09527)
- ♦ **EFPIA** European Federation of Pharmaceutical Industries and Associations (#07191)
- ♦ **EFPI** European Federation of Parquet Importers (#07187)
- ♦ **EFP-International** International Education for Peace Institute (#13230)
- ♦ **EFPM** European Fair Play Movement (#07025)
- ♦ **EFPN** European Governmental LGBTI Focal Points Network (#07401)
- ♦ EFPOS – European Federation of Psychosocial Oncology Societies (inactive)
- ♦ EFPPA / see European Federation of Psychologists Associations (#07199)
- ♦ **EFPP** European Federation for Psychoanalytic Psychotherapy (#07198)
- ♦ **EFPP** European Foundation for Plant Pathology (#07349)
- ♦ **EFPRA** European Fat Processors and Renderers Association (#07035)
- ♦ EFPRO – Association of European Fibre and Paper Research Organisations (inactive)
- ♦ **EFPSA** European Federation of Psychology Students' Associations (#07200)
- ♦ EFPSC – European Postal Financial Services Commission (inactive)
- ♦ **EFPS** European Federation of Productivity Services (#07196)
- ♦ EFPS – European Federation of Psychoanalytic Self-Psychology (no recent information)
- ♦ **EFPTA** European Federation of Psychology Teachers' Association (#07201)
- ♦ **EFPT** European Federation of Psychiatric Trainees (#07197)
- ♦ EFPW – European Federation for the Protection of Waters (inactive)
- ♦ **EFQM** EFQM – European Foundation for Quality Management (#05388)

♦ EFQM – European Foundation for Quality Management (EFQM) 05388

Main Office Av des Olympiades 2, 5th Floor, 1140 Brussels, Belgium. T. +3227753511. Fax +3227753535. E-mail: info@efqm.org.
Registered Office PO Box 6386, 5600 HJ Eindhoven, Netherlands.
URL: http://www.efqm.org/

History Oct 1989. Founded when the CEO/Presidents of 67 European companies subscribed to our Policy Document and declared their commitment to achieving EFQM mission and vision. **Aims** Support the management of European organizations in accelerating the process of developing quality strategies and implementing *total quality* programmes; stimulate and, where necessary, assist European partners to participate in the process of strengthening European quality management practices. **Structure** Governing Committee; Executive Committee; Chief Executive Officer. **Languages** Arabic, English, French, German, Spanish. **Staff** 21.00 FTE, paid. **Finance** Sources: members' dues. **Activities** Awards/prizes/competitions; events/meetings; training/education. **Events** *EFQM Forum* Lyon (France) 2022, *EFQM Forum* Lyon (France) 2022, *EFQM Forum* Brussels (Belgium) 2021, *EFQM Forum* Lyon (France) 2020, *EFQM Forum* Helsinki (Finland) 2019. **Publications** *EFQM Newsletter*. **Information Services** *databank containing information on EFQM members and information of interest to them (accessible to members only)*; *Excellence One* – online learning platform.

Members General; Additional; Associated. European companies, universities and institutes (800) in 36 countries and territories:
Argentina, Austria, Belarus, Belgium, Croatia, Cyprus, Czechia, Denmark, Finland, France, Germany, Gibraltar, Greece, Hungary, Iceland, Ireland, Italy, Latvia, Liechtenstein, Luxembourg, Malta, Netherlands, Norway, Poland, Portugal, Romania, Russia, Serbia, Slovenia, South Africa, Spain, Sweden, Switzerland, Türkiye, UK, Ukraine.
Included in the above, 5 companies and organizations listed in this Yearbook:
European Organization for Quality (EOQ, #08112); *European Telecommunications Standards Institute (ETSI, #08897)*; *Eurotunnel (#09193)*; *Joint Research Centre (JRC, #16147)* (Petten (Netherlands)); *The Conference Board in Europe (#04583)*.
NGO Relations Member of (1): *EFMD – The Management Development Network (#05387)*. Instrumental in setting up (1): *European Quality Platform (no recent information)*. In liaison with technical committees of: *International Organization for Standardization (ISO, #14473)*. [2022.05.08/XF0758/fy/**F**]

- ♦ **EFRA** European Federation of Radio Operated Model Automobiles (#07204)
- ♦ EFRA / see Flame Retardants Europe (#09791)
- ♦ **EFRAG** European Financial Reporting Advisory Group (#07254)

♦ EFRAT – International Organization for Saving Jewish Babies 05389

Exec Sec 10 Ha-iluy Street, PO Box 34204, 9134101 Jerusalem, Israel. T. +97225454502 – +97225454500. E-mail: tamar@efrat.org.il – efrat@efrat.org.il.
Pres address not obtained.
URL: http://www.efrat.org.il/

History Former names and other names: *Committee for the Rescue of Israel's Babies (CRIB)* – former. **Aims** Eliminate non-medical *abortions* through education, legislation and support of pregnant women.
Members Branches in 14 countries:
Argentina, Australia, Belgium, Brazil, Chile, France, Israel, Mexico, Panama, Spain, Switzerland, UK, Uruguay, USA.
[2021.05.18/XF5757/**F**]

- ♦ **EFRC** European Forum for Reciprocating Compressors (#07328)
- ♦ EFRE – European Federation for Renewable Energy (inactive)
- ♦ EFR – Environment Fellowship of Rotarians (internationally oriented national body)
- ♦ EFR – European Fast Reactor Associates (inactive)
- ♦ **EFR** European Financial Services Round Table (#07255)
- ♦ **EFRJ** European Forum for Restorative Justice (#07332)
- ♦ **EFRO** Europees Fonds voor Regionale Ontwikkeling (#08342)
- ♦ **EFRP** Evropako Forumo e Romango thaj e Phirutnengo (#08402)
- ♦ EFRP / see PensionsEurope (#18291)
- ♦ **EFRS** European Federation of Radiographer Societies (#07203)
- ♦ EFRSWSP – European Federation of Rudolf Steiner Waldorf School Parents (inactive)
- ♦ **EFRTC** European Federation of Railway Trackworks Contractors (#07205)
- ♦ EFSAC – European Fire and Security Advisory Council (inactive)
- ♦ EFSA – Ecumenical Foundation of Southern Africa (internationally oriented national body)
- ♦ **EFSA** European Federation of Sea Anglers (#07211)
- ♦ **EFSA** European Food Safety Authority (#07287)
- ♦ **EFSA** European Forum of Securities Associations (#07333)
- ♦ **EFSAS** European Foundation for South Asian Studies (#07350)
- ♦ **EFSCA** European Fire Service Colleges' Association (#07260)
- ♦ **EFSD** European Foundation for the Study of Diabetes (#07351)
- ♦ **EFSE** The European Fund for Southeast Europe (#07368)
- ♦ **EFS** European Federation of Sexology (#07213)
- ♦ EFS – European Fusarium Seminar (meeting series)
- ♦ **EFSG** European Fire and Security Group (#07259)
- ♦ **EFSHT** European Federation of Societies of Hand Therapy (#07215)
- ♦ EFSI – European Federation of the Scientific Image (no recent information)
- ♦ **EFSI** European Federation for Services to Individuals (#07212)
- ♦ **efsli** European Forum of Sign Language Interpreters (#07334)
- ♦ **EFSMA** European Federation of Sports Medicine Associations (#07219)
- ♦ **EFSM** European Federation of Societies for Microsurgery (#07216)
- ♦ EFSM / see European Federation of Sports Medicine Associations (#07219)
- ♦ **EFSN** European Fire Sprinkler Network (#07262)
- ♦ EF-Sortsmyndigheden (#04404)
- ♦ EFSP – European Federation for Somato-Psychotherapy (no recent information)
- ♦ **EFSPI** European Federation of Statistics in the Pharmaceutical Industry (#07220)
- ♦ EFSP / see Integrated Marketing Communications Council of Europe (#11369)
- ♦ EFSP / see South Pacific Evangelical Alliance (#19886)
- ♦ EFSQ / see International Association on Social Quality (#12168)
- ♦ **EFSS** European Federation of Surgical Specialties (#07222)
- ♦ EFSTA – European Fiscal Standards Association (unconfirmed)
- ♦ **EFSUMB** European Federation of Societies for Ultrasound in Medicine and Biology (#07217)
- ♦ **EFSZ** Europäisches Fremdsprachenzentrum (#06491)
- ♦ EFTA / see European Flexographic Industry Association
- ♦ EFTA-Benelux – European Flexographic Technical Association Benelux (internationally oriented national body)
- ♦ **EFTA CMP** Committee of Members of Parliament of EFTA Countries (#04269)

♦ EFTA Court 05390

Cour de l'AELE

Registrar Rue du Fort Thüngen 1, L-1499 Luxembourg, Luxembourg. T. +352421081. Fax +352434389. E-mail: eftacourt@eftacourt.int – registry@eftacourt.int.
URL: http://www.eftacourt.int/

History 1 Jan 1994. Established on entry into force of the Agreement on the European Economic Area (EEA) and the *Agreement between EFTA States on the Establishment of a Surveillance Authority and a Court of Justice*, both signed 2 May 1992, Porto (Portugal). The EFTA Court was set up under the latter agreement as an independent institution with judicial function in accordance with the *European Economic Area (EEA, #06957)* with respect to the Member States of *EFTA (#05391)* party thereto. Was initially based in Geneva (Switzerland); moved to Luxembourg on 1 Sep 1996. **Aims** Fulfil the judicial function within the EFTA system, interpreting the Agreement on the European Economic Area with regard to the EFTA States party to the agreement. **Structure** Comprises 3 judges, appointed by common accord of the Governments of the EEA EFTA States for a term of 6 years. Judges elect a President from among their number for a term of 3 years. Remains permanently in session. **Languages** English, German, Icelandic, Norwegian. **Staff** 20.00 FTE, paid. **Finance** Sources: contributions of member/participating states. **Activities** Conflict resolution; guidance/assistance/consulting. **Publications** *The EEA and the EFTA Court – Decentred Integration* (2014); *EFTA Court Texts relating to the Organisation, Jurisdiction and Procedure of the Court* (2008) in English, German, Icelandic, Norwegian; *The EFTA Court – Legal Framework and Case Law* (2008); *The EFTA Court Ten Years On – 1994-2004* (2005).
Members Member States EFTA States party to EEA Agreement and the Agreement between the EFTA States on the Establishment of a Surveillance Authority and a Court of Justice (3):
Iceland, Liechtenstein, Norway. [2021.11.04/XF5096/**F***]

- ♦ **EFTA** European Fair Trade Association (#07026)
- ♦ **EFTA** European Family Therapy Association (#07031)

♦ EFTA – European Free Trade Association 05391

Association européenne de libre-échange (AELE) – Europäische Freihandelsassoziation

Headquarters Rue de Varembé 9-11, 1211 Geneva 20, Switzerland. T. +41223322600. Fax +41223322677. E-mail: mail.gva@efta.int.
Brussels Office Ave des Arts 19H, 1000 Brussels, Belgium. T. +3222861711. Fax +3222861750. E-mail: mail.bxl@efta.int.
URL: http://www.efta.int/

History 4 Jan 1960, Stockholm (Sweden), on signature of the *Stockholm Convention*, by the governments of Austria, Denmark, Norway, Portugal, Sweden, Switzerland and the UK, following initial decision by government officials of these countries, Jun 1959, Saltsjöbaden (Sweden). The Stockholm Convention (hereafter referred to as the Convention) entered into force on 3 May 1960. Finland became an associate member in Jun 1961; and was formally approved as a full member 4 Nov 1985, with effect from 1 Jan 1986. Iceland became a full member in Mar 1970 and Liechtenstein in Sep 1991. Six members have left EFTA to become members of the *European Communities (EC, inactive)*, now the first "pillar" of the *European Union (EU, #08967)*: Denmark and the UK at the end of 1972; Portugal as of 31 Dec 1985; Austria, Finland and Sweden as of 31 Dec 1994. Guidelines for developing the EFTA-EC relationship and creation of *European Economic Area (EEA, #06957)* – originally referred to as *European Economic Space (EES)* – were set out in the Luxembourg Declaration of 1984. Exploratory talks on free movement of goods, services, capital and labour throughout the 19-country area began in 1989; they also covered increased cooperation in other fields such as education, the environment, social policy and research and development. The first meeting of EFTA-EC negotiators for formal negotiations on the establishment of a European Economic Area encompassing all EFTA and EC countries took place on 20 Jun 1990, with the aim of concluding negotiations in 1991 so that the EEA Agreement could come into force on 1 Jan 1993, at the same time as the EC single market. The EEA Agreement was finally concluded on 21 Oct 1991, signed 2 May 1992 and entered into force on 1 Jan 1994 for all EC and EFTA countries except Switzerland, which rejected the Agreement in a referendum on 1 Jan 1994. Updated EFTA Convention, the *Vaduz Convention*, signed at EFTA Ministerial meeting, 21 Jun 2001, Vaduz (Liechtenstein) and entered into force 1 Jun 2002, principally covers relations between EFTA members of EEA and Switzerland with the European Union so that all EFTA members benefit from privileged trading relations. The legal texts of the EEA Enlargement were signed 11 Nov 2003, and as of 1 May the 10 new EU Members States are also members of the EEA.
Aims Remove import duties, quotas and other obstacles to trade in Western Europe and uphold liberal, non-discriminatory practices in world trade; promote in the EFTA area and in each member state a sustained expansion of economic activity, full employment, increased productivity and the rational use of resources, financial stability and continuous improvement in living standards; secure conditions of fair competition in trade between member states; avoid significant disparity between member states in the conditions of supply of raw materials produced within the EFTA area; contribute to harmonious development and expansion of world trade and to progressive removal of barriers to this; create a single market in Western Europe.
Structure Council (meets twice a year at ministerial level and once a month at level of officials – Heads of Permanent Missions in Geneva (Switzerland) to EFTA). Council is assisted by the following:
- *'Committee on Third-Country Relations'*, set up Oct 1996, replacing the Group on Third Country Relations – oversees functioning and development of free trade and cooperation agreements with third countries.
- *'Economic Committee'*, set up 1964 – exchanges views on economic policy in Member States and engages in dialogue on such matters with the EU.
- *'Committee of Origin and Customs Experts (COCE)'* – oversees cooperation in the customs field, particularly in relation to free trade agreements.
- *'Committee on Technical Barriers to Trade'*, set up 12 Jul 1984 – advises the Council on standardization policy, conformity assessment policy, relations with other European quality infrastructure organizations and international aspects of technical regulatory work.
- *'Committee of Trade Experts'*, set up 1960 – deals with policies to facilitate trade by technical and legislative means.
- *'Budget Committee'*, set up in 1960.

EFTA
05391

alphabetic sequence excludes
For the complete listing, see Yearbook Online at

- *'Board of Auditors'*.
- EFTA Consultative Committee (CC), established Feb 1961 – provides a forum for representatives of industry and labour in the EFTA states to exchange views among themselves and with the Council.
- *Committee of Members of Parliament of EFTA Countries (EFTA CMP, #04269)*, set up in 1977 following 15 years of informal meetings – provides a forum in which MPs of EFTA states can discuss issues of concern among themselves and, on occasion, with EFTA Ministers.

Complemented by *Committee of Members of Parliament of the EFTA States Party to the EEA (EFTA MPS, #04270)*.

Joint Committees with each of EFTA's third-country partners manage and develop the Free Trade Agreements and Declarations on Cooperation.

'Expert Groups' (7): Legal Experts; Public Procurement; Services, Establishment and Capital Movement; Intellectual Property; Efficient Trade Procedures; Price Compensation; State Aid.

State Aid Experts; Public Procurement; Intellectual Property; Price Compensation; Services, Investment and Establishment; Legal Experts; Efficient Trade Procedures, meets regularly with: European Commission Directorates-General on Information Society and on Internal Market; *United Nations Economic Commission for Africa (ECA, #20554)*, in particular on *United Nations Centre for Trade Facilitation and Electronic Business (UN/CEFACT, #20527)*, *E-business Board for European Standardization (eBES, inactive)* and *European PRO Committee (EUROPRO, #08280)*; representatives of Central and Eastern European countries.

EFTA Standing Committee, comprising representatives from Iceland, Liechtenstein and Norway, with observers from Switzerland and EFTA Surveillance Authority, serves as the forum in which the EEA EFTA States consult one another and arrive at a position before meeting with the EU side in the EEA Joint Committee. It is assisted by 5 Subcommittees and a number of working and expert groups:

- *'Subcommittee I – Goods'*, with 16 Working Groups: Competition Policy; Customs Matters; Efficient Trade Procedures; Energy Matters; Feedingstuffs; Fisheries; Intellectual Property; Medicinal Products; Phytosanitary Matters; Plant Health; Processed Agricultural Products; Product Liability; Public Procurement; State Aid; Technical Barriers to Trade; Veterinary Matters.
- *'Subcommittee II – Free Movement of Capital and Services and Company Law'*, with 6 Working Groups: Audio-visual Services; Company Law; Financial Services; Information and Telecommunication Services; Postal Services; Transport.
- *'Subcommittee III – Free Movement of Persons'*, with 3 Working Groups: Free Movement of Workers and Employment; Mutual Recognition of Diplomas; Social Security.
- *'Subcommittee IV – Flanking and Horizontal Policies'*, with 16 Working Groups: Budgetary Matters; Civil Protection; Consumer Protection; Cultural Affairs; Disabled, Elderly and Social Exclusion; Education, Training and Youth; EFTA CCC; Enterprise and Entrepreneurship; Environment; Gender Equality and Family Policy; Heads of National Statistical Institutes; Health and Safety at Work and Labour Law; Interchange of Data between Administrations; Public Health; Research and Development; Tourism.
- *'Subcommittee V – Legal and Institutional Matters'*, with one Working Group: Ad-hoc Working Group on EEA Enlargement.
- Advisory committees established to facilitate communication with social partners and parliaments of EFTA States and the EU.

'EFTA Secretariat', based in Geneva, is headed by the Secretary-General who is assisted by 2 Deputy Secretaries General in Geneva and Brussels (Belgium). It was restructured, 1 Jan 1995, on accession of Austria, Finland and Sweden to the European Union. The Geneva Office deals chiefly with third country matters. EFTA Brussels Office, opened 11 Apr 1988, following EFTA Council decision, 12 Nov 1987, is an integral part of EFTA Secretariat, dealing with EEA matters. EFTA Luxembourg (Luxembourg) Office coordinates statistical cooperation with Eurostat.

To ensure implementation of the Agreement among the EFTA EEA states, the *EFTA Surveillance Authority (ESA, #05392)*, *EFTA Court (#05390)* and *Standing Committee of the EFTA States (#19953)* have been established. Their setting up was proposed, 14 Apr 1992, in two internal agreements which were signed on 2 May 1992, just before that on the EEA. In addition, MPS, set up 20 May 1992, Reykjavik (Iceland), on signature of an Agreement by EFTA states, serves as consultative body to the Standing Committee and as an information channel on the EEA between EFTA and the national parliaments of its member countries. Committee members form half of *EEA Joint Parliamentary Committee (EEA JPC, #05382)*, for which EFTA provides the Secretariat, the remaining 33 members being members of the European Parliament.

Languages English. **Staff** 60.00 FTE, paid. **Finance** Expenses covered by member states in proportions determined by GNP.

Activities Unites in one free trade area the markets of Iceland, Liechtenstein, Norway and Switzerland and also constitutes a platform for Iceland, Norway and Liechtenstein to participate in the EEA with the 15 member states of the European Union. EFTA Council: manages relations between EFTA states under the Convention; decides on policies to promote overall objectives of the Association and to facilitate development of links with other states (who are not members of the EU, or 'third countries'), unions of states or international organizations. Free trade in industrial goods among members commenced in 1966, when import duties were abolished. Finland abolished import duties in Dec 1967. Much of EFTA's work is carried out through informal mechanisms, with discussion among heads of national delegations, even in the case of disputes (when there is rarely need to resort to official complaints procedure). Current major activities are in the fields of:

- *'Free Movement of Goods'* – technical barriers to trade; origin rules and customs matters; efficient trade procedures; veterinary matters (including feeding stuffs and phytosanitary matters); energy; state aid; public procurement; competition policy; intellectual property.
- *'Free Movement of Capital and Services and Company Law'* – financial services; transport (including inland transport/inland waterways, maritime transport, civil aviation); new technology services (including telecommunications, audio-visual and information services); postal services.
- *'Free Movement of Persons'* – mutual recognition of diplomas; social security; European employment services (EURES).
- *'Flanking and Horizontal Policies'* – research and development; education, training and youth; small and medium-sized enterprises; environment; civil protection; social policy; consumer protection; tourism; culture.
- *'Legal and Institutional Questions'*.
- *'Translation and Publication'*.

'Mutual Recognition of Tests and Inspections' – EFTA Secretariat services: *Convention for the Mutual Recognition of Inspections in Respect of the Manufacture of Pharmaceutical Products (PIC, 1970)*; *Pharmaceutical inspection cooperation scheme (PIC/S)*; *Scheme for the mutual recognition of evaluation reports on pharmaceutical products (PER Scheme)*; *Convention on the Control and Marking of Articles of Precious Metals (Hallmarking convention, 1972)*.

'Standardization, Testing and Certification Policy' – pursued: through *Committee on Technical Barriers to Trade (TBT)*; through close contact with European standardization organizations; in cooperation with the European Community, the latter dating from the Luxembourg (Luxembourg) Declaration of 9 Apr 1984. Standardization mandates are mainly granted to the European standards organizations CEN, CENELEC and ETSI.

/European Economic Area/:

Establishment of a single market in Western Europe was substantially realized, 1 Jan 1973, when Free Trade Agreements (FTAs) between Austria, Iceland, Portugal, Sweden and Switzerland and the EEC came into force and when the latter was also enlarged by the entry of Denmark, Ireland and UK. Similar agreements came into force between Norway and the EEC on 1 Jul 1973 and between Finland and the EEC on 1 Jan 1974. Under these agreements, import duties on almost all industrial products were abolished from 1 Jul 1977, effectively creating an *EEC-EFTA Free Trade Zone* for free industrial trade between EFTA and countries of *European Community (inactive)*. The current *'European Economic Area'*, established 2 May 1992, comprises the internal market of the EU and the 3 EEA-EFTA countries. Together, these 28 countries represent a single market in services, capital and manufactured goods for over 455 million people. EEA also resulted in the creation of a single labour market and provides for participation by EFTA countries in various EU programmes, funds and projects in fields not directly related to trade such as research and development, the environment, education and training. Under the Agreement: the *European Commission (EC, #06633)* informally seeks advice from experts in EFTA countries when drawing up new legislation in the field covered by the Agreement; experts from EFTA states are ensured wide participation when the Commission exercises its executive powers, for example in amending certain annexes to existing EU legislation; EEA-EFTA states participate fully in EU's Internal Market through adoption of corresponding legislation and are associated with all activities of the EU in relation to the operation of the internal market, including involvement in all relevant EU committees; EEA-EFTA states fully contribute to and participate in all EU Programmes in the fields of research and development, information services, environment, education, training and youth, social policy, consumer protection, small and medium-sized enterprises, tourism, audiovisual sector, civil protection, culture. The rules of origin to the EEA Agreement – protocol 4 – were most recently amended from 1 Jan 1997, when the system of pan-European cumulation entered into force.

/Free Trade Agreements with/:

- *'Turkey'*, signed 10 Dec 1991;
- *'Israel'*, signed 17 Sep 1992.
- *'Morocco'*, signed 19 Jun 1997 and entered into force, 1999;
- *Palestine Liberation Organization (PLO)*, interim FTA signed 30 Nov 1998 and entered into force, 1999;
- *'North Macedonia'*, signed 19 Jun 2000;
- *'Croatia'*, signed 21 Jun 2001;
- *'Jordan'*, signed 21 Jun 2001;
- *'Mexico'*, signed 1 Jul 2001;
- *'Singapore'*, signed in 2002 and entered into force, 2003;
- *'Chile'*, signed in 2003 and entered into force, 2004;
- *'Lebanon'*, signed 24 Jun 2004, and entered into force, 2007;
- *'Tunisia'*, signed 17 Dec 2004;
- *'Korea Rep'*, signed 15 Dec 2005;
- *Southern African Customs Union (SACU, #19842)*, signed 2006, and entered into force, 2008;
- *'Egypt'*, entered into force, 2007;
- *'Canada'*, signed 2008;
- *'Colombia'*, signed 2008.

/Declarations of Cooperation with/:

- *'Albania'*, 10 Dec 1992;
- *'Egypt'*, 8 Dec 1995;
- *'Ukraine'*, 19 Jun 2000;
- *Gulf Cooperation Council (GCC, #10826)*, 23 May 2000;
- *Southern Common Market (#19868)*, 15 Dec 2000;
- *'Serbia-Montenegro'*, 12 Dec 2000;
- *'Algeria'*, 12 Dec 2002;
- *'Peru'*, 24 Apr 2006;
- *'Colombia'*, 17 May 2006;
- *'Mongolia'*, 2007.

/Formal launch of free trade negotiations with/:

- *'Canada'*, 1998;
- *'Thailand'*, 2005;
- *Gulf Cooperation Council (GCC, #10826)*;
- *'Colombia'*, 2007;
- *'Peru'*, 2007;
- *'Algeria'*, 2007.

/Mutual Recognition Agreements (MRAs) signed with/:

- *'USA'*.

/Technical assistance to other countries/:

- Joint EFTA-EU activities, including participation in the EU MEDSTAT programme for statistical assistance to Mediterranean countries.
- Projects related to EFTA Free Trade Agreements and Declarations of Cooperation and financed by EFTA states.

Events *Meeting* Geneva (Switzerland) 2014, *Conference on SMEs and Standardization* Brussels (Belgium) 2013, *Seminar on the EEA (European Economic Area)* Brussels (Belgium) 2013, *Ministerial Meeting* Geneva (Switzerland) 2013, *Summer Ministerial Meeting* Trondheim (Norway) 2013. **Publications** *EFTA Bulletin*. *EFTA Fact Sheets* – series. *Convention Establishing the European Free Trade Association*; *EFTA Trader's ABC* – includes translations in Bulgarian, Czech, Romanian – also on CD-ROM; *Guide to the Implementation of EDI-EDIFACT* – includes translations in Bulgarian, Czech, Romanian; *Principles and Elements of Free Trade Relations – 40 Years of EFTA Experience*. Annual Report. Occasional papers.

Members Member countries (4):
Iceland, Liechtenstein, Norway, Switzerland.

Partner countries through FTAs (" indicates part of European Union) (40):
Austria (*), Belgium (*), Bulgaria (*), Chile, Croatia, Cyprus (*), Czechia (*), Denmark (*), Estonia (*), Finland (*), France (*), Germany (*), Greece (*), Hungary (*), Ireland (*), Israel, Italy (*), Jordan, Korea Rep, Latvia (*), Lebanon, Lithuania (*), Luxembourg (*), Malta (*), Mexico, Morocco, Netherlands (*), North Macedonia, Palestine, Poland (*), Portugal (*), Romania (*), Singapore, Slovakia (*), Slovenia (*), Spain (*), Sweden (*), Tunisia, Türkiye, UK (*).

FTA with: SACU. Partner countries through Declarations on Cooperation (6):

Partner countries through Declarations on Cooperation (6):
Albania, Algeria, Colombia, Peru, Serbia, Ukraine.

Declarations on Cooperation with:
GCC; MERCOSUR.

IGO Relations Permanent observer status with: *World Intellectual Property Organization (WIPO, #21593)*. Observer to: *World Trade Organization (WTO, #21864)*. Special status with: *OECD (#17693)*, participating in the work of OECD Committees for trade, economic policy, economic development and review, competition law and policy, environment. Participates in the activities of: *UNCTAD (#20285)*. Accredited by: *United Nations Framework Convention on Climate Change – Secretariat (UNFCCC, #20564)*. Instrumental in setting up: *Convention on Jurisdiction and the Enforcement of Judgements in Civil and Commercial Matters (Lugano Convention, 1988)*. **NGO Relations** Agreement with: *Comité européen de normalisation (CEN, #04162)*. In liaison with technical committees of: *International Organization for Standardization (ISO, #14473)*. Observer to: *European Federation of National Associations of Measurement, Testing and Analytical Laboratories (EUROLAB, #07168)*. Close contacts with other European standards organizations, especially: *European Committee for Electrotechnical Standardization (CENELEC, #06647)*; *European Cooperation for Accreditation (EA, #06782)*; *European Telecommunications Standards Institute (ETSI, #08897)*. [2021/XD0766/t/**D***]

♦ **EFTA MPS** Committee of Members of Parliament of the EFTA States Party to the EEA (#04270)

♦ EFTA Surveillance Authority (ESA) 05392

Autorité de surveillance AELE

Headquarters Avenue des Arts 19H, 1000 Brussels, Belgium. T. +3222861811. Fax +3222861800. E-mail: registry@eftasurv.int.
URL: http://www.eftasurv.int/

History 1994, as an independent international organization with respect to *European Economic Area (EEA, #06957)*, having been proposed under Article 108 of 'Agreement on the European Economic Area', signed 2 May 1992, Porto (Portugal). Separate 'Agreement between the EFTA States on the Establishment of a Surveillance Authority and a Court of Justice' signed 2 May 1992 in Porto (Portugal). Both agreements entered into force 1 Jan 1994. **Aims** Ensure fulfillment by EFTA states of their obligations under EEA Agreement; ensure application of the rules of EEA Agreement on competition; monitor application of the EEA Agreement by other Contracting Parties. To this end: take decisions and other measures in cases provided for in EEA Agreement; formulate recommendations, deliver opinions and issue notices or guidelines on matters dealt with in EEA Agreement; cooperate, exchange information and consult with the European Commission. **Structure** Independent Board or College, comprising one member from each EFTA country but completely independent of governments and other EEA institutions. Departments: Internal Market Affairs; Competition and State Aid; Legal and Executive Affairs; Administration. Secretariat in Brussels (Belgium). **Languages** English. **Staff** 66.00 FTE, paid. *Administrative Tribunal of the International Labour Organization (ILO Tribunal, #00118)* is competent to settle disputes. **Finance** Contributions from member states. **Activities** Monitoring/evaluation; guidance/assistance/consulting; networking/liaising; knowledge management/information dissemination. **Publications** Annual Report. Internal Market Scoreboards.

Members 3 EFTA countries:
Iceland, Liechtenstein, Norway.

IGO Relations Close cooperation with European Union counterpart: *European Commission (EC, #06633)*. **NGO Relations** Member of: *European Policy Centre (EPC, #08240)*. [2021/XE3052/**E***]

♦ **EFTBA** European Federation of Thoroughbred Breeders' Associations (#07226)
♦ **EFTC** European Federation of Therapeutic Communities (#07225)
♦ **EFTCO** European Federation of Tank Cleaning Organizations (#07224)
♦ EFT – Europese Federatie van Taxi's (inactive)
♦ **EFTF** European Frequency and Time Forum (#07360)
♦ **EFTP** European Federation of Tall People (#07223)
♦ **EFTRE** European Forum for Teachers of Religious Education (#07337)
♦ **EFTTA** European Fishing Tackle Trade Association (#07267)
♦ **EFUCA** European Federation of UNESCO Clubs, Centres and Associations (#07231)
♦ **EFU** Europäische Frauen-Union (#09022)
♦ EFU – Europäische Freiwilligenuniversität (see: #02978)
♦ **EFUF** European Forum on Urban Forestry (#07339)
♦ **EFUG** European Focused Ion Beam Users Group (#07277)
♦ EF Ungdomsorkester / see European Union Youth Orchestra (#09024)

- ♦ **Efus** European Forum for Urban Security (#07340)
- ♦ EFVA / see European Vending and Coffee Service Association (#09049)
- ♦ **EfVET** European Forum of Technical and Vocational Education and Training (#07338)
- ♦ EFWMF / see Forum of Worldwide Music Festivals (#09933)
- ♦ **EFWPSA** European Federation of Branches of the World's Poultry Science Association (#07063)
- ♦ EFWZ – Europäischer Fonds für Währungspolitische Zusammenarbeit (inactive)
- ♦ EFXN – European Fragile X Network (unconfirmed)
- ♦ EFYC / see European Choral Association – Europa Cantat (#06541)
- ♦ **EFYE** European First Year Experience Network (#07263)
- ♦ EFYSO – European Federation of Youth Service Organizations (inactive)
- ♦ **EGA** European Golf Association (#07399)
- ♦ EGA / see International Gaucher Alliance (#13701)
- ♦ ÉGALE – Egalité Laïcité Europe (internationally oriented national body)

♦ Egalité 05393

Égalité pour les gais et lesbiennes dans les institutions européennes
Contact L130/03/224, 1049 Brussels, Belgium. E-mail: info@egalite-online.eu.
URL: http://www.egalite-online.eu/

History 1993. Former names and other names: *Equality for Gays And Lesbians In The European institutions (EGALITE)* – former. **Aims** Secure, within European Union bodies and institutions, non-discriminatory treatment for same-sex couples; campaign for the rights of LGBTI++ persons in Europe. **Structure** General Assembly; Board. **Languages** English, French. **Staff** Voluntary. **Finance** Sources: members' dues. **Activities** Events/meetings; networking/liaising; training/education. **Members** Individuals (400). Membership countries not specified. **NGO Relations** Member of (2): *ILGA-Europe (#11118)*; *ILGA World (International Lesbian, Gay, Bisexual, Trans and Intersex Association, #11120)*. [2020/XJ7046/**E**]

- ♦ Égalité pour les gais et lesbiennes dans les institutions européennes (#05393)
- ♦ Egalité Laïcité Europe (internationally oriented national body)
- ♦ Egalité maintenant (#05518)
- ♦ EGA / see Medicines for Europe (#16633)
- ♦ **EGAM** European Grassroots Antiracist Movement (#07407)
- ♦ EGAN / see EGAN – Patients Network for Medical Research and Health (#05394)
- ♦ **EGAN** EGAN – Patients Network for Medical Research and Health (#05394)

♦ EGAN – Patients Network for Medical Research and Health (EGAN) . 05394

Secretariat Koninginnelaan 23, 3762 DA Soest, Netherlands. T. +31356034040. E-mail: egan@egan.eu.
URL: http://www.egan.eu/

History Jun 1992, Copenhagen (Denmark). Set up following proposal 1991, Leuven (Belgium), at 23rd Annual General Meeting of *European Society of Human Genetics (ESHG, #08624)*. Constitution adopted May 1995, Berlin (Germany). Former names and other names: *European Alliance of Genetic Support Groups (EAGS)* – former; *European Alliance of Patient and Parent Organizations for Genetic Services and Innovation in Medicine (EAGS)* – former; *European Genetic Alliances' Network (EGAN)* – former (2000). Registration: Banque-Carrefour des Entreprises, No/ID: 0872.813.819, Start date: 30 Mar 2005, Belgium. **Aims** Represent patients with genetic and congenital conditions. **Structure** General Assembly; Board of Directors; Advisory Board; Secretariat. **Languages** English. **Staff** 1.50 FTE, voluntary. **Finance** Members' dues. Other sources: sponsorships; project subsidies. **Activities** Awareness raising; training/education; research/documentation; events/meetings. **Events** *Annual general meeting / Annual Meeting* Barcelona (Spain) 2008, *Central and Eastern European summit on preconception health and prevention of birth defects* Budapest (Hungary) 2008, *Annual general meeting / Annual Meeting* Nice (France) 2007, *Annual general meeting / Annual Meeting* Amsterdam (Netherlands) 2006, *Annual general meeting / Annual Meeting* Prague (Czech Rep) 2005. **Publications** *Biomedical Research and Orphan Medicinal Products* (1998) by C Smit et al; *Biomedical Research and Patenting: Ethical, Social and Legal Aspects* (1996) by C Smit et al; *Ethical Code* (1996).
Members Full; Associate. Nongovernmental organizations established in the field: European/condition specific; national umbrella organizations; European sections of international organizations. National alliances in 3 countries:
Netherlands, Sweden, UK.
Disease-specific organizations (12):
DEBRA International (#05021); *Dystonia Europe (#05151)*; *European Alliance of Neuromuscular Disorders Associations (EAMDA, #05876)*; *European Cancer Patient Coalition (ECPC, #06433)*; *European Federation of Crohn's and Ulcerative Colitis Associations (EFCCA, #07095)*; *European Federation of Hereditary Ataxias (Euro-ATAXIA, #07138)*; *European Haemophilia Consortium (EHC, #07444)*; *European Network for Research on Alternating Hemiplegia (ENRAH, #07987)*; Heart-EU; *International Gaucher Alliance (IGA, #13701)*; *International Pompe Association (IPA, #14618)* (Europe); *Retina International (RI, #18926)*.
Regional alliance:
Central and Eastern European Genetic Network (CEE GN, #03692).
NGO Relations Represented in: EURARENET; ESHG. Member of: *European Patients' Academy on Therapeutic Innovation (EUPATI, #08170)*; *International Genetic Alliance (IGA, #13709)*. Links with over 200 parent and patient organizations, including: *European Forum for Good Clinical Practice (EFGCP, #07313)*; *EURORDIS – Rare Diseases Europe (#09175)*; *Sight and Life (#19269)*; *World Alliance of Organizations for the Prevention and Treatment of Genetic and Congenital Conditions (WAO, #21085)*; national organizations. [2018/XD4708/y/**D**]

- ♦ **EGARA** European Group of Automotive Recycling Associations (#07417)
- ♦ **EGAS** European Group on Atomic Systems (#07416)
- ♦ **EGATIN** European Group Analytic Training Institutions Network (#07413)
- ♦ **EGATS** EUROCONTROL Guild of Air Traffic Services (#05669)
- ♦ **EGBA** European Gaming and Betting Association (#07375)
- ♦ **EGBA** European Green Belt Association (#07408)
- ♦ **EGB** Europäischer Gewerkschaftsbund (#08927)
- ♦ **EGB** European Guitar Builders (#07441)
- ♦ EGCMA / see Association des fabricants européens d'appareils de contrôle et de régulation (#02592)
- ♦ EGCOA / see Golf Course Association Europe (#10677)
- ♦ EGD – Education Globale et Développement (internationally oriented national body)
- ♦ **EGDF** European Games Developer Federation (#07373)
- ♦ **EGDF** European Guide Dog Federation (#07440)
- ♦ **EGDU** Associazione Europea delle Giuriste e dei Giuristi per la Democrazia e i Diritti dell'Uomo nel Mondo (#06105)
- ♦ EGEA (meeting series)
- ♦ **EGEA** European Garage Equipment Association (#07377)
- ♦ **EGEA** European Geography Association for Students and Young Geographers (#07388)
- ♦ **EGEC** European Geothermal Energy Council (#07391)
- ♦ **EGE** European Group on Ethics in Science and New Technologies (#07420)
- ♦ **EG** Euroguidance (#05691)
- ♦ EG – Europäischen Gemeinschaften (inactive)
- ♦ EG – Europese Gemeenschappen (inactive)
- ♦ EGEUS – European Group of Endoscopy Ultrasonography (inactive)
- ♦ **EGF** EUROGENDFOR (#05683)
- ♦ **EGF** European Genetics Foundation (#07386)
- ♦ EGF – European Geopolitical Forum (unconfirmed)
- ♦ **EGF** European Go Federation (#07398)
- ♦ **EGF** European Grassland Federation (#07406)
- ♦ EGF – European Growth Federation (no recent information)
- ♦ EGF / see European Structural Integrity Society (#08844)
- ♦ **EGF** Europeiska Grafologförbundet (#08616)
- ♦ **EGFL** European Study Group for Rehabilitation and Functional Surgery Following Laryngectomy (#08852)
- ♦ **EGGA** European General Galvanizers Association (#07383)
- ♦ EGGVP / see Access VetMed (#00054)
- ♦ **EGHN** European Garden Heritage Network (#07378)
- ♦ **EGIAN** European Group of International Accounting Networks and Associations (#07426)
- ♦ **EG-ICE** European Group for Intelligent Computing in Engineering (#07425)
- ♦ EGI / see EGI Foundation (#05395)
- ♦ **EGI.eu** EGI Foundation (#05395)
- ♦ **EGI** Europäisches Gewerkschaftsinstitut (#08928)
- ♦ EGI / see European Institute for Gender Equality (#07557)

♦ EGI Foundation (EGI.eu) 05395

Dir Science Park 140, 1098 XG Amsterdam, Netherlands. T. +31208932007. E-mail: contact@egi.eu.
URL: http://www.egi.eu/

History 8 Feb 2010, Amsterdam (Netherlands). Former names and other names: *European Grid Infrastructure* – former; *European Grid Initiative (EGI)* – former; *Stichting European Grid Initiative* – former. Registration: Netherlands. **Aims** Empower researchers from all disciplines to collaborate and to carry out data- and compute-intensive science and innovation. **Structure** Council; Executive Board. **Languages** English. **Staff** 30.00 FTE, paid. https://www.egi.eu/about/egi-foundation/team/. **Finance** Sources: donations; government support; members' dues. Other sources: European and governmental subsidies. URL: https://www.egi.eu/about/egi-council/joining-the-egi-council/ **Activities** Events/meetings; knowledge management/information dissemination. **Events** *Digital Infrastructures for Research Conference* Brussels (Belgium) 2017, *Digital Infrastructures for Research Conference* Brussels (Belgium) 2017, *Conference* Lisbon (Portugal) 2015, *Community Forum* Helsinki (Finland) 2014, *Iberian Grid Infrastructure Conference* Madrid (Spain) 2013. **Publications** *Director's Letters* (12 a year) in English; *Inspired* (4 a year). Brochures.
Members Participants: National Grid Initiatives (NGIs); Associated Participants: European International Research Organizations (EIROs). Participants in 25 countries:
Belgium, Bulgaria, Croatia, Czechia, Estonia, France, Germany, Greece, Hungary, Italy, Lithuania, Netherlands, North Macedonia, Poland, Portugal, Romania, Serbia, Slovakia, Slovenia, Spain, Sweden, Switzerland, Türkiye, UK, Ukraine.
EISCAT Scientific Association; EMSO ERIC; *European Organization for Nuclear Research (CERN, #08108)*; IS-ENES; SeaDataNet.
NGO Relations Member of (2): *Association of European-level Research Infrastructure Facilities (ERF-AISBL, #02518)*; *Knowledge4Innovation (K4I, #16198)*. [2020.11.27/XJ3938/fy/**F**]

- ♦ **EGIN** European Geographic Information Network (#07387)
- ♦ **EGIN** European Graphic/Media Industry Network (#07405)
- ♦ EGK – Europäische Güterzugfahrplankonferenz (inactive)
- ♦ EGKS – Europäische Gemeinschaft für Kohle und Stahl (inactive)
- ♦ **EGKS** European Gamma Knife Society (#07376)
- ♦ EGKS – Europese Gemeenschap voor Kolen en Staal (inactive)
- ♦ Eglantyne Jebb Office for the Protection of Children of Non-European Origin (inactive)
- ♦ Eglise de Dieu Ministérielle de Jesus – Christ Internationale (religious order)
- ♦ Eglise Grecque Melkite Catholique (#16707)
- ♦ Eglise internationale chrétienne – Maison de Galilée (internationally oriented national body)
- ♦ Eglise méthodiste épiscopale d'Afrique (internationally oriented national body)
- ♦ Eglise et paix (#03916)
- ♦ Eglise protestante africaine (internationally oriented national body)
- ♦ Eglise de scientologie (#03922)
- ♦ EGL – Organisation de la CEPGL pour l'énergie des pays de grands lacs (no recent information)
- ♦ **EGLSF** European Gay and Lesbian Sport Federation (#07382)
- ♦ **egma** European Gay and Lesbian Managers Association (#07381)
- ♦ EGMA – European GeoMembranes Association (inactive)
- ♦ EGM – European Glass Container Manufacturers' Committee (inactive)
- ♦ **EGMF** European Garden Machinery Industry Federation (#07379)

♦ Egmont Group of Financial Intelligence Units 05396

Secretariat PO Box 8071, Ottawa ON K1G 3H6, Canada. T. +16473494116. E-mail: mail@egmontsecretariat.org.
URL: http://www.egmontgroup.org/

History 9 Jun 1995, Brussels (Belgium). Established at founding meeting in Egmont-Arenberg Palace, from which name derives. **Aims** Connect Financial Intelligence Units across the globe to help combat money laundering and the financing of terrorism. **Structure** An informal gathering of Financial Intelligence Units (FIUs). Administrative functions shared on a rotating basis. Permanent Secretariat set up in Ottawa (Canada). **Events** *Meeting* Seoul (Korea Rep) 2008, *Meeting* Guernsey (UK) 2004, *Meeting* Sydney, NSW (Australia) 2003, *Meeting* The Hague (Netherlands) 2001, *Meeting* Madrid (Spain) 1997. **Publications** *Egmont Group International Bulletin*. Annual Report. **Members** Financial Intelligence Units in 167 countries and territories. Membership countries not specified. **IGO Relations** Member of: *Asia/Pacific Group on Money Laundering (APG, #01921)*. Observer to: *Middle East and North Africa Financial Action Task Force (MENAFATF, #16779)*. [2022.02.09/XM2427/**F***]

- ♦ Egmont Institute (internationally oriented national body)
- ♦ EGMONT – Royal Institute for International Relations / see Egmont Institute
- ♦ EGMP – Europees Genootschap voor Munt- en Penningkunde (internationally oriented national body)
- ♦ **EGN** European Geoparks Network (#07389)
- ♦ EGOA – Europäische Gesellschaft für Osteoarthrologie (inactive)
- ♦ **EGÖD** Europäischer Gewerkschaftsverband für den Öffentlichen Dienst (#07202)
- ♦ EGO – European Gaming Organization (no recent information)
- ♦ EGO – European Gravitational Observatory (internationally oriented national body)
- ♦ EGOLF / see European Group of Organisations for Fire Testing, Inspection and Certification (#07427)
- ♦ **EGOLF** European Group of Organisations for Fire Testing, Inspection and Certification (#07427)
- ♦ **EGOS** European Group for Organizational Studies (#07428)
- ♦ **EGoS** European Group of Surveyors (#07436)
- ♦ EGPA – European Group for Prisoners Abroad (inactive)
- ♦ **EGPA** European Group for Public Administration (#07430)
- ♦ **EGPA** European LGBT Police Association (#07686)
- ♦ EGPAF – Elizabeth Glaser Pediatric AIDS Foundation (internationally oriented national body)
- ♦ **EGP** European Green Party (#07409)
- ♦ **EGPL** European Group of Public Law (#07431)
- ♦ **EGPRN** European General Practice Research Network (#07384)
- ♦ EGPRW / see European General Practice Research Network (#07384)
- ♦ EGRD – Europäische Gemeinschaft der Religionen – Im Dialog (internationally oriented national body)
- ♦ **EGREPA** European Group for Research into Elderly and Physical Activity (#07432)
- ♦ EGR – Europäische Gesellschaft für Radiologie (inactive)
- ♦ **EGRIE** European Group of Risk and Insurance Economists (#07433)
- ♦ EG-SEA-AI / see European Group for Intelligent Computing in Engineering (#07425)
- ♦ **EGS** Europäische Gesellschaft für Schriftpsychologie und Schriftexpertise (#08616)
- ♦ **EGS** European Galactosaemia Society (#07372)
- ♦ EGS – European Geophysical Society (inactive)
- ♦ **EGS** European Glaucoma Society (#07393)

♦ egta – association of television and radio sales houses 05397

Dir Gen Rue Washington 34, boite 2, 1050 Brussels, Belgium. T. +3222903131. E-mail: info@egta.com.
URL: http://www.egta.com/

EGTA
05397
alphabetic sequence excludes
For the complete listing, see Yearbook Online at

History 1974. Founded by sales houses and commercial departments of public TV channels. Statutes adopted, 1990. Rebranded with present title, 2004. Former names and other names: *European Group of Television Advertising (EGTA)* – former; *Groupement européen de la publicité télévisée* – former; *EGTA – Association of Television and Radio Sales Houses* – former. Registration: Eu Transparency Register, No/ID: 1977807375-62. **Aims** Assist and empower television and radio sales houses in their efforts to monetize audio/video content through advertising solutions. **Structure** General Assembly (annual); Board; Executive Committee. **Languages** English. **Staff** 14.00 FTE, paid. **Finance** Sources: members' dues. **Activities** Knowledge management/ information dissemination; networking/liaising; politics/policy/regulatory. **Events** *Nordic Regional Meeting* Helsinki (Finland) 2013, *Annual General Assembly* Ljubljana (Slovenia) 2013, *Annual General Assembly* Paris (France) 2012, *Annual General Meeting* Munich (Germany) 2011, *Conference* Brussels (Belgium) 2010. **Publications** Briefs; books; guidelines; reports.
Members Radio and TV sales houses or commercial departments in 40 countries:
Austria, Belgium, Bulgaria, Canada, Croatia, Czechia, Denmark, Estonia, Finland, France, Georgia, Germany, Greece, Hungary, Iceland, Ireland, Italy, Japan, Kazakhstan, Latvia, Lithuania, Luxembourg, Morocco, Netherlands, Norway, Poland, Portugal, Romania, Russia, Slovakia, Slovenia, South Africa, Spain, Sweden, Switzerland, Türkiye, UK, Ukraine, USA, Uzbekistan.
Included in the above, 1 organization listed in this Yearbook:
European Broadcasting Union (EBU, #06404).
IGO Relations Recognized by: *European Commission (EC, #06633).* **NGO Relations** Member of (3): *EU Platform for Action on Diet, Physical Activity and Health (inactive); European Advertising Standards Alliance (EASA, #05829); European Interactive Digital Advertising Alliance (EDAA, #07582).* [2022.10.19/XD3705/y/**E**]

♦ EGTA / see egta – association of television and radio sales houses (#05397)
♦ EGTA – European Guitar Teachers Association (no recent information)
♦ **EGTB** Europäische Gesellschaft für Technische Bildung (#08757)
♦ **EGTC – AMPHICTYONY** European Grouping of Territorial Cooperation – Twinned Cities and Areas in the Mediterranean (#07423)
♦ **EGTL** European Group on Tort Law (#07437)
♦ **EGTMA** European Golf and Travel Media Association (#07400)
♦ **EGTM** European Group on Tumour Markers (#07438)
♦ **EGU** European Geosciences Union (#07390)
♦ **EGU** European Gliding Union (#07395)
♦ **EGVIA** European Green Vehicles Initiative Association (#07410)
♦ **EGVIAfor2Zero** European Green Vehicles Initiative Association for the 2Zero partnership (#07411)
♦ EGV / see International Mastic Asphalt Association (#14119)
♦ **EGWA** European Greenways Association (#07412)
♦ Egyptian Arab Land Bank (internationally oriented national body)
♦ Egyptian Council for Foreign Affairs (internationally oriented national body)
♦ Egyptian Freemasonry / see Ancient and Primitive Rite of Memphis-Misraïm (#00815)
♦ Egyptian Organization for Human Rights (internationally oriented national body)
♦ EGZE / see European Society of Dental Ergonomics (#08577)
♦ EGZ – Europäische Gesellschaft für Zusammenarbeit (inactive)
♦ EG-Zusammenarbeit der Fachverbände der Schaltgeräte Hersteller / see European Coordinating Committee of Manufacturers of Electrical Switchgear and Controlgear (#06790)
♦ **EHAC** European HEMS and Air Ambulance Committee (#07474)
♦ eHA – eHealth Africa (internationally oriented national body)
♦ **EHA** European Helicopter Association (#07472)
♦ **EHA** European Hematology Association (#07473)
♦ **EHA** European Huntington Association (#07509)
♦ EHA / see European Hydrogen Alliance (#07511)
♦ **EHA** European Hydrogen Alliance (#07511)
♦ EHA / see European Migraine and Headache Alliance (#07801)
♦ **EHAHRD-Net** East and Horn of Africa Human Rights Defenders Network (#05259)
♦ **EHBEA** European Human Behaviour and Evolution Association (#07506)
♦ **EHB** European Homograft Bank (#07498)
♦ **EHC** European Haemophilia Consortium (#07444)
♦ EHC / see European Handcycling Federation (#07447)
♦ **EHCI** Every Home for Christ International (#09214)
♦ EHC International / see Every Home for Christ International (#09214)
♦ **EHDN** European Huntington's Disease Network (#07510)
♦ EHDRA – European HD Radio Alliance (inactive)
♦ **EHEA** European Higher Education Area (#07483)
♦ eHealth Africa (internationally oriented national body)
♦ EHEC – European Hydrogen Energy Conference (meeting series)
♦ **EHEDG** European Hygienic Engineering Design Group (#07512)
♦ Ehegruppen END (#20112)
♦ Ehemalige des Europäischen Öffentlichen Dienstes / see Seniors of the European Public Service (#19229)
♦ **EHEN** European Housing Ecology Network (#07503)
♦ **EHES** European Historical Economics Society (#07490)
♦ EHFA / see EuropeActive (#05772)
♦ **EHFCN** European Healthcare Fraud and Corruption Network (#07453)
♦ **EHF** European Habitats Forum (#07443)
♦ **EHF** European Handball Federation (#07446)
♦ **EHF** European Handcycling Federation (#07447)
♦ **EHF** European Headache Federation (#07451)
♦ **EHF** European Hockey Federation (#07494)
♦ EHF – European Hotel Forum (unconfirmed)
♦ **EHF** European Housing Forum (#07504)
♦ **EHF** European Hovercraft Federation (#07505)
♦ **EHF** European Humanist Federation (#07507)
♦ **EHFF** European Health Futures Forum (#07456)
♦ EHF-FHE / see European Humanist Federation (#07507)
♦ **EHFG** European Health Forum Gastein (#07455)
♦ **EHHA** European Holiday Home Association (#07495)
♦ **EHH** European Historic Houses Association (#07491)
♦ **EHHF** European Heritage Heads Forum (#07478)
♦ EHI / see EHI Retail Institute
♦ EHIA – European Herbal Infusions Association (inactive)
♦ **EHI** Association of the European Heating Industry (#02514)
♦ **EHIBCC** European Health Industry Business Communications Council (#07457)
♦ **EHIMA** European Hearing Instrument Manufacturers Association (#07465)
♦ EH – Institut international d'économie humaine (inactive)
♦ EHI Retail Institute (internationally oriented national body)
♦ Ehlers-Danlos National Foundation / see Ehlers-Danlos Society
♦ Ehlers-Danlos Society (internationally oriented national body)
♦ **EHLF** European Heritage Legal Forum (#07479)
♦ **EHLTF** European Heart and Lung Transplant Federation (#07466)
♦ EHMA – Association of European Manufacturers of Heatmeters and Meters applied within the District Cooling Industry (inactive)
♦ EHMA / see European Harbour Masters' Committee (#07449)
♦ **EHMA** European Health Management Association (#07458)
♦ **EHMA** European Hotel Managers Association (#07502)
♦ **EHMC** European Harbour Masters' Committee (#07449)
♦ EHMF – European Health Managers Forum (no recent information)
♦ **EHMSG** European Helicobacter and Microbiota Study Group (#07471)
♦ **EHN** European Heart Network (#07467)
♦ **EHN** European Horse Network (#07499)
♦ EHN / see International Haemovigilance Network (#13768)
♦ **EHNS** European Head and Neck Society (#07452)
♦ EHO – Europe HOpes (internationally oriented national body)
♦ EHOG – Association of the European Host Operators Groups (inactive)
♦ **EHPA** European Heat Pump Association (#07469)
♦ EHPA / see European Herbal and Traditional Medicine Practitioners Association (#07475)
♦ EHPBA / see European-African Hepato-Pancreato-Biliary Association (#05840)
♦ **EHP** Euroheat and Power (#05694)
♦ **EHP** European Health Parliament (#07459)
♦ **EHP** European Humanist Professionals (#07508)
♦ **EHPM** European Federation of Associations of Health Product Manufacturers (#07052)
♦ **EHPRG** European High Pressure Research Group (#07486)
♦ **EHPS** European Health Psychology Society (#07462)
♦ EHPSG / see European Helicobacter and Microbiota Study Group (#07471)
♦ **EHPU** European Hang Gliding and Paragliding Union (#07448)
♦ **EHRA** Eurasian Harm Reduction Association (#05609)
♦ **EHRA** European Heart Rhythm Association (#07468)
♦ EHRA – European Human Rights Association (unconfirmed)
♦ EHRC – Estonian Human Rights Centre (internationally oriented national body)
♦ **EHRC** European Holstein and Red-Holstein Confederation (#07496)
♦ EHRC – European Humanities Research Centre, Oxford (internationally oriented national body)
♦ EHRF – European Human Rights Foundation (inactive)
♦ **EHRG** European Hedgehog Research Group (#07470)
♦ EHRI – European Holocaust Research Infrastructure (unconfirmed)
♦ **EHRS** European Hair Research Society (#07445)
♦ **EHRS** European Histamine Research Society (#07489)
♦ EHSA – European Homeland Security Association (no recent information)
♦ EHSA – European Home Systems Association (inactive)
♦ EHSC – European Home Study Council (inactive)
♦ **EHS** EuroHaptics Society (#05692)
♦ **EHS** European Hernia Society (#07480)
♦ **EHS** European Hip Society (#07488)
♦ **EHS** European Hobbes Society (#07493)
♦ **EHSF** European Hidradenitis Suppurativa Foundation (#07482)
♦ EHSG / see European Helicobacter and Microbiota Study Group (#07471)
♦ EHTB / see European Academy for Industrial Management (#05796)
♦ **EHTEL** European Health Telematics Association (#07463)
♦ EHTF / see European Heart and Lung Transplant Federation (#07466)
♦ **EHTG** European Hereditary Tumour Group (#07476)
♦ EHTN – End Human Trafficking Now (internationally oriented national body)
♦ **EHTPA** European Herbal and Traditional Medicine Practitioners Association (#07475)
♦ **EHTTA** European Historic Thermal Towns Association (#07492)
♦ EHU International – European Humanities University (internationally oriented national body)
♦ EHV – Europäische Heizkessel-Vereinigung (inactive)
♦ **EHV** Europäischer Heilbäderverband (#08805)
♦ EHV – Europäischer Holzhandelsverband (inactive)
♦ EIAA – European Interactive Advertising Association (inactive)
♦ EIA – Entente internationale de l'acier (inactive)
♦ EIA – Entente internationale anti-communiste (inactive)
♦ EIA – Environmental Investigation Agency (internationally oriented national body)
♦ EIA – European Information Association (inactive)
♦ EIA – European Intermodal Association (inactive)
♦ **EIA** European Irrigation Association (#07603)
♦ EIAO / see Inter-Parliamentary Assembly on Orthodoxy (#15959)
♦ **EIARD** European Initiative for Agricultural Research for Development (#07537)
♦ **EIAS** European Institute for Asian Studies (#07545)
♦ **EIASM** European Institute for Advanced Studies in Management (#07544)
♦ EIBA / see KNX Association (#16202)
♦ **EIBA** Académie européenne de commerce international (#07585)
♦ EIBA / see European International Business Academy (#07585)
♦ **EIBA** European International Business Academy (#07585)
♦ EIB Association – European Installation Bus Association (inactive)
♦ EIBC – European Independent Business Confederation (inactive)
♦ EIBE – European Institute for Business Ethics (internationally oriented national body)
♦ **EIB** Europaeiske Investeringsbank (#07599)
♦ **EIB** Europäische Investitionsbank (#07599)
♦ EIB – European Institute of Bioethics (internationally oriented national body)
♦ EIB / see European Institute of Public Administration (#07569)
♦ **EIB** European Investment Bank (#07599)
♦ EIB – Europees Instituut voor Bio-ethiek (internationally oriented national body)
♦ **EIB** Europeiska Investeringsbanken (#07599)
♦ **EIB** Europese Investeringsbank (#07599)
♦ **EIBF** European and International Booksellers Federation (#07584)
♦ EIBG / see Intelligent Building Group (#11374)
♦ EIBI / see European Technology and Innovation Platform Bioenergy (#08881)

♦ EIB Institute 05398

Dean Boulevard Konrad Adenauer 98-100, L-2950 Luxembourg, Luxembourg. T. +352437975000.
Street Address Boulevard J F Kennedy 37C, L-1855 Luxembourg, Luxembourg.
URL: http://institute.eib.org/

History Set up 1 Jan 2012, within the *EIB Group*, also consisting of *European Investment Bank (EIB, #07599)* and *European Investment Fund (EIF, #07601).* **Aims** Promote and support social, cultural and academic initiatives with European stakeholders and the public at large; act as a catalyst for economic and social development within EU Member States. **Structure** Steering Group; Team, headed by Dean. **Activities** Financial and/or material support; training/education; events/meetings. **NGO Relations** *European Regional Science Association (ERSA, #08346).* [2019/XM6008/j/**E***]

♦ **EIBIR** European Institute for Biomedical Imaging Research (#07546)
♦ EICA / see European Investment Casters' Federation (#07600)
♦ **EICAR** European Institute for Computer Anti-Virus Research (#07548)
♦ EICC / see Responsible Business Alliance
♦ EICCAM – European Information Centre for Complementary and Alternative Medicine (inactive)
♦ EiCCC – Europäisches Institut Conflict-Culture-Cooperation (internationally oriented national body)
♦ **EICEE** Educational Initiative for Central and Eastern Europe (#05366)
♦ EIC – Energy Industries Council (unconfirmed)
♦ **EIC** Euro-Mediterranean Irrigators Community (#05723)
♦ **EIC** European Implementation Collaborative (#07520)
♦ **EIC** European International Contractors (#07586)
♦ **EIC** European Iron Club (#07602)
♦ **EIC** Events Industry Council (#09212)
♦ **EICF** European Investment Casters' Federation (#07600)
♦ **EICPA** Eurasian Institute of Certified Public Accountants (#05610)

♦ EICR – European Institute of Cultural Routes (internationally oriented national body)
♦ EICTA / see DIGITALEUROPE (#05073)
♦ EIC TESLIANUM – Energy Innovation Center TESLIANUM (internationally oriented national body)
♦ **EICTV** Escuela Internacional de Cine y Televisión (#12572)
♦ EIDA – Eurasian International Development Association (no recent information)

♦ EIDD – Design for All Europe 05399

Pres Kraussstr 10-12, 4020 Linz, Austria. E-mail: info@dfaeurope.eu.
URL: http://dfaeurope.eu/

History Apr 1993, Dublin (Ireland), as *European Institute for Design and Disability (EIDD)*. EU Transparency Register: 208300337606-85. **Aims** Enhance quality of life through design for all. **Structure** General Assembly (annual); Executive Board. **Languages** English. **Staff** Part-time, voluntary. **Finance** National networks; *European Commission (EC, #06633)*. Annual budget: euro 20,000. **Activities** Events/meetings; guidance/assistance/consulting. **Events** *Annual General Assembly* Rijeka (Croatia) 2020, *Annual General Assembly* Katowice (Poland) 2019, *Annual General Assembly* Bratislava (Slovakia) 2018, *Annual General Assembly* Saint-Étienne (France) 2017, *Annual General Assembly* Porto (Portugal) 2016. **Publications** *EIDD Newsletter* (4 a year). Information Services: EIDD network database.
Members Organizations in 19 countries:
Australia, Austria, Belgium, Bulgaria, Croatia, Denmark, Estonia, Finland, France, Germany, Italy, Lithuania, Norway, Poland, Portugal, Slovakia, Spain, Sweden, UK.
IGO Relations *European Cooperation in Science and Technology (COST, #06784)*. **NGO Relations** Member of: *European Disability Forum (EDF, #06929)*. [2020/XE2720/jv/**E**]

♦ EIDD / see EIDD – Design for All Europe (#05399)

♦ Eidetics Academy 05400

Exec Dir General Delivery, Guelph ON N1H 6J5, Canada. E-mail: ecogenesis1@hotmail.com.

History 1969, Toronto ON (Canada), as *International Association for Eidetics (EIDETICS) – Fondation internationale d'eidétique*. Current title adopted, 2000. **Aims** Assist organizations and individuals to grow using the science of Eidetics, combining information and communication breakthroughs, *visual concepts* and materials to help in understanding emotions, *imagery* and *perceptions* in oneself, as well as leaders, managers, entrepreneurs, employees, consumers, patients, students and in the marketplace. **Languages** English, French, German. **Staff** 2.00 FTE, paid. **Finance** Student fees. **Activities** Training/education. **Publications** *Creating Whole Organization Synergy – the Eidetic Reference Book* (2000); *Eidetics and Organizational Systems* (1998); *Eidetics Whole Organization Development (EIDETICS)*.
Members Individuals in 2 countries:
Belgium, Canada. [2017/XD5778/v/**F**]

♦ EIDETICS / see Eidetics Academy (#05400)
♦ **EIDHR** European Instrument for Democracy and for Human Rights (#07576)
♦ EIDP – European Institute for Democratic Participation (internationally oriented national body)
♦ EIDQ Association (inactive)
♦ EIDWT – International Conference on Emerging Internet, Data & Web Technologies (meeting series)
♦ **EIED** Ecole Inter-Etats des Douanes de la CEMAC (#05297)
♦ **EI** Education International (#05371)
♦ **EIEIM** European Initiative for Exercise in Medicine (#07538)
♦ **EI** Emmanuel International (#05443)
♦ EI – Encourage International (internationally oriented national body)
♦ EI – Energy Institute (internationally oriented national body)
♦ EI – Epilepsy International (inactive)
♦ EIER-ETSHER / see Institut International d'Ingénierie de l'Eau et de l'Environnement (#11313)
♦ **EIESP** European Institute of Education and Social Policy (#07551)
♦ EI – Europe Institute, Vienna (internationally oriented national body)
♦ EI – Evaluation International (internationally oriented national body)
♦ EI – Eyesight International (internationally oriented national body)
♦ EIF / see Centre for European Integration Research
♦ **EIFAAC** European Inland Fisheries and Aquaculture Advisory Commission (#07540)
♦ EIFAC / see European Inland Fisheries and Aquaculture Advisory Commission (#07540)
♦ EIF – Centre for European Integration Research (internationally oriented national body)
♦ EIFD – European Institute of Financial Directors (internationally oriented national body)
♦ **EIFEC** European Institute for Export Compliance (#07553)
♦ **EIfEL** European Institute for E-Learning (#07552)
♦ **EIF** Enhanced Integrated Framework (#05484)
♦ **EIF** European Illustrators Forum (#07517)
♦ **EIF** European Internet Forum (#07591)
♦ **EIF** European Investment Fund (#07601)
♦ **EIFI** European Industrial Fasteners Institute (#07524)
♦ **EIFLE** European Institute for Family Life Education (#07554)
♦ **EIFL** Electronic Information for Libraries (#05425)
♦ eIFL.net / see Electronic Information for Libraries (#05425)
♦ **EIFP** European Institute for Fire Protection (#07555)
♦ **EIFRF** European Interreligious Forum for Religious Freedom (#07596)
♦ EIFSA / see World Inline Figure Skating Association (#21584)
♦ **EIFS** European Institute for Futures Studies (#07556)
♦ **EIGA** European Industrial Gases Association (#07525)
♦ **EIGCA** European Institute of Golf Course Architects (#07558)
♦ **EIGE** European Institute for Gender Equality (#07557)
♦ EIG EUMETNET / see Network of European Meteorological Services (#17022)
♦ The Eight / see Group of Eight (#10745)
♦ **EIHA** European Industrial Hemp Association (#07526)
♦ EIHC / see HealthLink360
♦ **EIH** European Institute for Health (#07559)
♦ EIHR – European Institute for Development of Human Resources, Willemstad (internationally oriented national body)
♦ EIIC / see European Society of Cataract and Refractive Surgeons (#08539)
♦ EII – Earth Island Institute (internationally oriented national body)
♦ **Eii** European Interferometry Initiative (#07583)
♦ **EIiF** European Industrial Insulation Foundation (#07527)
♦ EIIL – European Institute for Industrial Leadership (internationally oriented national body)
♦ **EIIRBO** European Institute for Intervention and Research on Burn Out (#07564)
♦ **EIIR** European Institute of Interdisciplinary Research (#07563)
♦ EIIS – European Institute for International Studies (internationally oriented national body)
♦ EIIW – Europäisches Institut für Internationale Wirtschaftsbeziehungen (internationally oriented national body)
♦ EIJS – European Institute of Japanese Studies, Stockholm (internationally oriented national body)
♦ **EILA** Entente Internationale des Maîtres Luthiers et Archetiers d'Art (#15542)
♦ **EILD** European Institute for Local Development (#07565)
♦ EILST – European Institute of Law, Science, and Technology (internationally oriented national body)
♦ EIL / see Worldwide Network of the Experiment in International Living (#21930)
♦ **EIM** European Rail Infrastructure Managers (#08324)
♦ EIM – Evangelistic International Ministries (internationally oriented national body)
♦ **EIMM** European Institute of Molecular Magnetism (#07566)
♦ **EINA** European Industrial Nitrocellulose Association (#07528)
♦ **EIN** Ecosocialist International Network (#05330)
♦ **EIN** European Ideas Network (#07514)
♦ **EIN** European Implementation Network (#07521)
♦ Einheits-System für Elektronische Rechentechnik (inactive)
♦ **EINIRAS** European Information Network on International Relations and Area Studies (#07534)
♦ Einstein Center for International Studies (internationally oriented national body)
♦ EIO – European Institute of Oncology, Milan (internationally oriented national body)
♦ **EIONET** European Environment Information and Observation Network (#07002)
♦ **EIOPA** European Insurance and Occupational Pensions Authority (#07578)
♦ **EIPA** European Industrial Packaging Association (#07529)
♦ **EIPA** European Institute of Public Administration (#07569)
♦ EIPA – Europe Israel Press Association (unconfirmed)
♦ EIPA / see INSOL Europe (#11231)
♦ **EIP** Association mondiale pour l'école instrument de paix (#21184)
♦ **EIPC** European Institute of Printed Circuits (#07568)
♦ EIPCP – European Institute for Progressive Cultural Policies (internationally oriented national body)
♦ EIPDAS – Educational Innovation Programme for Development in the Arab States (inactive)
♦ **EIP** Effective Institutions Platform (#05384)
♦ **EIPEN** European Interprofessional Education Network (#07595)
♦ **EIP** Euroopan Investointipankki (#07599)
♦ **EIP** European Immunogenicity Platform (#07519)
♦ **EIP** European Insolvency Practitioners Association (#07543)
♦ **EIP** European Institute of Peace (#07567)
♦ **EIP** Excellence in Pediatrics Institute (#09221)
♦ **EIPG** European Industrial Pharmacist Group (#07530)
♦ **EIPIN** European Intellectual Property Institutes Network (#07580)
♦ EIPM – European Institute of Purchasing Management (internationally oriented national body)
♦ **EIPPEE** Evidence Informed Policy and Practice in Education in Europe (#09217)
♦ EIPPEE Network / see Evidence Informed Policy and Practice in Education in Europe (#09217)
♦ EIRA – European Industrial Regions Association (inactive)
♦ **EIRENE** International Christian Peace Service (#12564)
♦ **e-IRG** e-Infrastructure Reflection Group (#11208)
♦ **EIRMA** European Industrial Research Management Association (#07531)

♦ EIROforum 05401

Contact address not obtained. E-mail: info@eiroforum.org.
Chair of Coordination Group c/o European Space Agency, Postbus 299, 2200 AG Noordwijk, Netherlands.
URL: http://www.eiroforum.org/

History 12 Nov 2002, Brussels (Belgium). Founded when charter was signed. **Aims** Promote quality and impact of *European scientific* research. **Structure** Council; Coordination Group. Thematic Working Groups (5). **Languages** English. **Finance** Organizations cover their share for common activities. Additional project support from: *European Commission (EC, #06633)*. **Activities** Advocacy/lobbying/activism; events/meetings; knowledge management/information dissemination; networking/liaising; research/documentation; training/education. **Publications** *Science in School* – European Science Teaching Journal. Science Policy Papers. Brochure.
Members Regional organizations (8):
European Consortium for the Development of Fusion Energy (EUROfusion, #06753); European Molecular Biology Laboratory (EMBL, #07813); European Organization for Astronomical Research in the Southern hemisphere (ESO, #08106); European Organization for Nuclear Research (CERN, #08108); European Space Agency (ESA, #08798); European Synchrotron Radiation Facility (ESRF, #08868); European X-Ray Free-Electron Laser Facility (European XFEL, #09127); Institute Max von Laue – Paul Langevin (ILL, #11283).
IGO Relations Statement of Intent with: *European Commission (EC, #06633)*. **NGO Relations** Member of (1): *Initiative for Science in Europe (ISE, #11214).* [2023.02.13/XF7127/y/**F**]

♦ Eiropadome (#06801)
♦ Eiropas Arejas Darbibas Dienesta (#07018)
♦ Eiropas Aviacijas Drosibas Agentura (#08978)
♦ Eiropas Dzives standartu Petniecibas, Integracijas un Civilas Sabiedribas Akademija (#05799)
♦ Eiropas Ekonomikas un Sociala Lietu Komiteja (#06963)
♦ Eiropas Jaunatnes Cilvektiesību Sadarbības Tikls (internationally oriented national body)
♦ Eiropas Komisija (#06633)
♦ Eiropas Kopienu Tiesa / see Court of Justice of the European Union (#04938)
♦ Eiropas lauksaimniecibas un lauku konsultantu asociacija (#07303)
♦ Eiropas Liberaldemoratiska reformu partija / see Alliance of Liberals and Democrats for Europe Party (#00703)
♦ Eiropas Liberalu un Demokratu Apvienibas Grupa / see Renew Europe (#18840)
♦ Eiropas Narkotiku un Narkomñijas Uzraudzibas Centrs (#07820)
♦ Eiropas Ombuds (#08084)
♦ Eiropas Parlaments (#08146)
♦ Eiropas Perifero Piejuras Regionu Konference (#04638)
♦ Eiropas Revizijas Palata (#06854)
♦ Eiropas Savieniba (#08967)
♦ Eiropas Savienibas Padome (#04895)
♦ Eiropas Savienibas Publikaciju birojs (#18562)
♦ Eiropas Savieni-bas Tiesas (#04938)
♦ Eiropas Tautas Partijas – Kristigie Demokrati (#10775)
♦ Eiropas Tehnologijas Instituta / see European Institute of Innovation and Technology (#07562)
♦ Eiropas Tiesiskas Sadarbības tikls Civillietas un Komerclietas (#07616)
♦ **EISA** Electoral Institute for Sustainable Democracy in Africa (#05415)
♦ **EISA** European Imaging and Sound Association (#07518)
♦ EISA – European Independent Steelworks Association (inactive)
♦ EISA – European Initiative for Sustainable Development in Agriculture (inactive)
♦ **EISA** European International Studies Association (#07589)
♦ EISA – European IT Services Association (inactive)

♦ EIS-AFRICA 05402

Exec Dir Intl Business Gateway, Cnr New Road & 6th Road,, Midrand, 1682, South Africa. T. +27112386300. E-mail: info@eis-africa.org.
URL: https://www.eis.africa/

History Registration: Start date: 2000, South Africa. **Aims** Promote cooperative management of *environmental* information systems (EIS) in Africa. **Structure** General Meeting (annual). Board of Directors. **Languages** English, French. **Finance** Sources: members' dues. **Activities** Serves as Africa's representative on continent-wide and global initiatives. **Events** *AfricaGIS Conference* Abidjan (Côte d'Ivoire) 2021, *AfricaGIS Conference* Kigali (Rwanda) 2019, *AfricaGIS Conference* Addis Ababa (Ethiopia) 2017, *AfricaGIS Conference* Addis Ababa (Ethiopia) 2013, *AfricaGis conference* Cairo (Egypt) 2011. **Publications** *EIS Newsletter* (12 a year). Technical reports; books. **IGO Relations** Partner of: *Group on Earth Observations (GEO, #10735)*. Cooperates with: *African Regional Institute for Geospatial Information Science and Technology (AFRIGIST, #00433); Department for International Development (DFID, inactive); FAO (#09260); International Bank for Reconstruction and Development (IBRD, #12317)* (World Bank); *Regional Centre for Mapping of Resources for Development (RCMRD, #18757); UNEP (#20299); UNDP (#20292); United Nations Economic Commission for Africa (ECA, #20554); United Nations Institute for Training and Research (UNITAR, #20576); United States Agency for International Development (USAID)*. **NGO Relations** Member of: *International Society for Photogrammetry and Remote Sensing (ISPRS, #15362)*. Cooperates with: *African Association of Remote Sensing of the Environment (AARSE, #00216); Committee on Earth Observation Satellites (CEOS, #04249); World Resources Institute (WRI, #21753)*. Liaises with: *International Society for Photogrammetry and Remote Sensing (ISPRS, #15362).*
[2021/XM1690/**D**]

♦ **EISCAT** European Incoherent Scatter Scientific Association (#07522)
♦ EISCAT Scientific Association / see European Incoherent Scatter Scientific Association (#07522)

EISC European Interparliamentary
05402
alphabetic sequence excludes
For the complete listing, see Yearbook Online at

♦ **EISC** European Interparliamentary Space Conference (#07594)
♦ **EIS** European Ichthyological Society (#07513)
♦ EIS – European Invertebrate Survey (inactive)
♦ EISF / see Global Interagency Security Forum (#10430)
♦ EISIC – European Intelligence and Security Informatics Conference (meeting series)
♦ EISIS – European Institute for a Sustainable Information Society (internationally oriented national body)
♦ **EISMV** Ecole inter-Etats des Sciences et Médecine Vétérinaires (#15982)
♦ **EISN** European Influenza Surveillance Network (#07532)
♦ EISSEAS / see European Institute for Asian Studies (#07545)
♦ EISS / see European Influenza Surveillance Network (#07532)
♦ **EISS** European Initiative for Security Studies (#07539)
♦ **EISS** European Institute of Social Security (#07571)
♦ **EITA** European Isotopes Transport Association (#07604)
♦ EITC – European Inland Transport Council (inactive)

♦ EIT Climate-KIC 05403

CEO Kattenburgerstraat 7, 1018 JA Amsterdam, Netherlands.
Belgium Branch Rue Guimard 7, 1050 Brussels, Belgium. E-mail: ckbrussels@climate-kic.org.
URL: https://www.climate-kic.org/

History 2010. A public-private partnership comprising the Climate-KIC Association and the Climate-KIC Holding. An Innovation Community of *European Institute of Innovation and Technology (EIT, #07562).* Registration: Kamer van Koophandel, No/ID: KVK 52000117, Netherlands. **Aims** Contribute to creating a prosperous, inclusive, climate-resilient society with a circular, zero-carbon economy. **Structure** Assembly; Governing Board; Executive Team. **Activities** Research/documentation; training/education. **NGO Relations** Member of (1): *Climate Chain Coalition (CCC, #04008).* [2023/AA1337/F]

♦ EIT Digital 05404

Contact Rue Guimard 7, 1040 Brussels, Belgium. E-mail: info@eitdigital.eu.
URL: http://www.eitdigital.eu/

History 2010. An Innovation Community of *European Institute of Innovation and Technology (EIT, #07562).* Former names and other names: *EIT Digital – Driving Europe's Digital Transformation* – full title. Registration: Banque-Carrefour des Entreprises, No/ID: 0831.431.639, Start date: 21 Oct 2010, Belgium; EU Transparency Register, No/ID: 848163332915-94, Start date: 19 Oct 2018. **Aims** Strengthen Europe's position in the digital world by delivering breakthrough digital innovations to the market and breeding entrepreneurial talent for economic growth and improved quality of life; help business and entrepreneurs to be at the frontier of digital innovation, by providing them with technology, talent and growth support. **Structure** General Assembly; Supervisory Board; Management Committee. **Languages** English. **Staff** 3.00 FTE, paid. **Activities** Advocacy/lobbying/activism; events/meetings; guidance/assistance/consulting; training/education. **Events** *Conference* Brussels (Belgium) 2019, *Meeting* Oulu (Finland) 2019. **Members** Partners (over 250). Membership countries not specified. **NGO Relations** Member of (1): *University Industry Innovation Network (UIIN, #20699).* [2021/XM7786/F]

♦ EIT Digital – Driving Europe's Digital Transformation / see EIT Digital (#05404)
♦ EIT / see European Institute of Innovation and Technology (#07562)
♦ **EIT** European Institute of Innovation and Technology (#07562)

♦ EIT Food 05405

CEO Ubicenter A Philipssite 5/34, 3001 Heverlee, Belgium. T. +3216170070. E-mail: info@eitfood.eu.
URL: https://www.eitfood.eu/

History An Innovation Community of *European Institute of Innovation and Technology (EIT, #07562).* Registration: Banque-Carrefour des Entreprises, No/ID: 0672.423.992, Start date: 15 Mar 2017, Belgium; EU Transparency Register, No/ID: 944733432021-08, Start date: 11 Jul 2018. **Aims** Make the food system more sustainable, healthy and trusted. **Structure** Supervisory Board; Management Team. **Events** *Annual Meeting* Brussels (Belgium) 2022, *The Future of Food Conference* Brussels (Belgium) 2022. [2023/AA1338/F]

♦ EIT Health 05406

CEO Mies-van-der-Rohe-Str 1C, 80807 Munich, Germany. T. +4989215474820. E-mail: info@eithealth.eu.
URL: https://eithealth.eu/

History 2015. An Innovation Community of *European Institute of Innovation and Technology (EIT, #07562).* Registration: Bavaria District court, No/ID: VR 206069, Start date: 6 Jul 2015, Germany, Munich; EU Transparency Register, No/ID: 781385241347-65, Start date: 11 Feb 2021. **Aims** Promote research, education, entrepreneurship and innovation in healthy living and active ageing, including the promotion of sustainable healthcare in Europe. **Structure** Partner Assembly; Supervisory Board; Management Board. Advisory Boards. **Finance** Sources: contributions of member/participating states; grants. Supported by: *European Institute of Innovation and Technology (EIT, #07562).* Annual budget: 320,000,000 EUR (2020). **Activities** Research/documentation; training/education. **Events** *Summit* Stockholm (Sweden) 2022, *Summit* Stockholm (Sweden) 2021, *Summit* Stockholm (Sweden) 2020, *Summit* Paris (France) 2019. [2022.02.15/AA1339/F]

♦ **EITI** Extractive Industries Transparency Initiative (#09229)

♦ EIT InnoEnergy 05407

CEO Kennispoort, John F Kennedylaan 2, 5612 AB Eindhoven, Netherlands. E-mail: info@innoenergy.com.
URL: https://www.innoenergy.com/

History An Innovation Community of *European Institute of Innovation and Technology (EIT, #07562).* Former names and other names: *KIC InnoEnergy SE* – legal name. Registration: Kamer van Koophandel, No/ID: KVK 51418886, Netherlands; EU Transparency Register, No/ID: 462849021886-85, Start date: 23 May 2016. **Aims** Build a sustainable, long-lasting operational framework amongst the three actors of the knowledge triangle in the energy sector: industry, research and higher education, while ensuring that the integration of the three is more efficient and has a higher impact on innovation (talent, technology, companies) than the three standing alone. **Activities** Events/meetings; research/documentation. **Events** *Joint Workshop on Data and Innovation* Brussels (Belgium) 2020. [2021/AA1340/F]

♦ EIT – International Conference on Electrical Impedance Tomography (meeting series)

♦ EIT Manufacturing 05408

CEO Paris-Saclay, Nano-INNOV, 2 Boulevard Thomas Gober, 91120 Palaiseau, France. E-mail: office@eitmanufacturing.eu.
URL: https://eitmanufacturing.eu/

History An Innovation Community of *European Institute of Innovation and Technology (EIT, #07562).* Registration: RNA, No/ID: W913012329, Start date: 2019, France. **Aims** Bring European manufacturing actors together in innovation ecosystems that add unique value to European products, processes, services and inspire the creation of globally competitive and sustainable manufacturing. **Structure** Supervisory Board; Management Team. [2021/AA1341/F]

♦ EITN – European Institute for Theoretical Neuroscience (unconfirmed)

♦ EIT RawMaterials 05409

CEO Tauentzienstr 11, 10789 Berlin, Germany. E-mail: info@eitrawmaterials.eu.
Main Website: https://eitrawmaterials.eu/

History 2015. An Innovation Community of *European Institute of Innovation and Technology (EIT, #07562).* Registration: Berlin District Court, No/ID: VR 34088, Start date: 18 May 2015, Germany. **Aims** Enable sustainable competitiveness of the European minerals, metals and materials sector along the value chain by driving innovation, education and entrepreneurship. **Structure** Regional Steering Committees; Executive Board; IP Committee; Educational Committee; Management Team. **Activities** Awareness raising; capacity building; certification/accreditation; events/meetings; financial and/or material support; guidance/assistance/consulting; networking/liaising; politics/policy/regulatory; projects/programmes; research and development; research/documentation; training/education. [2021.02.09/AA1342/F]

♦ EITS – European Institute of Tele-Surgery (internationally oriented national body)
♦ **EIT UM** EIT Urban Mobility (#05410)

♦ EIT Urban Mobility (EIT UM) 05410

CEO Torre Glories, Diagonal 211 – 25th floor, 08018 Barcelona, Spain.
COO address not obtained.
URL: https://www.eiturbanmobility.eu/

History Jan 2019. An Innovation Community of *European Institute of Innovation and Technology (EIT, #07562).* Registration: Spain; EU Transparency Register, No/ID: 667858034535-07, Start date: 9 Apr 2019. **Aims** Encourage positive changes in the way people move around cities in order to make them more liveable places. **Structure** Management Team. **Activities** Events/meetings; training/education. **Events** *Tomorrow.Mobility World Congress* Barcelona (Spain) 2022. **NGO Relations** Partner of (1): *International Road Federation (IRF, #14758).* [2022/AA1343/F]

♦ EIUA – European Institute of Urban Affairs, Liverpool (internationally oriented national body)
♦ EIUC / see Global Campus of Human Rights (#10269)
♦ EIVHGI – Europäischer Interessenverband Handel-Gewerbe-Industrie (internationally oriented national body)
♦ **EIWH** European Institute of Women's Health (#07574)
♦ **EIZ** Ekumenska inicijativa zena (#05351)
♦ EJA – Equality and Justice Alliance (unconfirmed)
♦ EJA – Esperanta Jura Asocio (no recent information)
♦ **EJA** European Jewish Association (#07608)
♦ **EJA** European Juggling Association (#07618)
♦ EJAF – Elton John AIDS Foundation (internationally oriented national body)
♦ **EJAL** Escuela Judicial de América Latina (#05537)
♦ EJCC – European Jewish Community Centre (unconfirmed)
♦ **EJC** European Jewish Congress (#07609)
♦ **EJC** European Journalism Centre (#07612)
♦ **EJC PISE** European Joint Committee on Plasma and Ion Surface Engineering (#07610)
♦ EJD / see European Junior Doctors Association (#07620)
♦ **EJD** European Junior Doctors Association (#07620)
♦ **EJDM** Europäische Vereinigung von Juristinnen und Juristen für Demokratie und Menschenrechte in der Welt (#06105)
♦ **EJEA** European Japan Experts Association (#07606)
♦ Ejército Azul de la Nuestra Señora de Fatima (religious order)
♦ Ejército de Salvación (#19041)
♦ EJF – Environmental Justice Foundation (internationally oriented national body)
♦ EJF – European Jewish Fund (unconfirmed)
♦ **EJF** European Justice Forum (#07621)
♦ EJFS / see Environmental Justice Foundation
♦ EJJF / see Ju-Jitsu European Union (#16163)
♦ EJJP – European Jews for a Just Peace (unconfirmed)
♦ **EJJU** European Ju Jitsu Union (#07619)
♦ EJJU / see Ju-Jitsu European Union (#16163)
♦ **EJN** Economic Justice Network for Churches in Eastern and Southern Africa (#05317)
♦ **EJN** Ethical Journalism Network (#05554)
♦ **EJN** European Judicial Network (#07615)
♦ **EJN** Europe Jazz Network (#09160)
♦ **EJPA** European Judges and Prosecutors Association (#07614)
♦ **EJTA** European Journalism Training Association (#07613)
♦ EJTEMM – European Joint Theoretical/Experimental Meeting on Membranes (meeting series)
♦ **EJTN** European Judicial Training Network (#07617)
♦ **EJU** European Judo Union (#20399)
♦ **EJVS** Edward Jenner Vaccine Society (#05377)
♦ EKAH – Evropaiki Kinotita Anfraka ke Haliva (inactive)
♦ EK-BYGG – Nordisk Embetsmann Komité for Samarbeid innen Byggesektoren (inactive)
♦ **EKC** European Kurash Confederation (#07631)
♦ **EKEK** Europäische Konferenz für Evangelische Kirchenmusik (#05753)
♦ EKEME – Greek Centre of European Studies and Research (internationally oriented national body)
♦ EKEM – Elliniko Kentro Evropaikon Meleton (internationally oriented national body)
♦ EK – Europa Klubo (internationally oriented national body)
♦ EK – Evropaiki Kinotites (inactive)
♦ **EK** Evropaiko Kinovulio (#08146)
♦ **EKF** European Karate Federation (#07624)
♦ **EKF** European Kendo Federation (#07625)
♦ **EKF** European Kyudo Federation (#07633)
♦ **EKG** European Kansei Group (#07622)
♦ **EKHA** European Kidney Health Alliance (#07626)
♦ EKI – Equip KIDS International (internationally oriented national body)
♦ **EKI** Europäische Kammer der Ingenieure (#06514)
♦ Ekklesia Foundation for Gender Education (internationally oriented national body)

♦ Ekklesia Society 05411

Gen Sec PO Box 5343, Frisco TX 75035, USA. T. +19724462267. Fax +19727674960. E-mail: gensec@ekk.org.
African Office address not obtained. T. +23442555368. Fax +23442555368.
URL: http://www.ekk.org/

History 1996, Carrollton, TX (USA). Comes within the framework of *Anglican Communion (#00827),* although not part of the official ecclesiastical structure. **Aims** Make disciples of *Jesus Christ,* conforming to the *Lambeth Quadrilateral* which affirms the authority of the *Scriptures,* faith of the historic Creeds, Sacraments as instituted by Jesus and historic *Apostolic* ministry. **Structure** Board; Archbishops Council; General Secretary; Regional Secretaries. **Finance** No membership fee; members may contribute a free will offering according to their financial ability when they join. Other sources: donations. Annual budget: approx US$ 200,000. **Activities** Religious activities; networking/liaising; guidance/assistance/consulting; events/meetings; projects/programmes. **Events** *Meeting* Nassau (Bahamas) 2000. **Publications** *Are We There Yet – the journey to be like Jesus*; *Christ and the World of Religions*; *Genuine Godliness and True Piety*; *Here and Coming – as is is in heaven*; *Relaiming Our Anglican Heritage*; *To Mend the Net*; *Ways of Faithfulness*; *Wild Vine – Fruitful Vine.* **Members** Individuals, clergy and dioceses affirming the Chicago Quadrilateral. Bishops (170) overseeing more than 40 million of the world's 80 million Anglicans, in 35 countries and territories:
Argentina, Aruba, Australia, Bahamas, Barbados, Bolivia, Brazil, Burundi, Central African Rep, Chile, Congo DR, Costa Rica, Egypt, Ghana, India, Jamaica, Japan, Kenya, Malaysia, Mexico, Nigeria, Pakistan, Papua New Guinea, Paraguay, Peru, Philippines, Rwanda, Singapore, Sudan, Tanzania UR, Trinidad-Tobago, Uganda, UK, USA, Windward Is. [2022/XF5943/v/F]

♦ EKLM / see European Federation of Tall People (#07223)
♦ EKMA – European Knowledge Media Association (no recent information)

♦ EKOenergy 05412

Program Manager c/o Finnish Asn for Nature Conservation, Itälahdenkatu 22 b, FI-00210 Helsinki, Finland. T. +358505687385. E-mail: info@ekoenergy.org.
Main Website: https://www.ekoenergy.org/

History 2013, Finland. Proposed 2010. Former names and other names: *EKOenergy ecolabel* – alias. **Aims** Promote the use of *sustainable renewable energy* worldwide, in particular by helping energy consumers make an additional positive impact. **Structure** Board; Advisory Group; Secretariat. **Languages** Chinese, Dutch, English, Finnish, French, German, Italian, Russian, Spanish, Turkish. Materials are available in over 20 languages. **Staff** 3.00 FTE, paid; 10.00 FTE, voluntary. **Finance** Sources: sale of products. Other source: through Erasmus+ programme of *European Union (EU, #08967).* Annual budget: 400,000 EUR (2022). **Activities** Certification/accreditation. Active in more than 70 countries in all continents. **Publications** *EKOenergy Newsletter* (every 3 weeks).

Members Founding members of the ecolabel in 14 countries:
Estonia, Finland, Georgia, Germany, Greece, Hungary, Iceland, India, Ireland, Netherlands, Portugal, Spain, Türkiye, UK.
IGO Relations Member of (1): *International Renewable Energy Agency (IRENA, #14715).* **NGO Relations** Member of (2): *Climate Action Network Europe (CAN Europe, #04001); Global 100% RE (#10160).* [2023.02.14/XM5634/**F**]

- ♦ EKOenergy ecolabel / see EKOenergy (#05412)
- ♦ Ekologian Pohjoismainen Kollegio (inactive)
- ♦ EKOM / see Eurasian Coalition on Male Health (#05603)
- ♦ Ekonomicheskij Sud Sodruzhestva Neezavismyh Gosudarstv (#05315)
- ♦ EKP – Europanemzet Közösségri Párt (internationally oriented national body)
- ♦ **EKPF** European Kidney Patients' Federation (#07627)
- ♦ EKRA – European Kidney Research Association (inactive)
- ♦ EK-R / NÄRP / NERP / see Arko Cooperation
- ♦ **EKS** Europäische Konvention für Stahlbau (#06779)
- ♦ **EKS** Europäische Kulturstiftung (#06868)
- ♦ **EKS** European Knee Society (#07628)
- ♦ EKTI – Euroopan Kestävän Tietoyhteiskunnan Instituutti (internationally oriented national body)
- ♦ EKU / see European Karate Federation (#07624)
- ♦ Ekumeniska Förbundet av Konferensinstitut i Europa (#17706)
- ♦ Ekumenska inicijativa zena (#05351)
- ♦ **EKV** Europäischer Kartellverband Christlicher Studentenverbände (#07076)
- ♦ EKWC – Europees Keramisch Werkcentrum (internationally oriented national body)
- ♦ **EKZ** Europäisches Kulturzentrum (#06472)
- ♦ eLab Europe / see eLabEurope
- ♦ eLabEurope (internationally oriented national body)
- ♦ **ELACTA** European Lactation Consultants Alliance (#07638)
- ♦ ELA – Earth Law Alliance (unconfirmed)
- ♦ ELA – Earthlife Africa (internationally oriented national body)
- ♦ ELA – Equipo Latinoamericano de Justicia y Género (internationally oriented national body)
- ♦ **ELA** European Labour Authority (#07635)
- ♦ **ELA** European Laser Association (#07654)
- ♦ **ELA** European Lawyers Association (#07661)
- ♦ **ELA** European Leucodystrophy Association (#07684)
- ♦ **ELA** European Lift Association (#07695)
- ♦ **ELA** European Logistics Association (#07710)
- ♦ **ELAG** European Library Automation Group (#07692)
- ♦ ELAII – Encuentro Latinoamericano de Informatica e Industrias de Información (meeting series)
- ♦ ELAM – Escuela Latinoamericana de Matematica (meeting series)
- ♦ ELANET – European Local Authorities Telematic Network (no recent information)
- ♦ eLAN / see European Landscape Architecture Students Association (#07641)
- ♦ **ELAPDIS** Escuela Latinoamericana de Pensamiento y Diseño Sistémico (#05538)
- ♦ **ELARD** European LEADER Association for Rural Development (#07663)
- ♦ **ELASA** European Landscape Architecture Students Association (#07641)
- ♦ **ELAS** European Ligand Assay Society (#07697)
- ♦ Elava Läänemere Fond (internationally oriented national body)
- ♦ **ELAW** Environmental Law Alliance Worldwide (#05503)
- ♦ eLBA – European Lotto Betting Association (unconfirmed)
- ♦ ELB – NGO Environment Liaison Board (inactive)
- ♦ **ELCA** European Landscape Contractors Association (#07642)
- ♦ ELCA / see European Lift and Lift Component Association (#07696)
- ♦ **ELCA** European Lift and Lift Component Association (#07696)
- ♦ **ELCA** European Lighting Clusters Alliance (#07698)
- ♦ ELCA – Evangelical Lutheran Church in America (internationally oriented national body)
- ♦ Elcano Royal Institute for International and Strategic Studies (internationally oriented national body)
- ♦ ELC – European Lamp Companies Federation (inactive)
- ♦ **ELC** European Language Council (#07646)
- ♦ **ELC** European Leadership Centre (#07664)
- ♦ ELC / see EU Specialty Food Ingredients (#09200)
- ♦ ELCSA – Evangelical Lutheran Church of Southern Africa (internationally oriented national body)
- ♦ **ELCWP** European Lung Cancer Working Party (#07717)
- ♦ ELDA – European Laser Disc Association (inactive)
- ♦ ELDC – European Lead Development Committee (inactive)
- ♦ Elderhostel / see Road Scholar – Elderhostel
- ♦ Elderhostel – Exploritas / see Road Scholar – Elderhostel
- ♦ The Elders / see The Elders Foundation (#05413)

♦ The Elders Foundation 05413

Chair 3 Tilney Street, London, W1K 1BJ, UK. T. +442070134646. E-mail: connect@theelders.org.
URL: http://www.theelders.org/

History May 2007, South Africa. May 2007, Ulusaba (South Africa), at first meeting, following discussions and negotiations since 1999 and formal proposal, Aug 2006, Virgin Is. Set up by group of humanitarians, lead by Nelson Mandela (1918-2013) and on the initiative of Richard Branson. Also referred to as *The Elders* and *Global Elders.* **Aims** Use collective experience, moral courage and ability to rise above parochial concerns of nation, race and creed, to help make the world a more peaceful, healthy and equitable place; contribute *wisdom*, independent *leadership* and *moral courage* to attempts to solve *world problems*; use influence and experience to persuade and facilitate action on a broad range of issues; act as "honest brokers" in *conflict resolution*; amplify the message on *crisis* situations; act as an independent voice of reason and wisdom at the shoulder of governments and other organizations; act as a role model in leading, guiding, creating and supporting initiatives, both publicly and behind the scenes. **Structure** Elders (12). Advisory Council. **Finance** Donations. **Activities** Usually meets at least twice a year at various locations.
Members Universally recognized and respected individuals (12), currently from 11 countries:
Algeria, Bangladesh, Brazil, China, Ghana, India, Ireland, Mozambique, Norway, South Africa, USA.
NGO Relations Supports and member of: *Girls not Brides (#10154).* [2019/XM7093/fv/**F**]

- ♦ **ELDH** European Association of Lawyers for Democracy and World Human Rights (#06105)
- ♦ ELDO – European Space Vehicle Launcher Development Organization (inactive)
- ♦ ELDR / see Alliance of Liberals and Democrats for Europe Party (#00703)
- ♦ ELDR Group / see Renew Europe (#18840)
- ♦ ELDR / see Renew Europe – Committee of the Regions (#18841)
- ♦ **ELDSNet** European Legionnaires' Disease Surveillance Network (#07681)
- ♦ **ELEC** European League for Economic Cooperation (#07669)
- ♦ ELEC – European Lean Educator Conference (meeting series)
- ♦ Election Network Society in the Arab Region (unconfirmed)
- ♦ Election-Watch.EU (internationally oriented national body)

♦ Electoral Commissions Forum of SADC Countries (ECF-SADC) 05414

Main Office PO Box 00284, Gaborone, Botswana. E-mail: info@ecfsadc.org.
URL: https://www.ecfsadc.org/

History 27 Jul 1998, Cape Town (South Africa). Former names and other names: *SADC Electoral Commissions Forum (SADC-ECF)* – former. **Aims** Strengthen cooperation and support among member countries on electoral issues and *democracy* building; promote conditions conducive to free, fair and transparent elections in SADC countries; promote democracy as a political system of responsible and accountable government through the electoral process; encourage active participation of citizens which are informed about the electoral process. **Structure** Conference (annual), is supreme policy-making body. Executive Committee, comprising Chairperson, Vice Chairperson and 5 members. President; Vice President. Secretariat. **Languages** English, Portuguese. **Finance** Members' dues. Other sources: fund raising activities; government grants and donations. **Activities** focus on the following areas to enhance training and capacity building: electoral systems design; electoral legal framework; electoral processes; project management; communication skills; election management; electoral planning; election observation missions; conflict management; voter education. **Events** *Annual General Conference* Swakopmund (Namibia) 2022, *Annual Meeting* Dar es Salaam (Tanzania UR) 1999. **Publications** *Principles of Electoral Management, Monitoring and Observation* – guidelines, jointly with EISA.
Members Electoral commissions in 14 countries and territories:
Angola, Botswana, Lesotho, Malawi, Mauritius, Mozambique, Namibia, Seychelles, South Africa, Swaziland, Tanganyika, Tanzania UR, Zambia, Zimbabwe. [2022/XF5658/**F***]

- ♦ Electoral Institute of South Africa / see Electoral Institute for Sustainable Democracy in Africa (#05415)
- ♦ Electoral Institute of Southern Africa / see Electoral Institute for Sustainable Democracy in Africa (#05415)

♦ Electoral Institute for Sustainable Democracy in Africa (EISA) 05415

Contact PO Box 740, Auckland Park, 2006, South Africa. T. +27113816000. Fax +27114826163. E-mail: info@eisa.org.
Exec Dir 14 Park Road, Richmond, Johannesburg, 2092, South Africa.
URL: http://www.eisa.org.za/

History 1996. Former names and other names: *Electoral Institute of South Africa* – former (1996); *Electoral Institute of Southern Africa* – former. **Aims** Promote credible elections, citizen participation and the strengthening of political institutions for sustainable democracy in Africa; operate in accordance with the Declaration of Principles for International Election Observation. **Structure** Board of Directors; Head Office in Johannesburg (South Africa); Field Offices (7). **Languages** English, French, Portuguese, Swahili. **Staff** 70.00 FTE, paid. **Finance** Sources: donations; fees for services. Annual budget: 10,000,000 USD. **Activities** Capacity building; events/meetings; guidance/assistance/consulting; publishing activities; research and development. **Events** *Symposium* Abidjan (Côte d'Ivoire) 2021, *Symposium* Johannesburg (South Africa) 2019, *Symposium* Johannesburg (South Africa) 2018, *Symposium* Johannesburg (South Africa) 2017, *Symposium* Johannesburg (South Africa) 2016. **Publications** *Journal of African Elections.* Annual Report; symposium, conference, seminar and workshop reports and proceedings; election observation mission reports; handbooks; occasional papers; election updates. **Members** Partnership with Election Management Bodies, political parties, civil society organizations and government institutions. Membership countries not specified. **IGO Relations** Cooperation agreement with: *International Institute for Democracy and Electoral Assistance (International IDEA, #13872).* **NGO Relations** Member of (1): *ACE Electoral Knowledge Network (#00066).* [2022/XG9790/j/**D**]

♦ Electrical Engineering STudents' European assoCiation (EESTEC) .. 05416

Secretariat c/o Mekelweg 4, 2628 CD Delft, Netherlands. Fax +31152781002. E-mail: vc-ea@eestec.net – board@eestec.net.
URL: http://www.eestec.net/

History 1986, Eindhoven (Netherlands). Current statutes adopted May 2019. Registration: Start date: 2002, Netherlands; Swiss Civil Code, Start date: 1995, End date: 2002, Switzerland. **Aims** Promote and develop international contacts and exchange of ideas among students of electrical engineering and computer science (EECS). **Structure** Board; Regions; Branches. **Languages** English. **Staff** 12.50 FTE, voluntary. **Finance** Sources: donations; grants. Private companies; universities. **Activities** Events/meetings; networking/liaising. **Events** *Spring Congress* Krakow (Poland) 2021, *Spring Congress* Delft (Netherlands) 2020, *Autumn Congress* Munich (Germany) 2020, *Spring Congress* Athens (Greece) 2019, *Annual Congress* Krakow (Poland) 2018. **Publications** *EESTEC Magazine.*
Members Institutions (54) in 25 countries:
Albania, Austria, Belgium, Bosnia-Herzegovina, Croatia, Finland, France, Germany, Greece, Hungary, Ireland, Italy, Montenegro, Netherlands, North Macedonia, Poland, Portugal, Romania, Russia, Serbia, Slovenia, Spain, Switzerland, Türkiye, UK.
NGO Relations Member of (1): *Informal Forum of International Student Organizations (IFISO, #11193).* Partner of (2): *Board of European Students of Technology (BEST, #03294); European Students of Industrial Engineering and Management (ESTIEM, #08846).* [2021.03.19/XD5487/**D**]

- ♦ Electrical Safety Foundation International (internationally oriented national body)
- ♦ Electric Drive Transportation Association (internationally oriented national body)
- ♦ Electriciens sans frontières (internationally oriented national body)
- ♦ ELECTRI-CITY.MOBI (unconfirmed)
- ♦ Electric Mine Conference (meeting series)
- ♦ Electric Mine Consortium (unconfirmed)

♦ Electric Power Council of the CIS 05417

Chairman 9 Leninsky prospect, Moscow MOSKVA, Russia, 119049. T. +74957106602 – +74957105687. Fax +74956258605. E-mail: mail@energo-cis.org.
Chief Specialist External Relations address not obtained.
URL: http://www.energo-cis.org/

History Established by Heads of State of member countries of *Commonwealth of Independent States (CIS, #04341)*, Feb 1992. **Aims** Help ensure sustainable power supply to the CIS countries, through common technological basis for power generation and transmission as well as parallel operation of national power systems. **Structure** Executive Committee.
Members States (11):
Armenia, Azerbaijan, Belarus, Kazakhstan, Kyrgyzstan, Moldova, Russia, Tajikistan, Turkmenistan, Ukraine, Uzbekistan.
IGO Relations *Energy Charter Conference (#05466).* **NGO Relations** *Union of the Electricity Industry – Eurelectric (#20379).* [2017.06.01/XE4429/**E***]

- ♦ Electric Rocket Propulsion Society (internationally oriented national body)
- ♦ Electric Vehicle Association of the Americas / see Electric Drive Transportation Association

♦ Electric Vehicle Association of Asia Pacific (EVAAP) 05418

SG c/o The Korean Society of Automotive Engineers, 13F, Paradise Venture Tower, 21 Teheran-ro 52-gil, Gangnam-gu, Seoul 06212, Korea Rep. T. +8225643971. Fax +8225643973. E-mail: conf@ksae.org.
Pres address not obtained.
URL: http://www.evaap.org/

History 1990. A regional association of *World Electric Vehicle Association (WEVA, #21374).* **Aims** As a non-profit professional association, promote the development and use of electric and hybrid vehicles; encourage and facilitate exchange of information among members and with international organizations of similar purpose; provide information for public dissemination, educational and government bodies. **Structure** General Meeting. Board of Directors, comprising up to 8 members. **Languages** English. **Finance** Members' dues. **Activities** Events/meetings. **Events** *International Electric Vehicle Symposium* Sacramento, CA (USA) 2023, *International Electric Vehicle Symposium* Oslo (Norway) 2022, *International Electric Vehicle Symposium* Nanjing (China) 2021, *International Electric Vehicle Symposium* Kobe (Japan) 2018, *International Electric Vehicle Symposium* Montréal, QC (Canada) 2016. **Publications** *EVAAP Newsletter* (4 a year).
Members Full; Associate. Organizations in 4 countries:
China, Japan, Korea Rep, Singapore. [2022/XD2375/**D**]

- ♦ Electric Vehicle Union (unconfirmed)
- ♦ Electrification Council of Central America / see Secretaria Ejecutiva del Consejo de Electrificación de América Central (#19191)

♦ Electroacoustic Music Studies Network (EMS) 05419

Exec Dir Sorbonne Maison de la recherche, 28 rue Serpente, 75006 Paris, France. E-mail: info@ems-network.org.
URL: http://www.ems-network.org/

History following meetings, starting 2003. Formally set up, 2006. **Aims** Encourage better understanding of electroacoustic music in terms of its genesis, its evolution, its current manifestations and its impact. **Structure** Organizing Committee; Executive Committee. **Languages** English, French. **Finance** Members' dues. **Activities** Co-organizes annual conference. **Events** *Conference* Leicester (UK) 2021, *Conference* Mexico City (Mexico) 2019, *Annual Conference / Conference* Sheffield (UK) 2015, *Annual Conference / Conference* Berlin (Germany) 2014, *Annual Conference / Conference* Lisbon (Portugal) 2013. **Publications** Proceedings. [2015.06.01/XM2931/**D**]

♦ Electroceramics Network 05420

Coordinator IRCER – Univ de Limoges, 12 rue Atlantis, 87068 Limoges CEDEX, France.
URL: https://electroceramics.org/

History 2017. Heir of the Electroceramics Conferences, which started in 1984. Founded in order to join *European Ceramic Society (ECerS, #06507)*. **Structure** International Committee. **Activities** Events/meetings. **Events** *Electroceramics Conference* Vilnius (Lithuania) 2024, *Electroceramics Conference* Krakow (Poland) 2022, *Electroceramics Conference* Darmstadt (Germany) 2020, *Electroceramics Conference* Hasselt (Belgium) 2018, *Electroceramics Conference* Limoges (France) 2016. [2023.02.20/AA2081/**F**]

♦ Electrochemical Society (ECS) 05421

Exec Dir 65 South Main St, Bldg D, Pennington NJ 08534-2839, USA. T. +16097371902. Fax +16097372743. E-mail: chris.jannuzzi@electrochem.org – ecs@electrochem.org.
URL: http://www.electrochem.org/

History 1902, USA, as American Electrochemical Society. Present name adopted, 1930. **Aims** Advance theory and practice of electrochemistry, solid state science and allied subjects; encourage research and dissemination of knowledge; assure the availability of adequate training and education of fundamental and applied scientists and engineers in the field. **Structure** Board of Directors; Management Team; Standing Committees (11); Subcommittees (3); Symposium Planning Advisory Board; Divisions (13). **Activities** Events/meetings; training/education. **Events** *Spring Meeting* Montréal, QC (Canada) 2029, *Spring Meeting* Seattle, WA (USA) 2026, *Fall Meeting* Chicago, IL (USA) 2025, *Spring Meeting* Montréal, QC (Canada) 2025, *Fall Meeting* Honolulu, HI (USA) 2024. **Publications** *Interface* (4 a year) – magazine; *ECS Electrochemistry Letters*; *ECS Journal of Solid State Science and Technology*; *ECS Solid State Letters*; *Electrochemical and Solid-State Letters*; *Journal of The Electrochemical Society*. *ECS Proceedings Volumes* – meeting papers; *ECS Transactions* – proceedings. Monographs.
Members Individuals (over 7,000); Institutional (about 100) in 65 countries. Institutional in 9 countries:
Canada, China, Germany, India, Italy, Japan, Sweden, Switzerland, USA.
NGO Relations Member of: *ORCID (#17790)*. [2020/XN7789/**C**]

♦ Electroencephalography and Clinical Neuroscience Society (ECNS) 05422

Treas Dept of Psychiatry, East Tennessee State Univ, Box 70567, 807 Univ Pkwy, Johnson City TN 37614, USA. T. +14234398010. Fax +14234392210.
URL: http://www.ecnsweb.com/

History 1998, on merger of (USA) American Medical EEG Association (AMEEGA) and (USA) American Psychiatric Electrophysiology Association (APEA). Commonly referred to as *EEG and Clinical Neuroscience Society (ECNS)*. **Aims** Further the clinical practice of classic electroencephalography (EEG) from the professional, scientific, and economic standpoints. **Structure** Board; Committees. **Activities** Awards/prizes/competitions; events/meetings. **Events** *Joint Annual Meeting* Halifax, NS (Canada) 2022, *BACI : International Conference on Basic and Clinical Multimodal Imaging* Naples (Italy) 2021, *Joint Annual Meeting* Toronto, ON (Canada) 2020, *BACI : International Conference on Basic and Clinical Multimodal Imaging* Chengdu (China) 2019, *BACI : International Conference on Basic and Clinical Multimodal Imaging* Bern (Switzerland) 2017. **Publications** *Clinical EEG and Neuroscience* – journal. **Members** Individuals. Membership countries not specified. **NGO Relations** Joint meetings with: *International Society for Brain Electromagnetic Topography (ISBET, #14984)*; *International Society for Neuroimaging in Psychiatry (ISNIP, #15297)*. [2017.01.16/XJ8111/**D**]

♦ The Electromagnetics Academy (internationally oriented national body)

♦ Electronic Business Group (EBG) 05423

CEO 57 Av Franklin Delano Roosevelt, 75008 Paris, France. T. +33173030193. E-mail: contact@ebg.net.
URL: http://www.ebg.net/

History 1998, Paris (France). **Aims** Boost innovation, new technologies, Internet and *digital medias*. **Structure** General Assembly; International Board; Committees (8). **Languages** English, French. **Staff** 40.00 FTE, paid. **Finance** Sources: members' dues. Other sources: partnerships. **Activities** Events/meetings; publishing activities; research and development. **Events** *The Digital Benchmark* Amsterdam (Netherlands) 2020, *The Digital Benchmark* Berlin (Germany) 2019, *General Assembly* Paris (France) 2019, *Meeting on Performances* Paris (France) 2019, *General Assembly* Paris (France) 2018. **Publications** White papers. **IGO Relations** French government. **NGO Relations** None. [2020/XM2932/**D**]

♦ Electronic Commerce Code Management Association (ECCMA) 05424

Exec Dir 2980 Linden St Ste E2, Bethlehem PA 18017, USA. T. +16108615990. Fax +16106254657. E-mail: info@eccma.org.
URL: http://www.eccma.org/

History Founded Apr 1999, on the suggestion of *UNDP (#20292)* to merge the Dun and Bradstreet Standard Product and Services Classification (SPSC) with the United Nations Common Coding System (UNCCS). **Aims** Develop and maintain open solutions for faster, better and cheaper access to authoritative master data; foster the development, growth and adoption of International Standards for Master Data Quality, through an international association of industry and government master data managers working collaboratively to increase the quality and lower the cost of descriptions of individuals, organizations, goods and services. **Structure** Board of Directors. **Languages** Arabic, Chinese, English, French, German, Polish, Spanish. **Staff** 11-50 paid. **Finance** Members' dues. Project consultancy. **Activities** Events/meetings; standards/guidelines; training/education. **Publications** Papers. **Members** Global membership. Membership countries not specified. **NGO Relations** *Information Quality International (IQ International, #11197)*. [2019.03.12/XM4139/**E**]

♦ Electronic Commerce Europe (no recent information)
♦ Electronic Communications Committee (see: #04602)
♦ Electronic Data Interchange Forum for Companies with Interests in Computing and Electronics / see Global Network for B2B Integration in High Tech Industries (#10481)
♦ Electronic Document Systems Association / see Xplor International (#21968)
♦ Electronic Frontier Foundation (internationally oriented national body)
♦ Electronic Imaging – the Visual Arts and Beyond (meeting series)
♦ Electronic Industry Citizenship Coalition / see Responsible Business Alliance
♦ Electronic Industry Code of Conduct / see Responsible Business Alliance

♦ Electronic Information for Libraries (EIFL) 05425

Dir Mindaugo str 23, LT-03214 Vilnius, Lithuania. E-mail: info@eifl.net.
Registered Office Marisplantsoen 9, 3431 GZ Nieuwegein, Netherlands.
URL: http://www.eifl.net/

History 1 Jan 1999. Founded by Open Society Institute. Former names and other names: *eIFL.net* – former. Registration: No/ID: KVK 34186245, Netherlands; EU Transparency Register, No/ID: 13020287260-60, Start date: 30 Nov 2011. **Aims** Enable access to knowledge through libraries in developing and transition countries to support sustainable development. **Structure** Management Board; Advisory Board; Office. **Languages** English. **Staff** 12.00 FTE, paid. **Finance** Sources: grants. Annual budget: 984,217 EUR (2021). **Activities** Advocacy/lobbying/activism; awareness raising; capacity building; networking/liaising; projects/programmes. **Events** *General Assembly* 2020, *General Assembly* Bishkek (Kyrgyzstan) 2019, *General Assembly* Doha (Qatar) 2018, *General Assembly* Tbilisi (Georgia) 2017, *General Assembly* Chisinau (Moldova) 2016. **Publications** *EIFL E-Newsletter* (6 a year). Annual Report.
Members Library consortia and projects in 53 countries and territories:
Armenia, Azerbaijan, Belarus, Bosnia-Herzegovina, Botswana, Bulgaria, Cambodia, Chile, China, Colombia, Congo DR, Côte d'Ivoire, Croatia, Czechia, Estonia, Ethiopia, Fiji, Georgia, Ghana, Hungary, Kazakhstan, Kenya, Kosovo, Kyrgyzstan, Laos, Latvia, Lesotho, Lithuania, Malawi, Maldives, Moldova, Mongolia, Myanmar, Namibia, Nepal, North Macedonia, Palestine, Poland, Romania, Senegal, Serbia, Slovakia, Slovenia, South Africa, Sudan, Syrian AR, Tanzania UR, Thailand, Uganda, Ukraine, Uzbekistan, Zambia, Zimbabwe.

Consultative Status Consultative status granted from: *UNESCO (#20322)* (Consultative Status); *World Intellectual Property Organization (WIPO, #21593)* (Permanent Observer Status). **NGO Relations** Member of (6): *African Library and Information Associations and Institutions (AfLIA, #00363)*; *Confederation of Open Access Repositories (COAR, #04573)*; *Copyright for Creativity (C4C, #04832)*; *Global Sustainability Coalition for Open Science Services (SCOSS, #10616)*; *International Coalition of Library Consortia (ICOLC, #12615)*; *International Federation of Library Associations and Institutions (IFLA, #13470)*. [2021.06.17/XJ0357/**E**]

♦ Electronic lexicography in the 21st century (meeting series)

♦ Electronic Literature Organization (ELO) 05426

Office Coordinator Washington State Univ Vancouver, The Creative Media and Digital Culture Program, 14204 NE Salmon Creek Ave, Vancouver WA 98686, USA. T. +13605469101. E-mail: eliterature.org@gmail.com.
Pres address not obtained.
URL: http://eliterature.org/

History Founded 1999, Chicago IL (USA). A US 501c(3) non-profit organization. **Aims** Foster and promote the reading, writing and understanding of literature as it develops and persists in a changing *digital* environment. **Structure** Board of Directors. **Finance** Sources: donations; grants. **Activities** Awards/prizes/competitions; events/meetings; knowledge management/information dissemination. **Events** *Conference* Coimbra (Portugal) 2023, *Conference* Como (Italy) 2022, *Conference* Vancouver, WA (USA) 2021, *Conference* Orlando, FL (USA) 2020, *Conference* Cork (Ireland) 2019. [2019/XM7913/**C**]

♦ Electronic Money Association (unconfirmed)
♦ Electronic Privacy Information Center (internationally oriented national body)

♦ Electronic Publishing Trust for Development (EPT) 05427

Sec 61 New Atlas Wharf, 3 Arnhem Place, London, E14 3SS, UK. T. +442070017848. E-mail: eptoffice9@gmail.com.
URL: http://epublishingtrust.net/

History 1996. **Aims** Facilitate open access to the world's scholarly literature; support electronic publication of reviewed bioscience journals from countries experiencing difficulties with traditional publication. [2018/XJ7075/**F**]

♦ Electronic Retailing Association Europe / see ERA Global – Electronic Retailing Association (#05525)
♦ Electronics Technicians Association International (internationally oriented national body)

♦ Electronics Watch 05428

Dir Kingsfordweg 151, 1043 GR Amsterdam, Netherlands. T. +447480050341. E-mail: info@electronicswatch.org.
URL: http://electronicswatch.org/

History 2015. Registration: Handelsregister, No/ID: 62721445, Netherlands. **Aims** Help public sector organizations work together and collaborate with civil society monitors in production regions to protect the rights of workers in their electronics supply chains. **Structure** Board of Trustees; Advisory Group. **Languages** Catalan, English, French, German, Spanish. **Staff** 7.00 FTE, paid. **Activities** Advocacy/lobbying/activism; awareness raising; capacity building; events/meetings; knowledge management/information dissemination; monitoring/evaluation; projects/programmes; training/education. **Events** *Freedom of Association* 2021, *Occupational Health and Safety* 2020, *Annual Conference* Barcelona (Spain) 2019, *Annual Conference* Amsterdam (Netherlands) 2018.
Members Affiliates (over 400) in 12 countries:
Australia, Austria, Belgium, Denmark, Germany, Netherlands, Norway, Spain, Sweden, Switzerland, UK, USA. [2022.05.04/XM8017/**F**]

♦ Electron Microscopy Society of Southern Africa / see Microscopy Society of Southern Africa
♦ **Electrounion** International Trade Union "Elektroprofsoyuz" (#15710)
♦ **ELEE** European Landscape Education Exchanges (#07643)
♦ ELEF / see LUPUS EUROPE (#16524)
♦ **ELENA** European Legal Network on Asylum (#07679)
♦ **ELEN** European Language Equality Network (#07647)
♦ Elephant Action League / see Earth League International (#05166)

♦ Elephant Protection Initiative Foundation (EPI Foundation) 05429

Communications Dir address not obtained. T. +442038653126. E-mail: info@elephantprotectioninitiative.org.
CEO address not obtained.
Main Website: http://www.elephantprotectioninitiative.org/

History Registration: Companies House, No/ID: 11594608, Start date: 28 Sep 2018, England and Wales; Charity Commission, No/ID: 1182805, England and Wales. **Aims** Secure the harmonious coexistence of people and elephants with herds able to travel across their range; support the international moratorium on elephant ivory trade and prevent Africa's ivory stockpiles from leaking onto the illegal market. **Structure** Leadership Council. **Languages** English, French, Portuguese. **Activities** Active in all member countries.
Members Signatory states (23):
Angola, Benin, Botswana, Chad, Congo Brazzaville, Côte d'Ivoire, Eritrea, Ethiopia, Gabon, Gambia, Guinea, Kenya, Liberia, Malawi, Mali, Niger, Nigeria, Sierra Leone, Somalia, South Sudan, Tanzania UR, Uganda, UK.
Partner organizations include 20 organizations listed in this Yearbook:
African Conservation Foundation (ACF); *Africa Nomads Conservation (ANC)*; *African Parks (AP, #00411)*; *African Wildlife Foundation (AWF, #00498)*; *Big Life Foundation (Big Life, #03233)*; *Born Free Foundation*; *Conservation International (CI)*; *Environmental Investigation Agency (EIA)*; *Fauna & Flora International (FFI, #09277)*; *HALO Trust*; *International Fund for Animal Welfare (IFAW, #13693)*; *Save the Elephants (STE)*; *Sheldrick Wildlife Trust (SWT)*; *Space for Giants*; *The Nature Conservancy (TNC)*; *TUSK*; *UNDP (#20292)*; *WildAid*; *Wildlife Conservation Society (WCS)*; *WildlifeDirect*. [2023.02.14/XM5136/y/**F**]

♦ Elephants Without Borders (internationally oriented national body)
♦ Elephants for Peace (internationally oriented national body)
♦ ELEPP – European Livestock Exporters and Producers Platform (unconfirmed)
♦ **EL** European Left (#07676)
♦ EL / see European State Lotteries and Toto Association (#08833)
♦ Elevage du bétail économique des pays nordiques (#17275)
♦ Elevages sans frontières (internationally oriented national body)
♦ eLex – Electronic lexicography in the 21st century (meeting series)
♦ **ELFAA** European Low Fares Airline Association (#07713)
♦ **ELFAC** European Large Families Confederation (#07651)
♦ **ELFA** European Law Faculties Association (#07656)
♦ ELF – Earth Liberation Front (internationally oriented national body)
♦ **ELF** Esperanto-Ligo Filatelista (#05545)
♦ **ELF** European Lacrosse Federation (#07637)
♦ ELF – European Landworkers' Federation (inactive)
♦ **ELF** European Liberal Forum (#07689)
♦ **ELF** European Locksmith Federation (#07708)
♦ **ELF** European Lung Foundation (#07718)
♦ ELF – International Conference of English as a Lingua Franca (meeting series)
♦ ELGA – European Leather Fair Federation (unconfirmed)
♦ ELG / see European Young Women's Christian Association (#09135)
♦ **ELGGN** European Low Grade Glioma Network (#07714)
♦ **ELGI** European Lubricating Grease Institute (#07716)
♦ **ELGIP** European Large Geotechnical Institutes Platform (#07652)
♦ **ELGRA** European Low Gravity Research Association (#07715)
♦ **ELHN** European Labour History Network (#07636)
♦ **ELHUA** European Life and Health Underwriters' Association (#07693)
♦ **ELIA** European Language Industry Association (#07648)

♦ **ELIA** European League of Institutes of the Arts (#07670)
♦ ELIAMEP – Hellenic Foundation for European and Foreign Policy (internationally oriented national body)
♦ **ELIAS** European Librarians in African Studies (#07691)
♦ ELI – Environmental Law Institute (internationally oriented national body)
♦ **ELI ERIC** Extreme Light Infrastructure ERIC (#09230)
♦ **ELI** European Law Institute (#07658)
♦ Elie Wiesel Foundation for Humanity (internationally oriented national body)
♦ **ELIG** European Learning Industry Group (#07674)

♦ Eliminate Child Labour in Tobacco Foundation (ECLT Foundation) . . 05430

Contact Rue François Versonnex 7, 1207 Carouge GE, Switzerland. T. +41223061444. E-mail: eclt@eclt.org.
URL: http://www.eclt.org/

History 5 Apr 2002, Geneva (Switzerland). **Aims** Prevent and address child labour in tobacco agriculture with the primary purpose of protecting and improving lives of children and eliminating child labour in tobacco-growing areas. **Structure** Board; Secretariat, headed by Executive Director. **Languages** English. **Staff** 12.00 FTE, paid. **Finance** Grants; donations. **Activities** Financial and/or material support; advocacy/lobbying/activism; knowledge management/information dissemination. Active in 5 countries: Kyrgyzstan; Malawi; Mozambique; Tanzania UR; Uganda. Active in: Kyrgyzstan, Malawi, Mozambique, Tanzania UR, Uganda. **Publications** *Understanding, Identifying, and Eliminating Child Labour in Tobacco Growing – A Field Practitioner's Guide.* Annual Report.
Members Representatives of tobacco growers, leaf companies and manufacturers. Members in 10 countries:
Denmark, Germany, Japan, Portugal, Sweden, Switzerland, Thailand, Türkiye, UK, USA.
Included in the above, 1 organization listed in this Yearbook:
International Tobacco Growers' Association (ITGA, #15694).
Consultative Status Consultative status granted from: *ECOSOC (#05331)* (Special). **IGO Relations** Main advisor: *ILO (#11123).* [2018.07.20/XF6620/fy/**F**]

♦ ELINET Association / see European Literacy Policy Network (#07702)
♦ **ELINET** European Literacy Policy Network (#07702)
♦ eLISA Consortium / see LISA Consortium (#16490)
♦ ELISAD – European Association of Libraries and Information Services on Addictions (inactive)
♦ **ELISAN** European Local Inclusion and Social Action Network (#07707)
♦ **ELITA** European Liver and Intestine Transplant Association (#07705)
♦ ELITE – European Federation of Associations for Teaching of Mother Tongues to Foreigners (no recent information)
♦ E.L.I.T.E. – European Laboratory for Industrial and Territorial Excellence (internationally oriented national body)
♦ ELIX – Conservation Volunteers Greece (internationally oriented national body)
♦ ELIX-CVG – ELIX – Conservation Volunteers Greece (internationally oriented national body)

♦ ELIXIR 05431

Contact Wellcome Genome Campus, Hinxton, CB10 1SD, UK. T. +441223492670. E-mail: info@elixir-europe.org.
URL: http://www.elixir-europe.org/

History 12 Jan 2014. Founded when ELIXIR Consortium Agreement went into force. **Aims** Coordinate life science data resources so that they form a single infrastructure for users in industry and academia. **Structure** Board; Scientific Advisory Board; Heads of Nodes Committee; Technical Coordinators; Training Coordinators. **Staff** 20.00 FTE, paid. **Activities** Knowledge management/information dissemination; research/documentation; training/education. **Events** *ELIXIR All Hands Meeting* Dublin (Ireland) 2023, *ELIXIR All Hands Meeting* Amsterdam (Netherlands) 2022, *Board Meeting* Tallinn (Estonia) 2022, *ELIXIR All Hands Meeting* Hinxton (UK) 2021, *ELIXIR All Hands Meeting* Hinxton (UK) 2020.
Members Nodes in 20 countries:
Belgium, Czechia, Denmark, Estonia, Finland, France, Germany, Hungary, Ireland, Israel, Italy, Luxembourg, Netherlands, Norway, Portugal, Slovenia, Spain, Sweden, Switzerland, UK.
Observer (1):
Greece.
Regional node:
EMBL's European Bioinformatics Institute (EMBL-EBI, #05433). [2023/XM5464/**F***]

♦ Elizabeth Glaser Pediatric AIDS Foundation (internationally oriented national body)
♦ Ellel Ministries International (internationally oriented national body)
♦ Ellen MacArthur Foundation (internationally oriented national body)
♦ Elliniko Kentro Evropaikon Meleton (internationally oriented national body)
♦ Elliniko Simvulio gia tous Prosfiges (internationally oriented national body)
♦ Elliott School of International Affairs (internationally oriented national body)
♦ **ELLKA** Eiropas lauksaimniecibas un lauku konsultantu asociacija (#07303)
♦ **ELLS** Euroleague for Life Sciences (#05702)
♦ **ELLV** Europäischer Leichtathletik-Lehrer-Verband (#06292)
♦ ELLV / see European Athletics Coaches Association (#06292)
♦ ELMA – European Association for Length Measuring Instruments and Machines (no recent information)
♦ **ELMA** European Lecithin Manufacturers Association (#07675)
♦ **ELMA** European Letterbox Marketing Association (#07683)
♦ **ELMA** European Live Music Association (#07704)
♦ **ELMC** European Law Moot Court Society (#07659)
♦ ELM – European Laboratory Medicine (inactive)
♦ ELMF / see European Garden Machinery Industry Federation (#07379)
♦ **ELMLE** European League for Middle Level Education (#07671)
♦ ELMO – European Laundry and Dry Cleaning Machinery Manufacturers Organization (no recent information)
♦ **ELMO** European Lifestyle Medicine Organization (#07694)
♦ **ELNET** European Leadership Network (#07667)
♦ **ELN** European Leadership Network (#07666)
♦ **ELN** European LeukemiaNet (#07685)
♦ ELN – European Life Network (internationally oriented national body)
♦ **ELNI** Environmental Law Network International (#05504)
♦ **ELNIT Association** International Association of Users and Developers of Electronic Libraries and New Information Technologies (#12252)
♦ ELOA – European Lead Oxide Association (inactive)
♦ **ELO** Electronic Literature Organization (#05426)
♦ **ELO** European Landowners' Organization (#07639)
♦ ELONETCE / see Association Justice and Environment, z.s. (#02774)
♦ **ELPA** European Litter Prevention Association (#07703)
♦ **ELPA** European Liver Patients 'Association (#07706)
♦ **ELP** European Logistics Platform (#07711)
♦ **ELP** Europos Liaudies Partijos – Krikscioniu Demokratu (#10775)
♦ ELPHA – European Live Poultry and Poultry Hatching Egg Association (unconfirmed)
♦ ElPub – International Conference on Electronic Publishing (meeting series)
♦ **ELRA** European Land Registry Association (#07640)
♦ **ELRA** European Language Resources Association (#07650)
♦ ELRA – European Leisure and Recreation Association (inactive)
♦ **ELRC** European Language Resource Coordination (#07649)
♦ **ELSA** Endoscopic and Laparoscopic Surgeons of Asia (#05462)
♦ **ELSA** European Laboratory for Structural Assessment (#07634)
♦ **ELSA** European Land and Soil Alliance (#07645)
♦ **ELSA** The European Law Students' Association (#07660)
♦ **ELSA** European League of Stuttering Associations (#07673)
♦ ELSD / see European Society for Lasers and Energy Based Devices (#08640)
♦ ELSE – European Life Science Editors (inactive)
♦ **ELS** European Laryngological Society (#07653)
♦ **ELS** European Leptospirosis Society (#07682)
♦ ELS – European Lotteries Sports (inactive)
♦ **ELSIA** European Lead Sheet Industry Association (#07668)
♦ ELSI – European Legal Studies Institute (internationally oriented national body)
♦ **ELSNIT** Euro-Latin Study Network on Integration and Trade (#05701)
♦ ELSO – European Life Scientist Organization (inactive)
♦ ELSO – Extracorporeal Life Support Organization (internationally oriented national body)
♦ ELSPA – Entertainment Leisure Software Publishers Association (inactive)
♦ **ELS** Poslanecky Klub Evropské Lidové Strany – Krest'anskych Demokrat (#10775)
♦ **ELS** Poslanecky Klub Evrópske l'Udovej Strany – Krest'anskych Demokratov (#10775)
♦ **ELS** Poslanska Skupina Evropske Ljudske Stranke – Krscanskih Demokratov (#10775)
♦ ELTAC – European Largest Textile and Apparel Companies (inactive)
♦ **ELTA** European Legal Technology Association (#07680)
♦ ELTA / see European Liver and Intestine Transplant Association (#07705)
♦ **ELTI** European Association of Long-Term Investors (#06112)
♦ ELTI – European Leaf Tobacco Interbranch (unconfirmed)
♦ Elton John AIDS Foundation (internationally oriented national body)
♦ **ELVHIS** Europäischer Leit-Verband der Hersteller von Gas-Infrarot- Hellstrahlern (#05758)
♦ ELWCHG / see Study Group on International Labor and Working Class History
♦ **ELW** European Lawyers for Workers Network (#07662)
♦ EMA / see Global Connections
♦ EMAA – European Martial Arts Association (internationally oriented national body)
♦ EMAA / see International Mastic Asphalt Association (#14119)
♦ EM Academy – The Electromagnetics Academy (internationally oriented national body)
♦ **EMACAPAP** Eastern Mediterranean Association for Child and Adolescent Psychiatry and Allied Professions (#05240)
♦ **EMAC** European Marketing Academy (#07745)
♦ EMAC – European Meeting on Ancient Ceramics (meeting series)
♦ EMA – Electronic Money Association (unconfirmed)
♦ **EMA** Erasmus Mundus Students and Alumni Association (#05527)
♦ **EMA** Euro-Mediterranean-Arab Association (#05717)
♦ **EMA** European Magnetism Association (#07725)
♦ **EMA** European Management Association (#07729)
♦ **EMA** European Marketing Association (#07746)
♦ **EMA** European Masters Athletics (#07750)
♦ EMA – European Meat Association (inactive)
♦ **EMA** European Medical Association (#07761)
♦ **EMA** European Medicines Agency (#07767)
♦ EMA – European Metallizers Association (inactive)
♦ **EMA** European Midwives Association (#07800)
♦ **EMA** European Museum Academy (#07835)
♦ **EMA** European Mycological Association (#07845)
♦ EMA – Europe Must Act (unconfirmed)
♦ EMAGOLD – European Gold Manufacturers Association (no recent information)
♦ EMALS – Euro-Mediterranean Association of Life Sciences (internationally oriented national body)
♦ **EMAN** Environmental Management Accounting Network (#05505)
♦ **EMAN** Euro-Mediterranean Academic Network (#05716)
♦ **EMAN** European Mycotoxins Awareness Network (#07847)
♦ **EMANI** European Mutual Association for Nuclear Insurance (#07842)
♦ EMAP – Embajada Mundial de Activistas por la Paz (unconfirmed)
♦ **EMAS** European Menopause and Andropause Society (#07782)
♦ **EMAS** European Microbeam Analysis Society (#07791)
♦ **EMASH** European Medical Association on Smoking and Health (#07762)
♦ Emaús Europa (#05444)
♦ Emaús Internacional (#05445)
♦ EMAU / see World Archery Europe (#21108)
♦ **EMAV** European Manufacturers of Autogenous Vaccines and Sera (#07731)
♦ **EMBAC** Executive MBA Council (#09223)
♦ **EMBA** European Milk Bank Association (#07804)
♦ Embajada Mundial de Activistas por la Paz (unconfirmed)
♦ **EMBARC** European Multicentre Bronchiectasis Audit and Research Collaboration (#07828)
♦ EMBARC Network / see European Multicentre Bronchiectasis Audit and Research Collaboration (#07828)
♦ **EMBC** European Molecular Biology Conference (#07812)
♦ EMB – Europäischer Metallgewerkschaftsbund (inactive)
♦ **EMB** European Marine Board (#07738)
♦ **EMB** European Milk Board (#07805)
♦ EMB-IVZW / see European Marine Board (#07738)

♦ EMBL Alumni Association 05432

Chairman Meyerhofstrasse 1, 69117 Heidelberg, Germany. T. +4962213878102. Fax +4962213878211. E-mail: alumni@embl.org.
URL: http://www.embl.org/alumni/

History 1999. Founded as the alumni association of *European Molecular Biology Laboratory (EMBL, #07813).* **Aims** Advance EMBL and the relevance of life science research in the scientific community and society at large. **Structure** Board; Alumni Relations Team. **Languages** English. **Staff** 4.00 FTE, paid. **Finance** Sources: sponsorship. Supported by: *European Molecular Biology Laboratory (EMBL, #07813).* **Activities** Networking/liaising. Active in: Austria, Belgium, Denmark, Finland, France, Germany, Greece, Ireland, Italy, Netherlands, Norway, Portugal, Spain, Sweden, Switzerland, UK, USA. **Events** *Yesterday, today and tomorrow* Heidelberg (Germany) 2004. **Members** As of Jan 2022, individuals (about 5,000) in 77 countries and territories. Membership countries not specified. [2022.11.10/XJ3330/**E**]

♦ **EMBL-EBI** EMBL's European Bioinformatics Institute (#05433)
♦ **EMBL** European Molecular Biology Laboratory (#07813)

♦ EMBL's European Bioinformatics Institute (EMBL-EBI) 05433

Dir Wellcome Genome Campus, Hinxton, Cambridge, CB10 1SD, UK. T. +441223494444. Fax +441223494468. E-mail: doffice@ebi.ac.uk.
Dir address not obtained.
URL: http://www.ebi.ac.uk/

History 1993, Hinxton (UK). Founded as an outstation of *European Molecular Biology Laboratory (EMBL, #07813).* **Aims** Provide freely available data and bioinformatics services to the scientific community; contribute to advancement of biology through investigator-driven research; provide advanced bioinformatics training to scientists at all levels; disseminate cutting-edge technologies to industry; support coordination of biological data provision throughout Europe. **Languages** English. **Staff** 708.00 FTE, paid. **Finance** Supported by: *European Commission (EC, #06633); European Molecular Biology Laboratory (EMBL, #07813);* national funding agencies and councils; *Wellcome Trust.* **Activities** Knowledge management/information dissemination; research and development; research/documentation; training/education. **Events** *Conference on therapeutic applications of computational biology and chemistry* Hinxton (UK) 2010, *TACBAC : conference* *on therapeutic applications of computational biology and chemistry* Hinxton (UK) 2010, *Conference on stem cell proteomics* Hinxton (UK) 2009, *Workshop on understanding protein structures* Hinxton (UK) 2009, *SME Bioinformatics Forum* Vienna (Austria) 2009. **NGO Relations** Instrumental in setting up (1): *Global Organisation for Bioinformatics Learning, Education and Training (GOBLET, #10516).* [2022.05.06/XK0942/j/**E**]

- ♦ **EMBL Staff Association** European Molecular Biology Laboratory Staff Association (#07814)
- ♦ **EMBMT** Eastern Mediterranean Blood and Marrow Transplantation Group (#05242)
- ♦ **EMBnet** European Molecular Biology Network (#07815)
- ♦ Embodied and Situated Language Processing Conference (meeting series)
- ♦ **EMBO** European Molecular Biology Organization (#07816)
- ♦ emBOLDen Alliances (internationally oriented national body)
- ♦ Embrace the Middle East (internationally oriented national body)
- ♦ **EMBRC-ERIC** European Marine Biological Resource Centre (#07737)
- ♦ **EMBRN** European Mast Cell and Basophil Research Network (#07748)
- ♦ **EMBS** Committee for European Marine Biology Symposia (#04255)
- ♦ **EMCA** European Memory Clinics Association (#07778)
- ♦ **EMCA** European Mosquito Control Association (#07823)
- ♦ EMCCC – European Multidisciplinary Colorectal Cancer Congress (meeting series)
- ♦ EMCC / see EMCC Global (#05434)
- ♦ **EMCC** EMCC Global (#05434)
- ♦ EMCC – European Municipal Credit Community (inactive)

♦ EMCC Global (EMCC) 05434

Contact 63A Scepterstrasse, 1050 Brussels, Belgium.
URL: https://www.emccglobal.org/

History 1992. Former names and other names: *European Mentoring Council (EMC)* – former (1992 to 2001); *European Mentoring and Coaching Council (EMCC)* – former. **Aims** Develop, promote and set the expectation of best practice in mentoring and coaching across Europe and beyond. **Structure** Council, consisting of members representing Affiliated Countries; International Executive Board. **Languages** English. **Staff** Voluntary. **Activities** Events/meetings. **Events** *Annual Conference* Dublin (Ireland) 2019, *Research Conference* Oxford (UK) 2019, *Annual Conference* Amsterdam (Netherlands) 2018, *Research Conference* Chester (UK) 2018, *Research Conference* London (UK) 2017. **Publications** *International Journal of Mentoring and Coaching.*

Members Individuals (over 5,000) in 62 countries. Membership countries not specified.
Affiliated countries (22):
Belgium, Croatia, Czechia, Denmark, Finland, France, Germany, Greece, Hungary, Ireland, Italy, Luxembourg, Morocco, Netherlands, Norway, Poland, Serbia, Sweden, Switzerland, Türkiye, UK, Ukraine.
NGO Relations Member of (1): *EFMD – The Management Development Network (#05387).* [2022.06.23/XE4640/v/**E**]

- ♦ **EMCDDA** European Monitoring Centre for Drugs and Drug Addiction (#07820)
- ♦ EMCEF – European Mine, Chemical and Energy Workers' Federation (inactive)
- ♦ EMC / see EMCC Global (#05434)
- ♦ EMCEMO – Euro-Mediterraan Centrum voor Migratie and Ontwikkeling (internationally oriented national body)
- ♦ **EMC** European Maccabi Confederation (#07720)
- ♦ **EMC** European Marketing Confederation (#07747)
- ♦ EMC – European Marketing Council (inactive)
- ♦ **EMC** European Methodist Council (#07787)
- ♦ EMC – European Mineralogical Conference (meeting series)
- ♦ **EMC** European Music Council (#07837)
- ♦ EMC / see European Society for Muscle Research (#08657)
- ♦ **EMC** Europe Makes Ceramics (#09161)
- ♦ EMCF – Edna McConnel Clark Foundation (internationally oriented national body)
- ♦ EMCF – European Monetary Cooperation Fund (inactive)
- ♦ **EMCO** Eastern Mediterranean Council of Optometry (#05243)
- ♦ EMCO – International Board of Cooperation for the Developing Countries (inactive)
- ♦ EmCon – International Conference on Emerging Contaminants (meeting series)
- ♦ **EMCRF** European and Mediterranean Cereal Rusts Foundation (#07769)
- ♦ EMCSR – European Meeting on Cybernetics and Systems Research (meeting series)
- ♦ EMCWP – European Mediterranean Commission on Water Planning (no recent information)
- ♦ **EMCY** European Union of Music Competitions for Youth (#09003)
- ♦ EMDA / see Network for European Monitoring and Development Assistance
- ♦ EMDA – Network for European Monitoring and Development Assistance (internationally oriented national body)
- ♦ EMDA Network Organisation / see Network for European Monitoring and Development Assistance
- ♦ EMD – European Management Development Centre, Huizen (internationally oriented national body)
- ♦ **EMDN** European Mitochondrial Disease Network (#07809)

♦ EMDR Europe Association 05435

Contact Im Oberstadel 5, 8405 Winterthur ZH, Switzerland. E-mail: secretary@emdr-europe.org.
Exec Assistant Via Vitruvio 43, 20128 Milan MI, Italy.
URL: http://emdr-europe.org/

History 1999. Originally set up within *EMDR International Association (EMDRIA).* Registration: EU Transparency Register, No/ID: 371321942417-65, Start date: 21 Apr 2021. **Aims** Establish, maintain and promote the highest standards of excellence and integrity in *eye* movement desensitization and reprocessing (EMDR) practice, research and education. **Structure** A grouping of national associations. **Languages** English. **Staff** 1.00 FTE, paid. **Finance** Sources: members' dues. **Activities** Awards/prizes/competitions; certification/accreditation; events/meetings; networking/liaising; research/documentation; standards/guidelines; training/education. **Events** *Annual Conference* Winterthur (Switzerland) 2021, *Annual Conference* Krakow (Poland) 2019, *Annual Conference* Strasbourg (France) 2018, *Annual Conference* Barcelona (Spain) 2017, *Annual Conference* The Hague (Netherlands) 2016.

Members National associations in 36 countries:
Albania, Armenia, Austria, Azerbaijan, Belgium, Bosnia-Herzegovina, Croatia, Czechia, Denmark, Finland, France, Georgia, Germany, Greece, Hungary, Iceland, Ireland, Israel, Italy, Lithuania, Luxembourg, Malta, Netherlands, Norway, Poland, Portugal, Romania, Russia, Serbia, Slovakia, Spain, Sweden, Switzerland, Türkiye, UK, Ukraine.
NGO Relations Member of (2): *Lifelong Learning Platform – European Civil Society for Education (LLLP, #16466); Mental Health Europe (MHE, #16715).* Associate member of: *European Federation of Psychologists Associations (EFPA, #07199).* [2021.09.02/XE4638/**E**]

- ♦ EMDRIA – EMDR International Association (internationally oriented national body)
- ♦ EMDR International Association (internationally oriented national body)
- ♦ **EMDS** European Macrophage and Dendritic Cell Society (#07722)
- ♦ **EMEA** European ME Alliance (#07757)
- ♦ EMEA / see European Medicines Agency (#07767)
- ♦ EMEAP – Executives' Meeting of East Asian and Pacific Central Banks (meeting series)
- ♦ EMEA Power Transmission Distributors Association / see European Power Transmission Distributors Association (#08265)
- ♦ EMEA Satellite Operators Association / see Global Satellite Operators' Association (#10586)

♦ EMEA Synthetic Turf Council (ESTC) 05436

CEO Rue Belliard 40, 1040 Brussels, Belgium. T. +3224369633. E-mail: info@estc.info.
URL: https://www.estc.info/

History Jun 2010, Brussels (Belgium). Former names and other names: *European Synthetic Turf Organisation (ESTO)* – former (2010 to 2019). Registration: Banque-Carrefour des Entreprises, No/ID: 0828.241.824, Start date: 3 Aug 2010, Belgium. **Aims** Ensure quality turf and to provide information that can help clients and end-users find the most appropriate solutions in synthetic turf systems. **Structure** Council. **Languages** English. **Staff** 1.00 FTE, paid. **Finance** Sources: members' dues. Annual budget: 300,000 EUR. **Activities** Awards/prizes/competitions; events/meetings. **Events** *Congress* Brussels (Belgium) 2021, *Congress* Rome (Italy) 2015.

Members Full; Associate. Membership countries not specified. Affiliate members:
CIRFS – European Man-made Fibres Association (#03944); European Tyre Recycling Association (ETRA, #08961); International Federation of Association Football (#13360); International Hockey Federation (#13802); Synthetic Turf Council (STC); World Rugby (#21757).
NGO Relations Member of (1): *Federation of European and International Associations Established in Belgium (FAIB, #09508).* Instrumental in setting up (1): *Synthetic Turf Council International (STCI).* [2021/XJ8848/ty/**D**]

- ♦ **EMECA** European Major Exhibition Centres Association (#07726)
- ♦ EMEC – European Marine Equipment Council (inactive)
- ♦ EMeF – EuroMediteranski Forum (internationally oriented national body)
- ♦ EMEF – Euro-Mediterranean Forum (internationally oriented national body)
- ♦ EMEFTA – Euro-Mediterranean Free-Trade Area (unconfirmed)
- ♦ **EMENA** European MEN Alliance (#07779)
- ♦ **EMEP** Cooperative Programme for Monitoring and Evaluation of the Long-range Transmission of Air Pollutants in Europe (#04800)
- ♦ Emerald Network (see: #19949)
- ♦ Emergeing Tech Commercializaion / see MANCEF (#16563)
- ♦ EMERGENCY (internationally oriented national body)
- ♦ Emergency Architects (internationally oriented national body)
- ♦ Emergency Economic Committee for Europe (inactive)
- ♦ Emergency Medical Services / see European EMS Leadership Network (#06980)
- ♦ Emergency Nutrition Network (internationally oriented national body)
- ♦ Emergency Preparedness and Disaster Relief Coordination Office / see PAHO/WHO Health Emergencies Department (#18023)

♦ Emergency, Prevention, Preparedness and Response (EPPR) 05437

Mailing Address Fram Centre, Postboks 6606, Stakkevollan, 9296 Tromsø, Norway. E-mail: eppr@arctic-council.org.
URL: https://eppr.org/

History 1991. Established as a programme of *Arctic Environmental Protection Strategy (AEPS, inactive).* Currently under the auspices of *Arctic Council (#01097).* **Aims** Protect the Arctic environment from the threat or impact of activities in the Arctic that may result in an accidental release of pollutants; promote sustainable development in the Arctic area; provide a framework for future cooperation in responding to the threat of *environmental* emergencies in the *Arctic* region. **Structure** Secretariat rotates with Chair. **Activities** Current projects include: development of a Circumpolar map of natural resources at risk from oil spills; source control management and prevention strategies for high risk activities in the Arctic. **Events** *Annual Meeting* Oulu (Finland) 2013, *Annual Meeting* Tromsø (Norway) 2013, *Annual Meeting* Copenhagen (Denmark) 2012, *Annual Meeting* Keflavik (Iceland) 2012, *Annual Meeting* Oslo (Norway) 2011. **Publications** *Arctic Guide; Field Guide for Oil Spill Response.* Reports.

Members Full in 8 countries:
Canada, Denmark, Finland, Iceland, Norway, Russia, Sweden, USA.
Permanent participants (6):
Aleut International Association (AIA); Arctic Athabaskan Council (AAC); Gwich'in Council International (GCI); Inuit Circumpolar Council (ICC, #15995); Russian Association of Indigenous Peoples of the North (RAIPON); Saami Council (#19012).
IGO Relations Cooperates with Arctic Council Working Groups: *Protection of the Arctic Marine Environment (PAME, #18547); Arctic Monitoring and Assessment Programme (AMAP, #01100); Conservation of Arctic Flora and Fauna (CAFF, #04728).* [2021/XK1391/y/**E***]

♦ Emergency Telecommunications Cluster (ETC) 05438

Coordinator c/o WFP, Via Cesare Giulio Viola 68, Parco dei Medici, 00148 Rome RM, Italy. E-mail: global.etc@wfp.org.
URL: http://www.etcluster.org/

History A cluster of *Inter-Agency Standing Committee (IASC, #11393).* **Aims** Provide shared communications services in humanitarian emergencies. **Structure** Leadership, headed by *World Food Programme (WFP, #21510).* Secretariat. **Activities** Humanitarian/emergency aid; training/education.

Members Membership open to all Inter-Agency Standing Committee (IASC) members. Members include 19 organizations listed in this Yearbook:
Action Against Hunger (#00086); Communicating with Disaster Affected Communities Network (CDAC Network, #04379); FAO (#09260); GVF (#10842); Inter-Agency Standing Committee (IASC, #11393); International Committee of the Red Cross (ICRC, #12799); International Organization for Migration (IOM, #14454); International Telecommunication Union (ITU, #15673); NetHope (#16979); Oxfam International (#17922); Plan International (#18386); Save the Children Federation (SCF); Télécoms sans frontières (TSF); UNDP (#20292); UNHCR (#20327); UNICEF (#20332); United Nations Office for the Coordination of Humanitarian Affairs (OCHA, #20593); WHO (#20950); World Vision International (WVI, #21904). [2017/XM5765/y/**E**]

- ♦ Emerge Poverty Free (internationally oriented national body)
- ♦ EMERG – European Mediterranean Regulators Groups (unconfirmed)
- ♦ Emerging Europe Alliance for Business Services, Innovation and Technology (unconfirmed)
- ♦ Emerging Europe Alliance – Emerging Europe Alliance for Business Services, Innovation and Technology (unconfirmed)
- ♦ Emerging Market Investors Association (unconfirmed)
- ♦ Emerging Markets Private Equity Association / see Global Private Capital Association (#10556)
- ♦ Emerging Markets Traders Association / see EMTA (#05449)

♦ Emerging Nanopatterning Methods Consortium (NaPa) 05439

Coordinator VTT Technical Research Centre, PO Box 1000, FI-02044 Espoo, Finland. T. +35820722111. Fax +358207227001.
URL: http://www.phantomsnet.net/NAPA/

Aims Integrate European know-how in *nanolithography* into a single integrated project. **Activities** Organizes meetings and training courses. **Events** *Meeting / Plenary Meeting* Barcelona (Spain) 2007, *Plenary Meeting* Copenhagen (Denmark) 2006, *Plenary Meeting* Glasgow (UK) 2006, *Plenary Meeting* Berlin (Germany) 2005, *Plenary Meeting* Lausanne (Switzerland) 2005.

Members Core partners (8) in 5 countries:
Finland, France, Germany, Ireland, Switzerland.
Participating groups (27) in 13 countries:
Austria, Denmark, France, Germany, Ireland, Italy, Netherlands, Poland, Russia, Spain, Sweden, Switzerland, UK. [2007/XM2745/**F**]

- ♦ EMES European Research Network / see EMES International Research Network (#05440)

♦ EMES International Research Network 05440

Managing Dir c/o Univ de Liège, Bd du Rectorat B33 – box 4, 4000 Liège, Belgium. T. +3243662751. Fax +3243662851.
URL: http://www.emes.net/

History 20 Apr 2002, Brussels (Belgium), as *European EMES Network – Réseau européen EMES* after working informally since 1996. Subsequently known as *EMES European Research Network.* Registered in accordance with Belgian law. EU Transparency Register: 788210432236-83. **Aims** Promote cooperation among European researchers working on the "Third Sector" also referred to as the social economy, the "économie solidaire" or the Non-Profit Sector. **Structure** Board of Directors; Coordination Unit. **Languages** English, French. **Staff** 1.50 FTE, paid. **Finance** Research projects; grants from partner foundations. **Activities** Research/documentation; projects/programmes; events/meetings. **Events** *EMES International Conference on Social Enterprise* Teruel (Spain) 2021, *EMES International Conference on Social Enterprise* Sheffield (UK) 2019, *EMES International Conference on Social Enterprise* Louvain-la-Neuve (Belgium) 2017, *EMES International Conference on Social Enterprise* Helsinki (Finland) 2015, *EMES International Conference on Social Enterprise / European Conference* Liège (Belgium) 2013. **Publications** Books. Conference papers; working papers; position papers.
Members Individual (over 300); Institutional (14). Institutions in 10 countries:

Belgium, Denmark, France, Ireland, Italy, Korea Rep, Norway, Portugal, Spain, UK.
Included in the above, 1 organization listed in this Yearbook:
European Research Institute on Cooperative and Social Enterprises (EURICSE).
NGO Relations *ISTR European Third-Sector Network (see: #15510).* Sister organization: *Red de Investigadores Latinoamericanos de Economia Social y Solidaria (RILESS, no recent information).* Partners include: *Euclid Network (#05574).* Member of: *European Federation of Citizen Energy Cooperatives (REScoop.eu, #07077).* [2019/XF6660/**F**]

- ♦ EMESUA – European Mail and Express Services Users' Association (inactive)
- ♦ EMETA – European Medical Trade Association (no recent information)
- ♦ EM / see European Movement International (#07825)
- ♦ **EMEYF** Europe and Middle East Young Friends (#09162)
- ♦ EMFA / see Alternative Investment Management Association (#00752)
- ♦ EMFA – European Moulded Fibre Association (unconfirmed)
- ♦ EMF / see Central and Eastern European Media Centre Foundation (#03694)
- ♦ EMF / see Covered Bond and Mortgage Council (#04940)
- ♦ EMF-ECBC / see Covered Bond and Mortgage Council (#04940)
- ♦ EMFEMA / see European Manufacturers of Feed Minerals Association (#07733)
- ♦ **EMFEMA** European Manufacturers of Feed Minerals Association (#07733)
- ♦ EMF – Encuesta Mundial de Fecundidad (inactive)
- ♦ EMF – Enquête mondiale sur la fécondité (inactive)
- ♦ **EMF** Espace Mathématique Francophone (#05541)
- ♦ EMF – Europäische Motel-Föderation (inactive)
- ♦ **EMF** European Materials Forum (#07751)
- ♦ EMF – European Metalworkers' Federation (inactive)
- ♦ **EMF** European Microlight Federation (#07794)
- ♦ **EMF** European Milk Forum (#07806)
- ♦ EMF – European Mime Federation (inactive)
- ♦ **EMF** European Minifootball Federation (#07808)
- ♦ EMF – European Motel Federation (inactive)
- ♦ **EMF** European Mountain Forum (#07824)
- ♦ **EMF** European Multicultural Foundation (#07830)
- ♦ **EMF** European Museum Forum (#07836)
- ♦ **EMF-FCP** Central and Eastern European Media Centre Foundation (#03694)
- ♦ EMFK – Europäisches Mennonitisches Friedenskomitee (internationally oriented national body)
- ♦ **E-MFP** European Microfinance Platform (#07793)
- ♦ EMF / see World Economic Forum (#21367)
- ♦ **EMG** Environmental Management Group (#05506)
- ♦ **EMG** Europäische Märchengesellschaft (#05755)
- ♦ EMG – European Mobility Group (unconfirmed)
- ♦ **EMGF** Eastern Mediterranean Gas Forum (#05244)
- ♦ EMG Meeting – European Metabolic Group Meeting (meeting series)
- ♦ **EMGM** European Meningococcal Disease Society (#07780)
- ♦ EMGS – Environmental Mutagenesis and Genomics Society (internationally oriented national body)
- ♦ **EMHA** European Migraine and Headache Alliance (#07801)
- ♦ **EMH** European Maritime Heritage (#07741)
- ♦ **EMH** European Membrane House (#07776)
- ♦ **EMHF** European and Mediterranean Horseracing Federation (#07770)
- ♦ **EMHF** European Men's Health Forum (#07783)
- ♦ **EMHG** European Malignant Hyperthermia Group (#07727)
- ♦ **EMHRF** Euro-Mediterranean Foundation of Support to Human Rights Defenders (#05720)
- ♦ EMHRN / see EuroMed Rights (#05733)
- ♦ EMIA – Emerging Market Investors Association (unconfirmed)
- ♦ **EMI** Earthquakes and Megacities Initiative (#05167)
- ♦ EMI – Engineering Ministries International (internationally oriented national body)
- ♦ EMI – Entraide médicale internationale (internationally oriented national body)
- ♦ **EMI** Entraide missionnaire internationale (#14170)
- ♦ EMI – European Manager Institute (internationally oriented national body)
- ♦ EMI – European Monetary Institute (inactive)
- ♦ **EMI** European Movement International (#07825)
- ♦ EMIFMA – European Medical Imaging Film Manufacturers (no recent information)
- ♦ **EMIG** Ecole des mines, de l'industrie et de la géologie (#19132)
- ♦ **EMIG** European Mucosal Immunology Group (#07826)

♦ Emily Dickinson International Society 05441

Sec Univ Clermont-Auvergne, UFR LCC, 34 avenue Carnot, 63000 Clermont-Ferrand, France.
URL: http://www.emilydickinsoninternationalsociety.org/

History 1988. Registration: Start date: 1988, USA, Massachusetts. **Aims** Promote, perpetuate and enhance the study and appreciation of Emily Dickinson worldwide. **Structure** Board. **Activities** Awards/prizes/competitions; events/meetings. **Events** *Triennial International Conference* Seville (Spain) 2022, *Triennial International Conference* Asilomar, CA (USA) 2019, *Triennial International Conference* Paris (France) 2016, *Triennial International Conference* College Park, MD (USA) 2013, *Triennial International Conference* Oxford (UK) 2010. **Publications** *Emily Dickinson Bulletin* (2 a year); *Emily Dickinson Journal* (2 a year). **NGO Relations** Member of (1): *American Literature Association (ALA, #00786).* [2021/XN7864/**E**]

- ♦ **EMIRAcle** European Manufacturing and Innovation Research Association (#07734)
- ♦ Emirates Centre for Strategic Studies and Research (internationally oriented national body)
- ♦ Emirghaniya (religious order)
- ♦ **EMIRI** Energy Materials Industrial Research Initiative (#05472)
- ♦ **EMISCO** European Muslim Initiative for Social Cohesion (#07839)

♦ Emissaries of Divine Light (The Emissaries) 05442

Dir 100 Sunrise Ranch Rd, Loveland CO 80538, USA. T. +19706794200. Fax +19706794248.
Sec – European Office Mickleton House, Mickleton, Chipping Campden, GL55 6SF, UK. T. +441386438525.
URL: http://www.emissaries.org/

History 1932, Nashville TN (USA), by Lloyd Arthur Meeker – pen-name *Uranda* – subsequently with Martin Exeter and Michael Exeter and more recently by a Board of Trustees. Expanded into an international *Emissary Network*, inter alia through *Foundation of Universal Unity*, set up Jul 1981, Vancouver (Canada), at 8th International Human Unity Conference. For a while from 1984 hosted associate organization *Emissary Foundation International, 'Emissary Foundation'* being the USA branch. Also known as: *Emissaries International*; *Society of Emissaries*; *Comunidad Internacional Emisaria*. **Aims** Bring about an understanding of eternal creative laws and principles that restore wholeness to human experience. **Structure** Board of Trustees. Operates as spiritually-based network of people united by the aims of the organization. **Languages** English, French, German, Italian, Russian, Spanish. **Staff** 100.00 FTE, paid. **Finance** Sources: donations; revenue from classes; sale of literature; income from events; sale of farm and garden produce. **Activities** Events/meetings; projects/programmes; training/education. **Publications** *Journal of the Creative Field* (4 a year). *Becoming a Sun* (2016) by David Karchere; *Seven Steps to the Temple of Light* (4th ed 1977) by Uranda. Books; booklets; transcripts of weekly addresses; audio and videotapes. **Information Services** *EmNet* – international teleconference and electronic bulletin board service.
Members In 8 countries:
Australia, Cameroon, Canada, Netherlands, New Zealand, Norway, South Africa, UK.
Emissary Centres (4) worldwide. Members in 3 countries:
Australia, Canada, USA.
Also members in Africa (countries not specified).
IGO Relations Associated with Department of Global Communications of the United Nations. [2018.09.19/XF5247/**F**]

- ♦ **The Emissaries** Emissaries of Divine Light (#05442)
- ♦ Emissaries International / see Emissaries of Divine Light (#05442)
- ♦ **EMLA** European Medical Laser Association (#07763)
- ♦ EMLC / see European Midwives Association (#07800)
- ♦ **EML** European Muslims League (#07841)
- ♦ **EMLG** European Molecular Liquids Group (#07817)
- ♦ EMLMF – Euro-Mediterranean Legal Metrology Forum (no recent information)
- ♦ **EMLO** European Maritime Law Organization (#07742)
- ♦ **EMLTD** European and Mediterranean League Against Thrombotic Diseases (#07771)
- ♦ **EMMA** European Magazine Media Association (#07723)
- ♦ EMMA – European Manufactured Marble Association (inactive)
- ♦ **emma** European Media Management Education Association (#07758)
- ♦ EMMA – European Moulding Manufacturers Association (inactive)
- ♦ Emmanuel Community (religious order)
- ♦ Emmanuel Gemeenschap (religious order)

♦ Emmanuel International (EI) 05443

Contact 1730 Scugog St, Port Perry ON L9L 1E2, Canada. T. +19059040633.
URL: http://www.ei-international.org/

History 1975. Founded by Rev George Middleton, as an international, interdenominational and evangelical organization. Former names and other names: *Emmanuel Relief and Rehabilitation International* – former. **Aims** Encourage, strengthen and assist *Churches* worldwide to meet the *spiritual* and physical needs of the *poor* in accordance with the Holy Scriptures; promote and facilitate Church partnerships worldwide by coordinating and channelling available resources for mutual benefit and ministry effectiveness; recruit, train, support and enable personnel to participate in the above programs. **Structure** International Board; Council. **Finance** Financed through individual and church-based support, non-government agency and government funding. **Activities** Events/meetings; projects/programmes; religious activities. Active in: Brazil, Haiti, Malawi, Philippines, South Africa, Tanzania UR, Uganda. **Events** *International Board Meeting* Port Perry, ON (Canada) 2022, *Meeting* 1993.
Members National affiliates and offices in 10 countries.
Brazil, Canada, Haiti, Malawi, Philippines, South Africa, Tanzania UR, Uganda, UK, USA.
NGO Relations Member of (1): *Global Connections.* [2022.11.10/XF5047/**F**]

- ♦ Emmanuel Relief and Rehabilitation International / see Emmanuel International (#05443)
- ♦ **EMMA for Peace** Euro Mediterranean Music Academy for Peace (#05725)

♦ Emmaüs Europe 05444

Emmaus Europe – Emaús Europa

Chief Exec 47 avenue de la Résistance, 93100 Montreuil, France. T. +33141582570. E-mail: contact@emmaus-europe.org.
Events Manager address not obtained.
URL: http://emmaus-europe.org/

History 21 May 2005, Paris (France). Registration: EU Transparency Register, No/ID: 487800623288-65, Start date: 6 Sep 2016. **Aims** Strengthen and preserve Emmaus' identity in Europe so as to: fight all forms of *exclusion* and social, racial, political, economic, religious, philosophical, ethnic and other kinds of *discrimination*; work to ensure that the *rights* of the poorest members of society are recognized and used. **Structure** General Assembly; Board; Regional Executive Committee; Team. **Activities** Advocacy/lobbying/activism; training/education.
Members Groups (about 350) in 20 countries:
Albania, Belgium, Bosnia-Herzegovina, Croatia, Denmark, Finland, France, Georgia, Germany, Italy, Latvia, Netherlands, Poland, Portugal, Romania, Spain, Sweden, Switzerland, UK, Ukraine.
NGO Relations Member of (3): *European Anti-Poverty Network (EAPN, #05908)*; *Migreurop (#16802)*; *Re-Use and Recycling European Union Social Enterprises (RREUSE, #18931).* [2021/XM6858/**E**]

♦ Emmaus International 05445

Emmaüs International – Emaús Internacional

Contact 47 av de la Résistance, 93104 Montreuil CEDEX, France. T. +33141582550 – +33141582551. Fax +33148187988. E-mail: contact@emmaus-international.org.
URL: http://www.emmaus-international.org/

History First Emmaus community set up Nov 1949, Paris (France), by Abbé Pierre (1912-2007) and the first world meeting of communities held 1969, Bern (Switzerland). At this meeting the 'Universal Manifesto of the Emmaus Movement' was adopted. Statutes adopted 1971, Montréal QC (Canada). **Aims** Serve as a link between member associations and secure their mutual aid while respecting their individual autonomy; support *emergency* and long term actions to assist those who suffer most; fight against causes of human *suffering*, *poverty* and *injustice*; awake consciences to human suffering; take social action, without political, racial, philosophical or spiritual discrimination. **Structure** General Assembly (every 4 years); Administrative Committee; Executive Committee; Secretariat. Continental movements in: Africa; America; Asia; *Emmaüs Europe (#05444).* **Languages** English, French, Spanish. **Staff** 20.00 FTE, paid. **Finance** Sources: contributions; donations; members' dues; revenue from activities/projects. Annual budget: 3,500,000 EUR (2019). **Activities** Advocacy/lobbying/activism; events/meetings. Active in all member countries. **Events** *General Assembly* Piriapolis (Uruguay) 2022, *General Assembly* Jesolo (Italy) 2016, *General Assembly* Anglet (France) 2012, *General Assembly* Ouagadougou (Burkina Faso) 2003, *General Assembly* Orléans (France) 1999.
Members Local (410) and national associations of communities in 41 countries:
Albania, Angola, Argentina, Bangladesh, Belgium, Benin, Bolivia, Bosnia-Herzegovina, Brazil, Burkina Faso, Burundi, Cameroon, Chile, Colombia, Congo DR, Côte d'Ivoire, Croatia, Denmark, Finland, France, Georgia, Germany, Guatemala, India, Italy, Latvia, Lebanon, Netherlands, Peru, Poland, Portugal, Romania, South Africa, Spain, Sweden, Switzerland, Togo, UK, Ukraine, Uruguay, USA.
Consultative Status Consultative status granted from: *ECOSOC (#05331)* (Special). **IGO Relations** Accredited by (1): *United Nations Office at Vienna (UNOV, #20604).* **NGO Relations** Member of (3): *Centre de recherche et d'information pour le développement, Paris (CRID)*; *Conference of Non-Governmental Organizations in Consultative Relationship with the United Nations (CONGO, #04635)*; *Coordination SUD.* Supports (1): *Global Call for Action Against Poverty (GCAP, #10263).* [2022.10.19/XE4714/**E**]

- ♦ EMME Chiro Fed – Eastern Mediterranean and Middle East Chiropractic Federation (no recent information)
- ♦ **EMMEN** European Modern Music Education Network (#07811)
- ♦ EMM – Entente médicale méditerranéenne (no recent information)
- ♦ EMM – Episcopal Migration Ministries (internationally oriented national body)
- ♦ EMMF – Episcopal Medical Missions Foundation (internationally oriented national body)
- ♦ **EMMI** European Money Markets Institute (#07819)
- ♦ EMMP – Encuentro Mundial de Movimientos Populares (meeting series)
- ♦ EMMS International (internationally oriented national body)
- ♦ **EMNA** European Mutual-Help Network for Alcohol-Related Problems (#07843)
- ♦ **EMN** Euroacademia Multidisciplinaria Neurotraumatologica (#05628)
- ♦ **EMN** Euro-Academy of Multidisciplinary Neurotraumatology (#05628)
- ♦ **EMN** European Microfinance Network (#07792)
- ♦ **EMN** European Migration Network (#07802)
- ♦ **EMN** European Mycological Network (#07846)
- ♦ **EMN** European Myeloma Network (#07849)
- ♦ **EMNI** European Mediation Network Initiative (#07760)
- ♦ **EMO** European Mortar Industry Organization (#07822)
- ♦ EMO – European Music Office (no recent information)
- ♦ EMOGEO – International and Interdisciplinary Conference on Emotional Geographies (meeting series)
- ♦ EMORI – Euro-Mediterranean Observatory on Risks Management (internationally oriented national body)
- ♦ EMOTA – European eCommerce and Omni-Channel Trade Association (inactive)
- ♦ EMOVA – European Management Office for Veterinary Associations (internationally oriented national body)

- EMPAC – European Metal Packaging (inactive)
- **EMPA** European Maritime Pilots' Association (#07743)
- **EMPA** European/Mediterranean Planetarium Association (#07772)
- **EMPA** European Melamine Producers Association (#07775)
- EMPA – European Metalworking Plantmakers Association (inactive)
- **EMPA** European Military Press Association (#07803)
- **EMPA** European Mollusc Producers' Association (#07818)
- EMPA / see Parliamentary Assembly – Union for the Mediterranean (#18216)
- EMPASI (unconfirmed)
- EMPEA / see Global Private Capital Association (#10556)
- EMP – European Myeloma Platform (inactive)
- EMP – European Society of Mathematical Physics (inactive)
- **EMPG** European Mathematical Psychology Group (#07754)
- EMPHA – European Manufacturers Paper Honeycomb Association (unconfirmed)
- **EMPHNET** Eastern Mediterranean Public Health Network (#05245)
- EMP – International Conference on Energy, Materials and Photonics (meeting series)
- Empire Fencing Federation / see Commonwealth Fencing Federation (#04328)
- Empire Forestry Association / see Commonwealth Forestry Association (#04329)
- Empire Parliamentary Association / see Commonwealth Parliamentary Association (#04355)
- Empire Press Union / see CPU Media Trust (#04941)
- Employed community Pharmacists in Europe / see European Association of Employed community Pharmacists in Europe (#06025)

♦ Employee Assistance European Forum (EAEF) 05446

Sec address not obtained. E-mail: info@eaef.org.
URL: http://eaef.org/

History 2002. **Aims** Develop employee assistance and work-life services in Europe. **Events** *Conference* Paris (France) 2019, *Conference* Bucharest (Romania) 2016, *Annual Conference* Madrid (Spain) 2015. **IGO Relations** *European Agency for Safety and Health at Work (EU-OSHA, #05843).* **NGO Relations** *Asia Pacific Employee Assistance Roundtable (APEAR, #01891); European Network for Workplace Health Promotion (ENWHP, #08037).* [2016/XM4612/**F**]

- Employee Assistance Professionals Association / see International Employee Assistance Professionals Association (#13264)
- Employers' Organization of the Metal Trades in Europe / see Council of European Employers of the Metal, Engineering and Technology-Based Industries (#04887)
- EMPM – European Media Packaging Manufacturers (inactive)
- Empowering Widows In Development / see Widows Rights International
- Empower International Ministries (internationally oriented national body)
- Empowers Africa (internationally oriented national body)
- EmpowerWomen / see Empower Women (#05447)

♦ Empower Women 05447

Contact c/o UN Women, 405 East 42nd St, New York NY 10017, USA. E-mail: empower.women@unwomen.org.
URL: http://www.empowerwomen.org/

History Launched 23 Sep 2013, as a platform, also referred to as *Knowledge Gateway on Women's Economic Empowerment.* Also referred to as *EmpowerWomen.* Grew into a global movement. **Aims** Empower women to achieve their full economic potential by inspiring both women and men to become advocates, change makers and leaders in their community. **Structure** Team. **Activities** Advocacy/lobbying/activism. **IGO Relations** Partners include: *Equal Futures Partnership (no recent information);* Government of Canada; *ILO (#11123); International Development Research Centre (IDRC, #13162); International Trade Centre (ITC, #15703); OECD (#17693); UN Women (#20724); UNCTAD (#20285); UNDP (#20292); UNIDO (#20336); United Nations Capital Development Fund (UNCDF, #20524); The World Bank Group (#21218); World Tourism Organization (UNWTO, #21861).* **NGO Relations** Partners include: *Cherie Blair Foundation for Women; International Knowledge Network of Women in Politics (iKNOW Politics, #13989); United Nations Global Compact (#20567); Women in Informal Employment: Globalizing and Organizing (WIEGO, #21003); Women's World Banking (WWB, #21037); World Pulse.* [2018/XM6724/**F**]

- Empresa Privada y Responsabilidad Social en las Américas (internationally oriented national body)

♦ Empty Nose Syndrome International Association (ENSIA) 05448

Contact address not obtained. T. +37126024437 – +14843268780.
Facebook: https://www.facebook.com/ENSIAssociation/

History 2014. Registration: No/ID: 40008243457, Start date: 18 Oct 2015, Latvia; 501(c)(3), USA. **Aims** Provide support and information to individuals affected by Empty Nose Syndrome. **Structure** Executive Board. **Publications** *ENSIA Newsletter.* **NGO Relations** Member of (1): *EURORDIS – Rare Diseases Europe (#09175)* (as Associate member). [2018/XM7453/**C**]

- EMRA / see Serving Europe (#19248)
- EMRC – European Marketing Research Centre, Brussels (internationally oriented national body)
- EMRC International Association / see European Marketing Research Centre, Brussels
- **EMRF Foundation** European Magnetic Resonance Forum Foundation (#07724)
- **EMRI** Erasmus Course on Magnetic Resonance Imaging (#05526)
- EMR – Institut für Europäisches Medienrecht (internationally oriented national body)
- **EMRO** European Media Research Organizations (#07759)
- **EMRO** WHO Regional Office for the Eastern Mediterranean (#20944)
- **E-MRS** European Materials Research Society (#07753)
- EMSA – European Marine Step Association (inactive)
- **EMSA** European Maritime Safety Agency (#07744)
- **EMSA** European Medical Students' Association (#07764)
- **EMSA** European Mobile Seed Association (#07810)
- **EMSC** European-Mediterranean Seismological Centre (#07774)
- **EMSCI** European Multicenter Study about Spinal Cord Injury (#07827)
- **EMSCO** European Myelodysplastic Syndromes Cooperative Group (#07848)
- **EMSEA** European Marine Science Educators Association (#07740)
- **EMS** Electroacoustic Music Studies Network (#05419)
- EMS / see European Macrophage and Dendritic Cell Society (#07722)
- **EMS** European Mathematical Society (#07755)
- **EMS** European Membrane Society (#07777)
- **EMS** European Meteorological Society (#07786)
- **EMS** European Microscopy Society (#07795)
- EMSG / see European Macrophage and Dendritic Cell Society (#07722)
- **EMSL** European Microwave Signature Laboratory (#07797)
- EMSN / see Marfan Europe Network (#16573)
- EMSO ERIC / see European Multidisciplinary Seafloor and water-column Observatory (#07831)
- **EMSO** European Multidisciplinary Seafloor and water-column Observatory (#07831)
- **EMSOS** European Musculo-Skeletal Oncology Society (#07834)
- EMSP – Ecole multinationale supérieure des postes, Abidjan (no recent information)
- **EMSP** European Multiple Sclerosis Platform (#07833)
- EMSSA / see Microscopy Society of Southern Africa
- EMSU – Europäische Mittelstands-Union (no recent information)

♦ EMTA 05449

Exec Dir 405 Lexington Ave, Ste 5304, New York NY 10174, USA. T. +16466764290.
Office Manager address not obtained.
URL: http://www.emta.org/

History 1990. Former names and other names: *LDC Debt Traders Association* – former (1990 to 1992); *Emerging Markets Traders Association* – former (1992 to 2000); *EMTA – Trade Association for the Emerging Markets* – full title (2000). **Aims** As a trade group for the *emerging markets trading* and *investment* community: promote orderly development of fair, efficient and transparent trading markets for emerging markets instruments; help integrate emerging markets into global capital markets. **Structure** Board of Directors; Executive Committee. **Languages** English, Portuguese, Spanish. **Staff** 8.00 FTE, paid. **Activities** Events/meetings. **Publications** *EMTA Bulletin* (4 a year); *EMTA Quarterly CDS Volume Survey* (4 a year); *EMTA Quarterly Emerging Markets Debt Trading Volume Survey* (4 a year); *EMTA Annual CDS Volume Survey* (annual); *EMTA Annual Emerging Markets Debt Trading Volume Survey* (annual). **Members** Full – members actively trading emerging markets instruments (20); Buy-Side – members investing in emerging markets instruments (66); Associate – members actively trading emerging markets instruments, but smaller and less active than full members (32); Affiliate – members with a strong interest in the emerging markets trading industry, but do not trade or invest (31). Membership countries not specified. [2022.05.05/XF7209/y/**F**]

- **EMTA** European Metropolitan Transport Authorities (#07789)
- EMTA / see European Music Therapy Confederation (#07838)
- EMTAR / see European Association for Modern Arabic Literature (#06123)
- EMTA – Trade Association for the Emerging Markets / see EMTA (#05449)
- **EMTC** European Music Therapy Confederation (#07838)
- **EMTG** European Meniscal Transplantation Group (#07781)
- **EMTICS** European Multicentre Tics in Children Studies (#07829)
- EMTO – Euro-Mediterranean Tourism Organization (no recent information)
- EMTS / see European Musculo-Skeletal Oncology Society (#07834)
- EMUC / see Maritime Development Center
- **EMU** Europäische Musikschul-Union (#05756)
- **EMU** European Economic and Monetary Union (#06961)
- **EMU** European Metal Union (#07785)
- **EMU** European Mineralogical Union (#07807)
- **EMUNI** Euro-Mediterranean University (#05728)
- **EMVA** European Machine Vision Association (#07721)
- EMV – Europese Middenstandsvereniging (inactive)
- **EMVO** European Medicines Verification Organisation (#07768)
- **EMWA** European Medical Writers Association (#07765)
- EMW / see East meets West (#05260)
- **EMW** East meets West (#05260)
- EMW – Evangelisches Missionswerk in Deutschland (internationally oriented national body)
- **EMWIS** Euro-Mediterranean Information System on Know-how in the Water Sector (#05722)
- EMYC / see European Methodist Youth and Children's Council (#07788)
- **EMYC** European Methodist Youth and Children's Council (#07788)
- EMYO – European Meeting of Young Ophthalmologists (meeting series)
- EMZ – Europäisches Migrationszentrum (internationally oriented national body)
- **ENAAT** European Network Against the Arms Trade (#07861)
- Enabel (internationally oriented national body)
- Enabel – Belgian Development Agency / see Enabel

♦ Enabling Education Network (EENET) 05450

Mailing Address PO Box 422, Hyde, SK14 9DT, UK. T. +4403300583339. E-mail: info@eenet.org.uk – consultancy@eenet.org.uk.
URL: http://www.eenet.org.uk/

History Apr 1997. Founded following initiatives of *Save the Children UK (SC UK).* Registration: Community Interest Company, No/ID: 07023142, Start date: 2009, England. **Aims** Encourage and support innovation and critical thinking on inclusion, equity and rights in education through a global information sharing and learning network; provide high quality consultancy services. **Structure** Steering Group; Managing Director; Programme Officer. **Languages** English. **Staff** 0.00 FTE, paid; 1.00 FTE, voluntary. Team of freelance consultants based in countries around the world. **Finance** Sources: contributions; donations; fees for services; grants; international organizations. **Activities** Events/meetings; guidance/assistance/consulting; knowledge management/information dissemination; networking/liaising; research and development. **Events** *Workshop on exploring inclusive education* Bandung (Indonesia) 2011, *International special education congress* Manchester (UK) 2000, *Seminar on inclusive education* Agra (India) 1998. **Publications** *Enabling Education Review* (annual) in Arabic, English, French, Portuguese, Spanish – newsletter; main edition in English, selected editions in other languages mentioned above, Braille and audiotape. For other publications, see: https://www.eenet.org.uk/eenets-resources/. **Information Services** *Documents and video library* – Online library with over 800 items on a wide range of topics relating to inclusive education.
Members Individuals and organizations in 150 countries and territories:
Afghanistan, Albania, Angola, Argentina, Armenia, Australia, Austria, Bahamas, Bahrain, Bangladesh, Barbados, Belarus, Belgium, Belize, Benin, Botswana, Brazil, Bulgaria, Burkina Faso, Burundi, Cambodia, Cameroon, Canada, Cape Verde, Cayman Is, Chile, China, Colombia, Congo Brazzaville, Congo DR, Costa Rica, Côte d'Ivoire, Croatia, Cuba, Cyprus, Czechia, Denmark, Djibouti, Ecuador, Egypt, El Salvador, Eritrea, Eswatini, Ethiopia, Fiji, Finland, France, Gambia, Georgia, Germany, Ghana, Greece, Grenada, Guatemala, Guinea, Guinea-Bissau, Guyana, Haiti, Honduras, Hungary, Iceland, India, Indonesia, Iran Islamic Rep, Iraq, Ireland, Israel, Italy, Jamaica, Japan, Jordan, Kenya, Korea Rep, Kuwait, Kyrgyzstan, Laos, Lebanon, Lesotho, Liberia, Luxembourg, Madagascar, Malawi, Malaysia, Maldives, Mali, Malta, Mauritania, Mauritius, Mexico, Moldova, Mongolia, Morocco, Mozambique, Myanmar, Namibia, Nepal, Netherlands, Nicaragua, Nigeria, North Macedonia, Norway, Oman, Pakistan, Palestine, Panama, Papua New Guinea, Paraguay, Peru, Philippines, Poland, Portugal, Qatar, Romania, Russia, Rwanda, Samoa, Saudi Arabia, Senegal, Serbia, Sierra Leone, Singapore, Somalia, South Africa, Spain, Sri Lanka, St Lucia, Sudan, Suriname, Sweden, Switzerland, Syrian AR, Tajikistan, Tanzania UR, Thailand, Tunisia, Uganda, UK, Ukraine, United Arab Emirates, Uruguay, USA, Uzbekistan, Vanuatu, Venezuela, Vietnam, Virgin Is UK, Yemen, Zambia, Zimbabwe.
[2020.11.11/XF4261/**F**]

- EnablingOpenScholarship (unconfirmed)
- **eNACSO** European NGO Alliance for Child Safety Online (#08049)

♦ Enactus 05451

Main Office 444 S Campbell Ave, Springfield MO 65806, USA. E-mail: contact@enactus.org.
URL: http://enactus.org/

History 1975, USA. Former names and other names: *Students in Free Enterprise (SIFE)* – former (1975 to 2012). **Aims** Bring together top *leaders* of today and tomorrow to create a better, more *sustainable* world through the positive power of *business.* **Structure** Board of Directors. International Advisory Council of Board Chairs. **Finance** Corporate, organizational and individual support. Global revenue (annual): US$ 21,300,000. **Events** *Booster Enactus Seminar* Paris (France) 2016. **Publications** Annual Report. Fact sheets; brochures.
Members Universities (around 1,600) in 39 countries:
Australia, Azerbaijan, Brazil, Canada, China, Egypt, Eswatini, France, Germany, Ghana, Guatemala, India, Ireland, Japan, Kazakhstan, Kenya, Korea Rep, Kyrgyzstan, Malaysia, Mexico, Morocco, Netherlands, New Zealand, Nigeria, Philippines, Poland, Puerto Rico, Russia, Senegal, Singapore, South Africa, Tajikistan, Thailand, Tunisia, UK, Ukraine, USA, Vietnam, Zimbabwe. [2022/XJ5903/**F**]

- ENA – EcoNews Africa (internationally oriented national body)
- **ENAEE** European Network for Accreditation of Engineering Education (#07859)
- ENA – Engage Now Africa (internationally oriented national body)
- **ENA** Europeana Network Association (#05899)
- ENA / see European Industrial Nitrocellulose Association (#07528)
- ENA – European NanoBusiness Association (no recent information)
- ENA – European Narcolepsy Association (no recent information)
- ENA – European Needlemakers' Association (inactive)
- ENA – European Neuroscience Association (inactive)
- ENA – European Nightlife Association (unconfirmed)

♦ **ENA** European NORM Association (#08056)
♦ **ENA** European Nurserystock Association (#08062)
♦ **ENA** European Nutraceutical Association (#08067)
♦ **ENAI** European Network for Academic Integrity (#07856)
♦ **ENAJ** European Network of Agricultural Journalists (#07864)
♦ **ENAME** Eastern Mediterranean Association of Medical Editors (#05241)
♦ ENAR – Election Network Society in the Arab Region (unconfirmed)
♦ **ENAR** European Network against Racism (#07862)
♦ **ENAS** European Network of Academic Sports Services (#07857)
♦ **ENASP** European Network of Agricultural Social Protection Systems (#07865)
♦ ENASTE / see International Network for Academic Steiner Teacher Education (#14226)
♦ **ENAT** European Network for Accessible Tourism (#07858)
♦ **ENATW** European Network Against Trafficking in Women for Sexual Exploitation (#07863)
♦ **ENBCS** European Network of Buddhist Christian Studies (#07869)
♦ **ENBF** European Noise Barrier Federation (#08052)
♦ **ENBIS** European Network for Business and Industrial Statistics (#07871)
♦ **ENBR** European Network for Better Regulation (#07868)
♦ **ENBRI** European Network of Building Research Institutes (#07870)
♦ ENCA / see European Natural Sausage Casings Association (#07854)
♦ **ENCA** European Network of Childbirth Associations (#07876)
♦ **ENCA** European Network of Heads of Nature Conservation Agencies (#07917)
♦ enCAFE – European Network for Comparative Analysis on Food and Eating (unconfirmed)
♦ **ENCALS** European Network for the Cure of ALS (#07889)

♦ ENCATC 05452

SG Ave Maurice 1, 1050 Brussels, Belgium. T. +3222012912. E-mail: info@encatc.org.
Pres Univ of Salento, Dept Management and Economics, Via per Monteroni, 73100 Lecce BT, Italy.
URL: http://www.encatc.org/

History Dec 1992, Warsaw (Poland). Current statutes adopted Nov 2020. Former names and other names: *European Network of Cultural Administration Training Centres (ENCATC)* – former; *Réseau européen des centres de formation d'administrateurs culturels* – former; *ENCATC – the European network on cultural management and policy* – full title. Registration: Banque-Carrefour des Entreprises, No/ID: 0464.174.494, Start date: 1 Oct 1998; EU Transparency Register, No/ID: 357467010010-25, Start date: 8 Nov 2012. **Aims** As the European network on cultural management and policy, stimulate *education* in Europe and beyond, engaging and responding to new developments in politics, economics, societies and technology. **Structure** General Assembly (annual); Board; Secretary General. **Languages** English, French. **Staff** 3.00 FTE, paid. **Finance** Sources: members' dues. Project funding through various sources, including: *European Cultural Foundation (ECF, #06868)*; UNESCO. Supported by: *European Union (EU, #08967)*. **Activities** Awards/prizes/competitions; events/meetings; networking/liaising; publishing activities; research and development; training/education. **Events** *ENCATC Congress* Brussels (Belgium) / Antwerp (Belgium) 2022, *ENCATC Congress* Brussels (Belgium) 2021, *Annual Conference* Brussels (Belgium) 2020, *Annual Conference* Dijon (France) 2019, *Annual Conference* Bucharest (Romania) 2018. **Publications** *ENCATC Digest Newsletter*; *ENCATC Newsletter*; *encatcSCHOLAR* – e-bulletin; *European Journal of Cultural Management and Policy*. *ENCATC Book Series on Cultural Management and Cultural Policy Education*. *The Story of ENCATC: 25 Years of Cultural Management and Policy in Europe*. Ad-hoc articles; reports; policy papers. **Information Services** *Members' Handbook* – database. **Members** Full; Associate; Supporting; Individual; Honorary. Members (over 130) in over 39 countries and territories. Membership countries not specified. **Consultative Status** Consultative status granted from: *UNESCO (#20322)* (Associate Status). [2021.09.03/XF3372/y/**F**]

♦ ENCATC – the European network on cultural management and policy / see ENCATC (#05452)
♦ ENCATE – European Network for Countering Antisemitism through Education (unconfirmed)
♦ **ENCC** European Network of Cultural Centres (#07888)
♦ **ENCePP** European Network of Centres for Pharmacoepidemiology and Pharmacovigilance (#07875)
♦ **ENCES** European Network for Copyright in support of Education and Science (#07885)
♦ **ENC** European Neighbourhood Council (#07855)
♦ **enc** European Network of Communities (#07881)
♦ **ENC** European Neuropeptide Club (#08044)
♦ ENC – European Nitrogen Cycle Meeting (meeting series)
♦ **ENC** European Nursing Council (#08063)
♦ **ENCFC** European Network Child Friendly Cities (#07877)
♦ **ENCG** European Network of Crystal Growth (#07887)
♦ **ENCI** European Network for Cancer Immunotherapy (#07872)
♦ **ENCJ** European Network of Councils for the Judiciary (#07886)
♦ ENCLS / see European Society of Comparative Literature (#08561)
♦ **ENCOD** European Coalition for Just and Effective Drug Policies (#06596)
♦ Encompass World Partners (internationally oriented national body)
♦ **ENCORD** European Network of Construction Companies for Research and Development (#07884)
♦ **ENCORE** Environmental Conference of the Regions of Europe (#05500)
♦ **ENCoRE** European Network for Conservation/Restoration Education (#07883)
♦ Encounter of Worldviews (internationally oriented national body)
♦ Encourage International (internationally oriented national body)
♦ ENCP / see European Community Psychology Association (#06682)
♦ **EN.CPS** European Network for Civil Peace Services (#07880)
♦ **ENCR** European Network of Cancer Registries (#07873)
♦ **ENCS** European Network for Cyber Security (#07890)
♦ Encuentro Europeo de Farmacia (meeting series)
♦ Encuentro Indígena de las Américas (unconfirmed)
♦ Encuentro Latinoamericano de Informatica e Industrias de Información (meeting series)
♦ Encuentro Mundial de Movimientos Populares (meeting series)
♦ Encuesta Mundial de Fecundidad (inactive)
♦ ENCWP / see European Association of Creative Writing Programmes (#05996)

♦ Encyclopedia of Life (EOL) 05453

Secretariat Smithsonian Institution, PO Box 37012, MRC 106, Washington DC 20013-7012, USA.
URL: http://eol.org/

History 2007, as a project. New governance model ratified, 6 Jan 2011, with new structure fully operational since Jul 2012. **Aims** Increase awareness and understanding of living *nature* through an Encyclopedia of Life that gathers, generates, and shares knowledge in an open, freely accessible and trusted digital resource. **Structure** Council. Executive Committee headed by Executive Chair. Secretariat, headed by Director of Operations. Working Groups (4): Content; Biodiversity Informatics; Scanning and Digitization; Learning and Education. **Finance** Supported by: *MacArthur Foundation*; Alfred P Sloan Foundation; several institutions. **IGO Relations** Participates in: *Global Biodiversity Information Facility (GBIF, #10250)*. [2013/XJ7095/**E**]

♦ **enda** Environnement et développement du Tiers-monde (#05510)

♦ ENDA Europe (EE) 05454

Address not obtained.
URL: http://www.enda-europe.org/

History Founded 1977, as *Enda Tiers Monde – Délégation en Europe*, a network of *Environnement et développement du Tiers-monde (enda, #05510)*. Registered in accordance with French law of 1901. **Aims** Support the fight against *poverty* and the promotion of *sustainable development* in Europe. **NGO Relations** Member of: *Coordination SUD*. [2015/XJ1852/**D**]

♦ **ENDA** European Nurse Directors Association (#08060)
♦ enda-ia – enda inter-arabe (internationally oriented national body)
♦ enda inter-arabe (internationally oriented national body)

♦ Endangered Species International (ESI) 05455

Headquarters 2112 Hayes St, San Francisco CA 94117, USA. E-mail: info@endangeredspeciesinternational.org.
URL: http://www.endangeredspeciesinternational.org/

History 2006. **Aims** Reverse the trend of human-induced species extinction, saving endangered animals and preserving wild places. **Structure** Headquarters in San Francisco CA (USA); Offices in: France; Switzerland; Congo Brazzaville; Philippines. **Languages** English, French, Spanish. **Staff** 60.00 FTE, paid; 150.00 FTE, voluntary. **Finance** Donations and grants. Budget (annual): US$ 400,000-700,000. **Activities** Advocacy/lobbying/activism; projects/programmes; awareness raising. **Publications** Irregular. **IGO Relations** *United Nations (UN, #20515)*. **NGO Relations** Partner of: *1% for the Planet*. [2015.08.29/XJ9181/**F**]

♦ Endangered Wildlife Trust (internationally oriented national body)
♦ ENDA-Third World / see Environnement et développement du Tiers-monde (#05510)
♦ ENDA-Tiers monde / see Environnement et développement du Tiers-monde (#05510)
♦ Enda Tiers Monde – Délégation en Europe / see ENDA Europe (#05454)
♦ enda TM / see Environnement et développement du Tiers-monde (#05510)
♦ ENDCAP (unconfirmed)
♦ End Child Prostitution in Asian Tourism / see End Child Prostitution, Child Pornography and Trafficking of Children for Sexual Purposes (#05456)

♦ End Child Prostitution, Child Pornography and Trafficking of Children for Sexual Purposes (ECPAT) 05456

ECPAT International 328/1 Phaya Thai Road, Ratchathewi, Bangkok, 10400, Thailand. T. +6622153388. Fax +6622158272. E-mail: info@ecpat.net.
URL: http://www.ecpat.org

History 10 Aug 1990, Bangkok (Thailand). Founded as a campaign to combat child prostitution in Asian tourism following a consultation on child prostitution, May 1990, Chiang Mai (Thailand). Became an international NGO, 1996, when full name was adopted to better reflect the organization's geographic expansion and broader mandate. Former names and other names: *End Child Prostitution in Asian Tourism* – former; *ECPAT International* – alias. **Aims** End sexual exploitation of children. **Structure** International Assembly (meets every 3 years); International Board of Trustees; International Secretariat in Bangkok (Thailand). **Languages** English, French, Spanish. **Staff** 26.00 FTE, paid. **Finance** Contributions from governments of Ireland, Netherlands and Sweden. Private donations and contributions from agencies, including the following organizations listed in this Yearbook: *Defence for Children International (DCI, #05025)*; Netherlands International; *Oak Foundation*; *Swedish International Development Cooperation Agency (Sida)*; *Terre des hommes Foundation (Tdh Foundation, #20132)*, Netherlands; *UNICEF (#20332)*. **Activities** Awareness raising; advocacy/lobbying/activism; training/education; events/meetings. **Events** *International Assembly* Paris (France) 2011, *World Congress* Rio de Janeiro (Brazil) 2008, *International Assembly* Bangkok (Thailand) 2005, *International Assembly* Bangkok (Thailand) 2002, *World congress on commercial and other forms of sexual exploitation of children* Yokohama (Japan) 2001. **Publications** Annual Report; country overviews; regional overviews; journals; thematic research reports; training resources and toolkits; brochures.
Members Organizations (113) in 99 countries and territories:
Albania, Argentina, Armenia, Australia, Austria, Azerbaijan, Bangladesh, Belarus, Belgium, Benin, Bhutan, Bolivia, Bosnia-Herzegovina, Botswana, Brazil, Bulgaria, Burkina Faso, Burundi, Cambodia, Cameroon, Canada, Chile, Colombia, Costa Rica, Côte d'Ivoire, Czechia, Dominican Rep, Ecuador, Estonia, Ethiopia, Finland, France, Gambia, Georgia, Germany, Ghana, Greece, Guatemala, Guinea, India, Indonesia, Iraq, Italy, Japan, Jordan, Kazakhstan, Kenya, Korea Rep, Kyrgyzstan, Lebanon, Liberia, Luxembourg, Malawi, Malaysia, Mauritius, Mexico, Moldova, Mongolia, Morocco, Mozambique, Nepal, Netherlands, New Zealand, Nicaragua, Niger, Nigeria, North Macedonia, Norway, Pakistan, Palestine, Paraguay, Peru, Philippines, Poland, Romania, Russia, Rwanda, Samoa, Serbia, Sierra Leone, South Africa, Spain, Sri Lanka, Sweden, Switzerland, Taiwan, Tanzania UR, Thailand, Togo, Türkiye, Uganda, UK, Ukraine, Uruguay, USA, Uzbekistan, Vietnam, Zambia, Zimbabwe.
Consultative Status Consultative status granted from: *ECOSOC (#05331)* (Special). **IGO Relations** Associated with Department of Global Communications of the United Nations. **NGO Relations** Member of (10): *Child Rights Connect (#03884)*; *Consortium for Street Children (CSC)* (as Observer Member of); *End Corporal Punishment (#05457)*; *European Financial Coalition against Commercial Sexual Exploitation of Children Online (EFC, #07249)*; *Global Partnership to End Violence Against Children (End Violence Against Children, #10533)*; *International Coalition for the Optional Protocol to the Convention on the Rights of the Child on a Communications Procedure (Ratify OP3CRC, #12617)*; *International Corporate Accountability Roundtable (ICAR, #12968)*; *Movimiento Mundial por la Infancia de Latinoamérica y El Caribe (MMI-LAC, #16873)*; *Religious in Europe Networking Against Trafficking and Exploitation (RENATE, #18833)*; *WePROTECT Global Alliance (#20860)* (as Board Member of). Partner of (1): *Adventure Travel Trade Association (ATTA, #00135)*. [2019.12.13/XF2222/**F**]

♦ End Corporal Punishment 05457

Contact The Foundry, 17 Oval Way, London, SE11 5RR, UK. E-mail: secretariat@end-violence.org.
URL: https://endcorporalpunishment.org/

History Apr 2001, Geneva (Switzerland). Former names and other names: *Global Initiative to End All Corporal Punishment of Children* – former. Registration: Charity Commission, England and Wales. **Aims** End legalized violence against children through universal prohibition and elimination of all corporal punishment. **Staff** 6.00 FTE, paid. **Activities** Advocacy/lobbying/activism; monitoring/evaluation; research/documentation. **Publications** *Global Initiative Newsletter*. Reports; leaflets; briefings; technical publications.
Members Supporters individuals; international and national organizations. International organizations include 41 organizations listed in this Yearbook:
- *ActionAid (#00087)*;
- *Africa Network Campaign on Education for All (ANCEFA, #00302)*;
- *Association for the Prevention of Torture (APT, #02869)*;
- *Child Helpline International (CHI, #03870)*;
- *Child Rights Connect (#03884)*;
- *Consortium for Street Children (CSC)*;
- *Defence for Children International (DCI, #05025)*;
- *Disability Council International (DisabCouncil, #05093)*;
- *Disabled Peoples' International (DPI, #05097)*;
- *EDU (#05363)*;
- *End Child Prostitution, Child Pornography and Trafficking of Children for Sexual Purposes (ECPAT, #05456)*;
- *EveryChild*;
- *Harm Reduction International (HRI, #10861)*;
- *HealthRight International*;
- *Human Rights Watch (HRW, #10990)*;
- *Inclusion International (#11145)*;
- *Inter-American Children's Institute (IACI, #11406)*;
- *International Association for Adolescent Health (IAAH, #11683)*;
- *International Disability Alliance (IDA, #13176)*;
- *International Federation for Parent Education (IFPE, #13499)*;
- *International Federation of Medical Students' Associations (IFMSA, #13478)*;
- *International Federation of Social Workers (IFSW, #13544)*;
- *International Foster Care Organization (IFCO, #13663)*;
- *International Pediatric Association (IPA, #14541)*;
- *International Prepaid Communications Association (IPCA, no recent information)*;
- *International Society for Social Pediatrics and Child Health (ISSOP, #15448)*;
- *International Women's Rights Action Watch Asia Pacific (IWRAW Asia Pacific, #15902)*;
- *Pan-American Federation for Information Technology in Agriculture (PanAFITA, #18102)*;
- *Plan International (#18386)*;
- *Rights International (RI)*;
- *Right to Education Initiative (RTE, #18942)*;
- *RI Global (#18948)*;
- *Save the Children International (#19058)*;
- *Sightsavers International (#19270)*;
- *SOS-Kinderdorf International (#19693)*;
- *Terre des Hommes International Federation (TDHIF, #20133)*;
- *WAVE Trust – Worldwide Alternatives to Violence*;
- *World Congress on Family Law and the Rights of Children and Youth (WCFLCR)*;
- *World Network of Users and Survivors of Psychiatry (WNUSP, #21672)*;
- *World Organisation Against Torture (OMCT, #21685)*.

IGO Relations Participant in Fundamental Rights Platform of: *European Union Agency for Fundamental Rights (FRA, #08969).* **NGO Relations** Member of (5): *Child Rights Connect (#03884); Global Partnership to End Violence Against Children (End Violence Against Children, #10533)* (CSO Forum); *International Coalition for the Optional Protocol to the Convention on the Rights of the Child on a Communications Procedure (Ratify OP3CRC, #12617)*; International NGO Council on Violence Against Children; NGO Panel for the Global Study on Children Deprived of Liberty. Cooperates with (1): *Global Partnership on Children with Disabilities (GPcwd, #10529).* [2020/XJ3476/y/**E**]

♦ Endeavor Global (internationally oriented national body)
♦ **END** Equipes Notre-Dame (#20112)
♦ END – European Nuclear Disarmament (inactive)
♦ End Female Genital Mutilation European Network / see End FGM European Network (#05458)

♦ End FGM European Network 05458

Dir Mundo B, Rue d'Edimbourg 26, 1050 Brussels, Belgium. T. +3228930907. E-mail: info@endfgm.eu.
Communications Officer address not obtained.
URL: http://www.endfgm.eu/

History 2014. Founded, continuing the work of the *End FGM European Campaign*, under the leadership of *Amnesty International (AI, #00801).* Former names and other names: *End Female Genital Mutilation European Network* – full title. Registration: EU Transparency Network, No/ID: 488509127575-64. **Aims** Ensure sustainable European action to end *female genital mutilation* (FGM). **Structure** Board. **Languages** English. **Staff** 5.00 FTE, paid. **Finance** Supported by: *European Commission (EC, #06633)* (Rights, Equality and Citizenship Programme); *Sigrid Rausing Trust*; *Wallace Global Fund.* **Activities** Advocacy/lobbying/activism; events/meetings; knowledge management/information dissemination; politics/policy/regulatory. **Events** *Network General Assembly* Brussels (Belgium) 2022. **Publications** Strategic Plan; training material; booklets; guides; guidelines; directives.
Members Full; Associate. Organizations in 11 EU countries:
Belgium, Cyprus, Finland, France, Germany, Ireland, Italy, Netherlands, Portugal, Spain, UK.
Included in the above, 5 organizations listed in this Yearbook:
Equilibres and Populations (Equipop); Foundation for Women's Health Research and Development (FORWARD); Italian Association for Women in Development ONLUS (AIDOS); Mediterranean Institute of Gender Studies (MIGS); TERRE DES FEMMES (#20131).
Associate organizations in 11 countries:
Belgium, France, Germany, Greece, Ireland, Malta, Netherlands, Spain, Sweden, Switzerland, UK.
NGO Relations Partner of: *ActionAid (#00087)* – Sweden; *Association for Emergency Aid and Solidarity Development Cooperation (WADI); Equilibres and Populations (Equipop); Finnish League for Human Rights; Foundation for Women's Health Research and Development (FORWARD); International Action Against Female Circumcision (INTACT); International Centre for Reproductive Health (ICRH); Italian Association for Women in Development ONLUS (AIDOS); Médecins du Monde – International (MDM, #16613); Mediterranean Institute of Gender Studies (MIGS);* national organizations; *Orchid Project; Save a Girl – Save a Generation; TERRE DES FEMMES (#20131); Wassu-UAB Foundation; We Will Speak Out (WWSO).* [2022.02.09/XM5255/y/**F**]

♦ The END Fund 05459

CEO 2 Park Avenue, 18th Floor, New York NY 10016, USA. T. +16466909775. E-mail: info@end.org.
URL: https://end.org/

History Registration: 501(c)(3) charitable organization, No/ID: EIN 27-3941186, USA; Companies Housse, No/ID: 06350698, Start date: 22 Aug 2007, England and Wales; Charity Commission, No/ID: 1122574, England and Wales. **Aims** Ensure people at risk of neglected tropical diseases can live healthy and prosperous lives. **Structure** International Board. **Activities** Advocacy/lobbying/activism; healthcare. **NGO Relations** Member of (1): *Humentum (#10993).* [2022/AA2837/f/**F**]

♦ End Human Trafficking Now (internationally oriented national body)

♦ Ending Clergy Abuse (ECA) 05460

Contact 5017 37TH Avenue SW, Seattle WA 98126, USA. T. +12064120165. E-mail: contactus@ecaglobal.org.
URL: https://www.ecaglobal.org/

History Jun 2018, Geneva (Switzerland). Proposed Aug 2017, by Barbara Blaine. Former names and other names: *The Accountability Project (TAP)* – former (2017 to 2018). **Aims** Compel the Roman Catholic Church to end clergy abuse, especially child sexual abuse, so as to protect children and to seek justice for victims. **Structure** Board of Directors. **Activities** Advocacy/lobbying/activism; events/meetings. **Publications** *ECA Global Newsletter* (12 a year).
Members Full in 10 countries:
Chile, France, Germany, Italy, Jamaica, Peru, Poland, Switzerland, UK, USA. [2021/AA2090/**F**]

♦ Ending Clerical Abuse / see Ending Clerical Abuse (#05461)

♦ Ending Clerical Abuse (ECA) 05461

USA 5017 37th Avenue SW, Seattle WA 98126, USA. T. +12064120165. E-mail: contactus@ecaglobal.org.
URL: http://www.ecaglobal.org/

History Started Aug 2017. Full title: *Ending Clerical Abuse (ECA) – Global Justice Project.* Registered as a US 503c3 non-profit corporation. **Aims** Compel the Roman *Catholic* Church to end clerical abuse, especially child *sexual* abuse, so as to protect children and seek justice for victims. **Structure** Team. **Activities** Advocacy/lobbying/activism; knowledge management/information dissemination; guidance/assistance/consulting; networking/liaising; events/meetings. **Publications** *ECA Global Newsletter* (12 a year).
Members Individuals in 10 countries:
Chile, Ecuador, France, Germany, Jamaica, Mexico, Poland, Spain, UK, USA.
IGO Relations *United Nations Convention on the Rights of the Child (CRC, 1989).* [2019/XM6723/**F**]

♦ Ending Violence Against Migrants (internationally oriented national body)
♦ ENDL – European Network on Digital Labour (unconfirmed)
♦ End-of-Life Research Group (internationally oriented national body)
♦ Endomesogiaki Epitropi (#11521)
♦ Endoscopica International (inactive)

♦ Endoscopic and Laparoscopic Surgeons of Asia (ELSA) 05462

Secretariat Nat Univ Hosp, 5 Lower Kent Ridge Road, Advanced Surgery Training Ctr, Level 2, Kent Ridge Wing 2, Singapore 110974, Singapore. T. +6567722897. Fax +6567746077.
URL: http://www.elsa-soc.org/

History Nov 1990. Officially registered in Singapore (Singapore), Jun 1991. **Aims** Promote clinical practice, teaching and research activities dealing with endoscopic surgery or minimally invasive surgery. **Structure** Executive Committee; oard of Governors; Secretariat. **Languages** English. **Finance** Members' dues. Profits from workshops and congresses. **Activities** Annual Asian or Asian Pacific scientific meetings; regional workshops, courses and symposia. **Events** *Asia Pacific Congress* Hong Kong (Hong Kong) 2021, *Annual Congress* Singapore (Singapore) 2020, *Asia Pacific Congress* Chiang Mai (Thailand) 2019, *Annual Congress* Kuala Lumpur (Malaysia) 2018, *Asia Pacific Congress* Cebu City (Philippines) 2017. **Publications** *Asian Journal of Endoscopic Surgery.*
Members Individuals in 35 countries and territories:
Argentina, Australia, Bahrain, Bangladesh, Brazil, Brunei Darussalam, China, Germany, Hong Kong, India, Indonesia, Israel, Italy, Japan, Korea Rep, Macau, Malaysia, Mongolia, Myanmar, Nepal, New Zealand, Pakistan, Peru, Philippines, Russia, Saudi Arabia, Singapore, Sri Lanka, Taiwan, Thailand, Türkiye, UK, United Arab Emirates, USA, Vietnam.
NGO Relations Member of: *International Federation of Societies of Endoscopic Surgeons (IFSES, #13546).* [2015/XD3540/v/**D**]

♦ Endo-Urological Society / see Endourology Society (#05463)
♦ Endo-Urology Society / see Endourology Society (#05463)

♦ Endourology Society 05463

Exec Sec 4100 Duff Place, Lower Level, Seaford NY 11783, USA. E-mail: admin@endourology.org.
URL: http://www.endourology.org/

History 1 May 1984, Germany FR. Officially instituted following initial meeting held 1983, London UK). Former names and other names: *Endo-Urology Society* – alias; *Endo-Urological Society* – alias; *International Endo-Urological Society* – alias. Registration: Start date: 18 Apr 1985, USA. **Aims** Facilitate scientific dialogue among endo-urologists worldwide. **Structure** Board of Directors; Executive Committee. Committees. **Activities** Awards/prizes/competitions; events/meetings; research/documentation; training/education. **Events** *World Congress of Endourology and Uro-Technology* San Diego, CA (USA) 2022, *World Congress of Endourology and Uro-Technology* Seoul (Korea Rep) 2022, *World Congress of Endourology and Uro-Technology* Hamburg (Germany) 2021, *World Congress of Endourology and Uro-Technology* Hamburg (Germany) 2020, *World Congress of Endourology* Abu Dhabi (United Arab Emirates) 2019. **Publications** *Journal of Endourology* (10 a year); *Journal of Endourology Case Reports*; *Journal of VideoUrology.* [2021/XD8379/**D**]

♦ **ENDOV** European Network on Volunteer Development (#08032)
♦ End Poverty 2015 / see UN Millennium Campaign (#20709)
♦ ENDS / see Both ENDS (#03307)
♦ **End Violence Against Children** Global Partnership to End Violence Against Children (#10533)

♦ End Water Poverty (EWP) 05464

Global Coordinator c/o WaterAid, 47-49 Durham Street, London, SE11 5JD, UK. T. +442077934960. E-mail: info@endwaterpoverty.org.
URL: https://endwaterpoverty.org/

History 2007. **Aims** Campaign and advocate to decision makers, the media and other development organizations to take action to end the water and sanitation crisis. **Structure** Steering Committee; International Secretariat. Task Teams; Forums.
Members Charities; non-profits; NGOs; networks; trade unions; interest groups. Members (185) in 35 countries:
Bangladesh, Benin, Cameroon, Canada, Central African Rep, Congo DR, Ethiopia, Finland, France, Germany, Ghana, India, Ireland, Kenya, Liberia, Malawi, Malta, Morocco, Nepal, Netherlands, Niger, Nigeria, Pakistan, Philippines, Rwanda, South Africa, Spain, Sri Lanka, Sudan, Switzerland, Togo, Uganda, UK, USA, Zimbabwe.
Included in the above, 37 organizations listed in this Yearbook:
- *Action Against Hunger (#00086);*
- *African Rural Development Movement (ARUDMO, #00447);*
- *Biodiversity Conservancy International;*
- *Canadian Physicians for Aid and Relief (CPAR);*
- *CARE International (CI, #03429);*
- *Catholic Agency for Overseas Development (CAFOD);*
- *Centro UNESCO del Pais Vasco (UNESCO Etxea);*
- *Christian Engineers in Development (CED);*
- *Community Based Impact Assessment Network for Eastern Africa (CIANEA, #04390);*
- *Free World Foundation (FWF);*
- *fresh20;*
- *Fundación Ecologia y Desarrollo (ECODES);*
- *Gender and Water Alliance (GWA, #10102);*
- *Green Ark Committee (GRC, #10712);*
- *Green Cross International (GCI, #10715);*
- *HELVETAS Swiss Intercooperation;*
- *Hope International Development Agency;*
- *Humanitarian and Charitable ONE Trust (HACOT);*
- *Human Rights and Justice Group International (Justice Group);*
- *Improve International;*
- *IRC (#16016);*
- *Oxfam International (#17922);*
- *PATH (#18260);*
- *Plan International (#18386);*
- *Samaritan's Purse (#19047);*
- *Save the Children UK (SC UK);*
- *Sightsavers International (#19270);*
- *SIMAVI;*
- *Tearfund, UK;*
- *Water 1st International;*
- *WaterAid (#20822);*
- *WaterCan;*
- *Water for People (WFP);*
- *Wherever the Need (WTN);*
- *World Federation of Khoja Shia Ithna-Asheri Muslim Communities (World Federation of KSIMC, #21449);*
- *World Toilet Organization (WTO, #21854);*
- *World Wide Fund for Nature (WWF, #21922).*

NGO Relations *Sanitation and Water for All (SWA, #19051).* [2023/XJ5803/y/**F**]

♦ **ENDYL** European Network of Democratic Young Left (#07892)
♦ **ENEA** European Neuroendocrine Association (#08040)
♦ ENE – Conference on the Early Neolithic of Europe (meeting series)
♦ **ENEF** European Network on the Economics of the Firm (#07896)
♦ ENEITA – European Nursing Education Information Technology Association (inactive)
♦ **ENEMO** European Network of Election Monitoring Organizations (#07900)
♦ **ENEN** European Nuclear Education Network (#08057)
♦ ENEP – European Network of Environmental Professionals (inactive)
♦ **ENEPRI** European Network of Economic Policy Research Institutes (#07894)
♦ **ENERCA** European Network for Rare and Congenital Anaemias (#07982)
♦ **ENeRG** European Network for Research in Geo-Energy (#07989)
♦ **ENERGIA** International Network on Gender and Sustainable Energy (#14272)
♦ Energie-Cités / see Energy Cities (#05467)
♦ Energistics Consortium (inactive)
♦ Energistics – Energistics Consortium (inactive)

♦ Energy 4 Impact 05465

CEO 5th Floor, Totara Park House, 34-36 Grays Inn Road, London, WC1X 8HR, UK. T. +442072428602. Fax +442072428602. E-mail: info@energy4impact.org.
URL: https://energy4impact.org/

History 31 Aug 2002, Johannesburg (South Africa). Founded during World Summit on Sustainable Development, organized by *United Nations Commission on Sustainable Development (CSD, inactive).* Former names and other names: *Global Village Energy Partnership (GVEP International)* – former (2002). Registration: Charity Commission, No/ID: 1119168, Start date: 2007, England and Wales. **Aims** Increase access to modern *energy* services to reduce poverty in the world's developing countries. **Structure** Trustee Board. Management Team. Regional Hubs/Offices. **Languages** English, French, Spanish. **Staff** 50.00 FTE, paid. **Finance** Supported by: government of Russia, and by the following organizations: Barclays Bank; *Department for International Development (DFID, inactive); European Union (EU, #08967); International Bank for Reconstruction and Development (IBRD, #12317);* UK Aid Network. **Activities** Projects/programmes. **Events** *Conference* Santa Cruz (Bolivia) 2003. **Publications** *Energy 4 Impact Newsletter.* Annual Review; guides; studies; reports.
Members Not a membership organization. **NGO Relations** Partners include: *Aga Khan Foundation (AKF, #00545); Practical Action (#18475); Renewable Energy and Energy Efficiency Partnership (REEEP, #18837); UNLEASH.* Member of: *Aspen Network of Development Entrepreneurs (ANDE, #02310).* Supports: *SEED (#19213); Sustainable Energy for All (SEforALL, #20056).* [2017/XJ3084/**F**]

♦ Energy Academy Europe (internationally oriented national body)

♦ Energy Charter Conference 05466

SG Bd de la Woluwe 46, 1200 Brussels, Belgium. T. +3227759819. Fax +3227759801. E-mail: secgen@encharter.org – info@encharter.org.
Sec address not obtained.
URL: https://www.energycharter.org/

History Established under the provisions of *Energy Charter Treaty (ECT, 1994)* and the *'Energy Charter Protocol on Energy Efficiency and Related Environmental Aspects'*, signed Dec 1994, Lisbon (Portugal), and entered into force Apr 1998. The Treaty was signed or acceded to by 55 states and the European Union. Roots date back to a political initiative launched in the early 1990s, at a time when the end of the Cold War offered an unprecedented opportunity to overcome economic divisions, and there was a recognized need to ensure that a commonly accepted foundation was established by developing energy cooperation among the states of the Eurasian continent. The Treaty's common "rules of the game" for the energy sector are designed to encourage investment and trade, to ensure reliable transit, to promote energy efficiency use, and to provide neutral mechanisms for the resolution of disputes. The Energy Charter Treaty was developed on the basis of the Energy Charter Declaration of 1991. Whereas the later document was drawn up as a declaration of political intent to promote energy cooperation, the Energy Charter Treaty is a legally- binding political instrument. The fundamental aim of the Treaty is to strengthen the rule of law on energy issues, by creating a level playing field of rules to be observed by all participating governments, thereby mitigating risks associated with energy-related investments and trade. In May 2015 a new political declaration, the *International Energy Charter*, was adopted or signed by 75 states and international organizations, and addresses the energy challenges of the 21st century and reflects the efforts to extend the global reach of the Energy Charter. The International Energy Charter remains open for signature by all states willing to accept those principles. **Aims** Find balanced solutions to key energy challenges among a diverse range of member countries across Europe and Asia, including producers, consumers and transit states, participating in the Charter on an equal basis. **Structure** Chairmanship held by a different country every year since 2014. Committees (2); Groups (4); Subsidiary Bodies (6); Secretariat. **Languages** English, French, German, Italian, Russian, Spanish. **Staff** 26.00 FTE, paid. **Finance** Secretariat financed by contributions of members of the Conference, calculated in line with UN practice. Some voluntary contributions, including from the EU. **Activities** Events/meetings; management of treaties and agreements; politics/policy/regulatory. Manages the following treaties/agreements: *Energy Charter Protocol on Energy Efficiency and Related Environmental Effects (1994)*. **Events** *OPEC-ECS-OFID Annual Legal Workshop* Vienna (Austria) 2020, *Meeting* Brussels (Belgium) 2019, *OPEC-ECS-OFID Annual Legal Workshop* Vienna (Austria) 2019, *Meeting* Tokyo (Japan) 2016, *Annual Policy Conference* Odessa (Ukraine) 2010. **Publications** *The Energy Charter Treaty and Related Documents.*
Members States parties to the Treaty (55):
Afghanistan, Albania, Armenia, Australia (not yet ratified), Austria, Azerbaijan, Belarus (not yet ratified), Belgium, Bosnia-Herzegovina, Bulgaria, Croatia, Cyprus, Czechia, Denmark, Estonia, Finland, France, Georgia, Germany, Greece, Hungary, Iceland, Ireland, Italy, Japan, Jordan, Kazakhstan, Kyrgyzstan, Latvia, Liechtenstein, Lithuania, Luxembourg, Malta, Moldova, Mongolia, Montenegro, Netherlands, North Macedonia, Norway (not yet ratified), Poland, Portugal, Romania, Russia (not yet ratified), Slovakia, Slovenia, Spain, Sweden, Switzerland, Tajikistan, Türkiye, Turkmenistan, UK, Ukraine, Uzbekistan, Yemen.
Also parties to the Treaty, 2 regional organizations:
European Atomic Energy Community (Euratom, inactive); European Union (EU, #08967).
Observers (49):
Afghanistan, Algeria, Bahrain, Bangladesh, Benin, Burkina Faso, Burundi, Cambodia, Canada, Chad, Chile, China, Colombia, Egypt, Eswatini, Gambia, Guatemala, Guyana, Indonesia, Iran Islamic Rep, Iraq, Jordan, Kenya, Korea Rep, Kuwait, Mali, Mauritania, Morocco, Niger, Nigeria, Oman, Pakistan, Palestine, Panama, Qatar, Rwanda, Saudi Arabia, Senegal, Serbia, Sierra Leone, Syrian AR, Tanzania UR, Tunisia, Uganda, United Arab Emirates, USA, Venezuela, Vietnam, Yemen.
International Organizations (15):
ASEAN (#01141); Baltic Sea Region Energy Cooperation (BASREC, #03148); East African Community (EAC, #05181); Economic Community of Central African States (ECCAS, #05311); Economic Community of West African States (ECOWAS, #05312); Electric Power Council of the CIS (#05417); European Bank for Reconstruction and Development (EBRD, #06315); G5 Sahel (#10060); International Bank for Reconstruction and Development (IBRD, #12317) (World Bank); *International Energy Agency (IEA, #13270); International Renewable Energy Agency (IRENA, #14715); OECD (#17693); Organization of Black Sea Economic Cooperation (BSEC, #17857); United Nations Economic Commission for Europe (UNECE, #20555); World Trade Organization (WTO, #21864).*
IGO Relations Accredited by (1): *United Nations Framework Convention on Climate Change – Secretariat (UNFCCC, #20564).* Observer status with (2): *ECOSOC (#05331); United Nations (UN, #20515)* (General Assembly). Related meetings organized by observers and by: *Council of the European Union (#04895); United Nations Commission on International Trade Law (UNCITRAL, #20531).* **NGO Relations** Member of (1): *European Policy Centre (EPC, #08240).* [2021/XE2744/y/**E***]

♦ Energy Charter Protocol on Energy Efficiency and Related Environmental Effects (1994 treaty)
♦ Energy Charter Treaty (1994 treaty)

♦ Energy Cities 05467

France Office 2 chemin de Palente, 25000 Besançon, France. T. +33381653680. E-mail: info@energy-cities.eu.
Belgium Office Renewable Energy House, Rue d'Arlon 63-65, 1040 Brussels, Belgium.
URL: https://energy-cities.eu/

History Former names and other names: *Energie-Cités* – alias; *Association of European Municipalities Towards Urban Energy Efficiency* – former; *Association de municipalités européennes pour la maîtrise de l'énergie en milieu urbain* – former; *Association of European Local Authorities Promoting Local Sustainable Energy Policies* – former; *Association des autorités locales européennes pour une politique énergétique locale durable* – former; *European Association of Local Authorities Inventing their Energy Future* – former; *Association européenne des autorités locales qui inventent leur futur énergétique* – former. Registration: RNA, No/ID: W251001130, Start date: 14 Sep 1990, France; No/ID: 0545.937.081, Start date: 1 Jan 1999, Belgium; EU Transparency Register, No/ID: 11514322965-05, Start date: 7 Jan 2010. **Aims** Strengthen the role and skills of local authorities in the field of sustainable energy; represent local authorities' interests and influence the policies and proposals made by European Union institutions in the fields of energy, environmental protection and urban policy; develop and promote municipalities' initiatives through exchange of experiences, transfer of know-how and implementation of joint projects. **Structure** General Meeting (annual); Executive Committee. **Languages** English, French. **Staff** 25.00 FTE, paid. **Finance** Sources: members' dues. Other sources: European and private funding. **Activities** Knowledge management/information dissemination; projects/programmes; research/documentation; training/education. **Events** *Joint Session* Brussels (Belgium) 2022, *Decarb Cities Forum* Vienna (Austria) 2020, *General Assembly* Heidelberg (Germany) 2019, *Annual Seminar* Aberdeen (UK) 2015, *Annual Seminar* Brussels (Belgium) 2014. **Publications** Newsletter (12 a year). Guides; handbooks; proceedings; book contributions. **Members** Municipal authorities (around 1,000) in over 30 countries. Membership countries not specified. **IGO Relations** Close cooperation with: *European Commission (EC, #06633)* (DG Energy; DG Mobility and Transport; DG Climate; DG Regional Policy). Involved in European programmes, including: Horizon 2020; *INTERREG V (#15966); Local Initiative Facility for the Environment (LIFE, inactive).* **NGO Relations** Member of (2): *Coalition for Energy Savings (#04056); Network of Associations of Local Authorities of South-East Europe (NALAS, #16997)* (as Associate member of). In partnership with networks of local authorities: *Climate Alliance (#04005); Council of European Municipalities and Regions (CEMR, #04891); EUROCITIES (#05662)* and its Mobility Forum; *European Federation of Agencies and Regions for Energy and the Environment (FEDARENE, #07041).* [2022.02.11/XE3526/**E**]

♦ Energy Community 05468

Dir Am Hof 4, Level 5-6, 1010 Vienna, Austria. T. +4315352222. Fax +431535222211. E-mail: contact@energy-community.org.
URL: http://www.energy-community.org/

History Established 1 Apr 2005, Vienna (Austria), by the Treaty establishing the Energy Community, signed Oct 2005, Athens (Greece), and entered into force Jul 2006. Parties to the Treaty are the *European Union (EU, #08967)* and 8 Contracting Parties from South East Europe and the Black Sea region: Albania; Bosnia-Herzegovina; Kosovo; Macedonia; Moldova; Montenegro; Serbia; Ukraine. **Aims** Extend the EU internal energy market to South East Europe and beyond on the basis of a legally binding framework; create a stable regulatory and market framework in order to attract investment in power generation and networks, create and integrated energy market, enhance security of supply, improve the environmental situation and enhance competition at regional level. **Structure** Ministerial Council (meets annually); Permanent High Level Group (meets 4 times a year); Regulatory Board; Secretariat based in Vienna (Austria). **Languages** English. **Staff** 36.00 FTE, paid. **Finance** All Parties to the Treaty contribute to the Energy Community budget, out of which nearly 95% originates from the *European Union (EU, #08967).* Donors Community is an integral part of the Energy Community process. Donors are institutions, organizations or government agencies for development wishing to contribute to the success of the Energy Community. Donors have agreed to coordinate their assistance to state and regional initiatives in order to achieve the common, overall objective of establishing a regionally integrated market. Donors Community includes:
– *Deutsche Gesellschaft für Internationale Zusammenarbeit (GIZ);*
– *European Bank for Reconstruction and Development (EBRD, #06315);*
– *European Commission (EC, #06633);*
– *European Investment Bank (EIB, #07599);*
– *INOGATE Programme (#11225);*
– *International Bank for Reconstruction and Development (IBRD, #12317)* (World Bank);
– *Kreditanstalt für Wiederaufbau (KfW);*
– Norwegian Ministry of Foreign Affairs;
– *Swedish International Development Cooperation Agency (Sida);*
– *United Nations Economic Commission for Europe (UNECE, #20555);*
– *United States Agency for International Development (USAID);*
– *Western Balkans Investment Framework (WBIF, #20910).*

Activities Politics/policy/regulatory; capacity building. **Events** *Workshop on Integrating Critical Energy Network Protection into Effective Disaster Risk Reduction Policies* Vienna (Austria) 2019, *Meeting* Brussels (Belgium) 2008, *Meeting* Tirana (Albania) 2008, *Meeting* Belgrade (Serbia) 2007, *Meeting* Belgrade (Serbia) 2007. **Publications** Implementation reports; special monitoring reports; annual activity reports; policy guidelines.
Members Parties to the Treaty include governments of 8 countries and territories:
Albania, Bosnia-Herzegovina, Kosovo, Moldova, Montenegro, North Macedonia, Serbia, Ukraine.
Also Party to the Treaty:
European Union (EU, #08967).
Observers – governments of 4 countries:
Armenia, Georgia, Norway, Türkiye. [2020/XM2029/**E***]

♦ Energy Coordinating Group (inactive)
♦ Energy Delta Institute (internationally oriented national body)

♦ Energy Drinks Europe (EDE) 05469

SG Rue de l'Association 50, 1000 Brussels, Belgium. T. +3222091144. Fax +3222097342. E-mail: secretariat@energydrinkseurope.org – info@energydrinkseurope.org.
URL: http://www.energydrinkseurope.org/

History Set up 2010. EU Transparency Register: 496000315769-13. **Aims** Take leadership on all issues related to energy drinks; engage in an open dialogue with public stakeholders; promote the responsible marketing of energy drinks. **Structure** Officers; Secretariat. [2020/XM6911/**D**]

♦ Energy-Economic Information System for the Latin American and Caribbean Region (see: #16313)

♦ Energy Efficiency Industrial Forum (EEIF) 05470

Contact CECED, Bd Brand Whitlock 114, 1200 Brussels, Belgium. T. +3227387810.
URL: http://www.eeif.eu/

Aims Act as a platform of European industries providing a full range of energy-efficient products and services. **Members** Organizations (9):
APPLiA – Home Appliance Europe (#00877); COGEN Europe (#04085); European Alliance of Companies for Energy Efficiency in Buildings (EuroACE, #05865); European Copper Institute (ECI, #06796); European Federation of Intelligent Energy Efficiency Services (EFIEES, #07145); European Insulation Manufacturers Association (EURIMA, #07577); European Partnership for Energy and the Environment (EPEE, #08157); Federation of European Rigid Polyurethane Foam Associations (PU Europe, #09538); LightingEurope (#16472). [2017/XM5447/ty/**F**]

♦ Energy Efficiency in Industrial Processes (EEIP) 05471

Business Dir Avenue des Klauwaerts 6, 1050 Brussels, Belgium. T. +3227404363. Fax +3228080244. E-mail: mail@ee-ip.org.
URL: http://www.ee-ip.org/

History Set up as a platform for business and policy in Europe. Active since Nov 2010 with official launch 12 Apr 2011, at *European Commission (EC, #06633).* Registered in accordance with Belgian law. EU Transparency Register: 66629495136-40. **Aims** Facilitate an open and inclusive dialogue within industry and between industry and policy. **Structure** Executive Board. Advisory Board. **Finance** Mainly through partnership arrangements. **Events** *Round Table on Financing Industrial Energy Efficiency* Brussels (Belgium) 2017. **Publications** *Energy Efficiency: Business and Industry* – magazine. **NGO Relations** Associate partner of: *Covenant of Mayors for Climate and Energy (#04939).* [2016/XJ4623/t/**F**]

♦ Energy and Environment Group (see: #20292)
♦ Energy Industries Council (unconfirmed)
♦ Energy Innovation Center TESLIANUM (internationally oriented national body)
♦ Energy Institute (internationally oriented national body)

♦ Energy Materials Industrial Research Initiative (EMIRI) 05472

Managing Dir Rue de Ransbeek 310, 1120 Brussels, Belgium. T. +3222642785.
URL: http://www.emiri.eu/

History Sep 2012. Registered in accordance with Belgian law. **Aims** Promote research and innovation on advanced materials needed for low-carbon energy applications. **Structure** General Assembly; Steering Committee. **Languages** English, French. **Finance** Members' dues.
Members Industry; Research; Associate. Research partners include 3 organizations listed in this Yearbook:
EUREC (#05619); European Materials Research Society (E-MRS, #07753); European Technology Platform on Advanced Engineering Materials and Technologies (EuMaT, #08887). [2019.06.04/XJ8459/ty/**F**]

♦ Energy Organization of the Great Lakes Countries (no recent information)

♦ Energypact Foundation 05473

Exec Dir Lassingleithnerplatz 2/3, 1020 Vienna, Austria.
URL: http://www.energypact.org/

History Founded, 2007, Switzerland. Currently based in Vienna (Austria). **Aims** Promote the balanced use of *energy* sources with the objective of reconciling innovation, economic development and the *protection* of the *environment.* **Structure** Executive Board. Committees (3): Security Diplomacy; Industry Engagement; Scientific and Technology. **Activities** Awareness raising; training/education; research/documentation; events/meetings. **Events** *Vienna Cyber Security Week Conference* Vienna (Austria) 2019, *Vienna Cyber Security Week Conference* Vienna (Austria) 2018. **Publications** *Energypact Foundation Newsletter.* [2019/XM7985/f/**F**]

♦ Energy Peace Partners (internationally oriented national body)
♦ Energy Peat Europe (no recent information)

♦ Energy Poverty Action (EPA) 05474

Contact c/o DBSA, 1258 Lever Road, Midrand, 1682, South Africa.

History Initiated at *World Economic Forum (WEF, #21367)* annual meeting, 2005, by 3 partners in Canada, South Africa and Sweden. *World Energy Council (WEC, #21381)* joined, 2007, Rome (Italy); and *World Business Council for Sustainable Development (WBCSD, #21254)* in 2008. **Aims** Deliver business expertise and best practices to reduce energy poverty by developing innovative, scaleable and replicable energy projects. **Structure** EPA Management Unit (EPAMU), hosted by *Development Bank of Southern Africa (DBSA).* [2010/XJ0684/**E**]

♦ Energy Regulators Association of East Africa (EREA) 05475

Exec Sec 8th Floor Mafao House, Old Moshi Road, PO Box 1669, Arusha, Tanzania UR. T. +255272520170. E-mail: info@energyregulators.org.
URL: http://www.energyregulators.org/

History 2008. Set up through Memorandum of Understanding, May 2009. Constitution signed 17 Dec 2013. **Aims** Pool expertise in regulatory matters relating to the energy sector, including but not limited to facilitating development of good policy proposals and legislation on energy regulation, in line with international trends and best regulatory practices. **Structure** General Assembly; Executive Committee; Secretariat; Secretariat Bureau; Portfolio Committees (3). **Languages** English. **Finance** National regulatory institutions; development partners. **Activities** Capacity building; monitoring/evaluation; guidance/assistance/consulting; networking/liaising; events/meetings. **Events** *Africa Regional Energy Regulators Summit* Arusha (Tanzania UR) 2022, *Annual General Assembly* Bujumbura (Burundi) 2022, *Annual General Assembly* Arusha (Tanzania UR) 2021, *Annual General Assembly* Arusha (Tanzania UR) 2020.
Members National Regulatory Institutions in 5 countries:
Burundi, Kenya, Rwanda, Tanzania UR, Uganda.
Associate (1):
South Sudan.
IGO Relations *East African Community (EAC, #05181)*; *Eastern Africa Power Pool (EAPP, #05226)*; *Regional Association of Energy Regulators for Eastern and Southern Africa (RAERESA, #18751).* [2022/XM6469/**D**]

♦ Energy Regulators Regional Association (ERRA) 05476

Head of Secretariat Logodi utca 44/b, Budapest 1012, Hungary. T. +36703925986. E-mail: secretariat@erranet.org.
URL: http://www.erranet.org/
History Dec 2000, Bucharest (Romania). Constitution signed by 15 members, Dec 2000. Constitution modified: 23 Feb 2001; 6 May 2003; 17 May 2006; 23 May 2007; 23 Apr 2008; 8 Apr 2009; 18 May 2011; Apr 2019. Registration: Start date: Apr 2001, Hungary. **Aims** Increase exchange of information and experience among its members; expand access to energy regulatory experience around the world. **Structure** General Assembly; Presidium; Financial Committee; Secretariat. **Languages** English, Russian. **Staff** 6.00 FTE, paid. **Finance** Sources: meeting proceeds; members' dues. Other sources: tuition fees. Supported by: *European Commission (EC, #06633)* (E-XK1784 – INOGATE Programme); *United States Agency for International Development (USAID)*; US National Association of Regulatory Utility Commissioners. **Activities** Events/meetings; knowledge management/information dissemination; training/education. **Events** *Energy Market Surveillance Seminar* Budapest (Hungary) 2021, *Seminar on Energy Policy and Regulation for High-Level Policy Makers and Commissioners* Budapest (Hungary) 2021, *World Forum on Energy Regulation (WFER)* Istanbul (Turkey) 2015, *European Utility Week Conference* Vienna (Austria) 2015, *Energy Investment and Regulation Conference* Baku (Azerbaijan) 2014. **Publications** *ERRA Newsletter* (2 a year). Issue papers; video presentations; podcasts. **Information Services** *Online Library.*
Members Full (34); Associate (14). Full in 34 countries:
Albania, Armenia, Austria, Azerbaijan, Bosnia-Herzegovina, Bulgaria, Cameroon, Croatia, Czechia, Estonia, Georgia, Hungary, Kazakhstan, Kyrgyzstan, Latvia, Lithuania, Moldova, Mongolia, Mozambique, Nigeria, North Macedonia, Oman, Pakistan, Palestine, Poland, Romania, Russia, Saudi Arabia, Serbia, Slovakia, Thailand, Türkiye, Ukraine, United Arab Emirates.
Associate (14) in 11 countries:
Algeria, Azerbaijan, Bosnia-Herzegovina, Egypt, France, Ghana, Jordan, Kosovo, Peru, United Arab Emirates, USA.
Regional Affiliate:
ECOWAS Regional Electricity Regulatory Authority (ERERA, #05337) (Energy Regulators Association of East Africa (EREA)).
NGO Relations Member of (1): *International Confederation of Energy Regulators (ICER, #12859).* [2022/XJ4638/**D**]

- ♦ Energy and Resources Institute (internationally oriented national body)
- ♦ Energy Services Network Association / see OSGP Alliance (#17903)

♦ Energy Technologies Europe 05477

SG Av Adolphe Lacomblé 59, 1030 Brussels, Belgium. T. +3227432986. Fax +3227432990.
Policy Officer address not obtained.
LinkedIn: https://www.linkedin.com/company/eppsa – -european-power-plant-suppliers-association
History 2001, as *European Boilermakers Association (EBA).* Subsequently changed name to *European Power Plant Suppliers Association (EPPSA).* Present title adopted May 2018. Registered in accordance with Belgian law. EU Transparency Register: 18146381379-29. **Aims** Provide innovative energy technologies for sustainable, reliable and affordable energy systems. **Structure** General Assembly (annual); Board of Directors; Committees (2); Secretariat, based in Brussels (Belgium). **Languages** English. **Staff** 1.00 FTE, paid; 0.50 FTE, voluntary. **Finance** Members' dues. **Activities** Events/meetings. **Events** *Annual Technology Meeting* Brussels (Belgium) 2014, *Annual Technology Meeting* Brussels (Belgium) 2013, *Annual Technology Meeting* Brussels (Belgium) 2012, *Meeting* Brussels (Belgium) 2011. **Publications** Annual Report; policy papers; press releases; technical brochures.
Members Full in 6 countries:
Austria, Belgium, Finland, Germany, Italy, UK.
NGO Relations Member of: *Industry4Europe (#11181).* [2021/XD8173/**D**]

♦ Energy Transitions Commission (ETC) 05478

Dir address not obtained. E-mail: info@energy-transitions.org.
Chair address not obtained.
URL: https://www.energy-transitions.org/
History 2016. **Aims** Achieve net-zero emissions by mid-century, in line with the Paris climate objective of limiting global warming to well below 2°C and ideally to 1.5°C. **Structure** Commissioners; Core Team; Regional teams. **Activities** Advocacy/lobbying/activism; knowledge management/information dissemination; research/documentation. **Members** Leaders from the energy landscape. Membership countries not specified. [2022/AA2513/v/**C**]

♦ Energy Union 05479

Contact DG for Energy, European Commission, 1049 Brussels, Belgium. T. +3222991111. E-mail: tim.mcphie@ec.europa.eu – lynn.rietdorf@ec.europa.eu.
URL: https://ec.europa.eu/energy/en/topics/energy-strategy/energy-union/
History Framework Strategy for a Resilient Energy Union with a Forward-Looking Climate Change Policy, adopted 25 Feb 2015, by *European Commission (EC, #06633).* **Aims** Give EU consumers – household and businesses – secure, sustainable, competitive and affordable energy. **Publications** *State of the Energy Union Report* (annual). [2022/XM4280/**E***]

- ♦ Energy Watch Group (unconfirmed)
- ♦ ENERI – European Network of Research Ethics and Research Integrity (unconfirmed)
- ♦ **ENERO** European Network of Environmental Research Organizations (#07902)
- ♦ **ENETS** European Neuroendocrine Tumor Society (#08041)
- ♦ **ENEX** European News Exchange (#08047)
- ♦ **ENFA** European Network of Fibromyalgia Associations (#07908)
- ♦ Enfance Missionnaire – Oeuvre Pontificale de l'Enfance Missionnaire (see: #16827)
- ♦ Enfance et partage (internationally oriented national body)
- ♦ Enfance Tiers Monde (internationally oriented national body)
- ♦ Enfants et développement / see Planète Enfants & Développement
- ♦ Enfants de Dieu / see The Family International (#09253)
- ♦ Enfants du Globe (internationally oriented national body)
- ♦ Enfants du Monde (internationally oriented national body)
- ♦ Pour les enfants pauvres (internationally oriented national body)
- ♦ Enfants réfugiés du monde (internationally oriented national body)
- ♦ Enfants de la rue du Vietnam / see Education for Development
- ♦ Enfants solidaires d'Afrique et du monde (internationally oriented national body)
- ♦ ENFC – European Nitrogen Fixation Conference (meeting series)
- ♦ **ENF** Europe of Nations and Freedom Group (#09163)
- ♦ **ENFiD** European Network of Filipino Diaspora (#07909)
- ♦ **ENFSI** European Network of Forensic Science Institutes (#07910)
- ♦ **ENGA** European Non-GMO Industry Association (#08053)
- ♦ **ENGAGE** European Network of Engineering for Agriculture and Environment (#07901)
- ♦ **ENGAGe** European Network of Gynaecological Cancer Advocacy Groups (#07916)
- ♦ Engage Now Africa (internationally oriented national body)
- ♦ EngenderHealth (internationally oriented national body)
- ♦ ENG / see European Academy of Allergy and Clinical Immunology (#05779)
- ♦ ENG – European Nursing Group (inactive)
- ♦ ENGIM / see European Association of Music and Imagery (#06126)

♦ Engineering Association of Mediterranean Countries (EAMC) 05480

Sec Via XXSettembre 5, 00187 Rome RM, Italy. T. +39685354739.
URL: https://www.eamc-engs.org/
History Launched 8 May 2014, Lecce (Italy), under the auspices of *World Federation of Engineering Organizations (WFEO, #21433).* **Aims** Develop a partnership between European and Arabian Mediterranean engineering associations; foster collaboration and mutually beneficial programmes. **Structure** General Assembly; Executive Board. Technical Committees. **Events** *General Assembly* Lisbon (Portugal) 2019.
Members National in 16 countries and territories:
Albania, Algeria, Cyprus, Egypt, Greece, Italy, Lebanon, Libya, Malta, Morocco, Palestine, Portugal, Slovenia, Spain, Syrian AR, Tunisia.
International organizations (4):
European Council of Civil Engineers (ECCE, #06810); *European Council of Engineers Chambers (ECEC, #06819)*; *Federation of Arab Engineers (FAE, #09420)*; *Réseau méditerranéen des écoles d'ingénieurs (RMEI, #18899).*
NGO Relations *Council of Associations of Long Cycle Engineers of a University or Higher School of Engineering of the European Union (CLAIUEU, #04869)*; *European Council of Engineers Chambers (ECEC, #06819)*; *European Council of Civil Engineers (ECCE, #06810)*; *Fédération Européenne d'Associations Nationales d'Ingénieurs (FEANI, #09558)*; *Federation of Arab Engineers (FAE, #09420).* [2019/XM8599/y/**E**]

- ♦ Engineering & Construction Risk Institute (internationally oriented national body)
- ♦ Engineering Ministries International (internationally oriented national body)
- ♦ Engineering World Health (internationally oriented national body)
- ♦ Engineers Against Poverty (internationally oriented national body)

♦ Engineers Without Borders International (EWB International) 05481

Ingénieurs sans frontières international (ISF international) – Ingenieurs Zonder Grenzen Internationaal (IZG Internationaal)
Pres 1031 33rd St, Ste 210, Denver CO 80205, USA. T. +112345678. E-mail: admin@ewb-international.org.
URL: http://www.ewb-international.org/
History Nov 2002. Former names and other names: *EWF International* – alias. Registration: 501(c)(3) organization, No/ID: EIN: 59-3821454, Start date: 2012, USA, Colorado. **Aims** Facilitate collaboration, information exchange and assistance among member associations; help member associations develop their capacity to assist poor communities in their respective countries and create a new generation of global engineers. **Structure** Board of Directors. **Languages** English. **Staff** 2.00 FTE, paid. **Activities** Financial and/or material support; guidance/assistance/consulting; projects/programmes. **Events** *Global Engineer International Forum* Reston, VA (USA) 2014, *Annual Conference* Boulder, CO (USA) 2003, *International forum on sustainable resources* Boulder, CO (USA) 2003.
Members National organizations in 69 countries and territories:
Argentina, Australia, Austria, Bangladesh, Belgium, Bolivia, Brazil, Burundi, Cambodia, Cameroon, Canada, Chile, Colombia, Congo Brazzaville, Côte d'Ivoire, Denmark, Ecuador, Egypt, Ethiopia, Finland, Gabon, Germany, Ghana, Greece, Honduras, Hong Kong, India, Iran Islamic Rep, Iraq, Israel, Jordan, Kenya, Korea Rep, Kosovo, Kuwait, Lebanon, Malaysia, Mexico, Nepal, Netherlands, New Zealand, Nigeria, North Macedonia, Norway, Pakistan, Palestine, Panama, Peru, Philippines, Portugal, Qatar, Rwanda, Saudi Arabia, Sierra Leone, Singapore, South Africa, Sri Lanka, Sudan, Sweden, Switzerland, Syrian AR, Tanzania UR, Türkiye, Uganda, UK, United Arab Emirates, USA, Venezuela, Zambia.
National organizations currently being established in 15 countries and territories:
Azerbaijan, Costa Rica, Egypt, Estonia, Ethiopia, Hungary, Indonesia, Mozambique, Papua New Guinea, Romania, Serbia, Somalia, Tunisia, Vietnam, Zimbabwe.
Consultative Status Consultative status granted from: *ECOSOC (#05331)* (Special). **NGO Relations** Member of: *Global WASH Cluster (GWC, #10651).* [2022.03.18/XF6973/**F**]

- ♦ Engineers' Council for Professional Development / see ABET
- ♦ Engineers Without Frontiers (internationally oriented national body)
- ♦ Engineers Without Frontiers USA / see Engineers for a Sustainable World
- ♦ Engineers for a Sustainable World (internationally oriented national body)
- ♦ Engineers of the World (internationally oriented national body)
- ♦ **ENGIP** European Network of Gastrointestinal Pathology (#07912)
- ♦ **ENGL** European Network of GMO Laboratories (#07914)
- ♦ English Academy of Southern Africa (internationally oriented national body)
- ♦ English International Association of Lund (internationally oriented national body)
- ♦ English and International Golf Greenkeepers Association / see British and International Golf Greenkeepers Association

♦ English-Speaking Union (ESU) 05482

Union pour l'héritage anglais
Head of Programmes Dartmouth House, 37 Charles Street, London, W1J 5ED, UK. T. +442075291550. E-mail: esu@esu.org.
URL: http://www.esu.org/
History 1918, by Sir Evelyn Wrench. Incorporates: *Atlantic Union*, set up 1897; *American and British Commonwealth Association*, formed 1941. UK Registered Charity: 273136. **Aims** Within the countries of the *Commonwealth*, the USA, Europe and elsewhere, promote mutual advancement of education of English-speaking people worldwide, in particular respecting their heritage, traditions and aspirations and current events and issues affecting them and their inter-relationships; promote study of the English language as a means of international communication of knowledge and understanding.
Structure Comprises 2 parallel and autonomous bodies, coordinated by *ESU International Council* set up 1974, comprising Chairman, Deputy Chairman, Honorary Treasurer, Secretary-General and Executive Secretary:
I. *English Speaking Union of the Commonwealth* – for international branches and for England and Wales, with headquarters in London (UK). Patron: H M Queen Elizabeth. President: H R H Prince Philip. Vice-Presidents (3, leaders of Britain's main political parties). Annual General Meeting. Board of Governors; Executive Committee of 7 members. Chairman; 2 Deputy Chairmen; Honorary Treasurer; Honorary Secretary; Director General. Local branches. Committees (8): National Council for England and Wales; Management and Development; Dartmouth House Limited Board of Governors; Investment; Education; English Language Council; Centre for Speech and Debate Committee; Books-Across-the-Sea Committee. Sub-Committees (7): Secondary School Exchange Scholarship; Lindemann Trust; Professional Scholarships; World Schools Debating; Library; Cultural Affairs; Promotions.
II. USA branch, with headquarters in New York NY (USA).
Languages English. **Staff** 27.50 FTE, paid. **Finance** Sources: donations; members' dues; sponsorship. Other sources: support from numerous sources. Annual budget: 1,825,697 GBP. **Activities** Organizes: Annual Summer Conference, from 1962 onwards, always in Oxford (UK); international educational exchanges of young people and adults; current affairs meetings, courses and conferences for people to learn about each other's countries; international internship programme for young people from Eastern Europe; international competitions, book exchanges and cultural seminars and events. These include: public speaking and debating competitions; English Language Awards for new ideas in teaching and learning English; Duke of Edinburgh English Language Book Competition; Lindemann Fellowships in Physical Sciences; John Smith Memorial Mace (international university debating competition); President's Award for Non-Book Materials. Sponsors language research and English language testing. **Events** *Annual General Meeting* Seattle, WA (USA) 2013, *Triennial World Members Conference / Triennial World Members' Conference* Istanbul (Turkey) 2012, *Triennial World Members Conference / Triennial World Members' Conference* Edinburgh (UK) 2008, *Triennial World Members' Conference* UK 2005, *European conference* Strasbourg (France) 2004. **Publications** *ESU Magazine* (4 a year). Annual Report.
Members International Membership in 62 countries and territories:

Albania, Argentina, Armenia, Australia, Austria, Bangladesh, Belarus, Belgium, Bermuda, Bhutan, Brazil, Bulgaria, Canada, Chile, China, Cyprus, Czechia, Denmark, Estonia, Finland, France, Georgia, Germany, Hong Kong, Hungary, Iceland, India, Japan, Korea Rep, Latvia, Lebanon, Lithuania, Madagascar, Malaysia, Malta, Mauritius, Mexico, Moldova, Monaco, Mongolia, Morocco, Nepal, New Zealand, Nigeria, Norway, Pakistan, Philippines, Poland, Portugal, Romania, Russia, Serbia, Sierra Leone, Sri Lanka, Tajikistan, Thailand, Türkiye, UK, Ukraine, USA, Vanuatu, Yemen.
Consultative Status Consultative status granted from: *ECOSOC (#05331)* (Ros A). **IGO Relations** *Commonwealth Secretariat (#04362).* **NGO Relations** Member of: *Commonwealth Consortium for Education (CCfE, #04318); Council of Commonwealth Societies (CCS, #04878).* [2020/XC0529/y/**C**]

- ♦ ENG / see Network of Aquaculture Centres in Asia-Pacific (#16991)
- ♦ **ENGS** European Network of Green Seniors (#07915)
- ♦ **ENGSO** European Non-Governmental Sports Organization (#08054)
- ♦ ENGVA / see NGVA Europe (#17130)
- ♦ **ENGV** European Network on Gender and Violence (#07913)
- ♦ **ENHA** European Nutrition for Health Alliance, The (#08069)

♦ Enhanced Heavily Indebted Poor Countries Initiative (HIPC Initiative) 05483

Contact World Bank, 1818 H St NW, Washington DC 20433, USA. T. +12024731000. Fax +12024776931.
History 1996, as *Heavily Indebted Poor Countries Initiative (HIPC Initiative)*, on agreement by governments to a proposal of *International Bank for Reconstruction and Development (IBRD, #12317)* and *International Monetary Fund (IMF, #14180)*. New name adopted, Oct 1999. **Aims** Reduce to a *sustainable* level the external debt of the world's poorest, most heavily indebted countries; place debt relief within an overall framework of *poverty* reduction. **Finance** Cost: under the original framework, about US$ 12,500 million in present value terms; under the new framework, potentially over US$ 29,300 million, about half from bilateral and half from multilateral creditors. *HIPC Trust fund* provides debt relief on debt owed to participating multilateral institutions; it consists of contributions from participating multilateral creditors and bilateral donors and can pre-pay or purchase a portion of the debt and cancel such debt, or pay debt service as it comes due. To date the Fund has obtained US$ 2,500 million in bilateral contributions and pledges from about 20 countries and the World Bank has transferred over US $1,300 million to its component of the Fund. Assistance from IMF is through special PRGF grants paid into an escrow account and used to cover debt service payments to the IMF. **Activities** Open to countries only eligible for highly concessional assistance from *International Development Association (IDA, #13155)* and from the IMF's Poverty Reduction and Growth Facility (PRGF) (previously the Enhanced Structural Adjustment Facility). Under the original framework, debt reduction was calculated on projections of debt stock at the completion point. Under the enhanced framework, relief is committed based on actual data at the decision point, not only adding greater certainty to the calculations but, in most cases, increasing the amount of relief actually provided; the benefits of export and central government revenue accrue fully to the country, allowing for greater investment in poverty reduction strategies. All creditors participate in providing exceptional assistance beyond current mechanisms as required to reach debt sustainability, sharing the costs and providing relief on a basis proportional to their share of the debt after the full application of traditional forms of debt relief. Multilateral institutions participate through action to reduce the present value of their claims.
Members About 35 countries could ultimately qualify for HIPC assistance. Countries currently receiving HIPC relief (23):
Benin, Bolivia, Burkina Faso, Cameroon, Chad, Gambia, Guinea, Guinea-Bissau, Guyana, Honduras, Madagascar, Malawi, Mali, Mauritania, Mozambique, Nicaragua, Niger, Rwanda, Sao Tomé-Principe, Senegal, Tanzania UR, Uganda, Zambia.
IGO Relations *Commonwealth Secretariat (#04362).* [2009/XK2047/**E***]

♦ Enhanced Integrated Framework (EIF) 05484

Exec Dir c/o WTO, Rue de Lausanne 154, 1211 Geneva 2, Switzerland. T. +41227396650. E-mail: eif.secretariat@wto.org.
URL: http://www.enhancedif.org/
Aims Assist Least Developed Countries (LDCs) to use trade as an engine for development and poverty reduction. **Finance** Trust fund donors: governments of Australia, Belgium, Canada, Denmark, Estonia, Finland, France, Germany, Hungary, Iceland, Ireland, Japan, Korea Rep, Luxembourg, Netherlands, Norway, Saudi Arabia, Spain, Sweden, Switzerland, Turkey, UK, USA; *European Commission (EC, #06633).* **Activities** Guidance/assistance/consulting; financial and/or material support; knowledge management/information dissemination.
Members LDCs (51):
Afghanistan, Angola, Bangladesh, Benin, Bhutan, Burkina Faso, Burundi, Cambodia, Cape Verde, Central African Rep, Chad, Comoros, Congo DR, Djibouti, Equatorial Guinea, Eritrea, Ethiopia, Gambia, Guinea, Guinea-Bissau, Haiti, Kiribati, Laos, Lesotho, Liberia, Madagascar, Malawi, Maldives, Mali, Mauritania, Mozambique, Myanmar, Nepal, Niger, Rwanda, Samoa, Sao Tomé-Principe, Senegal, Sierra Leone, Solomon Is, Somalia, South Sudan, Sudan, Tanzania UR, Timor-Leste, Togo, Tuvalu, Uganda, Vanuatu, Yemen, Zambia.
Partner agencies (8):
International Monetary Fund (IMF, #14180); International Trade Centre (ITC, #15703); The World Bank Group (#21218); UNCTAD (#20285); UNDP (#20292); UNIDO (#20336); World Tourism Organization (UNWTO, #21861); World Trade Organization (WTO, #21864).
Other strategic partners (7):
Common Market for Eastern and Southern Africa (COMESA, #04296); Commonwealth Secretariat (#04362); FAO (#09260); International Islamic Trade Finance Corporation (ITFC); *Pacific Islands Forum Secretariat (#17970); Standards and Trade Development Facility (STDF, #19948);* UN Department of Economic and Social Affairs (UNDESA). [2019/XM7595/y/**F**]

- ♦ **ENHCC** European Network of Health Care Chaplaincy (#07919)
- ♦ ENH – European Network for Housing and Urban Development (unconfirmed)
- ♦ ENHPS / see Schools for Health in Europe network foundation (#19133)
- ♦ **ENHR** European Network for Housing Research (#07924)
- ♦ **ENHSA** European Network of Heads of Schools of Architecture (#07918)
- ♦ ENHS – European Natural Hygiene Society (inactive)
- ♦ Enhumanity Group / see New Humanity Group
- ♦ ENIAC / see Association for European NanoElectronics ActivitieS (#02525)
- ♦ ENIA – European Nickel Industry Association (inactive)
- ♦ ENIAR – European Network for Indigenous Australian Rights (internationally oriented national body)
- ♦ **ENIC** European Network of National Information Centres on Academic Recognition and Mobility (#07950)
- ♦ **ENICPA** European Network of Information Centres for the Performing Arts (#07933)
- ♦ **ENID** European Network of Indicator Designers (#07931)
- ♦ **ENIEC** European Network on Intercultural Elderly Care (#07934)
- ♦ ENI – European Network for Ichthyosis (unconfirmed)
- ♦ **ENIL** European Network on Independent Living (#07929)
- ♦ ENI-NET Association for the Promotion of Neuroscience / see Network of European Neuroscience Institutes (#17025)
- ♦ **ENINET** Network of European Neuroscience Institutes (#17025)
- ♦ **ENIP** European Network on Indigenous Peoples (#07932)
- ♦ ENIQ Network / see Nuclear Generation II and III Association (#17618)
- ♦ **ENIRDELM** European Network for Improving Research and Development in Educational Leadership and Management (#07927)
- ♦ ENIRDEM / see European Network for Improving Research and Development in Educational Leadership and Management (#07927)
- ♦ **ENISA** European Union Agency for Network and Information Security (#08971)
- ♦ **ENIUGH** European Network in Universal and Global History (#08029)

♦ Enlace Continental de Mujeres Indigenas de las Americas (ECMIA) 05485

Main Office Horacio Urteaga 534, Of 203, 15072, Lima, Peru. E-mail: secretaria@ecmia.org.
URL: http://ecmia.org/
History 1995. **Aims** Participate and politically influence the defence and promotion of human *rights* of indigenous women on national and international levels. **Activities** Events/meetings. **Events** *Encuentro Continental de Mujeres Indígenas de Las Américas* Mexico City (Mexico) 2020, *Encuentro Continental de Mujeres Indígenas de Las Américas* Guatemala (Guatemala) 2015, *Encuentro Continental de Mujeres Indígenas de Las Américas* Morelos, PUE (Mexico) 2011, *Encuentro Continental de Mujeres Indígenas de Las Américas* Québec, QC (Canada) 2007, *Encuentro Continental de Mujeres Indígenas de Las Américas* Lima (Peru) 2004.
Members Full in 22 countries:
Argentina, Belize, Bolivia, Brazil, Canada, Chile, Colombia, Costa Rica, Ecuador, El Salvador, Guatemala, Guyana, Honduras, Mexico, Nicaragua, Panama, Paraguay, Peru, Suriname, Uruguay, USA, Venezuela. [2022.02.15/XJ2950/**F**]

- ♦ Enlace Latino / see Latin Link (#16399)

♦ Enlarged Partial Agreement on Cultural Routes 05486

Accord partiel élargi sur les Itinéraires culturels (APE)
Contact c/o Council of Europe, Av de l'Europe, 67075 Strasbourg CEDEX, France. T. +35224125032.
Contact address not obtained.
URL: http://www.coe.int/en/web/culture-and-heritage/cultural-routes
History Cultural Routes programme launched by *Council of Europe (CE, #04881)*, 1987. *Committee of Ministers of the Council of Europe (#04273)* adopted Resolution CM/Res (2010)53, establishing an Enlarged Partial Agreement (EPA), Dec 2010. Rules for the award of the Cultural Route certification revised by Resolution CM/Res (2013)67. **Aims** Reinforce the potential of Cultural Routes for cultural co-operation, sustainable territorial development and social cohesion, with a particular focus on themes of symbolic importance for European unity, history, culture and values and the discovery of less well-known destinations. **Structure** Governing Board. Technical Body: *European Institute of Cultural Routes (EICR).* **Events** *Annual Advisory Forum* Aranjuez (Spain) 2015.
Members Cultural Routes/Signatories to the Agreement in 24 countries:
Andorra, Armenia, Austria, Azerbaijan, Bulgaria, Cyprus, France, Germany, Greece, Hungary, Italy, Lithuania, Luxembourg, Monaco, Montenegro, Norway, Portugal, Romania, Russia, Serbia, Slovakia, Slovenia, Spain, Switzerland. [2016/XM4295/**F***]

♦ Enlarged Partial Agreement on Sport (EPAS) 05487

Accord partiel élargi sur le sport (APES)
Exec Sec DGII Democracy/Anti-discrimination/ Children and Sport Values, Council of Europe, Agora, 1 quai Jacoutot, 67075 Strasbourg, France. T. +33390215376. Fax +33388412429. E-mail: sport.epas@coe.int – sport@coe.int.
URL: http://www.coe.int/epas/
History Established within *Council of Europe (CE, #04881)*, on adoption on Resolution 2007 (8), taking over activities of Committee for the Development of Sport. **Aims** Promote development of sport in modern society, while emphasizing its positive values; develop and monitor policies and standards, and help with capacity building and exchange of good practice. **Structure** Governing Board; Consultative Committee; Statutory Committee; Secretariat. **Languages** English, French. **Staff** 8.00 FTE, paid. **Finance** Sources: members' dues. Annual budget: 814,100 EUR. **Activities** Capacity building; guidance/assistance/consulting; monitoring/evaluation; standards/guidelines. **Events** *Conference of Ministers* 2020, *Ministerial Conference* Tbilisi (Georgia) 2018. **Publications** *Handbook on Good Practices* – collection; *Sport Policy and Practice* – collection.
Members Member States (40):
Albania, Andorra, Armenia, Austria, Azerbaijan, Belarus, Belgium, Bosnia-Herzegovina, Bulgaria, Croatia, Cyprus, Estonia, Finland, France, Georgia, Greece, Hungary, Iceland, Israel, Italy, Latvia, Liechtenstein, Lithuania, Luxembourg, Malta, Monaco, Montenegro, Morocco, Netherlands, North Macedonia, Norway, Poland, Portugal, Russia, San Marino, Serbia, Slovenia, Switzerland, Türkiye, Ukraine.
Consultative Committee Members (25):
- *European Association for Sport Management (EASM, #06219);*
- *European Athlete Student Network (EAS, #06290);*
- *European Athletics (#06291);*
- *European Elite Athletes Association (EU Athletes, #06977);*
- *European Fair Play Movement (EFPM, #07025);*
- *European Gay and Lesbian Sport Federation (EGLSF, #07382);*
- *European Network of Sport Education (ENSE, #08012);*
- *European Non-Governmental Sports Organization (ENGSO, #08054);*
- *European Olympic Committees (EOC, #08083);*
- *European Paralympic Committee (EPC, #08140);*
- *European Physical Education Association (EUPEA, #08206);*
- *European University Sports Association (EUSA, #09036);*
- *Fédération internationale de SAMBO (FIAS, #09655);*
- *Football Against Racism in Europe (FARE Network, #09853);*
- *International Council of Sport Science and Physical Education (ICSSPE, #13077);*
- *International Dance Organization (IDO, #13131);*
- *International Federation for Sports Officials (IFSO, #13555);*
- *International School Sport Federation (ISF, #14792);*
- *International Sport and Culture Association (ISCA, #15587);*
- *Peace and Sport;*
- *Play the Game (#18404);*
- *Special Olympics International (SOI, #19910)* (Europe Eurasia);
- *Sports Rights Owners Coalition (SROC, #19929);*
- *TAFISA Europe (#20087);*
- *Union of European Football Associations (UEFA, #20386).* [2021.10.26/XM3416/y/**F***]

- ♦ **ENL** Europe des nations et des libertés (#09163)
- ♦ **ENLIGHT** ENLIGHT – The European Network for Light ion Hadron Therapy (#05488)

♦ ENLIGHT – The European Network for Light ion Hadron Therapy (ENLIGHT) 05488

Coordination Office c/o CERN, Espl. des Particules 1, 1211 Geneva 23, Switzerland. T. +41227671791. E-mail: enlight@cern.ch.
URL: https://enlight.web.cern.ch/
History 2002. Functions within *European Organization for Nuclear Research (CERN, #08108).* Former names and other names: *ENLIGHT – The European Network for Light ion Hadron Therapy – A multidisciplinary platform aimed at a coordinated effort towards ion beam research in Europe* – full title. **Aims** Develop strategies for securing the funding necessary to conduct research in areas needed for highly effective hadron therapy and to establish and implement common standards and protocols for treating *patients.* **Structure** Advisory Committee. **Languages** English. **Activities** Events/meetings; training/education. **Events** *ENLIGHT Annual Meeting* Bergen (Norway) 2020, *ENLIGHT Annual Meeting* Caen (France) 2019, *Annual Meeting* London (UK) 2018. [2021/XM7974/**F**]

- ♦ ENLIGHT – The European Network for Light ion Hadron Therapy – A multidisciplinary platform aimed at a coordinated effort towards ion beam research in Europe / see ENLIGHT – The European Network for Light ion Hadron Therapy (#05488)
- ♦ **ENLR** Europäische Netzwerk für die Entwicklung des ländlichen Raums (#07995)
- ♦ **ENMat** European Network of Materials Research Centres (#07943)
- ♦ **ENMCA** European Network of Medical Competent Authorities (#07944)
- ♦ **ENMC** European Network of Maritime Clusters (#07942)
- ♦ **ENMC** European Neuromuscular Centre (#08042)
- ♦ ENMCR / see Children's Rights European Academic Network (#03878)
- ♦ **ENMESH** European Network for Mental Health Service Evaluation (#07946)
- ♦ **ENM** European Nursing Module Network (#08064)
- ♦ Enmiendas al Protocolo sobre la prevención de la contaminación del Mar Méditerraneo causada por vertidos desde buques y aeronaves (1995 treaty)
- ♦ **ENMIX** European Nanoporous Materials Institute of Excellence (#07851)
- ♦ ENMOD Convention – Convention on the Prohibition of Military or Any other Hostile Use of Environmental Modification Techniques (1976 treaty)

- ENMS – European Nuclear Medicine Society (inactive)
- ENNA – European Nanoscience and Nanotechnology Association (unconfirmed)
- **ENNA** European Network of NGOs in Afghanistan (#07952)
- **ENNA** European Network of Nursing Academies (#07953)
- **ENNE** European Network of Nursing in Higher Education (#07954)
- ENN – Emergency Nutrition Network (internationally oriented national body)
- **ENN** European Narratology Network (#07853)
- **ENNHRI** European Network of National Human Rights Institutions (#07949)
- **ENNS** European Neural Network Society (#08039)
- **ENOC** European Network of Ombudspersons for Children (#07959)
- **ENOHE** European Network for Ombudsmen in Higher Education (#07958)
- **ENoLL** European Network of Living Labs (#07938)
- **ENoMW** European Network of Migrant Women (#07947)
- **ENOPE** European Network on Patient Empowerment (#07965)
- **ENOP** European Network of Organizational and Work Psychologists (#07960)
- **ENoP** European Network of Political Foundations (#07972)
- **ENORB** European Network on Religion and Belief (#07985)
- **ENOR** European Network for Oxysterol Research (#07962)
- ENO Schoolnet Association (unconfirmed)
- **ENOS** European Network on Occupational Social Work (#07955)
- **ENOS** European Network of Outdoor Sports (#07961)
- Enosi Evropaikon Tamievtirion / see European Savings and Retail Banking Group (#08426)
- Enosi Evropaikon Viomihanion Metapiisis Frouton ke Lahanikon / see European Association of Fruit and Vegetable Processors (#06049)
- Enosis Aneksartiton Evropaikon Halivurgion (inactive)
- eNOTE – European Network Of Tissue Establishments (unconfirmed)
- **ENOTHE** European Network of Occupational Therapy in Higher Education (#07956)
- Enough – Project to End Genocide and Crimes Against Humanity (internationally oriented national body)
- E-nous – European Network of Utilitarian Scholars (internationally oriented national body)
- ENOVO – European Network of Older-Volunteer Organizations (internationally oriented national body)
- ENOV – Réseau européen des bénévoles seniors / see European Network of Older-Volunteer Organizations
- **ENPA** European Network for Psychological Anthropology (#07977)
- **ENPA** European Newspaper Publishers' Association (#08048)
- **EnPAx** Environmental Peacebuilding Association (#05509)
- **ENPC** European Nursery Products Confederation (#08061)
- **ENPER** European Network for Plant Endomembrane Research (#07968)
- **ENP** European Network of Policewomen (#07970)
- **ENPHE** European Network of Physiotherapy in Higher Education (#07967)
- **ENPLAC** Exchange Network of Parliaments of Latin America and The Caribbean (#18696)
- **ENPODHE** European Network of Podiatry in Higher Education (#07969)
- **ENPOSS** European Network for the Philosophy of the Social Sciences (#07966)
- **ENPP** European Network for Positive Psychology (#07973)
- **Enpr-EMA** European Network of Paediatric Research at the European Medicines Agency (#07963)
- **ENPS** European Network for Psychosocial Support (#07978)
- ENPUD – Eurasian Network of People Who Use Drugs (unconfirmed)
- **ENQA** European Association for Quality Assurance in Higher Education (#06183)
- **ENQI** European Network for Qualitative Inquiry (#07980)
- Enquête mondiale sur la fécondité (inactive)
- **ENRAH** European Network for Research on Alternating Hemiplegia (#07987)
- Enraiza Derechos (internationally oriented national body)
- **ENRD** European Network for Rural Development (#07995)
- **EnR** European Energy Network (#06988)
- **ENRF** European Nursing Research Foundation (#08065)
- **ENRIO** European Network of Research Integrity Offices (#07990)
- **EN RLMM** European Network on Regional Labour Market Monitoring (#07983)
- **ENROAC** European Network for Research in Organisational and Accounting Change (#07991)
- **ENRS** European Network Remembrance and Solidarity (#07986)
- ENRS – European Network for Ricoeur Studies (unconfirmed)
- **ENRSP** European Network for Research on Supplementary Pensions (#07993)
- **ENRWA** European Network of Registers of Wills Association (#07984)
- **ENSAC** European Network of School-Age Childcare (#07997)
- **ENSACT** European Network for Social Action (#08003)
- **ENSA** European Network of Social Authorities (#08004)
- **ENSA** European Network for Social Intelligence (#08010)
- **ENSA** European Neutron Scattering Association (#08045)
- **ENSA** European Nursing Students Association (#08066)
- ENSA / see European Plant-Based Foods Association (#08210)
- **ENSA** European Plant-Based Foods Association (#08210)
- **ENSCA** European Natural Sausage Casings Association (#07854)
- ENSCOPE (unconfirmed)
- ENSDHE – European Network on Staff Development in Higher Education (inactive)
- **ENSEC** European Network for Social and Emotional Competence (#08006)
- ENSEC – European Nuclear Steelmaking Club (inactive)
- **ENSE** European Network of Sport Education (#08012)
- Enseignantes de Sainte Dorothée, Filles des Saints Coeurs (religious order)

♦ Enseignants sans frontières (ESF) 05489

Leraars zonder Grenzen

Secretariat Drève de Nivelles 166 bte 3, 1150 Brussels, Belgium. E-mail: info@esfbelgique.org.
URL: http://www.esfbelgique.org/

History 7 Nov 1994, Brussels (Belgium). Registration: Banque-Carrefour des Entreprises, Belgium. **Aims** Promote cooperation networks among teachers by respecting each one's cultural identity in the spirit of the Universal Declaration of Human Rights; promote an active pedagogy based on the autonomy of the learners and the development of all their abilities. **Structure** Board. **Languages** French. **Finance** Sources: donations; members' dues. Occasional public subventions. **Activities** Events/meetings; training/education.
Members Adhering members (50): organizations in 8 countries:
Belgium, Benin, Burkina Faso, Burundi, Madagascar, Mexico, Rwanda, Senegal.
NGO Relations Member of (1): *Belgian Platform for Education and Development (Educaid.be).*
[2022.03.08/XF4966/F]

- Enseignement à Distance pour l'Afrique (#05103)
- Ensemble contre les mines (internationally oriented national body)
- Ensemble Contre la Peine de Mort / see ECPM
- Ensemble, les enfants peuvent faire bouger les choses (internationally oriented national body)
- **ENS** European Nail Society (#07850)
- **ENS** European Network on Statelessness (#08013)
- ENS – European Neurological Society (inactive)
- **ENS** European Nuclear Society (#08059)
- ENSFH / see ENSH-Global Network for Tobacco Free Health Care Services (#05490)
- ENSG / see European Nursing Students Association (#08066)
- ENSH / see ENSH-Global Network for Tobacco Free Health Care Services (#05490)
- **ENSH-Global** ENSH-Global Network for Tobacco Free Health Care Services (#05490)

♦ ENSH-Global Network for Tobacco Free Health Care Services (ENSH-Global) 05490

Contact Barwon Health, The Corporate Office, PO Box 281, Geelong VIC 3220, Australia. E-mail: info@tobaccofreehealthcare.org.
URL: http://www.ensh.org/

History Founded within a European-funded initiative (1999-2005). Former names and other names: *European Network for Smoke-Free Hospitals (ENSH)* – former; *Réseau européen hôpitaux sans tabac* – former; *European Network for Smoke/Tobacco-Free Healthcare Services (ENSH)* – former; *ENSFH* – former. Registration: Start date: 2010, Belgium; Swiss Civil Code, Start date: 2015, Switzerland. **Aims** Advocate for and support implementation of tobacco control policies in healthcare services that are in accordance with FCTC/COP4 (8) Guidelines for implementation of Article 14 of the WHO Framework Convention on Tobacco Control; encourage, support and promote engagement in tobacco control measures in accordance with the provision of Article 2.1 of the Convention; engage health professionals and healthcare services worldwide to engage with and fulfil their obligations towards tobacco. **Activities** Advocacy/lobbying/activism; networking/liaising. **Events** *Workshop* Vienna (Austria) 2017, *International conference on health promoting hospitals and health services* Hersonissos (Greece) 2009, *International conference on health promoting hospitals* Palanga (Lithuania) 2006.
Members Full in 18 countries and territories:
Australia, Austria, Belgium, Estonia, Finland, France, Georgia, Germany, Ireland, Korea Rep, Norway, Romania, Spain, Sweden, Switzerland, Taiwan, UK, USA.
NGO Relations Member of: *European Network for Smoking and Tobacco Prevention (ENSP, #08002).*
[2015.09.16/XM1377/F]

- **ENSHPO** European Network of Safety and Health Professional Organisations (#07996)
- **ENSIA** Empty Nose Syndrome International Association (#05448)
- **ENSIE** European Network of Social Integration Enterprises (#08009)
- **ENSIE** European Network for the Study of Islam and Esotericism (#08017)
- **ENSIS** European Network for Social Innovation and Solidarity (#08008)
- **ENSLT** European Network of Sign Language Teachers (#08000)
- Ensophion of Humanity / see New Humanity Group
- ENSP / see European Network for Smoking and Tobacco Prevention (#08002)
- **ENSP** European Network for Smoking and Tobacco Prevention (#08002)
- **ENSREG** European Nuclear Safety Regulators Group (#08058)
- ENSR / see European Network for Social and Economic Research (#08005)
- **ENSR** European Network for Social and Economic Research (#08005)
- ENSSEE / see European Network of Sport Education (#08012)
- **ENSSER** European Network of Scientists for Social and Environmental Responsibility (#07999)
- ENSSHE / see European Network of Sport Education (#08012)
- **ENS@T** European Network for the Study of Adrenal Tumours (#08016)
- **ENSWaP** European Network of Steiner Waldorf Parents (#08014)
- **ENTE** European Network for Traveller Education (#08028)
- Ente Internazionale per la Standardizzazione delle Fibre Man-made (#03369)
- Entente balkanique (inactive)
- Entente baltique (inactive)

♦ Entente Council 05491

Conseil de l'Entente (CE)

Exec Sec Angle avenue Verdier-rue de Tessières, 01 BP 3734, Abidjan 01, Côte d'Ivoire. T. +22520331001 – +22520331417. Fax +22520331149. E-mail: conseildelentente@conseildelentente.org.
URL: http://www.conseildelentente.org/

History 29 May 1959, Abidjan (Côte d'Ivoire), comprising Dahomey (currently Benin), Côte d'Ivoire, Niger and Upper Volta (currently Burkina Faso), superseding *Union Sahel-Benin*, which had been created some months earlier. Togo joined the institution in 1966. The aim of the Entente Council was initially political, but at present it is strictly economic. Also referred to in English as *Council of the Entente* and as *Council of the Entente States*. Statutes registered in *'UNTS 1/18820'*. **Aims** Promote economic development of the region; harmonize and strengthen policies and economies of member states on the basis of friendship, brotherhood and solidarity. **Structure** Conference of Heads of State and Government (twice a year); Council of Foreign Ministers (meeting prior to Conference of Heads of State); Secretariat General. Specialized institutions: *Centre régional de formation pour entretien routier (CERFER, no recent information)*; *Mutual Aid and Loan Guaranty Fund of the Entente Council (EC-Fund, no recent information)*. Other training centres include: *Centre des formation technique de transporteurs routiers (CFTTR, inactive)*, Niamey (Niger), currently the responsibility of the government of Niger; *Centre de formation dans les transports routiers et les activités auxiliaires (CFTRA, no recent information)*, Ouagadougou. Conference of Heads of State constitutes the Board of Directors of FEGECE, which was created Jun 1966, Abidjan (Côte d'Ivoire), to deal with the issuing of guarantees for loans contracted by member states, replacing *'Solidarity Fund – Fonds de solidarité'*, created by same agreement as the Council itself. The Fund carries out all economic activities of the Council, working through a Management Committee and Administrative Secretariat. Chairmanship rotates among Heads of State. **Languages** French. **Finance** Annual contributions from member states. Subsidies and grants; investment returns and commission from guarantee operations. **Activities** Member states work on harmonization and cooperation in the fields of: duty and tax; economic and social development; education; information; working practices; justice; public works – transport and communications; health. Rural development programme comprising 19 projects in stockbreeding, food production and water supply; cooperates in regional telecommunications network. **Publications** Annual report.
Members Governments of 5 countries:
Benin, Burkina Faso, Côte d'Ivoire, Niger, Togo.
IGO Relations Participates in the activities of: *UNCTAD (#20285)*. Signatory to: *Agreement between the Central African States Concerning the Creation of a Special Fund for the Conservation of Wild Fauna (1983)*; *Agreement for Cooperation and Consultation between the Central African States for the Conservation of Wild Fauna (1983)*. Under Lomé Conventions, links with: *European Commission (EC, #06633).* [2020/XD0453/D*]

♦ Entente Européenne d'Aviculture et de Cuniculture (EE) 05492

European Association of Poultry, Pigeon, Cage Bird, Rabbit and Cavy Breeders – Association Européenne pour l'Elevage de Volailles, de Pigeons, d'Oiseaux, de Lapins et de Cobayes – Europäischer Verband für Geflügel-, Tauben-, Vogel-, Kaninchen- und Caviazucht

Pres Schürenstr 19, 8903 Birmensdorf ZH, Switzerland.
Gen Sec Kirchweg 7, 5647 Oberrüti AG, Switzerland.
URL: http://www.entente-ee.com/

History 1938. Registration: EU Transparency Register, No/ID: 313879841820-64, Start date: 16 Mar 2021. **Aims** Unite all small livestock organizations in Europe. **Structure** Annual General Meeting; Executive Committee. Sections. **Finance** Sources: members' dues. **Activities** Events/meetings. **Events** *EE Meeting* Netherlands 2027, *EE Meeting* Konjic (Bosnia-Herzegovina) 2022, *EE Meeting* Vienna (Austria) 2021, *EE Meeting* Prague (Czechia) 2020, *EE Meeting* Trogir (Croatia) 2019.
Members Individuals (about 2500000 individuals) in 31 countries:
Austria, Belgium, Bosnia-Herzegovina, Bulgaria, Croatia, Czechia, Denmark, Finland, France, Germany, Greece, Hungary, Ireland, Italy, Latvia, Lithuania, Luxembourg, Netherlands, Norway, Poland, Portugal, Romania, Russia, Serbia, Slovakia, Slovenia, Spain, Sweden, Switzerland, Türkiye, UK. [2023/AA1484/v/D]

- Entente européenne du commerce en gros des deux-roues (inactive)
- Entente internationale de l'acier (inactive)
- Entente internationale anti-communiste (inactive)
- Entente Internationale des Luthiers et Archetiers / see International Society of Violin and Bow-Makers (#15542)
- Entente Internationale des Maîtres Luthiers et Archetiers d'Art (#15542)
- Entente internationale des partis radicaux et des partis démocrates similaires (inactive)
- Entente juvénile (inactive)
- Entente médicale internationale / see Artsen Zonder Vakantie
- Entente médicale méditerranéenne (no recent information)

♦ Entente mondiale des femmes (inactive)
♦ Entente mondiale des femmes pour la paix (inactive)
♦ Entente scientifique internationale pour l'adoption d'une langue auxiliaire (inactive)
♦ **ENTEP** European Network on Teacher Education Policies (#08019)
♦ **ENTER** European Network on Training, Evaluation and Research in Mental Health (#08022)
♦ ENTER – European Network for Transfer and Exploitation of EU Project Results (internationally oriented national body)
♦ Enterprise for the Americas Initiative / see Enterprise for the Americas Initiative and Tropical Forest Conservation Act
♦ Enterprise for the Americas Initiative and Tropical Forest Conservation Act (internationally oriented national body)
♦ Enterprise Asia (unconfirmed)
♦ Enterprise Development International (internationally oriented national body)
♦ Enterprise Ethereum Alliance (unconfirmed)

♦ Enterprise Europe Network (EEN) 05493

Contact Head of Sector A13, c/o EASME, Covent Garden Building, Place Charles Rogier 16, 1210 Brussels, Belgium. E-mail: easme-een-communication@ec.europa.eu.
URL: http://een.ec.europa.eu/

History Launched Feb 2008, by *European Commission (EC, #06633)* – Directorate General for Enterprise and Industry. Builds on the former *Euro Info Centres (EIC, inactive)* and *Innovation Relay Centres Network (IRC Network, inactive)*, established in 1987 and 1995 respectively. Currently functions within *Executive Agency for Small and Medium-sized Enterprises (EASME)*. **Aims** Help SMEs make the most of business opportunities. **Staff** 3000.00 FTE, paid. **Finance** Financed by: *European Union (EU, #08967)* COSME programme. **Activities** Knowledge management/information dissemination; networking/liaising; capacity building; events/meetings; guidance/assistance/consulting. **Events** *Robotics and Artificial Intellignence Cross-Sectoral Innovation Conference* Oslo (Norway) 2021, *Applied Artificial Intelligence Conference* Vienna (Austria) 2020, *Annual Conference* Helsinki (Finland) 2019, *Forum Europe* Paris (France) 2019, *Singapore-Malta Forum* Singapore (Singapore) 2019. **Members** Partner organizations (about 600) in about 60 countries. Membership countries not specified. [2020/XM1584/**E**]

♦ Enterprise VPN User Organization / see European Virtual Private Network Users Association (#09066)
♦ Entertainment Leisure Software Publishers Association (inactive)
♦ ENT / see European Textile Network (#08903)
♦ **ENTIS** European Network of Teratology Information Services (#08020)
♦ ENTMA08 – European Network of Training in the Management of Aggression (unconfirmed)
♦ **ENTO** European Network of Training Organizations for Local and Regional Authorities (#08023)
♦ **ENTOG** European Network of Trainees in Obstetrics and Gynaecology (#08021)

♦ Entomological Society of Southern Africa (ESSA) 05494

Entomologiese Vereniging van Suidelike Afrika (EVSA)

Admin Officer PO Box 13162, Hatfield, 0028, South Africa. T. +27125431291. E-mail: admin@entsocsa.co.za.
Honorary Sec address not obtained. E-mail: chrisr@unisa.ac.za.
URL: http://www.entsocsa.co.za/

History 1937. **Aims** Promote entomology in Africa and communication between entomologists. **Structure** Executive Committee. **Languages** Afrikaans, English. **Staff** 2.00 FTE, paid. **Finance** Sources: meeting proceeds; subscriptions. **Activities** Southern African Development Community member states. **Events** *Biennial Congress* Tshipise (South Africa) 2021, *Biennial Congress* Durban (South Africa) 2019, *Biennial Congress* Grahamstown (South Africa) 2015, *Biennial Congress* Potchefstroom (South Africa) 2013, *Biennial Congress* Bloemfontein (South Africa) 2011. **Publications** *Rostrum* (3 a year); *African Entomology* (2 a year); *Memoirs of the Entomology Society of Southern Africa* (irregular). Congress proceedings.
Members Individual (Ordinary; Student/Retired/Honorary Life); Institutional; Sustaining. Institutions (41) and individuals (437) in 24 countries and territories:
Angola, Australia, Belgium, Benin, Botswana, Brazil, Eswatini, France, Germany, Ghana, Hong Kong, Italy, Japan, Kenya, Lesotho, Madagascar, Mauritius, Namibia, Netherlands, South Africa, UK, USA, Zambia, Zimbabwe.
[2020.05.05/XF5190/**F**]

♦ Entomologiese Vereniging van Suidelike Afrika (#05494)
♦ Entraide aux boursiers d'Afrique / see Solidarité étudiants du Monde
♦ Entraide aux étudiants africains / see Solidarité étudiants du Monde
♦ Entraide et fraternité (internationally oriented national body)
♦ Entraide médicale internationale (internationally oriented national body)
♦ Entraide missionnaire internationale (#14170)
♦ Entraide ouvrière internationale / see SOLIDAR (#19680)
♦ Entraide protestante Suisse (internationally oriented national body)
♦ Entraide universitaire internationale / see World University Service (#21892)
♦ Entraide universitaire mondiale (#21892)
♦ Entreculturas (internationally oriented national body)
♦ Entrenamiento en Vía Aérea Latinoamérica (unconfirmed)
♦ Entrepobles (internationally oriented national body)
♦ Entrepobos (internationally oriented national body)

♦ Entrepreneurs de l'audiovisuel européen (EAVE) 05495

European Audiovisual Entrepreneurs

Exec Rue de Luxembourg 238c, L-8077 Bertrange, Luxembourg. T. +3524452101. Fax +35244521070. E-mail: eave@eave.org.
URL: http://www.eave.org/

History 27 Oct 1987, Brussels (Belgium), as an initiative of the *MEDIA Programme (MEDIA, inactive)* of the European Union. Originally registered in accordance with Belgian law. Since 2005 registered in accordance with Luxembourg law. **Aims** Provide professional training and culture for European cinema, television and multimedia producers; innovate and improve systems of production and co-production; stimulate cooperation and create collaborative action favouring communication and production at a European level in the audiovisual field; manage creation of the resulting European network. **Structure** General Assembly (annual). Administrative Board, comprising 5 to 26 members. Executive Committee, consisting of 5 members of the Administrative Board. **Languages** English. **Staff** 5.50 FTE, paid. **Finance** MEDIA Programme; MEDIA Mundus; Film Fund Luxembourg (Luxembourg); public and private organizations in the countries that host EAVE sessions. **Activities** Organizes: continuous professional training programme; European and international programmes. **Events** *TIES THAT BIND Asia – Europe Producers Workshop* Singapore (Singapore) 2020, *Producers Workshop* Leipzig (Germany) 2019, *Marketing Workshop* Luxembourg (Luxembourg) 2019, *TIES THAT BIND Asia – Europe Producers Workshop* Luxembourg (Luxembourg) 2019, *Producers Workshop* Serbia 2019.
Members Full; Honorary. National Coordinators in 24 countries:
Austria, Belgium, Bosnia-Herzegovina, Cyprus, Czechia, Denmark, Estonia, Finland, France, Germany, Iceland, Ireland, Italy, Luxembourg, Malta, Netherlands, North Macedonia, Poland, Romania, Russia, Serbia, Spain, Sweden, UK.
[2020/XF0825/v/**F**]

♦ Entrepreneurs without Frontiers Foundation (internationally oriented national body)

♦ Entrepreneurship Research and Education Network of Central European Universities (ERENET) 05496

Sec Szugló utca 134, Budapest 1141, Hungary. E-mail: info@erenet.org.
South-Eastern Europe Sec Zmaj Jovina 12, Belgrade, PAK 11000, Serbia. T. +381112623055. Fax +381112181471. E-mail: office@ien.bg.ac.rs.
URL: http://www.erenet.org/

History 1 May 2004, as an open network without legal status. **Structure** Steering Committee. **Events** *Annual meeting* Budapest (Hungary) 2011. **Publications** *ERENET Journal*.
Members Full in 41 countries:
Albania, Armenia, Austria, Azerbaijan, Belarus, Belgium, Bosnia-Herzegovina, Bulgaria, Canada, China, Croatia, Cyprus, Czechia, Denmark, Estonia, Finland, France, Georgia, Germany, Greece, Hungary, Iran Islamic Rep, Israel, Italy, Moldova, Montenegro, Netherlands, North Macedonia, Poland, Portugal, Romania, Russia, Serbia, Slovakia, Slovenia, Switzerland, Türkiye, UK, Ukraine, USA, Venezuela. [2019/XJ4705/**F**]

♦ Entrepreneurs du Monde (internationally oriented national body)

♦ Entrepreneurs Organization (EO) 05497

Global Headquarters 500 Montgomery St, Ste 700, Alexandria VA 22314, USA. T. +17035196700. Fax +17035191864. E-mail: info@eonetwork.org.
URL: http://www.eonetwork.org/

History 1987. Originally founded as *Young Entrepreneurs' Organization (YEO, inactive)*, which included *World Entrepreneurs' Organization (inactive)*. Rebranded under current title, 2005. **Aims** Engage leading entrepreneurs to learn and grow. **Structure** Board of Directors comprising 9 elected members of the organization. Regional offices (4): Kuala Lumpur (Malaysia); Victoria (Canada); Berlin (Germany); Panama (Panama). **Languages** English. **Staff** 60.00 FTE, paid. **Finance** Members' dues. Grants and sponsorship. **Activities** Brings entrepreneurs together through forums, conferences, chapter events and 2 annual Global Universities. Also offers executive education, business growth resources and other benefits. **Events** *Global Leadership Conference* Washington, DC (USA) / Barcelona (Spain) 2022, *GLC Momentum – Global Leadership Conference* Alexandria, VA (USA) 2021, *Global Leadership Conference* Cape Town (South Africa) 2020, *Asia Bridge Forum* Hiroshima (Japan) 2020, *Global Leadership Conference* Macau (Macau) 2019. **Publications** *Octane* (4 a year) – magazine.
Members Chapters (123), comprising over 8,000 members, in 38 countries and territories:
Australia, Bahrain, Brazil, Canada, China, Colombia, Costa Rica, Dominican Rep, Ecuador, El Salvador, Germany, Guatemala, Hong Kong, India, Indonesia, Japan, Korea Rep, Malaysia, Mexico, Nepal, Netherlands, New Zealand, Oman, Pakistan, Panama, Philippines, Qatar, Russia, Saudi Arabia, Singapore, South Africa, Spain, Switzerland, Taiwan, Thailand, UK, United Arab Emirates, USA. [2021/XM1228/**F**]

♦ Entrepreneurs of the World (internationally oriented national body)
♦ Entreprise Works / VITA (internationally oriented national body)
♦ Entretiens universitaires réguliers pour l'administration en Europe / see Association Europa
♦ **ENTSO-E** European Network of Transmission System Operators for Electricity (#08026)
♦ ENTSO / see European Network of Transmission System Operators for Electricity (#08026)
♦ **ENTSOG** European Network of Transmission System Operators for Gas (#08027)
♦ Entwicklungsprogramm der Vereinten Nationen (#20292)
♦ Entwicklungswerkstatt Austria (internationally oriented national body)
♦ Entwicklungszusammenarbeit mit der Dritten Welt (internationally oriented national body)
♦ ENU – European Naturist Union (inactive)
♦ ENUIGH – European Network in European and Global History (internationally oriented national body)
♦ **ENUSP** European Network of ex- Users and Survivors of Psychiatry (#07906)
♦ **ENViL** European Network for Visual Literacy (#08031)

♦ Environic Foundation International (EFI) 05498

Pres 12035 Stonewick Place, Glen Allen VA 23059-7152, USA. T. +18043609130. Fax +18043609131. E-mail: info@environicfoundation.org.
URL: http://www.environicfoundation.org/

History 1970, Notre Dame IN (USA) and Washington DC (USA) (simultaneously), initially to organize the International Youth Conference on the Human Environment, 1971, Canada. **Aims** Be an agent of change, moving people from destructive to constructive social, economic and environmental practices by providing education that motivates people to engage in common purpose for the attainment of sustainable societies. **Structure** Board of Advisors of 25 to 30 members. Board of Trustees of 9 members. President. **Languages** English. **Staff** 2.00 FTE, paid. **Finance** Program grants; contributions from individuals, foundations and corporations. **Activities** Development, training and support for "Sustainable Societies" courses for colleges and universities; organizes workshops and lectures. **Events** *Annual meeting* Washington, DC (USA) 1998, *International youth conference on the human environment* New Zealand 1991, *Conference on geospatial economy* Japan 1990, *International conference on geospace and geopolitan planning* Netherlands 1990, *International conference on underground space and earth sheltered buildings* Shanghai (China) 1988. **Publications** *Environing Newsletter*. **Members** Not a membership organization. **Consultative Status** Consultative status granted from: *ECOSOC (#05331)* (Special). **IGO Relations** Consultative Status with United Nations. **NGO Relations** Contacts with: *SYLVA-WORLD for Development and the Protection of Forests and the Environment*.
[2008.06.01/XF4776/fv/**F**]

♦ Environment Africa (internationally oriented national body)
♦ Environmental Action Programme for Central and Eastern Europe (inactive)
♦ Environmental Ambassadors – Environmental Ambassadors for Sustainable Development (internationally oriented national body)
♦ Environmental Ambassadors for Sustainable Development (internationally oriented national body)

♦ Environmental Coalition on Standards (ECOS) 05499

Exec Dir Mundo B, Rue d'Edimbourg 26, 1050 Brussels, Belgium. T. +3228944668 – +3228944657. E-mail: info@ecostandard.org.
Head of Communications address not obtained. T. +3228930976.
URL: http://www.ecostandard.org/

History 2001. Former names and other names: *European Environmental Citizens' Organisation for Standardisation (ECOS)* – former (2001 to 2021); *Organisation européenne environnementale citoyenne de normalisation* – former (2001 to 2021). Registration: Banque-Carrefour des Entreprises, No/ID: 0475.593.473, Start date: 30 May 2001, Belgium; EU Transparency Register, No/ID: 96668093651-33, Start date: 21 May 2010. **Aims** Advocate for environmentally friendly technical standards, policies and laws; ensure the environmental voice is heard when they are developed and drive change by providing expertise to policymakers and industry players, leading to the implementation of strong environmental principles. **Structure** General Assembly (annual); Executive Committee; Task Forces; Secretariat, based in Brussels (Belgium). **Languages** Dutch, English, French, German, Irish Gaelic, Italian, Polish, Portuguese, Romanian, Spanish, Swedish. **Staff** 30.00 FTE, paid. **Finance** Sources: grants; members' dues; private foundations. Supported by: *EFTA (#05391)*; *European Commission (EC, #06633)*. **Activities** Advocacy/lobbying/activism; events/meetings; research/documentation; standards/guidelines; training/education. **Events** *Ecodesign as a Tool for Change* Brussels (Belgium) 2022, *Making Sustainable Products the Norm* Brussels (Belgium) 2021, *Circularity in Construction – Can EU fix it?* 2020, *Conference on Plastic in a Circular Economy* Brussels (Belgium) 2019, *Workshop on the Use of Standards in Policy* Brussels (Belgium) 2018. **Publications** Position papers; press releases; reports.
Members National organizations (45) in 26 countries:
Austria, Belgium, Bulgaria, Croatia, Cyprus, Czechia, Denmark, France, Germany, Greece, Hungary, Ireland, Italy, Latvia, Lithuania, Luxembourg, Netherlands, Norway, Poland, Portugal, Slovakia, Spain, Sweden, Switzerland, UK, USA.
European umbrella organizations (9):
Bellona Europa; *European Environmental Bureau (EEB, #06996)*; *European Federation for Transport and Environment (T and E, #07230)*; *Friends of the Earth Europe (FoEE, #10001)*; *Health and Environment Alliance (HEAL, #10879)*; *Health Care Without Harm (HCWH, #10875)* (Europe); *Re-Use and Recycling European Union Social Enterprises (RREUSE, #18931)*; *World Wide Fund for Nature (WWF, #21922)* (European Policy Office); *Zero Waste Europe (#22035)*.
IGO Relations Cooperates with (1): *European Commission (EC, #06633)*. **NGO Relations** Memorandum of Understanding with (1): *Association européenne pour la coordination de la représentation des consommateurs pour la normalisation (ANEC, #02561)*. Member of (2): *GoodElectronics (#10679)*; *Green Cooling Initiative (GCI)*. Cooperates with (6): *1% for the Planet*; *Comité européen de normalisation (CEN, #04162)*; *European Committee for Electrotechnical Standardization (CENELEC, #06647)*; *European Telecommunications Standards Institute (ETSI, #08897)*; *International Electrotechnical Commission (IEC, #13255)*; *International Organization for Standardization (ISO, #14473)*. [2022.05.13/XD8172/y/**D**]

♦ Environmental Compliance and Enforcement Network for Accession (inactive)
♦ Environmental Conference of the European Regions / see Environmental Conference of the Regions of Europe (#05500)

♦ Environmental Conference of the Regions of Europe (ENCORE) 05500

Gen Secretariat Bavarian State Min Environment Consumer Protection, Rosenkavalierplatz 2, Postfach 810140, 81901 Munich, Germany. T. +498992142202. Fax +498992143611. E-mail: europa@stmuv.bayern.de.

Exec Chair Eastern and Midland Regional Assembly, Kildare County Council Ireland, Coiseanna Hill, College Road, Clane, CO. KILDARE, W91 W2R0, Ireland.

URL: http://www.encoreweb.eu/

History Dec 1993, Brussels (Belgium). Former names and other names: *Environmental Conference of the European Regions* – former. **Aims** Promote political cooperation between regional Environment Ministers of the European Union, so as to contribute to effective implementation of EU environmental policy and improve environmental governance and sustainable development in the regions of Europe. **Structure** Conference (every 2 years); Steering Committee; Steering Group; Permanent Secretariat. **Languages** English. **Staff** None. **Finance** Self-financing. **Activities** Awareness raising; events/meetings; management of treaties and agreements; networking/liaising; politics/policy/regulatory. **Events** *ENCORE Conference* Tullamore (Ireland) 2021, *ENCORE Conference* Herning (Denmark) 2018, *ENCORE Conference* Pörtschach-Wörthersee (Austria) 2016, *ENCORE Conference* Munich (Germany) 2014, *ENCORE Conference* Assen (Netherlands) / Groningen (Netherlands) 2012. **Publications** Declarations.

Members Steering Group members (20) in 15 countries:
Austria, Belgium, Czechia, Denmark, Finland, France, Germany, Ireland, Italy, Netherlands, Poland, Slovenia, Spain, Sweden, UK. [2021.06.04/XM0650/c/**F**]

♦ Environmental Consultants and Operative Studies Group / see Arab Foundation for Marine Environment (#00962)
♦ Environmental Defense / see Environmental Defense Fund
♦ Environmental Defense Council / see Environmental Defense Fund
♦ Environmental Defense Fund (internationally oriented national body)
♦ Environmental Design Research Association (internationally oriented national body)
♦ Environmental Development Action / see Environnement et développement du Tiers-monde (#05510)
♦ Environmental Development Action in the Third World (#05510)

♦ Environmental Education Association of Southern Africa (EEASA) .. 05501

Pres c/o Environmental Learning Research Centre, Dept of Education, Rhodes Univ, PO Box 94, Grahamstown, 6140, South Africa. T. +27466037473. E-mail: eeasa@eeasa.org.za.

Street address 3230 Lucas Avenue, behind the Alumni Block, c/o Environmental Learning Research Centre, Grahamstown, 5140, South Africa.

URL: http://eeasa.org.za/

History 1982, South Africa, at international conference held at Treverton College. Registered in accordance with the South African law. **Aims** Support environmental education in southern Africa. **Structure** General Business Meeting (annual, during conference). Council (elected), including Presidents, Secretary and Treasurer; may also co-opt members as necessary. Office Bearers. **Languages** English. **Staff** 0.50 FTE, paid. **Finance** Members' dues (2010): Corporate – South African Rand 6,500; Overseas – South African Rand 475; Affiliate – South African Rand 385; Individuals – South African Rand 175. Other sources: donations; sponsorship; sales of publications. **Activities** Acts as the responsible body for consultation on and coordination of matters of public and professional interest in the field of environmental education; promotes interdisciplinary and multidisciplinary studies of the environment; promotes, organizes and sponsors activities and research and disseminates information regarding environmental education; organizes World Environmental Education Congress. Members in the regions form conference committees which propose and are appointed to host the EEASA Annual Conference and workshops. **Events** *Annual Conference* Kempton Park (South Africa) 2016, *Annual Conference* Grahamstown (South Africa) 2012, *Annual Conference* Kitwe (Zambia) 2010, *World Environmental Education Congress* Botswana 2009, *Annual Conference* Gaborone (Botswana) 2009. **Publications** *Environmental Education Bulletin* (2 a year); *Southern African Journal of Environmental Education* (annual). Monographs. (occasional).

Members Members (about 400), including teachers, field workers, academics, development workers, resource developers, conservation officials, industry trainers and extension workers, in 20 countries and territories:
Angola, Australia, Botswana, Eswatini, Hong Kong, Japan, Kenya, Latvia, Lesotho, Malawi, Mauritius, Mozambique, Namibia, Seychelles, South Africa, Tanzania UR, UK, USA, Zambia, Zimbabwe. [2017/XD2795/**D**]

♦ Environmental Evaluators Network (EEN) 05502

Réseau des Evaluateurs Environnementaux

Contact address not obtained.

URL: http://www.environmentalevaluators.net/

History 2006. Founded by US Environmental Protection Agency (EPA) and the National Fish and Wildlife Foundation (NFWF). **Aims** Advance practice, policy and theory of evaluating environmental programs, policies and other interventions through more systematic and collective learning. **Structure** Includes *European Environmental Evaluators Network (EEEN)*. **Activities** Events/meetings. **Events** *European Environmental Evaluators Network Forum* Helsinki (Finland) 2020, *European Environmental Evaluators Network Forum* Brussels (Belgium) 2018, *European Environmental Evaluators Network Forum* Edinburgh (UK) 2017, *European Environmental Evaluators Network Forum* Copenhagen (Denmark) 2016, *European Environmental Evaluators Network Forum* Florence (Italy) 2015. **NGO Relations** Member of (1): *International Organisation for Cooperation in Evaluation (IOCE, #14426)*. [2020/XJ6579/**F**]

♦ Environmental Foundation for Africa (internationally oriented national body)
♦ Environmental & Health Sciences Consortium / see International Environmental & Health Sciences Consortium (#13279)
♦ Environmental Investigation Agency (internationally oriented national body)
♦ Environmentalists for Nuclear Energy (internationally oriented national body)
♦ Environmental Justice Foundation (internationally oriented national body)
♦ Environmental Justice Foundation Charitable Trust / see Environmental Justice Foundation
♦ Environmental Justice Foundation Limited / see Environmental Justice Foundation
♦ Environmental Justice Foundation Stichting / see Environmental Justice Foundation

♦ Environmental Law Alliance Worldwide (ELAW) 05503

Alianza Mundial de Derecho Ambiental – Miedzynarodowe Stowarzyszenie Prawa Ochrony Srodowiska – Loka Viyaptha Parisara Neethi Santhanaya – Pandaigdigang Alyansa Para sa Batas Pangkalikasan

US Office 1412 Pearl St, Eugene OR 97401, USA. T. +15416878454. Fax +15416870535. E-mail: elawus@elaw.org.

URL: http://www.elaw.org/

History Founded 1989. **Aims** Facilitate development and practice of public interest environmental law throughout the world by exchanging legal, scientific and technical information as well as ideas, precedents and strategies across national boundaries. **Staff** 15.00 FTE, paid. Voluntary. **Finance** Supported by foundations, government organizations and individuals. **Activities** Knowledge management/information dissemination; guidance/assistance/consulting; networking/liaising; events/meetings. **Events** *Public interest environmental law conference* Eugene, OR (USA) 1995, *Public interest environmental law conference* Eugene, OR (USA) 1994. **Publications** *ELAW Advocate* (4 a year). **Members** Individuals in about 70 countries. Membership countries not specified. [2015.08.26/XF5517/**F**]

♦ Environmental Law Institute (internationally oriented national body)

♦ Environmental Law Network International (ELNI) 05504

Réseau international de droit de l'environnement – Internationales Netzwerk Umweltrecht

Contact c/o TH Bingen, Berlinstr 109, 55411 Bingen, Germany. T. +4969433951. Fax +496943057629. E-mail: julian.schenten@h-da.de.

URL: http://www.elni.org/

History 1990. **Aims** Promote international communication and cooperation of those working in the field of environmental law. **Structure** Board; Coordinating Bureau. **Finance** Sources: members' dues. **Activities** Events/meetings. **Publications** *elni Review* – online journal. *Publications of Environmental Law Network International* – book series. **Members** Individuals and organizations (about 350). Membership countries not specified. [2022.10.18/XF5703/**F**]

♦ Environmental Legal Organizations' Network Central and Eastern Europe / see Association Justice and Environment, z.s. (#02774)
♦ Environmentally Compatible Air Transport System / see ECATS International Association (#05278)

♦ Environmental Management Accounting Network (EMAN) 05505

Contact CSM – Leuphana Univ, Scharnhorststr 1, 21335 Lüneburg, Germany. T. +4941316772181. Fax +4941316772186.

URL: http://www.eman-eu.net/

History 1997. **Aims** Promote exchange among academics and practitioners on sustainability and environmental accounting, information management, reporting and communication; analyse current practice, theory and literature; develop and disseminate new approaches, including policies, procedures, methods and organizations. **Structure** Steering Committee. Regional chapters (4): Africa; Americas; Asia-Pacific; Europe. **Events** *Two decades of corporate environmental and sustainability accounting* Lüneburg (Germany) 2016, *Conference* Geneva (Switzerland) 2015, *Annual Conference* San Sebastian (Spain) 2015, *Annual Conference* Rotterdam (Netherlands) 2014, *Annual Conference* Dresden (Germany) 2013. **Publications** Books; volumes; journals.

Members Researchers, consultants, business people and policy advisers (countries not specified). Steering Committee members in 6 countries:
Denmark, Finland, Germany, Italy, Netherlands, UK. [2012.06.28/XF6869/**F**]

♦ Environmental Management Group (EMG) 05506

Secretariat UNEP/EMG, Int'l Environment House, 11-13 Chemin des Anemones, Châtelaine, 1219 Geneva, Switzerland. T. +41229178628. Fax +41227973420. E-mail: emg@unep.ch.

URL: http://www.unemg.org/

History 2001, pursuant to *United Nations (UN, #20515)* General Assembly resolution 53/242 of Jul 1999. **Aims** Achieve effective coordination and joint action in key areas of environmental and *human settlements* concern. **Structure** Chaired by Executive Director of *UNEP (#20299)*. Secretariat. **Activities** Furthers inter-agency cooperation in support of the implementation of the international environmental and human settlement agenda; identifies issues warranting joint efforts, and finds ways of engaging its collective capacity in coherent management responses to those issues. **Events** *Meeting* Geneva (Switzerland) 2005, *Meeting* Geneva (Switzerland) 2004, *Meeting* Geneva (Switzerland) 2004, *Meeting* Nairobi (Kenya) 2004, *Meeting* New York, NY (USA) 2004. **Publications** Texts; documents. **Members** Specialized agencies, programmes and organs of the United Nations system. **IGO Relations** Represents members to: *United Nations Commission on Sustainable Development (CSD, inactive)*; *United Nations Human Settlements Programme (UN-Habitat, #20572)* Governing Council; UNEP Governing Council. **NGO Relations** *One UN Climate Change Learning Partnership (UN CC:Learn, #17735)*. [2014.01.30/XE4203/**E***]

♦ Environmental Mutagenesis and Genomics Society (internationally oriented national body)
♦ Environmental Mutagen Society / see Environmental Mutagenesis and Genomics Society

♦ Environmental Paper Network (EPN) 05507

Contact PO Box 7091, Asheville NC 28802, USA. T. +18282518558. E-mail: info@environmentalpaper.org – luisa@environmentalpaper.org.

URL: http://environmentalpaper.org/

History Started 2002. **Aims** Empower and motivate consumers, corporations, organizations and governments to protect forests, climate, air, water and communities through more *sustainable* production and consumption of pulp and paper. **Structure** Organized into 3 non-hierarchical hubs, each with its own Steering Committee and staff: North America; China; International. **Activities** Projects/programmes.

Members Civil society organizations (over 140) in 29 countries:
Argentina, Australia, Austria, Bangladesh, Belgium, Brazil, Canada, China, Czechia, Estonia, Finland, France, Germany, Ghana, Indonesia, Italy, Japan, Netherlands, Norway, Poland, Portugal, Romania, Russia, Spain, Sweden, Switzerland, UK, Uruguay, USA.

Included in the above, 22 organizations listed in this Yearbook:
- *Both ENDS (#03307)*;
- *Canopy*;
- *Earth Day Network (EDN, #05164)*;
- *Earthworks*;
- *Environmental Defense Fund (EDF)*;
- *Environmental Investigation Agency (EIA)*;
- *Fern (#09736)*;
- *Forest Peoples Programme (FPP, #09865)*;
- *GLOBAL 2000*;
- *Global Exchange (GX)*;
- *Global Witness (GW)*;
- *Greenpeace International (#10727)*;
- *Green Sports Alliance (GSA)*;
- *Japan Tropical Forest Action Network (JATAN)*;
- *Mighty Earth*;
- *Pro Regenwald*;
- *Rainforest Action Network (RAN, #18614)*;
- *Save the Rhino International (SRI, #19061)*;
- *TROPICA VERDE*;
- *Wetlands International (#20928)*;
- *World Wide Fund for Nature (WWF, #21922)*;
- *Youth and Environment Europe (YEE, #22012)*. [2020/XM7754/y/**F**]

♦ Environmental Partnership for Central Europe / see Environmental Partnership for Sustainable Development (#05508)

♦ Environmental Partnership for Sustainable Development (EPSD) ... 05508

Dir Udolni 33 st, 602 00 Brno, Czechia. T. +420515903111.

URL: http://www.environmentalpartnership.org/

History 1991, as *Environmental Partnership for Central Europe (EPCE)*. **Aims** Support development of environmental *NGOs* and community initiatives, thus strengthening the move of the Central European countries towards more *market-oriented* economies and greater *democracy*. **Finance** Donations and sponsors in 1996 include: *Charities Aid Foundation (CAF)*; *Charles Stewart Mott Foundation*; *Foundation for a Civil Society (FCS)*; *German Marshall Fund of the United States (GMF)*; *International Institute for Energy Conservation – Europe (IIEC-Europe, see: #13875)*; *The Prince of Wales International Business Leaders Forum (PWIBLF, inactive)*; *Rockefeller Brothers Fund (RBF)*; *United States Agency for International Development (USAID)*; *World Wide Fund for Nature (WWF, #21922)*. **Activities** Financial and/or material support; guidance/assistance/consulting; projects/programmes. **Publications** Annual Report.

Members Offices in 6 countries:
Bulgaria, Czechia, Hungary, Poland, Romania, Slovakia. [2016.02.12/XF4317/**F**]

♦ Environmental Peacebuilding Association (EnPAx) 05509

Pres c/o ELI, 1730 M Street NW, Suite 700, Washington DC 20036, USA. E-mail: association@environmentalpeacebuilding.org.

URL: https://www.environmentalpeacebuilding.org/

History Apr 2018. Registration: Nonprofit corporation 501(c)(6), USA, District of Columbia. **Aims** Bring together researchers, practitioners, and decision makers working on issues of environment, conflict and peace. **Structure** Board of Directors; Interest Groups. **Finance** Sources: members' dues. **Activities** Events/meetings; training/education. **Events** *International Conference on Environmental Peacebuilding* Switzerland 2022.

Members Individuals (about 400); Institutional (23) in 70 countries. Membership countries not specified.
Alliance for Peacebuilding; *Center for Conservation Peacebuilding (CPeace)*; *Conservation International (CI)*; *Consortium on Gender, Security & Human Rights*; *EcoPeace Middle East (#05325)*; *Energy Peace Partners (EPP)*; *Environmental Law Institute (ELI)*; *Global Green Growth Institute (GGGI, #10392)*; *IMPACT (#11136)*; *International Alert (#11615)*; *International Institute for Sustainable Development (IISD, #13930)*. [2023.02.14/AA1163/y/**C**]

♦ Environmental Policy and Society (internationally oriented national body)

- ♦ Environmental Training Network for Latin America and the Caribbean (inactive)
- ♦ Environment Congress for Asia and the Pacific (meeting series)
- ♦ Environment and Development Resource Centre (internationally oriented national body)
- ♦ Environment and Development Service for NGOs / see Both ENDS (#03307)
- ♦ Environment and Development Service for Third World Citizens' Groups / see Both ENDS (#03307)
- ♦ Environment for Europe / see European ECO Forum (#06955)
- ♦ Environment Fellowship of Rotarians (internationally oriented national body)

♦ Environnement et développement du Tiers-monde (enda) 05510

Environmental Development Action in the Third World – Medio Ambiente y Desarrollo del Tercer Mundo

Contact Complexe SICAP Point E, Bât B – 1er étage, Avenue Cheikh Anta Dlop X Canal IV, BP 33 70 Dakar, Senegal. T. +221338699948 – +221335699949. Fax +221338605133. E-mail: se@endatiersmonde.org.

URL: http://endatiersmonde.org/

History 1972, Dakar (Senegal), as a joint programme of UNEP, *United Nations African Institute for Economic Development and Planning (#20518)* and *Swedish International Development Cooperation Agency (Sida)*. Also referred to as: *ENDA-Third World – ENDA-Tiers monde (enda TM)*; *Environmental Development Action*. Since 2008, an network of national organizations. EU Transparency Register: 192055335104-57. **Aims** Build societies in which everyone can participate in collective regulation as fully responsible individuals; promote the empowerment and strengthening of community participation and social movements; work for the respect of human rights, pluralism, cultural diversity, gender equality and equity between generations; mobilize in favour of the decompartmentalization and articulation of knowledge and actions at the local, regional and global levels; through training, action research, advocacy and strategic alliance building, contribute to the formulation of public policies for sustainable development and to a culture of peace and non-violence. **Structure** General Assembly (every 3 years); Administrative Council; Executive Secretariat. **Languages** English, French, Portuguese, Spanish.

Finance Government support from: Switzerland; Austria; Netherlands; Luxembourg; France. Supporters include:
- *Alliance Sud, Swiss Alliance of Development Organisations Swissaid – Catholic Lenten Fund – Bread for All – Helvetas – Caritas – Interchurch Aid*;
- *AQUADEV (inactive)*;
- *Brothers to All Men (BAM, #03339)*;
- *Caritas Internationalis (CI, #03580)* (Germany);
- *Comité Catholique contre la Faim et pour le Développement-Terre Solidaire (CCFD-Terre Solidaire)*;
- *Catholic Organization for Relief and Development (Cordaid)*;
- *Centre de coopération internationale en recherche agronomique pour le développement (CIRAD, #03733)*;
- *European Commission (EC, #06633)*;
- *HORIZONT 3000*;
- *ICCO – Interchurch Organization for Development Cooperation*;
- *International Development Research Centre (IDRC, #13162)*;
- *Oxfam International (#17922)* (Belgium);
- *Oxfam Novib*;
- *Terre des hommes Foundation (Tdh Foundation, #20132)*;
- United Nations.

Activities Training/education; advocacy/lobbying/activism. knowledge management/information dissemination. **Events** *African regional seminar on local governance* Saly (Senegal) 2008, *International conference on traditional medicine* Dakar (Senegal) 2004, *International colloquium on women, knowledge, science and sustainable development / Congress* Dakar (Senegal) 2003, *Joint meeting on sustainable local development and participative governance* Paris (France) 2002, *Colloque sur la gouvernance locale, l'économie sociale et les pratiques populaires face à la globalisation* Louvain-la-Neuve (Belgium) 2001. **Publications** *Passerelles entre le commerce et le dévelopement durable* (6 a year) – review; *African Environment – Environnement africain* (4 a year) in English, French; *Claire de lune*; *Etudes et Recherches*; *Outils et juex pédagogiques*.

Members Associations (17) in 13 countries:
Bolivia, Brazil, Colombia, Dominican Rep, Ethiopia, France, India, Madagascar, Mali, Morocco, Senegal, Tunisia, Vietnam.
Included in the above, 2 regional organizations listed in this Yearbook:
ENDA Europe (EE, #05454); *enda inter-arabe (enda-ia)*.

Consultative Status Consultative status granted from: *ECOSOC (#05331)* (General); *UNEP (#20299)*; *UNCTAD (#20285)* (General Category); *UNICEF (#20332)*; *UNIDO (#20336)*; *Organisation internationale de la Francophonie (OIF, #17809)*. **IGO Relations** Accredited to the Conference of the Parties of: *Secretariat of the United Nations Convention to Combat Desertification (Secretariat of the UNCCD, #19208)*. Accredited by: *United Nations Framework Convention on Climate Change – Secretariat (UNFCCC, #20564)*. Member of: *Observatoire du Sahara et du Sahel (OSS, #17636)*. Associated with Department of Global Communications of the United Nations.

NGO Relations Coordinates: *African NGO Habitat Caucus (Africaucus, no recent information)*. Partner of: *Climate Technology Centre and Network (CTCN, #04023)*; *Rainwater Partnership (no recent information)*. Supports: *Global Call for Action Against Poverty (GCAP, #10263)*. Member of:
- *Centre de recherche et d'information pour le développement, Paris (CRID)*;
- *Climate Action Network (CAN, #03999)*;
- *Coalition for an Effective African Court on Human and Peoples' Rights (African Court Coalition, #04055)*;
- *Council of Non-Governmental Organizations for Development Support (#04911)*;
- *Drynet (#05140)*;
- *EarthAction (EA, #05159)*;
- *Environment Liaison Centre International (ELCI, no recent information)*;
- *EuroMed Non-Governmental Platform (#05730)*;
- *Freshwater Action Network (FAN, inactive)*;
- *GEF CSO Network (GCN, #10087)*;
- *Global Gender and Climate Alliance (GGCA, no recent information)*;
- *International Network for Sustainable Energy (INFORSE, #14331)*;
- *International Union for Conservation of Nature and Natural Resources (IUCN, #15766)*;
- *LEDS Global Partnership (LEDS GP, #16435)*;
- *Settlements Information Network Africa (SINA, #19250)*;
- *Sustainable Development Communications Network (SDCN, inactive)*;
- *Transparency, Accountability and Participation Network (TAP Network, #20222)*;
- *WomenAction 2000 (no recent information)*;
- *World Social Forum (WSF, #21797)*.

[2022/XD7793/y/**F**]

- ♦ Environnement sans frontière (internationally oriented national body)
- ♦ ENVIRO-PROTECT – International Association for the Protection of the Environment in Africa (no recent information)
- ♦ **ENWHP** European Network for Workplace Health Promotion (#08037)
- ♦ ENYGF – European Nuclear Young Generation Forum (meeting series)
- ♦ **ENYSSP** European Network of Young Specialists in Sport Psychology (#08038)
- ♦ Enzyme Technical Association (unconfirmed)
- ♦ EOA / see Global Sourcing Association
- ♦ **EOA** European Oilseed Alliance (#08080)
- ♦ **EOA** European Olympic Academies (#08082)
- ♦ **EOA** European Ostomy Association (#08120)
- ♦ EOA – European Ostrich Association (no recent information)
- ♦ **EOCA** European Outdoor Conservation Association (#08121)
- ♦ EOCCD – European Organization for the Control of Circulatory Diseases (no recent information)
- ♦ **EOCC** European Organic Certifiers Council (#08094)
- ♦ **EOC** European Olympic Committees (#08083)
- ♦ **EOC** European Orchid Council (#08093)
- ♦ EOCN / see European Oncology Nursing Society (#08086)
- ♦ **EOEF** European Offender Employment Forum (#08077)
- ♦ **EO** Entrepreneurs Organization (#05497)
- ♦ **EOFed** European Orchestra Federation (#08092)
- ♦ EOF – European Oriental Federation (inactive)
- ♦ **EOF** Europees Ontwikkelingsfonds (#06914)
- ♦ EOFFI / see International Society of Fish and Shellfish Immunology (#15122)
- ♦ **EOGAN** European Oil and Gas Archives Network (#08079)
- ♦ EOG Association for Conservation / see European Outdoor Conservation Association (#08121)
- ♦ **EOG** European Outdoor Group (#08122)
- ♦ **EO and Glycols** Ethylene Oxide and Derivates Producers Association (#05556)
- ♦ EOHCS / see European Observatory on Health Systems and Policies (#08072)
- ♦ EOHR – Egyptian Organization for Human Rights (internationally oriented national body)
- ♦ **EOI** Europäisches Ombudsman Institut (#08085)
- ♦ EOI / see SOLIDAR (#19680)
- ♦ **EOL** Encyclopedia of Life (#05453)
- ♦ EOLSS International Editorial Council / see UNESCO-EOLSS Joint Committee
- ♦ **EOM** European Society for Environmental and Occupational Medicine (#08597)
- ♦ **EOMF** European Observatory of Mountain Forests (#08073)
- ♦ EOMW – European Oral Microbiology Workshop (meeting series)
- ♦ EONN / see European Monitoring Centre for Drugs and Drug Addiction (#07820)
- ♦ **EONS** European Oncology Nursing Society (#08086)
- ♦ **EOOS** European Ocean Observing System (#08075)
- ♦ EOP – Economics of Payments (meeting series)
- ♦ EOP – European Observatory for Plurilingualism (internationally oriented national body)
- ♦ EOPM – European Organization of Pakistani Minorities (internationally oriented national body)
- ♦ **EOPS** European Ophthalmic Pathology Society (#08089)
- ♦ EOPS – European Organization of Petrol and Service Stations (inactive)
- ♦ EOQC / see European Organization for Quality (#08112)
- ♦ **EOQ** European Organization for Quality (#08112)
- ♦ EORCU – European Ozone Research Coordinating Unit (internationally oriented national body)
- ♦ EORG – Europese Organisatie ter Bescherming van de Rechtspositie van Gedetineerden (internationally oriented national body)
- ♦ **EORNA** European Operating Room Nurses Association (#08087)
- ♦ **EORS** European Orthopaedic Research Society (#08119)
- ♦ **EORTC** European Organisation for Research and Treatment of Cancer (#08101)
- ♦ **EOSCA** European Oilfield Speciality Chemicals Association (#08078)
- ♦ EOS – Earth Observing System (internationally oriented national body)
- ♦ **EOSE** European Observatoire of Sport and Employment (#08071)
- ♦ EOS – EnablingOpenScholarship (unconfirmed)
- ♦ **EOS** Europäische Organisation der Sägewerke (#08114)
- ♦ **EOS** European Optical Society (#08091)
- ♦ **EOS** European Organisation for Security (#08102)
- ♦ **EOS** European Organization of the Sawmill Industry (#08114)
- ♦ **EOS** European Orthodontic Society (#08118)
- ♦ EOS International (internationally oriented national body)
- ♦ **EOTA** European Organisation for Technical Assessment (#08103)
- ♦ EOTC – European Organisation for Conformity Assessment (inactive)
- ♦ **EOU** European Ornithologists' Union (#08117)
- ♦ EOUG / see International Oracle Users Community (#14416)
- ♦ EOVS / see International Observatory of Violence in the School Environment (#14389)
- ♦ EO/WFCW / see European Organization of the World Organization of Workers (#08116)
- ♦ **EO/WOW** European Organization of the World Organization of Workers (#08116)
- ♦ **EOZ** Europese Organisatie der Zagerijen (#08114)
- ♦ EP2DS – International Conference on Electronic Properties of Two-Dimensional Systems (meeting series)
- ♦ EPA / see Oomoto
- ♦ **EPAA** European Partnership for Alternative Approaches to Animal Testing (#08155)
- ♦ EPAA – European Primary Aluminium Association (inactive)
- ♦ **EPACA** European Public Affairs Consultancies' Association (#08294)
- ♦ **EPAC** European Partners against Corruption (#08153)
- ♦ **EPACL** Equipe panafricaine de coordination des laïcs (#05523)
- ♦ EPACT – European Promotion Association for Composite Tanks and Tubulars (inactive)
- ♦ **EPAD** European Prevention of Alzheimer's Dementia Consortium (#08271)
- ♦ EPA – Ecole du patrimoine africain (internationally oriented national body)
- ♦ EPA – Eglise protestante africaine (internationally oriented national body)
- ♦ **EPA** Energy Poverty Action (#05474)
- ♦ **EPA** Europäisches Patentamt (#08166)
- ♦ EPA / see European Association of Polyol Producers (#06157)
- ♦ **EPA** European Association of Polyol Producers (#06157)
- ♦ EPA – European Palaeontological Association (inactive)
- ♦ **EPA** European Parents' Association (#08142)
- ♦ **EPA** European Parking Association (#08144)
- ♦ EPA – European Parliamentary Association (internationally oriented national body)
- ♦ **E-P-A** European Pathway Association (#08168)
- ♦ **EPA** European Perlite Association (#08189)
- ♦ **EPA** European Photochemistry Association (#08204)
- ♦ **epa** european playwork association (#08236)
- ♦ **EPA** European Privacy Association (#08278)
- ♦ EPA – European Probiotic Association (inactive)
- ♦ EPA – European Projects Association (unconfirmed)
- ♦ **EPA** European Prosthodontic Association (#08287)
- ♦ **EPA** European Psychiatric Association (#08290)
- ♦ **EPAG** European Pharmaceutical Aerosol Group (#08195)
- ♦ EPAGMA – European Peat and Growing Media Association (inactive)
- ♦ **EPAL** European Pallet Association (#08133)
- ♦ **EPAM** European NGO Platform Asylum and Migration (#08051)
- ♦ EPAN / see European Public Administration Network (#08293)
- ♦ EPAQ / see European Association for Panels and Profiles (#06142)
- ♦ Epargne sans frontière (internationally oriented national body)
- ♦ **EPAS** Enlarged Partial Agreement on Sport (#05487)
- ♦ **EPATH** European Professional Association for Transgender Health (#08283)
- ♦ **EPA/UNEPSA** European Paediatric Association (#08124)
- ♦ **EPAW** European Platform Against Windfarms (#08221)
- ♦ **EPBA** European Portable Battery Association (#08255)
- ♦ **EPBA** European Professional Beekeepers Association (#08284)
- ♦ **EPB** European Polar Board (#08238)
- ♦ **EPBF** European Paintball Federation (#08132)
- ♦ **EPBF** European Pocket Billiard Federation (#08237)
- ♦ EPBP – European Partners for Blindness Prevention (inactive)
- ♦ EPBRS / see European Biological Rhythms Society (#06337)
- ♦ **EPBRS** European Platform for Biodiversity Research Strategy (#08222)
- ♦ **EPBS** European Association for Professions in Biomedical Science (#06170)
- ♦ EPC / see European Plastics Converters (#08216)
- ♦ EPCAA / see International Pharmaceutical Congress Advisory Association (#14564)
- ♦ **EPCA** European Payments Consulting Association (#08174)
- ♦ **EPCA** European Personal Construct Association (#08190)
- ♦ **EPCA** European Petrochemical Association, The (#08192)
- ♦ EPCA – European Polyolefin Clingfilm Association (inactive)
- ♦ **EPCA** European Popular Culture Association (#08254)

EPCAS European Party
05510

- ♦ **EPCAS** European Party Caterer Association (#08161)
- ♦ **EPCCS** European Primary Care Cardiovascular Society (#08273)
- ♦ EPCE / see Environmental Partnership for Sustainable Development (#05508)
- ♦ **EPC** European Pancreatic Club (#08136)
- ♦ **EPC** European Paralympic Committee (#08140)
- ♦ **EPC** European Payments Council (#08175)
- ♦ **EPC** European Pellet Council (#08179)
- ♦ **EPC** European Policy Centre (#08240)
- ♦ **EPC** European Producers Club (#08281)
- ♦ **EPC** European Publishers Council (#08304)
- ♦ **EPC** Euro Pony Club (#09172)
- ♦ **EPCG** European Pulp and Paper Chemicals Group (#08306)
- ♦ **EPCIA** European Passive Components Industry Association 1100041302
- ♦ **EPCN** European Pond Conservation Network (#08253)
- ♦ EPCOS – European Phase Change and Ovonics Symposium (meeting series)
- ♦ **EPCRA** European Pentecostal and Charismatic Research Association (#08182)
- ♦ EPCR – European Professional Club Rugby (unconfirmed)
- ♦ **EPCS** European Public Choice Society (#08295)
- ♦ **epda** European Brand and Packaging Design Association (#06396)
- ♦ **EPDA** European Parkinson's Disease Association (#08145)
- ♦ **EPDA** European Plastics Distributors Association (#08217)
- ♦ **EPDA** – European Professional Drivers Association (unconfirmed)
- ♦ **EPDCC** European Pressure Die Casting Committee (#08268)
- ♦ EPDC / see European Plastics Distributors Association (#08217)
- ♦ **EPDE** European Platform for Democratic Elections (#08224)
- ♦ **EPD** European Partnership for Democracy (#08156)

♦ EPDIC Committee (EPDiCom) 05511
Chairman Dept of Civil/Environmental/Mechanical Engineering, Univ of Trento, Via Mesiano 77, 38123 Trento TN, Italy. T. +39461282417. Fax +39461281999.
URL: http://epdic.ing.unitn.it/
History 1998, Budapest (Hungary), during 6th *European Powder Diffraction Conference (EPDIC)*. **Aims** Steer organization of EPDIC events. **Structure** Committee. **Languages** English. **Staff** Voluntary. **Finance** Sources: participation fees; sponsorship; additional fees. **Activities** Awards/prizes/competitions. **Events** *European Powder Diffraction Conference* Edinburgh (UK) 2018, *European Powder Diffraction Conference* Bari (Italy) 2016, *European Powder Diffraction Conference* Aarhus (Denmark) 2014, *European Powder Diffraction Conference / Conference* Grenoble (France) 2012, *European powder diffraction conference / Conference* Darmstadt (Germany) 2010. **Publications** Proceedings. **NGO Relations** Special Interest Group of: *European Crystallographic Association (ECA, #06867)*. Collaborations and partnerships with various scientific organizations, including: *International Centre for Diffraction Data (ICDD)*. [2014.11.18/XJ6668/c/E]

- ♦ **EPDiCom** EPDIC Committee (#05511)
- ♦ **EPDLA** European Polymer Dispersions and Latex Association (#08250)
- ♦ EPDWA / see European Drinking Water Cooler Association
- ♦ **EPEA** European Prison Education Association (#08276)
- ♦ E and P – Échanges et Partenariats (internationally oriented national body)
- ♦ EPECS – European Patients Empowerment for Customised Solutions (internationally oriented national body)
- ♦ **EPEE** European Partnership for Energy and the Environment (#08157)
- ♦ **EPE** – Energy Peat Europe (no recent information)
- ♦ **EPE** European Partners for the Environment (#08154)
- ♦ **EPE** European Power Electronics and Drives Association (#08261)
- ♦ **EPEGA** European Poultry, Egg and Game Association (#08258)
- ♦ EPEMA – European Play Equipment Manufacturers Association (inactive)
- ♦ EPEMED – European Personalised Medicine Association (no recent information)
- ♦ **EPEN** – Ecologistas en Pro de la Energia Nuclear (internationally oriented national body)
- ♦ **EPERC** European Pressure Equipment Research Council (#08269)
- ♦ EPER – Entraide protestante Suisse (internationally oriented national body)
- ♦ EPETMA – European Polyester Terephthalate Film Manufacturers Association (inactive)
- ♦ **EP** Europäisches Parlament (#08146)
- ♦ **EP** Europaparlamentet (#08146)
- ♦ **EP** Europa-Parlamentet (#08146)
- ♦ **EP** European Parliament (#08146)
- ♦ **EP** – European People (internationally oriented national body)
- ♦ **EP** Europees Parlement (#08146)
- ♦ **EPEX** European Performance Co-Extruders (#08188)
- ♦ **EPFA** European Phenolic Foam Association (#08199)
- ♦ EPFA / see International Plasma and Fractionation Association (#14597)
- ♦ EPF – Episcopal Peace Fellowship (internationally oriented national body)
- ♦ **EPF** European Panel Federation (#08137)
- ♦ EPF – European Paper Forum (inactive)
- ♦ **EPF** European Parliamentary Forum for Sexual & Reproductive Rights (#08149)
- ♦ **EPF** European Passengers' Federation (#08162)
- ♦ **EPF** European Patients' Forum (#08172)
- ♦ EPF – European Peering Forum (meeting series)
- ♦ **EPF** European Photocatalysis Federation (#08203)
- ♦ EPF – European Policy Forum (internationally oriented national body)
- ♦ **EPF** European Polymer Federation (#08251)
- ♦ **EPF** European Powerlifting Federation (#08262)
- ♦ **EPF** European Property Federation (#08286)
- ♦ **EPF** European Psychoanalytical Federation (#08292)
- ♦ EPF / see Europe Foundation (#09158)
- ♦ **EPF** Europe Foundation (#09158)
- ♦ **EPFIF** European Pension Fund Investment Forum (#08181)
- ♦ EPFL / see European Leagues (#07672)
- ♦ EPFMA – European Polyvinyl Film Manufacturers Association (inactive)
- ♦ E and P Forum / see International Association of Oil and Gas Producers (#12053)
- ♦ **EPFSF** European Parliamentary Financial Services Forum (#08148)
- ♦ EPFU – European Powered Flying Union (unconfirmed)
- ♦ EPGA / see European Poultry and Game Association (#08259)
- ♦ EPGA / see European Poultry, Egg and Game Association (#08258)
- ♦ EPG – Annual Environmental Politics and Governance Conference (meeting series)
- ♦ EP/GDG / see EUROGIRO – Giro, Postbank, Commercial Bank Payment Institutions Organizations Worldwide (#05687)
- ♦ EPG – Europäische Parlamentarische Gesellschaft (internationally oriented national body)
- ♦ **EPG** European Placenta Group (#08209)
- ♦ **EPG** European Poultry and Game Association (#08259)
- ♦ EPG / see European Pulp Industry Sector Association (#08305)
- ♦ **EPHAC** European Public Health and Agriculture Consortium (#08296)
- ♦ EPHA Environment Network / see Health and Environment Alliance (#10879)
- ♦ **EPHA** European Public Health Alliance (#08297)
- ♦ **EPHAR** Federation of European Pharmacological Societies (#09527)
- ♦ **EPhEU** European Association of Employed community Pharmacists in Europe (#06025)
- ♦ **EphMRA** European Pharmaceutical Market Research Association (#08196)
- ♦ **EPHSA** – European Public Health Students Association (inactive)

- ♦ EPIA / see SolarPower Europe (#19676)
- ♦ EPICA – Ecumenical Program on Central America and the Caribbean (internationally oriented national body)
- ♦ EPIC-Africa (unconfirmed)
- ♦ EPIC – Electronic Privacy Information Center (internationally oriented national body)
- ♦ **EPICENTER** European Policy Information Center (#08241)
- ♦ **Epicentre** Groupe européen d'expertise en épidémiologie pratique (#10738)
- ♦ Epicentrum Foundation / see People in Need
- ♦ EPIC / see European Packaging Institutes Consortium (#08123)
- ♦ **EPIC** European Packaging Institutes Consortium (#08123)
- ♦ **EPIC** European Parliamentarians and Industrialists Council (#08147)
- ♦ **EPIC** European Photonics Industry Consortium (#08205)
- ♦ EPIC – European Process Intensification Conference (meeting series)
- ♦ Epicurean World Master Chefs Society / see World Master Chefs Society (#21639)
- ♦ Epididymis – International Conference on the Epididymis (meeting series)
- ♦ EPI – European Paper Institute (inactive)
- ♦ **EPIF** European Payment Institutions Federation (#08173)
- ♦ **EPI Foundation** Elephant Protection Initiative Foundation (#05429)
- ♦ **epi** Institute of Professional Representatives before the European Patent Office (#11288)
- ♦ Epilepsie euro services / see HandiCapacités

♦ Epilepsy Alliance Europe (EAE) 05512
Secretariat Office 0208, Nesta Business Centre, 4-5 Burton Hall Road, Sandyford, Dublin, CO. DUBLIN, Ireland. T. +35312108850. Fax +35312108450. E-mail: info@epilepsyallianceeurope.org.
URL: http://www.epilepsyallianceeurope.org/
History Set up 2015, under the auspices of *International League Against Epilepsy (ILAE, #14013)* and *International Bureau for Epilepsy (IBE, #12414)*. Registered in accordance with Irish law. EU Transparency Register: 18456627532-50. **Aims** Promote the rights of people with epilepsy; improve epilepsy care; disseminate awareness and knowledge about the complex spectrum of epileptic diseases; promote research in epilepsy and its comorbidities; establish epilepsy as a healthcare priority in Europe. **Structure** Board of Directors. **Events** *Epilepsy Colloquium* Lyon (France) 2019. **Publications** *EAE Newsletter*.
[2022/XM5650/**E**]

- ♦ Epilepsy International (inactive)
- ♦ **EPIM** European Programme for Integration and Migration (#08285)
- ♦ **EPIN** European Policy Institutes Network (#08242)
- ♦ **EPIP** European Policy for Intellectual Property (#08243)

♦ Episcopal Church in Jerusalem and the Middle East 05513
Cyprus and Gulf Diocese 2 Grigori Afxentiou Street, CY-1517 Nicosia, Cyprus. T. +35722671220. E-mail: info@cypgulf.org.
Egypt/North Africa/Horn of Africa Diocese 5 Michael Lutfallah Street, Zamalek, Cairo, Egypt. T. +20227380821. E-mail: info@dioceseofegypt.org.
URL: https://www.episcopalchurch.org/anglican-province/episcopal-church-jerusalem-m iddle-east
History 1841, as an autonomous member Church of *Anglican Communion (#00827)*. Restructured Jan 1976. **Aims** Serve the local Anglican (Palestinian and Arab) Christians; serve the entire community (Christian, Muslim and Jewish) through its various ministries. **Structure** Central Synod, under Diocesan Bishop. The Diocese includes Jerusalem, Palestinian National Authority, Israel, Jordan, Lebanon and Syria. The Province consists of the Dioceses of Jerusalem, Cyprus and the Gulf, Egypt and Iran. **Activities** Maintains Parishes (29) with 7,000 Communicants; institutions of educational and medical services (37). Reconciliation work, especially in Israel and Palestine. Annual Church Council Meeting. **Events** *Clergy conference* Cyprus 1996. **Publications** Newsletter.
Members Individuals in 35 countries and territories:
Bahamas, Bahrain, Cyprus, Egypt, France, Georgia, Germany, Greece, Holy See, Honduras, India, Iran Islamic Rep, Iraq, Ireland, Israel, Italy, Jordan, Korea DPR, Korea Rep, Kuwait, Lebanon, Nepal, Netherlands, Norway, Oman, Pakistan, Palestine, Philippines, South Africa, Sudan, Sweden, Switzerland, UK, United Arab Emirates, USA.
NGO Relations Working relations with: *World Council of Churches (WCC, #21320)*. Represented on the: *Anglican Consultative Council (ACC, #00828)*. Every diocese represented at the: *Lambeth Conference of Bishops of the Anglican Communion (#16224)*. Primates meet at: *Primates Meeting of the Anglican Communion (#18497)*. Links with various others.
[2019/XF5106/v/**F**]

- ♦ Episcopal Church Missionary Community / see New Wineskins Missionary Network
- ♦ Episcopal Conference of the Indian Ocean (#04592)
- ♦ Episcopal Conference of the Pacific (#04659)
- ♦ Episcopal Medical Missions Foundation (internationally oriented national body)
- ♦ Episcopal Migration Ministries (internationally oriented national body)
- ♦ Episcopal Pacifist Fellowship / see Episcopal Peace Fellowship
- ♦ Episcopal Peace Fellowship (internationally oriented national body)
- ♦ Episcopal Relief and Development (internationally oriented national body)

♦ Episcopal Secretariat of Central America 05514
Secrétariat épiscopal d'Amérique centrale – Secretariado Episcopal de América Central (SEDAC)
Pres Calle 22, Av 3-5, Barrio México, San José, San José, San José, 1000, Costa Rica. T. +50622213053 – +50622231729.
URL: http://www.sedac.info/
History Founded 26 Sep 1970, as *Episcopal Secretariat of Central America and Panama – Secrétariat épiscopal d'Amérique centrale et Panama – Secretariado Episcopal de América Central y Panama*. **Structure** Plenary Assembly (annual); Presidential Council; President; Secretary General. **Activities** Transmits to members documents of common interest proceeding from various religious organizations and, when appropriate, those arising from the pastoral communities and social and religious investigations. **Events** *Annual General Assembly* 1994, *Annual General Assembly* 1993, *General Assembly* San Salvador (El Salvador) 1992.
Members Bishops in 6 countries:
Costa Rica, El Salvador, Guatemala, Honduras, Nicaragua, Panama.
[2017/XD8880/**D**]

- ♦ Episcopal Secretariat of Central America and Panama / see Episcopal Secretariat of Central America (#05514)
- ♦ **EPIS** European Pulp Industry Sector Association (#08305)
- ♦ **EPITA** European Pancreas and Islet Transplant Association (#08135)
- ♦ EPITEL – Association for European Public Information by Television (inactive)
- ♦ Epitropi ton Evropaikon Kinotiton / see European Commission (#06633)
- ♦ Epitropi ton Nision (#16061)
- ♦ Epitropi tis Vorias Falassas (#17604)
- ♦ Epitropi tu Atlantiku Tosu (#03007)
- ♦ Epitropi ton Viomihanion Vamvakos ke Sinafon Inon tis EK / see European Federation of Cotton and Allied Textiles Industries (#07093)
- ♦ **EPIZONE** EPIZONE European Research Group (#05515)

♦ EPIZONE European Research Group (EPIZONE) 05515
Contact address not obtained. E-mail: epizone.bvr@wur.nl.
URL: https://www.epizone-eu.net/
History May 2012. Developed out of the EPIZONE EU Network of Excellence for Epizootic Disease Diagnosis and Control (2006-2012). **Aims** As an network of veterinary research institutes working on epizootic animal diseases, play a key role in research on prevention, detection and control of animal diseases and zoonoses so as to reduce the risks and harm to animal health and the risks to public health in the EU and beyond. **Finance** Sources: members' dues. **Activities** Events/meetings; knowledge management/information dissemination; research/documentation; training/education. **Events** *EPIZONE Annual Meeting* Barcelona (Spain) 2022, *EPIZONE Annual Meeting* Ghent (Belgium) 2021, *EPIZONE Annual Meeting* Barcelona (Spain) 2020, *EPIZONE Annual Meeting* Berlin (Germany) 2019, *EPIZONE Annual Meeting* Vienna (Austria) 2018.

Members Full partners in 12 countries:
Belgium, Denmark, France, Germany, Italy, Netherlands, Poland, Russia, Spain, Sweden, Switzerland, UK.
Associate member in 1 country:
USA. [2020/AA0743/j/**E**]

♦ **EPL Association** Europhysics Letters Association (#09169)
♦ **EPLAW** European Patent Lawyers Association (#08165)
♦ **EPL** European Petrochemical Luncheon International Association (#08193)
♦ **EPLF** Association of European Producers of Laminate Flooring (#02533)
♦ **EPL** Grupa Europejskiej Partii Ludowej – Chrzexcijanscy Demokraci (#10775)
♦ **EPLN** European Prison Litigation Network (#08277)
♦ **EPLO** European Peacebuilding Liaison Office (#08176)
♦ **EPLO** European Public Law Organization (#08299)
♦ **EPMA** European Association for Predictive, Preventive and Personalised Medicine (#06163)
♦ **EPMA** European Pari Mutuel Association (#08143)
♦ EPMA – European Pencil Manufacturer's Association (inactive)
♦ **EPMA** European Powder Metallurgy Association (#08260)
♦ EPMESC – International Conference on Enhancement and Promotion of Computational Methods in Engineering and Science (meeting series)
♦ EPMF / see European Powder Metallurgy Association (#08260)
♦ **EPMF** European Precious Metals Federation (#08267)
♦ EPMI – European Printer Manufacturers and Importers (no recent information)
♦ **EPMWR** European Platform for Migrant Workers' Rights (#08225)
♦ **EPN** Ecumenical Pharmaceutical Network (#05350)
♦ **EPN** Environmental Paper Network (#05507)
♦ **EPN** EUREF Permanent Network (#05620)
♦ **EPN** European Council of Practical Nurses (#06838)
♦ EPN – European Professionals Network (unconfirmed)
♦ **EPNOE** European Polysaccharide Network of Excellence (#08252)
♦ **EPNoSL** European Policy Network on School Leadership (#08245)
♦ **EPNS** European Paediatric Neurology Society (#08126)
♦ **EPOA** European Palm Oil Alliance (#08134)
♦ **EPOA** European Pride Organizers Association (#08272)
♦ EPOC – European Pherology Organizations Confederation (inactive)
♦ **EPODIN** European Patient Organisation for Dysimmune and Inflammatory Neuropathies (#08169)
♦ **EPO** European Patent Office (#08166)
♦ **EPO** European Pet Organization (#08191)
♦ EPOG / see European Paediatric Ophthalmological Society (#08127)
♦ **EPOMM** European Platform on Mobility Management (#08226)
♦ EPOS – Environmental Policy and Society (internationally oriented national body)
♦ **EPOS** European Association of Patients Organizations of Sarcoidosis and other Granulomatous Disorders (#06144)
♦ **EPOS** European Paediatric Ophthalmological Society (#08127)
♦ **EPOS** European Paediatric Orthopaedic Society (#08128)
♦ **EPOS** European Plate Observing System (#08220)
♦ **EPoSS** European Technology Platform on Smart Systems Integration (#08892)
♦ EPPA – European Paper Packaging Alliance (unconfirmed)
♦ EPPA – European Poker Players' Association (no recent information)
♦ EPPA / see European Trade Association of PVC Window System Supplies (#08924)
♦ **EPPA** European Trade Association of PVC Window System Supplies (#08924)
♦ **EPP-CoR** Group of the European People's Party in the Committee of the Regions (#10776)
♦ EPP – Energy Peace Partners (internationally oriented national body)
♦ **EPP** Euroopan Kansanpuolueen Rhymä – Kristillisdemokraatit (#10775)
♦ **EPP** Det Europaeiske Folkepartis Gruppe – Kristelige Demokrater (#10775)
♦ **EPP** Európai Néppart – Kereszténydemokratak – Képviselócsoport (#10775)
♦ **EPP** European People's Party (#08185)
♦ EPPF – European Profiles and Panels Producers Federation (inactive)
♦ **EPP** Group of the European People's Party – Christian Democrats (#10775)
♦ **EPP** Klub Zastupnika Europske Pucke Stranke – Krscanski Demokrati (#10775)
♦ **EPPM** Association of Engineering, Project, and Production Management (#02488)
♦ **EPPM** European Platform for Photodynamic Medicine (#08227)
♦ EPPN – European Paediatric Psychology Network (unconfirmed)
♦ **EPPO** European and Mediterranean Plant Protection Organization (#07773)
♦ **EPPO** European Public Prosecutor's Office (#08300)
♦ Epposi / see DigitalHealthEurope (#05078)
♦ **EPPR** Emergency, Prevention, Preparedness and Response (#05437)
♦ EPPSA / see Energy Technologies Europe (#05477)
♦ **EPPSP** European Parliament Platform for Secularism in Politics (#08152)

♦ EPP Women 05516

HQ Administrator c/o EPP, Rue du Commerce 10, 1000 Brussels, Belgium. T. +3223092867. Fax +3223008013. E-mail: eppwomen@epp.eu.
Pres address not obtained.
URL: http://www.eppwomen.eu/

History Founded as *European Union of Christian Democratic Women (EUCDW) – Union européenne des femmes démocrates-chrétiennes (UEFDC) – Union Europea de Mujeres Demócrata Cristianas (UEMDC).* Subsequently referred to as *Women of the EPP/EUCD – Femmes du PPE/UEDC – Mujeres del PPE/UEDC.* Previously also referred to as *EPP Women's Association.* **Aims** Support national member organizations and strengthen the role of women in politics; promote gender awareness and gender justice in EPP member parties, EPPW member organizations and EU and national politics. **Structure** Presidency, General Board; Congress. Specialized organization of: *European People's Party (EPP, #08185).* **Languages** English. **Activities** Events/meetings. **Events** *Congress* Vienna (Austria) 2019, *Congress* Ljubljana (Slovenia) 2018, *Congress* Berlin (Germany) 2017, *Congress* Sofia (Bulgaria) 2016, *Congress* Munich (Germany) 2015.
Members Women's organizations (about 60) from EPP political parties which are members of the EPP in 36 countries and territories:
Albania, Austria, Belarus, Belgium, Bosnia-Herzegovina, Bulgaria, Croatia, Cyprus, Czechia, Denmark, Estonia, Finland, France, Germany, Greece, Hungary, Ireland, Italy, Kosovo, Latvia, Lithuania, Luxembourg, Malta, Moldova, Netherlands, North Macedonia, Norway, Poland, Romania, Serbia, Slovakia, Slovenia, Spain, Sweden, Switzerland, Ukraine.
[2018.03.09/XD2142/**E**]

♦ EPP Women's Association / see EPP Women (#05516)
♦ EPP Youth / see Youth of the European People's Party (#22014)
♦ **EPRA** European Phenolic Resins Association (#08200)
♦ **EPRA** European Platform of Regulatory Authorities (#08229)
♦ **EPRA** European Public Real Estate Association (#08301)
♦ **EPRC** European Paper Recycling Council (#08139)
♦ EPRC – European Policies Research Centre, University of Strathclyde (internationally oriented national body)
♦ **EPR** European Platform for Rehabilitation (#08230)
♦ EPRG – European Pharmacovigilance Research Group (inactive)
♦ **EPRM** European Partnership for Responsible Minerals (#08159)
♦ **EPRO** European Association of Plastics Recycling and Recovery Organizations (#06153)
♦ EPRO – European Pentecostal Relief Organization (inactive)
♦ EPRS – European Paediatric Respiratory Society (inactive)
♦ **EPRUMA** European Platform for the Responsible Use of Medicines in Animals (#08231)
♦ EPRW – European Pesticide Residue Workshop (meeting series)
♦ **EPSA** European Pharmaceutical Students' Association (#08197)
♦ **EPSA** European Philosophy of Science Association (#08202)
♦ **EPSA** European Platform & Stairlift Association (#08233)
♦ **EPSA** European Political Science Association (#08247)
♦ EPSA – European Primary Schools Association (inactive)
♦ **EPSA** European Producers of Specialty Aluminas (#08282)
♦ EPSC / see European Federation of Public Service Unions (#07202)
♦ **EPSC** European Political Strategy Centre (#08248)
♦ **EPSC** European Process Safety Centre (#08279)
♦ **EPSD** Environmental Partnership for Sustainable Development (#05508)
♦ **EPS** Economists for Peace and Security (#05322)
♦ **EPSE** European Polycarbonate Sheet Extruders (#08249)
♦ EPS / see European Biological Rhythms Society (#06337)
♦ EPS – European Palm Society (internationally oriented national body)
♦ **EPS** European Peptide Society (#08186)
♦ EPS – European Phycological Society (inactive)
♦ **EPS** European Physical Society (#08207)
♦ EPSG / see European Biological Rhythms Society (#06337)
♦ EPSG – European Public Support Group (internationally oriented national body)
♦ **EPSI** European Platform for Sport Innovation (#08232)
♦ **EPSMA** European Power Supplies Manufacturer's Association (#08263)
♦ EPSMA – European Pressure Sensitive Manufacturers Association (inactive)
♦ **EPSM** European Association of Payment Service Providers for Merchants (#06145)
♦ EpsNet / see ECPR European Political Science Network (#05339)
♦ **EpsNet** ECPR European Political Science Network (#05339)
♦ EPSO / see European Partnership of Supervisory Organisations in Health Services and Social Care (#08160)
♦ **EPSO** European Partnership of Supervisory Organisations in Health Services and Social Care (#08160)
♦ **EPSO** European Plant Science Organization (#08211)
♦ **EPSRC** European Plastic Surgery Research Council (#08218)
♦ EPSR – European Plan Science Retreat (meeting series)
♦ **EPSSE** European Philosophical Society for the Study of Emotions (#08201)
♦ **EpSSG** European paediatric Soft tissue sarcoma Study Group (#08129)
♦ **EPSU** European Federation of Public Service Unions (#07202)
♦ **EPTA** European Parliamentary Technology Assessment (#08150)
♦ EPTA / see European Penitentiary Training Academies Network (#08180)
♦ **EPTA** European Penitentiary Training Academies Network (#08180)
♦ **EPTA** European Pentecostal Theological Association (#08184)
♦ **EPTA** European Piano Teachers' Association (#08208)
♦ **EPTA** European Power Tool Association (#08264)
♦ **EPTA** European Pultrusion Technology Association (#08307)
♦ **EPTDA** European Power Transmission Distributors Association (#08265)
♦ **EPT** Electronic Publishing Trust for Development (#05427)
♦ **EPTO** European Passenger Transport Operators (#08163)
♦ EPTO – European Peer Training Organization (internationally oriented national body)
♦ EPTRI – European Paediatric Translational Research Infrastructure (unconfirmed)
♦ **EPTS Foundation** European Platform of Transport Sciences (#08234)
♦ **EPUAP** European Pressure Ulcer Advisory Panel (#08270)
♦ **EPU** Europartner Umwelt (#08154)
♦ EPU – European Parliamentary Union (inactive)
♦ EPU – European Payments Union (inactive)
♦ EPU – European Picture Union (inactive)
♦ **EPU** European Polio Union (#08246)
♦ EPU – European Pressphoto Union (inactive)
♦ **EPUF** EuroMed Permanent University Forum (#05731)

♦ ePURE 05517

SG Rue de la Loi 223, 1040 Brussels, Belgium. T. +3226576679. E-mail: info@epure.org.
URL: http://www.epure.org/

History 2010, as *European Producers Union of Renewable Ethanol (ePURE),* by merger of *European Bioethanol Fuel Association (eBIO, inactive)* and *European Union of Ethanol Producers (UEPA, inactive).* Full title: *ePure – European Renewable Ethanol.* Registration: AISBL, Belgium. **Aims** Represent and support companies that produce *renewable ethanol* in the *European Union* for all end-uses, ie fuel, potable and industrial uses; represent companies with an interest in ethanol *production.* **Structure** General Assembly; Board of Directors; Executive Committee; Secretariat, headed by Secretary General. **Languages** English. **Staff** 6.00 FTE, paid. **Finance** Members' dues. **Activities** Knowledge management/information dissemination; advocacy/lobbying/activism; events/meetings.
Members Producing – companies with production plants in Europe; Associate – companies operating throughout the ethanol value chain. Producing (22) members in 12 countries:
Austria, Belgium, Denmark, Finland, France, Germany, Hungary, Netherlands, Slovakia, Spain, Sweden, UK.
Associate (32) in 15 countries:
Austria, Belgium, Czechia, Denmark, France, Germany, Hungary, India, Italy, Lithuania, Sweden, Switzerland, Türkiye, UK, USA.
IGO Relations Registered industry representative with: *European Commission (EC, #06633).* **NGO Relations** Liaison Organization of: *Comité européen de normalisation (CEN, #04162).* Member of: *European Bioeconomy Alliance (EUBA, #06334). Global Renewable Fuels Alliance (GRFA, #10566).* Associate member of: *CO2 Value Europe (CVE, #04042).* [2017/XJ2859/**D**]

♦ ePure – European Renewable Ethanol / see ePURE (#05517)
♦ **EPV** European Primate Veterinarians (#08274)
♦ EPVR / see European Platform for Rehabilitation (#08230)
♦ EPW – European Plastic Window Association (inactive)
♦ **EPWS** European Platform of Women Scientists (#08235)
♦ EQAC – Educational Quality Accrediting Commission (internationally oriented national body)
♦ EQA – European Quality Alliance (inactive)
♦ EQA – European Quality Assurance Association of Expanded Polystyrene Foam Manufacturers for Food Packaging (inactive)
♦ **EQA** European Quilt Association (#08316)
♦ **EQALM** European Organisation for External Quality Assurance Providers in Laboratory Medicine (#08098)
♦ **EQANIE** European Quality Assurance Network for Informatics Education (#08310)
♦ EQAR Association / see European Quality Assurance Register for Higher Education (#08311)
♦ **EQAR** European Quality Assurance Register for Higher Education (#08311)
♦ **EQAVET** European Quality Assurance in Vocational Education and Training (#08312)
♦ **EQCS** European Quality Control System (#08313)
♦ EQNet / see International Certification Network (#12532)
♦ Equadiff (meeting series)
♦ Equal Access International (internationally oriented national body)
♦ **EQUAL** European Quadricycle League (#08309)
♦ **EQUAL** European Quality Link (#08314)
♦ Equal Futures Partnership (no recent information)
♦ Equality Diversity Inclusion Conference – Equality, Diversity and Inclusion International Conference (meeting series)
♦ Equality, Diversity and Inclusion International Conference (meeting series)
♦ E-Quality: Experts on Gender and Ethnicity / see Atria – Institute for Gender Equality and Women's History

- ♦ Equality Fund (internationally oriented national body)
- ♦ Equality for Gays And Lesbians In The European institutions / see Egalité (#05393)
- ♦ E-Quality: Information Centre for Gender, Family and Diversity Issues / see Atria – Institute for Gender Equality and Women's History
- ♦ E-Quality: Information Centre for Gender Issues in a Multicultural Society / see Atria – Institute for Gender Equality and Women's History
- ♦ Equality and Justice Alliance (unconfirmed)
- ♦ E-Quality: Knowledge Centre for Gender, Family and Diversity Issues / see Atria – Institute for Gender Equality and Women's History

♦ Equality Now 05518

Egalité maintenant – Igualdad Ya

Contact 125 Maiden Ln, 9th Fl Ste B, New York NY 10026, USA. E-mail: info@equalitynow.org.
URL: http://www.equalitynow.org/

History 1992. Established as an international human rights organization with a *'Women's Action Network'* (USA). Registration: EU Transparency Register, No/ID: 170784531762-42. **Aims** Work to achieve legal and systemic change that addresses violence and discrimination against *women* and girls around the world. **Structure** Board of Directors; Advisory Council. Offices in: New York NY (USA); Nairobi (Kenya); London (UK). **Languages** Arabic, English, French, Spanish. **Staff** 49.00 FTE, paid. New York NY (USA) 16; London (UK) 15; Nairobi (Kenya) 15; Beirut (Lebanon) 3. **Finance** Sources: contributions; grants; private foundations. Supported by: *New Field Foundation*; *Oxfam Novib*; *UN Trust Fund to End Violence against Women (UN Trust Fund, #20716)*. Annual budget: 6,100,000 USD. **Activities** Advocacy/lobbying/activism; knowledge management/information dissemination. **Publications** *Women's Action*. Annual Report; AGLDF Report; Incest Report. **Members** Groups and individuals (35,000) in over 160 countries. Membership countries not specified. **Consultative Status** Consultative status granted from: *African Commission on Human and Peoples' Rights (ACHPR, #00255)* (Observer); *ECOSOC (#05331)* (Special). **NGO Relations** Member of: *Advocacy Network for Africa (ADNA)*; *Girls not Brides (#10154)*; *Global Campaign for Equal Nationality Rights (#10265)*; *Network of East-West Women (NEWW, #17006)*. Partner of: *Safe World for Women (inactive)*. [2020.08.27/XF3215/**F**]

- ♦ Equal Rights Beyond Borders (internationally oriented national body)

♦ Equal Rights Coalition (ERC) 05519

Coalition pour les droits égaux – Coalición por la Igualdad de Derechos

Co-Chair address not obtained. T. +13432037700. E-mail: media@international.gc.ca.
Co-Chair address not obtained. T. +56228274397. E-mail: prensa@minrel.gob.cl.
URL: https://equalrightscoalition.org/

History Launched Jul 2016, Montevideo (Uruguay), at Global LGBTI Human Rights Conference. **Aims** Promote and protect human rights of *lesbian*, *gay*, *bisexual*, *transgender* and *intersex* (LGBTI) people worldwide. **Structure** Co-Chairs (2). **Events** *ERC Global Conference* 2021, *ERC Global Conference* London (UK) 2020, *ERC Global Conference* Vancouver, BC (Canada) 2018. **Members** Governments (over 30). Membership countries not specified. [2021/XM6031/**E***]

- ♦ Equal Rights – Equal Responsibilities / see International Alliance of Women (#11639)
- ♦ Equal Rights International (inactive)

♦ Equal Rights Trust 05520

Dir 314-320 Gray's Inn Road, London, WC1X 8DP, UK. T. +442076102786. Fax +442034417436. E-mail: info@equalrightstrust.org.
URL: http://www.equalrightstrust.org/

History Office opened Jan 2007. Company limited by guarantee incorporated in England: No 5559173. UK Registered Charity: No 1113288. **Aims** Combat discrimination and advance equality worldwide; promote a unified human rights framework on equality, approaching each aspect of inequality in the context of other relevant aspects and developing strategies for translating the principles of equality into practice. **Structure** Board of Trustees of 17 members. **Languages** English. **Staff** 10.50 FTE, paid. 1 intern. **Finance** Financial year 2014-2015, work funded by: American Jewish World Service; Arcus; Astraea Lesbian Foundation for Justice; *Comic Relief*; *European Commission (EC, #06633)*; Open Society Foundations; *Swedish International Development Cooperation Agency (Sida)*; UK Foreign and Commonwealth Office; UN Voluntary Fund for Victims of Torture; *UN Women (#20724)*; *UNHCR (#20327)*; US Department of State – Bureau of Population, Refugees and Migration. Annual audited accounts for financial year ending Sep 2014 signed off in Dec 2014. Total income realized in that financial year was pounds1,461,545, adding to pounds103,381 brought forward from the previous year. **Activities** Advocacy/lobbying/activism; capacity building; networking/liaising; projects/programmes; events/meetings. Active in: Azerbaijan, Bangladesh, Belarus, Bosnia-Herzegovina, China, Croatia, Egypt, Guyana, India, Indonesia, Iran Islamic Rep, Jordan, Kazakhstan, Kenya, Kyrgyzstan, Madagascar, Malaysia, Moldova, Myanmar, Nepal, Nigeria, Pakistan, Russia, Serbia, Solomon Is, South Sudan, Sudan, Tajikistan, Thailand, Türkiye, Turkmenistan, UK, Ukraine, Uzbekistan, Yemen, Zambia. **Publications** *Equal Rights Review* (2 a year) – 14 vols to date. Country Reports; Thematic Reports. **Members** Not a membership organization. **Consultative Status** Consultative status granted from: *Council of Europe (CE, #04881)* (Participatory Status); *ECOSOC (#05331)* (Special). **IGO Relations** Cooperates with: Fundamental Rights Platform of: *European Union Agency for Fundamental Rights (FRA, #08969)*. Member of: Steering Committee of Global Campaign for Equal Nationality Rights with *UN Women (#20724)* and *UNHCR (#20327)*. **NGO Relations** Member of: *Global Campaign for Equal Nationality Rights (#10265)*; *European Network on Statelessness (ENS, #08013)*. [2019/XJ1801/**F**]

- ♦ Equator Initiative / see World Network of Indigenous Peoples and Local Community Land and Sea Managers (#21670)

♦ Para Equestrian (PE) 05521

Secretariat c/o FEI, HM King Hussein I Building, Chemin de la Joliette 8, 1006 Lausanne VD, Switzerland. T. +41213104747. Fax +41213104760. E-mail: info@horsesport.org.
URL: http://www.ipec-athletes.de/

History Aug 1991, Denmark, within *International Paralympic Committee (IPC, #14512)*, as *International Paralympic Equestrian Committee (IPEC)*. Current title adopted when joined *Fédération Équestre Internationale (FEI, #09484)*, 2003. **Aims** Within the framework of IPC, govern, educate, develop and support international equestrian *sport* for the *disabled*. **Structure** Committee; sub-committees. **Languages** English. **Staff** All voluntary. **Finance** IPC; sponsors. **Activities** Offers courses. Organizes: workshops; world championships; international competitions; Paralympics Games. **Events** *European congress on therapeutic riding* Gothenburg (Sweden) 1996. **Publications** Rulebooks; classification manual; Dressage Tests; information leaflets.
Members Competitions are open to all nationalities. IPC membership. Organizations in 44 countries and territories:
Australia, Austria, Bahamas, Belgium, Brazil, Canada, Chile, Croatia, Czechia, Denmark, Finland, France, Germany, Greece, Hong Kong, Hungary, Ireland, Israel, Italy, Japan, Malaysia, Netherlands, New Zealand, Norway, Pakistan, Peru, Philippines, Poland, Portugal, Russia, Singapore, Slovakia, Slovenia, South Africa, Spain, Sudan, Sweden, Switzerland, Taiwan, UK, Uruguay, USA, Venezuela, Zimbabwe. [2013/XE2504/**E**]

♦ Equestrian Educational Network (EEN) 05522

Contact Freiherr-von-Langen-Str 13, 48361 Warendorf, Germany.
URL: http://equestrian-educational-network.eu/

History Oct 1999, Strömsholm (Sweden). **Aims** Improve equestrian education in Europe by facilitating international information exchange about current methods and new developments; enable the direct exchange of students and teachers between approved equestrian training centres. **Structure** General Assembly. **Activities** Events/meetings. **Events** *Global Equestrian Educational Conference (GEEC)* Ypäjä (Finland) 2017.
Members Full in 8 countries:
Finland, France, Germany, Netherlands, Norway, Portugal, Sweden, UK.
IGO Relations *European Commission (EC, #06633)*. **NGO Relations** Member of *European Horse Network (EHN, #07499)*. [2016/XJ9446/**F**]

- ♦ Equestrian Order of the Holy Sepulchre of Jerusalem (religious order)
- ♦ Equilibres and Populations (internationally oriented national body)
- ♦ **Equinet** European Network of Equality Bodies (#07903)
- ♦ **EQUINET** Network for Equity in Health in East and Southern Africa (#17011)
- ♦ Equipas de Nossa Senhora (#20112)
- ♦ Equipe Cousteau (internationally oriented national body)

♦ Equipe panafricaine de coordination des laïcs (EPACL) 05523

Pan African Laity Coordination Board

Coordinator c/o SECAM, 4 Senchi Street, PO Box 9156, No 19 First Close, Airport Residential Area, Accra, Ghana. T. +23321778871. Fax +23321772857.
URL: http://www.secam-sceam.org/

History 1971, coming under the Doctrinal and Pastoral Commission of *Symposium of Episcopal Conferences of Africa and Madagascar (SECAM, #20077)*. **Aims** Promote commitment of the laity towards growth of the *Church* in Africa and towards development of the whole African person in his totality, taking into account the requirements of his material, intellectual moral, spiritual and religious needs. **Structure** Board, consisting of: Regional Coordinators; the Bishop responsible for lay apostolate in each region; Secretary General. **Languages** English, French, Portuguese. **Members** Individuals in 52 African countries. Membership countries not specified. [2008/XF0611/v/**F**]

- ♦ Equipes internationales de renaissance chrétienne (inactive)
- ♦ Equipes Notre-Dame (#20112)
- ♦ Equipes Notre-Dame "International" / see Teams of Our Lady (#20112)
- ♦ Equipes Saint-Vincent (internationally oriented national body)
- ♦ **EQuiP** European Association for Quality in General Practice/Family Medicine (#06184)
- ♦ **EQUIP** European Society for Quality and Safety in Family Practice (#08718)
- ♦ Equip KIDS International (internationally oriented national body)
- ♦ Equipo de Conferencias de Trabajadores de América Latina (inactive)
- ♦ Equipo Latinoamericano de Justicia y Género (internationally oriented national body)
- ♦ Equipo Nizkor (internationally oriented national body)
- ♦ Equipop – Equilibres and Populations (internationally oriented national body)
- ♦ Equipos Cristianos de Acción por la Paz (internationally oriented national body)

♦ Equipos Docentes de Latinoamérica y el Caribe (EDAL) 05524

Coordinator Caraz 161, San Antonio, Miraflores, Lima, Peru. T. +5114447754.
URL: http://www.equiposdocentes-al.com/

History as an organization of teams of Christian educators working in public schools. **Aims** Promote quality education for all. [2010/XM3923/**D**]

- ♦ Equipos de Nuestra Señora (#20112)
- ♦ Equipo Técnico Multidisciplinario de América Central (see: #11123)
- ♦ Equitas – Centre international d'éducation aux droits humains (internationally oriented national body)
- ♦ Equitas – International Centre for Human Rights Education (internationally oriented national body)
- ♦ Equité (internationally oriented national body)
- ♦ Equiterre (internationally oriented national body)
- ♦ ERAB / see European Foundation for Alcohol Research (#07342)
- ♦ **ERAB** European Foundation for Alcohol Research (#07342)
- ♦ ERAC – European Regional Aerodromes Community (unconfirmed)
- ♦ ERA Club / see International Evoked Response Audiometry Study Group (#13320)
- ♦ ERA-CODICE – Esperanto Radikala Asocio – Coordination pour l'intégration démocratique culturelle européenne (internationally oriented national body)
- ♦ ERA / see Comprehensive System International Rorschach Association (#04421)
- ♦ **ERA-EDTA** European Renal Association – European Dialysis and Transplant Association (#08353)
- ♦ ERA-ENVHEALTH (inactive)
- ♦ **ERA** Europäische Rechtsakademie (#00035)
- ♦ **ERA** European Radioecology Alliance (#08321)
- ♦ **ERA** European Radon Association (#08322)
- ♦ **ERA** European Ramblers' Association (#08328)
- ♦ **ERA** European Regions Airline Association (#08347)
- ♦ **ERA** European Rental Association (#08358)
- ♦ **ERA** European Retail Academy (#08386)
- ♦ ERA – European Retail Alliance (inactive)
- ♦ ERA – European Rifle Association (inactive)
- ♦ **ERA** European Rolfing Association (#08398)
- ♦ **ERA** European Rotogravure Association (#08404)
- ♦ ERA – European Rum Association (no recent information)
- ♦ ERA – European Rural Alliance (inactive)
- ♦ ERA / see European Union Agency for Railways (#08973)
- ♦ ERA – Europea Rum Associazione (no recent information)
- ♦ ERA Europe / see ERA Global – Electronic Retailing Association (#05525)
- ♦ ERA – Event Riders Association (no recent information)

♦ ERA Global – Electronic Retailing Association (ERA Global) 05525

CEO c/o Kanzlei Oberndoerfer, Maximilianstrasse 7b, 82319 Starnberg, Germany. T. +4981515566480. Fax +4981515566479.
Registered Address Chée d'Alsemberg 999, 1180 Brussels, Belgium.
URL: https://era-global.org

History Regional organization of *Electronic Retailing Association (ERA International, inactive)*. Former names and other names: *European Electronic Retailing Association* – former; *Electronic Retailing Association Europe (ERA Europe)* – legal name. Registration: Banque-Carrefour des Entreprises, No/ID: 0867.005.301, Start date: 31 Aug 2004, Belgium. **Aims** Represent the global multi-channel home shopping industry. **Structure** General Assembly; Board of Directors. **Languages** English, French. **Activities** Advocacy/lobbying/activism; awards/prizes/competitions; certification/accreditation; events/meetings; publishing activities. **Events** *Conference* Amsterdam (Netherlands) 2021, *Conference* Las Vegas, NV (USA) 2021, *Digital Week* Munich (Germany) 2021, *Multi-Channel Home Shopping Conference* Amsterdam (Netherlands) 2020, *Annual Meeting* Frankfurt-Main (Germany) 2020. **Publications** *ERA GLOBAL Journal* (weekly); *ERA GLOBAL Newsletter* (4 a year); *ERA GLOBAL Weekly Journal*.
Members Companies in 32 countries and territories:
Australia, Austria, Canada, China, Colombia, Cyprus, France, Germany, Greece, Hong Kong, Hungary, Ireland, Israel, Italy, Liechtenstein, Luxembourg, Mexico, Netherlands, New Zealand, Romania, Russia, San Marino, Serbia, Slovenia, South Africa, Spain, Switzerland, Taiwan, Thailand, UK, United Arab Emirates, USA. [2021.03.23/XM3701/**C**]

- ♦ **ERA Global** ERA Global – Electronic Retailing Association (#05525)
- ♦ ERAHS – East Asia Research Association for Agricultural Heritage Systems (unconfirmed)
- ♦ ERAIFT – Ecole régionale post-universitaire d'aménagement et de gestion intégrés des forêts et territoires tropicaux (internationally oriented national body)
- ♦ ERASMUS Academic Network / see Network for Innovation in Career Guidance and Counselling in Europe (#17038)

♦ Erasmus Course on Magnetic Resonance Imaging (EMRI) 05526

Contact Dept of Radiology – UZ Brussel, Laarbeeklaan 101, 1090 Brussels, Belgium. Fax +3224775362.
URL: https://www.emricourse.org/

History 1991, Brussels (Belgium). Registration: No/ID: ZVR 034846925, Austria. **Aims** Advance the knowledge and clinical use of magnetic resonance imaging in relation to other imaging methods, aimed at improving medical care for patients. **Activities** Training/education. [2020/AA0362/**F**]

- ♦ Erasmus Mundus Association / see Erasmus Mundus Students and Alumni Association (#05527)

♦ **Erasmus Mundus Students and Alumni Association (EMA)** **05527**
Contact Rue Joseph II 120, 1000 Brussels, Belgium. E-mail: vice.president@em-a.eu – president@em-a.eu – service@em-a.eu.
URL: http://www.em-a.eu/
History Jun 2006, Belgium. Founded on the initiative of *European Commission (EC, #06633)* – DG Education and Culture. Former names and other names: *Erasmus Mundus Association* – alias. Registration: AISBL, Start date: 2015, Belgium. **Aims** Spread awareness about Erasmus Mundus and Erasmus+ critical role in creating mutual understanding between nations and cultures; promote excellence of Erasmus Mundus, Erasmus+ and European education in general; create space for dialogue on quality of higher education; offer learning and professional opportunities. **Structure** General Assembly; Steering Committee; Chapters; Service Teams; Networks; Country and Programme Representatives. **Languages** English. **Staff** None. **Finance** *European Union (EU, #08967)*. **Activities** Research/documentation; guidance/assistance/consulting. **Events** *General Assembly* Brussels (Belgium) 2020, *ARISE (ASEAN Region International Student Engagement) Conference* Singapore (Singapore) 2019, *General Assembly* Vienna (Austria) 2019, *General Assembly* Brussels (Belgium) 2017, *General Assembly* Lugano (Switzerland) 2016. **Members** Individuals (approx 10,000). Membership countries not specified. **IGO Relations** *Asia-Europe Foundation (ASEF, #01270)*. **NGO Relations** *AIESEC (#00593)*; *Eastern European University Association (EEUA)*; *Eastern Partnership Civil Society Forum (EaP CSF, #05247)*; *Erasmus Student Network (ESN, #05529)*; *Erasmus+ Student and Alumni Alliance (ESAA, #05528)*; *garagErasmus Foundation (garagErasmus, #10070)*; *Organisation for Cooperation, Exchange And Networking among Students (OCEANS, #17802)*. [2020/XJ0107/**E**]

♦ **Erasmus+ Student and Alumni Alliance (ESAA)** **05528**
Contact c/o GIZ and partners, Rue de al Charité 33, 1210 Brussels, Belgium. T. +4922129492400. E-mail: service@esaa-eu.org – info@esaa-eu.org.
URL: http://www.esaa-eu.org/
History Mar 2015, Brussels (Belgium). Set up by *garagErasmus Foundation (garagErasmus, #10070)*, *Organisation for Cooperation, Exchange And Networking among Students (OCEANS, #17802)*, *Erasmus Student Network (ESN, #05529)* and *Erasmus Mundus Students and Alumni Association (EMA, #05527)*. Former names and other names: *Erasmus+ Student and Alumni Association (ESAA)* – former. **Aims** Enhance cooperation among Erasmus+ students and alumni. **Structure** Liaison Group. **Languages** English. **Activities** Capacity building; events/meetings; networking/liaising; projects/programmes.
Members Organizations (4):
Erasmus Mundus Students and Alumni Association (EMA, #05527); *Erasmus Student Network (ESN, #05529)*; *garagErasmus Foundation (garagErasmus, #10070)*; *Organisation for Cooperation, Exchange And Networking among Students (OCEANS, #17802)*. [2022.05.16/XM6581/y/**E**]

♦ Erasmus+ Student and Alumni Association / see Erasmus+ Student and Alumni Alliance (#05528)

♦ **Erasmus Student Network (ESN)** **05529**
Dir Rue Joseph II 120, 1000 Brussels, Belgium. T. +3222567427. E-mail: director@esn.org – secretariat@esn.org.
Pres address not obtained. E-mail: president@esn.org.
URL: http://www.esn.org/
History 10 Feb 1990, Copenhagen (Denmark). Founded at 1st General Meeting, with financial support of the *European Commission (EC, #06633)*, the idea having first been suggested at an evaluation meeting for ex-Erasmus students organized by *ERASMUS Bureau (inactive)*, Jan 1989, Ghent (Belgium). Statutes adopted 10 Feb 1990; most recently modified 25 Mar 2009. Registration: No/ID: BE.0876.728.26, Start date: 30 Nov 2005, Belgium; EU Transparency Register, No/ID: 45445593026-68. **Aims** Work to improve the social and practical integration of international students. **Structure** General Assembly; Annual General Meeting; International Board; International Committees; National Platforms; National Boards; Liaison Offices. **Languages** English. **Staff** 13.00 FTE, paid. **Finance** Sources: members' dues; sale of products; sponsorship. Administrative grant from *European Commission (EC, #06633)* under Erasmus+. **Activities** Events/meetings; networking/liaising. **Events** *Meeting* Lisbon (Portugal) 2019, *ARISE (ASEAN Region International Student Engagement) Conference* Singapore (Singapore) 2019, *Western European Platform Meeting* Utrecht (Netherlands) 2019, *Northern European Platform Meeting* Vaasa (Finland) 2019, *Annual General Meeting* Playa de Aro (Spain) 2018. **Publications** *ESN Newsletter*. Survey; guidebook; other ad hoc publications.
Members Local student organizations (530) in 40 countries:
Albania, Austria, Azerbaijan, Belarus, Belgium, Bosnia-Herzegovina, Bulgaria, Croatia, Cyprus, Czechia, Denmark, Estonia, Finland, France, Georgia, Germany, Greece, Hungary, Iceland, Ireland, Italy, Latvia, Liechtenstein, Lithuania, Luxembourg, Malta, Netherlands, North Macedonia, Norway, Poland, Portugal, Romania, Serbia, Slovakia, Slovenia, Spain, Sweden, Switzerland, Türkiye, UK.
Consultative Status Consultative status granted from: *Council of Europe (CE, #04881)* (Participatory Status). **NGO Relations** Member of: *European Movement International (EMI, #07825)*; *European Youth Forum (#09140)*; *Generation Climate Europe (GCE, #10114)*; *Informal Forum of International Student Organizations (IFISO, #11193)*; *Lifelong Learning Platform – European Civil Society for Education (LLLP, #16466)*; *World Youth Student and Educational Travel Confederation (WYSE Travel Confederation, #21959)*. Courtesy member of: *European Association for International Education (EAIE, #06092)*. Instrumental in setting up: *Erasmus+ Student and Alumni Alliance (ESAA, #05528)*. [2022/XF1739/**F**]

♦ **ERASS** European Rheumatism and Arthritis Surgical Society (#08387)

♦ **ERAS Society** **05530**
Secretariat Olof Palmes gata 29, 4th floor, SE-111 22 Stockholm, Sweden.
URL: http://erassociety.org/
History 2001. ERAS stands for: *Enhanced Recovery After Surgery*. Former names and other names: *ERAS Society – Improving Perioperative Care Worldwide* – full title. **Aims** Develop peri-operative care; improve recovery through research, education, audit and implementation of evidence-based practice. **Structure** Board; Executive Committee. **Activities** Events/meetings; research/documentation; training/education. **Events** *World Congress* Madrid (Spain) 2022, *World Congress* New Orleans, LA (USA) 2020, *World Congress* Liverpool (UK) 2019, *Asia Congress* Singapore (Singapore) 2019, *Singapore Enhanced Recovery after Surgery Symposium* Singapore (Singapore) 2018. [2021/XM6389/**C**]

♦ ERAS Society – Improving Perioperative Care Worldwide / see ERAS Society (#05530)
♦ **ERB** European Network of Experimental and Representative Basins (#07905)
♦ **ERB** Euroregion Baltic (#09176)
♦ ERB Network / see European Network of Experimental and Representative Basins (#07905)
♦ **ERCA** European Respiratory Care Association (#08382)
♦ **ERCA** European Rubber Chemicals Association (#08410)
♦ **ERCA** European Rural Community Alliance (#08412)
♦ ErCam – Congregazione degli Eremiti Camaldolesi di Monte Corona (religious order)
♦ ERCE / see European Regional Centre for Ecohydrology of the Polish Academy of Sciences, Lodz (#08341)
♦ **ERCE PAS** European Regional Centre for Ecohydrology of the Polish Academy of Sciences, Lodz (#08341)
♦ **ERC** Equal Rights Coalition (#05519)
♦ **ERCES** European and International Research Group on Crime, Social Philosophy and Ethics (#07588)
♦ ERC – European Rail Circle (inactive)
♦ ERC – European Recycling Coalition (inactive)
♦ ERC – European Registrars Conference (meeting series)
♦ **ERC** European Research Centre for Book and Paper Conservation-Restoration (#08359)
♦ **ERC** European Research Council (#08364)
♦ **ERC** European Resuscitation Council (#08385)
♦ **ERC** European Rohingya Council (#08397)
♦ **ERCIM** European Research Consortium for Informatics and Mathematics (#08362)
♦ ERCIS – European Research Center for Information Systems (unconfirmed)
♦ ERCMC / see Centre for Economic Research on Mediterranean Countries
♦ **ERCOFTAC** European Research Community on Flow, Turbulence and Combustion (#08361)
♦ ERCOMER – European Research Centre on Migration and Ethnic Relations (internationally oriented national body)
♦ **ERCOM** European Research Centres of Mathematics (#08360)
♦ ERCP / see European Roundtable on Sustainable Consumption and Production Society (#08408)
♦ ERCS – European Red Cell Society (unconfirmed)
♦ **ERCSG** European Renal Cell Study Group (#08354)
♦ **ERCST** European Roundtable on Climate Change and Sustainable Transition (#08406)
♦ ERC-WFMH / see Mental Health Europe (#16715)
♦ **ERDF** European Regional Development Fund (#08342)
♦ Erdheim-Chester Disease Global Alliance (internationally oriented national body)
♦ **ERDN** European Rural Development Network (#08413)
♦ **EREA** Association of European Research Establishments in Aeronautics (#02539)
♦ **EREA** Energy Regulators Association of East Africa (#05475)
♦ EREC – European Renewable Energy Council (inactive)
♦ **EREF** European Renewable Energies Federation (#08355)
♦ **EReg** Association of European Vehicle and Driver Registration Authorities (#02550)
♦ EREH – European Reference Centre for First Aid Education (internationally oriented national body)
♦ EREM – International Symposium on Electrokinetic Remediation (meeting series)
♦ **ERENET** Entrepreneurship Research and Education Network of Central European Universities (#05496)
♦ **EREN** European Roma Equality Network (#08400)
♦ **ERERA** ECOWAS Regional Electricity Regulatory Authority (#05337)
♦ **ERES** European Rare-Earth and Actinide Society (#08329)
♦ **ERES** European Real Estate Society (#08332)
♦ ERFA / see European Association of Surface Heating and Cooling (#06241)
♦ **ERFA** European Rail Freight Association (#08323)
♦ **ERF-AISBL** Association of European-level Research Infrastructure Facilities (#02518)
♦ Erfassung der Europäischen Wirbellosen (inactive)
♦ **ERF** Economic Research Forum (#05318)
♦ **ERFEN** Programa para el Estudio Regional del Fenómeno El Niño en el Pacifico Sudeste (#18523)
♦ **ERF** European Racquetball Federation (#08317)
♦ ERF – European Refugee Fund (inactive)
♦ ERF – European Risk Forum (unconfirmed)
♦ **ERF** European Rotorcraft Forum (#08405)
♦ **ERF** European Union Road Federation (#09014)
♦ ERFF – European Retail Financial Forum (unconfirmed)
♦ **ERFMI** European Resilient Flooring Manufacturers' Institute (#08380)
♦ **ERFO** European Recovered Fuel Organisation (#08334)
♦ **ERFP** European Regional Focal Point for Animal Genetic Resources (#08343)
♦ **ERGaR** European Renewable Gas Registry (#08356)
♦ ERG / see Body of European Regulators for Electronic Communications (#03299)
♦ **ERGECD** European Research Group on Experimental Contact Dermatitis (#08367)
♦ ERG / see European Association of Schools of Social Work (#06200)
♦ ERG – International Conference on the Exact Renormalization Group (meeting series)
♦ ErgbAfrica (unconfirmed)
♦ **ERGOMAS** European Research Group on Military and Society (#08368)

♦ **ERGO Network** **05531**
Exec Dir Rue d'Edimbourg 26, 1050 Brussels, Belgium. T. +3228931049. E-mail: info@ergonetwork.org.
Netherlands Office Acaciastraat 7, 6573 WZ Beekbergen, Netherlands. T. +31247370150.
URL: http://www.ergonetwork.org/
History 2004, as an informal gathering. Full title: *European Roma Grassroots Organisations Network (ERGO Network)*. Registered in accordance with Bulgarian law, 2008. **Aims** Contribute toward Roma equal citizenship in Europe by building an active and effective network in which Roma participate to create a positive identity; address stigmatization and discrimination; advocate for effective supportive policies; end exclusive policies. **Structure** Board, comprising President, Vice-President, Treasurer and member. **Activities** Advocacy/lobbying/activism; networking/liaising; knowledge management/information dissemination.
Members Organizations (26) in 19 countries:
Albania, Belgium, Bulgaria, Croatia, Czechia, France, Germany, Hungary, Italy, Lithuania, Moldova, Netherlands, North Macedonia, Poland, Romania, Slovakia, Spain, Türkiye, UK.
IGO Relations Participant in Fundamental Rights Platform of: *European Union Agency for Fundamental Rights (FRA, #08969)*. **NGO Relations** Cooperates with: *Policy Center for Roma and Minorities*. Founding member of: *European Roma Policy Coalition (ERPC, no recent information)*. [2016/XJ6192/**F**]

♦ Ergonomics Research Society / see International Ergonomics Association (#13294)
♦ ERGOSHIP – Maritime Human Factors Conference (meeting series)
♦ **ERIA** Economic Research Institute for ASEAN and East Asia (#05319)
♦ ERIBA – European Institute for the Biology of Ageing (unconfirmed)
♦ **ERICA** European Research into Consumer Affairs (#08363)
♦ **ERICarts** European Institute for Comparative Cultural Research (#07547)
♦ ERICarts Institute / see European Institute for Comparative Cultural Research (#07547)
♦ ERIC / see European Carbon Dioxide Capture and Storage Laboratory Infrastructure (#06446)
♦ ERIC / see European Infrastructure for Translational Medicine (#07536)
♦ ERIC / see European Marine Biological Resource Centre (#07737)
♦ ERIC / see European Plate Observing System (#08220)
♦ **ERIC** European Research Institute of Catalysis (#08369)
♦ **ERICH** European Research Institute for Chaplains in Healthcare (#08370)
♦ ERIC / see Joint Institute for VLBI in Europe (#16135)
♦ **ERIDOB** European Researchers in Didactics of Biology (#08366)
♦ ERIDO – European Regional Industrial Development Organization (inactive)
♦ ERI – Earth Rights Institute (internationally oriented national body)
♦ ERI – EarthRights International (internationally oriented national body)
♦ **ERI** Edmund Rice International (#05362)
♦ ERI – Europäische Rum-Industrie (no recent information)
♦ **ERIG** European Research Institute for Gas and Energy Innovation (#08371)
♦ **ERIH** European Route of Industrial Heritage (#08409)
♦ Erik Castrén Institute of International Law and Human Rights (internationally oriented national body)
♦ Erikshjälpen (internationally oriented national body)
♦ ERIN – European Responsible Investment Network (unconfirmed)
♦ ER – International Conference on Conceptual Modeling (meeting series)
♦ ERIO – European Roma Information Office (internationally oriented national body)
♦ ERIPLAN – European Research Institute for Regional and Urban Planning (inactive)
♦ ERISA – European Regional Information Society Association (no recent information)
♦ **ERI SEE** Education Reform Initiative of South Eastern Europe (#05372)
♦ **ERIS** Escuela Regional de Ingenieria Sanitaria y Recursos Hidraulicos (#18811)
♦ ERIS / see Regional School of Sanitary Engineering and Hydraulic Resources (#18811)
♦ ERIT – Federation of European Professionals Working in the Field of Drug Abuse (inactive)
♦ Eritrean Evangelical Alliance for Africa and the Middle East (unconfirmed)
♦ Erklärung von Bern / see Public Eye
♦ **ERL** European Rugby League (#08411)
♦ **ERMA** European Resin Manufacturers' Association (#08381)
♦ **ERMCO** European Ready Mixed Concrete Organization (#08330)
♦ **ERME** European Society for Research in Mathematics Education (#08728)
♦ ERM – Enfants réfugiés du monde (internationally oriented national body)
♦ ERM – European Retina Meeting (meeting series)

- ♦ ERMR – International Conference on Electrorheological Fluids and Magnetorheological Suspensions (meeting series)
- ♦ **ERNACT** European Regions' Network for the Application of Communications Technology (#08348)
- ♦ ERNA – European Respiratory Nurses Association (no recent information)
- ♦ ERNA / see Food Supplements Europe (#09852)
- ♦ **ERNAM** Ecole régionale de la navigation aérienne et du management (#18809)
- ♦ **ERNAPE** European Research Network About Parents in Education (#08374)
- ♦ **ERNDIM** European Research Network for Evaluation and Improvement of Screening, Diagnosis and Treatment of Inherited Disorders of Metabolism (#08372)
- ♦ **ERN** European Reference Networks (#08337)
- ♦ **ERN** European Rivers Network (#08391)
- ♦ **ERNOP** European Research Network on Philanthropy (#08375)
- ♦ **ERNSI** European Research Network System Identification (#08376)
- ♦ **ERNWACA** Educational Research Network for Western and Central Africa (#05368)
- ♦ ERO / see European Communications Office (#06676)
- ♦ **ERO** European Regional Organization of the Fédération dentaire internationale (#08345)
- ♦ **EROPA** Eastern Regional Organization for Public Administration (#05249)
- ♦ **EROP** European Register for Osteopathic Physicians (#08350)
- ♦ ERPA Cosmetics / see European Cosmetic Responsible Person Association (#06800)
- ♦ **ERPA** European Cosmetic Responsible Person Association (#06800)
- ♦ **ERPA** European Rigid PVC-Film Association (#08389)
- ♦ **ERPA** European Rolling Paper Association (#08399)
- ♦ **ERPA** European Rural Poultry Association (#08416)
- ♦ ERPC / see European Paper Recycling Council (#08139)
- ♦ **ERP** Euroopa Rahvapartei – Kristlike Demokraatide Fraktsioon (#10775)
- ♦ **ERP** European Recycling Platform (#08336)
- ♦ ERPS – Electric Rocket Propulsion Society (internationally oriented national body)
- ♦ **ERPUG** European Road Profile Users' Group (#08394)
- ♦ ERPW – European Radiation Protection Week (meeting series)
- ♦ **ERRAC** European Rail Research Advisory Council (#08325)
- ♦ **ERRA** Energy Regulators Regional Association (#05476)
- ♦ ERRA – European Recovery and Recycling Association (inactive)
- ♦ **ERRC** European Roma Rights Centre (#08401)
- ♦ **ERRIN** European Regions Research and Innovation Network (#08349)
- ♦ **ERRMA** European Renewable Raw Materials Association (#08357)
- ♦ **ERRS** European Radiation Research Society (#08319)
- ♦ **ERSA** European Regional Science Association (#08346)
- ♦ ERSCP / see European Roundtable on Sustainable Consumption and Production Society (#08408)
- ♦ **ERSCP Society** European Roundtable on Sustainable Consumption and Production Society (#08408)
- ♦ ERS – Earth Restoration Service (internationally oriented national body)
- ♦ **ERS** European Respiratory Society (#08383)
- ♦ **ERS** European Rhinologic Society (#08388)
- ♦ ERSF – European Road Safety Federation (inactive)
- ♦ **ERSO** European Rope Skipping Organization (#08403)
- ♦ ERS/RAC / see Regional Activity Centre for Information and Communication of the Barcelona Convention (#18745)
- ♦ ERSS / see European Society of Cataract and Refractive Surgeons (#08539)
- ♦ ERSTE Foundation (internationally oriented national body)
- ♦ ERSTE Stiftung (internationally oriented national body)
- ♦ **ERSTU** European River/Sea Transport Union (#08390)
- ♦ ERTA – European Radio Taxi Association (unconfirmed)
- ♦ **ERT** European Round Table for Industry (#08407)
- ♦ **ERTF** European Roma and Travellers Forum (#08402)
- ♦ ERTICO / see ERTICO ITS Europe (#05532)
- ♦ ERTICO Intelligent Transport Systems – Europe / see ERTICO ITS Europe (#05532)
- ♦ ERTICO Intelligent Transport Systems and Services – Europe / see ERTICO ITS Europe (#05532)

♦ ERTICO ITS Europe 05532

CEO Blue Tower, 2nd Floor, Avenue Louise 326, 1050 Brussels, Belgium. T. +3224000700. Fax +3224000701. E-mail: info@mail.ertico.com.
URL: http://www.ertico.com/

History 1991. Former names and other names: *European Road Transport Telematics Implementation Coordination Organization (ERTICO)* – former (1991); *ERTICO Intelligent Transport Systems – Europe* – former; *ERTICO Intelligent Transport Systems and Services – Europe* – full title. Registration: No/ID: 0445.743.506, Start date: 14 Feb 1992, Belgium; EU Transparency Register, No/ID: 12971262634-76, Start date: 18 Nov 2009. **Aims** Represent the interests and expertise of partners involved in providing Intelligent *Transport* Systems and Services (ITS); facilitate the safe, secure, clean, efficient and comfortable *mobility* of people and goods in Europe and beyond. **Structure** General Assembly; Supervisory Board; Chairman's Advisory Committee; Finance and Administration Group; Strategy Committee. **Languages** English. **Staff** 35.00 FTE, paid. **Finance** Partners' (shareholders) annual fees: euro 30,000 for the private sector, euro 15,000 for public authorities; partners' entrance fees: euro 10,000; partners' capital share: euro 620. Other sources: project funding; *European Commission (EC, #06633)*. **Activities** Advocacy/lobbying/activism; events/meetings; research/documentation. **Events** *World Congress on Intelligent Transport Systems and Services* Dubai (United Arab Emirates) 2024, *ITS European Congress* Lisbon (Portugal) 2023, *World Congress on Intelligent Transport Systems and Services* Suzhou (China) 2023, *World Congress on Intelligent Transport Systems and Services* Los Angeles, CA (USA) 2022, *ITS European Congress* Toulouse (France) 2022. **Publications** *ERTICO – ITS Europe* (6 a year) – electronic newsletter. Annual Report; activity book; project brochures; booklets.
Members Partners (106) from 5 sectors industry; public authorities; infrastructure operators; users; others. Public authorities in 21 countries:
Austria, Belgium, Czechia, Denmark, Finland, France, Germany, Hungary, Ireland, Italy, Luxembourg, Netherlands, Norway, Poland, Portugal, Saudi Arabia, Slovenia, Spain, Sweden, Switzerland, UK.
Members include 3 organizations listed in this Yearbook:
European Automobile Manufacturers' Association (ACEA, #06300); Fédération Internationale de l'Automobile (FIA, #09613); International Road Transport Union (IRU, #14761).
IGO Relations Close collaboration and consultation with several Directorates-General of the European Commission. **NGO Relations** Member of (6): *Alliance for Internet of Things Innovation (AIOTI, #00697); eSafetyAware (#05533); European Organisation for Security (EOS, #08102); European Road Transport Research Advisory Council (ERTRAC, #08396); Forum for Mobility and Society (FMS, #09924); International Association of Trusted Blockchain Applications (INATBA)*. Partner of (1): *International Road Federation (IRF, #14758)*. Instrumental in setting up (1): *Network of National ITS Associations (ITS Nationals, #17049)*. In liaison with technical committees of: *International Organization for Standardization (ISO, #14473)*. Hosts: *Mobility as a Service Alliance (MaaS Alliance)*. [2022/XD2946/y/**F**]

- ♦ **ERTMS** European Rail Traffic Management System (#08327)
- ♦ **ERTRAC** European Road Transport Research Advisory Council (#08396)
- ♦ ERU / see Association for European Rural Universities (#02541)
- ♦ Eruoopa Parlament (#08146)
- ♦ ERUS – European Robotic Urology Society (inactive)
- ♦ ERV – Europese Rum Vereniging (no recent information)
- ♦ **ERVO** European Research Vessel Operators (#08379)
- ♦ Erwin Schrödinger International Institute for Mathematical Physics (internationally oriented national body)
- ♦ **ER-WPT** Europe Region World Physiotherapy (#09167)
- ♦ ERWUS / see European Consultants Unit (#06769)
- ♦ **ERYICA** European Youth Information and Counselling Agency (#09142)
- ♦ ESAAAE – Eastern and Southern Africa Association of Agricultural Economists (inactive)
- ♦ ESAA / see Erasmus+ Student and Alumni Alliance (#05528)
- ♦ **ESAA** Erasmus+ Student and Alumni Alliance (#05528)
- ♦ **ESAAG** East and Southern African Association of Accountants-General (#05262)
- ♦ ESAAM / see European Society of Preventive, Regenerative and Anti-Aging Medicine (#08714)
- ♦ **ESAAM** European Society of Preventive, Regenerative and Anti-Aging Medicine (#08714)
- ♦ **ESAAMLG** Eastern and Southern African Anti-Money Laundering Group (#05252)
- ♦ ESABO – Eastern and Southern African Business Organization (no recent information)
- ♦ ESABR / see International Society for Animal Genetics (#14921)
- ♦ **ESAC** European Space Astronomy Centre 1100002952
- ♦ **ESACIPAC** Eastern and Southern Africa Centre of International Parasite Control (#05250)
- ♦ ESACP – European Society for Analytical Cellular Pathology (inactive)
- ♦ **ESACT** European Society for Animal Cell Technology (#08520)
- ♦ **ESADA** Eastern and Southern African Dairy Association (#05253)
- ♦ ESADE – Escuela Superior de Administración y Dirección de Empresas (internationally oriented national body)
- ♦ **ESA** Economic Science Association (#05320)
- ♦ **ESAE** European Society of Association Executives (#08526)
- ♦ **ESA** EFTA Surveillance Authority (#05392)
- ♦ **ESA** Euratom Supply Agency (#05617)
- ♦ ESA – European School Magazine Association (inactive)
- ♦ **ESA** European Sealing Association (#08452)
- ♦ **ESA** European Snacks Association (#08498)
- ♦ **ESA** European Society for Aesthetics (#08511)
- ♦ **ESA** European Society for Agronomy (#08515)
- ♦ ESA / see European Society of Anaesthesiology and Intensive Care (#08518)
- ♦ **ESA** European Sociological Association (#08790)
- ♦ **ESA** European Space Agency (#08798)
- ♦ ESA – European Space Association (inactive)
- ♦ **ESA** European Spice Association (#08814)
- ♦ **ESA** European Sponsorship Association (#08818)
- ♦ ESA – European Sports Academy (unconfirmed)
- ♦ **ESA** European Strabismological Association (#08840)
- ♦ **ESA** European Sulphuric Acid Association (#08854)
- ♦ ESA – European Sunglass Association (inactive)
- ♦ **ESA** European Sunlight Association (#08857)
- ♦ **ESA** European Surgical Association (#08861)
- ♦ **ESA** European Suzuki Association (#08867)
- ♦ ESA – European Symposium on Algorithms (meeting series)
- ♦ ESA / see Euroseeds (#09179)

♦ eSafetyAware 05533

SG Rue de la Science 41, 1040 Brussels, Belgium. T. +3222350721. Fax +3224166572. E-mail: info@esafetyaware.eu.
Project Manager address not obtained.
URL: http://www.esafetyaware.eu/

History 2008, Brussels (Belgium). **Aims** Promote public awareness of eSafety systems and their benefits. **Structure** Board of 13 members, including President. **Languages** English. **Activities** Areas: public information campaigns; demonstration events; workshops and training events; international collaboration to stimulate consumer demand. **Events** *eSafety Challenge* Vienna (Austria) 2011, *eSafety Challenge* Millbrook (UK) 2010, *eSafety Challenge* Rome (Italy) 2009.
Members Categories: Full; Associate; Observer. Industry, public authorities, motoring clubs and other organizations (36). Membership countries not specified. Full members include 3 organizations listed in this Yearbook:
Full members include 3 organizations listed in this Yearbook:
ERTICO ITS Europe (#05532); European Automobile Manufacturers' Association (ACEA, #06300); Fédération Internationale de l'Automobile (FIA, #09613).
Observer members include 2 organizations listed in this Yearbook:
European New Car Assessment Programme (EURO NCAP, #08046); Fédération européenne des auto-écoles (EFA, #09560).
IGO Relations Support from: *European Commission (EC, #06633).* [2013/XJ0630/y/**D**]

- ♦ **ESAFF** Eastern and Southern Africa small scale Farmers' Forum (#05256)
- ♦ **ESAFORM** European Scientific Association for Material Forming (#08442)
- ♦ **ESAFS** East and Southeast Asia Federation of Soil Science Societies (#05261)
- ♦ ESAG – European Security Advocacy Group (internationally oriented national body)
- ♦ ESAG – European Society of Aesthetic Gynecology (unconfirmed)
- ♦ ESAG Foundation / see European Security Advocacy Group
- ♦ **ESAIC** European Society of Anaesthesiology and Intensive Care (#08518)
- ♦ ESAIDARM / see Macroeconomic and Financial Management Institute of Eastern and Southern Africa (#16539)
- ♦ **E-SALAMA** Eastern and Southern Africa Laboratory Managers Association (#05251)
- ♦ ESALIA – Eastern and Southern Africa Leather Industries Association (no recent information)
- ♦ ESAM – Enfants solidaires d'Afrique et du monde (internationally oriented national body)
- ♦ **ESAM** European Society of Aerospace Medicine (#08509)
- ♦ **ESAMI** Eastern and Southern African Management Institute (#05254)
- ♦ ESAMRDC / see African Minerals and Geosciences Centre (#00373)
- ♦ **ESAN** European Social Action Network (#08499)
- ♦ ESANN – European Symposium on Artificial Neural Networks, Computational Intelligence and Machine Learning (meeting series)
- ♦ **ESAO** European Society for Artificial Organs (#08525)
- ♦ ESAPAC / see Central American Institute of Public Administration (#03670)
- ♦ **ESAPA** European Soda Ash Producers Association (#08791)
- ♦ ESAP – European Society of Ambulatory Pediatrics (inactive)
- ♦ **ESAP** European Society for Analytic Philosophy (#08519)
- ♦ **ESAPS** European Society of Aesthetic Plastic Surgery (#08510)
- ♦ ESARBICA – Eastern and Southern Africa Regional Branch of the International Council on Archives (see: #12996)
- ♦ **ESARDA** European Safeguards Research and Development Association (#08417)
- ♦ **ESAR** European Society for translational Antiviral Research (#08764)
- ♦ ESARIPO / see African Regional Intellectual Property Organization (#00434)
- ♦ **ESAS** European Scientific Association on Schizophrenia and other Psychoses (#08443)
- ♦ **ESAS** European Society of Aesthetic Surgery (#08512)
- ♦ **ESAS** European Society for Applied Superconductivity (#08522)
- ♦ ESAS – European Symposium on Atomic Spectrometry (meeting series)
- ♦ **ESASI** European Society of Air Safety Investigators (#08516)
- ♦ **ESASO** European School for Advanced Studies in Ophthalmology (#08428)
- ♦ ESASTE – East and Southern African Society for Teacher Education (inactive)
- ♦ ESAT – European Seminar of Applied Thermodynamics (meeting series)
- ♦ **ESAURP** Eastern and Southern African Universities Research Programme (#05255)
- ♦ **ESAVS** European School of Advanced Veterinary Studies (#08429)
- ♦ ESBA / see European Small Business Alliance of Small and Medium Independent Enterprises (#08494)
- ♦ **ESBA** European Small Business Alliance of Small and Medium Independent Enterprises (#08494)
- ♦ **ESBB** European, Middle Eastern and African Society for Biopreservation and Biobanking (#07798)

- ♦ **ESBES** European Society of Biochemical Engineering Sciences (#08529)
- ♦ **ESB** European Society for Biomaterials (#08530)
- ♦ **ESB** European Society of Biomechanics (#08531)
- ♦ **ESB** European Soil Bureau (#08793)
- ♦ ESBG / see European Savings and Retail Banking Group (#08426)
- ♦ **ESBG** European Savings and Retail Banking Group (#08426)
- ♦ ESBN / see European Soil Bureau (#08793)
- ♦ ESBO – European Solid Board Organization (inactive)
- ♦ ESBP – European Society of Biochemical Pharmacology (inactive)
- ♦ **ESBRA** European Society for Biomedical Research on Alcoholism (#08532)
- ♦ **ESBS** European Skull Base Society (#08492)
- ♦ ESBVM – Ecumenical Society of the Blessed Virgin Mary (religious order)
- ♦ **ESCAA** European Seed Certification Agencies Association (#08460)
- ♦ **ESCAD** European Society for Cosmetic and Aesthetic Dermatology (#08570)
- ♦ Escadrille interaméricaine (inactive)
- ♦ ESCA – European Small Volume Car Manufacturers Alliance (unconfirmed)
- ♦ ESCA – European Sponsorship Consultants Association (inactive)
- ♦ ESCA / see International Speech Communication Association (#15578)
- ♦ **ESCAN** European Society for Cognitive and Affective Neuroscience (#08553)
- ♦ ESCAP Bibliographic Information Systems (no recent information)
- ♦ ESCAPE – European Symposium on Computer Aided Process Engineering (meeting series)
- ♦ **ESCAP** European Society of Child and Adolescent Psychiatry (#08543)
- ♦ **ESCAP** United Nations Economic and Social Commission for Asia and the Pacific (#20557)

♦ ESCAP/WMO Typhoon Committee (TC) 05534

Sec Avenida de 5 de Outubro, Coloane, Macau, Macau. T. +85388010531. Fax +85388010530. E-mail: info@typhooncommittee.org.
URL: http://www.typhooncommittee.org/

History 1968, Bangkok (Thailand), as an intergovernmental body under the auspices of the then United Nations Economic Commission for Asia and the Far East (ECAFE), currently *United Nations Economic and Social Commission for Asia and the Pacific (ESCAP, #20557)*, and *World Meteorological Organization (WMO, #21649)*. Also referred to as *Typhoon Committee*. **Aims** Integrate and enhance regional activities in the areas of *meteorological, hydrological* and *disaster* risk reduction of members within international framework to reduce loss of lives and minimize social, economic and environmental impacts by typhoon-related disasters and enhance beneficial typhoon-related effects. **Structure** *Typhoon Committee Secretariat (TCS)*, the executive arm of the Committee. **Languages** English. **Staff** 2.50 FTE, paid. **Finance** Trust Fund. Annual budget: about US$ 100,000. **Activities** Programmes/projects; training/education; events/meetings. **Events** *Session* Japan 2021, *Session* Guangzhou (China) 2019, *Session* Hanoi (Vietnam) 2018, *Meeting* Jeju (Korea Rep) 2017, *Session* Yokohama (Japan) 2017. **Publications** *ESCAP/WMO Typhoon Committee Newsletter*. *Typhoon Committee Operation Manual*. Project publications.
Members Governments of 14 countries and territories:
Cambodia, China, Hong Kong, Japan, Korea DPR, Korea Rep, Laos, Macau, Malaysia, Philippines, Singapore, Thailand, USA, Vietnam.
IGO Relations *Caribbean Disaster Emergency Management Agency (CDEMA, #03493)*; *International Civil Aviation Organization (ICAO, #12581)*; *Joint WMO-IOC Technical Commission for Oceanography and Marine Meteorology (JCOMM, #16151)*; *Secretariat of the Pacific Regional Environment Programme (SPREP, #19205)*; *UNDP (#20292)*; *United Nations Office for Disaster Risk Reduction (UNDRR, #20595)*. **NGO Relations** *Asian Disaster Preparedness Center (ADPC, #01426)*; *International Federation of Red Cross and Red Crescent Societies (#13526)*. [2020/XE1009/**E***]

♦ Escarre International Centre for the Ethnic Minorities and Nations . 05535

Centre Internacional Escarré per a les Minories Etniques i les Nacions (CIEMEN)
Contact Rocafort 242 bis 2n, 08029 Barcelona, Spain. T. +34934443800. Fax +34934443809.
History 1975, Barcelona (Spain). Founded by Aureli Argemí i Roca. Part of the *Mercator Network*. **Aims** Carry out research into, and defend the *rights* of, groups, *communities* and peoples finding themselves to a greater or lesser extent in the situation of a minority. **Activities** Organizes *Conferencia de Nacions sense Estat d'Europa (Conseu)*, grouping 25 stateless nations in Europe. **Events** *Symposium on languages and legislation in Europe* Gandia (Spain) 1995, *International days* Girona (Spain) 1995, *International days* Banyoles (Spain) 1994, *International congress on European cultures* Barcelona (Spain) 1990. **Publications** *Europa de les Nacions* (periodical). Maps of languages of Europe; maps of nations of Europe; linguistic rights collection; dialogues collection. **NGO Relations** Provides secretariat for: *Mercator – Linguistic Rights and Legislation (Mercator Legislation, no recent information)*. Member of: *Foro Social Mediterraneo (FSMed, no recent information)*; *World Social Forum (WSF, #21797)*. [2019/XF2962/**E**]

- ♦ **ESCAS** European Society for Central Asian Studies (#08541)
- ♦ Escazú Agreement – Regional Agreement on Access to Information, Public Participation and Justice in Environmental Matters in Latin America and the Caribbean (2018 treaty)
- ♦ ESCBC – European Student Conference on Behaviour and Cognition (meeting series)
- ♦ **ESCB** European System of Central Banks (#08870)
- ♦ **ESCCA** European Society for Clinical Cell Analysis (#08544)
- ♦ **ESCCAP** European Scientific Counsel Companion Animal Parasites (#08445)
- ♦ ESCC – European Symposium on Comminution and Classification (meeting series)
- ♦ ESCC – European Symposium on Computer and Communications (meeting series)
- ♦ ESCD / see European Society of Contact Dermatitis (#08567)
- ♦ **ESCD** European Society of Contact Dermatitis (#08567)
- ♦ **ESCD** European Society of Cosmetic Dentistry (#08571)
- ♦ **ESCE** European Society for Comparative Endocrinology (#08558)
- ♦ ESCEO / see European Society for Clinical and Economic Aspects of Osteoporosis, Osteoarthritis and Musculoskeletal Diseases (#08545)
- ♦ **ESCEO** European Society for Clinical and Economic Aspects of Osteoporosis, Osteoarthritis and Musculoskeletal Diseases (#08545)
- ♦ ESC / see European Economic and Social Committee (#06963)
- ♦ ESC / see European Pharmaceutical Students' Association (#08197)
- ♦ **ESC** European Seismological Commission (#08461)
- ♦ **ESC** European Shippers' Council (#08477)
- ♦ **ESC** European Shooting Confederation (#08481)
- ♦ **ESC** European Society of Cardiology (#08536)
- ♦ **ESC** European Society of Chemotherapy – Infectious Diseases (#08542)
- ♦ ESC – European Society of Chronobiology (no recent information)
- ♦ ESC / see European Society of Contraception and Reproductive Health (#08568)
- ♦ **ESC** European Society of Contraception and Reproductive Health (#08568)
- ♦ **ESC** European Society of Criminology (#08575)
- ♦ ESC – European Society of Cryosurgery (inactive)
- ♦ **ESC** European Sports Conference (#08821)
- ♦ ESC – European Studies Centre, Oxford (internationally oriented national body)
- ♦ ESCF / see European Cystic Fibrosis Society (#06879)
- ♦ **ESCF** European Sickle Cell Federation (#08484)
- ♦ ESCF – European Skin Cancer Foundation (internationally oriented national body)
- ♦ **ESCFS** European Society of Craniofacial Surgery (#08574)
- ♦ **ESCG** European Society of Comparative Gastroenterology (#08559)
- ♦ ESCGTA / see European Association of Geographers (#06054)
- ♦ ESCH / see European Society for Clinical Hemorheology and Microcirculation (#08546)
- ♦ **ESCHFOE** Europäische Schornsteinfegermeister-Föderation (#05761)
- ♦ **ESCHM** European Society for Clinical Hemorheology and Microcirculation (#08546)
- ♦ **ESCI** European Society for Clinical Investigation (#08547)
- ♦ **ESCIF** European Spinal Cord Injury Federation (#08815)
- ♦ **ES-CK** European Society Coudenhove-Kalergi (#08573)
- ♦ **ESCL** European Society of Comparative Literature (#08561)
- ♦ **ESCL** European Society for Construction Law (#08566)
- ♦ **ESCLG** European Spirits Companies Liaison Group (#08817)
- ♦ **ESCLH** European Society for Comparative Legal History (#08560)
- ♦ ESCM / see European Society of Clinical Microbiology and Infectious Diseases (#08548)
- ♦ **ESCM** European Society for Composite Materials (#08563)
- ♦ **ESCMID** European Society of Clinical Microbiology and Infectious Diseases (#08548)
- ♦ ESCNM – European Society for Classical Natural Medicine (no recent information)
- ♦ **ESCNP** European Society for Clinical Neuropharmacology (#08549)
- ♦ Escola de Cultura de Pau (internationally oriented national body)
- ♦ Escola Judicial da América Latina (#05537)
- ♦ Escolapios – Orden de los Clérigos Regulares Pobres de la Madre de Dios de las Escuelas Pias (religious order)
- ♦ Escola Superior d'Administració i Direcció d'Empreses (internationally oriented national body)
- ♦ **ESCOM** European Society for the Cognitive Sciences of Music (#08555)
- ♦ **ESCOP** European Scientific Cooperative on Phytotherapy (#08444)
- ♦ **ESCoP** European Society for Cognitive Psychology (#08554)
- ♦ **ESCORENA** European System of Cooperative Research Networks in Agriculture (#08871)
- ♦ **ESCORG** European Society of Cosmetic and Reconstructive Gynecology (#08572)
- ♦ **ESCPB** European Society for Comparative Physiology and Biochemistry (#08562)
- ♦ ESCP-EAP Alumni Association / see Association of ESCP Europe Students and Graduates (#02493)
- ♦ ESCP-EAP European School of Management / see ESCP Europe Business School (#05536)
- ♦ ESCP-EAP European School of Management – Paris London Madrid Berlin Turin / see ESCP Europe Business School (#05536)
- ♦ **ESCP Europe Alumni** Association of ESCP Europe Students and Graduates (#02493)
- ♦ **ESCP** European Society of Clinical Pharmacy (#08551)
- ♦ **ESCP** European Society of Coloproctology (#08556)
- ♦ **ESCP** European Society for Communicative Psychotherapy (#08557)

♦ ESCP Europe Business School 05536

Main Office 79 av de la République, 75543 Paris CEDEX 11, France. T. +33149232000. Fax +33143559963. E-mail: info.fr@escpeurope.eu.
URL: http://www.escpeurope.eu/

History 1819, as 'Ecole Spéciale de Commerce et d'Industrie'. Subsequently called 'Ecole Supérieure de Commerce'. Developed into ESCP, 1869. On merger with Ecole des Affaires de Paris (EAP), 1999, changed title into *ESCP-EAP European School of Management*. Former full title: *ESCP-EAP European School of Management – Paris London Madrid Berlin Turin*. Previously also referred to as *Ecole européenne des affaires – Escuela Europea de Administración de Empresas – Europäische Wirtschaftshochschule*. Current title adopted 2009. Campuses in Germany opened 1973; Spain 1988; Italy 2004. **Aims** Provide business education and a global perspective on management issues; contribute to the development of a European, cross-national management culture; remain faithful to Europe's humanistic values while anticipating the new ways of the world. **Structure** Campuses at: Paris (France); Berlin (Germany); London (UK); Madrid (Spain); Turin (Italy). Each campus has its own specific governance structure. Includes: *Association of ESCP Europe Students and Graduates (ESCP Europe Alumni, #02493)*. **Languages** English, French, German, Italian, Spanish. **Staff** 127 full-time faculty; over 80 affiliate faculty; about 700 part-time professors and working professionals; over 40 visiting professors. **Finance** Sources: tuition fees; subsidies from Paris (France) Chamber of Commerce and Industry and from Berlin (Germany) Government (Senate); donations and contributions from European industry; ESCP Europe Foundation. **Activities** Training/education. **Events** *International Congress on French Business History* Paris (France) 2019, *European management conference* Paris (France) 2000, *International congress* Madrid (Spain) 1997, *Annual conference* Paris (France) 1997, *European congress on continuing education and training* Berlin (Germany) / Warsaw (Poland) / Prague (Czechoslovakia) / Budapest (Hungary) / Vienna (Austria) 1992. **Publications** *ESCP Europe Newsletter*; *European Management Journal*; *International Journal of Cross Cultural Management*. Books; articles; conference proceedings. **Members** Not a membership organization. **NGO Relations** Member of: *EFMD – The Management Development Network (#05387)*; *Higher Education Sustainability Initiative (HESI)*; *Principles for Responsible Management Education (PRME, #18500)*; *United Nations Global Compact (#20567)*. [2018/XF1544/**E**]

- ♦ ESCR / see European Society of Cardiovascular Radiology (#08538)
- ♦ **ESCR** European Society of Cardiovascular Radiology (#08538)
- ♦ **ESCR-Net** International Network for Economic, Social and Cultural Rights (#14255)
- ♦ **ESCRS** European Society of Cataract and Refractive Surgeons (#08539)
- ♦ ESCSB – European Society for Comparative Skin Biology (inactive)
- ♦ ESCS / see European Society of Aesthetic Surgery (#08512)
- ♦ **ESCTAIC** European Society for Computing and Technology in Anaesthesia and Intensive Care (#08564)
- ♦ ESCTS – European School of Cardio-Thoracic Surgery (internationally oriented national body)
- ♦ Escuela Agricola Panamericana del Zamorano (internationally oriented national body)
- ♦ Escuela de Estudios Hispano-Americanos, Sevilla (internationally oriented national body)
- ♦ Escuela de Estudios Orientales (internationally oriented national body)
- ♦ Escuela Europea de Administración de Empresas / see ESCP Europe Business School (#05536)
- ♦ Escuela Europea de Oncologia (#08434)
- ♦ Escuela Internacional de Cine y Televisión (#12572)
- ♦ Escuela Internacional de la Cultura Ayurvédica (internationally oriented national body)
- ♦ Escuela Internacional de la Rosacruz (religious order)

♦ Escuela Judicial de América Latina (EJAL) 05537

Escola Judicial da América Latina
Dir Gen Rua Lidia Klinger 265 – c 4, Abranches, Curitiba PR, CEP 82 130-160, Brazil. T. +554291091936. Fax +554230172567.
URL: http://www.ejal.org/

Aims Enhance and promote continuing education and improvement of judges in Latin America. **Structure** General Assembly. Executive Committee. **Languages** Portuguese, Spanish.
Members Full in 20 countries:
Argentina, Bolivia, Brazil, Chile, Colombia, Costa Rica, Dominican Rep, Ecuador, El Salvador, Guatemala, Honduras, Mexico, Nicaragua, Panama, Paraguay, Portugal, Puerto Rico, Spain, Uruguay, Venezuela.
IGO Relations *Comunidade dos Paises de Lingua Portuguesa (CPLP, #04430)*. **NGO Relations** *Red Latinoamericana de Jueces (REDLAJ, #18714)* is a founding member. [2011/XJ3420/**D**]

- ♦ Escuela Latinoamericana de Matematica (meeting series)

♦ Escuela Latinoamericana de Pensamiento y Diseño Sistémico (ELAPDIS) 05538

Gen Dir address not obtained. E-mail: contacto@elapdis.org.
URL: http://www.elapdis.org/

History 2007, Mérida (Venezuela). 2007, Merida (Venezuela). **Aims** Promote understanding and sharing of methodologies, studies and theoretical problems related to systems thinking and design. **Languages** Spanish. **Staff** 9.00 FTE, paid. **Activities** Training/education.
Members Full in 8 countries:
Argentina, Bolivia, Brazil, Chile, Colombia, Mexico, Peru, Venezuela.
NGO Relations *World Organisation of Systems and Cybernetics (WOSC, #21686)*. [2020.03.03/XM6163/**D**]

- ♦ Escuela Regional de Ingenieria Sanitaria / see Regional School of Sanitary Engineering and Hydraulic Resources (#18811)
- ♦ Escuela Regional de Ingenieria Sanitaria y Recursos Hidraulicos (#18811)
- ♦ Escuela Superior de Administración y Dirección de Empresas (internationally oriented national body)

- ♦ Escuela Superior de Administración Pública América Central / see Central American Institute of Public Administration (#03670)
- ♦ ESCU / see European Seniors' Union (#08466)
- ♦ **ESCV** European Society for Clinical Virology (#08552)
- ♦ ESCVS / see European Society for Cardiovascular and Endovascular Surgery (#08537)
- ♦ **ESCVS** European Society for Cardiovascular and Endovascular Surgery (#08537)
- ♦ **ESCWA** United Nations Economic and Social Commission for Western Asia (#20558)
- ♦ **ESDA** European Society of Dirofilariosis and Angiostrongylosis (#08584)
- ♦ ESDA – European Sound Directors' Association (no recent information)
- ♦ ESDA – European Stamp Dealers Association (inactive)
- ♦ **ESDaP** European Society for Dermatology and Psychiatry (#08579)
- ♦ **ESDAR** European Society of Domestic Animal Reproduction (#08586)
- ♦ ESDC / see European Dance Council (#06886)
- ♦ ESDC / see European Scientific Diving Panel (#08446)
- ♦ **ESDC** European Security and Defence College (#04107)
- ♦ **ESDE** European Society of Dental Ergonomics (#08577)
- ♦ **ESDE** European Society for Diseases of the Esophagus (#08585)
- ♦ ESD – International Workshop on Electrostatic Storage Devices (meeting series)
- ♦ **ESDIP** European Society of Digital and Integrative Pathology (#08583)
- ♦ **ESDN** European Sustainable Development Network (#08864)
- ♦ **ESDO** European Society of Digestive Oncology (#08582)
- ♦ ESDO for Smart Grids / see European Distribution System Operators' Association for Smart Grids (#06931)
- ♦ ESDP / see European Association of Developmental Psychology (#06010)
- ♦ **ESDP** European Scientific Diving Panel (#08446)
- ♦ **ESDP** European Society for Dermatopathology (#08580)
- ♦ ESDP / see European Society for Developmental Perinatal and Paediatric Pharmacology (#08581)
- ♦ **ESDPPP** European Society for Developmental Perinatal and Paediatric Pharmacology (#08581)
- ♦ ESDRA – European Sled Dog Racing Association (inactive)
- ♦ ESDREMA – European Surgical Dressings Manufacturers' Association (inactive)
- ♦ **ESDR** European Society for Dermatological Research (#08578)
- ♦ ESDS – European Society for Dermatological Surgery (inactive)
- ♦ ESDS – European Spinal Deformities Society (inactive)
- ♦ **ESEAC** European Society for Electroanalytical Chemistry (#08588)
- ♦ **ESEA** Ecological Society for Eastern Africa (#05300)
- ♦ **ESEA** European Sport Economics Association (#08820)
- ♦ **ESEB** European Society for Evolutionary Biology (#08600)
- ♦ ESEC – European Software Engineering Conference (meeting series)
- ♦ **ES** Econometric Society (#05310)
- ♦ ESED / see European Society of Cosmetic Dentistry (#08571)
- ♦ ESED – European Society for Environment and Development (inactive)
- ♦ **ESEE** European Society for Ecological Economics (#08587)
- ♦ ESE / see Eureka Association (#05621)
- ♦ **ESE** European Society of Endocrinology (#08594)
- ♦ **ESE** European Society of Endodontology (#08595)
- ♦ ESEGO – European Society of Endosonography in Gynecology and Obstetrics (inactive)
- ♦ **ESEH** European Society for Environmental History (#08596)
- ♦ ESEI – École supérieure d'études internationales (internationally oriented national body)
- ♦ ESEI – European Society for Emerging Infections (no recent information)
- ♦ esela – esela – The legal network for social impact (inactive)
- ♦ esela – The legal network for social impact (inactive)
- ♦ ESEM / see Educating Students in Engineering and Medicine (#05364)
- ♦ **ESEM** Educating Students in Engineering and Medicine (#05364)
- ♦ **ESEM** European Seminar in Ethnomusicology (#08463)
- ♦ **ESERA** European Science Education Research Association (#08438)
- ♦ ESER – Einheits-System für Elektronische Rechentechnik (inactive)
- ♦ **ESER** Europäische Gesellschaft für Notfallradiologie (#08592)
- ♦ **ESER** European Society of Emergency Radiology (#08592)
- ♦ **ESES** European Society of Endocrine Surgeons (#08593)
- ♦ ESFA – Esports Federation of Africa (unconfirmed)
- ♦ **ESFAM** Association of European Manufacturers of Sporting Firearms (#02523)
- ♦ **ESFAM** École supérieure de la francophonie pour l'administration et le management (#05298)
- ♦ ESFAN / see TAFISA Europe (#20087)
- ♦ ESFAS – European Society of Foot and Ankle Surgeons (inactive)
- ♦ ESF Committee on Radio Astronomy Frequencies (see: #08441)
- ♦ ESF – Earth Society Foundation (internationally oriented national body)
- ♦ **ESF** Enseignants sans frontières (#05489)
- ♦ ESF – Environnement sans frontière (internationally oriented national body)
- ♦ ESF – Epargne sans frontière (internationally oriented national body)
- ♦ **ESF** Esperantic Studies Foundation (#05542)
- ♦ ESF – Espoir sans frontières (internationally oriented national body)
- ♦ **ESF** European Fire Service Sport Federation (#07261)
- ♦ **ESF** European Safety Federation (#08418)
- ♦ **ESF** European Science Foundation (#08441)
- ♦ **ESF** European Services Forum (#08469)
- ♦ **ESF** European Shiatsu Federation (#08476)
- ♦ **ESF** European Sign Federation (#08485)
- ♦ **ESF** European Simmental Federation (#08487)
- ♦ **ESF** European Social Fund (#08501)
- ♦ **ESF** European Softball Federation (#08792)
- ♦ **ESF** European Spring Federation (#08825)
- ♦ **ESF** European Squash Federation (#08826)
- ♦ **ESF** European Sumo Federation (#08855)
- ♦ **ESF** European Surfing Federation (#08860)
- ♦ **ESF** Européens Sans Frontières (#09154)
- ♦ ESFH / see European Society for Haemapheresis and Haemotherapy (#08614)
- ♦ **ESFH** European Society for Haemapheresis and Haemotherapy (#08614)
- ♦ ESFI – Electrical Safety Foundation International (internationally oriented national body)
- ♦ **ESFI** Etudes Sans Frontières International (#05561)
- ♦ ESF / see Information Security Forum (#11198)
- ♦ **ESFL** European Students For Liberty (#08847)
- ♦ ESFM / see International Society of Feline Medicine (#15116)
- ♦ ESF Network for European Communications and Transport Activities Research / see Network on European Communications and Transport Activity Research (#17016)
- ♦ **ESFN** European Social Franchising Network (#08500)
- ♦ **ESfO** European Society for Oceanists (#08669)
- ♦ **ESFRC** European Shadow Financial Regulatory Committee (#08474)
- ♦ **ESFR** European Society on Family Relations (#08602)
- ♦ **ESFS** European Science Fiction Society (#08440)
- ♦ ESGA / see European Senior Golf Association (#08464)
- ♦ **ESGA** European Senior Golf Association (#08464)
- ♦ ESGA – European Society of Golf Course Architects (inactive)
- ♦ **ESGA** European Special Glass Association (#08807)
- ♦ **ESGAR** European Society of Gastrointestinal and Abdominal Radiology (#08605)
- ♦ **ESGCO** European Study Group on Cardiovascular Oscillations (#08849)
- ♦ ESGCP / see European Cell Proliferation Society (#06459)
- ♦ **ESGCT** European Society of Gene and Cell Therapy (#08608)
- ♦ **ESGE** European Society of Gastrointestinal Endoscopy (#08606)
- ♦ **ESGE** European Society for Gynaecological Endoscopy (#08611)
- ♦ **ESGENA** European Society of Gastroenterology and Endoscopy Nurses and Associates (#08604)
- ♦ ESG – European Shredder Group (no recent information)
- ♦ **ESG** European Society of Glass Science and Technology (#08610)
- ♦ **ESG** European Society of Gynecology (#08613)
- ♦ **ESGHM** European Society of Gender Health and Medicine (#08607)
- ♦ **ESGLD** European Study Group on Lysosomal Diseases (#08850)
- ♦ **ESGO** European Society of Gynaecological Oncology (#08612)
- ♦ ESGOI – European Society for Gynaecologic and Obstetric Investigation (internationally oriented national body)
- ♦ **ESGPIHI** European Study Group on Pathogenesis and Immunology in Helicobacter Infections (#08851)
- ♦ ESGR / see European Society of Gastrointestinal and Abdominal Radiology (#08605)
- ♦ **ESGS** European Salivary Gland Society (#08423)
- ♦ ESGS – European Society for General Semantics (no recent information)
- ♦ ESGT / see European Society of Gene and Cell Therapy (#08608)
- ♦ **ESHA** European School Heads Association (#08431)
- ♦ ESHA – European Sexual Health Alliance (inactive)
- ♦ **ESHA** European Small Hydropower Association (#08495)
- ♦ ESHDV – European Society for the History of Dermatology and Venerology (no recent information)
- ♦ **ESHE** European Society for the study of Human Evolution (#08744)
- ♦ **ESHET** European Society for the History of Economic Thought (#08620)
- ♦ **ESH** European School of Haematology (#08430)
- ♦ ESH – European Society for Hospital Sterile Supply (inactive)
- ♦ **ESH** European Society of Hypertension (#08627)
- ♦ **ESH** European Society of Hypnosis (#08629)
- ♦ **ESHG** European Society of Human Genetics (#08624)
- ♦ **ESHHS** European Society for the History of the Human Sciences (#08621)
- ♦ **ESHIMT** European Society for Hybrid, Molecular and Translational Imaging (#08626)
- ♦ **ESHLT** European Society for Heart and Lung Transplantation (#08619)
- ♦ **ESHMS** European Society of Health and Medical Sociology (#08618)
- ♦ **ESHNR** European Society of Head and Neck Radiology (#08617)
- ♦ **ESHO** European Society for Hyperthermic Oncology (#08628)
- ♦ **ESHP** European Society of Handwriting Psychology (#08616)
- ♦ **ESHPh** European Society for the History of Photography (#08622)
- ♦ **ESHRE** European Society of Human Reproduction and Embryology (#08625)
- ♦ **ESHRS** European Society of Hair Restoration Surgery (#08615)
- ♦ **ESHS** European Society for the History of Science (#08623)
- ♦ ESI / see Tecnalia Research and Innovation Foundation
- ♦ **ESIA** European Semiconductor Industry Association 1100041302
- ♦ ESIA – European Standard International Association (unconfirmed)
- ♦ ESIB / see European Students' Union (#08848)
- ♦ ESIB – National Unions of Students in Europe / see European Students' Union (#08848)
- ♦ ESI CEE – ESI Center Eastern Europe (internationally oriented national body)
- ♦ ESI Center Bulgaria / see ESI Center Eastern Europe
- ♦ ESI Center Eastern Europe (internationally oriented national body)
- ♦ ESIC – European Steel Industry Confederation (inactive)
- ♦ **ESICM** European Society of Intensive Care Medicine (#08632)
- ♦ **ESID** European Society for Immunodeficiencies (#08630)
- ♦ ESIDOG – European Society for Infectious Diseases in Obstetrics and Gynaecology (no recent information)
- ♦ ESI – Earth Security Initiative (internationally oriented national body)
- ♦ **ESI** Endangered Species International (#05455)
- ♦ ESI – Erwin Schrödinger International Institute for Mathematical Physics (internationally oriented national body)
- ♦ **ESI** European Scientific Institute (#08449)
- ♦ **ESI** European Scientific Institute (#08448)
- ♦ ESI – European Squirrel Initiative (internationally oriented national body)
- ♦ **ESI** European Stability Initiative (#08828)
- ♦ ESIFB – European Society for Intermediate Filament Biology (inactive)
- ♦ ESIF / see Solar Heat Europe (#19674)
- ♦ **ESIG** European Solvents Industry Group (#08796)
- ♦ **ESIL** European Society of International Law (#08634)
- ♦ **ESIM** European Society of Integrative Medicine (#08631)
- ♦ E-SIN / see European Small Islands Federation (#08496)
- ♦ **ESIN** European Small Islands Federation (#08496)
- ♦ **ESIP** European Social Insurance Platform (#08503)
- ♦ **ESIR** European Society for Isotope Research (#08636)
- ♦ ESIR / see European Society for Sexual Medicine (#08733)
- ♦ ESISC – European Strategic Intelligence and Security Centre (internationally oriented national body)
- ♦ **ESIS** European Structural Integrity Society (#08844)
- ♦ **ESIST** European Association for Studies in Screen Translation (#06227)
- ♦ **ESITIS** European Society for Intercultural Theology and Interreligious Studies (#08633)
- ♦ ESJJF – European Sport Jiu Jitsu Federation (unconfirmed)
- ♦ ESJK – Europäische Sport Jungens Konferenz (inactive)
- ♦ **ESJV** European Society for Jet Ventilation (#08637)
- ♦ ESKA / see European Association of Abnormal Road Transport and Mobile Cranes (#05923)
- ♦ **ESKA** European Shotokan Karate-do Association (#08482)
- ♦ ESKA / see European Society of Sports Traumatology, Knee Surgery and Arthroscopy (#08741)
- ♦ ESLA – European Service-Learning Association (inactive)
- ♦ **ESLA** European Speech and Language Therapy Association (#08812)
- ♦ ESLARED – Fundación Escuela Latinoamericana de Redes (internationally oriented national body)
- ♦ **ESLAS** European Society for Laser Aesthetic Surgery (#08639)
- ♦ **ESLAV** European Society for Laboratory Animal Veterinarians (#08638)
- ♦ ESLCCC – European Symposium on Late Complications After Childhood Cancer (meeting series)
- ♦ ESLD / see European Society for Lasers and Energy Based Devices (#08640)
- ♦ **ESLD** European Society for Lasers and Energy Based Devices (#08640)
- ♦ **ESLHO** European Scientific foundation for Laboratory Hemato Oncology (#08447)
- ♦ ESLI – Esperanta Sak-Ligo Internacia (inactive)
- ♦ **ESLO** European Society of Lingual Orthodontics (#08641)
- ♦ ESLP Conference – Embodied and Situated Language Processing Conference (meeting series)
- ♦ **ESMAC** European Society for Movement Analysis in Adults and Children (#08656)
- ♦ **ESMA** European Sales and Marketing Association (#08422)
- ♦ **ESMA** European Securities and Markets Authority (#08457)
- ♦ **ESMA** European Social Marketing Association (#08504)
- ♦ ESMA – European Society for Mathematics and the Arts (internationally oriented national body)
- ♦ ESMA / see European Specialist Printing Manufacturers Associations (#08809)
- ♦ **ESMA** European Specialist Printing Manufacturers Associations (#08809)
- ♦ **ESMA** European Speciality Minerals Association (#08811)
- ♦ ESMA / see European Stadium and Safety Management Association (#08830)

♦ **ESMB** European Society for Marine Biotechnology (#08645)
♦ **ESMD** European Society of Microscope Dentistry (#08653)
♦ **ESM** Earth Science Matters Foundation (#05169)
♦ ESME – eSports Middle East (unconfirmed)
♦ **ESM** European Society for Microcirculation (#08651)
♦ **ESM** European Society for Mycobacteriology (#08659)
♦ **ESM** European Stability Mechanism (#08829)
♦ ESMGS – European Society for Male Genital Surgery (no recent information)
♦ **ESMHD** European Society for Mental Health and Deafness (#08649)
♦ ESMH – European Society of Medical Hypnosis (no recent information)
♦ **ESMI** European Society for Molecular Imaging (#08655)

♦ ESMIG 05539

Managing Dir Bd A Reyers 80, 1030 Brussels, Belgium. T. +3222066876. E-mail: secretariat@esmig.eu.
Marketing and Communications Officer address not obtained. E-mail: communications@esmig.eu.
URL: http://www.esmig.eu/

History 2008. Replaces *Association of European Electricity Meter Manufacturers (CITEF, inactive)*. Former names and other names: *European Smart Metering Industry Group (ESMIG)* – former (2008 to 2014); *ESMIG – European Association of Smart Energy Solution Providers* – full title (2014). Registration: EU Transparency Register, No/ID: 71326222148-95, Start date: 13 Aug 2009. **Aims** Advocate for a regulatory framework that accelerates the introduction of innovative products and services which are fundamental to the smart energy and water systems of Europe's future. **Structure** General Assembly (twice a year); Executive Committee; Groups (5). **Languages** English. **Staff** 3.00 FTE, paid. **Finance** Sources: members' dues. Annual budget: 550,000 EUR. **Activities** Advocacy/lobbying/activism; events/meetings; knowledge management/information dissemination. **Events** *Energy Data at your Fingertips?!* Brussels (Belgium) 2020, *Europe energy market transformation and the impact of smart and disruptive digital technologies* Brussels (Belgium) 2018, *Workshop on ten Conditions for a Successful Smart Meter Roll- Out* Brussels (Belgium) 2018, *C-Level Summit* Brussels (Belgium) 2014, *Is the European Roll-Out of Smart Meters on Track Joint Workshop* Brussels (Belgium) 2012. **Publications** *ESMIG Newsletter* (weekly); *ESMIG Annual Book* (annual). Reports; studies; best practices; articles; brochures. **Members** International companies (19). Membership countries not specified. **NGO Relations** Member of (1): *DLMS User Association (#05109)*. Cooperates with (2): *Association européenne de fabricants de compteurs d'eau et d'énergie thermique (AQUA, #02567)*; *Association of European Manufacturers of Gas Meters, Gas Pressure Regulators, Safety Devices and Stations (FARECOGAZ, #02521)*. [2021.06.09/XJ0004/**D**]

♦ ESMIG – European Association of Smart Energy Solution Providers / see ESMIG (#05539)
♦ **ESMINT** European Society of Minimally Invasive Neurological Therapy (#08654)
♦ **ESMIT** European School of Multimodality Imaging & Therapy (#08432)
♦ **ESMO** European Society for Medical Oncology (#08648)
♦ **ESMR** European Society for Muscle Research (#08657)
♦ **ESMRMB** European Society of Magnetic Resonance in Medicine and Biology (#08644)
♦ ESMRN – European Society of Magnetic Resonance in Neuropaediatrics (inactive)
♦ ESMS / see European Society of Health and Medical Sociology (#08618)
♦ ESMS – European Society for Mass Spectrometry (inactive)
♦ **ESMS** European Society for Micrographic Surgery (#08652)
♦ ESMST / see European Membrane Society (#07777)
♦ ESMT / see ESMT Berlin
♦ ESMT Berlin (internationally oriented national body)
♦ **ESMTB** European Society for Mathematical and Theoretical Biology (#08646)
♦ **ESMT** Ecole supérieure multinationale des télécommunications de Dakar (#16898)
♦ ESMT / see International Society for Medical Shockwave Therapy (#15258)
♦ ESM Treaty – European Stability Mechanism Treaty (2011 treaty)
♦ **ESNA** European Society for New Methods in Agricultural Research (#08666)
♦ ESNA – European Society for Nineteenth-Century Art (unconfirmed)
♦ ESNA – European Society of Nuclear Methods in Agriculture (inactive)
♦ **ESNAM** European Society for Nanomedicine (#08660)
♦ ESNA / see OSGP Alliance (#17903)
♦ **ESNCH** European Society of Neurosonology and Cerebral Hemodynamics (#08665)
♦ **ESN** Erasmus Student Network (#05529)
♦ ESN / see European Board of Neonatology (#06363)
♦ **ESN** European Sensory Network (#08467)
♦ ESN / see European Services Forum (#08469)
♦ ESN – European Shortsea Network (unconfirmed)
♦ **ESN** European Social Network (#08505)
♦ **ESN** European Society of Nematologists (#08661)
♦ **ESN** European Society for Neurochemistry (#08662)
♦ **ESN** European Speechwriter Network (#08813)
♦ **ESN** Federation of the European Societies of Neuropsychology (#09547)
♦ ESNICVD / see European Society for Noninvasive and Preventive Cardiology (#08668)
♦ **ESNIPC** European Society for Noninvasive and Preventive Cardiology (#08668)
♦ ESNM / see European Society of Neurogastroenterology and Motility (#08663)
♦ **ESNM** European Society of Neurogastroenterology and Motility (#08663)
♦ **ESNO** European Specialist Nurses Organisation (#08808)
♦ **ESNR** European Society of Neuroradiology (#08664)
♦ ESNS – European Sport Nutrition Society (unconfirmed)
♦ ESOA – European Society of Obstetric Anaesthesiology (no recent information)
♦ ESOA – European Society of Osteoarthrology (inactive)
♦ ESOA / see Global Satellite Operators' Association (#10586)
♦ ESoCE / see European Society of Concurrent Enterprising Network (#08565)
♦ **ESoCE-NET** European Society of Concurrent Enterprising Network (#08565)
♦ **ESOC** European Space Operations Centre (#08800)
♦ ESOC – European Symposium on Organic Chemistry (meeting series)
♦ **ESOCITE** Sociedad Latinoamericana de Estudios Sociales de la Ciencia y la Tecnologia (#19407)
♦ ESOEPE / see European Network for Accreditation of Engineering Education (#07859)
♦ **ESO** Europäische Schiffer Organisation (#08491)
♦ **ESO** European Organization for Astronomical Research in the Southern hemisphere (#08106)
♦ **ESO** European School of Oncology (#08434)
♦ ESO – European School of Osteopathy (internationally oriented national body)
♦ **ESO** European Senior Organization (#08465)
♦ **ESO** European Stroke Organisation (#08843)
♦ ESO – European Supercentenarian Organisation (unconfirmed)
♦ **ESOI** European Society of Oncologic Imaging (#08670)
♦ ESOLA / see International Society for Oral Laser Applications (#15326)
♦ ESOMAR / see World Association of Research Professionals (#21182)
♦ **ESOMAR** World Association of Research Professionals (#21182)
♦ ESONE – Committee for European Studies on Norms for Electronics (inactive)
♦ ESON EGTC / see European Observation Network on Territorial Development and Cohesion (#08070)
♦ **ESONT** European Society of Ophthalmic Nurses and Technicians (#08672)
♦ **ESO-OEB** European Skippers Organisation (#08491)
♦ ESOPES – European Society for Out-Patient Eye Surgery (no recent information)
♦ **ESOP** European Society of Oncology Pharmacy (#08671)

♦ Esophageal ATresia Global Support Groups (EAT) 05540

Sec Sommerrainstr 61, 70374 Stuttgart, Germany.
Chair address not obtained.
URL: http://www.we-are-eat.org/

History Former names and other names: *Federation of Esophageal Atresia and Tracheo-Esophageal Fistula Support Groups (EAT)* – legal name. Registration: Baden-Württemberg District court, No/ID: VR 720961, Start date: 23 Nov 2011, Germany, Stuttgart. **Aims** Ensure that member organizations share knowledge and experience, address issues associated with Esophageal atresia which can be more effectively tackled internationally. **Structure** Board.
Members Full in 11-3 countries:
Argentina, Australia, Austria, Belgium, France, Germany, Italy, Netherlands, South Africa, Spain, Switzerland, Türkiye, UK.
Associate member in 1 country:
Canada.
NGO Relations Member of (2): *EURORDIS – Rare Diseases Europe (#09175)*; *Rare Diseases International (RDI, #18621)*. [2023/XM7448/**D**]

♦ ESOP / see International Society of Pharmacovigilance (#15356)
♦ ESOPRS / see European Society of Ophthalmic Plastic and Reconstructive Surgery (#08673)
♦ **ESOPRS** European Society of Ophthalmic Plastic and Reconstructive Surgery (#08673)
♦ ESOR – European Symposium on Organic Reactivity (meeting series)
♦ **ESORIB** European School of Oral Rehabilitation, Implantology and Biomaterials (#08435)
♦ **ESO Staff Association** European Southern Observatory Staff Association (#08797)
♦ **ESOT** European Society for Organ Transplantation (#08676)
♦ Espace Afrique international (internationally oriented national body)
♦ Espace économique européen (#06957)

♦ Espace Mathématique Francophone (EMF) 05541

Pres address not obtained.
URL: http://www.cfem.asso.fr/emf

History Organized since 2000. **Aims** Promote reflection exchanges within the French-speaking world on the key issues of mathematics education in current societies, at primary, secondary and higher levels, as well as on issues relating to initial and in-service teacher training. **Structure** Executive Board; Scientific Committee. **Languages** French. **Activities** Events/meetings. **Events** *EMF : Colloque Espace Mathématique Francophone* Cotonou (Benin) 2021, *EMF : Colloque Espace Mathématique Francophone* Paris (France) 2018, *EMF : Colloque Espace Mathématique Francophone* Algiers (Algeria) 2015, *EMF : Colloque Espace Mathématique Francophone* Geneva (Switzerland) 2012, *EMF : Colloque Espace Mathématique Francophone* Dakar (Senegal) 2009. **NGO Relations** Recognized by: *International Commission on Mathematical Instruction (ICMI, #12700)*. [2019/XM8434/c/**F**]

♦ ESPACI – European Society of Paediatric Allergy and Clinical Immunology (inactive)
♦ Espacio Económico Europeo (#06957)
♦ **ESPACOMP** European Society for Patient Adherence, COMpliance and Persistence (#08690)
♦ ESPA – European Shoe Press Association (no recent information)
♦ **ESPA** European Society for Paediatric Anaesthesiology (#08677)
♦ **ESPA** European Spas Association (#08805)
♦ **ESPA** European Spinal Psychologists Association (#08816)
♦ **ESPA** European Stabiliser Producers Association (#08827)
♦ **ESPAnet** Network for European Social Policy Analysis (#17030)
♦ ESPAS – Eastern and Middle European Confederation of National Societies of Plastic Aesthetic Restorative Surgery and Aesthetic Medicine (no recent information)
♦ ESPA / see Sterile Barrier Association (#19983)
♦ **ESPC** European Society of Protective Clothing (#08716)
♦ **ESPCG** European Society of Primary Care Gastroenterology (#08715)
♦ **ESPCH** European Society for Person Centered Healthcare (#08695)
♦ ESPCI – European Symposium on Paediatric Cochlear Implantation (meeting series)
♦ ESP Conference – Teaching English for Specific Purposes (meeting series)
♦ **ESPCOP** European Society for Perioperative Care of the Obese Patient (#08694)
♦ **ESPCR** European Society for Pigment Cell Research (#08707)
♦ **ESPD** European Society for Pediatric Dermatology (#08691)
♦ **ESPD** European Society for Photodermatology (#08703)
♦ **ESPE** European Society for Paediatric Endocrinology (#08678)
♦ **ESPE** European Society for Population Economics (#08709)
♦ **ESPEN** European Society for Clinical Nutrition and Metabolism (#08550)
♦ Esperanta Jura Asocio (no recent information)
♦ Esperanta Sak-Ligo Internacia (inactive)

♦ Esperantic Studies Foundation (ESF) 05542

Exec Dir 638 Greenwood Cir, Cary NC 27511, USA. T. +19197448003. E-mail: admin@esperantic.org.
Registered Address 1110 H Street, N.W., Suite 840, Washington DC 20005, USA.
URL: http://www.esperantic.org/

History 1968. Registration: USA, District of Columbia. **Aims** Mission Work to further understanding and practice of linguistic justice in a multicultural world. **Structure** Board of Directors; Advisory Board. **Languages** English, Esperanto. **Staff** 0.50 FTE, paid. **Finance** Sources: donations. Annual budget: 200,000 USD (2021). **Activities** Awards/prizes/competitions; events/meetings; knowledge management/information dissemination; research and development; training/education. **Publications** *Information for Interlinguists (IFI)*. Studies; books; articles. **Members** Not a membership organization. [2022/XF5477/f/**F**]

♦ Esperantista Virina Asocio en Afriko (unconfirmed)
♦ Esperantist Law Association (no recent information)
♦ Esperantist Music League (no recent information)
♦ Esperantist Ornithologists' Association (no recent information)
♦ Esperantists Association of Doctors (inactive)

♦ Esperanto Academy 05543

Académie d'espéranto – Akademio de Esperanto

Sec 72 quai de la Loire, 75019 Paris, France. E-mail: sekretario.akademio@gmail.com – sekretario@akademio-de-esperanto.org.
URL: http://www.akademio-de-esperanto.org/

History Founded 1905, Boulogne-sur-Mer (France), under the name *Lingva Komitato*. Reorganized and present name adopted 1948. Statutes revised 1964; 2009; 2015. **Aims** Control development of the international *language* Esperanto and give advice in case of doubt about the correct use of this language. **Structure** Akademio itself elects members for a term of 9 years. **Languages** Esperanto. **Staff** Voluntary. **Finance** Sources: international Esperanto movement. Annual budget: euro 2,000. **Activities** Networking/liaising; meeting activities. **Events** *Annual Meeting* Seoul (Korea Rep) 2017, *Annual Meeting* Nitra (Slovakia) 2016, *Annual Meeting* Lille (France) 2015, *Annual Meeting* Buenos Aires (Argentina) 2014, *Annual Meeting* Reykjavik (Iceland) 2013. **Publications** *Aktoj de la Akademio*; *Oficiala Bulteno*; *Oficialaj Informoj*.
Members Individuals (40) representing 22 countries:
Brazil, China, Cuba, Czechia, Finland, France, Germany, Hungary, India, Israel, Italy, Japan, Korea Rep, Luxembourg, Netherlands, Norway, Poland, Russia, Spain, UK, Ukraine, USA. [2020.02.12/XC0536/v/**F**]

♦ Esperanto-Asociación Internacional de Juristas (inactive)
♦ Esperanto Cultural Centre (internationally oriented national body)

♦ ESPERANTO + EDUKADO (ILEI) 05544

Main Office Nieuwe Binnenweg 176, 3015 BJ Rotterdam, Netherlands. E-mail: ilei.sekretario@gmail.com – mamduhi@gmail.com.
Pres Grande-Rue 9, cp 9, 2416 Les Brenets NE, Switzerland. T. +41796970966. E-mail: ilei.prezidanto@gmail.com.
URL: http://www.ilei.info/

Esperanto Family History
05544

History 12 Aug 1949, Bournemouth (UK). Founded in succession to *World Association of Esperantist Teachers (inactive)*, set up in 1908, and which lapsed during World War II. Current Statutes and By-Laws adopted 2011, Copenhagen (Denmark). Former names and other names: *International League of Esperantist Teachers* – former; *Internacia Ligo de Esperantistaj Instruistoj (ILEI)* – former; *Ligue internationale des enseignants espérantistes* – former; *International League of Esperanto Instructors* – former. **Aims** Promote education which leads to respect for mankind and *understanding* among peoples worldwide; collaborate with teachers to introduce Esperanto into schools. **Structure** Congress (annual); Executive Board; Sections (39); Representatives (12); contact persons (15). **Languages** Esperanto. **Staff** 7.00 FTE, voluntary. **Finance** Sources: contributions. Supported by: *Universal Esperanto Association (UEA, #20676)*. **Activities** Events/meetings; knowledge management/information dissemination; networking/liaising. **Events** *Congress* Lignano Sabbiadoro (Italy) 2023, *Congress* Cotonou (Benin) 2021, *Congress* Edinburgh (UK) 2021, *Congress* Rotterdam (Netherlands) 2020, *Congress* Cacak (Serbia) 2019. **Publications** *Internacia Pedagogia Revuo* (4 a year); *Juna Amiko* (4 a year). *Fantaziajoj Kaj Kantoj por Infanoj* (1995); *Kunvojagu* (1993); *Tendaraj Tagoj 1* (1993) – textbook for children; *Teorio Kaj Praktiko De Lingvo Instruado* (1992); *Universala Deklaracio pri Homrajtoj* (3rd ed 1961); *Esperanto en Britaj Lernejoj* (1959); *Struktura Kaj Socilingvistika Espoloro de Esperanto*.
Members Individuals in 70 countries and territories:
Albania, Argentina, Armenia, Australia, Austria, Bangladesh, Belgium, Benin, Bosnia-Herzegovina, Brazil, Bulgaria, Burundi, Cameroon, Canada, Chile, China, Colombia, Congo DR, Costa Rica, Côte d'Ivoire, Croatia, Cuba, Czechia, Denmark, Dominican Rep, Estonia, Finland, France, Germany, Hungary, Iceland, India, Indonesia, Iran Islamic Rep, Israel, Italy, Japan, Kenya, Korea Rep, Lithuania, Madagascar, Mexico, Mongolia, Nepal, Netherlands, New Zealand, Niger, Nigeria, Norway, Poland, Portugal, Romania, Russia, San Marino, Senegal, Serbia, Slovenia, South Africa, Spain, Sweden, Switzerland, Taiwan, Tanzania UR, Togo, UK, Ukraine, Uruguay, USA, Venezuela, Vietnam.
NGO Relations Member of (2): *International Federation of Language Teacher Associations (#13468)*; *Universal Esperanto Association (UEA, #20676)*.

[2023/XC2216/**C**]

♦ Esperanto Family History Association / see Foundation for East European Family History Societies
♦ Esperanto-Kulturzentrum (internationally oriented national body)
♦ Esperanto-Liga der Pfadfinder (#19309)
♦ Esperanto-Liga für Philatelie (#05545)

♦ Esperanto-Ligo Filatelista (ELF) 05545
Ligue philatélique espérantiste – Liga Filatélica Esperantista – Esperanto-Liga für Philatelie – Philatelic Esperanto League
Pres via Ghirlandaio 18/1, 34138 Trieste TS, Italy. E-mail: testudo.ts@gmail.com.
URL: http://www.kolektado.esperanto.cc/
History 6 Jul 1964. Also known as *Amika Rondo de Esperantaj-Kolektantoj (AREK)*. **Aims** Promote the collection of philatelic material concerning Esperanto and provide assistance to collectors. **Structure** Chairman and Vice-Chairman elected by postal vote of members every 3 years. **Languages** English, Esperanto, Italian. **Staff** 7.00 FTE, voluntary. **Finance** Grants from members. Annual budget: euro 1,000. **Activities** Events/meetings. **Events** *Meeting* Buenos Aires (Argentina) 2014, *Meeting* Reykjavik (Iceland) 2013, *Meeting* Trieste (Italy) 2013, *Meeting* Hanoi (Vietnam) 2012, *Meeting* Prague (Czech Rep) 2011. **Publications** *La Verda Lupeo/Fenikso* (3 a year) in Esperanto.
Members Individuals (about 120) in 27 countries:
Austria, Belgium, Brazil, Bulgaria, China, Croatia, Czechia, Denmark, Finland, France, Germany, Israel, Italy, Japan, Korea Rep, Lithuania, Mexico, Netherlands, Poland, Serbia, Slovakia, Spain, Sweden, Switzerland, UK, USA, Venezuela.
NGO Relations Affiliated member of: *Universal Esperanto Association (UEA, #20676)*.

[2020.03.14/XD3132/v/**D**]

♦ Esperanto Maritime League (inactive)
♦ Esperanto-Propaganda Asocio de Oomoto / see Oomoto
♦ Esperanto Radikala Asocio – Coordination pour l'intégration démocratique culturelle européenne (internationally oriented national body)
♦ Esperanto Weltbund (#20676)
♦ Esperanto Women's Association in Africa (unconfirmed)
♦ **ESPES** European Society of Paediatric Endoscopic Surgeons (#08679)
♦ **ESP** European Schools Project Association (#08436)
♦ **ESP** European Society of Pathology (#08689)
♦ **ESP** European Society for Photobiology (#08702)
♦ ESPGAN / see European Society for Paediatric Gastroenterology, Hepatology and Nutrition (#08680)
♦ **ESPGHAN** European Society for Paediatric Gastroenterology, Hepatology and Nutrition (#08680)
♦ **ESPHI** European Society for Paediatric Haematology and Immunology (#08681)
♦ ESPHO – European Society of Public Health Ophthalmology (no recent information)
♦ ESPIC / see European Society of Paediatric and Neonatal Intensive Care (#08683)
♦ **ESPID** European Society for Paediatric Infectious Diseases (#08682)
♦ ESPID – European Society for the Study and Prevention of Infant Death (inactive)
♦ **ESPI** European Space Policy Institute (#08801)
♦ **ESPKU** European Society for Phenylketonuria and Allied Disorders (#08697)
♦ ESPLAF – European Strategic Planning Federation (no recent information)
♦ **ESPLAT** European Society of Psychology Learning and Teaching (#08717)
♦ **ESPMH** European Society for Philosophy of Medicine and Health Care (#08698)
♦ ESPN / see European Society for Clinical Nutrition and Metabolism (#08550)
♦ **ESPN** European Society for Paediatric Nephrology (#08684)
♦ **ESPN** European Society for Paediatric Neurosurgery (#08685)
♦ **ESPNIC** European Society of Paediatric and Neonatal Intensive Care (#08683)
♦ **ESPNR** European Society for the Study of Peripheral Nerve Repair and Regeneration (#08745)
♦ **ESPO** European Sea Ports Organisation (#08453)
♦ **ESPO** European Society of Pediatric Otorhinolaryngology (#08692)
♦ ESPO – European Society for Psychosocial Oncology (inactive)
♦ Espoir pour un enfant (internationally oriented national body)
♦ Espoir mondial (internationally oriented national body)
♦ Espoir sans frontières (internationally oriented national body)
♦ Espoir sans frontières (internationally oriented national body)
♦ **ESPON** European Observation Network on Territorial Development and Cohesion (#08070)
♦ Espoo Convention – Convention on Environmental Impact Assessment in a Transboundary Context (1991 treaty)
♦ ESPORG – European Secure Parking Organisation (unconfirmed)
♦ Esports Europe / see European Esports Federation (#07007)
♦ Esports Federation of Africa (unconfirmed)
♦ eSports Middle East (unconfirmed)
♦ Esports World Federation (unconfirmed)
♦ **ESPP** European Society for Philosophy and Psychology (#08699)
♦ **ESPP** European Sustainable Phosphorus Platform (#08866)
♦ **ESPRAS** European Society of Plastic, Reconstructive and Aesthetic Surgery (#08708)
♦ **ESPR** European Society of Paediatric Radiology (#08686)
♦ **ESPR** European Society for Paediatric Research (#08687)
♦ **ESPR** European Society for Philosophy of Religion (#08700)
♦ **ESPREVMED** European Society of Preventive Medicine (#08713)
♦ **ESPRit** European Society of Periodical Research (#08693)
♦ **ESPRM** European Society of Physical and Rehabilitation Medicine (#08706)
♦ ESPRO – European Forum for Sustainable Property Development (internationally oriented national body)
♦ ESPT / see European Society of Pharmacogenomics and Personalised Therapy (#08696)
♦ **ESPT** European Society of Pharmacogenomics and Personalised Therapy (#08696)
♦ **ESPU** European Society for Paediatric Urology (#08688)
♦ ESQH – European Society for Quality in Healthcare (inactive)
♦ ESQR – European Society for Quality Research (unconfirmed)
♦ **ESRAD** European Society for Research in Adult Development (#08724)
♦ ESRADI – European Society of Reproductive and Developmental Immunology (inactive)
♦ **ESRA** European Safety and Reliability Association (#08419)
♦ **ESRA** European Shakespeare Research Association (#08475)
♦ ESRA / see European Society of Regional Anaesthesia and Pain Therapy (#08722)
♦ **ESRA** European Society of Regional Anaesthesia and Pain Therapy (#08722)
♦ **ESRA** European Street Rod Association (#08841)
♦ **ESRA** European Sugar Refineries Association (#08853)
♦ **ESRA** European Survey Research Association (#08862)
♦ ESRA – European Synthetic Rubber Association (no recent information)
♦ ESRA / see The Organization for Professionals in Regulatory Affairs (#17885)
♦ **ESRB** European Systemic Risk Board (#08872)
♦ ESRD / see United Nations Office for Disaster Risk Reduction (#20595)
♦ **ESREA** European Society for Research on the Education of Adults (#08725)
♦ **ESRE** Association of European Space Research Establishments (#02545)
♦ **ESReDA** European Safety, Reliability and Data Association (#08420)
♦ **ESR** European Society of Radiology (#08720)
♦ **ESR** European Society of Rheology (#08730)
♦ **ESRF** European Skin Research Foundation (#08490)
♦ ESRF / see European Squash Federation (#08826)
♦ ESRF – European Stroke Research Foundation (internationally oriented national body)
♦ **ESRF** European Synchrotron Radiation Facility (#08868)
♦ **ESRI** European Society for Reproductive Immunology (#08723)
♦ ESRI – European Studies Research Institute, Salford (internationally oriented national body)
♦ **esrii** European Society for Research on Internet Interventions (#08727)

♦ ESRIN 05546
Contact c/o ESRIN Headquarters, Via Galileo Galilei, Casella Postale 64, 00044 Frascati RM, Italy. T. +396941801. Fax +39694180280. E-mail: contactesa@esa.int.
URL: http://www.esa.int/
History 1966, as *European Space Research Institute – Institute européen de recherches spatiales*, in the framework of *European Space Research Organization (ESRO) – Organisation européenne de recherches spatiales* whose Convention entered into force on 20 Mar 1964 and was terminated by the Convention of *European Space Agency (ESA, #08798)*, to carry out research activities on interplanetary plasma physics. First permanent building for experiments completed and occupied in Feb 1969. In 1973, became ESA centre for management of scientific and technical information databases, providing access to 200 research and technology databases worldwide. Following internal reorganization, 1992, now focuses on data handling in the field of earth observation, previously the work of *Earthnet Programme Office (EPO, inactive)*, set up in 1978, within the framework of ESRIN. Since 1997, also responsible for ESA's non-operational data handling activities as well as for the maintenance of the ESA Web site. Since 1999, headquarters of the *'Vega Small Launcher Programme Department'*. **Aims** Provide the ground segment required for acquisition, preprocessing, archiving and distribution of *satellite* remote sensing data; develop Earth observation data user applications and novel algorithms; develop informatics applications and operate the resulting services and infrastructures for all ESA's establishments; implement the Vega Small Launcher Programme. **Structure** Departments (4) operate under delegation by the ESA Directorate of Earth Observation Programmes, by the Directorate of Operations and Infrastructure and by the Directorate of Launchers. **Staff** 180.00 FTE, paid. **Finance** Member States' quotas.
Activities /Earth Observation Programmes/ – *'Science and Applications Department'* responsible for: ensuring the interface with scientific public services and commercial user communities and for ensuring scientific support and providing applications expertise to other EO departments in the development and exploitation phase of all missions and programmes; Global Monitoring for Environment and Security "Initial Services" (GMES). *'Ground Segment Department'* responsible for acquisition, processing, archiving and distribution of data from ESA's Earth Observation Missions ERS-1, ERS-2, PROBA, Envisat and of data from other satellites such as Landsat, NOAA, MOS and JERS operated by non-ESA administrations (third party missions). Acts as user interface and payload data exploitation centre and operates worldwide catalogue, help and order desk, browse and product central services. /Launchers/ – *'VEGA Small Launcher Programme'* – management office set up 1999.
/Operations and Infrastructure/ – *'Information Systems Department'* – responsible for infrastructure management and support.
Events *ERS/ENVISAT symposium* Bergen (Norway) 2010, *GRID and e-collaboration workshop for the earth science community* Frascati (Italy) 2008, *Long term data preservation workshop* Frascati (Italy) 2008, *ERS/ENVISAT symposium* Montreux (Switzerland) 2007, *International GOCE user workshop* Frascati (Italy) 2006. **Publications** Articles in ESA Bulletin and other journals. **Information Services** *Earthnet Online INterferometric SAR Sample Images (INSI Collection)* – interferometry pages, sample images pages; *Earthnet Online Multimission User Information Services (MUIS)* – integrated service providing access to centralized and (later) decentralized online Earth observation data.
Members Member States of European Space Agency (17):
Austria, Belgium, Denmark, Finland, France, Germany, Greece, Ireland, Italy, Luxembourg, Netherlands, Norway, Portugal, Spain, Sweden, Switzerland, UK.
ESA State with special agreement:
Canada.

[2010/XE6746/j/**E***]

♦ ESRLA / see International Society for Religion, Literature and Culture (#15417)
♦ ESRLC / see International Society for Religion, Literature and Culture (#15417)
♦ ESRO – European Space Research Organization (inactive)
♦ ESRO / see European Space Research and Technology Centre (#08802)
♦ **ESRS** European Sleep Research Society (#08493)
♦ **ESRS** European Society for Rural Sociology (#08731)
♦ ESRS – European Synchrotron Radiation Society (no recent information)
♦ **ESRU** European Society of Residents in Urology (#08729)
♦ **ESSA** Entomological Society of Southern Africa (#05494)
♦ ESSA / see ESSA – The International Security Association (#05547)
♦ **ESSA** ESSA – The International Security Association (#05547)
♦ **ESSA** European Salmon Smokers Association (#08424)
♦ ESSA / see European Salt Producers Association (#08425)
♦ **ESSA** European Social Simulation Association (#08506)
♦ ESSA – European Sociology Students' Association (inactive)
♦ **ESSA** European State Studs Association (#08834)
♦ ESSA / see Internatioanl Betting Integrity Association (#11527)

♦ ESSA – The International Security Association (ESSA) 05547
Address not obtained.
URL: http://www.ecb-s.com/
History Officially registered as *European Security Systems Association (ESSA)*. Also referred to as *International Security Association*. Current statutes adopted Nov 2011. Registered in accordance with German law. EU Transparency Register: 573358933303-45. **Aims** Improve and guarantee the quality of products, components and materials from the security systems, fire protection and life safety segments. **Structure** General Assembly; Executive Committee; Managing Director. **Finance** Members' dues. **Activities** Certification/accreditation; events/meetings; networking/liaising.
Members Full; Extraordinary. Members in 38 countries:
Austria, Bangladesh, Belgium, Bosnia-Herzegovina, Brazil, Bulgaria, China, Croatia, Czechia, Finland, France, Germany, Greece, Hungary, India, Indonesia, Ireland, Italy, Japan, Korea Rep, Kosovo, Lithuania, Malaysia, Netherlands, New Zealand, North Macedonia, Norway, Poland, Romania, Russia, Serbia, Slovenia, Spain, Sweden, Switzerland, UK, Ukraine, USA.
NGO Relations Liaison Organization of: *Comité européen de normalisation (CEN, #04162)*.

[2018/XM4806/**D**]

♦ ESSA / see Pack2Go Europe (#18014)

- ESSA – Sport Betting Integrity / see Internatioanl Betting Integrity Association (#11527)
- ESSCD – European Society for Study of Coeliac Disease (unconfirmed)
- ESSC – European Shooting Sport Council (unconfirmed)
- ESSC European Society for Soil Conservation (#08739)
- ESSC – European Space Sciences Committee (see: #08441)
- ESSCS – European Society for the Study of Cognitive Systems (inactive)

ESSDERC/ESSCIRC Steering Committee 05548
Exec Sec c/o IMEC, Kapeldreef 75, 3001 Leuven, Belgium. T. +3216281328. Fax +3216281214. **Chair** Texas Instruments Deutschland GmbH, Haggertystrasse 1, 85356 Freising, Germany.
History ESSDERC stands for *European Solid-State Device Research Conference*; ESSCIRC stands for *European Solid-State Circuits Conference*. **Aims** Provide a *European* forum to present and discuss recent advances in *solid-state devices* and *technologies*. **Structure** Steering Committee. **Events** *European Solid State Device Research Conference / Annual Conference* Graz (Austria) 2015, *European Solid-State Circuits Conference* Graz (Austria) 2015, *European Solid State Device Research Conference* Venice (Italy) 2014, *European Solid-State Circuits Conference* Venice (Italy) 2014, *European Solid State Device Research Conference* Bucharest (Romania) 2013. **Publications** Conference proceedings.
Members Individuals in 13 countries:
Austria, Belgium, France, Germany, Greece, Italy, Japan, Korea Rep, Netherlands, Sweden, Switzerland, UK, USA.
[2014.11.04/XJ6457/c/E]

- ESSD European Society for Social Drug Research (#08736)
- ESSD European Society for Swallowing Disorders (#08755)
- ESSE European Society for the Study of English (#08743)
- ESS ERIC / see European Social Survey (#08507)
- ESS – Europaeisk Sammenslutning for Samarbejde (inactive)
- ESS Europaeisk Selskab for Skriftpsykologi (#08616)
- ESS European Shock Society, The (#08480)
- ESS European Social Survey (#08507)
- ESS European Society for Sonochemistry (#08740)
- ESS European Society of Surgery (#08751)
- ESS – European Sociobiological Society (inactive)
- ESS European Spallation Source ERIC (#08804)
- ESSFI / see SSE International Forum (#19937)
- ESSFN European Society for Stereotactic and Functional Neurosurgery (#08742)
- ESS Forum International (#19937)
- ESS Forum International – Red Internacional de Economia Social y Solidaria / see SSE International Forum (#19937)
- ESSIC / see International Society for the Study of Bladder Pain Syndrome (#15466)
- ESSIC International Society for the Study of Bladder Pain Syndrome (#15466)
- ESSIR / see European Society for Sexual Medicine (#08733)
- ESSIR – European Society for the Study of International Relations (inactive)
- ESSKA 2000 / see European Society of Sports Traumatology, Knee Surgery and Arthroscopy (#08741)
- ESSKA European Society of Sports Traumatology, Knee Surgery and Arthroscopy (#08741)
- ESSL European Severe Storms Laboratory (#08471)
- Essl Foundation (internationally oriented national body)
- Essl Foundation MGE gemeinnützige Privatstiftung / see Essl Foundation
- ESSMA European Stadium and Safety Management Association (#08830)
- ESSM European Society for Sexual Medicine (#08733)
- ESSNA European Specialist Sports Nutrition Alliance (#08810)
- ESSN – European Senior Service Network (inactive)
- ESSO European Society of Surgical Oncology (#08753)
- ES-SO European Solar Shading Organization (#08794)
- ESSOP / see International Society for Social Pediatrics and Child Health (#15448)
- ESSOR (internationally oriented national body)
- ESSPD European Society for the Study of Personality Disorders (#08746)
- ESSP European Society of Social Psychiatry (#08738)
- ESSPPMM / see Purine and Pyrimidine Society (#18579)
- ESSR / see European Society of Musculoskeletal Radiology (#08658)
- ESSR European Society of Musculoskeletal Radiology (#08658)
- ESSR European Society for Surgical Research (#08754)
- ESSSAT European Society for the Study of Science and Theology (#08747)
- ESSSB – European Symposium on Suicide and Suicidal Behaviour (meeting series)
- ESSSE European Society for Surgery of Shoulder and Elbow (#08752)
- ESST Association interuniversitaire européenne Société, science et technologie (#07597)
- ESST European Society for Sugar Technology (#08750)
- ESSTS European Society for Study of Tourette Syndrome (#08748)
- ESSU – European Services Strategy Unit (internationally oriented national body)
- ESSWE European Society for the Study of Western Esotericism (#08749)
- ESTAC – European Symposium on Thermal Analysis and Calorimetry (meeting series)
- ESTAD – European Steel Technology and Application Days (meeting series)
- ESTA ESTA Healthcare (#05549)
- ESTA / see European Association of Abnormal Road Transport and Mobile Cranes (#05923)
- ESTA European Association of Abnormal Road Transport and Mobile Cranes (#05923)
- ESTA European Security Transport Association (#08458)
- ESTA European Smoking Tobacco Association (#08497)
- ESTA European Steel Tube Association (#08837)
- ESTA European String Teachers Association (#08842)

ESTA Healthcare (ESTA) 05549
General Manager Hanikerweg 16, 5943 NB Lomm, Netherlands. T. +31643072487. E-mail: info@estahealthcare.com.
URL: https://www.estahealthcare.com/
History 1959, Netherlands. Registration: No/ID: 67716032, Netherlands. **Aims** Provide business development through member interaction and by offering European Healthcare Solutions by way of partnership with selected suppliers. **Structure** Management. **Languages** English. **Staff** 2.00 FTE, paid. **Activities** Events/meetings. **Events** *Annual meeting* Vienna (Austria) 2006, *Annual meeting* Milan (Italy) 2005, *Annual meeting* Stockholm (Sweden) 2004, *Annual meeting* Utrecht (Netherlands) 2003, *Annual meeting* Reykjavik (Iceland) 2002. **Publications** *ESTA News Bulletin* – internal bulletin.
Members Companies in 14 countries:
Czechia, Denmark, Finland, France, Germany, Iceland, Ireland, Italy, Netherlands, Norway, Poland, Sweden, Switzerland, UK.
[2020/XD2930/t/D]

- ESTAL European association for Surface Treatment on Aluminium (#06242)
- ESTC EMEA Synthetic Turf Council (#05436)
- ESTC – European Sialendoscopy Training Centre (internationally oriented national body)
- ESTD European Society for Trauma and Dissociation (#08767)
- ESTEC European Space Research and Technology Centre (#08802)
- ESTELA European Solar Thermal Electricity Association (#08795)
- ESTEP European Steel Technology Platform (#08836)
- ESTER European Graduate School for Training in Economic and Social Historical Research (#07404)
- ESTES European Society for Trauma and Emergency Surgery (#08768)
- EST – The European Society of Telemetry (internationally oriented national body)
- EST – European Society of Toxicology (inactive)
- EST European Society for Translation Studies (#08766)
- ESTHER Ecole inter-Etats des techniciens supérieurs de l'hydraulique et de l'équipement rural (#15981)

- ESTIEM European Students of Industrial Engineering and Management (#08846)
- ESTI European Society of Thoracic Imaging (#08759)
- ESTI – European Society of Transport Institutes (inactive)
- ESTIF (#19674)
- ESTIV European Society for Toxicology In Vitro (#08763)
- ESTL European Space Tribology Laboratory (#08803)
- ESTM European School of Transfusion Medicine (#08437)
- ESTO / see EMEA Synthetic Turf Council (#05436)
- Estonian Foreign Policy Institute (internationally oriented national body)
- Estonian Human Rights Centre (internationally oriented national body)
- Estonian Institute for Human Rights (internationally oriented national body)

Estonian World Council (EWCI) 05550
Conseil mondial estonien – Ulemaailmne Eesti Kesknoukogu
Pres 7648 Melotte St, San Diego CA 92119, USA.
URL: http://uekn.org/
History 1954; formally incorporated, 1982. **Aims** Unite, represent and exchange information among central organizations of Estonians abroad; maintain relations with Estonia. **Structure** Board of Directors; Executive Committee. **Languages** English, Estonian. **Staff** 0.50 FTE, paid. **Finance** Members' dues. Contributions. Annual budget: US$ 50,000. **Activities** Financial and/or material support; networking/liaising. **Events** *Annual Meeting* 2020, *Quadrennial Meeting* Tallinn (Estonia) 2019, *Quadrennial meeting* Toronto, ON (Canada) 2000, *Quadrennial meeting* Stockholm (Sweden) 1996.
Members Regular; Affiliate. Organizations in 12 countries:
Australia, Canada, Czechia, Finland, Germany, Latvia, Lithuania, Russia, Sweden, UK, Ukraine, USA.
[2019.02.11/XE1372/E]

- ESTP European Society on Tattoo and Pigment research (#08756)
- ESTP European Society of Toxicologic Pathology (#08762)
- Estrategia Andina, Centroamericana y Amazónica / see Red Latinoamericana sobre Deuda, Desarrollo y Derechos (#18711)
- Estrategia Internacional para la Reducción de Desastres / see United Nations Office for Disaster Risk Reduction (#20595)
- ESTRO European SocieTy for Radiotherapy and Oncology (#08721)
- ESTROT European SocieTy of Tissue Regeneration in Orthopaedics and Traumatology (#08761)
- ESTS European Set Theory Society (#08470)
- ESTS / see European Society for Study of Tourette Syndrome (#08748)
- ESTS European Society for Textual Scholarship (#08758)
- ESTS European Society of Thoracic Surgeons (#08760)
- ESTSS European Society for Traumatic Stress Studies (#08769)
- Estuarine and Brackish-Water Biological Association / see Estuarine and Coastal Sciences Association (#05551)
- Estuarine and Brackish Water Sciences Association / see Estuarine and Coastal Sciences Association (#05551)

Estuarine and Coastal Sciences Association (ECSA) 05551
Sec School of Biological and Marine Sciences, Univ of Plymouth, Drake Circus, Plymouth, PL4 8AA, UK.
URL: https://esca.international/
History Founded 1971, as *Estuarine and Brackish-Water Biological Association*. Name changed in 1972 to *Estuarine and Brackish Water Sciences Association*. Present name adopted 1989. UK Registered Charity: 264006. **Aims** Promote and advance multidisciplinary research into all aspects of estuaries and coasts; apply science and technology for their sustainable environmental management. **Structure** General Meeting (annual). **Languages** English. **Staff** Voluntary. **Finance** Members' dues. Annual budget: pounds10,000. **Activities** Events/meetings; financial and/or material support. **Events** *Annual Symposium* Hull (UK) 2021, *Annual Symposium* Hull (UK) 2020, *Meeting on the forth and Tay Estuaries* Edinburgh (UK) 2019, *Annual General Meeting* London (UK) 2018, *Annual Symposium* Perth, WA (Australia) 2018. **Publications** *ECSA Newsletter* (3 a year); *ECSA Bulletin* (2 a year); *Estuarine and Coastal Shelf Science* – journal. Handbooks; proceedings of meetings and symposia.
Members Professional scientists and estuarine and coastal managers in 32 countries:
Argentina, Australia, Belgium, Canada, Chile, China, Denmark, Finland, France, Germany, Greece, Iceland, India, Ireland, Italy, Japan, Lithuania, Netherlands, New Zealand, Nigeria, Norway, Poland, Portugal, Russia, Singapore, Slovenia, South Africa, Spain, Sweden, Thailand, UK, USA.
[2019.12.12/XD3543/D]

- Estuarine Research Federation / see Coastal and Estuarine Research Federation

Estudio Colaborativo Latino Americano de Malformaciones Congénitas (ECLAMC) 05552
Latin American Collaborative Study of Congenital Malformations
Main Office CEMIC – Dir de Investigación, Galvan 4102, 1431 Buenos Aires, Argentina. T. +541145457934. Fax +541152990414. E-mail: eclamc@eclamc.org.
Rio Office Fundaçao Oswaldo Cruz, Av Brasil 4365, Pav Leônidas Deane, Sala 617, Rio de Janeiro RJ, 21040-900, Brazil. T. +552138658141. Fax +552122604282. E-mail: castilla@centroin.com.br.
URL: http://www.eclamc.org/
History 1967. **Aims** Conduct research and prevention of *birth defects*. **Structure** Coordinator and a coordinating team direct activities from headquarters in Rio de Janeiro (Brazil) and Buenos Aires (Argentina). **Finance** Research grants from national research councils of Argentina and Brazil. **Activities** Research on clinical epidemiology of birth defects; surveillance of birth defects. **Events** *Annual meeting* Mangaratiba (Brazil) 1996, *Annual meeting* Solis (Uruguay) 1995, *Annual Meeting* Santiago (Chile) 1994, *Annual Meeting* Mangaratiba (Brazil) 1993, *Annual Meeting* Torres (Brazil) 1992. **Publications** Meeting proceedings. Occasional books.
Members Individuals in 12 countries:
Argentina, Bolivia, Brazil, Chile, Colombia, Costa Rica, Dominican Rep, Ecuador, Paraguay, Peru, Uruguay, Venezuela.
IGO Relations WHO (#20950); Pan American Health Organization (PAHO, #18108). **NGO Relations** Regional member of: *International Clearinghouse for Birth Defects Surveillance and Research (ICBDSR, #12594)*.
[2018/XF2565/v/E]

- ESUCB – European Symposium on Ultrasonic Characterization of Bone (meeting series)
- ESU English-Speaking Union (#05482)
- ESU – European School of Urology (see: #06264)
- ESU European Seniors' Union (#08466)
- ESU European Showmen's Union (#08483)
- ESU European Students' Union (#08848)
- ESU – European Sumo Union (no recent information)
- ESUOE – European Society of Urological Oncology (inactive)
- ESUR European Society of Urogenital Radiology (#08770)
- ESUR – European Society for Urological Research (inactive)
- ESVCE European Society of Veterinary Clinical Ethology (#08774)
- ESVC European Society of Veterinary Cardiology (#08773)
- ESVCN European Society of Veterinary and Comparative Nutrition (#08776)
- ESVCP European Society of Veterinary Clinical Pathology (#08775)
- ESVDC European Society for Vocational Designing and Career Counseling (#08788)
- ESVD European Society of Veterinary Dermatology (#08777)
- ESVE European Society of Veterinary Endocrinology (#08778)
- ESV – Equipes Saint-Vincent (internationally oriented national body)
- ESV Europäische Sparkassenvereinigung (#08426)
- ESV / see European Savings and Retail Banking Group (#08426)
- ESV European Society for Virology (#08787)
- ESVIM European Society of Veterinary Internal Medicine (#08779)
- ESV – International Technical Conference on the Enhanced Safety of Vehicles (meeting series)

- ♦ **ESVM** European Society for Vascular Medicine (#08771)
- ♦ **ESVN** European Society of Veterinary Neurology (#08781)
- ♦ **ESVNU** European Society of Veterinary Nephrology and Urology (#08780)
- ♦ **ESVO** European Society of Veterinary Ophthalmology (#08783)
- ♦ ESVONC / see European Society of Veterinary Oncology (#08782)
- ♦ **ESVONC** European Society of Veterinary Oncology (#08782)
- ♦ **ESVOT** European Society of Veterinary Orthopaedics and Traumatology (#08784)
- ♦ **ESVP** European Society of Veterinary Pathology (#08785)
- ♦ **ESVS** European Society for Vascular Surgery (#08772)
- ♦ **ESVV** European Society for Veterinary Virology (#08786)
- ♦ **ESWA** European Sex Workers' Rights Alliance (#08472)
- ♦ **ESWA** European Single Ply Waterproofing Association (#08488)
- ♦ ESWC – European STAMP Workshop and Conference (meeting series)
- ♦ **ESWDA** European Sports Workforce Development Alliance (#08823)
- ♦ ESW – Engineers for a Sustainable World (internationally oriented national body)
- ♦ **ESWET** European Suppliers of Waste to Energy Technology (#08858)
- ♦ ESWF – Esports World Federation (unconfirmed)
- ♦ **ESWI** European Scientific Working Group on Influenza (#08450)
- ♦ ESWM – European Society for Wood Mechanics (inactive)
- ♦ **ESWRA** European Social Work Research Association (#08508)
- ♦ **ESWTR** European Society of Women in Theological Research (#08789)
- ♦ ESYC – European Sports Youth Conference (inactive)
- ♦ **ETAD** Ecological and Toxicological Association of Dyes and Organic Pigments Manufacturers (#05302)
- ♦ ETA – Enzyme Technical Association (unconfirmed)
- ♦ ETA / see European Tennis Federation (#08898)
- ♦ ETA – European Thermographic Association (inactive)
- ♦ **ETA** European Thyroid Association (#08913)
- ♦ ETA / see european tube manufacturers association (#08953)
- ♦ **ETA** European Tugowners Association (#08956)
- ♦ **ETAF** European Tax Adviser Federation (#08875)
- ♦ **ETAG** European Travel and Tourism Advisory Group (#08946)
- ♦ ETA-I – Electronics Technicians Association International (internationally oriented national body)
- ♦ ETA International / see Electronics Technicians Association International
- ♦ Etaireai DIOGENIS – Etaireia DIOGENIS – Protovoulia Dialogou gia tin Politiki ton Narkotikon stin Notioanatoliki Evropi (internationally oriented national body)
- ♦ Etaireia DIOGENIS – Protovoulia Dialogou gia tin Politiki ton Narkotikon stin Notioanatoliki Evropi (internationally oriented national body)
- ♦ ETAN / see East Timor and Indonesia Action Network
- ♦ ETAN – East Timor and Indonesia Action Network (internationally oriented national body)
- ♦ ETA Network / see Educational Theatre Association
- ♦ ETAPC – European Technical Association for Protective Coatings (inactive)
- ♦ ETA / see Taxpayers Association of Europe (#20102)
- ♦ Etats ACP / see Organisation of African, Caribbean and Pacific States (#17796)
- ♦ Etats africains de la Charte de Casablanca (inactive)
- ♦ Etats-unies d'Afrique (unconfirmed)
- ♦ **ETBF** European Tenpin Bowling Federation (#08899)
- ♦ ETC (internationally oriented national body)
- ♦ **ETC** Emergency Telecommunications Cluster (#05438)
- ♦ **ETC** Energy Transitions Commission (#05478)
- ♦ ETC – European Tea Committee (inactive)
- ♦ ETC – European Testing Conference (meeting series)
- ♦ **ETC** European Theatre Convention (#08905)
- ♦ **ETC** European Timber Council (#08914)
- ♦ ETC – European Training- and Research Centre for Human Rights and Democracy (internationally oriented national body)
- ♦ **ETC** European Travel Commission (#08943)
- ♦ **ETC Group** Action Group on Erosion, Technology and Concentration (#00091)
- ♦ ETC International Group / see ETC
- ♦ ETC / see INTERREG V (#15966)
- ♦ **ETCMA** European Traditional Chinese Medicine Association (#08930)
- ♦ ETC Netherlands / see ETC
- ♦ ETCO / see European Donation and Transplant Coordination Organisation (#06939)
- ♦ ETCR – European Training Centre for Railways (internationally oriented national body)
- ♦ ETCS – European Tissue Culture Society (inactive)
- ♦ ETCS – European Train Control System (see: #08327)
- ♦ **ETDB** Economic Cooperation Organization Trade and Development Bank (#05314)
- ♦ **ETDF** European Training and Development Federation (#08933)
- ♦ ETEC – European Timber Exporters' Convention (inactive)
- ♦ **ETE** Evropaiki Trapeza Ependiseon (#07599)
- ♦ **ETEN** European Teacher Education Network (#08876)
- ♦ ETES – European Tissue Engineering Society (inactive)
- ♦ **ET** European Society for Catholic Theology (#08540)
- ♦ ET / see Eurotransplant International Foundation (#09192)
- ♦ ETFA – European Technological Forecasting Association (inactive)
- ♦ ETF – European Taxidermy Federation (inactive)
- ♦ ETF – European Teleconferencing Federation (inactive)
- ♦ ETF – European Telemarketing Federation (inactive)
- ♦ **ETF** European Trainers Federation (#08932)
- ♦ **ETF** European Training Foundation (#08934)
- ♦ ETF – European Transport Forum (meeting series)
- ♦ **ETF** European Transport Workers' Federation (#08941)
- ♦ ETF / see Resort Development Organisation (#18913)
- ♦ **ETFRN** European Tropical Forest Research Network (#08950)
- ♦ **ETHA** European Thrombosis and Haemostasis Alliance (#08911)

♦ Ethereum Foundation 05553

Exec Dir Zeughausgasse 7a, 6300 Zug, Switzerland. E-mail: press@ethereum.org.
URL: https://ethereum.foundation/

Aims Support Ethereum and related technologies. **Structure** Executive Board. **Activities** Events/meetings. **Events** *DEVCON Meeting* Osaka (Japan) 2019. [2020/AA0103/f/**F**]

♦ Ethical Journalism Network (EJN) 05554

Co-Sec International House, Holborn Viaduct, London, EC1A 2BN, UK. E-mail: contactus@ethicaljournalismnetwork.org.
URL: https://ethicaljournalismnetwork.org/

History Current articles of the Association adopted Apr 2015. Registration: Companies House, No/ID: 08558686, Start date: 6 Jun 2013, England and Wales; Charity Commission, No/ID: 1166150, Start date: 2016, England and Wales. **Aims** Strengthen the craft of journalism and promote for the public benefit high ethical standards in media through education, training and publication of useful research. **Structure** General Meeting; Board of Trustees; Secretariat. **Activities** Advocacy/lobbying/activism; knowledge management/information dissemination; networking/liaising; training/education. **Publications** *EJN Weekly Bulletin* (weekly). Infographics; podcasts; publications; videos.
Members Groups of journalists, editors, press owners and media support groups (over 70), including the following 26 organizations listed in this Yearbook:
- *Alliance of Independent Press Councils of Europe (AIPCE, #00689)*;
- *Arab Reporters for Investigative Journalism (ARIJ, #01036)*;
- *ARTICLE 19 (#01121)*;
- *Asia-Pacific Broadcasting Union (ABU, #01863)*;
- *Association of Commercial Television in Europe (ACT, #02436)*;
- *Child Rights International Network (CRIN, #03885)*;
- *European Broadcasting Union (EBU, #06404)*;
- *European Federation of Journalists (EFJ, #07152)*;
- *European Journalism Centre (EJC, #07612)*;
- *European Magazine Media Association (EMMA, #07723)*;
- *European Publishers Council (EPC, #08304)*;
- *Federation of African Journalists (FAJ, #09404)*;
- *Fundación Gabo*;
- *Globethics.net Foundation (#10669)*;
- *International Association of Women in Radio and Television (IAWRT, #12271)*;
- *International Media Support (IMS, #14128)*;
- *International Press Institute (IPI, #14636)*;
- *International Women's Media Foundation (IWMF, #15901)*;
- *Internews Europe (#15953)*;
- *Organization of News Ombudsmen and Standards Editors (ONO, #17879)*;
- *Public Media Alliance (PMA, #18568)*;
- *Reporters sans frontières (RSF, #18846)*;
- *South East European Network for Professionalisation of the Media (SEENPM, #19817)*;
- *South East Europe Media Organisation (SEEMO, #19823)*;
- *Thomson Foundation*;
- *World Association of Newspapers and News Publishers (WAN-IFRA, #21166)*. [2023.02.28/AA1487/y/**F**]

- ♦ Ethical Trading Initiative (internationally oriented national body)
- ♦ Ethic étapes (internationally oriented national body)
- ♦ ETHIC / see European Masterbatchers and Compounders (#07749)
- ♦ **ethics** International Society of Healthcare Ethics and Compliance Professionals (#15155)
- ♦ De l'éthique sur l'étiquette / see Clean Clothes Campaign (#03986)
- ♦ Ethnos360 (internationally oriented national body)

♦ Ethnos Asia Ministries 05555

Office GPO Box 2821, Bangkok, 10501, Thailand. T. +6622585808. Fax +6626612917. E-mail: info@ethnos-asia.org.
URL: http://ethnosasia.org/

Aims Strengthen and serve the Body of Christ in access-restricted nations in Asia. **NGO Relations** Founding member of: *Asian Solidarity Economy Coalition (ASEC, #01754)*. [2018.02.12/XJ5926/**D**]

- ♦ **ETHRA** European Tobacco Harm Reduction Advocates (#08918)

♦ Ethylene Oxide and Derivates Producers Association (EO and Glycols) 05556

Manager c/o CEFIC, Rue Belliard 40, 1040 Brussels, Belgium. T. +3224369487.
URL: https://www.petrochemistry.eu/sector-group/ethylene-oxide/

History as a sector group of *Conseil européen de l'industrie chimique (CEFIC, #04687)*. **Structure** Business Group; Working Groups (2): Distribution; Production. Toxicology Task Force. [2021/XE2169/**E**]

- ♦ eTIC-CEC / see European Federation for Managers in Technologies of Information and Communication (#07163)
- ♦ **eTIC-CEC** European Federation for Managers in Technologies of Information and Communication (#07163)
- ♦ ETIC – Extreme Traveler International Congress (meeting series)
- ♦ **ETICS** European Testing Inspection Certification System (#08901)
- ♦ ETI – Ethical Trading Initiative (internationally oriented national body)
- ♦ **ETI** Euro-Toques International (#09190)
- ♦ ETIG Group / see International Travel Insurance Alliance e.V. (#15728)
- ♦ Etihad Konfidiraliat al'Ifriqyah Lielriadha (#02360)

♦ ETIM International 05557

Registered Address Aekerlaethofstraat 29, 6269 DG Margraten, Netherlands. E-mail: info@etim-international.com.
URL: http://www.etim-international.com/

History Set up as a joined force to promote one *European Technical Information Model (ETIM)*. Registration: KVK, No/ID: 86818775, Netherlands. **Aims** Secure the *intellectual property* of the ETIM product classification; secure integrity and basic *uniformity* throughout Europe; establish one standard for the electro technical-, mechanical- and sanitary industry; coordinate cooperation with other *standardization* organizations; start initiatives of concern to the European Commission.
Members Full in 24 countries:
Australia, Austria, Belgium, Canada, Denmark, Estonia, Finland, France, Germany, Hungary, Italy, Lithuania, Mexico, Netherlands, New Zealand, Norway, Poland, Portugal, Slovenia, Spain, Sweden, Switzerland, UK, USA. [2023.02.13/XJ8931/**E**]

- ♦ ET – International Conference on Endothelin (meeting series)
- ♦ **ETIP Bioenergy** European Technology and Innovation Platform Bioenergy (#08881)
- ♦ **ETIP-DG** European Technology & Innovation Platform on Deep Geothermal (#08882)
- ♦ **ETIP PV** European Technology and Innovation Platform for Photovoltaics (#08883)
- ♦ **ETIP PV** European Technology and Innovation Platform Photovoltaics (#08884)

♦ ETIP Smart Networks for Energy Transition (ETIP SNET) 05558

Contact c/o Zabala Innovation Consulting, Rue Belliard 20, 1040 Brussels, Belgium. T. +3225138122. E-mail: info@etip-snet.eu.
URL: http://www.etip-snet.eu/

History Set up as *European Technology and Innovation Platform* by *European Commission (EC, #06633)*. **Aims** Guide research, development and innovation to support Europe's energy transition. **Structure** Governing Board; Executive Committee; Secretariat. Working Groups; National Stakeholder Coordination Group. **Activities** Events/meetings. **Events** *High Level Use Cases Seminar* Brussels (Belgium) 2022, *Workshop* Brussels (Belgium) 2021, *Workshop* Brussels (Belgium) 2021, *Workshop* Brussels (Belgium) 2021, *Western Region Workshop* Madrid (Spain) 2018. **Publications** *ETIP SNET Newsletter* (4 a year). [2019/XM7697/**F**]

- ♦ **ETIP SNET** ETIP Smart Networks for Energy Transition (#05558)
- ♦ **ETIPWind** European Technology and Innovation Platform on Wind Energy (#08885)
- ♦ **ETIRA** European Toner and Inkjet Remanufacturers Association (#08920)
- ♦ ETIS / see ETIS – Global IT Association for Telecommunications (#05559)

♦ ETIS – Global IT Association for Telecommunications 05559

Managing Dir ETIS Secretariat, Av Louise 65/11, 1050 Brussels, Belgium. T. +3222230771. Fax +3222192628. E-mail: wdm@etis.org – mh@etis.org.
URL: http://www.etis.org/

History Founded as *Information Systems for Telecommunications '92 (ISTEL92)* following meeting, Nov 1988, Reading (UK). Became *European Telecommunications Informatics Services (ETIS)* in late 1990s. Registration: Start date: 12 Jun 1991, Netherlands, The Hague; Banque-Carrefour des Entreprises, No/ID: 0536.130.183, Start date: 1 Jan 2008, Belgium. **Aims** Enable telecommunications *service providers* to improve their business performance by effective use of *information technology*. **Structure** Management Board; Council; Central Office; Working Groups. **Languages** English. **Staff** 4 FTE; over 500 experts part-time. **Finance** Members' dues. **Activities** Knowledge management/information dissemination; events/meetings. **Events** *Community Gathering* Brussels (Belgium) 2021, *Community Gathering* Brussels (Belgium) 2020, *Community Gathering* Vienna (Austria) 2019, *Community Gathering* Lisbon (Portugal) 2018, *Community Gathering* Copenhagen (Denmark) 2015. **Publications** Surveys.
Members Full in 29 countries:
Austria, Belgium, Bulgaria, Croatia, Cyprus, Czechia, Denmark, Estonia, Germany, Greece, Hungary, Ireland, Italy, Latvia, Lithuania, Montenegro, Netherlands, North Macedonia, Norway, Poland, Portugal, Romania, Russia, Slovakia, Spain, Sweden, Switzerland, Türkiye, UK.
NGO Relations Cooperates with: *European Telecommunications Network Operators' Association (ETNO, #08895)*; *TeleManagement Forum (TM Forum, #20123)*. [2021/XD5836/**D**]

- ♦ ETKON – Internationale Etikettenkonferenz (meeting series)
- ♦ ETLA – European Trade Law Association (no recent information)
- ♦ **ETLC** European Trade Union Liaison Committee on Tourism (#08929)
- ♦ ETL – Institute for European Tort Law (internationally oriented national body)
- ♦ ETMA – European Television Magazines Association (no recent information)
- ♦ **etma** european tube manufacturers association (#08953)
- ♦ ETMC – European Transport Maintenance Council (inactive)
- ♦ ETM / see eu can aid (#05570)
- ♦ **ETNA** European Transcultural Nurses' Association (#08936)
- ♦ **ETN** Europäisches Textil-Netzwerk (#08903)
- ♦ **ETN** European Textile Network (#08903)
- ♦ **ETN** European Turbine Network (#08957)
- ♦ **ETNO** European Telecommunications Network Operators' Association (#08895)
- ♦ **ETOA** European Tour Operators Association (#08922)

♦ ETO Consortium (ETOs) 05560

Secretariat c/o FIAN International, Willy-Brandt-Platz 5, 69115 Heidelberg, Germany. T. +4962216530030. Fax +4962216530033.
Twitter: https://twitter.com/etobligations

History 2007. ETOs stands for *extraterritorial obligations*. Subtitle: *ETOs for human rights beyond borders*. **Aims** Address the gaps in *human rights* protection that have opened up through the neglect of *extraterritorial obligations* (ETOs). **Structure** Steering Group, consisting of representatives of global CSOs and regional representatives (Latin America and Caribbean; Sub-Saharan Africa; Asia, Australia, Oceania; Europe and North America). **Events** *Conference* Lancaster (UK) 2009. **Publications** Newsletter (3 a year).

Members Human rights related Civil Society Organizations and academics (about 80). Organizations include 33 listed in this Yearbook:
- *Amnesty International (AI, #00801);*
- *Arab NGO Network for Development (ANND, #01016);*
- *Avocats Sans Frontières (ASF, #03050);*
- *Brot für die Welt;*
- *Center for International Environmental Law (CIEL);*
- *Center for Women's Global Leadership (CWGL);*
- *Centre for Human Rights, Pretoria;*
- *European Center for Constitutional and Human Rights (ECCHR);*
- *FIAN International (#09743);*
- *Focus on the Global South (Focus, #09807);*
- *Folkekirkens Nødhjaelp (FKN);*
- *Foundation for a Free Information Infrastructure (FFII, #09956);*
- *Global Initiative for Economic, Social and Cultural Rights (GI-ESCR);*
- *Greenpeace International (#10727);*
- *Habitat International Coalition (HIC, #10845);*
- *Human Rights Watch (HRW, #10990);*
- *Inclusive Development International (IDI);*
- *Institute for Agriculture and Trade Policy (IATP);*
- *Institute of Tropical Medicine Antwerp (IMT);*
- *International Baby Food Action Network (IBFAN, #12305);*
- *International Commission of Jurists (ICJ, #12695);*
- *International Federation for Human Rights (#13452);*
- *International Network for Economic, Social and Cultural Rights (ESCR-Net, #14255);*
- *International Peace Information Service (IPIS);*
- *Oxfam GB;*
- *People's Health Movement (PHM, #18305);*
- *Plataforma Interamericana de Derechos Humanos, Democracia y Desarrollo (PIDHDD, #18395);*
- *Public Eye;*
- *Quaker United Nations Office (QUNO, #18588);*
- *Robert F Kennedy Human Rights;*
- *Share the World's Resources (STWR);*
- *Transnational Institute (TNI, #20219);*
- *World Organisation Against Torture (OMCT, #21685).*

[2022/XJ9387/y/**B**]

- ♦ **ETOP** European Thoracic Oncology Platform (#08910)
- ♦ **ETOs** ETO Consortium (#05560)
- ♦ ETOs for human rights beyond borders / see ETO Consortium (#05560)
- ♦ ETOUR – Turismforskningsinstitutet (internationally oriented national body)
- ♦ **ETP4HPC** European Technology Platform for High Performance Computing (#08889)
- ♦ **ETPA** European Transpersonal Psychology Association (#08938)
- ♦ **ETP** Eiropas Tautas Partijas – Kristigie Demokrati (#10775)
- ♦ **ETP** European Travel Press (#08944)
- ♦ **ETPFG** European Two-Phase Flow Group (#08960)
- ♦ **ETPG** European Test Publishers Group (#08902)
- ♦ ETPOA / see Trade Promotion Europe (#20184)
- ♦ ETPO – European Trade Promotion Organization (no recent information)
- ♦ ETPPA – European Third Party Providers Association (unconfirmed)
- ♦ **ETP SMR** European Technology Platform for Sustainable Mineral Resources (#08894)
- ♦ ETRA – European Textile Rental Association (inactive)
- ♦ **ETRA** European Transport Research Alliance (#08939)
- ♦ ETRA – European Twowheel Retailers Association (inactive)
- ♦ **ETRA** European Tyre Recycling Association (#08961)
- ♦ ETRC / see European Travel Retail Confederation (#08945)
- ♦ **ETRC** European Travel Retail Confederation (#08945)
- ♦ **ETRIA** European TRIZ Association (#08949)
- ♦ **ETRMA** European Tyre and Rubber Manufacturers' Association (#08963)
- ♦ **ETRO** European Thrombosis Research Organization (#08912)
- ♦ **ETRS** European Tissue Repair Society (#08916)
- ♦ **ETRTO** European Tyre and Rim Technical Organisation (#08962)
- ♦ ETSA – European Telecommunication Services Association (inactive)
- ♦ **ETSA** European Textile Services Association (#08904)
- ♦ **ETSA** European Thermal Spray Association (#08908)
- ♦ **ETSA** European Training and Simulation Association (#08935)
- ♦ **ETS** Association of European Team Sports (#02546)
- ♦ ETSC – European Telemetry Standardisation Committee (internationally oriented national body)
- ♦ **ETSC** European Transport Safety Council (#08940)
- ♦ **ETSC** European Tuberous Sclerosis Complex Association (#08955)
- ♦ **ETS** European Teratology Society (#08900)
- ♦ **ETS** European Thermoelectric Society (#08909)
- ♦ **ETS** European Tissue Symposium (#08917)
- ♦ ETS – European Trauma Society (inactive)
- ♦ **ETS** European Turfgrass Society (#08959)
- ♦ **ETSF** European Theoretical Spectroscopy Facility (#08907)
- ♦ **ETSGA** European Traditional Sports and Games Association (#08931)
- ♦ **ETSG** European Trade Study Group (#08925)
- ♦ ETSHER – Ecole inter-Etats des techniciens supérieurs de l'hydraulique et de l'équipement rural (inactive)
- ♦ **ETSI** European Telecommunications Standards Institute (#08897)
- ♦ ETSO / see European Network of Transmission System Operators for Electricity (#08026)
- ♦ **ETSON** European Technical Safety Organisations Network (#08880)
- ♦ ETTFA / see International Tourism Trade Fairs Association (#15697)
- ♦ **ETTF** European Timber Trade Federation (#08915)
- ♦ Ett Internationellt Nätverk för det goda livet / see Cittaslow (#03958)
- ♦ Ettore Majorana Centre for Scientific Culture (internationally oriented national body)
- ♦ Ettore Majorana International Centre for Scientific Culture / see Ettore Majorana Centre for Scientific Culture
- ♦ ETTSA / see eu travel tech (#09205)
- ♦ ETTUC – European Teachers Trade Union Committee (inactive)
- ♦ **ETTU** European Table Tennis Union (#08873)
- ♦ **ETTW** Europeans throughout the World (#08839)
- ♦ **ETUCE** European Trade Union Committee for Education (#08926)
- ♦ **ETUC** European Trade Union Confederation (#08927)

♦ Etudes Sans Frontières International (ESFI) 05561

Studies Without Borders International
Pres address not obtained.
URL: http://www.esf-international.org/esfi/

Aims Support motivated *young people* from war and crisis regions with their studies in order to enable them to implement their own *development* projects. **Structure** Support Groups (3): Organizational Development; Fundraising and Public Relations; Programme.
Members Chapters in 5 countries:
Canada, France, Germany, Italy, Spain.

[2017/XJ5108/**F**]

- ♦ Etudiants démocrates européens (#06901)
- ♦ **ETU** European Taekwondo Union (#08874)
- ♦ **ETU** European Triathlon Union (#08948)
- ♦ ETUF-TCL – European Trade Union Federation for Textiles, Clothing and Leather (inactive)
- ♦ **ETUI** European Trade Union Institute (#08928)
- ♦ ETUI-REHS / see European Trade Union Institute (#08928)
- ♦ **ETV** Europäischer Tabakwaren-Grosshandelsverband (#08919)
- ♦ ETW / see eu can aid (#05570)
- ♦ ETWTC / see European Tyre and Rim Technical Organisation (#08962)

♦ EU40 05562

Managing Dir Rue d'Arlon 40, 1000 Brussels, Belgium. T. +3227214489 – +3227256369. E-mail: eu40team@eu40.eu.
URL: http://www.eu40.eu/

History Set up as the platform of young members of *European Parliament (EP, #08146)* and of the EU national parliaments. Registration: Banque-Carrefour des Entreprises, No/ID: 0808.009.505, Start date: 19 Nov 2008, Belgium; EU Transparency Register, No/ID: 139277512966-23, Start date: 21 Feb 2014. **Aims** Serve *young* members under the age of 40; strengthen their role inside the *European Parliament*. **Structure** Board. **Activities** Events/meetings; training/education. **Members** Members of the European Parliament, countries not specified. **NGO Relations** Partner of (1): *European Health Parliament (EHP, #07459)*.

[2020/XM7358/v/**E**]

- ♦ **EUAA** European Ayurveda Association (#06306)
- ♦ **EUAA** European Union Agency for Asylum (#08968)
- ♦ **EU-ABC** EU-ASEAN Business Council (#05566)
- ♦ **EUABC** Unión Europea de Asociaciones de Entrenadores de Baloncesto (#20383)
- ♦ **EUACA** European Airport Coordinators Association (#05852)
- ♦ **EuACA** European Artists' Association (#05917)
- ♦ **EUA-CDE** EUA Council for Doctoral Education (#05563)
- ♦ **EUAC** European Union of Aquarium Curators (#08975)

♦ EUA Council for Doctoral Education (EUA-CDE) 05563

Head Rue du Rhône 114, Case Postale 3174, 1211 Geneva 3, Switzerland. T. +41225520296. E-mail: info@eua-cde.org.
Office Manager address not obtained.
URL: https://eua-cde.org/

History 2008. Founded at the initiative of and integral part of *European University Association (EUA, #09027)*. **Aims** Contribute to the development of doctoral education and research training in Europe. **Structure** Steering Committee; Secretariat. **Activities** Events/meetings; knowledge management/information dissemination. **Members** Universities and institutions (270) in 38 countries. Membership countries not specified. **NGO Relations** Signatory to agreement of *Coalition for Advancing Research Assessment (CoARA, #04045)*.

[2023/AA3082/**E**]

- ♦ **EuADS** European Association for Data Science (#06005)
- ♦ **EUA** Euroasian Universities Association (#05641)
- ♦ EUA – European Union of Alysh (unconfirmed)
- ♦ **EUA** European University Association (#09027)

♦ EU Agencies Network (EUAN) 05564

Contact address not obtained. E-mail: coordination@euan.europa.eu.
URL: https://euagencies.eu/

History 2012. Founded as an informal network. **Aims** Enhance the value of individual EU Agencies and Joint Undertakings by deepening their collaboration, so as to provide EU citizens, businesses and institutions the right foundation to achieve their priorities.
Members EU Agencies (48):
- *Agency for the Cooperation of Energy Regulators (ACER, #00552);*
- *Bio-based Industries Joint Undertaking (BBI JU, #03239);*
- *Body of European Regulators for Electronic Communications (BEREC, #03299);*
- *Centre de traduction des organes de l'Union européenne (CdT, #03790);*
- *Clean Sky Joint Undertaking (Clean Sky JU, #03990);*
- *Community Plant Variety Office (CPVO, #04404);*
- *ECSEL Joint Undertaking (ECSEL JU, inactive);*
- *Eurojust (#05698);*
- *European Agency for Safety and Health at Work (EU-OSHA, #05843);*
- *European Banking Authority (EBA, #06311);*
- *European Centre for Disease Prevention and Control (ECDC, #06476);*
- *European Centre for the Development of Vocational Training (Cedefop, #06474);*
- *European Chemicals Agency (ECHA, #06523);*
- *European Defence Agency (EDA, #06895);*
- *European Environment Agency (EEA, #06995);*
- *European Fisheries Control Agency (EFCA, #07266);*
- *European Food Safety Authority (EFSA, #07287);*
- *European Foundation for the Improvement of Living and Working Conditions (Eurofound, #07348);*
- *European High Performance Computing Joint Undertaking (EuroHPC JU, #07485);*
- *European Institute for Gender Equality (EIGE, #07557);*
- *European Institute of Innovation and Technology (EIT, #07562);*
- *European Insurance and Occupational Pensions Authority (EIOPA, #07578);*
- *European Joint Undertaking for ITER and the Development of Fusion Energy (Fusion for Energy, #07611);*
- *European Labour Authority (ELA, #07635);*
- *European Maritime Safety Agency (EMSA, #07744);*
- *European Medicines Agency (EMA, #07767);*
- *European Monitoring Centre for Drugs and Drug Addiction (EMCDDA, #07820);*
- *European Police Office (Europol, #08239);*
- *European Public Prosecutor's Office (EPPO, #08300);*
- *European Securities and Markets Authority (ESMA, #08457);*
- *European Training Foundation (ETF, #08934);*
- *European Union Agency for Asylum (EUAA, #08968);*
- *European Union Agency for Fundamental Rights (FRA, #08969);*
- *European Union Agency for Law Enforcement Training (CEPOL, #08970);*
- *European Union Agency for Network and Information Security (ENISA, #08971);*
- *European Union Agency for Railways (#08973);*
- *European Union Agency for the Operational Management of Large-Scale IT Systems in the Area of Freedom, Security and Justice (eu-LISA, #08972);*

- *European Union Agency for the Space Programme (EUSPA, #08974);*
- *European Union Aviation Safety Agency (EASA, #08978);*
- *European Union Institute for Security Studies (EUISS, #08994);*
- *European Union Intellectual Property Office (EUIPO, #08996);*
- *European Union Satellite Centre (SatCen, #09015);*
- *Frontex, the European Border and Coast Guard Agency (#10005);*
- *Fuel Cells and Hydrogen Joint Undertaking (FCH JU, #10013);*
- *Innovative Medicines Initiative (IMI, #11221);*
- *SESAR Joint Undertaking (SJU, #19249);*
- *Shift2Rail Joint Undertaking (Shift2Rail JU, #19261);*
- *Single Resolution Board (SRB, #19287).* [2021/AA1421/y/**E**]

♦ EU Alliance for a democratic, social and sustainable European Semester (EU Semester Alliance) 05565

Contact c/o EAPN, Square de Meeûs 18, 1050 Brussels, Belgium. E-mail: team@eapn.eu.
URL: http://www.semesteralliance.net/

Aims Support progress towards a more democratic, social and sustainable Europe 2020 Strategy, through strengthening civil dialogue engagement in the European Semester at national and EU levels. **Structure** Coordinated by *European Anti-Poverty Network (EAPN, #05908).* **Activities** Advocacy/lobbying/activism; capacity building.
Members Organizations (15):
AGE Platform Europe (#00557); Caritas Europa (#03579); European Anti-Poverty Network (EAPN, #05908); European Association of Service Providers for Persons with Disabilities (EASPD, #06204); European Disability Forum (EDF, #06929); European Environmental Bureau (EEB, #06996); European Federation for Diaconia (Eurodiaconia, #07099); European Federation of National Organisations Working with the Homeless (#07174); European Public Health Alliance (EPHA, #08297); European Women's Lobby (EWL, #09102); Housing Europe – The European Federation for Public Cooperative and Social Housing (Housing Europe, #10956); International Council of Hides, Skins and Leather Traders Associations (ICHSLTA, #13029); Platform for International Cooperation on Undocumented Migrants (PICUM, #18401).
National Alliances (3) in 3 countries:
Bulgaria, Denmark, Ireland. [2016/XM5293/y/**E**]

- ♦ **EUAN** EU Agencies Network (#05564)
- ♦ **EuARe** European Academy of Religion (#05812)
- ♦ EuAsC2S – Eurasia Conference on Chemical Sciences (meeting series)

♦ EU-ASEAN Business Council (EU-ABC) 05566

Exec Dir Suite 29, Level 30, Six Battery Road, Singapore 049909, Singapore. E-mail: info@eu-asean.eu.
URL: http://www.eu-asean.eu/

History 5 May 2011, Jakarta (Indonesia). Founded at 1st ASEAN-EU Business Summit, by European Chambers of Commerce and Business Associations in 6 ASEAN countries. Memorandum of Understanding between chamber Presidents signed 4 May 2011, Jakarta (Indonesia). Registration: Singapore; EU Transparency Register, No/ID: 614220318268-60. **Aims** Promote changes in policies, rules and regulations so that European businesses can more easily invest and develop their businesses in the region to the benefit of the local economies and populations as well as their own shareholders. **Structure** General Assembly; Executive Board; Supervisory Board. **Languages** English. **Activities** Advocacy/lobbying/activism; capacity building; events/meetings; healthcare; politics/policy/regulatory; projects/programmes; publishing activities; research/documentation. Active in: Brunei Darussalam, Cambodia, Indonesia, Laos, Malaysia, Myanmar, Philippines, Singapore, Thailand, Vietnam. **Events** *ASEAN-EU Business Summit* Singapore (Singapore) 2021, *ASEAN-EU Health Summit* Singapore (Singapore) 2021, *ASEAN-EU Business Summit* Singapore (Singapore) 2020, *Seminar on ASEAN's Fight against COVID-19* Singapore (Singapore) 2020, *ASEAN-EU Business Summit* Bangkok (Thailand) 2019. **Members** Businesses. Membership countries not specified. **Consultative Status** Consultative status granted from: *ASEAN (#01141).* [2021.09.08/XJ6834/**E**]

- ♦ **EU ASE** European Alliance to Save Energy (#05882)
- ♦ **EUAS** European Association of Jewish Survivors of the Holocaust (#06099)

♦ EU-ASIA Centre (EAC) 05567

Contact Square Gutenberg 34, 1000 Brussels, Belgium. T. +3222307863. E-mail: info@eu-asiacentre.eu.
URL: http://www.eu-asiacentre.eu/

History 2011. EU Transparency Register: 707568010386-43. **Aims** Promote closer relations between the EU and Asia. **Structure** Advisory Board. **Languages** English. **Staff** 2.00 FTE, paid. **Finance** Grants from various bodies. **Activities** Events/meetings. **Publications** Reports; articles; papers. **IGO Relations** *Economic Research Institute for ASEAN and East Asia (ERIA, #05319).* **NGO Relations** Partners include: *Asia-Europe Foundation University Alumni Network (ASEFUAN, #01271); GIGA – German Institute of Global and Area Studies; ISEAS – Yusof Ishak Institute (ISEAS); Korea Institute for International Economic Policy (KIEP); UNU Institute on Comparative Regional Integration Studies (UNU-CRIS, #20717); Young Professionals in Foreign Policy (YPFP, #21997);* national institutions. [2019.06.05/XM5303/**E**]

- ♦ EU-Asia Financial Services Roundtable (unconfirmed)
- ♦ EU Association – European Union Association (internationally oriented national body)
- ♦ **EUATC** European Union of Associations of Translation Companies (#08977)
- ♦ **EU Athletes** European Elite Athletes Association (#06977)
- ♦ **EuAWE** European Association of Wine Economists (#06275)
- ♦ EUB / see Public Eye
- ♦ **eu.bac** European Building Automation and Controls Association (#06409)
- ♦ **EUBA** European Bentonite Producers Association (#06328)
- ♦ **EUBA** European Bioeconomy Alliance (#06334)
- ♦ EUBCE – European Biomass Conference and Exhibition (meeting series)
- ♦ **EUBC** European Boxing Confederation (#06387)
- ♦ **EUBF** European Bailiffs' Foundation (#06307)
- ♦ EUBGF / see World Backgammon Federation (#21213)
- ♦ **EUBIA** European Biomass Industry Association (#06339)

♦ Eubios Ethics Institute 05568

Dir American Univ of Sovereign Nations, Los Angeles CA 91356, USA. T. +19494399307. E-mail: asianbioethics@yahoo.co.nz – office@eubios.info.
URL: http://www.eubios.info/

History 1990, Christchurch (New Zealand). Established in Christchurch (New Zealand) and Tsukuba (Japan) simultaneously. Added a location in Bangkok (Thailand), 2005, and Los Angeles CA (USA), 2013. **Aims** Stimulate discussion of ethical issues. **Languages** English. **Staff** 10.00 FTE, voluntary. **Finance** Sources: donations. Annual budget: 20,000 USD. **Activities** Events/meetings; knowledge management/information dissemination; publishing activities; training/education. Active in: Cambodia, India, Indonesia, Japan, New Zealand, Thailand, USA. **Events** *LBD – Youth Looking Beyond Disaster Forum* Kathmandu (Nepal) 2015, *LBD – Youth Looking Beyond Disaster Forum* Scottsdale, AZ (USA) 2015, *LBD – Youth Looking Beyond Disaster Forum* Manila (Philippines) 2014, *LBD – Youth Looking Beyond Disaster Forum* Yogyakarta (Indonesia) 2014, *LBD – Youth Looking Beyond Disaster Forum* Kobe (Japan) 2013. **Publications** *Eubios Journal of Asian and International Bioethics* (6 a year). [2021.06.07/XM2698/j/**E**]

- ♦ EUBL – Europa Unuigo de Blindaj Laboruloj (inactive)

♦ EUBrasil Association 05569

Contact Residence Palace, Rue de la Loi 155, Mail Box 51, 1040 Brussels, Belgium. E-mail: eubrasil@eubrasil.eu – presidencia@eubrasil.eu.
URL: http://www.eubrasil.eu/

History 2004. Officially founded 10 Feb 2008, Brussels (Belgium). **Aims** Support development of successful *business* relations between the *European Union* and Brazil; promote political and cultural links. **Structure** Board of Directors; Advisory Board. **Languages** English, Portuguese. **Staff** 6.00 FTE, paid. **Finance** Private sector support. **Activities** Standards/guidelines; networking/liaising; research/documentation; events/meetings; knowledge management/information dissemination.
Members Individuals from the European Parliament and National Congress of Brazil; Companies. Individuals in 14 countries:
Austria, Belgium, Brazil, Czechia, France, Germany, Italy, Luxembourg, Netherlands, Portugal, Romania, Spain, Sweden, UK.
IGO Relations *European Parliament (EP, #08146).* **NGO Relations** *European Telecommunications Network Operators' Association (ETNO, #08895); Konrad Adenauer Foundation (KAF);* national organizations. [2015.07.15/XJ9802/**E**]

- ♦ **EUBREN** European Biomass Research Network (#06340)
- ♦ **EUBS** European Underwater and Baromedical Society (#08965)
- ♦ EUBW – European Union for Blind Workers (inactive)
- ♦ EUCAEA / see European Network of Engineering for Agriculture and Environment (#07901)
- ♦ **EUCA** European Union Control Association (#08982)
- ♦ **EucA** European University College Association (#09028)
- ♦ EUCA – Fédération européenne des associations de torréfacteurs du café (inactive)
- ♦ **EUCAM** European Centre for Monitoring Alcohol Marketing (#06492)
- ♦ **EUCAM** Europe-Central Asia Monitoring (#09151)

♦ eu can aid (ECA) 05570

Contact Council of the EU – Bureau JL 02 CG 39, Rue de la Loi 175, 1048 Brussels, Belgium. T. +3222818377. Fax +3222818378. E-mail: info@eucanaid.eu.
Vice-Pres address not obtained.
URL: http://www.eucanaid.eu/

History 25 Mar 1968, Brussels (Belgium). Former names and other names: *Europe – Third World Association (ETW)* – former; *Association Europe – Tiers-monde (ETM)* – former; *Asociación Europa – Tercer Mundo* – former; *Vereinigung Europa – Dritte Welt* – former; *Associação Europa – Terceiro Mundo* – former; *Associazione Europa – Terzo Mondo* – former; *Vereniging Europa – Derde Wereld* – former; *Foreningen Europa – Tredje Verden* – former; *Europa – Tredje Världenföreningen* – former. Registration: Banque-Carrefour des Entreprises, No/ID: 0408.299.229, Start date: 25 Mar 1968, Belgium. **Aims** Provide assistance to communities in need in the developing Countries by funding micro-projects or, more rarely, by providing emergency aid; heighten awareness of developing Countries issues among European Union staff. **Structure** General Assembly (annual); Committee; Project Group; Awareness Raising Group. **Languages** English, French. **Staff** Voluntary. **Finance** Sources: fundraising; members' dues. Annual budget: 200,000 EUR (2020). **Activities** Awareness raising; capacity building; financial and/or material support; projects/programmes; training/education. **Publications** *Periodical Information Sheet* (2 a year). **Members** Staff (about 550) of EU institutions in Brussels (European Commission, European Council, European Parliament). Individuals, mainly in Belgium. Other membership countries not specified. **NGO Relations** Member of: *Federation of European and International Associations Established in Belgium (FAIB, #09508).* [2021.09.01/XD0539/**F**]

- ♦ **EuCAN** European Concept for Accessibility Network (#06695)
- ♦ EUCAPA – European Capsules Association (no recent information)
- ♦ **EuCAPT** European Centre for AstroParticle Theory (#06470)
- ♦ **EUCAR** European Council of Automotive Research and Development (#06806)

♦ EUCARPIA 05571

SG Plantum NL, Vossenburchkade 68, 2805 PC Gouda, Netherlands. E-mail: eucarpia@ipk-gatersleben.de.
URL: https://www.eucarpia.eu/

History 2 Jul 1956, Wageningen (Netherlands). Statutes modified: 7 Jul 1959, Cologne (Germany FR); 23 May 1962, Paris (France); 26 Jun 1974, Budapest (Hungary); 24 Jun 1983, Wageningen; 2 Aug 1995, Jyväskylä (Finland); 30 Aug 2016, Zurich (Switzerland). Former names and other names: *European Association for Research on Plant Breeding* – former; *Association européenne pour l'amélioration des plantes* – former; *Europäische Gesellschaft für Züchtungsforschung* – former. **Aims** Contribute to development in the field of *plant* breeding by promoting scientific and technical cooperation, excluding any activity connected with a commercial interest. **Structure** General Assembly; Board; Executive Committee; Sections (12), headed by Chairpersons; Subsections; Working Groups. **Languages** English, French, German. **Staff** 3.00 FTE, voluntary. **Finance** Sources: gifts, legacies; members' dues; subsidies. Other sources: testamentary dispositions; all other acquisitions and revenues. **Activities** Knowledge management/information dissemination. **Events** *General Congress* Leipzig (Germany) 2024, *Fodder Crops and Amenity Grasses* Brno (Czechia) 2023, *Symposium on Fruit Breeding and Genetics* Dresden (Germany) 2023, *Ornamentals Symposium* Genoa (Italy) 2023, *Cereal Breeding – Challenges and Opportunities for Global Improvement* Szeged (Hungary) 2023. **Publications** *EUCARPIA Bulletin* (annual). Congress proceedings; proceedings of Section meetings.
Members Individuals in 56 countries:
Albania, Argentina, Australia, Austria, Belarus, Belgium, Bosnia-Herzegovina, Brazil, Bulgaria, Canada, China, Côte d'Ivoire, Croatia, Czechia, Denmark, Estonia, Finland, France, Germany, Greece, Hungary, Iceland, Iran Islamic Rep, Ireland, Israel, Italy, Japan, Kazakhstan, Latvia, Lithuania, Mali, Mexico, Moldova, Netherlands, New Zealand, Norway, Peru, Poland, Portugal, Romania, Russia, Serbia, Slovakia, Slovenia, South Africa, Spain, Sweden, Switzerland, Syrian AR, Thailand, Togo, Tunisia, Türkiye, UK, Ukraine, USA.
Consultative Status Consultative status granted from: *ECOSOC (#05331)* (Ros C); *FAO (#09260)* (Liaison Status). **IGO Relations** Instrumental in setting up (1): *European Cooperative Programme for Plant Genetic Resources (ECPGR, #06787).* [2022.10.20/XD0556/v/**D**]

- ♦ **EuCAS** European and Central Asian Safety Network (#06465)
- ♦ **EUCASS** European Conference for Aero-Space Sciences (#06728)
- ♦ **EUCAST** European Committee on Antimicrobial Susceptibility Testing (#06642)
- ♦ EUCATEL – European Conference of Associations of Telecommunications Industries (inactive)
- ♦ **EUCDA** Europäische Union Christlich Demokratischer Arbeitnehmer (#08981)
- ♦ EUCD – European Union of Christian Democrats (inactive)
- ♦ **EuCDN** European Community Development Network (#06679)
- ♦ EUCDW / see EPP Women (#05516)
- ♦ **EUCDW** European Union of Christian Democratic Workers (#08981)
- ♦ **EUCDW** Europese Unie van Christen Demokratische Werknemers (#08981)
- ♦ **EUCEB** European Certification Board for Mineral Wool Products (#06510)
- ♦ EUCED – European Network for Economic Cooperation and Development (internationally oriented national body)
- ♦ EUCE/ESC / see European Studies Center, Pittsburgh PA
- ♦ **EUCEET Association** European Civil Engineering Education and Training (#06565)
- ♦ **EUCE** Network of European Union Centres of Excellence (#17031)
- ♦ **EUCEN** European University Continuing Education Network (#09030)
- ♦ **EUCEPA** Comité européen de liaison pour la cellulose et le papier (#07688)
- ♦ **EUCEPA** European Liaison Committee for Pulp and Paper (#07688)
- ♦ **EUCETSA** European Committee of Environmental Technology Suppliers Associations (#06648)
- ♦ **EuCF** European Coaching Federation (#06587)
- ♦ **EUCG** European Union Cyclists' Group (#08984)
- ♦ EuCham – European Chamber (unconfirmed)
- ♦ Eucharistic Youth Movement (religious order)
- ♦ Euchem / see European Chemical Society (#06524)
- ♦ EUCHEMAP / see European Committee for Process Equipment and Plant Manufacturers (#06662)
- ♦ **EUCHEMAP** European Committee for Process Equipment and Plant Manufacturers (#06662)
- ♦ **EuCheMS** European Chemical Society (#06524)
- ♦ **EUCHIS** European Chitin Society (#06539)
- ♦ **EuCIA** European Composites Industry Association (#06692)
- ♦ EUCID – European Union of Clinicians in Implant Dentistry (inactive)
- ♦ **EuCIE** European Confederation of Inclusive Enterprises (#06704)
- ♦ EUCIS-LLL / see Lifelong Learning Platform – European Civil Society for Education (#16466)

♦ EU Civil Society Contact Group (CSCG) 05572
Coordinator c/o Social Platform, Square de Meeûs 18, 1050 Brussels, Belgium. T. +3225111711. Fax +3225111909.
URL: http://www.act4europe.org/
History 14 Feb 2002. **Aims** Encourage and promote a transparent and structured civil dialogue that is accessible, properly facilitated, inclusive, fair and respectful of the autonomy of NGOs; promote lasting access to information, access to justice in matters of concern to civil society, consultation and integration of all levels of civil society in the European project. **Languages** English. **Staff** 0.50 FTE, paid. **Activities** Represents the views and interests of rights and value based civil society organizations across the European Union on major issues affecting CSCG's sectors of activity. *'Act4Europe Campaign'* encouraged more active participation of national NGOs in the Future of Europe debate and in the development and realization of the participatory citizenship concept. Commissioned study: Civil Dialogue – Making It Work Better.
Members Rights and value based NGO sectors covering: environment; social; development; human rights; lifelong learning; public health; culture; women. International organizations (8), listed in this Yearbook: *Confédération européenne des ong d'urgence et de développement (CONCORD, #04547)*; *Culture Action Europe (CAE, #04981)*; *European Public Health Alliance (EPHA, #08297)*; *European Women's Lobby (EWL, #09102)*; *Human Rights and Democracy Network (HRDN, #10980)*; *Lifelong Learning Platform – European Civil Society for Education (LLLP, #16466)*; *The Green 10 (#10711)*. [2010/XM1640/y/**F**]

♦ EU CLG / see CLG Europe
♦ EUCLID / see BOBCATSSS Association (#03296)

♦ Euclid Consortium (EC) 05573
Dir c/o IAP, 98 B Bv Arago, 75014 Paris, France.
URL: https://www.euclid-ec.org/
History Founded in conjunction with *European Space Agency (ESA, #08798)* to coordinate the teams involved in the Euclid astronomy and astrophysics space mission. The Consortium, with ESA and industry partners comprises the *Euclid Collaboration*. Earlier meetings of the Consortium took place as part of the ESA's *Euclid Mission Conference* series. **Aims** Bring together teams of researchers in theoretical physics, particle physics, astrophysics and space astronomy, and also engineers, technicians, and management and administrative staffs working in public research laboratories and contributing to the Euclid mission. **Structure** Euclid Consortium Lead (ECL); Euclid Consortium Board (ECB). **Events** *Euclid Consortium Meeting* Barcelona (Spain) 2020, *Euclid Consortium Meeting* Helsinki (Finland) 2019, *Euclid Consortium Meeting* Bonn (Germany) 2018, *Euclid Consortium Meeting* London (UK) 2017, *Euclid Consortium Meeting* Lisbon (Portugal) 2016.
Members Full in 17 countries:
Austria, Belgium, Canada, Denmark, Finland, France, Germany, Italy, Japan, Netherlands, Norway, Portugal, Romania, Spain, Switzerland, UK, USA. [2022/AA3306/**E**]

♦ EUCLIDE Pôle universitaire Euclide (#05575)
♦ EUCLID Euclid University (#05575)
♦ EUCLID – European Association for Library and Information Education and Research (inactive)

♦ Euclid Network 05574
Exec Dir Saturnusstraat 14, 2516 AH The Hague, Netherlands. E-mail: team@euclidnetwork.eu.
URL: http://www.euclidnetwork.eu/
History 2007. Founded on the initiative of national organizations from France, Sweden and the UK. Registration: No/ID: 858326619, Start date: 2017, Netherlands; Companies House, No/ID: 6433321, England and Wales; EU Transparency Register, No/ID: 4361690830-63. **Aims** Empower civil society and social enterprise to drive positive change. **Structure** General Meeting (bi-annual); Board; Directors (11). **Languages** English. **Staff** 7.00 FTE, paid. **Finance** Sources: members' dues. Supported by: *European Union (EU, #08967)* (EU Programme for Employment and Social Innovation (EASI)). **Activities** Advocacy/lobbying/activism; capacity building; knowledge management/information dissemination; networking/liaising. **Events** *Impact Days Meeting* The Hague (Netherlands) 2022, *Meeting* Helsinki (Finland) 2019, *Summit* The Hague (Netherlands) 2018, *Annual General Meeting* Brussels (Belgium) 2017, *Round Table on Growing Leaders in the Shrinking Civic Space* Brussels (Belgium) 2017. **Publications** EU Funding Toolkit; EU3leader Framework; reports. **Information Services** Euclid Network Knowledge Centre.
Members Organizations (over 100,000) in 20 countries:
Austria, Bulgaria, Croatia, Cyprus, Denmark, France, Germany, Greece, Ireland, Italy, Netherlands, Portugal, Russia, Scotland, Serbia, Slovenia, Spain, Sweden, Türkiye, UK. [2022/XJ8212/**E**]

♦ Euclid University (EUCLID) 05575
Pôle universitaire Euclide (EUCLIDE)
Headquarters Bureau EUCLIDE au Campus ENAM, Avenue de France, Quartier Sica Saidou, BP 157, Bangui, Central African Rep. T. +23621615923. E-mail: info@euclid.int.
US Liaison Office 1101 30th St NW, Suite 500, Washington DC 20007, USA. T. +12022633628. Fax +12024660502.
URL: https://m.euclid.int/
History 16 Apr 2008, New York, NY (USA). Constituted and defined by the multilateral Memorandum of Understanding which entered into force on 16 Apr 2008, and by Framework Agreement, which entered into force on 3 Sep 2009. Developed out of a consortium of universities, set up 2005. Founding Participating Parties: St Vincent-Grenadines; Sierra Leone; Eritrea; Uganda. Registration: No/ID: 49006/49007, Central African Rep. **Aims** Contribute to sustainable development and capacity building of Participating States by training government staff and groups of special interest for Participating States. **Structure** Governing Board; Executive Board; Oversight Council; Advisory Board. **Languages** English, French. **Staff** 100.00 FTE, paid. **Finance** Sources: donations; revenue from activities/projects; sale of publications. Student fees. **Activities** Capacity building; events/meetings; knowledge management/information dissemination. **Publications** *Intergovernmental Research and Policy Journal (IRPJ)*. Books.
Members Participating States (11):
Burundi, Central African Rep, Comoros, Eritrea, Gambia, Senegal, Sierra Leone, St Vincent-Grenadines, Timor-Leste, Uganda, Vanuatu.
IGO Relations Cooperates with (5): *Africa Leather and Leather Products Institute (ALLPI, #00185)*; *African Training and Research Centre in Administration for Development (CAFRAD, #00486)*; *Association of Caribbean States (ACS, #02411)*; *Economic Community of West African States (ECOWAS, #05312)*; *International Anti-Corruption Academy (IACA, #11654)*. **NGO Relations** Memorandum of Understanding with (1): *Islamic Chamber of Commerce, Industry and Agriculture (ICCIA, #16036)*. Member of (4): *Academic Council on the United Nations System (ACUNS, #00020)*; *Association of African Universities (AAU, #02361)*; *Association of Universities of Asia and the Pacific (AUAP, #02968)*; *United Nations Academic Impact (UNAI, #20516)*. Instrumental in setting up (1): *International Institute for Inter-Religious Diplomacy (3IRD, inactive)*. Affiliated institution: *International Organization for Sustainable Development (IOSD)*. [2022/XJ1185/**F***]

♦ EUCMOS – European Congress on Molecular Spectroscopy (meeting series)
♦ EUCO – Association de l'industrie européenne du coco (inactive)

♦ EUCOBAT 05576
SG Excelsiorlaan 91, 1730 Zaventem, Belgium. T. +3227204080. Fax +3227202060. E-mail: info@eucobat.eu.
URL: http://www.eucobat.eu/
History Full title: *European Compliance Organizations for Batteries*. Registered in accordance with Belgian law. EU Transparency Register: 924840110791-74. **Aims** Ensure that all *waste batteries* are collected and *recycled* in an ecologically sound way; contribute to a better environment. **Structure** General Assembly; Board of Directors. Working Groups (3): Technical; Statistical; Policy.
Members Full in 14 countries:
Belgium, Czechia, Denmark, Finland, France, Germany, Ireland, Luxembourg, Netherlands, Norway, Portugal, Romania, Spain, Türkiye. [2021/XM5385/**D**]

♦ EUCOCO Sahara Coordination des comités européens de soutien au peuple sahraoui (#04824)
♦ EUCO European Cultures in Business and Corporate Communication (#05754)
♦ EUCOFEL – Union européenne du commerce de gros, d'expédition, d'importation et d'exportation en fruits et légumes (inactive)
♦ euCognition / see EUCognition – European Society for Cognitive Systems (#05577)

♦ EUCognition – European Society for Cognitive Systems 05577
Coordination office Anatolia College/ACT, Kennedy Street, PO Box 21021, Pylaia, 555 10 Thessaloniki, Greece. E-mail: coordination@eucognition.org.
URL: http://www.eucognition.org/
History Set up, 2006 as *European Network for the Advancement of Artificial Cognitive Systems (euCognition)*, which ended 2008. Follow-up programme ran from 2009 to 2011. EUCogIII ran from Nov 2011 – Dec 2014, when it ceased to be funded by *European Commission (EC, #06633)* research funding. **Aims** Connect researchers in artificial cognitive systems and related areas to reflect on the challenges of the discipline and disseminate their research. **Structure** Coordination Council. **Languages** English. **Staff** None. **Finance** Currently funded by *European Association of Cognitive Systems*. **Activities** Events/meetings; networking/liaising; research and development. **Events** *Joint Action Meeting* London (UK) 2017, *Members' Conference* Falmer (UK) 2013, *Members Conference* Palma (Spain) 2013, *Members Conference / Members' Conference* Odense (Denmark) 2012, *Members Conference / Members' Conference* Vienna (Austria) 2012. **Members** Researchers (about 1,000). Membership countries not specified. [2018.02.12/XJ7102/**F**]

♦ EUCOJUST – International Association for European Cooperation on Justice and Home Affairs (inactive)
♦ EUCOLAIT Association européenne du commerce des produits laitiers et dérivés (#06003)
♦ EUCOLAIT / see European Association of Dairy Trade (#06003)
♦ EucoLight European Association of lighting WEEE compliance schemes (#06108)
♦ EUCOMEDC (inactive)
♦ EUCOM — United States European Command (internationally oriented national body)
♦ EUCONEC – European Conference of the Industry of Electrical Capacitors (inactive)
♦ EUConsult European Association of Consultants to and about Not-For-Profit Organisations (#05988)
♦ EUCOPE European Confederation of Pharmaceutical Entrepreneurs (#06718)
♦ EUCOPRO European Association for Co-Processing (#05991)
♦ EUCORA – Europees Centrum voor Opleiding en Vervolmaking in Kunstambachten en Historische Restauratie (internationally oriented national body)
♦ Eucor – Le Campus européen (#05578)
♦ EU-CORD European Christian Organisations in Relief and Development (#06545)
♦ EUCORD European Cooperative for Rural Development (#06788)
♦ EU-CORD Network / see European Christian Organisations in Relief and Development (#06545)
♦ EUCOR / see Eucor – The European Campus (#05578)

♦ Eucor – The European Campus 05578
Eucor – Le Campus européen
Coordination Univ de Strasbourg, Maison Universitaire Internationale, 11 presqu'île André Malraux, 67100 Strasbourg, France. T. +33368858293 – +33368858295. E-mail: info@eucor-uni.org.
Secretariat Albert-Ludwigs-Univ Freiburg, Fahnenbergplatz, 79085 Freiburg, Germany.
URL: http://www.eucor-uni.org/
History 1989. Created with the structure of an *European Grouping of Territorial Cooperation*. Former names and other names: *European Confederation of Upper Rhine Universities (EUCOR)* – former; *Confédération européenne des universités du Rhin supérieur* – former; *Europäische Konföderation der Oberrheinischen Universitäten* – former. Registration: EU Transparency Register, No/ID: 356735030804-64. **Aims** Promote *cooperation* in all fields of *education* and *research* by fostering teacher and student exchanges, by launching research programmes in common and by favouring cross-frontier study courses, together with reciprocal recognition of study attainments. **Structure** Comprises 5 universities: Universität Basel; Albert-Ludwigs-Universität Freiburg; Université de Haute-Alsace; Karlsruher Institut für Technologie; Université de Strasbourg. Coordination Office in Strasbourg (France); Secretariat in Freiburg (Germany). **Languages** French, German. **Staff** 5.70 FTE, paid. **Finance** Sources: members' dues. **Activities** Projects/programmes; research/documentation; training/education.
Members Universities (5) in 3 countries:
France, Germany, Switzerland. [2022.05.12/XD3169/**D**]

♦ EuCornea European Society of Cornea and Ocular Surface Disease Specialists (#08569)
♦ EU Corporate Leaders Group / see CLG Europe
♦ EU Covenant of Mayors for Climate and Energy / see Covenant of Mayors for Climate and Energy (#04939)
♦ EUCPN European Crime Prevention Network (#06858)
♦ EUCREA Europe / see International Association for the Arts, the Media and Creativity by and with Disabled People (#11713)
♦ EUCREA International International Association for the Arts, the Media and Creativity by and with Disabled People (#11713)
♦ EUCROF European CRO Federation (#06863)
♦ EUCU.NET European Children's Universities Network (#06532)

♦ EU Customs Union 05579
Contact DG Taxation and Customs Union, c/o European Commission, Rue de la Loi 200, 1049 Brussels, Belgium. T. +3222991111. Fax +3222950756.
European Commission Taxation and Customs: http://ec.europa.eu/taxation_customs/index_en.htm
History Established 1958, when the then 6 member states of the European Economic Community, currently *European Community (inactive)*, set up the customs (or tariff) union to reach common rates of customs duties and to apply common trade provisions to third countries in stages. *Common Customs Tariff (CCT)* was introduced in 1968, by which time customs duties and restrictions in internal trade had been abolished, creating what was then called the *'Common Market'*. Internal border controls were maintained mainly for VAT and excise duty control purposes until coming into force of the *European Single Internal Market* in Jan 1993. By this time, common customs legislation had been introduced on a case-by-case basis to implement the common tariff, replacing existing purely national laws. This was amended and consolidated into the *Community Customs Code* (Council Regulation EEC No 2913/92 establishing Community Customs Code) and implementing provisions (Commission Regulation EEC No 2454/93 of 2 Jul 1993) in 1994, to provide a common framework for import and export procedures. There are currently no customs controls in internal single market commerce, while common tariffs and trade measures are applied at external frontiers of the *European Union (EU, #08967)* according to common unified customs management legislation. The strategy for the Customs Union adopted by *European Commission (EC, #06633)*, 8 Feb 2001, as a communication to *Council of the European Union (#04895)*, *European Parliament (EP, #08146)* and *European Economic and Social Committee (EESC, #06963)*, was replaced by the Strategy for the Evolution of the Customs Union of 1 Apr 2008. It follows the process of reforms launched by the adoption of the Modernized Customs Code (Regulation EC No 450/2008 of EP and Council of 23 Apr 2008) and the Decision No 70/2008/EC of the EP and of the Council of 15 Jan 2008 on a paperless environment for customs and trade, by modernizing customs working methods, developing staff competences and reallocating resources in an efficient and effective way. **Aims** Develop and manage the Customs Union; develop and implement tax policy across the EU for the benefit of citizens, businesses and member states. **Structure** Directorate General for Taxation and Customs Union (DG TAXUD) of the European Commission has overall responsibility for management. DG for Trade is responsible for tariff rates and commercial policy and trade defence. **Languages** Czech, Danish, Dutch, English, Estonian, Finnish, French, German, Hungarian, Irish Gaelic, Italian, Latvian, Lithuanian, Maltese, Polish, Portuguese, Slovakian, Slovene, Spanish, Swedish. **Staff** 543.00 FTE, paid. **Finance** DG for Taxation and Customs Union is allocated part of EC budget. Budget (annual): euro 135 million (commitment appropriations). **Activities** Manages, defends and develops the customs union as a vital part of protecting the external borders of the EU; tackles tax obstacles that currently prevent individuals and companies from operating freely across borders and from exploiting the full benefits of the Internal Market; encourages changes to tax systems so that they support Community objectives such as competitiveness and sustainable development; responds to international challenges associated with customs and tax policies; facilitates better cooperation between member states to combat tax customs fraud; engages in open dialogue with stakeholders and interested parties. Cooperation; programmes. **Publications** Taxation and customs documents; reports; taxation working papers; studies; videos. **Information Services** AEO; Customs Offices; EBTI; ECICS; EORI; EXPORT; QUOTA; SEED; SURVEILLANCE; SUSPENSIONS; TARIC; Taxes in Europe – Tax Reforms; TIC ON EUROPA; TIN ON EUROPA; TRANSIT; VIES.

Members States of the European Union (27):
Austria, Belgium, Bulgaria, Croatia, Cyprus, Czechia, Denmark, Estonia, Finland, France, Germany, Greece, Hungary, Ireland, Italy, Latvia, Lithuania, Luxembourg, Malta, Netherlands, Poland, Portugal, Romania, Slovakia, Slovenia, Spain, Sweden.
Customs unions with non-EU states (4):
Andorra, Monaco, San Marino, Türkiye. [2014/XK0128/**E***]

- EU Cyclists' Group / see European Union Cyclists' Group (#08984)
- **EuDA** European Dredging Association (#06946)
- **EUDAT CDI** EUDAT Collaborative Data Infrastructure (#05580)

♦ EUDAT Collaborative Data Infrastructure (EUDAT CDI) 05580

Head of Secretariat Keilaranta 14, FI-02150 Espoo, Finland. E-mail: info@eudat.eu.
URL: https://www.eudat.eu/

History Sep 2016. **Aims** Offer heterogeneous research data management services and storage resources. **Structure** Council; Board; Secretariat. **Events** *Conference* Athens (Greece) 2022, *Digital Infrastructures for Research Conference* Brussels (Belgium) 2017.
Members European data centres and research organizations (28) in 14 countries:
Czechia, Denmark, Finland, France, Germany, Greece, Italy, Netherlands, Norway, Poland, Portugal, Spain, Sweden, UK.
Common Language Resources and Technology Infrastructure (CLARIN, #04295); European Organization for Nuclear Research (CERN, #08108).
NGO Relations Memorandum of Understanding with (1): *Association of European Research Libraries (#02540).* [2022/AA1126/y/**F**]

- EUDAT – European Association for the Development of Databases in Education and Training (inactive)
- **EUDCA** European Data Centre Association (#06888)
- **EUDEC** European Democratic Education Community (#06898)

♦ EU Defence Environmental Network (DEFNET) 05581

Address not obtained.

History 2001. Set up as an informal group of environmental focal-points and specialists from ministries of defence of member states of *European Union (EU, #08967).* Restructured in 2004 and 2006. **Aims** Provide a forum for, and increase information sharing and communication of, best practice on the protection of the environment; assist ministries of defence of EU Member States in identifying consequences for the *military* of EU environmental law; contribute to EU environmental law-making and policy-making by bringing in military interests. **Structure** Plenary meeting (annual), usually in the country holding EU presidency for environmental matters. Chairperson; Secretariat headed by Deputy Chairperson. **Languages** English. **Staff** Voluntary. **Finance** No budget. **Events** *European Conference of Defence and the Environment (ECDE)* Stockholm (Sweden) 2019, *European Conference of Defence and the Environment (ECDE)* Helsinki (Finland) 2015, *Meeting* Lithuania 2013, *Meeting* Cyprus 2012, *Meeting* Poland 2011. **Publications** Fact sheets – online. **Members** Membership is open to civil-servants or military staff in active service working for one of the EU Member States. Observer status is granted to the United States of America (representative from the Department of Defence). **NGO Relations** Supports (1): *European Conference of Defence and the Environment (ECDE).* [2014.06.01/XM3111/**F***]

- **EUDemocrats** Alliance for a Europe of Democracies (#00678)
- EU – Dental Liaison Committee / see Council of European Dentists (#04886)
- **EuDES** European Dry Eye Society (#06949)
- EUD – Europa-Union Deutschland (internationally oriented national body)
- **EUD** European Union of the Deaf (#08985)
- EUD – European Union of Dentists (inactive)
- **EUDF** European Diabetes Forum (#06916)
- EUDICE – Association européenne pour le développement de l'information et la connaissance de l'environnement (inactive)
- Eudistes – Congrégation de Jésus et Marie (religious order)
- Eudisti – Congregazione di Gesù e Maria (religious order)
- EU-DLC / see Council of European Dentists (#04886)
- **EUDN** European Development Research Network (#06915)

♦ EU Dog & Cat Alliance 05582

Contact address not obtained. T. +447902658685. E-mail: info@dogandcatwelfare.eu.
URL: http://www.dogandcatwelfare.eu/

History 2014. Registration: EU Transparency Register, No/ID: 790258914732-21, Start date: 4 Nov 2014. **Aims** Build a better Europe for dogs and cats.
Members Organizations in 26 countries:
Austria, Belgium, Bulgaria, Croatia, Cyprus, Czech Rep, Denmark, Estonia, Finland, France, Germany, Greece, Hungary, Ireland, Italy, Latvia, Lithuania, Malta, Netherlands, Poland, Portugal, Romania, Slovenia, Spain, Sweden, UK.
[2022.11.02/XM5497/**D**]

- **EUDY** European Union of Deaf Youth (#08986)
- EUD Youth Commission / see European Union of Deaf Youth (#08986)
- EUEJ – European Union of Environmental Journalists (no recent information)
- EUEN / see The Federation of International Employers (#09644)
- **eu.ESCO** European Association of Energy Service Companies (#06027)
- **EU** Euroopan Unioni (#08967)
- **EU** Europaeiske Union (#08967)
- **EU** Europäische Union (#08967)
- **EU** European Union (#08967)
- **EU** Europeiska Unionen (#08967)
- **EU** Europese Unie (#08967)
- **EUEW** European Union of Electrical Wholesalers (#08987)
- **EU-EYE** European Alliance for Vision Research and Ophthalmology (#05890)
- EU-EYE / see European Vision Institute (#09069)
- **EUFA** European Fisheries Alliance (#07264)
- **EUFALDA** European Federation of Airline Dispatchers Associations (#07044)
- EUFAMI / see European Federation of Associations of Families of People with Mental Illness (#07051)
- **EUFAMI** European Federation of Associations of Families of People with Mental Illness (#07051)
- **EUFAPA** European Federation of Adapted Physical Activity (#07038)
- **EUFASA** European Union Foreign Affairs Spouses' Associations (#08991)
- **EUFASD** European FASD Alliance (#07032)
- **EUFAS** European Federation of Addiction Societies (#07039)
- **EUFCA** European Floor Coverings Association (#07271)
- **EUF-CE** European University Foundation – Campus Europae (#09031)

♦ EU Federation for the Factoring and Commercial Finance Industry (EUF) 05583

Main Office c/o FCI, 4 Rue François Vander Elst, 1950 Kraainem, Belgium. E-mail: info@euf.eu.com.
URL: http://euf.eu.com/

History 2009, as a subdivision of *International Factors Group (IFG).* Since Jan 2016, a subdivision of *FCI (#09278).* EU Transparency Register: 39275004756-35. **Aims** Act as a platform between the factoring and commercial finance industry and key legislative decision makers across Europe; enhance availability of finance to business, with a particular emphasis on the SME community. **Structure** Executive Committee; Coordination Team; Committees (3). **Languages** English. **Staff** 0.20 FTE, paid. **Finance** Members' dues. Event proceeds. Annual budget: euro 140,000. **Activities** Advocacy/lobbying/activism; Awareness raising; events/meetings; guidance/assistance/consulting; knowledge management/information dissemination; monitoring/evaluation. **Publications** *EUF Newsletter.* White papers; studies.
Members Full in 15 countries:
Austria, Belgium, Czechia, Denmark, France, Germany, Greece, Ireland, Italy, Netherlands, Poland, Portugal, Spain, Sweden, UK. [2019.12.11/XM5581/t/**E**]

- EU Federation of National Organizations of Importers and Exporters of Fish (#04194)
- **EUFED** European Union Federation of Youth Hostel Associations (#08988)
- **EUFEMED** European Federation for Exploratory Medicines Development (#07116)
- **EUFEPS** European Federation for Pharmaceutical Sciences (#07192)
- EUFETEC – European Feed Technology Center (inactive)
- **EUF** EU Federation for the Factoring and Commercial Finance Industry (#05583)
- **EUF** Europaeiske Udviklingsfonds (#06914)
- **EUF** Europäische Union der Fliesenfachverbände (#05762)
- **EUF** European Underwater Federation (#08966)
- EUFFI – European Foundation For Financial Inclusion (unconfirmed)
- **EUFIC** European Food Information Council (#07284)
- EUFJE – European Union Forum of Judges for the Environment (unconfirmed)
- EuFMD / see European Commission for the Control of Foot-and-Mouth Disease (#06635)
- **EUFMD** European Commission for the Control of Foot-and-Mouth Disease (#06635)
- **EuFN** European Focused Ion Beam Network (#07276)
- EUFODA – European Food Distributors Association (inactive)
- **EUFOREA** European Forum for Research and Education in Allergy and Airway Diseases (#07330)
- **EUFORES** European Forum for Renewable Energy Sources (#07329)
- **EUFOR** European Union Force in Bosnia and Herzegovina (#08990)
- **EUFORGEN** European Forest Genetic Resources Programme (#07296)
- EUFOS – European Federation of Otorhinolaryngological Societies (inactive)
- **EUFRAS** European Forum for Agricultural and Rural Advisory Services (#07303)
- EUFRES – European Forum for Religious Education in Schools (internationally oriented national body)
- **EUFRIN** European Fruit Research Institute Network (#07363)
- **EUFUS** European Focused Ultrasound Charitable Society (#07278)
- **EUGA** European Urogynaecological Association (#09041)
- EUGEO / see Association of European Geographical Societies (#02512)
- **EUGEO** Association of European Geographical Societies (#02512)
- EUG – European Union of Geosciences (inactive)
- EUGIC – European Urban Green Infrastructure Conference (meeting series)
- EUGINE – European Engine Power Plants Association (internationally oriented national body)
- **EUGIN** European Group of the Institutes of Navigation (#07424)
- **EUGLOH** European University Alliance for Global Health (#09026)
- EUGMS / see European Geriatric Medicine Society (#07392)
- **EuGMS** European Geriatric Medicine Society (#07392)
- **EUGOGO** European Group of Graves' Orbitopathy (#07421)
- EU Green Diplomacy Network / see Green Diplomacy Network (#10716)
- **EUGridPMA** European Policy Management Authority for Grid Authentication in e-Science (#08244)
- EUGROPA / see European Paper Merchants Association (#08138)
- **Eugropa** European Paper Merchants Association (#08138)
- **EUHA** European University Hospital Alliance (#09032)
- **EUHEA** European Health Economics Association (#07454)
- EU Health Coalition (unconfirmed)
- EUHOFA / see International Association of Hotel School Directors (#11942)
- **EUHOFA International** Association internationale des directeurs d'écoles hôtelières (#11942)
- **EuHPN** European Health Property Network (#07461)

♦ EUI Alumni Association 05584

Contact Univ of Cagliari, Via Università 40, 09124 Cagliari, Italy.
URL: http://www.eui.eu/Alumni/

History 1986. **Aims** Promote and reinforce contacts and mutual assistance between members in the spirit of the Convention setting up the European University Institute; maintain close links to the EUI and its researchers and other European and international institutions and organizations. **Structure** General Assembly (at least once a year); Executive Committee. **Languages** English, Italian. **Staff** 2.00 FTE, paid. **Finance** Members' dues. Donations. **Activities** Networking/liaising; events/meetings. **Events** *Seminar on Politics in a Gray Zone* Singapore (Singapore) 2015. **Publications** *The Building-up of the EUI Alumni Association 1986-2006* (2006) by F Torres et al.
Members Individuals in 55 countries and territories:
Argentina, Australia, Austria, Belgium, Brazil, Bulgaria, Canada, Chile, China, Colombia, Croatia, Cyprus, Czechia, Denmark, Egypt, Eritrea, Estonia, Finland, France, Germany, Greece, Hong Kong, Hungary, Ireland, Italy, Japan, Latvia, Lebanon, Lithuania, Luxembourg, Macau, Malta, Mexico, Netherlands, New Zealand, Norway, Philippines, Poland, Portugal, Romania, Senegal, Serbia, Singapore, Slovakia, Slovenia, Spain, Sweden, Switzerland, Taiwan, Tunisia, Türkiye, UK, United Arab Emirates, Uruguay, USA.
IGO Relations *European University Institute (EUI, #09034).* [2018/XE3167/v/**E**]

- **EU-IBD** European Invasive Bacterial Diseases Surveillance Network (#07598)
- EU-IBIS / see European Invasive Bacterial Diseases Surveillance Network (#07598)
- EUI – École Universitaire Internationale (internationally oriented national body)
- **EUI** European University Institute (#09034)
- **EU-IPFF** European Idiopathic Pulmonary Fibrosis and Related Disorders Federation (#07515)
- **EUIPO** European Union Intellectual Property Office (#08996)
- **EUISS** European Union Institute for Security Studies (#08994)
- EU-Japan Centre for Industrial Cooperation (internationally oriented national body)
- **EUJC** European Union of Judges in Commercial Matters (#08998)
- **EUJS** European Union of Jewish Students (#08997)
- EÜK – Europäisches Übersetzer-Kollegium (internationally oriented national body)
- **EUKN** European Urban Knowledge Network (#09039)
- **EUKO** Europäische Kulturen in der Wirtschaftskommunikation (#05754)
- EUKPF / see European Blackball Association (#06349)
- **EuKTS** European Knowledge and Technology Transfer Society (#07629)
- **EULAC** Asociación de Editoriales Universitarias de América Latina y el Caribe (#02121)
- **EU-LAC Foundation** European Union – Latin America and the Caribbean Foundation (#08999)
- EU-LAC Summit – European Union-Latin American and Caribbean Summit (meeting series)
- **EuLA** European Lime Association (#07699)
- **EULAR** European Alliance of Associations for Rheumatology (#05862)
- EULAS – European Union of Local Authority Staffs (inactive)

♦ EU-LAT Network 05585

Red EU-LAT

Exec Sec Rue de la Linière 11, 1060 Brussels, Belgium. T. +3225361912. Fax +3225361915. E-mail: info@eulatnetwork.org.
URL: https://eulatnetwork.org/

History Founded 11 Oct 2017, on merger of *Copenhagen Initiative for Central America and Mexico (CIFCA, inactive)* and *Grupo Sur (inactive).* Full title: *EU-LAT Network – Advocacy Network Europe – Latin America – Red EU-LAT – Red de Incidencia Europa – Latinoamérica.* Registered in accordance with Belgian law. EU Transparence Register: 996162612544-01. **Aims** Promote participatory *European policies* that contribute to the comprehensive respect of human *rights, gender* equality, democratization and a fair, inclusive and sustainable model of society in *Latin America.* **Structure** General Assembly; Board of Directors; Executive Secretariat. **Staff** 1.00 FTE, paid. **Finance** Members' dues.
Members Full (40) in 12 countries:
Belgium, Denmark, France, Germany, Greece, Ireland, Italy, Luxembourg, Netherlands, Spain, Sweden, UK.
Included in the above, 31 organizations listed in this Yearbook:
- *ActionAid (#00087);*
- *Asociación Entrepueblos;*
- *Associazione di Cooperazione Rurale in Africa e America Latina (ACRA);*
- *Broederlijk Delen;*
- *CNCD Opération 11 11 11;*
- *Coalition of the Flemish North South Movement – 11 11 11;*

- *Commission justice et paix (CJP);*
- *Comunità Impegno Servizio Volontariato (CISV);*
- *Cooperacció, Spain;*
- *Copenhagen Initiative for Central America and Mexico (CIFCA, inactive);*
- *Diakonia;*
- *Entraide et fraternité;*
- *FIAN International (#09743);*
- *Fonds voor Ontwikkelingssamenwerking – Socialistische Solidariteit (FOS);*
- *Fundación Mundubat (Mundubat);*
- *Greek Committee for International Democratic Solidarity (EEDDA);*
- *Humanistisch Instituut voor Ontwikkelingssamenwerking (Hivos);*
- *Ibis – Denmark;*
- *INTERMON OXFAM;*
- *International Federation for Human Rights (#13452);*
- *Mani Tese (MT);*
- *Protection International (PI, #18548);*
- *Secretariado Internacional Cristiano de Solidaridad con América Latina 'Oscar A Romero' (SICSAL);*
- *Swedish Development Partner (IM);*
- *Swedish NGO Centre for Development Cooperation (Forum Syd);*
- *Third World Solidarity Action (ASTM);*
- *Transnational Institute (TNI, #20219);*
- *Trocaire – Catholic Agency for World Development;*
- *We Effect;*
- *World Organisation Against Torture (OMCT, #21685);*
- *WSM.* [2019.10.02/XM8680/y/**F**]

♦ EU-LAT Network – Advocacy Network Europe – Latin America / see EU-LAT Network (#05585)
♦ EULEC – European Live Electronic Centre (internationally oriented national body)
♦ **EULETA** European Legal English Teachers' Association (#07677)
♦ EU-Lex IPG / see International Practice Group (#14632)

♦ EU-LIFE 05586

Exec Dir Room 427 – CRG PRBB Bldg, Dr Aiguader 88, 08003 Barcelona, Spain. T. +34933160169. E-mail: contact@eu-life.eu.
URL: https://eu-life.eu/

History 2013. An alliance of leading research centres in life sciences. **Aims** Contribute to the improvement of research by influencing European science policies and by developing, implementing and disseminating best practices in the organisation and management of research institutes. **Structure** Board of Directors; Strategy Group; Working Groups; Task forces; EU-LIFE Office. **Events** *Anniversary Conference* Lisbon (Portugal) 2023.
Members Full (15) in countries:
Austria, Belgium, Czechia, Denmark, Finland, France, Germany, Greece, Italy, Netherlands, Poland, Portugal, Spain, Switzerland, UK.
European Institute of Oncology, Milan (EIO); International Institute of Molecular and Cell Biology, Warsaw (IIMCB).
NGO Relations Signatory to Agreement of *Coalition for Advancing Research Assessment (CoARA, #04045).* [2023/AA3079/y/**D**]

♦ **eu-LISA** European Union Agency for the Operational Management of Large-Scale IT Systems in the Area of Freedom, Security and Justice (#08972)
♦ **EULITA** European Legal Interpreters and Translators Association (#07678)
♦ EUL/NGL / see The Left in the European Parliament (#16436)
♦ **EUMABOIS** Comité européen des constructeurs de machines à bois (#04152)
♦ **EuMA** European Microwave Association (#07796)
♦ EUMA / see European Opiate Addiction Treatment Association (#08090)
♦ **EUMA** European Union of Mountaineering Associations (#09002)
♦ EUMA / see International Management Assistants (#14081)
♦ **EUMAPRINT** European Committee of Printing and Paper Converting Machinery Manufacturers (#06661)
♦ **EUMASS** European Union of Insurance and Social Security Medicine (#08995)
♦ **EuMaT** European Technology Platform on Advanced Engineering Materials and Technologies (#08887)
♦ **EuMBC** European Masterbatchers and Compounders (#07749)
♦ **EuMB** European Matrix Biology (#07756)
♦ **EUMCA** European Medicinal Cannabis Association (#07766)
♦ EUMC – European Union Military Committee (inactive)
♦ **EUM** Entraide universitaire mondiale (#21892)
♦ **EuMEP** European Middle East Project (#07799)
♦ **EUMEPS** European Manufacturers of Expanded Polystyrene (#07732)
♦ **EUMETNET** Network of European Meteorological Services (#17022)
♦ **EUMETSAT** European Organisation for the Exploitation of Meteorological Satellites (#08096)
♦ **EUMETSAT Staff Association Committee** European Organisation for the Exploitation of Meteorological Satellites Staff Association Committee (#08097)
♦ EUM – European University of International Management and Business (internationally oriented national body)
♦ **EuMGA** European Myasthenia Gravis Association (#07844)
♦ EuMHA – European MHealth Alliance (inactive)
♦ **EUMH Alliance** European Alliance for Mental Health – Employment & Work (#05875)
♦ EUMH-WE / see European Alliance for Mental Health – Employment & Work (#05875)

♦ EUMICON 05587

Dir-Gen Wiedner Hauptstr 63 / B 3 16, 1045 Vienna, Austria. T. +435909003308. Fax +43590900113308. E-mail: office@eumicon.com.
Head Office Av de Tervuren 168, Boite 15, 1150 Brussels, Belgium.
URL: http://www.eumicon.com/

History 2012. Former names and other names: *European Mineral Resources Confederation* – full title. Registration: EU Transparency Register, No/ID: 992490647231-71, Start date: 25 Jul 2022. **Aims** Foster a dialogue on raw materials; provide solutions. **Structure** Officers. **Languages** English, German. **Staff** 1.50 FTE, voluntary. **Finance** Sources: members' dues. **Activities** Awareness raising; events/meetings. **Events** *European Mineral Resources Conference* Vienna (Austria) 2018, *EUMICON : European Mineral Resources Conference* Leoben (Austria) 2012. **Publications** *Eumicon Newsletter.* **Members** Companies (about 160). Membership countries not specified. **IGO Relations** *OECD (#17693)*; ministries. **NGO Relations** *Association européenne des métaux (EUROMETAUX, #02578); European Aluminium (#05893); European Association of Mining Industries, Metal Ores and Industrial Minerals (EUROMINES, #06122); European Steel Association (EUROFER, #08835)*; umbrella organizations. [2022/XM5208/**D**]

♦ EuMIGT – Association of European Manufacturers of Industrial Gas Turbines (inactive)
♦ EUMM – European Union Monitoring Commission (inactive)

♦ EUMOS 05588

Communications Officer Jules Bordetlaan 164, 1140 Brussels, Belgium. E-mail: info@eumos.eu.
URL: http://eumos.eu/

History Former names and other names: *EUMOS – European Safe Logistics Association* – full title; *European Association for Safe Logistics* – alias. Registration: No/ID: 0544.758.136, Start date: 27 Jan 2014, Belgium; EU Transparency Register, No/ID: 107758833349-94, Start date: 17 Dec 2018. **Aims** Make available know-how related to *cargo transport* safety, including packing, storage, loading and cargo securing; represent member interests following the common objective of ensuring safe logistics in Europe. **Structure** General Assembly; Management Board; Advisory Board; Secretariat. **Languages** English. **Staff** Operations run by service providers. **Finance** Sources: members' dues. **Activities** Advocacy/lobbying/activism; awards/prizes/competitions; events/meetings; networking/liaising; projects/programmes; publishing activities; research/documentation; standards/guidelines. Active in all member countries. **Events** *International Conference* Frankfurt-Main (Germany) 2023, *Symposium* Valencia (Spain) 2019.
Members Full in 35 countries:
Austria, Belgium, Bulgaria, Canada, Croatia, Cyprus, Czechia, Denmark, Estonia, Finland, France, Germany, Greece, Hungary, Ireland, Italy, Latvia, Lithuania, Luxembourg, Malaysia, Malta, Netherlands, Poland, Portugal, Romania, Russia, Slovakia, Slovenia, South Africa, Spain, Sweden, Switzerland, Türkiye, UK, USA. [2023/XM7341/**D**]

♦ EUMOS – European Safe Logistics Association / see EUMOS (#05588)
♦ EUMOTIV – Association européenne d'études de motivation économique, commerciale et industrielle (inactive)
♦ EUMS – European Mechanical Circulatory Support Summit (meeting series)
♦ EUMS / see European Union of Medical Specialists (#09001)
♦ EUMS – European Union Military Staff Office (inactive)
♦ EUMT – Europäische Union gegen den Missbrauch der Tiere (inactive)
♦ **EUNAAPA** European Network for Action and Physical Activity (#07860)
♦ **EUNEC** European Network of Education Councils (#07898)
♦ **EUNET** European Network for Education and Training (#07899)
♦ **EUnetHTA** European Network for Health Technology Assessment (#07921)
♦ **EUNETHYDIS** European Network for Hyperkinetic Disorders (#07925)
♦ **EuNet MERYC** European Network for Music Educators and Researchers of Young Children (#07948)

♦ EU Network of Nurse Regulators 05589

Secretariat 3 Empress Mews, London, SE5 9BT, UK. T. +7942639159.
URL: http://nurse-regulators.eu/

History Founded 2010. EU Transparency Register: 167225026406-15.
Members Full in 3 countries:
Ireland, Spain, UK. [2019/XM8688/**F**]

♦ **EUN** European Schoolnet (#08433)

♦ EUNICE Network 05590

Contact TU Munich, Lehrstuhl für Kommunikationsnetze, Arcisstr 21, Blg 9-1st Fl, Rm 1946, 80290 Munich, Germany. T. +498928923500. Fax +498928923523.

History Former names and other names: *European Network of Universities and Companies in Information and Communication Technology* – former. **Aims** Foster mobility of students, faculty members and research scientists working in the field of information and *communication technology*; promote educational and research cooperation among member institutions. **Activities** Training/education. **Events** *Eunice Open European Summer School and Conference* Rennes (France) 2014, *Conference on Information and Communications Technologies* Budapest (Hungary) 2012.
Members Universities and schools (18) in 10 countries:
Finland, France, Germany, Hungary, Italy, Netherlands, Norway, Russia, Spain, UK. [2016/XJ3077/**F**]

♦ **EUNIC** European Union National Institutes for Culture (#09004)
♦ **EUNIDA** European Network of Implementing Development Agencies (#07926)
♦ **EUNIRPA** European Non-Integrated Wire Rod Processors Association (#08055)
♦ **EUNIS** European University Information Systems Organization (#09033)
♦ **EUnited** European Engineering Industries Association (#06991)
♦ EUnited Turbines / see European Association of Gas and Steam Turbine Manufacturers (#06050)
♦ **EUniverCities** EUniverCities Network (#05591)

♦ EUniverCities Network (EUniverCities) 05591

Secretariat address not obtained. E-mail: eunivercities@exeter.ac.uk.
URL: https://eunivercitiesnetwork.com/

History 2012. **Aims** Exchange and spread knowledge, expertise and experience about city-university cooperation across urban Europe. **Activities** Events/meetings; projects/programmes. **Events** *Meeting* Exeter (UK) 2022, *Meeting* Innsbruck (Austria) 2022, *Meeting* Aveiro (Portugal) 2019, *Meeting* Malaga (Spain) 2019, *Meeting* Trondheim (Norway) 2018.
Members Medium-sized cities and universities. Members in 12 countries:
Austria, Belgium, France, Germany, Italy, Poland, Portugal, Romania, Spain, Sweden, Switzerland, UK. [2023.02.13/XM8039/**F**]

♦ **EUniWell** European University for Well-Being (#09037)
♦ **EU-NN** European Narcolepsy Network (#07852)
♦ **EU Non-Proliferation Network** European Network of Independent Non-Proliferation Think Tanks (#07930)
♦ **EUNOPS** European Network of Palm Scientists (#07964)
♦ EUNOS / see European Neuro-Ophthalmological Society (#08043)
♦ **EUNOS** European Neuro-Ophthalmological Society (#08043)
♦ E-UNSAT – European Conference on Unsaturated Soils (meeting series)
♦ **EU-OEA** Ocean Energy Europe (#17649)
♦ EUomo / see Europa Uomo (#05770)
♦ **EUON** European Union Observatory for Nanomaterials (#09007)
♦ **EU-OSHA** European Agency for Safety and Health at Work (#05843)
♦ EuOTA – European Ozone Trade Association (unconfirmed)
♦ **EuPA** European Proteomics Association (#08288)
♦ EUPA – European Union of Pankration Athlima (inactive)
♦ EUPA – European Union for the Protection of Animals (inactive)
♦ **EUpALS** European Organization for Professionals and Patients with ALS (#08111)
♦ **EUPAN** European Public Administration Network (#08293)
♦ Euparal / see Global Flooring Alliance (#10362)
♦ **EuParl** European Information and Research Network on Parliamentary History (#07535)
♦ **EUPATI** European Patients' Academy on Therapeutic Innovation (#08170)
♦ **EUPAVE** European Concrete Paving Association (#06697)
♦ **EuPC** European Plastics Converters (#08216)
♦ **EUPEA** European Physical Education Association (#08206)
♦ EUPE – European Union for Packaging and the Environment (inactive)
♦ **EUPET** European Association for Unoriented Polyester Films (#06261)
♦ **EuPF** European Plastic Films (#08213)
♦ **EuPFI** European Paediatric Formulation Initiative (#08125)
♦ **EUPHA** European Public Health Association (#08298)
♦ **EUPHE** European Union of Private Higher Education (#09009)
♦ **EuPIA** European Printing Ink Association (#08275)
♦ **EUPJ** European Union for Progressive Judaism (#09010)
♦ **EUPLAN** European Platelet Network (#08219)
♦ **EUPLAT** European Association of Public e-Tendering Platform Providers (#06181)
♦ **EUPO** European Community University Professors in Ophthalmology (#06685)
♦ **EUPOS** European Position Determination System (#08256)

♦ EUPPA – European Potato Processors' Association 05592

Main Office c/o Kellen, Av de Tervuren 188-A, Box 4, 1150 Brussels, Belgium. T. +3227611670. E-mail: euppa@kellencompany.com – mail@euppa.eu.
URL: http://www.euppa.eu/

History 16 Oct 1962, as *Union européenne des industries de transformation de la pomme de terre (UEITP) – European Association of Potato Processing Industry – Europäische Vereinigung der Kartoffelverarbeitenden Industrien – Unione Europea delle Industrie Trasformatrici di Patate – Europese Unie van Industriën van Aardappelprodukten – Europaeiske Union for Kartoffelforarbejdningsindustrierne.* Previously also referred to as *European Union of the Potato Processing Industry – Europäische Union der Kartoffelverarbeitenden Industrien.* Current title launched 1 Feb 2010, when new statutes were adopted. Registered in accordance with Belgian law. **Aims** Defend the industry's interests. **Structure** General Assembly; Executive Committee; Commissions (2). **Languages** English. **Staff** 2.00 FTE, paid. **Finance** Members' dues. Projects. **Activities** Research/documentation. **Events** *General Assembly* Brussels (Belgium) 2013, *General Assembly* Baarlo (Netherlands) 2012, *General Assembly* Marseille (France) 2011, *General Assembly* Potsdam (Germany) 2010, *General Assembly* Parma (Italy) 2009. **Publications** *Factors that Affect Fat Uptake during French Fries Production* (2007) by B De Meulenaer and J Van Camp. Leaflet.
Members National Secretaries in 6 countries:

Belgium, France, Germany, Italy, Netherlands, UK.
Associated members in 1 country:
Poland.
IGO Relations Recognized by: *European Commission (EC, #06633)*. **NGO Relations** Member of: *European Committee on the Rules and Usages of Inter-European Trade in Potatoes (European RUCIP Committee, #06666)*. Affiliated member of: *FoodDrinkEurope (#09841)*. [2019.12.12/XD0898/**D**]

- EUPPFL / see European Leagues (#07672)
- **EUPRA** European Peace Research Association (#08177)
- **EUPRERA** European Public Relations Education and Research Association (#08302)
- EUPR / see European Union of Public Relations (#09011)
- **EUPR** European Union of Public Relations (#09011)
- euPrevent / EMR Foundation / see euPrevent Foundation (#05593)
- euPrevent / Euregio Meuse-Rhine Foundation – crossing borders in health / see euPrevent Foundation (#05593)

♦ euPrevent Foundation 05593

Dir PO Box 33, 6400 AA Heerlen, Netherlands. T. +31636062039. E-mail: info@euprevent.eu.
URL: http://www.euprevent.eu/

History Former names and other names: *euPrevent / Euregio Meuse-Rhine Foundation – crossing borders in health* – full title; *euPrevent / EMR Foundation* – alias. Registration: Handelsregister, No/ID: 50357468, Netherlands. **Aims** Support cross-border cooperation among professionals and organizations engaged in maintaining, promoting and improving public health in the border region between the Netherlands, Belgium and Germany. **Structure** Board.
Members Full in 3 countries:
Belgium, Germany, Netherlands. [2023.02.28/XM7370/f/**F**]

- **EUPRIO** Association of European University Public Relations and Information Officers (#02549)
- EUPRO – European Union of Physics Research Organizations (inactive)
- EU ProSun (unconfirmed)
- EU ProSun Glass (unconfirmed)
- **EUproVET** European Providers of Vocational Education and Training (#08289)
- EuPR / see Plastics Recyclers Europe (#18394)
- EUPSA / see European Paediatric Surgeons' Association (#08130)
- **EUPSA** European Paediatric Surgeons' Association (#08130)
- **EUPSF** European Patient Safety Foundation (#08171)
- EUPSYCA – European Working Group for Psychosomatic Cancer Research (inactive)
- EU PVSEC – European Photovoltaic Solar Energy Conference (meeting series)
- **EURAAC** European Association of Acarologists (#05924)
- **EurAAP** European Association on Antennas and Propagation (#05937)
- Eura Audit International / see EuraAudit International (#05594)

♦ EuraAudit International 05594

Secretariat 24 rue de Londres, 75009 Paris, France. T. +33144159523. E-mail: secretariat@euraaudit.org.
URL: http://www.euraaudit.org/

History Also referred to as *Eura Audit International*. An association of independent *accountancy* firms. **Structure** Board of Directors, comprising President, General Secretary, 2 Vice-Presidents, Treasurer, 2 Honorary Presidents and 14 members. Committees (3): Multidisciplinary; IAS-IFRS; Organization. **Events** *Annual Congress* London (UK) 2017, *Annual Congress* Lisbon (Portugal) 2009, *Annual Congress* Sofia (Bulgaria) 2008. **Members** Audit and Chartered Accountancy offices (250). Membership countries not specified. **IGO Relations** Recognized by: *Asian Development Bank (ADB, #01422)*; *Banque ouest africaine de développement (BOAD, #03170)*; *The World Bank Group (#21218)*. [2018/XJ1405/**F**]

- EURAB – European Research Advisory Board (inactive)
- EURABIA – European Coordinating Committee of Friendship Societies with the Arab World (inactive)
- EURAC – European Academy of Bozen/Bolzano (internationally oriented national body)
- **EurAc** European Network for Central Africa (#07874)

♦ EURACHEM 05595

Sec Elena Sanchez, c/o LGC Limited, Queens Road, Teddington, TW11 0LY, UK. E-mail: secretariat@eurachem.org.
URL: http://www.eurachem.org/

History Nov 1989. **Aims** Provide a focus for analytical *chemistry* in *Europe* and a framework in which analytical chemists can collaborate to improve validity of chemical measurements; develop infrastructure and promote best practice. Promote: awareness of quality problems; development of validated methods; measurement traceability underpinned by reference materials; proficiency testing schemes; quality systems based on European standards. **Structure** General Assembly. Committee, comprising all members, associate members and observers reporting to national EURACHEM groups. Executive Committee, consisting of Chair, Vice-Chair, Past Chair, Chairmen of the working groups and 6 members co-opted from the General Assembly. Working Groups (4): Education and Training; Measurement Uncertainty and Traceability; Analytical Quality Assurance at Universities; PT-Mirror Group. **Finance** Members' dues (annual): euro 400 per country. No annual budget. Members contribute in kind to EURACHEM activities. **Activities** Organizes workshops and seminars. Collaborative projects managed by 2 or more participating institutes. **Events** *International Workshop on Proficiency Testing in Analytical Chemistry, Microbiology and Laboratory Medicine* Windsor (UK) 2023, *Annual Meeting* Prague (Czechia) 2021, *Annual Meeting* Bucharest (Romania) 2020, *Annual Meeting* Tartu (Estonia) 2019, *Annual Meeting* Dublin (Ireland) 2018. **Publications** *EURACHEM Newsletter* (annual). **Information Services** *EURACHEM Networking Scheme* – promotes pan-European collaboration on projects aimed at improving the quality of analytical measurements.
Members National representatives in 33 countries:
Albania, Austria, Belgium, Bulgaria, Croatia, Cyprus, Czechia, Denmark, Finland, France, Germany, Greece, Hungary, Iceland, Ireland, Italy, Lithuania, Luxembourg, Malta, Netherlands, Norway, Poland, Portugal, Romania, Russia, Slovakia, Slovenia, Spain, Sweden, Switzerland, Türkiye, UK, Ukraine.
Regional organization, listed in this Yearbook:
European Commission (EC, #06633).
International observers (9), listed in this Yearbook:
AOAC INTERNATIONAL (#00863); *Cooperation on International Traceability in Analytical Chemistry (CITAC, #04797)* (Consultative Committee for Amount of Substance – Metrology in Chemistry CCQM of); *European Association of National Metrology Institutes (EURAMET, #06129)*; *European Chemical Society (EuChemS, #06524)*; *European Cooperation for Accreditation (EA, #06782)*; *European Federation of National Associations of Measurement, Testing and Analytical Laboratories (EUROLAB, #07168)*; *International Laboratory Accreditation Cooperation (ILAC, #13995)*; *International Organization for Standardization (ISO, #14473)* (Committee on Reference Materials of); *International Union of Pure and Applied Chemistry (IUPAC, #15809)*.
IGO Relations Participates as observer in the activities of: *Codex Alimentarius Commission (CAC, #04081)*. [2022/XF5280/y/**F**]

- **EURACOAL** European Association for Coal and Lignite (#05978)
- EUR-ACOM / see Association of Europe's Coalfield Regions (#02585)
- **EURACOM** Association of Europe's Coalfield Regions (#02585)
- **EURACT** European Academy of Teachers in General Practice (#05817)
- **EURADA** European Association of Regional Development Agencies (#06187)
- **EURAD** Europe Against Drugs (#05774)
- EURADH – European Adhesion Conference (meeting series)
- **EURADIA** European Alliance for Diabetes Research (#05868)

♦ Euradopt 05596

Secretariat c/o Wereldkinderen, Regulusweg 11, 2516 AC The Hague, Netherlands. T. +31703506699. Fax +31703547867. E-mail: mail@euradopt.org.
URL: http://portal.euradopt.org/

History Founded 27 Mar 1993, The Hague (Netherlands), by adoption agencies in nine countries. Also referred to as *Association of Authorized European Adoption Agencies*. **Aims** Advocate *intercountry adoption* as an option in *child welfare* when pursued in the best interests of the child; establish common ethical rules and promote their application in international adoptions; promote cooperation between governments and adoption organizations; improve legislation and other measures for the *protection* of *childhood*. **Structure** Council; Executive Board; Chair rotates between countries every 2 years. **Finance** Members' dues. **Events** *Sustainability of Intercountry Adoption from Different Perspectives* Copenhagen (Denmark) 2022, *General Meeting* Utrecht (Netherlands) 2016, *The relevance of adoption – improving the life for children who cannot live with their family* Utrecht (Netherlands) 2016, *General Meeting* Stockholm (Sweden) 2014, *General Meeting* Berlin (Germany) 2012.
Members European adoption agencies (26) in 12 countries:
Belgium, Denmark, Finland, France, Germany, Iceland, Italy, Luxembourg, Netherlands, Norway, Spain, Sweden.
Included in the above, 1 organization listed in this Yearbook:
Netherlands Intercountry Child Welfare Organization (NICWO, no recent information).
IGO Relations Observer in the meetings of *The Hague Conference on Private International Law (HCCH, #10850)*. [2020/XF2582/y/**F**]

- **EURADOS** European Radiation Dosimetry Group (#08318)
- **EuRA** European Relocation Association (#08352)
- EURA – European Renderers Association (inactive)
- **EURA** European Urban Research Association (#09040)
- **EURAF** European Agroforestry Federation (#05848)
- EurAfrik (internationally oriented national body)
- **EurAgEng** European Society of Agricultural Engineers (#08513)
- EURAG – European Federation of the Elderly / see EURAG – European Federation of Older Persons (#05597)

♦ EURAG – European Federation of Older Persons 05597

Fédération européenne des personnes âgées (EURAG) – Federación Europea para los Ancianos – Bund der Älteren Generation Europas – Federazione Europea delle Persone Anziane

SG Leckova 1520, 149 00 Prague 4, Czechia.
Pres Parkstrasse 25-c, 61476 Kronberg, Germany.
URL: http://eurag-europe.net/

History Founded 1962, as *European Federation for the Self-Help of the Elderly*, as an informal working party of European old-age associations. Incorporated, 1966, in Luxembourg. Subsequently changed into *European Federation for the Welfare of the Elderly* and *EURAG – European Federation of the Elderly*. Current English title adopted 1 Jun 2002. **Aims** Promote maintenance of an independent life; strengthen participation in decision-making and support European integration; promote self-help; improve elderly people's situation and integration in society; safeguard financial security; prevent discrimination on grounds of age; develop potentials. **Structure** General Assembly (every 3 years); General Council; Presidential Board; Permanent Committees. **Languages** English, German. **Staff** None. **Finance** Members' dues. Other sources: subsidies; project funding. **Activities** Guidance/assistance/consulting; events/meetings; networking/liaising. **Events** *Meeting* Lausanne (Switzerland) 2020, *Conference* Moscow (Russia) 2019, *Congress* Darlowo (Poland) 2017, *International Conference* Ljubljana (Slovenia) 2016, *Congress* Berlin (Germany) 2015. **Publications** *AGE Platform* in English, French; *EURAG-Information* in English, German. Studies; reports.
Members Ordinary non-profit associations; Special individuals, public authorities and private associations; Supporting; Honorary individuals appointed by the Presidential Board who have acquired particular merit in the service of the older generation. Members in 27 countries:
Albania, Austria, Belgium, Bulgaria, Croatia, Czechia, Estonia, France, Germany, Hungary, Iceland, Ireland, Israel, Italy, Latvia, Lithuania, Luxembourg, Netherlands, Poland, Romania, Russia, Slovakia, Slovenia, Spain, Switzerland, UK, Ukraine.
Consultative Status Consultative status granted from: *ECOSOC (#05331)* (Ros A). **IGO Relations** Accredited by: *United Nations (UN, #20515)*; *United Nations Office at Geneva (UNOG, #20597)*; *United Nations Office at Vienna (UNOV, #20604)*. **NGO Relations** Member of: *AGE Platform Europe (#00557)*; *Conference of INGOs of the Council of Europe (#04607)*; *International Institute on Ageing, United Nations – Malta (INIA, #13860)*; *International Social Security Association (ISSA, #14885)*; *Social Platform (#19344)*. Cooperates with: *International Federation on Ageing (IFA, #13345)*. Supports: *European Alliance for the Statute of the European Association (EASEA, #05886)*. [2019.02.14/XD0716/**D**]

- **EURAG** Fédération européenne des personnes âgées (#05597)
- **EURAGRI** EURopean AGricultural Research Initiative (#05847)
- **EurAI** European Association for Artificial Intelligence (#05943)
- **EURALARM** Association of European Manufacturers of Fire and Security Systems (#02520)
- **EURALEX** European Association for Lexicography (#06107)
- **EURAMAL** European Association for Modern Arabic Literature (#06123)
- **EURAMAS** European Association for Multi-Agent Systems (#06124)
- **EURAMED** European Alliance for Medical Radiation Protection Research (#05874)
- **EURAMES** European Association for Middle Eastern Studies (#06120)
- **EURAMET** European Association of National Metrology Institutes (#06129)
- **EURAM** European Academy of Management (#05800)
- **EURAMI** European Aero-Medical Institute (#05834)
- EURAMI e V – Centre for Education, Information, Research and Supply / see European Aero-Medical Institute (#05834)

♦ eurammon 05598

Managing Dir Lyoner Str 18, 60528 Frankfurt-Main, Germany. T. +496966031277. Fax +496966032276.
URL: https://eurammon.com/

History 1996. Name derives from the combination of "Europe" and "ammonia". **Aims** Provide a platform for information and knowledge sharing; boost general awareness and acceptance of natural *refrigerants*, promote their use in the interests of a healthy *environment* and thereby continue developing a sustainable approach to refrigeration. **Structure** Executive Board. **Languages** English. **Activities** Events/meetings. **Events** *Symposium* 2022, *Symposium* Schaffhausen (Switzerland) 2019, *Symposium* Schaffhausen (Switzerland) 2017. **NGO Relations** Partners include: *Eurovent (#09194)*; *International Institute of Ammonia Refrigeration (IIAR)*; *Southern African Refrigerated Distribution Association (SARDA)*. [2022/XM5819/**D**]

- EURANDOM – European Institute for Statistics, Probability, Stochastic Operations Research and its Applications (internationally oriented national body)
- **EURAO** European Radio Amateurs' Organization (#08320)
- EURAPA – European Association for Prevention of Addicts (no recent information)
- **EURAPAG** European Association of Paediatric and Adolescent Gynaecology (#06140)
- **EURAPS** European Association of Plastic Surgeons (#06154)
- EurAqua / see European Network of Freshwater Research Organisations (#07911)
- **EurAqua** European Network of Freshwater Research Organisations (#07911)
- EURASAP – European Association for the Science of Air Pollution (inactive)
- **EURASC** European Academy of Sciences (#05813)
- **EURASCO** European Federation of Agricultural Exhibitions and Show Organizers (#07043)
- **EurASEAA** European Association of Southeast Asian Archaeologists (#06216)
- EurAseC – Eurasian Economic Community (inactive)
- **EURASEM** European Association for Experimental Mechanics (#06034)
- **EURAS** Eurasian Universities Union (#05615)
- **EURAS** European Academy for Standardisation (#05815)
- EURAS – European Anodisers' Association (inactive)
- **EURASHE** European Association of Institutions of Higher Education (#06086)

♦ **Eurasia Business and Economics Society (EBES)** **05599**

Main Office Aksemsettin Mah Kocasinan Cad No 8/4, Fatih, 34080 Istanbul/Istanbul, Türkiye. T. +902122205451. Fax +902122205452. E-mail: ebes@ebesweb.org.
URL: http://www.ebesweb.org/

History 2008. **Aims** Promote academic research in the field of economics, finance and business; encourage intellectual development of scholars; provide network opportunities for conference attendees for making long lasting academic cooperation. **Structure** Executive Board; Advisory Board. **Languages** English. **Staff** 5.00 FTE, paid; 50.00 FTE, voluntary. **Events** *Conference* Istanbul (Türkiye) 2023, *Conference* Lisbon (Portugal) 2023, *Conference* Madrid (Spain) 2023, *Conference* Berlin (Germany) 2022, *Conference* Istanbul (Türkiye) 2022. **Publications** *EBES Newsletter* (4 a year); *Eurasian Business Review (EABR)* (4 a year); *Eurasian Economic Review (EAER)* (4 a year). **Members** Individuals (2,587) in 87 countries. Membership countries not specified. **NGO Relations** Member of (1): *Global Labor Organization (GLO, #10445).* [2023.02.15/XJ9458/**C**]

♦ Eurasia Conference on Chemical Sciences (meeting series)
♦ Eurasia Foundation (internationally oriented national body)

♦ **Eurasia Foundation (EF)** **05600**

Fondation Eurasie

Address not obtained.
URL: http://www.eurasia.org/

History 1992, USA, as a public-private partnership. Initially founded to promote civil society, private enterprise and democratic institutions in the countries of the former Soviet Union. **Aims** Mobilize public and private resources to help citizens participate in building their future by strengthening their communities and improving their civic and economic *wellbeing*. **Structure** Management Team; Board of Trustees; Advisory Council. Regional organizations: *Eurasia Foundation of Central Asia (EFCA)*; *New Eurasia Foundation – Russia*; *New Eurasia Establishment – Belarus*. **Finance** Grant from: *United States Agency for International Development (USAID)*. **Events** *High-level economic forum on global economic crisis* Yerevan (Armenia) 2009. **NGO Relations** Member of: *InsideNGO (inactive)*. Together with: *Madariaga – College of Europe Foundation (inactive)*, set up: *New Eurasia Foundation (FNE, inactive)*. Supports: *Foundation for a Civil Society (FCS)*; *Internews International (inactive)*; *Voluntary Organizations Initiative in Central and Eastern Europe and Eurasia (VOICE International, no recent information)*; *World Free Press Institute (WFPI)*; *National Peace Foundation (NPF)*; *Freedom House*; *European Roma Rights Centre (ERRC, #08401).* [2017/XG6410/f/**F**]

♦ Eurasia Foundation (from Asia) / see Eurasia Foundation
♦ Eurasia Foundation of Central Asia (internationally oriented national body)
♦ **Eurasia IDEA Network** Eurasia International Digital Exchange Advocacy Network (#05601)

♦ **Eurasia International Digital Exchange Advocacy Network (Eurasia IDEA Network)** **05601**

Contact address not obtained. E-mail: eurasiacivilnet@gmail.com.

History 2009. **Aims** Strengthen solidarity within civil society in the region and with supporters around the world in response to threats and challenges faced by civil society, civic activists and human rights defenders in the region. **Members** Civil society activists in Eurasia; international organizations. Membership countries not specified. [2010/XJ2108/**F**]

♦ **Eurasian Association of Contitutional Review Bodies (EACRB)** **05602**

Contact Constitutional Council of the Republic of Kazakhstan, 39 Kunayev street, Esil district, Nur-Sultan, Kazakhstan, 010000. E-mail: okr@ksrk.gov.kz.
URL: http://www.concourt.am/

History Constituent conference held 24 Oct 1997. Original title: *Conference of Constitutional Control Organs of the Countries of Young Democracy (CCCOCYD).* **Aims** Promote generally accepted constitutional values, maintaining a permanent dialogue and sharing experience on the issues of ensuring the supremacy of constitution. **Languages** English, Russian. **IGO Relations** Participates in: *World Conference on Constitutional Justice (WCCJ, #21298).* [2019.10.23/XJ4109/**F**]

♦ Eurasian Center for Food Security (internationally oriented national body)

♦ **Eurasian Coalition on Male Health (ECOM)** **05603**

Exec Dir Mardi 3, 10113 Tallinn, Estonia. T. +37256082060.
Registered Seat Oismäe tee 36-8, 13511 Tallinn, Estonia.
URL: http://ecomnetwork.org/

History Also known under the acronym *EKOM*. Registered in accordance with Estonian law. **Aims** Create favourable conditions in the Eastern Europe and Central Asia region to ensure that men having sex with men (MSM) and *transgender* people have access to services in the field of sexual and reproductive health, mainly related to but not limited by *HIV* prevention, treatment, care and support, and that those are evidence-based and human rights oriented. **Structure** General Assembly; Steering Committee; Secretariat.
Members Full (45) in 14 countries:
Armenia, Azerbaijan, Belarus, Estonia, Georgia, Kazakhstan, Kyrgyzstan, Moldova, Netherlands, Russia, Spain, Tajikistan, Ukraine, USA.
NGO Relations Cooperates with: *MPact Global Action for Gay Men's Health and Rights (MPact, #16875).* [2015/XJ9368/**D**]

♦ **Eurasian Colorectal Technologies Association (ECTA)** **05604**

Sec Medizinische Uni Graz, Auenbruggerplatz 29, 8036 Graz, Austria. T. +4331638581190. Fax +433163826845.

History Founded 2007. **Aims** Promote and teach the use, and discourage the abuse, of advanced technologies for both *diagnosis* and treatment of large bowel *diseases* in European and Asian countries, in strict cooperation with the existing national and international colorectal societies; close the gap and raise the standard of colorectal surgery in the continents of Europe and Asia. **Structure** Governing Council, including Honorary President, President and 2 Vice-Presidents. Sections (3): Scientific and Biennial Congress Commission; Scientific Exchange Between Countries and Cooperation with Developing Countries; Young Surgeons. **Languages** Chinese, English, Italian. **Events** *Biennial Meeting* Seoul (Korea Rep) 2017, *Biennial Meeting* Moscow (Russia) 2015, *Biennial Meeting* Singapore (Singapore) 2013, *Biennial Meeting* Turin (Italy) 2011, *Biennial Meeting* Guangzhou (China) 2009. **Publications** *Techniques in Coloproctology* – official journal. **Members** in Europe and Asia (countries not specified). [2014/XJ5046/v/**C**]

♦ **Eurasian Commonwealth** International Organization for Promoting Public Diplomacy, Science, Education and Youth Cooperation (#14464)

♦ **Eurasian Development Bank (EDB)** **05605**

Head Office 220 Dostyk Ave, Almaty, Kazakhstan, 050051. T. +77272444044. Fax +77272508158. E-mail: info@eabr.org.
URL: http://www.eabr.org/

History 12 Jan 2006, Astana (Kazakhstan). Established following signing of Agreement on Establishment of the Bank. **Aims** Facilitate the development of market economies, economic growth and the expansion of trade and other economic ties through investment activities. Foster *economic* growth and integration processes in the Eurasian region. **Structure** Council; Management Board. Manages *Eurasian Foundation for Stabilization and Development (EFSD)*, formerly *EurAsEC Anti-Crisis Fund*, set up 2009. **Finance** Charter capital: US$ 7,000 million, including US$ 1,500 million of paid-in capital and US$ 5,500 million of callable capital. **Activities** Financial and/or material support; guidance/assistance/consulting; research/documentation; events/meetings; networking/liaising.
Members States (6; " indicates founding):
Armenia, Belarus, Kazakhstan (*), Kyrgyzstan, Russia (*), Tajikistan.
Consultative Status Consultative status granted from: *ECOSOC (#05331)* (Permanent Observer Status). **IGO Relations** Observer status with (1): *United Nations (UN, #20515)* (General Assembly). Memorandum of Understanding with (1): *International Investment Bank (IIB, #13951).* Member of (1): *Eurasian Group on Combating Money Laundering and Financing of Terrorism (EAG, #05608).* Cooperates with (1): *FAO Investment Centre (#09264).* Participates in the activities of: *UNCTAD (#20285).* **NGO Relations** Member of: *Global Infrastructure Connectivity Alliance (GICA, #10419).* Supports: *"Eurasian Economic Club of Scientists" Association (EECSA, no recent information).* [2022/XM3837/**F***]

♦ **Eurasian Dialogue** **05606**

Co-Founder Rue de Carouge 36bis, 1205 Geneva, Switzerland.
URL: http://www.eurasiandialogue.org/

History Set up 2011, Geneva (Switzerland). Registered in accordance with Swiss Civil Code. **Aims** Foster improved cultural and academic relations between Central Asia and Europe. **Structure** Executive Board. **Languages** English. **Staff** 5.00 FTE, voluntary. **Activities** Publishing activities; research/documentation. Active in: Belgium, Switzerland, UK. **Publications** *Perspectives on Central Asia* (3 a year) – bulletin.
Members Individuals in 3 countries:
Belgium, Switzerland, UK. [2015.06.10/XJ9670/**F**]

♦ Eurasian Economic Community (inactive)

♦ **Eurasian Economic Union (EAEU)** **05607**

Postal address 3/5 Smolensky Boulevard, bld 1, Moscow MOSKVA, Russia, 119121. E-mail: info@eecommission.org.
Chairman 2 Letnikovskaya St, bld 2, Moscow MOSKVA, Russia, 115114. T. +74956692400ext4133. Fax +74956692415.
URL: http://www.eaeunion.org/

History Proposed 1994. Agreement on *Customs Union (inactive)* signed 1995. Treaty on Customs Union and Common Economic Space signed 26 Jan 1999, Moscow (Russia). *Eurasian Economic Community (EurAseC, inactive)* set up, 10 Oct 2000, Astana (Kazakhstan). Agreement on formation of *Common Economic Space* signed 19 Sep 2003. Customs Union and Common Economic Space operational since 2010. Agreement on the Eurasian Economic Commission signed Nov 2011, and became functional Feb 2012. *Treaty on the Eurasian Economic Union*, signed 29 May 2014, and became into force 1 Jan 2015, when it replaced *Eurasian Economic Community (EurAseC, inactive)*. **Aims** Create proper conditions for sustainable economic development of Member States in order to improve living standards of their populations; seek creation of a common market for goods, services, capital and labour within the Union; ensure comprehensive modernization, cooperation and competitiveness of national economies within the global economy. **Structure** *Supreme Eurasian Economic Council (SEAC)* (meets at least annually), consisting of Heads of Member States; *Eurasian Intergovernmental Council*, (meets at least twice a year), consisting of Heads of governments of Member States; *Eurasian Economic Commission*, comprising Council and Board; *Court of the Eurasian Economic Union*, functions as permanent judicial body. **Languages** Russian. **Finance** Funded from the budget of the Union. **Events** *Anti-Counterfeiting* Nur-Sultan (Kazakhstan) 2021, *High-Level Eurasian Seminar* Rome (Italy) 2019, *International Conference on Key Principles of Creation of National Systems of Identification and Traceability of Farm Livestock* Moscow (Russia) 2014.
Members Member States (5):
Armenia, Belarus, Kazakhstan, Kyrgyzstan, Russia.
Consultative Status Consultative status granted from: *World Intellectual Property Organization (WIPO, #21593).* **IGO Relations** Memorandum of Understanding with: *World Customs Organization (WCO, #21350).* [2017.08.04/XM4174/**E***]

♦ Eurasianet (internationally oriented national body)
♦ EurAsian Geophysical Society (internationally oriented national body)

♦ **Eurasian Group on Combating Money Laundering and Financing of Terrorism (EAG)** **05608**

Exec Sec 31/1 Staromeonetniy per., Moscow MOSKVA, Russia, 119017. T. +74959503332. Fax +74959503332. E-mail: info@eurasiangroup.org.
URL: http://www.eurasiangroup.org/

History 6 Oct 2004, Moscow (Russia). Established as a FATF-style regional body for the countries of the Eurasian region. Founding conference attended by six founding countries: Belarus, Kazakhstan, China, Kyrgyzstan, Russia and Tajikistan. In 2005 and 2010 the group was expanded to include Uzbekistan (2005), Turkmenistan (2010) and India (2010) which previously had observer status. **Aims** Ensure effective interaction and cooperation at regional level and integration of EAG Member States into the international system of anti-money laundering and combating financing of terrorism in accordance with the Recommendations of the FATF and the anti-money laundering and combating financing of terrorism standards of other international organizations, to which EAG Member States are party. **Structure** Plenary (twice a year); Working Groups (3); Secretariat located in Moscow (Russia). **Languages** Chinese, English, Russian. **Staff** 13.00 FTE, paid. **Activities** Events/meetings; guidance/assistance/consulting; monitoring/evaluation; projects/programmes; research/documentation; standards/guidelines; training/education. Active in all member countries. **Events** *Plenary Meeting* Moscow (Russia) 2020, *Plenary Meeting* Ashgabat (Turkmenistan) 2019, *Plenary Meeting* Moscow (Russia) 2019, *Plenary Meeting* Minsk (Belarus) 2018, *Plenary Meeting* Nanjing (China) 2018. **Publications** *EAG Bulletin*. Mutual evaluation reports; typologies reports; press releases.
Members Governments of 9 countries:
Belarus, China, India, Kazakhstan, Kyrgyzstan, Russia, Tajikistan, Turkmenistan, Uzbekistan.
Observers governments of 15 countries:
Afghanistan, Armenia, France, Germany, Iran Islamic Rep, Italy, Korea Rep, Moldova, Mongolia, Montenegro, Poland, Serbia, Türkiye, Ukraine, USA.
Organizations (23):
– *Asian Development Bank (ADB, #01422);*
– *Asia/Pacific Group on Money Laundering (APG, #01921);*
– Bureau for the Coordination of the Fight against Organized Crime (BCBOP);
– *Central Asian Regional Information and Coordination Centre for Combating Illicit Trafficking of Narcotic Drugs, Psychotropic Substances and Their Precursors (CARICC, #03683);*
– *Collective Security Treaty Organization (CSTO, #04103);*
– *Committee of Experts on the Evaluation of Anti-Money Laundering Measures and the Financing of Terrorism (MONEYVAL, #04257);*
– *Commonwealth of Independent States Anti-Terrorism Center (CIS ATC, #04342);*
– *Commonwealth of Independent States (CIS, #04341)* (Executive Committee);
– Counter-Terrorism Committee (UN CTC);
– *Egmont Group of Financial Intelligence Units (#05396);*
– *Eurasian Development Bank (EDB, #05605);*
– *Eurasian Economic Union (EAEU, #05607)* (Eurasian Economic Commission);
– *European Bank for Reconstruction and Development (EBRD, #06315);*
– *Financial Action Task Force (FATF, #09765);*
– *International Bank for Reconstruction and Development (IBRD, #12317)* (World Bank);
– *International Criminal Police Organization – INTERPOL (ICPO-INTERPOL, #13110);*
– *International Monetary Fund (IMF, #14180);*
– *Middle East and North Africa Financial Action Task Force (MENAFATF, #16779);*
– *New Development Bank (NDB, #17081);*
– *Organization for Security and Cooperation in Europe (OSCE, #17887);*
– *Shanghai Cooperation Organization (SCO, #19256);*
– United Nations Analytical Support and Sanctions Monitoring Team;
– *United Nations Office on Drugs and Crime (UNODC, #20596).*
IGO Relations Observer status with (5): *Asia/Pacific Group on Money Laundering (APG, #01921); Committee of Experts on the Evaluation of Anti-Money Laundering Measures and the Financing of Terrorism (MONEYVAL, #04257); Egmont Group of Financial Intelligence Units (#05396); Middle East and North Africa Financial Action Task Force (MENAFATF, #16779); United Nations (UN, #20515)* (General Assembly). Member of (1): *Financial Action Task Force (FATF, #09765)* (as an Associate Member). [2023.02.26/XM1039/y/**F***]

♦ **Eurasian Harm Reduction Association (EHRA)** **05609**

Eurzaijos Zalos Mazinimo Asociacijos

Exec Dir Verkiu g 34B, office 701, LT-08221 Vilnius, Lithuania. T. +37062010630. E-mail: info@harmreductioneurasia.org.
Events Officer address not obtained. E-mail: irena@harmreductioneurasia.org.
URL: https://harmreductioneurasia.org/

History Set up 2017. Successor to *Eurasian Harm Reduction Network (EHRN, inactive)*. Current statutes signed 27 Nov 2017. EU Transparency Register: 932938331141-28. **Aims** Create in Central and Eastern Europe and Central Asia (CEECA) region a favourable environment for sustainable harm reduction programmes and decent lives of people who use drugs. **Structure** General Assembly; Steering Committee; Secretariat; Executive Director. **Languages** English, Russian. **Staff** 13.00 FTE, paid. **Activities** Knowledge management/information dissemination; training/education; advocacy/lobbying/activism; events/meetings; research/documentation. **Events** *European Harm Reduction Conference* Prague (Czechia) 2021. **Publications** Guides.

Members Full (251) in 26 countries:
Albania, Armenia, Belarus, Bosnia-Herzegovina, Bulgaria, Croatia, Czechia, Estonia, Georgia, Hungary, Kazakhstan, Kosovo, Kyrgyzstan, Latvia, Lithuania, Moldova, Montenegro, North Macedonia, Poland, Romania, Russia, Serbia, Slovakia, Slovenia, Tajikistan, Ukraine.
NGO Relations *International Network of People who Use Drugs (INPUD, #14301).* [2019.02.20/XM6968/**D**]

♦ Eurasian Institute of Certified Public Accountants (EICPA) 05610

Global Office Seifullin av 597A, Office 703, Almaty, Kazakhstan, 050000. T. +77272501889. Fax +77272543920. E-mail: info@cpaeurasia.org.
URL: http://cpaeurasia.org/
History Replaced *Eurasian Council of Certified Accountants and Auditors (ECCAA).* **Aims** Develop the professions of accountants and auditors; promote high professional standards and international financial reporting standards (IFRS). **Structure** Board; Executive Director. **Languages** Russian. **Staff** 1.00 FTE, paid. **Finance** Members' dues; certificate fees.
Members Chambers of professional accountants and auditors in 5 countries:
Kazakhstan, Kyrgyzstan, Tajikistan, Ukraine, Uzbekistan.
NGO Relations Affiliated with: *International Federation of Accountants (IFAC, #13335).* [2020/XJ8731/**D**]

♦ Eurasian International Development Association (no recent information)

♦ Eurasian Media Forum Foundation (EAMF) 05611

Contact 13 Republic Square, Office 504, Almaty, Kazakhstan, 050013. T. +77272506504. Fax +77272506505.
History 2001, Kazakhstan. Founded on the initiative of Dariga Nazarbayeva. **Aims** Facilitate professional development of Eurasian media; promote international understanding of Eurasian issues; provide a platform for discussion on the role and place of the Eurasian continent on global development and peace building processes; build new partnerships. **Languages** English, Kazakh, Russian. **Events** *Annual Conference / Annual Forum* Astana (Kazakhstan) 2015, *Annual Conference / Annual Forum* Astana (Kazakhstan) 2014, *Annual Conference / Annual Forum* Astana (Kazakhstan) 2013, *Annual Conference / Annual Forum* Astana (Kazakhstan) 2012, *Annual Conference / Annual Forum* Almaty (Kazakhstan) 2010. **IGO Relations** *NATO (#16945).* **NGO Relations** Partners include: *EastWest Institute (EWI, #05264); International Academy of Television Arts and Sciences (IATAS).* [2020/XJ3113/f/**F**]

♦ Eurasian Network of People Who Use Drugs (unconfirmed)
♦ Eurasian Patent Convention (1994 treaty)

♦ Eurasian Patent Office (EAPO) 05612

Office eurasien des brevets – Eurasische Patentamt – Evraziiskoe patentnoe vedomstvo (EAPV)
Pres 2 Maly Cherkassky per, Moscow MOSKVA, Russia, 109012. T. +74954116161. Fax +74956212423. E-mail: info@eapo.org.
URL: http://www.eapo.org/
History 12 Aug 1995, Moscow (Russia). Founded within the framework of *Eurasian Patent Organization (EAPO, #05613).* First patent applications officially filed 1 Jan 1996. Accountable to the Administrative Council of the Organization, the Office being both the Organization's executive body and its secretariat. Relevant convention: *Eurasian Patent Convention (1994).* 9 Sep 2019, adoption and signature of Protocol to the Eurasian Patent Convention on the Protection of Industrial Designs, Nur-Sultan (Kazakhstan). New regional system of the legal protection of industrial designs created by the Protocol on the basis of EAPO. First Eurasian industrial design applications filed 1 June 2021. **Aims** Provide a uniform application procedure for physical and legal persons to protect their inventions and industrial designs on the basis of a single Eurasian patent valid in the territory of the states party to the Eurasian Patent Convention (EAPC, patent for invention) and Protocol to the Eurasian Patent Convention on the Protection of Industrial Designs (indistrial design patent). **Structure** Departments (11). **Languages** Russian. **Finance** Self-financing through fees for: filing of Eurasian applications; examination; Eurasian patent grant and publication; maintenance of Eurasian patents; registration and certification of Eurasian patent attorneys. Other sources: additional fees; revenue from services rendered. **Activities** Certification/accreditation.
Members Contracting parties to the Eurasian Patent Convention (8):
Armenia, Azerbaijan, Belarus, Kazakhstan, Kyrgyzstan, Russia, Tajikistan, Turkmenistan.
IGO Relations Cooperates with (5): *African Intellectual Property Organization (#00344); African Regional Intellectual Property Organization (ARIPO, #00434); European Patent Office (EPO, #08166); European Union Intellectual Property Office (EUIPO, #08996); World Intellectual Property Organization (WIPO, #21593).* **NGO Relations** Cooperates with (1): *International Association for the Protection of Intellectual Property (#12112).* [2022.12.02/XD6971/**E***]

♦ Eurasian Patent Organization (EAPO) 05613

Secretariat 2 Maly Cherkassky per, Moscow MOSKVA, Russia, 109012. T. +74954116161. Fax +74956212423. E-mail: info@eapo.org.
URL: http://www.eapo.org/index_eng.html
History 12 Aug 1995. Established following signature of *Eurasian Patent Convention (1994)* signed 9 Sep 1994, Moscow (Russia). *Administrative Council of the Eurasian Patent Organization* first met in extraordinary session on 2 Oct 1995, Geneva (Switzerland). Rules of procedure of the Administrative Council and by-laws of the Organization adopted at first full meeting of the Council, 30 Nov – 1 Dec 1995, Moscow. Membership of the Convention is open to any state which is member of the United Nations and signatory to *Paris Convention for the Protection of Industrial Property, 1883 (1883)* and *Patent Cooperation Treaty (PCT, 1970).* **Aims** Establish an inter-state system for protection of inventions in the territory of the former USSR; perform the administrative tasks associated with the functioning of the system and granting of single Eurasian patents. **Structure** Administrative Council (meets in ordinary session annually), comprises Chairman, 2 Deputy Chairmen, a plenipotentiary representative (head of the national patent office) and a deputy representative of each contracting state. Sessions are attended by representatives of WIPO, who have the deliberative vote and, on invitation, by (non-voting) observers from other international organizations or states. Council: appoints President of *Eurasian Patent Office (EAPO, #05612);* recommends appointment of its Vice-Presidents; organizes permanent and ad hoc working groups 'in the practice of the Administrative Council', including Budget Working Group. The Office is both the executive body and the secretariat of the Organization. Headquarters are in Moscow (Russia), as defined in an agreement between the Organization and the Government of the Russian Federation, signed 4 Oct 1996, in force 15 Apr 1998. **Languages** Russian. **Finance** Office is self-financing through fees and revenue for services rendered. **Activities** Politics/policy/regulatory; standards/guidelines. **Events** *Administrative Council Extraordinary Meeting* Moscow (Russia) 2021, *Annual Meeting* Moscow (Russia) 2014, *Seminar on Protection of Intellectual Property* Chisinau (Moldova) 2013, *Annual Meeting* Moscow (Russia) 2013. **Publications** Annual Report; conference proceedings.
Members Contracting parties to the Eurasian Patent Convention, governments of 8 countries:
Armenia, Azerbaijan, Belarus, Kazakhstan, Kyrgyzstan, Russia, Tajikistan, Turkmenistan.
IGO Relations Permanent observer status with: *World Intellectual Property Organization (WIPO, #21593).* [2022.02.15/XD6732/**D***]

♦ Eurasian Regional Association of Zoos and Aquariums (EARAZA) .. 05614

Exec Dir Moscow Zoo, B Gruzinskaya 1, Moscow MOSKVA, Russia, 123242. T. +74992556364. Fax +74992556364. E-mail: earazazoos@yandex.ru.
URL: http://www.earaza.ru/
History Founded 1994. **Aims** Promote and strengthen cooperation in the professional activities of zoological institutions of the former Soviet Union. **Structure** Presidium; Executive Office; EARAZA Zoo Information Center (ZIC) serves as advisory office; Working Groups (8). **Languages** English, Russian. **Staff** 3.00 FTE, paid. **Finance** Sources: members' dues. Annual budget: 3,000,000 RUB (2020). **Activities** Events/meetings; knowledge management/information dissemination; research/documentation; training/education. **Publications** *Birds of Prey and Owls in Zoos and Breeding Stations* (annual); *EARAZA Informational Issue* (annual) in Russian; *Scientific Research in Zoological Gardens* (annual). Conference proceedings. Information Services: Database of all animal species included in international and European studbooks. **Members** Full (68); Associate (20); Candidate (9). Members in 22 countries. Membership countries not specified. **NGO Relations** Also links with other zoos and zoological institutions of East Europe. [2021.06.30/XJ3562/**D**]

♦ Eurasian Regional Branch of the International Council on Archives (see: #12996)
♦ Eurasian Student Association / see International Organization for Promoting Public Diplomacy, Science, Education and Youth Cooperation (#14464)
♦ Eurasian Sugar Assocation (unconfirmed)

♦ Eurasian Universities Union (EURAS) 05615

Avrasya Üniversiteler Birligi
Organizational Advancement Besyol Mah, Inonu Cad No 38, Istanbul/Istanbul, Türkiye. T. +902124116168. E-mail: pinarelbasan@euras-edu.org.
URL: http://www.euras-edu.org/
History 2008. **Aims** Connect universities and higher education institutions belonging to different geo-political and cultural backgrounds; seek ways to enhance their dialogue and exchange of best practices. **Structure** General Assembly; Executive Board. **Languages** English, Turkish. **Activities** Events/meetings; training/education. **Events** *EURIE : Eurasia International Higher Education Summit* Istanbul (Turkey) 2020, *EURIE : Eurasia International Higher Education Summit* Istanbul (Turkey) 2019, *EURIE : Eurasia International Higher Education Summit* Istanbul (Turkey) 2018, *EURIE : Eurasia International Higher Education Summit* Istanbul (Turkey) 2016, *Regional Conference* Istanbul (Turkey) 2015. **Publications** *EURAS Academic Journal.* **Members** Universities (over 120) in over 50 countries. Membership countries not specified. [2020.03.03/XM4279/**D**]

♦ Eurasian Women's Forum (meeting series)
♦ Eurasia Partnership Foundation / see Europe Foundation (#09158)
♦ Eurasia Reiyukai (unconfirmed)
♦ EURASICA – Eurasian Regional Branch of the International Council on Archives (see: #12996)
♦ EURASIP / see European Association for Signal Processing (#06205)
♦ **EURASIP** European Association for Signal Processing (#06205)
♦ Eurasische Patentamt (#05612)
♦ **EURASLIC** European Association of Aquatic Sciences Libraries and Information Centres (#05939)
♦ **EURASNET** European Alternative Splicing Network (#05892)
♦ EURASYP – European Association for Specialty Yeast Products (unconfirmed)
♦ EURATEX / see EURATEX – The European Apparel and Textile Confederation (#05616)
♦ **EURATEX** EURATEX – The European Apparel and Textile Confederation (#05616)

♦ EURATEX – The European Apparel and Textile Confederation (EURATEX) 05616

Contact Rue Belliard 40, Bte 2, 1040 Brussels, Belgium. T. +3222854883. E-mail: info@euratex.eu.
URL: http://www.euratex.eu/
History 1 Jan 1996, by merger of *European Clothing Association (ECLA, inactive), Comité de coordination des industries textiles de la Communauté européenne (COMITEXTIL, inactive)* and *European Largest Textile and Apparel Companies (ELTAC, inactive). Committee of the Wool Textile Industries in the EEC (inactive)* merged into EURATEX, Jan 2008. Previously also referred to as *European Apparel and Textile Organization (EURATEX) – Organisation européenne de l'habillement et du textile.* Registration: EU Transparency Register, No/ID: 7824139202-85; Belgium. **Aims** Promote competitiveness and sustainable growth of industrial T and C pipelines in Europe by promoting interests of the industry towards European and international institutions. **Structure** General Assembly; Board of Directors; Management Team. **Languages** English. **Staff** 9.00 FTE, paid. **Finance** Members' dues. **Activities** Research and development; events/meetings. Library. **Events** *Convention* Porto (Portugal) 2022, *TEXAPP Project Final Conference* Brussels (Belgium) 2018, *Convention* Valencia (Spain) 2018, *ETP Annual Conference* Brussels (Belgium) 2017, *Personal Protective Equipment Conference* Brussels (Belgium) 2017. **Publications** *EURATEX Bulletin* (4 a year). **Information Services** *Centre d'Informations Textile-Habillement (CITH).*
Members Full in 19 countries:
Austria, Belgium, Bulgaria, Croatia, Denmark, Finland, France, Germany, Greece, Hungary, Italy, Lithuania, Poland, Portugal, Slovenia, Spain, Switzerland, Türkiye, UK.
Included in the above, 5 organizations listed in this Yearbook:
Association internationale des utilisateurs de fils de filaments artificiels et synthétiques et de soie naturelle (AIUFFASS, #02750); CIRFS – European Man-made Fibres Association (#03944); EDANA, the voice of non-wovens (EDANA, #05353); European Federation of Cotton and Allied Textiles Industries (#07093); Fédération européenne des industries de corderie ficellerie et de filets (EUROCORD, #09573).
Associated/corresponding members in 5 countries:
Belarus, Belgium, Egypt, Germany, Serbia.
Included in the above, 2 organizations listed in this Yearbook:
European Carpet and Rug Association (ECRA, #06452); European Textile Services Association (ETSA, #08904).
Consultative Status Consultative status granted from: *ECOSOC (#05331)* (Ros C); *UNCTAD (#20285)* (Special Category). **IGO Relations** In role of replacing COMITEXTIL, recognized by: *European Commission (EC, #06633).* Cooperates with: *European Union Intellectual Property Office (EUIPO, #08996).* Observer to: *OSPAR Commission for the Protection of the Marine Environment of the North-East Atlantic (OSPAR Commission, #17905).* **NGO Relations** In role of replacing COMITEXTIL, in liaison with technical committees of: *International Organization for Standardization (ISO, #14473).* Member of: *Alliance for a Competitive European Industry (ACEI, #00670); European Platform for Chemicals Using Manufacturing Industries (CheMI, #08223); Industry4Europe (#11181); International Apparel Federation (IAF, #11659).* Cooperates with: *Groupement International de l'Etiquetage pour l'Entretien des Textiles (GINETEX, #10761).* [2020/XE2137/y/**D**]

♦ Euratom Apgades Agentura (#05617)
♦ Euratom Ellatasi Ügynökség (#05617)
♦ Euratom – European Atomic Energy Community (inactive)
♦ Euratomin Hankintakeskus (#05617)
♦ Euratomi Tarneagentuur (#05617)
♦ Euratomo Tiekimo Agentura (#05617)
♦ Euratoms Försörjningsbyrå (#05617)
♦ Euratoms Forsyningsagentur (#05617)

♦ Euratom Supply Agency (ESA) 05617

Agence d'approvisionnement d'Euratom – Agencia de Abastecimiento de Euratom – Euratom-Versorgungsagentur – Agência de Aprovisionamento da Euratom – Agenzia di Approvvigionamento dell'Euratom – Voorzieningsagentschap van Euratom – Euratoms Försörjningsbyrå – Euratoms Forsyningsagentur – Euratomin Hankintakeskus – Zasobovaci Agentura Euratomu – Zasobovacia Agentúra Euratomu – Euratom Ellatasi Ügynökség – Agencja Dostaw Euratomu – Agencija za Oskrbo Euratom – Euratomi Tarneagentuur – Euratom Apgades Agentura – Euratomo Tiekimo Agentura – Agenzija Ghall-Provvista ta' l-Euratom – Gniomhaireacht Solathair Euratom – Agentia de Aprovizionare a Euratom – Agencija Euratoma za Opskrbu
Head Office Complexe Euroforum, Rue Henri Schnadt 1, L-2530 Luxembourg, Luxembourg. E-mail: esa-aae@ec.europa.eu.
Website: https://euratom-supply.ec.europa.eu/index_en
History 1957, Rome (Italy). Established by *Treaty Establishing the European Atomic Energy Community (Treaty of Rome, 1957)* which set up *European Atomic Energy Community (Euratom, inactive).* Operative since 1 June 1960. Current Statutes established 12 Feb 2008 by *Council of the European Union (#04895)* decision. **Aims** Ensure a regular and equitable supply of nuclear materials (ores, source material and special fissile material) for all users in the European Atomic Energy Community; pursue the objective of long, medium and short term security of supply of nuclear materials, particularly nuclear fuel, for power and non-power uses, by means of the common supply policy. **Structure** Has legal personality and financial autonomy. Governance is defined in the statutes laid down by *Council of the European Union (#04895).* Acts under the supervision of *European Commission (EC, #06633),* which: adopts budget; appoints Director-General; issues directives; possesses the right of veto. Advisory Committee comprises 58 representatives of EU member states, nuclear materials producers and users. The Agency comes within the area of competence of *European Court of Auditors (#06854),* the Courts of First Instance and of Justice and other institutions of *European Union (EU, #08967).* **Languages** EU languages. **Staff** 17.00 FTE, paid. **Finance** Sources: international organizations. Supported by: *European Union (EU, #08967).* Annual budget: 228,000 EUR (2023).

Activities Politics/policy/regulatory. 1. Ensuring short, medium future supply: Ensure regular and equal access to supplies of nuclear materials for all users in the *European Atomic Energy Community (Euratom, inactive)*. To this end, it uses its right of option on nuclear materials produced in the Euratom Community Member States and its exclusive right to conclude contracts for supply of nuclear materials, coming from inside or outside the Community and it monitors transactions related to services in the nuclear fuel cycle.
Management of contracts on nuclear materials and/or services in the nuclear fuel cycle encompass:
– concluding nuclear materials and fuel supply contracts, pursuant to Article 52 of the Euratom Treaty;
– acknowledging notifications of contracts for supply of small quantities of nuclear materials and of transactions related to the provision of services in the nuclear fuel cycle, pursuant to Articles 74 and 75 of the Euratom Treaty respectively.
The Agency checks that contracts are compatible with provisions and objectives of the Euratom Treaty and with the Community's supply policy and that they comply with international obligations of the European Community. To ensure long term supply, ESA aims to prevent excessive dependence of Community users on any single external supplier, service provider or design through appropriate diversification.
The Commission agreement is required for exports of nuclear materials produced in the Community (under Article 59) and for supply contracts of more than 10 years duration (by virtue of Article 60 and 62).
If the Agency refuses a contract, this decision may be referred to the European Commission, whose decision may be challenged before *Court of Justice of the European Union (CJEU, #04938)*.
The Advisory Committee is consulted on all major policy issues of relevance to the Agency's area of work and on its annual report and budgetary matters. It acts as a link between the Agency and producer and user industries and as a forum for discussion and for formulation of advice on nuclear supply and trade matters.
2. Monitoring of developments in the nuclear fuel market:
ESA has a market observatory role and a duty to provide the Euratom Community with expertise, information and advice on any subject connected with the operation of the nuclear market. To this end, ESA monitors the market in order to identify trends likely to affect the Union's security of supply of nuclear materials and services. It aims to provide a wide range of information on nuclear market developments, as well as making reports on the EU market, average prices, total supply and demand etc. available to the public.
3. Monitoring of (and contribution to) the secure supply of medical radioisotopes:
Leads the actions towards securing the supply of source materials for the radioisotopes production, thus actively contributing to the European Commission's Strategic Agenda for Medical Ionising Radiation Applications (SAMIRA). The Agency undertakes measures to ensure security of supply of high-enriched uranium (HEU) and high-assay low-enriched uranium (HALEU) that are required to feed the production of medical radioisotopes and to fuel research reactors. ESA also monitors the production chain of medical radioisotopes through the European Observatory on the Supply of Medical Radioisotopes.
Publications *All Users Spot Uranium Price Index* (4 a year); *Spot Uranium Price Index type* (4 a year); *Uranium Market Report* (4 a year); *MAC-3 Uranium Price Index* (annual); *Multiannual Uranium Price Index* (annual). Annual Report.
Members Not a membership organization. All EU member states except Luxembourg and Malta participate in the Agency's capital and are represented on the Advisory Committee – governments of 25 countries:
Austria, Belgium, Bulgaria, Croatia, Cyprus, Czechia, Denmark, Estonia, Finland, France, Germany, Greece, Hungary, Ireland, Italy, Latvia, Lithuania, Netherlands, Poland, Portugal, Romania, Slovakia, Slovenia, Spain, Sweden.
[2022.10.11/XF1965/F*]

♦ Euratom-Versorgungsagentur (#05617)
♦ EURAU – European Symposium on Research in Architecture and Urban Design (meeting series)
♦ Eu-Ray European Association of Surface Heating and Cooling (#06241)
♦ EurBee European Association for Bee Research (#05952)
♦ EURBICA – European Regional Branch of the International Council on Archives (see: #12996)

♦ EURead 05618
Contact c/o Stiftung Lesen, Römerwall 40, 55131 Mainz, Germany. T. +4961312889090. Fax +496131230333. E-mail: joerg.maas@stiftunglesen.de.
URL: http://www.euread.com/
History 2000. Formal legal structure adopted, 2014. **Aims** Promote *reading*; exchange knowledge, experiences and concepts; jointly develop new strategies for the promotion of reading. **Structure** Annual General Meeting. **Languages** English. **Activities** Advocacy/lobbying/activism; awareness raising; events/meetings; projects/programmes; research/documentation. Global Network for Early Years Bookgifting. **Events** *Annual General Meeting* Brussels (Belgium) 2022, *Annual General Meeting* Brussels (Belgium) 2020, *Annual General Meeting* Brussels (Belgium) 2019, *Annual General Meeting* Brussels (Belgium) 2018.
Members Full in 22 countries and territories:
Austria, Belgium, Bulgaria, Czechia, Denmark, Finland, Germany, Greece, Hungary, Ireland, Italy, Lithuania, Malta, Netherlands, Norway, Poland, Portugal, Scotland, Spain, Switzerland, Türkiye, UK.
[2023.02.16/XM5163/F]

♦ EUREAU / see European Federation of National Associations of Water and Waste Water Services (#07170)
♦ EurEau Fédération européenne des associations nationales de services d'eau et assainissement (#07170)

♦ EUREC 05619
SG Place du champs de Mars 2, 1050 Brussels, Belgium. T. +3223184051. E-mail: info@eurec.be.
URL: http://www.eurec.be/
History 1991. Founded as a grouping of the type *European Economic Interest Grouping (EEIG, #06960)*. Former names and other names: *EUREC – Association of European Renewable Energy Research Centres* – full title; *European Renewable Energy Centres Agency (EUREC Agency)* – former (1991). Registration: EU Transparency Register, No/ID: 8156981516-21. **Aims** Identify research needs and enable R and D for innovative and integrated renewable energy solutions; promote sound policy making in renewable energy R and D; enable innovation and technology transfer by connecting research and industry through projects development; promote development of a highly qualified and trained workforce for the renewable energy sector; support international R and D cooperation in renewable energy. **Structure** Board of Management; Policy Contact Group; Steering Committee for European Master in Renewable Energy; Secretariat. **Languages** English. **Staff** 5.00 FTE, paid. **Finance** Members' dues. Other sources: co-funding from EU projects; fees related to European Master in Renewable Energy and European Master in Sustainable Energy System Management. **Activities** Research and development; training/education; knowledge management/information dissemination. **Events** *Workshop on Sustainability and Circularity in Renewable Energy Technology* Brussels (Belgium) 2022, *Rescuing Europe from energy dependency* Brussels (Belgium) 2019, *Workshop on Myths and Realities of Renewable Energies* Brussels (Belgium) 2019, *European Conference on the Role of Renewables* Brussels (Belgium) 2014, *European Workshop on LCA for Algal Biofuels* Brussels (Belgium) 2014.
Members Research and Development groups (41) in 15 countries:
Austria, Belgium, Finland, France, Germany, Greece, Italy, Netherlands, Portugal, Romania, Spain, Sweden, Switzerland, Türkiye, UK.
IGO Relations Cooperates with: *Group on Earth Observations (GEO, #10735)*. **NGO Relations** Member of: *European Alliance for Innovation (EAI, #05872)*; *Energy Materials Industrial Research Initiative (EM-IRI, #05472)*; *European Technology and Innovation Platform Photovoltaics (ETIP PV, #08884)*; *Knowledge4Innovation (K4I, #16198)*. Instrumental in setting up: *European Technology and Innovation Platform for Photovoltaics (ETIP PV, #08883)*; *European Technology Platform on Renewable Heating and Cooling (RHC-Platform, #08891)*.
[2020/XE2728/E]

♦ EurECA European Educators' Christian Association (#06968)
♦ EUREC Agency / see EUREC (#05619)
♦ EURECA-PRO European University on Responsible Consumption and Production (#09035)
♦ EUREC – Association of European Renewable Energy Research Centres / see EUREC (#05619)
♦ EurECCA European Cabin Crew Association (#06428)
♦ EUREC European Network of Research Ethics Committees (#07988)
♦ EURECO European Association for Knowledge Economy (#06101)
♦ Eurefap (no recent information)
♦ EUREFAS European Refurbishment Association (#08340)
♦ EUREF European Reference Organization for Quality Assured Breast Screening and Diagnostic Services (#08338)

♦ EUREF Permanent Network (EPN) 05620
Head Royal Observatory of Belgium, Av Circulaire 3, 1180 Brussels, Belgium. T. +3223730292. Fax +3223749822. E-mail: epncb@oma.be.
URL: http://epncb.oma.be/
History Set up Oct 1995, by EUREF, the Reference Frame Sub-Commission for Europe of *International Association of Geodesy (IAG, #11914)*. Originally based on a partnership with site operators of continuously operating GNSS sites, but currently a well-defined organization. **Aims** Maintain and provide access to: European Terrestrial Reference System 89 (ETRS89), used as the standard precise GNSS coordinate system throughout Europe for all *geo-referencing* activities (INSPIRE); several multi-disciplinary applications such as monitoring of the troposphere and ground deformations. **Structure** Coordination Group; Permanent GNSS stations; Operational Centres; Local Data Centres; Regional Data Centers; Real-time Broadcasters; Local Analyses Centres; Product coordinators. **Languages** English. **Staff** 14.00 FTE, paid. **Finance** National funding. **Activities** Monitoring/evaluation. **Events** *Annual Symposium* Gothenburg (Sweden) 2023, *Annual Symposium* Zagreb (Croatia) 2022, *Annual Symposium* Ljubljana (Slovenia) 2021, *Annual symposium* Tallinn (Estonia) 2019, *Annual Symposium* Amsterdam (Netherlands) 2018. **Publications** Articles.
[2014.06.01/XJ2491/E]

♦ EUREG – European Association for Interregional Cooperation (no recent information)
♦ EUREGHA European Regional and Local Health Authorities (#08344)
♦ EUREGIO (internationally oriented national body)
♦ Euregionales Netzwerk für Patientensicherheit und Infektionsschutz (internationally oriented national body)

♦ Eureka Association (Eureka) 05621
Head Secretariat Avenue de Tervueren 2, 1040 Brussels, Belgium. T. +3227770950. Fax +3227707495. E-mail: info@eurekanetwork.org.
URL: http://www.eurekanetwork.org/
History 29 Apr 1985, Paris (France). *EUREKA Initiative* launched Jul 1985. Agreement signed 30 Jun 1986, London (UK). Ultimate objective is of forming a *Technological Community* or *European Technological Area*. Former names and other names: *EUREKA Organization* – former; *Organisation EUREKA* – former; *Eureka Network – innovation beyond borders* – full title. Registration: Banque-Carrefour des Entreprises, No/ID: 0429.585.680, Start date: 21 Oct 1986, Belgium; EU Transparency Register, No/ID: 978266733477-05, Start date: 4 Jan 2019. **Aims** Foster cooperative projects in research and innovation. **Structure** Ministerial Conference (annual), comprising one minister from each member country and commissioner from *European Commission (EC, #06633)*. High Level Group (HLG); Executive Group. National Project Coordinators (NPCs). National Information Points (NIPs). Secretariat (ESE). **Languages** English. **Staff** 16.00 FTE, paid. **Finance** Sources: contributions of member/participating states. **Activities** Projects/programmes. **Events** *Global Innovation Summit* Estoril (Portugal) 2022, *Innovation Week Meeting* Helsinki (Finland) 2018, *Digital Innovation Forum* Amsterdam (Netherlands) 2017, *EURIPIDES Annual Forum* Stockholm (Sweden) 2016, *Innovation Week Meeting* Stockholm (Sweden) 2016. **Publications** *EUREKA News* (2 a year) – magazine. Project promotion sheets; brochures; folders; CD-Rom. **Information Services** *EUREKA Database* – comprising publicly available information on all EUREKA projects and proposals provided by the National Project Coordinators.
Members Participating countries (41):
Austria, Belgium, Bulgaria, Canada, Croatia, Cyprus, Czechia, Denmark, Estonia, Finland, France, Germany, Greece, Hungary, Iceland, Ireland, Israel, Italy, Korea Rep, Latvia, Lithuania, Luxembourg, Malta, Monaco, Netherlands, North Macedonia, Norway, Poland, Portugal, Romania, Russia, San Marino, Serbia, Slovakia, Slovenia, Spain, Sweden, Switzerland, Türkiye, UK, Ukraine.
Participating regional integration EU entity (1):
European Commission (EC, #06633).
National Information Points in 2 countries:
Albania, Bosnia-Herzegovina.
NGO Relations Member of (1): *Knowledge4Innovation (K4I, #16198)*. Partner of (1): *Inside Industry Association (Inside, #11230)*. In cooperation with technical committees of: *Comité européen de normalisation (CEN, #04162)*.
[2022/XF0279/F*]

♦ Eureka Eureka Association (#05621)
♦ Eureka Network – innovation beyond borders / see Eureka Association (#05621)
♦ EUREKA Organization / see Eureka Association (#05621)
♦ EUREL – Association européenne des réserves naturelles libres (inactive)
♦ EUREL / see Convention of National Associations of Electrical Engineers of Europe (#04788)
♦ EUREL Convention of National Associations of Electrical Engineers of Europe (#04788)

♦ EUREL Network 05622
Dir UMR 7354 DRES, 5 allée du Général Rouvillois, 67083 Strasbourg CEDEX, France. T. +33368856109. E-mail: eurel@misha.cnrs.fr.
URL: https://www.eurel.info/
History 2003, Strasbourg (France). EUREL stands for *EURope RELigion*, as a website of information on the legal and sociological status of religion, published by a group of expert members of a scientific network. **Aims** Provide accurate and up-to-date information on the social and legal status of *religion* in *Europe* from an *interdisciplinary* perspective, intended for the international scientific community, public authorities and political forces; gather comparative information concerning the enlarged Europe (EU member states, candidate countries and other European countries) and non-European countries. **Structure** Carried out by a joint research centre of the "Centre national de la recherche scientifique (CNRS)", the University of Strasbourg (UMR 7354 DRES) and a research centre of PSL/"Ecole Pratique des Hautes Etudes" (GSRL, Paris). Gathers at least one correspondent for each of the participating countries. **Languages** English, French. **Staff** 2.00 FTE, paid; 35.00 FTE, voluntary. **Finance** Funded by CNRS, University of Strasbourg and PSL/Ecole Pratique des Hautes Etudes. Annual budget: 4,000 EUR (2022). **Activities** Knowledge management/information dissemination; research/documentation. **Events** *Colloque Biennal* Lausanne (Switzerland) 2023, *Colloque Biennal International* Porto (Portugal) 2021, *Colloque Biennal International* Porto (Portugal) 2020, *Colloque Biennal International* Oslo (Norway) 2018, *Colloque Biennal International* Luxembourg (Luxembourg) 2016. **Publications** *Eurel Newsletter* (2 a year); *News Flash*. *Nonreligion in Late Modern Societies* (2022) by Dr Anne-Laure Zwilling and Dr Helge Arsheim; *Religion and Prison: an Overview of Contemporary Europe* (2020).
Members Full in 33 countries:
Austria, Belgium, Bulgaria, Canada, Croatia, Cyprus, Czechia, Denmark, Estonia, Finland, France, Germany, Greece, Hungary, Ireland, Italy, Latvia, Lithuania, Luxembourg, Montenegro, Netherlands, Norway, Poland, Portugal, Romania, Russia, Slovakia, Slovenia, Spain, Sweden, Switzerland, Türkiye, UK.
[2022.05.05/XM5247/F]

♦ EurelPro – European Association of Pension Schemes for Liberal Professions (inactive)
♦ EUREMAIL – Conférence permanente de l'industrie européenne productrice d'articles émaillés (inactive)
♦ EURENEW – European Treaty on Renewable Energy (unconfirmed)
♦ EURepack – European Reusable Packaging and Reverse Logistics Consortium (unconfirmed)
♦ EUREPGAP / see GLOBALG.A.P (#10386)
♦ EUREPRO – International Association for Prepress Industry (inactive)
♦ EURES – European Group for Research on Spatial Problems (inactive)
♦ EUREs – European Reticulo-Endothelial Society (inactive)
♦ EurEta European Higher Engineering and Technical Professionals Association (#07484)
♦ EURETINA – European Retina, Macula and Vitreous Society / see EURETINA – European Society of Retina Specialists (#05623)

♦ EURETINA – European Society of Retina Specialists 05623
Europäische Gesellschaft für Netzhautspezialisten
Secretariat Temple House, Temple Road, Blackrock, Dublin, CO. DUBLIN, A94 Y5W5, Ireland. T. +35312100092. Fax +35312091112. E-mail: euretina@euretina.org.
SG Sackler Fac of Medicine, Tel Aviv Univ, PO Box 39040, 6997801 Tel Aviv, Israel.
URL: http://www.euretina.org/
History Jun 2000. Former names and other names: *EURETINA – European Retina, Macula and Vitreous Society* – former (Jun 2000 to May 2003). Registration: Germany. **Aims** Promote sharing of knowledge among European vitreoretinal and macula specialists over new diagnostic developments, advances in vitreoretinal surgery, new drugs, and changes in the treatment of macular degeneration; educate young vitreoretinal

surgeons and encourage the pursuit of its subspecialty among newly qualified ophthalmologists. **Structure** General Assembly (annual, during scientific meeting); Board; Executive Committee. **Languages** English. **Finance** Sources: members' dues; revenue from activities/projects; sponsorship. **Activities** Awards/prizes/competitions; events/meetings; financial and/or material support; training/education. **Events** *Annual Congress* Hamburg (Germany) 2022, *Annual Congress* 2021, *Winter Meeting* Vilnius (Lithuania) 2021, *Annual Congress* 2020, *Winter Meeting* Vilnius (Lithuania) 2020. **Publications** *Ophtalmological* – official journal. **Members** Active Individual (3,385) in 111 countries. Membership countries not specified. [2021.08.31/XD9265/v/**D**]

- ♦ **EUR** Europäische Union der Rechtspfleger (#09012)
- ♦ EurExcel – European Association of Innovating SMEs (unconfirmed)
- ♦ **EurHeCA** European Health professionals Competent Authorities (#07460)
- ♦ **EURH** Europäische Union der Richter in Handelssachen (#08998)
- ♦ **EURH** Europese Unie der Rechters in Handelszaken (#08998)

♦ EURHODIP 05624

Coordinator c/o Escuela Superior de Hosteleria de Seville, Camino de los Descubrimientos 2, 41092 Seville, Sevilla, Spain. T. +34673832519. E-mail: bruxelles@eurhodip.com.
Head Office c/o MAI, Rue Washington 40, 1050 Brussels, Belgium.
URL: http://www.eurhodip.com/

History 1988. Founded by 20 European hospitality schools. Full title: *European Hotel Diploma (EURHODIP)*. Current statutes, registered Feb 2007, Brussels (Belgium), and approved Nov 2007, Brussels. Registration: Banque-Carrefour des Entreprises, No/ID: 0889.338.263, Start date: 10 May 2007, Belgium; EU Transparency Register, No/ID: 273251838549-15, Start date: 12 Jun 2020. **Aims** Promote European hospitality and *tourism* education and training; provide services for continuous improvement of quality education in a global perspective. **Structure** General Assembly (at least every 2 years); Board of Directors; Executive Board. **Languages** English, French. **Finance** Sources: gifts, legacies; grants; meeting proceeds; members' dues. **Activities** Awards/prizes/competitions; events/meetings. **Events** *Annual Conference* Leeuwarden (Netherlands) 2021, *Annual Conference* Leeuwarden (Netherlands) 2020, *Annual Conference* Istanbul (Turkey) 2019, *Annual Conference* Porec (Croatia) 2018, *Annual Conference* Seville (Spain) 2017. **Publications** *Eurhodip Magazine* (annual). *White Paper on Euroformation* (2003). **Members** Members (130) in 35 countries. Membership countries not specified. **IGO Relations** Cooperates with (1): *European Commission (EC, #06633)*. **NGO Relations** Member of (1): *Federation of European and International Associations Established in Belgium (FAIB, #09508)*. [2021.05.19/XJ3640/**F**]

- ♦ **EURHO** European Rural History Organisation (#08414)
- ♦ EURIBOR-EBF / see European Money Markets Institute (#07819)
- ♦ **Euribron** Insurance Broker Network (#11361)
- ♦ **EuRIC** European Recycling Industries' Confederation (#08335)
- ♦ EURICOM – European Institute of Communication and Culture (internationally oriented national body)
- ♦ **EURICPA** European Intelligent Cash Protection Association (#07581)
- ♦ EURICSE – European Research Institute on Cooperative and Social Enterprises (internationally oriented national body)
- ♦ **EURid** European Registry of Internet Domain Names (#08351)
- ♦ EURIFI – European Association of Furniture Technology Institutes (inactive)
- ♦ **EURIMA** European Insulation Manufacturers Association (#07577)
- ♦ **EURIMAGES** European Support Fund for the Co-Production and Distribution of Creative Cinematographic and Audiovisual Works (#08859)
- ♦ Eurimages Support Fund / see European Support Fund for the Co-Production and Distribution of Creative Cinematographic and Audiovisual Works (#08859)
- ♦ Eurim – European Informatics Market (internationally oriented national body)
- ♦ EURINCAD – Fédération européenne des indépendants et des cadres (inactive)
- ♦ **EURING** European Union for Bird Ringing (#08979)
- ♦ EU-Rio Group Institutionalized Ministerial Meeting (inactive)
- ♦ EURIPA – European Information Providers' Association (inactive)
- ♦ **EURIPA** European Rural and Isolated Practitioners Association (#08415)
- ♦ EURISA – European Investment Services Association (inactive)
- ♦ EURISC – European Institute for Risk, Security and Communication Management (internationally oriented national body)
- ♦ EURISCOAL – European Importers and Suppliers of Coal (inactive)
- ♦ EURIS – European Union of Research Institutes for Shoes (no recent information)
- ♦ EURISOL / see European Insulation Manufacturers Association (#07577)
- ♦ EURISOL – European Federation of the Electro-Ceramic Industry (inactive)
- ♦ EURIST – European Institute for Sustainable Transport (internationally oriented national body)

♦ Eurisy 05625

SG 52 rue Jacques Hillariet, 75012 Paris, France. T. +33147348175. E-mail: eurisy@eurisy.org.
URL: http://www.eurisy.org/

History 23 May 1989, France, as *European Association for the International Space Year* on the initiative of Founder President, the late Hubert Curien. Subsequently known under full title of *Promotion of Education and Information Activities for the Advancement of Space Technology and its Applications in Europe (EURISY)*. Currently only known under acronym. Registered in accordance with French law. **Aims** Facilitate and support full access of society to the benefits of satellites; act collectively to bridge space and society; raise awareness and inform society about benefits of innovative *satellite* services; support emergent final user communities in their appropriation of satellite services; support integrated cooperation on a European level. **Structure** General Assembly (annual); Council; General Management; Secretariat, headed by Secretary-General. **Languages** English. **Finance** Members' dues. Other sources: grants; sponsorship. **Activities** Financial and/or material support; knowledge management/information dissemination; events/meetings. **Events** *Conference on Satellite Applications Enhancing of Life in Cities* Ghent (Belgium) 2018, *Conference on Valuing and Managing Biodiversity* Lille (France) 2012, *Workshop on Leisure and Sustainable Development on the Coast* Bergen (Norway) 2011, *Workshop on Tackling Socio-Economic Disparities Using Satellite Information and Services* Brussels (Belgium) 2010, *Conference on Local and Regional Authorities using Satellite Information and Services to Mitigate and Adapt to Climate Change* Ljubljana (Slovenia) 2010. **Publications** *Eurisy Newsletter* (3 a year). Brochure; position papers; reports.

Members Full; Associate. Members include most space agencies and government offices in charge of space affairs in Europe, and international organizations dealing with space matters. Full in 16 countries:
Austria, Belgium, Cyprus, Germany, Greece, Hungary, Ireland, Italy, Malta, Morocco, Netherlands, Norway, Poland, Romania, Türkiye, UK.

Included in the above, 1 organization listed in this Yearbook:
European Space Agency (ESA, #08798).

IGO Relations Cooperates with: *European Committee of the Regions (CoR, #06665)*; *Network of European Regions Using Space Technologies (NEREUS, #17029)*. Observer status with: *Committee on the Peaceful Uses of Outer Space (COPUOS, #04277)*. Partner of: *Group on Earth Observations (GEO, #10735)*. **NGO Relations** Cooperates with: *Assembly of European Regions (AER, #02316)*; *Association of European Border Regions (AEBR, #02499)*; *Council of European Municipalities and Regions (CEMR, #04891)*; *SMEunited (#19327)*; *European Association of Remote Sensing Companies (EARSC, #06190)*; *European Association of Remote Sensing Laboratories (EARSeL, #06191)*; *Global Satellite Operators' Association (GSOA, #10586)*; *Galileo Services (GS, #10064)*. Member of: *International Astronautical Federation (IAF, #12286)*. [2018.09.05/XD2644/y/**F**]

- ♦ **Euritas** European Association of Public IT Service Providers (#06179)
- ♦ **EURITS** European Union for Responsible Incineration and Treatment of Special Waste (#09013)
- ♦ **EURLSSG** European Restless Legs Syndrome Study Group (#08384)
- ♦ **Eurlyaid – EAECI** Eurlyaid – European Association on Early Childhood Intervention (#05626)
- ♦ Eurlyaid / see Eurlyaid – European Association on Early Childhood Intervention (#05626)

♦ Eurlyaid – European Association on Early Childhood Intervention (Eurlyaid – EAECI) 05626

Sec-Treas address not obtained. E-mail: info@eurlyaid.eu.
URL: http://www.eurlyaid.eu/

History 1989, Rotterdam (Netherlands), as *European Network on Early Intervention (Eurlyaid)*. Subsequently known as *European Association on Early Intervention (EAEI)*. Present name adopted, 2003. **Aims** Increase quality of life for parents and children with special needs through early childhood intervention; stimulate growth and development of early childhood intervention on a European level; increase sensitivity to the values and ethics of early childhood intervention. **Languages** English.

Members in 18 countries:
Austria, Belgium, Canada, Cyprus, Czechia, Finland, France, Germany, Greece, Ireland, Italy, Luxembourg, Netherlands, Norway, Portugal, Spain, Switzerland, UK. [2018.09.17/XF6246/**F**]

- ♦ EURMIG – European Union Recreational Marine Industry Group (inactive)
- ♦ EURNEX Association / see EUropean rail Research Network of EXcellence (#08326)
- ♦ **EURNEX** EUropean rail Research Network of EXcellence (#08326)
- ♦ Euro 11 / see Eurogroup (#05689)
- ♦ EurO3zon (unconfirmed)
- ♦ Euro8ball / see European 8-Ball Pool Federation (#05777)

♦ Euroacademia 05627

Office Via Don Giorgio Bigongiari 149, 55100 Lucca LU, Italy. T. +3958353199. E-mail: office@euroacademia.eu.
Brussels Office Rue Edmond Delcourt 41, 1070 Brussels, Belgium. T. +32488205596.
URL: http://euroacademia.eu/

History Registered in accordance with the laws of: France; Italy; Belgium; Austria. **Aims** Become a hub for *academic* interaction on and about *Europe*; provide the framework for constructive and inclusive cooperation, networking, project building and dissemination of information and research. **Structure** Advisory Board. **Activities** Events/meetings; networking/liaising; knowledge management/information dissemination. **Events** *International Conference on Re-Inventing Eastern Europe* Berlin (Germany) 2014.

Members Full in 35 countries and territories:
Albania, Armenia, Austria, Belgium, Croatia, Cyprus, Czechia, Egypt, Estonia, France, Georgia, Germany, Greece, Hungary, India, Israel, Italy, Lebanon, Luxembourg, Netherlands, North Macedonia, Northern Cyprus, Poland, Portugal, Romania, Russia, Serbia, Spain, Sweden, Switzerland, Taiwan, Türkiye, UK, Ukraine, USA. [2017/XM5113/**F**]

- ♦ Euroacademia Multidisciplinaria Neurotraumatologica (#05628)

♦ Euro-Academy of Multidisciplinary Neurotraumatology (EMN) 05628

Euroakademie für Multidisziplinäre Neurotraumatologie – Euroacademia Multidisciplinaria Neurotraumatologica (EMN)

Gen Sec Oberstarzt, Neurosurgery BWK Ulm, Oberer Eselsberg 40, 89081 Ulm, Germany. T. +4973117102200. Fax +4973117102205.
Pres Dept of Neurosurgery, Univ of Medicine and Pharmacy, 5K Colonia Borhanci Street, 400481 Cluj-Napoca, Romania.
URL: https://emn-neurotrauma.org/

History Registered in accordance with German law. **Aims** Advance neurotraumatology in research, practical application and teaching. **Structure** Executive Committee; Presidium; Advisory Board; Committees. **Languages** English. **Finance** Members' dues. **Activities** Events/meetings; training/education. **Events** *Annual Congress* Zagreb (Croatia) 2015, *Annual Congress* Ulm (Germany) 2014, *Annual Congress* St Petersburg (Russia) 2013, *Annual Congress* Cluj-Napoca (Romania) 2012, *Annual Congress* Newcastle upon Tyne (UK) 2011. **Publications** Books; manuals; abstracts in *European Journal of Trauma and Emergency Surgery*. **Members** Ordinary; corresponding. Membership countries not specified. **IGO Relations** None. [2019/XE4580/**E**]

- ♦ **EuroACE** European Alliance of Companies for Energy Efficiency in Buildings (#05865)
- ♦ **Euro-ACS** European Association of Curriculum Studies (#06001)
- ♦ EuroAction / see European Union of Deaf Youth (#08986)
- ♦ Euro Action – ACORD / see ACORD – Agency for Cooperation and Research in Development (#00073)
- ♦ EUROADBEAD – International Association of European Manufacturers of Glass Beads for Safety Road Markings and Other Industrial Purposes (inactive)
- ♦ EUROADSAFE – European Road Safety Equipment Federation (inactive)
- ♦ Euroadvocaten / see Globaladvocaten (#10173)
- ♦ Euro-African Management Research Centre (internationally oriented national body)
- ♦ Euro-African Management Research Consult / see Euro-African Management Research Centre
- ♦ EURO-AIM – European Association for an Audiovisual Independent Market (inactive)
- ♦ **EURO-AIR** European Association of Air Heater Manufacturers (#05933)
- ♦ Euroakademie für Multidisziplinäre Neurotraumatologie (#05628)

♦ Euroalliages 05629

SG Av de Tervuren 168, 1150 Brussels, Belgium. T. +3227756301. E-mail: euroalliages@euroalliages.be.
URL: http://www.euroalliages.com/

History 1 Jan 1993, Brussels (Belgium). Founded to take over activities of *Liaison Committee of Ferroalloy Industries in the European Economic Community (inactive)*, set up 1957. New statutes registered: Nov 1995; Sep 2005; Nov 2012. Former names and other names: *EUROALLIAGES – Association of European Ferro-Alloy Producers* – full title. Registration: Banque Carrefour des Entreprises, No/ID: 0448.969.547, Start date: 27 Nov 1992, Belgium; EU Transparency Register, No/ID: 19153965510-75, Start date: 17 Mar 2011. **Aims** Promote safe, environmentally friendly and competitive production of *ferro-alloys* and *silicon* in Europe. **Structure** General Assembly (annual); Board of Directors; Secretariat. **Languages** English, French. **Staff** 5.00 FTE, paid. **Finance** Sources: members' dues.

Members Companies/groups of companies (20) belonging to the European Economic Area (EEA), in 12 countries:
Belgium, Bosnia-Herzegovina, Finland, France, Germany, Iceland, North Macedonia, Norway, Poland, Slovakia, Spain, Sweden.

NGO Relations Member of (3): *AEGIS Europe*; *Association européenne des métaux (EUROMETAUX, #02578)*; *Industry4Europe (#11181)*. Instrumental in setting up (1): *European Silica Fume Committee (#08486)*. [2023.02.14/XD3671/**D**]

- ♦ EUROALLIAGES – Association of European Ferro-Alloy Producers / see Euroalliages (#05629)
- ♦ Euroamerica Foundation (internationally oriented national body)
- ♦ Euro-American Association of Economic Development / see Euro-American Association of Economic Development Studies
- ♦ Euro-American Association of Economic Development Studies (internationally oriented national body)

♦ Euro American Association on Telematics and Information Systems (EATIS) 05630

Pres Univ of Valencia, Av de Blasco Ibañez 13, 46010 Valencia, Spain. E-mail: jjsamper@uv.es.
Scientific Director Federal Univ of Sergipe, Av Marechal Rondon, s/n Jd Rosa Elze, São Cristóvão SE, Brazil. E-mail: rogerio@ufs.br.
URL: http://eatis.org/

History 2006. Also referred to as *EATIS.org*. **Aims** Promote academic and research collaboration among European and American continent universities. **Structure** Steering Committee; Scientific Program Committee. **Languages** English, Portuguese, Spanish. **Staff** Part-time, voluntary. **Finance** Institutional support; registration fees. **Activities** Events/meetings; networking/liaising. **Events** *Conference* Aveiro (Portugal) 2020, *Conference* Fortaleza (Brazil) 2018, *Conference* Cartagena de Indias (Colombia) 2016, *Conference* Valparaiso (Chile) 2014, *Conference* Valencia (Spain) 2012. **Publications** Papers; conference proceedings. **Members** Researchers and professors affiliated to over 65 universities or research institutions in 31 countries. Membership countries not specified. **NGO Relations** National societies; universities. [2020.03.03/XJ6417/**C**]

- ♦ Euro-Arab Center for Studies, Paris (internationally oriented national body)

♦ Euro-Arab Chambers of Commerce (internationally oriented national body)
♦ Euroarab Foundation for Higher Studies (internationally oriented national body)
♦ Euro-Arab Network of NGOs for Development and Integration (internationally oriented national body)
♦ Euro-Arab Veterinary Association (#02975)

♦ Euro Area Business Cycle Network (EABCN) 05631

Network Coordinator Fac of Economics, Univ of Cambridge, Austin Robinson Bldg, Cambridge, CB3 9DD, UK.
URL: http://www.eabcn.org/

Aims Bring together researchers from Central Banks and other policy institution with those in academia to help shape the European business cycle agenda. **Structure** Steering Committee; Scientific Committee. **Activities** Events/meetings; training/education. **Events** *Conference* Oslo (Norway) 2015, *Money is Back Conference* London (UK) 2012, *Conference on Disaggregating the Business Cycle* Luxembourg (Luxembourg) 2012, *Workshop* Budapest (Hungary) 2010, *Workshop on forecasting techniques* Frankfurt-Main (Germany) 2010.
Members Central banks and institutions in 20 countries and territories:
Austria, Belgium, Czechia, England, Finland, France, Germany, Hungary, Ireland, Italy, Luxembourg, Netherlands, Norway, Poland, Portugal, Slovenia, Spain, Sweden, Switzerland, Ukraine.
Regional organizations (3):
Center for Economic and Policy Research (CEPR); European Central Bank (ECB, #06466); European Commission (EC, #06633) (DG ECFIN). [2019.10.21/XJ3674/**F**]

♦ Euro ARGILLA – European Clay Producers' Federation (inactive)
♦ **euroart** euroart – the European Federation of Artists' Colonies (#05632)

♦ euroart – the European Federation of Artists' Colonies (euroart) ... 05632

Contact Bergstr 13, 27726 Worpswede, Germany. T. +4942148406191. E-mail: office@euroart.eu.
SG 17 chemin du Bornage, 77630 Barbizon, France.
Registered Address Markt 7a, 3080 Tervuren, Belgium.
URL: https://www.euroart.eu/

History 1994, Brussels (Belgium). Founded under the auspices of *European Parliament (EP, #08146)* and *European Commission (EC, #06633)*. Registration: Banque-Carrefour des Entreprises, No/ID: 0728.451.885, Start date: 13 Jun 2019, Belgium. **Aims** Protect the past of artists' colonies and create the possibility of a new – joint – artistic future. **Structure** Steering Committee; Scientific Advisory Committee. **Activities** Events/meetings; networking/liaising.
Members Organizations, associated organizations and personal members (about 70) in 13 countries:
Austria, Belgium, Denmark, Finland, France, Germany, Hungary, Italy, Lithuania, Netherlands, Norway, Poland, Russia.
Consultative Status Consultative status granted from: *Council of Europe (CE, #04881)* (Participatory Status). [2023/AA2425/**E**]

♦ Euro Asia Civil Engineering Forum (EACEF) 05633

Co-Founder Uni Stuttgart – Fak 2 – ILEK, Pfaffenwaldring 7, 70569 Stuttgart, Germany.
URL: http://eacef.com/

History 2006, Stuttgart (Germany). **Aims** Be a forum of exchange between engineers and academics from Europe and Asia; promote international collaboration on sustainable building, green technology, and green construction with respect to global warming. **Activities** Events/meetings; knowledge management/information dissemination; research/documentation. **Events** *International Conference* Yogyakarta (Indonesia) 2022, *International Conference* Yogyakarta (Indonesia) 2021, *International Conference* Stuttgart (Germany) 2019, *International Conference* Seoul (Korea Rep) 2017, *International Conference* Surabaya (Indonesia) 2015. [2021/AA2052/**F**]

♦ Euro-Asia Management Studies Association (EAMSA) 05634

Contact School of Management Fribourg, Chemin du Musée 4, 1700 Fribourg, Switzerland. E-mail: y.j.ha@sheffield.ac.uk.
URL: http://www.eamsa.org/

History 1984, Berlin West (Germany FR), as *Euro-Japanese Management Studies Association*. Present name adopted 1987. **Aims** Promote research in the field of economics and management of enterprises or other organizations in Europe and Asia; promote the exchange of research results, practical experience and ideas; disseminate research results; facilitate joint international research in the field. **Structure** Board, comprising President, 2 Vice Presidents, Executive Secretary, Website Manager and organizing host of the next annual meeting. Advisory Committee of 15 members. **Languages** English. **Staff** Voluntary. **Finance** Members' dues. Donations. **Events** *Annual Conference* Tokyo (Japan) 2022, *Annual Conference* Dornbirn (Austria) 2019, *Annual Conference* Seoul (Korea Rep) 2018, *Annual Conference* Copenhagen (Denmark) 2017, *Annual Conference* Bangkok (Thailand) 2014. **Publications** *Journal of Asian Business and Management*.
Members Full in 28 countries and territories:
Australia, Austria, Canada, China, Finland, France, Germany, Hong Kong, Hungary, India, Israel, Italy, Japan, Korea Rep, Luxembourg, Malaysia, Netherlands, New Zealand, Poland, Portugal, Singapore, Spain, Sweden, Switzerland, Taiwan, Thailand, UK, USA. [2022/XD8261/**D**]

♦ Euro-Asian Accrediting Association of Evangelical Schools / see Euro-Asian Accrediting Association of Evangelical Seminaries (#05635)

♦ Euro-Asian Accrediting Association of Evangelical Seminaries (EAAA) 05635

Sec PO Box 62, Rivne, 33028, Ukraine. E-mail: office@e-aaa.info.
URL: http://www.e-aaa.org/

History 1997. Former names and other names: *Euro-Asian Accrediting Association of Evangelical Schools* – former. **Aims** Accredit evangelical higher educational institutions in accordance with generally accepted standards in the *Christian education* system; improve education; strengthen partnership; develop theology. **Structure** General Assembly (every 2 years); EAAA Council; Executive Committee. **Languages** English, Russian. **Staff** 6.00 FTE, paid. **Finance** Sources: donations; fees for services; members' dues. **Activities** Certification/accreditation; events/meetings; guidance/assistance/consulting; publishing activities; research/documentation; training/education. Eastern Europe and Central Asia. **Events** *General Assembly* 2021, *International Theological Conference* Lviv (Ukraine) 2019, *International Theological Conference on Methodologies of Theological Research* Kiev (Ukraine) 2018, *Conference on Information Support of the Educational process in theological education* Kremenchuk (Ukraine) 2018, *Conference on Theological Education* Kiev (Ukraine) 2017. **Publications** *Bible Pulpit News* (4 a year); *EAAA News* (4 a year); *Theological Reflections: Euro-Asian Journal of Theology* (2 a year). Books.
Members Full (52): theological educational institutions. Associate (3): theological educational organizations. Members (55) in 11 countries:
Armenia, Austria, Belarus, Kazakhstan, Kyrgyzstan, Lithuania, Moldova, Netherlands, Russia, Ukraine, USA.
NGO Relations Member of (1): *International Council for Evangelical Theological Education (ICETE, #13020)*. [2021.09.07/XE4551/**E**]

♦ Euro-Asian Association of Agricultural Engineers (EAAAE) 05636

SG VIM, 1st Institutsky proezd, 5 VIM, Moscow MOSKVA, Russia, 109428. T. +7951748700. Fax +7951714349. E-mail: vim@vim.ru.

History Founded 27 Apr 2000, St Petersburg (Russia). Officially formed 3 Oct 2000, Moscow (Russia). Regional association of: *International Commission of Agricultural and Biosystems Engineering (#12661)*. **Aims** Maintain the participation of agricultural engineers and scientists of former Soviet Union Republics, East-European countries and Asian countries. **Languages** English, Russian. **Events** *International scientific conference on ecology and agricultural machinery* St Petersburg (Russia) 2009.
Members in 3 countries:
Belarus, Russia, Ukraine. [2016/XD3726/**D**]

♦ Euro-Asian Association of Dermatovenereologists (unconfirmed)

♦ Euro-Asian Astronomical Society (EAAS) 05637

Co-Chair Inst of Astronomy Russia Acad Sci, Sternberg Astronomical Inst, Universitetskij Prospekt 13, Moscow MOSKVA, Russia, 119992. T. +74959393318. Fax +74959328841. E-mail: eaas@sai.msu.ru.
Co-Chair Inst of Astronomy, Russia Acad Sci, Pyatnitskaya St 48, Moscow MOSKVA, Russia, 119017. T. +74959531702. E-mail: ryabov-uran@ukr.net.
URL: http://www.sai.msu.su/EAAS/eng/index_eng.html

History Apr 1990. Registration: Russia. **Aims** Maintain development of astronomy; reinforce scientific contacts between astronomers of the former Soviet Union and their colleagues all over the world. **Structure** General Meeting; Council Board; Council Bureau; Inspection Commission. **Languages** English, Russian. **Staff** 1.50 FTE, paid. Several voluntary. **Finance** Sources: members' dues. **Activities** Events/meetings; knowledge management/information dissemination. **Events** *International Astrophysical Conference* Moscow (Russia) 2021, *General Meeting* Moscow (Russia) 2018, *General Meeting* Moscow (Russia) 2015, *International Conference on Astronomy from our Cosmic Neighborhood to Deepest Cosmology* Moscow (Russia) 2015, *International Conference on Astronomy in the Time of The Information Burst* Moscow (Russia) 2012. **Publications** *Astronomical and Astrophysical Transactions* (4 a year) in English; *Astrocourier* (up to 12 a year) in Russian.
Members Individuals (about 350) in 15 countries:
Armenia, Azerbaijan, Belarus, Bulgaria, Estonia, Georgia, Israel, Kazakhstan, Latvia, Moldova, Russia, Serbia, Tajikistan, Ukraine, Uzbekistan. [2022/XD5208/**D**]

♦ Euro-Asian Cooperation of National Metrological Institutions (COOMET) 05638

Head of Secretariat 93 Starovilensky Trakt, 220053 Minsk, Belarus. T. +375173787540. E-mail: coomet@belgim.by.
URL: http://www.coomet.org/

History Jun 1991, Warsaw (Poland). Established on signature of a memorandum of understanding by representatives of national metrological institutions of 4 countries and of *Commonwealth of Independent States (CIS, #04341)*. Former names and other names: *Organization of National Metrological Institutions of the States of Central and Eastern Europe* – former. **Aims** Contribute to effective resolution of problems concerning the uniformity of measures and to the uniformity of measurement procedures and its required accuracy; contribute to development of closer cooperation among national economies and elimination of technical barriers to international trade; bring into closer contact the activities of metrological services of the states of Euro-Asian states. **Structure** Committee (meets annually); President's Council; Secretariat provided by the institution of the President; Technical Committees; Subcommitees. **Languages** English, Russian. **Finance** No financial means of its own. **Activities** Knowledge management/information dissemination; monitoring/evaluation; projects/programmes; standards/guidelines; training/education. **Events** *Committee Meeting* Minsk (Belarus) 2021, *Committee meeting* Minsk (Belarus) 2021, *Committee Meeting* Minsk (Belarus) 2020, *Committee Meeting* Dresden (Germany) 2019, *Committee Meeting* Sarajevo (Bosnia-Herzegovina) 2018. **Publications** Project reports; documents; recommendations; programs; information materials; strategy.
Members Full – national metrological institutions of (Central and Eastern) European and Asian countries; Associate – (marked *) similar institutions of countries in other regions or participating in another regional metrology organization and having interest in cooperation within COOMET. Members in 21 countries:
Armenia, Azerbaijan, Belarus, Bosnia-Herzegovina (*), Bulgaria, China (*), Cuba (*), Georgia, Germany (*), Kazakhstan, Korea Rep (*), Kyrgyzstan, Lithuania, Moldova, Romania, Russia, Slovakia, Tajikistan, Türkiye (*), Ukraine, Uzbekistan.
IGO Relations Follows recommendations of: *International Organization of Legal Metrology (#14451); Metre Convention (1875)*. **NGO Relations** Follows recommendations of: *International Organization for Standardization (ISO, #14473)*. [2021.09.07/XD3547/**D***]

♦ Euro-Asian Council for Standardization, Metrology and Certification / see EuroAsian Interstate Council for Standardization, Metrology and Certification (#05639)
♦ Euro-Asian Federation of the Unions of the Evangelical Christians-Baptists (no recent information)

♦ EuroAsian Interstate Council for Standardization, Metrology and Certification (EASC) 05639

Exec Sec Meleja str 3, 220013 Minsk, Belarus. T. +375173684201 – +375173684220. Fax +375172151353. E-mail: easc@easc.org.by.
URL: http://www.easc.by/

History 13 Mar 1992. Former names and other names: *Euro-Asian Council for Standardization, Metrology and Certification* – former; *Intergovernmental Council on Standardization, Metrology and Certification* – former. **Aims** Carry out agreed policy in the area of standardization, metrology, accreditation and certification for the member states of the Commonwealth of Independent States. **Structure** Permanent Staff; President; Permanent Responsible Secretary. **Languages** Russian. **Finance** Sources: contributions of member/participating states. **Activities** Events/meetings. **Events** *Half-Yearly Meeting* Almaty (Kazakhstan) 2012, *Half-Yearly Meeting* Baku (Azerbaijan) 2011, *Half-Yearly Meeting* Turkmenbashi (Turkmenistan) 2011, *Half-Yearly Meeting* Gabala (Azerbaijan) 2010, *Half-Yearly Meeting* Kiev (Ukraine) 2010. **Publications** Interstate Standards (over 26,500 documents).
Members Presidents of national bodies for standardization, metrology and certification of the 11 CIS states and Georgia:
Armenia, Azerbaijan, Belarus, Georgia, Kazakhstan, Kyrgyzstan, Moldova, Russia, Tajikistan, Turkmenistan, Ukraine, Uzbekistan. [2022.02.15/XD6326/**D***]

♦ Euro-Asian Jewish Congress (EAJC) 05640

Pres 56 Kunaev Str, Almaty, Kazakhstan.
SG address not obtained. E-mail: eajc@mail.ru.
URL: http://www.eajc.org/

History 2002, Moscow (Russia). **Aims** Defend rights and legitimate interests of the Jewish people; promote and represent the Jewish community of the Euro-Asian region. **Publications** *Jews of Euro-Asia*. **NGO Relations** Regional branch of: *World Jewish Congress (WJC, #21599)*. [2014/XM1700/**F**]

♦ Euroasian Universities Association (EUA) 05641

Exec Board Room B-106, Leninskie Gory, GSP-1, Moscow State Univ, MV Lomonosov, Moscow MOSKVA, Russia, 119991. T. +74959392769. E-mail: eau_msu@rector.msu.ru.
URL: http://www.eau-msu.ru/

History 1989, Moscow (Russia). Former names and other names: *Universities Association of the Union of Soviet Socialist Republics* – former. **Structure** Congress; Council; Executive Committee. **Events** *Congress* Moscow (Russia) 2019, *Transatlantic Dialogue* Esch-sur-Alzette (Luxembourg) 2017, *Congress* St Petersburg (Russia) 2015, *Congress* Moscow (Russia) 2011, *Congress* Astana (Kazakhstan) 2009. **Publications** *Eurasian universities in XXI century* – monograph series.
Members Universities (128) in 13 countries:
Armenia, Azerbaijan, Belarus, Georgia, Kazakhstan, Kyrgyzstan, Latvia, Moldova, Russia, Tajikistan, Turkmenistan, Ukraine, Uzbekistan.
NGO Relations Joint meetings with: *International Association of Academies of Sciences (IAAS, #11679)*. [2022/XJ7105/**D**]

♦ Euro-Asia Tourism Studies Association (EATSA) 05642

Main Office 16 rue Philibert de la Mare, 21000 Dijon, France.
URL: https://www.eatsa-researches.org/

Aims Promote research and education in the field of tourism, hospitality and recreation studies in Asia and Europe, with special emphasis on international comparisons and the exchange of research results, practical experiences and ideas. **Structure** General Assembly; Direction Board. **Finance** Sources: members' dues. **Activities** Events/meetings; knowledge management/information dissemination; networking/liaising; research/documentation. **Events** *Annual Conference* Budapest (Hungary) / Veszprém (Hungary) 2022, *Annual Conference* Japan 2021, *Annual Conference* Sardinia (Italy) 2020, *Annual Conference* Konya (Turkey) / Antalya (Turkey) 2019, *Annual Conference* Dijon (France) / Château-Chinon (France) 2018. [2017.12.08/XM5500/**C**]

♦ **EURO** Association of European Operational Research Societies (#02528)
♦ **Euro-ATAXIA** European Federation of Hereditary Ataxias (#07138)

♦ **Euro Atlantic Diplomacy Society (EAD Society)** **05643**
Contact address not obtained. E-mail: office@eadsociety.com.
URL: http://www.eadsociety.com/
History 2013. **Aims** Provide a platform through which university students and youth can deepen their understanding of the mission and activities undertaken by international organizations. **Structure** Departments: Executive Board; Academic Council; Public Relations; Human Resources; Secretariat and Liaison; Research; Legal Matters/Advisory; Charity. **Languages** English, French. **Activities** Events/meetings; training/education. **Events** *Model NATO Youth Summit – MoNYS* Stockholm (Sweden) / Riga (Latvia) 2015, *Model NATO Youth Summit – MoNYS* Podgorica (Montenegro) 2014, *Model NATO Youth Summit – MoNYS* Brussels (Belgium) 2013, *Model NATO Youth Summit – MoNYS* Brussels (Belgium) 2012. **Consultative Status** Consultative status granted from: *ECOSOC (#05331)* (Special). **IGO Relations** *European Union (EU, #08967)*; *NATO (#16945)*; regional governments; *Visegrad Group (#20794)*. **NGO Relations** *Atlantic Treaty Association (ATA, #03010)*; *European Geopolitical Forum (EGF)*; *OneEurope (#17730)*; national organizations. [2021/XM4373/**C**]

♦ Euro-Atlantic Disaster Relief Coordination Centre / see Euro-Atlantic Disaster Response Coordination Centre (#05644)

♦ **Euro-Atlantic Disaster Response Coordination Centre (EADRCC)** ... **05644**
Centre euro-atlantique de coordination des réactions en cas de catastrophe
Contact NATO Headquarters, International Staff Operations Div, V Bldg V-119, 1110 Brussels, Belgium. T. +3227072670. Fax +3227072677. E-mail: eadrcc@hq.nato.int.
URL: http://www.nato.int/eadrcc/
History Established 29 May 1998, on approval by Ministers of Foreign Affairs of *Euro Atlantic Partnership Council (EAPC, #05646)* within the framework of *NATO (#16945)*. Together with *Euro-Atlantic Disaster Response Unit (EADRU, #05645)*, based on a proposal by the Russian Federation for enhanced practical cooperation in the field of international disaster relief and on NATO policy on cooperation for disaster assistance in peacetime. Office officially opened 3 Jun 1998. Former title in English: *Euro-Atlantic Disaster Relief Coordination Centre (EADRCC)*. **Aims** In close consultation with UN-OCHA, coordinate EAPC response to any disaster occurring within the geographical area of EAPC, the Mediterranean Dialogue and Istanbul Cooperation Initiative countries; promote and contribute to interoperability through joint training and exercises; develop appropriate plans and procedures for the use of EADRU. **Structure** Based at NATO Headquarters, Brussels (Belgium); part of NATO's international staff. Open to representatives of the United Nations and of NATO military authorities. **Languages** English, French. **Staff** 8 full-time, paid; 3 international; 5 voluntary. **Finance** by EAPC members, through Voluntary National Contribution. **Activities** Humanitarian/emergency aid; training/education.
Members Governments of 50 countries:
Albania, Armenia, Austria, Azerbaijan, Belarus, Belgium, Bosnia-Herzegovina, Bulgaria, Canada, Croatia, Czechia, Denmark, Estonia, Finland, France, Georgia, Germany, Greece, Hungary, Iceland, Ireland, Italy, Kazakhstan, Kyrgyzstan, Latvia, Lithuania, Luxembourg, Malta, Moldova, Montenegro, Netherlands, North Macedonia, Norway, Poland, Portugal, Romania, Russia, Serbia, Slovakia, Slovenia, Spain, Sweden, Switzerland, Tajikistan, Türkiye, Turkmenistan, UK, Ukraine, USA, Uzbekistan.
Mediterranean Dialogue countries (7):
Algeria, Egypt, Israel, Jordan, Mauritania, Morocco, Tunisia.
Istanbul Cooperation Initiative countries (4):
Bahrain, Kuwait, Qatar, United Arab Emirates.
Partner countries (8):
Afghanistan, Australia, Iraq, Japan, Korea Rep, Mongolia, New Zealand, Pakistan.
IGO Relations Close consultation with: *United Nations Office for the Coordination of Humanitarian Affairs (OCHA, #20593)*. [2013.06.01/XE3461/**E***]

♦ **Euro-Atlantic Disaster Response Unit (EADRU)** **05645**
Contact NATO Headquarters, V-Bldg, V-119, 1110 Brussels, Belgium. T. +3227072670. Fax +3227072677. E-mail: eadrcc@hq.nato.int.
URL: http://www.nato.int/
History 29 May 1998, on approval by Ministers of Foreign Affairs of *Euro Atlantic Partnership Council (EAPC, #05646)*, within the framework of *NATO (#16945)*. Together with *Euro-Atlantic Disaster Response Coordination Centre (EADRCC, #05644)*, based on a proposal by the Russian Federation. **Aims** Enhance practical *cooperation* in the field of international disaster relief and on *NATO* policy on cooperation for disaster assistance in peacetime. **Structure** A non-standing, multi-national mix of national civil and military elements – qualified personnel of rescue, medical and other units – volunteered by EAPC member countries and varying in composition and size in response to requirements of any given situation. **Activities** Expected to be deployed in case of major natural or technological disaster in any EAPC country on request from the country concerned or in support of a relevant international organization. National elements remain under national control while deployed in a stricken country as an asset of the *Local Emergency Management Agency*. [2011.10.07/XK1868/**E***]

♦ **Euro Atlantic Partnership Council (EAPC)** **05646**
Conseil de partenariat euro-atlantique (CPEA)
Contact c/o NATO, Box 1300, 1110 Brussels, Belgium. T. +3227075038 – +3227075057. E-mail: natodoc@hq.nato.int.
URL: https://www.nato.int/cps/en/natohq/topics_67979.htm
History 20 Dec 1991, Brussels (Belgium), at inaugural meeting, with the title *North Atlantic Cooperation Council (NACC) – Conseil de coopération Nord-Atlantique (CCNA)*, sometimes referred to by the acronym *COCONA*. Set up following decision Nov 1991, Rome (Italy), of a summit meeting of *NATO (#16945)*. Comprises a forum of the *North Atlantic Council (NAC, #17572)* with its cooperation partners. Ministerial level representatives of 16 NATO countries, 6 Central and Eastern European countries and the 3 Baltic States participated in the inaugural meeting; the republics of the former USSR which form the *Commonwealth of Independent States (CIS, #04341)* became participants in the process in Mar 1992, Georgia joined in Apr 1992 and Albania in Jun 1992. Finland also began attending as an observer in 1992. Slovenia and Macedonia joined in 1996. Current title adopted May 1997, upon replacing the North Atlantic Cooperation Council. **Aims** Function as a multilateral forum for *NATO* members and Partner countries of the Euro-Atlantic area to discuss political and security-related issues and develop cooperation on these and other issues. **Structure** Meetings. *Partnership for Peace (PfP, #18240)*, set up in Jan 1994, comes within EAPC framework. **Languages** English, French, Russian. **Activities** Guidance/assistance/consulting. **Events** *Security forum* Astana (Kazakhstan) 2009, *Workshop on combating illicit brokering in small arms and light weapons* Brussels (Belgium) 2009, *Ministerial meeting* Brussels (Belgium) 1994, *Ministerial meeting* Istanbul (Turkey) 1994, *Meeting* Brussels (Belgium) 1993.
Members NATO member countries (28) and partner countries (22). Governments of 50 countries:
Albania, Armenia, Austria, Azerbaijan, Belarus, Belgium, Bosnia-Herzegovina, Bulgaria, Canada, Croatia, Czechia, Denmark, Estonia, Finland, France, Georgia, Germany, Greece, Hungary, Iceland, Ireland, Italy, Kazakhstan, Kyrgyzstan, Latvia, Lithuania, Luxembourg, Malta, Moldova, Montenegro, Netherlands, North Macedonia, Norway, Poland, Portugal, Romania, Russia, Serbia, Slovakia, Slovenia, Spain, Sweden, Switzerland, Tajikistan, Türkiye, Turkmenistan, UK, Ukraine, USA, Uzbekistan.
IGO Relations Cooperates with: *Organization for Security and Cooperation in Europe (OSCE, #17887)*. Instrumental in setting up: *Euro-Atlantic Disaster Response Coordination Centre (EADRCC, #05644)*; *Euro-Atlantic Disaster Response Unit (EADRU, #05645)*. **NGO Relations** Instrumental in setting up: *PfP Consortium of Defence Academies and Security Studies Institutes (#18345)*. [2018/XC0004/**C***]

♦ **EUROAVIA** European Association of Aerospace Students (#05930)
♦ **EUROBAN** European Banana Action Network (#06310)

♦ **Euro Banking Association (EBA)** **05647**
Association bancaire pour l'Euro (ABE)
Main Office 40 rue de Courcelles, 75008 Paris, France. T. +33153670700. Fax +33153670707. E-mail: association@abe-eba.eu.
SG address not obtained.
URL: https://www.abe-eba.eu/
History 17 Sep 1985, Paris (France), as *ECU Banking Association Association bancaire pour l'Ecu*. Statutes revised 24 May 2002. EU Transparency Register: 889545625082-48. **Aims** Foster dialogue and experience exchange amongst payments industry practitioners towards a pan-European vision for payments. **Structure** General Meeting; Board. Oversight by: *European Central Bank (ECB, #06466)*. Association supervises subsidiary ABE Administration SA, an *'Administration Company'*. **Finance** Members' dues. Other sources: voluntary contributions; sale of contributions or services. **Activities** Events/meetings; guidance/assistance/consulting; networking/liaising; training/education. **Events** *Meeting* Stockholm (Sweden) 2019, *Meeting* Brussels (Belgium) 2016, *Annual Forum* Amsterdam (Netherlands) 2015, *Annual Forum / EBAday Forum* Helsinki (Finland) 2014, *Seminar* Amsterdam (Netherlands) 2013. **Publications** Reports; brochures.
Members Banks (169) and Associate members (20) from European Union countries, or EU branches of banks from non-EU countries. Members in 21 countries:
Austria, Belgium, Cyprus, Denmark, Finland, France, Germany, Greece, Hungary, Ireland, Italy, Luxembourg, Netherlands, Norway, Portugal, Slovenia, Spain, Sweden, Switzerland, UK, USA.
NGO Relations Member of: *European Committee for Banking Standards (ECBS, inactive)*; *European Payments Council (EPC, #08175)*. [2019/XE0613/**E**]

♦ **EUROBAT** Association of European Automotive and Industrial Battery Manufacturers (#02498)
♦ EUROBATS – Agreement on the Conservation of Populations of European Bats (1991 treaty)

♦ **Eurobesitas** **05648**
Pres Quai Perdonnet 14, 1800 Vevey VD, Switzerland. T. +41219235333. Fax +41219235336. E-mail: eurobesitas@bluewin.ch.
URL: http://www.eurobesitas.ch/
History 1993. Registered in accordance with Belgian law. **Aims** Promote the study of *obesity*; give support, information and/or treatment to obese people. **Languages** French. **Events** *Journées sur l'obésité et la nutrition appliquées à la santé / Meeting* Paris (France) 1999.
Members Individuals in 10 countries:
Belgium, Czechia, Denmark, France, Germany, Italy, Netherlands, Norway, Sweden, UK. [2015/XD5682/v/**D**]

♦ EuroBIC – European Biological Inorganic Chemistry Conference (meeting series)
♦ EUROBIOMATEX – European Science-Industry Consortium for Biomaterials and Health Care (unconfirmed)
♦ EUROBIT – European Association of Manufacturers of Business Machines and Information Technology Industry (inactive)
♦ **EUROBITUME** European Bitumen Association (#06348)
♦ Eurobot Association (unconfirmed)
♦ Eurobot – Eurobot Association (unconfirmed)

♦ **euRobotics** **05649**
SG BluePoint, Bd A Reyers 80, 1030 Brussels, Belgium. T. +3227068198. E-mail: secretariat@eu-robotics.net.
URL: http://www.eu-robotics.net/
History 17 Sep 2012. Founded on merger of *European Robotics Research Network (EURON, inactive)* and *European Robotics Technology Platform (EUROP)*. Registration: Belgium; EU Transparency Register, No/ID: 526825515147-41. **Aims** Boost European robotics research, development and innovation; foster a positive perception of robotics. **Structure** General Assembly; Board of Directors; Boards (2). **Languages** English. **Staff** 4.00 FTE, paid. **Finance** Members' dues. **Activities** Events/meetings. **Events** *European Robotics Forum (ERF2024)* 2024, *European Robotics Forum* Rotterdam (Netherlands) 2022, *European Robotics Forum* 2021, *European Robotics Forum* Bucharest (Romania) 2019, *European Robotics Forum* Vienna (Austria) 2015. **Publications** *euRobotics Newsletter*. Press releases.
Members Industry; Research; Associate. Members (250). Membership countries not specified. Included in the above, 1 organization listed in this Yearbook:
Included in the above, 1 organization listed in this Yearbook:
CLAWAR Association (#03981); *European Educational Research Association (EERA, #06967)*.
IGO Relations *European Commission (EC, #06633)*. [2021/XJ7523/**F**]

♦ **EuroBSDcon Foundation** **05650**
Stichting EuroBSDcon
Registered Address pa MKB Assist BV, Ringveste 1, 3992 DD Houten, Netherlands.
URL: https://eurobsdconfoundation.org/
History 28 Dec 2011. Founded to provide a legal setting for the EuroBSDcon conferences, organized since 2001. Registration: Stichting, No/ID: 54254515, Netherlands. **Aims** Gather users and developers working on and with 4.4BSD (Berkeley Software Distribution) based operating systems family and related projects. **Structure** Board. **Activities** Events/meetings. **Events** *European BSD Conference* Vienna (Austria) 2020, *European BSD Conference* Lillehammer (Norway) 2019, *European BSD Conference* Bucharest (Romania) 2018, *European BSD Conference* Paris (France) 2017, *European BSD Conference* Belgrade (Serbia) 2016. [2020/AA0682/c/**F**]

♦ EUROBUILD – European Organization for the Promotion of New Techniques and Methods in Building (inactive)
♦ EUROCADRES – Conseil des cadres européens (#05651)
♦ EUROCADRES – Consejo de los Cuadros Europeos (#05651)

♦ **EUROCADRES – Council of European Professional and Managerial Staff** **05651**
EUROCADRES – Conseil des cadres européens – EUROCADRES – Consejo de los Cuadros Europeos – EUROCADRES – Rat der Europäischen Fach- und Führungskräfte
Exec Officer Bd du Roi Albert II 5, 1210 Brussels, Belgium. T. +3222240734. E-mail: secretariat@eurocadres.eu.
Pres address not obtained.
URL: http://www.eurocadres.eu/
History 24 Feb 1993, Luxembourg. Founded under the auspices of *European Trade Union Confederation (ETUC, #08927)*. Registration: EU Transparency Register, No/ID: 803183412905-34. **Aims** Represent professionals and managers at European level; aim for a stronger knowledge-based Europe with real freedom of mobility and quality of working life. **Structure** Congress (every 4 years); General Assembly (annual); Praesidium; Executive Committee. Set up: *FEMANET (inactive)*. **Languages** English. **Staff** 3.00 FTE, paid; 2.00 FTE, voluntary. **Finance** Sources: members' dues; revenue from activities/projects. Supported by: *European Commission (EC, #06633)*. Annual budget: 450,000 EUR. **Activities** Advocacy/lobbying/activism; events/meetings; networking/liaising; research/documentation. **Events** *Congress* Madrid (Spain) 2021, *Annual General Assembly* Brussels (Belgium) 2015, *Annual General Assembly* Brussels (Belgium) 2014, *Congress* Brussels (Belgium) 2013, *Annual General Assembly* Brussels (Belgium) 2012. **Publications** Annual Report; guidelines; manuals; brochures; leaflets. **Members** National trade union organizations representing 6 million professional and managerial staff. Membership countries not specified. **IGO Relations** Recognized by: *European Commission (EC, #06633)* (as European Social Partner). Member of: Advisory Committee on Equal Opportunities for Women and Men; Advisory Committee on Free Movement of Workers. Participation at: Tripartite Social Summit for Growth and Employment. **NGO Relations** Member of (1): *European Alliance for Mental Health – Employment & Work (EUMH Alliance, #05875)*. *Association of National Organisations for Supervision in Europe (ANSE, #02821)*; *Association of Nordic Engineers (ANE, #02828)*; *CEC European Managers (#03623)*; EU Liaison Committee of *European Federation of Psychologists Associations (EFPA, #07199)*; *European Higher Engineering and Technical Professionals Association (EurEta, #07484)*; *European Students' Union (ESU, #08848)*; *Fédération Européenne d'Associations Nationales d'Ingénieurs (FEANI, #09558)*; *International Federation of Social Workers (IFSW, #13544)*. [2022.02.01/XE2199/t/**E**]

♦ EUROCADRES – Rat der Europäischen Fach- und Führungskräfte (#05651)

♦ EUROCAE 05652

Headquarters 9-23 rue Paul Lafargue, Le Triangle Building, 93200 Saint-Denis, France. E-mail: eurocae@eurocae.net.
URL: http://www.eurocae.net/

History 1963, Lucerne (Switzerland). Founded on adoption of a memorandum of understanding at first General Assembly. Former names and other names: *European Organization for Civil Aviation Electronics* – former (1963 to 1990); *Organisation européenne pour l'équipement électronique de l'aviation civile* – former (1963 to 1990); *Organisation européenne pour l'équipement de l'aviation civile* – former (1990); *European Organization for Civil Aviation Equipment (EUROCAE)* – former (1990). **Aims** Focus on *electronic* equipment for air transport, dealing exclusively with aviation standardization for both airborne and ground systems and equipment. **Structure** General Assembly (annual); President; Council; Technical Committee; Technical Working Groups; General Secretariat. **Languages** English. **Staff** 10.00 FTE, paid. **Finance** Sources: members' dues. **Activities** Capacity building; networking/liaising; politics/policy/regulatory; research and development; standards/guidelines. **Events** *Annual Symposium* Saint-Denis (France) 2021, *Annual General Assembly* Budapest (Hungary) 2004, *Annual General Assembly* Paris (France) 2003, *Annual General Assembly* Barcelona (Spain) 2002, *Annual General Assembly* Milan (Italy) 2001. **Publications** Technical documents.
Members Full; Corresponding; International. Civil aviation authorities, airports, airlines, industry and users including electronic equipment and equipment manufacturers, aircraft constructors and administrations. Full members in 15 countries:
Austria, Belgium, Denmark, Finland, France, Germany, Ireland, Italy, Netherlands, Norway, Romania, Spain, Sweden, Switzerland, UK. [2021.02.17/XD0819/y/**D**]

- ♦ **EUROCALL** European Association for Computer Assisted Language Learning (#05985)

♦ EUROCAM 05653

SG Rue du Trône 194, 1050 Brussels, Belgium. E-mail: secretariat@cam-europe.eu.
URL: http://www.cam-europe.eu/

History Set up as a platform for the entire *Complementary and Alternative Medicine* sector in the EU. Also known under the title *European stakeholder group for Complementary and Alternative Medicine*. Registered in accordance with Dutch law: 67945864, under full title *Stichting EUROCAM*. EU Transparency Register: 659086014916-83. **Aims** Influence the decision making of the European Union (EU) institutions and Member States to support and provide the means for the integration of the Complementary and Alternative Medicine (CAM) into European *healthcare* systems; promote and facilitate CAM's role in enhancing and maintaining citizens'health; highlight the health promotion and illness prevention aspects of CAM for EU public health policy and programmes. **Structure** Executive Committee; General Board. **Languages** English, French, German. **Staff** 3.00 FTE, paid. **Finance** Members' dues. Donations. **Activities** Networking/liaising; politics/policy/regulatory. **Events** *Conference on Complementary and Alternative Medicine* Brussels (Belgium) 2012.
Members Affiliated partners (12):
European Ayurveda Association (EUAA, #06306); European Central Council of Homeopaths (ECCH, #06467); European Committee for Homeopathy (ECH, #06651); European Council of Doctors for Plurality in Medicine (ECPM, #06816); European Federation and Forum for Osteopathy (EFFO, #07128); European Federation of Homeopathic Patients' Associations (EFHPA, #07139); European Federation of Patients' Associations for Anthroposophic Medicine (EFPAM, #07189); European Herbal and Traditional Medicine Practitioners Association (EHTPA, #07475); European Traditional Chinese Medicine Association (ETCMA, #08930); International Council of Medical Acupuncture and Related Techniques (ICMART, #13046); Internationale Vereinigung Anthroposophischer Ärztegesellschaften (IVAA, #13314); International Federation of Anthroposophic Arts and Eurythmy Therapies (IFAAET).
National Associated partners (3).
NGO Relations Member of: *European Public Health Alliance (EPHA, #08297).* Also collaborates with: *European Coalition on Homeopathic and Anthroposophic Medicinal Products (ECHAMP, #06595).* [2019.12.12/XJ6012/y/**F**]

- ♦ **Eurocare** European Alcohol Policy Alliance (#05856)
- ♦ **Eurocarers** European Association Working for Carers (#06277)

♦ Eurocarillon 05654

Contact address not obtained. E-mail: stadsbeiaardier@planet.nl.

History 1995, Bruges (Belgium). **Aims** Further the art of the *carillon* in *Europe*, promote the carillon as a full-fledged *concert* instrument. **Events** *Annual Festival* Bournville (UK) 2006, *Annual Festival* Amsterdam (Netherlands) 2005, *Annual Festival* Cobh (Ireland) 2003, *Annual Festival* Bruges (Belgium) 2002, *Annual Festival* Prague (Czech Rep) 2001. [2009/XF5878/**F**]

- ♦ Euro-Caritas / see Caritas Europa (#03579)
- ♦ **Euro-CASE** European Council of Applied Sciences, Technologies and Engineering (#06804)
- ♦ EUROCASTANEA – European Chestnut Network (unconfirmed)
- ♦ Eurocat – European Association on Catalysis (no recent information)

♦ EUROCAT – European Surveillance of Congenital Anomalies 05655

Coordinator European Commission, Joint Research Centre, Ispra, Via Fermi 2749, 21027 Ispra MB, Italy. T. +390332789246. E-mail: jrc-eurocat@ec.europa.eu.
URL: https://eu-rd-platform.jrc.ec.europa.eu/eurocat_en

History 1979. Founded by DG-XII 'Science and Technology' of *European Commission (EC, #06633)*, following 1975-1976 feasibility studies. 1991, status changed from research project to surveillance service under the coordination of DG-V 'Employment, Industrial Relations and Social Affairs, Health and Safety'. Evolved as a network of population-based registries for surveillance of congenital anomalies in Europe, which surveys about 25% of the European births. Central Registry, including central database, initially located at the Catholic University of Louvain (Belgium), then at the Scientific Institute for Public Health in Brussels (Belgium), subsequently at the London School of Hygiene and Tropical Medicine (UK), and finally at the University of Ulster, Northern Ireland (UK). 2015, Central Registry and European-level coordination activities of EUROCAT network transferred to the EC's Joint Research Centre (JRC), as an objective of the Administrative Arrangements (AA) signed by JRC and DG SANTE to implement EC's strategy in the field of rare diseases. Former names and other names: *Concerted Action on Congenital Anomalies and Twins* – former (1979); *European Registration of Congenital Anomalies* – former. **Aims** Provide essential epidemiologic information on congenital anomalies in Europe; facilitate early warning of teratogenic exposures; evaluate effectiveness of primary prevention; assess impact of developments in prenatal screening; act as an information and resource centre regarding clusters, exposures or risk factors of concern; provide a ready collaborative network and infrastructure for research related to causes and prevention of congenital anomalies and treatment and care of affected children; act as a catalyst for the setting up of registries throughout Europe collecting comparable, standardized data. **Structure** Annual Registry Leaders Meeting; Management Committee; Working Groups. **Languages** English. **Staff** 2.00 FTE, paid. **Finance** Sources: grants. Supported by: *European Communities (EC, inactive)* (Joint Research Centre budget). **Activities** Events/meetings; monitoring/evaluation. Surveys about 1.5 million births a year in Europe. **Events** *European Symposium* Zagreb (Croatia) 2013, *Registry Ledars Meeting* Zagreb (Croatia) 2013, *Registry Leaders Meeting* Budapest (Hungary) 2012, *Registry Leaders Meeting* Dublin (Ireland) 2010, *Registry Leaders Meeting* Bilbao (Spain) 2009. **Publications** Proceedings; reports. see also https://eu-rd-platform.jrc.ec.europa.eu/eurocat/publications_en **Information Services** *EUROCAT Database* – standardized central database on over 900,000 cases of congenital anomaly (updated annually).
Members Congenital anomaly registries in 22 countries:
Austria, Belgium, Bulgaria, Croatia, Czechia, Denmark, Finland, France, Germany, Ireland, Italy, Latvia, Malta, Netherlands, Norway, Poland, Portugal, Spain, Sweden, Switzerland, UK, Ukraine. [2022.11.04/XD1298/**D**]

- ♦ **EUROCBCA** European Confederation of Business Centre Associations (#06699)
- ♦ EUROCEAN – Association européenne océanique (inactive)
- ♦ EurOcean – European Centre for Information on Marine Science and Technology (internationally oriented national body)
- ♦ **EUROCEF** Comité européen d'action spécialisée pour l'enfant et la famille dans leur milieu de vie (#04150)
- ♦ EUROCEI – Centro Europeo de Empresas e Innovación (internationally oriented national body)
- ♦ EUROCENTRES / see Foundation for Language and Educational Centres (#09964)
- ♦ **EUROCENTRES** Foundation for Language and Educational Centres (#09964)

♦ Eurocer-Building 05656

SG De Baander 50, 3823 VK Amersfoort, Netherlands. T. +31337851116. Fax +31334564096.
URL: http://www.eurocer-building.com/

History 1 Jan 1994. Articles of Association: 1st edition – 13 Feb 1995; 2nd edition – 16 May 1997; 3rd edition – 28 Jul 2004. Former names and other names: *eurocer-building – European Association of Certification Bodies, Testing Laboratories and Inspection Bodies for the Building and Construction Industry* – full title. Registration: Netherlands. **Aims** Provide a point of reference for the members dealing with the needs of the building and construction industry, including all certification, testing and inspection aspects of design, services, products, buildings and construction. **Structure** General Assembly; Management Board; Conformity Assessment Bodies; President; Secretary-General. **Languages** English. **Activities** Certification/accreditation; events/meetings. **Events** *What quality for construction products – expectations and opportunities* Paris (France) 2002.
Members Certification bodies, testing laboratories and inspection bodies (9) active for the building and construction industry, in 7 countries:
Belgium, France, Italy, Lithuania, Netherlands, Portugal, Spain.
NGO Relations Member of: *European Accreditation Advisory Board (EAAB, see: #06782).* Observer of: *European Federation of National Associations of Measurement, Testing and Analytical Laboratories (EUROLAB, #07168).* [2014.06.20/XD7066/**D**]

- ♦ eurocer-building – European Association of Certification Bodies, Testing Laboratories and Inspection Bodies for the Building and Construction Industry / see Eurocer-Building (#05656)
- ♦ EuroCG – European Workshop on Computational Geometry (meeting series)
- ♦ **EUROCHAMBRES** Association des chambres de commerce et d'industrie européennes (#02423)
- ♦ EUROCHEMIC – Société européenne pour le traitement chimique des combustibles irradiés (inactive)

♦ Eurochild 05657

Finance Dir Av des Arts 7/8, 1210 Brussels, Belgium. T. +3225117083. Fax +3225117298. E-mail: info@eurochild.org.
URL: http://www.eurochild.org/

History 2004. Evolved from *European Forum for Child Welfare (EFCW, inactive).* Former names and other names: *Eurochild – Promoting the Welfare and Rights of Children and Young People* – former; *Eurochild – pour la promotion du bien-être et des droits des enfants et des jeunes* – former; *Eurochild – Giving a voice to children in Europe* – former; *Eurochild – Putting children at the heart of Europe* – full title. Registration: Banque-Carrefour des Entreprises, No/ID: 0866.544.946, Start date: 26 Jul 2004, Belgium; EU Transparency Register, No/ID: 79360311166-84, Start date: 18 Feb 2009. **Aims** Promote the *rights* and well-being of *children* and young people in Europe. **Structure** General Assembly (annual); Board. **Languages** English, French. **Staff** 16.00 FTE, paid. **Finance** Sources: members' dues; private foundations. Supported by: *European Commission (EC, #06633).* **Activities** Advocacy/lobbying/activism; events/meetings; guidance/assistance/consulting; knowledge management/information dissemination; research/documentation. **Events** *General Assembly* Brussels (Belgium) 2022, *General Assemblies and Members Day* Brussels (Belgium) 2021, *General Assembly* Brussels (Belgium) 2019, *General Assembly* Brussels (Belgium) 2018, *Annual Conference* Opatija (Croatia) 2018. **Publications** *Info Flash* (bi-weekly); *e-News Bulletin* (12 a year). Annual Report; policy papers; conference reports; fact sheets; discussion papers; press releases; flyers.
Members Full (142); Associate (45); Honorary (4). Members in 35 countries:
Albania, Austria, Belgium, Bulgaria, Croatia, Cyprus, Czechia, Denmark, Estonia, Finland, France, Germany, Greece, Hungary, Ireland, Italy, Kosovo, Latvia, Lithuania, Luxembourg, Malta, Netherlands, North Macedonia, Poland, Portugal, Romania, Serbia, Slovakia, Slovenia, Spain, Sweden, Switzerland, Türkiye, UK, Ukraine.
Included in the above, 18 organizations listed in this Yearbook:
Active – Sobriety, Friendship and Peace (inactive); Alliance for Childhood European Network Group (AFC-ENG, #00666); Ariel Foundation International (AFI, #01106); Children and Families Across Borders (CFAB); Children's Rights European Academic Network (CREAN, #03878); Defence for Children International (DCI, #05025); Diversity, Early Childhood Education and Training (DECET, #05106); European Association for Children in Hospital (EACH, #05970); European Council for Steiner Waldorf Education (ECSWE, #06844); European Non-Governmental Sports Organization (ENGSO, #08054) (Youth); *Home-Start International; International Association for Steiner/Waldorf Early Childhood Education (IASWECE, #12185); International Child Development Initiatives (ICDI); International Foster Care Organization (IFCO, #13663); Learning for Well-being Foundation (L4WB, #16431); SOS-Kinderdorf International (#19693); UNESCO (#20322)* (Centre at University of Ulster); *World Organization for Early Childhood Education (OMEP, #21689).*
Consultative Status Consultative status granted from: *Council of Europe (CE, #04881)* (Participatory Status); *ECOSOC (#05331)* (Special). **IGO Relations** Cooperates with (2): *European Union Agency for Fundamental Rights (FRA, #08969); UNICEF (#20332).* **NGO Relations** Member of (8): *Child Rights Connect (#03884); Child Rights International Network (CRIN, #03885); Conference of INGOs of the Council of Europe (#04607); European Anti-Poverty Network (EAPN, #05908); European Public Health Alliance (EPHA, #08297); Federation of European and International Associations Established in Belgium (FAIB, #09508); Global Coalition to End Child Poverty (#10292); Social Platform (#19344).* Cooperates with (10): *ChildFund Alliance (#03868); ERGO Network (#05531); EuroHealthNet (#05693); European Disability Forum (EDF, #06929); European Federation of National Organisations Working with the Homeless (#07174); European Youth Forum (#09140); Inclusion Europe – European Association of Societies of Persons with Intellectual Disability and their Families (Inclusion Europe, #11144); Plan International (#18386)* (EU Office); *Save the Children International (#19058); SOS-Kinderdorf International (#19693).* [2022.12.07/XJ3812/y/**F**]

- ♦ Eurochild – Giving a voice to children in Europe / see Eurochild (#05657)
- ♦ Eurochild – Promoting the Welfare and Rights of Children and Young People / see Eurochild (#05657)
- ♦ Eurochild – pour la promotion du bien-être et des droits des enfants et des jeunes / see Eurochild (#05657)
- ♦ Eurochild – Putting children at the heart of Europe / see Eurochild (#05657)
- ♦ Euro-Children (internationally oriented national body)

♦ EURO-CHINA 05658

Founding Pres/Intl Coordinator/CEO 39 av Princesse Grace, 98000 Monte Carlo, Monaco. T. +377607937322. Fax +37793303132. E-mail: euro-china@libello.com.
URL: http://www.tuttocina.it/eurochina/

History 12 Mar 1986, Geneva (Switzerland). Founded under the auspices of *European Union (EU, #08967)* and *United Nations (UN, #20515).* Statutes modified Oct 2000, Menton (France). Former names and other names: *European Centre for the Promotion of Innovation Technologies (ECPIT)* – former (12 Mar 1986); *Centre européen pour la promotion des innovations technologiques (CEPIT)* – former (12 Mar 1986); *European Advisory Council for Technology Trade (EACT)* – former; *Conseil consultatif européen pour les échanges technologiques* – former. Registration: France. **Aims** Promote economic and cultural understanding and cooperation between Europe and China by means of a wide range of programmes, projects and professional services, so as to encourage synergy in economic trade, technological and cultural progress. **Structure** International Board, led by President; China Liaison Offices in Shanghai. **Languages** Danish, English, French, German, Italian, Mandarin Chinese, Spanish. **Staff** 60.00 FTE, voluntary. **Finance** Sources: fees for services; investments; members' dues; private foundations; sale of publications. Services: surveys; consultancy; research. **Activities** Events/meetings; guidance/assistance/consulting; knowledge management/information dissemination; research/documentation; training/education. **Events** *Business forum* Hangzhou (China) 2007, *Business forum* Shanghai (China) 2006, *Business forum* Shanghai (China) 2005, *Business forum* Hangzhou (China) 2002, *Joint ventures and the big Chinese market* Èze (France) 1992. **Publications** Newsletters; bulletins; books.
Members Management and trade advisers, researchers, marketing, legal and financial experts, joint venture experts, technology transfer experts, internationalization and regional development experts. Correspondents in 24 countries:
Belgium, Brunei Darussalam, Cambodia, China, Denmark, France, Germany, Indonesia, Israel, Italy, Laos, Luxembourg, Malaysia, Monaco, Myanmar, Norway, Philippines, Singapore, Spain, Sweden, Switzerland, Thailand, Timor-Leste, Vietnam.

Consultative Status Consultative status granted from: *ECOSOC (#05331)* (Ros C); *UNCTAD (#20285)* (Special Category). **IGO Relations** Accredited by (1): *United Nations Office at Vienna (UNOV, #20604)*. Affiliated with (4): European Advisory Council for Technology Trade (EACT); Marco Polo Society; World Trade Advisory Council (WTAC); *World Trade Organization (WTO, #21864)*. Support received from: *Asian Development Bank (ADB, #01422)*; *European Bank for Reconstruction and Development (EBRD, #06315)* (World Bank); *European Commission (EC, #06633)*; United Nations *(UN, #20515)*. **NGO Relations** Affiliated with (1): *European Institute for Futures Studies (EIFS, #07556)*. [2022.02.15/XE0665/**F**]

♦ EUROCHIPS / see Children of Prisoners Europe (#03875)

♦ Euro Chlor 05659

Exec Dir c/o CEFIC, Rue Belliard 40 – Bte 15, 1040 Brussels, Belgium. T. +3224369500 – +3224369501. Fax +3224369550. E-mail: eurochlor@cefic.be.
URL: http://www.eurochlor.org/

History 1989. Founded as a sector group of *Conseil européen de l'industrie chimique (CEFIC, #04687)*, now an autonomous affiliated organization. Former names and other names: *Bureau international technique du chlore (BITC)* – former (1953); *EURO CHLOR Federation* – former. **Aims** Serve the chlor- *alkali industry* and its derivatives, the authorities and the public in Western *Europe* in matters of *safety*, *environment* and health connected with the production, transportation, handling and use of *chlorine* and chlorine derivatives. **Structure** Management Committee; Committees; Working Groups. Includes *European Chlorinated Solvent Association (ECSA, #06540)* and Chlorinated Paraffins, previously sector groups of CEFIC. **Events** *International Chlorine Technology Conference* Warsaw (Poland) 2022, *International Chlorine Technology Conference* Warsaw (Poland) 2021, *General Assembly* Brussels (Belgium) 2020, *International Chlorine Technology Conference* Warsaw (Poland) 2020, *Annual General Assembly* Bordeaux (France) 2018. **Publications** *Technical Recommendations (GEST)*. Brochures. **Members** Full – European chlorine and derivatives producers. Associate – non-chlorine producers in Western Europe. Technical Correspondents – chlorine producers outside Western Europe, consumers of chlorine worldwide, equipment supply companies worldwide. Membership countries not specified. **IGO Relations** Official observer to: *Baltic Marine Environment Protection Commission – Helsinki Commission (HELCOM, #03126)*; *OSPAR Commission for the Protection of the Marine Environment of the North-East Atlantic (OSPAR Commission, #17905)*. **NGO Relations** Member of: *European Biocidal Product Forum (EBPF, #06332)*; *Network of Reference Laboratories for Monitoring of Emerging Environmental Pollutants (NORMAN Network, #17053)*; *World Chlorine Council (WCC, #21274)*. [2021/XE0876/**E**]

♦ EURO CHLOR Federation / see Euro Chlor (#05659)
♦ EUROCHOR – Union of European Choral Federations (inactive)
♦ **EuroCHRIE** European Council on Hotel, Restaurant and Institutional Education (#06823)

♦ Eurochurch.net (ECN) 05660

Team Administrator Rowheath Pavillion, Heath Road, Bourneville, Birmingham, B30 1HH, UK.
URL: http://www.eurochurch.net/

History Founded 1981, as *European Church Growth Association (ECGA)*. Was previously referred to as *European Church Growth Movement*. **Aims** Provide a platform for dialogue and sharing to facilitate missional thinking and church planting in Europe. **Structure** Leadership Team. **Languages** Dutch, English, French, German, Italian, Norwegian, Spanish. **Staff** 0.50 FTE, paid. **Events** *Conference* Tallinn (Estonia) 2014, *Conference* Cologne (Germany) 2012, *Conference* Rome (Italy) 2009, *Conference* Lisbon (Portugal) 2008, *The changing shape of mission in Europe – what are the big questions at the heart of the church in Europe?* Kristiansand (Norway) 2005. **Members** Membership countries not specified. [2013.06.27/XD9193/**D**]

♦ Euro Cidadão Acção Serviço / see European Citizen Action Service (#06555)
♦ Eurociett / see World Employment Federation Europe (#21377)
♦ EuroCIM – European Causal Inference Meeting (meeting series)

♦ EUROCINEMA 05661

General Delegate Rue des Chartreux 19, Bte 12, 1000 Brussels, Belgium. T. +3227325830. Fax +3227333657. E-mail: eurocinema@eurocinema.eu.
URL: https://eurocinema.eu/

History 1991, Brussels (Belgium). Former names and other names: *Association of Producers of Cinema and Television (EUROCINEMA)* – full title; *Association de Producteurs de Cinéma et de Télévision* – full title. Registration: EU Transparency Register, No/ID: 43245696854-79. **Aims** Represent the interests of *film* and *audiovisual* producers in the *European Union*; serve as a platform for the European audiovisual sector. **Structure** General Delegate; Assistant. **Languages** English, French. **Staff** 2.00 FTE, paid. **NGO Relations** Member of (3): *Culture First Coalition (inactive)*; INCD Europe; *International Network for Cultural Diversity (INCD, no recent information)*. [2022.02.01/XE4706/**E**]

♦ **EuroCIO** European CIO Association (#06550)
♦ EuroCité (internationally oriented national body)

♦ EUROCITIES 05662

SG Square de Meeûs 1, 1000 Brussels, Belgium. T. +3225520888. Fax +3225520889. E-mail: info@eurocities.eu.
URL: http://www.eurocities.eu/

History Idea for EUROCITIES suggested at 2 conferences in 1986, Rotterdam (Netherlands) and 1989, Barcelona (Spain), when ad hoc working groups were set up. Became a formal network, 1991. First Brussels (Belgium) office opened, 1992. Original title: *European Association of Metropolitan Cities*. Registration: Banque-Carrefour des Entreprises, No/ID: 0447.820.987, Start date: 11 May 1992, Belgium; EU Transparency Register, No/ID: 12493392840-79, Start date: 18 Dec 2009. **Aims** Work in all areas of interest for cities; facilitate learning experiences between cities; represent cities' interests towards the European Union. **Structure** General Meeting (annual); Executive Committee; Thematic Forums (6); Working Groups (over 40). **Languages** English. **Staff** 42.00 FTE, paid. **Finance** Members' dues (50% of budget) to run Secretariat; EU funding (50% of budget) to develop projects/programmes. **Activities** Politics/policy/regulatory; networking/liaising. **Events** *Conference* Espoo (Finland) 2022, *Environment Forum* Grenoble (France) 2022, *Integrating Cities Conference* Utrecht (Netherlands) 2022, *Annual Conference* Leipzig (Germany) 2021, *Culture Forum* Tampere (Finland) 2021. **Publications** *EUROCITIES FLASH* (10 a year). Annual Report; position/policy papers; reports; flyers; brochures.
Members Full member cities (119) in 29 countries:
Austria, Belgium, Bulgaria, Croatia, Cyprus, Czechia, Denmark, Estonia, Finland, France, Germany, Greece, Hungary, Iceland, Ireland, Italy, Latvia, Lithuania, Luxembourg, Netherlands, Norway, Poland, Portugal, Romania, Slovakia, Slovenia, Spain, Sweden, UK.
Associated partner cities (47) in 19 countries:
Belgium, Bulgaria, Croatia, Cyprus, Finland, France, Germany, Greece, Italy, Lithuania, Netherlands, Norway, Portugal, Russia, Spain, Sweden, Switzerland, Türkiye, UK.
Associated member cities (18) in 9 countries:
Albania, Armenia, Bosnia-Herzegovina, Georgia, North Macedonia, Serbia, Switzerland, Türkiye, Ukraine.
Associated business partners (7) in 4 countries:
Denmark, France, Germany, Sweden.
NGO Relations Member of (5): *Culture Action Europe (CAE, #04981)*; *European Alliance for Culture and the Arts (#05866)*; *European Heritage Alliance 3.3 (#07477)*; *European Housing Forum (EHF, #07504)*; *European Policy Centre (EPC, #08240)*. [2020/XF5216/**F**]

♦ Euro Citizen Action Service / see European Citizen Action Service (#06555)
♦ Euro citoyen action service / see European Citizen Action Service (#06555)
♦ Euro Cittadino Azione Servizio / see European Citizen Action Service (#06555)
♦ Euro Ciudadano Acción Servicio / see European Citizen Action Service (#06555)
♦ **EURO-CIU** European Association of Cochlear Implant Users (#05979)
♦ EUROCLAMP – European Clamping Tools Association (no recent information)

♦ EUROCLASSICA 05663

Pres address not obtained.
URL: https://www.edugroup.at/praxis/portale/euroclassica.html

History Founded 2 Sep 1991, Nîmes (France), by 11 associations. Also referred to in French as *Fédération européenne des associations de professeurs de langues et de civilisations classiques*. Registered in accordance with Luxembourg law. **Aims** Bring together associations of teachers of classical languages and civilization in Europe and promote their cooperation; ensure promotion and defence of the study of classical languages and civilization; assert publicly the contemporary relevance of classical languages and civilizations; encourage cooperation with associations outside Europe which have similar aims. **Structure** General Assembly (annual, at Conference); Executive Committee. **Languages** English, French. **Finance** Members' dues. **Activities** Events/meetings; training/education; networking/liaising; research/documentation; certification/accreditation. **Events** *Annual Conference* Split (Croatia) / Mostar (Bosnia-Herzegovina) 2021, *Annual Conference* Split (Croatia) / Mostar (Bosnia-Herzegovina) 2020, *Annual Conference* Antwerp (Belgium) 2019, *Annual Conference* London (UK) 2018, *Annual Conference* Leiden (Netherlands) 2017. **Publications** *EUROCLASSICA Newsletter* in English, French. Reference works; textbooks.
Members Associations in 25 countries:
Austria, Belgium, Croatia, Czechia, Denmark, Finland, France, Germany, Greece, Hungary, Italy, Lithuania, Luxembourg, Malta, Netherlands, North Macedonia, Norway, Poland, Portugal, Romania, Russia, Spain, Sweden, Switzerland, UK.
Associate groups (3):
American Classical League (ACL); *European Association of Teachers of Ancient Greek (EATAG, #06248)*; *European Association of University Classics Teachers (Eurosophia, #06260)*. [2019.12.16/XD4980/y/**D**]

♦ **EUROCLIO** European Association of History Educators (#06069)
♦ EuroCloud / see Cloud Community Europe (#04027)
♦ EuroCloud Europe / see Cloud Community Europe (#04027)
♦ **Euro-CNS** European Confederation of Neuropathological Societies (#06715)

♦ EuroCollectNet (ECN) 05664

Contact Route d'Arlon 205, L-1150 Luxembourg, Luxembourg. T. +352288018. Fax +3522880189. E-mail: info@eurocollectnet.com.
URL: https://www.eurocollectnet.com/

History Also referred to as *EuroCollectNet Lawyers – International Debt Recovery*. Registered in accordance with Luxembourg law. **Structure** Board of Directors.
Members Individuals in 37 countries and territories:
Andorra, Armenia, Australia, Austria, Belgium, Bosnia-Herzegovina, Brazil, Croatia, Cyprus, Czechia, Denmark, England, France, Germany, Greece, Hungary, Iceland, Ireland, Italy, Liechtenstein, Lithuania, Luxembourg, Malta, Monaco, Montenegro, Netherlands, Poland, Portugal, Romania, Russia, Scotland, Serbia, Slovakia, Slovenia, Spain, Switzerland, Türkiye.
NGO Relations Member of: *Association of International Law Firm Networks (AILFN, #02753)*; *FCIB (#09279)*. [2019/XM8854/v/**F**]

♦ EuroCollectNet Lawyers – International Debt Recovery / see EuroCollectNet (#05664)
♦ EUROCOM (inactive)
♦ EuroCom – Gesellschaft für Europäische Kommunikation (internationally oriented national body)

♦ EuroCommerce (EC) 05665

Dir-Gen Av des Nerviens 85, 1040 Brussels, Belgium. T. +3227370598. E-mail: bastings@eurocommerce.eu.
URL: http://www.eurocommerce.eu/

History 29 Jan 1993, Brussels (Belgium). Founded by merger of *Confédération européenne du commerce de détail (CECD, inactive)*, *European Multiple Retailers' Association (GEDIS, inactive)* and *Federation of European Wholesale and International Trade Associations (FEWITA, inactive)*. *European Retail Round Table (ERRT, inactive)* merged into EuroCommerce, Nov 2019. Former names and other names: *Association européenne du commerce* – former. Registration: Banque-Carrefour des Entreprises, No/ID: 0449.507.896, Start date: 29 Jan 1993, Belgium; EU Transparency Register, No/ID: 84973761187-60, Start date: 19 Feb 2009. **Aims** Speak on behalf of retail, wholesale and international *trade*, small and medium-sized *enterprises* and major *distributors*, food and non-food sectors for the whole of Europe – European Union, EFTA and the countries of Central Europe; provide permanent representation for the *commercial* sector vis-à-vis the institutions of the European Union. **Structure** General Assembly; Board of Administration. **Languages** English, French, German. **Staff** 18.00 FTE, paid. **Finance** Sources: members' dues. **Activities** Advocacy/lobbying/activism. **Events** *Conference on Corporate Sustainability Due Diligence* Brussels (Belgium) 2022, *Conference on Embracing Transformation and Uncertainties* Brussels (Belgium) 2022, *Conference on Circular Economy* Brussels (Belgium) 2018, *Meeting on Celebrating Retail and Wholesale* Brussels (Belgium) 2018, *European Retail Conference* Brussels (Belgium) 2017. **Publications** Ad hoc online publications.
Members National associations, affiliates and companies in 28 countries:
Austria, Belgium, Bulgaria, Croatia, Cyprus, Czechia, Denmark, Estonia, Finland, France, Germany, Greece, Hungary, Iceland, Ireland, Italy, Latvia, Luxembourg, Netherlands, Norway, Poland, Portugal, Romania, Slovakia, Slovenia, Spain, Sweden, Switzerland.
Affiliate members include the following 7 organizations listed in this Yearbook:
Chamber of Commerce, Industry and Agriculture Belgium – Luxembourg – Africa-Caribbean-Pacific (CBL-ACP); *Direct Selling Europe (DSE, #05092)*; *Ecommerce Europe (#05307)*; *European Direct Selling Association (SELDIA, #06928)*; *European DIY-Retail Association – Global Home Improvement Network (EDRA-GHIN, #06933)*; *European Travel Retail Confederation (ETRC, #08945)*; *European Union of Electrical Wholesalers (EUEW, #08987)*.
NGO Relations Member of (2): *Circular Plastics Alliance (#03936)*; *Federation of European and International Associations Established in Belgium (FAIB, #09508)*. [2022.08.02/XD3738/y/**D**]

♦ EuroCom – Society for European Communication (internationally oriented national body)
♦ EUROCOM – Union européenne des marchands en combustibles (inactive)
♦ EUROCON – European Conference on Electronics Reliability in Electrical and Electronic Components and Systems (meeting series)
♦ **Euroconstruct** European Forecasting Group for the Construction Industry (#07292)

♦ Euroconsumers 05666

Luxembourg Office Ave Guillaume 13-b, L-1651 Luxembourg, Luxembourg.
Belgian Office Rue de Hollande 13, 1060 Brussels, Belgium. T. +3225423338.
URL: http://www.euroconsumers.org/

History 1990. Registered in accordance with Belgian law. EU Transparency Register: 284568937633-32. Registration: AISBL/IVZW, Belgium; Société anonyme, No/ID: B33093, Luxembourg. **Aims** Promote and defend the interest of consumers; provide solutions to their problems. **Structure** General Assembly (annual). Council. **Finance** Members' dues. **Events** *Euroconsumers International Forum* Luxembourg (Luxembourg) 2020.
Members National organizations in 5 countries:
Belgium, Brazil, Italy, Portugal, Spain.
NGO Relations Member of: *European Registry of Internet Domain Names (EURid, #08351)*. [2020/XF5717/**F**]

♦ EUROCONTROL 05667

Dir Gen Rue de la Fusée 96, 1130 Brussels, Belgium. E-mail: infocentre@eurocontrol.int.
URL: http://www.eurocontrol.int/

History 13 Dec 1960, Brussels (Belgium). Established on signature of *EUROCONTROL International Convention Relating to Cooperation for the Safety of Air Navigation (1960)* by representatives of 6 governments (in order of signing): Federal Republic of Germany, Belgium, France, United Kingdom, Luxembourg, Netherlands. Convention entered into force 1 Mar 1963. Ireland adhered to the Convention on 1 Jan 1965. Two Protocols signed, 6 Jul 1970 and 21 Nov 1978, Brussels, relating to tax issues and still in force (as amended by Article XXXVIII of amending Protocol of 1981). Protocol amending EUROCONTROL Convention of 1960 ("Amended Convention") as well as Multilateral Agreement relating to Route Charges, signed, 12 Feb 1981, Brussels, and entered into force, 1 Jan 1986. 27 Jun 1997, Brussels, 27 EUROCONTROL Member States signed Protocol consolidating EUROCONTROL Convention ("Revised Convention"). Ratification process of Revised Convention currently ongoing. 8 Oct 2002, Brussels, EUROCONTROL Member States and European Community signed Protocol on the Accession of the European Community to EUROCONTROL Convention. Former names and other names: *EUROCONTROL – Supporting European Aviation* – full title; *European Organisation for the Safety of Air Navigation (EUROCONTROL)* – former; *Organisation européenne pour la sécurité de la navigation aérienne* – former; *Europese Organisatie voor de Veiligheid van de Luchtvaart* – former. Registration: Banque-Carrefour des Entreprises, No/ID: 0923.980.032, Start date: 1 Mar 1963, Belgium. **Aims** As a pan-European, civl-military organization: support Member States to achieve safe, efficient and environmentally-friendly air traffic operations across Europe; deliver a Single European Sky that will meet the safety, capacity and performance challenges of European aviation in the 21st century. **Structure** Permanent Commission; Provisional Council; Enlarged Committee For Route Charges; Agency. Advisory and consultative groups Air Navigation Services Board; Audit Board; Civil-Military Stakeholder Committee; Maastricht Coordination Group; Military ATM Board; Standing Committee on Finance; Pension Fund Supervisory Board; Performance Review Commission. Network Management Board; Single Sky Committee. **Languages** English, French. **Staff** 1800.00 FTE, paid. Staff from 41 nationalities working at different sites. Dual internal Social Dialogue process: between Management and elected Staff Committees; between Management and 3 recognized Trade Unions: *Trade Union Eurocontrol Maastricht (TUEM, #20187)*; Union Syndicale France; *Union syndicale du service public européen (#20486)*. *Administrative Tribunal of the International Labour Organization (ILO Tribunal, #00118)* is competent to hear disputes between officials and EUROCONTROL. **Finance** Contributions from each member state (76%) and bank loans. Maastricht Upper Area Control Centre and Central Route Charges Office are financed separately. Annual budget: 865,000,000 EUR. **Activities** Research and development; training/education; advocacy/lobbying/activism. Core activities spread over 5 main areas: Network Manager; pan-European Single Sky; *EUROCONTROL Central Route Charges Office (CRCO)*; *EUROCONTROL Maastricht Upper Area Control Centre (MUAC, #05670)*; Centre; SESAR and Research. **Events** *Annual Safety Forum* Brussels (Belgium) 2022, *Annual Safety Forum* Brussels (Belgium) 2021, *Global Resilience Summit* Brussels (Belgium) 2021, *Annual Safety Forum* Brussels (Belgium) 2020, *Digitally Connected Airports Confererence* Brussels (Belgium) 2020. **Publications** *HindSight Magazine* (2 a year); *Skyway* (2 a year) – magazine. Annual Report.

Members Governments (41):
Albania, Armenia, Austria, Belgium, Bosnia-Herzegovina, Bulgaria, Croatia, Cyprus, Czechia, Denmark, Estonia, Finland, France, Georgia, Germany, Greece, Hungary, Ireland, Italy, Latvia, Lithuania, Luxembourg, Malta, Moldova, Monaco, Montenegro, Netherlands, North Macedonia, Norway, Poland, Portugal, Romania, Serbia, Slovakia, Slovenia, Spain, Sweden, Switzerland, Türkiye, UK, Ukraine.
Comprehensive Agreement States (2):
Israel, Morocco.

IGO Relations Close cooperation with, amongst other: *Agency for the Safety of Aerial Navigation in Africa and Madagascar (#00556)*; *Arab Civil Aviation Organization (ACAO, #00920)*; *European Union Aviation Safety Agency (EASA, #08978)*; *European Commission (EC, #06633)* – DG MOVE; *European Council (#06801)*; *European Defence Agency (EDA, #06895)*; *European Economic and Social Committee (EESC, #06963)*; *European Parliament (EP, #08146)*; *European Space Agency (ESA, #08798)*; *European Union (EU, #08967)*; *International Civil Aviation Organization (ICAO, #12581)*; *NATO (#16945)*. Various agreements with international organizations, including: *European Union Agency for the Space Programme (EUSPA, #08974)*. **NGO Relations** Close cooperation with: *Airports Council International (ACI, #00611)*; *Civil Air Navigation Services Organisation (CANSO, #03963)*; *International Air Transport Association (IATA, #11614)*; *International Council of Aircraft Owner and Pilot Associations (IAOPA, #12988)*; *International Federation of Air Line Pilots' Associations (IFALPA, #13349)*; *International Federation of Air Traffic Controllers' Associations (IFATCA, #13350)*; national organizations. Member of: *European Telecommunications Standards Institute (ETSI, #08897)*; *SESAR Joint Undertaking (SJU, #19249)*. [2022/XD0823/**D***]

♦ Euro Contrôle Route (ECR) 05668

Coordinator Aleje Jerozolimskie 94, 00-807 Warsaw, Poland. T. +48222204414.
Sec Rue de la Régence 39, 1000 Brussels, Belgium.
URL: https://www.euro-controle-route.eu/

History 5 Oct 1999. "Road transport inspection" working group set up, 1994, by *Benelux Union (#03207)* countries. Relations established with France 1997. Official start of ECR when Administrative Arrangement was signed. **Aims** Improve road safety, sustainability, fair competition and labour conditions in road transport by activities related to compliance with existing regulations. **Structure** Steering Committee; Executive Committee; Secretariat. Working Groups.

Members European Transport Inspection Services of 14 countries:
Austria, Belgium, Bulgaria, Croatia, France, Germany, Hungary, Ireland, Luxembourg, Netherlands, Poland, Romania, Spain, UK.
Observers (3):
Czechia, Portugal, Slovenia.

NGO Relations Cooperates with (1): *European Roads Policing Network (ROADPOL, #08395)*. [2022/AA2186/**F***]

♦ EUROCONTROL Guild of Air Traffic Services (EGATS) 05669

Exec Sec EGATS Secretariat, Horsterweg 11, Airport, 6199 AC Maastricht, Netherlands. E-mail: board@egats.org.
Pres address not obtained.
URL: http://www.egats.org/

History Dec 1972. Registered in accordance with Dutch law. **Aims** Contribute to *safety* and efficiency in air traffic *control*. **Structure** General Meeting (annual); Executive Board. **Languages** English. **Finance** Members' dues. Support from *EUROCONTROL (#05667)* for some activities. **Activities** Guidance/assistance/consulting; research and development; networking/liaising. **Events** *Annual General Meeting* Maastricht (Netherlands) 2019, *Annual General Meeting* Maastricht (Netherlands) 2005, *ATC : annual European air traffic control conference* Maastricht (Netherlands) 1999, *Annual Forum* Maastricht (Netherlands) 1999, *ATC : annual European air traffic control conference* Maastricht (Netherlands) 1998. **Publications** *Output* (2 a year).

Members Ordinary and Candidate: Eurocontrol operations personnel; Corporate: associations, industries and other organizations who contribute their support; Affiliate: individuals who support the Guild with financial donations. Members in 22 countries:
Austria, Belgium, Bulgaria, Cyprus, Denmark, France, Germany, Greece, Hungary, Ireland, Italy, Luxembourg, Netherlands, North Macedonia, Norway, Portugal, Slovenia, Spain, Sweden, Switzerland, Türkiye, UK.

IGO Relations *International Civil Aviation Organization (ICAO, #12581)*. **NGO Relations** Member of: *International Federation of Air Traffic Controllers' Associations (IFATCA, #13350)*. [2019.11.07/XE0578/**E**]

♦ EUROCONTROL International Convention Relating to Cooperation for the Safety of Air Navigation (1960 treaty)

♦ EUROCONTROL Maastricht Upper Area Control Centre (MUAC) 05670

Centre de contrôle de l'espace aérien supérieur, Maastricht

Dir Horsterweg 11, AIRPORT, 6199 AC Maastricht, Netherlands. T. +31433661234. Fax +31433661300. E-mail: muac.info@eurocontrol.int.
URL: http://www.eurocontrol.int/muac/

History 28 Feb 1964. Permanent Commission of *EUROCONTROL (#05667)* took official decision to set up first international control facility, on Dutch territory. Upper airspace covering Belgium and Luxembourg placed under EUROCONTROL responsibility, 3 Mar 1964. MUAC became operational 29 Feb 1972. Operated by EUROCONTROL on behalf of Belgium, Netherlands, Luxembourg and Germany on the basis of Agreement Relating to the Provision and Operation of Air Traffic Services and Facilities by EUROCONTROL at the Maastricht Upper Area Control Centre (Maastricht Agreement), signed 25 Nov 1986. Former names and other names: *International Civil-Military Air Traffic Control Centre* – former. **Aims** Provide control for the upper airspace (above 24,500 feet) of Belgium, Luxembourg, Netherlands and north-west Germany. **Structure** Management Board; Director. Member States retain their regulatory competence. **Languages** English. **Staff** 750.00 FTE, paid. Staff from 31 different nationalities. Mainly represented by *Trade Union Eurocontrol Maastricht (TUEM, #20187)* and Staff Committee Servants. **Finance** Sources: contributions of member/participating states. Funded separately from EUROCONTROL budget. Contributions by member states via cost-sharing formula. **Activities** Monitoring/evaluation. **Publications** Annual Report; fact sheets.

Members Member States (4):
Belgium, Germany, Luxembourg, Netherlands. [2022.10.16/XK0154/**E***]

♦ EUROCONTROL – Supporting European Aviation / see EUROCONTROL (#05667)
♦ **EURO COOP** European Community of Consumer Cooperatives (#06678)
♦ **EuroCOP** European Confederation of Police (#06719)
♦ Eurocophar (inactive)
♦ **EUROCOPYA** European Federation of Joint Management Societies of Producers for Private Audiovisual Copying (#07151)
♦ **EUROCORD** Fédération européenne des industries de corderie ficellerie et de filets (#09573)

♦ Eurocorps 05671

Corps européen – Eurocuerpo – Eurokorps – Eurocorps

Commanding General Quartier Aubert-de-Vincelles, 4 rue du Corps Européen, BP 70082, 67020 Strasbourg CEDEX, France. T. +33388432003. Fax +33388432005.
URL: http://www.eurocorps.org/

History 22 May 1992, La Rochelle (France). Established during the La Rochelle Summit, by the governments of France and Germany. Inaugural ceremony 5 Nov 1993, Strasbourg (France). Belgium joined 25 Jun 1993 and Spain 1 Jul 1994. Became fully operational 30 Nov 1995. Luxembourg adhered 7 May 1996. Poland became 6th framework nation, 1 Jan 2016. Since 1993, available to *Western European Union (WEU, inactive)*, and by the "SACEUR Agreement" available to *NATO (#16945)*.
Reorganization completed in accordance with *'Declaration of Cologne'*, 5 Jun 1999, around which time it was decided to transform Eurocorps into a 'Rapid Reaction Corps, available to both *European Union (EU, #08967)* and NATO. Transformation started and by Apr 2001, Eurocorps member states had offered the corps as a *'NATO Rapid Deployable Corps Headquarters'*. Sep 2002, certified as a NATO *'High Readiness Force (Land) Headquarters'*. Jun 2006, certified as a NRL Land Component Command. Certified as a *'Joint Task Force (JTF)'*, 2014. Certified as European Union Battle Group (EUBG) (F) Headquarter, 2016. Certification process preparing to be a Land Component Command (LCC) for NRF 2020 is ongoing.
Aims Based on a modular engagement plan: carry out missions of *humanitarian aid* and population assistance following natural or technical *disasters*; execute advisory or training missions; participate in peace-restoring or *peace-keeping* missions; engage as a mechanized army corps in high-intensity combat operations. **Structure** Multinational Army Corps Headquarters Staff with a Multinational Command Support Brigade and a Multinational Support Battalion. French/German Brigade – subordinated for operations, training and exercises. Organized as a rapid reaction corps after which it mirrors a NATO structure similar to a Rapid Deployable Corps Headquarters. In operations, national units from framework nations, earmarked for this specific assignment, and units from troop contributing nations are placed under operational command of HQ Eurocorps for the duration of deployment. Relevant treaties: *Treaty of Strasbourg* (Feb 2009) specifically for Eurocorps; *Treaty for Collaboration in Economic, Social and Cultural Matters and for Collective Self-defence (Brussels Treaty, 1948)*; *North Atlantic Treaty (1949)*. **Languages** Dutch, English, French, German, Polish, Spanish. **Staff** Garrisoned in Strasbourg (France): about 1,000 soldiers and 70 civilians from the 10 nations. **Finance** Supported by the 5 framework nations. **Activities** Humanitarian/emergency aid; conflict resolution. Missions include: 4 contingents to Bosnia-Herzegovina to *NATO-led Stabilization Force in Bosnia and Herzegovina (SFOR, inactive)* (1998-2000); Head of *KFOR (#16187)* mission in Kosovo (2000); Command of *International Security Assistance Force (ISAF, inactive)* in Kabul, Afghanistan (Aug 2004-Feb 2005); NRF stand-by period (1 Jun 2006-31 Dec 2006); NRF stand-by (2010); Committed in different HQs of ISAF (2012); Command the European Union Training Mission (EUTM) in Mali (2015); Stand-by period as Force Headquarters for EU Battle Group (F) HQ EUBG 16/2 and 17/1 (2016/17); Command the European Union Training Mission (EUTM) in the Central African Republic (2016/17).

Members Framework nations (5) – NATO and European Union:
Belgium, France, Germany, Luxembourg, Spain.
Associated Nations (5) – NATO AND European Union ; NATO :
Greece (*), Italy (*), Poland (*), Romania (*), Türkiye (**). [2022/XF2645/**F***]

♦ **Euro Cos humanisme et santé** Groupe pluri-professionnelle européen de reflexion et de formation en santé (#10766)
♦ Euro Cos and Santé / see Groupe pluri-professionnelle européen de reflexion et de formation en santé (#10766)
♦ **EUROCOTON** Fédération européene de l'industrie textile du coton et des fibres connexes (#07093)
♦ Euro Council / see Eurogroup (#05689)
♦ EuroCPR – European Communications Policy Research Conference (meeting series)
♦ Eurocréation pépinières / see Pépinières Européenes de Création

♦ euroCRIS 05672

Contact Heyendaalseweg 141, 6525 AJ Nijmegen, Netherlands. E-mail: eurocris@eurocris.org.
URL: http://www.eurocris.org/

History 2002. Founded deriving from informal platform group set up 1991. Registration: EU Transparency Register, No/ID: 881660532836-18, Start date: 9 Oct 2018. **Aims** Develop quality *Current Research Information Systems* (CRIS); act as custodian of the Common *European* Research Information Format (CERIF) – EU Recommendation; advance *interoperability* in the research community through CERIF. **Structure** Board; Task Groups (6). **Languages** English. **Staff** 0.50 FTE, paid. Voluntary. **Finance** Members' dues. Additional sponsoring by Institutional members; project funding. **Activities** Events/meetings; knowledge management/information dissemination. **Events** *Membership Meeting* Espoo (Finland) 2019, *Conference* Umeå (Sweden) 2018, *Conference* St Andrews (UK) 2016, *Membership Meeting* Paris (France) 2015, *Conference* Rome (Italy) 2014. **Publications** Annual Report; conference proceedings; seminar reports.

Members Institutional; Personal; Affiliate. Institutional in 43 countries:
Australia, Austria, Belgium, Brazil, Bulgaria, Canada, Colombia, Croatia, Czechia, Denmark, Finland, France, Germany, Greece, Hungary, Iceland, Iran Islamic Rep, Ireland, Israel, Italy, Kenya, Latvia, Montenegro, Netherlands, North Macedonia, Norway, Pakistan, Peru, Poland, Portugal, Russia, Serbia, Slovakia, Slovenia, Spain, Sweden, Switzerland, Türkiye, Uganda, UK, Ukraine, United Arab Emirates, USA.
Included in the above, 4 organizations listed in this Yearbook:
ESI Center Eastern Europe (ESI CEE); *European Plate Observing System (EPOS, #08220)*; *European Science Foundation (ESF, #08441)*; *Nordicom (#17374)*.
Personal in 46 countries:
Australia, Austria, Belgium, Bosnia-Herzegovina, Brazil, Bulgaria, Chile, China, Colombia, Denmark, Estonia, Finland, France, Georgia, Germany, Greece, India, Iran Islamic Rep, Israel, Italy, Japan, Kenya, Korea Rep, Latvia, Liechtenstein, Lithuania, Mexico, Netherlands, New Zealand, Nigeria, Norway, Peru, Poland, Portugal, Puerto Rico, Romania, Serbia, Slovakia, Spain, Sri Lanka, Sweden, Switzerland, Türkiye, UK, United Arab Emirates, USA.
Affiliate in 18 countries:
Austria, Belgium, Bulgaria, China, Finland, Germany, Greece, Iran Islamic Rep, Ireland, Lithuania, Netherlands, Portugal, Russia, Slovakia, Spain, Switzerland, UK, USA.

NGO Relations Cooperates with: *Alliance for Permanent Access (#00712)*; *Committee on Data for Science and Technology (CODATA, #04247)*; *Confederation of Open Access Repositories (COAR, #04573)*; *European Association of Research Managers and Administrators (EARMA, #06195)*; *European Research Consortium for Informatics and Mathematics (ERCIM, #08362)*; *European Science Foundation (ESF, #08441)*; *European University Information Systems Organization (EUNIS, #09033)*; Joint Information Systems Committee (JISC); VIVO – Research and Expertise Across Cornell; national organizations. [2018/XJ4287/**F**]

♦ EuroCTO Club 05673

Secretariat address not obtained. E-mail: secretariat@eurocto.eu.
URL: https://www.eurocto.eu/

History 14 Dec 2006. **Aims** Exchange experiences among the most experienced operators in CTO and complex procedures; test new technologies and strategies for CTO recanalization; issue 'state of the art' recommendations; promote scientific research and teaching courses; draw information from a dedicated registry. **Structure** Board. **Activities** Events/meetings; knowledge management/information dissemination; research/documentation; training/education. **Publications** *EuroCTO Club Newsletter*.

Members Individuals: Founding; Full and Coordinator; Full; Associated; Non-European Affiliated; Non-European Associate; Honorary. Members in 34 countries:
Armenia, Austria, Belgium, Bulgaria, Croatia, Czechia, Denmark, Egypt, Estonia, Finland, France, Germany, Greece, Hungary, Iran Islamic Rep, Iraq, Italy, Latvia, Lithuania, Netherlands, Norway, Poland, Portugal, Romania, Saudi Arabia, Serbia, South Africa, Spain, Sweden, Switzerland, Tunisia, Türkiye, UK, Ukraine. [2020/AA0748/v/**F**]

♦ Eurocuerpo (#05671)
♦ Euro-Currency Standing Committee / see Committee on the Global Financial System (#04258)
♦ EuroDAC – European Design Automation Conference (meeting series)

- ♦ EuroDAC / see Partner Community Council (#18228)
- ♦ **EURODAD** European Network on Debt and Development (#07891)

♦ EURODEFENSE Network 05674

SG Case 44 – 1 place Joffre, 75700 Paris SP 07, France. T. +33144424215. E-mail: info@eurodefense.eu – eurodefense.reseau@gmail.com.
URL: https://eurodefense.eu/

History 2001. *'EuroDéfense Association'* (French national association) set up Mar 1994, to promote the European security and defence identity. The founders decided to expand their ideas to the rest of Europe, thus contributing to the formation of a sister organization in Germany, and subsequently other countries followed. **Aims** Promote a European *security* and *defence* identity; contribute to developing a sense of European defence by concrete initiatives; help establish and reinforce links with fellow associations in each WEU country. **Structure** EURODEFENSE Council, managed by rotating Presidency. **Languages** English, French. **Activities** Awareness raising; events/meetings; guidance/assistance/consulting; knowledge management/information dissemination; monitoring/evaluation; networking/liaising; research/documentation. **Events** *Annual International Conference* Lisbon (Portugal) 2021, *Annual International Conference* Vienna (Austria) 2020, *Annual International Conference* Bucharest (Romania) 2019, *Annual International Conference* London (UK) 2017, *Annual International Conference* Paris (France) 2016. **Publications** Reports; surveys; articles; letters.
Members Associations in 15 countries:
Austria, Belgium, Denmark, Finland, France, Germany, Greece, Hungary, Italy, Luxembourg, Netherlands, Portugal, Romania, Spain, UK. [2021.09.09/XJ4779/**F***]

- ♦ **EuroDendro** European Working Group for Dendrochronology (#09110)
- ♦ Eurodesk Näverket (#05675)
- ♦ Eurodesk-Nettverket (#05675)
- ♦ Eurodesk Netvarket (#05675)
- ♦ Eurodesk Netwerk (#05675)

♦ Eurodesk Network 05675

Réseau Eurodesk – Red Eurodesk – Eurodesk Netzwerk – Rede Eurodesk – Eurodesk Netwerk – Eurodesk Netvarket – Eurodesk-Nettverket – Eurodesk-Verkosto – Eurodesk Näverket – Evróvisir Upplsinganetio

Dir Eurodesk Brussels Link, Rue aux Fleurs 32, 1000 Brussels, Belgium. T. +3222077700. Fax +3222077709. E-mail: info@eurodesk.eu.
URL: http://www.eurodesk.eu/

History 1990, Scotland. Founded with the support of *European Commission (EC, #06633)*, originally within the framework of *Youth for Europe (inactive)* and currently part of Erasmus++. Registration: Banque-Carrefour des Entreprises, No/ID: 0464.801.531, Start date: 31 Dec 1998, Belgium; EU Transparency Register, No/ID: 078783114207-72, Start date: 12 Aug 2014. **Aims** Provide *European information* for *young people* and those who work with them in order to foster mobility and active participation of young people. **Structure** General Assembly (twice a year); Executive Committee; Brussels Link Office in Brussels (Belgium). **Languages** English. **Staff** 8.00 FTE, paid. **Finance** Co-financed by: *European Commission (EC, #06633)* and Erasmus++. **Activities** Guidance/assistance/consulting; knowledge management/information dissemination. **Publications** *Eurodesk Annual Overview.*
Members National partners in 37 countries:
Austria, Bulgaria, Belgium, Croatia, Cyprus, Czechia, Denmark, Estonia, Finland, France, Georgia, Germany, Greece, Hungary, Iceland, Ireland, Italy, Latvia, Liechtenstein, Lithuania, Luxembourg, Malta, Montenegro, Netherlands, North Macedonia, Norway, Poland, Portugal, Romania, Serbia, Slovakia, Slovenia, Spain, Sweden, Switzerland, Türkiye, Ukraine.
Included in the above, 1 organization listed in this Yearbook:
Youth Society for Peace and Development of the Balkans (YSPDB).
IGO Relations Member of: Advisory Group of Partnership between the *European Commission (EC, #06633)* and *Council of Europe (CE, #04881)* in the Field of Youth. [2022.05.04/XF4907/y/**F**]

- ♦ Eurodesk Netzwerk (#05675)
- ♦ Eurodesk-Verkosto (#05675)
- ♦ EURODET – Europäische Detektiv-Akademie (internationally oriented national body)
- ♦ Eurodiaconia – Association of Diaconal Organizations in Europe (inactive)
- ♦ **Eurodiaconia** European Federation for Diaconia (#07099)
- ♦ EURODIDAC / see Worlddidac Association (#21361)

♦ EURODIF Corporation 05676

Société EURODIF

Address not obtained.

History 27 Nov 1973. Convention signed 20 Mar 1980, Paris (France), and entered into force 25 Jul 1982. Statutes registered in *'UNTS 1/21849'*. Name derives from *European Gaseous Diffusion Uranium Enrichment Consortium.* **Aims** Construct and exploit *factories* employing *gaseous diffusion* for separation of *uranium isotopes.* **Structure** Supervisory Board; Executive Management Board. **Finance** Capital: euro 152.500 million, owned by shareholding companies. **Events** *Joint international meeting* Antwerp (Belgium) 1986.
Members Private companies in 4 countries:
Belgium, France, Italy, Spain.
NGO Relations Member of: *Association for the Development of International Nuclear Instruction (no recent information).* [2010/XF2159/e/**F***]

- ♦ **EuroDIG** European Dialogue on Internet Governance (#06917)
- ♦ **euro.digital** European Association of Leading Digital Enterprises (#06106)
- ♦ EuroDIG Support Association / see European Dialogue on Internet Governance (#06917)
- ♦ **EURODOC** European Council of Doctoral Candidates and Junior Researchers (#06815)
- ♦ **EURODURG** European Drug Utilization Research Group (#06948)
- ♦ **EuroEAP Society** European Society for Electromechanically Active Polymer Transducers and Artificial Muscles (#08589)
- ♦ EURO-EDU / see Interdisciplines
- ♦ Euro-ELSO / see EuroELSO (#05677)

♦ EuroELSO 05677

Contact INTERPLAN, Sachsenstrasse 6, 20097 Hamburg, Germany. E-mail: euroelso@interplan.de.
Pres address not obtained.
URL: https://www.euroelso.net/

History Set up as the European branch of *Extracorporeal Life Support Organization (ELSO).* Former names and other names: *Euro-ELSO* – alias. **Aims** Provide support to institutions delivering *extracorporeal life support.* **Structure** Steering Committee. **Activities** Events/meetings; knowledge management/information dissemination; research/documentation; training/education. **Events** *Annual congress* Lisbon (Portugal) 2023, *Annual congress* London (UK) 2022, *Annual Congress* 2021, *Annual Congress* Barcelona (Spain) 2019, *Annual Congress* Prague (Czechia) 2018. **Publications** *EuroELSO Newsletter, Perfusion Journal.* Webinars. **NGO Relations** *European Board of Cardiovascular Perfusion (EBCP, #06356).* [2022/XM8402/**D**]

- ♦ Euroenviron (inactive)
- ♦ EuroEvoDevo / see European Society for Evolutionary Developmental Biology (#08601)

♦ EuroExpert 05678

SG c/o IfS, Hohenstaufenring 48/54, 50674 Cologne, Germany. T. +4922191277110. Fax +4922191277199. E-mail: secretary-general@euroexpert.org.
Registered Office 59 Bd de Verdun, L-2670 Luxembourg, Luxembourg.
URL: https://www.euroexpert.org/

History May 1998. Full title *Organisation for European Expert Associations.* Registration: Mémorial C, No/ID: F0002852, Start date: 1999, Luxembourg; EU Transparency Register, No/ID: 22720754078-66, Start date: 27 Aug 2010. **Aims** Develop, promote and converge common ethical and professional standards for experts within the EU; provide a point of contact between experts and European institutions; cooperate and relate with judicial and legal authorities, government departments, official and private bodies and other appropriate tribunals and organizations for purposes of accreditation and certification of experts; provide a forum for experts worldwide. **Structure** General Meeting (annual); Council; Secretariat in Cologne (Germany). **Languages** English. **Activities** Standards/guidelines; networking/liaising; certification/accreditation; events/meetings.
Members National organizations in 13 countries:
Austria, Croatia, Czechia, France, Germany, Italy, Poland, Portugal, Russia, Serbia, Spain, Switzerland, UK. [2021/XD9225/**D**]

- ♦ Euroexperts – European Real Estate Valuers (inactive)
- ♦ EUROFABE – European Federation of Associations of Business Economists (no recent information)
- ♦ **EurofamNet** European Family Support Network (#07030)
- ♦ **EuroFAWC** European Forum for Animal Welfare Councils (#07305)
- ♦ EUROFEDE – Fédération européenne de travailleurs de l'alimentation et industries connexes – OE/CMT (inactive)
- ♦ EuroFédération de psychanalyse (unconfirmed)
- ♦ EUROFED – European Federation of the International College of Surgeons (see: #12650)
- ♦ **Euro Fed Lipid** European Federation for the Science and Technology of Lipids (#07210)
- ♦ **EUROFEDOP** European Federation of Employees in Public Services (#07106)
- ♦ **EUROFEL** European Association of Feldspar Producers (#06037)
- ♦ **EUROFEMA** European Organic Fertilizers Manufacturers Association (#08095)
- ♦ EUROFER / see European Steel Association (#08835)
- ♦ **EUROFER** European Steel Association (#08835)
- ♦ **EUROFEU** Comité européen des constructeurs de matériel d'incendie et de secours (#06659)

♦ Eurofi 05679

SG 22 rue de Madrid, 75008 Paris, France. T. +33140829699. E-mail: contact@eurofi.net.
Brussels Av Herrmann Debroux 44, 1160 Brussels, Belgium.
URL: http://www.eurofi.net/

History 2000. Former names and other names: *EUROFI Association* – former; *Eurofi 2000* – former. Registration: EU Transparency Register, No/ID: 525103133519-45, Start date: 19 Dec 2018. **Aims** Serve as a thinkthank on *financial* regulation and supervision and as a renowned platform for exchanges between the financial services industry and the EU and international public authorities. **Structure** Board. **Finance** Members' dues. **Activities** Events/meetings; research/documentation. **Events** *Financial Forum* Berlin (Germany) 2020, *Financial Forum* Helsinki (Finland) 2019, *Financial Forum* Helsinki (Finland) 2019, *Financial Forum* Amsterdam (Netherlands) 2016, *Financial Forum* Luxembourg (Luxembourg) 2015. **Members** Global and European financial institutions (over 70). Membership countries not specified. **NGO Relations** *European Association of Long-Term Investors (ELTI, #06112); Long-Term Investors Club (LTIC, #16513).* [2020/XJ9426/**F**]

- ♦ Eurofi 2000 / see Eurofi (#05679)
- ♦ EUROFI Association / see Eurofi (#05679)
- ♦ EUROFIBREFILL – European Fibrefill Association (inactive)
- ♦ EUROFILLERS International Conference (meeting series)
- ♦ Eurofillers Polymerblends (meeting series)
- ♦ **EUROFIMA** EUROFIMA European Company for the Financing of Railroad Rolling Stock (#05680)
- ♦ EUROFIMA Europäische Gesellschaft für die Finanzierung von Eisenbahnmaterial (#05680)

♦ EUROFIMA European Company for the Financing of Railroad Rolling Stock (EUROFIMA) 05680

EUROFIMA Société européenne pour le financement de matériel ferroviaire – EUROFIMA Europäische Gesellschaft für die Finanzierung von Eisenbahnmaterial – EUROFIMA Società Europea per il Finanziamento di Materiale Ferroviario

CEO Rittergasse 20, 4051 Basel BS, Switzerland. T. +41612873340. Fax +41612873240.
URL: http://www.eurofima.org/

History 20 Nov 1956, on signature by 23 European countries of an international Convention, 20 Oct 1955, Basel (Switzerland). Under Basic Agreement of 30 Sep 1955, between the railways of the 23 countries parties to the Convention, the company would exist for 50 years from that date; extended, 15 Jun 1984, for a further 50 years (until 2056). Statutes adopted 20 Nov 1956; most recent statutes adopted 26 Mar 2010. Registered in accordance with Swiss Civil Code and pursuant to the Convention. **Aims** Facilitate for associated railways the acquisition of railway and equipment. **Structure** General Assembly (annual); Board of Directors. Meetings closed. **Languages** English, French, German. **Finance** Capital stock: Swiss Fr 2,600 million, 520 million are paid up. Shareholders are national railways of countries (figure indicates percentage shareholding): France (22.6); Germany (22.6); Italy (13.5); Belgium (9.8); Netherlands (5.8); Spain (5.22); Switzerland (5); Austria (2); Sweden (2); Luxembourg (2); Portugal (2); Czech Rep (1); Greece (2); Serbia (1.08); Hungary (0.7); Croatia (0.82); Slovakia (0.5); Bosnia-Herzegovina (0.51); Bulgaria (0.2); Slovenia (0.42); Macedonia Infrastructure (0.09); Montenegro (0.06); Macedonia Transport (0.02); Turkey (0.04); Denmark (0.02); Norway (0.02). Loans raised through banks or by public subscriptions. Balance sheet (31 Dec 2016): Swiss Fr 20,900,000. **Activities** Events/meetings. **Events** *Annual General Assembly* Luxembourg (Luxembourg) 2011, *Annual General Assembly* Venice (Italy) 2010, *Annual General Assembly* The Hague (Netherlands) 2009, *Annual General Assembly* The Hague (Netherlands) 2009, *Annual General Assembly* Stockholm (Sweden) 2008. **Publications** *EUROFIMA Annual Report* in English.
Members National railways of 25 countries:
Austria, Belgium, Bosnia-Herzegovina, Bulgaria, Croatia, Czechia, Denmark, France, Germany, Greece, Hungary, Italy, Luxembourg, Montenegro, Netherlands, North Macedonia, Norway, Portugal, Serbia, Slovakia, Slovenia, Spain, Sweden, Switzerland, Türkiye. [2018.06.12/XM1002/e/**F***]

- ♦ EUROFIMA Società Europea per il Finanziamento di Materiale Ferroviario (#05680)
- ♦ EUROFIMA Société européenne pour le financement de matériel ferroviaire (#05680)
- ♦ **EUROFINAS** European Federation of Finance House Associations (#07121)
- ♦ EuroFinUse / see BETTER FINANCE (#03219)
- ♦ **EuroFIR** European Food Information Resource (#07285)
- ♦ **EUROFISH** International Organisation for the Development of Fisheries and Aquaculture in Europe (#14427)
- ♦ EUROFLEX / see Flexible Packaging Europe (#09794)
- ♦ EUROFLEX – European Forum for the Flexible Packaging Industry / see Flexible Packaging Europe (#09794)
- ♦ EUROFLOUR – Association européenne des meuniers exportateurs (inactive)

♦ EUROFLUOR 05681

Contact c/o CEFIC, Rue Belliard 40, Box 15, 1040 Brussels, Belgium. T. +3224369509. E-mail: info@eurofluor.org.
URL: http://www.eurofluor.org/

History 1973, as a sector group of *Conseil européen de l'industrie chimique (CEFIC, #04687).* Full title: *EUROFLUOR – Comité Technique Européen du Fluor (CTEF) – European Technical Committee for Fluorine.* **Aims** Enhance *safety* around the *handling,* transportation and storage of *hydrofluoric acid.* **Structure** Committees (4). **Languages** English. **Staff** 2.00 FTE, paid. **Activities** Politics/policy/regulatory; Awareness raising; capacity building; events/meetings; guidance/assistance/consulting; knowledge management/information dissemination; networking/liaising; standards/guidelines; training/education. **Publications** Safety recommendations in several languages.
Members Producers and users of fluoride in 8 countries:
France, Germany, Italy, Netherlands, Spain, Sweden, Switzerland, UK. [2020/XE6020/**E**]

- ♦ EUROFLUOR – Comité Technique Européen du Fluor / see EUROFLUOR (#05681)
- ♦ **EuroFM** European Facility Management Network (#07021)
- ♦ **EURO FOIE GRAS** Fédération européenne du foie gras (#09569)
- ♦ EUROFOODWATER (unconfirmed)
- ♦ EUROFOR (inactive)
- ♦ **EUROFORGE** Comité de liaison des industries européennes de l'estampage et de la forge (#06649)
- ♦ **Eurofound** European Foundation for the Improvement of Living and Working Conditions (#07348)
- ♦ **EUROFRAME** European Forecasting Research Association for the Macro-Economy (#07294)
- ♦ **EuroFSA** European Fire Safety Alliance (#07258)
- ♦ Eurofuel / see European Liquid Heating Fuels Association (#07701)

♦ **Eurofuel** European Liquid Heating Fuels Association (#07701)
♦ Eurofunéraire – Fédération européenne des PME du funéraire (no recent information)
♦ **EUROfusion** European Consortium for the Development of Fusion Energy (#06753)

♦ Eurogas 05682

SG Rue d'Arlon 80, 1040 Brussels, Belgium. T. +3228944848. Fax +3228944800. E-mail: eurogas@eurogas.org – valentina.tonut@eurogas.org.
Head of Finance and Admin address not obtained.
Events Dir address not obtained.
URL: https://eurogas.org/

History Mar 1954, Amsterdam (Netherlands). Protocol adopted Mar 1954. Re-founded, 18 Apr 1990, Seville (Spain). Statutes amended Aug 2010. Current statutes adopted Aug 2016. Former names and other names: *Economic Research Committee of the Gas Industry* – former; *Comité d'études économiques de l'industrie du gaz (COMETEC-GAZ)* – former; *European Union of the Natural Gas Industry (EUROGAS)* – former (1990); *Union européenne de l'industrie du gaz naturel* – former (1990); *Europäische Vereinigung der Erdgaswirtschaft* – former (1990). Registration: Banque-Carrefour des Entreprises, No/ID: 0441.122.247, Start date: 23 Jul 1990, Belgium; EU Transparency Register, No/ID: 17909506129-41, Start date: 1 Jul 2011. **Aims** Strengthen the role of gas in the *energy* mix through ongoing dialogue with European industry players, global gas producers and relevant institutions and organizations. **Structure** General Assembly; Board. **Languages** English. **Staff** 10.00 FTE, paid. **Finance** Sources: members' dues. **Activities** Politics/policy/regulatory; research and development; events/meetings. **Events** *Annual Conference* Brussels (Belgium) 2022, *Eurogas TECH Conference* Brussels (Belgium) 2022, *Annual Conference* Brussels (Belgium) 2021, *Annual Conference* Brussels (Belgium) 2020, *Annual Conference* Brussels (Belgium) 2019. **Publications** *Eurogas Activity Report*. Brochures; studies.
Members Companies; associations/federations; international associations. Members (44) in 22 countries. Membership countries not specified. Included in the above, 2 organizations listed in this Yearbook:
Included in the above, 2 organizations listed in this Yearbook:
European Gas Research Group (#07380); *MARCOGAZ – Technical Association of the European Natural Gas Industry (#16572)*.
IGO Relations Recognized by: *European Commission (EC, #06633)* Energy Charter; *United Nations Economic Commission for Europe (UNECE, #20555)*. Accredited by: *United Nations Framework Convention on Climate Change – Secretariat (UNFCCC, #20564)*. **NGO Relations** Member of (3): *Federation of European and International Associations Established in Belgium (FAIB, #09508)*; *GasNaturally (#10074)*; *Industry4Europe (#11181)*. [2022/XD3621/**D**]

♦ EUROGENDFOR (EGF) 05683

Headquarters Via Giacomo Medici 87, 36100 Vicenza VICENZA, Italy.
URL: https://eurogendfor.org/

History 2006. Created following conclusions of the *European Council (#06801)* meeting, Dec 2000, Nice (France), which states that *European Union (EU, #08967)* should quickly be made operational in the area of security and defence. Status enshrined in Treaty of Velsen, 18 Oct 2007. Former names and other names: *European Gendarmerie Force (EUROGENDFOR)* – full title. **Aims** Serve as an operational, pre-organized, robust and rapidly deployable asset, able to perform all police tasks. **Structure** High Level Interdepartmental Committee (Comité InterMInistériel de haut Niveau – CIMIN); Commander. Permanent Headquarters, subdivided into 4 branches (Intelligence; Operations; Plans & Policy; Logistics) and 2 offices (Human Resources; Communication & Information Systems). EGF Forces.
Members EU Member States (7):
France, Italy, Netherlands, Poland, Portugal, Romania, Spain.
Partner (1):
Lithuania.
Observer (1):
Türkiye. [AA0620/**F***]

♦ EUROGENDFOR / see EUROGENDFOR (#05683)
♦ EUROGEO / see European Association of Geographers (#06054)
♦ **EUROGEO** European Association of Geographers (#06054)

♦ EuroGeographics 05684

SG/Exec Dir Rue du Nord 76, 1000 Brussels, Belgium. T. +32484663345. E-mail: contact@eurogeographics.org.
URL: http://www.eurogeographics.org/

History Jan 2001. Set up following merger of Sep 2000, Malmö (Sweden), on General Assembly of Sep 2000, Malmö (Sweden), when merger was decided between *Comité européen des responsables de la cartographie officielle (CERCO, inactive)* – set up 1979 within the framework of *Council of Europe (CE, #04881)*, and from Jan 1993 within the framework of *European Federation of European Coordination Networks of Scientific and Technical Cooperation (#07114)* – with its daughter organization, *Multipurpose European Ground Related Information Network (MEGRIN, inactive)*, set up 1993. Registration: Banque-Carrefour des Entreprises, No/ID: 0833.607.112, Start date: 9 Feb 2011, Belgium; EU Transparency Register, No/ID: 51080067776-74, Start date: 19 Jan 2012; RNA, No/ID: W771000277, Start date: 2 Jan 2001, End date: 21 Oct 2011, France. **Aims** Further development of the *European Spatial Data Infrastructure* through collaboration in the area of geographic information and representation of the Association's membership and its capabilities. **Structure** General Assembly (annual); Management Board; Executive Director; Knowledge Exchange Networks (7); Permanent Secretariat located in Brussels (Belgium). **Languages** Dutch, English, French, Irish Gaelic. **Staff** 9.00 FTE, paid. 5 consultants. **Finance** Members' dues. Other sources: funded projects funding; licensing revenue from services and products. **Activities** Knowledge management/information dissemination; awareness raising; capacity building; events/meetings; networking/liaising; projects/programmes. **Events** *General Assembly* Sarajevo (Bosnia-Herzegovina) 2022, *Open Data Workshop* Brussels (Belgium) 2018, *Extraordinary General Assembly* Leuven (Belgium) 2018, *General Assembly* Prague (Czechia) 2018, *General Assembly* Vienna (Austria) 2017. **Publications** *EuroGeographics Messenger Newsletter*. Annual Review.
Members Organizations (61) in 46 countries and territories:
Albania, Armenia, Austria, Azerbaijan, Belarus, Belgium, Bosnia-Herzegovina, Bulgaria, Croatia, Cyprus, Czechia, Denmark, Estonia, Finland, France, Georgia, Germany, Great Britain, Greece, Hungary, Iceland, Ireland, Italy, Kosovo, Latvia, Lithuania, Luxembourg, Malta, Moldova, Montenegro, Netherlands, North Macedonia, Northern Ireland, Norway, Poland, Portugal, Romania, Russia, Serbia, Slovakia, Slovenia, Spain, Sweden, Switzerland, Türkiye, Ukraine.
IGO Relations Cooperates with: *European Commission (EC, #06633)*; *European Environment Agency (EEA, #06995)*; *European Parliament (EP, #08146)*; *European Position Determination System (EUPOS, #08256)*; *Permanent Committee on Cadastre in the European Union (PCC, #18319)*; *Statistical Office of the European Union (Eurostat, #19974)*; *United Nations Committee of Experts on Global Geospatial Information Management (UN-GGIM, #20540)*. Provides Secretariat services for: *United Nations Committee of Experts on Global Geospatial Information Management (UN-GGIM, #20540)* – Europe. Partner of: *Group on Earth Observations (GEO, #10735)*. **NGO Relations** Member of: *European Geographic Information Network (EGIN, #07387)*; *Federation of European and International Associations Established in Belgium (FAIB, #09508)*. Cooperates with: *Council of European Geodetic Surveyors (#04890)*; *European Land Registry Association (ELRA, #07640)*; *European Spatial Data Research (EuroSDR, #08806)*; *European Umbrella Organization for Geographical Information (EUROGI, #08964)*; Public Sector Mapping Agencies (PSMA) Australia. [2021/XF6505/**F**]

♦ EuroGEOSS 05685

Contact address not obtained. E-mail: rtd-eurogeoss@ec.europa.eu.
URL: http://www.eurogeoss.eu/

History Launched 2017, as the regional initiative of *Group on Earth Observations (GEO, #10735)*. **Aims** Improve user uptake of *earth observation* assets; improve harvesting of *environmental information* from earth observation initiatives; respond to demands for earth observation data; better integrate European earth observation assets; integrate and scale up existing services. **Structure** Coordination Group. **Activities** Research and development; research/documentation; guidance/assistance/support; networking/liaising.
Members Governments (30):
Austria, Belgium, Bulgaria, Croatia, Cyprus, Czechia, Denmark, Estonia, Finland, France, Germany, Greece, Hungary, Iceland, Ireland, Italy, Latvia, Luxembourg, Malta, Netherlands, Norway, Portugal, Romania, Slovakia, Slovenia, Spain, Sweden, Switzerland, Türkiye, UK.
Regional entity:
European Commission (EC, #06633).
Contributing government (1):
Lithuania.
Participating organizations (10):
EuroGeoSurveys (#05686); *European Association of Remote Sensing Companies (EARSC, #06190)*; *European Centre for Medium-Range Weather Forecasts (ECMWF, #06490)*; *European Environment Agency (EEA, #06995)*; *European Global Ocean Observing System (EuroGOOS, #07396)*; *European Organisation for the Exploitation of Meteorological Satellites (EUMETSAT, #08096)*; *European Space Agency (ESA, #08798)*; *European Union Satellite Centre (SatCen, #09015)*; *Interbalkan Environment Center (i-BEC, #11458)*; *Network of European Meteorological Services (EUMETNET, #17022)*. [2018/XM6834/**E***]

♦ EuroGeoSurveys 05686

Gen Sec Rue Joseph II 36-38, 1000 Brussels, Belgium. T. +3228887553. Fax +3225035025. E-mail: info@eurogeosurveys.org.
URL: http://www.eurogeosurveys.org/

History 1995. Founded by the directors of the National Geological Survey Organizations of the then 15 member states of the European Union (EU) and those of Iceland, Norway and Switzerland. 31 Dec 2004, incorporated activities of *Forum of European Geological Surveys (FOREGS, inactive)*, which was originally referred to as *Western European Geological Surveys (WEGS)*. Former names and other names: *European Union of National Geological Surveys (EuroGeoSurveys)* – former; *European Association of National Geological Surveys (EuroGeoSurveys)* – former; *EuroGeoSurveys – The Association of the Geological Surveys of the European Union* – full title. Registration: No/ID: 0822.605.332, Start date: 26 Jan 2010, Belgium; EU Transparency Register, No/ID: 01224764261-72, Start date: 27 Sep 2010. **Aims** Provide public earth science knowledge to support the EU's competitiveness, social well-being, environmental management and international commitments. **Structure** Board of Directors; Executive Committee; National Delegates; Expert Groups; Thematic Working Groups; Secretariat. **Languages** English. **Staff** 9.00 FTE, paid. **Finance** Sources: members' dues. **Activities** Knowledge management/information dissemination; research/documentation. **Events** *General Meeting & Directors' Workshop* Brussels (Belgium) 2021, *EUREGEO : European Congress on Regional Geoscientific Cartography and Information Systems* Barcelona (Spain) 2015, *EUREGEO : European congress on regional geoscientific cartography and information systems* Bologna (Italy) 2012, *EUREGEO : European congress on regional geoscientific cartography and information systems* Munich (Germany) 2009. **Publications** *EuroGeoSurveys Strategic Research & Innovation Agenda* in English; *EuroGeoSurveys Strategy Document* in English.
Members Full in 36 countries:
Albania, Austria, Belgium, Bosnia-Herzegovina, Croatia, Cyprus, Czechia, Denmark, Estonia, Finland, France, Germany, Greece, Hungary, Ireland, Italy, Kosovo, Latvia, Lithuania, Luxembourg, Malta, Montenegro, Netherlands, Norway, Poland, Portugal, Romania, Russia, Serbia, Slovakia, Slovenia, Spain, Sweden, Switzerland, UK, Ukraine.
IGO Relations Partner of (3): *EuroGEOSS (#05685)*; *Global Soil Partnership (GSP, #10608)*; *Group on Earth Observations (GEO, #10735)*. **NGO Relations** Cooperates with (1): *International Association for Promoting Geoethics (IAPG, #12107)*. Affiliated with (1): *International Union of Geological Sciences (IUGS, #15777)*. [2021.02.22/XD6924/**D**]

♦ EuroGeoSurveys – The Association of the Geological Surveys of the European Union / see EurOGeoSurveys (#05686)
♦ EuroGeoSurveys / see EuroGeoSurveys (#05686)
♦ **EUROGI** European Umbrella Organization for Geographical Information (#08964)
♦ **EUROGIN** European Research Organization on Genital Infection and Neoplasia (#08378)
♦ EUROGIP (internationally oriented national body)
♦ EUROGIRO – Giro, Postbank and Commercial Bank Organizations in Europe / see EUROGIRO – Giro, Postbank, Commercial Bank Payment Institutions Organizations Worldwide (#05687)

♦ EUROGIRO – Giro, Postbank, Commercial Bank Payment Institutions Organizations Worldwide 05687

Main Office Toldbodgade 55-B, 1253 Copenhagen K, Denmark. E-mail: eurogiro@eurogiro.com.
URL: http://www.eurogiro.com/

History Founded Jul 1990, as *European Post Giro Directors Group (EP/GDG)*, following proposal, Jan 1989, by *Groupe de Paris (inactive)*, informal meetings having been held throughout the 1980s. Company founded in 1993. Subsequently changed title to *EUROGIRO – Giro and Postbank Organizations in Europe* and then *EUROGIRO – Giro, Postbank and Commercial Bank Organizations in Europe*. Also known by the title and tag line: *Eurogiro – your global payments community*. **Aims** Serve as a payment community to create business opportunities in particular with cross-border payments; establish common technological infrastructure for cross-border transfers; create common products and product lines to provide efficient, inexpensive, transparent services for users. **Structure** Board; Board Advisory Group; Technical User Group; General Community Meeting; European-Middle-East-African (EMEA) Customer Council; Asia Pacific Customer Council. **Languages** English. **Staff** 12.00 FTE, paid. **Finance** Company income. **Activities** Guidance/assistance/consulting. **Publications** *Eurogiro Newsletter* (4 a year).
Members Full (65) in 52 countries:
Albania, Australia, Austria, Bangladesh, Belgium, Bosnia-Herzegovina, Brazil, Bulgaria, Canada, Cape Verde, China, Croatia, Czechia, Denmark, France, Georgia, Germany, Greece, Hungary, India, Indonesia, Ireland, Israel, Italy, Japan, Korea Rep, Latvia, Lithuania, Luxembourg, Madagascar, Morocco, New Zealand, Philippines, Poland, Portugal, Romania, Saudi Arabia, Senegal, Serbia, Slovakia, Slovenia, Spain, Sri Lanka, Switzerland, Thailand, Togo, Tunisia, Türkiye, UK, Ukraine, USA, Vietnam.
IGO Relations Member of: *International Bank for Reconstruction and Development (IBRD, #12317)* (World Bank), Advisory Committee on Remittances in Public and Private Sector. Cooperates with: *Universal Postal Union (UPU, #20682)*. **NGO Relations** Cooperates with: *European Payments Council (EPC, #08175)*; *Society for Worldwide Interbank Financial Telecommunication (SWIFT, #19661)*. [2021/XE1691/e/**E**]

♦ EUROGIRO – Giro and Postbank Organizations in Europe / see EUROGIRO – Giro, Postbank, Commercial Bank Payment Institutions Organizations Worldwide (#05687)
♦ Eurogiro – your global payments community / see EUROGIRO – Giro, Postbank, Commercial Bank Payment Institutions Organizations Worldwide (#05687)
♦ EUROGITES – European Federation of Farm and Village Tourism / see European Federation of Rural Tourism (#07208)
♦ EUROGITES – European Federation of Rural Tourism / see European Federation of Rural Tourism (#07208)
♦ EUROGITES – Fédération européenne pour l'accueil touristique chez l'habitant à la campagne, à la ferme et au village / see European Federation of Rural Tourism (#07208)
♦ EUROGITES – Fédération européenne du tourisme rural / see European Federation of Rural Tourism (#07208)
♦ EUROGLACES / see EUROGLACES – European Ice Cream Association (#05688)
♦ **Euroglaces** EUROGLACES – European Ice Cream Association (#05688)

♦ EUROGLACES – European Ice Cream Association (Euroglaces) 05688

Contact c/o FEVIA, Rue de la Science 14, 1040 Brussels, Belgium. T. +3222138478. E-mail: info@euroglaces.eu.
URL: http://www.euroglaces.eu/

History 17 Oct 1961, as *Association of the Ice Cream Industries of the EEC – Association des industries des glaces alimentaires de la CEE (EUROGLACES) – Asociación de Industrias de Fabricantes de Helados de la CEE – Vereinigung des Speiseeisindustrie der EWG – Associazione fra le Industrie Alimentari del Gelato della CEE – Vereniging van Consumptieijsfabrikanten in de EEG – Sammenslutningen af Iskremindustrien IEF – Föreningen för Glassindustrin i EU – Syndesmos Viomichanion Pagotou tis EOK*. Subsequently changed title to *Association of the Ice Cream Industries of the EU – Association des industries des glaces alimentaires de l'UE – Asociación de Industrias de Fabricantes de Helados de la UE – Vereinigung des Speiseeisindustrie der EU – Associazione fra le Industrie Alimentari del Gelato della UE – Vereniging van Consumptieijsfabrikanten in de EU – Föreningen för Glassindustrin i EU*. Previously also referred to in French as *Association des industries des glaces alimentaires et crèmes glacées de la CEE*. EU Transparency Register: 31013503339-49. **Aims** Act as the voice of the European ice cream industry, helping its members to operate in the best possible regulatory and legislative framework at EU level; communicate the ice cream industry's values and concerns to a range

of audiences in the EU, including regulators, consumers and the media; track the latest developments in the EU legislation affecting the ice cream industry. **Structure** General Assembly; Board of Directors; Regulatory Affairs Committee; Secretary General. **Languages** English. **Events** *General Assembly* Copenhagen (Denmark) 2008, *General Assembly* Maastricht (Netherlands) 2007, *General Assembly* Nice (France) 2006, *General Assembly* Lisbon (Portugal) 2005, *General Assembly* Barcelona (Spain) 2004. **Publications** *Code of Practice for Edible Ices.*
Members National Federations in 10 countries:
Belgium, Bulgaria, France, Germany, Italy, Netherlands, Norway, Slovenia, Sweden, UK.
IGO Relations Recognized by: *European Commission (EC, #06633).* Participates as observer in the activities of: *Codex Alimentarius Commission (CAC, #04081).* **NGO Relations** In liaison with technical committees of: *International Organization for Standardization (ISO, #14473).* Member of: *FoodDrinkEurope (#09841).*
[2020/XE0171/**E**]

- ♦ EuroGOOS / see European Global Ocean Observing System (#07396)
- ♦ **EuroGOOS** European Global Ocean Observing System (#07396)
- ♦ **EuroGPR** European GPR Association (#07402)
- ♦ **EURO GRAPH** European Association of Graphic Paper Producers (#06060)
- ♦ **EUROGRAPHICS** European Association for Computer Graphics (#05986)
- ♦ Eurogroep (#05689)
- ♦ Euro Group / see Eurogroup (#05689)
- ♦ EUROGROUP / see European Small Business Alliance of Small and Medium Independent Enterprises (#08494)

♦ Eurogroup 05689

Eurogroupe – Eurogrupo – Euro-Gruppe – Eurogrupo – Eurogruppo – Eurogroep – Eurogruppen – Eurogruppen – Euroryhmä – An Grúpa Euro – Euroskupina – Euroskupina – Az eurócsoport – Eurogrupa – Evroskupina – Eurorühm – Eurogrupa – Grupp tal-Euro – Euroskupina – Eurogrupul
Address not obtained.
URL: http://www.consilium.europa.eu/
History First mentioned in the Presidency Conclusions of the *European Council (#06801)* of 12 and 13 Dec 1997. They stipulate that "the Ministers of the States participating in the euro area may meet informally among themselves to discuss issues connected with their shared specific responsibilities for the single currency. With Protocol 14 to *Treaty on European Union (Maastricht Treaty, 1992)* and to *Treaty of Lisbon (2007)* this arrangement was introduced in the Treaty. First operational meeting: 4 Jun 1998. Originally referred to informally as *Euro-X* and subsequently as *Euro Council (Euro 11) – Conseil de l'euro.* Also referred to as *Euro Group.* **Aims** Ensure close coordination of economic policies among the *euro* area member states; promote conditions for stronger economic growth. **Structure** An informal body gathering ministers of the euro area member states, which meets usually monthly before the Ecofin meeting of *Council of the European Union (#04895). European Commission (EC, #06633)* Commissioner for economic and financial affairs, taxation and customs and president of *European Central Bank (ECB, #06466)* also participate. President serves for term of 2.5 years. **Activities** Events/meetings, including Euro Summit meetings. **Events** *Eurogroup Meeting* Brussels (Belgium) 2019, *Eurogroup Meeting* Brussels (Belgium) 2019, *Eurogroup Meeting* Brussels (Belgium) 2019, *Eurogroup Meeting* Brussels (Belgium) 2019, *Eurogroup Meeting* Brussels (Belgium) 2019.
Members Finance ministers of 19 of the 28 member countries of the European Union:
Austria, Belgium, Cyprus, Estonia, Finland, France, Germany, Greece, Ireland, Italy, Latvia, Lithuania, Luxembourg, Malta, Netherlands, Portugal, Slovakia, Slovenia, Spain.
IGO Relations President is observer to Board of Governors of *European Stability Mechanism (ESM, #08829).*
[2016/XE3606/**E***]

- ♦ EUROGROUP (inactive)

♦ Eurogroup for Animals 05690

Eurogroup pour les animaux
CEO Rue Ducale 29, 1000 Brussels, Belgium. T. +3227400820. E-mail: info@eurogroupforanimals.org.
URL: http://www.eurogroupforanimals.org/
History Mar 1980, Brussels (Belgium). Former names and other names: *Eurogroup for Animal Welfare* – former. Registration: EU Transparency Register, No/ID: 6809935493-49; Belgium. **Aims** As a European animal advocacy umbrella organization, aim at building a Europe that cares for animals. **Structure** Annual General Meeting; Board. **Languages** English, French. **Staff** 25.00 FTE, paid. **Finance** Sources: contributions; donations; sponsorship. **Activities** Advocacy/lobbying/activism; networking/liaising. **Events** *Conference on global trade and farm animal welfare* Brussels (Belgium) 2009, *International forum on global aspects of farm animal welfare* Brussels (Belgium) 2008, *Meeting* Brussels (Belgium) 1995, *Annual plenary session* Brussels (Belgium) 1991, *Annual plenary session* Strasbourg (France) 1990. **Publications** *Eurobulletin* (weekly) – Members only newsletter; *Eurogroup for Animals Magazine* (12 a year). Annual Report; thematic publications; brochures.
Members National and international animal advocacy organizations (over 80) in 29 countries:
Australia, Austria, Belgium, Bulgaria, Croatia, Czechia, Denmark, Estonia, Finland, France, Germany, Greece, Ireland, Italy, Latvia, Lithuania, Luxembourg, Malta, Netherlands, Norway, Poland, Romania, Serbia, Slovakia, Spain, Sweden, Switzerland, UK, USA.
Consultative Status Consultative status granted from: *Council of Europe (CE, #04881)* (Participatory Status).
IGO Relations Accredited by (1): *International Whaling Commission (IWC, #15879).* Observer status with (1): *Standing Committee to the Bern Convention on the Conservation of European Wildlife and Natural Habitats (#19949).* Runs the secretariat of the European Parliament Intergroup for the Welfare and Conservation of Animals. **NGO Relations** Observer status with (1): *European Food Sustainable Consumption and Production Round Table (European Food SCP Roundtable, #07289).* Member of (3): *International Council on Animal Protection in OECD Programmes (ICAPO, #12992); Species Survival Network (SSN, #19916); TP Organics – European Technology Platform (TP Organics, #20180).* Cooperates with (1): *IFOAM Organics Europe (#11104).* In liaison with technical committees of: *International Organization for Standardization (ISO, #14473).*
[2022.03.21/XE3276/y/**E**]

- ♦ Eurogroup for Animal Welfare / see Eurogroup for Animals (#05690)
- ♦ Eurogroup pour les animaux (#05690)
- ♦ Eurogroupe (#05689)
- ♦ Eurogroupe (inactive)
- ♦ Eurogrupa (#05689)
- ♦ Eurogrupo (#05689)
- ♦ Euro-Gruppe (#05689)
- ♦ Eurogruppe (inactive)
- ♦ Eurogruppen (#05689)
- ♦ Eurogruppo (#05689)
- ♦ Eurogrupul (#05689)

♦ Euroguidance (EG) 05691

Contact Flemish Dept for Education and Training, EPOS, H Consciencegebouw, Koning Albert II-laan 15 3B, 1210 Brussels, Belgium. T. +3225539942.
URL: http://euroguidance.eu/
History Founded 1992, on the initiative of *European Commission (EC, #06633).* Also referred to as *Euroguidance Network.* Since 2014, part of the EC ERASMUS+ Programme. **Aims** Support competence development of the guidance community on the European dimension of lifelong guidance. **Finance** *European Commission (EC, #06633);* national funding sources. **Publications** *Euroguidance Insight* (2 a year) – newsletter.
Members Centres (over 40) in 36 countries:
Austria, Belgium, Bulgaria, Croatia, Cyprus, Czechia, Denmark, Estonia, Finland, France, Germany, Greece, Hungary, Iceland, Ireland, Italy, Latvia, Liechtenstein, Lithuania, Luxembourg, Malta, Montenegro, Netherlands, North Macedonia, Norway, Poland, Portugal, Romania, Serbia, Slovakia, Slovenia, Spain, Sweden, Switzerland, Türkiye, UK. [2019.06.18/XJ5442/**F**]

- ♦ Euroguidance Network / see Euroguidance (#05691)
- ♦ EUROGYPSUM / see European Association of Plaster and Plaster Product Manufacturers (#06152)
- ♦ **EUROGYPSUM** European Association of Plaster and Plaster Product Manufacturers (#06152)
- ♦ EuroHandelsinstitut / see EHI Retail Institute

♦ EuroHaptics Society (EHS) 05692

Contact address not obtained. E-mail: mharders@vision.ee.ethz.ch – a.m.wing@bham.ac.uk.
URL: http://www.eurohaptics.org/
History 2 Jul 2006, Paris (France). **Aims** Contribute to and promote the advancement of *Haptics* worldwide, focusing on *Europe.* **Events** *Conference* London (UK) 2016, *Conference* Paris (France) 2014, *Conference* Daejeon (Korea Rep) 2013, *EuroHaptics Conference* Istanbul (Turkey) 2013, *Conference / EuroHaptics Conference* Tampere (Finland) 2012.
[2013/XJ1546/**E**]

- ♦ Euro-HD Network / see European Huntington's Disease Network (#07510)

♦ EuroHealthNet 05693

Dir Rue Royale 146, 1000 Brussels, Belgium. T. +3222350320. Fax +3222350339. E-mail: info@eurohealthnet.eu.
URL: http://www.eurohealthnet.eu/
History 2003. Founded upon taking over activities of *European Network of Health Promotion Agencies (ENHPA, inactive).* Registration: Banque-Carrefour des Entreprises, No/ID: 0479.553.647, Start date: 7 Feb 2003, Belgium; EU Transparency Register, No/ID: 48562122691-12, Start date: 2 Dec 2009. **Aims** Address the factors that shape health and social inequalities, building the evidence base for public health and health-related policies and health promotion interventions. **Structure** General Council (annual); Executive Board; Office. Platforms (3): EuroHealthNet Practice, EuroHealthNet Policy, EuroHealthNet Research. **Languages** English. **Staff** 15.00 FTE, paid. **Finance** Sources: contributions of member/participating states; government support; members' dues; revenue from activities/projects. Other sources: EU joint actions, Horizon 2020, Horizon Europe, 3rd Health Programme, EU4Heamth, ESF+ Supported by: *European Commission (EC, #06633).* **Activities** Events/meetings; networking/liaising; politics/policy/regulatory. **Events** *General Council Meeting* Brussels (Belgium) 2022, *Seminar on Addressing Psychosocial Risks and Supporting Mental Health of Older Workers* Brussels (Belgium) 2022, *Seminar on Growing Strong in Times of Crisis* Brussels (Belgium) 2022, *Inter-Sectoral Health and Environment Research for InnovaTion Project Final Meeting* Brussels (Belgium) 2019, *Conference on Social Infrastructure Investment* Brussels (Belgium) 2018. **Publications** *Calls and Opportunities Newsletter, ENHPA Magazine, Health Highlights* – newsletter. Policy briefs; official statements; news releases; consultation responses; scientific publications.
Members Members and partners in 25 countries and territories:
Austria, Belgium, Denmark, England, Finland, France, Germany, Greece, Hungary, Ireland, Italy, Latvia, Luxembourg, Malta, Netherlands, Norway, Poland, Portugal, Romania, Scotland, Slovenia, Spain, Sweden, Switzerland, Wales.
NGO Relations Member of (3): *European Alliance for Mental Health – Employment & Work (EUMH Alliance, #05875); European Forum for Primary Care (EFPC, #07326)* (Associated); *European Public Health and Agriculture Consortium (EPHAC, #08296).* Instrumental in setting up (1): *Agency for Public Health Education Accreditation (APHEA, #00555).*
[2022.10.19/XF6831/**F**]

♦ Euroheat and Power (EHP) 05694

Managing Dir Cours Saint Michel 30a Boîte E, 1040 Brussels, Belgium. T. +3227402110. Fax +3227402119. E-mail: office@euroheat.org.
URL: http://www.euroheat.org/
History 19 May 1954, Paris (France). Statutes modified: Jun 1983, Lahti (Finland); Jun 1995, Stockholm (Sweden); Jun 1997, Arnhem (Netherlands); Jun 1999, Sheffield (UK); Jun 2001, Gdynia (Poland); 2009, Brussels (Belgium). Former names and other names: *International Union of Heat Distributors* – former; *Union internationale des distributeurs de chaleur (UNICHAL)* – former; *Internationaler Verband der Fernwärmeversorger* – former; *International Association for District Heating, District Cooling and Combined Heat and Power* – former; *Association internationale pour le chauffage urbain, le refroidissement à distance et la cogénération* – former; *Internationaler Verband für Fernheizung, Fernkühlung und Kraft-Wärme-Kopplung* – former. Registration: Banque-Carrefour des Entreprises, No/ID: 0463.158.172, Start date: 3 Feb 1998, Belgium; EU Transparency Register, No/ID: 88457577025-19, Start date: 26 Oct 2011. **Aims** Promote sustainable district heating and cooling in Europe. **Structure** General Assembly; Board of Directors; Companies' Electoral Forum; Working Groups; Task Forces; Certification Board; DHC+ Technology Platform. **Languages** English. **Staff** 14.00 FTE, paid. **Finance** Members' dues. Other sources: publications; events. **Activities** Advocacy/lobbying/activism; awareness raising; certification/accreditation; monitoring/evaluation; networking/liaising; research and development. **Events** *Congress* Turin (Italy) 2023, *Biennial Congress* Vilnius (Lithuania) 2021, *Conference* Brussels (Belgium) 2020, *Meeting on Vision 2050, Decarbonising District Energy for Our Cities* Brussels (Belgium) 2019, *ReUseHeat Policy Workshop on Waste Heat Recovery Investment* Brussels (Belgium) 2019. **Publications** *EHP Newsletter* (12 a year); *EHP and DHC+Highlights* (annual); *Country by Country* (every 2 years). Brochures; studies; reports.
Members Active; Supporting. Members in 33 countries:
Austria, Belgium, Bosnia-Herzegovina, Bulgaria, China, Croatia, Czechia, Denmark, Estonia, Finland, France, Germany, Greece, Hungary, Italy, Korea Rep, Latvia, Lithuania, Luxembourg, Netherlands, Norway, Poland, Portugal, Qatar, Russia, Serbia, Slovenia, Spain, Sweden, Switzerland, UK, Ukraine, United Arab Emirates.
NGO Relations Member of (6): *Asia Pacific Urban Energy Association (APUEA, #02073); Coalition for Energy Savings (#04056); European Forum for Renewable Energy Sources (EUFORES, #07329); European Technology Platform on Renewable Heating and Cooling (RHC-Platform, #08891); Federation of European and International Associations Established in Belgium (FAIB, #09508);* Knowledge for Innovation. Cooperates with (2): *Comité européen de normalisation (CEN, #04162); Covenant of Mayors for Climate and Energy (#04939).*
[2023/XD2727/**D**]

- ♦ EuroHIV – HIV/AIDS Surveillance in Europe / see European Network for HIV/AIDS Surveillance (#07923)
- ♦ EuroHIV – Surveillance du VIH/SIDA en Europe / see European Network for HIV/AIDS Surveillance (#07923)
- ♦ EURO-HKG – Europäische Gesellschaft zur Auswertung von Erfahrungen bei Planung, Bau und Betrieb von Hochtemperaturr-Reaktoren (inactive)
- ♦ EUROHORCs – European Union Research Organizations Heads of Research Councils (inactive)
- ♦ **EuroHPC JU** European High Performance Computing Joint Undertaking (#07485)
- ♦ **EuroHRN** European Harm Reduction Network (#07450)
- ♦ **EURO-HSP** European Federation of National HSP Associations (#07171)
- ♦ **EURO-INBO** Group of European Basin Organizations for the Implementation of the Water Framework Directive (#10771)
- ♦ Euro Inox – Euro Inox – The European Stainless Steel Development Association (inactive)
- ♦ Euro Inox – The European Stainless Steel Development Association (inactive)
- ♦ EuroInstitut du commerce / see EHI Retail Institute
- ♦ Euro-Institut – Institut pour la coopération transfrontalière (internationally oriented national body)
- ♦ Euro-Institut – Institut für Grenzüberschreitende Zusammenarbeit (internationally oriented national body)
- ♦ Euro-International Committee for Concrete (inactive)
- ♦ EuroInvestors / see BETTER FINANCE (#03219)
- ♦ **Euro IRP** European Association of Independent Research Providers (#06079)

♦ Euro-ISME 05695

Pres Centre de recherche, Académie Saint-Cyr Coetquidan, 56381 Guer CEDEX, France. E-mail: admin@euroisme.eu.
Treas 15 promenade Saint-Martin, 02000 Laon, France. T. +33785600039.
URL: http://www.euroisme.eu/
History Inaugural conference held Jun 2011, Paris (France). A chapter of: *International Society for Military Ethics (ISME).* Registration: Start date: Jan 2012, France. **Aims** Analyse, develop and promote best practice through the *armed forces* of the members of the European *defence* community. **Structure** General Assembly; Board of Directors. **Languages** English, French, German. **Activities** Awards/prizes/competitions; events/meetings; publishing activities. **Events** *Is military ethics keeping pace with the changing character of warfare?* Budapest (Hungary) 2022, *Annual Conference* Berlin (Germany) 2021, *Annual Conference* Vienna (Austria) 2019, *Annual Conference* Toledo (Spain) 2018, *Annual Conference* Brussels (Belgium) 2017. **Publications** *International Studies on Military Ethics* in English – book series. *EuroISME Occasional Papers.* Publication of winning theses. **Members** Membership countries not specified. **NGO Relations** Partner of (1): *International Committee of the Red Cross (ICRC, #12799).*
[2022/XM6666/**D**]

♦ **EurolSPA** European Internet Services Providers Association (#07592)
♦ **Euro-IX** European Internet Exchange Association (#07590)
♦ Euro-Japanese Management Studies Association / see Euro-Asia Management Studies Association (#05634)
♦ **EUROJESS** European Jesuits in Social Sciences (#07607)

♦ EUROJURIS International 05696

SG Keizer Karellaan 586, bus 9, 1082 Brussels, Belgium. E-mail: info@eurojuris.net.
Legal Seat Av des Dessus de Lives 2, 5101 Namur, Belgium. T. +3281343217. E-mail: info@eurojuris.net.
URL: http://www.eurojuris.net/

History as a grouping of the type *European Economic Interest Grouping (EEIG, #06960)*. Registration: Banque-Carrefour des Entreprises, No/ID: 0870.816.708, Start date: 27 Dec 2004. **Aims** Offer to law firms and their clients quality cross border *consultancy* in the field of *law* and *justice*. **Structure** General Secretariat (Brussels, Belgium). **Languages** English, French, German. **Staff** 1.00 FTE, paid. **Finance** Members' dues. **Activities** Projects/programmes; networking/liaising; events/meetings. **Events** *Congress* Madrid (Spain) 2022, *Congress* Paris (France) 2021, *Congress* Paris (France) 2020, *Congress* Frankfurt-Main (Germany) 2019, *Congress* Dubai (United Arab Emirates) 2018.
Members Law firms (over 700), comprising more than 6,000 lawyers. Individuals in 33 countries and territories:
Argentina, Australia, Brazil, Bulgaria, Canada, China, Costa Rica, Croatia, Cyprus, Czechia, Ecuador, Estonia, Greece, Hong Kong, Hungary, India, Ireland, Israel, Latvia, Lithuania, Luxembourg, Malta, Mexico, Montenegro, Poland, Romania, Singapore, Slovakia, Slovenia, Sweden, Türkiye, Ukraine, USA.
Organizations in 11 countries:
Austria, Belgium, Denmark, Finland, France, Germany, Netherlands, Norway, Spain, Switzerland, UK.
NGO Relations Member of: *Federation of European and International Associations Established in Belgium (FAIB, #09508)*. [2021/XF4022/**F**]

♦ Eurojurist / see Interlegal (#11517)

♦ Euro-jus Network 05697

Address not obtained.

History May 1993. **Aims** Inform and advise individuals and associations as to their *rights* in *European Community law* and under the *European Convention on Human Rights*. **Structure** Network of advisers based at national offices of the European Commission. UK Office: *Citizens' European Advisory Service (CEAS, no recent information)*. **Finance** Financed through non-governmental organizations' grants, donations and legal fees. **IGO Relations** *European Commission (EC, #06633)*. [2008/XF5138/**F**]

♦ Pro-Eurojust / see Eurojust (#05698)

♦ Eurojust 05698

Corporate Communications Office PO Box 16183, 2500 BD The Hague, Netherlands. Fax +31704125005.
Street address Johan de Wittlaan 9, 2517 JR The Hague, Netherlands.
URL: http://www.eurojust.europa.eu/

History Formally established by decision of *Council of the European Union (#04895)* of 28 Feb 2002 (2002/187/JHA), following recommendations of meeting of *European Council (#06801)*, Oct 1999, Tampere (Finland), decision of 6 Dec 2000, Brussels (Belgium), of Heads of State and Government of *European Union (EU, #08967)* and discussions of *European Parliament (EP, #08146)*, 28 Nov 2001. Intended to complement *European Police Office (Europol, #08239)*. Initially a provisional body with the title *Pro-Eurojust*; commenced operations as a permanent body under listed title, 1 Mar 2001. Mandate amended by Council Decision 2009/426/JHA of 16 Dec 2008. A decentralized agency of the European Union. **Aims** Enhance efficiency of national investigating and prosecuting authorities when dealing with serious cross-border organized crime. **Structure** Comprises high-level prosecutors, judges or police officers of equivalent competence, one from each EU Member State. Secretariats of *European Judicial Network (EJN, #07615)*, Genocide Network and JITs Network form part of the Eurojust administration. **Staff** 253.00 FTE, paid. **Activities** Events/meetings; knowledge management/information dissemination; management of treaties and agreements; politics/policy/regulatory. Manages the following treaties/agreements: *Convention on Mutual Legal Assistance in Criminal Matters between the Member States of the European Union (2000)*. **Events** *Meeting* Budapest (Hungary) 2014, *Meeting* Barcelona (Spain) 2009, *Meeting* The Hague (Netherlands) 2009, *Strategic meeting on cybercrime* Athens (Greece) 2008, *Strategic planning meeting* Noordwijk (Netherlands) 2006. **Publications** *Eurojust News*. Annual Report; strategic plans; judicial monitors; seminar outcomes. **Members** National authorities of governments of the European Union. **IGO Relations** Observer status with (1): *Financial Action Task Force (FATF, #09765)*. Cooperates with (1): *European Union Agency for the Operational Management of Large-Scale IT Systems in the Area of Freedom, Security and Justice (eu-LISA, #08972)*. Council of *Cooperation in the Field of Justice and Home Affairs (CJHA)*. Audited by: *European Court of Auditors (#06854)*. Close relations with a number of justice agencies, not all specified but including: Consultative Forum of Prosecutors General and Directors of Public Prosecution; *Frontex, the European Border and Coast Guard Agency (#10005)*; *European Anti-Fraud Office (#05906)*; *European Contact-point Network against Corruption (EACN, #06776)*; *European Counter Terrorism Centre (ectc, #06851)*; *European Cybercrime Centre (EC3)*; *European Judicial Network (EJN, #07615)*; *European Union Agency for Law Enforcement Training (CEPOL, #08970)*; *European Union Agency for Fundamental Rights (FRA, #08969)*; Europol. Also dialogue with: *European Commission (EC, #06633)*; European Council. Contacts with: *Group of States Against Corruption (#10789)*. **NGO Relations** Member of (3): *EU Agencies Network (EUAN, #05564)*; *Eurolib (#05703)*; *European Financial Coalition against Commercial Sexual Exploitation of Children Online (EFC, #07249)*. [2022/XF6206/**F***]

♦ Eurojustice (no recent information)
♦ Eurojust Network / see Interlegal (#11517)
♦ **Eurojute** European Association for the Trade in Jute and Related Products (#06256)
♦ Eurokansalaisen Toimintapaluelu Keskus / see European Citizen Action Service (#06555)
♦ EurOK – European Academy of Orthokeratology and Myopia Control (unconfirmed)
♦ Euro-Kinderen (internationally oriented national body)
♦ Eurokorps (#05671)
♦ **EUROLAB** European Federation of National Associations of Measurement, Testing and Analytical Laboratories (#07168)
♦ Euro-Labo – Association européenne pour les essais comparatifs (inactive)
♦ **EurolacTB** European-Latin-American-Caribbean-Tuberculosis Consortium (#07655)

♦ EuroLam Retina 05699

Secretariat 50 Edward Road West Bridgford, Nottingham, NG2 5GB, UK. T. +447830221032.
Secretariat address not obtained.
URL: https://www.eurolam.org/

History 23 May 2008, Vienna (Austria). **Aims** Establish personal contacts and promote scientific exchanges between specialists in vitreo-retinal diseases in *Europe* and *Latin America*; initiate, facilitate, and support research work and publications in this specialized field of *ophthalmology*; promote the diffusion of specific knowledge to general ophthalmologists in Europe and Latin America. **Structure** General Assembly; Board. **Finance** Sources: members' dues. **Activities** Events/meetings. **Events** *Macula and Retina Congress* Monterrey (Mexico) 2020, *Macula and Retina Congress* Quito (Ecuador) 2018, *Macula and Retina Congress* Fort Lauderdale, FL (USA) 2013, *Macular and Retina Congress* Miami, FL (USA) 2012, *Macular and Retina Congress* Miami, FL (USA) 2011. **NGO Relations** Member of (1): *International Council of Ophthalmology (ICO, #13057)*. [2020/XJ6499/**C**]

♦ **Eurolandscape** European Landscape Network (#07644)
♦ EUROLAT / see European-Latvian Institute
♦ **EUROLAT** Euro-Latin American Parliamentary Assembly (#05700)
♦ EUROLAT – European-Latvian Institute (internationally oriented national body)
♦ EUROLATEX – European Association of Latex Foam Industries (inactive)

♦ Euro-Latin American Parliamentary Assembly (EUROLAT) 05700

Assemblée parlementaire euro-latino américaine – Asamblea Parlamentaria Euro-Latinoamericana – Assembleia Parlamentar Euro-Latino-Americana

Co-Pres Europarl, Bât Altiero Spinelli 11E206, Rue Wiertz 60, 1047 Brussels, Belgium. E-mail: josejavier.fernandez@ep.europa.eu – prensa-es@europarl.europa.eu.
Co-Pres address not obtained.
URL: http://www.europarl.europa.eu/intcoop/eurolat/default_en.htm

History 2006. **Aims** Support, promote and consolidate in practical terms the Bi-regional Strategic Partnership by covering its 3 main concerns, namely: questions relating to democracy, external policy, governance, integration, peace and human rights; economic, financial and commercial affairs; social affairs, human exchange, the environment, education and culture. **Structure** Plenary Session (annual). A joint multilateral parliamentary assembly composed of 150 members, 75 from European Parliament and 75 from the Latin American component, including *Parlamento Latinoamericano (PARLATINO, #18203)*, *Andean Parliament (#00820)*, *Parlamento Centroamericano (PARLACEN, #18201)* and, as of April 2009, *Parlamento de MERCOSUR (PARLASUR, #18204)*. The Mexican and Chilean congresses are also represented in view of the existence of the Joint Parliamentary Committees EU/Mexico and EU/Chile. Executive Bureau (meeting at least twice a year), comprising 2 Co-Presidents (one European and one Latin American) and 14 Co-Vice-Presidents (7 from each side). Standing Committees (4): Political Affairs, Security and Human Rights; Economic, Financial and Commercial Affairs; Social Affairs, Human Exchanges, Environment, Education and Culture; Sustainable Development, Environment, Energy Policy, Research, Innovation and Technology. Working Group. Secretariat. **Languages** English, French, German, Irish Gaelic, Portuguese, Spanish. **Activities** Serves as a forum for parliamentary debate, control and review of all questions relating to the Bi-regional European Union, Latin America and Caribbean Strategic Partnership (established Jun 1999) as the parliamentary institution of that partnership and in line with the EuroLat Constituent Act; adopts and submits resolutions and recommendations to the various organizations, institutions and ministerial groups responsible for the development of the Bi-regional Strategic Association. **Events** *Ordinary Plenary Session* Buenos Aires (Argentina) 2022, *Ordinary Plenary Session* Brussels (Belgium) 2020, *Ordinary Plenary Session* Panama (Panama) 2019, *Ordinary Plenary Session* Vienna (Austria) 2018, *Ordinary Plenary Session* San Salvador (El Salvador) 2017. **IGO Relations** Invited to attend EUROLAT meetings: *Council of the European Union (#04895)*; *European Commission (EC, #06633)*; *European Union-Latin American and Caribbean Summit (EU-LAC Summit)*. [2021.10.26/XJ0185/**F***]

♦ Euro-Latin Study Network on Integration and Trade (ELSNIT) 05701

IDB Office in Europe Calle de Bailén 41, 28005 Madrid, Spain. T. +34913646950. E-mail: idbeurope@iadb.org – elsnit@iadb.org.
Contact c/o IDB, 1300 New York Avenue, Washington DC 20577, USA. T. +12026231000. Fax +12026233096. E-mail: mariapazr@iadb.org.
URL: http://www.iadb.org/en/topics/trade/euro-latin-study-network-on- integration-and-trade-elsnit,6368.html/

History 9 Oct 2002, Madrid (Spain), by *Inter-American Development Bank (IDB, #11427)*. **Aims** Generate research, studies and debate on integration and trade issues relevant to *Latin America* and the *Caribbean*. **Structure** Steering Committee, comprising representatives from IDB's Integration and Regional Programmes Department and Special Office in Europe, *European Commission (EC, #06633)* and 3 rotating European research centres. **Finance** Supported by: *Institute for the Integration of Latin America and the Caribbean (#11271)*. **Events** *Annual Conference* Paris (France) 2019, *Annual Conference* St Gallen (Switzerland) 2018, *Annual Conference* London (UK) 2017, *Annual Conference* Paris (France) 2016, *Annual Conference* Kiel (Germany) 2015. **Members** Membership countries not specified. [2016/XF6930/**F**]

♦ Euroleague for Life Sciences (ELLS) 05702

Contact Czech Univ Life Sciences, Kamýcká 129, 16500 Praha 6 – Suchol, 165 00 Prague, Czechia. E-mail: ells@czu.cz.
URL: http://www.euroleague-study.org/

History 2001. **Aims** Bring together universities cooperating in the fields of natural resource management, agricultural and forestry sciences, life sciences, veterinary sciences, food sciences, and environmental sciences. **Structure** Board. *Euroleague Student Association*. Rotating Secretariat. **Languages** English. **Staff** 0.50 FTE, paid. **Finance** Annual budget: about euro 100,000. **Activities** Training/education; awards/prizes/competitions; networking/liaising; events/meetings. **Events** *Scientific Student Conference* Hohenheim (Germany) 2023, *Scientific Student Conference* Prague (Czechia) 2022, *Conference* Copenhagen (Denmark) 2017, *International Relations Officers Meeting* Vienna (Austria) 2017, *Conference* Vienna (Austria) 2013.
Members Universities in 7 countries:
Austria, Czechia, Denmark, Germany, Netherlands, Poland, Sweden.
Partner universities in 4 countries:
China, Israel, New Zealand, USA. [2023/XJ8287/**F**]

♦ Eurolib 05703

Chair c/o EP Library, Spinelli 05D, Rue Wiertz 60, 1047 Brussels, Belgium.
Secretariat c/o Library and Documentation Service, Cedefop, PO Box 22427, 551 02 Thessaloniki, Greece. T. +302310490040.
URL: http://www.eurolibnet.eu/

History Founded Jun 1988, on the initiative of the Secretary General of *European Parliament (EP, #08146)*, as an informal grouping of institutional libraries. Agreement formalizing conduct of business adopted 18 Apr 1997, Dublin (Ireland). Full title: *EUROLIB – European Community and Associated Institutions Library Cooperation Group*. **Aims** Promote a wider awareness of the contribution EU institutions, EU agencies and and associated libraries make to the organizations they serve; enhance the professional performance of staff; help participating libraries achieve economies of investment in technology, acquisitions and services; develop common information tools; provide high-quality library services. **Structure** General Assembly (twice a year); Technical Meeting. Officers: Chair; 2 Vice-Chairs. **Languages** English, French. **Staff** Voluntary. **Finance** No budget. **Activities** Knowledge management/information dissemination; research/documentation; events/meetings. **Publications** *Eurolib Working Papers*.
Members Libraries and information services in European institutions, EU agencies and associated libraries (37):
- *Centro de Informação Europeia Jacques Delors (CIEJD)*;
- *College of Europe (#04105)*;
- *Council of Europe (CE, #04881)*;
- *Council of the European Union (#04895)*;
- *Court of Justice of the European Union (CJEU, #04938)*;
- *EUROCONTROL (#05667)*;
- *Eurojust (#05698)*;
- *European Agency for Safety and Health at Work (EU-OSHA, #05843)*;
- *European Central Bank (ECB, #06466)*;
- *European Centre for Disease Prevention and Control (ECDC, #06476)*;
- *European Centre for the Development of Vocational Training (Cedefop, #06474)*;
- *European Chemicals Agency (ECHA, #06523)*;
- *European Commission (EC, #06633)*;
- *European Committee of the Regions (CoR, #06665)*;
- *European Court of Auditors (#06854)*;
- *European Economic and Social Committee (EESC, #06963)*;
- *European Environment Agency (EEA, #06995)*;
- *European External Action Service (EEAS, #07018)*;
- *European Food Safety Authority (EFSA, #07287)*;
- *European Foundation for the Improvement of Living and Working Conditions (Eurofound, #07348)*;
- *European Institute for Gender Equality (EIGE, #07557)*;
- *European Institute of Public Administration (EIPA, #07569)*;
- *European Investment Bank (EIB, #07599)*;
- *European Maritime Safety Agency (EMSA, #07744)*;
- *European Medicines Agency (EMA, #07767)*;
- *European Monitoring Centre for Drugs and Drug Addiction (EMCDDA, #07820)*;
- *European Parliament (EP, #08146)*;
- *European Patent Office (EPO, #08166)*;
- *European Police Office (Europol, #08239)*;
- *European Research Council (ERC, #08364)* (Executive Agency);

- *European Training Foundation (ETF, #08934);*
- *European Union Agency for Fundamental Rights (FRA, #08969);*
- *European Union Agency for Law Enforcement Training (CEPOL, #08970);*
- *European University Institute (EUI, #09034);*
- *Joint Research Centre (JRC, #16147);*
- *Publications Office of the European Union (Publications Office, #18562);*
- *Single Resolution Board (SRB, #19287).* [2022/XF5592/y/F]

♦ EUROLIB – European Community and Associated Institutions Library Cooperation Group / see Eurolib (#05703)
♦ EUROLIBRI – Association of Publishers of European Legal and Economic Works (inactive)
♦ **EUROLICS** European Network for the Economics of Learning, Innovation, and Competence Building Systems (#07897)
♦ **Eurolife** Eurolife – Network of European Universities in Life Sciences (#05704)

♦ Eurolife – Network of European Universities in Life Sciences (Eurolife) 05704

Coordinator UMC Göttingen, Von-Siebold-Str 3, 37075 Göttingen, Germany. T. +495513968415. E-mail: eurolife@med.uni-goettingen.de.
URL: http://eurolifeuniversities.org/

History 1999. First Eurolife Collaboration Agreement signed and entered into force 1 Jan 2002. **Structure** Steering Committee. **Activities** Research/documentation; training/education. **Publications** *Eurolife Newsletter.*
Members Institutions in 8 countries:
Austria, France, Germany, Ireland, Netherlands, Spain, Sweden, UK. [2022/XJ8765/F]

♦ **EUROLIM** EUROLIM – Federation of Limousin Herd Books within the European Union (#05705)

♦ EUROLIM – Federation of Limousin Herd Books within the European Union (EUROLIM) 05705

Pres Home Farm, Cilycwm, Llandovery, SA20 0TG, UK. T. +441550720464.
URL: http://www.limousin.co.uk/international/eurolim.html

History 1989. **Aims** Encourage the promotion and expansion of the Limousin breed in the EU; improve the genetics of the Limousin breed within the EU; harmonize selection working methods and exchange research works and information; make it easier for each of the associations to apply EU Directives. **Structure** General Meeting (annual). Board, comprising President, 2 Vice-Presidents and Secretary. [2008/XJ8160/E]

♦ Eurolines Organisation 05706

Main Office Av de la Métrologie 6, 1130 Brussels, Belgium. T. +3222469140. Fax +3222165525.
URL: http://www.eurolines.com/

History 1985. Founded by operators of international regular coach lines. New statutes adopted 15 May 1997. Registration: AISBL/IVZW, No/ID: 0461.155.519, Start date: 15 May 1997, Belgium. **Aims** Promote commercial and technical cooperation among member coach line operators so as to develop international lines and promote members' interests and prosperity, but without interfering with their pool-operating agreements. **Structure** General Assembly (2 a year); Board; Executive Committee; Permanent Central Office/Secretariat in Brussels (Belgium). **Languages** English, French, German. **Staff** 2.00 FTE, paid. **Finance** Members' dues. **Activities** Standards/guidelines; advocacy/lobbying/activism. **Events** *General Assembly* Bucharest (Romania) 2015, *General Assembly* Bratislava (Slovakia) 2014, *General Assembly* Lisbon (Portugal) 2013, *General Assembly* Barcelona (Spain) 2012, *General Assembly* Munich (Germany) 2011. **Publications** Fact File.
Members Professional road passenger transport companies (31), operating regular international coach lines and affiliated to IRU. Members in 23 countries:
Austria, Belgium, Bosnia-Herzegovina, Bulgaria, Croatia, Czechia, Denmark, France, Germany, Hungary, Ireland, Italy, Lithuania, Netherlands, Portugal, Romania, Serbia, Slovakia, Slovenia, Spain, Sweden, Switzerland, UK. [2015.08.27/XD1166/F]

♦ Euro-Link for Lawyers / see World Link for Law (#21626)

♦ EuroLinux Alliance for a Free Information Infrastructure 05707

Address not obtained.

History 1999. **Aims** Protect and promote: Linux and commercial software and service activities for Linux in Europe; free software and open standards and open interfaces in Europe; competition and innovation in the information technology industry.
Members in 3 countries:
France, Germany, Italy.
NGO Relations *Association francophone des utilisateurs de Linux et des logiciels libres (AFUL, #02620).* [2009/XF6306/F]

♦ EUROLIPID – Fédération européenne pour l'étude des corps gras (inactive)
♦ **EUROLUX** European Group for Rooflights and Smoke-Ventilation (#07434)
♦ Euroma (internationally oriented national body)

♦ EuroMAB 05708

Contact c/o UNESCO MAB, 7 place de Fontenoy, 75007 Paris CEDEX 07, France. T. +33145684151. E-mail: mab@unesco.org.

History Comes within the framework of *Programme on Man and the Biosphere (MAB, #18526).* **Aims** Through the *Unesco* MAB programme: promote cooperation in *man* and *biosphere* research and training and development of biosphere *reserves* among countries of *Europe* and North America; support mutual programme development, exchange of *sustainable development* practices and use of biosphere reserves as learning sites within the UN Decade of Education on Sustainable Development. **Structure** Not an organization; a grouping of countries. Set up: *'Biosphere Integrated Monitoring Programme (BRIM)'.* **Finance** Through Unesco MAB Programme. Annual budget: US$ 2,000,000 (programme costs only). **Activities** Events/meetings; training/education; standards/guidelines; monitoring/evaluation; knowledge management/information dissemination. **Events** *Biennial Conference* Haapsalu (Estonia) 2015, *Biennial Conference* Lansdowne, ON (Canada) 2013, *Biosphere reserve coordinators meeting* Antalya (Turkey) 2007, *Biosphere Reserve Coordinators Meeting* Turkey 2007, *Biosphere reserve coordinators meeting* Hernstein (Austria) 2005. **Publications** Proceedings.
Members Covers 51 countries:
Albania, Andorra, Armenia, Austria, Azerbaijan, Belarus, Belgium, Bosnia-Herzegovina, Bulgaria, Canada, Croatia, Cyprus, Czechia, Denmark, Estonia, Finland, France, Georgia, Germany, Greece, Hungary, Iceland, Ireland, Israel, Italy, Latvia, Liechtenstein, Lithuania, Luxembourg, Malta, Moldova, Monaco, Montenegro, Netherlands, North Macedonia, Norway, Poland, Portugal, Romania, Russia, San Marino, Serbia, Slovakia, Slovenia, Spain, Sweden, Switzerland, Türkiye, UK, Ukraine, USA. [2017.06.01/XE2512/E]

♦ **EUROMABNET** European Monoclonal Antibodies Network (#07821)
♦ **EURoma** European Network on Social Inclusion and Roma under the Structural Funds (#08007)
♦ **EurOMA** European Operations Management Association (#08088)

♦ Euromaisiers 05709

Secretariat Av de Tervueren 13A, Bte 7, 1040 Brussels, Belgium. E-mail: secretariat@euromaisiers.eu.
URL: http://www.euromaisiers.eu/

History 18 Dec 1959, Paris (France). Current statutes adopted May 2004, Rotterdam (Netherlands). Former names and other names: *European Maize Milling Industry* – alias; *Groupement des associations des maïsiers des pays de la CEE (EUROMAISIERS)* – former; *Verband der Maisverarbeiter in den EWG-Ländern* – former; *Raggruppamento delle Associazioni degli Industriali del Mais de Paesi della CEE* – former; *Groepering van Associaties van de Maisverwerkende Industrieën van de EEG-Landen* – former. Registration: EU Transparency Register, No/ID: 97724634514-96. **Aims** Promote the manufacture and downstream distribution of healthy and natural maize-based ingredients for food products. **Structure** General Meeting; Presidium; Secretariat. **Events** *General Assembly* Gdansk (Poland) 2022, *Annual General Assembly* Lisbon (Portugal) 2014, *Annual General Assembly* Budapest (Hungary) 2013, *Annual General Assembly* Valencia (Spain) 2012, *Annual General Assembly* Paris (France) 2011.
Members Companies (21) and national organizations (1) in 10 countries:
Belgium, France, Germany, Hungary, Italy, Netherlands, Poland, Portugal, Spain, UK.
IGO Relations Recognized by: *European Commission (EC, #06633).* [2022.02.01/XE2941/t/E]

♦ EUROMALT / see Working Committee of the Malting Industry of the EU (#21055)
♦ EuroMam – European Quaternary Mammal Research Association (inactive)
♦ **EUROMAP** European Committee of Machinery Manufacturers for the Plastics and Rubber Industries (#06656)

♦ EUROMAR 05710

Sec c/o Institut de Biologie Structurale, 71 avenue des Martyrs, 38044 Grenoble CEDEX 9, France. T. +33457428562. Fax +33476501890.
Chair c/o Goethe University Frankfurt, Max von Laue Strasse 7, 60438 Frankfurt-Main, Germany. T. +496979829406. Fax +496979829404.
URL: http://www.euromar.org/

History 2 Apr 2005. Founded by representatives of *Groupement AMPERE (#10755), European Experimental Nuclear Magnetic Resonance Conference (EENC, inactive)* and the British Nuclear Magnetic Resonance Discussion Group (NMRDG). Serves as a division of *Groupement AMPERE.* **Structure** Board of Trustees; Programme Committee. **Activities** Events/meetings; awards/prizes/competitions. **Events** *European Conference on Magnetic Resonance* Glasgow (UK) 2023, *European Conference on Magnetic Resonance* Utrecht (Netherlands) 2022, *Annual European Magnetic Resonance Conference* Berlin (Germany) 2019, *Annual European Magnetic Resonance Conference* Nantes (France) 2018, *Annual European Magnetic Resonance Conference* Warsaw (Poland) 2017. [2022/XM1826/c/E]

♦ **Euromarches** European Marches Against Unemployment, Job Insecurity and Social Exclusions (#07735)

♦ EUROMARFOR 05711

Contact address not obtained. E-mail: euromarfor.pc@gmail.com.
URL: http://www.euromarfor.org/

History Established 15 May 1995, at WEU Ministerial Meeting, as the multinational military corps within the framework of *Western European Union (WEU, inactive)* responsible for sea operations. Previously acted as a *'FAWEU'* (Forces Answerable to WEU). **Aims** Fulfil missions defined in the Petersberg Declaration (1992), such as sea control, humanitarian missions, peacekeeping operations, crisis response operations and peace enforcement. **Languages** English, French, Italian, Portuguese, Spanish. **Activities** Humanitarian/emergency aid; conflict resolution.
Members Partner nations (4):
France, Italy, Portugal, Spain. [2019.12.16/XF3664/F*]

♦ **EUROMARINE** European Marine Research Network (#07739)
♦ Euromärsche gegen Erwerbslosigkeit, Ungeschützte Beschäftigung und Ausgrenzung (#07735)
♦ Euromarsen Tegen Werkloosheid, Armoede en Sociale Uitsluiting (#07735)
♦ **EUROMAT** European Gaming and Amusement Federation (#07374)

♦ Euromax 05712

Pres c/o Matchbox Media, Ste 8, Masons Yard, 175-177 Westbourne Street, Hove, BN3 5FB, UK. T. +441273978011. E-mail: administrator@euromax.org.
URL: http://www.euromax.org/

History 1989. **Aims** As the professional association of *European* large format *theatres*, promote cooperation amongst all sectors of the industry. **Structure** President; 2 Vice-Presidents (Theatres; Productions); Administrator. **Languages** English. **Staff** 0.50 FTE, paid; 3.00 FTE, voluntary. **Finance** Members' dues. **Events** *Meeting* 2021, *Meeting* 2020, *Meeting* Copenhagen (Denmark) 2019, *Meeting* Paris (France) 2015, *Meeting* The Hague (Netherlands) 2014. **Members** Membership countries not specified. [2022/XJ8180/F]

♦ **EUROMCONTACT** European Federation of National Associations and International Companies of Contact Lens and Contact Lens Care Product Manufacturers (#07167)
♦ Euro MDF Board – European Federation of Medium Density Fibreboard Manufacturers (inactive)

♦ EUROMECH – European Mechanics Society 05713

SG Inst de Mécanique des Fluides de Toulouse, allée Camille Soula, 31400 Toulouse, France.
URL: http://www.euromech.org/

History Sep 1964, Munich (Germany). Founded as interim committee, during International Congress of Applied Mechanics. Permanent committee set up 1967. New statutes adopted along present name, 3 Apr 1993. Former names and other names: *European Mechanics Committee* – former (1964 to 1989); *Comité européen de mécanique* – former (1964 to 1989); *European Mechanics Council* – former (1989 to 1993); *Conseil européen de mécanique* – former (1989 to 1993). **Aims** Promote development of mechanics as a branch of science and engineering, from fundamental research on behaviour of *fluids* and *solids* to applied research in engineering. **Structure** Council (meets annually); Advisory Board; Executive Committee; Conference Committees (5). **Languages** English. **Finance** Sources: gifts, legacies; grants; meeting proceeds; members' dues. **Activities** Events/meetings; knowledge management/information dissemination; research and development. **Events** *European Nonlinear Oscillations Conference* Lyon (France) 2022, *Colloquium on Granular Patterns in Oscillatory Flows* Genoa (Italy) 2021, *European Nonlinear Oscillations Conference* Lyon (France) 2021, *European Fluid Mechanics Conference* Zurich (Switzerland) 2021, *European Turbulence Conference* Zurich (Switzerland) 2021. **Publications** *EUROMECH Newsletter.*
Members Individual; Joint; Institutional, in 9 countries (Belgium/France and Portugal/Spain are joint countries):
Belgium, Czechia, France, Germany, Italy, Netherlands, Portugal, Spain, UK.
NGO Relations Affiliated with (1): *International Union of Theoretical and Applied Mechanics (IUTAM, #15823).* [2023.02.13/XD0808/F]

♦ Euromed Capital 05714

Contact 14 rue Le Peletier, 75009 Paris, France. E-mail: assoceuromed@gmail.com.

History 2005. Former names and other names: *Association Euromed Capital Forum* – former. Registration: France. **Aims** Promote information sharing between the different Private *Equity* agents and partners in the *Euro-Mediterranean* area, the investors, businessmen and international organizations. **Structure** Board of Directors, comprising Chairman, Secretary General and 12 members. **Activities** Organizes *Euromed Capital Forum.* **Events** *Euromed Capital Forum* 2022, *Private Equity Forum* Barcelona (Spain) 2018, *Private Equity Forum* Gammarth (Tunisia) 2013, *Private Equity Forum* Tunis (Tunisia) 2013, *Private Equity Forum* Tangiers (Morocco) 2009.
Members Full in 22 countries and territories:
Algeria, Belgium, Cyprus, Egypt, France, Greece, Israel, Italy, Jordan, Lebanon, Libya, Luxembourg, Malta, Monaco, Morocco, Palestine, Portugal, Slovenia, Spain, Syrian AR, Tunisia, Türkiye.
NGO Relations Member of: *ANIMA Investment Network (#00833).* [2017/XJ6605/F]

♦ EURO-MED Centre, Catania (internationally oriented national body)
♦ EuroMed CLEN / see French Language Network for International Clinical Epidemiology (#09992)
♦ EuroMed Droits (#05733)

♦ Euromed Feminist Initiative (EFI) 05715

Initiative Féministe Euroméditerranéenne (IFE)

Exec Dir 20 Rue Soufflot, 75005 Paris, France. T. +33146349280. E-mail: ife@efi-euromed.org.
URL: https://efi-ife.org/

History 2004, Paris (France). Founded as a feminist network. Formally enlarged under current title 2014. **Aims** Contribute to challenging the present *gender* power structures so to correct imbalances through fighting *discrimination* and oppression of *women* and bringing about positive changes for the whole society. **Structure** Board; Executive Committee. **Staff** 23.00 FTE, paid. **Activities** Advocacy/lobbying/activism; awareness raising.
Members Full in 14 countries and territories:
Algeria, Croatia, Egypt, Greece, Italy, Jordan, Lebanon, Morocco, North Macedonia, Palestine, Spain, Sweden, Tunisia, UK.
Consultative Status Consultative status granted from: *ECOSOC (#05331)* (Special). [2022.06.28/XM6196/C]

♦ Euromed Heritage (inactive)
♦ Euromed-IHEDN (internationally oriented national body)

♦ EuroMediteranski Forum (internationally oriented national body)
♦ Euro-Mediterraan Centrum voor Migratie and Ontwikkeling (internationally oriented national body)
♦ Euro-Mediterran-Arabischer Länderverein (#05717)

♦ Euro-Mediterranean Academic Network (EMAN) 05716

SG 16 rue Mazarine, 75006 Paris, France. E-mail: contact@g-i-d.org.
URL: http://g-i-d.org/en/euro-mediterranean-area/

History Formally set up 21 Jun 2010, Alexandria (Egypt), at the initiative of *Groupe interacadémique pour le développement (GID, #10746)*. Also referred to as *GID-EMAN*. **Aims** Foster *science* and *culture* so as to promote development and scientific excellence in the Mediterranean region. **Structure** General Assembly; Executive Committee. **Languages** English, French. **Staff** 1.00 FTE, paid. **Finance** Fundraising; GID contributions. **Activities** Training/education. **Events** *General Assembly* Dubrovnik (Croatia) 2015, *Parmenides Conference / General Assembly / Parmenides Conference* Dubrovnik (Croatia) 2015, *Parmenides Conference* Malta 2013, *Parmenides Conference* Valletta (Malta) 2013, *Parmenides Conference* Paris (France) 2012. **Publications** *Mediterranean Archaeology: a GID – EMAN advanced training course.*
Members Academies in 23 countries:
Albania, Algeria, Bosnia-Herzegovina, Croatia, Cyprus, Egypt, France, Greece, Israel, Italy, Jordan, Lebanon, Malta, Monaco, Montenegro, Morocco, Palestine, Portugal, Senegal, Slovenia, Spain, Tunisia, Türkiye.
NGO Relations Member of: *InterAcademy Partnership (IAP, #11376).* [2018.06.01/XJ7094/**F**]

♦ Euro-Mediterranean-Arab Association (EMA) 05717

Euro-Mediterran-Arabischer Länderverein
Managing Dir address not obtained.
URL: http://ema-hamburg.org/

History Set up as *Euro-Mediterranean Association for Cooperation and Development.* Registered in accordance with German law. **Aims** Promote and consolidate cooperation between Germany, the countries belonging to the Euro-Mediterranean partnership and the other Arabic states. **Structure** Members' Assembly; Executive Board. **Languages** Arabic, English, French, German. **Finance** Members' dues. **Activities** Networking/liaising. **Publications** *Mediterranes* – scientific magazine. **NGO Relations** *Arab Countries Water Utilities Association (ACWUA, #00934).* [2016.06.01/XJ6908/**E**]

♦ Euro-Mediterranean Association for Cooperation and Development / see Euro-Mediterranean-Arab Association (#05717)
♦ Euro-Mediterranean Association of Life Sciences (internationally oriented national body)
♦ Euro Mediterranean Biomedical Science Institute (internationally oriented national body)
♦ Euro-Mediterranean Centre for Climate Change (internationally oriented national body)
♦ Euro-Mediterranean Centre on Evaluation and Prevention of Seismic Risk (internationally oriented national body)

♦ Euro-Mediterranean Centre on Insular Coastal Dynamics (ICoD) . . . 05718

Head c/o IES, Univ of Malta, Msida, MSD 2080, Malta. T. +35623402340. Fax +35623402342.
URL: http://www.um.edu.mt/ies/entity/icod/

History May 1987, as *Euro-Mediterranean Centre on Marine Contamination Hazards – Centre euro-méditerranéen sur la contamination marine accidentelle*, within the framework of *Foundation for International Studies, University of Malta (FIS, inactive)*. A *'European Network of Specialist Centres'* of *Open Partial Agreement on the Prevention of, Protection against and Organization of Relief in Major Natural and Technological Disasters (EUR-OPA Major Hazards Agreement, #17762)*, within the framework of the *Council of Europe (CE, #04881)*. Present name adopted 1993. **Aims** Combat *marine* and *environmental degradation* at the *coast*; carry out research at a Euro-Mediterranean level on interactive processes at the coast, with special reference to insular environments; develop a better understanding of the interaction of the human/natural interface at the coast; contribute to civil protection at the coast; raise public awareness of, and academic interest in, pressing environmental issues on a local and regional scale. **Structure** Working Groups (3). **Languages** English. **Staff** 9.00 FTE, paid. **Finance** Main source: Council of Europe. Additional funding: local government grants; specific grants from collaborating organizations for joint organization of activities/training courses. **Activities** Research/documentation; training/education; knowledge management/information dissemination. **Events** *MEDCOAST : international conference on the Mediterranean costal environment / Biennial Conference* Qawra (Malta) 1997, *International conference on costings vs benefits of TBT-based and alternative antifoulants* Valletta (Malta) 1995, *Meeting of marine related universities* Valletta (Malta) 1995, *Meeting of Euro-Mediterranean marine centers* Valletta (Malta) 1994, *Clean seas conference* Valletta (Malta) 1993. **Publications** Monographs; proceedings; books; video. **IGO Relations** *European Centre for Research into Techniques for Informing the Population in Emergency Situations (CEISE); FAO (#09260); Intergovernmental Oceanographic Commission (IOC, #11496); UNEP (#20299); UNESCO (#20322); WHO (#20950).* **NGO Relations** *European Association of Marine Science and Technology (AESTM, no recent information); ICSC – World Laboratory (#11088).* [2011/XE1163/**E***]

♦ Euro-Mediterranean Centre on Marine Contamination Hazards / see Euro-Mediterranean Centre on Insular Coastal Dynamics (#05718)
♦ Euro-Mediterranean Centre for Research on Arid Areas (internationally oriented national body)
♦ Euro-Mediterranean Circle of Textile and Clothing Managers (#03828)
♦ Euro-Mediterranean CLEN / see French Language Network for International Clinical Epidemiology (#09992)

♦ Euro-Mediterranean Council for Burns and Fire Disaster (MBC) . . . 05719

Dir Gen c/o Div di Chirurgia Plastica e Terapia delle Ustioni, Ospedale Civico USL, Via C Lazzaro 58, 90127 Palermo PA, Italy. T. +39916663631 – +39916663707. Fax +3991596404. E-mail: mbcpa@medbc.com.
Pres American Univ of Beirut, Past and Reconstr Surgery, PO Box 113, Beirut, Lebanon. T. +9613340032.
URL: http://www.medbc.com/

History 1983, Palermo (Italy). Founded by Giovanni Dogo. Former names and other names: *Mediterranean Burns Club* – former; *Club méditerranéen des brûlures* – former; *Mediterranean Club for Burns and Fire Disaster* – former; *Club méditerranéen des brûlures et désastres du feu* – former. **Aims** Involve the intellectual forces of Mediterranean countries in an open exchange of opinion so as to analyse common themes, analogies and contrasts in the field of *prevention*, *treatment* and functional recovery of burns and in the field of fire disasters. **Structure** General Assembly; Officers: President, Secretary-General, Treasurer; Scientific Committee; Editorial Committee. Headquarters in Palermo (Italy). **Languages** English, French. **Finance** Sources: members' dues; subsidies. Subsidy by the Regional Parliament (Sicily). **Activities** Events/meetings; knowledge management/information dissemination; monitoring/evaluation; networking/liaising; research/documentation; training/education. **Events** *Meeting* Casablanca (Morocco) 2021, *International Conference on Burns and Fire Disasters* Casablanca (Morocco) 2006, *International Conference on Burns and Fire Disasters* Cyprus 2004, *International Conference on Burns and Fire Disasters* Tripoli (Libyan AJ) 2002, *International symposium on burns and fire disaster management* Jerusalem (Israel) 2000. **Publications** *Annals of the MBC* (4 a year). *Management of Mass Burns and Fire Disaster – Perspectives 2000* (1995) by M Masellis and S W A Gunn; *Management of Mass Burn Casualties and Fire Disasters* (1992) by M Masellis and S W A Gunn; *Multilingual Dictionary of Disaster Medicine and International Relief* (1989) by S W A Gunn; *Attacco alla Città* (1987) by S W A Gunn et al. Annual proceedings; videotape series; guidelines; training manuals; posters; pamphlets; slides. Available in English, French, Spanish, Turkish, Greek, Slav and Italian. Information Services: Electronic editing centre, graphic computer centre and animation computer centre include: clinical, bibliographical and didactic data; video material; bibliographic databank on burns, reconstructive surgery and fire disasters; clinical, therapeutic and nursing databank.
Members Individuals Founder; Ordinary; National Representative Members, in 20 countries:
Albania, Algeria, Bosnia-Herzegovina, Cyprus, Egypt, France, Greece, Israel, Italy, Lebanon, Libya, Malta, Morocco, Portugal, San Marino, Slovenia, Spain, Syrian AR, Tunisia, Türkiye.
Associate Members in 18 countries and territories:
Argentina, Austria, Bulgaria, China, Czechia, India, Japan, Kuwait, Lithuania, Peru, Poland, Québec, Romania, Russia, Saudi Arabia, Singapore, South Africa, USA.
IGO Relations *WHO (#20950)* Collaborating Centre (Jun 1997). Adviser and regional training centre to: *European Centre for Disaster Medicine (#06475).* Projects with: *TEMPUS IV (inactive).* **NGO Relations** Speciality member of: *International Federation of Surgical Colleges (IFSC, #13560).* Adviser and regional training centre to: *World Association for Disaster and Emergency Medicine (WADEM, #21133).* Instrumental in setting up: *International Association for Humanitarian Medicine Chisholm-Gunn (IAHM, #11946).* [2022.10.24/XF0944/v/**F**]

♦ Euro-Mediterranean Energy Forum (inactive)
♦ Euro-Mediterranean Federation against Enforced Disappearances (#09487)
♦ Euromediterranean Federation of Olive Oil Municipalities (inactive)
♦ Euro-Mediterranean Forum (internationally oriented national body)
♦ Euro-Mediterranean Foundation for Dialogue between Cultures / see Anna Lindh Euro-Mediterranean Foundation for the Dialogue between Cultures (#00847)

♦ Euro-Mediterranean Foundation of Support to Human Rights Defenders (EMHRF) 05720

Fondation euro-méditerranéenne de soutien aux défenseurs des droits de l'Homme
Contact Vestergade 16, 2nd Floor, 1456 Copenhagen K, Denmark.
URL: http://emhrf.org/

History Feb 2003, Malta. Founded at the General Assembly of *EuroMed Rights (#05733)*. Statutes adopted 29-31 Oct 2004. Officially launched 9 Dec 2004. Former names and other names: *Non-Governmental Platform for the Euro-Mediterranean Civil Forum – Plate-forme non gouvernementale EuroMed* – former; *NGO Platform for the Euromed Civil Forum* – former; *Foundation for the Euro-Mediterranean Civil Forum* – former. Registration: Start date: Oct 2004, Denmark. **Aims** Provide strategic financial assistance to regional, national and local human rights NGOs and institutes as well as individuals who promote, support, protect and monitor the observance of human rights in the South-Mediterranean region. **Structure** Board; Council of Representatives; Secretariat. **Languages** Arabic, English, French. **Staff** 8.00 FTE, paid. **Finance** Public and private donors. Annual budget: 2,850,000 EUR (2018). **Activities** Financial and/or material support. Active in: Algeria, Egypt, Israel, Jordan, Lebanon, Libya, Morocco, Palestine, Syrian AR, Tunisia. **Events** *Seminar / Discussion Seminar* Morocco 2014, *Seminar / Discussion Seminar* Brussels (Belgium) 2011. **Publications** *Annual Activity and Financial Report.* **Members** Not a membership organization. **NGO Relations** Member of (1): *ProtectDefenders.eu (#18546).* [2019.06.24/XF7051/f/**F**]

♦ Euro-Mediterranean Free-Trade Area (unconfirmed)

♦ Euro-Mediterranean Human Rights Monitor (Euro-Med Monitor) . . . 05721

Office Manager WTC II – c/o Regus Business Ctr, Route de Pré-Bois 29, 1215 Geneva, Switzerland. T. +41229295703. Fax +41229295703. E-mail: geneva@euromedmonitor.org.
URL: http://euromedmonitor.org/

History Set up Nov 2011. Registered in accordance with Swiss Civil Code: CH-660.0.748.015-1. EU Transparency Register: 326186932081-66. **Aims** Advocate for the human rights of all persons across Europe and the MENA region, particularly those who live under occupation, in the throes of war or political unrest and/or have been displaced due to persecution or armed conflict. **Structure** General Assembly; Board of Trustees; Steering Committee; Executive Director. Offices: Geneva (Switzerland); Gaza (West Bank-Gaza); Tunis (Tunisia); Tripoli (Libyan AJ). **Languages** Arabic, English, French. **Staff** 7.50 FTE, paid; 52.00 FTE, voluntary. **Finance** Donations, including from: *Friedrich-Ebert-Stiftung (FES).* **Activities** Advocacy/lobbying/activism; training/education; awareness raising; knowledge management/information dissemination; monitoring/evaluation. **Publications** *Euro-Med Monitor Newsletter.*
Members Full in 10 countries and territories:
Germany, Jordan, Lebanon, Libya, Palestine, Sweden, Switzerland, Tunisia, Türkiye, USA.
Also members in the Arab Gulf. Membership countries not specified.
IGO Relations None. **NGO Relations** *Asian Federation Against Involuntary Disappearances (AFAD, #01453); European Youth Human Rights Network (EYHR-Net); Friedrich-Ebert-Stiftung (FES); International Youth Foundation (IYF); International Coalition for the Responsibility to Protect (ICRtoP, #12620); Kvinna till Kvinna Foundation; World Solidarity Forum (WSF).* [2018.10.25/XM6946/**F**]

♦ Euro-Mediterranean Human Rights Network / see EuroMed Rights (#05733)

♦ Euro-Mediterranean Information System on Know-how in the Water Sector (EMWIS) 05722

Système euro-méditerranéen d'information sur les savoir-faire dans le domaine de l'eau (SEMIDE) – Sistema Euromediterraneo de información sobre la Pericia en el sector del Agua
Tech Coordinator – Manager UT Semide/EMWIS TU, BP 23, 06901 Sophia Antipolis CEDEX, France. T. +33492942291 – +33492942290. Fax +33492942295. E-mail: info@semide.org.
Contact 2229 route des Crêtes, Parc International d'Activitiés – Valbonne Sophia Antipolis, 06560 Valbonne, France.
URL: http://www.emwis.net/

History 10 Dec 1997, Naples (Italy). Established on approval by conference of water managers and major operators of a study led by French Ministry of the Environment and *International Office for Water (IOW, #14399)*. Set up to network systems in countries signatory to *Convention for the Protection of the Marine Environment and the Coastal Region of the Mediterranean (Barcelona Convention, 1976)*. National focal points set up following first meeting of EMWIS Management Committee, 17 Mar 1998, Paris (France). Implemented by an *European Economic Interest Grouping (EEIG, #06960)*, whose statutes were signed by IOW, 15 Jun 1998. Former names and other names: *Euro-Mediterranean Water Information System* – alias. **Aims** Facilitate access to information in the field by using modern communication means and networking already existing systems. **Structure** General Meeting. Management Committee comprises 13 countries, particularly those financing the Technical Unit, which is managed by a consortium of 3 operators representing France, Spain and Italy. Coordination Committee unites National Focal Points. EEIG managed by IOW. Based in Sophia-Antipolis (France). **Languages** Arabic, English, French. **Staff** 4.00 FTE, paid. **Finance** Contributions from countries comprising Technical Unit. Subsidy from *European Commission (EC, #06633).* **Activities** Events/meetings; networking/liaising; projects/programmes; research/documentation. **Events** *Workshop on Strengthening of National Information Systems and Harmonization of Data Collection towards a Shared Water Information System* Barcelona (Spain) 2012, *Euro-Mediterranean ministerial conference on water* Barcelona (Spain) 2010, *Atelier sur les apports des technologies spatiales pour le secteur de l'eau* Rome (Italy) 2010, *Conference of the water directors of the Euro-Mediterranean and Southeastern European countries* Athens (Greece) 2006, *Euro-mediterranean conference of the 35 water general directors* Rome (Italy) 2005. **Publications** *EMWIS Flash* (6 a year) in English – newsletter. Annual activity report; meeting proceedings.
Members Membership covers 35 countries and territories (" indicates focal points set up by respective government):
Algeria (*), Austria (*), Belgium (*), Cyprus (*), Czechia, Denmark, Egypt (*), Estonia, Finland, France (*), Germany, Greece (*), Hungary, Ireland, Israel (*), Italy (*), Jordan (*), Latvia, Lebanon (*), Lithuania, Luxembourg (*), Malta (*), Morocco (*), Netherlands, Palestine (*), Poland, Portugal (*), Slovakia, Slovenia, Spain (*), Sweden, Syrian AR (*), Tunisia (*), Türkiye (*), UK.
Regional integration EU entity:
European Union (EU, #08967).
IGO Relations Partner of (1): *Global Alliances for Water and Climate (GAfWaC, #10230).* [2021.09.02/XF4947/**F***]

♦ Euro-Mediterranean Irrigators Community (EIC) 05723

Head Office Paseo de la Habana 26, 2o Oficina 2, 28036 Madrid, Spain. T. +34915636318. Fax +34915636253. E-mail: eic@e-mic.org.
URL: http://www.e-mic.org/

History 2002. Registered in accordance with Spanish law. EU Transparency Register: 720377522563-06. **Aims** Facilitate information exchange, knowledge, plans, experiences, etc, among irrigators aimed at improving management and distribution of water from the legal, administrative and technician point of view. **Structure** General Assembly (annual); Board of Directors. **Languages** English, French, Spanish. **Events** *Capacity building symposium on integrated water management and irrigation* Istanbul (Turkey) 2004, *General Assembly* Istanbul (Turkey) 2004.
Members Organizations (10) in 10 countries:
Egypt, France, Germany, Greece, Italy, Morocco, Portugal, Spain, Tunisia, Türkiye. [2016.12.15/XJ3036/**F**]

♦ EURO-Mediterranean Lagoon Federation (EuroMedLag) 05724

Contact c/o ecotekne sp, Lecce-Monteroni sn, 73100 Lecce BT, Italy. T. +390832298606. E-mail: info.euromedlag@gmail.com.
URL: http://www.euromedlag.eu/

Aims Disseminate and promote ecological culture. **Structure** Board. **Activities** Events/meetings. **Events** *EUROLAG* Venice (Italy) 2020, *European Coastal Lagoons Symposium (EUROLAG)* Murcia (Spain) 2016, *European Coastal Lagoons Symposium (EUROLAG)* Lecce (Italy) 2013, *European Coastal Lagoons Symposium (EUROLAG)* Aveiro (Portugal) 2011. [2018/AA2011/**D**]

♦ Euro-Mediterranean Legal Metrology Forum (no recent information)

♦ Euro Mediterranean Music Academy for Peace (EMMA for Peace) .. 05725

Pres Via del Babuino 51, 00187 Rome RM, Italy. E-mail: info@emmaforpeace.org.
Honorary Pres address not obtained.
URL: http://www.emmaforpeace.org/

History Officially launched 2013, Warsaw (Poland), at 13th World Summit of Nobel Peace Laureates, under the patronage of *UNESCO (#20322)* and under the auspices of the Secretary General of *Council of Europe (CE, #04881)*. **Aims** Act as a network of music institutions, universities and philanthropic foundations brought together in the shared interest of music and the promotion of peace in the Mediterranean and Middle East regions. **Structure** Advisory Board; President; Honorary President. **Languages** Arabic, English, French. **Activities** Events/meetings. **IGO Relations** *UNESCO (#20322)*; *UNHCR (#20327)*; *UNICEF (#20332)*; *United Nations (UN, #20515)*. [2016.06.01/XM4246/**E**]

♦ Euro-Mediterranean Network for Co-operation (Mediter) 05726

Pres Rond-point Robert Schuman 9, 1040 Brussels, Belgium.
URL: http://euromediter.eu/

History Set up Jan 2011. EU Transparency Register: 59768738332-66. **Aims** Provide continuous training and production services to local Mediterranean stakeholders in the framework of EU programmes, in collaboration with existing networks in the area. **Structure** Board of Directors. **Activities** Training/education; networking/liaising; events/meetings.
Members Organizations in 6 countries:
France, Italy, Jordan, Lebanon, Malta, Tunisia.
Included in the above, 1 organization listed in this Yearbook:
Center of Arab Women for Training and Research, Tunis (CAWTAR, #03637). [2018/XM6871/**F**]

♦ Euro-Mediterranean Network of Experimental and Representative Basins / see European Network of Experimental and Representative Basins (#07905)
♦ Euro-Mediterranean Observatory on Risks Management (internationally oriented national body)
♦ Euro-Mediterranean Parliamentary Assembly / see Parliamentary Assembly – Union for the Mediterranean (#18216)
♦ Euro-Mediterranean Parliamentary Forum / see Parliamentary Assembly – Union for the Mediterranean (#18216)
♦ Euro-Mediterranean Partnership / see Union for the Mediterranean (#20457)
♦ Euro-Mediterranean Partnership Foreign Policy Institutes Network / see Euro-Mediterranean Study Commission (#05727)
♦ Euro-Mediterranean Regional and Local Assembly (#02313)

♦ Euro-Mediterranean Study Commission (EuroMeSCo) 05727

Dir c/o IEMed, Girona 20, 08010 Barcelona, Spain. T. +34932449850. E-mail: euromesco@iemed.org.
URL: https://www.euromesco.net/

History Feb 1994. Founded as an initiative of *Istituto Affari Internazionali, Roma (IAI)*, with the support of *European Commission (EC, #06633)*. Expanded Jun 1996. Former names and other names: *Mediterranean Study Commission (MeSCo)* – former; *Euro-Mediterranean Partnership Foreign Policy Institutes Network* – former. **Aims** Foster influential analysis and reflection on Euro-Mediterranean politics and policies; provide a platform for dialogue between researchers from the network, experts and key stakeholders; increase influence of think tanks and research institutes and actively contribute to policy shaping. **Structure** General Assembly; Steering Committee. Since 2010, Secretariat, located at *Institut Europeu de la Mediterrània (IEMed)*. **Languages** English, French. **Finance** Supported by: *European Union (EU, #08967)*; *Institut Europeu de la Mediterrània (IEMed)*. **Activities** Advocacy/lobbying/activism; events/meetings; knowledge management/information dissemination; networking/liaising; research/documentation. **Events** *Annual Conference and General Assembly* Tarragona (Spain) 2014, *Annual Conference and General Assembly* Paris (France) 2013, *Annual Conference and General Assembly* Barcelona (Spain) 2012, *Annual Conference and General Assembly* Barcelona (Spain) 2011, *Annual Conference and General Assembly* Amman (Jordan) 2008. **Publications** *EuroMeSCo Newsletter*; *Spot On*. Joint policy studies papers; briefs; reports.
Members Think tanks and research institutes (83) in 29 countries, of which 58 listed in this Yearbook:
Algeria, Austria, Belgium, Croatia, Cyprus, Czechia, Denmark, Egypt, Finland, France, Germany, Greece, Hungary, Israel, Italy, Jordan, Lebanon, Malta, Morocco, Netherlands, Palestine, Poland, Portugal, Slovenia, Spain, Sweden, Tunisia, Türkiye, UK.
- *Al Ahram Centre for Political and Strategic Studies (ACPSS)*;
- *Arab Forum for Alternatives (AFA)*;
- *Arab Reform Initiative (ARI, #01034)*;
- *Association of International Studies (AEI)*;
- *Austrian Institute for International Affairs (oiip)*;
- *Candid Foundation*;
- *Carnegie Europe (#03585)*;
- *Center for International Studies and Research (CERI)*;
- *Center for Middle Eastern Strategic Studies (ORSAM)*;
- *Center of Arab Women for Training and Research, Tunis (CAWTAR, #03637)*;
- *Centre des Etudes Méditerranéennes et Internationales (CEMI)*;
- *Centre for Economic Research on Mediterranean Countries (CREM)*;
- *Centre for European Studies, Ankara (CES)*;
- *Centre for International Information and Documentation, Barcelona (CIDOB Foundation)*;
- *Centre for Strategic Studies, Amman (CSS)*;
- *Centre of International Relations, Ljubljana (CIR)*;
- *Danish Institute for International Studies (DIIS)*;
- *Deutsche Gesellschaft für Auswärtige Politik (DGAP)*;
- *Deutsches Institut für Entwicklungspolitik (DIE)*;
- *Egmont Institute*;
- *Egyptian Council for Foreign Affairs (ECFA)*;
- *EuroMediteranski Forum (EMeF)*;
- *European Centre for Development Policy Management (ECDPM, #06473)*;
- *European Centre for Global Interdependence and Solidarity (North-South Centre, #06483)*;
- *European Council on Foreign Relations (ECFR, #06821)*;
- *European Neighbourhood Council (ENC, #07855)*;
- *European Policy Centre (EPC, #08240)*;
- *European University Institute (EUI, #09034)*;
- *Finnish Institute of International Affairs (FIIA)*;
- *Fondation méditerranéenne d'études stratégiques (FMES)*;
- *Foreign Policy Institute, Ankara (FPI)*;
- *German Marshall Fund of the United States (GMF)*;
- *Global Political Trends Center (GPoT)*;
- *Groupement d'études et de recherches sur la méditerranée (GERM)*;
- *Grupo de Estudios Europeos Mediterraneos (GREEM, no recent information)*;
- *Hellenic Foundation for European and Foreign Policy (ELIAMEP)*;
- *Institute for European Studies, Malta*;
- *Institute for World Economics of the Hungarian Academy of Sciences (IWE)*;
- *Institute of International Relations, Prague (IIR)*;
- *Institut français des relations internationales (IFRI)*;
- *Institut national des études de stratégie globale (INESG, no recent information)*;
- *Institut pro evropskou politiku (EUROPEUM)*;
- *Israel-Palestine: Creative Regional Initiatives (IPCRI)*;
- *Istituto Affari Internazionali, Roma (IAI)*;
- *Istituto di Studi sul Mediterraneo (ISMed)*;
- *Italian Institute for International Political Studies (ISPI)*;
- *Leonard Davis Institute for International Relations*;
- *Mediterranean Academy of Diplomatic Studies (MEDAC)*;
- *Moshe Dayan Centre for Middle Eastern and African Studies*;
- *Netherlands Institute of International Relations – Clingendael*;
- *Palestinian Academic Society for the Study of International Affairs (PASSIA)*;
- *Polish Institute of International Affairs (PIIA)*;
- *Real Instituto Elcano de Estudios Internacionales y Estratégicos*;
- *Royal Institute of International Affairs (RIIA)*;
- *Stiftung Wissenschaft und Politik (SWP)*;
- *Swedish Institute of International Affairs (SIIA)*;
- *Tampere Peace Research Institute (TAPRI)*;
- *Trans European Policy Studies Association (TEPSA, #20209).*

Observer members in 13 countries and including 14 organizations:
Austria, Belgium, Croatia, Egypt, France, Germany, Italy, Morocco, Poland, Slovenia, Spain, Sweden, Türkiye.
Casa Árabe; *Centre for European Policy Studies (CEPS, #03741)*; *Euromed-IHEDN*; *Euro-Mediterranean University (EMUNI, #05728)*; *European Union Institute for Security Studies (EUISS, #08994)*; *Europees Instituut, Gent*; *Fondation pour la recherche stratégique (FRS)*; *Fondazione Mediterraneo*; *GIGA – German Institute of Global and Area Studies*; *Institut de la Méditerranée (CMCI)*; *Institute for Development and International Relations (IRMO)*; *Institut Marocain des Relations Internationales (IMRI)*; *Peace Research Institute Frankfurt (PRIF)*; *Stockholm International Peace Research Institute (SIPRI, #19994).* [2021/XF4387/y/**E**]

♦ Euro-Mediterranean Tourism Organization (no recent information)

♦ Euro-Mediterranean University (EMUNI) 05728

Registered Address Trevisini Palace, Kidričevo nabrežje 2, 6330 Piran, Slovenia. T. +38659250050. E-mail: info@emuni.si.
URL: http://www.emuni.si/

History 9 Jun 2008, Piran (Slovenia). Former names and other names: *University Center for the Euro-Mediterranean Studies (Center EMUNI)* – former. Registration: Agency of the Republic of Slovenia for Public Legal Records and Related Services – AJPES, No/ID: 3487288000, Start date: 13 Feb 2009, Slovenia. **Aims** Develop academic and professional human resources in the region; generate scientific and scholarly knowledge and information; contribute to attaining the main goals of the Barcelona Process; support and strengthen existing cooperation networks among universities and institutes in the Euro-Mediterranean Partnership Countries; contribute to enhancement of intercultural dialogue in the region. **Structure** General Assembly; Management Board; Senate; President; Student Council. **Languages** Arabic, English, French, Slovene. **Staff** 8.50 FTE, paid. **Finance** Sources: government support; members' dues. Student fees. Supported by: *European Commission (EC, #06633)*. **Activities** Events/meetings; projects/programmes; publishing activities; training/education. **Events** *General Assembly* Barcelona (Spain) 2019, *Joint Conference* Maribor (Slovenia) 2012, *General Assembly* Lisbon (Portugal) 2011. **Publications** *International Journal of Euro-Mediterranean Studies*.
Members Full in 34 countries:
Albania, Algeria, Austria, Belgium, Bulgaria, Cyprus, Czechia, Egypt, Finland, France, Germany, Greece, Hungary, Israel, Italy, Jordan, Lebanon, Lithuania, Malta, Montenegro, Morocco, Netherlands, Norway, Palestine, Poland, Portugal, Romania, Russia, Slovakia, Slovenia, Spain, Tunisia, Türkiye, UK.
Included in the above, 16 organizations listed in this Yearbook:
Community of Mediterranean Universities (CMU, #04403); *Compostela Group of Universities (#04419)*; *European Association of Institutions of Higher Education (EURASHE, #06086)*; *European Students' Union (ESU, #08848)*; *Institute for Strategic and International Studies, Lisbon (IEEI)*; *Institut Europeu de la Mediterrània (IEMed)*; *International School for Advanced Studies, Trieste (ISAS)*; *International School for Social and Business Studies (ISSBS)*; *International School of Management (ISM)*; *International Telematic University UNINETTUNO*; *Mediterranean Organization for Promotion and Science (MOPS, #16670)*; *Mediterranean Universities Union (UNIMED, #16687)*; *Middle East Technical University (METU)*; *Mirovni inštitut*; *Programme for Palestinian-European-American Cooperation in Education (PEACE Programme, #18527)*; *Réseau méditerranéen des écoles d'ingénieurs (RMEI, #18899).*
IGO Relations Observer status with (1): *Parliamentary Assembly of the Mediterranean (PAM, #18212)*. Memorandum of Understanding with (2): *Anna Lindh Euro-Mediterranean Foundation for the Dialogue between Cultures (Anna Lindh Foundation, #00847)*; *United Nations Alliance of Civilizations (UNAOC, #20520)*. Cooperates with (1): *Assemblée Régionale et Locale Euro-Méditerranéenne (ARLEM, #02313)*. **NGO Relations** Member of (1): *Euro-Mediterranean Study Commission (EuroMeSCo, #05727)* (Observer). Instrumental in setting up (1): *Community of Mediterranean Universities (CMU, #04403).* [2021.03.02/XJ0418/y/**D**]

♦ Euro-Mediterranean Water Information System / see Euro-Mediterranean Information System on Know-how in the Water Sector (#05722)

♦ Euro-Mediterranean Women's Foundation 05729

Fondation des Femmes de l'Euro-Méditerranée

Pres Girona Str 20, 08010 Barcelona, Spain. E-mail: euromedwomen@iemed.org.
URL: http://www.euromedwomen.foundation/

History 2014. Founded by *Center of Arab Women for Training and Research, Tunis (CAWTAR, #03637)*, Fédération de la Ligue Démocratique des Droits des Femmes – Morocco, *Institut Europeu de la Mediterrània (IEMed)*, Interministerial Delegation to the Mediterranean (France), *International Mediterranean Women's Forum (IMWF, #14143)* and *Réseau Universitaire et Scientifique Euro-Méditerranéen sur le Genre et les Femmes (RUSEMEG, #18907)*. **Aims** Promote equal rights of women and men to participate in political, economic, civil and social life; eradicate all forms of violence and discrimination against women and girls; encourage a change in attitude and behaviour in favour of gender equality. **Structure** Managed by *Institut Europeu de la Mediterrània (IEMed)*. **Activities** Advocacy/lobbying/activism; capacity building; knowledge management/information dissemination; networking/liaising; research/documentation; training/education.
Members Associations; research and education centres; ministerial departments; local and regional authorities; media; enterprises and unions. Members (about 300) include:
Association of Organisations of Mediterranean Businesswomen (#02840); *Center of Arab Women for Training and Research, Tunis (CAWTAR, #03637)*; Fédération de la Ligue Démocratique des Droits des Femmes – Morocco; *Institut Europeu de la Mediterrània (IEMed)*; Interministerial Delegation to the Mediterranean (France); *International Mediterranean Women's Forum (IMWF, #14143)*; *Réseau Universitaire et Scientifique Euro-Méditerranéen sur le Genre et les Femmes (RUSEMEG, #18907).*
IGO Relations *Union for the Mediterranean (UfM, #20457).* [2022/XM5076/fy/**F**]

♦ Euro-Mediterranean Youth Platform (inactive)
♦ **EuroMedLag** EURO-Mediterranean Lagoon Federation (#05724)
♦ **Euro-Med Monitor** Euro-Mediterranean Human Rights Monitor (#05721)

♦ EuroMed Non-Governmental Platform 05730

Plate-forme non gouvernementale EuroMed

Registered Office 80 rue de Paris, 93000 Montreuil, France. T. +33142872864. Fax +33148701429.
History Charter adopted, Jun 2004, Limassol, Cyprus. Statutes adopted at 1st General Assembly, 1 Apr 2005, Luxembourg (Luxembourg). Current statutes amended and adopted, Dec 2009, Istanbul (Turkey). Registered in accordance with French law. **Aims** Set up a network and strengthen civil society's stakeholders from partner countries in the Barcelona Process, at local, national and regional levels, and promote their regional interests. **Structure** General Assembly (every 2 years). Board of 20 members. Executive Committee, comprising Chairperson, Vice-Chair, Secretary and Treasurer. **Languages** Arabic, English, French. **Events** *General Assembly* Istanbul (Turkey) 2009, *General Assembly* Madrid (Spain) 2007, *General Assembly* Luxembourg (Luxembourg) 2005.
Members Networks; foundations; international or regional non-governmental organizations. Members in 17 countries and territories:
Belgium, Denmark, Egypt, France, Greece, Israel, Italy, Jordan, Lebanon, Malta, Morocco, Netherlands, Palestine, Spain, Switzerland, Tunisia, UK.
Included in the above, 19 organizations listed in this Yearbook:

Arab Association for Human Rights (HRA, no recent information); Arab Institute for Human Rights (AIHR, #00983); Arab NGO Network for Development (ANND, #01016); Association des femmes de l'Europe méridionale (AFEM, #02594); Environnement et développement du Tiers-monde (enda, #05510); Euro-Mediterraan Centrum voor Migratie and Ontwikkeling (EMCEMO); EuroMed Rights (#05733); European Association for the Defence of Human Rights (AEDH, no recent information); European Environmental Bureau (EEB, #06996); Fondazione Mediterraneo; Heinrich Böll Foundation; Institut Europeu de la Mediterrània (IEMed); International Federation for Human Rights (#13452); Istituto per il Mediterraneo (IMED); Mediterranean Information Office for Environment, Culture and Sustainable Development (MIO-ECSDE, #16657); Oxfam International (#17922); Seydoux Foundation for the Mediterranean World; Union of Arab Community-Based Associations (Ittijah); World Organisation Against Torture (OMCT, #21685). [2012/XJ5985/y/F]

♦ EuroMed Permanent University Forum (EPUF) 05731

Secretariat URV – University of Tarragona, S Pau 4, 43003 Tarragona, Spain. T. +34977558528. Fax +34977559739. E-mail: epuf.info@gmail.com.
Facebook: https://www.facebook.com/EPUF.EuromedPermanentUniversityForum

History Oct 2006, Tampere (Finland), at 1st EuroMed Universities Rectors' Conference, when constitution act was conducted. Registered in accordance with Belgian law, Nov 2006. **Aims** Create a sustainable Higher Education Area in the EuroMed region. **Structure** General Assembly. Management Committee. President; Vice-President. Executive Secretariat, headed by Executive Secretary. **Activities** Annual *Euro-Mediterranean University Forum.* **Events** *Forum* Beirut (Lebanon) 2009, *Forum* Marseille (France) 2008, *Forum* Alexandria (Egypt) 2007, *Forum* Malta 2006.
Members Institutions (over 100) in 28 countries:
Albania, Algeria, Belgium, Bosnia-Herzegovina, Croatia, Cyprus, Czechia, Egypt, Estonia, Finland, France, Greece, Hungary, Israel, Italy, Jordan, Lebanon, Libya, Malta, Morocco, Palestine, Portugal, Slovenia, Spain, Syrian AR, Tunisia, Türkiye, UK.
Included in the above, 9 institutions listed in this Yearbook:
Anna Lindh Euro-Mediterranean Foundation for the Dialogue between Cultures (Anna Lindh Foundation, #00847); Beirut Arab University (BAU); Centre UNESCO de Catalunya (UNESCOCAT); Community of Mediterranean Universities (CMU, #04403); European Students' Union (ESU, #08848); Institut Europeu de la Mediterrània (IEMed); Mediterranean Universities Union (UNIMED, #16687); Regional Information Technology and Software Engineering Centre (RITSEC, #18789); Université de la Méditerranée, Marseille.
[2015/XJ7350/y/F]

♦ Euro+Med PlantBase 05732

Secretariat Freie Univ of Berlin, Botanic Garden and Botanical Museum Berlin, Königin Luise Strasse 6-8, 14195 Berlin, Germany. T. +493083850445. E-mail: e.raab-straube@bgbm.org.
URL: http://www.emplantbase.org/home.html

History Jan 1956, Leicester (UK). Founded as *Flora Europaea Organization (FEO) – Organisation de Flora Europaea (OFE) – Organización de Flora Europaea – Organisation für Flora Europaea.* Subsequently changed name to *Flora Europaea Residuary Body.* Project of EU Research Infrastructures. Secretariat moved to Berlin (Germany), 2004. Intellectual property rights vested with: *Society for the Management of Electronic Biodiversity Data (SMEBD, inactive).* **Aims** Provide an online, up-to-date and critically evaluated *taxonomic inventory* of the higher *plants* of the *European* and *Mediterranean* regions for the benefit of professional botanists, national and international authorities, conservationists, ecologists and environmental legislators. **Languages** English. **Finance** Sources: grants from official and private bodies. **Events** *General Meeting* Seville (Spain) 2005, *General Meeting* Palermo (Italy) 2001, *International conference* Reading (UK) 1988. **Information Services** *Euro+Med Plantbase* – online database.
Members Individuals in 52 countries:
Albania, Algeria, Armenia, Austria, Azerbaijan, Belarus, Belgium, Bosnia-Herzegovina, Bulgaria, Croatia, Czechia, Denmark, Egypt, Estonia, Finland, France, Georgia, Germany, Greece, Hungary, Iceland, Ireland, Israel, Italy, Jordan, Latvia, Lebanon, Libya, Lithuania, Luxembourg, Malta, Moldova, Montenegro, Morocco, Netherlands, North Macedonia, Norway, Poland, Portugal, Romania, Russia, Serbia, Slovakia, Slovenia, Spain, Sweden, Switzerland, Syrian AR, Tunisia, Türkiye, UK, Ukraine.
[2018.06.01/XD0968/v/E]

♦ euromedplatform – Euro-Mediterranean Youth Platform (inactive)

♦ EuroMed Rights 05733

EuroMed Droits

Program Director Vestergade 16, 2nd Floor, 1456 Copenhagen, Denmark. T. +4532641710. Fax +4532641702.
URL: http://www.euromedrights.org/

History Jan 1997, Copenhagen (Denmark). Created by *Danish Centre for Human Rights (inactive),* in response to the Barcelona Declaration and the establishment of the Euro-Mediterranean Partnership. Statutes approved at 2nd General Assembly, on 12-13 Dec 1997, Copenhagen. Former names and other names: *Euro-Mediterranean Human Rights Network (EMHRN)* – former; *Réseau euro-méditerranéen des droits de l'humains (REMDH)* – former. Registration: Denmark; EU Transparency Register, No/ID: 18343956476-47. **Aims** Promote human rights values and democratic reforms at regional and national levels in the Euro-Mediterranean area; develop and strengthen partnerships between NGOs in the area by creating network opportunities and encouraging civil society cooperation. **Structure** General Assembly (every 3 years); Executive Committee; Thematic and Country Working Groups. Secretariat in 3 offices: Copenhagen (Denmark); Brussels (Belgium); Tunis (Tunisia). **Languages** Arabic, English, French. **Staff** 35.00 FTE, paid. **Finance** Sources: donations. Annual budget: 5,470,000 EUR (2020). URL: https://euromedrights.org/about-us/who-we-are/#our-donors **Activities** Advocacy/lobbying/activism; capacity building; events/meetings; knowledge management/information dissemination; monitoring/evaluation; networking/liaising; projects/programmes; training/education. Euro-Mediterranean region. **Events** *General Assembly* Brussels (Belgium) 2018, *General Assembly* Brussels (Belgium) 2015, *General Assembly* Copenhagen (Denmark) 2012, *General Assembly* Barcelona (Spain) 2008, *General Assembly* Madrid (Spain) 2006. **Publications** *E-library.* Reports; factsheets; policy briefs; statements; press releases; newsletters.
Members Regular – national or regional nongovernmental organizations, academic institutions and national human rights institutions. National organizations in 23 countries and territories.
Algeria, Bulgaria, Cyprus, Czechia, Denmark, Egypt, Finland, France, Greece, Ireland, Israel, Italy, Jordan, Lebanon, Morocco, Portugal, Sahara West, Spain, Sweden, Syrian AR, Tunisia, Türkiye, UK.
Included in the above, 8 organisations listed in this Yearbook:
Arab Association for Human Rights (HRA, no recent information); Asociación para la Cooperación con el Sur – Las Segovias (ACSUR); Bruno Kreisky Foundation for Outstanding Achievements in the Area of Human Rights; Greek Committee for International Democratic Solidarity (EEDDA); Human Rights Centre; Sisterhood Is Global Institute (SIGI, #19298) (Jordan); *Tampere Peace Research Institute (TAPRI).*
Regional regular members (6):
AMERA International; Arabic Network for Human Rights Information (ANHRI, #00979); Arab Institute for Human Rights (AIHR, #00983); Cairo Institute for Human Rights Studies (CIHRS, #03397); European Association for the Defence of Human Rights (AEDH, no recent information).
Associate (non-voting) members (7):
Amnesty International (AI, #00801) (EU Office); *Association for the Prevention of Torture (APT, #02869); Human Rights Watch (HRW, #10990); International Bar Association's Human Rights Institute (IBAHRI, #12322); International Federation for Human Rights (#13452); Women's International League for Peace and Freedom (WILPF, #21024); World Organisation Against Torture (OMCT, #21685).*
IGO Relations Links with numerous human rights, women's rights and treaty bodies. **NGO Relations** Member of (2): *EuroMed Non-Governmental Platform (#05730); Human Rights and Democracy Network (HRDN, #10980).* Cooperates with (1): *Euro-Mediterranean Foundation of Support to Human Rights Defenders (EMHRF, #05720).* [2020.04.30/XF4881/y/F]

♦ EUROMED / see Union for the Mediterranean (#20457)
♦ **EuroMemo Group** European Economists for an Alternative Economic Policy in Europe (#06964)
♦ **EURO-MEMO-Gruppe** Arbeitsgruppe Alternative Wirtschaftspolitik für Europa (#06964)
♦ **EuroMeSCo** Euro-Mediterranean Study Commission (#05727)
♦ **EUROMETAL** Fédération européenne des associations de négociants en aciers, tubes et métaux (#09559)
♦ **EUROMETAUX** Association européenne des métaux (#02578)
♦ **EUROMET** European Mettray Organisation (#07790)
♦ Eurométrie-euroscopie (#05734)

♦ Eurometrika-Euroskopia 05734

Eurométrie-euroscopie

SG 5 rue Christine, 75006 Paris, France. T. +33143255960. Fax +33143259600. E-mail: euroskopia-eurometrika@orange.fr.
Registered Office c/o FAIB, Rue Washington 40, 1050 Brussels, Belgium.

History Dec 1991, Brussels (Belgium). Sub-title *Association internationale pour le développement et la communication.* Registered in accordance with Belgian law: 0447 524 445. **Aims** In the framework of world *interdependence* as a condition for harmonious development, promote *European* consciousness open to the rest of the world for real economic, social and cultural exchange and activities; promote a spirit of openness, particularly to the *Third World.* **Structure** General Assembly (annual). Administrative Council, comprising 17 members. Bureau, comprising President, several Vice-Presidents, Secretary-General, Secretary, Treasurer and their assistants. **Finance** Members' dues. **Activities** Represents *European Centre for Peace and Development (ECPD, #06496)* in Western Europe; provides advice in development and communication fields; carries out research, expertise, assessment and psycho-sociological studies; develops statistics. **Publications** Information Services: Information collection and dissemination; databases.
Members Individuals in 10 countries:
Albania, Congo DR, Croatia, France, Hungary, Mauritius, Morocco, North Macedonia, Romania, Serbia.
[2008.07.08/XF5527/v/F]

♦ **EUROM** European Federation of Precision Mechanical and Optical Industries (#07193)
♦ EUROM – European Observatory on Memories (unconfirmed)

♦ EUROMIC 05735

Exec Dir address not obtained.
Registered Office Rua Castilho 71, 2º Esq, 1250-068 Lisbon, Portugal.
URL: http://www.euromic.com/

History 1973, Paris (France). Registration: Portugal. **Aims** Act as the association of leading *destination management* companies. **Languages** English. **Staff** 1200.00 FTE, paid. **Finance** Members' dues. **Activities** Networking/liaising; events/meetings.
Members Membership by invitation only, and limited to one DMC per country. Destination Management Companies in 55 countries:
Argentina, Austria, Belgium, Brazil, Bulgaria, China, Costa Rica, Croatia, Cuba, Cyprus, Czechia, Denmark, Egypt, Estonia, France, Germany, Greece, Hungary, Iceland, India, Ireland, Israel, Italy, Japan, Jordan, Kazakhstan, Kenya, Korea Rep, Latvia, Lithuania, Malaysia, Malta, Mexico, Montenegro, Morocco, Netherlands, Norway, Poland, Portugal, Romania, Russia, Serbia, Slovenia, South Africa, Spain, Sweden, Switzerland, Taiwan, Tanzania UR, Thailand, Tunisia, Türkiye, UK, Ukraine, United Arab Emirates. [2021/XF6190/F]

♦ EUROMICRO 05736

Main Office PO Box 2043, 53743 St Augustin, Germany.
URL: http://www.euromicro.org/

History 1973. Former names and other names: *European Association for Microprocessing and Microprogramming* – former (1973); *EUROMICRO – European Organization for Information Technology and Microelectronics* – full title. **Aims** Support progress of information technology and microelectronics by annually holding 4 international scientific conferences. **Structure** General Meeting (annual); Board of Directors. **Languages** English. **Staff** 1.00 FTE, paid. **Activities** Events/meetings; knowledge management/information dissemination. **Events** *International Conference on Parallel, Distributed and Network-Based Processing* Valladolid (Spain) 2022, *Conference on Real-Time Systems* Barcelona (Spain) 2018, *Conference on Digital System Design* Prague (Czechia) 2018, *Conference on Software Engineering and Advanced Applications* Prague (Czechia) 2018, *Conference on Digital System Design* Vienna (Austria) 2017. **Publications** *Journal of Embedded Hardware Design; Journal of Embedded Software Design.* Conference and workshops proceedings.
Members Individuals in 34 countries and territories:
Argentina, Australia, Austria, Belgium, Brazil, Canada, China, Croatia, Czechia, Denmark, Estonia, Finland, France, Germany, Greece, Hungary, India, Ireland, Italy, Japan, Korea Rep, Netherlands, Norway, Poland, Portugal, Slovakia, Slovenia, Spain, Sweden, Switzerland, Taiwan, Türkiye, UK, USA.
NGO Relations Member of: *European Alliance for Innovation (EAI, #05872).* [2021/XD6345/v/D]

♦ EUROMICRO – European Organization for Information Technology and Microelectronics / see EUROMICRO (#05736)
♦ EUROMIL / see European Organisation of Military Associations and Trade Unions (#08099)
♦ **EUROMIL** European Organisation of Military Associations and Trade Unions (#08099)
♦ EUROMINE – Fédération européenne des associations de bois de mine (inactive)
♦ EUROMINERALS – Confederation of Learned/Engineering Societies in the Mineral Industry (inactive)
♦ **EUROMINES** European Association of Mining Industries, Metal Ores and Industrial Minerals (#06122)
♦ EuroMOF – International Conference on Metal Organic Frameworks and Porous Polymers (meeting series)

♦ Euromontana 05737

Dir Place du Champs de Mars 2, 1050 Brussels, Belgium. T. +3222804283. Fax +3222804285. E-mail: info@euromontana.org.
Pres address not obtained. E-mail: president@euromontana.org.
URL: http://www.euromontana.org/

History Founded 1995, Krakow (Poland), as an autonomous body, having existed as a working group of *European Confederation of Agriculture (CEA, inactive)* since 1974. Also referred to as *European Association for Mountain Areas – Association européenne pour les zones de montagne.* Previously also referred to as *Conférence européenne pour les problèmes économiques et sociaux des régions de montagne.* Registered in accordance with French law, 1996. EU Transparency Register: 5446623780-39. **Aims** Promote economic, social, cultural and environmental interests of *mountain* people; promote sustainable development of these regions. **Structure** General Assembly; Board of Directors. **Languages** English, French. **Staff** 2.00 FTE, paid. **Finance** Members' dues. Income from European projects. **Activities** Events/meetings; research/documentation; networking/liaising. **Events** *Attracting and Retaining Youth in the EU's Regions and Cities Workshop* Brussels (Belgium) 2022, *Communicating the Cohesion Policy to Citizens Workshop* Brussels (Belgium) 2022, *Montana174 Campaign Final Conference* Brussels (Belgium) 2022, *European Mountain Convention* Longobucco (Italy) 2022, *General Assembly* Brussels (Belgium) 2021. **Publications** Case studies; reports; proceedings; surveys; position papers.
Members Organizations (70) of 15 countries:
Austria, Bulgaria, Croatia, Czechia, France, Italy, North Macedonia, Norway, Portugal, Romania, Slovakia, Slovenia, Spain, Switzerland, UK.
Consultative Status Consultative status granted from: *ECOSOC (#05331)* (Special). **IGO Relations** Observer status with: *Convention for the Protection of the Alps (Alpine convention, 1991).* Member of: Civil Dialogue Group within *European Commission (EC, #06633). FAO (#09260)* Mountain Partnerships. Supports: Rural, Mountainous and Remote Areas Intergroup of *European Parliament (EP, #08146).* **NGO Relations** Member of: *European Mountain Forum (EMF, #07824); Intergroup on Rural, Mountainous and Remote Areas (RUMRA); Mountain Partnership (MP, #16862); TP Organics – European Technology Platform (TP Organics, #20180).* Partner of: *IFOAM Organics Europe (#11104).* Cooperates with: *Rurality – Environment – Development (RED, #19003).* [2020/XF3149/F]

♦ EUROMOT – Comité européen des associations de constructeurs de moteurs à combustion interne (inactive)
♦ **EUROMOT** European Association of Internal Combustion Engine Manufacturers (#06090)
♦ **EURO-MOULDERS** European Association of Manufacturers of Moulded Polyurethane Parts for the Automotive Industry (#06116)
♦ EUROMOVERS – EUROMOVERS Worldwide Alliance (unconfirmed)
♦ EUROMOVERS Worldwide Alliance (unconfirmed)
♦ **Euro-MRX Consortium** European Mental Retardation Consortium (#07784)
♦ Euro-Nairobi Centre for African Entrepreneurship Research and Development / see Centre for African Entrepreneurship Research and Development

♦ EURONATUR / see EuroNatur – European Nature Heritage Fund (#05738)

♦ EuroNatur – European Nature Heritage Fund 05738

Exec Dir Westendstrasse 3, 78315 Radolfzell, Germany. T. +49773292720. Fax +497732927222. E-mail: info@euronatur.org.
URL: https://www.euronatur.org/

History 1987, Germany FR. Former names and other names: *Stiftung Europäisches Naturerbe (EURONATUR)* – former. Registration: Germany. **Aims** Promote: *conservation* of biological *diversity* in Europe; conservation of *endangered species* and their habitats, with special emphasis on migratory species; sustainable development, especially in agriculture and tourism; transboundary cooperation in ecological projects and eco-political lobbying; ecological awareness. **Structure** Presiding Committee; Board of Trustees. Head Office, located in Radolfzell (Germany). **Languages** English, German. **Staff** 26.00 FTE, paid. **Finance** Sources: donations; fundraising; private foundations; sponsorship. Annual budget: 5,000,000 EUR. **Activities** Advocacy/lobbying/activism; events/meetings; knowledge management/information dissemination; projects/programmes. **Events** *European Rivers Summit* Brussels (Belgium) 2022, *European Rivers Summit* Lisbon (Portugal) 2021, *European Rivers Summit* Sarajevo (Bosnia-Herzegovina) 2018, *Seminar on the Drau-Mur biosphere reserve* Radenci (Slovenia) 1996. **Publications** *EuroNatur-Magazin* (4 a year) in German; *EuroNatur Newsletter* in English, German. Annual Report in English/German.
Members Partner organizations and projects in 16 countries:
Albania, Austria, Bosnia-Herzegovina, Bulgaria, Croatia, Germany, Greece, Hungary, Montenegro, North Macedonia, Poland, Romania, Serbia, Slovenia, Spain, Switzerland.
NGO Relations Observer status with (1): *ECNC Group (no recent information).* Member of (3): *Dinaric Arc Initiative (DAI, no recent information); EUROPARC Federation (#05768); International Union for Conservation of Nature and Natural Resources (IUCN, #15766).* Instrumental in setting up (1): *EECONET Action Fund (EAF, #05383)* (together with EUCC and Eurosite). Also links with national organizations. [2020.11.23/XF2835/f/**F**]

♦ EuroNCAP / see European New Car Assessment Programme (#08046)
♦ **EURO NCAP** European New Car Assessment Programme (#08046)
♦ EURONEM – European Association of Netting Manufacturers (inactive)
♦ EuroNeoNet – European Neonatal Network (inactive)

♦ Euronet Consulting 05739

Mailing Address 73 Rue Potagère, 1000 Brussels, Belgium. E-mail: info@euronetconsulting.com.
URL: http://www.euronetconsulting.com/

History 1990, Brussels (Belgium). Founded as a grouping of the type *European Economic Interest Grouping (EEIG, #06960).* **Aims** Provide development advisory services to international (public-funding) agencies/organizations. **Structure** General Assembly; Board of Management; Departments (2). **Languages** English, French. **Activities** Politics/policy/regulatory; capacity building; monitoring/evaluation; research and development; education/training; events/meetings.
Members Companies (8) in 6 countries:
Czechia, Denmark, France, Germany, Spain, UK.
Associate (11) in 9 countries:
Angola, Argentina, Burkina Faso, Chad, China, Ethiopia, Jordan, Mauritania, Türkiye. [2017/XJ3054/**F**]

♦ **Euronet MRPH** European Network of Medical Residents in Public Health (#07945)
♦ **EuroNet-TMS** European Network of Transfusion Medicine Societies (#08024)

♦ Euro-Network for Electronic Structure Calculations (Psi-k) 05740

Admin SciTech Daresbury, Warrington, WA4 4AD, UK. T. +441925603227. Fax +441925603634. E-mail: psik_admin@stfc.ac.uk – psik-coord@stfc.ac.uk.
URL: http://www.psi-k.net/

Structure Management Board; Working Groups (17). **Finance** Funded by: *European Commission (EC, #06633); European Science Foundation (ESF, #08441).* **Events** *Conference* Lausanne (Switzerland) 2022, *Conference* Lausanne (Switzerland) 2021, *Conference* Lausanne (Switzerland) 2020, *Conference* San Sebastian (Spain) 2015, *Conference* Berlin (Germany) 2010. **Publications** *Psi-k Newsletter.* [2019/XF5919/**F**]

♦ Euro Neuro (meeting series)
♦ **EURON** European Graduate School of Neuroscience (#07403)

♦ Euronews 05741

Contact 52 quai Rambaud, 69002 Lyon, France. T. +33428670000.
CEO address not obtained.
URL: http://www.euronews.com/

History Founded 7 Jun 1992, as Europe's only multilingual, pan-European news channel. Launched 1 Jan 1993 in 5 languages; began digital broadcast, 1999; became worldwide, 2004; launched first YouTube channels, 2007; launched sister channel 'Africanews', 2016, the first pan-African and multilingual media dedicated to sub-Saharan Africa. **Aims** Act as the European all-news channel covering world news 24 hours a day from a *European* viewpoint in 13 languages simultaneously: Arabic, English, French, German, Greek, Hungarian, Italian, Persian, Portuguese, Russian, Spanish, Turkish and Ukrainian. **Structure** Euronews SA: 25 shareholders. Since Jul 2015, Naguib Sawiris is the major shareholder with its company Media Global Networks (53%) plus public television channels and 3 local authorities. Africanews SAS, based in Congo Brazzaville is 100% Euronews SA. **Languages** Arabic, English, French, German, Hungarian, Irish Gaelic, Italian, Persian, Portuguese, Russian, Spanish, Turkish, Ukrainian. **Staff** 800.00 FTE, paid. **Finance** Financed by: contributions from its shareholders; an agreement with *European Commission (EC, #06633)* to produce and broadcast information programmes. Further income is derived from commercial activities – advertising, sponsorship, programme sales and distribution revenues. **Activities** Knowledge management/information dissemination.
Members Public broadcasting organizations in 21 countries:
Algeria, Belgium, Cyprus, Czechia, Egypt, Finland, France, Greece, Ireland, Italy, Malta, Morocco, Portugal, Romania, Russia, Slovenia, Sweden, Switzerland, Tunisia, Türkiye, Ukraine. [2015.11.13/XF1737/e/**F**]

♦ EuroNGI 05742

Chairman GET Telecom Paris, 37-39 rue Dareau, 75014 Paris, France. T. +33145818098. Fax +33145817158.
URL: http://eurongi.enst.fr/

Aims Create and maintain excellence in next generation *Internet design* and engineering. **Activities** Organizes conference and workshops. **Events** *Conference on next generation internet networks / Conference* Trondheim (Norway) 2007, *Conference on next generation internet design and engineering / Conference* Valencia (Spain) 2006. [2007/XM2615/**F**]

♦ EuroNGOs / see Inspire – the European Partnership for Sexual and Reproductive Health and Rights (#11232)
♦ EuroNICHE / see International Network for Humane Education (#14285)
♦ **Euro ONG Palestine** Association européenne des organisations non-gouvernementales travaillant sur la Palestine (#06135)
♦ Euro ONG Palestine / see European Association for Non-Governmental Organizations Working on Palestine (#06135)
♦ Euroopa Demokraatide ja Liberaalide Liidu Erakond (#00703)
♦ Euroopa Demokraatide ja Liberaalide liidu Fraktsioon / see Renew Europe (#18840)
♦ Euroopa Elu-uuringute, Integratsiooni ja Tsiviilühiskonna Akadeemia (#05799)
♦ Euroopa Justiitsvõrgustik Tsiviil- ja Kaubandusasjades (#07616)
♦ Euroopa Kemikaaliamet (#06523)
♦ Euroopa Komisjon (#06633)
♦ Euroopa Kontrollikoda (#06854)
♦ Euroopa Lennundusohutusamet (#08978)
♦ Euroopa Liberaalide, Demokraatide ja Reformistide Partei / see Alliance of Liberals and Democrats for Europe Party (#00703)
♦ Euroopa Liidu Kohus (#04938)
♦ Euroopa Liidu Nõukogu (#04895)
♦ Euroopa Liidu Väljaannete Talitus (#18562)
♦ Euroopa Liit (#08967)
♦ Euroopa Majandus- ja Sotsiaalkomitee (#06963)
♦ Euroopa Mereliste Äärealade Konverents (#04638)
♦ Euroopan alueiden komitea (#06665)
♦ Euroopan Ammatillisen Koulutuksen Kehittämiskeskus (#06474)
♦ Euroopa Narkootikuminde ja Narkomaania Seirekeskus (#07820)
♦ Euroopan Asianajajaliitto (#20365)
♦ Euroopan Hedelmä- ja Vihannesteollisuusyhdistys / see European Association of Fruit and Vegetable Processors (#06049)
♦ Euroopan Hiili- ja Teräsyhteisön perustamissopimus (1951 treaty)
♦ Euroopan huumausaineiden ja niiden väärinkäytön seurantakeskus (#07820)
♦ Euroopan Intergraatio-oikeuden Tutkimuksen Pohjoismainen Neuvosto (inactive)
♦ Euroopan Investointipankki (#07599)
♦ Euroopan jousimetsästysliitto ry (#06385)
♦ Euroopan kamarimusiikkipedagoginen yhdistys ry (#06516)
♦ Euroopan Kamikaalivirasto / see European Chemicals Agency (#06523)
♦ Euroopan Kansallisten Kielentutkimuslaitosten Yhteistyöelin / see European Federation of National Institutions for Language (#07172)
♦ Euroopan Kansanpuolueen Rhymä – Kristillisdemokraatit (#10775)
♦ Euroopan Kemikaalivirasto (#06523)
♦ Euroopan Kestävän Tietoyhteiskunnan Instituutti (internationally oriented national body)
♦ Euroopan Komissio (#06633)
♦ Euroopan Koulutuksen Tietoverkko (inactive)
♦ Euroopan Kuntien ja Alueiden Neuvosto (#04891)
♦ Euroopan Lentoturvallisuusvirasto (#08978)
♦ Euroopan liberaalidemokraattien Liiton Ryhmä / see Renew Europe (#18840)
♦ Euroopan liberaali demokraattinen puolue / see Alliance of Liberals and Democrats for Europe Party (#00703)
♦ Euroopan Liberaalidemokraattisten Puolueiden Liitto (#00703)
♦ Euroopan matemaattinen seura ry (#07755)
♦ Euroopan Oikeudellinen Verkosto Sivilli- ja Kauppaoikeus (#07616)
♦ Euroopan Oikeusasiamies (#08084)
♦ Euroopan Parlamentin Vihreä Ryhmä / see Group of the Greens – European Free Alliance (#10781)
♦ Euroopan Parlamentti (#08146)
♦ Euroopan Peripfeeristen Merellisten Alueiden Konferenssi (#04638)
♦ Euroopan Petostentorjuntavirasto (#05906)
♦ Euroopan Rakennustalousasiantuntijoiden (#06812)
♦ Euroopan saarien matkailu observatorio (#17645)
♦ Euroopan Seniorivpaanehtoisten Verkosto / see European Network of Older-Volunteer Organizations
♦ Euroopan Sosiaalirahasto (#08501)
♦ Euroopan Sosialidemokraattinen Puolue (#18249)
♦ Euroopan Sosialidemokraattisen Puolueen Parlamenttirhmä / see Group of the Progressive Alliance of Socialists and Democrats in the European Parliament (#10786)
♦ Euroopan Talous-ja Sosiaalikomitea (#06963)
♦ Euroopan, Tarkkuus – ja Optiikkateollisuuden Yhdistys (#07193)
♦ Euroopan Teknologiainstituutin / see European Institute of Innovation and Technology (#07562)
♦ Euroopan Tilintarkastustuomioistuin (#06854)
♦ Euroopan Uionin Mallasteollisuuden Yhteistyökomitea (#21055)
♦ Euroopan Ulkosuhdehallinnon Sivustolle (#07018)
♦ Euroopan Unioni (#08967)
♦ Euroopan unionin julkaisutoimisto (#18562)
♦ Euroopan Unionin Kuoro / see European Union Choir (#08980)
♦ Euroopan Unionin Neuvosto (#04895)
♦ Euroopan Unionin Nuorisofoorumi (inactive)
♦ Euroopan Unionin perusoikeuskirja (2000 treaty)
♦ Euroopan Unionin Tuomioistuimen (#04938)
♦ Euroopan Vesiviljelijöiden Liitto / see Federation of European Aquaculture Producers (#09491)
♦ Euroopan Virkamiesliitto / see European Public Service Union (#08303)
♦ Euroopan Vuoden Nainen (#20993)
♦ Euroopan Yhteisöjen Ensimmäisen Oikeusasteen Tuomioistuin (inactive)
♦ Euroopan Yhteisöjen Tuomioistuin / see Court of Justice of the European Union (#04938)
♦ Euroopa Ombudsman (#08084)
♦ Euroopa Parlamendi Sotsiaaldemokraatide Fraktsioon / see Group of the Progressive Alliance of Socialists and Democrats in the European Parliament (#10786)
♦ Euroopa Rahvapartei – Kristlike Demokraatide Fraktsioon (#10775)
♦ Euroopa Regioonide Komitee (#06665)
♦ Euroopa Ühenduste Kohus / see Court of Justice of the European Union (#04938)
♦ Euroopa Ülemkogu (#06801)
♦ Euroopa Välisteenistuse Veebisaidile (#07018)
♦ Eurooppalaiset Neoi Europeoi (#21984)
♦ Eurooppalaisten Paperipukkqliikkeiden Yhdistysten Liitto / see European Paper Merchants Association (#08138)
♦ Eurooppa-neuvosto (#06801)
♦ Euro-Orientation – European Association for Orientation, Vocational Guidance and Educational and Professional Information (inactive)
♦ Europa Asocio de la Fervojistoj (#02558)
♦ **EuropaBio** European Association of Bioindustries (#05956)
♦ Europa Bürger Dienstleitungsstelle / see European Citizen Action Service (#06555)

♦ Europacable 05743

SG Rue Marie de Bourgogne 58, 1000 Brussels, Belgium. E-mail: contact@europacable.eu.
URL: http://www.europacable.eu

History 1991. Founded as a grouping of the type *European Economic Interest Grouping (EEIG, #06960),* uniting 5 European organizations which now comprise ECBL business groups. Remained an EEIG until end 2020. Former names and other names: *European Confederation of Associations of Manufacturers of Insulated Wires and Cables (ECBL)* – former; *European Confederation of National Associations of Manufacturers of Insulated Wire and Cable (Europacable)* – full title. Registration: Banque-Carrefour des Entreprises, No/ID: 0746.714.017, Start date: 6 May 2020, Belgium; Companies House, No/ID: GE000049, Start date: 27 Apr 1993, End date: 31 Dec 2020, England; EU Transparency Register, No/ID: 4543103789-92, Start date: 15 Dec 2008. **Aims** Be recognized as a fully transparent lobby organization, representing the *wire* and *cable* industry in relevant EU policy debates; be a trusted source of technical information on wire and cable products; be actively engaged in relevant standardization processes; raise visibility of the European cable and wire industry. **Languages** English. **Finance** Sources: members' dues. **Activities** Advocacy/lobbying/activism; awareness raising; knowledge management/information dissemination; politics/policy/regulatory; standards/guidelines. **Events** *General Assembly* Brussels (Belgium) 2022. [2022.10.19/XD1095/**E**]

♦ Europa Cantat – Europäische Föderation Junger Chöre / see European Choral Association – Europa Cantat (#06541)
♦ Europa Cantat – European Federation of Young Choirs / see European Choral Association – Europa Cantat (#06541)
♦ Europa Cantat – Fédération européenne des jeunes chorales / see European Choral Association – Europa Cantat (#06541)

♦ EUROPAC – European Registry of Hereditary Pancreatitis and Familial Pancreatic Cancer (internationally oriented national body)

♦ Europa Cinemas 05744

Gen Dir 54 rue Beaubourg, 75003 Paris, France. T. +33142715370. Fax +33142714755. E-mail: info@europa-cinemas.org.
URL: http://www.europa-cinemas.org/

History 1992. Registered in accordance with French law. **Aims** Provide operational and financial support to cinemas that commit themselves to screen a significant number of European non-national *films*, to offer events and initiatives as well as promotional activities targeted at Young Audiences. **Structure** Board of Directors; Steering Committee; Experts Committee. Patronage Committee, comprising film-makers from all European countries. **Languages** English, French. **Staff** 15.00 FTE, paid. **Finance** Supported by: Centre National de la Cinématographie (CNC) (France); *European Support Fund for the Co-Production and Distribution of Creative Cinematographic and Audiovisual Works (EURIMAGES, #08859)*; Euromed Audiovisual and European Development Fund; French Ministry of Foreign Affairs. **Activities** Financial and/or material support; awards/prizes/competitions; events/meetings. **Events** *Conference* Lisbon (Portugal) 2019, *Annual Conference* Prague (Czech Rep) 2015, *Annual Conference* Athens (Greece) 2013, *Annual Conference* Paris (France) 2012, *Annual Conference* Athens (Greece) 2011. **Publications** *Europa Cinemas Guide* (annual).
Members Cinemas in 44 countries:
Afghanistan, Armenia, Austria, Belarus, Belgium, Bosnia-Herzegovina, Bulgaria, Croatia, Cyprus, Czechia, Denmark, Estonia, Finland, France, Germany, Greece, Hungary, Ireland, Italy, Kazakhstan, Kosovo, Latvia, Liechtenstein, Lithuania, Luxembourg, Malta, Moldova, Netherlands, North Macedonia, Norway, Poland, Portugal, Romania, Russia, Serbia, Slovakia, Slovenia, Spain, Sweden, Switzerland, Türkiye, UK, Ukraine, Uzbekistan. [2017/XF2728/F]

♦ Europacollege (#04105)
♦ EuropaColon / see Digestive Cancers Europe (#05070)
♦ EuroPACS – European Society for the Promotion of Picture Archiving and Communication Systems in Medicine / see European Society of Medical Imaging Informatics (#08647)
♦ **EUROPAD** European Opiate Addiction Treatment Association (#08090)
♦ **Europa Distribution** European Network of Independent Film Distributors (#07928)

♦ Europa Donna – The European Breast Cancer Coalition 05745

Coalition européenne contre le cancer du sein – Movimento Europeo contra el Cancer de Mama – Europäische Koalition gegen Brustkrebs – Movimento Europeo d'Opinione contro i Tumori del Seno

Exec Dir Piazza Amendola 3, 20149 Milan MI, Italy. T. +39236592280. Fax +39236592284. E-mail: info@europadonna.org.
URL: http://www.europadonna.org/

History 5 Feb 1993, Paris (France). Founded by Prof Umberto Veronesi, at meeting of *European Society of Breast Cancer Specialists (EUSOMA, #08534)*. Inaugural meeting: 24-25 Jun 1994, Milan (Italy). Registration: EU Transparency Register, No/ID: 13080161140-33, Start date: 13 Feb 2009. **Aims** Raise awareness of breast cancer; mobilize support of European women in pressing for improved breast cancer education, appropriate screening, optimal treatment and increased funding for research. **Structure** Executive Board. **Languages** English. **Staff** 4.00 FTE, paid. **Finance** Sources: grants; members' dues. **Activities** Advocacy/lobbying/activism; awareness raising; events/meetings; training/education. **Events** *European Breast Cancer Conference (EBCC)* Milan (Italy) 2024, *Pan-European Conference* Zagreb (Croatia) 2023, *European Breast Cancer Conference (EBCC)* Barcelona (Spain) 2022, *MBC Advocacy Seminar* 2021, *Pan-European Conference* Zagreb (Croatia) 2021. **Publications** *Europa Donna Newsletter*. Guides; brochures; booklets; proceedings.
Members National representatives in 47 countries:
Albania, Armenia, Austria, Belarus, Belgium, Bulgaria, Croatia, Cyprus, Czechia, Denmark, Estonia, Finland, France, Georgia, Germany, Greece, Hungary, Iceland, Ireland, Israel, Italy, Kazakhstan, Kyrgyzstan, Latvia, Lithuania, Luxembourg, Malta, Moldova, Monaco, Netherlands, North Macedonia, Norway, Poland, Portugal, Romania, Russia, Serbia, Slovakia, Slovenia, Spain, Sweden, Switzerland, Tajikistan, Türkiye, UK, Ukraine, Uzbekistan.
NGO Relations Member of (2): *European Patients' Forum (EPF, #08172)*; *Workgroup of European Cancer Patient Advocacy Networks (WECAN, #21054)*. Cooperates with (5): *European Cancer Organisation (ECO, #06432)*; *European Institute of Oncology, Milan (EIO)*; *European Organisation for Research and Treatment of Cancer (EORTC, #08101)*; *European School of Oncology (ESO, #08434)*; *European Society of Breast Cancer Specialists (EUSOMA, #08534)*. [2021.09.08/XF3629/F]

♦ Europae Archaeologiae Consilium (EAC) 05746

European Archaeological Council – Conseil Européen d'Archéologie

Assistant p/a Urban brussels, Mont des Arts 10-13, 1000 Brussels, Belgium. E-mail: info@e-a-c.org.
Pres address not obtained.
URL: http://www.european-archaeological-council.org/

History Nov 1999, Strasbourg (France). Founded following a series of informal meetings since 1995. Registration: Belgium. **Aims** Support management of the archaeological heritage throughout Europe; serve as a forum for national archaeological heritage management agencies. **Structure** General Assembly (annual); Board. **Languages** English, French. **Staff** 0.50 FTE, paid. **Finance** Sources: members' dues. **Activities** Knowledge management/information dissemination. **Events** *Heritage Symposium* Vienna (Austria) 2022, *Heritage Symposium* London (UK) 2021, *Heritage Symposium* Prague (Czechia) 2020, *Heritage Symposium* Dublin (Ireland) 2019, *Heritage Symposium* Sofia (Bulgaria) 2018. **Publications** *EAC Occasional Papers*. Meeting reports.
Members Full in 31 countries:
Albania, Austria, Belgium, Bulgaria, Croatia, Czechia, Denmark, Estonia, Finland, France, Germany, Greece, Hungary, Iceland, Ireland, Italy, Latvia, Lithuania, Malta, Netherlands, Norway, Poland, Portugal, Romania, Slovakia, Slovenia, Spain, Sweden, Switzerland, Türkiye, UK. [2022.05.04/XF5992/F]

♦ Europae Collegium / see College of Europe (#04105)
♦ Europaeiska Fristående Stålproducenternas Förbund (inactive)
♦ Europaeiska Gemenskapernas Domstol / see Court of Justice of the European Union (#04938)
♦ Europaeisk Center for Forebyggelse af og Kontrol med Sygdomme (#06476)
♦ Europaeisk Centrum for Detailhandel (inactive)
♦ Europaeiske Atomenergiefaellesskab (inactive)
♦ Europaeiske Auktionsholder Forening / see European Federation of Auctioneers (#07057)
♦ Europaeiske Borgmesterkonfoderation (inactive)
♦ Europaeiske Center for Private Hjaelpeorganisationer / see European Council for Non-Profit Organizations (#06834)
♦ Europaeiske Center for Udvikling af Erhvervsuddannelse (#06474)
♦ Europaeiske Fabrikantforning for Fabrikanter af Levnedsmiddelemulgatorer (#07281)
♦ Europaeiske Faellesskab (inactive)
♦ Europaeiske Faellesskab for EØF- Landenes Organisationer for Engroshandelen med OEI (#02555)
♦ Europaeiske Faellesskaber (inactive)
♦ Europaeiske Faellesskabers Domstol / see Court of Justice of the European Union (#04938)
♦ Europaeiske Faellesskabers Kor / see European Union Choir (#08980)
♦ Europaeiske Faellesskabers Ret (inactive)
♦ Europaeiske Faellesskabers Statistiske Kontor / see Statistical Office of the European Union (#19974)
♦ Europaeiske Filmhøjskole (internationally oriented national body)
♦ Det Europaeiske Folkepartis Gruppe – Kristelige Demokrater (#10775)
♦ Europaeiske Forbund af Fodderfabrikanter (#09566)
♦ Europaeiske Forbund for Importører af Tørrede Frugter, Konserves, Krydderier og Honning / see European Federation of the Trade in Dried Fruit, Edible Nuts, Processed Fruit and Vegetables, Processed Fishery Products, Spices, Honey and Similar Foodstuffs (#07229)
♦ Europaeiske Forbund for Industrien for Foder til Selskabscyr (#09571)
♦ Europaeiske Forening for Producenter af Encellede Proteiner (inactive)
♦ Europaeiske Forening af Professionelle Brandofficerer (no recent information)
♦ Europaeiske Forening af Speciallaeger / see European Union of Medical Specialists (#09001)
♦ Europaeiske Geografiske Selskab / see Association of European Geographical Societies (#02512)
♦ Europaeiske Graenseregioners Arbejdsfaellesskab (#02499)
♦ Europaeiske Investeringsbank (#07599)
♦ Europaeiske Katolske Center (internationally oriented national body)
♦ Europaeiske Kemikalieagentur / see European Chemicals Agency (#06523)
♦ Det Europaeiske Kemikalieagentur (#06523)
♦ Europaeiske Komité for Automobil-detailhandel og- reparation / see European Council for Motor Trades and Repairs (#06832)
♦ Europaeiske Kommuners og Regioners Råd (#04891)
♦ Europaeiske Kontor for Bekaempelse af Svig (#05906)
♦ Europaeiske Kul- og Stålfaelleskab (inactive)
♦ Europaeiske Laerersammenslutning (#02565)
♦ Europaeiske Liberal Demokratiske og Reform Parti / see Alliance of Liberals and Democrats for Europe Party (#00703)
♦ Europaeiske Medisk Forening (#07761)
♦ Europaeiske Miljøagentur (#06995)
♦ Europaeiske Ombudsmand (#08084)
♦ Europaeiske Organisation for Engroshandelen med Kød (inactive)
♦ Europaeiske Organisation for Frugt- og Grøntforarbejdningsindustri / see European Association of Fruit and Vegetable Processors (#06049)
♦ Europaeiske Organisation for Grøntkonservesindustri (inactive)
♦ Europaeiske Organisation af Herbergs- og Bistandsforeninger for Unge Arbejdere (inactive)
♦ Europaeiske Organisation for Sammenslutningerne af Diabetikerforretninger (no recent information)
♦ Europaeiske Overlaegeforening (#02577)
♦ Det Europaeiske Overvågningscenter for Narkotika og Narkotikamisbrug (#07820)
♦ Det Europaeiske Økonomiske og Sociale Udvalg (#06963)
♦ Europaeiske Råd (#06801)
♦ Europaeiske Rådet (#06801)
♦ Europaeiske Samarbejdsorganisation for Nationale Sproginstitutioner / see European Federation of National Institutions for Language (#07172)
♦ Europaeiske Sammenslutning af Erhvervsdrievende med Tilknytning til Vinindustrien (inactive)
♦ Europaeiske Sammenslutning af Nationale Foreninger for Frie Grundskoler (#06833)
♦ Europaeiske Sammenslutning af Ørredproducenter / see Federation of European Aquaculture Producers (#09491)
♦ Europaeiske Sammenslutning af Papir- Karton- og Emballogegrossister / see European Paper Merchants Association (#08138)
♦ Europaeiske Sammenslutning af Podologer (inactive)
♦ Europaeiske Sekretariat for Liberale Erhverv / see European Council of Liberal Professions (#06828)
♦ Europaeiske Socialdemokraters Gruppe / see Group of the Progressive Alliance of Socialists and Democrats in the European Parliament (#10786)
♦ De Europaeiske Socialdemokraters Gruppe Euroopan Parlamentin Sosialidemokraattinen Ryhmä / see Group of the Progressive Alliance of Socialists and Democrats in the European Parliament (#10786)
♦ De Europaeiske Socialdemokraters Parti (#18249)
♦ Europaeiske Socialfond (#08501)
♦ Europaeiske Sparekasseforening / see European Savings and Retail Banking Group (#08426)
♦ Europaeiske Tjenestemaends Fagforening / see European Public Service Union (#08303)
♦ Europaeiske Tjenestemandsforbund (#06567)
♦ Europaeiske Udvalg for Faglige Sammenslutninger af Importører og en Gros-Forhandlere af Naeringsmidler (inactive)
♦ Europaeiske Udvalg for Handelen med Stivelsesholdige Produkter og disses Biprodukter (inactive)
♦ Europaeiske Udviklingsfonds (#06914)
♦ Europaeiske Union (#08967)
♦ Europaeiske Union for Engros-Handelen med Aeg, Aeggeprodukter Fjerkrae og Vildt (#09021)
♦ Europaeiske Union for Handelen med Kvaeg og Kod (#20394)
♦ Europaeiske Union for Kartoffelforarbejdningsindustrierne / see EUPPA – European Potato Processors' Association (#05592)
♦ Europaeiske Union af Nationale Vandforsyningsforeninger / see European Federation of National Associations of Water and Waste Water Services (#07170)
♦ Europaeiske Unions charter om grundaeggende rettigheder (2000 treaty)
♦ Europaeiske Unions Domstol (#04938)
♦ Europaeiske Unions Kor / see European Union Choir (#08980)
♦ Europaeiske Unions Ungdomsforum (inactive)
♦ Europaeisk Federation af Bygnings- og Traeindustriarbejdere (#07065)
♦ Europaeisk Federation af Bygnings- og Treindustriarbejdere ØEF / see European Federation of Building and Woodworkers (#07065)
♦ Europaeisk Forbund for Små og Mellematore Virkaomheder (no recent information)
♦ Europaeisk Forening for Vegetabilsk Protein (#09047)
♦ Europaeisk Horeapparatakustiker Forbund / see European Association of Hearing Aid Professionals (#06066)
♦ Europaeisk Kristian Vänskap (inactive)
♦ Europaeisk Miljøsekretariat / see European Environmental Bureau (#06996)
♦ Europaeisk Råd for Unge Landmaend (#04689)
♦ Europaeisk Retligt Netvaerk for Civil- og Handelssager (#07616)
♦ Europaeisk Sammenslutning af Cellulose-, Papir- og Papindustrien (inactive)
♦ Europaeisk Sammenslutning for Databehandling i Havne (inactive)
♦ Europaeisk Sammenslutning for Databehandling i Skibsfart (inactive)
♦ Europaeisk Sammenslutning for Samarbejde (inactive)
♦ Europaeisk Sekretariat for Metalemballage Fabrikanter (inactive)
♦ Europaeisk Selskab for Skriftpsykologi (#08616)
♦ Europaeisk Sofartssikkerhedsagentur (#07744)
♦ Europaeisk Teknologisk Institut / see European Institute of Innovation and Technology (#07562)
♦ **EUROPAEM** European Academy for Environmental Medicine (#05790)
♦ Det Europaeske Luftfartssikkerhedsagentur (#08978)
♦ Europa Esperanto-Unio (#07006)
♦ **Europae Thesauri** Association Européenne des Trésors et Musées d'Eglises (#02583)

♦ Europaeum 05747

Dir c/o St Antony's College, 62 Woodstock Road, Oxford, OX2 6JF, UK. T. +441865284482. E-mail: euroinfo@europaeum.ox.ac.uk.
URL: http://www.europaeum.org/

History 1992, Oxford (UK). Founded on the setting up of a *European Studies Fund* as a trust fund at Oxford University. Phase I – Launch (1992-1996); Phase II – Consolidation (1996-2000); Phase III – Innovation (2000-2003); Phase IV – Extension (2003-2007); Phase V – Sustainability (2008-2012). **Aims** Serve as an 'international university without walls', in which future scholars and leaders of Europe will have an opportunity to share common learning and confront common concerns together. **Structure** Academic Council; Board of Trustees; Executive Committee. **Languages** English. **Staff** 4.00 FTE, paid. **Finance** Sources: contributions; donations; grants; members' dues. **Activities** Events/meetings; financial and/or material support; publishing activities; training/education. **Events** *Policy Seminar on Policy-Making inside Europe* Brussels (Belgium) 2021, *Chinese Investment in Europe* Mafra (Portugal) 2020, *Policy Seminar on the Balkan Completion* Zagreb (Croatia) 2020, *Europe in the Age of Xi and Trump* Geneva (Switzerland) 2019, *International conference on liberalism in East and West* Oxford (UK) 2009. **Publications** Annual Report and Accounts.
Members Universities (17) in 14 countries:
Belgium, Czechia, Denmark, Finland, France, Germany, Italy, Luxembourg, Netherlands, Poland, Portugal, Spain, Switzerland, UK.
Included in the above, 1 organization listed in this Yearbook:
Institut de hautes études internationales et du développement (IHEID).
NGO Relations Member of: *European Alliance for the Social Sciences and Humanities (EASSH, #05885).* [2020.09.09/XF3843/y/F]

- ♦ Europafactoring – Federation of European Factoring Associations (no recent information)
- ♦ Europa und Gesellschaft (#02586)
- ♦ Europagruppe der Filialbetriebe (inactive)
- ♦ Europa-Haus Marienberg (internationally oriented national body)
- ♦ Európai alkotmany létrehozasaról szóló szerzodés (2004 treaty)
- ♦ Európai Bizottsag (#06633)
- ♦ Európai Bor és Gasztronómiai Egyesületek Szövetse (#08076)
- ♦ Európai Életkutatasi, Integraciós és Civiltarsadalmi Adamémia (#05799)
- ♦ Európai Folklór Intézet (internationally oriented national body)
- ♦ Európai Gazdasagi és Szocialis Bizottsag (#06963)
- ♦ Európai Igazsagügyi Hálózat Polgari és Kereskedelmi Ügyekben (#07616)
- ♦ Europai Katolikus Informaciós Központ / see Jesuit European Social Centre (#16103)
- ♦ Europaiko Institouto Dikaiou, Epistimis and Technologias (internationally oriented national body)
- ♦ Európai Közösségek Birósaga / see Court of Justice of the European Union (#04938)
- ♦ Európai Kulturalis Varosok Hálózata / see Alliance de Villes Euro-méditerranéennes de Culture (#00726)
- ♦ Európai Külügyi Szolgâlat Honlapjan (#07018)
- ♦ Európai Liberalis, Demokrata és Reformpart / see Alliance of Liberals and Democrats for Europe Party (#00703)
- ♦ Európai Néppart – Kereszténydemokratak – Képviselócsoport (#10775)
- ♦ Europa Institute, Leiden (internationally oriented national body)
- ♦ Europa-Institut at Saarland University (internationally oriented national body)
- ♦ Europa-Institut – Sektion Rechtswissenschaft – der Universität des Saarlandes / see Europa-Institut at Saarland University
- ♦ Europainstitut, Wien (internationally oriented national body)
- ♦ Europa Institut der Wirtschaftsuniversität Vienna / see Europe Institute, Vienna
- ♦ Europa Instituut, Leiden (internationally oriented national body)
- ♦ Pro-Europa: International Union of Intellectual Refugees (inactive)
- ♦ Európai Ökociklus Társaság (#06954)
- ♦ Európai Ombudsman (#08084)
- ♦ Európai Parlament (#08146)
- ♦ Európai Repülésbiztonsagi Ügynökség (#08978)
- ♦ Europäische 11q Gruppe / see European Chromosome 11 Network (#06547)
- ♦ Europäische Agentur für Chemische Stoffe / see European Chemicals Agency (#06523)
- ♦ Europäische Agentur für die Sicherheit des Seeverkehrs (#07744)
- ♦ Europäische Agentur für Flugsicherheit (#08978)
- ♦ Europäische Akademie für Allergologie und Klinische Immunologie (#05779)
- ♦ Europäische Akademie für angewandte Forschung und Fortbildung – Bozen / see European Academy of Bozen/Bolzano
- ♦ Europäische Akademie Bayern (internationally oriented national body)
- ♦ Europäische Akademie Berlin (internationally oriented national body)
- ♦ Europäische Akademie für Bodenordnung (#05797)
- ♦ Europäische Akademie Bozen (internationally oriented national body)
- ♦ Europäische Akademie zur Erforschung von Folgen Wissenschaftlich-Technischer Entwicklungen (internationally oriented national body)
- ♦ Europäische Akademie der Ernährungswissenschaften (#00045)
- ♦ Europäische Akademie Hessen (internationally oriented national body)
- ♦ Europäische Akademie für Lebensforschung, Integration und Zivilgesellschaft (#05799)
- ♦ Europäische Akademie Nordrhein-Westfalen (internationally oriented national body)
- ♦ Europäische Akademie Otzenhausen (internationally oriented national body)
- ♦ Europäische Akademie, Schleswig Holstein (internationally oriented national body)
- ♦ Europäische Akademie für Städtische Umwelt, Berlin (internationally oriented national body)
- ♦ Europäische Akademie für Umweltmedizin (#05790)
- ♦ Europäische Akademie Wien (internationally oriented national body)
- ♦ Europäische Akademie der Wissenschaften und Künste (#05814)
- ♦ Europäische Allianz von Initiativen Angewandter Anthroposophie / see Alliance ELIANT (#00672)
- ♦ Europäische Allianz Katholischer Frauenverbände (#05864)
- ♦ Europäische Allianz der Kleinen und Mittleren Unternehmen (#08494)
- ♦ Europäische Arbeitsgemeinschaft der Circus- und Schausteller-Seelsorger aller Konfessionen / see International Group of Priests for Circus and Showmen of All Confessions (#13752)
- ♦ Europäische Arbeitsgemeinschaft für Fluorforschung und Kariesprophylaxe / see European Organization for Caries Research (#08107)
- ♦ Europäische Arbeitsgemeinschaft für Gerontopsychiatrie (#06057)
- ♦ Europäische Arbeitsgemeinschaft für Kariesforschung (#08107)
- ♦ Europäische Arbeitsgemeinschaft Kirche und Arbeitswelt / see European Contact Group – Ecumenical Network for Economic and Social Action (#06773)
- ♦ Europäische Arbeitsgemeinschaft 'Mut zur Ethik' (#09109)
- ♦ Europäische Arbeitsgemeinschaft der Niedergelassenen Ärzte (#05154)
- ♦ Europäische Arbeitsgemeinschaft für Pharma Biotechnologie (#06150)
- ♦ Europäische Arbeitsgemeinschaft für Psychosomatische Krebsforschung (inactive)
- ♦ Europäische Arbeitsgemeinschaft Schulmusik (#06127)
- ♦ Europäische Arbeitsgemeinschaft für Veterinärpathologen / see European Society of Veterinary Pathology (#08785)
- ♦ Europäische Arbeitsgemeinschaft für Weltreligionen in der Erziehung (#06279)
- ♦ Europäische Arbeitsgruppe Erforschung Normativer Systeme (#10741)
- ♦ Europäische Arbeitsgruppe für Lungenhochdruck (#18575)

♦ Europäische ARGE Landenentwicklung and Dorferneuerung (ARGE) 05748

European Association for Rural Development and Village Renewal

Contact Domgasse 4/2/5/16, 3100 St Pölten, Austria. T. +43274228559. Fax +4327422855920. E-mail: info@landentwicklung.org.
URL: http://www.landentwicklung.org/

History 1988. EU Transparency Register: 13857881394-50. **Aims** Promote international exchange of experience, in particular between countries and regions of *EU* member states and *transition countries* of the East. **Structure** Council. **Finance** Members' dues. **Activities** Awards/prizes/competitions; events/meetings. **Publications** *Dorferneuerung International*.

Members Full in 11 countries:
Austria, Belgium, Czechia, Germany, Hungary, Italy, Luxembourg, Poland, Slovakia, Slovenia, Switzerland.
[2018.01.17/XM5309/**D**]

- ♦ Europäische Association der Freizeiteinrichtungen der Kinder und Jugend (#06087)
- ♦ Europäische Atomgemeinschaft (inactive)
- ♦ Europäische Audiovisuelle Informationsstelle (#06294)
- ♦ Europäische Augenärztliche Gesellschaft für Kontaktlinsen (#06775)

♦ Europäische Autorenvereinigung "DIE KOGGE" (EADK) 05749

Association européenne des auteurs "DIE KOGGE" – European Authors' Association "DIE KOGGE"

Manager Stadtbibliothek Minden, Königswall 99, 32423 Minden, Germany. T. +495718379114. Fax +495718379130. E-mail: kogge@minden.de.
URL: http://www.diekogge.com/

History Founded 1924, Bremen (Germany), as "DIE KOGGE". Reorganized 1953, in Minden (Germany FR). Became, 1964, *Westeuropäische Autorenvereinigung "DIE KOGGE"*. Present name adopted 1973. **Aims** Improve literary life, through the exchange of thoughts and experiences. **Structure** Annual Meeting (always in Minden, Germany); Board of Directors. **Languages** German. **Events** *Annual meeting* Minden (Germany) 1997, *Annual meeting* Minden (Germany) 1996, *Annual meeting* Minden (Germany) 1995, *Annual meeting* Minden (Germany) 1994, *Annual meeting* Minden (Germany) 1993.

Members Individuals in 16 countries:
Austria, Belgium, Bulgaria, Croatia, Czechia, France, Georgia, Germany, Hungary, Italy, Netherlands, Poland, Romania, Slovakia, Switzerland, USA.
[2014.10.24/XE5935/v/**E**]

- ♦ Europäische Bank für Wiederaufbau und Entwicklung (#06315)
- ♦ Europäische Baptistische Mission / see EBM International (#05270)
- ♦ Europäische Bauern-Koordination / see European Coordination Via Campesina (#06795)
- ♦ Europäische Bausparkassenvereinigung (#07064)
- ♦ Europäische Behindertenaktion (#05825)
- ♦ Europäische Behörde für Lebensmittelsicherheit (#07287)
- ♦ Europäische Beobachtungsstelle für Drogen und Drogensucht (#07820)
- ♦ Europäische Beratervereinigung (#06769)
- ♦ Europäische Bestatter-Union (inactive)
- ♦ Europäische Bettwaren-Union (inactive)
- ♦ Europäische Bewährungshilfeorganisation / see Confederation of European Probation (#04530)
- ♦ Europäische Bewegung / see European Movement International (#07825)
- ♦ Europäische Bewegung (no recent information)
- ♦ Europäische Bewegung Christlicher Arbeiter (#06546)
- ♦ Europäische Bibliotheken für Theologie (#08906)
- ♦ Europäische Bildungs- und Aktionsgemeinschaft / see Europäische Akademie Nordrhein-Westfalen

♦ Europäische Bildungs-und Begegnungszentren (EBZ) 05750

European Centres for Culture and Communication

Contact Winterbachstrasse 38, 60320 Frankfurt-Main, Germany. T. +4917678851446. E-mail: email@bstwolf.eu.
URL: http://www.ebz-online.net/

History 1952, Ronco sopra Ascona (Switzerland). Several institutions were added throughout Europe since the foundation of the initial educational center. Former names and other names: *Andragogium* – former (1952 to 1977); *European Holiday Adult Education Centers* – former (1977); *Europäische Ferien-Heimvolkshochschule* – former (1977); *European Education and Meeting Centers* – former. **Aims** Help people to live together, to recognize prejudices, to reduce tensions and to resolve conflicts in a peaceful way; promote the European idea through cultural and political training. **Structure** General Assembly (at least annually). Managing Board, consisting of 1st President and 2 Assistant Presidents. **Finance** Sources: members' dues. Annual budget: 5,000 EUR.

Members Institutions in 6 countries:
Austria, France, Germany (2 institutions), Ireland, Italy, Sweden.
[2023.02.27/XF2365/**F**]

- ♦ Europäische Billard Konföderation (#04539)
- ♦ Europäische Binnenschiffahrts Union (#06318)
- ♦ Europäische Buddhistische Union (#06407)
- ♦ Europäische Bund der Nationalen Verbände von Spezialisten der Unternehmer und der Lieferanten von Materialen / see Experts for Specialised Construction and Concrete Systems (#09226)
- ♦ Europäische BürgerInnen Forum (#06562)
- ♦ Europäische Bürgerstiftungs-Initiative (#06680)
- ♦ Europäische Camac Vereinigung (no recent information)
- ♦ Europäische Charcot Stiftung / see European Charcot Foundation (#06518)
- ♦ Europäische charta der kommunalen selbstverwaltung (1985 treaty)
- ♦ Europäische charta der regional- oder minderheitensprachen (1992 treaty)
- ♦ Europäische Cheerleading Assoziation (#06520)
- ♦ Europäische Chemikalienagentur (#06523)
- ♦ Europäische Citizen's Band Föderation (#06556)
- ♦ Europäische Demokratische Anwälte (#03049)
- ♦ Europäische Demokratische Bewegung für Seelische Gesundheit (#06899)
- ♦ Europäische Demokratische Union (inactive)
- ♦ Europäische Detektiv-Akademie (internationally oriented national body)
- ♦ Europäische Eltern Organisation / see European Parents' Association (#08142)
- ♦ Europäische Endometriose Liga (#06982)
- ♦ Europäische Entwicklungsfond (#06914)
- ♦ Europäische Evangelikale Akkreditierungsvereinigung / see European Council for Theological Education (#06846)
- ♦ Europäische Evangelische Allianz (#07010)
- ♦ Europäische Fachgesellschaft für Umweltmedizin und Arbeitsmedizin (#08597)
- ♦ Europäische Fahrlehrer Assoziation (#09560)
- ♦ Europäische Fakultät für Bodenordnung / see European Academy of Land Use and Development (#05797)
- ♦ Europäische Ferien-Heimvolkshochschule / see Europäische Bildungs-und Begegnungszentren (#05750)
- ♦ Europäische Feuerstätten Arbeitsgemeinschaft (internationally oriented national body)
- ♦ Europäische Fluss-See-Transport Union (#08390)
- ♦ Europäische Föderation der Abfallwirtschaft / see European Federation of Waste Management and Environmental Services (#07232)
- ♦ Europäische Föderation der Akustischen Gesellschaften (inactive)
- ♦ Europäische Föderation der Aussenwerbung / see World Out of Home Organization (#21702)
- ♦ Europäische Föderation der Bau- und Holzarbeiter (#07065)
- ♦ Europäische Föderation der Bau- und Holzarbeiter in der EWG / see European Federation of Building and Woodworkers (#07065)
- ♦ Europäische Föderation der Bergbau-, Chemie- und Energiearbeitergewerkschaften (inactive)
- ♦ Europäische Föderation der Bergrinderrassen des Alpinen Systems / see Europäische Föderation der Rinderrassen des Alpensystems (#05752)
- ♦ Europäische Föderation der Berufsverbände von Psychologen / see European Federation of Psychologists Associations (#07199)
- ♦ Europäische Föderation für Betriebssport (#07083)
- ♦ Europäische Föderation Biotechnologie (#07062)
- ♦ Europäische Föderation der Chemiegewerkschaften (inactive)
- ♦ Europäische Föderation für Chemie-Ingenieur-Wesen (#07074)
- ♦ Europäische Föderation der Chöre der Union (#07075)
- ♦ Europäische Föderation der Entsorgungswirtschaft (#07232)
- ♦ Europäische Föderation für Firmen- und Betriebssport / see European Federation for Company Sport (#07083)
- ♦ Europäische Föderation Freier Radios (inactive)
- ♦ Europäische Föderation der Freizeitparks (inactive)
- ♦ Europäische Föderation der Gesellschaften für Meeresforschung und Marine Technology (inactive)
- ♦ Europäische Föderation der Gewerkschaften des Lebens-, Genussmittel-, Landwirtschafts- und Tourismussektors und Verwandter Branchen / see European Federation of Food, Agriculture and Tourism Trade Unions (#07125)
- ♦ Europäische Föderation der Grubenholzverbände (inactive)
- ♦ Europäische Föderation der Holzfaserplatten-Fabrikanten (inactive)
- ♦ Europäische Föderation der Importeure von Getrockneten Früchten, Konserven, Gewürzen und Honig / see European Federation of the Trade in Dried Fruit, Edible Nuts, Processed Fruit and Vegetables, Processed Fishery Products, Spices, Honey and Similar Foodstuffs (#07229)

♦ Europäische Föderation für Ingenieurbiologie (EFIB) 05751

European Federation for Soil Bioengineering – Fédération européenne pour le génie biologique – Federación Europea de Ingenieria del Paisaje – Federazione Europea per l'Ingegneria Naturalistica

SG Peter Jordan-Str 8, c/o Institut für Ingenieurbiologie, 1190 Vienna, Austria.

URL: http://www.efib.org/
History 1995. **Aims** Promote bioengineering. **Structure** Board of Directors, including President and Secretary-Treasurer. **Events** Congress Cascais (Portugal) 2012.
Members National organizations in 4 countries:
Germany, Italy, Spain, Switzerland. [2021/XD9308/**D**]

♦ Europäische Föderation für Katholische Erwachsenenbildung (#05966)
♦ Europäische Föderation Korrosion (#07090)
♦ Europäische Föderation der Landesgruppen der Weltvereinigung für Geflügelwissenschaft (#07063)
♦ Europäische Föderation von Morbus Crohn und Colitis Ulcerosa Vereinigungen (#07095)
♦ Europäische Föderation Nationaler Sprachinstitutionen / see European Federation of National Institutions for Language (#07172)
♦ Europäische Föderation der Öffentlich Bediensten (#07106)
♦ Europäische Föderation von Organisation der Angehörigen Psychisch Kranker (#07051)
♦ Europäische Föderation der Psychologenverbände (#07199)

♦ **Europäische Föderation der Rinderrassen des Alpensystems** 05752
European Federation of the Alpine System Bovine Breeds – Fédération Européen des Races Bovines de L'Arc Alpin (F.E.R.B.A.) – Federazione Europea Delle Razze Bovine del Sistema Alpino
Dir Fraz Favret, 11020 Gressan AO, Italy. T. +39165250984. Fax +39165251009.
URL: http://www.ferba.info/
History Founded 9 May 1992, Aosta (Italy). Also referred to as *Europäische Föderation der Bergrinderrassen des Alpinen Systems*. **Aims** Better coordinate commitments at European level, dealing with both the quantitative improvement of the production, and the quality of the produce. **Structure** General Assembly; Steering Committee.
Members Full in 5 countries:
Austria, France, Germany, Italy, Switzerland. [2017/XM7821/**D**]

♦ Europäische Föderation der Sperrholzindustrie (inactive)
♦ Europäische Föderation des Spielwaren-Gross- und Aussenhandels (inactive)
♦ Europäische Föderation des Spielwaren-Industrie (inactive)
♦ Europäische Föderation des Uhrengrosshandels (inactive)
♦ Europäische Föderation der Verbände der Spanplattenindustrie (inactive)
♦ Europäische Föderation der Verbände für den Unterricht von Muttersprachen an Fremdsprachler (no recent information)
♦ Europäische Föderation von Vereinen und Stiftungen zur Unterstützung von Opernhäusern und Festivals (inactive)
♦ Europäische Föderation der Zentren für Forschung und Information über das Sektenwesen (#07072)
♦ Europäische Forschungsgesellschaft für Ethik (#08726)
♦ Europäische Forum für Offen Systeme (no recent information)
♦ Europäische Forum für Religionslehrer (#07337)
♦ Europäische Frauensynode (meeting series)
♦ Europäische Frauen-Union (#09022)
♦ Europäische Freidenkervereinigung (#06048)
♦ Europäische Freie Allianz / see European Free Alliance (#07356)
♦ Europäische Freihandelsassoziation (#05391)
♦ Europäische Freiwilligenuniversität (see: #02978)
♦ Europäische Friedens-Aktion (internationally oriented national body)
♦ Europäische Gemeinschaft (inactive)
♦ Europäische Gemeinschaft der Bier-Grosshandels-Verbände der EG-Länder (#02555)
♦ Europäische Gemeinschaft der Köche / see Euro-Toques International (#09190)
♦ Europäische Gemeinschaft für Kohle und Stahl (inactive)
♦ Europäische Gemeinschaft der Religionen – Im Dialog (internationally oriented national body)
♦ Europäische Gemeinschaft der Werbewirtschaft (inactive)
♦ Europäische Gesellenzünfte / see Confederation of European Companions (#04522)
♦ Europäische Gesellschaft für Allgemeine Semantik (no recent information)
♦ Europäische Gesellschaft zur Auswertung von Erfahrungen bei Planung, Bau und Betrieb von Hochtemperaturr-Reaktoren (inactive)
♦ Europäische Gesellschaft für Baurecht (#08566)
♦ Europäische Gesellschaft für Bevölkerungswissenschaft (#06158)
♦ Europäische Gesellschaft für Chirurgische Forschung (#08754)
♦ Europäische Gesellschaft für chirurgische Onkologie (#08753)
♦ Europäische Gesellschaft für Diabetologie (#06228)
♦ Europäische Gesellschaft für die Geschichte der Photographie (#08622)
♦ Europäische Gesellschaft für die Geschichte der Psychiatrie (inactive)
♦ Europäische Gesellschaft für die Integration der Lebensmittelwissenschaft und-Technologie in die Lebensmittelversorgungskette / see ISEKI-Food Association (#16027)
♦ Europäische Gesellschaft zur Erforschung des Glücksspiels (#06231)
♦ Europäische Gesellschaft zur Erforschung der menschlichen Evolution (#08744)
♦ Europäische Gesellschaft zur Förderung von Bildarchivierungs und Kommunikationssystemen in der Medizin / see European Society of Medical Imaging Informatics (#08647)
♦ Europäische Gesellschaft zur Forschung in der Erwachsenenbildung (#08725)
♦ Europäische Gesellschaft für Freizeit (inactive)
♦ Europäische Gesellschaft für Gastroenterologie und Endoskopie / see European Association for Gastroenterology, Endoscopy and Nutrition (#06051)
♦ Europäische Gesellschaft für Gastrokamera-Diagnostik / see European Association for Gastroenterology, Endoscopy and Nutrition (#06051)
♦ Europäische Gesellschaft für Geographie / see Association of European Geographical Societies (#02512)
♦ Europäische Gesellschaft der Gesamten Inneren Medizin / see European Federation of Internal Medicine (#07147)
♦ Europäische Gesellschaft für Gesetzgebung / see International Association of Legislation (#11998)
♦ Europäische Gesellschaft für Gewebekulturen (inactive)
♦ Europäische Gesellschaft für Herbologie (#09089)
♦ Europäische Gesellschaft für hybride, molekulare und translationale Bildgebung (#08626)
♦ Europäische Gesellschaft für Ingenieurausbildung (#19462)
♦ Europäische Gesellschaft der Ingenieure und Industriellen (internationally oriented national body)
♦ Europäische Gesellschaft für Innere Medizin / see European Federation of Internal Medicine (#07147)
♦ Europäische Gesellschaft für Jüdische Studien / see European Association for Jewish Studies (#06098)
♦ Europäische Gesellschaft für Kartoffelforschung (#06160)
♦ Europäische Gesellschaft für Katholische Theologie (#08540)
♦ Europäische Gesellschaft für Kiefer-Gesichtschirurgie / see European Association for Cranio-Maxillo-Facial Surgery (#05995)
♦ Europäische Gesellschaft für Kinder- und Jugendpsychiatrie (#08543)
♦ Europäische Gesellschaft für Kinderneurochirurgie (#08685)
♦ Europäische Gesellschaft für Kinderradiologie (#08686)
♦ Europäische Gesellschaft für Klassische Naturheilkunde (no recent information)
♦ Europäische Gesellschaft für Klimatherapie (inactive)
♦ Europäische Gesellschaft für Klinische Physiologie der Atmung (inactive)
♦ Europäische Gesellschaft für Ländliche Soziologie (#08731)
♦ Europäische Gesellschaft für Luftfahrtpsychologie (#05950)
♦ Europäische Gesellschaft für Meinungs- und Marketing-Forschung / see World Association of Research Professionals (#21182)
♦ Europäische Gesellschaft für Netzhautspezialisten (#05623)

♦ Europäische Gesellschaft für Neuro-Linguistische Psychotherapie (#06131)
♦ Europäische Gesellschaft für Notfallradiologie (#08592)
♦ Europäische Gesellschaft für Nukleare Medizin (inactive)
♦ Europäische Gesellschaft für Oculoplastische Chirurgie (#08673)
♦ Europäische Gesellschaft für Optometrie (#08675)
♦ Europäische Gesellschaft für Osteoarthrologie (inactive)
♦ Europäische Gesellschaft für Pädiatrische Forschung (#08687)
♦ Europäische Gesellschaft für Phraseologie (#08705)
♦ Europäische Gesellschaft für Pneumologie (inactive)
♦ Europäische Gesellschaft für Radiologie (inactive)
♦ Europäische Gesellschaft für Rheumaorthopädie (#08387)
♦ Europäische Gesellschaft für Schriftpsychologie und Schriftexpertise (#08616)
♦ Europäische Gesellschaft für den Schutz des Bodens (#08739)
♦ Europäische Gesellschaft für seelische Gesundheit und Taubheit (#08649)
♦ Europäische Gesellschaft für Straight-Wire (unconfirmed)
♦ Europäische Gesellschaft zum Studium der Leberkrankheiten / see European Association for the Study of the Liver (#06233)
♦ Europäische Gesellschaft für das Studium von Literatur, Kultur und Umwelt (#06232)
♦ Europäische Gesellschaft für Technische Bildung (#08757)
♦ Europäische Gesellschaft für Theologische Forschung von Frauen (#08789)
♦ Europäische Gesellschaft für Toxikologie (inactive)
♦ Europäische Gesellschaft für Translationale Medizin (#08765)
♦ Europäische Gesellschaft für Trauma- und Akutchirurgie (#08768)
♦ Europäische Gesellschaft für Umwelt und Entwicklung (inactive)
♦ Europäische Gesellschaft für Unfallchirurgie (inactive)
♦ Europäische Gesellschaft für Veterinärpathologie / see European Society of Veterinary Pathology (#08785)
♦ Europäische Gesellschaft für Veterinärpathologie (#08785)
♦ Europäische Gesellschaft für Wirbeltier-Paläontologen / see European Association of Vertebrate Palaeontologists (#06266)
♦ Europäische Gesellschaft für Wirbeltierpaläontologie (#06266)
♦ Europäische Gesellschaft für Wissensökonomie (#06101)
♦ Europäische Gesellschaft für Zahnärztliche Ergonomie / see European Society of Dental Ergonomics (#08577)
♦ Europäische Gesellschaft für Züchtungsforschung / see EUCARPIA (#05571)
♦ Europäische Gesellschaft für Zusammenarbeit (inactive)
♦ Europäische Gewerkschafts-Föderation für den Landwirtschafts-, Nahrungsmittel- und Tourismussektor (#07125)
♦ Europäische Gruppe für Arbeiter Pastoral (#10740)
♦ Europäische Gruppe für Ethik der Naturwissenschaften und der neuen Technologien (#07420)
♦ Europäische Gruppe für Ethik der Naturwissenschaften und der neuen Technologien bei der Europäischen Kommission / see European Group on Ethics in Science and New Technologies (#07420)
♦ Europäische Gruppierung der Ruheständler und Rentner der Sparkassen, Banken und Ähnlichen Institutionen (#10777)
♦ Europäische Gussasphalt-Vereinigung / see International Mastic Asphalt Association (#14119)
♦ Europäische Güterzugfahrplankonferenz (inactive)
♦ Europäische Haliaeetus Gesellschaft (inactive)
♦ Europäische Handball Föderation (#07446)
♦ Europäische Hartpapier-Hülsen-Vereinigung (#06797)
♦ Europäische Heizkessel-Vereinigung (inactive)
♦ Europäische Hersteller von Diesel und Elektrischen Lokomotiven (inactive)
♦ Europäische Hochschule für Chemie, Polymere und Werkstoffe (internationally oriented national body)
♦ Europäische Hochschulkonferenz für Waldorfpädagogik / see International Network for Academic Steiner Teacher Education (#14226)
♦ Europäische Hochschullehrergruppe Technische Betriebsführung / see European Academy for Industrial Management (#05796)
♦ Europäische Holzwerkstoff-Platten Föderation / see European Panel Federation (#08137)
♦ Europäische Industriegruppe für Raumfahrtstudien / see Association of European Space Industry (#02544)
♦ Europäische Industriegruppe Verstärkte Kunststoffe – Verbundkunstoffe / see European Composites Industry Association (#06692)
♦ Europäische Industrievereinigung Feinmechanik und Optik (#07193)
♦ Europäische Interessengemeinschaft Holzbe- und Verarbeitungsmaschinen / see Combois (#04122)
♦ Europäische Investitionsbank (#07599)
♦ Europäische Investment-Vereinigung / see European Fund and Asset Management Association (#07365)
♦ Europäische Judo-Union (#20399)
♦ Europäische Junge Christliche Demokraten (inactive)
♦ Europäische Kammer der Ingenieure (#06514)
♦ Europäische Kapsel-Vereinigung (no recent information)
♦ Europäische Katholische Föderation von Bildungsstätten in Ländlichen Regionen (no recent information)
♦ Europäische Kernenergie-Gesellschaft (#08059)
♦ Europäische Kerzenverband (inactive)
♦ Europäische Koalition gegen Brustkrebs (#05745)
♦ Europäische Komitee für Verkehrssicherheit in den Streitkräften / see European Commission for Road Safety in Armed Forces (#06638)
♦ Europäische Kommission (#06633)
♦ Europäische Kommission der Hersteller von Elektrischen Installationsgeräten (#06646)
♦ Europäische Konfederation der Schuhindustrie (#04544)
♦ Europäische Konferenz der Binationalen/Bikulturellen Beziehungen (#06731)

♦ **Europäische Konferenz für Evangelische Kirchenmusik (EKEK)** 05753
European Conference for Protestant Church Music (ECPCM) – Conférence européenne des associations de musique d'église protestante (CEMEP)
Secretariat Hermannstrasse 12, 58638 Iserlohn, Germany. T. +49237140304. E-mail: secretariat@ecpcm.eu.
Pres Marklegade 20, 6240 Løgumkloster, Denmark. T. +4523609834. E-mail: president@ecpcm.eu.
URL: http://www.ECPCM.eu/
History Founded 1970, Frankfurt-Main (Germany FR). Previous statutes adopted Sep 1996, Gothenburg (Sweden) and amended Sep 1998, Bratislava (Slovakia); Sep 2000, Nîmes (France). Current statutes adopted Sep 2001, Strasbourg (France). **Aims** Promote protestant church music in Europe. **Structure** General Assembly (annual); Executive Committee; Secretariat. **Languages** English, French, German. **Staff** Voluntary. **Finance** Members' dues. **Activities** Events/meetings; knowledge management/information dissemination. **Events** *Conference* Palanga (Lithuania) 2018, *Conference* Strasbourg (France) 2015, *Conference* Sibiu (Romania) 2014, *Conference* Strasbourg (France) 2013, *Conference* Lausanne (Switzerland) 2012. **Publications** *Informations VI 2000*; *Informations VI 2005*.
Members Organizations and institutions (43) in 19 countries:
Austria, Czechia, Denmark, Estonia, Finland, France, Germany, Hungary, Italy, Latvia, Lithuania, Netherlands, Norway, Poland, Romania, Slovakia, Sweden, Switzerland, UK. [2017.03.09/XF1998/c/**F**]

♦ Europäische Konferenz der Hochschullehrer für Betriebswirtschaft (inactive)
♦ Europäische Konferenz der Industrie Elektrischer Kondensatoren (inactive)
♦ Europäische Konferenz Justitia et Pax / see Conference of European Justice and Peace Commissions (#04596)

Europäische Konferenz Molekularbiologie
05753

alphabetic sequence excludes
For the complete listing, see Yearbook Online at

- Europäische Konferenz für Molekularbiologie (#07812)
- Europäische Konferenz für Sozialwirtschaft (meeting series)
- Europäische Konferenz der Veranstalter Neuer Musik (#06736)
- Europäische Konferenz der Verkehrsminister / see International Transport Forum (#15725)
- Europäische Konferenz der Verwaltungen für Post und Telekommunikation (#04602)
- Europäische Konferenz der Weinbauregionen / see Assembly of European Wine Regions (#02317)
- Europäische Konföderation des Handels mit Farben, Wand- und Bodenbelägen (inactive)
- Europäische Konföderation der Jesuitenaltschüler (#04536)
- Europäische Konföderation der Laryngektomierten (#06709)
- Europäische Konföderation der Oberrheinischen Universitäten / see Eucor – The European Campus (#05578)
- Europäische Konföderation der Produktivgenossenschaften, der Sozialgenossenschaften und Beteiligungsunternehmen / see Confédération européenne des coopératives de travail associé, des coopératives sociales et des entreprises sociales et participatives (#04541)
- Europäische Konföderation Spielwaren (inactive)
- Europäische Konvention für Stahlbau (#06779)
- Europäische konvention über die gleichwertigkeit der reifezeugnisse (1953 treaty)
- Europäische konvention über urheber- und leistungsschutzrechtliche fragen im bereich des grenzüberschreitenden satellitenrundfunks (1994 treaty)
- Europäische Kooperation für anthroposophische Heilpädagogik und Sozialtherapie (#06783)
- Europäische Kooperative Longo Mai (#06786)
- Europäische Koordination Via Campesina (#06795)
- Europäische Krankenhaussozialpflegerverein (inactive)

♦ Europäische Kulturen in der Wirtschaftskommunikation (EUKO) . . . 05754

European Cultures in Business and Corporate Communication (EUCO)

Contact Hochschulstr 1, S1/03 182, 64289 Darmstadt, Germany. T. +496151163594. Fax +496151163694.

URL: http://www.wirtschaftskommunikation.net/

History 2000. Founded on the initiative of departments at University of Åbo Akademi in cooperation with the University of Regensburg and the Århus Business School. Former names and other names: *Research Network "European Cultures in Business and Corporate Communication"* – alias; *Forschungskooperation "Europäische Kulturen in der Wirtschaftskommunikation"* – alias. **Aims** Support international and interdisciplinary cooperation between linguistics, communication studies, psychology, economics, sociology, and other disciplines; improve the exchange of ideas and knowledge between academics and practitioners. **Activities** Events/meetings; research/documentation. **Events** *Interdisciplinary Conference* Nuremberg (Germany) 2024, *Interdisciplinary Conference* Lucerne (Switzerland) 2023, *Interdisciplinary Conference* Hamburg (Germany) 2022, *Interdisciplinary Conference* Turku (Finland) 2021, *Interdisciplinary Conference* Aarhus (Denmark) 2020. **Publications** *Europäische Kulturen in der Wirtschaftskommunikation – European Cultures in Business Communication* in English, German.

Members Scholars from 5 countries:
Denmark, Finland, Germany, Netherlands, Switzerland. [2022/AA2639/jv/**F**]

- Europäische Kulturgesellschaft (#08576)
- Europäische Kulturstiftung (#06868)
- Europäische LaktationsberaterInnen Allianz (#07638)
- Europäische Landarbeiter Föderation (inactive)
- Europäische Liberale, Demokratische und Reformpartei (#00703)
- Europäische Liga für Geistige Hygiene (inactive)
- Europäische Liga für Wirtschaftliche Zusammenarbeit (#07669)

♦ Europäische Märchengesellschaft (EMG) 05755

European Fairy Tale Association

Pres c/o Schloss Bentlage, Bentlager Weg 130, 48432 Rheine, Germany. T. +495971918420. Fax +495971918429. E-mail: info@maerchen-emg.de.

URL: http://www.maerchen-emg.de/

History 1956, Rheine (Germany), as *Society for the Preservation of the Fairy Tales of the European Peoples*. **Aims** Preserve *folk tales* and make people aware of them. **Finance** Members' dues. **Activities** Events/meetings; knowledge management/information dissemination. **Events** *International Congress* Binz (Germany) 2015, *International Congress* Rheine (Germany) 2014, *International Congress* Bad Brückenau (Germany) 2013, *International Congress* Lenzerheide (Switzerland) 2012, *International Congress* Senftenberg (Germany) 2011. **Publications** Books.

Members Individuals (over 2,500) in 24 countries:
Argentina, Austria, Belgium, Brazil, Canada, Denmark, Finland, France, Ireland, Israel, Italy, Japan, Liechtenstein, Luxembourg, Monaco, Netherlands, Norway, Russia, South Africa, Spain, Sweden, Switzerland, UK, USA. [2014.10.28/XF5843/v/**F**]

- Europäische Medizinische Assoziation (#07761)
- Europäische Medizin Laser Gesellschaft (#07763)
- Europäische Medizinstudierenden Vereinigung (#07764)
- Europäische Metall-Union (#07785)
- Europäische Meteorologische Gesellschaft (#07786)
- Europäische Mittelstands-Union (no recent information)
- Europäische Mittelstandsvereinigung (inactive)
- Europäische Motel-Föderation (inactive)

♦ Europäische Musikschul-Union (EMU) 05756

Union européenne des écoles de musique – European Music School Union

Contact Taubenstrasse 1, 10117 Berlin, Germany. E-mail: office@musicschoolunion.eu.

URL: http://www.musicschoolunion.eu/

History 1973, Saarbrücken (Germany FR). Current statutes adopted 1 Oct 1992. Registered in accordance with Swiss Civil Code. **Aims** Promote musical education and practice. **Structure** General Assembly (annual); Praesidium or Bureau; Secretary-General; Permanent Web Working Group. **Languages** English, French, German. **Staff** 1.00 FTE, voluntary. **Finance** Members' dues. **Activities** Knowledge management/information dissemination; networking/liaising; awareness raising; events/meetings. **Events** *Annual General Assembly* Differdange (Luxembourg) 2022, *Annual General Assembly* 2021, *Annual General Assembly* 2020, *Annual General Assembly* Stuttgart (Germany) 2020, *Annual General Assembly* Sofia (Bulgaria) / Plovdiv (Bulgaria) 2019. **Publications** *EMU Bulletin*; *EMU Letter*. *Statistical Information about the European Music School Union* (2006); *Manifesto – As Close as Music* (2003); *European Guide to Education in the Creative Arts* (2002); *EMU 2000 – Statistical Information about the European Music School Union* (2000); *Music Schools in Europe – Handbook of the European Union of Music Schools* (1995) in English, French, German. Booklets; reports.

Members Music schools (6,000) in 27 countries:
Austria, Azerbaijan, Belgium, Cyprus, Czechia, Denmark, Estonia, Finland, France, Germany, Hungary, Iceland, Ireland, Italy, Latvia, Liechtenstein, Luxembourg, Netherlands, Norway, Poland, Serbia, Slovakia, Slovenia, Spain, Sweden, Switzerland, UK.

NGO Relations Member of: *European Music Council (EMC, #07837)*. Associate member of: *International Music Council (IMC, #14199)*. [2019.12.19/XD1478/**D**]

- Europäischen Agentur für Netz- und Informationssicherheit (#08971)
- Europäische Nahrungsmittel- Grossenbandels-Vereingung (inactive)
- Europäische Naturisten Union (inactive)
- Europäischen Beratenden Verbrauchergruppe (#06771)
- Europäischen Christlichen Umweltnetzwerkes (#06543)
- Europäische Netz der Digitalen Städten (#07893)
- Europäische Netzwerk für die Entwicklung des ländlichen Raums (#07995)
- Europäischen Feuerwehr Sport Föderation (#07261)
- Europäischen Flüchtlingsfonds (inactive)
- Europäischen Gemeinschaften (inactive)
- Europäischen Gesellschaft der Entgiftungszentralen / see European Association of Poisons Centres and Clinical Toxicologists (#06155)
- Europäischen Gesellschaft für Umweltrecht (inactive)
- Europäischen Koordination für das Recht aller Ausländer auf Familienleben (#06794)
- Europäischen Monarchistischen Vereinigung (no recent information)
- Europäischen Netzes für die Rechte der Australischen Ureinwohner (internationally oriented national body)
- Europäischen Netzwerk für Lebensmittelinformation (#07285)
- Europäische Notfall- und Intensivmedizin Vereinigung (#09056)
- Europäische NROs für Sexuelle und Reproduktive Gesundheit und Rechte, Bevölkerung und Entwicklung / see Inspire – the European Partnership for Sexual and Reproductive Health and Rights (#11232)
- Europäischen Schieferverbandes (inactive)
- Europäischen Totentanz-Vereinigung (internationally oriented national body)
- Europäischen Verband der Stomatherapeuten (#06820)
- Europäischen Vereinigung für die Eisenbahn Interoperabilität (inactive)
- Europäischen Vereinigung der Förder- und Lagertechnik (#07752)
- Europäischen Zentrum für die Prävention und die Kontrolle von Krankheiten (#06476)
- Europäische Ökozentrum – Terre vivante (internationally oriented national body)
- Europäische Olympische Akademien (#08082)
- Europäische Ombudsstelle (#08084)
- Europäische Onkologie-Schule (#08434)
- Europäische Orchideen-Kommission / see European Orchid Council (#08093)
- Europäische ordnung der sozialen sicherheit (1964 treaty)
- Europäische ordnung der sozialen sicherheit, revidiert (1990 treaty)
- Europäische Organisation für Astronomische Forschung in der Südlichen Hemisphäre (#08106)
- Europäische Organisation für Bitumenschindeln (inactive)
- Europäische Organisation zur Erforschung und Behandlung von Krebs (#08101)
- Europäische Organisation für den Fertigbau (inactive)
- Europäische Organisation der Gemüsekonserven- Industrie (inactive)
- Europäische Organisation für Geoinformation (#08964)
- Europäische Organisation für Kernforschung (#08108)
- Europäische Organisation der Konfitüren- und Obstkonservenindustrie (inactive)
- Europäische Organisation der Militärverbände / see European Organisation of Military Associations and Trade Unions (#08099)
- Europäische Organisation für Molekularbiologie (#07816)
- Europäische Organisation zur Nutzung von Wettersatelliten (#08096)
- Europäische Organisation der Obersten Rechnungskontrollbehörden (#08115)
- Europäische Organisation der Obst- und Gemuseverarbeitenden Industrie / see European Association of Fruit and Vegetable Processors (#06049)
- Europäische Organisation für Qualität / see European Organization for Quality (#08112)
- Europäische Organisation für Reittourismus (inactive)
- Europäische Organisation der Sägewerke (#08114)
- Europäische Organisation für Technische Zulassungen / see European Organisation for Technical Assessment (#08103)
- Europäische Organisation der Tomatenkonserven-Industrie / see European Organisation of Tomato Industries (#08104)
- Europäische Organisation der Vereinigungen für Wohnheime und Hilfenfür Berufstätige Jugend (inactive)
- Europäische Organisation der Weltorganisation der Arbeitnehmer (#08116)
- Europäische Parlamentarische Gesellschaft (internationally oriented national body)
- Europäische Patentorganisation (#08167)
- Europäische Plattform für die Gewinnung unterirdischer Energie "Earth Energy" (unconfirmed)
- Europäische Polizeipräsidentenkonferenz (meeting series)
- Europäische Psychoanalytische Föderation (#08292)
- Europäischer Abbruchverband (#06902)
- Europäische Radsport-Union (#06876)
- Europäischer Aerosolverband (#09557)
- Europäischer Akademie für Unternehmensleitung und Betriebswirtschaft (#05801)
- Europäischer Alkohol-, Branntwein- und Spirituosenunion (inactive)
- Europäischer Anglerverband (#05900)
- Europäischer Anwaltsverein (#20365)

♦ Europäischer Arbeitskreis für Konzentrative Bewegungstherapie (EAKBT) 05757

European Association for Concentrative Movement Therapy

Secretariat Brosiweg 12b, 4143 Dornach SO, Switzerland. E-mail: kontakt@chkbt.ch.

URL: http://www.chkbt.ch/eakbt.html

History 21 Nov 2001, Salzburg (Austria).

Members Full in 6 countries:
Austria, Belgium, Germany, Italy, Slovakia, Switzerland.

NGO Relations Member of: *European Association for Psychotherapy (EAP, #06176)*. [2016.07.04/XJ5283/**D**]

- Europäischer Arbeitskreis für Landschaftspflege (inactive)
- Europäische Rat für die Baubranche (inactive)
- Europäischer Ausschuss für die Ausarbeitung von Standards im Bereich der Binnenschifffahrt (#04160)
- Europäischer Ausschuss der Diplom-Agraringenieure / see Confédération européenne des associations d'ingénieurs agronomes (#04538)
- Europäischer Ausschuss der Diplom-Agraringenieure der Europäischen Gemeinschaft / see Confédération européenne des associations d'ingénieurs agronomes (#04538)
- Europäischer Ausschuss für Feste Brennstoffe / see European Association for Coal and Lignite (#05978)
- Europäischer Ausschuss der Heiz- und Kochgeräte-Industrie (#04158)
- Europäischer Ausschuss von Nahrungsmittelimport und Grosshandelsverbänden (inactive)
- Europäischer Ausschuss der Nationalen Import- und Grosshandelsverbände für Tiefbau- und Fördergeräte (no recent information)
- Europäischer Ausschuss der Nationalen Verbände der Lederwaren und Reiseartikelhersteller und Verwandten Industrien (inactive)
- Europäischer Ausschuss der Regionen (#06665)
- Europäischer Ausschuss der Unternehmen aus dem Weinsektor (#04157)
- Europäischer Auswärtiger Dienst (#07018)
- Europäischer Baumpflegerat (#05911)
- Europäischer Beamtenbund (#06567)
- Europäischer Behälterglasindustrie-Verband (#09583)
- Europäischer Bergarbeiterverband (inactive)
- Europäischer Berufsfachverband für Gitarrelehrer und Gitarristen (no recent information)
- Europäischer Berufsimkerverband (#08284)
- Europäischer Briefmarken-Händlerverband (inactive)
- Europäischer Bund Christlicher Bau- und Holzarbeiterverbände (inactive)
- Europäischer Bund der Tabakeinzelhändler (#06725)
- Europäischer Coach-Verband (internationally oriented national body)
- Europäischer Cord-Samt-Verband (inactive)
- Europäischer CVJM Bund / see YMCA Europe (#21977)
- Europäischer Dachverband der Insolvenzpraktiker / see European Insolvency Practitioners Association (#07543)

♦ Europäischer Dachverband der Öffentlichen Kommunalen Energieversorgungsunternehmen / see European Federation of Local Energy Companies (#07156)
♦ Europäischer Dachverband der Präparatoren (inactive)
♦ Europäischer Dachverband Schwuler und Lesbischer Chöre / see LEGATO (#16441)
♦ Europäischer Dachverband der Unabhängigen Finanzberater und Finanzvermittler (#07122)
♦ Europäische Rechtsakademie (#00035)
♦ Europäische Regionale Organisation der FDI (#08345)
♦ Europäische Reisezugfahrplankonferenz (inactive)
♦ Europäischer Erfinderverband (inactive)
♦ Europäischer Erzieherbund (#02565)
♦ Europäischer Fachverband der Arzneimittel-Hersteller (#02543)
♦ Europäischer Fahrgastverband (#08162)
♦ Europäischer Federation Auktionatoren / see European Federation of Auctioneers (#07057)
♦ Europäischer Fernschulrat (inactive)
♦ Europäischer Flüssiggasverband / see Liquid Gas Europe (#16488)
♦ Europäischer Fonds für Währungspolitische Zusammenarbeit (inactive)
♦ Europäischer Gesamtverband des Schuhgrosshandels (inactive)
♦ Europäischer Gewerkschaftsausschuss Öffentlichen Dienst / see European Federation of Public Service Unions (#07202)
♦ Europäischer Gewerkschaftsbund (#08927)
♦ Europäischer Gewerkschaftsverband für den Öffentlichen Dienst (#07202)
♦ Europäischer Gewerkschaftsverband Textil, Bekleidung und Leder (inactive)
♦ Europäischer Gewichtheber Verband (#09090)
♦ Europäischer Glücksspielverband (no recent information)
♦ Europäischer Golf-Verband (#07399)
♦ Europäischer Heilbäderverband (#08805)
♦ Europäische Rheumaliga / see European Alliance of Associations for Rheumatology (#05862)
♦ Europäischer Holzhandelsverband (inactive)
♦ Europäischer Holzwerkstoffverband (#08137)
♦ Europäischer Hypothekenverband / see Covered Bond and Mortgage Council (#04940)
♦ Europäischer Interessenverband Handel-Gewerbe-Industrie (internationally oriented national body)
♦ Europäischer Kalkverband (#07699)
♦ Europäischer Kartellverband Christlicher Studentenverbände (#07076)
♦ Europäischer Keramik-Verbank (inactive)
♦ Europäischer Komitee für Regulierung Post (see: #04602)
♦ Europäischer Konföderation des Eisen- und Metallwaren Grosshandels (inactive)
♦ Europäischer Kongress über die Nutzung, Bewirtschaftung und Erhaltung historisch bedeutender Gebäude (meeting series)
♦ Europäischer Koordinierungsausschuss der Röntgen- und Elektromedizinischen Industrie / see European Coordination Committee of the Radiological, Electromedical Healthcare IT Industry (#06792)
♦ Europäischer Kunststofffenster-Verband (inactive)
♦ Europäischer Landjugendverband (#19007)
♦ Europäischer Lehrmittelverband / see Worlddidac Association (#21361)
♦ Europäischer Leichtathletik-Lehrer-Verband (#06292)

♦ Europäischer Leit-Verband der Hersteller von Gas-Infrarot-Hellstrahlern (ELVHIS) 05758

European Leading Association of Radiant Gas Heaters Manufacturers – Association européenne des fabricants de panneaux radiants lumineux à gaz

Secretariat Marienburgerstrasse 15, 50968 Cologne, Germany. T. +492213764830. Fax +492213764861. E-mail: info@figawa.de.
URL: http://www.elvhis.com/

History 1994. Former names and other names: *European Association of Luminous Radiant Gas Heaters Manufacturers* – former; *Association européenne principale des fabricants de panneaux radiants lumineux à gaz* – former; *Association européenne principale des fabricants des panneaux infrarouges lumineux à gaz* – former; *European Leading Association of High Intensity Gas Infrared Heater Manufacturers* – former. Registration: North Rhine-Westphalia District court, No/ID: VR 11347, Start date: 26 Aug 1993, Germany, Cologne; EU Transparency Register, No/ID: 933866423405-44, Start date: 14 Sep 2016. **Aims** Promote scientific research and provide information about infrared gas heaters, technical developments and its possible areas of use, in particular in the heating of large buildings, as well as the drafting and monitoring of European standards. **Structure** Board; General Secretariat.
Members Companies in 8 countries:
Canada, Czechia, France, Germany, Italy, Netherlands, Türkiye, UK.
NGO Relations In liaison with technical committees of: *Comité européen de normalisation (CEN, #04162).*
[2017/XD7972/**D**]

♦ Europäischer Markenverband (#06397)
♦ Europäischer Metallgewerkschaftsbund (inactive)
♦ Europäischer Methodistischer Jugendrat / see European Methodist Youth and Children's Council (#07788)
♦ Europäischer Milchindustrieverband (#06883)
♦ Europäischer Molkenprodukte Verband (#09093)
♦ Europäischer Musikrat (#07837)
♦ Europäischer Nierenpatientenverband / see European Kidney Patients' Federation (#07627)
♦ Europäischer Parfümerieverband (#07206)
♦ Europäischer Polyolefin-Klarsichtfolien Verband (inactive)
♦ Europäischer PVC-Hartfolien-Verband (#08389)
♦ Europäischer Radfahrer Verband (#06877)
♦ Europäischer Rat (#06801)
♦ Europäischer Rat für Druckgeräte Forschung (#08269)
♦ Europäischer Rat der Freien Berufe (#06828)
♦ Europäischer Rat der Junglandwirte (#04689)
♦ Europäischer Rat Methodistischer Kirchen (#07787)
♦ Europäischer Rat der Nationalen Verbände Freier Schulen (#06833)
♦ Europäischer Rat für Optometrie und Optik (#06835)
♦ Europäischer Rat für Rohleder (inactive)
♦ Europäischer Rat für Sozialwissenschaftliche Forschung über Lateinamerika (#04710)
♦ Europäischer Rat für Umweltrecht (no recent information)
♦ Europäischer Rat der Wein- und Gastronomie-Bruderschaften (#08076)
♦ Europäischer Rat der Wienstrassen (inactive)
♦ Europäischer Rat für Zahlungssysteme (inactive)
♦ Europäischer Rechnungshof (#06854)
♦ Europäischer Salzstudienausschuss / see European Salt Producers Association (#08425)
♦ Europäischer Schausteller Frauenbund (see: #08483)
♦ Europäischer Schiedsgerichtshof (#06853)
♦ Europäischer Schraubenverband (#07524)
♦ Europäischer Schulverband (#09479)
♦ Europäischer Sozialfonds (#08501)
♦ Europäischer Sportschiffahrtsverband (#06376)
♦ Europäischer Sprachenrat (#07646)
♦ Europäischer Sprengverband (#07117)
♦ Europäischer Stein-und Braunkohleverband / see European Association for Coal and Lignite (#05978)
♦ Europäischer Tabakwaren-Grosshandelsverband (#08919)
♦ Europäischer Transportbetonverband (#08330)
♦ Europäische Rum-Industrie (no recent information)
♦ Europäischer Verband der Amateurfahrer und Fahrerinnen des Trabersports (#05896)
♦ Europäischer Verband Ambulanter Pflegedienste (inactive)
♦ Europäischer Verband der Angestellten Ärzte (#07209)
♦ Europäischer Verband für Arbeitsstudien / see European Federation of Productivity Services (#07196)
♦ Europäischer Verband der Arzneimittelhersteller der Anthroposophischen Therapierichtung (#02568)
♦ Europäischer Verband für den Bauernhof und Land Tourismus / see European Federation of Rural Tourism (#07208)
♦ Europäischer Verband Beruflicher Bildungsträger (#06085)
♦ Europäischer Verband der Binnenhäfen (#07144)
♦ Europäischer Verband der Bürgermeister (inactive)
♦ Europäischer Verband der Bürgschaftsbanken / see European Association of Guarantee Institutions (#06061)
♦ Europäischer Verband der Büro- und Informationstechnischen Industrie (inactive)
♦ Europäischer Verband der Bürsten- und Pinsel-Industrie (#06406)
♦ Europäischer Verband des Chemiehandels (#09563)
♦ Europäischer Verband für Diakonie (#07099)
♦ Europäischer Verband für die Entwicklung des Schienenverkehrs (#06011)
♦ Europäischer Verband der Dienstleistungen für Familien (#07118)
♦ Europäischer Verband für das Dorf und für die Kleinstadt (#06848)
♦ Europäischer Verband der Eltern Hörgeschädigter Kinder (#09577)
♦ Europäischer Verband Energie – Chemie – Verschiedene Industrien (inactive)
♦ Europäischer Verband der Entcoffeinierer (inactive)
♦ Europäischer Verband für Erwachsenenbildung (#06018)
♦ Europäischer Verband der Erzeuger von Einzelligen Eiweissstoffen (inactive)
♦ Europäischer Verband der Fabrikanten von Sanitär-Keramik (#07073)
♦ Europäischer Verband der Flachglas-Hersteller / see Glass for Europe (#10157)
♦ Europäischer Verband Freikirchlicher Diakoniewerke (#06013)

♦ Europäischer Verband Freikirchlicher Diakoniewerke (evfdiakonie) 05759

Pres Albertinen-Diakoniewerk, Süntelstrasse 11a, 22457 Hamburg, Germany. T. +494055882811.
URL: http://www.evfdiakonie.org/

History 1907, as Freikirchliche Diakonie-Konferenz. Name changed to Verband Evangelisch-Freikirchlicher Diakonissen-Muterhäuser in Deutschland under der Schweiz in 1920. Present name adopted 1975. **Events** *Conference* Leichlingen (Germany) 2015, *Conference* Vienna (Austria) 2013, *Conference* Alicante (Spain) 2011, *Conference* l'Alfàs del Pi (Spain) 2011, *Conference* Hamburg (Germany) 2009.
Members Organizations (21) in 6 countries.
France, Georgia, Germany, Norway, Slovakia, Switzerland.
NGO Relations Member of: *European Federation for Diaconia (Eurodiaconia, #07099).*
[2018.06.14/XD1473/**D**]

♦ Europäischer Verband für Fremdenverkehrsfachleute (inactive)
♦ Europäischer Verband für Geflügel-, Tauben-, Vogel-, Kaninchen- und Caviazucht (#05492)
♦ Europäischer Verband des Gross- und Aussenhandels mit Milcherzeugnissen (#06003)
♦ Europäischer Verband der Hauskrankenpflege Organisationen (inactive)
♦ Europäischer Verband der Hersteller und Anwender von Spezialprodukten im Bauwesen / see Experts for Specialised Construction and Concrete Systems (#09226)
♦ Europäischer Verband der Hersteller von Erpölbohrgeräten (inactive)
♦ Europäischer Verband der Hersteller von Grosskochanlagen (#07068)
♦ Europäischer Verband der Hersteller von Gussheizungsgütern (inactive)
♦ Europäischer Verband der Hersteller von Hausgeräten / see APPLiA – Home Appliance Europe (#00877)
♦ Europäischer Verband der Hersteller von Heimtiernahrung (#09571)
♦ Europäischer Verband der Hersteller von Kunstoffolien – Hauptsächlich Polyäthylen (inactive)
♦ Europäischer Verband der Hersteller von Polyesterterephthalafolie (inactive)
♦ Europäischer Verband der Hersteller von Stahlheizkesseln (inactive)
♦ Europäischer Verband der Herz- und Lungentransplantierten (#07466)
♦ Europäischer Verband der Hilfsgewerbe der Weinwirtschaft (inactive)
♦ Europäischer Verband der Hochschulsprachenzentren (#04540)
♦ Europäischer Verband Höherer Berufe des Ingenieurwesens und der Technik (#07484)
♦ Europäischer Verband der Hörgeräte-Akustiker (#06066)
♦ Europäischer Verband für Industrielle Energiewirtschaft (inactive)
♦ Europäischer Verband der Industrien von Porzellan- Steingut- Geschirr- und Zierkeramik (#09574)
♦ Europäischer Verband der Industrie-Patentingenieure (#07042)
♦ Europäischer Verband der Jugendservice Organisationen (inactive)
♦ Europäischer Verband von Karton- und Faltschachtelherstellern / see Association of European Cartonboard and Carton Manufacturers (#02502)
♦ Europäischer Verband der Kies-, Sand- und Schotterproduzenten (#00558)
♦ Europäischer Verband für Kinesiologie (internationally oriented national body)
♦ Europäischer Verband der Konzessionäre von Gebührenpflichtigen Autobahnen und Bauwerken (#02559)
♦ Europäischer Verband des Kraftfahrzeuggewerbes / see European Council for Motor Trades and Repairs (#06832)
♦ Europäischer Verband der Künstleragenturen (#02554)
♦ Europäischer Verband für Landtourismus / see European Federation of Rural Tourism (#07208)
♦ Europäischer Verband für Lebensmittelverpackungen und Einweggeschirr / see Pack2Go Europe (#18014)
♦ Europäischer Verband der Lichtwerbung (#08485)
♦ Europäischer Verband lifestyle (internationally oriented national body)
♦ Europäischer Verband der Markenartikelindustrie / see European Brands Association (#06397)
♦ Europäischer Verband der Mischfutterindustrie (#09566)
♦ Europäischer Verband mittelständischer Energieunternehmer (internationally oriented national body)
♦ Europäischer Verband des Möbelhandels (#07132)
♦ Europäischer Verband der in öffentlichen Apotheken angestellten Apotheker (#06025)
♦ Europäischer Verband der Oralchirurgischen Gesellschaften (#07182)
♦ Europäischer Verband für Passiven Brandschutz (#06143)
♦ Europäischer Verband der Photographischen Industrie (inactive)
♦ Europäischer Verband für Produktivitätsförderung (#07196)
♦ Europäischer Verband für Psychotherapie (#06176)
♦ Europäischer Verband für Pultrusions Technik (#08307)
♦ Europäischer Verband der Rechtsanwalskammern bei den Obersten Gerichtshöfen (inactive)
♦ Europäischer Verband der Regelgerätehersteller (#02592)
♦ Europäischer Verband der Salmonidenzüchter / see Federation of European Aquaculture Producers (#09491)
♦ Europäischer Verband der Schmiedeindustrie (#06649)
♦ Europäischer Verband selbstständiger Zahntechniker / see Fédération européenne et internationale des patrons prothésistes dentaires (#09575)
♦ Europäischer Verband Selbstständiger Zahntechniker Labor Einhaber (#09575)

♦ Europäischer Verband der Standesbeamtinnen und Standesbeamten (EVS) 05760

European Association of Registrars – Association européenne des officiers de l'Etat civil (AEEC) – Associazione Europea delle Ufficialesse e degli Ufficiali dello Stato Civile

Pres c/o NVVB, Boerhaavelaan 14, 2713 HX Zoetermeer, Netherlands.

Europäischer Verband Talg
05760

alphabetic sequence excludes
For the complete listing, see Yearbook Online at

Contact c/o BDS, Bahnhofstr 14, 36364 Bad Salzschlirf, Germany. T. +496648931421. Fax +496648931422. E-mail: generalsekretaer-evs@standesbeamte.de.
URL: http://www.evs-eu.org/
History May 2000, Noordwijkerhout (Netherlands). Registration: Hesse District court, No/ID: VR 1690, Start date: 17 Aug 2004, Germany, Fulda; EU Transparency Register, No/ID: 205036743037-76, Start date: 7 Jun 2021. **Structure** Board. **Events** *Congress* Tallinn (Estonia) 2023, *Congress* Bratislava (Slovakia) 2022, *Congress* Bratislava (Slovakia) 2020, *Congress* Szczecin (Poland) 2019, *Congress* Iasi (Romania) 2018.
Members Full in 9 countries and territories:
Austria, Belgium, Germany, Italy, Netherlands, Poland, Romania, Scotland, Slovakia, Slovenia. [2023/XJ6698/**D**]

- ♦ Europäischer Verband der Talg und Schmalzindustrie (inactive)
- ♦ Europäischer Verband der UmweltberaterInnen (inactive)
- ♦ Europäischer Verband der Unterhaltungssoftware (#11380)
- ♦ Europäischer Verband der Veranstaltungs-Centren (#06032)
- ♦ Europäischer Verband für Verkehr und Umwelt (#07230)
- ♦ Europäischer Verband der Verleger von Jugendschriften (inactive)
- ♦ Europäischer Verband der Versorgungseinrichtungen des Öffentlichen Dienstes (#06180)
- ♦ Europäischer Verband der Walzwerksbauer (inactive)
- ♦ Europäischer Verband der Wellpappenfabrikanten (#07091)
- ♦ Europäischer Verband des Wild- und Geflügel-, Gross- und Aussenhandels / see European Poultry, Egg and Game Association (#08258)
- ♦ Europäischer Verband des Wild- und Geflügel- Gross- und Aussenhandels (#08259)
- ♦ Europäischer Verband für Wirkstoffe in der Tierernährung / see FEFANA – EU Association of Specialty Feed Ingredients and their Mixtures (#09720)
- ♦ Europäischer Verband für Wirkstoffe und Vormischung in der Tiernährung (#09720)
- ♦ Europäischer Verband der Zellstoff-, Papier und Pappeindustrie (inactive)
- ♦ Europäischer Verband für Zellstoff und Papiertechnik (#07688)
- ♦ Europäischer Verbindungsausschuss zur Koordinierung der Sozialen Wohnungswirtschaft / see Housing Europe – The European Federation for Public Cooperative and Social Housing (#10956)
- ♦ Europäischer Verbraucherschutzverband (#03360)
- ♦ Europäischer Verbraucherverband für Naturmedizin (no recent information)
- ♦ Europäischer Vereiniging der Eier-, Wild- und Geflügel-, Wirtschaft (#08258)
- ♦ Europäischer Vereinigung der Verbände der Lack-, Druckfarben- und Künstlerfarbenfabrikanten / see Conseil européen de l'industrie des peintures, des encres d'imprimerie et des couleurs d'art (#04688)
- ♦ Europäischer Verein Individueller Investoren (inactive)
- ♦ Europäischer Verein für Schulische und Berufliche Orientierung, Beratung und Information (inactive)
- ♦ Europäischer Verein für Unternehmensleitung und Betriebswirtschaft / see European Academy of Management and Business Economics (#05801)
- ♦ Europäischer Verein zur Verbrauchsabhängigen Energiekostenabrechnung (#05989)
- ♦ Europäischer Verein der Werkzeugmaschinenhändler (#06114)
- ♦ Europäischer Verein für Wirtschaftsprüfer / see European Accounting Association (#05820)
- ♦ Europäischer Verkehrssicherheitsrat (#08940)
- ♦ Europäischer Verleger-Verband (#09536)
- ♦ Europäischer Viehmärkteverband (#06109)
- ♦ Europäischer Windenergieverband / see WindEurope (#20965)
- ♦ Europäischer Wirtschaftsprüfer-Verband (inactive)
- ♦ Europäischer Wirtschafts- und Sozialausschuss (#06963)
- ♦ Europäischer Wirtschaftsverband Aussenhandel (inactive)
- ♦ Europäischer Wohnwagenverband (#06443)
- ♦ Europäischer Zentralverband der land- und forstwirtschaftlichen Lohnunternehmer und ländlichen Dienstleistungsunternehmern (#08105)
- ♦ Europäischer Zentralverband der Öffentlichen Wirtschaft / see SGI Europe (#19253)
- ♦ Europäischer Zentrum für Schiedsverfahren und Mediation (#06462)
- ♦ Europäischer Zwirnerei Verband (inactive)
- ♦ Europäisches abkommen zum schutz von fernsehsendungen (1960 treaty)
- ♦ Europäisches abkommen über soziale sicherheit (1972 treaty)
- ♦ Europäisches Aktionskomitee Freier Verbände / see European Council for Non-Profit Organizations (#06834)
- ♦ Europäisches Amt für Betrugsbekämpfung (#05906)
- ♦ Europäisches Amt für Jugend und Kinder (inactive)
- ♦ Europäisches Anwaltsverein / see AEA – International Lawyers Network (#00142)
- ♦ Europäisches Astronautenzentrum (#06287)
- ♦ Europäisches Atom-Forum / see nucleareurope (#17616)
- ♦ Europäisches Ausbildungszentrum für Handwerker im Denkmalschutz / see European Centre for Heritage Crafts and Professions (#06484)
- ♦ Europäisches auslieferungsübereinkommen (1957 treaty)
- ♦ Europäisches Ausschuss für Tenside und ihre organischen Zwischenprodukte (#06660)
- ♦ Europäisches Baumaschinen Komitee (#04254)
- ♦ Europäisches Bildungszentrum der Wohnungs- und Immobilienwirtschaft (internationally oriented national body)
- ♦ Europäisches Bioobst Forum (unconfirmed)
- ♦ Europäisches Bleiberatungs-Komitee (inactive)
- ♦ Europäisches Büro für Erwachsenenbildung / see European Association for the Education of Adults (#06018)
- ♦ Europäisches Büro für Funkangelegenheiten / see European Communications Office (#06676)
- ♦ Europäisches Büro für Kriegsdienstverweigerung (#06411)
- ♦ Europäisches Büro der Verbraucherverbände / see Bureau Européen des Unions de Consommateurs (#03360)
- ♦ Europäische Schausteller Jugend Union (see: #08483)
- ♦ Europäische Schausteller-Union (#08483)
- ♦ Europäische Schiffer Organisation (#08491)

♦ Europäische Schornsteinfegermeister-Föderation (ESCHFOE) 05761

Fédération européenne des maîtres ramoneurs – European Federation of Chimney Sweeps
SG Westerwaldstrasse 6, 53757 St Augustin, Germany. T. +49224134070. Fax +492241340710.
URL: http://www.eschfoe.com/
History 1954. Previously also referred to in English as *European Federation of Chimney Sweepers*. **Languages** English, French, German. **Staff** 2.00 FTE, paid. **Events** *Conference* Dietfurt (Germany) 2015, *Conference* Pörtschach (Austria) 2012, *Conference* Montreux (Switzerland) 2010, *Conference* Daventry (UK) 2002, *President conference* Budapest (Hungary) 2000.
Members National federations in 21 countries:
Austria, Belgium, Czechia, Denmark, Estonia, Finland, France, Germany, Hungary, Italy, Luxembourg, Netherlands, Norway, Poland, Slovakia, Slovenia, Spain, Sweden, Switzerland, UK, USA.
NGO Relations Member of: *SMEunited (#19327).* [2015.01.15/XD5767/**D**]

- ♦ Europäisches Chromosom 11 Netzwerk (#06547)
- ♦ Europäisches Chromosom 11q Netzwerk / see European Chromosome 11 Network (#06547)
- ♦ Europäische Schulleitervereinigung (#08431)
- ♦ Europäische Schulleitervereinigung im Sekundarbereich II / see European School Heads Association (#08431)
- ♦ Europäische Schwertransport- Automobilkranunion / see European Association of Abnormal Road Transport and Mobile Cranes (#05923)
- ♦ Europäische Schwertransporte und Kranarbeiten / see European Association of Abnormal Road Transport and Mobile Cranes (#05923)
- ♦ Europäisches Energie-Informations-Zentrum (inactive)
- ♦ Europäische Senioren Organisation (#08465)
- ♦ Europäische Senioren Union (#08466)
- ♦ Europäisches Forschungsinstitut für Kunstfasern (inactive)
- ♦ Europäisches Forschungsinstitut für Regional und Stadtplanung (inactive)
- ♦ Europäisches Forum Alpbach (#07304)
- ♦ Europäisches Forum älterer Freiwilliger / see European Network of Older-Volunteer Organizations
- ♦ Europäisches Forum der Altertums- und Denkmalschutzvereine (#07314)
- ♦ Europäisches Forum für angewandte Kriminalpolitik (internationally oriented national body)
- ♦ Europäisches Forum für Aussenwirtschaft, Verbrauchssteuern und Zoll (internationally oriented national body)
- ♦ Europäisches Forum für die Menschenrechte und die Rechte der Familie (#07315)
- ♦ Europäisches FORUM für den Entwicklungsdienst / see International Forum for Volunteering in Development (#13659)
- ♦ Europäisches Forum für Freiheit im Bildungswesen (#07311)
- ♦ Europäisches Forum für Komplementäre und Alternative Medizin Förderung der Integrierten Gesundheitsfürsorge / see European Federation for Complementary and Alternative Medicine (#07084)
- ♦ Europäisches Forum für Mehrsprachigkeit (internationally oriented national body)
- ♦ Europäisches Forum der Nationalen Laienkomittees (#07322)
- ♦ Europäisches Forum für Psychomotorik (#07327)
- ♦ Europäisches Forum für den Schulischen Religionsunterricht (internationally oriented national body)
- ♦ Europäisches Forum der Versicherungen gegen Arbeitsunfälle und Berufskrankheiten (#07317)
- ♦ Europäisches Fremdsprachenzentrum (#06491)
- ♦ Europäisches Fremdsprachenzentrum des Europarats / see European Centre for Modern Languages (#06491)
- ♦ Europäisches fürsorgeabkommen (1953 treaty)
- ♦ Europäisches Gartennetzwerk (#07378)
- ♦ Europäisches Gesellschaft für Agrarrecht und das Recht des Ländlichen Raumes (#04155)
- ♦ Europäisches Gewerkschaftsinstitut (#08928)
- ♦ Europäisches Gewerkschaftskomitee für Bildung und Wissenschaft (#08926)
- ♦ Europäisches Hochschulinstitut (#09034)
- ♦ Europäische Siebdruck-Herstellerverband / see European Specialist Printing Manufacturers Associations (#08809)
- ♦ Europäisches Informationsbüro für Kohlefragen (inactive)
- ♦ Europäisches Informationszentrum für Lebensmittel (#07284)
- ♦ Europäisches Institut für Berufsausbildung (inactive)
- ♦ Europäisches Institut Conflict-Culture-Cooperation (internationally oriented national body)
- ♦ Europäisches Institut für Gleichstellungsfragen (#07557)
- ♦ Europäisches Institut für Holzimprägnierung (#07575)
- ♦ Europäisches Institut für Internationale Wirtschaftsbeziehungen (internationally oriented national body)
- ♦ Europäisches Institut für Öffentliche Verwaltung / see European Institute of Public Administration (#07569)
- ♦ Europäisches Institut für Progressive Kulturpolitik (internationally oriented national body)
- ♦ Europäisches Institut für Soziale Sicherheit (#07571)
- ♦ Europäisches Institut für Telekommunikationsnormen (#08897)
- ♦ Europäisches Institut für Unternehmensführung / see INSEAD (#11228)
- ♦ Europäisches Institut für vergleichende Kulturforschung (#07547)
- ♦ Europäisches Institut für das Wohl des Kindes (internationally oriented national body)
- ♦ Europäisches Justizielles Netz für Zivil- und Handelssachen (#07616)
- ♦ Europäisches Katholisches Foyer (internationally oriented national body)
- ♦ Europäisches Komitee der Armaturenindustrie / see European Association for the Taps and Valves Industry (#06246)
- ♦ Europäisches Komitee der Bauökonomen (#06812)
- ♦ Europäisches Komitee der Brennerhersteller (inactive)
- ♦ Europäisches Komitee für Dampfkessel- Behälter- und Rohrleitungsbau (no recent information)
- ♦ Europäisches Komitee für die Erziehung der Frühreifen, Hochbegabten, Talentierten Kinder und Jugendlichen / see European Committee Promoting the Education of Gifted and Talented Young People (#06664)
- ♦ Europäisches Komitee für die Zusammenarbeit der Werkzeugmaschinen-Industrien / see European Association of the Machine tool Industries and related Manufacturing Technologies (#06113)
- ♦ Europäisches Komitee der Druck- und Papierverarbeitungsmaschinenindustrie (#06661)
- ♦ Europäisches Komitee für Elektrotechnische Normung (#06647)
- ♦ Europäisches Komitee der Fachverbände der Hersteller von Getrieben und Antriebselementen (#06643)
- ♦ Europäisches Komitee der Fachverbände der Hersteller von Verbrennungsmotoren (inactive)
- ♦ Europäisches Komitee zur Förderung Hochbegabter Kinder und Jugendlicher (#06664)
- ♦ Europäisches Komitee der Geratehersteller für Landwirtschaft und Garten (inactive)
- ♦ Europäisches Komitee der Grossanlagenbauer (no recent information)
- ♦ Europäisches Komitee für den Handel mit Stärkehaltigen Erzeugnissen und deren Verarbeitungserzeugnissen (inactive)
- ♦ Europäisches Komitee der Hersteller von Fahrzeugen, Geräten und Anlagen für den Brandschutz (#06659)
- ♦ Europäisches Komitee der Hersteller von Giessereimaschinen und Giessereiausrüstungen / see European Foundry Equipment Suppliers Association, The (#07353)
- ♦ Europäisches Komitee der Hersteller von Industrieöfen und Industrie-Wärmeanlagen / see The European Committee of Industrial Furnace, Heating and Metallurgical Equipment Associations (#06653)
- ♦ Europäisches Komitee der Hersteller von Kältetechnischen Erzeugnissen (inactive)
- ♦ Europäisches Komitee der Hersteller von Kompressoren, Vakuumpumpen und Druckluftwerkzeugen (#06657)
- ♦ Europäisches Komitee der Hersteller von Kunststoff und Gummimaschinen (#06656)
- ♦ Europäisches Komitee der Hersteller von Lufttechnischen und Trocknungs-Anlagen (inactive)
- ♦ Europäisches Komitee der Hersteller von Spannzeugen (no recent information)
- ♦ Europäisches Komitee der Herstellerverbände von Schweisszusätzen (inactive)
- ♦ Europäisches Komitee der Hersteller von Wäscherei- und Chemischreinigungsmaschinen (no recent information)
- ♦ Europäisches Komitee der Holzbearbeitungsmaschinenhersteller (#04152)
- ♦ Europäisches Komitee der Ingenieurfirmen (inactive)
- ♦ Europäisches Komitee für Jungbauern- und 4H-Clubs / see Rural Youth Europe (#19007)
- ♦ Europäisches Komitee für das Katholische Schulwesen (#04156)
- ♦ Europäisches Komitee des Kunst- und Gestaltenden Handwerks (inactive)
- ♦ Europäisches Komitee für Normung (#04162)
- ♦ Europäisches Komitee Ölhydraulik und Pneumatik / see European Fluid Power Committee (#07273)
- ♦ Europäisches Komitee zum Studium der Ursachen und Folgen des Zweiten Weltkrieges (inactive)
- ♦ Europäisches Komitee für Tenside und ihre organischen Zwischenstufen / see European Committee of Organic Surfactants and their Intermediates (#06660)
- ♦ Europäisches Komitee der Verbände der Landmaschinenhersteller / see European Agricultural Machinery Association (#05846)
- ♦ Europäisches Komitee der Waagenhersteller (#04151)
- ♦ Europäisches Kongress 'In der Begegnung Leben' (meeting series)
- ♦ Europäisches Konsortium für Ökologische Pflanzenzüchtung (#06761)
- ♦ Europäisches Koordinationszentrum für Sozialwissenschaftliche Forschung und Dokumentation (inactive)
- ♦ Europäisches Koordinierungsbüro der Internationalen Jugendorganisationen (inactive)
- ♦ Europäisches kulturabkommen (1954 treaty)

articles and prepositions
http://www.brill.com/yioo

Europäische Trainings
05761

♦ Europäisches Kulturzentrum (#06472)
♦ Europäisches Laboratorium für Molekularbiologie (#07813)
♦ Europäisches Management Forum / see World Economic Forum (#21367)
♦ Europäisches Mennonitisches Friedenskomitee (internationally oriented national body)
♦ Europäisches Migrationszentrum (internationally oriented national body)
♦ Europäisches Netz gegen Rassismus (#07862)
♦ Europäisches Netzwerk für das Alter (#05841)
♦ Europäisches Netzwerk für die Berufsanerkennung von Ärztinnen/Ärzten zuständigen Behörden (#07944)
♦ Europäisches Netzwerk für Fernlehre / see EDEN Digital Learning Europe (#05356)
♦ Europäisches Netzwerk der Fragiles X Vereine (unconfirmed)
♦ Europäisches Netzwerk der Gemeinschaften (#07881)
♦ Europäisches Netzwerk Grüner Senioren (#07915)
♦ Europäisches Netzwerk Kirche im Aufbruch (#07878)
♦ Europäisches Netzwerk von Myelom-Patientengruppen (inactive)
♦ Europäisches Netzwerk gegen Nationalismus, Rassismus, Faschismus und zur Unterstützung von Migranten und Flüchtlingen (#20511)
♦ Europäisches Netzwerk für Ökonomische Selbsthilfe und Lokale Entwicklung (#07895)
♦ Europäisches Netzwerk für Quarz (#08001)
♦ Europäisches Netzwerk der Schulgeographenverbände (#06054)
♦ Europäisches Netzwerk für Soziales Handeln (#08499)
♦ Europäisches Netzwerk für Sportausbildung (#08012)
♦ Europäisches Netzwerk für Textil / see European Textile Network (#08903)
♦ Europäisches niederlassungsabkommen (1955 treaty)
♦ Europäisches Observatorium für Gesundheitssysteme und Gesundheitspolitik (#08072)
♦ Europäisches Ombudsman Institut (#08085)
♦ Europäische Sonnenenergievereinigung / see EUROSOLAR – European Association for Renewable Energy (#09183)
♦ Europäisches Organisation für Umweltpolitik (inactive)
♦ Europäische sozialcharta (1961 treaty)
♦ Europäische sozialcharta – revidiert (1996 treaty)
♦ Europäische Sparkassenvereinigung (#08426)
♦ Europäisches Parlament (#08146)
♦ Europäisches Parlament – Fraktion der Europäischen Liberalen, Demokratischen und Reform Partei / see Renew Europe (#18840)
♦ Europäisches Parlament, Liberale und Demokratische Fraktion / see Renew Europe (#18840)
♦ Europäisches Patentamt (#08166)
♦ Europäische Sport Jungens Konferenz (inactive)
♦ Europäisches rahmenübereinkommen über die grenzüberschreitende zusammenarbeit zwischen gebietskörperschaften (1980 treaty)
♦ Europäisches Roma Rechtszentrum (#08401)
♦ Europäisches Satelittenkontrollzentrum (#08800)
♦ Europäisches Sekretariat der Freien Berufe / see European Council of Liberal Professions (#06828)
♦ Europäisches Sekretariat der Freien, Selbständigen und Sozialen Berufe / see European Council of Liberal Professions (#06828)
♦ Europäisches Sekretariat der Hersteller von leichten Metallverpackungen (inactive)
♦ Europäisches Soziales Netzwerk (#08505)
♦ Europäisches Städtenetzwerk Cities for Children / see Cities for Children (#03951)
♦ Europäisches Studienkomitee für Korrosion und Korrosionsschutz von Rohrleitungssystemen (#06670)
♦ Europäisches Studienkomitee für Korrosion und Korrosionsschutz von Rohrleitungssystemen – Trinkwasser, Abwasser, Gas und Öl / see European Committee for the study of corrosion and protection of pipes and pipeline systems (#06670)
♦ Europäisches Symposium zur Diagnostik der Beschwerdenvalidität (meeting series)
♦ Europäische Städte mit Interesse an Elektrofahrzeugen / see European Association of Cities Interested in the Use of Electric Vehicles (#05974)
♦ Europäische Stadt und Regionen Arbeiten an Neuen Verkehrslösungen / see POLIS (#18419)
♦ Europäisches Taubblinden Netzwerk (#06890)
♦ Europäisches Technologieinstitut / see European Institute of Innovation and Technology (#07562)
♦ Europäisches Textil-Netzwerk (#08903)
♦ Europäische Stiftung für Allergieforschung (internationally oriented national body)
♦ Europäische Stiftung für Berufsbildung (#08934)
♦ Europäische Stiftung für die Akkreditierung von Hotelschulen (#07341)
♦ Europäische Stiftung für Menschenrechte (inactive)
♦ Europäische Stiftung für Schlaganfallforschung (internationally oriented national body)
♦ Europäische Stiftung zur Verbesserung der Lebens- und Arbeitsbedingungen (#07348)
♦ Europäisches übereinkommen zur befreiung der von diplomatischen oder konsularischen vertretern errichteten urkunden von der legalisation (1968 treaty)
♦ Europäisches übereinkommen zur bekämpfung des terrorismus (1977 treaty)
♦ Europäisches übereinkommen betreffend auskünfte über ausländisches recht (1968 treaty)
♦ Europäisches übereinkommen zur einführung eines einheitlichen gesetzes über die schiedsgerichtsbarkeit (1966 treaty)
♦ Europäisches übereinkommen zur förderung der staatenübergreifenden freiwilligenarbeit für jugendliche (2000 treaty)
♦ Europäisches übereinkommen zur friedlichen beilegung von streitigkeiten (1957 treaty)
♦ Europäisches übereinkommen zum schutz des archäologischen erbes, revidiert (1992 treaty)
♦ Europäisches übereinkommen zum schutze des audio-visuellen erbes (2001 treaty)
♦ Europäisches übereinkommen zum schutz von haustieren (1987 treaty)
♦ Europäisches übereinkommen zum schutz von tieren in landwirtschaftlichen tierhaltungen (1976 treaty)
♦ Europäisches übereinkommen zum schutz der für versuche und andere wissenschaftliche zwecke verwendeten wirbeltiere (1986 treaty)
♦ Europäisches übereinkommen über den austausch von reagenzien zur blutgruppenbestimmung (1962 treaty)
♦ Europäisches übereinkommen über den austausch von reagenzien zur gewebstypisierung (1974 treaty)
♦ Europäisches übereinkommen über bestimmte internationale aspekte des konkurses (1990 treaty)
♦ Europäisches übereinkommen über die adoption von kindern (1967 treaty)
♦ Europäisches übereinkommen über die ahndung von zuwiderhandlungen im Strassenverkehr (1964 treaty)
♦ Europäisches übereinkommen über die akademische anerkennung von akademischen graden und hochschulzeugnissen (1959 treaty)
♦ Europäisches übereinkommen über die allgemeine gleichwertigkeit der studienzeiten an universitäten (1990 treaty)
♦ Europäisches übereinkommen über die anerkennung der rechtspersönlichkeit internationaler nichtstaatlicher organisationen (1986 treaty)
♦ Europäisches übereinkommen über die anerkennung und vollstreckung von entscheidungen über das sorgerecht für kinder und die wiederherstellung des sorgeverhältnisses (1980 treaty)
♦ Europäisches übereinkommen über die aufhebung des sichtsvermerkszwangs für flüchtlinge (1959 treaty)
♦ Europäisches übereinkommen über die au-pair-beschäftigung (1969 treaty)
♦ Europäisches übereinkommen über die ausübung von kinderrechten (1996 treaty)
♦ Europäisches übereinkommen über die berechnung von fristen (1974 treaty)
♦ Europäisches übereinkommen über die beschränkung der verwendung bestimmter detergentien in wasch- und reinigungsmitteln (1968 treaty)
♦ Europäisches übereinkommen über die entschädigung für opfer von gewalttaten (1983 treaty)
♦ Europäisches übereinkommen über die erlangung von auskünften und beweisen in verwaltungssachen im ausland (1978 treaty)
♦ Europäisches übereinkommen über die fortzahlung von stipendien an studierende im ausland (1969 treaty)
♦ Europäisches übereinkommen über die gemeinschaftsproduktion von kinofilmen (1992 treaty)
♦ Europäisches übereinkommen über die gleichwertigkeit der studienzeit an den universitäten (1956 treaty)
♦ Europäisches übereinkommen über die internationale beförderung von gefährlichen gütern auf binnenwasserstrassen (2000 treaty)
♦ Europäisches übereinkommen über die internationale geltung von strafurteilen (1970 treaty)
♦ Europäisches übereinkommen über die internationalen wirkungen der entziehung der fahrerlaubnis für kraftfahrzeuge (1976 treaty)
♦ Europäisches übereinkommen über die kontrolle des erwerbs und des besitzes von schusswaffen durch einzelpersonen (1978 treaty)
♦ Europäisches übereinkommen über die niederlassung von gesellschaften (1966 treaty)
♦ Europäisches übereinkommen über die obligatorische haftpflichtversicherung für kraftfahrzeuge (1959 treaty)
♦ Europäisches übereinkommen über die produkthaftpflicht bei personenschäden und tod (1977 treaty)
♦ Europäisches übereinkommen über die rechtshilfe in strafsachen (1959 treaty)
♦ Europäisches übereinkommen über die rechtsstellung der unehelichen kinder (1975 treaty)
♦ Europäisches übereinkommen über die rechtsstellung der wanderarbeitnehmer (1977 treaty)
♦ Europäisches übereinkommen über die regelung des personenverkehrs zwischen den mitgliedstaaten des Europarats (1957 treaty)
♦ Europäisches übereinkommen über die rückführung minderjähriger (1970 treaty)
♦ Europäisches übereinkommen über die staatsangehörigkeit (1997 treaty)
♦ Europäisches übereinkommen über die theoretische und praktische ausbildung von krankenschwestern und krankenpflegern (1967 treaty)
♦ Europäisches übereinkommen über die übermittlung von anträgen auf verfahrenshilfe (1977 treaty)
♦ Europäisches übereinkommen über die übertragung der strafverfolgung (1972 treaty)
♦ Europäisches übereinkommen über die überwachung bedingt verurteilter oder bedingt entlassener personen (1964 treaty)
♦ Europäisches übereinkommen über die unverjährbarkeit von verbrechen gegen die menschlichkeit und kriegsverbrechen (1974 treaty)
♦ Europäisches übereinkommen über die an verfahren vor den Europäischen gerichtshof für menschenrechte teilnehmenden personen (1996 treaty)
♦ Europäisches übereinkommen über die an verfahren vor der Europäischen kommission und dem Europäischen gerichtshof für menschenrechte teilnehmenden personen (1969 treaty)
♦ Europäisches übereinkommen über die zivilrechtliche haftung für durch kraftfahrzeuge verursachte schäden (1973 treaty)
♦ Europäisches übereinkommen über die zustellung von schriftstücken in verwaltungssachen im ausland (1977 treaty)
♦ Europäisches übereinkommen über fremdwährungsschulden (1967 treaty)
♦ Europäisches übereinkommen über gegenseitige hilfe auf dem gebiet der medizinischen spezialbehandlungen und der klimatischen einrichtungen (1962 treaty)
♦ Europäisches übereinkommen über das grenzüberschreitende fernsehen (1989 treaty)
♦ Europäisches übereinkommen über konsularische aufgaben (1967 treaty)
♦ Europäisches übereinkommen über den ort der zahlung von geldschulden (1972 treaty)
♦ Europäisches übereinkommen über rechtsschutz für dienstleistungen mit bedingtem zugang und der dienstleistungen zu bedingtem zugang (2001 treaty)
♦ Europäisches übereinkommen über den reiseverkehr von jugendlichen mit kollektivpass zwischen den mitgliedstaaten des Europarats (1961 treaty)
♦ Europäisches übereinkommen über den schutz von schlachttieren (1979 treaty)
♦ Europäisches übereinkommen über den schutz von tieren beim internationalen transport (1968 treaty)
♦ Europäisches übereinkommen über den sozialen schutz der landwirte (1974 treaty)
♦ Europäisches übereinkommen über staatenimmunität (1972 treaty)
♦ Europäisches übereinkommen über straftaten im zusammenhang mit kulturgut (1985 treaty)
♦ Europäisches übereinkommen über den übergang der verantwortung für flüchtlinge (1980 treaty)
♦ Europäisches übereinkommen zur verhütung von folter und unmenschlicher oder erniedrigender behandlung oder strafe (1987 treaty)
♦ Europäisches übereinkommen zur verhütung von rundfunksendungen, die von sendestellen ausserhalb der staatlichen hoheitsgebiete gesendet werden (1965 treaty)
♦ Europäisches Übersetzer-Kollegium (internationally oriented national body)
♦ Europäisches Übersetzer-Kollegium Nordrhein-Westfalen in Straelen / see Europäisches Übersetzer-Kollegium
♦ Europäisches Umweltbüro / see European Environmental Bureau (#06996)
♦ Europäisches Verband des Vereinigungen zum Erhalt des Industriellen und Technischen Erbes (#07053)
♦ Europäisches Verbindungskomitee Dienstleistungen von Allgemeinem Interesse (internationally oriented national body)
♦ Europäisches Verbindungskomitee des Speditions- und Lagereigewerbes im Gemeinsamen Markt / see CLECAT (#03993)
♦ Europäisches Volkshaus (internationally oriented national body)
♦ Europäisches Währungsinstitut (inactive)
♦ Europäisches Weltraum-Operationszentrum / see European Space Operations Centre (#08800)
♦ Europäisches Werkzeugkomitee (#04163)
♦ Europäisches WHO-Büro für Investitionen für Gesundheit und Entwicklung (see: #20945)
♦ Europäisches Zentrum / see European Centre for Social Welfare Policy and Research (#06500)
♦ Europäisches Zentrum für Anlagensicherheit / see European Process Safety Centre (#08279)
♦ Europäisches Zentrum für Arbeitnehmerfragen (#06505)
♦ Europäisches Zentrum für Ausbildung und Forschung auf dem Gebiet der Sozialen Wohlfahrt / see European Centre for Social Welfare Policy and Research (#06500)
♦ Europäisches Zentrum für Burgundische Studien (#05960)
♦ Europäisches Zentrum für Die Berufe in der Denkmalpflege (#06484)
♦ Europäisches Zentrum für die Förderung der Berufsbildung (#06474)
♦ Europäisches Zentrum für Föderalismus-Forschung (internationally oriented national body)
♦ Europäisches Zentrum fur Vermisste und Missbrauchte Kinder / see European Centre for Missing and Sexually Exploited Children
♦ Europäisches Zentrum für Mittelfristige Wettervorhersage (#06490)
♦ Europäisches Zentrum für Parlamentarische Wissenschaft und Dokumentation (#06495)
♦ Europäisches Zentrum für Presse- und Medienfreiheit (#06497)
♦ Europäisches Zentrum der Regionen (see: #07569)
♦ Europäisches Zentrum für Schadenersatz- und Versicherungsrecht (#06502)
♦ Europäisches Zentrum Venedig für die Berufe in der Denkmalpflege / see European Centre for Heritage Crafts and Professions (#06484)
♦ Europäisches Zentrum für Vermisste und Sexuell Ausgebeutete Kinder (internationally oriented national body)
♦ Europäisches Zentrum für Wohlfahrtspolitik und Sozialforschung (#06500)
♦ Europäische Teppichgemeinschaft / see European Carpet and Rug Association (#06452)
♦ Europäische Tierschutzunion (inactive)
♦ Europäische Tisch-Tennis Union (#08873)
♦ Europäische Trainings- und Forschungszentrum für Menschenrechte und Demokratie (internationally oriented national body)

- ♦ Europäische Transportarbeiter-Föderation (#08941)
- ♦ Europäische Triathlon Union (#08948)
- ♦ Europäische Tuben-Vereinigung / see european tube manufacturers association (#08953)
- ♦ Europäische Turnunion / see European Gymnastics (#07442)
- ♦ Europäische übereinkommen über den schutz von tieren beim internationalen transport – revidiert (2003 treaty)
- ♦ Europäische übereinkunft über die internationale patentklassifikation (inactive)
- ♦ Europäische übereinkunft über formerfordernisse bei patentanmeldungen (1953 treaty)
- ♦ Europäische Umweltagentur (#06995)
- ♦ Europäische Union (#08967)
- ♦ Europäische Union für das Agrément im Bauwesen (#20393)
- ♦ Europäische Union der Bierverbraucher (#06325)
- ♦ Europäische Union Christlich Demokratischer Arbeitnehmer (#08981)
- ♦ Europäische Union Christlicher Demokraten (inactive)
- ♦ Europäische Union der Film und Fernsehschaffenden (inactive)

♦ Europäische Union der Fliesenfachverbände (EUF) 05762

Union européenne des fédérations des entreprises de carrelage – Federation of European Tile-Fixers' Associations

Main Office c/o Swiss Tile Assoc, Keramikweg 3, 6252 Dagmersellen LU, Switzerland. E-mail: secretariat@euf-federation.com – info@euf-federation.com.
Registered Office address not obtained.
URL: https://www.euf-federation.com/

History 1958. Registration: Germany. **Aims** Promote dialogue, knowledge transfer and cooperation among member associations; support setting-up of new national associations; promote exchange of experience and initiation of projects; promote vocational training and further education; provide a platform for communication. **Structure** Legal seat in Saarbrücken (Germany). **Languages** English, French, German, Italian. **Staff** 5.00 FTE, paid. **Finance** Members' dues. **Activities** Events/meetings; projects/programmes. **Events** *Annual General Assembly* Stuttgart (Germany) 2022, *General assembly / Annual General Assembly* Castellón de la Plana (Spain) 2003.
Members in 12 countries:
Austria, Belgium, Czechia, France, Germany, Ireland, Italy, Luxembourg, Netherlands, Spain, Switzerland, UK.
[2021/XD8022/**D**]

- ♦ Europäische Union der Freien und Privaten Wohnungsunternehmen / see Build Europe (#03350)
- ♦ Europäische Union der Freien Wohnungsunternehmen / see Build Europe (#03350)
- ♦ Europäische Union der Gesellschaften der Wissenschaftsjournalisten (#09017)
- ♦ Europäische Union des Gross- und Aussenhandels mit Milcherzeugnissen / see European Association of Dairy Trade (#06003)
- ♦ Europäische Union des Grosshandels mit Eiern, Eiprodukten, Geflügel und Wild (#09021)
- ♦ Europäische Union des Handwerks und der Klein- und Mittelbetriebe / see SMEunited (#19327)
- ♦ Europäische Union des Hopfenhandels (inactive)
- ♦ Europäische Union Jüdischer Studenten / see European Union of Jewish Students (#08997)
- ♦ Europäische Union des Kartoffelgrosshandels / see European Potato Trade Association (#08257)
- ♦ Europäische Union des Kartoffelshandels (#08257)
- ♦ Europäische Union der Kartoffelverarbeitenden Industrien / see EUPPA – European Potato Processors' Association (#05592)
- ♦ Europäische Union für Lichtspiele (inactive)
- ♦ Europäische Union gegen den Missbrauch der Tiere (inactive)
- ♦ Europäische Union der Musiker (inactive)
- ♦ Europäische Union der Musikwettbewerbe für die Jugend (#09003)
- ♦ Europäische Union der Nationalen Musikwettbewerbe für die Jugend / see European Union of Music Competitions for Youth (#09003)
- ♦ Europäische Union der nationalen Vereinigungen der Wasserversorger / see European Federation of National Associations of Water and Waste Water Services (#07170)
- ♦ Europäische Union des Obst- und Gemüse- Gross- und Aussenhandels (inactive)
- ♦ Europäische Union der Pianofachverbände / see Union of European Piano Builders' Associations (#20391)
- ♦ Europäische Union Praktischer Tierärzte (#20405)
- ♦ Europäische Union der Privathochschulen (#09009)
- ♦ Europäische Union der Privatklinieken (#20397)
- ♦ Europäische Union der Rechtspfleger (#09012)
- ♦ Europäische Union der Richter in Handelssachen (#08998)
- ♦ Europäische Union der Sozialen Sicherung und Versicherungsmedizin (#08995)
- ♦ Europäische Union der Tapezierer, Dekorateure und Sattler (no recent information)
- ♦ Europäische Union der Unabhängigen Gewerkschaften (#06705)
- ♦ Europäische Union der Unabhängigen Schmierstoffverbände / see Union Européenne de l'Industrie des Lubrifiants (#20398)
- ♦ Europäische Union der Verbände der Gemindebediensteten (inactive)
- ♦ Europäische Union der Vereinigungen der Medizinalreferenten (inactive)
- ♦ Europäische Union der Zahnärzte (inactive)
- ♦ Europäische Verband von Polizistinnen (#07970)
- ♦ Europäische Verband für Schweisstechnik (#07233)
- ♦ Europäische vereinbarung über den austausch von programmen mit fernsehfilmen (1958 treaty)
- ♦ Europäische Vereinigung der Allgemeinärzte / see European Union of General Practitioners / Family Physicians (#08993)
- ♦ Europäische Vereinigung für Allgemeine Verzinkung (#07383)
- ♦ Europäische Vereinigung Älterer Studierender an den Universitäten (#07181)
- ♦ Europäische Vereinigung der Angehörigen Psychisch Kranker / see European Federation of Associations of Families of People with Mental Illness (#07051)
- ♦ Europäische Vereinigung der Ärzteverbände der besonderen Therapierichtungen (#06816)
- ♦ Europäische Vereinigung der Augenärzte (inactive)
- ♦ Europäische Vereinigung der Automaten-Verbände / see European Gaming and Amusement Federation (#07374)
- ♦ Europäische Vereinigung der Berufsfeuerwehroffiziere (no recent information)
- ♦ Europäische Vereinigung für Bestattungsdienste (#07131)
- ♦ Europäische Vereinigung Bildender Künstler aus Eifel und Ardennen (#07415)
- ♦ Europäische Vereinigung der Binnenschiffer (internationally oriented national body)
- ♦ Europäische Vereinigung der Braunviehzüchter (#06405)
- ♦ Europäische Vereinigung des Brennstoffhandels (inactive)
- ♦ Europäische Vereinigung der Briefumschlagfabrikanten (#09578)
- ♦ Europäische Vereinigung für Chemische und Molekulare Wissenschaften / see European Chemical Society (#06524)
- ♦ Europäische Vereinigung der Computer Hersteller / see Ecma International (#05288)
- ♦ Europäische Vereinigung der Datenbanken in der Aus- und Weiterbildung (inactive)
- ♦ Europäische Vereinigung für Dermato-Onkologie (#06008)
- ♦ Europäische Vereinigung für die Aluminium-Veredlung (#06242)
- ♦ Europäische Vereinigung gegen die Schädlichen Auswirkungen des Luftverkehrs (#20395)
- ♦ Europäische Vereinigung für Eifel und Ardennen (#07414)
- ♦ Europäische Vereinigung für Einkauf (inactive)
- ♦ Europäische Vereinigung der Eisenbahner (#02558)
- ♦ Europäische Vereinigung der Elektrokeramik-Industrie (inactive)
- ♦ Europäische Vereinigung der Erdgaswirtschaft / see Eurogas (#05682)
- ♦ Europäische Vereinigung für Erneuerbare Energien (#09183)
- ♦ Europäische Vereinigung der Fachärzte / see European Union of Medical Specialists (#09001)
- ♦ Europäische Vereinigung der Factoring-Verbände (no recent information)
- ♦ Europäische Vereinigung der Fleckviehzüchter (#08487)
- ♦ Europäische Vereinigung für Fleisch (inactive)
- ♦ Europäische Vereinigung für Fleischgrosshandel (inactive)
- ♦ Europäische Vereinigung der Fördertechnik / see European Materials Handling Federation (#07752)
- ♦ Europäische Vereinigung zur Förderung der Experimentellen Archäologie (#05926)
- ♦ Europäische Vereinigung für Geldtransporte und- Begleitung (#08458)
- ♦ Europäische Vereinigung Gemeindlicher Waldbesitzervertretungen (#07157)

♦ Europäische Vereinigung der Gemeinschaften zur Zertifizierung von Entsorgungsfachbetrieben (EVGE) 05763

European Federation of Associations for Certification of Specialised Waste Management Companies

Contact c/o bvse-Entsorgergemeinschaft, Fränkische Strasse 2, 53229 Bonn, Germany. T. +492289884931. Fax +49228884949. E-mail: baumann@egrw.de.
URL: http://evge.eu/

History 29 Oct 2004, Cologne (Germany). **Structure** Board of Directors.
Members Certifying agencies in (5) countries:
Austria, Czechia, Germany, Hungary, Slovakia.
[2019/XJ8134/**D**]

- ♦ Europäische Vereinigung der Genossenschaftsbanken (#05990)
- ♦ Europäische Vereinigung des Getreide-, Futter- und Düngemittelhandels / see Committee of the Trade in Cereals, Oilseeds, Pulses, Olive Oil, Oils and Fats, Animal Feed and Agrosupply of the EU (#04289)
- ♦ Europäische Vereinigung der Gewählten von Bergregionen (#06021)
- ♦ Europäische Vereinigung der Graveure und Flexografen (#02572)
- ♦ Europäische Vereinigung des Grosshandels für Papier, Pappe und Verpackung / see European Paper Merchants Association (#08138)
- ♦ Europäische Vereinigung für Grün und Blumen (#02570)
- ♦ Europäische Vereinigung für Hafeninformatik (inactive)
- ♦ Europäische Vereinigung für den Handel mit Juteprodukten (#06256)
- ♦ Europäische Vereinigung des Handels mit Büromöbeln, -Maschinen und -Bedarf (inactive)
- ♦ Europäische Vereinigung des Handels mit Trockenfrüchten, Konserven, Gewürzen, Honig und verwandten Waren / see European Federation of the Trade in Dried Fruit, Edible Nuts, Processed Fruit and Vegetables, Processed Fishery Products, Spices, Honey and Similar Foodstuffs (#07229)
- ♦ Europäische Vereinigung der Hersteller von Aluminium-Aerosoldosen / see International Organization of Aluminium Aerosol Container Manufacturers (#14437)
- ♦ Europäische Vereinigung der Hersteller von chirurgischem Nahtmaterial (#06243)
- ♦ Europäische Vereinigung der Hersteller Feuerfester Erzeugnisse (#08339)
- ♦ Europäische Vereinigung der Hersteller von Heizkörpern (inactive)
- ♦ Europäische Vereinigung der Hersteller Mitteldichter Faserplatten (inactive)
- ♦ Europäische Vereinigung von Herstellern und Distributeuren von Persönlichen Schutzausrüstungen (#08418)
- ♦ Europäische Vereinigung von Herstellern und Vertriebsgesellschaften biologischer Arzneimittel (no recent information)
- ♦ Europäische Vereinigung der Hersteller von Schul- und Büroschreibwaren (inactive)
- ♦ Europäische Vereinigung der Hersteller von Wasserzählern / see Association européenne de fabricants de compteurs d'eau et d'énergie thermique (#02567)
- ♦ Europäische Vereinigung der Hersteller von Wasserzählern und Wärmezählern (#02567)
- ♦ Europäische Vereinigung für Herz- und Gefässchirurgie / see European Society for Cardiovascular and Endovascular Surgery (#08537)
- ♦ Europäische Vereinigung des Holzbaus (#20164)
- ♦ Europäische Vereinigung der Holzleimbau-Industrie (no recent information)
- ♦ Europäische Vereinigung der Importeure von Büro- und Informationstechnik (inactive)
- ♦ Europäische Vereinigung der Industrie Flexibler Verpackung (inactive)
- ♦ Europäische Vereinigung der Institutionen für die Neuordnung des Ländlichen Raumes (#06198)
- ♦ Europäische Vereinigung für Interregionale Zusammenarbeit (no recent information)
- ♦ Europäische Vereinigung Junger Krankenhausverwalter / see European Medical Students' Association (#07764)
- ♦ Europäische Vereinigung von Juristinnen und Juristen für Demokratie und Menschenrechte in der Welt (#06105)
- ♦ Europäische Vereinigung für Kardiovaskuläre und Endovaskuläre Chirurgie (#08537)
- ♦ Europäische Vereinigung der Kartoffelverarbeitenden Industrien / see EUPPA – European Potato Processors' Association (#05592)
- ♦ Europäische Vereinigung der Kartonagenindustrie (inactive)
- ♦ Europäische Vereinigung der Kongressstädte (inactive)
- ♦ Europäische Vereinigung der Krankenhaus Apotheker (#06074)
- ♦ Europäische Vereinigung der Krankenhausdirektoren (#06073)
- ♦ Europäische Vereinigung der Krankenhausverwaltungsleiter / see European Association of Hospital Managers (#06073)
- ♦ Europäische Vereinigung für Krebsforschung (#05962)
- ♦ Europäische Vereinigung der Kühlhausunternehmen (inactive)
- ♦ Europäische Vereinigung für Leberforschung (#06233)
- ♦ Europäische Vereinigung der Leitenden Krankenhausärzte (#02577)
- ♦ Europäische Vereinigung der Leiter und Träger von Einrichtungen der Langzeitpflege (inactive)
- ♦ Europäische Vereinigung von Liebhaberorchestern (inactive)
- ♦ Europäische Vereinigung für das Management der Industrieforschung (#07531)
- ♦ Europäische Vereinigung des Milcheinzelhandel-Verbände (inactive)
- ♦ Europäische Vereinigung der Mittel-und Grossbetriebe des Einzelhandels (inactive)
- ♦ Europäische Vereinigung der Nationalen Baustoffhändler-Verbände (#06128)
- ♦ Europäische Vereinigung der Papiersackfabrikanten / see EUROSAC (#09177)
- ♦ Europäische Vereinigung der Patentrechtsanwälte (#08165)
- ♦ Europäische Vereinigung für Perinatale Medizin (#06148)
- ♦ Europäische Vereinigung für Personalführung / see European Association for People Management (#06146)
- ♦ Europäische Vereinigung für Pflanzliches Protein (#09047)
- ♦ Europäische Vereinigung für Pharmazeutische Marktforschung (#08196)
- ♦ Europäische Vereinigung für Physikalische Medizin und Funktionelle Neuerziehung / see European Society of Physical and Rehabilitation Medicine (#08706)
- ♦ Europäische Vereinigung der Podologen (inactive)
- ♦ Europäische Vereinigung der Privaten Luftverkehrs-Unternehmen (inactive)
- ♦ Europäische Vereinigung für Public Relations (#09011)
- ♦ Europäische Vereinigung für Public Relations – Internationale Dienstleistungs-Organisation / see European Union of Public Relations (#09011)
- ♦ Europäische Vereinigung für Pulverförmiges Aluminium (inactive)
- ♦ Europäische Vereinigung für Pulvermetallurgie / see European Powder Metallurgy Association (#08260)
- ♦ Europäische Vereinigung der Pumpenhersteller (#06182)
- ♦ Europäische Vereinigung der Raumplanerfakultregplan (#02542)
- ♦ Europäische Vereinigung der Rechtsfakultäten (#07656)
- ♦ Europäische Vereinigung der Restauratorenverbände / see European Confederation of Conservator-Restorers' Organisations (#06701)
- ♦ Europäische Vereinigung der Richter (#06100)
- ♦ Europäische Vereinigung der Rösterverbände (inactive)
- ♦ Europäische Vereinigung für Schiffahrts-Inforaltik (inactive)

- ♦ Europäische Vereinigung der Schleifmittel-Hersteller / see Federation of European Producers of Abrasives (#09532)
- ♦ Europäische Vereinigung Schmalweberei, Flechterei, und Elastische Gewebe (inactive)
- ♦ Europäische Vereinigung der Sonderabfallwirtschaft (inactive)
- ♦ Europäische Vereinigung für Soziale Medizin (no recent information)
- ♦ Europäische Vereinigung des Spielwaren-Detailhandels (inactive)
- ♦ Europäische Vereinigung der Sporthändlerverbände / see Sporting Goods Industry Data Harmonization Organization (#19924)
- ♦ Europäische Vereinigung für Sportpsychologie (#07218)
- ♦ Europäische Vereinigung der Staatlichen Lotterien und Totogesellschaften (#08833)
- ♦ Europäische Vereinigung der Steinzeugröhrenindustrie / see FEUGRES – European Clay Pipe Association (#09741)
- ♦ Europäische Vereinigung der Tabakwaren-Einzelhändlersverbände / see European Confederation of Tobacco Retailers (#06725)
- ♦ Europäische Vereinigung von Tageszeitungen in Minderheiten- und Regionalsprachen (#06002)
- ♦ Europäische Vereinigung für Thanatologie (inactive)
- ♦ Europäische Vereinigung für Thermographie (inactive)
- ♦ Europäische Vereinigung für Tiergesundheit und Gesundheitliche Sicherheit (#09581)
- ♦ Europäische Vereinigung für Tierproduktion (#07046)
- ♦ Europäische Vereinigung Tradizioneller Beherbergungsbetriebe / see Historic Hotels of Europe (#10930)
- ♦ Europäische Vereinigung Türkischer Akademiker (inactive)
- ♦ Europäische Vereinigung der Umweltwissenschaftlichen Berufe (no recent information)
- ♦ Europäische Vereinigung der Unternehmungen für Elektrische Anlagen / see EuropeOn (#09166)
- ♦ Europäische Vereinigung der Verbände Beratender Organisatoren (#07159)
- ♦ Europäische Vereinigung der Verbände von Finanzierungsbanken (#07121)
- ♦ Europäische Vereinigung der Verbände der Isolierunternehmungen (#09582)
- ♦ Europäische Vereinigung der Verbände kleiner und mittlerer Unternehmen / see European Entrepreneurs CEA-PME (#06994)
- ♦ Europäische Vereinigung der Verbände von Leasing-Gesellschaften (#07111)
- ♦ Europäische Vereinigung der Verbände der Reformhäuser (no recent information)
- ♦ Europäische Vereinigung der Verbände des Schuheinzelhandels (inactive)
- ♦ Europäische Vereinigung der Verbände der Überseeverdrangten und Ostvertriebenen (inactive)
- ♦ Europäische Vereinigung der Verbände der Unterhaltungsautomatenwirtschaft / see European Gaming and Amusement Federation (#07374)
- ♦ Europäische Vereinigung der Verkehrsunfallopfer Federazione Europea delle Vittime della Strada (#07207)
- ♦ Europäische Vereinigung für Verpackung und Umwelt (#08110)
- ♦ Europäische Vereinigung der Veterinäranatomen (#06268)
- ♦ Europäische Vereinigung für Wasseraufbereitung / see European Water and Wastewater Industry Association (#09087)
- ♦ Europäische Vereinigung für Wasserwirtschaft (#09080)
- ♦ Europäische Vereinigung der Werbeagenturen / see European Association of Communications Agencies (#05983)
- ♦ Europäische Vereinigung für Wirtschaftliche und Soziale Entwicklung (inactive)
- ♦ Europäische Verein für Unfallforschung und Unfall Analyse (#05925)
- ♦ Europäische Verkehrswissenschaftliche Gesellschaft (inactive)
- ♦ Europäische Verleger – Vereinigung für Recht und Wirtschaft (inactive)
- ♦ Europäische Vermikulit Gesellschaft (no recent information)
- ♦ Europäische Volkspartei (#08185)
- ♦ Europäische Volkspartei – Föderation der Christlich-Demokratischen Parteien der Europäischen Gemeinschaft / see European People's Party (#08185)
- ♦ Europäische Wandervereinigung (#08328)
- ♦ Europäische Warenbörse (#06674)
- ♦ Europäische Weiterbildungszentrum / see European Centre for Executive Development (#06479)
- ♦ Europäische Wirtschaftliche Interessenvereinigung (#06960)
- ♦ Europäische Wirtschaftshochschule / see ESCP Europe Business School (#05536)
- ♦ Europäische Wirtschaftskammer für Handel, Gewerbe und Industrie (#06959)
- ♦ Europäische Wirtschaftsvereinigung der Eisen- und Stahlindustrie / see European Steel Association (#08835)
- ♦ Europäische Wissenschaftsstiftung (#08441)
- ♦ Europäische Zentralbank (#06466)
- ♦ Europäische Zentralstelle für Kirchliche Hilfsaktionen (inactive)
- ♦ Europäische Zentrum für Minderheitenfragen (internationally oriented national body)
- ♦ Europäiska Föreningen för Vertebratpaleontologer (#06266)
- ♦ Europäisk Kromosom 11 Netvärk (#06547)
- ♦ Europäisk Kromosom 11q Netvärk / see European Chromosome 11 Network (#06547)
- ♦ Európai Szamvevoszék (#06854)
- ♦ Európai Tanacs (#06801)
- ♦ Európai Technológiai Intézet / see European Institute of Innovation and Technology (#07562)
- ♦ Európai Unió (#08967)
- ♦ as Európai Unió Bírósaganak (#04938)
- ♦ Európai Vegyianyag-ügynökség (#06523)
- ♦ Europa Klub Langer Menschen / see European Federation of Tall People (#07223)
- ♦ Europa Klubo (internationally oriented national body)
- ♦ Europa-Kommissionen (#06633)
- ♦ Europako Nekazarien Kordinakundea / see European Coordination Via Campesina (#06795)
- ♦ Europako Rromano Cacipasko Centro (#08401)
- ♦ EUROPALIA – Foundation Europalia International (internationally oriented national body)
- ♦ EUROPALUB – European Lubricants Statistics (inactive)
- ♦ EUROPAMA – European Packaging Machinery Association (no recent information)
- ♦ **EUR-OPA Major Hazards Agreement** Open Partial Agreement on the Prevention of, Protection against and Organization of Relief in Major Natural and Technological Disasters (#17762)
- ♦ Europamedborgamas Aktionsservice / see European Citizen Action Service (#06555)
- ♦ Europa Medica (inactive)

♦ Europa Medica 05764

Registered Office Av des Arts 39/1, 1040 Brussels, Belgium. T. +3222090201. Fax +3227375334.
URL: http://www.europamedica.org/

History Founded 1994. Also known as *Europa Medica GEIE-EESV*. A grouping of the type *European Economic Interest Grouping (EEIG, #06960)*. **Aims** Serve as a platform for the exchange of information within the medical insurance sector; represent and defend the mutual interest within the medical insurance sector; provide assistance for medical professionals settling, working or travelling within Europe. **Structure** General Assembly (annual); Management Committee. **Languages** English, French, Spanish. **Staff** None. **Finance** Members'dues; subscriptions. **Activities** Events/meetings.
Members Companies (7) in 6 countries:
Belgium, France, Netherlands, Spain, Sweden, UK. [2014.10.16/XF7125/F]

- ♦ Europa Medica GEIE-EESV / see Europa Medica (#05764)
- ♦ Europamuseum (#16907)

♦ EUROPAN 05765

Pres 16 bis rue François Arrago, 93100 Montreuil, France. T. +33962529598. E-mail: contact@europan-europe.eu.
URL: http://www.europan-europe.eu/

History 1988. Founded as a European programme of ideas competitions, followed by implementations, and open to young architects, urban planners and landscapers throughout Europe. **Aims** Provide a means of expressing new ideas in the field of *architecture, urbanism and landscape* through common themes to European countries; promote talented young architects, urban planners, landscapers by implementing significant architectural/urban/landscape works; provoke debate between professional networks and personalities in the fields of architecture, urbanism and landscape in the context of European-level events. **Structure** General Assembly; Council; National Secretariats. **Languages** English, French. **Staff** 3.00 FTE, paid. **Finance** Sources: members' dues. **Activities** Awards/prizes/competitions; events/meetings. Active in: Austria, Belgium, Croatia, Finland, France, Germany, Italy, Netherlands, Norway, Poland, Spain, Sweden, Switzerland. **Events** *E15/E16 Inter-sessions Forum* Montreuil (France) 2021, *16 Cities and Juries Forum* San Sebastian (Spain) 2021, *E15 Cities and Juries forum* Innsbruck (Austria) 2019, *E14/E15 Inter-sessions Forum* Brussels (Belgium) 2018, *E14 Cities and Juries Forum* Helsinki (Finland) 2017. **Publications** *Europan Results* (every 2 years). Implementation catalogues. [2022.05.04/XF2765/F]

♦ European Committee for Conservation of Bryophytes (ECCB) 05766

Chair Cuillin Views, 15 Earlish, Portree, IV51 9XL, UK.
URL: http://eccbbryo.nhmus.hu/

History 1990, Uppsala (Sweden), at 1st conference. **Aims** Provide a link between bryologists involved in conservation of bryophytes in different countries; identify priorities for bryophyte conservation throughout Europe and Macaronesia; increase publicity about threatened bryophytes; support relevant conservation authorities and those involved in the conservation of the flora and natural resources to take action to conserve bryophytes and encourage the study of bryophytes, particularly in areas which are poorly known. **Structure** Board; Chair; Vice-Chair; Secretary; Regional Coordinators. **Languages** English. **Staff** None. **Activities** Events/meetings; networking/liaising; awareness raising; knowledge management/information dissemination. **Events** *Conference* Budva (Montenegro) 2016, *Conference* Budapest (Hungary) 2012, *Conference* Cluj-Napoca (Romania) 2007, *Conference* Bispgården (Sweden) 2005, *Conference* Valencia (Spain) 2004. **Publications** *Red Data Book of European Bryophytes* (1995).
Members Full in 48 countries and territories:
Albania, Algeria, Andorra, Austria, Belarus, Belgium, Bosnia-Herzegovina, Bulgaria, Croatia, Cyprus, Czechia, Denmark, Estonia, Faeroe Is, Finland, France, Germany, Gibraltar, Greece, Holy See, Hungary, Iceland, Ireland, Italy, Latvia, Liechtenstein, Lithuania, Luxembourg, Malta, Moldova, Monaco, Montenegro, Netherlands, North Macedonia, Norway, Poland, Romania, Russia, San Marino, Serbia, Slovakia, Slovenia, Spain, Sweden, Switzerland, Türkiye, UK, Ukraine.
IGO Relations No formal contacts. **NGO Relations** No formal contacts. [2017.06.01/XM4753/D]

- ♦ Europanemzet Közzösségri Pàrt (internationally oriented national body)

♦ Europa Nostra 05767

SG Lange Voorhout 35, 2514 EC The Hague, Netherlands. E-mail: sqm@europanostra.org – info@europanostra.org.
Brussels Office Rue de Trèves 45, 1040 Brussels, Belgium. E-mail: bxl@europanostra.org.
URL: http://www.europanostra.org/

History 30 Nov 1963, Paris (France). Merged with the former *International Castles Institute (IBI, inactive)*, 1991. Former names and other names: *Europa Nostra – International Federation of Non-Governmental Associations for the Protection of Europe's Cultural and Natural Heritage* – former; *Europa Nostra – Fédération internationale des associations pour la sauvegarde du patrimoine culturel et naturel de l'Europe* – former; *Europa Nostra – Pan-European Non-Governmental Organization for the Protection of Europe's Architectural and Natural Heritage* – former; *Europa Nostra – Organisation pan-européenne non-gouvernmentale pour la sauvegarde du patrimoine architectural et naturel de l'Europe* – former; *Europa Nostra – Pan-European Federation of Non-Governmental Organizations for the Protection of Europe's Architectural and Natural Heritage* – former; *Europa Nostra – Fédération pan-européenne d'organisations non-gouvernementales pour la sauvegarde du patrimoine architectural et naturel de l'Europe* – former; *Europa Nostra – Pan-European Federation for Heritage* – former; *Europa Nostra – Fédération pan-européenne du patrimoine culturel* – former; *Europa Nostra – The Voice of Cultural Heritage in Europe* – full title; *La Voix du patrimoine culturel* – full title. Registration: EU Transparency Register, No/ID: 464201240893-11, Start date: 12 Jan 2020; Netherlands. **Aims** Put heritage and its benefits in the mainstream of public consciousness and illustrate its importance as a building block of European identity; make heritage a priority for public policies both at European and national levels; promote, at the European level, high standards of quality in the fields of heritage conservation, architecture, urban and rural planning; advocate a balanced and sustainable development of urban and rural, built and natural environment. **Structure** General Assembly (annual); Council; Board. **Languages** English, French. **Staff** 9.00 FTE, paid. **Finance** Sources: donations; grants; members' dues. **Activities** Advocacy/lobbying/activism; awards/prizes/competitions; events/meetings; research/documentation. **Events** *European Cultural Heritage Summit* Paris (France) 2019, *European Heritage Congress* Turku (Finland) 2017, *Annual Congress and General Assembly* Madrid (Spain) 2016, *Annual Congress and General Assembly* Oslo (Norway) 2015, *Annual Congress and General Assembly / General Assembly and Forum* Vienna (Austria) 2014. **Publications** *Scientific Bulletin* (annual); *European Cultural Heritage Review* (annual); *Europa Nostra Newsletter* (irregular) – electronic. Annual Report; annual awards publication.
Members Heritage NGOs (225) in 38 countries:
Albania, Andorra, Austria, Belgium, Bosnia-Herzegovina, Bulgaria, Croatia, Cyprus, Czechia, Denmark, Estonia, Finland, France, Germany, Greece, Hungary, Ireland, Italy, Latvia, Lithuania, Malta, Montenegro, Netherlands, North Macedonia, Norway, Poland, Portugal, Romania, Russia, Serbia, Slovakia, Slovenia, Spain, Sweden, Switzerland, Türkiye, UK, Ukraine.
Included in the above, 12 organizations listed in this Yearbook:
Alliance de Villes Euro-méditerranéennes de Culture (AVEC, #00726); Centre d'études, de recherche et d'histoire Compostellanes; Centre international du vitrail (CIV); European Association Architectural Heritage Restoration Firms (#05942); European Federation of Associations of Industrial and Technical Heritage (EFAITH, #07053); European Landowners' Organization (ELO, #07639); European Maritime Heritage (EMH, #07741); FEDECRAIL – European Federation of Museum and Tourist Railways (#09284); International Centre of the Roerichs (ICR); International Forum of Towns and Villages in Graz (ISG); PERSPECTIV – Association of Historic Theatres in Europe (PERSPECTIV, #18335); Rurality – Environment – Development (RED, #19003).
Associate Members (160) in 28 countries:
Albania, Belgium, Canada, Cyprus, Czechia, Denmark, Estonia, Finland, France, Germany, Greece, Hungary, Ireland, Italy, Lebanon, Luxembourg, Netherlands, Norway, Poland, Portugal, Russia, Slovakia, Spain, Sweden, Switzerland, Türkiye, UK, USA.
Individuals (1,430) in 43 countries:
Albania, Australia, Austria, Belgium, Brazil, Bulgaria, Canada, Croatia, Cyprus, Czechia, Denmark, Estonia, Finland, France, Georgia, Germany, Greece, Hungary, Ireland, Italy, Korea Rep, Latvia, Lithuania, Luxembourg, Malta, Moldova, Monaco, Montenegro, Netherlands, Norway, Poland, Portugal, Romania, Serbia, Slovakia, Slovenia, South Africa, Spain, Switzerland, Türkiye, UK, Ukraine, USA.
Consultative Status Consultative status granted from: *UNESCO (#20322)* (Consultative Status); *Council of Europe (CE, #04881)* (Participatory Status). **NGO Relations** Member of (5): *Africa Foundation*; *A Soul for Europe (ASF, #19697)*; *European Heritage Alliance 3.3 (#07477)*; *European Tourism Manifesto (#08921)*; *Permanent Forum of European Civil Society (#18322)*. Partner of (1): *European Federation of Fortified Sites (EFFORTS, #07127)*. Associate member of: *International National Trusts Organisation (INTO, #14214)*. [2020.03.03/XD0538/y/D]

- ♦ Europa Nostra – Fédération internationale des associations pour la sauvegarde du patrimoine culturel et naturel de l'Europe / see Europa Nostra (#05767)
- ♦ Europa Nostra – Fédération pan-européenne d'organisations non-gouvernementales pour la sauvegarde du patrimoine architectural et naturel de l'Europe / see Europa Nostra (#05767)
- ♦ Europa Nostra – Fédération pan-européenne du patrimoine culturel / see Europa Nostra (#05767)
- ♦ Europa Nostra – International Federation of Non-Governmental Associations for the Protection of Europe's Cultural and Natural Heritage / see Europa Nostra (#05767)
- ♦ Europa Nostra – Organisation pan-européenne non-gouvernmentale pour la sauvegarde du patrimoine architectural et naturel de l'Europe / see Europa Nostra (#05767)
- ♦ Europa Nostra – Pan-European Federation for Heritage / see Europa Nostra (#05767)
- ♦ Europa Nostra – Pan-European Federation of Non-Governmental Organizations for the Protection of Europe's Architectural and Natural Heritage / see Europa Nostra (#05767)
- ♦ Europa Nostra – Pan-European Non-Governmental Organization for the Protection of Europe's Architectural and Natural Heritage / see Europa Nostra (#05767)
- ♦ Europa Nostra – The Voice of Cultural Heritage in Europe / see Europa Nostra (#05767)

Europaparlamentet
05767

alphabetic sequence excludes
For the complete listing, see Yearbook Online at

♦ Europaparlamentet (#08146)
♦ Europa-Parlamentet (#08146)
♦ Europa-Parlamentet – Det Europaeiske Liberale og Demokratiske Partis Gruppe / see Renew Europe (#18840)
♦ Europa-Parlamentet – Europeiska Liberale Demokratiska och Reformististka Partigruppen / see Renew Europe (#18840)
♦ Europa-Parlamentet, Liberale og Demokratiske Gruppe / see Renew Europe (#18840)
♦ Europa plurilingue (internationally oriented national body)
♦ Europarat (#04881)
♦ Europarat der Karibik / see The Caribbean Council (#03482)

♦ EUROPARC Federation 05768

Fédération EUROPARC – Föderation EUROPARC

Main Office Waffnergasse 6, 93047 Regensburg, Germany. T. +4994159935980. Fax +4994159935989. E-mail: europarc@europarc.org.
Brussels Office Blvd L Schmidt 64, 1040 Brussels, Belgium. T. +3227390315. Fax +3227329499.
URL: http://www.europarc.org/

History 1973. Former names and other names: *Federation of Nature and National Parks of Europe* – former; *Fédération des parcs naturels et nationaux d'Europe* – former; *Föderation der Natur- und Nationalparke Europas* – former. Registration: No/ID: 0887.932.258, Start date: 1 Jan 2007, Belgium; EU Transparency Register, No/ID: 01380772294-53, Start date: 21 Sep 2009. **Aims** Protect Europe's variety of *wildlife*, habitats and *landscape*; assist European protected areas to achieve common aims across national frontiers; stimulate exchange of experience and ideas on the management of protected areas so as to improve their organization and function; promote Europe's protected natural and cultural *heritage* to the public, authorities and organizations. **Structure** General Assembly (annual, at Conference); Council; Directorate; Offices in:Brussels (Belgium), Regensburg (Germany); National and Regional Sections (7). **Languages** English, French, German. **Staff** 10.00 FTE, paid. **Finance** Sources: members' dues; revenue from activities/projects. **Activities** Awards/prizes/competitions; events/meetings; guidance/assistance/consulting; networking/liaising; projects/programmes; publishing activities. **Events** *Annual Conference* 2021, *General Assembly* 2021, *Annual Conference* Regensburg (Germany) 2020, *General Assembly* Regensburg (Germany) 2020, *Annual Conference and General Assembly* Jurmala (Latvia) 2019. **Publications** *Protected Areas In-Sight* (12 a year); *EUROPARC Newsletter* (2 a year); *Europäisches Bulletin – Natur- und Nationalparke – European Bulletin – Nature and National Parks – Bulletin européen – Parcs naturels and nationaux* (2 a year) in English, French, German. Reports; brochures; conference proceedings.

Members Protected areas; state or regional authorities; nature conservation NGOs. Members (about 400) in 38 countries:
Albania, Austria, Belarus, Belgium, Bosnia-Herzegovina, Bulgaria, Croatia, Czechia, Denmark, Estonia, Finland, France, Georgia, Germany, Greece, Hungary, Iceland, Ireland, Israel, Italy, Latvia, Lithuania, Luxembourg, Malta, Montenegro, Netherlands, Norway, Poland, Portugal, Romania, Russia, Serbia, Slovakia, Slovenia, Spain, Sweden, Switzerland, UK.

Consultative Status Consultative status granted from: *Council of Europe (CE, #04881)* (Participatory Status). **IGO Relations** Member of (1): *Standing Committee to the Bern Convention on the Conservation of European Wildlife and Natural Habitats (#19949)*. Cooperates with (3): *European Commission (EC, #06633)*; *UN Environment Programme World Conservation Monitoring Centre (UNEP-WCMC, #20295)*; *UNESCO (#20322)*. **NGO Relations** Member of (2): *International Federation for Sustainable Development and Fight to Poverty in the Mediterranean-Black Sea (FISPMED, #13562)*; *International Union for Conservation of Nature and Natural Resources (IUCN, #15766)*. [2021.09.01/XD5670/**E**]

♦ EUROPARKS – European Federation of Amusement and Leisure Parks (inactive)
♦ Europarne i Verden (#08839)

♦ Europartners Network 05769

Pres Elstar 5, 6922 BG Duiven, Netherlands. T. +31854852120. E-mail: info@europartners.org.
URL: http://www.europartners.org/

History 1902. **Aims** Develop leaders who will be able to equip *business* and professional people to develop, integrate and extend their *Christian faith* in their unique spheres of influence. **Activities** Organizes conferences, seminars and workshops. **Events** *Annual Conference* Jerusalem (Israel) 2016, *Annual Conference* Rotterdam (Netherlands) 2015, *Annual Conference* Prague (Czech Rep) 2014, *Annual Conference* Berlin (Germany) 2013, *Annual Conference* Jerusalem (Israel) 2012.

Members in 34 countries:
Albania, Armenia, Austria, Belarus, Belgium, Bulgaria, Croatia, Estonia, Finland, France, Germany, Greece, Hungary, Ireland, Israel, Italy, Latvia, Lithuania, Moldova, Netherlands, North Macedonia, Norway, Poland, Portugal, Romania, Russia, Serbia, Slovakia, Slovenia, Spain, Switzerland, Türkiye, UK, Ukraine.

NGO Relations Affiliate of: *CBMC International*. [2020/XF5614/**F**]

♦ Europartner Umwelt (#08154)
♦ Europa-Scouts (inactive)
♦ Europas Kvinder / see Association femmes d'Europe
♦ Europas-Latvijas Instituts Kulturas un Zinatnes Apmainai / see European-Latvian Institute
♦ Europas Maritime Udviklingscenter / see Maritime Development Center
♦ Europa y Sociedad (#02586)
♦ Europa e Società (#02586)
♦ Europa y sus Ciudadanos Actividades y Servicios / see European Citizen Action Service (#06555)
♦ EUROPATAT / see European Potato Trade Association (#08257)
♦ **EUROPATAT** European Potato Trade Association (#08257)
♦ EUROPATLAS – Fondation Europ'Atlas (unconfirmed)
♦ EUROPATLAS Stichting (unconfirmed)
♦ Europa – Tredje Världenföreningen / see eu can aid (#05570)
♦ Europa-Union Deutschland (internationally oriented national body)
♦ Pro-Europa: Union internationale des intellectuels réfugiés (inactive)
♦ Europa-Union der Vereine für Deutsche Schäferhunde / see Weltunion der Vereine für Deutsche Schäferhunde (#20858)
♦ Europa Unuigo de Blindaj Laboruloj (inactive)

♦ Europa Uomo 05770

Secretariat Leopoldstraat 34, 2000 Antwerp, Belgium. T. +3236459444. E-mail: europauomo@skynet.be.
URL: http://www.europa-uomo.org/

History 2002, Rome (Italy). Legally established Jun 2004, Milan (Italy). Former names and other names: *EUomo* – alias; *Europa Uomo – The European Prostate Cancer Coalition* – full title. Registration: Banque-Carrefour des Entreprises, No/ID: 0556.724.867, Start date: 13 Jun 2014, Belgium; End date: 2014, Italy; EU Transparency Register, No/ID: 489987524777-13, Start date: 28 Nov 2016. **Aims** Represent and support patient groups with *prostate diseases* in general and *cancer* in particular. **Structure** General Assembly; Executive Committee; Board and ex-officio members; Scientific Committee. **Languages** Dutch, English, French, German. **Staff** 1.00 FTE, paid; 10.00 FTE, voluntary. **Finance** Sources: grants; members' dues. **Activities** Advocacy/lobbying/activism; awareness raising; capacity building; events/meetings; knowledge management/information dissemination; training/education. **Events** *International EUomo Seminar* Warsaw (Poland) 2015. **Publications** *Update* (12 a year) in English. *EUPROMS 2.0* (2022) in English – A preview of findings from the econd Europa Uomo quality of life study; *EUPROMS* (2021) in English – Europa Uomo's study on quality of life after prostate cancer treatment. Summary of findings; *Europa Uomo Patient Reported Outcome Study (EUPROMS): Descriptive Statistics of a Prostate Cancer Survey from Patients for Patients* (2020) in English.

Members in 27 countries:
Armenia, Austria, Belgium, Bulgaria, Cyprus, Czechia, Denmark, Estonia, Finland, France, Germany, Hungary, Iceland, Ireland, Italy, Latvia, Lithuania, Netherlands, Norway, Poland, Portugal, Romania, Slovakia, Spain, Sweden, Switzerland, UK.

NGO Relations Member of (3): *European Cancer Organisation (ECO, #06432)* (Patient Advisory Committee); *European Patients' Forum (EPF, #08172)*; *Workgroup of European Cancer Patient Advocacy Networks (WECAN, #21054)*. [2022.10.19/XF7128/**F**]

♦ Europa Uomo – The European Prostate Cancer Coalition / see Europa Uomo (#05770)
♦ Europaverband der Rechtsanwälte und Steuerberater, Wirtschaftsprüfer und Unternehmensberater / see European Consultants Unit (#06769)
♦ Europaverband der Selbständigen (#06080)
♦ Europa Verduloj / see European Green Party (#07409)
♦ Europa Pro Vita (inactive)
♦ Europa Zentrum Baden-Württemberg (internationally oriented national body)
♦ Det Europæiske Regionsudvalg (#06665)
♦ Europæiske Union Ungdomsorkester (#09024)

♦ EuroPD 05771

Conference Secretariat In Conference Ltd, Unit 1, Q Court, Quality Street, Edinburgh, EH4 5BP, UK. T. +441313364203. E-mail: europd@in-conference.org.uk.
URL: http://www.europd.com/

History First meeting organized 1994, Berlin (Germany). Registered as a charity in accordance with German law. PD stands for *Peritoneal Dialysis*. **Structure** Scientific Programme Committee; Local Organising Committee. **Activities** Events/meetings. **Events** *European Peritoneal Dialysis Meeting* 2021, *European Peritoneal Dialysis Meeting* Glasgow (UK) 2020, *European Peritoneal Dialysis Meeting* Ljubljana (Slovenia) 2019, *European Peritoneal Dialysis Meeting* Dublin (Ireland) 2017, *European Peritoneal Dialysis Meeting* Krakow (Poland) 2015. [2017/XM5617/c/**E**]

♦ **EURO-PDT** European Society for Photodynamic Therapy (#08704)

♦ EuropeActive 05772

Exec Dir c/o House of Sport, Av des Arts 43, 1040 Brussels, Belgium. T. +32026499044. E-mail: thesecretariat@europeactive.eu.
Pres address not obtained.
URL: http://www.europeactive.eu/

History 28 Oct 2001, Frankfurt-Main (Germany). Evolved from *European Network Fitness Association (ENFA)*, set up 1996, Netherlands. Former names and other names: *European Health and Fitness Association (EHFA)* – former; *EuropeActive – the European Association for fitness and physical activity* – full title. Registration: Banque-Carrefour des Entreprises, Start date: 2008; EU Transparency Register, No/ID: 364892017621-92. **Aims** Represent interests of the European health, fitness and physical activity sector at EU level; help battle inactivity and obesity challenges across Europe; as a standards setting body, promote best practices in instruction and training through the European Register of Exercise Professionals (EREPS) and in the management and operations of fitness facilities. **Structure** General Assembly; Board; President; Executive Director; Head Office; Professional Standards Committee; Standards Council; Technical Expert Groups; Scientific Advisory Board. **Languages** English. **Staff** 12.00 FTE, paid. **Finance** Sources: grants; members' dues. Supported by: *European Commission (EC, #06633)*. Annual budget: 1,500,000 EUR (2020). **Activities** Events/meetings. **Events** *International Standards Meeting* 2022, *Annual Forum for Anti-Doping in Recreational Sport* Brussels (Belgium) 2022, *European Health & Fitness Forum (EHFF)* Cologne (Germany) 2022, *European Health & Fitness Forum (EHFF)* 2021, *International Standards Meeting* 2021. **Publications** *EuropeActive Newsletter* (12 a year); *EuropeActive Brussels Bulletin* (25 a year); *Annual European Health and Fitness Market Report*. **Information Services** *EuropeActive Knowledge Center*.

Members Fitness centres (over 35,000); national associations (24); market-leading suppliers; education providers; individuals. Members in 26 countries:
Austria, Belgium, Bulgaria, Croatia, Czechia, Denmark, Estonia, Finland, France, Germany, Greece, Hungary, Ireland, Italy, Latvia, Lithuania, Luxembourg, Netherlands, Norway, Poland, Portugal, Romania, Spain, Sweden, Switzerland, UK.

NGO Relations Member of (1): *European Sports Workforce Development Alliance (ESWDA, #08823)*. Liaison Organization of: *Comité européen de normalisation (CEN, #04162)*. [2021.02.19/XD8864/**D**]

♦ EuropeActive – the European Association for fitness and physical activity / see EuropeActive (#05772)

♦ EUROPEADE – International Association for European Folk Cultures 05773

EUROPEADE – Internationale Vereniging voor Europese Volksculturen

Exec Sec Potterstraat 167 bus 6, 9170 Sint-Pauwels, Belgium. T. +3232480727. E-mail: info@europeade.eu.
Pres address not obtained.
URL: http://www.europeade.eu/

History 1964, Antwerp (Belgium). Founded by Mon De Clopper (1922-1998). Registration: Banque-Carrefour des Entreprises, Start date: 1998, Belgium. **Aims** Promote respect and unity between the free European peoples, in a friendly atmosphere, and more specifically, by means of their folk cultures. **Structure** General Meeting; International Committee. **Languages** Dutch, English, French, German, Italian, Spanish. **Staff** 1.00 FTE, paid; 0.50 FTE, voluntary. **Finance** Sources: meeting proceeds; members' dues. **Events** *Annual Europeade* Klaipeda (Lithuania) 2022, *Annual Europeade* Klaipeda (Lithuania) 2021, *Annual Europeade* Sint-Pauwels (Belgium) 2020, *Annual Europeade* Frankenberg (Germany) 2019, *Annual Europeade* Viseu (Portugal) 2018. **Publications** *EUrOPEADE* in Dutch, English, French, German, Italian, Spanish.

Members Individuals in 30 countries:
Austria, Belgium, Bulgaria, Cyprus, Czechia, Denmark, Estonia, Finland, France, Georgia, Germany, Greece, Hungary, Ireland, Italy, Latvia, Lithuania, Luxembourg, Moldova, Netherlands, Poland, Portugal, Romania, Serbia, Slovenia, Spain, Sweden, Switzerland, UK, Ukraine. [2022.02.15/XD8356/v/**D**]

♦ EUROPEADE – Internationale Vereniging voor Europese Volksculturen (#05773)
♦ **Europea** Europe de l'enseignement agronomique (#09153)
♦ EUROPEA – Europe de l'Enseignement Agronomique AISBL / see EUROPEA – International (#05775)

♦ Europe Against Drugs (EURAD) 05774

Sec Gen Norway House, Rue Archimede 17, 1000 Brussels, Belgium. T. +32476967060. E-mail: eurad@eurad.net.
URL: http://www.eurad.net/

History Founded Oct 1989, Strasbourg (France), following a constitutive meeting, Apr 1988, Berlin West (Germany FR). EU Transparency Register: 24340297158-92. **Aims** Advocate a prevention and recovery oriented drug policy at national and international level. **Structure** Board; Secretariat. **Languages** English. **Staff** Council voluntary, supported by paid secretariat. **Finance** Sponsorship and donations. **Activities** Projects/programmes; events/meetings. **Publications** Net newsletter; leaflets; press releases.

Members Affiliated organizations (50) in 23 countries:
Argentina, Australia, Belgium, Bosnia-Herzegovina, Canada, Estonia, Finland, France, Ghana, Iceland, Ireland, Italy, Latvia, Nepal, Netherlands, New Zealand, Nigeria, Norway, Romania, Serbia, Sweden, Switzerland, UK.

Consultative Status Consultative status granted from: *ECOSOC (#05331)* (Special). **IGO Relations** Participant in Fundamental Rights Platform of *European Union Agency for Fundamental Rights (FRA, #08969)*. **NGO Relations** Member of: *Conference of Non-Governmental Organizations in Consultative Relationship with the United Nations (CONGO, #04635)*; *Vienna NGO Committee on Drugs (VNGOC, #20773)*. [2018/XF5271/y/**F**]

♦ Europe Agriculture Education Association / see EUROPEA – International (#05775)
♦ EuropeAid Amt für Zusammenarbeit (inactive)
♦ EuropeAid Byrån för samarbete (inactive)
♦ EuropeAid Cooperation Office (inactive)
♦ EuropeAid Dienst voor Samenwerking (inactive)
♦ EuropeAid office de coopération (inactive)
♦ EuropeAid Oficina de Cooperación (inactive)
♦ EuropeAid Samarbejdskontoret (inactive)
♦ EuropeAid Serviço de Cooperação (inactive)
♦ EuropeAid Ufficio di cooperazione (inactive)
♦ EuropeAid Yhteistyötoimisto (inactive)
♦ EUROPEA International / see Europe de l'enseignement agronomique (#09153)

♦ **EUROPEA – International** 05775
SG c/o EUROPEA-Austria, Frauentorgasse 72-74, 3430 Tulln, Austria. E-mail: europea.austria@aon.at.
Registered Address Ctre Technique Horticole, Chemin de Sibérie 4, 5030 Gembloux, Belgium.
URL: http://www.europea.org.
History Jan 1992, Strasbourg (France). Also referred to as *Europe Agriculture Education Association* and *EUROPEA – Europe de l'Enseignement Agronomique AISBL*. 1993, registered in accordance with Belgian law. **Aims** Encourage the development of *distance learning*; promote *foreign language teaching*. **Structure** General Assembly. Board, comprising President, 2 Vice-Presidents, Secretary, Vice-Secretary, Treasurer, Vice-Treasurer. **Events** *Seminar* Jyväskylä (Finland) 2019, *Meeting* Rotterdam (Netherlands) 2016, *Seminar* Maria Taferl (Austria) 2006, *Meeting and general assembly* Tampere (Finland) 2006, *Meeting and general assembly* Dillington (UK) 2005.
Members National networks representing agricultural colleges and institutes in 25 countries:
Austria, Belgium, Czechia, Denmark, Estonia, Finland, France, Germany, Hungary, Ireland, Italy, Latvia, Luxembourg, Malta, Netherlands, Norway, Poland, Portugal, Romania, Serbia, Slovakia, Spain, Sweden, Switzerland, UK. [2017/XF4722/**F**]

♦ **Europe Air Sports (EAS)** 05776
Programme Manager Pasuunatie 9 A 8, FI-00420 Helsinki, Finland. E-mail: info@europe-air-sports.org.
URL: http://www.europe-air-sports.org/
History 1988, Belgium. Sub-title: '*Association Coordinating Regulatory Matters for European National Aero Clubs and Associations of Member States of the European Civil Aviation Conference (ECAC) and the Fédération aéronautique internationale (FAI)*'. Registered in accordance with Dutch law, 29 Mar 1995. EU Transparency Register: 83743954330-47. **Aims** Represent the interests of pilots and light aircraft owners/operators in civil aviation regulatory developments. **Structure** Board; President. **Staff** 50.00 FTE, voluntary. **Activities** Politics/policy/regulatory; advocacy/lobbying/activism. **Events** *General Meeting* Cologne (Germany) 2006, *General Meeting* Friedrichshafen (Germany) 2005, *General Meeting* Cambridge (UK) 2004, *General Meeting* The Hague (Netherlands) 2003, *General Meeting* The Hague (Netherlands) 2003. **Publications** *EAS Newsletter*.
Members National aeroclubs in 18 countries:
Austria, Belgium, Cyprus, Czechia, Denmark, Finland, France, Germany, Italy, Luxembourg, Netherlands, Norway, Portugal, Slovenia, Sweden, Switzerland, Türkiye, UK.
Air sports organizations (6):
European Federation of Light, Experimental and Vintage Aircraft (EFLEVA, #07154); *European Gliding Union (EGU, #07395)*; *European Hang Gliding and Paragliding Union (EHPU, #07448)*; *European Microlight Federation (EMF, #07794)*; *European Powered Flying Union (EPFU)*; *PPL/IR Europe*. [2018/XF3746/y/**F**]

♦ European 11q Group / see European Chromosome 11 Network (#06547)

♦ **European 8-Ball Pool Federation (EEPF)** 05777
Sec 12 Helston Grove, Grove Hill West, Hemel Hempstead, HP2 6NU, UK. T. +441442244776. E-mail: secretary@euro8ball.com.
URL: http://www.euro8ball.com/home/
History Also referred to as *Euro8ball*. **Aims** Promote 8-Ball Pool in Europe. **Activities** Sporting activities. **NGO Relations** Member of: *World Eightball Pool Federation (WEPF, #21373)*. [2020/XD6961/**D**]

♦ European Academic Conference on Internal Audit and Corporate Governance (meeting series)

♦ **European Academies' Science Advisory Council (EASAC)** 05778
Exec Dir address not obtained.
Brussels Office c/o RASAB, Hertogsstraat 1, 1000 Brussels, Belgium. E-mail: info@easac.eu.
Main Website: http://www.easac.eu/
History 11 Jun 2001, Stockholm (Sweden). Registration: EU Transparency Register, No/ID: 133236011647-58, Start date: 26 Jul 2013. **Aims** Provide authoritative, evidence-based reports and assessments on scientific topics relevant to European policy needs. **Structure** Council; Bureau; Brussels Office; Secretariat. **Languages** English. **Staff** 8.00 FTE, paid. **Finance** Sources: members' dues. Supported by: *IAP – The Global Network of Science Academies (inactive)*. **Activities** Events/meetings; knowledge management/information dissemination. Active in all member countries. **Events** *Council Meeting* Halle (Saale) (Germany) 2021, *Council Meeting* Paris (France) 2021, *Council Meeting* Halle (Saale) (Germany) 2020, *Council Meeting* Halle (Saale) (Germany) 2020, *Council Meeting* Zagreb (Croatia) 2019. **Publications** Reports; statements; summaries.
Members National Science Academies in 28 countries:
Austria, Belgium, Bulgaria, Croatia, Cyprus, Czechia, Denmark, Estonia, Finland, France, Germany, Greece, Hungary, Ireland, Italy, Latvia, Lithuania, Netherlands, Norway, Poland, Portugal, Romania, Slovakia, Slovenia, Spain, Sweden, Switzerland, UK.
Organizational members (2):
Academia Europaea (#00011); *ALLEA – ALL European Academies (#00647)*.
NGO Relations Member of (1): *InterAcademy Partnership (IAP, #11376)*. Cooperates with (2): *ALLEA – ALL European Academies (#00647)*; *Federation of European Academies of Medicine (FEAM, #09490)*.
[2023.02.15/XE4415/y/**E**]

♦ European Academy for Advanced Research in Marketing / see European Marketing Academy (#07745)
♦ European Academy of Aesthetic Dentistry / see European Academy of Esthetic Dentistry (#05791)
♦ European Academy of Allergology and Clinical Immunology / see European Academy of Allergy and Clinical Immunology (#05779)
♦ European Academy of Allergy / see European Academy of Allergy and Clinical Immunology (#05779)

♦ **European Academy of Allergy and Clinical Immunology (EAACI)** ... 05779
Académie européenne d'allergologie et d'immunologie clinique – Europäische Akademie für Allergologie und Klinische Immunologie
Headquarters Hagenholzstr 111, 3rd Floor, 8050 Zurich ZH, Switzerland. T. +41442055533. Fax +41442055539. E-mail: info@eaaci.org – communications@eaaci.org.
URL: http://www.eaaci.org/
History Sep 1956, Florence (Italy). Founded at 3rd European Congress of Allergy, preliminary attempts having been made during 1st Congress, May-Jun 1950, Paris (France) and 2nd Congress, May 1953, Copenhagen (Denmark). Constitution and By-laws drawn up 1957, Utrecht (Netherlands). Former names and other names: *European Academy of Allergy (ENG)* – former; *Académie européenne d'allergie* – former; *European Academy of Allergology and Clinical Immunology* – former. Registration: EU Transparency Register, No/ID: 567788614987-34, Start date: 24 Nov 2014. **Aims** Formulate public health and research policies focusing on allergy at a European level. **Structure** Congress (annual); Executive Committee. **Languages** Czech, English, French, German, Portuguese, Spanish, Thai. **Staff** 11.00 FTE, paid. **Finance** Sources: meeting proceeds; members' dues; sponsorship. **Activities** Events/meetings; publishing activities; training/education. **Events** *Congress* Prague (Czechia) 2022, *EAACI-ESCD Skin Allergy Meeting* Copenhagen (Denmark) 2021, *Congress* Krakow (Poland) / Madrid (Spain) 2021, *Annual Congress* London (UK) 2020, *Pediatric Allergy and Asthma Meeting (PAAM)* Florence (Italy) 2019. **Publications** Newsletter; journal. Books; position papers; guidelines; scientific collaborations.
Members National Societies in 52 countries:
Albania, Algeria, Argentina, Australia, Austria, Azerbaijan, Belgium, Brazil, Bulgaria, Croatia, Cyprus, Czechia, Denmark, Estonia, Finland, France, Georgia, Germany, Greece, Hungary, Iceland, India, Ireland, Israel, Italy, Jordan, Kazakhstan, Korea Rep, Kosovo, Latvia, Lithuania, Luxembourg, Mexico, Mongolia, Netherlands, North Macedonia, Norway, Poland, Portugal, Romania, Russia, Saudi Arabia, Serbia, Slovakia, Slovenia, South Africa, Spain, Sweden, Switzerland, Türkiye, UK, Ukraine.
Included in the above, 3 organizations listed in this Yearbook:
Asia Pacific Association of Pediatric Allergy, Respirology and Immunology (APAPARI, #01849); *Australasian Society of Clinical Immunology and Allergy (ASCIA)*; *CIS Society of Allergology and Clinical Immunology (#03948)*.
NGO Relations Member of (2): *Biomedical Alliance in Europe (#03251)*; *European Chronic Disease Alliance (ECDA, #06548)*. [2022/XD0540/**D**]

♦ European Academy of Anaesthesiology (inactive)

♦ **European Academy of Andrology (EAA)** 05780
Communications Officer c/o Asszisztencia Kft, Szent Istvan krt 7, Budapest 1055, Hungary. E-mail: office@andrologyacademy.net.
Exec Sec Dept Growth & Reproduction, Rigshospitalet, Blegdamsvej 9, 2100 Copenhagen, Denmark.
Pres Dept of Experimental and Clinical Biomedical Sciences, University of Florence, Viale Pieraccini 6, 50139 Florence FI, Italy.
Main Website: http://www.andrologyacademy.net/
History 7 May 1992. Founded by a group of prominent European andrologists. Registration: Start date: 1992, Germany, Münster. **Aims** Raise scientific standards of andrology in Europe; improve education in andrology; develop strategies for increasing public awareness of andrology and the special problems relating to *male health, fertility and sexual disorders, male-specific cancers* and male *contraception*. **Structure** General Assembly; Executive Council; Committees. **Languages** English. **Staff** 2.00 FTE, paid; 20.00 FTE, voluntary. **Finance** Sources: members' dues; revenue from activities/projects; subscriptions. **Activities** Advocacy/lobbying/activism; awards/prizes/competitions; events/meetings; publishing activities; training/education. **Events** *European Congress of Andrology* Barcelona (Spain) 2022, *European Congress of Andrology* Münster (Germany) 2020, *European Congress of Andrology* Budapest (Hungary) 2018, *European Congress of Andrology* Rotterdam (Netherlands) 2016, *European Congress of Andrology* Barcelona (Spain) 2014. **Publications** *Andrology* (6 a year) in English – Scientific journal jointly published with ASA. Annual Reports; newsletters; monthly literature alerts. **Information Services** *Andrology Awareness Europe* – Website on Male Health for General Public.
Members Regular: Academicians; Honorary Academicians. Members in 47 countries:
Austria, Belgium, Bulgaria, Burkina Faso, Chile, China, Croatia, Czechia, Denmark, Egypt, Estonia, Finland, France, Germany, Greece, Hungary, Indonesia, Iran Islamic Rep, Iraq, Israel, Italy, Jordan, Latvia, Lithuania, Malaysia, Malta, Mexico, Moldova, Netherlands, Nigeria, North Macedonia, Norway, Poland, Portugal, Romania, Russia, Saudi Arabia, Serbia, Slovenia, South Africa, Spain, Sweden, Switzerland, Türkiye, UK, United Arab Emirates, USA.
Andrology Training Centres (28) in 17 countries:
Belgium (3 Centres), Croatia, Denmark, Egypt, Estonia, Germany (5 Centres), Greece, Hungary, Italy (6 Centres), Latvia, Netherlands, Poland, Russia, Spain, Sweden, UK, USA. [2022.05.17/XE4403/v/**E**]

♦ European Academy of Architecture (internationally oriented national body)

♦ **European Academy of Arts, Sciences and Humanities (EAASH)** 05781
Académie européenne des sciences, des arts et des lettres (AESAL) – Academia Europea de Ciencias, Artes y Letras (AECAL)
SG Résidence Le Monte Carlo, 3 bd Albert 1er, 06600 Antibes, France. Fax +33493340506. E-mail: nilemaire@wanadoo.fr.
URL: http://www.europeanacademysciencesartsandletters.com/
History 24 May 1980, following recommendations, 1973, at several international conferences. Also referred to in English as *European Academy of Letters, Sciences and Arts*. **Aims** Foster collaboration among nations in the fields of education, science, art and the humanities; in particular, establish a bridge between national academies of sciences, arts and humanities; analyse major *problems* of mankind which call for both a multidisciplinary and a multinational approach; cooperate with intergovernmental organizations to analyse and solve *world problems*. **Structure** Council of 18; Bureau; Committee of Patronage. Honorary Committee of representatives of governments and of intergovernmental organizations. Committee of official representatives of associated national academies. **Languages** Bulgarian, Czech, Danish, Dutch, English, French, German, Irish Gaelic, Italian, Norwegian, Polish, Portuguese, Russian, Serbo-Croatian, Slovakian, Slovene, Spanish, Swedish. **Staff** 9.00 FTE, voluntary. **Finance** Contributions from: Belgian Government; French Government; UNESCO; WHO. **Activities** Instrumental in setting up/organizes: *UNESCO-European Academy Joint Committee*; *Network of Academies of Mediterranean Countries (no recent information)*; *L'homme contre les virus (see: #05781)*; '*University and Health Development*' – international project; annual international symposium; international meetings; expert committees. **Events** *Annual International Symposium* Shanghai (China) 2010, *Annual international symposium* Paris (France) 2003, *Annual international symposium* Carthage (Tunisia) 2002, *Annual international symposium* Trieste (Italy) 2001, *EAASH annual international symposium / Annual International Symposium* Brussels (Belgium) 2000. **Publications** Proceedings of symposia.
Members Honorary; Titular; Associate. No more than 500 titular members under the age of 65; no numerical restriction on older members. Members co-opted from those most representative of the fields in question, especially from national and international academies; winners of major international prizes. Associate organizations in 24 countries and territories:
Argentina, Australia, Bolivia, Brazil, Canada, China, Djibouti, India, Indonesia, Israel, Japan, Jordan, Korea Rep, Kuwait, Madagascar, Mexico, Morocco, Philippines, Taiwan, Tunisia, Uruguay, USA, Venezuela, Vietnam.
Individuals, including 70 winners of the Nobel Prize, in 61 countries and territories:
Algeria, Andorra, Argentina, Australia, Austria, Belarus, Belgium, Bolivia, Brazil, Bulgaria, Canada, Chile, China, Congo Brazzaville, Croatia, Czechia, Denmark, Djibouti, Egypt, Finland, France, Germany, Greece, Hungary, India, Indonesia, Israel, Italy, Japan, Jordan, Korea Rep, Kuwait, Libya, Lithuania, Luxembourg, Madagascar, Mexico, Moldova, Monaco, Morocco, Norway, Poland, Portugal, Romania, Russia, Senegal, Serbia, Slovakia, Slovenia, Spain, Sweden, Switzerland, Taiwan, Tunisia, Türkiye, Ukraine, United Arab Emirates, Uruguay, USA, Venezuela, Vietnam.
Consultative Status Consultative status granted from: *ECOSOC (#05331)* (Ros C); *UNESCO (#20322)* (Consultative Status). **IGO Relations** Accredited by: *United Nations Office at Vienna (UNOV, #20604)*. Associated with Department of Global Communications of the United Nations. **NGO Relations** National academies (53).
[2012/XD0158/**E**]

♦ European Academy for Aviation Safety (inactive)
♦ European Academy Berlin (internationally oriented national body)
♦ European Academy of Bozen/Bolzano (internationally oriented national body)
♦ European Academy for Business Management / see European Academy of Management and Business Economics (#05801)
♦ European Academy of Business in Society / see Academy of Business in Society (#00032)

♦ **European Academy of Caring Science (EACS)** 05782
Chair address not obtained. E-mail: lisuhr@hst.aau.dk.
Contact address not obtained.
URL: http://www.eacs.nu/
Aims Serve the public and professions engaged in the caring sciences by advancing knowledge and practice through the generation, synthesis and dissemination of knowledge for caring. **Structure** Steering Group. **Activities** Events/meetings; research/documentation; networking/liaising. **Events** *Conference on Sustainable Caring for Health and Wellbeing* Vaasa (Finland) 2019, *Conference* Bodø (Norway) 2017, *Conference* Aarhus (Denmark) 2013, *Meeting* Stockholm (Sweden) 2012.
Members Core member institutions (9) in 3 countries:
Denmark, Sweden, UK. [2017/XJ6622/**D**]

♦ **European Academy of Childhood Disability (EACD)** 05783
Sec c/o Rehab Sciences, Group for Neuromotor Rehab, Tervuursevest 101, 3001 Leuven, Belgium. E-mail: secretary@eacd.org.
URL: http://www.eacd.org/
History Sep 1989, Oxford (UK). Registration: Charity Commission, No/ID: 1015225, England and Wales. **Aims** Improve health and participation of children with disabilities by promoting high quality research and implementation of the results of evidence based research into practice. **Structure** Committee Board; Executive Committee. **Languages** English. **Staff** No employed staff. **Finance** Members' dues. Other sources: profits from annual meetings. **Activities** Events/meetings; research/documentation. **Events** *Annual Meeting* Bruges (Belgium) 2024, *Annual Meeting* Ljubljana (Slovenia) 2023, *Annual Meeting* Barcelona (Spain) 2022, *Annual Meeting* 2021, *Annual Meeting* Poznań (Poland) 2020. **Publications** *EACD Newsletter*. Reports.
Members Paediatricians, neuropaediatricians, physiotherapists, occupational therapists, speech therapists, psychologists, nurses, social workers and special needs teachers. Members (about 500) in 42 countries and territories:
Australia, Austria, Belgium, Bosnia-Herzegovina, Bulgaria, Canada, China, Croatia, Denmark, Ecuador, Estonia, Finland, France, Germany, Greece, Hong Kong, Iceland, Ireland, Israel, Italy, Japan, Jordan, Kuwait, Latvia, Lebanon, Lithuania, Luxembourg, Malaysia, Netherlands, Norway, Poland, Portugal, Romania, Saudi Arabia, Slovenia, Spain, Sweden, Switzerland, Türkiye, UK, United Arab Emirates, USA.
National coordinators in 30 countries:

Austria, Belgium, Bosnia-Herzegovina, Bulgaria, Croatia, Denmark, Finland, France, Georgia, Germany, Greece, Ireland, Israel, Italy, Lithuania, Moldova, Netherlands, North Macedonia, Norway, Poland, Portugal, Romania, Serbia, Slovenia, Spain, Sweden, Switzerland, Türkiye, UK, Ukraine.

NGO Relations Together with *Australasian Academy of Cerebral Palsy and Developmental Medicine (AusACPDM)*, instrumental in setting up: *International Alliance of Academies of Childhood Disability (IAACD, #11619).* [2021/XE3616/**E**]

♦ European Academy of Chiropractic (see: #06538)

♦ European Academy for Continuing Medical Education (inactive)

♦ European Academy of Cosmetic Surgery (EACS) 05784

Contact address not obtained.

History Founded 1996. **Aims** Advocates for patient safety and satisfaction in the field of aesthetic surgery. **Structure** Board. **Finance** Members' dues. **Events** *World congress of cosmetic surgery* Manila (Philippines) 2004, *Annual Congress* Amsterdam (Netherlands) 2003, *International congress on cosmetics surgery and medicine* Buenos Aires (Argentina) 2003, *International symposium on applied esthetics* Buenos Aires (Argentina) 2003, *Beauty-full in Vienna* Vienna (Austria) 2002. **Publications** *European Cosmetic Surgery* – newsletter. **Members** Individuals. Membership countries not specified. [2016/XD7246/v/**D**]

♦ European Academy of Craniomandibular Disorders (EACD) 05785

Académie européenne des troubles cranio-faciaux

Sec Viale Col di Lana 27, 46100 Mantova MN, Italy.

URL: http://www.eacmd.org/

History 1984. **Aims** Foster knowledge on the etiology, diagnosis and treatment of orofacial and temporomandibular disorders. **Structure** Officers (change every year): President; Secretary. **Activities** Events/meetings. **Events** *Meeting* Bordeaux (France) 2018, *ICOT : International Conference of Orofacial Pain and Temporomandibular Disorders* London (UK) 2018, *Meeting* Barcelona (Spain) 2017, *Meeting* Amsterdam (Netherlands) 2015, *ICOT : International Conference of Orofacial Pain and Temporomandibular Disorders* Las Vegas, NV (USA) 2014. **Publications** *Journal of Orofacial Pain.*

Members Specialists in the field of orofacial pain and temporomandibular disorders (about 100) in 16 countries:

Austria, Belgium, Finland, France, Germany, Greece, Ireland, Italy, Netherlands, Norway, Portugal, Spain, Sweden, Switzerland, Türkiye, UK.

NGO Relations American Academy of Orofacial Pain (AAOP); *Asian Academy of Orofacial Pain and Temporomandibular Disorders (AAOT, #01296); European Academy of Orofacial Pain and Dysfunction (EAOPD, #05808); Ibero-Latin American Academy of Craniomandibular Disorders (ILADC).* [2018/XD3982/v/**D**]

♦ European Academy of Dental Sleep Medicine (EADSM) 05786

Sec c/o UZA, Wilrijkstraat 10, 2650 Edegem, Belgium. T. +3238215292. E-mail: info@eadsm.eu.

Registered Office Ghersburgstr 9, 83043 Bad Aibling, Germany.

URL: http://www.eadsm.eu/

History Officially founded 2 Apr 2006, Bad Reichenhall (Germany) as *European Dental Sleep Medicine Academy (EdeSA).* Current title adopted on reorganization of Academy, Feb 2008. **Aims** Offer a platform for dentists and medical colleagues, enabling interdisciplinary exchange to promote best practice in dental treatments for Sleep Related Breathing Disorders (SRDB) like Snoring, Obstructive Sleep Apnoea (OSAS). **Structure** Board. **Finance** Members' dues. **Activities** Events/meetings; training/education. **Publications** *Sleep and Breathing* – journal. **NGO Relations** Associate member of: *World Sleep Society (#21793).* [2019/XM8468/**D**]

♦ European Academy of Dentomaxillofacial Radiology / see European Academy of Dento Maxillo Facial Radiology (#05787)

♦ European Academy of Dento Maxillo Facial Radiology (EADMFR) . . 05787

Main Office c/o AIM Group, Grensstrat 7, 1831 Diegem, Belgium. T. +3227228234.

Registered Office Oude Haachtsesteenweg 107 box 3, 1831 Machelen, Belgium.

URL: http://eadmfr.info/

History 2004, Malmö (Sweden), during 9th European Congress of DentoMaxilloFacial Radiology. Registered in accordance with Belgian law, 21 Mar 2011. Also referred to as *European Academy of Dentomaxillofacial Radiology.* **Aims** Promote, advance and improve clinical practice, education and/or research specifically related to the specialty of dental and maxillofacial radiology within Europe; provide a forum for discussion, communication and the professional advancement of its members. **Structure** Central Council, consisting of representatives of each country. Executive Committee, comprising President, Vice-President/President Elect, Secretary, Treasurer, Immediate Past-President and 6 members. Committees (8): Specialisation; Education; Selection Criteria and Radiation Protection; Research and Scientific; Finance; Congress; Nominating; Junior. **Finance** Members' dues. **Events** *Congress* Leipzig (Germany) 2012, *Congress* Istanbul (Turkey) 2010, *Congress* Budapest (Hungary) 2008, *Congress* Budapest (Hungary) 2008, *Congress* Leuven (Belgium) 2006. **Publications** *EADMFR Newsletter.*

Members Full in 12 countries:

Belgium, Finland, Germany, Greece, Netherlands, Norway, Poland, Romania, Spain, Sweden, Türkiye, UK. [2018/XJ6933/**D**]

♦ European Academy of Dermatology and Venereology (EADV) 05788

Académie européenne de dermatologie et vénéréologie

Headquarters Via S Balestra 22B, 6900 Lugano TI, Switzerland. T. +41919734520. E-mail: leadership@eadv.org – eadvoffice@eadv.org.

URL: http://www.eadv.org/

History 3 Oct 1987, Luxembourg. Registration: EU Transparency Register, No/ID: 402959038681-39, Start date: 22 Jun 2020. **Aims** Further the knowledge of health professionals and advocates in the field of dermatology and venereology; advance patient care, education and research by providing a unique platform to bring people together and share ideas. **Structure** Board of Directors; Executive Committee. **Languages** English. **Staff** 33.00 FTE, paid. **Activities** Events/meetings; training/education. **Events** *International Spring Symposium* Seville (Spain) 2023, *International Spring Symposium* Ljubljana (Slovenia) 2022, *Annual Congress* Milan (Italy) 2022, *Annual Congress* 2021, *International Spring Symposium* 2021. **Publications** *Journal of the European Academy of Dermatology and Venereology (JEADV)* (12 a year); *EADV Newsletter* (4 a year).

Members Associate; Fellow; Junior; Senior; International Fellow; International Junior; Corporate; Honorary; Nurse and Medical Assistant; Student. Members in 116 countries and territories:

Afghanistan, Albania, Algeria, Angola, Argentina, Armenia, Aruba, Australia, Austria, Bahrain, Bangladesh, Belarus, Belgium, Bolivia, Bosnia-Herzegovina, Brazil, Brunei Darussalam, Bulgaria, Cambodia, Canada, Chile, China, Colombia, Costa Rica, Croatia, Cyprus, Czechia, Denmark, Ecuador, Egypt, Estonia, Finland, France, Georgia, Germany, Greece, Guatemala, Guiana Fr, Honduras, Hong Kong, Hungary, Iceland, India, Indonesia, Iran Islamic Rep, Iraq, Ireland, Israel, Italy, Japan, Jordan, Kazakhstan, Kenya, Korea Rep, Kosovo, Kuwait, Latvia, Lebanon, Lithuania, Luxembourg, Madagascar, Malawi, Malaysia, Maldives, Malta, Mauritius, Mexico, Moldova, Montenegro, Morocco, Nepal, Netherlands, New Zealand, Nigeria, North Macedonia, Norway, Oman, Pakistan, Palestine, Panama, Paraguay, Peru, Philippines, Poland, Portugal, Qatar, Romania, Russia, Rwanda, San Marino, Saudi Arabia, Serbia, Singapore, Slovakia, Slovenia, South Africa, Spain, Sri Lanka, Sudan, Sweden, Switzerland, Syrian AR, Taiwan, Tanzania UR, Thailand, Tunisia, Türkiye, UK, Ukraine, United Arab Emirates, Uruguay, USA, Uzbekistan, Venezuela, Vietnam, Yemen.

NGO Relations Cooperates with (9): *Associations and Conference Forum (AC Forum, #02909); European Association of Dermato-Oncology (EADO, #06008); European Society for Cosmetic and Aesthetic Dermatology (ESCAD, #08570);* European Society of Paediatric Dermatology (ESPaeD); *European Union of Medical Specialists (UEMS, #09001); Global Allergy and Asthma European Network (GA2LEN, #10179); International Alliance of Dermatology Patient Organizations (IAPDO, #11626); International League of Dermatological Societies (ILDS, #14018);* national societies. Supports (1): *European Skin Research Foundation (ESRF, #08490).* Sister societies: *European Dermatology Forum (EDF, #06907); European Society for Dermatological Research (ESDR, #08578).* Sub-specialty societies: *European Nail Society (ENS, #07850); European Skin-Care Nursing Network (ESNN, no recent information); European Society for Dermatology and Psychiatry (ESDaP, #08579); European Society for Dermatopathology (ESDP, #08580); European Society for the History of Dermatology and Venerology (ESHDV, no recent information); European Society for Micrographic Surgery (ESMS, #08652); European Society for Photodermatology (ESPD, #08703); European Society of Skin Cancer Prevention (EUROSKIN, #08735).* [2021.05.31/XF2928/v/**F**]

♦ European Academy of Design (EAD) 05789

Contact ImaginationLancaster, LICA Building, Lancaster Univ, Lancaster, LA1 4YD, UK. E-mail: imagination@lancaster.ac.uk.

URL: http://www.ead.lancs.ac.uk/

History Founded 1994. **Aims** Improve European-wide research collaboration and dissemination; promote publication and dissemination of research in design. **Structure** Executive Committee. **Finance** Members' dues. **Events** *Running with scissors* Dundee (UK) 2019, *Design for next* Rome (Italy) 2017, *Conference* Paris (France) 2015, *Conference* Gothenburg (Sweden) 2013, *Conference* Porto (Portugal) 2011. **Publications** *The Design Journal* (3 a year). Conference proceedings. **Members** Membership countries not specified. [2019.02.12/XE4581/**E**]

♦ European Academy of Diplomacy (internationally oriented national body)

♦ European Academy for Environmental Medicine (EUROPAEM) 05790

Académie européenne de médecine de l'environnement – Europäische Akademie für Umweltmedizin – Academia Europea per la Medicina per Ambiente Ecologico

Main Office Trierer Strasse 44, 54411 Hermeskeil, Germany. T. +4965039810880. Fax +4965039810881. E-mail: office@europaem.eu.

URL: https://europaem.eu/

History Germany. Registration: Germany. **Aims** Improve clinical environmental medicine in Europe. **Structure** General Meeting (annual). Board of Directors of up to 7 members, including 3 Chairmen. Scientific Board. **Finance** Members' dues. **NGO Relations** Member of: *EDC Free Europe (#05355); Health and Environment Alliance (HEAL, #10879).* [2018/XM2067/**E**]

♦ European Academy of Esthetic Dentistry (EAED) 05791

Contact Bahnhofstrasse 35, 8001 Zurich ZH, Switzerland. E-mail: info@eaed.org.

URL: http://www.eaed.org/

History 1986, Geneva (Switzerland). Also referred to as *European Academy of Aesthetic Dentistry.* **Aims** Promote excellence in dental aesthetics; provide leadership in the profession by defining *ethical standards*; foster interdisciplinary communication and research. **Activities** Events/meetings. **Events** *Annual Meeting* Munich (Germany) 2019, *Annual Meeting* Sorrento (Italy) 2018, *Meeting* Lisbon (Portugal) 2017, *Annual Meeting* Milan (Italy) 2017, *Annual Meeting* Copenhagen (Denmark) 2016. **Publications** *European Journal of Esthetic Dentistry.*

Members Active – individuals (72) in 17 countries:

Austria, Belgium, Brazil, Denmark, France, Germany, Greece, Ireland, Israel, Italy, Monaco, Poland, Spain, Switzerland, Türkiye, UK, USA.

NGO Relations *Asian Academy of Aesthetic Dentistry (#01293).* Member of: *International Federation of Esthetic Dentistry (IFED, #13417).* [2017.03.09/XE1979/v/**E**]

♦ European Academy of Facial Plastic Surgery (EAFPS) 05792

General Secretariat Nibelungenstr 87, 23562 Lübeck, Germany. Fax +4945158249981. E-mail: info@eafps.org.

URL: http://www.eafps.org/

History 1977, London (UK). Formerly also known as 'Joseph Society' and *European Academy of Facial Surgery.* **Aims** Stimulate study, research and scientific advancement in the field of plastic and reconstructive surgery in the face and neck. **Languages** English. **Staff** 0.50 FTE, paid. **Finance** Members' dues. Meeting registration fees. **Events** *Annual Conference* London (UK) 2022, *Annual Conference* Lübeck (Germany) 2020, *Annual Conference* Amsterdam (Netherlands) 2019, *Annual Conference* Regensburg (Germany) 2018, *Annual Conference* Lisbon (Portugal) 2017. **Publications** *Monographs in Facial Plastic Surgery* (4 a year).

Members Surgeons in 67 countries and territories:

Albania, Argentina, Australia, Austria, Bahrain, Belarus, Belgium, Brazil, Bulgaria, Canada, Colombia, Croatia, Cyprus, Denmark, Egypt, Estonia, Finland, France, Germany, Greece, Hong Kong, Hungary, Iceland, India, Iran Islamic Rep, Iraq, Ireland, Israel, Italy, Jordan, Kazakhstan, Korea Rep, Kuwait, Latvia, Lebanon, Liechtenstein, Luxembourg, Malaysia, Mauritius, Mexico, Monaco, Netherlands, New Zealand, North Macedonia, Norway, Oman, Poland, Portugal, Romania, Russia, Saudi Arabia, Serbia, Singapore, Slovakia, Slovenia, South Africa, Spain, Sweden, Switzerland, Taiwan, Thailand, Türkiye, UK, Ukraine, United Arab Emirates, USA, Venezuela.

NGO Relations Member of: *Confederation of European Otorhinolaryngology – Head and Neck Surgery (Confederation of European ORL-HNS, #04528); International Federation of Facial Plastic Surgery Societies (IFFPSS, #13422).* [2022/XD8088/v/**D**]

♦ European Academy of Facial Surgery / see European Academy of Facial Plastic Surgery (#05792)

♦ European Academy of Food Engineering (EAFE) 05793

Chair School of Food and Nutritional Science, Univ College Cork, Cork, CO. CORK, Ireland.

URL: http://efeacademy.eu/

Aims Emphasize the role of food engineering in food safety and supply, nutrition, diet and public health as the underpinning discipline for innovations, production and availability of a safe and healthy supply of foods. **Structure** Executive Group. **Activities** Events/meetings. **Events** *Food Engineering for Life Symposium* Cambridge, MA (USA) 2016.

Members Individuals in 18 countries:

Croatia, Denmark, France, Germany, Hungary, Iceland, Ireland, Israel, Italy, Netherlands, Norway, Poland, Portugal, Serbia, Spain, Sweden, Switzerland, Türkiye. [2016/XM5093/**D**]

♦ European Academy of Forensic Science / see European Network of Forensic Science Institutes (#07910)

♦ European Academy of Gynaecological Cancer (EAGC) 05794

Contact address not obtained. E-mail: bosze@eagc.eu.

URL: http://www.eagc.hu/

History 1999, Budapest (Hungary), by the *European Academy of Gynaecological Cancer Foundation (EAGCF).* **Aims** Organize comprehensive training in gynaecological oncology in Europe. **Structure** Executive Board, headed by Chairman. Advisory Board. **Languages** English. **Events** *Congress* Budapest (Hungary) 2010. **Publications** *CME Journal of Gynecologic Oncology. European Academy of Gynaecological Cancer Book Series.* **NGO Relations** *European School of Oncology (ESO, #08434).* [2013/XJ3773/**D**]

♦ European Academy of Gynaecological Endoscopy / see European Academy of Gynaecological Surgery (#05795)

♦ European Academy of Gynaecological Surgery (EAGS) 05795

Contact Diestsevest 43, 3000 Leuven, Belgium. T. +3216629629. Fax +3216629639. E-mail: info@europeanacademy.org.

URL: http://www.europeanacademy.org/

History Founded Sep 2004, as *European Academy of Gynaecological Endoscopy (EAGE),* at the instigation of *European Society for Gynaecological Endoscopy (ESGE, #08611).* Current title adopted Aug 2007. Also referred to as *+he Academy.* **Aims** Offer scientifically validated standards for training and education in gynaecological endoscopy. **Activities** Research/documentation; training/education; certification/accreditation. [2017/XM5592/**E**]

♦ European Academy for Industrial Management (AIM) 05796

Sec Gebroeders Nachtergaelestraat 23 bus 3, 9800 Deinze, Belgium.

History 1984. Former names and other names: *Europäische Hochschullehrergruppe Technische Betriebsführung (EHTB)* – former (1984 to 2000); *European Academy for Technical Plant Management* – former (1984 to 2000). Registration: No/ID: 40238814, Netherlands. **Aims** Be the leading organization in the EU concerning education of university students in engineering science in the field of Industrial Management. **Structure** Board. **Activities** Events/meetings; research/documentation; training/education. **Events** *Conference* Novi Sad (Serbia) 2021, *Conference* Berlin (Germany) 2020, *Conference* Madrid (Spain) 2019, *Conference* Madrid (Spain) 2019, *Conference* Riga (Latvia) 2018. [2020/AA0575/**F**]

♦ European Academy for International Training (internationally oriented national body)

♦ European Academy of Land Use and Development (EALD) 05797

Académie Européenne des Sciences du Foncier – Europäische Akademie für Bodenordnung

Contact PTH Royal Inst of Technology, Dept of Real Estate and Construction Management², SE-100 44 Stockholm, Sweden.

URL: https://www.landuseacademy.org/

History Former names and other names: *Faculté Européenne Des Sciences Du Foncier (FESF)* – former (2010); *European Faculty of Land Use and Development* – former (2010); *Europäische Fakultät für Bodenordnung* – former. **Aims** Contribute in a scientific way to the responsible and sustainable use of land. **Activities** Events/meetings. **Events** *International and Interdisciplinary Symposium* Vienna (Austria) 2021, *International and Interdisciplinary Symposium* Kaunas (Lithuania) 2019, *International and Interdisciplinary Symposium* Riga (Latvia) 2018, *International and Interdisciplinary Symposium* Ljubljana (Slovenia) 2016, *International Symposium* Oslo (Norway) 2015. [2021/AA2054/**D**]

♦ European Academy of Legal Theory (EALT) 05798

Académie européenne de théorie du droit – Europese Academie voor Rechtstheorie

Office Goeth-Uni Frankfurt/Main, Inst für Kriminalwissenschaften und Rechtsphilosophie, Grüneburgplatz 1, 60629 Frankfurt-Main, Germany. E-mail: legaltheory@univie.ac.at.

Co-Dir Facultés Universitaires – Saint-Louis Bxl, Blvd du Jardin botanique 43, 1000 Brussels, Belgium. T. +3222117876.

URL: http://www.legaltheory.eu/

History 1989, Brussels (Belgium). Founded by *European Association for the Teaching of Legal Theory (EATLT, #06250)* and 2 Belgian universities. Partnership with 2 universities ended 2009, and relaunched with new partners. **Aims** Promulgate and advance research and teaching in legal theory and their interrelations with legal practice. **Activities** Education; awards/prizes/competitions. **Publications** *European Academy of Legal Theory Series.*

Members Partner universities in 8 countries:

Austria, Belgium, Germany, Italy, Poland, Sweden, Switzerland, UK. [2014/XG9927/**E**]

♦ European Academy of Letters, Sciences and Arts / see European Academy of Arts, Sciences and Humanities (#05781)

♦ European Academy for Life Research, Integration and Civil Society 05799

Europäische Akademie für Lebensforschung, Integration und Zivilgesellschaft (EALIZ) – Evropska Akademie pro Vyskum Zivota, Integraci a Obcanskou Spolecnost – Európska Akadémia pre Vyskum Zivota, Integraciu a Obciansku Spolocnost – Európai Életkutatási, Integraciós és Civiltarsadalmi Adamémia – Europejska Akademie ds Badania Aspektów Zyciowych, Integracji oraz Spoteczenstwa Cywilnego – Evropska Adameija za Raviskovanje Zivljenja, Integracije in Civilno Druzbo – Euroopa Elu-uuringute, Integratsiooni ja Tsiviilühiskonna Akadeemia – Eiropas Dzives standartu Petniecibas, Integracijas un Civilas Sabiedribas Akademija – Europos Gyvenimo Tyrimo, Integracijos ir Pilietines Visuomenes Akademija – Academia Europeana Pentru Cercetare de Viata, Integrare si Societate Civila – Europska Akademija za Istrazivanje Zivota, Integraciju i Civilno Drustvo

Contact address not obtained. T. +432732705360. Fax +4327327053613.

History 2004. Legal status through *Verein zur Förderung der Europäischen Akademie für Lebensforschung, Integration und Zivilgesellschaft*, registered in accordance with Austrian law: ZVR 384154425. **Aims** Cooperate to achieve optimal European unity in the diversity, co-determination and joint construction of social transformation processes. **Structure** Board of Directors, comprising President, 2 Vice-Presidents, Secretary, Deputy Secretary, Treasurer and Deputy Treasurer. **Finance** Members' dues. **Events** *Conference on changing roles in Europe* Vienna (Austria) 2010. [2012/XJ5972/**D**]

♦ European Academy of Management (EURAM) 05800

Exec Officer EURAM Exec Office, Rue Fossé aux Loups 38, Letterbox 3, 1000 Brussels, Belgium. T. +3222066664. Fax +3225121929. E-mail: info@euram.academy.

Pres address not obtained.

URL: https://euram.academy/

History 21 Apr 2001, Barcelona (Spain). Registration: Banque-Carrefour des Entreprises, No/ID: 0864.204.177, Start date: 30 Jun 2003, Belgium. **Aims** Serve as a European forum for networking and research in general management, strategy, corporate governance, organizational theory, organizational behaviour and decision-making. **Structure** Board; Executive Committee. **Languages** English. **Finance** Sources: members' dues. **Events** *Leading Digital Transformation* Winterthur (Switzerland) 2022, *Annual Conference* Montréal, QC (Canada) 2021, *Annual Conference* Dublin (Ireland) 2020, *Annual Conference* Lisbon (Portugal) 2019, *Annual Conference* Reykjavik (Iceland) 2018. **Publications** *European Management Review* (4 a year); *EURAM Newsletter* (3 a year). **Members** Individuals (1,900) in over 50 countries. Membership countries not specified. [2023.02.14/XD8262/v/**D**]

♦ European Academy of Management and Business Economics 05801

Académie européenne de direction et économie de l'entreprise (AEDEM) – Academia Europea de Dirección y Economia de la Empresa – Europäischer Akademie für Unternehmensleitung und Betriebswirtschaft

Main Office Ciencias Económicas, Univ de Vigo, Campus de Marcosende, 36310 Vigo, La Coruña, Spain. E-mail: secretaria@redaedem.org.

URL: http://redaedem.org/

History as *European Association for Business Management – Association européenne de direction et économie de l'entreprise (AEDEM) – Asociación Europea de dirección y Economia de la Empresa – Europäischer Verein für Unternehmensleitung und Betriebswirtschaft – Associação Europeia de Direção e Economia da Empresa*. Previously also referred to in English as *European Academy for Business Management.* **Aims** Promote the development and application of business management. **Structure** General Assembly (annual). Board of Directors, comprising President, 8 Vice-Presidents, Secretary General, Treasurer, International Relations Coordinator, Vice International Relations Coordinator, Honorary President, 4 Honorary members and 6 voting members. Scientific Council, consisting of 5 Councillors (Business Management; Finances; Marketing; Production; Human Resources) and 5 Directors representing AEDEM's publications. Management Council, comprising Director, Secretary and 35 members. Editorial Committee. **Finance** Members' dues. **Activities** Organizes: Annual Congress; International Conference; national congress. **Events** *Annual congress* Tokyo (Japan) 2019, *Annual International Conference / International Conference* Paris (France) 2014, *Annual International Conference / International Conference* Aalen (Germany) 2013, *International Conference* Budapest (Hungary) 2012, *International Conference* Podgorica (Montenegro) 2011. **Publications** *AEDEM BIBLIOMETRICA* – journal; *Investigaciones Europeas de Dirección y Economia de la Empresa* – journal; *Revista de Economia y Empresa* – journal; *Revista Europea de Dirección y Economia de la Empresa* – journal. Annual meeting proceedings. **NGO Relations** *Sociedad Internacional de Gestión y Economia Fuzzy (SIGEF, #19386).* [2018/XD6181/**D**]

♦ European Academy for Medicine of Ageing (EAMA) 05802

Admin c/o Univ Hosp Gent, Dept Geriatric Medicine, De Pintelaan 185, 9000 Ghent, Belgium.

URL: http://www.eama.eu/

History Founded 1992, Sion (Switzerland), by *Group of European Professors in Medical Gerontology (GEPMG, inactive).* Registered in accordance with Belgian law: 0565 937 590. **Aims** Improve knowledge and skills in *geriatric* medicine for junior faculty members or promising candidates for future teachers in *geriatrics.* **Structure** Executive Board. **Languages** English. **Staff** 1.00 FTE, paid. **Finance** Supported by patrons, including: *WHO (#20950)*; *International Institute on Ageing, United Nations – Malta (INIA, #13860)*; *International Psychogeriatric Association (IPA, #14664).* Annual budget: about euro 230,000. **Activities** Training/education. **Members** Individuals (about 450) having received their EAMA diploma in 41 countries:

Argentina, Austria, Belgium, Brazil, China, Costa Rica, Cuba, Cyprus, Czechia, Denmark, Estonia, Finland, France, Germany, Greece, Hungary, Iceland, Israel, Italy, Japan, Lebanon, Lithuania, Mauritius, Mexico, Netherlands, Norway, Poland, Portugal, Qatar, Saudi Arabia, Senegal, South Africa, Spain, Sweden, Switzerland, Thailand, Tunisia, Türkiye, UK, Ukraine, USA. [2018/XE2188/v/**E**]

♦ European Academy of Neurology (EAN) 05803

Exec Dir Breite Gasse 4/7, 1070 Vienna, Austria. T. +4318890503. Fax +431889050313. E-mail: headoffice@ean.org.

URL: http://www.ean.org/

History Jun 2014. Set up by *European Federation of Neurological Societies (EFNS, inactive)* and *European Neurological Society (ENS, inactive).* Registration: ZVR, No/ID: 120490024, Austria; EU Transparency Register, No/ID: 308226821052-25, Start date: 14 Mar 2016. **Aims** Increase availability and standards of neurological services; advance development of neurology; encourage collaboration between European national neurological societies; support research and encourage research collaboration; strengthen the standard, availability and equality of neurological education; raise awareness. **Structure** Assembly of Delegates; Board. **Languages** English. **Staff** 7.00 FTE, paid. **Finance** Sources: donations; meeting proceeds; members' dues; sale of publications. **Activities** Events/meetings; research/documentation; awards/prizes/competitions. **Events** *Congress* Seville (Spain) 2025, *Congress* Helsinki (Finland) 2024, *Congress* Budapest (Hungary) 2023, *Congress* Vienna (Austria) 2022, *Congress* 2021. **Publications** *European Journal of Neurology (EJN).*

Members Institutional members in 44 countries:

Albania, Armenia, Austria, Azerbaijan, Belarus, Belgium, Bosnia-Herzegovina, Bulgaria, Croatia, Cyprus, Czechia, Denmark, Estonia, Finland, France, Georgia, Germany, Greece, Hungary, Iceland, Ireland, Italy, Latvia, Lithuania, Luxembourg, Moldova, Montenegro, Netherlands, North Macedonia, Norway, Poland, Portugal, Romania, Russia, Serbia, Slovakia, Slovenia, Spain, Sweden, Switzerland, Türkiye, UK, Ukraine, Uzbekistan.

Associate institutional members in 9 countries and territories:

Algeria, Egypt, Jordan, Lebanon, Libya, Morocco, Palestine, Syrian AR, Tunisia.

NGO Relations Member of (4): *Associations and Conference Forum (AC Forum, #02909)*; *Biomedical Alliance in Europe (#03251)*; *European Brain Council (EBC, #06391)*; *European Chronic Disease Alliance (ECDA, #06548).* [2022/XJ7482/**D**]

♦ European Academy of Nursing Science (EANS) 05804

Contact Regus EU Parliament, De Meeussquare 37, 1000 Brussels, Belgium. E-mail: contact@european-academy-of-nursing-science.com.

URL: http://www.european-academy-of-nursing-science.com/

History 1998. **Aims** Be the scientific community in Europe providing inspiration, collaboration and academic leadership in nursing. **Structure** Board. **Activities** Events/meetings; training/education; awards/prizes/competitions. **Events** *Winter Summit* Turku (Finland) 2018, *Winter Summit* Athens (Greece) 2015, *Summer Conference* Barcelona (Spain) 2015, *Annual Meeting* Utrecht (Netherlands) 2014. **Publications** *EANS Newsletter.* **Members** Individuals Full; Honorary; Student. Membership countries not specified. [2020/XJ9332/v/**D**]

♦ European Academy of Nutritional Sciences (#00045)

♦ European Academy of Occupational Health Psychology (EA-OHP) .. 05805

Pres address not obtained.

URL: http://www.eaohp.org/

Finance Members' dues. **Events** *Biennial Conference* Nicosia (Cyprus) 2020, *Biennial Conference* Lisbon (Portugal) 2018, *Biennial Conference* Athens (Greece) 2016, *Biennial Conference* London (UK) 2014, *Biennial Conference* Zurich (Switzerland) 2012. **Publications** *Occupational Health Psychologist* – newsletter. [2014/XJ3380/**E**]

♦ European Academy of Ophthalmology (EAO) 05806

Pres Dept Ophthalmology, Univ Vita-Salute, Scientific Inst San Raffaele, Via Olgettina 60, 20132 Milan MI, Italy. T. +39226432648. Fax +39226433643.

SG Univ of Coimbra, Centro Hospitalar Universitario Coimbra, Praceta Mota Pinto, 3000-075 Coimbra, Portugal. T. +351239701182 – +351239400449. Fax +351239826665.

Exec Vice-Pres Tel Aviv Univ, Sackler Fac of Medicine, Tel Aviv Medical Center, 6 Weizmann St, 64239 Tel Aviv, Israel. T. +97236927618. Fax +97236925693. E-mail: anatl@tlvmc.gov.il.

URL: http://www.eao.eu/

History 2003, as a working scientific group. **Aims** Coordinate, advise and promote education research and development in the science and practice of ophthalmology and related disciplines within Europe. **Structure** Board. **Languages** English. **Staff** 2.00 FTE, paid. **Finance** Members' dues. **Events** *Meeting* London (UK) 2014, *Meeting* Copenhagen (Denmark) 2013, *Meeting* Milan (Italy) 2012, *Meeting* Geneva (Switzerland) 2011, *Meeting* Paris (France) 2010.

Members Individuals (53) in 18 countries:

Austria, Belgium, Denmark, Finland, France, Germany, Greece, Hungary, Iceland, Israel, Italy, Netherlands, Poland, Portugal, Spain, Sweden, Switzerland, UK. [2019.03.11/XJ8372/v/**D**]

♦ European Academy of Optometry and Optics (EAOO) 05807

Events – Coordinator 42 Craven Street, London, WC2N 5NG, UK. T. +442077664385. Fax +442078396800. E-mail: admin@eaoo.info.

URL: http://www.eaoo.info/

History Registration: Companies House, No/ID: 6844057, Start date: 11 Mar 2009, England and Wales. **Aims** Advance optometry and optics; develop the scientific knowledge base; support and promote lifelong learning for optometrists, opticians, vision scientists and all those involved in eye health care across Europe. **Structure** Board of Trustees. **Languages** English. **Events** *Annual Conference* Helsinki (Finland) 2021, *Annual Conference* Helsinki (Finland) 2020, *Annual Conference* Rome (Italy) 2019, *Annual Conference* Zagreb (Croatia) 2018, *Annual Conference* Barcelona (Spain) 2017.

Members Full in 27 countries:

Austria, Belgium, Bulgaria, Croatia, Czechia, Denmark, Estonia, Finland, France, Germany, Hungary, Ireland, Israel, Italy, Latvia, Netherlands, Norway, Poland, Portugal, Serbia, Slovenia, Spain, Sweden, Switzerland, Türkiye, UK, USA.

European Federation of the Contact Lens and IOL Industries (EFCLIN, #07089). [2021/XJ7728/y/**D**]

♦ European Academy of Orofacial Pain and Dysfunction (EAOPD) 05808

Sec address not obtained.

Pres address not obtained.

URL: http://www.eaopd.org/

History Founded 14 Jul 2017, Geneva (Switzerland). Registered in accordance with Swiss Civil Code. **Aims** Improve the knowledge and skills of professionals working in the field of Orofacial Pain and Dysfunction (OPD). **Structure** General Assembly; Executive Board. **Activities** Events/meetings. **Events** *Annual Congress* Stockholm (Sweden) 2023, *Annual Congress* Naples (Italy) 2022, *Annual Congress* Lisbon (Portugal) 2021, *Annual Congress* Noordwijk (Netherlands) 2019, *ICOT : International Conference of Orofacial Pain and Temporomandibular Disorders* London (UK) 2018. **Members** Full; Student; Retiree; Affiliate. Membership countries not specified. **NGO Relations** *European Academy of Craniomandibular Disorders (EACD, #05785).* [2020/XM7059/**D**]

♦ European Academy of Orthokeratology and Myopia Control (unconfirmed)

♦ European Academy of Otology and Neuro-Otology (EAONO) 05809

Gen Sec c/o Radboud University Hospital, Philip van Leydenlaan 15, 6500 HB Nijmegen, Netherlands.

URL: http://www.eaono.org/

History 1996, Alghero (Italy). Founded during the 5th *International Conference on Cholesteatoma and Mastoid Surgery.* Inaugural meeting 1997, Sydney (Australia). Registration: Belgium. **Aims** Unite experts in otology, neuro-otology or skull base surgery in Europe; exchange and disseminate information about the anatomy, physiology, pathology, medical and surgical management of the ear, sensorineural systems of audition and equilibrium, trigeminal, facial, lower cranial nerves and related disorders as well as disorders of the nose, sinuses and pharynx related to skull base; stimulate basic and clinical research relating to these systems and disorders; encourage education and high quality training programmes. **Structure** General Assembly (every 2 years). Board elects Steering Committee, comprising President, Past-President, General Secretary, Chairman, 5 Regional Secretaries and Treasurer. **Finance** Members' dues. **Events** *Conference / EANO Week* London (UK) 2021, *Conference* London (UK) 2020, *International conference on cholesteatoma and ear surgery / International Meeting* Antalya (Turkey) 2008, *Workshop* Palma (Spain) 2008, *Workshop / Meeting* Cologne (Germany) 2006. **Publications** *O and N Journal.* **Members** Founder members (103) in 18 countries. Membership countries not specified. **NGO Relations** Member of: *Confederation of European Otorhinolaryngology – Head and Neck Surgery (Confederation of European ORL-HNS, #04528).* [2021/XE4250/**E**]

European Academy Otzenhausen 05809

♦ European Academy of Otzenhausen / see Europäische Akademie Otzenhausen

♦ European Academy of Paediatric Dentistry (EAPD) 05810
Académie européenne de pédodontie
Sec 2 Thivon St, Goudi, 115 27 Athens, Greece.
Contact 22 Kodrou str, Halandri, 152 31 Athens, Greece.
URL: http://www.eapd.eu/
History 1990. **Aims** Promote high standards of dental care for children; promote the specialty of paediatric dentistry in Europe; promote research into prevention of dental diseases in children; accredit training programmes in Europe. **Structure** Council; Executive Board; Committees (6). **Languages** English. **Staff** Voluntary. **Finance** Budget (annual): euro 20,000. **Activities** Events/meetings; certification/accreditation. **Events** Congress Gothenburg (Sweden) 2024, *Seminar* Prague (Czechia) 2023, *Congress* Lisbon (Portugal) 2022, *Seminar* Oslo (Norway) 2021, *Congress* Athens (Greece) 2020. **Publications** *European Archives of Paediatric Dentistry* (6 a year).
Members Individuals (about 560) in 53 countries:
Australia, Austria, Belgium, Bosnia-Herzegovina, Bulgaria, Canada, Croatia, Cyprus, Czechia, Denmark, Egypt, Finland, France, Germany, Greece, Guatemala, Hungary, Iceland, India, Indonesia, Iran Islamic Rep, Ireland, Israel, Italy, Jordan, Kuwait, Lithuania, Malaysia, Montenegro, Nepal, Netherlands, New Zealand, Norway, Oman, Poland, Portugal, Qatar, Romania, Russia, Saudi Arabia, Serbia, Singapore, Slovakia, Slovenia, Spain, Sweden, Switzerland, Thailand, Türkiye, UK, United Arab Emirates, USA, Venezuela.
IGO Relations *European Commission (EC, #06633).* **NGO Relations** Associate member of: *Platform for Better Oral Health in Europe (#18399);*
[2022/XD4414/D]

♦ European Academy of Paediatrics (EAP) 05811
Secretariat c/o Paragon Conventions, Avenue Louis-Casai 18, 1209 Geneva, Switzerland. T. +41225330948. Fax +41225802953. E-mail: secretariat@eapaediatrics.eu.
URL: http://www.eapaediatrics.eu/
History 12 Oct 1959, Montpellier (France). Founded at 17th Congress of *Association des pédiatres de langue française (APLF, #02855)*. New statutes adopted, 2006; revised 2008. Former names and other names: *Comité européen de liaison des pédiatres* – former (12 Oct 1959 to 12 Oct 1965); *European Confederation of National Syndicates and Professional Associations of Paediatricians (CESP)* – former (12 Oct 1965 to 1989); *Confédération européenne des syndicats nationaux et associations professionnelles de pédiatres* – former (12 Oct 1965 to 1989); *Confederation of European Specialists in Paediatrics (CESP)* – former (1989 to 2006); *Confédération européenne des spécialistes en pédiatrie* – former (1989 to 2006). Registration: Start date: 9 Aug 1972, Belgium; Start date: Aug 2008, Belgium; EU Transparency Register, No/ID: 517974629774-63. **Aims** Promote the health of children and young people in Europe; improve standards in training, service and research and represent the professional interests of paediatricians in the EU. **Structure** General Meeting (2 a year); Executive Committee; Secretariat in Brussels (Belgium). Working Groups. Also includes: *European Board of Paediatrics (EBP, #06368)*. **Languages** English, French. **Staff** 0.50 FTE, paid. **Finance** Sources: members' dues. **Activities** Events/meetings; knowledge management/information dissemination; training/education. **Events** *Congress* Padua (Italy) 2023, *Winter Meeting* Brussels (Belgium) 2022, *Winter Meeting* 2021, *Spring Meeting* Larnaca (Cyprus) 2021, *Congress* Porto (Portugal) 2021. **Publications** *EAP Journal*.
Members National associations in 31 countries:
Austria, Belgium, Bulgaria, Croatia, Cyprus, Czechia, Denmark, Estonia, Finland, France, Germany, Greece, Hungary, Iceland, Ireland, Italy, Latvia, Lithuania, Luxembourg, Malta, Netherlands, Norway, Poland, Portugal, Romania, Slovakia, Slovenia, Spain, Sweden, Switzerland, UK.
Associate in 9 countries:
Armenia, Bosnia-Herzegovina, Georgia, Moldova, Montenegro, North Macedonia, Serbia, Türkiye, Ukraine.
UEMS-Sub-Specialities:
European Board of Neonatology (EBN, #06363); European Paediatric Neurology Society (EPNS, #08126); European Society for Emergency Medicine (EuSEM, #08590); European Society for Paediatric Endocrinology (ESPE, #08678); European Society for Paediatric Gastroenterology, Hepatology and Nutrition (ESPGHAN, #08680); European Society for Paediatric Nephrology (ESPN, #08684); European Society of Paediatric and Neonatal Intensive Care (ESPNIC, #08683); Paediatric Rheumatology European Society (PRES, #18020); Section of Child and Adolescent Psychiatry UEMS; *SIOP Europe (SIOPE, #19288); Society for the Study of Inborn Errors of Metabolism (SSIEM, #19648).*
Affiliated and related organizations (8):
Association for Paediatric Education in Europe (APEE, #02847); European Confederation of Primary Care Paediatricians (ECPCP, #06721); European Public Health Alliance (EPHA, #08297); European Society for Paediatric Research (ESPR, #08687); European Society of Paediatric Radiology (ESPR, #08686); International Pediatric Association (IPA, #14541); International Society for Social Pediatrics and Child Health (ISSOP, #15448).
IGO Relations *European Commission (EC, #06633)* (DG V). **NGO Relations** Functions as the specialized section for European Union and EFTA countries within: *European Union of Medical Specialists (UEMS, #09001)*. Together with *European Society of Paediatric and Neonatal Intensive Care (ESPNIC, #08683)* and *European Society for Paediatric Research (ESPR, #08687)*, instrumental in setting up: *European Academy of Paediatrics Societies (EAPS)*. Endorses: *Steering Group on Influenza Vaccination (#19980)*. Member of: *European Public Health Alliance (EPHA, #08297)*. Associated member of: *European Forum for Primary Care (EFPC, #07326)*.
[2023/XD0690/y/D]

♦ European Academy of Paediatrics Societies (meeting series)
♦ European Academy of Paediatric Urology (see: #16883)
♦ European Academy of Rehabilitation Medicine (#00026)

♦ European Academy of Religion (EuARe) 05812
Registered Office Via San Vitale 114, c/o Fondazione per le Scienze Religiose Giovanni, 40125 Bologna BO, Italy. T. +3951239532. E-mail: eu_are@fscire.it – euare.bo@gmail.com.
URL: http://www.europeanacademyofreligion.org/
History 5 Dec 2016, Bologna (Italy). Statutes approved 21 Jun 2017. **Aims** Constitute an inclusive network; act as an open platform; provide a framework to foster research, communication, exchange and cooperation concerning important religious issues for the academic world and society at large. **Structure** General Assembly (annual); Executive Committee; Officers. **Languages** English. **Finance** Members' dues. **Activities** Events/meeting; research/documentation; networking/liaising. **Events** *Conference* Bologna (Italy) 2019, *Conference* Bologna (Italy) 2018, *Conference* Bologna (Italy) 2017. **Members** Individuals. Membership countries not specified. **NGO Relations** Cooperates with (1): *G20 Interfaith Forum Association (IF20, #10055)*.
[2020/XM6533/v/D]

♦ European Academy of Science, Arts and Humanities (no recent information)

♦ European Academy of Sciences (EURASC) 05813
Académie Européenne des Sciences
Registered Office Bvd de la Sauvenière 40, 4000 Liège, Belgium. T. +32425367118. Fax +3242541816.
URL: http://www.eurasc.org/
History Previously also known under the acronym *EAS*. Registered in accordance with Belgian law. **Aims** Promote excellence in science and technology and their essential roles in fostering social and economic development and progress; establish efficient collaboration among scientists, researchers, educators, engineers and public authorities worldwide. **Structure** General Assembly; Praesidium, consisting of Effective Members; Executive Committee; Scientific Committee; Technical Committee; Divisions (9). **Languages** English. **Staff** 0.50 FTE, paid; 46.00 FTE, voluntary. **Finance** Members' dues. **Activities** Knowledge management/information dissemination; research and development; events/meetings. **Events** *Symposium* Madrid (Spain) 2019, *The future of science in the 21st century – science and technology for the better future of humankind* Lisbon (Portugal) 2017, *Symposium* Brussels (Belgium) 2016, *Symposium* Brest (France) 2015, *Symposium* Porto (Portugal) 2014. **Publications** *Annals of the European Academy of Sciences* (2005, 2006). **Members** Effective and Associate. Membership countries not specified.
[2015.09.29/XM2925/D]

♦ European Academy of Sciences and Arts (EASA) 05814
Académie européenne des sciences et des arts – Europäische Akademie der Wissenschaften und Künste – Academia Scientiarum et Artium Europaea
Main Office St Peter-Bezirk 10, 5020 Salzburg, Austria. T. +43662841345. Fax +43662841343. E-mail: office@euro-acad.eu – presidential.office@euro-acad.eu.
URL: http://www.euro-acad.eu/
History 7 Mar 1990, Salzburg (Austria). Founded by Prof Dr Felix Unger, Franz Cardinal König and Prof Dr Nikolaus Lobkowicz. **Aims** Promote scientific and societal progress. **Structure** Senate, including Praesidium. **Languages** English, German. **Staff** 4.00 FTE, paid. **Activities** Awards/prizes/competitions; events/meetings; publishing activities. **Events** *Conference* Podgorica (Montenegro) 2019, *Annual RIN Baska Global Navigation Satellite Systems Conference* Baska (Croatia) 2018, *International Symposium on Justice and Solidarity* Kuopio (Finland) 2014, *International Conference on Religions and Ideologies, Peace or Violence* Ljubljana (Slovenia) / Celje (Slovenia) 2014, *International Conference on Transition to a new Society* Podgorica (Montenegro) 2014. **Publications** *30 Jahre Europäische Akademie/30 years of EASA* (2022) by Sir Josef Schopf; *Manifest for Europe*. Annual Report. **Members** Ordinary; Honorary. Membership countries not specified. **NGO Relations** Member of (4): *Alliance of International Science Organizations (ANSO, #00696); European Materials Forum (EMF, #07751)* (founding); *European Policy Centre (EPC, #08240); InterAcademy Partnership (IAP, #11376)*. Instrumental in setting up (1): *European-Latvian Institute (EUROLAT)*.
[2023.02.15/XE1704/v/E]

♦ European Academy for Standardisation (EURAS) 05815
Pres c/o Sonnenweg 3, 49324 Melle, Germany. T. +31553010170.
URL: https://www.euras.org/
History 1993, Hamburg (Germany). Registration: Lower Saxony District court, No/ID: VR r201484, Start date: 24 Mar 2016, Germany, Osnabrück. **Aims** Promote and achieve progress in the academic treatment of standardisation, involving the widest possible range of disciplines. **Structure** Board. **Activities** Events/meetings; knowledge management/information dissemination; research/documentation; standards/guidelines. **Events** *Annual Standardisation Conference* Aachen (Germany) 2021, *Annual Standardisation Conference* Rome (Italy) 2019, *EURAS Annual Standardisation Conference* Brussels (Belgium) 2013. **Members** Individuals. Membership countries not specified.
[2021/AA2057/v/D]

♦ European Academy of Surface Technology (EAST) 05816
Gen Sec Katharinenstr 17, 73525 Schwäbisch Gmünd, Germany. T. +497171100642. Fax +497171100654. E-mail: info@east-site.net.
URL: http://www.east-site.net/
History 1989. Founded as an international branch of the German Zentrum für Oberflächentechnik Schäbisch Gmünd, under the patronage of *European Parliament (EP, #08146), European Community (inactive)*, German Ministry of Research and Technology, and the State Ministry of Economic Affairs, Baden-Württemberg (Germany). Transformed into current form, 1998. Registration: No/ID: VR 847, Germany, Schwäbisch Gmünd. **Aims** Promote science, research, training and education in the fields of surface technology and related areas. **Structure** European Board; Executive Board. Office. **Activities** Events/meetings.
Members Full in 17 countries:
Austria, Belgium, Bulgaria, Denmark, Finland, France, Georgia, Germany, Greece, Hungary, Italy, Romania, Serbia, Spain, Switzerland, Türkiye, UK.
Associate in 5 countries:
Australia, Brazil, Canada, Japan, USA.
NGO Relations Member of: *International Union for Surface Finishing (IUSF, #15821)*.
[2022/XJ8605/D]

♦ European Academy of Teachers in General Practice (EURACT) 05817
Admin Sec Zavod za Razvoj Druzinske Medicine, Poljanski Nasip 58, 1000 Ljubljana, Slovenia. T. +38614386913. Fax +38614386910. E-mail: euract@woncaeurope.org.
URL: http://www.euract.eu/
History Founded Mar 1992, Scotland, deriving from the *Leeuwenhorst Group*, set up 1974, which was subsequently disbanded and was refounded in 1982 as *New Leeuwenhorst Group*. Current constitution approved 26 Apr 2009, St Petersburg (Russia). A network of *European Society of General Practice/Family Medicine (WONCA Europe, #08609)*. Registered in accordance with Dutch law. **Aims** Promote general practice teaching and *learning* by creating networks of teachers with common interests, gathering information on *curricula*, disseminating reports, publishing a journal, arranging courses and conferences and offering technical assistance and advice. **Structure** Council; Executive Board. **Languages** English. **Finance** Members' dues. **Activities** Guidance/assistance/consulting; knowledge management/information dissemination; networking/liaising; events/meetings; publishing activity. **Events** *Educational Conference* Slovenia 2023, *Meeting* Turku (Finland) 2006, *International workshop on tobacco and alcohol addiction* Barcelona (Spain) 2000, *European Network Organizations Open Conference* Palma (Spain) 1999, *International workshop on learning and teaching about family in general practice* Bled (Slovenia) 1997.
Members National Representatives in 38 countries:
Albania, Austria, Belgium, Bosnia-Herzegovina, Bulgaria, Croatia, Czechia, Denmark, Estonia, Finland, Georgia, Germany, Greece, Hungary, Ireland, Israel, Italy, Latvia, Lithuania, Malta, Moldova, Montenegro, Netherlands, North Macedonia, Norway, Poland, Portugal, Romania, Russia, Serbia, Slovakia, Slovenia, Spain, Sweden, Switzerland, Türkiye, UK, Ukraine.
IGO Relations Cooperates with: *WHO (#20950)*. **NGO Relations** Cooperates with: *European General Practice Research Network (EGPRN, #07384)*.
[2023/XE1936/E]

♦ European Academy for Technical Plant Management / see European Academy for Industrial Management (#05796)
♦ European Academy of Tumor Immunology (internationally oriented national body)
♦ European Academy of the Urban Environment, Berlin (internationally oriented national body)
♦ European Academy Vienna (internationally oriented national body)

♦ European Academy of Wind Energy (EAWE) 05818
Sec Kleiner Holzweg 2, 34121 Kassel, Germany. T. +491725713639.
URL: http://www.eawe.eu/
History 17 oct 2003. Current articles adopted 2010. **Aims** Formulate and execute joint R and D projects; coordinate high quality scientific research and education on wind energy at European level. **Structure** General Assembly. Executive Committee. Board, including President and Vice-President. **Activities** Organizes: annual PhD seminar; biannual Research Conference: annual Conference. Awards: Scientific Award; Excellent Young Wind Doctor Award. **Events** *Science from making torque from wind* Copenhagen (Denmark) 2014, *Seminar on Wind Energy in Europe* Zurich (Switzerland) 2012, *Seminar on Wind Energy in Europe* Delft (Netherlands) 2011, *Wind energy conference* Heraklion (Greece) 2010, *Seminar on wind energy in Europe* Trondheim (Norway) 2010.
Members Full; Associate; Honorary. Members in 11 countries:
Belgium, Denmark, France, Germany, Greece, Netherlands, Norway, Spain, Sweden, Switzerland, UK.
[2012/XJ5983/D]
♦ European Academy of Yuste Foundation / see Fundación Academia Europea e Iberoamericana de Yuste

♦ European Access Network (EAN) 05819
Secretariat Artevelde University of Applied Sciences, Hoogpoort 15, 9000 Ghent, Belgium.
Facebook: https://www.facebook.com/EuropeanAccessNetwork/
History 1991, Lille (France). Registration: England and Wales. **Aims** Encourage wider access to and participation in *higher education* and training in all European countries for those who are currently under-represented, whether for reasons of gender, ethnic origin, nationality, age, disability, low socio-economic status, vocational training, geographic location or earlier educational disadvantage. **Structure** General Meeting; Executive Committee. **Finance** Members' dues. Other sources: research income and sponsorship. **Activities** Networking/liaising; projects/programmes; knowledge management/information dissemination; research/documentation; training/education. **Events** *Annual Conference* Ghent (Belgium) 2019, *Annual Conference* The Hague (Netherlands) 2018, *World Congress on Access to Postsecondary Education* Campinas (Brazil) 2017, *Annual Conference* Giesen (Germany) 2017, *Annual Conference* Dublin (Ireland) 2016. **Publications** *Journal of Widening Participation and Lifelong Learning* (3 a year); *European Access News* (2 a year) – newsletter. Conference proceedings.
Members Staff in further, adult and higher education, local and national policy-makers, members of organizations relating to higher education, including employer organizations and trade unions. Individuals in 21 countries:

Australia, Belgium, Canada, Czechia, Estonia, Finland, France, Germany, Ireland, Latvia, Lithuania, Malta, Netherlands, Norway, Poland, Portugal, Russia, Spain, Sweden, UK, USA.
IGO Relations Supported by: *European Union (EU, #08967).* **NGO Relations** Involved with: *European University Continuing Education Network (EUCEN, #09030).* Affiliate member of: *International Association of Universities (IAU, #12246); SPACE Network (#19899).* [2020/XF4689/v/F]

♦ European Accounting Association (EAA) 05820
Association européenne de comptabilité
Administrative Coordinator c/o EIASM, Passage du Nord 19, 1000 Brussels, Belgium. T. +3222266660. Fax +3225121929. E-mail: eaa@eiasm.be.
Pres Tilburg School of Economics and Management and TiasNimbas Business School, Tilburg Univ, Warandelaan 2, PO Box 90153, 5000 LE Tilburg, Netherlands. T. +31134668623.
URL: http://www.eaa-online.org/
History 1977, Brussels (Belgium), under the auspices of *EFMD – The Management Development Network (#05387),* in close cooperation with *European Institute for Advanced Studies in Management (EIASM, #07544).* Registered in accordance with Belgian law. Previously also referred to as *European Association of Accountants – Association européenne d'experts comptables – Europäischer Verein für Wirtschaftsprüfer – Europese Vereniging van Accountants.* EU Transparency Register: 816374013997-80. **Aims** Create a European-wide community of accounting scholars and researchers; serve as a focal point of communication for members within and outside Europe. **Activities** Events/meetings; publishing activities; research and development; research/documentation. **Events** *Annual Congress* Bucharest (Romania) 2024, *Annual Congress* Espoo (Finland) 2023, *Annual Congress* Bergen (Norway) 2022, *Annual Congress* Bucharest (Romania) 2021, *Annual Congress* Bucharest (Romania) 2020. **Publications** *EAA Newsletter* (4 a year); *Accounting in Europe; European Accounting Review.* **Members** Institutional; Individual (2,588). Members in 60 countries. Membership countries not specified. **NGO Relations** *Association of International Accountants (AIA, #02654)* is member. Cooperates with: *European Finance Association (EFA, #07248); European International Business Academy (EIBA, #07585); European Marketing Academy (EMAC, #07745).* [2021/XD5801/D]

♦ European Accounting, Audit, Tax and Legal Association for medium-sized companies / see EuropeFides (#09156)
♦ European Accreditation Advisory Board (see: #06782)

♦ European Accreditation Agency for the Life Sciences (EAALS) 05821
Exec Sec 46 tour des Caves, 34120 Tourbes, France. E-mail: clues@abdn.ac.uk.
URL: http://www.eaals.eu/
History 2 Sep 2008, Lleida (Spain), by General Assembly of *Association for European Life Science Universities (ICA, #02519).* **Aims** Enhance the quality of degree programmes and higher educational institutions in life sciences and the rural environment, through quality assurance and international accreditation. **Structure** Board, reporting to ICA General Assembly. **Languages** English. **Staff** 0.50 FTE, paid. **Activities** Awards European Accreditation Agency for Higher Education in the Life Sciences Quality Label to degree programmes in higher education institutions. Makes recommendations for the continuing enhancement of their educational provision. **Publications** Handbook. [2010.08.25/XJ1735/E]

♦ European Accreditation of Certification (inactive)

♦ European Accreditation Committee in the Central Nervous System (EACIC) 05822
Contact Av Jacques Pastur 47, 1180 Brussels, Belgium. T. +32479987440. E-mail: eacic@ulb.ac.be.
Registered Office Rue Lens 13, 1000 Brussels, Belgium.
URL: http://www.eacic.eu/
History Founded within the framework of *LEONARDO DA VINCI (inactive)* (EUR/99/2091/1111b/FBC, Jan 2000-May 2000) from *European Commission (EC, #06633)* and in close collaboration with *European College of Neuropsychopharmacology (ECNP, #06612).* Registered in accordance with Belgian law. **Aims** Promote and encourage the development of continued medical education (CME) in the central nervous system throughout Europe; establish policies and high standards in CME; ensure CME plays an important role in the process of helping health care workers provide improved standards of clinical care to their patients. **Structure** General Assembly (annual); Steering Committee; Council; Secretariat. **Languages** English. **Staff** 2.00 FTE, paid. **Finance** Grants. Annual budget: about euro 60,000. **Activities** Events/meetings; publishing activities; training/educaiton. **Publications** Regular feedback reports on scientific accredited events.
Members in 9 countries:
Austria, Belgium, France, Germany, Italy, Netherlands, Sweden, UK, USA. [2018.06.01/XE4446/E]

♦ European Accreditation Council for Continuing Medical Education (EACCME) 05823
Secretariat c/o UEMS, Rue de l'Industrie 24, 1040 Brussels, Belgium. T. +3226495164. Fax +3226403730. E-mail: uems@skynet.be.
URL: http://www.eaccme.eu/
History Jan 2000, by *European Union of Medical Specialists (UEMS, #09001).* **Aims** Ensure mutual recognition of accreditation of EU-wide and international CME-CPD activities for live educational events through awarding European CME credits (ECMECs) to individual medical specialists, allowing the recognition and exchange of CME credits between all European countries; act as the central link between the National Accreditation Authorities (NAAs), the UEMS Specialist Sections and Boards (S&Bs), the European Specialty Accreditation Boards (ESABs) and the Providers of CME activities. **Languages** English. **Events** *Joint Conference on CME-CPD in Europe* Seville (Spain) 2022, *Virtual Joint Conference on CME-CPD in Europe* Seville (Spain) 2021, *Joint Conference on CME-CPD in Europe* Seville (Spain) 2020, *Joint Conference on CME-CPD in Europe* Brussels (Belgium) 2018, *Joint Conference on CME-CPD in Europe* Amsterdam (Netherlands) 2016. **NGO Relations** Collaborating centre of: *Global Allergy and Asthma European Network (GA2LEN, #10179).* [2017/XD7824/D]

♦ European Acoustics Association (EAA) 05824
Office c/o SEA, Serrano 144, 28006 Madrid, Spain.
URL: http://www.euracoustics.org/
History 1992. Became a grouping of the type *European Economic Interest Grouping (EEIG, #06960),* 2 Feb 1994, Liège (Belgium). From 1 Jan 1997, includes *Federation of Acoustical Societies of Europe (FASE, inactive),* set up 1972. Registration: EU Transparency Register, No/ID: 92630347278-84. **Aims** Promote development of the science of acoustics. **Structure** General Assembly; Board; Technical Committees; Office in Madrid (Spain). **Finance** Members' dues. Annual budget: euro 120,000. **Activities** Events/meetings; awards/prizes/competitions. **Events** *Joint Baltic-Nordic Acoustics Meeting (BNAM) & EUROREGIO Conference* Aalborg (Denmark) 2022, *EURONOISE : European Conference on Noise Control* Madeira (Portugal) 2021, *Forum Acusticum* Lyon (France) 2020, *EUROREGIO Conference* Aachen (Germany) 2019, *Spatial Audio Signal Processing Symposium* Paris (France) 2019. **Publications** *Acta Acustica* (6 a year) – journal.
Members National associations in 33 countries:
Austria, Belgium, Bulgaria, Croatia, Czechia, Denmark, Finland, France, Germany, Greece, Hungary, Iceland, Israel, Italy, Latvia, Lithuania, Morocco, Netherlands, North Macedonia, Norway, Poland, Portugal, Romania, Russia, Serbia, Slovakia, Slovenia, Spain, Sweden, Switzerland, Türkiye, UK, Ukraine.
IGO Relations Member of: *European Commission (EC, #06633)* – Noise Expert Group. **NGO Relations** Member of: *Initiative for Science in Europe (ISE, #11214).* Affiliate member of: *International Commission for Acoustics (ICA, #12658).* [2021/XF4375/F]

♦ European Actinide Research and Development Society (inactive)
♦ European Action Committee of the IUFO / see COFACE Families Europe (#04084)
♦ European Action in Disability / see European Action of the Disabled (#05825)

♦ European Action of the Disabled 05825
Action européenne des handicapés (AEH) – Europäische Behindertenaktion
Secretariat Markus Sittikus Strasse 20, 6845 Hohenems, Austria. T. +436642101882. E-mail: info@aeh-europe.de.
URL: http://www.aeh-europe.de/
History 18 May 1979, Luxembourg. Former names and other names: *European Action in Disability* – former. **Aims** Represent the interests of the *handicapped,* especially in the following areas: (a) complete social and professional integration/reintegration of handicapped persons; (b) extension of *preventive* measures aimed also at avoiding the worsening of handicaps; (c) informing the public about the problems of the handicapped. **Structure** General Assembly (every 3 years); Executive Board; General Secretariat, headed by Secretary General. **Languages** English, German. **Finance** Sources: members' dues. **Activities** Advocacy/lobbying/activism; guidance/assistance/consulting; knowledge management/information dissemination. **Events** *Conference* Brussels (Belgium) 2002, *Conference* Munich (Germany) 2002, *Conference* Viktorsberg (Austria) 2002, *European conference on employment for disabled people* Dresden (Germany) 1999, *Beschäftigung, Qualifizierung, Arbeitsassistenz* Salzburg (Austria) 1998. **Publications** *AEH Newsletter* (3-4 a year).
Members Associations and organizations (9) in 7 countries:
Austria, Belgium, France, Germany, Luxembourg, Netherlands, Slovenia.
Consultative Status Consultative status granted from: *Council of Europe (CE, #04881)* (Participatory Status).
IGO Relations Participant in Fundamental Rights Platform of: *European Union Agency for Fundamental Rights (FRA, #08969).* **NGO Relations** Member of (1): *European Disability Forum (EDF, #06929).* [2020.11.18/XF2615/y/F]

♦ European Action Research Committee on Children with Imprisoned Parents / see Children of Prisoners Europe (#03875)
♦ European Actuarial Academy (unconfirmed)
♦ European Actuarial Consultative Group / see Actuarial Association of Europe (#00105)
♦ European Adhesion Conference (meeting series)

♦ European Adhesive Tape Association (AFERA) 05826
SG c/o Lejeune Association Management, Laan van Nieuw Oost-Indië 131-G, 2593 BM The Hague, Netherlands. T. +31703123916. Fax +31703636348. E-mail: mail@afera.com.
URL: http://www.afera.com/
History 1958, Paris (France), as *Association des fabricants européens de rubans auto-adhésifs (AFERA) – European Self Adhesive Tapes Manufacturers Association.* Since 1 Jul 1999, based in The Hague (Netherlands). **Aims** Be the voice of the European adhesive tape industry. **Structure** General Assembly (annual); Steering Committee. Committees Marketing; Technical. Secretariat. **Languages** English. **Staff** 1.00 FTE, paid. **Finance** Members' dues. **Events** *Technical Seminar* Brussels (Belgium) 2023, *Technical Seminar* Brussels (Belgium) 2021, *Technical Seminar* Brussels (Belgium) 2020, *Annual General Assembly and Conference* Valencia (Spain) 2020, *Annual General Assembly and Conference* Lisbon (Portugal) 2019. **Publications** *Collection of Standardization Tables* in English, French; *Collection of Testing Methods* in English, French; *Glossary of Technical Terms* in English, French, German, Italian, Spanish.
Members Companies (110) in 17 countries:
Belgium, Czechia, Denmark, Finland, France, Germany, Greece, Hungary, Ireland, Israel, Italy, Netherlands, Slovenia, Spain, Switzerland, Türkiye, UK.
NGO Relations Member of: *European Platform for Chemicals Using Manufacturing Industries (CheMI, #08223); Global Tape Forum (GTF, #10621).* Supporter of: *European Paper Recycling Council (EPRC, #08139).* [2018/XD5876/D]

♦ European Administrative School / see European School of Administration (#08427)

♦ European Advanced Recycling Network (EARN) 05827
Contact Elektroaltgeräte Service, Landstrasse 91, 38644 Goslar, Germany. T. +495321683590. Fax +4953216835911. E-mail: office@earn-service.com.
URL: http://www.earn-electronics.com/
History 2003 by 4 companies to meet requirements of the Waste from Electrical and Electronic Equipment Directie (WEEE). **Aims** Minimize the customer's concerns and time spent to be compliant with WEEE legislation by offering a pan-European, complete package of services, securing efficient implementation and brand protection, in the most practical, economical and environmental manner. **Events** *Going green – CARE INNOVATION conference* Vienna (Austria) 2006. [2013.07.16/XM2783/F]

♦ European Advanced Translational Research Infrastructure in Medicine ERIC / see European Infrastructure for Translational Medicine (#07536)

♦ European Advertising Academy (EAA) 05828
Secretariat Nieuwe Achtergracht 166, 1018 WV Amsterdam, Netherlands. E-mail: info@icoria.org.
Pres European Univ Viadrina, Grosse Scharrnstr 59, 15230 Frankfurt-Oder, Germany.
URL: http://www.europeanadvertisingacademy.org/
History Founded 2005. **Aims** Provide a professional association to academics and practitioners interested in advertising and its applications that will promote, disseminate and stimulate high quality research in the field. **Structure** General Assembly (annual); Executive Committee; National Representatives. **Languages** English. **Staff** 9.00 FTE, paid. **Finance** Members' dues. **Activities** Knowledge management/information dissemination; events/meetings; networking/liaising. **Events** *Annual International Conference* Krems (Austria) 2019, *Annual International Conference* Krems (Austria) 2019, *Annual International Conference* Valencia (Spain) 2018, *Annual International Conference* Ghent (Belgium) 2017, *Annual International Conference* Ljubljana (Slovenia) 2016. **Publications** *Advances in Advertising Research* (annual). Conference proceedings.
Members Individuals (250) from 34 countries. Membership countries not specified. [2019.12.13/XM2348/D]

♦ European Advertising Lawyers Association / see Global Advertising Lawyers Alliance (#10171)

♦ European Advertising Standards Alliance (EASA) 05829
Alliance européenne pour l'éthique en publicité (AEEP)
Dir Gen Rue des Deux Eglises 26, 1000 Brussels, Belgium. T. +3225137806. Fax +3225132861. E-mail: info@easa-alliance.org.
URL: http://www.easa-alliance.org/
History 1991. Officially launched, May 1992. Statutes most recently modified, Mar 2002. Registration: No/ID: 0450.933.006, Start date: 13 Sep 1993, Belgium; EU Transparency Register, No/ID: 070638512780-81, Start date: 30 Jan 2014. **Aims** Promote and develop advertising self-regulation in Europe; support existing advertising self-regulatory systems; manage and coordinate cross-border complaints mechanism to ensure that cross-border complaints through a specific procedure are resolved speedily and effectively; provide information and research concerning advertising self-regulation. **Structure** General Assembly (annual); Executive Committee; Board of Directors; Secretariat. Self-Regulatory Committee; Central and Eastern European Council. **Languages** Dutch, English, French, German, Italian. **Staff** 7.00 FTE, paid. **Finance** Members' dues. Special projects. **Activities** Events/meetings; awards/prizes/competitions. **Events** *Spring Biannual Meeting* Paris (France) 2019, *Autumn Biannual Meeting* Stockholm (Sweden) 2019, *Meeting* Vienna (Austria) 2011, *Workshop* London (UK) 2000, *Workshop* Brussels (Belgium) 1998. **Publications** Annual Report; best practice recommendations; statistics reports; position papers; surveys.
Members Full; Associate. Self-Regulatory Organizations (SROs); Industry Associations. Full in 24 countries:
Austria, Belgium, Bulgaria, Cyprus, Czechia, Finland, France, Germany, Greece, Hungary, Ireland, Italy, Luxembourg, Netherlands, Poland, Portugal, Romania, Slovakia, Slovenia, Spain, Sweden, Switzerland, Türkiye, UK.
Industry members (15):
Advertising Information Group (AIG, #00137); Association of Commercial Television in Europe (ACT, #02436); Association of European Radios (AER, #02535); egta – association of television and radio sales houses (#05397); European Association of Communications Agencies (EACA, #05983); European Magazine Media Association (EMMA, #07723); European Newspaper Publishers' Association (ENPA, #08048); European Publishers Council (EPC, #08304); Federation of European Data & Marketing (FEDMA, #09499); IAB Europe (#11002); International Advertising Association (IAA, #11590); News Media Europe (NME, #17094); Search and Information Industry Association (Siinda, #19188); World Federation of Advertisers (WFA, #21407); World Out of Home Organization (WOO, #21702).
NGO Relations Founding member of: *International Council for Advertising Self-Regulation (ICAS, #12984).* Member of: *International Chamber of Commerce (ICC, #12534)* Code Revision Taskforce. [2019.02.13/XD3516/y/D]

European Advisory Board
05830

alphabetic sequence excludes
For the complete listing, see Yearbook Online at

♦ **European Advisory Board on Cat Diseases (ABCD)** **05830**
Chair address not obtained.
URL: http://www.abcdcatsvets.org/
History First meeting organized 2005, Lyon (France). **Aims** Establish a rational base for *vaccine* use in the cat; publish conclusions for the companion animal practitioners' scene. **Structure** Board. **Activities** Standards/guidelines; awards/prizes/competitions. **Publications** *ABCD Newsletter.*
Members Veterinarians (19) in 12 countries:
Austria, Belgium, France, Germany, Ireland, Italy, Netherlands, Poland, Spain, Sweden, Switzerland, UK.
NGO Relations *European Scientific Counsel Companion Animal Parasites (ESCCAP, #08445)*; *World Small Animal Veterinary Association (WSAVA, #21795).* [2018/XM6649/v/F]

♦ European Advisory Council for Mid-Life and Older Woman's Health / see European Advisory Council for Women's Health (#05831)
♦ European Advisory Council for Technology Trade / see EURO-CHINA (#05658)

♦ **European Advisory Council for Women's Health (EAC)** **05831**
Contact c/o European Inst of Women's Health, 9 Herbert Place, Dublin, 2, CO. DUBLIN, Ireland. T. +35316766717. Fax +35316766740. E-mail: info@eurohealth.ie.
URL: http://www.osteofound.org/activities/european_advisory_council.html
History 1996. Also referred to as *European Advisory Council for Mid-Life and Older Woman's Health.* **Aims** Make mid-life and older women's health a priority for research and health policy. **NGO Relations** Hosted by: *European Institute of Women's Health (EIWH, #07574).* [2009/XM0426/E]

♦ **European Aeroallergen Network (EAN)** **05832**
Contact Medical Univ of Vienna, Dept Oto-Rhino-Laryngology, Waehringer Guertel 18-20, 1090 Vienna, Austria.
URL: https://ean.polleninfo.eu/ean/
History Also referred to as *European Aerobiology Society (AES).* **Aims** Provide database for international scientific joint projects in aerobiology. **Finance** Data selling. Budget (annual): euro 50,000-150,000. **Activities** 'EAN Pollen Database' gathers information on almost 400 pollen counting stations throughout Europe. **Events** *General Meeting* Krakow (Poland) 2012, *General Meeting* Turku (Finland) 2008. **Publications** *EAN Newsletter.*
Members in 19 countries. Membership countries not specified. [2012.06.29/XM3231/F]

♦ European Aerobiology Society / see European Aeroallergen Network (#05832)

♦ **European Aerobiology Society (EAS)** **05833**
Pres address not obtained.
SG address not obtained.
URL: http://www.eas-aerobiology.eu/
History 14 Aug 2008, Finland. Founded during 4th European Symposium on Aerobiology, by 83 individuals and 5 associations. **Aims** Promote aerobiology and further its development; facilitate collaboration, research, education, information, technical development and practical application in the field; create a platform for individuals, associations, societies and institutions interested in aerobiology in Europe; elect the body responsible for organizing the European Symposia on Aerobiology; encourage collaboration with other areas of science. **Structure** General Assembly; Committee; Board; Working Groups. **Languages** English. **Staff** Voluntary. **Finance** Members' dues. **Activities** Education/training; events/meetings; standards/guidelines; knowledge management/information dissemination. **Events** *European Symposium on Aerobiology* Vilnius (Lithuania) 2024, *European Symposium on Aerobiology* Córdoba (Spain) 2020, *European Symposium on Aerobiology* Córdoba (Spain) 2020, *European Symposium on Aerobiology* Lyon (France) 2016, *Committee Meeting* Siauliai (Lithuania) 2015. **Publications** *EAS Newsletter* (1-3 a year).
Members Full in 28 countries:
Austria, Croatia, Czechia, Denmark, Estonia, Finland, France, Germany, Greece, Hungary, Italy, Latvia, Lithuania, Netherlands, Norway, Poland, Portugal, Romania, Russia, Serbia, Slovakia, Slovenia, Spain, Sweden, Switzerland, Türkiye, UK, Ukraine.
NGO Relations *European Federation of Allergy and Airways Diseases Patients' Associations (EFA, #07045)*; *International Association for Aerobiology (IAA, #11691)*; *International Ragweed Society (IRS, #14692)*; national societies. [2022/XM4297/D]

♦ European Aero-Medical Institute / see European Aero-Medical Institute (#05834)

♦ **European Aero-Medical Institute (EURAMI)** **05834**
Pres Wilhelm-Herter-Strasse 35, 72144 Dusslingen, Germany. T. +4970728909960. E-mail: office@eurami.org.
URL: http://www.eurami.org/
History 8 Sep 1992, Frankfurt-Main (Germany). At 2nd Meeting, 11 Feb 1993, Brussels (Belgium), EURAMI became a European Economic Interest Grouping (EEIG-EWIV), and first Statutes were adopted. Experiences of further work turned out, however, that some regulations of a European scientific community of interests do not correspond with the objectives and tasks of EURAMI, and therefore, at 4th meeting, 4 Mar 1994, London (UK), new Statutes were adopted and EURAMI was registered in accordance with German law, under the official name: *European Aero-Medical Institute (EURAMI) e V – Centre for Education, Information, Research and Supply.* **Aims** Within the framework of medical aspects of the air rescue component of rescue services / emergency medical aid: promote, harmonize and generalize air rescue worldwide; facilitate, develop and increase practical work of members; guarantee step by step an equally high level of air rescue throughout the world. **Structure** General Meeting. Executive Board. Permanent Secretary. Temporary Committees of Experts and Working Groups. **Finance** Members' dues. **Activities** Provides assistance in setting up national air rescue organizations; offers training courses; organizes and holds congresses and scientific events; participates in congresses. **Events** *Meeting* Lisbon (Portugal) 2011, *Meeting* Istanbul (Turkey) 2010, *Meeting* Athens (Greece) 2009, *Meeting* Prague (Czech Rep) 2008, *Meeting* Venice (Italy) 2007.
Members Individuals and air ambulance organizations (105) in 36 countries:
Australia, Belgium, Canada, Czechia, Denmark, Dominican Rep, Egypt, Finland, France, Germany, Greece, Hungary, Ireland, Italy, Kenya, Lithuania, Luxembourg, Malaysia, Malta, Mexico, Netherlands, Norway, Poland, Portugal, Saudi Arabia, Singapore, Slovenia, South Africa, Spain, Sweden, Switzerland, Thailand, Türkiye, UK, USA, Zimbabwe. [2018/XE1887/j/F]

♦ **European Aeronautics Science Network (EASN)** **05835**
Central Office Terweidenstraat 28, Budingen, 3440 Zoutleeuw, Belgium.
URL: http://www.easn.net/
History May 2008, emerging from 2 *European Commission (EC, #06633)* funded Coordination and Support Actions (CSAs). Registered in accordance with Belgian law. EU Transparency Register: 326503817586-97. **Aims** Advance aeronautics sciences and technologies; built up an open, unique European platform so as to structure, support and upgrade research activities of European aeronautics universities; facilitate them to respond to their key role within the European aeronautical research community in incubating new knowledge and breakthrough technologies. **Structure** General Assembly (annual); Board of Directors. Regional Contact Points (5): Central Europe; Central East Europe; North West Europe; Southern Europe; Western Europe. **Languages** English. **Staff** All voluntary. **Finance** Members' dues. **Activities** Research and development; events/meetings. **Events** *EASN International Conference* Barcelona (Spain) 2022, *EASN International Conference* Salerno (Italy) 2021, *EASN International Conference* Zoutleeuw (Belgium) 2020, *EASN International Conference* Athens (Greece) 2019, *EASN International Conference* Glasgow (UK) 2018. **Publications** *EASN Newsletter* (4 a year). Workshop proceedings; reports; dicussions.
Members Full in 38 countries:
Austria, Belgium, Bulgaria, Croatia, Cyprus, Czechia, Denmark, Estonia, Finland, France, Germany, Greece, Hungary, Iceland, Ireland, Israel, Italy, Latvia, Lithuania, Luxembourg, Malta, Montenegro, Netherlands, Northern Mariana Is, Norway, Poland, Portugal, Romania, Russia, Serbia, Slovakia, Slovenia, Spain, Sweden, Switzerland, Türkiye, UK, Ukraine.
NGO Relations Member of: *Initiative for Science in Europe (ISE, #11214).* [2021/XJ8717/F]

♦ **European Aerosol Assembly (EAA)** **05836**
Pres School of Earth and Environment, University of Leeds, Woodhouse Lane, Leeds, LS2 9JT, UK.
Gen Sec Dept of Civil and Environmental Engineering, Imperial College London, London, SW7 2AZ, UK.
URL: http://www.gaef.de/eaa/
History 1995. **Aims** Provide a forum for cooperation between national aerosol societies in Europe. **Structure** Council; Working Groups. **Languages** English. **Finance** Sources: members' dues. **Activities** Advocacy/lobbying/activism; events/meetings; knowledge management/information dissemination; networking/liaising; politics/policy/regulatory; training/education. **Events** *Annual European Aerosol Conference* Dublin (Ireland) 2021, *Annual European Aerosol Conference* Aachen (Germany) 2020, *Annual European Aerosol Conference* Gothenburg (Sweden) 2019, *Annual European Aerosol Conference* Zurich (Switzerland) 2017, *Annual European Aerosol Conference* Tours (France) 2016. **Publications** *Journal of Aerosol Science.*
Members Societies in 13 countries:
Belgium, Czechia, Finland, France, Germany, Greece, Hungary, Ireland, Israel, Italy, Netherlands, Spain, UK.
Regional member:
Nordic Society for Aerosol Research (NOSA, #17410). [2021/XD7001/y/D]

♦ European Aerosol Federation (#09557)

♦ **European Aerospace Cluster Partnership (EACP)** **05837**
Contact c/o Hamburg Aviation eV, Wexstr 7, 20355 Hamburg, Germany. E-mail: info@eacp-aero.eu.
URL: http://www.eacp-aero.eu/
History 6 May 2009. Founded as an informal and decentralized partnership. Registration: EU Transparency Register, No/ID: 151758339910-77, Start date: 12 Oct 2020. **Aims** Improve global competitiveness in Europe through intense inter-cluster collaboration. **Structure** General Assembly (annual). **Activities** Advocacy/lobbying/activism; knowledge management/information dissemination. **Events** *General Assembly* Hamburg (Germany) 2020, *General Assembly* Turin (Italy) 2019, *General Assembly* Delft (Netherlands) 2018, *General Assembly* Braunschweig (Germany) 2017.
Members Full in 18 countries:
Austria, Belgium, Czechia, Estonia, France, Germany, Ireland, Italy, Netherlands, Poland, Portugal, Romania, Spain, Sweden, Switzerland, Türkiye, UK, Ukraine. [2022.05.05/XM7316/F]

♦ **European Aerospace Quality Group (EAQG)** **05838**
Operations Manager Rue Montoyer 10, 1000 Brussels, Belgium. T. +3227758138. Fax +3227758131.
URL: http://www.eaqg.org/
History Set up as the European sector of *International Aerospace Quality Group (IAQG, #11594).* **Aims** Implement initiatives that make significant improvements in Quality and reductions in cost throughout the value stream by establishing and maintaining dynamic co-operation based on trust between International Aerospace companies. **Structure** General Meeting (2 a year). **Languages** English. **Staff** None paid. **Finance** Funded by IAQG. Budget (annual): around euro 150,000. **Events** *General Meeting* Rome (Italy) 2017, *General Meeting* Brussels (Belgium) 2016, *General Meeting* Manchester (UK) 2016.
Members Companies (35) and National Trade Organizations (8). National organizations in 8 countries:
Austria, France, Germany, Italy, Netherlands, Spain, Sweden, UK.
IGO Relations *European Union Aviation Safety Agency (EASA, #08978)*; *European Defence Agency (EDA, #06895).* [2016.06.23/XM4793/E]

♦ **Europeana Foundation** **05839**
Stichting Europeana
Gen Dir Prins Willem-Alexanderhof 5, 2595 BE The Hague, Netherlands. T. +31703140991. E-mail: info@europeana.eu.
URL: http://www.europeana.eu/
History First Europeana prototype set up Nov 2008, following 2005 call by 6 heads of state. Since May 2015, part of *European Commission (EC, #06633)* Digital Service Infrastructures. Functions as one of 3 pillars within the Europeana Initiative, along with *Europeana Network Association (ENA, #05899)* and Aggregators' Forum. Former names and other names: *European Digital Library* – former. Registration: Handelsregister, No/ID: KVK 27307531, Netherlands; EU Transparency Register, No/ID: 770007812381-96, Start date: 18 Dec 2013. **Aims** Transform the world with culture through making public *digital* collections of *museums*, galleries, libraries and *archives* from all across Europe. **Structure** Board of Directors; Supervisory Board; Advisory Board. **Languages** English. **Staff** 57.00 FTE, paid. **Finance** Largely funded by *European Commission (EC, #06633)*, with contributions from Ministries of Culture throughout Europe. Annual budget: about euro 6,000,000. **Activities** Research/documentation; knowledge management/information dissemination; events/meetings. **Events** *Annual General Meeting* Lisbon (Portugal) 2019, *EuropeanaTech Conference* Rotterdam (Netherlands) 2018, *Annual General Meeting* Vienna (Austria) 2018, *Annual General Meeting* Milan (Italy) 2017, *EuropeanaTech Conference* Paris (France) 2015. **Publications** Playbook; Strategy; Business Plan; Annual Report; Accounts.
Members Europeana Network Association has about 1,900 members from various European institutions, including:
Association of European Film Archives and Cinémathèques (#02511); *Association of European Research Libraries (#02540)*; *European Museum Academy (EMA, #07835)*; *European Museum Forum (EMF, #07836)*; *European Regional Branch of the International Council on Archives (EURBICA, see: #12996)*; *ICOM European Regional Alliance (ICOM-Europe, see: #13051)*; *International Association of Sound and Audiovisual Archives (IASA, #12172)*; *International Federation of Television Archives (IFTA, #13568)*; *MICHAEL Culture Association (#16742)*; *Network of European Museum Organizations (NEMO, #17024).*
IGO Relations *Common Language Resources and Technology Infrastructure (CLARIN, #04295).* **NGO Relations** Member of (1): *European Heritage Alliance 3.3 (#07477).* Partner of (1): *Globethics.net Foundation (#10669).* [2023/XM2445/fy/F]

♦ European-African Development Association (internationally oriented national body)

♦ **European-African Hepato-Pancreato-Biliary Association (E-AHPBA)** **05840**
Exec Dir c/o ACS Global, 14 Laurel Park Gardens, Glasgow, G13 1RA, UK. T. +441415302760.
URL: http://www.eahpba.org/
History 1999. Founded as a regional society of *International Hepato-Pancreato-Biliary Association (IHPBA, #13790).* Current title adopted when expanded to countries of the Middle East and Africa. Former names and other names: *European Hepato-Pancreato-Biliary Association (EHPBA)* – former (1999 to 2011). **Aims** Be the prime regional organization of the IHPBA devoted to relief of human suffering caused by hepato-pancreato-bilary (HPB) disorders. **Structure** Council; Committees (7); Management Office. **Languages** English. **Activities** Events/meetings; knowledge management/information dissemination; networking/liaising; research and development; training/education. **Events** *Biennial Congress* Dublin (Ireland) 2025, *Biennial Congress* Lyon (France) 2023, *Biennial Congress* Bilbao (Spain) 2021, *Biennial Congress* Amsterdam (Netherlands) 2019, *Biennial Congress* Mainz (Germany) 2017. **Publications** *HPB Journal.* **Members** Individuals (about 850). Membership countries not specified. [2021.05.27/XJ4014/E]

♦ **European Ageing Network (EAN)** **05841**
Réseau Européen du Vieillissement – Europäisches Netzwerk für das Alter
Exec Dir Na Pankráci 1618/30, 140 00 Prague, Czechia. T. +420777357832. Fax +420381213332. E-mail: info@ean.care.
Headquarters EDE asbl, c/ Résidence Grande Duchesse Joséphine Charlotte, 11 avenue Marie-Thérèse, L-2132 Luxembourg, Luxembourg.
URL: http://www.ean.care/
History 6 Apr 2018. Founded on merger of *European Association for Directors and Providers of Long-Term Care Services for the Elderly (EDE, inactive)* and *European Association of Homes and Services for the Ageing (EAHSA, inactive).* Registration: Luxembourg; EU Transparency Register, No/ID: 058359527245-73, Start date: 22 May 2017. **Aims** Improve the quality of life for older persons. **Structure** General Assembly; Executive Board. **Staff** 0.50 FTE, paid; 9.00 FTE, voluntary. **Events** *General Assembly* Vienna (Austria) 2021, *General Assembly* Lisbon (Portugal) 2020, *General Assembly* Matera (Italy) 2019, *General Assembly* Utrecht (Netherlands) 2019. **Publications** *EAN News.*
Members Umbrella associations, institutions or organizations dealing with or related to elderly care; academic institutions; individual professionals. Members in 28 countries:
Austria, Belgium, Croatia, Czechia, Denmark, Estonia, Finland, France, Germany, Hungary, Italy, Latvia, Lithuania, Luxembourg, Malta, Netherlands, Norway, Poland, Portugal, Romania, Russia, Serbia, Slovakia, Slovenia, Spain, Sweden, Switzerland, UK. [2020/XM7765/F]

♦ **European Age Management Network (EAMN)** **05842**
Address not obtained.
URL: http://www.eamn.fr/
History Jul 2010. Registered in accordance with French law. **Structure** General Assembly. Board of Directors of 5 members. [2013/XJ6357/**D**]

♦ European Agency for the Development and Health (#02562)
♦ European Agency for Development in Special Needs Education / see European Agency for Special Needs and Inclusive Education (#05844)
♦ European Agency for the Evaluation of Medicinal Products / see European Medicines Agency (#07767)
♦ European Agency for the Management of Operational Cooperation at the External Borders / see Frontex, the European Border and Coast Guard Agency (#10005)
♦ European Agency for Reconstruction (inactive)

♦ **European Agency for Safety and Health at Work (EU-OSHA)** **05843**
Agence européenne pour la sécurité et la santé au travail – Agencia Europea para la Seguridad y la Salud en el Trabajo
Dir 12 Santiago de Compostela, Edif Miribilla, 5th Floor, 48003 Bilbao, Biscay, Spain. T. +34944358400. Fax +34944358401. E-mail: information@osha.europa.eu.
Brussels Office Square de Meeûs 38/40, 1000 Brussels, Belgium.
URL: http://osha.europa.eu/
History 18 Jul 1994, by *Council of the European Union (#04895)*, having been proposed 30 Sep 1991, by *European Commission (EC, #06633)*. Operational since Sep 1996. Comprises one of the decentralized agencies set up under the *Treaty on European Union (Maastricht Treaty, 1992)* by the *European Union (EU, #08967)* to carry out specialized technical or scientific work on a wide range of subjects. Previously also referred to under the acronym *EASHW*. **Aims** Collect, analyse and communicate information on occupational safety and health across the EU; make Europe's workplaces safer, healthier and more productive, by promoting a culture of risk prevention and sharing good practice. **Structure** Management Board, consisting of representatives from all Members States representing the 3 key stakeholders groups (governments, employers' and worker organizations) as well as representatives of the European Commission and European Parliament; Executive Board of 8 Members; Director. **Languages** Bulgarian, Croatian, Czech, Danish, Dutch, English, Estonian, Finnish, French, German, Hungarian, Icelandic, Irish Gaelic, Italian, Latvian, Lithuanian, Maltese, Norwegian, Polish, Portuguese, Romanian, Slovakian, Slovene, Spanish, Swedish. **Staff** 67.00 FTE, paid. **Finance** Annual budget (2019): euro 15,700,000, of which euro 7,900,000 are operational expenditures. **Activities** Advocacy/lobbying/activism; events/meetings; knowledge management/information dissemination. **Events** *Youth first! Employment, skills and social policies that work for young Europeans in times of uncertainty* Brussels (Belgium) 2022, *Healthy Workplaces Campaign Partnership Meeting* Brussels (Belgium) 2019, *Meeting on Improving Occupational Safety and Health in Micro and Small Enterprises in Europe* Brussels (Belgium) 2019, *Healthy Workplaces Campaign Partnership Meeting* Brussels (Belgium) 2018, *Meeting on the Way Forward in Improving OSH in Europe's Micro and Small Enterprises* Brussels (Belgium) 2018. **Publications** *OSHmail* (12 a year) – electronic newsletter. Annual Report; series of specific reports on safety and health issues covered by work programmes; factsheets; conference proceedings; multimedia products.
Members Focal points in all EU and EFTA Member States and in (potential) candidate countries (36):
Austria, Belgium, Bulgaria, Croatia, Cyprus, Czechia, Denmark, Estonia, Finland, France, Germany, Greece, Hungary, Iceland, Ireland, Italy, Latvia, Liechtenstein, Lithuania, Luxembourg, Malta, Montenegro, Netherlands, North Macedonia, Norway, Poland, Portugal, Romania, Serbia, Slovakia, Slovenia, Spain, Sweden, Switzerland, Türkiye, UK.
International partners in 5 countries:
Australia, Canada, Japan, Korea Rep, USA.
International organization partners (6):
ILO (#11123); *International Commission on Occupational Health (ICOH, #12709)*; *International Occupational Hygiene Association (IOHA, #14391)*; *International Social Security Association (ISSA, #14885)*; *Pan American Health Organization (PAHO, #18108)*; *WHO (#20950)*.
IGO Relations Reports to: *European Court of Auditors (#06854)*. **NGO Relations** Member of (2): *EU Agencies Network (EUAN, #05564)*; *Eurolib (#05703)*. Partner of (1): *European Network for Workplace Health Promotion (ENWHP, #08037)*. Supports (1): *International Network on the Prevention of Accidents and Trauma at Work (Workingonsafety.net, #14306)*. Formal contacts with: *European Cleaning and Facility Services Industry (EFCI, #06571)*. [2021/XD5516/y/**D***]

♦ **European Agency for Special Needs and Inclusive Education** **05844**
Dir Ostre Stationsvej 33, C, 5000 Odense, Denmark. T. +4564410020. E-mail: secretariat@european-agency.org.
Brussels office Rue Montoyer 21, 1000 Brussels, Belgium. T. +3222136280. E-mail: brussels.office@european-agency.org.
URL: http://www.european-agency.org/
History 1996. Established at the end of the European Commission's Helios II programme, as an initiative of the Danish Government and endorsed by the member states' Education Ministers. Transferred to member states, 1999. As a formal European organization, serves as a permanent and systematic structure for European collaboration in the field of special needs and inclusive education. Former names and other names: *European Agency for Development in Special Needs Education* – former (1996 to 2014). Registration: EU Transparency Register, No/ID: 609904815975-13. **Aims** Improve the quality and effectiveness of inclusive education systems for all learners. **Structure** Representative Board; Management Board; National Coordinators. **Languages** English. **Staff** 35.00 FTE, paid. **Finance** Funded by Ministries of Education of member countries. Supported by: *European Union (EU, #08967)* (Erasmus+). **Activities** Knowledge management/information dissemination. **Events** *Agency Bi-annual Meeting* Athens (Greece) 2022, *Agency Bi-annual Meeting* 2021, *Agency Bi-annual Meeting* 2021, *Agency Bi-annual Meeting* 2020, *Agency Bi-annual Meeting* Budapest (Hungary) 2019. **Publications** *Agency eBulletin*. Reports; country policy reviews; tools; statistics.
Members Ministries of Education in 31 countries:
Austria, Belgium (Flemish, French and German communities), Bulgaria, Croatia, Cyprus, Czechia, Denmark, Estonia, Finland, France, Germany, Greece, Hungary, Iceland, Ireland, Italy, Latvia, Lithuania, Luxembourg, Malta, Netherlands, Norway, Poland, Portugal, Serbia, Slovakia, Slovenia, Spain, Sweden, Switzerland, UK. [2022.05.04/XE4512/**E**]

♦ European Aggregates Association / see Aggregates Europe (#00558)
♦ European Agreement on the Abolition of Visas for Refugees (1959 treaty)
♦ European Agreement on the Application of Article 23 of the 1949 Convention on Road Traffic (1950 treaty)
♦ European Agreement on 'au Pair' Placement (1969 treaty)
♦ European Agreement Concerning the International Carriage of Dangerous Goods by Inland Waterways (2000 treaty)
♦ European Agreement Concerning the International Carriage of Dangerous Goods by Road (1957 treaty)
♦ European Agreement Concerning Programme Exchanges by Means of Television Films (1958 treaty)
♦ European Agreement Concerning the Provision of Medical Care to Persons During Temporary Residence (1980 treaty)
♦ European Agreement Concerning the Work of Crews of Vehicles Engaged in International Road Transport, 1962 (1962 treaty)
♦ European Agreement Concerning the Work of Crews of Vehicles Engaged in International Road Transport, 1970 (1970 treaty)
♦ European Agreement on Continued Payment of Scholarships to Students Studying Abroad (1969 treaty)
♦ European Agreement on the Exchanges of Blood-grouping Reagents (1962 treaty)
♦ European Agreement on the Exchange of Therapeutic Substances of Human Origin (1958 treaty)
♦ European Agreement on the Exchange of Tissue-typing Reagents (1974 treaty)
♦ European Agreement on Important International Combined Transport Lines and Related Installations (1991 treaty)
♦ European Agreement on the Instruction and Education of Nurses (1967 treaty)
♦ European Agreement on Main Inland Waterways of International Importance (1996 treaty)
♦ European Agreement on Main International Railway Lines (1985 treaty)
♦ European Agreement on Main International Traffic Arteries (1975 treaty)
♦ European Agreement on Mutual Assistance in the Matter of Special Medical Treatments and Climatic Facilities (1962 treaty)
♦ European Agreement for the Prevention of Broadcasts Transmitted from Stations Outside National Territories (1965 treaty)
♦ European Agreement on the Protection of Television Broadcasts (1960 treaty)
♦ European Agreement on Regulations Governing the Movement of Persons between Member States of the Council of Europe (1957 treaty)
♦ European Agreement Relating to Persons Participating in Proceedings of the European Commission and Court of Human Rights (1969 treaty)
♦ European Agreement Relating to Persons Participating in Proceedings of the European Court of Human Rights (1996 treaty)
♦ European Agreement on the Restriction of the Use of Certain Detergents in Washing and Cleaning Products (1968 treaty)
♦ European Agreement on Road Markings (1957 treaty)
♦ European Agreement Supplementing the 1949 Convention on Road Traffic and the 1949 Protocol on Road Signs and Signals (1950 treaty)
♦ European Agreement Supplementing the Convention on Road Signs and Signals (1971 treaty)
♦ European Agreement Supplementing the Convention on Road Traffic (1971 treaty)
♦ European Agreement on Transfer of Responsibility for Refugees (1980 treaty)
♦ European Agreement on the Transmission of Applications for Legal Aid (1977 treaty)
♦ European Agreement on Travel by Young Persons on Collective Passports between the Member Countries of the Council of Europe (1961 treaty)

♦ **European Agricultural and Applied Economics Publications Foundation (EAAEP Foundation)** **05845**
Hon Sec Zuideinde 8b, PO Box 29703, 2761 DA Zevenhuizen, Netherlands.
URL: http://www.eaaep.org/
History Statutes updated 2013; 2019. Former names and other names: *Foundation to Publish ERAE* – former. Registration: Dutch Chamber of Commerce, No/ID: 41154716, Netherlands. **Aims** Support and enlarge publication possibilities for European researchers in the area of agricultural and applied economics and policy. **Structure** Board. **Languages** English. **Staff** 0.10 FTE, voluntary. **Finance** Sources: sale of publications. . Annual budget: 25,000 EUR. **Activities** Publishing activities. **Publications** *EuroChoices* – journal; *European Review of Agricultural Economics (ERAE)* – journal; *Q Open*. **NGO Relations** Memorandum of Understanding with (1): *European Association of Agricultural Economists (EAAE, #05932)*. [2021.05.18/XM4397/f/**F**]

♦ **European Agricultural Machinery Association (CEMA)** **05846**
SG Bluepoint, Blvd A Reyers 80, 1030 Brussels, Belgium. T. +3227068173. E-mail: secretariat@cema-agri.org.
URL: http://www.cema-agri.org/
History Oct 1959, Stresa (Italy). Former names and other names: *European Committee of Associations of Manufacturers of Agricultural Machinery* – former; *Comité européen des groupements de constructeurs du machinisme agricole (CEMA)* – former; *Comité Europeo de Asociaciones de Constructores de Maquinaria Agricola* – former; *Europäisches Komitee der Verbände der Landmaschinenhersteller* – former; *Comitato Europeo delle Associazioni dei Costruttori di Macchinario Agricolo* – former. Registration: Belgium; EU Transparency Register, No/ID: 489575310490-58, Start date: 21 Jan 2013. **Aims** Work towards a balanced legislative regulatory framework in the EU that supports competitiveness of the industry in Europe and enables the industry to provide smart solutions to help farmers worldwide grow food affordably and sustainably. **Structure** General Assembly; Board of Directors; Secretariat. Working Groups. **Languages** English. **Staff** 6.00 FTE, paid. **Activities** Awards/prizes/competitions; knowledge management/information dissemination; networking/liaising; research/documentation. **Events** *Seeding the Future of Sustainable Farming* Brussels (Belgium) 2021, *Conference on Agriculture 4.0 and Smart Farming in the Cloud* Brussels (Belgium) 2016, *Smart regulation for smart machines* Brussels (Belgium) 2015, *Meeting / Annual General Assembly* Brussels (Belgium) 2012, *Meeting* Brussels (Belgium) 2012.
Members Associations in 11 countries:
Austria, Belgium, Denmark, France, Germany, Italy, Netherlands, Poland, Spain, Türkiye, UK.
IGO Relations Recognized by: *European Commission (EC, #06633)*. **NGO Relations** Member of (3): *Agri-Food Chain Coalition (AFCC, #00577)*; *Alliance for Internet of Things Innovation (AIOTI, #00697)*; *Industry4Europe (#11181)*. Cooperates with (3): *Comité européen de normalisation (CEN, #04162)*; *European Professional Beekeepers Association (EPBA, #08284)*; *International Organization for Standardization (ISO, #14473)*. Associate member of: *European Network of Agricultural Journalists (ENAJ, #07864)*. [2022.10.20/XD0639/**D**]

♦ **EURopean AGricultural Research Initiative (EURAGRI)** **05847**
SG c/Dept of Chemistry and Bioscience, Fredrik Bajers Vej 7h, 9220 Aalborg Ø, Denmark. E-mail: bhe@bio.aau.dk.
URL: https://www.euragri.aau.dk/
Structure Board. **Activities** Events/meetings. **Events** *Conference* Ghent (Belgium) 2019, *Conference* Oslo (Norway) 2018. [2019/XM8033/**F**]

♦ European Agricultural Society and Show Organizers Consultative Committee / see European Federation of Agricultural Exhibitions and Show Organizers (#07043)

♦ **European Agroforestry Federation (EURAF)** **05848**
Pres address not obtained. E-mail: info@euraf.net.
SG address not obtained.
URL: https://euraf.isa.utl.pt/welcome/
History 15 Dec 2011. Set up during 1st Conference. Registration: EU Transparency Register, No/ID: 913270437706-82, Start date: 25 Mar 2020. **Aims** Promote the use of trees on farms as well as any kind of silvopastoralism throughout the different environmental regions of Europe. **Structure** General Assembly; Executive Committee; Executive Board. **Activities** Events/meetings; knowledge management/information dissemination; monitoring/evaluation; politics/policy/regulatory; research/documentation. Active in all member countries. **Events** *Conference* Nuoro (Italy) 2022, *Conference* Nuoro (Italy) 2021, *Conference* Nuoro (Italy) 2020, *Agroforestry as sustainable land use* Nijmegen (Netherlands) 2018, *General Assembly* Montpellier (France) 2016. **Publications** *EURAF Newsletter*.
Members Full in 20 countries:
Austria, Belgium, Bulgaria, Czechia, Denmark, France, Germany, Greece, Hungary, Ireland, Italy, Latvia, Netherlands, Poland, Portugal, Spain, Sweden, Switzerland, UK, Ukraine.
NGO Relations Member of (1): *TP Organics – European Technology Platform (TP Organics, #20180)*. [2022.10.27/XM4763/**D**]

♦ **European AIDS Clinical Society (EACS)** **05849**
Exec Sec Rue des Colonies 56, 1000 Brussels, Belgium. T. +3223161019. E-mail: info@eacsociety.org.
URL: http://www.eacsociety.org/
History 10 Nov 1995, Brussels (Belgium). Registration: Banque-Carrefour des Entreprises, No/ID: 0458.322.624, Start date: 11 Jul 1996, Belgium; EU Transparency Register, No/ID: 468777637658-12, Start date: 6 Apr 2020. **Aims** Promote excellence in standards of care, research and education in HIV infection and related co-infections; actively engage in the formulation of public health policy, so as to reduce HIV disease burden across Europe. **Structure** General Assembly; Regional Representatives; Governing Board; Bureau; Secretariat. **Languages** English. **Staff** 3.50 FTE, paid. **Finance** Sources: grants; meeting proceeds; members' dues. **Activities** Events/meetings; training/education. **Events** *European AIDS Conference* Warsaw (Poland) 2023, *Young Investigators Conference* Brussels (Belgium) 2022, *European AIDS Conference* London (UK) 2021, *Young Investigators Conference* Brussels (Belgium) 2020, *Standard of Care for HIV and Coinfections in Europe* Tbilisi (Georgia) 2020. **Publications** *EACS News*. *European Treatment Guidelines*.
Members Full and correspondants. Members in 40 countries:

Albania, Armenia, Austria, Azerbaijan, Belarus, Belgium, Bosnia-Herzegovina, Bulgaria, Croatia, Czechia, Denmark, Estonia, Finland, France, Georgia, Germany, Greece, Hungary, Iceland, Ireland, Italy, Latvia, Lithuania, Luxembourg, Moldova, Netherlands, North Macedonia, Norway, Poland, Portugal, Romania, Russia, Serbia, Slovakia, Slovenia, Spain, Sweden, Switzerland, UK, Ukraine.
NGO Relations Partner of (4): *European AIDS Treatment Group (EATG, #05850); European Civil Society Forum on HIV/AIDS (CSF, #06568); European Society of Clinical Microbiology and Infectious Diseases (ESCMID, #08548); EuroTEST (#09188).* [2022.05.17/XD4150/**D**]

♦ European AIDS Treatment Group (EATG) 05850

Exec Dir Av des Arts 56 – 4C, 1000 Brussels, Belgium. T. +3226269640. E-mail: office@eatg.org.
Registered Address Mettmanner Str 24-26, 40233 Düsseldorf, Germany.
URL: http://www.eatg.org/

History 1992, Berlin (Germany). Former names and other names: *Grupo Europeo de Tratamientos sobre SIDA* – former. Registration: North Rhine-Westphalia District Court, No/ID: VR 8542, Start date: 29 Oct 1998, Germany, Düsseldorf; Banque-Carrefour des Entreprises, No/ID: 0877.686.583, Start date: 5 Dec 2005, Belgium; EU Transparency Register, No/ID: 49959188061-85, Start date: 13 Feb 2012. **Aims** Advocate for the rights and interests of people living with, or affected by, HIV/AIDS and related co-infections within the WHO European region. **Structure** General Assembly (at least annually); Board of Directors; Office based in Brussels (Belgium). **Languages** English. **Staff** 8.00 FTE, paid. **Finance** Support: 80% private; 20% other. Annual budget: 1,500,000 EUR. **Activities** Advocacy/lobbying/activism; capacity building; events/meetings; networking/liaising; research and development; training/education. **Events** *International Workshop on HIV Pediatrics* Mexico City (Mexico) 2019, *International Workshop on HIV Pediatrics* Paris (France) 2017, *International Workshop on HIV Pediatrics* Durban (South Africa) 2016, *International Workshop on HIV Pediatrics* Vancouver, BC (Canada) 2015, *HIV in Europe conference* Stockholm (Sweden) 2009. **Publications** *EATG Newsletter*, *HIV and co-infections News Bulletin*. Brochures; educational material via COPE; training manuals; position papers.
Members Individuals in 48 countries:
Albania, Armenia, Austria, Belarus, Belgium, Bosnia-Herzegovina, Bulgaria, Canada, Croatia, Cyprus, Czechia, Denmark, Estonia, Finland, France, Georgia, Germany, Greece, Hungary, Iceland, Ireland, Israel, Italy, Kosovo, Kyrgyzstan, Latvia, Lithuania, Luxembourg, Moldova, Montenegro, Netherlands, North Macedonia, Poland, Portugal, Romania, Russia, Serbia, Slovenia, South Africa, Spain, Sweden, Switzerland, Tajikistan, Türkiye, UK, Ukraine, USA, Uzbekistan.
IGO Relations Collaborates with: *Joint United Nations Programme on HIV/AIDS (UNAIDS, #16149); WHO (#20950)*. Co-Chair of: *European Medicines Agency (EMA, #07767)* Patient and Consumer Working Party. Participant in Fundamental Rights Platform of *European Union Agency for Fundamental Rights (FRA, #08969)*.
NGO Relations Member of (14): *ACHIEVE (#00068); Civil Society Forum on Drugs (CSFD, #03968); Digital-HealthEurope (DHE, #05078); European Alliance for Responsible R and D and Affordable Medicines (#05879); European Forum for Good Clinical Practice (EFGCP, #07313); European Patients' Academy on Therapeutic Innovation (EUPATI, #08170); European Patients' Forum (EPF, #08172); European Public Health Alliance (EPHA, #08297); Federation of European and International Associations Established in Belgium (FAIB, #09508); ILGA World (International Lesbian, Gay, Bisexual, Trans and Intersex Association, #11120); International Alliance of Patients' Organizations (IAPO, #11633); International Treatment Preparedness Coalition (ITPC, #15729); Platform for International Cooperation on Undocumented Migrants (PICUM, #18401); TB Europe Coalition (TBEC, #20104)*. Co-Chair, and member of think Think Tank, of: *European Civil Society Forum on HIV/AIDS (CSF, #06568)*. Close cooperation with: *European Association for the Study of the Liver (EASL, #06233); Global Network of People Living with HIV/AIDS (GNP+, #10494); International Community of Women Living with HIV/AIDS (ICW, #12826); International Planned Parenthood Federation (IPPF, #14589).* [2021/XF3452/v/**F**]

♦ European AI Fund / see European Artificial Intelligence Society Fund (#05916)
♦ European Aikido Federation (inactive)

♦ European Air Law Association (EALA) 05851

Pres A310 Kamerlingh Onnes Gbw, Steenschuur 25, 2311 ES Leiden, Netherlands.
Treas Ehlers Ehlers and Partner, Widenmayerstrasse 29, 80538 Munich, Germany.
URL: http://www.eala.aero/

History 12 Oct 1988, London (UK). Founded on the initiative of Prof P D Dagtoglou. Registration: Companies House, No/ID: 6374877, England and Wales. **Aims** Promote study of the law and institutions of the European Union in relation to air *transport* and development of a common air transport policy. **Structure** General Meeting (annual); Committee of Management. **Languages** English. **Finance** Members' dues. **Activities** Events/meetings. **Events** *Annual Conference* Copenhagen (Denmark) 2021, *Annual Conference* Athens (Greece) 2020, *Annual Conference* Paris (France) 2019, *Annual Conference* Brussels (Belgium) 2018, *Annual Conference* Lisbon (Portugal) 2017. **Publications** Conference and Seminar papers.
Members Individual and Corporate in 36 countries and territories:
Albania, Australia, Austria, Belgium, Canada, Croatia, Czechia, Denmark, Faeroe Is, Finland, France, Germany, Greece, Iceland, Ireland, Italy, Lithuania, Luxembourg, Malta, Montenegro, Netherlands, Nigeria, Norway, Poland, Portugal, Romania, Russia, Serbia, Spain, Sweden, Switzerland, Türkiye, UK, Ukraine, United Arab Emirates, USA. [2020/XD2281/**D**]

♦ European Airlines Maintenance Training Committee / see European Aviation Maintenance Training Committee (#06303)
♦ European Airlines Presidents Association (no recent information)

♦ European Airport Coordinators Association (EUACA) 05852

Secretariat c/o Brussels Slot Coordination, New Terminal – 4th floor, TMA 530, BP 27, 1930 Zaventem, Belgium. E-mail: secretary@euaca.org.
URL: http://www.euaca.org/

History Registration: EU Transparency Register, No/ID: 500312626332-23; Belgium. **Aims** Deliver a professional, neutral, transparent, non discriminatory service to the aviation industry so as to contribute to efficient solutions to optimizing the use of capacity at European airports. **Structure** Plenary Session; Board; Secretariat.
Members Full in 27 countries and territories:
Austria, Belgium, Bulgaria, Croatia, Cyprus, Czechia, Denmark, Estonia, Faeroe Is, Finland, France, Germany, Greece, Hungary, Iceland, Ireland, Italy, Luxembourg, Malta, Netherlands, Norway, Poland, Portugal, Spain, Sweden, Switzerland, UK. [2022/XM5701/**D**]

♦ European Air Shippers' Council (inactive)

♦ European Air Transport Command (EATC) 05853

Contact PO Box 90102, 5600 RA Eindhoven, Netherlands. T. +31889510038. E-mail: pao@eatc-mil.com.
Street address Flight Forum 1550, bldg 601, 5657 EZ Eindhoven, Netherlands.
URL: https://eatc-mil.com/

History Born 1999. Ground rules set Sep 2010, subsequently inaugurated Eindhoven air base (Netherlands), by founding members, Netherlands, Belgium, France, Germany. **Aims** Improve the effectiveness and efficiency of the member nations *military* air transport efforts. **Structure** Multinational Air Transport Committee (MATraC); Advisory Group; Budget and Finance Committee. Headquarters, headed by Commander. Divisions (3): Operational; Functional; Policy and Support. **Activities** Training/education; standards/guidelines. **Publications** Manuals.
Members Asets (170) located at national air bases through 7 member nations:
Belgium, France, Germany, Italy, Luxembourg, Netherlands, Spain.
IGO Relations *Organisation Conjointe de Coopération en Matière d'Armement (OCCAR, #17801).* [2020/XM9010/**F***]

♦ European Airway Management Society (EAMS) 05854

Sec address not obtained. E-mail: secretary@eamshq.net.
URL: http://www.eamshq.net/162/

History Jun 2003, Glasgow (UK). Registered in accordance with German law, 22 Dec 2003. **Aims** Improve management of the patient's airway by anaesthetists and critical care personnel. **Structure** General Assembly (annual); Council; Board of Directors. **Languages** English. **Finance** Members' dues. **Activities** Training/education; events/meetings; knowledge management/information dissemination. **Events** *World Airway Management Meeting* Amsterdam (Netherlands) 2019, *Annual meeting / Meeting* Helsinki (Finland) 2010, *Annual meeting / Meeting* Milan (Italy) 2009, *Meeting* Copenhagen (Denmark) 2008, *Annual meeting / Meeting* Munich (Germany) 2007.
Members Individuals (about 250) in 29 members:
Albania, Argentina, Australia, Austria, Belgium, Bosnia-Herzegovina, Canada, China, Denmark, Finland, France, Germany, Greece, India, Ireland, Italy, Kuwait, Netherlands, Norway, Portugal, Saudi Arabia, South Africa, Spain, Sweden, Switzerland, Türkiye, UK, USA, Venezuela.
NGO Relations Specialty Organization of: *European Society of Anaesthesiology and Intensive Care (ESAIC, #08518).* [2019.02.12/XJ4173/v/**D**]

♦ **European AI & Society Fund** European Artificial Intelligence Society Fund (#05916)

♦ European ALARA Network (EAN) 05855

Coordinator c/o CEPN, 28 rue de la Redoute, 92260 Fontenay-aux-Roses, France. T. +33155521925. Fax +33155521921.
Chair SCK-CEN Mol, Boeretang 200, 2400 Mol, Belgium. T. +3214332853. Fax +3214321624.
URL: http://www.eu-alara.net/

History 1996. Founded by *European Commission (EC, #06633)*. Became a legal entity in 2005. 'ALARA' derives from the phrase 'as low as reasonably achievable'. **Aims** Promote wider and more uniform implementation of the ALARA principle for management of worker, public and patient exposures in all situations. **Structure** Steering Group; Administrative Board; Coordination Team. Includes: *European NORM Association (ENA, #08056)*. **Languages** English. **Finance** Originally sponsored by EC (DG Research); self-sustainable since 2005. **Activities** Events/meetings; knowledge management/information dissemination; publishing activities. **Events** *Workshop on Innovative ALARA Tools* Athens (Greece) 2019, *ALARA in emergency exposure situations* France 2019, *ALARA in emergency exposure situations* Lisbon (Portugal) 2017, *Workshop* Bern (Switzerland) 2016, *Education and training in radiation protection, improving ALARA culture through education and training* Rovinj (Croatia) 2014. **Publications** *European ALARA Newsletter* (2 a year). Workshop proceedings.
Members in 20 countries:
Austria, Belgium, Croatia, Czechia, Denmark, Finland, France, Germany, Greece, Iceland, Ireland, Italy, Netherlands, Norway, Portugal, Slovenia, Spain, Sweden, Switzerland, UK.
NGO Relations Formal cooperation agreements with: *European Federation for Non-Destructive Testing (EFNDT, #07179); European Federation of Organisations for Medical Physics (EFOMP, #07183); European Federation of Radiographer Societies (EFRS, #07203).* [2021/XF6609/**F**]

♦ European Alcohol, Brandy and Spirits Union (inactive)

♦ European Alcohol Policy Alliance (Eurocare) 05856

SG Rue Archimede 17, 3rd Floor, 1000 Brussels, Belgium. T. +3227360572. Fax +3227367351. E-mail: info@eurocare.org.
URL: http://www.eurocare.org/

History Oct 1990, Paris (France). Former names and other names: *European Council on Alcohol Research, Rehabilitation and Education* – former; *Advocacy for the Prevention of Alcohol related Harm in Europe* – former. Registration: No/ID: 0458.950.451, Start date: 10 Oct 1996, Belgium; EU Transparency Register, No/ID: 01546986656-22, Start date: 13 Sep 2011. **Aims** Provide a forum for *European Community* nongovernmental organizations and institutions working in the field of alcohol prevention, rehabilitation, research and education so as to establish closer cooperation and collaboration; as far as possible determine a common basis and aim among members of the European Community in support of these objectives; encourage understanding of social, cultural, economic and political response in Europe to the use of alcohol; facilitate collection, analysis, dissemination and utilization of data on alcohol consumption and related damage; develop preventative strategies appropriate to individual and community needs; stimulate development of an extended network of educational and training programmes for workers in medico-social centres, for the wider public and for students; represent members' views with the European Commission and the European Parliament. **Structure** General Assembly (annual); Board of Directors; Council. **Languages** English. **Staff** 3.00 FTE, paid. **Finance** Members' dues. **Activities** Events/meetings. **Events** *European Alcohol Policy Conference* Oslo (Norway) 2022, *European Alcohol Policy Conference* Oslo (Norway) 2020, *European Alcohol Policy Conference* Edinburgh (UK) 2018, *European Alcohol Policy Conference* Ljubljana (Slovenia) 2016, *European Alcohol Policy Conference* Brussels (Belgium) 2014. **Publications** *Marketing Alcohol to Young People* (2001); *Alcohol Problems in the Family* (1998); *Alcohol Policy and the Public Good – A Guide for Action* (1995); *Counterbalancing the Drinks Industry* (1995).
Members Organizations (about 60) in 19 countries:
Belgium, Denmark, Estonia, Finland, France, Germany, Ireland, Italy, Lithuania, Netherlands, Norway, Poland, Portugal, Slovenia, Spain, Sweden, Switzerland, Türkiye, UK.
Included in the above, 7 organizations listed in this Yearbook:
European Association for the Study of the Liver (EASL, #06233); European FASD Alliance (EUFASD, #07032); European Mutual-Help Network for Alcohol-Related Problems (EMNA, #07843); International Blue Cross (IBC, #12364); International Youth Health Organization (YHO, #15933); Nordiskt Alkohol- och Narkotikapolitiskt Samarbete (NordAN, #17536); United European Gastroenterology (UEG, #20506).
NGO Relations Member of: *European Public Health and Agriculture Consortium (EPHAC, #08296); European Public Health Alliance (EPHA, #08297).* Instrumental in setting up: *International Youth Health Organization (YHO, #15933).* [2022/XD4643/y/**D**]

♦ European Algae Biomass Association (EABA) 05857

Gen Manager Viale Belfiore 10, 50144 Florence FI, Italy. T. +39553241132. E-mail: info@eaba-association.org.
URL: https://www.eaba-association.org/en/

History Jun 2009. Registration: Italy. **Aims** Promote mutual interchange and cooperation in the field of algae biomass production and use, including biofuels uses and all other utilisations. **Structure** General Assembly; Steering Board. Committees (2): Scientific; Industry. Board of Auditors; Board of Arbitrators. **Languages** English. **Staff** 1.00 FTE, paid. **Finance** Members' dues. **Events** *AlgaEurope* Prague (Czechia) 2023, *AlgaEurope* Rome (Italy) 2022, *Conference* Florence (Italy) 2020, *Algae Based Biofuels Workshop* Brussels (Belgium) 2019, *Conference* Paris (France) 2019.
Members Industrial; Scientific; Individual; Observer; Candidate. Members (54) in 17 countries:
Australia, Austria, Belgium, Finland, France, Germany, Greece, Ireland, Israel, Italy, Mexico, Netherlands, Portugal, Slovenia, Spain, UK, USA.
NGO Relations In liaison with technical committees of: *Comité européen de normalisation (CEN, #04162).* [2022/XJ0436/**D**]

♦ European Aligner Society (EAS) 05858

Contact 48 London House, 172 Aldersgate Str, London, EC1A 4HU, UK. T. +442076007598.
URL: http://www.eas-aligners.com/

History 2013. **Aims** Bring together clinicians and manufacturers who are involved with *aligner therapy* and use their combined strengths to raise awareness, effectiveness and outcomes of aligner based treatment. **Structure** Board of Directors. **Events** *Summer Meeting* Porto (Portugal) 2022, *Congress* St Julian's (Malta) 2021, *Autumn Meeting* 2020, *Congress* Venice (Italy) 2018, *AlignerLab Workshop* Vienna (Austria) 2017. [2017/XM5809/**D**]

♦ European Aliphatic Isocyanates Producers Association (internationally oriented national body)
♦ European Allelopathy Society (no recent information)

♦ European Alliance for Access to Safe Medicines (EAASM) 05859

Exec Dir 1386 London Road, Leigh on Sea, SS9 2UJ, UK. T. +447540462867.
URL: http://www.eaasm.eu/

History 2007. Registration: Companies House, No/ID: 06384429, Start date: 28 Sep 2007, England; EU Transparency Register, No/ID: 861368611058-84, Start date: 29 Apr 2013. **Aims** As a pan-European *patient* safety organization: bring together all concerned with eliminating falsified medicines from the supply chain as well as unsafe medical practices. **Structure** Executive Board. **Activities** Advocacy/lobbying/activism. **Publications** *EAASM Newsletter*. Reports; articles; videos. **NGO Relations** Member of (3): *Alliance for Safe Online Pharmacies (ASOP Global); Alliance for Safe Online Pharmacy – EU (ASOP EU, #00720); EU Health Coalition*. Partners include: *European Depression Association (EDA, #06905); European Federation of Neurological Associations (EFNA, #07177); European Medical Association (EMA, #07761); European Parkinson's Disease Association (EPDA, #08145); GS1 (#10809); Healthcare Compliance Packaging Council Europe (HCPC Europe, #10874); Stroke Alliance for Europe (SAFE, #20012)*; national organizations. [2020/XM5029/**D**]

♦ European Alliance Against Depression e.V (EAAD) 05860
Contact Goerdelerring 9, 04109 Leipzig, Germany. T. +493419724440. Fax +493419724539. E-mail: contact@eaad.net.
URL: http://www.eaad.net/
History 2008. Registration: EU Transparency Register, No/ID: 98224959162-32. **Aims** Improve care; optimize treatment for *patients* with depressive *disorders*; prevent *suicidal* behaviour. **Structure** Board of Directors; Coordination Centre. **Activities** Advocacy/lobbying/activism; awareness raising; networking/liaising; projects/programmes; research/documentation. Community based intervention
Members National Chapters in 20 countries and territories:
Austria, Belgium, Canada, Chile, Croatia, France, Germany, Hungary, Ireland, Italy, Luxembourg, Netherlands, New South Wales, New Zealand, Norway, Poland, Portugal, Spain, Switzerland, Western Australia.
Associate Members in 8 countries and territories:
Albania, Belarus, Bulgaria, Greece, Italy, Kosovo, Queensland, Slovenia, UK. [2022.05.11/XM7126/**D**]

♦ European Alliance for Asian Studies 05861
Contact c/o IIAS, Rapenburg 59, 2311 GJ Leiden, Netherlands. T. +31715272227.
URL: https://asiascholars.eu/
History 1997, as *Strategic Alliance for Asian Studies*. **Aims** Unite forces in Europe on Asian Studies in order to establish scholarly excellence in central areas of research and expertise on Asia; build up high-quality, border-transcending research with a stronger focus on contemporary issues; create sustainable networks with Asian and other research institutions and scholars; strengthen links and communication between academic research on Asia and non-academic institutions and actors. **Structure** Cooperative framework of European institutes specializing in Asian studies. Secretariat ran by IIAS. **Activities** Works to step up the momentum and interaction between members and to provide a framework within which greater cooperation can occur; provides a coordinated framework for joint planning and for pooling of resources in conducting jointly organized projects; supports short-term fellowships for research in Asian studies, academic workshops and conferences and publications; sets up collaborative research programmes; stimulates researchers to publish their results; organizes Asia Updates, joint seminars and the ASEF/Alliance workshop series; cooperates on the *'Agenda Asia'* project. **Events** *Colloquium on Asian and European integration process in the new context of development challenges* Paris (France) 2010, *Workshop* Brussels (Belgium) 2006, *Workshop on communication and media in popular image building about Islam and the West* Leiden (Netherlands) 2005, *Workshop on the South Asian diaspora* Rotterdam (Netherlands) 2005, *Workshop on ports, pirates and hinterlands in East and Southeast Asia* Shanghai (China) 2005. **Publications** Information Services: Maintains database of conferences, workshops and seminars in the field of Asian studies.
Members International organizations (7), listed in this Yearbook:
Center for International Studies and Research (CERI); Centre for East Asian Studies, Madrid (CEAO); European Institute for Asian Studies (EIAS, #07545); GIGA Institut für Asien-Studien (IAS); International Institute for Asian Studies, Leiden (IIAS); NIAS-Nordisk Institut for Asienstudier (NIAS, #17132); School of Oriental and African Studies (SOAS).
IGO Relations *Asia-Europe Foundation (ASEF, #01270)*. **NGO Relations** *GIGA – German Institute of Global and Area Studies* is member. Sponsors: *European Conference on Agriculture and Rural Development in China (ECARDC, #06729)*. [2018/XF6608/y/**F**]

♦ European Alliance of Associations for Rheumatology (EULAR) 05862
Exec Dir Seestrasse 240, 8802 Kilchberg ZH, Switzerland. T. +41447163030. E-mail: eular@eular.org.
URL: http://www.eular.org/
History 1947, Copenhagen (Denmark). Founded at 1st European Congress on Rheumatology, as a regional league of *International League of Associations for Rheumatology (ILAR, #14016)*. Former names and other names: *Ligue européenne contre le rhumatisme* – former; *Europäische Rheumaliga* – former; *Evropejskaja Antirevmaticeskaja Liga* – former; *European League Against Rheumatism* – former. **Aims** Reduce the impact of rheumatic and musculoskeletal diseases (RMDs) on the individual and society; improve the social position and the quality of life of people with rheumatic and musculoskeletal diseases in Europe. **Structure** General Assembly; Board; Council; Committees; Communities; Study Groups; Task Forces. **Languages** English. **Staff** 40.00 FTE, paid. **Finance** Sources: members' dues. **Activities** Advocacy/lobbying/activism; awards/prizes/competitions; events/meetings; research and development; training/education. **Events** *European Congress of Rheumatology* Milan (Italy) 2023, *European Congress of Rheumatology* Copenhagen (Denmark) 2022, *European Congress of Rheumatology* Kilchberg (Switzerland) 2021, *European Congress of Rheumatology* Kilchberg (Switzerland) 2020, *Annual Congress* Madrid (Spain) 2019. **Publications** *Annals of the Rheumatic Diseases*; *RMD Open*.
Members National scientific societies, national organisations of people with rheumatic and musculoskeletal diseases (RMDs), and national organisations of health professionals in 44 countries:
Albania, Armenia, Austria, Belarus, Belgium, Bulgaria, Croatia, Cyprus, Czechia, Denmark, Estonia, Finland, France, Georgia, Germany, Greece, Hungary, Iceland, Ireland, Israel, Italy, Latvia, Lebanon, Lithuania, Malta, Moldova, Montenegro, Netherlands, North Macedonia, Norway, Poland, Portugal, Romania, Russia, San Marino, Serbia, Slovakia, Slovenia, Spain, Sweden, Switzerland, Türkiye, UK, Ukraine.
NGO Relations Member of (2): *Associations and Conference Forum (AC Forum, #02909)*; *Biomedical Alliance in Europe (#03251)*. Also links with national organizations. [2023.02.14/XD0795/**D**]

♦ European Alliance for Cardiovascular Health (EACH) 05863
Secretariat Square de Meeus 29, 1000 Brussels, Belgium. E-mail: each@escardio.org.
URL: https://www.cardiovascular-alliance.eu/
History 27 Sep 2021. Registration: EU Transparency Register, No/ID: 447156446198-44, Start date: 22 Apr 2022. **Aims** Call for a comprehensive EU policy response to improve the cardiovascular health of European citizens.
Members Partners (16):
Association internationale de la mutualité (AIM, #02721); *European Atherosclerosis Society (EAS, #06289)*; *European Chronic Disease Alliance (ECDA, #06548)*; *European Confederation of Pharmaceutical Entrepreneurs (EUCOPE, #06718)*; *European Congenital Heart Disease Organisation (ECHDO, #06738)*; *European Coordination Committee of the Radiological, Electromedical Healthcare IT Industry (COCIR, #06792)*; *European Federation of Pharmaceutical Industries and Associations (EFPIA, #07191)*; *European FH Patient Network (FH Europe, #07243)*; *European Heart Network (EHN, #07467)*; *European Kidney Health Alliance (EKHA, #07626)*; *European Society of Cardiology (ESC, #08536)*; *European Stroke Organisation (ESO, #08843)*; *Global Heart Hub (#10407)*; *MedTech Europe (#16692)*; *Stroke Alliance for Europe (SAFE, #20012)*; *World Heart Federation (WHF, #21562)*. [2022/AA2666/y/**D**]

♦ European Alliance of Catholic Women's Organisations (ANDANTE) . 05864
Alliance européenne d'organisations féminines catholiques – Europäische Allianz Katholischer Frauenverbände
Contact kfd-Bundesverband, Postfach 320640, 40421 Düsseldorf, Germany. E-mail: secretariat@andante-europa.net.
URL: http://www.andante-europa.net/
History 5 May 2006, Budapest (Hungary). **Aims** Promote the presence and participation of Catholic women in European society; acknowledge common values across the different cultures; work for the common good from a female perspective. **Structure** General Assembly (every 3 years); Coordinating Committee (CoCoA). **Languages** English, French, German. **Staff** Voluntary. **Finance** Members' dues. Private donations. **Activities** Events/meetings; training/education. **Events** *General Assembly* Hoddesdon (UK) 2016, *General Assembly* Bratislava (Slovakia) 2013, *General Assembly* Stadtbergen (Germany) 2012, *General Assembly* Strasbourg (France) 2010, *General Assembly* Sion (Switzerland) 2008. **Publications** Newsletter (2-4 a year).
Members Organizations (24) in 14 countries:
Albania, Austria, Czechia, Finland, France, Germany, Hungary, Latvia, Luxembourg, Netherlands, Romania, Slovakia, Switzerland, UK.
Consultative Status Consultative status granted from: *Council of Europe (CE, #04881)* (Participatory Status). [2021/XM2088/**F**]

♦ European Alliance for Community Networking (inactive)

♦ European Alliance of Companies for Energy Efficiency in Buildings (EuroACE) 05865
SG Rond-Point Schuman 6, 8th Floor, 1040 Brussels, Belgium. T. +3226391011. E-mail: info@euroace.org.
URL: http://www.euroace.org/
History 1998. Former names and other names: *European Association for the Conservation of Energy* – former. Registration: Banque-Carrefour des Entreprises, No/ID: 0898.506.941, Start date: 12 Jun 2008; EU Transparency Register, No/ID: 99005441548-23, Start date: 20 Apr 2009. **Aims** Work with EU institutions to help Europe move towards efficient use of energy in buildings, thereby contributing to the EU's commitments on job creation, energy security and sustainability. **Structure** General Assembly; Board; Working Groups; Secretariat. **Languages** English, French. **Staff** 5.00 FTE, paid. **Activities** Advocacy/lobbying/activism; networking/liaising; projects/programmes; research/documentation. Active within the European Union only. **Publications** Research reports. **Members** Companies (14). Membership countries not specified.
NGO Relations Member of (5): *Coalition for Energy Savings (#04056)*; *Energy Efficiency Industrial Forum (EEIF, #05470)*; *European Council for an Energy Efficient Economy (ECEEE, #06818)*; *Federation of European and International Associations Established in Belgium (FAIB, #09508)*; *Global Alliance for Buildings and Construction (GlobalABC, #10187)*. [2023.02.13/XF5799/y/**F**]

♦ European Alliance for Culture and the Arts 05866
Address not obtained.
URL: http://allianceforculture.com/
Aims Urge policy makers to re-think the European approach and include culture and the arts in the long-term strategic goals of the European project.
Members Organizations include the following 23 listed in this Yearbook:
- Association Européenne des Conservatoires, Académies de Musique et Musikhochschulen (AEC, #02560);
- ENCATC (#05452);
- EUROCITIES (#05662);
- European Broadcasting Union (EBU, #06404);
- European Choral Association – Europa Cantat (#06541);
- European Cities and Regions for Culture (LIKE, #06554);
- European Concert Hall Organisation (ECHO, #06696);
- European Early Music Network (EEMN, #06953);
- European Festivals Association (EFA, #07242);
- European League of Institutes of the Arts (ELIA, #07670);
- European Music Council (EMC, #07837);
- European Theatre Convention (ETC, #08905);
- European Union of Music Competitions for Youth (EMCY, #09003);
- European Union Youth Orchestra (EUYO, #09024);
- Fresh Arts Coalition Europe (FACE, #09995);
- IETM – International Network for Contemporary Performing Arts (#11098);
- International Society of Violin and Bow-Makers (ISVBM, #15542);
- Live DMA European Network (#16495);
- Network of European Museum Organizations (NEMO, #17024);
- Pearle – Live Performance Europe (#18284);
- Réseau européen pour la sensibilisation à l'opéra et à la danse (RESEO, #18878);
- Trans Europe Halles – A Network of Independent Cultural Centres (TEH, #20211);
- Worldwide Network of Artists Residencies (Res Artis, #21928). [2016/XM4837/y/**F**]

♦ European Alliance for Democratic Citizenship 05867
Address not obtained.
URL: http://www.futurelabeurope.eu/
History Initiated by the Körber Foundation. Affiliate of: *Network of European Foundations (NEF, #17019)*. **Aims** Promote active democratic citizenship among young Europeans. **Activities** Maintains *FutureLab*.
Members Participating organizations (10) in 7 countries:
Belgium, Estonia, Finland, Germany, Italy, Norway, Spain.
Included in the above, 3 organizations listed in this Yearbook:
Company of St Paul; *King Baudouin Foundation (KBF)*; *Robert Bosch Foundation*.
NGO Relations Operational partner: *European Policy Centre (EPC, #08240)*. [2015/XJ7143/y/**E**]

♦ European Alliance for Diabetes Research (EURADIA) 05868
Exec Dir Milnwood, 13 North Parade, Horsham, RH12 2BT, UK. T. +441403276363. Fax +441403276363. E-mail: secretariat@euradia.org.
URL: http://www.euradia.org/
History 2003, as an informal network under the title *European Research Area in Diabetes*. Current title adopted 2007, when registered as a legal entity in accordance with German law: VR 9885. Since 2013, a Charity registered in England and Wales: 1154726. EU Transparency Register: 97801907301-17. **Aims** Improve the lives of people affected by diabetes both now and in the future, through advocacy of diabetes research in Europe at the highest political and societal levels of influence, and by shaping the allocation of resources for diabetes research in Europe through increased awareness. **Structure** Executive Committee, comprising Chairman, Vice-Chairman, Honorary Treasurer and 2 members. **Events** *Symposium* Berlin (Germany) 2012. **Publications** *EURADIA Newsletter* (4 a year).
Members Companies (8); International federations (6):
European Association for the Study of Diabetes (EASD, #06228); *European Society for Paediatric Endocrinology (ESPE, #08678)*; *Foundation of European Nurses in Diabetes (FEND, #09953)*; *International Diabetes Federation Europe (IDF Europe, #13165)*; *Juvenile Diabetes Research Foundation International (JDRF International)*; *Primary Care Diabetes Europe (PCDE, #18495)*.
NGO Relations Member of: *European Coalition for Diabetes (ECD, #06592)*. [2018/XJ1856/y/**D**]

♦ European Alliance for Earth Sciences (GEO*8) 05869
Exec Sec GFZ German Research Centre for Geosciences, Telegrafenberg, 14473 Potsdam, Germany. T. +49331288 ext 1069. E-mail: contact@geo8.eu.
URL: https://geo8.eu/
History 4 Sep 2012, Potsdam (Germany). **Languages** English. **Activities** Events/meetings; projects/programmes. **Publications** Articles; workshop proceedings.
Members European Earth Science Institutions in 8 countries:
France, Germany, Italy, Netherlands, Poland, Spain, Switzerland, UK. [2022.06.10/AA2184/**D**]

♦ European Alliance of EU-critical Movements (TEAM) 05870
SG address not obtained.
URL: http://teameurope.co/
History Founded Mar 1997, Copenhagen (Denmark), when statutes were adopted, as *The European Anti-Maastricht Alliance*. **Aims** Provide a framework for cooperation and exchange of ideas among organizations concerned with the *undemocratic* character of the *European Union*. **Structure** General Meeting (annual); Council; Board. **Activities** Knowledge management/information dissemination; networking/liaising. **Events** *Annual General Meeting* London (UK) 2014, *Annual General Meeting* Riga (Latvia) 2013, *Annual General Meeting* Copenhagen (Denmark) 2012, *Annual General Meeting* Stockholm (Sweden) 2010, *Annual General Meeting* London (UK) 2009. **Publications** *Economic and Monetary Union Book*.
Members Full; Observer. Organizations (60) in 23 countries:
Austria, Czechia, Denmark, Estonia, Finland, France, Greece, Hungary, Iceland, Ireland, Italy, Latvia, Malta, Netherlands, Norway, Poland, Romania, Slovakia, Slovenia, Spain, Sweden, Switzerland, UK. [2016/XF4638/**E**]

♦ European Alliance of Genetic Support Groups / see EGAN – Patients Network for Medical Research and Health (#05394)

♦ European Alliance Group at the Committee of the Regions (EA-CoR) 05871
SG c/o CoR, Rue Belliard 101, 1040 Brussels, Belgium. T. +3222822251. Fax +3222822334.
URL: http://web.cor.europa.eu/ea/
Aims Ensure local and regional authorities achieve greater impact and influence in EU policy making; promote a decentralized EU and more autonomy of regional and local authorities as well as views of independents; promote balanced territorial and sustainable development, sustainability of rural areas, cultural and linguistic diversity. **Structure** Bureau; Secretariat.
Members Individuals in 11 countries:
Belgium, France, Hungary, Ireland, Italy, Lithuania, Poland, Romania, Slovakia, Spain, UK. [2019.12.20/XM4740/v/**E**]

♦ European Alliance of Initiatives for Applied Anthroposophy / see Alliance ELIANT (#00672)

♦ **European Alliance for Innovation (EAI)** **05872**

Main Office Begijnhoflaan 93a, 9000 Ghent, Belgium.
Operations Office c/o Slovak Uni, Vazovova 3, 811 07 Bratislava, Slovakia.
URL: http://www.eai.eu/

History Registration: VZW/ASBL, Belgium. **Aims** Address the global challenges of Europe's future competitiveness through innovation; promote and implement grassroots innovation including dissemination and personal recognition, educational and professional enhancement, research and technology transfer, intellectual property and standards, funding and business development, market trends and society. **Structure** *'EAI Community'*; *'Strategic Forum'*. Assembly of Members; Steering Board; Committees (3). **Languages** English. **Staff** 18.00 FTE, paid. **Finance** Sources: local government funds; *European Commission (EC, #06633)* programme funds; dissemination activities. **Activities** Knowledge management/information dissemination; research/documentation; training/education; standards/guidelines; events/meetings. Over 100 events held annually worldwide. **Events** *International Conference on Smart Objects and Technologies for Social Good (GOODTECHS)* Aveiro (Portugal) 2021, *International Conference on Digital Forensics and Cyber Crime* Singapore (Singapore) 2021, *International Conference on Smart Objects and Technologies for Social Good (GOODTECHS)* Antwerp (Belgium) 2020, *MONAMI – International Conference on Mobile Networks and Management* Ghent (Belgium) 2020, *International Conference on Collaborative Computing* London (UK) 2019. **Publications** *EAI Endorsed Transactions* – series of peer-reviewed research journals covering the latest specialist topics in ICT and related fields. **Information Services** *European Union Digital Library (EUDL)* – central repository of all scientific content published under the different venues of EAI publications, in line with the European Commission's Agenda 2020 objectives of providing a comprehensive Open Access publication portfolio in support of innovation.
Members Full in 37 countries:
Austria, Bangladesh, Belgium, Bosnia-Herzegovina, Bulgaria, Canada, China, Cyprus, Czechia, Denmark, Estonia, Finland, France, Germany, Greece, Hungary, India, Ireland, Israel, Italy, Kazakhstan, Latvia, Lithuania, Malta, Moldova, Netherlands, Pakistan, Poland, Portugal, Romania, Serbia, Slovakia, Slovenia, Spain, Sweden, UK, Vietnam.
Included in the above, 15 organizations listed in this Yearbook:
Ecologica International Association (#05299); *EUREC (#05619)*; *EUROMICRO (#05736)*; *European Business and Innovation Centre Network (EBN, #06420)*; *European Cooperation in Science and Technology (COST, #06784)*; *European Partners for the Environment (EPE, #08154)*; *European Regional Information Society Association (ERISA, no recent information)*; *European Research and Development Service for the Social Economy (DIESIS, #08365)*; *European Society for Engineers and Industrialists (SEII)*; *Institute for Computer Sciences, Social-Informatics and Telecommunications Engineering (ICST, #11248)*; *International Network for Small and Medium Sized Enterprises (INSME, #14325)*; *Mladiinfo International (#16834)*; *Peres Center for Peace, The*; *Taking IT Global (TIG)*; *United Nations Economic Commission for Europe (UNECE, #20555)* (Economic Cooperation and Integration Division). [2021/XJ2464/y/**F**]

♦ **European Alliance for Medical and Biological Engineering and Science (EAMBES)** **05873**

Communications Dir c/o KUL, Celestijnenlaan 200-A, 3001 Heverlee, Belgium. E-mail: manager@eambes.org.
URL: http://www.eambes.org/

History Founded by *International Federation for Medical and Biological Engineering (IFMBE, #13477)*. Statutes adopted 15 Jun 2003, Frankfurt-Main (Germany); updated 2008. Registration: Belgium. **Aims** Improve *health*, wealth and *well-being* by the application of medical and biological engineering and science. **Structure** General Council (meets annually), comprising Chair and elected representatives from each Division. Members in each membership category are organized into Divisions, each with their own Statutes and annual meetings (General Assemblies), which include: Division of Societies; Division of Academic Programmes or Institutions and Research Institutes; Division of Fellows. Executive Board, comprising President, President-Elect, Past-President, Secretary-General and Treasurer. Standing Committees (2): Nominating; Membership. Ad-Hoc Committees. Task Forces (2): Education; Research. **Languages** English. **Staff** 0.50 FTE, paid; 16.00 FTE, voluntary. **Finance** Members'dues. **Activities** Organizes workshops; serves and promotes Medical and Biological Engineering and Science (MBES) at European and national levels; fosters, coordinates and provides added value to activities of member organizations in MBES; collaborates where appropriate with national and international organisations; serves and promotes MBES education, training and accreditation programmes, as well as research and development; establishes recommendations for appropriate general responsibilities, organizational relationships and roles of those engaged in the field; establishes and maintains liaison with national and European governments and agencies; promotes public awareness of MBES; improves inter-society relations and cooperation in Europe within MBES and related fields; encourages and assists in formation of organizations for MBES where such organizations do not exist; recognizes individual and group achievements and contributions to the field. **Events** *NBC: Nordic-Baltic Conference on Biomedical Engineering and Medical Physics* Liepaja (Latvia) 2023, *MEDICON: Mediterranean Conference on Medical and Biological Engineering and Computing* Sarajevo (Bosnia-Herzegovina) 2023, *NBC: Nordic-Baltic Conference on Biomedical Engineering and Medical Physics* Tampere (Finland) 2017, *European medical and biological engineering conference* Prague (Czech Rep) 2005.
Members Categories Societies, including national organizations (25) and transnational societies (6); Academic Programmes or Institutions and Research Institutes (34); Fellows (34). Members in 27 countries:
Austria, Belgium, Bulgaria, Croatia, Cyprus, Czechia, Denmark, Estonia, Finland, France, Germany, Greece, Hungary, Israel, Italy, Moldova, Montenegro, Netherlands, Poland, Romania, Serbia, Slovakia, Spain, Sweden, Switzerland, UK, USA.
International organizations (3), listed in this Yearbook:
Educating Students in Engineering and Medicine (ESEM, #05364); *European Society for Artificial Organs (ESAO, #08525)*; *International Society for Medical Innovation and Technology (ISMIT, #15255)*.
IGO Relations *European Commission (EC, #06633)*. **NGO Relations** Member of: *Health First Europe (HFE, #10881)*; *International Federation for Medical and Biological Engineering (IFMBE, #13477)*. [2020/XJ3276/**F**]

♦ **European Alliance for Medical Radiation Protection Research (EURAMED)** **05874**

aligned approaches and responses to European research calls
Sec c/o EIBIR, Neutorgasse 9/12, 1010 Vienna, Austria. T. +4315334064. Fax +4315334064448.
URL: https://www.euramed.eu/

History Statutes adopted 1 Oct 2017. Registration: No/ID: ZVR 1619603266, Austria. **Aims** Improve medical care through sustainable research efforts in medical radiation protection; identify common research areas; serve as a platform for medical radiation protection research; develop aligned approaches and responses to European research calls. **Structure** General Assembly; Executive Board; Secretariat, hosted by *European Institute for Biomedical Imaging Research (EIBIR, #07546)*. Committees: Membership; Scientific. **Finance** Sources: members' dues; none. **Activities** Research/documentation; training/education. **Events** *ERPW : European Radiation Protection Week Conference* Estoril (Portugal) 2022, *European Radiation Protection Week (ERPW) Conference* Vienna (Austria) 2021.
Members Founding; Full; Associate; Corporate; Individual. Founding members (5):
European Association of Nuclear Medicine (EANM, #06136); *European Federation of Organisations for Medical Physics (EFOMP, #07183)*; *European Federation of Radiographer Societies (EFRS, #07203)*; *European SocieTy for Radiotherapy and Oncology (ESTRO, #08721)*; *European Society of Radiology (ESR, #08720)*.
Full in 7 countries:
Belgium, France, Germany, Greece, Ireland, Italy, Portugal. [2020/AA0777/**D**]

♦ European Alliance for Medicinal Cannabis (unconfirmed)

♦ **European Alliance for Mental Health – Employment & Work (EUMH Alliance)** **05875**

Address not obtained.
URL: https://eumhalliance.com/

History An informal coalition of European organizations. Former names and other names: *EUMH-WE* – alias. **Aims** Promote mental health and well-being in the workplace; advocate for equal access to the labour market for all people experiencing mental ill health; stimulate policy developments at EU level in these domains. **Structure** Governing Board. **Activities** Events/meetings; knowledge management/information dissemination; networking/liaising; research/documentation.
Members Organizations (8):
Association Européenne des Institutions Paritaires de la Protection Sociale (AEIP, #02575); *Association internationale de la mutualité (AIM, #02721)*; *EUROCADRES – Council of European Professional and Managerial Staff (#05651)*; *EuroHealthNet (#05693)*; *European Platform for Rehabilitation (EPR, #08230)*; *European Public Health Alliance (EPHA, #08297)*; GGZ Nederland; *Mental Health Europe (MHE, #16715)*. [2021/AA2736/y/**D**]

♦ European Alliance of Muscular Dystrophy Associations / see European Alliance of Neuromuscular Disorders Associations (#05876)

♦ **European Alliance of Neuromuscular Disorders Associations (EAMDA)** **05876**

Alliance européenne des associations de myopathes (AEMDA)
Pres Linhartova 1, 1000 Ljubljana, Slovenia. T. +38614720500. Fax +38614328142. E-mail: info@eamda.eu.
URL: http://www.eamda.eu/

History 29 Jun 1972, London (UK). Previous office locations: London (UK); Valetta (Malta). Former names and other names: *European Alliance of Muscular Dystrophy Associations* – former. **Aims** Comprise a platform for exchange of ideas and experience and for coordination of cooperative projects in the area of *neuromuscular disease*. **Structure** General Meeting (annual, at Conference); Executive Committee; EYO Committee. **Languages** English. **Staff** 1.00 FTE, voluntary. **Finance** Members' dues. **Activities** Events/meetings; training/education; knowledge management/information dissemination. **Events** *International Conference on NMD* Ljubljana (Slovenia) 2021, *International Conference on NMD* Ljubljana (Slovenia) 2020, *Annual General Meeting* Prague (Czechia) 2018, *Annual General Meeting* Zagreb (Croatia) 2017, *Annual General Meeting* Belgrade (Serbia) 2015. **Publications** *EAMDA Newsletter*. *Physiotherapy for Neuromuscular Diseases*; *Research into the Origin and Treatment of Muscular Dystrophy*. Conference, seminar and workshop reports; papers; brochures; surveys; newsletters; lists of on-going research; white papers on controversial or fast developing subjects; literature lists; diagnostic chart.
Members Associations in 32 countries:
Austria, Belgium, Bulgaria, Croatia, Cyprus, Czechia, Denmark, Estonia, Finland, France, Germany, Greece, Hungary, Ireland, Italy, Lithuania, Malta, Moldova, Netherlands, Norway, Poland, Romania, Russia, Serbia, Slovakia, Slovenia, Spain, Sweden, Switzerland, Türkiye, UK, Ukraine.
NGO Relations Member of: *European Disability Forum (EDF, #06929)*; *European Federation of Neurological Associations (EFNA, #07177)*; *EGAN – Patients Network for Medical Research and Health (EGAN, #05394)*; *EURORDIS – Rare Diseases Europe (#09175)*; *European Patients' Forum (EPF, #08172)*. Instrumental in setting up: *European Neuromuscular Centre (ENMC, #08042)*. [2022/XD3941/**D**]

♦ **European Alliance of News Agencies (EANA)** **05877**

Secretary General Wankdorfallee 5, 3000 Bern, Switzerland. E-mail: secretarygeneral@newsalliance.org.
Mailing Address Via Antonio Galli 10, 6900 Lugano TI, Switzerland.
URL: http://www.newsalliance.org/

History 21 Aug 1957, Strasbourg (France). Founded following meetings 1952, Brussels (Belgium) and 1956, Rome (Italy), and the setting up, Sep 1952, Geneva (Switzerland), of *Associated European Press Agencies – Agences de presse européennes associées*. Former names and other names: *European Alliance of Press Agencies (EAPA)* – former (21 Aug 1957); *Alliance européenne des agences de presse* – former (21 Aug 1957). Registration: Swiss Civil Code, No/ID: CH-035.6.031.208.5, Switzerland; EU Transparency Register, No/ID: 842844245143-68, Start date: 12 Jan 2022. **Aims** Serve as a forum for cooperation and exchange of information and experiences among European news agencies. **Structure** General Assembly (annual); Board. Membership limited to one agency per country. Meetings closed. **Languages** English. **Finance** Sources: contributions. **Activities** Events/meetings; knowledge management/information dissemination; training/education. Active in all member countries. **Events** *Spring Conference* Berlin (Germany) 2019, *Annual Conference* Madrid (Spain) 2014, *Annual General Assembly* Geneva (Switzerland) 2013, *General assembly / Annual General Assembly* Geneva (Switzerland) 2006, *Seminar* Geneva (Switzerland) 2006. **Publications** *EANA Newsletter* in English.
Members Agencies in 32 countries:
Albania, Andorra, Austria, Azerbaijan, Belgium, Bosnia-Herzegovina, Bulgaria, Croatia, Cyprus, Czechia, Denmark, Finland, France, Germany, Greece, Hungary, Italy, Netherlands, Norway, Poland, Portugal, Romania, Russia, Serbia, Slovakia, Slovenia, Spain, Sweden, Switzerland, Türkiye, UK, Ukraine.
Consultative Status Consultative status granted from: *ECOSOC (#05331)* (Ros A); *World Intellectual Property Organization (WIPO, #21593)* (Permanent Observer Status). [2022.02.16/XD0543/**D**]

♦ European Alliance of Patient and Parent Organizations for Genetic Services and Innovation in Medicine / see EGAN – Patients Network for Medical Research and Health (#05394)

♦ **European Alliance for Personalised Medicine (EAPM)** **05878**

Dir Avenue de l'Armee 10, 1040 Brussels, Belgium. T. +32472535104.
Registered Address Ulica Heroja Tomšiča 11, 2000 Maribor, Slovenia.
URL: http://euapm.eu/

History Mar 2012. **Aims** Improve patient care by accelerating the development, delivery and uptake of personalized healthcare including personalized medicine and diagnostics. **Structure** Board. **Finance** Members' dues. **Activities** Training/education; events/meetings. **Events** *Gobal Conference* Brussels (Belgium) 2021, *Presidency Conference* Brussels (Belgium) 2021, *Presidency Conference* Brussels (Belgium) 2020, *Congress* Brussels (Belgium) 2019, *Presidency Conference* Brussels (Belgium) 2019. **Publications** *EAPM Bulletin* (12 a year).
Members Members include the following 28 organizations listed in this Yearbook:
- *Association internationale de la mutualité (AIM, #02721)*;
- *Association of Schools of Public Health in the European Region (ASPHER, #02904)*;
- *ecancer Global Foundation*;
- *European Alliance for Personalised Medicine (EAPM, #05878)*;
- *European Association of Hospital Pharmacists (EAHP, #06074)*;
- *European Association of Nuclear Medicine (EANM, #06136)*;
- *European Association of Urology (EAU, #06264)*;
- *European Brain Council (EBC, #06391)*;
- *European Cancer Patient Coalition (ECPC, #06433)*;
- *European Centre for Public Health Genomics (ECPHG)*;
- *European Federation of Nurses Associations (EFN, #07180)*;
- *European Federation of Pharmaceutical Industries and Associations (EFPIA, #07191)*;
- *European Hematology Association (EHA, #07473)*;
- *European Kidney Health Alliance (EKHA, #07626)*;
- *European Oncology Nursing Society (EONS, #08086)*;
- *European Organisation for Research and Treatment of Cancer (EORTC, #08101)*;
- *European Parkinson's Disease Association (EPDA, #08145)*;
- *European Patients' Forum (EPF, #08172)*;
- *European Respiratory Society (ERS, #08383)*;
- *European Science Foundation (ESF, #08441)*;
- *European Society for Medical Oncology (ESMO, #08648)*;
- *European Society of Cardiology (ESC, #08536)*;
- *European Society of Pathology (ESP, #08689)*;
- *European Society of Radiology (ESR, #08720)*;
- *EURORDIS – Rare Diseases Europe (#09175)*;
- *Groupement International de la Répartition Pharmaceutique (GIRP, #10762)*;
- *International Diabetes Federation (IDF, #13164)*;
- *Pharmaceutical Group of the European Union (PGEU, #18352)*.

NGO Relations Member of (1): *European Society of Pharmacogenomics and Personalised Therapy (ESPT, #08696)*. [2021/XJ6848/y/**D**]

♦ European Alliance for Plant-based Foods (unconfirmed)
♦ European Alliance of Press Agencies / see European Alliance of News Agencies (#05877)
♦ European Alliance for the Promotion of Vision Research and Ophthalmology / see European Vision Institute (#09069)
♦ European Alliance for Research Excellence (unconfirmed)

♦ European Alliance for Responsible R and D and Affordable Medicines 05879

Coordinator c/o EPHA, Rue de Trèves 49, 1000 Brussels, Belgium.
URL: http://medicinesalliance.eu/

Aims Create and R and D system that is driven by public health needs delivers medicines that are universally accessible and affordable. **Finance** Members' dues. Other contributors: *Joanna Briggs Institute (JBI)*; *European Public Health Alliance (EPHA, #08297)*.
Members Consumer, patient and public health organizations in 25 countries:
Austria, Bulgaria, Cyprus, Denmark, Finland, France, Germany, Greece, Iceland, Ireland, Italy, Latvia, Lithuania, Netherlands, North Macedonia, Norway, Poland, Portugal, Romania, Slovenia, Spain, Sweden, Switzerland, UK, Ukraine.
Included in the above, 35 organizations listed in this Yearbook:
- *AIDS Action Europe (#00590)*;
- *Association de lutte contre le sida (AIDES)*;
- *Brot für die Welt*;
- *Bureau Européen des Unions de Consommateurs (BEUC, #03360)*;
- *Bureau international des Médecins sans frontières (MSF International, #03366)*;
- *Coalition International SIDA (Coalition PLUS)*;
- *Cochrane Collaboration (#04078)*;
- *Commons Network*;
- *East European and Central Asian Union of PLWH (ECUO, #05257)*;
- *European AIDS Treatment Group (EATG, #05850)*;
- *European Public Health Alliance (EPHA, #08297)*;
- *Farmacéuticos Mundi (FARMAMUNDI)*;
- *Global Health Advocates (#10400)*;
- *Health Action International (HAI, #10868)*;
- *Health and Trade Network (HaT, #10890)*;
- *International Society of Drug Bulletins (ISDB, #15066)*;
- *Knowledge Ecology International (KEI, #16200)*;
- *Medicines for Europe (#16633)*;
- *Medico International*;
- *Mundo Sano*;
- *Public Eye*;
- *Restless Development*;
- *Salud por Derecho*;
- *Universities Allied for Essential Medicines (UAEM, #20692)*;
- *WEMOS*. [2018/XM6408/y/**D**]

♦ European Alliance of Responsible Tourism and Hospitality (EARTH) 05880

Head Office Boulevard Charlemagne 74, 1000 Brussels, Belgium. T. +3225431043. E-mail: coordination.earth@gmail.com.
Pres address not obtained. E-mail: presidenteaitr@aitr.org.
URL: https://earthresponsible.wordpress.com/

History 16 Oct 2008. Founded by 27 organizations from 5 countries. Registration: No/ID: 0811.932.461, Start date: 27 May 2009, Belgium; EU Transparency Register, No/ID: 65750918967-37, Start date: 13 Jun 2012. **Aims** Promote the concept of responsible tourism and its principles and values by: promoting exchange of good practices along with tools available to both small and micro-enterprises for a sustainable and competitive tourism; conveying to members the core vision of the European Agenda on responsible and competitive tourism; approving and implementing a Corporate Social Responsibility (CSR) system. **Structure** Board. **Languages** English, French, German, Italian, Spanish. **Activities** Awareness raising; events/meetings; networking/liaising; training/education. **Events** *SENINTER Project Conference* Brussels (Belgium) 2017, *Conference on New European Common Qualifications of Heritage Interpretation in Tourism Sector* Brussels (Belgium) 2015, *European Conference on Transparency of CSR Skills in European Tourism* Brussels (Belgium) 2015, *European Conference on Responsible Tourism in a Sharing Economy* Brussels (Belgium) 2014.
Members Organizations in 7 countries:
Belgium, France, Germany, Ireland, Italy, Malta, Slovenia, Spain, UK.
Included in the above, 2 organizations listed in this Yearbook:
European Research and Development Service for the Social Economy (DIESIS, #08365); *Istituto per la Cooperazione Economica Internazionale (ICEI)*.
NGO Relations Member of (1): *European Tourism Manifesto (#08921)*. *International Social Tourism Organisation (ISTO, #14889)*. [2018/XM3899/y/**D**]

♦ European Alliance for Restless Legs Syndrome (EARLS) 05881

Contact Rue d'Egmont 11, 1000 Brussels, Belgium.
URL: http://www.earls.eu/

History Nov 2009, Brussels (Belgium). **Aims** Contribute to raising awareness of Restless Legs Syndrome (RLS). **Structure** Board; Advisory Board. **Languages** English. **Staff** Voluntary. **Finance** Ad hoc project-based funding, mostly from the pharmaceutical industry. Annual budget: 10,000 EUR. **Activities** Awareness raising.
Members Organizations in 7 countries:
Finland, France, Netherlands, Norway, Spain, Sweden, UK. [2022/XJ1654/**D**]

♦ European Alliance to Save Energy (EU ASE) 05882

Pres c/o BSE, Avenue Milcamps 41, 1030 Brussels, Belgium. E-mail: info@euase.eu.
URL: http://www.euase.eu/

History Dec 2010, at United Nations Climate Conference. EU Transparency Register: 37816636575-51. **Aims** Work towards a future where energy efficiency and end-users empowerment are central to the EU energy system and are fundamental drivers for job creation, sustainable growth, competitiveness, energy productivity, innovation, energy security and decarbonization. **Structure** Board.
Members Companies; NGOs and Foundations; Honorary members. Included in the above, 2 organizations listed in this Yearbook:
Alliance to Save Energy (ASE); *European Climate Foundation (ECF, #06574)*.
NGO Relations Sister organization: *Alliance to Save Energy (ASE)*. Member of: *Coalition for Energy Savings (#04056)*. Partner of: *Global Alliance for Energy Productivity (#10196)*. Associate partner of: *Covenant of Mayors for Climate and Energy (#04939)*. [2017/XJ2719/y/**E**]

♦ European Alliance on Skills for Employability 05883

Contact address not obtained.

Aims Provide technology access to train and certify young *unemployed* and older *workers* with information communication technology. **Structure** Managed and operated by e-Skills Certification Consortium (eSCC). Alliance Management Committee. **Activities** Events/meetings. **Events** *Employer Forum on Accessibility in the Workplace* Brussels (Belgium) 2011.
Members Companies and organizations in 5 countries:
Belgium, Germany, Ireland, Netherlands, Spain.
Included in the above, 1 organization listed in this Yearbook:
ICDL Europe (#11052). [2012/XM1666/y/**F**]

♦ European Alliance of SMA Groups / see SMA Europe (#19310)
♦ European Alliance for SMC / see European Alliance for SMC/BMC (#05884)

♦ European Alliance for SMC/BMC 05884

Sec Bd A Reyers 80, 1030 Brussels, Belgium. T. +3227068010. E-mail: info@smcbmc-europe.org.
URL: http://smcbmc-europe.org/

History 1993, as *European Alliance for SMC*. **Aims** Promote the use of *sheet moulding* compound (SMC) and bulk moulding compound (BMC) in the automotive, electrical, construction and sanitary industry. **Structure** Steering Committee. **Activities** Events/meetings; awards/prizes/competitions. **Events** *Light Composite Materials for a Sustainable Future Conference* Brussels (Belgium) 2012, *Seminar on composites in transport* Amsterdam (Netherlands) 2005.
Members Active (15) in 7 countries:
Belgium, France, Germany, Italy, Netherlands, Spain, UK.
NGO Relations Sectoral organization of: *European Composites Industry Association (EuCIA, #06692)*. [2019.10.08/XM0667/**F**]

♦ European Alliance for the Social Sciences and Humanities (EASSH) 05885

Dir 54 bd Raspail, 75006 Paris, France. E-mail: executive.secretary@eassh.eu.
URL: https://eassh.eu

History 20 Dec 2011, Paris (France). Revived Jan 2015, Paris (France). Registration: Répertoire des enterprises et des Establisséments (SIRENE), No/ID: 830 189 650, Start date: 3 Jun 2015, France, Paris; EU Transparency Register, No/ID: 754273928909-61. **Aims** Promote research on social sciences and humanities as a resource for Europe and the world. **Structure** General Assembly; Governing Board; Director. **Languages** English, French. **Finance** Sources: members' dues. **Activities** Events/meetings. Active in all member countries. **Events** *General Assembly* Brussels (Belgium) 2022.
Members Founding; Group of Higher Education and Research Institutions Associations and Academies; Groups of co-opted Individuals; Group of Individuals. Members in 16 countries:
Belgium, Croatia, Denmark, Finland, France, Hungary, Ireland, Italy, Netherlands, Norway, Portugal, Slovakia, Spain, Sweden, Switzerland, UK.
https://eassh.eu/Members.
European institutions include 25 organizations listed in this Yearbook:
- *Academia Europaea (#00011)*;
- *CARMEN – The Worldwide Medieval Network (CARMEN, #03584)*;
- *Common Language Resources and Technology Infrastructure (CLARIN, #04295)*;
- *Digital Research Infrastructure for the Arts and Humanities (DARIAH-EU, #05083)*;
- *Europaeum (#05747)*;
- *European Association for Chinese Studies (EACS, #05973)*;
- *European Association for the Study of Religions (EASR, #06235)*;
- *European Association of Development Research and Training Institutes (EADI, #06012)*;
- *European Confederation of Political Science Associations (ECPSA, #06720)*;
- *European Consortium for Humanities Institutes and Centres (ECHIC, #06755)*;
- *European Consortium for Political Research (ECPR, #06762)*;
- *European Educational Research Association (EERA, #06967)*;
- *European Group for Public Administration (EGPA, #07430)*;
- *European Language Council (ELC, #07646)*;
- *European Regional Science Association (ERSA, #08346)*;
- *European Science Foundation (ESF, #08441)*;
- *European Social Work Research Association (ESWRA, #08508)*;
- *European Society for Comparative Legal History (ESCLH, #08560)*;
- *European Society for Environmental History (ESEH, #08596)*;
- *European Society of Comparative Literature (ESCL, #08561)*;
- *European Sociological Association (ESA, #08790)*;
- *EvalHum (#09207)*;
- *Fédération internationale des associations d'études classiques (FIEC, #09607)*;
- *Net4Society (#16976)*;
- *Network of European Institutes for Advanced Studies (Netias, #17020)*. [2021.06.09/XJ6406/**D**]

♦ European Alliance for the Statute of the European Association (EASEA) 05886

Coordinator c/o Eur Civic Forum, Hameau de St-Hippolyte, 04300 Limans, France. T. +33492730598. E-mail: fr@forumcivique.org.
URL: http://www.easea.eu/

History as an informal alliance of NGOs. **Aims** Support the EP Written Declaration 84/2010 on establishing a European Statute for Mutuals, Associations and Foundations. **Structure** Coordinated by *European Civic Forum (ECF, #06563)*.
NGO Relations Supporting organizations include:
- *Association for Community Colleges (ACC, #02441)*;
- *Association des états généraux des étudiants de l'Europe (AEGEE-Europe, #02495)*;
- *Association des femmes de l'Europe méridionale (AFEM, #02594)*;
- *Centre international de formation européenne (CIFE, #03755)*;
- *Conference of Peripheral Maritime Regions of Europe (CPMR, #04638)*;
- *Erasmus Student Network (ESN, #05529)*;
- *EURAG – European Federation of Older Persons (#05597)*;
- *European Alternatives (EA, #05891)*;
- *European Anti-Poverty Network (EAPN, #05908)*;
- *European Association for the Defence of Human Rights (AEDH, no recent information)*;
- *European Association of History Educators (EUROCLIO, #06069)*;
- *European Association for Local Democracy (ALDA, #06110)*;
- *European Association of Service Providers for Persons with Disabilities (EASPD, #06204)*;
- *European Citizen Action Service (ECAS, #06555)*;
- *European Civic Forum (ECF, #06563)*;
- *European Council for Non-Profit Organizations (#06834)*;
- *European Esperanto Union (#07006)*;
- *European Expression*;
- *European Federalist Party (#07036)*;
- *European Forum for Freedom in Education (EFFE, #07311)*;
- *European League for Economic Cooperation (ELEC, #07669)*;
- *European Movement International (EMI, #07825)*;
- *European Network for Education and Training (EUNET, #07899)*;
- *European Non-Governmental Sports Organization (ENGSO, #08054)*;
- *European Public Health Alliance (EPHA, #08297)*;
- *Centre for European Volunteering (CEV, #03743)*;
- *European Youth Forum (#09140)*;
- *Fédération européenne des femmes actives en famille (FEFAF, #09568)*;
- *ILGA-Europe (#11118)*;
- *International Sport and Culture Association (ISCA, #15587)*;
- *Lifelong Learning Platform – European Civil Society for Education (LLLP, #16466)*;
- *Party of European Socialists (PES, #18249)*;
- *Santé mentale et exclusion sociale – Europa (SMES Europa, #19053)*;
- *SOLIDAR (#19680)*;
- *Standing Committee of European Doctors (#19955)*;
- *Union of European Federalists, The (UEF, #20385)*;
- *Young European Federalists (#21984)*. [2012.01.24/XJ4971/**E**]

♦ European Alliance of Subject-Specific and Professional Accreditation and Quality Assurance (EASPA) 05887

Pres c/o ASIIN, PO Box 10 11 39, 40002 Düsseldorf, Germany. T. +4922190097710 – +492219009770. Fax +4922190097799. E-mail: gf@asiin.de.
Street Address c/o ASIIN eV, Robert-Stolz-Str 5, 40470 Düsseldorf, Germany.
URL: http://www.easpa.eu/

History 29 Nov 2011, Düsseldorf (Germany), by *European Network for Accreditation of Engineering Education (ENAEE, #07859)*, *European Quality Assurance Network for Informatics Education (EQANIE, #08310)*, *Association Européenne des Conservatoires, Académies de Musique et Musikhochschulen (AEC, #02560)*, *European Chemistry Thematic Network (ECTN, #06526)*, *ISEKI-Food Association (#16027)*, *European Association for Public Administration Accreditation (EAPAA, #06177)*, *European Countries Biologists Association (ECBA, #06852)* and *European Physical Society (EPS, #08207)*. Registered in accordance with German law. **Aims** Provide a platform for the cooperation between European and international quality assurance networks and international organizations in the development and harmonization of their activities in the field of quality assurance and quality improvement in higher education. **Structure** General Assembly (annual); Executive Board. **Finance** Members' dues.
Members Full (8):
Association Européenne des Conservatoires, Académies de Musique et Musikhochschulen (AEC, #02560); *European Association for Public Administration Accreditation (EAPAA, #06177)*; *European Chemistry Thematic Network (ECTN, #06526)*; *European Countries Biologists Association (ECBA, #06852)*; *European Network for Accreditation of Engineering Education (ENAEE, #07859)*; *European Physical Society (EPS, #08207)*; *European Quality Assurance Network for Informatics Education (EQANIE, #08310)*; *ISEKI-Food Association (#16027)*.
Associate (2):
European Federation of Geologists (EFG, #07133); *International Centre of Excellence in Tourism and Hospitality Education (THE-ICE, #12491)*. [2015/XJ9468/ty/**D**]

♦ European Alliance for Television and Culture (EATC) 05888
Alliance européenne pour la télévision et la culture (AETC)
Projects Manager c/o EBU/UER TV Dept, Programme Collections and Exchange, Ancienne Route 17A, Case Postale 45, Grand Saconnex, 1218 Geneva, Switzerland. T. +35226478558. Fax +35226864298.
URL: http://www.ebu.ch/fr/eurovisiontv/fiction/pge.php
History Founded 26 Jun 1987, Geneva (Switzerland), under the auspices of *European Broadcasting Union (EBU, #06404)*. **Aims** Serve as the authoritative voice for public service media as a cornerstone of democratic society; provide media services and a centre of learning and knowledge sharing; operate EUROVISION (distributor and producer of quality content), and EURORADIO (news and music exchange). **Structure** General Assembly. **Finance** Members' dues. **Activities** Awards/prizes/competitions; events/meetings. **Events** *Meeting* Berlin (Germany) 2008, *Extraordinary general assembly* Geneva (Switzerland) 2002.
Members Active (73) broadcasting organizations within the European Broadcasting Area as defined by the ITU, or which are members of the Council of Europe. Active members in 56 countries (not specified). Associate (35) broadcasting organizations or groups thereof from a member country of the ITU outside the European Broadcasting Area which provide radio and/or television service with a major role in national broadcasting and whose membership is deemed useful for the EBU. Associate members in 21 countries (not specified).
Associate (35) broadcasting organizations or groups thereof from a member country of the ITU outside the European Broadcasting Area which provide radio and/or television service with a major role in national broadcasting and whose membership is deemed useful for the EBU. Associate members in 21 countries (not specified). [2014.11.10/XF2234/F]

♦ European Alliance for Transformative Therapies (TRANSFORM) . . . 05889
Secretariat address not obtained. E-mail: secretariat@transformalliance.eu.
URL: https://transformalliance.eu/
History Dec 2020. Founded as a multi-stakeholder Alliance that connects Members of *European Parliament (EP, #08146)* and policy-makers with patient groups, medical experts and associations, scientists, researchers, industry actors, networks and other relevant stakeholders. **Aims** Foster effective dialogue and provide evidence-based policy recommendations to enable safe and timely patient access to cell and gene therapies, whilst ensuring the sustainability of healthcare systems. **Structure** TRANSFORM MET Interest Group; Secretariat.
Members Organizations (13):
Childhood Cancer International Europe (CCI Europe, #03872); European Alliance for Vision Research and Ophthalmology (EU-EYE, #05890); European Association for Haemophilia and Allied Disorders (EAHAD, #06063); European Confederation of Pharmaceutical Entrepreneurs (EUCOPE, #06718); European Federation of Neurological Associations (EFNA, #07177); European Haemophilia Consortium (EHC, #07444); European Paediatric Translational Research Infrastructure (EPTRI); EURORDIS – Rare Diseases Europe (#09175); International Patient Organization for Primary Immunodeficiencies (IPOPI, #14533); Retina International (RI, #18926); SIOP Europe (SIOPE, #19288); Thalassaemia International Federation (#20139); World Duchenne Organization (WDO, #21366).
Observers – 1 organization and 2 individuals in 2 countries:
Belgium, UK.
European Medicines Agency (EMA, #07767). [2021/AA2340/y/E]

♦ European Alliance for Vision Research and Ophthalmology (EU-EYE) 05890
Secretariat Temple House, Temple Road, Blackrock, Dublin, CO. DUBLIN, Ireland. T. +35318669400. E-mail: info@eueye.org.
Head Office Rue de Grand-Bigard 14, 1082 Brussels, Belgium.
URL: http://www.eueye.org/
History 2015. Launched by 9 European subspecialty ophthalmology societies. Registration: Banque-Carrefour des Entreprises, No/ID: 0643.482.261, Start date: 19 Nov 2015, Belgium; EU Transparency Register, No/ID: 221589017973-83, Start date: 26 Jun 2015. **Aims** Increase awareness about research in vision science and ophthalmology; improve eye health in Europe. **Structure** General Assembly; Board; Executive Committee. **Finance** Sources: members' dues. URL: https://www.eueye.org/wp-content/uploads/2020/11/EU-EYE_Finance_2020.pdf **Activities** Training/education. Europe. **Publications** *Focus-EU* in English – e-newsletter providing overview of EU and global policy developments.
Members Organizations (11):
ANIRIDIA-NET (#00846); EURETINA – European Society of Retina Specialists (#05623); European Association for the Study of Diabetic Eye Complications (EASDEC, #06229); European Association for Vision and Eye Research (EVER, #06274); European Eye Bank Association (EEBA, #07020); European Glaucoma Society (EGS, #07393); European Paediatric Ophthalmological Society (EPOS, #08127); European Society of Cataract and Refractive Surgeons (ESCRS, #08539); European Society of Cornea and Ocular Surface Disease Specialists (EuCornea, #08569); European Vision Institute Clinical Research Network (EVICR.net, #09070); European Vision Institute (EVI, #09069). [2021.06.08/XM8692/y/D]

♦ European Alliance for Volunteering (inactive)
♦ European Alliance of YMCAs / see YMCA Europe (#21977)
♦ European ALS Consortium / see European Network for the Cure of ALS (#07889)

♦ European Alternatives (EA) 05891
Alternativs Européennes
Communications Officer Via dei Prati Fiscali 215, 00141 Rome RM, Italy. E-mail: info@euroalter.com.
London Office 501 The Nexus Building, Broadway, Letchworth Garden City, SG6 9BL, UK.
URL: https://euroalter.com/
History 2006. Based in London (UK) with sister legal entities in France, Italy and Germany. Constitution approved 2011. Registration: Companies House, No/ID: 06101658, Start date: 13 Feb 2007, England and Wales; Berlin District court, No/ID: VR 32369, Start date: 22 Apr 2013, Germany; EU Transparency Register, No/ID: 85223352533-24, Start date: 21 Oct 2009. **Aims** Promote alternative forms of *political subjectivity* and collective political action. **Structure** Board of Trustees; Advisory Board; Steering Committee. **Activities** Advocacy/lobbying/activism; events/meetings; research/documentation. **Events** *Annual General Meeting* Berlin (Germany) 2016. **Publications** *Europa Magazine* (6 a year). **Members** Individuals. Membership countries not specified. **IGO Relations** Participant in Fundamental Rights Platform of *European Union Agency for Fundamental Rights (FRA, #08969)*. **NGO Relations** Member of (3): *A Soul for Europe (ASF, #19697); Eastern Partnership Civil Society Forum (EaP CSF, #05247); From the Sea to the City.* Supports (1): *European Alliance for the Statute of the European Association (EASEA, #05886).* Signatory to: *Alter Summit.* [2023/XJ8235/v/F]

♦ European Alternative Splicing Network (EURASNET) 05892
Coordinator Max Planck Inst for Biophysical Chemistry, Dept of Cellular Biochemistry, Am Fassberg 11, 37077 Göttingen, Germany. T. +495512011405.
Archived website: https://eurasnet.webarchive.hutton.ac.uk/
History as a EU-funded Network of Excellence, with funding period 2006-2011. Since 2012 continues as an informal network. **Aims** Investigate and understand the principles of alternative splicing and how it affects human health. **Structure** Scientific Advisory Board. Coordinator. **Languages** English. **Finance** Funded as a Framework 6 Programme of *European Commission (EC, #06633)*. **Activities** Joint Programme of Activities (JPA) covers research, integration and dissemination, subdivided into 22 work packages (22). **Events** *International conference / Conference* Granada (Spain) 2011, *Seminar on guiding supervised learning by biological prior* Paris (France) 2010, *Symposium on alternative splicing and genetic disease* Paris (France) 2010, *Conference* Krakow (Poland) 2008. **Publications** *EURASNET Newsletter*. Pamphlet; brochure.
Members Research groups in 13 countries:
Argentina, Austria, Denmark, France, Germany, Israel, Italy, Poland, Portugal, Spain, Sweden, Switzerland, UK. [2013.06.01/XJ2289/E]

♦ European Aluminium 05893
Association européenne de l'aluminium
Dir Gen Av de Tervueren 168, 1150 Brussels, Belgium. T. +3227756363. E-mail: admin@european-aluminium.eu.
URL: http://www.european-aluminium.eu/
History 26 Mar 1981, Düsseldorf (Germany). Subsumed *Organisation of European Aluminium Refiners and Remelters (OEA, inactive)*. Former names and other names: *European Aluminium Assocation (EAA)* – former. Registration: Banque-Carrefour des Entreprises, No/ID: 0480.720.716, Start date: 1 Jan 1997, Belgium; EU Transparency Register, No/ID: 9224280267-20, Start date: 1 Aug 2008. **Aims** Promote the outstanding properties of aluminium; secure growth and optimize the contribution metal can make to meeting Europe's sustainability challenges. **Structure** General Assembly (twice a year); Executive Committee; Divisions (5), each having Executive Committee or Council; Industry Committees and Divisional Committees; Market Groups. **Languages** English. **Staff** 20.00 FTE, paid. **Finance** Sources: members' dues. **Activities** Events/meetings; knowledge management/information dissemination; research/documentation; training/education. **Events** *European Conference* Brussels (Belgium) 2015, *Safety Workshop* Brussels (Belgium) 2015, *Aluminium Recycling Congress* Vienna (Austria) 2015, *General Assembly* Brussels (Belgium) 2014, *Packaging Seminar* Helsinki (Finland) 2014. **Publications** *Digital Activity Report 2021-2022* (annual) in English. *Mid-Term Review of our Sustainability Roadmap* (2022) in English; *Circular Aluminium Action Plan* in English – a strategy for achieving aluminium's full potential for circularity by 2030; *Vision 2050* in English – European Aluminium's contribution to the EU's mid-century low carbon roadmap. Annual Activity Report; position papers; brochures; leaflets; lectures; press kit; videos.
Members Primary aluminium producers; downstream manufacturers of extruded, rolled and cast aluminium; producers of recycled aluminium and national aluminium associations representing over 600 plants in 21 countries:
Austria, Belgium, Bosnia-Herzegovina, Denmark, Finland, France, Germany, Greece, Hungary, Iceland, Ireland, Italy, Netherlands, Norway, Romania, Slovenia, Spain, Sweden, Switzerland, Türkiye, UK.
European association members (2):
European Aluminium Foil Association (EAFA, #05894); European association for Surface Treatment on Aluminium (ESTAL, #06242).
IGO Relations Also links with European institutions, agencies and bodies. **NGO Relations** Member of (7): *AEGIS Europe; Aluminium Stewardship Initiative (ASI, #00758); Association européenne des métaux (EUROMETAUX, #02578); European Affairs Platform (EAP, no recent information); European Policy Centre (EPC, #08240); Industry4Europe (#11181); METALS FOR BUILDINGS (#16737).* Partner of (1): *Metal Packaging Europe (MPE, #16736).* In liaison with technical committees of: *Comité européen de normalisation (CEN, #04162); Fédération européenne du verre d'emballage (FEVE, #09583); International Organization for Standardization (ISO, #14473).* Associate Expert Group of *Business and Industry Advisory Committee to the OECD (BIAC, #03385).* [2022.05.12/XD5149/ty/D]

♦ European Aluminium Assocation / see European Aluminium (#05893)

♦ European Aluminium Foil Association (EAFA) 05894
Exec Dir Am Mörsenbroicher Weg 200, 40470 Düsseldorf, Germany. T. +4921138732602. E-mail: enquiries@alufoil.org.
URL: http://www.alufoil.org/
History 1972, as successor of *Aluminium Foil Conference (AFCO, inactive)*. Current statutes approved 15 Oct 2004; amended 17 Jun 2016. EU Transparency Register: 138712718435-55. **Aims** Represent foil rollers, container and household foil manufacturers as well as flexible packaging producers. **Structure** General Assembly; Board; Executive Director. Groups (6): Container; *Flexible Packaging Europe (FPE, #09794)*; Rewinder; Roller (Foil Rollers); Closures; FPE German. **Languages** English. **Activities** Research/documentation; advocacy/lobbying/activism; events/meetings; awards/prizes/competitions. **Events** *Congress* Florence (Italy) 2004, *Congress* Istanbul (Turkey) 2003, *Congress* Madrid (Spain) 2002, *Congress* Düsseldorf (Germany) 2001, *Congress* Istanbul (Turkey) 2001. **Publications** *Infoil* in English, French, German, Italian, Spanish, Turkish – newsletter. *Alufoil File* – leaflet series.
Members Aluminium foil rollers, aluminium container manufacturers and converters. National groups and individual companies (104 companies) in 21 countries:
Austria, Belgium, Bulgaria, Croatia, Czechia, Denmark, Finland, France, Germany, Greece, Hungary, Italy, Luxembourg, Netherlands, Norway, Russia, Spain, Sweden, Switzerland, Türkiye, UK. [2019/XE0104/E]

♦ European Aluminium Holloware Manufacturer's Association (inactive)

♦ European Alzheimer's Disease Consortium (EADC) 05895
Chair Dept of Geriatric Psychiatry, Zentralinst für Seelische Gesundheit, Univ of Heidelberg, Postfach 12 21 20, 68072 Mannheim, Germany. T. +496211703672. Fax +496211703673.
URL: http://www.eadc.info/
History Jun 2001, Avignon (France). **Aims** Increase scientific understanding of Alzheimer's disease; prevent, slow or ameliorate the primary and secondary symptoms of Alzheimer's disease. **Structure** Steering Committee. Special Interest Groups. **Finance** Supported by: *European Commission (EC, #06633).* **Activities** Research/documentation; events/meetings. **Publications** *EADC Newsletter* (2 a year). Books.
Members Centres of excellence (50) in 15 countries:
Belgium, Denmark, Finland, France, Germany, Greece, Italy, Luxembourg, Netherlands, Poland, Romania, Spain, Sweden, Switzerland, UK.
NGO Relations Close cooperation with: *Alzheimer Europe (AE, #00761)*; national organizations. [2019/XF6935/F]

♦ European Amateur Baseball Confederation / see Confederation of European Baseball (#04518)
♦ European Amateur Boxing Association / see European Boxing Confederation (#06387)

♦ European Amateur Gentlemen Drivers Federation 05896
Fédération européenne des gentlemen amateurs et cavalières du trot (FEGAT) – Europäischer Verband der Amateurfahrer und Fahrerinnen des Trabersports
Vice-Pres/Gen Sec Pilar 4, 07500 Manacor, Spain. T. +34617581329. E-mail: agustimascaro@gmail.com.
URL: http://www.fegat.info/
History 1954. **Structure** Officers: President; Vice-President/General-Secretary; 2 Vice-Presidents. **Languages** Danish, English, Faroese, French, German, Icelandic, Italian, Norwegian, Swedish. **Activities** Organizes championships: European Championship for Gentlemen; European Championship for Ladies; FEGAT Cup; X Friendship Races.
Members in 16 countries:
Austria, Belgium, Czechia, Denmark, Finland, France, Germany, Hungary, Italy, Netherlands, Norway, Russia, Spain, Sweden, Switzerland, Ukraine. [2014/XD9146/D]

♦ European-American Centre for Policy Analysis / see RAND Europe

♦ European-American Consortium for Legal Education (EACLE) 05897
Contact c/o Centre for International and Comparative Law, Univ of Baltimore School of Law, 1420 N Charles St, Baltimore MD 21201-5779, USA.
URL: http://www.eacle.org/
History 2000. **Aims** Exchange students, faculty, scholarship and experience between European and American law faculties so that law students, lawyers and legal academics will have a broader understanding of the interrelated legal world. **Events** *Annual Conference* Baltimore, MD (USA) 2013, *Annual Conference* Ghent (Belgium) 2012, *Annual Conference* Long Island, NY (USA) 2011, *Annual Conference* Rotterdam (Netherlands) 2010, *Annual Conference* Santa Clara, CA (USA) 2009.
Members Law schools (10) in 6 countries:
Belgium, Finland, Italy, Netherlands, Poland, USA. [2012.07.13/XM3365/F]

♦ European Amputee Football Federation (EAFF) 05898
Contact 14 Lazienkowska Street, 00-449 Warsaw, Poland. T. +48533982629. E-mail: office@amputeefootball.eu.
URL: https://amputeefootball.eu/

History 2015. Registration: Charities Commission, No/ID: 1163840, England and Wales; Companies House, No/ID: CE004483, England and Wales. **Aims** Include and support people with amputations or limb defects; increase their access to amputee football opportunities; use football to improve their quality of life. **Structure** Board. **Activities** Awards/prizes/competitions; events/meetings; sporting activities. **Events** *Congress* 2020, *Congress* Poland 2019, *Congress* Warsaw (Poland) 2018, *Congress* Dublin (Ireland) 2017, *Congress* Dublin (Ireland) 2015.
Members Full in 18 countries and territories:
Albania, Azerbaijan, Belgium, England, France, Georgia, Germany, Greece, Ireland, Israel, Italy, Netherlands, Poland, Russia, Scotland, Spain, Türkiye, Ukraine. [2021/AA1996/**D**]

♦ Europeana Network Association (ENA) 05899

Vereniging Europeana Network
Contact c/o Europeana Foundation, Prins Willem-Alexanderhof 5, 2595 BE The Hague, Netherlands. E-mail: network@europeana.eu.
URL: https://pro.europeana.eu/europeana-network-association
History Along with *Europeana Foundation (#05839)*, one of 3 pillars of Europeana Initiative. Current statutes updated Feb 2018. Registration: Handelsregister, No/ID: KVK 62755692, Netherlands; EU Transparency Register, No/ID: 077220432108-21, Start date: 19 Jul 2018. **Aims** Expand and improve access to Europe's digital cultural heritage. **Structure** General Assembly; Members Council; Management Board. Task Forces; Working Groups.
Members Individuals in 96 countries and territories:
Albania, Algeria, Argentina, Armenia, Australia, Austria, Azerbaijan, Bangladesh, Barbados, Belarus, Belgium, Bosnia-Herzegovina, Botswana, Brazil, Bulgaria, Canada, Chile, China, Colombia, Costa Rica, Côte d'Ivoire, Croatia, Cyprus, Czechia, Denmark, Ecuador, Egypt, Estonia, Finland, France, Georgia, Germany, Ghana, Greece, Hungary, Iceland, India, Indonesia, Iran Islamic Rep, Ireland, Israel, Italy, Jamaica, Japan, Jordan, Kenya, Korea Rep, Kosovo, Latvia, Lebanon, Lithuania, Luxembourg, Malta, Mexico, Moldova, Mongolia, Montenegro, Morocco, Nepal, Netherlands, New Zealand, Nigeria, North Macedonia, Norway, Pakistan, Palestine, Peru, Philippines, Poland, Portugal, Qatar, Romania, Russia, Saudi Arabia, Serbia, Singapore, Slovakia, Slovenia, South Africa, Spain, Sri Lanka, Sudan, Sweden, Switzerland, Taiwan, Thailand, Tunisia, Türkiye, UK, Ukraine, United Arab Emirates, Uruguay, USA, Venezuela, Vietnam, Zimbabwe. [2023/AA3104/v/**E**]

♦ European Anglers Alliance (EAA) 05900

Alliance européenne des pêcheurs à la ligne – Europäischer Anglerverband
SG Rue de la Loi 81A, 1000 Brussels, Belgium. T. +3227251115. E-mail: info@eaa-europe.eu.
Pres address not obtained.
URL: http://www.eaa-europe.eu/
History 1994, Brussels (Belgium). Statutes adopted, 22 Mar 1997; revised 2012. Registration: Germany; EU Transparency Register, No/ID: 60105502183-69. **Aims** Safeguard the *aquatic* environment, *fish* stocks and the recreational angling of Europe; protect interest of all those who fish with a rod and line for recreational purposes. **Structure** General Assembly (annual); Board; Subgroups (2); Task Forces (3). Integrated *Federation of Nordic Anglers' Associations (NSU, inactive)*. **Languages** English. **Staff** 1.00 FTE, paid. **Finance** Sources: members' dues. Annual budget: 150,000 EUR (2022). **Activities** Advocacy/lobbying/activism; events/meetings; politics/policy/regulatory. **Publications** Position papers; resolutions; leaflets.
Members Organizations in 12 countries:
Austria, Denmark, Finland, France, Germany, Italy, Netherlands, Norway, Slovenia, Sweden, Switzerland, UK.
Associate members in 5 countries:
Estonia, Latvia, Scotland, Spain, Wales.
IGO Relations Member of: *European Commission (EC, #06633)* – Marine Strategy Framework Directive Coordination Group DG ENV; *Standing Committee to the Bern Convention on the Conservation of European Wildlife and Natural Habitats (#19949)*; Water Framework Directive Strategic Coordination Group DG ENV; Working Group Invasive Alien Species DG ENV; Co-ordination Group for Biodiversity and Nature DG ENV. Provides secretariat to: *European Parliament (EP, #08146)* Forum on Recreational Fisheries and Aquatic Environment. **NGO Relations** Member of (5): Aquaculture Advisory Council (AAC); *Baltic Sea Advisory Council (BSAC, #03139)*; *Mediterranean Advisory Council (MEDAC, #16639)*; *North Sea Advisory Council (NSAC, #17603)*; *North Western Waters Advisory Council (NWWAC, #17607)*. [2022.05.04/XF3944/**F**]

♦ European Anglers Federation (EAF) 05901

Pres 9bis rue Nationale, 94500 Champigny-sur-Marne, France. T. +33608976116. E-mail: info@euroangler.eu.
Social Headquarters Korompai utca 17, Budapest 1124, Hungary.
URL: http://www.euroangler.eu/
History Founded 22 Jun 2005, Visegrad (Hungary), as *European Anglers Forum*. Statutes adopted Sep 2007. EU Transparency Register: 79676742514-50. **Aims** Provide a framework for cooperation between national anglers federations. **Structure** Board.
Members Full in 10 countries:
Belgium, Croatia, Czechia, France, Germany, Hungary, Italy, Poland, Slovakia, Switzerland. [2019/XM8693/**D**]

♦ European Anglers Forum / see European Anglers Federation (#05901)
♦ European Animal Fat Processors Association (inactive)
♦ European Animal Health Study Centre (#03745)

♦ European Animal Protein Association (EAPA) 05902

SG Boulevard Baudouin 18, 4th Floor, 1000 Brussels, Belgium. T. +3222035141. Fax +3222033244. E-mail: devries@skypro.be – info@eapa.biz.
Chairman address not obtained.
URL: http://eapa.biz/
History 1988. Registration: EU Transparency Register, No/ID: 065456717887-82, Start date: 18 Jun 2015. **Aims** Represent companies that specialize in the production and supply of high quality natural animal proteins. **Events** *How safe plasma can help to reduce the usage of antibiotics on European farms?* Cologne (Germany) 2015.
Members Companies: animal protein producers in 10 countries:
Belgium, Denmark, France, Germany, Italy, Netherlands, Poland, Spain, Sweden, UK.
IGO Relations Observer status with: *Codex Alimentarius Commission (CAC, #04081)*. [2019/XD8408/**D**]

♦ European Animal Research Association (EARA) 05903

Communications Manager 3.04 Labs Atrium, The Stables Market, Chalk Farm Road, London, NW1 8AH, UK. T. +442033553095. Fax +442034117808. E-mail: info@eara.eu.
Exec Dir Spaces European District, Rue Belliard 40, 1040 Brussels, Belgium.
URL: http://eara.eu/
History 2014. Registration: EU Transparency Register, No/ID: 331480324807-34. **Aims** Enhance understanding and awareness of research involving animals across Europe, allowing for a more constructive dialogue with all stakeholders and a more favourable climate for research in Europe. **Structure** Governing Board. **Languages** English. **Staff** 4.00 FTE, paid. **Finance** Sources: members' dues. Annual budget: 350,000 EUR. **Activities** Advocacy/lobbying/activism; knowledge management/information dissemination; research/documentation. **Publications** *EARA Communications Handbook*. **Information Services** *EARA Study of EU-based websites 2020*.
Members Research institutions in 31 countries:
Australia, Austria, Belgium, Brazil, Canada, Czechia, Denmark, Finland, France, Georgia, Germany, Greece, Hungary, Israel, Italy, Luxembourg, Malta, Mauritius, Netherlands, New Zealand, Poland, Portugal, Romania, Serbia, Slovenia, South Africa, Spain, Switzerland, Türkiye, UK, USA.
Included in the above, 11 organizations listed in this Yearbook:
AAALAC International; *AnimalhealthEurope (#00837)*; *Animal Research Tomorrow (#00840)*; *Association of Primate Veterinarians (APV)*; *Australian and New Zealand Council for the Care of Animals in Research and Teaching (ANZCCART)*; *European College of Laboratory Animal Medicine (ECLAM, #06611)*; *European Federation of Animal Technologists (EFAT)*; *European Primate Veterinarians (EPV, #08274)*; *European Society for Laboratory Animal Veterinarians (ESLAV, #08638)*; *Federation of European Neuroscience Societies (FENS, #09522)*; *International Council for Laboratory Animal Science (ICLAS, #13039)*.
IGO Relations Observer status with (2): *Convention on International Trade in Endangered Species of Wild Fauna and Flora (CITES, 1973)*; *European Union (EU, #08967)*. [2022.05.19/XM6312/y/**D**]

♦ European Anodisers' Association (inactive)

♦ European Anthropological Association (EAA) 05904

Association européenne d'anthropologie
Gen Sec Eötvös Lorand Univ, Fac of Science, Dept of Biological Anthropology, Pazmany Péter Sétany 1/c, Budapest 1117, Hungary. E-mail: makac@amu.edu.pl.
URL: http://eaa.elte.hu/
History 1975. **Aims** Promote research and teaching in anthropology. **Structure** General Assembly; Council; Board. **Languages** English. **Staff** Voluntary. **Finance** Sources: members' dues. **Activities** Events/meetings; knowledge management/information dissemination; training/education. **Events** *Biennial Congress* Odense (Denmark) 2018, *Biennial Congress* Zagreb (Croatia) 2016, *Biennial Congress* Moscow (Russia) 2014, *Biennial Congress* Ankara (Turkey) 2012, *Biennial Congress* Poznań (Poland) 2010. **Publications** *European Anthropological Association Newsletter*, *International Journal of Anthropology*. *EAA Biennial Books* – in 5 vols.
Members Individuals in 48 countries:
Argentina, Armenia, Australia, Austria, Belarus, Belgium, Bosnia-Herzegovina, Bulgaria, Canada, Chile, China, Colombia, Croatia, Czechia, Denmark, Egypt, France, Georgia, Germany, Greece, Hungary, India, Israel, Italy, Japan, Latvia, Lithuania, Mexico, Moldova, Netherlands, North Macedonia, Norway, Peru, Poland, Portugal, Russia, Slovakia, Slovenia, South Africa, Spain, Sweden, Switzerland, Türkiye, UK, Ukraine, USA, Venezuela, Zambia.
IGO Relations Programmes of: *UNESCO (#20322)*; *WHO (#20950)*; *European Commission (EC, #06633)*. **NGO Relations** Member of: *International Association of Human Biologists (IAHB, #11945)*. [2022.05.10/XD2478/v/**D**]

♦ European Anthroposophic Manufacturers Association (#02568)
♦ European Anti-Ageing Association (inactive)
♦ European Anti-Arms Trade Network / see European Network Against the Arms Trade (#07861)

♦ European Antibullying Network (EAN) 05905

Registered Office Wittebroodhof 12, 9052 Ghent, Belgium. E-mail: info@antibullying.eu – eansecretariat@antibullying.eu.
URL: http://www.antibullying.eu/
History Jan 2013, Athens (Greece). Founded to meet the need for a collective, organized and coordinated response to bullying on a European level, in the framework of the homonym EU-funded project (Daphne III). Officially launched June 2014, during the project's final conference in Athens (Greece). Registration: Banque-Carrefour des Entreprises, No/ID: 0628.590.286, Start date: 8 Mar 2015, Belgium. **Aims** Bring together organizations and stakeholders working in and across Europe to combat the phenomenon of bullying, cyber-bullying and school violence, both in prevention as well as intervention; as an umbrella organization, coordinate anti-bullying actions and initiatives on the European level; campaign and advocate for a common European strategy; produce and promote exchange of good practices, enforce capacity building and provide tools and trainings to professionals in the field; raise awareness among the general public and empower children and young people as well as parents and teachers on how to tackle bulling. **Structure** General Assembly; Board of Directors; Secretariat. **Languages** English. **Staff** None paid. **Finance** Sources: members' dues; revenue from activities/projects. Supported by: *European Union (EU, #08967)*. Annual budget: 30,000 EUR (2021). **Activities** Advocacy/lobbying/activism; awareness raising; capacity building; events/meetings; research/documentation. Active in all member countries. **Events** *International Conference* Brussels (Belgium) 2019, *International Conference* Athens (Greece) 2018, *International Conference* Citta di Castello (Italy) 2017, *International Conference* St Julian's (Malta) 2016, *International Conference* Brussels (Belgium) 2015. **Publications** *EAN Strategy Position Paper* (2014); *European Guide of Antibullying Good Practices* (2014).
Members Founding; Full; Honorary; Associate; Affiliate. Organizations (23) in 15 countries.
Bosnia-Herzegovina, Bulgaria, Croatia, Cyprus, Finland, Greece, Hungary, Ireland, Italy, Lithuania, Malta, North Macedonia, Romania, Spain, UK (Cyprus). [2022.12.01/XM5198/**F**]

♦ European Anti-Fraud Office 05906

Office européen de lutte antifraude (OLAF) – Oficina Europea de Lucha Contra el Fraude – Europäisches Amt für Betrugsbekämpfung – Organismo Europeu de Luta Antifraude – Ufficio Europeo per la Lotta Antifrode – Europees Bureau voor Fraudebestrijding – Europeiska Byrån för Bedrägerbekämpning – Europaeiske Kontor for Bekaempelse af Svig – Euroopan Petostentorjuntavirasto
Dir-Gen European Commission, 1049 Brussels, Belgium. T. +3222954859. Fax +3222960853.
URL: https://ec.europa.eu/anti-fraud/
History 28 Apr 1999, by *European Commission (EC, #06633)* Decision 1999/352. Commenced activities 1 Jun 1999. Successor to *European Commission Anti-Fraud Unit (UCLAF, inactive)*. Amendments: Commission Decisions: 2013/478/EU, 27 Sep 2013; (EU) 2015/512, 25 Mar 2015; (EU) 2015/2418, 18 Dec 2015. Reorganized 1 Feb 2012. Regulation No 883/2013, 11 Sep 2013. **Aims** Detect, investigate and stop fraud with EU funds. **Structure** Director-General; Directorates (4). **Languages** English, French. **Staff** 445.00 FTE, paid. **Finance** EC Budget. **Activities** Monitoring/evaluation; knowledge management/information dissemination. **Events** *Conference on Fighting Illicit Tobacco* Brussels (Belgium) 2018, *Conference on the Anti-Fraud Information System and OLAF's Support to Customs Agencies* Vienna (Austria) 2018, *Conference on the Evaluation of Regulation 883/2013* Brussels (Belgium) 2017, *Conference on a new and holistic approach to fighting corruption* Laxenburg (Austria) 2010, *Meeting* Brussels (Belgium) 2004. **Publications** Reports.
Members EU Member States (27):
Austria, Belgium, Bulgaria, Croatia, Cyprus, Czechia, Denmark, Estonia, Finland, France, Germany, Greece, Hungary, Ireland, Italy, Latvia, Lithuania, Luxembourg, Malta, Netherlands, Poland, Portugal, Romania, Slovakia, Slovenia, Spain, Sweden.
IGO Relations Partners: *European Police Office (Europol, #08239)*; *International Criminal Police Organization – INTERPOL (ICPO-INTERPOL, #13110)*; *World Customs Organization (WCO, #21350)*. Member of: *European Anti-Fraud Office (#05906)*. Instrumental in setting up: *International Anti-Corruption Academy (IACA, #11654)*; *OLAF Anti-Fraud Communicators Network (OAFCN, #17714)*. Contacts with: *Group of States Against Corruption (#10789)*. [2019.07.16/XF5674/**F***]

♦ The European Anti-Maastricht Alliance / see European Alliance of EU-critical Movements (#05870)

♦ European Antimicrobial Resistance Surveillance Network (EARS-Net) 05907

Senior Expert ECDC, Tomtebodavägen 11A, Solna, SE-171 83 Stockholm, Sweden. T. +46858601172. Fax +46858601001. E-mail: ears-net@ecdc.europa.eu.
URL: http://www.ecdc.europa.eu/en/activities/surveillance/EARS-Net/Pages/index.aspx
History 1 Apr 1998, as *European Antimicrobial Resistance Surveillance System (EARSS)*, initially funded by *European Commission (EC, #06633)* Directorate General for Health and Consumer Affairs (DG SANCO) and Dutch Ministry of Health, Welfare and Sports (RIVM). Current name adopted Jan 2010, when activities were transferred to *European Centre for Disease Prevention and Control (ECDC, #06476)*. **Aims** Maintain a comprehensive surveillance and information system on antimicrobial resistance based on a network of national surveillance systems providing European reference data on antimicrobial resistance for public *health* purposes. **Structure** Managed and coordinated by *European Centre for Disease Prevention and Control (ECDC, #06476)*. Supported by a Coordination Group composed of individual experts selected among the nominated disease specific contact points. National coordinators are nominated by the participating countries. **Languages** English. **Finance** Funded by *European Centre for Disease Prevention and Control (ECDC, #06476)*. **Activities** Knowledge management/information dissemination. **Events** *Plenary Meeting* Stockholm (Sweden) 2010, *Plenary Meeting* Strasbourg (France) 2009, *Plenary Meeting* Athens (Greece) 2008, *Plenary Meeting* Stockholm (Sweden) 2007, *Plenary Meeting* Rome (Italy) 2005. **Publications** *EARS-Net Reporting Protocol* (2010). **Information Services** *EARS-Net* – interactive database. **Members** Participants in 26 EU countries, Norway and Iceland. **IGO Relations** Collaborates with: European Surveillance of Antimicrobial Consumption (ESAC); *WHO (#20950)*. **NGO Relations** *European Committee on Antimicrobial Susceptibility Testing (EUCAST, #06642)*. [2013/XF4869/**F**]

♦ European Antimicrobial Resistance Surveillance System / see European Antimicrobial Resistance Surveillance Network (#05907)

♦ European Anti-Poverty Network (EAPN) 05908

Dir Boulevard Bischoffsheim 11, 1000 Brussels, Belgium. T. +3222265850. Fax +3222265869. E-mail: team@eapn.eu.
Events Manager address not obtained.
Office Manager address not obtained.

URL: http://www.eapn.eu/
History Dec 1990, Brussels (Belgium). Former names and other names: *Réseau européen des associations de lutte contre la pauvreté et l'exclusion sociale* – former. Registration: Banque-Carrefour des Entreprises, No/ID: 0446.777.149, Start date: 26 Feb 1992, Belgium; EU Transparency Register, No/ID: 3945154610-54, Start date: 4 Nov 2008. **Aims** Work for a social Europe free of poverty and social exclusion with access to economic, social and cultural rights for all. **Structure** General Assembly (annual); Executive Committee; Bureau. **Languages** English, French, German, Spanish. **Staff** 6.00 FTE, paid. **Finance** Main source: *European Commission (EC, #06633)* – 80% of budget. Other sources: contributions in kind; funding from foundations. **Activities** Monitoring/evaluation; advocacy/lobbying/activism; events/meetings; knowledge management/ information dissemination; awareness raising. **Events** *Annual Policy Conference* Brussels (Belgium) 2022, *European Meeting of People Experiencing Poverty (PeP)* Brussels (Belgium) 2022, *Annual Policy Conference* Brussels (Belgium) 2021, *Meeting of People Experiencing Poverty* Brussels (Belgium) 2021, *Meeting of People Experiencing Poverty* Brussels (Belgium) 2019. **Publications** *Flash* (6 a year) – newsletter. Position papers; reports; books; letters; videos; press releases.
Members National networks in 32 countries:
Austria, Belgium, Bulgaria, Croatia, Cyprus, Czechia, Denmark, Estonia, Finland, France, Germany, Greece, Hungary, Iceland, Ireland, Italy, Latvia, Lithuania, Luxembourg, Malta, Netherlands, North Macedonia, Norway, Poland, Portugal, Romania, Serbia, Slovakia, Slovenia, Spain, Sweden, UK.
European and international organizations (13):
AGE Platform Europe (#00557); Emmaüs Europe (#05444); Eurochild (#05657); European Consumer Debt Network (ECDN, #06772); European Federation for Diaconia (Eurodiaconia, #07099); European Federation of National Organisations Working with the Homeless (#07174); European Food Banks Federation (FEBA, #07280); European Network against Racism (ENAR, #07862); International Federation of Social Workers (IFSW, #13544); International Movement ATD Fourth World (#14193); Platform for International Cooperation on Undocumented Migrants (PICUM, #18401); Salvation Army (#19041); Santé mentale et exclusion sociale – Europa (SMES Europa, #19053).
Consultative Status Consultative status granted from: *Council of Europe (CE, #04881)* (Participatory Status).
NGO Relations Member of (3): *EU Alliance for a democratic, social and sustainable European Semester (EU Semester Alliance, #05565); SDG Watch Europe (#19162); Social Platform (#19344).* Supports (1): *European Alliance for the Statute of the European Association (EASEA, #05886).* [2021/XF2456/y/**F**]

♦ European Apparel and Textile Organization / see EURATEX – The European Apparel and Textile Confederation (#05616)

♦ European Aquaculture Society (EAS) 05909

Société européenne d'aquaculture
Exec Dir Slijkensesteenweg 4, 8400 Ostend, Belgium. T. +3259323859.
URL: http://www.aquaeas.eu/
History Founded 30 Apr 1976, Bredene (Belgium), as an affiliated society of the then *'World Mariculture Society (WMS)'*, currently *World Aquaculture Society (WAS, #21099).* Originally referred to as *European Mariculture Society.* Registered in accordance with Belgian law. **Aims** Promote contacts at European level among all involved in marine and freshwater aquaculture; facilitate circulation of information; promote sponsorship of multidisciplinary research; enhance cooperation among governmental, scientific and commercial organizations and individuals on all matters dealing with aquaculture. **Structure** General Assembly (annual); Board of Directors. **Languages** English. **Staff** 2.00 FTE, paid. **Finance** Members' dues. **Activities** Events/ meetings. **Events** *Aquaculture Europe Conference* Rimini (Italy) 2022, *Aquaculture Europe Conference* 2021, *Aquaculture Europe Conference* Funchal (Portugal) 2021, *Aquaculture Europe Conference* Cork (Ireland) 2020, *Aquaculture Europe Conference* Berlin (Germany) 2019. **Publications** *Aquaculture Europe* (6 a year) – PDF newsletter; *Aquaculture Europe Magazine* (2 a year). *EMS/WAS Special Publications* – series. *Aquaculture International* – online; *European Aquaculture Trade Directory; International Aquaculture Trade Directory.* Proceedings of conferences, symposia and seminars.
Members Sponsors; Institutions; Individuals; Students ('young persons' under 30). Members in 40 countries and territories:
Austria, Belgium, Brazil, Canada, Chile, Croatia, Czechia, Denmark, Finland, France, Germany, Greece, Hungary, Iceland, Iran Islamic Rep, Ireland, Israel, Italy, Japan, Latvia, Libya, Malta, Martinique, Mexico, Netherlands, Norway, Poland, Portugal, Romania, Serbia, Slovenia, South Africa, Spain, Sweden, Switzerland, Thailand, Türkiye, Uganda, UK, USA.
IGO Relations Observer status with: *International Council for the Exploration of the Sea (ICES, #13021).* **NGO Relations** Member of: *European Aquaculture Technology and Innovation Platform (EATiP, #05910); European Forum of Farm Animal Breeders (EFFAB, #07310).* Supports: *Asian Fisheries Society (AFS, #01483).* [2021/XD0076/**D**]

♦ European Aquaculture Technology and Innovation Platform (EATiP) 05910

Gen Sec Square de la Paix 28, 4031 Liège, Belgium. T. +3243382995. E-mail: secretariat@eatip.eu.
Exec Sec address not obtained.
URL: http://www.eatip.eu/
History Registration: No/ID: 0808.986.136, Start date: 9 Jan 2009, Belgium; EU Transparency Register, No/ID: 118286121781-91, Start date: 13 May 2016. **Aims** Establish a strong relationship between aquaculture and the consumer; assure a sustainable aquaculture industry; consolidate the role of aquaculture in society. **Structure** General Assembly; Board of Directors; Operating Council; Thematic Areas (8); Secretariat, headed by Secretary General. **Activities** Research and development; knowledge management/information dissemination. **Events** *General Meeting* Liège (Belgium) 2020, *General Meeting* Brussels (Belgium) 2019, *General Meeting* Brussels (Belgium) 2018, *General Meeting* Brussels (Belgium) 2017, *General Meeting* Brussels (Belgium) 2016.
Members Commercial companies; Research institutes; organizations. Commercial companies in 8 countries:
Belgium, Denmark, France, Greece, Netherlands, Norway, Spain, UK.
Research institutes in 12 countries:
Belgium, Denmark, France, Greece, Hungary, Ireland, Italy, Netherlands, Norway, Portugal, Spain, UK.
Organizations include the following 6 listed in this Yearbook:
COPA – european farmers (COPA, #04829); European Aquaculture Society (EAS, #05909); European Bureau for Conservation and Development (EBCD, #06412); European Mollusc Producers' Association (EMPA, #07818); Fédération européenne des fabricants d'aliments composés pour animaux (FEFAC, #09566); Federation of European Aquaculture Producers (FEAP, #09491).
Observers (2):
European Commission (EC, #06633); European Investment Bank (EIB, #07599). [2020/XJ4691/y/**F**]

♦ European Aquarium and Terrarium Association (unconfirmed)
♦ European Arbitration Convention (treaty)
♦ European Arbitration Court / see European Court of Arbitration (#06853)

♦ European Arboricultural Council (EAC) 05911

Conseil européen de l'arboriculture – Europäischer Baumpflegerat
Sec Haus der Landschaft, Alexander-von-Humboldt-Str 4, 53604 Bad Honnef, Germany. T. +492224770747. Fax +492224770777. E-mail: secretary@eac-arboriculture.com – office@eac-arboriculture.com.
URL: http://www.eac-arboriculture.com/
History 1993. Registration: Germany. **Aims** Improve the health and care for *trees* of environmental importance; advance the profession of arboriculture. **Structure** General Meeting (annual). Executive Committee, consisting of Chairman, 1st Vice Chairman, 2nd Vice-Chairmen, Immediate Past Chairman. Committees (4): Education and Certification; Publication and Work Practice; Public Relations and Marketing; European Arboriculture Online. Working Groups (7): Exam Rules Board; Accreditation Board; Question Bank Board; Planting Guide; Safety Guide; Guide for ETW; ECOT – European City of the Trees. Liaison Officer with Europe (Brussels, Belgium). Secretary; Treasurer. **Languages** English. **Staff** 0.50 FTE, paid. **Finance** Members' dues. **Activities** Serves as a forum for delegates from various arboricultural organizations throughout Europe with the object of elevating the status and advancing the profession by liaising on matters ranging from research and education to successful tree establishment and improvement of working practice. Main areas of concern: research on urban trees; education and training; safety practices with pruning tools and chain saws; tree management; disease and pest control; tree planting in urban conditions; harmonization in tree care procedures in Europe. **Events** *Annual General Meeting* Vilnius (Lithuania) 2020. **Publications** *EAC Newsletter* in English. *A Guide to Safe Work Practice; European Tree and Palm Planting Guide; European Tree Pruning Guide; European Treeworker Handbook* – in 9 languages.
Members Representatives organizations in 22 countries:
Austria, Belgium, Croatia, Czechia, Denmark, Estonia, Finland, France, Germany, Italy, Latvia, Netherlands, Norway, Poland, Romania, Russia, Slovakia, Spain, Sweden, Switzerland, UK, Ukraine.
Included in the above, 2 organizations listed in this Yearbook:
International Society of Arboriculture (ISA, #14936); UNEP (#20299). [2021/XD6069/y/**D**]

♦ European Archaeological Council (#05746)

♦ European Architectural Endoscopy Association (EAEA) 05912

Contact Vienna Univ of Technology, Karlsplatz 13, 1040 Vienna, Austria. T. +4315880125050. Fax +4315880141799.
URL: http://info.tuwien.ac.at/eaea/
History 1992. **Aims** Argue for the significance of endoscopy in exploring and representing architecture and space; function as a platform for experimentation, research, communications development, user participation and teaching by means of endoscopy and environmental simulation. **Structure** Each member acts as Secretariat for a 2-year term (the year before and following a conference). **Languages** English. **Finance** Running expenses are the responsibility of the member acting as a secretariat. **Activities** include: (1) Visualization and application in architecture and town planning: built environments; road-design; housing areas; urban spaces; interior spaces; etc; (2) Implementation of endoscopy in design work; (3) Research on environmental simulation and experience of environment in motion; (4) Observation of technical developments. Organizes conference (every 2 years). **Events** *Biennial Conference* Lódz (Poland) 2015, *Biennial Conference* Milan (Italy) 2013, *Biennial Conference* Delft (Netherlands) 2011, *Biennial Conference* Cottbus (Germany) 2009, *Biennial conference* Moscow (Russia) 2007. **Publications** *EAEA Newsletter.*
Members Full endoscopy laboratories operating in Europe; Associate endoscopy laboratories operating in non-European countries and individuals in all countries. Members in 13 countries:
Australia, Austria, Czechia, Denmark, Finland, Germany, Japan, Netherlands, Russia, Slovakia, Sweden, Switzerland, USA. [2013/XD3834/**D**]

♦ European Architectural History Network (EAHN) 05913

Contact EAHN Office, Middle East Technical Univ, Fac of Architecture, Dumlupinar Bulvari No 1, 06800 Ankara/Ankara, Türkiye. E-mail: office@eahn.org – news@eahn.org.
URL: http://www.eahn.org/
History 2005. **Aims** Support research and education by providing a public forum for the dissemination of knowledge about the histories of architecture. **Structure** Business Meeting (annual); Council. **Languages** English. **Finance** Members' dues. Private sources. **Activities** Events/meetings; training/education; knowledge management/information dissemination. **Events** *International Conference* Madrid (Spain) 2022, *International Conference* Edinburgh (UK) 2021, *International Conference* Edinburgh (UK) 2020, *Thematic Conference* Sydney, NSW (Australia) 2019, *Symposium* Helsinki (Finland) 2018. **Publications** *Architectural Histories* – journal. **Members** Individuals (1,146) in 50 countries. Membership countries not specified. [2019/XJ0993/**D**]

♦ European Architectural Students Assembly (meeting series)
♦ European Area Committee of YMCAs / see YMCA Europe (#21977)

♦ European Arenas Association (EAA) 05914

Contact Ahoy-weg 10, 3084 BA Rotterdam, Netherlands. E-mail: management@europeanarenas.com.
URL: http://www.europeanarenas.com/
History Jun 1990. Registration: EU Transparency Register, No/ID: 088905531785-87, Start date: 14 Jun 2018. **Aims** Create a common interest forum for members of leading venues throughout Europe. **Structure** Executive Committee. **Languages** English. **Staff** 1.00 FTE, paid. **Finance** Members' dues; business partners. **Activities** Knowledge management/information dissemination; training/education; events/meetings. **Events** *General Meeting* Paris (France) 2017, *Congress* Rotterdam (Netherlands) 2011, *Stadia and Arena Convention* Barcelona (Spain) 2000.
Members Arenas (35) in 21 countries:
Austria, Belgium, Czechia, Estonia, Finland, France, Germany, Hungary, Italy, Latvia, Lithuania, Luxembourg, Netherlands, Norway, Poland, Portugal, Serbia, Spain, Sweden, Switzerland, UK. [2021/XD6195/**D**]

♦ European Armenian Federation for Justice and Democracy (internationally oriented national body)
♦ European Armsport Federation / see European Armwrestling Federation (#05915)

♦ European Armwrestling Federation (EAF) 05915

Head Office Sofia Park Trading Zone, Building 16V, fl 1 – Office 1-2, 1766 Sofia, Bulgaria. E-mail: office@waf-armwrestling.com – eaf@europe.com.
URL: http://www.eaf-armwrestling.com/
History Also referred to in English as *European Armsport Federation.* **Structure** Congress (annual). Executive Board, comprising President, 3 Vice-Presidents and General Secretary. Standing Committees (7). Secretariat. **Languages** English. **Finance** Members' dues. **Activities** Organizes championships and tournaments.
Members National associations in 29 countries:
Armenia, Austria, Azerbaijan, Belarus, Belgium, Bulgaria, Czechia, Denmark, Finland, France, Georgia, Germany, Greece, Hungary, Israel, Italy, Latvia, Lithuania, Netherlands, Norway, Romania, Russia, Slovakia, Spain, Sweden, Switzerland, Türkiye, UK, Ukraine.
NGO Relations *World Armwrestling Federation (WAF, #21110).* [2019/XD7482/**D**]

♦ European Arrest Warrant (2001 treaty)
♦ European Article Numbering Association / see GS1 (#10809)
♦ European Artificial Intelligence Fund / see European Artificial Intelligence Society Fund (#05916)

♦ European Artificial Intelligence Society Fund (European AI & Society Fund) 05916

Dir c/o NEF – Philanthropy House, Rue Royale 94, 1000 Brussels, Belgium. T. +3222352413. E-mail: info@europeanaifund.org – info@nef-europe.org.
URL: https://europeanaifund.org/
History Former names and other names: *European Artificial Intelligence Fund (European AI Fund)* – former (2020 to 2023). **Aims** Shape the direction of AI in Europe. **Structure** Hosted by *Network of European Foundations (NEF, #17019).* Steering Committee. **Finance** Supported by: *Charles Stewart Mott Foundation;* Fondation Nicolas Puech; *Ford Foundation (#09858); King Baudouin Foundation (KBF);* Luminate; *Mozilla Foundation; Oak Foundation; Open Society Foundations (OSF, #17763); Robert Bosch Foundation; Stiftung Mercator.* **Activities** Financial and/or material support. **NGO Relations** Supports (1): *AlgorithmWatch.* [2023/AA2311/f/**F**]

♦ European Artists' Association (EuACA) 05917

Secretariat c/o CEPE, Avenue E Van Nieuwenhuyse 6, 1160 Brussels, Belgium. T. +3226767480. Fax +3226767490. E-mail: secretariat@cepe.org.
URL: http://www.artists-colours.org/
History Set up as a sector group of *Conseil européen de l'industrie des peintures, des encres d'imprimerie et des couleurs d'art (CEPE, #04688).* **Aims** Represent members' non-commercial collective interests that their continuity and success are ensure; advocate on behalf of members to ensure continuity; promote the image of the sector impartially. **Activities** Standards/guidelines; events/meetings; guidance/assistance/consulting.
Members Full in 9 countries:
Belgium, Denmark, France, Germany, Italy, Netherlands, Spain, Switzerland, UK. [2017/XM5700/**E**]

♦ European Arts and Entertainment Alliance (EAEA) 05918

Contact address not obtained. T. +3222345652. Fax +3222350861. E-mail: johannes.studinger@uniglobalunion.org.
URL: http://www.iaea-globalunion.org/
History Previously referred to as *European Entertainment Alliance (EEA).*
Members International organizations (2):
International Federation of Actors (#13337); International Federation of Musicians (#13486).
NGO Relations Regional organization of: *International Arts and Entertainment Alliance (IAEA, #11676).* Recognized by: *European Trade Union Confederation (ETUC, #08927).* [2014/XF5730/**F**]

♦ European Asbestos Removal Association (EARA) 05919

Address not obtained.
URL: http://www.eara.nl/

History 1 Jul 1980. **Aims** Provide technical guidance on all technical requirements of legislation concerning asbestos. **Structure** Governing Council of 14 members. Officers: Chairman; Deputy Chairman; 4 Committee Chairmen; Treasurer; Site Audit Chairman; ATaC Chairman. Committees (4): Technical; Training; Vetting; PR. Asbestos Testing and Consulting Division (ATaC). **Languages** English. **Activities** Runs management courses; provides training. **Publications** *ARCA News*. Guide; members' directory.
Members Full; Associate; Analytical. Members in 8 countries:
Belgium, Denmark, Germany, Gibraltar, Ireland, Luxembourg, Netherlands, UK. [2012/XD6361/D]

♦ European Asphalt Pavement Association (EAPA) 05920

Association européenne des producteurs d'enrobés bitumineux
SG Rue du Commerce 77, 1040 Brussels, Belgium. T. +3225025888. Fax +3225022358. E-mail: info@eapa.org.
URL: http://eapa.org/

History 1973. Articles revised and approved at Council Meeting: 6 Jun 1990, Solna (Sweden); 19 Jun 2006, Brussels (Belgium); 5 Nov 2013, Brussels (Belgium). Former names and other names: *Association Européenne des Producteurs d'Enrobés Bitumineux* – alias. Registration: Banque Carrefour des Entreprises, No/ID: 0885.290.789, Start date: 24 Sep 2006, Belgium; Eu Transparency Register, No/ID: 094579310230-47, Start date: 4 Dec 2012. **Aims** Promote use of asphalt in the creation and maintenance of a sustainable European *road network*. **Structure** Council; Executive Committee. **Languages** English. **Staff** 2.00 FTE, paid. **Finance** Sources: members' dues. **Activities** Knowledge management/information dissemination; events/meetings. **Events** *Joint Congress* Vienna (Austria) 2022, *Joint Congress* Brussels (Belgium) 2021, *Joint Congress* Madrid (Spain) 2020, *Symposium* Paris (France) 2019, *Joint Meeting* Berlin (Germany) 2018. **Publications** Congress and symposia proceedings; statements.
Members Associations in 15 countries:
Croatia, Czechia, Denmark, Estonia, Finland, France, Germany, Hungary, Ireland, Norway, Slovenia, Spain, Sweden, Türkiye, UK.
NGO Relations Member of (8): *Construction 2050 Alliance (#04760)*; *Construction Products Europe AISBL (#04761)*; *European Construction Forum (ECF, #06765)*; *European Council for Construction Research, Development and Innovation (ECCREDI, #06813)*; *European Road Transport Research Advisory Council (ERTRAC, #08396)*; *European Union Road Federation (ERF, #09014)*; Global Asphalt Pavement Alliance; *Industry4Europe (#11181)*. In liaison with technical committees of: *Comité européen de normalisation (CEN, #04162)*. [2020/XD8990/D]

♦ European Asphalt Technology Association (EATA) 05921

Contact c/o ENTPE, 3 rue Maurice Audin, 69518 Vaulx-en-Velin CEDEX, France.
URL: http://www.eata2015.org/

History Founded 2003. **Aims** Provide a forum for high quality peer reviewed papers on all aspects of asphalt technology; publish high quality fundamental and applied research in the field; bring together theory and practice; give a better understanding of existing practice; describe and make comparisons with new developments. **Activities** Events/meetings. **Events** *Meeting* Vienna (Austria) 2021, *Meeting* Granada (Spain) 2019, *Meeting* Stockholm (Sweden) 2015, *Meeting* Braunschweig (Germany) 2013, *Meeting* Parma (Italy) 2010. [2015/XJ3115/D]

♦ European Assembly of Citizens (EAC) 05922

Assemblée européenne des citoyens (AEC)
Pres 21ter rue Voltaire, 75011 Paris, France. T. +33143790923 – +33143716212. Fax +33143793209.
URL: http://www.aechca.fr/

History in the 1980s, as a result of dialogue between civic movements in Eastern Europe and disarmament movements in Western Europe. **Aims** Promote dialogue among individuals who share the same values. Concerns: peace; disarmament; anti-racism; civic mediation. **Events** *International seminar* Arzano (France) 1998. **Publications** *Réseaux de citoyens* – liaison bulletin, common publication with AITEC, CEDETIM and CEDIDELP. **IGO Relations** *Council of Europe (CE, #04881)*. **NGO Relations** Affiliated to: *Helsinki Citizens' Assembly (hCa, #10905)*. Instrumental in setting up: *Maison des citoyens du monde (MCM)*. Founding member of: *Initiatives Pour un Autre Monde (IPAM)*. [2019/XF4172/F]

- ♦ European Asset Management Association (inactive)
- ♦ European Assistive Technology Information Network / see Global Assistive Technology Information Network (#10240)
- ♦ European Associated Centre in Flood Problems / see European Centre for Mitigation of Natural Risks
- ♦ European Association, The / see European Association for the Advancement of Social Sciences (#05928)

♦ European Association of Abnormal Road Transport and Mobile Cranes (ESTA) 05923

Director Lotte Beesestraat 4, 2331 KJ Leiden, Netherlands. T. +31715724705. Fax +31715724968. E-mail: director@estaeurope.eu – officemanager@estaeurope.eu.
Office Manager address not obtained.
URL: http://estaeurope.eu/

History 1976. Former names and other names: *European Association for the Transport of Heavy Loads* – former; *Europäische Schwertransporte und Kranarbeiten (ESKA)* – former; *European Association for Special Transport and Rigging* – former; *European Association of Heavy Haulage Transport and Mobile Cranes* – former; *Association européenne pour les transports exceptionnels et les grues automobiles* – former; *Europäische Schwertransport- Automobilkranunion (ESTA)* – former. Registration: Chamber of commerce, No/ID: 27347721, Netherlands; EU Transparency Register, No/ID: 870060728390-52, Start date: 19 Sep 2017. **Aims** Connect and represent the European Abnormal Transport and Mobile Crane Industry by maintaining a knowledge base with the aim of improving sustainability, safety and efficiency and to inspire the next generation. **Structure** Board of Directors; Sections (2): Transport, Cranes. **Languages** Dutch, English, French, German. **Staff** 10.00 FTE, paid. **Activities** Awards/prizes/competitions; events/meetings; knowledge management/information dissemination; networking/liaising. **Events** *Autumn Meeting* Helsinki (Finland) 2021, *Spring Meeting* Paris (France) 2021, *Spring Meeting* Amsterdam (Netherlands) 2020, *Meeting* Helsinki (Finland) 2020, *Meeting* Piacenza (Italy) 2019. **Publications** *ESTA Newsletter* (5 a year) – The Newsletter is published in English, French, German, Spanish and Italian.
Members National organizations in 21 countries:
Austria, Belgium, Bulgaria, China, Czechia, Denmark, Finland, France, Germany, Greece, Ireland, Israel, Italy, Netherlands, Norway, Poland, Spain, Sweden, Switzerland, Türkiye, UK. [2023.02.14/XD0803/D]

- ♦ European Association of the Academic Study of Religions (inactive)

♦ European Association of Acarologists (EURAAC) 05924

Pres Univ Politécnica de Valencia, Instituto Agroforestal Mediterraneo, Camino de Vera, s/n, 46022 Valencia, Spain. E-mail: fjferrag@eaf.upv.es – tsagkarakou@nagref.gr.
URL: http://euraac.webs.upv.es/

History 1987, Amsterdam (Netherlands). **Aims** Organize meetings for dissemination of knowledge among acarologists; provide a means for personal contact among workers in this field; provide support for instructional workshops for those wishing to specialize in this discipline; represent the views of European acarologists in approaches to official bodies in matters pertaining to the interests of acarology. **Structure** Executive Committee, comprising President, President-Elect, Secretary, Treasurer and 5 members, with the possibility to co-opt further members. **Languages** English. **Staff** Voluntary. **Finance** Members' dues. **Activities** Organizes symposium (every 4 years). **Events** *Quadrennial Symposium* Bari (Italy) 2021, *Quadrennial Symposium* Bari (Italy) 2020, *Quadrennial Symposium* Valencia (Spain) 2016, *Quadrennial symposium* Vienna (Austria) 2012, *Quadrennial symposium* Montpellier (France) 2008. **Publications** *EURAAC News Letters*. Proceedings from symposia.
Members Individuals and organizations in 41 countries:
Argentina, Australia, Austria, Belarus, Belgium, Brazil, Bulgaria, Canada, China, Czechia, Denmark, Egypt, Finland, France, Georgia, Germany, Greece, Hungary, Iran Islamic Rep, Ireland, Israel, Italy, Japan, Kenya, Malta, Netherlands, New Zealand, Norway, Poland, Portugal, Russia, Serbia, Slovakia, South Africa, Spain, Sweden, Switzerland, Türkiye, UK, Ukraine, USA. [2015/XD7872/D]

♦ European Association for Accident Research and Analysis 05925

Europäische Verein für Unfallforschung und Unfall Analyse (EVU)
Main Office Inffeldgasse 11/2, 9010 Graz, Austria. T. +433168739401. Fax +433168739402. E-mail: info@evuonline.org.
URL: http://www.evuonline.org/

History Registration: No/ID: 22 VR 2768, Germany, Wiesbaden. **Events** *Congress* Haifa (Israel) 2021, *Congress* Barcelona (Spain) 2019, *Congress* Dubrovnik (Croatia) 2018, *Congress* Haarlem (Netherlands) 2017, *Congress* Bratislava (Slovakia) 2016. [2020/XD9467/D]

- ♦ European Association of Accountants / see European Accounting Association (#05820)
- ♦ European Association of Addiction Therapy (no recent information)
- ♦ European Association of the Adhesive and Sealant Industry / see Fédération européenne des industries de colles et adhésifs (#09572)

♦ European Association for the Advancement of Archaeology by Experiment (EXAR) 05926

Europäische Vereinigung zur Förderung der Experimentellen Archäologie
Pres Pfahlbaumuseum Unteruhldingen, Strandpromenade 6, 88690 Uhldingen-Mühlhofen, Germany. T. +497556928900. Fax +4975569289010. E-mail: mail@pfahlbauten.de.
URL: http://www.exar.org/

History Founded 2002, Oldenburg (Germany), during the 10th Congress of Experimental Archaeology. **Aims** Advance works of archaeology by experiment. **Structure** Board. **Finance** Members' dues. **Activities** Events/meetings. **Events** *Conference* Brandenburg an der Havel (Germany) 2022, *Conference* Perl (Germany) 2021, *Conference* Vienna (Austria) 2019, *Conference* Uhldingen-Mühlhofen (Germany) 2018, *Conference* Xanten (Germany) 2017. **Publications** *Experimentelle Archäologie in Europa – Bilanz – Experimental Archaeology in Europe – Bilanz* – yearbook.
Members Individuals (about 80) in 8 countries:
Austria, France, Germany, Italy, Netherlands, Slovakia, Switzerland, UK. [2019.02.26/XD9134/v/D]

- ♦ European Association for the Advancement of Radiation Curing by UV, EB and Laser Beams / see RadTech Europe (#18606)

♦ European Association for the Advancement of Science and Technology (EUROSCIENCE) 05927

Association européenne pour la promotion de la science et de la technologie (EUROSCIENCE)
SG 1 Quai Lezay Marnésia, 67000 Strasbourg, France. T. +33388241150. E-mail: office@euroscience.org.
URL: http://www.euroscience.org/

History 15 Mar 1997, Strasbourg (France). Statutes revised: 2002; 2014. Registration: France; EU Transparency Register, No/ID: 960231515423-37. **Aims** Contribute to European integration through promotion of a threefold citizenship among scientists and scientific institutions in Europe – European, disciplinary and national/regional; enhance the contribution of science to the well-being and prosperity of mankind; influence shaping of policies for science in Europe; raise awareness of the issues linking science to society. **Structure** General Assembly (every 2 years); Governing Board; Executive Committee; ESOF Committee; Work Groups; Local Sections; Secretariat located in Strasbourg (France). **Languages** English. **Staff** 3.00 FTE, paid. **Finance** Sources: donations; international organizations; meeting proceeds; members' dues; private foundations; revenue from activities/projects; sale of publications; sponsorship. **Activities** Awards/prizes/competitions; events/meetings; guidance/assistance/consulting; politics/policy/regulatory; publishing activities; research/documentation. **Events** *ESOF : Euroscience Open Forum* Leiden (Netherlands) 2022, *ESOF : Euroscience Open Forum* Trieste (Italy) 2020, *ESOF : Euroscience Open Forum* Toulouse (France) 2018, *SFSA : Science Forum South Africa* Pretoria (South Africa) 2017, *SFSA : Science Forum South Africa* Pretoria (South Africa) 2016. **Publications** *Euroscientist* – journal.
Members Full; Associate; Founder; Corporate. Individuals and institutions in 59 countries:
Albania, Armenia, Australia, Austria, Belarus, Belgium, Bulgaria, Cameroon, Canada, China, Croatia, Cuba, Czechia, Denmark, Estonia, Finland, France, Georgia, Germany, Ghana, Greece, Hungary, Iceland, India, Indonesia, Ireland, Israel, Italy, Japan, Kenya, Korea Rep, Laos, Latvia, Lithuania, Luxembourg, Malta, Mexico, Moldova, Monaco, Netherlands, Nigeria, Norway, Pakistan, Poland, Portugal, Romania, Russia, Serbia, Singapore, Slovakia, Slovenia, South Africa, Spain, Sweden, Switzerland, Türkiye, UK, Ukraine, USA.
Corporate in 10 European countries. Membership countries not specified.
Founding members (150) in 26 countries. Membership countries not specified. [2022.05.17/XD6860/D]

♦ European Association for the Advancement of Social Sciences (EA) 05928

Gesellschaft zur Förderung der Europäischen Soziologie
Chairman Wällischgasse 8, 1030 Vienna, Austria. T. +43171393137139110.
URL: http://europeanassociation.eu/

History 1989. Also referred to as *European Association, The*. Took over activities of *Interdisciplinary Centre for Comparative Research in the Social Sciences (ICCR, inactive)*, 2017. Registered in accordance with Austrian law. **Aims** Improve society through high-quality research and efficient dissemination. **Structure** General Assembly (annual); Board; *ICCR Foundation*. **Activities** Research/documentation; events/meetings; knowledge management/information dissemination. **Events** *Conference* Niamey (Niger) 2007. **Publications** *INNOVATION – The European Journal of Social Sciences: Innovation* (4 a year); *EA Newsletter* (4-6 a year). Books; research reports; working papers. [2018.09.04/XD8788/D]

- ♦ European Association of Advertising Agencies / see European Association of Communications Agencies (#05983)

♦ European Association of Aerial Surveying Industries (EAASI) 05929

SG Nervierslaan 54, 1780 Wemmel, Belgium. E-mail: info@eaasi.eu – secretary.general@eaasi.eu.
URL: https://www.eaasi.eu/

History Registration: Banque-Carrefour des Entreprises, No/ID: 0730.835.414, Start date: 18 Jul 2019, Belgium. **Aims** Increase the influence of the European Aerial Surveying Industry on political and administrative decisions that affect it; promote use of aerial surveying data by educating decision makers; ensure a predictable quality level of services by certification; serve as a platform for communication and cooperation among members to enact positive change. **Structure** General Meeting; Board. **Events** *EAASI Partners Summit* Malaga (Spain) 2021, *Summit* Brussels (Belgium) 2019. **NGO Relations** Member of (1): *European Umbrella Organization for Geographical Information (EUROGI, #08964)*. [2023/AA1407/D]

- ♦ European Association of Aeronautical and Astronautical Students / see European Association of Aerospace Students (#05930)
- ♦ European Association of Aerospace Industries (inactive)

♦ European Association of Aerospace Students (EUROAVIA) 05930

Pres Kluyverweg 1, 2629 HS Delft, Netherlands. E-mail: ib@euroavia.eu.
URL: http://euroavia.eu/

History 16 Mar 1959, Aachen (Germany). Former names and other names: *European Association of Aeronautical and Astronautical Students* – former (16 Mar 1959 to 1992). Registration: Kamer van Koophandel, No/ID: 27184119, Start date: 1999, Netherlands. **Aims** Promote European cooperation in the aerospace field by providing opportunities for members to meet, exchange and learn on all levels; interact with aerospace stakeholders; address the aerospace formative skills gap. **Structure** International Board; Senior Council; Working Groups (10); Local Groups, each with its own Local Board. **Languages** English. **Staff** Voluntary. **Finance** Sources: members' dues; sponsorship. Other sources: particular projects financed by sponsors or participation fees. **Activities** Awards/prizes/competitions; events/meetings; training/education. **Events** *AMEAC : Annual Meeting of the EUROAVIA Congress* Naples (Italy) 2022, *Extra Meeting of the EUROAVIA Congress (ExMEAC)* Naples (Italy) 2022, *Electronic Control System Symposium* Patras (Greece) 2022, *Fly – In Workshop* Rzeszów (Poland) 2022, *Fly – In Workshop* Tampere (Finland) 2022. **Publications** *EUROAVIA Magazine* (annual); *EUROAVIA Newsletter* (about 12 a year) in English. Congress proceedings; manuals.
Members Local Groups (42), totalling over 3,000 members, in 19 countries:
Belgium, Croatia, Egypt, Finland, France, Germany, Greece, India, Italy, Netherlands, Poland, Portugal, Romania, Serbia, Spain, Sweden, Türkiye, UK, Ukraine.
NGO Relations Member of (2): *Council of European Aerospace Societies (CEAS, #04882)* (as Associate Member); *Informal Forum of International Student Organizations (IFISO, #11193)*. [2022.12.08/XD1120/D]

♦ European Association Against Fibre Pollution (inactive)

♦ European Association against Violence against Women at Work . . . 05931

Association européenne contre les violences faites aux femmes au travail (AVFT)

Contact 51 bvd Auguste Blanqui, 75013 Paris, France. T. +33145842424. Fax +33145834393. E-mail: contact@avft.org.
URL: http://www.avft.org/

History 1985, Paris (France). Registered in accordance with French law. **Aims** Defend the rights and integrity of women; sensitize the appropriate groups about violence against women, especially about *sexist* and sexual violence and *discrimination* in the workplace. **Structure** General Assembly. Administrative Council. **Staff** 3.50 FTE, paid; 7.00 FTE, voluntary. **Finance** Budget (annual): about euro 152,450. **Activities** Provides free concrete help, guidance and follow up through a hotline, counselling, legal and other advice. Organizes: colloquia; campaigns. Conducts: training seminars; research. Maintains a documentation centre om women's rights. **Events** *Sexual harassment* Paris (France) 1999. **Publications** *La Lettre de l'AVFT* (4 a year); *Projects féministes* (periodical). *Agir contre les vidences sexuelles et sexistes dans les relations de travail* (2002) – guide. Moral reports. [2017/XF4159/**F**]

♦ European Association of Agencies to Promote the Global Ocean Observing System / see European Global Ocean Observing System (#07396)

♦ European Association of Agricultural Economists (EAAE) 05932

Mailing Address PO Box 8130, Bode 56, 6700 EW Wageningen, Netherlands. T. +31317484065. E-mail: eaae@wur.nl.
Main: http://www.eaae.org/

History 28 Aug 1975, Uppsala (Sweden). Founded following 1st European Congress. **Aims** Further knowledge and understanding of agricultural economics, especially in the European context; promote exchange of experience, ideas and information among agricultural economists. **Structure** General Meeting; Board; Liaison Officers. **Languages** English. **Staff** 3.00 FTE, voluntary. **Finance** Sources: members' dues. **Activities** Events/meetings; knowledge management/information dissemination. **Events** *Triennial Congress* Rennes (France) 2023, *Triennial Congress* Prague (Czechia) 2021, *Triennial Congress* Prague (Czechia) 2020, *Seminar on Enhancing the Environmental and Climate Ambition of the EU Farming Sector* Brussels (Belgium) 2019, *Seminar on the Evaluation of New CAP Instruments* Budapest (Hungary) 2018. **Publications** *EuroChoices* (3 a year); *EAAE Newsflash* in English; *European Review of Agricultural Economics (ERAE)* – journal. Congress and seminar proceedings; books.

Members Active membership granted to all attending congress and lasts to following congress (3 years). Individuals (1,025) in 54 countries:
Albania, Algeria, Australia, Austria, Belarus, Belgium, Bosnia-Herzegovina, Bulgaria, Canada, Croatia, Cyprus, Czechia, Denmark, Egypt, Estonia, Finland, France, Germany, Greece, Hungary, Iceland, India, Ireland, Israel, Italy, Japan, Korea Rep, Latvia, Lithuania, Luxembourg, Malta, Moldova, Montenegro, Morocco, Netherlands, New Zealand, North Macedonia, Norway, Poland, Portugal, Romania, Russia, Serbia, Slovakia, Slovenia, South Africa, Spain, Sweden, Switzerland, Tunisia, Türkiye, UK, Ukraine, USA.
National liaison officers in 17 countries:
Austria, Belgium, Bulgaria, Denmark, Finland, France, Germany, Hungary, Italy, North Macedonia, Norway, Poland, Portugal, Slovakia, Slovenia, Switzerland, UK.

Consultative Status Consultative status granted from: *ECOSOC (#05331)* (Ros C); *FAO (#09260)* (Liaison Status). **IGO Relations** Liaison officers with: *European Commission (EC, #06633)*; *FAO (#09260)* – European Commission on Agriculture (ECA); *International Bank for Reconstruction and Development (IBRD, #12317)*; *OECD (#17693)*. **NGO Relations** Memorandum of Understanding with (1): *European Agricultural and Applied Economics Publications Foundation (EAAEP Foundation, #05845)*. [2021.02.18/XD4654/v/**D**]

♦ European Association of Agrochemical Companies (unconfirmed)
♦ European Association of Air Conditioning Stockholders (inactive)

♦ European Association of Air Heater Manufacturers (EURO-AIR) 05933

Gen Sec FIGAWA, Marienburger Strasse 15, 50968 Cologne, Germany. T. +492213764830. Fax +492213764861. E-mail: info@figawa.de.
Pres c/o Winterwarm BV, Industrieweg 8, 7102 DZ Winterswijk, Netherlands.
URL: http://www.euro-air.com/

History Founded 1995. EU Transparency Register: 859925523408-38. **Aims** Promote and represent the common interests of the European *industry* in construction of air heaters in their dealings with all relevant authorities, particularly through appropriate cooperation with the existing specialist organizations, official bodies and other offices in Europe and through collaboration in legal measures.

Members Companies in 6 countries:
Belgium, Denmark, Germany, Italy, Netherlands, UK.

NGO Relations Cooperates with: *Comité européen de normalisation (CEN, #04162)*. [2019/XD7444/**D**]

♦ European Association of Air Medical Escorts (unconfirmed)

♦ European Association of Airport and Seaport Police (EAASP) 05934

Contact Herik 13, 1273 AW Huizen, Netherlands. T. +31358871087. E-mail: info@eaasp.org – secretary@eaasp.org.
URL: https://eaasp.org/

History Feb 1973, London (UK). Registration: EU Transparency Register, No/ID: 050313823462-21, Start date: 29 Sep 2016. **Aims** Prevent criminal activity affecting international transport of passengers and cargo; encourage and develop exchange of information among law enforcement agencies at air and sea ports; study policy methodology and endorse best practice; reduce loss of property in transit; improve inter-agency cooperation to counter the threat posed by international terrorism and serious and organized crime; develop and improve security strategies at international air and sea ports; promote exchange of experience and expertise in the field of emergency and disaster management at air and sea ports. **Structure** Executive Committee. **Languages** English. **Staff** 6.00 FTE, voluntary. **Finance** Members 'dues: euro 80. **Events** *Annual Conference* London (UK) 2020, *Annual Conference* Lisbon (Portugal) 2019, *Annual Conference* The Hague (Netherlands) 2018, *Annual Conference* Athens (Greece) 2015, *Annual Conference* Dubrovnik (Croatia) 2014.

Members in 17 countries and territories:
Austria, Belgium, Bulgaria, Channel Is, Denmark, Estonia, Finland, Germany, Gibraltar, Malta, Netherlands, Norway, Portugal, Russia, Switzerland, UK, USA. [2020/XD8982/**D**]

♦ European Association of Aluminium Aerosol Container Manufacturers / see International Organization of Aluminium Aerosol Container Manufacturers (#14437)
♦ European Association of Amateur Orchestras (inactive)

♦ European Association for American Studies (EAAS) 05935

SG Liechtensteinerstrasse 33, 37 6800 Feldkirch, PH Voralberg, 6800 Feldkirch, Austria. T. +43552231199. E-mail: secretary-general@eaas.eu.
Pres School of Arts English and Languages, 2 University Square, Belfast, BT7 1NN, UK. T. +44028973261.
URL: http://www.eaas.eu/

History 1953, Salzburg (Austria). Formal constitution agreed upon in 1954. Articles (new constitution) adopted in Apr 1977, Oxford (UK); amended Apr 1980, Amsterdam (Netherlands), and 2006. **Aims** Encourage the study of and research in all areas of American culture and society; promote cooperation and intercommunication between European students of the United States of America. **Structure** General Meeting and Conference (every 2 years); Board. **Languages** English. **Staff** None. **Finance** Sources: members' dues. **Activities** Awards/prizes/competitions; events/meetings; projects/programmes. **Events** *EAAS Conference* Thessaloniki (Greece) 2021, *Biennial Conference* Warsaw (Poland) 2020, *Biennial Conference* London (UK) 2018, *Joint Congress* Seoul (Korea Rep) 2018, *Biennial Conference* The Hague (Netherlands) 2014. **Publications** *European Journal of American Studies*. Conference proceedings.

Members National associations; joint national associations (Belgium-Luxembourg American Studies Association; Czech and Slovak Association for American Studies). Individuals in those European countries where no national association exists. Members in 28 countries:
Belarus, Belgium, Bulgaria, Canada, Czechia, Denmark, Finland, France, Germany, Greece, Hungary, Iceland, Ireland, Italy, Luxembourg, Netherlands, Norway, Poland, Portugal, Romania, Russia, Slovakia, Spain, Sweden, Switzerland, Türkiye, UK, USA.
Included in the above, 2 organizations listed in this Yearbook:
Association française d'études américaines (AFEA); *Deutsche Gesellschaft für Amerikastudien (DGfA)*.
Affiliate member (1):
Israel Association of American Studies (IAAS). [2022.05.11/XD7618/**D**]

♦ European Association of Amusement Suppliers Industry (EAASI) . . 05936

Address not obtained.
URL: http://www.eaasi.org/

Aims Represent the European ride manufacturers. **Structure** Managing Committee, comprising President, 2 Vice-Presidents, General Secretary-Treasurer and Secretary. **Events** *General Assembly* Munich (Germany) 2011.

Members National organizations in 10 countries:
Belgium, France, Germany, Italy, Luxembourg, Netherlands, Russia, Spain, Switzerland, UK. [2011/XD8776/t/**D**]

♦ European Association for Animal Production / see European Federation of Animal Science (#07046)

♦ European Association on Antennas and Propagation (EurAAP) 05937

Secretariat Avenue du Port 86C, Box 204, 1000 Brussels, Belgium. T. +3227325692. E-mail: contact@euraap.org.
URL: https://www.euraap.org/

History Founded by EU FP6 *Antenna Centre of Excellence (ACE)*, a Network of Excellence running under Information Society Technologies (IST) research area of the EU FP6. Registration: Banque-Carrefour des Entreprises, No/ID: 0880.326.270, Start date: 29 Mar 2006, Belgium. **Aims** Maintain, develop and broaden on a non-profit basis, the European objectives activities initiated by the European Network of Excellence ACE. **Structure** Delegate Assembly; Board of Directors; Working Groups (9). **Languages** English. **Staff** None. Activities carried out on voluntary basis. **Finance** Main sources: conference fees; European School of Antennas (ESoA). **Activities** Events/meetings; financial and/or material support; knowledge management/information dissemination; standards/guidelines; networking/liaising; research and development. **Events** *European Conference on Antennas and Propagation (EuCAP)* Stockholm (Sweden) 2025, *European Conference on Antennas and Propagation* Glasgow (UK) 2024, *European Conference on Antennas and Propagation* Florence (Italy) 2023, *European Conference on Antennas and Propagation* Madrid (Spain) 2022, *European Conference on Antennas and Propagation* Düsseldorf (Germany) 2021. **Publications** Conference papers.

Members Individuals (1,171) in 57 countries and territories:
Albania, Algeria, Australia, Austria, Belgium, Bolivia, Brazil, Canada, China, Colombia, Croatia, Cyprus, Czechia, Denmark, Egypt, Finland, France, Georgia, Germany, Greece, Hong Kong, Hungary, India, Iran Islamic Rep, Ireland, Israel, Italy, Japan, Kazakhstan, Korea Rep, Lebanon, Luxembourg, Malaysia, Mexico, Netherlands, Nigeria, Norway, Pakistan, Poland, Portugal, Qatar, Russia, Saudi Arabia, Serbia, Singapore, Slovenia, South Africa, Spain, Sweden, Switzerland, Taiwan, Tunisia, Türkiye, UK, Ukraine, United Arab Emirates, USA. [2023/XM3342/**D**]

♦ European Association for Apitherapy (inactive)

♦ European Association for Aquatic Mammals (EAAM) 05938

Association européenne pour les mammifères marins

Sec Rue de la Science 14b, 1000 Brussels, Belgium. T. +3228992930. E-mail: information@eaam.org.
URL: https://eaam.org/

History 1972, Harderwijk (Netherlands). Founded as an interest group. Registration: No/ID: 0508.695.615, Start date: 24 Dec 2012, Belgium; EU Transparency Register, No/ID: 394562126660-68, Start date: 6 Apr 2017. **Aims** Promote free exchange of knowledge and further scientific progress pertaining to treatment, management, conservation and scientific research of aquatic mammals. **Structure** Board. **Languages** English. **Staff** 5.00 FTE, voluntary. **Finance** Sources: members' dues. **Activities** Events/meetings; standards/guidelines; training/education. **Events** *We are back !* 2022, *Conference* 2021, *Annual Symposium* Valencia (Spain) 2020, *Annual Symposium* Albufeira (Portugal) 2019, *Annual Symposium* Pomezia (Italy) 2018. **Publications** *EAAM Newsletter* (3-4 a year); *Aquatic Mammals*. Brochures; pamphlets; leaflets; charts; diagrams.

Members Full (over 140) zoologists, veterinarians, members of the medical profession and individuals devoting a significant part of their professional activity to teaching, research or practice of aquatic mammal zoology, medicine and conservation; Associate persons who have a strong interest in aquatic mammals but not qualifying for full membership. Institutional membership (22) organizations staff who spend a significant amount of time on the keeping of live aquatic mammals, or studies on live or dead aquatic mammals. Personal, Retired and Honorary members in 22 countries and territories:
Australia, Bahamas, Belgium, Canada, Denmark, Dominican Rep, Finland, France, Germany, Hong Kong, Israel, Italy, Malta, Netherlands, Portugal, Singapore, South Africa, Spain, Sweden, Switzerland, UK, USA.

NGO Relations Member of (2): *Alliance of Marine Mammal Parks and Aquariums (AMMPA)*; *European Tourism Manifesto (#08921)*. [2022/XD6162/**D**]

♦ European Association of Aquatic Sciences Libraries and Information Centres (EURASLIC) 05939

Exec Sec Rudjer Boskovic Inst, Bijenicka cesta 54, PO Box 180, HR-10002 Zagreb, Croatia. T. +38514680086. Fax +38514561095.
Pres address not obtained.
URL: http://www.euraslic.org/

History 1988, Plymouth (UK). Regional group of *International Association of Aquatic and Marine Science Libraries and Information Centers (IAMSLIC, #11707)*. Registered in accordance with French law, Apr 1990, Paris (France). **Aims** Promote exchange of ideas and views on issues of mutual concern in the field; collect and present views and proposals; encourage cooperation within Europe and build links with national, regional and international aquatic sciences libraries and information networks; undertake joint projects to improve flow, exchange and dissemination of aquatic information. **Structure** Executive Board. **Languages** English. **Finance** Members' dues. **Activities** Events/meetings; training/education; knowledge management/information dissemination. **Events** *Biennial Conference* Zagreb (Croatia) 2019, *Biennial Conference* Bremen (Germany) 2017, *Biennial Conference* Rome (Italy) 2015, *Biennial Conference* Varna (Bulgaria) 2013, *Biennial Conference* Lyon (France) 2011. **Publications** *EURASLIC Newsletter* (annual). Conference proceedings.

Members Personal; Institutional; Sponsored. Members in 21 countries:
Belgium, Bulgaria, Croatia, Denmark, Estonia, France, Germany, Greece, Iceland, Ireland, Israel, Italy, Latvia, Poland, Portugal, Russia, Spain, Sweden, Switzerland, UK, Ukraine.

IGO Relations Formal contact with: *FAO (#09260)*; *Intergovernmental Oceanographic Commission (IOC, #11496)*; *International Oceanographic Data and Information Exchange (IODE, #14396)* and the IODE Group of Experts on Marine Information Management (GEMIM). [2020.03.10/XD2936/**D**]

♦ European Association of Archaeologists (EAA) 05940

Association européenne d'archéologie (AEA)

Senior Manager Letenska 4, 118 01 Prague, Czechia. T. +4202733701679. Fax +420257014411. E-mail: administrator@e-a-a.org – secretary@e-a-a.org.
Sec address not obtained.
URL: https://www.e-a-a.org/

History 22 Sep 1994, Ljubljana (Slovenia). Founded 1994, when Statutes were adopted. Statutes revised: 26 Sep 1998, Gothenburg (Sweden); Sep 2017; Sep 2019; Sep 2022. Registration: EU Transparency Register, No/ID: 361044932292-22. **Aims** Promote: development of archaeological research and exchange of information in Europe; management and interpretation of European archaeological heritage; proper ethical and scientific standards for archaeological work; the interests of professional archaeologists in Europe; cooperation with other organisations with similar aims; interest in archaeological remains as evidence of the human past and contributing to our knowledge of human culture and to discourage a focus upon any commercial value that may attach to such material; friendship and peaceful cooperation of archaeologists; work for protection of archaeological remains and cultural heritage, including the prevention of related illegal activities. **Structure** Annual Meeting; Executive Board; Nomination Committee; Secretariat. **Languages** English. **Staff** 3.30 FTE, paid. **Finance** Sources: members' dues. **Activities** Awards/prizes/competitions; events/meetings. **Events** *Annual Meeting* Rome (Italy) 2024, *Annual Meeting* Belfast (UK) 2023, *Annual Meeting* Budapest (Hungary) 2022, *Annual Meeting* Kiel (Germany) 2021, *Annual Meeting* 2020. **Publications** *European Journal of Archaeology* (4 a year); *The European Archaeologist* (4 a year). *THEMES in Contemporary Archaeology*. **Members** Regular; Family; Student; Retired; Corporate; Life. Members (over 2,500) in 70 countries. Membership countries not specified. **Consultative Status** Consultative status granted from: *Council of Europe (CE, #04881)* (Participatory Status). **IGO Relations** Observer status with (1): *Intergovernmental Negotiating Committee for a Legally Binding Agreement on Forests in Europe (INC-Forests, inactive)*. **NGO Relations** Member of (1): *European Heritage Alliance 3.3 (#07477)*. [2022.10.20/XD7466/**D**]

♦ European Association for Architectural Education (EAAE) 05941

Association européenne pour l'enseignement de l'architecture (AEEA)

Secretariat KU Leuven, Fac Architectuur, Paleizenstraat 65/67, 1030 Brussels, Belgium. T. +32093986470. E-mail: secretariat@eaae.be.

URL: http://www.eaae.be/

History 1975. Former names and other names: *Association européenne des écoles d'architecture* – alias. Registration: Belgium. **Aims** Promote exchange of ideas and people in the architecture education and research sector; explore development of architectural education in Europe; provide a representative forum for teachers and students to meet and confer; enable schools throughout Europe to explore new ways of helping future architects to acquire skills to meet the future needs of society; facilitate exchange of staff and students among schools; make specific proposals on creation of greater complementarity and closer relations within education. **Structure** General Assembly (annual); Council; Permanent Secretariat, headed by Secretary-General. **Languages** English, French. **Finance** Sources: members' dues. **Activities** Awards/prizes/competitions; events/meetings; knowledge management/information dissemination; training/education. Set up: *European Network of Heads of Schools of Architecture (ENHSA, #07918).* **Events** *Annual Conference and General Assembly* Madrid (Spain) 2022, *EAAE-ARCC International Conference* Miami, FL (USA) 2022, *Deans Summit* Oslo (Norway) 2021, *Annual Conference* Prague (Czechia) 2021, *EAAE – ARCC International Conference* Valencia (Spain) 2020. **Publications** *EAAE News Sheet* (3 a year) in English, French; *STOA* (annual) – journal; *Transactions on Architectural Education – Cahiers de l'enseignement de l'architecture* (periodical). *AEEA Index* in English, French; *Guide to European Schools of Architecture.* Forum and workshop reports; guides. **Information Services** *AEEA Databank.*

Members Active schools of architecture in 38 countries:
Albania, Austria, Azerbaijan, Belgium, Bulgaria, Croatia, Cyprus, Czechia, Denmark, Estonia, Finland, France, Germany, Greece, Hungary, Iceland, Ireland, Italy, Kosovo, Latvia, Liechtenstein, Lithuania, Macedonia, Montenegro, Netherlands, Norway, Poland, Portugal, Romania, Serbia, Slovakia, Slovenia, Spain, Sweden, Switzerland, Türkiye, UK, Ukraine.

Associate in 4 countries:
Italy, Lebanon, Russia, USA.

Individuals in 3 countries:
France, Nigeria, Türkiye.

NGO Relations Supports setting up of: *African Association for Education in Architecture and Planning (no recent information).* Close links with North American counterparts. [2022.10.24/XD2391/D]

♦ European Association of Architectural Heritage Firms / see European Association Architectural Heritage Restoration Firms (#05942)

♦ European Association Architectural Heritage Restoration Firms . . . 05942

Association Européenne des Entreprises de Restauration du Patrimoine Architectural (AEERPA)

Main Office Calle Gran Via 6-4, 28013 Madrid, Spain. T. +34639201090.

Facebook: https://www.facebook.com/aeerpa/

History Dec 1992, Strasbourg (France). Former names and other names: *European Association of Architectural Heritage Firms* – alias; *Association européenne des entreprises du patrimoine architectural* – alias; *European Association of Firms Specializing in the Restoration of the Architectural Heritage* – alias. **Aims** Protect architectural heritage and related professions. **Structure** General Assembly; Administrators Board. **Languages** Dutch, English, French, Spanish. **Staff** 1.00 FTE, paid. **Activities** Events/meetings. **Events** *General Assembly* Avignon (France) 2013, *General Assembly* Granada (Spain) 2012, *General Assembly* Geneva (Switzerland) 2011, *General Assembly* Sibiu (Romania) 2010, *Meeting* Strasbourg (France) 2003. **Publications** *AEERPA Newsletter* (annual). White book on economic benefits from heritage restoration in Europe.

Members Full in 11 countries:
Belgium, Croatia, France, Germany, Netherlands, Portugal, Romania, Spain, Switzerland, Türkiye, UK.

NGO Relations Member of (3): *Europa Nostra (#05767); European Heritage Alliance 3.3 (#07477); International Council on Monuments and Sites (ICOMOS, #13049).* [2019/XD4318/D]

♦ European Association for Artificial Intelligence (EurAI) 05943

Pres address not obtained.

Vice-Pres Dept of Computer Science and Engineering, Univ of Bologna, Viale Risorgimento 2, 40136 Bologna BO, Italy. T. +39512093790.

URL: http://www.eurai.org/

History Jul 1982, Paris (France). Former names and other names: *European Coordinating Committee for Artificial Intelligence (ECCAI)* – former. Registration: Banque-Carrefour des Entreprises, Belgium; EU Transparency Register, No/ID: 724852331101-36. **Aims** Promote research, education and applications of artificial intelligence in Europe. **Structure** General Assembly (annual); Board of Directors; Technical Secretariat. **Languages** English. **Staff** 7.00 FTE, voluntary. **Finance** Sources: meeting proceeds; revenue from activities/projects; sponsorship. **Activities** Awards/prizes/competitions; events/meetings; training/education. **Events** *Conference* Vienna (Austria) 2022, *Conference* Santiago de Compostela (Spain) 2020, *Biennial Conference* Stockholm (Sweden) 2018, *Biennial Conference* The Hague (Netherlands) 2016, *Biennial Conference* Prague (Czech Rep) 2014. **Publications** *AI Communications – The European Journal on Artificial Intelligence* (periodical). Conference proceedings.

Members Scientific European associations concerned with artificial intelligence in 26 countries:
Austria, Bulgaria, Czechia, Denmark, Finland, France, Germany, Greece, Hungary, Ireland, Israel, Italy, Latvia, Lithuania, Norway, Poland, Portugal, Romania, Russia, Slovakia, Slovenia, Spain, Sweden, Switzerland, UK, Ukraine.

Regional member (1):
BNVKI-AIABN: Benelux Association for Artificial Intelligence (BNVKI-AIABN, #03292).

NGO Relations Member of (1): *European Forum for ICST (#07316).* Affiliated with (1): *World Organisation of Systems and Cybernetics (WOSC, #21686).* [2023.02.14/XD9186/D]

♦ European Association of Artist Managers (#02554)

♦ European Association for Asian Art and Archaeology (EAAA) 05944

Secretariat Dept of Asian Studies, Fac of Arts, Univ of Ljubljana, Askerceva 2, 1000 Ljubljana, Slovenia. E-mail: info@ea-aaa.eu.

URL: http://ea-aaa.eu/

History Statutes adopted Nov 2012; supplemented Sep 2013; changed Aug 2017. Registration: Slovenia. **Aims** Encourage and promote all academic and scholarly activities related to Asian art and archaeology in European countries. **Structure** General Assembly; Board; Executive Committee. **Activities** Events/meetings; training/education; publishing activities; research/documentation; networking/liaising; knowledge management/information dissemination. **Events** *Conference* Ljubljana (Slovenia) 2020, *Conference* Zurich (Switzerland) 2017, *Conference* Olomouc (Czech Rep) 2014. **Publications** *EAAA Monograph Series.* [2020.03.11/XM7533/D]

♦ European Association for Astronomy Education (EAAE) 05945

Pres address not obtained.

Sec address not obtained. E-mail: rkollegium@gmail.com.

URL: http://www.eaae-astronomy.org/

History 25 Nov 1995, Athens (Greece), following adoption of a declaration, 25-30 Nov 1994, Garching (Germany), by participants at a workshop organized by *European Organization for Astronomical Research in the Southern hemisphere (ESO, #08106).* **Aims** Improve and promote astronomical education. **Structure** General Assembly; Executive Council, including President, Vice-President, Secretary, Treasurer, Editor and Honorary President; standing committees (2); working groups (7); national representatives. Secretariat located at Administrative Centre of ESO, Garching (Germany). **Finance** Members' dues. **Activities** Organizes Summer school. **Events** *General Assembly* Noordwijk (Netherlands) 2002, *Youth astronomical conference* Varna (Bulgaria) 2002, *General Assembly* Stockholm (Sweden) 1998. **Publications** *EAAE Newsletter.*

Members Teachers of astronomy, and others interested in its teaching, in 17 countries:
Austria, Belgium, Denmark, Finland, France, Germany, Greece, Ireland, Italy, Luxembourg, Netherlands, Norway, Portugal, Spain, Sweden, Switzerland, UK.

NGO Relations Cooperates with: *European/Mediterranean Planetarium Association (EMPA, #07772).* [2018/XD5502/D]

♦ European Association of Attorneys / see AEA – International Lawyers Network (#00142)

♦ European Association for an Audiovisual Independent Market (inactive)

♦ European Association for Audiovisual Media Education (EAAME) . . 05946

Association européenne pour l'éducation aux médias audiovisuels (AEEMA)

Chair address not obtained. E-mail: info@aeema.net.

History Founded 2 Dec 1989, Paris (France), under the joint auspices of *European Commission (EC, #06633)* and the Council of Europe. Operational from Jan 1990. Registered in accordance with Belgian law. As of 2016, assumed ceased to exist. **Aims** Coordinate activities of audiovisual media education professionals at a European level so as to develop the identity of the audiovisual media; foster the idea of an audiovisual culture among the public at large; promote teaching of sound and image languages; persuade young people, the general public, public and political authorities and the professions of the need for such education; prepare young people to use new means of communication; encourage a critical approach to audiovisual media; open job opportunities; exchange information on methods of training and audiovisual creation; develop firm links among educators in the field. **Structure** General Meeting (annual, at conference). Board (meets twice a year), comprising up to 2 members per community represented. **Languages** English, French. **Staff** 1.00 FTE, paid. **Finance** Members' dues. Other sources: own projects; co-productions with members; support from *Audiovisual Eureka (AVE, inactive),* Council of Europe and European Commission. **Activities** Events/meetings; training/education; knowledge management/information dissemination. **Events** *Annual General Assembly* Brussels (Belgium) 1996, *Joint international seminar* Brussels (Belgium) 1996, *Annual General Assembly* 1995, *International seminar* Bad Marienberg (Germany) 1990. **Publications** *European Index of Audiovisual Media Education Experts.*

Members Organizations and individuals in 37 countries:
Australia, Austria, Belgium, Burkina Faso, Canada, Cyprus, Czechia, Denmark, Egypt, Finland, France, Germany, Greece, Hungary, India, Iran Islamic Rep, Ireland, Israel, Italy, Luxembourg, Malta, Netherlands, Norway, Poland, Portugal, Romania, Russia, Serbia, Slovakia, Slovenia, South Africa, Spain, Sweden, Switzerland, Türkiye, UK, USA.

Consultative Status Consultative status granted from: *Council of Europe (CE, #04881)* (Participatory Status). **IGO Relations** *European Council (#06801).* [2016/XD2338/D]

♦ European Association of Auditors and Tax Consultants (inactive)

♦ European Association of Authorised Representatives (EAAR) 05947

Contact Suite 115, Wey House 15 Church Street, Weybridge, KT13 8NA, UK. T. +447798631554. E-mail: info@eaarmed.org – mail@obelis.net.

URL: http://www.eaarmed.org/

History 2002, as a grouping of the type *European Economic Interest Grouping (EEIG, #06960).* Registered under English law, number GE192. EU Transparency Register: 293779123135-32. **Aims** Enhance the quality of European Authorised Representation; provide an understanding of European Authorised Representatives' responsibilities to other stakeholders. **Activities** Events/meetings. **Events** *European Symposium on New Medical Device Regulations* Brussels (Belgium) 2018, *Assembly Meeting* Paris (France) 2014, *Assembly Meeting* Brussels (Belgium) 2013, *Assembly Meeting* London (UK) 2013, *Assembly Meeting* Paris (France) 2012. **Members** Membership countries not specified. [2019/XJ8135/D]

♦ European Association of Automotive Suppliers (CLEPA) 05948

Association Européenne des Fournisseurs Automobiles

SG Cours Saint-Michel 30g, 1040 Brussels, Belgium. T. +3227439130. E-mail: info@clepa.be.

URL: http://www.clepa.eu/

History 16 Mar 1959, Geneva (Switzerland). Former names and other names: *Liaison Committee for the Manufacture of Automobile Equipment and Spare Parts* – former; *Comitato di Collegamento dei Costruttori di Componenti e Ricambi* – former; *Liaison Committee for the Automotive Equipment and Parts Industry* – former; *Comité de liaison de la construction d'équipement et de pièces d'automobiles* – former; *Verbindungsausschuss der Kraftfahrzeugteile- und Zubehörindustrie* – former; *Comitato di Collegamento dei Costruttori di Componenti e Parti per Autoveicoli* – former; *Verbindingscomité voor de Bouw van Uitrustingen en Onderdelen* – former; *Liaison Committee for the Automotive Components and Equipment Industry* – former (1995 to 1996); *Comité de liaison de la construction d'équipements et de pièces d'automobiles (CLEPA)* – former (1995 to 1996); *Verbindingscomité voor de Industrie van Onderdelen Uitrustingen voor Voertuigen* – former (1995 to 1996); *Association of European Automotive Components and Parts Industry* – former (1996 to 1997); *Association of European Automotive Components and Parts Industry* – former (1997 to 1998). Registration: Banque-Carrefour des Entreprises, No/ID: 0455.664.329, Start date: 30 Mar 1995, Belgium; EU Transparency Register, No/ID: 91408765797-03, Start date: 6 May 2011. **Aims** Be the leading provider of highly efficient and sustainable mobility worldwide. **Structure** General Assembly (annual); Board of Directors; Steering Committee; Working Groups; Experts Groups; Task Forces. **Languages** English. **Finance** Sources: members' dues. **Activities** Advocacy/lobbying/activism; networking/liaising; research/documentation. **Events** *Aftermarket Conference* Brussels (Belgium) 2022, *Annual General Assembly* Brussels (Belgium) 2022, *Materials Regulations Meeting* Brussels (Belgium) 2022, *Aftermarket Conference* Brussels (Belgium) 2021, *Aftermarket Conference* Brussels (Belgium) 2021. **Publications** *CLEPA Newsletter* (12 a year). Position papers.

Members Corporate (120); Associate (11); National Trade (13). National associations in 13 countries:
Belgium, Denmark, France, Germany, Italy, Luxembourg, Netherlands, Poland, Portugal, Slovenia, Spain, Sweden, UK.

Associate members include the following 5 organizations listed in this Yearbook:
Association of European Automotive and Industrial Battery Manufacturers (EUROBAT, #02498); Association of European Wheel Manufacturers (EUWA, #02552); Association of Plastics Manufacturers in Europe (Plastics Europe, #02862); European Association of Manufacturers of Moulded Polyurethane Parts for the Automotive Industry (EURO-MOULDERS, #06116); Glass for Europe (#10157).

Consultative Status Consultative status granted from: *ECOSOC (#05331)* (Ros A). **IGO Relations** Participates in the work of: *United Nations Economic Commission for Europe (UNECE, #20555).* **NGO Relations** Member of (6): *Circular Plastics Alliance (#03936); European Green Vehicles Initiative Association (EGVIA, #07410); European Road Transport Research Advisory Council (ERTRAC, #08396); Federation of European and International Associations Established in Belgium (FAIB, #09508); Forum for Mobility and Society (FMS, #09924); Industry4Europe (#11181).* Instrumental in setting up (1): *International Green Automotive Lightweight Technology Alliance (IALTA).* In liaison with technical committees of: *Comité européen de normalisation (CEN, #04162); International Organization for Standardization (ISO, #14473).* Partner of: *European Automotive Research Partners Association (EARPA, #06301);* European Automotive and Telecoms Alliance; European Forum for Manufacturing (EFM); *International Federation of Automotive Engineering Societies (#13369).* [2020/XD2920/y/D]

♦ European Association of Avian Veterinarians (EAAV) 05949

Contact Frankfurter Str 91, 35392 Giessen, Germany.

URL: http://www.eaav.org/

History 1990. Founded as a European Committee of *Association of Avian Veterinarians (AAV, #02389)* As of 2014, constituted as an independent body. **Structure** Board, comprising President, Past-President, President-Elect, Secretary, Treasurer and Webmaster. **Events** *International Conference on Avian Herpetological and Exotic Mammal Medicine (ICARE)* Munich (Germany) 2024, *International Conference on Avian Herpetological and Exotic Mammal Medicine* Budapest (Hungary) 2022, *International Conference on Avian Herpetological and Exotic Mammal Medicine* Budapest (Hungary) 2021, *International Conference on Avian Herpetological and Exotic Mammal Medicine* London (UK) 2019, *International Conference on Avian Herpetological and Exotic Mammal Medicine* Venice (Italy) 2017.

Members Individuals in 19 countries:
Austria, Belgium, Czechia, Denmark, France, Germany, Israel, Italy, Luxembourg, Netherlands, Nigeria, Norway, Portugal, Spain, St Kitts-Nevis, Switzerland, Türkiye, UK, United Arab Emirates. [2022/XM3201/v/E]

♦ European Association of Aviation Personnel Schools / see International Association of Aviation Personnel Schools (#11721)

♦ European Association for Aviation Psychology (EAAP) 05950

Association Européenne pour la Psychologie Aéronautique – Europäische Gesellschaft für Luftfahrtpsychologie – Europese Vereniging voor Luchtvaartspsychologie

Contact Van Speykstraat 49B, NL-9726 BK, Groningen, Netherlands. E-mail: secretarygeneral@eaap.net.

URL: http://www.eaap.net/

History 31 Oct 1956, Scheveningen (Netherlands). Former names and other names: *Western European Association for Aviation Psychology (WEAAP)* – former; *Association de l'Europe occidentale pour la psychologie aéronautique* – former; *Westeuropäische Gesellschaft für Luftfahrt-Psychologie* – former. Registration: Chamber of Commerce, No/ID: 40531390, Netherlands, Amsterdam. **Aims** Promote the study of psychology and the scientific pursuit of applied psychology in the field of aviation. **Structure** General Assembly (at least every 2 years); Board; Working Groups (4). **Languages** English. **Finance** Sources: donations; members' dues. **Activities** Events/meetings. **Events** *Biennial Conference* Gibraltar 2022, *Biennial Conference* Gibraltar 2021, *Biennial Conference* Gibraltar 2020, *Biennial Conference* Dubrovnik (Croatia) 2018, *Biennial Conference* Lisbon (Portugal) 2016. **Publications** *Aviation Psychology and Applied Human Factors*; *EAAP Newsletter*. Congress proceedings.
Members Individuals Full and Associate; Corporate and/or governmental. Members in 50 countries and territories:
Argentina, Australia, Austria, Belgium, Bolivia, Brazil, Bulgaria, Canada, China, Costa Rica, Croatia, Czechia, Denmark, Ecuador, Estonia, Finland, France, Germany, Greece, Greenland, Hong Kong, Hungary, Iceland, India, Ireland, Italy, Latvia, Mauritius, Netherlands, New Zealand, Norway, Oman, Pakistan, Poland, Portugal, Qatar, Romania, Russia, Singapore, Slovakia, Slovenia, South Africa, Spain, Sweden, Switzerland, Taiwan, Türkiye, UK, United Arab Emirates, USA.
NGO Relations Associate member of: *European Federation of Psychologists Associations (EFPA, #07199)*. [2021/XD3432/v/D]

♦ European Association for Banking and Financial History 05951

SG Hanauer Landstr 126-128, 60314 Frankfurt-Main, Germany. T. +4969365084650.
URL: http://www.eabh.info/
History Nov 1990. Former names and other names: *European Association for Banking History (EABH)* – former (1990). Registration: Germany. **Aims** Promote dialogue between European bankers, academics and archivists. **Structure** Board of Management, including Chairman, Deputy Chairman, Chairman of the Board of Patrons, Chairman of the Academic Advisory Council, Treasurer and 3 members. Board of Patrons, comprising Chairman, Deputy Chairman and 17 members. Academic Advisory Council, consisting of Chairman, 2 Deputy Chairman, 1 ex-officio member and 17 members. **Languages** English. **Staff** 2.00 FTE, paid. **Finance** Members' dues. **Activities** Organizes: symposia; workshops; colloquia; residential training courses; studies. Awards prizes: Biennial Prize for the Best Submitted Article for Financial History Research; Annual Cultural Heritage Prize. Provides consultation services. Main areas (3): presentation of academic research into banking and financial history in publications and colloquia; exchange of information on issues and problems of bank archives; use of research findings for practical application in banks. **Events** *Annual Meeting* Sofia (Bulgaria) 2022, *Annual Meeting* 2021, *Annual Conference* Paris (France) 2017, *Annual Conference* Vienna (Austria) 2016, *Annual Conference* Rüschlikon (Switzerland) 2014. **Publications** *EABH Bulletin* (2 a year); *Financial History Review* (2 a year) – journal. *Studies in Banking History* – series. *Handbook on the History of European Banks* (1994). Workshop proceedings; brochures. **Information Services** *European Guide on Banking and Business Archives* – online database.
Members Banks (86) in 29 countries:
Albania, Austria, Belgium, Bulgaria, Croatia, Cyprus, Czechia, Denmark, Finland, France, Germany, Greece, Hungary, Iceland, Ireland, Italy, Lithuania, Luxembourg, Malta, Netherlands, Portugal, Romania, Slovakia, Slovenia, Spain, Sweden, Switzerland, Türkiye, UK.
International organizations (2):
Bank for International Settlements (BIS, #03165); *European Central Bank (ECB, #06466)*. [2019/XD5923/D]

- ♦ European Association for Banking History / see European Association for Banking and Financial History (#05951)
- ♦ European Association for Battery Electric Vehicles / see Going-Electric (#10673)
- ♦ European Association for Battery, Hybrid and Fuel Cell Electric Vehicles (#06024)
- ♦ European Association of Bead and Lath Producers (unconfirmed)

♦ European Association for Bee Research (EurBee) 05952

Contact Forschungsstelle für Bienenkunde, Univ Bremen, 82498, Cartesium 4-47, 28334 Bremen, Germany. T. +4942121864243. E-mail: dorothea.brueckner@uni-bremen.de.
URL: http://www.eurbee.org/
History 2002, Cardiff (UK). Registered in accordance with German law. **Aims** Encourage networking on all aspects of honeybee biology and politics. **Structure** Board, comprising President, Past President and Secretary. **Languages** English. **Finance** Members' dues. **Activities** Events/meetings; networking/liaising. **Events** *Biennial Conference* Belgrade (Serbia) 2022, *Biennial Conference* Belgrade (Serbia) 2020, *Biennial Conference* Ghent (Belgium) 2018, *Biennial Conference* Cluj-Napoca (Romania) 2016, *Biennial Conference* Murcia (Spain) 2014. **Publications** *EurBee Newsletter*. Abstracts. [2017.06.01/XM0382/D]

♦ European Association for Behavioural and Cognitive Therapies (EABCT) 05953

Secretariat c/o DGVT, Postfach 13 43, 72003 Tübingen, Germany. E-mail: office@eabct.eu.
URL: http://www.eabct.eu/
History 1970, Munich (Germany). Former names and other names: *European Association for Behaviour Therapy (EABT)* – former. Registration: Netherlands. **Aims** Provide an international forum within Europe for discussion of matters relevant to empirically based principles and practice of behavioural approaches in health, education and related fields both at an individual and a community level. **Structure** General Meeting; Governing Body (Committee); Board of Directors. **Languages** English. **Staff** Voluntary. **Finance** Members' dues. Other sources: income from congresses and workshops. **Activities** Events/meetings; knowledge management/information dissemination. **Events** *EABCT Congress* Antalya (Türkiye) 2023, *EABCT Congress* Barcelona (Spain) 2022, *EABCT Congress* Belfast (UK) 2021, *EABCT Congress* Athens (Greece) 2020, *Annual General Meeting* Sofia (Bulgaria) 2018. **Publications** *EABCT Newsletter*.
Members Full: associations in 39 countries:
Albania, Austria, Belgium, Bosnia-Herzegovina, Bulgaria, Croatia, Cyprus, Czechia, Denmark, Estonia, Finland, France, Georgia, Germany, Greece, Hungary, Iceland, Ireland, Israel, Italy, Kosovo, Latvia, Lithuania, Montenegro, Netherlands, North Macedonia, Norway, Poland, Portugal, Romania, Russia, Serbia, Slovenia, Spain, Sweden, Switzerland, Türkiye, UK, Ukraine.
Affiliate: associations in 6 countries:
Canada, Egypt, Lebanon, Morocco, Palestine, Russia.
IGO Relations *WHO (#20950)*; *WHO Regional Office for Europe (#20945)*. **NGO Relations** Member of (1): *World Confederation of Cognitive and Behavioural Therapies (WCCBT, #21292)*. Contacts with: *Association for Behavioural and Cognitive Therapies (ABCT)*; *Asociación Latinoamericana de Analisis y Modificación del Comportamiento (ALAMOC, #02179)*; *World Federation for Mental Health (WFMH, #21455)*. [2021/XD2637/D]

♦ European Association for Behaviour Analysis (EABA) 05954

Pres Panteion Univ of Athens, Dept of Psychology, 136 Syggrou Ave, 176 71 Athens, Greece.
URL: http://www.europeanaba.org/
Events *Conference* Tampere (Finland) 2022, *Conference* Tampere (Finland) 2020, *Conference* Würzburg (Germany) 2018, *Conference* Enna (Italy) 2016, *Conference* Stockholm (Sweden) 2014. **Members** Membership countries not specified. [2014/XJ8075/D]

- ♦ European Association for Behaviour Therapy / see European Association for Behavioural and Cognitive Therapies (#05953)

♦ European Association for Biblical Studies (EABS) 05955

Information Officer address not obtained. E-mail: information@eabs.net – secretary@eabs.net.
Registered Address Johannisstrasse 1-4, 48143 Münster, Germany.
URL: http://www.eabs.net/
History 1996, Dublin (Ireland). Current constitution adopted Aug 2011, Thessaloniki (Greece). Registered in accordance with German law. **Aims** Encourage the flow of biblical scholarship between European countries and make it easier for scholars and students in Central and Eastern Europe to participate with their colleagues in Western Europe and beyond in the exchange of knowledge and ideas. **Structure** Committee, comprising Officers (President, Executive Officer, Secretary, Treasurer, Information Officer, Graduate Representative) and members at large. **Languages** English, German. **Finance** Members' dues. **Activities** Organizes: annual conference; annual student conference. Runs about 40 research groups. **Events** *Annual Meeting* Siracusa (Italy) 2023, *Annual Meeting* Toulouse (France) 2022, *Annual Meeting* Wuppertal (Germany) 2021, *Annual Meeting* Wuppertal (Germany) 2020, *Annual Meeting* Warsaw (Poland) 2019. [2012.11.14/XD7863/D]

- ♦ European Association for Bioeconomic Studies (inactive)

♦ European Association of Bioindustries (EuropaBio) 05956

Senior Manager Av des Arts 53, 1000 Brussels, Belgium.
URL: http://www.europabio.org/
History 1996, Brussels (Belgium). Founded within the framework of *Conseil européen de l'industrie chimique (CEFIC, #04687)*. Now an autonomous affiliated organization. Former names and other names: *Senior Advisory Group on Biotechnology (SAGB)* – former. Registration: Banque-Carrefour des Entreprises, No/ID: 0477.520.310, Start date: 17 Feb 2002, Belgium; EU Transparency Register, No/ID: 1298286943-59, Start date: 8 Jan 2009. **Aims** Promote an innovative and dynamic biotechnology-based industry in Europe. **Structure** Board of Directors; Executive Committee; Councils; Working Groups; Task Forces. **Languages** English, French. **Staff** 14.00 FTE, paid. **Finance** Sources: members' dues. **Activities** Awards/prizes/competitions; events/meetings. **Events** *EFIB : European Forum for Industrial Biotechnology and the Bioeconomy* Rotterdam (Netherlands) 2023, *EFIB : European Forum for Industrial Biotechnology and the Bioeconomy* Vilnius (Lithuania) 2022, *EFIB : European Forum for Industrial Biotechnology and the Bioeconomy* Vienna (Austria) 2021, *EFIB : European Forum for Industrial Biotechnology and the Bioeconomy* Brussels (Belgium) 2020, *EFIB : European Forum for Industrial Biotechnology and the Bioeconomy* Brussels (Belgium) 2019. **Members** Corporate; Associate; National Associations. Membership countries not specified. **Consultative Status** Consultative status granted from: *World Intellectual Property Organization (WIPO, #21593)* (Observer Status). **IGO Relations** Observer status with (1): *OECD (#17693)*. **NGO Relations** Member of (8): Alliance for Safe Biologic Medicines (ASBM) (Associate); *EU Health Coalition*; *European Bioeconomy Alliance (EUBA, #06334)*; *European Food Sustainable Consumption and Production Round Table (European Food SCP Roundtable, #07289)*; *European Policy Centre (EPC, #08240)*; *European Technology Platform for Sustainable Chemistry (SusChem, #08893)* (Founding); *Federation of European and International Associations Established in Belgium (FAIB, #09508)*; *Industry4Europe (#11181)*. Cooperates with (2): *Business and Industry Advisory Committee to the OECD (BIAC, #03385)*; *Comité européen de normalisation (CEN, #04162)*. Supports (1): *SPRU – Science and Technology Policy Research*. Instrumental in setting up (2): *International Biotechnology Forum (IBF, no recent information)*; *International Council of Biotechnology Associations (ICBA)*. Stakeholder in: *European Network for Health Technology Assessment (EUnetHTA, #07921)*. [2022.05.04/XF1061/tv/E]

♦ European Association for Biometrics (EAB) 05957

Secretariat Prins Hendriklaan 22, 1404 AT Bussum, Netherlands. E-mail: secretariat@eab.org.
URL: https://eab.org/
History Registration: Handelsregister, No/ID: KVK 55450555, Netherlands. **Aims** Tackle the complex challenges facing ID in Europe, ranging from migration to privacy rights. **Structure** Supervisory Board; Management Team. Special Interest Groups; Committees; Working Groups. **Activities** Awards/prizes/competitions; events/meetings; knowledge management/information dissemination.
Members Government members in 5 countries:
Denmark, Germany, Netherlands, Norway, USA.
Academia in 10 countries:
Austria, Belgium, France, Germany, Norway, Poland, Serbia, Spain, Switzerland, UK.
Also Industry and Individual members. Membership countries not specified. [2021/AA1375/D]

♦ European Association for Body Psychotherapy (EABP) 05958

Association Européenne de Psychothérapie Corporelle

Secretariat Tintorettostraat 29/1, 1077 RP Amsterdam, Netherlands. T. +31630439755. E-mail: secretariat@eabp.org – secretariatasst@eabp.org.
URL: http://www.eabp.org/
History 20 Dec 1988, Oslo (Norway). Former names and other names: *Europese Vereniging voor Lichaamsgerichte Psychotherapie* – legal name. Registration: Chamber of Commerce, No/ID: 67477135, Start date: 2016, Netherlands, Amsterdam; Start date: 1988, End date: 2016, Switzerland. **Aims** Connect professional (body) psychotherapists; exchange expertise working with the body and mine; enable collaboration with people from associated disciplines. **Structure** General Assembly; Board of Directors; Committees (6); Secretariat. **Languages** English. **Staff** 1.00 FTE, paid. **Finance** Members' dues. Other sources: congress proceeds; journal sales. **Activities** Certification/accreditation; knowledge management/information dissemination; publishing activities; events/meetings. **Events** *European Congress for Body Psychotherapy* Sofia (Bulgaria) 2023, *European Congress for Body Psychotherapy* 2021, *Biennial Congress* Bologna (Italy) 2020, *European Congress for Body Psychotherapy* Berlin (Germany) 2018, *Biennial Congress* Athens (Greece) 2016. **Publications** *EABP Newsletter* (6 a year) – electronic; *International Body Psychotherapy Journal* (2 a year) – joint publication with USABP.
Members Full; Organizational; Candidate; Associate; Student; Honorary. Members (692; " indicates National Associations) in 23 countries and territories:
Australia, Austria (*), Belgium, Denmark, Finland, France, Germany (*), Greece (*), Israel (*), Italy (*), Japan, Kosovo, Lithuania, Netherlands (*), Norway, Poland, Portugal, Russia, Serbia (*), Sweden, Switzerland (*), UK (*).
NGO Relations Member of, and sends representatives to: *European Association for Psychotherapy (EAP, #06176)*. Sister organization: US Association of Body Psychotherapy (USABP). *European Federation for Bioenergetic Analysis Psychotherapy (EFBA-P, #07061)* is member. [2021/XD4724/D]

♦ European Association for Bronchology and Interventional Pulmonology (EABIP) 05959

Sec 5th Pulmonary Dept, Dr Suat Seren Training/Research Hosp for Thoracic Medicine and Surgery, Yenisehir, 35110 Izmir/Izmir, Türkiye. T. +905326614522.
Registered Office Amalienstrasse 5, 69126 Heidelberg, Germany.
URL: http://www.eabip.org/
History 8 Jun 2001, Portugal, during a scientific meeting. Previously also referred to as *EAB*. Registered in accordance with German law. **Aims** Enhance multidisciplinary and international collaboration so as to develop, evaluate, and disseminate techniques, procedures, and cases that will benefit patients with various pulmonary diseases like lung cancer, COPD, asthma, pleural processes, and other thoracic disorders. **Structure** General Assembly. Executive Committee. **Finance** Members' dues. **Events** *European Congress for Bronchology and Interventional Pulmonology* Athens (Greece) 2021, *European Congress for Bronchology and Interventional Pulmonology* Dubrovnik (Croatia) 2019, *European Congress for Bronchology and Interventional Pulmonology* Dubrovnik (Croatia) 2017, *European Congress for Bronchology and Interventional Pulmonology* Barcelona (Spain) 2015, *European Congress for Bronchology and Interventional Pulmonology* Cesme (Turkey) 2013. **Publications** *Respiration* (6 a year) – journal. **NGO Relations** Member of: *World Association for Bronchology and Interventional Pulmonology (WABIP, #21121)*. [2015/XM8223/D]

- ♦ European Association of Building and Construction Experts / see Association of European Experts in Building and Construction (The) (#02510)

♦ European Association of Burgundy Studies 05960

Centre européen d'études bourguignonnes (CEEB) – Europäisches Zentrum für Burgundische Studien

SG Université de Liège, Quai Roosevelt 1B A4, 4000 Liège, Belgium.
Asst SG address not obtained. E-mail: ceeb.14.16@gmail.com.
URL: http://ceeb.hypotheses.org/
History 1960. Also referred to in English as *European Centre for Burgundian Research*. Previously referred to in French as *Centre européen d'études burgondo-médianes*. **Aims** Promote exchanges among all interested in the period of the Dukes of Burgundy and the first Habsbourgs, at the junction between *mediaeval* and modern times in the Western world, especially covering the area between the North Sea, the Rhine and Danube and the Mediterranean Sea, where political, economic and cultural relationships appeared most intense. **Activities** Organizes symposia. **Events** *Annual Meeting* Prague (Czechia) 2019, *Annual Meeting* Vienna (Austria) 2018, *Annual Meeting* Lons-le-Saunier (France) / Arlay (France) 2017, *Annual Meeting* Münster (Germany) 2016, *Annual Meeting* Morlanwelz (Belgium) / Brussels (Belgium) 2015. **Publications** Series (annual).
Members Professional and amateur historians, whatever their specialization, in 17 countries:
Austria, Belgium, Canada, Czechia, France, Germany, Ireland, Italy, Japan, Luxembourg, Netherlands, Poland, Portugal, Russia, Switzerland, UK, USA. [2017/XE5941/v/E]

- ♦ European Association for Business Management / see European Academy of Management and Business Economics (#05801)

♦ European Association of Business and Management Teachers (inactive)
♦ European Association of Campus Security (inactive)

♦ European Association for Cancer Education (EACE) 05961

Sec Inst of Urology, Rambam Health Care Campus, HaAliya HaShniya St 8, 3109601 Haifa, Israel. T. +97247771891. E-mail: secretary@eaceonline.com.
URL: http://www.eaceonline.com/

History 1987. **Aims** Improve clinical outcomes through education and training of individuals involved within the cancer and *palliative* care continuum; facilitate communication and networking between those involved in cancer education. **Structure** General Meeting (annual, at Scientific Meeting); Board; Local Organizing Committee; Scientific Committee. **Languages** English. **Staff** 10.00 FTE, voluntary. **Finance** Members' dues. Annual budget: euro 8,000. **Activities** Training/education; events/meetings; awards/prizes/competitions. **Events** *Scientific Meeting* Krakow (Poland) 2022, *Scientific Meeting* Krakow (Poland) 2021, *Scientific Meeting* Krakow (Poland) 2020, *Scientific Meeting* Porto (Portugal) 2019, *Scientific Meeting* Haifa (Israel) 2018. **Publications** *Journal of Cancer Education* (4 a year) – jointly with 'American Association for Cancer Education'.

Members Organizations and individuals engaged in cancer education in 18 countries:
Australia, Austria, Belgium, Canada, Cyprus, Denmark, France, Germany, India, Italy, Lithuania, Netherlands, Poland, Portugal, Sweden, UK, USA, Vietnam.

IGO Relations *WHO (#20950)* Collaborating Centre for Cancer Education (WHO-CCCE). **NGO Relations** American Association for Cancer Education (AACE). [2021/XD1694/**D**]

♦ European Association for Cancer Research (EACR) 05962

Association européenne de recherche sur le cancer – Asociación Europea para Investigación del Cancer – Europäische Vereinigung für Krebsforschung – Associazione Europea per le Ricerche sul Cancro

Address not obtained.
URL: http://www.eacr.org/

History 9 Jan 1968, Amsterdam (Netherlands). Registration: Charity Commission, No/ID: 7682372, Start date: 24 Jun 2011, England and Wales; Companies House, No/ID: 07682372, England and Wales; EU Transparency Register, No/ID: 372265125077-82; Netherlands. **Aims** Advance cancer research, from basic research to prevention, treatment and care; grow as an influential organization with a strong strategic position in the European cancer continuum through interaction with stakeholders; provide a forum to raise the profile of cancer research and cancer researchers in Europe and the need for sustained political and economic support; gain, value and support increasing numbers of members through services, activities, scientific meetings, fellowships and opportunities for communication. **Structure** General Assembly, Board of 5 officers and 7 members (4-year terms). **Languages** English. **Staff** 7.00 FTE, paid. **Finance** Members' dues. Grants to support educational activities. **Activities** Events/meetings; awards/prizes/competitions; financial and/or material support. **Events** *Innovative Cancer Science Congress* Turin (Italy) 2023, *Innovative Cancer Science Congress* Seville (Spain) 2022, *Congress* 2021, *Joint Conference on Molecular Pathology Approach to Cancer* 2021, *Joint Conference on Cancer Imaging* Oxford (UK) 2021. **Publications** *e-news Bulletin* (bi-weekly); *European Journal of Cancer* (periodical) – official journal; *EACR Yearbook*.

Members Individuals (over 9,000) with academic qualifications and having held an appointment or worked actively in cancer research. Members in 81 countries and territories, predominantly European. Membership countries not specified. Affiliate – Society Members in 14 countries:
Affiliate – Society Members in 14 countries:
Belgium, Croatia, Denmark, France, Germany, Hungary, Ireland, Israel, Italy, Portugal, Serbia, Spain, Türkiye, UK.

NGO Relations Partner organization of: *European Alliance for Personalised Medicine (EAPM, #05878)*. Cooperates with: *European Society for Medical Oncology (ESMO, #08648)*. [2020/XD0547/**D**]

♦ European Association of Cardboard Manufacturers (inactive)
♦ European Association of Cardiothoracic Anaesthesiology / see European Association of Cardiothoracic Anaesthesiology and Intensive Care (#05963)

♦ European Association of Cardiothoracic Anaesthesiology and Intensive Care (EACTAIC) 05963

Main Office c/o AIM Italy, Via Flaminia 1068, 00189 Rome RM, Italy. E-mail: eactaic@aimgroup.eu.
URL: http://www.eactaic.org/

History 1986. Former names and other names: *European Association of Cardiothoracic Anaesthesiology (EACTA)* – former. **Aims** Be a forum in Europe for international scientific discussions and exchange of ideas in the field of cardiothoracic anaesthesia and related topics; promote education and development in this field. **Structure** Representative Council; Board of Directors, Committees (3): Scientific, Congress, Education; Subspecialty Committees; Task Forces. **Languages** English. **Staff** 3.00 FTE, paid. **Finance** Sources: members' dues; sponsorship. **Activities** Awards/prizes/competitions; events/meetings; financial and/or material support; training/education. **Events** *Annual Congress* Naples (Italy) 2022, *Annual Congress* 2021, *Annual Meeting* Rome (Italy) 2020, *Annual Meeting* Ghent (Belgium) 2019, *Annual Meeting* Manchester (UK) 2018. **Publications** *EACTA Newsletter*, *Journal of Cardiothoracic and Vascular Anesthesia (JCVA)*. Meeting abstracts.

Members Individuals in 47 countries:
Australia, Austria, Belgium, Bosnia-Herzegovina, Bulgaria, Canada, China, Croatia, Czechia, Denmark, Estonia, Finland, France, Georgia, Germany, Greece, Hungary, India, Iran Islamic Rep, Ireland, Israel, Italy, Japan, Jordan, Latvia, Lithuania, Luxembourg, Malta, Netherlands, Norway, Poland, Portugal, Romania, Russia, Serbia, Slovakia, Slovenia, Spain, Suriname, Sweden, Switzerland, Türkiye, UK, Ukraine, United Arab Emirates, USA, Uzbekistan.

NGO Relations Member of: *European Board of Cardiovascular Perfusion (EBCP, #06356)*. Speciality organization of: *European Society of Anaesthesiology and Intensive Care (ESAIC, #08518)*. Links with *European Association of Cardiovascular Imaging (EACVI, see: #08536)*. [2021.06.25/XD1431/v/**D**]

♦ European Association for Cardio-Thoracic Surgery (EACTS) 05964

Association européenne pour la chirurgie cardio-thoracique

Secretariat EACTS House, Madeira Walk, Windsor, SL4 1E4, UK. T. +441753832166. Fax +441753620407. E-mail: info@eacts.co.uk.
SG Thoracic Surgery, Room BD 569 Erasmus MC, PO Box 2040, 3000 CA Rotterdam, Netherlands. E-mail: secretary.general@eacts.co.uk.
URL: http://www.eacts.org/

History 1986. Registration: Charity Commission, No/ID: 1140274, England and Wales. **Aims** Promote scientific exchange between cardiac and thoracic surgeons in Europe. **Structure** General Assembly; Council. Organizational and Standing Committees. Officers. **Languages** English. **Finance** Members' dues. Income from annual meeting. **Activities** Events/meetings; awards/prizes/competitions; training/education. **Events** *Annual Meeting* Milan (Italy) 2022, *Annual Meeting* Barcelona (Spain) 2021, *Annual Meeting* Barcelona (Spain) 2020, *Annual Meeting* Lisbon (Portugal) 2019, *Annual Meeting* Milan (Italy) 2018. **Publications** *European Journal of Cardio-Thoracic Surgery* (12 a year) – printed and electronic; *MultiMedia Manual of Cardiothoracic Surgery* – journal. **Information Services** *Interactive Cardiovascular and Thoracic Surgery* – electronic publication platform.

Members Full in 48 countries:
Argentina, Australia, Austria, Belgium, Brazil, Bulgaria, Canada, Chile, Croatia, Cyprus, Czechia, Denmark, Estonia, Finland, France, Germany, Ghana, Greece, Hungary, Iceland, India, Iran Islamic Rep, Ireland, Israel, Italy, Japan, Latvia, Libya, Lithuania, Monaco, Netherlands, Norway, Poland, Portugal, Romania, Russia, Saudi Arabia, Serbia, Singapore, Slovakia, Slovenia, Spain, Sweden, Switzerland, Türkiye, UK, Ukraine, USA.

NGO Relations Member of: *Biomedical Alliance in Europe (#03251)*; *Associations and Conference Forum (AC Forum, #02909)*; *European Board of Cardiovascular Perfusion (EBCP, #06356)*. Together with: *European Society for Cardiovascular and Endovascular Surgery (ESCVS, #08537)* and *European Society of Thoracic Surgeons (ESTS, #08760)*, set up: *European Board of Cardiothoracic Surgery (EBCTS, #06355)*; *European Cardiovascular and Thoracic Surgery Institute of Accreditation (ECTSIA, #06450)*; *European School of Cardio-Thoracic Surgery (ESCTS)*. [2020/XD1717/**D**]

♦ European Association of Cardiovascular Imaging (see: #08536)
♦ European Association for Cardiovascular Prevention and Rehabilitation / see European Association of Preventive Cardiology (#06164)

♦ European Association of Career Guidance (EACG) 05965

Pres 36 Stasinou Str, Office 104, Strovolos, CY-2003 Nicosia, Cyprus. T. +35722283600. E-mail: makrides.g@ucy.ac.cy – career.eu@ucy.ac.cy.
URL: http://www.eacg.eu/

History 2010, Cyprus, following a European funded project *CAREER-EUshop* (2008-2010). **Aims** Enable information and experience exchange by career guidance counsellors and HR practitioners. **Structure** General Assembly; Management Board. **Languages** English. **Staff** 2.00 FTE, paid; 3.00 FTE, voluntary. **Finance** Members' dues. Proceeds from activities. Budget (annual): euro 30,000. **Activities** Training/education; events/meetings; knowledge management/information dissemination. Active in: Belgium, Bulgaria, Cyprus, Greece. **Publications** Conference proceedings; guidelines. **Members** Individuals (45). Membership countries not specified. **NGO Relations** *European Association of ERASMUS Coordinators (EAEC, #06030)*. [2016.07.23/XM4911/**E**]

♦ European Association of Care and Help at Home (inactive)
♦ European Association of Carton and Cartonboard Manufacturers / see Association of European Cartonboard and Carton Manufacturers (#02502)
♦ European Association of the Casing-Dressing Industry and Trade / see European Natural Sausage Casings Association (#07854)
♦ European Association on Catalysis (no recent information)

♦ European Association for Catholic Adult Education 05966

Fédération européenne pour l'éducation catholique des adultes (FEECA) – Europäische Föderation für Katholische Erwachsenenbildung – Associazione Europea per l'Educazione Cattolica degli Adulti – Europese Federatie voor Katholiek Volwassenenvorming – Europeiska Samarbetsorganet för Katolsk Vuxenutbildning – Evropska Federacija za Versko Izobrazevanje Odraslih – Katholikus Felnottképzés Europai Szövetsége

Dir Gen c/o Katholische Erwachsenenbildung, Rheinweg 34, 53113 Bonn, Germany. T. +49228902470. Fax +492289024729. E-mail: office@feeca.eu.
URL: https://feeca.eu/

History 2 May 1963, Lucerne (Switzerland). Founded at 3rd International Conference of Catholic Education Movements, when statutes were adopted. Statutes most recently amended 14 Nov 2012, Vienna (Austria). **Aims** Further exchange of experience and ideas among Catholics engaged in adult education in European countries; strengthen cooperation in research and teaching methods; facilitate international meetings of members; maintain contacts with other European and international adult education organizations and institutions; ensure continuing education for adults. **Structure** General Assembly (annual); Executive Board. **Languages** English, German. **Staff** 1 FTE in cooperation with catholic organizations has European Office for Catholic Youth and Adult Education in Brussels (Belgium). **Finance** Members' dues. Gifts. **Activities** Events/meetings; training/education. **Events** *Congress* Cologne (Germany) 2015, *Congress* Strasbourg (France) 2014, *Congress* Miercurea Ciuc (Romania) 2013, *Biennial General Assembly* Szombathely (Hungary) 2004, *Congress* Prague (Czech Rep) 2003.

Members National associations of Catholic education, or regional/linguistic groupings within a country where no national association exists, in 10 countries:
Austria, Czechia, France, Germany, Hungary, Italy, Lithuania, Luxembourg, Romania, Switzerland.

NGO Relations Member of: *Lifelong Learning Platform – European Civil Society for Education (LLLP, #16466)*. Links with a number of organizations of Christian Churches, including: *Commission of the Bishops' Conferences of the European Union (COMECE, #04205)*; *European Association for the Education of Adults (EAEA, #06018)*; *Evangelische Arbeitsgemeinschaft für Erwachsenenbildung in Europa (EAEE, inactive)*. [2020/XD0548/**D**]

♦ European Association of CCP Clearing Houses / see European Association of Central Counterparty Clearing Houses (#05967)

♦ European Association of Central Counterparty Clearing Houses (EACH) 05967

Address not obtained.
URL: http://www.eachccp.eu/

History 1991, as *European Association of Clearing Houses*. Present name adopted 2000. Also referred to as *European Association of CCP Clearing Houses*. Registered in accordance with Belgian law. EU Transparency Register: 36897011311-96. **Aims** Ensure that the evolving discussions on clearing and settlement in Europe and globally, are fully informed by the expertise and opinions of those responsible for providing central counterparty clearing services. **Structure** Plenary Assembly; Board; Secretariat. Committees; Working Groups. **Languages** English. **Staff** None. **Finance** None. **Activities** Advocacy/lobbying/activism. **Events** *Meeting* Paris (France) 2005, *Meeting* Barcelona (Spain) 2004, *Meeting* Warsaw (Poland) 2004, *Meeting* Brussels (Belgium) 2003, *Meeting* Edinburgh (UK) 2003. **Publications** Papers; reports; position papers.

Members Senior executives specializing in clearing or risk management from European clearing houses, the majority either divisions of, wholly-owned or majority-owned by exchanges and a minority not controlled by an exchange or exchanges. Members operate in 23 countries:
Austria, Belgium, Denmark, Estonia, Finland, France, Germany, Greece, Hungary, Iceland, Ireland, Italy, Latvia, Lithuania, Luxembourg, Norway, Poland, Russia, Serbia, Spain, Sweden, Switzerland, UK.

IGO Relations *European Commission (EC, #06633)*. **NGO Relations** Close cooperation with: *European Central Securities Depositories Association (ECSDA, #06468)*; *Federation of European Securities Exchanges (FESE, #09542)*. [2017/XD9133/**D**]

♦ European Association of Centres of Medical Ethics (EACME) 05968

Association européenne des centres d'éthique médicale (AECEM)

Sec VU University Medical Center Amsterdam, Dept of Ethics, Law and Humanities, Van der Boechorststraat 7, 1081 BT Amsterdam, Netherlands.
Registered Office Maastricht Univ, FHML Health/Ethics/Society, Postbus 616, 6200 MD Maastricht, Netherlands. T. +31433882145.
URL: http://www.eacmeweb.com/

History 1985. Statutes adopted 26 Sep 1986, Maastricht (Netherlands). Statutes revised 13 Apr 2015. Registration: Netherlands. **Aims** Promote public critical concern regarding ethical issues involved in developing biomedical sciences; provide members with information, documentation and other research tools on problems of ethics and health; coordinate collaborative research and exchange results; contribute to the European debate on bioethics; promote teaching of ethics among all involved in health care. **Structure** Assembly of Participants (annual); Supervisory Board; Executive Board. **Languages** English. **Staff** 1.00 FTE, paid. **Finance** Sources: donations; gifts, legacies; members' dues. **Activities** Events/meetings; financial and/or material support. **Events** *Conference* Cluj-Napoca (Romania) 2021, *Webinar* 2020, *Conference* Cluj-Napoca (Romania) 2020, *Conference* Oxford (UK) 2019, *Conference* Amsterdam (Netherlands) 2018. **Publications** *EACME News* (weekly). Conference reports.

Members Full (institutional) in 15 countries:
Belgium, Bulgaria, Czechia, France, Germany, Italy, Netherlands, Norway, Portugal, Romania, Slovakia, Spain, Sweden, Switzerland, UK.

Associate (institutions and individuals) in 13 countries:
Austria, Bulgaria, France, Germany, Iceland, Italy, Luxembourg, Portugal, Russia, Serbia, Sweden, Switzerland, UK.

Honorary in 2 countries:
Belgium, Switzerland.

IGO Relations Cooperates with (2): *European Commission (EC, #06633)*; *WHO (#20950)*. **NGO Relations** Statement of collaboration with: *European Society for Philosophy of Medicine and Health Care (ESPMH, #08698)*; *International Association of Bioethics (IAB, #11725)*. [2021/XD2114/**D**]

♦ European Association of Certified Turnaround Professionals (EACTP) 05969

Contact c/o PKF Cooper Parry, Sky View, Argosy Road, East Midlands Airport, Castle Donington, Derby, DE74 2SA, UK. T. +402082863025. E-mail: secretariat@eactp.eu.
URL: http://www.eactp.eu/

Aims Establish a European-wide accreditation programme for all turnaround professionals across the continent. **Structure** Executive Board. Committees (3): Standards and Admissions; Certification Oversight; Education and Training. **Finance** Members' dues. **Activities** Certification/accreditation. **Publications** Newsletter. **Members** Individuals. Membership countries not specified. **NGO Relations** In association with: *Turnaround Management Association – Global (TMA Global).* [2015/XM4223/t/**D**]

- ♦ European Association of Certified Valuators and Analysts (unconfirmed)
- ♦ European Association of Chemical Distributors (#09563)
- ♦ European Association for Chemical and Molecular Sciences / see European Chemical Society (#06524)
- ♦ European Association of Chemistry and the Environment / see Association of Chemistry and the Environment (#02426)
- ♦ European Association of the Chewing Gum Industry (inactive)
- ♦ European Association for Child and Adolescent Psychiatry / see European Society of Child and Adolescent Psychiatry (#08543)

♦ European Association for Children in Hospital (EACH) 05970

Association européenne pour les enfants à l'hôpital

Coodinator address not obtained.
URL: http://www.each-for-sick-children.org/

History 1993, Austria. Founded following a conference May 1988, Leiden (Netherlands). **Aims** Improve the rights and needs of children before, during or after a stay in hospital and other healthcare services. **Structure** Coordinating Committee (Executive), comprising one delegate per nation. Officers: Coordinator; General Secretary; Treasurer. **Languages** English. **Staff** 3.00 FTE, voluntary. **Finance** Sources: members' dues. **Activities** Advocacy/lobbying/activism; awareness raising; healthcare; management of treaties and agreements; networking/liaising. Manages the following treaties/agreements: *United Nations Convention on the Rights of the Child (CRC, 1989).* **Events** *Conference* Frankfurt-Main (Germany) 2018, *Conference* Utrecht (Netherlands) 2016, *Conference* Prague (Czech Rep) 2014, *Conference* Manchester (UK) 2012, *Conference* Dublin (Ireland) 2010.

Members Full: national organizations in 11 countries:
Austria, Czechia, Finland, Germany, Iceland, Ireland, Netherlands, Portugal, Sweden, Switzerland, UK (Scotland).
Associate: national organizations in 6 countries:
Austria, Croatia, France, Italy, Japan, Slovenia.
Individuals in 7 countries:
Croatia, Czechia, Greece, Hungary, Italy, Netherlands, Spain.
Honorary in 1 country:
Germany.

NGO Relations Member of (1): *Child Rights Connect (#03884).* [2023.02.14/XD5967/**D**]

- ♦ European Association of Children's Museums / see Hands On ! International Association of Children's Museums (#10856)

♦ European Association for Chinese Law (EACL) 05971

Association européenne pour l'étude du droit chinois

Contact address not obtained. E-mail: dominique.grisay@gmail.com.

History 10 Sep 1984, Strasbourg (France). Registered in accordance with Belgian law. **Aims** Further and coordinate study and knowledge of Chinese law. **Structure** General Assembly (annual). Executive Board. Standing Committees (6): Standard Contracts; Banking and Monetary Affairs; Arbitration; Maritime Law; Legal Terminology; Administrative Law. **Languages** English. **Staff** 5.00 FTE, voluntary. **Finance** Members' dues. Donations. **Activities** Provides: information; computerized documentation; research facilities; courses in Chinese law and legal terminology. Projects: Seminar for European jurists; Research and translation service; Reference library. **Events** *Annual General Assembly* Brussels (Belgium) 1989, *General assembly / Annual General Assembly* Strasbourg (France) 1988, *General assembly / Annual General Assembly* Strasbourg (France) 1987, *Annual General Assembly* Oxford (UK) 1986, *Meeting* Strasbourg (France) 1986. **Publications** *EACL Information Bulletin* (4 a year) – for members. *Chinese Law* – series.

Members Legal and sinological academics; legal practitioners. Members in 14 countries and territories:
Austria, Belgium, China, Denmark, France, Germany, Hong Kong, Ireland, Italy, Netherlands, Spain, Switzerland, UK, USA. [2013/XD5880/**D**]

♦ European Association for Chinese Philosophy (EACP) 05972

Treas Vrtaca 7, 1000 Ljubljana, Slovenia. T. +38631792574.
Sec Campus I – 3 Stock – A351, Uni Trier, FB II – Sinologie, Universitätsring 15, 54296 Trier, Germany.
URL: http://www.ea-cp.eu/

History Founded Feb 2014, Ljubljana (Slovenia). Statutes adopted Oct 2014. Registered in accordance with Slovenian law. **Aims** Encourage and advance all academic and scholarly activities related to Chinese philosophy in all European countries; create and maintain a platform for a fruitful cooperation and exchange of ideas; open a dialogue between scholars of Asian, especially Chinese intellectual history; offer a platform for the presentation and discussion of recent topical researches. **Structure** General Assembly; Board; Executive Committee. **Finance** Members' dues. **Activities** Events/meetings; guidance/assistance/support; publishing activities; networking/liaising; knowledge management/information dissemination. **Events** *Biennial Conference* Ghent (Belgium) 2019, *Biennial Conference* Basel (Switzerland) 2017. **Publications** *EACP Newsletter.* [2019/XM7536/**D**]

♦ European Association for Chinese Studies (EACS) 05973

Association européenne d'études chinoises (AEEC)

Pres c/o DSAAM, Università Ca' Foscari, Dorsoduro 3246, 30123 Venice VE, Italy.
URL: http://www.chinesestudies.eu/

History 1975. Constitution adopted by General Assembly, 1976, Paris (France). Constitution revised: 2000, Turin (Italy); 2016, St Petersburg (Russia). Former names and other names: *Association européenne de sinologie* – alias. **Aims** Promote and foster all scholarly activities related to *sinology* in Europe. **Structure** General Assembly (every 2 years); Board; Executive Committee. **Languages** Chinese, English, French. **Staff** Voluntary. **Finance** Members' dues. Other sources: public and private grants; income from special events; contributions. **Activities** Awards/prizes/competitions; events/meetings; financial and/or material support; training/education. **Events** *Biennial Conference* Tallinn (Estonia) 2024, *Biennial Conference* Olomouc (Czechia) 2022, *Biennial Conference* Leipzig (Germany) 2021, *Biennial Conference* Leipzig (Germany) 2020, *Biennial Conference* Glasgow (UK) 2018. **Publications** *EACS Newsletter* (annual); *Journal of the European Association for Chinese Studies.* Surveys of Sinology in European countries.

Members Individuals in 33 countries and territories:
Australia, Austria, Belgium, Bulgaria, Canada, China, Croatia, Czechia, Denmark, Finland, France, Georgia, Germany, Greece, Holy See, Hungary, Ireland, Italy, Netherlands, Norway, Poland, Portugal, Romania, Russia, Serbia, Slovakia, Slovenia, Spain, Sweden, Switzerland, Taiwan, UK, USA.

NGO Relations Member of: *European Alliance for the Social Sciences and Humanities (EASSH, #05885); International Union for Oriental and Asian Studies (IUOAS, inactive).* Through IUOAS, affiliated with: *International Council for Philosophy and Human Sciences (CIPSH, #13061).* [2022/XD9877/v/**D**]

- ♦ European Association of Christian Democratic Local Administrators (no recent information)
- ♦ European Association of Christian Teachers / see SIESC – European Federation of Christian Teachers (#19267)

♦ European Association of Cities Interested in the Use of Electric Vehicles 05974

Association européenne des villes intéressées par l'utilisation de véhicules électriques (CITELEC)

Head Office c/o VUB-FirW-ETEC, Pleinlaan 2, 1050 Brussels, Belgium. E-mail: citelec@vub.ac.be.
Sec Auwegemvaart 110, 2800 Mechelen, Belgium.
Pres Via A Maspoli 15, 6850 Mendrisio TI, Switzerland.

History 2 Feb 1990, Brussels (Belgium). Founded when statutes were adopted. Statutes modified, 2006. Former names and other names: *Europäische Städte mit Interesse an Elektrofahrzeugen* – alias. Registration: Belgium. **Aims** Bring together towns interested in electric, hybrid and fuel cell vehicles in urban centres; inform the public and decision-makers, define requirements, organize training and carry out studies on the impact of traffic on atmospheric pollution; study standardization in the field. **Structure** General Assembly. Administrative Council, comprising 5 to 15 members. Bureau, consisting of President, 2 Vice-Presidents, Secretary and Treasurer. **Languages** Dutch, English, French. **Staff** 1.00 FTE, paid. **Finance** Members' dues: towns euro 440 – euro 1,925 based on number of inhabitants; associate members euro 880; transport companies based on number of inhabitants in town served; individuals euro 100. **Activities** Projects: evaluation of the introduction of electric vehicles in several European cities; action of hybrid buses and electric minibuses; demonstrations; development of electrically propelled vehicle standardization and regulation. **Events** *General Assembly* Stavanger (Norway) 2009, *General Assembly* Geneva (Switzerland) 2008, *General Assembly* Monte Carlo (Monaco) 2006, *General Assembly* Brussels (Belgium) 2005, *Forum and conference / Trans European Meeting* Monte Carlo (Monaco) 2002. **Publications** *EVFOCUS.*

Members Active communes situated in countries participating in COST. Associate communes, companies, research centres, individuals in any country. Honorary. Towns (about 50) in 11 countries:
Austria, Belgium, France, Italy, Monaco, Netherlands, Norway, Spain, Sweden, UK, USA.

IGO Relations *European Commission (EC, #06633); European Cooperation in Science and Technology (COST, #06784).* **NGO Relations** Joint publication with: *European Association for Electromobility (AVERE, #06024).* [2019/XD2337/**D**]

♦ European Association of the Civil Commerce of Weapons 05975

Association Européenne de Commerce d'Armes Civiles (AECAC)

SG Gisselberger Str 10, 35037 Marburg, Germany. E-mail: info@aecac.eu.
Registered Seat Rue F Pelletier 82, 1030 Brussels, Belgium.
URL: http://www.aecac.eu/

History 1992. Registration: Banque-Carrefour des Entreprises, No/ID: 0879.973.211, Start date: 14 Mar 2006, Belgium; EU Transparency Register, No/ID: 54608658341-02, Start date: 14 Mar 2012. **Aims** Lower barriers that exist in the sector to small and medium-sized enterprises who are involved in gun and *hunting* trading.

Members Full in 14 countries:
Austria, Belgium, Cyprus, Denmark, Finland, France, Germany, Greece, Ireland, Italy, Luxembourg, Netherlands, Spain, Sweden.

NGO Relations Member of (2): *Conservation Force (#04729)* (Associate); *World Forum on Shooting Activities (WFSA, #21523).* Partner of (1): *Association of European Manufacturers of Sporting Firearms (ESFAM, #02523).* [2020/XG6986/**D**]

- ♦ European Association of Clearing Houses / see European Association of Central Counterparty Clearing Houses (#05967)

♦ European Association of Clinical Anatomy (EACA) 05976

SG Dépt d'Anatomie – Service de Radiologie Guilloz,n CHU Nancy Univ de Lorraine Hôpital Central, 29 av Maréchal de Lattre de Tassigny, CO No 34, 54035 Nancy CEDEX, France. T. +33383851687. Fax +33383859725.
URL: http://www.eaca-aeac.org/

History 1988. **Aims** Promote anatomic research applied to everyday medical practice, surgery and medical imaging; facilitate development of scientific relations; strengthen friendly bonds within the economic and geographic unity of the Europe of tomorrow. **Structure** General Assembly; Board. **Languages** English. **Staff** 11.00 FTE, voluntary. **Finance** Members' dues. **Events** *Biennial European Congress* Madrid (Spain) 2019, *Biennial European Congress* Warwick (UK) 2017, *IALM Intersocietal Symposium* Venice (Italy) 2016, *Biennial European Congress* Rouen (France) 2015, *Biennial European Congress* Lisbon (Portugal) 2013. **Publications** *Surgical and Radiologic Anatomy – Journal of Clinical Anatomy.*

Members Full in 26 countries:
Albania, Algeria, Austria, Belgium, Bulgaria, Canada, China, Côte d'Ivoire, Czechia, France, Germany, India, Italy, Japan, Korea Rep, North Macedonia, Portugal, Romania, Senegal, South Africa, Spain, Switzerland, Tunisia, Türkiye, UK, USA. [2015.08.28/XD8027/**D**]

- ♦ European Association for Clinical Neuropharmacology / see European Society for Clinical Neuropharmacology (#08549)
- ♦ European Association of Clinical Pathologists (inactive)

♦ European Association for Clinical Pharmacology and Therapeutics (EACPT) 05977

Chairperson c/o Batiment CBRS – Fac de médecine, 2 rue du Prof Descottes, 87000 Limoges CEDEX, France.
URL: http://www.eacpt.org/

History 1993. Founded following the activities of a "Working Party" formed in the early 1980s under the auspices of the WHO in Europe. **Aims** Promote the utilization of clinical pharmacological services in health care delivery; improve and harmonize the teaching of the rational use of drugs at both undergraduate and postgraduate levels; contribute with clinical pharmacological expertise to policy decisions regarding drug regulation in Europe; utilize the skills of clinical pharmacology and therapeutics in counteracting misuse of prescription drugs and other chemical substances; promote problem- and patient-oriented drug information for physicians and other health professionals; increase the input of clinical pharmacological skills in the clinical evaluation of drugs; promote high professional standards in drug prescribing and high ethical standards in clinical drug research; enable individual countries to benefit from the diversification of clinical pharmacology and therapeutics in Europe; encourage collaboration with other agencies interested in clinical pharmacology and therapeutics. **Structure** Council of 62 delegates. Executive Committee, composed of Chairman, Vice-Chairman, Treasurer, Secretary and 7 Councillors. **Languages** English. **Staff** 2.00 FTE, paid. **Finance** Members' dues: national societies pay euro 5 for each individual member. **Activities** Arranges scientific meetings, workshops and courses in clinical pharmacology and therapeutics in Europe. Organizes summer schools. **Events** *Congress* Lille (France) 2027, *Congress* Helsinki (Finland) 2025, *Congress* Rotterdam (Netherlands) 2023, *Congress* Athens (Greece) 2022, *Congress* Athens (Greece) 2021. **Publications** *Basic and Clinical Pharmacology and Toxicology* – journal.

Members National societies in 29 countries:
Austria, Belgium, Bosnia-Herzegovina, Bulgaria, Croatia, Czechia, Denmark, Estonia, Finland, France, Georgia, Germany, Greece, Hungary, Israel, Italy, Lithuania, Netherlands, Norway, Portugal, Romania, Russia, Serbia, Slovakia, Spain, Sweden, Switzerland, Türkiye, UK.

NGO Relations Observer at: *European Federation for Pharmaceutical Sciences (EUFEPS, #07192).* Member of: *International Union of Basic and Clinical Pharmacology (IUPHAR, #15758).* Close links with: *International Society of Pharmacovigilance (ISoP, #15356).* [2022/XD5711/**D**]

♦ European Association for Coal and Lignite (EURACOAL) 05978

SG Rue de la Science 14b, 1040 Brussels, Belgium. T. +3227753170. E-mail: euracoal@euracoal.org.
Pres address not obtained.
Vice-Pres address not obtained.
URL: https://www.euracoal.eu/

History 21 Mar 1953. Former names and other names: *Association of the Coal Producers of the European Community* – former (21 Mar 1953); *Comité d'étude des producteurs de charbon d'Europe occidentale (CEPCEO)* – former (21 Mar 1953); *Comité de Estudios de los Productores de Carbón de la Europa Occidental* – former (21 Mar 1953); *Studienausschuss des Westeuropäischen Kohlenbergbaus* – former (21 Mar 1953); *Studie-Comité van de Westeuropese Steenkolenproducenten* – former (21 Mar 1953); *European Solid Fuels' Association* – former; *Comité européen des combustibles solides (CECSO)* – former; *Comité Europeo de Combustibles Sólidos* – former; *Europäischer Ausschuss für Feste Brennstoffe* – former; *Association européenne du charbon et du lignite* – former; *Europäischer Stein-und Braunkohleverband* – former. Registration: Banque-Carrefour des Entreprises, No/ID: 0408.290.816, Start date: 23 Oct 2002, Belgium; EU Transparency Register, No/ID: 19853116579-64, Start date: 6 Sep 2011. **Aims** Highlight the important role of coal to secure the energy supply within the EU; Demonstrate coal's contribution to security of supply, to national and regional added value and to the protection of the environment, so as to create a satisfactory framework for coal extraction and utilization in Europe. **Structure** General Assembly; Executive Committee; Energy & Environment

Policy Committee; Market Committee; Technical Research Committee. Meetings closed. **Languages** English, French, German, Polish. **Staff** 3.00 FTE, paid. **Finance** Sources: members' dues. **Activities** Events/meetings; politics/policy/regulatory. **Events** *Plenary assembly* Brussels (Belgium) 2020, *Plenary assembly* Brussels (Belgium) 1998, *Plenary Assembly* Brussels (Belgium) 1994, *Plenary Assembly* Brussels (Belgium) 1992. **Publications** *Market Reports* (2 a year). *Coal Industry across Europe* (7th ed 2020). Brochures.
Members Full and Associate members comprising national federations, national associations, companies or institutes which have an interest in coal and/or lignite. Members in 14 countries:
Bosnia-Herzegovina, Bulgaria, Czechia, Germany, Greece, Hungary, Poland, Romania, Serbia, Slovakia, Slovenia, Spain, Türkiye, Ukraine.
IGO Relations Accredited by (2): *Central Commission for the Navigation of the Rhine (CCNR, #03687); European Commission (EC, #06633).* **NGO Relations** Member of (3): *European Energy Forum (EEF, #06986)* (as Associate); *Federation of European and International Associations Established in Belgium (FAIB, #09508); Industry4Europe (#11181).* [2020.11.25/XD3429/**E**]

♦ European Association of Cochlear Implant Users (EURO-CIU) 05979

Association européenne des porteurs d'un implant cochléaire

Pres Rue Emile Lavandier 16, L-1924 Luxembourg, Luxembourg. T. +352441746. Fax +35244222225.
URL: http://www.eurociu.org/

History 1995. **Aims** Support *deaf* people with cochlear implants. **Structure** General Assembly; Board; Executive Committee. **Languages** English, French, German. **Staff** 1.00 FTE, paid. **Finance** Members' dues. Donations. **Activities** Events/meetings; knowledge management/information dissemination. **Events** *Annual General Assembly* Wroclaw (Poland) 2019, *International Symposium* Wroclaw (Poland) 2019, *Annual General Assembly* Barcelona (Spain) 2018, *International Symposium* Helsinki (Finland) 2017, *Annual General Assembly* Varese (Italy) 2016.
Members Associations in 19 countries:
Austria, Belgium, Cyprus, Czechia, Denmark, Estonia, Finland, France, Germany, Greece, Hungary, Italy, Luxembourg, Netherlands, Norway, Spain, Sweden, Switzerland, UK.
NGO Relations Member of: *European Disability Forum (EDF, #06929).* [2018/XD6966/**D**]

♦ European Association for Cognitive Ergonomics (EACE) 05980

Association européenne d'ergonomie cognitive

Address not obtained.
URL: http://www.eace.net/

History Founded Aug 1987, Paris (France), a series of conferences having been initiated from 1982. **Aims** Gather together European researchers working to bring cognitive sciences and technical *information processing* system developments into close relationship so that: capacities and limits of the human information processing system may be taken into account when designing technical systems; learning and utilization of these technical systems may be helped by appropriate aids. **Structure** Executive Committee. **Languages** English. **Staff** 9.00 FTE, voluntary. **Finance** Members' dues. **Activities** Events/meetings. **Events** *ECCE : European Conference on Cognitive Ergonomics* Siena (Italy) 2021, *ECCE : European Conference on Cognitive Ergonomics* Siena (Italy) 2020, *ECCE : European Conference on Cognitive Ergonomics* Belfast (UK) 2019, *ECCE : European Conference on Cognitive Ergonomics* Utrecht (Netherlands) 2018, *ECCE : European Conference on Cognitive Ergonomics* Umeå (Sweden) 2017. **Publications** Books; conference proceedings.
Members Full confirmed researchers. Probationers registered doctoral students with demonstrated capacity for research in the field, all domiciled in Europe. Other persons outside Europe may become correspondents. Individuals in 25 countries:
Austria, Belgium, Bulgaria, Canada, Denmark, Finland, France, Germany, Greece, Hungary, Ireland, Israel, Italy, Luxembourg, Netherlands, Norway, Poland, Portugal, Romania, Russia, Spain, Sweden, Switzerland, UK, USA. [2017/XD1715/v/**D**]

♦ European Association for the Coir Industry (inactive)
♦ European Association of Coleopterology (#02125)
♦ European Association of Coloproctology (inactive)

♦ European Association for Commonwealth Literature and Language Studies (EACLALS) 05981

Chair School of English, Communication, Philosophy, 1 / 30 John Percival Bldg, Colum Drive, Cardiff, CF10 3EU, UK. E-mail: contact@eaclals.com – info@eaclals.eu.
URL: https://www.eaclals.com/

History 1971, as a regional branch of *Association for Commonwealth Literature and Language Studies (ACLALS, #02439).* Constitution revised 28 Apr 2011, Istanbul (Turkey). Former names and other names: *European Branch Association for Commonwealth Literature and Language Studies* – former. **Aims** Encourage and promote Commonwealth and post-colonial studies in European universities and schools; promote exchanges between scholars and, whenever possible, between students; promote young academics in the field of Commonwealth (Post-colonial) literatures in Europe. **Structure** Executive Committee; Standing Committee. **Languages** English. **Finance** Members' dues. **Activities** Events/meetings; networking/liaising; knowledge management/information dissemination. **Events** *Triennial Conference* Paris (France) 2023, *Triennial Conference* Cardiff (UK) 2021, *Triennial Conference* Cardiff (UK) 2020, *Triennial Conference* Oviedo (Spain) 2017, *Triennial Conference* Innsbruck (Austria) 2014. **Publications** *EACLALS Newsletter* (2 a year). Conference proceedings.
Members Ordinary; Student; Associate (individuals residing out of Europe). Individuals in 39 countries and territories:
Australia, Austria, Belgium, Brazil, Canada, Croatia, Cyprus, Czechia, Denmark, Finland, France, Germany, Hong Kong, India, Ireland, Italy, Japan, Latvia, Malta, Mauritius, Netherlands, New Zealand, Norway, Poland, Portugal, Romania, Senegal, Singapore, Slovakia, Slovenia, South Africa, Spain, Sri Lanka, Sweden, Switzerland, UK, United Arab Emirates, USA, Zimbabwe.
NGO Relations Links with other regional branches of ACLALS: East African Association for Commonwealth Literature and Language Studies (EAACLALS); *Southern African Association for Commonwealth Literature and Language Studies (SAACLALS, see: #02439); South Pacific Association for Commonwealth Literature and Language Studies (SPACLALS, see: #02439); West Indian Association for Commonwealth Literature and Language Studies (WIACLALS, #20921)*; national associations. [2022/XE4590/v/**E**]

♦ European Association of Communication Directors (EACD) 05982

Pres Square de Meeûs 37, 1000 Brussels, Belgium. T. +3222192290. Fax +3222192292. E-mail: info@eacd-online.eu.
URL: http://www.eacd-online.eu/

History Founded 8 Nov 2006, Brussels (Belgium), by over 100 founding members from 23 countries. **Aims** Attract, inspire and engage current and future communication leaders to drive excellence in the profession; offer professionals a platform to connect, deepen their expertise, share best practice, and establish and promote relevant standards. **Structure** Annual General Assembly, in Brussels (Belgium); Board of Directors; Steering Committee; Working Groups (10); Regional Groups (33). **Languages** English. **Finance** Members' dues. **Activities** Advocacy/lobbying/activism; events/meetings; guidance/assistance/consulting; awards/prizes/competitions. **Events** *EACD Summit* Brussels (Belgium) 2021, *EACD Summit* Berlin (Germany) 2019, *EU Public Affairs Conference on How Brussels Works* Brussels (Belgium) 2017, *European Communication Summit* Brussels (Belgium) 2017, *General Assembly* Brussels (Belgium) 2017. **Publications** *Communication Director* (4 a year) in English – magazine; *EACD Newsletter. European Communication Monitor Survey.* Service brochures.
Members In-house communication and public relations professionals (over 2,300) in 54 countries and territories:
Albania, Australia, Austria, Belgium, Bosnia-Herzegovina, Bulgaria, Canada, Croatia, Cyprus, Czechia, Denmark, Egypt, Estonia, Finland, France, Georgia, Germany, Greece, Hong Kong, Hungary, Iceland, India, Ireland, Italy, Kazakhstan, Kenya, Latvia, Liechtenstein, Luxembourg, Malaysia, Malta, Montenegro, Nepal, Netherlands, Norway, Poland, Portugal, Qatar, Romania, Russia, Serbia, Singapore, Slovakia, Slovenia, South Africa, Spain, Sweden, Switzerland, Tunisia, Türkiye, UK, Ukraine, United Arab Emirates, USA. [2016.06.01/XM0176/**D**]

♦ European Association for Communication in Healthcare / see International Association for Communication in Healthcare (#11792)

♦ European Association of Communications Agencies (EACA) 05983

Dir Gen Avenue Defacqz 78, 1060 Brussels, Belgium. T. +3227400714. E-mail: info@eaca.eu.
URL: https://eaca.eu/

History 24 Sep 1960, Oslo (Norway). Founded following preliminary meetings 1957-1959. Former names and other names: *European Association of Advertising Agencies (EAAA)* – former; *Association européenne des agences de publicité* – former; *Europäische Vereinigung der Werbeagenturen* – former. Registration: Banque-Carrefour des Entreprises, No/ID: 0422.332.060, Start date: 23 Dec 1981, Belgium; EU Transparency Register, No/ID: 397482431021-09, Start date: 3 Apr 2018. **Aims** Promote: honest, effective advertising; high professional standards; awareness of the contribution of advertising in a free market economy; close cooperation between agencies, advertisers and media in European advertising bodies; an optimal external and internal operating environment for advertising agencies. **Structure** Council (once a year); Board of Directors; President; Director-General; Secretariat. Each group of members constitutes a committee, each with its own Chairman who is a member of the Board ex officio. **Languages** English. **Staff** 7.00 FTE, paid. **Finance** Sources: members' dues. **Activities** Advocacy/lobbying/activism; awards/prizes/competitions; events/meetings; politics/policy/regulatory; training/education. **Events** *Seminar on how to Specialise in Regulation and Competition Policy in the Digital Economy* Brussels (Belgium) 2019, *Evolution Lab Meeting* Brussels (Belgium) 2018, *Evolution Lab Meeting* Brussels (Belgium) 2017, *A4UExpo : affiliate marketing conference* Amsterdam (Netherlands) 2009, *Congress* Bergen (Norway) 1999. **Publications** *EACA Newsletter* (12 a year). **Members** Membership organized into 5 councils: International Agencies' Council (IAC) – the 9 largest international agencies in Europe; National Associations' Council (NAC) – the national agency associations in 30 European markets; Integrated Marketing Communications Council of Europe (IMCC) – 8 national associations of leading sales promotion agencies in Europe; Media Agencies' Council (MAC) – 8 international media networks; Health Communications Council (HCC) – key players in European Health Communications. **Consultative Status** Consultative status granted from: *World Intellectual Property Organization (WIPO, #21593)* (Permanent Observer Status). **IGO Relations** Officially recognized by: *European Commission (EC, #06633); FAO (#09260).* **NGO Relations** Member of (3): *Creative Media Business Alliance (CMBA, #04947); European Interactive Digital Advertising Alliance (EDAA, #07582); Global Alliance for Responsible Media (GARM, #10224).* [2022.10.19/XD0561/**D**]

♦ European Association for Comparative Economic Studies (EACES) . 05984

Pres Inst for Economics of Hungarian Ac of Sciences, Budaörsiút 45, Budapest 1112, Hungary. T. +3613092652.
Sec address not obtained.
URL: http://www.eaces.eu/

History 29 Sep 1990, Verona (Italy). Founded 29 Sept 1990, Verona (Italy). Registered in accordance with German law. **Aims** Promote and coordinate international collaboration in the field of comparative study of economic systems, with specific focus on European transition processes. **Structure** General Assembly (every 2 years); Executive Committee; Managing Board; Advisory Board. **Languages** English. **Staff** Voluntary. **Finance** Members' dues. **Activities** Events/meetings; awards/prizes/competitions. **Events** *Biennial Conference and General Assembly* 2021, *Biennial Conference and General Assembly* Naples (Italy) 2020, *Biennial Conference and General Assembly* Warsaw (Poland) 2018, *World Congress of Comparative Economics* St Petersburg (Russia) 2017, *Biennial Conference and General Assembly* Regensburg (Germany) 2016. **Publications** *EACES Newsletter* (4 a year) – internal; *Economic Systems; European Journal for Comparative Economics (EJCE).*
Members Full in 28 countries:
Albania, Austria, Belgium, Bulgaria, Croatia, Czechia, Denmark, Estonia, Finland, France, Germany, Greece, Hungary, Israel, Italy, Japan, Netherlands, Poland, Portugal, Romania, Russia, Serbia, Slovakia, Slovenia, Spain, UK, Ukraine, USA. [2017.10.26/XD6402/**D**]

♦ European Association for Comparative Tests (inactive)

♦ European Association for Computer Assisted Language Learning (EUROCALL) 05985

SG Ulster Univ, Cromore Road, Coleraine, BT52 1SA, UK. T. +442870123992. E-mail: secretary@eurocall-languages.org.
URL: http://www.eurocall-languages.org/

History 1993, Hull (UK). UK Registered Charity: 1041889. **Aims** Promote the use of *foreign languages* within Europe: provide a European focus for all aspects of the use of technology for language learning; enhance quality, dissemination and efficiency of computer assisted language learning materials. **Structure** Executive Committee. **Languages** English. **Staff** 0.50 FTE, paid. **Finance** Members' dues. Conference surpluses. **Activities** Knowledge management/information dissemination; research/documentation; events/meetings. **Events** *Annual Conference* Paris (France) 2021, *Annual Conference* Copenhagen (Denmark) 2020, *Annual Conference* Louvain-la-Neuve (Belgium) 2019, *Annual Conference* Jyväskylä (Finland) 2018, *Annual Conference* Groningen (Netherlands) 2014. **Publications** *ReCALL Journal* (3 a year); *EUROCALL Review* – online. Conference Short Papers.
Members Individual; Corporate; Benefactor; Student. Individuals in 36 countries and territories:
Australia, Austria, Belgium, Canada, Cyprus, Czechia, Denmark, Estonia, Finland, France, Germany, Greece, Hong Kong, Hungary, Iceland, Ireland, Israel, Italy, Japan, Kosovo, Latvia, Mexico, Netherlands, New Zealand, Norway, Poland, Portugal, Romania, Singapore, Spain, Sweden, Switzerland, Taiwan, Türkiye, UK, USA.
Corporate members in 20 countries and territories:
Austria, Belgium, Canada, Cyprus, Czechia, Denmark, Finland, France, Germany, Greece, Ireland, Italy, Netherlands, Portugal, Russia, Spain, Sweden, Switzerland, Türkiye, UK.
NGO Relations Member of: *WorldCALL (#21256).* Affiliated with: *International Association for Language Learning Technology (IALLT)* [2020/XD6727/**D**]

♦ European Association for Computer Graphics (EUROGRAPHICS) ... 05986

Association européenne pour les graphiques sur l'ordinateur

Sec Postfach 2926, 38629 Goslar, Germany. Fax +4953216762998. E-mail: secretary@eg.org.
Registered Office c/o Fiduciaire A Richard SA, Avenue de Frontenex 32, 1207 Geneva, Switzerland.
URL: https://www.eg.org/

History 1980. Registered in accordance with Swiss Civil Code. **Aims** Contribute and promote the advancement of computer graphics, primarily in Europe, by all suitable means. **Structure** General Assembly (annual); Executive Committee. **Languages** English. **Staff** 40.00 FTE, voluntary. **Finance** Members' dues. **Activities** Events/meetings; training/education. **Events** *Annual Conference* Vienna (Austria) 2021, *Annual Conference* Genoa (Italy) 2019, *EuroVis : Symposium on Visualization* Brno (Czechia) 2018, *Symposium on Rendering* Karlsruhe (Germany) 2018, *Annual Symposium on Geometry Processing* Paris (France) 2018. **Publications** *Computer Graphics Forum* (9 a year). Workshop proceedings series; conference proceedings.
Members Individuals in 43 countries and territories:
Australia, Austria, Belgium, Brazil, Bulgaria, Canada, China, Colombia, Cyprus, Czechia, Denmark, Finland, France, Germany, Greece, Hong Kong, Hungary, India, Ireland, Israel, Italy, Japan, Korea Rep, Lithuania, Malta, Mexico, Netherlands, New Zealand, Norway, Poland, Portugal, Russia, Singapore, Slovenia, South Africa, Spain, Sweden, Switzerland, Taiwan, Thailand, Türkiye, UK, USA.
Also in Caribbean. [2018.09.04/XD8998/v/**D**]

♦ European Association for Computer Science Logic (EACSL) 05987

Pres TU Dortmund, Fak für Informatik, 44227 Dortmund, Germany.
URL: http://www.eacsl.org/

History 14 Jul 1992, Wadern (Germany). **Aims** Promote computer science logic in the areas of scientific research and education; support both basic and application oriented research. **Structure** Executive Board; Scientific Council. **Languages** English, German. **Finance** Members' dues. **Activities** Events/meetings; training/education; awards/prizes/competitions. **Events** *Annual Conference* Göttingen (Germany) 2022, *Annual Conference* Ljubljana (Slovenia) 2021, *Annual Conference* Barcelona (Spain) 2020, *Annual Conference* Birmingham (UK) 2018, *Annual Conference* Stockholm (Sweden) 2017. **Publications** Conference proceedings.
Members Individuals in 22 countries:
Australia, Belgium, Canada, Croatia, Czechia, Denmark, Finland, France, Germany, Israel, Italy, Netherlands, New Zealand, Norway, Poland, Portugal, Russia, Spain, Sweden, Switzerland, UK, USA.
NGO Relations Member of (1): *International Federation for Computational Logic (IFCoLog, #13397).* Sponsors: *Workshop on Logic, Language, Information and Computation (WoLLIC).* [2019.02.13/XD6173/v/**D**]

♦ European Association for Concentrative Movement Therapy (#05757)

- ♦ European Association of Concert Managers / see Association Européenne des Agents Artistiques (#02554)
- ♦ European Association for the Conservation of Energy / see European Alliance of Companies for Energy Efficiency in Buildings (#05865)
- ♦ European Association for the Conservation of the Geological Heritage / see International Association for the Conservation of the Geological Heritage (#11810)
- ♦ European Association of Conservatories (#02560)
- ♦ European Association for Construction Labour Research / see European Institute for Construction Labour Research (#07549)
- ♦ European Association for Construction Repair, reinforcement and protection (unconfirmed)

♦ European Association of Consultants to and about Not-For-Profit Organisations (EUConsult) 05988

Exec Sec c/o Dohnensteig 5A, 13467 Berlin, Germany. T. +493040536845.
URL: http://www.euconsult.org/

History 1991, Amsterdam (Netherlands). **Aims** Provide a forum for consultants to the not-for-profit sector, encouraging collaboration, stimulating ethical and professional behaviour, and developing technical and business skills of members. **Structure** Annual General Meeting; Board. **Languages** English. **Staff** None. **Finance** Members' dues. Conference fees. **Activities** Events/meetings. **Events** *Summer Conference* Berlin (Germany) 2022, *Summer Conference* Strasbourg (France) 2015, *Winter Workshop* London (UK) 2014, *Summer Conference* Vienna (Austria) 2014, *Summer Conference* Copenhagen (Denmark) 2013.
Members Consulting firms in 12 countries:
Austria, Belgium, Denmark, France, Germany, Ireland, Italy, Netherlands, Portugal, Spain, Switzerland, UK.
[2019.10.18/XD6820/**D**]

- ♦ European Association for Consultation Liaison Psychiatry and Psychosomatics (inactive)
- ♦ European Association of Consumer Electronics Manufacturers (inactive)

♦ European Association for the Consumption-based Billing of Energy Costs (EVVE) 05989

Association européenne pour le décompte des coûts énergétiques sur la base de la consommation – Europäischer Verein zur Verbrauchsabhängigen Energiekostenabrechnung

Managing Dir Heilsbachstrasse 24, 53123 Bonn, Germany. T. +49228351496. Fax +49228358371. E-mail: info@evve.com.
Dir Gen address not obtained.
URL: http://www.evve.com/

History 1993, Copenhagen (Denmark). Registration: No/ID: 20 VR 8062, Germany, Bonn; EU Transparency Register, No/ID: 74838936515-43. **Aims** Promote introduction of consumption-based billing of energy costs Europe-wide; solve problems arising in this specific branch to economic, juridical and technological benefit of all members; represent interests of members with institutions of the European Community and its member states. **Structure** General Meeting (annual); Board; Presidency. **Languages** English, French, German. **Staff** 3.00 FTE, paid. **Finance** Sources: members' dues. Annual budget: 430,000 EUR. **Events** *Annual general meeting* Vienna (Austria) 2019, *Shaping the Future of Energy Efficiency in Buildings – Cost Effective and Sustainable* Brussels (Belgium) 2018, *Annual General Meeting* Rome (Italy) 1999, *European workshop on energy cost allocation in buildings* Brussels (Belgium) 1997. **Publications** *Guidelines for the Billing of Heating, Air-Conditioning and Hot Water Heating Costs according to the Actual Consumption.*
Members Full in 8 countries:
Austria, Denmark, France, Germany, Luxembourg, Netherlands, Slovenia, Spain.
Associate (1) in 1 country:
Germany.
IGO Relations Projects with *European Commission (EC, #06633).* [2021.09.07/XD5626/**D**]

- ♦ European Association for Contemporary History / see Association internationale d'histoire contemporaine de l'Europe (#02705)
- ♦ European Association of Contract Research Organizations (inactive)
- ♦ European Association for the Control of Structures (no recent information)
- ♦ European Association for Cooperation (inactive)

♦ European Association of Co-operative Banks (EACB) 05990

Groupement européen des banques coopératives (GEBC) – Europäische Vereinigung der Genossenschaftsbanken

Secretariat Rue de l'Industrie 26-38, 1040 Brussels, Belgium. T. +3222301124. Fax +3222300649. E-mail: secretariat@eacb.coop.
URL: http://www.eacb.coop/

History 1 Oct 1970, Brussels (Belgium). Former names and other names: *Association of Co-operative Savings and Credit Institutions of the EEC* – former (1 Oct 1970); *Groupement des coopératives d'épargne et de crédit de la CEE* – former (1 Oct 1970); *Vereinigung der Spar- und Kreditgenossenschaften der EWG* – former (1 Oct 1970); *Association of Co-operative Banks of the EC* – former (1993); *Groupement des banques coopératives de la CE* – former (1993); *Vereinigung der Genossenschaftsbanken der EG* – former (1993); *Banques coopératives* – alias. Registration: EU Transparency Register, No/ID: 4172526951-19; AISBL/IVZW, No/ID: 0896.081.149, Belgium. **Aims** Represent, promote and defend the values of the cooperative banking model in Europe and on global stage. **Structure** Board; Executive Committee; General Secretariat. **Languages** English, French, German. **Staff** 13.00 FTE, paid. **Finance** Members' dues. **Activities** Advocacy/lobbying/activism; events/meetings; research/documentation. **Events** *Convention on Cooperative Banks* Brussels (Belgium) 2020, *Convention on Cooperative Banks* Brussels (Belgium) 2017, *European Forum on Co-operative Banks & SMEs* Brussels (Belgium) 2016, *Convention on Cooperative Banks* Brussels (Belgium) 2015, *European Forum on Co-operative Banks & SMEs* Brussels (Belgium) 2014. **Publications** *Roadmap for Co-operative Banks.* Annual Report; position papers; press releases.
Members Full members: cooperative banks (20) in 15 countries:
Austria, Bulgaria, Cyprus, Finland, France, Germany, Greece, Italy, Luxembourg, Netherlands, Poland, Portugal, Romania, Slovenia, Spain.
Associate members in 7 countries:
Belgium, Canada, Denmark, Japan, Lithuania, Switzerland, UK.
NGO Relations Member of: *Cooperatives Europe (#04801); European Financial Reporting Advisory Group (EFRAG, #07254); European Payments Council (EPC, #08175); International Co-operative Alliance (ICA, #12944).* Together with *European Banking Federation (EBF, #06312)* and *European Savings and Retail Banking Group (ESBG, #08426),* set up: *European Banking Industry Committee (EBIC, #06314); European Committee for Banking Standards (ECBS, inactive); European Payments Council (EPC, #08175).* [2020/XE8512/**D**]

- ♦ European Association for the Coordination of Consumer Representation in Standardization (#02561)

♦ European Association for Co-Processing (EUCOPRO) 05991

Pres Holcim Group Services, Government Relations, Rue Vilain XIIII no 53-55, 7th Floor, 1000 Brussels, Belgium. E-mail: contact@eucopro.org.
URL: http://www.eucopro.org/

History EU Transparency Register: 75111426376-95. **Aims** Represent pre-treatment companies that prepare alternative fuels and raw materials, mainly from hazardous waste, so as to recover them in co-processing processes, such as cement kiln. **Structure** General Assembly; Board of Directors; Bureau.
Members Companies (16) in 11 countries:
Austria, Belgium, France, Germany, Greece, Italy, Netherlands, Poland, Romania, Slovakia, Spain. [2019/XM0046/**D**]

♦ European Association of Corporate Treasurers (EACT) 05992

Chair 46 rue d'Amsterdam, 75009 Paris, France. E-mail: secretary@eact.eu.
URL: https://eact.eu/

History 2002. Registration: EU Transparency Register, No/ID: 674630747738-35, Start date: 26 Sep 2022. **Aims** Be the voice of treasury professionals in Europe. **Structure** Board of Directors (meets twice a year). **Languages** English. **Staff** 2.00 FTE, paid. **Activities** Awareness raising; events/meetings; knowledge management/information dissemination; networking/liaising; politics/policy/regulatory. **Events** *Annual Summit* La Hulpe (Belgium) 2019, *Meeting* Brussels (Belgium) 2011. **Publications** *Journeys to treasury* in English – The treasury – and the treasurer – of 2025 is likely to be almost unrecognisable to that of a decade earlier.
Members National associations (23) in 21 countries:
Austria, Belgium, Croatia, Czechia, Finland, France, Germany, Greece, Hungary, Ireland, Italy, Luxembourg, Netherlands, Poland, Romania, Slovakia, Slovenia, Spain, Sweden, Switzerland, UK.
Russian member currently suspended.
NGO Relations Member of (1): *International Group of Treasury Associations (IGTA, #13759).*
[2022/XM1512/**D**]

♦ European Association for Counselling (EAC) 05993

Association européenne de counselling

Admin Office 23 Cranwell Court, Newcastle upon Tyne, NE3 2UX, UK. E-mail: office@eac.eu.com.
Registered Office Rue de la Concorde 53, 1050 Brussels, Belgium.
URL: http://www.eac.eu.com/

History 1992. Statutes adopted 1998. Registration: Banque-Carrefour des Entreprises, No/ID: 0463.515.092, Start date: 18 Jun 1998, Belgium. **Aims** Further develop the profession of counselling in Europe and ensure its official recognition; form partnerships in policy development at national and European Union levels; establish a European accreditation standard for individuals and training course providers. **Structure** Annual General Meeting; Executive Council. **Languages** English. **Staff** 0.50 FTE, paid. **Finance** Sources: members' dues. **Activities** Certification/accreditation; events/meetings; politics/policy/regulatory. **Events** *General Assembly* Rome (Italy) 2022, *Crisis Communication – Connecting and Disconnecting in Modern Era* Belgrade (Serbia) 2019, *Resource Orientation & Peer Support* Cologne (Germany) 2018, *Counselling children and adolescents – new insights* St Julian's (Malta) 2014, *Conference* Valletta (Malta) 2014. **Publications** *Counselling in Europe; Training, Standards, Research, 'Culture' & Information about 39 Countries* (2021) by Dr Dirk Rohr; *EAC Accredited Member Register.*
Members Individuals and organizations in 19 countries:
Belgium, Cyprus, France, Germany, Greece, Hungary, Ireland, Israel, Italy, Malaysia, Malta, Netherlands, Portugal, Russia, Serbia, Spain, Sweden, Switzerland, UK.
NGO Relations Member of (1): *Geneva Global Health Hub (G2H2, #10122).* [2022.10.07/XD5687/**D**]

♦ European Association of Counselling Psychology (EACP) 05994

Contact address not obtained. E-mail: eacp.membership@gmail.com – ejcop.contact@gmail.com.
URL: http://www.eacp.eu/

History 2006. Registered in accordance with UK law. **Aims** Support development and application of counselling psychology across Europe. **Structure** Council; Officers. **Activities** Awards/prizes/competitions. **Publications** *European Journal of Counselling Psychology (EJCoP).*
Members Full; Associate; Affiliate. Members in 8 countries:
Cyprus, Greece, Ireland, Italy, Malta, Portugal, Spain, UK.
NGO Relations Affiliated to: *International Union of Psychological Science (IUPsyS, #15807).*
[2019.06.10/XJ5135/**D**]

- ♦ European Association for Country Planning Institutions / see European Association for Rural Development Institutions (#06198)
- ♦ European Association of Craft, Small and Medium-Sized Enterprises / see SMEunited (#19327)

♦ European Association for Cranio-Maxillo-Facial Surgery (EACMFS) 05995

Société européenne de chirurgie cranio-maxillo-faciale

Secretariat Administrator PO Box 85, Midhurst, GU29 9WS, UK. T. +441730810951. E-mail: secretariat@eacmfs.org.
URL: http://www.eacmfs.org/

History 1970, Zurich (Switzerland). Founded as *European Association for Maxillo-Facial Surgery (EAMFS) – Société européenne de chirurgie maxillo-faciale – Europäische Gesellschaft für Kiefer-Gesichtschirurgie.* Registration: Swiss Civil Code, Switzerland. **Aims** Promote the theory and practice of cranio-maxillo-facial surgery; develop equivalent standards of training in the speciality in Europe. **Structure** General Assembly (every 2 years); Council; Executive Committee. **Languages** English. **Staff** One paid; voluntary. **Finance** Members' dues. **Activities** Training/education; knowledge management/information dissemination; networking/liaising. **Events** *Congress* Amsterdam (Netherlands) 2028, *Congress* Athens (Greece) 2026, *Congress* Rome (Italy) 2024, *FACE AHEAD – Young Surgeons CMF Summit* Barcelona (Spain) 2022, *Congress* Madrid (Spain) 2022. **Publications** *Journal of Cranio-Maxillo-Facial Surgery.*
Members Individuals Active; Associate; Trainees; Retired; Honorary. Members in 52 countries and territories:
Armenia, Australia, Austria, Belarus, Belgium, Brazil, Bulgaria, Canada, Côte d'Ivoire, Croatia, Cyprus, Denmark, Egypt, Estonia, Finland, France, Germany, Greece, Hong Kong, Hungary, Iceland, India, Iran Islamic Rep, Ireland, Israel, Italy, Japan, Korea Rep, Latvia, Lithuania, Malaysia, Moldova, Montenegro, Netherlands, Nigeria, Norway, Philippines, Poland, Portugal, Romania, Russia, Saudi Arabia, Serbia, Slovakia, Slovenia, South Africa, Spain, Sweden, Switzerland, Türkiye, UK, USA.
[2021/XD4426/v/**D**]

♦ European Association of Creative Writing Programmes (EACWP) ... 05996

Community Manager address not obtained. E-mail: info@eacwp.org.
Pres address not obtained.
URL: http://eacwp.org/

History 2005, as *European Network of Creative Writing Programmes (ENCWP).* New statutes and current title adopted Sep 2010. **Aims** Foster exchange of students, teachers and scholars and disseminate information, ideas and knowledge in the field of creative writing. **Structure** Board. **Languages** English. **Staff** 1.00 FTE, paid. Voluntary. **Finance** Members' dues. Grants. **Activities** Training/education; events/meetings; projects/programmes. **Events** *Symposium* Arnhem (Netherlands) 2020, *Symposium* Barcelona (Spain) 2019, *Symposium* Brussels (Belgium) 2018, *Symposium* Vienna (Austria) 2017, *Symposium* Turin (Italy) 2016.
Members Institutional; Individual; Non-European Observer; Honorary. Institutional (28) in 15 countries:
Argentina, Austria, Belgium, Czechia, Denmark, Finland, France, Italy, Lebanon, Netherlands, Norway, Portugal, Spain, Türkiye, UK.
IGO Relations *European Commission (EC, #06633)* Erasmus+. [2016.06.01/XM4611/**D**]

- ♦ European Association for Creativity by Disabled People / see International Association for the Arts, the Media and Creativity by and with Disabled People (#11713)

♦ European Association for Creativity and Innovation (EACI) 05997

Chairman address not obtained.
Sec address not obtained.
URL: http://www.eaci.net/

History 27 Oct 1993. Founded deriving from *Periscope (inactive)* of European creativity and innovation practitioners which had existed since 1985. Registration: Netherlands. **Aims** Foster creativity in innovation. **Structure** General Assembly; General Board; Executive Board; Office in Antwerp (Belgium). **Languages** Dutch, English, French, German. **Staff** 2.00 FTE, paid. **Finance** Sources: members' dues. **Activities** Events/meetings; knowledge management/information dissemination; monitoring/evaluation; networking/liaising; projects/programmes; research and development; training/education. **Events** *Conference* Faro (Portugal) 2011, *Conference* Brussels (Belgium) 2009, *Conference* Copenhagen (Denmark) 2007, *Transformations* Lódz (Poland) 2005, *The cross-cultural innovation concept* Mainz (Germany) 2003. **Publications** *Creativity and Innovation Management Journal.*
Members Individual; Corporate. Members in 19 countries:
Belgium, Brazil, Canada, Denmark, France, Germany, Italy, Japan, Korea Rep, Malta, Mexico, Netherlands, Norway, Poland, Portugal, Sweden, UK, USA, Vietnam. [2019/XD4201/**D**]

♦ European Association of Credit Rating Agencies (EACRA) 05998

Main Office 84 avenue de la République, 75011 Paris, France. E-mail: office@eacra.fr.
URL: http://eacra.eu/

History Nov 2009. Current articles adopted Apr 2014. Registration: No/ID: W751202513, France; EU Transparency Register, No/ID: 24205924101-57. **Aims** Offer opportunities for EU-based CRAs to meet. **Structure** General Assembly; Board. **Finance** Members' dues. **Activities** Events/meetings. **Events** *Meeting* Vienna (Austria) 2017. **Publications** Position papers.
Members Corporate; Associate. Members in 5 countries:
Germany, Italy, Spain, Switzerland, Türkiye. [2022/XM6652/**D**]

♦ **European Association for Critical Animal Studies (EACAS)** **05999**

Contact address not obtained. E-mail: eacas.eu@gmail.com.
URL: http://www.eacas.eu/

History 2015. Founded by Richard Twine and Tereza Vandrovcová. **Aims** Bring together european CAS scholars and activists who are interested in the field of Critical Animal Studies. **Structure** Non-hierarchical association of academics and activists. **Activities** Events/meetings. **Events** *Conference* Lowestoft (UK) 2021, *Conference* Barcelona (Spain) 2019, *European Conference for Critical Animal Studies* Lund (Sweden) 2017, *European Conference of Critical Animal Studies* Lisbon (Portugal) 2015, *European Conference of Critical Animal Studies* Karlsruhe (Germany) 2013. [2022.05.10/XM7852/**D**]

♦ **European Association of Cultural Researchers (ECURES)** **06000**

SG ERICarts, Ulmenallee 24a, 50999 Cologne, Germany. T. +4922365097972.
Pres Univ of Barcelona, Gran Via de les Corts Catalanes 585, 08007 Barcelona, Spain. E-mail: annavillar-roya@ub.edu.
URL: http://www.ecures.org/

History Founded 1993, Bonn (Germany). **Aims** Advance cultural research through conferences, publications and other means; assist members in their comparative research projects. **Structure** Assembly of Members; Board; Secretariat located at ERICarts Institute. **Languages** English. **Staff** 1.00 FTE, paid; 1.00 FTE, voluntary. **Finance** Revenue from shares in *European Institute for Comparative Cultural Research (ERICarts, #07547)*; projects. **Activities** Events/meetings; publishing activities; projects/programmes. **Events** *General Assembly* Paris (France) 2019. **Members** (113) in 34 countries. Membership countries not specified. **IGO Relations** *Council of Europe (CE, #04881)*; *UNESCO (#20322)*. **NGO Relations** *European Institute for Comparative Cultural Research (ERICarts, #07547)*. Standing member of: *Association of the Compendium of Cultural Policies and Trends (CCPT Association, #02442)*. [2020.03.05/XM1782/**D**]

♦ **European Association of Curriculum Studies (Euro-ACS)** **06001**

Contact Univ of Minho, Research Ctr in Education, Gualtar Campus, 4710-057 Braga, Portugal. T. +351253601200. Fax +351253604248. E-mail: euroacs@ie.uminho.pt.
URL: http://webs.ie.uminho.pt/euroacs/

History Launched 18 Oct 2013. **Aims** Contribute to development of collaborative research efforts among scholars interested in Curriculum Studies; promote curriculum research in Europe. **Structure** Officers: President; Vice-President; Secretary; Treasurer. **Languages** English. **Staff** 4.00 FTE, paid; 1.00 FTE, voluntary. **Finance** Conference fees; proceeds from publications. Budget (annual): euro 10,000. **Events** *European Conference* Maynooth (Ireland) 2019, *European Conference* Tallinn (Estonia) 2017, *European Conference* Adana (Turkey) 2015, *European Conference* Braga (Portugal) 2013. **Publications** *International Journal of Curriculum Studies* (2 a year).
Members Full in 19 countries:
Australia, Belgium, Brazil, Canada, Cyprus, Denmark, Estonia, Finland, Germany, Ireland, Luxembourg, Netherlands, Norway, Portugal, South Africa, Spain, Türkiye, UK, USA.
NGO Relations *International Association for the Advancement of Curriculum Studies (IAACS, #11685)*; national associations. [2014.09.23/XJ6761/**D**]

♦ **European Association of Daily Newspapers in Minority and Regional Languages (Midas)** **06002**

Europäische Vereinigung von Tageszeitungen in Minderheiten- und Regionalsprachen – Associazione Europea dei Quotidiani in Lingua Minoritaria e Regionale

Sec European Academy Bozen/Bolzano, Drusus Allee 1/Viale Druso 1, 39100 Bolzano, Italy. T. +39471055210. Fax +39471055299.
URL: http://www.midas-press.org/

History Founded 28 Jul 2001, Palma (Spain). Also referred as to *Minority Dailies Association*. Registered in accordance with Italian law. **Aims** Coordinate strategies and stimulate cooperation in the areas of information exchange, printing and marketing; organize campaigns; obtain support from EU institutions for minority languages and their print media. **Structure** General Assembly. Governing Board, comprising President and 6 members. Court of Arbitration. General Secretary. **Finance** Members' dues. Third party funds. **Activities** Awards prizes: Midas Prize for Journalism; Otto von Habsburg Prize for Journalism. **Events** *General Assembly* Flensburg (Germany) 2013, *General Assembly* Bratislava (Slovakia) 2012, *General Assembly* Bolzano (Italy) 2011, *General Assembly* Vilnius (Lithuania) 2010, *General Assembly* Barcelona (Spain) 2009. **Publications** *Minority Dailies Association MIDAS: European Association of Daily Newspapers in Minority and Regional Languages, 10-year Anniversary* (2010); *Minority Dailies Associations MIDAS: European Association of Daily Newspapers in Minotiry and Regional Languages 2001-2005* (2005); *European Network of Print-Media: Future Co-operation of Minority Dailies* (2001) – conference proceedings.
Members Newspapers (29) in 12 countries:
Croatia, Czechia, Denmark, Finland, Germany, Italy, Latvia, Lithuania, Romania, Slovakia, Spain, Switzerland.
NGO Relations Affiliate member of: *World Association of Newspapers and News Publishers (WAN-IFRA, #21166)*. [2013.11.26/XJ2817/**D**]

♦ **European Association of Dairy Trade** **06003**

Association européenne du commerce des produits laitiers et dérivés (EUCOLAIT) – Europäischer Verband des Gross- und Aussenhandels mit Milcherzeugnissen – Unione Europea dei Commercianti dei Prodotti Lattiero Caseari – Europese Vereniging van Groothandelsondernemingen in Zuivelprodukten

Secretariat Rue Belliard 199, 1040 Brussels, Belgium. T. +3222374372. E-mail: info@eucolait.eu.
SG address not obtained.
Office Manager address not obtained.
URL: http://www.eucolait.eu/

History 29 Sep 1959, Bonn (Germany). Former names and other names: *European Union of Importers, Exporters and Dealers in Dairy Products* – former; *Union européenne du commerce des produits laitiers et dérivés (EUCOLAIT)* – former; *Europäische Union des Gross- und Aussenhandels mit Milcherzeugnissen* – former; *Unione Europea dei Commercianti dei Prodotti Lattiero Caseari* – former; *Europese Vereniging van Groothandelsondernemingen in Zuivelprodukten* – former. Registration: Banque Carrefour des Entreprises, No/ID: 0867.635.405, Start date: 3 Feb 1983, Belgium; EU Transparency Register, No/ID: 5159980776-55, Start date: 12 Dec 2008. **Aims** Promote the interests of the dairy trade towards the European Institutions. **Structure** Statutory General Assembly (annual); Board of Directors. **Languages** English, French, German. **Staff** 4.00 FTE, paid. **Finance** Sources: members' dues. **Activities** Events/meetings; knowledge management/information dissemination; politics/policy/regulatory; projects/programmes. **Events** *General Assembly* Brussels (Belgium) 2021, *General Assembly* Edinburgh (UK) 2019, *General Assembly* Prague (Czechia) 2018, *General Assembly* Amsterdam (Netherlands) 2017, *General Assembly* Dublin (Ireland) 2016. **Information Services** *Info-Service* – Rapid information service (daily if necessary) covering current issues and matters of urgency (exclusively for members).
Members Full in 16 countries:
Austria, Belgium, Czechia, Denmark, Estonia, Finland, France, Germany, Ireland, Italy, Lithuania, Netherlands, Poland, Portugal, Spain, UK.
IGO Relations Accredited by (1): *European Commission (EC, #06633)* (Product Committees have regular meetings in the presence of Commission representatives). **NGO Relations** Member of (2): *European Liaison Committee for Agricultural and Agri-Food Trades (#07687)*; *Federation of European and International Associations Established in Belgium (FAIB, #09508)*. [2022.05.10/XD0882/t/**D**]

♦ European Association of Dance Historians / see European Association for Dance History (#06004)

♦ **European Association for Dance History (EADH)** **06004**

Association européenne des historiens de la danse (AEHD)

Chair 9 St Margarets Avenue, Torquay, TQ1 4LW, UK. E-mail: committee@eadh.com.
URL: http://www.eadh.com/

History 1989, France, as *European Association of Dance Historians (EADH)*. **Aims** Promote education of the general public in the history of dance; develop research in the history of dance. **Structure** Committee; Council. **Languages** English, French. **Staff** 7.00 FTE, paid. **Finance** Members' dues. **Activities** Events/meetings; training/education; research/documentation. **Events** *Colonial dancing in Europe, European dancing in the colonies* Porto (Portugal) 2019, *Dutch dancing in the 20th century* Leiden (Netherlands) 2018, *Conference* London (UK) 2018, *The golden ages of Spanish dance – crossing boundaries in Europe and beyond* Seville (Spain) 2018, *Relations between music and dance* Dresden (Germany) 2017. **Publications** *Choreologica* – journal.
Members Categories: Active – European residents and either hold a degree or equivalent in dance history research, or show published evidence of genuine dance history scholarship; Associate – open to all non-Europeans or others who do not hold appropriate qualifications; Joint – 2 persons residing at same address; Corporate – libraries, dance archives and other institutions with dance related interests; Student Honorary Life. Individuals in 16 countries:
Austria, Belgium, Czechia, Denmark, Finland, France, Germany, Hungary, Iceland, Italy, Netherlands, Portugal, Spain, Sweden, UK, USA.
NGO Relations Formal contact with: *World Dance Council (WDC, #21353)*. [2019.12.12/XN3669/**D**]

♦ European Association for Data and Cloud (unconfirmed)
♦ European Association of Data Protection Professionals (unconfirmed)

♦ **European Association for Data Science (EuADS)** **06005**

Office Univ of Luxembourg – Campus Belval, Avenue de l'Université 2, L-4366 Esch-sur-Alzette, Luxembourg. E-mail: contact@euads.org.

History 2016. Registered in accordance with Luxembourg law. **Aims** Provide a setting for fostering communication and cooperation among all stakeholders of data science. **Structure** Board of Administration. **Activities** Research/documentation; knowledge management/information dissemination; events/meetings; training/education. **Events** *European Conference on Data Analysis* Bayreuth (Germany) 2019, *European Conference on Data Analysis* Paderborn (Germany) 2018, *European Conference on Data Analysis* Wroclaw (Poland) 2017, *European Conference on Data Analysis* Colchester (UK) 2015, *European Conference on Data Analysis* Bremen (Germany) 2014.
Members Institutions (5) in 3 countries:
Germany, Luxembourg, UK. [2017/XM5854/**D**]

♦ European Association of Decaffeinators (inactive)

♦ **European Association for Decision Making (EADM)** **06006**

Sec-Treas Behavioural Science Inst, Radboud Univ Nijmegen, PO Box 9104, 6500 HE Nijmegen, Netherlands.
URL: http://www.eadm.eu/

History Aug 1969, as *Subjective Probability, Utility and Decision Making (SPUDM)*. Registered in accordance with Dutch law. Present name adopted Aug 1993. **Aims** Advance and diffuse knowledge about human judgement and decision making. **Structure** Board, comprising President, President-Elect, Secretary/Treasurer and 2 members. **Languages** English. **Staff** Voluntary. **Finance** Members' dues. **Activities** Organizes conferences, workshops. Sponsors the 'Bruno de Finetti Award', for promising young researchers. **Events** *SPUDM : Subjective Probability, Utility, and Decision Making Conference* Warwick (UK) 2021, *SPUDM : Subjective Probability, Utility, and Decision Making Conference* Amsterdam (Netherlands) 2019, *SPUDM : Subjective Probability, Utility, and Decision Making Conference* Haifa (Israel) 2017, *SPUDM : Subjective Probability, Utility, and Decision Making Conference* Budapest (Hungary) 2015, *SPUDM : Subjective Probability, Utility, and Decision Making Conference* Barcelona (Spain) 2013. **Publications** *EADM Bulletin* (3 a year). Conference' proceedings.
Members in 26 countries and territories:
Australia, Austria, Belgium, Canada, Croatia, Czechia, Finland, France, Germany, Greece, Hong Kong, Hungary, Israel, Italy, Japan, Netherlands, Norway, Poland, Russia, Slovenia, Spain, Sweden, Switzerland, Türkiye, UK, USA. [2014/XD6619/**D**]

♦ European Association for the Defence of Human Rights (no recent information)

♦ **European Association of Dental Public Health (EADPH)** **06007**

Sec UCL, Dept of Epidemiology and Public Health, 1-19 Torrington Place, London, WC1E 7HB, UK. T. +447752784342. E-mail: secretary@eadph.org.
URL: http://www.eadph.org/

History 1996. Registered in accordance with German law, 1999. **Aims** Promote oral health and health strategies within Europe. **Structure** Council. Executive Board, comprising President, Vice-President, Co-President, Immediate Past President, Secretary, Treasurer, Associate Editor and 3 Executive Officers. Two Auditors. **Languages** English. **Staff** Voluntary. **Finance** Members' dues. **Events** *Annual Congress* Ghent (Belgium) 2019, *Annual Congress* Palma (Spain) 2018, *Annual Congress* Budapest (Hungary) 2016, *Annual Congress* Istanbul (Turkey) 2015, *Annual Congress* Gothenburg (Sweden) 2014. **Publications** *EADPH Newsletter* – in Community Dental Health.
Members Individuals in 29 countries and territories:
Australia, Austria, Belgium, Cyprus, Czechia, Denmark, Finland, France, Germany, Greece, Hong Kong, Hungary, Iceland, Ireland, Israel, Italy, Kuwait, Lithuania, Netherlands, Norway, Poland, Portugal, Romania, Spain, Sweden, Switzerland, Türkiye, UK, USA.
NGO Relations Member of: *Platform for Better Oral Health in Europe (#18399)*; *World Federation of Public Health Associations (WFPHA, #21476)*. [2014/XD6442/v/**D**]

♦ **European Association of Dermato-Oncology (EADO)** **06008**

Europäische Vereinigung für Dermato-Onkologie

Communications Manager Friedenstr 58, 15366 Neuenhagen bei Berlin, Germany. E-mail: info@eado.org.
Registered Headquarters Max-Högger-Strasse 6, 8048 Zurich ZH, Switzerland. T. +41442444700.
URL: http://www.eado.org/

History 1998. Registration: EU Transparency Register, No/ID: 973644438148-14, Start date: 14 May 2020. **Aims** Promote, coordinate and improve clinical and laboratory research activities in the field of skin cancer. **Structure** General Assembly (annual); Board; Executive Committee. **Activities** Events/meetings; training/education. **Events** *Congress* Vienna (Austria) 2028, *Congress* Barcelona (Spain) 2027, *Congress* Prague (Czechia) 2026, *Congress* Athens (Greece) 2025, *Congress* Rome (Italy) 2023. **Members** Full in 70 countries. Membership countries not specified. [2022.05.13/XD8165/**D**]

♦ European Association of Development Agencies / see European Association of Regional Development Agencies (#06187)

♦ **European Association for Developmental Care (EADCare)** **06009**

Association Européenne pour les Soins de Soutien au Développement (AESSD)

Contact Service du Développement et de la Croissance, Dept femme/enfant/adolescent, Hôp Universitaires de Genève, Rue Willy Donzé 6, 1205 Geneva, Switzerland. T. +41223724352. Fax +41223724315. E-mail: contact@eadcare.org.
URL: http://www.eadcare.org/

History Current statutes adopted 15 Dec 2010. Registered in accordance with Swiss Civil Code. **Aims** Promote developmental care; reunite and federate multi-disciplinary teams involved in the field of developmental care for premature, term-born babies, infants, children and adolescents based on a variety of approaches; create a reference base supporting clinical applications, training, research and scientific publications. **Structure** Annual General Meeting; Committee. **Languages** English, French. **Finance** Members' dues. **Activities** Training/education; events/meetings. **Events** *Stockholm Conference on Ultra-Early Intervention* Stockholm (Sweden) 2020, *Symposium for Developmental Care in Neonatology and Pediatrics* Madrid (Spain) 2019, *Stockholm Conference on Ultra-Early Intervention* Stockholm (Sweden) 2019, *Stockholm Conference on Ultra-Early Intervention* Stockholm (Sweden) 2018, *Symposium for Developmental Care in Neonatology and Pediatrics* Paris (France) 2017. [2020.02.14/XM8436/**D**]

♦ **European Association of Developmental Psychology (EADP)** **06010**

Sec c/o Fachb Erziehungswissenschaft, Erzabt-Klotz-Str 1, 5020 Salzburg, Austria.
URL: http://www.eadp.info/

History Statutes adopted 24 Jun 1994. Current constitution adopted 26 Oct 2010. Former names and other names: *European Society for Developmental Psychology (ESDP)* – former (1994). Registration: Netherlands. **Aims** Foster study of developmental science throughout Europe for public benefit; support and train young European researchers; promote exchange of related information between members and learned national and international organizations; promote excellence. **Structure** Council. **Languages** English. **Staff**

None. **Finance** Members' dues. **Activities** Events/meetings; awards/prizes/competitions. **Events** *European Conference on Developmental Psychology* Turku (Finland) 2023, *European Conference on Developmental Psychology* St Petersburg (Russia) 2021, *European Conference on Developmental Psychology* Athens (Greece) 2019, *European Conference on Developmental Psychology* Utrecht (Netherlands) 2017, *European Conference on Developmental Psychology* Braga (Portugal) 2015. **Publications** *European Journal of Developmental Psychology* (6 a year).
Members Individuals (a) with university degree or equivalent in an area relevant to study of human development; (b) professionals active in human development or who have published research contributing to its understanding. Members (365) in 34 countries:
Australia, Austria, Belgium, Brazil, Bulgaria, Canada, Croatia, Cyprus, Denmark, Estonia, Finland, France, Germany, Greece, Hungary, Israel, Italy, Japan, Latvia, Lithuania, Netherlands, Norway, Poland, Portugal, Romania, Russia, Slovenia, Spain, Sweden, Switzerland, Türkiye, UK, Ukraine, USA.
NGO Relations *International Society for the Study of Behavioural Development (ISSBD, #15465).* Associate member of: *European Federation of Psychologists Associations (EFPA, #07199).* [2022/XD6314/**D**]

♦ European Association for the Development of Databases in Education and Training (inactive)

♦ European Association for the Development of Railway Transport .. 06011

Association européenne pour le développement du transport ferroviaire (AEDTF) – Asociación Europea para el Desarrollo del Transporte Ferroviario – Europäischer Verband für die Entwicklung des Schienenverkehrs – Associazione Europea per lo Sviluppo del Trasporto Ferroviario
Pres 12 rue de la Libération, 38610 Gières, France. T. +33476893565. E-mail: info@aedtf.org – president@aedtf.org.
URL: https://www.aedtf.ch/
History Statutes adopted 18 Dec 1988, Grenoble (France); modified 22 Apr 1989; 11 Dec 1993; 27 Jan 1996; 25 Jan 1997; 25 Jan 2003. Registration: France. **Aims** Develop and promote railway transport in Europe. **Structure** General Assembly; Administration Council; Bureau. **Languages** English, French, German, Italian, Polish, Spanish. **Staff** Voluntary. **Finance** Adhesions. **Events** *Annual General Assembly* Grenoble (France) 2002. **Publications** *Lettre d'Infos de l'AEDTF* (2 a year).
Members Associations; Collectivities; Enterprises; Individuals. Associations in 24 countries:
Austria, Belgium, Czechia, Denmark, Estonia, Finland, France, Germany, Greece, Hungary, Ireland, Italy, Latvia, Lithuania, Luxembourg, Netherlands, Poland, Portugal, Slovakia, Slovenia, Spain, Sweden, Switzerland, UK.
Included in the above, 1 organization listed in this Yearbook:
Association internationale des journalistes ferroviaires (AIJF, no recent information). [2017.10.11/XD7591/**D**]

♦ European Association of Development Research and Training Institutes (EADI) 06012

Association européenne des instituts de recherche et de formation en matière de développement
Exec Sec Kaiser-Friedrich-Str 11, 53113 Bonn, Germany. T. +492282618101. Fax +492282618103. E-mail: postmaster@eadi.org.
URL: http://www.eadi.org/
History Sep 1975, Linz (Austria). Founded on adoption of constitution at Constituent General Assembly, following founding conference, 1974, Ghent (Belgium). Constitution amended by General Assembly, 2002, Ljubljana; 2005, Bonn (Germany). Registration: Vereinsregister, No/ID: VR 7686, Germany, Bonn. **Aims** Promote research and training activities in development, as approached through social sciences and interdisciplinary studies. **Structure** General Assembly (every 3 years); Executive Committee; Management Committee; Sub-Committees; Task Groups; Working Groups (22). **Languages** English, French. **Staff** 6.00 FTE, paid. **Finance** Members' dues. Other sources: subventions, mainly from German Federal Government, North Rhine Westphalia; sale of publications. Convenors generally responsible for financing their Working Groups. **Activities** Guidance/assistance/consulting; events/meetings; research/documentation; training/education. **Events** *General Conference* Lisbon (Portugal) 2023, *General Conference* Bonn (Germany) 2021, *General Conference* The Hague (Netherlands) 2020, *Directors Meeting* Vienna (Austria) 2018, *General Conference* Bergen (Norway) 2017. **Publications** *EADI Research Monitor* (12 a year); *EADI e-newsletter* (12 a year); *European Journal of Development Research (EJDR)* (5 a year); *Courses and Training in Development* – selected from institutional members. *EADI Book Series* – conference papers, seminar and meeting reports and long-term reflections by working groups. Annual report; brochures; conference and seminar proceedings. Information Services: EADI Research Portal. **Information Services** *Devtrain* – database for Development Training Opportunities.
Members Institutional; Associate. Members (125) in 26 countries:
Austria, Belgium, Croatia, Czechia, Denmark, Finland, France, Germany, Greece, Hungary, Ireland, Italy, Luxembourg, Malta, Netherlands, Norway, Poland, Portugal, Romania, Serbia, Slovenia, Spain, Sweden, Switzerland, Türkiye, UK.
Full institutional: institutes concerned with development research and training; full individual: individuals (about 100) professionally active in the field. Members in 30 countries:
Austria, Belgium, Bulgaria, Canada, Denmark, Finland, France, Georgia, Germany, Ghana, India, Ireland, Italy, Korea Rep, Malaysia, Mexico, Netherlands, Nigeria, Norway, Poland, Portugal, Russia, Singapore, Spain, Sweden, Switzerland, Uganda, UK, USA, Zimbabwe.
Included in the above, 71 institutes listed in this Yearbook:
- *Arnold Bergstraesser Institut für Kulturwissenschaftliche Forschung (ABI);*
- *Austrian Institute for International Affairs (oiip);*
- *Austrian Research Foundation for Development Cooperation (ÖFSE);*
- *Center for Development Research, Bonn (ZEF);*
- *Centre européen de recherche en économie du développement (DIAL);*
- *Centre for African and Development Studies (CEsA);*
- *Centre for Development and the Environment, Oslo (SUM);*
- *Centre for Development Studies, Dublin (CDS, no recent information);*
- *Centre for Development Studies, Groningen (CDS);*
- *Centre for Global Development, Leeds (CGD);*
- *Centre for International Development Issues, Nijmegen (CIDIN);*
- *Centre for International Information and Documentation, Barcelona (CIDOB Foundation);*
- *Centre for Studies and Research on International Development, Clermont-Ferrand (CERDI);*
- *Centre for Tropical and Subtropical Agriculture and Forestry (CeTSAF);*
- *Centre of African Studies, Edinburgh (CAS);*
- *Centro di Studi di Politica Internazionale (CeSPI);*
- *Chr Michelsen Institute – Development Studies and Human Rights (CMI);*
- *Commissione Cooperazione Internazionale per lo Sviluppo (CICOPS);*
- *Commission for Research Partnerships with Developing Countries (KFPE);*
- *Dag Hammarskjöld Foundation (DHF, #04995);*
- *Danish Institute for International Studies (DIIS);*
- *Department of Peace and Development Research, Gothenburg University (PADRIGU);*
- *Deutsche Gesellschaft für Internationale Zusammenarbeit (GIZ);*
- *Deutsches Institut für Entwicklungspolitik (DIE);*
- *Development Policy and Practice;*
- *Development Studies Association (DSA);*
- *European Centre for Development Policy Management (ECDPM, #06473);*
- *Groupement d'intérêt scientifique pour l'étude de la mondialisation et du développement (GEMDEV);*
- *Hungarian International Development Assistance (HUN-IDA);*
- *ILO (#11123);*
- *Institut de recherche pour le développement (IRD);*
- *Institut d'études du développement, Louvain-la-Neuve (DVLP);*
- *Institute for Development and International Relations (IRMO);*
- *Institute for Development Research and Development Policy;*
- *Institute for Housing and Urban Development Studies (IHS);*
- *Institute for International Scientific and Technological Cooperation;*
- *Institute for International Studies, Warsaw;*
- *Institute for World Economics of the Hungarian Academy of Sciences (IWE);*
- *Institute of Development Studies, Brighton (IDS);*
- *Institute of Development Studies, Helsinki (IDS);*
- *Institute of International Relations, Prague (IIR);*
- *Institute of Studies in International Development and Cooperation (no recent information);*
- *Institut für Entwicklung und Frieden, Duisburg (INEF);*
- *Instituto Complutense de Estudios Internacionales (ICEI);*
- *Institut universitaire d'études du développement, Genève (IUED, inactive);*
- *Instituut voor Ontwikkelingsbeleid en -beheer, Universiteit Antwerpen (IOB);*
- *Internationaler Hilfsfonds (IH);*
- *International Institute for Environment and Development (IIED, #13877);*
- *International Institute for Geo-Information Science and Earth Observation (ITC, inactive);*
- *International Institute of Social Studies, The Hague (ISS);*
- *International Security and Development Center (ISDC);*
- *Istituto Agronomico per l'Oltremare, Italy (IAO);*
- *Les Afriques dans le monde (LAM);*
- *Món-3 – Universitaris pel Tercer Món;*
- *Natural Resources Institute (NRI);*
- *Netherlands Organization for International Cooperation in Higher Education (NUFFIC);*
- *NIAS-Nordisk Institut for Asienstudier (NIAS, #17132);*
- *Nordic Africa Institute (NAI, #17168);*
- *Norsk Forening for Utviklingsforskning (NFU);*
- *Norwegian Institute of International Affairs (NUPI);*
- *OECD Development Centre (#17692);*
- *Overseas Development Institute (ODI);*
- *Oxfam GB;*
- *Research Centre on Development and International Relations (DIR);*
- *Research School for Resource Studies for Development (CERES);*
- *Royal Tropical Institute (KIT);*
- *Society for International Development (SID, #19581);*
- *United Nations Research Institute for Social Development (UNRISD, #20623);*
- *United Nations University – Maastricht Economic and Social Research Institute on Innovation and Technology (UNU-MERIT, #20647);*
- *UNU World Institute for Development Economics Research (UNU-WIDER, #20722);*
- *Vienna Institute for International Dialogue and Cooperation (VIDC).*

IGO Relations Close relations with: *European Commission (EC, #06633); OECD (#17693); UNCTAD (#20285); UNDP (#20292); UNESCO (#20322).* **NGO Relations** Institutional member of: *Academic Council on the United Nations System (ACUNS, #00020); Society for International Development (SID, #19581).* Member of: *European Alliance for the Social Sciences and Humanities (EASSH, #05885); International Science Council (ISC, #14796); International Partnership on Religion and Sustainable Development (PaRD, #14524).* Hosted by: GDI-DIE; ZEF Bonn (Germany). [2022/XD4827/y/**D**]

♦ European Association of Diaconal Institutions of the Free Churches 06013

Europäischer Verband Freikirchlicher Diakoniewerke (evfdiakonie)
Pres Albertinen-Diakoniewerk, Süntelstrasse 11a, 22457 Hamburg, Germany. T. +494055882811.
URL: http://www.evfdiakonie.org/
Members Institutions in 11 countries:
Austria, Denmark, Finland, France, Germany, Hungary, Netherlands, Norway, Sweden, Switzerland, UK.
NGO Relations Member of: *World Federation of Diaconal Associations and Diaconal Communities (DIAKONIA, #21429).* Together with African members of DIAKONIA, comprises: *DIAKONIA Region Africa/Europe (DRAE, see: #21429).* [2018.06.14/XD5678/**E**]

♦ European Association for Digital Humanities (EADH) 06014

Sec Blijde-Inkomststraat 21 – box 3311, 3000 Leuven, Belgium. T. +3216372139. E-mail: secretary@eadh.org.
Pres address not obtained.
URL: http://eadh.org/
History 1973. Former names and other names: *Association for Literary and Linguistic Computing (ALLC)* – former (1973 to 2012). **Aims** Bring together and represent Digital Humanities in Europe across the entire spectrum of disciplines that research, develop and apply digital humanities methods and technology. **Structure** General Meeting (annual); Executive Committee; Sub-Committees. **Languages** English. **Staff** Voluntary. **Finance** Sources: members' dues. Annual budget: 12,000 EUR. **Activities** Awards/prizes/competitions; events/meetings; research/documentation; training/education. **Events** *Digital Humanities Conference* Ottawa, ON (Canada) 2020, *Digital Humanities Conference* Utrecht (Netherlands) 2019, *Digital Humanities Conference* Mexico City (Mexico) 2018, *Digital Humanities Conference* Montréal, QC (Canada) 2017, *Digital Humanities Conference* Krakow (Poland) 2016. **Publications** *DSH – The Journal of Digital Scholarship in the Humanities.* **Information Services** *Discussion Forum* – digital seminar. **Members** Individuals. Membership countries not specified. **NGO Relations** Instrumental in setting up (1): *Alliance of Digital Humanities Organizations (ADHO, #00671).* Constituent organizations include: *Association for Computers and the Humanities (ACH, #02446); Australasian Association for Digital Humanities (aaDH);* national associations. Affiliate organizations include: *Consortium for the Maintenance of the Text Encoding Initiative (TEI Consortium, #04753).* Associated with: *Digital Humanities in the Nordic and Baltic Countries (DHNB, #05080).* [2022/XE0829/v/**D**]

♦ European Association for Digital Transition (unconfirmed)
♦ European Association for Directors and Providers of Long-Term Care Services for the Elderly (inactive)
♦ European Association of Directors of Social Services / see European Social Network (#08505)

♦ European Association for Distance Learning (EADL) 06015

Main Office 11 Thorpe Lane, Cawood, Selby, YO8 3SG, UK. E-mail: enquiries@eadl.info.
URL: http://www.eadl.org/
History Apr 1985, Dublin (Ireland). Founded by merger of *European Council for Education by Correspondence (CEC, inactive)*, set up 1963, Brussels (Belgium), and *European Home Study Council (EHSC, inactive)*, set up 1968. Former names and other names: *Association of European Correspondence Schools (AECS)* – former (Apr 1985 to Jun 1999). **Aims** Promote: knowledge of distance education, its potential and achievements; professional and ethical standards in the field; research into methods and cooperation in exchange of ideas and results; interests of members and students; cooperation with national councils and associations. **Structure** General Meeting (annual at Conference); Executive Committee; Research and Development Committee. **Languages** English. **Staff** 1.00 FTE, voluntary. **Finance** Sources: meeting proceeds; members' dues; sale of publications. **Activities** Awards/prizes/competitions; events/meetings; training/education. **Events** *Annual Conference* Brussels (Belgium) 2023, *Annual Conference* Copenhagen (Denmark) 2022, *Annual Conference* Selby (UK) 2021, *Annual Conference* Berlin (Germany) 2020, *Annual Conference* Manchester (UK) 2018. **Publications** *EADL Headlines* (6 a year). *A guide to quality in online teaching and learning for digital sharing (FUN)* (1st ed 2018); *ISO 29990 Quality Guide*; *Quality Guidelines to Improve the Quality of Distance Learning Institutes in Europe.* Conference papers.
Members Ordinary (66); Associate (7); Individual (2); Start-up (6); Honorary (5). Members in 23 countries:
Austria, Belgium, Cyprus, Czechia, Denmark, Estonia, France, Germany, Hungary, India, Iraq, Ireland, Italy, Netherlands, Norway, Poland, Portugal, Spain, Switzerland, Türkiye, UK, Ukraine, USA. [2022.10.20/XD5920/**D**]

♦ European Association of Distance Teaching Universities (EADTU) .. 06016

Managing Dir Parkweg 27, 6212 XN Maastricht, Netherlands. T. +31433118712. E-mail: secretariat@eadtu.eu.
URL: http://www.eadtu.eu/
History 23 Jan 1987, Heerlen (Netherlands). Registration: EU Transparency Register, No/ID: 016107725457-79, Start date: 16 Jan 2017; Netherlands. **Aims** Promote distance higher education and e-Bologna in Europe; support contacts among academic staff of participating institutions and cooperation in research, course-development, course-transfer and credit-transfer; develop new methods and techniques, including new technologies and media; organize common projects in cooperation with European authorities. **Structure** General Assembly; Supervisory Board; Rectors Conference; Associations Conference; Student Council; Office. **Languages** English. **Staff** 5.50 FTE, paid. **Finance** Members' dues. Other sources: projects. **Activities** Events/meetings; training/education; knowledge management/information dissemination. **Events** *Annual Conference* Madrid (Spain) 2019, *Policy Forum on European MOOCs* Brussels (Belgium) 2016, *Annual Conference* Paris (France) 2013, *Annniversary Conference / Annual Conference* Paphos (Cyprus) 2012, *Annual Conference* Eskisehir (Turkey) 2011. **Publications** *Dictionary of Distance Education Terminology*; *Directory of Media, Methods and Technology in EADTU Member Institutions*; *Directory of Study Centres in Europe*; *Mini Directory.* Reports; working papers; conference proceedings.
Members Full members, representing open universities, national consortia of dual mode institutions or associations, in 22 countries:
Austria, Belgium, Cyprus, Czechia, Denmark, Finland, France, Germany, Greece, Ireland, Italy, Latvia, Lithuania, Netherlands, Norway, Poland, Portugal, Slovenia, Spain, Switzerland, Türkiye, UK.

Associate in 2 countries:
Ecuador, Israel.
NGO Relations Instrumental in setting up: *EDEN Digital Learning Europe (EDEN, #05356)*. Affiliate member of: *Open Education Consortium (#17751)*. [2020/XD0972/**D**]

♦ European Association on Early Intervention / see Eurlyaid – European Association on Early Childhood Intervention (#05626)

♦ European Association for Earthquake Engineering (EAEE) 06017

Association européenne de génie sismique

SG City – Univ of London, Northampton Square, London, EC1V 0HB, UK. T. +442070408956.
URL: http://www.eaee.org/

History 1 Oct 1964, Skopje (Yugoslavia). Statutes most recently revised, Jul 2010. **Aims** Promote regional cooperation among scientists and engineers in the field of earthquake engineering; advance the research front; contribute and support all related research and educational activities. **Structure** General Assembly of Delegates (every 4 years, at Conference); Executive Committee; Specialized Task Groups (8). **Languages** English. **Staff** 0.50 FTE, paid. **Finance** Members' dues. Other sources: conference fees; donations; sale of publications. Office expenses met by country hosting secretariat; conference expenses met by host country. **Activities** Events/meetings; knowledge management/information dissemination. **Events** *European Conference on Earthquake Engineering and Seismology* Bucharest (Romania) 2022, *Quadrennial Conference* Bucharest (Romania) 2022, *Quadrennial Conference* Thessaloniki (Greece) 2018, *European Conference on Earthquake Engineering and Seismology* Istanbul (Turkey) 2014, *Quadrennial Conference* Ohrid (Macedonia) 2010. **Publications** *Bulletin of Earthquake Engineering* (12 a year); *EAEE Newsletter* (annual).
Members Individuals; National Associations or Committees (for Europe and vicinity only); Organizations. Members in 33 countries:
Algeria, Austria, Bosnia-Herzegovina, Bulgaria, Croatia, Cyprus, Czechia, Egypt, France, Georgia, Germany, Greece, Hungary, Iceland, Iran Islamic Rep, Israel, Italy, Montenegro, Netherlands, North Macedonia, Norway, Poland, Portugal, Romania, Russia, Serbia, Slovakia, Slovenia, Spain, Switzerland, Türkiye, UK, Ukraine.
NGO Relations *European Seismological Commission (ESC, #08461)* represented on Executive Committee. [2019.04.23/XD5079/**D**]

♦ European Association of Earth Science Editors (inactive)
♦ European Association of Eco-Counsellors (inactive)
♦ European Association of Editors of Biological Periodicals / see European Association of Science Editors (#06201)
♦ European Association of Editors of Periodicals in Chemistry and Physics (inactive)

♦ European Association for the Education of Adults (EAEA) 06018

Association européenne pour l'éducation des adultes – Asociación Europea para la Educación de Adultos – Europäischer Verband für Erwachsenenbildung

SG Mundo-J, Rue de l'Industrie 10, 1000 Brussels, Belgium. T. +3228932522. E-mail: eaea-office@eaea.org.
Communications Officer Bulevardi 21, FI-00180 Helsinki, Finland. T. +358405112475. E-mail: eaea-info@eaea.org.
URL: http://www.eaea.org/

History 1953, Geneva (Switzerland). Founded by *European Centre for Culture (ECC, #06472)* and representatives from a number of European countries. Former names and other names: *European Bureau of Adult Education (EBAE)* – former (1953 to 2000); *Bureau européen de l'éducation populaire (BEEP)* – former (1953 to 2000); *Oficina Europea de Educación Popular* – former (1953 to 2000); *Europäisches Büro für Erwachsenenbildung* – former (1953 to 2000); *Europees Bureau voor Volksontwikkeling* – former (1953 to 2000). Registration: Banque-Carrefour des Entreprises, No/ID: 0472.146.213, Belgium; EU Transparency Register, No/ID: 3334854676-12. **Aims** Link and represent European organizations directly involved in adult learning; promote adult learning and access to and participation in non-formal adult education for all, particularly for groups currently under-represented. **Structure** General Assembly; Executive Board; President. Board meetings open to members. **Languages** English, Finnish, French, German, Italian, Polish. **Staff** 7.00 FTE, paid. **Finance** Sources: members' dues; revenue from activities/projects. Supported by: *European Commission (EC, #06633)*. **Activities** Advocacy/lobbying/activism; awards/prizes/competitions; awareness raising; capacity building; events/meetings; knowledge management/information dissemination; networking/liaising; projects/programmes; training/education. **Events** *General Assembly and Annual Conference* Mechelen (Belgium) 2022, *Annual General Assembly* Brussels (Belgium) 2021, *Annual General Assembly* Bratislava (Slovakia) 2020, *Annual General Assembly* Copenhagen (Denmark) 2019, *Annual General Assembly* Tallinn (Estonia) 2018. **Publications** *EAEA Newsletter* (6 a year). Policy statements and recommendations; constitution; work plan; activity reports; guidelines.
Members Organizations (120) representing more than 60 million learners in 45 countries:
Armenia, Austria, Azerbaijan, Belarus, Belgium, Bosnia-Herzegovina, Bulgaria, Croatia, Cyprus, Czechia, Denmark, Estonia, Finland, France, Georgia, Germany, Greece, Hungary, Iceland, Ireland, Israel, Italy, Kosovo, Latvia, Liechtenstein, Lithuania, Malta, Moldova, Montenegro, Netherlands, North Macedonia, Norway, Poland, Portugal, Romania, Russia, Serbia, Slovakia, Slovenia, Spain, Sweden, Switzerland, Türkiye, UK, Ukraine.
Consultative Status Consultative status granted from: *UNESCO (#20322)* (Consultative Status); *Council of Europe (CE, #04881)* (Participatory Status). **IGO Relations** Cooperates with (3): *European Commission (EC, #06633)*; *European Parliament (EP, #08146)*; *UNESCO Institute for Lifelong Learning (UIL, #20305)*. **NGO Relations** Member of (6): *Confédération européenne des ong d'urgence et de développement (CONCORD, #04547)* (as associated member of); *Eastern Partnership Civil Society Forum (EaP CSF, #05247)*; *International Council for Adult Education (ICAE, #12983)* (as regional member of); *Lifelong Learning Platform – European Civil Society for Education (LLLP, #16466)*; *SDG Watch Europe (#19162)*; *Social Platform (#19344)* (Associate member). Cooperates with (4): *ALL DIGITAL (#00646)*; *European Basic Skills Network (EBSN, #06321)*; *Institut für Internationale Zusammenarbeit des Deutschen Volkshochschul-Verbandes (DVV-International)*; *Nordic Network for Adult Learning (#17349)*. Also links with national education centres. [2022.05.12/XD0601/y/**D**]

♦ European Association for Education in Electrical and Information Engineering (EAEEIE) 06019

Main Office c/o ESSTIN, 2 rue Jean Lamour, 54500 Vandoeuvre-les-Nancy, France. E-mail: info@eaeeie.org.
URL: http://www.eaeeie.org/

History 1990. Registration: Start date: 6 Jul 1990, France. **Aims** Foster good practice in education for electrical and information engineering; determine corresponding educational criteria in order to establish common standards of education; promote continuing education as a necessary means for maintaining professional effectiveness of engineers; improve understanding of educational practices throughout the EU; develop credit transfer schemes between collaborating establishments; foster a strong technological research base and develop educational research. **Structure** General Assembly. Council, comprising President, Secretary General, Treasurer, 4 Honorary Presidents, 2 Honorary members, 3 Executive Committee members, 3 members of Academic Affairs, 19 Coopted members and 13 Elected members. Executive Committee. **Languages** Czech, Danish, Dutch, English, Estonian, Finnish, French, German, Hungarian, Irish Gaelic, Italian, Latvian, Lithuanian, Maltese, Polish, Portuguese, Slovakian, Slovene, Spanish, Swedish. **Staff** Voluntary. **Finance** Members' dues. **Activities** Includes: *'Innovation for Education in Information Technology through Multimedia and Communication Networks (INEIT-MUCON Thematic Network)'*; *'Thematic Harmonization in Electrical and Information Engineering in Europe (THEIRE)'* – designs, develops and disseminates web-based courses in Electrical and Information Engineering (EIE) in Higher Education; *'EIE-Surveyor: Reference Point of Electrical and Information Engineering in Europe'* – reflection and proposition on generic competences and subject-specific competences, methodology for accreditation, multinational degrees and the situation of implementation of the Bologna process and implementation of quality assessment methodologies in EIE in higher education. **Events** *Annual Conference* Coimbra (Portugal) 2022, *Annual Conference* Ruse (Bulgaria) 2019, *Annual Conference* Copenhagen (Denmark) 2015, *Annual Conference* Cesme (Turkey) 2014, *Annual Conference* Chania (Greece) 2013. **Publications** Conference proceedings; monographs.
Members Institutional members in 11 countries:
Belgium, Finland, France, Italy, Latvia, Lithuania, Norway, Poland, Portugal, Spain, USA.
Full in 21 countries:
Belgium, Bulgaria, Czechia, Estonia, Finland, France, Germany, Greece, Iceland, Ireland, Italy, Latvia, Lithuania, Luxembourg, Netherlands, Poland, Portugal, Romania, Spain, UK, Ukraine.
IGO Relations Contributes to: *SOCRATES Programme (inactive)*. [2022/XD7546/**D**]

♦ European Association for Education and Research in Commercial Distribution (EAERCD) 06020

Pres Inst for Retail Studies, Univ of Stirling, Stirling, FK9 4LA, UK. T. +441786467399. Fax +441786465290.
URL: http://www.eaercd.org/

History 1990. **Aims** Serve as a forum for academics involved in teaching and research in the distributive trades. **Structure** A virtual organization. Secretariat. **Languages** English. **Staff** 0.50 FTE, voluntary. **Events** *International Conference on Research in the Distributives Trades* Valencia (Spain) 2013, *Conference* Parma (Italy) 2011, *International conference on research in the distributive trades / Conference* Guildford (UK) 2009, *International conference on research in the distributive trades / Conference* Saarbrücken (Germany) 2007, *International conference on education and themes in commercial distribution* Uxbridge (UK) 2006. **Publications** *EAERCD Newsletter*, *International Review of Retail, Distribution and Consumer Research*.
Members Individuals in 23 countries:
Austria, Belgium, Canada, Chile, Czechia, Denmark, Finland, France, Germany, Greece, Ireland, Italy, Japan, Korea Rep, Latvia, Netherlands, Norway, Singapore, Spain, Sweden, Switzerland, UK, USA. [2010.06.01/XD7760/v/**D**]

♦ European Association for Education and Research in Public Relations / see European Public Relations Education and Research Association (#08302)

♦ European Association of Elected Representatives from Mountain Regions 06021

Association européenne des élus de montagne (AEM) – Asociación Europea de Autoridades Politicas de Regiones de Montaña – Europäische Vereinigung der Gewählten von Bergregionen – Associação Européia dos Eleitos de Montanha – Associazione Europea degli Eletti della Montagna – Evropaiki Enosi Eklegmenon ton Orinon Periohon

SG Maison des Parcs et de la Montagne, 256 Rue de République, 73000 Chambéry, France. T. +33689595381.
Facebook: https://www.facebook.com/Association-Europ%C3%A9enne-des-%C3%A9lus-de-Montagne-AEM-PRO-MONTE-335792263129497/

History 11 Mar 1991, Strasbourg (France). Registered in accordance with French law. **Aims** Strengthen links between elected representatives of mountain regions and promote solidarity among these regions and the *local authorities* and organizations of which they are comprised; represent and defend their interests; work for a European mountain policy which covers legal, economic, social and cultural problems and fully respects the environment. **Structure** General Meeting (annual); Executive Committee; Brussels (Belgium) office hosted by Piemonte Region Delegation in Brussels. **Languages** English, French, German, Italian, Portuguese, Slovakian, Spanish. **Staff** 3.00 FTE, paid. **Finance** Members' dues. Annual budget: euro 170,000. **Activities** Advocacy/lobbying/activism; politics/policy/regulatory. Management of treaties and agreements: *Convention for the Protection of the Alps (Alpine convention, 1991)*. **Events** *General Assembly* Le Grand-Bornand (France) 2013, *Quadrennial international congress of integrated management in high watersheds* Megève (France) 2010, *General Assembly* Turin (Italy) 2009, *General Assembly* Brussels (Belgium) 2008, *Rencontre des élus de montagne* Megève (France) 2006. **Publications** *Pro Monte* in English, French – newsletter.
Members Full members of the European Parliament, of national or local parliaments or of local mountain communities or their representative organizations. Associate similar from regions which although not mountainous have similar characteristics; Observer. Members in 11 countries:
Austria, Bulgaria, France, Germany, Italy, Poland, Portugal, Slovakia, Slovenia, Spain, Switzerland.
Consultative Status Consultative status granted from: *Council of Europe (CE, #04881)* (Participatory Status).
IGO Relations Observer at: *Congress of Local and Regional Authorities of the Council of Europe (#04677)*. Cooperates with: *European Committee of the Regions (CoR, #06665)*. [2017.03.08/XD3684/**D**]

♦ European Association of Electrical Contractors / see EuropeOn (#09166)

♦ European Association of Electrical and Electronic Waste Take Back Systems (WEEE Forum) 06022

Dir Gen Bluepoint Conference and Business Centre, Bd Auguste Reyers 80, 1030 Brussels, Belgium. T. +3227068701. E-mail: info@weee-forum.org.
URL: http://www.weee-forum.org/

History Apr 2002. WEEE stands for *waste electrical and electronic equipment*. Registration: Banque-Carrefour des Entreprises, No/ID: 0883.940.313, Start date: 3 Oct 2006, Belgium; EU Transparency Register, No/ID: 702397445-73, Start date: 24 Jun 2008. **Aims** Strive for excellence in *waste electrical* and *electronic equipment* (WEEE) collective take-back systems; serve as a forum for cooperation and ideas exchange at international level. **Structure** General Assembly (annual); Board of Directors. **Languages** English. **Staff** 5.00 FTE, paid. **Finance** Members' dues. EU funded projects. **Activities** Research and development; standards/guidelines. **Events** *Conference / Biennial Forum* London (UK) 2012, *Conference / Biennial Forum* Zurich (Switzerland) 2010, *Conference / Biennial Forum* Vienna (Austria) 2008. **Publications** *Eye on WEEE*.
Members Organizations in 30 countries:
Australia, Austria, Belgium, Canada, Cyprus, Czechia, Denmark, Estonia, France, Germany, Greece, Hungary, Iceland, Ireland, Italy, Lithuania, Luxembourg, Malta, Netherlands, New Zealand, Norway, Poland, Portugal, Romania, Slovakia, Slovenia, Spain, Sweden, Switzerland, UK.
NGO Relations Member of: *Federation of European and International Associations Established in Belgium (FAIB, #09508)*. Technical Liaison Partner with: *European Committee for Electrotechnical Standardization (CENELEC, #06647)*. [2021/XM3297/**F**]

♦ European Association of the Electricity Transmission and Distribution Equipment and Services Industry (T and D EUROPE) 06023

SG BluePoint Bldg, Blvd A Reyers 80, 1030 Brussels, Belgium. T. +3222066867. E-mail: secretariat@tdeurope.eu.
URL: http://www.tdeurope.eu/

History Mar 2008. Founded on merger of *Committee of Associations of European Transformer Manufacturers (COTREL, inactive)* and high voltage part of *European Coordinating Committee of Manufacturers of Electrical Switchgear and Controlgear (CAPIEL, #06790)* HV. Registration: EU Transparency Register, No/ID: 90453504235-64. **Aims** Promote the common technical, industrial, economic and environmental interests of the European electricity transmission and distribution manufacturing, and product derived solutions industry; work towards future-proofing electricity networks in Europe. **Structure** Executive Committee; Strategy Areas (4). **Languages** English. **Staff** 1.50 FTE, paid. **Finance** Members' dues. **Activities** Monitoring/assessment; politics/policy/regulatory; knowledge management/information dissemination; networking/liaising.
Members Full: national organizations in 12 countries:
Austria, Belgium, France, Germany, Italy, Netherlands, Norway, Portugal, Spain, Switzerland, Türkiye, UK.
Corporate (6); Associate (3). Membership countries not specified.
NGO Relations Cooperation agreement with: *European Committee for Electrotechnical Standardization (CENELEC, #06647)*; *European Network of Transmission System Operators for Electricity (ENTSO-E, #08026)*. [2022/XM1288/t/**E**]

♦ European Association for Electromobility (AVERE) 06024

European Association for Battery, Hybrid and Fuel Cell Electric Vehicles

SG Rue Montoyer 24, 1000 Brussels, Belgium. T. +32228800609. E-mail: chair@avere.org.
Pres address not obtained.
URL: http://www.avere.org/

History 17 Apr 1978, Brussels (Belgium). Founded as *European Electric Road Vehicle Association – Association européenne des véhicules électriques routiers (AVERE)*, under the sponsorship of the Commission of the European Communities, currently *European Commission (EC, #06633)*. Subsequently changed title to *Association européenne des véhicules électriques – batteries, hybrides et piles à combustible (AVERE) – European Association for Battery, Hybrid and Fuel Cell Electric Vehicles*. Registration: Banque-Carrefour des Entreprises, No/ID: 0418.362.879, Start date: 6 Dec 1978, Belgium; EU Transparency Register, No/ID: 269727723042-29, Start date: 17 Aug 2016. **Aims** Promote the use of battery, hybrid and fuel cell electric vehicles – individually and in fleets and for priority uses, so as to achieve greener *mobility* for cities and countries. **Structure** General Assembly (annual); Bureau; Secretary General. **Languages** English, French.

Staff 6.00 FTE, paid. **Finance** Members' dues. Budget (annual): about euro 120,000. **Activities** Events/meetings; advocacy/lobbying/activism; knowledge management/information dissemination; networking/liaising. **Events** *International Electric Vehicle Symposium* Sacramento, CA (USA) 2023, *International Electric Vehicle Symposium* Oslo (Norway) 2022, *E-Mobility Conference* Brussels (Belgium) 2021, *International Electric Vehicle Symposium* Nanjing (China) 2021, *E-Mobility Conference* Brussels (Belgium) 2020. **Publications** *AVERE Information Service* (4 a year) – bibliography; *EV-Focus* (4 a year) – magazine; *World Electric Vehicle Journal* (4 a year). Technical reports; symposium proceedings.
Members National associations in 15 countries and territories:
Belgium, Bulgaria, Finland, France, Germany, Greece, Hungary, Italy, Netherlands, Norway, Poland, Romania, Scotland, Slovakia, Spain.
Network members (2):
European Association of Cities Interested in the Use of Electric Vehicles (#05974); Union of the Electricity Industry – Eurelectric (#20379).
IGO Relations *International Energy Agency (IEA, #13270)* – Hybrid and Electric Vehicle Implementing Agreement. **NGO Relations** Member of: *Federation of European and International Associations Established in Belgium (FAIB, #09508); World Electric Vehicle Association (WEVA, #21374).* Partners include: *POLIS (#18419).* Cooperates with: *Electric Drive Transportation Association (EDTA); Electric Vehicle Association of Asia Pacific (EVAAP, #05418).* [2021/XD6958/y/**D**]

♦ European Association of Electronic and Electrical Engineers (inactive)
♦ European Association E.L.I.T.E. / see European Laboratory for Industrial and Territorial Excellence

♦ European Association of Employed community Pharmacists in Europe (EPhEU) 06025

Europäischer Verband der in öffentlichen Apotheken angestellten Apotheker
SG c/o Verband Angestellter Apotheker Österreichs, Spitalgasse 31/4, 1090 Vienna, Austria. T. +43140414419. Fax +43140414414. E-mail: epheu@vaaoe.at.
URL: http://www.epheu.eu/
History Founded 2012. Also referred to as *Employed community Pharmacists in Europe.* Registered in accordance with Austrian law. **Aims** Represent the occupational, legal, social, socio-political and cultural interests of the profession of employed pharmacists in Europe. **Structure** General Assembly; Executive Board. **Finance** Members' dues.
Members Members in 12 countries:
Austria, Belgium, Croatia, France, Germany, Hungary, Luxembourg, Monaco, Montenegro, Norway, Poland, UK.
NGO Relations Observer member of: *Common Wisdom Projects (CWP, inactive).* [2019/XM4462/**D**]

♦ European Association for Endoscopic Surgery and Other Interventional Techniques (EAES) 06026

Exec Dir PO Box 335, 5500 AH Veldhoven, Netherlands. T. +31402525288. Fax +31402523102. E-mail: info@eaes.eu.
URL: http://www.eaes.eu/
History Oct 1990, Paris (France). Registration: France. **Aims** Evaluate endoscopic surgery and interventional techniques in Europe; coordinate training of surgeons in these techniques; promote scientific studies. **Structure** Annual Congress; Executive Office; Committees (3). **Languages** English. **Staff** 3.50 FTE, paid. **Finance** Members' dues. **Activities** Monitoring/evaluation; training/education; research/documentation. **Events** *Congress* Rome (Italy) 2023, *Congress* Krakow (Poland) 2022, *Congress* Barcelona (Spain) 2021, *Winter Meeting* Veldhoven (Netherlands) 2021, *WCES : Biennial World Congress of Endoscopic Surgery* Yokohama (Japan) 2020. **Publications** Articles.
Members Corporate (companies) and individual medical practitioners (3,063) in 94 countries and territories:
Albania, Argentina, Armenia, Aruba, Australia, Austria, Azerbaijan, Bahrain, Bangladesh, Belarus, Belgium, Bosnia-Herzegovina, Brazil, Bulgaria, Canada, Chile, China, Colombia, Croatia, Cyprus, Czechia, Denmark, Ecuador, Egypt, Estonia, Finland, France, Georgia, Germany, Greece, Hong Kong, Hungary, Iceland, India, Indonesia, Iran Islamic Rep, Iraq, Ireland, Israel, Italy, Japan, Jordan, Kazakhstan, Kenya, Korea Rep, Kosovo, Kuwait, Latvia, Lebanon, Libya, Lithuania, Malaysia, Malta, Mexico, Moldova, Mongolia, Morocco, Myanmar, Namibia, Netherlands, New Zealand, Nigeria, North Macedonia, Norway, Oman, Pakistan, Palestine, Panama, Peru, Philippines, Poland, Portugal, Qatar, Romania, Russia, Saudi Arabia, Serbia, Singapore, Slovakia, Slovenia, South Africa, Spain, Sudan, Sweden, Switzerland, Thailand, Türkiye, UK, Ukraine, United Arab Emirates, USA, Uzbekistan, Venezuela, Yemen.
NGO Relations Member of: *Federación Latinoamericana de Cirurgia (FELAC, #09349); International Federation of Societies of Endoscopic Surgeons (IFSES, #13546); United European Gastroenterology (UEG, #20506).* [2021/XD3539/**D**]

♦ European Association of Energy Service Companies (eu.ESCO) 06027

Dir Governmental Relations Diamant Bldg, Boulevard A Reyers 80, 1030 Brussels, Belgium. T. +3227068202. E-mail: info@eu-esco.org.
URL: http://www.euesco.org/
History Founded 2009, by *European Building Automation and Controls Association (eu.bac, #06409).* **Aims** Boost the energy services market by increasing its transparency and its trustworthiness; represent energy service companies offering energy performance contracting vis-à-vis European institutions, other relevant European stakeholders, member states and public authorities. **Structure** Chair. **Languages** English. **Staff** 1.00 FTE, paid. **Finance** Members' dues. **Activities** Knowledge management/information dissemination; events/meetings; training/education; awareness raising; networking/liaising. **Events** *Europe Conference* Vienna (Austria) 2015, *European Utility Week Conference* Vienna (Austria) 2015, *Europe Conference* Barcelona (Spain) 2014, *Europe Conference* Copenhagen (Denmark) 2013, *Europe Conference* London (UK) 2012. **Publications** Documents; press releases; position papers. **Members** Private companies limited to the European Union. Membership countries not specified. **NGO Relations** Cooperates with: *Covenant of Mayors for Climate and Energy (#04939); EUROCITIES (#05662).* [2015.09.08/XJ7602/**D**]

♦ European Association of Engravers and Flexographers (#02572)
♦ European Association of Environmental Economists / see European Association of Environmental and Resource Economists (#06028)
♦ European Association for Environmental Management Education (inactive)

♦ European Association of Environmental and Resource Economists (EAERE) 06028

Contact Via della Libertà 12, Building Porta dell'Innovazione (2nd Floor), 30175 Venice VE, Italy. T. +390412346065. E-mail: eaere@eaere.org.
URL: https://www.eaere.org/
History Apr 1990, Venice (Italy). Former names and other names: *European Association of Environmental Economists* – former. Registration: Italy; EU Transparency Register, No/ID: 99844686327-88. **Aims** Contribute to development and application of environmental and resource economics as a science in Europe; improve communication and contact between teachers, researchers and students; develop and encourage cooperation between university level teaching and research institutions. **Structure** General Assembly; Council. **Languages** English. **Finance** Sources: members' dues. **Activities** Events/meetings; training/education. **Events** *Annual Conference* Limassol (Cyprus) 2023, *Annual Conference* Rimini (Italy) 2022, *Annual Conference* Berlin (Germany) 2021, *Annual Conference* Berlin (Germany) 2020, *Annual Conference* Manchester (UK) 2019. **Publications** *Environmental and Resource Economics (ERE); Review of Environmental Economics and Policy (REEP).*
Members Individuals (over 1,000) in 77 countries and territories:
Afghanistan, Algeria, Australia, Austria, Bangladesh, Belgium, Benin, Bosnia-Herzegovina, Brazil, Bulgaria, Cameroon, Canada, Chile, China, Colombia, Costa Rica, Croatia, Cyprus, Czechia, Denmark, Egypt, Ethiopia, Finland, France, Germany, Ghana, Greece, Hong Kong, Hungary, Iceland, India, Indonesia, Iran Islamic Rep, Ireland, Israel, Italy, Japan, Kenya, Korea Rep, Lebanon, Lithuania, Luxembourg, Malawi, Malta, Mexico, Montenegro, Nepal, Netherlands, New Zealand, Nigeria, Norway, Peru, Philippines, Poland, Portugal, Romania, Russia, Rwanda, Serbia, Slovakia, Slovenia, South Africa, Spain, Sri Lanka, Sweden, Switzerland, Taiwan, Tanzania UR, Thailand, Trinidad-Tobago, Türkiye, Turkmenistan, UK, Ukraine, Uruguay, USA, Vietnam.
IGO Relations Partner of (4): *European Chemicals Agency (ECHA, #06523);* European Climate Pact; *Intergovernmental Panel on Climate Change (IPCC, #11499); United Nations Framework Convention on Climate Change (UNFCCC, 1992).* **NGO Relations** Observer status with (7): African Association of Environmental and Resource Economists (AFAERE); *Asian Association of Environmental and Resource Economics (AAERE, #01322); Association of Environmental and Resource Economists (AERE); European Archives Centre (inactive); International Institute for Environment and Development (IIED, #13877); International Society for Ecological Economics (ISEE, #15069);* Latin American Association of Environmental and Resource Economists (LAERE). [2022.10.18/XD3002/v/**D**]

♦ European Association of E-Pharmacies (EAEP) 06029

Public Affairs Manager Erik de Rodeweg 11-13, 5975 WD Sevenum, Netherlands. E-mail: info@eaep.com.
URL: https://www.eaep.com/
History Former names and other names: *European Association of Mail Service Pharmacies (EAMSP)* – former; *Association européenne des e-pharmacies* – former; *Verband der europäischen Online-Apotheken* – former. Registration: No/ID: 14070032, Netherlands, Noorderpoort; EU Transparency Register, No/ID: 22824156875-36. **Aims** Represents the voice of e-pharmacies on the European continent; improve the health of Europe's citizens and strengthen the European healthcare system. **Languages** English. **Publications** *EAEP newsletter.*
Members Companies in 13 countries:
Austria, Belgium, Bulgaria, Czechia, France, Germany, Ireland, Italy, Netherlands, Norway, Slovakia, Spain, Switzerland.
NGO Relations Member of (3): *Alliance for Safe Online Pharmacy – EU (ASOP EU, #00720); EU Health Coalition; European Connected Health Alliance (ECHAlliance, #06741).* [2023.02.14/XM5030/**D**]

♦ European Association of ERASMUS Coordinators (EAEC) 06030

Pres 36 Stasinou Street, Office 104, Strovolos, CY-2003 Nicosia, Cyprus.
URL: http://www.eaecnet.com/
History Founded Jun 2004, Lódz (Poland). Launched Jun 2005, Cyprus, at 1st ERACON. Registered in accordance with the law of Cyprus. **Aims** Enable exchange of information and experience among European Erasmus+ Programme Coordinators; promote mobility of *students* and academic and administrative staff in the *EU*; circulate provisions on the Bologna Process and its updates in *academic* circles; promote principles of and participation in LLP European Commission Programme; support raising educational standards and quality in the EU; prepare project proposals to be funded by the European Commission; cooperate as a partner in European projects. **Structure** General Assembly; Management Board. **Languages** English. **Staff** 3.00 FTE, paid. **Finance** Members' dues. Activities surplus. **Activities** Publishing activities; networking/liaising; events/meetings. **Events** *Conference* Paphos (Cyprus) 2019, *Conference* Murcia (Spain) 2018, *Conference* Maribor (Slovenia) 2017, *Conference* Thessaloniki (Greece) 2016, *Conference* Porto (Portugal) 2015. **Publications** *EAEC Newsletter* (2-3 a year). Conference Abstract Booklet; leaflets.
Members Institutional; Individual. Members in 20 countries:
Belgium, Bulgaria, Cyprus, Czechia, Denmark, France, Germany, Greece, Latvia, Lithuania, Malta, Netherlands, Poland, Portugal, Romania, Slovakia, Slovenia, Spain, Türkiye, UK. [2018/XM3309/**E**]

♦ European Association of Establishments for Veterinary Education (EAEVE) 06031

Association Européenne des Etablissements d'Enseignement Vétérinaire (AEEEV)
Office Manager Hietzinger Kai 87, 1130 Vienna, Austria. T. +4315123394. E-mail: office@eaeve.org.
Pres Univ of Lyon, 92 Rue Pasteur, 69007 Lyon, France.
URL: http://www.eaeve.org/
History The European System of Evaluation of Veterinary Training was conceived as a peer assessment programme and was started and financed (1985-1993) by the European Commission (EC) on the recommendation of the Advisory Committee on Veterinary Training (ACVT), which later recommended a permanent system be set up. EAEVE was requested by the EC to set up and run the system on a self-financing basis in 1994. Registration: EU Transparency Register, No/ID: 300212020206-59. **Aims** Evaluate, promote and further develop the quality and standard of veterinary medical establishments and their teaching within, but not limited to, the member states of the European Union; act as final arbiter in the European System of Evaluation of Veterinary Training (ESEVT). **Structure** General Assembly (GA); Executive Committee (ExCom); Parent organization of European Committee on Veterinary Education (ECOVE); Committee of Internal Quality Assurance (CIQA) directs development, implementation, revision and improvement of quality in the ESEVT; Office in Vienna (Austria). **Languages** English. **Staff** 2.50 FTE, paid. **Finance** Sources: members' dues. **Activities** Certification/accreditation; monitoring/evaluation; training/education. **Events** *Annual General Assembly* Nantes (France) 2020, *Annual General Assembly* Zagreb (Croatia) 2019, *Annual General Assembly* Hannover (Germany) 2018, *Annual General Assembly* London (UK) 2017, *Annual General Assembly* Uppsala (Sweden) 2016. **Publications** Online publications.
Members Veterinary Educational Establishments existing in Europe (101 of 110) in 39 countries:
Albania, Austria, Belgium, Bosnia-Herzegovina, Bulgaria, Croatia, Czechia, Denmark, Estonia, Finland, France, Germany, Greece, Hungary, Ireland, Israel, Italy, Japan, Jordan, Latvia, Lithuania, Netherlands, North Macedonia, Norway, Poland, Portugal, Romania, Russia, Serbia, Slovakia, Slovenia, Spain, Sweden, Switzerland, Thailand, Tunisia, Türkiye, UK, Ukraine.
IGO Relations Observer status with (1): *European Commission (EC, #06633)* (Advisory Committee on Veterinary Training). Cooperates with (1): *OIE – World Organisation for Animal Health (#17703).* **NGO Relations** Cooperates with (6): *European Board of Veterinary Specialisation (EBVS, #06375); Federation of Veterinarians of Europe (#09713);* International Accreditors' Working Group (IAWG); *International Veterinary Students' Association (IVSA, #15851); Réseau des établissements d'enseignement vétérinaire de la Méditerranée (REEV-Med, #18871);* Veterinary Continuous Education in Europe (VETCEE). Affiliate Member of: *European Association for Quality Assurance in Higher Education (ENQA, #06183).* Founding member of: *European Coordination Committee for Veterinary Training (ECCVT, #06793).* Listed in: *European Quality Assurance Register for Higher Education (EQAR, #08311).* [2021.06.09/XD2333/**D**]

♦ European Association for ETICS / see European Association for External Thermal Insulation Composite Systems (#06035)

♦ European Association of Event Centers (EVVC) 06032

Europäischer Verband der Veranstaltungs-Centren
Head Office Niddastrasse 74, 60329 Frankfurt-Main, Germany. T. +4969915096980. Fax +4969915096989. E-mail: info@evvc.org.
URL: http://www.evvc.org/
History 24 Oct 1955, Hannover (Germany FR), as *International Federation of City, Sport and Multipurpose Halls – Fédération internationale des salles municipales de sports et polyvalentes.* Later became *International Association of Municipal, Sports and Multipurpose Centres – Union internationale des salles municipales, des halls de sport et des salles polyvalentes – Internationaler Verband der Stadt-, Sport- und Mehrzweckhallen (VDSM).* Previously also known under the French title *Association européenne des centres de manifestations.* Statutes adopted 11 Jun 1956; modified: 1973, 1974, 1987, 1992, 2009, 2017. Present name adopted 1997. Present logo adopted 2008. **Aims** Act as a platform for exchange of experience and information among members; make financial matters of events branch-accessible and transparent to the public; help members communicate with the media and decision makers in their towns and regions. **Structure** General Assembly; Board of Directors; Head Office; Working Groups. **Languages** English, German. **Staff** 5.00 FTE, paid. **Finance** Members' dues. Partners. **Activities** Events/meetings; training/education; guidance/assistance/consulting; knowledge management/information dissemination; awards/prizes/competitions. **Events** *Management Meting* Bregenz (Austria) 2017, *Annual General Assembly* Berlin (Germany) 2014, *Annual General Assembly* Frankfurt-Main (Germany) 2013, *Annual General Assembly* Berlin (Germany) 2012, *Management Symposium* Salzburg (Austria) 2012. **Publications** E-mail newsletter (12 a year). In-house index of members and partners.
Members City halls; municipal halls; sports and multipurpose halls; arenas, special event locations; congress centres. Members (about 300) in 7 countries:
Austria, Bosnia-Herzegovina, Czechia, Germany, Liechtenstein, Luxembourg, Switzerland.
NGO Relations Member of: *Joint Meetings Industry Council (JMIC, #16140).* Cooperates with: *International Association of Venue Managers (IAVM); International Congress and Convention Association (ICCA, #12892).* [2019.10.16/XD1824/**D**]

♦ European Association for Evolutionary Political Economy (EAEPE) . 06033

Gen Sec Fac di Economia, Dipto di Economia, Univ Roma Tre, 3o p – st 3-11, Via Silvio D'amico 111, 00145 Rome RM, Italy.
URL: http://eaepe.org/

History Founded Jun 1988. **Aims** Promote evolutionary, institutional, dynamic and realistic approaches to economic theory and policy. **Structure** Membership Meeting; Council; Board of Trustees; Honorary Presidents; Secretariat. **Languages** English. **Staff** No paid staff. **Finance** Members' dues. Annual budget: about euro 50,000. **Activities** Events/meetings; awards/prizes/competitions; training/education; research/documentation. **Events** *Annual Conference* Naples (Italy) 2022, *Annual Conference* Naples (Italy) 2021, *Annual Conference* Rome (Italy) 2020, *Annual Conference* Warsaw (Poland) 2019, *Annual Conference* Nice (France) 2018. **Publications** *EAEPE Newsletter*, *Journal of Institutional Economics*. *Routledge Series*. *Elgar Companion to Institutional and Evolutionary Economics* (1995) – in 2 vols, with USA national association. Conference proceedings; conference papers.

Members Full in 52 countries and territories:
Albania, Argentina, Australia, Austria, Belarus, Belgium, Brazil, Bulgaria, Canada, Chile, China, Croatia, Czechia, Denmark, Estonia, Ethiopia, Finland, France, Germany, Greece, Hong Kong, Hungary, India, Ireland, Israel, Italy, Jamaica, Japan, Korea Rep, Latvia, Lithuania, Malta, Netherlands, New Zealand, Nigeria, Norway, Pakistan, Philippines, Poland, Portugal, Romania, Russia, Serbia, Slovakia, Slovenia, South Africa, Spain, Sweden, Switzerland, Türkiye, UK, Ukraine.

NGO Relations Member of: *International Confederation of Associations for Pluralism in Economics (ICAPE, #12849)*. [2017.10.26/XD1319/**D**]

♦ European Association for the Exchange of Technical Literature in the Field of Ferrous Metallurgy (inactive)

♦ European Association for Experimental Mechanics (EURASEM) 06034

Sec Lab of Optics and Experimental Mechanics (FEUP/INEGI), Dept of Mechanics, Fac of Engineering of Univ of Porto, Rua Dr Roberto Frias, 4200-465 Porto, Portugal. T. +351225081718. Fax +351225081440.
Pres VUB, MeMC Mechanics on Materials and Construction, Pleinlaan 2 bldg Kb, 1050 Brussels, Belgium. T. +3226292840. Fax +3226292928.
URL: http://eurasem.org/

History 1959, Delft (Netherlands), as *Permanent Committee for Stress Analysis*. Changed title to *European Permanent Committee for Experimental Mechanics*, 1990. Present name adopted 1998. **Aims** Further international collaboration in the field of experimental mechanics. **Structure** International Conference (every 4 years, as a rule 2 years after the International Congress of Applied Mechanics); Permanent Committee. **Languages** English, French, German. **Finance** No financial responsibilities with respect to International Conferences; puts no funds at disposal of organizations or of the country organizing International Conference. **Activities** Training/education; knowledge management/information dissemination; research and development; standards/guidelines. **Events** *International Conference on Experimental Mechanics (ICEM)* Krakow (Poland) 2022, *ICEM : International Conference on Experimental Mechanics* Krakow (Poland) 2021, *ICEM : International Conference on Experimental Mechanics* Krakow (Poland) 2020, *ICEM : International Conference on Experimental Mechanics* Brussels (Belgium) 2018, *ICEM : International Conference on Experimental Mechanics* Rhodes Is (Greece) 2016.

Members National organizations represented in the Permanent Committee in 19 countries:
Austria, Belgium, Denmark, Estonia, France, Germany, Greece, Ireland, Israel, Italy, Netherlands, Norway, Poland, Portugal, Romania, Spain, Sweden, Switzerland, UK. [2020/XE0606/**D**]

♦ European Association of Experimental Social Psychology / see European Association of Social Psychology (#06210)
♦ European Association of Exploration Geophysicists (inactive)
♦ European Association for Extended Reality / see EuroXR (#09197)

♦ European Association for External Thermal Insulation Composite Systems (EAE) 06035

Managing Dir Boulevard Reyers 80, 1030 Brussels, Belgium. E-mail: info@ea-etics.com.
URL: http://www.ea-etics.eu/

History 2008. Former names and other names: *European Association for ETICS* – alias. Registration: EU Transparency Register, No/ID: 150628337276-48, Start date: 10 Feb 2020. **Aims** Promote system approach; expand the market; engage in political and technical lobbying; conduct research and testing. **Structure** General Meeting; Board. **Activities** Events/meetings. **Events** *European ETICS Forum* Prague (Czechia) 2021, *European ETICS Forum* Warsaw (Poland) 2017, *European ETICS Forum* Milan (Italy) 2015, *Forum* Strasbourg (France) 2012, *Forum* Brussels (Belgium) 2010.

Members Ordinary in 12 countries:
Austria, Belgium, Czechia, France, Germany, Italy, Netherlands, Poland, Romania, Slovakia, Türkiye, UK.
Extraordinary – sector associations (6):
European Association of Bead and Lath Producers (Europrofiles); *European Association of Technical Fabrics producers (TECH-FAB Europe)*; *European Insulation Manufacturers Association (EURIMA, #07577)*; *European Manufacturers of Expanded Polystyrene (EUMEPS, #07732)*; *European Phenolic Foam Association (EPFA, #08199)*; *Federation of European Rigid Polyurethane Foam Associations (PU Europe, #09538)*.

NGO Relations Member of (4): *Construction 2050 Alliance (#04760)*; *Construction Products Europe AISBL (#04761)* (Associate); *European Council for Construction Research, Development and Innovation (ECCREDI, #06813)*; *PolyStyreneLoop Cooperative (PS Loop)*. In liaison with technical committees of: *Comité européen de normalisation (CEN, #04162)*. [2020/XM7410/y/**D**]

♦ European Association of Faculties of Pharmacy (EAFP) 06036

Association européenne des facultés de pharmacie

Pres Dept of Pharmacy Fac of Medicine and Surgery, Univ of Malta, Msida, MSD 2080, Malta. T. +35623402896.
Gen Sec Fac of Pharmacy, Campus Universitario Cartuja, Univ of Granada, 18071 Granada, Spain.
URL: http://eafponline.eu/

History 12 Oct 1992, Paris (France). EU Transparency Register: 23748726738-26. **Aims** Harmonize pharmacy curricula and education standards in Europe; promote exchange of students, faculty and staff; engage in common teaching and research projects. **Structure** General Assembly (annual). Executive Committee (meets at least annually), comprising President, Vice-President, General Secretary, Treasurer and 7 members. **Languages** English. **Staff** 11.00 FTE, voluntary. **Finance** Members' dues. Other sources: grants and subsidies from European and national organizations; subsidies and donations from local authorities and commercial enterprises. Budget (annual): euro 25,000 – euro 30,000. **Activities** Research/documentation. **Events** *Annual Conference* Malta 2020, *Annual Conference* Krakow (Poland) 2019, *Annual Conference* Parma (Italy) 2018, *Annual Conference* Helsinki (Finland) 2017, *Annual Conference* Paris (France) 2016. **Publications** *Euro Pharmacy Faculties News* (4 a year).

Members Active; Associate; Individual. Individuals in 25 countries:
Austria, Belgium, Bosnia-Herzegovina, Bulgaria, Croatia, Czechia, Denmark, Estonia, Finland, France, Germany, Greece, Hungary, Iceland, Ireland, Italy, Malta, Norway, Poland, Romania, Serbia, Slovenia, Spain, Switzerland, UK.

NGO Relations Observer at: *European Federation for Pharmaceutical Sciences (EUFEPS, #07192)*. [2015/XD5710/**D**]

♦ European Association of Fashion Retailers (inactive)
♦ European Association of Fatty Acid Producing Companies / see European Oleochemicals and Allied Products Group (#08081)

♦ European Association of Feldspar Producers (EUROFEL) 06037

SG c/o IMA Europe, Rue des Deux Eglises 26, Box 2, 1000 Brussels, Belgium. T. +3222104410. Fax +3222104429.
URL: http://www.ima-europe.eu/about-ima-europe/associations/eurofel/

History Jun 1996, Brussels (Belgium). Registered in accordance with Belgian law. **Aims** Promote the interests of the European feldspar industry; study scientific, technical, documentary and institutional questions of interest to the industry, particularly with respect to public health, the environment, standardization of working conditions and hygiene, definition of technical standards and information regarding national and European Community regulations. **Structure** General Assembly (annual); Administrative Council. **Languages** English. **Finance** Members'dues.

Members Full organizations and companies involved in extraction, treatment or sales of feldspar in Europe. Associate other organizations or individuals with an interest in and contributing to the Association. Full members in 8 countries:
Finland, France, Germany, Italy, Portugal, Spain, Sweden, Türkiye.

NGO Relations Member of: *Industrial Minerals Association – Europe (IMA Europe, #11179)*. Shares office staff with: *European Association of Plaster and Plaster Product Manufacturers (EUROGYPSUM, #06152)*; *Calcium Carbonate Association – Europe (CCA-Europe, #03399)*; *European Association of Industrial Silica Producers (EUROSIL, #06082)*; *European Bentonite Producers Association (EUBA, #06328)*; *European Borates Association (EBA, #06382)*; *European Kaolin and Plastic Clays Association (KPC Europe, #07623)*; *European Lime Association (EuLA, #07699)*; *European Speciality Minerals Association (ESMA, #08811)*; *International Diatomite Producers Association (IDPA, #13172)*; *Scientific Association of European Talc Industry (Eurotalc, #19146)*; IMA Europe. [2016.10.19/XD5486/**D**]

♦ European Association of Fibre Drum Manufacturers 06038

Syndicat européen de l'industrie des fûts de fibres (SEFFI) – Verband der Europäischen Fiberfassindustrie

Sec Boval House, 24 Mount Prade, Harrogate, HG1 1BX, UK. T. +447770633320. Fax +447053642594. E-mail: seffi@theipa.co.uk.
URL: http://www.seffi.org/

History Founded 1991. **Aims** Promote benefits of fibre drums; represent the industry at European and international levels. **Structure** General Assembly (annual); Working Groups (3). **Languages** English. **Staff** 3.00 FTE, paid. **Activities** Standards/guidelines; guidance/assistance/consulting; events/meetings. **Events** *Annual General Meeting* Budapest (Hungary) 2019, *Meeting* Düsseldorf (Germany) 2015, *Annual General Meeting* Rome (Italy) 2015, *Annual General Meeting* Rome (Italy) 2015, *International Conference on Industrial Packaging* Vancouver, BC (Canada) 2015. **Publications** *Notes on National Reuse, Recycling and Disposal Legislation*.

Members Companies involved in the production of fibre drums in 11 countries:
Finland, France, Germany, Ireland, Italy, Netherlands, Spain, Sweden, Switzerland, Türkiye, UK.

IGO Relations *International Civil Aviation Organization (ICAO, #12581)*; *International Maritime Organization (IMO, #14102)*. **NGO Relations** *European Industrial Packaging Association (EIPA, #07529)*; *International Fibre Drum Institute (IFDI)*. [2018.08.06/XD4911/t/**D**]

♦ European Association of Firms Specializing in the Restoration of the Architectural Heritage / see European Association Architectural Heritage Restoration Firms (#05942)

♦ European Association of Fisheries Economists (EAFE) 06039

Sec AZTI Marine Research, Txatxarramendi Ugartea z/g, 48395 Sukarrieta, Álava, Spain.
Pres Univ of Western Brittany, 12 rue de Kergoat – Bat B, CS 93837, 29238 Brest CEDEX 3, France.
URL: http://www.umr-amure.fr/eafe/html/index_01.php

History 12 Jan 1989, Brussels (Belgium). Registered in accordance with French law. **Aims** Promote cooperation in economic research in fisheries and *aquaculture*; assist in dissemination of information about fisheries economics among members; further understanding of fisheries economics; serve as a channel of communication with other interested bodies. **Structure** General Meeting; Bureau. **Languages** English. **Finance** Members' dues. Other sources: support from corporate membership. **Activities** Events/meetings. **Events** *New management issues within the reformed Common Fishery Policy – implementation and socio-economic impacts* Salerno (Italy) 2015, *Conference / Annual Meeting and Conference* Edinburgh (UK) 2013, *Conference* Hamburg (Germany) 2011, *Annual Meeting and Conference* Helsinki (Finland) 2010, *Annual meeting and conference* Malta 2009.

Members Corporate (5) institutions and representative groups in the EEA with an interest in fisheries and fisheries economics research. Individual (102) and Student (2) economists working in fisheries in academia, industry or the public sector, from or working in a member state of the EEA. Corporate in 5 countries:
Denmark, France, Netherlands, Spain, UK.
Individuals and students in 20 countries:
Belgium, Canada, Denmark, Finland, France, Germany, Greece, Iceland, Ireland, Italy, Japan, Latvia, Lithuania, Netherlands, Norway, Portugal, Spain, Sweden, Türkiye, UK.

IGO Relations European Commission (DG Maritime Affairs Fisheries); FAO; OECD. [2015.06.01/XF0936/**E**]

♦ European Association of Fishing Ports and Auctions (inactive)

♦ European Association of Fish Pathologists (EAFP) 06040

Gen Sec Croatian Veterinary Inst, Lab for Fish and Molluscs Diseases, Savska 143, HR-10000 Zagreb, Croatia. T. +38516123663.
URL: http://www.eafp.org/

History 25 Oct 1979, Munich (Germany). **Aims** Promote rapid exchange of experience and information on aquatic disease problems and related topics. **Structure** Council. **Languages** English. **Staff** Voluntary. **Finance** Members' dues. **Activities** Events/meetings; training/education. **Events** *International Conference on Diseases of Fish and Shellfish* Aberdeen (UK) 2023, *International Conference on Diseases of Fish and Shellfish* Porto (Portugal) 2019, *International Conference on Diseases of Fish and Shellfish* Belfast (UK) 2017, *International Conference on Diseases of Fish and Shellfish* Las Palmas de Gran Canaria (Spain) 2015, *International Conference on Diseases of Fish and Shellfish* Tampere (Finland) 2013. **Publications** *EAFP Bulletin* (6 a year). Conference proceedings.

Members Sustaining (organizations), libraries and individuals in 55 countries and territories:
Argentina, Australia, Austria, Belgium, Brazil, Canada, Chile, China, Côte d'Ivoire, Croatia, Cyprus, Czechia, Denmark, Egypt, Faeroe Is, Finland, France, Germany, Greece, Hungary, Iceland, India, Indonesia, Iran Islamic Rep, Ireland, Israel, Italy, Japan, Korea Rep, Latvia, Malaysia, Malta, Netherlands, New Zealand, Norway, Philippines, Poland, Portugal, Romania, Russia, Serbia, Slovenia, South Africa, Spain, Sweden, Switzerland, Syrian AR, Taiwan, Thailand, Tunisia, Türkiye, UK, Ukraine, USA, Vietnam. [2022/XD3773/**D**]

♦ European Association of Fish Producers Organizations (EAPO) 06041

Association Européenne des Organisations de Producteurs dans le secteur de la pêche – Asociación Europea de Organizaciones de Productores de Pesca – Europese Vereniging van Producentenorganisaties in de Visserijsector

SG Hendrik Baelskaai 20 bus 0-2, 8400 Ostend, Belgium. T. +3259432005. Fax +3259322840. E-mail: info@eapo.com.
URL: http://www.eapo.com/

History Founded 2 Dec 1980. Previously also referred to in Dutch as *Europese Vereniging van Visproducerende Organisaties*. EU Transparency Register: 46491656228-65. **Aims** Improve relationships between European fish producers; solve the European fish marketing problems. **Structure** General Assembly; Executive Committee.

Members Full in 10 countries:
Belgium, Denmark, France, Germany, Ireland, Netherlands, Poland, Spain, Sweden, UK.

NGO Relations *Market Advisory Council (MAC, #16584)*. [2019/XD7968/**D**]

♦ European Association of Flexible Polyurethane Foam Blocks Manufacturers (EUROPUR) 06042

Association européenne des fabricants de blocs de mousse souple de polyuréthane – Verband der Europäischen Hersteller von Polyurethan-Weichblockschaum

SG Av de Cortenbergh 71, 1000 Brussels, Belgium. T. +3227418281. Fax +3227366072. E-mail: info@europur.org.
Pres address not obtained.
URL: http://www.europur.com/

History 1966. Registration: Banque-Carrefour des Entreprises, No/ID: 0451.703.066, Start date: 23 Dec 1993, Belgium. **Aims** Establish permanent liaison between member associations; promote joint study of matters of common interest; ensure promotion and representation of the polyurethane foam industry at the international level and in particular with European economic institutions; liaise with associations representing related industries, suppliers' industry and client sectors. **Structure** General Assembly (annual); Board of Directors; Executive Committee; Technical Committee; Secretariat, headed by Secretary General. **Languages** English. **Staff** 1.50 FTE, paid. **Finance** Sources: members' dues. Annual budget: 150,000 EUR. **Activities** Events/

European Association Flower
06042

alphabetic sequence excludes
For the complete listing, see Yearbook Online at

meetings; networking/liaising. **Events** *Annual Conference* Berlin (Germany) 2022, *Annual General Assembly* Lisbon (Portugal) 2019, *Annual General Assembly* Brussels (Belgium) 2016, *Annual General Assembly* Frankfurt-Main (Germany) 2015, *Annual General Assembly* Vienna (Austria) 2014. **Publications** Fact sheet; guidelines; review.
Members Ordinary national associations and individual member companies in 29 countries:
Austria, Belgium, Denmark, Estonia, Finland, France, Germany, Ghana, Greece, Hungary, Ireland, Italy, Kosovo, Lithuania, Netherlands, Norway, Poland, Portugal, Romania, Russia, Serbia, Slovenia, South Africa, Spain, Sweden, Switzerland, Türkiye, UK, Ukraine.
Associate suppliers of raw materials from the chemical industry and producers of manufacturing equipment, in 12 countries:
Belgium, Denmark, France, Germany, Hungary, Italy, Netherlands, Norway, Poland, Spain, Switzerland, UK.
NGO Relations Member of (1): *Circular Plastics Alliance (#03936)*. Cooperates with (1): *European Association of Manufacturers of Moulded Polyurethane Parts for the Automotive Industry (EURO-MOULDERS, #06116)*. Defends common interests together with: *Federation of European Rigid Polyurethane Foam Associations (PU Europe, #09538)* and *European Diisocyanate and Polyol Producers Association (ISOPA, #06926)*.
[2022/XD1562/**D**]

♦ European Association for Flower Growers (unconfirmed)
♦ European Association for Flowers and Landscaping (#02570)

♦ European Association of Folklore Festivals (EAFF) 06043

Contact 47 Nikola Gabrovski Str, PO Box 27 A, 5002 Veliko Turnovo, Bulgaria. T. +35962621541. E-mail: office@eaff.eu.
URL: http://eaff.eu/

History 2007, Veliko Tarnovo (Bulgaria). Set up 2007, Vilko Tarnovo (Bulgaria). **Aims** Preserve, develop and make popular the folklore of the different European nations by organizing festivals and using the modern television, computer and other information technologies. **Activities** Events/meetings. **Publications** *Review of EAFF*.
Members Festivals in 42 countries:
Albania, Armenia, Austria, Azerbaijan, Belarus, Bosnia-Herzegovina, Brazil, Bulgaria, China, Croatia, Czechia, Estonia, Finland, France, Georgia, Germany, Greece, Hungary, India, Israel, Italy, Kazakhstan, Korea Rep, Latvia, Lithuania, Malta, Montenegro, Morocco, Netherlands, North Macedonia, Poland, Romania, Russia, Serbia, Slovakia, Spain, Tunisia, Türkiye, UK, United Arab Emirates, Uzbekistan, Vietnam.
Groups in 28 countries:
Armenia, Belarus, Brazil, Bulgaria, Canada, Croatia, Cyprus, Estonia, Georgia, India, Indonesia, Iran Islamic Rep, Ireland, Israel, Latvia, Lithuania, Malaysia, Moldova, Mongolia, Paraguay, Poland, Romania, Russia, Slovakia, Slovenia, Sweden, Ukraine, USA.
IGO Relations Consultant to: *Intergovernmental Committee for the Safeguarding of the Intangible Cultural Heritage (#11477)*. Accredited to: *UNESCO (#20322)* – Intangible Cultural Heritage. **NGO Relations** Member of: *International Mask Arts and Culture Organization (IMACO, #14111)*; *International Dance Council (#13130)*; *International Organization of Folk Art (IOV World, #14447)*.
[2018/XM6513/**D**]

♦ European Association for Food Safety (SAFE Consortium) 06044

SG Rue Vanderborght 20, 1081 Brussels, Belgium.
Scientific Secretary address not obtained.
URL: http://www.safeconsortium.org/

History Oct 2002. **Aims** Promote food safety in Europe through coordination, development and dissemination of scientific research. **Structure** General Meeting (annual); Executive Board. **Languages** English. **Events** *ENG Annual Global Food Safety Summit* Amsterdam (Netherlands) 2015, *Workshop on Keeping Safety and Integrity in the Food Chain* Bilbao (Spain) 2015, *Annual General Meeting* Brussels (Belgium) 2015, *Congress* Istanbul (Turkey) 2011, *Congress* Girona (Spain) 2009.
Members Organizations (13) in 10 countries:
Iceland, Italy, Lithuania, Norway, Poland, Portugal, Romania, Slovakia, Spain, Switzerland.
IGO Relations *European Commission (EC, #06633)*; *European Food Safety Authority (EFSA, #07287)*. **NGO Relations** Member of: *FOODforce (#09843)*.
[2021/XD8756/**D**]

♦ European Association of Football Teams Physicians (inactive)

♦ European Association for Forensic Child and Adolescent Psychiatry, Psychology and Other Involved Professions (EFCAP) 06045

Contact PO Box 909, 5600 AX Eindhoven, Netherlands. E-mail: info@efcap.eu.
Contact address not obtained.
URL: https://www.efcap.eu/

History 1997, The Hague (Netherlands). **Aims** Improve facilities and facilitate joint international scientific research to promote interdisciplinary training and interdisciplinary education; exchange data obtained from research, and practical experiences and innovative research and treatment methods; gather information on and contribute to national and European policy, in so far as this policy affects young people; raise awareness of the need for constant change in criminal and civil justice systems, so as to provide for the interests and development requirements of children and young people. **Structure** Board; Advisory Board; National Groups in Finland, Netherlands, Portugal and UK. **Languages** English. **Staff** 2.00 FTE, voluntary. **Finance** Sources: none. **Activities** Knowledge management/information dissemination. **Events** *Conference* Eindhoven (Netherlands) 2021, *Conference* Eindhoven (Netherlands) 2020, *Congress* Porto (Portugal) 2016, *Youth, risk and mental health – multiple roads to recovery* Manchester (UK) 2014, *Congress* Berlin (Germany) 2012.
[2021/XD9246/**D**]

♦ European Association for Forensic Entomology (EAFE) 06046

Pres c/o IRCGN, Faune Flore Forensique, 5 bd de l'Hautil, 95037 Cergy-Pontoise CEDEX, France. E-mail: president@eafe.org.
Contact c/o INCC Labo Microtraces, 100 Chaussée de Vilvorde, 1120 Brussels, Belgium.
URL: http://www.eafe.org/

History 2002. **Aims** Promote the use of entomology in forensic casework in Europe. **Activities** Events/ meetings. **Events** *Conference* Crete (Greece) 2023, *Conference* Alcala de Henares (Spain) 2022, *Conference* Portsmouth (UK) 2021, *Conference* Portsmouth (UK) 2020, *Conference* Bordeaux (France) 2019. **Members** Individuals. Membership countries not specified.
[2022/XM3741/**D**]

♦ European Association of Former Members of Parliament of the Member States of the Council of Europe / see European Association of Former Parliamentarians (#06047)

♦ European Association of Former Parliamentarians (FP-AP) 06047

Association Européenne des Anciens Parlementaires (FP-AP)

Sec Palais de la Nation, Place de la Nation 1, 1009 Brussels, Belgium. T. +32474296795. E-mail: fpap.secretariat@gmail.com.
SG address not obtained.
Seat Assemblée Nationale, 126 rue de l'Université, 75355 Paris 07 SP, France.
URL: https://www.fpap-europe.org/

History 1994. Informal group initially set up 1987, Strasbourg (France), by representatives of Belgium, Germany, France and Italy. Former names and other names: *European Association of Former Members of Parliament of the Member States of the Council of Europe* – former; *Association européenne des anciens parlementaires des pays membres du Conseil de l'Europe* – former. **Aims** Promote the European ideal, based on individual and political liberties, the primacy of law and true democracy; contribute to European construction. **Structure** General Assembly; Bureau; Restricted Bureau. **Languages** English, French. **Finance** Sources: members' dues. **Activities** Events/meetings; politics/policy/regulatory; research/documentation. **Events** *Annual General Assembly* Brussels (Belgium) 2021, *Annual General Assembly* Brussels (Belgium) 2020.
Members Full in 21 countries:
Andorra, Austria, Belgium, Cyprus, Finland, France, Germany, Greece, Ireland, Italy, Luxembourg, Malta, Netherlands, Norway, Poland, Portugal, Spain, Sweden, Switzerland, Türkiye, UK.
Observer in 1 country:
Lithuania.
Regional member:
European Parliament Former Members Association (FMA, #08151).
[2021.05.25/XJ7783/**E**]

♦ European Association for Forwarding, Transport, Logistics and Customs Services / see CLECAT (#03993)
♦ European Association for Free Nature Reserves (inactive)

♦ European Association of the Free Thought (EAFT) 06048

Association Européenne de la Pensée Libre (AEPL) – Asociación Europea de Pensamiento Libre (AEPL) – Europäische Freidenkervereinigung (EFDV) – Associazione Europea del Pensiero Libero (AEPL) – Europese Vereniging van het Vrije Denken (EVVD)

Contact address not obtained. E-mail: presidentaepl@outlook.com.
URL: http://www.aepl.eu/

History 2007. Registered in accordance with Belgian law. **Aims** Promote propagation of the principles developed by the 18th century *Enlightenment*; stimulate debate about European topics; promote a secular Europe. **Languages** Dutch, English, French, German, Italian, Spanish. **Staff** None paid. **Finance** Members' dues. **Activities** Knowledge management/information dissemination.
Members Full (about 1,900) in 17 countries:
Austria, Belgium, Bulgaria, Estonia, Finland, France, Germany, Italy, Latvia, Luxembourg, Netherlands, North Macedonia, Poland, Portugal, Spain, Switzerland, UK.
IGO Relations Partner of: *European Commission (EC, #06633)*; *European Parliament (EP, #08146)*. **NGO Relations** Member of Advisory Board of: *European Parliament Platform for Secularism in Politics (EPPSP, #08152)*.
[2020.03.03/XJ5952/**D**]

♦ European Association of Freight Villages / see European Logistic Platforms Association (#07709)
♦ European Association of Fruit Juice Industries / see European Fruit Juice Association (#07362)

♦ European Association of Fruit and Vegetable Processors (PROFEL) . 06049

Organisation Européenne des Industries Transformatrices de Fruits et Légumes

Contact Av des Nerviens 9-31, 1040 Brussels, Belgium. T. +3225008759. E-mail: profel@profel-europe.eu.
URL: http://www.profel-europe.eu/

History 16 Nov 1978. Founded on merger of *Organisation européenne des industries de la conserve de légumes (OECL, inactive)*, set up 28 May 1958, and *European Organization of Preserved and Tinned Fruit Industries (OEICCF, inactive)*. Former names and other names: *Organisation européenne des industries transformatrices de fruits et légumes (OEITFL)* – former; *Association of European Fruit and Vegetable Processing Industries* – former; *Organización Europea de Industrias Transformadoras de Frutas y Hortalizas* – former; *Europäische Organisation der Obst- und Gemuseverarbeitenden Industrie* – former; *Organizzazione Europea delle Industrie di Trasformazione di Frutta e Ortaggi* – former; *Europese Organisatie der Groenten en Fruitverwerkende Industrie* – former; *Europaeiske Organisation for Frugt- og Grøntforarbejdningsindustri* – former; *Euroopan Hedelmä- ja Vihannesteollisuusyhdistys* – former; *Enosi Evropaikon Viomihanion Metapiisis Frouton ke Lahanikon* – former; *Organization of European Industries Transforming Fruit and Vegetables* – former. Registration: EU Transparency Register, No/ID: 609308836770-29. **Aims** Represent the processed fruit and vegetable sector in Europe. **Structure** General Assembly; Executive Committee; Secretariat. Sections (6): Canned Vegetables; Frozen Vegetables; Dried Vegetables; Deciduous Fruit; Fruit Jams; Frozen Fruit. **Languages** English, French, Italian, Spanish. **Events** *Conference* Brussels (Belgium) 2018, *International conference on fruit, vegetable and potato processing* Bruges (Belgium) 2005, *General Assembly* Brussels (Belgium) 2002.
Members National Associations; Companies. Members in 11 countries:
Austria, Belgium, Finland, France, Germany, Greece, Hungary, Italy, Netherlands, Spain, UK.
IGO Relations Recognized by: *European Commission (EC, #06633)*. **NGO Relations** Affiliated member of: *FoodDrinkEurope (#09841)*. Member of: *CIUS – European Sugar Users (#03961)*.
[2021.06.08/XD1547/t/**D**]

♦ European Association of Functional Re-education and Professional Training Centres in Precision Orthopedics and Skilled Shoe-making for Young Physically Handicapped (inactive)
♦ European Association of Furniture Technology Institutes (inactive)

♦ European Association of Gas and Steam Turbine Manufacturers (EUTurbines) 06050

SG Lyoner Str 18, 60528 Frankfurt-Main, Germany. T. +496966031309. Fax +496966032309.
Brussels Office Blue Point, Blvd A Reyers 80, 1030 Brussels, Belgium. T. +3227068211. Fax +3227068210.
URL: http://www.euturbines.eu/

History 2004. Former names and other names: *EUnited Turbines* – former (2004). Registration: EU Transparency Register, No/ID: 75093131694-63. **Aims** Serve as the voice of the European gas and steam turbine manufacturers; strengthen the competitive position of the industry and keep its leading role in the global market place. **Languages** English. **Finance** Sources: members' dues. **Activities** Events/meetings. **Events** *Conference on Energy Related Research* Brussels (Belgium) 2012. **Members** Corporations. Membership countries not specified. **NGO Relations** Member of (2): *European Energy Forum (EEF, #06986)*; *Industry4Europe (#11181)*. Technical Liaison Partner with: *European Committee for Electrotechnical Standardization (CENELEC, #06647)*.
[2021.06.09/XJ8179/**D**]

♦ European Association for Gastrocamera Diagnosis / see European Association for Gastroenterology, Endoscopy and Nutrition (#06051)
♦ European Association for Gastroenterology and Endoscopy / see European Association for Gastroenterology, Endoscopy and Nutrition (#06051)

♦ European Association for Gastroenterology, Endoscopy and Nutrition (EAGEN) 06051

Admin Office Destination Services, Nuellerstr 48, 42115 Wuppertal, Germany. T. +492028702991. Fax +492022572291. E-mail: eage@d-s-europe.com.
Sec MU – Internal Med, Auenbruggerplatz 15, 8036 Graz, Austria. Fax +433163853428.
URL: http://www.eagen.org/

History Feb 1970, Berlin (Germany). Founded on the initiative of Hiroshi Oshima. Former names and other names: *European Association for Gastrocamera Diagnosis* – former (1970); *Association européenne du diagnostic de la gastrocamera* – former (1970); *Europäische Gesellschaft für Gastrokamera-Diagnostik* – former (1970); *European Association for Gastroenterology and Endoscopy (EAGE)* – former; *Europäische Gesellschaft für Gastroenterologie und Endoskopie* – former; *European Society for Gastrocamera Diagnosis and Endoscopy* – former (1979). **Aims** Exchange experience and ideas in the field of gastroenterology and endoscopy; promote scientific research and postgraduate training, and improved standards of practice. **Structure** General Assembly of members (annual, in conjunction with scientific meeting) elects Executive Committee consisting of President (2 years), 2 Secretaries and a Treasurer (5-year terms), which nominates 8-member Programme Committee and appoints auxiliary advisory committee. **Languages** English. **Staff** 400.00 FTE, paid. **Finance** Members' dues. **Activities** *European Postgraduate School in Gastroenterology*. **Events** *Board Meeting* Vienna (Austria) 2017, *Meeting on gastroenterology and hepatology* Vienna (Austria) 1998, *Annual Congress* Birmingham (UK) 1997, *Annual Congress* Paris (France) 1996, *Annual Congress* Berlin (Germany) 1995. **Publications** *European Journal for Gastroenterology and Hepatology*.
Members Individuals in 33 countries:
Australia, Austria, Belgium, Chile, Czechia, Denmark, Finland, France, Germany, Greece, Hungary, Iceland, Ireland, Israel, Italy, Korea DPR, Korea Rep, Kuwait, Luxembourg, Malaysia, Malta, Netherlands, Norway, Poland, Portugal, Saudi Arabia, Slovenia, South Africa, Spain, Sweden, Switzerland, Türkiye, UK.
NGO Relations Through: *United European Gastroenterology (UEG, #20506)*, a consortium of 7 European associations, organizes an annual scientific meeting in the field (the first in Feb 1991). The other 5 associations are: *International Society for Digestive Surgery (ISDS, #15060)* (European chapter); *European Association for the Study of the Liver (EASL, #06233)*; *European Pancreatic Club (EPC, #08136)*; *European Society of Gastrointestinal Endoscopy (ESGE, #08606)*; *European Society for Paediatric Gastroenterology, Hepatology and Nutrition (ESPGHAN, #08680)*.
[2022/XD3972/v/**D**]

♦ European Association for Gastrointestinal Emergencies and Intensive Care (inactive)

♦ The European Association for Gender Research, Education and Documentation (ATGENDER) 06052

Sec PO Box 164, 3500 AD Utrecht, Netherlands. T. +31302536013.
URL: https://atgender.eu/

History Sep 2009. Founded following agreement between *Association of Institutions for Feminist Education and Research in Europe (AOIFE, inactive), Women's International Studies Europe (WISE, inactive)* and *Advanced Thematic Network in European Women's Studies (ATHENA, inactive)*. **Aims** Provide a professional association for academics in the interdisciplinary field of Women's, Gender, Transgender, Sexuality and Queer Studies, Feminist Research and professionals that promote women's, sexual and LGBTQI rights, equality and diversity in Europe. **Structure** Board of Directors. **Languages** Danish, Dutch, English, Finnish, French, German, Greek, Italian, Polish, Serbian, Swedish, Turkish. **Staff** 1.00 FTE, paid. **Finance** Sources: members' dues. In 2012 co-funded by: *European Union (EU, #08967)* Lifelong Learning Programme. **Activities** Events/meetings; knowledge management/information dissemination; publishing activities. **Events** *European Feminist Research Conference* Milan (Italy) 2022, *Spring Conference* London (UK) 2020, *Spring Conference* Gijón (Spain) 2019, *European Feminist Research Conference* Göttingen (Germany) 2018, *Spring Conference* Vilnius (Lithuania) 2017. **Publications** *ATGender News* (irregular). *Teaching with Gender.* Brochure.
Members Institutions (59) in 21 countries:
Austria, Belgium, Croatia, Czechia, Denmark, Finland, France, Germany, Hungary, Ireland, Italy, Kosovo, Lithuania, Netherlands, Norway, Portugal, Serbia, Spain, Sweden, Switzerland, UK. [2021.05.27/XM2545/E]

♦ European association for gender surgery (unconfirmed)

♦ European Association of Geochemistry (EAG) 06053

Business Office Wijnbouw 7, 3991 NL Houten, Netherlands. E-mail: office@eag.eu.com.
Headquarters IPGP Gopel Bur 566, 1 rue Jussieu, 75238 Paris CEDEX 05, France.
URL: http://www.eag.eu.com/

History 1985. Registered in accordance with French law. **Aims** Promote geochemistry internationally and in particular provide a forum for the presentation of geochemistry, exchange of ideas, publications and recognition of scientific excellence. **Languages** English. **Staff** 2.00 FTE, paid. **Activities** Events/meetings; publishing activities; awards/prizes/competitions; financial and/or material support. **Events** *Goldschmidt Conference* Houten (Netherlands) 2020, *Goldschmidt Conference* Barcelona (Spain) 2019, *Goldschmidt Conference* Boston, MA (USA) 2018, *Goldschmidt Conference* Paris (France) 2017, *Goldschmidt Conference* Yokohama (Japan) 2016. **Publications** *Geochemical Perspectives.* Geochemical Perspectives Letters.
Members Individuals (2900), including 70% in Europe. Membership countries not specified. **NGO Relations** Organizes Goldschmidt Conference with: *Geochemical Society.* [2017.03.08/XD0992/D]

♦ European Association of Geographers (EUROGEO) 06054

Réseau européen des associations de professeurs de géographie – Europäisches Netzwerk der Schulgeographenverbände

Pres Univ of Zaragoza, Pedro Cerbuna 12, 50009 Saragossa, Spain. E-mail: president@eurogeography.eu.
Registered Office 3 Sint Blasiusstraat, 8020 Waardamme, Belgium.
URL: http://www.eurogeography.eu/

History 1979. Former names and other names: *European Standing Conference of Geography Teachers' Associations (ESCGTA)* – former (1979 to Jan 1995); *Conférence permanente européenne des associations de professeurs de géographie (CEPG)* – former (1979 to Jan 1995); *European Network of Geography Teachers' Associations (EUROGEO)* – former (Jan 1995 to 2008). Registration: Banque-Carrefour des Entreprises, No/ID: 0817.975.363, Start date: 21 Aug 2009, Belgium; EU Transparency Register, No/ID: 528257519840-30, Start date: 7 Dec 2015. **Aims** Develop, support and promote policies designed to advance the status of geography; establish and promote cross-border cooperation in the field; promote education and training in geography from a European perspective; represent nationally and internationally members' views. **Structure** Standing Conference (convened normally every year). **Finance** Sources: contributions; revenue from activities/projects; sponsorship; subsidies. Subsidies from international organizations including *European Commission (EC, #06633).* **Activities** Advocacy/lobbying/activism; events/meetings; guidance/assistance/consulting; training/education. **Events** *Annual Conference* Madrid (Spain) 2021, *Annual Conference* Madrid (Spain) 2020, *Annual Conference* Ljubljana (Slovenia) 2019, *Annual Conference* Paris (France) 2019, *Annual General Meeting* Paris (France) 2019. **Publications** *European Journal of Geography. EUROGEO Books Series.* Books; proceedings.
Members Participating associations in 27 countries:
Albania, Belgium, Czechia, Denmark, Finland, France, Germany, Iceland, Ireland, Italy, Latvia, Lithuania, Luxembourg, Malta, Netherlands, Norway, Poland, Portugal, Romania, Russia, Slovakia, Slovenia, Spain, Sweden, Switzerland, UK, Ukraine.
Consultative Status Consultative status granted from: *Council of Europe (CE, #04881)* (Participatory Status); *ECOSOC (#05331)* (Special). **NGO Relations** Member of (1): *International Platform for Citizen Participation (IPCP, #14599).* [2021.09.01/XF1798/F]

♦ European Association of Geoscientists and Engineers (EAGE) 06055

CEO De Molen 42, 3994 DB Houten, Netherlands. T. +31889955055. Fax +31306343524. E-mail: eage@eage.org.
URL: http://www.eage.org/

History 1 Jan 1995. Founded by merger of *European Association of Exploration Geophysicists (EAEG, inactive)* and *European Association of Petroleum Geoscientists and Engineers (EAPG, inactive)*, which became respectively the Geophysical and Petroleum Divisions of EAGE. Registration: Netherlands. **Aims** Promote development and application of geosciences and related engineering subjects; promote innovation and technical progress. **Structure** Business Meeting (annual, at Conference); Board; Technical Divisions; Committees (7); Advisory Council; Head Office in Houten (Netherlands); Regional Offices in Bogota (Colombia), Dubai (United Arab Emirates), Kuala Lumpur (Malaysia) and Moscow (Russia). Asia Pacific. **Languages** English. **Staff** 60.00 FTE, paid. **Finance** Members' dues: Active, euro 50; Student, Retired, euro 25. **Activities** Awards/prizes/competitions; events/meetings; publishing activities; training/education. **Events** *EAGE Conference on Petroleum Geostatistics* Porto (Portugal) 2023, *Annual Conference* Vienna (Austria) 2023, *EAGE Conference on Digital Innovation for a Sustainable Future* Bangkok (Thailand) 2022, *International Petroleum Technology Conference (IPTC)* Dhahran (Saudi Arabia) 2022, *Annual Conference* Madrid (Spain) 2022. **Publications** *First Break* (12 a year) – magazine; *Geophysical Prospecting* (6 a year) – journal of the Geophysical Division; *Near Surface Geophysics* (6 a year); *Basin Research* (4 a year) – journal; *Petroleum Geoscience* (4 a year) – journal of the Petroleum Division. Regional newsletters; workshop proceedings; extended abstracts of workshops and conference papers; books. **Information Services** *EarthDoc* – online geoscience database; *Learning Geoscience* – education portal.
Members Active; Student; Honorary; Emeritus. Members include members of the former EAEG and EAPG and may belong to either or both of the 2 divisions. Individuals (about 19,000) in 102 countries and territories:
Albania, Algeria, Angola, Argentina, Australia, Austria, Azerbaijan, Bahrain, Bangladesh, Belarus, Belgium, Bolivia, Botswana, Brazil, Brunei Darussalam, Bulgaria, Cameroon, Canada, Chile, China, Colombia, Congo DR, Croatia, Cyprus, Czechia, Denmark, Ecuador, Egypt, Estonia, Faeroe Is, Finland, France, Gabon, Germany, Ghana, Greece, Greenland, Hong Kong, Hungary, Iceland, India, Indonesia, Iran Islamic Rep, Iraq, Ireland, Israel, Italy, Japan, Kazakhstan, Korea Rep, Kuwait, Latvia, Lebanon, Libya, Lithuania, Luxembourg, Malaysia, Malta, Mexico, Morocco, Myanmar, Namibia, Netherlands, New Zealand, Niger, Nigeria, Norway, Oman, Pakistan, Peru, Philippines, Poland, Portugal, Qatar, Romania, Russia, Saudi Arabia, Senegal, Serbia-Montenegro, Singapore, Slovakia, Slovenia, South Africa, Spain, Sudan, Sweden, Switzerland, Syrian AR, Taiwan, Tanzania UR, Thailand, Trinidad-Tobago, Tunisia, Türkiye, UK, Ukraine, United Arab Emirates, USA, Uzbekistan, Venezuela, Vietnam, Zimbabwe.
NGO Relations Associated with: *Balkan Geophysical Society (BGS, #03074); EurAsian Geophysical Society (EAGO); European Geosciences Union (EGU, #07390); Scandinavian Visualization Society (Scanviz);* national associations. Together with *American Association of Petroleum Geologists (AAPG), Society of Economic Geologists (SEG, #19546)* and *Society of Petroleum Engineers (SPE, #19616),* sponsors *International Petroleum Technology Conference (IPTC).* [2021/XD4765/v/D]

♦ European Association of Geosynthetic product Manufacturers (EAGM) 06056

Sec Postbus 109, 9670 AC Winschoten, Netherlands. E-mail: info@eagm.eu.
Contact address not obtained.
URL: http://www.eagm.eu/

History Registration: Handelsregister, No/ID: KVK 83348794, Netherlands; EU Transparency Register, No/ID: 274194344591-38, Start date: 18 Nov 2021. **Aims** Promote the knowledge and the usage of European synthetic products and underline the sustainable benefits when applying these products; establish free circulation of geosynthetic products within the European Community, in a market where products have to comply with the same criteria and standards in each individual country; promote and maintain a high level of quality for geosynthetic products, to be subject to equal and objective parameters, assuring customers that products from EAGM members are of a proven high level of quality; strive for a full acceptance of geosynthetic products and solutions as equal or better than "conservative" building methods. **Structure** Board, composed of President, Vice-President and Treasurer. **Activities** Advocacy/lobbying/activism; awareness raising; events/meetings; guidance/assistance/consulting; networking/liaising; publishing activities; standards/guidelines.
Members Companies (22). Membership countries not specified. [2023.02.14/XM7657/D]

♦ European Association of Geriatric Psychiatry (EAGP) 06057

Association européenne de psychiatrie gériatrique – Europäische Arbeitsgemeinschaft für Gerontopsychiatrie

Executive Secretariat Alexianer Krefeld GmbH, Diessemer Bruch 81, 47805 Krefeld, Germany.
Pres Inst of Mental Health, Univ of Nottingham, Jubilee Campus, Univ of Nottingham Innovation Park, Triumph Road, Nottingham, NG7 2TU, UK.
URL: http://www.eagp.com/

History 1971. Formally registered in 1987. **Aims** Advance research, practice and education in the field of geriatric psychiatry. **Structure** Membership Meeting (annual); Board. **Languages** English, French, German. **Finance** Members' dues. **Activities** Networking/liaising; events/meetings; knowledge management/information dissemination. **Events** *Annual Symposium* Santiago de Compostela (Spain) 2010, *Annual symposium* Tours (France) 2009, *Annual Symposium* Kos (Greece) 2008, *Annual Symposium* Santiago de Compostela (Spain) 2007, *Annual Symposium* Cologne (Germany) 2006. **Publications** *International Journal of Geriatric Psychiatry* – official journal. Symposium proceedings.
Members Full in 29 countries and territories:
Australia, Austria, Belgium, Canada, Czechia, Denmark, Finland, France, Germany, Greece, Hong Kong, Hungary, Israel, Italy, Latvia, Malta, Montenegro, Netherlands, Norway, Palestine, Poland, Portugal, Romania, Serbia, Spain, Sweden, Switzerland, Türkiye, UK.
IGO Relations *WHO (#20950).* **NGO Relations** Cooperates with: *International Psychogeriatric Association (IPA, #14664).* [2016.06.21/XD7205/D]

♦ European Association for Gestalt Therapy (EAGT) 06058

Office Manager Skulebakken 22, 3760 Neslandsvatn, Norway. T. +4795839146. E-mail: info@eagt.org.
URL: http://www.eagt.org/

History Founded 5 May 1985, Germany FR, by 21 representatives of Gestalt organizations in 36 European countries nd in 4 non-European countries. Registered in accordance with Dutch law. **Aims** Promote Gestalt Therapy in Europe; combine and exchange knowledge and resources; foster a high professional standard of Gestalt Therapy; encourage research. **Structure** General Board; Executive Committee. **Languages** English. **Staff** 8.00 FTE, voluntary. **Finance** Members' dues. **Activities** Standards/guidelines; research/documentation. **Events** *Triennial Congress* Budapest (Hungary) 2019, *The expressive interaction with music* Ghent (Belgium) 2017, *Triennial Congress* Taormina (Italy) 2016, *Triennial Congress* Krakow (Poland) 2013, *Triennial Congress* Berlin (Germany) 2010.
Members Individuals – Gestalt therapists and practitioners in organizations; Organizational – training institutes, national organizations for Gestalt Therapy and professional organizations. Members in 46 countries and territories:
Armenia, Australia, Austria, Belarus, Belgium, Bermuda, Bosnia-Herzegovina, Bulgaria, Canada, Croatia, Cyprus, Czechia, Denmark, Estonia, Faeroe Is, Finland, France, Georgia, Germany, Greece, Hungary, Ireland, Israel, Italy, Latvia, Lithuania, Luxembourg, Malta, Montenegro, Nepal, Netherlands, North Macedonia, Norway, Poland, Romania, Russia, Serbia, Slovakia, Slovenia, Spain, Sweden, Switzerland, Türkiye, UK, Ukraine, USA. [2019/XD3266/D]

♦ European Association of Golf Historians and Collectors (EAGHC) . . . 06059

Association Européenne des Historiens and Collectionneurs de Golf

Contact 20 avenue Notre Dame, 06000 Nice, France. E-mail: admin@golfika.com.
URL: http://www.golfika.com/

History Registration: Start date: May 2006, France. **Aims** Offer a place to individuals interested in golf history and/or collection of golf artefacts; exchange and share information. **Structure** General Meeting; Board. **Languages** English, French. **Staff** Voluntary. **Finance** Sources: members' dues. **Events** *Annual Meeting* Landskrona (Sweden) 2022, *Annual Meeting* Arnhem (Netherlands) 2019, *Annual Meeting* Pau (France) 2018, *Annual Meeting* St Andrews (UK) 2017, *Annual Meeting* Billund (Denmark) 2016. **Publications** *Golfika* – magazine. [2023.02.14/XM7570/D]

♦ European Association for Grain Legume Research (inactive)

♦ European Association of Graphic Paper Producers (EURO GRAPH) . 06060

Dir Gen Av Louise 250, 1050 Brussels, Belgium. T. +3226392600. Fax +3226392601. E-mail: office@euro-graph.org.
URL: http://www.euro-graph.org/

History Replaced *Association of Newsprint Manufacturers in the EEC (inactive)* and *European Association of Manufacturers of Magazine Papers (inactive).* Former title: *CEPIPRINT.* Previously also known as *Association of European Publication Paper Producers.* Present name adopted, 2012, when merged with *European Association of Fine Paper Producers (CEPIFINE, inactive).* A Participating Industry Sector of *Confederation of European Paper Industries (CEPI, #04529).* Originally registered in accordance with Swiss Civil Code. Relocated from Zurich (Switzerland) to Brussels (Belgium), 2002, after which it was registered in accordance with Belgian law. **Aims** Represent and raise public awareness regarding graphic paper industry sectors. **Structure** General Assembly (2 a year); Board. **Languages** English. **Finance** Members' dues. **Activities** Knowledge management/information dissemination; standards/guidelines.
Members Companies belonging to 27 independent groups, in 16 countries:
Austria, Belgium, Denmark, Finland, France, Germany, Italy, Netherlands, Norway, Poland, Portugal, Slovakia, Spain, Sweden, Switzerland, UK. [2018.01.30/XE1776/E]

♦ European Association of Guarantee Institutions 06061

Association européenne de Cautionnement (AECM) – Asociación Europea de Instituciones de Garantia – Associazione Europea degli Organismi di Garanzia

SG Av d'Auderghem 22-28, 1040 Brussels, Belgium. T. +3226405177. Fax +3226405177. E-mail: info@aecm.eu.
Events Manager address not obtained.
URL: http://www.aecm.eu/

History Founded 1992, as *European Association of Mutual Guarantee Societies – Association européenne du cautionnement mutuel (AECM) – Asociación Europea de Caución Mutua – Europäischer Verband der Bürgschaftsbanken – Associação Europeia de Caucionamento Mútuo – Europese Vereniging voor Onderlinge Borgstelling – Associazione Europea di Garanzia Mutua – Kölczönär Garanciabistosítók Egyesülete.* Registered in accordance with Belgian law. EU Transparency Register: 67611102869-33. **Aims** Provide loan guarantees for SMEs who have an economically sound project but cannot provide sufficient bankable collateral. **Structure** General Assembly (annual); Board of Directors. **Languages** English, French, German, Italian, Spanish. **Staff** 4.00 FTE, paid. **Finance** Members' dues. **Activities** Events/meetings; training/education. **Events** *Annual Event* Vienna (Austria) 2022, *Annual Event* Brussels (Belgium) 2021, *Annual Seminar* Antwerp (Belgium) 2019, *Annual Seminar* Warsaw (Poland) 2018, *Annual Seminar* Madrid (Spain) 2017. **Publications** *AECM Newsletter, Overview of European Guarantee Schemes.* Annual audited statistical report. **IGO Relations** *European Commission (EC, #06633); International Finance Corporation (IFC, #13597)* – World Bank Group; *OECD (#17693).* **NGO Relations** Member of: *SME Finance Forum (#19323).* [2021/XD3893/D]

♦ European Association of Gynaecologists and Obstetricians (inactive)

♦ **European Association for Haematopathology (EAHP)** **06062**
Association européenne d'hématopathologie
Sec/Treas PO Box 557, 2300 AN Leiden, Netherlands. T. +31715191033. E-mail: secretariat@european-association-for-haematopathology.org.
Office Address Van Hout Bldg – 2nd Floor, Pompoenweg 9, 2321 DK Leiden, Netherlands.
URL: https://www.european-association-for-haematopathology.org/
Aims Study diseases of the haematopoietic and lymphoid systems; promote the exchange and dissemination of knowledge concerning the diagnosis and treatment of these diseases. **Activities** Organizes congresses, joint meetings and tutorials. **Events** *Congress* Florence (Italy) 2022, *International Workshop on Bone Marrow Pathology* Lund (Sweden) 2022, *Congress* Leiden (Netherlands) 2021, *Congress* Dubrovnik (Croatia) 2020, *International Workshop on Bone Marrow Pathology* Frankfurt-Main (Germany) 2019.
Members Individuals (418) in 53 countries and territories:
Angola, Argentina, Australia, Austria, Belgium, Brazil, Bulgaria, Cameroon, Canada, China, Croatia, Cyprus, Czechia, Denmark, Egypt, Finland, France, Germany, Greece, Hong Kong, Hungary, Iceland, Iran Islamic Rep, Ireland, Israel, Italy, Japan, Korea Rep, Kuwait, Latvia, Lebanon, Malaysia, Mexico, Monaco, Netherlands, North Macedonia, Norway, Poland, Portugal, Romania, Russia, Saudi Arabia, Singapore, Slovakia, Slovenia, Spain, Sweden, Switzerland, Taiwan, Thailand, Türkiye, UK, USA.
[2022/XD2008/v/**D**]

♦ **European Association for Haemophilia and Allied Disorders (EAHAD)** **06063**
CEO Cours Saint Michel 30b, Hive5 – Securex Bldg, 1040 Brussels, Belgium. T. +32485861683. E-mail: info@eahad.org.
Communications Officer address not obtained.
URL: http://www.eahad.org/
History 7 Jun 2007, Vienna (Austria). Registration: EU Transparency Register, No/ID: 027577048901-13, Start date: 9 Feb 2023. **Aims** Ensure the provision of the highest quality of *clinical care*; educate the *medical* community and the general public; promote scientific research. **Structure** Executive Committee; Committees (3). **Languages** English, French. **Staff** 4.00 FTE, paid. **Finance** Sources: meeting proceeds. Main source of funding is the annual scientific congress. Annual budget: 800,000 EUR (2022). **Activities** Advocacy/lobbying/activism; events/meetings; healthcare; research/documentation; training/education. **Events** *Annual Congress* Manchester (UK) 2023, *Annual Congress* 2022, *Annual Congress* Brussels (Belgium) 2021, *Annual Congress* The Hague (Netherlands) 2020, *Annual Congress* Prague (Czechia) 2019. **Publications** *EAHAD Newsletter*, *Haemophilia*. **Members** Individuals (107): ordinary members (medical doctors); allied health professionals; junior and honorary members. Membership countries not specified. **NGO Relations** Cooperates with (1): *European Haemophilia Consortium (EHC, #07444)*.
[2023.02.15/XJ8079/**D**]

♦ European Association of Headteachers of Jewish Schools (inactive)
♦ European Association for Health Development / see Association européenne pour le développement et la santé (#02562)

♦ **European Association for Health Information and Libraries (EAHIL)** **06064**
Co-Pres c/o GIH Library, PO Box 5626, SE-114 86 Stockholm, Sweden. E-mail: eahil-secr@list.ecompass.nl.
URL: http://www.eahil.eu/
History Aug 1987, Brighton (UK). Statutes modified: 21 Feb 1991; Oct 1994; Nov 1998; May 2001. Former names and other names: *Association européenne pour l'information et les bibliothèques de santé (AEIBS)* – alias. **Aims** Improve library services to health professions by cooperation and shared experience across national boundaries. **Structure** Council; Executive Board; Special Interest Groups. **Languages** English. **Staff** Voluntary. **Finance** Sources: meeting proceeds; sponsorship. **Activities** Events/meetings; knowledge management/information dissemination; networking/liaising. **Events** *European Conference of Medical and Health Libraries* 2024, *EAHIL Workshop* Trondheim (Norway) 2023, *European Conference of Medical and Health Libraries* Rotterdam (Netherlands) 2022, *EAHIL Workshop* Istanbul (Turkey) 2021, *European Conference of Medical and Health Libraries* Lódz (Poland) 2020. **Publications** *Journal of the European Association for Health Information and Libraries* (4 a year).
Members Individuals, institutions and associations in 59 countries:
Australia, Austria, Belarus, Belgium, Bosnia-Herzegovina, Brazil, Bulgaria, Canada, Chile, Croatia, Cuba, Cyprus, Czechia, Denmark, Estonia, Ethiopia, Finland, France, Germany, Greece, Hungary, Iceland, Ireland, Israel, Italy, Jordan, Kyrgyzstan, Latvia, Lithuania, Moldova, Netherlands, New Zealand, Nigeria, North Macedonia, Norway, Poland, Portugal, Qatar, Romania, Russia, Saudi Arabia, Serbia, Slovakia, Slovenia, South Africa, Spain, Sweden, Switzerland, Tajikistan, Tanzania UR, Tunisia, Türkiye, Uganda, UK, Ukraine, United Arab Emirates, USA, Uzbekistan, Zimbabwe.
NGO Relations Member of (2): *European Bureau of Library, Information and Documentation Associations (EBLIDA, #06413)*; *International Federation of Library Associations and Institutions (IFLA, #13470)*.
[2021.06.15/XD0911/**D**]

♦ **European Association of Health Law (EAHL)** **06065**
Chair Fac of Law, Univ of Bergen, PO Box 7806, 5020 Bergen, Norway. E-mail: eurohealthlaw@gmail.com – administration@eahl.eu.
Main Website: http://www.eahl.eu/
History Apr 2008, Edinburgh (UK). Proposed Aug 2006, Toulouse (France), during 16th World Congress for Medical Law, when Advisory Board was created. Constitution adopted at founding conference. Registration: Handelsregister, No/ID: KVK 34299335, Netherlands; EU Transparency Register, No/ID: 958197144450-41, Start date: 21 Oct 2021. **Aims** Strengthen the health and human rights interface throughout Europe; serve as an indispensable source of advice and guidance for the future of health law and policies in Europe. **Structure** General Assembly; Board of Directors; Advisory Board; Reflection Committee; National Contact Points; Chief Liaison Officer; EAHL Administration. **Languages** English. **Staff** 1.00 FTE, paid. **Finance** Sources: members' dues. **Activities** Events/meetings; guidance/assistance/consulting; networking/liaising; publishing activities; research/documentation; training/education. **Events** *Conference20-22/04/2022* Ghent (Belgium) 2022, *Conference* Toulouse (France) 2019, *Conference* Bergen (Norway) 2017, *Health law and cross border health care in Europe* Prague (Czech Rep) 2015, *Conference* Riga (Latvia) 2014. **Publications** *EAHL Newsletter*. **Members** Individual; Institutional; Associate. Membership countries not specified.
[2022.10.12/XM4220/**D**]

♦ European Association of Hearing Aid Acousticians / see European Association of Hearing Aid Professionals (#06066)
♦ European Association of Hearing Aid Audiologists / see European Association of Hearing Aid Professionals (#06066)
♦ European Association of Hearing Aid Dispensers / see European Association of Hearing Aid Professionals (#06066)

♦ **European Association of Hearing Aid Professionals (AEA)** **06066**
Association Européenne des Audioprothésistes – Europäischer Verband der Hörgeräte-Akustiker
SG Rue Washington 40, 1050 Brussels, Belgium. E-mail: general.secretary@aea-audio.org – info@aea-audio.org.
Pres address not obtained. E-mail: president@aea-audio.org.
URL: http://www.aea-audio.org/
History 1968. In English previously referred to as *European Association of Hearing Aid Audiologists*, *European Association of Hearing Aid Dispensers* and *European Association of Hearing Aid Acousticians*. Previously also referred to as *Associazione Europea Audio-Protesisti – Europese Vereniging van Hoorapparaten – Europaeisk Horeapparatakustiker Forbund*. Registration: Banque-Carrefour des Entreprises, No/ID: 0810.047.889, Start date: 25 Feb 2009, Belgium; EU Transparency Register, No/ID: 321294817975-44, Start date: 25 Jun 2015. **Aims** Serve as the European umbrella association of national professional associations representing Hearing Aid Professionals from member countries. **Structure** General Assembly (annual); Board; Technical Working Group (European Committee for Audiology and Technology ECAT). **Languages** English, French, German. **Finance** Members' dues. **Activities** Standards/guidelines; training/education; events/meetings. **Events** *General Assembly* Lübeck (Germany) 2019, *General Assembly* Brussels (Belgium) 2015, *General Assembly* Brussels (Belgium) 2014, *General Assembly* Brussels (Belgium) 2013, *General Assembly* Bucharest (Romania) 2009. **Publications** Recommendations; guidelines; documents.
Members Full in 13 countries:
Austria, Belgium, France, Germany, Greece, Italy, Malta, Netherlands, Poland, Portugal, Romania, Spain, Switzerland.
IGO Relations Recognized by: *European Commission (EC, #06633)*; *WHO (#20950)* – World Hearing Forum.
NGO Relations Member of: *Federation of European and International Associations Established in Belgium (FAIB, #09508)*.
[2020.03.07/XD5537/t/**D**]

♦ European Association of Heavy Haulage Transport and Mobile Cranes / see European Association of Abnormal Road Transport and Mobile Cranes (#05923)

♦ **European Association for Heritage Interpretation (Interpret Europe)** **06067**
Managing Dir Carl-von-Ossietzky-Strasse 3, 14471 Potsdam, Germany. T. +38641911112. E-mail: mail@interpret-europe.net – office@interpret-europe.net.
URL: http://interpret-europe.net/
History Jul 2010, Slovenia. Informal networking activities initiated in 1999. Registration: No/ID: VR 700462, Start date: 8 Oct 2010, Germany; EU Transparency Register, No/ID: 937661834903-18, Start date: 21 May 2019. **Aims** Foster and further good practice and research in heritage interpretation throughout Europe. **Structure** General Assembly; Supervisory Committee; Advisory Group; Executive Management. **Languages** English. **Staff** 2.00 FTE, paid. **Finance** Sources: donations; grants; meeting proceeds; members' dues; revenue from activities/projects. Supported by: *European Union (EU, #08967)*. **Activities** Events/meetings; standards/guidelines. **Events** *Conference* Potsdam (Germany) 2021, *Conference* Witzenhausen (Germany) 2020, *Conference* Sarajevo (Bosnia-Herzegovina) 2019, *Conference* Köszeg (Hungary) 2018, *Conference* Inverness (UK) 2017. **Publications** *Interpret Europe* (4 a year) – newsletter; *Bridging the Gap* – journal.
Members Individuals and organizations in 30 countries:
Australia, Austria, Belgium, Bulgaria, Canada, Costa Rica, Croatia, Cyprus, Denmark, Finland, France, Germany, Greece, Hungary, Ireland, Israel, Italy, Latvia, Malta, Netherlands, Norway, Poland, Romania, Slovenia, Spain, Sweden, Switzerland, Türkiye, UK, USA.
NGO Relations Member of (3): Climate Heritage Network; *Culture Action Europe (CAE, #04981)*; *European Heritage Alliance 3.3 (#07477)*.
[2022.05.10/XM4019/**D**]

♦ European Association for Higher Education in Biotechnology (inactive)
♦ European Association of Historical Associations (inactive)

♦ **European Association of Historic Towns and Regions (Heritage Europe)** **06068**
Association européenne des villes et régions historiques
SG The Guildhall, Gaol Hill, Norwich, NR2 1JS, UK. T. +441603496400. Fax +441603496417. E-mail: european-association@historic-towns.org.
URL: http://www.historic-towns.org/
History 8 Oct 1999, Strasbourg (France). Former names and other names: *EAHTR* – former. Registration: Private company limited by guarantee, No/ID: 4411400, Start date: 8 Apr 2002, England. **Aims** Promote the interests of historic towns through international cooperation and sharing good practice in sustainable management of historic areas. **Structure** General Assembly; Bureau. **Languages** English. **Staff** part-time. **Finance** Funded by: subscription payments; EU Culture Programme grant. Support from Norwich City Council; *Council of Europe (CE, #04881)*. **Activities** focus on sustainable management of historic towns and cities, covering tourism, transportation, retailing, living and design and conservation. Develops a programme of conferences, cultural events and research; identifies and shares experience and good practice. Participates either as lead partner or partner. Current European projects include: HerO – Heritage as Opportunity; Sustainable Management Strategies for Vital Historic Urban Landscapes. **Events** *International Symposium* Innsbruck (Austria) 2007, *International Symposium* Paris (France) 2007, *International Symposium* Verona (Italy) 2007, *Annual symposium / International Symposium* Dubrovnik (Croatia) 2006, *Symposium on heritage led regeneration / International Symposium* Gothenburg (Sweden) 2005. **Publications** *The Chronicle* – newsletter.
Members Full; Associate; Reciprocal. Represents over 1200 cities in 32 countries:
Austria, Belgium, Bulgaria, Croatia, Czechia, Finland, France, Germany, Greece, Ireland, Malta, Netherlands, North Macedonia, Portugal, Romania, Russia, Slovakia, Slovenia, Türkiye, UK.
European Walled Towns (EWT, #09079).
IGO Relations *Council of Europe (CE, #04881)*. **NGO Relations** Member of (1): *European Heritage Alliance 3.3 (#07477)*.
[2020/XD7708/**D**]

♦ **European Association of History Educators (EUROCLIO)** **06069**
Exec Dir Riouwstr 139, 2585 HP The Hague, Netherlands. T. +31703817836. E-mail: secretariat@euroclio.eu.
URL: https://euroclio.eu/
History 21 Apr 1993. Founded on request of *Council of Europe (CE, #04881)*. Former names and other names: *European Association of Teachers of History* – former; *European Standing Conference of History Teachers' Associations* – former; *Conférence Permanente Européenne des Associations de Professeurs d'Histoire* – former. **Aims** Support development of responsible and innovative history, citizenship and heritage education by promoting critical thinking, multi-perspectivity, mutual respect and inclusion of controversial issues. **Structure** General Assembly (annual); Board; Secretariat. **Languages** English. **Staff** 4.00 FTE, paid. **Finance** Operational support funded through EU projects. **Activities** Capacity building; events/meetings; training/education. **Events** *Annual Conference* Vilnius (Lithuania) 2023, *Annual Conference* Bologna (Italy) / Ferrara (Italy) 2022, *General Assembly and Annual Conference* Marseille (France) 2018, *General Assembly and Annual Conference* San Sebastian (Spain) 2017, *Joint Conference on Multiperspectivity and Tolerance in History Teaching* Seoul (Korea Rep) 2017. **Publications** *EUROCLIO Monthly Newsletter*. Annual Report; special reports.
Members Full: National History Teachers' Associations and Institutes in 48 countries and territories:
Albania, Armenia, Austria, Azerbaijan, Belarus, Bosnia-Herzegovina, Bulgaria, Croatia, Cyprus, Czechia, Denmark, England, Estonia, Finland, France, Georgia, Germany, Hungary, Iceland, Ireland, Italy, Kosovo, Kyrgyzstan, Latvia, Lithuania, Luxembourg, Malta, Moldova, Montenegro, Netherlands, North Macedonia, Northern Ireland, Norway, Poland, Portugal, Romania, Russia, Scotland, Serbia, Slovakia, Slovenia, Spain, Sweden, Switzerland, Tajikistan, Türkiye, Ukraine, Wales.
Associated members (organizations, institutes and universities) in 13 countries:
Australia, Austria, Cyprus, Denmark, Germany, Greece, Israel, Morocco, Netherlands, Poland, Spain, Türkiye, UK.
Included in the above, 4 organizations listed in this Yearbook:
Cummings Center for Russian and East European Studies; *European Educational Publishers Group (EEPG, #06966)*; *Georg Eckert Institute for International Textbook Research*; *International Society for History Didactics (ISHD, #15167)*.
Consultative Status Consultative status granted from: *Council of Europe (CE, #04881)* (Participatory Status); *UNESCO (#20322)* (Consultative Status). **IGO Relations** *United Nations Alliance of Civilizations (UNAOC, #20520)*; *European Commission (EC, #06633)*; *European Wergeland Centre (EWC, #09092)*; *Organization for Security and Cooperation in Europe (OSCE, #17887)*; *UNDP (#20292)*; *UNESCO (#20322)*. Member of: *Anna Lindh Euro-Mediterranean Foundation for the Dialogue between Cultures (Anna Lindh Foundation, #00847)*. **NGO Relations** Member of (5): *Democracy and Human Rights Education in Europe (DARE Network, #05031)*; *Eastern Partnership Civil Society Forum (EaP CSF, #05247)*; *European Civic Forum (ECF, #06563)*; *European Heritage Alliance 3.3 (#07477)*; *Lifelong Learning Platform – European Civil Society for Education (LLLP, #16466)*. Cooperates with (1): *EUSTORY (#09202)*. Supports (1): *European Alliance for the Statute of the European Association (EASEA, #05886)*.
[2023/XF2601/y/**F**]

♦ **European Association for the History of Medicine and Health (EAHMH)** **06070**
Association européenne pour l'histoire de la médecine et de la santé
Sec History of Medicine Unit, 90 Vicent Drive, Univ Birmingham, Edgbaston, Birmingham, B15 2TT, UK. T. +441214158122.
URL: http://www.eahmh.net/
History 1991, Strasbourg (France). **Aims** Promote and foster research and education in the history of medicine and health; encourage scientific cooperation between individuals and national and international societies. **Structure** Scientific Board, including President, Vice-President, Past-President, President-Elect, Chairperson, Secretary and Treasurer. **Languages** English. **Finance** Members' dues. **Events** *Biennial Conference* Birmingham (UK) 2019, *Biennial Conference* Bucharest (Romania) 2017, *Biennial Conference* Cologne (Germany) 2015, *Biennial Conference* Lisbon (Portugal) 2013, *Biennial Conference* Utrecht (Netherlands) 2011. **Publications** Series; conference' proceedings.

Members Full in 33 countries:
Algeria, Australia, Austria, Belgium, Brazil, Canada, Croatia, Czechia, Denmark, Finland, France, Germany, Greece, Hungary, Ireland, Israel, Italy, Japan, Latvia, Mexico, Netherlands, New Zealand, Norway, Poland, Portugal, Russia, Slovenia, Spain, Sweden, Switzerland, Türkiye, UK, USA.
NGO Relations Active in promoting: *International Network for the History of Homeopathy (#14281)*; *International Network for the History of Hospitals (INHH, #14282)*; *International Network for the History of Public Health (INHPH, #14284)*. [2014/XD5927/**D**]

♦ European Association for the History of Psychiatry (inactive)

♦ European Association for Holocaust Studies 06071

Sec c/o Inst of European Studies, Jagiellonian Univ, ul Jodlowa 13, 30-252 Krakow, Poland. E-mail: info@eahs.eu.
URL: http://www.eahs.eu/
History Pilot meeting 2003, Oxford (UK) and inaugural conference, 2011 (Poland). Formal founding meeting held 2015, Krakow (Poland). Registration: Start date: Oct 2015, Poland. **Aims** Promote the field of Holocaust studies in Europe. **Structure** General Assembly; Executive Board; Audit Committee. **Languages** English, Polish. **Staff** 3.00 FTE, paid. **Finance** Members' dues. Other sources: donations; sponsorship; inheritance; subventions; research grants; shares; deposits; conference fees. **Activities** Research/documentation; training/education; publishing activities; events/meetings; knowledge management/information dissemination. **Members** Individuals. Membership countries not specified. [2017/XM0377/**D**]

♦ European Association for Home Economics (EAHE) 06072

Contact address not obtained. E-mail: eahe@ifhe.ch.
URL: https://eahe.ifhe.ch/
History Legal body of the European region of *International Federation for Home Economics (IFHE, #13447)*. **Structure** Executive Committee. [2021/AA2040/**D**]

♦ European Association of Homes and Services for the Ageing (inactive)
♦ European Association for Horse Assisted Education / see International Association for Horse Assisted Education (#11939)
♦ European Association of Hospital Administrators / see European Association of Hospital Managers (#06073)
♦ European Association of Hospital and Health Services Social Workers (inactive)

♦ European Association of Hospital Managers (EAHM) 06073

Association européenne des directeurs d'hôpitaux (AEDH) – Europäische Vereinigung der Krankenhausdirektoren (EVKD)
SG Rue des Mérovingiens 5, L-8070 Bertrange, Luxembourg. T. +3524241421.
URL: http://www.eahm.eu.org/
History 24 Oct 1970, Strasbourg (France). Former names and other names: *European Association of Hospital Administrators* – former; *Europäische Vereinigung der Krankenhausverwaltungsleiter* – former. Registration: France, Alsace et Moselle. **Aims** Promote hospital services, particularly administration, in European countries by developing new ideas and exchanging information on practical results achieved by research in all appropriate fields; safeguard these interests in international organizations concerned. **Structure** General Assembly (annual); Executive Committee. **Languages** English, French, German. **Staff** 1.00 FTE, paid. **Finance** Sources: members' dues. **Activities** Events/meetings. **Events** *Annual Congress* Budapest (Hungary) 2022, *Annual Congress* Budapest (Hungary) 2020, *Annual Congress* Ghent (Belgium) 2019, *Annual Congress* Cascais (Portugal) 2018, *Biennial Congress* Bologna (Italy) 2016. **Publications** *Hospital* (5 a year) in English – journal, with summaries in French and German. Reports of Congress and General Assembly.
Members National associations or groups of hospital administrators in 23 countries:
Austria, Belgium, Bulgaria, Croatia, Denmark, Finland, France, Germany, Hungary, Iceland, Ireland, Italy, Lithuania, Luxembourg, Netherlands, Norway, Poland, Portugal, Slovakia, Spain, Sweden, Switzerland, UK.
NGO Relations Member of (1): *Integrating Healthcare Enterprise International (IHE International, #11372)*. [2021/XD4621/**D**]

♦ European Association of Hospital Pedagogues / see Hospital Organization of Pedagogues in Europe (#10949)

♦ European Association of Hospital Pharmacists (EAHP) 06074

Association européenne des pharmaciens des hôpitaux – Europäische Vereinigung der Krankenhaus Apotheker
Managing Director Bd Brand Whitlock 87, Box 11 – 4th Floor, 1200 Brussels, Belgium. T. +3226692513. Fax +3226692529. E-mail: info@eahp.eu.
Pres Univ Hosp Motol, V Uvalu 84, 150 06 Prague, Czechia.
URL: http://www.eahp.eu/
History 6 Mar 1972, The Hague (Netherlands). Proposed 1969, Strasbourg (France). Founded 1972 when statutes were signed. Officially became an international not-for-profit organization, 1 Aug 2011. **Aims** Provide continuing education for hospital pharmacists. **Structure** General Assembly (annual); Board of Directors. **Languages** English. **Staff** 8.00 FTE, paid. **Finance** Sources: grants; meeting proceeds; members' dues. **Activities** Certification/accreditation; events/meetings; training/education. **Events** *Annual Congress* Lisbon (Portugal) 2023, *Annual Congress* Vienna (Austria) 2022, *Annual Congress* Brussels (Belgium) 2021, *Annual Congress* Gothenburg (Sweden) 2020, *Annual General Assembly* Edinburgh (UK) 2019. **Publications** *European Journal of Hospital Pharmacist* (6 a year) in English; *EAHP Survey of Hospital Pharmacy Practice across Europe.*. *EAHP Medicines Shortages Report 2018* in English; *EAHP's 2019 Medicines Shortages Report* in English. Annual Report; position papers; ad hoc publications.
Members Hospital pharmacists (23,000) grouped in national hospital pharmacy organizations in 35 countries:
Austria, Belgium, Bosnia-Herzegovina, Bulgaria, Croatia, Czechia, Denmark, Estonia, Finland, France, Germany, Greece, Hungary, Iceland, Ireland, Italy, Latvia, Lithuania, Luxembourg, Malta, Montenegro, Netherlands, North Macedonia, Norway, Poland, Portugal, Romania, Serbia, Slovakia, Slovenia, Spain, Sweden, Switzerland, Türkiye, UK.
NGO Relations Member of (4): *European Public Health Alliance (EPHA, #08297)*; *Federation of European and International Associations Established in Belgium (FAIB, #09508)*; *Integrating Healthcare Enterprise International (IHE International, #11372)*; *International Pharmaceutical Federation (#14566)*. Also links with national organizations. [2021.06.08/XD5630/**D**]

♦ European Association of Hospital Teachers / see Hospital Organization of Pedagogues in Europe (#10949)
♦ European Association of Hotel School Directors / see International Association of Hotel School Directors (#11942)

♦ European Association of Hotel and Tourism Schools 06075

Association européenne des écoles d'hôtellerie et de tourisme (AEHT)
SG PO Box 71, L-9201 Diekirch, Luxembourg. T. +35226803003. Fax +35226803103. E-mail: secretariat@aeht.lu.
Pres Quinta da Boavista, 3000-076 Coimbra, Portugal. T. +351239007000. Fax +351239007139.
URL: http://www.aeht.eu/
History May 1988, Illkirch-Graffenstanden (France). May 1988, Illkirch-Graffenstaden (France). Head office moved to Diekirch (Luxembourg), Oct 2000. **Aims** Promote a European outlook among Hotel and Tourism schools by: encouraging contacts between schools throughout Europe; promoting better knowledge of other countries' education systems; facilitating exchanges of teachers and students; forging closer links between schools and the profession; sharing teaching methods and materials, skills and knowledge. **Structure** General Assembly. Praesidium, comprising President, 5 Vice-Presidents, Treasurer, Secretary-General, Interpreter/translator and Webmaster. **Languages** English, French. **Staff** 1.00 FTE, paid. Voluntary. **Finance** Members' dues. Subvention. **Activities** Organizes: annual conference; training seminars for teaching staff; conferences for students, teachers and directors; 'Christmas in Europe' Festival gastronomy for peace; professional placements for students; refresher placements for teachers in units of the hotel groups. **Events** *Annual Conference* Senigallia (Italy) 2022, *Annual Conference* Tallinn (Estonia) 2021, *Annual Conference* Aveiro (Portugal) 2020, *Annual Conference* Split (Croatia) 2019, *Annual Conference* Leeuwarden (Netherlands) 2018. **Publications** *AEHT Yearbook*.
Members Schools in 40 countries:
Albania, Austria, Belgium, Bosnia-Herzegovina, Bulgaria, Croatia, Cyprus, Czechia, Denmark, Estonia, Finland, France, Germany, Greece, Hungary, Iceland, Ireland, Italy, Latvia, Lithuania, Luxembourg, Malta, Monaco, Montenegro, Netherlands, North Macedonia, Norway, Poland, Portugal, Romania, Russia, Serbia, Slovakia, Slovenia, Spain, Sweden, Switzerland, Türkiye, UK, Ukraine. [2020/XD3708/**D**]

♦ European Association of Human Ecology (inactive)
♦ European Association for Humanistic Psychology (inactive)

♦ European Association for Hydrogen and fuel cells and Electro-mobility in European Regions (HyER) 06076

Secretariat Avenue Palmerston 3, 1000 Brussels, Belgium. T. +3222854094.
History 14 Apr 2008, Brussels (Belgium). Former names and other names: *European Regions and Municipalities Partnership for Hydrogen and Fuel Cells (HyRaMP)* – former. Registration: EU Transparency Register, No/ID: 16329274008-54. **Aims** Provide European regions and municipalities with a representative body coherent, distinguishable and influential with respect to the 'European Joint Technology Initiative for Fuel Cells and Hydrogen (FCHJTI)' and all relevant stakeholders and decision makers at both public and private level. **Structure** Board; Secretariat. **Events** *Seminar on Decarbonising Heavy Duty Road Transport* Brussels (Belgium) 2018, *Workshop on Crossborder Cooperation to Accelerate the Deployment of Alternative Fuels* Brussels (Belgium) 2018, *Annual General Meeting* Copenhagen (Denmark) 2014, *Regional Power for Clean Transport Conference* Oslo (Norway) 2013.
Members Regions and municipalities of 9 countries:
France, Germany, Italy, Latvia, Norway, Portugal, Spain, Sweden, UK. [2021/XJ3430/**D***]

♦ European Association for Hypno Psychotherapy (internationally oriented national body)

♦ European Association for e-Identity and Security (EEMA) 06077

Dir Special Projects Payton House, Packwood Court, Guild Street, Stratford-upon-Avon, CV37 6RP, UK. T. +441386793028. E-mail: info@eema.org.
Project Manager address not obtained.
Registered Office Rue Washington 40, 1050 Brussels, Belgium.
URL: http://www.eema.org/
History Mar 1987. Former names and other names: *European Electronic Mail Association* – former (Mar 1987 to 9 Jun 1992); *European Electronic Messaging Association (EEMA)* – former (9 Jun 1992); *European Forum for Advanced Business Communications* – former; *EEMA European Forum for Electronic Business* – former (28 Jul 1999). Registration: Banque-Carrefour des Entreprises, No/ID: 0434.956.809, Start date: 18 Aug 1988; EU Transparency Register, No/ID: 606078725523-08, Start date: 24 Jan 2017. **Aims** Provide business and technical networking opportunities at both local and regional levels in the broad areas associated with *digital* identity and its applications, including security. **Structure** General Assembly (annual, at Conference); Board of Management; Executive Office, headed by Executive Director. **Languages** English. **Staff** 1.50 FTE, paid. **Finance** Sources: meeting proceeds; members' dues; revenue from activities/projects; sponsorship. **Activities** Events/meetings; knowledge management/information dissemination; publishing activities; training/education. **Events** *Annual Conference* London (UK) 2022, *Annual Conference* London (UK) 2021, *Annual Conference* Brussels (Belgium) 2020, *ISSE : Information Security Solutions Europe Conference* Stratford-upon-Avon (UK) 2020, *ISSE : Information Security Solutions Europe Conference* Brussels (Belgium) 2019. **Publications** *EEMA Communiqué* (12 a year) – news digest. Conference proceedings. **Members** Service providers; user companies; academic institutions; software and hardware companies; government bodies; consultants. Members (100). Membership countries not specified. **Consultative Status** Consultative status granted from: *ECOSOC (#05331)* (Ros A). **NGO Relations** Member of (1): *Federation of European and International Associations Established in Belgium (FAIB, #09508)*. [2021.06.10/XD0833/**D**]

♦ European Association of Importers of Finished Products (inactive)
♦ European Association of Independent Airlines (inactive)

♦ European Association of Independent Performing Arts (EAIPA) 06078

Contact Gumpendorfer Str 63B, 1060 Vienna, Austria. T. +4314038794. E-mail: info@eaipa.eu.
URL: http://www.eaipa.eu/
History Founded 2018. **Aims** Improve the framework conditions of individual performing artists, artist groups, independent theatres and other artistic companies as well as of all professional groups and infrastructures associated with the industry and in regard to their structural, social, legal, financial, political, organizational, artistic and cultural aspects.
Members Full in 14 countries:
Austria, Bulgaria, Czechia, Germany, Hungary, Iceland, Italy, Romania, Slovakia, Slovenia, Spain, Sweden, Switzerland, Ukraine. [2022/XM7850/**D**]

♦ European Association of Independent Research Providers (Euro IRP) 06079

Address not obtained.
URL: http://euroirp.com/
History 2005. Registered in England: 4824438. **Aims** Enhance awareness and reputation of independent research; change perception that research is free; work with regulators and investors to promote awareness and acceptance of payment structures; improve regulatory and fiscal environment in which independent research firms operate. **Structure** Board. **Finance** Members' dues. **Publications** Articles. **NGO Relations** *Asian Association of Independent Research Providers (Asia IRP)*. [2017/XM6037/**D**]

♦ European Association of Independents 06080

Confédération européenne des indépendants (CEDI) – Europaverband der Selbständigen – Confederazione Europea dei Lavoratori Autonomie
SG Hüttenbergstrasse 38-40, 66538 Neunkirchen, Germany. T. +496821306240. Fax +496821306241. E-mail: info@esd-ev.de.
URL: http://www.bvd-cedi.de/
History 14 Dec 1973, Luxembourg. Founded at the instigation of the German national association. **Aims** Represent independent and self employed workers, *business* and trade – small and medium sized enterprises. **Languages** French, German, Italian. **Events** *Meeting* Berlin (Germany) 2004, *Meeting* Brussels (Belgium) 2004, *Meeting* Paris (France) 2004, *Meeting* Vienna (Austria) 2004, *Meeting* Brussels (Belgium) 2003.
Members Full federations in 8 countries:
Austria, Belgium, France, Germany, Italy, Luxembourg, Netherlands, Portugal.
Contacts in 14 countries:
Andorra, Austria, Georgia, Hungary, Luxembourg, Poland, Portugal, Romania, Russia, Spain, Switzerland, Türkiye, UK, USA.
IGO Relations Recognized by: *European Commission (EC, #06633)*. [2016/XD3857/**D**]

♦ European Association of Independent Vehicle Traders (EAIVT) 06081

Managing Dir Chée de Louvain 1188, 1200 Brussels, Belgium. T. +49463618071. Fax +494636976172. E-mail: info@eaivt.org.
URL: http://www.eaivt.org/
History Registration: Banque-Carrefour des Entreprises, Belgium; EU Transparency Register, No/ID: 846066722763-87. **Aims** Support the independent automotive trade. **Structure** General Assembly (annual); Executive Board. **Languages** English. **Finance** Sources: members' dues. **Events** *International Markets Congress* Noordwijk (Netherlands) 2023, *International Markets Congress* Athens (Greece) 2022, *International Markets Congress* London (UK) 2019, *International Markets Congress* Dubrovnik (Croatia) 2018, *Forum* Marseille (France) 2018. **Publications** *Member Info*. **Members** Members and Partners in over 25 countries. Membership countries not specified. [2022.06.07/XD7739/t/**D**]

♦ European Association of Individual Investors (inactive)
♦ European Association of Industrial Container Reconditioners / see European Reconditioners of Industrial Packaging (#08333)
♦ European Association for Industrial Marketing and Marketing Management / see European Marketing Association (#07746)
♦ European Association of Industrial Measurements (inactive)

European Association Industrial
06082
alphabetic sequence excludes
For the complete listing, see Yearbook Online at

♦ **European Association of Industrial Silica Producers (EUROSIL) 06082**
SG Rue des Deux Eglises 26, Box 2, 1000 Brussels, Belgium. T. +3222104422.
URL: http://www.eurosil.eu/
History May 1991, France. Former names and other names: *European Association of Silica Producers* – former (May 1991). Registration: Crossroads Bank for Enterprises, No/ID: 0459.769.904, Start date: 6 Dec 1996, Belgium; EU Transparency Register, No/ID: 312840210910-27, Start date: 28 Mar 2013. **Aims** Promote development and utilization of industrial silica; represent interests of members; provide members with a forum in which to tackle regulatory, technical, health and safety and environmental issues at EU and national levels. **Structure** General Assembly (annual); Management Board. **Languages** English. **Staff** 8.00 FTE, paid. **Finance** Sources: members' dues.
Members Companies (47) in 10 countries:
Belgium, France, Germany, Italy, Netherlands, Norway, Portugal, Spain, Sweden, UK.
NGO Relations Member of (1): *Industrial Minerals Association – Europe (IMA Europe, #11179)*. Shares office staff with: *Calcium Carbonate Association – Europe (CCA-Europe, #03399); European Association of Feldspar Producers (EUROFEL, #06037); European Bentonite Producers Association (EUBA, #06328); European Borates Association (EBA, #06382); European Kaolin and Plastic Clays Association (KPC Europe, #07623); European Lime Association (EuLA, #07699); European Speciality Minerals Association (ESMA, #08811); International Diatomite Producers Association (IDPA, #13172); Scientific Association of European Talc Industry (Eurotalc, #19146).* [2022/XF3411/t/F]

♦ European Association of Industries of Branded Products / see European Brands Association (#06397)
♦ European Association 'Inédits' (#02574)
♦ European Association for Information Development and Environment Awareness (inactive)
♦ European Association of Information Services (no recent information)

♦ **European Association for Injury Prevention and Safety Promotion (EuroSafe) 06083**
Address not obtained.
URL: http://www.eurosafe.eu.com/
History Replaces *European Consumer Safety Association (ECOSA, inactive)*. **Aims** Reduce both intentional and unintentional fatal and non-fatal injuries through increased coordination and strategies that combine and build upon existing strengths and capacities. **Structure** Executive Committee, including General Secretary. **Activities** Projects/programmes. **Events** *European Conference on Injury Prevention and Safety Promotion* Luxembourg (Luxembourg) 2019, *European Conference on Injury Prevention and Safety Promotion* Amsterdam (Netherlands) 2017, *Joint Seminar on the Use of Injury Data* Vienna (Austria) 2016, *Associated and Collaborating Partners Meeting* Vienna (Austria) 2012, *European conference on injury prevention and safety promotion* Budapest (Hungary) 2011. **Publications** *EuroSafe Alert*. **Consultative Status** Consultative status granted from: *WHO (#20950)* (Official Relations). **NGO Relations** Instrumental in setting up: *European Child Safety Alliance (ECSA, #06534).* [2020/XM1437/D]

♦ European Association of Innovating SMEs (unconfirmed)

♦ **European Association of Innovation Consultants (EAIC) 06084**
Association européenne des consultants en innovation
SG Square de Meeûs 35, 1000 Brussels, Belgium. T. +32479202959. E-mail: info@eaic.eu.
URL: https://www.eaic.eu/
History 6 Jul 2021, Belgium. Developed out of European Working Group of Innovation Consultants (EGWIC). Registration: Banque-Carrefour des Entreprises, No/ID: 0770.820.594, Start date: 6 Jul 2021, Belgium; EU Transparency Register, No/ID: 552465444550-96, Start date: 2 Nov 2021. **Aims** Gather active Innovation Consultants in the field of European research and innovation projects; facilitate exchange of experience and good practices among members; promote professional skills and expertise in European R&I projects. **Structure** General Assembly (annual); Board; Working Groups; Task Forces. **Languages** English. **Staff** 0.50 FTE, paid. **Publications** *Next Generation EU guide on Recovery and Resilience Plans* (4 a year) in English.
Members Companies in 31 countries:
Andorra, Austria, Belgium, Bulgaria, Croatia, Cyprus, Czechia, Denmark, Estonia, Finland, France, Germany, Greece, Ireland, Israel, Italy, Lithuania, Luxembourg, Moldova, Netherlands, Norway, Poland, Portugal, Romania, Slovenia, Spain, Sweden, Switzerland, Türkiye, UK, USA. [2022.05.12/AA2187/D]

♦ European Association of Insolvency Practitioners Organizations / see European Insolvency Practitioners Association (#07543)

♦ **European Association of Institutes for Vocational Training 06085**
Association européenne des centres de formation professionelle – Europäischer Verband Beruflicher Bildungsträger (EVBB)
SG Av de la Renaissance 1, 1000 Brussels, Belgium.
URL: http://www.evbb.eu/
History Founded 1992, Düsseldorf (Germany). EU Transparency Register: 283282925136-45. **Aims** Improve the quality of vocational education and training in Europe; increase efforts being carried out in education at European and global level. **Structure** Executive Committee; General Secretariat. **Languages** English, French, German. **Staff** 7.00 FTE, paid. **Finance** Members' dues. Other sources: conference fees; project related income. **Activities** Events/meetings; training/education. **Events** *Annual Conference / International Conference* Brussels (Belgium) 2015, *Annual Conference / International Conference* Zagreb (Croatia) 2014, *Annual Conference / International Conference* Athens (Greece) 2013, *Annual Conference / International Conference* Frankfurt-Main (Germany) 2012, *Annual Conference / International Conference* Istanbul (Turkey) 2011. **Publications** *The Sofia Declaration* (2018); *The Bratislava Declaration*; *The Maltese Declaration*. Conference proceedings; position papers.
Members Vocational training institutes (over 60) in 30 countries:
Austria, Belgium, Bosnia-Herzegovina, Bulgaria, China, Croatia, Denmark, Estonia, France, Georgia, Germany, Greece, Hungary, Israel, Italy, Kosovo, Latvia, Lithuania, Malta, Norway, Poland, Portugal, Romania, Russia, Slovakia, Sri Lanka, Switzerland, Tunisia, Türkiye, Vietnam.
IGO Relations Member of: *European Economic and Social Committee (EESC, #06963)* Liaison Group. **NGO Relations** Member of: *European Entrepreneurs CEA-PME (#06994); European Movement International (EMI, #07825); Digital Skills and Jobs Coalition*; European Alliance for Apprenticeships (EAfA). [2019.12.12/XM0207/t/D]

♦ European Association for Institutional Research / see EAIR, The European Higher Education Society (#05153)

♦ **European Association of Institutions of Higher Education (EURASHE) 06086**
Association Européenne des Institutions d'Enseignement Supérieur
SG Ravensteingalerij 27/3, 1000 Brussels, Belgium. T. +3222114197. Fax +3222114199. E-mail: eurashe@eurashe.eu.
URL: http://www.eurashe.eu/
History Founded Feb 1990, Patras (Greece), at founding conference. Current Statutes adopted, 26 Apr 2007, Copenhagen (Denmark). Registered in accordance with Belgian law. EU Transparency Register: 622449913391-69. **Aims** Provide a platform to exchange information, projects and views on future developments in higher education policies in the EU and the EHEA. **Structure** General Assembly; Board; Secretariat in Brussels (Belgium). **Languages** English. **Staff** 5.00 FTE, paid. **Finance** Members' dues. EU funding. Annual budget (2016): euro 460,000. **Activities** Politics/policy/regulatory; training/education; events/meetings. **Events** *European Quality Assurance Forum* Aveiro (Portugal) 2023, *Annual Conference* Brussels (Belgium) 2022, *European Quality Assurance Forum* Timisoara (Romania) 2022, *European Quality Assurance Forum* Brussels (Belgium) 2021, *Annual Conference* Porto (Portugal) 2021. **Publications** Conference reports; policy position papers; surveys; studies; reports.
Members Individual institutions, national associations, associate and affiliate members. Members in 40 countries and territories:
Armenia, Austria, Belarus, Belgium, Canada, Croatia, Cyprus, Czechia, Denmark, Egypt, Estonia, Finland, France, Georgia, Germany, Greece, Hungary, Ireland, Kazakhstan, Kyrgyzstan, Latvia, Lithuania, Macau, Malta, Moldova, Netherlands, Norway, Poland, Portugal, Romania, Russia, Serbia, Slovenia, Spain, Switzerland, Tajikistan, UK, Ukraine, United Arab Emirates, USA.
IGO Relations Cooperates with: *European Commission (EC, #06633); European Parliament (EP, #08146).* Bologna Follow-Up Group (BFUG) of: *European Higher Education Area (EHEA, #07483).* **NGO Relations** Founding member of: *European Quality Assurance Register for Higher Education (EQAR, #08311); Euro-Mediterranean University (EMUNI, #05728).* Member of: *Lifelong Learning Platform – European Civil Society for Education (LLLP, #16466).* Cooperates with: *Academic Cooperation Association (ACA, #00019); BUSINESSEUROPE (#03381); Education International (EI, #05371); European Association for International Education (EAIE, #06092); European Association for Quality Assurance in Higher Education (ENQA, #06183); European Consortium for Accreditation in Higher Education (ECA, #06748); European Students' Union (ESU, #08848); European University Association (EUA, #09027); European University Continuing Education Network (EUCEN, #09030); Universities of Applied Sciences Network (UASNET, #20693).* [2019/XD2600/D]

♦ **European Association of Institutions of Non-formal Education of Children and Youth (EAICY) 06087**
Association européenne des institutions de loisirs des enfants et des jeunes – Europäische Association der Freizeiteinrichtungen der Kinder und Jugend – Evropska Asociace Zarizeni pro Volny Cas Deti a Mladeze – Evropejskaja Associacija Ucrezdenij Svobodnogo Vremeni Detej i Molodezi
Gen Sec Konstitucijos av 25, LT-08105 Vilnius, Lithuania.
Contact address not obtained.
URL: http://www.eaicy.eu/
History Nov 1991, Prague (Czechia). Statutes adopted 21 Nov 1996, Prague. Former names and other names: *European Association for Leisure Time Institutions of Children and Youth (EAICY)* – former (Nov 1991); *Association européenne des institutions de loisirs des enfants et des jeunes* – former (Nov 1991); *Europäische Association der Freizeiteinrichtungen der Kinder und Jugend* – former (Nov 1991); *Evropska Asociace Zarizeni pro Volny Cas Deti a Mladeze* – former (Nov 1991); *Evropejskaja Associacija Ucrezdenij Svobodnogo Vremeni Detej i Molodezi* – former (Nov 1991); *European Association for the Leisure Time Institutions of Children and Youth of Great Cities* – alias. Registration: Czech Rep. **Aims** Develop and coordinate special programmes and activities in the field of non-formal education. **Structure** General Assembly (every 2 years); Praesidium; Control Commission; Office in Vilnius (Lithuania). **Languages** English, French, German, Russian. **Staff** Voluntary. **Finance** Members' dues. Other sources: donations; participation fees for various activities; subsidies from the Council of Europe. **Activities** Events/meetings; knowledge management/information dissemination. **Events** *International seminar* Vilnius (Lithuania) 2002, *International seminar* Prague (Czech Rep) 2001, *Members assembly* Prague (Czech Rep) 2001, *International meeting of youth* Krakow (Poland) 2000, *International conference on youth and society* Vilnius (Lithuania) 2000. **Publications** *Youth of Europe* (3 a year) in Czech, English, Russian – bulletin. Books; pamphlets.
Members Full organizations and individuals; Honorary individuals, in 19 countries:
Belarus, Bulgaria, Croatia, Czechia, Estonia, France, Georgia, Germany, Hungary, Italy, Kazakhstan, Latvia, Lithuania, Moldova, Netherlands, Poland, Russia, Slovakia, Ukraine.
NGO Relations Member of: *Conference of INGOs of the Council of Europe (#04607).* [2017.03.14/XD6034/D]

♦ European Association of Insurance Company Managers (#02556)
♦ European Association of Insurers of Industries / see Federation of European Risk Management Associations (#09539)
♦ European Association for Integrating Food Science and Engineering Knowledge into the Food Chain / see ISEKI-Food Association (#16027)

♦ **European Association for Integrative Psychotherapy (EAIP) 06088**
Main Office Willowholme, Upper Albert Road, Glenageary, Dublin, CO. DUBLIN, Ireland. E-mail: eaipdublin@gmail.com.
URL: http://www.europeanintegrativepsychotherapy.com/
History Feb 1993. **Aims** Promote and extend the practice and development of integrative psychotherapy in Europe; promote post-graduate and post-qualification training in the field, training of supervisors and trainers and the highest standards of clinical and ethical practice; promote research and education in the theory and practice of integrative psychotherapy and exchange and understanding of the different theoretical and practical approaches. **Structure** General Meeting (annual). Board of Directors, consisting of President, Vice-President, General Secretary, Treasurer and 2 representatives of each organizational member. Representatives (3): External Relations; Training Standards; Ethics. **Languages** English, French, German. **Staff** 6.00 FTE, voluntary. **Finance** Members' dues. **Activities** Provides accreditation of member organizations' training courses; represents members with national, European and international associations and with other professions, institutions and governments. **Events** *Annual General Meeting* Ljubljana (Slovenia) 2013, *Annual General Meeting* Athens (Greece) 2012, *Annual General Meeting* Athens (Greece) 2004, *Annual General Meeting* Paris (France) 2003, *Annual General Meeting* UK 2002.
Members Full (20); Provisional (2); Associate. Members in 12 countries:
Austria, Croatia, France, Germany, Ireland, Italy, Netherlands, Poland, Romania, Slovenia, Sweden, Switzerland.
[2011.11.07/XD4723/D]

♦ **European Association of Intellectual Disability Medicine (MAMH) .. 06089**
Admin Office afd HAG/AVG, PO Box 2040, 3000 CA Rotterdam, Netherlands. T. +31107043341.
History Apr 1991, Amsterdam (Netherlands), as *Medical Aspects of Mental Handicap (MAMH)*. Registered in accordance with Dutch law. **Aims** Collect and exchange knowledge regarding causes, prevention and treatment of different types of learning disability; stimulate and support applied scientific research in the field; initiate, support and promote education in medical care of people with a learning disability. **Structure** General Meeting (annual); Board, including President, Secretary and Treasurer. **Finance** Members' dues. **Events** *General Meeting* Rome (Italy) 2011, *General Meeting* Bristol (UK) 2010, *General Meeting* Amsterdam (Netherlands) 2009, *General Meeting* Potsdam (Germany) 2008, *General Meeting* Maastricht (Netherlands) 2006.
Members Full in 13 countries:
Belgium, Denmark, Finland, Germany, Hungary, Italy, Netherlands, Norway, Romania, Sweden, Türkiye, UK, Ukraine.
NGO Relations Close contacts with: *Inclusion International (#11145); International Association for the Scientific Study of Intellectual and Developmental Disabilities (IASSIDD, #12153).* [2017/XD9373/D]

♦ European Association for Interaction between University Institutions (inactive)

♦ **European Association of Internal Combustion Engine Manufacturers (EUROMOT) 06090**
General Manager Rue Joseph Stevens 7, 1000 Brussels, Belgium. T. +3228932142. E-mail: info@euromot.eu – secretariat@euromot.eu.
URL: https://www.euromot.eu/
History 21 Jan 1991, London (UK). Founded to supersede *Comité européen des associations de constructeurs de moteurs à combustion interne (EUROMOT, inactive)*. Former names and other names: *Association of European Manufacturers of Internal Combustion Engines* – former (29 Jan 1991 to 1998). Registration: EU Transparency Register, No/ID: 6284937371-73; AISBL/IVZW, Belgium. **Aims** Unite manufacturers of reciprocating internal combustion engines, whether petrol, diesel, gas or dual fuel, with applications ranging from hand-held and self-propelled forestry/garden care equipment to road vehicles, off-road equipment, rail locomotives, ships and power plants; strengthen the competitive capacity of the European internal combustion engine industry with regard to its significance in all areas of possible application. **Structure** General Assembly (annual); Board; General Secretariat. Working groups (5): Small Petrol Engines; Non-Road Mobile Machinery Engines; Marine Engines; Stationary Engines; Communications, Media and Government Relations. **Languages** English. **Staff** 2.00 FTE, paid. **Finance** Members' dues. **Activities** Advocacy/lobbying/activism; capacity building; standards/guidelines; politics/policy/regulatory; events/meetings; research/documentation; networking/liaising. **Events** *Briefing* Brussels (Belgium) 2000, *Briefing* Brussels (Belgium) 1999, *Briefing* Brussels (Belgium) 1998, *Briefing* Brussels (Belgium) 1997, *Briefing* Brussels (Belgium) 1996. **Publications** *EUROMOT Briefing Papers* – series. Other papers; standards; guidelines; activity report.
Members Manufacturers in 15 countries:
Austria, Belgium, Denmark, Finland, France, Germany, Italy, Japan, Netherlands, Norway, Spain, Sweden, Switzerland, UK, USA.
Consultative Status Consultative status granted from: *International Maritime Organization (IMO, #14102); ECOSOC (#05331)* (Roster). **NGO Relations** Member of (1): *Industry4Europe (#11181).* Cooperates with (2): *Comité européen de normalisation (CEN, #04162); International Organization for Standardization (ISO, #14473).* Also links with a number of national organizations active in the field. [2023/XD3107/D]

♦ European Association for Internal Communication (FEIEA) 06091

Pres Av do Brasil 35, 1o B, 1700-062 Lisbon, Portugal. T. +351964242428.
URL: http://www.feiea.eu/

History 22 Aug 1955, Copenhagen (Denmark). Founded at the third European Congress, the first having been organized in 1948 in Paris by the French association. New statutes adopted, 13 Nov 2019. Former names and other names: *Federation of European Internal Editors Associations* – former; *Fédération des associations européennes de journalistes d'entreprises* – former; *Verband der Europäischen Arbeitsgemeinschaften von Werkschriftleitern* – former; *Federation of European Internal Communications Associations (FEIEA)* – former; *Federation of European Industrial Editors Associations* – former; *Fédération des associations européennes de la presse d'entreprise* – former. Registration: Crossroads Bank for Enterprises, No/ID: 0412.916.924, Start date: 25 Jan 1973, End date: 1 Jan 1975, Belgium; Portugal. **Aims** Connect, inspire and develop internal communicators across Europe, driving recognition of the value of internal communication and the strategic impact our profession has on outstanding organizational performance. **Structure** Council (meets annually); quarterly Council virtual meetings; Executive Committee meets monthly (virtual) **Languages** English. **Staff** 0.00 FTE, paid; 12.00 FTE, voluntary. **Finance** Sources: meeting proceeds; members' dues. **Activities** Advocacy/lobbying/activism; awards/prizes/competitions; certification/accreditation; events/meetings; guidance/assistance/consulting; training/education. **Events** *Award Ceremony* Zurich (Switzerland) 2019, *Award Ceremony* Ljubljana (Slovenia) 2018, *Conference* Vienna (Austria) 2010, *Congress* Sweden 2006, *Congress* Brussels (Belgium) 2005.

Members National federations in 8 countries:
Belgium, Denmark, Italy, Portugal, Slovakia, Slovenia, Switzerland, UK. [2023.02.14/XD0938/**D**]

♦ European Association of Internal Medicine / see European Federation of Internal Medicine (#07147)

♦ European Association for International Education (EAIE) 06092

Exec Dir PO Box 11189, 1001 GD Amsterdam, Netherlands. T. +31203445100. Fax +31203445119. E-mail: news@eaie.org.
Street address Herengracht 487, 1017 BT Amsterdam, Netherlands.
URL: http://www.eaie.org/

History Dec 1989, Amsterdam (Netherlands). Founded at first major European conference for professionals in the field of international higher education exchange. Registration: Chamber of Commerce, No/ID: 40536784, Netherlands, Amsterdam. **Aims** Help members succeed professionally; contribute to developments in international higher education from a European perspective. **Structure** Board; General Council; Committees (4); Expert Communities (15). **Languages** English. **Staff** 26.00 FTE, paid. **Finance** Members' dues. **Activities** Training/education; events/meetings; knowledge management/information dissemination. **Events** *Annual Conference* Rotterdam (Netherlands) 2023, *Annual Conference* Barcelona (Spain) 2022, *Community Exchange Meeting* Amsterdam (Netherlands) 2021, *Annual Conference* Gothenburg (Sweden) 2021, *Community Exchange Meeting* Amsterdam (Netherlands) 2020. **Publications** *Forum* (3 a year) – magazine. *Pathways to Practice* – series. **Members** Individuals in 85 countries and territories. Membership countries not specified.
IGO Relations Courtesy associates: *Council of Europe (CE, #04881)*; *OECD (#17693)*.
NGO Relations Courtesy associates include the following organizations listed in this Yearbook:
- *Academic Cooperation Association (ACA, #00019)*;
- *African Network for Internationalization of Education (ANIE, #00391)*;
- *AIESEC (#00593)*;
- *Asia-Pacific Association for International Education (APAIE, #01844)*;
- *Association of African Universities (AAU, #02361)*;
- *Association of International Education Administrators (AIEA)*;
- *Associations and Conference Forum (AC Forum, #02909)*;
- *British Council*;
- *Canadian Bureau for International Education (CBIE)*;
- *Centre for International Mobility (CIMO)*;
- *Deutscher Akademischer Austauschdienst (DAAD)*;
- *EFMD – The Management Development Network (#05387)*;
- *Erasmus Student Network (ESN, #05529)*;
- *European Association of Institutions of Higher Education (EURASHE, #06086)*;
- *European Students' Union (ESU, #08848)*;
- *European University Association (EUA, #09027)*;
- *Federazione Internazionale Cronometristi (FIC, #09717)*;
- *Forum européen de l'orientation académique (FEDORA, inactive)*;
- *IDP Education*;
- *Institute of International Education (IIE)*;
- *International Association for Educational Assessment (IAEA, #11861)*;
- *International Association of Universities (IAU, #12246)*;
- *International Association of University Presidents (IAUP, #12248)*;
- *International Education Association of Australia (IEAA)*;
- *International Education Association of South Africa (IEASA)*;
- *Mexican Association for International Education (AMPEI)*;
- *NAFSA – Association of International Educators*;
- *Netherlands Organization for International Cooperation in Higher Education (NUFFIC)*;
- *Rui Foundation*;
- *UK Council for International Student Affairs (UKCISA)*. [2023/XD2394/v/**D**]

♦ European Association of the International League of Societies for Persons with Mental Handicap / see Inclusion Europe – European Association of Societies of Persons with Intellectual Disability and their Families (#11144)
♦ European Association for the International Space Year / see Eurisy (#05625)
♦ European Association for Interregional Cooperation (no recent information)

♦ European Association for Investors in Non-listed Real Estate Vehicles (INREV) 06093

Main Office Ito Tower 8th fl, Gustav Mahlerplein 62, 1082 MA Amsterdam, Netherlands. T. +31202358600. E-mail: info@inrev.org.
URL: http://inrev.org/

History Incorporated Sep 2002 and launched May 2003. Registration: No/ID: 34178762, Netherlands; EU Transparency Register, No/ID: 47748145557-46. **Aims** Improve the accessibility of non-listed investment industry by promoting greater transparency, accessibility, professionalism and standards of best practice. **Structure** Management Board. **Languages** English. **Staff** 16.99 FTE, paid. **Finance** Members' dues. **Activities** Events/meetings; training/education. **Events** *Annual Conference* Athens (Greece) 2022, *Annual Conference* 2021, *Advanced Tax Round Table* Berlin (Germany) 2019, *Annual Conference* Venice (Italy) 2019, *Autumn Conference* Madrid (Spain) 2018. **Publications** *IQ Magazine* (4 a year); *INREV Annual Index*. Surveys.
Members Full (353). Members in 23 countries and territories:
Canada, Cyprus, Denmark, Estonia, Finland, France, Germany, Greece, Hong Kong, Ireland, Italy, Japan, Luxembourg, Netherlands, Norway, Portugal, Singapore, Spain, Sweden, Switzerland, UK, United Arab Emirates, USA.
NGO Relations Member of: *European Real Estate Forum (#08331)*; *International Ethics Standards Coalition (IES Coalition, #13307)*; *International Property Measurement Standards Coalition (IPMSC, #14656)*. [2022/XJ5366/**D**]

♦ European Association of Israel Studies (EAIS) 06094

Contact Institute of the Middle & Far East, room 1.10, Jagiellonian Univ, 2a Oleandry Street, 30-063 Krakow, Poland. E-mail: info@israelstudies.eu.
URL: http://www.israelstudies.eu/

Aims Promote, encourage and support the independent, academic study of Israel across Europe. **Structure** Executive Committee. **Finance** Sources: members' dues. **Activities** Research/documentation. **Events** *Annual Conference* Beersheba (Israel) 2023, *Annual Conference* Oxford (England) 2022, *Annual Conference* Bucharest (Romania) 2021, *Annual Conference* Prague (Czechia) 2019, *Annual Conference* London (UK) 2018. [2023.02.19/XM7854/**E**]

♦ European Association of Japanese Resource Specialists (EAJRS) .. 06095

Nihon Shiryô Senmonka Oshu Kyôkai

Chair c/o Japanese Studies KUL, Blijde-Inkomststraat 21, Box 3318, 3000 Leuven, Belgium. E-mail: eajrs@eajrs.net.
URL: http://www.eajrs.net/

History 1989, West Berlin (Germany). Founded following discussions resulting from British Library's 3rd Oriental Studies colloquium, Sep 1988, London (UK). **Aims** Promote development and dissemination of *information* and *library* resources for Japanese studies in Europe; support those professionally interested in provision of resources for the study of Japan. **Structure** General Meeting. Board. Officers: President, Secretary, Treasurer, Organizer of the Next Conference. Steering Committee (meets at Annual Conference). **Finance** Funding received from: *Japan Foundation* and other organizations, for annual conferences. **Activities** Provides a forum for the exchange of information between librarians, museum curators and researchers interested in Japanese materials of all kinds. Publishing activity. Conferences (held annually). **Events** *Conference* Lisbon (Portugal) 2022, *Conference* St Petersburg (Russia) 2021, *Conference* St Petersburg (Russia) 2020, *Annual Conference* Sofia (Bulgaria) 2019, *Annual Conference* Kaunas (Lithuania) 2018. **Publications** *EAJRS Newsletter* (2 a year).
Members Librarians, curators, information specialists and academics with an interest in library matters in 22 countries:
Australia, Austria, Belgium, Bulgaria, Czechia, Denmark, Finland, France, Germany, Hungary, Italy, Japan, Netherlands, New Zealand, Norway, Poland, Russia, Spain, Sweden, Switzerland, UK, USA.
NGO Relations Member of: *European Association for Japanese Studies (EAJS, #06096)*. [2022/XE2104/v/**E**]

♦ European Association for Japanese Studies (EAJS) 06096

Secretariat c/o Freie Univ Berlin, Inst of East Asian Studies, Japanese Studies, Hittorfstr 18, 14195 Berlin, Germany. T. +493083850929. Fax +4930838450931. E-mail: office@eajs.eu.
URL: http://www.eajs.eu/

History 1973, Oxford (UK). **Aims** Stimulate interest and encourage research in Japanese studies in all countries of Europe. **Structure** Council. **Languages** English, Japanese. **Staff** 0.50 FTE, paid. **Finance** Sources: international organizations; members' dues; private foundations. Supported by: *Japan Foundation*; *Toshiba International Foundation*. **Activities** Events/meetings; publishing activities. **Events** *Triennial Conference* Ghent (Belgium) 2023, *Workshop for Doctoral Students* Olomouc (Czechia) 2022, *Triennial Conference* Ghent (Belgium) 2021, *Workshop for Doctoral Students* Leuven (Belgium) 2021, *Workshop for Doctoral Students* Berlin (Germany) 2020. **Publications** *Bulletin of the European Association for Japanese Studies* (annual). Meeting reports; conference programmes; scholarship reports.
Members Individuals and institutions (1,000) in 40 countries and territories:
Australia, Austria, Belarus, Belgium, Bulgaria, Canada, Croatia, Czechia, Denmark, Egypt, Estonia, Finland, France, Germany, Greece, Hong Kong, Hungary, Israel, Italy, Japan, Korea Rep, Lithuania, Luxembourg, Netherlands, New Zealand, Norway, Poland, Portugal, Romania, Russia, Serbia, Singapore, Slovenia, Spain, Sweden, Switzerland, Türkiye, UK, Ukraine, USA.
NGO Relations Cooperates with (3): *European Association of Japanese Resource Specialists (EAJRS, #06095)*; *Nordic Association for Japanese and Korean Studies (NAJAKS, #17195)*; *Society for East Asian Archaeology (SEAA, #19544)*. [2022.02.15/XD0339/**D**]

♦ European Association of Jesuit Alumni / see Confédération européenne des Anciens et Anciennes Elèves des établissements de la Compagnie de Jésus (#04536)
♦ European Association of Jewish Child Survivors of the Holocaust / see European Association of Jewish Survivors of the Holocaust (#06099)

♦ European Association of Jewish Community Centres (EAJCC) 06097

Association européenne des centres communautaires juifs (AECCJ)

Contact c/o Standard Fsju, 39 Rue Broca, 75005 Paris, France.
URL: http://www.eajcc.eu/

History Registered in accordance with French law. **Events** *Conference* Marseille (France) 2012, *Conference* London (UK) 2010, *European conference of Jewish community centers* Bucharest (Romania) 2008, *European conference of Jewish community centers* Paris (France) 2003. **NGO Relations** Member of: *JCC Global (#16093)*. Associate member of: *European Council of Jewish Communities (ECJC, #06825)*. [2013/XD8536/**D**]

♦ European Association for Jewish Culture (no recent information)

♦ European Association for Jewish Studies (EAJS) 06098

Administrator Clarendon Inst Bldg, Walton Street, Oxford, OX1 2HG, UK. T. +441865610433. E-mail: admin@eurojewishstudies.org.
Sec address not obtained.
URL: http://eurojewishstudies.org/

History Founded 1981, Oxford (UK). Previously also known in French, German and Italian: *Association européenne des études juives – Europäische Gesellschaft für Jüdische Studien – Associazione Europea per lo Studio del Giudaismo*. UK Registered Charity: 7119740. **Aims** Advance scholarly Jewish studies in Europe for public benefit; advance research in Jewish studies and teaching of jewish studies at European universities and other places of higher education and learning. **Structure** Executive Committee; Permanent Secretariat in Oxford (UK). **Languages** English, French, German, Italian. **Staff** 1.00 FTE, paid. **Finance** Members' dues. Private donations; private and public funding. **Activities** Events/meetings. **Events** *Congress* Frankfurt-Main (Germany) 2023, *Seeking for the roots of Jewish traditions* Krakow (Poland) 2018, *Jewish and non-Jewish cultures in contact – new research perspectives* Paris (France) 2014, *Congress* Ravenna (Italy) 2010, *Past and present perspectives in Jewish studies* Moscow (Russia) 2006. **Publications** *European Journal of Jewish Studies (EJJS)* (2 a year). *Directory of Jewish Studies in Europe*. Congress proceedings.
Members Full; Associate; Student individuals in 30 countries:
Austria, Belgium, Brazil, Canada, Czechia, Denmark, Finland, France, Germany, Hungary, Ireland, Israel, Italy, Japan, Lithuania, Netherlands, Norway, Poland, Romania, Russia, Serbia, Slovakia, Slovenia, Spain, Sweden, Switzerland, Türkiye, UK, Ukraine, USA.
NGO Relations Joint publication with: *Leopold Zunz Centre for the Study of European Jewry (LZZ)*. [2016/XD3745/v/**D**]

♦ European Association of Jewish Survivors of the Holocaust (EUAS) 06099

Pres Postbus 87131, 1080 JC Amsterdam, Netherlands.
URL: http://www.eu-as.org/

History 11 Nov 2001, Prague (Czech Rep), as *European Association of Jewish Child Survivors of the Holocaust*. Co-founders included Jana Draska (1930-2009). **Aims** Represent the interests of European child survivors of the Holocaust.
Members In 15 countries:
Belarus, Bosnia, Croatia, Czechia, France, Germany, Italy, Latvia, Lithuania, Montenegro, Poland, Russia, Slovakia, Slovenia, Sweden, UK. [2018/XM0363/**D**]

♦ European Association of Judges (EAJ) 06100

Association européenne des magistrats – Asociación Europea de Jueces – Europäische Vereinigung der Richter – Associazione Europea dei Magistrati

Pres Palazzo di Giustizia, 1 Piazza Cavour, 00193 Rome RM, Italy. T. +390668832213. Fax +39066871195. E-mail: secretariat@iaj-uim.org.
URL: http://www.iaj-uim.org/

History Regional group of *International Association of Judges (IAJ, #11978)*. Current statutes adopted 10 May 2003, Dubrovnik (Croatia); amended 16 May 2014, Limassol (Cyprus). Registration: EU Transparency Register, No/ID: 61342526458-86, Start date: 22 Aug 2011. **Aims** Promote closer European cooperation in all areas pertaining to the judiciaries of the member states and international and supranational judiciaries. **Structure** General Assembly; Executive Committee; President. **Languages** English, French. **Finance** Sources: contributions. Supported by: *International Association of Judges (IAJ, #11978)*. **Activities** Events/meetings. **Events** *Meeting* 2021, *Meeting* Copenhagen (Denmark) 2019, *Meeting* Berlin (Germany) 2018, *Meeting* Chisinau (Moldova) 2017.
Members Associations in 44 countries:
Albania, Armenia, Austria, Azerbaijan, Belgium, Bosnia-Herzegovina, Bulgaria, Croatia, Cyprus, Czechia, Denmark, Estonia, Finland, France, Georgia, Germany, Greece, Hungary, Iceland, Ireland, Israel, Italy, Latvia, Liechtenstein, Lithuania, Luxembourg, Malta, Moldova, Montenegro, Netherlands, North Macedonia, Norway, Poland, Portugal, Romania, Serbia, Slovakia, Slovenia, Spain, Sweden, Switzerland, Türkiye, UK, Ukraine.

IGO Relations Observer status with (2): *Commission européenne pour l'efficacité de la justice (CEPEJ, #04213)*; *Consultative Council of European Judges (CCJE, #04767)*. Cooperates with (3): *Council of Europe (CE, #04881)*; *Organization for Security and Cooperation in Europe (OSCE, #17887)*; *United Nations (UN, #20515)*. **NGO Relations** Cooperates with (4): *Central and Eastern European Law Initiative (CEELI, #03693)*; *European Network of Councils for the Judiciary (ENCJ, #07886)*; *Groupement européen pour la circulation des oeuvres (GRECO, inactive)*; *International Bar Association (IBA, #12320)*. [2022.02.01/XD5965/**E**]

♦ European Association for Knowledge Economy (EURECO) 06101
Europäische Gesellschaft für Wissensökonomie

Contact Maria-Cebotari-Str 6a, 5020 Salzburg, Austria. T. +436763135044. E-mail: office@eureco.info.

URL: https://www.eureco.info/

History 2010, Salzburg (Austria). Registration: Vereinsbehörde – Landespolizeidirektion Salzburg, No/ID: 1267680384, Austria, Salzburg. **Aims** Promote research and science in the field of knowledge economy. **Structure** Board, headed by Director General; Secretary General heads Administration; Advisory Board. **Languages** English, German. **Staff** 20.00 FTE, voluntary. **Activities** Events/meetings; knowledge management/information dissemination; networking/liaising; politics/policy/regulatory; research/documentation; training/education. Active in: Austria, Croatia, Czechia, Germany, Hungary, Italy, Netherlands, Slovakia, Slovenia, Switzerland. **Publications** *Journal of the European Association for Knowledge Economy. Innovatives Wissensmanagement – Innovative Knowledge Management* in English, German.

Members Full in 6 countries:
Austria, Czechia, Germany, Hungary, Netherlands, Switzerland. [2022.02.14/AA1329/**D**]

♦ European Association for Korean Language Education (unconfirmed)

♦ European Association of Labour Economists (EALE) 06102
Association européenne des économistes du travail

Sec School of Business and Economics, Research Ctr for Education and the Labour Market, Maastricht Univ, PO Box 616, 6200 MD Maastricht, Netherlands. T. +31433883647. Fax +31433884914. E-mail: eale-sbe@maastrichtuniversity.nl.

URL: http://www.eale.nl/

History Sep 1989, Turin (Italy). Founded at inaugural conference. **Aims** Promote advancement of knowledge in the field and application of labour economics in Europe and elsewhere. **Structure** Executive Committee; Network of Correspondents. **Languages** English. **Staff** 0.50 FTE, paid. **Finance** Members' dues. Support from national and international organizations, including: Federal Agency of Labour (Germany); Italian Central Bank. **Activities** Events/meetings. **Events** *Annual Conference* Bergen (Norway) 2024, *Annual Conference* Prague (Czechia) 2023, *Annual Conference* Padua (Italy) 2022, *Annual Conference* Padua (Italy) 2021, *Annual Conference* Berlin (Germany) 2020. **Publications** *EALE Newsletter*; *Labour Economics* – official journal. Information Services: Database.

Members Individuals and institutions in 38 countries and territories:
Australia, Austria, Belgium, Bulgaria, Canada, Croatia, Cyprus, Czechia, Denmark, Estonia, Finland, France, Germany, Greece, Hong Kong, Hungary, Iceland, Ireland, Italy, Japan, Lithuania, Luxembourg, Netherlands, New Zealand, Norway, Poland, Portugal, Romania, Russia, Slovakia, Slovenia, Spain, Sweden, Switzerland, Türkiye, UK, Ukraine, USA. [2022/XD2501/**D**]

♦ European Association for Language Testing and Assessment (EALTA) 06103

Sec Euroexam International, Test Development Centre, Tabor utca 5, Budapest 1012, Hungary.
Pres Tromgassli 6, 3303 Jegenstorf BE, Switzerland.

URL: http://www.ealta.eu.org/

History Constitution adopted, 23 Apr 2004; revised 4 Jun 2005; 8 Jun 2009; 9 Sep 2013; 05 Jun 2017; 26 May 2018; 31 May 2019; 22 May 2020. **Aims** Promote understanding of theoretical principles of language testing and assessment, and improvement and sharing of testing and assessment practices throughout Europe. **Structure** Executive Committee; Membership Committee; Committee for Conference Organization. **Languages** English. **Staff** 10.00 FTE, voluntary. **Finance** Formed with financial support from *European Community (inactive)* (ENLTA project Dec 2003 – Nov 2005). Since then, self-supporting. **Activities** Events/meetings; guidance/assistance/consulting; training/education. **Events** *Annual Conference* Budapest (Hungary) 2022, *Annual Conference* 2021, *Annual Conference* Dublin (Ireland) 2019, *Annual Conference* Bochum (Germany) 2018, *Annual Conference* Sèvres (France) 2017. **Publications** *Developments in language education: A memorial volume in honour of Sauli Takala* (2019); *Profile-G: A computer program for profile analysis* (2019); *Putting the CEFR to good use: Selected articles by the presenters of the IATEFL, TEASIG ane EALTA Conference* (2011). **Members** Individual (1,197); Associate (204); Institutional (67); Expert (25). Membership countries not specified. **Consultative Status** Consultative status granted from: *Council of Europe (CE, #04881)* (Participatory Status). [2021.06.09/XJ0939/**D**]

♦ European Association of Latex Foam Industries (inactive)
♦ European Association for the Law of East-West Commerce (inactive)

♦ European Association of Law and Economics (EALE) 06104

Managing Dir c/o Economics Dept, Viale Filopanti 1, 40126 Bologna BO, Italy. E-mail: contact@eale.org.
Registered Address c/o Universiteitstraat 4, 9000 Ghent, Belgium.

URL: http://www.eale.org/

History 1984, Lund (Sweden). Former names and other names: *European Foundation for Law and Economics (EFLE)* – alias. Registration: Belgium. **Aims** Further research and teaching in law and economics; provide assistance for scholars embarking on this field. **Structure** Advisory Board of up to 10 members; Management Board of 6 members; President; Secretary. **Languages** English. **Staff** None. **Finance** None. **Activities** Organizes conferences, seminars and workshops. **Events** *Annual Conference* Barcelona (Spain) 2021, *Annual Conference* 2020, *Biennial Joint Conference* Milan (Italy) 2019, *Annual Conference* Tel Aviv (Israel) 2019, *Annual Conference* Milan (Italy) 2018. **Publications** *EALE Newsletter*. *Geneva Papers on Risk and Insurance* – series. *Governance by Legal and Economic Measures* (1993) by P Andersen et al; *Economic Analysis of Law – A Collection of Applications* (1991) by W Weigel; *Law and Economics: Some Further Insights* (1991) by R Pardolesi and R Van den Bergh; *Essays in Law and Economics: Corporations, Accident Prevention and Compensation of Losses* (1989) by M Faure and R Van den Bergh; *Law and Economics and the Economics of Legal Regulations* (1986) by Graf J M von der Schulenburg and G Skogh. Between 1994-2003, annual conference proceedings published in the 'International Review of Law and Economics (IRLE)'; conference proceedings.

Members Individuals (about 360) Full and Associate (A), in 19 countries:
Belgium, Canada (A), Croatia, Denmark, France, Germany, Greece, Hungary, Iceland, Ireland, Italy, Netherlands, Norway, Poland, Spain, Sweden, Switzerland, UK, USA (A).

NGO Relations Organizes seminar every 2 years jointly with: *Geneva Association (#10119)*. [2020/XD2265/v/**D**]

♦ European Association of Lawyers for Democracy and World Human Rights (ELDH) 06105
Association européenne des juristes pour la démocratie et les droits de l'homme dans le monde (AJDH) – Asociación Europea de los Juristas por la Democracia y los Derechos Humanos en el Mundo – Europäische Vereinigung von Juristinnen und Juristen für Demokratie und Menschenrechte in der Welt (EJDM) – Associazione Europea delle Giuriste e dei Giuristi per la Democrazia e i Diritti dell'Uomo nel Mondo (EGDU)

SG Platanenstr 13, 40233 Düsseldorf, Germany. T. +49211444001. Fax +49211444027.

URL: http://eldh.eu/

History 1 May 1993, Paris (France). Former names and other names: *AELDH* – former; *AEJDH* – former; *AEGDU* – former. Registration: Germany. **Aims** Promote human rights, peace, disarmament and understanding between peoples; fight against racism and fascism; fight against discrimination; promote equal entitlement of women and men and respect children's rights; protect the environment; carry out fact-finding missions. **Structure** General Assembly (every 2 years); Executive Committee; Secretariat, located in Düsseldorf (Germany). **Languages** English, French, German. **Staff** 6.00 FTE, voluntary. **Finance** Members' dues. Other sources: donations; grants; subscriptions. **Activities** Research/documentation; standards/guidelines; politics/policy/regulatory; events/meetings; monitoring/evaluation. **Events** *Under pressure of the troika – the impact on collective labour rights in Southern Europe and Ireland* Madrid (Spain) 2015, *Conference* Belgrade (Serbia) 2014, *Migrants – outlaws everywhere; The alien as an enemy, homeless, excluded* Berlin (Germany) 2013, *Conference* Berlin (Germany) 2012, *Conference* London (UK) 2012. **Publications** Conference' proceedings; reports.

Members National associations of democratic lawyers in 11 countries and territories:
Belgium, Bulgaria, England, France, Germany, Greece, Italy, North Macedonia, Spain, Switzerland, Türkiye.
Individual members in 10 countries:
Albania, Austria, Belgium, Finland, Hungary, Latvia, Russia, Serbia, Spain, Sweden.

NGO Relations Member of: *European Network against Racism (ENAR, #07862)*. [2022/XD6002/**D**]

♦ European Association of Leading Digital Enterprises (euro.digital) . 06106

SG Rond Point Schuman 6, 1040 Brussels, Belgium.

URL: https://euro.digital/

History EU Transparency Register: 728566135580-48. **Aims** Represent the IT Demand side to the outside world in positioning towards the European IT lawmaking, regulatory processes and vendors. **Structure** Board of Directors. **Members** National associations. Membership countries not specified. [2019/XM8552/**D**]

♦ European Association for Legal and Fiscal Studies (no recent information)
♦ European Association of Legislation / see International Association of Legislation (#11998)
♦ European Association for Leisure Time Institutions of Children and Youth / see European Association of Institutions of Non-formal Education of Children and Youth (#06087)
♦ European Association for the Leisure Time Institutions of Children and Youth of Great Cities / see European Association of Institutions of Non-formal Education of Children and Youth (#06087)
♦ European Association for Length Measuring Instruments and Machines (no recent information)

♦ European Association for Lexicography (EURALEX) 06107
Association européenne de lexicographie

Assistant Sec-Treas Inst voor de Nederlandse taal, Rapenburg 61, 2311 GJ Leiden, Netherlands. T. +31715141648. E-mail: info@euralex.org.

URL: http://www.euralex.org/

History 12 Sep 1983, Exeter (UK). Founded at inaugural meeting. Constitution agreed at General Meeting, 13 Sep 1986; amended at General Meetings 8 Aug 1992, 3 Sep 1994, 18 Jul 2008 and 20 July 2018. **Aims** Promote scholarly and professional activities related to lexicography, including the training of *dictionary* makers and dictionary users. **Structure** General Meeting (every 2 years); Executive Board. **Languages** English. **Staff** Voluntary. **Finance** Sources: members' dues. **Activities** Events/meetings; training/education. **Events** *Biennial Congress* Mannheim (Germany) 2022, *Biennial Congress* Komotini (Greece) 2021, *Biennial Congress* Alexandroupoli (Greece) 2020, *Biennial Congress* Ljubljana (Slovenia) 2018, *Biennial Congress* Tbilisi (Georgia) 2016. **Publications** *International Journal of Lexicography* (4 a year); *EURALEX Newsletter*. *EURALEX Proceedings 1983-2020 (ISSN 2521-7100)*.

Members Personal; Honorary; Institutional; International Friendship Fund (IFF). Individuals in 53 countries and territories:
Afghanistan, Albania, Australia, Austria, Barbados, Belgium, Brazil, Bulgaria, Canada, China, Croatia, Czechia, Denmark, Egypt, Estonia, Finland, France, Georgia, Germany, Greece, Hong Kong, Hungary, Iceland, India, Iran Islamic Rep, Ireland, Israel, Italy, Japan, Kenya, Korea Rep, Latvia, Lithuania, Luxembourg, Malaysia, Netherlands, New Zealand, Norway, Pakistan, Poland, Portugal, Romania, Russia, Serbia, South Africa, Spain, Sweden, Switzerland, Tanzania UR, UK, Ukraine, USA, Vietnam.

NGO Relations Accredited by (5): *African Association for Lexicography (AFRILEX)*; *Asian Association for Lexicography (ASIALEX, #01328)*; *Australasian Association for Lexicography (AUSTRALEX)*; Dictionary Society of North America (DSNA); *NORDTERM (#17552)*. [2021.06.10/XD3475/**D**]

♦ European Association of Libraries and Information Services on Addictions (inactive)
♦ European Association for Library and Information Education & Research / see BOBCATSSS Association (#03296)
♦ European Association for Library and Information Education and Research (inactive)
♦ European Association lifestyle (internationally oriented national body)

♦ European Association of lighting WEEE compliance schemes (EucoLight) 06108

Secretariat Diamant Bldg, Bd A Reyers 80, 1030 Brussels, Belgium. T. +32487344876.

URL: http://www.eucolight.org/

History 2015. EU Transparency Register: 239813917190-50. Registered in accordance with Belgian law. Registration: AISBL/IVZW, Belgium. **Aims** Promote the development of a better regulatory framework and the efficient collection and *recycling* of waste lamps. **Structure** General Assembly; Board of Directors; Secretariat; Working Groups.

Members Full in 18 countries:
Austria, Belgium, Czechia, Denmark, Estonia, Finland, France, Germany, Hungary, Italy, Netherlands, Poland, Portugal, Romania, Slovakia, Slovenia, Spain, UK.
Affiliate member:
LightingEurope (#16472).

NGO Relations Technical Liaison Partner of: *European Committee for Electrotechnical Standardization (CENELEC, #06647)*. [2020/XM4827/**D**]

♦ European Association of Linguists and Language Teachers (no recent information)

♦ European Association of Livestock Markets 06109
Association européenne des marchés aux bestiaux (AEMB) – Europäischer Viehmärkteverband

Contact c/o UECBV, Rue de la Loi 81A, Box 9, 4th Flr, 1040 Brussels, Belgium. T. +3222304603. Fax +3222309400. E-mail: info@uecbv.eu.

URL: http://www.aemb.eu/

History 14 Jun 1983, Brussels (Belgium). Registration: Start date: 19 Oct 1983, Belgium; EU Transparency Register, No/ID: 156178926045-44. **Aims** Encourage scientific research and technical progress for the purpose of promoting the improvement and modernization of market buildings, equipment and facilities; develop an information and consultation network; represent members at the international and European Community level. **Structure** General Assembly (annual). Board (meeting 3 times a year). Specialized Sections. **Languages** English, French, German. **Staff** 3.00 FTE, paid. **Finance** Membership contributions. **Events** *Annual general assembly* Ribeiras de Lea (Spain) 2011, *Annual General Assembly* Aberdeen (UK) 2010, *Annual General Assembly* Kilkenny (Ireland) 2009, *Annual General Assembly* Wolvega (Netherlands) 2008, *Annual General Assembly* Laissac (France) 2007. **Publications** *Directory of the EEC-Livestock Markets*; *European Code of Practice*.

Members Livestock markets in 8 countries:
Belgium, Denmark, France, Ireland, Netherlands, Portugal, Spain, UK.

NGO Relations Member of: *Union européenne du commerce du bétail et de la viande (UECBV, #20394)*. [2020/XD7367/**D**]

♦ European Association of Local Authorities of Coal Mining Areas / see Association of Europe's Coalfield Regions (#02585)
♦ European Association of Local Authorities Inventing their Energy Future / see Energy Cities (#05467)

♦ European Association for Local Democracy (ALDA) 06110
Association européenne pour la démocratie locale

SG Rue Belliard 20, 1040 Brussels, Belgium. T. +3224302048. E-mail: aldabrussels@aldaintranet.org – aldabrussels@alda-europe.eu.
Strasbourg Office Council of Europe, 1 Avenue de l'Europe, 67075 Strasbourg, France. T. +33390214593. Fax +33390215517. E-mail: aldastrasbourg@aldaintranet.org – alda@aldaintranet.org.
Communication Department Viale Milano 66, 36100 Vicenza VICENZA, Italy. T. +39444540146. Fax +39444231043.

URL: http://www.alda-europe.eu/

History 1999. Founded under the auspices of *Congress of Local and Regional Authorities of the Council of Europe (#04677)*. Former names and other names: *Association of the Local Democracy Agencies (ALDA)* – former; *Association des agences de la démocratie locale (AADL)* – former. **Aims** Promote good governance and citizens participation at local level, throughout the enlarged Europe. **Structure** General Assembly (annual); Board; Bureau. **Languages** English, French, Italian. **Staff** 20.00 FTE, paid. **Finance** Members' dues. Public and private donors, including *European Commission (EC, #06633)*. **Activities** Events/meetings; training/ education; awareness raising; advocacy/lobbying/activism. **Publications** *ALDA Email Newsletter* (12 a year) in Arabic, English, French, Italian, Russian, Serbian. Annual Activity Report; brochures; project reports.
Members Local and regional authorities; international and national association of local authorities; Civil Society Organizations (CSOs); universities and educational institutions; individuals. Total members (300). individuals. Municipalities; provinces or counties; associations of local authorities in 30 countries:
Albania, Armenia, Belgium, Bosnia-Herzegovina, Bulgaria, Croatia, Denmark, France, Georgia, Greece, Italy, Kosovo, Latvia, Malta, Moldova, Montenegro, Morocco, North Macedonia, Poland, Portugal, Romania, Serbia, Slovakia, Slovenia, Spain, Switzerland, Tunisia, Türkiye, UK, Ukraine.
Civil Society Organizations in 37 countries:
Albania, Algeria, Armenia, Austria, Azerbaijan, Belarus, Belgium, Bulgaria, Cyprus, Czechia, Estonia, Finland, France, Germany, Greece, Hungary, Iceland, Israel, Italy, Lithuania, Moldova, Montenegro, Morocco, Netherlands, North Macedonia, Poland, Portugal, Romania, Russia, Serbia, Slovakia, Slovenia, Spain, Sweden, Türkiye, UK, Ukraine.
Included in the above, 18 organizations listed in this Yearbook:
Association of Cities and Regions for Sustainable Resource Management (ACR+, #02433); *Balkan Assist*; *BalticFem*; *Civilscape (#03966)*; *Comitato Internazionale per lo Sviluppo dei Popoli (CISP)*; *European Academy of Bozen/Bolzano (EURAC)*; *European Association for Viewers Interests (EAVI, #06272)*; *European Projects Association (EPA)*; *Europejskie Centrum Współpracy Mlodziezy (ECWM)*; *Foster Europe*; *Globus et Locus*; *Institut international des droits de l'Homme et de la paix*; *International Association for the Advancement of Innovative Approaches to Global Challenges (IAAI, #11687)*; *Istituto per la Cooperazione Economica Internazionale (ICEI)*; *Istituto Scientifico Biomedico Euro Mediterraneo (ISBEM)*; *Oxfam Trading*; *Peipsi Koostöör Keskus (Peipsi CTC)*; *Slovenian Global Action (SLOGA)*.
Universities in 5 countries:
Georgia, Italy, Morocco, Slovenia, Ukraine.
Local democracy agencies in 8 countries:
Albania, Armenia, Bosnia-Herzegovina, Georgia, Kosovo, Montenegro, Serbia, Ukraine.
Consultative Status Consultative status granted from: *Council of Europe (CE, #04881)* (Participatory Status).
IGO Relations Institutional partner of: *Congress of Local and Regional Authorities of the Council of Europe (#04677)*. Partner of: *European Commission (EC, #06633)* – within structured dialogue of Europe for Citizens Programme. Observer to: *Assemblée Régionale et Locale Euro-Méditerranéenne (ARLEM, #02313)*; *Conference of the Regional and Local Authorities for the Eastern Partnership (CORLEAP, #04645)*; *European Committee of the Regions (CoR, #06665)*. Participant in Fundamental Rights Platform of: *European Union Agency for Fundamental Rights (FRA, #08969)*. **NGO Relations** Member of (9): *Association of Cities and Regions for Sustainable Resource Management (ACR+, #02433)*; *Central and Eastern European Citizens Network (CEE CN, #03689)*; *Citizens for Europe (CFEU, #03956)*; *CIVICUS: World Alliance for Citizen Participation (#03962)*; *Conference of INGOs of the Council of Europe (#04607)*; *Confédération européenne des ong d'urgence et de développement (CONCORD, #04547)*; *Eastern Partnership Civil Society Forum (EaP CSF, #05247)*; *Energy Cities (#05467)*; *European Partnership for Democracy (EPD, #08156)*. Participant in: *Civil Society Europe*. Supports: *Covenant of Mayors for Climate and Energy (#04939)*. [2020/XD9329/y/**D**]

♦ European Association of Logic, Language and Information / see Association of Logic, Language and Information (#02789)

♦ European Association for Logistics and Transportation in Healthcare (EALTH) 06111

Gen Manager Garocentre Sud, Chemin de la Reconversion 19, 7110 Houdeng-Goegnies, Belgium.
URL: https://www.ealth.org/

History 14 Nov 2011. Registration: Banque-Carrefour des Entreprises, No/ID: 501.659.848, Start date: 30 Nov 2012, Belgium; EU Transparency Register, No/ID: 257135610488-90. **Aims** Represent interests of companies involved in the healthcare product supply chain in Europe. **Structure** Annual Meeting; Board of Directors. **Languages** Dutch, English, French, German. **NGO Relations** Member of (1): *European Technology Platform ALICE (ALICE, #08888)*. [2023.03.01/XM7511/**D**]

♦ European Association of Logotherapy and Existential Analysis (no recent information)

♦ European Association of Long-Term Investors (ELTI) 06112

SG Rue Montoyer 51, 1000 Brussels, Belgium. E-mail: secretariat@eltia.eu.
URL: http://www.eltia.eu/

History Launched 5 Jul 2013, Paris (France). Also referred to as *European Long-Term Investors*. Registered in accordance with Belgian law, 30 Jul 2013: 0544 292 437. EU Transparency Register: 977980112556-82. **Aims** Promote long-term investment in close alignment with the objectives and initiatives developed by the European Union to foster sustainable, smart and inclusive growth and job creation. **Structure** Governance and Management Board. **Languages** English. **Staff** 2.00 FTE, paid. **Finance** Members' dues. Annual budget (2016): over euro 60,000. **Activities** Events/meetings. **Events** *Annual General Assembly* Vilnius (Lithuania) 2018, *Annual General Assembly* Warsaw (Poland) 2017, *Annual General Assembly* Madrid (Spain) 2016, *Annual General Assembly* Zagreb (Croatia) 2015, *Annual General Assembly* Prague (Czech Rep) 2014.
Members Full – national official financial institutions. Associate – multilateral and regional financial institutions and non-banking institutions. Full (20) in 19 countries:
Austria, Belgium, Bulgaria, Croatia, Czechia, France, Germany, Greece, Hungary, Ireland, Italy, Latvia, Lithuania, Luxembourg, Malta, Poland, Portugal, Slovenia, Spain.
Associate (7) in 4 countries:
Germany, Greece, Lithuania, Türkiye.
Regional Associate members (2):
Council of Europe Development Bank (CEB, #04897); *Nordic Investment Bank (NIB, #17327)*.
Multilateral Associate member:
Long-term Infrastructure Investors Association (LTIIA, #16512).
Permanent Observer:
European Investment Bank (EIB, #07599).
NGO Relations *Confrontations for a European Participative Democracy (Confrontations Europe)*; *Eurofi (#05679)*; *Long-term Infrastructure Investors Association (LTIIA, #16512)*; *Long-Term Investors Club (LTIC, #16513)*. [2019/XJ9424/y/**D**]

♦ European Association of Luminous Radiant Gas Heaters Manufacturers / see Europäischer Leit-Verband der Hersteller von Gas-Infrarot- Hellstrahlern (#05758)
♦ European Association of the Machine Tool Industries / see European Association of the Machine tool Industries and related Manufacturing Technologies (#06113)

♦ European Association of the Machine tool Industries and related Manufacturing Technologies (CECIMO) 06113

Dir Gen Blvd Brand Whitlock 165, 1200 Brussels, Belgium. E-mail: information@cecimo.eu.
URL: http://www.cecimo.eu/

History 13 Jul 1950, Brussels (Belgium). Former names and other names: *European Association of the Machine Tool Industries* – former (1950); *Comité européen de coopération des industries de la machine-outil (CECIMO)* – former (1950); *Comité Europeo de Cooperación de las Industrias de la Maquina-Herramienta* – former (1950); *Europäisches Komitee für die Zusammenarbeit der Werkzeugmaschinen-Industrien* – former (1950); *Comité Europeu de Cooperação das Indústrias da Maquina-Ferramenta* – former (1950); *Comitato Europeo di Cooperazione tra Industrie delle Macchine Utensili* – former (1950); *European Committee for Cooperation of the Machine Tool Industries* – former (1950). Registration: No/ID: 0447.050.135, Start date: 30 Apr 1991, Belgium; EU Transparency Register, No/ID: 79464041975-17, Start date: 9 Jul 2009. **Aims** Represent globally the common position of the European machine tool industry and promote their presence, mainly through EMO exhibitions; maintain a Market Intelligence Service gathering and distributing statistical and economic data and reports; support European and international standardization; promote innovation and exploitation of research results; promote cooperation with other international organizations. **Structure** Central Committee (meets twice a year); Bureau; Sub-Committees; Secretariat. Meetings closed. **Languages** English. **Staff** 8.00 FTE, paid. **Finance** Sources: members' dues. **Events** *Fall Meetings* Brussels (Belgium) 2022, *Spring Meeting* Brussels (Belgium) 2020, *Fall Meeting* Paris (France) 2020, *AMEC : Additive Manufacturing European Conference* Brussels (Belgium) 2019, *Fall Meeting* Brussels (Belgium) 2019. **Publications** *International Statistics of Machine Tools* (annual); *Statistical Overview* (annual). *Extent of Liability when using the General ECE Supply Conditions*; *The Machine Tool Industry in Western Europe*. Other studies reserved for members' private use.
Members National associations of machine tool manufacturers, representing over 1300 industrial enterprises, in 15 countries:
Austria, Belgium, Czechia, Denmark, Finland, France, Germany, Italy, Netherlands, Portugal, Spain, Sweden, Switzerland, Türkiye, UK.
IGO Relations Recognized by: *European Commission (EC, #06633)*. Participates in the work of: *United Nations Economic Commission for Europe (UNECE, #20555)*. **NGO Relations** Member of (5): *Alliance for Internet of Things Innovation (AIOTI, #00697)*; *European Factories of the Future Research Association (EFFRA, #07023)*; *European Policy Centre (EPC, #08240)*; *Federation of European and International Associations Established in Belgium (FAIB, #09508)*; *Industry4Europe (#11181)*. Cooperation agreement with: *European Committee for Electrotechnical Standardization (CENELEC, #06647)*. In liaison with technical committees of: *International Organization for Standardization (ISO, #14473)*. Associate Expert Group of *Business and Industry Advisory Committee to the OECD (BIAC, #03385)*. [2022/XD0629/t/**D**]

♦ European Association of Machine Tool Merchants (EAMTM) 06114

Association européen des marchands de machines-outils – Europäischer Verein der Werkzeugmaschinenhändler

Permanent SG Villalaan 83, 1190 Brussels, Belgium. T. +3225341515. E-mail: info@eamtm.com.
Pres address not obtained.
URL: http://www.eamtm.eu/

History 1973. Expanded from *British Association of Used Machine Tool Merchants*. Former names and other names: *Association of European Machine Tool Merchants* – former. Registration: Banque-Carrefour des Entreprises, No/ID: 0457.158.228, Start date: 1 Jun 1995, Belgium; EU Transparency Register, No/ID: 310983522681-08, Start date: 13 Jul 2016. **Aims** Represent the interests of machine tool merchants in Europe and elsewhere. **Structure** Council. **Languages** Dutch, English, French, German, Spanish. **Staff** 1.00 FTE, paid. **Finance** Sources: members' dues. **Events** *Annual Conference* Vouliagmeni (Greece) 2019, *Annual Conference* Palma (Spain) 2018, *Annual Conference* Badesi (Italy) 2017, *Annual Conference* Albufeira (Portugal) 2016, *Annual Conference* Edinburgh (UK) 2015.
Members Machine tool merchants in 16 countries:
Belgium, Denmark, Finland, France, Germany, India, Italy, Japan, Netherlands, Poland, Slovakia, Spain, Sweden, Switzerland, UK, USA. [2022.05.18/XD1527/**D**]

♦ European Association for Machine Translation (EAMT) 06115

Secretariat Schützenweg 57, 4123 Allschwil BL, Switzerland.
Secretary address not obtained.
URL: http://www.eamt.org/

History 1991. Registered in accordance with Swiss Civil Code. **Aims** Serve those interested in machine translation and *computer*-based translation tools. **Structure** Officers: President; Secretary; Treasurer. **Languages** English. **Staff** Voluntary. **Finance** Members' fees: student – euro 10; individual – euro 35; non-profit organization – euro 115; corporate organization – euro 230. **Activities** Organizes workshops and conferences. **Events** *Annual Conference* Allschwil (Switzerland) 2020, *Biennial Machine Translation Summit* Dublin (Ireland) 2019, *Annual Conference* Alicante (Spain) 2018, *Annual Conference* Prague (Czechia) 2017, *Annual Conference* Riga (Latvia) 2016. **Publications** *Compendium of Translation Software* (2 a year) – electronic only.
Members Associations and individuals in 24 countries:
Austria, Belgium, Bulgaria, Croatia, Czechia, Denmark, Estonia, Finland, France, Germany, Greece, Hungary, Ireland, Italy, Luxembourg, Malta, Netherlands, Norway, Poland, Slovenia, Spain, Sweden, Switzerland, UK.
NGO Relations Regional Association of: *International Association for Machine Translation (IAMT, #12008)*. [2020/XD6309/**D**]

♦ European Association of Mail Service Pharmacies / see European Association of E-Pharmacies (#06029)
♦ European Association of Management Training Centres (inactive)
♦ European Association of Manufacturers of Business Machines and Information Technology Industry (inactive)
♦ European Association of Manufacturers and Distributors of Educational Materials / see Worlddidac Association (#21361)
♦ European Association of the Manufacturers of Gas Pressure Regulators and Safety Devices (inactive)

♦ European Association of Manufacturers of Moulded Polyurethane Parts for the Automotive Industry (EURO-MOULDERS) 06116

Association européenne des fabricants de pièces moulées de polyuréthane destinées à l'industrie automobile

SG Av de Cortenbergh 71, 1000 Brussels, Belgium. T. +3227418281. Fax +3227366072. E-mail: info@euromoulders.org.
URL: http://www.euro-moulders.org/

History Jun 1998. Founded by 10 member companies. Registration: Banque-Carrefour des Entreprises, No/ID: 0464.563.385, Start date: 20 Sep 1998, Belgium. **Aims** Establish permanent liaison among member companies; promote joint study of common interests; ensure promotion and representation of polyurethane moulded foam for *automotive* industry at international level, in particular liaising with European economic institutions; liaise with associations representing related industries, suppliers and client sectors; organize response to development of EU directives – such as 'End of Live Vehicles' directive – and to general regulations affecting the industry. **Structure** General Assembly (annual); Board of Directors; Executive Committee; Technical Committee. **Languages** English. **Staff** 1.50 FTE, paid. **Finance** Sources: members' dues. Annual budget: 200,000 EUR. **Activities** Events/meetings; knowledge management/information dissemination; networking/liaising. **Events** *Annual Conference* Berlin (Germany) 2022, *General Assembly* Lisbon (Portugal) 2019, *General Assembly* Krakow (Poland) 2018, *General Assembly* Milan (Italy) 2017, *General Assembly* Brussels (Belgium) 2016.
Members Full: companies (10) in 6 countries:
Belgium, France, Germany, Italy, Spain, Türkiye.
Associate in 8 countries:
Belgium, France, Germany, Hungary, Netherlands, Spain, Switzerland, UK.
NGO Relations Member of (2): *Circular Plastics Alliance (#03936)*; *European Association of Automotive Suppliers (CLEPA, #05948)* (Associate). [2021.02.17/XD6707/t/**D**]

♦ European Association of Manufacturers of Polycarbonate Sheet (inactive)
♦ European Association of Manufacturers of Radiators (inactive)
♦ European Association of Marine Science and Technology (no recent information)
♦ European Association for Maxillo-Facial Surgery / see European Association for Cranio-Maxillo-Facial Surgery (#05995)
♦ European Association of Mayanists (#02126)
♦ European Association of Media Personnel (see: #09682)
♦ European Association for Mediated Learning and Cognitive Modifiability (no recent information)

♦ European Association Medical Devices of Notified Bodies (TEAM-NB) 06117

Dir Bd Frère Orban 35A, 4000 Liège, Belgium. T. +3242545588.
URL: http://www.team-nb.org/

History 6 Nov 2001. Also referred to as *European Association of Notified Bodies for Medical Devices*. EU Transparency Register: 731188910513-57. **Aims** Promote high technical and ethical standards in the functioning of notified bodies; protect legal and commercial interests of notified bodies functioning in the medical device directives; improve communication in the field. **Languages** English. **Events** *Meeting* Brussels (Belgium) 2006.

Members Agencies (24) in 12 countries:
Denmark, France, Germany, Greece, Ireland, Italy, Netherlands, Norway, Slovenia, Sweden, Türkiye, UK.
[2018.06.01/XM0369/D]

♦ European Association of medium-sized energy companies (internationally oriented national body)

♦ European Association for Mental Health in Intellectual Disability (EAMHID) 06118

Pres Square Ambiorix 32, 1000 Brussels, Belgium. T. +3222304761. E-mail: president@eamhid.eu.
URL: https://eamhid.eu/

History 1993. Former names and other names: *European Association for Mental Health in Mental Retardation (MHMR)* – former. **Aims** Promote cooperation and exchange of knowledge in the field of mental health care for intellectually disabled people with special emphasis on improving standards of service provision. **Structure** Assembly; Executive Committee; Officers; Special Working Groups. **Languages** English. **Finance** Member's dues. Other sources: gifts; subsidies. **Activities** Events/meetings; guidance/assistance/consulting; research/documentation; training/education. **Events** *Congress* Helsinki (Finland) 2023, *Congress* Berlin (Germany) 2021, *Congress* Barcelona (Spain) 2019, *Congress* Luxembourg (Luxembourg) 2017, *Congress* Florence (Italy) 2015. **Publications** *Journal of Intellectual Disability Research (JIDR). Practice Guidelines for the Assessment and Diagnosis of Mental Health Problems in Adults with Intellectual Disability.* Congress and symposium proceedings.

Members Individuals and organizations in 15 countries:
Australia, Austria, Belgium, Canada, Croatia, Denmark, Finland, Germany, Italy, Luxembourg, Netherlands, Norway, Portugal, South Africa, UK. [2020/XD3509/D]

♦ European Association for Mental Health in Mental Retardation / see European Association for Mental Health in Intellectual Disability (#06118)
♦ European Association of Metallurgical Slags Producers and Processors / see EUROSLAG
♦ European Association of Metals (#02578)

♦ European Association of Methodology (EAM) 06119

Pres Utrecht Univ, Domplein 29, 3512 JE Utrecht, Netherlands.
URL: http://www.eam-online.org/

History 27 Feb 2004, Frankfurt-Main (Germany). Registered in accordance with German law. **Aims** Promote research and development of empirical research methods in the field of behavioural, social, educational, health and economic sciences and in the field of evaluation research. **Structure** General Assembly; Executive Committee. **Languages** English. **Staff** None. **Finance** Members' dues. **Events** *Biennial Conference* Valencia (Spain) 2021, *Biennial Conference* Valencia (Spain) 2020, *Biennial Conference* Jena (Germany) 2018, *Biennial Conference* Palma (Spain) 2016, *Biennial Conference* Utrecht (Netherlands) 2014. **Publications** *Methodology – European Journal of Research Methods in the Behavioural and Social Sciences.* **Members** Full in 45 countries. Membership countries not specified. [2015.02.24/XM3042/D]

♦ European Association of Metropolitan Cities / see EUROCITIES (#05662)
♦ European Association for Microprocessing and Microprogramming / see EUROMICRO (#05736)

♦ European Association for Middle Eastern Studies (EURAMES) 06120

Pres Center for Research on the Arab World, Uni Mainz, 55099 Mainz, Germany. Fax +4961313924736.
URL: http://www.eurames.de/

History Founded 11 Jul 1990, Paris (France). Constitution amended 4 Jul 2000. **Aims** Further European cooperation in Middle East studies. **Structure** Council (meets annually); Secretariat. **Languages** English, French, German. **Staff** 2.00 FTE, paid. **Finance** Grant from *European Commission (EC, #06633)*. **Activities** Knowledge management/information dissemination; research/documentation; events/meetings; training/education. **Events** *Conciliating revelation and science in the Abrahamic traditions* London (UK) 2012, *Council Meeting* Berlin (Germany) 2011, *EURAMES Triennial Conference* Exeter (UK) 2011, *World congress for Middle Eastern studies* Barcelona (Spain) 2010, *Triennial Conference* Freiburg-Breisgau (Germany) 2007. **Publications** *EURAMES Info Service* (weekly); *Eurames Newsletter. European Expertise on the Middle East and Africa* (1993) by Emma Murphy et al. Information Services: Directory of individuals and organizations in Europe concerned with the Middle East – database. **Information Services** *European Directory of Middle East Studies* – database.

Members Societies in 23 countries:
Belarus, Belgium, Bulgaria, Cyprus, Czechia, Denmark, Finland, France, Germany, Greece, Ireland, Italy, Netherlands, Norway, Poland, Portugal, Romania, Russia, Spain, Sweden, Switzerland, Türkiye, UK, Ukraine.
Individuals in 20 countries and territories:
Algeria, Bahrain, Canada, Egypt, Iran Islamic Rep, Iraq, Israel, Jordan, Kuwait, Lebanon, Morocco, Oman, Palestine, Saudi Arabia, Sudan, Syrian AR, Tunisia, United Arab Emirates, USA, Yemen.
Included in the above, 5 organizations listed in this Yearbook:
British Society for Middle Eastern Studies (BRISMES); Deutsche Arbeitsgemeinschaft Vorderer Orient für Gegenwartsbezogene Forschung und Dokumentation (DAVO); Deutsche Morgenländische Gesellschaft (DMG); European Association of Middle East Librarians (MELCom International, #06121); Nordic Society for Middle Eastern Studies (nsmes, #17419).

NGO Relations Located at: *Zentrum für Forschung zur Arabischen Welt (ZEFAW).* [2019.02.12/XD3031/y/D]

♦ European Association of Middle East Librarians (MELCom International) 06121

Sec Middle East Centre Librarian, St Antony's College, Univ of Oxford, 68 Woodstock Rd, Oxford, OX2 6JF, UK. T. +441865284780. E-mail: melcomintl.secretary@gmail.com.
Pres Bamberg Univ Library, Feldkirchenstr 21, 96052 Bamberg, Germany. T. +9518631530. E-mail: melcominternational.president.ub@uni-bamberg.de.
URL: http://www.melcominternational.org/

History 1979. Former names and other names: *Middle East Librarian Committee* – former (1979 to 1993). **Aims** Promote cooperation among individuals and institutions concerned with all aspects of Middle East librarianship, collections development, book trade and publishing. **Structure** Board; Scientific Advisory Board; Grants Committee. **Languages** English, French. **Staff** Part-time, voluntary. **Finance** Sources: meeting proceeds; members' dues. **Activities** Events/meetings. **Events** *Annual Conference* Naples (Italy) 2019, *Annual Conference* Budapest (Hungary) 2018, *Annual Conference* Cambridge (UK) 2017, *Annual Conference* Leiden (Netherlands) 2016, *Annual Conference* Constantine (Algeria) 2015.

Members Individuals (over 360) in 40 countries:
Algeria, Armenia, Azerbaijan, Belgium, Bosnia-Herzegovina, Bulgaria, Canada, Croatia, Cyprus, Egypt, Finland, France, Germany, Hungary, Indonesia, Iran Islamic Rep, Iraq, Israel, Italy, Japan, Jordan, Kuwait, Lebanon, Morocco, Netherlands, North Macedonia, Palestine, Qatar, Russia, Saudi Arabia, Serbia, Spain, Switzerland, Syrian AR, Tunisia, Türkiye, UK, United Arab Emirates, USA, Uzbekistan.

NGO Relations Member of (1): *European Association for Middle Eastern Studies (EURAMES, #06120).*
[2021.06.10/XD7957/v/D]

♦ European Association of Mining Industries, Metal Ores and Industrial Minerals (EUROMINES) 06122

Contact Av de Tervuren 168, Boîte 15, 1150 Brussels, Belgium. T. +3222050840. E-mail: secretariat@euromines.be.
URL: http://www.euromines.org/

History 20 May 1996. Former names and other names: *International Association of European Mining Industries, Metal Ores and Industrial Minerals* – former (1996). Registration: Banque-Carrefour des Entreprises, No/ID: 0459.110.403, Start date: 20 May 1996, Belgium; EU Transparency Register, No/ID: 62722978644-95, Start date: 23 Apr 2012. **Aims** Study problems encountered by the extractive industry in Europe, including technological and environmental aspects; at an opportune time, present the results of research to international, European and national authorities and to the general public. **Structure** General Assembly (annual); Steering Committee. **Languages** Croatian, Czech, Dutch, English, French, German, Irish Gaelic, Polish, Romanian, Slovakian, Spanish. **Staff** 6.00 FTE, paid. **Finance** Members' dues. **Activities** Training/education; knowledge management/information dissemination. **Events** *General Assembly* Brussels (Belgium) 2021, *EU-Latin America Mining and Exploration Convention* Madrid (Spain) 2018, *Non-Energy Extractive Industry Platform Meeting* Brussels (Belgium) 2017, *Conference on Mine Closure* Cornwall (UK) 2013, *General Assembly* Stockholm (Sweden) 2013. **Publications** *Euromines* in Spanish – newsletter. Annual Report.

Members Direct: Associations in 14 countries:
Austria, Bulgaria, Czechia, Finland, Germany, Greece, Hungary, Norway, Portugal, Romania, Slovakia, Sweden, Türkiye, UK.
Direct: Companies in 6 countries:
France, Netherlands, Poland, Spain, Sweden, UK.
Associate: associations (2) in 1 country:
Germany.
Associated: companies (5) in 4 countries:
Canada, France, Germany, UK.

IGO Relations *European Commission (EC, #06633); International Bank for Reconstruction and Development (IBRD, #12317); OECD (#17693); UNEP (#20299); United Nations (UN, #20515).* **NGO Relations** *Barytes Association, The (#03180); Business and Industry Advisory Committee to the OECD (BIAC, #03385); Comité européen de normalisation (CEN, #04162); EUMICON (#05587); Federation of European Mineral Engineering Programs (FEMP, #09517); Industry4Europe (#11181); International Council on Mining and Metals (ICMM, #13048); World Wide Fund for Nature (WWF, #21922).* Member of: *European Network on Silica (NEPSI, #08001); Federation of European and International Associations Established in Belgium (FAIB, #09508).*
[2021/XD5228/ty/D]

♦ European Association for Modern Arabic Literature (EURAMAL) ... 06123

Pres c/o Univ degli Studi di Napoli L'Orientale, Dipto Asia Africa e Mediterraneo, Piazza S Domenico Maggiore 12, Palazzo Corigliano, 80134 Naples NA, Italy.
Sec c/o Sofia Univ of St Kliment Ohridski, Fac of Classical and Modern Philology, Dept Arabic and Semitic Studies, 79 Todor Alexandrov Blvd, 1303 Sofia, Bulgaria. E-mail: braykh@gmail.com.
URL: http://folk.uio.no/guthst/euramal_start.html

History as *European Meeting of Teachers of Arabic (EMTAR).* **Aims** Promote, encourage and support interest and scholarly research in modern Arabic literature; increase cooperation and information exchange between individuals and organizations in the field. **Structure** General Meeting (every 2 years); Council. **Languages** Arabic, English, French, German, Italian. **Finance** Members' dues. Other sources: mixed funding for conferences and proceedings. **Events** *Conference* Oslo (Norway) 2016, *Conference* Madrid (Spain) 2014, *Literature and the Arab Spring – analyses and perspectives* Paris (France) 2012, *Conference* Rome (Italy) 2010, *Conference* Rome (Italy) 2010. **Publications** *Arabic Literature in a Posthuman World* (2019); *New Geographies: Texts and Contexts in Modern Arabic Literature!* (2018); *La littérature à l'heure du Printemps arabe* (2016); *Desire, Pleasure and the Taboo: New Voices and Freedom of Expression in Contemporary Arabic Literature* (2014); *From New Values to New Aesthetics: Turning Points in Modern Arabic Literature – vols 1-2* (2011); *The Creativity of Exile and the Diaspora: Middle Eastern Writers Re-Thinking Literature, Society, Politics* (2008); *Identity: Remembered, Discovered, Invented* (2006); *Intertextuality in Modern Arabic Literature since 1967* (2006); *La poétique de l'espace dans la littérature arabe moderne* (2002); *Literary Innovation in Modern Arabic Literature: Schools and Journals* (2000); *Writing the Self: Autobiographical writing in modern Arabic literature* (1998); *Love, Marriage and Sexuality in Modern Arabic Literature* (1994).

Members Individuals in 18 countries:
Bulgaria, Egypt, France, Germany, Iran Islamic Rep, Italy, Lebanon, Morocco, Netherlands, Norway, Poland, Romania, Russia, Spain, Sweden, Switzerland, UK, USA. [2019.12.16/XM2750/v/D]

♦ European Association of Mollusc Producers / see European Mollusc Producers' Association (#07818)
♦ European Association of Motorcycle Manufacturers / see Association des constructeurs européens de motocycles (#02450)
♦ European Association for Mountain Areas / see Euromontana (#05737)
♦ European Association of Mozzarella Manufacturers (inactive)
♦ European Association for Multiagent Systems / see European Association for Multi-Agent Systems (#06124)

♦ European Association for Multi-Agent Systems (EURAMAS) 06124

Sec IRIT, Université Paul Sabatier, 118 Route de Narbonne, 31062 Toulouse CEDEX 9, France.
URL: http://www.euramas.org/

History Also referred to as *European Association for Multiagent Systems.* Registered in accordance with French law. **Aims** Promote European science and *technology* in the area of multiagent systems. **Structure** General Assembly. Board of Directors, including Chair, Deputy Chair and Secretary. **Activities** Organizes: European Workshop on Multiagent Systems (EUMAS); European Summer School on Multiagent Systems (EASSS). **Events** *European Conference on Multi-Agent Systems* Bergen (Norway) 2018, *European Conference on Multi-Agent Systems* Paris (France) 2017, *European workshop on Multi-agent Systems* Maastricht (Netherlands) 2011. [2012/XJ5226/D]

♦ European Association of Musculo-Skeletal Transplantation (inactive)

♦ European Association of Museums of the History of Medical Sciences (EAMHMS) 06125

Association européenne des musées de l'histoire des sciences médicales (AEMHSM)

Pres c/o BMMC, Charitéplatz 1, 10117 Berlin, Germany.
URL: http://www.eamhms.org/

History 1983, Saint-Julien-en-Beaujolais (France). Registered in accordance with French law. **Aims** Provide links among individuals and institutions studying and housing historic objects of medical and historical significance. **Structure** General Meeting (every 2 years). Council (meets annually), composed of 11-15 members including the Bureau: President, 2 Vice-Presidents; Secretary-General; Vice Secretary-General; Treasurer; Vice-Treasurer. **Languages** English, French. **Finance** Members' dues. **Activities** Organizes: biennial congress and workshops on conservation; exhibitions. **Events** *Biennial Congress* Barcelona (Spain) 2018, *Biennial Congress* Groningen (Netherlands) 2016, *Biennial Congress* London (UK) 2014, *Biennial Congress* Berlin (Germany) 2012, *Biennial Congress* Copenhagen (Denmark) 2010. **Publications** *Bulletin* (2 a year) in English, French. Congress proceedings. Information Services: Central register of holdings, personnel and specialist advice.

Members Institutes and individuals in 31 countries:
Argentina, Australia, Austria, Belarus, Belgium, Canada, China, Croatia, Cyprus, Denmark, Estonia, France, Germany, Italy, Japan, Latvia, Lithuania, Netherlands, Norway, Poland, Portugal, Romania, Russia, Slovenia, Spain, Sweden, Switzerland, UK, Ukraine, USA, Vietnam. [2016/XD2156/D]

♦ European Association of Music Conservatories, Academies and High Schools / see Association Européenne des Conservatoires, Académies de Musique et Musikhochschulen (#02560)
♦ European Association of Music Festivals / see European Festivals Association (#07242)

♦ European Association of Music and Imagery (EAMI) 06126

Contact address not obtained.
URL: http://www.music-and-imagery.eu/

History Set up as a continuation of the more loosely organized *European Network of Music and Guided Imagery (ENGIM).* Preliminary version of EAMI set up, Sep 2014, Berlin (Germany). Constitutional assembly Sep 2016, Athens (Greece). Registered in accordance with Danish law: 36156341. **Aims** Inform about, stimulate and enhance practice, education and research in the Bonny Method of Guided Imagery and Music (GIM). **Structure** Board. **Finance** Members' dues. **Activities** Events/meetings; training/education. **Events** *European Conference* Fredericia (Denmark) 2022, *European Conference* Fredericia (Denmark) 2020, *European Conference* Termonfeckin (Ireland) 2018. [2021/XM6259/D]

♦ European Association for Music in Schools (EAS) 06127

Association européenne pour la musique à l'école – Europäische Arbeitsgemeinschaft Schulmusik

Pres LUCA School of Arts, Lemmensinstituut, Lemmensberg 3, 3000 Leuven, Belgium. E-mail: info@eas-music.org.
URL: http://www.eas-music.org/

History 1990, Lübeck (Germany). **Aims** Advocate for high quality music education accessible to all. **Structure** General Assembly (annual); Executive Committee. **Languages** English. **Staff** Voluntary. **Finance** Sources: members' dues. **Activities** Advocacy/lobbying/activism; events/meetings; projects/programmes. **Events** *Conference* Lyon (France) 2023, *Conference* Belgrade (Serbia) 2022, *Conference* Freiburg-Breisgau (Germany) 2021, *Music for all* Padua (Italy) 2020, *The school I'd like* Malmö (Sweden) 2019. **Publications** *EAS E-Newsflash. European perspectives on Music Education* – (annual) book series.

Members Full; Sponsor; Honorary. Individuals and institutions in 37 countries and territories:
Albania, Austria, Belgium, Bulgaria, Croatia, Cyprus, Czechia, Denmark, Estonia, Finland, France, Germany, Greece, Hungary, Iceland, Ireland, Italy, Kosovo, Latvia, Lithuania, Luxembourg, Montenegro, Netherlands, North Macedonia, Norway, Poland, Portugal, Scotland, Serbia, Slovakia, Slovenia, Spain, Sweden, Switzerland, Türkiye, UK, Ukraine.
NGO Relations Member of (2): *European Music Council (EMC, #07837)*; *International Music Council (IMC, #14199)*. [2021.10.21/XD7037/**D**]

- ♦ European Association of Mutual Guarantee Societies / see European Association of Guarantee Institutions (#06061)
- ♦ European Association of Myasthenia Gravis Patients' Associations / see European Myasthenia Gravis Association (#07844)

♦ European Association of National Builders' Merchants Associations 06128

Union européenne des fédérations nationales des négociants en matériaux de construction (UFEMAT) – Europäische Vereinigung der Nationalen Baustoffhändler-Verbände

Gen Sec Altitude II, Brusselsesteenweg 524 B6, 1731 Zellik, Belgium. T. +3224662483. Fax +3224632646. E-mail: marnix@fema.be – ufemat@ufemat.eu.
URL: http://www.ufemat.eu/

History 18 Apr 1959, Brussels (Belgium), as *Union of National Federations of Building Materials Merchants in the EEC – Union des fédérations nationales des négociants en matériaux de construction de la CEE*. Includes activities of *EUROFORUM (inactive)*. **Aims** Provide information on the different aspects of the industry, and showcase common interests. **Structure** Officers: President; Vice-President. **Languages** English, French, German. **Activities** Monitors developments in distribution, management, training and advanced training, technology, product development, logistics and legislation. Organizes regular meetings with the building materials industry. **Events** *Congress* Montreux (Switzerland) 2022, *Congress* Montreux (Switzerland) 2019, *Congress* Lisbon (Portugal) 2018, *Congress* Stockholm (Sweden) 2017, *Congress* Berlin (Germany) 2016.
Members National organizations in 15 countries:
Austria, Belgium, Denmark, France, Germany, Hungary, Ireland, Italy, Luxembourg, Netherlands, Portugal, Slovakia, Sweden, Switzerland, UK.
IGO Relations Recognized by: *European Commission (EC, #06633)*. [2017/XD3359/**D**]

- ♦ European Association of National Geological Surveys / see EuroGeoSurveys (#05686)
- ♦ European Association of the National IBD Study Groups / see European Crohn's and Colitis Organisation (#06864)

♦ European Association of National Metrology Institutes (EURAMET) . 06129

GS Bundesallee 100, 38116 Braunschweig, Germany. T. +495315921960. Fax +495315921969. E-mail: secretariat@euramet.org.
Management Support Unit Hampton Road, Teddington, TW11 0LW, UK. E-mail: msu@npl.co.uk.
URL: http://www.euramet.org/

History 1 Jul 2007. Successor to *European Collaboration on Measurement Standards (EUROMET, inactive)*. Registered in accordance with German law. EU Transparency Register: 83842168796-93. **Aims** Develop and disseminate an integrated, cost effective and internationally competitive measurement infrastructure for Europe. **Structure** General Assembly; Board of Directors; Technical Committees; EMPIR Committee; Research Council; Secretariat. **Languages** English. **Events** *Annual General Assembly* Braunschweig (Germany) 2021, *Annual General Assembly* Borås (Sweden) 2019, *Annual General Assembly* Bucharest (Romania) 2018, *Annual Meeting* Paris (France) 2018, *Annual General Assembly* Madrid (Spain) 2017. **Members** National metrology institutes (NMIs). Membership countries not specified. **IGO Relations** *European Federation of National Associations of Measurement, Testing and Analytical Laboratories (EUROLAB, #07168)*. Observer member of: *Intra-Africa Metrology System (AFRIMETS, #15992)*. **NGO Relations** Member of (2): *EURACHEM (#05595)*; *European Accreditation Advisory Board (EAAB, see: #06782)*. [2019/XM3658/**D**]

♦ European Association of National Productivity Centres (EANPC) ... 06130

Association européenne des centres nationaux de productivité (AECNP) – Asociación Europea de Centros Nacionales de Productividad

SG c/o RKW, Düsseldorfer Str 40-A, 65760 Eschborn, Germany. E-mail: secretariat@eanpc.eu.
URL: https://www.eanpc.eu/

History 17 Jan 1966, Paris (France). Founded following meetings from 1953 to 1961 of the Productivity Committee of *European Productivity Agency (EPA, inactive)*, attached to *Organization for European Economic Cooperation (OEEC, inactive)*, and from 1961 to 1965 of *OECD (#17693)*. During reorganization of the latter, representatives of national productivity centres decided to form their own association. Statutes modified: 1981, 1991. Registration: Start date: 14 Nov 1966, Belgium. **Aims** Facilitate and intensify exchange of information and experience and encourage cooperation among participating centres, especially in the field of scientific research; establish liaison with non-European productivity centres and their international organizations, and with international organizations dealing in social and economic affairs. **Structure** Managing Board (meeting at least twice a year at General Assembly); Executive Bureau; Working Groups; Liaison Committees. **Languages** English, French. **Staff** 2.00 FTE, paid. **Finance** Members' dues. Commissioned projects. **Activities** Knowledge management/information dissemination; networking/liaising. **Events** *European Management Conference* Athens (Greece) 2014, *European productivity conference* Antalya (Turkey) 2010, *European productivity conference / Half-yearly Meeting* Zilina (Slovakia) 2007, *European productivity conference* Espoo (Finland) 2006, *Impact of training on productivity in the work-place* Grimsby (UK) 2005. **Publications** *Epi* (3 a year); *Europroductivity* (3 a year). Reports of activities; survey reports.
Members Full; Associate; Corresponding. Members in 12 countries:
Austria, Belgium, Cyprus, Czechia, Finland, Germany, Hungary, Italy, Netherlands, Romania, Slovakia, Türkiye.
IGO Relations Recognized by: *European Commission (EC, #06633)*. [2019/XD0573/**D**]

- ♦ European Association for Negotiation and Mediation (unconfirmed)
- ♦ European Association of Netting Manufacturers (inactive)
- ♦ European Association of Neuro-Linguistic Programming (unconfirmed)

♦ European Association for Neuro-Linguistic Psychotherapy (EANLPt) 06131

Association européenne pour la psycho-thérapie neuro-linguistique – Asociación Europea de Psicoterapia Neuro-Lingüística – Europäische Gesellschaft für Neuro-Linguistische Psychotherapie – Europeese Vereniging voor Neuro-Linguïstische Psychotherapie

Main Office Widerhofergasse 4, 1094 Vienna, Austria. T. +4313176780. Fax +4313176781 – +4313176722. E-mail: info@eanlpt.org.
SG Ferdinand-Raimund-Gasse 10-12, 2345 Brunn-Gebirge, Austria. T. +43676849112218. E-mail: friendly@schuetz.at.
URL: http://www.eanlpt.org/

History 1995, Vienna (Austria). **Aims** Promote the psychotherapeutic application of NLP (Neuro-Linguistic Psychotherapy NLPt) in Europe as an accredited and recognized method of psychotherapy; support high quality training standards for NLPt and represent the method in European Government bodies and within the EAP; support formation of a worldwide platform for neurolistic psychotherapy with highly respected standards and procedures. **Structure** General Assembly; Country Board; Executive; Training Standards Committee. **Languages** English. **Staff** 0.50 FTE, paid. **Finance** Sources: members' dues. Other sources: ECP fees. Annual budget: 12,000 EUR. **Events** *Conference* Zagreb (Croatia) 2019, *Conference* Bari (Italy) 2018, *Conference* Bucharest (Romania) 2018, *Conference* Odessa (Ukraine) 2017, *Conference* Vienna (Austria) 2017.
Members National organizations (25) and training institutes (7) in 19 countries:
Austria, Belgium, Croatia, Denmark, Finland, France, Germany, Greece, Hungary, Ireland, Italy, Latvia, Netherlands, Poland, Russia, Slovenia, Switzerland, UK, Ukraine.
NGO Relations Cooperates with (1): *European Association for Psychotherapy (EAP, #06176)*. [2022.02.15/XD7526/**D**]

♦ European Association for Neuro-Oncology (EANO) 06132

Sec c/o WMA GmbH, Alser Strasse 4, 1090 Vienna, Austria. T. +431405138331. E-mail: office@eano.eu.
URL: http://www.eano.eu/

History 1994, Brussels (Belgium). Founded following activities initiated in 1990. Part of: *World Federation of Neuro-Oncology Societies (WFNOS, #21462)*. **Languages** English. **Staff** 0.50 FTE, paid. **Events** *EANO Meeting* Glasgow (UK) 2024, *EANO Meeting* Rotterdam (Netherlands) 2023, *EANO Meeting* Vienna (Austria) 2022, *EANO Meeting* 2021, *EANO Meeting* Glasgow (UK) 2020.
Members Individuals (600) in 36 countries:
Argentina, Australia, Austria, Belgium, Bulgaria, Canada, Czechia, Denmark, Egypt, Finland, France, Germany, Greece, Hungary, Ireland, Israel, Italy, Japan, Latvia, Luxembourg, Malaysia, Netherlands, Norway, Poland, Portugal, Russia, Serbia, Slovakia, Slovenia, South Africa, Spain, Sweden, Switzerland, Türkiye, UK, USA.
NGO Relations Instrumental in setting up: *International Brain Tumour Alliance (IBTA, #12393)*. [2021/XD6855/v/**D**]

♦ European Association of Neuroscience Nurses (EANN) 06133

Pres Zwanenveld 37-18, 6538 XX Nijmegen, Netherlands. T. +31243449540. Fax +31243614914.
Sec 22 Camm Str, Walkley, Sheffield, S6 3TR, UK.
URL: http://www.eann.info/

History 1979. **Aims** Enhance and develop the competence of European neuroscience nurses by improving information exchange between nurses across Europe. **Structure** Executive Committee, comprising Honorary Officers – Chairman, Vice-Chairman, Secretary, Treasurer – and one representative of each member country. **Languages** English. **Staff** Voluntary. **Finance** Members' dues. **Activities** Events/meetings; awards/prizes/competitions. **Events** *Quadrennial Congress* Belgrade (Serbia) 2015, *Meeting* Helsinki (Finland) 2014, *Meeting* Vienna (Austria) 2013, *Meeting* Istanbul (Turkey) 2012, *Quadrennial Congress* Blankenberge (Belgium) 2011.
Members Associations and individuals in 19 countries:
Belgium, Croatia, Denmark, Finland, France, Germany, Greece, Iceland, Italy, Malta, Netherlands, Norway, Poland, Serbia, Spain, Sweden, Switzerland, Türkiye, UK. [2019/XD1029/**D**]

- ♦ European Association of Neurosurgery / see European Association of Neurosurgical Societies (#06134)

♦ European Association of Neurosurgical Societies (EANS) 06134

Association européenne de sociétés de neurochirurgie

Exec Dir c/o Artion, Ethnikis Antistaseos 74, Kamalaria, 551 33 Thessaloniki, Greece. E-mail: info@eans.org.
Registered Office Rue d'Egmont 11, 1000 Brussels, Belgium. Fax +3225141430.
URL: http://www.eans.org/

History 1972, Prague (Czechia). Continental Association of: *World Federation of Neurosurgical Societies (WFNS, #21466)*. Registered in accordance with Belgian law. Former names and other names: *European Association of Neurosurgery* – alias. Registration: Crossroads Bank for Enterprises, No/ID: 0443.413.229, Start date: 1 Sep 1990, Belgium; EU Transparency Register, No/ID: 626408448688-50, Start date: 31 Jan 2023. **Aims** Act as the primary advocate for neurosurgery, neurosurgeons and their patients in Europe and beyond; facilitate free interchange of neurosurgical knowledge and experience among members, and thereby enable members to enhance the care that they deliver to their patients. **Structure** EANS Council; Open Executive Committee; Board of Officers. Sections (6): Functional Neurosurgery; Neuro-oncology; Radiosurgery; Spinal Surgery; Trauma and Critical Care; Vascular. **Languages** English. **Staff** 0.20 FTE, paid. **Finance** Sources: meeting proceeds; members' dues; sponsorship. Annual budget: 2,000,000 EUR (2022). **Activities** Events/meetings; training/education. **Events** *Congress* Belgrade (Serbia) 2022, *Young Neurosurgeons Meeting* Florence (Italy) 2022, *Congress* Hamburg (Germany) 2021, *Congress* Thessaloniki (Greece) 2020, *Congress* Dublin (Ireland) 2019. **Publications** *Acta Neurochirurgica* – journal.
Members National Societies in 39 countries:
Armenia, Austria, Azerbaijan, Belgium, Bosnia-Herzegovina, Bulgaria, Croatia, Cyprus, Czechia, Denmark, Estonia, Finland, France, Georgia, Germany, Greece, Hungary, Israel, Italy, Kazakhstan, Kosovo, Latvia, Lithuania, Netherlands, North Macedonia, Norway, Poland, Portugal, Romania, Russia, Serbia, Slovakia, Slovenia, Spain, Sweden, Switzerland, Türkiye, UK, Ukraine.
Individuals (about 1,300) worldwide. Membership countries not specified.
NGO Relations Member of (1): *European Brain Council (EBC, #06391)*. [2023/XD6367/**D**]

- ♦ European Association of Next Generation Telecommunications Innovators (unconfirmed)
- ♦ European Association for Non-Governmental Organizations on the Question of Palestine / see European Association for Non-Governmental Organizations Working on Palestine (#06135)

♦ European Association for Non-Governmental Organizations Working on Palestine 06135

Association européenne des organisations non-gouvernementales travaillant sur la Palestine (Euro ONG Palestine)

Chair Rue Stévin 115, 1000 Brussels, Belgium. T. +3222310174. Fax +3222310174.

History as *European Association for Non-Governmental Organizations on the Question of Palestine – Association européenne des organisations non-gouvernementales sur la question de la Palestine (Euro ONG Palestine)*. Statutes adopted 29 Mar 1992. **Aims** Ensure liaison among members and facilitate common action to: reach a just, durable and *peaceful* solution of the Palestinian question based on United Nations resolutions; promote economic and social development in the occupied territories; achieve respect for protective international charters and conventions and promote *human rights* and the rights of the *child* with respect to Palestinians. **Structure** General Assembly. Coordinating Committee, comprising President, Vice-President, Treasurer and Secretary. **Languages** English, French. **Staff** 1.00 FTE, paid. **Finance** Members' contributions. Subsidies from: Belgian government; *European Union (EU, #08967)*. **Activities** Organizes: campaigns; conferences; missions of civilian observers. **Events** *Seminar on durum wheat improvement in the Mediterranean region* Saragossa (Spain) 2000, *Conférence sur les territoires occupés de Palestine* Brussels (Belgium) 1992.
Members Representatives of organizations in 9 countries:
Belgium, Denmark, France, Greece, Italy, Luxembourg, Norway, Spain, UK.
Included in the above, 1 organization listed in this Yearbook:
CIMADE.
NGO Relations Represented at: *International Coordinating Committee for NGOs on the Question of Palestine (ICCP, inactive)*. [2010/XE3184/y/**E**]

- ♦ European Association of Notified Bodies for Medical Devices / see European Association Medical Devices of Notified Bodies (#06117)

♦ European Association of Nuclear Medicine (EANM) 06136

Association européenne de médecine nucléaire

Exec Dir Schmalzhofgasse 26, 1060 Vienna, Austria. T. +4318904427. Fax +43189044279. E-mail: office@eanm.org.
URL: http://www.eanm.org/

History 1 Jan 1988. Founded upon decision made 4 Sep 1986, by merger of *European Nuclear Medicine Society (ENMS, inactive)* and *Society of Nuclear Medicine – Europe (SNME, inactive)*. Registration: No/ID: 063483520, Austria; EU Transparency Register, No/ID: 348978437245-85, Start date: 7 Feb 2020. **Aims** Advance science and education in nuclear medicine for the benefit of public health and humanity; promote exchange of information in the field and education and training in nuclear medicine techniques. **Structure** Assembly of Members (annual); Assembly of Delegates (annual); Executive Committee; Advisory Council. **Languages** English. **Staff** 6.00 FTE, paid. **Finance** Sources: meeting proceeds; members' dues. **Activities** Awards/prizes/competitions; events/meetings; training/education. Education through *European School of Multimodality Imaging & Therapy (ESMIT, #08432)*. **Events** *Annual Congress* Vienna (Austria) 2026, *Annual Congress* Barcelona (Spain) 2025, *Annual Congress* Vienna (Austria) 2023, *Annual Congress* Barcelona (Spain) 2022, *Annual Congress* Vienna (Austria) 2021. **Publications** *EJNMMI Journal* (14 a year); *EANM News. Technologist's Guides*.
Members Ordinary; Associate; Corporate; Emeritus; Junior; Technologists; Society members; Affiliate Society. Members (3,700) in 88 countries and territories:
Algeria, Argentina, Armenia, Australia, Austria, Bahrain, Bangladesh, Belgium, Bosnia-Herzegovina, Brazil, Bulgaria, Burkina Faso, Canada, Chile, China, Colombia, Costa Rica, Croatia, Cyprus, Czechia, Denmark, Egypt, Estonia, Finland, France, Georgia, Germany, Greece, Hong Kong, Hungary, Iceland, India, Indonesia, Iran Islamic Rep, Ireland, Israel, Italy, Japan, Jordan, Kazakhstan, Korea Rep, Kosovo, Kuwait, Latvia, Lebanon, Lithuania, Luxembourg, Malaysia, Malta, Mexico, Monaco, Mongolia, Montenegro, Morocco, Namibia, Netherlands, New Zealand, Nigeria, North Macedonia, Norway, Oman, Pakistan, Philippines, Poland, Portugal, Romania, Russia, Saudi Arabia, Senegal, Serbia, Singapore, Slovakia, Slovenia, South Africa, Spain, Sweden, Switzerland, Syrian AR, Taiwan, Thailand, Tunisia, Türkiye, UK, Ukraine, United Arab Emirates, Uruguay, USA, Uzbekistan.

NGO Relations Member of (3): *Biomedical Alliance in Europe (#03251); European Alliance for Medical Radiation Protection Research (EURAMED, #05874); European Cancer Organisation (ECO, #06432)*. Partner of (1): *Multidisciplinary European Low Dose Initiative Association (MELODI Association, #16882)*. Shareholder in: *European Institute for Biomedical Imaging Research (EIBIR, #07546)*. Participating organization of: *European Alliance for Personalised Medicine (EAPM, #05878)*. [2022/XD1720/v/D]

♦ European Association of Nurses in HIV/AIDS Care (inactive)
♦ European Association of Operators of Toll Road Infrastructures (#02559)

♦ European Association for Oral Medicine (EAOM) 06137

Treas address not obtained.
Pres address not obtained. E-mail: s.porter@ucl.ac.uk.
URL: http://www.eaom.eu/

History 1998. **Aims** Improve clinical care in the field of oral medicine; promote education and research in oral medicine in Europe; promote the exchange of scientific information. **Structure** General Meeting (every 2 years). General Assembly. Board (Council), comprising Executive Committee (President, Past-President, President-Elect, Secretary-General and Treasurer) and 5 regional representatives. **Languages** English. **Staff** Voluntary. **Finance** Members' dues. Congress proceeds. **Activities** Awards/prizes/competitions. **Events** *Biennial Congress* Turin (Italy) 2016, *Biennial Congress* Antalya (Turkey) 2014, *Biennial Congress* Athens (Greece) 2012, *Biennial Congress* London (UK) 2010, *Biennial Congress* Salzburg (Austria) 2008. **Publications** Congress proceedings.

Members Individuals 37 countries:
Albania, Australia, Austria, Brazil, Croatia, Czechia, Denmark, Estonia, Finland, France, Germany, Greece, Hungary, Iceland, Iran Islamic Rep, Ireland, Israel, Italy, Japan, Kuwait, Latvia, Lithuania, Netherlands, Norway, Portugal, Romania, Saudi Arabia, Serbia, Slovenia, Spain, Sweden, Switzerland, UK, USA.

NGO Relations Associate member of: *Platform for Better Oral Health in Europe (#18399)*. Close contacts with: American Academy of Oral Medicine; *International Academy of Oral Medicine (IAOM, #11562)*. [2017/XD8475/v/D]

♦ European Association for Organic Agriculture and Health (inactive)

♦ European Association of Organic Geochemists (EAOG) 06138

Sec Labo de Géologie de Lyon, Univ Lyon 1, Campus de la Doua, 69622 Villeurbanne, France.
URL: http://www.eaog.org/

History 1983, The Hague (Netherlands). **Aims** Promote studies and research on recent sediment, petroleum and coal geochemistry and environmental (organic) geochemistry including biological and non-biological processes and interactions in recent and ancient geologic regimes. **Structure** International Meeting, including a membership Assembly (every 2 years); Board. **Languages** English. **Staff** 6.00 FTE, voluntary. **Finance** Members' dues. Other sources: meeting proceeds; industrial sponsorship. **Activities** Events/meetings; financial and/or material support. **Events** *International Meeting on Organic Geochemistry (IMOG)* Montpellier (France) 2023, *International Meeting on Organic Geochemistry (IMOG)* Montpellier (France) 2021, *International Conference* Gothenburg (Sweden) 2019, *International Conference* Florence (Italy) 2017, *International Meeting on Organic Geochemistry (IMOG 2015)* Prague (Czech Rep) 2015. **Publications** *Organic Geochemistry* – journal. *Advances in Organic Geochemistry* – series.

Members Individuals in 40 countries:
Algeria, Australia, Austria, Belgium, Brazil, Canada, Chile, China, Croatia, Czechia, Denmark, Egypt, Finland, France, Germany, Greece, Hungary, India, Indonesia, Israel, Italy, Japan, Korea Rep, Kuwait, Mexico, Morocco, Netherlands, New Zealand, Nigeria, Norway, Oman, Poland, Russia, Saudi Arabia, Spain, Switzerland, Türkiye, UK, USA, Venezuela.

NGO Relations *European Association of Geoscientists and Engineers (EAGE, #06055)*; Organic Division of *Geochemical Society*. [2022/XD2024/v/D]

♦ European Association of Organizations for Home Care and Help at Home (inactive)
♦ European Association for Orientation, Vocational Guidance and Educational and Professional Information (inactive)

♦ European Association for Osseointegration (EAO) 06139

Association européenne pour l'osséointégration

Exec Dir 38 rue croix des petits champs, 75001 Paris, France. T. +33142366220. E-mail: info@eao.org.
Contact Av du Bourgmestre E Demunter, Bte 10, 1090 Brussels, Belgium.
URL: http://www.eao.org/

History Founded 1991, Munich (Germany). Current constitution adopted, 15 Sep 2001, Milan (Italy). UK Registered Charity: 1099474. **Aims** As the leading association within the field of implant *dentistry* in Europe, improve the quality of patient care by bridging the gap between science and clinical practice. **Structure** General Assembly; Board of Directors; Committees. **Languages** English. **Staff** 5.00 FTE, paid. **Finance** Members' dues. **Activities** Events/meetings; training/education. **Events** *Annual Congress* Geneva (Switzerland) 2022, *Annual Congress* Milan (Italy) 2021, *Annual Congress* Paris (France) 2020, *Annual Congress* Lisbon (Portugal) 2019, *Annual Congress* Vienna (Austria) 2018. **Publications** *Clinical Oral Implants Research* (12 a year) – journal; *Inspyred* (2 a year). **Members** Full; Young Professional; Honorary; Student; Over 65. Membership countries not specified. [2019/XD3629/D]

♦ European Association of Paediatric and Adolescent Gynaecology (EURAPAG) 06140

SG Oppenheimer Strasse 33, 60594 Frankfurt-Main, Germany. T. +496934878257. E-mail: secretarygeneral@eurapag.com.
Seat Moto, V Uvalu 84, 150 06 Prague 5, Czechia.
URL: http://www.eurapag.com/

History Resolution about foundation 8 May 2007, Sao Paulo (Brazil), during 15th World Congress of Paediatric and Adolescent Gynaecology. Officially set up 28 Mar 2008, Prague (Czech Rep). Registered in accordance with Czech law, 15 Apr 2008. **Aims** Promote education and research in the field adolescent and paediatric gynaecology. **Structure** Delegate Assembly (every 3 years, during European Congress). Executive Board, comprising President, President-Elect, Vice-President, Secretary-General, Treasurer and 4 members. **Languages** English. **Staff** Voluntary. **Finance** Members' dues. **Events** *European Congress* Thessaloniki (Greece) 2024, *European Congress* Rotterdam (Netherlands) 2021, *European Congress* Rotterdam (Netherlands) 2020, *European Congress* Vilnius (Lithuania) 2017, *European Congress* London (UK) 2014.

Members National organizations in 19 countries:
Belgium, Bulgaria, Cyprus, Czechia, Finland, Germany, Greece, Hungary, Italy, Kazakhstan, Latvia, Lithuania, Poland, Russia, Serbia, Slovakia, Switzerland, UK, Ukraine.
Individuals in 5 countries:
France, Ireland, Norway, Portugal, Sweden. [2021/XJ6887/D]

♦ European Association for Paediatric Education / see Association for Paediatric Education in Europe (#02847)

♦ European Association for Palliative Care (EAPC) 06141

Association européenne pour les soins palliatifs (AESP) – Associazione Europea per le Cure Palliative

CEO Luchthavenlaan 10, 1800 Vilvoorde, Belgium. T. +353879677176. E-mail: info@eapcnet.eu.
URL: http://www.eapcnet.eu/

History Dec 1988, Milan (Italy). Founded on the initiative of Prof Vittorio Ventafridda and the Floriani Foundation. Former names and other names: *EAPC Onlus* – former. Registration: Banque-Carrefour des Entreprises, No/ID: 0660.570.295, Start date: 29 Jul 2016, Belgium; End date: 2016, Italy; EU Transparency Register, No/ID: 006087021537-90, Start date: 26 Apr 2016. **Aims** Promote development of high quality palliative care across the life span by fostering and sharing palliative care education, research, policy and evidence-based practice. **Structure** Annual General Meeting; Board of Directors; Executive Committee; Chief Executive Office; Reference Groups (9) Task Forces (17). **Languages** English. **Staff** 5.50 FTE, paid. **Finance** Sources: members' dues. **Activities** Awards/prizes/competitions; events/meetings; research and development; training/education. **Events** *World Congress* Rotterdam (Netherlands) 2023, *World Research Congress* Vilvoorde (Belgium) 2022, *World Congress* Helsinki (Finland) 2021, *World Congress* Vilvoorde (Belgium) 2021, *World Research Congress* Vilvoorde (Belgium) 2020. **Publications** *Palliative Medicine* (10 a year) – official research journal; *Journal of Palliative Medicine* (6 a year) – official journal; *EAPC Newsletter*. Recommendations; white papers; statements. **Information Services** *EAPC Blog;*.

Members National Associations (56) in 33 countries:
Albania, Australia, Austria, Belgium, Croatia, Cyprus, Czechia, Denmark, Finland, France, Germany, Greece, Hungary, Iceland, Ireland, Italy, Latvia, Lithuania, Luxembourg, Macedonia, Netherlands, New Zealand, Norway, Poland, Portugal, Romania, Slovakia, Slovenia, Spain, Sweden, Switzerland, UK, Ukraine.
Individual members in 40 countries. Membership countries not specified.

Consultative Status Consultative status granted from: *Council of Europe (CE, #04881)* (Participatory Status). **NGO Relations** Member of (3): *Civil Society Forum on Drugs (CSFD, #03968); European Cancer Organisation (ECO, #06432); Worldwide Hospice Palliative Care Alliance (WHPCA, #21924)*. Associated member of: *European Forum for Primary Care (EFPC, #07326)*. [2022.10.19/XD3047/D]

♦ European Association for Panels and Profiles (PPA-Europe) 06142

SG Europark Fichtenhain A 13 a, D-47807, Krefeld, Germany. T. +492151936300. Fax +4921519363029. E-mail: info@epaq.eu.
URL: http://www.ppa-europe.eu/

History 2003. Founded as *European Quality Assurance Association for Panels and Profiles (EPAQ)*. Registration: EU Transparency Register, No/ID: 1083333660-35, Start date: 21 Nov 2008. **Aims** Represent manufacturers of panels and profiles made of metal; establish quality rules for panels and profiles made of metal, based upon harmonized European *standards*. **Structure** General Assembly; Managing Committee; Committees (4); Secretariat in Krefeld (Germany). **Languages** English, French, German. **Staff** 2.50 FTE, paid. **Finance** Members' dues. Annual budget: euro 300,000. **Activities** Events/meetings; standards/guidelines. **Events** *Congress* Prague (Czechia) 2021, *Congress* 2020, *Annual Congress* Marseille (France) 2019, *Annual Congress* Thessaloniki (Greece) 2018, *Annual Congress* Hamburg (Germany) 2017.

Members Full in 15 countries:
Austria, Belgium, Finland, France, Germany, Iceland, Italy, Liechtenstein, Netherlands, Russia, Slovenia, Spain, Switzerland, Türkiye, UK.

NGO Relations Member of: *Construction Products Europe AISBL (#04761); METALS FOR BUILDINGS (#16737)*. Cooperates with: *European Organisation for Technical Assessment (EOTA, #08103)*. In liaison with technical committees of: *Comité européen de normalisation (CEN, #04162)*. [2019/XM2447/D]

♦ European Association of Parental Alienation Practitioners (inactive)
♦ European Association of Paritarian Institutions / see Association Européenne des Institutions Paritaires de la Protection Sociale (#02575)
♦ European Association of Paritarian Institutions of Social Protection (#02575)

♦ European Association for Passive Fire Protection (EAPFP) 06143

Association européenne pour la protection passive contre l'incendie – Europäischer Verband für Passiven Brandschutz

Main Office Unit 34 BASE Inno Ctr, Broxhead House, 60 Barbados Road, Bordon, GU35 0FX, UK. T. +441420471616. E-mail: admin@eapfp.com.
URL: http://www.eapfp.com/

History 1988. Former names and other names: *European Association for Specialist Fire Protection (EASFP)* – former alias; *European Association Structural Fire Protection* – former alias. **Aims** Group European manufacturers and contractors involved in passive fire protection to steelwork, timber and other specialist applications. **Structure** Officers: President; Secretary. **Languages** English. **Staff** 7.00 FTE, paid. **Finance** Subscriptions. **Events** *Annual General Meeting* Bruges (Belgium) 2022, *Annual General Meeting* Vienna (Austria) 2019, *Annual General Meeting* Brussels (Belgium) 2018, *Joint conference on fire safe products in construction* Luxembourg (Luxembourg) 2007, *Joint conference on fire safe products in construction* Kirchberg (Luxembourg) 1999.

Members Full; Associate. Members in 10 countries:
Belgium, Cyprus, Denmark, Germany, Liechtenstein, Netherlands, Norway, Russia, Spain, UK.

NGO Relations In liaison with technical committees of: *Comité européen de normalisation (CEN, #04162)*. Member of: *Construction Products Europe AISBL (#04761); Industry4Europe (#11181)*. [2020/XD5868/D]

♦ European Association of Patients Organizations of Sarcoidosis and other Granulomatous Disorders (EPOS) 06144

Office PO Box 30 43, 40650 Meerbusch, Germany. T. +4921598153025. Fax +4921598153026. E-mail: info@sarcoidosis.biz.
URL: http://www.sarcoidosis.biz/

History 2001. Former names and other names: *Sarcoidosis Europe* – former (1 Jan 2018). Registration: Handelsregister, No/ID: KVK 34144599, Netherlands. **Aims** Stimulate international research; provide a forum for the exchange of ideas, experiences and expertise. **Events** *European PF Patient Summit* Gentbrugge (Belgium) 2021.

Members Full in 7 countries:
Belgium, France, Germany, Ireland, Netherlands, Switzerland, UK.

NGO Relations Member of (2): *EURORDIS – Rare Diseases Europe (#09175); World Association of Sarcoidosis and other Granulomatous Disorders (WASOG, #21183)*. [2022.05.10/XM1562/D]

♦ European Association of Payment Service Providers for Merchants (EPSM) 06145

Office Ludwigstr 8, 80539 Munich, Germany. T. +4989206021135. Fax +4989206021610. E-mail: office@epsm.eu.
URL: http://www.epsm.eu/

History Registered in accordance with German law. EU Transparency Register: 75870078560-90. Registration: Bavaria District court, No/ID: VR 18893, Start date: 8 Apr 2005, Germany, Munich; EU Transparency Register, No/ID: 75870078560-90, Start date: 11 Apr 2012. **Aims** Represent the interests of European companies providing payment services or services for payment service providers for merchants. **Structure** General Meeting; Board/Executive Committee; Advisory Council. **Languages** English. **Staff** 2.50 FTE, paid. **Finance** Sources: members' dues. **Activities** Events/meetings; knowledge management/information dissemination; networking/liaising; guidance/assistance/consulting. **Publications** *EPSM Market Research Newsletter* (12 a year).

Members Full (68) in 15 countries:
Austria, Belgium, Czechia, Denmark, France, Germany, Greece, Ireland, Latvia, Luxembourg, Netherlands, Slovakia, Sweden, Switzerland, UK.

NGO Relations Member of (1): *European Payment Institutions Federation (EPIF, #08173)* (Observer). [2022/XM5840/D]

♦ European Association of Pension Schemes for Liberal Professions (inactive)

♦ European Association for People Management (EAPM) 06146

International Manager c/o CIPD UK, 151 The Broadway, London, SW19 1JQ, UK. E-mail: eapmsecretary@eapm.org.
URL: http://www.eapm.org/

History 19 Oct 1962, Paris (France). Founded on the initiative of *OECD (#17693)*. Former names and other names: *European Association for Personnel Management (EAPM)* – former; *Association européenne pour la direction du personnel (AEDP)* – former; *Asociación Europea de Dirección de Personal* – former; *Europäische Vereinigung für Personalführung* – former. Registration: Swiss Civil Code, Switzerland. **Aims** As an umbrella body of national Human Resources (HR) organizations in Europe: promote and develop knowledge of human resource issues and activities, and their importance to industry, commerce and both public and private sector administration; provide encouragement and support to the organizational development of national HR associations in Europe. **Structure** Delegates Assembly (annual); Executive Committee. **Languages** English. **Staff** 1.00 FTE, paid. Voluntary. **Finance** Sources: members' dues. **Activities** Events/meetings; networking/liaising; projects/programmes. **Events** *Delegates Assembly* Istanbul (Türkiye) 2022, *Biennial Congress* Vilnius (Lithuania) 2021, *Biennial Congress* Bled (Slovenia) 2019, *Biennial Congress* Paris (France) 2017, *Meeting* Istanbul (Turkey) 2016.

Members Full (32); Corresponding (2). National HR associations or professional institutes in 34 countries:
Armenia, Austria, Belgium, Bulgaria, Croatia, Cyprus, Czechia, Denmark, Estonia, Finland, France, Georgia, Germany, Greece, Hungary, Iceland, Ireland, Israel, Italy, Latvia, Lithuania, Netherlands, North Macedonia, Norway, Poland, Portugal, Romania, Slovakia, Slovenia, Spain, Sweden, Switzerland, Türkiye, UK.

IGO Relations *ILO (#11123)* (Special List). **NGO Relations** Instrumental in setting up (1): *World Federation of People Management Associations (WFPMA, #21474)* (and member of). [2022.05.11/XD0554/D]

♦ European Association of Percutaneous Cardiovascular Interventions (EAPCI) 06147

Pres William Harvey Research Inst, Barts & London School of Medicine and Dentistry, Queen Mary University of London, Charterhouse Square, London, EC1M 6BQ, UK. E-mail: eapci@escardio.org.
URL: https://www.escardio.org/Sub-specialty-communities/European-Association-of-Percutaneous-Cardiovascular-Interventions-(EAPCI)

History Officially launched after a vote by General Assembly of *European Society of Cardiology (ESC, #08536)* at the World Congress of Cardiology, Barcelona (Spain), 2006. Created from a joint venture between the now dissolved ESC Working Group on Interventional Cardiology and EuroPCR. **Aims** Reduce the burden of cardiovascular disease in Europe through percutaneous cardiovascular interventions. **Structure** Executive Board; Committees (10). **Languages** English. **Activities** Events/meetings; training/education. **Events** *EuroPCR Congress* Paris (France) 2019, *EuroPCR Congress* Paris (France) 2018, *EuroPCR Congress* Paris (France) 2017, *EuroPCR Congress* Paris (France) 2016, *EuroPCR Congress* Paris (France) 2015. **Publications** *EuroIntervention Journal. PCR-EAPCI Textbook.* **Members** over 5,000. Membership countries not specified.
NGO Relations Registered branch of: *European Society of Cardiology (ESC, #08536).* [2020/XM2426/**D**]

♦ European Association of Perinatal Medicine (EAPM) 06148

Association européenne de médecine périnatale – Europäische Vereinigung für Perinatale Medizin

Secretariat c/o MCA Events, Via Bonaventura Zumbini n 29, 20143 Milan MI, Italy. T. +39234934404. Fax +39234934397. E-mail: info@europerinatal.eu.
URL: http://www.europerinatal.eu/

History 30 Mar 1968, West Berlin (Germany). Founded at conclusion of 1st European Congress of Perinatal Medicine. New constitution and by-laws approved in Jul 1993, Amsterdam (Netherlands). Amendments made: Sep 1996, Glasgow (UK); Jun 2000, Porto (Portugal). Most recent constitution and by-laws approved, May 2006, Amsterdam (Netherlands). **Aims** Promote research and disseminate information to improve the quality and supply of perinatal care in Europe; contribute to the improvement of pre- and postgraduate teaching as well as continue education in the profession; propose guidelines and standardize criteria for audit, evaluation and clinical care; foster collaboration between various disciplines involved in perinatal care. **Structure** General Assembly (every 2 years at Congress); Executive Board; Committees (2). **Languages** English, French, German, Spanish. **Staff** 1.00 FTE, paid. **Finance** Sources: meeting proceeds; members' dues. **Activities** Awards/prizes/competitions; events/meetings; training/education. **Events** *European Congress of Perinatal Medicine* Lisbon (Portugal) 2022, *European Congress on Intrapartum Care* 2021, *European Congress of Perinatal Medicine* Lisbon (Portugal) 2021, *European Congress of Perinatal Medicine* Lisbon (Portugal) 2020, *European Congress on Intrapartum Care* Turin (Italy) 2019. **Publications** *Journal of Maternal-Fetal and Neonatal Medicine* (12 a year). Study group booklets and guidelines; congress proceedings.
Members National societies (marked *) and individuals in 65 countries:
Albania, Algeria, Argentina, Armenia, Australia, Austria, Belgium, Brazil, Bulgaria, Canada, Chile, Croatia (*), Cyprus, Czechia, Denmark, Ecuador, Egypt, Estonia, Finland (*), France (*), Georgia, Germany (*), Greece, Hungary, Iceland, India, Indonesia, Ireland, Israel, Italy (*), Japan, Jordan, Kuwait, Latvia, Lebanon, Lithuania, Luxembourg, Malaysia, Malta, Mexico, Monaco, Netherlands, New Zealand, North Macedonia, Norway, Pakistan, Philippines, Poland, Portugal (*), Romania, Russia, Saudi Arabia, Serbia, Singapore, Slovakia, Slovenia, South Africa, Spain, Sweden, Switzerland, Thailand, Türkiye, UK (*), Ukraine, USA.
NGO Relations Cooperates with (1): *International Cooperation Agency for Maternal and Infant Health (Matres Mundi International).* Instrumental in setting up (1): *International Academy of Perinatal Medicine (IAPM, #11568).* Representative body at: *European Board and College of Obstetrics and Gynaecology (EBCOG, #06357).* Associated with: *International Association of the Diabetes and Pregnancy Study Groups (IADPSG, #11846).* [2021.02.18/XD0576/**D**]

♦ European Association of Personality Psychology (EAPP) 06149

Sec address not obtained. E-mail: secretary@eapp.org.
URL: http://www.eapp.org/

History 1984, Groningen (Netherlands), following proposals in May 1982, Tilburg (Netherlands). Registered in accordance with Dutch law. **Aims** Promote and develop empirical and theoretical personality psychology in Europe and, by exchange of information between European members and associations elsewhere, throughout the world. **Structure** Members' Assembly (annual); Board of Directors; Executive Committee. **Languages** English. **Staff** None. **Finance** Members' dues. **Activities** Events/meetings. **Events** *Biennial Conference* Madrid (Spain) 2022, *Biennial Conference* Madrid (Spain) 2020, *Biennial Conference* Zadar (Croatia) 2018, *Biennial Conference* Timisoara (Romania) 2016, *Biennial Conference* Lausanne (Switzerland) 2014. **Publications** *EAPP Newsletter* (26 a year); *European Journal of Personality and Personality Science* – official journal. *Advances in Personality Psychology* – book series.
Members Individuals of doctorate level (230) in 36 countries:
Armenia, Australia, Austria, Belgium, Bulgaria, Canada, Chile, China, Croatia, Czechia, Denmark, Estonia, Finland, Germany, Greece, Hungary, Israel, Italy, Japan, Latvia, Lithuania, Malaysia, Netherlands, Norway, Poland, Portugal, Romania, Russia, Serbia, Slovakia, Slovenia, Spain, Sweden, Switzerland, UK, USA.
NGO Relations Member of: *International Union of Psychological Science (IUPsyS, #15807).* Associate member of: *European Federation of Psychologists Associations (EFPA, #07199).* [2020.03.04/XD3760/v/**D**]

♦ European Association for Personnel Management / see European Association for People Management (#06146)
♦ European Association of Persons Responsible for Regulatory Compliance of Medical Devices (unconfirmed)
♦ European Association of Petroleum Geoscientists and Engineers (inactive)

♦ European Association of Pharma Biotechnology (EAPB) 06150

Association européenne de pharma biotechnologie – Europäische Arbeitsgemeinschaft für Pharma Biotechnologie

Address not obtained.
URL: http://www.eapb.org/

History Founded 2 Apr 2000, Berlin (Germany). Acts as Associated section of *European Society of Biochemical Engineering Sciences (ESBES, #08529).* Dissolved 31 Jul 2017. **Aims** Advance biotechnology in pharmaceutical sciences, specifically as applied to medicinal drugs, industrial materials, processes, products and their associated issues. **Structure** General Meeting (every 2 years); Board; Executive Committee; Working/Special Interest Groups (3). Regulatory; Regenerative Medicine; Biotech-Entrepreneurship. **Languages** English, German. **Staff** 9.00 FTE, voluntary. **Finance** Members' dues (annual). **Activities** Networking/liaising; events/meetings. **Events** *Science to Market Conference* Frankfurt-Main (Germany) 2016, *Annual Science to Market Conference / S2M Conference* Berlin (Germany) 2014, *Science to Market Conference* Cologne (Germany) 2013, *World congress on emulsions* Lyon (France) 2010, *World meeting on pharmaceutics, biopharmaceutics and pharmaceutical technology / World Meeting* Valletta (Malta) 2010. **Publications** *European Biotechnology Science and Industry News (EBSIN)* (12 a year) – members' journal. Results and presentations from webinars.
Members Individuals – scientists in biotechnology and pharmaceutical companies. Corporate/University/Research Institute – companies, departments of companies, organizations from academia and industry, especially pharmaceutical industry and related sciences involved in pharma biotechnology. Members (about 1,700) in 27 countries:
Austria, Belgium, Canada, Denmark, Finland, France, Germany, Greece, Hungary, India, Ireland, Italy, Japan, Luxembourg, Netherlands, New Zealand, Poland, Portugal, Russia, Slovakia, Slovenia, Spain, Sweden, Switzerland, Türkiye, UK, USA. [2015.09.17/XD9028/**D**]

♦ European Association of Pharmaceutical Full-line Wholesalers / see Groupement International de la Répartition Pharmaceutique (#10762)
♦ European Association of Pharmaceutical Wholesalers / see Groupement International de la Répartition Pharmaceutique (#10762)
♦ European Association of the Photographic Industry (inactive)

♦ European Association for Physician Health (EAPH) 06151

Contact address not obtained. E-mail: info@eaph.eu.
URL: http://www.eaph.eu/

History Nov 2008. Constitution adopted, 29 Oct 2009. **Aims** Encourage a universally higher standard of support for doctors in difficulty across the continent. **Structure** Officers include: Chair; Vice-Chair. **Events** *Conference* Oslo (Norway) 2019, *Conference* Paris (France) 2017, *Doctors resilience, building European networks through research and practice* Barcelona (Spain) 2015, *Membership Meeting* Salzburg (Austria) 2011, *Membership Meeting* Barcelona (Spain) 2010. [2012/XJ1396/**D**]

♦ European Association of Physiotherapist Photographers and Film-Makers (inactive)
♦ European Association of Pianomaker Unions / see Union of European Piano Builders' Associations (#20391)
♦ European Association for Planned Giving (internationally oriented national body)

♦ European Association of Plaster and Plaster Product Manufacturers (EUROGYPSUM) 06152

SG Rue de la Presse 4, 1000 Brussels, Belgium. T. +3222271111. Fax +3222272780. E-mail: secretariat@eurogypsum.org – info@eurogypsum.org.
URL: http://www.eurogypsum.org/

History 1961. Current bylaws adopted 23 Aug 2011. Former names and other names: *Working Community of the European Gypsum Industries* – former (1961 to 1996); *Association européenne de l'industrie du plâtre* – former (1961 to 1996); *Arbeitsgemeinschaft der Europäischen Gipsindustrie* – former (1961 to 1996); *Association of European Gypsum Industries (EUROGYPSUM)* – former (1996); *Association des industries européennes du plâtre* – former (1996); *Verband der Europäischen Gipsindustrien* – former (1996). Registration: Banque Carrefour des Entreprises, No/ID: 0850.834.906, Start date: 8 Jan 1996, Belgium; EU Transparency Register, No/ID: 26369367005-58, Start date: 24 Oct 2011. **Aims** Promote on a European scale, development of the plaster, gypsum and anhydrite industries along with building components derived from these. **Structure** General Assembly (annual); Board of Directors; Working Groups; Committees. **Languages** English. **Staff** 2.00 FTE, paid. **Finance** Sources: members' dues. Annual budget: 500,000 EUR. **Events** *Eurogypsum's 60 Years Celebration* Brussels (Belgium) 2022, *Biennial Congress* Strasbourg (France) 2010, *Biennial Congress* Brussels (Belgium) 2008, *Biennial Congress* Edinburgh (UK) 2006, *Biennial Congress* Taormina (Italy) 2004. **Publications** Position papers; policy papers; fact sheets; proceedings.
Members Ordinary (11 associations) representing 16 countries:
Austria, Belgium, Denmark, Finland, France, Germany, Ireland, Italy, Luxembourg, Netherlands, Norway, Poland, Spain, Sweden, Türkiye, UK.
Extraordinary members (4) in 2 countries:
Cyprus, Portugal.
IGO Relations Recognized by: *European Commission (EC, #06633).* **NGO Relations** Member of (5): *Construction 2050 Alliance (#04760); Construction Products Europe AISBL (#04761)* (Associate); *Federation of European and International Associations Established in Belgium (FAIB, #09508); Industry4Europe (#11181); Society of European Affairs Professionals (SEAP, #19553).* In liaison with technical committees of: *Comité européen de normalisation (CEN, #04162); International Organization for Standardization (ISO, #14473).* [2022.05.18/XD7010/**D**]

♦ European Association of Plastic Packaging Manufacturers (inactive)

♦ European Association of Plastics Recycling and Recovery Organizations (EPRO) 06153

EPRO Office Konigin Astridlaan 59 bus 5, 1780 Wemmel, Belgium.
URL: http://www.epro-plasticsrecycling.org/

History Registration: No/ID: 0480.245.812, Start date: 7 Mar 2003, Belgium; EU Transparency Register, No/ID: 376025921978-72, Start date: 27 May 2016. **Aims** Serve as a platform for cooperation and exchange of information between European plastics recycling organizations. **Activities** Awards/prizes/competitions; events/meetings. **Events** *General Meeting* Ghent (Belgium) 2016, *General Meeting* Madrid (Spain) 2007, *General Meeting* Catania (Italy) 2006, *General Meeting* Oslo (Norway) 2004.
Members National organizations in 14 countries:
Austria, Belgium, Finland, France, Germany, Iceland, Italy, Norway, Portugal, South Africa, Spain, Sweden, Switzerland, UK.
NGO Relations Member of (1): *Circular Plastics Alliance (#03936).* [2022/XD7933/**D**]

♦ European Association of Plastic Surgeons (EURAPS) 06154

Association européenne des chirurgiens plasticiens

SG Central Office, c/o Chair of Plastic Surgery, Sapienza Univ of Rome, Via di Grottarossa 1035-39, 00189 Rome RM, Italy. T. +39633776691. E-mail: office@euraps.org.
URL: http://www.euraps.org/

History 1989. **Aims** Promote excellence in plastic surgery in Europe; stimulate research and investigation, at the European level as well as to coordinate various forms of teaching; preserve the unity of plastic surgery by illustrating its different aspects. **Structure** Board, consisting of President, Vice-President, Secretary General, Treasurer and Council members representing European countries with an important participation. **Languages** English. **Finance** Members' dues. Other source: Annual Meeting. **Activities** Knowledge management/information dissemination; events/meetings; training/education; awards/prizes/competitions. **Events** *Annual Meeting* Palma (Spain) 2025, *Annual Meeting* Athens (Greece) 2024, *Annual Meeting* Stockholm (Sweden) 2023, *Annual Meeting* Naples (Italy) 2022, *Annual Meeting* Rome (Italy) 2021. **Publications** *European Journal of Plastic Surgery.*
Members Individuals in 24 countries:
Austria, Belgium, Canada, Croatia, Finland, France, Germany, Greece, Hungary, Israel, Italy, Japan, Korea Rep, Netherlands, Norway, Portugal, Romania, Slovenia, Spain, Sweden, Switzerland, Türkiye, UK, USA. [2015.02.04/XD2045/v/**D**]

♦ European Association of Podologists (inactive)
♦ European Association of Poison Control Centres / see European Association of Poisons Centres and Clinical Toxicologists (#06155)

♦ European Association of Poisons Centres and Clinical Toxicologists (EAPCCT) 06155

Gen Sec c/o UMC Utrecht, Toxicology / Brain Ctr, Postbus 85500, 3508 GA Utrecht, Netherlands.
Registered Office Rue Bruyn 4, 1120 Brussels, Belgium.
URL: http://www.eapcct.org/

History 28 Sep 1964, Tours (France). Former names and other names: *European Association of Poison Control Centres* – former (1964 to 1992); *Association européenne des centres anti-poisons* – former (1964 to 1992); *Europäischen Gesellschaft der Entgiftungszentralen* – former. Registration: Belgium; EU Transparency Register, No/ID: 772116923142-95. **Aims** Advance knowledge and understanding of the diagnosis and treatment of all forms of poisoning. **Structure** Board. **Languages** English. **Staff** 0.50 FTE, paid. Voluntary. **Finance** Members' dues (2014): Full – euro 165; Associate – euro 120. **Activities** Events/meetings; knowledge management/information dissemination; training/education. **Events** *International Congress* Palma (Spain) 2023, *Annual International Congress* Tallinn (Estonia) 2022, *Annual International Congress* Pavia (Italy) 2021, *Annual International Congress* Tallinn (Estonia) 2020, *Annual International Congress* Naples (Italy) 2019. **Publications** *European Association of Poison Control Centres Newsletter* (2-3 a year). *Clinical Toxicology; Current Awareness in Clinical Toxicology.* Meeting reports.
Members Individuals with university training, interested in clinical toxicology and related fields and currently working in the poisons field; poison centres. Members in 57 countries and territories:
Armenia, Australia, Austria, Azerbaijan, Belgium, Brazil, Bulgaria, Croatia, Czechia, Denmark, Ecuador, Estonia, Finland, France, Georgia, Germany, Ghana, Greece, Hong Kong, Iceland, India, Iran Islamic Rep, Ireland, Israel, Italy, Jamaica, Korea Rep, Lithuania, Luxembourg, Malta, Moldova, Myanmar, Netherlands, North Macedonia, Norway, Pakistan, Poland, Portugal, Romania, Russia, Senegal, Serbia, Slovakia, Slovenia, South Africa, Spain, Sri Lanka, Sudan, Sweden, Switzerland, Trinidad-Tobago, Tunisia, Türkiye, UK, Uruguay, USA, Zimbabwe.
NGO Relations Member of, and joint activities with: *EUROTOX (#09191); International Union of Toxicology (IUTOX, #15824).* Close collaboration with American Academy of Clinical Toxicologists (AACT). [2022/XD0577/**D**]

♦ European Association of Political Consultants (EAPC) 06156

Exec Sec Ecuador 3, 41120 Gelves, Sevilla, Spain. T. +4369911991155. E-mail: chematalero@gmail.com.
URL: http://www.eapc.eu/

History 14 Sep 1996, Vienna (Austria). A branch of *International Association of Political Consultants (IAPC, #12094).* **Aims** Develop, support and maintain the democratic process; increase exchange of information and experience between political consultants. **Structure** General Assembly (annual). Board, including President, Vice-President, Treasurer and Executive Secretary. **Languages** English. **Finance** Members' dues. **Events** *Conference* Vienna (Austria) 2022, *Conference* Vienna (Austria) 2021, *Conference* Tbilisi (Georgia) 2020, *Conference* Athens (Greece) 2019, *Conference* London (UK) 2018. **Publications** *Election Time* (annual); *Europe and Us* – newsletter.

European Association Polyol
06157

alphabetic sequence excludes
For the complete listing, see Yearbook Online at

Members Regular; Associate; Honorary individuals (62) in 23 countries and territories:
Argentina, Austria, Brazil, Canada, Denmark, Finland, France, Germany, Italy, Lithuania, Malta, Netherlands, Portugal, Romania, Russia, Slovenia, Spain, Sweden, Switzerland, Türkiye, UK, Ukraine, USA. [2011.06.01/XD9376/**D**]

♦ European Association of Polyol Producers (EPA) 06157

Secretariat Av de Tervueren 13 A – Bte 7, 1040 Brussels, Belgium. T. +3227365354. Fax +3227323427. E-mail: epa@ecco-eu.com.
URL: http://www.polyols-eu.org/

History 1991, as *European Polyol Association (EPA)*. Registered in accordance with Belgian law. EU Transparency Register: 96540262048-16. **Aims** Represent the interests of the principal European producers of polyols (sugar alcohols) at the level of the European Union and other European and international bodies. **Languages** English. **Staff** 0.50 FTE, paid. **Finance** Members' dues.
Members Full in 5 countries:
Belgium, France, Germany, Netherlands, UK.
IGO Relations Participates as observer in the activities of: *Codex Alimentarius Commission (CAC, #04081)*.
NGO Relations Member of: *EU Specialty Food Ingredients (#09200)*. [2019/XD3680/**D**]

♦ European Association for Population Studies (EAPS) 06158

Association européenne pour l'étude de la population – Europäische Gesellschaft für Bevölkerungswissenschaft – Evropejskaja Associacija po Demograficeskim Issledovanijam
Exec Dir POB 11676, 2502 AR The Hague, Netherlands. T. +31703565230. E-mail: eaps@nidi.nl.
Street address Lange Houtstraat 19, 2511 CV The Hague, Netherlands.
URL: http://www.eaps.nl/

History 31 Mar 1983, The Hague (Netherlands), when statutes were adopted. Has been assigned the functions previously carried out by *European Centre for Population Studies (ECPS, inactive)*, set up 21-23 May 1953, Paris (France). Registered in accordance with Dutch law. **Aims** Foster cooperation between persons interested or engaged in European populations studies; stimulate interest in population matters among governments, national and international organizations and the general public. **Structure** General Assembly (every 4 years); Council; Executive Dir. **Languages** English. **Staff** 1.00 FTE, paid. **Finance** Members' dues. Other sources: donations; gifts; legacies. **Activities** Events/meetings; training/education. **Events** *European Population Conference* Groningen (Netherlands) 2022, *European Population Conference* Padua (Italy) 2020, *European Population Conference* Brussels (Belgium) 2018, *European Population Conference* Mainz (Germany) 2016, *European Population Conference* Budapest (Hungary) 2014. **Publications** *European Journal of Population* (4 a year); *European Studies of Population* (irregular).
Members Individuals; affiliated institutions, including members of CICRED located in Europe. Members in 50 countries and territories:
Albania, Armenia, Australia, Austria, Azerbaijan, Belarus, Belgium, Bosnia-Herzegovina, Bulgaria, Canada, China, Croatia, Czechia, Denmark, Estonia, Finland, France, Georgia, Germany, Greece, Hungary, Indonesia, Ireland, Israel, Italy, Japan, Latvia, Lithuania, Luxembourg, Mexico, Moldova, Netherlands, North Macedonia, Norway, Poland, Portugal, Romania, Russia, Serbia, Slovakia, Slovenia, Spain, Sweden, Switzerland, Türkiye, UK, Ukraine, USA, Uzbekistan.
NGO Relations Works in consultation with: *International Union for the Scientific Study of Population (IUSSP, #15814)*. [2022/XD6970/**D**]

♦ European Association of Porcine Health Management (EAPHM) . . . 06159

Contact Rue Victor Oudart 7, 1030 Brussels, Belgium. T. +3225337020. E-mail: info@eaphm.org.
URL: http://www.eaphm.org/

History 2010. Registration: Banque-Carrefour des Entreprises, No/ID: 0834.060.537, Start date: 25 Feb 2011, Belgium. **Aims** Provide European practitioners with a platform for sharing information and developing and improving their skills and competences. **Structure** Annual General Meeting; Board; Executive Committee. **Languages** English. **Staff** 5.00 FTE, voluntary. **Finance** Sources: meeting proceeds; members' dues; sponsorship. **Activities** Events/meetings; healthcare; networking/liaising; standards/guidelines. **Events** *Congress* Bern (Switzerland) 2020, *European Symposium on Porcine Health Management* Utrecht (Netherlands) 2019, *European Symposium on Porcine Health Management* Barcelona (Spain) 2018, *European Symposium on Porcine Health Management* Prague (Czechia) 2017, *European Symposium on Porcine Health Management* Dublin (Ireland) 2016. **Publications** *EAPHM Newsletter* (24 a year). **Members** Porcine veterinarians. Membership countries not specified. [2022.05.10/XM5470/**D**]

♦ European Association of Potato Processing Industry / see EUPPA – European Potato Processors' Association (#05592)

♦ European Association for Potato Research (EAPR) 06160

Association européenne pour la recherche sur la pomme de terre – Europäische Gesellschaft für Kartoffelforschung
Main Office PO Box 500, 1, 3001 Leuven, Belgium. T. +3216229427. Fax +3216229450. E-mail: info@eapr.net.
URL: http://www.eapr.net/

History 12 Aug 1956, Lund (Sweden). Founded following preliminary conferences: 1951, Denmark; 1953, UK; 1955, Netherlands. Formally constituted 1960. Registration: Netherlands. **Aims** Improve cooperation between research workers concerned with subjects related to the potato; promote exchange of scientific and general information among European and non-European countries on culture and use of the potato. **Structure** General Meeting (every 3 years); Council. Sections. **Languages** English. **Staff** 8.00 FTE, voluntary. **Finance** Members' dues. **Activities** Knowledge management/information dissemination; research/documentation. **Events** *Triennial Conference* Krakow (Poland) 2022, *Triennial Conference* Krakow (Poland) 2021, *Triennial Conference* Warsaw (Poland) 2020, *Triennial joint meeting* Rostock (Germany) 2018, *Triennial Conference* Paris (France) 2017. **Publications** *Potato Research* (4 a year). Conference proceedings.
Members Sustaining (collective); Ordinary (individual). About 625 members in 60 countries:
Algeria, Australia, Austria, Belarus, Belgium, Bosnia-Herzegovina, Brazil, Bulgaria, Canada, Chile, China, Croatia, Cyprus, Czechia, Denmark, Ecuador, Eritrea, Estonia, Finland, France, Germany, Greece, Hungary, Iceland, India, Iran Islamic Rep, Iraq, Ireland, Israel, Italy, Japan, Kenya, Korea Rep, Latvia, Liechtenstein, Lithuania, Mauritius, Mexico, Nepal, Netherlands, New Zealand, Norway, Peru, Poland, Portugal, Romania, Russia, Saudi Arabia, Slovakia, Slovenia, South Africa, Spain, Sweden, Switzerland, Togo, Tunisia, Türkiye, UK, Uruguay, USA. [2021/XD0555/**D**]

♦ European Association of Poultry, Pigeon, Cage Bird, Rabbit and Cavy Breeders (#05492)
♦ European Association of Practising Criminal Defence Lawyers / see European Criminal Bar Association (#06859)

♦ European Association for Practitioner Research on Improving Learning (EAPRIL) 06161

Acting Managing Dir Peterseliegang 1, Box 1, 3000 Leuven, Belgium. T. +3216231900. E-mail: info@eapril.org.
Events Manager address not obtained.
URL: http://www.eapril.org/

History 2009. Former names and other names: *European Association for Practitioner Research on Improving Learning in education and professional practice (EAPRIL)* – full title. Registration: Banque-Carrefour des Entreprises, No/ID: 0821.385.805, Start date: 28 Nov 2009, Belgium. **Aims** Support practice and research in lifelong learning (educational and professional) in interacting, collaborating and benefiting from each other's roles and strengths with the aim of contributing to the professional development of both. **Structure** General Assembly; Executive Board; Office. **Languages** English. **Staff** 1.00 FTE, paid. **Finance** Sources: meeting proceeds; members' dues. **Activities** Awards/prizes/competitions; events/meetings; financial and/or material support; knowledge management/information dissemination. **Events** *Conference* Nijmegen (Netherlands) 2022, *Conference* Kufstein (Austria) 2021, *Conference* Kufstein (Austria) 2020, *Conference* Tartu (Estonia) 2019, *Conference* Portoroz (Slovenia) 2018. **Publications** Conference proceedings; special issues in international journals. EAPRIL members' platform. **NGO Relations** Member of (1): *Skillman Network (#19306)* (Alliance). Sister organization: *European Association for Research on Learning and Instruction (EARLI, #06194)*. [2022/XJ6064/**D**]

♦ European Association for Practitioner Research on Improving Learning in education and professional practice / see European Association for Practitioner Research on Improving Learning (#06161)

♦ European Association for Precision Livestock Farming (EA-PLF) . . . 06162

Secretariat c/o MV Congressi, Via Marchesi 26/d, 43126 Parma PR, Italy. T. +3905212901 ext 43. Fax +390521291314. E-mail: secretariat@eaplf.eu.
URL: https://www.eaplf.eu/

History Took over activities of EU-PLF project, funded by *European Commission (EC, #06633)*, running Nov 2012 – Oct 2016. **Events** *European Conference on Precision Livestock Farming* Vienna (Austria) 2022, *European Conference on Precision Livestock Farming* Cork (Ireland) 2019, *European Conference on Precision Livestock Farming* Prague (Czech Rep) 2011, *European Conference on Precision Livestock Farming* Wageningen (Netherlands) 2009, *European Conference on Precision Livestock Farming* Uppsala (Sweden) 2005. [2022/AA2972/**E**]

♦ European Association for Predictive, Preventive and Personalised Medicine (EPMA) 06163

Association Européenne de Médecine Prédictive et Personnalisée
SG Dept of Radiology, Univ of Bonn, Sigmund-Freud-Str 25, 53105 Bonn, Germany. T. +4922828715982. Fax +4922828715983.
Pres c/o EMA, Av des Volontaires 19, 1160 Brussels, Belgium. T. +3227342980. Fax +3227342023.
URL: http://www.epmanet.eu/

History Registered in accordance with Belgian law, 9 Mar 2009: 810-056-403. **Aims** Promote education, innovation and legislation in predictive, preventive and personalised medicine. **Structure** Board of Directors; Advisory Boards (2); Editorial Board. **Languages** English. **Finance** Sources: budgets of national EPMA committees; budgets of European projects; publication proceeds; congress proceeds. **Activities** Research/documentation; training/education/ events/meetings; guidance/assistance/consulting; networking/liaising. **Events** *Congress* Nürburg (Germany) 2019, *Congress* Malta 2017, *World Congress* Brussels (Belgium) 2013, *Educational Workshop* Budapest (Hungary) 2012, *World Congress* Bonn (Germany) 2011. **Publications** *EPMA Journal. Advances in Predictive, Preventive and Personalised Medicine* – book series. Books.
Members National Boards in 45 countries and territories:
Australia, Austria, Belgium, Bulgaria, Canada, China, Croatia, Cyprus, Czechia, Denmark, Estonia, Finland, France, Georgia, Germany, Greece, Hungary, India, Ireland, Israel, Italy, Japan, Korea Rep, Lithuania, Luxembourg, Malta, Mexico, Montenegro, Netherlands, New Zealand, North Macedonia, Poland, Portugal, Romania, Russia, Serbia, Slovakia, Spain, Sweden, Switzerland, Taiwan, Türkiye, UK, Ukraine, USA.
Institutional members in 10 countries:
China, Czechia, Estonia, Germany, Italy, Korea Rep, Luxembourg, Poland, Russia, Switzerland.
NGO Relations Cooperates with: *European Federation of Clinical Chemistry and Laboratory Medicine (EFLM, #07080)*; *European, Middle Eastern and African Society for Biopreservation and Biobanking (ESBB, #07798)*; *European Society of Predictive Medicine (EUSPM, #08711)*; *European Society of Radiology (ESR, #08720)*; national organizations. [2018.06.01/XJ6429/**D**]

♦ European Association for Prevention of Addicts (no recent information)

♦ European Association of Preventive Cardiology (EAPC) 06164

Main Office CS 80179 Biot, 2035 route des Colles, Les Templiers, 06903 Sophia Antipolis CEDEX, France. T. +33492947600. Fax +33492947601.
URL: https://www.escardio.org/Sub-specialty-communities/European-Association-of-Preventive-Cardiology-(EAPC)

History Aug 2004, Munich (Germany). Founded on merger of ESC Working Group on Cardiac Rehabilitation and Exercise Physiology and ESC Working Group on Epidemiology and Prevention. Registered branch of *European Society of Cardiology (ESC, #08536)*. Former names and other names: *European Association for Cardiovascular Prevention and Rehabilitation (EACPR)* – former (2004 to 28 Aug 2016). **Aims** Promote excellence in research, practice, education and policy in cardiovascular health, primary and secondary prevention. **Events** *ESC Preventive Cardiology Congress* Malaga (Spain) 2023, *ESC Preventive Cardiology Congress* Ljubljana (Slovenia) 2021, *ESC Preventive Cardiology Congress* Malaga (Spain) 2020, *EuroPrevent Annual Congress* Lisbon (Portugal) 2019, *EuroPrevent Annual Congress* Ljubljana (Slovenia) 2018. **Publications** *European Journal of Preventive Cardiology*. [2023/XJ4093/**E**]

♦ European Association of Printing Managers (inactive)

♦ European Association of Private International Law (EAPIL) 06165

SG Rue Alphonse Weicker 4, L-2721 Luxembourg, Luxembourg. E-mail: secretary.general@eapil.org.
URL: https://eapil.org/

History 2019. Registration: Luxembourg. **Aims** Promote the study and development of private international law. **Structure** General Assembly; Scientific Council; Board of Administration. **Finance** Sources: members' dues. **Activities** Events/meetings; knowledge management/information dissemination. **Events** *Conference* Aarhus (Denmark) 2021. **Publications** *EAPIL Newsletter*. [2021/AA1373/**D**]

♦ European Association of Producers of Cast Iron Heating Materials (inactive)
♦ European Association of Producers and Distributors of Natural Medicines (no recent information)

♦ European Association of Producers of Flame Retardant Olefinic Cable Compounds (FROCC) 06166

Sec SACO AEI Polymers Ltd, Sandwich Industrial Estate, Sandwich, CT13 9LY, UK. T. +441304616171.
Pres Borealis Polymers Oy, Muovintie 19, FI-06101 Porvoo, Finland. T. +3589394900.
URL: http://frocc.org/

Aims Promote use of *fire retardant*, zero halogen compounds in cable applications. **Structure** Executive Committee. **Activities** Advocacy/lobbying/activism; research/documentation.
Members Companies (5) in 4 countries:
Denmark, Germany, Italy, UK.
NGO Relations Member of (1): *Fire Safe Europe (FSEU, #09780)*. [2021.06.15/XM5823/**D**]

♦ European Association of Producers of Publications for Youth (inactive)

♦ European Association of Producers of Steel for Packaging 06167

Association professionelle des producteurs européens d'aciers pour emballage (APEAL)
SG Av Ariane 5, Bldg Integrale E3, Ground floor, 1200 Brussels, Belgium. T. +3225379151. E-mail: info@apeal.be.
URL: http://www.apeal.org/

History 1986. Former names and other names: *Association professionnelle des producteurs européens d'aciers pour emballage* – former. Registration: Banque Carrefour des Entreprises, No/ID: 0480.186.424, Start date: 25 Feb 2003, Belgium; EU Transparency Register, No/ID: 70036906501-10, Start date: 30 Aug 2011. **Aims** Make a positive contribution to development of EU policy relating to steel for packaging, particularly in the areas of packaging, waste, recycling and recovery; inform and work closely with relevant stakeholders to ensure widespread understanding and support for steel as a sustainable packaging solution. **Structure** Working Groups. **Languages** English. **Staff** 4.00 FTE, paid. **Events** *Conference* Brussels (Belgium) 2018, *Steel packaging congress* Düsseldorf (Germany) 2008, *Steel packaging congress* Düsseldorf (Germany) 2005, *Steel packaging congress* Düsseldorf (Germany) 2002, *Steel packaging congress* Düsseldorf (Germany) 1996. **Publications** *Steel for Packaging Update* – e-newsletter. Press releases; position papers; reports; studies; brochures; videos.
Members Producers in 6 countries:
Belgium, France, Germany, Italy, Netherlands, Slovakia. [2021.09.01/XD1198/t/**D**]

♦ European Association for Product and Process Modelling in the Building Industry (EAPPM) 06168

Chairman Technische Univ Dresden, Inst für Bauinformatik, 01062 Dresden, Germany. T. +49351463332966 – +49351463333527. Fax +49351463333975.
URL: http://www.ecppm.org/

History 1994. **Aims** Sponsor and oversee organization of the biennial European Conference on Product and Process Modelling in the Building Industry (ECPPM); develop and promote application of applied *computer science* and information technology methods. **Structure** Steering Committee, comprising Chairman, Vice-Chairman and 18 members. **Languages** English. **Staff** 18.00 FTE, voluntary. **Finance** Voluntary donations.

Activities Works on the following EU research projects on Applied Computer Sciences in Construction Engineering:
- *'BidSaver'* – Business Integrator Dynamic Support Agents for Virtual Enterprise;
- *'CE-NET II'* – Concurrent Enterprising Network of Excellence;
- *'e-College'* – Advanced Infrastructure for Pan-European Collaborative Engineering;
- *'e-COGNOS'* – Methodology, tools and architecture for electronic COnsistent knowledGe maNagement across prOjects and between enterpriSes in the construction domain;
- *'Genesis'* – Development of a decision support methodology to improve logistics performance of globally acting production networks and to apply Value System Designer (VSD) process method to innovation processes, specifically new product development and concurrent engineering processes;
- *'Globemen'* – Global Engineering and Manufacturing in Enterprise Networks;
- *'Gnosis'* – The virtual factory;
- *'ICCI'* – Innovation coordination, transfer and deployment through networked Cooperation in the Construction Industry;
- *'ICSS'* – Integrated Client-Server System for a Virtual Enterprise in Building Industry;
- *'I-Mass'* – Information Management and interoperability of content for distributed systems of high volume data repositories through multi agent systems.
- *'inteliGrid'* – interoperability of virtual organizations on a Complex Semantic Grid, a European research project developing grid technologies to provide an interoperability platform to engineering.
- *'ISTforCE'* – Intelligent Services and Tools for Concurrent Engineering;
- *'KM Forum'* – European Knowledge Management Forum;
- *'Manbuild'* – industry driven goal is to create a new paradigm for building production by combining efficient manufacturing in factories and construction sites and open an system for products and components.
- *'OSMOS'* – Open System for Inter-Enterprise Information Management in Dynamic Virtual Environments;
- *'ProdAEC'* – European Network for the Promotion of the Standards and eBusiness in the AEC sector;
- *'PRODCHAIN'* – Development of a decision support methodology;
- *'VL'* – Virtual Laboratory;
- *'ArKoS'* – Architecture for Collaborative Scenarios;
- *'E-Sharing'*;
- *'IuK Bau'* – design, develop and evaluate a mobile information- and communication system to support the controlling and monitoring of construction progress in SMEs.
- *'LIAISON'* – Location based services for the enhancement of working environments.
- *'DataMiningGrid'* – Provision of a set of general-purpose data mining tools and services for Grid computing environments.
- *'InteliGrid'* – Interoperability of Virtual Organizations on Complex Semantic Grid.
- *'OASIS'* – Open Advanced System for dISaster and emergency management.
- *'ATHENA'* – Advanced Technologies for interoperability of Heterogeneous Enterprise Networks and their Applications.
- *'INTELCITIES'* – Intelligent Cities.
- *'InPro'* – Open Information Environment for Knowledge-based Collaborative Processes throughout the Lifecycle of a Building.
- *'BauVOGrid'* – Grid Platform for the Virtual Organization in Construction.

Events *Conference* Trondheim (Norway) 2022, *Biennial Conference* Copenhagen (Denmark) 2018, *Biennial Conference* Reykjavik (Iceland) 2012, *Biennial Conference – ECPPM* Cork (Ireland) 2010, *Biennial conference / Biennial Conference – ECPPM* Nice (France) 2008. **Publications** *EAPPM e-Newsletter* (annual).
Members Individuals from universities, research institutes and industries, in 23 countries:
Australia, Austria, Bulgaria, Czechia, Denmark, Finland, France, Germany, Greece, Iceland, Ireland, Italy, Japan, Netherlands, New Zealand, Portugal, Russia, Slovenia, Spain, Sweden, Switzerland, UK, USA.
IGO Relations *European Commission (EC, #06633).* **NGO Relations** Participates in annual conferences of: *International Council for Research and Innovation in Building and Construction (CIB, #13069).*
[2016/XD7812/tv/**D**]

♦ European Association of Professional Beauticians (#04549)
♦ European Association of Professional Fire Brigade Officers (no recent information)
♦ European Association of Professional Secretaries / see International Management Assistants (#14081)

♦ European Association of Professionals Working in the Drug Field (ITACA) 06169

Contact address not obtained. T. +39686381988. Fax +39686382176. E-mail: itacaitalia@itacaitalia.it.
History Previously also referred to as *European Society of Professionals Working with Drug Dependences.* Also referred to as *ITACA Europe.* **Aims** Foster open-minded collaboration and debate between people from different national and professional backgrounds in order to develop common strategies, techniques and good practice which are evidence based and protect human rights. **Structure** Board, comprising President, Vice-President, Secretary, Treasurer and 4 members. **Activities** Events/meetings. **Events** *CLAT : Latin conference on harm reduction* Barcelona (Spain) 2005, *International congress on addiction* Vienna (Austria) 2004, *CLAT : Latin conference on harm reduction* Perpignan (France) 2003, *CLAT : Latin conference on harm reduction* Barcelona (Spain) 2001.
Members National delegations in 6 countries (" responsible for Nordic countries):
France, Greece, Italy, Norway, Portugal, Spain. [2010/XD9052/t/**D**]

♦ European Association for Professions in Biomedical Science (EPBS) 06170

Gen Sec Place Jean-Jacobs 3, 1000 Brussels, Belgium. E-mail: generalsecretary@epbs.net – epbs@epbs.net.
Pres address not obtained.
URL: http://www.epbs.net/
History May 1999, The Hague (Netherlands). Registration: Banque-Carrefour des Entreprises, Start date: 2006, Belgium. **Aims** Promote maintenance of highest standards of practice, suppport training and education, and develop the ethical and professional values of Biomedical Scientists throughout Europe. **Structure** General Governing Body; Management Body. **Languages** English. **Staff** 7.00 FTE, voluntary. **Activities** Events/meetings; networking/liaising; politics/policy/regulatory. **Events** *GGB Meeting* Helsinki (Finland) 2022, *Conference* Genoa (Italy) 2019, *Annual Meeting* Figueira da Foz (Portugal) 2018, *Annual Meeting* Salzburg (Austria) 2017, *Student Forum* Salzburg (Austria) 2017. **Publications** Policy statements.
Members Full in 21 countries:
Austria, Belgium, Croatia, Cyprus, Denmark, Estonia, Finland, France, Germany, Greece, Iceland, Ireland, Italy, Malta, Netherlands, Norway, Portugal, Spain, Sweden, Switzerland, UK.
NGO Relations Liaison Organization of: *Comité européen de normalisation (CEN, #04162).*
[2021.02.19/XJ8139/t/**D**]

♦ European Association of Programmes in Health Services Studies / see European Health Management Association (#07458)

♦ European Association for Programming Languages and Systems (EAPLS) 06171

SG c/o Infomatics Dept, N-6-11Bush House, 30 Aldwych, London, WC2B 4BG, UK.
URL: http://www.eapls.org/
History 24 Sep 1996, Aachen (Germany). Founded following discussions initiated by Reinhard Wilhelm in 1992. Registration: Netherlands. **Aims** Promote research in the area of programming languages and systems; promote cooperation among researchers in programming. **Structure** Membership Meeting (annual). Board, comprising President, Vice-President, General Secretary and 5 members. Scientific Council of at least 3 members. **Languages** English. **Staff** Voluntary. **Finance** Members' dues. Grants from TMR Programme of the European Commission. **Activities** Provides facilities to enable research in the field of programming languages and systems. **Events** *ETAPS : European Joint Conferences on Theory and Practice of Software* Paris (France) 2023, *ETAPS : European Joint Conferences on Theory and Practice of Software* Munich (Germany) 2022, *ETAPS : European Joint Conferences on Theory and Practice of Software* Luxembourg (Luxembourg) 2021, *ETAPS : European Joint Conferences on Theory and Practice of Software* Dublin (Ireland) 2020, *ETAPS : European Joint Conferences on Theory and Practice of Software* Prague (Czechia) 2019. **Publications** *Journal of Functional and Logic Programming.* Annual Report. **Members** Individuals (500) and corporations. Membership countries not specified. **NGO Relations** Member of: *European Forum for ICST (#07316).* Joint conference with: *European Association of Software Science and Technology (EASST, #06213); European Association for Theoretical Computer Science (EATCS, #06253).* [2021/XD7486/**D**]

♦ European Association of Promoters of Commercial Centres (inactive)
♦ European Association for the Promotion of Cogeneration / see COGEN Europe (#04085)
♦ European Association for the Promotion of Hand Hygiene (inactive)
♦ European Association for the Promotion of Health / see European network for health promotion and economic development (#07920)
♦ European Association for the Promotion of Poetry (inactive)
♦ European Association for the Promotion of Research into the Dynamic Behaviour of Materials and its Applications / see DYMAT Association (#05148)
♦ European Association for the Promotion of Sustainable and Responsible Fisheries / see Blue Fish Europe (#03284)
♦ European Association for the Protection of Encrypted Works and Services / see Audiovisual Anti-Piracy Alliance (#03015)

♦ European Association of Psychological Assessment (EAPA) 06172

Pres Humboldt-University Berlin, Unter den Linden 6, 10099 Berlin, Germany. E-mail: president@eapa.science.
URL: http://www.eapa-homepage.org/
History 7 Jun 1990, Madrid (Spain). Registration: Spain. **Aims** Promote scientific interest in, and study of, psychological assessment in Europe (diagnostic processes, assessment of personality, intelligence and behaviour, observational and neuropsychological assessment as well as assessment in the different applied fields such as clinical and health, education, work or evaluation research); create opportunities for scientific exchanges worldwide. **Structure** Members' Assembly; Executive Committee. **Languages** English. **Staff** Voluntary. **Finance** Sources: members' dues. **Activities** Awards/prizes/competitions; events/meetings; training/education. **Events** *Biennial Conference* Warsaw (Poland) 2023, *Biennial Conference* Brussels (Belgium) 2019, *Biennial Conference* Lisbon (Portugal) 2017, *Biennial Conference* Zurich (Switzerland) 2015, *Biennial Conference* San Sebastian (Spain) 2013. **Publications** *European Journal of Psychological Assessment (EJPA)* (6 a year); *Newsletter of the European Association of Psychological Assessment; Psychological Test Adaptation and Development (PTAD)* – official journal.
Members Founder; Full; Honorary. Individuals (mostly university teachers and professors) in 33 countries and territories:
Argentina, Australia, Austria, Belarus, Belgium, Croatia, Czechia, Denmark, France, Germany, Greece, Hungary, Iceland, India, Ireland, Israel, Italy, Netherlands, New Zealand, Nigeria, Norway, Portugal, Romania, Russia, Serbia, Slovenia, Spain, Sweden, Switzerland, Taiwan, Türkiye, UK, USA.
NGO Relations Member of (1): *International Union of Psychological Science (IUPsyS, #15807).* Cooperates with (2): *European Association of Personality Psychology (EAPP, #06149); International Society for the Study of Individual Differences (ISSID, #15476).* Associate of: *European Federation of Psychologists Associations (EFPA, #07199).* [2021.06.09/XD6275/v/**D**]

♦ European Association for Psychological Type (EAPT) 06173

Dir Weerstraat 66, 2880 Bornem, Belgium.
URL: http://www.eapt.org/
History Founded 2005, by Lieve Vermeulen and Georg Stueer. **Aims** Offer a European Platform for Psychological Type. **Structure** Virtual organization. National Supporting Associations. **Languages** English, German. **Events** *International Conference* Amsterdam (Netherlands) 2016, *European Type Conference / International Conference* Paris (France) 2012, *International Conference* Berlin (Germany) 2010, *International Conference* Copenhagen (Denmark) 2008, *International Conference* Brussels (Belgium) 2006.
Members Organizations (4):
Association Francophone des Types Psychologiques (AFTP); British Association for Psychological Type; German Association for Psychological Type (DGAT); *Type Association Benelux (TAB, #20272).*
[2016/XJ6505/y/**D**]

♦ European Association of Psychology and Law (EAPL) 06174

Treas address not obtained. E-mail: eapl@eapl.eu.
Sec address not obtained. T. +31433883275.
URL: http://www.eapl.eu/
History 1992, Oxford (UK), following a decision made Nuremberg (Germany), 1990. **Aims** Promote and develop research improvements in legal procedures teaching and practice in the field of psychology and law within Europe; increase cooperation in the field. **Structure** Executive Committee. Special Committees (2). **Finance** Members' dues. **Activities** Special Committees (2): Psychology and Law in Eastern Europe; Relation of Research and Practice. **Events** *Uses and Limits of psychological expertise in legal processes* Santiago de Compostela (Spain) 2019, *Conference* Turku (Finland) 2018, *Conference* Mechelen (Belgium) 2016, *Conference* Toulouse (France) 2016, *Conference* Nürburg (Germany) 2015. **Publications** *Psychology, Crime and Law* – journal. **Members** Full; Affiliate; Honorary. Membership countries not specified. **NGO Relations** *Nordic Network for research on Psychology and Law (NNPL, #17364).* [2015/XD1497/**D**]

♦ European Association of Psychosomatic Medicine (EAPM) 06175

Administration address not obtained. E-mail: info@eapm.eu.com – contact@eapm.eu.com.
URL: http://www.eapm.eu.com/
History Apr 2012, Austria. Founded on merger of *European Association for Consultation Liaison Psychiatry and Psychosomatics (EACLPP, inactive)* and *European Network of Psychosomatic Medicine (ENPM),* which previously co-organized *European Conference on Psychosomatic Research (ECPR, inactive).* **Aims** Promote and integrate psychosomatic (biopsychosocial) approach to health and disease. **Structure** General Assembly; Executive Council; Advisory Body; Arbitration Panel. **Languages** English. **Staff** 0.50 FTE, paid. **Finance** Sources: meeting proceeds; members' dues. **Activities** Awareness raising; knowledge management/information dissemination; networking/liaising; research/documentation; training/education. **Events** *Annual Meeting* Lausanne (Switzerland) 2024, *Annual Meeting* Wroclaw (Poland) 2023, *Annual Meeting* Vienna (Austria) 2022, *Annual Meeting* Nürburg (Germany) 2021, *Annual Scientific Meeting* Vienna (Austria) 2020. **Publications** *EAPM Newsletter, Journal of Psychosomatic Research* – official journal. Guidelines; monographs.
Members Full in 39 countries:
Australia, Austria, Belgium, Brazil, Bulgaria, Canada, Costa Rica, Croatia, Denmark, Finland, France, Germany, Greece, Hungary, Iran Islamic Rep, Ireland, Israel, Italy, Latvia, Lithuania, Malta, Netherlands, New Zealand, Norway, Philippines, Poland, Portugal, Qatar, Romania, Russia, Saudi Arabia, Singapore, Slovenia, Spain, Sweden, Switzerland, Türkiye, UK, USA.
[2023.02.14/XJ6003/**D**]

♦ European Association for Psychotherapy (EAP) 06176

Association européenne de psychothérapie – Europäischer Verband für Psychotherapie
Main Office Mariahilferstrasse 1d/13, 1060 Vienna, Austria. T. +436995131729. Fax +436995122604. E-mail: eap.headoffice@europsyche.org – eap.admin@europsyche.org – info@europsyche.org.
URL: http://www.europsyche.org/
History 30 Jun 1991, Vienna (Austria). Based on the *'Strasbourg Declaration for Psychotherapy 1990'.* **Aims** Support professional interests of psychotherapy organizations and psychotherapists; influence development and regulation of psychotherapy standards in Europe; make information and documentation available to political organizations and government departments; promote high standards of education and training; promote collaboration and exchange of ideas among different psychotherapy orientations; encourage contact with related services; support research. **Structure** General Meeting (annual); Executive Committee; Board. Committees (10): National Umbrella Organisations; Membership; European Training Standards; European Wide Organisations; Ethics; Training Accreditation; Advisory; Scientific Research; Statutes; Nominations; Grandparenting Advisory Panel. **Languages** English, German. **Staff** 2.00 FTE, paid. **Finance** Sources: members' dues. **Activities** Certification/accreditation; events/meetings; research/documentation; training/education. **Events** *Conference on Refugees* Pristina (Kosovo) 2022, *Hope of Psychotherapy for our Endangered World* Vienna (Austria) 2022, *Conference on Refugees* Pristina (Kosovo) 2020, *Conference on Initiating Practice Related Research* Vienna (Austria) 2020, *Sense and Sensibility in Psychotherapy* Belgrade (Serbia) 2018. **Publications** *International Journal of Psychotherapy* (3 a year).
Members National Awarding Organizations; National Umbrella Organizations; National Delegates in 42 countries:
Albania, Austria, Belarus, Belgium, Bosnia-Herzegovina, Bulgaria, Croatia, Cyprus, Czechia, Denmark, Estonia, Finland, France, Germany, Greece, Hungary, Iceland, Ireland, Italy, Latvia, Liechtenstein, Lithuania, Luxembourg, Malta, Moldova, Monaco, Netherlands, North Macedonia, Norway, Poland, Portugal, Romania, Russia, Serbia, Slovakia, Slovenia, Spain, Sweden, Switzerland, Türkiye, UK, Ukraine.
European Wide Accrediting Organizations (16):

European Association Public
06177

alphabetic sequence excludes
For the complete listing, see Yearbook Online at

Europäischer Arbeitskreis für Konzentrative Bewegungstherapie (EAKBT, #05757); European Association for Body Psychotherapy (EABP, #05958); European Association for Gestalt Therapy (EAGT, #06058); European Association for Hypno Psychotherapy (EAHP); European Association for Integrative Psychotherapy (EAIP, #06088); European Association for Neuro-Linguistic Psychotherapy (EANLPt, #06131); European Association for Psycho Organic Analysis (EAPOA, no recent information); European Association for Reality Therapy (EART); European Association for Transactional Analysis (EATA, #06257); European Confederation of Psychoanalytic Psychotherapies (ECPP, #06722); European Family Therapy Association (EFTA, #07031); European Federation for Bioenergetic Analysis Psychotherapy (EFBA-P, #07061); European Federation for Psychoanalytic Psychotherapy (EFPP, #07198); European Federation of Centres for Positive Psychotherapy (EFCPP, #07071); Federation of European Psychodrama Training Organizations (FEPTO, #09535); Network of the European Associations for Person-Centred and Experiential Psychotherapy and Counselling (PCE Europe, #17013).
Consultative Status Consultative status granted from: *Council of Europe (CE, #04881)* (Participatory Status). **NGO Relations** Member of (1): *European Council of Liberal Professions (#06828).* Instrumental in setting up (1): *World Council for Psychotherapy (WCP, #21337).* [2022.10.19/XD4072/y/**D**]

♦ European Association for Public Administration Accreditation (EAPAA) 06177

Secretariat c/o Univ Twente, PO Box 217, 7500 AE Enschede, Netherlands. T. +31534894408. E-mail: secretariat@eapaa.org.
SG Radboud Univ, Fac Managementwetenschappen, Sectie Bestuurskunde/Politicologie, Postbus 9108, 6500 HK Nijmegen, Netherlands. T. +31243611973. E-mail: sg@eapaa.org.
URL: https://www.eapaa.eu/
History 12 Dec 1999, Enschede (Netherlands). Registration: Netherlands. **Aims** Accredit study programmes in Europe in the field of public administration and management. **Structure** General Meeting (annual); Board; Accreditation Committee; Executive Committee; Secretariat. **Finance** Fees for accreditation procedures. **Activities** Accreditation/certification. **Events** *Annual Meeting* Speyer (Germany) 2014, *Meeting* Belgrade (Serbia) 2013, *Meeting* Edinburgh (UK) 2013, *Annual Meeting* Toulouse (France) 2010, *General meeting / Annual Meeting* St Julian's (Malta) 2009. **NGO Relations** Founding member of: *European Alliance of Subject-Specific and Professional Accreditation and Quality Assurance (EASPA, #05887).* Member of: *International Association of Schools and Institutes of Administration (IASIA, #12147).* Registered with: *European Quality Assurance Register for Higher Education (EQAR, #08311).* Cooperates with: *European Group for Public Administration (EGPA, #07430); Network of Institutes and Schools of Public Administration in Central and Eastern Europe (NISPAcee, #17039).* [2019/XD4757/**D**]

♦ European Association of Public Banks (EAPB) 06178

Association européenne de banques publiques
Main Office Av de la Joyeuse Entrée 1-5, 1040 Brussels, Belgium. T. +3222869060. Fax +3222310347. E-mail: info@eapb.eu.
URL: http://www.eapb.eu/
History Founded 4 May 2000. Full title: *European Association of Public Banks – European Association of Public Banks and Funding Agencies (EAPB) – Association européenne de banques publiques et d'institutions communales de financement.* Registration: EU Transparency Register, No/ID: 8754829960-32; Belgium. **Aims** Highlight the importance of public banks for the economic structure of Europe; promote their common interests; encourage cross-border cooperation between public sector banks in Europe. **Structure** General Assembly (annual); Administrative Board; Managing Board. Committees (3): Legal; Economic and Financial Affairs; Competition. Ad-hoc working groups. **Languages** English, French, German. **Staff** 11.00 FTE, paid. **Finance** Members' dues. **Activities** Knolwedge managenet/information dissemination; events/meetings; monitoring/evaluation. **Events** *Chief Executives Officers Conference* Brussels (Belgium) 2021, *General Assembly* Brussels (Belgium) 2021, *Chief Executives Officers Conference* Brussels (Belgium) 2019, *CEO Conference* Brussels (Belgium) 2018, *Workshop on Public Banks Implementing Financial Instruments in EU Cohesion Policy within the Multiannual Financial Framework* Brussels (Belgium) 2018. **Publications** *EAPB Newsletter* (12 a year). Online information bulletin; Annual Report; books.
Members National federations (3) and banks (37) in 21 countries:
Austria, Belgium, Bosnia-Herzegovina, Bulgaria, Croatia, Denmark, Finland, Germany, Hungary, Italy, Latvia, Netherlands, North Macedonia, Norway, Poland, Romania, Serbia, Slovakia, Slovenia, Sweden, Switzerland.
NGO Relations Member of: *European Parliamentary Financial Services Forum (EPFSF, #08148).* Instrumental in setting up: *European Banking Industry Committee (EBIC, #06314).* [2019/XD3984/**D**]

♦ European Association of Public Banks – European Association of Public Banks and Funding Agencies / see European Association of Public Banks (#06178)

♦ European Association of Public IT Service Providers (Euritas) 06179

Head Office c/o Höhne, In der Maur and Partner Rechtsanwälte GmbH & Co KG, Mariahilfer Str 20, 1070 Vienna, Austria. E-mail: euritas@brz.gv.at.
URL: http://www.euritas.eu/
History 2010. Initial activities started 2007. Registration: EU Transparency Register, No/ID: 503557320277-45. **Structure** Management Board; General Committee; Joint Advisory Group; Head Office. **Activities** Events/meetings; projects/programmes.
Members in 9 countries:
Austria, Belgium, Croatia, Denmark, Germany, Italy, Malta, Netherlands, Switzerland. [2023.02.27/XM8699/**D**]

♦ European Association of Public Relations and Communications Students (no recent information)

♦ European Association of Public Sector Pension Institutions (EAPSPI) 06180

Association Européenne des institutions de retraite du secteur public (AEIRSP) – Europäischer Verband der Versorgungseinrichtungen des Öffentlichen Dienstes (EVVOD)
SG Denningerstrasse 37, 81925 Munich, Germany. T. +498992357575. Fax +498992358599. E-mail: info@eapspi.eu.
URL: http://www.eapspi.eu/
History Nov 1990, Bordeaux (France). Former names and other names: *European Club of Local Government Staff Pension Funds* – former (1990 to 1997). Registration: Start date: 2007, Germany; EU Transparency Register, No/ID: 453224331082-90. **Aims** Share and exchange expertise and innovations in the pensions field; provide a voice for public sector pension institutions in Europe. **Structure** General Assembly (annual); Board; General Secretariat; Pensions Policy Committee; Task Forces. **Languages** English, French, German. **Staff** 1.00 FTE, paid. **Finance** Sources: members' dues. Annual budget: 278,219 EUR (2022). **Events** *Annual Conference* Stockholm (Sweden) 2021, *Annual Conference* Helsinki (Finland) 2020, *Annual Conference* Munich (Germany) 2019, *Annual Conference* Lisbon (Portugal) 2018, *Annual Conference* Oslo (Norway) 2017. **Publications** Meetings reports.
Members Organizations in 15 countries:
Austria, Belgium, Denmark, Finland, France, Germany, Ireland, Netherlands, Norway, Portugal, Slovenia, Spain, Sweden, Switzerland, UK. [2022.02.18/XD8159/**D**]

♦ European Association of Public e-Tendering Platform Providers (EUPLAT) 06181

Contact address not obtained. E-mail: info@euplat.org.
URL: http://www.euplat.org/
History Registration: Belgium; EU Transparency Register, No/ID: 861294931424-64. **Aims** Discuss and represent common interests of commercial e-tendering platforms serving EU public contracting authorities and economic operations. **Activities** Advocacy/lobbying/activism; certification/accreditation; guidance/assistance/consulting; knowledge management/information dissemination. [2023.02.14/XM5671/**F**]

♦ European Association of Publishers of Women's or Family Periodicals (inactive)
♦ European Association of Pulp Manufacturers (inactive)

♦ European Association of Pump Manufacturers (EUROPUMP) 06182

Association européenne des constructeurs de pompes – Europäische Vereinigung der Pumpenhersteller – Associazione Europea dei Produttori di Pompe
SG BluePoint Brussels, Bd Auguste Reyers 80, 1030 Brussels, Belgium. T. +3222066866. E-mail: secretariat@europump.org.
URL: http://www.europump.eu/
History 20 Mar 1959, Brussels (Belgium). Current statutes adopted Aug 1993. Former names and other names: *European Committee of Pump Manufacturers* – former (1959). Registration: No/ID: 0463.618.725, Start date: 2 Jul 1998, Belgium; EU Transparency Register, No/ID: 0757172464-29, Start date: 3 Oct 2008. **Aims** Study the problems involved in the development of the pump *industry* and promote its progress. **Structure** General Assembly (annual); Executive Council; Secretariat. Commissions (4): Technical; Marketing/PR; Standards; SME Network. **Languages** English. **Finance** Members' dues. Sale of publications. **Events** *Joint Conference – CEIR – EUROPUMP – PNEUROP* Marseille (France) 2023, *Joint Conference* Brussels (Belgium) 2022, *Annual Meeting and General Assembly* Brussels (Belgium) 2021, *Annual Meeting and General Assembly* Brussels (Belgium) 2020, *Annual Meeting and General Assembly* Naples (Italy) 2019. **Publications** *World Pumps* (periodical). *Guide on NPSH* (1997); *Guide on the Application of the EU Machine Directrice of Pumps* (1995); *This is Europump* (1994); *Multilingual Component Names* (1989); *Multilingual Pump Names* (1982); *Multilingual Pump Applications* (1978). Annual comparative study of inter-company ratios. Annual economic survey and report.
Members National associations in 17 countries:
Austria, Belgium, Czechia, Denmark, Finland, France, Germany, Greece, Italy, Netherlands, Poland, Romania, Russia, Sweden, Switzerland, Türkiye, UK.
IGO Relations Recognized by: *European Commission (EC, #06633).* [2020/XD0652/**D**]

♦ European Association for Quality Assurance in Higher Education (ENQA) 06183

Director Rue de l'Industrie 10, 1000 Brussels, Belgium. T. +3227355659. E-mail: secretariat@enqa.eu.
URL: https://www.enqa.eu/
History 2000. Originating from European Pilot Project for Evaluating Quality in Higher Education (1994-1995) and further supported by Recommendation of *Council of Europe (CE, #04881)* (98/561/EC), 24 Sep 1998. Former names and other names: *European Network for Quality Assurance in Higher Education* – former (2000 to 2004). Registration: Belgium; EU Transparency Register, No/ID: 940278813607-60. **Aims** As the designated stakeholder organisation of quality assurance agencies in the EHEA, represent their interests internationally, support them nationally and provide them with comprehensive services and networking opportunities; promote innovation in quality assurance and enhance quality assurance processes. **Structure** General Assembly (bi-annual); Board; Secretariat; Appeals and Complaints Committee; Agency Review Committee. **Languages** English. **Staff** 7.30 FTE, paid. **Finance** Sources: grants; members' dues. Other sources: project funding. Supported by: *European Commission (EC, #06633).* **Activities** Events/meetings; knowledge management/information dissemination. **Events** *European Quality Assurance Forum* Aveiro (Portugal) 2023, *General Assembly* Brussels (Belgium) 2022, *Members Forum* Cardiff (UK) 2022, *General Assembly* Stockholm (Sweden) 2022, *European Quality Assurance Forum* Timisoara (Romania) 2022. **Publications** *Standards and Guidelines for Quality Assurance in the European Higher Education Area (ESG).* Occasional papers; reports.
Members Members in 31 countries:
Armenia, Austria, Belgium, Bulgaria, Croatia, Cyprus, Denmark, Estonia, Finland, France, Georgia, Germany, Greece, Holy See, Hungary, Ireland, Italy, Kazakhstan, Latvia, Lithuania, Netherlands, Norway, Poland, Portugal, Romania, Slovenia, Spain, Sweden, Switzerland, Türkiye, UK.
Members operating across Europe (2):
European Association of Establishments for Veterinary Education (EAEVE, #06031); Institutional Evaluation Programme (EUA).
Affiliates in 30 countries and territories:
Albania, Andorra, Azerbaijan, Bosnia-Herzegovina, Curaçao, Czechia, France, Germany, Hong Kong, Iceland, Israel, Italy, Jordan, Kazakhstan, Kosovo, Luxembourg, Malta, Mauritania, Mexico, Moldova, Montenegro, Netherlands, North Macedonia, Northern Cyprus, Serbia, Slovakia, Spain, UK, Ukraine, Uzbekistan.
Affiliates operating across Europe (10):
Association for Dental Education in Europe (ADEE, #02467); Central and Eastern European Network of Quality Assurance Agencies in Higher Education (CEENQA, #03696); EFMD – The Management Development Network (#05387); EQ-Arts; *European Consortium for Accreditation in Higher Education (ECA, #06748); European Council for Business Education (ECBE, #06807); European Council for Theological Education (ECTE, #06846); European Council on Chiropractic Education (ECCE, #06809);* MusiQuE – Music Quality Enhancement, Foundation for Quality Enhancement and Accreditation in Higher Music Education; Réseau Figure (Le Réseau Formation en InGénierie d'Universités de Recherche).
IGO Relations Member of (1): Bologna Follow-Up Group. Cooperates with (1): *Asean Quality Assurance Network (AQAN, #01227).* **NGO Relations** Member of (1): *European Quality Assurance Register for Higher Education (EQAR, #08311).* Cooperates with (6): *Arab Network for Quality Assurance in Higher Education (ANQAHE, #01014); Asia-Pacific Quality Network (APQN, #02004); BUSINESSEUROPE (#03381); Education International (EI, #05371); European Association of Institutions of Higher Education (EURASHE, #06086); European Students' Union (ESU, #08848).* [2022.11.10/XF5877/y/**F**]

♦ European Association for Quality in General Practice/Family Medicine (EQuiP) 06184

Manager Egå Engvej 60, 8250 Aarhus, Denmark. T. +4528864863. E-mail: equip.we@gmail.com.
URL: https://equip.woncaeurope.org/
History Founded as a network organization within *European Society of General Practice/Family Medicine (WONCA Europe, #08609).* **Aims** Contribute to the achievement of high levels of quality of care for patients in general practice in all European countries. **Structure** Executive Board. **Events** *Assembly* Zagreb (Croatia) 2016, *Assembly* Stockholm (Sweden) 2012. **Publications** Books; articles; leaflets.
Members National delegates in 28 countries:
Austria, Belgium, Croatia, Denmark, Estonia, Finland, France, Germany, Greece, Hungary, Iceland, Ireland, Israel, Italy, Latvia, Malta, Netherlands, Norway, Poland, Portugal, Romania, Russia, Slovenia, Spain, Sweden, Switzerland, Türkiye, UK. [2019.10.22/XJ0627/**E**]

♦ European Association of Quality Intermediary Organizations in Mobility / see European Association of Quality Organisations in Mobility (#06185)
♦ European Association for Quality Language Services / see Evaluation and Accreditation of Quality in Language Services (#09209)

♦ European Association of Quality Organisations in Mobility (EAQOM) 06185

Founding Member Chée de Wemmel 77, 1090 Brussels, Belgium.
URL: https://eaqom.org/
History 13 Sep 2018, Brussels (Belgium). Founded by the *IntoQuality Project.* Former names and other names: *European Association of Quality Intermediary Organizations in Mobility (EAQOM)* – former. Registration: Banque Carrefour des Entreprises, No/ID: 0719.614.393, Start date: 30 Jan 2019, Belgium. **Aims** Define and promote responsible organizational, logistical and evaluation practices in the planning, execution and follow-up of European mobilities in view of allowing mobile Europeans to benefit from international and intercultural exchanges, experiences, training and learning. **Activities** Advocacy/lobbying/activism; knowledge management/information dissemination; networking/liaising; research/documentation.
Members Founding in 6 countries:
Austria, Belgium, Bulgaria, Germany, Italy, Portugal.
Associate in 1 country:
Bulgaria. [2020/AA1369/**D**]

♦ European Association on Radiation / see RadTech Europe (#18606)
♦ European Association of Radiology (inactive)
♦ European Association of Railway Equipment Manufacturers (inactive)
♦ European Association for Railway Interoperability (inactive)

♦ European Association of Real Estate Professions (CEPI) 06186

Association européenne des Professions immobilières

Office Manager Av de Tervueren 36, Boîte 2, 1040 Brussels, Belgium. T. +3227354990. Fax +3227359988. E-mail: secretariat@cepi.eu.
Dir Gen address not obtained.
URL: http://www.cepi.eu/

History 24 Apr 1990, Brussels (Belgium). Founded when statutes were adopted, within the framework of *Fédération internationale des professions immobilières (FIABCI, #09653)*. Statutes modified: 15 Apr 2005, Riga (Latvia). Previously constituent bodies *Confédération européenne des administrateurs de biens (CEAB, inactive)* and *European Property Agents Group (EPAG, inactive)* merged into CEPI, 8 Feb 2011, when new statutes were adopted. Merged with *European Confederation of Real Estate Agents (CEI, inactive)*, Mar 2015. Statutes most recently modified, 2 Oct 2020, at the web-based Extraordinary General Assembly. Former names and other names: *Conseil FIABCI Communauté économique européenne (FIABCI-CEE)* – former; *FIABCI Communauté européenne (FIABCI-CE)* – former; *Conseil européen des professions immobilières (CEPI)* – former; *European Council of Real Estate Professions* – former; *CEPI-CEI* – former (Mar 2015). Registration: Banque-Carrefour des Entreprises, No/ID: 0446.801.202, Start date: 25 Feb 1992, Belgium; EU Transparency Register, No/ID: 1094652600-90, Start date: 3 Nov 2008. **Structure** General Meeting; Board of Directors; Presidency; Secretariat; Professional Divisions; Management Team; Permanent Technical Committees; Working groups. **Languages** English, French. **Finance** Sources: members' dues. **Activities** Advocacy/lobbying/activism; research/documentation; training/education. **Events** *General Assembly* Brussels (Belgium) 2021, *General Assembly* Brussels (Belgium) 2021, *General Assembly* Brussels (Belgium) 2020, *General Assembly* Brussels (Belgium) 2020, *General Assembly* London (UK) 2019. **Publications** *CEPI Brussels Flash*; *CEPI Information*; *CEPI Meets*; *CEPI Newsletter*; *CEPI Podcast*.

Members Associations in 21 countries:
Andorra, Austria, Belgium, Bulgaria, Czechia, Denmark, Finland, Georgia, Germany, Greece, Ireland, Italy, Lithuania, Luxembourg, Netherlands, Poland, Romania, Slovakia, Spain, Switzerland, UK. [2022.05.11/XD2937/t/**D**]

- ♦ European Association for Reality Therapy (internationally oriented national body)
- ♦ European Association of Reference Laboratories (no recent information)
- ♦ European Association of Refrigeration Enterprises (inactive)
- ♦ European Association of Régies de quartier (internationally oriented national body)

♦ European Association of Regional Development Agencies (EURADA) 06187

Association européenne des agences de développement régionales

Dir Rue Montoyer 24 – 5th floor, 1000 Brussels, Belgium. T. +3222870832. E-mail: info@eurada.org.
URL: http://www.eurada.org/

History 27 Nov 1991. Statutes adopted 4 Dec 1991. Registered according to Belgian law. Derives from *European Cooperation Network of Development Agencies*, set up 1989 within the framework of *Regions and Cities of Europe (RECITE Programme, inactive)*, following first Congress of Development Agencies, 1988, Athens (Greece). Previously referred to as *European Association of Development Agencies – Association européenne des agences de développement*. EU Transparency Register: 827929825168-90. **Aims** Bring together and disseminate good practice in economic development for the benefit of members. **Structure** General Assembly (annual); Board of Directors; Executive Committee. **Languages** English, French. **Staff** 3.00 FTE, paid. **Finance** Members dues. **Activities** Events/meetings. **Events** *Workshop* Brussels (Belgium) 2022, *IN4WOOD Final Conference* Brussels (Belgium) 2019, *Seminar on Industry 4.0 in Cities and Regions in the Context of the Knowledge Exchange Platform* Brussels (Belgium) 2019, *Annual European employment week* Brussels (Belgium) 2009, *AGORADA plus conference* Brussels (Belgium) 2008. **Publications** *EURADA Information Bulletin*. Position papers.

Members Regular Associate. Regular in 18 countries:
Austria, Belgium, Bulgaria, Croatia, Czechia, Finland, France, Greece, Hungary, Ireland, Italy, Netherlands, Poland, Portugal, Romania, Slovenia, Spain, UK.
Associate in 3 countries:
Bosnia-Herzegovina, Serbia, Türkiye.
Partnership forum members in 7 countries:
Czechia, France, Germany, Greece, Italy, Spain, Ukraine.
IGO Relations *Cohesion Fund (#04087)*; *European Regional Development Fund (ERDF, #08342)*. **NGO Relations** Member of: *ANIMA Investment Network (#00833)*. [2022/XF2353/**D**]

♦ European Association of Regional and Local Authorities for Lifelong Learning (EARLALL) 06188

Association européenne des autorités régionales et locales pour l'apprentissage tout au long de la vie

Business Manager Rue des Deux Eglises 27, 1000 Brussels, Belgium. T. +3222854545. E-mail: earlall@earlall.eu.
Pres address not obtained.
URL: http://www.earlall.eu/

History 11 Oct 2001, Brussels (Belgium), on the initiative of *'Regione Toscana'*. Registered in accordance with Belgian law. EU Transparency Register: 137489015927-79. **Aims** Reach a high degree of collaboration between members in the field of European lifelong learning policies; establish close cooperation with institutions of the European Union. **Structure** General Assembly; Board. **Languages** English. **Staff** 2.00 FTE, paid. **Finance** Members' dues. **Activities** Networking/liaising; politics/policy/regulatory. **Events** *General Assembly* Varazdin (Croatia) 2022, *General Assembly* 2020, *General Assembly* Brussels (Belgium) 2019, *Project Development Workshop* Brussels (Belgium) 2019, *General Assembly* San Sebastian (Spain) 2015. **Publications** Position papers; project results.

Members Full: Regional Governments at the second level of government (12) in 8 countries:
Bulgaria, Croatia, France, Germany, Italy, Norway, Spain, Sweden.
Observer:
Sweden.
NGO Relations Member of: *Lifelong Learning Platform – European Civil Society for Education (LLLP, #16466)*. [2021/XD9024/y/**D**]

♦ European Association of Regional Television (CIRCOM Regional) .. 06189

Association européenne des télévisions régionales

SG c/o HRT, Prisavlje 3, 10000 Zagreb, Croatia. E-mail: circom@circom-regional.eu.
Deputy SG France 3 Alsace, Place de Bordeaux – BP 428, 67005 Strasbourg CEDEX, France. T. +33388566809.
URL: http://www.circom-regional.eu/

History Founded 1983. **Aims** Promote the development of regional television; facilitate cooperation between regional television stations, particularly through co-production projects; strengthen vocational training; examine and debate issues affecting regional television. **Structure** Board of Directors. **Languages** English, French. **Finance** Members' dues. Supported by public service broadcasters and the international Board members. **Activities** Awards/prizes/competitions; training/education. **Events** *Annual Conference* Dundalk (Ireland) 2015, *Annual Conference* Cavtat (Croatia) 2014, *Annual Conference* Santiago de Compostela (Spain) 2013, *Annual Conference* Malmö (Sweden) 2012, *Annual Conference* Timisoara (Romania) 2011.

Members Regional television stations (250) in 30 countries:
Albania, Austria, Belgium, Bosnia-Herzegovina, Bulgaria, Croatia, Czechia, Denmark, Finland, France, Georgia, Germany, Greece, Hungary, Ireland, Italy, Malta, Netherlands, North Macedonia, Norway, Poland, Portugal, Romania, Serbia, Slovakia, Slovenia, Spain, Sweden, Switzerland, UK.
NGO Relations Member of: *Permanent Conference of Mediterranean Audiovisual Operators (COPEAM, #18320)*. Partner of: *International Radio and Television Union (#14689)*. Instrumental in setting up: *International Public Television (INPUT, #14674)*. [2022/XD7113/**D**]

- ♦ European Association of Registrars (#05760)
- ♦ European Association for Regression Therapy / see Earth Association for Regression Therapy (#05160)

♦ European Association of Remote Sensing Companies (EARSC) 06190

Association européenne des sociétés de télédétection

SG Rue de la Loi 26, 7ème étage, 1040 Brussels, Belgium. E-mail: secretariat@earsc.org.
Chairman Springfield Drive, Leatherhead, KT22 7LP, UK. T. +441372759784.
URL: http://www.earsc.org/

History 1989. Registration: Banque-Carrefour des Entreprises, No/ID: BE 0447243442, Belgium; EU Transparency Register, No/ID: 928649113568-51. **Aims** As an industrial trade association: represent European Earth Observation, geo-information and service companies; foster development of the European geo-information service industry; stimulate a sustainable market for geo-information services using remote sensing data. **Structure** General Assembly (annual, in Brussels); Administrative Council; Board of Directors; Working Groups (3). **Languages** English. **Staff** 12.00 FTE, paid. **Finance** Sources: members' dues; revenue from activities/projects. **Activities** Advocacy/lobbying/activism; awards/prizes/competitions; awareness raising; capacity building; events/meetings; knowledge management/information dissemination; networking/liaising. **Events** *Forum for Innovation and Research in European Earth Observation* Brussels (Belgium) 2022, *Workshop on Boosting the Market for EO Services in the Digital Economy* Brussels (Belgium) 2017, *Workshop on Improving EO Services Industry Involvement in EU Space Programmes and Initiatives* Brussels (Belgium) 2017, *Workshop on PCP/PPI in Horizons2020 Projects on Earth Observation CDTI/SOST* Brussels (Belgium) 2015, *Workshop on the impact of GMES (global monitoring for environment and security) governance models on industry* Brussels (Belgium) 2009. **Publications** *EARSC Monthly Report*; *EOmag*. *Industry Survey Report*. Annual Report; position papers. **Information Services** *earsc-portal*; *EOpages* – brokerage platform to help potential customers find suppliers while service providers are able to promote their products.

Members Full (135 companies); Observer (8); Trial (15). Members in 25 countries:
Austria, Belgium, Bulgaria, Croatia, Czechia, Denmark, Finland, France, Germany, Greece, Ireland, Italy, Luxembourg, Netherlands, Norway, Poland, Portugal, Romania, Slovakia, Slovenia, Spain, Sweden, Switzerland, UK, USA.
IGO Relations Partner of (2): *EuroGEOSS (#05685)*; *Group on Earth Observations (GEO, #10735)*. **NGO Relations** Member of (3): European and Latin American Technology Based Business Network (ELAN Network); *European Geographic Information Network (EGIN, #07387)*; *European Umbrella Organization for Geographical Information (EUROGI, #08964)*. Also links with national associations. [2022.05.10/XD7393/**D**]

♦ European Association of Remote Sensing Laboratories (EARSeL) .. 06191

Association européenne de laboratoires de télédétection

Admin Dir Am Dill 169, 48163 Münster, Germany.
Registered Office 6 rue de la Toussant, 67000 Strasbourg, France.
URL: http://www.earsel.org/

History Aug 1977, Strasbourg (France). Founded as a Study Group of the *Council of Europe (CE, #04881)*. Co-sponsored by *European Space Agency (ESA, #08798)* and *European Commission (EC, #06633)*. **Aims** Encourage European research and facilitate scientific exchange between participating laboratories; identify priority areas for research and foster cooperation. **Structure** General Assembly; Bureau; Council; Special Interest Groups (16). **Languages** English, French, German. **Staff** 0.50 FTE, paid. **Finance** Sources: members' dues; sponsorship. **Activities** Events/meetings. Active in all member countries. **Events** *EARSeL Symposium* Bucharest (Romania) 2023, *EARSeL Symposium* Paphos (Cyprus) 2022, *Annual General Assembly and Symposium* Warsaw (Poland) 2021, *Annual General Assembly and Symposium* Salzburg (Austria) 2019, *Annual General Assembly and Symposium* Chania (Greece) 2018. **Publications** *European Journal of Remote Sensing*. *EARSeL Book Series on Remote Sensing*. Symposium proceedings.

Members Full (130): research laboratories in Europe and associated member countries of the European Union. Members in 27 countries:
Austria, Belgium, Bulgaria, Canada, Croatia, Cyprus, Czechia, Denmark, Estonia, Finland, France, Germany, Greece, Hungary, Italy, Luxembourg, Netherlands, Norway, Poland, Portugal, Romania, Russia, Spain, Sweden, Switzerland, Türkiye, UK.
Observers: laboratories outside Europe and industrial firms. Observers in 1 country:
Israel.
IGO Relations Partner of: *Group on Earth Observations (GEO, #10735)*. **NGO Relations** Member of: *International Society for Photogrammetry and Remote Sensing (ISPRS, #15362)*. Observer status with: *European Umbrella Organization for Geographical Information (EUROGI, #08964)*. Cooperates with: *Eurisy (#05625)*. [2022/XD7186/**D**]

- ♦ European Association for Research into Adapted Physical Activity / see European Federation of Adapted Physical Activity (#07038)

♦ European Association for Research on Adolescence (EARA) 06192

Association européenne pour la recherche en adolescence

Sec Università di Bologna, Dipartimento di Psicologia, Viale Berti Pichat 5, 40127 Bologna BO, Italy. T. +39547338508.
URL: http://www.earaonline.org/

History 1991. Founded following a series of informal meetings. Registration: France. **Aims** Promote and safeguard high quality basic and applied psychological research in Europe on all aspects of adolescence. **Structure** General Assembly (every 2 years, at Conference). Executive Council of 12 members. Executive Committee, comprising President, President-Elect and up to 4 members. **Languages** English. **Finance** Members' dues. Grants. **Activities** Research topics: adolescent socialization; adolescents at risk; adolescent mental health; adolescents identity formation; research methodology. **Events** *Conference* Dublin (Ireland) 2022, *Conference* Porto (Portugal) 2020, *Biennial Conference* Ghent (Belgium) 2018, *Biennial Conference* Chiclana de la Frontera (Spain) 2016, *Biennial Conference* Cesme (Turkey) 2014. **Publications** *EARA News* (2 a year).

Members Full; Associate; Student. Psychologists, psychiatrists and sociologists (150) in 28 countries:
Austria, Belgium, Bosnia-Herzegovina, Croatia, Cyprus, Czechia, Denmark, Estonia, Finland, France, Germany, Greece, Hungary, Italy, Netherlands, Norway, Poland, Portugal, Romania, Russia, Serbia, Slovenia, Spain, Sweden, Switzerland, Türkiye, UK, Ukraine. [2022/XD5585/v/**D**]

- ♦ European Association for Research and Application of Laser and Related Technologies in Medicine, Surgery and Therapy / see European Medical Laser Association (#07763)
- ♦ European Association for Research and Development in Higher Education (inactive)

♦ European Association for Research in Industrial Economics (EARIE) 06193

Association européenne de la recherche en économie industrielle

Exec Sec c/o EIASM, Place De Brouckère 31 – 2nd floor, 1000 Brussels, Belgium. T. +3222266660. Fax +3225121929. E-mail: earie@eiasm.be.
URL: http://www.earie.org/

History 1974, London (UK). **Aims** Provide a professional society for academics and professionals in the field of industrial economics. **Structure** Executive Committee. **Languages** English. **Finance** Members' dues. **Activities** Events/meetings; knowledge management/information dissemination; networking/liaising; awards/prizes/competitions. **Events** *Annual Conference* Vienna (Austria) 2022, *Annual Conference* Bergen (Norway) 2021, *Annual Conference* Bologna (Italy) 2020, *Annual Conference* Barcelona (Spain) 2019, *Annual Conference* Athens (Greece) 2018. **Publications** *International Journal of Industrial Organization (IJIO)*.

Members Individuals (400-550) in 40-50 countries. Membership countries not specified. **NGO Relations** Member of: *EFMD – The Management Development Network (#05387)*. [2017.06.01/XD7210/tv/**D**]

♦ European Association for Research on Learning and Instruction (EARLI) 06194

Communications Manager Peterseliegang 1, Box 1, 3000 Leuven, Belgium. T. +3216231900. E-mail: info@earli.org.
URL: http://www.earli.org/

History 1985. Registration: Banque-Carrefour des Entreprises, Belgium. **Aims** Promote, develop and advance empirical and theoretical research into learning and instruction; exchange information between European members and organizations worldwide. **Structure** General Assembly (annual); Members' Meeting (biennial); Executive Committee; Head Office, led by Managing Director. **Languages** English. **Staff** 2.80 FTE, paid. **Finance** Sources: meeting proceeds; members' dues; private foundations; revenue from activities/projects; sale of publications; sponsorship. . **Activities** Events/meetings; networking/liaising; training/education. . **Events** *Biennial Conference* Thessaloniki (Greece) 2023, *JURE Conference* Thessaloniki (Greece) 2023, *Special Interest Group on Researcher Education and Careers Meeting* Helsinki (Finland) 2022, *Special*

Interest Group on Early Childhood Education Meeting Utrecht (Netherlands) 2022, *Special Interest Group on Inquiry Learning and Special Interest Group on Argumentation, Dialogue and Reasoning Joint Meting* Utrecht (Netherlands) 2022. **Publications** *Educational Research Review*; *Frontline Learning Research*; *Learning and Instruction*. *New Perspectives on Learning and Instruction.*
Members Full membership requires PhD degree or enrollment in a PhD programme, research activity in a university or research centre in the field or professional involvement in research on innovations in teaching and learning. JURE membership requires subscription to a master or PhD programme. Individuals (about 2,500) in 39 countries and territories:
Australia, Austria, Belgium, Bulgaria, Canada, Czechia, Denmark, Finland, France, Germany, Greece, Hong Kong, Hungary, India, Indonesia, Ireland, Israel, Italy, Japan, Korea Rep, Luxembourg, Malaysia, Malta, Montenegro, Netherlands, New Zealand, Norway, Peru, Philippines, Poland, Portugal, Romania, Serbia, Spain, Sweden, Switzerland, Türkiye, UK, USA.
NGO Relations Sister organization: *European Association for Practitioner Research on Improving Learning (EAPRIL, #06161)*. Founding member of: *World Education Research Association (WERA, #21372)*.
[2022.10.31/XD2680/v/**D**]

♦ European Association of Research Managers and Administrators (EARMA) 06195

Sec Rue Joseph II 36-38, 4th Floor, 1000 Brussels, Belgium. T. +32499408301. E-mail: earma@earma.org.
URL: http://www.earma.org/
History 13 Jan 1995, Genoa (Italy). Registration: Banque-Carrefour des Entreprises, No/ID: 0477.806.558, Start date: 4 Jul 2002, Belgium. **Aims** Increase efficiency and maximize the impact of publicly-funded research within the European Research Area, by improving quality and professionalism of research management and administration throughout Europe. **Structure** General Assembly (annual); Board; Working Groups; Secretariat. **Languages** English. **Staff** 2.00 FTE, paid. **Finance** Members' dues. **Activities** Events/meetings; training/education; networking/liaising; advocacy/lobbying/activism; politics/policy/regulatory. **Events** *Annual Conference* Prague (Czechia) 2023, *Annual Conference* Oslo (Norway) 2022, *Annual Conference* Brussels (Belgium) 2021, *Annual Conference* Brussels (Belgium) 2020, *Annual Conference* Bologna (Italy) 2019. **Publications** *EARMA Newsletter*, *LINK* – magazine.
Members Institutional (120) and Ordinary (about 180 individuals). Institutional in 43 countries:
Albania, Austria, Belgium, Canada, Cyprus, Czechia, Denmark, Finland, France, Germany, Hungary, Iceland, Ireland, Israel, Italy, Japan, Kazakhstan, Korea Rep, Latvia, Lithuania, Luxembourg, Malaysia, Malta, Netherlands, Norway, Poland, Portugal, Qatar, Romania, Russia, Saudi Arabia, Serbia, Singapore, Slovenia, Spain, St Kitts-Nevis, Sweden, Switzerland, Tajikistan, Türkiye, UK, United Arab Emirates, USA.
Ordinary in 34 countries:
Australia, Austria, Belgium, Botswana, Bulgaria, Canada, Côte d'Ivoire, Czechia, Denmark, Estonia, Finland, France, Germany, Hungary, Ireland, Israel, Italy, Japan, Kenya, Luxembourg, Netherlands, Norway, Pakistan, Poland, Portugal, Romania, Slovakia, South Africa, Spain, Sweden, Switzerland, Türkiye, UK, USA.
NGO Relations Member of: *International Network of Research Management Societies (INORMS, #14317)*. Cooperates with: *Association of Commonwealth Universities, The (ACU, #02440)*; *euroCRIS (#05672)*; *European Association for the Transfer of Technologies, Innovation and Industrial Information (TII, #06259)*; *International Network for Small and Medium Sized Enterprises (INSME, #14325)*; *Society of Research Administrators International (SRA)*; *Southern African Research and Innovation Management Association (SARIMA)*; *West African Research and Innovation Management Association (WARIMA, #20895)*; national organizations.
[2020/XD5905/**D**]

♦ European Association for Research on Obesity in Childhood (EAROC) 06196

Main Office Alser Str 14/4, 1090 Vienna, Austria. E-mail: info.earoc@gmail.com.
URL: http://www.earoc.org/
History 2007. **Aims** Promote and support research in the field of childhood obesity; encourage the establishment of an evidence-based approach to tackling childhood obesity. **Structure** Executive Board. **Events** *International Symposium on the Morbidly Obese Adolescent* Vienna (Austria) 2011, *Symposium on lipids in children / Symposium* Vienna (Austria) 2008.
[2018/XJ5368/**D**]

- ♦ European Association for Research on Plant Breeding / see EUCARPIA (#05571)
- ♦ European Association for REsearch on SERvices / see European Network for REsearch on SERvices (#07992)

♦ European Association of Research and Technology Organizations (EARTO) 06197

SG Rue Joseph II 36-38, 1000 Brussels, Belgium. T. +3225028698. Fax +3225028693. E-mail: secretariat@earto.eu.
URL: http://www.earto.eu/
History 1999, Brussels (Belgium). Founded upon merger of *European Association of Contract Research Organizations (EACRO, inactive)* and *Federation of European Industrial Cooperative Research Organizations (FEICRO, inactive)*. Registration: EU Transparency Register, No/ID: 977869932377-59; Belgium. **Aims** Promote and defend the interests of Research and Technology Organizations (RTOs) in Europe by reinforcing their profile and position as key players in minds of EU decision-makers; ensure European research and development and innovation programmes are best attuned to their interests; provide added-value services to members to improve operational practices and business performance; provide information and advice to make best use of funding opportunities. **Structure** Executive Board; Secretariat. **Languages** English. **Staff** 4.00 FTE, paid. **Finance** Sources: members' dues. **Activities** Awards/prizes/competitions; events/meetings; knowledge management/information dissemination. **Events** *Annual Conference* Barcelona (Spain) 2022, *High-Level Conference on the Role of Technology Infrastructures in the new Pact for Research and Innovation* Brussels (Belgium) 2022, *Policy Meeting* Brussels (Belgium) 2022, *Policy Meeting* 2021, *Annual Conference* Brussels (Belgium) 2021. **Publications** *EARTO Newsletter* (12 a year); *Impact Delivered* (annual). Policy papers; press statements.
Members Individual; Association; Corresponding. Members in 27 countries:
Argentina, Austria, Belgium, Brazil, Canada, Cyprus, Denmark, Finland, France, Germany, Greece, Ireland, Italy, Korea Rep, Lithuania, Luxembourg, Norway, Poland, Portugal, Romania, Slovenia, Spain, Sweden, Switzerland, Taiwan, Thailand, UK.
NGO Relations Member of (1): *European Federation of National Associations of Measurement, Testing and Analytical Laboratories (EUROLAB, #07168)*.
[2022.05.23/XD7223/**D**]

- ♦ European Association of Reserve Non Commissioned Officers / see Confédération Interalliée des Sous-Officiers de Réserve (#04556)
- ♦ European Association for Rett Syndrome / see Rett Syndrome Europe (#18928)
- ♦ European Association of Roofing Tile and Brick Manufacturers / see Tiles and Bricks Europe (#20163)
- ♦ European Association of the Rubber Industry / see European Tyre and Rubber Manufacturers' Association (#08963)

♦ European Association for Rural Development Institutions 06198

Association européenne des institutions d'aménagement rural (AEIAR) – Europäische Vereinigung der Institutionen für die Neuordnung des Ländlichen Raumes – Associazione Europea delle Organizzazioni Operanti nel Settore delle Strutture e delle Trasformazioni Fondiario-Agrarie – Europese Vereniging van de Instellingen voor de Inrichting van het Platteland
SG c/o Vlaamse Landmaatschappij, Koning Albert II laan 15, 1210 Brussels, Belgium. T. +3225436946. Fax +3225437399.
URL: http://www.aeiar.eu/
History 23 Jun 1965, Brussels (Belgium), by 12 institutions from the then 6 European Community countries. Previously referred to in English as *European Association for Country Planning Institutions*. **Aims** Improve *agrarian* structures to enable sustainable *land management*; improve living, working and environmental conditions to reinforce the economy of rural areas. **Structure** General Assembly. Administration Board. Working Groups (2). General Secretariat. **Languages** English, French, German. **Staff** 10.00 FTE, paid. **Finance** Members' dues. Expertise fees. **Activities** Congresses and study-days; Advice. **Events** *Meeting* Luxembourg (Luxembourg) 1996.
Members National and regional associations in 11 countries:
Belgium, Croatia, France, Germany, Greece, Hungary, Italy, Lithuania, Luxembourg, Netherlands, Poland.
Included in the above, 1 organization listed in this Yearbook:
Terres d'Europe (no recent information).
NGO Relations Cooperates with: *Rurality – Environment – Development (RED, #19003)*.
[2019/XD0551/y/**E**]

- ♦ European Association for Rural Development and Village Renewal (#05748)
- ♦ European Association for Safeguards Research and Development / see European Safeguards Research and Development Association (#08417)
- ♦ European Association for Safe Logistics / see EUMOS (#05588)
- ♦ European Association of Sauces and Vinegar (no recent information)

♦ European Association of Schools of Occupational Medicine (EASOM) 06199

SG c/o Service de Santé, 32 rue Glesener, L-1630 Luxembourg, Luxembourg.
URL: http://www.easom.eu/
History 19 Mar 1993, Berlin (Germany). Registration: Netherlands. **Aims** Promote the highest standards of education and training in occupational medicine in Europe through exchange of knowledge, skills and experience of teaching and training between member schools. **Structure** Board. **Languages** English, French, German. **Staff** None. **Finance** Members' dues. Initial funding from *European Community Action Scheme for the Mobility of University Students (ERASMUS, inactive)*. **Activities** Events/meetings; knowledge management/information dissemination; networking/liaising; training/education. EASOM Summer School. **Events** *General assembly* Linz (Austria) 1998, *Quality improvement in education and training in occupational health services* Stockholm (Sweden) 1996. **Publications** *EASOM News Bulletin* (2 a year). Position papers. Information Services: Establishing a database for audiovisual teaching materials.
Members Full (30): schools of occupational medicine; Associate (3): individuals involved in occupational medicine teaching; Sustaining (1): organizations interested in supporting education and training in occupational medicine. Members in 20 countries:
Austria, Belgium, Croatia, Czechia, Finland, France, Germany, Greece, Ireland, Italy, Netherlands, North Macedonia, Norway, Portugal, Romania, Serbia, Slovenia, Spain, Switzerland, UK.
IGO Relations Cooperates with official organizations on all aspects of occupational physicians' training: *European Commission (EC, #06633)*; *WHO (#20950)*; *WHO Regional Office for Europe (#20945)*.
[2022/XD3167/**D**]

- ♦ European Association of Schools of Political Studies of the Council of Europe / see Association of Schools of Political Studies of the Council of Europe (#02902)

♦ European Association of Schools of Social Work (EASSW) 06200

Association Européenne des Ecoles de Travailleurs Sociaux
Treas Inst of Social Work, Heidelberglaan 7, 3584 CS Utrecht, Netherlands. T. +31884819220.
URL: http://www.eassw.org/
History Founded as a regional association of *International Association of Schools of Social Work (IASSW, #12149)*, with the title *European Regional Group for Social Work Education (ERG)*, also referred to as *European Group for Social Work Education*. Present name adopted 1994. Became an independent association 1 Dec 1995. **Aims** Promote social development; develop high quality education, training and knowledge for social work practice, social services and social welfare policies in Europe. **Structure** General Assembly (every 2 years); Executive Committee. **Finance** Members' dues. Other sources: subsidies; grants; projects; consultations; sale of publications; revenues from seminars, workshops, congresses. **Activities** Provides assistance for: European exchange programmes of member schools; creation of curricula development and implementation of new schools in social work; development of European networks and research projects. Represents and promotes the interests of social work education on the European level. Provides a European forum for members. **Events** *Biennial Congress* Madrid (Spain) 2019, *Biennial Congress* Paris (France) 2017, *Biennial Congress* Milan (Italy) 2015, *Biennial Congress* Dubrovnik (Croatia) 2009, *IFSW European seminar* Parma (Italy) 2007. **Publications** *EASSW Bulletin*. *EASSW directory of schools of social work*. Proceedings of conferences.
Members National or sub-regional associations of schools of social work and individual schools of social work (about 300); individual teachers of social work education. Members in 33 countries:
Albania, Austria, Belarus, Belgium, Bosnia-Herzegovina, Bulgaria, Croatia, Czechia, Denmark, Estonia, Finland, France, Germany, Greece, Hungary, Iceland, Ireland, Italy, Luxembourg, Netherlands, North Macedonia, Norway, Poland, Portugal, Romania, Russia, Slovakia, Slovenia, Spain, Sweden, Switzerland, UK, Ukraine.
Consultative Status Consultative status granted from: *Council of Europe (CE, #04881)* (Participatory Status).
NGO Relations Member of: *European Network for Social Action (ENSACT, #08003)*. Cooperates with: European branches of *International Council on Social Welfare (ICSW, #13076)*; *Formation d'éducateurs sociaux européens (FESET, #09873)*; *International Federation of Social Workers (IFSW, #13544)*.
[2014/XE0668/**D**]

- ♦ European Association for the Science of Air Pollution (inactive)

♦ European Association of Science Editors (EASE) 06201

Association européenne de rédacteurs d'ouvrages scientifiques
Sec The Brambles, Ryton Road, Dymock, GL18 2DG, UK. T. +447721521927. E-mail: secretary@ease.org.uk.
URL: http://www.ease.org.uk/
History 1982, Pau (France). Founded through merger of *European Life Science Editors (ELSE, inactive)*, set up 12 Apr 1967, Amsterdam (Netherlands), and of *European Association of Earth Science Editors (EDITERRA, inactive)*, formed 2 Dec 1968, Paris (France). Former names and other names: *European Association of Editors of Biological Periodicals* – former. Registration: Companies House, No/ID: 04049507, Start date: 2000, England and Wales. **Aims** Improve the global standard and quality of science editing by promoting the value of science editors and supporting professional development, research and collaboration. **Structure** Board of Directors; Council; Editorial Board. **Languages** English. **Staff** 0.50 FTE, paid. **Finance** Sources: meeting proceeds; revenue from activities/projects; sponsorship; subscriptions. Annual budget: 50,000 GBP (2021). **Activities** Events/meetings; politics/policy/regulatory; training/education. **Events** *General Assembly and Conference* Istanbul (Türkiye) 2023, *General Assembly and Conference* Valencia (Spain) 2022, *General Assembly and Conference* Dymock (UK) 2021, *Conference* Dymock (UK) 2020, *General Assembly and Conference* Bucharest (Romania) 2018. **Publications** *European Science Editing* (4 a year). *Science Editors' Handbook* (2nd ed 2013); *EASE Guidelines for Authors and Translators*. Position papers.
Members Individuals (about 700) in 50 countries and territories:
Australia, Austria, Bahrain, Bangladesh, Belgium, Bosnia-Herzegovina, Brazil, Bulgaria, Canada, China, Colombia, Croatia, Czechia, Denmark, Ecuador, Estonia, Finland, France, Germany, Hong Kong, India, Iran Islamic Rep, Ireland, Israel, Italy, Japan, Korea Rep, Mexico, Nepal, Netherlands, New Zealand, Nigeria, Norway, Peru, Poland, Portugal, Romania, Russia, Serbia, Slovenia, Spain, Sweden, Switzerland, Thailand, Türkiye, UK, Ukraine, United Arab Emirates, USA, Venezuela.
NGO Relations Member of (3): *Association of Learned and Professional Society Publishers (ALPSP, #02786)*; *International Union of Biological Sciences (IUBS, #15760)*; *International Union of Geological Sciences (IUGS, #15777)*.
[2022.10.18/XD0248/v/**D**]

- ♦ European Association of Search and Database Publishing (inactive)

♦ European Association for Secure Transactions (EAST) 06202

Exec Dir 3 Walker Street, Edinburgh, EH3 7JY, UK. T. +441315100268. E-mail: coordinator@easteam.eu.
URL: https://www.association-secure-transactions.eu/
History 2004. Former names and other names: *European ATM Security Team* – former (2004 to 2017). Registration: EU Transparency Register, No/ID: 480357824530-10. **Aims** Improve public/private sector cross-border cooperation in the fight against organized cross-border *crime*. **Activities** Events/meetings; knowledge management/information dissemination.
Members National; Associate. National members in 35 countries:
Austria, Belgium, Brazil, Bulgaria, Canada, Cyprus, Czechia, Denmark, Finland, France, Germany, Greece, Hungary, Indonesia, Ireland, Italy, Liechtenstein, Luxembourg, Malta, Mexico, Netherlands, Norway, Poland, Portugal, Romania, Russia, Serbia, Slovakia, South Africa, Spain, Sweden, Switzerland, Türkiye, UK, Ukraine.
Associate members in 53 countries and territories:

Australia, Belarus, Belgium, Brunei Darussalam, Bulgaria, Cambodia, Canada, Colombia, Croatia, Cyprus, Czechia, Denmark, Egypt, Finland, France, Germany, Greece, Hong Kong, Hungary, Iceland, Indonesia, Iran Islamic Rep, Israel, Italy, Japan, Luxembourg, Macau, Malaysia, Malta, Mexico, Myanmar, Netherlands, New Zealand, Norway, Philippines, Poland, Portugal, Romania, Russia, Singapore, Slovenia, South Africa, Spain, Switzerland, Taiwan, Thailand, Türkiye, UK, United Arab Emirates, Uruguay, USA, Vietnam.
IGO Relations Cooperates with (3): *ASEANAPOL (#01138)*; *Council of Europe (CE, #04881)*; *International Criminal Police Organization – INTERPOL (ICPO-INTERPOL, #13110).* [2021.02.22/XM8695/**D**]

♦ European Association of Securities Dealers (inactive)
♦ European Association of Senior Hospital Physicians (#02577)

♦ European Association of Service-Learning in Higher Education (EASLHE) 06203

Registered Address Prinsstraat 14, 2000 Antwerp, Belgium. E-mail: contact@easlhe.eu.
URL: https://www.easlhe.eu/

History 21 Sep 2019, Antwerp (Belgium). Founded at 2nd European Conference of Service-Learning in Higher Education, succeeding the European Network of Service-Learning in Higher Education, which had been founded, 2017, Galway (Ireland). Registration: Banque Carrefour des Entreprises, No/ID: 0735.468.351, Start date: 22 Aug 2019, Belgium. **Aims** Promote service-learning in higher education in Europe; foster scholarly activities related to it. **Structure** General Assembly; Board of Directors. **Languages** English. **Staff** 19.00 FTE, voluntary. **Finance** Sources: members' dues. **Activities** Advocacy/lobbying/activism; guidance/assistance/consulting; knowledge management/information dissemination; networking/liaising; research/documentation; training/education. **Events** *European Conference on Service-Learning in Higher Education* Rotterdam (Netherlands) 2022, *European Conference on Service-Learning in Higher Education* Bucharest (Romania) 2021, *European Conference on Service-Learning in Higher Education* 2020, *European Conference on Service-Learning in Higher Education* Antwerp (Belgium) 2019, *European Conference on Service-Learning in Higher Education* Madrid (Spain) 2018. **Publications** *EASLHE Newsletter Learn to engage – engage to learn* in English. *Practical guide on e-Service-Learning in response to COVID-19* (2020) in English.
Members Full in 11 countries:
Austria, Belgium, Croatia, Germany, Italy, Netherlands, Portugal, Romania, Slovakia, Spain, UK. [2022/AA1371/**D**]

♦ European Association of Service Providers for Persons with Disabilities (EASPD) 06204

Asociación Europea de Suministradores de Servicios para Personas con Minusvalias – Europese Vereniging van Voorzieningen voor Personen met een Handicap – Associazione Europea di Centri che Offrono Servizi per Persone Handicappate
SG Rue du Commerce 72, 1040 Brussels, Belgium. T. +3222337720. E-mail: info@easpd.eu.
URL: http://www.easpd.eu/

History 1996. Current statutes adopted 11 Dec 2004, Brussels (Belgium). Took over activities from *Providers' European Network (PEN, inactive)*. Former names and other names: *European Association for Service Providers for Persons with Disability* – alias. Registration: No/ID: 0478.078.455, Start date: 22 Feb 1999, Belgium; EU Transparency Register, No/ID: 120906010805-50, Start date: 12 Mar 2013. **Aims** Promote equal opportunities for people with disabilities through effective and high-quality service systems. **Structure** General Assembly (meets at least twice a year); Board; Executive Committee; Standing Committees (4); Interest Groups (6); Secretariat. **Languages** Dutch, English, French, German, Italian, Romanian, Spanish. **Staff** 10.00 FTE, paid. **Finance** Members' dues. Project funding from *European Commission (EC, #06633)*; Brussels (Belgium) Capital Region. **Activities** Events/meetings; research/documentation. **Events** *DDSkills Conference* Brussels (Belgium) 2022, *EURECO Platform Forum* Brussels (Belgium) 2022, *Inclusive University Digital Education Project Final Conference* Brussels (Belgium) 2022, *Risk Management in NGOs – Why Does it Matter?* Brussels (Belgium) 2022, *Conference* Brussels (Belgium) 2021. **Publications** *Newsletter* (annual); *Newsflashes* (8 a year). Annual Report; position papers on quality of life; conference and workshop reports; action plans; conference proceedings; leaflets; best practices on employment; press releases; news.
Members Categories: Umbrella Member Organization (UMO); Single Agency Member Organization (SAMO); Observers; Corresponding Partner (outside membership addressing research units, university departments, authorities and individuals in any part of the world). Membership open to governmental organizations and schools/centres providing education to people with disabilities and to all member countries of the Council of Europe. Represents service provider organizations (over 8,000) in European countries. UMOs in 14 countries:
Austria, Belgium, Estonia, Finland, France, Germany, Greece, Hungary, Ireland, Luxembourg, Netherlands, North Macedonia, Portugal, UK.
SAMOs in 22 countries:
Austria, Belgium, Bulgaria, Croatia, Cyprus, Czechia, France, Germany, Greece, Hungary, Ireland, Italy, Lithuania, Moldova, Netherlands, North Macedonia, Portugal, Romania, Slovenia, Spain, Sweden, UK.
Included in the above, 4 organizations listed in this Yearbook:
Baltic Sea Forum (#03142); *European Action of the Disabled (#05825)*; *European Cooperation in Anthroposophical Curative Education and Social Therapy (ECCE, #06783)*; *European Union of Supported Employment (EUSE, #09018).*
Consultative Status Consultative status granted from: *Council of Europe (CE, #04881)* (Participatory Status).
IGO Relations Member of: *European Economic and Social Committee (EESC, #06963)*; *European Parliament (EP, #08146)*. Cooperates with: *European Union Agency for Fundamental Rights (FRA, #08969)*. *ILO (#11123)*.
NGO Relations Member of: *Civil Society Europe*; *EU Alliance for a democratic, social and sustainable European Semester (EU Semester Alliance, #05565)*; *European Coalition for Community Living (ECCL, #06590)*; *European Federation of Family Employment (EFFE, #07118)*; *Global Partnership for Disability and Development (GPDD, #10530)*; *Social Platform (#19344)*; *Social Services Europe (#19347)*. Instrumental in setting up: *Federation of European Social Employers (FESE, #09545)*. Cooperates with: *International Association for the Scientific Study of Intellectual and Developmental Disabilities (IASSIDD, #12153)*. Supports: *European Alliance for the Statute of the European Association (EASEA, #05886).* [2020/XD7283/y/**D**]

♦ European Association for Service Providers for Persons with Disability / see European Association of Service Providers for Persons with Disabilities (#06204)
♦ European Association for Shipping Informatics (inactive)
♦ European Association of Ships in Bottles (unconfirmed)
♦ European Association SIBIU2020 for Education and Culture (unconfirmed)

♦ European Association for Signal Processing (EURASIP) 06205

Pres EE Dept, ESAT/SISTA, KU Leuven, Kasteelpark Arenberg 10, 3001 Leuven, Belgium. T. +3216321060. Fax +3216321970.
URL: http://www.eurasip.org/

History 1 Sep 1978, Florence (Italy). Former names and other names: *European Association for Signal, Speech and Image Processing (EURASIP)* – former (1 Sep 1978). **Aims** Improve communication between groups and individuals that work within the multidisciplinary, fast growing field of Signal Processing in Europe and elsewhere. **Structure** General Assembly (every 2 years); Administrative Committee (AdCom); Advisory Committee. **Languages** English. **Staff** 20.00 FTE, voluntary. **Finance** Sources: members' dues. Annual budget: 80,000 USD. **Activities** Events/meetings; knowledge management/information dissemination; training/education. **Events** *EUSIPCO : European Signal Processing Conference* Amsterdam (Netherlands) 2021, *EUSIPCO : European Signal Processing Conference* Amsterdam (Netherlands) 2020, *European Conference on Networks and Communications* Piscataway, NJ (USA) 2020, *EUSIPCO : European Signal Processing Conference* La Coruña (Spain) 2019, *European Conference on Networks and Communications* Valencia (Spain) 2019. **Publications** *EURASIP Newsletter* (10 a year); *Applied Signal Processing*; *Audio, Speech and Music Processing*; *Bioinformatics and Systems Biology*; *Embedded Systems*; *Image Communication*; *Information Security*; *Signal Processing*; *Speech Communication*; *Wireless Communications and Networking*. *Signal Processing and Communications* – book series. Conference proceedings.
Members Institutional; Individual; Student. Members in 26 countries:
Austria, Belgium, Canada, Denmark, Egypt, Finland, France, Germany, Greece, Hungary, India, Israel, Italy, Japan, Montenegro, Morocco, Netherlands, Norway, Portugal, Serbia, Spain, Sweden, Switzerland, Tunisia, UK, USA.
NGO Relations Accredited by (3): *Institute of Electrical and Electronics Engineers (IEEE, #11259)*; *International Computer Science Conventions (ICSC)*; *SPIE (#19919).* [2021.06.14/XD9544/**D**]

♦ European Association for Signal, Speech and Image Processing / see European Association for Signal Processing (#06205)
♦ European Association of Silica Producers / see European Association of Industrial Silica Producers (#06082)
♦ European Association of Single-Cell Protein Producers (inactive)

♦ European Association of Sinological Librarians (EASL) 06206

Chair Asian Library, Leiden Univ Libraries, PO Box 9501, 2300 RA Leiden, Netherlands. T. +31715273443.
Visiting Address Witte Singel 27, 2311 BG Leiden, Netherlands.
URL: http://www.easl.org/

Events *Annual Conference* Zurich (Switzerland) 2016, *Annual Conference* Oxford (UK) 2015, *Annual Conference* Stockholm (Sweden) 2014, *Annual Conference* Leiden (Netherlands) 2013, *Annual Conference* Paris (France) 2012. **Publications** *Bulletin of the European Association of Sinological Librarians.* [2019.10.07/XD5714/**D**]

♦ European Association for Skills and Knowledge (inactive)

♦ European Association of Small and Medium sized Enterprises (SME Safety) 06207

Contact Rue Jacques de Lalaing 4, 1040 Brussels, Belgium. T. +3222850726. E-mail: info@sme-safety.eu.
URL: http://www.sme-safety.eu/

History Registered in accordance with Belgian law. **Aims** Safeguard the interests of European SMEs in the safety sector in the international regulatory and policy domain; represent members' interests and views vis-à-vis European and international standardization bodies; inform members on the development of standards and legislation in the safety sector. **Structure** General Assembly; Administrative Council. **Events** *Joint Workshop on Personal Protective Equipment* Brussels (Belgium) 2019.
Members Full in 7 countries:
Czechia, France, Germany, Hungary, Italy, Poland, Spain.
Regional member:
European Builders Confederation (EBC, #06408).
NGO Relations Member of: *Small Business Standards (SBS, #19311)*. Liaison Organization of: *Comité européen de normalisation (CEN, #04162).* [2015/XJ9360/**D**]

♦ European Association for SME Transfer (Transeo) 06208

SG Av Maurice Destenay 13, 4000 Liège, Belgium. T. +3242200180. E-mail: info@transeo-association.eu.
URL: http://www.transeo-association.eu/

History 9 Dec 2010, Brussels (Belgium), following European Conference on SME Transfer (Transeo Conference), May 2009, Spa (Belgium). Registered in accordance with Belgian law. EU Transparency Register: 14605998391-97. **Aims** Encourage, sustain and promote collaboration and exchange of good practices and information in the field of *small and medium enterprise* (SME) transfer among *European* professionals in private, (semi-)public and academic sectors, so as to stimulate the *business* transfer market at both local and international levels. **Structure** General Assembly; Board of Directors; Secretariat. **Languages** English. **Events** *General Assembly* Paris (France) 2013. **Publications** E-Newsletter.
Members Active; Supporting. Members in 15 countries:
Belgium, Canada, Croatia, Denmark, Finland, France, Germany, Italy, Luxembourg, Morocco, Netherlands, Norway, Poland, Spain, Sweden.
IGO Relations *European Commission (EC, #06633)* – DG Grow. [2018.02.09/XJ2285/**E**]

♦ European Association of Social Anthropologists (EASA) 06209

Association Européenne des Anthropologues Sociaux
Sec c/o RAI, 50 Fitzroy Street, London, W1T 5BT, UK.
URL: http://www.easaonline.org/

History 14 Jan 1989, Italy. Founded at inaugural meeting. Current constitution amended most recently Jul 2016. Registration: Charity Commission, No/ID: 1108186, England and Wales; Companies House, No/ID: 05181210, England and Wales. **Aims** Improve understanding of world societies by promoting education and research in social anthropology; encourage professional communication and cooperation between European social anthropologists. **Structure** General Meeting (annual); Forum of Members; Executive Committee. **Languages** English, French. **Staff** All honorary posts. **Finance** Sources: grants; members' dues. **Activities** Events/meetings. **Events** *Conference* Belfast (UK) 2022, *Biennial Conference* 2020, *Why the World Needs Anthropologists Symposium* Prague (Czechia) 2020, *Why the World Needs Anthropologists Symposium* Oslo (Norway) 2019, *Biennial Conference* Stockholm (Sweden) 2018. **Publications** *Social Anthropology – Anthropologie Sociale* (4 a year) – journal; *Newsletter* (3 a year). *EASA Book Series.*
Members Founder; Ordinary; Honorary; Associate; Students. Individual social anthropologists in 79 countries and territories:
Albania, Argentina, Australia, Austria, Bahrain, Bangladesh, Belarus, Belgium, Bosnia-Herzegovina, Brazil, Bulgaria, Canada, Chile, China, Colombia, Croatia, Cyprus, Czechia, Denmark, Ecuador, Egypt, Estonia, Finland, France, Germany, Ghana, Greece, Guatemala, Hungary, Iceland, India, Indonesia, Iran Islamic Rep, Ireland, Israel, Italy, Japan, Jordan, Kenya, Korea Rep, Latvia, Lebanon, Lithuania, Luxembourg, Malta, Mexico, Morocco, Netherlands, New Zealand, North Macedonia, Norway, Pakistan, Peru, Philippines, Poland, Portugal, Romania, Russia, San Marino, Serbia, Singapore, Slovakia, Slovenia, South Africa, Spain, Sudan, Sweden, Switzerland, Syrian AR, Taiwan, Thailand, Togo, Trinidad-Tobago, Türkiye, UK, Ukraine, Uruguay, USA, Vietnam.
NGO Relations Member of (2): *Initiative for Science in Europe (ISE, #11214)*; *World Council of Anthropological Associations (WCAA, #21317)*. Affiliated with (1): *European Network for Psychological Anthropology (ENPA, #07977)*. Instrumental in setting up (1): *Les collections africaines en Europe (no recent information)*. Sister organization: *Société internationale d'ethnologie et de folklore (SIEF, #19481).* [2022/XD3384/v/**D**]

♦ European Association for Social and Cultural Progress (inactive)
♦ European Association of Social Medicine (no recent information)

♦ European Association of Social Psychology (EASP) 06210

Exec Officer Universiteitssingel 40, PO Box 616, 6200 MD Maastricht, Netherlands. E-mail: office@easp.eu.
URL: http://www.easp.eu/

History 1964. Former names and other names: *European Association of Experimental Social Psychology (EAESP)* – former (1964 to 2008). Registration: Start date: 1964, Netherlands. **Aims** Secure promotion and development of theoretical and experimental social psychology within Europe and exchange of information between European members and other associations throughout the world. **Structure** Members' Meeting (every 3 years); Executive Committee; Working groups; Committees. **Languages** English. **Staff** 0.50 FTE, paid; 7.00 FTE, voluntary. **Finance** Members' dues. Other sources: donations; legacies; proceeds of publications; subventions; interest. **Activities** Events/meetings; training/education; research/documentation. **Events** *Triennial General Meeting* Krakow (Poland) 2023, *Triennial General Meeting* Krakow (Poland) 2021, *Triennial General Meeting* Krakow (Poland) 2020, *Triennial General Meeting* Granada (Spain) 2017, *Triennial General Meeting* Amsterdam (Netherlands) 2014. **Publications** *European Bulletin of Social Psychology*; *European Journal of Social Psychology*; *European Review of Social Psychology*. *European Monographs in Social Psychology.*
Members Individuals expected to make a substantial contribution to the development of experimental and/or theoretical social psychology (900) in 29 countries:
Austria, Belgium, Bulgaria, Croatia, Czechia, Denmark, Estonia, Finland, France, Germany, Greece, Hungary, Italy, Lithuania, Montenegro, Netherlands, Norway, Poland, Portugal, Romania, Russia, Serbia, Slovakia, Slovenia, Spain, Sweden, Switzerland, UK, Ukraine.
Postgraduate students (237) – individuals studying for a doctoral degree in social psychology, based at an institute of higher education in Europe. Membership countries not specified.
NGO Relations Member of: *Initiative for Science in Europe (ISE, #11214)*. Affiliated to: *International Union of Psychological Science (IUPsyS, #15807).* [2021/XD4267/**D**]

♦ European Association for the Social Rehabilitation of Dying (inactive)

♦ European Association of Societies of Aesthetic Plastic Surgery (EASAPS) 06211

Contact 13 rue Le Corbusier, 92100 Boulogne, France. T. +33607037685. Fax +33141109860. E-mail: info@easaps.org.
URL: http://www.easaps.org/

History 2006, Lille (France). **Aims** Harmonize scientific-level *legislation* on cosmetic surgery throughout Europe. **Structure** Steering Committee. **Languages** English. **Staff** 0.50 FTE, voluntary. **Finance** Sources: members' dues. Annual budget: 15,000 EUR. **Events** *Biennial Meeting* Gothenburg (Sweden) 2024, *Biennial Meeting* Lisbon (Portugal) 2022, *Biennial Meeting* Lisbon (Portugal) 2021, *Biennial Meeting* Bruges (Belgium) 2019, *Biennial Meeting* Bucharest (Romania) 2017. **Publications** *Aesthetic Plastic Surgery* – journal.
Members Individuals (2700) in 13 countries:
Bulgaria, France, Hungary, Israel, Italy, Lithuania, Portugal, Romania, Russia, Spain, Switzerland, Türkiye, UK.
IGO Relations *European Commission (EC, #06633).* **NGO Relations** Instrumental in setting up (1): *European Society of Aesthetic Plastic Surgery (ESAPS, #08510).* [2021/XM8289/**D**]

♦ European Association for Sociology of Sport (EASS) 06212

Pres University of Copenhagen, Nørre Allé 51, 2200 Copenhagen, Denmark.
SG University of Barcelona, Gran Via de les Corts Catalanes 585, 08007 Barcelona, Spain.
URL: http://www.eass-sportsociology.eu/

History 16 Nov 2001, Vienna (Austria). **Aims** Promote cooperation between experts dealing with social issues related to physical activity and sport in Europe. **Structure** General Assembly (every 2 years). Executive Board. **Events** *The Role of Sport Sociology in Interdisciplinary Research* Tübingen (Germany) 2022, *Sports in the face of the global health crisis of COVID-19 – Great social challenges* Córdoba (Spain) 2021, *Conference* Southampton (UK) 2020, *Conference* Bø (Norway) 2019, *Sport, Discriminations and Inclusion* Bordeaux (France) 2018. **Publications** *European Journal for Sport and Society (ejss)* (4 a year). [2022/XM0014/**D**]

♦ European Association of Software Science and Technology (EASST) 06213

Pres Univ of Leicester, University Rd, Leicester, LE1 7RH, UK.
URL: http://www.easst.org/

History Registered in accordance with German law. **Aims** Promote development of science and engineering on software intensive-systems that play an increasing role in Europe's way into the information society. **Structure** General Assembly (annual). Board, comprising President, Vice-President, Treasurer, Secretary and 4 further members. **Finance** Members' dues. **Events** *General Assembly* Uppsala (Sweden) 2017, *ETAPS: European joint conferences on theory and practice of software* York (UK) 2009, *International conference on foundations of software science and computation structures* York (UK) 2009, *International conference on fundamental approaches to software engineering* York (UK) 2009, *International conferences on tools and algorithms for the construction and analysis of systems* York (UK) 2009. **Publications** *EASST Newsletter* (irregular). **NGO Relations** Joint conference with: *European Association for Programming Languages and Systems (EAPLS, #06171); European Association for Theoretical Computer Science (EATCS, #06253).* Member of: *European Forum for ICST (#07316).* [2017/XM0362/**D**]

♦ European Association for Solar Energy / see EUROSOLAR – European Association for Renewable Energy (#09183)
♦ European Association of South Asian Archaeologists / see European Association for South Asian Archaeology and Art (#06214)

♦ European Association for South Asian Archaeology and Art (EASAA) 06214

Pres address not obtained.
URL: http://easaa.org/

History 1970. Former names and other names: *Association of South Asian Archaeologists in Western Europe* – former (1970 to 1991); *European Association of South Asian Archaeologists* – former (1991); *Association européenne des archéologues d'Asie du Sud* – former (1991). **Aims** Unite scholars working in the disciplines of South Asian archaeology, art history, architecture and heritage. **Structure** Meeting (every 2 years); Executive Committee. Host of each meeting acts as President. Semi-Permanent Secretary. Organizing Committee. **Languages** English. **Staff** Voluntary. **Finance** No members' dues. Conference registration fees. **Activities** Events/meetings; networking/liaising. **Events** *Biennial Conference* Barcelona (Spain) 2022, *Biennial Conference* Barcelona (Spain) 2021, *Biennial Conference* Barcelona (Spain) 2020, *Biennial Conference* Naples (Italy) 2018, *Biennial Conference* Cardiff (UK) 2016. **Publications** Meeting proceedings.
Members Individuals representing 10 countries:
Austria, Finland, France, Germany, Italy, Netherlands, Poland, Spain, Sweden, UK. [2020.03.05/XD8801/v/**D**]

♦ European Association for South Asian Studies (EASAS) 06215

Secretariat Büro EG, Adolfstr 39, 53111 Bonn, Germany. E-mail: anne.schnellen_easas@gmx.de.
Pres University of Vienna, Dept of South Asian/Tibetan/Buddhist Studies, Bereich Südasienkunde, Spitalgasse 2, Uni Campus AAKh, Hof 2-1, 1090 Vienna, Austria.
Vice-Pres University of Turin, Fac di Lingue e Letterature Straniere, Studio al Piano Terreno, Via Giulia di Barolo 3/a, Turin TO, Italy.
URL: http://www.easas.eu/

History Founded 1968, Cambridge (UK); reconstituted 1996, Copenhagen (Denmark); again 2009, Bonn (Germany). **Aims** Support and promote South Asian Studies in all countries of Europe. **Structure** Council. **Languages** English, German. **Staff** None. **Finance** Members' dues. **Events** *European Conference on South Asian Studies* Turin (Italy) 2023, *European Conference on South Asian Studies* Vienna (Austria) 2021, *European Conference on South Asian Studies* Vienna (Austria) 2020, *European Conference on South Asian Studies* Paris (France) 2018, *European Conference on South Asian Studies* Warsaw (Poland) 2016. **Publications** *EASAS Newsletter. SAMAJ-EASAS Special Issue.*
Members Ordinary; Corresponding; Corporate; Associate; Honorary. Members in 33 countries:
Australia, Bangladesh, Belgium, Bulgaria, Canada, China, Denmark, Finland, France, Germany, Hungary, India, Ireland, Israel, Italy, Japan, Lithuania, Nepal, Netherlands, New Zealand, Norway, Pakistan, Poland, Portugal, Russia, Singapore, South Africa, Sri Lanka, Sweden, Switzerland, Türkiye, UK, USA. [2016.12.22/XD4889/**D**]

♦ European Association of Southeast Asian Archaeologists (EurASEAA) 06216

Contact address not obtained. E-mail: euraseaa@nomadit.co.uk – contact@euraseaa-poznan2017.pl.
Facebook: https://www.facebook.com/EurASEAA14/

History 1986. **Events** *Conference* Poznań (Poland) 2017, *International Conference / Conference* Paris (France) 2015, *Conference* Dublin (Ireland) 2012, *Conference* Berlin (Germany) 2010, *International conference / Conference* Leiden (Netherlands) 2008. **Members** No fixed membership, membership lasts for the duration of the conference. [2017/XD8843/**D**]

♦ European Association for South-East Asian Studies (EUROSEAS) . . 06217

Secretariat PO Box 9515, 2300 RA Leiden, Netherlands. E-mail: euroseas@kitlv.nl.
URL: http://www.euroseas.org/

History 18 May 1992. **Aims** Enhance Southeast Asian studies in Europe; assist European scholars wanting to integrate their work on Southeast Asia with other specialists in the field and in establishing contacts with specialists in the Southeast Asia region itself; provide scholars from Southeast Asia and other areas outside Europe with greater access to European research facilities; support existing institutions; make international funding agencies aware of this branch of study. **Structure** General Meeting (at least every 4 years, at conference). Board, comprising 2 members from each of 7 geographical regions in Europe plus one representative of other countries. Executive Committee, comprising Chairman, Vice-Chairman, Secretary and 2 advisers. Advisory Council comprising up to 8 scholars from Southeast Asia. Secretariat. **Languages** English. **Staff** 0.50 FTE, paid. **Finance** Members' dues: Individual euro 35; MA Student euro 17.50; Corporate euro 70. Subsidies. Budget (annual): about euro 102,100. **Activities** Organizes interdisciplinary conferences; initiates and coordinates fund raising and research; provides general information for individuals and institutions worldwide. **Events** *Conference* Paris (France) 2022, *Conference* Olomouc (Czechia) 2021, *Conference* Berlin (Germany) 2019, *Conference* Vienna (Austria) 2015, *Conference* Lisbon (Portugal) 2013. **Publications** *European Newsletter of Southeast Asian Studies (ENSEAS)* (2 a year). *European Directory of South-East Asian Studies* (1997). Conference abstracts.
Members Individual scholars, scholarly associations, institutions and other organizations focused on SE Asia. Members in 25 countries:
Australia, Austria, Belgium, Brunei Darussalam, Denmark, Finland, France, Germany, Indonesia, Ireland, Italy, Luxembourg, Malaysia, Netherlands, Norway, Philippines, Poland, Portugal, Russia, Singapore, Spain, Sweden, Switzerland, UK, USA.
IGO Relations *NIAS-Nordisk Institut for Asienstudier (NIAS, #17132).* **NGO Relations** Provides secretariat for: *European Vietnam Studies Network (EUROVIET, no recent information).* [2020/XD4093/**D**]

♦ European Association for Special Education (no recent information)
♦ European Association for Specialist Fire Protection / see European Association for Passive Fire Protection (#06143)
♦ European Association for Special Transport and Rigging / see European Association of Abnormal Road Transport and Mobile Cranes (#05923)
♦ European Association for Specialty Yeast Products (unconfirmed)
♦ European Association for Spectral Imaging / see International Association for Spectral Imaging (#12176)

♦ European Association of Sport Employers (EASE) 06218

Gen Sec c/o WOS, Postbus 185, 6800 AD Arnhem, Netherlands. T. +31264824450. E-mail: ease@easesport.eu.
URL: http://www.easesport.eu/

History Jan 2003. Registered in accordance with French law. **Aims** Promote and develop representation in Europe; participate in *European Sectoral Social Dialogue Committee (ESSDC)*; negotiate at European level on behalf of employers in sports. **Structure** Board; Permanent Committees (3). **Languages** English. **Staff** 1.00 FTE, paid. **Activities** Networking/liaising.
Members Full in 6 countries:
France, Ireland, Netherlands, Spain, Sweden, UK.
European organization (1):
Rugby Europe (#18998).
NGO Relations Member of: *European Sports Workforce Development Alliance (ESWDA, #08823).* [2020.03.06/XM2667/**D**]

♦ European Association of Sporting Ammunition Manufacturers / see Association of European Manufacturers of Sporting Ammunition (#02522)

♦ European Association for Sport Management (EASM) 06219

SG PO Box 450304, 50878 Cologne, Germany. T. +4922149826093. E-mail: office@easm.net.
URL: http://www.easm.net/

History 1993. **Aims** Promote, stimulate and encourage studies, research, scholarly writing and professional development in the field of sport management. **Structure** Board. **Languages** English. **Staff** 0.50 FTE, paid. **Finance** Members' dues. Other sources: conference proceeds; allowances; congress proceeds; international projects. **Activities** Events/meetings; certification/accreditation; training/education; guidance/assistance/consulting; awards/prizes/competitions. **Events** *EASM Virtual Conference* Cologne (Germany) 2021, *EASM Conference* London (UK) 2021, *Sport Management Virtual Conference* 2020, *Sport Management Conference* Seville (Spain) 2019, *Annual Conference / Annual Congress* Dublin (Ireland) 2015. **Publications** *European Sport Management Quarterly.*
Members Organizations in 5 countries and territories:
Belgium, Hong Kong, Italy, Portugal, UK.
Individuals in 40 countries and territories:
Albania, Argentina, Australia, Austria, Belgium, Bulgaria, Canada, Cyprus, Czechia, Denmark, Estonia, Finland, France, Germany, Greece, Hong Kong, Hungary, India, Ireland, Italy, Japan, Latvia, Lithuania, Luxembourg, Netherlands, New Zealand, Nigeria, Norway, Poland, Portugal, Romania, Russia, San Marino, Spain, Sweden, Switzerland, Taiwan, Türkiye, UK, USA.
IGO Relations Member of (1): *Enlarged Partial Agreement on Sport (EPAS, #05487)* (Consultative Committee). **NGO Relations** Member of (3): *European Network of Sport Education (ENSE, #08012); International Council of Sport Science and Physical Education (ICSSPE, #13077); World Association for Sport Management (WASM, #21194).* [2021/XD7749/**D**]

♦ European Association of State Lotteries / see European State Lotteries and Toto Association (#08833)
♦ European Association of State Lotteries and Lottos / see European State Lotteries and Toto Association (#08833)

♦ European Association of State Territorial Representatives (EASTR) . 06220

Association européenne de représentants territoriaux de l'état (AERTE)

Gen Sec Fort de Charenton, 94706 Maisons-Alfort CEDEX, France. T. +33157440788.
URL: http://www.aerte-asso.org/

History 2000, to give a juridical basis to the European days, started in 1993. Registered in accordance with Belgian law: 28862/2000. **Aims** Allow exchange of experiences between state territorial representatives from European countries. **Structure** Board of Directors; Executive Board; Associated Partners. **Languages** English, French. **Staff** 2.00 FTE, paid. **Finance** Members' dues. **Activities** Events/meetings. **Events** *European Days* Istanbul (Turkey) 2015, *European Days* Liège (Belgium) 2014, *European Days* Bergen (Norway) 2013, *European Days* Paris (France) 2012, *Euro-Mediterranean Observatory of State Territorial Action* Marrakech (Morocco) 2011.
Members Full in 15 countries:
Belgium, Finland, France, Germany, Hungary, Italy, Morocco, Netherlands, Norway, Poland, Romania, Slovakia, Sweden, Switzerland, Türkiye. [2018.08.24/XM2938/**E**]

♦ European Association of State Veterinary Officers (EASVO) 06221

Union européenne des vétérinaires fonctionnaires (UEVF)

Contact c/o FVE, Rue Victor Oudart 7, 1030 Brussels, Belgium. T. +3225337020. E-mail: info@fve.org.
URL: http://www.fve.org/about_fve/sections/EASVO.php

History 9 Oct 1980, Avignon (France). Founded as a specialist interest group of *Federation of Veterinarians of Europe (#09713).* **Aims** Promote, preserve and protect the proper ethical standards and professional interests of veterinarians directly employed by the national or regional governments of European countries; present the views of these state veterinary officers to the Federation of Veterinarians of Europe, European Union institutions, national and regional governments and other organizations; promote professional and fraternal relations between state veterinary officers in different countries. **Structure** Meeting (2 a year); Executive Committee, consisting of President, 2 Vice-Presidents, Secretary and Treasurer. **Languages** English. **Staff** Voluntary. **Finance** Sources: members' dues. Annual budget: 2,500 GBP. **Activities** Events/meetings. **Events** *General Assembly* Brussels (Belgium) 2019, *Meeting* Basel (Switzerland) 2010, *Meeting* Brussels (Belgium) 2009, *Meeting* Vienna (Austria) 2008, *Meeting* Krakow (Poland) 2007. **Publications** Minutes of meetings.
Members Delegates of veterinary associations in 22 countries:
Austria, Belgium, Czechia, Denmark, Estonia, Finland, France, Germany, Greece, Iceland, Ireland, Italy, Latvia, Lithuania, Netherlands, Norway, Poland, Portugal, Spain, Sweden, Switzerland, UK. [2022.05.11/XD6579/v/**D**]

♦ European Association of Steel Drum Manufacturers 06222

Syndicat européen de l'industrie des fûts en acier (SEFA) – Verband der Europäischen Stahlfassindustrie

Pres c/o Agoria, Diamant Building, Bd A Reyers 80, 1030 Brussels, Belgium. T. +33490965853. Fax +33490965853.
URL: http://www.sefa.be/

History 1953. Previously also referred to as *European Syndicate on Steel Drums – Syndicat européen des fûts en acier (SEFA)* and *European Secretariat of the Steel Drums Industry – Secretariat européen des fûts en acier – Vereniging van de Europese Industrie van Stalen Vaten.* Registered in accordance with Belgian law. Current statutes adopted 17 Jun 2006. **Aims** Promote general interests of the new Steeldrum Industry. **Structure** General Assembly (annual). Board, comprising President, Chairman, 7 Vice-Chairmen and 2 Permanent Committee Vice-Chairmen. Transport and Regulatory Committee; Ad hoc Working Groups. **Languages** English. **Finance** Members' dues. **Events** *International conference on industrial packaging* San Francisco, CA (USA) 2006.
Members Associate; Supplier. National groups in 14 countries:
Belgium, Czechia, Denmark, Finland, France, Germany, Iran Islamic Rep, Israel, Italy, Netherlands, Spain, Türkiye, UK, United Arab Emirates.

IGO Relations Recognized by: *European Commission (EC, #06633).* **NGO Relations** In liaison with the technical committees of: *International Organization for Standardization (ISO, #14473).* Member of: *European Industrial Packaging Association (EIPA, #07529); International Confederation of Drum Manufacturers (ICDM, #12857).* [2010.06.01/XD9667/t/**D**]

♦ European Association of Steel Heating Boiler Manufacturers (inactive)

♦ European Association for Storage of Energy (EASE) 06223

SG Av Adolphe Lacomblé 59/8, 1030 Brussels, Belgium. T. +3227432982. E-mail: info@ease-storage.eu.

Communications – Events Manager address not obtained.

URL: http://www.ease-storage.eu/

History 2011. Registration: Banque-Carrefour des Entreprises, No/ID: 0841.068.588, Start date: 16 Nov 2011, Belgium; EU Transparency Register, No/ID: 43859808000-87, Start date: 7 Feb 2012. **Aims** Actively support deployment of energy storage as an indispensable instrument in order to improve the flexibility of and deliver services to the energy system with respect to EU energy and climate policy. **Structure** General Assembly; Executive Board; Secretariat. Committees (3): Technology; Strategy; Communications. **Activities** Advocacy/lobbying/activism; awards/prizes/competitions; knowledge management/information dissemination; networking/liaising; research/documentation. **Events** *Energy Storage Global Conference (ESGC)* Brussels (Belgium) 2023, *Energy Storage Global Conference* Brussels (Belgium) 2022, *Energy Storage Global Conference* Brussels (Belgium) 2021, *Energy Storage Global Conference* Brussels (Belgium) 2020, *Energy Storage Global Conference* Brussels (Belgium) 2018. **NGO Relations** Member of: *Federation of European and International Associations Established in Belgium (FAIB, #09508).* Cooperates with: *Association of European Automative and Industrial Battery Manufacturers (EUROBAT, #02498); European Hydrogen Alliance (EHA, #07511); Gas Infrastructure Europe (GIE, #10073); Union of the Electricity Industry – Eurelectric (#20379)*; national organizations. [2021/XJ7991/**D**]

♦ European Association for the Streamlining of Energy Exchange-gas (EASEE-gas) 06224

Association européenne pour la rationalisation des échanges d'énergie-gaz

SG Av de Tervueren 188A, PO Box 4, 1150 Brussels, Belgium. T. +3227611633. E-mail: easee-gas@kellencompany.com.

Headquarters Tour Pacific, 11-13 Cours Valmy, 92977 Paris La Défense CEDEX, France.

URL: https://easee-gas.eu/

History 14 Mar 2002, Paris (France). Registration: France; EU Transparency Register, No/ID: 807289724401-47. **Aims** Deliver efficient and harmonized solutions that support business processes across different actors in the gas value chain; facilitate transition to a sustainable and integrated energy system in Europe. **Structure** General Meeting of Members (GMoM); Board of Directors; Coordination Committee, Working groups (3) and Task Forces. Managed by office in Brussels (Belgium). **Languages** English. **Staff** 1.00 FTE, paid. **Finance** Sources: members' dues. **Activities** Events/meetings; guidance/assistance/consulting; knowledge management/information dissemination; networking/liaising; standards/guidelines. **Events** *Annual General Meeting of Members GMoM* Barcelona (Spain) 2023, *Annual General Meeting of Members GMoM* Porto (Portugal) 2019. **Publications** *EASEE-gas Newsletter* (4 a year). Annual Report.

Members Full (69) and service providers (15) in 18 countries:

Austria, Belgium, Czechia, France, Germany, Italy, Lithuania, Luxembourg, Netherlands, Norway, Poland, Portugal, Russia, Slovakia, Spain, Sweden, Switzerland, UK.

Included in the above, 9 organizations listed in this Yearbook:

Agency for the Cooperation of Energy Regulators (ACER, #00552); Association of the European Heating Industry (EHI, #02514); Eurogas (#05682); European Federation of Energy Traders (EFET, #07108); Gas Infrastructure Europe (GIE, #10073); International Association of Oil and Gas Producers (IOGP, #12053); International Federation of Industrial Energy Consumers, Europe (IFIEC – Europe, #13456); MARCOGAZ – Technical Association of the European Natural Gas Industry (#16572); Union of the Electricity Industry – Eurelectric (#20379).

NGO Relations Liaison Organization of: *Comité européen de normalisation (CEN, #04162).* [2023/XD8898/y/**D**]

♦ European Association for Structural Dynamics (EASD) 06225

Secretariat c/o System Dynamics Lab, Dep Mech Engineering, Univ of Thessaly, Leoforos Anthinon, Pedion Areos, 383 34 Volos, Greece. T. +302421074006. Fax +302421074012. E-mail: costasp@mie.uth.gr – costasp@uth.gr.

URL: http://www.easd.uth.gr/

History 1990, to organize *European Conference on Structural Dynamics (EURODYN).* **Events** *EURODYN : International Conference on Structural Dynamics* Athens (Greece) 2020, *EURODYN : International Conference on Structural Dynamics* Rome (Italy) 2017, *EURODYN : International Conference on Structural Dynamics* Porto (Portugal) 2014, *EURODYN : International Conference on Structural Dynamics* Leuven (Belgium) 2011, *EURODYN : International Conference on Structural Dynamics* Southampton (UK) 2008. [2014/XM1671/**F**]

♦ European Association Structural Fire Protection / see European Association for Passive Fire Protection (#06143)

♦ European Association of Students of Classical Philology (no recent information)

♦ European Association for Studies of Australia (EASA) 06226

Acting Treas 1 Chemin du Haut de St-Pierre, 14250 Tilly-Sur-Seulles, France.

URL: http://www.easa-australianstudies.net/

History Founded 1989. **Aims** Promote research in and teaching of Australian studies at European tertiary institutions. **Structure** General Meeting. Board, comprising President, General Secretary, Treasurer and 4 further members. **Languages** English. **Staff** Voluntary. **Finance** Members' dues. **Events** *Biennial Conference* Barcelona (Spain) 2018, *Biennial Conference* Veszprém (Hungary) 2015, *Conference on Transculturation and Aesthetics* Bergen (Norway) 2012, *Biennial conference* Presov (Slovakia) 2011, *Biennial conference* Palma (Spain) 2009. **Publications** *EASA Newsletter* (2 a year).

Members Ordinary; Associate; Corporate; Affiliated; Honorary. Scholars, students and teachers in 24 countries:

Australia, Austria, Belgium, Croatia, Czechia, Denmark, France, Germany, Hungary, Ireland, Italy, Luxembourg, New Zealand, Norway, Poland, Portugal, Serbia, Slovakia, Slovenia, Spain, Sweden, Switzerland, UK, USA.

NGO Relations Links with a number of national organizations active in the field. [2016/XD7518/v/**D**]

♦ European Association for Studies in Screen Translation (ESIST) ... 06227

Pres Univ of Macerata, Dept of Humanities, Via Illuminati 4, 62100 Macerata MC, Italy. T. +393477949441.

Vice-Pres Univ of Westminster, 309 Regent St, Marylebone, London, W1B 2UW, UK.

URL: http://www.esist.org/

History Founded 1995, Cardiff (UK). **Aims** Facilitate exchange of information and promote professional standards in the training and practice of screen translation. **Structure** General Meeting; Executive Board. **Languages** English. **Staff** Voluntary. **Finance** Members' dues. **Activities** Events/meetings; knowledge management/information dissemination; awards/prizes/competition; training/education; projects/programmes; networking/liaising. **Events** *International Conference on Media for All* Stockholm (Sweden) 2019, *Conference* Berlin (Germany) 2016, *Workshop* Poznań (Poland) 2016, *International Conference on Media for All* Sydney, NSW (Australia) 2015, *Conference* Bydgoszcz (Poland) 2014.

Members Full individuals in 31 countries and territories:

Argentina, Australia, Austria, Belgium, Brazil, Bulgaria, Canada, China, Croatia, Denmark, Finland, France, Germany, Greece, Hong Kong, India, Ireland, Italy, Netherlands, Norway, Pakistan, Poland, Portugal, Slovenia, South Africa, Spain, Sweden, Switzerland, UK, USA, Venezuela.

NGO Relations Member of: *International Network of Translation and Interpreting Studies Associations (INTISA, #14335).* [2017/XD7464/v/**D**]

♦ European Association on the Study of Acute Abdominal Pain (inactive)

♦ European Association for the Study of Bioprostheses (inactive)

♦ European Association for the Study of Diabetes (EASD) 06228

Association européenne pour l'étude du diabète – Europäische Gesellschaft für Diabetologie

Managing Dir Rheindorfer Weg 3, 40591 Düsseldorf, Germany. T. +492117584690. Fax +4921175846929. E-mail: secretariat@easd.org.

URL: http://www.easd.org/

History 1965, Montecatini (Italy). Registration: Switzerland. **Aims** Encourage and support research in the field of diabetes; ensure rapid diffusion of acquired knowledge and facilitate its application.

Structure General Assembly; Board – also board of *European Foundation for the Study of Diabetes (EFSD, #07351).* Study Groups:

- AIDPIT – Artificial Insulin Delivery, Pancreas and Islet Transplantation;
- D&CVD – Diabetes and Cardiovascular Disease;
- DCSG – Diabetes and Cancer;
- DESG – Diabetes Education;
- DFSG – Diabetic Foot;
- DIAB IMAGE – Biomedical Imaging in Diabetes;
- DNSG – Diabetes and Nutrition;
- DPSG – Diabetes Pregnancy;
- EASDec – Eye Complications;
- EDEG – European Diabetes Epidemiology;
- EDNSG – European Diabetic Nephropathy;
- EGIR – European Group for the Study of Insulin Resistance;
- ExPAS – Exercise and Physical Activity;
- HSRHE-SG – Health Services Research and Health Economics;
- IHSG – International Hypoglycaemia;
- INCSG – Incretin;
- ISG – Islet;
- MSSG – Study Group on Metabolic Surgery;
- NAFLD – Non-alcoholic fatty liver disease;
- NEURODIAB – Diabetes Neuropathy;
- PCDE – Study Group on Primary Care Research in Diabetology;
- PSAD – Psychosocial Aspects of Diabetes;
- RM-SG – Reactive Metabolites in Diabetes;
- SGGD – Study Group on Genetics of Diabetes.

Languages English. **Staff** None. **Finance** Sources: donations; members' dues. **Activities** Awards/prizes/competitions; events/meetings; research/documentation; training/education. **Events** *Annual Meeting* Madrid (Spain) 2024, *Annual Meeting* Hamburg (Germany) 2023, *Annual Meeting* Stockholm (Sweden) 2022, *Annual Meeting* 2021, *Annual Meeting* Glasgow (UK) 2021. **Publications** *Diabetologia* – official journal. **Members** Individual (Standard; Student; Postdoc/Fellow; Allied Health Professionals/Nurse); Corporate; Honorary. Membership countries not specified. **NGO Relations** Member of (1): *European Diabetes Forum (EUDF, #06916).* [2020/XD0559/v/**D**]

♦ European Association for the Study of Diabetic Eye Complications (EASDEC) 06229

Sec c/o Moorfields Eye Hospital, 162 City Road, London, EC1V 2PD, UK. E-mail: secretary@easdec.org.

URL: http://www.easdec.org/

History 1990, within *European Association for the Study of Diabetes (EASD, #06228).* **Aims** Promote diabetic *retinopathy* research. **Structure** Board, comprising President, Past-President, Vice-President, Secretary and Treasurer. **Languages** English. **Staff** Voluntary. **Finance** None. **Events** *Meeting* Coimbra (Portugal) 2023, *Meeting* Belfast (UK) 2022, *Meeting* Odense (Denmark) 2021, *Meeting* Barcelona (Spain) 2020, *Meeting* Amsterdam (Netherlands) 2019.

Members Individuals in 39 countries:

Austria, Belgium, Bulgaria, Canada, Croatia, Denmark, Egypt, Estonia, Finland, France, Germany, Greece, Hungary, Iceland, Ireland, Israel, Italy, Latvia, Lithuania, Luxembourg, Morocco, Netherlands, North Macedonia (former Yugoslav Rep of), Norway, Poland, Portugal, Romania, Russia, San Marino, Serbia, Slovakia, Slovenia, Spain, Sweden, Switzerland, Tunisia, Türkiye, UK, USA.

NGO Relations Member of: *European Alliance for Vision Research and Ophthalmology (EU-EYE, #05890).* [2014.06.01/XD6356/v/**E**]

♦ European Association for the Study of Dreams (EASD) 06230

Association européenne pour l'étude du rêve

Sec Assoc Oniros, Chitry Mont Sabot, 58190 Neuffontaines, France. T. +33386248641. Fax +33957795326. E-mail: eujo_ca@yahoo.ca – oniros@oniros.fr.

Registered Office Rue Xavier de Bue 3, Boîte 7, 1180 Brussels, Belgium. T. +3223765854.

URL: http://www.oniros.fr/

History 1987. Registered in accordance with Belgian law, 1991. Closely associated with French national organization 'ONIROS'; sometimes referred to as *ONIROS/EASD.* **Aims** Valorize the dream with the public opinion, as well as the scientific community; carry out studies and research on the dream, in a multidisciplinary perspective, while respecting the rights of human beings and of animals. **Structure** General Assembly (annual). Management Council (meets once a year), consisting of 3 to 15 members, including President, Treasurer, Secretary General and Assistant Secretary. **Events** *Dream and/or reality* Luxembourg (Luxembourg) 1994, *Extraordinary general assembly / Congress* Luxembourg (Luxembourg) 1994, *Congress* Aarhus (Denmark) 1987. **Publications** *Oniros* (2 a year).

Members Full; Adhering; Honorary. Members in 12 countries:

Belgium, Chad, France, Germany, Italy, Luxembourg, Mexico, Netherlands, Sweden, Switzerland, UK, USA. [2014/XD1489/**D**]

♦ European Association for Study of Economic, Commercial and Industrial Motivation (inactive)

♦ European Association for the Study of Gambling (EASG) 06231

Association européenne pour l'étude des jeux de hasard – Asociación Europea para el Estudio de los Juegos de Azar – Europäische Gesellschaft zur Erforschung des Glücksspiels

SG Pieter Calandlaan 317-319, 1068 NH Amsterdam, Netherlands. E-mail: easg@easg.org.

URL: http://www.easg.org/

History Current constitution adopted 27 Jan 2004, London (UK). **Aims** Provide a forum for the study, discussion and dissemination of knowledge about gambling in Europe; promote comparative study of historical, economical, mathematica, social and psychological aspects of gambling. **Structure** General Meeting; Executive Committee. **Languages** English. **Staff** 2.00 FTE, voluntary. **Finance** Members' dues. Conference sponsorships. **Activities** Events/meetings; guidance/assistance/consulting. **Events** *European Conference on Gambling Studies and Policy Issues* Oslo (Norway) 2022, *European Conference on Gambling Studies and Policy Issues* Oslo (Norway) 2020, *European Conference on Gambling Studies and Policy Issues* Valletta (Malta) 2018, *European Conference on Gambling Studies and Policy Issues* Lisbon (Portugal) 2016, *Seminar on Match Fixing* Amsterdam (Netherlands) 2015.

Members Full in 25 countries:

Austria, Belgium, Denmark, Finland, France, Germany, Greece, Hungary, Iceland, Italy, Lithuania, Luxembourg, Netherlands, Norway, Poland, Portugal, Romania, Slovenia, South Africa, Spain, Sweden, Switzerland, UK, USA, Venezuela. [2021/XD6312/**D**]

♦ European Association for the Study of Literature, Culture and Environment (EASLCE) 06232

Europäische Gesellschaft für das Studium von Literatur, Kultur und Umwelt

Pres address not obtained. E-mail: contact@easlce.eu – president@easlce.eu.

URL: http://www.easlce.eu/

History Registration: Start date: 2004, Germany. **Aims** Provide an international forum for the promotion of research and education in the fields of literary, cultural and environmental studies. **Structure** General Meeting (annual); Advisory Board; Executive Committee of 3 officers. **Languages** English. **Staff** 0.50 FTE, paid. **Finance** Sources: members' dues. **Events** *Biennial Conference* Granada (Spain) 2022, *Biennial Conference* Brussels (Belgium) 2016, *Biennial Conference* Tartu (Estonia) 2014, *Biennial Conference* Santa Cruz de Tenerife (Spain) 2012, *Biennial Conference* Bath (UK) 2010. **Publications** *EASLCE Newsletter* (2 a year); *Ecozon@* (2 a year) – journal.

European Association Study
06233

alphabetic sequence excludes
For the complete listing, see Yearbook Online at

Members Full in 19 countries:
Austria, Belgium, Canada, Denmark, Estonia, France, Germany, Iran Islamic Rep, Ireland, Italy, Lithuania, Netherlands, Norway, Poland, Portugal, Spain, Türkiye, UK, USA. [2021.03.22/XJ6573/D]

♦ European Association for the Study of the Liver (EASL) 06233

Europäische Vereinigung für Leberforschung

Address not obtained.
URL: http://www.easl.eu/

History 24 Apr 1966, Germany FR. Current constitution adopted 2016. Former names and other names: *Association européenne pour l'étude du foie* – former; *Europäische Gesellschaft zum Studium der Leberkrankheiten* – former. Registration: EU Transparency Register, No/ID: 597006135119-96; Switzerland. **Aims** Promote communication between European workers interested in the liver and its disorders. **Structure** Businees Meeting (annual); Governing Board; Scientific Committee; Ethics Committee. **Languages** English. **Staff** 20.00 FTE, paid. **Finance** Members' dues. Other sources: profit share from publication; annual meeting; UEGF annual meeting; voluntary contributions. **Activities** Events/meetings; research and development; training/education. **Events** *International Liver Congress* London (UK) 2022, *International Liver Congress* Geneva (Switzerland) 2021, *International Liver Congress (ILC)* London (UK) 2020, *International Symposium on Coagulation in Liver Diseases* Groningen (Netherlands) 2019, *Annual Congress* Vienna (Austria) 2019. **Publications** *Journal of Hepatology* (12 a year); *EASL Newsletter*.

Members National associations in 33 countries:
Armenia, Austria, Belarus, Belgium, Bosnia-Herzegovina, Bulgaria, Croatia, Czechia, Denmark, France, Georgia, Germany, Greece, Hungary, Ireland, Israel, Italy, Latvia, Lithuania, Netherlands, Poland, Portugal, Romania, Russia, Serbia, Slovakia, Slovenia, Spain, Sweden, Switzerland, Türkiye, UK, Ukraine.

NGO Relations Regional association of: *International Association for the Study of the Liver (IASL, #12203)*. Member of: *Biomedical Alliance in Europe (#03251)*; *Associations and Conference Forum (AC Forum, #02909)*; *European Alcohol Policy Alliance (Eurocare, #05856)*; *European Board of Gastroenterology and Hepatology (EBGH, #06359)*; *European Cancer Organisation (ECO, #06432)*; *European Chronic Disease Alliance (ECDA, #06548)*. Through: *European Public Health Alliance (EPHA, #08297)*; *United European Gastroenterology (UEG, #20506)*, a consortium of 7 European associations, organizes an annual scientific meeting in that field (the first in Feb 1991). The other 5 associations are: *European Association for Gastroenterology, Endoscopy and Nutrition (EAGEN, #06051)*; *European Pancreatic Club (EPC, #08136)*; *European Society of Gastrointestinal Endoscopy (ESGE, #08606)*; *European Society for Paediatric Gastroenterology, Hepatology and Nutrition (ESPGHAN, #08680)*; *International Society for Digestive Surgery (ISDS, #15060)* (European chapter). Collaborates with: *European AIDS Treatment Group (EATG, #05850)*; *International Network on Health and Hepatitis in Substance Users (INHSU, #14276)*. Instrumental in setting up: *European Liver Patients 'Association (ELPA, #07706)*. [2021/XD0560/D]

♦ European Association for the Study of Obesity (EASO) 06234

Exec Dir Level 2, 8 Waldegrave Road, Teddington, TW11 8GT, UK. T. +442037517967. E-mail: enquiries@easo.org.
URL: http://www.easo.org/

History 1986. Registration: Charity Commission, No/ID: 1111288, England and Wales; EU Transparency Register, No/ID: 020025124702-06, Start date: 24 Nov 2016. **Aims** Be the voice of the European obesity community, representing scientists, health care practitioners, physicians, public health experts and patients; reduce the burden of unhealthy weight; support development of a unified evidence-based approach to tackling obesity across disciplines and countries; advocate obesity as an urgent and relevant health priority to policymakers, NGOs, research funders, health professionals, media, industry and the public; identify and articulate effective solutions to these stakeholders. **Structure** Executive Committee; Officers; Working Groups (3). **Languages** English. **Staff** 1.00 FTE, paid. Several functions outsourced to consultants and agencies. **Finance** Sources: donations; fees for services; meeting proceeds; members' dues; sale of publications. **Activities** Advocacy/lobbying/activism; awards/prizes/competitions; events/meetings; networking/liaising; standards/guidelines; training/education. **Events** *European Congress on Obesity* Dublin (Ireland) 2023, *Zoom Forward 22* Maastricht (Netherlands) 2022, *European Congress on Obesity* 2021, *European Congress on Obesity* 2020, *European and International Congress on Obesity* 2020.

Members National professional membership associations in 32 countries:
Austria, Belgium, Bulgaria, Croatia, Czechia, Denmark, Finland, France, Georgia, Germany, Greece, Hungary, Iceland, Ireland, Israel, Italy, Montenegro, Netherlands, North Macedonia, Norway, Poland, Portugal, Romania, Russia, Serbia, Slovakia, Slovenia, Spain, Sweden, Switzerland, Türkiye, UK.

IGO Relations Official relations with: *WHO Regional Office for Europe (#20945)*. **NGO Relations** Member of (4): *Biomedical Alliance in Europe (#03251)*; *EU Health Coalition*; *EU Platform for Action on Diet, Physical Activity and Health (inactive)*; *European Cancer Organisation (ECO, #06432)*. [2022.03.04/XD4770/D]

♦ European Association for Study and Reflection on Consumer Problems (inactive)

♦ European Association for the Study of Religions (EASR) 06235

Gen Sec Inst HSD, Stockholms universitet, SE-106 91 Stockholm, Sweden.
URL: http://www.easr.eu/

History May 2000, Krakow (Poland). Registration: Netherlands. **Aims** Promote the academic study of religions through the international collaboration of all scholars normally resident in Europe whose research has a bearing on the subject. **Structure** General Assembly (annual); Committee. **Languages** English. **Staff** Voluntary. **Finance** Members' dues. **Activities** Events/meetings. **Events** *Conference* Kiev (Ukraine) 2023, *Conference* Cork (Ireland) 2022, *Annual Conference* Pisa (Italy) 2021, *Annual Conference* Tartu (Estonia) 2019, *Annual Conference* Bern (Switzerland) 2018. **Publications** Conference papers occasionally published by host of conference.

Members National associations in 25 countries:
Austria, Belgium, Czechia, Denmark, Estonia, Finland, France, Germany, Greece, Hungary, Italy, Latvia, Luxembourg, Netherlands, Norway, Poland, Portugal, Romania, Slovakia, Spain, Sweden, Switzerland, Türkiye, UK, Ukraine.
Individuals in 4 countries:
Bulgaria, Japan, Russia, Slovenia.

NGO Relations Regional association of: *International Association for the History of Religions (IAHR, #11936)*. Member of: *European Alliance for the Social Sciences and Humanities (EASSH, #05885)*. [2021/XD7997/D]

♦ European Association for Study of Safety Problems in Production and Use of Propellant Powders (inactive)

♦ European Association for the Study of Science and Technology (EASST) 06236

Association européenne pour l'étude de la science et de la technologie

Pres Bodemsweg 2, 6225 ND Maastricht, Netherlands. E-mail: easst@univie.ac.at.
URL: http://easst.net/

History 1981. Constitution adopted 1994, Budapest (Hungary); amended Oct 1996, Bielefeld (Germany) and Sep 2010, Trento (Italy). **Aims** Foster scholarly study of science and technology, including their historical development and their role in society. **Structure** Council. **Languages** English. **Staff** 0.50 FTE, paid. **Finance** Sources: meeting proceeds; members' dues. **Activities** Awards/prizes/competitions; events/meetings. **Events** *Biennial International Conference* Madrid (Spain) 2022, *Locating and timing Matters: Significance and Agency of STS in Emerging Worlds* Prague (Czechia) 2020, *Biennial International Conference* Lancaster (UK) 2018, *Biennial International Conference* Barcelona (Spain) 2016, *Biennial International Conference* Torun (Poland) 2014. **Publications** *EASST Review* (4 a year); *Science & Technology Studies (S&TS Journal)* (4 a year) – online.

Members Individuals in 43 countries:
Argentina, Australia, Austria, Belarus, Belgium, Bolivia, Brazil, Bulgaria, Canada, Croatia, Denmark, Estonia, Finland, France, Germany, Greece, Hungary, India, Ireland, Italy, Japan, Latvia, Lithuania, Luxembourg, Mexico, Netherlands, New Zealand, North Macedonia, Norway, Philippines, Poland, Portugal, Romania, Russia, Slovenia, South Africa, Spain, Sweden, Switzerland, Türkiye, UK, Ukraine, USA. [2020/XD7400/v/D]

♦ European Association for the Study of Theatre and Performance (EASTAP) 06237

Pres 20 avenue Trudaine, 75009 Paris, France. T. +33607768867.
Contact address not obtained.
URL: http://eastap.com/

History 2017, Paris (France). **Aims** Promote the diversity of theatre and performance methodologies and research in Europe, bringing together scholars and artists. **Structure** General Assembly; Executive Committee. **Languages** English, French. **Staff** Voluntary. **Finance** Sources: members' dues. **Activities** Advocacy/lobbying/activism; events/meetings; knowledge management/information dissemination; research/documentation. **Events** *Theatrical Minds* Milan (Italy) 2022, *Congress* Lisbon (Portugal) 2019, *Congress* Paris (France) 2018. **Publications** *European Journal of Theater and Performance*.

Members Organizations in 3 countries:
France, Italy, UK.
Individuals in 19 countries:
Belgium, Brazil, Canada, Chile, Croatia, Denmark, Finland, France, Germany, Italy, Japan, Netherlands, Norway, Poland, Slovenia, Spain, Sweden, UK, USA. [2022/XM7753/D]

♦ European Association for Substance Abuse Research (EASAR) 06238

Chairperson IFT Inst für Therapieforschung, Leopoldstr 175, 80804 Munich, Germany. T. +498936080430. Fax +498936080419.
URL: http://www.easar.com/

History Founded 1994, in close cooperation with *WHO Regional Office for Europe (#20945)*, and in consultation with *European Monitoring Centre for Drugs and Drug Addiction (EMCDDA, #07820)*. **Aims** Stimulate and strengthen European cooperation in any field of research of abuse of psycho-active substances in order to improve prevention and treatment, and contribute in this manner to the wellbeing of people. **Structure** Board. **Languages** English. **Staff** None. **Activities** Networking/liaising; research/documentation; training/education; events/meetings. **Events** *Annual Conference* Velence (Hungary) 2019, *Annual Conference* Vienna (Austria) 2018, *Annual Conference* Nunspeet (Netherlands) 2017, *Annual Conference* Middelfart (Denmark) 2016, *Annual Conference* Bangor (UK) 2015.

Members Research institutes and research supporting organizations (22) in 14 countries:
Austria, Czechia, Denmark, France, Germany, Greece, Hungary, Netherlands, Poland, Slovenia, Spain, Sweden, Switzerland, UK.

NGO Relations Member of: *European Federation of Addiction Societies (EUFAS, #07039)*. [2018.07.27/XD5299/D]

♦ European Association of Sugar Producers (#04159)

♦ European Association of Sugar Traders (ASSUC) 06239

SG Rue de Trêves 49-51, Box 14, 1040 Brussels, Belgium. T. +3222310638. Fax +3227326766. E-mail: assuc@assuc.eu.
URL: http://www.assuc.eu/

History 9 Dec 1959. Former names and other names: *Association of Professional Organizations of the Sugar Trade for EEC Countries* – former (9 Dec 1959); *Association des organisations professionnelles du commerce des sucres pour les pays de la CEE* – former (9 Dec 1959); *Association of Professional Organizations of the Sugar Trade for EU Countries* – former; *Association des organisations professionnelles du commerce des sucres pour les pays de l'UE* – former; *Vereinigung der Berufsorganisationen des Zuckerhandels für die Länder der EU* – former; *Associazione delle Organizzazioni Professionali del Commercio degli Zuccheri per i Paesi Membri della UE* – former; *Vereniging van Beroepsorganisaties van de Suikerhandel in de Landen van de EU* – former; *Sammenslutningen af Faglige Organisationer for Sukkerhandelen i EF-Landene* – former. Registration: EU Transparency Register, No/ID: 73074372526-61. **Aims** Promote visibility of the professional sector of the sugar trade; represent and defend general interests of members; facilitate cooperation among operators in the sugar trade sector at European level; provide a networking platform for traders (importers, exporters, dealers, brokers and distributors) in sugar and its derivatives. **Structure** General Assembly (annual), in Brussels (Belgium); Board of Directors. **Languages** English. **Finance** Members' dues. **Activities** Monitoring/evaluation; networking/liaising; knowledge management/information dissemination; guidance/assistance/consulting; events/meetings. **Events** *Annual General Assembly* Brussels (Belgium) 2013, *Annual General Assembly* Brussels (Belgium) 2012, *Annual General Assembly* Brussels (Belgium) 1996, *Annual General Assembly* Brussels (Belgium) 1993, *Annual General Assembly* Brussels (Belgium) 1992. **Publications** *ASSUC Newsletter*. Annual Report.

Members Full; Affiliated. Members in 18 countries:
Algeria, Belgium, Bulgaria, Denmark, Finland, France, Germany, Hungary, Italy, Lithuania, Malta, Netherlands, Poland, Romania, Spain, Sweden, Switzerland, UK.

IGO Relations Recognized by: *European Commission (EC, #06633)*; *International Sugar Organization (ISO, #15623)*; *World Trade Organization (WTO, #21864)*. **NGO Relations** Member of: *Joint Secretariat of Agricultural Trade Associations (#16148)*. [2020/XE0166/t/E]

♦ European Association for Supervision / see European Association for Supervision and Coaching (#06240)

♦ European Association for Supervision and Coaching (EASC) 06240

Treas EASC Office, Waldstr 32, 10551 Berlin, Germany. T. +493039847555. Fax +493039847555. E-mail: office@easc-online.eu.
URL: http://www.easc-online.eu/

History 1994. Founded as *European Association for Supervision (EAS)*. Current title adopted 2010. Registration: Berlin District court, No/ID: VR 34044, Start date: 12 Oct 1994, Germany, Charlottenburg. **Aims** Assure quality in coaching and supervision. **Structure** General Assembly; Managing Board. **Events** *Congress* Barcelona (Spain) 2022, *Congress* 2021, *Congress* Eichstätt (Germany) 2018, *Congress* Bratislava (Slovakia) 2016, *Congress* Berlin (Germany) 2015. **Members** Individuals (532) in 15 countries. Membership countries not specified. **NGO Relations** Partners: *Association of National Organisations for Supervision in Europe (ANSE, #02821)*; *International Organization Development Association (IODA, #14444)*; national associations. [2021/XJ9090/D]

♦ European Association for the Support of TV Programmes Exports (no recent information)

♦ European Association of Surface Heating and Cooling (Eu-Ray) ... 06241

Gen Manager c/o Bodentechnik, Seestrasse 40, 8802 Kirchberg SG, Switzerland. T. +41447152760. Fax +41447152750. E-mail: info@eu-ray.com.
URL: http://www.eu-ray.com/

History 1990, as *European Radiant Floor Heating Association (ERFA)*. Present name adopted 2002, when most recent statutes were adopted. **Aims** Promote the use of surface heating and cooling; develop and maintain governmental programme, international standards and regulations; conduct studies of general interest. **Structure** General Assembly (annual). Executive Board. Working Groups. **Languages** English. **Staff** 1.00 FTE, paid. Consultants. **Finance** Members' dues. Other sources: income from investments; contributions; donations. **Events** *Annual General Assembly* Frankfurt-Niederrad (Germany) 2011, *Annual General Assembly* Vienna (Austria) 2010, *Annual General Assembly* Baveno (Italy) / Stresa (Italy) 2009, *Annual General Assembly* Barcelona (Spain) 2008, *Annual General Assembly* Helsinki (Finland) 2007.

Members Companies; individuals; associations. Members in 11 countries:
Austria, Belgium, Finland, France, Germany, Italy, Netherlands, Spain, Switzerland, UK, USA. [2013/XD7442/D]

♦ European association for Surface Treatment on Aluminium (ESTAL) 06242

Association européenne du traitement de surface sur aluminium – Europäische Vereinigung für die Aluminium-Veredlung

SG Wyssgerbistr 4, 6442 Gersau SZ, Switzerland. T. +41447722277. E-mail: secretariat@estal.org.
Pres address not obtained. E-mail: president@estal.org.
URL: http://www.estal.org/

History 1989. Previously also referred to as *Association for European Surface Treatment on Aluminium*. Takes over activities of *European Aluminium Coaters' Association (EUROCOAT, inactive)* and *European Anodisers' Association (EURAS, inactive)*. Registered in accordance with Swiss Civil Code. Registration: EU Transparency Register, No/ID: 709577927547-05, Start date: 20 Jun 2017. **Aims** Defend members' interests at international level; actively contribute towards finding solutions to technical, economic and ecological issues associated with the production and utilisation of surface treated aluminium; encourage the sharing of knowledge and development of new technologies among members. **Structure** General Assembly; Executive Committee; Steering Committee. Director; Secretariat. Committees. **Languages** English. **Finance** Members'

dues. **Activities** Events/meetings; advocacy/lobbying/activism. **Events** *Congress* Budapest (Hungary) 2021, *Congress* Istanbul (Turkey) 2019, *Congress* Toledo (Spain) 2017, *Congress* Porto (Portugal) 2015, *Annual Congress* Krakow (Poland) 2013.
Members Active: national trade associations in 10 countries:
Austria, Belgium, Germany, Hungary, Netherlands, Portugal, Spain, Switzerland, Türkiye, UK.
Associate: companies in 5 countries:
Denmark, Finland, Poland, Slovakia, Sweden.
NGO Relations Instrumental in setting up: *QUALANOD (#18589)*. Member of: *European Aluminium (#05893)*. [2020/XD9183/**D**]

♦ European Association of Surgical Sciences (no recent information)

♦ European Association of the Surgical Suture Industry (EASSI) 06243

Europäische Vereinigung der Hersteller von chirurgischem Nahtmaterial
SG Reinhardtstr 29b, 10117 Berlin, Germany. T. +493024625517. Fax +493024625599. E-mail: info@eassi.eu.
SG address not obtained.
URL: http://www.eassi.eu/
History 1972. Re-established 2006. Registration: Berlin District court, No/ID: VR 34202, Germany, Charlottenburg; EU Transparency Register, No/ID: 557917345246-94, Start date: 10 Feb 2022. **Aims** Represent the interests of European manufacturers of surgical sutures and meshes. **Structure** Working Groups. **Languages** English. **Staff** 0.50 FTE, paid. **Finance** Sources: members' dues. **Activities** Politics/policy/regulatory; standards/guidelines.
Members Full in 7 countries:
Czechia, France, Germany, Italy, Spain, Switzerland, UK.
NGO Relations Member of (1): *MedTech Europe (#16692)*. [2022/XD3503/t/**D**]

♦ European Association for Survey Research / see European Survey Research Association (#08862)
♦ European Association of Sustainability Professionals (unconfirmed)
♦ European Association of Synthetic Biology Students and Postdocs / see European Synthetic Biology Society (#08869)
♦ European Association of Syrups Producers (inactive)

♦ European Association of Systems Medicine (EASyM) 06244

Contact c/o JRC for Computational Biomedicine, RWTH Aachen Univ, Pauwelsstr 19, 52074 Aachen, Germany. E-mail: info.easym@gmail.com.
URL: http://www.easym.eu/
History Set up 30 Sep 2015, Brussels (Belgium). Registered in accordance with German law. **Aims** Foster systems medicine approaches in experimental medicine and clinical research. **Structure** Executive Board: Communication Office; Education Task Group. **Languages** English. **Staff** 1.00 FTE, paid. **Finance** Members' dues. Other sources: donations; sponsorship; registration fees. **Activities** Events/meetings; training/education. **Events** *International Conference in Systems and Network Medicine* Washington, DC (USA) 2019, *Conference* Utrecht (Netherlands) 2018, *Conference* Berlin (Germany) 2016. **Members** Institutional (4); Individual (over 100). Membership countries not specified. [2018.10.05/XM5622/**D**]

♦ European Association for Table Football (inactive)

♦ European Association of Taiwan Studies (EATS) 06245

Contact address not obtained. E-mail: info@eats-taiwan.eu.
URL: http://www.eats-taiwan.eu/
History 2004. **Aims** Promote Taiwan studies and research in Europe. **Structure** General Assembly; Board. **Activities** Training/education; awards/prizes/competitions; events/meetings. **Events** *Annual Conference* Brno (Czechia) 2021, *Annual Conference* Brussels (Belgium) 2020, *Annual Conference* Nottingham (UK) 2019, *Annual Conference* Zurich (Switzerland) 2018, *Annual Conference* Venice (Italy) 2017. **Publications** *EATS Newsletter*, *International Journal of Taiwan Studies*. [2020/XM7535/**D**]

♦ European Association for Tapes, Braids, Elastic Materials (inactive)

♦ European Association for the Taps and Valves Industry (CEIR) 06246

SG BluePoint, Bd Auguste Reyers 80, 1030 Brussels, Belgium. T. +3222066866. E-mail: secretariat@ceir.eu.
URL: http://www.ceir.eu/
History 16 Apr 1959. Founded to unify the valve industry associations in the original 6 European Economic Community countries, following contacts on European cooperation since 1947. Reorganized 17 Oct 1986, Dubrovnik (Yugoslavia). Former names and other names: *European Committee for the Valve Industry* – former (16 Apr 1959); *Comité européen de l'industrie de la robinetterie (CEIR)* – former (16 Apr 1959); *Europäisches Komitee der Armaturenindustrie* – former (16 Apr 1959). Registration: EU Transparency Register, No/ID: 54018122087-60. **Aims** Harmonize national technical and economic regulations; exchange economic and technical information and ensure reciprocal contacts between specialists, organizations and their member-firms, thus contributing to an improvement in market conditions and a growth in productivity; promote *standardization* of European *specifications*, preparing recommendations within the framework of international standards bodies; improve quality of products; strive for standardization of conditions of sale and commerce. **Structure** General Assembly (at least annual); Board; Committees (3); Working Groups; General Secretariat. **Languages** English, French, German. **Finance** Members' dues. **Activities** Research/documentation; events/meetings. **Events** *Joint Conference – CEIR – EUROPUMP – PNEUROP* Marseille (France) 2023, *Joint Conference* Brussels (Belgium) 2022, *Annual Congress* Brussels (Belgium) 2021, *Annual Congress* Brussels (Belgium) 2020, *Annual Congress* Barcelona (Spain) 2019. **Publications** *CEIR Bulletin* (5 a year); *CEIR – newsletter*. Position papers; guides; press releases.
Members National associations in 10 countries:
Finland, France, Italy, Portugal, Russia, Spain, Sweden, Switzerland, Türkiye, UK.
Companies in 6 countries:
Denmark, Germany, Portugal, Spain, Switzerland, Türkiye.
IGO Relations Recognized by: *European Commission (EC, #06633)*. [2022/XD0656/t/**D**]

♦ European Association of Tax Law Professors (EATLP) 06247

Sec Rietlandpark 301, 1019 DW Amsterdam, Netherlands. T. +31644634060. E-mail: eatlp@ibfd.org.
URL: http://www.eatlp.org/
History 10 Jun 1999, Stockholm (Sweden). Statutes adopted Nov 1999, Amsterdam (Netherlands). Former names and other names: *Association of European Tax Law Professors* – alias. Registration: Netherlands; EU Transparency Register, No/ID: 199090913475-87. **Aims** Contribute to development of European tax law, and of academic teaching and research programmes on European, international, domestic and comparative taxation. **Structure** General Assembly (annual); Executive Board; Academic Committee of European Taxation. **Languages** English. **Staff** 0.25 FTE, paid; 6.00 FTE, voluntary. **Finance** Sources: members' dues. **Events** *Annual Congress* Antwerp (Belgium) 2024, *Annual Congress* Luxembourg (Luxembourg) 2023, *Annual Congress* Vienna (Austria) 2022, *Annual Congress* 2021, *Annual Congress* Vienna (Austria) 2020. **Publications** *Taxation of Cross-Border Pensions* – journal. *EATLP International Tax Series*.
Members Full; Associate. Members in 39 countries:
Austria, Belgium, Brazil, Canada, China, Colombia, Croatia, Czechia, Denmark, Finland, France, Germany, Greece, Hungary, Ireland, Israel, Italy, Japan, Kazakhstan, Luxembourg, Malta, Netherlands, North Macedonia, Norway, Poland, Portugal, Romania, Russia, Serbia, Slovakia, Slovenia, South Africa, Spain, Sweden, Switzerland, Türkiye, UK, Ukraine, USA. [2023.02.16/XD7938/**D**]

♦ European Association of Teachers (#02565)

♦ European Association of Teachers of Ancient Greek (EATAG) 06248

Contact 1 Sandy Court, Seamill, Kilbride, WEST KA23 9NT, UK. T. +441294822709.
History Founded 9 Jun 1989, Kourion (Cyprus). **Aims** Encourage exchange of ideas and development of cooperation at European level.
Members Individuals in 22 countries:
Albania, Austria, Belgium, Bulgaria, Croatia, Cyprus, Czechia, Estonia, France, Germany, Greece, Ireland, Latvia, Malta, Netherlands, Poland, Portugal, Romania, Slovakia, Slovenia, Spain, UK.
NGO Relations Member of: *EUROCLASSICA (#05663)*. [2015/XD5460/**D**]

♦ European Association of Teachers of History / see European Association of History Educators (#06069)
♦ European Association of Teachers of Spanish (#02127)

♦ European Association for the Teaching of Academic Writing (EATAW) 06249

Editor Coventry University, Priory Street, Coventry, CV1 5FB, UK. T. +442476887904.
URL: http://www.eataw.eu/
History Founded, 1 Jul 2007, Bochum (Germany). Informally founded, 2001, Groningen (Netherlands). Registered in accordance with Swiss Civil Code. **Aims** As a scholarly forum, bring together those involved or interested in the teaching, tutoring, research, administration and development of academic writing in higher education in Europe. **Structure** Board. **Languages** English. Contributions to conferences accepted in any European language. **Finance** None. **Activities** Networking/liaising; events/meetings; awareness raising; training/education; projects/programmes; standards/guidelines. **Events** *Biennial Conference* Gothenburg (Sweden) 2019, *Biennial Conference* London (UK) 2017, *Biennial Conference* Tallinn (Estonia) 2015, *Biennial Conference* Budapest (Hungary) 2013, *Biennial Conference* Limerick (Ireland) 2011.
Members Full (680) in 42 countries and territories:
Argentina, Armenia, Australia, Austria, Azerbaijan, Belgium, Bulgaria, Canada, Czechia, Denmark, Estonia, France, Georgia, Germany, Greece, Hong Kong, Hungary, Iran Islamic Rep, Israel, Italy, Latvia, Lithuania, Malaysia, Mexico, Montenegro, Netherlands, New Zealand, Norway, Poland, Portugal, Romania, Russia, Serbia, South Africa, Sweden, Switzerland, Taiwan, Thailand, Türkiye, UK, Ukraine, USA. [2018.10.10/XJ4427/**D**]

♦ European Association for the Teaching of Legal Theory (EATLT) 06250

Association européenne pour l'enseignement de la théorie du droit (AEETD)
Pres Law Dept, Queen Mary Univ of London, Mile End Road, London, E1 4NS, UK. T. +32496213513.
URL: http://www.legaltheory.be/
History 1989, Edinburgh (UK), following congress of *Internationale Vereinigung für Rechts- und Sozialphilosophie (IVR, #13318)*. Registered in accordance with Belgian law. **Structure** Board. **Languages** English. **Activities** Training/education; awards/prizes/competitions. **Publications** *The European Academy of Legal Theory Series*.
Members Individuals in 10 countries:
Austria, Belgium, France, Germany, Italy, Netherlands, Poland, Sweden, Switzerland, UK.
NGO Relations Instrumental in setting up: *European Academy of Legal Theory (EALT, #05798)*. [2018.09.10/XD2355/v/**D**]

♦ European Association for Technical Communication (tekom Europe) 06251

CEO Rotebühlstr 64, 70178 Stuttgart, Germany. T. +49711657040. Fax +497116570499. E-mail: info@tekom.eu.
URL: https://www.technical-communication.org/
History 2013. Registration: EU Transparency Register, No/ID: 194995512904-93, Start date: 10 Feb 2014; No/ID: VR 721237, Start date: 17 Dec 2013, Germany. **Aims** Promote professional and business interests of all persons involved in technical communication. **Structure** Assembly of Delegates; Executive Board. **Activities** Training/education; events/meetings; knowledge management/information dissemination; networking/liaising; awards/prizes/competitions. **Events** *Annual Meeting* Vienna (Austria) 2019.
Members National organizations in 13 countries:
Austria, Belgium, Bulgaria, Denmark, France, Germany, Hungary, Israel, Poland, Romania, Sweden, Switzerland, Türkiye.
Corporate member in 1 country:
Italy. [2020/XM8697/**D**]

♦ European Association of Technical Fabrics producers (unconfirmed)
♦ European Association for Technical Orthopaedics and Orthopaedic Rehabilitation (inactive)
♦ European Association for Technology Transfer and Training (no recent information)
♦ European Association for Telematic Applications (inactive)

♦ European Association for Terminology (EAFT) 06252

Association européenne de terminologie (AET) – Asociación Europea de Terminologia – Associazione Europea per la Terminologia – Europese Vereniging voor Terminologie (EVT) – Europeiska Terminologiföreningen
Secretariat c/o TERMCAT, Mallorca 272 – 1st Floor, 08037 Barcelona, Spain. T. +34934526161. E-mail: term@eaft-aet.net.
URL: http://www.eaft-aet.net/
History 3 Oct 1996, Kolding (Denmark). Registration: Netherlands. **Aims** Promote *plurilingualism* in Europe through terminology; provide a platform for promoting and professionalizing terminological activities. **Structure** General Assembly; Board; Advisory Council. Working Groups (3). Secretariat. **Finance** Sources: members' dues. **Events** *Terminology Summit* Dublin (Ireland) 2021, *Terminology Summit* Barcelona (Spain) 2014, *Seminar on the Applications of Cognitive Terminological Theories in Terminology Management* Zagreb (Croatia) 2013, *Terminology Summit* Oslo (Norway) 2012, *Terminology summit* Budapest (Hungary) 2010. **NGO Relations** Cooperates with (1): *Réseau Lexicologie, Terminologie, Traduction (Réseau LTT, #18897)*. In liaison with technical committees of: *International Organization for Standardization (ISO, #14473)*. [2022/XD6502/**D**]

♦ European Association for Textile Polyolefins (inactive)

♦ European Association for Theoretical Computer Science (EATCS) .. 06253

Association européenne d'informatique théorique
Sec Palazzo Battibocca, Via del Bastione 1, School of Science & Technology, 62032 Camerino MC, Italy. T. +390737402567. Fax +390737402561.
URL: http://www.eatcs.org/
History 1972, Paris (France). **Aims** Facilitate exchange of ideas and results among theoretical computer scientists; stimulate cooperation between theoretical and practical community in computer science. **Structure** General Assembly (annual, during Colloquium); Council; Board. **Languages** English. **Staff** None. **Finance** Members' dues. Sales of publications. **Activities** Events/meetings; awards/prizes/competitions. **Events** *International Colloquium on Automata Languages and Programming (ICALP)* Paris (France) 2022, *International Colloquium on Automata, Languages, and Programming (ICALP)* Glasgow (UK) 2021, *International Colloquium on Automata Languages and Programming* Camerino (Italy) 2020, *International Colloquium on Automata Languages and Programming* Patras (Greece) 2019, *Symposium on Parallelism in Algorithms and Architectures* Vienna (Austria) 2018. **Publications** *Bulletin of the EATCS* (3 a year); *Theoretical Computer Science (TCS)* – journal. *EATCS Monographs in Theoretical Computer Science* – series; *EATCS Texts in Theoretical Computer Science* – series.
Members Individuals in 50 countries and territories:
Albania, Armenia, Australia, Austria, Belgium, Brazil, Bulgaria, Canada, Chile, China, Czechia, Denmark, Estonia, Finland, France, Georgia, Germany, Greece, Hong Kong, Hungary, Iceland, India, Ireland, Israel, Italy, Japan, Korea Rep, Latvia, Lithuania, Netherlands, New Zealand, Norway, Philippines, Poland, Portugal, Romania, Russia, Singapore, Slovakia, South Africa, Spain, Sweden, Switzerland, Taiwan, Türkiye, UK, Ukraine, Uruguay, USA, Vietnam.
NGO Relations Member of (1): *European Forum for ICST (#07316)*. Joint conference with: *European Association for Programming Languages and Systems (EAPLS, #06171)*; *European Association of Software Science and Technology (EASST, #06213)*. Sponsors: *Workshop on Logic, Language, Information and Computation (WoLLIC)*. [2021/XD9086/v/**D**]

♦ European Association for Thermal and Climatic Medicine (inactive)

♦ European Association of Thermology (EAT) 06254

Association européenne de thermologie (AET)
Treas Hernalser Hauptstr 209/14, 1170 Vienna, Austria. T. +4314805423.
Pres UCL Inst of Immunity and Transplantation, royal Free Campus, Rowland Hill Street, London, NW3 2PF, UK. T. +442077940500 ext 22516. E-mail: eurothermology@gmail.com.
URL: http://www.eurothermology.org/

History 1972, Strasbourg (France). Registered under Austrian law 2003. **Aims** Coordinate European and international standards in scientific applications of *temperature*, thermal imaging and measurements in *biology* and *medicine*. **Structure** Board. **Languages** English. **Staff** Voluntary. **Finance** Members' dues. **Events** *Congress* Wroclaw (Poland) 2021, *Congress* London (UK) 2018, *Congress* Madrid (Spain) 2015, *Congress* Porto (Portugal) 2012, *International conference on thermal engineering and thermogrammetry* Budapest (Hungary) 2011. **Publications** *Thermology International* (4 a year) – journal.
Members Ordinary in 16 countries:
Austria, Czechia, Finland, Germany, Greece, Hungary, Italy, Netherlands, Norway, Poland, Portugal, Russia, Slovakia, Spain, Sweden, UK.
Extraordinary in 5 countries:
Brazil, Lebanon, Netherlands, UK, USA.
NGO Relations Member of: *International College of Thermology (ICT, no recent information).*
[2020/XD3112/**D**]

♦ European Association of Tissue Banks (EATB) 06255
Main Office c/o DGFG, Feodor-Lynen-Str 21, 30625 Hannover, Germany. E-mail: office@eatcb.eu.
URL: http://www.eatb.org/
History 1991, Berlin (Germany). Former names and other names: *European Association of Tissue and Cell Banks (EATCB)* – full title (2019). **Aims** Promote cooperation, research and development in the field in Europe; publish standards to ensure that the conduct of tissue banking meets acceptable norms of technical and ethical performance. **Structure** Board. **Languages** English. **Finance** Members' dues. **Activities** Standards/guidelines; training/education; events/meetings; knowledge management/information dissemination; projects/programmes. **Events** *Congress* Zagreb (Croatia) 2023, *Congress* Warsaw (Poland) 2022, *Online Congress* 2021, *Congress* Gdansk (Poland) 2020, *Congress* Leiden (Netherlands) 2019. **Publications** *EATB Newsletter*. Conference proceedings; standards; educational material.
Members Full in 32 countries:
Australia, Austria, Belgium, Brazil, Bulgaria, Croatia, Czechia, Denmark, Estonia, Finland, France, Germany, Greece, Hungary, Iran Islamic Rep, Ireland, Israel, Italy, Japan, Lebanon, Luxembourg, Netherlands, Norway, Poland, Portugal, Slovakia, South Africa, Spain, Switzerland, Thailand, UK, USA.
NGO Relations Member of (1): *World Union of Tissue Banking Associations (WUTBA, #21888).*
[2023/XD3791/**D**]

♦ European Association of Tissue and Cell Banks / see European Association of Tissue Banks (#06255)
♦ European Association of Tolled Motorway, Bridge and Tunnel Concessionaires / see Association Européenne des Concessionnaires d'Autoroutes et d'Ouvrages à Péage (#02559)
♦ European Association for Tourism and Leisure Education / see Association for Tourism and Leisure Education and Research (#02956)
♦ European Association Trade-Commerce-Industry / see Europäischer Interessenverband Handel-Gewerbe-Industrie
♦ European Association Trade-Crafts-Industry (internationally oriented national body)
♦ European Association for the Trade in Jute Products / see European Association for the Trade in Jute and Related Products (#06256)
♦ European Association for the Trade in Jute Products and Related Products / see European Association for the Trade in Jute and Related Products (#06256)

♦ European Association for the Trade in Jute and Related Products (Eurojute) 06256
Association européenne pour le commerce des produits de jute – Asociación Europea para el Comercio de los Productos del Yute – Europäische Vereinigung für den Handel mit Juteprodukten
SG PO Box 93002, 2509 AA The Hague, Netherlands. T. +31703490750. Fax +31703490775. E-mail: info@eurojute.com.
Street Address Bezuidenhoutseweg 12, 2594 AV The Hague, Netherlands.
URL: http://www.eurojute.org/
History 23 Apr 1970, Antwerp (Belgium). Former names and other names: *European Association for the Trade in Jute Products (EATJP)* – former; *European Association for the Trade in Jute Products and Related Products (EAJP)* – former. **Aims** Improve relations among national associations and individual firms concerned with *trade* in jute products; carry out scientific examination of problems affecting this trade; facilitate exchange of information; protect members' interests and represent the trade, including at the international level, especially to ensure liberalization of trade and reduction of tariffs. **Structure** General Meeting (twice a year); Board; Chief Executive Officer (Secretary). **Languages** English. **Finance** Sources: members' dues. **Activities** Networking/liaising. **Events** *Annual General Meeting* Lisbon (Portugal) 2019, *Annual General Meeting* Bologna (Italy) 2018, *Annual General Meeting* Barcelona (Spain) 2017, *Annual General Meeting* Groningen (Netherlands) 2016, *Meeting* Milan (Italy) 2015.
Members Individual enterprises in 8 countries:
Belgium, Denmark, Italy, Netherlands, Romania, Spain, Switzerland, UK.
Consultative Status Consultative status granted from: *FAO (#09260)* (Liaison Status); *UNCTAD (#20285)* (Special Category).
[2020.06.23/XD4045/t/**D**]

♦ European Association of Traditional Chinese Medicine (inactive)
♦ European Association for Training Centres for Socio-Educational Care Work / see Formation d'éducateurs sociaux européens (#09873)
♦ European Association of Training Programmes in Hospital and Health Services Administration / see European Health Management Association (#07458)

♦ European Association for Transactional Analysis (EATA) 06257
Association européenne d'analyse transactionnelle
Exec Sec Silvanerweg 8, 78464 Konstanz, Germany. T. +49753195270. Fax +49753195271. E-mail: office@eatanews.org.
URL: http://www.eatanews.org/
History 1976. **Aims** Bring together the numerous training activities in Transactional Analysis (TA) in Europe in a federated structure to ensure quality and standards and help create powerful national TA organizations. **Structure** Council (meets annually); Committees (5). **Languages** English. **Activities** Awards/prizes/competitions; events/meetings. **Events** *Theory Development and Research Conference* Belgrade (Serbia) 2021, *World Conference for Transactional Analysis* Birmingham (UK) 2020, *Annual Congress* Cherkassy (Ukraine) 2019, *Theory Development and Research Conference* London (UK) 2018, *World Conference for Transactional Analysis* Berlin (Germany) 2017. **Publications** *EATA Newsletter* (3 a year).
Members Regular; Associate. Associations (36) comprising 7,800 individuals in 30 countries:
Armenia, Austria, Belgium, Bosnia-Herzegovina, Bulgaria, Croatia, Czechia, Finland, France, Georgia, Germany, Hungary, Italy, Kazakhstan, Kyrgyzstan, Montenegro, Netherlands, North Macedonia, Norway, Poland, Romania, Russia, Serbia, Slovenia, Spain, Sweden, Switzerland, Türkiye, UK, Ukraine.
[2022.10.20/XD6974/y/**D**]

♦ European Association for Transcultural Group Analysis (EATGA) . . . 06258
Association Européenne pour l'Analyse Transculturelle de Groupe (AEATG)
Sec Via Modestino 1, 20144 Milan MI, Italy.
URL: http://www.eatga.net/
History 1986. Registered in accordance with Belgian law. **Aims** promote research on cultural groups; promote intercultural exchanges. **Structure** General Assembly. Board of Directors. Officers: President; Vice-President; Secretary; Treasurer. **Languages** Languages of participants. **Staff** Voluntary. **Finance** Members' dues. **Activities** Organizes seminars, workshops and study days. **Events** *European intercultural seminar / European Seminar* Heidelberg (Germany FR) 1989. **Publications** *EATGA Newsletter* (annual).
Members Individuals in 7 countries:
Austria, Belgium, France, Germany, Italy, Switzerland, UK.
[2010.06.01/XD7620/v/**D**]

♦ European Association for the Transfer of Technologies, Innovation and Industrial Information (TII) 06259
Association européenne pour le transfert des technologies, de l'innovation et de l'information industrielle
SG 67 rue du Château, L-1329 Luxembourg, Luxembourg. T. +352428873. E-mail: cr@tii.org.
URL: http://www.tii.org/
History 4 May 1984, Luxembourg, with the support of Commission of the European Communities (currently European Commission). Registered in accordance with Luxembourg law. **Aims** Represent the technology transfer and innovation-support professions in Europe. **Structure** Board of Management, consisting of representatives from each European Union country and one member representing non-EU members. Secretariat located in Luxembourg (Luxembourg). **Languages** English, French. **Staff** 2.50 FTE, paid. **Finance** Financed in roughly equal parts by: members' dues; contracts with EU; sale of services. **Activities** Training/education; events/meetings. **Events** *Annual General Meeting* Brussels (Belgium) 2018, *Annual Conference* Singapore (Singapore) 2015, *Annual Conference* Utrecht (Netherlands) 2014, *Annual Conference* Beijing (China) 2013, *Annual Conference* Copenhagen (Denmark) 2012. **Publications** *The Business Platform: Entrepreneurship and Management in the Early Stages of a Firm's Development.* **Members** Technology transfer specialists; Public and private consultants; Chambers of commerce and industry; Universities; Research centres; Business and innovation centres; Regional development agencies; Governmental ministries or agencies; International organizations. Members (200) in 41 countries. Membership countries not specified. **IGO Relations** Recognized by: *European Commission (EC, #06633).* **NGO Relations** Partner of: *European Association of Research Managers and Administrators (EARMA, #06195).*
[2019/XD8790/t/**D**]

♦ European Association for the Transport of Heavy Loads / see European Association of Abnormal Road Transport and Mobile Cranes (#05923)
♦ European Association for Trauma and Emergency Surgery (inactive)
♦ European Association of Treasures and Churchesmuseums (#02583)
♦ European Association of Turkish Academics (inactive)
♦ European Association of Underwater Games (inactive)
♦ European Association of Universities and Colleges of Art, Design and Media / see The Global Association of Art and Design Education and Research (#10241)
♦ European Association of Universities, Schools and Colleges of Optometry (inactive)

♦ European Association of University Classics Teachers (Eurosophia) 06260
Association européenne de professeurs de langues anciennes de l'enseignement supérieur (APLAES) – Federación Europea de los Profesores de Lenguas Clasicas de la Enseñanza Superior
Sec Université Jean Monnet, UFR arts lettres, 33 rue du 11 novembre, 42023 Saint-Étienne CEDEX 2, France.
URL: http://www.aplaes.org/
History 6 Dec 1967. Registration: France. **Aims** Promote the spread of classical *humanism* at European universities; contribute to the development and improvement of the teaching and learning of the Greek and Latin languages, literature and civilisations; enable university teachers to strengthen their scientific, pedagogical and professional cooperation. **Structure** General Assembly (annual). Council; Bureau. **Languages** English, French. **Events** *Congress* Aix-en-Provence (France) 2013, *Congress* Orléans (France) 2012, *Congress* Nantes (France) 2011, *Congress* Toulouse (France) 2010, *Congress* Bordeaux (France) 2009. **Publications** *Eurosophia Newsletter.* **Members** Organizations and individuals. Membership countries not specified. **IGO Relations** *Council of Europe (CE, #04881).* **NGO Relations** Member of: *EUROCLASSICA (#05663).*
[2021/XD9292/**D**]

♦ European Association for Unoriented Polyester Films (EUPET) 06261
Pres Industriepark Hoechst, F821, 65926 Frankfurt-Main, Germany. E-mail: info@coexpan-montonate.it.
SG c/o EuPC, Avenue de Cortenbergh 71, Box 4, 1000 Brussels, Belgium. T. +3227324124. Fax +3227324218.
URL: http://www.eupet.org/
History 1994, as *European Unsaturated PET Film Manufacturers Association.* Previously also referred to as *European Unoriented PET Film Manufacturers Association.* New name adopted, 2000. **Languages** English, German. **Staff** 2.00 FTE, paid.
Members Full in 6 countries:
France, Germany, Italy, Poland, Switzerland, UK.
[2012.07.25/XD4805/**D**]

♦ European Association of Urban Historians / see European Association for Urban History (#06262)

♦ European Association for Urban History (EAUH) 06262
Association Européenne d'Histoire Urbaine
Sec address not obtained. E-mail: mail@eauh.eu – eauh@uantwerpen.be.
Chair address not obtained.
URL: http://www.eauh.eu/
History 1989. Former names and other names: *European Association of Urban Historians* – former; *European Association for Urban History Ry* – legal name. Registration: Finland. **Aims** Promote interest for and research in urban history. **Structure** Board, comprising President, Secretary, Treasurer and 13 members, plus Corresponding members. **Languages** English, French. **Staff** Part-time, voluntary. **Finance** Conference organizers raise money for event. Fund for bursaries. **Events** *International Conference* Antwerp (Belgium) 2022, *International Conference* Antwerp (Belgium) 2021, *International Conference* Antwerp (Belgium) 2020, *International Conference* Rome (Italy) 2018, *International Conference* Helsinki (Finland) 2016. **Members** No formal membership. **NGO Relations** Partner of (1): *International Students of History Association (ISHA, #15613).*
[2021/XD8791/**D**]

♦ European Association for Urban History Ry / see European Association for Urban History (#06262)

♦ European Association of Urban Missions (EAUM) 06263
Arbeitsgemeinschaft Europäischer Stadtmissionen (AGES)
Pres Slezska diakonie Na Nivach 7, 737 01 Cesky Tesin, Czechia.
Treas Evangelische Stadtmission Freiburg e V, Adelhauser Strasse 27, 79098 Freiburg, Germany.
URL: http://www.stadtmissioneuropa.eu/
History Constitution adopted at 1st conference, 25 Sep 1974, Geneva (Switzerland); revised 27 May 1995, Gothenburg (Sweden). **Events** *Conference* Stockholm (Sweden) 2012, *Conference* Zurich (Switzerland) 2008, *Conference* London (UK) 2004, *Conference* Berlin (Germany) 2001, *Conference* Prague (Czech Rep) 1998.
Members Full in 9 countries:
Czechia, England, Finland, France, Germany, Netherlands, Norway, Sweden, Switzerland.
NGO Relations *City Mission World Association (CMWA, inactive).*
[2012/XJ1970/**D**]

♦ European Association of Urological Nurses / see European Association of Urology Nurses (#06265)

♦ European Association of Urology (EAU) 06264
Central Office PO Box 30016, 6803 AA Arnhem, Netherlands. T. +31263890680. Fax +31263890674. E-mail: info@uroweb.org.
SG Sheffield Hallam Univ, Fac of Health and Wellbeing – City Campus, Howard Street, Sheffield, S1 1WB, UK.
Street Address Mr E N van Kleffensstraat 5, 6842 CV Arnhem, Netherlands.
URL: http://www.uroweb.org/
History 1972. Restructured and reorganized: Aug 1993; Sep 1996. **Aims** Raise the level of urological care throughout Europe and beyond. **Structure** General Assembly; Board; EAU Offices (12) include: *European School of Urology (ESU, see: #06264).* All offices are supported by EAU Central Office, headed by 2 Executive Managers. EAU Section Office, comprising 13 Sections: Robotic Urology (ERUS), previously Oncological Urology (ESOU), previously Urological Research (ESUR), previously Andrological Urology (ESAU), previously Female and Functional Urology (ESFFU), formed on merger of *European Society of Female Urology (inactive)* and *European Society of Neuro-Urology (ESNU, inactive)*; Genitourinary Reconstructive Surgeons (ESGURS), previously Infections in Urology (ESIU), previously Uro-Technology (ESUT), previously Transplantation Urology (ESTU), previously Urological Imaging (ESUI), previously Uropathology (ESUP), previously Urolithiasis (EULIS), previously Office Urologist (ESUO). **Languages** English. **Staff** 60.00 FTE, paid. **Finance** Members' dues. **Activities** Research/documentation; training/education; knowledge management/information dissemination; events/meetings. **Events** *European Multidisciplinary Congress on Urological Cancers (EMUC)* Marseille (France) 2023, *Annual Congress* Milan (Italy) 2023, *ERUS : European robotic urology symposium* Barcelona (Spain) 2022, *Meeting* Barcelona (Spain) 2022, *European Multidisciplinary Congress on Urological Cancers (EMUC)* Budapest (Hungary) 2022. **Publications** *European Urology* (12 a year) – journal; *European Urology Today (EUT)* (4-6 a year) – newsletter; *European Urology Focus* – journal; *European Urology Oncology* – journal. Guidelines; historia; recommendations.

Members Active; Junior; Active International; Affiliate; Senior; Honorary. Medical professional (over 18,000) in 82 countries and territories:
Albania, Argentina, Armenia, Australia, Austria, Azerbaijan, Bangladesh, Belarus, Belgium, Brazil, Bulgaria, Canada, Colombia, Costa Rica, Côte d'Ivoire, Croatia, Cyprus, Czechia, Denmark, Egypt, Estonia, Finland, France, Georgia, Germany, Greece, Hong Kong, Hungary, Iceland, India, Indonesia, Iran Islamic Rep, Iraq, Ireland, Israel, Italy, Japan, Jordan, Kazakhstan, Korea Rep, Latvia, Lebanon, Libya, Lithuania, Luxembourg, Malaysia, Malta, Mexico, Moldova, Monaco, Morocco, Netherlands, New Zealand, North Macedonia, Norway, Pakistan, Poland, Portugal, Puerto Rico, Romania, Russia, Saudi Arabia, Senegal, Serbia, Singapore, Slovakia, Slovenia, South Africa, Spain, Sudan, Sweden, Switzerland, Syrian AR, Taiwan, Tunisia, Türkiye, UK, Ukraine, United Arab Emirates, Uruguay, USA, Yemen.
NGO Relations Member of (2): *European Alliance for Personalised Medicine (EAPM, #05878)*; *European Cancer Organisation (ECO, #06432)*. Cooperates with (1): *European Organisation for Research and Treatment of Cancer (EORTC, #08101)*. [2021/XD6052/v/D]

♦ European Association of Urology Nurses (EAUN) 06265

Manager PO Box 30016, 6803 AA Arnhem, Netherlands. T. +31263890680. Fax +31263890674. E-mail: eaun@uroweb.org – info@uroweb.org.
URL: http://nurses.uroweb.org/

History 2000. Former names and other names: *European Association of Urological Nurses (EAUN)* – former (2000). **Aims** Foster the highest standards of urological nursing care throughout Europe; facilitate continued development of urological nursing in all its aspects. **Languages** English. **Activities** Training/education; events/meetings. **Events** *Meeting* Amsterdam (Netherlands) 2022, *Meeting* 2021, *Meeting* Amsterdam (Netherlands) 2020, *Meeting* Barcelona (Spain) 2019, *Meeting* Copenhagen (Denmark) 2018. **Publications** *EAUN Newsletter*. *Guidelines for Urology Nurses*. **Members** Individuals (over 3,000) in 40 countries and territories. Membership countries not specified. **NGO Relations** Member of (2): *European Cancer Organisation (ECO, #06432)*; *European Specialist Nurses Organisation (ESNO, #08808)*. [2022/XJ3902/D]

♦ European Association for Use of the By-Products of Coal-Fired Power Stations / see European Coal Combustion Products Association (#06588)

♦ European Association of Vertebrate Palaeontologists (EAVP) 06266

Association européenne de paléontologues des vertébrés – Asociación Europea de Paleontólogos de Vertebrados – Europäische Gesellschaft für Wirbeltierpaläontologie – Associazione Europea dei Paleontologi dei vertebrati – Europees Genootschap van Vertebratenpaeontologen – Europäiska Föreningen för Vertebratpaleontologer

Hon Pres Geowissenschaftliche Abteilung, Staatliches Museum, Erbprinzenstrasse 13, 76133 Karlsruhe, Germany. E-mail: eavp@eavp.org.
URL: http://www.eavp.org/

History Jul 2003, Basel (Switzerland). Founded during the 8th *European Workshop on Vertebrate Palaeontology*. Statutes revised: 2015. Former names and other names: *Europäische Gesellschaft für Wirbeltier-Paläontologen* – alias. Registration: Germany. **Languages** English, French, German. **Events** *Conference* Benevento (Italy) 2022, *Conference* 2021, *Conference* Benevento (Italy) 2020, *Conference* Brussels (Belgium) 2019, *Conference* Lisbon (Portugal) 2018. **Members** Individuals and institutions. Membership countries not specified. [2021/XJ8023/D]

♦ European Association of Veterinarians in Education, Research and Industry (EVERI) 06267

Contact c/o FVE, Rue Victor Oudart 7, 1030 Brussels, Belgium. T. +3225337020. E-mail: despoina@fve.org.
URL: https://everi.fve.org/

History 16 Nov 1973, Genval (Belgium). Former names and other names: *Federation of European Veterinarians in Industry and Research (FEVIR)* – former (1973 to 2005); *Fédération européenne des vétérinaires de l'industrie et de la recherche* – former (1973 to 2005); *Federación de Veterinarios Europeos de la Industria y la Investigación* – former (1973 to 2005). Registration: EU Transparency Register, No/ID: 629998914866-31. **Aims** Provide members with updated information on European Union policy and legislation related to animals, animal products, feed, medicated feed and veterinary medicinal products; establish working relations with EU decision-makers; participate in the policy-making of other European associations; serve as a communication platform for members. **Structure** General Assembly (annual); Board of Directors. **Events** *General Assembly* Bratislava (Slovakia) 2019, *General Assembly* Brussels (Belgium) 2019, *General Assembly* Bergen (Norway) 2018, *General Assembly* Rome (Italy) 2018, *Joint meeting* Brussels (Belgium) 1999.
Members Full national organizations in 3 countries:
Belgium, Germany, UK.
IGO Relations Recognized by: *European Commission (EC, #06633)*. **NGO Relations** Member of (1): *Federation of Veterinarians of Europe (#09713)*. *International Veterinary Students' Association (IVSA, #15851)* is member. [2022.05.11/XD5334/t/D]

♦ European Association of Veterinary Anatomists (EAVA) 06268

Association européenne des anatomistes vétérinaires – Asociación Europea de Anatomistas Veterinarios – Europäische Vereinigung der Veterinäranatomen – Societas Europaea Anatomorum Veterinariorum

SG Dept of Anatomy/Histology/Embryology, Fac of Veterinary Medicine, Univ of Veterinary and Pharmazeutical Sciences, Palackeho 1-3, 612 42 Brno, Czechia. T. +420604206455. Fax +420541562217.
URL: http://www.eava.eu/

History Founded Aug 1963, Hannover (Germany FR), following suggestion at 5th Congress of *World Association of Veterinary Anatomists (WAVA, #21202)*, 4-8 Sep 1961, Vienna (Austria). Founding Assembly: 6 Apr 1964, Vienna. Statutes adopted 4-7 Aug 1965, Giessen (Germany FR); amended 24 Aug 1990, Leipzig (Germany). **Aims** Afford those persons in European or neighbouring countries engaged in the study of anatomy of domestic animals the opportunity to come together for the advancement of these studies. **Structure** General Assembly (every 2 years, at Congress); Executive Committee. **Languages** English. **Staff** Voluntary. **Finance** Members' dues. Other sources: government grants; support from public authorities, organizations or individuals; proceeds from activities. **Activities** Events/meetings; awards/prizes/competitions. **Events** *Biennial General Assembly* Vienna (Austria) 2016, *Biennial General Assembly* Cluj-Napoca (Romania) 2014, *Biennial General Assembly* Stara Zagora (Bulgaria) 2012, *Biennial general assembly / Congress* Paris (France) 2010, *Biennial general assembly / Congress* Budapest (Hungary) 2008. **Publications** *Vademecum – Societas Europaea Anatomorum Veterinariorum* (1996).
Members Individuals (Full or Honorary – 312) in 46 countries:
Argentina, Austria, Belgium, Bosnia-Herzegovina, Brazil, Bulgaria, Canada, Croatia, Czechia, Denmark, Egypt, Estonia, Finland, France, Germany, Greece, Hungary, India, Iran Islamic Rep, Ireland, Israel, Italy, Japan, Lithuania, Moldova, Morocco, Netherlands, New Zealand, North Macedonia, Poland, Portugal, Romania, Russia, Saudi Arabia, Serbia, Slovakia, Slovenia, Spain, Sweden, Switzerland, Türkiye, UK, Ukraine, USA, Venezuela, Zimbabwe.
NGO Relations Member of: *World Association of Veterinary Anatomists (WAVA, #21202)*. [2015.01.09/XD0586/v/D]

♦ European Association of Veterinary Diagnostic Imaging (EAVDI) . . . 06269

Sec Langford Vets, Univ of Bristol, Langford House, Langford, Bristol, BS40 5DU, UK. E-mail: secretary@eavdi.org.
URL: http://www.eavdi.org/

History 6 Sep 1992, Switzerland. 6 Sep 1992, Ebnat-Kappel (Switzerland), as a continuation of the *'British Veterinary Radiology Association (BVRA)'*, founded in the 1960's, which became *'European Veterinary Radiological Association (EVRA)'* in 1991. **Aims** Promote study and development of veterinary radiography, radiology, ultrasonography, nuclear medicine, computed tomography, magnetic resonance imaging and radiotherapy and other veterinary applications of diagnostic imaging or radiobiology. **Structure** Annual General Meeting; Board of Officers. Divisions (meeting annually) each have their own Board comprising 3 officers: Chairman; Secretary; Treasurer. Screening Sub-Committee for Scholarships and Travel Grants. **Languages** English. **Staff** Voluntary. **Finance** Members' dues. **Activities** Training/education; awards/prizes/competitions. Set up: *European College of Veterinary Diagnostic Imaging (ECVDI, #06623)*. **Events** *Annual General Assembly* Windsor (UK) 2018, *Annual General Assembly* Wroclaw (Poland) 2016, *EVDI : Annual European Veterinary Diagnostic Imaging Meeting* Wroclaw (Poland) 2016, *EVDI : Annual European Veterinary Diagnostic Imaging Meeting* Utrecht (Netherlands) 2014, *Autumn Meeting* Loughborough (UK) 2013. **Publications** *EAVDI Yearbook*.

Members Ordinary; Student; Honorary individuals in 26 countries:
Austria, Belgium, Denmark, Finland, France, Germany, Greece, Hungary, Iran Islamic Rep, Ireland, Israel, Italy, Morocco, Netherlands, Norway, Poland, Portugal, Romania, Slovenia, South Africa, Spain, Sweden, Switzerland, Türkiye, UK, USA.
NGO Relations Member of: *International Veterinary Radiology Association (IVRA, #15850)*. [2018/XD5566/v/D]

♦ European Association of Veterinary Laboratory Diagnosticians (EAVLD) 06270

Sec Animal and Plant Health Agency, Woodham Lane, Addlestone, KT15 3NB, UK.
URL: http://www.eavld.org/

History 2008. Founded following the activities of *Collaborating Veterinary Laboratories (CoVetLab)*. Statutes adopted 2009. **Aims** Improve veterinary and public health by providing a platform for communication among veterinary laboratory diagnosticians; promote highest standards in European veterinary laboratories. **Structure** General Meeting (every 2 years); Governing Board. **Finance** Members' dues. **Events** *Congress* Seville (Spain) 2022, *Congress* Seville (Spain) 2020, *Congress* Brussels (Belgium) 2018, *Congress* Prague (Czechia) 2016, *Congress* Pisa (Italy) 2014. **NGO Relations** Memorandum of Understanding with (2): *European College of Veterinary Microbiology (ECVM, #06625)*; *European Society of Clinical Microbiology and Infectious Diseases (ESCMID, #08548)*. Sister organizations: American Association of Veterinary Laboratory Diagnosticians (AAVLD); *World Association of Veterinary Laboratory Diagnosticians (WAVLD, #21205)*. [2022/XJ7440/D]

♦ European Association for Veterinary Pharmacology and Toxicology (EAVPT) 06271

Pres c/o Royal Veterinary College, Royal College St, London, NW1 0TU, UK.
URL: http://www.eavpt2012.nl/

History 29 Jun 1978, Hannover (Germany FR). **Aims** Create a forum for the exchange of knowledge and ideas in the fields of experimental and clinical veterinary pharmacology, toxicology and therapeutics. **Structure** Congress (every 3 years). Board of National Coordinators, President, Senior Vice-President, Junior Vice-President, Secretary and Treasurer. **Languages** English. **Staff** Part-time, voluntary. **Finance** Members' dues. **Activities** Organizes congress and workshop. **Events** *Congress* Bruges (Belgium) 2023, *Congress* Lviv (Ukraine) 2022, *Congress* Wroclaw (Poland) 2018, *Congress* Nantes (France) 2015, *Congress* Noordwijkerhout (Netherlands) 2012. **Publications** *EAVPT Newsletter*, *Journal of Veterinary Pharmacology and Therapeutics*. Congress proceedings.
Members Veterinary pharmacologists in any country. Full in 43 countries:
Argentina, Australia, Austria, Belgium, Bulgaria, Canada, Chile, China, Colombia, Czechia, Denmark, Egypt, Finland, France, Germany, Greece, Hungary, Indonesia, Ireland, Israel, Italy, Japan, Korea Rep, Mexico, Monaco, Netherlands, Nigeria, Norway, Pakistan, Poland, Portugal, Scotland, Serbia-Montenegro, South Africa, Spain, Sri Lanka, Sudan, Sweden, Switzerland, UK, Ukraine, United Arab Emirates, USA. [2018/XD2169/D]

♦ European Association for Veterinary Specialization (no recent information)

♦ European Association for Viewers Interests (EAVI) 06272

SG Rond Point Schuman 9/16, 1040 Brussels, Belgium. T. +3222303006. E-mail: eavi@eavi.eu.
URL: http://www.eavi.eu/

History Registration: Banque-Carrefour des Entreprises, No/ID: 0872.621.797, Start date: 5 Dec 2004, Belgium; EU Transparency Register, No/ID: 211406234638-53, Start date: 23 Apr 2019. **Aims** Support the adoption of initiatives that enable citizens to read, write and participate in public life through the media. **Languages** English. **Activities** Awareness raising; events/meetings; knowledge management/information dissemination; networking/liaising; projects/programmes; training/education. **Events** *Session* Brussels (Belgium) 2021, *International Conference* Budapest (Hungary) 2011, *International Conference* Madrid (Spain) 2009, *International Conference* Rome (Italy) 2008, *International Conference* Lucca (Italy) 2004. **Publications** *EAVI Newsletter* (6 a year). *The Media Coach book* (2021) in English. **IGO Relations** Partner of (4): *Council of Europe (CE, #04881)*; *European Audiovisual Observatory (#06294)*; *UNESCO (#20322)*; *United Nations Alliance of Civilizations (UNAOC, #20520)*. **NGO Relations** Member of (1): *European Association for Local Democracy (ALDA, #06110)*. [2021.12.03/XJ8996/D]

♦ European Association of Violin and Bow Makers 06273

Association européenne des maîtres luthiers et archetiers – Verband Europäischer Geigen- und Bogenbau-Meister – Associazione Europea Maestri Liutai e Archettai (AEL)

Pres Rheinstr 73, 65185 Wiesbaden, Germany.
Sec Bischof Blum Platz 9, 65366 Geisenheim, Germany. T. +496722971982. Fax +496722971984.
URL: http://www.ael-violins.com/

History 1987, Sofia (Bulgaria), as *European Union of Violin and Bow Makers (UEL)*. Present name adopted 1993. **Aims** Promote the art of violin making as a European cultural wealth; offer a platform on European violin makers can exchange opinions and experiences; maintain links with other national and international associations active in the field. **Structure** Board, including President, Vice-President, Secretary and Treasurer. **Languages** English, German, Italian. **Staff** 35.00 FTE, paid. **Events** *Meeting* Mittenwald (Germany) 2006, *Meeting* Cremona (Italy) 2005, *Meeting* Cremona (Italy) 2004, *Meeting* Cremona (Italy) 2003, *Meeting* Cremona (Italy) 2002.
Members Individuals in 12 countries:
Austria, Belgium, Denmark, France, Germany, Italy, Netherlands, Portugal, Spain, Sweden, Switzerland, UK. [2011.09.30/XD8384/D]

♦ European Association for Virtual Reality and Augmented Reality / see EuroXR (#09197)
♦ European Association of Visceral Surgery (no recent information)

♦ European Association for Vision and Eye Research (EVER) 06274

Sec Viale Matteotti 7, 50121 Florence FI, Italy. T. +395550238. Fax +3955570227. E-mail: eversecretary@oic.it.
Registered Seat Kapucijnenvoer 33, 3000 Leuven, Belgium. T. +3216233849. Fax +3216234097.
URL: http://everassociation.org/

History 1997, by merger of: *Association for Eye Research (AER, inactive)*; *European Community Ophthalmic Research Association (ECORA, inactive)*; *Joint European Research Meetings on Ophthalmology and Vision for the European Vision and Eye Research (Jermov for Ever, inactive)*. Registered in accordance with Belgian law: BE-0465-214-572. **Aims** Encourage research and disseminate knowledge concerning the eye and vision. **Structure** Annual General Assembly; Board; Executive Committee. Scientific Sections (11); Special Committees. **Languages** English. **Staff** 2.00 FTE, paid. **Finance** Members' dues. Other sources: subsidies; incomes from activities. **Events** *Annual International Meeting on Ophthalmology and Vision* Nice (France) 2021, *Annual International Meeting on Ophthalmology and Vision* Nice (France) 2020, *Annual International Meeting on Ophthalmology and Vision* Nice (France) 2019, *Annual International Meeting on Ophthalmology and Vision* Nice (France) 2018, *Annual International Meeting on Ophthalmology and Vision* Nice (France) 2017. **Members** Effective; Non-voting. Members (over 850) in 48 countries. Membership countries not specified. **NGO Relations** Member of: *European Alliance for Vision Research and Ophthalmology (EU-EYE, #05890)*. [2022/XD6469/D]

♦ European Association for the Visual Studies of Man (inactive)
♦ European Association for Waste Water Management (inactive)
♦ European Association of Water and Heat Meter Manufacturers (#02567)
♦ European Association of Water Meters Manufacturers / see Association européenne de fabricants de compteurs d'eau et d'énergie thermique (#02567)
♦ European Association of Wine Cities / see Réseau Européen des Villes du Vin (#18881)

♦ European Association of Wine Economists (EuAWE) 06275

Contact ISVV, 210 chemin de Leysotte, 33140 Villenave-d'Ornon, France. T. +33557575804. E-mail: contact@euawe.com.
URL: http://www.euawe.com/

History Jan 2020. Follows *Vineyard Data Quantification Society (VDQS)*. **Aims** Develop knowledge in the field of wine economics. **Structure** Board; Scientific Committee; Steering Committee; Honorary Committee. **Activities** Events/meetings; knowledge management/information dissemination. **Events** *Conference* Vila Real (Portugal) 2022. [2021/AA2274/D]

♦ European Association of Women Executives / see Femmes chefs d'entreprises mondiales (#09733)
♦ European Association for Women and Health Research (no recent information)
♦ European Association of Women Resource Centres (no recent information)

♦ European Association for Women in Science, Engineering and Technology (WITEC) 06276

Femmes dans la science, l'ingénierie et la technologie – Mujeres en la ciencia, la tecnologia y la ingenieria – Frauen in Naturwissenschaft, Ingenieurwesen und Technologie – Donne nella scienza, tecnologia, ingegneria – Vrouwen in techniek en exact – Kvinnor inom teknisk och naturvetenskaplig sektor – Kvinder i videnskab og teknologi – Naiset tieteen ja tekniikan aliolla

Secretariat WITEC Sweden, Vapensmedsgatan 6, SE-415 74 Gothenburg, Sweden. T. +46723091919. E-mail: info@witec.se.
Main Website: https://www.witeceu.com/

History 1988. Founded as a sectoral University-Enterprise Training Partnership (UETP). Formerly known as *Women in Technology in the European Community.* 2001, established as a non-profit European association. **Aims** Increase the number of girls and women studying science, engineering and technology; develop women's technical and entrepreneurial skills through training initiatives and projects; create information exchanges and networking opportunities for women in science, engineering and technology; promote and support research into areas relating to women in non-traditional fields; promote regional, national and international awareness and interest in the field. **Structure** General Meeting (annual); Executive Committee, comprising President, Secretary and Treasurer. Secretariat; National Networks. **Languages** English, Swedish. **Staff** across Europe. **Activities** Events/meetings; guidance/assistance/consulting; knowledge management/ information dissemination; networking/liaising; projects/programmes; training/education. Europe. **Events** *General Meeting* Magdeburg (Germany) 2005, *Conference / Meeting* Hungary 2003, *Conference* Netherlands 2003, *Conference* Estonia 2002, *European database of women experts in science engineering and technology set – opportunities across Europe* London (UK) 2000. **Publications** *WITEC E-Newsletter. Case Studies of Good Practice; European Documentation Guide of Best Practice in Vocational Training; European Handbook of Women Experts; Guideline for Action; Women as Industrial Placement.* **Information Services** *European Database of Women Experts in Science, Engineering and Technology (SET)* – enables users to find a broad range of information about women experts across Europe.
Members National networks in 9 countries:
Austria, Germany, Greece, Hungary, Italy, Netherlands, Spain, Sweden, UK. [2023.02.24/XF5120/**F**]

♦ European Association Working for Carers (Eurocarers) 06277

Secretariat Rue Père de Deken 14, 1040 Brussels, Belgium. T. +32456141950. E-mail: info@ eurocarers.org.
URL: http://www.eurocarers.org/

History Dec 2006, Luxembourg. Originated from2 European networks: Carmen, a network on integrated care; Eurofamcare, a research network on carers of older persons. Registration: EU Transparency Register, No/ID: 887457714435-80. **Aims** Be the leading authority on carers and their contribution to the sustainability of health and long-term care systems across the EU. **Structure** General Assembly; Board; Secretariat. **Languages** English, French, Italian, Spanish. **Staff** 6.00 FTE, paid. **Finance** Members' dues. Other sources: EaSI operating grant (DG EMPL); EU core action grants; sponsors. **Activities** Research/documentation; politics/policy/regulatory; advocacy/lobbying/activism; networking/liaising; awareness raising; knowledge management/information dissemination; projects/programmes; capacity building; events/meetings. **Events** *Annual General Meeting* Brussels (Belgium) 2018, *Global Forum on Incontinence* Rome (Italy) 2018, *Annual General Meeting* Brussels (Belgium) 2017, *Annual General Meeting* Brussels (Belgium) 2016, *Annual General Meeting* Helsinki (Finland) 2014. **Publications** *EuCa Newsletter.* Policy and strategy documents; position papers; presentations fact sheet; video library. **Members** Over 60 carers' organizations as well as relevant research and development organizations. Membership countries not specified. **IGO Relations** *European Commission (EC, #06633); European Parliament (EP, #08146)* Interest Group on Carers. **NGO Relations** Associate member of: *European Forum for Primary Care (EFPC, #07326); International Alliance of Carer Organizations (IACO, #11623); Social Platform (#19344).* Partnership agreement with: *European Patients' Forum (EPF, #08172).* Strong collaboration with: *AGE Platform Europe (#00557); EuroHealthNet (#05693); European Forum for Primary Care (EFPC, #07326); European Social Network (ESN, #08505).*
[2021/XJ9300/**D**]

♦ European Association of Work and Organizational Psychology (EAWOP) 06278

SG Dept of Organizational Psychology, Erasmus Univ Rotterdam, Burgemeester Oudlaan 50, 3062 PA Rotterdam, Netherlands. E-mail: admin@eawop.org.
Treas Univ of Bucharest, Sos Panduri 90, 050663 Bucharest, Romania.
URL: http://www.eawop.org/

History 1991, Rouen (France). Founded at 5th European Congress for Work and Organizational Psychology. Statutes amended 1997. **Aims** Promote and support development and application of work and organizational psychology in Europe; facilitate links between scientists and professionals in the field across Europe. **Structure** General Assembly; Constituent Council; Executive Committee. Task Forces. Secretariat. **Languages** English. **Staff** 0.50 FTE, paid. **Finance** Sources: members' dues. **Activities** Events/meetings; training/ education. **Events** *Congress* Katowice (Poland) 2023, *Congress* Glasgow (UK) 2022, *Congress* Glasgow (UK) 2021, *Congress* Turin (Italy) 2019, *Congress* Dublin (Ireland) 2017. **Publications** *European Journal of Work and Organizational Psychology* (6 a year); *Organizational Psychology Review* (4 a year); *EAWOP in Practice* – e-journal.
Members Professional associations in 24 countries:
Austria, Belgium, Denmark, Estonia, Finland, France, Germany, Greece, Ireland, Italy, Latvia, Lithuania, Malta, Netherlands, Norway, Poland, Portugal, Romania, Slovenia, Spain, Sweden, Switzerland, UK, Ukraine.
NGO Relations Agreement of Cooperation with: *European Federation of Psychologists Associations (EFPA, #07199).* Affiliate of: *International Union of Psychological Science (IUPsyS, #15807).* [2021/XD7795/**D**]

♦ European Association for World Religions in Education (EAWRE) .. 06279

Association européenne de réflexion sur les religions du monde dans l'éducation – Europäische Arbeitsgemeinschaft für Weltreligionen in der Erziehung

Secretariat Centrum für Religiöse Studien, Westfälische Wilhelms-Uni, Hammerstr 95, 48153 Münster, Germany. T. +492518326110. Fax +492518326111. E-mail: crs@uni-muenster.de.
Chairman Molenveltlaan 21, 2071 BR Santpoort, Netherlands. T. +31235376075.

History 1990. Restructuring, 2010. **Aims** Contribute to more appropriate, accurate, adequate and empathetic teaching of world religions, according to self-understanding and scholarly knowledge, on all levels of education; contribute to a fair recognition of the factual, cultural and religious variety in Europe. **Structure** General Meeting (annual). Board, comprising President, Chairman, Vice-Chairman, Secretary, Deputy Secretary, Treasurer and 2 members. **Finance** Members' dues. Sponsoring; projects. **Activities** Carries out work in 3 major forms all aimed at supporting teachers in realizing a solid and effective teaching of world religions: publication of theoretical and practical literature for teachers; organization of teachers conferences on a European level; advisory services. Organizes conferences and workshops. **Events** *Annual general meeting and conference* Thessaloniki (Greece) 2006, *Annual general meeting and conference* Amsterdam (Netherlands) 2005, *Annual general meeting and conference* Lancaster (UK) 2004, *Annual general meeting and conference* Strasbourg (France) 2003, *Annual General Meeting and Conference* Crete (Greece) 2002. **Publications** *Calendar of Religious Festivals* (annual) in English, French, German. *Religious Diversity at Home in Various Countries; Religious Education, Europe and Young People.*
Members Individuals from different religious backgrounds and academic disciplines in 15 countries:
Austria, Belgium, Denmark, Finland, France, Germany, Greece, Hungary, Italy, Netherlands, Norway, Sweden, Türkiye, UK, Ukraine.
IGO Relations Occasional cooperation with Education Committee of *Council of Europe (CE, #04881).* **NGO Relations** Member of: *Coordinating Group for Religion in Education (CoGREE, #04823).* [2019/XD6819/**D**]

♦ European Association of Writers, 1941 (inactive)
♦ European Association for Young Dentists (unconfirmed)

♦ European Association of Young Economists (EAYE) 06280

Chair Dept Social Economics – UGent, Sint-Pietersplein 6, 9000 Ghent, Belgium.
URL: http://www.eaye.eu/

History Set up evolving out of the Spring Meeting of Young Economists (SMYE), starting 1996. **Aims** Facilitate the interaction between young non-tenured researchers in economics working on topics within economics. **Activities** Events/meetings; awards/prizes/competitions. **Events** *Spring Meeting* Bologna (Italy) 2021, *Spring Meeting* Bologna (Italy) 2020, *Spring Meeting* Brussels (Belgium) 2019, *Workshop on Social Networks* Paris (France) 2019, *Spring Meeting* Palma (Spain) 2018. [2015.06.01/XJ9588/**D**]

♦ European Association of Young Historians (inactive)
♦ European Association of Young Mediators (no recent information)

♦ European Association of Young Neurologists and Trainees (YNT) .. 06281

Pres Semmelweis University, Institute of Genomic Medicine and Rare Disorders, Tömo u 25-29, Budapest 1083, Hungary. T. +3614591483.
Sec address not obtained. E-mail: ynt.secretary@googlemail.com.
URL: http://www.eaynt.org/

History 8 Aug 1999, Lisbon (Portugal). Registered in accordance with Belgian law. **Aims** Promote clinical exchange; develop access to education and research; provide an informative service; foster the European culture. **Structure** General Assembly. Board, comprising President, Secretary, Treasurer, Vice-Presidents and officers for the specialist sections. **Languages** English. **Staff** 10.00 FTE, voluntary. **Finance** Private and commercial sponsorship. **Activities** Runs a clinical exchange programme, to create a fund providing grants for young neurologists. Collects and evaluates information on neurology training programmes. Facilitates access to scientific venues. **Events** *General Assembly* Helsinki (Finland) 2003, *General Assembly* Vienna (Austria) 2002, *General Assembly* Copenhagen (Denmark) 2000, *Meeting* Trest (Czech Rep) 2000, *General Assembly* Milan (Italy) 1999. **Publications** Books; reports; proceedings.
Members Full in 49 countries:
Albania, Argentina, Azerbaijan, Belarus, Belgium, Brazil, Bulgaria, Chile, Colombia, Croatia, Czechia, Denmark, Estonia, Finland, France, Georgia, Germany, Greece, Hungary, India, Indonesia, Ireland, Israel, Italy, Japan, Kazakhstan, Latvia, Lithuania, Malaysia, Moldova, Netherlands, Norway, Philippines, Poland, Portugal, Romania, Russia, Serbia, Slovakia, Slovenia, Spain, Sweden, Switzerland, Tajikistan, Türkiye, UK, Ukraine, USA, Uzbekistan. [2015/XD7274/**D**]

♦ European Association of Young Opera Friends (JUVENILIA) 06282

Main Office Via Silvio Pellico 6, 20121 Milan MI, Italy. E-mail: juvenilia.eu@gmail.com.
URL: https://juvenilia.eu/

History Feb 1998, Milan (Italy). Former names and other names: *European Network of Young Opera Friends* – former (1998). **Aims** Improve communication between clubs, opera companies and individuals in Europe. **Structure** General Assembly (annual). **Events** *General Assembly* Nürburg (Germany) 2006, *General Assembly* Paris (France) 2005, *General Assembly* Amsterdam (Netherlands) 2004, *General Assembly* Milan (Italy) 2003, *General Assembly* Madrid (Spain) 2002. **Publications** *JUVENILA Newsletter.*
Members in 9 countries:
Austria, Belgium, Czechia, France, Germany, Italy, Netherlands, Poland, Spain. [2021/XM1344/**D**]

♦ European Association of Youth Orchestras (inactive)
♦ European Association for Zoological Nomenclature (inactive)

♦ European Association of Zoos and Aquaria (EAZA) 06283

Exec Dir Postal Address Plantage Middenlaan 45, 1018 DC Amsterdam, Netherlands. E-mail: info@ eaza.net.
URL: http://www.eaza.net/

History 12 Feb 1988, Rockanje (Netherlands). Statutes adopted 9 Jun 1988. Former names and other names: *European Community Association of Zoos and Aquaria (ECAZA)* – former. Registration: EU Transparency Register, No/ID: 058910411877-30, Start date: 18 Sep 2013. **Aims** Facilitate cooperation within the European zoo and aquarium community with the aim of furthering its professional quality in keeping animals and presenting them for the education of the public, and of contributing to scientific research and conservation of global diversity. **Structure** General Meeting (annual); Council (meets twice a year); Executive Committee; Executive Office; Standing Committees (3), include: *European Endangered Species Programme (EEP);* Specialist Committees (7); Working Groups (8). **Languages** English. **Staff** 16.00 FTE, paid. **Activities** Training/ecucation; research/documentation; advocacy/lobbying/activism; awareness raising. **Events** *Annual Conference* Albufeira (Portugal) 2022, *Animal Welfare Forum* Apeldoorn (Netherlands) 2022, *Conservation Forum* Zagreb (Croatia) 2022, *Annual Conference* Amsterdam (Netherlands) 2021, *Education Conference* San Diego, CA (USA) 2021. **Publications** *Zooquaria* (4 a year).
Members Full (294); Temporary (12); Associate (35); Corporate (36). Zoos and aquaria in 43 countries and territories:
Armenia, Austria, Belgium, Bosnia-Herzegovina, Bulgaria, Chile, Croatia, Czechia, Denmark, Estonia, Finland, France, Georgia, Germany, Greece, Hungary, Ireland, Israel, Italy, Kazakhstan, Kuwait, Latvia, Lithuania, Luxembourg, Netherlands, Norway, Palestine, Poland, Portugal, Qatar, Romania, Russia, Serbia, Slovakia, Slovenia, Spain, Sweden, Switzerland, Türkiye, UK, Ukraine, United Arab Emirates, USA.
IGO Relations Member of: *Convention on the Conservation of Migratory Species of Wild Animals (Bonn Convention, 1979); Standing Committee to the Bern Convention on the Conservation of European Wildlife and Natural Habitats (#19949).* Cooperates with: *European Commission (EC, #06633); European Parliament (EP, #08146).* **NGO Relations** Member of (3): *International Union for Conservation of Nature and Natural Resources (IUCN, #15766); Turtle Conservation Fund (TCF, #20263); World Association of Zoos and Aquariums (WAZA, #21208).* Partner of (1): *Pan-African Association of Zoos and Aquaria (PAAZA, #18039).* [2022/XD2115/**D**]

♦ European Association of Zoo and Wildlife Veterinarians (EAZWV) .. 06284

Exec Dir PO Box 23, Liebefeld, 3097 Bern, Switzerland. T. +41313718242. Fax +41313718244. E-mail: secretariat@eazwv.org.
URL: http://www.eazwv.org/

History 16 May 1996, Rostock (Germany). Registration: EU Transparency Register, No/ID: 158270723530-82. **Aims** Promote advancement of veterinary knowledge and skill in the field of zoo and wild animals; improve husbandry of zoo animals and the management of wild animal populations. **Structure** General Assembly (annual); Board; Working Group. **Languages** English. **Staff** 1.00 FTE, paid. **Finance** Sources: members' dues. Annual budget: 30,000 EUR. **Events** *Zoo and Wildlife Health Conference* 2021, *Zoo and Wildlife Health Conference* Bern (Switzerland) 2020, *Joint Conference on Zoo and Wildlife Health* Kolmården (Sweden) 2019, *Joint Conference on Zoo and Wildlife Health* Prague (Czechia) 2018, *International Conference on Diseases of Zoo and Wild Animals* Barcelona (Spain) 2015. **Publications** *EAZWV News* (4 a year). *Transmissible Diseases Handbook.* Meeting proceedings.
Members Veterinarians (700) in 51 countries and territories:
Argentina, Australia, Austria, Belgium, Bosnia-Herzegovina, Brazil, Bulgaria, Canada, China, Croatia, Czechia, Denmark, Estonia, Finland, France, Germany, Greece, Hong Kong, Hungary, India, Indonesia, Iran Islamic Rep, Ireland, Israel, Italy, Laos, Lithuania, Luxembourg, Mozambique, Netherlands, Norway, Peru, Poland, Portugal, Qatar, Romania, Russia, Singapore, Slovenia, South Africa, Spain, Sweden, Switzerland, Trinidad-Tobago, Tunisia, Türkiye, UK, Ukraine, United Arab Emirates, USA, Vietnam.
NGO Relations Member of (3): *International Union for Conservation of Nature and Natural Resources (IUCN, #15766); Union européenne des vétérinaires praticiens (UEVP, #20405); World Association of Zoos and Aquariums (WAZA, #21208).* [2021/XD6921/v/**D**]

♦ European Associaton of Medical and Scientific Illustrators / see Association Européenne des Illustrateurs Médicaux et Scientifiques (#02573)

♦ European Astrobiology Institute (EAI) 06285

Administrator c/o ESF, 1 quai Lezay-Marnésia, BP 90015, 67080 Strasbourg, France. T. +33388767100. Fax +333388370532.
Chair address not obtained.
URL: https://europeanastrobiology.eu/

Aims Carry out research, training, outreach and dissemination activities in astrobiology in a comprehensive and coordinated manner, thereby securing a leading role for the European Research Area in the field. **Structure** General Assembly; Management Committee; Executive Committee; Board of Trustees. Working Groups. **Activities** Events/meetings; knowledge management/information dissemination; research/documentation; training/education. **Events** *BEACON: Biennial European Astrobiology Conference* Las Palmas de Gran Canaria (Spain) 2023, *BEACON: Biennial European Astrobiology Conference* Santa Cruz de la Palma (Spain) 2022.

Members Participating entities and institutions (25) in 12 countries:
Belgium, Czechia, Estonia, France, Germany, Hungary, Italy, Poland, Portugal, Spain, Sweden, UK. [2022/AA2682/j/D]

♦ European Astrobiology Network Association (EANA) 06286

Pres c/o Deutsches Zentrum für Luft- und Raumfahrt eV, Microgravity User Support Center, Geb 29, Linder Höhe, 51147 Cologne, Germany.
Sec Dept Earth Sciences, Freie Univ Berlin, Kaiserswerther Str 16-18, 14195 Berlin, Germany.
URL: http://www.eana-net.eu/

History 23 May 2001, Frascati (Italy). Founded during 1st European Workshop on Exo/Astrobiology by *European Space Agency (ESA, #08798)* at *ESRIN (#05546)*. A Steering Group was set up Oct 1999, London (UK). Former names and other names: *European Exo/Astrobiology Network Association* – former. **Aims** Coordinate centres of excellence in astrobiology or related fields of research in Europe, so as to share expertise and research facilities. **Structure** Executive Council. **Languages** English, French. **Staff** Voluntary. **Finance** Sources: members' dues. Other sources: regional and local funding from meeting countries. Supported by: *European Space Agency (ESA, #08798)*; *European Union (EU, #08967)*. **Activities** Awards/prizes/competitions; events/meetings; training/education. **Events** *Conference* 2021, *European Astrobiology Conference* Bologna (Italy) 2020, *European Astrobiology Conference* Orléans (France) 2019, *European Astrobiology Conference* Berlin (Germany) 2018, *European Astrobiology Conference* Aarhus (Denmark) 2017. **NGO Relations** NASA Astrobiology Institute (NAI). [2022/XM3461/D]

♦ European Astronaut Centre (EAC) 06287

Centre européen des astronautes – Europäisches Astronautenzentrum

Head PO Box 90 60 96, 51127 Cologne, Germany. T. +4922036001101. Fax +4922036001102.
Public Relations address not obtained.
URL: https://www.esa.int/About_Us/EAC/

History 10 May 1990, within the framework of *European Space Agency (ESA, #08798)*, following decision of ESA Ministers, Nov 1987, The Hague (Netherlands), to establish a manned "In-Orbit Infrastructure". Part of ESA Directorate of Human Spaceflight and Microgravity at *European Space Research and Technology Centre (ESTEC, #08802)*. **Aims** Coordinate European astronaut activities; select and train European astronauts to take part in missions on board the International Space Station (ISS); train international *space* station astronauts on ESA flight elements and payloads; implement 'European Astronauts Policy', including management of the single European Astronauts Corps; be the 'home base' of all European astronauts, defining and observing rules concerning their safety and medical surveillance. **Structure** Head of the Centre; Administration; Astronauts Division; Astronauts Training Division; Medical Support Office; Management Support Office. **Languages** English, French. **Staff** 100.00 FTE, paid. **Finance** Contributions of 18 ESA member states participating in the Columbus Programme: Austria; Belgium; Czech Rep; Denmark; Finland; France; Germany; Ireland; Italy; Luxembourg; Netherlands; Norway; Portugal; Romania; Spain; Sweden; Switzerland; UK. **Activities** Monitors the process guaranteeing that all astronauts are governed by same rules of selection; provides basic and specialized training to ESA astronauts; awards successful graduates with membership in *European Astronaut Centre (see: #06287)*. Provides specialized training to ISS astronauts using training facilities for the ESA contributions to the ISS: Columbus, Automated Transfer Vehicle and PayLoads and a large neutral buoyancy facility. **Events** *Conference on European astronaut activities* Madrid (Spain) 1993.
Members Member states of the European Space Agency (ESA) (19):
Austria, Belgium, Czechia, Denmark, Finland, France, Germany, Greece, Ireland, Italy, Luxembourg, Netherlands, Norway, Portugal, Romania, Spain, Sweden, Switzerland, UK.
ESA State with special agreement:
Canada.
Astronauts from 10 member states:
Belgium, Denmark, France, Germany, Italy, Netherlands, Spain, Sweden, Switzerland, UK. [2018/XE1543/E*]

♦ European Astronaut Centre (see: #06287)

♦ European Astronomical Society (EAS) 06288

Société européenne d'astronomie

Secretariat c/o Univ of Geneva, Dept of Astronomy, ISDC, Chemin d'Ecogia 16, 1290 Versoix GE, Switzerland. T. +41223792100 – +41223792110. Fax +41223792133. E-mail: execsec-eas@unige.ch – eas@unige.ch.
Main: http://eas.unige.ch/

History 11 Oct 1990, Davos (Switzerland). Founded at regional meeting of *International Astronomical Union (IAU, #12287)*, following several years preparatory activity. Registration: Switzerland; EU Transparency Register, No/ID: 743919128337-14. **Aims** Advance astronomy in Europe by providing: an independent forum for discussion; a means for action at a European level. **Structure** General Meeting (every year); Council. Includes Joint Astrophysics Division with EPS. **Languages** English. **Finance** Members' dues. **Activities** Advocacy/lobbying/activism; networking/liaising; events/meetings; awards/prizes/competitions; guidance/assistance/consulting; financial and/or material support. **Events** *Annual Meeting* Valencia (Spain) 2022, *Annual Meeting* Leiden (Netherlands) 2021, *European Solar Physics Meeting* Turin (Italy) 2021, *European Solar Physics Meeting* Turin (Italy) 2020, *Annual Meeting* Versoix (Switzerland) 2020. **Publications** *EAS Newsletter*. Reports.
Members Individual professional astronomers in 44 countries:
Armenia, Australia, Austria, Azerbaijan, Belgium, Brazil, Bulgaria, Chile, Croatia, Cyprus, Czechia, Denmark, Estonia, France, Georgia, Germany, Greece, Hungary, Iceland, India, Ireland, Israel, Italy, Japan, Kazakhstan, Latvia, Lithuania, Netherlands, Norway, Poland, Portugal, Romania, Russia, Serbia, Slovakia, Slovenia, South Africa, Spain, Sweden, Switzerland, Türkiye, UK, Ukraine, USA. [2021/XD3024/D]

♦ European Asylum Support Office / see European Union Agency for Asylum (#08968)
♦ European Atherosclerosis Group / see European Atherosclerosis Society (#06289)

♦ European Atherosclerosis Society (EAS) 06289

Société européenne d'athérosclérose

Exec Officer Head Office, Mässans Gata 10, Box 5243, SE-402 24 Gothenburg, Sweden. T. +46317602427. Fax +4631812022. E-mail: office@eas-society.org.
Pres Imperial College London, Department of Public Health, 74 Ferndale Road, London, SW4 7SE, UK.
URL: https://www.eas-society.org/default.aspx

History 29 Feb 1964, Paris (France). Constitution agreed 6 Jan 1967, Milan (Italy). Previously registered in accordance with Swiss Civil Code. Former names and other names: *European Atherosclerosis Group* – former (1964 to 1986); *Groupe européen d'athérosclérose* – former (1964 to 1986). Registration: No/ID: 802418-0427, Sweden, Västra Götaland County. **Aims** Share knowledge about the causes, natural history, treatment and prevention of atherosclerosis and related diseases; advance research, and improve management of these diseases in the clinic. **Structure** General Meeting (annual); Executive Committee. **Languages** English. **Staff** 5.00 FTE, paid. **Finance** Sources: contributions; grants; meeting proceeds; members' dues; revenue from activities/projects; sponsorship. **Activities** Events/meetings; networking/liaising; standards/guidelines; training/education. **Events** *Congress* Mannheim (Germany) 2023, *Congress* Milan (Italy) 2022, *Congress* Helsinki (Finland) 2021, *Congress* Gothenburg (Sweden) 2020, *Congress* Maastricht (Netherlands) 2019. **Publications** *Atherosclerosis*. Guidelines; consensus position papers. **Members** Individuals (2,500) in 118 countries; Societies. Membership countries not specified. **NGO Relations** Member of (2): *Biomedical Alliance in Europe (#03251)*; *European Alliance for Cardiovascular Health (EACH, #05863)*. Cooperates with (7): *European Federation of Clinical Chemistry and Laboratory Medicine (EFLM, #07080)*; *European Lipoprotein Club (#07700)*; *European Society for Vascular Medicine (ESVM, #08771)*; *European Society of Cardiology (ESC, #08536)*; *International Atherosclerosis Society (IAS, #12288)*; *International Federation of Clinical Chemistry and Laboratory Medicine (IFCC, #13392)*; National Lipid Association (NLA). [2022.05.04/XD0588/D]

♦ European Athlete Student Network (EAS) 06290

Head Office Apartment 4, Villanueva Building, 99 Hannieqa Street, Ghaxaq, GXQ 1025, Malta. E-mail: info@dualcareer.eu.
URL: http://www.dualcareer.eu/

History 2004, with the support of *European Commission (EC, #06633)*, during The European Year of Education Through Sport (EYES). Current statutes adopted 11 Sep 2014, Rome (Italy). Registered in accordance with UK law. Former names and other names: *EAS – The Dual Career Network* – alias. **Aims** Support European athletes in combining high performance sport and education. **Structure** General Assembly (annual); Executive Board. **Activities** Events/meetings; networking/liaising. **Events** *Annual Conference* Lisbon (Portugal) 2021, *Annual Conference* Rovaniemi (Finland) 2016, *Annual Conference* Amsterdam (Netherlands) 2015, *Annual Conference* Rome (Italy) 2014, *Annual Conference* Trondheim (Norway) 2013. **IGO Relations** Member of: *Enlarged Partial Agreement on Sport (EPAS, #05487)*. [2020/XJ9341/F]

♦ European Athletic Association / see European Athletics (#06291)

♦ European Athletics 06291

CEO Av. Louis-Ruchonnet 16, 1003 Lausanne VD, Switzerland. T. +41213134350. E-mail: office@european-athletics.org.
URL: http://www.european-athletics.org/

History 1 Nov 1969, Bucharest (Romania). Founded as a regional body of *World Athletics (#21209)*, replacing *European Committee of the International Amateur Athletic Federation – Comité Européen de la Fédération Internationale d'Athlétisme Amateur*, set up 7 Jan 1934. Statutes approved by IAAF, 31 Aug 1970. Current Constitution adopted 15 Oct 2005. Former names and other names: *European Athletic Association (EAA)* – former; *Association Européenne d'Athlétisme* – former. Registration: Swiss Civil Code, Switzerland; EU Transparency Register, No/ID: 914417720489-88. **Aims** Work to promote the sport of athletics (including track and field, cross country, road running, race walking and mountain running) throughout Europe. **Structure** Council; Commissions (5). **Languages** English, French. **Staff** 25.00 FTE, paid. **Finance** Sources: revenue from activities/projects; sponsorship. Television fees; marketing. **Activities** Awards/prizes/competitions; sporting activities. **Events** *Biennial Congress* Prague (Czechia) 2019, *Meeting* Oslo (Norway) 2015, *Biennial European Athletics Championship* Zurich (Switzerland) 2014, *Biennial European Juniors Championship* Gothenburg (Sweden) 2013, *Biennial European Athletics Championship* Helsinki (Finland) 2012. **Publications** *European Athletics Inside Track* (2 a year); *European Athletics Review* (annual); *Statistics Handbook* (annual).
Members National athletic federations in 51 European countries (Israel considered part of Europe instead of Asia for European Athletics purposes):
Albania, Andorra, Armenia, Austria, Azerbaijan, Belarus, Belgium, Bosnia-Herzegovina, Bulgaria, Croatia, Cyprus, Czechia, Denmark, Estonia, Finland, France, Georgia, Germany, Gibraltar, Greece, Hungary, Iceland, Ireland, Israel, Italy, Kosovo, Latvia, Liechtenstein, Lithuania, Luxembourg, Malta, Moldova, Monaco, Montenegro, Netherlands, North Macedonia, Norway, Poland, Portugal, Romania, Russia, San Marino, Serbia, Slovakia, Slovenia, Spain, Sweden, Switzerland, Türkiye, UK, Ukraine.
Consultative Status Consultative status granted from: *UNESCO (#20322)* (Consultative Status). **IGO Relations** Member of (1): *Enlarged Partial Agreement on Sport (EPAS, #05487)* (Consultative Committee). **NGO Relations** Represented in relevant European Athletics committees/commissions: *European Broadcasting Union (EBU, #06404)*. [2020.11.19/XD3885/E]

♦ European Athletics Coaches Association (EACA) 06292

Fédération d'Europe des entraîneurs d'athlétisme – Europäischer Leichtathletik-Lehrer-Verband (ELLV)

Pres Selwood, Zeals Row, Zeals, Warminster, BA12 6PE, UK. E-mail: secretary@athleticscoaches.eu – office@fwd.uk.com.
URL: http://www.athleticscoaches.eu/

History as *European Track and Field Coaches Association (ELLV)*. **Aims** Improve competitive and performance records of European IAAF members; coordinate European contribution to IAAF Development Program in coaching and related matters. **Structure** General Assembly (annual); Council. **Languages** English. **Staff** 1.00 FTE, voluntary. **Finance** Members' dues. **Activities** Events/meetings. **Events** *Annual Congress* Rome (Italy) 2015, *Annual Congress* Rome (Italy) 2014, *Annual Congress* Glasgow (UK) 2012, *Annual Congress* Glasgow (UK) 2011, *Annual Congress* Glasgow (UK) 2010.
Members Full in 47 countries:
Albania, Andorra, Armenia, Austria, Azerbaijan, Belarus, Belgium, Bosnia-Herzegovina, Bulgaria, Croatia, Cyprus, Czechia, Denmark, Estonia, Finland, France, Georgia, Germany, Greece, Hungary, Iceland, Ireland, Italy, Latvia, Liechtenstein, Lithuania, Luxembourg, Malta, Moldova, Monaco, Netherlands, North Macedonia, Norway, Poland, Portugal, Romania, Russia, San Marino, Serbia, Slovakia, Slovenia, Spain, Sweden, Switzerland, Türkiye, UK, Ukraine.
NGO Relations Member of: *International Council for Coaching Excellence (ICCE, #13008)*. Cooperates with: *World Athletics (#21209)*. [2019.04.29/XD1500/D]

♦ European ATM Security Team / see European Association for Secure Transactions (#06202)
♦ European Atomic Energy Community (inactive)

♦ European Atomic Energy Society (EAES) 06293

Société européenne d'énergie atomique (SEEA)

Contact address not obtained.

History 1954, London (UK). **Aims** Facilitate cooperation in the field of civil nuclear energy research work. **Structure** Council; Executive; Working Group; Waste Management Sub Group (WMSG); Research Reactor Operators Group (RROG). **Languages** English. **Staff** Voluntary. **Finance** Members pay own costs; host country funds conference. **Activities** Events/meetings. **Events** *Annual Joint-Meeting of Council and Working Group* Oxford (UK) 2010, *Annual Joint-Meeting of Council and Working Group* Ljubljana (Slovenia) 2006, *Annual Joint-Meeting of Council and Working Group* Holmenkollen (Norway) 2005, *Annual Joint-Meeting of Council and Working Group* Toledo (Spain) 2004, *Annual Joint-Meeting of Council and Working Group* Genval (Belgium) 2003.
Members National governments, commissions or research organizations (23):
Austria, Belgium, Czechia, Denmark, Finland, France, Germany, Greece, Hungary, Italy, Lithuania, Netherlands, Norway, Poland, Portugal, Romania, Russia, Slovakia, Slovenia, Spain, Sweden, Switzerland, UK. [2018.04.20/XD0589/D*]

♦ European Atomic Forum / see nucleareurope (#17616)
♦ European Atomized Aluminium Association (inactive)
♦ European Audio Phonological Centres Association (inactive)
♦ European Audio Video Association (inactive)
♦ European Audiovisual Entrepreneurs (#05495)

♦ European Audiovisual Observatory 06294

Observatoire européen de l'audiovisuel – Europäische Audiovisuelle Informationsstelle

Exec Dir Head Office, 76 allée de la Robertsau, 67000 Strasbourg, France. T. +33390216000. Fax +33390216019.
Communications Officer address not obtained.
URL: http://www.obs.coe.int/

History 1992, Strasbourg (France). Established as a partial and enlarged agreement of *Council of Europe (CE, #04881)*, following: decision of 2nd Ministerial Conference of *Audiovisual Eureka (AVE, inactive)*, 12 June 1992, Helsinki (Finland); adoption of Resolution (92) 70 of *Committee of Ministers of the Council of Europe (#04273)*, 15 Dec 1992; adoption of Resolution (97) 4 of Committee of Ministers, 20 Mar 1997; adoption of Resolution (2000) 7 of Committee of Ministers, 21 Sep 2000. **Aims** Provide a means of accessing reliable Europe-wide information about the European audiovisual sector – television, cinema, VOD, on demand audiovisual services, and also public policy on the audiovisual sector. **Structure** Executive Council, comprising representatives of each member State and the European Community, represented by the European Commission, with *Council of Europe (CE, #04881)* as Observer. Advisory Committee; Financial Committee; Bureau of the Executive Council; Audit Committee; Secretariat. **Languages** English, French, German. **Staff** 27.00 FTE, paid. **Finance** Sources: fees for services; members' dues; sale of products. **Activities** Events/meetings; knowledge management/information dissemination. **Events** *Meeting* Strasbourg (France) 2014, *Workshop on accompanying the transposition of the Audiovisual Media Services Directive in the year 2009* Saarbrücken (Germany) 2009, *Symposium* Leipzig (Germany) 1994, *International colloquium* Rennes (France) 1994. **Publications** *IRIS* (10 a year) – newsletter; *IRIS Plus* (3 a year) – thematic report; *IRIS Special* (2 a year); *FOCUS – World Film Market Trends* (annual); *Key Trends*; *The Yearbook Online Service*. Economic reports. **Information Services** *AVMSD*; *IRIS MERLIN*; *LUMIERE*; *LUMIEREVOD*; *MAVISE*.
Members Member States (40):

Albania, Armenia, Austria, Belgium, Bosnia-Herzegovina, Bulgaria, Croatia, Cyprus, Czechia, Denmark, Estonia, Finland, France, Georgia, Germany, Greece, Hungary, Iceland, Ireland, Italy, Latvia, Liechtenstein, Lithuania, Luxembourg, Malta, Montenegro, Morocco, Netherlands, North Macedonia, Norway, Poland, Portugal, Romania, Slovakia, Slovenia, Spain, Sweden, Switzerland, Türkiye, UK.
Additional members:
European Commission (EC, #06633); European Union (EU, #08967).
IGO Relations Permanent observer status with: *World Intellectual Property Organization (WIPO, #21593).* Observers of the Advisory Committee: *European Support Fund for the Co-Production and Distribution of Creative Cinematographic and Audiovisual Works (EURIMAGES, #08859).* Members of Advisory Committee include representatives of: European Commission; *European Investment Bank (EIB, #07599).*
NGO Relations Members of Advisory Committee include representatives of the following European professional organizations:
- *Association of Commercial Television in Europe (ACT, #02436);*
- *Association of European Film Archives and Cinémathèques (#02511);*
- *GIGAEurope AISBL (#10151);*
- *Comité des industries cinématographiques et audiovisuelles de l'Union européenne et de l'Europe extracommunautaire (CICCE, no recent information);*
- *European Audiovisual Production (CEPI, #06295);*
- *European Broadcasting Union (EBU, #06404);*
- *European Platform of Regulatory Authorities (EPRA, #08229);*
- *Federation of European Screen Directors (#09541);*
- *Fédération des Scénaristes d'Europe (FSE, #09703);*
- IAMCR;
- *Institut für Europäisches Medienrecht (EMR)* (Partner);
- *International Federation of Film Distributors Associations (#13428);*
- *International Federation of Film Producers' Associations (#13429);*
- *International Federation of Journalists (IFJ, #13462);*
- *International Union of Cinemas (#15763);*
- *International Video Federation (IVF, #15852).*

Acts as secretariat for: *European Film Agency Research Network (EFARN, #07246).* Cooperates with: *Balkanmedia Association (#03077); International Association for Media and Communication Research (IAMCR, #12022).* [2023.02.13/XF2493/**F***]

♦ European Audiovisual Production (CEPI) 06295

SG c/o Europe Analytica, Avenue des Arts 43, 5th Floor, 1040 Brussels, Belgium. E-mail: cepi@europe-analytica.com.
Registered Address 5 rue Cernuschi, 75017 Paris, France.
URL: https://www.cepi-producers.eu/

History Aug 1988, Paris (France). Former names and other names: *European Coordination of Independent Producers* – former (1990); *Coordination of European Independent Producers* – former; *Coordination européenne des producteurs indépendants (CEPI)* – former. Registration: EU Transparency Register, No/ID: 59052572261-62, Start date: 11 Sep 2009. **Aims** Represent independent television and cinema production on a European scale, protecting general interests and furthering development; strengthen exchange of information about audiovisual production; develop commercial relations; create a network of information and dialogue; promote interests of independent producers vis-a-vis European, national and international authorities. **Structure** General Assembly; Board. **Languages** English. **Staff** 2.00 FTE, paid. **Finance** Sources: members' dues. **Activities** Events/meetings.
Members Active; Associate; Benefactor. National Associations (16) in 15 countries:
Austria, Belgium, Denmark, Finland, France, Germany, Greece, Ireland, Italy, Netherlands, Norway, Portugal, Spain, Sweden, UK.
Consultative Status Consultative status granted from: *World Intellectual Property Organization (WIPO, #21593)* (Permanent Observer Status). **IGO Relations** Member of the Advisory Committee of: *European Audiovisual Observatory (#06294).* **NGO Relations** On Board of: *Vision 1250 (no recent information).* [2022/XD3689/**D**]

♦ European Audiovisual and Telecommunications Institute (internationally oriented national body)

♦ European Auditing Research Network (EARNet) 06296

Gen Sec c/o Aalto University, Audit Research Group – School of Business, Ekonominaukio 1, FI-02150 Espoo, Finland. T. +358403538058.
URL: https://ear-net.org/

History Apr 2000. **Aims** Foster research and the exchange of ideas among auditing scholars and research on a European level. **Structure** Scientific Committee; General Secretary. **Languages** English. **Activities** Events/meetings. **Events** *Biennial Symposium* Amsterdam (Netherlands) 2021, *Biennial Symposium* Parma (Italy) 2019, *Biennial Symposium* Leuven (Belgium) 2017, *Biennial Symposium* Lausanne (Switzerland) 2015, *Biennial Symposium* Trier (Germany) 2013. **Publications** *Auditing, Trust and Governance – Developing Regulation in Europe* (2008). **Members** Individuals (332) in 44 countries. Membership countries not specified. [2021/XJ3552/v/**F**]

♦ European Authors' Association "DIE KOGGE" (#05749)

♦ European Autoclaved Aerated Concrete Association (EAACA) 06297

Association européenne des fabricants de beton cellulaire – Verband der Europäischen Porenbetonindustrie

SG Hohes Steinfeld 1, 14797 Kloster Lehnin, Germany. E-mail: info@eaaca.org.
URL: http://www.eaaca.org/

History 1988. EU Transparency Register: 899865010107-44. **Aims** Promote the interests of producers of autoclaved aerated concrete (AAC) and their national associations across all of Europe. **Structure** Managing Board. **Languages** English. **Events** *Conference* Bydgoszcz (Poland) 2011, *Conference* London (UK) 2005, *Conference* Zurich (Switzerland) 1992.
Members Full in 17 countries:
Austria, Belgium, Bulgaria, Czechia, Denmark, Estonia, France, Germany, Hungary, Italy, Netherlands, Poland, Romania, Slovakia, Slovenia, Türkiye, UK.
NGO Relations Member of: *Fire Safe Europe (FSEU, #09780); Industry4Europe (#11181).* Associate member of: *Construction Products Europe AISBL (#04761).* In liaison with technical committees of: *Comité européen de normalisation (CEN, #04162).* [2020/XD3386/t/**D**]

♦ European Automated Clearing House Association (EACHA) 06298

SG Rue Washington 40, 1050 Brussels, Belgium. E-mail: info@eacha.org.
Pres address not obtained.
URL: http://www.eacha.org/

History 28 Sep 2006. Founded by 20 representatives from Automated Clearing Houses and retail payment processors in 16 countries. Registration: Banque-Carrefour des Entreprises, No/ID: 0886.371.251, Start date: 12 Jan 2007, Belgium. **Aims** Contribute to the Single Euro Payments Area (SEPA) project discussions and implementation, in the best interests of members; be a forum for sharing of information amongst members; advance the views of members on issues of general interest to the payment industry; work on specific issues as and when they arise such as developing common standards for SEPA interbank clearing and settlement activities. **Activities** Knowledge management/information dissemination; standards/guidelines. **Events** *Payments Forum* Madrid (Spain) 2022, *Payments Forum* Madrid (Spain) 2021, *Payments Forum* Madrid (Spain) 2020, *Payments Forum* Copenhagen (Denmark) 2019, *Payments Forum* Ljubljana (Slovenia) 2018.
Members Membership open to all institutions in Europe that function as Automated Clearing Houses. Founding members in 16 countries:
Belgium, Croatia, Denmark, France, Germany, Greece, Hungary, Italy, Netherlands, Norway, Poland, Portugal, Spain, Sweden, Switzerland, UK.
IGO Relations Working relations with: *European Central Bank (ECB, #06466).* **NGO Relations** Member of (1): *Federation of European and International Associations Established in Belgium (FAIB, #09508).* [2022/XM3473/**F**]

♦ European Automobile Clubs (unconfirmed)

♦ European Automobile Engineers Cooperation (EAEC) 06299

Pres Elisabethstrasse 26, 1010 Vienna, Austria. T. +431585274160. Fax +431585274199.

History Former names and other names: *European Automotive Engineers Cooperation* – former. **Activities** Events/meetings. **Events** *Congress* Minsk (Belarus) 2019, *Congress* Madrid (Spain) 2017, *Congress* Valencia (Spain) 2011, *Congress* Bratislava (Slovakia) 2009, *Automobile for the future* Budapest (Hungary) 2007.
Members Full in 24 countries:
Austria, Belarus, Belgium, Bulgaria, Croatia, Czechia, Finland, France, Germany, Hungary, Italy, Latvia, Lithuania, Netherlands, Poland, Romania, Russia, Serbia, Slovakia, Slovenia, Spain, Sweden, Switzerland, UK. [2011/XD9041/**D**]

♦ European Automobile Manufacturers' Association (ACEA) 06300

Association des constructeurs européens d'automobiles

Director-General Av des Nerviens 85, 1040 Brussels, Belgium. T. +3227325550. E-mail: info@acea.auto.
Main Website: http://www.acea.auto

History Feb 1991. Replaces *Committee of Common Market Automobile Constructors (CCMC, inactive)* and *Liaison Committee for the Motor Industry in the EEC Countries (inactive).* Former names and other names: *Association of European Automobile Manufacturers* – former. Registration: Banque Carrefour des Entreprises, No/ID: 0444.072.631, Start date: 14 May 1991, Belgium; EU Transparency Register, No/ID: 0649790813-47, Start date: 18 Dec 2008. **Aims** Represent the common interests of the 15 major European car, truck and bus manufacturers; dialogue at all levels with the European Union and others concerned with the industry, including the public; use the industry's experience and technical knowledge to cooperate with policy-makers, legislators and opinion-makers in advancing mutual understanding and contributing to realistic and effective legislation. **Structure** Board of Directors; President; Standing Committees; Network of national automobile manufacturers associations. Permanent Office based in Brussels (Belgium). Regional Offices (2): ACEA Beijing (China); ACEA Seoul (South Korea). **Languages** English. **Staff** 30.00 FTE, paid. **Activities** Events/meetings; knowledge management/information dissemination; research/documentation. **Events** *How to scale up zero-emission commercial vehicles?* Brussels (Belgium) 2020, *Putting the EU auto industry back on track post-COVID* Brussels (Belgium) 2020, *Leading the mobility transformation – the future of the EU auto industry* Brussels (Belgium) 2019, *Towards Zero Meeting on Safe Vehicles, Save Drivers and Safe Roads* Brussels (Belgium) 2018, *Powertrain Options for Commercial Vehicles Conference* Brussels (Belgium) 2017. **Publications** *European car registration figures on passenger cars and commercial vehicles* (12 a year). Diverse information material; industry report; economic report; country and regional reports; press releases; statistics on the automobile industry; tax guide; oil sequences.
Members European automobile manufacturers (15) with headquarters in 7 countries:
Belgium, France, Germany, Italy, Netherlands, Sweden, UK.
Associated organizations in 30 countries:
Austria, Belgium, Bulgaria, Croatia, Cyprus, Czechia, Denmark, Estonia, Finland, France, Germany, Greece, Hungary, Ireland, Italy, Latvia, Lithuania, Malta, Netherlands, Norway, Poland, Portugal, Romania, Slovakia, Slovenia, Spain, Sweden, Switzerland, Türkiye, UK.
Representations of related industries (2) listed in this Yearbook:
European Association of Automotive Suppliers (CLEPA, #05948); European Council for Motor Trades and Repairs (#06832).
IGO Relations Accredited by (1): *United Nations Framework Convention on Climate Change – Secretariat (UNFCCC, #20564).* **NGO Relations** Member of (7): *Alliance for a Competitive European Industry (ACEI, #00670); Circular Plastics Alliance (#03936); European Logistics Platform (ELP, #07711); Industry4Europe (#11181); International Organization of Motor Vehicle Manufacturers (#14455)* (Associate); *International Road Transport Union (IRU, #14761); Partnership for Clean Fuels and Vehicles (PCFV, #18231).* [2021.06.09/XD2552/y/**D**]

♦ European Automotive Engineers Cooperation / see European Automobile Engineers Cooperation (#06299)

♦ European Automotive Research Partners Association (EARPA) 06301

SG Rue Joseph II 36-38, 1000 Brussels, Belgium. T. +31888665761. E-mail: info@earpa.eu.
Event Organizer address not obtained.
URL: http://www.earpa.eu/

History Jul 2002. Registration: Banque-Carrefour des Entreprises, No/ID: 0477.987.492, Start date: 19 Dec 2001, Belgium; EU Transparency Register, No/ID: 91806074044-71, Start date: 23 Aug 2010. **Aims** Seek close cooperation with the automotive industry (OEMs and suppliers) and with European institutions and EU member states, so as to develop the future of R and D in Europe; contribute actively to the European Research Area and the future of EU Framework Programmes. **Structure** General Assembly (annual, at Conference); Executive Board; Secretariat; Foresight Groups (5). **Languages** English. **Staff** 2.00 FTE, paid. **Finance** Sources: members' dues. **Activities** Events/meetings; knowledge management/information dissemination; research and development. **Events** *EARPA Forum* Brussels (Belgium) 2023, *Spring Meeting* Brussels (Belgium) 2023, *Spring Meeting* Brussels (Belgium) 2022, *Future of Road Mobility Forum* Brussels (Belgium) 2021, *Future Of Road Mobility Forum* Brussels (Belgium) 2020. **Publications** *EARPA Newsletter.* Roadmaps; position papers (regular).
Members Large and small commercial automotive R and D organizations and national institutes and universities. Members (49) in 14 countries:
Austria, Belgium, Czechia, France, Germany, Greece, Ireland, Italy, Netherlands, Norway, Portugal, Slovakia, Slovenia, Spain, Sweden, UK.
NGO Relations *European Association of Automotive Suppliers (CLEPA, #05948); European Conference of Transport Research Institutes (ECTRI, #06737); European Council of Automotive Research and Development (EUCAR, #06806); European Road Transport Research Advisory Council (ERTRAC, #08396); Oil Companies' European Association for Environment, Health and Safety in Refining and Distribution (CONCAWE, #17708).* [2021/XD8893/**D**]

♦ European Automotive Services and Repairers Association (unconfirmed)

♦ European Automotive and Telecoms Alliance (EATA) 06302

Secretariat Avenue de Tervueren 188A, Box 4, 1150 Brussels, Belgium. T. +3227611603. E-mail: eata@kellencompany.com.
URL: https://eata.be/

History 2016. Founded following an initiative of Günther Oettinger. Registration: EU Transparency Register, No/ID: 255052934788-63. **Structure** General Assembly; Steering Committee; Secretariat. **NGO Relations** Founding Associations (6): *European Automobile Manufacturers' Association (ACEA, #06300) European Association of Automotive Suppliers (CLEPA, #05948) European Competitive Telecommunications Association (ECTA, #06689) European Telecommunications Network Operators' Association (ETNO, #08895) Global mobile Suppliers Association (GSA, #10476) GSM Association (GSMA, #10813).* [2020/XM8700/**D**]

♦ European Automotive Trim Suppliers (inactive)

♦ European Aviation Maintenance Training Committee (EAMTC) 06303

Sec Venestraat 53, 2266 AX Leidschendam, Netherlands. E-mail: admin@eamtc.org.
URL: http://www.eamtc.org/

History 1984. Former names and other names: *European Airlines Maintenance Training Committee* – former (1990). Registration: Handelsregister, No/ID: KVK 34287465, Start date: 2007, Netherlands. **Aims** Promote safety through training and best practice; present the training industry. **Structure** General Assembly; Executive Committee; Supervisory Board. Working Groups. **Activities** Training/education; events/meetings. **Events** *Meeting* Frankfurt-Main (Germany) 2017, *Meeting* Luleå (Sweden) 2017, *Meeting* Paris (France) 2016, *Meeting* Vergiate (Italy) 2016, *Meeting* Berlin (Germany) 2015.
Members Full in 36 countries and territories:
Australia, Austria, Bahrain, Bangladesh, Brazil, Bulgaria, Canada, Croatia, Denmark, Finland, France, Germany, Greece, Hong Kong, Iceland, Indonesia, Ireland, Italy, Kazakhstan, Kuwait, Lebanon, Lithuania, Luxembourg, Netherlands, New Zealand, Norway, Pakistan, Qatar, Russia, Spain, Sweden, Switzerland, Türkiye, UK, United Arab Emirates, USA.
IGO Relations Cooperates with (1): *European Union Aviation Safety Agency (EASA, #08978).* **NGO Relations** Cooperates with (3): *European Association for Aviation Psychology (EAAP, #05950); European Training and Simulation Association (ETSA, #08935); International Civil Aviation English Association (ICAEA, #12580).* [2021/XM4133/**D**]

♦ European Aviation Security Association / see Aviation Security Services Association – International (#03046)

♦ European Aviation Security Training Institute (EASTI) 06304

Institut européen pour la formation à la sûreté de l'aviation

Dir Rue de la Fusée, 90, 1130 Brussels, Belgium. T. +322471132811.

URL: http://www.easti.eu/

History Founded 19 Nov 1997, Brussels (Belgium), as a common venture of *European Civil Aviation Conference (ECAC, #06564)* and *International Civil Aviation Organization (ICAO, #12581)*. **Aims** Meet the continuing need for trained aviation security *personnel* in Europe and in other regions; provide specialized training to further enhance their ability to safeguard international *civil* aviation. **Structure** Board, comprising Directors General of ECAC member states and Executive Secretary of ECAC. **Languages** Dutch, English, French. **Finance** Self-supporting. **Activities** Training/education. **IGO Relations** Cooperates with: *Universal Postal Union (UPU, #20682)*. **NGO Relations** Cooperates with: *Airports Council International (ACI, #00611)*; *European Express Association (EEA, #07017)*; *Airlines International Representation in Europe (AIRE, #00608)*; *International Air Transport Association (IATA, #11614)*; *International Federation of Air Line Pilots' Associations (IFALPA, #13349)*. [2015.09.17/XE3683/j/E*]

♦ European AVM Alliance (EAA) 06305

Dir Gen Rond Point Schuman 6, Box 5, 1040 Brussels, Belgium. E-mail: contact@europeanavmalliance.org.

URL: https://www.europeanavmalliance.org/

History AVM stands for *Automated Valuation Models*. Registration: Banque-Carrefour des Entreprises, No/ID: 0754.573.292, Start date: 18 Sep 2020, Belgium; EU Transparency Register, No/ID: 004258218904-75, Start date: 24 Sep 2015. **Aims** Promote AVM awareness and disseminate a greater understanding of the benefits that AVMs can deliver; represent the interests of the AVM industry vis-a-vis European institutions and other market influencers; establish consistently high quality standards for AVMs across jurisdictions and to certify compliance for these standards through the EAA AVM Label. **Activities** Advocacy/lobbying/activism; standards/guidelines. **Publications** *European Standards for Statistical Valuation Methods for Residential Properties* (2nd ed 2019).

Members Full in 9 countries:
Austria, Germany, Greece, Italy, Netherlands, Norway, Spain, Sweden, UK.

NGO Relations Member of (1): *Federation of European and International Associations Established in Belgium (FAIB, #09508)*. [2023/XM8701/D]

♦ European Ayurveda Association (EUAA) 06306

Contact Römerstr 1-3, 74629 Pfedelbach, Germany. T. +497949590. E-mail: info@euroayurveda.com.

URL: http://www.euroayurveda.eu/

History Founded 2006. **Aims** Make Ayurveda – an ancient, traditional, holistic system of health promotion, maintenance and healing – available for everybody. **Structure** Board of Directors. **Events** *Meeting* Brussels (Belgium) 2018.

Members Full in 18 countries:
Andorra, Austria, Belgium, Croatia, Czechia, Germany, Greece, Hungary, Italy, Latvia, Netherlands, Poland, Portugal, Slovenia, Switzerland, Türkiye, UK, Ukraine.

NGO Relations Member of: *Association of Natural Medicine in Europe (ANME)*. Affiliated with: *EUROCAM (#05653)*. Participates in: *European Public Health Alliance (EPHA, #08297)*. [2019/XM7759/D]

♦ European Backgammon Federation / see World Backgammon Federation (#21213)
♦ European Backgammon Federation (no recent information)
♦ European Badminton Union / see Badminton Europe (#03058)
♦ European Baha'i Business Forum / see ebbf – ethical business building the future (#05269)

♦ European Bailiffs' Foundation (EUBF) 06307

Contact Avenue des Gaulous 33, 1040 Brussels, Belgium. T. +33637010557.

URL: http://www.cehj.eu/

History Founded Jan 2018. EU Transparency Register: 399887736699-71. **Aims** Improve cooperation of enforcement authorities in Europe. **Structure** Board; Secretariat.

Members Full in 7 countries and territories:
Belgium, France, Hungary, Italy, Luxembourg, Poland, Scotland.

Observing in 2 countries:
Albania, Bulgaria. [2019/XM8702/f/F]

♦ European Bakery Equipment Manufacturers Association (inactive)
♦ European Balloon Council / see European Balloon and Party Council (#06308)

♦ European Balloon and Party Council (EBPC) 06308

Dir-Gen Square de Meeus 35, 1000 Brussels, Belgium. T. +3228084852. E-mail: info@ebpcouncil.eu.

URL: https://www.ebpcouncil.eu/

History 2002. Former names and other names: *European Balloon Council (EBC)* – former. Registration: Banque-Carrefour des Entreprises, No/ID: 0737.916.216, Start date: 21 Nov 2019, Belgium; EU Transparency Register, No/ID: 831057748513-73, Start date: 3 Jan 2023. **Aims** Assist members in understanding the broad range of safety issues and helping to change standards in the balloon and party industry. **Structure** Steering Committee; Executive Committee; Operations Manager. **Languages** Dutch, English, French, German. **Staff** 1.00 FTE, paid.

Members Full in 10 countries:
Belgium, Denmark, Germany, Greece, Italy, Mexico, Netherlands, Türkiye, UK, USA.

Associate in 1 country:
Russia.

NGO Relations In liaison with technical committees of: *Comité européen de normalisation (CEN, #04162)*. [2023/XJ4960/D]

♦ European Bamboo Society (EBS) 06309

Association européenne du bambou

European Coordinator de Vlist 12, 3448 JK Woerden, Netherlands. E-mail: secretariaat@bamboepagina.nl.

URL: http://www.bamboepagina.nl/

History Founded in the late 1980s. **Aims** Promote bamboo and its uses. **Structure** Each member country managed by its own Board. **Languages** Dutch, English, French, German. **Staff** 0.00 FTE, paid. **Finance** Sources: donations; members' dues; sale of publications. Advertising revenue. **Activities** Events/meetings; publishing activities. **Events** *EBS EuroMeeting* Netherlands 2012, *EBS EuroMeeting* Switzerland 2010, *EBS EuroMeeting* Buisson (France) 2008, *EBS EuroMeeting* Frankfurt-Main (Germany) 2006, *General Meeting* UK 2005.

Members National societies in 10 countries (indicates other societies):
Australia (*), Belgium, China, France, Germany, Japan (*), Netherlands, New Zealand (*), UK, USA (*).

NGO Relations Also links with national societies. [2021.02.17/XD3236/D]

♦ European Banana Action Network (EUROBAN) 06310

Réseau d'action européen pour les bananes

Main Office c/o Bananalink, 49 Colegate, Norwich, NR3 1DD, UK. E-mail: coord.euroban@gmail.com – coord.euroban@googlemail.com.

URL: https://www.bananalink.org.uk/about/euroban/

History 1994. Former names and other names: *European Banana and Agro Industrial Product Action Network* – alias. **Aims** Promote sustainable production and trade in bananas worldwide. **Structure** Coordinated by *Banana Link*. **Languages** English, French, Spanish. **Staff** 2.5 – 4.5 FTE. **Finance** Members' dues. *European Commission (EC, #06633)* DG Development. **Activities** Politics/policy/regulatory; networking/liaising; events/meetings. **Events** *International banana conference* Brussels (Belgium) 2005. **Publications** *Banana Trade News Bulletin* (3 a year).

Members Organizations (35) in 13 countries:
Austria, Belgium, Denmark, France, Germany, Hungary, Ireland, Italy, Netherlands, Spain, Sweden, Switzerland, UK.

Included in the above, 15 organizations listed in this Yearbook:
ActionAid France – Peuples Solidaires; *Banafair*; *Banana Link*; *Centro de Estudios Rurales y de Agricultura Internacional (CERAI)*; *Centro Mondialità Sviluppo Reciproco (CMSR)*; *Christian Aid*; *Consorzio 'Cooperazione Terzo Mondo' Altromercato (Consorzeio CTM Altromercato)*; *Fairtrade International (FLO, #09240)*; *Global Justice Now*; *Ibis – Denmark*; *International Centre for Trade Union Rights (ICTUR, #12525)*; *International Union of Food, Agricultural, Hotel, Restaurant, Catering, Tobacco and Allied Workers Associations (IUF, #15772)*; *Max Havelaar Foundation*; *New Development Centre, Vecchiano*; *Oxfam Trading*.

NGO Relations Cooperates with (2): *Global Labor Justice-International Labor Rights Forum (GLJ-ILRF)*; *International Union of Food, Agricultural, Hotel, Restaurant, Catering, Tobacco and Allied Workers Associations (IUF, #15772)*. *Coordinadora Latinoamericano de Sindicatos Bananeros en Agroindustriales (COLSIBA, #04810)*; *Windward Islands Farmers' Association (WINFA, #20966)*. [2017.07.17/XF3874/y/F]

♦ European Banana and Agro Industrial Product Action Network / see European Banana Action Network (#06310)
♦ European Bank of Frozen Blood of Rare Groups / see Sanquin Bank of Frozen Blood (#19052)

♦ European Banking Authority (EBA) 06311

Exec Dir Tour Europlaza, 20 avenue André Prothin, CS 30154, 92927 Paris La Défense CEDEX, France. T. +332073821776. E-mail: info@eba.europa.eu.

URL: http://www.eba.europa.eu/

History 1 Jan 2011. Established by Regulation (EC) No 1093/2010 of *Council of the European Union (#04895)* and *European Parliament (EP, #08146)*, 24 Nov 2010. Has taken over responsibilities of *Committee of European Banking Supervisors (CEBS, inactive)*. Part of *European System of Financial Supervision (ESFS)*. A decentralized agency of *European Union (EU, #08967)*. **Aims** Contribute, through adoption of binding Technical Standards (BTS) and Guidelines, to creation of the European Single Rulebook in banking. **Structure** Board of Supervisors, composed of Chairperson, Alternate Chairperson, one representative each of Member State, one representative of each Observer State and one representative each of *European Commission (EC, #06633)*, *European Central Bank (ECB, #06466)*, *European Systemic Risk Board (ESRB, #08872)*, *European Insurance and Occupational Pensions Authority (EIOPA, #07578)* and *European Securities and Markets Authority (ESMA, #08457)*. Management Board, comprising Chairperson and representatives of national supervisory authorities and of EC. Joint Board of Appeal, with ESMA and EIOPA. Banking Stakeholder Group. **Activities** Standards/guidelines; guidance/assistance/consulting; monitoring/evaluation. **Events** *Joint ESAs High-Level Conference on Financial Education and Literacy* Brussels (Belgium) 2022. **Publications** Annual Report.

Members National supervisory authorities of 27 countries:
Austria, Belgium, Bulgaria, Croatia, Cyprus, Czechia, Denmark, Estonia, Finland, France, Germany, Greece, Hungary, Ireland, Italy, Latvia, Lithuania, Luxembourg, Malta, Netherlands, Poland, Portugal, Romania, Slovakia, Slovenia, Spain, Sweden.

Observers (3):
Iceland, Liechtenstein, Norway.

IGO Relations Audited by: *European Court of Auditors (#06854)*. **NGO Relations** Member of (1): *EU Agencies Network (EUAN, #05564)*. [2021/XJ2856/E*]

♦ European Banking Federation (EBF) 06312

Fédération bancaire de l'Union européenne (FBE)

CEO Ave des Arts 56, 1000 Brussels, Belgium. T. +3225083711. Fax +3225112328. E-mail: ebf@ebf.eu.

Frankfurt Office Weissfrauenstr 12-16, 60311 Frankfurt-Main, Germany.

URL: http://www.ebf.eu/

History 10 Jun 1960, Rome (Italy). Founded as *Banking Federation of the European Community – Fédération bancaire de la Communauté européenne*. Registration: Banque-Carrefour des Entreprises, No/ID: 0472.150.369, Start date: 29 Jun 2000; EU Transparency Register, No/ID: 4722660838-23, Start date: 19 Dec 2008. **Aims** As the voice of the European banking sector, bring together national banking associations from across Europe; promote a thriving European economy underpinned by a stable, secure and inclusive financial ecosystem, and a flourishing society where financing is available to fund the dreams of citizens, businesses and innovators. **Structure** Board; Executive Committee; Consultative Committees (15). **Languages** English. **Staff** 28.00 FTE, paid. **Finance** Members' dues. **Activities** Events/meetings. Represents interests of over 3,500 large and small European banks, from 32 national banking associations, together having assets of over euro 20,000,000,000,000 and over 2.3 million employees. **Events** *European Banking Summit* Brussels (Belgium) 2022, *EBF and UNEP FI Virtual Event* Brussels (Belgium) 2021, *European Banking Summit* Brussels (Belgium) 2021, *Digital Finance Summit* Brussels (Belgium) 2019, *Tax Conference* Brussels (Belgium) 2019. **Publications** *EBF Economic Outlook* (annual) – electronic; *EBF Facts and Figures* (annual); *EBF Letter* (annual) – electronic; *EBF Newsletter* (daily and weekly) – paper and electronic.

Members Full: banking associations representing commercial banks in 32 countries (EU and EFTA):
Austria, Belgium, Bulgaria, Croatia, Cyprus, Czechia, Denmark, Estonia, Finland, France, Germany, Greece, Hungary, Iceland, Ireland, Italy, Latvia, Liechtenstein, Lithuania, Luxembourg, Malta, Netherlands, Norway, Poland, Portugal, Romania, Slovakia, Slovenia, Spain, Sweden, Switzerland, UK.

Associates: banking associations in 11 countries:
Albania, Andorra, Azerbaijan, Bosnia-Herzegovina, Monaco, Montenegro, North Macedonia, Russia, Serbia, Türkiye, Ukraine.

IGO Relations Recognized by: *European Commission (EC, #06633)*. **NGO Relations** Founding member of: *International Banking Federation (IBFed, #12311)*. Member of: *Euro Institute (no recent information)*; *European Banking Industry Committee (EBIC, #06314)*; *European Financial Reporting Advisory Group (EFRAG, #07254)*; *European Parliamentary Financial Services Forum (EPFSF, #08148)*; *European Payments Council (EPC, #08175)*; *European Services Forum (ESF, #08469)*; *Federation of European and International Associations Established in Belgium (FAIB, #09508)*; *Institute of International Bankers*. Works closely with: *European Banking and Financial Services Training Association (EBTN, #06313)*. [2021/XE0185/E]

♦ European Banking and Financial Services Training Association (EBTN) 06313

Main Office c/o EBF, Av des Arts 56, 1000 Brussels, Belgium. E-mail: office@ebtn-association.eu.

URL: http://www.ebtn-association.eu/

History 1 Jan 1998. Founded upon merger of *European Bank Training Network (EBT Network, inactive)*, set up 4 Nov 1991, and *International Foundation for Computer-based Education in Banking and Finance (IFCEB, inactive)*. Registration: EU Transparency Register, No/ID: 223937834255-49. **Aims** Become the standard-setting body for accreditation, certification and qualification of knowledge, skills and competences in the European financial services sector. **Structure** Annual General Meeting; Board of Directors; Executive Committee; Executive Manager. **Languages** English. **Finance** Members' dues. Professional qualifications and certifications. **Activities** Accreditation/certification; training/education. **Events** *Meeting* Budapest (Hungary) 2018, *Triple E Conference* Brussels (Belgium) 2015, *International meeting* Lisbon (Portugal) 2010, *General Meeting* Copenhagen (Denmark) 2008, *Conference* Paris (France) 2007. **Publications** *EBTN Newsletter*.

Members Full (24) in 21 countries:
Belgium, Bulgaria, Cyprus, Finland, France, Germany, Greece, Hungary, Ireland, Italy, Malta, Netherlands, Poland, Portugal, Romania, Russia, Serbia, Slovakia, Slovenia, Spain, UK.

Included in the above, 3 organizations listed in this Yearbook:
International Banking Institute, Sofia (IBI); *International Banking Institute, St Petersburg (IBI)*; *International School of Banking and Finance*.

Associate (16) in 15 countries and territories:
Armenia, Azerbaijan, Bahrain, Bangladesh, Belgium, Egypt, Hong Kong, India, Kosovo, Kuwait, Lebanon, Moldova, North Macedonia, Togo, Vietnam.

Included in the above, 1 organization listed in this Yearbook:
World Savings Banks Institute (WSBI, #21764).

IGO Relations Works closely with: *European Commission (EC, #06633)*. **NGO Relations** Works closely with: *European Banking Federation (EBF, #06312)*. [2022/XF4531/y/F]

♦ European Banking Industry Committee (EBIC) 06314

Secretariat c/o European Banking Federation, Avenue des Arts 56, 1000 Brussels, Belgium. T. +3225083711. Fax +3222300649. E-mail: secretariat@ebic.org – info@ebic.org.

Chairman address not obtained.
URL: http://www.eubic.org/
History by *European Association of Co-operative Banks (EACB, #05990), European Banking Federation (EBF, #06312), European Savings and Retail Banking Group (ESBG, #08426), Covered Bond and Mortgage Council (CBMC, #04940); European Federation of Building Societies (EFBS, #07064), European Federation of Finance House Associations (EUROFINAS, #07121), European Federation of Equipment Leasing Company Associations (LEASEUROPE, #07111)* and *European Association of Public Banks (EAPB, #06178).* EU Transparency Register: 776974929089-90. **Aims** Provide advice and ensure a comprehensive consultation of market participants and representative industry view throughout the process of drafting, adopting, implementing and enforcing EU financial legislation. **Members** Founder members. [2019/XE4688/t/E]

♦ European Bank for Reconstruction and Development (EBRD) 06315

Banque européenne pour la reconstruction et le développement (BERD) – Europäische Bank für Wiederaufbau und Entwicklung (EBWE)

SG EBRD Headquarters, Five Bank Street, London, E14 4BG, UK. T. +442073386000. Fax +442073386100. E-mail: communications@ebrd.com – celaj@ebrd.com – warrenm@ebrd.com.
URL: http://www.ebrd.com/

History 8 Jan 1990, Paris (France). 8-9 Jan 1990, Paris (France), at constitutional conference comprising representatives of 34 countries, following proposals, Nov 1989, by President Mitterrand of France, and confirmation, 9 Dec 1989, Strasbourg (France), at summit conference of member countries of *European Community (inactive).* Statutes approved, Oct 1990, by *European Parliament (EP, #08146).* Inaugurated 15 Apr 1991, London (UK), on signature of a Headquarters Agreement. **Aims** Develop open and sustainable market economies in countries committed to, and applying, democratic principles. **Structure** Board of Governors (meets annually), consisting of one Governor and one Alternate for each EBRD member. Board of Directors; President; Executive Committee; Senior leadership group. Board Committees (3): Audit; Budget and Administrative Affairs; Financial and Operations Policies. Management Committees Asset and Liability; Crisis Management Team; Enforcement; Equity; Information Technology Governance; Operations; Procurement Complaints; Risk; Strategy and Policy. Administrative Tribunal. **Languages** English, French, German, Russian. **Staff** Headquarters: 951; local offices: 256. **Finance** Owned by 65 countries and *European Union (EU, #08967)* and *European Investment Bank (EIB, #07599).* Capital subscription totals: euro 28,882,070,000. **Activities** Financial and/or material support; guidance/assistance/consulting; advocacy/lobbying/activism. Up to end 2016, invested over 110,000,000,000 in 4,500 projects. Active in: Albania, Armenia, Azerbaijan, Belarus, Bosnia-Herzegovina, Bulgaria, Croatia, Cyprus, Czechia, Egypt, Estonia, Georgia, Greece, Hungary, Jordan, Kazakhstan, Kosovo, Kyrgyzstan, Latvia, Lithuania, Moldova, Mongolia, Montenegro, Morocco, North Macedonia, Poland, Romania, Russia, Serbia, Slovakia, Slovenia, Tajikistan, Tunisia, Türkiye, Turkmenistan, Ukraine, Uzbekistan. **Events** *Annual Meeting of the Initiative for Coal Regions in Transition in the Western Balkans and Ukraine* Brussels (Belgium) 2022, *Joint Workshop on Documentary Credits and Bank Guarantees* Vienna (Austria) 2019, *Meeting on Empowering Businesses to Engage with Sustainable Finance and the SDGs* Brussels (Belgium) 2018, *Annual CompNet Conference* Brussels (Belgium) 2017, *Trade Finance Practitioners (TFP) Trade Finance Forum* Vienna (Austria) 2017. **Publications** *Transition Report Update* (annual); *Transition Report* (annual); *EBRD Annual Report. Financing with the EBRD.* Reports; papers; profiles.
Members Open to all European countries and to non-European countries which are members of the International Monetary Fund. Currently governments of 65 countries:
Albania, Armenia, Australia, Austria, Azerbaijan, Belarus, Belgium, Bosnia-Herzegovina, Bulgaria, Canada, China, Croatia, Cyprus, Czechia, Denmark, Egypt, Estonia, Finland, France, Georgia, Germany, Greece, Hungary, Iceland, Ireland, Israel, Italy, Japan, Jordan, Kazakhstan, Korea Rep, Kosovo, Kyrgyzstan, Latvia, Liechtenstein, Lithuania, Luxembourg, Malta, Mexico, Moldova, Mongolia, Montenegro, Morocco, Netherlands, New Zealand, North Macedonia, Norway, Poland, Portugal, Romania, Russia, Serbia, Slovakia, Slovenia, Spain, Sweden, Switzerland, Tajikistan, Tunisia, Türkiye, Turkmenistan, UK, Ukraine, USA, Uzbekistan.
Regional institutional members (2):
European Investment Bank (EIB, #07599); European Union (EU, #08967).
IGO Relations Observer status with: *Global Forum on Transparency and Exchange of Information for Tax Purposes (#10379); International Fund for Agricultural Development (IFAD, #13692); World Trade Organization (WTO, #21864).* Works in close cooperation with: *International Bank for Reconstruction and Development (IBRD, #12317); International Finance Corporation (IFC, #13597); International Monetary Fund (IMF, #14180); Multilateral Investment Guarantee Agency (MIGA, #16888); OECD (#17693);* and with the United Nations and its Specialized Agencies and other related bodies, in particular with *United Nations Economic Commission for Europe (UNECE, #20555),* and any entity, whether public or private, concerned with the economic development of, and investment in, Central and Eastern European countries. Memorandum of Understanding with: *Nordic Investment Bank (NIB, #17327).* Relationship agreement signed with: *Council of Europe (CE, #04881); ILO (#11123); UNIDO (#20336).* Member of: *Committee of International Development Institutions on the Environment (CIDIE, no recent information); Consultative Group to Assist the Poor (CGAP, #04768); Environmental Action Programme for Central and Eastern Europe (EAP, inactive); Eurasian Group on Combating Money Laundering and Financing of Terrorism (EAG, #05608); Peace Implementation Council (#18279); Regional Cooperation Council (RCC, #18773).* Accredited by: *United Nations Framework Convention on Climate Change – Secretariat (UNFCCC, #20564).* Member of Steering Group of: *Anti-Corruption Network for Eastern Europe and Central Asia (ACN, #00853).* Instrumental in setting up: *Global Environment Facility (GEF, #10346); Northern Dimension Environmental Partnership (NDEP, #17584).* Supports: *CIS-7 Initiative (no recent information).* **NGO Relations** Member of: *Better Than Cash Alliance (#03220); Consultative Group to Assist the Poor (CGAP, #04768); Euro Institute (no recent information); European Policy Centre (EPC, #08240); Intelligent Building Group (IBG, #11374); International Council on Archives (ICA, #12996); International Office for Water (IOW, #14399).* Cooperates with: *International Union of Credit and Investment Insurers (Bern Union, #15767).* [2023/XF2441/y/F*]

♦ European Baptist Convention / see International Baptist Convention (#12318)

♦ European Baptist Federation (EBF) 06316

Fédération baptiste européenne

Gen Sec Baptist House, Postjesweg 150, 1061 AX Amsterdam, Netherlands. T. +31202103026. E-mail: office@ebf.org.
URL: http://www.ebf.org/

History 1949, Rüschlikon (Switzerland). A regional office of *Baptist World Alliance (BWA, #03176).* **Aims** Strengthen ties of fellowship, cooperation and friendship amongst the Baptists of Europe. **Structure** Council; Executive; Divisions (3). **Languages** English. **Staff** 4.00 FTE, paid. **Finance** Members' contributions; grants from BWA. Annual general budget: about euro 210,000; Annual aid budget: about euro 50,000. **Activities** Events/meetings; advocacy/lobbying/activism. **Events** *Meeting* Amsterdam (Netherlands) 2009, *Meeting* Prague (Czech Rep) 2005, *Meeting* Beirut (Lebanon) 2004, *Quinquennial Congress* Warsaw (Poland) 2003, *Convention* Vienna (Austria) 2000. **Publications** *European Baptist Press Service (EBPS).*
Members National Unions and Conventions (54), totalling about 826,000 baptists in 54 unions and conventions. Members in 48 countries and territories:
Albania, Armenia, Austria, Azerbaijan, Belarus, Belgium, Bosnia-Herzegovina, Bulgaria, Croatia, Czechia, Denmark, Egypt, England, Estonia, Finland, France, Georgia, Germany, Hungary, Iraq, Israel, Italy, Jordan, Latvia, Lebanon, Lithuania, Malta, Moldova, Netherlands, North Macedonia, Norway, Poland, Portugal, Romania, Russia, Scotland, Serbia, Slovakia, Slovenia, Spain, Sweden, Switzerland, Syrian AR, Türkiye, Turkmenistan, Ukraine, Uzbekistan, Wales.
Included in the above, 2 regional organizations:
European Baptist Women United (EBWU, #06317); International Baptist Convention (IBC, #12318).
NGO Relations Member of: *Conference of European Churches (CEC, #04593).* [2021/XD0591/y/D]

♦ European Baptist Mission / see EBM International (#05270)
♦ European Baptist Women's Union / see European Baptist Women United (#06317)

♦ European Baptist Women United (EBWU) 06317

Sec address not obtained.
URL: http://www.ebwu.org/

History 1948, London (UK). Founded within *Baptist World Alliance (BWA, #03176).* Former names and other names: *European Baptist Women's Union (EBWU)* – former; *Union européenne des femmes baptistes* – former. **Aims** Equip new leaders for national and international leadership; build a Europe-wide fellowship of women through their leaders; working with individual and community needs; uniting women in mission and ministry. **Structure** Executive Committee of 6 including President, Vice President, Secretary, Treasurer and two additional members. **Languages** English, Russian. **Staff** 3.00 FTE, voluntary. **Finance** Voluntary gifts. **Activities** Events/meetings. Organizes annual prayer and gift days. **Events** *Quinquennial Conference* Lviv (Ukraine) 2018, *Quinquennial Conference* Hannover (Germany) 2013, *Quinquennial Conference* Dalfsen (Netherlands) 2008, *Quinquennial Conference* Labin (Croatia) 2003, *Quinquennial Conference* Prague (Czech Rep) 1998. **Publications** *News and Views* (annual). *History of EBWU* (1998).
Members Full in 41 countries and territories:
Albania, Armenia, Austria, Azerbaijan, Belarus, Belgium, Bulgaria, Croatia, Czechia, Denmark, Estonia, Finland, France, Georgia, Germany, Hungary, Iraq, Israel, Italy, Jordan, Kosovo, Latvia, Lebanon, Malta, Moldova, Netherlands, Norway, Poland, Portugal, Romania, Russia, Serbia, Slovakia, Spain, Sweden, Switzerland, Tajikistan, Türkiye, UK, Ukraine, Uzbekistan.
Included in the above, one organization listed in this Yearbook:
International Baptist Convention (IBC, #12318).
Individuals in 5 countries:
Bosnia-Herzegovina, Egypt, Kazakhstan, Lithuania, North Macedonia. [2023.02.22/XD3821/D]

♦ European Barge Union (EBU) 06318

Union européenne de la navigation fluviale (UENF) – Europäische Binnenschiffahrts Union (EBU) – Europese Binnenvaart Unie (EBU)

SG Vasteland 12E, 3011 BM Rotterdam, Netherlands. T. +31107989880. Fax +31104129091. E-mail: info@ebu-uenf.org.
Registered Office Avenue Grandchamp 148, 1150 Brussels, Belgium.
URL: http://www.ebu-uenf.org/

History Founded 14 Dec 2001, by merger of *Consortium international de la navigation rhénane (CINR, inactive)* and *International Union for Inland Navigation (IBU, inactive).* EU Transparency Register: 36944616803-45. **Aims** Represent the interests of *inland navigation* on a pan European level; deal with problems arising out of the future development of the inland navigation industry and inland *waterway transport.* **Structure** General Assembly; Board of Directors; Secretariat; Technical Committees. **Languages** English. **Staff** 1.00 FTE, paid. **Finance** Members' dues. **Events** *Seminar* Brussels (Belgium) 2014, *Seminar* Brussels (Belgium) 2013, *Seminar* Strasbourg (France) 2012, *Seminar* Brussels (Belgium) 2011, *Seminar* Brussels (Belgium) 2010. **Publications** Annual Report.
Members Organizations in 9 countries:
Austria, Belgium, Czechia, France, Germany, Luxembourg, Netherlands, Romania, Switzerland.
Corresponding members (3) include 1 organization listed in this Yearbook:
European River/Sea Transport Union (ERSTU, #08390).
NGO Relations Member of: *European Inland Waterway Transport Platform (European IWT Platform, #07541).* [2019/XD8679/D]

♦ European Bar Human Rights Institute (#11240)
♦ European Baromedical Association / see European Baromedical Association for nurses, operators and technicians (#06319)

♦ European Baromedical Association for nurses, operators and technicians (EBAss) 06319

Sec Hyperbaric Health Pty Ltd, Level 2, Latrobe Private Hosp, Cnr Plenty Rd & Kingsbury Dr, Bundoora VIC 3083, Australia.
URL: https://ebass.org/

History Former names and other names: *European Baromedical Association* – legal name. Registration: Charity Commission, No/ID: 1183525, England and Wales; Banque Carrefour des Entreprises, No/ID: 864.646.023, Start date: 2 May 2002, End date: 6 Oct 2018, Belgium. **Structure** General Assembly; Board of Directors. Committees (4): Education; Safety; Communication; Accreditation. **Activities** Certification/accreditation; events/meetings; training/education. [2020/AA1368/D]

♦ European Bars Federation 06320

Fédération des Barreaux d'Europe (FBE) – Federación del los Colegios de Abogados de Europa – Verband Europäischer Rechtsanwaltkammern – Federação dos Barreau da Europa – Federazione degli Ordini Forensi di Europa

Gen Sec 3 rue du Général Frère, 67000 Strasbourg, France. T. +33388371266. Fax +33388368752. E-mail: fbe@fbe.org.
URL: http://www.fbe.org/

History 27 Jun 1986, Paris (France). Re-founded under current name, 23 May 1992 in Barcelona, as successor to Conference of Major European Bars. Current statutes adopted, 9 Oct 1999, Taormina (Italy). Former names and other names: *Conference of Principal Bars of Europe* – former (27 Jun 1986 to 23 May 1992); *European Bars Federation* – alias. Registration: France, Alsace. **Aims** Promote cooperation among European bars. **Structure** General Assembly; Presidency. **Languages** English, French, German, Italian, Spanish. **Finance** Members' dues. **Activities** Events/meetings; training/education. **Events** *General Congress* Palermo (Italy) 2022, *Congress* Sofia (Bulgaria) 2022, *General Congress* Barcelona (Spain) 2019, *Congress* Lisbon (Portugal) 2019, *Congress* Vienna (Austria) 2014.
Members Full in 18 countries:
Andorra, Austria, Belgium, Bulgaria, Czechia, France, Germany, Greece, Italy, Luxembourg, Netherlands, Poland, Portugal, Romania, Spain, Switzerland, Türkiye, UK.
Consultative Status Consultative status granted from: *Council of Europe (CE, #04881)* (Participatory Status).
NGO Relations Member of: *Conference of INGOs of the Council of Europe (#04607).* [2021/XD4083/D]

♦ European Baseball Confederation / see Confederation of European Baseball (#04518)
♦ European Baseball Federation / see Confederation of European Baseball (#04518)

♦ European Basic Skills Network (EBSN) 06321

Head of Secretariat Klauzal u 10, Budapest 1046, Hungary. E-mail: secretariat@basicskills.eu.
SG address not obtained.
URL: http://www.basicskills.eu/

History Jun 2010. Launched within the *European Commission (EC, #06633)* Working Group for the Implementation of the Action Plan for Adult Learning. Initial agreement for establishment of the network in 2008 between members of the Working Group which represented the educational authorities of all countries participating in the Lifelong Learning Programme. **Aims** Promote excellence in policy design and policy implementation for the field of adult basic skills, a field which has considerable impact on education, employment, social inclusion, the fight against poverty, and sustainable economic growth. **Structure** General Assembly; Executive Committee; Secretariat. **Languages** English. **Staff** 0.50 FTE, paid; 7.00 FTE, voluntary. **Finance** Sources: members' dues. **Events** *Annual Conference* Berlin (Germany) 2018, *Annual Conference* Luxembourg (Luxembourg) 2017, *Annual Conference* Ljubljana (Slovenia) 2016, *Annual Conference* The Hague (Netherlands) 2015, *Annual Conference* Budapest (Hungary) 2014. **Publications** *EBSn Quarterly* (4 a year).
Members Policy makers, policy providers, research institutions and national provider associations working in the field of basic skills for adults. Members (79) in 35 countries:
Armenia, Austria, Belgium, Croatia, Cyprus, Czechia, Denmark, Estonia, Finland, France, Germany, Greece, Hungary, Iceland, Ireland, Italy, Latvia, Liechtenstein, Lithuania, Luxembourg, Malta, Montenegro, Netherlands, North Macedonia, Norway, Poland, Portugal, Romania, Serbia, Slovakia, Slovenia, Spain, Sweden, Switzerland, UK.
Included in the above, 1 organization listed in this Yearbook:
Nordic Network for Adult Learning (#17349).
Associate members in 8 countries:
Argentina, Australia, Canada, Egypt, New Zealand, Singapore, Uganda, Vietnam. [2020.06.23/XJ6004/D]

♦ European Basketball Players' Union (internationally oriented national body)
♦ European Bat Research Symposium (meeting series)
♦ European Battery Recyclers Association / see European Battery Recycling Association (#06322)

♦ European Battery Recycling Association (EBRA) 06322

Secretariat Rue Royale 80, 1000 Brussels, Belgium. T. +32492972330. E-mail: info@ebra-recycling.org.
URL: http://www.ebrarecycling.org/

History 1998. Previously also referred to as *European Battery Recyclers Association.* **Aims** Promote the development of collection, treatment, sorting and recycling of spent batteries; encourage the activities and the flow of information concerning the techniques of collection, sorting, treatment and recycling; develop a dialogue with the administrations at European level and with the battery industry; establish standards for the quality of treatment and recycling. **Finance** Members' dues.
Members Full in 4 countries:
Belgium, France, Sweden, Switzerland. [2019/XD8335/**D**]

♦ European Bearing and Joint Manufacture Association (no recent information)

♦ European Beat Studies Network (EBSN) 06323

Contact address not obtained. E-mail: info@ebsn.eu.
URL: http://ebsn.eu/
History Founded 2010. **Aims** Promote and share critical and creative work in the Beat field. **Structure** Board. **Languages** English. **Staff** Voluntary. **Finance** Sources: conference fees; sponsorship; grants and donations. **Activities** Events/meetings; knowledge management/information dissemination; networking/liaising; publishing activities; research/documentation. **Events** *Annual Conference* Nicosia (Cyprus) 2019, *Annual Conference* Vienna (Austria) 2018. **Publications** Essays. **Members** Individuals (about 300). Membership countries not specified. [2020.03.11/XM7999/**F**]

♦ European Bedding Industries' Association (EBIA) 06324

SG Rue Montoyer 24, 1000 Brussels, Belgium. T. +3225290670. E-mail: info@europeanbedding.eu.
URL: http://www.europeanbedding.eu/
History Jan 2000. Registration: Banque-Carrefour des Entreprises, No/ID: 0472.057.725, Start date: 10 Apr 2000, Belgium; EU Transparency Register, No/ID: 422791133712-60, Start date: 22 Jan 2019. **Aims** Represent the European bedding industry; promote research related to sleeping comfort; increase cooperation between the members. **Structure** Board of Directors. **Activities** Awards/prizes/competitions; events/meetings. **Events** *General Assembly* Madrid (Spain) 2017, *General Assembly* Berlin (Germany) 2016.
Members Ordinary in 7 countries:
Belgium, France, Germany, Italy, Netherlands, Spain, UK. [2020/XM0383/t/**D**]

♦ European Bedding Manufacturers' Union (inactive)

♦ European Beer Consumers Union (EBCU) 06325

Union européenne des consommateurs de bière (UECB) – Europäische Union der Bierverbraucher
Chair 230 Hatfield Road, St Albans, AL1 4LW, UK.
Secretariat address not obtained. E-mail: secretary@ebcu.org.
URL: http://www.ebcu.org/
History 26 May 1990, Bruges (Belgium). EU Transparency Register: 570846710712-13. **Aims** Give voice to the beer consumer at European level, both within and beyond the European Union. **Structure** Executive Committee. **Languages** English. **Staff** Voluntary. **Finance** Members' dues. **Activities** Events/meetings; knowledge management/information dissemination; advocacy/lobbying/activism. **Publications** News published in members' publications.
Members Organizations and Associate Members in 15 countries:
Austria, Belgium, Czechia, Denmark, Finland, Germany, Ireland, Italy, Netherlands, Norway, Poland, Spain, Sweden, Switzerland, UK. [2019.12.19/XD3029/**D**]

♦ European Begg Society of Orthodontics (EBSO) 06326

Sec Viersener Str 23, 41061 Mönchengladbach, Germany. Fax +492161207010. E-mail: secr.ebso@yahoo.com.
URL: http://www.ebsocongress.com/
History 1967, Netherlands. **Aims** Promote excellence in light wire and Begg and Tip Edge. **Structure** European Council, comprising President, Past President, Secretary, Treasurer and 2 members. **Finance** Members' dues. **Events** *Biennial Congress* Bonn (Germany) 2019, *Biennial Congress* Amsterdam (Netherlands) 2017, *Biennial Congress* Leiden (Netherlands) 2015, *Biennial Congress* Ghent (Belgium) 2013, *Biennial Congress* Bad Oeynhausen (Germany) 2011. **Publications** *EBSO Newsletter.*
Members Full in 11 countries:
Belgium, Denmark, France, Germany, Ireland, Israel, Netherlands, Norway, Spain, Sweden, UK. [2017/XE2174/**E**]

♦ European Behavioural and Neural Genetics Society / see International Behavioural and Neural Genetics Society (#12332)

♦ European Behavioural Pharmacology Society (EBPS) 06327

Gen Sec Università degli studi di Verona, Policlinco G B Rossi, P le L A Scuro 10, 37134 Verona BL, Italy. T. +39458027277. Fax +39458027452.
Pres address not obtained.
URL: http://www.ebps.org/
History 6 Jul 1986, Antwerp (Belgium). **Aims** Advance development of behavioral pharmacology. **Structure** General Meeting (every 2 years); Committee. **Finance** Sources: members' dues. **Activities** Events/meetings. **Events** *Biennial Meeting* Mannheim (Germany) 2023, *Biennial Meeting* Maastricht (Netherlands) 2021, *Biennial Conference* Braga (Portugal) 2019, *Biennial Conference* Heraklion (Greece) 2017, *Biennial Conference* Verona (Italy) 2015. **Publications** *Behavioural Pharmacology.* **NGO Relations** Member of (1): *Federation of European Neuroscience Societies (FENS, #09522).* [2021/XD7092/**D**]

♦ European Belt Wrestling Confederation (unconfirmed)
♦ European Bentonite Association / see European Bentonite Producers Association (#06328)

♦ European Bentonite Producers Association (EUBA) 06328

SG c/o IMA-Europe, Rue des Deux Eglises 26, 1000 Brussels, Belgium. T. +3222104410. E-mail: secretariat@ima-europe.eu.
URL: http://www.ima-europe.eu/eubaindex.htm
History 12 Jan 1999, Brussels (Belgium), as *European Bentonite Association.* **Aims** Serve as the official body representing European bentonite producers. **Languages** English. **Staff** 7.50 FTE, paid.
Members Companies in 10 countries:
Austria, Cyprus, Denmark, Germany, Greece, Italy, Netherlands, Spain, UK, USA.
NGO Relations Member of: *Industrial Minerals Association – Europe (IMA Europe, #11179).* Shares office staff with: *Calcium Carbonate Association – Europe (CCA-Europe, #03399); European Association of Feldspar Producers (EUROFEL, #06037); European Association of Industrial Silica Producers (EUROSIL, #06082); European Borates Association (EBA, #06382); European Kaolin and Plastic Clays Association (KPC Europe, #07623); European Lime Association (EuLA, #07699); European Speciality Minerals Association (ESMA, #08811); International Diatomite Producers Association (IDPA, #13172); Scientific Association of European Talc Industry (Eurotalc, #19146);* IMA Europe. In liaison with technical committees of: *Comité européen de normalisation (CEN, #04162).* [2018.09.06/XD7539/**D**]

♦ European Betting Association / see European Gaming and Betting Association (#07375)
♦ European BIC Network / see European Business and Innovation Centre Network (#06420)
♦ European Bicycle Manufacturers Association (unconfirmed)

♦ European Bifurcation Club (EBC) 06329

Address not obtained.
URL: http://www.bifurc.net/
History 2005. **Aims** Develop new concepts, processes and devices for the treatment of *coronary* bifurcation lesions. **Events** *Annual Meeting* Barcelona (Spain) 2018, *Annual Meeting* Brussels (Belgium) 2018, *Annual Meeting* Rotterdam (Netherlands) 2016, *Annual Meeting* Bordeaux (France) 2014, *Annual Meeting* London (UK) 2013. [2012/XM3665/**E**]

♦ European Billiards Confederation (#04539)

♦ European Billiards and Snooker Association (EBSA) 06330

Gen Sec 8 Coedcelyn Road, Sketty, Swansea, SA2 8DS, UK. T. +447980927914.
URL: http://www.ebsa.tv/
History Current constitution adopted Jun 2011. **Aims** Act as the European governing body and conduct and promote European championships in billiards and snooker in accordance with the rules of the World Governing Body; foster and promote billiards and snooker throughout Europe. **Structure** Annual General Meeting; Executive Board; Statutory Sub-Committees. **Languages** English. **Staff** 3.00 FTE, voluntary. **Finance** Members' dues. **Activities** Sporting events; training/education.
Members Full in 46 countries and territories:
Albania, Austria, Belarus, Belgium, Bosnia-Herzegovina, Bulgaria, Croatia, Cyprus, Czechia, Denmark, England, Estonia, Finland, France, Germany, Gibraltar, Greece, Guernsey, Hungary, Iceland, Ireland, Isle of Man, Israel, Italy, Jersey, Latvia, Lithuania, Malta, Moldova, Netherlands, North Macedonia, Northern Ireland, Norway, Poland, Portugal, Romania, Russia, Scotland, Serbia, Slovakia, Spain, Sweden, Switzerland, Türkiye, Ukraine, Wales.
NGO Relations Regional association of: *International Billiards and Snooker Federation (IBSF, #12340); World Confederation of Billiards Sports (WCBS, #21291); World Professional Billiards and Snooker Association (WPBSA, #21740); World Snooker Federation (WSF, #21796).* [2019.04.25/XM2340/**D**]

♦ European Bioanalysis Forum (EBF) 06331

Contact Havenlaan 86C, b204, 1000 Brussels, Belgium. E-mail: admin@europeanbioanalysisforum.eu – info@europeanbioanalysisforum.eu.
URL: http://www.europeanbioanalysisforum.eu/
History 2006. Registered in accordance with Belgian law. **Aims** Implement a platform for discussion of science, day-to-day procedures, business tools, technologies and regulatory issues. **Structure** Steering Committee. **Activities** Events/meetings. **Events** *Open Symposium* Barcelona (Spain) 2017, *Workshop* Lisbon (Portugal) 2017, *Open Symposium* Barcelona (Spain) 2016, *Young Scientists Symposium* Barcelona (Spain) 2016, *Open Symposium* Barcelona (Spain) 2015. [2016/XJ8529/**F**]

♦ European Biochar Industry Consortium (unconfirmed)

♦ European Biocidal Product Forum (EBPF) 06332

Manager c/o CEFIC, Rue Belliard 40, Box 15, 1040 Brussels, Belgium. T. +3224369465. E-mail: cmi@cefic.be.
URL: https://specialty-chemicals.eu/ebpf/
History As a sector group of *Conseil européen de l'industrie chimique (CEFIC, #04687).* Took over activities of *European Producers of Biocidal Products (EPBP, inactive)* and *European Producers of Biocidal Active Substances (EPAS).* Also referred to as *European Biocides Products Forum.* **Aims** Serve as a forum for the exchange of views on environmental, toxicological and data protection issues relating to biocides and regulatory affairs.
Members Full: companies (53) in 12 countries:
Belgium, Czechia, Finland, France, Germany, Hungary, Italy, Netherlands, Spain, Switzerland, UK, USA.
Associate: organizations (16) in 9 countries:
Austria, Belgium, France, Germany, Netherlands, Spain, Sweden, Switzerland, UK.
Included in the above, 3 organizations listed in this Yearbook:
Conseil européen de l'industrie des peintures, des encres d'imprimerie et des couleurs d'art (CEPE, #04688); Euro Chlor (#05659); International Association for Soaps, Detergents and Maintenance Products (#12166). [2020/XM1237/y/**D**]

♦ European Biocides Products Forum / see European Biocidal Product Forum (#06332)

♦ European Biodiesel Board (EBB) 06333

SG Bd Saint Michel 34, 1040 Brussels, Belgium. T. +3227632477. Fax +3227630457. E-mail: info@ebb-eu.org – secretariat@ebb-eu.org.
URL: http://www.ebb-eu.org/
History Jan 1997. Registration: Banque-Carrefour des Entreprises, No/ID: 0851.156.192, Start date: 15 Apr 1997, Belgium; EU Transparency Register, No/ID: 84244281858-12, Start date: 18 Jun 2009. **Aims** Promote use of biodiesel in the European Union; fulfil international standards for sustainability in GHG emissions and sustainable feedstock. **Structure** Board. **Languages** English. **Staff** 5.00 FTE, paid. **Finance** Sources: members' dues. **Activities** Advocacy/lobbying/activism; research and development. **Events** *Conference* Brussels (Belgium) 2013, *European Biodiesel Conference* Rotterdam (Netherlands) 2011, *Conference* Brussels (Belgium) 2010.
Members Biodiesel producers (43) in 18 countries:
Austria, Belgium, Bulgaria, Cyprus, Czechia, Denmark, Finland, France, Germany, Greece, Ireland, Italy, Netherlands, Poland, Portugal, Romania, Slovakia, Spain.
NGO Relations Member of (1): *European Oilseed Alliance (EOA, #08080)* (Associate). In liaison with technical committees of: *Comité européen de normalisation (CEN, #04162).* [2022/XD8885/**D**]

♦ European Bioeconomy Alliance (EUBA) 06334

Contact c/o EuropaBio, Ave de l'Armée 6, 1040 Brussels, Belgium. E-mail: info@bioeconomyalliance.eu – hello@bioeconomyalliance.eu.
URL: http://bioeconomyalliance.eu/
Aims Make bioeconomy a pan-European political priority; mobilize opinion leaders with a view to mainstreaming bioeconomy as a viable and accepted alternative; create a level playing field for bio-based *products* and materials.
Members Organizations (11):
Bio-based Industries Consortium (BIC, #03238); Comité européen des fabricants de sucre (CEFS, #04159); Confederation of European Forest Owners (CEPF, #04525); COPA – european farmers (COPA, #04829); ePURE (#05517); European Association of Bioindustries (EuropaBio, #05956); European Bioplastics (#06342); FEDIOL – The EU Vegetable Oil and Proteinmeal Industry (#09718); Forest-Based Sector Technology Platform (FTP, #09861); General Confederation of Agricultural Cooperatives in the European Union (#10107); Primary Food Processors (PFP, #18496); Starch Europe (#19966).
NGO Relations Member of: *Bioenergy Europe (#03247).* [2018/XM5749/y/**D**]

♦ European BioElectromagnetics Association (EBEA) 06335

Pres address not obtained.
URL: http://www.ebea.org/
History 15 Dec 1989, Madrid (Spain). **Aims** Promote scientific study in Europe and advance understanding of the interaction of electromagnetic energy and acoustic energy with biological systems, by bringing together scientists of various backgrounds and by facilitating European integration of research; promote education in Europe on bioelectromagnetics; inform the public on advances possible in the field and on presence or absence of health risks of exposure to working and domestic environments. **Structure** Business Meeting (annual). Council (meets once a year), consisting of President, Vice-President, Executive Secretary-Treasurer and 9 members from at least 3 European countries. National sections. **Languages** English. **Staff** Voluntary. **Finance** Members' dues. Budget (annual): about euro 20,000. **Activities** Events/meetings. Proposes to set up: *European Bioelectromagnetics School.* **Events** *BioEM Annual Meeting* Nagoya (Japan) 2022, *BioEM Annual Meeting* Ghent (Belgium) 2021, *BioEM Annual Meeting* Oxford (UK) 2020, *BioEM Annual Meeting* Montpellier (France) 2019, *Annual Meeting* Portoroz (Slovenia) 2018. **Publications** *EBEA News* (4 a year). Annual Business report.
Members Ordinary; Associate; Student; Emeritus; Sustaining. Scientists and organizations in 41 countries:
Armenia, Australia, Belarus, Belgium, Bulgaria, Canada, China, Croatia, Czechia, Denmark, Estonia, Finland, France, Germany, Greece, Hungary, India, Ireland, Israel, Italy, Japan, Latvia, Lithuania, Netherlands, Norway, Poland, Portugal, Romania, Russia, Serbia, Slovakia, Slovenia, Spain, Sweden, Switzerland, Türkiye, Turkmenistan, UK, Ukraine, USA, Uzbekistan.
IGO Relations Collaborates with: *European Cooperation in Science and Technology (COST, #06784); WHO (#20950).* **NGO Relations** Collaborates with: *Bioelectrochemical Society (BES, #03244); The Bioelectromagnetics Society (BEMS, #03245); International Commission on Non-Ionizing Radiation Protection (ICNIRP, #12707); Union radio-scientifique internationale (URSI, #20475).* [2014/XD2563/**D**]

♦ European Bioenergy Business Forum (internationally oriented national body)
♦ European Bioethanol Fuel Association (inactive)
♦ European Biofeedback Association (no recent information)

European Biofuels Technology
06335

alphabetic sequence excludes
For the complete listing, see Yearbook Online at

♦ European Biofuels Technology Platform / see European Technology and Innovation Platform Bioenergy (#08881)

♦ European Biogas Association (EBA) 06336

Dir Renewable Energy House, Rue d'Arlon 63-65, 1040 Brussels, Belgium. T. +3224001087. Fax +3225461934. E-mail: info@europeanbiogas.eu.
URL: http://www.european-biogas.eu/

History 3 Feb 2009. Registration: EU Transparency Register, No/ID: 18191445640-83; Crossroads Bank for Enterprises, No/ID: 0811.023.928, Start date: 8 Apr 2009, Belgium. **Aims** Promote the deployment of sustainable biogas and biomethane production and use from anaerobic digestion (AD) and biomass gasification in Europe. **Structure** Executive Board; Company Advisory Council; Scientific Advisory Council. **Languages** Dutch, English, Finnish, French, German, Italian, Spanish. **Staff** 6.00 FTE, paid. **Activities** Advocacy/lobbying/activism; events/meetings; guidance/assistance/consulting; politics/policy/regulatory; research and development; research/documentation. **Events** *Annual Conference* Brussels (Belgium) 2022, *Annual Conference* Brussels (Belgium) 2021, *Annual Conference* Brussels (Belgium) 2020, *Annual Conference* Brussels (Belgium) 2020, *Annual Conference* Brussels (Belgium) 2019. **Publications** *Companies Cataglogues* (annual); *Success Stories* (annual); *EBA Newsletter*. Annual Report; specific publications on EBA topics of interest; position papers; press releases. **Members** Full: national associations; Associate: international companies, research institutes, individuals. Membership countries not specified. **NGO Relations** Member of (3): *European Forum for Renewable Energy Sources (EUFORES, #07329)*; *European Renewable Energies Federation (EREF, #08355)*; *European Renewable Gas Registry (ERGaR, #08356)*. [2022/XJ1480/**D**]

♦ European Biological Control Laboratory (internationally oriented national body)
♦ European Biological Inorganic Chemistry Conference (meeting series)
♦ European Biological Research Association (no recent information)

♦ European Biological Rhythms Society (EBRS) 06337

Sec Videnska 1083, 142 20 Prague 4, Czechia. T. +420241064528. Fax +420241062488. E-mail: info@ebrs-online.org.
URL: http://www.ebrs-online.org/

History 22 Nov 1978, Amsterdam (Netherlands). Officially constituted during 1st Symposium. Statutes and By-laws adopted 20 Nov 1978, Amsterdam; modified: Jul 1981, Giessen (Germany FR); 6 Sep 1990, Guildford (UK); 24 Jul 1993 Copenhagen (Denmark); 5 Sep 2005, Frankfurt-Main (Germany); 27 Aug 2009, Strasbourg (France); 2011, Oxford (UK). Former names and other names: *European Pineal Study Group (EPSG)* – former (22 Nov 1978 to 1990); *Groupe européen d'études de l'épiphyse* – former (22 Nov 1978 to 1990); *European Pineal Society (EPS)* – former (1990 to 2002); *European Pineal and Biological Rhythms Society (EPBRS)* – former (2002 to 2005). **Aims** Promote *chronobiology* and *chronomedicine*; study the circadian/seasonal organizations and mechanisms in a vertical approach that integrates molecular, cellular, system-physiological, behavioural and medical aspects. **Structure** General Assembly (every 2 years); Board. **Languages** English. **Staff** Part-time, voluntary. **Finance** Members' dues. Other sources: subventions from governments, governmental and non-governmental organizations and persons; annual contributions or donations of supporting members. **Activities** Research/documentation; events/meetings; knowledge management/information dissemination; publishing activities. **Events** *Congress* Zurich (Switzerland) 2022, *Congress* Zurich (Switzerland) 2021, *Congress* Lyon (France) 2019, *Congress* Amsterdam (Netherlands) 2017, *Congress* Manchester (UK) 2015. **Members** Ordinary; Trainee; Emeritus; Supporting; Honorary. Individuals in 43 countries and territories:
Algeria, Argentina, Australia, Austria, Belgium, Bosnia-Herzegovina, Brazil, Bulgaria, Canada, Czechia, Denmark, Egypt, Finland, France, Germany, Hong Kong, Hungary, India, Israel, Italy, Japan, Mexico, New Zealand, Norway, Pakistan, Peru, Poland, Romania, Russia, Serbia, Slovakia, Slovenia, South Africa, Spain, Sweden, Switzerland, Taiwan, Thailand, Türkiye, UK, Ukraine, USA, Zimbabwe.
NGO Relations Member of: *European Sleep Research Society (ESRS, #08493)*; *European Society of Endocrinology (ESE, #08594)*; *World Federation of Societies of Chronobiology (WFSC, #21484)*. [2022/XD9304/v/**D**]

♦ European Biomass Association / see Bioenergy Europe (#03247)

♦ European Biomass Combustion Network (CombNet) 06338

Coordinator c/o Procede Biomass BV, PO Box 328, 7500 AH Enschede, Netherlands. T. +31537112500. Fax +31537112599.
URL: http://www.combnet.com/

History 2005. **Publications** *ThermalNet* (2 a year). [2009/XM2248/**F**]

♦ European Biomass Conference and Exhibition (meeting series)

♦ European Biomass Industry Association (EUBIA) 06339

SG Scotland House, Rond-Point Schuman 6, 1040 Brussels, Belgium. T. +3222828440. E-mail: eubia@eubia.org.
Deputy Sec address not obtained.
URL: http://www.eubia.org/

History 1996. Registered in accordance with Belgian law. **Aims** Promote bioenergy and directly represent the biomass industry to EU institutions; promote international cooperation between industry and research sector in elaboration of industrial strategies and programmes on new biomass valorization technologies. **Structure** Officers: President; Secretary-General/Executive Vice-President; Deputy Secretary-General; Project Managers. **Languages** English, French. **Staff** 4.00 FTE, paid. **Activities** Policy/politics/regulatory; networking/liaising; research and development; events/meetings. **Events** *European Biomass Conference* Bologna (Italy) 2023, *European Biomass Conference* Marseille (France) 2022, *European Biomass Conference* Marseille (France) 2021, *European Biomass Conference* 2020, *European Biomass Conference* Lisbon (Portugal) 2019. **Members** Founding; Associate Utilities, Companies, Small Medium Enterprises, Institutes, Universities (about 40) in 17 countries:
Austria, Belgium, Chile, Croatia, Cyprus, Finland, France, Germany, Greece, Hungary, Italy, Pakistan, Poland, Portugal, Spain, Sweden, UK.
IGO Relations Member of: *Global Bioenergy Partnership (GBEP, #10251)*. *Joint Research Centre (JRC, #16147)* is member. **NGO Relations** Instrumental in setting up: *Alliance for Rural Electrification (ARE, #00719)*; *European Biomass Research Network (EUBREN, #06340)*. [2017.10.13/XE4133/t/**E**]

♦ European Biomass Research Network (EUBREN) 06340

Contact c/o EUBIA, Rond-Point Schuman 6, Scotland House, 1040 Brussels, Belgium. T. +3222828440.
URL: http://www.eubren.com/

History Set up with the help of *European Biomass Industry Association (EUBIA, #06339)*. **Aims** Promote mutual interchange and cooperation in the field of biomass production and use. **Structure** General Assembly (annual); Board.
Members Universities in 17 countries:
Austria, Belgium, Croatia, Cyprus, Denmark, Finland, France, Germany, Greece, Hungary, Italy, Poland, Portugal, Romania, Spain, Sweden, UK. [2016.06.16/XM4177/**F**]

♦ European Biomedical Research Association (inactive)

♦ European Biophysical Societies' Association (EBSA) 06341

Sec Chemistry Dept, Imperial College London, London, SW7 2AZ, UK. T. +442075945797.
URL: http://www.ebsa.org/

History 1984. **Aims** Advance and disseminate knowledge of the principles, recent developments and applications of biophysics; foster exchange of scientific information among European biophysicists and biophysicists in general. **Structure** General Assembly (in conjunction with European Biophysics Congress); Executive Committee. **Languages** English. **Finance** Members' dues. Sales of publication. **Activities** Events/meetings; training/education. **Events** *European Biophysics Congress* Stockholm (Sweden) 2023, *European Biophysics Congress* Vienna (Austria) 2021, *European Biophysics Congress* Madrid (Spain) 2019, *European Biophysics Congress* Edinburgh (UK) 2017, *European Biophysics Congress* Dresden (Germany) 2015. **Publications** *European Biophysics Journal*.
Members Biophysical societies in 31 countries:
Albania, Armenia, Austria, Belarus, Belgium, Croatia, Czechia, Denmark, Egypt, Finland, France, Germany, Hungary, Israel, Italy, Lithuania, Netherlands, Norway, Poland, Portugal, Romania, Russia, Serbia, Slovakia, Slovenia, Spain, Sweden, Switzerland, Türkiye, UK, Ukraine.
Associate member in 1 country:
Iran Islamic Rep.
NGO Relations *European Association for the Advancement of Science and Technology (EUROSCIENCE, #05927)*; *Initiative for Science in Europe (ISE, #11214)*; *International Union for Pure and Applied Biophysics (IUPAB, #15808)*. [2019.12.12/XD6479/**D**]

♦ European Bioplastics 06342

Managing Dir Marienstrasse 19-20, 10117 Berlin, Germany. T. +493028482350. Fax +493028482359. E-mail: info@european-bioplastics.org.
URL: http://www.european-bioplastics.org/

History 2 Nov 2005. Successor to *International Biodegradable Polymers Association and Working Groups (inactive)*. EU Transparency Register: 245070265-17. **Aims** Support and promote: growth and use of renewable raw materials in products and applications; innovation leading to lower environmental impact of durable and non-durable plastic products; independent third party certification and product labelling; separate collection of organic waste including compostable products and composting; identification and evaluation of other eco-efficient end-of-life options. **Structure** General Assembly (annual); Board. **Activities** Events/meetings. **Events** *Conference* Berlin (Germany) 2021, *Conference* Berlin (Germany) 2020, *Conference* Berlin (Germany) 2017, *Conference* Berlin (Germany) 2016, *Shaping smart solutions* Berlin (Germany) 2015. **Publications** *Bioplastics Bulletin*. Conference proceedings; papers.
Members Full in 18 countries:
Austria, Belgium, Brazil, China, Finland, France, Germany, Israel, Italy, Japan, Netherlands, Norway, Poland, Spain, Sweden, Switzerland, UK, USA.
NGO Relations Liaison Organization of: *Comité européen de normalisation (CEN, #04162)*. Member of: *European Bioeconomy Alliance (EUBA, #06334)*; *European Policy Centre (EPC, #08240)*; *International Sustainability and Carbon Certification (ISCC)*. [2020/XM3291/**D**]

♦ European Biosafety Association (EBSA) 06343

EBSA Office Kerkstraat 108, 9050 Ghent, Belgium. T. +3292334866. E-mail: ebsa-office@ebsaweb.eu.
Pres Federal Office of Public Health, Schwarzenburgstrasse 157, 3003 Bern, Switzerland.
URL: http://www.ebsaweb.eu/

History Jun 1996. Statutes revised in 2003. Current statutes adopted 2 Oct 2016. Registration: No/ID: BE 0475.189.538, Belgium; EU Transparency Register, No/ID: 539635916353-39. **Aims** Provide a forum for members to discuss and debate issues of concern in biological safety; represent those working in the field of biosafety and associated activities. **Structure** General Assembly (annual); Executive Council. **Languages** English. **Finance** Members' dues. **Activities** Events/meetings; knowledge management/information dissemination; training/education. **Events** *Annual Conference* Ghent (Belgium) 2022, *Annual Conference* Luxembourg (Luxembourg) 2021, *Annual Conference* Luxembourg (Luxembourg) 2020, *Annual Conference* Bucharest (Romania) 2019, *Annual Conference* Copenhagen (Denmark) 2018. **Publications** *EBSA Newsletter*. **Members** Individual (440); Corporate (20), representing over 40 countries. Membership countries not specified. **NGO Relations** Member of: *International Federation of Biosafety Associations (IFBA, #13373)*. [2020.03.03/XD5173/**D**]

♦ European Biostimulants Industry Council (EBIC) 06344

Contact c/o Prospero and Partners, Lange Winkelhaakstr 26, 2060 Antwerp, Belgium. T. +3232900123. E-mail: arnaud@prospero.ag – barbara@prospero.ag.
Contact c/o Prospero and Partners, 34 rue des Blondeaux, 94240 L'Hay-les-Roses, France. T. +33140910570.
URL: http://www.biostimulants.eu/

History Jun 2011. Founded as European Biostimulant Industry Consortium. Current title adopted when gained legal identity, 2013. Current statutes amended Nov 2018. Registration: EU Transparency Register, No/ID: 034239613511-14, Start date: 23 Apr 2014. **Aims** Foster the role of the biostimulants sector in helping agriculture to produce more with less. **Structure** General Assembly; Board; Secretariat. **Members** Companies. Membership countries not specified. [2019/XM8703/t/**D**]

♦ European Biotechnology Network 06345

SG Rue de la Science 14b, 1040 Brussels, Belgium. T. +3227337237. E-mail: office@european-biotechnology.net.
Pres address not obtained.
Office Manager address not obtained.
URL: http://www.european-biotechnology.net/

History Founded 2009. **Aims** Facilitate cooperation between professionals in biotechnology and the life sciences all over Europe. **Activities** Events/meetings. **Events** *Biotechnology in Application – Farm to Fork Meeting* Brussels (Belgium) 2011. **Publications** *European Biotechnology News Magazine* (4 a year). *European Biotechnology Industry Guide*. **Members** Biotech professionals from science and research, industry, academia, organizations, state agencies and authorities. Membership countries not specified. [2015.09.02/XJ0556/**D**]

♦ European Biotechnology Thematic Network Association (EBTNA) . . 06346

Gen Sec Univ of Perugia, Via del Giochetto, 06126 Perugia PG, Italy.
Pres Erciyes Univ, Rektörlügü, 38039 Kayseri/Kayseri, Türkiye.
URL: https://www.ebtna.eu/

History 1996. Registration: No/ID: 5773 Modl, Start date: 27 Nov 2006. **Aims** Present academic and industrial projects that help to establish connections between the biotech industry and science. **Structure** General Assembly; Administrative Council; Executive Board. **Languages** English. **Staff** 0.50 FTE, paid. **Finance** Sources: donations; fees for services; international organizations; meeting proceeds; members' dues; sale of publications; subscriptions. **Activities** Events/meetings; projects/programmes. **Events** *European Biotechnology Congress* Prague (Czechia) 2022, *European Biotechnology Congress* 2021, *European Biotechnology Congress* Prague (Czechia) 2020, *European Biotechnology Congress* Valencia (Spain) 2019, *European Biotechnology Congress* Athens (Greece) 2018. **Publications** Articles.
Members National Boards in 45 countries:
Albania, Austria, Azerbaijan, Belarus, Belgium, Brazil, Bulgaria, China, Croatia, Cyprus, Czechia, Ecuador, Egypt, France, Georgia, Germany, Greece, Hungary, Iceland, India, Iran Islamic Rep, Israel, Italy, Jordan, Kazakhstan, Korea Rep, Latvia, Lithuania, Mexico, Moldova, Morocco, Netherlands, North Macedonia, Pakistan, Poland, Portugal, Romania, Russia, Scotland, Slovakia, Slovenia, Spain, Sweden, Türkiye, UK.
Also in Latin America (countries not specified). [2023.02.13/XJ2742/**F**]

♦ European Bird Census Council (EBCC) 06347

Conseil pour le recensement des oiseaux d'Europe

Chairperson c/o The Lodge, Sandy, SG19 2DL, UK.
URL: http://www.ebcc.info/

History 1992. Founded upon merger of *European Ornithological Atlas Committee (EOAC, inactive)* and *International Bird Census Committee (IBCC, inactive)*. **Aims** Study the distribution, numbers and demography of European birds, applying rigorous and standardized procedures for data-gathering and interpretation in order to assure scientific validity; monitor distribution, numbers and demography so that changes may be both detected and, if possible, understood and so that the relevant agencies may be provided with a sound basis for the conservation and management of Europe's birds and their habitats. **Structure** Board, consisting of 2 Delegates per European country; Executive Committee of up to 10 members, including Chairman, Vice-Chairman, Secretary, Treasurer and Newsletter Editor. **Staff** None. **Activities** *'Pan-European Common Bird Monitoring Project'*, started Jan 2002, aims to use common birds as indicators of the general state of nature, using scientific data on changes in breeding populations across Europe. **Events** *Bird Numbers Conference* Lucerne (Switzerland) 2022, *Bird Numbers Conference* Evora (Portugal) 2019, *Bird Numbers Conference* Halle (Saale) (Germany) 2016, *Bird Numbers Conference* Cluj-Napoca (Romania) 2013, *Bird Numbers Conference* Caceres (Spain) 2010. **Publications** *Bird Census News*. *EBCC Atlas of European Breeding Birds*.
Members Authorities, organizations and individuals in 45 countries:
Albania, Andorra, Armenia, Austria, Azerbaijan, Belarus, Belgium, Bosnia-Herzegovina, Bulgaria, Croatia, Cyprus, Czechia, Denmark, Estonia, Finland, France, Georgia, Germany, Greece, Hungary, Iceland, Ireland, Italy, Latvia, Liechtenstein, Lithuania, Luxembourg, Malta, Moldova, Netherlands, North Macedonia, Norway, Poland, Portugal, Romania, Russia, Serbia, Slovakia, Slovenia, Spain, Sweden, Switzerland, Türkiye, UK, Ukraine. [2022/XD4367/**D**]

♦ European Bitumen Association (EUROBITUME) 06348

Association européenne du bitume

Dir Gen Bd du Souverain 165, 4th Floor, 1160 Brussels, Belgium. T. +3225669140. Fax +3225669149. E-mail: info@eurobitume.eu.

Office Manager address not obtained.

URL: https://www.eurobitume.eu/

History 1969, Brussels (Belgium). Most recent statutes adopted May 2020. Registration: Belgium. **Aims** Sustain a clear and positive technical image of the European bitumen industry; be its spokesman and acknowledged focal point. **Structure** General Assembly (2 a year); Board of Directors (BoD); HSE Committee; Communications (PRC); Technical Committee (TC). **Languages** English, French. **Staff** 1.00 FTE, paid. **Finance** Sources: members' dues. **Activities** Active in all member countries. **Events** *Joint Congress* Vienna (Austria) 2022, *Autumn Meeting* 2021, *Spring Meeting* 2021, *Joint Congress* Brussels (Belgium) 2021, *Autumn Meeting* 2020. **Publications** *Safe Delivery of Bitumen – Standard European* (2012) in English, Norwegian – electronic; *Life Cycle Inventory: Bitumen* (2011); *Safe Delivery of Bitumen Benelux, 3rd ed* (2011) in Dutch, French; *Safe Delivery of Bitumen – Version for Germany, 1st ed* (2011) – electronic; *Safe Delivery of Bitumen – Version for Portugal, 1st ed* (2011) – electronic; *Safe Delivery of Bitumen – Version for Spain, 1st ed* (2011) – electronic; *The Bitumen Industry – A Global Perspective – Production, chemistry, use, specification and occupational exposure, 2nd ed* (2011) – joint publication with Asphalt Institute. Position papers; congress reports; seminar and workshop proceedings.

Members 15 Core Members, 1 International Member & 11 Associate Members in 13 countries and territories:
Abidjan, Austria, Belgium, France, Germany, Italy, Netherlands, Portugal, Spain, Sweden, Switzerland, Taiwan, UK.

NGO Relations Member of (1): *European Union Road Federation (ERF, #09014).* [2022/XD3942/**D**]

♦ European Bitumen Shingle Organization (inactive)

♦ European Blackball Association 06349

Sec 43 Bushmills Road, Coleraine, BT52 2BP, UK. T. +44126556309. Fax +44126556309.

URL: http://www.eba-pool.org/

History as *European and United Kingdom Pool Federation (EUKPF).* [2014/XE3566/**E**]

♦ European Blind Union (EBU) 06350

Union Européenne des Aveugles (UEA)

Dir 6 rue Gager-Gabillot, 75015 Paris, France. T. +33147053820. Fax +33147053821. E-mail: ebusecretariat@euroblind.org – ebu@euroblind.org.

URL: http://www.euroblind.org/

History 27 Aug 1984, Hurdal (Norway). Founded when constitution was adopted. European regional branch of *World Blind Union (WBU, #21234).* Registration: EU Transparency Register, No/ID: 42378755934-87, Start date: 27 May 2011. **Aims** Represent all blind and partially-sighted people in Europe; promote advancement of the interests of blind and partially-sighted people, including those with additional disabilities with the goal of achieving their equal rights as citizens and full participation in society; provide a European forum for exchange of knowledge and experience in the field of blindness and low vision; promote prevention and cure of blindness. **Structure** General Assembly; Board; Central Office. **Languages** English, French, German, Russian. **Staff** 3.50 FTE, paid. **Finance** Sources: donations; fundraising; members' dues. **Activities** Events/meetings; knowledge management/information dissemination; research and development. **Events** *General Assembly* Heathrow (UK) 2015, *EBU deafblind conference* Plovdiv (Bulgaria) 2012, *General Assembly* Fredericia (Denmark) 2011, *Braille21 world congress* Leipzig (Germany) 2011, *An inclusive Europe conference* Vienna (Austria) 2010. **Publications** *EBU Newsletter* (12 a year); *EBU Focus Newsletter* (4 a year).

Members National members in 41 countries:
Albania, Armenia, Austria, Belarus, Belgium, Bosnia-Herzegovina, Bulgaria, Croatia, Cyprus, Czechia, Denmark, Estonia, Finland, France, Germany, Greece, Hungary, Iceland, Ireland, Italy, Kazakhstan, Lithuania, Luxembourg, Moldova, Montenegro, Netherlands, North Macedonia, Norway, Poland, Portugal, Romania, Russia, Serbia, Slovakia, Slovenia, Spain, Sweden, Switzerland, Türkiye, UK, Ukraine.

Associate members (2):
Kosovo.

International League of Blind Esperantists (#14017).

Consultative Status Consultative status granted from: *Council of Europe (CE, #04881)* (Participatory Status).

IGO Relations Participant in Fundamental Rights Platform of: *European Union Agency for Fundamental Rights (FRA, #08969).* **NGO Relations** Member of (4): *Conference of INGOs of the Council of Europe (#04607); European Disability Forum (EDF, #06929); European Women's Lobby (EWL, #09102)* (Supporting); *Social Platform (#19344).* Special cooperation with: *International Council for Education of People with Visual Impairment (ICEVI, #13015).* Links with most European and worldwide disability organizations. [2021/XE6441/y/**D**]

♦ European Blood Alliance (EBA) 06351

Exec Dir c/o BLSI, Clos Chapelle-aux-Champs 30, 1200 Brussels, Belgium. E-mail: info@europeanbloodalliance.eu.

Registered Address Plesmanlaan 125, 1066 CX Amsterdam, Netherlands.

URL: http://www.europeanbloodalliance.eu/

History 21 Sep 1998. Registration: EU Transparency Register, No/ID: 149855010621-40; Kamer van Koophandel, No/ID: 34210816, Netherlands, Amsterdam; Banque-Carrefour des Entreprises, No/ID: 0727.603.730, Belgium. **Aims** Improve the performance of blood establishments for the benefit of patients, based on scientific and ethical principles. **Structure** Board; Executive Committee; Secretariat. **Languages** English. **Staff** 1.00 FTE, paid. **Finance** Members' dues. **Activities** Events/meetings; awareness raising; knowledge management/information dissemination. **Events** *Workshop* Brussels (Belgium) 2009, *Risks, threats and decision-making in a complex environment* Stockholm (Sweden) 2007, *Blood centers role in transfusion recipient care* London (UK) 2006, *International blood and plasma conference* Lisbon (Portugal) 2005, *Harmonisation of processes* Québec, QC (Canada) 2005. **Publications** Members' newsletter; position papers.

Members Full; national blood services in 26 countries:
Austria, Belgium, Croatia, Denmark, Estonia, Finland, France, Germany, Greece, Hungary, Iceland, Ireland, Italy, Latvia, Lithuania, Luxembourg, Malta, Netherlands, Norway, Portugal, Romania, Slovenia, Spain, Sweden, Switzerland, UK.

Observer in 1 country:
Serbia.

NGO Relations Founding member of: *Alliance of Blood Operators (ABO, #00659).* Co-organizes: *European Conference on Donor Health and Management (ECDHM).* [2021/XF6974/**F**]

♦ European Blue Cross Youth Association (inactive)

♦ European Bluegrass Music Association (EBMA) 06352

Chairman address not obtained.

URL: http://www.ebma.org/

History Founded Feb 2001, Jena (Germany). **Aims** Further bluegrass music, musicians and bands in Europe; enhance bluegrass music's image. **Structure** General Assembly (annual); Board of Directors. **Languages** English. **Staff** None. **Finance** Members' dues. Other sources: sponsorship; income from sales. **Events** *Gathering / European Bluegrass Summit* Munich (Germany) 2015, *Summit / European Bluegrass Summit* Prague (Czech Rep) 2014, *Summit / European Bluegrass Summit* Prague (Czech Rep) 2013, *Summit / European Bluegrass Summit* Bühl (Germany) 2012, *Summit / European Bluegrass Summit* Bühl (Germany) 2011. **Publications** *Bluegrass Europe* (4 a year); *European Bluegrass Directory* (irregular).

Members Bands; associations; individuals. Members in 17 countries:
Austria, Belgium, Canada, Czechia, Denmark, Finland, France, Germany, Ireland, Italy, Netherlands, Norway, Spain, Sweden, Switzerland, UK, USA. [2018/XD8259/**D**]

♦ European Board for Accreditation in Cardiology (EBAC) 06353

Main Office Schanzenstrasse 36, Suite 31a, 51063 Cologne, Germany. T. +4922116998622. Fax +4922116998620. E-mail: contact@ebac-cme.org.

URL: http://www.ebac-cme.org/

History 2001. Founded as a joint initiative between *European Society of Cardiology (ESC, #08536)* and the Cardiology Section of *European Union of Medical Specialists (UEMS, #09001).* Since 2011, a limited liability company with *European Cardiology Section Foundation (ECSF, #06449).* **Aims** Stimulate, coordinate and facilitate high quality Continuing Medical Education (CME) in cardiology, both for individuals and institutions, so as to provide the highest possible standard of care for patients and populations. **Structure** Board, comprising 3 delegates mandated by *European Union of Medical Specialists (UEMS, #09001),* 3 delegated mandated by *European Society of Cardiology (ESC, #08536),* 1 delegate representing *Association for European Paediatric and Congenital Cardiology (AEPC, #02529)* and 1 representative of *European Society of Hypertension (ESH, #08627).* **Languages** English. **Activities** Certification/accreditation. **Events** *International Meeting on Intensive Cardiac Care* London (UK) 2012, *International meeting on intensive cardiac care* Tel Aviv (Israel) 2007. **Publications** *EBAC Newsletter.* **NGO Relations** Located at: *European Heart House (see: #08536).* [2020/XM2302/**D**]

♦ European Board of Anaesthesiology (EBA) 06354

Sec-Treas c/o UEMS, Rue de l'Industrie, 1040 Brussels, Belgium. T. +3226495164. Fax +3226403730. E-mail: secretary@eba-uems.eu – info@eba-uems.eu.

Pres address not obtained. E-mail: president@eba-uems.eu.

URL: http://www.eba-uems.eu/

History 1993, as part of *European Union of Medical Specialists (UEMS, #09001).* **Aims** Harmonize teaching in the member countries of the European Union and the European Free Trade Area. **Structure** Board (meets twice a year); President; Secretary; 2 elected representatives from each European country and free trade zone, representing their country's national societies; observers from other European countries. **Languages** English. **Finance** Members' dues.

Members Governments of 34 countries:
Austria, Belgium, Bulgaria, Croatia, Cyprus, Czechia, Denmark, Estonia, Finland, France, Germany, Greece, Hungary, Ireland, Italy, Latvia, Lithuania, Luxembourg, Malta, Montenegro, Netherlands, North Macedonia, Norway, Poland, Portugal, Romania, Russia, Serbia, Slovakia, Slovenia, Spain, Sweden, Switzerland, UK.

NGO Relations Joint meetings with: *European Society of Anaesthesiology and Intensive Care (ESAIC, #08518).* [2016/XD5614/**D**]

♦ European Board of Cardiothoracic Surgery (EBCTS) 06355

Exec Secretariat EACTS House, Madiera Walk, Windsor, SL4 1EU, UK. T. +441753832166. Fax +441753620407. E-mail: ebcts@eacts.co.uk.

URL: https://www.ebcts.org/

History 4 Oct 1996, by *European Association for Cardio-Thoracic Surgery (EACTS, #05964), European Society for Cardiovascular and Endovascular Surgery (ESCVS, #08537)* and *European Society of Thoracic Surgeons (ESTS, #08760).* Former names and other names: *European Board of Thoracic and Cardiovascular Surgeons (EBTCS)* – former. **Aims** Create a common high standard for the quality of thoracic and cardiovascular surgery throughout Europe. **Structure** Board of 9 members, including Chairman and Secretary. **Activities** Organizes examinations. [2023/XE4448/**E**]

♦ European Board of Cardiovascular Perfusion (EBCP) 06356

Gen Sec Kruidtuinlaan 32, 1000 Brussels, Belgium. E-mail: info@ebcp.eu.

URL: https://www.ebcp.eu/

History 1991. Registration: Banque-Carrefour des Entreprises, No/ID: 0696.823.650, Start date: 28 May 2018, Belgium; EU Transparency Register, No/ID: 768196943720-52, Start date: 27 Jul 2021. **Aims** Establish, monitor and maintain equality of standards in education and training in practice of perfusion and related studies for the benefit of the public; set out Essentials and Guidelines by which training programmes will be accredited by the Board and where such programmes will lead to qualifications recognized by all societies in Europe; develop an Advanced level of education and training programme to train the trainers in perfusion and thereby qualify the trainers to teach perfusion skills; establish a common perfusionists certification programme in Europe and thereby permit greater mobility of labour with recognition of professional competence; issue a European Certificate of competence in Perfusion to certify that the bearer has satisfied the Board by examination that the required standard of competence has been attained; liaise with the European commission to legalize these objectives through the appropriate health department. **Structure** Accreditation Committee; Certification Committee; Scientific Committee; Office. **Languages** English. **Staff** 0.00 FTE, paid; 45.00 FTE, voluntary. **Activities** Certification/accreditation; monitoring/evaluation; standards/guidelines; training/education. **Events** *Conference on Perfusion Education & Training (ECoPEaT)* Barcelona (Spain) 2021, *European Conference on Perfusion Education and Training* Lisbon (Portugal) 2019, *European Conference on Perfusion Education and Training* Amsterdam (Netherlands) 2015, *European Conference on Perfusion Education and Training* Lisbon (Portugal) 2011, *European conference on perfusion education and training* Lisbon (Portugal) 2008. **Publications** *2019 EACTS/EACTA/EBCP guidelines on cardiopulmonary bypass in adult cardiac surgery* (2019) in English.

Members Societies in 30 countries:
Belgium, Bulgaria, Croatia, Cyprus, Denmark, Finland, France, Germany, Greece, Ireland, Italy, Latvia, Lithuania, Luxembourg, Malta, Netherlands, North Macedonia, Norway, Poland, Portugal, Serbia, Slovenia, South Africa, Spain, Sweden, Switzerland, Türkiye, UK, Ukraine, United Arab Emirates.

Supporting members (2):
European Association for Cardio-Thoracic Surgery (EACTS, #05964); European Association of Cardiothoracic Anaesthesiology and Intensive Care (EACTAIC, #05963).

IGO Relations Liaises with: *European Commission (EC, #06633).* **NGO Relations** Represented on the Board: EACTA; EACTS; *European Society for Cardiovascular and Endovascular Surgery (ESCVS, #08537).* [2022.02.02/XE3912/**E**]

♦ European Board and College of Obstetrics and Gynaecology (EBCOG) 06357

Admin 7 Killeaton Park, Dunmurry, Belfast, BT17 9HE, UK. T. +442890610559. Fax +442890610584. E-mail: ebcogexams@gmail.com.

Registered Office c/o UEMS, 20 Ave de la Couronne, 1050 Brussels, Belgium.

URL: http://www.ebcog.org/

History 1996. Founded on merger of *European Board of Gynaecology and Obstetrics (EBGO, inactive)* and *European College of Obstetrics and Gynaecology (ECOG, inactive).* Merged with: *European Association of Gynaecologists and Obstetricians (EAGO, inactive).* Comes within *European Union of Medical Specialists (UEMS, #09001).* **Aims** Improve the health of women and their babies by promoting the highest possible standards of care in all European countries. **Structure** Council; Executive. Standing Committees. Subspeciality representatives from: *European Urogynaecological Association (EUGA, #09041); European Association of Perinatal Medicine (EAPM, #06148); European Society of Gynaecological Oncology (ESGO, #08612); European Society of Human Reproduction and Embryology (ESHRE, #08625).* **Activities** Certification/accreditation; events/meetings; training/education. **Events** *European Congress of Obstetrics and Gynaecology* Athens (Greece) 2021, *European Congress of Obstetrics and Gynaecology* Bergen (Norway) 2020, *Congress* Paris (France) 2018, *Congress* Istanbul (Turkey) 2016, *Congress / European Congress* Glasgow (UK) 2014.

Members National societies of 36 countries:
Albania, Austria, Belgium, Bulgaria, Croatia, Cyprus, Czechia, Denmark, Estonia, Finland, France, Germany, Greece, Hungary, Iceland, Ireland, Italy, Kosovo, Latvia, Lithuania, Malta, Netherlands, North Macedonia, Norway, Poland, Portugal, Romania, Russia, Slovakia, Slovenia, Spain, Sweden, Switzerland, Türkiye, UK, Ukraine.

NGO Relations Cooperates with (2): *European Federation for Colposcopy and Pathology of the Lower Genital Tract (EFC, #07081); International Society for Infectious Diseases in Obstetrics and Gynaecology (ISIDOG, #15200).* Instrumental in setting up (2): *European Network of Trainees in Obstetrics and Gynaecology (ENTOG, #08021); European Society for Gynaecological Endoscopy (ESGE, #08611).* Allied regional federation of: *Fédération Internationale de Gynécologie et d'Obstétrique (FIGO, #09638).* [2021/XE3795/**E**]

♦ European Board of Dermatology and Venereology (EBDV) 06358

Pres Dermatology Dept, Univ of Medical Sciences, 46 Przybyszewskiego St, 60-355 Poznań, Poland. E-mail: mczarnec@ump.edu.pl.

URL: http://www.uems-ebdv.org/ebdv/

History within *European Union of Medical Specialists (UEMS, #09001).* **Aims** Establish and maintain high *standards of training, education* and *qualification* of physicians practising as dermatologists and venereologists. **Structure** Council; Sections; Board. Officers: President; General Secretary; Treasurer. [2018/XE3707/**E**]

♦ European Board of Gastroenterology / see European Board of Gastroenterology and Hepatology (#06359)

♦ European Board of Gastroenterology and Hepatology (EBGH) 06359

Pres of Board School of Postgraduate Medicine, Univ of Hertfordshire, Hatfield, AL10 9AB, UK. T. +441707285219.
Pres of the Section Skane Univ Hosp, Getingevägen 4, SE-221 85 Lund, Sweden.
URL: http://www.eubog.org/

History Founded Sep 1992, as a part of the gastroenterology section of *European Union of Medical Specialists (UEMS, #09001)*. Original title: *European Board of Gastroenterology (EBG)*. **Aims** Serve patients throughout Europe by developing, supporting and encouraging doctors of the highest quality in the specialty of Gastroenterology and Hepatology. **Structure** Section, composed of 2 delegates from each of the 30 EUMS member countries and a representative from *European Junior Doctors Association (EJD, #07620)*; Board; Executive Committee; Sub-Committees (4). **Languages** English, French. **Staff** 1.00 FTE, paid. **Finance** Members' dues. Diploma fees. **Activities** Standards/guidelines; training/education; monitoring/evaluation; networking/liaising; knowledge management/information dissemination. **Events** *Meeting* Palermo (Italy) 2014, *Meeting* Berlin (Germany) 2013, *Meeting* London (UK) 2003, *Spring meeting / Meeting* Moscow (Russia) 2002, *Autumn meeting* Amsterdam (Netherlands) 2001. **Publications** *Accredited European Training Centres*; *The Blue Book 2017* in English, French.
Members in 28 countries:
Austria, Belgium, Bulgaria, Croatia, Cyprus, Czechia, Denmark, Estonia, Finland, France, Germany, Greece, Hungary, Ireland, Italy, Latvia, Lithuania, Luxembourg, Malta, Netherlands, Poland, Portugal, Romania, Slovakia, Slovenia, Spain, Sweden, UK.
Observers from 4 countries:
Belarus, Bosnia-Herzegovina, Russia, Ukraine.
Included in Observer organizations, 1 listed in this Yearbook:
European Association for the Study of the Liver (EASL, #06233).
NGO Relations Member of: *European Union of Medical Specialists (UEMS, #09001)* Council, CESMA.
[2018.08.02/XD4909/y/**E**]

♦ European Board of Medical Assessors (EBMA) 06360

Dir c/o Educational Dev Dept, P.O. Box 616, 6200 MD Maastricht, Netherlands. E-mail: ebma@rcsed.ac.uk.
URL: https://www.ebma.eu/

History Founded following discussions initiated in 2008-2009, following the *Bologna Accord for a European Higher Education Area*. **Aims** Promote the quality of the healthcare workforce by providing a series of assessment programmes for individuals and health education institutions. **Structure** Council of Participants; Board. **Activities** Events/meetings; training/education. **Events** *Annual Conference* Helsinki (Finland) 2022, *European Conference on Assessment in Medical Education* Lódz (Poland) 2019. [2022/AA3215/**D**]

♦ European Board of Medical Genetics / see European Board of Medical Genetics (#06361)

♦ European Board of Medical Genetics (EBMG) 06361

Office c/o Vienna Medical Academy, Alserstr 4, 1090 Vienna, Austria. T. +431405138335. Fax +4314078274. E-mail: office@ebmg.eu.
URL: https://www.ebmg.eu/413.0.html

History Jun 2012. Full title: *European Board of Medical Genetics – Verein zur Förderung der Entwicklung und Implementierung von Ausbildungsstandards in der Humangenetik*. Registration: non-for profit association, No/ID: 616719544, Start date: Jun 2014, Austria. **Aims** Serve the needs of *patients* who use genetic services in Europe through ensuring good standards of practice. **Structure** General Assembly; Executive Board; Boards of Professional Branches. **Members** Full; Supporting; Honorary. Membership countries not specified. **NGO Relations** Affiliated to: *European Society of Human Genetics (ESHG, #08624)*. [2020/XM4859/**E**]

♦ European Board of National Archivists (EBNA) 06362

Contact State Archives – Denmark, Rigsdagsgården 9, 1218 Copenhagen K, Denmark. E-mail: mailbox@sa.dk.

Aims Gather national archivists (Directors-General) of national archives services of EU member states. **Structure** Convenes twice a year under the chairmanship of the EU-Presidency in question. **Events** *Conference* Dublin (Ireland) 2013, *Conference* Vilnius (Lithuania) 2013, *Conference* Copenhagen (Denmark) 2012, *Conference* Nicosia (Cyprus) 2012, *Conference* Krakow (Poland) 2011. **Members** Directors-General of National Archives Services of the EU member states. [2021/XM0644/c/**F**]

♦ European Board of Neonatology (EBN) 06363

Secretariat Rue de Sablières 5, 1242 Satigny GE, Switzerland. E-mail: office@espr.eu.
URL: https://www.ebn-education.eu/

History Set up as the educational branch of *European Society for Paediatric Research (ESPR, #08687)*. Former names and other names: *European Society of Neonatology (ESN)* – former. **Aims** Continue, develop, and support professional education and training in neonatology so as to improve perinatal and neonatal care throughout Europe. **Structure** Council. **Activities** Events/meetings; training/education. **Events** *JENS : Congress of Joint European Neonatal Societies* 2021, *JENS : Congress of Joint European Neonatal Societies* Maastricht (Netherlands) 2019, *JENS : Congress of Joint European Neonatal Societies* Venice (Italy) 2017, *Annual Business Meeting* Budapest (Hungary) 2015, *JENS : Congress of Joint European Neonatal Societies* Budapest (Hungary) 2015. **NGO Relations** Cooperates with (1): *Union of European Neonatal and Perinatal Societies (UENPS, #20389)*. [2021/XM2830/**E**]

♦ European Board of Neurology (EBN) 06364

Secretariat Vienna Medical Ac, Alser Str 4, 1090 Vienna, Austria. T. +431405138314. Fax +4314078274. E-mail: gl@medacad.org.
URL: http://www.uems-neuroboard.org/ebn/

History Set up as a section within *European Union of Medical Specialists (UEMS, #09001)*.
[2014.10.30/XJ2871/**E**]

♦ European Board of Neuroradiology (EBNR) 06365

Contact Althardstrasse 70, 8105 Regensdorf ZH, Switzerland. E-mail: info@ebnr.org.
URL: http://www.ebnr.org/

History Former names and other names: *European Board of Neuroradiology – Diagnostic and Interventional (EBNR)* – full title. **Aims** Serve patients and medical professionals by certifying that its diploma holders have obtained and demonstrated a standard of knowledge and skill of Neuroradiology. **Structure** Board. **Languages** English. **Activities** Certification/accreditation; training/education. **NGO Relations** Accredited by (2): *European Society of Neuroradiology (ESNR, #08664)*; *European Union of Medical Specialists (UEMS, #09001)*. [2022.10.21/XM5502/**D**]

♦ European Board of Neuroradiology – Diagnostic and Interventional / see European Board of Neuroradiology (#06365)

♦ European Board of NLP (unconfirmed)

♦ European Board of Ophthalmology (EBO) 06366

Exec Officer Agenda, Temple House, Temple Road, Blackrock, CO. DUBLIN, Ireland. T. +35312100058. Fax +35312091112.
SG Dept of Opthalmology MUMC, Univ of Padova, via Giustiniani 2, 35128 Padua PD, Italy. T. +39498752350. Fax +39498755168.
URL: http://www.ebo-online.org/

History 1992, as a working group of the specialist section of *European Union of Medical Specialists (UEMS, #09001)*. **Aims** Guarantee highest standards of *care* in the field of ophthalmology in countries of the *European Union* by ensuring that training of ophthalmologists is raised to the highest possible level. **Structure** General Meeting (twice a year). Board, comprising: 2 representatives of each country (one representing the profession the other academia); one ex-officio member each from *European Community University Professors in Ophthalmology (EUPO, #06685)* and *European Junior Doctors Association (EJD, #07620)*. Executive Committee comprising President, 4 Vice-Presidents, Secretary-General and Treasurer. Working Committees (5): Residency Review; Education; Residency Exchange; Continuous Medical Education; Finance. **Languages** English. **Staff** 4.00 FTE, paid. **Finance** Main source: UEMS. **Activities** Training/education.
Members Members in 29 countries:
Austria, Belgium, Bulgaria, Cyprus, Czechia, Denmark, Estonia, Finland, France, Germany, Greece, Hungary, Iceland, Ireland, Italy, Latvia, Lithuania, Malta, Netherlands, Norway, Poland, Portugal, Romania, Slovakia, Slovenia, Spain, Sweden, Switzerland, UK.
Candidate members in 2 countries:
Croatia, Türkiye.
NGO Relations Member of: *International Council of Ophthalmology (ICO, #13057)*. [2013.09.12/XE2025/**E**]

♦ European Board of Oro-Maxillo-Facial Surgery (EBOMFS) 06367

Sec Haartamaninkatu 4E, HUS, FI-00029 Helsinki, Finland.
Pres 60 Maria de Molina, 4 Izqda, 28006 Madrid, Spain.
URL: http://www.ebomfs.net/

History within *European Union of Medical Specialists (UEMS, #09001)*. **Aims** Enhance oro-maxillo-facial surgery standards of training and practice. **Structure** Board, comprising President, Secretary, Chairman and Treasurer. **Activities** Organizes 'EBOMFS Recognition of Qualification'. [2016/XM2640/**E**]

♦ European Board of Paediatrics (EBP) 06368

Board européen de pédiatrie

Secretariat c/o Paragon Group, Avenue Louis-Casai 18, 1209 Geneva, Switzerland. T. +41225330948. Fax +41225802953. E-mail: secretariat@eapaediatrics.eu.
URL: https://www.eapaediatrics.eu/ebp-exams/

History 1994. Founded as a part of *European Academy of Paediatrics (EAP, #05811)* but following Statutes and rules of *European Union of Medical Specialists (UEMS, #09001)*. **Aims** Supervise training centres, educators and methods of *training* so as to ensure comparable theoretical and practical *education* for all European paediatricians; attain a high standard of care in paediatrics in countries of the European Union and EFTA by ensuring that training in theory, practice and research is at the highest level. **Structure** Delegates Meeting (twice a year). Board consists of 2 representatives of each UEMS member country. Executive Committee comprises Chairperson, Vice-Chairperson, Secretary and Treasurer, the 2 latter also being officers of EAP. **Languages** English, French. **Staff** 0.50 FTE, paid. **Finance** Members' dues. **Activities** Recommends setting up and maintenance of standards for specialist training and minimum standards to which training centres should conform; makes proposals for quality of training and syllabus; recommends procedures for free movement of paediatricians; assesses quality of training in countries of the European Community and other UEMS member countries; facilitates exchange of trainees; setting up *'European Board Quality Control'* as system of recognition of individual quality and issuing a certificate of quality giving right to the title *'Fellow of the European Board of Paediatrics'*; organizes annual meeting in Brussels (Belgium). **Events** *Meeting* Brussels (Belgium) 2002, *Meeting* Brussels (Belgium) 2000, *Meeting* Brussels (Belgium) 1999, *Meeting* Brussels (Belgium) 1998, *Meeting* Brussels (Belgium) 1997.
Members Official representatives in 28 countries:
Austria, Belgium, Cyprus, Czechia, Denmark, Estonia, Finland, France, Germany, Greece, Hungary, Ireland, Israel, Italy, Latvia, Lithuania, Luxembourg, Malta, Netherlands, Norway, Poland, Portugal, Slovakia, Slovenia, Spain, Sweden, Switzerland, UK.
Observer members in 3 countries:
Iceland, North Macedonia, Russia.
Associated members in 4 countries:
Croatia, Georgia, Israel, Türkiye.
NGO Relations Reports to CESP. [2014/XE2275/**E**]

♦ European Board of Paediatric Surgery (EBPS) 06369

Sec Dept Pediatric Surgery and Pediatric Urology, Univ Hosp of Goethe-Univ, Campus Niederrad, Theodor-Stern-Kai 7, 60590 Frankfurt-Main, Germany. T. +496963016659. Fax +496963017936.
Pres Dept Surgery and Urology for Children and Adolescents, Medical Univ of Gdansk, Nowe Ogrody 1-6 Str, 80-803 Gdansk, Poland. T. +48587640190. Fax +48587640361. E-mail: pczaud@gumed.edu.pl.
URL: http://www.uemspaedsurg.org/

History 1994, as part of the specialist section paediatric surgery of *European Union of Medical Specialists (UEMS, #09001)*. **Aims** Attain the highest standards of care in the field of paediatric surgery in the countries of the European Union. **Structure** General Council. **Languages** English. **Staff** Voluntary. **Finance** Members' dues. Annual budget: about euro 5,000. **Activities** Events/meetings; awards/prizes/competitions; training/education; knowledge management/information dissemination. **Publications** *EBPS Newsletter* (annual).
Members Full in 31 countries:
Austria, Belgium, Bulgaria, Croatia, Cyprus, Czechia, Denmark, Estonia, Finland, France, Germany, Greece, Hungary, Ireland, Italy, Latvia, Lithuania, Luxembourg, Malta, Netherlands, Norway, Poland, Portugal, Romania, Slovakia, Slovenia, Spain, Sweden, Switzerland, Türkiye, UK.
NGO Relations Together with: *European Board of Urology (EBU, #06374)*; *European Society for Paediatric Urology (ESPU, #08688)*; UEMS, set up: *Multidisciplinary Joint Committee on Paediatric Urology (JCPU, #16883)*. [2017.12.30/XD8526/**D**]

♦ European Board of Pathology (EBP) 06370

Pres Univ Gent, N Goormagtigh Inst voor PA – Blok A, De Pintelaan 185, 9000 Ghent, Belgium. T. +3292403663. Fax +3292404965. E-mail: europathol@gmail.com.
URL: http://www.europathol.org/

History as part of Section of Pathology of *European Union of Medical Specialists (UEMS, #09001)*. **Aims** Stimulate proper pathology practice in Europe. **Structure** Board, comprising Chairman and Secretary.
Members Individuals in 22 countries:
Austria, Belgium, Croatia, Denmark, Finland, France, Germany, Greece, Hungary, Ireland, Italy, Luxembourg, Netherlands, Norway, Poland, Portugal, Slovenia, Spain, Sweden, Switzerland, Türkiye, UK. [2016/XJ4526/v/**E**]

♦ European Board of Physical and Rehabilitation Medicine 06371

Bureau européen de médecine physique et de réadaptation

Pres Hôpital Nestlé, NE-05 / 5053, 1011 Lausanne VD, Switzerland.
SG Via Altolina 17, 06034 Foligno PG, Italy.
URL: http://www.euro-prm.org/

History 1991, as part of *European Union of Medical Specialists (UEMS, #09001)*. **Structure** Executive Committee, comprising President, Vice-President, Secretary, Vice-Secretary and Treasurer. **Events** *Biennial Congress* Athens (Greece) 2000.
Members Full in 18 countries:
Austria, Belgium, Denmark, Finland, France, Germany, Greece, Iceland, Ireland, Italy, Luxembourg, Netherlands, Norway, Portugal, Spain, Sweden, Switzerland, UK.
Associate in 6 countries:
Croatia, Cyprus, Hungary, Poland, Slovenia, Türkiye. [2014/XD8271/**E**]

♦ European Board of Plastic, Reconstructive and Aesthetic Surgery (EBOPRAS) 06372

SG Plastic Surgery and Burns Unit, Mater Dei Hospital, Msida, MSD 2090, Malta.
Pres Dept of Surgery, Oulu Univ Hosp, PO Box 21, FI-90029 Oulu, Finland.
URL: http://www.ebopras.org/

History Founded 19 Sep 1991. Approved by the Management Council of *European Union of Medical Specialists (UEMS, #09001)*, Mar 1992. **Aims** Promote optimum plastic surgical care for the people of the UEMS and UEMS associate / observer countries by means of: (a) Setting standards for training programmes in the specialty of plastic, reconstructive and aesthetic surgery; (b) Issuing clear definitions of the minimum standards for training institutions and for those responsible for the provision of plastic surgery training (At the invitation of participating institutions, their standards will be assessed by on-site investigation); (c) Conducting a European Board Examination; (d) Instituting exchange programmes for trainees between recognized institutions; (e) Maintaining high educational standards by organizing and / or supervising professional courses. Supports the EUMS in the aims of establishing closer relationships between national professional organizations of plastic surgeons and supporting and coordinating their activities, and of ensuring that ethical standards are determined and complied with by registered plastic surgeons. **Structure** Executive Committee; other Committees (4). **Languages** English. **Finance** Members' dues. **Activities** Awards/prizes/competitions; networking/liaising; certification/accreditation. **Events** *Congress* Vienna (Austria) 2005, *Meeting* Graz (Austria) 2001, *Congress* Rome (Italy) 2001, *Congress* Lisbon (Portugal) 1997, *Congress* Berlin (Germany) 1993.
Members Societies in 30 countries:

Armenia, Austria, Belgium, Croatia, Cyprus, Czechia, Denmark, Finland, France, Germany, Greece, Hungary, Ireland, Israel, Italy, Latvia, Luxembourg, Malta, Netherlands, Norway, Poland, Portugal, Romania, Slovakia, Slovenia, Spain, Sweden, Switzerland, Türkiye, UK.
Individuals in 3 countries:
Cyprus, Malta, North Macedonia. [2017.10.10/XF2916/E]

♦ European Board of Radiology (EBR) 06373

Contact C/ Passeig de Gràcia 86, planta 9, 08008 Barcelona, Spain. T. +34936794169. Fax +34936676694. E-mail: diploma@myebr.org.
URL: http://www.myebr.org/

History Set up as an initiative of *European Society of Radiology (ESR, #08720)*. Registered in accordance with Spanish law. **Aims** Serve *patients* and *medical* professionals by certifying that its diploma holders have obtained and demonstrated a standard of knowledge and skill. **Activities** Training/education; certification/accreditation. **NGO Relations** *European Society of Neuroradiology (ESNR, #08664)*. [2017/XM5503/D]

- ♦ European Boardsailing Association (inactive)
- ♦ European Board of Thoracic and Cardiovascular Surgeons / see European Board of Cardiothoracic Surgery (#06355)
- ♦ European Board of Urologists in Training / see European Society of Residents in Urology (#08729)

♦ European Board of Urology (EBU) 06374

Exec Dir Mr EN van Kleffensstraat 5, 6842 CV Arnhem, Netherlands. T. +31263890846. Fax +31263890848. E-mail: ebu@ebu.com.
URL: http://www.ebu.com/

History Founded 1990, by members of *European Union of Medical Specialists (UEMS, #09001)*, which had been set up in 1958 by national specialist medical organizations of European Community countries. Registered as a European foundation under the law of the Netherlands. **Aims** Study, promote and harmonize urological training in Europe, both on the basic and postgraduate level. **Structure** Board, consisting of 2 delegates from each member country; Executive Committee. Committees (4): Accreditation; Certification; Examination; Manpower. **Activities** Certification/accreditation; guidance/assistance/consulting; training/education. **Events** *Congress* Copenhagen (Denmark) 1996.
Members National urological organizations, urologists and medical educators in 30 countries:
Austria, Belgium, Croatia, Czechia, Denmark, Estonia, Finland, France, Georgia, Germany, Greece, Hungary, Ireland, Italy, Latvia, Lithuania, Luxembourg, Malta, Netherlands, Norway, Poland, Portugal, Romania, Slovakia, Slovenia, Spain, Sweden, Switzerland, Türkiye, UK.
Also included in the above, one international organization:
European Society of Residents in Urology (ESRU, #08729).
NGO Relations Represented on Board of: *European School of Urology (ESU, see: #06264)*. Together with: *European Board of Paediatric Surgery (EBPS, #06369)*; *European Society for Paediatric Urology (ESPU, #08688)*; UEMS, set up: *Multidisciplinary Joint Committee on Paediatric Urology (JCPU, #16883)*. [2016/XF3338/E]

♦ European Board of Veterinary Specialisation (EBVS) 06375

Contact Anaximandrou 96B, Nea Elvetia, 542 50 Thessaloniki, Greece. E-mail: info@ebvs.eu.
URL: https://ebvs.eu/

History 20 May 1993, Luxembourg, as *Interim Board of Veterinary Specialization (IBVS)*. Current title adopted, 11 Mar 1996. Registered in accordance with Dutch law. **Aims** Lead and promote veterinary specialist professional training and certification in Europe to advance animal health and wellbeing and public health. **Structure** Annual General Meeting; Board; Executive Committee. **Languages** English. **Staff** 1.00 FTE, paid. **Finance** Members' dues. Fees for processing applications for recognition of new colleges. **Activities** Certification/accreditation; monitoring/evaluation. **Events** *Annual General Meeting* Brussels (Belgium) 2014, *General Assembly and Meeting* Brussels (Belgium) 2012, *General Assembly and Meeting* Brussels (Belgium) 2012, *Annual meeting* Brussels (Belgium) 2008, *Annual meeting* Brussels (Belgium) 2007.
Members Colleges represented on EBVS (26):
- *European College for Veterinary Public Health (ECVPH, #06629);*
- *European College of Animal Reproduction (ECAR, #06605);*
- *European College of Animal Welfare and Behavioural Medicine (ECAWBM, #06606);*
- *European College of Aquatic Animal Health (ECAAH, #06607);*
- *European College of Bovine Health Management (ECBHM, #06608);*
- *European College of Equine Internal Medicine (ECEIM, #06609);*
- *European College of Laboratory Animal Medicine (ECLAM, #06611);*
- *European College of Porcine Health Management (ECPHM, #06613);*
- *European College of Poultry Veterinary Science (ECPVS, #06614);*
- *European College of Small Ruminant Health Management (ECSRHM, #06615);*
- *European College of Veterinary Anaesthesia and Analgesia (ECVAA, #06619);*
- *European College of Veterinary and Comparative Nutrition (ECVCN, #06621);*
- *European College of Veterinary Clinical Pathology (ECVCP, #06620);*
- *European College of Veterinary Dermatology (ECVD, #06622);*
- *European College of Veterinary Diagnostic Imaging (ECVDI, #06623);*
- *European College of Veterinary Emergency and Critical Care (ECVECC);*
- *European College of Veterinary Internal Medicine – Companion Animals (ECVIM – CA, #06624);*
- *European College of Veterinary Microbiology (ECVM, #06625);*
- *European College of Veterinary Neurology (ECVN, #06626);*
- *European College of Veterinary Ophthalmologists (ECVO, see: #08783);*
- *European College of Veterinary Pathologists (ECVP, #06627);*
- *European College of Veterinary Pharmacology and Toxicology (ECVPT, #06628);*
- *European College of Veterinary Surgeons (ECVS, #06630);*
- *European College of Zoological Medicine (ECZM, #06631);*
- *European Veterinary Dental College (EVDC, #09054).*

NGO Relations Founding member of: *European Coordination Committee for Veterinary Training (ECCVT, #06793)*. Cooperates with: American Board of Veterinary Specialties (ABVS); *European Association of Establishments for Veterinary Education (EAEVE, #06031)*; *Federation of Veterinarians of Europe (#09713)*. Links with veterinary specialist organizations across Europe. [2021/XF3984/y/F]

♦ European Boating Association (EBA) 06376

Association européenne de navigation de plaisance – Europäischer Sportschiffahrtsverband

Gen Sec c/o RYA House, Ensign Way, Hamble, SO31 4YA, UK. T. +442380604233. E-mail: eba@eba.eu.com.
URL: https://eba.eu.com/

History 1982. Former names and other names: *European Yachting Association* – former. Registration: EU Transparency Register, No/ID: 205999610833-45. **Aims** Serve the interests of pleasure boat owners in Europe. **Structure** General Assembly; Executive Committee. Secretary and Secretariat provided by British Royal Yachting Association (RYA). **Languages** English. **Staff** Full-time of British RYA. **Finance** Sources: members' dues. **Events** *General Meeting* Ghent (Belgium) 2018, *General Meeting* Helsinki (Finland) 2018, *General Meeting* Palma (Spain) 2017, *General Meeting* Stockholm (Sweden) 2017, *General Meeting* Vienna (Austria) 2016. **Publications** Position statements.
Members Open to national boating organizations in any European country. National boat user groups in 16 countries:
Austria, Belgium, Denmark, Finland, France, Germany, Iceland, Ireland, Italy, Netherlands, Norway, Spain, Sweden, Switzerland, Türkiye, UK.
Consultative Status Consultative status granted from: *ECOSOC (#05331)* (Ros A). **IGO Relations** Accredited by (1): *Comité européen pour l'élaboration de standards dans le domaine de la navigation intérieure (CESNI, #04160)*. [2023.02.22/XD4954/D]

♦ European Boating Industry (EBI) 06377

Main Office Square de Meeûs 35, 1000 Brussels, Belgium. T. +3228953608 – +3228953609. E-mail: office@europeanboatingindustry.eu.
URL: http://www.europeanboatingindustry.eu/

History Jun 2009. Founded as a successor to *European Confederation of Nautical Industries (ECNI, inactive)*. Registration: EU Transparency Register, No/ID: 74989093163-18. **Aims** Advance and represent a sustainable boating and nautical tourism industry. **Structure** General Assembly; Council; Executive Committee. **Languages** English, French. **Staff** 2.00 FTE, paid. **Finance** Sources: fees for services; members' dues. **Events** *General Assembly* Brussels (Belgium) 2021, *General Assembly* Brussels (Belgium) 2021, *General Meeting* Brussels (Belgium) 2018, *General Meeting* Brussels (Belgium) 2017, *Conference on Skippers Working Without Borders* Brussels (Belgium) 2016. **Publications** *EBI Newsletter* (12 a year). Articles; position papers; press releases.
Members National associations representing the recreational boating industry in 8 countries:
Belgium, Finland, France, Germany, Italy, Poland, Slovenia, Spain.
Members include 1 organization listed in this Yearbook:
International Marine Certification Institute (IMCI, #14091).
NGO Relations Member of (2): *European Tourism Manifesto (#08921)*; *Industry4Europe (#11181)*. Cooperates with (7): *European Anglers Alliance (EAA, #05900)*; *European Boating Association (EBA, #06376)*; *European Fishing Tackle Trade Association (EFTTA, #07267)*; *European Sailing Federation (EUROSAF, #08421)*; *International Council of Marine Industry Associations (ICOMIA, #13044)*; *PIANC (#18371)* (Navigation Task Group on Water Framework Directive and Marine Strategy Directive); *Sail for Europe (#19035)*. [2022.05.18/XJ2167/t/D]

♦ European Boatmen's Association (EBA) 06378

Sec Noorderlaan 21, Haven 28, 2030 Antwerp, Belgium. T. +3232059455. Fax +3232059431. E-mail: eba@brabo.com.
President's Office Angopi, Via Salaria 89, 00198 Rome RM, Italy.
URL: https://ebanet.org/

History Founded 26 Apr 1977, Paris (France). EU Transparency Register: 312071025265-71. **Aims** Improve and enhance the sector's professional standards.
Members National associations (14) in 13 countries:
Belgium, Croatia, France, Germany, Greece, Italy, Malta, Montenegro, Netherlands, Slovenia, Spain, Sweden, UK.
NGO Relations *International Boatmen's Linesmen's Association (IBLA).* [2020/XM8723/D]

♦ European Bobath Tutors Association (EBTA) 06379

Pres address not obtained.
Sec address not obtained.
URL: https://www.bobathtutors.com/

History 1971. Statutes registered, 9 Dec 1994, Beek (Netherlands). Registered in accordance with Dutch law. **Aims** Maintain the integrity of the Neuro Developmental Treatment (NDT)/Bobath concept for the treatment of children and adults with disability due to cerebral palsy and other allied neurological conditions and develop this concept in accordance with evolving scientific evidence; promote the availability and accessability of NDT/Bobath concept to all countries; maintain and improve the standards of training of NDT/Bobath tutors and courses. **Structure** General Meeting (every 2 years). Executive Committee, comprising President, Vice-President, Treasurer, Secretary and one member. Committees and Subcommittees. **Languages** English. **Finance** Members' dues. **Activities** Organizes regular meetings and educational programmes. **Events** *Congress* Ghent (Belgium) 2022, *Biennial Conference* Lausanne (Switzerland) 2021, *Biennial Conference* Lausanne (Switzerland) 2020, *Biennial Conference* Porto (Portugal) 2016, *Senior Tutors Workshop* Porto (Portugal) 2016.
Members National organizations (not more than one from each country) of therapists and physicians who are qualified tutors to teach the NDT/Bobath concept, in 17 countries:
Austria, Belgium, Denmark, Finland, France, Germany, Greece, Israel, Italy, Netherlands, Poland, Portugal, Slovenia, Spain, Sweden, UK, USA.
Associate members in 3 countries:
Brazil, South Africa, USA. [2022/XD6321/D]

- ♦ European Boilermakers Association / see Energy Technologies Europe (#05477)

♦ European Bone and Joint Infection Society (EBJIS) 06380

Head Office ZA La Pièce 2, 1180 Rolle VD, Switzerland. E-mail: elenida.shkarpa@ebjis.org.
URL: http://www.ebjis.org/

History 12 Nov 1982, as *Study Group on Bone and Joint Infection – Groupe d'etude de l'infection osseuse articulaire*. Present name adopted, 20 Apr 1993. **Aims** Promote knowledge of all infections affecting the musculoskeletal system; promote prevention and treatment of these infections. **Structure** Annual General Assembly; Board; Executive Committee. **Languages** English. **Staff** 1.00 FTE, voluntary. **Finance** Members' dues. Congress revenue. **Activities** Events/meetings; training/education. **Events** *Annual Meeting* Ljubljana (Slovenia) 2021, *Annual Meeting* Ljubljana (Slovenia) 2020, *Annual Meeting* Antwerp (Belgium) 2019, *Annual Meeting* Helsinki (Finland) 2018, *Annual Meeting* Nantes (France) 2017. **Publications** *EBJIS Newsletter*; *EBJIS Official Journal*. **Members** Physicians interested in musculoskeletal infections from a scientific or clinical point of view (365). Membership countries not specified. [2020.03.03/XD5273/D]

- ♦ European Bone Marrow Transplant Group / see European Society for Blood and Marrow Transplantation (#08533)

♦ European Bonsai Association (EBA) 06381

Chairman 38 St Philips Road, Upper Stratton, Swindon, SN2 7QH, UK. T. +441793822470. Fax +441793822470.
URL: http://www.ebabonsai.com/

Events *Annual Convention* Albi (France) 2019, *Annual Convention* Arco (Italy) 2018, *Annual Convention* Genk (Belgium) 2017, *Annual Convention* Székesfehérvar (Hungary) 2016, *Annual Convention* Vilnius (Lithuania) 2015.
Members in 20 countries:
Austria, Belgium, Croatia, Czechia, Denmark, France, Germany, Italy, Lithuania, Luxembourg, Monaco, Netherlands, Poland, Portugal, San Marino, Slovakia, Spain, Sweden, Switzerland, UK. [2013/XD4731/D]

- ♦ European Booksellers Federation / see European and International Booksellers Federation (#07584)

♦ European Borates Association (EBA) 06382

SG c/o IMA-Europe, Rue des Deux Eglises 26, Box 2, 1000 Brussels, Belgium. T. +3222104410. E-mail: secretariat@ima-europe.eu.
URL: http://ima-europe.eu/about-ima-europe/associations/eba/

History Founded 1998. Registered in accordance with Belgian law. **Aims** Serve as the representative body of the European borates industry. **Structure** Secretariat based at *Industrial Minerals Association – Europe (IMA Europe, #11179)*. **Languages** English. **Staff** 7.50 FTE, paid.
Members Companies in 7 countries:
France, Germany, Italy, Netherlands, Peru, Türkiye, UK.
NGO Relations Member of: *Industrial Minerals Association – Europe (IMA Europe, #11179)*. Cooperates with: *Calcium Carbonate Association – Europe (CCA-Europe, #03399)*; *European Association of Feldspar Producers (EUROFEL, #06037)*; *European Association of Industrial Silica Producers (EUROSIL, #06082)*; *European Bentonite Producers Association (EUBA, #06328)*; *European Kaolin and Plastic Clays Association (KPC Europe, #07623)*; *European Lime Association (EuLA, #07699)*; *European Speciality Minerals Association (ESMA, #08811)*; *International Diatomite Producers Association (IDPA, #13172)*; *Scientific Association of European Talc Industry (Eurotalc, #19146)*. [2018.09.06/XD6866/D]

♦ European Botanical and Horticultural Libraries Group (EBHL) 06383

Sec Linnean Society, Burlington House, London, W1J 0BF, UK. E-mail: info@ebhl.org.
Pres Lindley Library, 80 Vincent Square, London, SW1P 2PE, UK.
URL: https://ebhl.org/

History 30 Sep 1994, Kew (UK). Former names and other names: *Association des Bibliothèques Botaniques et Horticoles Européennes (EBHL)* – alias. **Aims** Promote and facilitate cooperation and communication between those working in botanical, horticultural and environmental libraries, archives and related institutions in Europe and internationally. **Structure** General Assembly (annual); Board. **Languages** English. **Staff** 7.00 FTE, voluntary. **Finance** Sources: members' dues. **Activities** Events/meetings. **Events** *Annual Meeting* Champex (Switzerland) 2019, *Annual Meeting* New York, NY (USA) 2018, *Annual Meeting* Geneva (Switzerland) 2017, *Annual Meeting* Edinburgh (UK) 2016, *Annual Meeting* Berlin (Germany) 2015.

European Botanic Gardens
06384

alphabetic sequence excludes
For the complete listing, see Yearbook Online at

Members Full in 14 countries:
Austria, Belgium, Croatia, Czechia, France, Germany, Italy, Netherlands, Norway, Spain, Sweden, Switzerland, UK, USA.
Associate members. Membership countries not specified.
Affiliate members in 1 country:
USA. [2022.05.19/XF4863/F]

♦ European Botanic Gardens Consortium (EBGC) 06384

Contact Descanso House, 199 Kew Road, Richmond, TW9 3BW, UK. E-mail: info@bgci.org.
URL: http://www.botanicgardens.eu/

History 1994. Convened by *Botanic Gardens Conservation International (BGCI, #03306)*. **Aims** Plan Europe-wide initiatives for botanic gardens, especially within the context of implementation of the Convention on Biological Diversity and other European biodiversity policies and strategies. **Structure** National Representatives. **Languages** English. **Activities** Events/meetings. **Events** *EUROGARD : European Botanic Gardens Congress* Budapest (Hungary) 2022, *EUROGARD : European Botanic Gardens Congress* Lisbon (Portugal) 2018, *EUROGARD : European Botanic Gardens Congress* Paris (France) 2015, *EUROGARD : European Botanic Gardens Congress* Chios (Greece) 2012, *EUROGARD : European Botanic Gardens Congress* Helsinki (Finland) 2009.
Members Full in 25 countries:
Austria, Belgium, Bulgaria, Croatia, Czechia, Denmark, Estonia, Finland, France, Germany, Greece, Hungary, Ireland, Italy, Latvia, Lithuania, Netherlands, Norway, Poland, Portugal, Romania, Slovenia, Spain, Switzerland, UK.
[2021.06.28/XM7954/D]

♦ European Bottled Watercooler Association / see Watercoolers Europe (#20825)
♦ European Bottom Fisheries Alliance (unconfirmed)

♦ European Bowhunting Association (EBA) 06385

Euroopan jousimetsästysliitto ry
Pres Al 25 15392 Holo, SE-153 92 Hölö, Sweden. E-mail: info@europeanbowhunting.org.
URL: http://www.europeanbowhunting.org/

History Finland. Registration: Finnish Register of Associations, No/ID: 201811, Finland. **Aims** Communicate the value of bowhunting as a tool for sustainable game management; improve ecological conditions and awareness. **Structure** General Assembly; Board. **Languages** English. **Staff** None. **Finance** Sources: members' dues. subsidies. **Members** Contacts and national members in 30 countries. Membership countries not specified. **NGO Relations** Associate member of: *Federation of Associations for Hunting and Conservation of the EU (#09459)*. [2022/XM8229/D]

♦ European Bowling Proprietors Association (EBPA) 06386

SG Urbergsgatan 90, SE-603 56 Norrköping, Sweden. T. +4611123870. Fax +4611126126. E-mail: info@ebpabowl.com – info@vilbergen-bowling.se.
Pres address not obtained.
URL: http://www.ebpabowl.com/

History Jan 5 1995, Helsinki (Finland). **Aims** Market all bowling centres in Europe; organize international tournaments. **Languages** English. **Activities** Sporting activities. **Publications** Catalogue.
Members Bowling Centers in 29 countries:
Austria, Belgium, Bulgaria, Cyprus, Czechia, Denmark, Egypt, Estonia, Finland, France, Germany, Greece, Guernsey, Ireland, Italy, Latvia, Lithuania, Luxembourg, Netherlands, Norway, Portugal, Russia, Slovenia, Spain, Sweden, Switzerland, Türkiye, UK, Ukraine. [2022/XD7522/D]

♦ European Boxing Confederation (EUBC) 06387

Pres Piazza Donegani, 06081 Assisi PG, Italy. T. +39758044720. E-mail: eubc.office@gmail.com.
URL: http://www.eubcboxing.org/

History Founded Jun 1970, Moscow (USSR), taking over the activities of the continental bureau of *International Boxing Association (IBA, #12385)*, set up 28 Nov 1946, London (UK). Original title *European Amateur Boxing Association (EABA)*. Previously also referred to in French as *Association européenne de boxe amateur*. Current title adopted on restructuring when merged with European regional bureau of AIBA, 2007, Chicago IL (USA). **Aims** Govern the sport of boxing in all its forms in Europe; organize European championships in different age groups and international tournaments in accordance with AIRBA Rules. **Structure** Congress (meets every 4 years); Executive Committee of 15 members and 3 observers; Bureau of 5 members. Commissions (6): Coaches; Competition; Medical; R/J; Women's Boxing; Youth. **Languages** English, French, Russian. **Staff** 1.00 FTE, paid. **Finance** Members' dues (annual). Other sources: AIBA subvention; hosting rights of European Championships; regular tournament hosting fees; television rights for European Championships. **Activities** Sporting activities. **Events** *Extraordinary General Assembly* Trabzon (Turkey) 2012, *Quadrennial Congress* Almaty (Kazakhstan) 2010, *Extraordinary General Assembly* Madrid (Spain) 2009, *Quadrennial Congress* Antalya (Turkey) 2006, *Quadrennial Congress* Yalta, Crimea (Ukraine) 2002.
Members National boxing associations/federations (one per country) in 49 countries and territories:
Albania, Andorra, Armenia, Austria, Azerbaijan, Belarus, Belgium, Bosnia-Herzegovina, Bulgaria, Croatia, Cyprus, Czechia, Denmark, England, Estonia, Finland, France, Georgia, Germany, Greece, Hungary, Iceland, Ireland, Israel, Italy, Latvia, Lithuania, Luxembourg, Moldova, Monaco, Montenegro, Netherlands, North Macedonia, Norway, Poland, Portugal, Romania, Russia, San Marino, Scotland, Serbia, Slovakia, Slovenia, Spain, Sweden, Switzerland, Türkiye, Ukraine, Wales. [2016/XD4226/D]

♦ European Boxing League (unconfirmed)

♦ European Boxing Union (EBU) 06388

Gen Sec Via Topino 37, 00199 Rome RM, Italy. T. +39685354249. Fax +3968413447.
Registered Office Ave Georges Eeckhoud 11, 1030 Brussels, Belgium.
URL: http://www.boxebu.com/

History Founded as a continental boxing federation of *World Boxing Council (WBC, #21242)*. Statutes modified: 2008, Budva (Montenegro); 2010, Madrid (Spain); 2011, Dublin (Ireland). **Aims** Develop and promote European professional boxing; control the different European championships; award titles of Champion. **Structure** General Meeting; Board of Directors (meets twice a year). **Languages** English, French. **Finance** Championship sanction fees. **Activities** Sporting activities. **Events** *General Assembly* La Coruña (Spain) 2020, *General Assembly* Sibenik (Croatia) 2019, *General Assembly* Belgrade (Serbia) 2017, *General Assembly* Brussels (Belgium) 2016, *General Assembly* Paris (France) 2015.
Members Full; Associate; Individual; Honorary. Boxing federations in 35 countries:
Austria, Belarus, Belgium, Bosnia-Herzegovina, Bulgaria, Croatia, Cyprus, Czechia, Denmark, Estonia, Finland, France, Georgia, Germany, Hungary, Ireland, Israel, Italy, Latvia, Lithuania, Luxembourg, Moldova, Monaco, Netherlands, Norway, Poland, Portugal, Romania, Russia, Serbia, Slovakia, Spain, Sweden, Switzerland, UK, Ukraine. [2015/XE2430/D]

♦ European Boxwood and Topiary Society (EBTS) 06389

Association Européenne pour le Buis et l'Art Topiaire – Europese Buxus- en Vormsnoeivereniging
Registered Address Rue du Village 5, 1490 Court-Saint-Etienne, Belgium. E-mail: info@ebts.org.
URL: https://www.ebts.org/

History 1996, UK. Registration: Banque-Carrefour des Entreprises, No/ID: 0809.650.783, Start date: 29 Jan 2009, Belgium. **Aims** Encourage appreciation, cultivation and knowledge of Boxwood and Topiary; further extend both historic and scientific research in the subject. **Structure** European council; each country responsible for running its own organization. **Languages** English, French. Languages of member organizations. **Staff** Voluntary. **Finance** Sources: members' dues. **Activities** Advocacy/lobbying/activism; guidance/assistance/consulting; research/documentation. **Publications** *Topiarius* (annual) – journal.
Members Full in 5 countries:
Belgium, France, Germany, Netherlands, UK.
Associate group:
Japan. [2023.02.16/XM7096/D]

♦ European Brain and Behaviour Society (EBBS) 06390

Société européenne du cerveau et du comportement
Sec Fac of Nursing, Univ of Athens, 123 Papadiamadopoulou str, Goudi, 115 17 Athens, Greece. E-mail: astam@nurs.uoa.gr – secretary@ebbs-science.org.
Secretariat Science Park 904, SILS-CNS, 1098 XH Amsterdam, Netherlands. T. +31205257621. Fax +31205257934.
URL: http://ebbs-science.org/

History 1968, Rotterdam (Netherlands). **Aims** Exchange information between European scientists interested in the relationship of brain mechanisms and behaviour. **Structure** General Meeting (annual); Committee. **Languages** English. **Staff** Voluntary. **Finance** Sources: members' dues. **Activities** Active in all member countries. **Events** *Annual General Meeting* Prague (Czechia) 2019, *Annual General Meeting* Bilbao (Spain) 2017, *Annual General Meeting* Verona (Italy) 2015, *Annual General Meeting* Munich (Germany) 2013, *Annual General Meeting* Seville (Spain) 2011. **Publications** EBBS publications series; meeting reports.
Members Ordinary and Associate in 41 countries:
Australia, Austria, Bangladesh, Belgium, Bulgaria, Canada, China, Croatia, Czechia, Denmark, Finland, France, Georgia, Germany, Greece, Hungary, Iceland, Iran Islamic Rep, Ireland, Israel, Italy, Japan, Netherlands, New Zealand, North Macedonia, Norway, Poland, Portugal, Romania, Russia, Saudi Arabia, Serbia, Slovakia, Slovenia, Spain, Sweden, Switzerland, Türkiye, UK, Ukraine, USA.
NGO Relations Member of: *Federation of European Neuroscience Societies (FENS, #09522)*; *International Brain Research Organization (IBRO, #12392)*. [2020.06.23/XD0595/v/D]

♦ European Brain Council (EBC) 06391

Exec Dir D'Egmont 11, 1000 Brussels, Belgium. T. +3225132757. E-mail: info@braincouncil.eu.
URL: http://www.europeanbraincouncil.org/

History 22 Mar 2002, Brussels (Belgium). Founded by *European Federation of Neurological Societies (EFNS, inactive)*. Registration: Banque-Carrefour des Entreprises, No/ID: 0864.644.340, Start date: 1 Feb 2004, Belgium; EU Transparency Register, No/ID: 31091478710-90, Start date: 4 May 2012. **Aims** Promote brain research in order to improve the quality of life of those living with brain disorders in Europe. **Structure** Board; Executive. **Languages** English. **Activities** Awareness raising; events/meetings; healthcare; networking/liaising; politics/policy/regulatory; research/documentation. **Events** *Brain Innovation Days* Brussels (Belgium) 2022, *European Brain Summit* Brussels (Belgium) 2021, *General Assembly* Brussels (Belgium) 2021, *Brain Innovation Days* Brussels (Belgium) 2020, *General Assembly* Brussels (Belgium) 2019. **Publications** *The Value of Treatment of Brain Disorders in Europe*. Cost studies.
Members Ordinary: professional and patient organizations (7):
European Academy of Neurology (EAN, #05803); *European College of Neuropsychopharmacology (ECNP, #06612)*; *European Federation of Neurological Associations (EFNA, #07177)*; *European Psychiatric Association (EPA, #08290)*; *Federation of European Neuroscience Societies (FENS, #09522)*; *Global Alliance of Mental Illness Advocacy Networks (GAMIAN)*; *International Brain Research Organization (IBRO, #12392)*.
Ordinary: Industrial partners. Membership countries not specified. Associate and Observer (8):
Associate and Observer (8):
Brains for Brain (#03315); *European Federation of Associations of Families of People with Mental Illness (EUFAMI, #07051)*; *European Medical Students' Association (EMSA, #07764)*; *European Stroke Organisation (ESO, #08843)*; *Federation of the European Societies of Neuropsychology (ESN, #09547)*; *International Federation of Clinical Neurophysiology (IFCN, #13393)* (European Chapter); *International League Against Epilepsy (ILAE, #14013)* (Commission for European Affairs); Network of National Brain Councils and National Action Groups.
NGO Relations Member of (5): *Biomedical Alliance in Europe (#03251)*; *EU Health Coalition*; *European Alliance for Personalised Medicine (EAPM, #05878)*; *Federation of European and International Associations Established in Belgium (FAIB, #09508)*; *Psychedelic Access and Research European Alliance (PAREA)* (Founding). Endorses: *Steering Group on Influenza Vaccination (#19980)*. [2022/XD8632/y/D]

♦ European Brain Foundation (EBF) 06392

Exec Dir Rue d'Egmont 11, 1000 Brussels, Belgium. T. +3225127639. E-mail: office@brainfoundation.eu.
Project Manager address not obtained.
URL: https://www.brainfoundation.eu/

History 11 Oct 2022. Officially launched at 2nd Brain Innovation Days. Registration: Banque-Carrefour des Entreprises, No/ID: 0776.850.927, Start date: 5 Nov 2021, Belgium. **Aims** Support research aiming at reducing the burden of brain disorders for European citizens. **Structure** Board of Directors.
[2023.03.01/AA3168/f/F]

♦ European Brain Injury Consortium (EBIC) 06393

Chair c/o Univ of Cambridge, Head Div of Anaesthesia, Box 93, Addenbrooke's Hosp, Cambridge, CB2 2QQ, UK. T. +441223217889.
URL: http://www.ebic.nl/

History UK. **Aims** Establish close collaboration between European neurotrauma centres and investigators in the management of Traumatic Brain Injury (TBI) and other types of acute brain damage; act as an advisory organ in both practical and theoretical issues concerning brain injury studies. **Structure** General Meeting (usually annually); Executive Committee. **Languages** English. **Finance** No fixed income. Sources: donations; consultancy activities. **Publications** Articles. [2018.02.23/XF5647/F]

♦ European Brain Injury Society (EBIS) 06394

Association européenne d'étude des traumatisés crâniens et de leur réinsertion
Pres Centre La Braise, Rue de la Vigne 56, 1070 Brussels, Belgium. T. +3225222003. Fax +3225236555. E-mail: ebis.secretariat@skynet.be.
Registered Office Rue de Londres 17, 1050 Brussels, Belgium.
URL: http://www.ebissociety.org/

History 1989, Brussels (Belgium), meetings having been arranged since 1986 by *COFACE Families Europe (#04084)*, the Ligue pour l'adaptation du diminué physique du travail (LADAPT) and a working group set up in 1986 for the study of severe head injury and social rehabilitation. Registered in accordance with Belgian law. **Aims** Study brain injured people and their *rehabilitation*. **Structure** General Assembly (annual). Board of Management (meets once a year), consisting of 15 members. Officers: President; Vice-Presidents; Secretary General; Treasurer. **Languages** English, French. **Finance** Members' dues. EC grants for projects. **Activities** Carries out studies and research. Organizes scientific and professional meetings. Collects and disseminates documentation in the field. Topics: evaluation; epidemiology; training and education; specific programmes for retraining and social reintegration; promotion of patient and family groups; development of regional coordinating networks; standardizing legislation; information and public awareness; prevention. **Events** *International congress* Paris (France) 2000, *The multi-disciplinarity management of the brain injured* Coimbra (Portugal) 1994, *Employment after traumatic brain injury* Northampton (UK) 1994, *The process of rehabilitation* Ottignies (Belgium) 1994, *Evaluation of the severely head injured* Paris (France) 1992. **Publications** *Handbook for use with Families of Head Injured People*. Head injury evaluation document. Information Services: Database on medical/scientific and social aspects of head injury.
Members Doctors, psychologists, social workers, lawyers and members of patient and family associations. Full and Founding in 15 countries:
Belgium, Côte d'Ivoire, Denmark, France, Germany, Greece, Ireland, Italy, Luxembourg, Netherlands, Portugal, Spain, Sweden, Switzerland, UK. [2017/XD2354/D]

♦ European Branch Association for Commonwealth Literature and Language Studies / see European Association for Commonwealth Literature and Language Studies (#05981)

♦ European Branded Clothing Alliance (EBCA) 06395

Mananging Dir c/o Hanover, Square de Meeûs 35 – 6th floor, 1000 Brussels, Belgium. T. +3225882616. E-mail: secretariat@ebca-europe.org.
URL: http://www.ebca-europe.org/

History Founded 2007. EU Transparency Register: 61866543669-46. **Aims** Provide a voice for retail clothing brands in Europe. **Members** Brands (about 60). Membership countries not specified. [2019/XM8531/D]

♦ European Brand and Packaging Design Association (epda) 06396

Gen Manager Bergstrasse 11, 40878 Ratingen, Germany. T. +4921021029940. Fax +4921021029941.
Head Office Grellingerstrasse 75, 4052 Basel BS, Switzerland.
URL: https://www.epda-design.com/

History Founded 1990, as *Packaging Design Association of Europe (PDA-Europe)*, subsequently *Packaging and Brand Design Association of Europe*. Changed title to *PDA – Pan European Brand Design Association*, 1996; *European Packaging Design Association*, 2012. Located in Switzerland. **Aims** Facilitate cooperation within the *industry* for design; promote the industry with users, concerned governmental institutions and European Community authorities. **Structure** General Assembly (annual); Executive Committee; Secretariat. **Languages** English. **Finance** Members' dues. Sponsorship fees. **Activities** Networking/liaising; advocacy/lobbying/activism; guidance/assistance/consulting; events/meetings. **Events** *Congress* Moscow (Russia) 2020, *Meet and Greet Meeting* Glasgow (UK) 2019, *Congress* Vienna (Austria) 2019, *Meet and Greet Meeting* Vienna (Austria) 2019, *Meet and Greet Meeting* Paris (France) 2018.
Members Commercial agencies in 16 countries:
Belgium, Finland, France, Germany, Greece, Italy, Japan, Netherlands, Norway, Poland, Russia, Spain, Sweden, Switzerland, Thailand, USA.
NGO Relations Member of: *International Council of Design (ICoD, #13013).* [2018.06.05/XD3139/**D**]

♦ European Brands Association 06397
Association des industries de marques (AIM) – Europäischer Markenverband
Main Office Avenue des Gaulois 9, 1040 Brussels, Belgium. T. +3227360305. Fax +3227346702.
URL: http://www.aim.be/
History 5 Oct 1967, Brussels (Belgium). Founded as *European Association of Industries of Branded Products – Association européenne des industries de produits de marque – Europäischer Verband der Markenartikelindustrie – Associazione Europea fra le Industrie di Prodotti di Marca – Europese Vereniging van Merkartikelfabrikanten*. Current name adopted 1996. Most recent statutes adopted in 2004. Registration: No/ID: 0408.298.635, Start date: 5 Oct 1967, Belgium; EU Transparency Register, No/ID: 1074382679-01, Start date: 26 Nov 2008. **Aims** Promote: common interests of branded product manufacturers; relations between manufacturers and retailers; action against counterfeiting; environment and packaging; logistics; trademark questions; branding, consumer and marketing issues. **Structure** General Assembly (annual). Board, half of whose members represent national associations and half corporate members. Steering Committee of 13 members, including President, Vice-President, Immediate Past-President, Treasurer, Director-General and Committee Chairmen. Specialized Committees and Task Forces (11). **Languages** English. **Staff** 7.00 FTE, paid. **Finance** Members' dues.
Members Corporate and national associations (about 1,800 companies) in 21 countries:
Austria, Belgium, Czechia, Denmark, Finland, France, Germany, Greece, Hungary, Ireland, Italy; Luxembourg, Netherlands, Norway, Portugal, Russia, Slovakia, Spain, Sweden, Switzerland, UK.
Consultative Status Consultative status granted from: *World Intellectual Property Organization (WIPO, #21593)* (Permanent Observer Status). **IGO Relations** Recognized by: *European Commission (EC, #06633).* Cooperates with: *European Union Intellectual Property Office (EUIPO, #08996).* **NGO Relations** Member of (2): *Circular Plastics Alliance (#03936); Industry4Europe (#11181).* Sectoral association of: *European Shippers' Council (ESC, #08477).* [2019/XD5569/t/**D**]

♦ European Brass Band Association (EBBA) 06398
Gen Sec Charles de Kerckhovelaan 17, 9000 Ghent, Belgium. E-mail: generalsecretary@ebba.eu.com.
Chairman address not obtained.
URL: http://www.ebba.eu.com/
History 1995. Registration: Corporate Court Ghent, No/ID: 0771336, Start date: 1995, Belgium; Mémorial Court, No/ID: F0003129, Start date: 1995, Luxembourg. **Aims** Further and promote the intrinsic, aesthetic and social values of brass bands in Europe. **Structure** General Meeting (annual); Executive Committee; Music Commission; Delegates. **Languages** English. **Staff** 0.50 FTE, voluntary. **Activities** Awards/prizes/competitions; events/meetings.
Members Full in 14 countries and territories:
Austria, Belgium, Denmark, England, France, Ireland, Lithuania, Netherlands, Northern Ireland, Norway, Scotland, Sweden, Switzerland, Wales. [2022.10.28/XD6896/**D**]

♦ European Brass Teachers Association (inactive)

♦ European Breakfast Cereal Association (CEEREAL) 06399
Acting Managing Dir Av des Nerviens 9-31, 1040 Brussels, Belgium. T. +3225495640. Fax +3225112905. E-mail: info@ceereal.eu.
URL: http://www.ceereal.eu/
History 10 Feb 1992. Took over the activities of *Federation of Associations of Oat- and Barley Millers in the EEC (inactive)*, which ceased to exist Jul 1992. Registration: Banque Carrefour des Entreprises, No/ID: 0762.867.386, Start date: 3 Feb 2021, Belgium; EU Transparency Register, No/ID: 234450341442-14, Start date: 15 Feb 2021. **Aims** Create a positive and balanced regulatory environment conducive to sustainable growth and innovation for EU breakfast cereal and oat milling companies; promote and defend members' interests to EU institutions, stakeholders and consumer and industry associations; promote breakfast as the most important meal of the day. **Structure** General Assembly; Board of Directors; Food Safety Working Group; Nutrition, Sustainability and Communications Working Group; Oat Millers Forum. **Languages** English. **Staff** 2.00 FTE, paid. **Finance** Sources: members' dues. **Activities** Politics/policy/regulatory.
Members National associations (9) in 8 countries:
Finland, France, Germany, Ireland, Italy, Portugal, Spain, UK.
Companies (10). Membership countries not specified.
IGO Relations As successor to Federation of Associations of Oat- and Barley Millers in the EEC, recognized by: *European Commission (EC, #06633).* **NGO Relations** Member of (3): *FoodDrinkEurope (#09841); Industry4Europe (#11181); Whole Grain Initiative (WGI, #20939).* [2022.05.31/XD3695/**D**]

♦ European Breast Cancer Council (EBCC) 06400
Contact c/o EORTC, Ave E Mounier 83, 1200 Brussels, Belgium. E-mail: info@ebccouncil.com.
URL: http://ebccouncil.com/
History 1998. Founded by *European Organisation for Research and Treatment of Cancer (EORTC, #08101)* Breast Cancer Group, *European Society of Breast Cancer Specialists (EUSOMA, #08534)* and *Europa Donna – The European Breast Cancer Coalition (#05745).* Former names and other names: *EBC Council* – alias; *Breast Cancer Working Group (BCWG)* – former (2012). **Aims** Raise awareness and improve prevention, diagnosis, treatment and care of breast cancer patients. **Activities** Events/meetings. **Events** *European Breast Cancer Conference (EBCC)* Barcelona (Spain) 2022, *European Breast Cancer Conference* Barcelona (Spain) 2020, *European Breast Cancer Conference* Brussels (Belgium) 2020, *European Breast Cancer Conference* Barcelona (Spain) 2018. **Publications** Position papers.
Members Organizations (3):
Europa Donna – The European Breast Cancer Coalition (#05745); European Organisation for Research and Treatment of Cancer (EORTC, #08101) (Breast Cancer Group); *European Society of Breast Cancer Specialists (EUSOMA, #08534).* [2020/AA1169/y/**E**]

♦ European Brewery Convention (EBC) 06401
Convention européenne de brasserie
Main Office c/o Brewers of Europe, Rue Caroly 23-25, 1050 Brussels, Belgium. T. +3225511810. Fax +3226609402. E-mail: info@brewersofeurope.org – info@europeanbreweryconvention.eu.
URL: https://europeanbreweryconvention.eu/
History 1947, Scheveningen (Netherlands). Recognized by Netherlands Royal Decree No 24 of 15 Sep 1949. Dissolved as a legal entity in 2008. Restructured as the scientific and technological, but autonomous part of *The Brewers of Europe (#03324).* Former names and other names: *Continental Brewery Centre* – former (1947); *Centre continental de brasserie* – former (1947). **Aims** Promote and develop brewing and malting science and technology, application of best practice in brewing and malting technology and transfer of knowledge from other industries into brewing and malting. **Structure** Executive Committee. **Languages** English, French, German. **Staff** 1.00 FTE, paid. **Finance** Members' dues. Annual budget: euro 220,000. **Activities** Research and development; networking/liaising; knowledge management/information dissemination; events/meetings. **Events** *EBC Congress* Madrid (Spain) 2022, *Biennial Congress* Antwerp (Belgium) 2019, *Biennial Congress* Ljubljana (Slovenia) 2017, *Biennial Congress* Porto (Portugal) 2015, *Biennial Congress* Luxembourg (Luxembourg) 2013. **Publications** *Analytica EBC; Analytica Microbiologica; Annual Reports on Field Trials of the Barley and Malt Committee; EBC Thesaurus on Brewing and Malting Terminology.* Good practice manuals; proceedings of congresses; monographs of symposia.

Members National organizations in 28 countries:
Austria, Belgium, Croatia, Cyprus, Czechia, Denmark, Finland, France, Germany, Greece, Hungary, Ireland, Italy, Lithuania, Luxembourg, Malta, Netherlands, Norway, Poland, Portugal, Romania, Slovakia, Slovenia, Spain, Sweden, Switzerland, Türkiye, UK. [2020.03.12/XD0596/**D**]

♦ European Bridge League (EBL) 06402
Ligue européenne de bridge
Headquarters Maison du Sport Intl, Av de Rhodanie 54, 1007 Lausanne VD, Switzerland. T. +41215447218.
Sec 12 rue Cristophe Colomb, 56860 Séné, France. T. +33645579360. E-mail: secretariat@europeanbridge.org.
URL: http://www.eurobridge.org/
History 1947, Copenhagen (Denmark). Founded as successor to *International Bridge League – Ligue internationale de bridge*, set up in 1933, Scheveningen (Netherlands). New Statutes adopted: Sep 1967; last amended: Jun 2016. Has taken over, Jan 1999, the activities of *European Union Bridge League (EUBL, inactive).* **Aims** Promote *contract bridge* in Europe; control contract bridge in Europe played under competitive conditions in affiliated countries; foster friendly relations among national associations in Europe. **Structure** Congress of Delegates; Executive Committee. **Languages** English. **Staff** 1.00 FTE, paid. **Finance** Sources: members' dues; revenue from activities/projects. **Activities** Awards/prizes/competitions. **Events** *Seminar* Budapest (Hungary) 2012.
Members Recognized national contract bridge organizations in 45 countries and territories:
Albania, Austria, Belarus, Belgium, Bosnia-Herzegovina, Bulgaria, Croatia, Cyprus, Czechia, Denmark, England, Estonia, Faeroe Is, Finland, France, Georgia, Germany, Greece, Hungary, Iceland, Ireland, Israel, Italy, Latvia, Lebanon, Lithuania, Malta, Monaco, Netherlands, Norway, Poland, Portugal, Romania, Russia, San Marino, Scotland, Serbia, Slovakia, Slovenia, Spain, Sweden, Switzerland, Türkiye, Ukraine, Wales.
NGO Relations Affiliated to: *World Bridge Federation (WBF, #21246)*, as one of 7 geographical zones. [2020.06.24/XD0597/**D**]

♦ European Bridge Press Association / see International Bridge Press Association (#12399)

♦ European Brief Therapy Association (EBTA) 06403
Sec address not obtained.
Pres address not obtained.
URL: http://www.ebta.nu/
History 1991, Paris (France). Founded on the initiative of Steve de Shazer and Insoo Kim Berg. **Structure** Board, composed of President, Treasurer, Secretary, Research Coordinator, Webmaster, non-voting Senior Adviser and 7 other members. **Finance** Members' dues. **Activities** Organizes conferences. **Events** *Annual Conference* Copenhagen (Denmark) 2021, *Annual Conference* Copenhagen (Denmark) 2020, *Annual Conference* Florence (Italy) 2019, *Annual Conference* Sofia (Bulgaria) 2018, *Annual Conference* Frankfurt-Main (Germany) 2017. **Publications** *EBTA Newsletter.* [2020/XD6895/**D**]

♦ European Broadcasting Convention (1933 treaty)
♦ European Broadcasting Office (inactive)

♦ European Broadcasting Union (EBU) 06404
Union européenne de radio-télévision (UER)
Dir Gen L'Ancienne Route 17A, PO Box 45, Grand-Saconnex, 1218 Geneva, Switzerland. T. +41227172005 – +41227172111. Fax +41227172010 – +41227172111. E-mail: dgo@ebu.ch – ebu@ebu.ch – info@ebu.ch.
URL: http://www.ebu.ch/
History 12 Feb 1950, Torquay (UK). Founded following the birth of radio broadcasting across Europe, and in succession to *International Broadcasting Union (inactive)*, set up 4 Apr 1925, Geneva (Switzerland). International co-operation disrupted during World War II and Cold War. *International Radio and Television Organization (OIRT, inactive)*, set up 28 Jun 1946, based in Prague (Czech Rep), represented broadcasters in Eastern Europe until it disbanded in 1992. EBU and its *Eurovision (inactive)* and *Euroradio (inactive)* operations merged with OIRT and its *Intervision (inactive)*, 1 Jan 1993, thus resulting in full reunification of European broadcasting. Former names and other names: *Union européenne de radiodiffusion* – former; *Unión Europea de Radiodifusión* – former; *Union der Europäischen Rundfunkorganisationen* – former. Registration: Banque-Carrefour des Entreprises, No/ID: 0850.059.993, Start date: 1 Jan 1950, Belgium; Switzerland; EU Transparency Register, No/ID: 93288301615-56, Start date: 19 Dec 2008. **Aims** Strive to secure a sustainable future for public service media; provide world-class content from news to sport and music; create a centre for learning and sharing based on founding ethos of solidarity and co-operation. **Structure** General Assembly; Executive Board; Statutory Expert Groups (2); Sectoral Assemblies and Committees (7); Operations Council; Committees (2); Groups (2); Operates: *Eurovision*; *Euroradio.* **Languages** English, French. **Staff** 425.00 FTE, paid. **Finance** Sources: members' dues. Operations are self-financed. Annual budget: 405,000,000 CHF. **Activities** Advocacy/lobbying/activism; events/meetings; guidance/assistance/consulting. **Events** *Connect Conference* Geneva (Switzerland) 2021, *Digital Radio Summit* Geneva (Switzerland) 2021, *Connect Conference* Geneva (Switzerland) 2020, *Digital Radio Summit* Geneva (Switzerland) 2020, *News Xchange Conference* Vienna (Austria) 2020. **Publications** *Diffusion* (weekly); *EBU Technical Review* (4 a year); *Technical Review: Best of* (annual). General and technical publications.
Members Active; Associate; Group. Active (69) in 56 countries:
Albania, Algeria, Andorra, Armenia, Austria, Azerbaijan, Belarus, Belgium, Bosnia-Herzegovina, Bulgaria, Croatia, Cyprus, Czechia, Denmark, Egypt, Estonia, Finland, France, Georgia, Germany, Greece, Holy See, Hungary, Iceland, Ireland, Israel, Italy, Jordan, Latvia, Lebanon, Libya, Lithuania, Luxembourg, Malta, Moldova, Monaco, Montenegro, Morocco, Netherlands, North Macedonia, Norway, Poland, Portugal, Romania, Russia, San Marino, Serbia, Slovakia, Slovenia, Spain, Sweden, Switzerland, Tunisia, Türkiye, UK, Ukraine.
Associate (31) in 20 countries and territories:
Australia, Bangladesh, Brazil, Canada, Chile, China, Cuba, Georgia, Hong Kong, India, Iran Islamic Rep, Japan, Korea Rep, Malaysia, Mauritius, New Zealand, Oman, South Africa, Syrian AR, USA.
Approved participants in 4 countries:
France, North Macedonia, Russia, Spain.
Included in the above, 3 organizations listed in this Yearbook:
Euronews (#05741); Radio Vaticana – Vatican News; TV5Monde (TV5, #20269).
Consultative Status Consultative status granted from: *ECOSOC (#05331)* (Ros C); *UNESCO (#20322)* (Associate Status); *World Intellectual Property Organization (WIPO, #21593)* (Permanent Observer Status). **IGO Relations** Observer to: *Intergovernmental Committee of the International Convention of Rome for the Protection of Performers, Producers of Phonograms and Broadcasting Organizations (#11474); European Audiovisual Observatory (#06294); Union for the International Registration of Audiovisual Works (#20444).* Collaborates with: *European Commission (EC, #06633).* Working relations with: *International Telecommunication Union (ITU, #15673)* and official relations with its Radiocommunication and Telecommunication Standardization Sectors. Official Relations with: *Council of Europe (CE, #04881); ILO (#11123); WHO (#20950).* Related union: Advisory Committee to the UNSG for *Internet Governance Forum (IGF, #15950); Arab States Broadcasting Union (ASBU, #01050).* Invited to sessions of Intergovernmental Council of: *International Programme for the Development of Communication (IPDC, #14651).* **NGO Relations** Member of (15): *Digital Radio Mondiale Consortium (DRM, #05082); Digital Television Action Group (DigiTAG, #05084); egta – association of television and radio sales houses (#05397); Ethical Journalism Network (EJN, #05554); European Alliance for Culture and the Arts (#05866); European Internet Forum (EIF, #07591); European Services Forum (ESF, #08469); European Telecommunications Standards Institute (ETSI, #08897); International Music Council (IMC, #14199)* (Associate); *Internet Corporation for Assigned Names and Numbers (ICANN, #15949)* (Governmental Advisory Committee); *Olympic Movement (#17719); Permanent Conference of Mediterranean Audiovisual Operators (COPEAM, #18320); SGI Europe (#19253); World Broadcasting Unions (WBU, #21247); WorldDAB (#21351).* Instrumental in setting up (1): *Joint Industry Audience Research Methodology Group (ARM, no recent information).* Sponsors: *Prix Jeunesse.* Arrangements with: *International Federation of Association Football (#13360); International Olympic Committee (IOC, #14408).* Houses: *DVB Project (#05147).* Joint television commission with: *European Gymnastics (#07442).* In liaison with technical committees of: *International Organization for Standardization (ISO, #14473).* Related unions: *African Union of Broadcasting (AUB, #00490); Asia-Pacific Broadcasting Union (ABU, #01863); Caribbean Broadcasting Union (CBU, #03465); International Association of Broadcasting (IAB, #11738); North American Broadcasters Association (NABA, #17561); Organización de Telecomunicaciones de Iberoamérica (OTI, #17851).* Together with related unions, organizes: *World Conference of Broadcasting Unions. European Alliance for Television and Culture (EATC, #05888)* organizes the 'Geneva-Europa Prizes for Television Writing'. [2022.03.04/XD0598/**D**]

♦ European Bromeliad Society (inactive)
♦ European Brown Breed Federation (no recent information)

♦ European Brown Swiss Federation 06405

Fédération européenne des éleveurs de la race brune – Europäische Vereinigung der Braunviehzüchter – Federazione Europea degli Allevatori della Razza Bruna – Evropsko Udruzenje Uzgjaca Smedjeg Goveda

Sec 149 rue de Bercy, 75595 Paris CEDEX 12, France. T. +33140044946. E-mail: eu.bs.federation@gmail.com.
URL: http://www.brown-swiss.org/

History 10 May 1964, Lucerne (Switzerland). Current constitution adopted 7 Feb 1980, Zurich (Switzerland). **Aims** Promote cooperation between various Brown Swiss *cattle breeding* organizations in order to promote the breed. **Structure** General Meeting (at least every 2 years); Committee (Board of Directors). **Languages** English, French, German, Italian. **Staff** 9.00 FTE, voluntary. **Finance** Members' dues. **Events** *World Conference / European Conference of Brown Cattle Breeders* Kempten (Germany) 2014, *World Conference* St Gallen (Switzerland) 2012, *European Conference of Brown Cattle Breeders* Novo Mesto (Slovenia) 2010, *European conference of brown cattle breeders* Clermont-Ferrand (France) 2006, *European conference of brown cattle breeders* Cham (Switzerland) 2002.
Members Full in 11 countries:
Austria, Bulgaria, France, Germany, Italy, Romania, Slovenia, Spain, Switzerland, UK, Ukraine.
NGO Relations *European Brown Breed Federation (no recent information).* [2019.11.08/XD2101/**E**]

♦ European Brushware Federation 06406

Fédération européenne de l'industrie de la brosserie et pinceauterie (FEIBP) – Europäischer Verband der Bürsten- und Pinsel-Industrie – Federazione Europea dell'Industria delle Spazzole e dei Pennelli – Europese Federatie van de Borstel- en Penseelindustrie

Mailing Address PO Box 4076, 5000 JB Tilburg, Netherlands. E-mail: info@feibp.eu.
URL: http://www.eurobrush.com/

History 27 Sep 1958, Brussels (Belgium). Former names and other names: *Executive Committee for the EEC of the European Brushware Federation* – former (1958); *Commission exécutive pour CEE de la Fédération européenne de l'industrie de la brosserie et pinceauterie* – former (1958). **Structure** General Assembly; Executive Committee; Executive Commission; Working groups (8): industrial brushes; toothbrushes; personal use brushes; household brushes; paintbrushes and rollers; fine paintbrushes; raw materials suppliers; professional hygiene brushes. **Languages** English, French, German. **Finance** Members dues. **Events** *Congress* Prague (Czechia) 2020, *Congress* Lucerne (Switzerland) 2019, *Congress* France 2018, *Congress* Germany 2017, *Congress* Scotland 2016.
Members National organizations in 19 countries:
Austria, Belgium, Croatia, Denmark, France, Germany, Hungary, Italy, Netherlands, Norway, Poland, Russia, Spain, Sweden, Switzerland, Tunisia, Türkiye, UK, United Arab Emirates.
IGO Relations Recognized by: *European Commission (EC, #06633).* **NGO Relations** Member of: *Confédération européenne des industries du bois (CEI Bois, #04545).* In liaison with technical committees of: *International Organization for Standardization (ISO, #14473).* [2020/XD0915/t/**D**]

♦ European Buddhist Union (EBU) 06407

Union bouddhiste d'Europe (UBE) – Europäische Buddhistische Union (EBU)

Pres 9 rue Saulnier, 75009 Paris, France. E-mail: info@europeanbuddhism.org.
Main Website: http://europeanbuddhism.org

History 1973, Neuilly (France). Founded by *International Zen Association (#15940).* Former names and other names: *Buddhist Union of Europe (BUE)* – alias. Registration: EU Transparency Register, No/ID: 173532529975-58, Start date: 2 Mar 2018. **Aims** Facilitate international exchange and promote spiritual friendship among European Buddhists; support social action and ideas motivated by Buddhist values; amplify the voice of Buddhism in Europe and worldwide. **Structure** General Assembly (once a year); Executive Council. **Languages** English. **Finance** Sources: donations; members' dues. **Activities** Events/meetings; publishing activities; religious activities. **Events** *Annual General Meeting* Pomaia (Italy) 2021, *Annual General Meeting* Pomaia (Italy) 2020, *Annual General Meeting* Barcelona (Spain) 2019, *Annual General Meeting* Ledbury (UK) 2018, *Annual General Meeting* Vienna (Austria) 2016. **Publications** *EBU Magazine*; *EBU Newsletter.* EBU Podcast.
Members National Buddhist associations and buddhist centres in 18 countries:
Austria, Belgium, Croatia, Finland, France, Germany, Hungary, Ireland, Italy, Netherlands, Norway, Poland, Portugal, Slovenia, Spain, Sweden, Switzerland, UK.
Consultative Status Consultative status granted from: *Council of Europe (CE, #04881)* (Participatory Status).
NGO Relations Member of: *World Fellowship of Buddhists (WFB, #21501).* [2021.08.31/XD5943/**D**]

♦ European Builders Confederation (EBC) 06408

SG Rond-point Schuman 2-4, 5th floor, 1040 Brussels, Belgium. T. +3225142323. Fax +3225140015. E-mail: secretariat@ebc-construction.eu.
URL: http://www.ebc-construction.eu/

History 1990, Paris (France). Former names and other names: *Confédération européenne de l'artisanat, des petites et moyennes entreprises du bâtiment* – former. Registration: Crossroads Bank for Enterprises, No/ID: 0461-747-219, Start date: 30 Oct 1997, Belgium; EU Transparency Register, No/ID: 09256701147-51, Start date: 16 Feb 2009. **Aims** Promote and defend the interests of participating associations and their members with the European institutions; provide information for members; promote and improve the image and standing of small and medium-sized building *enterprises* and *craft* organisations in Europe. **Structure** General Assembly (annual); Executive Board; Secretariat. Technical Committees (3): Economic; Technical; Social Affairs. **Languages** English, French, Italian, Spanish. **Staff** 5.00 FTE, paid. **Finance** Sources: members' dues. **Activities** Events/meetings. **Events** *Annual Congress* Brussels (Belgium) 2022, *Annual Congress* Rome (Italy) 2019, *Annual Congress* Paris (France) 2018, *Annual Congress* Zagreb (Croatia) 2017, *Roundtable on Opportunities from Energy Saving Obligations and Alternative Measures* Brussels (Belgium) 2016. **Publications** *The Construction voice* (12 a year); *EBC Newsletter* (4 a year). Annual Report; position papers; press releases.
Members National associations of construction industry SMEs in 15 countries:
Austria, Belgium, Croatia, France (2), Hungary, Ireland, Italy (2), Latvia, Luxembourg, Netherlands, Poland, Romania, Slovakia, Slovenia, Spain.
Associate in 1 countries:
Switzerland.
IGO Relations Cooperates with (1): *European Agency for Safety and Health at Work (EU-OSHA, #05843).* **NGO Relations** Partner of (14): Build up; Built4People; *Comité européen de normalisation (CEN, #04162)*; *Construction 2050 Alliance (#04760)*; European Alliance for Apprenticeships; *European Association of Small and Medium sized Enterprises (SME Safety, #06207)*; *European Council for Construction Research, Development and Innovation (ECCREDI, #06813)*; *European Housing Forum (EHF, #07504)*; European Social Dialogue Committee for Construction; High Level Construction Forum; *Small Business Standards (SBS, #19311)*; *SMEunited (#19327)*; Standing Committee on Construction; *WorldSkills Europe (#21790).* [2022.10.19/XD2807/**D**]

♦ European Builders of Diesel Engine and Electric Locomotives (inactive)

♦ European Building Automation and Controls Association (eu.bac) 06409

Managing Dir Boulevard A Reyers 80, 1030 Brussels, Belgium. T. +3227068202. Fax +3227068210. E-mail: info@eubac.org.
URL: http://www.eubac.org/

History 2003, Brussels (Belgium). EU Transparency Register: 20943263315-44. **Aims** Represent major European manufacturers of products and systems for home and building automation. **Structure** General Assembly; Board. **Languages** English, French, German. **Staff** 5.00 FTE, paid. **Events** *Why Indoor Environmental Quality (IEQ) Matters – Towards Healthier Buildings* Brussels (Belgium) 2022.
Members Companies in 11 countries:
Austria, Belgium, Denmark, France, Germany, Ireland, Netherlands, Spain, Sweden, Switzerland, UK.
NGO Relations Instrumental in setting up: *European Association of Energy Service Companies (eu.ESCO, #06027).* [2019/XJ7603/**D**]

♦ European Building Design Association (inactive)
♦ European Building and Services Association (no recent information)

♦ European Bulk Oil Traders' Association (EBOTA) 06410

Contact c/o HFW, Friary Court, 65 Crutched Friars, London, EC3N 2AE, UK. T. +442072648531. E-mail: info@ebota.eu.
Contact address not obtained.
URL: http://www.ebota.org

History Dec 2011. Conceived 2008. Registration: EU Transparency Register, No/ID: 59052498328-06, Start date: 12 Mar 2012. **Aims** Engage, for and on behalf of members, in issues impacting the bulk trading of oil liquids, petrochemicals, biofuels, LNG, LPG and other refined products, feedstocks and associated derivatives; focus on regulatory regimes impacting European oil trading. **Structure** Council; Working Groups (3); Secretariat. **Finance** Sources: members' dues. **Activities** Advocacy/lobbying/activism; events/meetings; monitoring/evaluation; politics/policy/regulatory; training/education. **Members** Companies. Full; Associate. Membership countries not specified. [2022.04.29/XM5644/t/**D**]

♦ European Bureau of Adult Education / see European Association for the Education of Adults (#06018)

♦ European Bureau for Conscientious Objection (EBCO) 06411

Bureau européen de l'objection de conscience (BEOC) – Europäisches Büro für Kriegsdienstverweigerung

Pres Rue van Elewyck 35, 1050 Brussels, Belgium. T. +3226485220. E-mail: ebco@ebco-beoc.org.
SG address not obtained.
URL: http://www.ebco-beoc.org/

History Jul 1979. Statutes adopted 31 Jul 1986. Registration: Banque-Carrefour des Entreprises, No/ID: 0428.899.653, Start date: 22 May 1986, Belgium; EU Transparency Register, No/ID: 32954646807-31, Start date: 28 Sep 2011. **Aims** Promote collective campaigns for release of *imprisoned* conscientious objectors; lobbying European governments and institutions for full recognition of the right to conscientious objection to *military* service. **Structure** General Assembly (annual); Board; Officers (6). **Languages** English, French, German. **Staff** Voluntary. **Finance** Members' dues. Assistance from *European Youth Foundation (EYF, #09141).* **Activities** Events/meetings; advocacy/lobbying/activism; training/education; research/documentation. **Events** *General Assembly* Brussels (Belgium) 2020, *International Meeting* London (UK) 2016, *International Meeting* Brussels (Belgium) 2015, *International Meeting* Geneva (Switzerland) 2015, *International Meeting* Brussels (Belgium) 2014. **Publications** *Conscientious Objection to Military Service in Europe* (annual) – survey.
Members Experts and national pacifist movements in 25 countries:
Armenia, Belarus, Belgium, Bulgaria, Cyprus, Finland, France, Georgia, Germany, Greece, Hungary, Italy, Netherlands, North Macedonia, Norway, Portugal, Romania, Russia, Serbia, Spain, Sweden, Switzerland, Türkiye, UK, Ukraine.
Organizations in 18 countries:
Austria, Belgium, Bulgaria, Finland, France, Germany, Greece, Italy, Netherlands, North Macedonia, Norway, Portugal, Russia, Serbia, Spain, Sweden, Switzerland, Türkiye.
Consultative Status Consultative status granted from: *Council of Europe (CE, #04881)* (Participatory Status).
IGO Relations Cooperates with: *European Youth Centres (EYCs, #09138).* **NGO Relations** Member of: *European Youth Forum (#09140). Youth Society for Peace and Development of the Balkans (YSPDB)* is associate member. [2021/XF0221/**F**]

♦ European Bureau for Conservation and Development (EBCD) 06412

Bureau européen pour la conservation et le développement

Dir Rue de la Science 10, 1000 Brussels, Belgium. T. +3222303070. Fax +3222308272. E-mail: ebcd.info@ebcd.org.
URL: http://www.ebcd.org/

History Founded Apr 1989, Brussels (Belgium). Registered in accordance with Belgian law. EU Transparency Register: 704526524109-47. **Aims** Promote conservation and sustainable use of natural renewable resources both in Europe and worldwide; support science-based solutions, full stakeholder participation, due consideration for the socio-economic aspects, and for cultural diversity. **Structure** Board. **Languages** English, French, German, Irish Gaelic, Spanish, Swedish. **Staff** 7.00 FTE, paid. **Finance** Sources: government agencies; associations; NGOs; projects financed by: *European Commission (EC, #06633).* Annual budget: about euro 500,000. **Activities** Politics/policy/regulatory; events/meetings. **Events** *Intergroup Meeting* Brussels (Belgium) 2018, *Meeting on Forests and Climate* Brussels (Belgium) 2017, *Intergroup Meeting* Brussels (Belgium) 2014, *Meeting on Islands Challenges* Brussels (Belgium) 2013, *International conference on aquaculture* Brussels (Belgium) 2008. **Publications** *EBCD Fisheries Newsletter.* Reports; analyses. **Members** Not a membership organization. **IGO Relations** Cooperates with: *FAO (#09260)*; FAO Committee on Fisheries (COFI); *Secretariat of the Convention on Biological Diversity (SCBD, #19197)*; *Secretariat of the Convention on International Trade in Endangered Species of Wild Fauna and Flora (CITES Secretariat, #19199)*; *UNEP (#20299)*; *UNESCO (#20322)*; *United Nations Framework Convention on Climate Change – Secretariat (UNFCCC, #20564).* **NGO Relations** Member of: *European Aquaculture Technology and Innovation Platform (EATiP, #05910)*; *International Union for Conservation of Nature and Natural Resources (IUCN, #15766)*; *Long Distance Advisory Council (LDAC, #16511)*; *North Sea Advisory Council (NSAC, #17603)*; *North Western Waters Advisory Council (NWWAC, #17607).* [2018.09.06/XF0875/**F**]

♦ European Bureau of Consumers' Unions / see Bureau Européen des Unions de Consommateurs (#03360)

♦ European Bureau of Library, Information and Documentation Associations (EBLIDA) 06413

Dir Koninklijke Bibliotheek, Prins Willem-Alexanderhof 5, 2595 BE The Hague, Netherlands. T. +31703140137.
URL: http://www.eblida.org/

History 13 Jun 1992, following meeting May 1991, London (UK). Concept originated Aug 1987, Brighton (UK), at conference of *International Federation of Library Associations and Institutions (IFLA, #13470).* Registered in accordance with Dutch law: 40412969. EU Transparency Register: 32997432484-79. **Aims** As an independent umbrella association of national library, information, documentation and archive associations and institutions in Europe, act as the representative voice of the library and information science profession in European matters, with a specific interest in European information issues, including copyright and licensing, culture and education and EU enlargement. **Structure** Council (annual); Executive Committee; Secretariat. Expert Groups. **Languages** Dutch, English, French, German, Spanish. **Staff** 1.00 FTE, paid. **Finance** Members' dues. Sponsorship. **Activities** Advocacy/lobbying/activism; events/meetings; knowledge management/information dissemination. **Events** *Annual Council Meeting and Conference* Athens (Greece) 2022, *Annual Council Meeting* 2021, *Annual Meeting* 2020, *Annual Meeting and Conference* Dublin (Ireland) 2019, *Annual Meeting* Strasbourg (France) 2018. **Publications** *EBLIDA News* (12 a year) – electronic. Annual Report.
Members Full (44): national library, information, documentation and archive associations within the European Union; Associate (77): similar associations in other European countries and individual libraries and institutes. Represents interests of over 90,000 members in 35 countries:
Austria, Belgium, Bosnia-Herzegovina, Bulgaria, Croatia, Cyprus, Czechia, Denmark, Estonia, France, Georgia, Germany, Greece, Hungary, Ireland, Italy, Latvia, Lithuania, Luxembourg, Malta, Moldova, Montenegro, Netherlands, Norway, Poland, Portugal, Romania, Serbia, Slovakia, Slovenia, Spain, Sweden, Switzerland, Türkiye, UK.
Included in the above, 2 organizations listed in this Yearbook:
European Association for Health Information and Libraries (EAHIL, #06064); *European Parliament (EP, #08146)* (Library).
Consultative Status Consultative status granted from: *World Intellectual Property Organization (WIPO, #21593)* (Permanent Observer Status). **IGO Relations** *Council of Europe (CE, #04881)*; *European Commission (EC, #06633)*; *European Parliament (EP, #08146)*; *UNESCO (#20322)*; *World Intellectual Property Organization (WIPO, #21593).* **NGO Relations** Member of: *Copyright for Creativity (C4C, #04832)*; *International Federation of Library Associations and Institutions (IFLA, #13470). European and International Booksellers Federation (EIBF, #07584)*; *European Network for Copyright in support of Education and Science (ENCES, #07885).* [2017.10.05/XD3055/**D**]

♦ European Bureau of Peace Brigades International / see Protection International (#18548)

♦ European Bureau for Youth and Childhood (inactive)

♦ European Burns Association (EBA) 06414

Europese Brandwondenvereniging

Secretariat PO Box 440, 5201 AK 's Hertogenbosch, Netherlands. T. +31736901415. E-mail: eba@congresscare.com.

URL: http://www.euroburn.org/

History 1981. Registration: No/ID: 0461.516.003, Start date: 2 Oct 1997, Belgium; No/ID: KVK 54062632, Start date: 2011, Netherlands. **Aims** Encourage cooperation in the field of burn care throughout the continent; promote burn prevention; study the prevention of burn injury and all other aspects of burn treatment. **Structure** Board; Committees (3). **Languages** English. **Finance** Members' dues. **Activities** Networking/liaising; knowledge management/information dissemination; research/documentation. **Events** *Congress* Nantes (France) 2023, *Congress* Turin (Italy) 2022, *Congress* Turin (Italy) 2021, *Congress* Helsinki (Finland) 2019, *Congress* Barcelona (Spain) 2017. **Publications** *EBA Newsletter*, *European Burn Journal* – formerly: European Journal of Burn Care.

Members Full (citizens of European countries); Associate (citizens of non-European countries); Industrial (commercial organizations). Individuals in 31 countries and territories:

Albania, Algeria, Austria, Belgium, Brazil, Croatia, Czechia, Denmark, Egypt, Estonia, Finland, France, Germany, Greece, Hungary, Ireland, Italy, Lithuania, Malaysia, Netherlands, Norway, Poland, Portugal, Romania, Slovakia, Slovenia, Spain, Sweden, Switzerland, Tunisia, USA.

Organizations in 23 countries and territories:

Australia, Austria, Belgium, Bulgaria, Czechia, Denmark, Finland, France, Germany, Hong Kong, Hungary, India, Ireland, Italy, Netherlands, Norway, Portugal, Romania, Singapore, Slovakia, Sweden, Türkiye, UK. [2023/XD6485/**D**]

♦ European Business Angels Network / see European Trade Association for Business Angels, Seed Funds, and other Early Stage Market Players (#08923)

♦ European Business Aviation Association (EBAA) 06415

SG Sq de Meeûs 37, 1000 Brussels, Belgium. T. +3223182800. E-mail: communications@ebaa.org.

URL: http://www.ebaa.org/

History Mar 1977, Netherlands. Former names and other names: *IBAA – Europe* – former; *International Business Aircraft Association – Europe* – former. Registration: No/ID: 0425.678.758, Start date: 20 Mar 1987, Belgium; EU Transparency Register, No/ID: 120566513356-64, Start date: 28 Mar 2014. **Aims** Represent, promote and protect the interests of business aviation in Europe, whether for carriage of passengers or goods; ensure that business/executive aviation interests are considered in discussions on civil air transport. **Structure** General Meeting (annual); Board of Governors. Associate Members Advisory Council. Airports, Handling and Ground Operations Committee. **Languages** Dutch, English, French, German, Portuguese, Spanish. **Staff** 7.00 FTE, paid. **Finance** Sources: members' dues. **Activities** Advocacy/lobbying/activism; events/meetings; knowledge management/information dissemination. **Events** *European Business Aviation Convention & Exhibition (EBACE)* Geneva (Switzerland) 2023, *European Business Aviation Summit* Brussels (Belgium) 2022, *EBACE : European Business Aviation Convention* Geneva (Switzerland) 2022, *Annual General Meeting* Brussels (Belgium) 2021, *EBACE : European Business Aviation Convention* Geneva (Switzerland) 2021. **Publications** *EBAA Newsletter* (10 a year); *Who's Who in the EBAA* (annual). Policy position papers; Intelligence reports.

Members National Organizations in 8 countries:

France, Germany, Italy, Malta, Norway, Russia, Switzerland, UK.

Member Companies in 67 countries and territories:

Algeria, Austria, Azerbaijan, Bahrain, Belgium, Bermuda, Brazil, Bulgaria, Canada, China, Curaçao, Cyprus, Czechia, Denmark, Egypt, Estonia, Finland, France, Georgia, Germany, Gibraltar, Greece, Guernsey, Hong Kong, Iceland, India, Indonesia, Ireland, Isle of Man, Israel, Italy, Japan, Jordan, Kenya, Latvia, Lebanon, Liechtenstein, Luxembourg, Maldives, Malta, Moldova, Monaco, Morocco, Netherlands, New Zealand, Nigeria, Norway, Pakistan, Poland, Portugal, Qatar, Romania, Russia, Saudi Arabia, Slovakia, Slovenia, Spain, Sweden, Switzerland, Tunisia, Türkiye, UK, Ukraine, United Arab Emirates, Uruguay, USA, Virgin Is UK.

NGO Relations Member of (2): *Air Transport Action Group (ATAG, #00614)*; *Council for Environmentally Friendly Aviation (CEFA, #04880)*. Founder member and member of Council of: *International Business Aviation Council (IBAC, #12418)*. [2022/XD0729/**D**]

♦ European Business Club Association (unconfirmed)

♦ European Business Congress / see International Business Congress (#12419)

♦ European Business Council for Africa (EBCAM) 06416

SG Rue Montoyer 24-b5, 1000 Brussels, Belgium. T. +3225120695. Fax +3225123766. E-mail: info@ebcam.eu – contact@ebcam.eu.

Chief Administration Officer address not obtained.

URL: https://www.ebcam.eu/

History 1973. Former names and other names: *Group of Seven for Economic Cooperation with Africa* – former; *Groupe des sept pour la coopération économique avec l'Afrique* – former; *Group of Seven for European Private Sector Cooperation with Africa (Group of Seven)* – former; *Groupe des sept pour la coopération du secteur privé européen avec l'Afrique (Groupe des sept)* – former; *Group of Seven for European Private Sector Cooperation with Africa, Caribbean and Pacific* – former; *Groupe des sept pour la coopération du secteur privé européen avec l'Afrique, les Caraïbes et le Pacifique* – former; *Business Council Europe – Africa – Mediterranean (BCEAM)* – former (1996); *Business Council Europe – Afrique – Méditerranée* – former (1996); *European Business Council for Africa and the Mediterranean (EBCAM)* – former. Registration: Banque-Carrefour des Entreprises, No/ID: 0890.388.239, Start date: 27 Jun 2007, Belgium. **Aims** Unite European *investors* and other operators engaged in economic activity in African, Caribbean and Pacific (ACP) countries; promote cooperation between the European *private sector* and *ACP countries* and private trade and investment in those countries; cooperate with other professional European groups; examine and encourage measures by which private European funding and technical expertise can be made available to the countries concerned and contribute to their economic and social *development*; assist European institutions and ACP governments on issues of concern to European private sector companies in ACP countries. **Structure** General Meeting (3 a year, usually in Brussels); Plenary Meeting (annual); Board; Secretariat in Brussels (Belgium). **Languages** English, French. **Finance** Entirely financed by member associations. **Activities** Liaising/networking; guidance/assistance/consulting. **Events** *Africa-EU-China: Avenues for a New Economic Partnership?* Brussels (Belgium) 2020, *Annual Plenary Meeting* Budapest (Hungary) 2010, *Annual Plenary Meeting* Athens (Greece) 2009, *Annual Plenary Meeting* Copenhagen (Denmark) 2008, *Annual Plenary Meeting* The Hague (Netherlands) 2007.

Members Full in 15 countries:

Belgium, Denmark, France, Germany, Greece, Hungary, Luxembourg, Monaco, Netherlands, Norway, Portugal, Spain, Sweden, Switzerland, UK.

Africa Association, Hamburg; *Chamber of Commerce, Industry and Agriculture Belgium – Luxembourg – Africa-Caribbean-Pacific (CBL-ACP)*; *Conseil français des investisseurs en Afrique (CIAN)*; *Invest Africa*; *Netherlands-African Business Council (NABC)*.

Consultative Status Consultative status granted from: *UNCTAD (#20285)* (General). **IGO Relations** Regular links with: *Organisation of African, Caribbean and Pacific States (OACPS, #17796)*. Cooperates with: *African Development Bank (ADB, #00283)*; *European Economic and Social Committee (EESC, #06963)*; *European Commission (EC, #06633)*; *European Development Fund (EDF, #06914)*; *International Finance Corporation (IFC, #13597)*. [2021/XF0560/y/**F**]

♦ European Business Council for Africa and the Mediterranean / see European Business Council for Africa (#06416)

♦ European Business Council for a Sustainable Energy Future (e5) . . 06417

Chief Exec Oberföhringer Str 175 a, 81925 Munich, Germany. T. +491779330369. Fax +498995720604. E-mail: info@e5.org.

Managing Dir address not obtained.

URL: http://www.e5.org/

History 8 Feb 1996, Brussels (Belgium). Founded to implement the *'Sustainable Energy Charter'*, drawn up by European business leaders, Mar 1995, at UN Climate Summit. Also referred to as *e-to-the-power-of-five*. **Aims** Open untapped business opportunities and create extra jobs while serving the cause of environmental and climate protection. Key elements (5): energy; environment; economy; employment; efficiency. Urge Europe to adopt new energy and transport policies so as to avoid ecological risks and long-term economic damage. **Structure** General Meeting. Executive Board, including Chairman. Advisory Committee. **Languages** English, German. **Staff** 3.00 FTE, paid; 4.00 FTE, voluntary. **Finance** Sources: members' dues. **Publications** *e5-News*. *e5 Basis Paper*, *Sustainable Energy Charter*. Statements; expert opinions.

Members Partner associations in 3 countries:

Australia, UK, USA.

Included in the above, 1 organization listed in this Yearbook:

Internation Council for Sustainable Energy (ICSE, #15947).

Scientific advisors (3), including 2 organizations listed in this Yearbook:

Global Climate Forum (GCF, #10287); *Wuppertal Institute for Climate, Environment and Energy*.

Full members include 6 organizations listed in this Yearbook:

COGEN Europe (#04085); *Community of European Railway and Infrastructure Companies (CER, #04396)*; *European Insulation Manufacturers Association (EURIMA, #07577)*; *International Network for Environmental Management (INEM, #14263)*; *Solar Heat Europe (SHE, #19674)*; *World Wide Fund for Nature (WWF, #21922)*.

IGO Relations Accredited by: *United Nations Framework Convention on Climate Change – Secretariat (UNFCCC, #20564)*. **NGO Relations** Member of (1): *Global Climate Forum (GCF, #10287)*. Instrumental in drawing up Charter: *International Institute for Energy Conservation – Europe (IIEC-Europe, see: #13875)*; *International Network for Environmental Management (INEM, #14263)*. [2019/XD5444/y/**D**]

♦ European Business Ethics Forum (meeting series)

♦ European Business Ethics Network (EBEN) 06418

Contact c/o Edhec Business School, 24 ave Gustave Delory, CS 50411, 59057 Roubaix CEDEX 1, France. E-mail: eben@edhec.edu.

URL: http://www.eben-net.org/

History Nov 1987, Brussels (Belgium). Founded in association with *EFMD – The Management Development Network (#05387)*, at the conclusion of 1st major European conference on business ethics. **Aims** Promote ethics in excellence in businesses; increase awareness about ethical challenges in the global marketplace; enable dialogue on the role of business in society. **Structure** General Assembly; Executive Committee. **Languages** English. **Staff** 6.00 FTE, voluntary. **Finance** Members' dues. Other sources: corporate sponsorship; surplus revenue from conferences. **Activities** Events/meetings; knowledge management/information dissemination; networking/liaising; publishing activities; training/education. **Events** *Annual Conference* Rimini (Italy) 2023, *Research Conference* Frankfurt-Main (Germany) 2022, *Annual Conference* St Petersburg (Russia) 2022, *Annual Conference* St Petersburg (Russia) 2021, *Annual Conference* St Petersburg (Russia) 2020. **Publications** *Journal of Business Ethics* (annual) – following Conference; *European Business Ethics E-Newsletter* (irregular). Conference proceedings.

Members Individual; Institutional; Students; Company; Reduced. Members (1,300) in 36 countries:

Australia, Austria, Belgium, Canada, Croatia, Cyprus, Czechia, Denmark, Estonia, Finland, France, Germany, Greece, Hungary, Ireland, Israel, Italy, Lithuania, Luxembourg, Malta, Mexico, Netherlands, Norway, Poland, Portugal, Russia, Slovakia, Slovenia, South Africa, Spain, Sri Lanka, Sweden, Thailand, Türkiye, UK, USA.

EBEN National Networks in 18 countries:

Austria, Denmark, Finland, France, Germany, Greece, Hungary, Iceland, Ireland, Israel, Italy, Netherlands, Norway, Portugal, Spain, Sweden, Türkiye, UK.

Including in the above, 1 organization listed in this yearbook:

amfori (#00797).

NGO Relations Partner of: *Globethics.net Foundation (#10669)*. [2021/XF0937/**F**]

♦ European Business and Financial Press Association / see European Business Press (#06423)

♦ European Business History Association (EBHA) 06419

Past Pres c/o GUG, Sophienstrasse 44, 60487 Frankfurt-Main, Germany. T. +496997203314. Fax +496997203357. E-mail: ahschneider@unternehmensgeschichte.de – secretary@ebha.org.

URL: http://www.ebha.org/

History 1994. **Aims** Promote research, teaching and general awareness of all aspects of European business and *management* history; encourage collaboration through projects and scholarships as well as exchange of students. **Structure** Council. **Languages** English. **Finance** Members' dues. **Activities** Events/meetings. **Events** *Annual Congress* Madrid (Spain) 2022, *Annual Congress* Tokyo (Japan) 2021, *World Congress of Business History (WCBH)* Tokyo (Japan) 2021, *World Congress of Business History (WCBH)* Tokyo (Japan) 2020, *Annual Congress* Rotterdam (Netherlands) 2019. **Publications** *EBHA Newsletter* (2 a year). Register of Members Booklet.

Members Individuals (321) in 32 countries:

Argentina, Austria, Belgium, Brazil, Canada, China, Denmark, Finland, France, Germany, Greece, Hungary, India, Ireland, Italy, Japan, Korea Rep, Malta, Mexico, Netherlands, Norway, Portugal, Romania, Russia, South Africa, Spain, Sweden, Switzerland, Thailand, Türkiye, UK, USA.

NGO Relations Member of: *International Economic History Association (IEHA, #13224)*. [2021/XD5924/v/**D**]

♦ European Business Initiative on Taxation (unconfirmed)

♦ European Business and Innovation Centre Network (EBN) 06420

Réseau européen des centres européens d'entreprise et d'innovation (CEEI)

CEO Av de Tervuren 168, Bte 25, 1150 Brussels, Belgium. T. +3227728900. Fax +3227729574. E-mail: info@ebn.eu.

URL: http://www.ebn.eu/

History 20 Nov 1984. Founded under the auspices of *European Commission (EC, #06633)*. Statutes adopted 22 Jan 1985 and subsequently updated. Former names and other names: *European BIC Network* – alias. Registration: No/ID: 0426.938.768, Start date: 20 Nov 1984, Belgium; EU Transparency Register, No/ID: 056070639177-60, Start date: 10 Aug 2020. **Aims** Support development and growth of innovative entrepreneurs, start-ups and SMEs. **Structure** General Assembly (annual, at Congress); Board of Directors; Executive Committee. **Languages** English. **Staff** 15.00 FTE, paid. **Finance** Members' dues. Other sources: contracts for services to the European Commission and other members; commercial services. **Activities** Certification/accreditation; projects/programmes; networking/liaising; education/training; guidance/assistance/consulting; knowledge management/information dissemination; advocacy/lobbying/activism. **Events** *Annual Congress* Brussels (Belgium) 2022, *Annual Congress* Brussels (Belgium) 2021, *Annual Congress* Brussels (Belgium) 2020, *Annual Congress* Rome (Italy) 2019, *Annual Congress* Esch-sur-Alzette (Luxembourg) 2018. **Publications** *EBN Impact Report*, *The Business Innovator Magazine*.

Members Full (BICs, 160); Associate (other organizations, 55); correspondents and members by reciprocity in 35 countries and territories:

Austria, Belgium, Bulgaria, Chile, China, Croatia, Cyprus, Czechia, Egypt, Finland, France, Germany, Greece, Hungary, India, Ireland, Italy, Lebanon, Luxembourg, Morocco, Netherlands, Norway, Poland, Portugal, Slovakia, Slovenia, South Africa, Spain, Sweden, Switzerland, Taiwan, Tunisia, UK, USA, Zimbabwe.

NGO Relations Member of: *ANIMA Investment Network (#00833)*; *European Alliance for Innovation (EAI, #05872)*; *World Alliance for Innovation (WAINOVA, #21082)*. [2022/XF1770/**F**]

♦ European Business Institute (internationally oriented national body)

♦ European Business Leaders' Convention (EBLC) 06421

SG c/o Miltton House, Sörnäisten Rantatie 15, FI-00530 Helsinki, Finland. E-mail: eblc@eblc.org.

Events Manager address not obtained.

URL: https://www.eblc.org/

History 2002. **Structure** Council; Board. **Activities** Events/meetings. **Events** *Northern Light Summit* Helsinki (Finland) 2022, *Coming Out of the Dark – Technologies and Policies to Take us Forward*. Helsinki (Finland) 2021, *The Corona World – What is the New Paradigm for Business?* Helsinki (Finland) 2020, *Northern Light Summit* Helsinki (Finland) 2019. [2021.09.02/AA0507/v/**C**]

♦ European Business Network for Social Cohesion / see CSR Europe (#04977)

♦ European Business Organisation Worldwide Network (EBO WWN) . . 06422

Secretariat c/o Intl Dept of Business Europe, Avenue de Cortenbergh 168, 1000 Brussels, Belgium. E-mail: info@eboworldwide.eu – eboworldwidenetwork@gmail.com.

URL: https://eboworldwide.eu/

European Business Press
06423

alphabetic sequence excludes
For the complete listing, see Yearbook Online at

History 2001. Former names and other names: *EBOWWN* – alias; *EBO Worldwide Network* – alias. Registration: Crossroads Bank for Enterprises, No/ID: 0835.733.786, Start date: 22 Apr 2011, Belgium; EU Transparency Register, No/ID: 941242711525-27, Start date: 7 Jul 2013. **Aims** Provide a platform for European business organizations at global and regional levels to share best practices. **Structure** Board of Directors; Secretariat. Chapters. **Finance** Supported by: *European Commission (EC, #06633)* (DG Enterprise and Industry). **Activities** Events/meetings. **Events** Annual General Meeting Brussels (Belgium) 2022, *Annual General Meeting* Brussels (Belgium) 2022, *Annual General Meeting* Brussels (Belgium) 2016, *Annual General Meeting* Brussels (Belgium) 2015, *Annual General Meeting* Brussels (Belgium) 2014. **Publications** Position papers.
Members Chapters in 47 countries and territories:
Argentina, Armenia, Australia, Benin, Brazil, Burkina Faso, Cambodia, Canada, Chile, China, Côte d'Ivoire, Dominican Rep, Ethiopia, Ghana, Hong Kong, India, Indonesia, Japan, Kazakhstan, Korea Rep, Laos, Macau, Macedonia, Malaysia, Mali, Moldova, Mongolia, Myanmar, Nepal, New Zealand, North Macedonia, Papua New Guinea, Paraguay, Philippines, Russia, Rwanda, Singapore, South Africa, Sri Lanka, Sudan, Taiwan, Tanzania UR, Thailand, Togo, Trinidad-Tobago, Ukraine, Vietnam.
[2022.10.19/XM5321/**F**]

♦ **European Business Press (EBP)** **06423**
SG Rozna Dolina, cX/17B, 1000 Ljubljana, Slovenia.
URL: http://www.business-press.org/
History 6 Oct 1962, Como (Italy), as *European Business Press Federation – Union de la presse économique et financière européenne (UPEFE)*, following preliminary meetings in 1960 and 1961. Previously also referred to in English as *European Business and Financial Press Association*. Current title adopted, 1999. **Aims** Develop a spirit of European solidarity among members; stimulate and facilitate work along such lines, especially in the field of economic and financial information and the defence of the common interests of the profession. **Structure** General Assembly (annual); Executive Committee. **Languages** English. **Staff** 0.50 FTE, paid. **Finance** Members' dues (annual): euro 1,500. **Activities** Annual meeting; seminars which aim to position the financial economic press as a source of information and seek convergence with communications needs of leading companies; training of journalists; surveys. Establishing an inventory of available research potential in the field of genetic toxicology. **Events** *General Assembly* Istanbul (Turkey) 2014, *Editors Seminar* Vienna (Austria) 2014, *Editors Seminar* Frankfurt-Main (Germany) 2013, *Publishers Seminar* Stockholm (Sweden) 2013, *General Assembly* Zurich (Switzerland) 2013. **Publications** *How to Reach Europe* (current ed 2013/2014) – directory. Information Services: Database of members.
Members Financial/economic newspapers and journals (45) in 26 countries:
Austria, Belgium, Bulgaria, Czechia, Denmark, Estonia, Finland, France, Germany, Greece, Italy, Latvia, Lithuania, Netherlands, Norway, Poland, Portugal, Russia, Slovakia, Slovenia, Spain, Sweden, Switzerland, Türkiye, UK, Ukraine.
NGO Relations Associate member of: *European Magazine Media Association (EMMA, #07723)*.
[2017/XD3366/**D**]

♦ European Business Press Federation / see European Business Press (#06423)

♦ **European Business Registry Association (EBRA)** **06424**
Pres Marnixlaan 30, 1000 Brussels, Belgium. E-mail: secretary@ebra.be.
URL: https://ebra.be/
History Jan 2019. Created on coalition of European Business Register (EBR) and *European Commerce Registers' Forum (ECRF, inactive)*. Registration: No/ID: 0725.426.475, Start date: 16 Apr 2019, Belgium. **Aims** Establish an international community of business registries that collaborate on common initiatives, develop and share knowledge; and collectively progress the business registry domain. **Structure** Board of Directors. **Activities** Events/meetings; monitoring/evaluation; networking/liaising; research/documentation.
Events *Annual Conference* Sundsvall (Sweden) 2022, *Annual Conference* Helsinki (Finland) 2021, *Annual Conference* Amsterdam (Netherlands) 2020, *Annual Conference* Tallinn (Estonia) 2019. **Publications** *The International Business Report. 2020 Case Study on the impact of the COVID-19 pandemic on Business Registries* – launched in collaboration with EBRA sister associations, the Corporate Registers Forum (CRF), the International Association of Commercial Administrators (IACA) and the Association of Registers of Latin America and the Caribbean (ASORLAC).. **Information Services** *The European Business Register Network (EBR)* – electronic network of National Business Registers and Information Providers from 17 European countries..
Members Full in 33 countries and territories:
Albania, Austria, Azerbaijan, Belgium, Bosnia-Herzegovina, Denmark, Estonia, Finland, France, Georgia, Germany, Gibraltar, Guernsey, Ireland, Isle of Man, Italy, Jersey, Kosovo, Latvia, Liechtenstein, Lithuania, Luxembourg, Malta, Moldova, Montenegro, Netherlands, North Macedonia, Norway, Serbia, Slovenia, Spain, Sweden, UK.
[2022/AA1047/**D**]

♦ European Business School, Dublin (internationally oriented national body)

♦ **European Business Schools Librarians's Group (EBSLG)** **06425**
Sec Vlerick Business School, Reep 1, 9000 Ghent, Belgium. T. +3292109727.
URL: http://www.ebslg.org/
History 1970. **Aims** Provide a forum for the directors of libraries of leading European business schools. **Structure** Annual General Meeting; Council. Groups (3): Northern European; Continental; Anglophone. **Languages** English. **Staff** Voluntary. **Finance** Sources: members' dues. **Activities** Events/meetings; knowledge management/information dissemination. **Events** *Joint Meeting* Vienna (Austria) 2020, *General Meeting* Glasgow (UK) 2017, *Joint Conference* Singapore (Singapore) 2016, *Joint Meeting* Singapore (Singapore) 2016, *General Meeting* St Gallen (Switzerland) 2015.
Members Full in 18 countries:
Austria, Belgium, Czechia, Denmark, Finland, France, Germany, Hungary, Ireland, Netherlands, Norway, Portugal, Russia, Slovenia, Spain, Sweden, Switzerland, UK.
NGO Relations Cooperates with (3): *Academic Business Library Directors (ABLD)*; *Asia Pacific Business School Librarians' Group (APBSLG, #01865)*; *Latin American Council of Business Schools (#16308)*.
[2021/XM3728/**D**]

♦ **European Business Services Alliance (EBSA)** **06426**
Secretariat c/o EFCA, Av des Arts 3-5, 1210 Brussels, Belgium. E-mail: secretariat@servicealliance.eu.
URL: http://servicealliance.eu/
History Registration: EU Transparency Register, No/ID: 939194528262-23. **Aims** Increase knowledge, visibility and recognition of the business services industry at the European level; promote the convergence of views and positions expressed by European Business Services associations so as to enhance our ability to make strong representations to the EU Institutions and other relevant European and international stakeholders.
Members Organizations (9):
Architects Council of Europe (ACE, #01086); *Confederation of European Security Services (CoESS, #04532)*; *European Cleaning and Facility Services Industry (EFCI, #06571)*; *European Federation of Engineering Consultancy Associations (EFCA, #07109)*; *European Federation of Management Consultancies Associations (#07159)*; *European Forum of Independent Professionals (EFIP)*; *European Textile Services Association (ETSA, #08904)*; *FoodServiceEurope (#09851)*; *World Employment Federation Europe (#21377)*.
[2022.10.18/XM8726/y/**D**]

♦ **European Business Summit (EBS)** **06427**
Dir Gen Rue du Belvédère 28, 1050 Brussels, Belgium. T. +3226453481. E-mail: esr@ebsummit.eu – info@ebsummit.eu.
URL: http://www.ebsummit.eu/
History Registration: Banque-Carrefour des Entreprises, No/ID: 0502.707.349, Start date: 23 Jan 2013, Belgium; EU Transparency Register, No/ID: 268958411031-65, Start date: 22 Apr 2013. **Aims** Bring politics and business together in order to discuss and pursue their common goals; provide European institutions with a platform where they can place their top priorities in the spotlight. **Structure** Steering Committee. **Activities** Events/meetings; research/documentation. **Events** *European Business Summit* Brussels (Belgium) 2022, *European Business Summit* Brussels (Belgium) 2022, *European Business Summit* Brussels (Belgium) 2021, *European Business Summit* Brussels (Belgium) 2020, *European Business Summit* Brussels (Belgium) 2019. **IGO Relations** *Eureka Association (Eureka, #05621)*; *European Investment Bank (EIB, #07599)*. **NGO Relations** Partners include: *AIESEC (#00593)*; *BUSINESSEUROPE (#03381)*; *Conseil européen de l'industrie chimique (CEFIC, #04687)*; *Enterprise Europe Network (EEN, #05493)*; *European Climate Foundation (ECF,*

#06574); *CropLife Europe (#04965)*; *European Federation of Pharmaceutical Industries and Associations (EFPIA, #07191)*; *European Youth Forum (#09140)*; *Federation of Regional Growth Actors in Europe (FEDRA, #09701)*; *GSM Association (GSMA, #10813)*; *Invest Europe – The Voice of Private Capital (Invest Europe, #15997)*; *Junior Enterprises Europe (JE Europe, #16169)*; *Project Management Institute (PMI, #18534)*.
[2021/XM5311/**F**]

♦ European Business Travel Association (inactive)
♦ European Button Industries Federation (inactive)

♦ **European Cabin Crew Association (EurECCA)** **06428**
Pres Av Louise 143/4, 1050 Brussels, Belgium. E-mail: contact@eurecca.eu.
URL: https://eurecca.eu/
History 2014, Brussels (Belgium). Registration: Belgium; EU Transparency Register, No/ID: 444629814963-15. **Aims** Improve general living and work conditions for flight attendants. **Structure** Conference (annual); Board; Executive Committee; Working Groups. **Languages** English, French, German, Portuguese, Spanish. **Activities** Advocacy/lobbying/activism; events/meetings. **Events** *Annual Conference* Lisbon (Portugal) 2022, *Annual Conference* Lisbon (Portugal) 2019, *Annual Conference* Lisbon (Portugal) 2018. **Publications** Position papers; press releases; expertise papers.
Members European cabin crew unions in 7 countries:
France, Germany, Greece, Italy, Netherlands, Portugal, Spain.
NGO Relations Liaison Organization of: *Comité européen de normalisation (CEN, #04162)*.
[2022.05.25/XM4808/**D**]

♦ European Cable Communications Association / see GIGAEurope AISBL (#10151)

♦ **European Calcified Tissue Society (ECTS)** **06429**
Exec Dir MAI, Rue Washington 40, 1050 Brussels, Belgium. E-mail: ects@ectsoc.org.
Registered Address 16 Albyn Place, Aberdeen, AB10 1PS, UK.
URL: http://www.ectsoc.org/
History 16 Sep 1981, Knokke (Belgium). Founded when previous Rules of Order were adopted. Current constitution adopted, 2001, when ECTS was incorporated as a limited company. Registration: Companies House, No/ID: SC220522, Start date: 22 Jun 2001, Scotland; Banque-Carrefour des Entreprises, No/ID: 0718.756.736, Start date: 16 Jan 2019, Belgium. **Aims** Advance scientific knowledge of the structure and function of calcified tissues and related subjects. **Structure** General Business Meeting (annual); Board of Directors. **Languages** English. **Staff** 0.50 FTE, paid. 0.5 FTE, supported by Bioscientifica Ltd. **Finance** Members' dues. Other sources: donations, grants. **Activities** Awards/prizes/competitions; research/documentation; knowledge management/information dissemination. **Events** *Congress* Marseille (France) 2024, *Congress* Liverpool (UK) 2023, *International Conference on Children's Bone Health* Dublin (Ireland) 2022, *Congress* Helsinki (Finland) 2022, *International Conference on Children's Bone Health* Dublin (Ireland) 2021. **Members** Scientists engaged in work on calcified tissues and related subjects for 2 years or more. Membership countries not specified. **NGO Relations** Member of: *Biomedical Alliance in Europe (#03251)*; *European Society of Endocrinology (ESE, #08594)*; *Federation of European and International Associations Established in Belgium (FAIB, #09508)*; *Initiative for Science in Europe (ISE, #11214)*; *International Federation of Musculoskeletal Research Societies (IFMRS, #13485)*. Joint meeting with: *International Bone and Mineral Society (IBMS, #12379)*.
[2021/XD6407/v/**D**]

♦ **European Calcium Silicate Producers Association (ECSPA)** **06430**
Europese Vereniging van Kalkzansteenproducenten
SG Blvd du Souverain 68, 1170 Brussels, Belgium. E-mail: info@ecspa.org.
URL: http://www.ecspa.org/
History 1989. Registration: Banque Carrefour des Entreprises, No/ID: 0894.543.995, Start date: 15 May 2007, Belgium; EU Transparency Register, No/ID: 97717061899-40, Start date: 25 Jun 2009. **NGO Relations** Member of (3): *Construction 2050 Alliance (#04760)*; *Construction Products Europe AISBL (#04761)*; *Industry4Europe (#11181)*. In liaison with technical committees of: *Comité européen de normalisation (CEN, #04162)*.
[2019/XD8007/**D**]

♦ **European Calcium Society (ECS)** **06431**
SG KU Leuven, Lab Molecular and Cellular Signalling, Campus Gasthuisberg O/N1, Herestraat 49 box 802, 3000 Leuven, Belgium. T. +3216330660. Fax +3216330732.
Pres Centre de Biologie du Dév – UMR 5547, Univ Paul Sabatier – bât 4R3b3, 118 route de Narbonne, 31062 Toulouse CEDEX 04, France. T. +33561556398.
URL: http://www.calciumsociety.org/
History 1997. Current statutes adopted May 2005. Registered in accordance with Belgian law. **Aims** Develop and sustain relationships between different generations of scientists working in the field of Ca2+ binding and signalling and the various proteins involved (the "calcium toolkit"). **Structure** General Assembly; Executive Board. **Languages** English. **Staff** 2.00 FTE, paid. **Finance** Members' dues. **Activities** Events/meetings; networking/liaising; awards/prizes/competitions; financial and/or material support. **Events** *International Calreticulin Workshop* Montréal, QC (Canada) 2019, *Biennial Symposium* Toulouse (France) 2012, *Biennial symposium* Warsaw (Poland) 2010, *General assembly* Warsaw (Poland) 2010, *General Assembly* Leuven (Belgium) 2008. **Publications** *ECS e-Bulletin* (12 a year); *ECS Newsletter* (2 a year); *Member's Directory* (annual). *Calcium: The Molecular Basis of Calcium Action in Biology and Medicine* (2000).
Members Individuals in 33 countries and territories:
Australia, Austria, Belgium, Brazil, Canada, China, Czechia, Denmark, Finland, France, Germany, Hungary, India, Ireland, Israel, Italy, Japan, Korea Rep, Luxembourg, Mexico, Netherlands, Norway, Poland, Portugal, Qatar, Serbia, Slovenia, Spain, Sweden, Switzerland, Taiwan, UK, USA.
IGO Relations *European Cooperation in Science and Technology (COST, #06784)*.
[2019.12.19/XD6274/**D**]

♦ European Camac Association (no recent information)
♦ European Campaign on Debt and Development / see European Network on Debt and Development (#07891)
♦ European CanCer Organisation / see European Cancer Organisation (#06432)

♦ **European Cancer Organisation (ECO)** **06432**
Chief Exec Rue d'Egmont 13, 1000 Brussels, Belgium. T. +3227750200. E-mail: info@ecco-org.eu.
URL: https://www.europeancancer.org/
History Founded by three European scientific cancer organisations, including *European Society for Medical Oncology (ESMO, #08648)* and *SIOP Europe (SIOPE, #19288)*. Statutes adopted 1987; amended 2 June 1994; 1 Nov 1995; 5 June 1996; 11 Sep 1999; 4 June 2002; 2007; 2015; 2019. Former names and other names: *European CanCer Organisation (ECCO)* – former (Sep 2007 to 2020); *Federation of European Cancer Societies (FECS)* – former; *Fédération des sociétés européennes oncologiques* – former. Registration: Banque-Carrefour des Entreprises, No/ID: 0450.934.093, Start date: 2 Jun 1994, Belgium; EU Transparency Register, No/ID: 51022176260-12, Start date: 20 Jul 2011. **Aims** Reduce the burden of cancer; improve outcomes and quality of care for cancer patients through multidisciplinarity and multiprofessionalism. **Structure** General Assembly (twice a year); Board of Directors; Patient Advisory Committee; Executive Committee. **Languages** English, French. **Finance** Benefits derived from Community 365 initiative. **Activities** Advocacy/lobbying/activism; events/meetings; politics/policy/regulatory. **Events** *European Cancer Summit* Brussels (Belgium) 2023, *European Cancer Summit* Brussels (Belgium) 2022, *European Cancer Summit* Brussels (Belgium) 2021, *European Cancer Summit* Brussels (Belgium) 2020, *European Cancer Summit* Brussels (Belgium) 2019.
Members Full members – international organizations (40):
– *Association of European Cancer Leagues (ECL, #02500)*;
– *Cardiovascular and Interventional Radiological Society of Europe (CIRSE, #03427)*;
– *European Association for Palliative Care (EAPC, #06141)*;
– *European Association for the Study of Obesity (EASO, #06234)*;
– *European Association for the Study of the Liver (EASL, #06233)*;
– *European Association of Nuclear Medicine (EANM, #06136)*;
– *European Association of Urology (EAU, #06264)*;
– *European Association of Urology Nurses (EAUN, #06265)*;
– *European Federation for Colposcopy and Pathology of the Lower Genital Tract (EFC, #07081)*;
– *European Head and Neck Society (EHNS, #07452)*;
– *European Hematology Association (EHA, #07473)*;

- *European Hereditary Tumour Group (EHTG, #07476)*;
- *European Oncology Nursing Society (EONS, #08086)*;
- *European Organisation for Research and Treatment of Cancer (EORTC, #08101)*;
- *European Pain Federation (EFIC, #08131)*;
- *European Pancreatic Club (EPC, #08136)*;
- *European Respiratory Society (ERS, #08383)*;
- *European School of Oncology (ESO, #08434)*;
- *European Society for Clinical Nutrition and Metabolism (ESPEN, #08550)*;
- *European Society for Hybrid, Molecular and Translational Imaging (ESHIMT, #08626)*;
- *European SocieTy for Radiotherapy and Oncology (ESTRO, #08721)*;
- *European Society for Sexual Medicine (ESSM, #08733)*;
- *European Society of Breast Cancer Specialists (EUSOMA, #08534)*;
- *European Society of Breast Imaging (EUSOBI, #08535)*;
- *European Society of Coloproctology (ESCP, #08556)*;
- *European Society of Digestive Oncology (ESDO, #08582)*;
- *European Society of Endocrinology (ESE, #08594)*;
- *European Society of Gynaecological Oncology (ESGO, #08612)*;
- *European Society of Oncologic Imaging (ESOI, #08670)*;
- *European Society of Oncology Pharmacy (ESOP, #08671)*;
- *European Society of Pathology (ESP, #08689)*;
- *European Society of Radiology (ESR, #08720)*;
- *European Society of Skin Cancer Prevention (EUROSKIN, #08735)*;
- *European Society of Surgical Oncology (ESSO, #08753)*;
- *International Papillomavirus Society (IPVS, #14511)*;
- *International Psycho-Oncology Society (IPOS, #14665)*;
- *Multinational Association of Supportive Care in Cancer (MASCC, #16895)*;
- *Organization of European Cancer Institutes (OECI, #17865)*;
- *Société internationale d'oncologie gériatrique (SIOG, #19493)*;
- *United European Gastroenterology (UEG, #20506)*.

Patient Advisory Committee members – international organisations (22):
- *Acute Leukemia Advocates Network (ALAN, #00107)*;
- *Childhood Cancer International (CCI, #03871)*;
- *Digestive Cancers Europe (DiCE, #05070)*;
- *Europa Donna – The European Breast Cancer Coalition (#05745)*;
- *Europa Uomo (#05770)*;
- *European Cancer Patient Coalition (ECPC, #06433)*;
- *European Liver Patients 'Association (ELPA, #07706)*;
- *EURORDIS – Rare Diseases Europe (#09175)*;
- *International Brain Tumour Alliance (IBTA, #12393)*;
- *International Kidney Cancer Coalition (IKCC, #13983)*;
- *International Neuroendocrine Cancer Alliance (INCA, #14348)*;
- *Leukemia Patient Advocates Foundation (LePAF)*;
- *Lung Cancer Europe (LuCE, #16523)*;
- *Lymphoma Coalition (LC, #16535)*;
- *MDS Alliance (#16608)*;
- *Melanoma Patient Network Europe (MPNE)*;
- *Myeloma Patients Europe (MPE, #16924)*;
- *Pancreatic Cancer Europe (PCE, #18172)*;
- *Sarcoma Patients EuroNet (SPAEN, #19054)*;
- *Thyroid Cancer Alliance (TCA, #20157)*;
- *World Bladder Cancer Patient Coalition (WBCPC, #21233)*;
- *Youth Cancer Europe (YCE, #22008)*.

NGO Relations Memorandum of Understanding with (1): *Sharing Progress in Cancer Care (SPCC)*. Member of (7): *Associations and Conference Forum (AC Forum, #02909)* (Founding); *Biomedical Alliance in Europe (#03251)*; *European Chronic Disease Alliance (ECDA, #06548)*; *European Public Health Alliance (EPHA, #08297)*; *European Society of Association Executives (ESAE, #08526)*; *Federation of European and International Associations Established in Belgium (FAIB, #09508)*; *Union for International Cancer Control (UICC, #20415)*. Hosts secretariat of: *Accreditation Council for Oncology in Europe (ACOE, #00063)*.
[2023/XD0532/y/**D**]

♦ European Cancer Patient Coalition (ECPC) 06433

Dir Rue de Montoyer 40, 1000 Brussels, Belgium. T. +3227214114. E-mail: administration@ecpc.org – info@ecpc.org.
URL: http://www.ecpc.org/

History 2003. Registration: Banque-Carrefour des Entreprises, No/ID: 0818.999.605, Start date: 1 Sep 2009; EU Transparency Register, No/ID: 57929627082-79, Start date: 7 Nov 2011. **Aims** Represent the views of cancer patients in the European *health care* debate; provide a forum for European cancer patients to exchange information and share best practice experiences; speak with a single voice for all cancer patients. **Structure** General Assembly (annual); Board; Head Office located in Brussels (Belgium). **Languages** English, French, Spanish. **Staff** 10.50 FTE, paid. **Finance** Project funding from *European Commission (EC, #06633)*; grants from 10 sustaining partners. **Activities** Knowledge management/information dissemination; training/ education; events/meetings; advocacy/lobbying/activism. **Events** *14 Million Reasons to Discuss Life after Cancer* Brussels (Belgium) 2021, *Ordinary General Assembly* Brussels (Belgium) 2021, *Annual General Meeting* Brussels (Belgium) 2020, *Annual Congress* Brussels (Belgium) 2019, *Workshop on Biomarkers and Patients' Access to Personalized Oncology Drugs in Europe* Brussels (Belgium) 2018. **Publications** *ECPC News*; *ECPC Newsletter*. Annual Report; newsletters; press releases; member briefs; position papers.
Members Organizations. Full in 31 countries:
Austria, Belgium, Bulgaria, Cyprus, Czechia, Denmark, Estonia, Finland, France, Germany, Greece, Hungary, Ireland, Italy, Latvia, Lithuania, Luxembourg, Malta, Netherlands, Norway, Poland, Portugal, Romania, Serbia, Slovakia, Slovenia, Spain, Sweden, Switzerland, UK, USA.
Included in the above, 6 organizations listed in this Yearbook:
Digestive Cancers Europe (DiCE, #05070); *Europa Uomo (#05770)*; *International Brain Tumour Alliance (IBTA, #12393)*; *Myeloma Patients Europe (MPE, #16924)*; *Thyroid Cancer Alliance (TCA, #20157)*; *Women against Lung Cancer in Europe (WALCE)*.
Associate in 37 countries and territories:
Armenia, Australia, Austria, Bosnia-Herzegovina, Brazil, Bulgaria, Canada, Croatia, Cyprus, Denmark, Germany, Greece, Iraq, Ireland, Israel, Italy, Latvia, Lithuania, Netherlands, New Zealand, Nigeria, North Macedonia, Peru, Poland, Romania, Russia, Serbia, Slovakia, Slovenia, Spain, Sweden, Switzerland, Taiwan, Türkiye, UK, Ukraine, USA.
IGO Relations Member of: Health Policy Forum of the Commission DG SANCO of *European Commission (EC, #06633)*; Working Group with Patients and Consumers *European Medicines Agency (EMA, #07767)*. Maintains links with: *Council of Europe (CE, #04881)*. **NGO Relations** Member of (7): *EGAN – Patients Network for Medical Research and Health (EGAN, #05394)*; *EU Health Coalition*; *European Alliance for Personalised Medicine (EAPM, #05878)*; *European Cancer Organisation (ECO, #06432)* (Patient Advisory Committee); *Federation of European and International Associations Established in Belgium (FAIB, #09508)*; *Rare Cancers Europe (RCE, #18620)*; *World Pancreatic Cancer Coalition (WPCC, #21708)*. Cooperates with: *Association of European Cancer Leagues (ECL, #02500)*; *European Hematology Association (EHA, #07473)*; *EURORDIS – Rare Diseases Europe (#09175)*; *European Patients' Forum (EPF, #08172)*; *DigitalHealthEurope (DHE, #05078)*; *Europa Uomo (#05770)*; *European Society for Medical Oncology (ESMO, #08648)*. [2021/XM1043/y/**F**]

♦ European Cancer Prevention Organization (ECPO) 06434

Belgian Headquarters Klein Hilststraat 5, 3500 Hasselt, Belgium. T. +3211275734. Fax +3211283677.
URL: http://www.ecpo.org/

History 11 Dec 1981, Brussels (Belgium). 11-12 Dec 1981, Brussels (Belgium), as *European Organization for Cooperation in Cancer Prevention Studies*. Registered in accordance with Belgian law, 27 Jan 1983. **Aims** Contribute to a decrease in the incidence of human cancer by assisting in research and studies into cancer prevention. **Structure** General Assembly (annual). Board, including President, Chairman and Treasurer. Working Groups. **Languages** English. **Staff** 1.00 FTE, paid; 3.00 FTE, voluntary. **Finance** Sources: EEC subsidies; cancer leagues; consultancy fees; royalties. **Activities** carried out under the guidance of the Scientific Advisory Committee and through Working Groups: Diet and Cancer; Hormonal and Sexual Factors and Cancer; Colon Cancer; AIDS and Cancer; Public Information and Cancer Prevention; Breast Cancer; Epidemiology and Cancer. **Events** *Annual Meeting / Annual Symposium* Genk (Belgium) / Hasselt (Belgium) 2014, *Annual Symposium* Brussels (Belgium) 2009, *Annual Symposium* Brussels (Belgium) 2008, *Annual world cancer congress* Shanghai (China) 2008, *Annual Symposium* Paris (France) 2007. **Publications** *ECP News*; *European Journal of Cancer Prevention*. Symposium proceedings.
Members Participating scientists (about 120) in 16 countries:
Belgium, Czechia, Denmark, Finland, France, Germany, Greece, Ireland, Italy, Luxembourg, Netherlands, Norway, Portugal, Sweden, Switzerland, UK.
Participating scientists also in the former USSR (countries not specified).
IGO Relations *WHO Regional Office for Europe (#20945)*. [2014/XD1507/**D**]

♦ European Cancer Rehabilitation and Survivorship Symposium (meeting series)
♦ European Candle Association (inactive)

♦ European Candle Institute (ECI) 06435

Address not obtained.
URL: http://www.eci-candles.com/

History Registered in accordance with Belgian law. **Aims** Promote the interest of the European candle industry. **Structure** General Assembly. Executive Board, including President and Vice-President. Technical Committee. Managing Director.
Members Candle manufacturing companies (3) in 2 countries:
Germany, Netherlands. [2011/XM4031/j/**F**]

♦ European Candle Manufacturers Association (ECMA) 06436

SG Avenye de Tervuren 188a, box 4, 1150 Brussels, Belgium. T. +3227731503. E-mail: ecma@kellencompany.com.
URL: https://candleseurope.com/

History 1 Jan 2021. Founded on merger of *Association of European Candle Makers (AECM, inactive)* and *European Candle Association (ECA, inactive)*. Registration: Banque-Carrefour des Entreprises, No/ID: 0773.950.330, Start date: 16 Sep 2021, Belgium. **Aims** Promote the safe use of candles; increase the knowledge and safety of candles; takes an active role in developing the regulatory and standardization environment. **Structure** Executive Board; Committees and Working Groups; Secretariat. **Events** *Annual Conference* Lisbon (Portugal) 2023.
Members Candle Producers in 17 countries:
Austria, Belgium, France, Germany, Ireland, Italy, Latvia, Lithuania, Netherlands, Poland, Portugal, Serbia, Spain, Sweden, Switzerland, UK, Ukraine.
National associations in 2 countries:
France, UK.
Associate in 9 countries:
Belgium, Bulgaria, Germany, Italy, Poland, Spain, Sweden, UK, USA. [2023/AA3273/t/**D**]

♦ European Canicross and Bikejöring Federation (ECF) 06437

Fédération européenne de canicross et de bikejöring

Pres Chemin du Congo 38, Desnié, 4910 Theux, Belgium. T. +3287376635.
URL: http://www.cani-cross.eu/

Aims Promote the sport of canicross and bikejöring in Europe; work towards standardization of competition rules. **Structure** General Assembly (annual); Board of Directors. **Languages** English, French. **Activities** Events/meetings.
Members National organizations (7) in 7 countries:
Austria, Belgium, France, Hungary, Italy, Poland, Switzerland. [2015.01.19/XM1920/**D**]

♦ European Canoe Association (ECA) 06438

SG Kneza Mislava 11, HR-10000 Zagreb, Croatia. T. +38514572008. Fax +38514572010. E-mail: ecaofficezagreb@gmail.com.
Pres 35 Killerton Park Drive, West Bridgford, Nottingham, NG 27 SB, UK. T. +441159811574. Fax +441159810714.
URL: http://www.canoe-europe.org/

History Dec 1993, Rome (Italy). **Aims** Promote canoe sport throughout Europe; increase information exchange between members. **Structure** Congress (every 2 years); Board; Executive Committee. **Languages** English, French, German. **Staff** 1.00 FTE, voluntary. **Activities** Events/meetings. **Events** *Biennial Congress* Belgrade (Serbia) 2019, *Biennial Congress* Bucharest (Romania) 2017, *Biennial Congress* Sofia (Bulgaria) 2015, *Biennial Congress* Zagreb (Croatia) 2013, *Biennial Congress* Porto (Portugal) 2011.
Members National federations in 44 countries:
Albania, Andorra, Armenia, Austria, Azerbaijan, Belarus, Belgium, Bosnia-Herzegovina, Bulgaria, Croatia, Cyprus, Czechia, Denmark, Estonia, Finland, France, Georgia, Germany, Greece, Hungary, Ireland, Israel, Italy, Latvia, Lithuania, Luxembourg, Malta, Moldova, Netherlands, North Macedonia, Norway, Poland, Portugal, Romania, Russia, Serbia, Slovakia, Slovenia, Spain, Sweden, Switzerland, Türkiye, UK, Ukraine.
NGO Relations Recognized by: *International Canoe Federation (ICF, #12437)*. [2020.03.03/XD5179/**D**]

♦ European Capital Markets Institute (ECMI) 06439

SG Place du Congrès 1, 1000 Brussels, Belgium. T. +3222293965. Fax +3222194151. E-mail: ecmi@ceps.eu.
URL: http://www.eurocapitalmarkets.org/

History 1 Oct 1993, Madrid (Spain). Registration: Banque-Carrefour des Entreprises, Belgium; EU Transparency Register, No/ID: 63505977233-67. **Aims** Provide a broad-based forum representing *academics* and *practitioners* to analyse specific issues related to European capital markets; sponsor inter-professional studies relating to cross-border activities and *investments*; make appropriate proposals and recommendations which contribute to the more effective functioning of European capital markets. **Structure** General Assembly (annual); Board; Advisory Board. **Languages** English. **Staff** None. **Finance** Sources: members' dues. **Activities** Events/meetings; research/documentation. **Events** *Annual Conference* Brussels (Belgium) 2022, *Annual Conference* Brussels (Belgium) 2021, *Corporate Sustainability Reporting: Setting an EU standard* Brussels (Belgium) 2021, *Greening the European Green Bond market* Brussels (Belgium) 2021, *How crisis-proof is the financial market infrastructure?* Brussels (Belgium) 2020. **Publications** *ECMI Newsletter* (3-4 a year). *ECMI Commentaries* – series; *ECMI Policy Brief* – series; *ECMI Research Papers* – series. Annual Report; books; statistical package.
Members Stock exchanges, universities, banks, brokers, investment banks, financial associations, professional firms and business schools (44) in 26 countries:
Austria, Belgium, Cyprus, Czechia, Denmark, Finland, France, Germany, Greece, Iceland, Ireland, Italy, Japan, Luxembourg, Malta, Netherlands, Norway, Poland, Portugal, Slovenia, Spain, Sweden, Switzerland, Türkiye, UK, USA.
International founding members (7), include the following 3 organizations listed in this Yearbook:
European Federation of Financial Analysts Societies (EFFAS, #07123); *Federation of European Securities Exchanges (FESE, #09542)*.
NGO Relations Coordinated by: *Centre for European Policy Studies (CEPS, #03741)*.
[2021.06.11/XE2372/jy/**E**]

♦ European Capitals and Cities of Sport Federation (ACES Europe) .. 06440

Fédération des associations des capitales et villes européennes du sport

Gen Sec Rond Point Robert Schuman 6, Bte 5, 1040 Brussels, Belgium. T. +3225880813. E-mail: aces@aces-europa.eu.
URL: http://www.aceseurope.eu/

History 2001. Registration: No/ID: 0831.576.545, Start date: 2 Dec 2010, Belgium; EU Transparency Register, No/ID: 35118309721-12, Start date: 28 Sep 2012. **Aims** Assign annual recognition of European Capital, City, Community, and Town of Sport. **Structure** Board. **Languages** English. **Finance** Annual budget: 150,000 EUR. **Activities** Awards/prizes/competitions; projects/programmes. **Publications** *European Cities of Sport*. **Members** Candidates of 28 EU countries and Turkey. **Consultative Status** Consultative status granted from: *UNESCO (#20322)* (Consultative Status). **IGO Relations** Recognized by: *European Commission (EC, #06633)* in the White Paper (Art 50). [2020/XM5106/**D**]

♦ European Capitals Trade Unions Network (ECTUN) 06441

Coordinator address not obtained.
URL: http://www.ectun.eu/

History Nov 1985, Rome (Italy). **Aims** Enhance a regular exchange of information, contacts and of best practices; establish spaces for dialogue among the trade union organisations of the capital cities and their regions. **Structure** Permanent Committee; Coordinator. **Activities** Events/meetings. **Events** *Conference* 2021, *Conference* Helsinki (Finland) 2020, *Conference* Sofia (Bulgaria) 2019, *Conference* Valletta (Malta) 2018, *Conference* London (UK) 2017.
Members Trade unions in 23 countries:
Austria, Belgium, Bulgaria, Cyprus, Denmark, Estonia, Finland, France, Germany, Greece, Hungary, Ireland, Italy, Latvia, Malta, Netherlands, Poland, Portugal, Romania, Russia, Spain, Sweden, UK. [2021/AA1904/**F**]

♦ European Capitals Universities Network / see Network of Universities from the Capitals of Europe (#17061)
♦ European Capsules Association (no recent information)

♦ European Captive Insurance and Reinsurance Owners' Association (ECIROA) 06442

Exec Manager Rue Edwad Steichen 10, L-2540 Luxembourg, Luxembourg.
URL: http://www.eciroa.org/
History 19 Aug 2008. Registration: Mémorial C, No/ID: F0007729, Start date: 15 Oct 2008, Luxembourg; EU Transparency Register, No/ID: 12749675101-70, Start date: 26 Jan 2011, Belgium. **Aims** Protect and support the captive industry; represent members in discussions with official, regulatory bodies. **Structure** General Meeting; Board of Directors; Executive Management. **Activities** Events/meetings. **Events** *Biennial European Captive Forum* Luxembourg (Luxembourg) 2021, *Biennial European Captive Forum* Luxembourg (Luxembourg) 2018, *Biennial European Captive Forum* Luxembourg (Luxembourg) 2016, *Biennial European Captive Forum* Luxembourg (Luxembourg) 2014. [2020/XM5574/**D**]

♦ European Caravan Federation (ECF) 06443

Fédération européenne de caravaning – Europäischer Wohnwagenverband
SG Hamburger Allee 14, 60486 Frankfurt-Main, Germany. T. +49697040390. Fax +496970403923. E-mail: info@e-c-f.com.
URL: http://www.e-c-f.com/
History 1964. Registration: EU Transparency Register, No/ID: 634929022403-73. **Aims** Represent internationally the caravanning industry in Europe. **Structure** General Assembly (annual); Board of Directors. **Languages** English, French, German. **Staff** 1.00 FTE, paid. **Finance** Sources: members' dues. Annual budget: 80,000 CHF. **Activities** Advocacy/lobbying/activism; events/meetings; standards/guidelines. **Events** *Annual Meeting* Ljubljana (Slovenia) 2022, *Annual Meeting* Düsseldorf (Germany) 2020, *Annual Meeting* Stockholm (Sweden) 2019, *Annual Meeting* Milan (Italy) 2015, *Annual Meeting* London (UK) 2014.
Members Full in 14 countries:
Austria, Belgium, Denmark, Finland, France, Germany, Italy, Netherlands, Norway, Slovenia, Spain, Sweden, Switzerland, UK.
NGO Relations Cooperates with (1): *International Organization for Standardization (ISO, #14473).* [2022.10.18/XD0106/**D**]

♦ European Carbohydrate Organization (ECO) 06444

Pres Dept of Organic Chemistry, Indian Inst of Science, Bangalore, Karnataka 560 012, Bangalore KARNATAKA 560 012, India. T. +918022932578. Fax +918023600529.
URL: http://www.internationalcarbohydrateorganisation.org/
Aims Encourage research, communication and education in glycoscience. **Structure** Officers: President; President-Elect; Secretary. President is national representative of the last country to host the symposium. **Activities** Organizes 'European Carbohydrate Symposium', Summer school and courses. **Events** *EUROCARB Biennial Symposium* Paris (France) 2021, *EUROCARB Biennial Symposium* Leiden (Netherlands) 2019, *EUROCARB Biennial Symposium* Barcelona (Spain) 2017, *EUROCARB Biennial Symposium / Biennial Symposium* Moscow (Russia) 2015, *EUROCARB Biennial Symposium* Tel Aviv (Israel) 2013. [2016/XM2018/**D**]

♦ European Carbon Association (ECA) 06445

Contact Poznan Univ of Technology, Inst of Chemistry and Technical Electrochemistry, Pitrowo 3, 60-965 Poznań, Poland. T. +48616653632.
URL: http://www.europeancarbon.eu/
History 1997. Statutes adopted 23 Nov 2001, Berlin (Germany). **Aims** Promote carbon research, development, applications and awareness across Europe. **Activities** Events/meetings; awards/prizes/competitions. **Events** *Annual World Conference on Carbon* London (UK) 2021, *Annual World Conference on Carbon* Kyoto (Japan) 2020, *Annual World Conference on Carbon* Lexington, KY (USA) 2019, *Annual World Conference on Carbon* Madrid (Spain) 2018, *Annual World Conference on Carbon* Melbourne, VIC (Australia) 2017.
Members Full in 6 countries:
France, Germany, Poland, Spain, UK, Ukraine.
NGO Relations *World Conference on Carbon.* [2015/XM4347/**E**]

♦ European Carbon Dioxide Association (inactive)

♦ European Carbon Dioxide Capture and Storage Laboratory Infrastructure (ECCSEL) 06446

Contact address not obtained. E-mail: info@eccsel.org.
URL: http://www.eccsel.org/
History Established Jun 2017, as a permanent pan-European distributed research infrastructure – *European Research Infrastructure Consortium (ERIC).* **Aims** Open access for researchers to a top quality European research infrastructure devoted to second and third generation Carbon Capture and Storage (CCS) technologies in an efficient and structured way to help enabling low to zero CO2 emissions from industry and power generation to combat global *climate change.* **Finance** Funding from *European Union (EU, #08967)* – Horizon 2020. **Activities** Research and development.
Members Member countries (5):
France, Italy, Netherlands, Norway, UK. [2018/XM6873/**F***]

♦ European Carbon and Graphite Association (ECGA) 06447

SG Av de Tervuren 168, Bte 11, 1150 Brussels, Belgium. T. +32477225303. E-mail: graphit@ecga.net.
URL: https://ecga.net/
History 1995. Registration: Banque-Carrefour des Entreprises, No/ID: 0454.645.631, Start date: 23 Jan 1995, Belgium; EU Transparency Register, No/ID: 66301488645-70. **Aims** Promote the benefit and value of carbon and graphite products and the industry to society; endeavour to uphold the industry's interests; raise public awareness accordingly. **Structure** General Assembly (annual); Administrative Council; Committees (4). **Languages** Dutch, English, French, German, Polish, Romanian. **Staff** 3.00 FTE, paid. **Finance** Sources: members' dues. **Activities** Advocacy/lobbying/activism; awareness raising; politics/policy/regulatory. **Publications** Annual Report; bulletins.
Members Founder companies (4) in 2 countries:
France, Germany.
Members in 18 countries:
Austria, Belgium, Finland, France, Germany, Italy, Luxembourg, Mozambique, Netherlands, Norway, Poland, Portugal, Slovakia, Spain, Sweden, Switzerland, UK, Ukraine.
IGO Relations Observer status with (1): *OECD (#17693).* **NGO Relations** Member of (2): *Federation of European and International Associations Established in Belgium (FAIB, #09508); Industry4Europe (#11181).* Associate Expert Group of *Business and Industry Advisory Committee to the OECD (BIAC, #03385).* [2023/XD4848/t/**D**]

♦ European Cardiac Arrhythmia Society (ECAS) 06448

Contact 2 Place Delibes, 13008 Marseille, France.
SG 39 rue Reuzo, 13008 Marseille, France.
URL: https://www.ecas-heartrhythm.org/
History Aug 2004, Marseille (France). Registration: Registre National des Associations, France. **Aims** Promote excellence in the care of patients with cardiac arrhythmias by improving the education of physicians and allied professionals in charge of arrhythmia patients; provide information on rythm disturbances to general public. **Structure** Executive Committee. **Languages** English. **Staff** 1.00 FTE, paid; 2.00 FTE, voluntary. **Finance** Sources: meeting proceeds; members' dues; sponsorship. **Activities** Advocacy/lobbying/activism; awards/prizes/competitions; events/meetings; knowledge management/information dissemination; research and development; standards/guidelines; training/education. **Events** *Annual Congress* Paris (France) 2020, *Annual Congress* Marseille (France) 2019, *Annual Congress* Paris (France) 2018, *Annual Congress* Rome (Italy) 2017, *Annual Congress* Paris (France) 2016. **Publications** *Journal of Interventional Cardiac Electrophysiology* (8 a year).
Members Senior; Founding; Affiliate; Associate; Honorary. Members in 42 countries and territories:
Argentina, Armenia, Austria, Belgium, Bosnia-Herzegovina, Brazil, Canada, Côte d'Ivoire, Croatia, Denmark, Egypt, Finland, France, Germany, Greece, Hong Kong, India, Iran Islamic Rep, Ireland, Israel, Italy, Japan, Latvia, Lebanon, Madagascar, Mexico, Morocco, Netherlands, Poland, Romania, Russia, Slovakia, South Africa, Spain, Sweden, Switzerland, Taiwan, Tunisia, Türkiye, UK, United Arab Emirates, USA. [2020/XM0709/**D**]

♦ European Cardiology Section Foundation (ECSF) 06449

Contact c/o Sparkasse KölnBonn, Stiftungs- und Vereinsmanagement, Hahnenstr 57, 50667 Cologne, Germany. E-mail: contact@e-cs-f.org.
URL: http://e-cs-f.org/
History 2010. Founded as the charitable foundation of *European Union of Medical Specialists (UEMS, #09001)* Cardiology Section. **Aims** Promote science and research, and education and professional training. **Structure** Board; Council. **Activities** Certification/accreditation; events/meetings; training/education. Sole stakeholder of *European Board for Accreditation in Cardiology (EBAC, #06353).* **NGO Relations** Cooperates with (3): *European Atherosclerosis Society (EAS, #06289); European Society of Cardiology (ESC, #08536); European Society of Hypertension (ESH, #08627).* [2021/AA0905/f/**F**]

♦ European Cardionephrology Association (no recent information)

♦ European Cardiovascular and Thoracic Surgery Institute of Accreditation (ECTSIA) 06450

Administrator Papworth Hospital, Cambridge, CB3 8RE, UK. T. +441480364299. Fax +441480364744.
History 13 Oct 2003, Vienna (Austria), by *European Association for Cardio-Thoracic Surgery (EACTS, #05964), European Society for Cardiovascular and Endovascular Surgery (ESCVS, #08537)* and *European Society of Thoracic Surgeons (ESTS, #08760).* **Aims** Encourage a culture of clinical performance monitoring. **Structure** Board of 6 members. [2007/XM0606/j/**E**]

♦ European Card Payment Association (ECPA) 06451

Gen Sec Rue d'Arlon 82, 1040 Brussels, Belgium. T. +33672832058. E-mail: general-secretary@europeancardpaymentassociation.eu.
URL: https://www.europeancardpaymentassociation.com/
History Founded Jun 2014. Registered in accordance with Belgian law. EU Transparency Register: 839751414764-22. **Aims** Monitor, evaluate and respond to relevant legislation proposed in the EEA. **Structure** Board.
Members Full in 10 countries:
Belgium, Bulgaria, Denmark, France, Italy, Netherlands, Norway, Portugal, Spain, UK.
Regional association (1):
PAN-Nordic Card Association (PNC, #18182). [2020/XM8727/**D**]

♦ European Carpet Association / see European Carpet and Rug Association (#06452)

♦ European Carpet and Rug Association (ECRA) 06452

Contact Rue Montoyer 24, 1000 Brussels, Belgium. T. +3223581674. E-mail: ecra@ecra.eu.
URL: http://www.ecra.eu/
History 2005, as *European Carpet Association (ECA) – Association européenne du tapis – Europäische Teppichgemeinschaft.* Registered in accordance with Belgian law. EU Transparency Register: 690030131158-90. **Aims** Defend, promote and support the interests of the European carpet and rug industry at the economic, social and technical level. **Structure** General Assembly (annual); Administrative Board. Director-General. **Languages** English. **Staff** 2.00 FTE, paid. **Finance** Members' dues. **Events** *Convention* Germany FR 1988, *Convention* Neuss (Germany FR) 1986.
Members National associations; individual firms in countries with no national association; individual firms having a turnover of more than euro 50,000. Members in 10 countries:
Austria, Belgium, Denmark, France, Germany, Netherlands, Spain, Switzerland, UK, USA.
NGO Relations Member of (5): *Circular Plastics Alliance (#03936); EURATEX – The European Apparel and Textile Confederation (EURATEX, #05616); European Floor Coverings Association (EUFCA, #07271); European Plastics Converters (EuPC, #08216); World Carpet and Rug Council (WCRC, #21261).* In liaison with technical committees of: *International Organization for Standardization (ISO, #14473).* [2019/XD5125/**D**]

♦ European Carton Makers Association (ECMA) 06453

Association européenne des fabricants de cartonnages pliants – Vereinigung der Europäischen Faltschachtel- Industrie
Managing Dir PO Box 85612, 2508 CH The Hague, Netherlands. T. +31703123911. E-mail: mail@ecma.org.
URL: http://www.ecma.org/
History Oct 1960, Cologne (Germany). A Participating Industry Sector of *Confederation of European Paper Industries (CEPI, #04529).* Registration: No/ID: KVK 40409444, Netherlands; EU Transparency Register, No/ID: 948591610750-02, Start date: 4 Mar 2013. **Aims** Be the recognized body of the European carton industry; act to influence the political and economic situation within the industry in Europe; enhance and improve the competitive environment for members. **Structure** Executive Committee; Secretariat in The Hague (Netherlands); Technical Advisor in Brussels (Belgium). **Languages** English. **Staff** 3.00 FTE, paid. **Finance** Sources: members' dues. **Activities** Awards/prizes/competitions; events/meetings; research/documentation. **Events** *Annual Congress* Krakow (Poland) 2022, *Annual Congress* Krakow (Poland) 2020, *Annual Congress* St Julian's (Malta) 2019, *Annual Congress* Riga (Latvia) 2018, *Annual Congress* Salzburg (Austria) 2017. **Publications** *ECMA Newsletter* (Monthly) in English – online. *ECMA Code of Folding Carton Design Styles; PRISM Report.* Braille guidelines.
Members National carton associations; carton manufacturers; members of branch multinationals; associate; overseas. National carton associations in 11 countries:
Austria, Belgium, Denmark, France, Germany, Italy, Spain, Sweden, Switzerland, Türkiye, UK.
Manufacturers in 21 countries:
Austria, Belgium, Croatia, Czechia, Denmark, Finland, France, Germany, Greece, Hungary, Iceland, Ireland, Italy, Netherlands, Norway, South Africa, Spain, Sweden, Switzerland, Türkiye, UK.
Members of branch multinationals in 10 countries:
Austria, Belgium, Denmark, France, Germany, Italy, Netherlands, Sweden, Switzerland, UK.
Associate members in 12 countries:
Austria, Belgium, Canada, Finland, France, Germany, Italy, Netherlands, Spain, Sweden, Switzerland, UK.
Overseas members in 6 countries:
Argentina, India, Japan, Russia, South Africa, USA.
NGO Relations Member of: *European Platform for Chemicals Using Manufacturing Industries (CheMI, #08223); International Confederation of Paper and Board Converters in Europe (CITPA, #12866).* Affiliated with: *Nordic Carton Association (NCA, no recent information).* Makes annual Pro Carton/ECMA Award – with *Association of European Cartonboard and Carton Manufacturers (PRO CARTON, #02502).* [2022.10.28/XD0603/t/**E**]

♦ European Car-Transport Group of Interest / see Association of European Vehicle Logistics (#02551)
♦ European Cartridge Collectors Club / see European Cartridge Research Association (#06454)

♦ European Cartridge Research Association (ECRA) 06454

Sec Oude Waalsdorperweg 63, 2597 AK The Hague, Netherlands. T. +31703740091. E-mail: secretary@ecra.info.
URL: http://www.ecra.info/
History 1964, Antwerp (Belgium), as *European Cartridge Collectors Club (ECCC).* **Aims** Further study in and research of historic and technical development of *ammunition.* **Structure** Language groups (5): Dutch; English; French; German, Spanish. **Languages** English, French, German, Spanish. **Staff** 4.00 FTE, voluntary. **Finance** Members'dues. Sales. **Activities** Organizes annual meeting. **Publications** Montly bulletin.

Members Organizations and individuals in 29 countries:
Argentina, Australia, Austria, Belgium, Bulgaria, Canada, Croatia, Czechia, Denmark, Finland, France, Germany, Greece, Iceland, Italy, Luxembourg, Netherlands, New Zealand, Norway, Poland, Portugal, Russia, South Africa, Spain, Sweden, Switzerland, UK, Uruguay, USA. [2018/XD9157/**D**]

♦ European Car and Truck Rental Association (inactive)
♦ European Cash Management Companies Association / see European Security Transport Association (#08458)

♦ European Casino Association (ECA) 06455

SG Square de Meeûs 38-40, 1000 Brussels, Belgium. T. +3224016130. E-mail: info@europeancasinoassociation.org.
URL: http://www.europeancasinoassociation.org/

History Early 1990s, as *European Casino Forum*. Registration: Banque-Carrefour des Entreprises, No/ID: 0878.519.102, Start date: 11 Jan 2006, Belgium; Eu Transparency Register, No/ID: 541453110746-37, Start date: 4 Mar 2013. **Aims** Address and promote issues related to casinos and/or casino operations. **Structure** General Assembly (twice a year); Board of Directors; Working Groups. **Activities** Knowledge management/information dissemination; awareness raising; politics/policy/regulatory. **Events** *International Casino Conference* London (UK) 2023, *Casino Industry Forum* Baden (Austria) 2022, *International Casino Conference* London (UK) 2020, *International Casino Conference* London (UK) 2019, *Industry Forum* Monte Carlo (Monaco) 2019.
Members National associations and casino operators in 28 countries:
Austria, Belgium, Czechia, Denmark, Estonia, Finland, France, Germany, Greece, Hungary, Italy, Latvia, Liechtenstein, Lithuania, Luxembourg, Monaco, Montenegro, Netherlands, Poland, Portugal, San Marino, Serbia, Slovakia, Slovenia, Spain, Sweden, Switzerland, UK. [2022/XJ7993/**D**]

♦ European Casino Forum / see European Casino Association (#06455)

♦ European Castor and Wheel Manufacturers Association (ECMA) . . . 06456

Secretariat Via Scarsellini 13, 20161 Milan MI, Italy. T. +39245418563. Fax +39245418545. E-mail: info@e-cma.eu.
URL: http://www.e-cma.eu/

History Oct 2004, Wermelskirchen (Germany). **Structure** Board, comprising President, 2 Vice-Presidents, Treasurer and 6 members. **Events** *Plenary Meeting* Bologna (Italy) 2009, *Plenary Meeting* Hannover (Germany) 2008, *Plenary Meeting* Milan (Italy) 2007.
Members Companies in 5 countries:
Belgium, Finland, Germany, Italy, Netherlands. [2015/XJ1668/**D**]

♦ European Cast Polymer Association (inactive)

♦ European Catalyst Manufacturers Association (ECMA) 06457

Contact c/o CEFIC, Av E Van Nieuwenhuyse 4, Box 1, 1160 Brussels, Belgium. T. +3226767211. Fax +3226767300. E-mail: bpi@cefic.be.
URL: http://www.cefic.org/

History 1983, as sector group and affiliate organization of *Conseil européen de l'industrie chimique (CEFIC, #04687)*. **Aims** Represent manufacturers of *metal oxide* catalysts in Western Europe. **Structure** Committee. Working Parties (5) deal with specific metals (nickel, cobalt and chromium) and metal oxides, with transport of catalysts, and problems of spent catalysts. **Activities** Programme on environmental and biological monitoring; assists with toxicology review; maintains links with common interest groups; represents views of the industry to regulatory authorities and international agencies.
Members Metal and metal oxide catalyst manufacturers (18) in 9 countries:
Belgium, Denmark, France, Germany, Italy, Luxembourg, Netherlands, Norway, UK. [2015/XD1069/**E**]

♦ European Catholic Centre / see European Catholic Home
♦ European Catholic Home (internationally oriented national body)
♦ European Causal Inference Meeting (meeting series)
♦ European Cavernoma Alliance (unconfirmed)
♦ European Cell Biology Organization (inactive)

♦ European Cell Death Organization (ECDO) 06458

Contact ECDO Secretariat, Dept of Molecular Biomedical Research, VIB-Univ of Ghent, Technologiepark 927, 9052 Zwijnaarde, Belgium. T. +3293313682. Fax +3293313511. E-mail: ecdo@dmbr.ugent.be.
URL: http://www.ecdo.eu/

History 1994. Statutes adopted Jan 1995. Statutes revised Nov 1999. **Aims** Share information on current developments in the field of cell death research; collect and disseminate information in cell death research; facilitate scientific links between the participating laboratories. **Structure** General Assembly (every 2 years). Executive Committee. Board of Directors, including President, President-Elect, Vice-President, General Secretary and Treasurer. **Events** *Joint Conference* Paris (France) 2023, *Euroconference on Apoptosis* Bonn (Germany) 2022, *Euroconference on Apoptosis* Dresden (Germany) 2019, *Euroconference on Apoptosis* St Petersburg (Russia) 2018, *Euroconference on Apoptosis* Leuven (Belgium) 2017. **Members** Individuals (approx 170). Membership countries not specified. [2014/XD8439/**D**]

♦ European Cell Proliferation Society (ECPS) 06459

Chairman Centre for Diabetes, Barts and The London School of Medicine and Dentistry, 4 Newark Street, London, E1 2AT, UK. T. +442078822357. Fax +442078822186.

History 1966, as *European Study Group for Cell Proliferation (ESGCP) – Groupe européen d'étude sur la prolifération cellulaire*. **Events** *Congress* St Julian's (Malta) 2010, *Meeting / Congress* Warsaw (Poland) 2007, *Meeting / Congress* London (UK) 2005, *Meeting / Congress* Prague (Czech Rep) 2004, *Meeting / Congress* Reims (France) 2002. **Publications** *Cell Proliferation* – journal. **Members** Membership countries not specified. [2010/XD9403/**E**]

♦ European Cellulose Insulation Association (ECIA) 06460

Chairman Dreve du Pressoir 38, Postbus 1190, 1190 Brussels, Belgium.
URL: https://www.ecia.eu/

History Inaugural meeting, Oct 2013, Brussels (Belgium). Registration: EU Transparency Register, No/ID: 109119138911-69, Start date: 9 Jul 2020. **Aims** Provide better energy and eco-efficiency by insulating the European buildings well with cellulose fiber insulation. **Structure** Board of Directors. **Events** *Annual Meeting* Antwerp (Belgium) 2019, *Annual Meeting* Athens (Greece) 2018, *Annual Meeting* Les Sables-d'Olonne (France) 2017, *Meeting* Brussels (Belgium) 2016, *Annual Meeting* Vienna (Austria) 2016.
Members Full in 9 countries:
Austria, Belgium, Czechia, Denmark, Finland, France, Germany, Spain, Switzerland.
Associate in 2 countries:
Finland, USA.
NGO Relations Liaison Organization of: *Comité européen de normalisation (CEN, #04162)*. Associate Member of *Construction Products Europe AISBL (#04761)*. [2020/XM4798/**D**]

♦ European Cement Research Academy (ECRA) 06461

Managing Dir P.O. Box 30 03 32, 40403 Düsseldorf, Germany. T. +492112398380. Fax +49211239838500. E-mail: info@ecra-online.org.
Events Manager Toulouser Allee 71, 40476 Düsseldorf, Germany.
URL: http://www.ecra-online.org/

History 2003. Registration: North-Rhine Westphalia District court, No/ID: HRB 47580, Start date: 21 Feb 2003, Germany, Düsseldorf. **Aims** Advance innovation in the cement industry within the context of sustainable development; communicate the latest knowledge and research findings in cement and concrete technology. **Structure** Technical Advisory Board. **Activities** Events/meetings; research/documentation. **Publications** *ECRA Newsletter* (3 a year). **Members** Cement producers (over 40). Membership countries not specified. [2021.09.07/XJ8755/**D**]

♦ European Center for Arbitration and Mediation 06462

Centre Européen d'Arbitrage et de Médiation – Centro Europeo de Arbitraje y de Mediación – Europäischer Zentrum für Schiedsverfahren und Mediation – Centro Europeo di Arbitrato e di Mediazione

SG 3 rue du Général Frère, CS 10033, 67081 Strasbourg CEDEX, France.
URL: http://www.cour-europe-arbitrage.org/

History Original title: *Centre européen d'arbitrage*. Registered in accordance with the law of Alsace-Moselle (France), 1959. **Aims** Study arbitration; promote the culture of arbitration; administer arbitration proceedings and mediation. **Structure** General meeting; Council; President; Vice Presidents; Secretary General; Treasurer. Includes: *European Court of Arbitration (#06853)*; Mediation Centre for Europe, the Mediterranean and the Middle East. **Languages** English, French, German, Italian, Spanish. **Finance** Members' dues. Administrative dues for arbitration and mediation services. **Activities** Organizes: training courses and discussions; conferences. **Publications** *International Bulletin*.
Members Delegations in 14 countries:
Austria, Belgium, Croatia, Egypt, France, Germany, Greece, Ireland, Italy, Lebanon, Spain, Switzerland, Tunisia, Türkiye. [2018/XE2782/**E**]

♦ European Center for Constitutional and Human Rights (internationally oriented national body)
♦ European Center for Economic and Policy Analysis and Affairs (unconfirmed)
♦ European Center for Human Rights (unconfirmed)
♦ European Center of International Hotel Management (internationally oriented national body)

♦ European Center for Not-for-Profit Law (ECNL) 06463

Exec Dir Riviervismarkt 5, 2513 AM The Hague, Netherlands. T. +31639029805. E-mail: info@ecnl.org.
URL: https://ecnl.org/

History Founded as the regional center of *International Center for Not-for-Profit Law (ICNL, #12471)* – European network. Former names and other names: *ICNL-Budapest* – former. Registration: KVK, No/ID: 73239518, Netherlands; EU Transparency Register, No/ID: 052513138393-62, Start date: 9 Jun 2020. **Aims** Promote the strengthening of a supportive legal environment for civil society in Europe, with a focus on Central and Eastern Europe, by developing expertise and building capacity in legal issues affecting not-for-profit organisations and public participation. **Structure** Board; Supervisory Board. **NGO Relations** Member of (2): *Eastern Partnership Civil Society Forum (EaP CSF, #05247)*; *Global NPO Coalition on FATF (#10508)*. Cooperates with (2): *Balkan Civil Society Development Network (BCSDN, #03070)*; *European Civic Forum (ECF, #06563)*. Affiliated with (1): *European Digital Rights (EDRi, #06924)*. [2022/XM2917/**D**]

♦ European Center for Preventing Addictions (internationally oriented national body)

♦ European Center of Sustainable Development (ECSDEV) 06464

Secretariat Piazzale Aldo Moro, 00185 Rome RM, Italy. T. +39692958486. E-mail: contact@ecsdev.org.
URL: http://ecsdev.org/

History 10 Feb 2010, Rome (Italy). **Aims** Plan and conduct scientific conferences and sustainability science research; disseminate research findings. **Structure** International Advisory Board; Secretariat. **Languages** English. **Staff** 5.00 FTE, voluntary. **Activities** Events/meetings; publishing activities; research and development; research/documentation; training/education. **Events** *International Conference on Sustainable Development* Rome (Italy) 2020, *International Conference on Sustainable Development* Rome (Italy) 2019, *International Conference on Sustainable Development* Rome (Italy) 2018. **Publications** *European Journal of Sustainable Development*. Conference proceedings. [2018.08.06/XM5740/**D**]

♦ European Center for Sustainable Finance (internationally oriented national body)
♦ European Center for Transitional Justice (unconfirmed)

♦ European and Central Asian Safety Network (EuCAS) 06465

Contact c/o IAEA – VIC, PO Box 100, 1400 Vienna, Austria. E-mail: eucas.contact-iaea@iaea.org.
URL: http://gnssn.iaea.org/main/EuCAS/

History Established 28 Sep 2016. Functions within *Global Nuclear Safety and Security Network (GNSSN, #10509)* of *International Atomic Energy Agency (IAEA, #12294)*. **Aims** Strengthen nuclear and *radiation* safety infrastructure at regional level. **Structure** Plenary; Steering Committee; Secretariat – provided by *International Atomic Energy Agency (IAEA, #12294)*. Working Groups. **Activities** Knowledge management/information dissemination; capacity building.
Members National Regulatory Bodies and Technical Safety Organizations of 20 countries:
Armenia, Belarus, Belgium, Bosnia-Herzegovina, Bulgaria, Czechia, France, Georgia, Germany, Greece, Kazakhstan, Lithuania, Malta, Moldova, Norway, Romania, Russia, Serbia, Slovakia, Tajikistan. [2017/XM6494/**F***]

♦ European Central Bank (ECB) 06466

Banque centrale européenne (BCE) – Europäische Zentralbank (EZB)

Pres Postfach 16 03 19, 60066 Frankfurt-Main, Germany. T. +496913440. Fax +496913446000. E-mail: info@ecb.europa.eu.
Street address Sonnemannstr 20, 60314 Frankfurt-Main, Germany.
Main: http://www.ecb.europa.eu/

History Established on approval by *Council of the European Union (#04895)*, in accordance with *Treaty on European Union (Maastricht Treaty, 1992)*, signed 7 Feb 1992. ECB Statutes, which are annexed as a Protocol to the Maastricht Treaty, were drawn up by *Committee of Governors of the Central Banks of the Member States of the European Economic Community (inactive)* before its dissolution. Functions as an integral part of the *European Communities (EC, inactive)*, the first "pillar" of the *European Union (EU, #08967)* and, together with national central banks, constitutes the *European System of Central Banks (ESCB, #08870)*, which was also established on 1 Jun 1998 in the context of the third stage of *European Economic and Monetary Union (EMU, #06961)*. Located in Frankfurt-Main (Germany), ECB assumed responsibility for monetary policy in the euro area on 1 Jan 1999. It replaces *European Monetary Institute (EMI, inactive)*, established 1 Jan 1994, which prepared a regulatory, organizational and logistic framework for the ESCB to perform its tasks in the third stage of EMU. Became responsible for the *Single Supervisory Mechanism (SSM)*, 1 Nov 2014. **Aims** Maintain price stability in the euro area. **Structure** Decision-making bodies: – *'Governing Council'* comprises all 6 members of the Executive Board and governors of National Central Banks (NCBs) without derogation, that participate fully in Monetary Union as part of the euro area. – *'Executive Board'* comprises President, Vice-President and 4 members, appointed by the European Council. – *'General Council'* comprises ECB President, ECB Vice-President and the governors of National Central Banks of all EU countries, whether or not participating in Monetary Union. As a transitional body, it will be dissolved once all EU Member States have introduced the single currency. – *'Supervisory Board'* comprises Chair, Vice-Chair, 4 ECB representatives and representatives of national supervisors. *Court of Justice of the European Union (CJEU, #04938)* is competent to settle any disputes. **Languages** Bulgarian, Croatian, Czech, Danish, Dutch, English, Estonian, Finnish, French, German, Greek, Hungarian, Irish Gaelic, Italian, Latvian, Lithuanian, Maltese, Polish, Portuguese, Romanian, Slovakian, Slovene, Spanish, Swedish. **Staff** 3546.00 FTE, paid. Staff organized through *International and European Public Services Organisation (IPSO, #13311)*. **Finance** The capital of the ECB comes from the NCBs of all EU Member States. **Activities** Events/meetings; politics/policy/regulatory. Defines and implements monetary policy; conducts foreign exchange operations; holds and manages the euro area's foreign currency reserves; promotes the smooth operation of payment systems. Specific tasks in the areas of: banking supervision; banknotes; statistics, macroprudential policy and financial stability; international and European cooperation. **Events** *Conference on Monetary Policy* Frankfurt-Main (Germany) 2020, *Forum on Central Banking* Frankfurt-Main (Germany) 2020, *Joint Conference on European Financial Integration* Brussels (Belgium) 2019, *Annual CompNet Conference* Brussels (Belgium) 2017, *Joint Conference on European Financial Integration* Brussels (Belgium) 2017. **Publications** *Convergence Report*; *Economic Bulletin*; *Financial Stability Review*; *International Journal of Central Banking (IJCB)* – in collaboration with BIS and G-10; *Weekly Financial Statement*. Annual Report; working papers; occasional papers.
Members Central banks in 19 of the 27 member countries of the European Union:
Austria, Belgium, Cyprus, Estonia, Finland, France, Germany, Greece, Ireland, Italy, Latvia, Lithuania, Luxembourg, Malta, Netherlands, Portugal, Slovakia, Slovenia, Spain.

IGO Relations Member of (2): *Bank for International Settlements (BIS, #03165)*; *Group of Twenty (G20, #10793)*. Participating in meetings of the Governing Council without right to vote: President of the Council of the European Union; a member of *European Commission (EC, #06633)*. President of ECB participates in meetings of the Council of the Union when matters relating to ESCB are discussed, in particular those of *Council of Finance Ministers of the European Union (Ecofin)* and *European Stability Mechanism (ESM, #08829)*. Upon invitation, participates in *Eurogroup (#05689)* meetings. Up to 2 members and 2 alternates in *Economic and Financial Committee (EFC)*. Reports annually to: *European Parliament (EP, #08146)*; Council of the European Union; European Commission; *European Council (#06801)*. Observer to: *International Monetary Fund (IMF, #14180)*. [2022.11.10/XF2923/**E***]

♦ European Central Bureau for Inter-Church Aid (inactive)

♦ European Central Council of Homeopaths (ECCH) 06467

Gen Sec address not obtained. E-mail: ecch@gn.apc.org.
URL: http://www.homeopathy-ecch.org/

History Jun 1990, Netherlands. Former names and other names: *European Council for Classical Homeopathy (ECCH)* – former (1990 to Jun 2009). Registration: EU Transparency Register, No/ID: 04627551301-91, Start date: 5 Mar 2009. **Aims** Improve the health of the European public by: developing highest standards of homeopathic practice among the homeopathic profession; promoting and protecting the rights of such professionals as regards establishment and freedom of movement between countries. **Structure** Council. **Languages** English. **Staff** 2.00 FTE, paid. **Finance** Members' dues. Annual budget: about pounds45,000. **Activities** Knowledge management/information dissemination. **Events** *Regulation Conference* London (UK) 2014, *Conference / Case Conference* Egmond aan Zee (Netherlands) 2003, *Case Conference* St Gallen (Switzerland) 2001, *Conference / Case Conference* Tromsø (Norway) 2000, *Conference / Case Conference* Barcelona (Spain) 1999. **Publications** *ECCH Newsletter*. Booklet; guidelines.

Members Organizations; individuals (). Members in 28 countries:
Armenia, Austria (*), Belgium, Bosnia-Herzegovina, Bulgaria, Croatia, Czechia, Denmark, Finland, France (*), Germany, Greece, Iceland (*), Ireland, Israel, Italy, Liechtenstein (*), Luxembourg (*), Netherlands, North Macedonia, Norway, Poland, Portugal, Serbia, Slovakia, Spain, Sweden, Switzerland, UK.

NGO Relations Associate member of: *European Public Health Alliance (EPHA, #08297)*. Member of: *European Coalition on Homeopathic and Anthroposophic Medicinal Products (ECHAMP, #06595)*. Liaison Organization of: *Comité européen de normalisation (CEN, #04162)*. Affiliated with: *EUROCAM (#05653)*. [2020/XD4977/**D**]

♦ European Central Inland Transport Organization (inactive)

♦ European Central Securities Depositories Association (ECSDA) 06468

Secretariat 75 Rue Royale, 1040 Brussels, Belgium. T. +3222309901. E-mail: info@ecsda.eu.
URL: http://ecsda.eu/

History 18 Nov 1997, Madrid (Spain). Took over membership of *Central and Eastern European Central Securities Depositories Association (CEECSDA, inactive)* when it dissolved, 31 Dec 2005. Registration: Banque-Carrefour des Entreprises, Belgium; EU Transparency Register, No/ID: 92773882668-44. **Aims** Promote a constructive dialogue between the CSD community, European public authorities and other stakeholders aiming at contributing to an efficient and risk-averse infrastructure for European *financial* markets. **Structure** General Meeting (annual); Board of Directors; Executive Committee; Working Groups (6). **Languages** English, French. **Staff** 4.00 FTE, paid. **Finance** Sources: members' dues. **Activities** Politics/policy/regulatory. **Publications** Position papers; reports; joint papers.

Members Full; Associate. National and international (") Central Securities Depositories in 38 countries:
Austria, Belgium (*), Bosnia-Herzegovina, Bulgaria, Croatia, Cyprus, Czechia, Denmark, Estonia, Finland, France, Germany, Greece, Hungary, Iceland, Italy, Kazakhstan, Latvia, Lithuania, Luxembourg (*), Malta, Moldova, Montenegro, Netherlands, North Macedonia, Norway, Poland, Portugal, Romania, Serbia, Slovakia, Slovenia, Spain, Sweden, Switzerland, Türkiye, UK, Ukraine.

NGO Relations Accredited by (3): *Africa and Middle East Depositories Association (AMEDA, #00190)*; *Asia Pacific Central Securities Depository Group (ACG, #01866)*; *European Society of Association Executives (ESAE, #08526)*. Member of (1): *International Association of Trusted Blockchain Applications (INATBA)*. [2022.05.10/XD6639/**D**]

♦ European Centre for Advanced Research in Economics / see European Centre for Advanced Research in Economics and Statistics

♦ European Centre for Advanced Research in Economics and Statistics (internationally oriented national body)

♦ European Centre for Advanced Studies in Thermodynamics (ECAST) 06469

Centre européen de réflexion et d'étude en thermodynamique (CERET)

Contact LRGP-ENSIC, 1 rue Grandville, 54000 Nancy, France. T. +33383175258 – +333(33649244716. Fax +33383322975.

History 14 Mar 1989, Paris (France). Registered in accordance with French law. **Aims** Contribute to cooperation in Europe between those concerned in research, teaching, information and applications of thermodynamics. **Structure** Governing Board; Bureau. **Languages** English, French. **Finance** Members' dues. Grants. **Activities** Events/meetings; awards/prizes/competitions. **Events** *JETC : Joint European Thermodynamics Conference* Barcelona (Spain) 2019, *JETC : Joint European Thermodynamics Conference* Budapest (Hungary) 2017, *JETC : Joint European Thermodynamics Conference* Nancy (France) 2015, *JETC : Joint European Thermodynamics Conference* Brescia (Italy) 2013, *JETC : joint European thermodynamics conference* Chemnitz (Germany) 2011.

Members Individuals in 5 countries:
Belgium, France, Germany, Netherlands, Switzerland. [2017.10.31/XE1679/v/**E**]

♦ European Centre for Allergy Research Foundation (internationally oriented national body)

♦ European Centre for Architecture and Information and Communication Technologies (internationally oriented national body)

♦ European Centre for AstroParticle Theory (EuCAPT) 06470

Dir Inst for Theoretical Physics, Univ of Amsterdam, Science Park 904, Postbus 94485, 1090 GL Amsterdam, Netherlands. T. +31205257658.
Central hub c/o CERN, 1211 Geneva 23, Switzerland.

History Founded 10 Jul 2019, by *European Organization for Nuclear Research (CERN, #08108)* and *Astroparticle Physics European Consortium (APPEC, #02998)*. **Aims** Coordinate and promote *theoretical physics* in the fields of astroparticle physics and cosmology in Europe. **Structure** Steering Committee. [2019/XM8670/**E**]

♦ European Centre for Atomic and Molecular Computations 06471

Centre Européen de Calcul Atomique et Moléculaire (CECAM)

Dir Ecole Polytechnique Fédérale Lausanne, Batochime (BCH), 1015 Lausanne VD, Switzerland. T. +41216931977. Fax +41216931985. E-mail: helpdesk@cecam.org.
URL: http://www.cecam.org/

History Oct 1969, Paris (France). **Aims** Promote fundamental research in simulation and modelling in the fields of molecular and condensed matter physics and chemistry, materials science, bio- and medicinal chemistry and statistical mechanics. **Structure** Council; Board of Directors; Scientific Advisory Council. **Languages** English. **Staff** 14.00 FTE, paid; 17.00 FTE, voluntary. CECAM-HQ Administration: 6. **Finance** Sources: members' dues. Annual budget: 1,000,000 EUR. **Activities** Awards/prizes/competitions; events/meetings; networking/liaising; projects/programmes; research and development; research/documentation; training/education. **Events** *Workshop on Protein Dynamics* Les Houches (France) 2021, *Workshop on Rheology of Gel Networks* Lyon (France) 2017, *Workshop on Challenges across Large-Scale Biomolecular and Polymer Simulations* Vienna (Austria) 2017, *International Workshop on Biomembranes* Espoo (Finland) 2016, *Workshop on Water at Interfaces, from Proteins to Devices* Vienna (Austria) 2016.

Members Institutions (25) in 15 countries:
Austria, Belgium, China, Finland, France, Germany, Ireland, Israel, Italy, Netherlands, Slovenia, Spain, Sweden, Switzerland, UK.
Nodes (17) in 10 countries:
Austria, Finland, France, Germany, Ireland, Israel, Italy, Netherlands, Spain, UK. [2020.12.02/XJ3449/**E**]

♦ European Centre for Buildings Rehabilitation / see European Centre for Rehabilitation of Buildings

♦ European Centre for Burgundian Research / see European Association of Burgundy Studies (#05960)

♦ European Centre for Business Innovation (internationally oriented national body)

♦ European Centre of Chemical Manufacturers' Federations (inactive)

♦ European Centre for Conflict Prevention / see Global Partnership for the Prevention of Armed Conflict Foundation

♦ European Centre for Conflict Prevention / see Global Partnership for the Prevention of Armed Conflict (#10538)

♦ European Centre for Conflict Prevention and Resolution / see Global Partnership for the Prevention of Armed Conflict Foundation

♦ European Centre for Conservation, Restoration and Renovation / see European Centre for Restoration Techniques

♦ European Centre for Continuing Education / see European Centre for Executive Development (#06479)

♦ European Centre for Corporate Engagement / see European Center for Sustainable Finance

♦ European Centre for Culture (ECC) 06472

Centre européen de la culture (CEC) – Centro Europeo de la Cultura – Europäisches Kulturzentrum (EKZ)

Main Office 40 rue Le-Corbusier, 1208 Geneva, Switzerland. T. +41227106600. Fax +41227880409. E-mail: info@ceculture.org.
URL: http://www.ceculture.org/

History 7 Oct 1950, Geneva (Switzerland). Founded by Denis de Rougemont and Raymond Silva and under the auspices of *European Movement International (EMI, #07825)*, following decision of the EM Congress, May 1948, The Hague (Netherlands), and as successor to *Bureau d'études pour un Centre européen de la culture*, set up Feb 1949. Current statutes adopted 21 Mar 1986. Statutes revised 28 Mar 1996. Ceased to exist Dec 2001 due to lack of finance, with 'Euroateliers', the educational workshops on European citizenship and on democracy continue to take place. Revived when current statutes adopted 26 May 2003. Former names and other names: *European Cultural Centre* – alias. Registration: Switzerland. **Aims** Identify the content of the common culture of Europeans in its unity and diversity; foster this cultural diversity in the united Europe; strengthen dialogue between European culture and the other cultures of the world; unite European cultural forces, providing a meeting place and means of coordination; study theoretical and practical problems posed by *cultural pluralism*; consider the interaction between *tradition* and *innovation* in the field of culture in the broadest sense; promote cultural exchanges with similar centres in other regions; promote dialogue between world cultures and on *civic* education. **Structure** General Assembly (at least twice a year). Board of Directors consisting of: President, Vice-President, Public Relations Officer, Programmes Officer, Members and correspondents Officer, Legal matters Officer, Finance Officer, 3 Members and 5 Associate Members. International Secretariat, comprising Executive President, Secretary-General and Administrator. **Languages** English, French, German. **Staff** 10.00 FTE, paid. **Finance** Sources: Government subsidies; private funds; subscriptions; sale of publications; grants from official and private bodies; gifts. Budget (annual): euro 800,000.

Activities Main topics of interest: the ultimate aims and values of European culture; future of regions within a federated Europe; future of Europe in a changing world; federalist approach; East-West and trans-Atlantic inter-cultural dialogues; dialogue between cultures; historical and cultural studies; employment, unemployment and leisure. Main programmes: publications; support for *'Intercultures'* (intercultural cooperation programmes); organization of *'Euroforums'* and of *'Euroateliers'* (educational workshops on European citizenship and on democracy); studies and research. Created or helped to create:
– *College of Europe (#04105)*, 1949, Bruges (Belgium);
– *European Festivals Association (EFA, #07242)*, 5 Dec 1951, Geneva (Switzerland), which the Centre manages;
– *European Council for Nuclear Research (CERN, inactive)*, 15 Feb 1952, following European Cultural Conference, 1949, Lausanne (Switzerland), which subsequently became, 28 Sep 1954, Paris (France),
– *European Organization for Nuclear Research (CERN, #08108)*;
– *European Association for the Education of Adults (EAEA, #06018)*, 1953, Geneva;
– *European Cultural Foundation (ECF, #06868)*, 16 Dec 1954, Geneva;
– *European Institute of the University of Geneva (inactive)*, 1963, Geneva;
– *Campagne d'éducation civique européenne (no recent information)*, 1960, directed by the European Communities from 1975 to 1980 and subsequently relaunched, 1986, by the Centre;
– *European Archives Centre (inactive)*, 10 Jul 1984, Geneva.

Events *Psychological and cultural aspects of European currency* 1998, *Intercultures* Brasov (Romania) 1997, *Forum of local and regional media* Trento (Italy) 1997, *Euroforum* Geneva (Switzerland) 1996, *Symposium on regionalism, federalism, ecologism / General Assembly and Symposium* Barcelona (Spain) 1995. **Publications** *Temps européens* (4 a year) in French – magazine; *ECC Newsletter* (2 a year) in English, French; *Festivals* (annual); *Season* (annual). *L'Europe en bref* – series (20 to date), paperback reference books and interactive IT programmes. **Members** Individuals; institutions, public organizations and companies, notably the national and international cultural institutions founded by the Centre. Membership countries not specified. **NGO Relations** Member of: *Fédération des Institutions Internationales établies à Genève (FIIG, #09599)*; *International Federation of Europe Houses (FIME, inactive)*; *Permanent Forum of European Civil Society (#18322)*. Adhering body of: *Robert Schuman Institute for Europe (IRSE, #18959)*. [2015/XD0703/**D**]

♦ European Centre for Democracy and Human Rights (unconfirmed)

♦ European Centre for Development Policy Management (ECDPM) . . . 06473

Centre européen de gestion des politiques de développement

Dir Head Office, Onze Lieve Vrouweplein 21, 6211 HE Maastricht, Netherlands. T. +31433502900. E-mail: info@ecdpm.org – sm@ecdpm.org.
Brussels Office Rue Archimède 5, 1000 Brussels, Belgium. T. +3222374310.
URL: http://www.ecdpm.org/

History 1986. Founded within the framework of cooperation between the European Communities and the African, Caribbean and the Pacific (ACP) group of countries. Registration: Netherlands; EU Transparency Register, No/ID: 738492215435-82. **Aims** Make policies in Europe and Africa work for inclusive and sustainable development. **Structure** Board of Governors; Board Executive Committee; Management Team; Director. **Languages** English, French. **Staff** 65.00 FTE, paid. **Finance** Sources: government support; revenue from activities/projects. **Activities** Events/meetings; guidance/assistance/consulting; knowledge management/information dissemination; networking/liaising; research/documentation; training/education. **Events** *Europe-wide global education congress* Maastricht (Netherlands) 2002. **Publications** *ECDPM Weekly Compass Newsletter* (weekly); *Great Insights* (4 a year). Discussion papers; policy papers; briefs; blogs. [2020.05.19/XF1236/**E**]

♦ European Centre for the Development of Vocational Training (Cedefop) 06474

Centre européen pour le développement de la formation professionnelle (Cedefop) – Centro Europeo para el Desarrollo de la Formación Profesional – Europäisches Zentrum für die Förderung der Berufsbildung – Centro Europeu para o Desenvolvimento da Formação Profissional – Centro Europeo per lo Sviluppo della Formazione Professionale – Europees Centrum voor de Ontwikkeling van de Beroepsopleiding – Europeiskt Centrum för Utveckling av Yrkesutbildning – Europaeiske Center for Udvikling af Erhvervsuddannelse – Euroopan Ammatillisen Koulutuksen Kehittämiskeskus

Headquarters Service post, Europe 123, 570 01 Thessaloniki, Greece. T. +302310490111. Fax +302310490049. E-mail: info@cedefop.europa.eu.
Brussels Office c/o European Commission, Rue de Spa 3 SPA3 04/94, 4th floor, Office 94, 1049 Brussels, Belgium. T. +3222991093.
URL: http://www.cedefop.europa.eu/

History 10 Feb 1975. Set up as an organization of the European Communities, by Regulation 337/75 of *Council of the European Union (#04895)*. Serves as one of the decentralized agencies set up by the *European Union (EU, #08967)* within the framework of *Treaty on European Union (Maastricht Treaty, 1992)* to carry out specialized technical or scientific work on a wide range of subjects. Linked closely with DG EMPL – DG for Employment, Social Affairs and Inclusion. **Aims** Support development of European vocational education and training (VET) in policies and contribute to their implementation. **Structure** Tripartite Governing Board, consisting 27 representatives of the governments of the Member States; 27 representatives of employers' organizations;

27 representatives of trade union organizations; 6 representatives of the Commission, appointed for a 3-year term, plus observers from Iceland and Norway. Director, appointed by the Commission for a 5-year term, renewable once. **Languages** EU languages. **Staff** 119.00 FTE, paid. **Finance** Sources: grants. Supported by: *European Commission (EC, #06633)*. **Activities** Awareness raising; guidance/assistance/consulting; knowledge management/information dissemination; networking/liaising; politics/policy/regulatory. **Events** *Brussels Seminar* Brussels (Belgium) 2022, *Youth first! Employment, skills and social policies that work for young Europeans in times of uncertainty* Brussels (Belgium) 2022, *ReferNet Annual Plenary Meeting* Thessaloniki (Greece) 2021, *Brussels Seminar* Brussels (Belgium) 2020, *Policy Learning Forum on Upskilling Pathways* Brussels (Belgium) 2020. **Publications** *Cedefop Newsletter*. Annual Report; flyers; briefing notes; research papers; country specific reports, data visualizations. https://www.cedefop.europa.eu/en/publications-and-resources. **Information Services** *VET-Bib* – Bibliographical database; *VET in Europe* – Overview of EU vocational education and training systems..

Members Member States of the European Union (27) send representatives to CEDEFOP's Governing Board:
Austria, Belgium, Bulgaria, Croatia, Cyprus, Czechia, Denmark, Estonia, Finland, France, Germany, Greece, Hungary, Ireland, Italy, Latvia, Lithuania, Luxembourg, Malta, Netherlands, Poland, Portugal, Romania, Slovakia, Slovenia, Spain, Sweden.
Observers from 2 countries:
Iceland, Norway.

IGO Relations Close and institutional links with: *European Commission (EC, #06633)*; *European Court of Auditors (#06854)*; *European Economic and Social Committee (EESC, #06963)*; *European Foundation for the Improvement of Living and Working Conditions (Eurofound, #07348)*; *European Labour Authority (ELA, #07635)*; *European Parliament (EP, #08146)*; *European Training Foundation (ETF, #08934)*. Scientific Advisor to: *European Quality Assurance in Vocational Education and Training (EQAVET, #08312)*. Contacts within the framework of the Work Programme with: *Council of Europe (CE, #04881)*; *ILO (#11123)*; *UNESCO (#20322)*.
NGO Relations Member of (1): *EU Agencies Network (EUAN, #05564)*. Library is member of: *Eurolib (#05703)*; *International Council on Archives (ICA, #12996)*. [2022.10.11/XE5357/**E***]

♦ European Centre for Digital Resources in Chinese Studies (internationally oriented national body)
♦ European Centre for Disaster Awareness with the Use of Internet, Cyprus (internationally oriented national body)

♦ European Centre for Disaster Medicine 06475

Centre européen pour la médecine des catastrophes – Centro Europeo para la Medicina de Catastrofes – Centro Europeo per la Medicina delle Catastrofi (CEMEC)

Main Office Via Scialoja 1, 47893 Cailungo, San Marino. T. +3780549994535. Fax +3780549903706. E-mail: cemec@iss.sm – cemec.info@iss.sm.
URL: http://www.cemec-sanmarino.eu/

History 27 Nov 1986, San Marino (San Marino). Operational from Oct 1987. One of the *'European Network of Specialist Centres'* of *Open Partial Agreement on the Prevention of, Protection against and Organization of Relief in Major Natural and Technological Disasters (EUR-OPA Major Hazards Agreement, #17762)*, in the overall framework of the *Council of Europe (CE, #04881)*. **Aims** Promote and develop training and research in the field of disaster medicine aimed at health personnel and volunteers involved with *emergency* situations. **Structure** General Assembly. Board of Directors; Scientific Committee. Officers: President; President of the Scientific Committee; Secretary General. **Languages** English, French, Italian. **Staff** 2.00 FTE, paid. **Activities** *'Training'*: European Master in Disaster Medicine (EMDM) – one-year post-university course reserved for doctors, in collaboration with universities of San Marino, Novara and Brussels; intensive courses on disaster medicine; international seminars and congresses; courses specific to veterinary actions in disasters; courses on ethical and psychological aspects of disasters. *'Research'* activities carried out in cooperation with other European specialized centres and other international organizations: /Child Trauma Network/. *'MID Project'* – tele mental health system adapting space telecommunications systems to enhance mental healthcare systems for populations affected by psychological and psychiatric trauma. **Events** *EUSEM Congress* San Marino (San Marino) 1998, *International symposium* San Marino (San Marino) 1996, *European conference on gender approaches to health in emergency situations* San Marino (San Marino) 1995. **Publications** *Le onde elettromagnetiche: rischi e certezze* (2001); *Advanced in Clinical Toxicology* (1997, 1998); *Accidental Radiation and Nuclear Emergencies* (1995); *Health and Medical Implications of a Nuclear Emergency* (1995); *Toxicological Emergencies* (1995); *Emergency Care* (1994); *Early Health Measures in Maxi-Emergencies* (1993); *Public Health in Disaster Medicine*; *The Evolution of Disaster Medicine*. Proceedings. **Information Services** *EMER-CHEM Project* – data base on computerized management of hazardous material incidents.

Members Full in 21 countries:
Albania, Algeria, Bangladesh, Belgium, Bulgaria, China, Egypt, France, Greece, India, Israel, Italy, Japan, Lebanon, Morocco, Netherlands, Spain, Sweden, Switzerland, Tunisia, USA.

IGO Relations A *WHO (#20950)* Collaborating Centre. *WHO (#20950)*. Cooperates with: Council of Europe; United Nations Department of Humanitarian Affairs. **NGO Relations** Adviser and regional training centre: *Euro-Mediterranean Council for Burns and Fire Disaster (MBC, #05719)*. [2016/XD1543/**E***]

♦ European Centre for Disease Prevention and Control (ECDC) 06476

Centre européen de prévention et de contrôle des maladies – Centro Europeo para la Prevención y el Control de las Enfermedades – Europäischen Zentrum für die Prävention und die Kontrolle von Krankheiten – Centro Europeu de Prevenção e Controlo das Doenças – Centro Europeo per la Prevenzione e il Controllo delle Malattie – Europees Centrum voor Ziektepreventie en -bestrijding – Europeiskt Centrum för Förebyggande och Kontroll av Sjukdomar – Europaeisk Center for Forebyggelse af og Kontrol med Sygdomme

Main Office Gustav III boulevard 40, SE-169 73 Solna, Sweden. T. +46858601000. Fax +46858601001. E-mail: info@ecdc.europa.eu.
Main: https://ecdc.europa.eu/

History 21 Apr 2004. Established by Regulation (EC) No 851/2004 of the *European Parliament (EP, #08146)* and of the *Council of the European Union (#04895)*. Became operational May 2005, Stockholm (Sweden). A decentralized agency of *European Union (EU, #08967)*. **Aims** Strengthen Europe's defences against infectious diseases by identifying, assessing and communicating current and emerging threats to human health. **Structure** Management Board; Advisory Forum; Director; Units (5). Includes the following surveillance networks: *European Antimicrobial Resistance Surveillance Network (EARS-Net, #05907)*; *European Diphtheria Surveillance Network (EDSN, #06927)*; *European Food- and Waterborne Disease and Zoonoses Surveillance Network (FWD-Net)*; *European Influenza Surveillance Network (EISN, #07532)*; *European Invasive Bacterial Diseases Surveillance Network (EU-IBD, #07598)*; *European Legionnaires' Disease Surveillance Network (ELDSNet, #07681)*; *European Network for HIV/AIDS Surveillance (#07923)*; *European Network for STI Surveillance (#08015)*; *European Tuberculosis Surveillance Network (#08954)*; *Healthcare-associated Infections Network (HAI-Net)*. **Languages** EU languages. **Activities** Capacity building; events/meetings; guidance/assistance/consulting; publishing activities; training/education. **Events** *ONE – Health Environment and Society Conference* Brussels (Belgium) 2022, *ESCAIDE : European Scientific Conference on Applied Infectious Disease Epidemiology* Stockholm (Sweden) 2022, *ESCAIDE : European Scientific Conference on Applied Infectious Disease Epidemiology* 2021, *ESCAIDE : European Scientific Conference on Applied Infectious Disease Epidemiology* Warsaw (Poland) 2020, *ESCAIDE : European Scientific Conference on Applied Infectious Disease Epidemiology* Stockholm (Sweden) 2019. **Publications** *Eurosurveillance* (weekly) – scientific journal. Scientific, technical and meeting reports; brochures.

Members All 27 EU Member States and the 3 EEA Member States (*):
Austria, Belgium, Bulgaria, Croatia, Cyprus, Czechia, Denmark, Estonia, Finland, France, Germany, Greece, Hungary, Iceland (*), Ireland, Italy, Latvia, Liechtenstein (*), Lithuania, Luxembourg, Malta, Netherlands, Norway (*), Poland, Portugal, Romania, Slovakia, Slovenia, Spain, Sweden.

IGO Relations Audited by: *European Court of Auditors (#06854)*. **NGO Relations** Member of (1): *EU Agencies Network (EUAN, #05564)*. Represented on Advisory Forum: *European Patients' Forum (EPF, #08172)*; *European Public Health Association (EUPHA, #08298)*; *European Society of Clinical Microbiology and Infectious Diseases (ESCMID, #08548)*; *Pharmaceutical Group of the European Union (PGEU, #18352)*; *Standing Committee of European Doctors (#19955)*. [2022.10.14/XJ3125/**E***]

♦ European Centre of Documentation and Compensation (inactive)
♦ European Centre for Ecological and Agricultural Tourism (inactive)

♦ European Centre for Ecotoxicology and Toxicology of Chemicals (ECETOC) 06477

Centre européen d'écotoxicologie et de toxicologie des produits chimiques

SG Rue Belliard 40, 1040 Brussels, Belgium. T. +3226753600. E-mail: info@ecetoc.org.
URL: http://www.ecetoc.org/

History 1978, Brussels (Belgium). Statutes most recently modified, 3 June 2020, Brussels (Belgium). Former names and other names: *European Chemical Industry Ecology and Toxicology Centre* – former; *Centre d'écologie et de toxicologie de l'industrie chimique européenne* – former. Registration: No/ID: 0418.344.469, Start date: 6 Mar 1978, Belgium; EU Transparency Register, No/ID: 446308349108-12, Start date: 16 Feb 2023. **Aims** Secure scientific evaluation of toxicological and ecotoxicological data affecting the chemical industry. **Structure** General Assembly (annual) always in Brussels (Belgium); Executive Board; Scientific Committee; Task Forces. **Languages** English. **Staff** 5.00 FTE, paid. **Finance** Sources: members' dues. Annual budget: 1,500,000 EUR. **Activities** Networking/liaising; research/documentation. **Events** *Annual General Meeting* Brussels (Belgium) 2022, *LRI Human Health Progress Review and Scoping Meeting* Brussels (Belgium) 2020, *LRI Human Health Progress Review and Scoping Meeting* Brussels (Belgium) 2019, *Annual Meeting* Brussels (Belgium) 2018, *LRI Human Health Progress Review and Scoping Meeting* Brussels (Belgium) 2018. **Publications** Annual Report; monographs; technical reports on toxicity, ecotoxicity and specific chemicals.

Members Full (30); Associate (5). Members in 11 countries:
Belgium, France, Germany, Italy, Japan, Netherlands, Norway, Spain, Switzerland, UK, USA.

NGO Relations Member of (1): *Network of Reference Laboratories for Monitoring of Emerging Environmental Pollutants (NORMAN Network, #17053)*. Cooperates with (1): *Conseil européen de l'industrie chimique (CEFIC, #04687)*. [2023/XE6634/**E**]

♦ European Centre for Educational Resilience and Socio-Emotional Health / see Centre for Resilience and Socio-Emotional Health (#03783)

♦ European Centre for Electoral Support (ECES) 06478

Head of Programmes Av Louise 222, 1050 Brussels, Belgium. T. +3223255558. Fax +3225026630. E-mail: info@eces.eu.
Exec Dir address not obtained.
URL: https://www.eces.eu/en/

History Sep 2010. Launched, Dec 2010, when first President of management board, Abbot Apollinaire Mulhongo Malu Malu, was invited to attend the European Development Days. Initiative from Fabio Bargiacchi, 1997, after participation in a mission in Bosnia organized by *Organization for Security and Cooperation in Europe (OSCE, #17887)*. Registration: Banque-Carrefour des Entreprises, No/ID: 0829.998:514, Start date: 6 Oct 2010, Belgium; EU Transparency Register, No/ID: 578467420707-73, Start date: 17 Feb 2016. **Aims** Promote sustainable democratic development through provision of advisory services, operational support and management of large projects in the electoral and democracy assistance field; continue to be the reference not-for-profit private European organisation to implement electoral support projects in line with the values and policies of the European Union and its Member states in the context of their development cooperation with their partner countries; support the partner countries of the EU and of its Member States to organize their electoral processes in a credible and transparent manner as the best contribution to prevent electoral conflicts and to promote stability toward inclusiveness and fair societies. **Structure** Management Board; Management Unit; Quality Support Management Cell; Coordination, External Relations and Communications Cell. Sections (3): Administration and Finance; Programs and Resources Mobilization; Operations and Project Implementation. **Languages** English, French, German, Italian, Portuguese, Spanish, Swedish. **Staff** 200.00 FTE, paid. **Finance** Sources: contributions; donations; grants. Supported by: *Australian Aid (inactive)*; EU Member States; *European Union (EU, #08967)*; *Organisation internationale de la Francophonie (OIF, #17809)*; *Swiss Agency for Development and Cooperation (SDC)*; *United States Agency for International Development (USAID)*; Universities. Annual budget: 8,954,847 EUR (2020). URL: https://www.eces.eu/en/funding-and-cocontributions **Activities** Awareness raising; capacity building; certification/accreditation; conflict resolution; events/meetings; financial and/or material support; knowledge management/information dissemination; monitoring/evaluation; politics/policy/regulatory; projects/programmes; standards/guidelines; training/education. Active in all member countries. **Publications** Copyrights; Guides; Handbooks. **NGO Relations** Member of: GEO Conference Steering Committee. Partner of: Central African School for Electoral Administration (EFEAC). [2021/XJ6402/**E**]

♦ European Centre of Employers and Enterprises of Public Services / see SGI Europe (#19253)
♦ European Centre of Employers and Enterprises of Public Services and of Services of General Interest / see SGI Europe (#19253)
♦ European Centre of Enterprises with Public Participation / see SGI Europe (#19253)
♦ European Centre of Enterprises with Public Participation and of Enterprises of General Economic Interest / see SGI Europe (#19253)
♦ European Centre for Ethnic and Regional Studies – University of Maribor (internationally oriented national body)
♦ European Centre for Ethnolinguistic Cartography (#03744)
♦ **European Centre** European Centre for Social Welfare Policy and Research (#06500)

♦ European Centre for Executive Development (CEDEP) 06479

Centre européen d'éducation permanente

Pres bd de Constance, 77300 Fontainebleau, France. T. +33164694444. Fax +33164227731. E-mail: info@cedep.fr.
Contact address not obtained.
URL: http://www.cedep.fr/

History 18 Nov 1971, Fontainebleau (France), as *Centre for Executive Development (CEDEP)* by 6 European companies, as an independent centre associated with *INSEAD (#11228)*. Also previously known as *European Centre for Continuing Education – Centre européen d'éducation permanente – Europäische Weiterbildungszentrum*. Registered in accordance to Belgian law. **Aims** Provide partner companies with *management* programmes, encouraging development of their managers.

Members Companies (27) in the industrial and services sectors in 8 countries:
Belgium, Denmark, France, India, Netherlands, Spain, UK, USA.

NGO Relations Member of: *EFMD – The Management Development Network (#05387)*. [2020/XE2613/**E**]

♦ European Centre for Federalist Action (inactive)
♦ European Centre on Forest Fires (internationally oriented national body)

♦ EUROPEAN CENTRE FOR INFORMATION POLICY and SECURITY (ECIPS) 06480

Pres address not obtained. T. +447493803249. E-mail: secretary-general@ecips.eu.
URL: https://www.ecips.eu/

History Originally set up 2013, UK. Relocated to Belgium, 2015. Registered in accordance with Belgian law as an international organization, Jun 2015: 634898256. **Aims** Ensure and promote mutual international assistance between all European organizations in the chain of Policy, Information, Security and Justice, which needs re-enforcement by creating both, a platform and policies, for innovative practices in the domain of Justice and Home Affairs (JHA). **Structure** *International Information Policy and Security Council (IIPSC)*; Executive Committee; General Secretariat; National Central Bureau; Advisory Board; Commission for the Control of Records. **Languages** Dutch, English, French. **Staff** 2000.00 FTE, paid. Reserve Force Officers: 56,000. **Finance** Members' dues. Proceeds through public activities. **Activities** Knowledge management/information dissemination; publishing activities. **Publications** Reports; summit proceedings.

Members States to which the provisions of Article 47 of the Statute of Membership shall apply (28):
Austria, Belgium, Bulgaria, Croatia, Cyprus, Czechia, Denmark, Estonia, Finland, France, Germany, Greece, Hungary, Ireland, Italy, Latvia, Lithuania, Luxembourg, Malta, Netherlands, Poland, Portugal, Romania, Slovakia, Slovenia, Spain, Sweden, UK. [2019.02.13/XM4386/**D**]

♦ European Centre for the French Language (internationally oriented national body)
♦ European Centre on Geodynamic Hazards of High Dams (internationally oriented national body)

♦ European Centre for Geodynamic and Morphodynamic Hazards, Strasbourg / see European Centre on Geomorphological Hazards (#06482)
♦ European Centre on Geodynamic Risks of High Dams / see European Centre on Geodynamic Hazards of High Dams

♦ European Centre for Geodynamics and Seismology (ECGS) 06481

Centre européen de géodynamique et de séismologie (CEGS)

Chairman 19 rue Josy Welter, L-7256 Walferdange, Luxembourg. T. +3523314871. Fax +35233148788. E-mail: info@ecgs.lu.
URL: http://www.ecgs.lu/

History 13 Jun 1988, within the framework of *Open Partial Agreement on the Prevention of, Protection against and Organization of Relief in Major Natural and Technological Disasters (EUR-OPA Major Hazards Agreement, #17762)*, under an agreement including signatories from 9 countries, *European Commission (EC, #06633)* and *Council of Europe (CE, #04881)*. **Aims** Develop European cooperation in scientific research in geodynamics and seismology, applied to the prevention of natural disasters, being earthquakes and volcanic eruptions. **Activities** Studies tectonic deformation in relation to seismology, using GPS and absolute gravity measurement. **Events** *Workshop on Earthquake Source Physics on Various Scales* Luxembourg (Luxembourg) 2012, *Seismicity patterns in the Euro-Med region* Luxembourg (Luxembourg) 2008, *Seth Chandler Wobble workshop* Luxembourg (Luxembourg) 2004, *Instrumentation and metrology in gravimetry* Luxembourg (Luxembourg) 2002, *Workshop on non-linear dynamics and earthquake predictions* Trieste (Italy) 1997. [2021/XE1071/**E***]

♦ European Centre on Geomorphological Hazards 06482

Centre Européen sur les Risques Géomorphologiques (CERG)

Main Office 3 rue de l'Argonne, 67083 Strasbourg, France. T. +33390240943. Fax +33390240900.

History 1988. Established as one of the *'European Network of Specialist Centres'* of *Open Partial Agreement on the Prevention of, Protection against and Organization of Relief in Major Natural and Technological Disasters (EUR-OPA Major Hazards Agreement, #17762)*, within the framework of the *Council of Europe (CE, #04881)*, on the initiative of Jean-Claude Flageollet (1931-2014). Former names and other names: *European Centre for Geodynamic and Morphodynamic Hazards, Strasbourg (ECGDH)* – former alias; *Centre européen sur les risques géo- et morphodynamiques, Strasbourg (CERD)* – former alias; *European Centre for Seismic and Geomorphological Hazards (CESG)* – former. Registration: France. **Aims** Develop multidisciplinary research in the field of geo-morphological and geo-hydrological hazards; disseminate methodology and techniques through advanced training courses and guidebooks; promote scientific and technical cooperation between CERG European members and exterior individuals or organizations. **Structure** General Assembly (annual). Executive Committee, comprising President, Vice-President, 3 Advisory Members, Executive Secretary and Deputy Executive Secretary. **Finance** Since 1988, research programmes supported by: *European Community (inactive)* and Council of Europe. Occasionally also supported by national research programmes and other administrations. **Activities** *'Training'*: Training School on Risk Management; European Intensive Summer Courses; Post-Graduate Training School; Master of Sciences "Natural and Man-Made Risks"; Be-Safe-Net website; implementation of didactic materials on geomorphological hazards. *'Research'*: seisme and landslides; inventory of existing databases on landslides; floods and muddy slurries; risk management in the framework of ADRIM and STRIM programmes; Earthquake-induced Landslides in the NW Apennines Programme; Debris Flows Modelling Programme; risk management. *'Other'*: programmes – Epoch; Teslec; Newtech; Alarm; supports preparation of EU proposals for members; technical expertises. *European-Mediterranean Seismological Centre (EMSC, #07774)* pinpoints the parameters of major earthquakes occurring in the Europe/Mediterranean region and gathers and disseminates information. *European Centre for Geomorphological Research (ECGH, no recent information)* develops and coordinates research programmes and training schemes in the field of landslides and erosion disasters, especially earthquake-induced, with a view to prevention and inclusion in alert system arrangements. Special unit promotes international cooperation for earthquake study. **Publications** *Geological and Geomorphological Studies in Seismic Hazard Assessment for Territorial Planning* (2000); *Occupation du sol et réponse hydrologique: utilisation de la télédétection* (1998). Symposia proceedings. **Members** Active; Corresponding researchers (75), including geologists, geomorphologists, engineering geologists, hydrologists and geotechnicians, in 23 laboratories and research centres of 14 European countries (not specified). [2016/XE1884/**E***]

♦ European Centre for Gerontological Documentation and Research (inactive)
♦ European Centre of Gerontology (internationally oriented national body)

♦ European Centre for Global Interdependence and Solidarity (North-South Centre) 06483

Centre européen pour l'interdépendance et la solidarité mondiales (Centre Nord-Sud) – Centro Europeu para a Interdependência e Solidariedade Globais

Exec Dir Rua de Sao Caetano 32, 1200-829 Lisbon, Portugal. T. +351213584030. Fax +351213584037 – +351213584072. E-mail: nscinfo@coe.int – rozenn.hemon@coe.int.
Chair address not obtained.
URL: http://www.nscentre.org/

History May 1989, Lisbon (Portugal). Set up by agreement of the Committee of Ministers of the *Council of Europe (CE, #04881)*, as an "Enlarged Partial Agreement", to enable member states to continue cooperation established during the *European Public Campaign on North-South Interdependence and Solidarity (North South Campaign)*, 1988. Commenced activities in May 1990. Abbreviated title: *North-South Centre of the Council of Europe – Centre Nord-Sud du Conseil de l'Europe – Centro Norte-Sul do Conselho da Europa.* Also referred to as: *European Centre for Global Interdependence and Solidarity of the Council of Europe (North-South Centre).* Also known under the acronym *NSC*. **Aims** Promote dialogue between North and South, fostering solidarity and raising awareness of global *interdependence*. **Structure** Executive Committee; Bureau; Secretariat, headed by Executive Director. **Languages** English, French. **Staff** 10.00 FTE, paid. **Finance** Member states' contributions according to GNP and population. Other sources: voluntary contributions from Member States or external partners. Annual budget: euro 705,000. **Activities** Training/education; awards/prizes/competitions; events/meetings; knowledge management/information dissemination. **Events** *World Forum on Intercultural Dialogue* Baku (Azerbaijan) 2019, *World Forum on Intercultural Dialogue* Baku (Azerbaijan) 2017, *World Forum on Intercultural Dialogue* Baku (Azerbaijan) 2015, *World Forum on Intercultural Dialogue* Baku (Azerbaijan) 2013, *World Forum on Intercultural Dialogue* Baku (Azerbaijan) 2011. **Publications** *One World Our World* – newsletter. Reports.

Members Governments of 21 countries:
Algeria, Andorra, Azerbaijan, Bosnia-Herzegovina, Bulgaria, Cape Verde, Croatia, Cyprus, Greece, Holy See, Liechtenstein, Luxembourg, Malta, Montenegro, Morocco, Portugal, Romania, San Marino, Serbia, Spain, Tunisia. [2022/XE3001/**E***]

♦ European Centre for Global Interdependence and Solidarity of the Council of Europe / see European Centre for Global Interdependence and Solidarity (#06483)
♦ European Centre for Health Policy (see: #20945)
♦ European Centre on Health of Societies in Transition / see ECOHOST – The Centre for Health and Social Change

♦ European Centre for Heritage Crafts and Professions 06484

Centre européen pour les métiers du patrimoine – Europäisches Zentrum für Die Berufe in der Denkmalpflege – Centro Europeo per i Mestieri del Patrimonio

Dir Via Trieste 43, 36016 Thiene VICENZA, Italy. T. +39445372329. E-mail: centroeuropeo@villafabris.eu.
URL: http://www.villafabris.eu/

History 1976, Venice (Italy). Established within the framework of *Council of Europe (CE, #04881)*. Former names and other names: *European Centre for Training Craftsmen in the Conservation of the Architectural Heritage* – former; *Centre européen de formation d'artisans pour la conservation du patrimoine architectural* – former; *Europäisches Ausbildungszentrum für Handwerker im Denkmalschutz* – former; *Centro Europeo di Formazione degli Artigiani per la Conservazione del Patrimonio Architettonico* – former; *Venice European Centre for the Skills of Architectural Heritage Conservation* – former; *Venice European Centre for the Trades and Professions of the Conservation of Architectural Heritage* – former; *Centre européen de Venise pour les métiers de la conservation du patrimoine architectural* – former; *Europäisches Zentrum Venedig für die Berufe in der Denkmalpflege* – former; *Centro Europeo di Venezia per i Mestieri della Conservazione del Patrimonio Architettonico* – former. **Aims** Offer training in the field of *restoration* and handicrafts; consolidate and develop activities at national and international levels. **Structure** Since 2008, located at Villa Fabris, Venice (Italy). **Languages** English, French, German, Italian. **Finance** Sources: contributions; government support; international organizations; private foundations. Annual budget: 516,460 EUR. **Activities** Events/meetings; projects/programmes; training/education. [2021.03.09/XF0197/t/**E***]

♦ European Centre for Humanitarian Health (internationally oriented national body)
♦ European Centre for Information on the Irradiation of Foodstuffs (inactive)
♦ European Centre for Information on Marine Science and Technology (internationally oriented national body)
♦ European Centre for Innovative Textiles (unconfirmed)

♦ European Centre of the International Council of Women (ECICW) .. 06485

Centre européen du Conseil international des femmes (CECIF)

Acting Pres address not obtained. E-mail: cecif.ecicw@gmail.com – president@ecicw-cecif.eu.
URL: http://www.icw-cif.com/

History 1961, Axenstein (Switzerland). Founded as a regional group of *International Council of Women (ICW, #13093)*. New Constitution adopted 15 Mar 2002, Malta. Registration: Start date: Jun 2002, France. **Aims** Achieve *equal rights* and opportunities for women and men in all fields of society; empower women to make their voices heard and promote their participation in *decision-making* at national and European levels; work for *peace* and defend *human rights*; build networks for cooperation between women's organizations in East and West European countries; study and monitor questions relating to the situation of women in Europe; present motions and statements and respond to initiatives from various European-level authorities. **Structure** General Assembly (2 a year); Board; Working Groups (3). **Finance** Sources: members' dues. **Activities** Events/meetings; training/education. Areas include: prevention of trafficking in women; housing; poverty; fair trade; pensions; social security; health; the environment; equality; refugees; ageing; osteoporosis; violence against children; violence against women and other areas of the Beijing (China) Platform for Action. Representatives report to member organizations. Contributed to *Charter of Fundamental Rights of the European Union (2000)*; has made proposals to the Constitutional Treaty of the Union. **Events** *General Assembly* Athens (Greece) 2006, *General Assembly* Kiev (Ukraine) 2006, *General Assembly* Freiburg (Germany) 2005, *General Assembly* Kiev (Ukraine) 2005, *General Assembly* Ukraine 2005.

Members National Councils in 29 member countries:
Austria, Azerbaijan, Belgium, Denmark, Finland, France, Germany, Greece, Hungary, Israel, Italy, Lebanon, Lithuania, Luxembourg, Malta, Monaco, Morocco, Netherlands, North Macedonia, Northern Cyprus, Romania, Russia, Slovenia, Spain, Switzerland, Tunisia, Türkiye, UK, Ukraine.

Consultative Status Consultative status granted from: *Council of Europe (CE, #04881)* (Participatory Status).
IGO Relations *European Commission (EC, #06633)*; *European Food Safety Authority (EFSA, #07287)*; *Comité directeur pour l'égalité entre les femmes et les hommes (CDEG, inactive)*. Participant in Fundamental Rights Platform of: *European Union Agency for Fundamental Rights (FRA, #08969)*. **NGO Relations** Founding member of: *European Women's Lobby (EWL, #09102)*. Signatory to Founding Statement of: *Alliance for Lobbying Transparency and Ethics Regulation (ALTER-EU, #00705)*. Representatives take part in activities of: EWL. [2022.10.19/XE5691/**E**]

♦ European Centre for International Political Economy (ECIPE) 06486

Dir Avenue des Arts 40, 1040 Brussels, Belgium. T. +3222891350. Fax +3222891359. E-mail: info@ecipe.org.
Stockholm Office Box 576, Frejgatan 13, SE-114 79 Stockholm, Sweden.
URL: http://ecipe.org/

History 2006, by Fredrik Erixon and Razeen Sally. EU Transparency Register: 954230536257-09. **Aims** Carry out research on *trade* policy and other international economic policy issues of importance to Europe. **Structure** Board of Trustees. **Finance** Base funding from Free Enterprise Foundation (Sweden). **Events** *Seminar on Food Security* Brussels (Belgium) 2022, *Seminar on Implementing the Global Corporate Minimum Tax* Brussels (Belgium) 2022, *Seminar on Unleashing the Internal Data Flow in the EU* Brussels (Belgium) 2016, *Conference on Understanding the Value of Transatlantic Data Flows* Brussels (Belgium) 2014, *Seminar on the Politics of Trade in the United States* Brussels (Belgium) 2014. [2018/XJ1087/**F**]

♦ European Centre for Jewish Leadership (internationally oriented national body)

♦ European Centre for Jewish Students (ECJS) 06487

Dir Rue du Cornet 22, 1040 Etterbeek, Belgium. T. +3222803765 – +3222801501. Fax +3222801435. E-mail: info@ecjs.org.
URL: http://www.ecjs.org/

History Founded Jan 2003. **Aims** Promote Jewish awareness; combat anti-Semitism. **Languages** English. **Staff** 1.00 FTE, paid; 3.00 FTE, voluntary. **Finance** Private donors. Budget (annual): euro 1 million. **Activities** Meeting activities. **Events** *Jewish European Professionals Event* Nice (France) 2014, *Jewish European Professionals Event* Bratislava (Slovakia) 2013, *Jewish European Professionals Event* Cascais (Portugal) 2013, *Jewish European Professionals Event* Valencia (Spain) 2013, *Jewish European Professionals Event* Thessaloniki (Greece) 2012. **Publications** *ECJS Newsletter* (12 a year). **NGO Relations** Member of: *UNITED for Intercultural Action – European Network Against Nationalism, Racism, Fascism and in Support of Migrants and Refugees (UNITED, #20511)*. [2014.06.01/XJ3886/**E**]

♦ European Centre for Judges and Lawyers 06488

Centre européen de la magistrature et des professions juridiques

Contact Onze Lieve Vrouweplein 22, 6211 HE Maastricht, Netherlands. T. +31433296222. E-mail: info@eipa.eu.
Contact Rue Nicolas Adames 8, L-1114 Luxembourg, Luxembourg. T. +3524262301. E-mail: info-lux@eipa.eu.
URL: https://www.eipa.eu/about-us/eipa-luxembourg/

History Jan 1992, Luxembourg. Founded on agreement with the government of Luxembourg, as an antenna of the *European Institute of Public Administration (EIPA, #07569)*, an activity within its Unit IV *'Community Legal Systems'*. **Aims** Train European *legal* experts; focus on legal activities for judges and other members of the legal *professions* as well as for *civil servants* and officials from the *European Union* institutions involved in legal issues. **Activities** Events/meetings; training/education. **Events** *EU Law for Non-Lawyers – Advanced* Luxembourg (Luxembourg) 2023, *EIPA Update on the European Green Deal: Where Do We Stand and What's Next?* Luxembourg (Luxembourg) 2022, *European Union Civil Service Law* Luxembourg (Luxembourg) 2022, *Introduction to EU Asylum and Migration Law* Luxembourg (Luxembourg) 2022, *Recent Trends in the Case Law of the Court of Justice of the EU* Luxembourg (Luxembourg) 2022. **Publications** Papers and briefings; book studies and reports; Practitioner Guide. [2022.10.25/XK1126/**E**]

♦ European Centre for Knowledge and Technology Transfer (Eurotex) 06489

Exec Dir Chée de Wavre 348, 1040 Brussels, Belgium. T. +3222306916. Fax +3222306916. E-mail: rv.eurotex@gmail.com.
URL: http://www.eurotex.org/

History 1999. Registration: Banque-Carrefour des Entreprises, No/ID: 0470.146.627, Start date: 8 Feb 2000, Belgium. **Aims** Promote knowledge and technology transfer between the EU and Eastern Europe and Central Asia (EECA) countries. **Structure** Governing Board; Advisory Board. **Languages** English. **Staff** 2.00 FTE, paid. **Finance** Financed through *European Commission (EC, #06633)* project grants. Annual budget: about euro 100,000. **Activities** Projects/programmes; knowledge management/information dissemination; events/meetings.

Members Full in 9 countries:
Armenia, Belgium, Denmark, France, Germany, Russia, Switzerland, UK, Ukraine.

IGO Relations *European Organization for Nuclear Research (CERN, #08108)*; *Joint Institute for Nuclear Research (JINR, #16134)*; national societies. [2021/XE4227/**E**]

♦ European Centre for Law and Justice (internationally oriented national body)
♦ European Centre on the Legislative Aspects of Disasters / see Higher Institute of Emergency Planning – European Centre Florival
♦ European Centre for Mathematics and Statistics in Metrology (unconfirmed)

♦ European Centre for Medium-Range Weather Forecasts (ECMWF) . 06490

Centre européen pour les prévisions météorologiques à moyen terme (CEPMMT) – Europäisches Zentrum für Mittelfristige Wettervorhersage (EZMW) – Centro Europeo per le Previsioni Meteorologiche a Medio Termine – Europees Centrum voor Weervoorspellingen op Middellange Termijn

Dir Gen Shinfield Park, Reading, RG2 9AX, UK. T. +441189499000. Fax +441189869450. E-mail: pressoffice@ecmwf.int.

Contact Robert-Schuman-Platz 3, 53175 Bonn, Germany.

Contact Tecnopolo di Bologna, Via Stalingrado 84/3, 40128 Bologna BO, Italy.

URL: http://www.ecmwf.int/

History 1 Nov 1975. Established with the signature of a Convention by which an Interim Committee was formed pending ratification of the Convention. Initiated under the programmes of *European Cooperation in Science and Technology (COST, #06784)*, instituted in 1971 by the EEC's *European Research Area Committee (ERAC)*. Centre inaugurated 15 Jun 1979. Statutes registered in *'UNTS 1/14669'*. **Aims** Develop capability for medium-range weather forecasting; provide numerical weather forecasts to Member and Cooperating States. **Structure** Council; Director-General; Advisory Committees. **Languages** English, French, German. **Staff** 400.00 FTE, paid. **Finance** Sources: contributions of member/participating states. Member States' contributions (2019): GBP 48,000,000. Annual budget: 112,300,000 GBP (2019). **Activities** Events/meetings; knowledge management/information dissemination; monitoring/evaluation; projects/programmes; research and development; training/education. **Events** *Workshop on Uncertainties at 183 Ghz* Paris (France) 2015, *ECAM : European conference on applications of meteorology* San Lorenzo de El Escorial (Spain) 2007, *RISK 2000 : international conference on space techniques for the management of major risks and their consequences* Paris (France) 2001, *Workshop on clouds, radiation transfer and the hydrological cycle* Reading (UK) 1990, *Meeting* Berlin (Germany FR) 1988. **Publications** *ECMWF Newsletter* (4 a year). Annual Report; scientific publications. **Information Services** *ECMWF Data Services* – Archive of meteorological data.

Members Member States (23) signatory to the Convention:

Austria, Belgium, Croatia, Denmark, Estonia, Finland, France, Germany, Greece, Iceland, Ireland, Italy, Luxembourg, Netherlands, Norway, Portugal, Serbia, Slovenia, Spain, Sweden, Switzerland, Türkiye, UK.

Cooperating States (12):

Bulgaria, Czechia, Georgia, Hungary, Israel, Latvia, Lithuania, Montenegro, Morocco, North Macedonia, Romania, Slovakia.

IGO Relations Partner of (2): *EuroGEOSS (#05685)*; *Group on Earth Observations (GEO, #10735)*. Cooperates with (8): *African Centre of Meteorological Applications for Development (ACMAD, #00242)*; *Convention on Long-range Transboundary Air Pollution (#04787)* (Executive Body); *European Organisation for the Exploitation of Meteorological Satellites (EUMETSAT, #08096)*; *European Space Agency (ESA, #08798)*; *Joint Research Centre (JRC, #16147)*; *Preparatory Commission for the Comprehensive Nuclear-Test-Ban Treaty Organization (CTBTO, #18482)*; *Regional Integrated Multi-Hazard Early Warning System for Africa and Asia (RIMES, #18790)*; *World Meteorological Organization (WMO, #21649)*. **NGO Relations** Member of (3): *European Meteorological Society (EMS, #07786)*; *International Centre for Earth Simulation (ICES Foundation)*; *ORCID (#17790)*. [2022.11.15/XE4022/**E***]

- ♦ European Centre for Minority Issues (internationally oriented national body)
- ♦ European Centre for Missing and Exploited Children / see European Centre for Missing and Sexually Exploited Children
- ♦ European Centre for Missing and Sexually Exploited Children (internationally oriented national body)
- ♦ European Centre for Mitigation of Natural Risks (internationally oriented national body)
- ♦ European Centre for Mobility Documentation (internationally oriented national body)

♦ European Centre for Modern Languages (ECML) 06491

Centre européen pour les langues vivantes (CELV) – Europäisches Fremdsprachenzentrum (EFSZ)

Exec Dir Nikolaiplatz 4, 8020 Graz, Austria. T. +43316323554. Fax +433163235544. E-mail: information@ecml.at.

URL: http://www.ecml.at/

History Established Apr 1994, by 8 founding states (Austria, France, Greece, Liechtenstein, Malta, Netherlands, Slovenia and Switzerland), under an *'Enlarged Partial Agreement on the European Centre for Modern Languages'* of *Council of Europe (CE, #04881)*. Under resolution 98 (11) of *Committee of Ministers of the Council of Europe (#04273)* became a permanent institution of the Council of Europe from 2 Jul 1998. Full title: *European Centre for Modern Languages of the Council of Europe – Centre européen pour les langues vivantes du Conseil de l'Europe – Europäisches Fremdsprachenzentrum des Europarats*. **Aims** Function as a catalyst for reform in the *teaching* and learning of languages; encourage excellence and innovation in language teaching; support member states in implementation of effective language education policies. **Structure** Governing Board; Bureau; National Nominating Authorities; National Contact Points; Programme Consultants. Includes: INGO Professional Network Forum on Language Education; Expert Networks. **Languages** English, French, German. Project outputs and other resources available in additional languages. **Staff** 11.00 FTE, paid. **Finance** Sources: members' dues. Annual budget: 1,474,000 EUR (2023). **Activities** Events/meetings; networking/liaising; training/education. **Events** *FemCities Conference* Graz (Austria) 2014, *Quality education and language competences for 21st century society* Graz (Austria) 2014, *Conference on Empowering Language Professionals* Graz (Austria) 2011, *Conference on media skills and competence* Tampere (Finland) 2005, *International workshop on foreign language teaching and learning in Central and Eastern European countries* Warsaw (Poland) 1997. **Publications** *European Language Gazette* – newsletter. *ECML Publication Series* – research and development work results. Thematic collections; resource websites; CD-ROM; field studies; expert reports.

Members States party to the Enlarged Partial Agreement, currently governments of 35 countries:

Albania, Andorra, Armenia, Austria, Belgium, Bosnia-Herzegovina, Bulgaria, Croatia, Cyprus, Czechia, Denmark, Estonia, Finland, France, Germany, Greece, Hungary, Iceland, Ireland, Latvia, Liechtenstein, Lithuania, Luxembourg, Malta, Montenegro, Netherlands, North Macedonia, Norway, Poland, Romania, Serbia, Slovakia, Slovenia, Sweden, Switzerland.

NGO Relations Also links with national authorities, national institutes and universities active in the field. [2022.11.30/XE2052/**E***]

- ♦ European Centre for Modern Languages of the Council of Europe / see European Centre for Modern Languages (#06491)

♦ European Centre for Monitoring Alcohol Marketing (EUCAM) 06492

Contact PO Box 9769, 3506 GT Utrecht, Netherlands. T. +31306565041. E-mail: eucam@eucam.info.

History 2007, Netherlands. Founded by STAP (Dutch Institute for Alcohol Policy). **Aims** Collect, exchange and promote knowledge and experience about alcohol marketing throughout Europe. **Activities** Research/documentation; knowledge management/information dissemination; events/meetings. **Publications** Newsletter.

Members Full in 6 countries:

Italy, Lithuania, Netherlands, Norway, Sweden, Switzerland.

NGO Relations *European Alcohol Policy Alliance (Eurocare, #05856)*. [2020.03.12/XM8772/**D**]

♦ European Centre for Nanostructured Polymers (ECNP) 06493

Contact Loc Pentima Bassa 21, Via G Giusti 9, 05100 Terni PG, Italy. T. +390744492939. Fax +390744492950. E-mail: info@ecnp-eu.org.

URL: http://www.ecnp-eu.org/

History Founded by *European Commission (EC, #06633)* – DG General Research. Operates under the auspices of the Nanofun-Poly European Network of Excellence. **Aims** Promote excellence in the priority sectors of the European Research Area (ERA), particularly with regard to polymer nanotechnologies. **Languages** English. **Staff** 12.00 FTE, paid. **Finance** Supported by European, national and regional research projects. **Activities** Events/meetings; research and development; training/education. **Events** *International Conference on Nanostructured Polymers and Nanocomposites* Lódz (Poland) 2022, *International Conference on Nanostructured Polymers and Nanocomposites* Lódz (Poland) 2021, *International Conference on Nanostructured Polymers and Nanocomposites* Lódz (Poland) 2020, *International Conference on Biobased and Biodegradable Polymers* Stockholm (Sweden) 2019, *International Conference* San Sebastian (Spain) 2018. **Publications** *Journal of Nanostructured Polymers and Nanocomposites*.

Members Full in 8 countries:

Czechia, France, Germany, Greece, Italy, Poland, Spain, Sweden.

IGO Relations *European Commission (EC, #06633)* – DG General Research. [2022/XM2449/e/**E**]

♦ European Centre of New Technologies for the Management of Natural and Technological Major Hazards (ECNTRM) 06494

Centre européen des nouvelles technologies pour la gestion des risques naturel et technologiques majeurs

Dir Davydkovskaja 7, Moscow MOSKVA, Russia, 121352. T. +74954009024. Fax +74999955695.

History 1990, as one of the *'European Network of Specialist Centres'* of *Open Partial Agreement on the Prevention of, Protection against and Organization of Relief in Major Natural and Technological Disasters (EUR-OPA Major Hazards Agreement, #17762)*, within the framework of the *Council of Europe (CE, #04881)* on the basis of EMERCOM of Russia. Previously referred to as *European Centre for Non-linear Dynamics and Theory of Seismic Risks – Centre européen sur la dynamique non linéaire et la théorie du risque sismique* or known under the acronym *ECNT*. **Aims** Carry out scientific and methodical maintenance of actions on safety and protection of the occupied territories against amazing factors of *emergency* situations. **Structure** Board; Head; Deputy Head. **Finance** Funds of OPA and Emercom of Russia. **Activities** Research and development; events/meetings. **Publications** *Civil Defense Technologies* – periodical magazine. Scientific reports; management manuals; recommendations. **NGO Relations** Based at: *International Institute of Earthquake Prediction Theory and Mathematical Geophysics (IIEPT / MITPAN, no recent information)*. [2016.06.28/XE1905/v/**E***]

- ♦ European Centre for Non-linear Dynamics and Theory of Seismic Risks / see European Centre of New Technologies for the Management of Natural and Technological Major Hazards (#06494)
- ♦ European Centre for Overseas Industrial Equipment and Development (inactive)

♦ European Centre for Parliamentary Research and Documentation (ECPRD) 06495

Centre européen de recherche et de documentation parlementaires (CERDP) – Europäisches Zentrum für Parlamentarische Wissenschaft und Dokumentation (EZPWD)

Co-Sec Parlement européen, Rue Wiertz 60, 1047 Brussels, Belgium. T. +3222842287. E-mail: ecprd@europarl.europa.eu.

Co-Sec Assemblée parlementaire du Conseil de l'Europe, 67075 Strasbourg CEDEX, France. T. +33388412911.

URL: http://www.ecprd.europarl.europa.eu/

History Jun 1977, Vienna (Austria). Established by *Conference of Speakers of the European Union Parliaments*. Re-structured and new statutes adopted Oct 1995, Strasbourg (France); statutes approved by the Secretaries General at the Conference of Speakers of European Assemblies, Jun 1996, Budapest (Hungary), and amended by the Secretaries General at the Conference of Presidents of Parliaments, 31 May 2006, Tallinn (Estonia). **Aims** Promote exchange of *information*, ideas, experience and good practice among administrations of parliaments in Europe; strengthen close cooperation among parliamentary services; collect, exchange and publicize studies produced by parliamentary services. **Structure** Responds to Secretaries General on the occasion of *Conference of Speakers of European Assemblies – Conférence des présidents des assemblées parlementaires européennes*, including Presidents of European Parliament and of Parliamentary Assembly of the Council of Europe. Conference of Correspondents (annual) comprises senior officials in the parliamentary assemblies. Executive Committee (meeting at least twice a year), comprises 2 Co-Directors plus 5 Correspondents appointed by the Conference of Correspondents. Coordinators for the Areas of Interests (4). Secretary General of *European Parliament (EP, #08146)* and Secretary General of *Parliamentary Assembly of the Council of Europe (PACE, #18211)* each appoint a Co-Director and a Co-Secretary. Secretariat, based at European Parliament, Brussels (Belgium). **Languages** English, French, German. **Staff** 1.00 FTE, paid. **Finance** Member chambers meet cost of participation of their officials. Operating costs covered by budgets of *European Parliament (EP, #08146)* and *Parliamentary Assembly of the Council of Europe (PACE, #18211)*. **Activities** Events/meetings; knowledge management/information dissemination; research/documentation. **Events** *EBA Seminar* Berlin (Germany) 2022, *Parliaments and the Whistleblowing Directive* Brussels (Belgium) 2022, *Remote Executive Committee Meeting* Brussels (Belgium) 2022, *Parliaments and the General Data Protection* Vienna (Austria) 2022, *Annual Conference of Correspondents* Yerevan (Armenia) 2022. **Publications** Information Services: Central secretariat acts as a clearinghouse.

Members Regional assemblies (2):

European Parliament (EP, #08146); *Parliamentary Assembly of the Council of Europe (PACE, #18211)*.

Parliamentary Assemblies of Member States of European Union and Council of Europe (47):

Albania, Andorra, Armenia, Austria, Azerbaijan, Belgium, Bosnia-Herzegovina, Bulgaria, Croatia, Cyprus, Czechia, Denmark, Estonia, Finland, France, Georgia, Germany, Greece, Hungary, Iceland, Ireland, Italy, Latvia, Liechtenstein, Lithuania, Luxembourg, Malta, Moldova, Monaco, Montenegro, Netherlands, North Macedonia, Norway, Poland, Portugal, Romania, Russia, San Marino, Serbia, Slovakia, Slovenia, Spain, Sweden, Switzerland, Türkiye, UK, Ukraine.

Countries with observer status in the Parliamentary Assembly of the Council of Europe (3):

Canada, Israel, Mexico.

Countries with status of Partners for Democracy within the Parliamentary Assembly of the Council of Europe (4):

Jordan, Kyrgyzstan, Morocco, Palestine. [2022.10.14/XE0233/y/**E***]

♦ European Centre for Peace and Development (ECPD) 06496

Centre européen pour la paix et le développement – Centro Europeo para la Paz y el Desarrollo – Evropejskij Centr Mira i Razvitija – Evropski Centar za Mir i Razvoj

Exec Dir Terazije 41, Belgrade, PAK 11000, Serbia. T. +381113246041 – +381113246042 – +381113246045. Fax +381113240673 – +381113234082. E-mail: office@ecpd.org.rs – ecpd@eunet.rs.

URL: http://www.ecpd.org.rs/

History Jul 1985. Founded by an international agreement concluded between *University for Peace (UPEACE, #20702)* established by the United Nations and the Government of Yugoslavia. **Aims** Organize and carry out *postgraduate* studies at specialist, master and doctoral levels, research activities and dissemination of knowledge which contribute to promotion of peace, development and international cooperation. **Structure** International Council; Academic Council; Executive Board; Executive Director. **Languages** Croatian, English, Serbian. **Staff** 81.00 FTE, paid. **Finance** Sources: contributions; government support; international organizations; private foundations; revenue from activities/projects; sale of publications. tuition fees. **Activities** Events/meetings; knowledge management/information dissemination; research/documentation; training/education. **Events** *International Conference on a New Human Concept of Security* Belgrade (Serbia) 2018, *International Conference on Future of the World between Globalization and Regionalization* Belgrade (Serbia) 2017, *Conference on Pharmacoeconomics* Opatija (Croatia) 2017, *International Conference on Reconciliation, Tolerance and Human Security in the Balkans* Belgrade (Serbia) 2014, *International Conference on Reconciliation, Tolerance and Human Security in the Balkans* Belgrade (Serbia) 2013. **Publications** *ECPD Survey* (4 a year); *The European Journal of Management and Public Policy* (2 a year) – ECPD Scientific Journal. Books; studies; monographs; proceedings of international meetings.

Members Centers in 20 countries:

Austria, Belgium, Bosnia-Herzegovina, Bulgaria, Croatia, Finland, France, Germany, Greece, Hungary, Italy, Luxembourg, Montenegro, Netherlands, North Macedonia, Romania, Russia, Slovenia, Spain, UK.

IGO Relations Cooperates with (9): *Inter-American Development Bank (IDB, #11427)*; *International Atomic Energy Agency (IAEA, #12294)*; *International Bank for Reconstruction and Development (IBRD, #12317)* (World Bank); *Regional Cooperation Council (RCC, #18773)*; *UNCTAD (#20285)*; *UNESCO (#20322)*; *UNIDO (#20336)*; *United Nations University (UNU, #20642)*; *WHO (#20950)*. Cooperative agreement with: *European Commission (EC, #06633)* (European Economic Commission); *International Development Law Organization (IDLO, #13161)*; *International Institute for the Unification of Private Law (UNIDROIT, #13934)*; *UN Interim Administration Mission in Kosovo (UNMIK, #20343)*; *United Nations Commission on International Trade Law (UNCITRAL, #20531)*. **NGO Relations** Cooperative agreement with: *Diplomatic Academy of Vienna (DA)*; International Centre for Local and Regional Development; *International Law Institute, Washington DC (ILI)*; numerous academic institutions. [2020.05.15/XE2861/**E**]

♦ European Centre for Press and Media Freedom (ECPMF) 06497

Europäisches Zentrum für Presse- und Medienfreiheit

Managing Dir Menckestr 27, 04155 Leipzig, Germany. T. +4934120040313. Fax +493415629663. E-mail: info@ecpmf.eu.

URL: http://www.ecpmf.eu/

History Founded 24 Jun 2015, Leipzig (Germany), by 25 representatives. Registered in accordance with German law. EU Transparency Register: 823710129179-63. **Aims** Secure the use of the European Charter on Freedom of the Press throughout Europe; gain recognition for it as a basis for the EU enlargement negotiations. **Structure** General Assembly; Supervisory Board; Executive Board; Expert Advisory Committees. **Activities** Knowledge management/information dissemination; research/documentation. **Events** *Free European Media Conference* Gdansk (Poland) 2022. **Publications** *ECPMF Newsletter*.
Members Individuals; organizations. Organizations include 3 listed in this Yearbook:
European Federation of Journalists (EFJ, #07152); *Institut für Europäisches Medienrecht (EMR)*; *South East Europe Media Organisation (SEEMO, #19823)*.
NGO Relations *International Press Institute (IPI, #14636)*; *Lie Detectors*. [2019/XM7757/y/**D**]

- European Centre for the Promotion of Innovation Technologies / see EURO-CHINA (#05658)

♦ European Centre for Public Affairs (ECPA) 06498

Exec Dir address not obtained. E-mail: secretariat@theecpa.eu.
URL: http://www.theecpa.eu/

History Founded 1986, Oxford (UK). EU Transparency Register: 750705410501-01. **Aims** Record, analyse and improve the conduct of public affairs. **Structure** Management Board of 36 members. **Finance** Members' dues. **Activities** Training/education. **Events** *Annual conference* Brussels (Belgium) 2010, *Conference on public affairs in the new Europe* Brussels (Belgium) 2010, *Annual conference* Brussels (Belgium) 2009, *INSIDE Brussels meeting* Brussels (Belgium) 2009, *Annual Conference* Brussels (Belgium) 2008. **Publications** *Public Affairs Newsletter* (12 a year); *Journal of Public Affairs*. *Occasional Papers* – series. Books; case studies.
Members Corporate. Membership countries not specified. [2019/XE4400/**F**]

- European Centre of Public Enterprises / see SGI Europe (#19253)
- European Centre for Public Health Genomics (unconfirmed)
- European Centre for the Regions, Barcelona (see: #07569)
- European Centre for Rehabilitation of Buildings (internationally oriented national body)
- European Centre for Research and Advanced Training in Scientific Computation (internationally oriented national body)
- European Centre for Research in Asia, Africa and Latin America (no recent information)
- European Centre for Research in Development Economics (internationally oriented national body)
- European Centre for Research on Federalism (internationally oriented national body)
- European Centre for Research, Networking, Education and Action training in Purchasing and Supply Chain Management / see European Institute of Purchasing Management
- European Centre for Research into Techniques for Informing the Population in Emergency Situations (internationally oriented national body)
- European Centre for Research and Training in Human Rights and Humanitarian Law (internationally oriented national body)
- European Centre for the Responsibility to Protect (internationally oriented national body)
- European Centre for Restoration Techniques (internationally oriented national body)
- European Centre of Retail Trade (inactive)
- European Centre for the Rights of Children with Disabilities (internationally oriented national body)

♦ European Centre for River Restoration (ECRR) 06499

Centre européen pour la réhabilitation des fleuves (CERF)
Contact c/o Jagersveld 28, 8222 AB Lelystad, Netherlands. E-mail: info@ecrr.org.
URL: http://www.ecrr.org/

History Founded 1995. Founding meeting, 1999, Silkeborg (Denmark). EU Transparency Register: 598486033693-78. **Aims** Foster communication between people working with river restoration in Europe; support the development of river restoration as an integral part of sustainable water management throughout Europe. **Structure** Board (meets at least twice a year); Secretariat. **Languages** English. **Staff** 1.00 FTE, paid. **Finance** Members' dues. **Events** *European River Symposium* Vienna (Austria) 2021, *European River Symposium* Vienna (Austria) 2016, *European River Restoration Conference* Vienna (Austria) 2014, *Conference on River Restoration / Conference* Vienna (Austria) 2013, *Seminar on forging targets and solutions for rivers and water ecosystem restoration / Conference* Ljubljana (Slovenia) 2011. **Publications** *ECRR Network eNews* (12 a year).
Members Individuals (nearly 1000); organizations (15). National and topic centres in 12 countries:
Finland, France, Italy, Netherlands, Norway, Poland, Romania, Russia, Spain, Sweden, UK, Ukraine.
Included in the above, 3 organizations listed in this Yearbook:
International Network of Basin Organizations (INBO, #14235); *Wetlands International (#20928)*; *World Fish Migration Foundation*.
NGO Relations *Global Water Partnership (GWP, #10653)* – Central and East Europe. [2020.03.05/XJ4186/**E**]

- European Centres for Culture and Communication (#05750)
- European Centre for Seismic and Geomorphological Hazards / see European Centre on Geomorphological Hazards (#06482)

♦ European Centre for Social Welfare Policy and Research (European Centre) 06500

Centre européen de recherche en politique sociale – Europäisches Zentrum für Wohlfahrtspolitik und Sozialforschung
Exec Dir Berggasse 17, 1090 Vienna, Austria. T. +43131945050. E-mail: ec@euro.centre.org.
URL: http://www.euro.centre.org/

History 1974, Vienna (Austria). Established on signature of an agreement between *United Nations (UN, #20515)* and the Federal Government of Austria (host government). Subsequent agreements, signed 1978 and 1981, reconfirmed the Centre as an autonomous intergovernmental organization affiliated to the United Nations. Statutes amended and present name adopted in 1989. Former names and other names: *European Centre for Social Welfare Training and Research (ECSWTR)* – former; *Centre européen de formation et de recherche en action sociale* – former; *Europäisches Zentrum für Ausbildung und Forschung auf dem Gebiet der Sozialen Wohlfahrt* – former; *Europäisches Zentrum* – alias; *ECSWPR* – former. Registration: No/ID: ZVR 583470062, Austria. **Aims** Foster collaboration between governments and organizations in the field of social welfare. **Structure** General Assembly; Board of Directors. **Languages** English, French, German. **Staff** 20.00 FTE, paid. **Finance** Sources: fees for services; government support. Contributions from host government and affiliated governments; third-party funds acquired for services provided. **Activities** Events/meetings; guidance/assistance/consulting; networking/liaising; politics/policy/regulatory; research and development. **Events** *Annual General Assembly* Vienna (Austria) 2021, *Annual General Assembly* Vienna (Austria) 2020, *Annual Meeting and General Assembly* Vienna (Austria) 2019, *Annual Meeting and General Assembly* Vienna (Austria) 2018, *Vienna EUROMOD Workshop* Vienna (Austria) 2018. **Publications** *Policy Briefs* in English, German; *The European Centre Newsletter* in English. Annual Report; reports; working papers; books; journal articles.
Members Governments of 42 countries, representing the UNECE Region:
Armenia, Austria, Azerbaijan, Belgium, Bosnia-Herzegovina, Bulgaria, Canada, Croatia, Cyprus, Czechia, Denmark, Finland, France, Germany, Greece, Hungary, Ireland, Israel, Italy, Kosovo, Latvia, Lithuania, Luxembourg, Malta, Moldova, Netherlands, North Macedonia, Norway, Poland, Portugal, Romania, Russia, Serbia, Slovakia, Slovenia, Spain, Sweden, Switzerland, Türkiye, UK, Ukraine, USA.
NGO Relations Member of (1): *European Association Working for Carers (Eurocarers, #06277)*. [2021.08.30/XE6139/**E***]

- European Centre for Social Welfare Training and Research / see European Centre for Social Welfare Policy and Research (#06500)

♦ European Centre for Space Law (ECSL) 06501

Exec Officer c/o ESA HQ, 24 rue du Général Bertrand, CS 30798, 75345 Paris CEDEX 7, France. T. +33153697128. E-mail: ecsl@esa.int.
URL: http://www.esa.int/ecsl

History 12 May 1989. Founded by *European Space Agency (ESA, #08798)*, on the basis of a Charter, last amended 2009. **Aims** Promote, foster and enhance knowledge about space law and policy in Europe and beyond. **Structure** General Meeting of Members (every 3 years); Board; Executive Officer. **Languages** English. **Staff** 1.00 FTE, paid. **Finance** Sources: donations; meeting proceeds; members' dues. Assured by ESA. **Activities** Events/meetings; training/education. **Events** *NOSA/ECSL/UiO Space Law Symposium* Oslo (Norway) 2022, *Annual Practitioners Forum* Paris (France) 2022, *Young Lawyers Symposium* Paris (France) 2022, *Annual Practitioners Forum* Paris (France) 2021, *Young Lawyers Symposium* Paris (France) 2021. **Publications** *ECSL Newsletter*; *Space Law in the News*. Proceedings of colloquia and workshops; books.
Members Individuals (students, academia, lawyers and practitioners). National points of contact in 18 countries:
Austria, Belgium, Czechia, Denmark, Estonia, Finland, France, Germany, Hungary, Italy, Luxembourg, Netherlands, Portugal, Romania, Slovakia, Spain, Switzerland, UK.
https://www.esa.int/About_Us/ECSL_-_European_Centre_for_Space_Law/ECSL_National_Points_of_Contact.
Corporate members: European institutions and industry working in the space sector (not specified).
NGO Relations Member of (1): *European Network of Independent Non-Proliferation Think Tanks (EU Non-Proliferation Network, #07930)*. Cooperates with (2): *Commission mondiale d'éthique des connaissances scientifiques et des technologies de l'UNESCO (COMEST, #04235)*; *International Institute of Space Law (IISL, #13926)*. Also links with national organizations. [2022.10.24/XE3937/**E**]

- European Centre for Studies of Sulphuric Acid / see European Sulphuric Acid Association (#08854)
- European Centre of Technological Safety (internationally oriented national body)
- European Centre for Theoretical Studies in Nuclear Physics and Related Areas, Villazzano (internationally oriented national body)

♦ European Centre of Tort and Insurance Law (ECTIL) 06502

Europäisches Zentrum für Schadenersatz- und Versicherungsrecht
Managing Dir Reichsratsstrasse 17/2, 1010 Vienna, Austria. T. +431427729650. Fax +431427729670. E-mail: ectil@ectil.org.
URL: http://www.ectil.org/

History Feb 1999, Vienna (Austria), to create a secure institutional basis for the drafting of the *'Principles of European Tort Law'* and to undertake research projects in the field of tort law. Registered in accordance with Austrian law. **Aims** Create a secure institutional basis for drafting of the Principles of European Tort Law; undertake research projets in the field of tort and insurance law. **Structure** General Meeting (annual); Supervisory Board; Board of Directors. **Languages** English, German. **Finance** Supporting members and sponsors. **Activities** Events/meetings; publishing activities. **Events** *Annual Conference on European Tort Law* Vienna (Austria) 2021, *Annual Conference on European Tort Law* Vienna (Austria) 2019, *Annual Conference on European Tort Law* Vienna (Austria) 2018, *Annual Conference on European Tort Law* Vienna (Austria) 2017, *Annual Conference on European Tort Law* Vienna (Austria) 2016. **Publications** *Journal of European Tort Law (JETL)* (3 a year); *Yearbook on European Tort Law*. *Principles of European Tort Law* – series together with European Group on Tort Law; *Tort and Insurance Law* – series. **Information Services** *Database on European Tort Law EuroTort* – online.
Members Ordinary individuals in 19 countries:
Austria, Belgium, Czechia, Denmark, France, Germany, Greece, Israel, Italy, Netherlands, Norway, Poland, Portugal, South Africa, Spain, Sweden, Switzerland, UK, USA.
Fellows in 32 countries:
Australia, Austria, Belgium, Bulgaria, China, Czechia, Denmark, Estonia, Finland, France, Germany, Greece, Hungary, Ireland, Israel, Italy, Latvia, Lithuania, Malta, Netherlands, New Zealand, Norway, Poland, Portugal, Romania, Slovenia, South Africa, Spain, Sweden, Switzerland, UK, USA.
NGO Relations Cooperates with: *European Group on Tort Law (EGTL, #07437)*; *Institute of European and Comparative Private Law (IECPL)*; *Institute for European Tort Law (ETL)*; Karl-Franzens-University, Graz (KFU); *Maastrichts Europees Instituut voor Transnationaal Rechtswetenschappelijk Onderzoek (METRO)*; national centres. Instrumental in setting up: *World Tort Law Society (WTLS, #21855)*. [2021/XE3924/v/**E**]

- European Centre for Traditional Culture / see European Folklore Institute
- European Centre for Traditional and Regional Cultures / see European Centre for Training and Regional Cooperation (#06503)
- European Centre for Training Craftsmen in the Conservation of the Architectural Heritage / see European Centre for Heritage Crafts and Professions (#06484)
- European Centre on Training and Formation of Local and Regional Authorities and Population in the Field of Natural and Technological Disasters (internationally oriented national body)

♦ European Centre for Training and Regional Cooperation (ECTARC) . 06503

Canolfan Hyfforddiant a Diwylliannau Rhanbarthol Ewrop
Main Office Parade Street, Llangollen, LL20 8RB, UK. T. +441978861514. Fax +441978861804. E-mail: ectarc@ectarc.com.
URL: http://www.ectarc.com/

History 1988, Llangollen (UK). Founded by *Assembly of European Regions (AER, #02316)* and *Conference of Peripheral Maritime Regions of Europe (CPMR, #04638)*, building upon the *European Centre for Folk Studies (ECFS)*. Original title: *European Centre for Traditional and Regional Cultures – Centre européen des cultures traditionnelles et régionales – Canolfan Diwylliannau Traddodiadol a Rhanbarthol Ewrop*. Registration: Charity Commission, England and Wales. **Aims** Contribute and influence the social, cultural and economic development of Wales through European activities designed to realize the individual potential and personal development of young people and adult learners'; develop existing and potential youth, training and education activities as its main business utilizing the opportunities offered by European Funding Programmes. **Structure** Board of Trustees, comprising Chairperson and representatives of supporting organizations. **Finance** Sources: funding from local and regional authorities in Europe; *European Social Fund (ESF, #08501)*; income from research and consultancy work, courses, conferences and youth and training programmes. **Activities** Manages programmes of interregional cooperation and training; provides expertise to support networks; develops strategic plans, studies, analyses and policy reviews; monitors and evaluates projects. Priority themes: Culture and economic development linkages; Regional and minority languages; Rural development, cultural tourism and cultural policies; Problems facing young people and measures to tackle them; Interregional cooperation and European networking. Organizes International Youth Programmes. **Events** *Conference* Llangollen (UK) 1999, *Conference – Culture, nation and region in Europe* Cardiff (UK) 1998, *Conference* Shannon (Ireland) 1997, *International conference on culture and economic development* Girona (Spain) 1995, *Conference on the Role of Regional Diversity in Building a United Europe* Trento (Italy) 1993. **Publications** Newsletter; magazine; occasional papers.
Members Individuals, organizations, local and regional authorities in 17 countries:
Austria, Belgium, Czechia, Denmark, France, Germany, Greece, Hungary, Ireland, Italy, Netherlands, Portugal, Russia, Serbia, Slovakia, Spain, Switzerland.
IGO Relations Observer status on: *Council of Europe (CE, #04881)*. **NGO Relations** Observer on AER. [2017/XE1371/**E**]

- European Centre on Urban Risks (internationally oriented national body)
- European Centre for the Validation of Alternative Testing Methods (inactive)

♦ European Centre for Women and Technology (ECWT) 06504

Secretariat Oslo Intl Hub, Oscars Gate 27, 0352 Oslo, Norway. T. +4792477960. E-mail: info@ecwt.eu.
URL: http://www.ecwt.eu/

History 9 May 2008. Founded on the initiative of the European branch of *International Taskforce on Women and Information and Communication Technologies (ITF, #15658)*. Statutes approved 18 Jul 2008. Registration: Norway. **Aims** Ensure, based on a multi-stakeholder partnership (MSP) of representatives from the business sector, government, the academia and the non-profit sector, a major break-through and a measurable and significant European increase in the participation of women in education, entrepreneurship, employment and leadership in ICT and related sectors until the gender gap is decreased in a rapid speed; collaborate with and give added value to already existing structures and organizations, by sharing knowledge and best practices and creating synergies, leveraging resources, research and progress. **Structure** Executive Group; High-level Advisory Committee; Working Groups (4); National Point of Contacts (N-POCs). **Languages** English,

Greek, Hungarian, Norwegian, Swedish. **Staff** 2.00 FTE, paid. **Activities** Advocacy/lobbying/activism; awareness raising; capacity building; events/meetings; guidance/assistance/consulting; knowledge management/information dissemination; monitoring/evaluation; networking/liaising; projects/programmes; research and development; training/education. As the leading European level platform, ensure the gender dimension of the Digital Agenda through finding ways and means for measurably and significantly increasing the number of girls and women in STEM and computing and integrating a critical mass of women in Europe in the design, research, innovation, production, and use of ICT. Active in: Armenia, Austria, Belgium, Bosnia-Herzegovina, Bulgaria, Croatia, Finland, France, Germany, Greece, Israel, Kosovo, Lithuania, Malta, Netherlands, North Macedonia, Norway, Poland, Portugal, Romania, Spain, Switzerland, United Arab Emirates. **Events** *Conference on women in science, innovation and technology in the digital age* Budapest (Hungary) 2011. **Members** Organizations and individuals. Membership countries not specified. [2022.11.01/XM8204/E]

♦ European Centre for Workers' Questions 06505

Centre européen pour les travailleurs – Europäisches Zentrum für Arbeitnehmerfragen (EZA)

SG Johannes-Albers-Allee 2, 53639 Königswinter, Germany. T. +49222329980. Fax +492223299822. E-mail: eza@eza.org.
URL: http://www.eza.org/

History Founded 29 Jan 1985. Registered in accordance with Luxembourg law. EU Transparency Register: 514122517027-14. **Aims** Promote social, economic and cultural *development* of European society through organizations of seminars and *educational* projects regarding European social questions. **Structure** Governing Body. **Languages** English, French, German, Italian, Polish, Portuguese, Spanish. **Staff** 6.00 FTE, paid. **Finance** Members' dues. Additional funding from: *European Commission (EC, #06633)*. Annual budget: about euro 3,000,000. **Activities** Training/education; research/documentation; events/meetings. **Events** *Seminar* Vienna (Austria) 2013, *Seminar* Doorn (Netherlands) 2009, *Seminar on immigration and undeclared employment* Barcelona (Spain) 2004, *Seminar on European social dialogue* Poland 2004, *Seminar on social partners, civil society and negotiations on the enlargement of the EU* Romania 2004. **Publications** *EZA Newsletter* in Croatian, English, French, German, Italian, Spanish. Seminar programme; Concept document.
Members Full (57) in 26 countries:
Austria, Belgium, Bulgaria, Croatia, Cyprus, Czechia, Denmark, Estonia, France, Germany, Greece, Hungary, Italy, Lithuania, Luxembourg, Malta, Netherlands, North Macedonia, Poland, Portugal, Romania, Slovakia, Slovenia, Spain, Switzerland, UK.
Included in the above, 6 organizations listed in this Yearbook:
Centro Internacional de Formação dos Trabalhadores da Indústria e Energia (CIFOTIE); European Christian Workers Movement (ECWM, #06546); European Federation of Employees in Public Services (EUROFEDOP, #07106); Europees Forum; Groupe européen de pastorale ouvrière (GEPO, #10740); World Organization of Workers (WOW, #21697).
Associate (4) in 4 countries:
Belgium, Germany, Latvia, Poland.
Observers (11) in 9 countries:
Albania, Bulgaria, Czechia, Germany, Malta, Netherlands, Serbia, Slovenia, Ukraine.
NGO Relations Member of: *Robert Schuman Institute for Developing Democracy in Central and Eastern Europe (RSI, #18958).* [2018.08.01/XE4572/y/E]

- ♦ European Centre of Youth Cooperation (internationally oriented national body)
- ♦ European Ceramic Association (inactive)
- ♦ European Ceramic Fibre Industry Association / see ECFIA (#05280)

♦ European Ceramic Industry Association (CERAME-UNIE) 06506

Dir Gen Rue Belliard 12, 1040 Brussels, Belgium. T. +3228083880. Fax +3225115174. E-mail: sec@cerameunie.eu.
Office Manager address not obtained.
URL: http://www.cerameunie.eu/

History 25 Oct 1962, Brussels (Belgium). Former names and other names: *Liaison Bureau of Ceramic Industries of the Common Market* – former; *Bureau de liaison des industries céramiques du Marché commun* – former; *Liaison Office of the European Ceramic Industries* – former; *Bureau de liaison des industries céramiques européennes* – former. Registration: Banque-Carrefour des Entreprises, No/ID: 0826.354.579, Start date: 2 Jun 2010, Belgium; EU Transparency Register, No/ID: 79465004946-12, Start date: 11 Jan 2011. **Aims** Study matters of common interest for the ceramic industry in scientific, technical, economic, legal and other areas in the framework of the European economic integration; develop and promote common positions on these issues with European Union authorities. **Structure** General Assembly. Board of Presidents, comprising Chairman, 2 Vice-Chairmen and Sector Presidents. Committee of Directors. Secretariat, headed by Secretary-General. Sectors (10): *Tiles and Bricks Europe (TBE, #20163); European Ceramic Tile Manufacturers' Federation (CET, #06508); Fédération européenne des industries de porcelaine et de faïence de table et d'ornementation (FEPF, #09574); European Federation of Ceramic Sanitaryware Manufacturers (#07073); European Refractories Producers Federation (#08339); European Technical Ceramics Federation (EuTeCer, #08878); FEUGRES – European Clay Pipe Association (FEUGRES e.V., #09741); Federation of European Producers of Abrasives (FEPA, #09532); European Expanded Clay Association (EXCA, #07013); European Enamel Authority (EEA)* (Associate member). **Languages** English, French, German. **Staff** 11.00 FTE, paid. **Activities** Events/meetings; networking/liaising. **Events** *European Ceramic Days* Brussels (Belgium) 2022, *European Ceramic Days* Brussels (Belgium) 2021, *European Ceramic Days* Brussels (Belgium) 2020, *European Ceramic Days* Brussels (Belgium) 2019, *European Ceramic Days* Brussels (Belgium) 2018. **Publications** *Courrier.*
Members Federations of national associations; direct members. National associations in 30 countries:
Austria, Belgium, Bulgaria, Croatia, Cyprus, Czechia, Denmark, Estonia, Finland, France, Germany, Greece, Hungary, Ireland, Italy, Latvia, Luxembourg, Netherlands, Norway, Poland, Portugal, Romania, Russia, Slovakia, Slovenia, Spain, Sweden, Switzerland, Türkiye, UK.
IGO Relations Accredited by (1): *European Commission (EC, #06633).* **NGO Relations** Member of (7): *AEGIS Europe; Construction 2050 Alliance (#04760); Construction Products Europe AISBL (#04761); European Network on Silica (NEPSI, #08001); European Platform for Chemicals Using Manufacturing Industries (CheMI, #08223); Federation of European and International Associations Established in Belgium (FAIB, #09508); Industry4Europe (#11181).* In liaison with technical committees of: *Comité européen de normalisation (CEN, #04162).* [2023/XE0347/ty/E]

♦ European Ceramic Society (ECerS) 06507

Sec Av Gouverneur Cornez 4, 7000 Mons, Belgium. T. +3265403421. Fax +3265403458. E-mail: ecers@bcrc.be.
URL: http://www.ecers.org/

History 1987. Together with *European Technical Ceramics Federation (EuTeCer, #08878)*, took over relevant activities of suspended *European Ceramic Association (AEC, inactive)*, 1989. Registration: Banque-Carrefour des Entreprises, No/ID: 0535.566.197, Start date: 8 May 2013, Belgium. **Aims** Coordinate and promote the study of ceramics. **Structure** Council; Executive Committee; Advisory Group; Working Groups (4). Networks (3): *Europe Makes Ceramics (EMC, #09161); Electroceramics Network (#05420);* Bioceramics Network. International Advisory Board. **Languages** English. **Staff** 2.00 FTE, paid. **Finance** Sources: members' dues. **Activities** Events/meetings; guidance/assistance/consulting; knowledge management/information dissemination; research/documentation; training/education. **Events** *Conference* Dresden (Germany) 2025, *Electroceramics Conference* Vilnius (Lithuania) 2024, *Conference* Lyon (France) 2023, *Conference* Krakow (Poland) 2022, *Electroceramics Conference* Krakow (Poland) 2022. **Publications** *Journal of the European Ceramic Society; Open Ceramics.*
Members Full in 28 countries:
Austria, Belgium, Croatia, Czechia, Denmark, Finland, France, Georgia, Germany, Greece, Hungary, Ireland, Italy, Latvia, Netherlands, Norway, Poland, Portugal, Romania, Russia, Serbia, Slovakia, Slovenia, Spain, Sweden, Switzerland, Türkiye, UK.
Associate members in 2 countries:
Iran Islamic Rep, Morocco. [2022.02.15/XD2096/D]

- ♦ European Ceramics Work Centre, Netherlands (internationally oriented national body)

♦ European Ceramic Tile Manufacturers' Federation (CET) 06508

SG Rue Belliard 12, 1040 Brussels, Belgium. T. +3228083880. Fax +3225115174.
URL: http://cerameunie.eu/members/sectors/

History 20 Feb 1959, Brussels (Belgium), as *Common Market Group of Ceramic Tile Producers – Groupement des producteurs de carreaux céramiques du Marché commun (CMC) – Vereinigung der Keramikfliesenhersteller des Gemeinsamen Markts – Raggruppamento dei Produttori di Piastrelle di Ceramica del Mercato Comune – Groepering van de Keramiektegel-Producenten van de Gemeenschappelijke Markt.* Present name adopted 1991. **Aims** Study jointly the problems that the application of EC/EU rules poses to the producers; further solutions to these problems; represent the interest of this *industrial* sector to *European Community/European Union* institutions. **Structure** General Assembly (meets twice a year); President; Secretariat, headed by Secretary-General; Technical Committee; Economic Committee. **Languages** English, French, German. **Finance** Members' dues. **Activities** Matters currently dealt with: Central and Eastern Europe; standardization; technological cooperation; environmental issues. **Events** *General Assembly* Izmir (Turkey) 2008, *General Assembly* Berlin (Germany) 2007, *General Assembly* Naples (Italy) 2006, *General Assembly* Dublin (Ireland) 2005, *General Assembly* Toledo (Spain) 2004.
Members Full in 22 countries:
Austria, Belgium, Czechia, Denmark, Finland, France, Germany, Greece, Hungary, Ireland, Italy, Luxembourg, Netherlands, Norway, Poland, Portugal, Slovakia, Spain, Sweden, Switzerland, Türkiye, UK.
IGO Relations Recognized by: *European Commission (EC, #06633).* **NGO Relations** Member of: *European Ceramic Industry Association (CERAME-UNIE, #06506); Industry4Europe (#11181); World Ceramic Tiles Forum (WCTF, #21266).* In liaison with technical committees of: *International Organization for Standardization (ISO, #14473).* [2018/XE0344/E]

♦ European Cereals Genetics Co-operative (EWAC) 06509

Contact c/o Crop Research Inst, Drnovska 507, 161 06 Prague 6, Czechia.
URL: http://www.ewac.eu/

History as *European Wheat Aneuploid Co-operative.* Inaugural meeting 1967, Cambridge (UK). Current title adopted, 2005, Prague (Czech Rep). **Aims** Foster cooperative research in cereal genetics, cytogenetics, genomics and molecular biology across Europe. **Activities** Organizes conferences. **Events** *Conference* Bucharest (Romania) 2018, *Conference* Lublin (Poland) 2015, *Conference* Novi Sad (Serbia) 2011, *Conference* Istanbul (Turkey) 2007, *Conference* Prague (Czech Rep) 2005. **Publications** *EWAC Newsletter.*
Members Individuals in 15 countries:
Bulgaria, Czechia, France, Germany, Hungary, Italy, Japan, Poland, Romania, Russia, Serbia, Spain, Türkiye, UK, Ukraine. [2017/XJ2208/D]

- ♦ European Cereals Union (inactive)
- ♦ European Certification Board for Logistics (inactive)

♦ European Certification Board for Mineral Wool Products (EUCEB) . . 06510

Bureau européen certification des produits en laine minérale

Permanent Office c/o Kellen, Avenue de Tervueren 188a, Postbox 4, 1150 Brussels, Belgium. T. +3227611683. E-mail: euceb@kellencompany.com.
URL: http://www.euceb.org/

History Jun 2000. Registration: Luxembourg. **Aims** Ensure that all the fibers produced by its members comply with note Q of the European Regulation (EC) 1272/2008. **Structure** General Assembly (annual); Management Board, headed by President; Quality Board; General Secretariat. **Languages** English. **Finance** Sources: members' dues. **Activities** Created the EUCEB-Trademark, granted to a manufacturer only, provided several prerequisites.
Members Companies (62) in 33 countries:
Austria, Belarus, Belgium, Brazil, Canada, China, Croatia, Czechia, Denmark, Finland, France, Germany, Greece, Hungary, Iceland, India, Ireland, Italy, Lithuania, Mexico, Netherlands, Norway, Poland, Romania, Russia, Serbia, Slovakia, Slovenia, Spain, Sweden, Switzerland, UK, USA. [2022.10.19/XD8752/D]

- ♦ European Certification Network / see International Certification Network (#12532)

♦ European Certification and Qualification Association (ECQA) 06511

Pres Piaristengasse 1, 3500 Krems, Austria. E-mail: ecqa_president@ecqa.org – info@ecqa.org.
URL: http://www.ecqa.org/

Aims Provide a world-wide unified certification schema for numerous professions; join experts from the market and support the definition and development of the knowledge required for job roles; define and verify quality criteria for training organizations and trainers to assure the sale level of trainings; centrally promote all certified job roles. **Structure** Board; Executive Board; Secretariat. **Languages** English. **Activities** Certification/accreditation; events/meetings. **Events** *ECQA Days* Ankara (Turkey) 2015, *ECQA Days* Kirchberg (Luxembourg) 2014, *ECQA Days* Cannes (France) 2013, *ECQA Days* Krems (Austria) 2012, *ECQA Days* Timisoara (Romania) 2011. **Publications** *ECQA Newsletter.*
Members Organizations in 27 countries and territories:
Austria, Belgium, Brazil, Bulgaria, Canada, China, Croatia, Denmark, Finland, France, Germany, Greece, Hungary, India, Ireland, Italy, Japan, Kosovo, Luxembourg, Netherlands, Poland, Romania, Russia, Slovenia, Spain, UK, USA.
Included in the above, 3 organizations listed in this Yearbook:
European Manufacturing and Innovation Research Association (EMIRAcle, #07734); International Network for Terminology (TermNet, #14332); International Software Consulting Network (ISCN, #15557).
NGO Relations Cooperates with: *European Manufacturing and Innovation Research Association (EMIRAcle, #07734);* Henry Tudor; INTACS; *International Software Consulting Network (ISCN, #15557); International Software Testing Qualifications Board (ISTQB, #15559).* [2019.09.26/XJ4925/D]

♦ European Cervical Cancer Association (ECCA) 06512

Contact Rue Jourdan 121, 1060 Brussels, Belgium. T. +3225382833. Fax +3225385833.
URL: http://www.ecca.info/

Aims Raise awareness of cervical cancer and its prevention among members of the general public, healthcare professionals and public health decision-makers in Europe. **Structure** Board of Directors of 6. **Publications** Reports; brochures.
Members Full in 36 countries:
Algeria, Austria, Belgium, Bosnia-Herzegovina, Bulgaria, Croatia, Cyprus, Czechia, Denmark, Estonia, Finland, France, Georgia, Germany, Greece, Hungary, Iceland, Ireland, Italy, Latvia, Lithuania, Netherlands, North Macedonia, Norway, Poland, Portugal, Romania, Russia, Serbia, Slovakia, Slovenia, Spain, Sweden, Türkiye, UK, Ukraine.
International Organizations (5):
Association of European Cancer Leagues (ECL, #02500); Axios International; Programs for Appropriate Technologies in Health (PATH); *Union for International Cancer Control (UICC, #20415).*
NGO Relations Member of: *The NCD Alliance (NCDA, #16963); Union for International Cancer Control (UICC, #20415).* [2014/XJ0526/y/D]

- ♦ European Cetacean Bycatch Campaign (internationally oriented national body)
- ♦ European Cetacean Organization / see European Cetacean Society (#06513)

♦ European Cetacean Society (ECS) 06513

Sec c/o Inst for Biodiversity Studies, Fac of Mathematics/Natural Sciences/information Technologies, Univ of Primorska, Glagoljaska 8, 6000 Koper, Slovenia.
URL: http://www.europeancetaceansociety.eu/

History Jan 1987, Hirtshals (Denmark). Also known as *European Cetacean Organization (ECO).* **Aims** Promote and coordinate scientific study and *conservation* of cetaceans; gather and disseminate information to members and to the general public. **Structure** Council; Working Groups (4); National Contact Persons. **Languages** English. **Staff** None. **Finance** Members' dues. **Activities** Knowledge management/information dissemination; events/meetings. **Events** *World Marine Mammal Conference* Barcelona (Spain) 2019, *Annual Conference* Liège (Belgium) 2014, *Annual Conference* Cadiz (Spain) 2011, *Annual Conference* Stralsund (Germany) 2010, *Annual Conference* Istanbul (Turkey) 2009. **Publications** *ECS Newsletter* (3 a year). *European Research on Cetaceans* – proceedings of Annual Conference. Proceedings of workshops.
Members Individuals (about 400) in 46 countries and territories:
Algeria, Argentina, Australia, Austria, Belgium, Brazil, Canada, Chile, China, Croatia, Czechia, Denmark, Faeroe Is, Finland, France, Germany, Greece, Hong Kong, Hungary, Iceland, India, Ireland, Israel, Italy, Japan, Malaysia, Maldives, Malta, Monaco, Morocco, Netherlands, Norway, Peru, Poland, Portugal, Russia, Singapore, Slovenia, South Africa, Spain, Sweden, Switzerland, Türkiye, UK, Ukraine, USA.

European Chamber
06513

alphabetic sequence excludes
For the complete listing, see Yearbook Online at

IGO Relations *UNEP (#20299)*; *European Commission (EC, #06633)*. Also advises the secretariats of: *Agreement on the Conservation of Small Cetaceans of the Baltic, North East Atlantic, Irish and North Seas (ASCOBANS, 1992)*; *Agreement on the Conservation of Cetaceans of the Black Sea, Mediterranean Sea and contiguous Atlantic Area (ACCOBAMS, 1996)*. **NGO Relations** Advises environmental groups such as: *Friends of the Earth International (FoEI, #10002)*; *Greenpeace International (#10727)*; *World Wide Fund for Nature (WWF, #21922)*. [2017.11.24/XD0965/v/**D**]

- European Chamber (unconfirmed)
- European Chamber of Commerce for Traditional Chinese Medicine (no recent information)

♦ European Chamber of Engineers (ECE) 06514

Chambre européenne d'ingénieurs (CEI) – Europäische Kammer der Ingenieure (EKI)

Pres Jade Hochschule, Ofener Strasse 16/19, 26121 Oldenburg, Germany. T. +494414086908.
Registered Office Clos du Chemin Creux 6-B, 1030 Brussels, Belgium.
URL: http://ece-engineers.com/

History Statutes adopted 2002. Registered in accordance with Belgian law. **Aims** Assist all European engineers in their legal, professional, economic, social and professional affairs. **Structure** Assembly; Board of Governors. [2013.11.29/XM4066/**D**]

- European Chamber of Extrajudicial Adjudicators and Experts of Europe (internationally oriented national body)

♦ European Chamber Music Academy (ECMA) 06515

Coordination c/o mdw – Uni für Musik und darstellende Kunst, Anton-von-Weber-Platz 1, 1030 Vienna, Austria. E-mail: office@ecma-music.com.
URL: http://www.ecma-music.com/

History Originated from the *Accademia Europea del Quartetto*, 2001. Subtitle: *Association for the Promotion of European Chamber Music*. Since 2007, registered in accordance with Austrian law. **Structure** Executive Committee. **Activities** Training/education. [2019/XM8050/**D**]

♦ European Chamber Music Teachers' Association (ECMTA) 06516

Gesellschaft Europäischer Kammermusik-Lehrer – Europeiska Kammarmusikpedagogiska Föreningen rf – Euroopan kamarimusiikkipedagoginen yhdistys ry

Sec Tatari 13, 10116 Tallinn, Estonia. E-mail: info@ecmta.eu.
URL: http://www.ecmta.eu/

History Founded 22 Feb 2007, Finland. **Aims** Preserve and develop European classical chamber music heritage. **Structure** Board of 7 members. **Languages** English, Finnish. **Activities** Events/meetings. **Events** *Annual Meeting* Vilnius (Lithuania) 2020, *Autumn Meeting* Vilnius (Lithuania) 2020, *Autumn Meeting* Leiston (UK) 2019, *Annual Meeting* Lisbon (Portugal) 2019, *Autumn Meeting* Nicosia (Cyprus) 2018. **Members** About 80 institutional, individual, ensemble and contributing members in over 20 countries. Membership countries not specified. **NGO Relations** Member of: *European Music Council (EMC, #07837)*. [2021/XJ0245/**D**]

- European Chambers of Commerce Group for Trade with Latin America (inactive)
- European Chapter of the Association for Computational Linguistics (see: #02445)

♦ European Chapter on Combinatorial Optimization (ECCO) 06517

Coordinator DEI "Guglielmo Marconi", Univ of Bologna, Viale Risorgimento 2, 40136 Bologna BO, Italy. T. +39512093022. Fax +39512093073. E-mail: ecco-secretary@grenoble-inp.fr.
URL: https://ecco.grenoble-inp.fr/

History 1987. Former names and other names: *EURO Working Group on Combinatorial Optimization* – alias. **Aims** Discuss recent and important issues in combinatorial optimization and its applications with European combinatorialists. **Structure** Advisory Board. **Languages** English. **Staff** 0.50 FTE, paid; 0.50 FTE, voluntary. **Finance** Sources: meeting proceeds. Supported by: *Association of European Operational Research Societies (EURO, #02528)*. Annual budget: 10,000 EUR. **Activities** Events/meetings. **Events** *Conference* St Petersburg (Russia) 2022, *Conference* Madrid (Spain) 2021, *Conference* St Petersburg (Russia) 2020, *Conference* St Julian's (Malta) 2019, *Conference* Fribourg (Switzerland) 2018. **Publications** Peer reviewed papers.
Members Individuals (over 1,300) interested in combinatorial optimization, either in theoretical aspects or in business, industry or public administration. Members in 57 countries:
Algeria, Australia, Austria, Bangladesh, Belarus, Belgium, Brazil, Bulgaria, Canada, China, Czechia, Denmark, Egypt, France, Germany, Ghana, Greece, Hungary, India, Iran Islamic Rep, Ireland, Israel, Italy, Japan, Jordan, Kazakhstan, Korea Rep, Kuwait, Lebanon, Lithuania, Marshall Is, Mexico, Mongolia, Nepal, Netherlands, Nigeria, Norway, Pakistan, Peru, Poland, Portugal, Romania, Russia, Saudi Arabia, Serbia, Singapore, Slovakia, Spain, Sweden, Switzerland, Thailand, Tunisia, Türkiye, UK, Ukraine, United Arab Emirates, USA. [2023.02.20/XF5398/cv/**F**]

♦ European Charcot Foundation (ECF) 06518

General Coordination SEAUTON Intl BVBA, Vaartdijk 3 box 002, 3018 Leuven, Belgium. T. +32473414583. E-mail: secretariat@charcot-ms.org.
Scientific Secretariat IRCCS Ospedale San Raffaele, Via Olgettina 60, 20132 Milan MI, Italy. T. +39226433092.
URL: http://www.charcot-ms.org/

History 1990. Former names and other names: *European Charcot Foundation for Multiple Sclerosis Research* – alias; *Fondation européenne Charcot* – former; *Europäische Charcot Stiftung* – former. Registration: Banque-Carrefour des Entreprises, No/ID: 0547.995.164, Start date: 27 Feb 2014, Belgium. **Aims** Realize a European dimension in *Multiple Sclerosis* (MS) research and capitalize on the resources of European cooperation and coordination to overcome this debilitating *disease*. **Structure** Board; Executive Board; Committees (7). **Languages** English. **Staff** 4.00 FTE, paid. **Finance** Sources: international organizations; private foundations. national multiple sclerosis societies and industries. **Activities** Events/meetings; knowledge management/information dissemination; research/documentation; training/education. **Events** *Annual Meeting* Baveno (Italy) 2022, *Annual Meeting* Baveno (Italy) 2021, *Annual Meeting* Milan (Italy) 2020, *Annual Meeting* Baveno (Italy) 2019, *Annual Meeting* Baveno (Italy) 2018. **Publications** Reports; symposia proceedings.
Members Full in 64 countries and territories:
Albania, Argentina, Australia, Austria, Belarus, Belgium, Brazil, Bulgaria, Canada, Chile, China, Costa Rica, Croatia, Cuba, Cyprus, Czechia, Denmark, Egypt, Estonia, Finland, France, Georgia, Germany, Greece, Hungary, Iceland, Iran Islamic Rep, Ireland, Israel, Italy, Japan, Korea Rep, Kuwait, Latvia, Lithuania, Luxembourg, Mexico, Moldova, Montenegro, Morocco, Netherlands, Nigeria, North Macedonia, Norway, Pakistan, Panama, Poland, Portugal, Puerto Rico, Romania, Russia, Saudi Arabia, Serbia, Slovakia, Slovenia, South Africa, Spain, Sweden, Switzerland, Thailand, Türkiye, UK, Ukraine, USA. [2022/XF2713/f/**F**]

- European Charcot Foundation for Multiple Sclerosis Research / see European Charcot Foundation (#06518)

♦ European Charities' Committee on Value-Added Tax (ECCVAT) 06519

Chairman Church House, Great Smith Street, London, SW1P 3AZ, UK. T. +442072221265. E-mail: info@eccvat.org.
URL: http://www.eccvat.org/

History 1992. Registration: EU Transparency Register, No/ID: 72562234730-60, Start date: 9 Dec 2010. **Aims** Research the impact of VAT and other taxes on charities and NGOs; represent charities and NGOs by informing EU institutions about this impact. **Activities** Advocacy/lobbying/activism; events/meetings; knowledge management/information dissemination; monitoring/evaluation; networking/liaising; research/documentation. **Events** *International philantropy conference* Brussels (Belgium) 2005.
Members Organizations in 5 countries, including 4 organizations listed in this Yearbook:
Belgium, Germany, Netherlands, Spain, UK.
EuroCom – Society for European Communication; *European Fundraising Association (EFA, #07367)*; *Philanthropy Europe Association (Philea, #18358)*; *Wellcome Trust*. [2021.05.26/XE4302/y/**E**]

- European Charter of the Cistercian Abbeys and Sites (#03854)
- European Chartered Accountants, Lawyers, Tax Advisors and Management Consultants / see European Consultants Unit (#06769)
- European Charter on Environment and Health (1989 treaty)
- European Charter of Local Self-government (1985 treaty)
- European Charter on Mountain Regions (1995 treaty)
- European Charter for Regional or Minority Languages (1992 treaty)

♦ European Cheerleading Association (ECA) 06520

Europäische Cheerleading Assoziation (ECA)

Contact Otto-Fleck-Schneise 12, 60528 Frankfurt-Main, Germany. T. +496996740267. E-mail: office@ecacheer.org.
URL: https://www.ecacheer.org/

History 1994. Statutes amended Feb 2010, Helsinki (Finland). Current statutes adopted Feb 2019, Barcelona (Spain). Registration: No/ID: VR 14973, Start date: 11 Sep 2012, Germany. **Aims** Promote cheerleading in Europe in cooperation with its member associations. **Structure** General Meeting; Board. **Languages** English, German. **Activities** Sporting activities; training/education.
Members Federations in 17 countries:
Belgium, Bosnia-Herzegovina, Croatia, Germany, Ireland, Italy, Latvia, Lithuania, Luxembourg, Montenegro, Netherlands, Russia, Slovenia, Spain, Switzerland, UK, Ukraine.
NGO Relations Member of (1): *European Dance Sport Federation (EDSF, #06887)*. Continental federation of: *International Federation of Cheerleading (IFC, #13386)*. [2021.02.17/XJ6340/**D**]

♦ European Chemical Employers Group (ECEG) 06521

Dir Gen Bd Auguste Reyers 80, 1030 Brussels, Belgium. T. +3222389774. E-mail: secretariat@eceg.org.
URL: http://www.eceg.org/

History Founded 2001, Brussels (Belgium). Registered in accordance with Belgian law, 2011. **Aims** Represent the chemicals, pharmaceuticals, rubber and plastics industries in Europe, and serve as a social partner and a consultation body of European Institutions and other stakeholders. **Languages** English. **Staff** 2.00 FTE, paid. **Finance** Members' dues. **Activities** Advocacy/lobbying/activism; politics/policy/regulatory; events/meetings. **Events** *Conference* Copenhagen (Denmark) 2013, *Conference* Dublin (Ireland) 2013, *Conference* Brussels (Belgium) 2011, *Conference* Potsdam (Germany) 2010, *Conference* Lisbon (Portugal) 2007. **Publications** Reports; position papers; statements; other documents.
Members National employers' federations in 18 countries:
Austria, Belgium, Bulgaria, Croatia, Czechia, Denmark, Finland, France, Germany, Hungary, Italy, Netherlands, Norway, Poland, Slovakia, Spain, Sweden, UK.
NGO Relations Cooperates with: *Conseil européen de l'industrie chimique (CEFIC, #04687)*. Previously part of Sector Social Dialogue Committee with *European Mine, Chemical and Energy Workers' Federation (EMCEF, inactive)*. [2019.12.18/XJ0895/**F**]

- European Chemical Industry Council (#04687)
- European Chemical Industry Ecology and Toxicology Centre / see European Centre for Ecotoxicology and Toxicology of Chemicals (#06477)
- European Chemical Marketing and Strategy Association (inactive)

♦ European Chemical Regions Network (ECRN) 06522

Network and Policy Coordinator Rue de Trèves 59, 1040 Brussels, Belgium. T. +32471528331. E-mail: office@ecrn.net – ecrn@ecrn.net.
URL: http://www.ecrn.net/

History 2004. Founded as a temporary project of *INTERREG V (#15966)*, under the 2000-2006 phase when it was known as INTERREG III, with 13 member regions from 7 European countries. Now a permanent organization. Registration: Banque-Carrefour des Entreprises, No/ID: 0712.938.716, Start date: 8 Nov 2018, Belgium; EU Transparency Register, No/ID: 290674324480-26, Start date: 14 Nov 2016. **Aims** Advocate for a stronger regional dimension in European strategies and policies related to the chemical industry. **Structure** General Assembly; Executive Board; Network Secretariat; Working Group. **Languages** English, French, Italian, Polish. **Activities** Advocacy/lobbying/activism; awareness raising; capacity building; events/meetings; knowledge management/information dissemination; monitoring/evaluation; networking/liaising; politics/policy/regulatory; projects/programmes. **Events** *General Assembly* Brussels (Belgium) 2021, *Conference on Building the Sustainable Chemical Industry of Tomorrow* Brussels (Belgium) 2020, *General Assembly* Brussels (Belgium) 2020, *General Assembly* Brussels (Belgium) 2016, *Congress* Milan (Italy) 2015. **Publications** *Who is Who of Chemical Regions*. Position papers.
Members Regions (10) from 6 EU countries:
Drenthe, Flanders, Groningen, Limburg, Lombardy, Masovian, Saxony-Anhalt, South Holland, Usti nad Labem, Wallonia.
IGO Relations Participates in: High Level Group on the Competitiveness of the European Chemical Industry of *European Commission (EC, #06633)*. **NGO Relations** Member of (1): *Circular Plastics Alliance (#03936)*. Cooperates with (2): *Conseil européen de l'industrie chimique (CEFIC, #04687)*; *European Environmental Bureau (EEB, #06996)*. [2022/XJ0670/**D**]

- European Chemical Road Transport Association / see European Chemical Transport Association (#06525)

♦ European Chemicals Agency (ECHA) 06523

Agence européenne des produits chimiques – Agencia Europea de Sustancias y Mezclas Quimicas – Europäische Chemikalienagentur – Agência Europeia dos Produtos Quimicos – Agenzia Europea per le Sostanze Chimiche – Europees Agentschap voor Chemische Stoffen – Europeiska Kemikaliemyndigheten – Det Europaeiske Kemikalieagentur – Euroopan Kemikaalivirasto – Evropska Agentura pro Chemické Latky – Európska Chemicka Agentúra – Európai Vegyianyag-ügynökség – Europejska Agencja Chemikaliów – Evropska Agencija za Kemikalije – Euroopa Kemikaaliamet – Europos cheminiu Medziagu Agentura – Agentjia Europeanā pentru Produse Chimice

Address not obtained.
URL: http://echa.europa.eu/

History 2007. Established as a decentralized agency of *European Union (EU, #08967)*. Operational as of 1 Jun 2008. Former names and other names: *Agence européenne des produits chimique* – former; *Agencia Europea de Sustancias y Preparados Quimicos* – former; *Europäische Agentur für Chemische Stoffe* – former; *Agência Europeia das Substâncias Quimicas* – former; *Agenzia Europea delle Sostanze Chimiche* – former; *Europaeiske Kemikalieagentur* – former; *Euroopan Kamikaalivirasto* – former. **Aims** Manage all REACH (Regulation for Registration, Evaluation, Authorization and Restriction of Chemicals), CLP (Regulation on Classification, Packaging and Labelling of substances and mixtures), Biocides, and Prior Informed Consent Chemicals tasks by carrying out or coordinating the necessary activities, so as to ensure a consistent implementation at Community level and provide Member States and the EU with the best possible scientific advice on questions related to the safety and the socio-economic aspects of the use of chemicals. **Structure** Management Board. Executive Director. Secretariat. Committees (4): Member State; Risk Assessment; Socio-economic Analysis; Biocidal Products. Forum; Board of Appeal. **Languages** English. **Staff** 463.00 FTE, paid. **Finance** Community Contributions; fees income of Registrations. Budget (2011): euro 99.8 million. **Activities** Responsible for the REACH Regulation, regulation on the Classification, Labelling and Packaging (CLP) of chemicals, Biocidal Products Regulation and Prior Inform Consent Chemicals management. **Events** *ONE – Health Environment and Society Conference* Brussels (Belgium) 2022, *Meeting* Brussels (Belgium) 2019, *Instrument for Pre-accession Assistance Conference* Helsinki (Finland) 2019, *Workshop on Update Needs Regarding the EU System for the Evaluation of Substances* Brussels (Belgium) 2018, *Global Helsinki Chemicals Forum* Helsinki (Finland) 2018.
Members Governments of 27 countries:
Austria, Belgium, Bulgaria, Croatia, Cyprus, Czechia, Denmark, Estonia, Finland, France, Germany, Greece, Hungary, Ireland, Italy, Latvia, Lithuania, Luxembourg, Malta, Netherlands, Poland, Portugal, Romania, Slovakia, Slovenia, Spain, Sweden.
IGO Relations Audited by: *European Court of Auditors (#06854)*; Internal Audit Service of the EU Commission. Took over activities of: *European Chemicals Bureau (inactive)*. **NGO Relations** Member of (1): *EU Agencies Network (EUAN, #05564)*. Accepts accredited stakeholders (list available on website). Maintains: *European Union Observatory for Nanomaterials (EUON, #09007)*. [2021/XM3659/**D***]

♦ European Chemical Society (EuCheMS) 06524

Société Européenne de Chimie

SG Rue du Trône 62, 1050 Brussels, Belgium. T. +3222892690. E-mail: secretariat@euchems.eu.
URL: http://www.euchems.eu/

History 1970. Since adoption of new constitution, 19-20 Sep 1996, includes European Communities Chemistry Council. Constitution revised 15 Oct 2004, Bucharest (Romania). Former names and other names: *Federation of European Chemical Societies (FECS)* – former; *Fédération des sociétés chimiques européennes* – former; *Föderation Europäischer Chemischer Gesellschaften* – former; *Federacija Evropejskih Himiceskih Obscestv* – former; *Euchem* – former; *European Association for Chemical and Molecular Sciences* – former (2004); *Association européenne pour les sciences chimiques et moléculaires* – former (2004); *Europäische Vereinigung für Chemische und Molekulare Wissenschaften* – former (2004). Registration: Banque-Carrefour des Entreprises, No/ID: 0880.955.582, Start date: 26 Apr 2006, Belgium; EU Transparency Register, No/ID: 03492856440-03, Start date: 17 Aug 2011. **Aims** Nurture a platform for scientific discussion; provide a single, unbiased European voice on key policy issues in chemistry and related fields. **Structure** General Assembly (annual); Executive Board. **Languages** Czech, Danish, Dutch, English, Estonian, EU languages, Finnish, French, German, Hungarian, Irish Gaelic, Italian, Latvian, Lithuanian, Maltese, Polish, Portuguese, Russian, Slovakian, Slovene, Spanish, Swedish. **Staff** 3.00 FTE, paid. **Finance** Sources: members' dues. Supported by: *European Federation of Managerial Staff in the Chemical and Allied Industries (FECCIA, #07160)*. **Activities** Awards/prizes/competitions; events/meetings; knowledge management/information dissemination; politics/policy/regulatory. **Events** *European Chemistry Congress* Lisbon (Portugal) 2022, *European Conference on Theoretical and Computational Chemistry* Chalkidiki (Greece) 2021, *European Chemistry Congress* Lisbon (Portugal) 2020, *Euroanalysis : Biennial European Conference on Analytical Chemistry* Istanbul (Turkey) 2019, *European Conference on Theoretical and Computational Chemistry* Perugia (Italy) 2019. **Publications** *Brussels News Updates (BNU)* (12 a year); *Chemistry in Europe* (4 a year).
Members National societies (41) in 33 countries:
Austria, Belgium, Bulgaria, Croatia, Cyprus, Czechia, Denmark, Estonia, Finland, France, Germany, Greece, Hungary, Ireland, Israel, Italy, Luxembourg, Montenegro, Netherlands, North Macedonia, Norway, Poland, Portugal, Romania, Russia, Serbia, Slovakia, Slovenia, Spain, Sweden, Switzerland, Türkiye, UK.
Consultative Status Consultative status granted from: *ECOSOC (#05331)* (Ros C). **NGO Relations** Observer to: *EURACHEM (#05595)*. Associated organization of: *International Union of Pure and Applied Chemistry (IUPAC, #15809)*. Partner of: *Conseil européen de l'industrie chimique (CEFIC, #04687)*. [2022.05.11/XD4925/**D**]

♦ European Chemical Society (no recent information)

♦ European Chemical Transport Association (ECTA) 06525

Contact Bd Auguste Reyers 80, 1030 Brussels, Belgium. T. +3223185827. E-mail: info@ecta.com.
URL: https://www.ecta.com/
History Oct 1997, Barcelona (Spain). Former names and other names: *European Chemical Road Transport Association (ECRTA)* – former (1997 to 1999). Registration: Belgium. **Aims** Provide chemical transport industry with an authoritative voice at European level; improve standards of efficiency, safety and quality as well as environmental and social impacts of the transport and logistics of chemical goods in Europe; manage the ECTA Responsible Care Scheme. **Structure** General Assembly (annual); Board of Directors; Executive Committee; Working Groups. **Languages** English. **Staff** 3.00 FTE, paid. **Finance** Sources: members' dues. **Activities** Events/meetings; research/documentation. **Events** *Annual General Meeting* Düsseldorf (Germany) 2015, *Annual General Meeting* Düsseldorf (Germany) 2014, *Annual General Meeting* Düsseldorf (Germany) 2013, *Annual General Meeting* Düsseldorf (Germany) 2012, *Annual General Meeting* Rotterdam (Netherlands) 2011. **Publications** *ECTA Newsletter*. Annual Report; best practices guidelines; reports. **Members** Transport and logistic-related companies across Europe. Membership countries not specified.
[2022.05.11/XD7172/**D**]

♦ European Chemistry Thematic Network (ECTN) 06526

Gen Sec c/o SEFI, Rue des Deux Eglises, 1000 Brussels, Belgium. E-mail: generalsecretary@ectn.eu – secretariat@ectn.eu.
Contact c/o EuChemS, Rue du Trône 62, 1050 Brussels, Belgium.
URL: http://ectn.eu/
History Set 2003, up following network activity of *European Chemistry and Chemical Engineering Education Network (EC2E2N, inactive)*. Full title: *European Chemistry Thematic Network Association (ECTN Association)* Registered in accordance with Belgian law. EU Transparency Register: 839118419891-83. **Structure** General Assembly; Administrative Council. **Events** *General Assembly* Amsterdam (Netherlands) 2023, *General Assembly* Budapest (Hungary) 2022, *General Assembly* Krakow (Poland) 2019, *General Assembly* Prague (Czechia) 2018, *Workshop on Glyphosate* Brussels (Belgium) 2017.
Members Full in 13 countries:
Austria, Belgium, Czechia, France, Germany, Ireland, Italy, Netherlands, Poland, Romania, Slovakia, Spain, UK.
NGO Relations Founding member of: *European Alliance of Subject-Specific and Professional Accreditation and Quality Assurance (EASPA, #05887)*. Member of: *International Union of Pure and Applied Chemistry (IUPAC, #15809)*. [2019/XJ9470/**E**]

♦ European Chemistry Thematic Network Association / see European Chemistry Thematic Network (#06526)

♦ European Chemoreception Research Organization (ECRO) 06527

Organisation européenne pour les recherches chimiosensorielles
Registered address place Mercelin Berthelot, 75005 Paris, France.
URL: https://www.ecro-online/
History 25 Aug 1970, Zeist (Netherlands). 1971, registered in accordance with French law. **Aims** Promote fundamental and applied research in chemosensory science, especially *olfaction* and taste in vertebrates and invertebrates. **Structure** Board. **Languages** English, French. **Staff** Voluntary. **Finance** Members dues. **Activities** Knowledge management/information dissemination; guidance/assistance/consulting; events/meetings. **Events** *Conference* Berlin (Germany) 2022, *Congress* Trieste (Italy) 2019, *Congress* Würzburg (Germany) 2018, *Congress* Cambridge (UK) 2017, *Congress* Athens (Greece) 2016. **Publications** *Chemical Senses* (12 a year). Annual Report.
Members Full in 31 countries:
Argentina, Australia, Austria, Belgium, Canada, China, Croatia, Czechia, Denmark, Finland, France, Germany, Hungary, Ireland, Israel, Italy, Japan, Lithuania, Netherlands, New Zealand, Norway, Poland, Qatar, Russia, South Africa, Spain, Sweden, Switzerland, Tunisia, UK, USA. [2022/XD4236/**D**]

♦ European Chess Union (ECU) 06528

Office Rainweidstrasse 2, 6333 Hünenberg ZG, Switzerland. Fax +41415880245. E-mail: ecu-office2014@gmail.com.
Pres Kipshidze Str 10 – ap 21, 0179 Tbilisi, Georgia. T. +995599559989. Fax +99532294962. E-mail: azmai@hotmail.com.
URL: http://www.europechess.org/
History Current statutes adopted, 18 Apr 1998, Budapest (Hungary)/Elista (USSR); amended 2003, Plovdiv (Bulgaria), 2005, Gothenburg (Sweden), 2010, Rijeka (Croatia), 2015, Bar (Montenegro) and 2017, Crete (Greece). Registration: Switzerland; EU Transparency Register, No/ID: 391036939479-80, Start date: 8 Sep 2020. **Aims** Safeguard and further the interests of chess in Europe. **Structure** General Assembly (annual); Board. **Languages** English, French, German. **Staff** 2.00 FTE, paid. **Finance** Members' dues. Other sources: Tournament fees; service fees; other revenues. **Activities** Events/meetings; sporting activities. **Events** *General Assembly* Batumi (Georgia) 2014, *General Assembly* Porto Carras (Greece) 2011, *General Assembly* Khanty-Mansiysk (Russia) 2010, *General Assembly* Novi Sad (Serbia) 2009, *General Assembly* Dresden (Germany) 2008. **Publications** Manual.
Members Members (54) in 54 countries and territories:
Albania, Andorra, Armenia, Austria, Azerbaijan, Belarus, Belgium, Bosnia-Herzegovina, Croatia, Cyprus, Czechia, Denmark, England, Estonia, Faeroe Is, Finland, France, Georgia, Germany, Greece, Guernsey, Hungary, Iceland, Ireland, Israel, Italy, Jersey, Kosovo, Latvia, Liechtenstein, Lithuania, Luxembourg, Malta, Moldova, Monaco, Montenegro, Netherlands, North Macedonia, Norway, Poland, Portugal, Romania, Russia, San Marino, Scotland, Serbia, Slovakia, Slovenia, Spain, Sweden, Switzerland, Türkiye, Ukraine, Wales.
Associated member (1):
International School Chess Union (ISCU, #14785).
IGO Relations Cooperates with: *European Parliament (EP, #08146)*. **NGO Relations** Collaborates with: *Fédération internationale des échecs (FIDE, #09627)*. [2018.01.24/XD8464/**D**]

♦ European Chestnut Network (unconfirmed)

♦ European Child-Friendly-Cities Network / see European Network Child Friendly Cities (#07877)

♦ European Childhood Obesity Group (ECOG) 06529

Secretariat c/o Business Solutions Europa, Rue Philippe Le Bon 15, 1000 Brussels, Belgium. T. +3225885671. E-mail: info@ecog-obesity.eu.
URL: http://www.ecog-obesity.eu/
History 1990, Brussels (Belgium). **Aims** Develop clinical and scientific knowledge of obesity in childhood; increase understanding of childhood obesity through studies, research and professional publications. **Structure** General Meeting (annual); Board of Directors; Scientific Advisor. **Languages** English. **Finance** Members' dues. **Events** *Congress* Vichy (France) 2022, *Congress* Budapest (Hungary) 2021, *Congress* Wadowice (Poland) 2019, *Congress* Rome (Italy) 2017, *Workshop* Thessaloniki (Greece) 2016. **Publications** *The ECOG Free Obesity eBook*. **Members** Researchers, practitioners and other professionals working on child obesity in 16 countries. Membership countries not specified. **IGO Relations** *WHO (#20950)*. **NGO Relations** Member of: *Safe Food Advocacy Europe (SAFE, #19026)*. [2016.06.01/XF6843/**F**]

♦ European Children's Film Association (ECFA) 06530

Association Européenne du Cinéma pour l'Enfance et la Jeunesse
SG Rue du Pavillon 3, 1030 Brussels, Belgium. T. +3222425409. Fax +3222427427. E-mail: mail@ecfaweb.org.
URL: http://www.ecfaweb.org/
History Oct 1988, Mons (Belgium). Registered in accordance with Belgian law. EU Transparency Register: 367368430590-77. **Aims** Support *cinema* for children in its cultural, economical, aesthetic, social, political and educational aspects; offer a communication panel to promote new ways of cooperation within Europe, East or West, in the field of young audience film production, distribution and exhibition. **Structure** Board. **Languages** English, French. **Staff** 0.50 FTE, voluntary. **Finance** Members' dues. Annual budget: about euro 7,500. **Activities** Events/meetings; awards/prizes/competitions; networking/liaising; guidance/assistance/consulting. **Events** *Annual General Meeting* Berlin (Germany) 2019, *Conference* Stockholm (Sweden) 2017, *ICEM/ECFA Conference* Oslo (Norway) 2003, *I am what I eat* Desenzano del Garda (Italy) 2002, *Conference* Cologne (Germany) 2001. **Publications** *ECFA Update* (6 a year) – newsletter; *ECFA Journal* (4 a year).
Members Film professionals and associations in 40 countries:
Albania, Australia, Austria, Belgium, Canada, China, Croatia, Czechia, Denmark, Estonia, Finland, France, Germany, Greece, Hungary, India, Ireland, Israel, Italy, Japan, Latvia, Lithuania, Luxembourg, Netherlands, North Macedonia, Norway, Poland, Portugal, Romania, Russia, Serbia, Slovakia, Slovenia, Spain, Sweden, Switzerland, Türkiye, UK, Ukraine, USA.
[2019/XD2027/**D**]

♦ European Children's Hospitals Organisation (ECHO) 06531

Secretariat Hosp Sant Joan de Déu, Passeig Sant Joan de Déu 2, Esplugues de Llobregat, 08950 Barcelona, Spain. E-mail: echoinfo@sjdhospitalbarcelona.org.
URL: https://www.echohospitals.org/
History EU Transparency Register: 601865937284-34. **Aims** Advocate for children's health and their access to the best quality care through the collaborative work of children's hospitals. **Structure** Board; Secretariat. **Activities** Advocacy/lobbying/activism; research/documentation; training/education. [2020/XM8858/**D**]

♦ European Children's Universities Network (EUCU.NET) 06532

Gen Sec c/o Vienna Univ Children's Office, Lammgasse 8/4, 1080 Vienna, Austria. E-mail: info@eucu.net – kinderbuero@univie.ac.at.
URL: http://www.eucu.net/
History Founded 2008, as a project co-funded by *European Commission (EC, #06633)*. Project ended 2010, but activities continued. Set up as a self-financed network, 2011. **Aims** Support existing programs with strategies for funding and sustainability; enhance further growth of Children's Universities. **Structure** Scientific Board; Presidents (3); General Secretary; International Liaison Coordinator. **Languages** English. **Staff** 5.00 FTE, paid. **Finance** Members' dues. Initially funded by: *European Commission (EC, #06633)* – Seventh Framework Programme for Research and Technological Development (FP7). **Activities** Events/meetings; publishing activities. **Events** *Conference* Vienna (Austria) 2014, *International conference* Vienna (Austria) 2009. **Publications** *The EUCUNET White Book*.
Members Individuals; institutions. Members in 30 countries:
Austria, Belgium, Brazil, Canada, Colombia, Croatia, Denmark, Estonia, Finland, France, Georgia, Germany, India, Ireland, Italy, Kenya, Lithuania, Luxembourg, Netherlands, North Macedonia, Poland, Portugal, Romania, Russia, Slovakia, Slovenia, Switzerland, Türkiye, UK, USA. [2014.11.06/XJ1404/**F**]

♦ European Child Rescue Alert and Police Network on Missing Children (AMBER Alert Europe) 06533

Contact Rondpoint Robert Schuman 9, 1040 Brussels, Belgium. T. +3228082159. Fax +3228082161. E-mail: info@amberalert.eu.
URL: http://www.amberalert.eu/
History AMBER Alert Netherlands set up Nov 2008. AMBER Alert Europe set up Mar 2013. EU Transparency Register: 488692317424-44. Registered in accordance with Dutch law: 852414183. **Aims** Assist in saving missing or at-risk children by connecting law enforcement with other police experts and with the public across Europe. **Structure** Board of Directors; Advisory Board. **Languages** Dutch, English, French, German. **Finance** Government grants; services; donations. **Activities** Networking/liaising; guidance/assistance/consulting; knowledge management/information dissemination; training/education. **Members** Official organizations, public authorities and business entities in 21 countries. Membership countries not specified. **IGO Relations** Links with members of: *European Parliament (EP, #08146)*. [2019.12.13/XM4359/y/**F**]

♦ European Child Safety Alliance (ECSA) 06534

Contact c/o RoSPA House, 28 Calthorpe Road, Edgbaston, Birmingham, B15 1RP, UK. T. +441212482000. E-mail: secretariat@childsafetyeurope.org.
URL: http://www.childsafetyeurope.org/
History within *European Association for Injury Prevention and Safety Promotion (EuroSafe, #06083)*. Now hosted by The Royal Society for the Prevention of Accidents (RoSPA). Previously known under the acronym *ECOSA*. **Aims** Advance child injury prevention throughout Europe. **IGO Relations** Partners: *European Commission (EC, #06633)*; *UNICEF (#20332)*; *WHO (#20950)*. **NGO Relations** Member of: *Health and Environment Alliance (HEAL, #10879)*. [2020/XM2068/**E**]

♦ European Chilled Food Federation (ECFF) 06535

Fédération européenne des plats frais refrigérés
Secretariat c/o AIDEPI, Viale del Poggio Fiorito 61, 00144 Rome RM, Italy. T. +3968091071. Fax +3968073186.
URL: http://www.ecff.net/
History Oct 1991. EU Transparency Register: 602672918933-28. **Aims** Promote quality and safety of production and distribution of chilled foods; represent the industry and its views to European decision makers and regulatory bodies. **Languages** English. **Publications** *ECFF Recommendations for Hygiene Manufacture of Chilled Foods*. Annual Report.
Members Companies and organizations in 7 countries:
Belgium, Finland, Germany, Italy, Netherlands, Spain, Switzerland, UK.
IGO Relations *EFTA (#05391)*; *European Union (EU, #08967)*. [2019/XD7853/**D**]

♦ European Chimneys Association (ECA) 06536

SG UNITAM, 39-41 rue Louis Blanc, 92400 Courbevoie, France. T. +33147176460. Fax +33147176461. E-mail: contact@unitam.fr.
URL: http://www.eca-europe.org/
History 1989. **Aims** Focus the experiences and strengths of European Chimney producers; represent chimney and chimney systems manufacturers in Europe. **NGO Relations** In liaison with technical committees of: *Comité européen de normalisation (CEN, #04162)*. [2015/XD8129/**D**]

♦ European China Law Studies Association (ECLS) 06537

Pres address not obtained.
Vice-Pres address not obtained.
Treas address not obtained.
URL: http://www.ecls.eu/

History 2006. **Structure** Board, comprising Chair, Vice-Chair/Treasurer and 4 members. **Events** *Annual Conference* Copenhagen (Denmark) 2022, *Annual Conference* Warsaw (Poland) 2021, *Annual Conference* Durham (UK) 2019, *Annual Conference* Turin (Italy) 2018, *Annual Conference* Leiden (Netherlands) 2017. **Members** Individuals. Membership countries not specified. [2022/XJ1345/v/**D**]

♦ European Chinese Kuo Shu Federation (inactive)

♦ European Chips and Snacks Association / see European Snacks Association (#08498)

♦ European Chiropractors' Union (ECU) 06538

Association européenne des chiropraticiens – Union Europäischer Chiropraktoren

Head Office De Vang 5, 4191 TM Geldermalsen, Netherlands. E-mail: info@chiropractic-ecu.org.
URL: http://www.chiropractic-ecu.org/

History May 1932, London (UK). Registration: EU Transparency Register, No/ID: 43612725310-63. **Aims** Promote the health benefits of chiropractic, high standards of education and excellence in conduct and practice; advocate the inclusion of chiropractic within health policies and health programmes. **Structure** General Assembly-Convention (annual); General Council; Executive Council. Academic arm: *European Academy of Chiropractic (EAC, see: #06538)*. **Languages** English. **Staff** 0.50 FTE, voluntary. **Finance** Sources: members' dues; sponsorship. **Events** *Convention* Utrecht (Netherlands) 2022, *Convention* Utrecht (Netherlands) 2020, *Annual Convention* Berlin (Germany) 2019, *Annual Convention* Oslo (Norway) 2016, *Annual Convention* Athens (Greece) 2015. **Publications** *Backspace* (2 a year) in English, Spanish – newsletter.

Members National chiropractors' associations and individuals in 23 countries:
Austria, Belgium, Cyprus, Czechia, Denmark, Estonia, Finland, Germany, Greece, Hungary, Iceland, Ireland, Italy, Liechtenstein, Luxembourg, Malta, Netherlands, Norway, Poland, Spain, Sweden, Switzerland, Türkiye.

NGO Relations Member of (2): *European Public Health Alliance (EPHA, #08297)*; *World Federation of Chiropractic (WFC, #21420)*. Cooperates with (1): *European Council on Chiropractic Education (ECCE, #06809)*. [2022.10.18/XD0619/**D**]

♦ European Chitin Society (EUCHIS) 06539

Pres Inst de Estudios Biofuncionales, Fac de Farmacia, Univ Complutense, Pasea de Juan XXIII no 1, 28040 Madrid, Spain.
Sec IPREM, Helioparc Pau Pyrenées, 2 avenue P Angot, 64053 Pau CEDEX 09, France.
Registered Address Claude Bernard Univ, Lab d'Etudes des Matériaux Plastiques et des Biomatériaux, 43 bv du 11 Novembre 1918, Villeurbanne, France.
URL: http://www.euchis.org/

History 1992, Villeurbanne (France). **Aims** Encourage basic and applied scientific studies of all aspects of chitin, including chitosan and derivatives of chitin and chitosan, and related *enzymes*; aid the dissemination of such studies; encourage and facilitate exchanges between European scientists working in the field of chitin; encourage the practical application of fundamental research in the field of chitin; act as a central organization for the standardization of matters relating to chitin. **Structure** General Assembly (every 2 years). Board of Directors. **Languages** English. **Staff** 1.00 FTE, paid. **Finance** Members' dues. Other sources: donations; income from sale of goods; subsidies; income from scientific meetings or congresses; advertising revenue. **Activities** Events/meetings; awards/prizes/competitions. **Events** *Conference* Münster (Germany) 2015, *International Conference on Chitin and Chitosan* Münster (Germany) 2015, *Conference* Porto (Portugal) 2013, *Conference* St Petersburg (Russia) 2011, *Conference* Venice (Italy) 2009. **Publications** *Chitin Newsletter* (2 a year).

Members Categories Active; Collective; Associated; Honorary; Donor. Individuals in 21 countries:
Belarus, Belgium, Denmark, Finland, France, Germany, Greece, Italy, Mexico, Netherlands, Norway, Poland, Portugal, Russia, Slovakia, Slovenia, Spain, Thailand, UK, Ukraine, USA. [2015/XE2047/v/**D**]

♦ European Chlorinated Solvent Association (ECSA) 06540

Contact CEFIC, Rue Belliard 40 – Bte 15, 1040 Brussels, Belgium. T. +3224369506. Fax +3226769550. E-mail: ecsa@cefic.be.
URL: http://www.eurochlor.org/

History 1989. A sector group of *Conseil européen de l'industrie chimique (CEFIC, #04687)* within *Euro Chlor (#05659)*. **Aims** Develop authoritative statements on issues related to chlorinated solvents based on best available data; sponsor research on *environmental* and *toxicological* issues; develop an *industry* programme supporting the safe *recycling* and ultimate *disposal* of chlorinated solvent residues. **Structure** Management Committee; Working Groups (5). **Languages** English. **Staff** 1.50 FTE, paid. **Finance** Members' dues. **Activities** Working Groups (5): Technical; Occupational and Environmental Health; Statistics; Communication and Outreach; Reach. **Publications** Sustainability report; technical documents on proper storage, handling, use, disposal and recycling of chlorinated solvents.

Members Full in 6 countries:
Belgium, Czechia, France, Germany, Switzerland, UK. [2019.10.07/XE1507/**E**]

♦ European Choral Association – Europa Cantat 06541

SG c/o Haus der Kultur, Weberstr 59a, 53113 Bonn, Germany. T. +492289125663. Fax +492289125658. E-mail: info@europeanchoralassociation.org.
URL: http://www.europeanchoralassociation.org/

History 15 May 1960, Geneva (Switzerland). Constitution adopted 9 Feb 1963, Bonn (Germany FR). New name adopted when merged with *Union of European Choral Federations (EUROCHOR, inactive)*. Former names and other names: *Europa Cantat – European Federation of Young Choirs (EFYC)* – former (15 May 1960 to Jan 2011); *Europa Cantat – Fédération européenne des jeunes chorales (FEJC)* – former (15 May 1960 to Jan 2011); *Europa Cantat – Europäische Föderation Junger Chöre (EFJC)* – former (15 May 1960 to Jan 2011). Registration: EU Transparency Register, No/ID: 236316930224-39; Start date: 9 Feb 1963, Germany FR. **Aims** Contribute to mutual understanding between European peoples, including their music, languages and cultural heritage; allow young people to get to know Europe in a different way by studying and performing choral *music* together with other Europeans and listening to other choirs. **Structure** General Assembly (annual); Board of Directors. **Languages** English, French, German. **Staff** 3.50 FTE, paid. Voluntary. **Finance** Supported by: *European Union (EU, #08967)* Creative Europe and Erasmus+ programmes; German Ministry for Family, Seniors, Women and Youth; City of Bonn. **Activities** Events/meetings; training/education; awards/prizes/competitions; projects/programmes. **Events** *Leading Voices – European Days for Vocal and Choral Leaders* Utrecht (Netherlands) 2022, *General Assembly* Utrecht (Netherlands) 2016, *General Assembly* Barcelona (Spain) 2014, *International seminar for children choir conductors* Marktoberdorf (Germany) 1998, *Annual General Assembly* Bonn (Germany FR) 1988. **Publications** Song books; CDs; reports; leaflets; Festival DVDs.

Members Choral and conductors' organizations, choirs in 28 countries:
Armenia, Austria, Belgium, Croatia, Czechia, Denmark, Estonia, Finland, France, Georgia, Germany, Greece, Hungary, Ireland, Israel, Italy, Liechtenstein, Lithuania, Luxembourg, Netherlands, Norway, Romania, Russia, Slovenia, Spain, Sweden, Switzerland, UK.

Individuals and choirs in 27 countries and territories:
Austria, Belgium, Bulgaria, Croatia, France, Germany, Greece, Hungary, Ireland, Israel, Italy, Latvia, Lebanon, Lithuania, Netherlands, Norway, Portugal, Russia, Serbia, Slovenia, Spain, Switzerland, Taiwan, Türkiye, UK, Ukraine, USA.

NGO Relations Member of: *Choral Festival Network (CFN, #03894)*; *Culture Action Europe (CAE, #04981)*; *European Alliance for Culture and the Arts (#05866)*; *European Music Council (EMC, #07837)*; *International Federation for Choral Music (IFCM, #13388)*; *International Music Council (IMC, #14199)*. Patron of: EuroChoir; *World Youth Choir (WYC, #21955)*. Links with a large number of organizations, including: *Europäische Musikschul-Union (EMU, #05756)*; *Musica International (#16911)*. [2021/XD4519/**D**]

♦ European Christian Convention (ECC) 06542

Main Office address not obtained. E-mail: mail@europan-christian-convention.eu.
URL: https://www.european-christian-convention.eu/

History 2017. Founded following discussions initiated in 2015. Registration: Banque-Carrefour des Entreprises, No/ID: 0672.994.314, Start date: 24 Mar 2017, Belgium. **Aims** Organize a large scale ecumenical gathering of Christians from across Europe. **Structure** Members' Assembly; Board.

Members National and regional bodies (32)
Belarus, Finland, Germany, Greece, Hungary, Latvia, Poland, Russia, Spain, Sweden, Switzerland.
Church and Peace (#03916); *Colloquy of European Parishes (#04119)*; *European Continental Province of the Moravian Church (#06777)*; *European Forum of National Laity Committees (#07322)*; *Fellowship of European Broadcasters (FEB, #09726)*; *Oikosnet Europe – Ecumenical Association of Academies and Laity Centres in Europe (EAALCE, #17706)*; *World Student Christian Federation (WSCF, #21833)*. [2022/AA3134/y/**D**]

♦ European Christian Endeavour Union (inactive)

♦ European Christian Environmental Network (ECEN) 06543

Europäischen Christlichen Umweltnetzwerkes

Sec c/o Conference of European Churches, Ecumenical Centre, Rue Joseph II 174, 1000 Brussels, Belgium. T. +3222301732. Fax +3222311413.
URL: http://www.ecen.org/

History 24 Oct 1998, Vilémov (Czechia). 24 Oct 1998, Vilemov (Czech Rep). **Aims** Increase cooperation and exchange of information between European *churches* and Christian groups involved in environmental work. **Structure** Assembly (at least every 2 years). Leadership Team, elected by the Assembly, conducts work of the Network between Assemblies and establishes working coalitions in which members work together on specific themes. **Languages** English. **Staff** 0.50 FTE, paid. Leadership Team all voluntary. **Finance** Members raise funds to cover envisaged expenses. **Activities** Working coalitions' areas of work: climate change; water; environmental management; eco-theology; education; worship; others. **Events** *Assembly* Elspeet (Netherlands) 2012, *Assembly* Prague (Czech Rep) 2010, *The true challenge of climate change* Milan (Italy) 2008, *Living in a new energy era* Flämslätt (Sweden) 2006, *Assembly* Basel (Switzerland) 2005. **Publications** *ECEN Newsletter*. *Time for God's Creation* (2006); *Listening to Creation Groaning* (2004); *Water – Source of Life* (2003). **Members** and friends in most European countries. Membership countries not specified. **NGO Relations** Coordinated by: *Conference of European Churches (CEC, #04593)*. [2013/XF5867/**F**]

♦ European Christian Friendship (inactive)

♦ European Christian Internet Conference (ECIC) 06544

Pres address not obtained.
URL: http://www.ecic.mobi/

History As a network of individuals working in the field of Christian internet activity. Constitution approved, 2013. **Structure** Steering Committee of 5 members. **Events** *European Christian Internet Conference (ECIC)* 2021, *European Christian Internet Conference (ECIC)* Aalborg (Denmark) 2019, *European Christian Internet Conference (ECIC)* London (UK) 2018, *European Christian Internet Conference (ECIC)* Warsaw (Poland) 2017, *European Christian Internet Conference (ECIC)* Gothenburg (Sweden) 2016. [2019/XJ4279/c/**F**]

♦ European Christian Mission (internationally oriented national body)

♦ European Christian Organisations in Relief and Development (EU-CORD) 06545

Dir Rue de l'Arbre Benit 44-46, Bte 6, 1050 Brussels, Belgium. T. +3224860174. E-mail: info@eu-cord.org.
URL: http://www.eu-cord.org/

History 1997. Former names and other names: *EU-CORD Network* – alias. Registration: Banque-Carrefour des Entreprises, No/ID: 0480.186.919, Start date: 28 Feb 2003, Belgium; EU Transparency Register, No/ID: 323804648361-77, Start date: 12 Dec 2022. **Aims** Support members and their national counterparts to develop partnership approaches, diversify funding options, and access funding from the European Union; advocate towards European policymakers on issues concerning humanitarian action, sustainable development, peacebuilding, and the role of faith-based organisations; communicate the added value of faith-based actors and the importance of engaging with faith communities towards the European Union and other civil society actors; develop the knowledge of members and their national civil society counterparts through mutual capacity building and learning. **Structure** General Assembly; Administrative Council; Programme Groups; Secretariat. **Languages** English, French. **Staff** 2.00 FTE, paid. **Finance** Sources: members' dues. Annual budget: 300,000 EUR (2022). **Activities** Advocacy/lobbying/activism; capacity building; events/meetings; knowledge management/information dissemination; politics/policy/regulatory. EU-CORD members are working in 87 countries across Africa, Asia, Middle East, South/Central America. **Publications** Annual Report.

Members Christian organizations (26) in 12 European countries:
Belgium, Denmark, Finland, Germany, Hungary, Ireland, Netherlands, Norway, Spain, Sweden, Switzerland, UK.
Included in the above, 13 organizations listed in this Yearbook:
Christian Outreach – Relief and Development (CORD); *Fida International*; *International Aid Services (IAS)*; *Läkarmissionen*; *Leprosy Mission International (TLMI, #16446)*; *MEDAIR*; *Mission Aviation Fellowship (MAF, #16829)*; *Mission East*; *Strømme Foundation (SF)*; *Tear*; *Tearfund, Belgium*; *Tearfund, UK*; *ZOA*.

NGO Relations Member of (4): *Confédération européenne des ong d'urgence et de développement (CONCORD, #04547)*; *International Disability and Development Consortium (IDDC, #13177)*; *International Partnership on Religion and Sustainable Development (PaRD, #14524)*; *SDG Watch Europe (#19162)*. [2022.05.18/XE4129/y/**E**]

♦ European Christian Workers Movement (ECWM) 06546

Mouvement des travailleurs chrétiens d'Europe (MTCE) – Movimiento de Trabajadores Christianos de Europa (MTCE) – Europäische Bewegung Christlicher Arbeiter (EBCA)

Coordinator c/o KWB, Urbain Britsierslaan 5, 1030 Brussels, Belgium. E-mail: coordination@mtceurope.org.
Registered Office Bd du Jubilée 124, 1080 Brussels, Belgium.
URL: http://mtceurope.org/

History Founded Dec 1993, Brussels (Belgium). Registered in accordance with Belgian law. **Aims** Provide workers with religious and socio-cultural training in an environment of Christian reverence. **Structure** General Assembly (annual); Administrative Board. **Languages** English, French, German, Spanish. **Staff** 0.25 FTE, paid. **Finance** Members' dues. Subvention from European Union for organization of seminars. **Activities** Events/meetings. **Events** *Impact of the Coronavirus Pandemic on Employment and Social Affairs – Experiences and Actions for Recovery* Lisbon (Portugal) 2022, *Meeting* Lisbon (Portugal) 2014, *Meeting* Haltern (Germany) 2013, *Meeting* Bratislava (Slovakia) 2012, *Meeting* London (UK) 2011.

Members National and sub-national organizations in 13 countries:
Austria, Belgium, Czechia, Denmark, France, Germany, Italy, Luxembourg, Portugal, Slovakia, Spain, Switzerland, UK.

NGO Relations Member of: *European Centre for Workers' Questions (#06505)*; *European Sunday Alliance (#08856)*. [2019.02.18/XF2597/**F**]

♦ European Chromosome 11 Network 06547

Réseau européen du chromosome 11 – Red Europea de la Chromosoma 11 – Europäisches Chromosom 11 Netzwerk – Europees Chromosoom 11 Netwerk – Europäisk Kromosom 11 Netvärk

Pres Winkel 1, 31167 Bockenem, Germany. E-mail: info@chromosome11.eu.
URL: http://www.chromosome11.eu/

History 11 Jun 1997. Former names and other names: *European Chromosome 11Q Network* – former; *Réseau européen du chromosome 11Q* – former; *Red Europea de la Chromosoma 11Q* – former; *Europäisches Chromosom 11q Netzwerk* – former; *Europees Chromosoom 11q Netwerk* – former; *Europäisk Kromosom 11q Netvärk* – former; *European 11q Group* – former; *Europäische 11q Gruppe* – former; *Europese 11q Groep* – former; *11Q Network* – former; *11Q Netzwerk* – former. Registration: Baden-Württemberg District court, No/ID: VR 510650, Start date: 8 Aug 2008, Germany. **Aims** Promote cooperation and exchange of information between families with anomalies on chromosome 11. **Structure** Board. **Languages** Dutch, English, French, German, Italian, Spanish. **Finance** Sources: members' dues; subsidies. **Events** *Conference* Pforzheim (Germany) 2019, *Conference* Pforzheim (Germany) 2014, *Conference* Pforzheim (Germany) 2011, *Conference* Pforzheim (Germany) 2009, *The future as an opportunity* Pforzheim (Germany) 2007. **Publications** Newsletter; conference proceedings; flyers.

Members Individuals in 14 countries and territories:
Austria, Belgium, Denmark, France, Germany, Ireland, Italy, Netherlands, Russia, Spain, Sweden, Switzerland, Taiwan, UK.

NGO Relations Member of (1): *EURORDIS – Rare Diseases Europe (#09175)*. Contacts with international and national organizations, including: *European Cytogeneticists Association (ECA, #06880)* Register of Unbalanced Chromosome Aberrations; national associations. Also member of national associations. [2020/XE4558/v/**E**]

♦ European Chromosome 11Q Network / see European Chromosome 11 Network (#06547)

♦ European Chronic Disease Alliance (ECDA) 06548

Office Rue du Luxembourg 22-24, 1000 Brussels, Belgium. T. +3222741070. E-mail: info@alliancechronicdiseases.org.
URL: http://www.alliancechronicdiseases.org/

History 2009. Founded by *European Society of Cardiology (ESC, #08536), European Cancer Organisation (ECO, #06432), European Society for Medical Oncology (ESMO, #08648), European Heart Network (EHN, #07467), European Kidney Health Alliance (EKHA, #07626), International Diabetes Federation (IDF, #13164) – Europea, European Association for the Study of the Liver (EASL, #06233), European Respiratory Society (ERS, #08383), Foundation of European Nurses in Diabetes (FEND, #09953)*. Former names and other names: *Chronic Disease Alliance* – alias. Registration: EU Transparency Register, No/ID: 696745644088-26, Start date: 14 Sep 2021. **Aims** Reverse the alarming rise in chronic diseases by providing leadership and policy recommendations based on contemporary evidence. **Structure** Informal alliance without legal status. **Languages** English. **Finance** Sources: members' dues. **Events** *Final Conference* Brussels (Belgium) 2017, *Chronic Diseases Summit* Brussels (Belgium) 2014. **Publications** Policy papers.
Members Organizations (12):
European Academy of Allergy and Clinical Immunology (EAACI, #05779); European Academy of Neurology (EAN, #05803); European Association for the Study of the Liver (EASL, #06233); European Cancer Organisation (ECO, #06432); European Heart Network (EHN, #07467); European Kidney Health Alliance (EKHA, #07626); European Respiratory Society (ERS, #08383); European Society for Medical Oncology (ESMO, #08648); European Society of Cardiology (ESC, #08536); European Society of Hypertension (ESH, #08627); International Diabetes Federation Europe (IDF Europe, #13165); United European Gastroenterology (UEG, #20506).
NGO Relations Member of (1): *European Alliance for Cardiovascular Health (EACH, #05863).* [2022/XJ5558/y/**D**]

♦ European Church Growth Association / see Eurochurch.net (#05660)
♦ European Church Growth Movement / see Eurochurch.net (#05660)
♦ European Cider and Fruit Wine Association (#02643)

♦ European Cigar Manufacturers Association (ECMA) 06549

SG PO Box 4076, 5004 JB Tilburg, Netherlands. T. +31135944125. Fax +31135944748.
URL: http://www.ecma.eu/

History Registered in accordance with Belgian law. EU Transparency Register: 92802501097-37. **Structure** General Assembly; Board of Directors. **Finance** Members' dues.
Members Full in 13 countries:
Belgium, Denmark, France, Germany, Hungary, Ireland, Italy, Luxembourg, Netherlands, Portugal, Spain, Switzerland, UK. [2014/XD8161/**D**]

♦ European Cinema Society / see European Film Academy (#07244)
♦ European Cinema Support Fund / see European Support Fund for the Co-Production and Distribution of Creative Cinematographic and Audiovisual Works (#08859)

♦ European CIO Association (EuroCIO) 06550

SG Rue de la Loi 221, 1040 Brussels, Belgium. E-mail: sg@eurocio-asso.org.
URL: http://www.eurocio.org/

History 7 Feb 2012. Registration: Banque Carrefour des Entreprises, No/ID: 0839.937.252, Start date: 5 Oct 2011, Belgium; EU Transparency Register, No/ID: 85172105610-37, Start date: 5 Apr 2011. **Aims** Support the work of *Chief Information Officers* (CIOs) in large international businesses through information exchange, meetings and senior level professional development services. **Structure** Board. **Activities** Training/education. **Events** *Annual Conference* Brussels (Belgium) 2018, *Annual Conference* Berlin (Germany) 2015, *Annual Conference* Brussels (Belgium) 2014, *Annual Conference* Brussels (Belgium) 2013, *Annual Conference* Brussels (Belgium) 2012. **Publications** *European CIO Association Newsletter*.
Members Full in 11 countries:
Belgium, Bulgaria, France, Germany, Greece, Hungary, Italy, Netherlands, Sweden, Türkiye, UK.
NGO Relations Member of: *European e-Skills Association (EeSA, #08489).* [2020/XJ5365/**D**]

♦ European Circle of Ethics Officers / see Cercle d'Ethique des Affaires

♦ European Circuit Society (ECS) 06551

Contact Elektro DTU, Electronics/Signal Processing, 348 Technical Univ of Denmark DTU, Bldg 348, 2800 Kongens Lyngby, Denmark. T. +4545253650. Fax +4545880117.

History 1993, Davos (Switzerland). **Aims** Promote the well-being of scientific activities within ECS scope in Europe; promote the scientific viability of ECS area as distinguished from other contiguous or partially overlapping areas; offer help to research funding organizations for the definition of programmes and for the evaluation of proposals within ECS fields of interest; give financial support to members and organizations in geographical areas where the economic situation endangers the scientific activities in ECS fields of interest. **Structure** Society Meeting (held during each ECCTD). Council, including President (2-year term) who is also the Conference Chair of the latest ECCTD. Members of Council are the chairmen of the past ECTD conferences. Members are participants of the latest ECCTD conference. **Languages** English. **Activities** Field of interest broadly defined as Circuits in all its usual aspects within Electrical/Electronic Engineering and Systems as related to circuits and includes in particular: Linear and Nonlinear Circuit Theory, with its mathematical and physical basis and its theoretical foundations; Circuit Design and Implementation, in particular the design and implementation of integrated circuits; Computer-Aided Design; Computational aspects of Circuit Analysis and Design; Analog, Digital and Mixed-Signal Processing; System theoretic methods related to all aforementioned disciplines; Applications of circuit-theoretic and related system-theoretic methods in other disciplines. **Events** *European Conference on Circuit Theory and Design* Sofia (Bulgaria) 2020, *European Conference on Circuit Theory and Design* Catania (Italy) 2017, *European Conference on Circuit Theory and Design* Trondheim (Norway) 2015, *European Conference on Circuit Theory and Design* Dresden (Germany) 2013, *European Conference on Circuit Theory and Design* Linköping (Sweden) 2011. **Publications** *International Journal of Circuit Theory and Applications*.
Members Individuals (participants of the latest ECCTD) in 38 countries:
Australia, Austria, Belarus, Belgium, Brazil, Canada, China, Czechia, Denmark, Egypt, Estonia, Finland, France, Germany, Greece, Hungary, Iceland, India, Ireland, Israel, Italy, Japan, Lebanon, Lithuania, Netherlands, Norway, Poland, Portugal, Romania, Russia, Serbia, Spain, Sweden, Switzerland, Türkiye, UK, Ukraine, USA. [2021/XD8351/v/**D**]

♦ European Circus Association (ECA) 06552

Director Am Kuckhofsweg 15, 41542 Dormagen, Germany. E-mail: eca@europeancircus.eu.
Registered Address Europalaan 2, 5591 CN Heeze, Netherlands.
URL: https://www.europeancircus.eu/

History 2002. Registration: EU Transparency Register, No/ID: 256514337978-12, Start date: 29 Apr 2020; No/ID: 32092926, Netherlands. **Aims** Defend common interests of circuses in Europe; promote circus arts and culture. **Structure** General Meeting; Executive Board; Advisory Board. **Languages** Dutch, English, French, German, Italian. **Staff** 2.00 FTE, voluntary. **Finance** Members' dues. Donations. **Activities** Events/meetings. **Events** *Annual Symposium* Monte Carlo (Monaco) 2010, *Annual symposium* Monte Carlo (Monaco) 2009, *Annual Symposium* Monte Carlo (Monaco) 2007, *Annual Symposium* Monte Carlo (Monaco) 2006, *Colloquium on clowns* Wiesbaden (Germany) 2005. **Publications** *ECA Information* (6 a year) in Dutch, English, French, German, Italian. Brochures.
Members Regular; Associate; Board; Donor. Members in 29 countries:
Australia, Austria, Belgium, Canada, China, Denmark, Finland, France, Germany, Hungary, Ireland, Italy, Japan, Latvia, Lithuania, Monaco, Netherlands, Norway, Poland, Portugal, Romania, Russia, South Africa, Spain, Sweden, Switzerland, UK, Ukraine, USA.
Included in the above, 2 organizations listed in this Yearbook:
Circus Federation of Australasia (CFA); Fédération européenne des écoles de cirque professionnelles (FEDEC, #09565).
NGO Relations Member of: *Fédération Mondiale du Cirque (#09689); Pearle – Live Performance Europe (#18284).* [2021/XM0574/y/**D**]

♦ European Cities Against Drugs (ECAD) 06553

SG Box 24 228, SE-104 51 Stockholm, Sweden. T. +46850829363. Fax +46850829466. E-mail: ecad@ecad.net.
Street Address Gyllenstiernsgatan 7, SE-115 26 Stockholm, Sweden.
URL: http://www.ecad.net/

History 1994, Stockholm (Sweden). Registration: Sweden; EU Transparency Register, No/ID: 098529124947-40, Start date: 8 Dec 2016. **Aims** Promote and develop through democratic means the fight against drugs, in order to contribute to a Europe free from drugs; provide experience and knowledge about the work against drugs and drug abuse at local, national and international levels. **Structure** Mayors' Conference (annual). Advisory Board acts as Executive Committee, consisting of delegates of 10 member cities, including at least 5 capital cities. Head Office in Stockholm (Sweden); regional offices in St Petersburg (Russia), Riga (Latvia), Burgas (Bulgaria), Istanbul (Turkey) and Malta. **Staff** 8.00 FTE, paid. **Finance** Members' dues. Special subsidy from City of Stockholm (Sweden). Budget (annual): Swedish Kr 4.5 million. **Activities** Events/meetings; knowledge management/information dissemination. **Events** *Annual Mayors Conference* Stavanger (Norway) 2016, *Annual Mayors Conference* Valletta (Malta) 2015, *Annual Mayors Conference / Annual Mayors' Conference* Stockholm (Sweden) 2014, *Annual Mayors Conference / Annual Mayors' Conference* Moscow (Russia) 2013, *Annual Mayors Conference / Annual Mayors' Conference* Killarney (Ireland) 2012. **Publications** *ECAD Newsletter* (10 a year) in English, Latvian, Lithuanian, Russian, Spanish, Swedish.
Members Cities (250) having signed the "Stockholm Resolution" in 26 countries:
Albania, Bosnia-Herzegovina, Bulgaria, Cyprus, Czechia, Estonia, Finland, Germany, Greece, Hungary, Iceland, Ireland, Italy, Latvia, Lithuania, Malta, Moldova, Netherlands, North Macedonia, Norway, Poland, Russia, Serbia, Sweden, Switzerland, Türkiye.
IGO Relations Relevant treaties: *Convention on Psychotropic Substances (1971); Single Convention on Narcotic Drugs, 1961 (1961); Single Convention on Narcotic Drugs, 1961, as amended by the Protocol amending the Single Convention on Narcotic Drugs, 1961 (1975); United Nations Convention against Illicit Traffic in Narcotic Drugs and Psychotropic Substances (1988).* **NGO Relations** Member of: *Civil Society Forum on Drugs (CSFD, #03968); Vienna NGO Committee on Drugs (VNGOC, #20773).* [2019/XF3540/**F**]

♦ European Cities on Drug Policy (inactive)
♦ European Cities Marketing / see City Destinations Alliance (#03960)

♦ European Cities and Regions for Culture (LIKE) 06554

LIKE – Association des villes et régions de européennes pour la culture
Main Office 18 Rue du Maréchal de Lattre de Tassigny, 59000 Lille, France.
URL: http://www.likeculture.eu/

History Founded Jul 1994, Lisbon (Portugal), following a series of informal meetings since 1992, *Association of European Cities and Regions for Culture – Association des villes et régions de la grande Europe pour la culture (Les Rencontres)*. Present name adopted, 2016. Registered in accordance with French law. **Aims** Promote awareness of the essential role played by elected *local government* officials in charge of culture; encourage contacts among these officials throughout Europe, at national, bilateral, multilateral and regional level; make elected officials more aware of cultural problems and European issues; promote exchange of information among them; establish common approaches and common proposals to put forward to national governments and international institutions in Europe and beyond. **Structure** General Assembly (annual, at 'Les Rencontres' Conference); Steering Committee; Board of Directors; Branch office in Brussels (Belgium). **Languages** English, French. **Staff** 32.50 FTE, paid. Temporary trainees and other employees for events. **Finance** Members' dues. Other sources: grants from French Ministries of Culture and Communication and of Foreign Affairs; grants from other foreign European Ministries. Subsidies from: *European Commission (EC, #06633)* – Culture Programme; French-speaking Community Federation and the French-speaking Community Commission of Belgium; PACA; Nord-Pas de Calais Region. **Activities** Events/meetings; training/education. **Events** *General Assembly / European Campus* Lille (France) 2014, *Extraordinary General Assembly* Umeå (Sweden) 2014, *Les Rencontres* Marseille (France) 2013, *Meeting – Les Rencontres / European Campus* Tampere (Finland) 2013, *European Campus* Paris (France) 2012. **Publications** *Les Rencontres* – information bulletin. Meeting reports; Green Paper; White Paper.
Members Full: local and regional authorities – elected officials in charge of culture from cities and regions, Directors of cultural affairs; Associate: managers of local or national arts and culture organizations, directors of European cultural institutions, organizations and networks. Members in 28 countries:
Austria, Belgium, Bosnia-Herzegovina, Bulgaria, Croatia, Cyprus, Czechia, Denmark, Finland, France, Germany, Greece, Hungary, Ireland, Israel, Italy, Lithuania, Netherlands, North Macedonia, Norway, Portugal, Romania, Slovakia, Slovenia, Spain, Sweden, Türkiye, UK.
NGO Relations Member of: *European Alliance for Culture and the Arts (#05866).* [2017/XD6067/**D**]

♦ European Cities and Regions Networking for Innovative Transport Solutions / see POLIS (#18419)
♦ European Cities and Regions Networking for New Transport Solutions / see POLIS (#18419)

♦ European Citizen Action Service (ECAS) 06555

Service d'action du citoyen européen – Actie Dienst voor de Europese Burger
Dir Av de la Toison d'Or 77, Floor 1, 1060 Brussels, Belgium. T. +3225480490. Fax +3225480499.
Pres Kroonwinningstraat 7a, 3500 Hasselt, Belgium.
URL: http://www.ecas.org/

History 8 May 1990, Brussels (Belgium), when statutes adopted by General Assembly. Previously referred to as *Europa y sus Ciudadanos Actividades y Servicios – Europa Bürger Dienstleitungsstelle – Ação Serviço Cidadão Europeu – Servizi e Azione per i Cittadini Europei – Dienst en Aktie voor de Europese Burgers – Hanlingsorgan for Borgernes Europa* and subsequently *Euro Citizen Action Service – Euro citoyen action service – Euro Ciudadano Acción Servicio – Aktiondienst Europäische Bürger – Euro Cidadão Acção Serviço – Euro Cittadino Azione Servizio – Aktie Service Europese Staatsburgers – Europeiske Borgere Aksjon Service – Aktivitetstjeneste Borger i Europa – Eurokansalaisen Toimintapaluelu Keskus – Europamedborgamas Aktionsservice – Evropolitis Drasi Ipiresia*. New statutes adopted 7 May 2015. Registered in accordance with Belgian law. EU Transparency Register: 47003483702-10. **Aims** Empower citizens in order to create a more inclusive and stronger European Union by: promoting and defending citizens' rights; developing and supporting mechanisms to increase citizens and citizen organizations' democratic participation in, and engagement with, the EU. **Structure** General Assembly; Board of Directors. **Languages** English, French. **Staff** 9.00 FTE, paid. **Finance** Sources: EU institutions; private foundations and donors; services. **Activities** Advocacy/lobbying/activism; awareness raising; capacity building; events/meetings; guidance/assistance/consulting; knowledge management/information dissemination; monitoring/evaluation; networking/liaising; projects/programmes; publishing activities; research/documentation; standards/guidelines; training/education. **Events** *Digital Democracy Day Meeting* Brussels (Belgium) 2021, *Conference on Online Disinformation : Finding the Silver Bullet in the Digital World* Brussels (Belgium) 2019, *Digital Democracy Day Meeting* Brussels (Belgium) 2019, *Meeting on the State of the Union Citizen's Rights* Brussels (Belgium) 2019, *Meeting on the State of the Union Citizen's Rights* Brussels (Belgium) 2018. **Publications** Reports; studies; guidellines; working papers; recommendations.
Members Governing (20); Ordinary (113). Non-profit organizations, public bodies and individuals in 35 countries:
Albania, Austria, Belgium, Bosnia-Herzegovina, Bulgaria, Canada, Croatia, Cyprus, Czechia, Denmark, Estonia, Finland, France, Germany, Greece, Hungary, Iceland, Ireland, Italy, Kosovo, Latvia, Lithuania, Malta, Moldova, Netherlands, North Macedonia, Poland, Portugal, Romania, Slovakia, Slovenia, Spain, Sweden, Switzerland, UK.
IGO Relations Contacts with: *European Commission (EC, #06633); European Economic and Social Committee (EESC, #06963); European Ombudsman (#08084); European Parliament (EP, #08146);* REFIT Platform for Better Regulation. **NGO Relations** Partners include: *Democracy International (DI); Erasmus Student Network (ESN, #05529); European Alternatives (EA, #05891); European Association for Local Democracy (ALDA, #06110); European Disability Forum (EDF, #06929); Institut pro evropskou politiku (EUROPEUM); Migration Policy Group (MPG, #16801); Union of European Federalists, The (UEF, #20385); VoteWatch Europe (#20811).* Member of: *Civil Society Europe.* [2020/XF1071/y/**F**]

♦ European Citizen's Band Federation (ECBF) 06556

Fédération européenne la Citizen's Band (FECB) – Europäische Citizen's Band Föderation – Federazione Europea della Citizen's Band
Gen Sec Chse Romaine 623, Bte 4, 1020 Brussels, Belgium. T. +32484658304. E-mail: secretary@ecbf.eu.

URL: http://www.ecbf.eu/
History 1976. Previously referred to as *Europe Citizen's Band Association* and as *Europe Citizen Band Federation (ECBF)*. Registered in accordance with Belgian, French and European Law. **Aims** Associate in a federation the European national Citizen's Band organizations; promote adequate initiatives to liberalize, promote, regulate and control CBs in Europe; constitute, on a European level, a representative body of the CB; work for universal recognition and acceptance of the ECBS as the official representative body within Europe. **Structure** General Assembly; Administrative Council. **Languages** English. **Staff** 10.00 FTE, voluntary. **Finance** Members' dues. Other sources: grants; gifts and legacies; profits; proceeds from services. **Activities** Research/documentation. **Events** *Congress* Brussels (Belgium) 2014, *Congress* Brussels (Belgium) 2010, *Congress* Brussels (Belgium) 2006, *Congress* Brussels (Belgium) 2005, *Congress* Paris (France) 2000.
Members Individuals. Associations and clubs in 17 countries and territories:
Andorra, Austria, Belgium, Catalunya, Croatia, France, Germany, Greece, Hungary, Italy, Monaco, Netherlands, Poland, Portugal, Romania, Spain, Sweden, UK.
IGO Relations *European Commission (EC, #06633).* **NGO Relations** Member of: *European Telecommunications Standards Institute (ETSI, #08897).* [2017/XD8559/**D**]

♦ European Citizen Science Association (ECSA) 06557

Verein der europäischen Bürgerwissenschaften
Coordinator c/o Museum für Naturkunde Berlin, Leibniz-Inst für Evolutions- un Biodiversitätsforschung, Bereichsleitung Wissenschaftskommunikation und Wissensforschung, Invalidenstr 43, 10115 Berlin, Germany. T. +493020938776.
URL: http://ecsa.citizen-science.net/
History Jun 2013, during EU Green Week. Initially set up as an informal network. Formally set up 2014, when registered in accordance with German law. EU Transparency Register: 479444018258-40. **Aims** Connect citizens and science through fostering active participation. Encourage the growth of the Citizen Science movement in Europe. **Structure** General Assembly; Executive Board; Board of Directors; Steering Committee; Headquarters; Working Groups; Advisory Board. **Languages** English, German. **Staff** 6.00 FTE, paid. **Finance** Members' dues. Other sources: H2020 projects; donations. **Activities** Research/documentation; networking/liaising; training/education; capacity building; knowledge management/information dissemination. **Events** *International Conference* Berlin (Germany) 2022, *International Conference* Trieste (Italy) 2020, *General Assembly* Brussels (Belgium) 2019, *International Conference* Geneva (Switzerland) 2018, *General Assembly* Berlin (Germany) 2016. **Publications** Policy papers; guidelines; documents. **Members** Full (over 200) in 27 countries. Membership countries not specified. **Consultative Status** Consultative status granted from: *UNEP (#20299).* **NGO Relations** Memorandum of Understanding with: *Association of European University Public Relations and Information Officers (EUPRIO, #02549)*; national organizations. [2019/XM5039/**D**]

♦ European Citizens' Initiative Campaign (ECI Campaign) 06558

General Coordinator Ida-Kerkovius-strasse 7, 79100 Freiburg, Germany. T. +4976148806364. E-mail: contact@citizens-initiative.eu.
Project Manager address not obtained. T. +48782784684.
URL: http://www.citizens-initiative.eu/
History After EU Constitutional Treaty was initially rejected by French and Dutch citizens in 2005, *Democracy International (#05032)* and *Association des états généraux des étudiants de l'Europe (AEGEE-Europe, #02495)* started setting up of the Initiative by collecting signatures across Europe. Legal basis of ECI set out in Art 11, Paragraph 4 of *Treaty on European Union (Maastricht Treaty, 1992)* and Art 24, Paragraph 1 of Treaty on the Functioning of the European Union. Specific practical arrangements and procedures for launching an ECI are set out in the ECI regulation 211/2011, applicable since 1 Apr 2012. **Aims** Work for the successful introduction and implementation of the European Citizen's Initiative *right* – a tool of participatory, transnational and digital *democracy.* **Structure** Coordination Team. **Finance** Financial and logistical support from various organizations, including: *Citizens of Europe*; *King Baudouin Foundation (KBF)*; *Heinrich Böll Foundation.* **Activities** Worked for inclusion of ECI in the draft EU Constitution and later revised *Treaty of Lisbon (2007).* Lobbied for citizen-friendly rules governing its use. Currently monitors implementation of ECI and provides guidance to groups and individuals on using the ECI. **Publications** *ECI Newsletter.*
Members Contributors (over 120 NGOs and foundations), including the following 24 organizations listed in this Yearbook:
- *Association des états généraux des étudiants de l'Europe (AEGEE-Europe, #02495)*;
- *Centre for European Volunteering (CEV, #03743)*;
- *Children of the Earth (COE)*;
- *Citizens of Europe*;
- *Confrontations for a European Participative Democracy (Confrontations Europe)*;
- *Democracy International (#05032)*;
- *European Emergency Number Association (EENA, #06978)*;
- *European Federation of Christian Student Associations (#07076)*;
- *European Forum for Freedom in Education (EFFE, #07311)*;
- *European Liberal Youth (LYMEC, #07690)*;
- *European Movement International (EMI, #07825)*;
- *Europeans throughout the World (ETTW, #08839)*;
- *European Union Federation of Youth Hostel Associations (EUFED, #08988)*;
- *European Youth Forum (#09140)*;
- *Fédération européenne des femmes actives en famille (FEFAF, #09568)*;
- *Federation of Young European Greens (FYEG, #09715)*;
- *Initiative and Referendum Institute Europe (IRI Europe)*;
- *International Falcon Movement – Socialist Educational International (IFM-SEI, #13327)*;
- *International Federation of Liberal Youth (IFLRY, #13469)*;
- *Mouvement international de la jeunesse agricole et rurale catholique (MIJARC, #16865)*;
- *Permanent Forum of European Civil Society (#18322)*;
- *Transnational Institute (TNI, #20219)*;
- *Young European Federalists (#21984)*;
- *Young European Socialists (YES, #21989).* [2017/XM3004/y/**F**]

♦ European Citizens' Mobility Forum (ECMF) 06559

Contact address not obtained. T. +3227432592.
Contact address not obtained. T. +3227432586.
URL: http://www.busandcoach.travel/en/smart_policies/european_citizens_mobility_for um/
History 15 May 2013, at *European Parliament (EP, #08146)*, at the recommendation of EU Smart Move High Level Group (HLG). **Aims** Support the practical implementation of the Smart Move High Level Group's Recommendations; propose new concrete actions to double the use and market share of collective passenger transport in the EU by 2025, through a detailed and targeted European Action Programme.
Members Representatives from EU institutions, civil society and stakeholders, business and trade associations. Members include 10 organizations listed in this Yearbook:
Eurolines Organisation (#05706); *European Commission (EC, #06633)*; *European Committee of the Regions (CoR, #06665)*; *European Disability Forum (EDF, #06929)*; *European Economic and Social Committee (EESC, #06963)*; *European Parliament (EP, #08146)*; *European Passenger Transport Operators (EPTO, #08163)*; *International Association of Public Transport (#12118)*; *International Road Transport Union (IRU, #14761)*; *POLIS (#18419).* [2015/XJ9320/**F**]

♦ European Citizens' Seminars 06560

Contact Krämperufer 4, 99084 Erfurt, Germany.
URL: http://www.citizenseminars.eu/
History 7 May 2006, Erfurt (Germany). Registered in accordance with German law. **Aims** Organize the seminars. **Structure** Board of 5 members. [2010/XJ2183/**E**]

♦ European Citric Acid Manufacturers Association (ECAMA) 06561

Contact c/o CEFIC, Av E Van Nieuwenhuyse 4, 1160 Brussels, Belgium. T. +3226767211. Fax +3226767301. E-mail: map@cefic.be.
URL: http://www.ecama.org/
History Founded 1981, as a sector group and affiliate organization of *Conseil européen de l'industrie chimique (CEFIC, #04687).* **Structure** General Assembly; Working Groups (2). **Publications** Monograph on citric acid and citrates. **Members** Producers of citric acid in Europe. Membership countries not specified. [2016.01.28/XE5994/**E**]

♦ European Civic Forum (ECF) 06563

Forum civique européen (FCE)
Dir 167 bd de la villette, 75010 Paris, France. T. +33180051910. E-mail: contact@civic-forum.eu.
URL: https://civic-forum.eu/
History 17 Dec 2005, Strasbourg (France). Founded as an informal network. Officially set up, Dec 2006, when statutes were adopted. Registration: France; EU Transparency Register, No/ID: 981872117501-10. **Aims** Encourage a civic and popular ownership of Europe by its citizens; trigger a real European civic dialogue based on clear thinking; encourage meetings and exchange programmes between associations and NGOs; carry out information and awareness campaigns for the European citizens. **Structure** General Assembly (annual); Steering Committee; Board of Directors. **Activities** Awards/prizes/competitions; events/meetings. **Events** *European Civic Academy* Florence (Italy) 2022. **Publications** Newsletter.
Members Associations (nearly 100) in 26 countries.
Belgium, Cyprus, Czechia, Denmark, Estonia, Finland, France, Georgia, Germany, Greece, Hungary, Ireland, Italy, Latvia, Lithuania, Luxembourg, Netherlands, North Macedonia, Poland, Portugal, Romania, Serbia, Slovakia, Slovenia, Spain, UK.
Listed in the above, 7 organizations listed in this Yearbook:
Association des états généraux des étudiants de l'Europe (AEGEE-Europe, #02495); *Association européenne des enseignants (AEDE, #02565)*; *Contact-2103 (#04775)*; *European Association for the Defence of Human Rights (AEDH, no recent information)*; *European Association of History Educators (EUROCLIO, #06069)*; *Permanent Forum of European Civil Society (#18322)*; *Pour la Solidarité (PLS)*; *We Are Europe!.*
Consultative Status Consultative status granted from: *Council of Europe (CE, #04881)* (Participatory Status).
NGO Relations Member of (1): *Civil Society Europe.* Supports (1): *European Alliance for the Statute of the European Association (EASEA, #05886).* [2023/XJ0438/y/**F**]

♦ European Civic Forum (ECF) 06562

Forum civique européen (FCE) – Europäische BürgerInnen Forum (EBF) – Foro Cívico Europeo (FCE)
Main Office St Johanns-Vorstadt 13, Postfach 1848, 4004 Basel BS, Switzerland. T. +41612620111. Fax +41612620246. E-mail: ch@forumcivique.org – contact@forumcivique.org.
URL: https://forumcivique.org/
History 1990. Founded following the fall of the Berlin Wall. Integrates activities of *European Federation of Free Radios (FERL, inactive).* **Aims** Exchange information between grass root groups in Eastern and Western Europe. **Structure** Informal network with branches in most of European countries (east and west). **Finance** Sources: contributions from participants and supporters; private donations; sale of publications; grants from various institutions, including *European Commission (EC, #06633)* and *Council of Europe (CE, #04881).* Budget (annual): about Swiss Fr 1 million. **Activities** Supports: exchange between Eastern and Western Europe; study on the exploitation of migrants in the extensive fruit and vegetable sector throughout Europe and in particular in Andalusia; campaign of support for the SOC agricultural workers union in Almeria which is active among migrants in the greenhouses there; migrants and refugees in Ukraine; studies and campaigns concerning agriculture, food and autonomy, in particular on seeds. **Events** *Annual congress / Congress* Forcalquier (France) 1997, *Annual Congress* Forcalquier (France) 1996, *Annual congress / Congress* Forcalquier (France) 1995, *Congress* Forcalquier (France) 1994, *Annual congress* Limans (France) 1993. **Publications** *Archipel* (12 a year) in French, German. Reports in English, French, German.
Members ECF Groups in 7 countries:
Austria, Belgium, France, Germany, Russia, Switzerland, Ukraine.
Individuals in 1 country:
Costa Rica.
IGO Relations *European Economic and Social Committee (EESC, #06963).* [2022/XF5376/**F**]

♦ European Civil Aviation Conference (ECAC) 06564

Conférence européenne de l'aviation civile (CEAC)
Exec Sec 3bis Villa Emile Bergerat, 92522 Neuilly-sur-Seine CEDEX, France. T. +33146418544. Fax +33176739857. E-mail: secretariat@ecac-ceac.org.
URL: http://www.ecac-ceac.org/
History 1954, Strasbourg (France). Founded at an intergovernmental conference which granted ECAC a status intermediate between complete independence and being a subordinate regional organization of *International Civil Aviation Organization (ICAO, #12581).* Constitution adopted 1955; completely revised 1993. **Aims** Promote continued development of a safe, efficient and sustainable European air *transport* system. **Structure** Plenary Sessions; Directors General of Civil Aviation (44); Coordinating Committee; Secretariat based in Paris (France). Associated Bodies: *European Aviation Security Training Institute (EASTI, #06304)*; *Joint Aviation Authorities Training Organisation (JAA TO, #16122).* **Languages** English, French. **Staff** 17.00 FTE, paid. **Finance** Sources: members' dues. **Activities** Events/meetings; training/education. **Events** *Triennial Plenary Session* Neuilly-sur-Seine (France) 2021, *Meeting* Bucharest (Romania) 2020, *Meeting* Neuilly-sur-Seine (France) 2020, *Subgroup on Immigration Meeting* Neuilly-sur-Seine (France) 2020, *Subgroup on Immigration Meeting* Paris (France) 2020. **Publications** *ECAC News* (4 a year). Session reports; manuals; documents; recommendations.
Members Governments of 44 countries:
Albania, Armenia, Austria, Azerbaijan, Belgium, Bosnia-Herzegovina, Bulgaria, Croatia, Cyprus, Czechia, Denmark, Estonia, Finland, France, Georgia, Germany, Greece, Hungary, Iceland, Ireland, Italy, Latvia, Lithuania, Luxembourg, Malta, Moldova, Monaco, Montenegro, Netherlands, North Macedonia, Norway, Poland, Portugal, Romania, San Marino, Serbia, Slovakia, Slovenia, Spain, Sweden, Switzerland, Türkiye, UK, Ukraine.
IGO Relations Memorandum of Understanding with (4): *African Civil Aviation Commission (AFCAC, #00248)*; *Arab Civil Aviation Organization (ACAO, #00920)*; *Economic Community of West African States (ECOWAS, #05312)*; *Latin American Civil Aviation Commission (LACAC, #16297).* [2021.08.31/XD0621/**F***]

♦ European Civil Engineering Education and Training (EUCEET Association) 06565

Pres Rue des deux Eglises 39, 1000 Brussels, Belgium.
URL: http://www.euceet.eu/
History 14 Jul 1997, Barcelona (Spain). Founded by Technical University of Civil Engineering, Bucharest (Romania). Under the auspices of *SOCRATES Programme (inactive)*, built EUCEET I (1 Sep 1998 – 31 Aug 2001); EUCEET I Dissemination (1 Oct 2001 – 30 Sep 2002); EUCEET II (1 Oct 2002 – 31 Dec 2005); EUCEET III (1 Oct 2006 – 31 Mar 2010). Association set up, 12 Mar 2007, Brussels (Belgium). **Aims** Contribute to development of civil engineering education in Europe by enhancing cooperation between universities, faculties and departments of civil engineering. **Structure** General Assembly (annual); Administrative Council; Permanent Secretariat. **Languages** English. **Staff** 1.00 FTE, paid. **Finance** Sources: members' dues. **Activities** Events/meetings; networking/liaising; projects/programmes; publishing activities. **Events** *Joint Conference* Pisa (Italy) 2023, *Joint Conference* Thessaloniki (Greece) 2021, *International Conference on Civil Engineering Education* Barcelona (Spain) 2018, *World Engineering Education Forum* Florence (Italy) 2015, *Conference* Moscow (Russia) 2013. **Publications** *EUCEET Newsletter* (4 a year).
Members Full in 28 countries and territories:
Albania, Belgium, Bulgaria, Cyprus, Czechia, Denmark, Estonia, Finland, France, Germany, Greece, Hungary, Ireland, Italy, Kosovo, Latvia, Lithuania, Netherlands, Poland, Romania, Russia, Slovakia, Slovenia, Spain, Taiwan, Türkiye, UK, Ukraine.
NGO Relations Associate organization of: *European Council of Civil Engineers (ECCE, #06810).* [2020.05.07/XK2347/**E**]

♦ European Civil Liberties Network (ECLN) 06566

Contact address not obtained. T. +442088021882. Fax +442088801727.
URL: http://www.ecln.org/
History 19 Oct 2005, Brussels (Belgium). **Aims** Provide a platform for groups working on civil liberties issues across Europe.
Members Organizations and individuals in 12 countries:
Belgium, Bulgaria, Denmark, Germany, Greece, Ireland, Italy, Netherlands, Norway, Spain, Switzerland, UK.
Included in the above, 2 organizations listed in this Yearbook:
Institute of Race Relations (IRR); *Statewatch.* [2009/XM0726/**F**]

♦ **European Civil Service Federation (ECSF)** **06567**
Fédération de la fonction publique européenne (FFPE) – Federación de la Función Pública Europea – Europäischer Beamtenbund – Federação da Função Publica Europêia – Federazione della Funzione Pubblica Europea – Bond van Europese Ambtenaren – Europaeiske Tjenestemandsforbund – Omospondias Evropaion Dimosion Liturgon
Main Office 70 Rue Joseph II, J70 1/88, 1049 Brussels, Belgium. T. +3222950012. Fax +3222981721. E-mail: ffpe.bxl@gmail.com – osp-ffpe-bxl@ec.europa.eu.
URL: http://www.ffpe-bxl.eu/
History 11 Jan 1962, Brussels (Belgium). Statutes amended 1 Jul 1974, and 29 Jun 2009. Registration: Belgium. **Aims** Foster the idea of a European civil service in the common interest of *staff* of international organizations operating in *Western Europe* or pursuing Western European regional objectives in an international context; uphold the interests of the European civil service and its members. **Structure** Council, composed of members nominated by Committees in each institution or organization, elects Bureau. General Assembly (annual) of all members in each institution. **Languages** Danish, Dutch, English, French, German, Irish Gaelic, Italian, Portuguese, Spanish. **Finance** Members' dues. **Events** *A new Europe for a new globalisation – NGOs and trade unions together from Seattle to Brussels* Brussels (Belgium) 2000. **Publications** *9 Mai* (3 a year).
Members Individuals in all Member States of the European Communities as well as in other countries where staff members of the European Communities are employed. Local committees in 12 countries:
Belgium, Denmark, France, Germany, Greece, Ireland, Italy, Luxembourg, Netherlands, Portugal, Spain, UK.
Individuals in 66 countries:
Algeria, Angola, Australia, Barbados, Belgium, Benin, Botswana, Brazil, Burundi, Cameroon, Canada, Central African Rep, Chad, Comoros, Congo Brazzaville, Côte d'Ivoire, Denmark, Djibouti, Eswatini, Ethiopia, Fiji, France, Gabon, Gambia, Germany, Ghana, Greece, Guinea, Guinea-Bissau, Indonesia, Ireland, Italy, Jamaica, Jordan, Kenya, Lesotho, Liberia, Luxembourg, Madagascar, Malawi, Mali, Mauritania, Mauritius, Morocco, Mozambique, Netherlands, Niger, Papua New Guinea, Portugal, Rwanda, Senegal, Sierra Leone, Solomon Is, Somalia, Spain, Sudan, Suriname, Switzerland, Tanzania UR, Togo, Tunisia, UK, USA, Vanuatu, Zambia, Zimbabwe.
IGO Relations Framework Agreement gives recognition of ECSF as an organization representing staff and right to negotiate on their behalf with: *Council of the European Union (#04895)*; *European Commission (EC, #06633)*; *European Economic and Social Committee (EESC, #06963)*. Negotiates with: *Council of Europe (CE, #04881)*. **NGO Relations** Member of: *Permanent Forum of European Civil Society (#18322)*.
[2022/XD0622/**E**]

♦ **European Civil Society Forum on HIV/AIDS (CSF)** **06568**
Contact European Commission, DG Health and Food Safety, Unit C3 Health Threats Unit, L-2990 Luxembourg, Luxembourg.
URL: http://ec.europa.eu/health/sti_prevention/hiv_aids/civil_society_forum /index_en.htm
History 2005, by *European Commission (EC, #06633)*. An informal advisory body to its European Think Tank on HIV/AIDS. **Aims** Facilitate participation of non-governmental organizations in policy development and implementation and information exchange activities on HIV/AIDS. **Activities** Politics/policy/regulatory; knowledge management/information dissemination.
Members National organizations in 20 countries:
Belgium, Bulgaria, Czechia, Denmark, France, Germany, Greece, Hungary, Latvia, Lithuania, Moldova, Netherlands, Poland, Portugal, Romania, Russia, Serbia, Sweden, UK, Ukraine.
International organizations (7):
AIDS Action Europe (#00590); *Caritas Europa (#03579)*; *European AIDS Treatment Group (EATG, #05850)*; *European Network for the Promotion of Rights and Health among Migrant Sex Workers (TAMPEP, #07976)*; *International Planned Parenthood Federation (IPPF, #14589)*; *Red Cross EU Office (#18643)*; *WHO Regional Office for Europe (#20945)*.
[2015.12.22/XM1783/y/**F**]

♦ European Civil Society Platform on Lifelong Learning / see Lifelong Learning Platform – European Civil Society for Education (#16466)

♦ **European Civil Society Platform for Multilingualism (ECSPM)** **06569**
Contact Lyngbyvej 31D – 2 th, 2100 Copenhagen, Denmark. T. +4526252112. E-mail: multilingualism@ecspm.org.
URL: http://ecspm.org/
History Launched 2009, as Civil Society Platform to Promote Multilingualism, as a cooperation headed by *European Commission (EC, #06633)*. Mandate completed 2011. Relaunched under same title 2012; third period started 2013. When mandate not renewed by European Commission 2014, restructured and adopted current title 2016. Registered in accordance with Danish law: CVR 37116866. EU Transparency Register: 432147321633-77. **Aims** Be a strong voice of Europe's civil society promoting language policies and for research on multilingualism in all aspects of social life. **Structure** General Assembly; Executive Committee; Secretariat. **Finance** Members' dues. **Activities** Awareness raising; guidance/assistance/consulting; events/meetings; research/documentation.
Members Full in 4 countries:
Germany, Greece, Netherlands, UK.
Regional/international members include 10 organizations listed in this Yearbook:
Association of Language Testers in Europe (ALTE, #02779); *Centre for the Study of Superdiversity (Babylon)*; *European Esperanto Union (#07006)*; *European Federation of National Institutions for Language (EFNIL, #07172)*; *Federal Union of European Nationalities (FUEN, #09396)*; *ICC – the international language association (ICC, #11050)*; *International Federation of Language Teacher Associations (#13468)*; *Literature Across Frontiers (LAF, #16492)*; *Mercator European Research Centre on Multilingualism and Language Learning (Mercator Research Centre, #16719)*; *Network to Promote Linguistic Diversity (NPLD, #17052)*.
NGO Relations *Cracking the Language Barrier (#04942)*; *Lifelong Learning Platform – European Civil Society for Education (LLLP, #16466)*.
[2018/XM7346/y/**F**]

♦ European Claimants Association (inactive)
♦ European Clamping Tools Association (no recent information)

♦ **European Clay Groups Association (ECGA)** **06570**
Contact ISTerre – UGA, CS 40700, 38058 Grenoble CEDEX 9, France.
History 1987, Seville (Spain). Founded during 6th EUROCLAY conference. **Aims** Stimulate research among, and distribute information to, European scientists working in the field of clay science and technology. **Structure** Council, including President and Secretary. **Events** *EUROCLAY : International Conference on Clay Science and Technology* Bari (Italy) 2023, *EUROCLAY : International Conference on Clay Science and Technology* Paris (France) 2019, *EUROCLAY : International Conference on Clay Science and Technology* Edinburgh (UK) 2015, *MECC – Mid-European Clay Conference* Dresden (Germany) 2014, *Euroclay quadrennial meeting / Quadrennial Meeting* Antalya (Turkey) 2011. **Publications** *ECGA Newsletter* (annual).
Members National groups (19) in 19 countries:
Belgium, Bulgaria, Czechia, France, Germany, Hungary, Israel, Italy, Kazakhstan, Netherlands, Poland, Portugal, Romania, Russia, Slovakia, Spain, Türkiye, UK, Ukraine.
NGO Relations *Association internationale pour l'étude des argiles (AIPEA, #02688)*.
[2022/XM2271/**D**]

♦ European Clay Pipe Association / see FEUGRES – European Clay Pipe Association (#09741)
♦ European Clay Producers' Federation (inactive)
♦ European Clean Clothes Campaign / see Clean Clothes Campaign (#03986)

♦ **European Cleaning and Facility Services Industry (EFCI)** **06571**
Secretariat Rue Belliard 205, 1040 Brussels, Belgium. T. +3222258330. Fax +3222258339. E-mail: secretariat@efci.eu.
URL: http://www.efci.eu/
History Founded 1988, as *European Federation of Cleaning Industries (EFCI) – Fédération européenne du nettoyage industriel (FENI)*. Registered in accordance with Belgian law. EU Transparency Register: 79863609229-39. **Aims** Unify representative national professional organizations of the cleaning industry. **Structure** General Assembly; Board of Directors; Committees (3); Secretariat. **Languages** English, French. **Staff** 3.00 FTE, paid. **Finance** Members' dues. **Activities** Monitoring/evaluation; training/education. **Events** *General Assembly* Stockholm (Sweden) 2014, *General Assembly* Berlin (Germany) 2013, *General Assembly* Rome (Italy) 2012, *General Assembly* Amsterdam (Netherlands) 2011, *General Assembly* Paris (France) 2010. **Publications** *Cleaning Industry – European Social Dialogue* in English, French; *The Cleaning Industry in Europe* in English – report. Training kits; manuals; guides.
Members National representative employers' associations in 15 countries:
Austria, Belgium, Cyprus, Finland, France, Germany, Italy, Luxembourg, Netherlands, Norway, Slovenia, Spain, Sweden, Switzerland, UK.
Individual companies in 8 countries:
Austria, Belgium, France, Germany, Greece, Ireland, Italy, UK.
IGO Relations Consultative Status with: *European Commission (EC, #06633)* (DG Employment and Social Affairs). Formal contacts with: *European Agency for Safety and Health at Work (EU-OSHA, #05843)*; *European Economic and Social Committee (EESC, #06963)*; *European Foundation for the Improvement of Living and Working Conditions (Eurofound, #07348)*. **NGO Relations** Agreement with: *UNI Global Union – Europa (UNI Europa, #20342)*, 17 Dec 1993, on adoption of a recommendation regarding the implementation of a European directive on working hours. Member of: *European Business Services Alliance (EBSA, #06426)*.
[2018.09.06/XD4142/t/**D**]

♦ **European Cleft Organisation (ECO)** **06572**
Exec Dir Verrijn Stuartlaan 28, 2288 EL Rijswijk, Netherlands. E-mail: info@europeancleft.org.
URL: http://www.europeancleft.org/
History Jul 2007. Registration: Handelsregister, No/ID: KVK 27299662, Netherlands. **Aims** Promote advancement of medical expertise and standards of care in the treatment of cleft *lip* and *palate* in Europe. **Structure** Board. **Languages** Dutch, English, French, Polish. **Activities** Advocacy/lobbying/activism; capacity building; standards/guidelines; training/education. **Publications** *Fendlipo* (4 a year) – newsletter. **NGO Relations** Member of (3): *European Patients' Forum (EPF, #08172)* (associate); *EURORDIS – Rare Diseases Europe (#09175)* (Associate); *Face Equality International (FEI, #09232)*.
[2020/XJ7441/**D**]

♦ **European Cleft Palate Craniofacial Association (ECPCA)** **06573**
Contact address not obtained.
URL: https://ecpca.eu/
History 2015, Gothenburg (Sweden). Founded during 10th European Craniofacial Congress. **Aims** Promote and support the management of cleft lip and palate deformities, and related craniofacial anomalies in Europe. **Structure** General Business Meeting; Board; Advisory Board. **Languages** English. **Events** *European Cleft Congress* Milan (Italy) 2024, *Quadrennial Congress* Utrecht (Netherlands) 2019.
[2021.02.17/AA0496/**D**]

♦ European Climate Forum / see Global Climate Forum (#10287)

♦ **European Climate Foundation (ECF)** **06574**
CEO Riviervismarkt 5, 2513 AM The Hague, Netherlands. T. +31707119600. E-mail: info@europeanclimate.org.
Brussels Office Rue de la Science 23, 1040 Brussels, Belgium. T. +3228949300.
URL: http://www.europeanclimate.org/
History 2008. Former names and other names: *Stichting European Climate Foundation* – full title. Registration: EU Transparency Register, No/ID: 64869491516-70; Netherlands. **Aims** Promote climate and energy policies that greatly reduce Europe's greenhouse gas emissions and help Europe play an international leadership role in mitigating *climate change*. **Structure** Management Board; Leadership Team. Offices: The Hague (Netherlands); Brussels (Belgium); Berlin (Germany); London (UK); Warsaw (Poland); Paris (France). **Languages** Dutch, English, French, German, Italian, Polish, Spanish. **Staff** 155.00 FTE, paid. **Finance** Sources: international organizations; private foundations. Supported by: *Oak Foundation*; *The William and Flora Hewlett Foundation*. **Activities** Financial and/or material support. Active in: Belgium, France, Germany, Netherlands, Poland, Spain, UK. **Events** *Conference* London (UK) 2020, *Conference on Integrative Economics* Paris (France) 2020, *Friends of the Paris Agreement – High Level Dialogue Meeting* Beijing (China) 2019, *Rescuing Europe from energy dependency* Brussels (Belgium) 2019, *Conference on Power Solutions Programme* Brussels (Belgium) 2012. **Publications** *Energy Price Monitor* (12 a year). Annual Report. **NGO Relations** Member of (7): *Coalition for Energy Savings (#04056)*; *European Alliance to Save Energy (EU ASE, #05882)*; *European Policy Centre (EPC, #08240)*; *Friends of Europe (#10003)*; *Global Military Advisory Council On Climate Change (GMACCC, #10474)*; *LEDS Global Partnership (LEDS GP, #16435)*; *Philanthropy Europe Association (Philea, #18358)*. Partner of (1): *ClimateWorks Foundation (#04024)*. Supports (1): *Climate Action Network Europe (CAN Europe, #04001)*.
[2020.10.15/XM2831/f/**F**]

♦ **European Climate Realist Network (ECRN)** **06575**
Contact address not obtained. E-mail: ecrteam@ecr.network.
URL: https://ecr.network/
History Sep 2018. **Aims** Strengthen the European climate realist movement; influence climate and energy policy on both national levels and on EU level. **Activities** Events/meetings; knowledge management/information dissemination. **Events** *Conference on Natural Variability and Tolerance* Oslo (Norway) 2019, *Conference on Natural Variability and Tolerance* Oslo (Norway) 2019.
Members Full in 10 countries:
Belgium, Denmark, France, Germany, Ireland, Netherlands, Norway, Portugal, Sweden, UK.
[2020/AA0704/**F**]

♦ **European Climate Research Alliance (ECRA)** **06576**
Sec Rue du Trône 98, 1050 Brussels, Belgium. T. +3225000983. Fax +3225000980.
URL: http://www.ecra-climate.eu/
History Officially launched 4 Oct 2011, Brussels (Belgium). EU Transparency Register: 276191631370-31. **Aims** Strengthen, expand and optimize EU climate research capabilities through the sharing of world-class national facilities in Europe and the collaborative realization of pan-EU programmes. **Structure** Executive Committee; Secretariat. **Events** *General Assembly* Brussels (Belgium) 2022, *General Assembly* Brussels (Belgium) 2019, *General Assembly* Brussels (Belgium) 2017.
Members Research institutions (21) in 10 countries:
Czechia, Denmark, Finland, France, Germany, Italy, Norway, Spain, Sweden, UK.
IGO Relations Observer to: *JPI Climate (#16156)*.
[2019/XM4307/**D**]

♦ European Clinical Pharmacists Association / see European Society of Clinical Pharmacy (#08551)

♦ **European Clinical Research Infrastructure Network (ECRIN)** **06577**
Dir Gen 5-7 rue Watt, 75013 Paris, France. T. +33180058646. E-mail: contact@ecrin.org.
URL: http://www.ecrin.org/
History 2004. Supported by European Commission funding from DG Research. Officially awarded the status of European Research Infrastructure Consortium (ERIC), a legal status designed to facilitate the joint establishment and operation of research infrastructures of European interest. Former names and other names: *ECRIN – Reciprocal Knowledge Programme (ECRIN-RKP)* – former (2004 to 2005); *ECRIN – Transnational Working Group (ECRIN-TWG)* – former (2006 to 2008); *ECRIN Preparation Phase for the Infrastructure (ECRIN-PPI)* – former (2008 to 2011); *ECRIN Integration Activity (ECRIN-IA)* – former (2012 to 2015); *ECRIN-ERIC* – alias. **Aims** Integrate national clinical research facilities into a pan-European infrastructure, able to provide support to multinational clinical research in any medical field, and for any category of clinical research; enhance European and international collaboration on non-commercial, multinational clinical trails; strengthen institutional capacity to develop and implement such trials through creation of tools and resources, and provision of services. **Structure** Assembly of Members; Network Committee; Scientific Board; Coordination Team; European Correspondent in each country hosted at the national hub. **Languages** English. **Staff** 25.00 FTE, paid. **Finance** Member States' contributions; European project support. Annual budget (2016): euro 2,000,000; plus additional project funding: euro 3,500,000. **Activities** Guidance/assistance/consulting; research and development; events/meetings. **Events** *International Clinical Trials Day Meeting* Paris (France) 2019, *International Clinical Trials Day Meeting* Lisbon (Portugal) 2017, *Meeting on Conducting Independent, Multinational Clinical Trials in Europe* Paris (France) 2015, *Annual Meeting* Trondheim (Norway) 2015. **Publications** Information Services: Maintains database with regulatory and ethical requirements for clinical trials.
Members Full in 9 countries:
Czechia, France, Germany, Hungary, Ireland, Italy, Norway, Portugal, Spain.
Observer in 3 countries:
Poland, Slovakia, Switzerland.
IGO Relations *European Commission (EC, #06633)*. Cooperates with: *OECD (#17693)*; *WHO (#20950)*. **NGO Relations** Member of (2): *European Forum for Good Clinical Practice (EFGCP, #07313)*; *European Institute for Innovation through Health Data (i-HD, #07561)*.
[2021/XM0039/**D**]

European Clothing Association
06577

alphabetic sequence excludes
For the complete listing, see Yearbook Online at

♦ European Clothing Association (inactive)
♦ European Cloud Alliance (unconfirmed)

♦ European Cloud User Coalition (ECUC) 06578

Moderator Neue Börsenstr 1, 60487 Frankfurt-Main, Germany. T. +496913643689. E-mail: info@ecuc.group.
URL: https://ecuc.group/

History Jan 2021. Registration: EU Transparency Register, No/ID: 443094047788-55, Start date: 5 Oct 2022. **Aims** Promote regulatory compliant use of public cloud in the European financial industry through technology standardization, developing common solutions and dialogue with the Cloud Service Providers (CSPs). **Structure** Rotating Moderators; Workstreams (4). **Activities** Knowledge management/information dissemination. **Members** Financial institutions. Membership countries not specified. [AA2923/**D**]

♦ European Club Association (ECA) 06579

Secretariat Rte de St-Cergue 9, 1260 Nyon VD, Switzerland. T. +41227615440. E-mail: info@ecaeurope.com.
URL: http://www.ecaeurope.com/

History Set up as the first independent body to directly represent clubs at European level, replacing *G-14 European Football Clubs Grouping (G-14, inactive)* and *European Club Forum*, both dissolved early 2008. Formal memorandum of understanding signed, 21 Jan 2008, with *International Federation of Association Football (#13360)* and *Union of European Football Associations (UEFA, #20386)*. Registration: Switzerland; EU Transparency Register, No/ID: 925747033224-18. **Aims** Serve as the official body for clubs to have a powerful voice in decision-making in the *football* world; give clubs direct access to major stakeholders; provide clubs with information, expert guidance and support on complex issues and day-to-day challenges. **Structure** General Assembly (twice a year); Executive Board; Working Groups (5). **Languages** English. **Staff** 9.00 FTE, paid. **Activities** Advocacy/lobbying/activism. **Events** *General Assembly* 2021, *General Assembly* Budapest (Hungary) 2021, *Session* Stockholm (Sweden) 2019, *General Assembly* Stockholm (Sweden) 2015, *General Assembly* Barcelona (Spain) 2014. **Publications** *ECA Club Management Guide*.

Members Ordinary: membership established every 2 years at the end of the UEFA season on the basis of UEFA ranking. Currently 105 clubs in the 53 countries and territories having national associations within UEFA:
Albania, Andorra, Armenia, Austria, Azerbaijan, Belarus, Belgium, Bosnia-Herzegovina, Bulgaria, Croatia, Cyprus, Czechia, Denmark, England, Estonia, Faeroe Is, Finland, France, Georgia, Germany, Greece, Hungary, Iceland, Ireland, Israel, Italy, Kazakhstan, Latvia, Liechtenstein, Lithuania, Luxembourg, Malta, Moldova, Montenegro, Netherlands, North Macedonia, Northern Ireland, Norway, Poland, Portugal, Romania, Russia, San Marino, Scotland, Serbia, Slovakia, Slovenia, Spain, Sweden, Switzerland, Türkiye, Ukraine, Wales.
Associate: having been an Ordinary member during the previous 2-year cycle; having won the UEFA Champions League at least once; participation in the current UEFA Champions League competition. Clubs with international sporting and/or financial operations can also apply for Associate membership. Currently 109 clubs in 50 of the above countries and territories:
Albania, Andorra, Armenia, Austria, Azerbaijan, Belarus, Belgium, Bosnia-Herzegovina, Bulgaria, Czechia, Denmark, England, Estonia, Faeroe Is, Finland, France, Georgia, Germany, Greece, Hungary, Iceland, Ireland, Israel, Italy, Kazakhstan, Latvia, Lithuania, Luxembourg, Malta, Moldova, Montenegro, Netherlands, North Macedonia, Northern Ireland, Norway, Poland, Portugal, Romania, Russia, San Marino, Scotland, Serbia, Slovakia, Slovenia, Spain, Sweden, Switzerland, Türkiye, Ukraine, Wales.

NGO Relations Cooperates with: *European Leagues (#07672)*; *Fédération internationale des footballeurs professionnels (FIFPRO, #09633)*; *International Federation of Association Football (#13360)*; *Union of European Football Associations (UEFA, #20386)*. [2020/XM3602/**E**]

♦ European Club of Companies (internationally oriented national body)

♦ European Club for Countertrade and Offset (ECCO) 06580

Operations Manager 176 av de Charles de Gaulle, 92522 Neuilly CEDEX, France. T. +33610600802. E-mail: info@ecco-offset.eu – ecco.offset@gmail.com.
Chairman address not obtained.
URL: http://www.ecco-offset.eu/

History 2010. Registration: France. **Aims** Create an international platform to share information and best practices in the field of offsets and countertrade activities. **Structure** Board; Executive Committee. **Languages** English, French, Spanish. **Staff** 1.00 FTE, paid. **Finance** Sources: meeting proceeds; members' dues. **Activities** Events/meetings; networking/liaising; training/education. **Events** *Symposium* Paris (France) 2016, *Symposium* London (UK) 2015, *Symposium* Paris (France) 2015, *Symposium* Paris (France) 2014, *Symposium* Vienna (Austria) 2014. **Publications** *ECCO News*. Guides.

Members Offset Obligators; Offset Stakeholders; Individuals. Members in 16 countries:
Austria, Belgium, Brazil, France, Germany, Greece, India, Lebanon, Malaysia, Norway, South Africa, Spain, Sweden, Switzerland, UK, USA.

NGO Relations Partner of (1): *Global Forum on Law, Justice and Development (GFLJD, #10373)*. [2022.02.15/XJ9602/t/**D**]

♦ European Club for Human Resources (EChr) 06581

General Secretariat Rue du Luxembourg 19-21, 1000 Brussels, Belgium. T. +3222136271.

History Registered in accordance with Belgian law. **Aims** Develop an international vision of human resources management from a European viewpoint. **Structure** Executive Committee, comprising President, General Secretary, 2 Vice-Presidents, Treasurer and 2 members. Scientific Committee. General Secretariat. **Activities** Meeting activities; studies. **Events** *Annual European employment week* Brussels (Belgium) 2009. **Publications** *European HR Barometer*. **IGO Relations** *ECOSOC (#05331)*; *European Commission (EC, #06633)*; *European Parliament (EP, #08146)*. [2017/XJ0329/**F**]

♦ European Club of Local Government Staff Pension Funds / see European Association of Public Sector Pension Institutions (#06180)

♦ European Club for Paediatric Burns (ECPB) 06582

Contact address not obtained. E-mail: ecpburns@gmail.com – support@ecpb.info.
URL: https://www.ecpb.info/

History 7 Sep 1991, Switzerland. **Aims** Standardize and optimize paediatric burn care; collect, evaluate and public multi-centre data; stimulate contact and exchange of physicians and personnel between paediatric burn centres; exchange information about current project; promote paediatric burn centres. **Activities** Organizes congresses and workshops. Grants the *'ECPB Zora Janzekovic Prize'*. **Events** *Workshop* Hannover (Germany) 2022, *World Congress* Machynlleth (UK) 2020, *Workshop* Lyon (France) 2015, *Triennial World Congress* Boston, MA (USA) 2014, *Triennial world congress* Zurich (Switzerland) 2011. **Members** Membership countries not specified. [2022/XF7129/**F**]

♦ European Club of Paediatric Dieticians 06583

Club européen des diététiciens de l'enfance (CEDE)

Pres 26 Grande Rue, 54700 Loisy, France.
URL: http://www.cede-nutrition.org/

History Mar 1996. **Aims** Act as reference for practical aspects of *nutrition* for healthy and sick children treated individually, collectively or in hospital; promote children's nutritional health; assert the profession of paediatric dietician through acknowledgement of its specificity. **Finance** Members' dues: euro 30 per year, per applicant. Sponsorship. **Activities** Working groups produce position papers on nutrition care, based on experience, technical skill, scientific knowledge and recommendations. **Events** *Meeting* Paris (France) 2012, *Meeting* Luxembourg (Luxembourg) 2011, *Meeting* Brussels (Belgium) 2010, *Meeting* Paris (France) 2009, *Meeting* Luxembourg (Luxembourg) 2008. **Publications** *CEDE News* (4 a year) in French – bulletin. **Members** Membership countries not specified. [2020/XF6174/**F**]

♦ European Club on Paediatric Intensive Care / see European Society of Paediatric and Neonatal Intensive Care (#08683)
♦ European Club for Paediatric Research (inactive)
♦ European Club of Young Cardiac Surgeons (no recent information)

♦ European Clusters Alliance 06584

Contact Rue Belliard 40, 1000 Brussels, Belgium. E-mail: contact@clustersalliance.eu.
URL: https://clustersalliance.eu/

History 20 Apr 2020, Brussels (Belgium). Former names and other names: *ECA* – alias. Registration: Banque-Carrefour des Entreprises, No/ID: 0751.557.681, Start date: 28 Jul 2020, Belgium; EU Transparency Register, No/ID: 632695640817-36, Start date: 3 Jan 2020. **Aims** Be the common voice of European industrial clusters, facilitating connections and opportunities to meet the challenges our economy faces.

Members National cluster associations (19) in 18 countries:
Austria, Belgium, Bulgaria, Czechia, Finland, France, Germany, Greece, Italy, Latvia, Moldova, Poland, Portugal, Romania, Slovakia, Spain, Sweden, Ukraine. [2022.05.11/AA1278/**D**]

♦ European CME Forum 06585

Programme Dir Maasdijk 409, 4264 AS Veen, Netherlands.
URL: https://cmeforum.org/

History 2008, UK. Registration: Handelsregister, No/ID: KVK 81103700, Netherlands. **Aims** Bring together all stakeholder groups with an interest in Continuing Medical Education (CME)/Continuing Professional Development (CPD) for healthcare professionals; facilitate multi-channel discussion in an independent and neutral environment to promote the advance of high quality CME in Europe and around the globe. **Activities** Events/meetings. **Events** *Annual European CME Forum* Barcelona (Spain) 2022, *Annual European CME Forum* Veen (Netherlands) 2021, *Annual European CME Forum* Veen (Netherlands) 2020, *Annual European CME Forum* Manchester (UK) 2019, *Annual European CME Forum* London (UK) 2018. **Publications** *Journal of European CME (JECME)*. [2021.11.30/AA2200/**F**]

♦ European CMT Federation (ECMTF) 06586

Pres Rue d'Egmont 11, 1000 Brussels, Belgium. E-mail: president@ecmtf.org – secretary@ecmtf.org – info@ecmtf.org.
Treas address not obtained.
URL: http://www.ecmtf.org/

History 2016, Italy. Registration: Tribunal de commerce, No/ID: 0700326736, Start date: 2018, Belgium. **Aims** Unite CMT advocacy groups across Europe; help raise awareness, support research and promote better care for people with *Charcot-Marie-Tooth disease*. **Structure** General Assembly; Board of Directors. **Languages** English. **Staff** 10.00 FTE, voluntary. **Finance** Sources: contributions; donations; fundraising; international organizations; members' dues. Annual budget: 150,000 EUR (2021). **Activities** Awareness raising; research and development.

Members National organizations (14) in 10 EU countries:
Austria, Belgium, France, Germany, Hungary, Italy, Netherlands, Romania, Spain, UK.
Associate: national organizations (2) in 2 non-EU countries:
China, Israel.

NGO Relations Member of (2): *European Federation of Neurological Associations (EFNA, #07177)*; *EURORDIS – Rare Diseases Europe (#09175)* (Associate). Cooperates with (1): *European Alliance of Neuromuscular Disorders Associations (EAMDA, #05876)*. [2022.05.16/XM7733/**D**]

♦ European Coaching Association (internationally oriented national body)

♦ European Coaching Federation (EuCF) 06587

Pres Widerhofergasse 4, 1090 Vienna, Austria. T. +4313174702. E-mail: info@eucf.org.
URL: http://www.eucf.org/

History Registered in accordance with Austrian law. **Structure** Officers: President; 2 Vice-President; Vice-President/Treasurer; Vice-President/Secretary. [2016/XM0967/**D**]

♦ European Coal Combustion Products Association (ECOBA) 06588

Sec. Gen. Deilbachtal 173, 45257 Essen, Germany. T. +492018128297. Fax +492018128364. E-mail: info@ecoba.org.
URL: http://www.ecoba.org/

History 30 Mar 1990, Germany FR. Former names and other names: *European Association for Use of the By-Products of Coal-Fired Power Stations* – former (1990 to 2002). **Aims** Promote coal combustion products (CCPs) as valuable raw and construction materials which can be utilized in environmentally compatible ways, especially among legislative and standardizing institutions; communicate the economic and ecological benefits of CCP utilization. **Structure** General Assembly; Governing Board; Committees (3); Working Groups (2). **Languages** English. **Staff** 1.00 FTE, paid. **Finance** Sources: members' dues. **Activities** Events/meetings; knowledge management/information dissemination; politics/policy/regulatory; research and development. **Events** *Ashtrans Europe Conference* Copenhagen (Denmark) 2021, *EUROCOALASH Conference* Thessaloniki (Greece) 2021, *EUROCOALASH Conference* Dundee (UK) 2019, *ASHTRANS Europe Conference* Barcelona (Spain) 2018, *ROMCEN International Conference* Bucharest (Romania) 2018. **Publications** *ECOBA Information Bulletin*. Conference proceedings.

Members Full (24) in 16 countries:
Czechia, Denmark, Estonia, Finland, France, Germany, Greece, Ireland, Italy, Netherlands, Poland, Portugal, Serbia, Spain, UK, Ukraine.
Affiliate in 7 countries:
Belgium, Germany, Israel, Japan, South Africa, UK, USA.
Honorary in 3 countries:
Netherlands, Poland, USA.
Informational in 2 countries:
India, Russia.
Associate in 4 countries:
Belgium, Germany, Portugal, Singapore.

IGO Relations Collaborates with: *European Commission (EC, #06633)* Directorates. **NGO Relations** In liaison with technical committees of: *Comité européen de normalisation (CEN, #04162)*. Member of: *American Coal Ash Association (ACAA, #00777)*. [2021.06.17/XD2981/**D**]

♦ European Coal Geology Group (ECGP) 06589

Contact address not obtained. T. +48322372848.
URL: http://www.ecc9.polsl.pl/

History Set up, following the activities of the Coal Group of the Geological Society of London, as an informal group of academics and applied scientists and technicians. **Structure** Permanent Committee of 8. **Events** *European Coal Conference* Gliwice (Poland) 2013, *European Coal Conference* Darmstadt (Germany) 2010, *European Coal Conference* Lviv (Ukraine) 2008, *European Coal Conference* Belgrade (Serbia-Montenegro) 2005, *European Coal Conference* Mons (Belgium) 2002. [2013/XJ6684/**D**]

♦ European Coal Information Agency (inactive)
♦ European Coalition for Chemical Recycling (unconfirmed)
♦ European Coalition of Cities Against Racism (see: #12610)

♦ European Coalition for Community Living (ECCL) 06590

Secretariat c/o ENIL, 7th Fl – Mundo J, Rue de l'Industrie 10, 1000 Brussels, Belgium.
URL: http://www.community-living.info/

History Founded Aug 2005, by *Autism-Europe (AE, #03040)*, Center for Policy Studies of *Central European University (CEU, #03717)*, *European Disability Forum (EDF, #06929)*, *Inclusion Europe – European Association of Societies of Persons with Intellectual Disability and their Families (Inclusion Europe, #11144)*, *Mental Health Europe (MHE, #16715)* and Open Society Foundations – Mental Health Initiative. An initiative of *European Network on Independent Living (ENIL, #07929)*. **Aims** Work towards the social inclusion of people with *disabilities* by promoting the provision of comprehensive, quality community-based services as an alternative to institutionalization. **Structure** Managed by *European Network on Independent Living (ENIL, #07929)*. **Languages** English. **Staff** 0.50 FTE, paid. **Finance** Project-based funding. Budget (annual): about euro 50,000. **Publications** *Briefing on Structural Funds Investments for People with Disabilities: Achieving the Transition from Institutional Care to Community Living* (2013); *Creating Successful Campaigns for Community Living* (2011).

Members Organizations in 26 countries and territories:

Armenia, Austria, Azerbaijan, Belgium, Bosnia-Herzegovina, Bulgaria, Croatia, Czechia, Estonia, Finland, Georgia, Germany, Greece, Hungary, Ireland, Kosovo, Latvia, Moldova, Netherlands, North Macedonia, Poland, Romania, Serbia, Slovakia, UK, Ukraine.
Included in the above, 5 regional organizations:
Autism-Europe (AE, #03040); European Association of Service Providers for Persons with Disabilities (EASPD, #06204); European Disability Forum (EDF, #06929); Inclusion Europe – European Association of Societies of Persons with Intellectual Disability and their Families (Inclusion Europe, #11144); Mental Health Europe (MHE, #16715).
Individuals in 3 countries:
Cyprus, Portugal, Spain.
NGO Relations Member of: European Expert Group on the Transition from Institutional to Community-based Care. [2015/XJ8278/y/**E**]

♦ European Coalition for Corporate Justice (ECCJ) 06591

Coordinator Rue D'Edimbourg 26, 1050 Brussels, Belgium. T. +3228931027.
URL: http://www.corporatejustice.org/
History Founded 2005, by European NGOs and national coalitions. EU Transparency Register: 48872621093-60. Registered as ASBL in Belgium since 2018, enterprise number: 0699 883 407. **Aims** Develop a common vision of corporate justice, build capacity and knowledge among civil society organizations, and influence corporate accountability policies. **Structure** General Assembly (annual); Steering Group; Secretariat. **Languages** English. **Staff** 3.00 FTE, paid. **Finance** Members' dues. External funding, currently including from: *Brot für die Welt; German Catholic Bishops' Organisation for Development Cooperation (MISEREOR); Joseph Rowntree Charitable Trust; Sigrid Rausing Trust.* **Activities** Politics/policy/regulatory; capacity building. **Publications** *A Human Rights Review of the EU Non-Financial Reporting Directive* (2019); *Assessments of National Action Plans (NAPs) on Business and Human Rights* (2017); *The EU's Business: Recommended actions for the EU and its Member States to ensure access to judicial remedy for business-related human rights impacts* (2015); *The Third Pillar: Access to Judicial Remedies for Human Rights Violations by Transnational Business* (2013) – in cooperation with ICAR and CORE; *Human Right Due Diligence – The Role of States* (2012) – in cooperation with ICAR and CNCA.
Members Civil Society Organizations (CSOs) platforms; individual NGOs. National CSO platforms in 12 countries:
Austria, Belgium, Denmark, France, Germany, Italy, Luxembourg, Netherlands, Norway, Spain, Switzerland, UK.
Organizations representing countries where no platform has been established, in 4 countries:
Czechia, Finland, Poland, Sweden.
European and international organizations (3):
Corporate Europe Observatory (CEO, #04839); Friends of the Earth Europe (FoEE, #10001); International Federation for Human Rights (#13452).
NGO Relations Member of: *GoodElectronics (#10679).* [2019.09.20/XM3440/y/**F**]

♦ European Coalition for Diabetes (ECD) 06592

Head Office Milnwood House, 13 North Parade, Horsham, RH12 2BT, UK. T. +441403276363.
URL: http://www.ecdiabetes.eu/
History Founded Nov 2009, as a relaunch of the *EU Diabetes Working Group (EUDWG)*, by *Foundation of European Nurses in Diabetes (FEND, #09953), European Alliance for Diabetes Research (EURADIA, #05868), International Diabetes Federation Europe (IDF Europe, #13165)* and *Primary Care Diabetes Europe (PCDE, #18495).* EU Transparency Register: 513172621753-81. **Aims** Improve prevention of diabetes, as well as the health and quality of life of European citizens living with diabetes, by influencing EU policy. **Structure** 4 Co-Chairs, with chairmanship rotating between Co-Chairs. **Languages** English. **Staff** 0.50 FTE, paid. **Finance** Financed by member organizations.
Members Organizations (4):
European Alliance for Diabetes Research (EURADIA, #05868); Foundation of European Nurses in Diabetes (FEND, #09953); International Diabetes Federation Europe (IDF Europe, #13165); Primary Care Diabetes Europe (PCDE, #18495). [2019/XJ1859/y/**E**]

♦ European Coalition for Economic Growth (ECEG) 06593

Pres Jasomirgottstr 3/11, 1010 Vienna, Austria. Fax +431505134999. E-mail: office@austriancenter.com – b.schier@e-growth.eu – office@e-growth.eu.
URL: http://www.e-growth.eu/
History Founded 2006, Vienna (Austria). Infrastructure provided by the Austrian Economics Center (AEC). **Aims** Act as an umbrella organization and a net-hub for all free market oriented and economic theory organizations in Europe; work closely with other institutes and think tanks of similar backgrounds. **Languages** English, German, Spanish. **Finance** Financed by individuals, corporations and foundations. **Activities** Research/documentation; training/education; politics/policy/regulatory; events/meetings. Active in: Europe (including eastern Europe); Caucasus region; Middle East; USA. **Events** *ICCC : international conference on climate change* Chicago, IL (USA) 2010, *ICCC : international conference on climate change* New York, NY (USA) 2009, *ICCC : international conference on climate change* New York, NY (USA) 2008.
Members Full in 22 countries:
Austria, Belgium, Bosnia-Herzegovina, Bulgaria, Czechia, Denmark, France, Georgia, Germany, Iceland, Italy, Lithuania, Norway, Poland, Romania, Russia, Slovakia, Sweden, Switzerland, Türkiye, UK, USA.
Included in the above, 4 organizations listed in this Yearbook:
Educational Initiative for Central and Eastern Europe (EICEE, #05366); International Policy Network (IPN); Ludwig von Mises Institute Europe (LVMI Europe, #16521); Taxpayers Association of Europe (TAE, #20102).
NGO Relations Member of: *Civil Society Coalition on Climate Change (CSCCC, #03967).*
[2015.09.08/XJ1333/y/**D**]

♦ European Coalition to End Animal Experiments (ECEAE) 06594

Coalition européenne pour mettre fin à l'expérimentation animale – Coalición Europea para la Abolición de los Experimentos con Animales
Contact LSCV Europe Head Office, 234 route de chez les Favre, 74270 Chessenaz, France. E-mail: info@eceae.org.
URL: http://www.eceae.org/
History 1990. Founded by animal welfare/rights societies throughout the European Union. Former names and other names: *European Coalition to End Cosmetic Tests on Animals* – former. Registration: RNA, No/ID: W743006265, Start date: 2 Sep 2019, France; EU Transparency Register, No/ID: 054680935509-93, Start date: 23 Jul 2019. **Aims** Work towards eliminating animal experiments. **Languages** English. **Staff** provided by: British Union for the Abolition of Vivisection (BUAV). **Finance** Sources: donations; members' dues. **Activities** Campaigns and lobbies for animal protection; responds to EU animal testing issues; produces scientific reports; participates in expert working groups meetings. Operates the Humane Cosmetics Standard (HCS). **Events** *Half-yearly meeting* Netherlands 1996, *Half-yearly meeting* Paris (France) 1996.
Members Groups (14) in 12 countries:
Austria, Croatia, Czechia, Denmark, France, Germany, Ireland, Italy, North Macedonia, Serbia, Spain, Switzerland.
Included in the above, 1 organization listed in this Yearbook:
Internationaler Bund der Tierversuchsgegner (IBT, no recent information).
IGO Relations Accredited stakeholder of: *European Chemicals Agency (ECHA, #06523).* [2020/XF2306/**F**]

♦ European Coalition to End Cosmetic Tests on Animals / see European Coalition to End Animal Experiments (#06594)

♦ European Coalition on Homeopathic and Anthroposophic Medicinal Products (ECHAMP) 06595

Public Affairs Manager Rue Washington 40, 1050 Brussels, Belgium. T. +3226499440. E-mail: office@echamp.eu.
Pres address not obtained.
URL: http://www.echamp.eu/
History Nov 1999. A grouping of the type *European Economic Interest Grouping (EEIG, #06960).* Registration: Banque-Carrefour des Entreprises, No/ID: 0467.826.644, Start date: 2 Dec 1999, Belgium; EU Transparency Register, No/ID: 85825114058-57, Start date: 25 Aug 2010. **Aims** Enable members to meet the demand from users and prescribers across the EU for homeopathic and anthroposophic medicinal products. **Structure** Assembly (annual, in country holding EU presidency); Board of Management; Secretariat, located in Brussels (Belgium). **Languages** English. **Staff** 1.00 FTE, paid. **Finance** Sources: contributions; members' dues. **Activities** Advocacy/lobbying/activism; capacity building. **Events** *Assembly* 2022, *Assembly* 2021, *Assembly* 2020, *Assembly* Dublin (Ireland) 2019, *Assembly* Marseille (France) 2018. **Publications** *ECHAMP Position Papers.* Annual Report.
Members Full Members; Corresponding Partners; Associate Partners. Full (54 companies) in 17 countries:
Austria, Belgium, Bulgaria, Denmark, Finland, France, Germany, Ireland, Italy, Lithuania, Netherlands, Norway, Poland, Portugal, Spain, Sweden, UK.
Corresponding (12), including the following 10 organizations listed in this Yearbook:
Association of Natural Medicine in Europe (ANME); European Central Council of Homeopaths (ECCH, #06467); European Committee for Homeopathy (ECH, #06651); European Council of Doctors for Plurality in Medicine (ECPM, #06816); European Federation for Naturopathy (EFN, inactive); European Federation of Homeopathic Patients' Associations (EFHPA, #07139); European Federation of Patients' Associations for Anthroposophic Medicine (EFPAM, #07189); International Association of Anthroposophic Pharmacists (IAAP); Internationale Vereinigung Anthroposophischer Ärztegesellschaften (IVAA, #13314); Nordic Cooperation Committee for complementary and alternative Medicine (NSK, #17254).
Associate (10 associations) in 10 countries:
Austria, Belgium, Denmark, Germany, Ireland, Netherlands, Portugal, Sweden, Switzerland, UK.
NGO Relations Member of (1): *Federation of European and International Associations Established in Belgium (FAIB, #09508).* Cooperates with (1): *EUROCAM (#05653).* [2022.10.20/XF6078/y/**F**]

♦ European Coalition for Israel (internationally oriented national body)

♦ European Coalition for Just and Effective Drug Policies (ENCOD) . . 06596

Treas Guldensporenstraat 61, 2140 Antwerp, Belgium. T. +32495122644. E-mail: office@encod.org – team@encod.org.
URL: http://www.encod.org/
History 1993. Former names and other names: *European NGO Council on Drugs* – former; *European NGO Council on Drugs and Development* – former; *Comité Europeo de ONGs sobre Drogas y Desarrollo* – former. Registration: Banque-Carrefour des Entreprises, No/ID: 0472.682.681, Start date: 31 Aug 2000, Belgium; EU Transparency Register, No/ID: 331952831201-01, Start date: 16 Apr 2018. **Aims** Obtain more transparency and democracy in the drug policy-making process; improve understanding of the causes and effects of the drugs trade; contribute to the elaboration of just and effective drugs control policies; bring about greater consistency between drugs control efforts and economic and social policies. **Structure** General Assembly (annual); Executive Committee; Secretariat. **Languages** Danish, Dutch, English, French, German, Italian, Spanish. **Staff** 30.00 FTE, voluntary. **Finance** Sources: donations; members' dues. Other sources: inheritances; loans. **Activities** Networking/liaising; awareness raising. **Events** *General Assembly* Slovenia 2014, *General Assembly* Bermeo (Spain) 2013, *General Assembly* Antwerp (Belgium) 2012, *General Assembly* Prague (Czech Rep) 2011, *General Assembly* Frankfurt-Main (Germany) 2010. **Publications** *The ENCOD Bulletin* (12 a year) in Dutch, English, French, German, Italian, Spanish.
Members Ordinary; Associate; Donor. Individuals in 36 countries:
Argentina, Australia, Austria, Bangladesh, Belgium, Bolivia, Chile, Colombia, Denmark, Finland, France, Germany, Hungary, India, Indonesia, Iran Islamic Rep, Ireland, Italy, Mali, Mexico, Moldova, Netherlands, New Zealand, Nigeria, North Macedonia, Norway, Peru, Portugal, Slovakia, Slovenia, Spain, Sweden, Switzerland, UK, Ukraine, USA. [2022/XE0770/v/**E**]

♦ European Coalition for Vision (unconfirmed)
♦ European Coal Organization (inactive)
♦ European Coal and Steel Community (inactive)

♦ European Coast Guard Functions Forum (ECGFF) 06597

Brussels c/o Frontex Liaison Office, Avenue d'Auderghem 20, 1040 Brussels, Belgium. E-mail: info@ecgff.eu.
URL: http://www.ecgff.eu/
History Launched 2009. **Aims** Study, contribute to and promote understanding and development of *maritime* issues of importance and of common interest related to Coast Guard Functions across borders and sectors, both civil and military; contribute to progress in CGF activities. **Structure** Plenary Conference; Chairmanship; Secretariat. **Events** *Plenary Conference* Lisbon (Portugal) 2017, *Plenary Conference* London (UK) 2016, *Plenary Conference* Helsinki (Finland) 2015, *Conference* Italy 2014, *Conference* Chios (Greece) 2013.
Members Heads of the Coast Guard Functions or equivalents or each EU maritime nation and associated Schengen countries. Participating countries (25):
Belgium, Bulgaria, Croatia, Cyprus, Denmark, Estonia, Finland, France, Germany, Greece, Iceland, Ireland, Italy, Latvia, Lithuania, Malta, Netherlands, Norway, Poland, Portugal, Romania, Slovenia, Spain, Sweden, UK.
Participating institutions:
European Commission (EC, #06633) (Maritime Affairs and Fisheries); *European Fisheries Control Agency (EFCA, #07266); European Maritime Safety Agency (EMSA, #07744); European Union Satellite Centre (SatCen, #09015); Frontex, the European Border and Coast Guard Agency (#10005);* Mobility and Transport.
IGO Relations *Frontex, the European Border and Coast Guard Agency (#10005).* [2016/XM4675/**F***]

♦ European Cockpit Association (ECA) 06598

Office Manager Rue du Commerce 22, 1000 Brussels, Belgium. T. +3227053293. Fax +3227050877. E-mail: eca@eurocockpit.be.
URL: http://www.eurocockpit.be/
History Founded 1990, by representatives of pilots and flight engineers from the then 12 European Community countries. Registered in accordance with Belgian law. EU Transparency Register: 39838147687-59. **Aims** Study scientific, technical, documentary and institutional problems of common interest to *civil aviation* airline pilots and cockpit crew and reinforce cooperation among them. **Structure** General Assembly (annual, in Nov, always in Brussels-Belgium); Executive Board; Secretariat. Working Groups. **Languages** English, French. **Staff** 8.00 FTE, paid. **Finance** Members' dues. **Activities** Guidance/assistance/consulting; knowledge management/information dissemination; events/meetings. **Events** *Conference* Brussels (Belgium) 2013, *General Assembly* Brussels (Belgium) 2013, *Meeting* Brussels (Belgium) 2010, *General Assembly* London (UK) 1994. **Publications** *Cockpit News* (12 a year) – newsletter.
Members Founding; adhering. Associations representing over 38,000 pilots in 36 countries:
Austria, Belgium, Bosnia-Herzegovina, Bulgaria, Croatia, Cyprus, Czechia, Denmark, Estonia, Finland, France, Germany, Greece, Hungary, Iceland, Ireland, Italy, Latvia, Lithuania, Luxembourg, Malta, Montenegro, Netherlands, North Macedonia, Norway, Poland, Portugal, Romania, Serbia, Slovenia, Spain, Sweden, Switzerland, Türkiye, UK, Ukraine.
IGO Relations *European Union Aviation Safety Agency (EASA, #08978).* **NGO Relations** Liaison Organization of: *Comité européen de normalisation (CEN, #04162).* Represents European interests of: *International Federation of Air Line Pilots' Associations (IFALPA, #13349).* [2019/XD2177/**D**]

♦ European Cocoa Association (ECA) 06599

SG Av des Gaulois 3, Box 6, 1040 Brussels, Belgium. T. +3226620006. Fax +3226620008. E-mail: officeadministrator@eurococoa.com – info@eurococoa.com.
URL: http://www.eurococoa.com/
History Sep 2000. Registration: Banque-Carrefour des Entreprises, No/ID: 0472.920.332, Start date: 28 Sep 2000, Belgium; EU Transparency Register, No/ID: 03804222429-10, Start date: 1 Oct 2009. **Aims** Serve as the voice of the European cocoa community and as a vantage point in relationship with other direct or indirect actors of the cocoa-chain. **Languages** English. **Staff** 6.00 FTE, paid. **Finance** Sources: members' dues. **Events** *European Cocoa Forum* 2025, *European Cocoa Forum* Rome (Italy) 2022, *European Cocoa Forum* Lisbon (Portugal) 2019, *Forum on Availability of Raw Materials in the Context of Current and Future EU Policies* Brussels (Belgium) 2018, *Forum on Life Cycle Assessment Use in Agro-Bulk Supply Chains and on Product Environment Footprint* Brussels (Belgium) 2017. **Publications** *ECA Newsletter* (4 a year); *European Cocoa Bean Usage* (4 a year); *Update* – for members only. Position papers.
Members Effective (23); Contributors (9). Members in 7 countries:
Belgium, France, Germany, Netherlands, Spain, Switzerland, UK.

European Code Social
06599

alphabetic sequence excludes
For the complete listing, see Yearbook Online at

IGO Relations Observer status with (1): *International Cocoa Organization (ICCO, #12627).* **NGO Relations** Member of (1): *Primary Food Processors (PFP, #18496).* Liaison Organization of: *Comité européen de normalisation (CEN, #04162); Federation of Cocoa Commerce (FCC, #09473).* Joint publication with: *Association of the Chocolate, Biscuit and Confectionery Industries of the EU (CAOBISCO, #02427).* [2022.02.15/XD8409/**D**]

- ♦ European Code of Social Security (1964 treaty)
- ♦ European Code of Social Security, Revised (1990 treaty)
- ♦ European Coffee Bureau (inactive)

♦ European Coffee Federation (ECF) 06600

Fédération européenne du café

SG Av des Nerviens 9-31, 1040 Brussels, Belgium. T. +3225495641. E-mail: info@ecf-coffee.org.
URL: http://www.ecf-coffee.org/

History 5 Jun 1980, Hamburg (Germany). Founded during International Coffee Congress, simultaneously with *Committee of European Coffee Associations (CECA, inactive)*, when it also federated with *European Federation of Associations of Coffee Roasters (EUCA, inactive)*, set up 3 Feb 1967, Hamburg. Took over activities of EUCA, CECA and *Association of Soluble Coffee Manufacturers of the European Community (inactive)*, 1 Jan 2006, and of *European Association of Decaffeinators (inactive)*, 1 Jan 2012. Registration: EU Transparency Register, No/ID: 958482431512-92. **Aims** Facilitate the development of an environment in which the European coffee trade and industry can meet the needs of consumers and society, while competing effectively to ensure the resilience and long-term sustainability of the coffee supply chain.; defend their interests in all member countries by exchange of views and experience. **Structure** General Assembly (annual); Secretariat in Brussels (Belgium). **Languages** English. **Staff** 2.00 FTE, paid. **Finance** Sources: members' dues; subscriptions. **Activities** Events/meetings. **Events** *Annual General Assembly* 2020, *Annual General Assembly and Congress* Athens (Greece) 2019, *Annual General Assembly and Congress* Amsterdam (Netherlands) 2018, *Annual General Assembly and Congress* Copenhagen (Denmark) 2017, *Annual General Assembly and Congress* Brussels (Belgium) 2015. **Publications** *European Coffee Report* (annual).
Members Associations in 14 countries:
Austria, Belgium, Denmark, Finland, France, Germany, Greece, Italy, Netherlands, Norway, Spain, Sweden, Switzerland, UK.
Company members in 9 countries:
Belgium, Estonia, Finland, France, Germany, Italy, Netherlands, Switzerland, UK.
NGO Relations Member of (2): *FoodDrinkEurope (#09841); Global Coffee Platform (GCP, #10298).* [2021.06.14/XD9764/**E**]

♦ European Coil Coating Association (ECCA) 06601

Managing Dir Av de Tervuren 273, 1150 Brussels, Belgium. T. +3225150020. E-mail: info@prepaintedmetal.eu.
URL: http://www.prepaintedmetal.eu/

History 1967. Statutes revised 2011; current statutes adopted Nov 2020. Registration: Banque-Carrefour des Entreprises, No/ID: 0414.448.930, Start date: 12 Sep 1974, Belgium; EU Transparency Register, No/ID: 8427163134-48, Start date: 3 Jul 2008. **Aims** Promote the use of pre-painted *metal* as an environmentally sound, cost effective and high quality method of *finishing.* **Structure** General Meeting (annual); Board of Directors; Executive Committee; Marketing, Sustainability and Technical Committees. **Languages** English, French. **Staff** 3.00 FTE, paid. **Finance** Sources: meeting proceeds; members' dues. **Activities** Certification/accreditation; events/meetings; knowledge management/information dissemination; research and development; standards/guidelines. **Events** *Spring Meeting* Marseille (France) 2022, *Congress* Brussels (Belgium) 2021, *Spring Meeting* Lucerne (Switzerland) 2021, *Congress* Brussels (Belgium) 2020, *Congress* Brussels (Belgium) 2019. **Publications** ECCA Collection; sustainability report; promotional material; technical reports; statistics.
Members European companies: coater; supplier; special (firms outside Europe, or institutes and associations).
European members in 21 countries:
Austria, Belgium, Czechia, Denmark, Finland, France, Germany, Greece, Italy, Luxembourg, Netherlands, Norway, Poland, Russia, Serbia, Slovakia, Spain, Sweden, Switzerland, Türkiye, UK.
IGO Relations Recognized by: *European Commission (EC, #06633).* **NGO Relations** Member of (3): *Federation of European and International Associations Established in Belgium (FAIB, #09508); Industry4Europe (#11181); METALS FOR BUILDINGS (#16737).* In liaison with technical committees of: *Comité européen de normalisation (CEN, #04162).* [2021.02.17/XD2718/**D**]

♦ European Coke Committee (ECC) 06602

No fixed address address not obtained.

History Original title: *European Cokemaking Committee.* **Structure** An informal group of coke oven managers and technologists. No headquarters or finance. Chairman and Secretariat rotate every 2 years. **Activities** Meetings for exchange of views and information of a technical and production nature. **Events** *Meeting* Taranto (Italy) 2011, *China international coking technology and coke market congress* Beijing (China) 2006, *European coke and iron-making congress / Meeting / Conference* Stockholm (Sweden) 2005, *Meeting* Dunkerque (France) 2003, *Meeting* Linz (Austria) 2001. [2015/XE3204/**E**]

- ♦ European Cokemaking Committee / see European Coke Committee (#06602)
- ♦ European Cold Rolled Section Association (internationally oriented national body)

♦ European Cold Storage and Logistics Association (ECSLA) 06603

SG Square de Meeûs 35, 1000 Brussels, Belgium. T. +3228939737. Fax +3228939788. E-mail: info@ecsla.eu.
URL: https://ecsla.eu/

History 1997. Founded as successor to *Association européenne des exploitations frigorifiques (AEEF, inactive).* Registration: No/ID: 0465.297.122, Start date: 11 Feb 1999, Belgium; EU Transparency Register, No/ID: 12075096931-04, Start date: 12 Oct 2011. **Aims** Represent cold logistics companies' interests, at the level of European and international institutions, so as to contribute to the development of a legislative and economic framework addressing the competitiveness of industry *food*, food quality and safety, consumer protection and respect for the environment. **Structure** General Meeting (annual); Board of Directors; Committees (4); Permanent Secretariat. **Languages** English. **Staff** 1.00 FTE, paid. **Finance** Sources: members' dues. **Activities** Politics/policy/regulatory; research/documentation. **Events** *Cold Chain Logistics Conference* Amsterdam (Netherlands) 2015, *Autumn Conference* Brussels (Belgium) 2015, *Cold Chain Logistics Conference* Maastricht (Netherlands) 2014, *Cold Chain Logistics Conference* Bruges (Belgium) 2013, *Annual General Meeting* Lyon (France) 2009. **Publications** *ECSLA Atlas* – directory of European public refrigeration enterprises. Activity reports; technical reports.
Members Ordinary national federations or individuals in any European country; Correspondent national federations outside Europe or organizations, individuals or concerns which might usefully collaborate.
Ordinary members in 9 countries:
Austria, Belgium, France, Germany, Greece, Italy, Netherlands, Spain, Switzerland.
IGO Relations Recognized by *European Commission (EC, #06633); European Parliament (EP, #08146).* **NGO Relations** Member of (2): *European Logistics Platform (ELP, #07711); SMEunited (#19327).* Partner in: *Global Cold Chain Alliance (GCCA, #10299).* [2022/XD6973/**D**]

- ♦ European Collaborative for Science, Industry and Technology Exhibitions / see European Network of Science Centres and Museums (#07998)
- ♦ European Collection of Animal Cell Cultures / see European Collection of Authenticated Cell Cultures (#06604)

♦ European Collection of Authenticated Cell Cultures (ECACC) 06604

Main Office Culture Collections, UK Health Security Agency, Porton Down, Salisbury, SP4 0JG, UK. T. +441980612512. E-mail: culturecollections@phe.gov.uk.
URL: https://www.phe-culturecollections.org.uk/

History 1985. Established as a cell culture collection to service the research community and provide an International Depository Authority recognized patent depository for Europe. Former names and other names: *European Collection of Animal Cell Cultures* – former (1985); *European Collection of Cell Cultures* – former. **Aims** Be a centre of expertise in all aspects of authenticated cell cultures by developing and maintaining a diverse collection, and producing a high level of specialist knowledge. **Languages** English. **Activities** Certification/accreditation; research and development; training/education. **Publications** Guides. Information Services: Database. **IGO Relations** Recognized as an International Deposit Authority (IDA) by *World Intellectual Property Organization (WIPO, #21593)*, for patent deposits under the terms of *Budapest Treaty on the International Recognition of the Deposit of Microorganisms for the Purposes of Patent Procedure (Budapest Treaty of 1977, 1977).* Recognized as an IDA by *Budapest Union for the International Recognition of the Deposit of Microorganisms for the Purposes of Patent Procedure (#03345).* [2021.10.21/XF1597/**F**]

- ♦ European Collection of Cell Cultures / see European Collection of Authenticated Cell Cultures (#06604)
- ♦ European Collectors and Modellers Association (no recent information)

♦ European College of Animal Reproduction (ECAR) 06605

Sec Veterinärstrasse 13, 80539 Munich, Germany. E-mail: secretary@ecarcollege.org – info@ecarcollege.org.
Pres c/o School of Veterinary Medicine, University College Dublin, Belfield, Dublin, CO. DUBLIN, Ireland.
URL: https://www.ecarcollege.org/

History 30 Oct 1999. Constitution adopted 1999; most recently revised Sep 2020. Former names and other names: *European College of Theriogenology* – alias. Registration: Austria. **Aims** Contribute significantly to the maintenance and enhancement of the quality of European Veterinary Specialists in Animal Reproduction across all European countries at the highest possible level so as to ensure that improved veterinary medical services will be provided to the public. **Structure** General Assembly (annual); Board. Committees (2): Credentials; Examination. **Finance** Sources: members' dues. **Activities** Events/meetings; training/education.
Members Diplomates – veterinarians fulfilling membership requirements; honorary. Individuals (150) in 20 countries:
Argentina, Austria, Belgium, Czechia, Denmark, Finland, France, Germany, Greece, Hungary, Italy, Netherlands, Norway, Portugal, South Africa, Spain, Sweden, Switzerland, UK, USA.
NGO Relations Organizations involved: *European Board of Veterinary Specialisation (EBVS, #06375); European Society of Domestic Animal Reproduction (ESDAR, #08586); European Veterinary Society for Small Animal Reproduction (EVSSAR, #09059).* [2023/XE4102/v/**E**]

♦ European College of Animal Welfare and Behavioural Medicine (ECAWBM) 06606

Secretary address not obtained. E-mail: secretary@ecawbm.org.
URL: http://www.ecawbm.com/

History Set up as *European College of Veterinary Behavioural Medicine – Companion Animals (ECVBM-CA).* EU Transparency Register: 770295426144-35. **Aims** Provide animal owners and their veterinarians with veterinarians specialized in animal welfare and behavioural medicine through qualified European Specialists. **Structure** General Meeting (annual). Board, comprising President, Vice-President, Secretary, Treasurer and 1 further member. **Events** *Annual Congress* Lisbon (Portugal) 2016, *International Veterinary Behaviour Meeting* Brazil 2015, *Annual Congress* Bristol (UK) 2015, *Annual Congress* Apt (France) 2014, *International Veterinary Behaviour Meeting* Lisbon (Portugal) 2013. **NGO Relations** Member of: *European Board of Veterinary Specialisation (EBVS, #06375).* [2019/XE4709/**E**]

♦ European College of Aquatic Animal Health (ECAAH) 06607

Sec c/o Veterinary Sciences, University of Messina, Via G Palatucci, 98168 Messina ME, Italy.
URL: https://ecaah.org/

History 2014. Founded when provisionally recognized by *European Board of Veterinary Specialisation (EBVS, #06375).* **Aims** Advance *veterinary* and related biological sciences and animal health care in Europe and increase the skills of those practising in this field. **Structure** Interim Executive Committee; Committees (5). **Languages** English. **Staff** None paid. **Finance** Members' dues. Other sources: donations; meeting proceeds. **Activities** Standards/guidelines; certification/accreditation; research/documentation; knowledge management/information dissemination. Active in: Europe.
Members Full (36) in 9 countries:
Belgium, Germany, Greece, Ireland, Italy, Netherlands, Norway, Spain, UK.
NGO Relations *European Board of Veterinary Specialisation (EBVS, #06375).* [2022/XJ9830/**E**]

- ♦ European College of Avian Medicine and Surgery / see European College of Zoological Medicine (#06631)

♦ European College of Bovine Health Management (ECBHM) 06608

Sec GD Animal Health Service, PO Box 9, 7400 AA Deventer, Netherlands. T. +31570660364. Fax +31570660190.
Pres Clinic for Ruminants, Bremgartenstrasse 109a, 3012 Bern, Switzerland. T. +41316312344.
Admin Office Clinic for Ruminants, Sonnenstrasse 16, 85764 Oberschleissheim, Germany. E-mail: admin@ecbhm.org.
URL: http://www.ecbhm.org/

History Founded 6 Nov 2003, Paris (France). **Aims** Advance health oriented bovine production management in Europe; increase competency of those who practice in the field. **Structure** General Meeting (annual); Board. **Languages** English, German. **Staff** 0.50 FTE, paid. **Finance** Members' dues. **Activities** Training/education. **Events** *Congress* Maribor (Slovenia) 2015, *Congress* Oviedo (Spain) 2014, *Congress* Bern (Switzerland) 2013, *Congress* Lisbon (Portugal) 2012, *Congress* Liège (Belgium) 2011.
Members Full in 25 countries:
Australia, Austria, Belgium, Canada, Czechia, Denmark, Finland, France, Germany, Greece, Hungary, Ireland, Israel, Italy, Netherlands, Norway, Portugal, Serbia, Slovakia, Slovenia, Spain, Sweden, Switzerland, UK, USA.
NGO Relations Member of: *European Board of Veterinary Specialisation (EBVS, #06375).* [2015/XE4710/**E**]

♦ European College of Equine Internal Medicine (ECEIM) 06609

Sec address not obtained. E-mail: secretary@eceim.info.
URL: https://www.eceim.info/

History 14 Sep 2000, Birmingham (UK). **Aims** Advance equine internal medicine in Europe; increase competency of those who practice in the field. **Structure** General Assembly (annual). Board, comprising President, Vice-President, Treasurer, Secretary and 1 further member. **Languages** English. **Events** *Congress* Copenhagen (Denmark) 2024, *Congress* Lyon (France) 2023, *Congress* Rome (Italy) 2022, *Congress* 2021, *Congress* Valencia (Spain) 2019. **NGO Relations** Member of (1): *European Board of Veterinary Specialisation (EBVS, #06375).* [2023/XE4711/**E**]

♦ European College of Gerodontology (ECG) 06610

Hon Sec Natl and Kapodistrian Univ of Athens, School of Dentistry, Div of Gerodontology, Thivon 2 Goudi, 115 27 Athens, Greece. E-mail: akossion@dent.uoa.gr.
URL: http://www.gerodontology.eu/

History Founded 5 Sep 1990, Amsterdam (Netherlands). **Aims** Provide a forum for contact between all those sharing an interest in *oral* care for the elders; foster international cooperation on research in gerodontology; establish a European body to which questions concerning oral health, oral health policies and educational aspects for gerodontology can be referred. **Structure** Board. **Languages** English. **Finance** Members' dues. Sponsors. **Activities** Events/meetings. **Events** *Annual Conference* Athens (Greece) 2020, *Annual Conference* Amersfoort (Netherlands) 2019, *Annual Conference* London (UK) 2018, *Annual Conference* Valletta (Malta) 2017, *Annual Conference* Paris (France) 2016. **Publications** *Gerodontology* – journal.
Members Individuals in 27 countries:
Austria, Belgium, Brazil, Canada, Croatia, Denmark, Finland, Germany, Greece, Hong Kong, Ireland, Israel, Italy, Japan, Malta, Netherlands, Norway, Poland, Portugal, Romania, Spain, Sweden, Switzerland, UK, United Arab Emirates, Uruguay, USA.
NGO Relations Associate member of: *Platform for Better Oral Health in Europe (#18399).* [2021/XD2673/v/**F**]

♦ European College of Laboratory Animal Medicine (ECLAM) 06611

Mailing Address 266 Banbury Road, No 314, Oxford, OX2 7DL, UK. E-mail: secretariat@eclam.eu.
Registered Address 71-75 Shelton St, Covent Garden, London, WC2H 9JQ, UK.
URL: https://eclam.eu/

History Nov 2000. Previously registered under French law. Registration: Companies House, No/ID: 11407024, England and Wales. **Aims** Further scientific progress in laboratory animal medicine; establish standards of specialist *veterinary* training and qualification. **Structure** Council. **Languages** English. **Staff** 1.00 FTE, paid. **Finance** Members' dues. **Activities** Training/education; certification/accreditation; events/meetings. **Events** *Joint Scientific Meeting* Barcelona (Spain) 2018, *Joint Scientific Meeting* Lyon (France) 2016, *Joint Scientific Meeting* Hannover (Germany) 2015, *Joint Scientific Meeting* Athens (Greece) 2014, *Joint Scientific Meeting* Cambridge (UK) 2013. **Publications** Newsletter.
Members Full in 11 countries:
Germany, Ireland, Israel, Italy, Netherlands, Norway, Spain, Sweden, Switzerland, UK, USA.
Also members in West Indies. Membership countries not specified.
NGO Relations Member of: *European Animal Research Association (EARA, #05903)*; *European Board of Veterinary Specialisation (EBVS, #06375)*; *International Association of Colleges of Laboratory Animal Medicine (IACLAM, #11787)*. [2020/XD7778/**E**]

♦ European College of Naturopathic Medicine (internationally oriented national body)

♦ European College of Neuropsychopharmacology (ECNP) 06612

Exec Dir Daltonlaan 400, 3584 BK Utrecht, Netherlands. T. +31857826670. E-mail: secretariat@ecnp.eu.
Deputy Exec Dir address not obtained.
URL: http://www.ecnp.eu/

History May 1985, Copenhagen (Denmark). Constituted May 1987, Basel (Switzerland). Former names and other names: *Collège européen de neuropsycho-pharmacologie* – former. **Aims** Stimulate high-quality experimental and *clinical* research and education in applied and translational neuroscience. **Structure** General Assembly; Executive Committee. Committees; Review Board. **Languages** English. **Staff** 14.00 FTE, paid. **Finance** Sources: donations; members' dues. **Activities** Awards/prizes/competitions; events/meetings; publishing activities; training/education. **Events** *ECNP Congress* Milan (Italy) 2024, *ECNP Congress* Barcelona (Spain) 2023, *ECNP Congress* Vienna (Austria) 2022, *Annual Congress* Lisbon (Portugal) 2021, *Annual Congress* Utrecht (Netherlands) 2020. **Publications** *European Neuropsychopharmacology*; *Neuroscience Applied*. Proceedings. **Members** Clinical psychiatrists, neuroscientists, neurologists and pharmacologists. Membership countries not specified. **NGO Relations** Member of (7): *Associations and Conference Forum (AC Forum, #02909)*; *Biomedical Alliance in Europe (#03251)*; *European Brain Council (EBC, #06391)*; *Federation of European Neuroscience Societies (FENS, #09522)*; *Global Alliance of Mental Illness Advocacy Networks – Europe (GAMIAN Europe, #10211)*; *International Union of Basic and Clinical Pharmacology (IUPHAR, #15758)*; *Psychedelic Access and Research European Alliance (PAREA)* (Founding). [2023.02.24/XF0392/v/**F**]

♦ European College of Porcine Health Management (ECPHM) 06613

Sec 82-b High Street, Sawston, Cambridge, CB22 3HJ, UK.
URL: http://www.ecphm.org/

History Current constitution and bylaws adopted May 2019. Registration: Companies House, No/ID: 06952287, England and Wales. **Aims** Advance health oriented porcine production management in Europe; increase the competency of those who practice in the field. **Structure** Board; Committees (3). **Events** *European Symposium on Porcine Health Management (ESPHM)* Thessaloniki (Greece) 2023, *European Symposium on Porcine Health Management (ESPHM)* Budapest (Hungary) 2022, *European Symposium on Porcine Health Management* Utrecht (Netherlands) 2019, *European Symposium on Porcine Health Management* Barcelona (Spain) 2018, *European Symposium on Porcine Health Management* Prague (Czechia) 2017. **Publications** *Porcine Health Management (PHM)* – journal. **NGO Relations** Member of: *European Board of Veterinary Specialisation (EBVS, #06375)*. [2023/XJ3526/**E**]

♦ European College of Poultry Veterinary Science (ECPVS) 06614

Sec address not obtained.
Registered Office Union Suite, The Union Building, 51-59 Rose Lane, Norwich, NR1 1BY, UK.
URL: http://www.ecpvs.com/

History Founded Feb 2008, when *European Board of Veterinary Specialisation (EBVS, #06375)* granted provisional recognition. Constitutional officially registered Dec 2008. Registration: Companies House, No/ID: 10991623, England and Wales. **Aims** Advance poultry veterinary science in Europe; increase the competency of those who practise in this field. **Structure** General Meeting (annual); Board; committees. **Languages** English. **Staff** Voluntary. **Finance** Fees of diplomats; donations. **Activities** Events/meetings. **Events** *Annual General Meeting* Utrecht (Netherlands) 2019, *Annual General Meeting* Valencia (Spain) 2018, *Annual General Meeting* Edinburgh (UK) 2017, *Annual General Meeting* Deventer (Netherlands) 2015. **Members** in Europe (membership countries not specified). **NGO Relations** Member of: *European Board of Veterinary Specialisation (EBVS, #06375)*. [2019/XM2903/**E**]

♦ European College of Small Ruminant Health Management (ECSRHM) 06615

Pres Victoria Cottage, Reeth, Richmond, DL11 6SZ, UK.
URL: http://www.ecsrhm.eu/

History 2008. **Aims** Advance veterinary knowledge in the field of small ruminant health management. **Structure** Officers: President; Past-President; Vice-President; Secretary; Treasurer. **Languages** English. **Activities** Acts as an institution to qualify members of the veterinary profession as specialists in small ruminant health management by establishing and defining the standard of qualification based on evidence-based medicine (EBM); develops graduate teaching programmes in small ruminant health management; develops and supervises EBM continuing education programmes for veterinarians interested in small ruminant health management; encourages members to pursue original scientific investigations and to contribute to relevant literature; works to define and describe the veterinary speciality of small ruminant health management; supervises the professional activities of members and ensures that such professional activities are guided by EBM; promotes collaboration with national veterinary associations, farmers' associations, government institutions and international agencies. **Events** *Annual General Meeting* Shrewsbury (UK) 2012, *Annual General Meeting* Athens (Greece) 2011, *Annual General Meeting* Lancaster (UK) 2010, *Annual General Meeting* Stavanger (Norway) 2009, *Annual General Meeting* Lancaster (UK) 2008. **NGO Relations** Member of: *European Board of Veterinary Specialisation (EBVS, #06375)*. [2012.06.01/XM2902/**E**]

♦ European College of Sport Science (ECSS) 06616

Ecole européenne de sciences du sport

Exec Dir Aachener Str 1053-1055, 50858 Cologne, Germany. T. +4922196262771. E-mail: office@sport-science.org.
Communications Assistant address not obtained.
URL: http://www.sport-science.org/

History 1995, Nice (France). **Aims** Promote science and research in the interdisciplinary fields of sport science and sports medicine. **Structure** Executive Board; Scientific Board; Scientific Committee; Advisory Board; Reviewing Panel. **Languages** English. **Staff** 5.00 FTE, paid. **Finance** Sources: fees for services; members' dues; sale of publications; sponsorship. **Activities** Awards/prizes/competitions; events/meetings; guidance/assistance/consulting; research/documentation. **Events** *Annual Congress* Paris (France) 2023, *Annual Congress* Seville (Spain) 2022, *Annual Congress* Cologne (Germany) 2021, *Annual Congress* Cologne (Germany) 2020, *Annual Congress* Prague (Czechia) 2019. **Publications** *European Journal of Sport Science* (10 a year). Conference abstracts. **Members** Student; Regular; Fellow. Membership countries not specified. **NGO Relations** Member of (2): *International Council of Sport Science and Physical Education (ICSSPE, #13077)*; *International Olympic Committee (IOC, #14408)*. [2022/XE4223/**E**]

♦ European College of Sports Medicine and Exercise Physicians (ECOSEP) 06617

Chair 34 G Seferi Str, 542 50 Thessaloniki, Greece. E-mail: contact@sportsmed.gr.
URL: http://www.ecosep.eu/

Aims Advance competency of sports physicians and the best possible care for their athletes and the citizens of Europe; collaborate with other sports medicine organizations; serve as source of information to the public. **Structure** Officers, including President; Committees (8). **Languages** English. **Staff** 10.00 FTE, paid. **Finance** Members' dues. **Events** *Biennial Congress* Athens (Greece) 2021, *Biennial Congress* Paris (France) 2019, *Biennial Congress* Dubai (United Arab Emirates) 2017, *Biennial Congress* Barcelona (Spain) 2015, *Biennial Congress* Frankfurt-Main (Germany) 2013. **Members** Full Sports and Exercise Physicians; Associate medical doctors and physios working or teaching in the sport medical field, and trainees in Sports and Exercise Medicine; Student. Membership countries not specified. [2020/XJ8279/v/**D**]

♦ European College for the Study and Evaluation of Bodily Damage (inactive)

♦ European College for the Study of Vulval Diseases (ECSVD) 06618

Address not obtained.
URL: http://www.ecsvd.eu/

History 1997, Paris (France). **Aims** Promote communication among medical doctors managing patients with vulval disease; increase research in the field of vulval disease. **Structure** Executive Council. Officers: President; Treasurer; Secretary. **Languages** English. **Events** *Congress* Vienna (Austria) 2020, *Congress* Copenhagen (Denmark) 2018, *Congress* Turin (Italy) 2016, *Congress* Birmingham (UK) 2014, *Congress* Amsterdam (Netherlands) 2012. **Members** Ordinary; Corresponding; Sponsor. Membership countries not specified. **NGO Relations** *International Society for the Study of Vulvovaginal Disease (ISSVD, #15491)*. [2020/XD8406/**D**]

♦ European College of Surgeons (inactive)
♦ European College of Theriogenology / see European College of Animal Reproduction (#06605)
♦ European College of Veterinary Anaesthesia / see European College of Veterinary Anaesthesia and Analgesia (#06619)

♦ European College of Veterinary Anaesthesia and Analgesia (ECVAA) 06619

Sec address not obtained.
URL: http://www.ecvaa.org/

History 26 Apr 1993. Founded as *European College of Veterinary Anaesthesia (ECVA)*, by *Association of Veterinary Anaesthetists (AVA, #02976)*. Inaugurated 1 Jan 1995. Registration: Start date: 22 May 1997, Netherlands. **Aims** Advance study, research into and practice of veterinary anaesthesia, analgesia and intensive care in Europe; increase the competence of veterinary anaesthesiologists. **Structure** General Assembly (annual); Board; Executive Committee. Credentials and Education Committee; Examination Committee. **Languages** English. **Staff** Voluntary. **Activities** Certification/accreditation; standards/guidelines; events/meetings; research/documentation. **Events** *World Congress* Venice (Italy) 2018, *Spring Meeting* Caceres (Spain) 2015, *World Congress* Kyoto (Japan) 2015, *Autumn Meeting* Vienna (Austria) 2014, *World Congress* Cape Town (South Africa) 2012. **Publications** *Veterinary Anaesthesia and Analgesia* (6 a year) – journal.
Members Diplomates (159), including 8 Honorary members. Members in 18 countries:
Argentina, Australia, Belgium, Brazil, Canada, France, Germany, Greece, Ireland, Italy, Netherlands, South Africa, Spain, Sweden, Switzerland, Tanzania UR, UK, USA.
NGO Relations Member of: *European Board of Veterinary Specialisation (EBVS, #06375)*. [2021/XD6038/v/**D**]

♦ European College of Veterinary Behavioural Medicine – Companion Animals / see European College of Animal Welfare and Behavioural Medicine (#06606)

♦ European College of Veterinary Clinical Pathology (ECVCP) 06620

Sec Laburnum Close, Congleton, CW12 4TX, UK. E-mail: secretariat@ecvcp.org.
Pres address not obtained.
URL: http://www.esvcp.org/

History by *European Society of Veterinary Clinical Pathology (ESVCP, #08775)*. **Aims** Certify veterinarians as specialists in veterinary clinical pathology. **Structure** Board, comprising President, Vice-President, Past-President, Secretary, Treasurer and 2 Councillors. Subcommittees (5): Examinations; Education; Credentials; Science; Laboratory Accreditation. **Languages** English. **Staff** Voluntary. **Finance** Members' dues. Donations. **Activities** Annual examination; annual continuing education; annual general meeting and congress. **Events** *Joint Congress* Vienna (Austria) 2020, *Joint Congress* Arnhem (Netherlands) 2019, *Annual Scientific Meeting* Athens (Greece) 2018, *Annual Scientific Meeting* Milan (Italy) 2014, *Annual Scientific Meeting* Berlin (Germany) 2013. **Publications** *ECVCP Newsletter* (2 a year).
Members Full in 16 countries:
Australia, Canada, Denmark, France, Germany, Greece, Hungary, Ireland, Israel, Italy, Norway, Spain, Sweden, Switzerland, UK, USA.
NGO Relations Member of: *European Board of Veterinary Specialisation (EBVS, #06375)*. [2021/XJ0388/**E**]

♦ European College of Veterinary and Comparative Nutrition (ECVCN) 06621

Sec address not obtained. E-mail: ecvcn@moesseler.de.
Pres address not obtained.
URL: http://www.esvcn.eu/

History 1998, by *European Society of Veterinary and Comparative Nutrition (ESVCN, #08776)*. **Aims** Advance veterinary and comparative nutrition; increase competence of those who practice in the field. **Structure** Officers: President; Vice-President; Past President; Treasurer; Secretary. **Languages** English. **Events** *Congress* Turin (Italy) 2019, *Congress* Munich (Germany) 2018, *Congress* Cirencester (UK) 2017, *Congress* Berlin (Germany) 2016, *Congress* Toulouse (France) 2015. **Members** Individuals (36) in 12 countries. Membership countries not specified. **NGO Relations** Member of: *European Board of Veterinary Specialisation (EBVS, #06375)*. [2019.12.12/XD8403/**D**]

♦ European College of Veterinary Dermatology (ECVD) 06622

Treas c/o Centre Hospitalier Vétérinaire Frégis, 43 Av Aristide Briand, 94110 Arcueil, France.
Sec Tierärztliche Spezialisten, Rodigallee 85, 22043 Hamburg, Germany.
URL: http://www.ecvd.org/

History 1992, London (UK). **Aims** Advance veterinary dermatology in Europe; increase the competence of those who practice in the field. **Structure** Annual General Meeting; Board; Committees (4). **Languages** English. **Staff** Voluntary. **Finance** Members' dues. Congress proceeds. Annual budget: about euro 20,000. **Activities** Training/education; certification/accreditation; research/documentation; knowledge management/information dissemination. **Events** *World Congress of Veterinary Dermatology* Boston, MA (USA) 2024, *European Veterinary Dermatology Congress* Gothenburg (Sweden) 2023, *Annual Congress* Porto (Portugal) 2022, *Annual Congress* 2021, *World Congress of Veterinary Dermatology* Sydney, NSW (Australia) 2020. **Publications** *Veterinary Dermatology* (6 a year) – journal.
Members Full: diplomats (110) in 23 countries:
Australia, Austria, Belgium, Croatia, Czechia, Denmark, Estonia, France, Germany, Greece, Ireland, Israel, Italy, Netherlands, Portugal, Russia, Slovakia, Slovenia, Spain, Sweden, Switzerland, UK, USA.
NGO Relations Member of: *European Board of Veterinary Specialisation (EBVS, #06375)*; *World Association for Veterinary Dermatology (WAVD, #21203)*. [2017.09.27/XE2706/v/**E**]

♦ European College of Veterinary Diagnostic Imaging (ECVDI) 06623

Sec Pixelvet, 51 Shoesmith Lane, Kings Hill, ME19 4FF, UK.
URL: http://www.ecvdi.org/

History 1993, on the initiative of *European Association of Veterinary Diagnostic Imaging (EAVDI, #06269)*, in response to recommendations of the Advisory Committee for Veterinary Training (ACVT) to *European Commission (EC, #06633)*. Registered in accordance with German law. **Aims** Stimulate further development in the field; improve the quality of: *animal health* care, through specialised knowledge and skills in veterinary diagnostic imaging; *general practice*, through contact between general practitioners and registered specialists; service to the public, including protection of general public, staff members and animals from unqualified "specialists". **Structure** General Meeting (annual). Board, consisting of President, Vice-President, Secretary, Treasurer and 6 members. Committees (5): Examination; Credential; Education; Nomination; Constitution. EBVS Representatives (2). **Languages** English. **Staff** Voluntary. **Finance** Members' dues: pounds200. **Activities** Provides training programmes to provide in-depth training in veterinary diagnostic imaging, related and applied sciences and areas of medical diagnostic imaging; offers Formal Programmes

European College Veterinary
06623

alphabetic sequence excludes
For the complete listing, see Yearbook Online at

(Residency) and Individual (Alternative) Programmes; establishes guidelines for post-graduate education and experience, prerequisite to becoming a European Specialist in Veterinary Diagnostic Imaging; examines and qualifies veterinary surgeons as specialists in veterinary diagnostic imaging; encourages research and other contributions to knowledge relating to the pathogenesis, diagnosis, therapy, prevention and control of animal diseases and promotes the communication and dissemination of this knowledge. Organizes: annual scientific conference; Annual General Meeting; annual candidate examinations to evaluate new graduates for becoming members. **Events** *EVDI : Annual European Veterinary Diagnostic Imaging Meeting* Wroclaw (Poland) 2016, *EVDI : Annual European Veterinary Diagnostic Imaging Meeting* Utrecht (Netherlands) 2014, *EVDI : Annual European Veterinary Diagnostic Imaging Meeting* Cascais (Portugal) 2013, *Meeting* Turkey 2013, *EVDI : Annual European Veterinary Diagnostic Imaging Meeting* Bursa (Turkey) 2012.
Members Individuals in 22 countries:
Australia, Austria, Belgium, Canada, Denmark, Finland, France, Germany, Greece, Ireland, Israel, Italy, Luxembourg, Netherlands, New Zealand, Norway, South Africa, Spain, Sweden, Switzerland, UK, USA.
Also members in West Indies. Membership countries not specified.
NGO Relations Member of: *European Board of Veterinary Specialisation (EBVS, #06375).* Affiliated to: *International Veterinary Radiology Association (IVRA, #15850).* [2012.06.01/XD5565/v/**E**]

♦ European College of Veterinary Emergency and Critical Care (unconfirmed)

♦ European College of Veterinary Internal Medicine – Companion Animals (ECVIM – CA) 06624

Exec Sec Postfach 60 05 05, 81205 Munich, Germany. T. +498921752448. Fax +498924401538. E-mail: secretariat@ecvim-ca.org.
URL: http://www.ecvim-ca.org/
History 28 Jun 1994, Utrecht (Netherlands), as an independent organization of *European Society of Veterinary Internal Medicine (ESVIM, #08779).* **Aims** Advance companion animal internal medicine in Europe; increase competency of those who practice in this field. **Structure** General Assembly (annual); Board; Executive Committee; Specialty Groups; Committees. **Languages** English. **Staff** 0.50 FTE, paid; 0.50 FTE, voluntary. **Finance** Members' dues. Other sources: job ads; congress fees. **Events** *Congress* Lyon (France) 2024, *Congress* Barcelona (Spain) 2023, *Congress* Gothenburg (Sweden) 2022, *Congress* Munich (Germany) 2021, *Congress* Munich (Germany) 2020.
Members Diplomats (476) in 22 countries and territories:
Australia, Austria, Belgium, Canada, Czechia, Denmark, Finland, France, Germany, Hong Kong, Ireland, Israel, Italy, Netherlands, New Zealand, Norway, South Africa, Spain, Sweden, Switzerland, UK, USA.
NGO Relations Member of: *European Board of Veterinary Specialisation (EBVS, #06375); Federation of European Companion Animal Veterinary Associations (FECAVA, #09497).* Affiliated with: *European Society of Veterinary Endocrinology (ESVE, #08778).* [2020/XE2705/v/**E**]

♦ European College of Veterinary Microbiology (ECVM) 06625

Sec Lab Services Ltd, Unit8, Mowat Industrial Estate, Sandown Rd, Watford, WD24 7UY, UK. E-mail: secretary@ecvmicro.org.
URL: http://ecvmicro.org/
Aims Contribute to the maintenance and enhancement of the quality of European veterinary specialists in veterinary microbiology across all European countries at the highest possible level so as to ensure that improved veterinary medical services will be provided to the public. **Structure** Annual General Meeting; Executive Committee. **Languages** English. **Finance** Members' dues. Other sources: Donations; income from educational meetings; investment income. **Activities** Training/education; events/meetings. **Members** Founding Diplomates; Practising Diplomates; Non-practising Diplomates; Retired Diplomates; Honorary Members; Associate Members. Membership countries not specified. **NGO Relations** Member of: *European Board of Veterinary Specialisation (EBVS, #06375).* [2019/XM5601/**E**]

♦ European College of Veterinary Neurology (ECVN) 06626

Pres Dept Small Animal Medicine, Univ of Leipzig, An den Tierkliniken 23, 04107 Leipzig, Germany. E-mail: president@ecvn.org – admin@ecvn.org.
Sec Aúna Especialidades Veterinarias, Algepser 22-1, Parque Empresarial Tàctica, Paterna, 46980 Valencia, Spain. E-mail: secretary@ecvn.org.
URL: http://www.ecvn.org/
History as academic college of *European Society of Veterinary Neurology (ESVN, #08781).* **Aims** Advance veterinary neurology in Europe and increase the competence of those who practice in this field by: establishing guidelines for post-graduate education; examining and authenticating veterinarians as specialists in veterinary neurology; encouraging research about the nervous system of animals, and promoting communication and dissemination of this knowledge. **Structure** Executive Committee; Credentials Committee; Examinations Committee. Officers: President; Vice-President; Secretary; Treasurer; Past-President; Member at Large. **Languages** English. **Finance** Annual fee of graduates; credentials submission; examination fees from candidates; sponsorship. **Activities** Supervises training, sets examinations for veterinary neurologists and awards diplomas to those successful. **Events** *Annual Symposium* Venice (Italy) 2021, *Annual Symposium* Venice (Italy) 2020, *Annual Symposium* Wroclaw (Poland) 2019, *Annual Symposium* Copenhagen (Denmark) 2018, *Annual Symposium* Helsinki (Finland) 2017. **Publications** *ESVN/ECVN Annual Newsletter.*
Members Graduates (diplomates – 97) of advanced course of study in 16 countries and territories:
Belgium, China, Czechia, Finland, France, Germany, Israel, Italy, Netherlands, New Zealand, Spain, Sweden, Switzerland, Taiwan, UK, USA.
NGO Relations Member of: *European Board of Veterinary Specialisation (EBVS, #06375).* [2019/XE2685/v/**E**]

♦ European College of Veterinary Ophthalmologists (see: #08783)
♦ European College of Veterinary Parasitology / see European Veterinary Parasitology College (#09058)

♦ European College of Veterinary Pathologists (ECVP) 06627

Admin Dir address not obtained.
URL: http://www.ecvpath.org/
History 28 Sep 1995, Edinburgh (UK). Founded following a proposal by *European Society of Veterinary Pathology (ESVP, #08785).* **Aims** Further scientific progress in veterinary pathology; establish standards of training, experience and examination for qualification as a specialist in veterinary pathology; further recognition of such qualified specialists by suitable certification and other means. **Structure** Council; Committees. **Languages** English. **Staff** Voluntary. **Finance** Sources: members' dues. **Activities** Certification/accreditation; research/documentation; training/education. **Events** *Annual Meeting* 2021, *Annual Meeting* Turin (Italy) 2020, *Annual Meeting* Cluj-Napoca (Romania) 2018, *Annual Meeting* Lyon (France) 2017, *Annual Meeting* Bologna (Italy) 2016. **Publications** *ECVP Newsletter* (annual); *Veterinary Pathology* – official journal.
Members Individuals (260) in 17 countries:
Austria, Belgium, Canada, Czechia, Denmark, Finland, France, Germany, Ireland, Italy, Netherlands, Norway, Portugal, Spain, Sweden, Switzerland, UK.
NGO Relations Member of (1): *European Board of Veterinary Specialisation (EBVS, #06375).* Cooperates with (2): *European Society of Toxicologic Pathology (ESTP, #08762); European Society of Veterinary Pathology (ESVP, #08785).* [2020/XD6078/v/**D**]

♦ European College of Veterinary Pharmacology and Toxicology (ECVPT) 06628

Sec 82b High Street, Sawston, Cambridge, CB22 3HJ, UK.
Pres address not obtained.
URL: http://www.ecvpt.org/
History Founded 1997. Registration: Companies House, No/ID: 07311080, England and Wales. **Aims** Provide a framework for specialization in veterinary pharmacology and toxicology. **Structure** Executive Board. Committees (4): Credentials; Nominations; Fiscal; Residency and Education. **Languages** English. **Staff** Voluntary. **Activities** Provides facilities for professional post-academic training and professional specialization (residency programme). Organizes seminars and workshops. **Events** *International Congress* Bruges (Belgium) 2023, *International Congress* Lviv (Ukraine) 2021, *Meeting* 2002. **Publications** *ECVPT Info* – website.
Members Residency Programme Directors; Resident Supervisors; Residents; Diplomates; Retired Diplomates; Non-practising Diplomates; Honorary; Associate. Individuals in 18 countries:
Argentina, Australia, Austria, Belgium, Canada, Finland, France, Germany, Greece, Ireland, Israel, Italy, Netherlands, Spain, Sweden, Switzerland, UK, USA.
Also members in the West Indies. Membership countries not specified.
NGO Relations *European Association for Veterinary Pharmacology and Toxicology (EAVPT, #06271); European Board of Veterinary Specialisation (EBVS, #06375).* [2022/XD6074/v/**D**]

♦ European College for Veterinary Public Health (ECVPH) 06629

Pres Salisburylaan 133, 9820 Merelbeke, Belgium.
URL: http://www.ecvph.org/
History 27 Feb 1999, Vienna (Austria), under the aegis of *Union européenne des vétérinaires hygiénistes (UEVH, #20404).* **Aims** Further scientific progress in veterinary public health and the subspecialities population medicine and *food science*; establish standards of training, experience and examination for qualification as specialist in veterinary public health; further recognition of qualified specialists. **Structure** Council, comprising President, 2 Vice-Presidents, Treasurer, Secretary and 3 further members. **Finance** Members' dues. **Activities** Organizes training programmes. **Events** *Annual General Meeting* Edinburgh (UK) 2019, *Annual General Meeting* Perugia (Italy) 2018, *Annual General Meeting* Liège (Belgium) 2017, *Annual General Meeting* Uppsala (Sweden) 2016, *Annual General Meeting* Belgrade (Serbia) 2015. **NGO Relations** Member of: *European Board of Veterinary Specialisation (EBVS, #06375).* [2016/XD7779/**E**]

♦ European College of Veterinary Surgeons (ECVS) 06630

Operations Manager c/o Vetsuisse Fac, Univ Zurich, Winterthurerstrasse 260, 8057 Zurich ZH, Switzerland. T. +41446358492. Fax +41446358991. E-mail: info@ecvs.org.
URL: http://www.ecvs.org/
History 11 Apr 1991, France. Received Permanent Recognition by *European Board of Veterinary Specialisation (EBVS, #06375)*, 2000. Former names and other names: *European College of Veterinary Surgery* – alias. Registration: Handelsregisteramt des Kantons Zürich, No/ID: CHE-107.612.251, Start date: 2 Jun 1994, Switzerland. **Aims** Advance veterinary surgery through the training of specialists to improve the health and welfare of animals committed to our care. **Structure** General Assembly; Board of Regents; Committees (6). **Languages** English. **Staff** 3.00 FTE, paid. **Finance** Sources: meeting proceeds; members' dues; sponsorship. **Activities** Events/meetings; training/education. Active in all member countries. **Events** *Annual Scientific Meeting* Valencia (Spain) 2024, *Annual Scientific Meeting* Krakow (Poland) 2023, *Annual Scientific Meeting* Porto (Portugal) 2022, *Annual Scientific Meeting* 2021, *Annual Scientific Meeting* Valencia (Spain) 2020. **Publications** *Veterinary Surgery.*
Members Individuals in 35 countries and territories:
Australia, Austria, Belgium, Canada, Costa Rica, Czechia, Denmark, Finland, France, Germany, Grenada, Hong Kong, Hungary, Ireland, Israel, Italy, Netherlands, New Zealand, Northern Ireland, Norway, Poland, Portugal, Qatar, Saudi Arabia, Scotland, Singapore, Slovakia, South Africa, Spain, St Kitts-Nevis, Sweden, Switzerland, UK, United Arab Emirates, USA.
NGO Relations Member of (1): *European Board of Veterinary Specialisation (EBVS, #06375).* [2021.09.07/XE2704/v/**E**]

♦ European College of Veterinary Surgery / see European College of Veterinary Surgeons (#06630)

♦ European College of Zoological Medicine (ECZM) 06631

Treas Klinik für Vogel und Reptilien, Univ Leipzig, Augustusplatz 10, 04109 Leipzig, Germany. E-mail: secretary@eczm.eu – admin@eczm.eu.
Pres address not obtained.
URL: http://www.eczm.eu/
History Aug 1993, on the initiative of *Association of Avian Veterinarians (AAV, #02389)*, as *European College of Avian Medicine and Surgery (ECAMS) – Europese Vereniging voor Inwendige Ziekten en Chirurgie bij Vogels.* Current title adopted on the initiative of *European Board of Veterinary Specialisation (EBVS, #06375)*, Apr 2009. New constitution adopted Mar 2009. Registered in accordance with Dutch law. **Aims** Advance avian medicine in Europe and increase the competency of those who practice in this field. **Structure** General Meeting (annual); Board; Executive Committee; Specialty Groups; Committees (5). **Languages** English. **Staff** 0.50 FTE, paid. **Finance** Members' dues: euro 150. **Activities** Knowledge management/information dissemination; certification/accreditation; training/education. **Events** *International Conference on Avian Herpetological and Exotic Mammal Medicine* Budapest (Hungary) 2022, *International Conference on Avian Herpetological and Exotic Mammal Medicine* Budapest (Hungary) 2021, *Joint Conference on Zoo and Wildlife Health* Kolmården (Sweden) 2019, *International Conference on Avian Herpetological and Exotic Mammal Medicine* London (UK) 2019, *Joint Conference on Zoo and Wildlife Health* Prague (Czechia) 2018.
Members 'Diplomates' Founding ECAMS; Founding ECZM; Full; Non-Practising; Retired; Honorary. Individuals in 18 countries:
Australia, Austria, Belgium, Croatia, Czechia, Denmark, France, Germany, Hungary, Italy, Netherlands, Norway, Spain, Sweden, Switzerland, UK, United Arab Emirates, USA.
NGO Relations Member of: *European Board of Veterinary Specialisation (EBVS, #06375).* [2014.06.25/XD6036/v/**D**]

♦ European Colloid and Interface Society (ECIS) 06632

Contact Dep Chemistry and CSGI, Univ Florence, via della Lastruccia 3, 50019 Florence FI, Italy. E-mail: pln@csgi.unifi.it.
Contact Dep Chemistry, Univ Porto, Rua do Campo Alegre 687, 4169-007 Porto, Portugal. E-mail: efm-arque@fc.up.pt.
URL: http://www.ecis-web.eu/
History 3 Oct 1986, Como (Italy), when statutes were adopted. **Aims** Advance colloid and interface science and promote cooperation between European scientists; cooperate with existing national societies in European countries and with other international organizations. **Structure** General Assembly (annual, at conference). Council, comprising Chairman, Vice-Chairman (Chairman-elect) and immediate Past-Chairman. General Secretariat. **Languages** English. **Staff** 0.50 FTE, voluntary. **Finance** Members' dues. **Activities** Collects and disseminates information on activities of national and international societies; organizes an annual conference in the field of colloid science; working parties survey and report on specific aspects or areas of colloid and interface science in a European context. **Events** *European Student Colloid Conference* Budapest (Hungary) 2022, *Annual Conference* Leuven (Belgium) 2019, *Annual Conference* Ljubljana (Slovenia) 2018, *Annual Conference* Madrid (Spain) 2017, *Annual Conference* Rome (Italy) 2016. **Publications** Conference proceedings.
Members Personal individual scientists in universities, research institutions or industries interested in colloid chemistry; Corporate companies interested in the advancement of colloid and interface science. Members in 35 countries and territories:
Australia, Austria, Belgium, Bulgaria, Canada, Croatia, Czechia, Denmark, Finland, France, Germany, Greece, Hungary, India, Ireland, Israel, Italy, Japan, Kazakhstan, Malta, Netherlands, Norway, Poland, Portugal, Romania, Russia, Serbia, Slovakia, Slovenia, Spain, Sweden, Switzerland, UK, Ukraine, USA. [2014/XD2306/**D**]

♦ European Colloquium on Geo-Chronology, Cosmo-Chronology and Isotope Geology (meeting series)
♦ European Colloquium of Indonesian and Malay Studies (meeting series)
♦ European Commercial Managers Federation (internationally oriented national body)

♦ European Commission (EC) 06633

Commission européenne – Comisión Europea – Europäische Kommission – Comissão Européia – Commissione Europea – Europese Commissie – Europeiska Kommissionen – Europa-Kommissionen – Euroopan Komissio – Evropaiki Epitropi – An Coimisiún Eorpach – Evropska Komise – Európska Komisia – Európai Bizottsag – Komisja Europejska – Evropska Komisija – Euroopa Komisjon – Eiropas Komisija – Europos Komisija – Il-Kummissjoni Ewropea – Europska Komisija – Comisia Europeana
Deputy SG c/o Secretariat General – EC, Rue de la Loi 200, 1049 Brussels, Belgium. T. +3222991111 – +3222994393. Fax +3222950138 – +322295013840.
Pres address not obtained.
URL: http://ec.europa.eu/

History 25 Aug 1952, with the name 'High Authority', as an executive body of *European Coal and Steel Community (ECSC, inactive)* created under the *Treaty Establishing the European Coal and Steel Community (Treaty of Paris, 1951)*. The twin treaties – *Treaty Establishing the European Economic Community (Treaty of Rome)* and *Treaty Establishing the European Atomic Energy Community (Treaty of Rome, 1957)* or 'Rome Treaties', in force from 1 Jan 1958 establishing the European Economic Community (EEC), subsequently becoming *European Community (inactive)*, and the *European Atomic Energy Community (Euratom, inactive)* – also set up Commissions for each of the new Communities. The present Commission came into existence as a single entity, with full legal title *Commission of the European Communities (CEC) – Commission des Communautés européennes (CCE) – Comisión de las Comunidades Europeas – Kommission der Europäischen Gemeinschaften – Comissão das Comunidades Européias – Commissione delle Comunità Europee – Commissie van de Europese Gemeenschappen – Kommissionen for de Europaeiske Faellesskaber – Epitropi ton Evropaikon Kinotiton*, Jul 1967, when the 'Merger' Treaty of 8 Apr 1965 came into force, since when it functioned a single organ common to the three, and then two, European Communities. The ECSC ceased to exist in Jul 2002, following expiration of the Paris Treaty when European Community became responsible for the steel sector.

The *Single European Act (SEA, 1986)* was signed Feb 1986, and ratified by member parliaments by 31 Mar 1987. It came into force 1 Jul 1987, amending and complementing the Paris and Rome Treaties. As well as covering social, economic and monetary cooperation and measures to make the Community more effective and democratic, it treated the institutionalization of foreign policy cooperation within *European Political Cooperation (EPC, inactive)*.

The *Treaty on European Union (Maastricht Treaty, 1992)* was signed on 7 Feb 1992; the Commission's current title was formally adopted by the Council of Ministers on 9 Nov 1993. The Maastricht Treaty expanded the former concept of the *European Communities (EC, inactive)* by making it the first "pillar" of the *European Union (EU, #08967)* and also replaced the title of the *'Council of the European Communities'* by *'Council of the European Union'* and of the *'European Economic Community (EEC)'* of the Treaty of Rome by the *'European Community'*, which title may be seen as officially referring to the old EEC only. Under the Treaty, *Common Foreign and Security Policy (CFSP / PESC)*, deriving from EPC, became the second "pillar" of the Union; while *Cooperation in the Field of Justice and Home Affairs (CJHA)* (interior policy) is the third "pillar".

The Maastricht Treaty confirmed the powers of the Commission conferred upon it by previous treaties and acts. It is to be called upon for advice by the Council when considering the request on any country for membership of the European Union.

The European Union was recognized as a legal entity by *Treaty of Amsterdam (1997)*, the successor to the Maastricht treaty, signed 2 Oct 1997. Within the single institutional framework of the Union, the Commission is responsible, with the Council, for ensuring consistency. Its composition and mode of operation were revised by the *Nice Treaty (2001)*, signed 26 Feb 2001, Nice, which came into effect 1 Feb 2003. Further revisions, especially regarding enlargement, were formalized in the *Treaty of Accession*, also known as *Treaty of Athens*, signed 16 Apr 2003, Athens, which entered into force with the accession of 10 new member states on 1 May 2004.

The *Treaty of Lisbon (2007)*, which came into force 1 Dec 2009, gave further power to the European Union and officially succeeded the European Community, changing the title of the Treaty of Rome to *Treaty on the Functioning of the European Union (TFEU, 1957)*.

Aims As the European Union's executive body: propose *legislation* which is then adopted by co-legislators, the European Parliament and the Council of Ministers; enforce European *law* – where necessary with the help of the Court of Justice of the EU; set objectives and priorities for action, outlined yearly in the Commission Work Programme and work towards delivering them; manage and implement EU *policies* and the *budget*; represent the Union outside Europe.

Structure The term 'Commission' refers to both the College of Commissioners as well as the institution itself. College of Commissioners includes one member of each Member State, and including President, First Vice-President, High Representative of the Union for Foreign Policy and Security Policy, and 5 Vice-Presidents. The Commission works according to the principle of collective responsibility with Commissioners – serving 5-year terms – having no individual decision-making powers. President is elected by *European Parliament (EP, #08146)* with Commission as a whole needing the Parliament's consent.

Departments/Directorates-General (DGs), each headed by a Director-General:
- Agriculture and Rural Development (AGRI);
- Budget (BUDG);
- Climate Action (CLIMA);
- Communication (COMM);
- Communications Networks, Content and Technology (CONNECT);
- Competition (COMP);
- Economic and Financial Affairs (ECFIN);
- Education and Culture (EAC);
- Employment, Social Affairs and Inclusion (EMPL);
- Energy (ENER);
- Environment (ENV);
- *Statistical Office of the European Union (Eurostat, #19974)*;
- Financial Stability, Financial Services and Capital Markets Union (FISMA);
- Health and Food Safety (SANTE);
- Humanitarian Aid and Civil Protection;
- Human Resources and Security (HR);
- Informatics (DIGIT);
- Internal Market, Industry, Entrepreneurship and SMEs (GROW);
- International Cooperation and Development (DEVCO);
- Interpretation (SCIC);
- *Joint Research Centre (JRC, #16147)*;
- Justice and Consumers (JUST);
- Maritime Affairs and Fisheries (MARE);
- Migration and Home Affairs (HOME);
- Mobility and Transport (MOVE);
- Neighbourhood and Enlargement Negotiations (NEAR);
- Regional and Urban Policy (REGIO);
- Research and Innovation (RTD);
- Secretariat-General (SG);
- Service for Foreign Policy Instruments (FPI);
- Taxation and Customs Union (TAXUD);
- Trade (TRADE);
- Translation (DGT).

'Services':
- Central Library;
- *European Anti-Fraud Office (#05906)*;
- European Commission Data Protection Officer;
- European Political Strategy Centre (EPSC);
- Historical Archives;
- Infrastructure and Logistics – Brussels (OIB);
- Infrastructure and Logistics – Luxembourg (OIL);
- Internal Audit Service (IAS);
- Legal Service (SJ);
- Office for Administration and Payment of Individual Entitlements (PMO);
- Publications Office (OP).

Languages Bulgarian, Croatian, Czech, Danish, Dutch, English, Estonian, Finnish, French, German, Hungarian, Irish Gaelic, Italian, Latvian, Lithuanian, Maltese, Polish, Portuguese, Romanian, Slovakian, Slovene, Spanish, Swedish. **Staff** 23000.00 FTE, paid. **Finance** EU Budget is proposed by European Commission and approved by national governments and European Parliament.

Activities Directorates-General: draft laws, but proposals become official only once the College of Commissioners adopts them; manage funding initiatives at EU level, and carry out public consultations and communication activities. The Commission also administers several executive agencies to help manage EU programmes. Overview of EU activities in all areas through which the Commission administers programmes and projects:
- Agriculture, fisheries and foods;
- Business;
- Climate action;
- Cross-cutting policies;
- Culture, education and youth;
- Economy, finance and tax;
- Employment and social rights;
- Energy and natural resources;
- Environment, consumers and health;
- External relations and foreign affairs;
- Justice, home affairs and citizens' rights;
- Regions and local development;
- Science and technology;
- EU explained;
- Transport and travel.

Through the above, cooperates with and on:
- *Euratom Supply Agency (ESA, #05617)*;
- *Natura 2000 Network (see: #06633)*;
- *European Economic Interest Grouping (EEIG, #06960)*;
- *European Crime Prevention Network (EUCPN, #06858)*;
- *Eureka Association (Eureka, #05621)*;
- *European Instrument for Democracy and for Human Rights (EIDHR, #07576)*;
- *European Environment Agency (EEA, #06995)*;
- *European Investment Bank (EIB, #07599)*;
- *Court of Justice of the European Union (CJEU, #04938)*;
- *European Central Bank (ECB, #06466)*;
- *European Economic and Monetary Union (EMU, #06961)*;
- *European Consumer Consultative Group (ECCG, #06771)*;
- *Committee of Permanent Representatives to the European Union (#04278)*;
- *EU Customs Union (#05579)*;
- *European Committee of the Regions (CoR, #06665)*;
- *European Cooperation in Science and Technology (COST, #06784)*;
- *European University Institute (EUI, #09034)*;
- *National Academic Recognition Information Centres (NARIC, #16937)*;
- *Board of Governors of the European Schools (#03295)*;
- *European Ombudsman (#08084)*.

The European Commission allocates part of the EU budget to companies and organisations in the form of calls for tender, grants or funds and other financing programmes. With a budget of euro 454,000 million (2014-2020), the European structural and investment funds (ESIFs) are the European Union's main investment policy tool:
European Regional Development Fund (ERDF, #08342); *European Social Fund (ESF, #08501)*; *Cohesion Fund (#04087)*; *European Agricultural Fund for Rural Development (EAFRD)*; *European Maritime and Fisheries Fund (EMFF)*.

Events *European Biomass Conference* Bologna (Italy) 2023, *European Conference on Connected Automated Driving* Brussels (Belgium) 2023, *EUROCEAN : European Conference on Marine Science and Ocean Technology* Vigo (Spain) 2023, *Conference on Persons with Disabilities* Brussels (Belgium) 2022, *EU-GCC Business Forum* Brussels (Belgium) 2022. **Publications** All publications go through *Publications Office of the European Union (Publications Office, #18562)*.

Members College of Commissioners, comprised of 1 Commissioner from each of the 27 member states:
Austria, Belgium, Bulgaria, Croatia, Cyprus, Czechia, Denmark, Estonia, Finland, France, Germany, Greece, Hungary, Ireland, Italy, Latvia, Lithuania, Luxembourg, Malta, Netherlands, Poland, Portugal, Romania, Slovakia, Slovenia, Spain, Sweden.
Enlargement: since 1 May 2004, 1 further country has applied for EU membership: Turkey. The EU assists this country in taking on EU laws and provides a range of financial assistance to improve their infrastructure and economy. North Macedonia became a candidate country in 2005. Potential countries:
Potential countries:
Albania (since 2003), Bosnia-Herzegovina (since 2003), Iceland (since 2009), Kosovo (since 2008), Montenegro (since 2006), Serbia (since 2003).

IGO Relations *EFTA (#05391)* – following negotiations between the EEC and EFTA, an agreement was signed, 2 May 1992, Porto (Portugal), on the implementation of: *European Economic Area (EEA, #06957)*. Although the agreement implied implementation by 1 Jan 1993, it actually came into force 1 Jan 1994. Under the agreement, the Commission informally seeks advice from experts in EFTA countries when drawing up new legislation in the field covered by the agreement; experts from EFTA states are ensured wide participation when the Commission exercises its executive powers, for example in amending certain annexes to existing EU legislation. EFTA participates fully in the Framework Programmes and EFTA countries participate in and pay up to 10% of the operating costs of a number of EU research and development programmes. Programmes in a number of fields are fully open to nationals of all EEA countries and, in the field of education, current and future programmes are also open. Members of the Commission are represented on: *EEA Council (#05379)*; *EEA Joint Committee (#05381)*.

The Commission negotiates in the name of the Union with:
- *Organisation of African, Caribbean and Pacific States (OACPS, #17796)* (in the framework of the Lomé Conventions);
- *Andean Community (#00817)*;
- *Asia-Pacific Economic Cooperation (APEC, #01887)*;
- EFTA;
- *NAFTA Secretariat (#16927)*;
- *Permanent Mechanism for Consultation and Political Coordination (Rio Group, inactive)*;
- *Southern Common Market (#19868)*.

Principal regional organizations in the framework of regional cooperation under the Lomé Conventions:
- *Agency for the Safety of Aerial Navigation in Africa and Madagascar (#00556)*;
- *Caribbean Community (CARICOM, #03476)*;
- *Caribbean Development Bank (CDB, #03492)*;
- *Comité permanent inter-Etats de lutte contre la sécheresse dans le Sahel (CILSS, #04195)*;
- *Common Market for Eastern and Southern Africa (COMESA, #04296)*;
- *Communauté économique des pays des Grands Lacs (CEPGL, #04375)*;
- *Desert Locust Control Organization for Eastern Africa (DLCO-EA, #05042)*;
- *Eastern and Southern African Management Institute (ESAMI, #05254)*;
- *Economic Community of Central African States (ECCAS, #05311)*;
- *Economic Community of West African States (ECOWAS, #05312)*;
- *Entente Council (#05491)*;
- *Commission de l'Océan Indien (COI, #04236)*;
- *Intergovernmental Authority on Development (IGAD, #11472)*;
- *Interafrican Bureau for Animal Resources (AU-IBAR, #11382)*;
- *International Centre for the Bantu Civilizations (CICIBA, inactive)*;
- *Northern Corridor Transit and Transport Coordination Authority (NCTTCA, #17582)*;
- *Organisation of Eastern Caribbean States (OECS, #17804)*;
- *Pacific Community (SPC, #17942)*;
- *Pacific Islands Forum Fisheries Agency (FFA, #17969)*;
- *Pacific Islands Forum Secretariat (#17970)*;
- *Southern African Development Community (SADC, #19843)*;
- *University of the South Pacific (USP, #20703)*;
- *University of the West Indies (UWI, #20705)*.

Developing countries outside the Lomé Conventions are linked with the Community under less global agreements. These countries are known collectively as *ALAMED* – Asia, Latin America, Mediterranean.

Permanent observer status with: *World Intellectual Property Organization (WIPO, #21593)*. *International Organization for Migration (IOM, #14454)*. Observer member of: *Committee of European Banking Supervisors (CEBS, inactive)*. Member of: *FAO Regional Office for Asia and the Pacific (RAP, #09266)*. Signatory to: *Convention on Biological Diversity (Biodiversity convention, 1992)*; *Cooperation Agreement for the Protection of North-East Atlantic Coasts and Waters Against Pollution (Lisbon Agreement, 1990)*; *European Declaration Against Racism and Xenophobia (1986)*; *Paris Memorandum of Understanding on Port State Control (Paris MOU, 1982)*; *WIPO Copyright Treaty (WCT, 1996)*.

Delegations, agreements, cooperation or other relationship with the following bodies:
- *ASEAN (#01141)*;
- *Association of Overseas Countries and Territories of the European Union (OCTA, #02843)*;
- *CIHEAM – International Centre for Advanced Mediterranean Agronomic Studies (CIHEAM, #03927)*;
- *Council of the Baltic Sea States (CBSS, #04870)*;
- *Council of Europe (CE, #04881)*, including observer to *European Population Committee (CAHP, inactive)* and joint sponsorship of *Schools for Health in Europe network foundation (SHE, #19133)*;
- *Current Agricultural Research Information System (CARIS, inactive)*;

European Commission
06633

alphabetic sequence excludes
For the complete listing, see Yearbook Online at

- *European Bank for Reconstruction and Development (EBRD, #06315)*;
- *International Agency for Research on Cancer (IARC, #11598)*;
- *International Atomic Energy Agency (IAEA, #12294)*;
- *International Information System for the Agricultural Sciences and Technology (AGRIS, #13848)*;
- *International Livestock Research Institute (ILRI, #14062)*;
- *International Maritime Organization (IMO, #14102)*;
- *International Monetary Fund (IMF, #14180)*;
- *International Telecommunication Union (ITU, #15673)*;
- *OECD (#17693)*;
- *Organization for Security and Cooperation in Europe (OSCE, #17887)*;
- *Transport Corridor from Europe-Caucasus-Asia (TRACECA, #20225)*;
- *UNESCO (#20322)*;
- *United Nations (UN, #20515)*.

The following intergovernmental organizations also have or indicate links with the Commission:
- *Association of European Public Postal Operators (PostEurop, #02534)*;
- *Bureau international des poids et mesures (BIPM, #03367)*;
- *Caribbean Agricultural Research and Development Institute (CARDI, #03436)*;
- *CGIAR System Organization (CGIAR, #03843)*;
- *Consultative Meeting of Contracting Parties to the London Convention/Meeting of Contracting Parties to the London Protocol (#04769)*;
- *Co-operation Group to Combat Drug Abuse and Illicit Trafficking in Drugs (Pompidou Group, #04796)*;
- *European Centre for Geodynamics and Seismology (ECGS, #06481)*;
- *European Initiative for Agricultural Research for Development (EIARD, #07537)*;
- *European Institute of Public Administration (EIPA, #07569)*;
- *European and Mediterranean Plant Protection Organization (EPPO, #07773)*;
- *EUROCONTROL (#05667)*;
- *European Organization for Nuclear Research (CERN, #08108)*;
- *European Safeguards Research and Development Association (ESARDA, #08417)*;
- *European Space Agency (ESA, #08798)*;
- *European Telecommunications Satellite Organization (EUTELSAT IGO, #08896)*;
- *European Youth Centres (EYCs, #09138)*;
- *Inter-American Drug Abuse Control Commission (#11429)*;
- *International Council for the Exploration of the Sea (ICES, #13021)*;
- *International Customs Tariffs Bureau (#13124)*;
- *International Energy Agency (IEA, #13270)*;
- *International Lead and Zinc Study Group (ILZSG, #14012)*;
- *International Trade Centre (ITC, #15703)*;
- *Internationale Kommission zum Schutz der Elbe (IKSE, #13249)*;
- *Joint Ministerial Committee of the Boards of Governors of the Bank and the Fund on the Transfer of Real Resources to Developing Countries (Development Committee, #16141)*;
- *Latin American Faculty of Social Sciences (#16316)*;
- *The Mediterranean Science Commission (CIESM, #16674)*;
- *Nordic Council (NC, #17256)*;
- *OECD Development Assistance Committee (DAC, see: #17693)*;
- *Organization of Arab Petroleum Exporting Countries (OAPEC, #17854)*;
- *OSPAR Commission for the Protection of the Marine Environment of the North-East Atlantic (OSPAR Commission, #17905)*;
- *Secretariat of the Convention of Wetlands (#19200)*;
- *UNEP (#20299)*;
- *UNCTAD (#20285)*;
- *United Nations Commission on the Status of Women (CSW, #20536)*;
- *WHO (#20950)*;
- *WHO Regional Office for Europe (#20945)*.

NGO Relations Observer to the Governing Board of: *European Union Agency for Law Enforcement Training (CEPOL, #08970)*. Official delegation from: *Sovereign Military Hospitaller Order of St John of Jerusalem, of Rhodes and of Malta (SMOM)*. In liaison with technical committees of: *International Organization for Standardization (ISO, #14473)*. Principal regional nongovernmental organizations in the framework of regional cooperation under the Lomé Conventions: *Caribbean Agricultural Trading Company (CATCO, inactive)*; *Caribbean Association of Industry and Commerce (CAIC, #03448)*; *Inter-African Electrical Engineering College (IEEC, inactive)*; *International Centre of Insect Physiology and Ecology (ICIPE, #12499)*. Although the Commission does not grant "Consultative Status" to organizations, it does list those European or international organizations of which it has official cognizance. However, a recent list of such organizations has not been available since the 1990s. [2020/XE2442/v/**E***]

♦ European Commission Against Racism and Intolerance (see: #04881)

♦ European Commission on Agriculture / see FAO/CIHEAM International Network for the Research and Development of Pasture and Forage Crops (#09257)

♦ European Commission on Agriculture / see Inter-Regional Cooperative Research Network on Buffalo (#15967)

♦ European Commission on Agriculture (ECA) 06634

Commission européenne d'agriculture – Comisión Europea de Agricultura

Headquarters c/o FAO Regional Office for Europe and Central Asia, Benczur utca 34, Budapest 1068, Hungary. T. +3614612000. Fax +3613517029. E-mail: fao-ro-europe@fao.org.

URL: http://www.fao.org/europe/commissions/eca/en/

History 1949, Rome (Italy), within the framework of *FAO (#09260)*, on the recommendation of a preparatory meeting of representatives of European Member Nations, 1949, Paris (France), as *European Committee on Agricultural Technology – Comité européen de technologie agricole*. Formally recognized as an Article VI-1 body and functions defined, 1951, by 6th Session, Resolution 87, of FAO Conference. Title changed to *European Committee on Agriculture – Comité européen d'agriculture* by decision of the Council at its 15th Session, 1952. Present title adopted in 1956. Terms of reference broadened by 9th Session of FAO Conference, 1957 (Resolution 26/57). **Aims** Assist Member Governments to undertake joint action and cooperation in *technological* agricultural problems, including: research; education extension; review of *nutrition* questions; questions relating to agricultural economy that do not come under the purview of FAO Committee on Commodity Problems; and related activities in or by countries of Member Governments in Europe. Encourage and facilitate cooperation between international governmental and nongovernmental organizations concerned with agricultural technology in Europe; make recommendations on all matters within its geographical and technical competence. **Structure** Open to all member Nations in the FAO European region. Member governments designate representatives who serve in a continuing capacity and elect Executive Committee – Chairman, Vice-Chairman and 5 members – from among themselves. **Languages** English, French, German, Spanish. **Activities** Events/meetings; projects/programmes; research/documentation. Arranges technical visits and study tours; supports preparation of country field projects on pluriactive development. Coordinates and monitors regional projects including: *European System of Cooperative Research Networks in Agriculture (ESCORENA, #08871)*; *Working Party on the Role of Women and the Agricultural Family in Rural Development*; *Standing Group on European Agricultural Policies*; *Joint FAO/ECE Working Party on Economics of the Agri-Food Sector and Farm Management*; *Joint FAO/ECE Working Party on Relations between Agriculture and the Environment*; *Joint FAO/ECE/Conference of European Statisticians Study Group on Food and Agricultural Statistics in Europe*. **Events** *Session* Budapest (Hungary) 2015, *Session* Bucharest (Romania) 2014, *Session* Baku (Azerbaijan) 2012, *Session* Yerevan (Armenia) 2010, *Session* Innsbruck (Austria) 2008.

Members Member Nations (53):
Albania, Andorra, Armenia, Austria, Azerbaijan, Belarus, Belgium, Bosnia-Herzegovina, Bulgaria, Croatia, Cyprus, Czechia, Denmark, Estonia, Finland, France, Georgia, Germany, Greece, Hungary, Iceland, Ireland, Israel, Italy, Kazakhstan, Kyrgyzstan, Latvia, Lithuania, Luxembourg, Malta, Moldova, Monaco, Montenegro, Netherlands, North Macedonia, Norway, Poland, Portugal, Romania, Russia, San Marino, Serbia, Slovakia, Slovenia, Spain, Sweden, Switzerland, Tajikistan, Türkiye, Turkmenistan, UK, Ukraine, Uzbekistan.
Regional integration EU entity (1):
European Union (EU, #08967).
Associate member (1):
Faeroe Is.

NGO Relations Instrumental in setting up:
- *European Cooperative Research Network on Flax and other Bast Plants (see: #08871)*;
- *European Cooperative Research Network on Recycling of Agricultural, Municipal and Industrial Residues in Agriculture (RAMIRAN)*;
- *European Cooperative Research Network on Soybean (inactive)*;
- *European Cooperative Research Network on Sunflower (see: #08871)*;
- *European Cooperative Research Network on Sustainable Rural Environment and Energy – Pollination Focus (SREN – Pollination Focus, inactive)*;
- *European Cooperative Research Network on Sustainable Rural Environmental and Energy (SREN, see: #08871)*;
- *European Cooperative Research Network on Trace Elements, Natural Antioxidants and Contaminants in Foods and Diets (inactive)*;
- *FAO/CIHEAM Inter-Regional Cooperative Research Network on Nuts (NUCIS, #09258)*;
- *FAO/CIHEAM International Network for the Research and Development of Pasture and Forage Crops (#09257)*;
- *FAO Inter-Regional Cooperative Research Network on Rice in the Mediterranean Climate Areas (MedRice Network, #09263)*;
- *Inter-Regional Cooperative Research Network on Buffalo (Buffalo Network, #15967)*;
- *Inter-Regional Cooperative Research Network on Cotton for the Mediterranean and Middle East Regions (#15968)*;
- *Inter-Regional Cooperative Research Network on Olives (#15969)*. [2019/XE9634/**E***]

♦ European Commission for the Control of the Danube (inactive)

♦ European Commission for the Control of Foot-and-Mouth Disease (EUFMD) 06635

Commission européenne de lutte contre la fièvre aphteuse

Sec FAO HQ, Room C-518, Viale delle Terme di Caracalla, 00153 Rome RM, Italy. T. +39657055528. Fax +39657055749.

URL: http://www.fao.org/ag/againfo/commissions/en/eufmd/eufmd.html

History 12 Jun 1954, Rome (Italy), on coming into force of Constitution approved by 7th Session of Conference of *FAO (#09260)*, (1953, Resolution 33). Constitution amended at the 9th (1962), 20th (1973), and 22nd (1977) Sessions of the Commission, and subsequently approved by the 39th (1962, Resolution 3/39), 61st (1973, Resolution 5/61) and 72nd (1977, Resolution 5/72) Sessions of FAO Council respectively. Europe is now free from FMD and, since 1992, no regular vaccination is permitted in the region. In response to these changed circumstances, objectives extended, Apr 1993, Rome. Referred to also under the English acronyms *EuFMD* and *FAO/EUFMD*. **Aims** Promote national and international action with respect to control measures against foot-and-mouth disease with a view to its ultimate eradication from Europe. Extended objectives: monitor the FMD situation in the surrounding area and worldwide and disseminate the information obtained; promote appropriate areas of research; provide a forum to coordinate prevention and control of FMD in Member Countries; establish effective surveillance and monitoring of the FMD situation in collaboration with surrounding countries; encourage the development and implementation of policies and strategies to ensure a prompt and effective response to outbreaks of FMD in these countries. **Structure** Session (open, every 2 years); Executive Committee (meets twice a year, meeting closed); Research Group of the Standing Technical Committee (meets annually). **Languages** English, French. **Staff** 2.00 FTE, paid. Staff funded by the EuFMD Commission plus project staff under the agreement with the EC for support to training and project operations promoting FMD control in the European neighbourhood region. **Finance** Contributions of Member Governments, plus agreement with EC for support to FMD surveillance and control operations. **Activities** Advises governments and makes recommendations on problems relating to prevention and control of foot-and-mouth disease and on national contingency plans. Collects and disseminates comprehensive information on outbreaks of the disease and, in collaboration with *World Reference Laboratory for Foot and Mouth Diseases (WRLFMD)*, arranges for rapid identification of virus. Sessions, held in Rome (Italy), annually in March from 1954 to 1973, biennially since then. **Events** *General Session* Rome (Italy) 2011, *General Session* Rome (Italy) 2009, *General Session* Rome (Italy) 2007, *Session* Rome (Italy) 2007, *Session* Rome (Italy) 2007.

Members Open to European Member Nations of the FAO and to European members of IOE which are members of the United Nations and accept the Constitution of the Commission. Other European States, members of the United Nations, may be accepted by Decision of the Commission's membership. Currently governments of 34 countries:
Albania, Austria, Belgium, Bulgaria, Croatia, Cyprus, Czechia, Denmark, Estonia, Finland, France, Germany, Greece, Hungary, Iceland, Ireland, Israel, Italy, Latvia, Lithuania, Luxembourg, Malta, Netherlands, Norway, Poland, Portugal, Romania, Serbia, Slovenia, Spain, Sweden, Switzerland, Türkiye, UK.
Observer:
European Union (EU, #08967).

IGO Relations *OIE – World Organisation for Animal Health (#17703)*; *Comisión Sudamericana para la Lucha contra la Fiebre Aftosa (COSALFA, #04143)*. [2011.03.01/XD0626/**E***]

♦ European Commission for Democracy through Law (Venice Commission) 06636

Commission européenne pour la démocratie par le droit (Commission de Venise)

Sec DG-I, Council of Europe, 67075 Strasbourg CEDEX, France. T. +33388412067. Fax +33388413738.

Pres address not obtained.

URL: http://venice.coe.int/

History 10 May 1990, Strasbourg (France), as a Partial Agreement of the *Council of Europe (CE, #04881)*. Became an Enlarged Partial Agreement by Resolution adopted by the Committee of Ministers, 21 Feb 2002. Also referred to as *Venice Commission of the Council of Europe – Commission de Venise du Conseil de l'Europe*. **Aims** Act as consultative body operating in the field of constitutional law understood in a broad sense; provide legal advice to member states and, in particular, help states wishing to bring their legal and institutional structures in line with European standards and international experiences in the fields of democracy, human rights and the rule of law; ensure dissemination and consolidation of a common constitutional heritage, playing a unique role in conflict management, and provide "emergency constitutional aid" to states in transition. **Structure** Commission; Scientific Council; Council for Democratic Elections; Joint Council on Constitutional Justice. Sub-Commissions (12). **Languages** English, French, Russian. **Staff** 28.00 FTE, paid. **Finance** Members' dues. Annual Budget: euro 4,600,000. **Activities** Politics/policy/regulatory; research/documentation; guidance/assistance/consulting; events/meetings. **Events** *European Conference of Electoral Management Bodies* Oslo (Norway) 2018, *High-Level Round Table on Reform of Criminal Procedure Legislation* Astana (Kazakhstan) 2014, *Plenary Session* Venice (Italy) 2014, *Plenary Session* Venice (Italy) 2013, *Plenary Session* Venice (Italy) 2013. **Publications** *Bulletin on Constitutional Case-law* (3 a year) in English, French. *Science and Technique of Democracy* – series. Annual Report; brochures. **Information Services** *CODICES* – database – comprises summaries of key decisions of constitutional courts and courts of equivalent jurisdiction of most countries of Europe and observer countries, published in 'Bulletin on Constitutional Case-Law', together with available full texts of these decisions, constitutions and laws on the courts; *Documentation Centre on Constitutional Justice* – Strasbourg (France).

Members Experts appointed because of international recognition of their experience in democratic institutions or their contribution to enhancement of law and political science. Members of 62 countries:
Albania, Algeria, Andorra, Armenia, Austria, Azerbaijan, Belgium, Bosnia-Herzegovina, Brazil, Bulgaria, Canada, Chile, Costa Rica, Croatia, Cyprus, Czechia, Denmark, Estonia, Finland, France, Georgia, Germany, Greece, Hungary, Iceland, Ireland, Israel, Italy, Kazakhstan, Korea Rep, Kosovo, Kyrgyzstan, Latvia, Liechtenstein, Lithuania, Luxembourg, Malta, Mexico, Moldova, Monaco, Montenegro, Morocco, Netherlands, North Macedonia, Norway, Peru, Poland, Portugal, Romania, Russia, San Marino, Serbia, Slovakia, Slovenia, Spain, Sweden, Switzerland, Tunisia, Türkiye, UK, Ukraine, USA.
Associate members in 1 country:
Belarus.
Observer status: 4 countries:
Argentina, Holy See, Japan, Uruguay.
Special status of cooperation in 2 countries and territories:
Palestine, South Africa.
Participating international organizations (2):
European Union (EU, #08967); *OSCE – Office for Democratic Institutions and Human Rights (OSCE/ODIHR, #17902)*.

IGO Relations Instrumental in setting up: *World Conference on Constitutional Justice (WCCJ, #21298)*. **NGO Relations** *Association des cours constitutionnelles Francophone (ACCF, #02459)*; *Association of European Election Officials (ACEEEO, #02508)*; Commonwealth Courts; *Eurasian Association of Contitutional Review Bodies (EACRB, #05602)*; *Southern African Judges Commission (SAJC, #19847)*; *Union of Arab Constitutional Courts and Councils (UACCC, #20351)*. [2019.12.11/XE1426/v/**E***]

♦ European Commission for the Efficiency of Justice (#04213)

♦ European Commission of Human Rights / see European Court of Human Rights (#06855)

- ♦ European Commission of Human Rights (inactive)
- ♦ European Commission on Looted Art / see Commission for Looted Art in Europe (#04234)

♦ European Commission of the Nobility 06637

Commission d'information et de liaison des associations nobles d'Europe (CILANE)

Contact Association d'Entraide de la Nobless Française, 9 rue du Chevalier de Saint Georges, 75008 Paris, France. T. +33142601506.

URL: http://www.cilane.eu/

History Apr 1959, following a series of meetings since 1957. **Aims** Contribute to maintaining the *traditional values* of the nobility and adapting them to developments in the modern world by: promoting friendship; encouraging mutual assistance and contacts; furthering exchange, particularly among youth. **Structure** Coordinator. Head Office in Paris (France). **Languages** English, French. **Finance** Members' dues. **Activities** Events/meetings. **Events** *Congress* Brussels (Belgium) 2021, *Congress* Brussels (Belgium) 2020, *Triennial Congress* Gödöllö (Hungary) 2014, *Triennial Congress* Malta 2011, *Triennial Congress* Paris (France) 2008.

Members Organizations and Pontifical Nobility (RNP) in 17 countries and territories:

Belgium, Croatia, Denmark, Finland, France, Germany, Hungary, Italy, Malta, Netherlands, Portugal, Réunion, Russia, Spain, Sweden, Switzerland, UK. [2020/XE4760/**E**]

♦ European Commission for Road Safety in Armed Forces (ECRAF) ... 06638

Policy Secretariat Sessvollmoen Garnison, 2058 Sessvollmoen, Norway. E-mail: secretary@ecraf.org – president@ecraf.org – vicepresident@ecraf.org.

Admin Sec Forces armées, Quartier Reine Elisabeth, Rue d'Evere, 1140 Brussels, Belgium. E-mail: info@ecraf.org.

URL: http://www.ecraf.org/

History as *European Committee for Road Safety in the Armed Forces (ECRAF) – Comité européen pour la sécurité routière dans les forces armées – Europäische Komitee für Verkehrssicherheit in den Streitkräften.* Present name adopted, 2009. Statutes adopted 21 Sep 2002, London (UK); 10-12 Sep 2009, Finland. **Aims** Create a forum for exchange of ideas and initiatives relating to road safety between armed forces in Europe. **Structure** Meeting (annual). Officers: President; Vice-President; Secretary. Working Group. **Languages** English, French, German. **Activities** Promotes adoption of best practice and develops standardized European armed forces road safety policy; evaluates and uses ideas to improve road safety in European armed forces in cooperation with other organizations and institutions; plans, organizes and directs shared international campaigns for road safety. **Events** *Annual Congress* Helsinki (Finland) 2016, *Annual Congress* Belgrade (Serbia) 2015, *Annual Congress* Trencin (Slovakia) 2014, *Annual Congress* Sarajevo (Bosnia-Herzegovina) 2013, *Annual Congress* Saragossa (Spain) 2012.

Members European armed forces and civilian road safety organizations in 30 countries:

Armenia, Austria, Belgium, Croatia, Cyprus, Czechia, Denmark, Estonia, Finland, France, Georgia, Germany, Greece, Hungary, Italy, Latvia, Lithuania, Netherlands, Norway, Poland, Portugal, Romania, Slovakia, Slovenia, Spain, Sweden, Switzerland, Türkiye, UK, Ukraine. [2022/XE4653/**E**]

♦ European Commission on Sexual Orientation Law (ECSOL) 06639

Coordinator Maxingstrasse 22-24/4/9, 1130 Vienna, Austria. E-mail: office@sexualorientationlaw.eu.

URL: http://www.sexualorientationlaw.eu/

History Originating in European Group of Experts on Combating Sexual Orientation Discrimination, 2002-2004. **Aims** Undertake specific projects and formulate reports; act as a forum for its members for exchange of information, collaboration, and discussion on important themes; conduct research into all aspects relating to sexual orientation law.

Members Individuals in European countries, including in 43 countries:

Albania, Andorra, Armenia, Austria, Azerbaijan, Belgium, Bosnia-Herzegovina, Bulgaria, Croatia, Cyprus, Czechia, Denmark, Estonia, Finland, France, Georgia, Germany, Greece, Hungary, Iceland, Ireland, Italy, Latvia, Lithuania, Luxembourg, Malta, Moldova, Montenegro, Netherlands, North Macedonia, Norway, Poland, Portugal, Romania, Russia, Serbia, Slovakia, Slovenia, Sweden, Switzerland, Türkiye, UK, Ukraine.

IGO Relations Participant in Fundamental Rights Platform of: *European Union Agency for Fundamental Rights (FRA, #08969).* [2014.10.31/XJ6185/**E**]

- ♦ European Committee for Advanced Analytic Autogenic Therapy / see European Committee for the Analytically Oriented Advanced Autogenic Training (#06641)

♦ European Committee for the Advancement of Thermal Sciences and Heat Transfer (EUROTHERM) 06640

Pres AGH Univ of Science and Technology, 30 Mickiewicza Ave, 30-059 Krakow, Poland. T. +48126172694.

Sec Inst Superior Técnico, Univ de Lisboa, Av Rovisco Pais, 1049-001 Lisbon, Portugal. T. +351218418194.

URL: http://www.eurothermcommittee.eu/

History 16 Oct 1986, Brussels (Belgium). Formally launched following decision of European scientific communities working in the field of thermal science and its applications at 8th International Heat Transfer Conference, 21 Aug 1986, San Francisco CA (USA). Derives from *European Heating Boilers Association (EBA, inactive)*, set up 1980, Århus (Denmark), by merger of *European Association of Producers of Cast Iron Heating Materials (CEFACEF, inactive)*, formed in 1959, with *European Association of Steel Heating Boiler Manufacturers (UECCA, inactive)*, created in 1960, with the provisional denomination *UECCA – CEFACEF.* **Aims** Promote and foster European cooperation in thermal sciences and heat transfer by supporting the organization and coordination of seminars and conferences in the field. **Structure** Committee of 30. President; Secretary. **Languages** English. **Staff** 2.00 FTE, voluntary. **Finance** Budget for prizes and awards supplied by seminar and conference organisers. **Activities** Awards/prizes/competitions; events/meetings. **Events** *European Thermal Sciences Conference (EUROTHERM2024)* Bled (Slovenia) 2024, *European Thermal Sciences Conference* Lisbon (Portugal) 2021, *European Thermal Sciences Conference* Lisbon (Portugal) 2020, *European Thermal Sciences Conference* Krakow (Poland) 2016, *Seminar on Nanoscale and Microscale Heat Transfer IV* Lyon (France) 2014. **Publications** Conference proceedings.

Members Representatives (maximum 2 per country, with exception of past Presidents of the Committee who retain membership of the Committee) appointed by and representing 16 European countries:

Austria, Belgium, Finland, France, Germany, Greece, Hungary, Ireland, Italy, Netherlands, Poland, Portugal, Slovenia, Spain, Sweden, UK.

IGO Relations Formal contacts with: *European Commission (EC, #06633)* (DGXII). [2022/XE1392/**E**]

- ♦ European Committee for Agricultural and Horticultural Tools and Implements (inactive)
- ♦ European Committee on Agricultural Technology / see European Commission on Agriculture (#06634)
- ♦ European Committee for Agricultural Training / see Comitato Europeo per la Formazione e l'Agricoltura
- ♦ European Committee on Agriculture / see European Commission on Agriculture (#06634)
- ♦ European Committee of Agronomists / see Confédération européenne des associations d'ingénieurs agronomes (#04538)
- ♦ European Committee of Air Handling and Air Conditioning Equipment Manufacturers (inactive)
- ♦ European Committee of Air Handling and Refrigeration Equipment Manufacturers / see Eurovent (#09194)

♦ European Committee for the Analytically Oriented Advanced Autogenic Training (ECAAT) 06641

Secretariat Piazza de Gasperi 41, 35131 Padua PD, Italy. T. +3949650861. E-mail: info@ecaat.org.

Pres Pyrkergasse 23, 1190 Vienna, Austria. T. +4313682366. Fax +431368166123.

URL: http://www.ecaat.org/

History 15 Dec 1982, Padua (Italy), as *European Committee for Advanced Analytic Autogenic Therapy.* **Aims** Promote autogenic *psychotherapy*, especially analytic advanced autogenic training. **Finance** Members' dues. **Activities** Events/meetings.

Members in 5 countries:

Austria, Germany, Italy, Japan, Switzerland. [2007/XM0424/**E**]

♦ European Committee on Antimicrobial Susceptibility Testing (EUCAST) 06642

Secretariat Lab for Antimicrobial Suceptibility Testing, c/o Clinical Microbiology, Central Hosp, SE-351 85 Växjö, Sweden. T. +46470589673 – +46470587460.

Chairman address not obtained.

URL: http://www.eucast.org/

History Statutes adopted Nov 1999; amended Apr 2007 and May 2011. A standing committee jointly organized by *European Society of Clinical Microbiology and Infectious Diseases (ESCMID, #08548), European Centre for Disease Prevention and Control (ECDC, #06476)* and European national breakpoint committees. **Structure** Steering Committee; General Committee; Subcommittees; National AST Committees; Development Laboratories; Network Laboratories. **Events** *General Committee Meeting* Copenhagen (Denmark) 2015, *General Committee Meeting* Berlin (Germany) 2013. **IGO Relations** *European Medicines Agency (EMA, #07767).* **NGO Relations** *European Antimicrobial Resistance Surveillance Network (EARS-Net, #05907).* [2015/XJ9265/**E**]

- ♦ European Committee of Associations of Manufacturers of Agricultural Machinery / see European Agricultural Machinery Association (#05846)

♦ European Committee of Associations of Manufacturers of Gears and Transmission Parts 06643

Comité européen des associations de constructeurs d'engrenages et d'éléments de transmission (EUROTRANS) – Europäisches Komitee der Fachverbände der Hersteller von Getrieben und Antriebselementen

Address not obtained.

URL: http://www.euro-trans.org/

History Founded 1969. EU Transparency Register: 8449553739-37. **Structure** General Secretariat; Board; Working Groups; EUROTRANS Trainings. **Languages** English. **Events** *Annual Meeting* Bari (Italy) 2014, *Annual Meeting* Hannover (Germany) 2013, *Annual Meeting* Paris (France) 2012, *Annual meeting* Hannover (Germany) 2011, *Annual meeting* Munich (Germany) 2010. **Publications** Glossaries.

Members National associations in 7 countries:

Belgium, Finland, France, Germany, Italy, Switzerland, UK.

IGO Relations *European Commission (EC, #06633).* [2013.11.25/XD2779/**D**]

- ♦ European Committee of Associations of Manufacturers of Internal Combustion Engines (inactive)
- ♦ European Committee of Associations of Manufacturers of Welding Products (inactive)
- ♦ European Committee for Big Game Hunting (inactive)
- ♦ European Committee of Boiler, Vessel and Pipework Manufacturers (no recent information)
- ♦ European Committee of Burner Manufacturers (inactive)
- ♦ European Committee for Business Support Services (inactive)
- ♦ European Committee for Catholic Education (#04156)
- ♦ European Committee of Chemical Plant Manufacturers / see European Committee for Process Equipment and Plant Manufacturers (#06662)

♦ European Committee on Computational Methods in Applied Sciences (ECCOMAS) 06644

Secretariat Int Ctr for Numerical Methods in Engineering, Edificio C-1, Campus Norte UPC, c/ Gran Capitan s/n, 08034 Barcelona, Spain. T. +34934054697. Fax +34932058347. E-mail: eccomas@cimne.upc.edu.

Sec Univ Politécnica de Catalunya, Campus Nord – Modulo C-2, 08034 Barcelona, Spain.

URL: http://www.eccomas.org/

History 1993. Former names and other names: *European Community on Computational Applications Methods in Applied Sciences* – alias. **Aims** Bring together European organizations with members interested in computational *mechanics* and *mathematics* applied to problems in mechanics and *engineering.* **Structure** General Assembly; Managing Board; Executive Committee. **Languages** English. **Activities** Events/meetings; awards/prizes/competitions. **Events** *International Conference on Isogeometric Analysis (IGA)* Banff, AB (Canada) 2022, *ECCOMAS : European Congress on Computational Methods in Applied Sciences and Engineering* Oslo (Norway) 2022, *International Conference on Textile Composites and Inflatable Stuctures* 2021, *Conference on Multibody Dynamics* Budapest (Hungary) 2021, *International Conference on Isogeometric Analysis (VIGA)* Lyon (France) 2021. **Publications** *ECCOMAS Newsletter.* Proceedings.

Members National organizations (20) in 14 countries:

Belgium, Finland, France (2), Germany (2), Greece (2), Ireland, Italy (2), Netherlands, Portugal, Russia, Spain (2), Switzerland, Türkiye, UK (2).

Regional organizations (3):

Central European Association of Computational Mechanics (CEACM, #03705); European Research Community on Flow, Turbulence and Combustion (ERCOFTAC, #08361); Nordic Association for Computational Mechanics (NoACM, #17187).

NGO Relations Affiliated to and cooperative arrangement with: *International Association for Computational Mechanics (IACM, #11800).* [2016.06.01/XE3174/y/**E**]

- ♦ European Committee for a Constructive Tomorrow (internationally oriented national body)
- ♦ European Committee of Constructors of Weighing Instruments (#04151)
- ♦ European Committee of Consulting Firms (inactive)
- ♦ European Committee for Cooperation of the Machine Tool Industries / see European Association of the Machine tool Industries and related Manufacturing Technologies (#06113)
- ♦ European Committee of the Cotton and Allied Textile Industries / see European Federation of Cotton and Allied Textiles Industries (#07093)

♦ European Committee on Crime Problems (CDPC) 06645

Comité européen pour les problèmes criminels (CDPC)

Sec Head of the Criminal Law Div, DG I – Human Rights and Rule of Law, Council of Europe, 67075 Strasbourg CEDEX, France. T. +33390215466. Fax +33388412794. E-mail: dgi-cdpc@coe.int.

URL: http://www.coe.int/cdpc/

History 1957, Strasbourg (France). Established within the framework of *Council of Europe (CE, #04881).* Former names and other names: *Council of Europe Steering Committee on Crime Problems* – alias. **Aims** Oversee and coordinate the Council of Europe's activities in the field of crime prevention and crime control. **Structure** Committee; Bureau; Council for Penological Co-operation (PC-CP); Committee of Experts on the Operation of European Conventions on Co-operation in Criminal Matters (PC-OC); Ad-hoc Drafting Groups; Secretariat of the Criminal Law Division. **Languages** English, French. **Staff** 7.00 FTE, paid. **Finance** Council of Europe General Budget. Annual budget: 750,000 EUR. **Activities** Events/meetings; guidance/assistance/consulting; knowledge management/information dissemination; monitoring/evaluation. **Events** *Plenary Session* Strasbourg (France) 2022, *Plenary Session* Strasbourg (France) 2022, *Plenary Session* Strasbourg (France) 2021, *Plenary Session* Strasbourg (France) 2020, *Plenary Session* Strasbourg (France) 2019. **Publications** *The White Paper on Transnational Organised Crime.*

Members Council of Europe member states (46):

Albania, Andorra, Armenia, Austria, Azerbaijan, Belgium, Bosnia-Herzegovina, Bulgaria, Croatia, Cyprus, Czechia, Denmark, Estonia, Finland, France, Georgia, Germany, Greece, Hungary, Iceland, Ireland, Italy, Latvia, Liechtenstein, Lithuania, Luxembourg, Malta, Moldova, Monaco, Montenegro, Netherlands, North Macedonia, Norway, Poland, Portugal, Romania, San Marino, Serbia, Slovakia, Slovenia, Spain, Sweden, Switzerland, Türkiye, UK, Ukraine.

IGO Relations Instrumental in setting up (1): *Committee of Experts on the Evaluation of Anti-Money Laundering Measures and the Financing of Terrorism (MONEYVAL, #04257).* [2022.12.01/XE1497/**E***]

- ♦ European Committee of Domestic Equipment Manufacturers / see APPLiA – Home Appliance Europe (#00877)
- ♦ European committee for drawing up standards in the field of inland navigation (#04160)
- ♦ European Committee for EC Agricultural Engineers / see Confédération européenne des associations d'ingénieurs agronomes (#04538)
- ♦ European Committee for Economic and Social Progress (inactive)
- ♦ European Committee for the Education of Children and Adolescents who are Intellectually Advanced, Gifted, Talented / see European Committee Promoting the Education of Gifted and Talented Young People (#06664)

European Committee Electrical
06646

alphabetic sequence excludes
For the complete listing, see Yearbook Online at

♦ European Committee of Electrical Installation Equipment Manufacturers (CECAPI) 06646

Comité européen des constructeurs d'appareillage électrique d'installation (CECAPI) – Europäische Kommission der Hersteller von Elektrischen Installationsgeräten

Contact BluePoint Brussels, Boulevard Auguste Reyers 80, 1030 Brussels, Belgium. E-mail: secretarygeneral@cecapi.org.
URL: http://www.cecapi.org/

History 30 Jun 1991. Founded when statutes were adopted, a Coordinating Commission having been in existence since 1967. Former names and other names: *European Committee of Manufacturers of Electrical Installation Equipment* – alias. Registration: Banque-Carrefour des Entreprises, No/ID: 0727.447.441, Start date: 23 May 2019, Belgium; EU Transparency Register, No/ID: 599743711223-32, Start date: 28 May 2013. **Aims** Encourage and develop relations between European manufacturers of electrical installation equipment and keep them informed on technical and economic questions of interest to the *profession*; arrange meetings between members to consider their views and seek common positions; act as official spokesman of the industry within Europe; work towards establishment of statutes of a future Association of European Manufacturers of Electrical Installation Equipment. **Structure** General Assembly; Steering Committee; Working Groups. **Languages** English. **Finance** Sources: members' dues. **Events** *Presidents Meeting / Presidents' Meeting* Belgium 2012, *Presidents' Meeting* Horgen (Switzerland) 2006, *Presidents meeting / Presidents' Meeting* Paris (France) 2005, *Presidents meeting / Presidents' Meeting* Ghent (Belgium) 2004, *Presidents meeting / Presidents' Meeting* Stresa (Italy) 2003.

Members Open to associations of EC and EFTA countries. National professional associations (10) in 9 countries:
Austria, Belgium, France, Germany, Italy, Portugal, Spain, Switzerland, UK.

NGO Relations Member of (1): *Forum for European Electrical Domestic Safety (FEEDS)*. Cooperation agreement with: *European Committee for Electrotechnical Standardization (CENELEC, #06647)*.
[2021/XD3659/**E**]

♦ European Committee for Electrotechnical Standardization (CENELEC) 06647

Comité européen de normalisation électrotechnique (CENELEC) – Europäisches Komitee für Elektrotechnische Normung

Dir Gen Rue de la Science 23, 1040 Brussels, Belgium. T. +3225500811. Fax +3225500819. E-mail: info@cencenelec.eu – media@cencenelec.eu.
Pres address not obtained.
URL: https://www.cencenelec.eu/

History 1 Jan 1973. Founded on merger of *European Committee for the Coordination of Electrotechnical Standards of EEC Member Countries (inactive)*, set up 20 Oct 1958, with *Comité européen de coordination des normes électriques (CENEL, inactive)*, a *'Group of Six'* having been in operation since 1959 and comprising national electrotechnical committees of the then 6 countries of the EEC. Registration: Banque-Carrefour des Entreprises, No/ID: 0412.958.890, Start date: 29 Dec 1972, Belgium; EU Transparency Register, No/ID: 58258552517-56, Start date: 18 Oct 2009. **Aims** Serve as the officially responsible body for standardization in the electrotechnical field in Europe. **Structure** General Assembly; Administration Board; Technical Board. Secretariat at CEN-CENELEC Management Centre (CCMC). **Languages** English, French, German. **Staff** 80.00 FTE, paid. **Finance** Sources: members' dues; revenue from activities/projects. Supported by: *EFTA (#05391)*; *European Union (EU, #08967)*. **Activities** Events/meetings; standards/guidelines. **Events** *Hearing for life – How Can Hearing Protection Support?* Brussels (Belgium) 2022, *Highlights in Circular Economy standardization in CEN and CENELEC* Brussels (Belgium) 2022, *The potential of European Standards to Support the European Strategy towards a Green and Sustainable Environment* Brussels (Belgium) 2022, *Trusted Chips: The Standardization Landscape and Opportunities for Europe* Brussels (Belgium) 2022, *Workshop on Personal Protective Equipment (PPE), Medical Devices (MD) Dual Use Products* Brussels (Belgium) 2022. **Publications** *On the Spot* (6 a year).

Members National Electrotechnical Committees (NECs) in 33 countries:
Austria, Belgium, Bulgaria, Croatia, Cyprus, Czechia, Denmark, Estonia, Finland, France, Germany, Greece, Hungary, Iceland, Ireland, Italy, Latvia, Lithuania, Luxembourg, Malta, Netherlands, North Macedonia, Norway, Poland, Portugal, Romania, Slovakia, Slovenia, Spain, Sweden, Switzerland, Türkiye, UK.
Affiliate status: National Standardization Organizations in 12 countries:
Albania, Belarus, Bosnia-Herzegovina, Egypt, Georgia, Israel, Jordan, Moldova, Montenegro, Serbia, Tunisia, Ukraine.

IGO Relations Designated as a European Standards Organization by: *European Commission (EC, #06633)*. **NGO Relations** Cooperation agreement with: *International Electrotechnical Commission (IEC, #13255)*. Sister organizations: *Comité européen de normalisation (CEN, #04162)*; *European Telecommunications Standards Institute (ETSI, #08897)*. Partner organizations:
- *APPLiA – Home Appliance Europe (#00877)*;
- *Association européenne pour la coordination de la représentation des consommateurs pour la normalisation (ANEC, #02561)*;
- *GIGAEurope AISBL (#10151)*;
- *Europacable (#05743)*;
- *European Association of the Electricity Transmission and Distribution Equipment and Services Industry (T and D EUROPE, #06023)*;
- *Orgalim – Europe's Technology Industries (#17794)*;
- *Environmental Coalition on Standards (ECOS, #05499)*;
- *European Trade Union Confederation (ETUC, #08927)*;
- *KNX Association (#16202)*;
- *Small Business Standards (SBS, #19311)*;
- *Union of the Electricity Industry – Eurelectric (#20379)*.

Partner Standardization Bodies (PSBs) – national standards bodies in countries outside Europe. Technical Liaison Partners:
- *Association of European Manufacturers of Fire and Security Systems (EURALARM, #02520)*;
- *Confederation of European Security Services (CoESS, #04532)*;
- *DIGITALEUROPE (#05073)*;
- *DLMS User Association (#05109)*;
- *European Association of Electrical and Electronic Waste Take Back Systems (WEEE Forum, #06022)*;
- *European Association of Gas and Steam Turbine Manufacturers (EUTurbines, #06050)*;
- *European Association of lighting WEEE compliance schemes (EucoLight, #06108)*;
- *European Distributed Energy Resources Laboratories (DERlab, #06930)*;
- *European Electronics Recyclers Association (EERA, #06975)*;
- *European Federation of Campingsite Organisations and Holiday Park Assocations (EFCO and HPA, #07066)*;
- *European Recycling Platform (ERP, #08336)*;
- *European Testing Inspection Certification System (ETICS, #08901)*;
- *European Vending and Coffee Service Association (EVA, #09049)*;
- *EuropeOn (#09166)*;
- *International Amateur Radio Union (IARU, #11646)*;
- *International Association of Public Transport (#12118)*;
- *LightingEurope (#16472)*;
- *OSGP Alliance (#17903)*;
- *SolarPower Europe (#19676)*;
- *Association of the European Rail Supply Industry (UNIFE, #02536)*. [2023/XD0634/**D**]

♦ European Committee of Environmental Technology Suppliers Associations (EUCETSA) 06648

Coordinator Diamant Bldg, Boulevard A Reyers 80, 1030 Brussels, Belgium. T. +3227722987. Fax +3227728015. E-mail: info@eucetsa.com.
URL: http://www.eucetsa.net/

History 1999. Registered in accordance with Belgian law. **Aims** Promote the international competitiveness of the environmental technology industry in Europe. **Structure** General Assembly. Board, comprising President, Vice-President and Secretary-General/Treasurer.

Members Regular; Associate. Trade associations (7) in 6 countries:
Belgium, Norway, Portugal, Spain, Sweden, Switzerland.

NGO Relations Member of: *European Partners for the Environment (EPE, #08154)*; *European Water Partnership (EWP, #09083)*. [2014/XM0959/**E**]

♦ European Committee for External Quality Assessment Programmes in Laboratory Medicine / see European Organisation for External Quality Assurance Providers in Laboratory Medicine (#08098)
♦ European Committee of Food and Packaging Machinery Manufacturers (inactive)

♦ European Committee of Forging and Stamping Industries 06649

Comité de liaison des industries européennes de l'estampage et de la forge (EUROFORGE) – Europäischer Verband der Schmiedeindustrie

SG Goldene Pforte 1, 58093 Hagen, Germany. T. +492331958813. Fax +49233151046.
Registered Office c/o Bluepoint Conference and Business Center, Bd A Reyers 80, 1030 Brussels, Belgium.
URL: http://www.euroforge.org/

History 1953, by national forging associations of UK, France and Germany. Registered in accordance with Belgian law. EU Transparency Register: 966874435557-34. **Aims** Represent the forging industries in Europe. **Structure** General Assembly (annual); Executive Board. Secretariat-General assured by Director of one of the national member associations. **Languages** English, French, German. **Events** *Triennial Congress* Berlin (Germany) 2014, *Triennial Congress* Hyderabad (India) 2011, *Triennial Congress* Chicago, IL (USA) 2008, *Triennial international forging congress / Triennial Congress* Nagoya (Japan) 2005, *Triennial international forging congress / Triennial Congress* Cologne (Germany) 2002.

Members National organizations in 11 countries:
Belgium, Czechia, Finland, France, Germany, Italy, Poland, Spain, Sweden, Türkiye, UK.

IGO Relations Recognized by: *European Commission (EC, #06633)*. [2019/XD2798/t/**E**]

♦ European Committee of Foundry Associations / see European Foundry Association, The (#07352)

♦ European Committee for Future Accelerators (ECFA) 06650

Comité européen pour les futurs accélérateurs

Chairperson CERN/DG, 1211 Geneva 23, Switzerland. T. +497612035713. Fax +497612035931. E-mail: council.secretariat@cern.ch.
Sec Av Gama Pinto, 2, Complexo Interdisciplinar (3is), 1649-003 Lisbon, Portugal.
URL: http://ecfa.web.cern.ch/

History 1963. Founded by *European Organization for Nuclear Research (CERN, #08108)*, as an independent association for the scientific community. **Aims** Contribute to long-range planning of high-energy physics facilities. **Structure** Plenary; Restricted EFCA Committee. **Languages** English. **Finance** No budget. Expenses of organizing events covered by Member States in each case. **Activities** Events/meetings. **Events** *Plenary Meeting* Geneva (Switzerland) 2022, *Plenary Meeting* Geneva (Switzerland) 2022, *Plenary Meeting* 2021, *Plenary Meeting* 2021, *Plenary Meeting* Geneva (Switzerland) 2021. **Publications** Reports; papers.

Members CERN Member States and Associate Member States (28):
Austria, Belgium, Bulgaria, Croatia, Cyprus, Czechia, Denmark, Finland, France, Germany, Greece, Hungary, Israel, Italy, Netherlands, Norway, Poland, Portugal, Romania, Serbia, Slovakia, Slovenia, Spain, Sweden, Switzerland, Türkiye, UK, Ukraine.
European Organization for Nuclear Research (CERN, #08108).
Observers in 2 countries:
Russia, USA.
Astroparticle Physics European Consortium (APPEC, #02998); *European Physical Society (EPS, #08207)*; *European Science Foundation (ESF, #08441)*; *Nuclear Physics European Collaboration Committee (NuPECC, #17620)*.

NGO Relations Cooperates with (1): *International Committee for Future Accelerators (ICFA, #12774)*.
[2023.02.20/XE0633/**E**]

♦ European Committee for the Handicrafts and Creative Arts (inactive)
♦ European Committee for Home-based Priority Action for the Child and the Family (#04150)

♦ European Committee for Homeopathy (ECH) 06651

Gen Sec Noorwegenstraat 49, Haven 8008X, 9940 Ghent, Belgium. E-mail: info@homeopathyeurope.org – generalsecretary@homeopathyeurope.org.
URL: http://homeopathyeurope.org/

History 16 Oct 1995, Brussels (Belgium). Registration: Belgium; EU Transparency Register, No/ID: 28998516721-93. **Aims** Fully integrate homeopathy within the European healthcare system. **Structure** General Assembly (every 2 years); Council; Subcommittees; Working Groups. **Languages** English. **Staff** 1.00 FTE, paid. **Finance** Sources: members' dues. Annual budget: 150,000 EUR. **Activities** Events/meetings; healthcare; politics/policy/regulatory; research/documentation; standards/guidelines; training/education. **Events** *General Assembly* Utrecht (Netherlands) 2022, *Spring meeting* Edinburgh (UK) 2019, *Autumn Meeting* Paris (France) 2019, *Spring Meeting* Athens (Greece) 2018, *Joint Homeopathic Symposium* Sofia (Bulgaria) 2018. **Publications** *ECH Newsletter*. *Homeopathic Thesaurus* (2016); *Homeopathy in Europe* (2016). Standards; guidelines; position papers; booklets.

Members Institutional (national homeopathic associations); Associate (various other homeopathic organisations). Associations in 28 countries:
Austria, Belgium, Bulgaria, Croatia, Cyprus, Czechia, Estonia, France, Germany, Greece, Hungary, Italy, Latvia, Lithuania, Moldova, Netherlands, Poland, Portugal, Romania, Russia, Serbia, Slovakia, Slovenia, Spain, Switzerland, Türkiye, UK, Ukraine.

IGO Relations *Council of Europe (CE, #04881)* – European Directorate for the Quality of Medicines and HealthCare; *European Commission (EC, #06633)* – DG SANTE; *European Parliament (EP, #08146)*; Homeopathic Medicinal Products Working Group of the Heads of Medicines Agencies; *WHO (#20950)*. **NGO Relations** Member of: *CAMDOC Alliance (#03402)*; *EUROCAM (#05653)*; *European Public Health Alliance (EPHA, #08297)*. Liaison Organization of: *Comité européen de normalisation (CEN, #04162)*.
[2022.10.20/XE2420/**E**]

♦ European Committee for Hyperbaric Medicine (ECHM) 06652

Pres Natl Ctr for Hyperbaric Medicine, Medical Univ of Gdansk, Powstania Styczniowego 9B, 81-519 Gdynia, Poland. E-mail: ecb@daneurope.org.
Gen Sec address not obtained.
URL: http://www.echm.org/

Events *Conference* Stockholm (Sweden) 2009, *Conference* Lille (France) 2004, *Conference* London (UK) 1998.
NGO Relations Member of: *European Diving Technology Committee (EDTC, #06932)*. [2022/XE4511/**E**]

♦ European Committee of Importers' and Wholesale Grocers' Associations (inactive)
♦ European Committee of Industrial Furnace and Heating Equipment Associations / see The European Committee of Industrial Furnace, Heating and Metallurgical Equipment Associations (#06653)
♦ European Committee of Industrial Furnace and Heating Equipment Manufacturers / see The European Committee of Industrial Furnace, Heating and Metallurgical Equipment Associations (#06653)

♦ The European Committee of Industrial Furnace, Heating and Metallurgical Equipment Associations (CECOF) 06653

SG Lyoner Strasse 18, 60528 Frankfurt-Main, Germany. T. +496966031414. E-mail: info@cecof.org.
URL: http://www.cecof.org/

History 1972. Former names and other names: *European Committee of Industrial Furnace and Heating Equipment Manufacturers* – former; *Comité Européen des Constructeurs de Fours et d'Equipements thermiques industriels (CECOF)* – former; *Europäisches Komitee der Hersteller von Industrieöfen und Industrie-Wärmeanlagen* – former; *European Committee of Industrial Furnace and Heating Equipment Associations (CECOF)* – former (2019). **Aims** Promote the European industrial furnace and heating equipment industry; protect its business interests; deal with all matters being of relevance to members, with particular focus on technical and marketing issues such as supporting trade fairs and standardization. **Structure** General Assembly; Presidency; General Secretariat; Commissions. **Languages** English. **Activities** Knowledge management/information dissemination; politics/policy/regulatory. **Events** *General Assembly* Graz (Austria) 2021, *General Assembly* Frankfurt-Main (Germany) 2020, *General Assembly* Turin (Italy) 2019, *General Assembly* Frankfurt-Main (Germany) 2018, *General Assembly* Helsinki (Finland) 2015.

Members National associations in 8 countries:
Austria, Belgium, France, Germany, Italy, Sweden, Türkiye, UK.
Individuals in 2 countries:
Romania, Switzerland.
Associated in 2 countries:
Japan, USA.

IGO Relations Recognized by: *European Commission (EC, #06633)*. **NGO Relations** Joint publication with: *European Foundry Equipment Suppliers Association, The (CEMAFON, #07353)*. [2021.06.21/XD3582/t/**D**]

♦ European Committee of Interior Designers (inactive)

♦ European Committee for Interoperable Systems (ECIS) 06654

Head Office Avenue Louise 65 – Box 2, 1050 Brussels, Belgium. T. +3227062415. Fax +3227062415. E-mail: info@ecis.eu.
URL: http://www.ecis.eu/

History 1989, Brussels (Belgium). Registered in accordance with Belgian law. EU Transparency Register: 32238324913-44. **Aims** Defend moral and material interests common to members; obtain by collective action measures likely to assist members in their activities; advocate and support a careful balance between strong *intellectual property* protection and rewards for *innovation*; promote initiatives favouring interoperability of *computer* and *communication* systems and products. **Structure** General Assembly; Executive Committee. National Working Groups Secretariat. **Finance** Members' dues: Sustaining: euro 20,000 upwards; Regular euro 10,000; Associate euro 1,000; Academic/Individual/Small Business euro 200. **Activities** Monitoring/evaluation; guidance/assistance/consulting; events/meetings. **Publications** *ECIS Newsletter*.
Members Computer hardware and software suppliers, computer users and service companies in 9 countries:
Denmark, Finland, France, Germany, Japan, Norway, Spain, UK, USA.
Consultative Status Consultative status granted from: *World Intellectual Property Organization (WIPO, #21593)* (Permanent Observer Status). [2019/XF5337/**F**]

♦ European Committee of Landscape Architects (inactive)

♦ European Committee on Legal Cooperation 06655

Comité européen de coopération juridique (CDCJ)

Sec c/o Council of Europe, DG "Human Rights and Rule of Law", DG I – Legal Co-operation Div, 67075 Strasbourg CEDEX, France. T. +33390214260. Fax +33390215663. E-mail: dgi-cdcj@coe.int.
Contact address not obtained.
URL: http://www.coe.int/cdcj/

History Comes within the framework of *Council of Europe (CE, #04881)* and reporting to *Committee of Ministers of the Council of Europe (#04273)*. **Aims** Oversee the Council of Europe's work in the field of public and private law and advise the Committee of Ministers on all questions within its area of competence; promote law reform and facilitate legal cooperation among Council of Europe member states. **Structure** Steering Committee (meets annually) in Strasbourg (France) at Council of Europe Headquarters; Bureau (meets at least twice a year). Subordinate bodies and working groups set up when appropriate and according to priority. **Languages** English, French. **Activities** Events/meetings; networking/liaising; standards/guidelines. **Events** *Plenary Meeting* Strasbourg (France) 2022, *Plenary Meeting* Strasbourg (France) 2022, *Plenary Meeting* Strasbourg (France) 2021, *Plenary Meeting* Strasbourg (France) 2021, *Plenary Meeting* Strasbourg (France) 2020. **Publications** *Evaluation report on Recommendation CM/Rec(2014)7 of the Committee of Ministers of the Council of Europe on the protection of whistleblowers – Rapport d'évaluation de la Recommandation CM/Rec(2014)7 du Comité des Ministres du Conseil de l'Europe sur la protection des lanceurs d'alerte* (2022) in English, French; *Evaluation report on Recommendation CM/Rec(2015)4 of the Committee of Ministers of the Council of Europe on preventing and resolving disputes on child relocation – Rapport d'évaluation de la Recommandation CM/Rec(2015)4 du Comité des Ministres du Conseil de l'Europe relative à la prévention et à la résolution des conflits sur le déménagement de l'enfant* (2022) in English, French; *Statelessness and the right to a nationality in Europe: progress, challenges and opportunities – Final Report of the International Conference and technical meeting of experts (Strasbourg, 23-24 September 2021) – Apatridie et le droit à une nationalité en europe : progrès, défis et opportunités – Rapport final de la Conférence internationale et réunion technique d'experts (Strasbourg, 23-24 septembre 2021)* (2022) in English, French; *Guidelines of the Committee of Ministers of the Council of Europe on online dispute resolution mechanisms in civil and administrative court proceedings – Lignes directrices du Comité des Ministres du Conseil de l'Europe sur les mécanismes de règlement en ligne des litiges dans les procédures judiciaires civiles et administratives* (2021) in English, French; *Guidelines of the Committee of Ministers of the Council of Europe on the efficiency and the effectiveness of legal aid schemes in the areas of civil and administrative law – Lignes directrices du Comité des Ministres du Conseil de l'Europe sur les mécanismes de règlement en ligne des litiges dans les procédures judiciaires civiles et administratives* (2021) in English, French; *Report on the review of the implementation of the European Convention on the Legal Status of Children born out of Wedlock (ETS No. 085) – Rapport sur l'examen de la mise en œuvre de la Convention européenne sur le statut juridique des enfants nés hors mariage (STE n° 085)* (2021) in English, French; *Study on the feasibility of a new, binding or non-binding, European legal instrument on the profession of lawyer – possible added-value and effectiveness – Etude sur la faisabilité d'un nouvel instrument juridique européen, contraignant ou non, sur la profession d'avocat – valeur ajoutée et efficacité potentielles* (2021) in English, French – more information at https://www.coe.int/en/web/cdcj/profession-of-lawyer; *Guidelines of the Committee of Ministers of the Council of Europe on electronic evidence in civil and administrative proceedings – Lignes directrices du Comité des Ministres du Conseil de l'Europe sur les preuves électroniques dans les procédures civiles et administratives* (2019) in English, French – Also available in Polish and Russian (unofficial translation).
Members All 46 member states of the Council of Europe.
Albania, Andorra, Armenia, Austria, Azerbaijan, Belgium, Bosnia-Herzegovina, Bulgaria, Croatia, Cyprus, Czechia, Denmark, Estonia, Finland, France, Georgia, Germany, Greece, Hungary, Iceland, Ireland, Italy, Latvia, Liechtenstein, Lithuania, Luxembourg, Malta, Moldova, Monaco, Montenegro, Netherlands, North Macedonia, Norway, Poland, Portugal, Romania, San Marino, Serbia, Slovakia, Slovenia, Spain, Sweden, Switzerland, Türkiye, UK, Ukraine.
Also, Observers with the Council of Europe in 5 countries:
Canada, Holy See, Japan, Mexico, USA.
Observer organizations (10), listed in this Yearbook:
European Union (EU, #08967) (including, as appropriate, the Fundamental Rights Agency); *International Commission on Civil Status (ICCS, #12671)*; *International Institute for the Unification of Private Law (UNIDROIT, #13934)*; *International Law Commission (ILC, #14004)*; *OECD (#17693)*; *Office of the United Nations High Commissioner for Human Rights (OHCHR, #17697)*; *Organization for Security and Cooperation in Europe (OSCE, #17887)*; *OSCE – Office for Democratic Institutions and Human Rights (OSCE/ODIHR, #17902)*; *The Hague Conference on Private International Law (HCCH, #10850)*; *UNHCR (#20327)*.
Observers to the CDCJ (ISS + non-member states with which the Council of Europe has a Neibourghood Partnership including relevant co-operation activities):
Morocco, Tunisia.
Council of Bars and Law Societies of Europe (CCBE, #04871); *International Commission of Jurists (ICJ, #12695)*; *International Social Service (ISS, #14886)*. [2022.11.30/XE1302/y/**E***]

♦ European Committee of Liquid Applied Waterproofing Systems (inactive)

♦ European Committee of Machinery Manufacturers for the Plastics and Rubber Industries (EUROMAP) 06656

Comité européen des constructeurs de machines pour plastiques et caoutchouc – Comité Europeo de Constructores de Maquinaria para Plasticos y Caucho – Europäisches Komitee der Hersteller von Kunststoff und Gummimaschinen – Comitato Europeo Costruttori Macchine per Materie Plastiche e Gomma

Address not obtained.
URL: http://www.euromap.org/

History May 1964, Hannover (Germany). **Aims** Study and, as far as possible, solve problems involved in the development of the *industry*. **Structure** Assembly (annual). Executive Committee. **Languages** English, French, German, Italian, Spanish. **Finance** Members' dues. **Activities** Sponsors 4 major European plastics exhibitions; assists in the creation of industrial standards concerning construction and safety of plastics and rubber processing machinery; monitors and analyses national trends in machinery sales and production; produces leaflets and technical literature; oversees public relations aspects of the European market. **Events** *Annual General Assembly* Zurich (Switzerland) 2002.
Members National organizations in 9 countries:
Austria, France, Germany, Italy, Luxembourg, Spain, Switzerland, Türkiye, UK.
IGO Relations Recognized by: *European Commission (EC, #06633)*. **NGO Relations** Member of (1): *Circular Plastics Alliance (#03936)*. *Association of Plastics Manufacturers in Europe (Plastics Europe, #02862)*; *European Plastics Converters (EuPC, #08216)*. [2014/XD0643/t/**D**]

♦ European Committee of Manufacturers of Compressors, Vacuum Pumps and Pneumatic Tools (PNEUROP) 06657

Comité européen des constructeurs de compresseurs, pompes à vide et outils à air comprimé – Europäisches Komitee der Hersteller von Kompressoren, Vakuumpumpen und Druckluftwerkzeugen

SG c/o Orgalim, BluePoint Brussels, Bd A Reyers 80, 1030 Brussels, Belgium. T. +3222066866. E-mail: secgen@pneurop.eu – secretariat@pneurop.eu.
URL: http://www.pneurop.eu/

History 1958. Founded by national associations of France, Germany and UK. Official founding, 1960. Currently referred to as *European Committee of Manufacturers of Compressors, Vacuum Technology, Pneumatic Tools, Air Treatment Equipment and Condensate Treatment Equipment*. Registration: Banque-Carrefour des Entreprises, No/ID: 0477.331.852, Start date: 9 May 2002, Belgium; EU Transparency Register, No/ID: 67236492080-88, Start date: 28 Jul 2009. **Aims** Study the technical development of the industry and foster its progress. **Structure** Plenary Meeting (annual); Council. President. Committees. **Languages** English. **Finance** Fees for services (General Secretariat). **Events** *Joint Conference – CEIR – EUROPUMP – PNEUROP* Marseille (France) 2023, *Joint Conference* Brussels (Belgium) 2022, *Plenary Meeting* Brussels (Belgium) 2020, *Plenary Meeting* Lucerne (Switzerland) 2019, *Plenary Meeting* Brussels (Belgium) 2018.
Members National trade associations of manufacturers of compressors, vacuum pumps and pneumatic tools in 101 countries:
Austria, Belgium, Finland, France, Germany, Italy, Sweden, Switzerland, Türkiye, UK.
IGO Relations Recognized by: *European Commission (EC, #06633)*. **NGO Relations** In liaison with technical committees of: *International Organization for Standardization (ISO, #14473)*. [2021/XD2934/**D**]

♦ European Committee of Manufacturers of Compressors, Vacuum Technology, Pneumatic Tools, Air Treatment Equipment and Condensate Treatment Equipment / see European Committee of Manufacturers of Compressors, Vacuum Pumps and Pneumatic Tools (#06657)
♦ European Committee of Manufacturers of Domestic Heating and Cooking Appliances (#04158)
♦ European Committee of Manufacturers of Electrical Installation Equipment / see European Committee of Electrical Installation Equipment Manufacturers (#06646)

♦ European Committee of Manufacturers of Electrical Machines and Power Electronics (CEMEP) 06658

Comité européenne de constructeurs de machines électriques et d'électronique de puissance

Main Office c/o ORGALIME, Diamant Bldg, 80 Bd A Reyers, 1030 Brussels, Belgium. T. +3227068237 – +3227068230. Fax +3227068253. E-mail: cemep@cemep.eu.
URL: http://cemep.eu/

History 1 Jan 1991. Founded succeeding the 2 section committees Coordinating Committee for Common Market Associations of Manufacturers of Rotating Electrical Machinery – Comité de coordination des constructeurs de machines tournantes électriques du Marché commun (COMEL) and COCOS, which were disbanded 31 Dec 1990. A European sector committee of *Orgalim – Europe's Technology Industries (#17794)*. Registration: EU Transparency Register, No/ID: 779609618363-91. **Aims** Represent European manufacturers of electrical machines and power electronics equipment and systems. **Events** *Conference* Milan (Italy) 2022.
Members National organizations in 9 countries:
Belgium, Finland, France, Germany, Italy, Poland, Portugal, Spain, UK.
IGO Relations Recognized by: *European Commission (EC, #06633)*. [2022/XE2857/**E**]

♦ European Committee of the Manufacturers of Fire Protection Equipment and Fire Fighting Vehicles 06659

Comité européen des constructeurs de matériel d'incendie et de secours (EUROFEU) – Europäisches Komitee der Hersteller von Fahrzeugen, Geräten und Anlagen für den Brandschutz

SG bvfa – Bundesverband Technischer Brandschutz eV, Koellikerstrasse 13, 97070 Würzburg, Germany. T. +499313539225. Fax +499313539229. E-mail: info@eurofeu.org.
URL: http://www.eurofeu.org/

History 1969, Frankfurt-Main (Germany). Former names and other names: *European Committee of the Manufacturers of Fire Protection and Safety Equipment and Fire Fighting Vehicles* – former. Registration: EU Transparency Register, No/ID: 588863229596-57, Start date: 15 Jan 2018. **Aims** Establish and promote common policies on matters affecting the fire trade in Europe and lobby on behalf of the trade with authorities, public bodies and international organizations; promote and maintain high standards of design and manufacture; establish uniform nomenclature and definitions; exchange technical information; establish standards, and technical, testing and servicing requirements; promote fire protection and disaster control. **Structure** General Assembly (every 2 years); Presidium; General Secretariat. **Languages** English. **Staff** 2.00 FTE, paid. **Finance** Sources: members' dues. **Activities** Knowledge management/information dissemination; standards/guidelines. **Events** *General Assembly* Lübeck (Germany) / Bad Oldesloe (Germany) 2016, *General Assembly* Altenrhein (Switzerland) 2014, *Biennial General Assembly* Rome (Italy) 2012, *General Assembly* Rome (Italy) 2012, *General Assembly* London (UK) 2010. **Publications** Position papers; technical papers; booklet.
Members National trade organizations in 7 countries:
Belgium, France, Germany, Ireland, Italy, Spain, Switzerland.
Individual in 5 countries:
Luxembourg, Netherlands, Sweden, UK, USA.
IGO Relations Recognized by: *European Commission (EC, #06633)*; *United Nations Framework Convention on Climate Change (UNFCCC, 1992)*. Accredited by: *United Nations Framework Convention on Climate Change – Secretariat (UNFCCC, #20564)*. **NGO Relations** Cooperates with: *European Fire and Security Group (EFSG, #07259)*, together with *Association of European Manufacturers of Fire and Security Systems (EURALARM, #02520)*; *Eurosafe (#09178)*. In liaison with technical committees of: *Comité européen de normalisation (CEN, #04162)*; *International Organization for Standardization (ISO, #14473)*. [2023.02.14/XD3134/**D**]

♦ European Committee of the Manufacturers of Fire Protection and Safety Equipment and Fire Fighting Vehicles / see European Committee of the Manufacturers of Fire Protection Equipment and Fire Fighting Vehicles (#06659)
♦ European Committee of Manufacturers of Refrigeration Equipment (inactive)
♦ European Committee for Materials and Products for Foundries / see European Foundry Equipment Suppliers Association, The (#07353)
♦ European Committee for Mental Health (inactive)
♦ European Committee on Milk-Butterfat Recording / see International Committee for Animal Recording (#12746)
♦ European Committee for Motor Trades and Repairs / see European Council for Motor Trades and Repairs (#06832)
♦ European Committee of National Federations of the Leather, Travel Goods and Allied Industries (inactive)
♦ European Committee of National Organizations of Importers and Distributors of Construction and Handling Equipment (no recent information)

♦ European Committee of Organic Surfactants and their Intermediates 06660

Comité européen des agents de surface et leurs intermédiaires organiques (CESIO) – Europäisches Ausschuss für Tenside und ihre organischen Zwischenprodukte

SG CEFIC, Rue Belliard 40, bte 15, 1040 Brussels, Belgium. T. +3224369300. E-mail: info@cesio.eu.
URL: https://www.cesio.eu/

History 1974, Brussels (Belgium). Founded as sector group of *Conseil européen de l'industrie chimique (CEFIC, #04687)*. Former names and other names: *European Committee for Surface Active Agents and their Organic Intermediates* – alias; *Europäisches Komitee für Tenside und ihre organischen Zwischenstufen* – former. **Aims** Provide an international forum for discussion and resolution of problems affecting European *industry* for organic surfactants and their intermediates. **Structure** General Assembly (annual); Executive Committee; Technical and Regulatory Affairs Management Team. **Languages** English. **Events** *World Surfactant Congress* Rome (Italy) 2023, *World Congress* Munich (Germany) 2019, *World Congress* Istanbul (Turkey) 2015, *World Congress* Barcelona (Spain) 2013, *World congress* Vienna (Austria) 2011.

Members Companies (11), Associate (2) and associations (8) in 12 countries:
Belgium, France, Germany, Italy, Netherlands, Norway, Poland, Portugal, Spain, Sweden, Switzerland, UK.
NGO Relations Member of (1): *International Association for Soaps, Detergents and Maintenance Products (#12166).* [2023.02.25/XD0018/E]

♦ European Committee for Postal Regulation (see: #04602)
♦ European Committee for the Prevention of Torture and Inhuman or Degrading Treatment or Punishment (#04164)

♦ European Committee of Printing and Paper Converting Machinery Manufacturers (EUMAPRINT) 06661

Comité européen des constructeurs de machines pour les industries graphiques et papetières – Europäisches Komitee der Druck- und Papierverarbeitungsmaschinenindustrie – Comitato Europeo fra i Costruttori di Macchine Grafiche e Cartotecniche

SG SWISSMEM, Graphic Machinery Division, Fingstweidstrasse 102, Postfach, 8037 Zurich ZH, Switzerland. T. +41443844814. Fax +41443844242.
URL: http://www.eumaprint.com/

History Founded 1957. **Aims** Collect and disseminate printing machinery statistics furnished by members. **Structure** President (2-year term) chosen on a rotation basis from industry representatives from the various member countries. **Languages** English. **Staff** 1.00 FTE, voluntary. **Activities** Research/documentation. **Publications** Compilation of statistics (2 a year).
Members National trade associations in 6 countries:
France, Germany, Italy, Spain, Switzerland, UK.
NGO Relations Cooperates with: *Orgalim – Europe's Technology Industries (#17794).*
[2015.01.05/XD5379/t/D]

♦ European Committee for Process Equipment and Plant Manufacturers (EUCHEMAP) 06662

Sec Process Plant and Equipment Assn within VDMA, Lyoner Strasse 18, 60528 Frankfurt-Main, Germany. T. +496966031393. Fax +496966031421.
URL: http://www.euchemap.com/

History 1965, as *European Committee of Chemical Plant Manufacturers (EUCHEMAP) – Comité européen des constructeurs de matériel pour l'industrie chimique.* **Aims** Promote the interchange of information and opinion between the member associations; consider all matters affecting the suppliers of the *chemical* and allied industries in Europe.
Members National organizations in 8 countries:
Belgium, France, Germany, Italy, Netherlands, Spain, Switzerland, UK.
IGO Relations Recognized by: *European Commission (EC, #06633).* **NGO Relations** In liaison with technical committees of: *International Organization for Standardization (ISO, #14473).* [2012.06.29/XD2667/E]

♦ European Committee of Professional Diving Instructors (CEDIP) ... 06663

Association européenne des moniteurs de plongée professionnels – Europese Vereniging van Professionele Duikinstructeurs

Contact SIAS, Via L Cagnola 7, 24050 Ghisalba BG, Italy. T. +393296263749. E-mail: contact@cedip.com.
URL: http://www.cedip.org/

History 1992. Registered in accordance with Belgian law. **Aims** Defend the interests of divers and diving instructors. **Structure** General Assembly (annual); Director Committee. **Languages** English, French. **Staff** 1.00 FTE, paid; 1.00 FTE, voluntary. **Finance** Members' dues. **Activities** Training/education; standards/guidelines.
Members Organizations in 14 countries:
Austria, Belgium, Bosnia-Herzegovina, France, Germany, Italy, Luxembourg, Poland, Russia, Serbia, Slovenia, Spain, Switzerland, Ukraine.
Individuals in 14 countries and territories:
Bolivia, Canada, China, Croatia, Djibouti, Egypt, Mauritius, Monaco, Neth Antilles, Polynesia Fr, Seychelles, Slovakia, Slovenia, Vietnam. [2018.11.01/XD6706/D]

♦ European Committee Promoting the Education of Gifted and Talented Young People (EUROTALENT) 06664

Comité européen pour l'éducation des enfants et adolescents précoces surdoués et talentueux – Comité Europeo para la Educación de Alumnos Superdotados y con Talento – Europäisches Komitee zur Förderung Hochbegabter Kinder und Jugendlicher – Associazione Europea per l'Educazione die Fanciulli Precoci e dei Giovani con Alto Potenziale – Europees Comité voor de Educatie van Intellectueel Vroegrijpe, Hoogbegaafde en Getalenteerde Kinderen en Adolescenten

Pres Centro Huerta del Rey, calle Pio del Rio Hortega 10, bajo local 6, 47014 Valladolid, Spain. T. +34635540274. E-mail: c_h_rey@cop.es.
Gen Sec 8 rue du Sable, 67200 Strasbourg, France. T. +33388272014.
URL: http://www.eurotalent.org/

History Founded May 1988, Tours (France). Former titles: *European Committee for the Education of Children and Adolescents who are Intellectually Advanced, Gifted, Talented – Comité européen pour l'éducation des enfants et adolescents précoces surdoués, talentueux (EUROTALENT) – Comité Europeo para la Educación de Niños y Adolescentes Precoces, Super Dotatos y Talentosos – Europäisches Komitee für die Erziehung der Frühreifen, Hochbegabten, Talentierten Kinder und Jugendlichen – Comitato Europeo per l'Educazione dei Fangiulii ed Adolescenti Precoci, Super Dotati, Talentati – Europees Comité voor de Educatie van Intellectueel Vroegrijpe, Hoogbegaafde en Getalenteerde Kinderen en Adolescenten.* Previously referred to in French as *Comité européen pour l'éducation des enfants et adolescents précoces: doués, talentueux et désavantagés, pour filles et garçons.* **Aims** Inform the European Institutions, the Council of Europe, media, public opinion, economic and social world and parents about specific needs of gifted children and adolescents; develop education and training of those concerned – administrative staff, school councillors, psychologists, teachers, social workers. **Structure** General Assembly (annual during end of January, in Paris, France). **Languages** English, French, German, Italian, Spanish. **Staff** 7.00 FTE, voluntary. **Finance** Members' dues. **Activities** Events/meetings; training/education; networking/liaising; capacity building; advocacy/lobbying/activism. **Events** *International congress* Milan (Italy) 1993, *International congress* Barcelona (Spain) 1989. **Publications** Newsletters (several a year). **Members** National associations in Europe (13); individual members in Europe; associations and individuals from countries outside Europe. Membership countries not specified. **Consultative Status** Consultative status granted from: *Council of Europe (CE, #04881)* (Participatory Status). **NGO Relations** Cooperates with: *World Council for Gifted and Talented Children (WCGTC, #21328).*
[2022/XF1304/F]

♦ European Committee for the Protection of the Population Against the Hazards of Chronic Toxicity (inactive)
♦ European Committee of Pump Manufacturers / see European Association of Pump Manufacturers (#06182)

♦ European Committee of the Regions (CoR) 06665

Comité européen des régions (CdR) – Comité Europeo de las Regiones – Europäischer Ausschuss der Regionen – Comité das Regiões Europeu – Comitato europeo delle regioni – Europees Comité van de Regio's – Europeiska regionkommittén – Det Europæiske Regionsudvalg – Euroopan alueiden komitea – Coiste Eorpach na Réigiún – Európsky výbor regiónov – Régiók Európai Bizottsága – Europejski Komitet Regionów – Evropski odbor regij – Euroopa Regioonide Komitee – Evropski odbor regija – Comitetul European al Regiunilor

Secretary-General Rue Belliard 99-101, Etterbeek, 1040 Brussels, Belgium. T. +3222822211 – +3222822005. Fax +3222822325. E-mail: cor-info-point@cor.europa.eu.
URL: https://cor.europa.eu/en

History 1 Nov 1993, Brussels (Belgium). Established within the framework of the *European Union (EU, #08967)* under the *Treaty on European Union (Maastricht Treaty, 1992).* Scope enlarged under *Treaty of Amsterdam (1997)* and *Nice Treaty (2001).* 1st plenary session: 9-10 Mar 1994, Brussels. Since the *Treaty of Lisbon (2007)* came into force 2009, acts as an advisory body to *European Parliament (EP, #08146), Council of the European Union (#04895)* and *European Commission (EC, #06633).* Former names and other names: *Committee of the Regions of the European Communities* – former (1 Nov 1993); *Comité des régions des Communautés européennes* – former (1 Nov 1993); *Committee of the Regions of the European Union* – former; *Comité des régions de l'Union européenne* – former; *Comité van de Regio's van de Europese Unie* – former. **Aims** Represent local and regional authorities across the European Union and advise on new laws that have an impact on regions and cities (70% of all EU legislation); bring EU citizens closer to the EU institutions' work; coordinate action between the European, national, regional and local levels. **Structure** Plenary Session (in Brussels), composed of 329 full members and 329 alternate members, appointed for 4 years (https://cor.europa.eu/en/members/Pages/default.aspx). The number of CoR members from each Member State is as follows: Austria 12, Belgium 12, Bulgaria 12, Croatia 9, Cyprus 6, Czech Republic 12, Denmark 9, Estonia 7, Finland 9, France 24, Germany 24, Greece 12, Hungary 12, Ireland 9, Italy 24, Latvia 7, Lithuania 9, Luxembourg 6, Malta 5, Netherlands 12, Poland 21, Portugal 12, Romania 15, Slovakia 9, Slovenia 7, Spain 21, Sweden 12. Council; Bureau. Commissions (6): CIVEX – Citizenship, Governance, Institutional Affairs and External Relations; COTER – Territorial Cohesion Policy; ECON – Economic Policy; ENVE – Environment, Climate Change and Energy; NAT – Natural Resources; SEDEC – Social Policy, Education, Employment, Research and Culture. Members organized through 6 Political groups, each with its own secretariat: *Group of the European People's Party in the Committee of the Regions (EPP-CoR, #10776); Party of European Socialists (PES, #18249)* – CoR; *Renew Europe – Committee of the Regions (Renew Europe, #18841); European Alliance Group at the Committee of the Regions (EA-CoR, #05871); European Conservatives and Reformists Group – Committee of the Regions (ECR-CoR, #06746);* the Greens. Joint Services of the Economic and Social Committee and the Committee of the Regions (Translation; Logistics). International Cooperation through *Conference of the Regional and Local Authorities for the Eastern Partnership (CORLEAP, #04645).* Administration headed by the Secretary-General. **Languages** EU languages. **Staff** Since 1 Jan 1995, CoR and *European Economic and Social Committee (EESC, #06963)* have shared some services. **Activities** Events/meetings; politics/policy/regulatory. **Events** *EuroPCom : European Conference on Public Communication* Brussels (Belgium) 2022, *European Week of Regions and Cities Meeting* Brussels (Belgium) 2022, *Meeting* Brussels (Belgium) 2022, *Meeting* Brussels (Belgium) 2022, *Montana174 Campaign Final Conference* Brussels (Belgium) 2022. **Publications** *Regions and Cities of Europe* (5 a year) – newsletter, in 7 EU languages. *Committee of the Regions and the Presidency of the European Union* – in 2 EU languages; *Committee of the Regions Political Priorities* – in 7 EU languages; *CoR at a Glance* – in 24 official EU languages; *Key Dates* – in 7 EU languages. Occasional thematic brochures.
Members Individuals (329 full members and 329 alternates) representing local and regional authorities, from regional ministers and presidents to local councillors and mayors, from 6 political families, in the 27 European Union countries:
Austria, Belgium, Bulgaria, Croatia, Cyprus, Czechia, Denmark, Estonia, Finland, France, Germany, Greece, Hungary, Ireland, Italy, Latvia, Lithuania, Luxembourg, Malta, Netherlands, Poland, Portugal, Romania, Slovakia, Slovenia, Spain, Sweden.
IGO Relations Cooperates with (3): *Baltic Sea States Subregional Cooperation (BSSSC, #03150); Conférence des assemblées législatives régionales d'Europe (CALRE, #04582); REGLEG (#18823).* **NGO Relations** Cooperates with (7): *Arco Latino (#01094); Assembly of European Regions (AER, #02316); Association of European Border Regions (AEBR, #02499); Conference of Peripheral Maritime Regions of Europe (CPMR, #04638); Council of European Municipalities and Regions (CEMR, #04891); EUROCITIES (#05662); European Association of Elected Representatives from Mountain Regions (#06021).* [2021.12.22/XE3088/E*]

♦ European Committee for Road Safety in the Armed Forces / see European Commission for Road Safety in Armed Forces (#06638)
♦ European Committee on Romani Emancipation (unconfirmed)

♦ European Committee on the Rules and Usages of Inter-European Trade in Potatoes (European RUCIP Committee) 06666

Comité européen sur des règlements et usages du commerce intereuropéen de pommes de terre (Comité européen RUCIP)

Contact Rue de Trèves 49-51, 1040 Brussels, Belgium. T. +3227771585. Fax +3227771586. E-mail: info@rucip.eu.
URL: http://www.rucip.eu/

History Founded within *European Potato Trade Association (EUROPATAT, #08257).* **Structure** Composed of: *European Potato Trade Association (EUROPATAT, #08257); EUPPA – European Potato Processors' Association (#05592); Intercoop Europe (ICE, #11464).* **Activities** Politics/policy/regulatory.
Members in 10 countries:
Belgium, Czechia, France, Germany, Ireland, Italy, Netherlands, Spain, Switzerland, UK. [2016.12.22/XE9983/t/E]

♦ European Committee of Safe Manufacturers Associations / see Eurosafe (#09178)
♦ European Committee for Scientific Research on the Origins and Consequences of the Second World War (inactive)
♦ European Committee for Social Cohesion / see European Committee on Social Cohesion, Human Dignity and Equality (#06667)

♦ European Committee on Social Cohesion, Human Dignity and Equality (CDDECS) 06667

Secretariat c/o Council of Europe, Agora Bldg, 67075 Strasbourg CEDEX, France. T. +33388412167. Fax +33388412718.
URL: http://www.coe.int/en/web/cddecs/

History Established as *European Committee for Social Cohesion – Comité européen pour la cohésion sociale (CDCS)* within the framework of *Council of Europe (CE, #04881).* Replaced *Comité européen de sécurité sociale (CDSS, inactive),* the previous *Steering Committee for Social Affairs (inactive)* and the subsequent *Comité directeur pour l'emploi et le travail (CDEM, inactive)* and *Steering Committee on Social Policy (inactive).* Current name adopted, 2014. Relevant instruments: *European Social Charter (1961); European Code of Social Security (1964); European Convention on Social Security (1972); Additional Protocol to the European Social Charter, 1988 (1988); European Code of Social Security, Revised (1990); European Social Charter – Revised (1996).* **Aims** Oversee and coordinate the intergovernmental work of the Council of Europe in the fields of social cohesion, human dignity, equality and anti-discrimination; advise the Committee of Ministers (CM) on all questions within these areas. **Structure** Committee; Bureau. **Activities** Management of treaties and agreements: European Code of Social Security; European Code of Social Security (revised); European Convention on Social Security and *Protocol to the European Convention on Social Security (1994); European Agreement on 'au Pair' Placement (1969).* **Events** *Council of Europe and the role of national human rights institutions, equality bodies and ombudsman offices in promoting equality and social inclusion* Helsinki (Finland) 2015, *Meeting* Strasbourg (France) 2004, *Meeting* Strasbourg (France) 2003, *Meeting* Strasbourg (France) 2003, *Meeting* St Julian's (Malta) 2002.
Members Governments of the 47 member countries of the Council of Europe:
Albania, Andorra, Armenia, Austria, Azerbaijan, Belgium, Bosnia-Herzegovina, Bulgaria, Croatia, Cyprus, Czechia, Denmark, Estonia, Finland, France, Georgia, Germany, Greece, Hungary, Iceland, Ireland, Italy, Latvia, Liechtenstein, Lithuania, Luxembourg, Malta, Moldova, Monaco, Montenegro, Netherlands, North Macedonia, Norway, Poland, Portugal, Romania, Russia, San Marino, Serbia, Slovakia, Slovenia, Spain, Sweden, Switzerland, Türkiye, UK, Ukraine.
Observers, governments of 5 non-member states:
Canada, Holy See, Japan, Mexico, USA.
Observer organizations (4), and 2 representatives of NGOs in consultative status of the Council of Europe, listed in this Yearbook:
BUSINESSEUROPE (#03381); EFTA (#05391); European Commission (EC, #06633); European Trade Union Confederation (ETUC, #08927); ILO (#11123); OECD (#17693).
IGO Relations *European Network of National Observatories on Childhood (ChildONEurope, #07951).*
[2015/XK1855/y/E*]

♦ European Committee of Social Rights (ECSR) 06668

Comité européen des droits sociaux

Exec Sec DGI Human Rights and Rule of Law, Council of Europe, 67075 Strasbourg CEDEX, France. T. +33388412892. Fax +33388413700. E-mail: social.charter@coe.int.

URL: http://www.coe.int/socialcharter/

History A *Council of Europe (CE, #04881)* monitoring body, governed by Article 25 of the *European Social Charter (1961).* **Aims** Supervise application of the European Social Charter through a reporting system and a collective complaints procedure. **Structure** Composed of 14 independent and impartial members. Holds 7 sessions a year. **Languages** English, French. **Finance** Council of Europe budget. **Activities** Monitoring/ evaluation; awareness raising; training/education. **Publications** Conclusions (annual); decisions on collective complaints; information and visibility materials. **Information Services** *Case-law on HUDOC Database.*

Members 47 Member States of the Council of Europe:

Albania, Andorra, Armenia, Austria, Azerbaijan, Belgium, Bosnia-Herzegovina, Bulgaria, Croatia, Cyprus, Czechia, Denmark, Estonia, Finland, France, Georgia, Germany, Greece, Hungary, Iceland, Ireland, Italy, Latvia, Liechtenstein, Lithuania, Luxembourg, Malta, Moldova, Monaco, Montenegro, Netherlands, North Macedonia, Norway, Poland, Portugal, Romania, Russia, San Marino, Serbia, Slovakia, Slovenia, Spain, Sweden, Switzerland, Türkiye, UK, Ukraine.

IGO Relations Cooperates with: organizations of the European Union and the United Nations; human rights institutions; equality bodies; national governments. **NGO Relations** Cooperates with international NGOs enjoying participatory status with the Council of Europe, particularly NGOS which make up the Human Rights Committee of the Conference of INGOs, as well as organizations entitled to lodge complaints with ECSR.

[2018.10.15/XE3916/**E***]

♦ European Committee for Sports History (CESH) 06669

SG Univ of Alcala, Fac of Education, C/ Madrid 1, 19001 Guadalajara, Spain.

URL: http://www.cesh-site.eu/

History Sep 1995, Bordeaux (France). **Aims** Coordinate European projects on the history of physical education and sport. **Structure** Officers: President; Secretary General; Treasurer. **Languages** Czech, Danish, Dutch, English, Estonian, Finnish, French, German, Hungarian, Irish Gaelic, Italian, Latvian, Lithuanian, Maltese, Polish, Portuguese, Slovakian, Slovene, Spanish, Swedish. **Staff** 3.00 FTE, voluntary. **Finance** Members' dues. **Activities** Events/meetings; awards/prizes/competitions. **Events** *International Congress* Bucharest (Romania) 2022, *International Congress* Lisbon (Portugal) 2021, *International Congress* Lausanne (Switzerland) 2019, *International Congress* Hannover (Germany) 2018, *International Congress* Strasbourg (France) 2017. **Publications** *CESH Newsletter*, *European Studies in Sports History* – journal. *Annual of CESH* – in 5 vols. Congress proceedings.

Members Individuals (90) in 30 countries:

Australia, Austria, Belgium, Canada, Croatia, Cyprus, Czechia, Denmark, Finland, France, Germany, Greece, Israel, Italy, Japan, Montenegro, Netherlands, New Zealand, Norway, Poland, Portugal, Romania, Russia, Serbia, Slovenia, Spain, Sweden, Switzerland, UK, USA.

National organization (1) in one country:

Italy.

[2020/XE2573/**E**]

- ♦ European Committee for Standardization (#04162)
- ♦ European Committee for the study of corrosion and protection of pipes and pile systems – Drinking water, waste water, gas and oil / see European Committee for the study of corrosion and protection of pipes and pipeline systems (#06670)

♦ European Committee for the study of corrosion and protection of pipes and pipeline systems 06670

Comité Européen pour l'etude de la corrosion et la protection des canalisations (CEOCOR) – Europäisches Studienkomitee für Korrosion und Korrosionsschutz von Rohrleitungssystemen

SG c/o Synergrid, Galerie Ravenstein 4, Boîte 2, 1000 Brussels, Belgium. T. +3222371111. Fax +3222304480.

URL: http://www.ceocor.lu/

History 1956. Became an international organization, 1981, Brussels (Belgium), as a committee of *International Water Services Association (IWSA, inactive).* Original title: *Committee on the Study of Corrosion and Protection of Canalizations – Comité d'étude de la corrosion et de la protection des canalisations.* Previously also known as *International Corrosion Committee*; *Committee for the Study of Corrosion and the Protection of Pipework*; *Committee on the Study of Corrosion and Protection of Pipes.* Current full title *European Committee for the study of corrosion and protection of pipes and pile systems – Drinking water, waste water, gas and oil – Comité Européen pour l'etude de la corrosion et la protection des canalisations – Eaux potables, Eaux usées, Gaz et Pétrole – Europäisches Studienkomitee für Korrosion und Korrosionsschutz von Rohrleitungssystemen – Trinkwasser, Abwasser, Gas und Öl.* Registration: Belgium. **Aims** Provide the basis for scientific and technical guidance in the fields of corrosion by studies, recommendations and publications; contribute to formulation of European standards. **Structure** General Assembly (annual); Board of Directors; Standing Committee; Working Groups. **Languages** English, French, German. **Staff** Voluntary. **Finance** Members' dues. **Activities** Events/meetings; research/documentation; standards/guidelines. **Events** *Autumn Days Meeting* Brussels (Belgium) 2022, *Congress* Zurich (Switzerland) 2022, *Annual Conference* Madrid (Spain) 2021, *Annual Conference* Madrid (Spain) 2020, *Autumn Days* Brussels (Belgium) 2019. **Publications** Congress proceedings; practical guides; recommendations; scientific articles.

Members National associations in 20 countries:

Australia, Austria, Belgium, Canada, Czechia, Denmark, Finland, France, Germany, Greece, Italy, Luxembourg, Netherlands, Poland, Slovakia, Slovenia, Spain, Sweden, Switzerland, UK.

NGO Relations *European Federation of Corrosion (EFC, #07090)* – EUROCORR; *NACE International – The Corrosion Society (#16925)*; national institutions.

[2021/XE0670/**E**]

- ♦ European Committee for the Study of Salt / see European Salt Producers Association (#08425)
- ♦ European Committee of Sugar Manufacturers / see Comité européen des fabricants de sucre (#04159)
- ♦ European Committee for Surface Active Agents and their Organic Intermediates / see European Committee of Organic Surfactants and their Intermediates (#06660)

♦ European Committee for Surface Treatment 06671

Comité européen des traitements de surfaces (CETS)

Sec c/o VOM Belgie, Kapeldreef 60, 3001 Leuven, Belgium. T. +3216401420. Fax +3216298319. E-mail: info@cets-eu.be.

Pres c/o SEA, Federation House, 10 Vyse Street, Birmingham, B18 6LT, UK. E-mail: info@sea.org.uk.

URL: http://cets-eu.be/

History 1981. Since 2010, registered in accordance with Belgian law: 0827 987 545. EU Transparency Register: 5774391386-55. **Aims** Provide a scientific and engineering voice at the European Union on proposals for environmental, health and safety legislation. **Structure** General Assembly; Board; Sections (2). **Languages** English, French. **Staff** Voluntary. **Finance** Members' dues. **Activities** Knowledge management/ information dissemination; standards/guidelines; research/documentation. **Events** *General Assembly* Gothenburg (Sweden) 2009, *General Assembly* Barcelona (Spain) 2008, *General Assembly* Brussels (Belgium) 2007, *Meeting* Seville (Spain) 2002.

Members Full (18 associations; 2 institutes). Members in 14 countries:

Austria, Belgium, Denmark, Finland, France, Germany, Ireland, Italy, Netherlands, Norway, Poland, Spain, Sweden, UK.

Institutes include 1 organization listed in this Yearbook:

Nickel Institute (#17133).

IGO Relations Accredited stakeholder at: *European Chemicals Agency (ECHA, #06523).*

[2021/XJ3257/**E**]

- ♦ European Committee of Teachers of Landscape Higher Education (inactive)

♦ European Committee of Textile Machinery Manufacturers 06672

Comité européen des constructeurs de matériel textile (CEMATEX) – Comité Europeo de los Constructores de Maquinaria Textil – Komitee der Europäischen Hersteller von Textilmaschinen – Comitato Europeo dei Costruttori di Macchinario Tessile – Europees Comité van Constructeurs van Textiel-Machines

Contact c/o Swissmem, Pfingstweidstrasse 102, 8005 Zurich ZH, Switzerland. E-mail: info@ cematex.com.

URL: http://www.cematex.com/

History 20 Oct 1952, Zurich (Switzerland). **Aims** Study problems concerned with the development and evolution of the *industry.* **Structure** Plenary Meeting (twice a year). Central Committee elects Board. Meetings closed. **Languages** Dutch, English, French, German, Italian, Spanish, Swedish. **Staff** 1.00 FTE, paid. **Activities** Organizes *International Textile Machine Association Exhibition (ITMA).* **Events** *ITMA* Milan (Italy) 2023, *ITMA Exhibition* Barcelona (Spain) 2011, *ITMA Asia* Shanghai (China) 2008, *ITMA Exhibition* Munich (Germany) 2007, *ITMA Exhibition* Birmingham (UK) 2003.

Members National associations in 9 countries:

Belgium, France, Germany, Italy, Netherlands, Spain, Sweden, Switzerland, UK.

IGO Relations Recognized by: *European Commission (EC, #06633).* **NGO Relations** In liaison with technical committees of: *International Organization for Standardization (ISO, #14473).*

[2022/XD0655/**D**]

- ♦ European Committee for Trade in Starch Products and Derivatives (inactive)
- ♦ European Committee for Training and Agriculture (internationally oriented national body)

♦ European Committee for Treatment and Research in Multiple Sclerosis (ECTRIMS) 06673

Secretariat c/o Congrex, Reinacherstr 131, 4053 Basel BS, Switzerland. T. +41616867779. Fax +41616867788. E-mail: secretariat@ectrims.eu.

SG address not obtained.

URL: http://www.ectrims.eu/

History 1979. **Aims** Facilitate communication, create synergies, and promote and enhance research and learning among professionals for the ultimate benefit of people affected by MS. **Structure** Council; Executive Committee. **Languages** English. **Staff** 1.00 FTE, paid. **Finance** Sources: meeting proceeds; sponsorship. **Events** *Congress* Amsterdam (Netherlands) 2022, *Congress* 2021, *Congress* Basel (Switzerland) 2020, *Joint Meeting* Washington, DC (USA) 2020, *Congress* Stockholm (Sweden) 2019. **Publications** None.

Members Full in 34 countries:

Austria, Belarus, Belgium, Bulgaria, Croatia, Cyprus, Czechia, Denmark, Finland, France, Germany, Greece, Hungary, Iceland, Ireland, Israel, Italy, Latvia, Lithuania, Luxembourg, Netherlands, North Macedonia, Norway, Poland, Portugal, Romania, Russia, Serbia, Slovenia, Spain, Sweden, Switzerland, Türkiye, UK.

NGO Relations Cooperates with (8): American Committee for Treatment and Research in Multiple Sclerosis (ACTRIMS); *Comité Latinoamericano para el Tratamiento y la Investigación en Esclerosis Múltiple (LACTRIMS, #04190)*; *European Charcot Foundation (ECF, #06518)*; *European Multiple Sclerosis Platform (EMSP, #07833)*; *Magnetic Imaging in Multiple Sclerosis (MAGNIMS, #16548)*; *Multiple Sclerosis International Federation (MSIF, #16899)*; *Pan-Asian Committee for Treatment and Research in Multiple Sclerosis (PACTRIMS, #18163)*; *Rehabilitation in Multiple Sclerosis (RIMS, #18826).*

[2022/XF5459/**F**]

- ♦ European Committee for Umami (unconfirmed)
- ♦ European Committee for the Valve Industry / see European Association for the Taps and Valves Industry (#06246)
- ♦ European Committee for Water Resources Management / see European Water Resources Association (#09085)
- ♦ European Committee of Wine Companies (#04157)
- ♦ European Committee of Woodworking Machinery Manufacturers (#04152)
- ♦ European Committee of Workers Cooperative Productive Societies / see Confédération européenne des coopératives de travail associé, des coopératives sociales et des entreprises sociales et participatives (#04541)
- ♦ European Committee of Workers' Cooperatives / see Confédération européenne des coopératives de travail associé, des coopératives sociales et des entreprises sociales et participatives (#04541)
- ♦ European Committee of Writers (inactive)
- ♦ European Committee for Young Farmers' and 4H Clubs / see Rural Youth Europe (#19007)
- ♦ European Committee for Young Farmers' Clubs Federations / see Rural Youth Europe (#19007)

♦ European Commodities Exchange 06674

Bourse de Commerce Européenne – Bolsa de Comercio Europea – Europäische Warenbörse – Borsa Europea del Commercio

SG 10 place Gutenberg, BP 70012, 67081 Strasbourg CEDEX, France. T. +33388752508.

URL: http://www.bourse-europeenne.com/

History Inaugurated 1961. Previously also referred to as *Bolsa Europea de Productos Basicos – Borsa Merci Europea – Europese Warenbeurs* and in Spanish as *Asociación de Bolsas Europeas de Comercio de Cereales.* **Aims** Offer the opportunity for players in the *cereal* sector to meet each other face to face, discuss the market's future, establish contacts and consolidate relationships of reciprocal trust. **Languages** English, French, German, Italian, Spanish. **Events** *Annual Meeting* Copenhagen (Denmark) 2021, *Annual Meeting* Berlin (Germany) 2020, *Annual Meeting* Vienna (Austria) 2019, *Annual Meeting* Rouen (France) 2018, *Annual Meeting* Brussels (Belgium) 2017.

Members Full in 12 countries:

Austria, Belgium, Czechia, Denmark, France, Germany, Italy, Netherlands, Poland, Spain, Türkiye, UK.

[2021/XF1550/**F**]

- ♦ European Communication Association (inactive)

♦ European Communication Research and Education Association (ECREA) 06675

Pres Chée de Waterloo 1151, 1180 Brussels, Belgium. E-mail: president@ecrea.eu.

Gen Sec address not obtained. E-mail: generalsecretary@ecrea.eu – info@ecrea.eu.

URL: http://www.ecrea.eu/

History 20 Sep 1997, Amsterdam (Netherlands). Officially launched, 31 Mar 2000, Brussels (Belgium). Nov 2005, merged with *European Communication Association (ECA, inactive).* Former names and other names: *European Consortium for Communications Research (ECCR)* – former (20 Sep 1997 to Nov 2005); *Consortium européen pour la recherche en communication* – former (20 Sep 1997 to Nov 2005); *Europees Consortium voor Communicatie-onderzoek* – former (20 Sep 1997 to Nov 2005). Registration: Belgium. **Aims** Promote cooperation between European researchers and research groups on communication information and *mass media.* **Structure** General Assembly (annual); Executive Board. **Finance** Members' dues. **Activities** Events/meetings; knowledge management/information dissemination. **Events** *European Communication Conference* Aarhus (Denmark) 2022, *ECREA Journalism Conference* Utrecht (Netherlands) 2022, *European Communication Conference* Braga (Portugal) 2021, *European Communication Conference* Braga (Portugal) 2020, *Conference* Vienna (Austria) 2019. **Publications** *The Role of the Mass Media in Hostile Conflicts from World War I to the War on Terror* (2013); *Towards a Sustainable Information Society: Deconstructing WSIS* (2005); *The European Information Society: A Reality Check* (2003); *Reclaiming the Media: Communication Rights and Democratic Media Roles.* Online newsletter; conference proceedings.

Members Institutional; Individual; Associate Institutional. Institutional in 30 countries:

Austria, Belgium, Bosnia-Herzegovina, Bulgaria, Cyprus, Czechia, Denmark, Estonia, Finland, France, Germany, Greece, Hungary, Ireland, Italy, Latvia, Lithuania, Netherlands, Norway, Portugal, Romania, Russia, Serbia, Slovakia, Spain, Sweden, Switzerland, Türkiye, UK, Ukraine.

Individuals in 54 countries and territories:

Albania, Australia, Austria, Belgium, Bosnia-Herzegovina, Brazil, Bulgaria, Cameroon, Canada, China, Colombia, Croatia, Czechia, Denmark, Egypt, Finland, France, Georgia, Germany, Greece, Hong Kong, Hungary, India, Iran Islamic Rep, Ireland, Israel, Italy, Jamaica, Kazakhstan, Kuwait, Lebanon, Lithuania, Malaysia, Malta, Mexico, Netherlands, North Macedonia, Norway, Peru, Philippines, Poland, Portugal, Romania, Slovenia, South Africa, Spain, Sweden, Switzerland, Türkiye, UK, Ukraine, United Arab Emirates, USA, Zimbabwe.

Associate in 16 countries:

Austria, Belgium, Croatia, Estonia, Finland, France, Norway, Poland, Romania, Russia, Slovenia, Spain, Sweden, Türkiye, UK, USA.

NGO Relations Member of: *International Federation of Communication Associations.*

[2017.06.01/XF5766/**F**]

♦ European Communications Office (ECO) 06676

Bureau européen des communications

Dir Nyropsgade 37, 4th Floor, 1602 Copenhagen, Denmark. T. +4533896300. Fax +4533896330. E-mail: eco@eco.cept.org.

URL: http://www.cept.org/eco/
History 6 May 1991. Established, on basis of a Memorandum of Understanding. *Convention for the establishment of the European Radiocommunications Office*, signed by the members of *Conférence européenne des administrations des postes et des télécommunications (CEPT, #04602)*, entered into force 1 Mar 1996. A permanent office of CEPT. Jan 2001, merged with *European Telecommunications Office (ETO, inactive)*. **Aims** Provide advice and support to CEPT and its three Committees; help it to develop and deliver its policies and decisions in an effective and transparent way. **Structure** Office Council. Headquarters based in Copenhagen (Denmark). **Languages** English. **Staff** 12.00 FTE, paid. **Finance** Sources: contributions of member/participating states. **Activities** Guidance/assistance/consulting; knowledge management/information dissemination; networking/liaising. **Events** *CEPT annual conference / CEPT Conference / Annual CEPT Conference* Montreux (Switzerland) 2009, *CEPT annual conference / CEPT Conference / Annual CEPT Conference* Strasbourg (France) 2008, *CEPT annual conference / CEPT Conference* Berlin (Germany) 2006, *CEPT annual conference / CEPT Conference / Annual CEPT Conference* Barcelona (Spain) 2005, *CEPT annual conference / CEPT Conference / Annual CEPT Conference* Nice (France) 2003. **Publications** Technical Reports; documents.
Members CEPT Administrations which have signed the ECO Convention (36):
Austria, Belgium, Bosnia-Herzegovina, Bulgaria, Croatia, Cyprus, Czechia, Denmark, Estonia, Finland, France, Germany, Greece, Holy See, Hungary, Iceland, Ireland, Italy, Latvia, Liechtenstein, Lithuania, Luxembourg, Malta, Monaco, Montenegro, Netherlands, Norway, Poland, Portugal, Romania, Slovakia, Spain, Sweden, Switzerland, Türkiye, UK.
IGO Relations Permanent office of: Committee for ITU Policy (Com-ITU); *Conférence européenne des administrations des postes et des télécommunications (CEPT, #04602)*; *Electronic Communications Committee (ECC, see: #04602)*; *European Committee for Postal Regulation (CERP, see: #04602)* (CERP). **NGO Relations** Member of (1): *European Telecommunications Standards Institute (ETSI, #08897)*.
[2022.10.11/XE0218/**E***]

- European Communications Policy Research Conference (meeting series)
- European Communities (inactive)
- European Communities Biologists Association / see European Countries Biologists Association (#06852)
- European Communities Choir / see European Union Choir (#08980)
- European Communities Trade Mark Association / see ECTA (#05341)
- European Communities Trade Mark Practitioners' Association / see ECTA (#05341)
- European Community (inactive)
- European Community of Advertising Organizations (inactive)

♦ European Community Association of Ship Brokers and Agents (ECASBA) 06677

Contact 7th Floor, Walsingham House, 35 Seething Lane, London, EC3N 4AH, UK. T. +442076233113. E-mail: generalmanager@fonasba.com.
Chairman Verenigde Nederlandse Cargadoors, Postbus 54200, 3008 JE Rotterdam, Netherlands. T. +31104020336. E-mail: mtecasbachair@fonasba.com.
URL: http://www.ecasba.com/
History 1993. Originally established 1990 as a sub-committee of *Federation of National Associations of Shipbrokers and Agents (FONASBA, #09694)*. Registration: EU Transparency Register, No/ID: 570356124662-33. **Aims** Represent the common interests of ship agents and ship brokers towards the European Union. **Structure** Advisory Panel. **Languages** English. **Staff** 1.50 FTE, paid. **Finance** Sources: members' dues. **Events** *Seminar* Brussels (Belgium) 2020, *Seminar* Brussels (Belgium) 2020, *Seminar* Brussels (Belgium) 2017.
Members in 21 countries:
Belgium, Bulgaria, Croatia, Cyprus, Denmark, Finland, France, Germany, Greece, Hungary, Ireland, Italy, Malta, Netherlands, Poland, Portugal, Slovenia, Spain, Sweden, Türkiye, UK.
NGO Relations Member of (1): *Maritime Industries Forum (MIF, no recent information)*.
[2023.02.14/XE4262/**E**]

- European Community Association of Zoos and Aquaria / see European Association of Zoos and Aquaria (#06283)
- European Community Banana Trade Association (inactive)
- European Community Biodiversity Clearing House Mechanism (inactive)
- European Community Club of Advanced Engineering for Agriculture / see European Network of Engineering for Agriculture and Environment (#07901)
- European Community Cocoa Trade Organisation (inactive)
- European Community on Computational Applications Methods in Applied Sciences / see European Committee on Computational Methods in Applied Sciences (#06644)
- European Community of Consulting Engineers (inactive)

♦ European Community of Consumer Cooperatives (EURO COOP) 06678

Communauté européenne des coopératives de consommateurs
SG Rue du Trône 4, 1000 Brussels, Belgium. T. +3222850070. Fax +3222310757. E-mail: info@eurocoop.coop.
URL: http://www.eurocoop.coop/
History 11 Jun 1957. Absorbed *European Union of Production and Wholesale Centres of Consumers' Cooperative Societies (inactive)* in 1970. Previous statutes adopted 4 Nov 1970 and amended: 12 May 1975; 2 May 1988; 4 May 1993; 3 May 1995; 12 May 1997; 1 Juin 2006. Current statutes adopted 1 Jun 2006. Secretariat in Brussels (Belgium) since 1962. EU Transparency Register: 3819438251-87. **Aims** Represent and uphold the structure and ethics of consumer cooperative enterprises at European level. **Structure** Members' Assembly (annual); Board; Ad-hoc Working Groups (3). **Languages** English, French. **Staff** 5.00 FTE, paid. **Finance** Members' dues. **Activities** Knowledge management/information dissemination; politics/policy/regulatory; events/meetings. **Events** *General Assembly* Manchester (UK) 2019, *Coop Logistics Seminar* Tampere (Finland) 2017, *General Assembly* Tampere (Finland) 2017, *European nutrition and lifestyle conference* Brussels (Belgium) 2011. **Publications** Position papers; reports; press releases.
Members National Unions, grouping over 5,000 local and regional consumer cooperatives representing 32 million consumers. Members in 19 countries:
Bulgaria, Cyprus, Czechia, Denmark, Estonia, Finland, Germany, Hungary, Iceland, Israel, Italy, Netherlands, Norway, Romania, Slovakia, Spain, Sweden, UK, Ukraine.
IGO Relations Member of: Stakeholder Advisory Group of *European Food Safety Authority (EFSA, #07287)*. Contacts with: *European Commission (EC, #06633)* through a number of advisory committees and various Directorates-General. Associate member of: *European Consumer Consultative Group (ECCG, #06771)*. **NGO Relations** Member of: *Cooperatives Europe (#04801)*; *EU Platform for Action on Diet, Physical Activity and Health (inactive)*; *European Food Sustainable Consumption and Production Round Table (European Food SCP Roundtable, #07289)*; European Retail Forum for Sustainability; *TP Organics – European Technology Platform (TP Organics, #20180)*; *Transatlantic Consumer Dialogue (TACD, #20203)*.
[2020/XD0678/**D**]

- European Community of Cooks / see Euro-Toques International (#09190)
- European Community Deafblind Secretariat / see European Deafblind Network (#06890)
- European Community Dental Students Committee / see European Dental Students Association (#06904)

♦ European Community Development Network (EuCDN) 06679

Coordinator address not obtained.
URL: http://eucdn.net/
History 1990. Former names and other names: *Combined European Bureau for Social Development (CEBSD)* – former (1990); *Oficina Europea Combinada para el Desarrollo Social* – former (1990). Registration: No/ID: 27-S-156304, Netherlands, The Hague. **Aims** Promote community and social development in Europe by: setting up exchanges of good practice, especially on participation; providing training; disseminating information/discussion material; bringing community development to the attention of policy makers. **Structure** Board of 9 members (meets 4 times a year), each with an executive role. **Languages** English, French. **Staff** 1.00 FTE, paid. **Finance** Members' dues. Budget (annual): euro 120,000. **Activities** Runs exchange projects; organizes conferences; runs training programmes; facilitates e-group on community development; promotes policy lessons from good practice in community development. **Events** *Eastern European conference* Budapest (Hungary) 2004, *Dialogue with communities* UK 2004. **Publications** *CEBSD Bulletin* (6 a year). *Including the Excluded: From Practice to Policy in European Community Development* (2005); *Alcantara – building bridges between cultures* (1999); *Neighbourhood Economy at Work* (1999); *Setting the Scene: Community-based responses to urban deprivation in five European countries* (1997); *Social Inclusion and Citizenship in Europe: The Contribution of Community Development* (1997). Books; reports. Information Services: Resource Database.
Members Partners and Associates in 19 countries:
Belgium, Bulgaria, Czechia, Denmark, Estonia, France, Germany, Hungary, Ireland, Italy, Netherlands, Norway, Poland, Romania, Slovakia, Slovenia, Spain, Sweden, UK.
NGO Relations Member of: *Social Platform (#19344)*.
[2020/XD7763/**D**]

- European Community Federation of Youth Hostel Associations / see European Union Federation of Youth Hostel Associations (#08988)
- European Community Foreign Affairs Spouses' Association / see European Union Foreign Affairs Spouses' Associations (#08991)

♦ European Community Foundation Initiative (ECFI) 06680

Europäische Bürgerstiftungs-Initiative
Coordinating Dir c/o Assn of German Foundations, Mauerstr 93, 10117 Berlin, Germany. T. +493089794757. E-mail: info@communityfoundations.eu.
URL: http://communityfoundations.eu/
History Jan 2016. Launched as an umbrella initiative for community foundations and their support organizations, conceived as a long-term project. **Aims** Strengthen community foundations in Europe by providing support for existing umbrella organizations in their respective countries. **Structure** Management Team; Advisory Group. **Languages** English, German. **Staff** Part-time. **Finance** Financing from various foundation, including: *Charles Stewart Mott Foundation*; *Robert Bosch Foundation*; Körber Foundation; Lipoid Foundation. **Activities** Training/education; events/meetings. **Events** *Conference* UK 2017. **Publications** Guides. **Members** Not a membership organization. **NGO Relations** *Worldwide Initiatives for Grantmaker Support (WINGS, #21926)*.
[2022/XM4736/**F**]

- European Community of Interests – Woodworking and Woodprocessing Machinery / see Combois (#04122)
- European Community Investment Partners (inactive)
- European Community Liaison Committee of Historians / see European Union Liaison Committee of Historians (#09000)
- European Community Network for the Implementation and Enforcement of Environmental law / see European Union Network for the Implementation and Enforcement of Environmental Law (#09005)
- European Community Network of the National Academic Recognition Information Centres / see National Academic Recognition Information Centres (#16937)
- European Community Organization of Socialist Youth / see Young European Socialists (#21989)

♦ European Community Organizing Network (ECON) 06681

Europska siet komunitneho organizovani
Main Office Námestie mládeže 587/17, 960 01 Zvolen, Slovakia. E-mail: organizing.europe@gmail.com.
URL: http://econnet.eu/
Aims Guided by the values of justice, compassion, democratic participation, and by appreciation of ethnic, racial and spiritual diversity, promote, support, and expand community organizing in Europe. **Activities** Provides training, consulting and another resources to member organizations and to other groups and NGO's wanting to implement community organizing. Organizes: exchanges among organizers and volunteers; annual meeting for training and exchange of experience and best practice. **Events** *Annual Meeting* Budapest (Hungary) 2014.
Members Full, organizations (16) in 8 countries:
Bosnia, Bulgaria, Germany, Hungary, Moldova, Poland, Slovakia, Ukraine.
Associate, organizations (2) in 2 countries:
Sweden, Ukraine.
NGO Relations Affiliate member of: *Central and Eastern European Citizens Network (CEE CN, #03689)*.
[2021/XJ0969/**F**]

- European Community on Protection of Marine Life

♦ European Community Psychology Association (ECPA) 06682

Chairwoman Alma Mater Studiorum Univ of Bologna, Viale Europa 115, 47023 Cesena FC, Italy. T. +390547338517. E-mail: ecpa.psychassociation@gmail.com.
Registered Address Grasmarkt 105 / 18 (Agora Gallery), 1000 Brussels, Belgium.
URL: http://www.ecpa-online.com/
History Former names and other names: *European Network of Community Psychologists (ENCP)* – former. **Aims** Represents a scientific and professional community strongly committed to engage with communities and to build with them social change. **Structure** Association Board, comprising President, Treasurer, Members and Past President. **Languages** English, Italian, Polish, Portuguese, Slovakian. **Staff** 25.00 FTE, voluntary. No paid staff. **Finance** Sources: members' dues. **Activities** Awareness raising; capacity building; monitoring/evaluation; research and development; research/documentation; training/education. **Events** *Conference* Bratislava (Slovakia) 2021, *European Conference on Community Psychology* Oslo (Norway) 2021, *Conference and Workshop in Community Psychology in Slovakia* Bratislava (Slovakia) 2020, *Conference* Newcastle upon Tyne (UK) 2017, *Beyond the crisis – building community and critical visions to achieve justice, fairness and well-being* Naples (Italy) 2013. **Publications** Articles. **NGO Relations** Member of (1): *European Federation of Psychologists Associations (EFPA, #07199)* (Associate member).
[2021.06.15/XJ1263/**D**]

- European Community Regional Secretariat of the World Federation of the Deaf / see European Union of the Deaf (#08985)
- European Community Sea Ports Organisation / see European Sea Ports Organisation (#08453)

♦ European Community Shipowners' Associations (ECSA) 06683

Associations d'armateurs des Communautés européennes
SG Bvd du Régent 43-44, 1000 Brussels, Belgium. T. +3225106120. E-mail: mail@ecsa.eu.
URL: http://www.ecsa.eu/
History 1965, Paris (France). Former names and other names: *Comité des associations d'armateurs du Marché commun* – former; *Committee of Shipowners' Associations of the European Communities* – former; *Comité des associations d'armateurs des Communautés européennes (CAACE)* – former; *Ausschuss der EWG-Reederverbände* – former; *Comitato delle Associazioni di Armatori delle Comunità Europee* – former; *Comité van Rederverenigingen van de Europese Gemeenschappen* – former. Registration: EU Transparency Register, No/ID: 59004966537-01, Start date: 1 Sep 2011. **Aims** Study and provide a useful forum for discussions on all matters relating to the *maritime industry* including all aspects of an EC/EU *shipping* policy; seek a common position among members and promote their policies with the authorities of the *European Union*; generally, defend the common interests of the shipping industries of EU Member States. **Structure** General Assembly (annual); Board of Directors; Secretariat; Committees; Working Groups. **Staff** 10.80 FTE, paid. **Finance** Sources: members' dues. **Activities** Advocacy/lobbying/activism; events/meetings; knowledge management/information dissemination; politics/policy/regulatory. **Events** *Annual General Assembly* Antwerp (Belgium) 2010, *Annual General Assembly* Antwerp (Belgium) 2010, *Workshop on seafarer training, recruitement and exchange of good practice* Brussels (Belgium) 2010, *Workshop on various technical, administrative and financial challenges involved in shifting to LNG* Lisbon (Portugal) 2010, *Annual General Assembly* Paris (France) 2009. **Publications** *ECSA Newsletter*. Annual Report; press releases; position papers.
Members National shipowners' associations in 19 countries:
Belgium, Cyprus, Denmark, Estonia, Finland, France, Germany, Greece, Ireland, Italy, Lithuania, Luxembourg, Malta, Netherlands, Norway, Portugal, Slovenia, Spain, Sweden.
IGO Relations Observer status with (1): *Baltic Marine Environment Protection Commission – Helsinki Commission (HELCOM, #03126)*. Recognized by: *European Commission (EC, #06633)*. **NGO Relations** Member of (2): *European Services Forum (ESF, #08469)*; *International Maritime Statistics Forum (IMSF, #14105)*. Participant of: *WATERBORNE (#20823)*.
[2022/XE0306/**E**]

♦ European Community of Students of Economics (inactive)
♦ European Community Studies Association / see European Union Studies Association

♦ European Community Studies Association (ECSA) 06684

Pres Univ Internacional de Catalunya, Fac of Humanities, Edifici Alfa, Campus Barcelona, Immaculada 22, 08017 Barcelona, Spain. T. +34932541800. Fax +34934187673. E-mail: ebanus@uic.es.
URL: http://www.uic.es/en/ecsa/

History 1987, as an umbrella association for the different associations dealing with European studies around the world. **Aims** Promote teaching and university research on European integration; develop cooperation among its members and, through them, the widest possible cooperation between universities worldwide; manage transnational programmes of research and technical assistance; disseminate information on university activities relating to teaching and research on European integration. **Structure** Board (elected for 2 years) of 5 members, chaired by President. **Languages** English, French. **Staff** None. **Finance** Grants via the Jean Monnet Programme of *European Commission (EC, #06633)*. **Activities** Organizes World Conference (every 2 years), always in Brussels (Belgium). Stimulates networks of academic cooperation. Carries out studies in the area of European integration. Builds academic networks in organizing transnational research projects. **Events** *Biennial world conference* Brussels (Belgium) 2006, *Conference on the WTO after Hong Kong* Vienna (Austria) 2006, *Biennial world conference* Brussels (Belgium) 2004, *Biennial world conference* Brussels (Belgium) 2002, *Conference on the future constitution of Europe* Vienna (Austria) 2002. **Publications** *European Union Review. East Central Europe and the European Union: From Eruope Agreements to a Member Status* (1997); *Poland and the European Union – Between Association and Membership* (1997); *Hungary – From Europe Agreement to a Member Status in the European Union* (1996); *Who's Who in European Integration Studies (in Non EU States)* (1996); *Who's Who in European Integration Studies (in EU States)* (4th ed 1995); *Federalism, Subsidiarity and Democracy in the European Union* (1994); *East-Central European States and the EC: Legal Adaptations tot the Market Economy* (1993); *Legal, Economic and Administrative Adaptations of Central European Countries to the EC* (1993).

Members Associations dealing with European studies (59) and individuals. National associations in 45 countries and territories:
Argentina, Australia, Austria, Belgium, Brazil, Bulgaria, Canada, Chile, China, Croatia, Cyprus, Czechia, Denmark, Estonia, Finland, France, Germany, Greece, Hong Kong, Hungary, India, Ireland, Israel, Italy, Japan, Korea Rep, Lithuania, Macau, Malta, Morocco, Netherlands, New Zealand, Norway, Poland, Portugal, Russia, Slovakia, Spain, Sweden, Switzerland, Taiwan, Thailand, Türkiye, UK, USA.
International organization (1):
Finnish European Studies Association (FESA). [2011.06.01/XK1944/y/**E**]

♦ European Community Studies Center / see European Union Studies Center, New York

♦ European Community University Professors in Ophthalmology (EUPO) 06685

Office Kapucijnenvoer 33, 3000 Leuven, Belgium. T. +3216332398. Fax +3216332678.
Sec address not obtained.
URL: http://www.eupo.eu/

History May 1988, Lisbon (Portugal), during congress of *European Society of Ophthalmology (SOE, #08674)*. **Aims** Promote medical education, research and patient care relating to the field of ophthalmology; maintain and raise standards of ophthalmology and in patient care. **Structure** General Assembly (annual), Council; Board. **Languages** English. **Staff** 11.00 FTE, voluntary. **Finance** Members' dues. **Activities** Training/education; events/meetings. **Events** *Course* Nice (France) 2014, *Course* Copenhagen (Denmark) 2013, *Course* Leuven (Belgium) 2012, *Course* Geneva (Switzerland) 2011, *Course* Athens (Greece) 2010.

Members Individuals (280) in 19 countries:
Austria, Belgium, Czechia, Denmark, Finland, France, Germany, Greece, Hungary, Ireland, Italy, Netherlands, Poland, Portugal, Serbia, Spain, Sweden, Switzerland, UK.

NGO Relations Close links with the monospecialist section of ophthalmology: *European Union of Medical Specialists (UEMS, #09001)*. Formal contacts with EOS. [2016/XE0741/v/**D**]

♦ European Community of Wholesale Beer Trade Associations of Member Countries of the EEC / see Association européenne des associations du commerce de gros de bière et boissons des pays de l'Europe (#02555)
♦ European Community Wholesalers and International Traders Association (inactive)
♦ European Community of Young Horticulturists (#04376)
♦ European Community Youth Orchestra / see European Union Youth Orchestra (#09024)
♦ European Company for the Chemical Processing of Irradiated Fuels (inactive)

♦ European Company Lawyers Association (ECLA) 06686

Association européenne des juristes d'entreprises (AEJE)

Managing Dir Avenue Louise 326, 1050 Brussels, Belgium. T. +32280854560. E-mail: info@ecla.eu.
URL: https://ecla.online/

History 1983, as a series of regular consultations among national associations. Formally constituted, 25 Jun 1990, on approval of articles of association. Registered in accordance with Belgian law. EU Transparency Register: 382239613871-43. **Aims** Represent members at European and international levels; create centres for study, documentation and contact to improve exchange of professional information; promote legal research. **Structure** General Assembly; Executive Board; General Manager. **Languages** English, French. **Staff** 1.50 FTE, paid. **Finance** Members' dues (annual) euro 1,000. **Activities** Organizes working sessions and conferences; contributes to seminars, courses and conferences organized by members at national level or by other international organizations. **Events** *European forum for in-house counsel* Brussels (Belgium) 2009, *European forum for in-house counsel* Brussels (Belgium) 2008, *European forum for in-house counsel* Brussels (Belgium) 2007, *European forum for in-house counsel / Conference* Brussels (Belgium) 2006, *Conference* Paris (France) 2005. **Publications** *The In-House Counsel Newsletter* (4 a year).

Members Associations (21) in 20 countries:
Austria, Belgium, Croatia, Czechia, Denmark, England, Estonia, Finland, France, Germany, Ireland, Italy, Lithuania, Norway, Poland, Portugal, Slovenia, Spain, Sweden, Wales. [2019/XD2301/**D**]

♦ European Competence Network on Mastocytosis (ECNM) 06687

Address not obtained.
URL: https://ecnm.meduniwien.ac.at/

Aims Provide the best available information for patients and doctors; provide access to important diagnostic tests for all patients; establish standards for the diagnosis and treatment of mastocytosis; establish reference centres and centres of excellence in Europe; facilitate referrals to specialists in these centres for all patients, either through doctor-doctor telenet-contact, or direct referral if required. **Structure** Board. **Events** *Annual Meeting* Basel (Switzerland) 2022, *Annual Meeting* Brno (Czechia) 2021, *Working Conference on Eosinophil Disorders and Related Syndromes* Vienna (Austria) 2021, *Annual Meeting* Vienna (Austria) 2020, *Working Conference on Mast Cell Disorders* Vienna (Austria) 2020. [2015/XJ5372/**F**]

♦ European Competition Lawyers Association (ECLA) 06688

Contact address not obtained.
URL: http://www.competitionlawyers.org/

History 2017. **Aims** Promote scientific and practical legal discussion about competition law development; allow the exchange of national and international practical experiences in competition law procedures and advocacy; connect dedicated competition lawyers so as to allow continuing professional and social relationship; provide a forum to meet and discuss. **Activities** Events/meetings; networking/liaising. **Events** *Seminar* Stockholm (Sweden) 2022, *Seminar* Madrid (Spain) 2021, *Annual Conference* Madrid (Spain) 2020, *Annual Conference* Prague (Czechia) 2019, *Annual Conference* Lisbon (Portugal) 2018. **Members** Individuals. Membership countries not specified. [2022/XM7626/v/**D**]

♦ European Competitive Telecommunications Association (ECTA) ... 06689

Office Manager Rue de Trèves 49-51, Office 5A, 1040 Brussels, Belgium. T. +3222900100. Fax +3222900105. E-mail: info@ectaportal.com.
URL: http://www.ectaportal.com/

History Jun 1998, UK. EU Transparency Register: 24627752238-32. **Aims** Assist and encourage market liberalization and competition; represent the telecommunications industry to key government and regulatory bodies; maintain a forum for networking and business development throughout Europe. **Structure** Board of Directors. **Languages** English. **Staff** 3.00 FTE, paid. **Finance** Members' dues. **Activities** Events/meetings; politics/policy/regulatory; networking/liaising; research and development. **Events** *Annual Regulatory Conference* Brussels (Belgium) 2019, *Annual Regulatory Conference* Brussels (Belgium) 2018, *Annual Regulatory Conference* Brussels (Belgium) 2014, *Conference on Single Market for Telecoms* Brussels (Belgium) 2013, *Annual Regulatory Conference* Brussels (Belgium) 2012. **Publications** *ECTA Review.*

Members Full in 23 countries:
Austria, Belgium, Bulgaria, Denmark, Finland, France, Germany, Greece, Hungary, Ireland, Italy, Latvia, Netherlands, Poland, Portugal, Russia, Serbia, Slovakia, Slovenia, Spain, Sweden, Türkiye, UK.

NGO Relations Associate member of: *European Internet Forum (EIF, #07591).* [2019.12.12/XD8308/**D**]

♦ European Complement Network (ECN) 06690

Sec Ctr Complement Inflammation/Research, Dept of Medicine, Imperial College 5N1 – 5th Floor, Commonwealth Bldg – Hammersmith Campus, London, W12 0NN, UK. T. +442083832398.
URL: http://www.ecomplement.org/

Aims Promote communication between complement *laboratories* in Europe. **Structure** Committee; Chair. **Staff** Voluntary. **Events** *European Congress on Complement in Human Disease* Madrid (Spain) 2019, *European Congress on Complement in Human Disease* Copenhagen (Denmark) 2017, *European congress on complement in human disease* Leiden (Netherlands) 2011, *European congress on complement in human disease / Congress* Visegrad (Hungary) 2009, *European congress on complement in human disease / Congress* Cardiff (UK) 2007. **Publications** Congress proceedings. **NGO Relations** Close collaboration with: *International Complement Society (#12833).* [2017/XM0710/**F**]

♦ European Complex Systems Society / see Complex Systems Society (#04418)
♦ European Compliance Organizations for Batteries / see EUCOBAT (#05576)
♦ European Composers' Forum (inactive)

♦ European Composer and Songwriter Alliance (ECSA) 06691

SG Av de la Toison d'Or 60C, 1060 Brussels, Belgium. T. +3225440333. E-mail: info@composeralliance.org.
URL: http://composeralliance.org/

History 7 Mar 2007, Brussels (Belgium). Regrouping 3 federations of composer associations: *Alliance of Popular Composer Organisations in Europe (APCOE, inactive); European Composers' Forum (ECF, inactive); Federation of Film and Audiovisual Composers of Europe (FFACE, inactive).* Registration: Belgium; EU Transparency Register, No/ID: 71423433087-91. **Aims** Defend and promote music authors' rights at national, European and international levels; serve as a platform for communication and debate among European composer federations so as to formulate shared policies and lobby for their implementation. **Structure** Assembly; Board of Directors. Committees: Popular Music (APCOE); Art and Contemporary Music (ECF); Film and Audio-visual Music (FFACE). **Languages** English. **Staff** 4.00 FTE, paid. **Finance** Sources: grants; international organizations; members' dues; sponsorship. Supported by: Creative Europe; *European Union (EU, #08967).* Annual budget: 374,128 EUR (2020). **Activities** Advocacy/lobbying/activism; awards/prizes/competitions; awareness raising; events/meetings; networking/liaising. **Events** *Creators Conference* Brussels (Belgium) 2020, *Winter Session* Brussels (Belgium) 2020, *Winter Session* Brussels (Belgium) 2019, *Autumn Session* Stockholm (Sweden) 2019, *Creators Conference* Belgrade (Serbia) 2018.

Members Composer and songwriter associations of any genre of music creation, in 26 countries:
Austria, Belgium, Croatia, Denmark, Estonia, Finland, France, Germany, Greece, Hungary, Iceland, Ireland, Italy, Luxembourg, Netherlands, North Macedonia, Norway, Poland, Portugal, Romania, Serbia, Slovenia, Spain, Sweden, Switzerland, UK.
Supportive members in 7 countries:
Austria, France, Israel, Italy, Netherlands, Switzerland, UK.

Consultative Status Consultative status granted from: *World Intellectual Property Organization (WIPO, #21593)* (Observer Status). **NGO Relations** Member of: *European Music Council (EMC, #07837); International Music Council (IMC, #14199).* Partner of: *International Council of Music Authors (#13052).* [2020.07.10/XJ0268/**D**]

♦ European Composites Industry Association (EuCIA) 06692

Contact c/o Agoria, BluePoint Brussels, Bd A Reyers 80, 1030 Brussels, Belgium. T. +3227068010. E-mail: contact@eucia.eu.
URL: http://www.eucia.eu/

History 14 Nov 1960, as *European Organization of Reinforced Plastic Associations – Composite Materials (GPRMC) – Groupement européen des plastiques renforcés – Matériaux Composites – Europäische Industriegruppe Verstärkte Kunststoffe – Verbundkunststoffe.* Became new legal entity and adopted current title, 5 Dec 2004, Edinburgh (UK). **Aims** Represent national composites associations and industry specific sectors, targeting end-segments sectors or potential product groups or processes at EU level. **Structure** General Assembly (annual); Board of Directors; General Manager. **Languages** English, French, German. **Staff** 1.00 FTE, paid. **Finance** Members' dues. Sponsoring members. **Activities** Advocacy/lobbying/activism; politics/policy/regulatory; research and development; knowledge management/information dissemination; events/meetings. **Events** *Meeting on Lightweight, Durable and Sustainable Composites* Brussels (Belgium) 2017, *Composites Europe conference* Essen (Germany) 2010, *Composites Europe conference* Stuttgart (Germany) 2009, *Annual Athens summit on global climate and energy security* Athens (Greece) 2008, *Composites Europe conference* Essen (Germany) 2008.

Members National organizations in 10 countries:
Belgium, Denmark, Finland, France, Germany, Italy, Netherlands, Norway, Türkiye, UK.
Sectorial organizations (4):
European Alliance for SMC/BMC (#05884); European Pultrusion Technology Association (EPTA, #08307); European UP/VE Resin Association (#09038); GlassFibreEurope (#10158).

IGO Relations Recognized by: *European Commission (EC, #06633); Statistical Office of the European Union (Eurostat, #19974).* **NGO Relations** Supports: *Association of Plastics Manufacturers in Europe (Plastics Europe, #02862); Conseil européen de l'industrie chimique (CEFIC, #04687)* Unsaturated Polyester and Styrene Sector Groups. Member of: *Industry4Europe (#11181).* [2020.03.10/XE3157/ty/**D**]

♦ European Composites, Plastics and Polymer Processing Platform (ECP4) 06693

Contact address not obtained. E-mail: info@ecp4.eu.
URL: https://www.ecp4.eu/

Aims Bring innovation partners together to identify opportunities for collaborative Research and Development efforts which yield industrial innovation. **Structure** Board of Directors. **Activities** Events/meetings; guidance/assistance/consulting; networking/liaising.

Members Full in 13 countries:
Austria, Belgium, Czechia, Denmark, Finland, France, Germany, Ireland, Italy, Lithuania, Netherlands, Portugal, Spain.
European Plastics Converters (EuPC, #08216); European Resilient Flooring Manufacturers' Institute (ERFMI, #08380); The European Plastic Pipes and Fittings Association (TEPPFA, #08215).

NGO Relations Member of (1): *Circular Plastics Alliance (#03936).* [2020/AA1037/y/**F**]

♦ European Compost Network (ECN) 06694

Exec Dir Im Dohlenbruch 11, 44795 Bochum, Germany. T. +492344389447. E-mail: info@compostnetwork.info.
URL: http://www.compostnetwork.info/

History within the framework of *ORBIT Association (inactive).* As of 2010, ECN and ORBIT merged and adopted new structure under current title. Current statutes adopted 2014. Registered in accordance with German law: VR 4604. EU Transparency Register: 26513411360-51. **Aims** Promote the adoption of sustainable systems for organic waste management through technological development and improvement of practices. **Structure** Board; Secretariat. **Languages** English. **Staff** 2.00 FTE, paid. **Activities** Events/meetings; guidance/assistance/consulting. **Events** *Workshop on the Road to an Urban Bioeconomy* Brussels (Belgium) 2018. **Publications** *ECN News. ECN ISSUE Papers.* Quality manual. Information Services: Shares knowledge and information through: E-mail; exchange of reports and articles; workshops; website including web-based discussion fora.

European Comprehensive Cancer
06694

alphabetic sequence excludes
For the complete listing, see Yearbook Online at

Members Biowaste organizations, enterprises, universities research institutions, municipal authorities and environmental non-profit organizations in 30 countries:
Austria, Belgium, Bulgaria, Cyprus, Czechia, Denmark, Estonia, Finland, France, Germany, Greece, Hungary, Ireland, Italy, Latvia, Lithuania, Luxembourg, Malaysia, Netherlands, Norway, Poland, Portugal, Romania, Russia, Serbia, Slovenia, Spain, Sweden, Switzerland, UK.
NGO Relations Member of: *European Environmental Bureau (EEB, #06996).* [2019/XF6885/**F**]

♦ European Comprehensive Cancer Centre Alliance / see Descartes Cancer Consortium (#05041)
♦ European Computer Competence Certificate Foundation / see European Digital Competence Certificate Foundation
♦ European Computer Driving Licence Foundation / see ICDL Europe (#11052)
♦ European Computer Leasing and Trading Association (inactive)
♦ European Computer Manufacturers Association / see Ecma International (#05288)
♦ European Computer Measurement Association (inactive)
♦ European Computing Services Association (inactive)

♦ European Concept for Accessibility Network (EuCAN) 06695

Coordinator c/o Info-Handicap, Av de la gare 65, L-1611 Luxembourg, Luxembourg. T. +352621359820.
URL: http://www.eca.lu/
History Preparatory work started May 1985. First draft called 'European Concept for Accessibility' presented 1996. Coordination task transferred from Dutch CCPT to Luxembourg Info-Handicap, 1999. Also known under the acronym *ECA*. Functions as an independent network without legal status. **Aims** Facilitate networking and promote the concepts of accessibility and design for all. **Structure** Open network. **Languages** English. **Staff** No paid staff. **Finance** No budget. Publications financed via ad-hoc sponsoring. **Publications** Manuals.
Members Full in 21 countries:
Austria, Belgium, Czechia, Finland, France, Germany, Greece, Hungary, Ireland, Israel, Italy, Lithuania, Luxembourg, Netherlands, Norway, Portugal, Serbia, Spain, Sweden, Switzerland, UK. [2016.10.20/XJ8522/**F**]

♦ European Concert Hall Organisation (ECHO) 06696

SG S A Palais des Beaux-Arts de Bruxelles, Rue Ravenstein 23, 1000 Brussels, Belgium. T. +3225078431. Fax +3225078515. E-mail: echo@bozar.be.
URL: https://www.concerthallorganisation.eu/
History 1994. Registration: Crossroads Bank for Enterprises, No/ID: 0473.482.734, Belgium. **Aims** Serve as a forum for exchange of ideas, experiences and ambitions. **Structure** General Assembly; Management Board. Other Boards (2): Financial Board; Artistic Board. Departments (8). **Languages** English. **Staff** 3-4 in each concert hall. **Finance** Sources: members' dues. **Activities** Capacity building; events/meetings; projects/programmes; training/education. **Events** *The Art of Music Education* Hamburg (Germany) 2022, *The Art of Music Education* Hamburg (Germany) 2020, *The Art of Music Education* Hamburg (Germany) 2018, *The Art of Music Education* Hamburg (Germany) 2016, *The Art of Music Education* Hamburg (Germany) 2014.
Members Concert halls and arts centres 11 countries:
Austria, Belgium, France, Germany, Greece, Hungary, Luxembourg, Netherlands, Spain, Sweden, UK.
NGO Relations Member of (2): *Culture Action Europe (CAE, #04981); European Alliance for Culture and the Arts (#05866).* [2021/XD6068/**D**]

♦ European Concrete Paving Association (EUPAVE) 06697

Communication and Office Manager Bd du Souverain 68, Bte B-13, 1170 Brussels, Belgium. T. +3226455231. E-mail: info@eupave.eu.
URL: http://www.eupave.eu/
History 2007. Registration: Banque Carrefour des Entreprises, No/ID: 0896.192.304, Start date: 4 Dec 2007, Belgium; EU Transparency Register, No/ID: 76295483387-66. **Aims** Promote all aspects of cement and concrete products to *transport* infrastructure and related areas, in particular the specific contributions of cement and concrete to road safety, fuel consumption, congestion reduction and sustainable construction. **Structure** General Assembly; Board; Technical and Promotion Committee. **Languages** English. **Staff** 1.00 FTE, paid; 1.00 FTE, voluntary. **Finance** Sources: meeting proceeds; members' dues. Annual budget: 120,000 EUR. **Activities** Advocacy/lobbying/activism; knowledge management/information dissemination. **Events** *International Symposium on Concrete Roads* Krakow (Poland) 2023, *International Symposium on Concrete Roads* Berlin (Germany) 2018, *International Symposium on Concrete Roads* Prague (Czech Rep) 2014, *International symposium on concrete roads* Seville (Spain) 2010, *International symposium on concrete roads* Lisbon (Portugal) 1998. **Publications** *EUPAVE Newsletter.* Technical brochures; position papers.
Members Full (23) and Associate in 14 countries:
Austria, Belgium, France, Germany, Italy, Netherlands, Poland, Portugal, Slovenia, Spain, Switzerland, Türkiye, UK, USA.
Included in the above, 2 organizations listed in this Yearbook:
CEMBUREAU – The European Cement Association (CEMBUREAU, #03634); European Ready Mixed Concrete Organization (ERMCO, #08330).
NGO Relations Member of (2): *European Union Road Federation (ERF, #09014); Industry4Europe (#11181).* [2022/XJ6753/y/**D**]

♦ European Concrete Platform / see Concrete Europe (#04433)

♦ European Concrete Societies Network (ECSN) 06698

Contact c/o Österreichische Bautechnik Vereinigung, Karlsgasse 5, 1040 Vienna, Austria. E-mail: office@bautechnik.pro.
URL: http://www.ecsn.net/
History 1996, Wiesbaden (Germany). **Aims** Encourage cooperation between members and thereby promote development of concrete technology and use of concrete in Europe. **Structure** Board; Chairman; Secretariat. **Finance** Members' dues. **Activities** Knowledge management/information dissemination; networking/liaising; awards/prizes/competitions. **Events** *Meeting* Dublin (Ireland) 2010, *European symposium on service life and serviceability of concrete structures* Espoo (Finland) 2006.
Members National organizations in 11 countries:
Austria, Belgium, Czechia, Finland, Germany, Ireland, Italy, Netherlands, Norway, Sweden, UK. [2019/XF5979/**F**]

♦ European Confederation of Agriculture (inactive)
♦ European Confederation of Agronomist Associations (#04538)
♦ European Confederation of Associations of Manufacturers of Insulated Wires and Cables / see Europacable (#05743)
♦ European Confederation of Auxiliary Occupations in the Wine Trade (inactive)
♦ European Confederation of Biologists / see Confederation of European Biopathologists (#04520)

♦ European Confederation of Business Centre Associations (EUROCBCA) 06699

Sec Avenue Louise 149/24 – 12th floor, 1050 Brussels, Belgium. T. +3225357536. Fax +3225357537.
URL: http://www.eurocbca.com/
History 2007. Constitution signed 2008, Spain. **Aims** Represent owners and providers of business centres and services offices in Europe. **Structure** Board of Directors, comprising President, Treasurer, Secretary and 2 Vocals.
Members Full in 6 countries:
Belgium, France, Germany, Italy, Spain, UK. [2016/XJ5321/**D**]

♦ European Confederation of Care Home Organizations / see European Confederation of Care-Home Organizations (#06700)

♦ European Confederation of Care-Home Organizations (ECHO) 06700

Confédération européenne des propriétaires de maisons de repos
General Manager European Office, Avenue Marnix, 30 VI Floor, 1000 Brussels, Belgium. T. +3222896230. Fax +3222896235. E-mail: echo@echo-eu.com.
URL: http://www.echo-eu.com/
History 8 Apr 1992, Brussels (Belgium). Registered in accordance with Belgian law. Also referred to as *European Confederation of Care Home Organizations (ECHO).* **Aims** Promote the dignity of private establishments for the *elderly* in European Union countries; support interests of members, their residents and staff, through dialogue with national governments, European Commission, media, social services, health authorities and other appropriate individuals and organizations; promote education and training of all working on care in private homes for the elderly; support and encourage practical means of developing and improving techniques and practices in these establishments. **Structure** General Assembly (annual). Board, consisting of 2 representatives per member country (only one having right to vote), includes President, Vice-President, Secretary and Treasurer. **Languages** English, French. **Staff** Voluntary. **Finance** Members' dues. **Activities** Exchange of ideas, information and experience; biennial congress and other meetings, exhibitions and events. **Events** *General Meeting* Baarn (Netherlands) 2011, *Congress* Valencia (Spain) 2011, *General Assembly* Barcelona (Spain) 2006, *General Assembly* Hannover (Germany) 2006, *General Assembly* Helsinki (Finland) 2006.
Members National associations in 11 countries:
Belgium, Bulgaria, Finland, France, Germany, Greece, Italy, Netherlands, Poland, Portugal, UK.
NGO Relations Member of: *European Health Chamber; Health First Europe (HFE, #10881).* [2015/XD3304/**D**]

♦ European Confederation of Catholic Rural People's Schools (no recent information)

♦ European Confederation of Conservator-Restorers' Organisations (ECCO) 06701

Confédération européenne des organisations de conservateurs-restaurateurs
Office Admin Rue Coudenberg 70, 1000 Brussels, Belgium. E-mail: tprjtmun@gmail.com – info@ecco-eu.org.
URL: http://www.ecco-eu.org/
History 14 Oct 1991, Brussels (Belgium). Previously also known in German as *Europäische Vereinigung der Restauratorenverbände.* Registered in accordance with Belgian law. **Aims** Promote conservation-restoration of works of cultural heritage; promote and develop a high level of training, research and practice in the field; work toward legal recognition of professional status at national and European level; ensure representation of the profession and defence of its interests with European and international organizations. **Structure** General Assembly (annual); Committee; Bureau; Working Groups. **Languages** English, French. **Staff** 1.00 FTE, paid. **Finance** Members' dues. **Activities** Advocacy/lobbying/activism; training/education. **Events** *Annual General Assembly* Berlin (Germany) 2019, *Annual General Assembly* Lisbon (Portugal) 2013, *Annual General Assembly* Brussels (Belgium) 2006, *Annual General Assembly* Brussels (Belgium) 2005, *Annual General Assembly* Brussels (Belgium) 2004. **Publications** *EECO 20th Anniversary Special Printed Edition* (2012); *Competences for Access to the Conservation-Restoration Profession* (2011); *ECCO Professional Guidelines III* (2004); *Acteurs du Patrimoine Européen et Législation (APEL)* (2001) – survey of the legal and professional responsabilities of conservator-restorers as regards the other parties involved in the preservation and conservation of cultural heritage. Reports.
Members Full (22) and Associate (3), representing over 5,000 members in EU countries and EFTA countries. Full in 19 countries:
Austria, Belgium, Bulgaria, Croatia, Denmark, Finland, France, Germany, Greece, Hungary, Ireland, Italy, Norway, Portugal, Slovakia, Slovenia, Spain, Sweden, Switzerland.
International organization:
Associate members in 3 countries:
Czechia, Malta, Romania.
NGO Relations Member of (2): *European Council of Liberal Professions (#06828); European Heritage Alliance 3.3 (#07477).* In liaison with technical committees of: *European Network for Conservation/Restoration Education (ENCoRE, #07883).* [2019/XD4130/y/**D**]

♦ European Confederation of Corn Growers / see European Confederation of Maize Production (#06711)
♦ European Confederation of Corn Production / see European Confederation of Maize Production (#06711)
♦ European Confederation of Deacons (no recent information)

♦ European Confederation of Directors' Associations (ecoDa) 06702

Confédération Européenne des Associations d'Administrateurs
Dir Gen Av des Arts 41, 1040 Brussels, Belgium. T. +3222315811. E-mail: contact@ecoda.org.
URL: http://www.ecoda.org/
History Dec 2004, by Institute of Directors (UK), Association des administrateurs (Belgium), and Institut Français des Administrateurs (France). Registered in accordance with Belgian law. EU Transparency Register: 37854527418-86. **Aims** Promote the interests of supervisory board members. **Structure** General Assembly; Board of Directors; Committees (3). **Languages** English. **Staff** 2.00 FTE, paid. **Activities** Events/meetings; training/education; advocacy/lobbying/activism. **Events** *Conference on Board Governance and Emerging Risks in the C21* Brussels (Belgium) 2015, *Joint Conference on Striking the Right Balance in Corporate Governance and Shareholder Engagement* Brussels (Belgium) 2015, *Conference on Building Corporate Governance Reform for Long Term Sustainable Growth* Madrid (Spain) 2015, *Annual Conference* Brussels (Belgium) 2009. **Publications** *ECODA Newsletter.* Position papers; studies; reports.
Members Full: associations representing individual Company Directors in 20 countries:
Albania, Belgium, Croatia, Estonia, Finland, France, Germany, Italy, Latvia, Lithuania, Luxembourg, Netherlands, Norway, Portugal, Romania, Slovenia, Spain, Sweden, Switzerland, UK.
Affiliate in 3 countries:
Albania, North Macedonia, UK.
Corporate associates in 3 countries:
Belgium, Denmark, UK.
NGO Relations Member of: *Global Network of Director Institutes (GNDI, #10486).* [2019.02.12/XJ0661/**E**]

♦ European Confederation of Distributors, Producers and Importers of Medicinal Plants (inactive)
♦ European Confederation for the Employment of Handicapped Persons (no recent information)
♦ European Confederation of Equipment Distributors (no recent information)
♦ European Confederation of Executives and Managerial Staff / see CEC European Managers (#03623)
♦ European Confederation of Fire Protection Associations / see Confederation of Fire Protection Associations (#04552)
♦ European Confederation of Flax and Hemp (#04546)
♦ European Confederation of the Footwear Industry (#04544)
♦ European Confederation of Free Trade Unions in the Community / see European Trade Union Confederation (#08927)

♦ European Confederation of Fuel Distributors (ECFD) 06703

Confédération européenne des négociants en combustibles et carburants – Europese Confederatie van Brandstoffenhandelaars
Contact c/o Brafco, Rue Léon Lepage 4, 1000 Brussels, Belgium. T. +3225024200. E-mail: jmattart@fuel-distributors.eu.
Gen Sec address not obtained.
URL: http://www.ecfd.be/
History 2003. Former names and other names: *European Conference of Fuel Distributors* – former (2003 to 2014). Registration: EU Transparency Register, No/ID: 48067211204-09. **Aims** Defend the interest of members at European level, safeguarding the independence, resilience and profitability of businesses supplying petroleum products for households and motorists of the European Union. **Structure** General Assembly; Executive Committee. **Activities** Advocacy/lobbying/activism; events/meetings; publishing activities; research/documentation.
Members National federations of heating oil distributors and independent petrol station owners (5) in 5 countries:
Austria, Belgium, France, Germany, UK. [2022.05.09/XM3458/**F**]

♦ European Confederation of Hardware Wholesale Trade (inactive)

♦ European Confederation of Inclusive Enterprises (EuCIE) **06704**

Contact address not obtained.
URL: http://www.eucie.org/

History 2017, Brussels (Belgium). Constitutive Charter signed at *European Parliament (EP, #08146)*. Former names and other names: *European Confederation of Inclusive Enterprises employing persons with disabilities* – full title. Registration: EU Transparency Register, No/ID: 017234935125-06, Start date: 3 Jul 2019. **Aims** Co-build an inclusive European society through sustainable *employment* for people with *disabilities*. **Structure** Board. **Activities** Advocacy/lobbying/activism; events/meetings. **Events** *Congress* Valencia (Spain) 2017.
Members Full in 3 countries:
France, Germany, Spain. [2020/XM6600/**D**]

♦ European Confederation of Inclusive Enterprises employing persons with disabilities / see European Confederation of Inclusive Enterprises (#06704)
♦ European Confederation for Independent and Local Radios and Televisions (no recent information)

♦ European Confederation of Independent Trade Unions (CESI) **06705**

Confédération européenne des syndicats indépendants – Confederación Europea de Sindicatos Independientes – Europäische Union der Unabhängigen Gewerkschaften – Confederazione Europea dei Sindacati Indipendenti

SG Av des Arts 19AD, 1000 Brussels, Belgium. T. +3222821870. Fax +3222821871. E-mail: info@cesi.org.
URL: http://www.cesi.org/

History 1990. Constitution adopted 26 Nov 1992, Brussels (Belgium) at 1st Congress. Most recent constitution adopted by 8th Congress, 2020, Brussels. Registration: Banque-Carrefour des Entreprises, Belgium; EU Transparency Register, No/ID: 32738888445-74. **Aims** Represent trade union organizations in EU member states, EU accession candidates and countries in the scope of the Council of Europe; protect and promote better working and living conditions; stimulate and encourage further development of social dimension of the EU. **Structure** Congress (every 4 years); Board; Praesidium. Sectoral Committees (Trade Councils); Horizontal Commissions; General secretariat in Brussels (Belgium). *Europe Academy* acts as internal research and training institution for members. *CESI Youth* represents the interests of youth organizations and young affiliates of member organizations. **Languages** English, French, German, Italian, Spanish. **Staff** 8.00 FTE, paid. **Activities** Advocacy/lobbying/activism; events/meetings; networking/liaising; politics/policy/regulatory; projects/programmes; research/documentation; training/education. **Events** *Youth Forum* Brussels (Belgium) 2016, *Beyond the crisis – developing sustainable alternatives* Brussels (Belgium) 2009, *Congress* Brussels (Belgium) 2008, *Congress* Brussels (Belgium) 2000. **Publications** Conference proceedings; research; work and project outcomes.
Members European umbrella trade union organizations and national trade union organizations in 26 countries and territories:
Albania, Austria, Belgium, Bosnia, Finland, France, Germany, Hungary, Ireland, Italy, Kosovo, Latvia, Lithuania, Luxembourg, Malta, Montenegro, Netherlands, North Macedonia, Poland, Portugal, Romania, Serbia, Slovakia, Spain, Switzerland, Ukraine.
Consultative Status Consultative status granted from: *Council of Europe (CE, #04881)* (Participatory Status).
IGO Relations Relations with: *European Committee of the Regions (CoR, #06665)*; *European Agency for Safety and Health at Work (EU-OSHA, #05843)*; *European Commission (EC, #06633)*; *European Economic and Social Committee (EESC, #06963)*; *European Foundation for the Improvement of Living and Working Conditions (Eurofound, #07348)*; *European Parliament (EP, #08146)*; *ILO (#11123)*; *OECD (#17693)*. **NGO Relations** Member of: *European Movement International (EMI, #07825)*; *European Policy Centre (EPC, #08240)*; *European Sunday Alliance (#08856)*; *European Women's Lobby (EWL, #09102)*; *European Youth Forum (#09140)*. [2022.05.24/XD5459/ty/**D**]

♦ European Confederation of Independent Winegrowers (ECIW) **06706**

Confédération Européenne des Vignerons Indépendants (CEVI)

Main Office Immeuble Le Chanzy, 18 Avenue Winston Churchill, 94220 Charenton-le-Pont, France. T. +33153663299. E-mail: info@cevi-eciw.eu.
URL: http://www.cevi-eciw.eu/

History 2002. Founded by French, Swiss and Portuguese federations. **Aims** Defend and promote the *profession* of independent winegrower within a European and international framework. **Languages** English, French.
Members National federations of independent winegrowers in 11 countries:
Bulgaria, Canada, France, Hungary, Italy, Luxembourg, Montenegro, Portugal, Slovenia, Spain, Switzerland.
NGO Relations Observer to: *Wine in Moderation (WIM, #20967)*. [2022/XJ8692/**D**]

♦ European Confederation of Institutes of Internal Auditing (ECIIA) .. **06707**

Confédération européenne des instituts d'audit interne

Address not obtained.
URL: http://www.eciia.eu/

History 1982. Registration: Banque-Carrefour des Entreprises, No/ID: 0474.676.329, Start date: 7 Jan 2001, Belgium; EU Transparency Register, No/ID: 849170014736-52, Start date: 21 Oct 2014. **Aims** Support the position of internal control professionals in the EU and member countries; promote the application of the global institute of Internal Audit Standards and Code of Ethics to all internal audit activity in the public and the private sector. **Structure** General Assembly. Management Board. **Languages** English. **Events** *Conference* Brussels (Belgium) 2022, *Conference* Estoril (Portugal) 2020, *Conference* Luxembourg (Luxembourg) 2019, *Conference* Madrid (Spain) 2018, *Conference* Basel (Switzerland) 2017. **Publications** *European Governance* – magazine.
Members National Institutes of Internal Audit (35):
Armenia, Austria, Belgium, Bosnia-Herzegovina, Bulgaria, Croatia, Cyprus, Czechia, Denmark, Estonia, Finland, France, Germany, Greece, Hungary, Iceland, Ireland, Israel, Italy, Latvia, Lithuania, Luxembourg, Morocco, Netherlands, North Macedonia, Norway, Poland, Portugal, Serbia, Slovenia, Spain, Sweden, Switzerland, Türkiye, UK.
NGO Relations Member of: *Federation of European and International Associations Established in Belgium (FAIB, #09508)*. [2021/XD5132/**D**]

♦ European Confederation of International Trading Houses Associations (CITHA) **06708**

Headquarters Avenue des Nerviens 85 – 3rd floor, 1040 Brussels, Belgium. E-mail: info@citha.eu.
Germany c/o BDEx, Am Weidendamm 1A, 10117 Berlin, Germany. T. +493072625793. Fax +493072625794.

History 1955, as *Stockholm Club*. Formal body founded, 1971, Milan (Italy), with the title *Confederation of International Trading Houses Associations (CITHA) – Confederación de Asociaciones de Empresas de Comercio Internacional*. Formally constituted 1973, London (UK). Previously also referred to as *Coordinating Committee of International Trading Houses Associations*. **Aims** Represent international trading houses' associations and their members; promote and justify liberalization of trade; act as coordinating body for national associations; support studies and information exchange on technical problems. **Structure** General Assembly (annual); Board (meeting at least annual). **Languages** Dutch, English, French, German. **Staff** 2.00 FTE, paid. **Finance** Members' dues: euro 1,200. **Activities** Conventions; symposia. East-West Trade Committee. **Events** *Annual General Assembly* Paris (France) 2010, *Annual General Assembly* Basel (Switzerland) 2009, *Annual General Assembly* Sopot (Poland) 2008, *Annual General Assembly* Madrid (Spain) 2007, *Annual General Assembly* Istanbul (Turkey) 2006.
Members International trading house associations; Associate members: enterprises engaged in international trade. Members in 9 countries:
Austria, France, Germany, Hungary, Italy, Spain, Switzerland, Türkiye, UK.
Consultative Status Consultative status granted from: *ECOSOC (#05331)* (Ros C); *UNCTAD (#20285)* (General Category). [2019/XD9219/**D**]

♦ European Confederation of Iron and Steel Industries / see European Steel Association (#08835)
♦ European Confederation of Jesuit Alumni / see Confédération européenne des Anciens et Anciennes Elèves des établissements de la Compagnie de Jésus (#04536)
♦ European Confederation of Jesuit Alumni/ae (#04536)
♦ European Confederation of Junior Enterprises / see Junior Enterprises Europe (#16169)
♦ European Confederation of Language Centres in Higher Education (#04540)

♦ European Confederation of Laryngectomees (CEL) **06709**

Confédération européenne des laryngectomisés – Confederación Europea de los Laringectomizados – Europäische Konföderation der Laryngektomierten – Confederazione Europea dei Laringectomizzati – Europese Confederatie van de Gelaryngectomeerden

SG Elper Höhe 7a, 45701 Herten, Germany. T. +49236642732. E-mail: neukoe@web.de.
Pres Thomas Mann Str 40, 53111 Bonn, Germany. T. +4922833889302.

History 14 Jun 1965, Milan (Italy). Previously referred to as *Confederation of European Laryngectomees – Konföderation der Europäischen Laryngektomierten*. Statutes amended 22 Sept 2006. Registered in accordance with French law. **Aims** Promote rehabilitation work in the areas of speech training, medical and health care and vocational training; familiarize the European public with the interests and problems of laryngectomees. **Structure** Delegates' Meeting. Executive Committee, comprising President, Vice-President, Secretary-General, Treasurer and 2 Assessors. **Languages** German. **Staff** Voluntary. **Activities** Exchange of experiences on all organizational levels as well as contacts with the relevant executive and legislative bodies of Europe. **Events** *European Congress* Crikvenica (Croatia) 2006, *European Congress* Dresden (Germany) 2003, *European Congress* Bredsten (Denmark) 1997, *Congress / International Conference* Munich (Germany) 1993, *Congress / International Conference* Amsterdam (Netherlands) 1990.
Members Organizations and member associations (26) in 19 countries:
Armenia, Austria, Belgium, Croatia, Denmark, Finland, France, Germany, Greece, Iceland, Italy, North Macedonia, Norway, Poland, Portugal, Slovenia, Spain, Sweden, Switzerland. [2014/XD2129/**D**]

♦ European Confederation of Local Intermediate Authorities **06710**

Confédération Européenne des Pouvoirs Locaux Intermédiaires (CEPLI)

Secretariat Rue Montoyer 24, 1000 Brussels, Belgium. T. +3222317141. Fax +3222317003. E-mail: contact@cepli.eu.
SG address not obtained.
URL: http://www.cepli.eu/

History 2008, by a charter. Constitutive meeting Jul 2008, Avignon (France). Constitution ratified, Jun 2011, Rome (Italy). **Aims** Increase involvement and participation in the European decision-making process; reinforce the consistency and visibility of activities in the European area; facilitate cooperation between intermediary local authorities; establish continuous exchange of information and good practices between regional authorities. **Structure** Political Conference. Bureau, comprising President, Premier Vice-President, Secretary-General and Treasurer. Secretariat. Technical Working Groups. **Languages** English, French. **Events** *Political Conference* Ploiesti (Romania) 2013, *Political Conference* Brussels (Belgium) 2012, *Political Conference* Rome (Italy) 2011, *Political Conference* Berlin (Germany) 2010, *Political Conference* Caceres (Spain) 2009.
Members Unions of local authorities of 11 countries and territories:
Bulgaria, Flanders, France, Germany, Greece, Hungary, Italy, Poland, Romania, Spain, Wallonia.
Associate members (2):
Arco Latino (#01094); *Partenalia (#18223)*. [2015/XJ5874/**D***]

♦ European Confederation of Local Public Sector Energy Distribution Companies / see European Federation of Local Energy Companies (#07156)

♦ European Confederation of Maize Production **06711**

Confédération Européenne de la Production de Maïs (CEPM)

Permanent Secretariat 23-25 av de Neuilly, 75116 Paris, France. T. +33147234832. Fax +33140709344.
Contact Square de Meeus 21, 1050 Brussels, Belgium. T. +3222303868.
URL: http://www.cepm.org/

History 1985, as *European Confederation of Corn Growers – Confédération européenne des producteurs de maïs (CEPM)*. Originally also referred to in English as *European Confederation of Corn Production*. **Aims** Represent and defend the interests of all or part of maize chains: corn, maize silage, maize seeds and sweet corn. **Structure** Assembly (annual); Board. **Languages** English, French. **Finance** Members' dues. **Activities** Events/meetings; advocacy/lobbying/activism. **Events** *General Assembly* Paris (France) 2006. **Publications** *Corn Market*; *Newsletter CEPM*. Activity reports.
Members Full in 10 countries:
Bulgaria, France, Germany, Hungary, Italy, Poland, Portugal, Romania, Slovakia, Spain. [2019.07.09/XD3439/**D**]

♦ European Confederation of Major Musical Associations (inactive)
♦ European Confederation of Medical Experts in the Assessment and Compensation of Physical Injury (#04543)

♦ European Confederation of Medical Mycology (ECMM) **06712**

Pres c/o Congress Care, PO Box 440, 5201 AK 's Hertogenbosch, Netherlands. E-mail: president@ecmm.info – office@ecmm.info.
Gen Sec address not obtained. E-mail: secretary@ecmm.info.
Registered Address c/o Steiger-Zumstein & Partners AG, Nauenstr 49, 4052 Basel BS, Switzerland.
URL: https://www.ecmm.info/

History Statutes adopted 25 Nov 1993, Paris (France); updated 9 Jun 1997, Salsomaggiore (Italy), 27 Oct 2007, Turin (Italy), and 24 Apr 2017 (Vienna (Austria). Former names and other names: *Confédération européenne de mycologie médicale (CEMM)* – former. Registration: No/ID: CHE-114.577.192, Switzerland; Start date: 7 Feb 1997, France. **Aims** Promote the science and practice of all aspects of medical mycology throughout Europe; initiate, facilitate and coordinate research and other scientific activities on an international basis throughout Europe; facilitate the discussion and dissemination of the results of international collaborative research; collaborate with other organizations with similar objectives. **Structure** Council (meets annually); Executive Committee. **Languages** English. **Staff** Voluntary. **Finance** Sources: members' dues. **Activities** Events/meetings. **Events** *International Congress on Trends in Medical Mycology (TIMM)* Athens (Greece) 2023, *ECMM Congress* Aberdeen (UK) 2021, *International Congress on Trends in Medical Mycology (TIMM)* Aberdeen (UK) 2021, *ECMM Congress* Nice (France) 2019, *International Congress on Trends in Medical Mycology (TIMM)* Nice (France) 2019.
Members National societies in 22 countries:
Austria, Belgium, Croatia, Czechia, Finland, France, Germany, Greece, Hungary, Ireland, Israel, Italy, Netherlands, Poland, Portugal, Romania, Russia, Serbia, Spain, Sweden, Türkiye, UK.
Regional member:
Nordic Society for Medical Mycology (NSMM, #17417).
NGO Relations Partner of (1): *Global Action For Fungal Infections (GAFFI, #10166)*. Affiliated with (1): *International Society for Human and Animal Mycology (ISHAM, #15181)*. [2021/XD4365/**D**]

♦ European Confederation of Modern Pentathlon (ECMP) **06713**

SG Prospekt Mira 146-160, Moscow MOSKVA, Russia, 129366.
URL: http://www.pentathloneu.org/

History 19 Apr 1991. **Aims** Develop Modern Pentathlon in Europe. **Structure** General Assembly; Executive Board. **Languages** English. **Staff** 1.00 FTE, voluntary. **Finance** Through budget of *World Penthathlon (UIPM, #21720)*. **Activities** Sporting activities. **Events** *Congress* Sofia (Bulgaria) 2014, *Congress* Warsaw (Poland) 2005.
Members National federations who are members of UIPM in 35 countries:
Armenia, Austria, Belarus, Bulgaria, Croatia, Cyprus, Czechia, Denmark, Estonia, Finland, France, Georgia, Germany, Great Britain, Greece, Hungary, Ireland, Israel, Italy, Kosovo, Latvia, Lithuania, Moldova, Monaco, Netherlands, Poland, Portugal, Romania, Russia, Slovakia, Spain, Sweden, Switzerland, Türkiye, Ukraine.
NGO Relations *World Penthathlon (UIPM, #21720)*. [2018.09.27/XM0503/**D**]

♦ European Confederation of National Associations of Manufacturers of Insulated Wire and Cable / see Europacable (#05743)

♦ European Confederation of National Bakery and Confectionery Organizations (CEBP) **06714**

Sec House of the European Economy, Rue Jacques de Lalaing 4, 1040 Brussels, Belgium. E-mail: office@cebp.eu.
SG C/ Raimundo Fernandez Villaverde 6-61-izq, 28003 Madrid, Spain. T. +34915346996. E-mail: secgen@cebp.eu.
URL: http://www.cebp.eu/

History 6 Apr 1960. Founded as *Association des organisations nationales de la boulangerie et de la pâtisserie de la CEE (AONBP)*. Name subsequently changed to *Confédération des organisations nationales de la boulangerie, pâtisserie, glacerie, chocolaterie, confiserie de la CEE (CEBP)*, then *Association des organisations nationales de la boulangerie, de la pâtisserie, de la confiserie, de la chocolaterie artisanales de la CEE* and then to listed title. The organization still retains its acronym *'CEBP'*. Registration: Belgium. **Aims** Coordinate the activities of member organizations and represent its members with the institutions of the European Community; promote scientific research and technological progress in the fields involved, through exchange of information, experience and documentation. **Structure** General Assembly (annual); Board of 4 members; Secretariat. **Languages** English, French, German, Spanish. **Activities** Events/meetings; advocacy/lobbying/activism; networking/liaising. **Events** *General Assembly* Madrid (Spain) 2003, *General Assembly* Brussels (Belgium) 2002, *General Assembly* Spain 1996, *General Assembly* Spain 1995, *General Assembly* Brussels (Belgium) 1994. **Publications** *CEBP Bulletin on News in the Countries*; *CEBP Express Update on EU Legislation*.
Members National organizations in 14 countries:
Austria, Belgium, Denmark, Finland, France, Germany, Greece, Hungary, Luxembourg, Netherlands, Romania, Spain, Sweden, Switzerland.
IGO Relations Recognized by: *European Commission (EC, #06633)*. **NGO Relations** Member of: *SMEunited (#19327)*. [2020/XE0152/**E**]

♦ European Confederation of National Syndicates and Professional Associations of Paediatricians / see European Academy of Paediatrics (#05811)
♦ European Confederation of Nautical Industries (inactive)

♦ European Confederation of Neuropathological Societies (Euro-CNS) 06715

Secretariat Academic Medical Ctr, Univ Amsterdam, Meibergdreef 9, 1105 AZ Amsterdam, Netherlands. E-mail: office.euro.cns@gmail.com.
Sec Dept Neuropathology and Pathology, Sheffield Univ Medical School, Neuropathology – 'E' Floor, Royal Hallmashire Hosp, Sheffield, S10 2JF, UK. T. +441142712949. Fax +441142711711.
URL: http://www.euro-cns.org/
History 1993. **Aims** Improve quality of care of patients with neurological diseases by setting and maintaining high standards of training and practice in neuropathology throughout Europe. **Structure** Council; Executive Committee. **Languages** English. **Staff** 2.00 FTE, paid. **Finance** Members' dues. **Activities** Training/education; events/meetings. **Events** *European Congress of Neuropathology* Odense (Denmark) 2021, *European Congress of Neuropathology* Odense (Denmark) 2020, *European Congress of Neuropathology* Bordeaux (France) 2016, *European Congress of Neuropathology* Edinburgh (UK) 2012, *European Congress of Neuropathology* Athens (Greece) 2008. **Publications** *Clinical Neuropathology* (6 a year) – official journal.
Members National societies in 16 countries:
Austria, Belgium, Bulgaria, France, Germany, Greece, Hungary, Ireland, Italy, Netherlands, Poland, Portugal, Romania, Slovenia, Spain, Switzerland, Türkiye, UK.
Regional organizations (2):
Baltic Association of Neuropathologists (BAN, #03099); *Scandinavian Society of Neuropathology (#19113)*.
NGO Relations Subsection of Section of Pathology of: *European Union of Medical Specialists (UEMS, #09001)*. Member of: *Federation of European Neuroscience Societies (FENS, #09522)*. [2019.02.13/XD6835/y/**D**]

♦ European Confederation of the Office Furniture, Machines and Accessories Trade (inactive)

♦ European Confederation of Outdoor Employers (EC-OE) 06716

Communications Manager Wolfshaegen 180, 3040 Huldenberg, Belgium. E-mail: info@ec-oe.eu – admin@ec-oe.eu.
URL: http://ec-oe.eu/
History Current statutes adopted Mar 2019. Registration: Crossroads Bank for Enterprises, No/ID: 0806.394.850, Start date: 27 Jun 2008, Belgium; EU Transparency Register, No/ID: 787572614995-24, Start date: 24 Nov 2014. **Aims** Look after the interests of entrepreneurs established within the European Union that professionally offer and execute outdoor activities and related activities and that offer guidance to the participants of these activities; represent, promote commercial outdoor activities, both to the public at large as to national and supra national authorities. **Structure** Annual General Meeting; Board of Directors. **Activities** Advocacy/lobbying/activism; knowledge management/information dissemination; networking/liaising.
Members Full in 10 countries:
Belgium, Czechia, France, Germany, Greece, Ireland, Netherlands, Portugal, Spain, Switzerland.
Associate in 3 countries:
Estonia, Hungary, Lithuania. [2022.10.19/XM8774/**D**]

♦ European Confederation of Paint, Printing Ink and Artists' Colours Manufacturers' Associations / see Conseil européen de l'industrie des peintures, des encres d'imprimerie et des couleurs d'art (#04688)

♦ European Confederation of Pest Control Associations 06717

Confédération européenne des associations de pesticides appliqués (CEPA)
Dir Gen Seringenstraat 37, 1950 Kraainem, Belgium. T. +3227313281 – +322(32475989198. Fax +3227315843.
URL: http://www.cepa-europe.org/
History 1974. **Aims** Be the principal representative of the European pest management industry towards the European and international institutions; contribute to the scientific development of products, methods and processes resulting in the destruction of parasites and harmful pests in all (non-agricultural) spheres; encourage the investigation and study of all problems concerning the destruction of pests by organizing cooperation and exchanges between European and international bodies, governments and departments of general interest; contribute to the professional training development in the framework of its activity. **Structure** General Assembly. Officers: President; Vice-President; Treasurer; Director General. **Languages** English, French. **Staff** 2.00 FTE, paid. **Finance** Members' dues. Industry sponsorship. **Activities** Promotion of the benefits pest management brings to health and the environment; organization of industry training; collation of industry data; coordination of external and internal communication of the industry; development of technical positions on emerging issues; organization of industry events. **Events** *EUROPEST conference* Budapest (Hungary) 2010, *European pest management day meeting / General Assembly* London (UK) 2007, *General Assembly* Dublin (Ireland) 2006, *General Assembly* Venice (Italy) 2005, *General Assembly* Berlin (Germany) 2004.
Members Full national trade member associations in 15 countries:
Austria, Belgium, Bulgaria, Czechia, France, Germany, Hungary, Ireland, Italy, Netherlands, Poland, Portugal, Spain, Switzerland, UK.
Companies in 6 countries:
Estonia, Finland, Greece, Latvia, Lithuania, Sweden.
Associate in 2 countries:
France, Germany. [2014/XD6797/**D**]

♦ European Confederation of Pharmaceutical Entrepreneurs (EUCOPE) 06718

Confédération européenne des entrepreneurs pharmaceutiques
SG Rue Marie de Bourgogne 58, 1000 Brussels, Belgium. T. +3228426982. Fax +3228426983. E-mail: office@eucope.org.
URL: http://www.eucope.org/
History 2008, Brussels (Belgium). Registration: Banque Carrefour des Entreprises, No/ID: 0807.963.676, Start date: 25 Nov 2008, Belgium; EU Transparency Register, No/ID: 87600691525-93, Start date: 15 Apr 2009. **Aims** Promote companies and associations active in research, development, production and distribution of pharmaceutical products and enhance their scientific, technical, economic and legal objectives. **Structure** Executive Board; Working Groups. **Members** Companies. Membership countries not specified. **NGO Relations** Member of (2): *EU Health Coalition*; *European Alliance for Cardiovascular Health (EACH, #05863)*. [2022.05.10/XJ4662/**D**]

♦ European Confederation for Physical Therapy (inactive)
♦ European Confederation for Plant Protection Research (inactive)

♦ European Confederation of Police (EuroCOP) 06719

Head of Office Rue Principale 59a, L-5480 Wormeldange, Luxembourg. T. +352434961. Fax +35243496133. E-mail: contact@eurocop-police.org.
URL: https://eurocop.org/
History Nov 2002, Røskilde (Denmark). Set up by merger of *Union internationale des syndicats de police (UISP, inactive)* and *Standing Committee of Police in Europe (SCOPE, inactive)*. Registration: EU Transparency Register, No/ID: 303115848497-82, Start date: 30 Dec 2022. **Aims** Promote, defend and develop the police profession and the role of the police service as a civil, democratically controlled public body; assist member organizations in relation to issues affecting employment conditions and duties of police officers and police services of Europe. **Structure** Congress (every 5 years); Committee; Executive Committee; Secretariat. **Languages** English. **Staff** 1.50 FTE, paid. **Finance** Sources: subscriptions. Annual budget: 300,000 EUR. **Activities** Events/meetings; guidance/assistance/consulting; knowledge management/information dissemination; politics/policy/regulatory. **Events** *Spring Meeting* Gibraltar 2022, *Autumn Meeting* Torremolinos (Spain) 2022, *Autumn Meeting* Edinburgh (UK) 2021, *Spring Meeting* Luxembourg 2021, *Congress* Luxembourg 2020. **Publications** *Newsletter* (4 a year).
Members National organizations (32), representing about 300,000 individuals, in 23 countries and territories:
Belgium, Czechia, Denmark, Finland, Gibraltar, Greece, Iceland, Ireland, Italy, Kosovo, Latvia, Lithuania, Luxembourg, Malta, Netherlands, Northern Ireland, Norway, Portugal, Slovakia, Spain, Sweden, Switzerland, UK.
Consultative Status Consultative status granted from: *Council of Europe (CE, #04881)* (Participatory Status).
NGO Relations Member of (3): *European Trade Union Confederation (ETUC, #08927)*; *International Council of Police Representative Associations (ICPRA, #13063)*; *NGO Committee on Disarmament, Peace and Security, New York NY (#17106)*. [2023/XD9121/**D**]

♦ European Confederation of Political Science Associations (ECPSA) 06720

Secretariat c/o Univ Osnabrück, Seminarstr 33, FB 1 – Sozialwissenschaften, 49074 Osnabrück, Germany. E-mail: secretariat.ecpsa@gmail.com.
URL: http://www.ecpsa.org/
History Nov 2007, Berlin (Germany). **Aims** Promote the discipline of political science throughout Europe. **Structure** Executive Committee. **Events** *Annual General Meeting* Valencia (Spain) 2008.
Members Full in 19 countries:
Bosnia-Herzegovina, Croatia, Finland, France, Germany, Greece, Hungary, Lithuania, Norway, Poland, Portugal, Romania, Russia, Serbia, Slovenia, Spain, Sweden, Switzerland, Türkiye.
NGO Relations Member of: *European Alliance for the Social Sciences and Humanities (EASSH, #05885)*. [2017/XM2979/**D**]

♦ European Confederation of Primary Care Paediatricians (ECPCP) 06721

Confédération Européenne de Pédiatrie Ambulatoire (CEPA)
Pres 11 quai Général Sarrail, 69006 Lyon, France.
URL: http://www.ecpcp.eu/
History 2009. Founded as an evolution of *European Society of Ambulatory Pediatrics (ESAP, inactive)*. Registration: France. **Aims** Advocate the role of paediatricians as primary care doctors for children from conception to adulthood through good medical practice as well as through health education and promotion of children and adolescents, taking their families and social environment into account; promote paediatric primary care. **Structure** General Assembly; Executive Bureau; Executive Committee. **Languages** English. **Finance** Members' dues. **Activities** Health care; advocacy/lobbying/activism; research/documentation; training/education. **Events** *Spring Meeting* Helsinki (Finland) 2022, *General Assembly* 2021, *Extraordinary General Assembly* Madrid (Spain) 2020, *Spring Meeting* Bratislava (Slovakia) 2019, *Autumn Meeting* Lyon (France) 2019.
Members Paediatricians (over 30,000) from 22 paedriatric societies in 18 countries:
Austria, Croatia, Cyprus, Czechia, Finland, France, Germany, Hungary, Israel, Italy, Latvia, Lithuania, Luxembourg, Portugal, Slovakia, Slovenia, Spain, Switzerland.
IGO Relations *WHO (#20950)* Copenhagen. **NGO Relations** *European Academy of Paediatrics (EAP, #05811)*; *European Paediatric Association (EPA/UNEPSA, #08124)*; Global Consortium for Paediatric Education (GCPEC). [2022/XM6654/v/**D**]

♦ European Confederation of Private Employment Agencies / see World Employment Federation Europe (#21377)

♦ European Confederation of Psychoanalytic Psychotherapies (ECPP) 06722

Vice-Pres address not obtained.
Pres address not obtained.
URL: http://ecpp.org/
History 13 Jul 2003, Lviv (Ukraine). Registered in accordance with Austrian law. **Aims** Bring together all psychoanalytic psychotherapists and psychotherapeutic organizations based on the concepts of transference and resistance. **Structure** General Meeting (every 2 years). Board, including President, at least 2 Vice-Presidents, Treasurer and Secretary. Committees (3): Certification and Accreditation; Executive; Ethics. **Events** *Congress* Vienna (Austria) 2018, *General Assembly* Kiev (Ukraine) 2010. **Members** Organizations; Individuals. Membership countries not specified. **NGO Relations** Member of: *European Association for Psychotherapy (EAP, #06176)*. [2016/XJ5285/**D**]

♦ European Confederation of Public Sector Energy Distribution Companies / see European Federation of Local Energy Companies (#07156)
♦ European Confederation of Pulp, Paper and Board Industries (inactive)
♦ European Confederation of Real Estate Agents (inactive)
♦ European Confederation of Retail Tobacconists / see European Confederation of Tobacco Retailers (#06725)
♦ European Confederation for Retail Trade (inactive)
♦ European Confederation of Roller Skating (#04550)

♦ European Confederation of Search and Selection Associations (ECSSA) 06723

SG Av du Port 86C, Box 302, 1000 Brussels, Belgium. T. +49228916111. Fax +49228916151. E-mail: info@ecssa.org.
URL: http://www.ecssa.org/
History 2004. Founded by the French, German and Italian associations of Executive Recruitment Consultants. **Aims** Develop the *Recruitment* and Search and Selection industry on a European level through professional ethics and standards; become a dynamic forum for networking and exchange of information and views between members; promote interests of the industry among different European organizations. **Structure** Chairman; Vice-Chairmen; Secretary General. **Languages** English. **Staff** No permanently employed staff.
Members National organizations (7) in 7 countries:
Belgium, France, Germany, Italy, Luxembourg, Spain, UK. [2020.06.24/XM3091/**D**]

♦ European Confederation of the Shoe Retailers Associations (inactive)

♦ European Confederation of Soil Science Societies (ECSSS) 06724

Pres c/o HEPIA, Route de Presinge 150, 1254 Jussy, Switzerland.
URL: https://soilscience.eu/
History Sep 2004, Freiburg (Germany). Constitution adopted 2006. Statutes updated: 2018. Registration: EU Transparency Register, No/ID: 083729347629-95, Start date: 15 Sep 2022. **Aims** Foster collaboration and cooperation amongst national societies of soil science in Europe and amongst European soil scientists in all branches of soil sciences and their applications; give support to the above in the pursuit of their activities. **Structure** Council; Executive Committee. **Languages** English. **Staff** None. **Finance** Sources: meeting proceeds. **Activities** Events/meetings. **Events** *EUROSOIL Congress* Geneva (Switzerland) 2021, *EUROSOIL Congress* Geneva (Switzerland) 2020, *EUROSOIL Congress* Istanbul (Turkey) 2016, *EUROSOIL congress* Bari (Italy) 2012, *EUROSOIL congress / EUROSOIL* Vienna (Austria) 2008.
Members Presidents of national organizations in 43 countries:
Albania, Armenia, Austria, Azerbaijan, Belarus, Belgium, Bosnia-Herzegovina, Bulgaria, Croatia, Cyprus, Czechia, Denmark, Estonia, Finland, France, Georgia, Germany, Greece, Hungary, Iceland, Ireland, Italy, Latvia, Lithuania, Luxembourg, Malta, Moldova, Netherlands, North Macedonia, Norway, Poland, Portugal, Romania, Russia, Serbia, Slovakia, Slovenia, Spain, Sweden, Switzerland, Türkiye, UK, Ukraine.
IGO Relations *European Commission (EC, #06633)* (Research). **NGO Relations** Member of (1): *International Union of Soil Sciences (IUSS, #15817)* (Regional). [2022/XM1541/**D**]

♦ European Confederation of Spirits Producers / see spiritsEUROPE (#19921)
♦ European Confederation of Sport and Health (no recent information)
♦ European Confederation of Telemedical Organizations in Dermatology (inactive)

♦ European Confederation of Tobacco Retailers 06725

Confédération européenne des détaillants en tabacs (CEDT) – Europäischer Bund der Tabakeinzelhändler

Contact Rue Montoyer 31, 1000 Brussels, Belgium. T. +3227721305. Fax +3227724401. E-mail: info@cedt.eu.
SG Federazione Italiana Tabaccai, Via Leopoldo Serra 32, 00153 Rome RM, Italy. T. +396585501. E-mail: fit@tabaccai.it.
URL: https://www.cedt.eu/index.php?VPPage=home

History 2 Oct 1963, Vienna (Austria). Founded as *European Federation of Tobacco Retail Organizations – Fédération européenne des organisations des détaillants en tabacs (FEODT)*. Restructured, 1970, with adoption of current English title and with French title *Confédération européenne des organisations des détaillants en tabacs*. Sometimes also referred to as *European Confederation of Retail Tobacconists (ECRT) – Europäische Vereinigung der Tabakwaren-Einzelhändlersverbände*. A grouping of the type *European Economic Interest Grouping (EEIG, #06960)* since 1999. Registration: Banque-Carrefour des Entreprises, No/ID: 0466.774.787, Start date: 19 Jul 1999, Belgium. **Aims** Promote commercial interests of tobacco retailers in Europe; cooperate closely with all organizations that can contribute positively to the benefit of these retailers and their clients; stimulate national tobacco retail trade organizations; follow developments relevant to the trade, within and outside the European Union; make proposals and recommendations at national and European level; encourage exchange of economic and technical information; support organizations of smokers' interests. **Structure** General Assembly (annual), in the presence of the Central Board (President, Vice-President, Secretary and Treasurer) and 2 official representatives of national trade organizations. Working groups. Secretariat in Brussels (Belgium). **Languages** English, French. **Staff** 3.00 FTE, paid. **Finance** Members' dues. **Activities** Monitors European legislative activity; provides information to the press and to members. **Events** *General Assembly* Vienna (Austria) 1996, *European conference* Amsterdam (Netherlands) 1995, *General Assembly* Vienna (Austria) 1987. **Publications** Circulars to members.
Members National organizations in 6 countries:
France, Greece, Italy, San Marino, Spain, Switzerland.
IGO Relations Recognized by: *European Commission (EC, #06633).* [2021/XD0760/**D**]

♦ European Confederation for Trade in Paint, Wall- and Floorcoverings (inactive)
♦ European Confederation of Upper Rhine Universities / see Eucor – The European Campus (#05578)

♦ European Confederation of Watercolour Societies (ECWS) 06726

Coordinator c/o Ass Italiana Acquerellisti, Via Ciardi n 25, 20148 Milan MI, Italy. E-mail: info@acquerello-aia.it – info@ecws.eu.
URL: http://www.ecws.eu/

History 14 Mar 1998. **Aims** Internationally promote the *art* of watercolour *painting*; foster cooperation among national and regional watercolour societies; promote the artistic activities of member societies. **Structure** Council (meets annually). **Languages** English. **Staff** 0.50 FTE, voluntary. **Finance** No budget. **Activities** Events/meetings. **Events** *Symposium* Palma (Spain) 2020, *Symposium* Haapsalu (Estonia) 2019, *Symposium* Krakow (Poland) 2018, *Symposium* Salamanca (Spain) 2017, *Symposium* Avignon (France) 2016. **Publications** Exhibition catalogue.
Members Associations (15) in 13 countries:
Belgium, Denmark, Estonia, Finland, France, Germany, Iceland, Ireland, Italy, Norway, Poland, Spain, Sweden. [2021.02.22/XJ5373/**D**]

♦ European Confederation of the Wholesale Footwear Trade (inactive)
♦ European Confederation of the Wholesale Leather Trade (inactive)
♦ European Confederation of Wholesalers in Painting, Earth and Wall Sheeting (inactive)
♦ European Confederation of Woodworking Industries (#04545)
♦ European Confederation of Worker Cooperatives, Social Cooperatives and Social and Participative Enterprises (#04541)
♦ European Confederation of Workers' Cooperatives, Social Cooperatives Participative Enterprises / see Confédération européenne des coopératives de travail associé, des coopératives sociales et des entreprises sociales et participatives (#04541)
♦ European Confederation of Young Entrepreneurs / see Young Entrepreneurs for Europe (#21982)
♦ European Confederation of Youth Club Organizations / see European Confederation of Youth Clubs (#06727)

♦ European Confederation of Youth Clubs (ECYC) 06727

Confédération européenne des organisations des centres de jeunes

Main Office Rue des Tanneurs 186, 1000 Brussels, Belgium. E-mail: ecyc@fcjmp.be.
Representative at UNESCO Féd française des MJC, 15 rue de la Condamine, 75017 Paris, France.
URL: http://www.ecyc.org/

History Sep 1976, Copenhagen (Denmark). Former names and other names: *European Confederation of Youth Club Organizations* – alias. Registration: EU Transparency Register, No/ID: 541150616964-09. **Aims** Promote close cooperation, particularly socio-cultural, among non-governmental youth club centre organizations in Europe; increase social awareness and international understanding of all those involved, and specifically promote active programmes; promote understanding of socio-political processes and encourage active involvement of young people in their own communities. **Structure** General Assembly; Bureau. **Languages** English, French. **Staff** 2.00 FTE, paid; 5.00 FTE, voluntary. **Finance** Members' dues. Other sources: European Commission; European Youth Foundation. **Activities** Projects/programmes; training/education; events/meetings; research and development; networking/liaising. **Events** *General Assembly and Conference* Antwerp (Belgium) 2008, *General Assembly and Conference* Luxembourg 2007, *General Assembly and Conference* Sibiu (Romania) 2007, *General Assembly and Conference* Vienna (Austria) 2006, *General Assembly and Conference* Hamburg (Germany) 2005. **Publications** *ECYC News Bulletin* (6 a year). Manuals; research projects.
Members National associations of youth clubs, totalling 18,000 youth clubs with over 3.5 million individual members in the age group 10-25 years. Full in 20 countries and territories:
Armenia, Austria, Azerbaijan, Belgium, Cyprus, Denmark, Finland, Flanders, Hungary, Iceland, Ireland, Luxembourg, Norway, Romania, Russia, Spain, Sweden, Switzerland, UK, Wales.
Consultative Status Consultative status granted from: *Council of Europe (CE, #04881)* (Participatory Status).
IGO Relations *UNESCO (#20322).* Special links with: *European Commission (EC, #06633).* Regular relations with: *European Youth Centres (EYCs, #09138); European Youth Foundation (EYF, #09141).* **NGO Relations** Member of: *European Youth Forum (#09140).* [2022/XD7453/**D**]

♦ European Confederation of Youth Travel Organizations (inactive)
♦ European Conference on Advances in Databases and Information Systems (meeting series)

♦ European Conference for Aero-Space Sciences (EUCASS) 06728

Sec Chaussée De Waterloo 72, 1640 St-Genesius-Rode, Belgium.
Pres address not obtained.
URL: http://www.eucass.eu/

History Registration: Banque-Carrefour des Entreprises, No/ID: 0882.078.804, Start date: 27 Jun 2006, Belgium. **Aims** Improve the vitality of scientific communication, the quality of technical activities, and stimulate exchanges between European scientists and engineers. **Events** *EUCASS : European Conference for Aerospace Sciences* Lille (France) 2021, *EUCASS : European Conference for Aerospace Sciences* Madrid (Spain) 2019, *EUCASS : European Conference for Aerospace Sciences* Milan (Italy) 2017, *EUCASS : European Aerospace Conference* Krakow (Poland) 2015, *EUCASS : European Conference for Aerospace Sciences* Munich (Germany) 2013. **Publications** *EUCASS Science News Bulletin.* **NGO Relations** Member of: *Federation of European and International Associations Established in Belgium (FAIB, #09508); Initiative for Science in Europe (ISE, #11214); International Astronautical Federation (IAF, #12286).* Partners include: *Council of European Aerospace Societies (CEAS, #04882); EUROMECH – European Mechanics Society (#05713); European Aeronautics Science Network (EASN, #05835); European Committee on Computational Methods in Applied Sciences (ECCOMAS, #06644); European Physical Society (EPS, #08207); European Research Community on Flow, Turbulence and Combustion (ERCOFTAC, #08361); Von Karman Institute for Fluid Dynamics (VKI, #16182).* [2021/XJ8716/**F**]

♦ European Conference on Agriculture and Rural Development in China (ECARDC) 06729

Secretariat Fac of Technology, Delft Univ, PO Box 5015, 2600 GA Delft, Netherlands. E-mail: ecardc@gmail.com.
URL: http://www.ecardc.org/

Aims Provide an international forum to meet, discuss and share information and experiences about China's rural development among scholars, development agencies, international donors, and professionals in development aid. **Structure** Steering Committee; Partner Institutions. **Finance** Sponsored by: *European Alliance for Asian Studies (#05861).* **Events** *Conference* China 2015, *ECARDC Conference* Tianjin (China) 2015, *ECARDC Conference / Conference* Würzburg (Germany) 2013, *Conference* Aarhus (Denmark) 2011, *ECARDC conference* Aarhus (Denmark) 2011. [2013/XM4029/**E**]

♦ European Conference on Applications of Polar Dielectrics (meeting series)

♦ European Conference of Arab Horse Organizations (ECAHO) 06730

Exec Sec Na Blatech 242, 277 11 Libis, Czechia. T. +420602876396. E-mail: office@ecaho.org.
Registered Office Goethestr 61, 9008 St Gallen, Switzerland.
URL: http://ecaho.org/

History Registration: Swiss Civil Code, No/ID: CHE-283 245 416, Switzerland. **Structure** Annual General Meeting; Executive Committee; Commissions (3): EAHSC, EAHSpC, EAHRIC; Committees. **Activities** Awards/prizes/competitions; training/education. **Events** *Annual General Meeting* Abu Dhabi (United Arab Emirates) 2022, *Annual General Meeting* Brussels (Belgium) 2021, *Annual General meeting* Paris (France) 2020, *Annual General Meeting* Rome (Italy) 2019, *Annual General Meeting* Munich (Germany) 2018. **Publications** *ECAHO Bulletin.*
Members Full in 29 countries:
Austria, Bahrain, Belgium, Czechia, Denmark, Egypt, France, Germany, Hungary, Iran Islamic Rep, Israel, Italy, Jordan, Kuwait, Morocco, Netherlands, Norway, Oman, Palestine, Poland, Qatar, Russia, Saudi Arabia, Spain, Sweden, Switzerland, Syrian AR, UK, United Arab Emirates.
Associate (Observers) in 8 countries:
Iran Islamic Rep, Lebanon, Libya, Morocco, Poland, Russia, Slovakia, Tunisia. [2020.08.18/XJ8285/**C**]

♦ European Conference on Argumentation (meeting series)
♦ European Conference of Associations of Telecommunications Industries (inactive)

♦ European Conference of Binational/Bicultural Relationships (ECB) . 06731

Fédération européenne des couples bi-nationaux/bi-culturelles – Europäische Konferenz der Binationalen/Bikulturellen Beziehungen

Contact Verband binationaler Familien und Partnerschaften, Ludolfusstr 2-4, 60487 Frankfurt-Main, Germany. T. +49697137560. Fax +49697075092. E-mail: frankfurt@verband-binationaler.de.
Contact 11 Villa Curial, 75019 Paris, France.
URL: http://www.ecbn.eu/

History Statutes adopted, 6 May 1990, Frankfurt-Main (Germany); revised, 13 Sep 1998, Zurich (Switzerland). Registered in accordance with German law.
Members Associate members in 5 countries:
Austria, France, Germany, Netherlands, Switzerland.
NGO Relations Member of: *European Coordination for Foreigners' Right to Family Life (COORDEUROP, #06794).* [2014/XG7312/**D**]

♦ European Conference on Chemistry and the Environment (meeting series)

♦ European Conference on Christian Education (ECCE) 06732

Conférence européenne sur l'éducation chrétienne (CEEC)

Pres address not obtained.
URL: http://www.ecceweb.org/

History 1968, Boldern (Switzerland), in link with the former *World Council of Christian Education (WCCE, inactive)* in Europe. Statutes amended, Apr 1992, Schiers (Switzerland). Revised 2004. **Aims** Serve as a forum for the exchange of ideas, experiences and models, as well as encourage developments in the fields of Sunday School and Christian Education. **Structure** Assembly (every 3 years, with triennial European conference). Steering Group (meets annually), comprising 5 representatives plus a Treasurer of the 5 European regions, including President, Vice-President and Secretary. Regions (5): British Isles; Northern Europe; Latin countries; Middle Europe; Eastern Europe. **Languages** English. **Staff** Voluntary. **Finance** Members' conference fees. **Events** *Conference* Broxbourne (UK) 2016, *Weaving the future* Helsinki (Finland) 2013, *Conference* Järvenpää (Finland) 2013, *Conference* Paris (France) 2010, *Triennial conference / Conference* St Pölten (Austria) 2007.
Members Individuals in 27 countries:
Austria, Azerbaijan, Belarus, Belgium, Bulgaria, Czechia, Denmark, Estonia, Finland, France, Germany, Hungary, Ireland, Italy, Latvia, Lithuania, Netherlands, Norway, Poland, Portugal, Romania, Russia, Slovakia, Spain, Sweden, Switzerland, UK. [2018/XF5713/v/**F**]

♦ European Conference of Christian Radios (no recent information)
♦ European Conference on Clinical Haemorheology (meeting series)
♦ European Conference on Computer Supported Cooperative Work (meeting series)
♦ European Conference on Computer Vision (meeting series)
♦ European Conference on Conflict Prevention / see Global Partnership for the Prevention of Armed Conflict (#10538)
♦ European Conference on Controlled Fusion and Plasma Physics (meeting series)
♦ European Conference on Cooperatives (meeting series)
♦ European Conference on Craft and Small Enterprises (meeting series)
♦ European Conference on Cyber Warfare and Security (meeting series)
♦ European Conference of Defence and the Environment (meeting series)
♦ European Conference on Digital Libraries / see International Conference on Theory and Practice of Digital Libraries (#12887)
♦ European Conference on Domestic Violence (meeting series)
♦ European Conference on Donor Health and Management (meeting series)
♦ European Conference on Electronics Reliability in Electrical and Electronic Components and Systems (meeting series)
♦ European Conference of Engineering Societies of Western Europe and the United States of America (inactive)
♦ European Conference on Few- and Several-Body Problems in Nuclear Physics (meeting series)
♦ European Conference on Flood Risk Management (meeting series)
♦ European Conference on Fluid-Particle Separation (meeting series)
♦ European Conference of Fuel Distributors / see European Confederation of Fuel Distributors (#06703)
♦ European Conference on Fungal Genetics (meeting series)
♦ European Conference on Games Based Learning (meeting series)
♦ European Conference on Heat Treatment (meeting series)
♦ European Conference on Heat Treatment and Surface Engineering (meeting series)
♦ European Conference on the Impact of Artificial Intelligence and Robotics (meeting series)
♦ European Conference of the Industry of Electrical Capacitors (inactive)

♦ European Conference on Information Systems (ECIS) 06733

Contact c/o AIS, PO Box 2712, Atlanta GA 30301-2712, USA.
URL: http://aisel.aisnet.org/ecis/

Structure Standing Committee. **Events** *Conference* Istanbul (Turkey) 2016, *Conference* Münster (Germany) 2015, *Digital work, digital life* Tel Aviv (Israel) 2014, *Conference* Utrecht (Netherlands) 2013, *Conference* Barcelona (Spain) 2012. **Publications** Conference proceedings available since 2000. **Members** Membership countries not specified. **NGO Relations** Sponsored by: *Association for Information Systems (AIS, #02645).* [2015/XF7047/c/**F**]

♦ European Conference on Innovation and Entrepreneurship (meeting series)
♦ European Conference on Integrated Optics (meeting series)

♦ European Conference Justitia et Pax / see Conference of European Justice and Peace Commissions (#04596)
♦ European Conference on Knowledge Management (meeting series)
♦ European Conference of Landscape Architecture Schools / see European Council of Landscape Architecture Schools (#06826)
♦ European Conference on Laser Interaction with Matter (meeting series)
♦ European Conference on e-Learning (meeting series)
♦ European Conference on Management Leadership and Governance (meeting series)
♦ European Conference on Mental Health (meeting series)
♦ European Conference of Ministers of Transport / see International Transport Forum (#15725)
♦ European Conference on Mixing (meeting series)
♦ European Conference on Molecular Electronics (meeting series)

♦ European Conference of National Ethics Committees (COMETH) . . . 06734

Conférence européenne des comités nationaux d'éthique

Contact Bioethics Unit – DG I Human Rights and Rule of Law, Council of Europe, 67075 Strasbourg CEDEX, France. T. +33388412268 – +33388412220.
URL: http://www.coe.int/bioethics/

History Founded as *Standing Conference of European Ethics Committees.* Previously also referred to as *European Standing Conference of European National Ethics Committees.* **Aims** Promote cooperation between national ethics committees (or similar bodies) set up in Council of Europe Member States; help countries wishing to set up a national ethics committee; promote public debate on ethical issues raised by progress in the fields of biology, medicine and public health. **Structure** Standing Bureau. Secretariat provided by Bioethics Unit of Council of Europe. **Languages** English, French. **Staff** 3.00 FTE, paid. **Activities** Networking/liaising; events/meetings; research/documentation. **Events** *Biennial Meeting* Berlin (Germany) 2007, *Biennial Meeting* Dubrovnik (Croatia) 2005, *Biennial Meeting* Strasbourg (France) 2003, *Biennial Meeting* Paphos (Cyprus) 2001, *Biennial Meeting* Strasbourg (France) 2000.
Members Representatives of national bioethics committees (or equivalent) in 47 countries:
Albania, Andorra, Armenia, Austria, Azerbaijan, Belgium, Bosnia-Herzegovina, Bulgaria, Croatia, Cyprus, Czechia, Denmark, Estonia, Finland, France, Georgia, Germany, Greece, Hungary, Iceland, Ireland, Italy, Latvia, Liechtenstein, Lithuania, Luxembourg, Malta, Moldova, Monaco, Montenegro, Netherlands, North Macedonia, Norway, Poland, Portugal, Romania, Russia, San Marino, Serbia, Slovakia, Slovenia, Spain, Sweden, Switzerland, Türkiye, UK, Ukraine. [2014.06.01/XF3119/F]

♦ European Conference on Optical Communication (meeting series)
♦ European Conference on Organized Films (meeting series)
♦ European Conference of Phaleristic Societies (meeting series)

♦ European Conference on Politics and Gender (ECPG) 06735

Address not obtained.
URL: https://ecpg.eu/

History 2009, Belfast (UK). Registration: Charity, Switzerland. **Aims** Offer a platform for exchange and dialogue about how understanding gender is central to understand politics and where diversity and plurality in analytical perspectives and methodologies is enhanced. **Activities** Awards/prizes/competitions; events/meetings. **Events** *Conference* Amsterdam (Netherlands) 2019, *Conference* Amsterdam (Netherlands) 2019, *Conference* Lausanne (Switzerland) 2017, *Conference* Uppsala (Sweden) 2015, *Conference* Barcelona (Spain) 2013. **Publications** *European Journal of Politics and Gender (EJPG).* [2019/AA0796/c/E]

♦ European Conference of Postal and Telecommunications Administrations (#04602)

♦ European Conference of Promoters of New Music (ECPNM) 06736

Union européenne des organisateurs de musique nouvelle – Europäische Konferenz der Veranstalter Neuer Musik

SG c/o Gaudeamus Muziekweek, Loevenhoutsedijk 301, 3552 XE Utrecht, Netherlands. T. +31308200111.
URL: http://www.ecpnm.com/

History 1981. **Aims** Promote contacts and cooperation between organizers – on local, national and international levels – of events of music of the 20th and 21st century with the main focus on music composed after 1950. **Structure** General Assembly (annual); Executive Committee. **Finance** Members' dues. **Activities** Networking/liaising; events/meetings. **Events** *Annual General Assembly* Rattenberg (Austria) 2010, *General Assembly* Gothenburg (Sweden) 2009, *Annual General Assembly* Cagliari (Italy) 2008, *Annual General Assembly* Oslo (Norway) 2006, *Extraordinary general assembly* Salzburg (Austria) 2006. **Publications** *News Bulletin* (12 a year); *Calendar of Events* (annual). Brochure.
Members Full: corporate bodies; Extraordinary: interested persons and groups such as musicians, musicologists, journalists, editors and others. Members in 33 countries and territories:
Albania, Austria, Belgium, Bulgaria, Croatia, Czechia, Denmark, Estonia, Finland, France, Germany, Greece, Hungary, Ireland, Italy, Kosovo, Latvia, Lithuania, Luxembourg, Netherlands, North Macedonia, Norway, Poland, Portugal, Romania, Russia, Serbia, Slovakia, Spain, Sweden, Switzerland, UK, Ukraine.
Included in the above, 4 organizations listed in this Yearbook:
Calouste Gulbenkian Foundation; European Live Electronic Centre (EULEC); Internationales Musikinstitut Darmstadt (IMD); Mediterranean Music Centre, Lamia.
Associate in members in 15 countries:
Austria, Bulgaria, France, Germany, Greece, Hungary, Ireland, Latvia, Netherlands, Portugal, Russia, Sweden, Switzerland, UK, Ukraine.
NGO Relations Associate member of: *International Music Council (IMC, #14199).* Member of: *European Festivals Association (EFA, #07242); European Music Council (EMC, #07837).* [2018/XF2361/y/F]

♦ European Conference for Protestant Church Music (#05753)
♦ European Conference of Psychoanalysts (meeting series)
♦ European Conference of Radio and Electronic Equipment Associations (inactive)
♦ European Conference on Religion and Peace / see European Council of Religious Leaders – Religions for Peace (#06840)
♦ European Conference on Research Methodology for Business and Management Studies (meeting series)
♦ European Conference on Satellite Communications (inactive)
♦ European Conference of Social Economy (meeting series)
♦ European Conference on Social Media (meeting series)
♦ European Conference on Software Architecture (meeting series)
♦ European Conference on the Spectroscopy of Biological Molecules (meeting series)
♦ European Conference on Supercritical CO2 (meeting series)
♦ European Conference of Support and Solidarity with the Saharawi People / see Coordination des comités européens de soutien au peuple sahraoui (#04824)
♦ European Conference on Symbolic and Quantitative Approaches to Reasoning with Uncertainty (meeting series)
♦ European Conference on Symptom Validity Assessment (meeting series)

♦ European Conference of Transport Research Institutes (ECTRI) 06737

SG c/o POLIS, Rue du Trône 98, 1050 Brussels, Belgium. T. +3225005688. Fax +3225005689. E-mail: office@ectri.org.
URL: http://www.ectri.org/

History Apr 2003. Founded by 15 national transport research institutes and universities from 13 European countries. Registration: Banque-Carrefour des Entreprises, No/ID: 0831.370.370, Start date: 25 Nov 2010, Belgium; EU Transparency Register, No/ID: 54191854341-51, Start date: 12 Oct 2010. **Aims** Be the leading European research association for sustainable and multimodal mobility. **Structure** General Assembly (twice a year); Board; Thematic Groups (6); Task Forces (3); Secretariat. **Languages** English, French. **Staff** 3.00 FTE, paid. **Finance** Sources: members' dues. Other funds. Annual budget: 403,000 EUR (2022). **Activities** Events/meetings; guidance/assistance/consulting. **Events** *General Assembly* Brussels (Belgium) 2021, *General Assembly* Brussels (Belgium) 2021, *Young Researchers Seminar* Portoroz (Slovenia) 2021, *General Assembly* Brussels (Belgium) 2020, *General Assembly* Brussels (Belgium) 2020. **Publications** *European Transport Research Review (ETRR)* – journal. Position papers; reports.
Members Transport research organizations and institutes (28) in 19 countries:
Austria, Belgium, Czechia, Finland, France, Germany, Greece, Hungary, Ireland, Italy, Latvia, Norway, Poland, Portugal, Slovakia, Slovenia, Spain, Sweden, UK.
NGO Relations Partner of (7): Cooperative, connected and automated mobility (CCAM) partnership; *European Road Transport Research Advisory Council (ERTRAC, #08396); European Technology Platform ALICE (ALICE, #08888); European Transport Research Alliance (ETRA, #08939);* National Academies Transportation Research Board (TRB); Towards zero emission road transport (2Zero) partnership; *WATERBORNE (#20823).* [2022.02.14/XM0720/F]

♦ European Conference of Triga Reactor Users (meeting series)
♦ European Conference on Underwater Acoustics (meeting series)
♦ European Conference on Unsaturated Soils (meeting series)
♦ European Conference of Wine Producing Regions / see Assembly of European Wine Regions (#02317)
♦ European Conference of Youth Cards / see European Youth Card Association (#09137)

♦ European Congenital Heart Disease Organisation (ECHDO) 06738

Registered Address Borrestraat 51, 1050 Brussels, Belgium. E-mail: board@echdo.eu.
URL: https://www.echdo.eu/

History 2007. Registration: Banque-Carrefour des Entreprises, No/ID: 0821.091.637, Start date: 25 Sep 2009, Belgium. **Aims** Share information and experiences in order to improve the care and treatment for all people affected by CHD everywhere in Europe. **Structure** General Assembly; Board. **Events** *Annual General Meeting* Reykjavik (Iceland) 2019.
Members Full in 19 countries:
Austria, Belgium, Bulgaria, Cyprus, Estonia, Finland, Germany, Greece, Hungary, Iceland, Ireland, Italy, Netherlands, Norway, Poland, Romania, Spain, Sweden, UK.
NGO Relations Member of (3): *European Alliance for Cardiovascular Health (EACH, #05863); European Patients' Forum (EPF, #08172)* (Full); *EURORDIS – Rare Diseases Europe (#09175).* [2019/XM1563/D]

♦ European Congenital Heart Surgeons Association (ECHSA) 06739

Treas address not obtained.
URL: http://www.echsa.org/

History 1992, as *European Congenital Heart Surgeons Foundation.* Current title adopted 2003. Registered in accordance with Finnish law. **Aims** Advance surgery for congenital heart defects; improve treatment of patients with congenital heart diseases in Europe; promote research and treatment related directly or indirectly to congenital heart diseases irrespective of the patients race, religion, origin, wealth or other discriminative factors. **Structure** General Meeting; Board. **Finance** Members' dues. **Activities** Knowledge management/information dissemination; research/documentation; events/meetings. **Events** *Spring Meeting* Copenhagen (Denmark) 2015, *Fall Meeting* Bergamo (Italy) 2014, *Spring Meeting* Madrid (Spain) / Toledo (Spain) 2014, *Spring Meeting* Paris (France) 2013, *Fall Meeting* Vienna (Austria) 2013. **Information Services** *European Congenital Heart Defects Database (ECHDD).*
Members Individuals in 27 countries:
Austria, Belgium, Bulgaria, Canada, Czechia, Denmark, Finland, France, Germany, Greece, Ireland, Italy, Kuwait, Malaysia, Netherlands, Norway, Poland, Portugal, Russia, Saudi Arabia, Slovakia, Spain, Sweden, Switzerland, Türkiye, Ukraine, USA.
NGO Relations *World Society for Pediatric and Congenital Heart Surgery (WSPCHS, #21809).* [2015/XJ9357/D]

♦ European Congenital Heart Surgeons Foundation / see European Congenital Heart Surgeons Association (#06739)
♦ European Congress of Entomology (meeting series)

♦ European Congress of Ethnic Religions (ECER) 06740

Contact Vivulskio 27-4, LT-03114 Vilnius, Lithuania. T. +37052162966. E-mail: trinkunas@romuva.lt – info@ecer-org.eu.
URL: http://ecer-org.eu/

History Jun 1998, Vilnius (Lithuania), as *World Congress of Ethnic Religions (WCER) – Congrès mondial des religions ethniques.* **Aims** Serve as an international body that will assist Ethnic Religious groups in various countries and will oppose discrimination against such groups. **Structure** Steering Committee. **Events** *Congress* Prague (Czech Rep) 2013, *Congress* Odense (Denmark) 2012, *Congress* Bologna (Italy) 2010, *Congress* Nagpur (India) 2009, *Congress* Poznań (Poland) 2008. **Publications** *The Oaks* – newsletter. [2013/XM1704/c/F]

♦ European Congress on Hypnosis in Psychotherapy and Psychosomatic Medicine (meeting series)
♦ European Congress of Magnetic Resonance in Neuropediatrics (meeting series)
♦ European Congress on Molecular Spectroscopy (meeting series)
♦ European Congress of Pathology / see European Society of Pathology (#08689)
♦ European Congress for Persons with Disabilities – Living in the Encounter (meeting series)
♦ European Congress on the Use, Management and Conservation of Buildings of Historical Value (meeting series)

♦ European Connected Health Alliance (ECHAlliance) 06741

Contact address not obtained. E-mail: info@echalliance.com.
URL: http://www.echalliance.com/

History 2012. Resulted from the merger between *European MHealth Alliance (EuMHA, inactive)* and *European Connected Health Campus (ECHCampus, inactive).* Registration: Community Interest Company, No/ID: NI610694, Northern Ireland; Finland; EU Transparency Register, No/ID: 918355124862-52, Start date: 13 Dec 2016. **Aims** Provide leadership, education and focus supporting European and global implementation of connected health technologies; secure and engage in collaborative research and development; support strategic and tactical marketing and business development needs of members; develop and provide educational opportunities, in support of broad scale deployments connected health. **Structure** Board of Directors; International Advisory Panel. **Events** *Digital Health and Wellness Summit* Barcelona (Spain) 2021, *Digital Health Society Summit* Helsinki (Finland) 2019, *WoHIT : HIMSS Europe World of Health IT Conference* Barcelona (Spain) 2017, *WoHIT : HIMSS Europe World of Health IT Conference* Barcelona (Spain) 2016. **NGO Relations** Member of (1): *EU Health Coalition.* Partner of (1): *Digital Health Society (DHS).* [2021/XJ8779/D]

♦ European Consensus Platform for 3R-Alternatives to Animal Experimentation / see European Consensus-Platform for Alternatives (#06742)

♦ European Consensus-Platform for Alternatives (ecopa) 06742

Sec Boskant 101, 2350 Vosselaar, Belgium. E-mail: info@ecopa.eu.
Main Website: https://www.ecopa.eu/

History 10 Nov 2002, Brussels (Belgium). Founded following 1st meeting Sep 1999, Bologna (Italy). Former names and other names: *European Consensus Platform for 3R-Alternatives to Animal Experimentation* – full title. Registration: Banque-Carrefour des Entreprises, Belgium; EU Transparency Register, No/ID: 592558413934-02, Start date: 11 Jul 2014. **Aims** Promote "the three Rs" in the use of *animals* in research, testing, education and training in Europe: *Replacement* of animals; *Reduction* of the number of animals used; *Refinement* to reduce suffering and increase animal welfare. **Structure** General Assembly (annual); Board. **Languages** English. **Staff** Voluntary. **Finance** Sources: members' dues. **Activities** Events/meetings; financial and/or material support; knowledge management/information dissemination. **Events** *Annual Meeting* Rome (Italy) 2019, *Symposium* Paris (France) 2018, *Workshop* Helsinki (Finland) 2017, *Annual Meeting* Madrid (Spain) 2011, *Annual meeting* Brussels (Belgium) 2006.
Members National platforms in 7 countries:
Finland, France, Germany, Italy, Norway, Spain, Switzerland.
Associated platforms in 2 countries:
Austria, Romania. [2022.05.04/XF6960/F]

♦ European Conservation Agriculture Federation (ECAF) 06743

Fédération européenne pour la promotion de l'agriculture durable

Secretariat Rond Point Schuman 6, bte 5, 1040 Brussels, Belgium. T. +3222347891. Fax +3222347911. E-mail: egonzalez@ecaf.org.
URL: http://www.ecaf.org/

History 14 Jan 1999, Brussels (Belgium). Registration: No/ID: 0468.087.455, Start date: 14 Jan 1999, Belgium; EU Transparency Register, No/ID: 043446618888-27, Start date: 23 Sep 2015. **Aims** Improve technology transfer to farms; promote agricultural and environmental policies supportive of sustainable soil management; improve information exchange in the research, policy and practitioner communities; research, develop, evaluate and promote soil management systems to improve crop production and protection of the environment. **Structure** General Assembly (annual); Council; Executive Director. **Languages** English, French, Spanish. **Staff** 7.00 FTE, paid. **Finance** Financed mainly by EU and LIFE+ projects. Annual budget: 237,000 EUR. **Activities** Projects/programmes; events/meetings; training/education. **Events** *Green Carbon Conference* Brussels (Belgium) 2014, *European congress on conservation agriculture* Madrid (Spain) 2010, *World congress on conservation agriculture* Madrid (Spain) 2001. **Publications** *Conservation Agriculture: Making Climate Change Mitigation and Adaptation Real in Europe* (2017) by Gonzalez-Sanchez et al; *Making Sustainable Agriculture Real in CAP 2020: The Role of Conservation Agriculture* (2012) by Basch et al. Bulletins; technical reports; books. **Information Services** *Conservation agriculture: Making sustainable agriculture real* – database.

Members National organizations in 15 countries:
Denmark, Finland, France, Germany, Greece, Ireland, Italy, Moldova, Portugal, Russia, Slovakia, Slovenia, Spain, Switzerland, UK.

IGO Relations *Centre de coopération internationale en recherche agronomique pour le développement (CIRAD, #03733)*; *Deutsche Gesellschaft für Technische Zusammenarbeit (GTZ, inactive)*; *European Commission (EC, #06633)*; *European Parliament (EP, #08146)*; *FAO (#09260)*; *International Bank for Reconstruction and Development (IBRD, #12317)* (World Bank). **NGO Relations** *African Conservation Tillage Network (ACT, #00265)*. [2020/XD7163/D]

♦ European Conservatives Group (EC) 06744

Groupe des démocrates européens (GDE)

Secretariat c/o Parliamentary Assembly, Conseil de l'Europe, Bureau 5117, 67075 Strasbourg CEDEX, France. T. +33388412677. Fax +33388412786. E-mail: coepa.del@parliament.uk.
URL: http://www.edgpace.org/

History Founded 1969, as a political group of the *Parliamentary Assembly of the Council of Europe (PACE, #18211)*. Original title: *Group of Independent Representatives*. Subsequent English title, adopted Sep 1980: *European Democrat Group (EDG)*. Current Statutes adopted 1 Jul 1993, Strasbourg (France). **Aims** As a centre-right coalition of members of the Parliamentary Assembly of the Council of Europe, promote the respect of individual liberty and human rights and responsibilities under the rule of law, pluralist democracy and the support of a free market economy. **Structure** Bureau, consisting of President, Senior Vice-President, Secretary General-Treasurer, Vice-Presidents, Honorary President and 2 Joint Secretaries. Working Party of the Bureau, comprising President, Senior Vice-President, Secretary General-Treasurer and 4 other members. Secretariat. Auditors (2). **Languages** Dutch, English, French, German, Italian, Portuguese, Russian, Spanish, Turkish. **Staff** 1.00 FTE, paid. **Finance** Contributions of *Council of Europe (CE, #04881)*. **Activities** Organizes seminars. **Events** *Seminar on where is Russia heading?* Strasbourg (France) 1994. **Publications** None.

Members Representatives and substitutes of the Council of Europe's Parliamentary Assembly. As at 14 Apr 2008, Individuals (97) from 21 countries:
Armenia, Azerbaijan, Bosnia-Herzegovina, Czechia, Denmark, Estonia, France, Greece, Iceland, Italy, Latvia, Lithuania, Monaco, Norway, Poland, Portugal, Russia, Slovakia, Türkiye, UK, Ukraine. [2017/XF1521/v/F]

♦ European Conservatives and Reformists Group (ECR) 06745

SG c/o Eur Parl, Rue Wiertz – ATR 02K022, 1047 Brussels, Belgium. T. +3222841394 – +3222844532.
Strasbourg Office Allée du Printemps – LOW T04 139, 67070 Strasbourg, France. T. +33388176786.
URL: http://www.ecrgroup.eu/

History Jun 2009. A group in *European Parliament (EP, #08146)*. **Aims** Bring about major reform of the EU based on Eurorealism, decentralisation of powers, more openness and a focus on supporting Europe's economic growth. **Structure** Chairmanship; Bureau. **Events** *Meeting* London (UK) 2017, *Meeting* Brussels (Belgium) 2013, *Meeting* Brussels (Belgium) 2013, *Meeting* Brussels (Belgium) 2013, *Meeting* Brussels (Belgium) 2013.

Members MEPs (currently 74) in 16 countries:
Belgium, Bulgaria, Croatia, Czechia, Denmark, Finland, Germany, Greece, Ireland, Italy, Latvia, Lithuania, Netherlands, Poland, Romania, Slovakia. [2017.10.12/XJ2312/F]

♦ European Conservatives and Reformists Group – Committee of the Regions (ECR-CoR) 06746

SG c/o CoR, Rue Belliard 101, 1040 Brussels, Belgium. T. +3222822375. E-mail: ecr@cor.europa.eu.
Communications/Policy Advisor address not obtained.
URL: http://web.cor.europa.eu/ecr/

History 10 Apr 2013. Officially announced during the 11-12 April 100th plenary session of the *European Committee of the Regions (CoR, #06665)*. **Aims** Ensure that decisions are taken as close to the citizens as possible and at the EU level only when necessary; ensure a strong voice for local and regional government in guiding EU policies in relation to efficient and modern public services; encourage greater localism, an improved environment and minimal regulation; endeavour to achieve cost effective and efficient administration of the Committee of the Regions. **Publications** *ECR Group Newsletter*.

Members Individuals in 8 countries:
Czechia, Denmark, Finland, Lithuania, Netherlands, Poland, Slovakia, UK.

IGO Relations *Conference of the Regional and Local Authorities for the Eastern Partnership (CORLEAP, #04645)*. [2021/XM4741/v/E]

♦ European Conservatives and Reformists Party (ECR) 06747

Registered Office Rue du Trône 4, 1000 Brussels, Belgium. T. +3222806039. E-mail: info@ecrparty.eu.
URL: https://ecrparty.eu/

History 1 Oct 2009. Former names and other names: *Alliance of European Conservatives and Reformists (AECR)* – former (2009 to 2016); *Alliance of Conservatives and Reformists in Europe (ACRE)* – former (2016 to 2019). Registration: Banque Carrefour des Entreprises, No/ID: 0820.208.739, Start date: 30 Oct 2009, Belgium. **Aims** Advance the principles set out in the Prague Declaration of Principles and/or any other subsequent documents. **Structure** Council; Conference; Executive Board. **Languages** English. **Events** *Brussels Summit* Brussels (Belgium) 2018, *Faith and Freedom Summit* Brussels (Belgium) 2018.

Members Parties; Individual; Affiliated Organizations. Members in 21 countries:
Albania, Armenia, Azerbaijan, Belarus, Croatia, Czechia, Faeroe Is, Finland, Georgia, Iceland, Italy, Latvia, Lithuania, Luxembourg, Montenegro, Northern Cyprus, Poland, Romania, Slovakia, Türkiye, UK.

Regional partners in 8 countries:
Australia, Canada, Colombia, Israel, Morocco, New Zealand, Tunisia, USA.

IGO Relations *European Parliament (EP, #08146)*. **NGO Relations** *European Conservatives and Reformists Group (ECR, #06745)*. [2020/XM4324/D]

♦ European Consortium for Accreditation in Higher Education (ECA) . 06748

Chair NVAO, Parkstraat 83, 2514 JG The Hague, Netherlands. E-mail: secretariat@ecahe.eu.
URL: http://ecahe.eu/

History Nov 2003, Córdoba (Spain). Renewed June 2008, Krakow (Poland). Registration: Handelsregister, No/ID: 60488360, Start date: Apr 2014, Netherlands. **Aims** Achieve mutual recognition of accreditation and quality assurance decisions; enhance conditions for mutual recognition, especially for joint programmes; provide a platform for mutual learning and disseminating experiences with accreditation and accreditation-like practices; provide transparent information on quality; facilitate internationalization of institutions and students. **Structure** Board; Financial Committee; Working Groups; Certification Group; Secretariat. **Languages** English. **Finance** Sources: members' dues. **Activities** Certification/accreditation; events/meetings; publishing activities; training/education. **Events** *Members Seminar* Paris (France) 2022, *Winter Seminar* The Hague (Netherlands) 2021, *Meeting* Tel Aviv (Israel) 2020, *Seminar* The Hague (Netherlands) 2020, *Meeting* Valladolid (Spain) 2020. **Publications** *ECA Newsletter* (2 a year). Guides; frameworks; handbooks; position papers. **Information Services** *ECA Experts Exchange Portal*; *ECA trainings*; *Internationalisation Platform with Good Practices in Internationalisation and Certificates*.

Members Organizations (17) in 12 countries and territories:
Belgium, Croatia, Denmark, France, Germany, Netherlands, Poland, Portugal, Romania, Slovenia, Spain, Sweden.

Observers in 2 countries:
Australia, Israel.

NGO Relations Cooperates with (3): *Asia-Pacific Quality Network (APQN, #02004)*; *Central and Eastern European Network of Quality Assurance Agencies in Higher Education (CEENQA, #03696)*; *International Network of Quality Assurance Agencies in Higher Education (INQAAHE, #14312)*. Associate Member of: *European Association for Quality Assurance in Higher Education (ENQA, #06183)*. [2023.02.14/XM1754/F]

♦ European Consortium of Anchors Producers (ECAP) 06749

SG Via L in Polonia 29b, 24128 Bergamo BG, Italy.
Registered Office Via Monte Grappa 7, 24121 Bergamo BG, Italy.
URL: http://www.ecap-sme.org/

History Feb 2001. Registration: EU Transparency Register, No/ID: 089769923883-95, Start date: 14 Oct 2016. **Aims** Represent SMEs anchors and fixing systems producers and safeguard their interests in *standardization*, legally, technically and on a services front. **Structure** Board of Directors. **Languages** English, French, German, Italian, Spanish. **Staff** 2.00 FTE, paid. **Finance** Sources: members' dues. **Activities** Advocacy/lobbying/activism; standards/guidelines; research/documentation; guidance/assistance/consulting.

Members Full in 8 countries:
Belgium, Denmark, France, Germany, Italy, Spain, Switzerland, UK.

IGO Relations Member of: *European Commission (EC, #06633)* Action Plan "Construction 2020". **NGO Relations** Observer status with (1): *European Organisation for Technical Assessment (EOTA, #08103)*. Member of (2): *Construction Products Europe AISBL (#04761)*; *Small Business Standards (SBS, #19311)*. Cooperates with (1): *Comité européen de normalisation (CEN, #04162)*. [2021/XM2906/D]

♦ European Consortium for Arts Therapies Education (ECArTE) 06750

Chair Royal Central School of Speech and Drama, Eton Avenue, London, NW3 3HY, UK.
URL: http://www.ecarte.info/

History 1991, with the support of *European Community Action Scheme for the Mobility of University Students (ERASMUS, inactive)*. Registered in accordance with Dutch law. **Aims** Represent arts therapies at European level; work towards mutual recognition of courses; act as an instrument for quality assurance; promote and instigate relevant research at European level; use expertise to set up new courses; maintain a framework for staff and student exchange; collect information. **Structure** General Assembly (annual); Executive Board; Working Groups. **Languages** English. **Staff** 5.00 FTE, voluntary. Several part-time, paid. **Finance** Members' dues. Other sources: conference proceeds; sale of publications; project funding. **Activities** Events/meetings; publishing activities. **Events** *International Congress* Alcala de Henares (Spain) 2019, *International Congress* Krakow (Poland) 2017, *International Congress* Palermo (Italy) 2015, *International Congress* Paris (France) 2013, *International Congress* Lucca (Italy) 2011. **Publications** *Cultural Landscapes* (2017); *Dimensions of Reflection in the Arts Therapies* (2015); *Arts Therapies and the Intelligence of Feeling* (2013); *Arts Therapies and the Space Between* (2011); *The Space Between: the Potential for Change: Selected Proceedings of the 10th European Arts Therapies Conference, London, September 2009* (2011); *Arts in Arts Therapies: a European Perspective* (2009); *European Arts Therapy: Grounding the Vision – to advance theory and practice* (2006); *Arts Therapy: Recognized Discipline or Soul-Graffiti? – Approaches, Applications, Evaluations* (2003); *Arts – Therapies – Communication* – in 3 vols.

Members Full (34); Associate (1); Partner. Members in 13 European countries:
Belgium, Estonia, Finland, France, Germany, Ireland, Lithuania, Netherlands, Norway, Slovenia, Spain, Sweden, UK. [2017.10.23/XF6925/F]

♦ European Consortium on Chronic Respiratory Insufficiency (ECCRI) 06751

Secretariat c/o VSCA, Lt gen van Heutszlaan 6, 3743 JN Baarn, Netherlands. T. +3155480480. E-mail: info@vsca.nl.
URL: http://www.vsca.nl/

History Founded Mar 1993, Lyon (France). Also referred to as *European Consortium on Chronic Respiratory Insufficiency in Neuromuscular Disorders*. **Aims** Establish cooperation between professionals involved in management of chronic respiratory insufficiency; work for the structural improvement of care for people who make use of chronic (intermittent) respiratory support in the Netherlands and abroad, from the perspective of the care recipient. **Languages** Dutch. **Finance** Supported by: *European Alliance of Neuromuscular Disorders Associations (EAMDA, #05876)*.

Members Individuals (35) in 13 countries:
Austria, Belgium, Denmark, Finland, France, Germany, Italy, Netherlands, Norway, Spain, Sweden, Switzerland, UK. [2014.06.01/XF5353/F]

♦ European Consortium on Chronic Respiratory Insufficiency in Neuromuscular Disorders / see European Consortium on Chronic Respiratory Insufficiency (#06751)

♦ European Consortium for Church and State Research 06752

Contact Derecho Eclesiastico del Estado, Fac de Derecho, Univ de Alcala, c/Libreros 27, 28801 Alcala de Henares, Madrid, Spain. T. +34918854319. Fax +34918854348. E-mail: european.consortium@uah.es.
URL: http://www.churchstate.eu/

History Founded 12 Dec 1989, Milan (Italy), at *Istituto di Diritto Internazionale, Università degli Studi di Milano (no recent information)*. **Aims** Promote development of studies in the field of relations between States and *religious denominations* in Europe from a historical, political and, particularly, juridical point of view. **Structure** General Assembly; Executive Committee. **Languages** English, French. **Staff** 6.00 FTE, voluntary. **Finance** Members' dues. **Events** *Annual Meeting* Alcala de Henares (Spain) 2015, *Annual Meeting* Vienna (Austria) 2014, *Annual Meeting* Strasbourg (France) 2013, *Annual Meeting* Budapest (Hungary) 2012, *Annual Meeting* Oxford (UK) 2011. **Publications** *European Journal for Church and State Research* (annual); *European Consortium for Church and State Research Newsletter*. *Law and Religion Studies*. Meeting proceedings.

Members Universities and other cultural institutions in 23 countries:
Austria, Belgium, Cyprus, Czechia, Estonia, Finland, France, Germany, Greece, Hungary, Ireland, Italy, Latvia, Luxembourg, Malta, Netherlands, Poland, Portugal, Romania, Slovenia, Spain, Sweden, UK.

NGO Relations Member of: *European Academy of Religion (EuARe, #05812)*; *International Association of Legal Science (IALS, #11997)*. [2019.12.19/XF5327/F]

♦ European Consortium for Communications Research / see European Communication Research and Education Association (#06675)

♦ European Consortium for the Development of Fusion Energy (EUROfusion) 06753

Headquarters Boltzmannstr 2, 85748 Garching, Germany. T. +498932994201.
Communications Office address not obtained. T. +498932994123.
URL: http://www.euro-fusion.org/

History Launched 9 Oct 2014, by *European Commission (EC, #06633)*. Manages the European fusion research activities on behalf of *European Atomic Energy Community (Euratom, inactive)*. Substitutes *European Fusion Development Agreement (EFDA, inactive)* and *EFDA JET (inactive)*. **Aims** Prepare for ITER experiments; develop concepts for the fusion power demonstration plant DEMO. **Structure** General Assembly; Coordinator; Scientific and Technical Advisory Committee. Programme Management Unit, Garching (Germany) and Culham (UK); ITER Physics Department; Power Plant Physics and Technology Department. **Languages** English. **Finance** Grant Agreement of euro 424,000,000 from Euratom Horizon 2020 programme and about the same amount from Member States. Budget (2014-2018): euro 850,000,000. **Activities** Research and development. **Events** *General Assembly* Madrid (Spain) 2016. **Publications** *Fusion in Europe* (4 a year) – newsletter.

Members National research organizations (30) in 28 countries:
Austria, Belgium, Bulgaria, Croatia, Cyprus, Czechia, Denmark, Estonia, Finland, France, Germany, Greece, Hungary, Ireland, Italy, Latvia, Lithuania, Netherlands, Poland, Portugal, Romania, Slovakia, Slovenia, Spain, Sweden, Switzerland, UK, Ukraine.

NGO Relations *EIROforum (#05401)*. [2019/XJ8839/E*]

♦ **European Consortium for Emergency Contraception (ECEC)** **06754**
Office c/o EEIRH, 1 Moldovei St, 540493 Targu-Mures, Romania. E-mail: info@ec-ec.org – cpuig@eeirh.org.
URL: http://www.ec-ec.org/
History Jun 2012, Athens (Greece). **Aims** Expand knowledge about and access to emergency contraception (EC) in European countries; promote standardization of EC service delivery in a European context; ensure equitable access to EC within Europe; serve as an authoritative source of information on and a voice for expanded access to EC in the region. **Structure** Board; Advisory Committee. Hosted at: East European Institute for Reproductive Health (EEIRH). **Languages** English. **Activities** Networking/liaising; research/documentation; knowledge management/information dissemination; training/education. **Publications** Guidelines. **NGO Relations** Partner of (1): *International Consortium for Emergency Contraception (ICEC, #12911).*
[2020/XJ7172/E]

♦ **European Consortium for Humanities Institutes and Centres (ECHIC)** **06755**
Secretariat Dipto di Studi Umanistici, Corso Cavour 2, 62100 Macerata MC, Italy. T. +397332584062.
URL: http://www.echic.org/
History Founding conference 2011, Dublin (Ireland), following meetings organized since 2008. Registered in accordance with Italian law. **Aims** Canvass the need for humanities research; speak on behalf of the humanities and develop a language for the (position of) humanities institutes in European universities today. **Structure** General Assembly; Executive Council; President. **Languages** English. **Activities** Events/meetings; networking/liaising. **Publications** *ECHIC Newsletter.*
Members Full in 20 countries:
Belgium, Croatia, Estonia, France, Germany, Greece, Hungary, Iceland, Ireland, Italy, Montenegro, Netherlands, North Macedonia, Norway, Poland, Portugal, Romania, Spain, Sweden, UK.
NGO Relations Member of: *European Alliance for the Social Sciences and Humanities (EASSH, #05885).* Regional member of: *International Council for Philosophy and Human Sciences (CIPSH, #13061).* Affiliate member of: *Consortium of Humanities Centers and Institutes (CHCI).* Affiliated institutes include: *European Science Foundation (ESF, #08441).* [2018.09.06/XM6596/D]

♦ **European Consortium of Innovative Universities (ECIU)** **06756**
SG c/o Univ of Twente, PO Box 217, 7500 AE Enschede, Netherlands.
Head of Brussels Office Rue du Luxembourg 3, 1000 Brussels, Belgium.
URL: http://www.eciu.org/
History 18 Nov 1997, Twente (Netherlands). Registration: Handelsregister, Netherlands; EU Transparency Register, No/ID: 526221434040-38. **Aims** As a consortium of research universities, focus on: collaboration in innovative teaching and learning; enhancement of university-society interaction; internationalization of the student and staff experience; active engagement in policy development and practice within the evolving European Higher Education Area. **Structure** Rectors' and Presidents' Meeting (annual); Executive Board; Central Secretariat; Brussels Office; ECIU University Project Management; Local Ambassadors; Expert Groups; Work Packages. **Languages** English. **Staff** 4.00 FTE, paid. ECIU Foundation Plus: 300. **Finance** Sources: members' dues. Supported by: *European Commission (EC, #06633)* (DG EAC). **Activities** Politics/policy/regulatory; research and development; research/documentation; training/education. **Events** *Annual Conference* Brussels (Belgium) 2020, *Board Meeting* Barcelona (Spain) 2019, *ECIU Rectors and Presidents Meeting* Dublin (Ireland) 2019. **Publications** *ECIU Magazine.*
Members Universities in 14 countries:
Denmark, Finland, France, Germany, Ireland, Italy, Lithuania, Mexico, Netherlands, Norway, Poland, Portugal, Spain, Sweden.
[2022.05.05/XF5811/F]

♦ European Consortium on Landscape Economics (#04745)

♦ **European Consortium for Mathematics in Industry (ECMI)** **06757**
Exec Dir DTU COMPUTE – Dept Applied Mathematics and Computer Science, Technic Univ Denmark, Asmussens Allé, Bldg 303B – room 012, 2800 Lyngby, Denmark. T. +4545253061. Fax +4522162755. E-mail: director@ecmi-indmath.org.
Pres address not obtained.
URL: http://www.ecmi-indmath.org/
History 26 Jun 1987, Rotterdam (Netherlands). **Aims** Promote the use of mathematical models in industry; educate industrial *mathematicians* to meet the growing demand for such experts; ensure the transfer of knowledge and skills and effectively use scarce academic resources in Europe. **Structure** Council. **Languages** English. **Staff** 20.00 FTE, paid. **Finance** Members' dues. **Activities** Guidance/assistance/consulting; events/meetings; training/education. **Events** *Biennial Conference* Wuppertal (Germany) 2021, *Biennial Conference* Limerick (Ireland) 2020, *Biennial Conference* Budapest (Hungary) 2018, *Biennial Conference* Santiago de Compostela (Spain) 2016, *Biennial Conference* Taormina (Italy) 2014. **Publications** *Journal of Mathematics in Industry. European Consortium for Mathematics in Industry* – series. Annual Report; scientific papers.
Members Full membership industrial companies/non-academic organizations and university departments/other academic groups. Associate membership individuals. Centres in 10 countries:
Austria, Denmark, Finland, France, Germany, Ireland, Italy, Netherlands, Norway, UK.
NGO Relations Member of (1): *International Council for Industrial and Applied Mathematics (ICIAM, #13032).*
[2021/XF2384/t/F]

♦ **European Consortium for Ocean Research Drilling (ECORD)** **06758**
Dir CEREGE-CNRS, Europôle Méditerranéen de l'Arbois, BP 80, 13545 Aix-en-Provence, France. T. +33442971545. E-mail: ema@cerege.fr.
URL: http://www.ecord.org/
History Oct 2003, to provide a structure to participate in *International Ocean Discovery Program (IODP, #14393).* **Aims** Coordinate Europe's participation in IODP; extend the scientific capability by providing support for mission-specific platform (MSP) operations. **Structure** Council; Facility Board (EFB); Managing Agency (EMA); Science Operator (ESO); ECORD Outreach Task Force (EOTF); Science and Support Advisory Committee (ESSAC); Industry Liaison Panel (ECORD ILP). **Languages** English. **Events** *Meeting* Paris (France) 2008. **Publications** *ECORD Newsletter.*
Members National Funding Agencies in 15 countries:
Austria, Canada, Denmark, Finland, France, Germany, Ireland, Italy, Netherlands, Norway, Portugal, Spain, Sweden, Switzerland, UK.
NGO Relations Supports: *International Ocean Discovery Program (IODP, #14393).* [2019.06.03/XM2947/E]

♦ **European Consortium for Organic Animal Breeding (Eco-AB)** **06759**
Contact FiBL, Ackerstrasse, 5070 Frick AG, Switzerland. T. +41628657290. Fax +41628657273. E-mail: anet.spengler@fibl.org.
Chair Stichting Bio-KI, Badelochstraat 17, 3813 DS Amersfoort, Netherlands.
URL: http://www.eco-ab.org/
History 29 May 2006, Odense (Denmark). Registered in accordance with German law, with head office in Glonn (Germany). **Aims** Provide a platform for discussion, knowledge exchange and experience in all issues relating to animal breeding in organic animal *farming* systems; initiate and support organic animal breeding programmes; develop scientific concepts for organic animal breeding; provide independent, competent expertise for the development of credible and practical standards for animal breeding in organic systems. **Structure** General Meeting (at least annual); Board. **Languages** English, German. **Staff** 1.00 FTE, paid. **Finance** Members' dues. Annual budget: about euro 7,000. **Activities** Knowledge management/information dissemination; standards/guidelines. **Events** *General Meeting* Hamburg (Germany) 2012, *General Meeting* Stavanger (Norway) 2011, *General Meeting* Wageningen (Netherlands) 2011, *General Meeting* Leipzig (Germany) 2010, *General Meeting* Bristol (UK) 2009. **Publications** Position papers; theses. **Members** Research scientists and practitioners involved or interested in animal breeding issues relating to the principles of organic animal farming. Membership countries not specified. [2016.12.14/XM3026/F]

♦ **European Consortium of the Organic-Based Fertilizer Industry (ECOFI)** **06760**
Contact c/o Prospero and Parnters, lange Winkelhaakstr 26, 2060 Antwerp, Belgium. T. +3232900123.
URL: http://www.ecofi.info/
History Founded Mar 2014, by 12 companies. EU Transparency Register: 275714913510-19. **Aims** Promote the contribution made by the organic-based fertilizers sector to the emergence of a knowledge-intensive, environmentally sustainable and high-employment economy in Europe. **Structure** Board; Secretariat. **Events** *Summit of the Organic and organo-mineral Fertilisers Industries in Europe (SOFIE)* Brussels (Belgium) 2023.
[2019/XM8775/t/D]

♦ **European Consortium for Organic Plant Breeding (ECO-PB)** **06761**
Europäisches Konsortium für Ökologische Pflanzenzüchtung
Chairperson Research Inst of Organic Agriculture FiBL, Ackerstrasse 113, 5070 Frick AG, Switzerland. T. +41628650443.
URL: http://www.eco-pb.org/
History Founded 20 Apr 2001, Driebergen (Netherlands). Registered in accordance with German law. EU Transparency Register: 329523333979-86. **Aims** Protect the environment, nature and biodiversity by furthering organic agriculture through plant breeding directed at the needs of organic farming systems. **Structure** General Assembly (annual); Board of Directors. **Languages** English, German. **Staff** 0.50 FTE, paid. **Finance** Members' dues. **Activities** Events/meetings; politics/policy/regulatory. **Events** *European Workshop on Organic Seed Regulation* Brussels (Belgium) 2013. **Publications** *ECO-PB Newsletter.* Position paper on organic plant breeding; position paper on European seed law revision; translation of dossier on new breeding techniques; survey of seed companies; reports; proceedings; papers.
Members Founding (7); Full (13); Associate (24). Members in 15 countries:
Austria, Belgium, Denmark, Finland, France, Germany, Greece, Hungary, Italy, Latvia, Luxembourg, Netherlands, Portugal, Switzerland, UK.
NGO Relations Member of: *TP Organics – European Technology Platform (TP Organics, #20180).*
[2019/XM3003/F]

♦ **European Consortium for Political Research (ECPR)** **06762**
Consortium européen de recherches en sciences politiques – Evropejskij Konsorcium Politiceskih Issledovanij
Dir Harbour House, Hythe Quay, Colchester, CO2 8JF, UK. T. +441206630020. E-mail: membership@ecpr.eu.
URL: http://www.ecpr.eu/
History Set up 1970, by representatives of 8 European political science institutions, with help of a 5-year grant from *Ford Foundation (#09858).* UK Registered Charitable Incorporated Organisation (CIO): 1167403. **Aims** Promote development of *political science* in Europe and the rest of the world by fostering collaboration between individuals active in the field. **Structure** Council (meets annually); Board of Trustees (Executive Committee); Management Team. **Languages** English. **Staff** 16.50 FTE, paid. **Finance** Members' dues. Other sources: publication sales and subscriptions; event fees. **Activities** Events/meetings; training/education; publishing activities; research/documentation. **Events** *Human Rights and Foreign Policy / Joint Human Rights Conference* London (UK) 2021, *Annual General Conference* Colchester (UK) 2020, *Annual Joint Sessions of Workshops* Colchester (UK) 2020, *Human Rights and Foreign Policy / Joint Human Rights Conference* London (UK) 2020, *Annual General Conference* Wroclaw (Poland) 2019. **Publications** *European Journal of International Relations (EJIR); European Journal of Political Research (EJPR); European Political Science (EPS); European Political Science Review (EPSR); Political Data Yearbook (PDY); Political Research Exchange (PRX). Comparative European Politics* – book series.
Members Institutions in 20 European countries:
Austria, Belgium, Cyprus, Denmark, Finland, France, Germany, Greece, Iceland, Ireland, Italy, Luxembourg, Malta, Netherlands, Norway, Portugal, Spain, Sweden, Switzerland, UK.
Included in the above, 16 organizations listed in this Yearbook:
Austrian Institute for International Affairs (oiip); Central European University (CEU, #03717); College of Europe (#04105); Eastern Mediterranean University; European Centre for Minority Issues (ECMI); European University at St Petersburg (EUSP); European University Institute (EUI, #09034); GIGA – German Institute of Global and Area Studies; Institut de hautes études internationales et du développement (IHEID); Institute of International Relations, Prague (IIR); International Research Institute of Stavanger (IRIS); Moskovskij Gosudarstvennyj Institut Mezdunarodnyh Otnosenij (MGIMO); Norwegian Institute of International Affairs (NUPI); Peace Research Institute Frankfurt (PRIF); School of Oriental and African Studies (SOAS); Swedish Institute of International Affairs (SIIA).
Associate members (outside Europe) in 10 countries:
Australia, Brazil, Canada, Colombia, Japan, Mexico, New Zealand, Singapore, Taiwan, USA.
NGO Relations Member of: *European Alliance for the Social Sciences and Humanities (EASSH, #05885); International Science Council (ISC, #14796).* [2018.06.01/XD3988/D]

♦ **European Consortium for Sociological Research (ECSR)** **06763**
Sec c/o MZES – AB-A, Univ of Mannheim, 68131 Mannheim, Germany. E-mail: ecsr@ecsrnet.eu.
URL: http://www.ecsrnet.eu/
History Founded 1991. **Aims** Promote theory-driven empirical research in sociology in Europe. **Structure** Council; Executive Board. **Activities** Events/meetings; training/education; awards/prizes/competitions. **Events** *Annual conference* Paris (France) 2018, *Conference on globalization, social inequality and the life course* Groningen (Netherlands) 2007, *Annual conference / Conference* Prague (Czech Rep) 2006, *Annual conference / Conference* Paris (France) 2005, *Annual Conference* Granada (Spain) 2004. **Publications** *European Sociological Review* – journal.
Members Research institutes and university departments (over 90) in 24 countries:
Austria, Belgium, Bulgaria, Czechia, Denmark, Estonia, Finland, France, Germany, Hungary, Ireland, Israel, Italy, Lithuania, Luxembourg, Netherlands, Norway, Romania, Slovakia, Slovenia, Spain, Sweden, Switzerland, UK. [2019/XF4606/D]

♦ **European Constitutional Law Network (ECLN)** **06764**
Contact c/o Humboldt Univ Berlin, Walter Hallstein-Inst for European Constitutional Law, Unter den Linden 6, 10099 Berlin, Germany. T. +493020933440. Fax +493020933449.
History 1998, Berlin (Germany). Founded on the initiative of Prof Ingolf Pernice. **Aims** Facilitate, encourage and foster the growing interest in the idea of European Constitutionalism by strengthening communication and exchange of ideas with academic partners from the Member or future Member States of the EU, USA and China. **Structure** Informal structure. **Events** *Conference* Thessaloniki (Greece) 2015, *Conference* Florence (Italy) 2013, *Conference* New York, NY (USA) 2012, *Conference* Madrid (Spain) 2010, *Conference* Sofia (Bulgaria) 2008. **Publications** *ECLN Series.*
Members Individuals in 24 countries:
Austria, Belgium, Bulgaria, Croatia, Czechia, Denmark, Finland, France, Germany, Greece, Hungary, Ireland, Italy, Lithuania, Netherlands, Norway, Poland, Portugal, Russia, Spain, Sweden, Switzerland, UK, USA. [2015/XJ4141/F]

♦ EuropeanConstitution.eu (unconfirmed)

♦ European Construction, built environment and energy efficient building Technology Platform / see European Construction Technology Platform (#06768)

♦ **European Construction Forum (ECF)** **06765**
Contact c/o FIEC, Ave Louise 225, 1050 Brussels, Belgium. T. +3225145535. Fax +3225110276.
URL: http://www.ecf.be/
Aims Work for the establishment and recognition of a single comprehensive policy approach for the European construction sector through raising the awareness of decision makers at European level to the specific issues affecting the sector as a whole.
Members European organizations (11):
Architects Council of Europe (ACE, #01086); CEMBUREAU – The European Cement Association (CEMBUREAU, #03634); Concrete Europe (#04433); European Asphalt Pavement Association (EAPA, #05920); European Construction Industry Federation (#06766); European Council of Civil Engineers (ECCE, #06810); European Federation of Building and Woodworkers (EFBWW, #07065); European Federation of Engineering Consultancy Associations (EFCA, #07109); European Insulation Manufacturers Association (EURIMA, #07577); Royal Institution of Chartered Surveyors (RICS, #18991). [2014.10.06/XF4470/y/F]

♦ European Construction Industry Federation 06766

Fédération de l'industrie européenne de la construction (FIEC) – Verband der Europäischen Bauwirtschaft

Dir Gen Av Louise 225, 1050 Brussels, Belgium. T. +3225145535. Fax +3225110276. E-mail: info@fiec.eu.

URL: https://www.fiec.eu/

History 1905, Liège (Belgium). Current Statutes adopted Jun 2017, Stockholm (Sweden). Former names and other names: *International Federation of Building and Public Works* – former; *Fédération internationale du bâtiment et des travaux publics* – former; *International Federation of European Contractors of Building and Public Works* – former; *Fédération internationale des entrepreneurs européens de bâtiment et de travaux publics* – former; *Fédération internationale des entrepreneurs de la construction* – former; *International European Construction Federation* – former; *Fédération internationale européenne de la construction* – former; *Internationaler Europäischer Bauverband* – former. Registration: Banque Carrefour des Entreprieses, No/ID: 0688.919.140, Start date: 26 Jan 2018, Belgium; RNA, No/ID: W751069921, Start date: 15 Oct 1984, End date: 29 Jun 2018, France; EU Transparency Registry, No/ID: 92221016212-42, Start date: 14 Jul 2011. **Aims** Represent, without discrimination, construction enterprises of all sizes from all building and civil engineering specialties, engaged in all kinds of working methods. **Structure** General Assembly; Steering Committee; Commissions (3). **Languages** English, French, German. **Staff** 7.00 FTE, paid. **Finance** Sources: members' dues. **Activities** Advocacy/lobbying/activism. **Events** *General Assembly* Brussels (Belgium) 2021, *General Assembly* Brussels (Belgium) 2020, *Annual Conference and General Assembly* Paris (France) 2019, *Meeting on Construction 4.0* Brussels (Belgium) 2018, *Annual Conference and General Assembly* Stockholm (Sweden) 2017. **Publications** *FIEC Newsletter* (weekly); *FIEC Statistical Report* (annual); *Key Figures* (annual). *FIEC in a Nutshell*. Annual Report. Information Services: Documentation centre.

Members National employers' organizations (33) in EU, EFTA and Central/Eastern Europe. Members in 28 countries:

Austria, Belgium, Bulgaria, Croatia, Cyprus, Czechia, Denmark, Estonia, Finland, France, Germany, Greece, Hungary, Ireland, Italy, Latvia, Lithuania, Luxembourg, Netherlands, Norway, Portugal, Romania, Slovakia, Slovenia, Spain, Sweden, Switzerland, Türkiye.

IGO Relations Special relationship with: *ILO (#11123)*. Recognized by: *European Commission (EC, #06633)*. Participates in the work of: *United Nations Economic Commission for Europe (UNECE, #20555)*. **NGO Relations** Member of (8): *Comité européen de normalisation (CEN, #04162)* (Associate); *Confederation of International Contractors Associations (CICA, #04558)*; *Construction 2050 Alliance (#04760)*; *European Council for Construction Research, Development and Innovation (ECCREDI, #06813)*; *European Services Forum (ESF, #08469)*; *Federation of European and International Associations Established in Belgium (FAIB, #09508)*; *Global Alliance for Buildings and Construction (GlobalABC, #10187)*; *WorldSkills Europe (#21790)* (Associate). Instrumental in setting up (2): *European Construction Forum (ECF, #06765)*; *International Organization for Standardization (ISO, #14473)*. Associate Expert Group of *Business and Industry Advisory Committee to the OECD (BIAC, #03385)*. Close links with: *European International Contractors (EIC, #07586)*, having complementary tasks agreed in protocol agreement signed 1984 and a common Vice-President. Signatory of first edition of 'Conditions of Contract (International) for Works of Civil Engineering Construction'. These Conditions have received approval and ratification of: *Associated General Contractors of America (AGC)*; *Federación Interamericana de la Industria de la Construcción (FIIC, #09333)*; *International Federation of Asian and Western Pacific Contractors' Associations (IFAWPCA, #13359)*; *International Road Federation (IRF Global, #14759)*. Sectoral Social Partner in European Sectoral Social Dialogue, together with: *European Federation of Building and Woodworkers (EFBWW, #07065)*. Special links with: *International Organisation of Employers (IOE, #14428)*. [2021/XD1910/t/**D**]

♦ European Construction Institute (ECI) 06767

Chair BRE, Bucknalls Lane, Watford, WD25 9XX, UK. T. +443330430643. E-mail: eci@bre.co.uk.

URL: http://www.eci-online.org/

History 1990. **Aims** Bring together clients, contractors and consultants to achieve a continuous improvement in the efficiency, excellence and international competitiveness of European construction through research, development cooperation and implementation. **Structure** Board of Advisors; Executive Board. Committees (2): Central Programme; External Relations. Central Operations Unit. Regional Units (3): Benelux; German; UK. **Finance** Members' dues. **Activities** Knowledge management/information dissemination; events/meetings; awards/prizes/competitions. **Events** *Annual Conference* Amsterdam (Netherlands) 2015, *Annual Conference* London (UK) 2013, *Annual Conference* Düsseldorf (Germany) 2012, *Annual conference* London (UK) 2007, *Annual Conference* Delft (Netherlands) 2006. **Publications** *ECI News* (3 a year) – newsletter. Conference proceedings; task force reports; papers; books; guides.

Members Clients, Contractors, Consultants from over 65 based companies in 8 countries:

Belgium, France, Germany, Italy, Netherlands, Norway, Spain, UK. [2020/XF3920/j/**E**]

♦ European Construction Technology Platform (ECTP) 06768

SG ECTP Secretariat, 290 route des Lucioles, BP 209, 06904 Sophia Antipolis CEDEX, France. E-mail: secretariat@ectp.org.

Chairman c/o Bouygues, Av de Cortenbergh 52, 1000 Brussels, Belgium.

URL: http://www.ectp.org/

History 2004. Former names and other names: *European Construction, built environment and energy efficient building Technology Platform* – full title. Registration: EU Transparency Register, No/ID: 60598725719-66, Start date: 22 Apr 2011. **Aims** Develop new research, development and innovation strategies so as to raise the sector to a higher level of performance and competitiveness. **Structure** Plenary Assembly; Steering Committee; Thematic Committees; Working Groups; General Secretariat. **Languages** English. **Staff** 1.00 FTE, paid. **Finance** Sources: members' dues. **Activities** Advocacy/lobbying/activism; events/meetings. **Events** *When EU construction shapes high-tech sustainable built environment* Brussels (Belgium) 2018, *Conference* Brussels (Belgium) 2016, *Construction and built environment future horizons* Brussels (Belgium) 2014, *Workshop* Madrid (Spain) 2014, *Conference* Warsaw (Poland) 2011. **Publications** *ECTP Newsletter*. Action plans; strategies; road maps; position papers. **Members** Organizations (about 140): Construction companies; suppliers; designers and consultants; research bodies; clients; users; associations. Membership countries not specified. **IGO Relations** *European Commission (EC, #06633)*. **NGO Relations** Member of (1): *Alliance for Internet of Things Innovation (AIOTI, #00697)*. *Forum of European National Highway Research Laboratories (FEHRL, #09910)* is member. [2019.12.12/XM2694/**F**]

♦ European Consultants Association / see European Consultants Unit (#06769)

♦ European Consultants Unit (ECU) 06769

Europäische Beratervereinigung

European Office Wittelsbacherstrasse 20, 82319 Starnberg, Germany. T. +49815115990. Fax +4981513853. E-mail: ecu@ecu-online.org.

URL: http://www.ecu-online.org/

History Oct 1988, as *European Chartered Accountants, Lawyers, Tax Advisors and Management Consultants – Organisation européenne des conseils d'entreprises en droit, audit, gestion et développement – Europaverband der Rechtsanwälte und Steuerberater, Wirtschaftsprüfer und Unternehmensberater (ERWUS)*. Present name adopted 1989. Also referred to as: *ECU-Europe*; *European Consultants Association*; *European International Consultants Association (OICE)*. **Aims** Improve relationship between professionals and cooperation between groups of professionals worldwide; improve relationship between public institutions, unions and organizations worldwide; develop concepts to improve cooperation with the business sector; act as a an economic adviser in Europe. **Activities** Organizes Meetings. **Events** *Eurocongress* Krakow (Poland) 2000, *International relations, cooperation teams, insolvency law and public tenders* Munich (Germany) 1999, *Eurocongress* Thessaloniki (Greece) 1999, *International marketing and international enterprise transfer* Berlin (Germany) 1998, *International law of taxation and succession* Riva del Garda (Italy) 1998. **Publications** *Fax News* (4 a year); *Advisor in Europe* (annual). Information Services: Databank for a consultant-search-service; information network.

Members Organizations in 17 countries:

Austria, Belgium, Bulgaria, France, Germany, Greece, Hungary, Italy, Luxembourg, Netherlands, Portugal, Russia, Slovakia, Spain, Sweden, Switzerland, UK. [2012/XF5434/**F**]

♦ European Consultation on Refugees and Exiles / see European Council on Refugees and Exiles (#06839)

♦ European Consultative Commission (inactive)

♦ European Consumer Centres Network (ECC-Net) 06770

Réseau des centres européens des consommateurs

Contact c/o European Commission, DG Health and Consumer Protection, 1049 Brussels, Belgium. T. +3222991111.

URL: http://ec.europa.eu/ecc-net/

History 2005, resulting from the merger between *European Extrajudicial Network (EEJ-Net)* (or Clearing Houses) with the ECCs (or Euroguichets). **Aims** Provide information on consumer rights; assist in resolving disputes when the consumer and trader involved are based in 2 different European countries. **Structure** ECCs hosted by public bodies or non-profit-making organizations designated by a respective Member State and approved by *European Commission (EC, #06633)*. **Finance** Co-financed by grants from *European Union (EU, #08967)* and participating countries. **Activities** Knowledge management/information dissemination; conflict resolution; events/meetings. **Publications** Reports; promotional materials.

Members National European Consumer Centres in 30 countries:

Austria, Belgium, Bulgaria, Croatia, Cyprus, Czechia, Denmark, Estonia, Finland, France, Germany, Greece, Hungary, Iceland, Ireland, Italy, Latvia, Lithuania, Luxembourg, Malta, Netherlands, Norway, Poland, Portugal, Romania, Slovakia, Slovenia, Spain, Sweden, UK.

IGO Relations Cooperates with other EU-wide networks, including: Consumer Protection Cooperation Network; *European Judicial Network (EJN, #07615)*; FIN-Net; SOLVIT. [2019.07.11/XF6565/y/**F**]

♦ European Consumer Consultative Group (ECCG) 06771

Groupe consultatif européen des consommateurs (GCEC) – Europäischen Beratenden Verbrauchergruppe (EBVG)

Contact European Commission, DG for Justice and Consumers, 1049 Brussels, Belgium. E-mail: ec-consumer-consultative-group@ec.europa.eu.

URL: http://ec.europa.eu/consumers/empowerment/eccg_en.htm

History 9 Oct 2003, by *European Commission (EC, #06633)*, by Commission Decision 2003/709/EC. Decision repealed by Commission Decision 2009/705/EC, 14 Sep 2009. Replaces *Consumers' Committee (CC, inactive)*. **Aims** Serve as a discussion forum for problems relating to consumer interests within the European Union; advise, guide and inform the Commission on developments in consumer policies; serve as a source of information and soundboard for national organizations. **Activities** Events/meetings; networking/liaising; knowledge management/information dissemination.

Members Representatives of national consumer organizations in 27 countries:

Austria, Belgium, Bulgaria, Croatia, Cyprus, Czechia, Denmark, Estonia, Finland, France, Germany, Greece, Hungary, Ireland, Italy, Latvia, Lithuania, Luxembourg, Malta, Netherlands, Poland, Portugal, Romania, Slovakia, Slovenia, Spain, Sweden.

Representatives of 2 international organizations:

Association européenne pour la coordination de la représentation des consommateurs pour la normalisation (ANEC, #02561); *Bureau Européen des Unions de Consommateurs (BEUC, #03360)*.

Observers in 2 countries:

Iceland, Norway.

Associate members (2):

COFACE Families Europe (#04084); *European Community of Consumer Cooperatives (EURO COOP, #06678)*. [2017/XM2632/y/**E***]

♦ European Consumer Debt Network (ECDN) 06772

Coordinator c/o Maison des Associations Internationales, Rue Washington 40, 1050 Brussels, Belgium. E-mail: secretary@ecdn.eu.

Pres address not obtained. E-mail: president@ecdn.eu.

URL: http://www.ecdn.eu/

History Nov 2007. Founded by 8 national organizations active in the fight against over-indebtedness and financial exclusion. Registration: Banque-Carrefour des Entreprises, No/ID: 0893.346.244, Start date: 9 Nov 2007, Belgium; EU Transparency Register, No/ID: 124530543759-62, Start date: 3 Aug 2021. **Aims** Be a key force in bringing forward a social Europe that promotes and safeguards the *financial* inclusion and well-being of all its inhabitants while at the same time taking seriously its responsibility for and contributing to a social world; network with all relevant stakeholders in the field; support in building debt counseling services; promote tools for financial education; research over-indebtedness and the impact of debt advice; inform about debt regulation. **Structure** General Assembly (annual); Management Committee. **Languages** English. **Staff** 1.00 FTE, paid. **Finance** Sources: members' dues; revenue from activities/projects. **Activities** Events/meetings. **Events** *General Assembly* Strasbourg (France) 2022, *General Assembly* Amsterdam (Netherlands) 2019, *Conference on Debt Advice in a Cashless Society* Copenhagen (Denmark) 2018, *General Assembly* Copenhagen (Denmark) 2018, *General Assembly* Vienna (Austria) 2017. **Publications** *ECDN Newsletter*, *Money Matters*.

Members Organizations in 19 countries:

Austria, Bulgaria, Czechia, Finland, France, Germany, Iceland, Ireland, Italy, Luxembourg, Netherlands, Norway, Poland, Portugal, Romania, Slovakia, Spain, Sweden, Switzerland.

NGO Relations Member of (3): *European Anti-Poverty Network (EAPN, #05908)*; *Federation of European and International Associations Established in Belgium (FAIB, #09508)*; *Social Platform (#19344)*. [2022.10.19/XJ1815/**D**]

♦ European Consumer Safety Association (inactive)
♦ European Consumers' Organisation (#03360)
♦ European Contact Group for Church and Society / see European Contact Group – Ecumenical Network for Economic and Social Action (#06773)

♦ European Contact Group – Ecumenical Network for Economic and Social Action (ECG) 06773

Contact address not obtained. T. +420222211799. Fax +420222211799.

URL: http://www.ecgnet.cz/

History 1965, under the name *European Contact Group for Church and Society*, as the regional group for Western Europe of *World Council of Churches (WCC, #21320)*, within Unit II as part of the network of *Urban Rural Mission*. Previously referred to as *European Contact Group on Urban Industrial Mission (ECG) – Communauté européenne de travail Eglise et société industrielle – Europäische Arbeitsgemeinschaft Kirche und Arbeitswelt*. **Aims** Reflect on the responses of the Churches to urban industrial society; develop Urban Industrial and Rural Mission (UIRM) work by the exchange of ideas, experience and through training staff members; enable UIRM groups to meet around areas of common interest and concern; organize specific programmes of bi- and multi-lateral exchanges of workers, activists and community leaders; support all those who struggle for a more just society, especially the *marginalized*; develop new UIRM initiatives in *Central* and *Eastern Europe*. **Structure** General Assembly (every 2 years). Executive Committee (meets three times a year). Programme Development Secretary. **Languages** English, French, German. **Staff** 3.00 FTE, paid. **Finance** Members' dues. Other sources: grants from churches, foundations, agencies, *European Commission (EC, #06633)*. **Activities** Promotion and evaluation of training courses, workshops and other training events; participation in VETURI international network for new initiatives in diaconal training; specific training for central and eastern Europe; organisation of personal study and sabbatical leave. Main action-research and learning programmes: Workplace and employment/unemployment based activity; Urban and rural locality, community and local economy based activity. Information and documentation service. **Events** *General Meeting* Bochum (Germany) 2005, *General Meeting* Great Yarmouth (UK) 2003, *General Meeting* Most (Czech Rep) 2003, *General Meeting* Nürburg (Germany) 1999, *Consultation* Portugal 1991. **Publications** *ECG eNews* (periodical) in English, French, German. *ECG Working Papers*.

Members National movements, ecumenical networks and churches, organizations and individuals concerned with urban, industrial and rural issues in 27 European countries:

Albania, Austria, Belgium, Czechia, Denmark, Estonia, Finland, France, Germany, Greece, Hungary, Iceland, Ireland, Italy, Latvia, Lithuania, Luxembourg, Netherlands, Norway, Poland, Portugal, Romania, Slovakia, Spain, Sweden, Switzerland, UK.

NGO Relations Joint projects with: *Work and Economy Research Network in the European Churches (WEN, #21051)*. Cooperates with: *Ecumenical Forum of European Christian Women (EFECW, #05347)*; *Conference of European Churches (CEC, #04593)*; *Transnationals Information Exchange (TIE)*; *European Network of the Unemployed (ENU, no recent information)* (now an autonomous body). [2014/XE8606/**E**]

♦ European Contact Group on Urban Industrial Mission / see European Contact Group – Ecumenical Network for Economic and Social Action (#06773)

♦ European Contact Lens Forum (ECLF) 06774

Secretariat Rue de Tamines 10, 1060 Brussels, Belgium. T. +3225373711. Fax +3225373711. E-mail: info@eclf.eu.
URL: http://www.eclf.eu/

Aims Provide an exchange platform between all contact lens specialists, academics and the industry; promote contact lenses to the European eye care professionals; address issues around the safe use and sale of contact lenses with the EU decision-makers and other professionals; promote education and the expansion of the European contact lens and lens care markets. **Activities** Events/meetings; networking/liaising. **Events** *Seminar* Amsterdam (Netherlands) 2012. **Publications** Position papers.

Members Organizations (5):
European Contact Lens Society of Ophthalmologists (ECLSO, #06775); European Council of Optometry and Optics (ECOO, #06835); European Federation of National Associations and International Companies of Contact Lens and Contact Lens Care Product Manufacturers (EUROMCONTACT, #07167); European Federation of the Contact Lens and IOL Industries (EFCLIN, #07089); International Association of Contact Lens Educators (IACLE, #11815). [2015/XM4348/y/F]

♦ European Contact Lens Society of Ophthalmologists (ECLSO) 06775

Société européenne des ophtalmologistes contactologues – Europäische Augenärztliche Gesellschaft für Kontaklinsen

Pres Univ Hosp Antwerp, Wilrijkstraat 10, 2650 Edegem, Belgium. T. +32476414734.
Contact 19 Allées Jean Jaurès, 31015 Toulouse CEDEX 6, France. T. +33534452645. Fax +33561420009. E-mail: regist-eclso@europa-organisation.com.
URL: http://www.eclso.eu/

History 1969, Munich (Germany). Current statutes adopted 17 Apr 1982; amended 22 May 1993; 16 Sep 1994. Registration: Germany. **Aims** Promote research on ocular surface disease and contact lens related medical applications and pathology; increase communication between member societies. **Structure** General Assembly (annual); Board (Praesidium). **Languages** English, French, German. **Staff** 7.00 FTE, voluntary. **Finance** Sources: members' dues. **Activities** Events/meetings; knowledge management/information dissemination. **Events** *Annual Congress* Paris (France) 2022, *Annual Congress* Paris (France) 2021, *Annual Congress* Paris (France) 2020, *Annual Congress* Mandelieu-La Napoule (France) 2018, *Annual Congress* London (UK) 2017. **Publications** *ECLSO Newsletter*.

Members Ophtalmologists with principal activity in the field of ocular surface and contact lenses; national groups of ophthalmologists; Associate: eye care professionals. Members in 30 countries:
Austria, Belgium, Brazil, Bulgaria, Canada, Croatia, Czechia, France, Germany, Greece, Hungary, Iran Islamic Rep, Israel, Italy, Latvia, Lithuania, Moldova, Morocco, Netherlands, Poland, Portugal, Romania, Serbia, Slovenia, Spain, Switzerland, Tunisia, Türkiye, UK, USA.

NGO Relations Member of (2): *European Contact Lens Forum (ECLF, #06774); International Medical Contact Lens Council (IMCLC, #14131).* [2021/XD6897/D]

♦ European Contact-point Network against Corruption (EACN) 06776

Pres Federal Bureau of Anti-Corruption (BAK), Herrengasse 7, 1010 Vienna, Austria. T. +431531266849 – +431531266873. E-mail: secretariat@epac-eacn.org.
URL: http://www.epac-eacn.org/

History Established as the formal network comprising Anti-Corruption Authorities (ACAs) of *European Union (EU, #08967)* Member States, based on *European Partners against Corruption (EPAC, #08153)* structures. Constitution adopted, 2009, Nova Gorica (Slovenia). Constituted within framework of European Union Council Decision 2008/852/JHA, 24 Oct 2008. **Aims** Improve cooperation between authorities mandated with the prevention of, and fight against, corruption in the EU; foster closer relations between Member States and EU institutions. **Structure** General Assembly; Secretariat. Includes *European Partners against Corruption (EPAC, #08153).* **Languages** English. **Finance** Sources: contributions. **Activities** Events/meetings; knowledge management/information dissemination; monitoring/evaluation; networking/liaising; standards/guidelines. **Events** *Annual Conference* Rust (Austria) 2018, *Annual Conference* Lisbon (Portugal) 2017, *Annual Conference* Krakow (Poland) 2013, *Annual Conference* Barcelona (Spain) 2012, *Annual Conference* Laxenburg (Austria) 2011. **Publications** *Setting Standards for Europe Handbook: Anti-Corruption Authority Standards and Police Oversight Principles* (2012).

Members Anti-Corruption Authorities (50) of 21 countries:
Austria, Belgium, Bulgaria, Estonia, Finland, France, Germany, Greece, Hungary, Ireland, Latvia, Luxembourg, Malta, Netherlands, Poland, Portugal, Romania, Slovakia, Slovenia, Sweden, UK.

IGO Relations Memorandum of Understanding with: *International Anti-Corruption Academy (IACA, #11654); International Association of Anti-Corruption Authorities (IAACA, #11703); The World Bank Group (#21218)* – Integrity Vice Presidency (INT). [2020/XJ4608/E*]

♦ European Containerboard Industry Trade Organization / see CEPI ContainerBoard (#03824)
♦ European Containerboard Organization / see CEPI ContainerBoard (#03824)
♦ European Container Glass Federation (#09583)
♦ European Continental International Federation Amateur Unifight / see International Federation Amateur Unifight (#13353)

♦ European Continental Province of the Moravian Church 06777

Evangelische Brüder-Unität – Evangelische Broeder-Uniteit

Herrnhut Office Zittauer Str 20, 02747 Herrnhut, Germany. T. +4935873487-0. Fax +4935873487-99. E-mail: info@ebu.de.
Bad Boll Office Moravian Mission Soc, Badwasen 6, 73087 Bad Boll, Germany. T. +49716494210. Fax +497164942199. E-mail: brueder-unitaet.bb@ebu.de.
Zeist Office Zusterplein 20, 3703 CB Zeist, Netherlands. T. +31306924833. Fax +31306919639.
URL: http://www.ebu.de/

History 1732, Herrnhut (Germany). Registration: No/ID: KVK 41178135, Netherlands, Amsterdam. **Events** *Anniversary International Meeting* Herrnhut (Germany) 2022, *World mission conference* Herrnhut (Germany) 2001.

Members Covers 8 countries:
Albania, Denmark, Estonia, Germany, Latvia, Netherlands, Sweden, Switzerland.

NGO Relations Member of (2): *Conference of European Churches (CEC, #04593); World Council of Churches (WCC, #21320).* [2021.09.01/XE2619/E]

♦ European Continuous Casting Conference (meeting series)

♦ European Controllers Cup (ECC) 06778

Sec address not obtained. E-mail: joulesy2@aol.com.
URL: http://www.eccfootball.org/

History Competition organized since early 1960s, with an international committee founded 1972. Also referred to as *ECC Football*. **Aims** Solve problems and assist the organizing committees of the tournament. **Structure** Anual General Meeting/Captains' Meeting; Executive Committee. **Activities** Sporting activities. **Events** *Captains Meeting* Lisbon (Portugal) 2018.

Members Teams in 28 countries:
Austria, Belgium, Bulgaria, Canada, Croatia, Czechia, Denmark, Finland, France, Germany, Greece, Hungary, Iceland, Ireland, Italy, Kazakhstan, Latvia, Netherlands, Norway, Poland, Portugal, Romania, Russia, Serbia, Spain, Switzerland, UK, USA. [2019/XM7955/F]

♦ European Control Manufacturers' Association / see Association des fabricants européens d'appareils de contrôle et de régulation (#02592)
♦ European Control Manufacturers Association (#02592)
♦ European Convention on the Abolition of Legalisation of Documents Executed by Diplomatic Agents or Consular Officers (1968 treaty)
♦ European Convention on the Academic Recognition of University Qualifications (1959 treaty)
♦ European Convention on the Adoption of Children (1967 treaty)
♦ European Convention on the Adoption of Children – Revised (2008 treaty)
♦ European Convention on the Calculation of Time-limits (1974 treaty)
♦ European Convention on Certain International Aspects of Bankruptcy (1990 treaty)
♦ European Convention on Cinematographic Co-production (1992 treaty)
♦ European Convention on Civil Liability for Damage Caused by Motor Vehicles (1973 treaty)
♦ European Convention on the Compensation of Victims of Violent Crimes (1983 treaty)
♦ European Convention on Compulsory Insurance Against Civil Liability in Respect of Motor Vehicles (1959 treaty)
♦ European Convention Concerning the Social Security of Workers Engaged in International Transport (1956 treaty)

♦ European Convention for Constructional Steelwork (ECCS) 06779

Convention européenne de la construction métallique (CECM) – Europäische Konvention für Stahlbau (EKS)

SG Avenue des Ombrages 32, Boîte 20, 1200 Brussels, Belgium. T. +3227620429. Fax +3227620935. E-mail: eccs@steelconstruct.com.
URL: http://www.steelconstruct.com/

History 17 Oct 1955. Registration: Start date: 28 Jul 1969, Netherlands. **Aims** Prepare recommendations and guidelines for the design and execution of *steel* structures; promote coordination and cooperation with related organizations; undertake research and publish practical results. **Structure** General Assembly; Executive Board; Management Working Group; Promotion Management Board; Technical Management Board; Recruitment Committee; Joint Commission. **Languages** English, French, German. **Staff** 2.50 FTE, paid. **Finance** Sources: members' dues; revenue from activities/projects; sale of publications. **Activities** Advocacy/lobbying/activism; awards/prizes/competitions; events/meetings; financial and/or material support; networking/liaising; research/documentation; training/education. **Events** *Eurosteel Conference on Steel and Composite Structures* Amsterdam (Netherlands) 2023, *Eurosteel Conference on Steel and Composite Structures* Sheffield (UK) 2021, *Eurosteel Conference on Steel and Composite Structures* Sheffield (UK) 2020, *Eurosteel Conference on Steel and Composite Structures* Copenhagen (Denmark) 2017, *Annual Meeting* Stockholm (Sweden) 2016. **Publications** *ECCS Newsletter* (12 a year); *Steel Construction – Design and Research* (4 a year) – journal. Manuals; recommendations; codes; symposium proceedings.

Members Full; Individual; Associate; International; Supporting; Company. Full national organizations in 18 countries:
Austria, Czechia, Denmark, Finland, France, Germany, Hungary, Italy, Luxembourg, Netherlands, Norway, Poland, Portugal, Romania, Spain, Sweden, Switzerland, Türkiye.
Associate national organizations in 3 countries:
Belgium, France, Germany.
Supporting (2) in 2 countries:
Luxembourg, UK.
Included in the above, 1 organization listed in this Yearbook:
European General Galvanizers Association (EGGA, #07383).

IGO Relations Recognized by: *European Commission (EC, #06633).* **NGO Relations** Member of (2): *Construction 2050 Alliance (#04760); European Council for Construction Research, Development and Innovation (ECCREDI, #06813).* Founding member of: *Liaison Committee of International Associations of Civil Engineering (#16453)* and member of its *Joint Committee on Structural Safety (JCSS, #16126)*, together with *International Association for Bridge and Structural Engineering (IABSE, #11737); International Association for Shell and Spatial Structures (IASS, #12162); International Council for Research and Innovation in Building and Construction (CIB, #13069); Réunion internationale des laboratoires d'essais et de recherches sur les matériaux et les constructions (RILEM, #18930).* In liaison with technical committees of: *Comité européen de normalisation (CEN, #04162); International Institute of Welding (IIW, #13935); International Organization for Standardization (ISO, #14473).* [2022/XD0699/y/F]

♦ European Convention on Consular Functions (1967 treaty)
♦ European Convention on the Control of the Acquisition and Possession of Firearms by Individuals (1978 treaty)
♦ European Convention on Customs Treatment of Pallets Used in International Transport (1960 treaty)
♦ European Convention on the Equivalence of Diplomas Leading to Admission to Universities (1953 treaty)
♦ European Convention on the Equivalence of Periods of University Study (1956 treaty)
♦ European Convention on Establishment (1955 treaty)
♦ European Convention on Establishment of Companies (1966 treaty)
♦ European Convention on the Exercise of Children's Rights (1996 treaty)
♦ European Convention on Extradition (1957 treaty)
♦ European Convention on Foreign Money Liabilities (1967 treaty)
♦ European Convention on the General Equivalence of Periods of University Study (1990 treaty)
♦ European Convention on Human Rights / see European Court of Human Rights (#06855)
♦ European Convention on Information on Foreign Law (1968 treaty)
♦ European Convention on the International Classification of Patents for Inventions (inactive)
♦ European Convention on International Commercial Arbitration (1961 treaty)
♦ European Convention on the International Effects of Deprivation of the Right to Drive a Motor Vehicle (1976 treaty)
♦ European Convention on the International Validity of Criminal Judgments (1970 treaty)
♦ European convention on inter-regional cooperation (inactive)
♦ European Convention on the Legal Protection of Services Based On, or Consisting Of, Conditional Access (2001 treaty)
♦ European Convention on the Legal Status of Children Born out of Wedlock (1975 treaty)
♦ European Convention on the Legal Status of Migrant Workers (1977 treaty)
♦ European Convention of Library Suppliers and Information Providers (meeting series)
♦ European Convention on Mutual Assistance in Criminal Matters (1959 treaty)
♦ European Convention on Nationality (1997 treaty)
♦ European Convention on the Non-applicability of Statutory Limitation to Crimes Against Humanity and War Crimes (1974 treaty)
♦ European Convention on the Obtaining Abroad of Information and Evidence in Administrative Matters (1978 treaty)
♦ European Convention on Offences Relating to Cultural Property (1985 treaty)
♦ European Convention on Orchids (meeting series)
♦ European Convention for the Peaceful Settlement of Disputes (1957 treaty)
♦ European Convention on the Place of Payment of Money Liabilities (1972 treaty)
♦ European Convention for the Prevention of Torture and Inhuman or Degrading Treatment or Punishment (1987 treaty)
♦ European Convention on Products Liability in Regard to Personal Injury and Death (1977 treaty)
♦ European Convention on the Promotion of a Transnational Long-term Voluntary Service for Young People (2000 treaty)
♦ European Convention for the Protection of Animals During International Transport (1968 treaty)
♦ European Convention for the Protection of Animals During International Transport – Revised (2003 treaty)
♦ European Convention for the Protection of Animals Kept for Farming Purposes (1976 treaty)
♦ European Convention for the Protection of Animals for Slaughter (1979 treaty)
♦ European Convention on the Protection of the Archaeological Heritage (1969 treaty)
♦ European Convention on the Protection of the Archaeological Heritage, Revised (1992 treaty)
♦ European Convention on the Protection of the Audiovisual Heritage (2001 treaty)
♦ European Convention for the Protection of Pet Animals (1987 treaty)
♦ European Convention for the Protection of Vertebrate Animals Used for Experimental and other Scientific Purposes (1986 treaty)
♦ European Convention Providing a Uniform Law on Arbitration (1966 treaty)
♦ European Convention on the Punishment of Road Traffic Offences (1964 treaty)
♦ European Convention on Recognition and Enforcement of Decisions Concerning Custody of Children and on Restoration of Custody of Children (1980 treaty)

♦ European Convention on the Recognition of the Legal Personality of International Non-Governmental Organisations (1986 treaty)
♦ European Convention Relating to the Formalities Required for Patent Applications (1953 treaty)
♦ European Convention Relating to Questions on Copyright Law and Neighbouring Rights in the Framework of Transfrontier Broadcasting by Satellite (1994 treaty)
♦ European Convention on the Repatriation of Minors (1970 treaty)
♦ European Convention on the Service Abroad of Documents Relating to Administrative Matters (1977 treaty)
♦ European Convention on Social and Medical Assistance (1953 treaty)
♦ European Convention on the Social Protection of Farmers (1974 treaty)
♦ European Convention on Social Security (1972 treaty)
♦ European Convention on Spectator Violence and Misbehaviour at Sports Events and in Particular at Football Matches (1985 treaty)
♦ European Convention on State Immunity (1972 treaty)
♦ European Convention on the Supervision of Conditionally Sentenced or Conditionally Released Offenders (1964 treaty)
♦ European Convention on the Suppression of Terrorism (1977 treaty)
♦ European Convention on the Transfer of Proceedings in Criminal Matters (1972 treaty)
♦ European Convention on Transfrontier Television (1989 treaty)

♦ European Convention of Young People in Alcoholics Anonymous (EURYPAA) 06780

Contact address not obtained. E-mail: info@eurypaa.org – secretary@eurypaa.org.
URL: https://www.eurypaa.org/

Structure Advisory Board. **Activities** Events/meetings. **Events** *All Europe Young People in Alcoholics Anonymous Convention* Warsaw (Poland) 2022, *All Europe Young People in Alcoholics Anonymous Convention* Warsaw (Poland) 2021, *All Europe Young People in Alcoholics Anonymous Convention* Warsaw (Poland) 2020, *All Europe Young People in Alcoholics Anonymous Convention* Barcelona (Spain) 2019, *All Europe Young People in Alcoholics Anonymous Convention* Vilnius (Lithuania) 2018. [2021/AA1625/**D**]

♦ European Cookware Manufacturers' Association (inactive)

♦ European Cool Roofs Council (ECRC) 06781

Secretariat Dreve du Pressoir, 1190 Brussels, Belgium. T. +2821036159. E-mail: ecrc@coolroofcouncil.eu.
URL: http://coolroofcouncil.eu/

History 2011. Foundation supported by IEE Project COOL ROOFS (IEE/07/475/SI2.499428). **Aims** Develop scientific knowledge and research in relation to "cool roof" technology; promote the use of cool roof products and materials in Europe. **Structure** Board of Directors; Committees (3). **Languages** English. **Staff** 3.00 FTE, paid; 4.00 FTE, voluntary. **Finance** Members' dues. **Activities** Standards/guidelines; events/meetings. **Members** Companies (17); universities and research institutes (8). Membership countries not specified. Included in the above, 1 organization listed in this Yearbook: **NGO Relations** Associated partner of: *Covenant of Mayors for Climate and Energy (#04939).* [2018.06.01/XJ9348/**D**]

♦ European Cooperation for Accreditation (EA) 06782

Exec Sec 75 avenue Parmentier, 75544 Paris CEDEX 11, France. T. +33140212462. Fax +33140212400. E-mail: secretariat@european-accreditation.org.
Sec address not obtained.
URL: http://www.european-accreditation.org/

History 27 Nov 1997, Vienna (Austria), by merger of *European Accreditation of Certification (EAC, inactive)* and *European Cooperation for Accreditation of Laboratories (EAL, inactive).* Registered in accordance with Dutch law, Jun 2000. Activities of Secretariat declared in Paris (France), Jan 2010. EU Transparency Register: 369088318746-31. **Aims** Coordinate and lead the European accreditation infrastructure to allow results of conformity assessment services in one country to be accepted by Regulators and the market place in another country without further examination. **Structure** General Assembly (at least annual); Executive Committee; *European Accreditation Advisory Board (EAAB, see: #06782)*; Permanent Secretariat; Committees (6). **Languages** English. **Staff** 7.00 FTE, paid. **Finance** Members' dues. Operational and action grants from: *EFTA (#05391); European Commission (EC, #06633).* **Activities** Certification/accreditation; politics/policy/regulatory. **Events** *General Assembly* Luxembourg (Luxembourg) 2020, *General Assembly* Zagreb (Croatia) 2020, *General Assembly* Budapest (Hungary) 2019, *General Assembly* Rome (Italy) 2019, *Laboratory Committee Meeting* Warsaw (Poland) 2019. **Publications** Promotion and information documents; procedural and policy documents.

Members Full: nationally-recognized accreditation bodies in 36 European countries or candidates to accession:
Albania, Austria, Belgium, Bulgaria, Croatia, Cyprus, Czechia, Denmark, Estonia, Finland, France, Germany, Greece, Hungary, Iceland, Ireland, Italy, Latvia, Lithuania, Luxembourg, Malta, Montenegro, Netherlands, North Macedonia, Norway, Poland, Portugal, Romania, Serbia, Slovakia, Slovenia, Spain, Sweden, Switzerland, Türkiye, UK.
Associate: accreditation bodies located in countries listed as potential candidate members or covered by the EU Neighbourhood policy (ENP) (12):
Algeria, Belarus, Bosnia-Herzegovina, Egypt, Georgia, Israel, Jordan, Kosovo, Moldova, Morocco, Tunisia, Ukraine. [2021/XF4529/**F**]

♦ European Cooperation in Anthroposophical Curative Education and Social Therapy (ECCE) 06783

Coopération européenne pour la pédagogie curative et la sociothérapie anthroposophiques – Europäische Kooperation für anthroposophische Heilpädagogik und Sozialtherapie

Vice-Pres Brugakker 4118, 3704 ZB Zeist, Netherlands. T. +31650204989.
Management Assistant Hasenoehrlstrasse 12, 1100 Vienna, Austria.
Registered Office Asselkouter 34, 9820 Merelbeke, Belgium.

History 26 Mar 1992, Netherlands. Founded by the (Netherlands) "Council for Curative Education and Social Therapy". Registration: End date: 2016, Netherlands; Start date: 2016, Belgium. **Aims** Represent persons with special needs and look after their interests on a European level, and doing this out of anthroposophy. **Structure** Board. **Languages** English, French, German. **Staff** 0.50 FTE, paid. **Finance** Members' dues. Annual budget: euro 15,000. **Activities** Training/education; projects/programmes; networking/liaising; events/meetings. **Events** *European Congress* Belgrade (Serbia) 2018, *European Congress* Brussels (Belgium) 2015, *European congress* The Hague (Netherlands) 2008, *European Congress* Strasbourg (France) 2002, *International conference* Dornach (Switzerland) 2001. **Publications** *ECCE LINK* – newsletter. Brochure.

Members Organizations in 18 countries:
Austria, Belgium, Czechia, Denmark, Finland, France, Germany, Hungary, Ireland, Italy, Netherlands, Norway, Portugal, Romania, Spain, Sweden, Switzerland, UK.

IGO Relations *European Commission (EC, #06633).* **NGO Relations** Associated member of: *Inclusion Europe – European Association of Societies of Persons with Intellectual Disability and their Families (Inclusion Europe, #11144).* Full Member of: *European Disability Forum (EDF, #06929).* Also member of: *Alliance ELIANT (#00672); European Association of Service Providers for Persons with Disabilities (EASPD, #06204).* [2018.06.01/XD7027/**D**]

♦ European Cooperation Centre (unconfirmed)
♦ European Cooperation in the Field of Scientific and Technical Research / see European Cooperation in Science and Technology (#06784)
♦ European Cooperation Fund / see Network of European Foundations (#17019)
♦ European Cooperation for Informatics (inactive)
♦ European Cooperation in Maritime Research / see European Council for Maritime Applied R and D (#06829)
♦ European Cooperation and Partnership Network (unconfirmed)

♦ European Cooperation in Science and Technology (COST) 06784

Coopération européenne dans le domaine de la recherche scientifique et technique

Dir Av du Boulevard 21, 1210 Brussels, Belgium. T. +325333800. E-mail: communications@cost.eu.
Main Website: http://www.cost.eu/

History 1971, Brussels (Belgium). Established by the Ministerial Conferences, comprising Ministerial representatives of the then 19 participating states, as an intergovernmental European framework for international cooperation between nationally funded research activities. Currently used by the scientific communities of 36 European countries. Previously came within the remit of *Council of the European Union (#04895)* and of *European Commission (EC, #06633).* There was no statute establishing COST as it worked with flexible, pragmatic operating rules agreed by COST member states. As of 1 Oct 2014, legal entity implementing all activities under Horizon 2020, based on the Framework Partnership Agreement with the European Commission is *COST Association*, set up Sep 2013 as an international not-for-profit. Former names and other names: *European Cooperation in the Field of Scientific and Technical Research (COST)* – former. Registration: Banque-Carrefour des Entreprises, No/ID: 0829.090.573, Start date: 8 Sep 2010, Belgium; EU Transparency Register, No/ID: 480090715925-32, Start date: 16 Feb 2015. **Aims** Strengthen Europe in scientific and technical research through support of European cooperation and interaction between European researchers; maximize European synergy and added value in non-competitive and pre-normative research; enable scientists to collaborate in a wide spectrum of activities in research and technology; providesnetworking opportunities for researchers and innovators in order to strengthen Europe's capacity to address scientific, technological and societal challenges. **Structure** Ministerial Conference (every 5-6 years). *COST Association* integrates governance, management and implementation functions into a single structure. It comprises Committee of Senior Officials (CSO) – acts as General Assembly; Executive Board; Administration. COST National Coordinators (CNC); COST Scientific Committee. **Languages** English. **Staff** 65.00 FTE, paid. **Finance** Funded by the European Union **Activities** Networking/liaising. **Events** *COST Action CA19102 – Language In The Human-Machine Era Conference* Leeuwarden (Netherlands) 2023, *COST Action CA19102 – Language In The Human-Machine Era Meeting* Jyväskylä (Finland) 2022, *COST Action CA19102 – Language In The Human-Machine Era Meeting* Jyväskylä (Finland) 2021, *EVBRES COST Network (CA-17117) Evidence-Based Research Conference* Oulu (Finland) 2021, *European Conference on Trapped Ions* Stockholm (Sweden) 2021.

Members COST Member States (41- " indicates states which are not members of the European Union):
Albania (*), Armenia, Austria, Belgium, Bosnia-Herzegovina (*), Bulgaria, Croatia, Cyprus, Czechia, Denmark, Estonia, Finland, France, Georgia, Germany, Greece, Hungary, Iceland (*), Ireland, Italy, Latvia, Lithuania, Luxembourg, Malta, Moldova (*), Montenegro (*), Netherlands, North Macedonia (*), Norway (*), Poland, Portugal, Romania, Serbia (*), Slovakia, Slovenia, Spain, Sweden, Switzerland (*), Türkiye (*), UK (*), Ukraine.
Cooperating Member State:
Israel.
Partner Member:
South Africa.

IGO Relations Instrumental in setting up (1): *European Centre for Medium-Range Weather Forecasts (ECMWF, #06490).* [2023.03.02/XE0506/**E***]

♦ European Cooperation in Social Science Information and Documentation (inactive)

♦ European Cooperation for Space Standardization (ECSS) 06785

Exec Sec PO Box 299, 2200 AG Noordwijk, Netherlands. T. +31715655748. E-mail: ecss-secretariat@esa.int.
URL: http://www.ecss.nl/

History 1993. Founded upon signing of terms of reference. **Aims** Develop, promote and maintain a single set of standards for use in European space activities. **Structure** Steering Board; Executive Secretariat; Technical Authority; Working Groups. Secretariat provided by: *European Space Agency (ESA, #08798).* **Languages** English. **Publications** Standards; handbooks; technical memoranda. **NGO Relations** Cooperation agreement with: *Comité européen de normalisation (CEN, #04162); European Committee for Electrotechnical Standardization (CENELEC, #06647).* Recognizes: *Association of European Space Industry (EUROSPACE, #02544).* In liaison with technical committees of: *International Organization for Standardization (ISO, #14473).* [2023.02.14/XD5049/**D**]

♦ European Cooperative Association of International Civil Servants / see Association coopérative financière des fonctionnaires internationaux (#02455)

♦ European Cooperative Longo Mai 06786

Coopérative européenne Longo Maï – Europäische Kooperative Longo Mai

Contact St Johanns-Vorstadt 13, BP 1848, 4001 Basel BS, Switzerland. E-mail: info@prolongomai.ch.
Pro Longo maï (PLM): https://www.prolongomaif.ch/

History Jun 1973, Saint-Rémy-de-Provence (France). **Aims** Save the *desertification* of *poor regions.* **Activities** Sheep farming and agriculture on a communal basis. Radio station. Flying school. Contacts with Central America. Reception and defence of refugees. **Members** Communes and individuals. [2021/XF7619/**F**]

♦ European Cooperative Programme for Crop Genetic Resources Networks / see European Cooperative Programme for Plant Genetic Resources (#06787)

♦ European Cooperative Programme for Plant Genetic Resources (ECPGR) 06787

Programme coopératif européen sur les ressources phytogénétiques – Programa Cooperativo Europeo de Recursos Fitogenéticos

Sec c/o Alliance Bioversity CIAT, Via di San Domenico 1, 00153 Rome RM, Italy. T. +3966118231 – +3966118291. Fax +39661979661. E-mail: ecpgr@cgiar.org.
URL: http://www.ecpgr.cgiar.org/

History 1980. Established on recommendations of: *EUCARPIA (#05571), FAO (#09260); UNDP (#20292).* Tenth phase of 5 years (2019-2023) approved Jan 2019. Phase XI 2024-2028. Former names and other names: *European Cooperative Programme for Crop Genetic Resources Networks (ECP/GR)* – former; *Programme coopératif européen de réseaux sur les ressources phytogénétiques des cultures* – former; *Programa Cooperativo Europeo para Redes de Recursos Fitogenéticos* – former. **Aims** Ensure long-term *conservation* and facilitate utilization of plant genetic resources in Europe. **Structure** Steering Committee; Executive Committee; Crop Working Groups (20); Thematic Working Groups (4); Secretariat. **Languages** English. **Staff** 4.00 FTE, paid. **Finance** Sources: contributions of member/participating states. Phase X 2019-2023: about euro 2,688,250. **Activities** Financial and/or material support; knowledge management/information dissemination. **Events** *Steering Committee Meeting* Alnarp (Sweden) 2022, *Ad Hoc Meeting of the Steering Committee* 2020, *Meeting* Thessaloniki (Greece) 2018, *Meeting* Visegrad (Bosnia-Herzegovina) 2016, *Meeting* Vienna (Austria) 2012. **Publications** *ECPGR Information Bulletin*; *Genetic Resources Journal* in English – open access peer-reviewed journal. Proceedings; reports. **Information Services** *AEGIS – A European Genebank Integrated System*; *EURISCO – European Search Catalogue for Plant Genetic Resources.*

Members Governments of 33 countries:
Albania, Austria, Belarus, Bulgaria, Croatia, Cyprus, Czechia, Denmark, Estonia, Finland, France, Georgia, Germany, Greece, Hungary, Iceland, Ireland, Italy, Latvia, Lithuania, Montenegro, Netherlands, Norway, Portugal, Romania, Serbia, Slovakia, Slovenia, Spain, Sweden, Switzerland, Türkiye, UK.

IGO Relations Secretariat provided by: *Bioversity International (#03262).* [2022.10.19/XE2562/**E***]

♦ European Cooperative Research Network on Buffalo / see Inter-Regional Cooperative Research Network on Buffalo (#15967)
♦ European Cooperative Research Network on Flax and other Bast Plants (see: #08871)
♦ European Cooperative Research Network on Nuts / see FAO/CIHEAM Inter-Regional Cooperative Research Network on Nuts (#09258)
♦ European Cooperative Research Network on Olives / see Inter-Regional Cooperative Research Network on Olives (#15969)
♦ European Cooperative Research Network on Pasture and Fodder Crops / see FAO/CIHEAM International Network for the Research and Development of Pasture and Forage Crops (#09257)
♦ European Cooperative Research Network on Rice / see FAO Inter-Regional Cooperative Research Network on Rice in the Mediterranean Climate Areas (#09263)

- ♦ European Cooperative Research Network on Sunflower (see: #08871)
- ♦ European Cooperative Research Network on Sustainable Rural Environmental and Energy (see: #08871)

♦ European Cooperative for Rural Development (EUCORD) 06788

Exec Dir Chaussée de Vleurgat 206, Bte 5, 1000 Brussels, Belgium. T. +3226488937. E-mail: info@eucord.org.
URL: http://www.eucord.org/

History Former names and other names: *European Development Cooperatie* – legal name. Registration: Handelsregister, Start date: May 2003, Netherlands. **Aims** Help people living in *poverty* in developing countries to improve their well being, by engaging the private sector in delivering services to rural communities so as to ensure healthy families and sustainable livelihoods; actively promote partnerships between civil society organizations, corporations that are investing in developing countries, and development agencies. **Structure** Supervisory Board. **Languages** English, French. **Staff** 5.00 FTE, paid. **Finance** Sources: international organizations; private foundations. **Activities** Active in: Burundi, Congo DR, Ethiopia, Ghana, Guinea, Kenya, Mali, Nigeria, Rwanda, Senegal, Sierra Leone, Tanzania UR, Uganda. **IGO Relations** Partner of (5): *Common Fund for Commodities (CFC, #04293); FAO (#09260); International Crops Research Institute for the Semi-Arid Tropics (ICRISAT, #13116); UNIDO (#20336); United States Agency for International Development (USAID).* **NGO Relations** Partner of (4): Africa Enterprise Challenge Fund (AECF); *Alliance for a Green Revolution in Africa (AGRA, #00685); European Marketing Research Centre, Brussels (EMRC); West and Central African Council for Agricultural Research and Development (WECARD, #20907).* Affiliated with (1): *Winrock International.*
[2022.02.11/XM3817/F]

♦ European Cooperative Youth Network (ECYON) 06789

Address not obtained.
URL: http://www.ecyon.net/

Aims As a community of youth organizations, youth workers and young activists from various parts of Europe, cooperate by sharing best practices and ideas, developing partnerships, creating joint projects, initiating campaigns, and supporting each other in diverse areas. **NGO Relations** *OneEurope (#17730).*
[2020/XM4744/F]

- ♦ European Coordinating Committee for Artificial Intelligence / see European Association for Artificial Intelligence (#05943)
- ♦ European Coordinating Committee for Clinical Haemorheology / see European Society for Clinical Hemorheology and Microcirculation (#08546)
- ♦ European Coordinating Committee of Friendship Societies with the Arab World (inactive)

♦ European Coordinating Committee of Manufacturers of Electrical Switchgear and Controlgear (CAPIEL) 06790

SG Espace Hamelin, 11-17 rue de l'Amiral Hamelin, 75016 Paris, France. T. +33145057077. Fax +33147046857. E-mail: info@capiel.eu.
URL: https://www.capiel.eu/

History 11 Apr 1959. High-voltage part of CAPIEL merged with *Committee of Associations of European Transformer Manufacturers (COTREL, inactive)* into *European Association of the Electricity Transmission and Distribution Equipment and Services Industry (T and D EUROPE, #06023)*, Mar 2008. Current statutes adopted Jun 2011. Former names and other names: *Coordinating Committee for Common Market Associations of Manufacturers of Industrial Electrical Switchgear and Controlgear* – former (11 Apr 1959); *Comité de coordination des associations de constructeurs d'appareillage industriel électrique du Marché commun (CAPIEL)* – former (11 Apr 1959); *EG-Zusammenarbeit der Fachverbände der Schaltgeräte Hersteller* – former (11 Apr 1959); *Comitato di Coordinazione delle Associazioni dei Costruttori di Apparecchiature Industriali Elettriche del Mercato Comune* – former (11 Apr 1959); *Coördinatie Comité voor de Samenwerking der Fabrikanten van Schakelapparatuur in de EG* – former (11 Apr 1959); *Coordinating Committee for the Associations of Manufacturers of Industrial Electrical Switchgear and Controlgear in the European Union* – former; *Comité de coordination des associations de constructeurs d'appareillage électrique industriel de l'Union Européenne (CAPIEL)* – former; *Koordinierendes Komitee der Fachverbände der Schaltgerätehersteller in der Europäischen Union* – former; *Comitato di Coordinamento della Associazioni dei Costruttori di Apparecchiature elettriche industriali dell'Unione Europea* – former; *Coördinatie Comité voor de Samenwerking der Fabrikanten van Schakelapparatuur in de Europese Unie* – former. Registration: EU Transparency Register, No/ID: 492532816900-02; France. **Aims** Promote and support the common technical, industrial, economical, environmental and political interests of the European low voltage switchgear and controlgear industry (products, systems and assemblies). **Structure** Plenary Committee; Steering Committee. Project Groups. **Languages** English. **Events** *International conference on wadi hydrology* Amman (Jordan) 2003. **Publications** Position papers.

Members National organizations in 8 countries:
Austria, Belgium, Finland, France, Germany, Italy, Spain, UK.

IGO Relations Recognized by: *European Commission (EC, #06633).* **NGO Relations** Cooperation agreement with: *European Committee for Electrotechnical Standardization (CENELEC, #06647).* [2022/XE0423/E]

- ♦ European Coordinating Group on Homeworking / see European Homeworking Group (#07497)
- ♦ European Coordinating Group for National Institutions for the Promotion and Protection of Human Rights / see European Network of National Human Rights Institutions (#07949)
- ♦ European Coordinating Group for the Textile Industry (inactive)
- ♦ European Coordination of Associations and Individuals for Freedom of Conscience (internationally oriented national body)
- ♦ European Coordination Bureau of International Youth Organizations (inactive)
- ♦ European Coordination Centre for Research and Documentation in Social Sciences (inactive)

♦ European Coordination Committee on Human Rights Documentation (ECCHRD) 06791

Comité de coordination européen sur la documentation des droits de l'homme

Contact PO Box 1155, SE-221 05 Lund, Sweden. T. +46462221215. Fax +46462221222.
Street Address Raoul Wallenberg Inst, Stora Grabrödersg 17 B, SE-221 05 Lund, Sweden.
URL: http://www2.law.uu.nl/english/sim/library/ecchrd/ecchrd.html

Events *Meeting* Strasbourg (France) 2014, *Meeting* Sarajevo (Bosnia-Herzegovina) 2013, *Meeting* Berlin (Germany) 2012, *Meeting* Budapest (Hungary) 2011, *Meeting* Vienna (Austria) 2010. [2010.06.30/XE3258/E]

♦ European Coordination Committee of the Radiological, Electromedical Healthcare IT Industry (COCIR) 06792

SG BluePoint Brussels, Bd A Reyers 80, 1030 Brussels, Belgium. T. +32217068960. Fax +32217068969. E-mail: info@cocir.org.
URL: http://www.cocir.org/

History 1959. Founded by medical engineering industries of 5 European countries. Former names and other names: *European Coordination Committee of the Radiological and Electromedical Industries* – former; *Comité européen de coordination des industries radiologiques et électromédicales (COCIR)* – former; *Comité Europeo de Coordinación de las Industrias Radiológicas y Electromédicas* – former; *Europäischer Koordinierungsausschuss der Röntgen- und Elektromedizinischen Industrie* – former; *Comitato Europeo di Coordinamento delle Industrie Radiologiche ed Elettromedicali* – former; *Europees Coördinerend Comité van Röntgen- en Elektromedische Industrie* – former; *Europeiska Röntgen- och Elektromedicinska Industrins Samordningskommitté* – former; *European Coordination Committee of the Radiological, Electromedical and Medical IT Industries* – former. Registration: Banque Carrefour des Entreprises, No/ID: 0478.589.387, Start date: 22 Oct 2002, Belgium; EU Transparency Agency, No/ID: 0478.589.387, Start date: 17 Jan 2012. **Aims** Act as European organization of trade associations representing *manufacturers* of medical electric equipment; represent and promote members' interests; support development of *standards* regarding *safety* of patients and users; implement a European Quality System assessment scheme; communicate with *European Union* policy-makers on economic, regulatory and technical issues related to healthcare; work with organizations promoting harmonized standards and regulatory control worldwide and encourage free trade; cooperate with governments and EU authorities in achieving the above. **Structure** Council; Board; Office. Committees: Information; Technical; Economic Affairs. Working Groups appointed by Council. **Finance** Sources: members' dues. **Activities** Advocacy/lobbying/activism; events/meetings. **Events** *General Assembly* Brussels (Belgium) 2022, *Joint Workshop on the European Health Data Space Proposal* Brussels (Belgium) 2022, *General Assembly* Brussels (Belgium) 2021, *General Assembly* Brussels (Belgium) 2020, *General Assembly* Brussels (Belgium) 2019. **Publications** *COCIR Newsletter* – online. Brochure.

Members Corporate; national associations (13). National associations in 11 countries:
Belgium, France, Germany, Hungary, Italy, Netherlands, Portugal, Spain, Sweden, Türkiye, UK.

IGO Relations Recognized by: *European Commission (EC, #06633).* **NGO Relations** Member of (5): *EU Health Coalition; European Alliance for Cardiovascular Health (EACH, #05863); Federation of European and International Associations Established in Belgium (FAIB, #09508); Global Diagnostic Imaging, Healthcare IT, and Radiation Therapy Trade Association (DITTA, #10319); Industry4Europe (#11181).* Associate expert of: *Business and Industry Advisory Committee to the OECD (BIAC, #03385).* Cooperation agreement with: *European Committee for Electrotechnical Standardization (CENELEC, #06647).* Shareholder in *European Coordination Committee of the Radiological, Electromedical Healthcare IT Industry (COCIR, #06792).* Stakeholder in: *European Network for Health Technology Assessment (EUnetHTA, #07921).* [2022/XE0642/t/E]

- ♦ European Coordination Committee of the Radiological and Electromedical Industries / see European Coordination Committee of the Radiological, Electromedical Healthcare IT Industry (#06792)
- ♦ European Coordination Committee of the Radiological, Electromedical and Medical IT Industries / see European Coordination Committee of the Radiological, Electromedical Healthcare IT Industry (#06792)

♦ European Coordination Committee for Veterinary Training (ECCVT) . 06793

Main Office Rue Victor Oudart 7, 1030 Brussels, Belgium. E-mail: despoina@fve.org.
URL: https://eccvt.fve.org/

History 2004. Founded by *European Association of Establishments for Veterinary Education (EAEVE, #06031), European Board of Veterinary Specialisation (EBVS, #06375)* and *Federation of Veterinarians of Europe (#09713).* **Aims** Coordinate members' views on veterinary education. **Structure** Supervised by members' executive committees/boards. Rotating chairmanship. Secretariat provided by FVE. **Publications** *ECCVT Newsletter.*

Members Organizations (3):
European Association of Establishments for Veterinary Education (EAEVE, #06031); European Board of Veterinary Specialisation (EBVS, #06375); Federation of Veterinarians of Europe (#09713).
[2021/XM5602/y/E]

- ♦ European Coordination of Film Festivals (no recent information)

♦ European Coordination for Foreigners' Right to Family Life (COORDEUROP) 06794

Coordination européenne pour le droit des étrangers à vivre en famille – Coordinación Europea por el Derecho de los Extranjeros de Vivir en Familia – Europäischen Koordination für das Recht aller Ausländer auf Familienleben – Coordinamento Europeo per il Diritto degli Stranieri a Vivere in Famiglia – Coordenação Europeia para o Direito dos Estrangeiros a Viverem em Famililia

Address not obtained.

History 1993. Registration: Belgium. **Aims** Take all initiatives in favour of the right to live in family for people of third countries residing in one of the States of the European Union. **Structure** General Assembly (every 2 years, annual up to 2002). Council, composed of 12 to 24 members. Executive Committee. **Languages** English, French, Italian, Spanish. **Staff** None. **Finance** Members' dues. Other sources: contributions; income of projects. **Events** *General Assembly* Frankfurt-Main (Germany) 2005, *General Assembly* Paris (France) 2002, *General Assembly* Rome (Italy) 2002, *General Assembly* Paris (France) 2001, *General Assembly* Brussels (Belgium) 2000.

Members Full in 6 countries:
Belgium, France, Germany, Greece, Italy, Spain.
Included in the above, 4 organizations listed in this Yearbook:
Centre d'information et d'études sur les migrations internationales (CIEMI); Churches' Commission for Migrants in Europe (CCME, #03912); CIMADE; European Conference of Binational/Bicultural Relationships (ECB, #06731).

NGO Relations Member of: *European Platform for Migrant Workers' Rights (EPMWR, #08225).*
[2014/XE3419/y/E]

- ♦ European Coordination For Freedom of Conscience / see European Coordination of Associations and Individuals for Freedom of Conscience
- ♦ European Coordination of Independent Producers / see European Audiovisual Production (#06295)
- ♦ European Coordination, International Young Catholic Students – International Movement of Catholic Students (inactive)
- ♦ European Coordination IYCS-IMCS – European Coordination, International Young Catholic Students – International Movement of Catholic Students (inactive)
- ♦ European Coordination of MJC, Youthclubs and Youth Associations / see Contact-2103 (#04775)
- ♦ European Coordination of Support for the Sahrawi People (#04824)

♦ European Coordination Via Campesina (ECVC) 06795

Coordination Européenne Via Campesina – Coordinadora Europea Via Campesina – Europäische Koordination Via Campesina – Coordenadora Européia Via Campesina – Europese Vereniging Via Campesina – Coordenadora Europea Via Campesina

Contact Rue de la Sablonnière 18, 1000 Brussels, Belgium. T. +3222173112. Fax +3222184509. E-mail: info@eurovia.org.
URL: http://www.eurovia.org/

History 1986, as *European Farmers Coordination – Coordination paysanne européenne (CPE) – Coordinadora Campesina Europea – Europäische Bauern-Koordination – Coordenadora Agricola Européia – Europese Boeren Vereniging – Coordenadora Labrega Europea – Europako Nekazarien Kordinakundea – Sambandet av Europeiske Bønder.* Enlarged and launched under current title, Jun 2008. EU Transparency Register: 28920471149-55. **Aims** Change the present framework of the European *agriculture* policy, presently linked with the international trade rules (WTO) of 1994 into the food sovereignty framework, which responds to food, climate and biodiversity challenges; maintain *sustainable* family farms in all regions of Europe to ensure food security, quality food production and respect for the environment; maintain strong rural communities; ensure fair farm prices; stop the concentration in bigger farms; develop new rules for international trade. **Structure** Coordination Committee of 10 members. **Languages** English, French, German, Italian, Spanish. **Staff** 3.00 FTE, paid. **Activities** Advocacy/lobbying/activism; events/meetings. **Events** *Conference on a CAP for Small Farmers and Citizens* Brussels (Belgium) 2018, *General assembly* Brussels (Belgium) 1999.

Members Full: organizations (27) in 18 countries:
Austria, Belgium, Denmark, Finland, France, Georgia, Germany, Greece, Italy, Netherlands, Norway, Portugal, Romania, Spain, Sweden, Switzerland, Türkiye, UK.
International associated member:

IGO Relations Member of: advisory committees of DG AGRI and DG SANCO of *European Commission (EC, #06633).* **NGO Relations** Member of: *European Food Sovereignty Movement (NYELENI, #07288)* and its European Movement for Food Sovereignty and another CAP (Foodsovcap); *Seattle to Brussels Network (S2B, #19190); TP Organics – European Technology Platform (TP Organics, #20180); La Via Campesina (#20765).*
[2020/XF2076/y/F]

- ♦ European COPD Coalition (inactive)

♦ European Copper Institute (ECI) 06796

Chief Exec Av de Tervueren 168, Box 10, 1150 Brussels, Belgium. T. +3227777070. Fax +3227777079. E-mail: eci@copperalliance.eu.
URL: http://www.copperalliance.eu/

History 1996. Headquartered in Brussels (Belgium) since 1998. Registration: Companies House, No/ID: a, Start date: 25 Jan 1996, England and Wales; EU Transparency Register, No/ID: 04134171823-87, Start date: 10 Jun 2009. **Aims** As a member of the Copper Alliance, develop and defend markets for copper; make a positive contribution to society's sustainable development goals. **Structure** Board of Directors. **Languages** English. **Staff** 12.00 FTE, paid. **Finance** Administrative costs shared by membership. **Activities** Advocacy/lobbying/activism; knowledge management/information dissemination. **Publications** Applications brochure; papers on various health, sustainability and environmental issues.
Members ICA Producer members; European industrial companies. Members in 9 countries:
Belgium, Bulgaria, Finland, Germany, Ireland, Norway, Poland, Spain, Sweden.
IGO Relations Accredited by (1): *United Nations Framework Convention on Climate Change – Secretariat (UNFCCC, #20564)*. **NGO Relations** Member of (6): *Association européenne des métaux (EUROMETAUX, #02578)*; *Coalition for Energy Savings (#04056)*; *Construction Products Europe AISBL (#04761)*; *Energy Efficiency Industrial Forum (EEIF, #05470)*; *Forum for European Electrical Domestic Safety (FEEDS)*; *METALS FOR BUILDINGS (#16737)*. Functions as regional office of: *International Copper Association (ICA, #12962)*. Supporting member of: *European Forum for Renewable Energy Sources (EUFORES, #07329)*. Associate member of: *Fédération internationale pour la sécurité des usagers de l'électricité (FISUEL, #09658)*. Liaison Organization of: *Comité européen de normalisation (CEN, #04162)*. [2020.11.18/XE3262/jy/**E**]

♦ European Co-Production Association (no recent information)
♦ European Corduroy Federation (inactive)

♦ European Core and Tube Association (ECTA) 06797
Association européenne des tubes carton – Europäische Hartpapier-Hülsen-Vereinigung
   Main Office Grosse Friedberger Str 44-46, 60313 Frankfurt-Main, Germany. T. +496929724943. Fax +4969296532. E-mail: info@ecta.info.
   URL: http://www.ecta.info/
Activities EUROTUBE Conference. **Events** *EUROTUBE Conference* Hamburg (Germany) 2021, *EUROTUBE Conference* Tel Aviv (Israel) 2019.
Members National associations and companies (approx 65) in 17 countries:
Austria, Belgium, Czechia, Finland, France, Germany, Hungary, Ireland, Israel, Italy, Lebanon, Lithuania, Netherlands, Spain, Sweden, Switzerland, UK.
NGO Relations International branch federation of: *International Confederation of Paper and Board Converters in Europe (CITPA, #12866)*. [2020/XM4623/**D**]

♦ European Cork Federation 06798
Confédération européenne du liège (CELiège)
   SG Apart 100, 2900-365 Santa Maria de Lamas, Portugal. T. +351227442544. Fax +351227442547.
   Pres c/o AECORK, C/ Miquel Vincke y Meyer Nº 13, 17200 Palafrugell, Girona, Spain.
   URL: http://celiege.eu/
History 21 Nov 1989, Paris (France). Created 9 Nov 1962, Paris (France). Former names and other names: *EEC Cork Confederation: Industry and Commerce* – former; *Confédération du liège de la CEE: Industrie et commerce* – former. **Aims** Study technical, economic, social and fiscal problems of interest to the cork sector; study and adopt general rules; collect and disseminate documentation concerning the cork sector and certifications SYSTECODE and SUBERCODE. **Structure** General Assembly (annual); Management Board. **Languages** French. **Staff** 18.00 FTE, paid. **Finance** Sources: members' dues.
Members Full in 6 countries:
France, Germany, Italy, Portugal, Spain, UK.
NGO Relations In liaison with technical committees of: *International Organization for Standardization (ISO, #14473)*. [2008.06.01/XE0428/**D**]

♦ European Corporate Governance Institute (ECGI) 06799
Institut européen de corporate governance
   Contact c/o Royal Academies of Belgium, Palace of the Academies, Rue Ducale 1, 1000 Brussels, Belgium. T. +3225502340.
   URL: http://www.ecgi.global/
History Successor to *European Corporate Governance Network (ECGN, inactive)*. EU Transparency Register: 313390020603-18. **Aims** Improve corporate governance through fostering independent scientific research and related activities. **Structure** General Assembly (annual); Board of Directors. **Languages** English. **Activities** Research/documentation; knowledge management/information dissemination; events/meetings. **Events** *Global Corporate Governance Colloquium* Frankfurt-Main (Germany) 2019, *General Assembly* Berlin (Germany) 2018, *Global Corporate Governance Colloquium* Cambridge, MA (USA) 2018, *General Assembly* Lausanne (Switzerland) 2017, *Conference of the EU-Asia Corporate Governance Dialogue* Singapore (Singapore) 2017. **Publications** *Working Paper Series*.
Members Academic; Institutional; Practitioner; Research; Patrons. Members in 57 countries and territories:
Albania, Australia, Austria, Belarus, Belgium, Bosnia-Herzegovina, Brazil, Bulgaria, Canada, China, Croatia, Cyprus, Denmark, Egypt, Estonia, Finland, France, Germany, Greece, Hong Kong, India, Indonesia, Ireland, Israel, Italy, Japan, Jordan, Korea Rep, Lithuania, Luxembourg, Malta, Mexico, Mongolia, Netherlands, New Zealand, Norway, Pakistan, Peru, Poland, Portugal, Romania, Russia, Rwanda, Saudi Arabia, Singapore, Slovakia, Slovenia, South Africa, Spain, Sweden, Switzerland, Trinidad-Tobago, Türkiye, UK, Ukraine, United Arab Emirates, USA. [2019/XE4418/j/**E**]

♦ European Corporate Security Association (internationally oriented national body)

♦ European Cosmetic Responsible Person Association (ERPA) 06800
   Main Office 30 Bvd Brand Whitlock, 1200 Brussels, Belgium. E-mail: info@erpacosmetics.com.
   URL: http://www.erpacosmetics.com/
History 18 Jan 2011. Former names and other names: *ERPA Cosmetics* – alias. Registration: EU Transparency Register, No/ID: 846662328834-63. **Aims** Support efforts to protect the safety of European individuals who use cosmetic products by promoting high standards of services and professional conduct among the European Responsible Persons. **Structure** An organization of the type *European Economic Interest Grouping (EEIG, #06960)*. **Events** *Annual Congress on Regulations and Compliance for Cosmetics* Brussels (Belgium) 2023, *Annual Congress on Regulations and Compliance for Cosmetics* Brussels (Belgium) 2022, *Annual Congress on Regulations and Compliance for Cosmetics* Brussels (Belgium) 2021, *International Congress on Regulations and Compliance in Cosmetics* Brussels (Belgium) 2019, *International Congress on Regulations and Compliance in Cosmetics* Brussels (Belgium) 2018. **Members** Founder; Core; Association; International. Membership countries not specified. [2023/XM6044/**E**]

♦ European Cosmetic, Toiletry and Perfumery Association / see Cosmetics Europe – The Personal Care Association (#04852)

♦ European Council 06801
Conseil européen – Consejo Europeo – Europäischer Rat – Conselho Europeu – Consiglio Europeo – Europese Raad – Europaeiske Rådet – Europaeiske Råd – Eurooppa-neuvosto – Evropaïko Simvulio – Chomhairle Eorpach – Evropska Rada – Európska Rada – Európai Tanacs – Rada Europejska – Evropski Svet – Euroopa Ülemkogu – Eiropadome – Europos Vadovu Taryba – Kunsill Ewropew – Europsko Vijece – Consiliul European
   Gen Sec Bâtiment Justus Lipsius, Rue de la Loi 175, 1048 Brussels, Belgium. T. +3222816111. Fax +3222816934. E-mail: press.office@consilium.europa.eu.
   URL: http://www.consilium.europa.eu/
History Dec 1974, Paris (France). Established by Heads of State or Government of the then 10 members of the *European Communities (EC, inactive)*, institutionalizing a previously informal series of meetings and functioning as the *European Summit* of *Council of the European Union (#04895)*. Further institutionalized by the *Single European Act (SEA, 1986)*, signed Feb 1986, ratified by member parliaments by 31 Mar 1987, which came into force 1 Jul 1987. Article D of *Treaty on European Union (Maastricht Treaty, 1992)*, signed 7 Feb 1992, gives the European Council the role of providing impetus for development of the *European Union (EU, #08967)* and defining its general political guidelines, and of producing an annual report on the Union's progress. Although it had not been an official institution of the European Communities, the Council became one of the institutions of the European Union when the EU came into operation. The *Treaty of Amsterdam (1997)*, signed 2 Oct 1997 following agreement among the Heads of State and Government 16-17 Jun 1997, Amsterdam (Netherlands), at a meeting of the Council, gave a legal personality to the European Union, allowing it to negotiate as one entity. The Amsterdam treaty includes a revised section on common foreign and security policy which provides for the European Council to decide on common strategies to be implemented by the EU in areas where member states share important interests. *Laeken Declaration*, signed at a meeting of the Council, 15 Dec 2001, Brussels (Belgium), and the associated *Convention on the Future of Europe (inactive)*, anticipated the creation of an *'Area of Freedom, Security and Justice'*. The Convention completed its work 10 Jul 2003. Following changes introduced by the *Treaty of Lisbon (2007)*, the European Council became one of the EU's main institutions and under article 68 of *Treaty on the Functioning of the European Union (TFEU, 1957)*, became responsible for defining strategic guidelines for the area of freedom, security and justice. **Aims** Determine the EU's general political direction and priorities – essentially setting the policy agenda for the EU. **Structure** Comprises Heads of state or government of EU countries, President of *European Commission (EC, #06633)* and High Representative for Foreign Affairs and Security Policy. Convened and chaired by President, who is elected by the Council itself. Meets 4 times a year in 'EU summits', always in Brussels (Belgium), with additional meetings possibly convened by President. General Secretariat, headed by Secretary-General – shared with *Council of the European Union (#04895)*. **Languages** EU languages. **Staff** 3048.00 FTE, paid. **Finance** On budget of the European Union. **Activities** Decides on the EU's overall direction and political priorities, but not does pass laws, but conclusions instead; deals with complex or sensitive issues that cannot be resolved at lower levels of intergovernmental cooperation; sets the EU's common foreign and security policy, taking into account EU strategic interests and defence implications; nominates and appoints candidates to certain high profile EU level roles, such as *European Central Bank (ECB, #06466)* and *European Commission (EC, #06633)*. Has a formal role in the EU's annual European semester process – a cycle of economic and fiscal policy coordination. **Events** *Meeting* Brussels (Belgium) 2014, *Meeting* Brussels (Belgium) 2014, *Special Meeting* Brussels (Belgium) 2014.
Members Heads of State or Government of the Member States of the European Union (27):
Austria, Belgium, Bulgaria, Croatia, Cyprus, Czechia, Denmark, Estonia, Finland, France, Germany, Greece, Hungary, Ireland, Italy, Latvia, Lithuania, Luxembourg, Malta, Netherlands, Poland, Portugal, Romania, Slovakia, Slovenia, Spain, Sweden.
IGO Relations Receives an annual report from: *European Central Bank (ECB, #06466)*. Cooperates with and on: *European Economic and Monetary Union (EMU, #06961)*; *European Parliament (EP, #08146)*; *NATO (#16945)*. [2020/XE7976/**E***]

♦ European Council of Academies of Applied Sciences, Technologies and Engineering / see European Council of Applied Sciences, Technologies and Engineering (#06804)
♦ European Council on African Studies (no recent information)
♦ European Council on Alcohol Research, Rehabilitation and Education / see European Alcohol Policy Alliance (#05856)

♦ European Council for Alkylphenols and Derivatives (CEPAD) 06802
   Contact CEFIC, Rue Belliard 40, Boîte 15, 1040 Brussels, Belgium.
   URL: http://cepad.cefic.org/
History Set up as a sector group of *Conseil européen de l'industrie chimique (CEFIC, #04687)*. Acronym is derived from previous french name. Former names and other names: *Conseil européen des phénols alkylés et dérivés (CEPAD)* – former. **Aims** Provide a forum to represent the association and its members' interests; develop and promote initiatives on their behalf. **Languages** English. **Activities** Research/documentation.
Members Full (4) and Associate (2) in 5 countries:
Belgium, France, Germany, Sweden, Switzerland. [2021.05.26/XE3726/**E**]

♦ European Council of American Chambers of Commerce (ECACC) ... 06803
   Vice-Chair c/o AmCham Slovenia, Dunajska 156, WTC, 1000 Ljubljana, Slovenia. T. +38682051350.
   E-mail: ace@amcham.si.
   URL: http://www.amchamsineurope.com/
History 1963, as *Council of American Chambers of Commerce in Europe*. Present name adopted in 1985. Previously referred to in English as *Council of American Chambers of Commerce Europe and Mediterranean*, and in French as *Conseil européen des chambres de commerce américaines*. Also known as *AmChams in Europe*. **Aims** Promote commercial, financial and industrial relations between the *USA* and host countries; present the views of the *business* community in members' areas to agencies and organizations in USA; when appropriate, represent members' interests to host country governments and to regional intergovernmental organizations. **Structure** Executive Council; Board of Directors. **Languages** English. **Finance** Members' dues. **Activities** Events/meetings. **Events** *Conference* Washington, DC (USA) 1993, *Conference* Brussels (Belgium) 1991, *Annual fall meeting* 1988, *Meeting* Washington, DC (USA) 1988, *Annual fall meeting* Paris (France) 1987. **Publications** *European American Business*.
Members American Chambers of Commerce in 43 countries:
Albania, Armenia, Austria, Azerbaijan, Belgium, Bosnia-Herzegovina, Bulgaria, Croatia, Cyprus, Denmark, Estonia, Finland, France, Georgia, Germany, Gibraltar, Greece, Hungary, Ireland, Israel, Italy, Kosovo, Latvia, Lithuania, Luxembourg, Malta, Moldova, Montenegro, Netherlands, North Macedonia, Norway, Poland, Romania, Russia, Serbia, Slovakia, Slovenia, Spain, Sweden, Switzerland, Türkiye, UK, Ukraine.
Consultative Status Consultative status granted from: *World Intellectual Property Organization (WIPO, #21593)* (Permanent Observer Status). [2019.05.06/XE0732/**E**]

♦ European Council of Applied Sciences and Engineering / see European Council of Applied Sciences, Technologies and Engineering (#06804)

♦ European Council of Applied Sciences, Technologies and 06804
Engineering (Euro-CASE)
   SG Le Ponant, Bât A, 19 rue Leblanc, 75015 Paris, France. E-mail: mail@euro-case.org.
   URL: http://www.euro-case.org/
History 1992. Founded on the initiative of members of France's *Conseil pour les Applications de l'Académie des Sciences (CADAS)*. Former names and other names: *European Council of Applied Sciences and Engineering* – former (1992); *European Council of Academies of Applied Sciences, Technologies and Engineering* – alias. Registration: France. **Aims** Provide impartial, independent and balanced advice on technological issues with a clear European dimension. **Structure** Board; Executive Committee; Permanent Secretariat in Paris (France). **Languages** English. **Staff** 2.00 FTE, paid. **Finance** Members' dues. **Activities** Events/meetings; awards/prizes/competitions. **Events** *Annual Conference* Brussels (Belgium) 2022, *Annual Conference* London (UK) 2021, *Annual Conference* Zagreb (Croatia) 2020, *Annual Conference* Oslo (Norway) 2019, *Annual Conference* Zurich (Switzerland) 2018. **Publications** *Euro-CASE Reports* – series. *European IST Prize Winners Book*. Annual Report.
Members Full and Associate: academies of applied sciences, technology and engineering in 23 European countries:
Austria, Belgium, Croatia, Czechia, Denmark, Finland, France, Germany, Greece, Hungary, Ireland, Italy, Netherlands, Norway, Poland, Portugal, Romania, Serbia, Slovenia, Spain, Sweden, Switzerland, UK.
NGO Relations Academic partner of: *Federation of European Academies of Medicine (FEAM, #09490)*. [2022/XD5547/**D**]

♦ European Council of Artists (ECA) 06805
Conseil européen des artistes
   Coordinator c/o Council of Danish Artists, Hillerídgade 30a 1 sal, 2200 Copenhagen N, Denmark.
   Pres Artists Fed, PO Box 637, 121 Reykjavik, Iceland.
History Founded May 1995, Ebeltoft (Denmark). **Aims** Communicate with and influence European policies of concern to artists; secure close mutual relations with the political institutions of Europe. **Structure** Congress (annual). Executive Committee. **Languages** English. **Staff** 1.50 FTE, paid. **Activities** Meeting activities. **Events** *Annual Conference* Vilnius (Lithuania) 2012, *Annual conference and congress / Annual Conference* Madrid (Spain) 2011, *Annual conference and congress / Annual Conference* Zagreb (Croatia) 2010, *Annual Conference* Floriana (Malta) 2009, *Annual conference and congress* Valletta (Malta) 2009. **Publications** Electronic newsletters; conference proceedings; reports.
Members Organizations in 26 countries and territories:
Austria, Belgium, Croatia, Cyprus, Czechia, Denmark, England, Estonia, Faeroe Is, Finland, Georgia, Germany, Hungary, Iceland, Lapland, Latvia, Lithuania, Malta, Poland, Portugal, Romania, Scotland, Slovakia, Slovenia, Spain, Sweden.
NGO Relations Member of: *On the Move (OTM, #16868)*. [2017/XF4351/**F**]

♦ **European Council of Automotive Research and Development (EUCAR)** **06806**

Dir Avenue des Nerviens 85, 1040 Brussels, Belgium. T. +3227387352. Fax +3227387312. E-mail: eucar@eucar.be.
URL: http://www.eucar.be/

History 27 May 1994. Legally a part of *European Automobile Manufacturers' Association (ACEA, #06300)* but with independence in its subject areas. Registration: EU Transparency Register, No/ID: 733099334608-76. **Aims** Strengthen the competitiveness of European automotive manufacturers through strategic collaborative research and innovation. **Structure** Council, headed by rotating Chairman. Working Groups. **Languages** English. **Staff** 4.00 FTE, paid. **Activities** Events/meetings; research/documentation. **Events** *Annual Conference* Brussels (Belgium) 2012, *Annual Conference* Brussels (Belgium) 2008, *Freight transport meeting* Brussels (Belgium) 2008, *Annual Conference* Brussels (Belgium) 2007, *Annual Conference* Brussels (Belgium) 2006. **Publications** Annual Project Book. **Members** Vehicle manufacturers (14). Membership countries not specified. **NGO Relations** Member of: *European Green Vehicles Initiative Association (EGVIA, #07410)*; *European Road Transport Research Advisory Council (ERTRAC, #08396)*; *European Technology Platform ALICE (ALICE, #08888)*; iMobility Forum. [2021/XD7974/E]

♦ European Council for Blood Pressure and Cardiovascular Research / see European Council for Cardiovascular Research (#06808)
♦ European Council for Building Professionals (inactive)

♦ **European Council for Business Education (ECBE)** **06807**

Pres Rue J Coosemans 30, 1030 Brussels, Belgium.
URL: http://www.ecbe.eu/

History Jul 1995, Paris (France). Registered in accordance with Belgian law. **Aims** Encourage and support continuous improvement in the quality of business education worldwide; translate excellence in business education into reality for students entering the global market place. **Structure** Board of Directors, comprising President, Secretary, President-Elect, Treasurer, Secretary, Treasurer and 6 members. **Languages** English. **Staff** 4.00 FTE, paid. **Finance** Members' dues. **Activities** Organizes: annual conference; seminars. Participates in international conferences. Accreditation evaluation; involvement in European projects; quality assurance in education; consulting, advising and assisting in developing institutions. **Events** *Annual Conference* Brussels (Belgium) 2020, *Annual Conference* Brussels (Belgium) 2019, *Annual Conference* Madrid (Spain) 2018, *Annual Conference* Vienna (Austria) 2013, *Annual conference* Barcelona (Spain) 2012. **Publications** Conference proceedings.
Members Accredited in 13 countries:
Czechia, France, Hungary, North Macedonia, Peru, Poland, Romania, Russia, Serbia, Slovenia, Spain, Switzerland, USA.
Included in the above, 2 organizations listed in this Yearbook:
European Center of International Hotel Management (CMH); *Institut européen de management international (IEMI)*.
Candidate in 1 country:
Czechia.
Members in 23 countries:
Bahrain, Belgium, Cyprus, Egypt, Greece, Guatemala, Iceland, India, Kazakhstan, Kenya, Lebanon, North Macedonia, Romania, Russia, Serbia, Singapore, Slovenia, Spain, Sweden, Switzerland, UK, Ukraine, USA.
IGO Relations *European Commission (EC, #06633)*. **NGO Relations** Affiliate member of: *European Association for Quality Assurance in Higher Education (ENQA, #06183)*. [2021/XJ1734/y/D]

♦ **European Council for Cardiovascular Research (ECCR)** **06808**

Main Office c/o The Conference Collective, 8 Waldegrave Road, Teddington, TW11 8HT, UK. T. +442089777997. E-mail: eccr@conferencecollective.co.uk.
URL: http://www.eccr.org/

History Oct 1997, as *European Council for Blood Pressure and Cardiovascular Research (ECCR)*. Bye-laws amended 17 Oct 1998, 16 Oct 1999. UK Registered Charity: 1078280. **Aims** Promote clinical and experimental research in hypertension and cardiovascular disease in Europe. **Structure** General Meeting (annual). Executive Committee, comprising President, President-Elect, Treasurer, Secretary, Programme Coordinator and 5 members. **Languages** English. **Staff** None. **Finance** Financed by: Corporate members; conference registration fees. **Events** *Meeting* Treviso (Italy) 2019, *Annual Meeting* La Colle-sur-Loup (France) 2010, *Annual meeting* La Colle-sur-Loup (France) 2010, *Annual Meeting* La Colle-sur-Loup (France) 2009, *Annual meeting* La Colle-sur-Loup (France) 2009.
Members Individuals (185) in 15 countries:
Belgium, Czechia, Denmark, France, Germany, Ireland, Israel, Italy, Netherlands, Norway, Poland, Spain, Sweden, Switzerland, UK. [2020/XD7389/v/D]

♦ European Council of Chemical Manufacturers' Federations / see Conseil européen de l'industrie chimique (#04687)

♦ **European Council on Chiropractic Education (ECCE)** **06809**

Treas Charlottenstrasse 32, 40210 Düsseldorf, Germany. E-mail: info@cce-europe.org.
Pres address not obtained.
URL: http://www.cce-europe.org/

History 1986. Registration: North Rhine-Westphalia District court, No/ID: VR 2732, Start date: 29 Aug 1990, Germany, Düsseldorf. **Aims** As an autonomous organization concerned with accreditation (and re-accreditation) of the education and training of chiropractors, assure the quality of chiropractic education and training against a set of educational standards. **Structure** Council (meets annually); Executive Committee; Commission on Accreditation; Quality Assurance Committee. **Languages** English. **Staff** 1.00 FTE, paid. **Finance** Members' dues. Other sources: supported by ECU; donations. **Activities** Certification/accreditation. **Events** *Annual Meeting* Paris (France) 2013, *Annual Meeting* Brussels (Belgium) 2012, *Annual Meeting* Frankfurt-Main (Germany) 2011, *Annual Meeting* Brussels (Belgium) 2010, *Annual Meeting* Frankfurt-Main (Germany) 2009. **Publications** *Accreditation Procedures and Standards for Chiropractic Education*; *Evaluation Team Manual*.
Members Accredited institutions (12) in 6 countries:
Denmark, France, South Africa, Spain, Switzerland, UK.
Included in the above, 1 organization listed in this Yearbook:
AECC University College.
NGO Relations Member of (2): *Councils on Chiropractic Education International (CCEI, #04916)*; *World Federation of Chiropractic (WFC, #21420)*. [2021/XD2717/D]

♦ **European Council of Civil Engineers (ECCE)** **06810**

Conseil européen des ingénieurs civils

Gen Sec PO Box 13641, NTUA – Patission Street Complex, 28th October and Stournari Street, 106 82 Athens, Greece. E-mail: ecce_sps@otenet.gr.
Registered Office c/o ICE, 1 Great George Street, Westminster, London, SW1P 3AA, UK.
URL: http://www.ecceengineers.eu/

History 12 Dec 1985, Madrid (Spain). Founded at a meeting of representatives of professional engineering organizations, when constitution and rules were adopted. Registration: Companies House, No/ID: 02916733, Start date: 7 Apr 1994, England. **Aims** Promote the highest technical and ethical standards; provide a source of impartial advice; promote cooperation with other pan-European organizations in the construction industry. **Structure** General Assembly; Executive Board. **Languages** English. **Staff** 1.00 FTE, paid. **Finance** Sources: members' dues. **Activities** Events/meetings; guidance/assistance/consulting. **Events** *General Meeting* Athens (Greece) 2020, *General Meeting* Lisbon (Portugal) 2019, *General Meeting* Podgorica (Montenegro) 2019, *General Meeting* London (UK) 2018, *General Meeting* Tallinn (Estonia) 2018. **Publications** *ECCE E-Journal*. Annual Report. Technical briefings; position papers; books.
Members Full in 23 countries:
Austria, Bulgaria, Croatia, Cyprus, Czechia, Estonia, Georgia, Greece, Hungary, Latvia, Lithuania, Malta, Montenegro, Poland, Portugal, Russia, Serbia, Slovakia, Slovenia, Spain, Türkiye, UK, Ukraine.
Associate in 2 countries:
Japan, USA.
European Construction Forum (ECF, #06765); *Fédération Européenne d'Associations Nationales d'Ingénieurs (FEANI, #09558)*; *World Federation of Engineering Organizations (WFEO, #21433)*.
NGO Relations Member of (5): *Consejo de las Asociaciones Profesionales de Ingenieros Civiles de Lengua Oficial Portuguesa y Castellana (CECPC-CICPC, #04702)*; *Construction 2050 Alliance (#04760)*; *Engineering Association of Mediterranean Countries (EAMC, #05480)*; *European Construction Forum (ECF, #06765)*; *European Council for Construction Research, Development and Innovation (ECCREDI, #06813)*. Cooperates with (2): *European Council of Engineers Chambers (ECEC, #06819)*; *Fédération Européenne d'Associations Nationales d'Ingénieurs (FEANI, #09558)*. Instrumental in setting up and member of: *World Council of Civil Engineers (WCCE, #21321)*. Associated organization: *European Civil Engineering Education and Training (EUCEET Association, #06565)*. [2020/XD1133/D]

♦ European Council for Classical Homeopathy / see European Central Council of Homeopaths (#06467)
♦ European Council for Clinical Laboratories Medicine (no recent information)
♦ European Council for Clinical and Laboratory Standardization (inactive)
♦ European Council of Coloproctology (inactive)
♦ European Council of Conscripts Organizations (inactive)

♦ **European Council for the Conservation of Fungi (ECCF)** **06811**

Sec c/o Swiss Federal Research Institute WSL, RU Biodiversity and Conservation Biology, Zürcherstrasse 111, 8903 Birmensdorf ZH, Switzerland. E-mail: senn@wsl.ch.
URL: http://www.wsl.ch/eccf/

History 1985, Oslo (Norway). Currently serves as conservation body of *European Mycological Association (EMA, #07845)*. **Aims** Promote the conservation of fungi; promote the attention for the conservation of fungi to all governmental bodies and non-governmental organizations, as well as to politicians and mycologists; stimulate studies and publications on the changes in the mycoflora on a local, regional, national and European level; stimulate studies and discussions on the factors and processes responsible for these observed changes in the mycoflora; stimulate the publication of national and regional Red Data Lists of threatened fungi; promote international cooperation in research, monitoring programmes and in the publication of an European Red Data List of threatened fungi. **Structure** Conservation Board. **Languages** English. **Activities** Monitoring/evaluation; knowledge management/information dissemination; events/meetings. **Events** *Conservation Workshop* Cambridge (UK) 2020, *Meeting* Porto Carras (Greece) 2011, *International meeting on fungal conservation / Meeting* Whitby (UK) 2009, *Meeting* St Petersburg (Russia) 2007, *Meeting* Córdoba (Spain) 2005. **Publications** *ECCF Newsletter* (annual). *Fungal Conservation – Issues and Solutions* (2001); *Signalarter: Indikatorer på skyddsvärd skog Flora over Kryptogamer* (2001); *Fungi of Europe: Investigation, Recording and Conservation* (1993). Red Data Lists of endangered fungi; meeting proceedings.
Members in 36 countries:
Armenia, Austria, Azerbaijan, Belarus, Belgium, Bulgaria, Czechia, Denmark, Estonia, Finland, France, Georgia, Germany, Greece, Hungary, Iceland, Ireland, Italy, Latvia, Lithuania, Luxembourg, Moldova, Netherlands, North Macedonia, Norway, Poland, Portugal, Romania, Russia, Serbia, Slovakia, Slovenia, Spain, Sweden, Switzerland, UK.
IGO Relations Member of: *Standing Committee to the Bern Convention on the Conservation of European Wildlife and Natural Habitats (#19949)*. **NGO Relations** Affiliate member of: *Planta Europa (#18388)*. [2020.03.03/XD7967/D]

♦ **European Council of Construction Economists** **06812**

Conseil européen des économistes de la construction (CEEC) – Europäisches Komitee der Bauökonomen – Euroopan Rakennustalousasiantuntijoiden

Gen Sec 8 av Percier, 75008 Paris, France. T. +31478691616. E-mail: info@ceecorg.eu.
URL: http://www.ceecorg.eu/

History 29 Jun 1979, London (UK). **Aims** Link professionals in Europe to share relevant best practices, information and experience; promote the profession of construction economist, common knowledge and international standards. **Structure** Officers: President; 2 Vice-Presidents; General Secretary. **Languages** English, French. **Staff** None. **Finance** Members' dues. Subscriptions. **Activities** Networking/liaising; knowledge management/information dissemination; standards/guidelines; events/meetings. **Events** *Half-Yearly Conference* Budapest (Hungary) 2010, *Half-Yearly Conference* Helsinki (Finland) 2010, *Half-Yearly Conference* Brussels (Belgium) 2009, *Half-Yearly Conference* Limassol (Cyprus) 2009, *Half-Yearly Conference* Munich (Germany) 2008.
Members National organizations in 14 countries:
Czechia, Denmark, Estonia, Finland, France, Germany, Hungary, Ireland, Netherlands, Poland, Portugal, Spain, Switzerland, UK.
Observer in 1 country:
Canada.
IGO Relations Recognized by: *European Commission (EC, #06633)*. **NGO Relations** Member of: *International Cost Management Standard Coalition (ICMS Coalition, #12978)*. [2019.08.19/XD2581/E]

♦ **European Council for Construction Research, Development and Innovation (ECCREDI)** **06813**

Contact Rue du Lombard 42, 1000 Brussels, Belgium. T. +3226557711. E-mail: info@eccredi.org.
URL: http://www.eccredi.org/

History 19 Dec 1995, Brussels (Belgium), on signature of a Memorandum of Understanding by representatives of European federations concerned with construction, in its widest sense. **Aims** Contribute to competitiveness, quality, safety and environmental performance of the construction sector and to overall sustainability of the built environment by advocating for effective construction research, technical and process development and innovation. **Structure** Council. **Languages** English. **Finance** Members' dues. **Activities** Guidance/assistance/consulting; events/meetings; advocacy/lobbying/activism. **Events** *Conference on B4E building for a European future* Maastricht (Netherlands) 2004.
Members Regional organizations (15), representing principal interests within construction (contractors, engineering consultants, architects and designers, product and materials producers, building control organizations, social housing providers and research bodies):
Architects Council of Europe (ACE, #01086); *Association of European Experts in Building and Construction (The) (AEEBC, #02510)*; *Committee for European Construction Equipment (CECE, #04254)*; *European Asphalt Pavement Association (EAPA, #05920)*; *European Association for External Thermal Insulation Composite Systems (EAE, #06035)*; *European Builders Confederation (EBC, #06408)*; *European Construction Industry Federation (#06766)*; *European Convention for Constructional Steelwork (ECCS, #06779)*; *European Council of Civil Engineers (ECCE, #06810)*; *European Demolition Association (EDA, #06902)*; *European Federation of Engineering Consultancy Associations (EFCA, #07109)*; *European Large Geotechnical Institutes Platform (ELGIP, #07652)*; *European Network of Building Research Institutes (ENBRI, #07870)*; *European Network of Construction Companies for Research and Development (ENCORD, #07884)*; *Union européenne pour l'agrément technique dans la construction (UEAtc, #20393)*.
IGO Relations *European Commission (EC, #06633)*. [2019.12.12/XD5432/y/D]

♦ European Council for Cooperation in Welding / see European Federation for Welding, Joining and Cutting (#07233)
♦ European Council of Crafts and Small and Medium-Sized Enterprises (inactive)

♦ **European Council of Deaf Researchers of Sign Language (ECDRSL)** **06814**

Address not obtained.

History As of 2009 activities reduced to workshop organizing. As of 2013, inactive. **Aims** Promote and share the experience and expertise in the field of research among with other deaf researchers in Europe. **Structure** Board, comprising President, Secretary, Treasurer, 2 members. **Languages** English, International Sign Language. **Staff** None. **Finance** Members' dues. **Activities** Organizes workshops. **Events** *Workshop for the deaf researchers in sign language* Jyväskylä (Finland) 2005, *International deaf researchers of sign language workshop* Bristol (UK) 1997. **Publications** *ECDRSL Newsletter* (2 a year). [2013.12.13/XD6674/d/D]

♦ **European Council of Doctoral Candidates and Junior Researchers (EURODOC)** **06815**

Conseil européen des doctorants et jeunes docteurs

Main Office Rue d'Egmont 11, 1000 Brussels, Belgium. E-mail: secretary@eurodoc.net – board@eurodoc.net.
URL: http://www.eurodoc.net/

History 2 Feb 2002, Girona (Spain). Registration: No/ID: 0873.895.764, Start date: 1 May 2005, Belgium; EU Transparency Register, No/ID: 832797511955-47, Start date: 25 Sep 2013. **Aims** Represent and consolidate the community of doctoral candidates and junior researchers in Europe in their pursuit of a decent professional life. **Structure** General Meeting (annual); Administrative Board; Advisory Board; Secretariat. **Languages** English. **Staff** Voluntary. **Finance** Members' dues. **Events** *Eurodoc Conference* Prague (Czechia) 2021, *Eurodoc Conference* Warsaw (Poland) 2020, *Annual Conference* Brussels (Belgium) 2019, *Annual Conference* Oslo (Norway) 2017, *Annual Conference* Cluj-Napoca (Romania) 2015. **Publications** *EURODOC Newsletter* (12 a year). Policy papers; speeches; reports; communications; commentaries; discussion papers.
Members National organizations (28) in 26 countries:
Austria, Azerbaijan, Belgium, Bulgaria, Croatia, Czechia, Denmark, Finland, France, Germany, Hungary, Italy, Latvia, Lithuania, Luxembourg, Netherlands, Norway, Poland, Portugal, Serbia, Slovakia, Slovenia, Spain, Sweden, Switzerland, Ukraine.
Consultative Status Consultative status granted from: *Council of Europe (CE, #04881)* (Participatory Status).
IGO Relations *European Commission (EC, #06633)* EURAXESS. **NGO Relations** Observer member of: *Initiative for Science in Europe (ISE, #11214).* [2021/XJ4113/D]

♦ European Council of Doctors for Plurality in Medicine (ECPM) 06816

Conseil européen des médecins pour le pluralisme thérapeutique – Consejo Europeo Medico para la Pluralidad Medica – Europäische Vereinigung der Ärzteverbände der besonderen Therapierichtungen – Federazione dei Medici Europei per il Pluralismo in Medicina – Europese Federatie van Artsenverenigingen voor het Therapeutisch Pluralisme

Secretariat Brombacherstrasse 5, 4057 Basel BS, Switzerland. T. +41613032366. Fax +41613032367.
Pres Otto Wagner Spital, Sanatoriumsstrasse 2, 1140 Vienna, Austria. E-mail: schunder@gamed.or.at.
URL: http://www.camdoc.eu/

Structure General Assembly. Steering Committee, including President. **Languages** French, German.
Members Associations (45) in 8 countries:
Austria, Belgium, France, Germany, Italy, Netherlands, Spain, Switzerland.
Included in the above, 7 organizations listed in this Yearbook:
European Society of Medical Hypnosis (ESMH, no recent information); Internationale Forschungsgemeinschaft für Bioelektronische Funktionsdiagnostik und Therapie; Internationale Gesellschaft für Ganzheitliche Zahn-Medizin (GZM, #13239); Internationale Gesellschaft für Homöopathie und Homotoxikologie (IGHH); Internationale Medizinische Gesellschaft für Neuraltherapie nach Huneke-Regulationstherapie; International Society of Medical Doctors for Biophysical Information Therapy (BIT, #15253); Medizinische Gesellschaft für System- und Regulationsdiagnostik (EAV, #16689).
NGO Relations Member of: *CAMDOC Alliance (#03402); European Coalition on Homeopathic and Anthroposophic Medicinal Products (ECHAMP, #06595); European Public Health Alliance (EPHA, #08297).* Affiliated with: *EUROCAM (#05653).* [2015/XD7632/y/D]

♦ European Council on Eating Disorders (ECED) 06817

Contact Div of Mental Health, St George's – Univ of London, Hunter Wing, Level 6, London, SW17 0RE, UK. T. +442087255528 – +442087255529. Fax +442087253538.
URL: http://www.eced.co.uk/

History Nov 1989. **Aims** Establish links and maintain contact between individuals and institutions throughout Europe who work with eating disorder sufferers in any context; provide a forum to share information and ideas about treatment of eating disorders and further and improve understanding of effective *therapies*; improve knowledge and research into eating disorders and encourage research collaboration between different European countries. **Structure** General Council (meets every 2 years); Steering Committee of 3 members. **Languages** English. **Staff** 1.00 FTE, paid. **Finance** Supported by private institutions. **Activities** Develops database; organizes inter-European meetings; provides centralized source of papers. Organizes *'Interdisciplinary Eating Disorders Conference'* in different countries. **Events** *General Meeting* Paris (France) 2019, *General Meeting* Vilnius (Lithuania) 2017, *General Meeting* Heidelberg (Germany) 2015, *General Meeting* Oslo (Norway) 2013, *General meeting* Florence (Italy) 2011.
Members Full in 28 countries:
Austria, Belgium, Bulgaria, Croatia, Cyprus, Czechia, Denmark, Estonia, Finland, France, Germany, Greece, Hungary, Iceland, Ireland, Italy, Luxembourg, Netherlands, North Macedonia, Norway, Poland, Portugal, Slovenia, Spain, Sweden, Switzerland, Türkiye, UK. [2013/XD5747/D]

♦ European Council for Education by Correspondence (inactive)

♦ European Council for an Energy Efficient Economy (ECEEE) 06818

Exec Dir Sveavägen 98, 4tr, SE-113 50 Stockholm, Sweden. T. +4686731130. E-mail: eceee@eceee.org.
URL: http://www.eceee.org/

History 1993. Current by-laws adopted, 18 Nov 2011, Brussels (Belgium). Registered in accordance with Norwegian law, 1998; registered in accordance with Swedish law since 2005. **Aims** Stimulate energy efficiency through information exchange and pan-European cooperation. **Structure** General Assembly (annual); Board. **Languages** English. **Staff** 3.00 FTE, paid. **Finance** Members' dues (fees and core member contributions). Sponsorships. **Activities** Training/education; networking/liaising; events/meetings; politics/policy/regulatory; knowledge management/information dissemination. **Events** *Industrial Efficiency* Gothenburg (Sweden) 2020, *Annual General Assembly* Brussels (Belgium) 2013, *Annual General Assembly* Brussels (Belgium) 2012, *Annual General Assembly* Brussels (Belgium) 2011, *Annual General Assembly* Paris (France) 2004. **Publications** *eceee news* – online newsletter. Proceedings; reports; position papers.
Members Organizations (over 75) and individuals (over 600). Members in 22 countries:
Austria, Belgium, Bulgaria, Canada, China, Czechia, Denmark, Finland, France, Germany, India, Italy, Japan, Netherlands, Norway, Portugal, Slovenia, Spain, Sweden, Switzerland, UK, USA.
Included in the above, 2 international organizations listed in this Yearbook:
European Insulation Manufacturers Association (EURIMA, #07577); World Wide Fund for Nature (WWF, #21922).
IGO Relations Accredited by: *United Nations Framework Convention on Climate Change – Secretariat (UNFCCC, #20564).* Observer status in: *United Nations Framework Convention on Climate Change (UNFCCC, 1992).* Cooperates with: *European Commission (EC, #06633).* **NGO Relations** Member of: *Coalition for Energy Savings (#04056).* Provided support to setting up of: *Buildings Performance Institute Europe (BPIE, #03354).* [2020/XE4503/E]

♦ European Council of Engineers Chambers (ECEC) 06819

Secretariat Karslgasse 9/2, 1040 Vienna, Austria. T. +431505580751. E-mail: office@ecec.net.
Brussels Office c/o CEPLIS, Coudenberg 70, 1000 Brussels, Belgium. T. +3225114439.
URL: http://www.ecec.net/

History 2003, Vienna (Austria), following activities initiated in 1998. Statutes adopted Sep 2003, Vienna (Austria); amended Nov 2004, Brussels (Belgium); Nov 2005, Warsaw (Poland); Nov 2006, Rome (Italy); Nov 2009, Sofia (Bulgaria); 2010, Ljubljana (Slovenia); 2013, Athens (Greece). EU Transparency Register: 52510694541-69. **Aims** Secure quality and safety of design and construction; stimulate sustainability of design and construction; enhance international mobility of European chartered engineers; provide relevant information and communication. **Structure** General Assembly; Executive Board; Informal working groups. **Activities** Events/meetings. **Events** *International Conference on Damage Mechanics* Belgrade (Serbia) 2012.
Members Chambers in 16 countries and territories:
Austria, Bulgaria, Croatia, Cyprus, Czechia, Germany, Greece, Hungary, Italy, Montenegro, North Macedonia, Poland, Serbia, Slovakia, Slovenia, Spain.
NGO Relations Member of: *Engineering Association of Mediterranean Countries (EAMC, #05480); European Council of Liberal Professions (#06828); World Federation of Engineering Organizations (WFEO, #21433).* Partner of: *European Council of Civil Engineers (ECCE, #06810); European Federation of Engineering Consultancy Associations (EFCA, #07109); Fédération Européenne d'Associations Nationales d'Ingénieurs (FEANI, #09558).* [2022/XM4067/D]

♦ European Council of Enterostomal Therapy (ECET) 06820

Conseil européen de stomathérapie (CES) – Europäischen Verband der Stomatherapeuten

Secretariat c/o CAP Partner, Nordre Fasanvej 113, 2, 2000 Frederiksberg, Denmark. T. +4570200305. Fax +4570200315. E-mail: info@ecet-stomacare.eu – info@cap-partner.eu.
Pres Richard-Zach-Gasse 31, 8045 Graz, Austria. T. +43316896029000. Fax +43316896029999. E-mail: president@ecet-stomacare.eu.
URL: https://ecet-stomacare.eu/

History Jun 2003, Munich (Germany). Founded during 7th European congress of *World Council of Enterostomal Therapists (WCET, #21327).* Registration: Belgium. **Aims** Promote the highest standards of patient care, research and education among nurses throughout Europe. **Structure** General Meeting (annual); Board. **Events** *Congress* Rome (Italy) 2019, *Building bridges – from West to East, from South to North – ostomy, continence, wound* Berlin (Germany) 2017, *Congress* Brussels (Belgium) 2015, *Congress* Paris (France) 2013, *Congress* Bologna (Italy) 2011. [2020.06.26/XJ3202/D]

♦ European Council on Environmental Law (no recent information)
♦ European Council for Fatwa and Research (see: #09682)

♦ European Council on Foreign Relations (ECFR) 06821

Main Office Unter den Linden 17, 10117 Berlin, Germany. E-mail: communications@ecfr.eu – press@ecfr.eu.
Registered Office 4th Floor, Tennyson House, 159-165 Great Portland St, London, W1W 5PA, UK.
URL: http://ecfr.eu/

History Oct 2007. Registration: Charity Commission, No/ID: 1143536, England and Wales; EU Transparency Register, No/ID: 339569615567-89; Charitable Entity, No/ID: 127/603/54318, Germany. **Aims** Conduct research on European foreign and security policy; provide a safe meeting space for decision-makers, activists and influencers to share ideas; promote informed debate about Europe's role in the world. **Structure** Council; Board of Trustees; Management Team. National Offices (7). **Languages** Bulgarian, English, French, German, Italian, Polish, Spanish. **Staff** 60.00 FTE, paid. **Finance** Support from: foundations; governments; corporations; individuals. **Activities** Events/meetings. **Events** *Annual Meeting* Berlin (Germany) 2020, *Annual Meeting* Lisbon (Portugal) 2019, *Annual Meeting* Paris (France) 2018, *Meeting on Ensuring a Comprehensive EU Approach to Crises* Brussels (Belgium) 2012. **Publications** *ECFR Newsletter* (weekly). Reports; briefs; memos; Foreign Policy scorecard. **Members** Individuals (over 300). Member countries not specified. **NGO Relations** Member of: *Euro-Mediterranean Study Commission (EuroMeSCo, #05727).* Associate member of: *Policy Association for an Open Society (PASOS, #18416).* [2020.06.22/XJ4764/D]

♦ European Council on Global Health / see Global Health Europe (#10404)

♦ European Council for High Ability (ECHA) 06822

Sec c/o Cente for Talented Youth, DCU Glasnevin Campus, Dublin, 9, CO. DUBLIN, Ireland. E-mail: admin@echa-site.eu.
URL: https://echa-site.eu/

History 1987, Utrecht (Netherlands). Former names and other names: *European Council for High Ability – Its Study and Development* – full title. Registration: No/ID: 8260 97 741, Netherlands. **Aims** Act as a communications network to promote exchange of information among people interested in high ability – educators, researchers, psychologists, parents and the highly able themselves; advance study and development of potential excellence in people. **Structure** General Committee, consisting of President, Secretary, Treasurer and 4 members. **Languages** English. **Activities** Offers 2-year Advanced Diploma in the Education of the Highly Able (with University of Nijmegen, Netherlands and University of Münster, Germany); forms special interest groups and a network of national correspondents; initiates and stimulates international applied research. **Events** *ECHA Thematic Conference* 2025, *Conference* 2024, *Thematic Conference on Teaching Highly Able Students* Haifa (Israel) 2023, *Conference* The Hague (Netherlands) 2022, *Conference* Porto (Portugal) 2021. **Publications** *ECHA News* (2 a year); *High Ability Studies* (2 a year). Books.
Members Individuals in 52 countries and territories:
Australia, Austria, Belgium, Bermuda, Bosnia-Herzegovina, Brazil, Bulgaria, Canada, Chile, China, Croatia, Cyprus, Czechia, Denmark, Estonia, Finland, France, Germany, Greece, Hong Kong, Hungary, India, Indonesia, Ireland, Israel, Italy, Japan, Latvia, Liechtenstein, Lithuania, Luxembourg, Malta, Netherlands, New Zealand, Norway, Peru, Poland, Portugal, Romania, Russia, Serbia, Singapore, Slovenia, Spain, Sweden, Switzerland, Taiwan, Türkiye, UK, Ukraine, USA, Uzbekistan.
NGO Relations Affiliate federation of: *World Council for Gifted and Talented Children (WCGTC, #21328).* [2021/XD3810/v/D]

♦ European Council for High Ability – Its Study and Development / see European Council for High Ability (#06822)

♦ European Council on Hotel, Restaurant and Institutional Education (EuroCHRIE) 06823

Admin 26 St Ronan's Road, Harrogate, HG2 8LE, UK. T. +447920450175. E-mail: admin@eurochrie.org.
URL: http://www.eurochrie.org/

History Regional federation of *International Council on Hotel, Restaurant and Institutional Education (CHRIE).* **Aims** Advance quality of education for all members and constituencies through proactive professional development, research, coalitions and networks. **Structure** Executive Committees (5); Directors (8). Country Area Consultants (21) assist members locally. **Languages** English. **Staff** Voluntary. **Finance** Sources: meeting proceeds; members' dues. **Activities** Awards/prizes/competitions; awareness raising; events/meetings; financial and/or material support; guidance/assistance/consulting; knowledge management/information dissemination; networking/liaising; publishing activities; research and development; research/documentation; training/education. **Events** *Annual EuroCHRIE Conference* Apeldoorn (Netherlands) 2022, *Annual EuroCHRIE Conference* Aalborg (Denmark) 2021, *Annual EuroCHRIE Conference* Aalborg (Denmark) 2020, *APacCHRIE & EuroCHRIE Joint Conference* Hong Kong 2019, *Annual EuroCHRIE Conference* Dublin (Ireland) 2018. **Publications** *Journal of Hospitality and Tourism Education* (4 a year); *Journal of Hospitality and Tourism Research* (3 a year); *Journal of Hospitality and Tourism Cases.* **Members** Full (300) in 39 countries. Membership countries not specified. [2023.02.16/XE4567/E]

♦ European Council of Information Associations (no recent information)

♦ European Council of Interior Architects (ECIA) 06824

Pres Quai de Willebroeck 37, 1000 Brussels, Belgium. T. +3222122620. E-mail: info@ecia.net – president@ecia.net – secretary.general@ecia.net.
SG address not obtained.
URL: http://ecia.net/

History 16 Oct 1992, Brussels (Belgium). **Aims** Act as the common voice of Interior Architects on European and international level, promoting this profession as a vital part of society and economy. **Structure** General Assembly (annual); Executive Board; Working Groups. **Languages** English, French. **Staff** 3.00 FTE, voluntary. **Finance** Sources: grants; members' dues. Creative Europe Programme Supported by: *European Commission (EC, #06633).* **Activities** Advocacy/lobbying/activism; awards/prizes/competitions; awareness raising; capacity building; certification/accreditation; events/meetings; knowledge management/information dissemination; networking/liaising; politics/policy/regulatory; projects/programmes; research/documentation; standards/guidelines; training/education. Europe. **Events** *Congress* Helsinki (Finland) 1999, *Meeting on European women working in interior architecture and architecture* Paris (France) 1999, *Europe habitable* Barcelona (Spain) 1996. **Publications** *ECIA Newsletter. The Charter of Interior Architecture* (2021) in English.
Members Organizations in 15 countries:
Austria, Belgium, Estonia, Finland, France, Germany, Iceland, Italy, Malta, Netherlands, Norway, Slovakia, Spain, Sweden, Switzerland. [2022.05.12/XD3510/D]

♦ European Council of International Schools / see Educational Collaborative for International Schools (#05365)

♦ European Council of Jewish Communities (ECJC) 06825

Conseil européen des communautés juives (CECJ)

Contact 38 Rue de Berri, 75008 Paris, France. T. +33970466707. E-mail: paris@ecjc.org.
URL: http://www.ecjc.org/

History 1964, Geneva (Switzerland), as successor body to *Standing Conference of European Jewish Community Services*, which first met in 1960, Geneva. Name subsequently changed to *European Council of Jewish Community Services (ECJCS) – Conseil européen des services communautaires juifs (CESCJ)*. Widened to include further affiliates, 29-31 Jan 1993, Riga (Latvia); 12 Sep 1993, London (UK). Present name adopted 12 Sep 1993, London. Constitution amended 12 Sep 1993, London; Jul 2000, Milan (Italy); Apr 2002, Brussels (Belgium). 29 May 2011, new statutes adopted. Registered in accordance with Swiss law. **Aims** Strengthen Jewish communal life in an enlarged Europe through: social, cultural, educational and community building activities; fostering close cooperation among Jewish communities; initiating joint projects responding to common needs and planning their implementation. Provide a forum for inter-European planning and cooperation; enhance the quality of Jewish life through development of community institutions; provide specific training in skills to implement policy-making, budgeting, staff development and other communal management issues; improve communication throughout Europe and embody exchange of information and ideas among lay and professional groups, building a functional network among lay and professional leaders of Jewish NGOs throughout Western, Central and Eastern Europe, including the former USSR; promote coordination, cooperation and joint venture projects among Jewish and other NGOs and also partner institutions; develop relations on behalf of Jewish NGOs with the European institutions; alleviate poverty and distress for Jewish people in Europe; promote new communications media, information technology and training for Jewish communities. **Structure** General Meeting (annual). Council, composed of representatives from each member organization or community (one vote per country). Executive Officers Committee, consisting of President, Vice-Presidents (up to 6), Treasurer, Secretary and Executive Director. **Languages** English. **Staff** 2-5 (project oriented). **Finance** Members' dues. Ad hoc sources; project grants. **Activities** Formal and informal education, leadership training, social welfare, restitution and cultural activities ranging from local to pan-European scale. Priorities: (i) *'Network Development'*, Regional cooperation projects in Europe. (ii) *'Initiation and Coordination of New Programmes'*, through *European Centre for Jewish Leadership (Le'atid Europe)*. (iii) *'Relations with European Institutions'*. (iv)*European Jewish Welfare Fund (Carelink, no recent information)*. (v) *'Communication'*. (vi) *'Foundations'*. Organizes: European Conference on Jewish Education (Arachim); Conference on social welfare services and others. Co-organizes the European Day of Jewish Culture and European Jewish Cultural Itinerary. **Events** *European conference of Jewish community centers* Vilnius (Lithuania) 2006, *Arachim Pan European conference on Jewish education* 2005, *General assembly* Budapest (Hungary) 2004, *European conference of Jewish community centers* Paris (France) 2003, *Annual General Meeting* Prague (Czech Rep) 2003. **Publications** *Connection* (every 2-4 weeks) – e-magazine; *Fax-Link: The European Bulletin Board. ECJC Series – Current Trends in European Jewry* – 4 vols. *Hungarian Jewry in Profile*.

Members Communities and organizations (68) representing over 4 million people in 40 countries (" indicates Associated):

Austria, Azerbaijan, Belarus, Belgium, Bosnia-Herzegovina, Bulgaria, Croatia, Czechia, Denmark, Estonia, Finland, France, Georgia, Germany, Greece, Hungary, Italy, Kazakhstan, Latvia, Lithuania, Luxembourg, Moldova, Morocco (*), Netherlands, North Macedonia, Norway, Poland, Portugal, Romania, Russia, Serbia, Slovakia, Slovenia, Spain, Sweden, Switzerland, Tunisia (*), Türkiye, UK, Ukraine.

Included in the above, 3 organizations listed in this Yearbook:

European Association of Jewish Community Centres (EAJCC, #06097); European Union of Jewish Students (EUJS, #08997); International Association of Jewish Studies and Jewish Culture (no recent information).

NGO Relations Member of: *Commission for Looted Art in Europe (#04234); International Council on Jewish Social and Welfare Services (INTERCO, #13035); JCC Global (#16093); World Jewish Restitution Organization (WJRO, #21601).* [2022/XD4461/y/**D**]

♦ European Council of Jewish Community Services / see European Council of Jewish Communities (#06825)

♦ European Council of Kitchen Constructors (no recent information)

♦ European Council of Landscape Architecture Schools (ECLAS) 06826

Secretariat TU-Vienna Inst 260, Erzherzog Johann Platz 1, 1040 Vienna, Austria. T. +4315880126125. Fax +4315880126199. E-mail: info@eclas.org.

Pres Kreutzwaldi 58a, 51014 Tartu, Estonia.

URL: http://eclas.org/

History Founded as *European Conference of Landscape Architecture Schools*, following two meetings in Berlin (Germany), 1989 and Vienna (Austria), 1990. First ECLAS Meeting 1991, Wageningen (Netherlands). Current title adopted, 2000, Dubrovnik (Croatia). Registered in accordance with Dutch law. **Aims** Foster and develop scholarship in landscape architecture throughout Europe by strengthening contacts and enriching the dialogue between members of Europe's landscape academic community and by representing the interests of this community within the wider European social and institutional context. **Structure** General Assembly; Executive Committee. **Languages** English. **Staff** None. **Finance** Members' dues. **Activities** Events/meetings. **Events** *Annual Conference* Vienna (Austria) 2021, *Annual Conference* Uppsala (Sweden) 2020, *Joint Conference* Ås (Norway) 2019, *Annual Conference* Ghent (Belgium) 2018, *Annual Conference* London (UK) 2017. **Publications** *Journal of Landscape Architecture (JoLA)*. Book series; conference proceedings.

Members Full in 29 countries:

Austria, Belgium, Bulgaria, Croatia, Czechia, Denmark, Estonia, Finland, France, Germany, Greece, Hungary, Iceland, Ireland, Italy, Latvia, Netherlands, Norway, Poland, Portugal, Romania, Serbia, Slovakia, Slovenia, Spain, Sweden, Türkiye, UK, Ukraine. [2017.10.27/XD8294/**D**]

♦ European Council of Legal Medicine (ECLM) 06827

Vice-Pres/Honorary Sec Inst Médico-Légal, 173 rue de Bercy, 75012 Paris, France.

Pres address not obtained.

URL: http://www.eclm.eu/

Events *General Assembly* Venice (Italy) 2016, *IALM Intersocietal Symposium* Venice (Italy) 2016, *General Assembly* Istanbul (Turkey) 2012, *General Assembly* Funchal (Portugal) 2011, *General Assembly* Lisbon (Portugal) 2009.

Members Full in 14 countries:

Denmark, Finland, Germany, Greece, Iceland, Italy, Luxembourg, Netherlands, Norway, Portugal, Spain, Sweden, Switzerland, UK.

NGO Relations *Sevilla Working Party on Legal Medicine in Europe (no recent information).* [2020.03.04/XD4175/**D**]

♦ European Council of Liberal Professions 06828

Conseil européen des professions libérales (CEPLIS) – Europäischer Rat der Freien Berufe

Dir Gen Rue du Tabellion 66, 1050 Brussels, Belgium. T. +3225114439. E-mail: secretariat@ceplis.org.

Registered Address Coudenberg 70, 1000 Brussels, Belgium.

URL: https://ceplis.org/

History 1974. Former names and other names: *European Secretariat of the Liberal, Independent and Social Professions* – former (1974); *Secrétariat européen des professions libérales, indépendantes et sociales* – former (1974); *Europäisches Sekretariat der Freien, Selbständigen und Sozialen Berufe* – former (1974); *Europees Secretariat der Vrije, Zelfstandige en Sociale Beroepen* – former (1974); *European Secretariat for the Liberal Professions* – former; *Secrétariat européen des professions libérales (SEPLIS)* – former; *Secretariado Europeo de las Profesiones Liberales* – former; *Europäisches Sekretariat der Freien Berufe* – former; *Segretariato Europeo delle Libere Professioni* – former; *Europees Secretariaat voor de Vrije Beroepen* – former; *Europaeiske Sekretariat for Liberale Erhverv* – former. Registration: Banque-Carrefour des Entreprises, No/ID: 0476.478.846, Start date: 28 Jun 2001, Belgium. **Aims** Coordinate and defend the moral, cultural, scientific and material interests of liberal professions. **Structure** General Assembly; Executive Board; Secretariat General. **Languages** English, French. **Staff** 4.00 FTE, paid. **Finance** Members' tuition fees. **Activities** Advocacy/lobbying/activism; events/meetings; guidance/assistance/consulting; knowledge management/information dissemination. **Events** *General Assembly* Brussels (Belgium) 2018, *General Assembly* Valletta (Malta) 2017, *General Assembly* Brussels (Belgium) 2016, *General Assembly* Dublin (Ireland) 2016, *General Assembly* Venice (Italy) 2015. **Publications** *CEPLIS Telegram* in English, French; *Lettre CEPLIS* in English, French.

Members Interprofessional associations; international and regional (European) organizations; Correspondant members; Observers. Members in 11 countries:

Austria, Belgium, Croatia, France, Ireland, Italy, Luxembourg, Malta, Romania, Spain, UK.

Included in the above, 14 organizations listed in this Yearbook:

Confederation of European Biopathologists (CEB, #04520); Council of European Geodetic Surveyors (#04890); European Association for Psychotherapy (EAP, #06176); European Confederation of Conservator-Restorers' Organisations (ECCO, #06701); European Council of Engineers Chambers (ECEC, #06819); European Council of Podiatrists (ECP); European Federation of Clinical Chemistry and Laboratory Medicine (EFLM, #07080); European Federation of Psychologists Associations (EFPA, #07199); European Federation of Tourist Guide Associations (#07228); European Higher Engineering and Technical Professionals Association (EurEta, #07484); European Speech and Language Therapy Association (ESLA, #08812); Fédération Européenne d'Associations Nationales d'Ingénieurs (FEANI, #09558); International Federation of Automobile Experts (IFAE, #13368).

IGO Relations Recognized by: *European Commission (EC, #06633).* **NGO Relations** Member of (1): *World Union of Professions (WUP, #21882).* [2022/XD8437/ty/**E**]

♦ European Council of Literary Translators' Associations (#04686)

♦ European Council of Management / see European Management Association (#07729)

♦ European Council for Maritime Applied R and D (ECMAR) 06829

Secretariat Rue de la Loi 67, 3rd Floor, 1000 Brussels, Belgium. E-mail: info@ecmar.eu.

URL: http://www.ecmar.eu/

History 1953, as *International Cooperation in Ship Research (ICSR)*. Name changed to *European Cooperation in Maritime Research (ECMAR)*, 1989. Current title adopted, 2007. Registered in accordance with Belgian law. EU Transparency Register: 862403321757-69. **Aims** Promote interest within European Maritime Applied Research and Development organizations; develop a maritime R and D strategy; enhance cooperation between members by (virtual) networks and by organizing conferences and workshops; coordinate studies and activities to promote maritime applied R and D. **Structure** General Assembly (annual). Council of 7 members. Director. **Languages** English. **Staff** 1.50 FTE, paid. **Finance** Members' dues. Budget (annual): about euro 70,000.

Members Full in 14 countries:

Austria, Bulgaria, Denmark, Finland, France, Germany, Italy, Netherlands, Norway, Poland, Romania, Spain, Sweden, UK.

NGO Relations Participant of: *WATERBORNE (#20823).* [2018/XD8337/**D**]

♦ European Council of Medical Orders (ECMO) 06830

Conseil Européen des Ordres des Médecins (CEOM)

Sec Gen c/o CNOM, 4 rue Léon Jost, 75855 Paris CEDEX 17, France. T. +3224016158. E-mail: secretariat@ceom-ecmo.eu.

URL: https://www.ceom-ecmo.eu/

History 22 Jun 1971, Paris (France). Functioning rules defined in Agreement adopted Jun 2011. Former names and other names: *Conférence internationale des ordres et des organismes d'attributions similaires (CIO)* – former; *Conférence européenne des ordres et des organismes d'attributions similaires* – former; *Europese Conferentie van Orde van Geneesheren* – former. **Aims** Promote the practice of high quality medicine respectful of patients' needs within the European Union and the European Free Trade Association. **Structure** Plenary Meeting (twice a year); Board; Secretariat. **Languages** English, French. **Staff** 40.00 FTE, paid. **Finance** No budget. **Events** *Plenary Meeting* Madrid (Spain) 2018, *Plenary Meeting* Bucharest (Romania) 2013, *Plenary Meeting* Brussels (Belgium) 2012, *Plenary Meeting* Ljubljana (Slovenia) 2012, *Plenary Meeting* Turin (Italy) 2011. **Publications** E-publications.

Members Medical organizations in 16 countries:

Austria, Belgium, Cyprus, France, Germany, Greece, Ireland, Italy, Luxembourg, Netherlands, Portugal, Romania, Slovenia, Spain, Switzerland, UK.

NGO Relations Partner of (12): *Association européenne des médecins des hôpitaux (AEMH, #02577); CAMDOC Alliance (#03402); EANA – European Working Group of Physicians in Private Practice (#05154); European Federation of Salaried Doctors (#07209); European Forum of Medical Associations and WHO (EFMA, #07320); European Junior Doctors Association (EJD, #07620); European Medical Students' Association (EMSA, #07764); European Network of Medical Competent Authorities (ENMCA, #07944); European Union of General Practitioners / Family Physicians (#08993); Standing Committee of European Doctors (#19955); Symposium of the Central and Eastern European Chambers of Physicians (ZEVA); World Medical Association (WMA, #21646).* [2023/XF2629/**F**]

♦ European Council for Modelling and Simulation (ECMS) 06831

Pres Wilhelmshaven/Oldenburg/Elsfleth, Friedrich-Paffrath-Str 101, 26389 Wilhelmshaven, Germany. E-mail: ecms@scs-europe.net.

URL: http://www.scs-europe.net/

History 18 Jul 1990, Calgary (Canada), as *Continental Europe Simulation Council (CESC)*, within the framework of *Society for Modeling Simulation International (SCSI, #19598)*, at annual meeting of SCSI Board of Directors, and following setting up of an SCSI European Office, 1986. Name changed to *European Simulation Council (EuSC)* in 1992, after the dissolution of UK Simulation Council. Became an independent organization in 2004, when adopted present title. **Aims** Promote research and development priorities in modelling and simulation in Europe; promote corporate interests/priorities of European simulationists on the international scene. **Structure** Annual Meeting; Steering Committee. **Languages** English. **Finance** Financed through conferences and workshops. **Activities** Events/meetings. **Events** *European Conference on Modelling and Simulation* Caserta (Italy) 2019, *European Conference on Modelling and Simulation* Wilhelmshaven (Germany) 2018, *European Conference on Modelling and Simulation* Budapest (Hungary) 2017, *European Conference on Modelling and Simulation* Regensburg (Germany) 2016, *European Conference on Modelling and Simulation* Varna (Bulgaria) 2015. **Publications** Conference proceedings. Information Services: Digital library.

Members Individual and corporate in 28 countries:

Austria, Belarus, Belgium, Cyprus, Denmark, Estonia, Finland, France, Germany, Greece, Hungary, Iceland, Ireland, Italy, Latvia, Lithuania, Luxembourg, Montenegro, Netherlands, Norway, Portugal, Russia, Serbia, Spain, Sweden, Switzerland, UK, Ukraine.

IGO Relations *WHO (#20950).* **NGO Relations** Acts as interface between SCSI and: *Arbeitsgemeinschaft Simulation (ASIM, #01083)*; Dutch Benelux Simulation Society; *Federation of European Simulation Societies (EUROSIM, #09544); Scandinavian Simulation Society (SIMS, #19100); Société francophone de simulation (FRANCOSIM, no recent information)*; UK Simulation Society. [2018/XE1200/**E**]

♦ European Council for Motor Trades and Repairs 06832

Conseil européen du commerce et de la réparation automobiles (CECRA)

Dir Gen CECRA, Boulevard de la Woluwe 42, Boîte 6, 1200 Brussels, Belgium. T. +3227719656. Fax +3227726567. E-mail: mail@cecra.eu.

URL: http://www.cecra.eu/

History 1983, as *European Committee for Motor Trades and Repairs – Comité européen du commerce et de la réparation automobiles – Europäischer Verband des Kraftfahrzeuggewerbes – Comitato Europeo del Commercio e de la Riparazione Automotoristica – Europees Komitee voor de Automobielhandel en -Herstelling – Europaeiske Komité for Automobil-detailhandel og- reparation*. Registered in accordance with Belgian law. EU Transparency Register: 33885548180-35. **Aims** Carry out scientific, economic, technical and administrative studies of all problems which relate to the activities of selling and repairing *cars* and which concern international economic integration, in particular within the *European Union*, together with the research into and application of solutions to such problems. **Structure** General Meeting. Board of Directors, consisting or the representatives of each of the European Union member states. Executive Bureau, comprising President, Vice President-Treasurer and 1 or 2 Vice Presidents, one of whom is the Executive-Vice President Divisions (4); Working Groups (5). **Finance** Members' dues. **Activities** Research/documentation; knowledge management/information dissemination; events/meetings; networking/liaising. **Events** *General Meeting* Brussels (Belgium) 2016, *European Truck Dealer Meeting* Brussels (Belgium) 2014, *General Assembly* Brussels (Belgium) 2014.

Members Full in 18 countries:

Austria, Belgium, Czechia, Denmark, Finland, France, Germany, Ireland, Luxembourg, Netherlands, Norway, Portugal, Slovakia, Slovenia, Spain, Sweden, Switzerland, UK.

European Dealer Councils in 6 countries:

Belgium, France, Germany, Italy, Netherlands, UK.

Observer in 2 countries:

Iceland, Israel.

IGO Relations Recognized by: *European Commission (EC, #06633).* **NGO Relations** Member of: *Alliance for the Freedom of Car Repair in the EU (AFCAR, #00682).* In liaison with technical committees of: *Comité européen de normalisation (CEN, #04162).* [2019/XE0652/t/**E**]

♦ European Council of National Associations of Independent Schools (ECNAIS) 06833

Conseil européen des associations nationales d'écoles indépendantes – Consejo Europeo de Asociaciones Nacionales de Escuelas Independientes – Europäischer Rat der Nationalen Verbände Freier Schulen – Conselho Europeu das Associações Nacionais de Escolas Independentes – Europees Samenwerkingsverband van Nationale Organisaties van Onafhankelijke Scholen – Europaeiske Sammenslutning af Nationale Foreninger for Frie Grundskoler – Europeiska Rådet av Nationella Friskoleförbund – Wurooppalaisten Yrsityskoulujen Liittojen Neuvosto

SG c/o AEEP, Av Defensores de Chaves 32, 1o Esq, 1000-119 Lisbon, Portugal. T. +351217955390. Fax +351217964075. E-mail: secretariat@ecnais.org.
Headquarters Fredrikinkatu 61 A, 3 krs, FI-00100 Helsinki, Finland.
URL: http://www.ecnais.org/

History 1988. Articles and memorandum of association adopted 13 Oct 1989. Registration: Start date: 2018, Finland; Companies House, No/ID: 02492855, Start date: 1990, End date: 2019, England and Wales. **Aims** Promote the rights of pluralism in national education systems and of parental choice of education for their children; promote the role of independent schools in a modern democratic society; further the interests of all kinds of independent education, whatever the religious, social and philosophical principles on which such education is founded. **Structure** General Meeting (annual). Management Committee, consisting of one representative of each country of association membership, plus up to 3 co-opted members who may be representatives of international associations of independent schools. Honorary Officers: Chairman; Secretary; Treasurer. **Languages** English. **Finance** Members' dues. **Activities** Knowledge management/information dissemination; events/meetings. **Events** *ECNAIS Conference* Stockholm (Sweden) 2020, *ECNAIS Conference* Istanbul (Turkey) 2019, *ECNAIS Conference* Kiev (Ukraine) 2018, *ECNAIS Conference* Rome (Italy) 2017, *ECNAIS Conference* Athens (Greece) 2016. **Publications** *ECNAIS Bulletin* (3-4 a year). Brochures; pamphlets; leaflets; charts; diagrams.

Members National associations of independent schools in 17 countries:
Austria, Belarus, Bulgaria, Czechia, Denmark, Finland, France, Greece, Hungary, Iceland, Netherlands, Poland, Portugal, Romania, Spain, Türkiye, Ukraine.
Associate members in 4 countries:
Australia, Netherlands, Switzerland, UK.

NGO Relations Member of: *Lifelong Learning Platform – European Civil Society for Education (LLLP, #16466).* [2021/XD2665/**D**]

♦ European Council for Non-Destructive Testing (inactive)

♦ European Council for Non-Profit Organizations 06834

Comité européen des associations d'intérêt général (CEDAG)

Pres c/o UNIPSO, Rue du Congrès 37-41 – bte 3, 1000 Brussels, Belgium. E-mail: cedag@cedag-eu.org.
URL: http://www.cedag.eu/

History Founded 15 Nov 1989, as *European Council for Voluntary Organizations – Comité européen des associations d'intérêt général – Europäisches Aktionskomitee Freier Verbände – Comité Europeo de Asociaciones de Interés General – Comitato Europeo delle Associazioni d'Interesse Generale – Europees Comité van Verenigingen voor Algemeen Belang – Europaeiske Center for Private Hjaelpeorganisationer – Comité Europeu das Associações de Interesse Geral – Evropaiki Epitropi Ton Organosseon Kinu Kalu – Kansalaisjärjestöjen Euroopan Yhdistys – Rådet för Föreningar i Europa.* From 2004, only new English and original French title are used. Registered in accordance with Belgian law, 1992. Statutes modified, 13 May 1996. EU Transparency Register: 1815241602-21. **Aims** Provide a voice for the associative sector in Europe. **Structure** General Assembly (annual); Administrative Council (meets at least twice a year). **Languages** English, French. **Staff** Voluntary. **Finance** Members' dues. **Activities** Events/meetings. **Events** *Meeting on how can social profit organisations use EU social policy to shape their environment* Brussels (Belgium) 2010, *The value of not-for-profit organisations , best practice in corporate social responsibility* Brussels (Belgium) 2003, *Towards stronger partnerships in an enlarged Europe* Warsaw (Poland) 2003, *Conference* Brussels (Belgium) 2002, *General Assembly* Brussels (Belgium) 1999. **Publications** *Never without the Associations: Which Civil Dialogue in an Enlarged Europe* (2003) in English, French; *Bilan annuel de la vie associative dans les pays de l'Uion européenne (Allemagne, Espagne, France, Italie)* (1999); *Associations and Lotteries* (1995); *Associations and New Sources of Funding* (1995); *Associations' Activities and European Laws on Competition and Taxation* (1994); *Associations and European Structural Funds* (1994); *European Citizenship and Democracy* (1992) in English, French; *The Associations and Europe, Associations and Realization of the Internal Market* (1990). Reports; conference proceedings; brochure.

Members in 7 countries:
Belgium, Czechia, France, Hungary, Luxembourg, Portugal, Sweden.

IGO Relations *European Commission (EC, #06633); European Economic and Social Committee (EESC, #06963); European Parliament (EP, #08146).* **NGO Relations** Founding member of: *Social Economy Europe (SEE, #19335); Social Services Europe (#19347).* Associate member of: *Social Platform (#19344).* Supports: *European Alliance for the Statute of the European Association (EASEA, #05886).* [2018.09.06/XD2928/y/**D**]

♦ European Council for Nuclear Research (inactive)
♦ European Council of Nursing Regulators / see European Nursing Council (#08063)

♦ European Council of Optometry and Optics (ECOO) 06835

Conseil européen de l'optométrie et de l'optique – Europäischer Rat für Optometrie und Optik

SG Rond Point Schuman 6, Box 5, 1040 Brussels, Belgium. T. +32474078709. E-mail: secretariat@ecoo.info.
Head Office Winkelbüel 2, 6043 Adligenswil LU, Switzerland.
URL: http://www.ecoo.info/

History Nov 1992, Paris (France). Founded on merger of *Common Market Opticians' Group (inactive)*, set up 8 Jun 1960, Luxembourg, and *Pan European Group of Optometrists (inactive)* of *World Council of Optometry (WCO, #21335).* Registration: EU Transparency Register, No/ID: 03999415319-19, Start date: 16 Feb 2011. **Aims** Improve vision and eye health by providing high-quality, cost-effective optometric and optical services across Europe. **Structure** General Assembly; Executive Committee; Committees (2). **Languages** English. **Staff** 1.00 FTE, paid. **Finance** Sources: grants; members' dues. **Activities** Events/meetings. **Events** *Spring Meeting* Rome (Italy) 2019, *Annual General Assembly* Malmö (Sweden) 2018, *Spring Meeting* Zagreb (Croatia) 2018, *Spring Meeting* Barcelona (Spain) 2017, *Annual General Assembly* Prague (Czechia) 2017. **Publications** *ECOO Newsletter.* Press releases; position papers; studies.

Members National optometric organizations in 22 countries:
Austria, Belgium, Bulgaria, Cyprus, Czechia, Denmark, Finland, Germany, Hungary, Ireland, Italy, Malta, Netherlands, Norway, Poland, Portugal, Slovakia, Slovenia, Spain, Sweden, Switzerland, UK.

NGO Relations Member of (1): *European Public Health Alliance (EPHA, #08297).* [2022.10.19/XD3694/**D**]

♦ European Council of the Paint, Printing Ink and Artists' Colours Industry (#04688)

♦ European Council for Pastoral Care and Counselling (ECPCC) 06836

SG Kirchplatztreff, Kirchplatz 2, 95444 Bayreuth, Germany.
URL: http://www.ecpcc.info/

History Founded within *International Council on Pastoral Care and Counselling (ICPCC, #13059).* **Aims** Further learning and dialogue in the field of pastoral care and counselling in Europe. **Structure** General Assembly; Steering Committee. **Languages** English. **Staff** 7.00 FTE, voluntary. **Finance** Congress financed through congress fees. No annual budget. **Events** *Quadrennial Conference* Balatonszárszó (Hungary) 2022, *Quadrennial Conference* Balatonszárszó (Hungary) 2021, *Quadrennial Conference* Järvenpää (Finland) 2017, *Quadrennial Conference* Göttingen (Germany) 2013, *Quadrennial Conference* Leuven (Belgium) 2009. **Publications** *Interreligious Encounter on Cura Animarum: ECPCC and ICPCC documents and reports from 1972-1988* (2013). **Members** Not a membership organization. **NGO Relations** Contacts with: *International Council on Pastoral Care and Counselling (ICPCC, #13059).* [2020/XJ4185/**E**]

♦ European Council for Payment Systems (inactive)
♦ European Council for Plasticisers and Intermediates / see European Plasticisers (#08214)
♦ European Council of Police Trade Unions / see European Council of Police Unions (#06837)

♦ European Council of Police Unions (ECPU) 06837

Conseil européen des syndicats de police (CESP) – Consejo Europeo de Sindicatos de Policia (CESP)

Contact 52 rue Crozatier, 75012 Paris, France. E-mail: info@cesp.eu.
Main Website: http://www.cesp.eu/

History Dec 1988, Avila (Spain). Former names and other names: *European Council of Police Trade Unions* – alias. Registration: EU Transparency Register, No/ID: 387010543645-11, Start date: 22 Jul 2021. **Aims** Work for understanding between police and citizens; make citizens and their representatives aware of the problems of the police; bring together police officers belonging to affiliated *trade unions*; ensure the proper performance of their duty and help improve and standardize their working conditions; defend the moral and material interests of affiliated trade unions and their members before the competent European courts; establish all lawful systems of trade union action not prejudicial to public order safety; promote the right to organize for police officers in the Council of Europe member states and oppose any restriction on that right. **Structure** Congress (every 3 years); Executive Bureau. Works for the adoption of a *'European Police Charter'* and respect of *European Social Charter (1961).* **Languages** English, French. **Staff** 10.00 FTE, paid. **Finance** Sources: donations; members' dues. Annual budget: 55,000 EUR (2021). **Events** *Congress* Santander (Spain) 2012, *Congress* Novi Sad (Serbia) 2008, *Congress* Varna (Bulgaria) 2005, *Meeting* Velenje (Slovenia) 2005, *Meeting* Gdansk (Poland) 2004.

Members Trade union organizations (15), representing 250,000 police officers, in 14 countries:
Albania, Bosnia-Herzegovina, Cyprus, France, Germany, Greece, Italy, Lithuania, Montenegro, Netherlands, North Macedonia, Portugal, Romania, Spain.

Consultative Status Consultative status granted from: *Council of Europe (CE, #04881)* (Participatory Status). **NGO Relations** Member of (1): *Conference of INGOs of the Council of Europe (#04607).* [2022.05.16/XD2676/**D**]

♦ European Council of Practical Nurses (EPN) 06838

Pres The Finnish Union of Practical Nurses, Ratamestarinkatu 12, FI-00520 Helsinki, Finland. T. +35892727910. Fax +358927279120.

History 1980. **Aims** Create a common identity for practical nurses; promote common interests; safeguard the members social and professional interests. **Events** *Congress* Helsinki (Finland) 1998.

Members National associations in 6 countries and territories:
Denmark, Faeroe Is, Finland, Iceland, Luxembourg, Norway. [2015.06.25/XD6531/**D**]

♦ European Council of Real Estate Professions / see European Association of Real Estate Professions (#06186)

♦ European Council on Refugees and Exiles (ECRE) 06839

Conseil européen sur les réfugiés et les exilés (ECRE)

Main Office Avenue des Arts 7/8, 1210 Brussels, Belgium. T. +3223290040.
Senior Communication Coordinator address not obtained. T. +32472230041.
URL: http://www.ecre.org/

History 1974. Former names and other names: *European Consultation on Refugees and Exiles* – former (1974 to 1994); *Consultation européenne sur les réfugiés et les exilés* – former (1974 to 1994). Registration: Belgium; EU Transparency Register, No/ID: 43750202163-43. **Aims** Protect and advance the rights of refugees, asylum seekers and displaced persons. **Structure** General Conference (annual); Board; Secretariat, headed by Secretary-General. Includes: *European Legal Network on Asylum (ELENA, #07679).* **Languages** English. **Staff** 14.00 FTE, paid. **Finance** Members' dues. Grants from: *European Commission (EC, #06633)*; international organizations and foundations. **Activities** Guidance/assistance/consulting; research/documentation; advocacy/lobbying/activism; networking/liaising; events/meetings; publishing activities. **Events** *General Conference* Brussels (Belgium) 2022, *General Conference* Brussels (Belgium) 2021, *General Conference* Brussels (Belgium) 2019, *General Conference* Belgrade (Serbia) 2018, *Meeting on the Protection of Refugees and on Addressing Forced Displacement in the EU Post-2020 Multiannual Financial Framework (MFF)* Brussels (Belgium) 2018. **Publications** *ECRE Weekly Bulletin*; *ECRE Weekly Legal Updates.* Policy notes; memorandums; comments; briefs; reports. **Information Services** *The Asylum Information Database (AIDA)*; *The European Database of Asylum Law (EDAL)*; *The European Legal Network on Asylum (ELENA).*

Members National agencies (85) in 35 countries:
Austria, Azerbaijan, Belgium, Bosnia-Herzegovina, Bulgaria, Croatia, Cyprus, Czechia, Denmark, Estonia, Finland, France, Georgia, Germany, Greece, Hungary, Ireland, Italy, Kosovo, Lithuania, Luxembourg, Malta, Netherlands, North Macedonia, Norway, Poland, Portugal, Romania, Russia, Serbia, Slovakia, Spain, Sweden, Switzerland, Türkiye, UK, Ukraine.
Included in the above, 33 organizations listed in this Yearbook:
- *Amnesty International (AI, #00801)*;
- *Arbeiterwohlfahrt International (AWO International)*;
- *Caritas Europa (#03579)* (various national societies);
- *Churches' Commission for Migrants in Europe (CCME, #03912)*;
- *Conference of European Churches (CEC, #04593)*;
- *Coordination et initiatives pour réfugiés et étrangers (CIRE)*;
- *Danish Refugee Council (DRC)*;
- *DIAKONIE – Evangelischer Flüchtlingsdienst*;
- *Dutch Refugee Council*;
- *France terre d'asile (FTDA)*;
- *Greek Council for Refugees (GCR)*;
- *Helsinki Citizens' Assembly (hCa, #10905)*;
- *HIAS*;
- *International Catholic Migration Commission (ICMC, #12459)*;
- *International Cities of Refuge Network (ICORN, #12578)*;
- *International Eurasia-Press Fund (IEPF, #13309)*;
- *International Federation of Red Cross and Red Crescent Societies (#13526)* (varous national societies);
- *International Labor Communications Association (ILCA)*;
- *International Rehabilitation Council for Torture Victims (IRCT, #14712)*;
- *International Rescue Committee (IRC, #14717)* (various societies);
- *Irish Refugee Council*;
- *Italian Council for Refugees (CIR)*;
- *Jesuit Refugee Service (JRS, #16106)*;
- *Norwegian Organization for Asylum Seekers (NOAS)*;
- *Norwegian Refugee Council (NRC)*;
- *Organisation suisse d'aide aux réfugiés (OSAR)*;
- *Portuguese Refugee Council (CPR)*;
- *Refugee Council (#18739)* (various national societies);
- *Refugee Studies Centre, Oxford (RSC)*;
- *Scottish Refugee Council (SRC)*;
- *Spanish Commission for Refugee Assistance (CEAR)*;
- *UNHCR (#20327)* (Memorial Human Rights Centre).

Consultative Status Consultative status granted from: *Council of Europe (CE, #04881)* (Participatory Status). **IGO Relations** Participant in Fundamental Rights Platform of: *European Union Agency for Fundamental Rights (FRA, #08969).* Member of: *Frontex, the European Border and Coast Guard Agency (#10005)* Consultative Forum. Also links with European Union institutions and informal fora, including the intergovernmental consultations on asylum, refugee and migration policies. **NGO Relations** Member of: *European NGO Platform Asylum and Migration (EPAM, #08051)*; *European Policy Centre (EPC, #08240).* Also links with NGOs working on asylum and immigration (not specified). [2020/XF2696/y/**F**]

♦ European Council of Religious Leaders – Religions for Peace (ECRL) 06840

SG c/o Dept of Theology, Univ of Winchester, Sparkford Road, Winchester, SO22 4NR, UK. E-mail: secretariat@ecrl.eu.
URL: http://ecrl.eu/

History Inaugurated 2002, Oslo (Norway), as one of 4 regional Inter-Religious Councils (IRCs) within *Religions for Peace (RfP, #18831).* Originally also referred to as *World Conference on Religion and Peace*; *European Conference on Religion and Peace.* **Aims** As a coalition of Senior religious leaders of Europe's historic religions, Christianity, Judaism and Islam with Buddhists, Hindus, Sikhs and Zoroastrians in Europe: cooperate on conflict prevention and transformation, peaceful coexistence and reconciliation; encourage members of their respective communities to do the same. **Structure** Council; Executive Committee; Secretariat in Bushey (UK).

Languages English. **Staff** 1.00 FTE, paid. **Finance** Members' dues. Supported by: Norwegian Ministry of Foreign Affairs; foundations; religious institutions. **Activities** Events/meetings. **Events** *Annual Roundtable and Business Meeting* Brussels (Belgium) 2014, *European Conference on Religion and Peace* 1996. **Publications** *Different Faiths – Common Action: A Strategy for European Council of Religious Leaders 2013-2018.* Annual Report; Council Declarations.
Members Institutional religious bodies, institutions and organizations; Individual. Members in 21 countries and territories:
Austria, Belgium, Bosnia-Herzegovina, Croatia, Czechia, Denmark, Finland, France, Germany, Holy See, Ireland, Italy, Kosovo, Netherlands, Norway, Romania, Russia, Spain, Sweden, Switzerland, UK.
Included in the above, one organization listed in this Yearbook:
Russian Orthodox Church (#19010).
NGO Relations Member of: *Joint Learning Initiative on Faith and Local Communities (JLI, #16139).* [2020/XK0704/y/**E**]

♦ European Council for Research on Strabismus / see European Strabismological Association (#08840)
♦ European Council for Rural Law (#04155)
♦ European Council of Shopping Places (unconfirmed)

♦ European Council of Skeptical Organizations (ECSO) 06841

Chairman Hungarian Skeptic Society, Pf 2, Budapest 1580, Hungary. E-mail: info@szkeptikustarsasag.hu.
Contact Arheilger Weg 11, 64380 Rossdorf, Germany. T. +496154695023. Fax +496154695022.
URL: http://www.ecso.org/
History 25 Sep 1994, Ostend (Belgium), on signature of an agreement which came into force 1 Jan 1995. Non-profit organization 2004. **Aims** Protect the public from the promulgation of claims and therapies which have not been subjected to critical testing; investigate extraordinary claims which are on the fringe of or contradict current scientific knowledge, such as phenomena commonly identified as paranormal or pseudoscientific – although none will be rejected in advance of objective evaluation; promote scientific inquiry, critical thinking, science education and public policy based on good practice in science and medicine, including alternative medicine. **Structure** Council (meets annually, usually at Congress); Board. **Languages** English. **Finance** Members' dues. **Activities** Events/meetings; knowledge management/information dissemination. **Events** *Conference* Ghent (Belgium) 2019, *Conference / European Sceptics Conference* London (UK) 2015, *Conference* Stockholm (Sweden) 2013, *World Skeptics Congress* Berlin (Germany) 2012, *Conference / European Sceptics Conference* Budapest (Hungary) 2010.
Members National organizations in 13 countries:
Belgium, Czechia, Finland, France, Germany, Hungary, Ireland, Italy, Netherlands, Slovakia, Spain, Sweden, UK.
NGO Relations Together with *Gesellschaft zur wissenschaftlichen Untersuchung von Parawissenschaften (GWUP)*, instrumental in setting up *Centre for Inquiry – Europe.* Member of: *International Network of Skeptical Organizations (no recent information).* [2015/XD4973/**D**]

♦ European Council for Small Business and Entrepreneurship (ECSB) 06842

Secretariat c/o University of Turku, School of Economics, Turun yliopisto, FI-20014 Turku, Finland. T. +358505126956. E-mail: info@ecsb.org – ecsb@utu.fi.
URL: https://ecsb.org/
History 19 Sep 1988. **Aims** As a research-driven non-profit organisation, facilitate the creation and dissemination of new knowledge through research and the open exchange of ideas between academia, education, policy and practice. **Structure** Board of Directors; Executive Committee. **Finance** Sources: members' dues. **Events** *Nordic Conference on Small Business Research* Odense (Denmark) 2022, *3E (ECSB Entrepreneurship Education) Conference* Turku (Finland) 2021, *RENT : Conference on Research in Entrepreneurship and Small Business* Turku (Finland) 2021, *3E (ECSB Entrepreneurship Education) Conference* Trondheim (Norway) 2020, *RENT : Conference on Research in Entrepreneurship and Small Business* Turku (Finland) 2020. **NGO Relations** Member of (2): *EFMD – The Management Development Network (#05387); International Council for Small Business (ICSB, #13075).* Joint conferences with: *European Institute for Advanced Studies in Management (EIASM, #07544).* [2021.05.25/XM3120/**E**]

♦ European Council for Social Research on Latin America (#04710)

♦ European Council of Spatial Planners (ECTP-CEU) 06843

Conseil européen des urbanistes
Administrator M.A.I., Rue Washington 40, 1050 Brussels, Belgium. T. +32470350432. E-mail: secretariat@ectp-ceu.eu.
URL: http://www.ectp-ceu.eu/
History 8 Nov 1985. Replaced *Liaison Committee between the Associations and the National Institutes of Town Planners in the Member Countries of the European Community (inactive).* Founded on signing of International Agreement and Declaration. Statutes amended in 1988. Former names and other names: *European Council of Town Planners (ECTP)* – former. Registration: Banque-Carrefour des Entreprises, No/ID: 0419.378.312, Start date: 26 Apr 1979, Belgium. **Aims** Enable free movement of town planners in member countries of the *European Union*, through mutual recognition of their qualifications and skills; represent and promote the town planning profession recognizing its specific characteristics, its ethics, its values and foundations in land management policy, among European institutions, national political institutions, economic and social powers and citizens. **Structure** General Assembly (2 a year); Council (meets twice a year); Executive Committee; Working Groups. **Languages** English, French. **Staff** 1.00 FTE, paid. Voluntary. **Finance** Sources: members' dues. Annual budget: 45,000 EUR. **Activities** Awards/prizes/competitions; events/meetings; networking/liaising. **Events** *Spring General Assembly* Bergen (Norway) 2020, *Spring General Assembly* Madrid (Spain) 2019, *Autumn General Assembly* Plymouth (UK) 2019, *Biennial Conference on Towns and Town Planners in Europe* Plymouth (UK) 2019, *Autumn General Assembly* Leuven (Belgium) 2018. **Publications** *15 Steps Towards Territorial Cohesion; A Centenary of Spatial Planning in Europe; The Charter of European Planning; Try It This Way* – checklist on sustainable urban development. Annual Report.
Members Full associations (20) in 18 countries:
Belgium, Cyprus, Czechia, Denmark, France, Greece, Hungary, Ireland, Italy, Malta, Netherlands, Norway, Poland, Portugal, Romania, Slovenia, Spain, UK.
Corresponding associations (3) in 3 countries:
Germany, Iceland, Türkiye.
Observer associations (2) in 2 countries:
Estonia, Serbia.
Consultative Status Consultative status granted from: *Council of Europe (CE, #04881)* (Participatory Status).
NGO Relations Member of (3): *European Heritage Alliance 3.3 (#07477); Federation of European and International Associations Established in Belgium (FAIB, #09508); Global Planners Network (GPN, #10548).* Partner of (1): *World Urban Campaign (WUC, #21893).* [2022/XE5983/**D**]

♦ European Council for Steiner Waldorf Education (ECSWE) 06844

Acting Managing Dir Rue du Trône 194, 1050 Brussels, Belgium. T. +3226440043. E-mail: info@ecswe.eu.
Acting Pres address not obtained.
URL: https://ecswe.eu/
History 1991. Former names and other names: *European Council of Steiner Waldorf Schools (ECSWS)* – former. Registration: Banque-Carrefour des Entreprises, No/ID: 0898.707.869, Start date: 20 Jun 2008, Belgium; EU Transparency Register, No/ID: 256252314853-30, Start date: 3 Nov 2014. **Aims** Support Steiner Waldorf education and promoting freedom in education in Europe. **Structure** Council; Board. **Languages** English. Translations to all member languages. **Staff** 3.00 FTE, paid; 3.00 FTE, voluntary. **Finance** Sources: grants; members' dues. Supported by: *European Union (EU, #08967).* **Activities** Advocacy/lobbying/activism; awareness raising; capacity building; events/meetings; knowledge management/information dissemination; networking/liaising; politics/policy/regulatory; projects/programmes; publishing activities; training/education. **Events** *Meeting* 2023, *Meeting* 2022, *Meeting* Ghent (Belgium) 2022, *Meeting* Lisbon (Portugal) 2022, *Meeting* Frankfurt-Main (Germany) 2021. **Publications** *ECSWE Newsletter. Assessment as Dialogue: Twenty inspiring practices from classrooms and schools around Europe* (1st 2021) in English. **Information Services** *Translations of existing materials on Steiner Waldorf Education* in English.
Members Full national associations (27) representing 28 countries:
Armenia, Austria, Belgium, Croatia, Czechia, Denmark, Estonia, Finland, France, Germany, Hungary, Ireland, Italy, Latvia, Lithuania, Luxembourg, Netherlands, Norway, Poland, Portugal, Russia, Slovakia, Slovenia, Spain, Sweden, Switzerland, UK, Ukraine.
NGO Relations Member of (5): *Alliance ELIANT (#00672); Alliance for Childhood European Network Group (AFC-ENG, #00666); Eurochild (#05657); International Network for Academic Steiner Teacher Education (INASTE, #14226); Lifelong Learning Platform – European Civil Society for Education (LLLP, #16466).* Partner of (6): *European Network of Steiner Waldorf Parents (ENSWaP, #08014); Freunde der Erziehungskunst Rudolf Steiners; Goetheanum; International Association for Steiner/Waldorf Early Childhood Education (IASWECE, #12185); International Forum for Steiner/Waldorf-Education (Hague Circle, #13653); Learning for Well-being Foundation (L4WB, #16431).* [2023.02.28/XE3263/**E**]

♦ European Council of Steiner Waldorf Schools / see European Council for Steiner Waldorf Education (#06844)

♦ European Council for Student Affairs (ECStA) 06845

Conseil européen de la vie étudiante
Secretariat c/o CNOUS, 60 bd du Lycée, 92170 Vanves, France. T. +33171229747. E-mail: ecsta@cnous.fr – ecsta@studentenwerke.de.
URL: http://www.ecsta.org/
History Feb 1999, Brussels (Belgium). Registration: No/ID: 0465.297.617, Start date: 11 Feb 1999, Belgium. **Aims** Promote social infrastructure within higher education institutions in Europe; promote cooperation between organizations responsible for this sector in Europe; promote mobility of students in the European Higher Education Area. **Structure** General Assembly (annual); Board of Management. Acts as contact and advisory body for: *European Commission (EC, #06633); Council of Europe (CE, #04881); Council of the European Union (#04895); UNESCO (#20322).* **Languages** English, French. **Staff** None. **Finance** Members' dues. **Activities** Advocacy/lobbying/activism; guidance/assistance/consulting; events/meetings. **Events** *Transatlantic Dialogue* Esch-sur-Alzette (Luxembourg) 2017, *Conference* Aix-en-Provence (France) 2011, *Conference* Bonn (Germany) 2010, *Conference* Rome (Italy) 2009, *Conference* Nancy (France) 2008.
Members in 12 countries:
Austria, Belgium, Denmark, France, Germany, Ireland, Italy, Luxembourg, Norway, Portugal, Switzerland, Türkiye.
IGO Relations *European Commission (EC, #06633);* Ministries of Education and Higher Education in participating countries. [2020/XD7238/**D**]

♦ European Council of Teachers of Mathematics (no recent information)
♦ European Council of Telecommunications Users' Associations (inactive)

♦ European Council for Theological Education (ECTE) 06846

Coordinator Via dei Lucumoni 33, 01015 Sutri VITERBO, Italy. T. +39761419001. Fax +39761419001. E-mail: office@ecte.eu.
URL: https://ecte.eu/
History 31 Oct 1979, Switzerland. 31 Oct 1979, Chrischona (Switzerland). An autonomous body within *World Evangelical Alliance (WEA, #21393).* Former names and other names: *Europäische Evangelikale Akkreditierungsvereinigung* – former (2017); *Association évangélique européenne d'accréditation* – former (2017); *European Evangelical Accrediting Association (EE AA)* – former (2017). Registration: Germany. **Aims** Bring member schools to a process of self-*evaluation* and accreditation; provide networking and service to member schools. **Structure** General Assembly. Council of 8 members. Student Council set up Oct 2008. Visitation Evaluation Team (VET) comprising academics, administrators and evangelical leaders. **Languages** English. **Staff** 0.50 FTE, paid; 3.00 FTE, voluntary. **Finance** Members' dues. **Activities** Organizes training conferences. **Events** *Biennial general convention / Biennial Convention* London (UK) 2011, *General assembly / Biennial Convention* Sopron (Hungary) 2009, *Biennial Convention* Rome (Italy) 2007, *Biennial Convention* Prague (Czech Rep) 2005, *Biennial general convention / Biennial Convention* Bergneustadt (Germany) 2001. **Publications** *The Theological Educator* – online journal. *Manual of Accreditation* (1995); *Directory of Evangelical Theological Schools in Europe* (1992).
Members Evangelical theological schools in 23 countries:
Austria, Belgium, Bulgaria, Croatia, Denmark, Estonia, Finland, France, Germany, Greece, Israel, Italy, Lebanon, Netherlands, Norway, Romania, Serbia, Slovakia, Spain, Sweden, Switzerland, UK, Ukraine.
NGO Relations Charter member of: *International Council for Evangelical Theological Education (ICETE, #13020).* Member of: *International Network of Quality Assurance Agencies in Higher Education (INQAAHE, #14312).* Associate of: *European Evangelical Alliance (EEA, #07010); European Association for Quality Assurance in Higher Education (ENQA, #06183).* [2020/XD1826/**E**]

♦ European Council on Tolerance and Reconciliation (ECTR) 06847

SG Al Przyjaciol 8/, 00-565 Warsaw, Poland. T. +48226226603. Fax +48226294816. E-mail: office@ectr.eu.
Brussels Office Avenue Maurice 32, 1050 Brussels, Belgium.
URL: http://ectr.eu/
History Oct 2008, by Aleksander Kwasniewski, former President of Poland, and Moshe Kantor, President of *European Jewish Congress (EJC, #07609).* **Aims** Foster understanding and tolerance among peoples of various ethnic origin; educate on techniques of reconciliation; facilitate post-conflict social apprehensions; monitor chauvinistic behaviour; propose protolerance initiatives and legal solutions. **Structure** Board. **Activities** Awards/prizes/competitions; advocacy/lobbying/activism. [2015/XJ9664/**D**]

♦ European Council of Town Planners / see European Council of Spatial Planners (#06843)

♦ European Council for the Village and Small Town (ECOVAST) 06848

Conseil européen pour le village et la petite ville – Europäischer Verband für das Dorf und für die Kleinstadt
Pres Sherborne, Ingleden Park Road, Tenterden, TN30 6NS, UK. T. +441580762379.
Treas Bildungszentrum für Natur-Umwelt-ländliche Räume Schleswig-Holstein, Hamburger Chaussee 25, 24220 Flintbek, Germany. T. +494347704793.
URL: http://www.ecovast.org/
History Founded 1984, Bellnhausen-Gladenbach (Germany FR). Registered in Alsace (France). **Aims** Further the well-being of *rural* communities and the safeguarding of the rural heritage throughout Europe; foster economic, social and cultural vitality and administrative identity of rural communities throughout Europe; safeguard and promote the sensitive and imaginative renewal of built and natural environments of such communities. **Structure** General Assembly; Executive Committee; International Working Groups; National Sections. **Languages** English, French, German. **Staff** Voluntary. **Finance** Sources: members' dues. **Activities** Capacity building; events/meetings. **Events** *General Assembly* Croatia 2018, *General Assembly* Köszeg (Hungary) 2013, *Biennial Conference* Witzenhausen (Germany) 2012, *General Assembly* Vienna (Austria) 2011, *Biennial Conference* Isle of Wight 2010. **Publications** *ECOVAST Newsletter. Landscape Identification: A Guide to Good Practice* (2006); *Traditional Rural Architecture: A Strategy for Europe* (2006); *Agriculture and Forestry: Sustaining their Future in Europe* (1997) in English, French, German; *Heritage Trails Manual* (1997). Conference proceedings; position papers.
Members Non-governmental and governmental organizations at local, regional, national and international levels; individuals. Members in 13 countries:
Austria, Croatia, Germany, Hungary, Italy, Luxembourg, North Macedonia, Poland, Portugal, Romania, Russia, Slovakia, UK.
IGO Relations Cooperates with: *European Commission (EC, #06633)* – DG Agri and DG Regio. **NGO Relations** Member of (1): *European Heritage Alliance 3.3 (#07477).* [2017/XD0517/**D**]

♦ European Council of Vinyl Manufacturers (ECVM) 06849

Gen Manager Av de Cortenbergh 71, 3rd Floor, 1000 Brussels, Belgium. T. +3223295105.
URL: http://www.pvc.org/en/p/ecvm/
History As a division of *Association of Plastics Manufacturers in Europe (Plastics Europe, #02862).* **Aims** Represent European PVC resin producing companies. **Structure** Vinyls Committee. Value Chain Platforms (3): *PVCMed Alliance (#18583); PVC4Pipes (#18582); PVC4Cables (#18581).* **Languages** English. **Staff** 3.00 FTE, paid. **Events** *VinylPlus Sustainability Forum* Brussels (Belgium) 2020, *VinylPlus Sustainability Forum* Prague (Czechia) 2019, *VinylPlus Sustainability Forum* Madrid (Spain) 2018, *VinylPlus Sustainability Forum* Berlin (Germany) 2017, *VinylPlus Sustainability Forum* Cannes (France) 2015. **Publications** *ECVM Newsletter.*
Members PVC resin producers in 6 countries:
Belgium, Germany, Netherlands, Portugal, Spain, UK.
NGO Relations Member of: *PVC4Pipes (#18582).* Associate Member of: *Construction Products Europe AISBL (#04761).* Instrumental in setting up: *VinylPlus (#20780).* [2019.07.10/XE1205/**E**]

♦ European Council for Voluntary Organizations / see European Council for Non-Profit Organizations (#06834)

♦ European Council of Wine Roads (inactive)

♦ European Council of WIZO Federations (ECWF) 06850

Conseil Européen des Fédérations WIZO (CEFW)

Contact c/o WIZO-France, 10 rue St Augustin, 75002 Paris, France. E-mail: info@ecwf.online.
URL: https://ecwf.online/

History Jan 1992, Paris (France), within *Women's International Zionist Organization (WIZO, #21030)*. **Aims** Strengthen bonds among national federations in Europe so as to work together to unite European *women* and enable them to act in favour of *human rights* and women's human rights. **Structure** Conference (annual); Board of Executives. **Languages** English. **Finance** Members' dues. Other sources: subsidies granted by the *European Commission (EC, #06633)*; regional and/or municipal councils of places where the annual conference is held. **Activities** Politics/policy/regulatory; networking/liaising; events/meetings. **Events** *Annual Conference / General Meeting* Amsterdam (Netherlands) 2014, *Annual Conference / General Meeting* Berlin (Germany) 2013, *Annual Conference / General Meeting* Stockholm (Sweden) 2012, *General Meeting* London (UK) 2011, *General Meeting* London (UK) 2010.

Members Individuals in 17 countries:
Austria, Belgium, Czechia, Denmark, Estonia, Finland, France, Germany, Greece, Hungary, Italy, Lithuania, Netherlands, Spain, Sweden, Switzerland, UK.

Consultative Status Consultative status granted from: *Council of Europe (CE, #04881)* (Participatory Status).
NGO Relations Member of: *European Women's Lobby (EWL, #09102)*; *Conference of INGOs of the Council of Europe (#04607)*. [2022/XE2645/E]

♦ European Council of Young Farmers (#04689)

♦ European Counter Terrorism Centre (ectc) 06851

Centre européen de la lutte contre le terrorisme

Head c/o EUROPOL, PO Box 90850, 2509 LW The Hague, Netherlands. T. +31703025000. Fax +31703455896.
URL: http://www.europol.europa.eu/content/ectc/

History 1 Jan 2016, within the Operations Department of *European Police Office (Europol, #08239)*. Also referred to as *European Counter Terrorist Centre (ECTC)*. **Aims** Be a central information hub in the fight against terrorism in the EU, providing analysis for ongoing investigations and contributing to a coordinated reaction in the event of major terrorist attacks. **Staff** 44.00 FTE, paid. **Activities** Knowledge management/information dissemination; advocacy/lobbying/activism. [2016/XM4388/E*]

♦ European Counter Terrorist Centre / see European Counter Terrorism Centre (#06851)

♦ European Countries Biologists Association (ECBA) 06852

Association des biologistes des pays européens

Headquarters c/o Soc of Biology, Charles Darwin House, 12 Roger Street, London, WC1N 2JU, UK. T. +442076852567. E-mail: ecba@ecba.eu.
URL: http://www.ecba.eu/

History Oct 1975, Bonn (Germany FR), as *European Communities Biologists Association – Association des biologistes des Communautés européennes – Vereinigung der Biologen der Europäischen Gemeinschaften – Associazione dei Biologi delle Comunità Europee*. New name adopted 1998. **Aims** Represent *professional* interests and ensure professional competence of biologists within the *European Communities*; provide information on professional matters concerning biologists; promote cooperation among national biologists' associations throughout Europe; facilitate free movement of biologists within the European Communities; promote exchange of teachers of biologists within the European Communities; promote recognition of the essential role of biology in the education of the public at all levels of the education system; advise the European Commission and the public in general of biological issues of public concern. **Structure** Council (meets annually). Steering Committee (meets twice a year), consisting of Chairman, Treasurer and Secretary. Commissioners appointed for specific purposes. **Finance** Dues from national associations. **Activities** Launching of the EuroBiol professional title. Organizes workshops. **Events** *Council Meeting* Utrecht (Netherlands) 2010, *Council Meeting* Nicosia (Cyprus) 2009, *Council Meeting* Berlin (Germany) 2008, *Council Meeting* London (UK) 2007, *Council Meeting* Antalya (Turkey) 2006. **Publications** *Eurobioletter* (periodical). Reports.

Members National associations Full; Associate; Affiliate. Individuals (professional biologists) of countries not represented in ECBA Observers. Full members National associations in 12 countries:
Full members National associations in 12 countries:
Belgium, Denmark, Finland, France, Germany, Greece, Ireland, Italy, Netherlands, Portugal, Spain, UK.
Associate members National associations in 3 countries:
Austria, Norway, Sweden.
Affiliate members National associations in 2 countries:
Italy, Spain.
Observers in 1 country:
Switzerland.

NGO Relations Founding member of: *European Alliance of Subject-Specific and Professional Accreditation and Quality Assurance (EASPA, #05887)*. Member of: *European Council of Liberal Professions (#06828)*. [2011.07.26/XE4533/E]

♦ European Court of Arbitration 06853

Cour européenne d'arbitrage (CEA) – Corte Europea de Arbitraje – Europäischer Schiedsgerichtshof – Corte Arbitrale Europea

Secretariat/International Registrars c/o Ordre des Avocats de Strasbourg, 3 rue Général Frère, 67000 Strasbourg, France. T. +33368781453. E-mail: info@cour-europe-arbitrage.org.
Pres Viale Cassiodoro 3, 20145 Milan MI, Italy. T. +3924989361. E-mail: president@cour-europe-arbitrage.org.
URL: http://www.cour-europe-arbitrage.org/

History Founded in the 1950s. Regulations first amended and entered into force Jan 2015; most recently amended July 2022. A division of *European Center for Arbitration and Mediation (#06462)*. Founded under patronage inter alia of: *Council of Europe (CE, #04881)*. Former names and other names: *European Arbitration Court* – alias; *Europees Arbitragehof* – former. **Aims** Promote the culture of arbitration and mediation; administer international and domestic arbitration and mediation. **Structure** Includes: *Mediation Centre for Europe, the Mediterranean and the Middle East*; *International School of Arbitration and Mediation of the Mediterranean and the Middle East*. **Languages** English, French, German, Italian, Spanish. **Staff** Officers operate through own staff. **Finance** Sources: contributions; members' dues. Other sources: administrative fees for arbitral proceedings and mediation proceedings. **Activities** Events/meetings; training/education. **Events** *MED-MID : Annual Mediterranean and Middle East Conference* 2020, *MED-MID : Annual Mediterranean and Middle East Conference* Paris (France) 2019, *MED-MID : Annual Mediterranean and Middle East Conference* Larnaca (Cyprus) 2018, *MED-MID : Annual Mediterranean and Middle East Conference* Milan (Italy) 2017, *MED-MID : Annual Mediterranean and Middle East Conference* Madrid (Spain) 2016. **Publications** *Med-Mid Arbitration and Mediation Reports*; *Rules of the Court*. Leaflets.

Members Chapters in 14 countries:
Belgium/Brussels Capital Region, Cyprus, France, Germany, Greece, Iran Islamic Rep, Iraq (Kurdistan), Italy, Kuwait, Lebanon, Romania, Spain, Syrian AR, Türkiye.

NGO Relations Member of (1): *International Federation of Commercial Arbitration Institutions (IFCAI)*. [2023.02.15/XF4195/F]

♦ European Court of Auditors 06854

Tribunal de Cuentas Europeo – Evropsky Ucetni Dvur – Den Europaeiske revisionsret – Europäischer Rechnungshof – Euroopa Kontrollikoda – Cour des comptes européenne – Cúirt Iniúchóirí na Heorpa – Europski Revizorski Sud – Corte dei conti europea – Eiropas Revizijas Palata – Europos Audito Rumai – Európai Szamvevoszék – Il-Qorti Ewropea Ta' l-Awdituri – Europese Rekenkamer – Tribunal de Contas Europeu – Curtea de Conturi Europeana – Európsky Dvor Auditorov – Evropsko Racunsko Sodisce – Euroopan Tilintarkastustuomioistuin – Europeiska revisionsrätten

Contact Rue Alcide De Gasperi 12, L-1615 Luxembourg, Luxembourg. T. +35243981. E-mail: eca-info@eca.europa.eu.
URL: http://www.eca.europa.eu/

History 22 Jul 1975. Established by the Treaty of Brussels. Became operational in Oct 1977. Originally within the framework of the *European Communities (EC, inactive)*, the status of the Court was enhanced to institution (1 Nov 1993) of *European Union (EU, #08967)* under the *Treaty on European Union (Maastricht Treaty, 1992)*, signed 7 Feb 1992, which set out the terms of the EU, since which time the Court has been referred to under its present title. The Court is thus one of 5 institutions of the European Union and a common institution to: *European Community (inactive)* (previously 'European Economic Community – EEC'); *European Atomic Energy Community (Euratom, inactive)*; and *European Coal and Steel Community (ECSC, inactive)*. (Note that the ECSC ceased to exist in Jul 2002, following expiration of the Paris Treaty; the European Community became responsible for the steel sector). Prior to 1975 the Court's functions were carried out by 2 separate bodies: EEC and Euratom Audit Board (Commission de contrôle) and ECSC Auditor General (Commissaire aux comptes). The Court's role was confirmed and strengthened on 1 May 1999 with the entry into force of the *Treaty of Amsterdam (1997)*, which empowered the Court to carry out sound financial management audits, emphasized its role in the fight against fraud and allowed it to have recourse to the Court of Justice in order to protect its prerogatives with regard to the other EU institutions. The *Nice Treaty (2001)* of 1 Feb 2003 confirmed the principle that there should be one member from each Member State, which allowed the Court the option of being organized in chambers and highlighted the importance of the Court's cooperation with national audit bodies. The *Treaty of Lisbon (2007)* again affirmed mandate and status as EU institution. Former names and other names: *Court of Auditors of the European Communities* – former; *Cour des comptes des Communautés européennes* – former; *Rechnungshof der Europäischen Gemeinschaften* – former; *Corte dei Conti delle Comunità Europee* – former; *Rekenkamer van de Europese Gemeenschappen* – former. **Aims** Contribute to improving EU *financial* management; promote accountability and transparency; act as the independent guardian of the financial interests of the citizens of the Union; check if EU budget has been implemented correctly and that EU funds have been raised and spent legally and in accordance with the principles of sound financial management. **Structure** Court comprises one member from each EU member state, appointed by Council of Ministers for 6-year terms after consultation with *European Parliament (EP, #08146)*. Members elect President from among themselves (3-year term). Court enjoys organizational autonomy and has adopted its own rules of procedure. Chambers (5): I – sustainable use of natural resources; II – investment for cohesion, growth and inclusion; III – external action, security and justice; IV – regulation of markets and competitive economy; V – financing and administering the Union. Horizontal committees (2): Audit Quality Control Committee, dealing with audit policies, standards and methodology, audit support and development and audit quality control; Administrative Committee, dealing with all administrative matters and decisions on communication and strategy. Members of each Chamber elect a Dean. **Languages** EU languages. **Staff** 873.00 FTE, paid. **Finance** On the general budget of the European Union. Annual budget: 162,141,175 EUR (2022). **Activities** Acts as external auditor of European Union finances.

Members Individuals (27), one for each of the 27 EU member States:
Austria, Belgium, Bulgaria, Croatia, Cyprus, Czechia, Denmark, Estonia, Finland, France, Germany, Greece, Hungary, Ireland, Italy, Latvia, Lithuania, Luxembourg, Malta, Netherlands, Poland, Portugal, Romania, Slovakia, Slovenia, Spain, Sweden.

IGO Relations Funds and organizations within the Court's area of competence include:
– *Agency for the Cooperation of Energy Regulators (ACER, #00552)*;
– *Body of European Regulators for Electronic Communications (BEREC, #03299)*;
– *Centre de traduction des organes de l'Union européenne (CdT, #03790)*;
– *Community Plant Variety Office (CPVO, #04404)*;
– Education, Audiovisual and Culture Executive Agency;
– *Euratom Supply Agency (ESA, #05617)*;
– *Eurojust (#05698)*;
– *Frontex, the European Border and Coast Guard Agency (#10005)*;
– *European Agency for Safety and Health at Work (EU-OSHA, #05843)*;
– *European Union Aviation Safety Agency (EASA, #08978)*;
– *European Banking Authority (EBA, #06311)*;
– *European Centre for the Development of Vocational Training (Cedefop, #06474)*;
– *European Centre for Disease Prevention and Control (ECDC, #06476)*;
– *European Chemicals Agency (ECHA, #06523)*;
– *European Defence Agency (EDA, #06895)*;
– *European Environment Agency (EEA, #06995)*;
– European Fisheries Control Agency;
– *European Food Safety Authority (EFSA, #07287)*;
– *European Foundation for the Improvement of Living and Working Conditions (Eurofound, #07348)*;
– *European Union Agency for the Space Programme (EUSPA, #08974)*;
– *European Institute for Gender Equality (EIGE, #07557)*;
– *European Institute of Innovation and Technology (EIT, #07562)*;
– *European Insurance and Occupational Pensions Authority (EIOPA, #07578)*;
– *European Maritime Safety Agency (EMSA, #07744)*;
– *European Police Office (Europol, #08239)*;
– *European Research Council (ERC, #08364)*;
– *European Securities and Markets Authority (ESMA, #08457)*;
– *European Training Foundation (ETF, #08934)*;
– *European Union Agency for Fundamental Rights (FRA, #08969)*;
– *European Union Agency for Network and Information Security (ENISA, #08971)*;
– *European Union Agency for Railways (#08973)*;
– *European Union Intellectual Property Office (EUIPO, #08996)*;
– Executive Agency for Competitiveness and Innovation;
– Executive Agency Health and Consumers;
– Research Executive Agency (REA).

NGO Relations Member of (2): *Association for Human Resources Management in International Organizations (AHRMIO, #02634)*; *International Organization of Supreme Audit Institutions (INTOSAI, #14478)*. Cooperates with (1): *European School of Administration (EUSA, #08427)*. Instrumental in setting up (1): *Syndicat autonome du personnel de la Cour des comptes européenne (inactive)*. Library is member of: *Eurolib (#05703)*; European Archives Group. [2022.10.17/XF8309/F*]

♦ European Court of Human Rights 06855

Cour européenne des droits de l'homme

Pres Council of Europe, 67075 Strasbourg CEDEX, France. T. +33388412018. Fax +33388412730. E-mail: echrinfo@echr.coe.int.
Registrar address not obtained.
URL: http://www.echr.coe.int/

History Apr 1959, Strasbourg (France). Established by *Council of Europe (CE, #04881)*, under the terms of *Convention for the Protection of Human Rights and Fundamental Freedoms (1950)*, also known as *'European Convention on Human Rights'*, in conjunction with *European Commission of Human Rights (inactive)*. Effective from 1 Nov 1998, the Court was restructured in accordance with *Protocol no 11 to the Convention for the Protection of Human Rights and Fundamental Freedoms (1994)*, signed 11 May 1994, as a single permanent Court to replace the part-time, two-tier system of Commission and Court. This restructuring was to resolve the growing difficulty experienced in coping with an ever-increasing volume of cases by eliminating the time-consuming examination of cases by two separate bodies and was designed to ensure better access to the system for the individual, resolve cases quickly and improve efficiency. **Aims** Under Article 19 of the Convention, signed 1950, in force 1953, ensure the observance of engagements undertaken by contracting parties. Under Articles 32, 33, 34 and 47, jurisdiction extends to all matters concerning interpretation and application of the Convention – allegations of breaches of Convention provisions referred to the Court by any Contracting State, by an individual, group of individuals or nongovernmental organization claiming to be a *victim* of a *violation* by one of the Contracting Parties of the rights protected under the Convention, and requests for advisory opinions. **Structure** Under Protocol No 11, effective 1 Nov 1998, the Court is composed of a number of judges equal to the number of Contracting Parties (currently 46), and sits permanently in Strasbourg (France). Judges elected for non-renewable term of 9 years, from a list of 3 candidates nominated by the contracting party concerned. They sit in their individual capacity and enjoy full independence in the discharge of their duties. Plenary Court adopts Rules of Court and sets up the Chambers. Sections (5) reflect the different legal systems among contracting parties and aim at geographical and gender balance. Cases are examined by Committees, Chambers, or by the Grand Chamber. Inadmissible applications examined by single judge. Three-judge Committee may rule by unanimous vote on admissibility and merits of cases already covered by well-established case-law of the Court. Application may also be assigned to a 7-judge Chamber which rules

by majority vote, mostly on admissibility and merits of case. Chambers may relinquish jurisdiction in favour of Grand Chamber when case raises serious questions affecting interpretation of Convention or its Protocols, or when resolution of a question before Chamber may have a result inconsistent with previous Court judgement. Parties may object to relinquishment of jurisdiction and may request referral to Grand Chamber within 3 months of judgement delivery. Such a request is heard by panel of 5 judges of Grand Chamber. *Committee of Ministers of the Council of Europe (#04273)* is responsible for supervising execution of the Court's judgements. **Languages** English, French. **Staff** 622 FTE, permanent; 22 FTE, temporary. **Finance** Under Article 50 of the Convention, the expenses of the Court are borne by the Council of Europe. Annual budget: 74,510,300 EUR (2022). **Activities** Events/meetings. Since its creation, until 1 Jan 2022, The Court has delivered more than 24,511 judgements and reviewed almost 957,300 applications. **Events** *Colloquium on Comparative Human Rights* Strasbourg (France) 2018, *Conference on European Convention on Human Rights and General International Law* Strasbourg (France) 2015, *International judicial conference* San Francisco, CA (USA) 2000. **Publications** *Facts and Figures* (annual); *Overview* (annual); *Information Note on the Court's Case-Law* (11 a year). Annual Report.
Members Convention ratified by 46 countries:
Albania, Andorra, Armenia, Austria, Azerbaijan, Belgium, Bosnia-Herzegovina, Bulgaria, Croatia, Cyprus, Czechia, Denmark, Estonia, Finland, France, Georgia, Germany, Greece, Hungary, Iceland, Ireland, Italy, Latvia, Liechtenstein, Lithuania, Luxembourg, Malta, Moldova, Monaco, Montenegro, Netherlands, North Macedonia, Norway, Poland, Portugal, Romania, San Marino, Serbia, Slovakia, Slovenia, Spain, Sweden, Switzerland, Türkiye, UK, Ukraine.
The Russian Federation left the organization on 16 September 2022.
NGO Relations No official relations. [2022.11.07/XF0438/**F***]

♦ European Covered Bond Council (ECBC) 06856

SG Rue de la Science 14 A, 2nd floor, 1040 Brussels, Belgium. T. +3222854030. E-mail: info@hypo.org.
URL: https://hypo.org/ecbc

History 2004. Set up as a part of European Mortgage Federation (EMF). Merged with EMF, Jun 2014, and united under *Covered Bond and Mortgage Council (CBMC, #04940)*. CBMC replaced EMF as the legal name under which bother entities operate, but in practice both brands are maintained and used for identification. **Aims** Represent and promote the interests of covered bond market participants at the international level. **Structure** Plenary; Steering Committee; Working Groups (6); Secretariat. **Languages** English. **Staff** 7.00 FTE, paid. **Finance** Members' dues. **Events** *Covered Bond Congress* Munich (Germany) 2019, *Plenary Meeting* Munich (Germany) 2019, *Plenary Meeting* Riga (Latvia) 2019, *Asian Covered Bond Forum* Singapore (Singapore) 2019, *Asian Covered Bond Forum* Singapore (Singapore) 2018. **Publications** *European Covered Bond Fact Book*. **Information Services** *ECBC Covered Bond Comparative Database*. **Members** Covered bond market participants (over 120). Membership countries not specified. [2021/XJ6397/**E**]

♦ European Credit Research Institute (ECRI) 06857

General Manager c/o CEPS, Place du Congrès 1, 1000 Brussels, Belgium. T. +3222293911. Fax +3222194151. E-mail: ecri@ceps.eu – info@ecri.eu.
Events/Membership Coordinator address not obtained.
URL: http://www.ecri.eu/

History Mar 1999. Registration: Banque-Carrefour des Entreprises, No/ID: 0476.488.843, Start date: 24 Jan 2002, Belgium. **Aims** Provide in-depth analysis and insight into the structure, evolution and regulation of consumer *financial* services markets in Europe. **Structure** Executive Committee. Coordinated by: *Centre for European Policy Studies (CEPS, #03741)*. **Languages** English, French. **Staff** 2.00 FTE, paid. **Finance** Sources: fundraising; members' dues; sale of publications. **Activities** Events/meetings; monitoring/evaluation; publishing activities; research/documentation. **Events** *Combating money laundering in the EU: time to get serious* Brussels (Belgium) 2021, *Effectiveness of AML Policies – Transaction Monitoring* Brussels (Belgium) 2021, *Instant payments: Forcing a breakthrough in European market integration?* Brussels (Belgium) 2021, *Moratoria on loan repayments: status-quo and phase-out!* Brussels (Belgium) 2021, *The role of credit bureaus in EU credit markets today* Brussels (Belgium) 2002. **Publications** *ECRI Statistical Package* (annual); *ECRI Commentaries*; *ECRI Policy Briefs*; *ECRI Quarterly Newsletter*. Research reports. Information Services: Statistical databases. **Members** Corporate (9). Membership countries not specified. [2021.06.11/XE4323/j/**E**]

♦ European Cricket Council / see International Cricket Council Europe Region (#13106)

♦ European Crime Prevention Network (EUCPN) 06858

Main Office Rue du Commerce 96, 1000 Brussels, Belgium. E-mail: eucpn@ibz.eu.
URL: http://www.eucpn.org/

History May 2001. Established by a decision of *Council of the European Union (#04895)* to promote crime prevention activity in member states across the EU. This founding legislation was repealed and replaced by a new Council decision, 30 Nov 2009. Former names and other names: *Réseau européen de prévention de la criminalité (REPC)* – former. **Aims** Promote crime prevention knowledge and practices among EU Member States. **Structure** Board of National Representatives; Rotating Chair (every 6 months); Executive Committee; Secretariat based in Brussels (Belgium). **Languages** English. **Staff** 8.00 FTE, paid. **Finance** Support from: *European Union (EU, #08967)* – Internal Security Fund. **Activities** Events/meetings; awards/prizes/competitions; knowledge management/information dissemination; training/education. **Events** *Conference* Brussels (Belgium) 2020, *Best Practices Conference* Helsinki (Finland) 2019, *Meeting* Vienna (Austria) 2018, *Annual Conference* Brussels (Belgium) 2010, *Annual conference on best practices in crime prevention* Stockholm (Sweden) 2009. **Publications** *EUCPN Newsletter* (6 a year); *Toolbox* (2 a year); *Monitor* (annual). Pilot study.
Members Full in 27 countries:
Austria, Belgium, Bulgaria, Croatia, Cyprus, Czechia, Denmark, Estonia, Finland, France, Germany, Greece, Hungary, Ireland, Italy, Latvia, Lithuania, Luxembourg, Malta, Netherlands, Poland, Portugal, Romania, Slovakia, Slovenia, Spain, Sweden. [2022/XF6557/**F***]

♦ European Criminal Bar Association (ECBA) 06859

Secretariat 25 Bedford Row, London, WC1R 4HD, UK. E-mail: secretariat@ecba.org.
URL: http://www.ecba.org/

History May 1997, Strasbourg (France). Founded during a Conference at the European Commission of Human Rights, and under the initiative of Prof Franz Salditt on behalf of Deutscher Anwaltverein (Germany) and Rock Tansey QC on behalf of the Criminal Bar Association of England and Wales. Former names and other names: *European Association of Practising Criminal Defence Lawyers* – former (1997). **Aims** Be a leading group of independent criminal defence lawyers in the Council of Europe promoting the fundamental rights of persons under criminal investigation, suspects, accused and convicted persons; build a widespread association of criminal defence lawyers, from all member states; become a leading lobbyist and consultant on criminal law and justice in Europe; promote the interests of members in their professional development and in professional matters of common concern. **Structure** Executive Committee; Advisory Board. **Languages** English. **Staff** 0.50 FTE, paid. **Finance** Sources: meeting proceeds; members' dues. **Activities** Advocacy/lobbying/activism; events/meetings. **Events** *EFCL Annual Conference* Frankfurt-Main (Germany) 2023, *Spring Conference* Warsaw (Poland) 2023, *Spring Conference* Riga (Latvia) 2022, *Autumn Conference* St Julian's (Malta) 2022, *Autumn Conference* Berlin (Germany) 2021. **Publications** Press releases; statements. **Members** in all EU member states as well as other countries (not specified). **NGO Relations** Accredited by (1): *Academy of European Law (#00035)*. [2022.05.12/XM1538/**D**]

♦ European Criminal Law Academic Network (ECLAN) 06860

Réseau académique de droit pénal européen
Coordinator IEE-ULB, Av Franklin Roosevelt 39, 1050 Brussels, Belgium. T. +3226503072. Fax +3226503068. E-mail: aweyembe@ulb.ac.be.
Coordinator UL, Faculté de Droit/Economie/Finance, 4 rue Alphonse Weicker, L-2721 Luxembourg, Luxembourg. T. +3524666446887.
URL: http://www.eclan.eu/

History Founded 2004, by *Institut d'études européennes, ULB (IEE)* and the *'Université Libre de Bruxelles'*. Began activities 1 Dec 2004. **Aims** Create and intensify contacts between academics and researchers specialized in EU Criminal Law; facilitate collaboration and synergies between universities in this field. **Structure** Management Committee; Advisory Board; Coordinators; ECLAN Team; National Contact Points. **Languages** English. **Finance** Financed through: *European Commission (EC, #06633)*; Belgian Ministry of Justice; Ministry of Justice of Luxembourg. **Activities** Networking/liaising; research/documentation; publishing activities; events/meetings; knowledge management/information dissemination. **Events** *Colloquium* Brussels (Belgium) 2005. **Publications** *New Journal of European Criminal Law*. Articles.
Members Individuals in 32 countries:
Austria, Belgium, Bosnia-Herzegovina, Bulgaria, Croatia, Cyprus, Czechia, Denmark, Estonia, Finland, France, Germany, Greece, Hungary, Iceland, Ireland, Italy, Latvia, Lithuania, Luxembourg, Malta, Netherlands, Norway, Poland, Portugal, Romania, Slovakia, Slovenia, Spain, Sweden, Switzerland, UK. [2019.10.02/XM0646/**F**]

♦ European Crisis Management Academy (ECMA) 06861

Contact Crisis Research Center, Leiden Univ, Dept of Public Administration, Postbus 9555, 2300 RB Leiden, Netherlands. T. +31715273723. Fax +31715273979.
URL: http://www.ecm-academy.nl/

History Jun 2000, by the Crisis Research Centre of Leiden University (Netherlands) and the Centre for Crisis Management Research and Training of Swedish National Defence College (Stockholm). **Aims** Strengthen European security through assisting in development of *safe*, robust and *sustainable societies* and *policies*; improve the knowledge base for an enhanced capacity of dealing with national and transnational crises in the European framework; facilitate exchange of ideas and best practices between practitioners and academics. **Structure** General Assembly. Governing Council of 15 members, elected by General Assembly. Secretariat in Leiden (Netherlands). **Finance** No membership fee. **Activities** Organizes: conferences; study projects; summer school; training seminars. **Events** *Future challenges for crisis management in Europe* Stockholm (Sweden) 2006, *Conference* Slovenia 2004, *Foundations for cooperative European crisis management – establishing common ground* Stockholm (Sweden) 2001, *Conference* The Hague (Netherlands) 1999. **Members** Individuals crisis managers and academics. Membership countries not specified. [2011/XE4249/v/**E**]

♦ European Critical Care Foundation (ECCF) 06862

Contact c/o Fiduciaire Verifid, Rue du Rhône 100, 1211 Geneva 3, Switzerland.
URL: http://euroccf.org/

History 2009. Registered in accordance with Swiss Civil Code. **Aims** Improve delivery of critical care, raise awareness of factors that lead to unequal and inequitable outcomes, and trigger action in European institutions to overcome those barriers. **Structure** Board; Scientific Advisory Council. **Languages** English, French. **Finance** Set up with a grant of unrestricted funding from Eli Lilly. **Activities** Funds or initiates research proposals. **Publications** Articles. [2019.08.02/XJ4552/f/**F**]

♦ European CRO Federation (EUCROF) 06863

Secretariat p/a GroenHoed, Pelmolenlaan 2, 3447 GW Woerden, Netherlands. T. +393498586648. E-mail: info@eucrof.eu.
Pres address not obtained. E-mail: president@eucrof.eu.
URL: http://www.eucrof.eu

History Oct 2005. Bylaws adopted 7 Sep 2010. Registration: Netherlands; EU Transparency Register, No/ID: 898445414948-91. **Aims** Promote *clinical research*; support close relations and information exchange among member associations. **Structure** General Assembly; Executive Board; Full Members' Board; Working Groups (12), **Languages** English. **Activities** Events/meetings; training/education. **Events** *Conference* Madrid (Spain) 2022, *Science, technology and regulations coming together for better patients' health* Amsterdam (Netherlands) 2020, *Conference* Vienna (Austria) 2018, *Conference* Paris (France) 2015, *Conference* Brussels (Belgium) 2013. **Publications** *EUCROF Newsletter*. Position papers.
Members Full in 12 countries:
Belgium, Czechia, France, Germany, Greece, Italy, Netherlands, Romania, Slovakia, Spain, Türkiye, UK.
Associate in 12 countries:
Albania, Austria, Bulgaria, Croatia, Denmark, Georgia, Serbia, Spain, Sweden, Switzerland, UK, Ukraine.
Partner members in 3 countries:
Algeria, Egypt, Israel.
NGO Relations Member of (1): *European Forum for Good Clinical Practice (EFGCP, #07313)*. [2021.02.17/XJ8947/**D**]

♦ European Crohn's and Colitis Organisation (ECCO) 06864

Exec Dir Ungargasse 6/13, 1030 Vienna, Austria. T. +43171022420. Fax +4317102242001. E-mail: ecco@ecco-ibd.eu.
URL: https://www.ecco-ibd.eu/

History 24 Mar 2001, Vienna (Austria). Founded following a series of meetings held since 1999. Former names and other names: *European Association of the National IBD Study Groups* – former. **Aims** Strive for an optimization of care for patients with inflammatory *bowel* disease. **Structure** General Assembly; Governing Board. Committees/Working Groups (11): Scientific; Surgery; Education; Clinicians; Paediatricians; Guidelines; Epidemiology; Young Physicians; Nurses; Dieticians; Histopathologists. **Languages** English. **Activities** Events/meetings; training/education; financial and/or material support. **Events** *Congress* Copenhagen (Denmark) 2023, *Congress* Stockholm (Sweden) 2022, *Annual Congress* Vienna (Austria) 2021, *Annual Congress* Vienna (Austria) 2020, *Meeting* Vienna (Austria) 2019. **Publications** *Journal of Crohn's and Colitis (JCC)* (12 a year); *ECCO News* (4 a year).
Members National study groups in 36 countries:
Austria, Belgium, Bosnia-Herzegovina, Bulgaria, Croatia, Cyprus, Czechia, Denmark, Estonia, Finland, France, Germany, Greece, Hungary, Ireland, Israel, Italy, Latvia, Lithuania, Malta, Moldova, Netherlands, Norway, Poland, Portugal, Romania, Russia, Serbia, Slovakia, Slovenia, Spain, Sweden, Switzerland, Türkiye, UK, Ukraine.
NGO Relations Member of: *Associations and Conference Forum (AC Forum, #02909)*; *United European Gastroenterology (UEG, #20506)*. [2021/XM3303/**D**]

♦ European Crop Care Association (ECCA) 06865

Mailing Address Weverstraat 18, 1761 Borchtlombeek, Belgium. T. +32476824364. E-mail: secretary@ecca-org.eu.
Registered Office Rue des Chevaliers 14, 1050 Brussels, Belgium.
URL: http://www.ecca-org.eu/

History 18 Feb 1993, Eghezée (Belgium). Registration: Banque-Carrefour des Entreprises, No/ID: 0450.933.303, Start date: 18 Oct 1993, Belgium; EU Transparency Register, No/ID: 059443622722-41, Start date: 18 Jul 2016. **Aims** Inform members about European and national legislation affecting their professional activities, particularly those concerned with obtaining and renewing authorization for sale of plant protection products; seek common solutions to legal, financial, scientific and technical problems arising due to European Union and national requirements, with a view to facilitating or developing members' economic activity. **Structure** General Assembly (annual); Council. **Languages** English. **Staff** 0.50 FTE, paid. **Finance** Members' dues. **Activities** Guidance/assistance/consulting; standards/guidelines. **Events** *Regulatory Conference* Ghent (Belgium) 2019, *Conference* Brussels (Belgium) 2015.
Members Companies selling their own plant protection products in 12 countries:
Belgium, France, Germany, Ireland, Italy, Netherlands, Poland, Portugal, Serbia, Slovenia, Spain, UK.
IGO Relations EU Advisory Group on the Food Chain and Animal and Plant Health; *European Commission (EC, #06633)*; *FAO (#09260)*; national registration authorities. **NGO Relations** *AgroCare (#00580)*. [2020/XD3518/**D**]

♦ European Crop Protection Association / see CropLife Europe (#04965)
♦ European Croquet Federation (#09564)

♦ European Crowdfunding Network (ECN) 06866

Exec Dir Neo Bldg, Rue Montoyer 24, 1000 Brussels, Belgium. T. +4917649281117. E-mail: info@eurocrowd.org.
Registered Office Avenue du Champ de Courses 18, 1301 Wavre, Belgium.
URL: http://eurocrowd.org/

History 2011. Registration: Banque-Carrefour des Entreprises, No/ID: 0525.640.723, Start date: 2 Apr 2013, Belgium; EU Transparency Register, No/ID: 789197248108-13, Start date: 14 Nov 2022. **Aims** Promote adequate transparency, (self) regulation and governance while offering a combined voice in policy discussion and *public opinion* building. **Structure** Steering Council; Board of Directors; Advisory Board; Secretariat. Work Groups. **Staff** 0.50 FTE, paid. **Activities** Events/meetings. **Events** *Annual Convention* Brussels (Belgium) 2022, *Annual Convention* Brussels (Belgium) 2021, *Annual Convention* Brussels (Belgium) 2020, *Annual Convention* Brussels (Belgium) 2019, *Annual Convention* Brussels (Belgium) 2018.

Members Full in 16 countries:
Austria, Belgium, Finland, France, Germany, Greece, Italy, Luxembourg, Malta, Netherlands, Portugal, Spain, Sweden, Switzerland, Türkiye, UK.
NGO Relations Member of (1): *International Association of Trusted Blockchain Applications (INATBA).* [2022/XM4734/**F**]

♦ European Cruise Council / see CLIA Europe (#03995)

♦ European Crystallographic Association (ECA) 06867

Sec William Perkin Bldg, School Engineering Physical Sciences, Heriot-Watt Univ, Edinburgh, EH14 4AS, UK. T. +441314518036. Fax +441314513180. E-mail: secretary@ecanews.org.
Pres Dipto Chimica Generale ed Inorganica/Chimica Analitica/Chimica Fisica, Univ di Parma, Parco Area delle Scienze 17A, 43100 Parma PR, Italy. T. +39521905421. Fax +39521905557. E-mail: president@ecanews.org.
URL: http://www.ecanews.org/

History 27 Aug 1997, Lisbon (Portugal). Founded as a regional associate of *International Union of Crystallography (IUCr, #15768)*, replacing *European Crystallographic Committee*, set up 1972, charter adopted 14 Jul 1998. Registered in accordance with Dutch law. Registration: Netherlands. **Aims** Contribute to the advancement of crystallography in all its aspects, including related topics concerning non-crystalline states; promote European cooperation in the field. **Structure** Council (meets annually) – IUCR may send an observer to Council meetings; Executive Committee; General Interest Groups; Special Interest Groups. **Languages** English. **Staff** None. **Finance** Sources: gifts, legacies; members' dues; sponsorship; subsidies. **Activities** Awards/prizes/competitions; events/meetings; research and development; training/education. **Events** *ECM : European Crystallographic Meeting* Padua (Italy) 2024, *ECM : European Crystallographic Meeting* Versailles (France) 2022, *ECM : European Crystallographic Meeting* Vienna (Austria) 2019, *High-Pressure Workshop* Vienna (Austria) 2019, *ECM : European Crystallographic Meeting* Oviedo (Spain) 2018. **Publications** *ECANEWS* – electronic newsletter. Handbook.
Members National (adhering bodies); Affiliate (legal bodies); Individual. Members in 36 countries:
Algeria, Austria, Belgium, Bulgaria, Croatia, Czechia, Denmark, Egypt, Estonia, Finland, France, Germany, Greece, Hungary, Ireland, Israel, Italy, Latvia, Morocco, Netherlands, North Macedonia, Norway, Poland, Portugal, Russia, Serbia, Slovakia, Slovenia, South Africa, Spain, Sweden, Switzerland, Tunisia, Türkiye, UK, Ukraine.
NGO Relations *EPDIC Committee (EPDiCom, #05511)* acts as SIG. [2021.06.08/XD5194/**D**]

♦ European Cultural Alliance (inactive)
♦ European Cultural Centre / see European Centre for Culture (#06472)
♦ European Cultural Centre of Delphi (internationally oriented national body)
♦ European Cultural Convention (1954 treaty)

♦ European Cultural Foundation (ECF) 06868

Fondation européenne de la culture (FEC) – Fundación Europea de la Cultura (FEC) – Europäische Kulturstiftung (EKS) – Europese Culturele Stichting (ECS)
Main Office Jan van Goyenkade 5, 1075 HN Amsterdam, Netherlands.
URL: http://www.culturalfoundation.eu/

History 16 Dec 1954, Geneva (Switzerland). Founded on the initiative of Denis de Rougemont under the auspices of *European Centre for Culture (ECC, #06472).* Moved to Amsterdam (Netherlands), 1960. **Aims** Promote cultural cooperation in Europe so as to achieve a unified Europe in which cultural diversity can flourish; foster within Europe a sense of belonging for all its people; emphasize cultural concerns as important in maintaining human rights and democracy. **Structure** Advisory Council; Board. **Languages** Dutch, English, French, German. **Staff** 17.00 FTE, paid. **Finance** Dutch national lotteries; private and public funds, including from: *Humanistisch Instituut voor Ontwikkelingssamenwerking (Hivos); UNICEF (#20332); Nordic Council (NC, #17256).* **Activities** Advocacy/lobbying/activism; awards/prizes/competitions; projects/programmes. **Events** *IDEA Workshop* Madrid (Spain) 2017, *Conference on a new cultural policy for Europe* Rotterdam (Netherlands) 2004, *Conference on art for social change* Utrecht (Netherlands) 2004, *Which languages for Europe seminar* Oegstgeest (Netherlands) 2000, *Which languages for Europe conference* Amsterdam (Netherlands) / Leiden (Netherlands) 1998. **Publications** Ezines (digital newsletters). Annual Report; country reports; books.
Members Network of Fora in 13 countries:
Austria, Bulgaria, Czechia, Finland, Germany, Greece, Hungary, Ireland, Poland, Portugal, Sweden, Switzerland, UK.
IGO Relations Working relations with: *Council for Cultural Cooperation (inactive); Council of Europe (CE, #04881); European Commission (EC, #06633); European Parliament (EP, #08146).* Agreement with: *Council of Europe (CE, #04881).* **NGO Relations** Member of (3): *Culture Action Europe (CAE, #04981); European Heritage Alliance 3.3 (#07477); Philanthropy Europe Association (Philea, #18358).* Instrumental in setting up: *Association for Teacher Education in Europe (ATEE, #02949); Centre for European Policy Studies (CEPS, #03741); East/West Parliamentary Practice Project (EWPPP, no recent information); European Institute of Education and Social Policy (EIESP, #07551); European Institute for the Media (EIM, no recent information); European Translation School (no recent information); Fund for Central and East European Book Projects (CEEBP, #10040); Institute for European Environmental Policy (IEEP, #11261).* Associated institute: *Institut für die Wissenschaften vom Menschen (IWM, #11239).* [2019/XF0704/fy/**F**]

♦ European Cultural Network for Development Cooperation 06869

Réseau culturel européen de coopération au développement
SG address not obtained. T. +33610404542. E-mail: reseauculturedev@gmail.com.
URL: http://reseauculturel.org/

History as *Mouvement pour la chambre des beaux arts de Méditerranée.* Subsequently called *Mediterranean Chamber of Fine Arts – Chambre des beaux arts de Méditerranée.* Current title adopted Oct 2010. Registered in accordance with French law. **Aims** Reinforce the cultural dimension of development; preserver cultural diversity; promote cultural policies for development; offer training opportunities. **Structure** Board; Bureau; Regional Offices (5); International Secretariat in Paris (France). **Languages** Albanian, Arabic, English, French, Irish Gaelic, Spanish. **Staff** 1.50 FTE, paid. **Finance** Financed by: *European Commission (EC, #06633); UNESCO (#20322);* French Ministry of Employment and Social Affairs; Conseil Régional Ile de France; private donors. **Activities** Training/education; financial and/or material support; awards/prizes/competitions; events/meetings. **Events** *Forum interrégional* Amman (Jordan) 2000. **Publications** *COOPLUS. De la tradition au design* in Arabic, French, Greek, Turkish – guide. CD-ROMs.
Members Full in 40 countries and territories:
Albania, Algeria, Armenia, Belgium, Bosnia-Herzegovina, Burkina Faso, Cameroon, Côte d'Ivoire, Denmark, Egypt, France, Georgia, Greece, Iceland, Iran Islamic Rep, Italy, Jordan, Kazakhstan, Kosovo, Kyrgyzstan, Lebanon, Mali, Morocco, Niger, North Macedonia, Oman, Palestine, Qatar, Russia, Senegal, Serbia, Sweden, Switzerland, Syrian AR, Tanzania UR, Tunisia, Türkiye, Ukraine, United Arab Emirates, Uzbekistan.
Consultative Status Consultative status granted from: *UNESCO (#20322)* (Consultative Status). **IGO Relations** Member of: *Intergovernmental Committee for the Safeguarding of the Intangible Cultural Heritage (#11477).* **NGO Relations** Member of: *Centre de recherche et d'information pour le développement, Paris (CRID).* Partner to: *International Dance Council (#13130);* National Ballet of Kosovo. Instrumental in setting up: *Council of European Dentists (CED, #04886);* 'Ullyssa-art' network and its successor 'PRODECOM'. [2019/XE3639/**E**]

♦ European Cultural Organization for Social Education (internationally oriented national body)

♦ European Cultural Parliament (ECP) 06870

Verein für ein Europäisches Kulturparlament
SG Hohenzollerndamm 81, 14199 Berlin, Germany. T. +491701644950. Fax +493082407211. E-mail: contact@kulturparlament.com.
Registered Office c/o Ernst Klett AG, Postfach 10 60 16, 70049 Stuttgart, Germany.
Events Manager Burgunderstr 21, 71717 Beilstein, Germany.
URL: http://www.kulturparlament.com/

History 2001, Strasbourg (France). **Aims** Strengthen the role of cultural and artistic ideas and initiatives in Europe; strengthen the dialogue between citizens in Eastern and Western Europe and between the various arts sectors. **Structure** Senate, comprising Board and Preparatory Committee. **Finance** Supported by the Governments of Finland, Flanders, Luxembourg, Romania and a large number of national and international organizations, including: *British Council; Calouste Gulbenkian Foundation; Company of St Paul; Council of Europe (CE, #04881); International Fund for the Promotion of Culture (IFPC, inactive);* Körber Foundation; *Robert Bosch Foundation.* **Activities** *'Sibiu Declaration'*, 7 Oct 2007. **Events** *Seminar* Berlin (Germany) 2020, *Session* Dilijan (Armenia) 2019, *Transatlantic Dialogue* Esch-sur-Alzette (Luxembourg) 2017, *Session* Rotterdam (Netherlands) 2017, *Session* Batumi (Georgia) 2016. **Publications** *Sibiu-Rpoert* (annual). ECP Research Group report (annual).

Members Individuals (about 160) in 42 countries:
Albania, Armenia, Austria, Azerbaijan, Belarus, Belgium, Bosnia-Herzegovina, Bulgaria, Croatia, Cyprus, Czechia, Denmark, Estonia, Finland, France, Georgia, Germany, Greece, Hungary, Iceland, Ireland, Italy, Latvia, Lithuania, Luxembourg, Malta, Netherlands, North Macedonia, Norway, Poland, Portugal, Romania, Russia, Serbia, Slovakia, Slovenia, Spain, Sweden, Switzerland, Türkiye, UK, Ukraine.
NGO Relations Member of (1): *A Soul for Europe (ASF, #19697).* Links with a national and international organizations, including: *Directors Across Borders (DAB); European Cultural Foundation (ECF, #06868); Culture Action Europe (CAE, #04981); European League of Institutes of the Arts (ELIA, #07670); EUSTORY (#09202); Verein für Sprach- und Kulturaustausch in Mittel-, Ost- und Südosteuropa (MitOst).* [2022/XM3100/v/**F**]

♦ European Cultural Tourism Network (ECTN) 06871

Registered Office Avenue Prekelinden 64 bte 5, 1200 Brussels, Belgium. E-mail: info@culturaltourism-net.eu.
URL: http://www.culturaltourism-network.eu/

History 2009, Brussels (Belgium). Founded following merger of the network set up by ECTN INTERREG IIIC operation led by Wales and CHRON INTERREG IIIB CADSES (Network for European Cultural Tourism Authorities and Regions – NECTAR), led by EKPOL – Social and Cultural Council of the then Magnesia Prefecture, now of Thessalie Region (Greece). Registration: No/ID: 0812.251.967, Start date: 12 Jun 2009, Belgium. **Aims** Bring together tourism and cultural industry professionals working in different regions of Europe to exchange experience and information on best practice and to develop new approaches and innovation; facilitate development of transnational and inter-regional cooperation projects; create new and innovative approaches and tools; ensure improved cooperation and integration between the tourism and cultural sectors; develop and improve training opportunities; enable exchange of experience and best practice; develop common responses to European Commission and other EU institutions consultations; link with other networks; facilitate sharing of research. **Structure** Board. Working Groups (3): Research; Practitioners; Policy. **Languages** English. **Staff** 1.00 FTE, paid. **Finance** Sources: members' dues. **Activities** Guidance/assistance/consulting; events/meetings; awards/prizes/competitions; networking/liaising; projects/programmes; financial and/or material support. **Events** *International Conference for Cultural Tourism in Europe* Krk (Croatia) 2020, *Annual Conference* Granada (Spain) 2019, *Annual Conference* Paphos (Cyprus) 2018, *Annual Conference* Sibiu (Romania) 2017, *Annual Conference* Guimarães (Portugal) 2016. **Publications** *ECTN Newsletter.*
Members Full (20) in 17 countries:
Albania, Bulgaria, Croatia, Cyprus, Germany, Greece, Hungary, Ireland, Italy, Latvia, Montenegro, Poland, Portugal, Romania, Serbia, Spain, Sweden.
Associate (10) in countries:
Albania, Croatia, Georgia, Greece, Poland, Romania, Spain, Sweden, UK, Ukraine.
NGO Relations Member of (2): *European Heritage Alliance 3.3 (#07477); European Tourism Manifesto (#08921).* [2020/XM3065/**F**]

♦ European Culture Collections Curators' Organization / see European Culture Collections' Organization (#06872)

♦ European Culture Collections' Organization (ECCO) 06872

Sec BCCM/IHEM Fungi: Human and Animal Health, Sciensano, J Wytsmanstr 14, 1050 Brussels, Belgium. T. +3226425509. Fax +3226425541.
Pres Westerdijk Fungal Biodiversity Institute, Uppsalalaan 8, 3584 CT Utrecht, Netherlands. T. +31302122600. Fax +31302122601.
URL: http://www.eccosite.org/

History May 1982, Göttingen (Germany). Former names and other names: *European Culture Collections Curators' Organization (ECCCO)* – former. **Aims** Increase communication and stimulate collaborative study between culture collections; unite *curators* and managers of national culture collections located in Europe for collaboration and exchange of points of view with respect to operation of collections and services provided and to technical, legal and administrative developments. **Structure** General Assembly; Executive Board. **Languages** English. **Staff** 8.00 FTE, voluntary. **Finance** Sources: members' dues. **Activities** Events/meetings; financial and/or material support; guidance/assistance/consulting; knowledge management/information dissemination; management of treaties and agreements; politics/policy/regulatory; standards/guidelines. *Convention on Biological Diversity (Biodiversity convention, 1992).* **Events** *Annual Conference* Turin (Italy) 2019, *Annual Conference* Moscow (Russia) 2018, *Annual Conference* Brno (Czechia) 2017, *Annual Conference* Aberdeen (UK) 2016, *Annual Conference* Paris (France) 2015. **Publications** *ECCO core Material Transfer Agreement* (2009); *European Culture Collections: Microbial Biodiversity in Safe Hands* (1999); *Biotechnology Resources in Europe; Patent Depositories in Europe.*
Members Individual (scientists); Corporate (public and private entities); Sustaining (members that make financial donations); Honorary (individuals). Collections which are Corporate Member are largely devoted to cultures (microorganisms, plasmids, animal, human, hybridoma and plant cell cultures, viruses, algae and protozoa), and must be registered with WDCM, produce a catalogue of holdings and supply cultures to the scientific community. Members are based in countries with societies affiliated to FEMS. Members (82) in 26 countries:
Austria, Belgium, Bulgaria, Czechia, Denmark, Estonia, Finland, France, Germany, Greece, Hungary, Italy, Latvia, Netherlands, Norway, Poland, Portugal, Romania, Russia, Slovakia, Slovenia, Spain, Sweden, Switzerland, Türkiye, UK.
IGO Relations All European *'International Depositary Authorities (IDA)'* under *Budapest Treaty on the International Recognition of the Deposit of Microorganisms for the Purposes of Patent Procedure (Budapest Treaty of 1977, 1977)* subscribe to ECCO. [2020.07.06/XD4656/y/**D**]

♦ European Cultures in Business and Corporate Communication (#05754)
♦ European Customs Union Study Group (inactive)

♦ European Cutting Tools Association (ECTA) 06873

Association européenne d'outils de coupe
SG c/o VDMA Precision Tools, Lyoner Strasse 18, 60528 Frankfurt-Main, Germany. T. +496966031467. Fax +496966032467. E-mail: ecta@vdma.org.
URL: http://www.ecta-tools.org/

History Nov 1974, London (UK). **Aims** Improve cooperation between European manufacturers of engineers' cutting and clamping tools; represent the industry to EU authorities. **Activities** Sections – Information Dissemination; Observation of International Raw Materials Markets; Reporting about Regional and Technical Changes in Customer Industries; Annual "ECTA European Cutting Tool Conference". **Events** *World Cutting Tools Conference* Munich (Germany) 2019, *Annual Conference* Stresa (Italy) 2018, *Annual Conference* Barcelona (Spain) 2017, *Annual Conference* London (UK) 2015, *Annual Conference* Montreux (Switzerland) 2014.
Members National organizations in 8 countries:
France, Germany, Italy, Netherlands, Spain, Sweden, Switzerland, UK.
IGO Relations Recognized by: *European Commission (EC, #06633).* [2018/XD2900/**D**]

♦ European Cybercrime Training and Education Group (ECTEG) 06874

Address not obtained.
URL: http://www.ecteg.eu/

History Originally created 2007, as *Europol Working Group on the Harmonisation of Cybercrime Investigation Training*, by *European Police Office (Europol, #08239)*, in support of the *European Commission (EC, #06633)* "Falcone" project. Adopted current title, 11 Nov 2009. Remained an informal group until Nov 2016, when it officially became an international non-profit association. Registered in accordance with Belgian law, 25 Dec 2016. **Structure** Board; Advisory Group. **Finance** Funded by *European Commission (EC, #06633).* **Activities** Guidance/assistance/support; knowledge management/information dissemination; standards/guidelines; networking/liaising; training/education.
Members Law enforcement agencies in 14 countries:
Austria, Belgium, Cyprus, Finland, France, Germany, Ireland, Italy, Netherlands, Norway, Poland, Portugal, Spain, Sweden.
Academic institutions in 7 countries:
Belgium, Cyprus, France, Germany, Ireland, Spain, UK.
Other organizations include 2 national organizations in 2 countries:
France, UK.
Other organizations include 2 organizations listed in this Yearbook:

European Cycle Logistics
06875

alphabetic sequence excludes
For the complete listing, see Yearbook Online at

Organization for Security and Cooperation in Europe (OSCE, #17887); United Nations Office on Drugs and Crime (UNODC, #20596).
IGO Relations Close cooperation with: *European Police Office (Europol, #08239)* – EC3; *European Union Agency for Law Enforcement Training (CEPOL, #08970).* **NGO Relations** *Global Forum on Cyber Expertise (GFCE, #10371).* [2018/XM7842/y/E]

♦ European Cycle Logistics Federation (ECLF) 06875

Contact c/o Chittenden Horley Ltd, 456 Chester Road, Manchester, M16 9HD, UK. E-mail: enquiry@eclf.bike.
Main Website: https://eclf.bike/

History Registration: Companies House, No/ID: 08953330, Start date: 21 Mar 2014, England and Wales. **Aims** Promote the use of cycles and related low-emission vehicles for the delivery of goods and services; create a better urban environment and contribute positively to local economies. **Activities** Knowledge management/information dissemination; projects/programmes. **Events** *Conference* Dublin (Ireland) 2019, *Symposium* Berlin (Germany) 2018, *Conference* Vienna (Austria) 2017. **NGO Relations** Cooperates with (1): *Cycling Industries Europe (CIE, #04988).* [2022/AA1997/D]

♦ European Cycling Union 06876

Union européenne de cyclisme (UEC) – Europäische Radsport-Union

SG Postfach 339, 8703 Erlenbach ZH, Switzerland. T. +41449120446. Fax +41449120446. E-mail: uec@bluewin.ch.
URL: http://www.uec.ch/

Structure Directors Committee, comprising President, 3 Vice-Presidents, Secretary-General, Treasurer and 2 further members. Commissions (5). **Activities** Commissions (5): BMX; Indoor Cycling; Mountain-Bike; Trial; Track. Organizes championships and competitions.
Members National organizations (47) in 47 countries:
Albania, Andorra, Armenia, Austria, Azerbaijan, Belarus, Belgium, Bosnia-Herzegovina, Bulgaria, Croatia, Cyprus, Czechia, Denmark, Estonia, Finland, France, Georgia, Germany, Greece, Hungary, Ireland, Israel, Italy, Latvia, Liechtenstein, Lithuania, Luxembourg, Malta, Moldova, Monaco, Netherlands, North Macedonia, Norway, Poland, Portugal, Romania, Russia, San Marino, Serbia, Slovakia, Slovenia, Spain, Sweden, Switzerland, Türkiye, UK, Ukraine.
NGO Relations Continental confederation of: *Union Cycliste Internationale (UCI, #20375).* [2010/XM1254/D]

♦ European Cyclists' Federation (ECF) 06877

Fédération européenne des cyclistes – Europäischer Radfahrer Verband

Mailing Address Mundo Madou, Rue de la Charité 22, 1210 Brussels, Belgium. T. +3223290380. E-mail: office@ecf.com.
CEO address not obtained.
URL: http://www.ecf.com/

History 1983, Copenhagen (Denmark). Founded following discussions at International Cycle Planning Conference – *Velo-city* – in Bremen (Germany FR). Current statutes adopted 30 Mar 2012. Former names and other names: *Organisation cycliste européenne (CO)* – former. Registration: No/ID: 0460.439.895, Start date: 19 Jan 1997, Belgium; EU Transparency Register, No/ID: 28451455737-18, Start date: 27 Apr 2011. **Aims** Promote and protect interests of everyday and tourist cycling throughout Europe; represent cycling interests with European and international organizations. **Structure** General Meeting (annual); Board; Secretariat in Brussels (Belgium), headed by Secretary-General. **Languages** English. **Staff** 18.00 FTE, paid. **Finance** Sources: grants; members' dues; sponsorship. **Activities** Advocacy/lobbying/activism; events/meetings; knowledge management/information dissemination; networking/liaising. **Events** *Velo-City Conference* Ghent (Belgium) 2024, *Velo-City Conference* Leipzig (Germany) 2023, *Velo-City Conference* Ljubljana (Slovenia) 2022, *EuroVelo and Cycling Tourism Conference* Barcelona (Spain) 2021, *Velo-City Conference* Lisbon (Portugal) 2021. **Publications** *ECF Newsletter* (12 a year); *EuroVelo Newsletter* (12 a year). Position papers; research reports; policy papers; resolutions; briefing papers; news articles.
Members Full; Associate. Organizations in 47 countries and territories:
Albania, Australia, Austria, Belarus, Belgium, Bosnia-Herzegovina, Bulgaria, Canada, China, Croatia, Cyprus, Czechia, Denmark, Estonia, Finland, France, Georgia, Germany, Greece, Hungary, Iceland, India, Ireland, Israel, Italy, Latvia, Lithuania, Luxembourg, Netherlands, Norway, Philippines, Poland, Portugal, Romania, Russia, Serbia, Slovakia, Slovenia, Spain, Sweden, Switzerland, Taiwan, Thailand, Türkiye, UK, Ukraine, USA.
Consultative Status Consultative status granted from: *ECOSOC (#05331)* (Ros A). **IGO Relations** Accredited by (1): *European Commission (EC, #06633).* NGO representation to: *International Transport Forum (ITF, #15725).* Advises: *United Nations Economic Commission for Europe (UNECE, #20555).* Regular contact with members of: *European Parliament (EP, #08146).* **NGO Relations** Member of (4): *European Federation for Transport and Environment (T and E, #07230); European Greenways Association (EGWA, #07412); European Tourism Manifesto (#08921); Partnership on Sustainable, Low Carbon Transport Foundation (SLoCaT Foundation, #18244).* Instrumental in setting up (1): *Cities for Cyclists (inactive).* In liaison with technical committees of: *Comité européen de normalisation (CEN, #04162); International Organization for Standardization (ISO, #14473).* [2022/XD0793/D]

♦ European Cylinder Makers / see European Cylinder Makers Association (#06878)

♦ European Cylinder Makers Association (ECMA) 06878

SG Eaton Close, Eaton Hill, Baslow, DE45 1SB, UK. T. +447717288580.
URL: http://ecma.info/

History Former names and other names: *European Cylinder Makers (ECM)* – former. **Aims** Promote the common interest of the industry with regard to supranational, international and national organizations and with regard to the participants of the international market. **Structure** General Assembly; Chairman; Secretary General. **Members** Membership countries not specified. **NGO Relations** In liaison with technical committees of: *Comité européen de normalisation (CEN, #04162); International Organization for Standardization (ISO, #14473).* [2023.02.14/XD5012/D]

♦ European Cystic Fibrosis Society (ECFS) 06879

Main Office Kastanieparken 7, 7470 Karup, Denmark. T. +4586676260. Fax +4586676290. E-mail: info@ecfs.eu.
URL: http://www.ecfs.eu/

History 1969, Grindelwald (Switzerland). Constitution amended, 4 Jun 1997, Davos (Switzerland); Jun 1998, Berlin (Germany). Former names and other names: *European Working Group for Cystic Fibrosis (EWGCF)* – former (1969 to 1997); *Groupe européen de recherches sur la fibrose cystique* – former (1969 to 1997); *European Society for Cystic Fibrosis (ESCF)* – former (1997 to Jun 1998). **Aims** Improve survival and quality of life for people with cystic fibrosis (CF) by promoting high quality research, education and care. **Structure** General Meeting (annual); Governing Board. **Languages** English. **Staff** 10.00 FTE, paid. **Events** *European Cystic Fibrosis Conference* Vienna (Austria) 2023, *European Cystic Fibrosis Conference* Rotterdam (Netherlands) 2022, *European Cystic Fibrosis Conference* Karup (Denmark) 2021, *European Cystic Fibrosis Conference* Karup (Denmark) 2020, *European Cystic Fibrosis Conference* Lyon (France) 2020. **Publications** *Journal of Cystic Fibrosis.*
Members Active (over 1,000); Corresponding. Individuals in 44 countries:
Argentina, Australia, Austria, Belgium, Brazil, Bulgaria, Canada, Croatia, Czechia, Denmark, Ecuador, France, Germany, Greece, Hungary, Ireland, Israel, Italy, Latvia, Lithuania, Luxembourg, Netherlands, New Zealand, North Macedonia, Norway, Oman, Pakistan, Poland, Portugal, Romania, Russia, Saudi Arabia, Serbia, Slovakia, Slovenia, South Africa, Spain, Sweden, Switzerland, UK, Ukraine, United Arab Emirates, Uruguay, USA.
NGO Relations Member of: *European Network of Paediatric Research at the European Medicines Agency (Enpr-EMA, #07963).* [2021/XD4672/v/E]

♦ European Cytogeneticists Association (ECA) 06880

Association des cytogénéticiens européens (ACE)

Gen Sec 27 rue du Fbg St Jacques, APHP Centre, Universite Paris Cité, 75014 Paris, France.
URL: http://www.e-c-a.eu/

History Registered in accordance with French law. **Aims** Represent and promote fundamental research and applications in the field of cytogenetics. **Structure** General Meeting (annual); Board of Directors; Scientific Programme Committee; Permanent Working Groups. **Activities** Events/meetings. **Events** *European Cytogenetics Conference* Montpellier (France) 2023, *European Cytogenomics Conference* 2021, *European Cytogenetics Conference* Salzburg (Austria) 2019, *European Cytogenetics Conference* Florence (Italy) 2017, *European Cytogenetics Conference* Strasbourg (France) 2015. **Publications** *ECA Newsletter.*
Members Active; Associate; Honorary. Individuals in 78 countries and territories:
Albania, Armenia, Australia, Austria, Bahrain, Belarus, Belgium, Bolivia, Bosnia-Herzegovina, Brazil, Bulgaria, Canada, Chile, China, Croatia, Curaçao, Cyprus, Czechia, Denmark, Egypt, Estonia, Finland, France, Georgia, Germany, Greece, Hungary, Iceland, India, Iran Islamic Rep, Iraq, Ireland, Israel, Italy, Japan, Jordan, Kazakhstan, Korea Rep, Kuwait, Latvia, Lebanon, Libya, Lithuania, Luxembourg, Malaysia, Malta, Morocco, Netherlands, New Zealand, Nigeria, North Macedonia, Norway, Pakistan, Peru, Poland, Portugal, Qatar, Romania, Russia, Saudi Arabia, Senegal, Serbia, Slovakia, Slovenia, South Africa, Spain, Sweden, Switzerland, Syrian AR, Taiwan, Tunisia, Türkiye, UK, Ukraine, United Arab Emirates, Uruguay, USA, Yemen.
NGO Relations Member of: *European Rare Chromosomes Network on the Internet (Eurochromnet, inactive); International Federation of Human Genetics Societies (IFHGS, #13451).* [2022/XD7109/v/D]

♦ European Cytokine Society (ECS) 06881

Sec-Treas Pavillon Hardy A, Hôpital Cochin, 27 rue Faubourg St Jacques, 75014 Paris, France.
URL: http://www.europeancytokinenetwork.com/

History 1993. **Aims** Increase educational, scientific and multidisciplinary activities in the field of cytokine research; promote actions to integrate basic cytokine research and clinical applications in Europe. **Events** *International conference on cytokine medicine* Manchester (UK) 2003. **Publications** *European Cytokine Network* – journal. **NGO Relations** *International Cytokine and Interferon Society (ICIS, #13127).* [2010/XD8228/D]

♦ European Cytological Congress (meeting series)
♦ European Cytoskeletal Club / see European Cytoskeleton Forum (#06882)

♦ European Cytoskeleton Forum (ECF) 06882

Pres Francis Crick Inst, 1 Midland Road, London, NW1 1AT, UK. T. +442072693733. Fax +442072693581.
URL: https://www.europeancytoskeletalforum.org/

History 1980. Former names and other names: *European Cytoskeletal Club* – former (1980 to 1993). **Aims** Promote and disseminate scientific knowledge concerning the structure and function of cytoskeletal elements. **Structure** Board. **Languages** English. **Staff** None. **Finance** Meetings financed by: The Company of Biologists; *European Commission (EC, #06633); European Molecular Biology Organization (EMBO, #07816);* local industries; national science foundations. **Activities** Meeting activities. **Events** *Meeting* Hannover (Germany) 2021, *Meeting* Hannover (Germany) 2020, *Meeting* Prague (Czechia) 2018, *Meeting* Helsinki (Finland) 2017, *Systems-level view of cytoskeletal function* Rehovot (Israel) 2014. **Publications** Meeting reports.
Members Individuals (over 500) in 17 countries:
Austria, Belgium, Denmark, Finland, France, Germany, Greece, Israel, Italy, Luxembourg, Netherlands, Norway, Portugal, Spain, Sweden, Switzerland, UK. [2020/XF0703/v/F]

♦ European Dairy Association (EDA) 06883

Association laitière européenne – Europäischer Milchindustrieverband

Main Office Avenue d'Auderghem 22-28, 1040 Brussels, Belgium. T. +3225495040. Fax +3225495049.
URL: http://eda.euromilk.org/

History 1 Jan 1995. Founded following merger of *EC Dairy Trade Association (inactive)* with *Association of Preserved Milk Manufacturers of the EEC (inactive).* Registration: EU Transparency Register, No/ID: 42967152383-63; Belgium. **Aims** Define, prepare, implement and defend action to be conducted by the dairy industry in the context of the European Union; defend and represent at international level the common interests of the dairy industry of EU member states. **Structure** General Assembly (annual); Board; Committees; Working Groups; Task Forces. Secretariat. **Languages** English, French, German. **Staff** 8.00 FTE, paid. **Events** *Annual Convention* Madrid (Spain) 2020, *Joint Annual Congress* Vienna (Austria) 2019, *Joint Annual Congress* Dublin (Ireland) 2018, *Joint Annual Congress* Stockholm (Sweden) 2017, *Joint Annual Congress* Nice (France) 2016. **Publications** *EDA Major Issues* (2 a year).
Members Full in 21 countries:
Austria, Belgium, Croatia, Czechia, Denmark, Estonia, Finland, France, Germany, Greece, Ireland, Italy, Latvia, Luxembourg, Netherlands, Poland, Portugal, Slovenia, Spain, Sweden, UK.
Associate in 1 country:
Serbia.
IGO Relations Recognized by: *European Commission (EC, #06633).* Participates as observer in the activities of: *Codex Alimentarius Commission (CAC, #04081).* **NGO Relations** Special section: *Association de l'industrie de la fonte de fromage de l'UE (ASSIFONTE, #02642).* Affiliated member of: *FoodDrinkEurope (#09841).* Member of: *Industry4Europe (#11181).* [2020/XD5662/t/D]

♦ European Dairy Farmers 06884

General Manager Grüner Kamp 19-21, 24768 Rendsburg, Germany. E-mail: manager@dairyfarmer.net.
URL: https://www.dairyfarmer.net/

History 1990, Stoneleigh (UK). Registration: Schleswig-Holstein District court, No/ID: VR 6495 Kl, Start date: 22 Jan 2009, Germany, Kiel. **Aims** Connect dairy farmers and other players in the dairy sector across Europe. **Structure** General Assembly; Council. **Activities** Advocacy/lobbying/activism; events/meetings; knowledge management/information dissemination; networking/liaising. **Events** *Annual EDF Congress* Cork (Ireland) 2022, *Annual EDF Congress* Cork (Ireland) 2021, *Annual EDF Congress* Cork (Ireland) 2020, *Annual EDF Congress* Kolding (Denmark) 2019, *Annual EDF Congress* Santiago de Compostela (Spain) 2018.
Members National branches in 15 countries:
Belgium, Czechia, Denmark, Finland, France, Germany, Ireland, Italy, Netherlands, Portugal, Slovakia, Spain, Sweden, Switzerland, UK. [2021/AA2243/D]

♦ European Dana Alliance for the Brain (EDAB) 06885

Administration The Dana Centre, 165 Queen's Gate, London, SW7 5HD, UK. T. +442079424532.
Exec Dir c/o The Dana Foundation, 505 Fifth Avenue, 6th Floor, New York NY 10017, USA. T. +12122234040. Fax +12123178721.
URL: http://www.edab.net/

History Jan 1997, London (UK). **Aims** Raise awareness of brain *disease* and brain-related *disorders*; promote research in the field. **Structure** Offices in Lausanne (Switzerland) and London (UK). **Activities** Events/meetings. **Events** *Semaine du cerveau* Mont-Saint-Aignan (France) 2010, *Semaine internationale du cerveau* Paris (France) 2006.
Members Full in 19 countries:
Austria, Belgium, Czechia, Denmark, Finland, France, Germany, Hungary, Israel, Italy, Netherlands, Norway, Poland, Spain, Sweden, Switzerland, UK, Ukraine, USA. [2018/XE2977/E]

♦ European Dance Council (EDC) 06886

Office Weidestr 120 b, 22083 Hamburg, Germany. T. +494063606570. E-mail: kk@dancecouncil.eu.
URL: http://dancecouncil.eu/

History Set up 3 Apr 2007, as *European Social Dance Council (ESDC).* Current statutes adopted 2013. Registered in accordance with German law: VR 21709. **Structure** General Assembly; Executive Board.
Members Full in 5 countries:
Austria, Belgium, Czechia, Germany, Netherlands. [2018/XM6914/D]

♦ European Dance Sport Federation (EDSF) 06887

Pres Saksaganskoho 7/13, Kiev, 01033, Ukraine. T. +380442392335. Fax +380442890251. E-mail: office@dancesporteurope.org.
URL: http://idsa.com.ua/edsf/eng/

History 13 Dec 2006, Kiev (Ukraine). Registered in accordance with Ukrainian law. **Aims** Promote development of dance sport and other styles of dance; protect legal creative, sport, social and other interests of members. **Structure** Annual General Assembly; Managing Committee. **Languages** English. **Staff** 3.00 FTE, paid. **Finance** Sources: members' dues. **Activities** Awards/prizes/competitions; events/meetings; training/education.
Members Full; Associate; Provisional. Members in 35 countries:
Albania, Austria, Belarus, Belgium, Bosnia-Herzegovina, Croatia, Cyprus, Czechia, Denmark, Estonia, Finland, France, Germany, Greece, Hungary, Iceland, Ireland, Israel, Italy, Latvia, Lithuania, Luxembourg, Malta, Netherlands, North Macedonia, Norway, Poland, Portugal, Romania, Serbia, Slovakia, Slovenia, Spain, Sweden, Switzerland.
NGO Relations Member of (1): *International Dance Sport Association (IDSA, #13132).* [2020/XJ6348/D]

♦ European Data Centre Association (EUDCA) **06888**

Contact address not obtained. E-mail: info@eudca.org.
URL: http://www.eudca.org/

History Founded 2011. Registered in accordance with Belgian law: BE0847628857. EU Transparency Register: 073113537074-85. **Aims** Represent interests of the European commercial data centre operator community, both politically and commercially. **Structure** General Assembly; Board. **Members** Companies. Membership countries not specified. [2019/XM8765/**D**]

♦ European Data Protection Board (EDPB) **06889**

Contact Rue Wiertz 60, 1047 Brussels, Belgium. E-mail: edpb@edpb.europa.eu.
Office Address Rue Montoyer 30, 1000 Brussels, Belgium.
URL: https://edpb.europa.eu/

History Created by the EU General Data Protection Regulation (GDPR), adopted 27 Apr 2016, and published in the EU Official Journal, 4 May 2016. **Aims** Ensure the consistent application in the European Union of the General Data Protection Regulation and of the European Law Enforcement Directive. **Structure** Board; Secretariat, provided by European Data Protection Supervisor (EDP). **Events** *EDPS Conference* Brussels (Belgium) 2022.

Members Data protection agencies of 27 countries:
Austria, Belgium, Bulgaria, Croatia, Cyprus, Czechia, Denmark, Estonia, Finland, France, Germany, Greece, Hungary, Ireland, Italy, Latvia, Lithuania, Luxembourg, Malta, Netherlands, Poland, Portugal, Romania, Slovakia, Slovenia, Spain, Sweden.
European Data Protection Supervisor (EDPS).
Members without voting rights in 3 EEA countries:
Iceland, Liechtenstein, Norway. [2021/AA1573/**E***]

♦ European Deaf-Blind Network / see European Deafblind Network (#06890)

♦ European Deafblind Network (EDbN) **06890**

Réseau européen pour les sourds-aveugles – Red Europea para la Sordoceguera – Europäisches Taubblinden Netzwerk – Network Europeo sulla Sordocecità

Pres Carrer Leiva 2 D, baixos, 08014 Barcelona, Spain. T. +34933317366. E-mail: edbn@edbn.org.
URL: https://edbn.org/

History Founded 1987, Dublin (Ireland), as *European Community Deafblind Secretariat (ECDBS)*. Previously also referred to as *European Deaf-Blind Network*. Current title adopted 1994. EU Transparency Register: 521959826374-31. **Aims** Improve the situation of deafblind people in Europe with the objective of achieving their equal rights and full participation in society; act as a European forum for exchange of knowledge and experience in the area of deafblindness. **Structure** Board; Management Committee. **Staff** 2.00 FTE, paid. **Finance** Members' dues. Subventions from *European Commission (EC, #06633)*. Budget (annual): about euro 100,000. **Activities** Knowledge management/information dissemination; research/documentation. **Events** *Annual Seminar and Meeting* Groningen (Netherlands) 2006, *European family conference* Salou (Spain) 2006, *Parents conference* Poland 2002, *Annual seminar and meeting* Portugal 2001, *Annual seminar and meeting* Osimo (Italy) 2000. **Publications** *EDbN Newsletter* (2 a year).

Members Full; Associate; Honorary. Organizations in 17 countries:
Austria, Belgium, Denmark, Finland, France, Germany, Greece, Ireland, Italy, Malta, Netherlands, Poland, Portugal, Spain, Sweden, Switzerland, UK.

NGO Relations Member of: *Deafblind International (DbI, #05014)*; *European Disability Forum (EDF, #06929)*. [2020/XF3648/**F**]

♦ European Deafblind Union (EDBU) **06891**

Pres Andrija Madulica 34, HR-10000 Zagreb, Croatia. T. +38514828549. E-mail: tsanya@mac.com – edbu@edbu.eu.
URL: http://www.edbu.eu/

History 22 Oct 2003, Fredericia (Denmark). Registration: Banque Carrefour des Entreprises, No/ID: 0689.665.743, Start date: 1 Feb 2018, Belgium; EU Transparency Register, No/ID: 521959826374-31, Start date: 18 Mar 2017. **Aims** Work for equality and full participation of deafblind persons in all European countries; promote awareness of deafblindness as a unique disability. **Structure** General Assembly; Executive Committee; Working Groups. **Languages** English. **Finance** Sources: members' dues. **Activities** Advocacy/lobbying/activism; awareness raising; events/meetings; knowledge management/information dissemination; networking/liaising; projects/programmes; training/education. **Events** *Annual General Assembly* Budapest (Hungary) 2019, *Annual Conference* Tampere (Finland) 2017, *General Assembly* Tampere (Finland) 2017, *General Assembly* Plovdiv (Bulgaria) 2012, *General Assembly* Zagreb (Croatia) 2008. **Publications** *EDBU Newsletter*.

Members Full in 20 countries:
Belgium, Bulgaria, Croatia, Czechia, Denmark, Finland, France, Germany, Hungary, Iceland, Italy, Kazakhstan, Norway, Poland, Russia, Slovenia, Spain, Sweden, Switzerland, UK.
Associate in 4 countries:
Finland, Italy, Norway, Russia.
Individual in 3 countries:
Finland, France, Greece.

IGO Relations *European Commission (EC, #06633)*; *European Parliament (EP, #08146)*. **NGO Relations** Member of: *European Disability Forum (EDF, #06929)*; European Platform of Deafness, Hard of Hearing and Deafblindness (EUPDHHD). [2020.03.03/XM3660/**D**]

♦ European Deaf Champions League / see Deaf Champions League (#05015)

♦ European Deaf Sport Organization (EDSO) **06892**

Main Office Rue de la Loi 26/15, 1040 Brussels, Belgium. E-mail: info@edso.eu.
URL: http://www.edso.eu/

History 7 Jul 1983, Antibes (France). Regional confederation of *International Committee of Sports for the Deaf (ICSD, #12805)*. **Aims** Provide deaf athletes the opportunity to compete at European level. **Structure** Congress (every 2 years); Executive Committee; Technical Directors; Commissions (4). **Languages** English, International Sign Language. **Staff** On honorary basis. **Finance** Members' dues. Participation fees. **Activities** Sporting activities. **Events** *Biennial Congress* Mechelen (Belgium) 2022, *Biennial Congress* Copenhagen (Denmark) 2020, *Biennial Congress* Heraklion (Greece) 2018, *Biennial Congress* Yerevan (Armenia) 2016, *Biennial Congress* Antalya (Turkey) 2014. **Publications** *EDSO Bulletin* (annual).

Members National associations in 42 countries:
Armenia, Austria, Azerbaijan, Belarus, Belgium, Bosnia-Herzegovina, Bulgaria, Croatia, Cyprus, Czechia, Denmark, Estonia, Finland, France, Georgia, Germany, Great Britain, Greece, Hungary, Iceland, Ireland, Israel, Italy, Latvia, Lithuania, Malta, Moldova, Netherlands, North Macedonia, Norway, Poland, Portugal, Romania, Russia, Serbia, Slovakia, Slovenia, Spain, Sweden, Switzerland, Türkiye, Ukraine. [2020/XD0383/**E**]

♦ European Deaf Students' Union (EDSU) **06893**

Pres Rue de la Loi 26/15, 1040 Brussels, Belgium. E-mail: edsu.edsu@gmail.com.
URL: https://edsunion.wixsite.com/edsu

History 2011. First conceived as a Focus Group of *European Union of Deaf Youth (EUDY, #08986)*. Became an official working group under EUDY, 2012; an independent organization, 2014; a legally recognized NGO, 2017. **Aims** Represent deaf student organizations at European level; promote, advance, protect rights and opportunities for deaf students in Europe. **Structure** General Assembly; Board. **Languages** English. **Activities** Awareness raising; knowledge management/information dissemination; networking/liaising; training/education. **NGO Relations** Associate member of: *European Students' Union (ESU, #08848)*. [2022.02.15/XM5626/**D**]

♦ European Declaration Against Racism and Xenophobia (1986 treaty)

♦ European Decontamination Institute (EDI) **06894**

Secretariat Rue des Colonies 11 – 1, 1000 Brussels, Belgium. T. +3228085258. E-mail: info@decontaminationinstitute.org.
URL: https://www.decontaminationinstitute.org/

History Founded 2013. EU Transparency Register: 027027432669-16. **Aims** Look after, promote and protect the interests of the decontamination industry in Europe; set and promote the interests of the decontamination industry in Europe; be involved in and have an impact on health and safety legislation; be involved in improving the legislation concerning the removal and depositing of hazardous waste. **Structure** General Assembly; Board of Directors; Secretariat. Working Groups. **Languages** English. **Finance** Members' dues. **Activities** Standards/guidelines; knowledge management/information dissemination; advocacy/lobbying/activism; training/education.

Members Full in 19 countries:
Australia, Belgium, Croatia, Denmark, Finland, France, Germany, Ireland, Italy, Luxembourg, Netherlands, New Zealand, Poland, Russia, Serbia, South Africa, Spain, Sweden, USA.

NGO Relations *European Demolition Association (EDA, #06902)*. [2020.02.05/XM8777/**D**]

♦ European Decorative and Stationery Plastics Foils Association (inactive)

♦ European Defence Agency (EDA) **06895**

Chief Exec Rue des Drapiers 17-23, 1050 Brussels, Belgium. T. +3225042800. Fax +3225042815. E-mail: info@eda.europa.eu.
URL: http://www.eda.europa.eu/

History 12 Jul 2004, Brussels (Belgium). Founded by Joint Action 2004/551/CFSP of *Council of the European Union (#04895)*, following proposals, 17 Nov 2003, at meeting of Defence Ministers of *European Union (EU, #08967)*. An EU agency set up under Common Security and Defence Policy. Former names and other names: *Armaments and Research Agency* – former. **Aims** Support development of defence capabilities and military cooperation among EU Member States; stimulate defence research and technology and strengthen the European defence industry; act as a military interface to EU policies. **Structure** Ministerial Steering Board, headed by Head of Agency. Chief Executive; Deputy Chief Executive. Operational Directorates (3): Industry, Synergies and Enablers (ISE) Capability, Armament and Planning (CAP); Research, Technology and Innovation (RTI). **Languages** English. **Staff** 170.00 FTE, paid. **Finance** Annual budget: 32,500,000 EUR (2018). **Activities** Networking/liaising; projects/programmes. **Events** *Annual Conference* Brussels (Belgium) 2022, *European Defence Innovation Day* Brussels (Belgium) 2022, *Annual Conference* Brussels (Belgium) 2021, *Military Mobility Symposium* Brussels (Belgium) 2021, *Annual Conference* Brussels (Belgium) 2020. **Publications** *European Defence Matters* – webzine. Annual Report.

Members Within the framework of the European Union, governments of 26 countries:
Austria, Belgium, Bulgaria, Croatia, Cyprus, Czechia, Estonia, Finland, France, Germany, Greece, Hungary, Ireland, Italy, Latvia, Lithuania, Luxembourg, Malta, Netherlands, Poland, Portugal, Romania, Slovakia, Slovenia, Spain, Sweden.
Administrative Agreements with 4 non-EU countries:
Norway, Serbia, Switzerland, Ukraine.

IGO Relations Cooperates with other stakeholders including: Council of the European Union – relevant working parties and General Secretariat; *European Commission (EC, #06633)*; *NATO (#16945)*; *Organisation Conjointe de Coopération en Matière d'Armement (OCCAR, #17801)*. Audited by: *European Court of Auditors (#06854)*. **NGO Relations** Member of (1): *EU Agencies Network (EUAN, #05564)*. Recognizes: *Unmanned Vehicle Systems International (UVS International, #20708)*. In cooperation with technical committees of: *Comité européen de normalisation (CEN, #04162)*. Links with *European Organisation for Security (EOS, #08102)*; *International Aerospace Quality Group (IAQG, #11594)*; industry, academic, research and other institutions (not specified). [2020/XF7202/**F***]

♦ European Defence Community (inactive)

♦ European Dehydrators Association **06896**

Commission intersyndicale des déshydrateurs européens (CIDE) – Asociación de Deshidratadores Europeos – Arbeitsgemeinschaft Europäischer Trocknungsbetriebe – Commissione Intersindicale dei Disidratatori Europei – Europese Vereniging van Groenvoeder-Drogerijen – Sammenslutning af Europaeiske Tørrerier

SG Rue Froissart 57, 1040 Brussels, Belgium. E-mail: ericguillemot@aol.com.
URL: http://www.europeanforage.org/

History 17 Mar 1959, Paris (France). Registration: Belgium; EU Transparency Register, No/ID: 174907913450-05, Start date: 14 Apr 2014. **Aims** Establish a permanent link between member unions. **Structure** General Meeting (annual). **Languages** English, Irish Gaelic. **Staff** 1.00 FTE, paid. **Finance** Members' dues. **Activities** Exchange of data on dehydration: techniques, production, import-export trade, prices, trade standards. **Events** *Annual General Meeting* Berlin (Germany) 2003, *Annual General Meeting* Dublin (Ireland) 2002, *Annual General Meeting* Germany 2002, *Annual General Meeting* Dublin (Ireland) 2001, *Annual General Meeting* Venice (Italy) 2001.

Members National unions in 7 countries:
France, Germany, Italy, Latvia, Netherlands, Spain, UK.

IGO Relations Recognized by: *European Commission (EC, #06633)*. [2020/XD0790/**D**]

♦ European Delirium Association (EDA) **06897**

Sec c/o Evangelisches Klinikum Bethel, Bethesdaweg 12, 33617 Bielefeld, Germany. E-mail: info@europeandeliriumassociation.org.
URL: http://europeandeliriumassociation.org/

History Initially founded as an informal body; legal status obtained in 2015. Registration: Amtsgericht, No/ID: VR4565, Start date: 2015, Germany, Bielefeld. **Structure** General Assembly (annual); Board; Executive Committee. **Finance** Sources: meeting proceeds; members' dues. **Events** *Annual Meeting* Birmingham (UK) 2023, *Annual Meeting* Monza (Italy) 2022, *Annual Meeting* Barcelona (Spain) 2021, *Annual Meeting* Barcelona (Spain) 2020, *Annual Meeting* Edinburgh (UK) 2019. **Publications** *Annals of Delirium*. [2020/XJ4187/**D**]

♦ European Democracy Forum (internationally oriented national body)
♦ European Democrat Group / see European Conservatives Group (#06744)

♦ European Democratic Education Community (EUDEC) **06898**

Contact Helmholtzstr 25, 04177 Leipzig, Germany. E-mail: info@eudec.org.
URL: http://www.eudec.org/

History Feb 2008, Leipzig (Germany). Registration: No/ID: VR 4704, Start date: 16 Mar 2009, Germany. **Aims** Promote and support democratic education across Europe. **Structure** Assembly/Annual General Meeting; Council; Oversight Committee. **Languages** English. **Staff** 0.16 FTE, paid. **Finance** Sources: donations; members' dues. Annual budget: 21,000 EUR. **Activities** Events/meetings; guidance/assistance/consulting; training/education. **Events** *Conference* Sofia (Bulgaria) 2023, *Conference* Leiston (UK) 2022, *Conference* Sofia (Bulgaria) 2020, *Conference* Kiev (Ukraine) 2019, *Confererence* Vinnitsa (Ukraine) 2019.

Members Full in 37 countries and territories:
Albania, Austria, Belgium, Bulgaria, Croatia, Czechia, Denmark, Finland, France, Germany, Greece, Ireland, Israel, Italy, Lithuania, Luxembourg, Monaco, Netherlands, Norway, Peru, Poland, Portugal, Romania, Serbia, Slovakia, Slovenia, South Africa, Spain, Sri Lanka, Sweden, Switzerland, Taiwan, Thailand, Türkiye, UK, Ukraine, USA.

NGO Relations Member of (1): *European Forum for Freedom in Education (EFFE, #07311)*. Cooperates with (2): *Australasian Democratic Education Community (ADEC)*; *International Democratic Education Conference (IDEC)*. [2022.11.09/XM6486/**D**]

♦ European Democratic Lawyers (#03049)

♦ European Democratic Movement for Mental Health **06899**

Mouvement démocratique européen pour la santé mentale – Europäische Demokratische Bewegung für Seelische Gesundheit – Movimento Europeo Democratico per la Salute Mentale

Contact c/o Casa Basaglia Haus, Via N Sauro 8, Sinigo, 39012 Merano, Italy. T. +39473247700. Fax +39473247701.

History May 2008, Rome (Italy). **Aims** Work for the judicial and social *equalization* of people with a psycho-social *disability*; combat stigmatization of and discrimination against these people. **Structure** Managing Board. **NGO Relations** *European Network of ex- Users and Survivors of Psychiatry (ENUSP, #07906)*. [2009/XJ0037/**F**]

European Democratic Party
06900

alphabetic sequence excludes
For the complete listing, see Yearbook Online at

♦ **European Democratic Party (EDP)** **06900**
Parti démocrate européen (PDE) – Partito Democratico Europeo
Contact Rue de l'Industrie 4, 1000 Brussels, Belgium. E-mail: contact@pde-edp.eu.
URL: http://pde-edp.eu/
History 2004, Brussels (Belgium). Also referred to as *European Democrat Party*. Registered in accordance with Belgian law. **Aims** Assure a close and lasting collaboration between members; promote and organize initiatives; support and coordinate actions of party members at European Parliament elections; develop close working relations between and among party members, their parliamentary, European, national and regional groups, groups in the parliamentary assemblies and parties with the same political platform outside the European Union; work towards federal unification and integration of Europe; fully support representation of regional and local interests and relevant application of the principle of subsidiarity. **Structure** Congress (every 2 years). Council. Presidency, comprising 2 Co-Presidents, 4 Vice-Presidents, Secretary-General and Delegate-General. **Languages** English, French, Italian. **Staff** 1.00 FTE, paid. **Finance** Members' dues. Co-financement from grants of *European Parliament (EP, #08146)*.
Members Parties in 8 countries:
Belgium, Cyprus, France, Italy, Poland, San Marino, Slovakia, Spain.
Individual members in 10 countries:
Belgium, Cyprus, France, Ireland, Italy, Poland, Romania, San Marino, Slovakia, Spain.
IGO Relations Represented at: *European Committee of the Regions (CoR, #06665)*; *Council of Europe (CE, #04881)*; *European Parliament (EP, #08146)*. **NGO Relations** Member of: *European Movement International (EMI, #07825)*. Affiliated with: *Institute of European Democrats (IED, #11260)*. [2014.01.27/XM0245/**E**]

♦ European Democrat Party / see European Democratic Party (#06900)
♦ European Democrats / see Group of the European People's Party – Christian Democrats (#10775)

♦ **European Democrat Students (EDS)** **06901**
Etudiants démocrates européens
SG Rue du Commerce 10, 1000 Brussels, Belgium. E-mail: secgen@edsnet.eu.
URL: http://www.edsnet.eu/
History Founded 13 May 1961, Vienna (Austria), as *International Union of Christian-Democratic and Conservative Students (ICCS) – Union internationale des étudiants démocrates-chrétiens et conservateurs*, at the 3rd International Student Conference, Vienna (Austria), as the official students' organization of *European People's Party (EPP, #08185)*. Name changed, 1970, to *European Union of Christian-Democratic and Conservative Students (ECCS) – Union européenne des étudiants démocrates-chrétiens et conservateurs* to align its member-organizations more closely with efforts to build a united Europe. Current name adopted 5 Jun 1975. 1997/1998, merged with *United Students for Europe (USE, inactive)*. **Aims** Follow and advocate the principles of personal freedom, democracy, human rights and the rule of law, on a worldwide scale; develop contacts, exchanges and political cooperation among Centre-Right, Christian Democrat, Conservative and Liberal students and youth in Europe; work for a free, democratic and united Europe, inside and outside the European Union; form a better understanding of cultural and political situations worldwide; promote the principles of market economy; exchange information on education policy and other political matters. **Structure** Council (meets 5 times a year); Executive Bureau; Secretariat; Working Groups. **Languages** English. **Staff** 1.00 FTE, paid. **Finance** Members' dues. Other sources: European Commission; *European Youth Foundation (EYF, #09141)*; sponsors and donors. **Activities** Politics/policy/regulatory; advocacy/lobbying/activism; networking/liaising; events/meetings; training/education. **Events** *Alumni Congress* Vienna (Austria) 2011, *Seminar* Malta 2005, *Winter university* Strasbourg (France) / Frankfurt-Main (Germany) 2005, *Seminar* Riga (Latvia) 2004, *Seminar* Warsaw (Poland) 2004. **Publications** *BullsEye* (4 a year) – magazine. *Students on the Right Way – European Democrat Students 1961-2017*. Annual report; occasional publications.
Members Student and youth organizations (43), representing over 1.6 million students, in 33 countries and territories:
Austria, Belarus, Belgium, Bulgaria, Croatia, Cyprus, Czechia, Denmark, Estonia, Finland, France, Georgia, Germany, Greece, Hungary, Israel, Italy, Kosovo, Latvia, Lithuania, Malta, Moldova, North Macedonia, Norway, Portugal, Romania, Serbia, Slovakia, Slovenia, Spain, Sweden, UK, Ukraine.
Consultative Status Consultative status granted from: *Council of Europe (CE, #04881)* (Participatory Status).
IGO Relations Consultative Status with: *UNESCO (#20322)*. Recognized by: *European Commission (EC, #06633)* (DGXXII). **NGO Relations** Regional member association of *International Young Democrat Union (IYDU, #15928)*. Member of: *European Youth Forum (#09140)*; *Robert Schuman Institute for Developing Democracy in Central and Eastern Europe (RSI, #18958)*. Instrumental in setting up: *European Democrat Union (EDU, inactive)*; European Youth Forum. [2019.12.12/XD4591/**D**]

♦ European Democrat Union (inactive)

♦ **European Demolition Association (EDA)** **06902**
Association européenne de démolition – Europäischer Abbruchverband – Europese Vereniging van Sloopwerken
SG Atrium Bldg – Regus BC – Rabuso, Rue des Colonies 11-1, 1000 Brussels, Belgium. T. +3228082760. E-mail: info@europeandemolition.org.
URL: http://www.europeandemolition.org/
History 1978. Registration: EU Transparency Register, No/ID: 437180632625-02, Start date: 19 Sep 2018. **Aims** Promote and protect the interests of the demolition industry in Europe; exchange information on techniques, working methods and training; harmonize health and safety legislation; maintain contacts with similar organizations in other parts of the world; set and promote European standards on demolition techniques and promote recycling of demolition debris; harmonize the rules in Europe concerning the removal, depositing and recycling of demolition debris. **Structure** General Assembly; Board of Directors; Executive Board; Secretariat. **Languages** English, French, German. **Staff** 9.00 FTE, paid. **Finance** Sources: members' dues. **Activities** Advocacy/lobbying/activism; events/meetings; guidance/assistance/consulting; research/documentation; standards/guidelines. **Events** *Annual Convention* Paris (France) 2022, *Annual Convention* Belgrade (Serbia) 2021, *Annual Convention* Belgrade (Serbia) 2020, *Annual Convention* Paris (France) 2020, *Annual Convention* Vienna (Austria) 2018. **Publications** *EDA Newsletter*. Annual Industry Report.
Members Full associations of demolition contractors; individuals. Members in 33 countries:
Austria, Belgium, Bosnia-Herzegovina, Bulgaria, Croatia, Cyprus, Czechia, Denmark, Estonia, Finland, France, Georgia, Germany, Greece, Hungary, Ireland, Italy, Japan, Luxembourg, Malta, Netherlands, Norway, Poland, Portugal, Romania, Russia, Spain, Sweden, Switzerland, Türkiye, UK, USA.
IGO Relations Recognized by: *European Commission (EC, #06633)*. **NGO Relations** Member of (2): *Construction 2050 Alliance (#04760)*; *European Council for Construction Research, Development and Innovation (ECCREDI, #06813)*. [2021/XD5528/**D**]

♦ European Dental Dealers' Association / see Association of Dental Dealers in Europe (#02466)

♦ **European Dental Hygienists Federation (EDHF)** **06903**
Pres Malmskillnadsgatan 48 – 5tr, SE-111 84 Stockholm, Sweden. E-mail: info@edhf.eu – jeannine.byrne@hotmail.com.
URL: http://www.edhf.eu/
Aims Strengthen the dental hygienist profession by working towards recognition of the profession in all European countries and in EU directives; collaborate about dental hygienist education. **Structure** Board.
Members Full in 15 countries:
Austria, Czechia, Denmark, Finland, Germany, Ireland, Italy, Malta, Netherlands, Norway, Portugal, Slovakia, Spain, Sweden, Switzerland.
NGO Relations Member of (1): *Platform for Better Oral Health in Europe (#18399)*. [2017/XJ8435/**D**]

♦ European Dental Sleep Medicine Academy / see European Academy of Dental Sleep Medicine (#05786)
♦ European Dental Society (no recent information)

♦ **European Dental Students Association (EDSA)** **06904**
President c/o Academisch Centrum Tandheelkunde Amsterdam, Gustav Mahlerlaan 3004, 1081 LA Amsterdam, Netherlands. E-mail: board@edsaweb.org – president@edsaweb.org.
Gen Sec address not obtained. E-mail: secretary@edsaweb.org.
URL: http://www.edsaweb.org/
History Nov 1988, Paris (France). Former names and other names: *European Community Dental Students Committee (EDS)* – former (Nov 1988). Registration: EU Transparency Register, No/ID: 320613219208-18, Start date: 15 Oct 2015. **Aims** Express European dental students' opinions on educational, professional and social aspects of dentistry. **Structure** General Assembly (twice a year); Leadership; National Delegates; Working Groups and Taskforces. **Languages** English. **Finance** Sources: fundraising; members' dues; sponsorship. **Activities** Events/meetings; networking/liaising; projects/programmes; research/documentation; training/education. **Events** *Meeting* Istanbul (Türkiye) 2023, *Meeting* Lublin (Poland) 2022, *Meeting* Palma (Spain) 2022, *Meeting* Amsterdam (Netherlands) 2021, *Meeting* Košice (Slovakia) 2021. **Publications** *EDSA Newsletter* (6 a year); *EDSA Magazine* (2 a year).
Members Full in 31 countries:
Albania, Austria, Bosnia-Herzegovina, Bulgaria, Croatia, Czechia, Denmark, Estonia, Finland, France, Georgia, Germany, Ireland, Italy, Latvia, Lithuania, Malta, Netherlands, North Macedonia, Norway, Poland, Portugal, Romania, Russia, Serbia, Slovakia, Slovenia, Spain, Sweden, Türkiye, UK. [2022/XE3053/**E**]

♦ European Deontological Association of Graphologists (#02468)

♦ **European Depression Association (EDA)** **06905**
Pres c/o European Medical Assoc, Av des Volontaires 19, 1160 Brussels, Belgium. T. +3227342980. Fax +3227342135. E-mail: info@eddas.eu – info@europeandepressionday.eu.
URL: http://www.europeandepressionday.eu/
History 2004. **Aims** Raise awareness and promote better understanding of the impact of depression on people's lives; challenge stigma and discrimination; provide a voice for those who experience depression. **Structure** Board. **Languages** English. **Staff** Voluntary. **Finance** Members' dues. Sponsoring. Budget (annual): about euro 50,000. **Activities** Events/meetings.
Members Organizations; patients; researchers; healthcare professionals. Members in 18 countries:
Austria, Belgium, Croatia, Czechia, France, Germany, Greece, Hungary, Italy, Lithuania, Poland, Portugal, Serbia, Slovakia, Slovenia, Spain, Switzerland, UK.
NGO Relations Member of: *Alliance for Safe Online Pharmacy – EU (ASOP EU, #00720)*. Partner of: *European Alliance for Access to Safe Medicines (EAASM, #05859)*. [2020/XM1602/**F**]

♦ **European Dermato-Epidemiology Network (EDEN)** **06906**
Chairman London School of Hygiene and Tropical Medicine, St John's Inst of Dermatology, Keppel Street, London, WC1E 7HT, UK. T. +442079272680.
URL: https://www.dermepi.eu/
History 1995, Marseille (France). Former names and other names: *European Dermatology Epidemiology Network (EDEN)* – former. **Aims** Promote high quality research into epidemiology and conduct clinical research; improve the role of epidemiology in dermatology; share expertise; contact isolated groups and encourage them to join in. **Structure** Executive Committee; Steering Committee. **Languages** English. **Staff** None. **Finance** Voluntary contributions; specifically project-based budgeting. **Activities** Knowledge management/information dissemination; training/education. **Events** *Forum* Rotterdam (Netherlands) 2021, *Forum* Berlin (Germany) 2018, *Forum* Madrid (Spain) 2017, *International Congress on Dermato-Epidemiology* Malmö (Sweden) 2012, *International Congress on Dermato-Epidemiology* Nottingham (UK) 2008.
Members Full in 7 countries:
France, Germany, Italy, Netherlands, Spain, Sweden, UK. [2015.06.01/XF4526/**F**]

♦ European Dermatology Epidemiology Network / see European Dermato-Epidemiology Network (#06906)

♦ **European Dermatology Forum (EDF)** **06907**
Exec Dir c/o Dept of Dermatology, Zurich Univ Hosp, Rämistrasse 100, 8091 Zurich ZH, Switzerland.
URL: http://www.euroderm.org/
History 1997. Registration: Switzerland. **Aims** Improve *health care* for *skin patients* in Europe; prepare and spread guidelines for better care of dermatological diseases; strengthen the position and health economic impact of dermatology; improve and harmonize undergraduate teaching and postdoctoral education in dermatology; stimulate clinical research. **Structure** Annual General Scientific Meeting; Board of Directors. **Languages** English. **Staff** 0.50 FTE, paid. **Finance** Sources: members' dues. Support from drug companies. **Activities** Events/meetings; standards/guidelines; training/education. **Events** *Meeting* Montreux (Switzerland) 2022, *Meeting* Zurich (Switzerland) 2021, *Meeting* Montreux (Switzerland) 2020, *Meeting* Montreux (Switzerland) 2019, *Meeting* St Gallen (Switzerland) 2018. **Publications** *White Book: The Challenge of Skin Disease in Europe* (2020). **Members** Mostly heads of academic departments (200), representing 30 countries in Europe. Membership countries not specified. **NGO Relations** Member of (1): *International League of Dermatological Societies (ILDS, #14018)*. Sister organizations: *European Academy of Dermatology and Venereology (EADV, #05788)*; *European Society for Dermatological Research (ESDR, #08578)*; *European Union of Medical Specialists (UEMS, #09001)*. [2021.05.21/XF6210/**F**]

♦ European Desalination Association (inactive)

♦ **European Desalination Society (EDS)** **06908**
SG Univ Campus Bio-Medico of Rome, Fac of Engineering, Via Alvaro del Portillo 21, 00128 Rome RM, Italy. T. +393488848406. Fax +19285433036. E-mail: europeandesalination@gmail.com – info@edsoc.com.
Main: http://www.edsoc.com/
History 1993. Founded on merger of *European Desalination Association (EDA, inactive)* with the *Working Party on Fresh Water from the Sea* of *European Federation of Chemical Engineering (EFCE, #07074)*. **Aims** Promote awareness of the true value of water and its augmentation by desalination; encourage research, development and appropriate use of desalination, desalination technology and water re-use; encourage and promote its environmentally responsible and efficient use; promote European business development in desalination and related technology and European exports, research and technology. **Structure** Board of Directors. **Languages** English. **Staff** 2.50 FTE, paid. **Finance** Members' dues. Event sponsorship. **Activities** Events/meetings; training/education. **Events** *Conference* Las Palmas de Gran Canaria (Spain) 2022, *Conference on Membranes in Drinking and Industrial Water Production* Leeuwarden (Netherlands) 2017, *EUROMED Conference* Tel Aviv (Israel) 2017, *IDA International Conference on Water Reuse and Recycling* Nice (France) 2016, *International Conference on Thermal Energy Systems* Naples (Italy) 2015. **Publications** *Desalination and Water Treatment* (12 a year) – journal. *Desalination Directory*. Conference proceedings.
Members Individual and corporate, including universities, companies, research institutes, government agencies and concerned individuals. Members in 41 countries and territories:
Algeria, Argentina, Australia, Austria, Bahrain, Belgium, Bermuda, Bulgaria, Croatia, Cyprus, Czechia, Denmark, Egypt, France, Germany, Gibraltar, Greece, Israel, Italy, Kazakhstan, Kuwait, Lebanon, Libya, Malta, Mexico, Morocco, Netherlands, Norway, Oman, Philippines, Poland, Russia, Saudi Arabia, Spain, Sweden, Switzerland, Tunisia, Türkiye, UK, United Arab Emirates, USA.
NGO Relations Member of: *European Water Partnership (EWP, #09083)*; *International Desalination Association (IDA, #13152)*. Cooperates with *International Water Association (IWA, #15865)*. Affiliated with: *Water Science and Technology Association (WSTA, #20838)*. [2022/XD5497/**D**]

♦ European DesertNet / see Association of the Network for International Research on Desertification (#02823)
♦ European Design for Ageing Network / see Include Network (#11143)

♦ **European Design for All e-Accessibility Network (EDeAN)** **06909**
Contact c/o FORTH-ICS, N Plastira 100, Vasilika Vouton, 700 13 Heraklion, Greece. E-mail: iosif@ics.forth.gr.
URL: http://www.edean.org/
History 2002, in accordance with one of the specific goals of the eEurope 2002 Action Plan of *European Commission (EC, #06633)*. Inactive since 2012. **Aims** Raise the profile of Design for All and emphasize its importance in achieving greater e-Accessibility. **Structure** Annually rotating Secretariat. Special Interest Groups (SIGs, 6): Policy and Legislation; Standardization; Best practice in DfA training; Benchmarking; Technological Development; All members. **Languages** English. **Staff** Voluntary. **Finance** Activities supported by *European Commission (EC, #06633)*-funded projects. **Activities** Awareness raising; knowledge management/information dissemination. **Events** *Conférence internationale sur l'accessibilité et les systèmes de suppléance* Paris (France) 2011. **Publications** *EDeAN Newsletter*.
Members National Contact Centres (NCCs) in 24 countries:
Austria, Belgium, Cyprus, Czechia, Denmark, Estonia, Finland, France, Germany, Greece, Hungary, Ireland, Italy, Lithuania, Malta, Netherlands, Norway, Portugal, Romania, Slovakia, Slovenia, Spain, Sweden, UK.
IGO Relations *European Commission (EC, #06633)* – GD Information Society. [2017.06.01/XJ2172/d/**E**]

♦ **European Design and Automation Association (EDAA)** **06910**
Sec address not obtained.
URL: http://www.edaa.com/
History 1993. Registration: Belgium. **Aims** Operate for educational, scientific and technical purposes for the benefit of the international electronics design and design automation community. **Structure** General Assembly (annual). Board, including Chairman, Vice-Chairman, Treasurer, Secretary. **Languages** English. **Staff** Voluntary. **Events** *Design, Automation and Test in Europe Conference (DATE)* Antwerp (Belgium) 2023, *Design, Automation and Test in Europe Conference (DATE)* 2022, *Design, Automation and Test in Europe Conference (DATE)* 2021, *Design, Automation and Test in Europe Conference (DATE)* Grenoble (France) 2020, *Design, Automation and Test in Europe Conference (DATE)* Florence (Italy) 2019. [2021/XD6497/**D**]

♦ European Design Automation Conference (meeting series)

♦ **European Designing Out Crime Association (E-DOCA)** **06911**
Contact Van Diemenstraat 374, 1013 CR Amsterdam, Netherlands.
URL: http://www.e-doca.eu/
History Chapter of *International CPTED Association (ICA, #13101)*. **Aims** Implement, promote and further develop crime prevention through environmental design and designing out crime in Europe. **Structure** Run by *'Stichting Veilig Ontwerp en Beheer (SVOC)'* (Netherlands). **Languages** Czech, Danish, Dutch, English, Estonian, Finnish, French, German, Hungarian, Irish Gaelic, Italian, Latvian, Lithuanian, Maltese, Polish, Portuguese, Slovakian, Slovene, Spanish, Swedish. **Finance** Members' dues.
Members Individuals in 22 countries:
Austria, Belgium, Cyprus, Czechia, Denmark, Estonia, Finland, France, Germany, Greece, Hungary, Ireland, Italy, Kenya, Netherlands, Norway, Poland, South Africa, Spain, Sweden, Switzerland, UK. [2015/XM0589/**E**]

♦ European Dessert Mixes Manufacturers' Association (no recent information)
♦ European Destinations of Excellence / see EDEN Network (#05357)

♦ **European and Developing Countries Clinical Trials Partnership (EDCTP)** **06912**
Europe Office PO Box 93015, 2509 AA The Hague, Netherlands. T. +31703440880. Fax +31703440899. E-mail: info@edctp.org – media@edctp.org.
Africa Office PO Box 19070, Tygerberg, 7505, South Africa. T. +27219380690. Fax +27219380569.
URL: http://www.edctp.org/
History Founded 2003, as a European response to the global health crisis caused by the three main poverty-related diseases of HIV/AIDS, tuberculosis and malaria. Formed by a *European Parliament (EP, #08146)* and *European Council (#06801)* decision in order to pool resources. Set up under the European Commission's Sixth Framework Programme (FP6) for research and technological development. First EDCTP programme ended Dec 2015; 2nd EDCTP programme (EDCTP2; 2014-2024) started 2 Dec 2014 and funded under Horizon 2020, the EU Framework Programme for Research and Innovation, with a contribution by European Union. **Aims** Accelerate development of new or improved *drugs, vaccines, microbicides* and diagnostics against *HIV/AIDS, tuberculosis* and *malaria*, as well as neglected and/or emergent infectious *diseases*, especially relevant for *Sub-Saharan* Africa, through funding clinical research in phases I-IV, with a focus on phase III clinical trials. **Structure** General Assembly; Strategic Advisory Committee; Secretariat. **Languages** English, French, Portuguese. **Staff** 30.00 FTE, paid. **Finance** Member state donors; *European Union (EU, #08967)*; third party donors, including: *Bill and Melinda Gates Foundation (BMGF)*. **Activities** Events/meetings. **Events** *EDCTP Forum* Maputo (Mozambique) 2021, *EDCTP Forum* Lisbon (Portugal) 2018, *EDCTP Forum* Lusaka (Zambia) 2016, *EDCTP Forum* Berlin (Germany) 2014, *High-Level Conference on EDCTP2 Programme* Cape Town (South Africa) 2014. **Publications** *e-Alert* in English – newsletter; *EDCTP Newsletter* in English, French, Portuguese. Annual Report, in English, French, Portuguese.
Members States participating as members of EDCTP Association (legal implementation instrument for EDCPT2) (28):
Austria, Burkina Faso, Cameroon, Congo Brazzaville, Denmark, Finland, France, Gabon, Gambia, Germany, Ghana, Ireland, Italy, Luxembourg, Mali, Mozambique, Netherlands, Niger, Norway, Portugal, Senegal, South Africa, Spain, Sweden, Tanzania UR, Uganda, UK, Zambia.
Partners in 63 countries:
Angola, Austria, Belgium, Benin, Botswana, Burkina Faso, Burundi, Cameroon, Cape Verde, Central African Rep, Chad, Comoros, Congo Brazzaville, Congo DR, Côte d'Ivoire, Denmark, Equatorial Guinea, Eritrea, Eswatini, Ethiopia, France, Gabon, Gambia, Germany, Ghana, Greece, Guinea, Guinea-Bissau, Ireland, Italy, Kenya, Lesotho, Liberia, Luxembourg, Madagascar, Malawi, Mali, Mauritania, Mauritius, Mozambique, Namibia, Netherlands, Niger, Nigeria, Norway, Portugal, Rwanda, Sao Tomé-Principe, Senegal, Seychelles, Sierra Leone, Somalia, South Africa, Spain, Sudan, Sweden, Switzerland, Tanzania UR, Togo, Uganda, UK, Zambia, Zimbabwe. [2021/XM2652/**F**]

♦ European Developmental Biology Organization (inactive)
♦ European Development Cooperatie / see European Cooperative for Rural Development (#06788)

♦ **European Development Finance Institutions (EDFI)** **06913**
Main Office Rue de la Loi 81A, 1040 Brussels, Belgium. T. +3222302369. Fax +3222300405. E-mail: edfi@edfi.eu.
URL: http://www.edfi.eu/
History A grouping of the type *European Economic Interest Grouping (EEIG, #06960)*. EU Transparency Register: 410540760-32. **Aims** Represent the interests of bilateral institutions operating in developing and reforming economies, mandated by their governments to foster growth in *sustainable* businesses, help reduce poverty and improve people's lives, and contribute to achieving the Sustainable Development Goals by promoting economically, environmentally and socially sustainable development through financing and investing in profitable private sector enterprises; strength information flow and cooperation between members and other bilateral, multilateral and regional development finance institutions. **Structure** General Meeting (meets annually), consisting of Chief Executives of all EDFI Member Institutions. Board of Directors; Brussels (Belgium) Office; General Committee; ad hoc working groups. **Languages** English. **Staff** 1.00 FTE, paid. **Finance** Members' dues. **Activities** Financial and/or material support. **Events** *TGAIS : The Global African Investment Summit* London (UK) 2015, *Annual General Meeting* Luxembourg (Luxembourg) 2008, *Annual General Meeting* The Hague (Netherlands) 2007, *Annual meeting / Annual General Meeting* Oslo (Norway) 2006, *Annual meeting / Annual General Meeting* Edinburgh (UK) 2005. **Publications** *EDFI Monthly Newsletter*. Annual Report.
Members Development banks (15) in 13 countries:
Austria, Belgium, Denmark, Finland, France, Germany, Italy, Netherlands, Norway, Spain, Sweden, Switzerland, UK.
Included in the above, 11 development banks listed in this Yearbook:
Belgian Corporation for International Investment (BMI); *CDC Group* (CDC Group); *Compañia Española de Financiación de Desarrollo (COFIDES)*; *DEG – Deutsche Investitions- und Entwicklungsgesellschaft*; *Investerin-gsfonden for Udviklingslande (IFU)*; *Italian Corporation for International Joint Ventures (SIMEST)*; *Nederlandse Financierings-Maatschappij voor Ontwikkelingslanden (FMO)*; *Norwegian Investment Fund for Developing Countries (Norfund)*; *Société de promotion et de participations pour la coopération économique, Paris (PROPARCO)*; *Swedfund – International*; *Teollisen Yhteistyön Rahasto (FINNFUND)*. [2019/XF3991/y/**F**]

♦ **European Development Fund (EDF)** **06914**
Fonds européen de développement (FED) – Fondo Europeo de Desarrollo (FED) – Europäische Entwicklungsfond (EEF) – Fundo Europeu de Desenvolvimento (FED) – Fondo Europeo de Sviluppo (FES) – Europees Ontwikkelingsfonds (EOF) – Europaeiske Udviklingsfonds (EUF)
Dir Gen c/o EC-DG EuropeAid (DEVCO), Rue de la Loi 41, 1049 Brussels, Belgium. T. +3222988624. Fax +3222996407.
Info Point – Coordinator Rue de la Loi 43, 1040 Brussels, Belgium. T. +3222999814. Fax +3222965833.
URL: https://international-partnerships.ec.europa.eu/
History 1957, Brussels (Belgium). Established under provisions of the *Treaty on the Functioning of the European Union (TFEU, 1957)* within the framework of associations with its *Association of Overseas Countries and Territories of the European Union (OCTA, #02843)* for a period of 5 years, and within the framework of *European Union (EU, #08967)*; these provisions were renewed under the *Yaoundé Conventions*, the first signed 20 Jul 1963 and entered into force 1 Jul 1964, the second signed 29 Jul 1969 and expired 31 Jan 1975.
The Yaoundé Convention set up *'Associated States of Africa and Madagascar (ASAM) – Etats africains et malgache associés au Marché Commun'*, subsequently *Association of the European Economic Community and the African and Malagasy States (EAMA, inactive)*. Provisions of the Yaoundé Conventions were extended to all member countries of *Organisation of African, Caribbean and Pacific States (OACPS, #17796)* by the signing of *ACP-EEC Convention (Lomé convention, 1975)*, 28 Feb 1975. *Second ACP-EEC Convention (Lomé II, 1979)*, signed 31 Oct 1979. *Third ACP-EEC Convention (Lomé III, 1984)*, signed 8 Dec 1984 and entered into force in Mar 1985.
The *Fourth ACP-EEC Convention (Lomé IV, 1989)*, was signed 15 Dec 1989 and came into force 1 Mar 1990, for 10 years, but the related (7th) EDF remained funded for only 5 years. The convention was amended on 4 Nov 1995, Mauritius, and adjusted to the new treaty establishing the European Community and the European Union. The Lomé Convention was replaced by the *ACP-EU Partnership Agreement (Cotonou agreement, 2000)*, signed 23 Jun 2000 for a period of 20 years, and revised, 25 Jun 2005 and 4 Nov 2010. The association agreement with the remaining OCTs was renewed on 27 Nov 2001 for a period until 2011, with agreement amended on 19 Mar 2007.
Previous: 9th EDF, supplemented by the transferred balances from the previous EDFs, covered the period 2000-2007. 10th EDF covered 2008-2013.
The EDF is set up as an intergovernmental fund, replaced every 5 years, and administered by the *European Commission (EC, #06633)* or, for the investment facility which includes interest subsidies and a revolving fund for risk capital and loans. The *European Council (#06801)* of 15-16 Dec 2005 decided on a 10th EDF, which will be aligned on the financial perspectives of *European Communities (EC, inactive)* and will cover the 6-year period 2008-2013. As of Jan 2011, EDF serves as one of 3 "geographical" instruments for the DG Development and Cooperation – EuropeAid.
11th EDF (2014-2020) created by intergovernmental agreement, signed Jun 2013 and entered into force 1 Mar 2015.
Aims Provide aid for 79 African, Caribbean and Pacific (ACP) partner countries of the Union and for the Overseas Countries and Territories of Member States; stimulate economic development, social and human development, regional cooperation and integration. **Structure** EDF Committee, comprising representatives of member states, is chaired by a representative of the European Commission. **Finance** Not part of the EU budget. Audited by the Court of Auditors of the European Communities. Budget (2014-2020): euro 30,500 million. **Activities** Financial and/or material support. **Events** *International Symposium on the Future of Manufacturing Industries in Japan, Korea, Germany and France* Tokyo (Japan) 2013. **Members** Not a membership organization.
IGO Relations European institutions:
– *Council of the European Union (#04895)*;
– *European Economic and Social Committee (EESC, #06963)*;
– *European Parliament (EP, #08146)*.
Multinational fora and organizations, notably development funding and trade organizations, such as the United Nations (and its "system") and including the following bodies:
– *Arab Fund for Economic and Social Development (AFESD, #00965)*;
– *Arab Fund for Technical Assistance to African Countries (AFTAAC, #00966)*;
– *International Bank for Reconstruction and Development (IBRD, #12317)*;
– *International Cocoa Organization (ICCO, #12627)*;
– *International Monetary Fund (IMF, #14180)*;
– *OECD (#17693)*;
– *OPEC Fund for International Development (OFID, #17745)*;
– *UNIDO (#20336)*;
– *United Nations Economic Commission for Africa (ECA, #20554)*.
Organizations involved with the implementation of regional cooperation:
– *Agency for the Safety of Aerial Navigation in Africa and Madagascar (#00556)*;
– *Caribbean Community (CARICOM, #03476)*;
– *Comité permanent inter-Etats de lutte contre la sécheresse dans le Sahel (CILSS, #04195)*;
– *Economic Community of West African States (ECOWAS, #05312)*;
– *Commission de l'Océan Indien (COI, #04236)*;
– *Organisation of Eastern Caribbean States (OECS, #17804)*;
– *Organisation pour la mise en valeur du fleuve Sénégal (OMVS, #17815)*;
– *Pacific Islands Forum Secretariat (#17970)*;
– *Southern African Development Community (SADC, #19843)*.
NGO Relations Supports: *African Malaria Network Trust (AMANET, #00365)*; *Africare (#00516)*; *International Trypanotolerance Centre (ITC, #15739)*; *Oceania Customs Organisation (OCO, #17658)*.
Links with the following multinational charitable NGOs:
– *Caritas Internationalis (CI, #03580)*;
– *HelpAge International (#10904)*;
– *International Red Cross and Red Crescent Movement (#14707)*;
– *Japanese Organization for International Cooperation (no recent information)*;
– *Oxfam GB*. [2019/XF4360/f/**F***]

♦ European Development Institute (unconfirmed)
♦ European Development Platform (internationally oriented national body)

♦ **European Development Research Network (EUDN)** **06915**
Secretariat c/o Development Economics, Platz der Göttinger, Sieben 3, 37073 Göttingen, Germany. T. +49551397487. Fax +49551398173. E-mail: eudn.network@uni-goettingen.de.
URL: http://www.eudn.eu/
History Dec 2000, Tokyo (Japan), at 2nd annual Conference of *Global Development Network (GDN, #10318)*, serving as its European hub. **Aims** Make European development expertise available to researchers in other regions; strengthen cooperation among researchers within Europe and developing countries. **Structure** Executive Committee. **Languages** English. **Staff** Voluntary. **Finance** No core funding. **Activities** Events/meetings; training/education. **Events** *Commons and Development* Paris (France) 2016, *Conference* Paris (France) 2014.
Members Individuals. Full (91) in 12 countries:
Belgium, Denmark, France, Germany, Greece, Italy, Netherlands, Norway, Sweden, Switzerland, UK, USA.
Associate (32) in 9 countries:
Belgium, France, Germany, Italy, Netherlands, Spain, Sweden, Switzerland, UK.
NGO Relations *Global Development Network (GDN, #10318)*. [2017.06.01/XJ6589/v/**F**]

♦ **European Diabetes Forum (EUDF)** **06916**
Exec Dir South Ctr Titanium, Marcel Broodthaers Square 8/5, 1060 Brussels, Belgium. E-mail: info@eudf.org.
URL: https://www.eudf.org/
History 2018. Founded by *European Association for the Study of Diabetes (EASD, #06228)*, *European Foundation for the Study of Diabetes (EFSD, #07351)*; *Foundation of European Nurses in Diabetes (FEND, #09953)* and Juvenile Diabetes Research Foundation (JDRF). Registration: Banque Carrefour des Entreprises, No/ID: 0745.472.021, Start date: 17 Mar 2020, Belgium; EU Transparency Register, No/ID: 235585541427-10, Start date: 15 Feb 2021. **Aims** Ensure the translation of research into policy actions towards better diabetes care at national level. **Structure** General Assembly; Board; Executive Director.
Members Full; Associate.
European Association for the Study of Diabetes (EASD, #06228); *European Foundation for the Study of Diabetes (EFSD, #07351)*; *Foundation of European Nurses in Diabetes (FEND, #09953)*; *International Diabetes Federation Europe (IDF Europe, #13165)*; *International Society for Pediatric and Adolescent Diabetes (ISPAD, #15344)*; Juvenile Diabetes Research Foundation (JDRF); *Primary Care Diabetes Europe (PCDE, #18495)*; *Société Francophone du Diabète (SFD, #19468)*. [2021/AA1362/y/**F**]

♦ European Diabolo Association (unconfirmed)
♦ European Diagnostic Manufacturers Association (inactive)
♦ European Dialogue (internationally oriented national body)

♦ **European Dialogue on Internet Governance (EuroDIG)** **06917**
SG Holbeinstr 6, 04229 Leipzig, Germany. T. +4934124743008. E-mail: office@eurodig.org.
Pres Schächlistr 19, 8953 Dietikon ZH, Switzerland.
URL: https://www.eurodig.org/

History 2008. Legal form: *EuroDIG Support Association.* Registration: EU Transparency Register, No/ID: 546442133048-22, Start date: 29 Oct 2018. **Aims** Promote the engagement of Europeans in multistakeholder dialogue in order to share their expertise and best practice and, where possible, identify common ground. **Structure** General Assembly; Board; Secretariat. **Events** *EuroDIG : European Dialogue on Internet Governance* Leipzig (Germany) 2020, *EuroDIG : European Dialogue on Internet Governance* The Hague (Netherlands) 2019, *EuroDIG : European Dialogue on Internet Governance* Tbilisi (Georgia) 2018, *EuroDIG : European Dialogue on Internet Governance* Tallinn (Estonia) 2017, *EuroDIG : European Dialogue on Internet Governance* Brussels (Belgium) 2016. **IGO Relations** *Council of Europe (CE, #04881); European Commission (EC, #06633).* **NGO Relations** *European Broadcasting Union (EBU, #06404); European Telecommunications Network Operators' Association (ETNO, #08895); Internet Corporation for Assigned Names and Numbers (ICANN, #15949); Internet Society (ISOC, #15952); RIPE Network Coordination Centre (RIPE NCC, #18951).* [2020/XM8778/F]

♦ European Dialysis Exhibitors Association (inactive)
♦ European Dialysis and Transplant Association – European Renal Association / see European Renal Association – European Dialysis and Transplant Association (#08353)

♦ European Dialysis and Transplant Nurses Association – European Renal Care Association (EDTNA/ERCA) 06918

Association européenne d'infirmières et infirmiers de dialyse et de transplantation – Association européenne pour les soins des reins

Address not obtained.
URL: http://www.edtnaerca.org/

History 1971, Florence (Italy). **Aims** Achieve a high level of quality care and support for patients and their families; promote the advancement of renal care through education and continuous professional development; develop and continually update standards for renal care; promote awareness of the social, cultural and ethical implications involved in the provision of renal care; initiate, promote and conduct research in renal care; encourage communication and cooperation; be the recognized multi-disciplinary renal care association in Europe; establish collaborations with other associations and organizations. **Structure** Executive Committee, comprising President, Treasurer, Secretary and 3 members. Supervisory Board. Consultants. Conference Scientific Programme Committee. **Languages** English. **Finance** Members' dues. Annual Conference. **Activities** Interest Groups (7): Anaemia; CKD; Nutrition; PD; Social Workers; Technicians; Transplant. **Events** *Annual Conference* Amsterdam (Netherlands) 2022, *Annual Conference* Ljubljana (Slovenia) 2021, *Annual Conference* Ljubljana (Slovenia) 2020, *Annual Conference* Prague (Czechia) 2019, *Annual Conference* Genoa (Italy) 2018. **Publications** *EDTNA/ERCA Newsletter* (3 a year) – in 15 languages. Handbooks; guides; guidelines. **Members** Individuals (about 2,300) Member; E-Member; Conference; Corporate. Members in 72 countries. Membership countries not specified. **IGO Relations** *WHO (#20950).* **NGO Relations** Member of: *European Kidney Health Alliance (EKHA, #07626); European Specialist Nurses Organisation (ESNO, #08808).* [2017/XD7017/v/D]

♦ European Digestive Surgery (EDS) 06919

Sec Dept of Surgery, Klinikum rechts der Isar, Technical University Munich, Ismaninger Str 22, 81675 Munich, Germany. T. +498941402121. E-mail: secretary@edsurgery.org.
URL: http://www.edsurgery.org/

History Founded 1995. **Aims** Support young surgeons in europe, especially in Eastern European countries. **Structure** Council. **Languages** English. **Staff** 1.00 FTE, paid. **Finance** Members' dues. Support from: *United European Gastroenterology (UEG, #20506).* **Activities** Organizes postgraduate courses and workshops. **Events** *Postgraduate Courses* Kiev (Ukraine) 2014, *Postgraduate Courses* Istanbul (Turkey) 2013, *Postgraduate Courses* Thessaloniki (Greece) 2012, *Postgraduate Courses* Lublin (Poland) 2011, *Postgraduate Courses* Cluj-Napoca (Romania) 2010. **Publications** *Digestive Surgery* (6 a year). **Members** Individuals (about 1,200) in 66 countries. Membership countries not specified. **NGO Relations** *International Society for Digestive Surgery (ISDS, #15060); United European Gastroenterology (UEG, #20506).* [2017/XD8023/D]

♦ European Digital Cinema Forum (EDCF) 06920

Gen Sec Huis ter Heideweg 18, 3705 LZ Zeist, Netherlands. T. +492734571106. E-mail: admin@edcf.net.
URL: http://www.edcf.net/

History Netherlands. Registration: Netherlands; EU Transparency Register, No/ID: 69839146871-20. **Aims** Discuss key issues surrounding European Digital Cinema; provide a basis of common understanding across all European territories of the business and technical matters of digital cinema. **Structure** Board. **Languages** English. **Finance** Sources: members' dues. **Publications** Guides. [2020.10.15/XJ0243/F]

♦ European Digital Competence Certificate Foundation (internationally oriented national body)
♦ European Digital Dealers Association (no recent information)

♦ European Digital Finance Association (EDFA) 06921

SG Rue des Pères Blancs 4, 1040 Brussels, Belgium. E-mail: office@europeandigitalfinance.eu.
URL: https://www.europeandigitalfinance.eu/

History Feb 2020. Registration: No/ID: 0747.637.792, Start date: 26 May 2020, Belgium; EU Transparency Register, No/ID: 497284939842-90, Start date: 6 Oct 2020. **Aims** Advocate for innovative, more affordable and secure financial services.
Members Finance companies federated in 13 national associations:
Belgium, Bulgaria, Czechia, France, Hungary, Ireland, Italy, Netherlands, Poland, Portugal, Romania, Slovakia, Spain.
[2020/AA1121/D]

♦ European Digital Learning Network (DLEARN) 06922

Secretariat Via Domenico Scarlatti 30, 20124 Milan MI, Italy. T. +39287284807. E-mail: info@dlearn.eu.
URL: http://dlearn.eu/

History Launched Jan 2016. EU Transparency Register: 756728721690-51. **Aims** Embrace the challenges brought by the digital transformation in terms of digital skills mismatch and digital learning opportunities. **Structure** Scientific Committee. **Activities** Training/education; events/meetings; research/documentation. **Publications** *Dlearn Quarterly Newsletter.*
Members Full in 12 countries:
Belgium, Bulgaria, Cyprus, Greece, Ireland, Italy, Malta, Poland, Portugal, Romania, Slovenia, Spain.
Included in the above, 1 organization listed in this Yearbook: [2019/XM6542/F]

♦ European Digital Library / see Europeana Foundation (#05839)
♦ European Digital Media Association / see DOT Europe (#05125)

♦ European Digital Reading Lab (EDRLab) 06923

Contact 14 rue Alexandre Parodi, 75010 Paris, France. T. +33140411189. E-mail: contact@edrlab.org.
URL: https://www.edrlab.org/

History 2015. Registration: France; EU Transparency Register, No/ID: 293351620135-49. **Aims** Deploy an open, interoperable and accessible digital publishing ecosystem in Europe. **Structure** Board of Directors. **Finance** Sources: members' dues. **Activities** Awareness raising; events/meetings; networking/liaising; research and development; standards/guidelines. **Events** *Digital Publishing Summit* Paris (France) 2020, *Digital Publishing Summit* Paris (France) 2019, *Digital Publishing Summit* Berlin (Germany) 2018, *Digital Publishing Summit* Brussels (Belgium) 2017, *Digital Publishing Summit* Bordeaux (France) 2016. **Publications** *EDRLab Newsletter.*
Members Full in 10 countries:
Canada, Denmark, France, Germany, Italy, Netherlands, Poland, Switzerland, UK, USA.
NGO Relations Member of (1): *World Wide Web Consortium (W3C, #21935).* [2022.02.08/XM8782/F]

♦ European Digital Rights (EDRi) 06924

Exec Dir Rue Belliard 12, 1040 Brussels, Belgium. E-mail: brussels@edri.org.
URL: http://edri.org/

History Current constitution adopted 8 Jun 2002, Berlin (Germany). Registration: Banque-Carrefour des Entreprises, No/ID: 0866.466.752, Start date: 2 Jul 2004, Belgium; EU Transparency Register, No/ID: 16311905144-06, Start date: 28 Jan 2011. **Aims** Promote, protect and uphold civil rights in the field of information- and communication technology. **Structure** General Assembly (annual); Board. **Events** *Privacy Camp Annual Conference* Brussels (Belgium) 2019. **Publications** *EDRi-gram* – newsletter.

Members Organizations (nearly 50) in 21 countries:
Austria, Belgium, Bulgaria, Czechia, Denmark, Finland, France, Germany, Iceland, Ireland, Italy, Netherlands, North Macedonia, Poland, Portugal, Romania, Slovakia, Spain, Sweden, Türkiye, UK.
Access Now (#00052); Amnesty International (AI, #00801); ARTICLE 19 (#01121); Committee to Protect Journalists (CPJ, #04280) (Observer); *Electronic Frontier Foundation (EFF); Electronic Privacy Information Center (EPIC); European Center for Not-for-Profit Law (ECNL, #06463); Free Software Foundation Europe (FSFE); NOYB – European Center for Digital Rights (NOYB, #17613); Privacy International (PI, #18504); Reporters sans frontières (RSF, #18846); Statewatch.*
Consultative Status Consultative status granted from: *World Intellectual Property Organization (WIPO, #21593)* (Permanent Observer Status). **IGO Relations** Participant in Fundamental Rights Platform of: *European Union Agency for Fundamental Rights (FRA, #08969).* Member of: *European Economic and Social Committee (EESC, #06963)* Liaison Group. **NGO Relations** Member of (3): *Copyright for Creativity (C4C, #04832); Global Net Neutrality Coalition (#10480); Transatlantic Consumer Dialogue (TACD, #20203).* Partner of (1): *European Association for the Defence of Human Rights (AEDH, no recent information).* [2023/XF6794/y/F]

♦ European Digital SME Alliance 06925

Main Office 123 Rue du Commerce, 1000 Brussels, Belgium. E-mail: office@digitalsme.eu.
Registered Office Rue Jacques de Lalaing 4, 1040 Brussels, Belgium.
URL: http://www.digitalsme.eu/

History Dec 2007. Former names and other names: *Pan European ICT and eBusiness Network for SME (PIN-SME)* – former (Dec 2007). Registration: No/ID: 0899.786.252, Start date: 13 Aug 2008, Belgium; EU Transparency Register, No/ID: 082698126468-52, Start date: 24 Mar 2017. **Structure** General Assembly. Administrative Council, headed by President. Other officers: General Secretary; Vice-Presidents; Treasurer. **Events** *Forum on ICT Standardisation* Brussels (Belgium) 2019.
Members Full in 7 countries:
Bulgaria, Denmark, France, Germany, Italy, Spain, UK.
Associate in 2 countries:
Kosovo, Serbia.
NGO Relations Member of (3): *Alliance for Internet of Things Innovation (AIOTI, #00697); Small Business Standards (SBS, #19311); SMEunited (#19327).* [2019/XM2751/D]

♦ European Digital Video Broadcasting Project / see DVB Project (#05147)

♦ European Diisocyanate and Polyol Producers Association (ISOPA) 06926

Main Office Rue Belliard 65, 1040 Brussels, Belgium. T. +3227863553. E-mail: main@isopa.org.
Main Website: http://www.isopa.org/

History Nov 1987. Founded as a sector group of *Conseil européen de l'industrie chimique (CEFIC, #04687).* Now an autonomous affiliated organization. Former names and other names: *European Isocyanate Producers Association* – former; *European Di-isocyanate Producers Association* – former. Registration: Banque-Carrefour des Entreprises, No/ID: 0649.434.695, Start date: 26 Feb 2016, Belgium; EU Transparency Register, No/ID: 00770563312-18, Start date: 10 Mar 2010. **Aims** Resolve health, safety and environmental questions specifically related to diisocyanates and polyols production in Europe. **Structure** Organizing Committee; Sub-Committees (5); Full-time Secretariat. **Activities** Knowledge management/information dissemination; research and development. **Events** *Polyurethane world congress* Amsterdam (Netherlands) 1997, *Polyurethanes world congress* Vancouver, BC (Canada) 1993.
Members Diisocyanate producers (6) in 4 countries:
Belgium, Germany, Hungary, Switzerland.
NGO Relations Member of (4): *Circular Plastics Alliance (#03936); Federation of European and International Associations Established in Belgium (FAIB, #09508); Industry4Europe (#11181); Modern Building Alliance (#16842).* In liaison with technical committees of: *International Organization for Standardization (ISO, #14473).*
[2022.10.19/XE1237/E]

♦ European Diphtheria Surveillance Network (EDSN) 06927

Contact c/o ECDC, SE-169 73 Stockholm, Sweden. T. +46858601000. Fax +46858601001. E-mail: info@ecdc.europa.eu.
URL: http://ecdc.europa.eu/en/healthtopics/diptheria/edsn/Pages/index.aspx

History 1 Nov 2006. Founded as a 38-month programme. As of Feb 2010, a surveillance network of *European Centre for Disease Prevention and Control (ECDC, #06476).* Former names and other names: *DIPNET – Diphtheria Surveillance Network* – former. **Aims** Integrate surveillance, which covers all diphtheria diseases caused by toxigenic C diphtheriae and C ulcerans from an epidemiology and laboratory point of view. **Activities** Epidemiological and microbiological surveillance data on diphtheria collected through *European Surveillance System (TESSy).*
Members Full in 30 countries:
Austria, Belgium, Bulgaria, Croatia, Cyprus, Czechia, Denmark, Estonia, Finland, France, Germany, Greece, Hungary, Iceland, Ireland, Italy, Latvia, Liechtenstein, Lithuania, Luxembourg, Malta, Netherlands, Norway, Poland, Portugal, Romania, Slovakia, Slovenia, Spain, Sweden. [2022.05.11/XJ2540/F]

♦ European Direct Marketing Association (inactive)

♦ European Direct Selling Association (SELDIA) 06928

Exec Dir Av de Tervueren 14 – Bte 1, 1040 Brussels, Belgium. T. +3227361014. Fax +3227363497. E-mail: seldia@seldia.eu.
URL: http://www.seldia.eu/

History 1968. Inaugural meeting: 12 Jun 1969, Brussels (Belgium). New statutes registered 3 May 1998. Former names and other names: *Fédération européenne pour la vente et le service à domicile (FEVSD)* – former (1968 to Apr 1991); *Federation of European Direct Selling Associations (FEDSA)* – former (Apr 1991 to 2010). Registration: Banque-Carrefour des Entreprises, No/ID: 0420.029.202, Start date: 21 Dec 1979, Belgium; EU Transparency Register, No/ID: 1710335466-15, Start date: 3 Oct 2008. **Aims** Be the voice of the European Direct Selling sector; represent national direct selling associations, corporate members, service providers to direct selling companies and people who are engaged in direct selling in Europe. **Structure** General Assembly (annual); Board of Directors; CEO Council; Committees (3). **Languages** English, French. **Staff** 3.00 FTE, paid. **Finance** Sources: members' dues. **Activities** Advocacy/lobbying/activism; events/meetings; networking/liaising; standards/guidelines. **Events** *European Direct Selling Conference* Brussels (Belgium) 2022, *European Direct Selling Conference* Brussels (Belgium) 2021, *European Direct Selling Conference* Brussels (Belgium) 2020, *European Direct Selling Conference* Brussels (Belgium) 2018, *European Direct Selling Conference* Brussels (Belgium) 2016.
Members Corporate (14); National associations (25) in 25 countries:
Bulgaria, Croatia, Czechia, Denmark, Estonia, Finland, France, Greece, Hungary, Ireland, Italy, Latvia, Lithuania, Luxembourg, Netherlands, Norway, Poland, Portugal, Romania, Slovakia, Slovenia, Spain, Sweden, Türkiye, Ukraine.
IGO Relations Recognized by (1): *European Commission (EC, #06633).* **NGO Relations** Member of (5): *EuroCommerce (EC, #05665); European Society of Association Executives (ESAE, #08526); Federation of European and International Associations Established in Belgium (FAIB, #09508); Federation of European Data & Marketing (FEDMA, #09499); World Federation of Direct Selling Associations (WFDSA, #21431).*
[2023.02.14/XD4404/D]

♦ European Dirofilaria Society / see European Society of Dirofilariosis and Angiostrongylosis (#08584)

♦ European Disability Forum (EDF) 06929

Forum européen des personnes handicapées

Secretariat Ave des Arts 7-8, 1210 Brussels, Belgium. T. +3222824600. Fax +3222824609. E-mail: info@edf-feph.org.
Dir address not obtained.
URL: http://www.edf-feph.org/

History 6 May 1996, Brussels (Belgium). Founded as the European umbrella organization representing the interests of 80 million disabled citizens in Europe, to continue the work of *European Forum of Disabled People (FORUM, inactive)* which ceased to exist on completion of *Handicapped People in Europe Living Independently in Open Society (HELIOS, inactive).* Created by disabled people and parents of disabled people who cannot represent themselves. Commenced operations as an independent organization, 1 Jan 1997. Registration: Belgium; Eu Transparency Register, No/ID: 57868523887-16. **Aims** Ensure disabled people full access to fundamental and *human rights* through their active involvement in policy development and implementation in Europe. **Structure** General Assembly (annual); Board. **Languages** English. **Staff** 9.00 FTE, paid. **Finance** Members' dues. Other sources: subsidy from *European Commission (EC, #06633)*; donations. **Activities** Advocacy/lobbying/activism; events/meetings. **Events** *Annual General Assembly* Athens (Greece) 2022, *Conference on Persons with Disabilities* Brussels (Belgium) 2022, *European Accessibility Summit* Brussels (Belgium) 2022, *Annual General Assembly* Zagreb (Croatia) 2020, *Conference on Persons with Disabilities* Brussels (Belgium) 2019. **Publications** *Disability Voice EU* (4 a year) – magazine; *EDF Member's Mailing*. Annual Report; position papers; case studies; alternative reports.

Members Full: National Councils in 29 countries:
Austria, Belgium, Bulgaria, Croatia, Cyprus, Czechia, Denmark, Estonia, Finland, France, Germany, Greece, Hungary, Iceland, Ireland, Italy, Latvia, Lithuania, Luxembourg, Malta, Norway, Poland, Portugal, Romania, Slovakia, Slovenia, Spain, Sweden, UK.
Full – NGOs (24):
- *Autism-Europe (AE, #03040)*;
- *Brain Injured and Families European Confederation (BIF-EC, #03314)*;
- *Cerebral Palsy – European Community Association (CP-ECA, #03832)*;
- *DEBRA International (#05021)*;
- *Disabled Peoples' International (DPI, #05097)* (Europe);
- *European Action of the Disabled (#05825)*;
- *European Alliance of Neuromuscular Disorders Associations (EAMDA, #05876)*;
- *European Association of Cochlear Implant Users (EURO-CIU, #05979)*;
- *European Blind Union (EBU, #06350)*;
- *European Cooperation in Anthroposophical Curative Education and Social Therapy (ECCE, #06783)*;
- *European Deafblind Network (EDbN, #06890)*;
- *European Deafblind Union (EDBU, #06891)*;
- *European Down Syndrome Association (EDSA, #06942)*;
- *European Dyslexia Association – International Organisation for Specific Learning Disabilities (EDA, #06951)*;
- *European Federation of Hard of Hearing People (EFHOH, #07136)*;
- *European League of Stuttering Associations (ELSA, #07673)*;
- *European Network of ex- Users and Survivors of Psychiatry (ENUSP, #07906)*;
- *European Network on Independent Living (ENIL, #07929)*;
- *European Union of the Deaf (EUD, #08985)*;
- *Fédération Européenne des Parents d'Enfants Déficients Auditifs (FEPEDA, #09577)*;
- *Inclusion Europe – European Association of Societies of Persons with Intellectual Disability and their Families (Inclusion Europe, #11144)*;
- *International Federation for Spina Bifida and Hydrocephalus (IF SBH, #13552)*;
- *International Federation of Persons with Physical Disability (FIMITIC, #13504)*;
- *Retina International (RI, #18926)*.

Ordinary member NGOs (10), listed in this Yearbook:
Association de recherche et de formation sur l'insertion en Europe (ARFIE, #02887); *Association internationale aphasie (AIA, #02668)*; *EIDD – Design for All Europe (#05399)*; *European Federation of Crohn's and Ulcerative Colitis Associations (EFCCA, #07095)*; *European Multiple Sclerosis Platform (EMSP, #07833)*; *European Paralympic Committee (EPC, #08140)*; *European Union of Supported Employment (EUSE, #09018)*; *International Association for the Arts, the Media and Creativity by and with Disabled People (EUCREA International, #11713)*; *Mental Health Europe (MHE, #16715)*; *Social Firms Europe (CEFEC, #19338)*.
Associate (47) in 22 countries:
Albania, Belgium, Bosnia-Herzegovina, Bulgaria, Croatia, France, Hungary, Ireland, Israel, Italy, Malta, Montenegro, Netherlands, North Macedonia, Norway, Poland, Serbia, Slovakia, Spain, Sweden, Switzerland, UK.
Included in the above, 15 organizations listed in this Yearbook:
Christian Blind Mission (CBM) (EU Liaison Office); *COFACE Families Europe (#04084)*; *European Federation of Hereditary Ataxias (Euro-ATAXIA, #07138)*; *European Guide Dog Federation (EGDF, #07440)*; *European Ostomy Association (EOA, #08120)*; *European Polio Union (EPU, #08246)*; *European Spinal Cord Injury Federation (ESCIF, #08815)*; *EuroPsy Rehabilitation (no recent information)*; *International Federation of Hard-of-Hearing Young People (IFHOHYP, #13436)*; *Leonard Cheshire Disability (#16443)*; *Nordic Handicap Federation (NHF, #17308)*; *The Dysmelia Network (DysNet, #05149)*.
Observer – national federations in 5 countries:
Albania, Croatia, North Macedonia, Serbia, Türkiye.
Sponsoring member in 1 country:
Netherlands.
Individuals (32) in 17 members:
Belgium, Congo DR, Croatia, Denmark, France, Germany, Greece, Ireland, Italy, Luxembourg, Netherlands, Portugal, Slovenia, Spain, Türkiye, UK, USA.
Consultative Status Consultative status granted from: *ECOSOC (#05331)*; *ILO (#11123)* (Special List); *Council of Europe (CE, #04881)* (Participatory Status). **IGO Relations** Member of: *European Economic and Social Committee (EESC, #06963)* Liaison Group with Civil Society. Participant in Fundamental Rights Platform of: *European Union Agency for Fundamental Rights (FRA, #08969)*. **NGO Relations** Social partners: *BUSINESSEUROPE (#03381)*; *European Trade Union Confederation (ETUC, #08927)*. Member of: *Civil Society Europe*; *EU Alliance for a democratic, social and sustainable European Semester (EU Semester Alliance, #05565)*; *European Policy Centre (EPC, #08240)*; *European Telecommunications Standards Institute (ETSI, #08897)*; *European Women's Lobby (EWL, #09102)*; *International Disability Alliance (IDA, #13176)*; *SDG Watch Europe (#19162)*; *Social Platform (#19344)*. Instrumental in setting up: *European Coalition for Community Living (ECCL, #06590)*. Represented in: *European Citizens' Mobility Forum (ECMF, #06559)*.
[2021/XF4532/y/**F**]

♦ European Disposables and Nonwovens Association / see EDANA, the voice of nonwovens (#05353)
♦ European Distance Education Network / see EDEN Digital Learning Europe (#05356)
♦ European Distance and E-Learning Network / see EDEN Digital Learning Europe (#05356)

♦ European Distributed Energy Resources Laboratories (DERlab) 06930

Secretariat Manager c/o Fraunhofer IEE, Königstor 59, 34119 Kassel, Germany. T. +495617294277. E-mail: office@der-lab.net.
URL: http://www.der-lab.net/
History Founded 2008, by 11 European laboratories. Registered in accordance with German law. **Aims** Develop joint requirements and quality criteria for the connection and operation of distributed energy resources (DER); support consistent development of DER technologies. **Structure** Board; Office located in Kassel (Germany). **Languages** English, German. **Activities** Research and development; training/education; guidance/assistance/consulting; events/meetings. **Publications** *DERlab Public Activity Report* (annual). Guides; technical White Books. **Information Services** *Database of DER and Smart Grid Research Infrastructure*; *Database of DER Interconnection Specifications*.
Members over 30 in 21 countries:
Austria, Belgium, Bulgaria, Cyprus, Czechia, Denmark, Finland, France, Germany, Greece, Ireland, Italy, Luxembourg, Netherlands, Poland, Portugal, Romania, Spain, Switzerland, UK, USA.
NGO Relations Technical Liaison Partner of: *European Committee for Electrotechnical Standardization (CENELEC, #06647)*.
[2020.03.03/XJ4948/**D**]

♦ European Distribution System Operators' Association for Smart Grids (EDSO) 06931

SG Rue de la Loi 82, 1040 Brussels, Belgium. T. +3227371340. E-mail: info@edsoforsmartgrids.eu.
URL: http://www.edsoforsmartgrids.eu/
History May 2010, Italy. Former names and other names: *ESDO for Smart Grids* – former. Registration: Banque-Carrefour des Entreprises, No/ID: 0825.054.581, Belgium. **Aims** Promote and enable customer empowerment and increase in the use of clean energy sources through electrification, development of smart and digital grid technologies in real-life situations, new market designs and regulation. **Structure** Assembly; Board of Directors; Executive Committee; Committees, Secretariat. **Languages** English. **Staff** 10.00 FTE, paid. **Finance** Sources: members' dues. Annual budget: 1,000,000 EUR. **Activities** Advocacy/lobbying/activism; events/meetings; knowledge management/information dissemination; politics/policy/regulatory; projects/programmes; research and development. **Events** *Projects in the Spotlight Event* 2022, *Global DSO Event* Brussels (Belgium) 2022, *InnoGrid Session* Brussels (Belgium) 2022, *Seminar on Cybersecurity* Brussels (Belgium) 2022, *Stakeholder and Innovation Council Seminar* Brussels (Belgium) 2021. **Publications** Reports; recommendations; position papers; guidance; videos; podcasts.
Members European Distribution System Operators (36); Associations (3). Members in 23 countries:
Austria, Belgium, Cyprus, Czechia, Finland, France, Germany, Greece, Hungary, Ireland, Italy, Latvia, Lithuania, Netherlands, Poland, Portugal, Romania, Slovakia, Slovenia, Spain, Sweden, UK, Ukraine.
[2022.05.10/XM4924/**D**]

♦ European Distributor Alliance Council / see Partner Community Council (#18228)

♦ European Diving Technology Committee (EDTC) 06932

Sec 83 Boundary Lane, St Leonards Ringwood, St Leonards, BH24 2SF, UK. T. +441202855648. Fax +441202897067. E-mail: secretary@adc-uk.info.
URL: http://www.edtc.org/
History Mar 1973, as the result of an initiative taken by the United Kingdom's Society for Underwater Technology (SUT). Registered in accordance with German law. **Aims** Increase safety of *professional* diving in Europe. **Structure** Executive Board, comprising Chairman, Vice-Chairman, Secretary/Treasurer and 3 members. Legal seat in Kiel (Germany). **Finance** None. **Events** *Meeting / Conference* Belgium 2012, *Meeting* Oslo (Norway) 2012, *Meeting* Marseille (France) 2011, *Meeting* Prague (Czech Rep) 2010, *Meeting* Copenhagen (Denmark) 2009.
Members Categories Medical; Industry; Government; Unions. Members in 19 countries:
Austria, Belgium, Croatia, Czechia, Denmark, Estonia, Finland, France, Germany, Italy, Netherlands, Norway, Poland, Portugal, Spain, Sweden, Switzerland, Türkiye, UK.
Included in the above, 4 organizations, listed in this Yearbook:
European Committee for Hyperbaric Medicine (ECHM, #06652); *IMCA International Marine Contractors Association (IMCA, #11127)*; *International Diving Schools Association (IDSA, #13183)*; *International Transport Workers' Federation (ITF, #15726)*.
Observer organizations in 3 countries:
Australia, Canada, South Africa.
Included in the above, 1 organization listed in this Yearbook:
European Underwater Federation (EUF, #08966).
[2013/XE4566/y/**E**]

♦ European DIY-Retail Association / see European DIY-Retail Association – Global Home Improvement Network (#06933)

♦ European DIY-Retail Association – Global Home Improvement Network (EDRA-GHIN) 06933

Gen Sec An der Rechtschule 1-3, 50667 Cologne, Germany. T. +4922127059555. Fax +4922127759579.
URL: http://www.edra-ghin.org/
History Apr 2002, Berlin (Germany), by French and Germany national DIY associations, as *European DIY-Retail Association (EDRA)*. 2010, became an independent organization. Current title adopted Jan 2016, Warsaw (Poland). EU Transparency Register: 897456530168-43. **Aims** Represent the interests of the European home improvement sector; improve quality of legislation for the DIY sector; provide a global network for member organizations. **Structure** Board; President; General Secretary. **Languages** English, French, German. **Staff** 5.00 FTE, paid. **Finance** Members' dues. **Activities** Networking/liaising; advocacy/lobbying/activism. **Events** *Global DIY Summit* Copenhagen (Denmark) 2022, *Virtual DIY Summit* 2021, *Global DIY Summit* Copenhagen (Denmark) 2021, *Global DIY Summit* Dublin (Ireland) 2019, *Global Summit* Barcelona (Spain) 2018. **Publications** *EDRA/GHIN Newsletter*. Annual brochure.
Members Full in 69 countries and territories:
Albania, Andorra, Argentina, Australia, Austria, Belarus, Belgium, Bosnia-Herzegovina, Botswana, Brazil, Bulgaria, Canada, Chile, China, Colombia, Croatia, Cyprus, Czechia, Denmark, Egypt, Estonia, Eswatini, Finland, France, Germany, Greece, Hungary, Iceland, Ireland, Italy, Japan, Kazakhstan, Latvia, Lesotho, Lithuania, Luxembourg, Madagascar, Malawi, Malta, Mexico, Morocco, Mozambique, Namibia, Netherlands, New Zealand, North Macedonia, Norway, Pakistan, Peru, Poland, Portugal, Romania, Russia, Serbia, Slovakia, Slovenia, South Africa, Spain, Sweden, Switzerland, Taiwan, Thailand, Türkiye, UK, Ukraine, Uruguay, USA, Vietnam, Zambia.
NGO Relations Member of: *EuroCommerce (EC, #05665)*.
[2018.10.09/XM2101/**D**]

♦ European DNA Profiling Group (EDNAP) 06934

Sec Dept of Forensic Medicine, Fac of Health and Medical Sciences, Univ of Copenhagen, 11 Frederik V's Vej, 2100 Copenhagen, Denmark. T. +4535326110. Fax +4535326270.
URL: http://www.isfg.org/EDNAP/
History 1988, London (UK). 1991, accepted as a working group of *International Society for Forensic Genetics (ISFG, #15128)*. **Aims** Harmonize *DNA technology* for *crime* investigation in Europe. **Structure** Secretary. **Languages** English. **Staff** None. **Finance** No budget. **Activities** Events/meetings; knowledge management/information dissemination; research/documentation. **Events** *Meeting* Innsbruck (Austria) 2018, *Meeting* Rome (Italy) 2018, *Meeting* Athens (Greece) 2017, *Meeting* Vilnius (Lithuania) 2017, *Meeting* Rome (Italy) 2016. **Publications** Books; reports.
Members Institutes in 16 countries:
Austria, Belgium, Denmark, Finland, France, Germany, Greece, Ireland, Italy, Netherlands, Norway, Portugal, Spain, Sweden, Switzerland, UK.
[2019.12.11/XE1808/**E**]

♦ European Doctoral Programmes Association in Management and Business Administration (EDAMBA) 06935

General Secretariat c/o EIASM, Passage du Nord 19, 1000 Brussels, Belgium. T. +3222266660 – +3222266661. Fax +3225121929.
URL: http://www.edamba.eu/
History May 1991, Stockholm (Sweden). **Aims** Promote and facilitate cooperation among doctoral programmes of *universities* and business schools in management and business administration by managing a network to exchange information, PhD candidates and promote research cooperation. **Structure** General Meeting (annual) of PhD directors or representatives of member schools. Executive Committee of 7. **Languages** English. **Finance** Self-financed. **Activities** Training/education; events/meetings. **Events** *Annual Meeting* Brussels (Belgium) 2022, *Annual Meeting* Brussels (Belgium) 2021, *Annual Meeting* Brussels (Belgium) 2020, *Annual Meeting* Oxford (UK) 2019, *Annual Meeting* Cologne (Germany) 2018. **Publications** *Book of Thesis Competition*; *EDAMBA Guide in Doctoral Programmes*. Proceedings of Annual Meeting and Supervisor's Workshops.
Members Universities and business schools (60) in 21 countries:
Austria, Croatia, Czechia, Denmark, Finland, France, Germany, Greece, Hungary, Ireland, Italy, Netherlands, Norway, Poland, Russia, Slovakia, Slovenia, South Africa, Spain, Sweden, UK.
NGO Relations Member of: *EFMD – The Management Development Network (#05387)*.
[2019/XD4157/**D**]

♦ European Doctors Orchestra (internationally oriented national body)

♦ European Documentary Network (EDN) 06936

Contact Herengracht 244, 1016 BT Amsterdam, Netherlands.
Registered Office Vognmagergade 10 – 1st Floor, 1120 Copenhagen K, Denmark. T. +4533131122. Fax +4533131144.
URL: https://edn.network/
History Jul 1996. Registration: EU Transparency Register, No/ID: 918627716960-50. **Aims** Inform members about possibilities for documentary coproduction and other kinds of collaboration across the borders; strengthen networking among documentary professionals worldwide. **Structure** General Assembly; Executive Committee. **Languages** English. **Staff** 6.00 FTE, paid. **Finance** Members' dues. Other sources: support from Danish Film Institute. Activities financed by various sources. **Activities** Guidance/assistance/consulting; networking/liaising; events/meetings. **Events** *General Assembly* Amsterdam (Netherlands) 2015, *General Assembly* Copenhagen (Denmark) 2015, *General Assembly* Amsterdam (Netherlands) 2014, *General Assembly* Amsterdam (Netherlands) 2013, *General Assembly* Amsterdam (Netherlands) 2012. **Publications** *EDN Financing Guide Documentaries* (annual); *EDN Newsletter*. **Members** Film makers; producers; production companies; distributors, associations; film institutions and boards; universities and festivals; broadcasters and film and television agencies. Members (nearly 1,000) in over 60 countries. Membership countries not specified.
[2017/XF4894/y/**F**]

♦ European Documentation Centre / see Institute for European Studies, Malta

♦ European Documentation Centres (EDC Network) 06937

Centres de documentation européenne (Réseau CDE) – Europese Documentatiecentra (RDC Netwerk)
Contact address not obtained. Fax +3222980401.
URL: https://european-union.europa.eu/contact-eu/meet-us_en

History 1963. Established by *European Commission (EC, #06633)*. **Aims** Help universities and research institutes promote and develop education and research on European integration; encourage them to take part in the debate on Europe; help ordinary citizens learn about the Union's policies.
Members Documentation centres (400) in universities, research centres and libraries in 26 member countries of the European Union:
Austria, Belgium, Bulgaria, Cyprus, Czechia, Denmark, Estonia, Finland, France, Germany, Greece, Hungary, Ireland, Italy, Latvia, Lithuania, Malta, Netherlands, Poland, Portugal, Romania, Slovakia, Slovenia, Spain, Sweden, UK.
[2011.06.01/XF6582/**F**]

♦ European Documentation Centre, University of Navarra / see Centre for European Studies – University of Navarra
♦ European Documentation and Research Centre, Valletta / see Institute for European Studies, Malta

♦ European Domestic Glass (EDG) 06938

Deputy SG Av Louise 89 – Bte 5, 1050 Brussels, Belgium. T. +3225384449. Fax +3225378469.
History 1966, UK. Former names and other names: *European Domestic Glass Group* – former; *European Domestic Glass Committee (EDG)* – former; *Comité européen du verre domestique* – former. Registration: EU Transparency Register, No/ID: 733257915694-82; Belgium. **Aims** Provide a forum for manufacturers and others concerned in the pan-European domestic glassware industry. **Languages** English. **Staff** 1.00 FTE, paid. **Activities** Knowledge management/information dissemination; events/meetings. **Events** *Conference* Kosta (Sweden) 2014, *Conference* Arques (France) 2012, *Conference / Biennial Conference* Istanbul (Turkey) 2008, *Conference / Biennial Conference* Deggendorf (Germany) 2005, *Conference / Biennial Conference* Lisbon (Portugal) 2002.
Members Trade association, manufacturers and associated industries, and multinational companies in 9 countries:
Austria, Bulgaria, Czechia, France, Germany, Ireland, Italy, Slovenia, Türkiye.
NGO Relations Member of: *AEGIS Europe*; *Glass Alliance Europe (#10156)*; *Industry4Europe (#11181)*.
[2019/XD7047/**D**]

♦ European Domestic Glass Committee / see European Domestic Glass (#06938)
♦ European Domestic Glass Group / see European Domestic Glass (#06938)

♦ European Donation and Transplant Coordination Organisation (EDTCO) 06939

Contact Carrer Joan Maragall 12, 08360 Canet de Mar, Barcelona, Spain. T. +34937942658. Fax +34937942658. E-mail: etco-edc@esot.org.
URL: https://www.esot.org/EDTCO/home
History 1982, as *European Transplant Coordinators Organization (ETCO)*. Previously also referred to as *European Foundation for Transplant Coordinators*. Current title adopted following merger with European Donation Committee, a section of *European Society for Organ Transplantation (ESOT, #08676)*, Sep 2011. Registered in accordance with Dutch law, 1983. **Aims** Support health care professionals to provide clinically effective programmes on organ and tissue donation, procurement and transplantation. **Structure** Congress (every 2 years). Conference of Members (annual). Executive Council, comprising President, Vice President, Treasurer, Secretary and 3 Councillors. Administrative Council, consisting of Committee Chairmen and one national key member per country. *'Standing Committees'* (4): Certification; Web Page and Journal; National Key Member; Education. Extra Standing Committees (5): New Members/New Areas; Legal and Ethical; Tissues; Quality; Clinical Coordinators. Congress and Meetings Committees (3): Local Organizing; Scientific Programme; Congress and Fundraising. **Languages** English. **Staff** 0.50 FTE, paid. **Finance** Members' dues. Other sources: financial support from associations and companies. **Activities** Events/meetings; training/education. **Events** *Biennial Congress* Berlin (Germany) 2009, *Annual meeting* Latvia 2008, *Biennial Congress* Prague (Czech Rep) 2007, *Annual meeting* Wroclaw (Poland) 2006, *Biennial congress / Annual Meeting* Geneva (Switzerland) 2005. **Publications** *ETCO News* (3 a year); *Organs and Tissues* – journal.
Members Ordinary; Corresponding; Honorary; Sponsors; Institutional. Individuals in 42 countries:
Argentina, Armenia, Australia, Austria, Belgium, Brazil, Bulgaria, Canada, Costa Rica, Croatia, Czechia, Denmark, Estonia, Finland, France, Georgia, Germany, Greece, Hungary, Indonesia, Israel, Italy, Japan, Kazakhstan, Kuwait, Latvia, Lebanon, Lithuania, Luxembourg, Malta, Mexico, Moldova, Netherlands, Norway, Poland, Portugal, Romania, Serbia, South Africa, Tunisia, Türkiye, Ukraine.
Associate members in 6 countries and territories:
Australia, Hong Kong, Israel, Japan, USA, Venezuela.
IGO Relations Health division of: *Council of Europe (CE, #04881)*. **NGO Relations** Cooperates with: *European Shock Society, The (ESS, #08480)*. European and Scandinavian organ exchange organizations: *European Homograft Bank (EHB, #07498)*; *Scandiatransplant Association (#19066)*. Other regional and international organizations: *Asia Pacific Association of Surgical Tissue Banking (APASTB, #01854)*; *European Renal Association – European Dialysis and Transplant Association (ERA-EDTA, #08353)*; *International Society for Heart and Lung Transplantation (ISHLT, #15157)*; *International Transplant Nurses Society (ITNS)*; *Middle East Society for Organ Transplantation (MESOT, #16790)*; *The Transplantation Society (TTS, #20224)*.
[2017/XD1896/v/**D**]

♦ European Door and Shutter Federation (EDSF) 06940

Contact Neumarktstrasse 2 b, 58095 Hagen, Germany. T. +49233120080. Fax +492331200840. E-mail: info@edsf.com.
URL: http://www.edsf.com/
History 1985. **Aims** Educate about door products; distribute product information and industry best practices for installation, use, service and maintenance; speak for the interest of European manufacturers to relevant institutions/organizations; further advance of EU standards worldwide. **Structure** General Assembly; Board. **Languages** English. **Activities** Monitoring/evaluation; events/meetings. **Events** *General Assembly* Plovdiv (Bulgaria) 2019, *Door Forum* Munich (Germany) 2015, *General Assembly* Verona (Italy) 2014, *General Assembly* Prague (Czech Rep) 2013, *General Assembly* Madrid (Spain) 2011.
Members Organizations; Manufacturers. Members in 13 countries:
Austria, Bulgaria, Czechia, Denmark, Finland, France, Germany, Italy, Netherlands, Poland, Spain, Sweden, Switzerland.
[2020.03.16/XD3502/**D**]

♦ European Down and Feather Association (EDFA) 06941

CEO Thomas-Mann-Strasse 9, 55122 Mainz, Germany. T. +496131588560. E-mail: info@edfa.eu.
Pres 2 Westcliffe Road, Ruskington, NG34 9AY, UK. T. +447740281203.
URL: http://www.edfa.eu/
History Founded 1982. Previously referred to as *Association of European Bedfeather and Bedding Industries – Association européenne des industries de plumes et articles de literie – Verband der Europäischen Bettfedern- und Bettwarenindustrie*. **Aims** Promote the interests of the European bedfeather and bedding industry. **Structure** Board.
Members National organizations (19) in 13 countries:
Austria, Denmark, Finland, France, Germany, Ireland, Italy, Netherlands, Poland, Russia, Spain, Switzerland, UK.
[2013/XD2963/**D**]

♦ European Down Syndrome Association (EDSA) 06942

Association européenne pour le syndrome de Down
Pres Mundo Madou, Av des Arts 7-8, 1210 Brussels, Belgium. E-mail: info@edsa.eu.
Treas address not obtained.
URL: http://www.edsa.eu/
History Founded Nov 1987, Verviers (Belgium). Registered in accordance with Belgian law. **Aims** Promote development of a network of associations for Down syndrome, in all European nations, respecting the diversity of cultures and peoples, the common denominator being the improvement of the quality of life for persons with Down syndrome and their families. **Structure** General Assembly (every 3 years); Board. **Languages** English. **Staff** None. **Finance** Members' dues. **Activities** Awareness raising; advocacy/lobbying/activism; guidance/assistance/consulting; networking/liaising. **Events** *Congress* Istanbul (Turkey) 2016, *World congress* Dublin (Ireland) 2009, *European Conference* Sarajevo (Bosnia-Herzegovina) 2009, *World Congress* Palma (Spain) 2005, *World Congress* Durban (South Africa) 2004. **Publications** *EDSA Newsletter* (12 a year).
Members Organizations (36) in 32 countries:
Albania, Austria, Belgium, Bosnia-Herzegovina, Croatia, Cyprus, Czechia, Denmark, France, Germany, Greece, Hungary, Iceland, Ireland, Italy, Kosovo, Luxembourg, Malta, Morocco, Netherlands, North Macedonia, Poland, Portugal, Romania, Russia, Slovenia, Spain, Sweden, Switzerland, Türkiye, UK, Ukraine.
NGO Relations Member of: *Down Syndrome International (DSi, #05128)*; *European Disability Forum (EDF, #06929)*.
[2022/XD1837/**D**]

♦ European Dragon Boat Federation (EDBF) 06943

SG Lisnavagh, Rathvilly, CO. CARLOW, Ireland. E-mail: secretary@edbf.org.
URL: http://www.edbf.org/
History 5 May 1990, Mechelen (Belgium). **Aims** Develop the sport of dragon boat racing in its modern era; ensure that festival based dragon boating retains its traditions and remains a sport and recreation to be enjoyed at all levels, by as many people as possible. **Structure** Executive Committee; Commissions (5). **Languages** English. **Staff** 8.00 FTE, voluntary. **Finance** Sources: meeting proceeds; members' dues. **Activities** Sporting activities. **Events** *Annual General Assembly* Murcia (Spain) 2014, *Annual General Assembly* Amsterdam (Netherlands) 2009, *Annual General Assembly* Budapest (Hungary) 2008, *Annual General Assembly* Kiev (Ukraine) 2006.
Members Full in 21 countries:
Armenia, Austria, Cyprus, Czechia, France, Germany, Hungary, Ireland, Italy, Moldova, Netherlands, Norway, Poland, Russia, Serbia, Slovakia, Spain, Sweden, Switzerland, UK, Ukraine.
Temporary in 4 countries:
Albania, Georgia, Israel, Lithuania.
[2021.09.16/XD9448/**D**]

♦ European Drama Encounters (internationally oriented national body)

♦ European Draught Horse Federation 06944

Fédération Européenne du Cheval de Trait pour la promotion de son Utilisation (FECTU)
Pres Haaptstrooss 21, L-7475 Schoos, Luxembourg. E-mail: info@fectu.org.
URL: http://www.fectu.org/
History 1 Nov 2003. Registered in accordance with Luxembourg law. **Aims** Encourage cooperation between organizations involved in promotion and advancement of the working heavy horse and other draught animals. **Structure** General Meeting (annual); Board. **Languages** English, French, German. **Finance** Members' dues. **Publications** *Draught Animal News*; *FECTU-INFO* – newsletter.
Members National associations or clubs (20) in 14 countries:
Austria, Belgium, Denmark, Finland, France, Germany, Luxembourg, Norway, Poland, Portugal, Spain, Sweden, Switzerland, UK.
NGO Relations Member of: *European Horse Network (EHN, #07499)*; *TP Organics – European Technology Platform (TP Organics, #20180)*.
[2022/XM4016/y/**D**]

♦ European Draughts Confederation (EDC) 06945

Pres Largo Lauro de Bosis 15, c/o FID – CONI, 00135 Rome RM, Italy. E-mail: information@europedraughts.org.
URL: http://europedraughts.org/
History 13 Aug 1988, Tallinn (Estonia). Statutes adopted May 2003; amended: Aug 2005; Nov 2007; 9 Oct 2021. **Aims** Unite people of various nationalities wishing to promote draughts; promote draughts in European countries and as a sport among young people; coordinate and stimulate activities of draughts clubs. **Structure** General Assembly; Executive Board. **Activities** Advocacy/lobbying/activism; awards/prizes/competitions; networking/liaising.
Members Federations in 28 countries and territories:
Armenia, Azerbaijan, Belarus, Belgium, Bulgaria, Croatia, Cyprus, Czechia, England, Estonia, France, Georgia, Germany, Hungary, Israel, Italy, Latvia, Lithuania, Moldova, Netherlands, Poland, Portugal, Russia, Slovenia, Switzerland, Türkiye, Ukraine, Wales.
NGO Relations Continental federation of: *Fédération Mondiale du Jeu de Dames (FMJD, #09690)*.
[2021.09.02/AA1110/**D**]

♦ European Dredging Association (EuDA) 06946

Association européenne de dragage
SG Av Grandchamp 148, 1150 Brussels, Belgium. T. +3226468183. Fax +3226466063. E-mail: info@euda.be.
Chairman address not obtained.
URL: http://www.european-dredging.info/
History 6 Dec 1993. Registration: Banque-Carrefour des Entreprises, No/ID: 0451.688.517, Start date: 16 Dec 1993; EU Transparency Register, No/ID: 2492574893-58, Start date: 30 Dec 2008. **Aims** Act as the voice of the European dredging industry and represent its interests with European institutions. **Structure** Annual General Meeting; Board of Directors; International Secretariat. Committees (3): Social; Environmental; Market Access. **Languages** Dutch, English, French. **Staff** 1.50 FTE, paid. **Finance** Sources: members' dues. **Activities** Events/meetings; knowledge management/information dissemination; politics/policy/regulatory; research and development. **Events** *Annual Conference* Brussels (Belgium) 2022, *Annual Conference* Brussels (Belgium) 2019, *Annual Conference* Brussels (Belgium) 2018, *Annual Meeting* Brussels (Belgium) 2017, *Annual Meeting* Brussels (Belgium) 2016. **Publications** *EuDa news*. Annual Report; studies; position papers; brochures.
Members Leading European dredging companies and their national federations in 7 countries:
Belgium, Denmark, Germany, Ireland, Italy, Netherlands, UK.
IGO Relations Links with various European institutions, including: European Sustainable Shipping Forum (ESSF) of *European Commission (EC, #06633)*. Observer to: *Baltic Marine Environment Protection Commission – Helsinki Commission (HELCOM, #03126)*. **NGO Relations** Member of (3): *Federation of European and International Associations Established in Belgium (FAIB, #09508)*; *International Chamber of Shipping (ICS, #12535)* (Associate); *WATERBORNE (#20823)*. Sister organizations: *Central Dredging Association (CEDA, #03688)*; *International Association of Dredging Companies (IADC, #11852)*; *PIANC (#18371)*.
[2022/XD4370/**D**]

♦ European Drinking Water Cooler Association (internationally oriented national body)
♦ European Driving Schools Association (#09560)

♦ European Drought Centre (EDC) 06947

Coordinator Hydrology and Qantitative Water Management Group, Wageningen Univ, PO Box 47, 6700 AA Wageningen, Netherlands. T. +31683596767. Fax +31317419000.
Coordinator Dept of Geosciences, Univ of Oslo, PO Box 1047, Blindern, 0316 Oslo, Norway. T. +4722857214. Fax +4722854215.
URL: http://europeandroughtcentre.com/
History May 2004, Bratislava (Slovakia), during a joint meeting of *FRIEND/Alpine and Mediterranean Hydrology (FRIEND/AMHY, see: #13826)* and *FRIEND/Northern European (see: #13826)*. A virtual centre of expert groups and organizations in Europe. **Aims** Promote collaboration and capacity building between drought scientists and the user community; enhance European cooperation on drought research and drought management in order to mitigate the impacts of drought on society, economy and the environment. **Structure** 2 Coordinators. Core Group of 8 members and webmaster. Network Groups. **Activities** Disseminates information or provides access to information. Network Group on Training. **Events** *International Conference on Drought* Valencia (Spain) 2015. **Publications** *Hydrological Drought – Processes and Estimation Methods for Streamflow and Groundwater – Development in Water Science* (2004).
Members Individuals in 17 countries:
Austria, Canada, Czechia, Ethiopia, France, Netherlands, Nigeria, Norway, Poland, Russia, Saudi Arabia, Slovakia, Spain, Türkiye, UK, Ukraine, USA.
Individuals whose membership is under consideration in 22 countries:
Algeria, Argentina, Bulgaria, Cuba, Denmark, Egypt, Germany, Greece, Hungary, Indonesia, Iran Islamic Rep, Italy, Malaysia, Morocco, Nepal, New Zealand, Palestine, Portugal, Romania, Serbia, South Africa, Sweden.
IGO Relations Formal links with: *UNESCO (#20322)*. Takes part in discussion group on drought of *United Nations Office for Disaster Risk Reduction (UNDRR, #20595)*.
[2019/XM0926/v/**E**]

♦ European Druggists' Confederation (inactive)

♦ European Drug Utilization Research Group (EURODURG) 06948

Sec Dept of Clinical Pharmacy, Univ of Szeged, Szikra utca 8, Szeged 6725, Hungary. T. +3662342572.

Chair Strathclyde Inst of Pharmacy and Biomedical Sciences, Univ of Strathclyde, Room 501a Robertson Wing, Taylor Street, Glasgow, G4 0NR, UK. T. +441415482113. Fax +441415522562.

URL: http://www.pharmacoepi.org/eurodurg/

History 1 Sep 1994, Huddinge (Sweden), on approval of draft constitution. Constitution accepted by General Assembly, 30 Jun 1996, Balatonvilagos (Hungary), at 1st Congress. Since 2010 serves as European chapter of the Special Interest Group within *International Society for Pharmacoepidemiology (ISPE, #15355)*. **Aims** Provide a forum for open exchange of scientific information and development of policy, education and advocacy for the field of pharmacoepidemiology, including pharmacovigilance, drug utilization research, outcomes research, comparative effectiveness research and therapeutic risk management. **Structure** General Assembly (every 2 years, normally at a scientific meeting); Executive Committee; Working Groups (5). **Languages** English. **Staff** Voluntary. **Finance** Financial support from: *International Society for Pharmacoepidemiology (ISPE, #15355)*. **Activities** Events/meetings; training/education; projects/programmes. **Events** *Conference* Szeged (Hungary) 2020, *Conference* Edinburgh (UK) 2017, *Conference* Milan (Italy) 2016, *Conference* Groningen (Netherlands) 2014, *Conference* Antwerp (Belgium) 2011. **Publications** *EURODURG Bulletin* (annual). *Drug Utilisation Research: methods and applications* (2016).

Members National groups in 21 countries:

Armenia, Austria, Belgium, Croatia, Czechia, Denmark, Estonia, France, Germany, Greece, Hungary, Italy, Kosovo, Lithuania, Norway, Portugal, Russia, Slovakia, Spain, Sweden, UK.

IGO Relations Formal contacts with: *WHO (#20950)* Collaborating Center for Drug Statistics Methodology.

[2019.12.14/XD5582/**E**]

♦ European Dry Eye Society (EuDES) 06949

SG address not obtained.

URL: https://www.dryeye-society.com/

History 3 Nov 2020. **Aims** Attend to the unmet needs of dry eye patients in Europe. **Structure** Bureau; Executive Committee. **Activities** Events/meetings. **Events** *Meeting* Munich (Germany) 2023.

[2022/AA2966/**D**]

♦ European DX Council (EDXC) 06950

SG address not obtained.

URL: http://edxcnews.wordpress.com/

History 1967, Copenhagen (Denmark). Also referred to as *Association of Shortwave-Listeners and DX Organizations in Europe*. **Aims** Promote goodwill and closer cooperation between DX – *long-distance radio* – clubs and organizations and promotę DX-ing in Europe; improve contacts between DX *listeners* and *radio stations*. **Structure** Board of Deputies. **Languages** English. **Staff** 1.00 FTE, voluntary. **Finance** Members' dues. **Events** *Annual Conference* Escaldes-Engordany (Andorra) 2019, *Annual Conference* Bratislava (Slovakia) / Vienna (Austria) 2018, *Annual Conference* Tampere (Finland) 2017, *Annual Conference* Manchester (UK) 2016, *Annual Conference* St Petersburg (Russia) 2015. **Publications** *Club List* (annual); *Radio Countries List*. Reporting guide.

Members Full in 10 countries:

Denmark, Finland, Germany, Hungary, Ireland, Italy, Russia, Spain, Sweden, UK.

Included in the above, 1 organization listed in this Yearbook:

Worldwide DX Club.

Observer clubs in 2 countries:

Germany, USA.

[2019.02.13/XD4257/**E**]

♦ European Dyslexia Association – International Organisation for Specific Learning Disabilities (EDA) 06951

Pres 61 Compass Court North, Royal Canal Park, Ashtown, D15E657, Dublin, CO. DUBLIN, Ireland. E-mail: chair@eda-info.eu – eda-info@eda-info.eu.

Registered Address c/o Bureau Felix and Felix sprl, Chée de Tubize 135, 1440 Braine-le-Château, Belgium.

URL: http://www.eda-info.eu/

History 18 Oct 1987. Took over resources and materials of *Dyslexia and Literacy International (inactive)*, 2020. Registration: Banque-Carrefour des Entreprises, No/ID: 0432.894.271, Start date: 4 Jan 1988, Belgium; EU Transparency Register, No/ID: 225738324922-97, Start date: 5 Dec 2016. **Aims** Be the voice of people with dyslexia, dyscalculia and other co-occurring specific learning difficulties. **Structure** General Assembly (at least annually); Board of Directors. **Languages** English, French, German. **Staff** Voluntary. **Finance** Sources: meeting proceeds; members' dues; revenue from activities/projects. Supported by: *European Union (EU, #08967)*. Annual budget: 10,000 EUR. **Activities** Advocacy/lobbying/activism; awareness raising; knowledge management/information dissemination; networking/liaising. **Events** *General Assembly* 2022, *Dyslexia@Work Conference* Brussels (Belgium) 2022, *General Assembly* 2021, *General Assembly* Växjö (Sweden) 2019, *All-European Dyslexia Conference* Modena (Italy) 2016. **Publications** *Guidance Criteria for Education of Professionals and Teachers Working with Persons with Dyslexia* (2013); *The EDA Questionnaire: The Rights of the Dyslexic Child* (2004); *The International Book of Dyslexia* (1997); *Dyslexia – Primary School Provision in Europe* (1995); *Early Recognition Report* (1993).

Members Organizations (43) in 25 countries:

Austria, Belgium, Czechia, Denmark, Finland, France, Germany, Greece, Ireland, Israel, Italy, Lithuania, Luxembourg, Malta, Netherlands, Norway, Poland, Romania, San Marino, Slovenia, Spain, Sweden, Switzerland, Türkiye, UK.

Consultative Status Consultative status granted from: *UNESCO (#20322)* (Consultative Status).

[2022.10.19/XD1038/**D**]

♦ European Dystonia Federation / see Dystonia Europe (#05151)

♦ European Early Childhood Education Research Association (EECERA) 06952

Contact c/o CREC, St Thomas Children's Ctr, Bell Barn Road, Attwood Green, Birmingham, B15 2AF, UK. T. +441214640020. E-mail: enquiries@eecera.org.

URL: http://www.eecera.org/

History 1990. **Aims** Promote and disseminate multi-disciplinary research on early childhood and its applications to policy and practice. **Structure** Board of Trustees. **Languages** English. **Activities** Events/meetings; publishing activities. **Events** *Annual Conference* Zagreb (Croatia) 2021, *Annual Conference* Zagreb (Croatia) 2020, *Annual Conference* Athens (Greece) 2019, *Multilingual Childhoods International Research Conference* Hamar (Norway) 2019, *Annual Conference* Budapest (Hungary) 2018. **Publications** *European Early Childhood Education Research Journal (EECERJ)* (6 a year). **Members** Individuals (282) from 35 countries. Membership countries not specified. **NGO Relations** *Pacific Early Childhood Education Research Association (PECERA, #17946)*.

[2017.11.23/XM4587/**D**]

♦ European Early Music Network (EEMN) 06953

Réseau Européen de la Musique Ancienne (REMA)

Exec Sec c/o CMBV, 22 av de Paris, BP 20353, 78003 Versailles CEDEX, France. E-mail: info@rema-eemn.net.

URL: http://www.rema-eemn.net/

History 2000, France. Registration: France. **Aims** Promote Early Music and help raise its profile in Europe. **Structure** General Assembly (annual); Executive Committee; Board. **Languages** English, French. **Staff** 2.00 FTE, paid. **Finance** Sources: members' dues. Supported by: *European Commission (EC, #06633)*; French Ministry for Culture. Annual budget: 100,000 EUR. **Activities** Events/meetings; knowledge management/information dissemination. **NGO Relations** Member of (4): *European Alliance for Culture and the Arts (#05866)*; *European Music Council (EMC, #07837)*; *International Music Council (IMC, #14199)*; *Pearle – Live Performance Europe (#18284)* (Associate member).

[2022.02.09/XJ4451/**F**]

♦ European Ecocycles Society (ECOCYCLES) 06954

Európai Ökociklus Társaság

Main Office Matrai ut 36, Gyöngyös 3200, Hungary. E-mail: info@ecocycles.net.

URL: https://www.ecocycles.net/

Aims Promote knowledge concerning *ecological* cycles and further its development; facilitate collaboration; create a platform for students and scientists; encourage collaboration with other areas related to environmental and health issues. **Structure** Committee. **Finance** Members' dues. **Activities** Events/meetings. **Publications** *ECOCYCLES* – journal. **NGO Relations** *Observatory on Tourism in the European Islands (OTIE, #17645)*.

[2020/XM6218/**D**]

♦ European ECO Forum 06955

Co-Chair c/o EEB, Bvd de Waterloo 34, 1000 Brussels, Belgium. T. +3222891090. Fax +3222891099.

Co-Chair ECO Accord, PO Box 43, Moscow MOSKVA, Russia, 129090.

URL: http://www.eco-forum.org/

History Sep 1993, Bratislava (Slovakia), as an NGO working group *Environment for Europe*. **Aims** Improve and broaden pan-European *NGO* networks and coalitions and enhance their involvement and the legitimization of their contribution towards *protection* of *nature* and the *environment*. **Structure** Coordination Board. **Activities** Conference Issue Groups (6): Biodiversity; Environmental Action Programme for Central and Eastern Europe; Energy and Climate; Transport; Consumption and Production Patterns; Public Participation. **Events** *Meeting* Aarhus (Denmark) 1998, *NGO environmental conference* Aarhus (Denmark) 1998, *Meeting* Brussels (Belgium) 1996, *Meeting* Groznjan (Croatia) 1995. **Publications** *ECO Forum Newsletter* (irregular). **Members** Contact NGOs (200). Membership countries not specified. **NGO Relations** Member of: *EarthAction (EA, #05159)*.

[2019/XF4967/**F**]

♦ European Ecological Centre – Terre vivante (internationally oriented national body)

♦ European Ecological Federation (EEF) 06956

Contact Dept Community Ecology, Helmholtz Centre for Environmental Research – UFZ, Theodor-Lieser-Strasse 4, 06120 Halle (Saale), Germany. T. +49345558-5313. Fax +49345558-5329.

URL: http://www.europeanecology.org/

History Sep 1989, Siena (Italy). **Aims** Enable cooperation between European ecological societies so as to promote the science of ecology in Europe. **Structure** Council elects Executive Board, comprising President, 2 Vice-Presidents, General Secretary, Meetings Coordinator and 3 further members. **Languages** English. **Staff** through member organization. **Finance** Members' contributions. Budget (annual): about euro 2,000. **Activities** Events/meetings; awards/prizes/competitions. **Events** *Triennial Congress* Lisbon (Portugal) 2019, *Triennial Congress* Rome (Italy) 2015, *Triennial Congress* Avila (Spain) 2011, *Triennial Congress* Leipzig (Germany) 2008, *Triennial Congress* Izmir (Turkey) 2005. **Publications** *Web-ecology* – electronic journal.

Members National organizations in 20 countries:

Austria, Belgium, Czechia, Estonia, France, Germany, Greece, Hungary, Netherlands, North Macedonia, Norway, Poland, Portugal, Romania, Slovakia, Spain, Sweden, Switzerland, Türkiye, UK.

Included in the above, 1 organization listed in this Yearbook:

Nordic Society Oikos (NSO, #17423).

NGO Relations Affiliated with: *International Association for Ecology (INTECOL, #11856)*. [2018/XD2230/**D**]

♦ European eCommerce and Omni-Channel Trade Association (inactive)

♦ European Economic Area (EEA) 06957

Espace économique européen (EEE) – Espacio Económico Europeo (EEE)

Contact c/o EFTA, Rue Joseph II 12-16, 1000 Brussels, Belgium. T. +3222861711. Fax +3222861750. E-mail: mail.bxl@efta.int.

URL: http://www.efta.int/eea/

History 2 May 1992, Porto (Portugal), on signature of an Agreement between the *European Community (inactive)* and the member countries of *EFTA (#05391)*. Entered into force on 1 Jan 1994, for 5 countries on EFTA side (Sweden, Finland, Austria, Norway and Iceland) and the then 12 EU member states. For Liechtenstein, EEA Agreement entered into force on 1 May 1995. Switzerland remains outside following a referendum, Dec 1992. Sweden, Finland and Austria transferred from EFTA to the *European Union (EU, #08967)* on 1 Jan 1995. Cyprus, Czech Rep, Estonia, Hungary, Latvia, Lithuania, Malta, Poland, Slovakia and Slovenia joined 1 May 2004. Bulgaria and Romania joined 2007. Croatia joined 2014. EEA now consists of the 28 EU member states together with Iceland, Liechtenstein and Norway. It extends the *EU Customs Union (#05579)* single market to the 3 participating EFTA / EEA countries. **Aims** Promote a continuous and balanced strengthening of *trade* and economic relations between the Contracting Parties so as to create a homogenous European Economic Area. **Structure** EEA institutions ensure that EEA rules are observed and enforced and that EEA remains a homogenous economic area. Political direction is provided by *EEA Council (#05379)*, which meets twice a year. *EEA Joint Committee (#05381)* comprises representatives of EU and EFTA states. It is responsible for implementation and effective operation of the EEA Agreement and meets once a month at the senior official level. *EEA Consultative Committee (EEA CC, #05378)* works to strengthen contacts between social partners in European Union and EFTA states. *EEA Joint Parliamentary Committee (EEA JPC, #05382)* provides an opportunity for debate and dialogue between the EFTA Parliamentary Committee and *European Parliament (EP, #08146)*. *European Commission (EC, #06633)* and *EFTA Surveillance Authority (ESA, #05392)* carry out surveillance of implementation of the EEA Agreement. *EFTA Court (#05390)* and *Court of Justice of the European Union (CJEU, #04938)* provide judicial control. **Languages** English. **Staff** About 100 at secretariat, of whom one-third are based in Geneva (Switzerland) and two-thirds in Brussels (Belgium) and Luxembourg (Luxembourg). **Finance** Budget divided between operational and administrative costs, to which states contribute. Operational expenditure is total EU programme budget less administrative expenditure. Budget comprises commitments and payments. **Activities** Extends the EC Internal Market to the 3 participating EFTA countries. EEA Agreement includes harmonized legislation for the 4 freedoms: free movement of goods, services, capital and persons. However, it does not cover all EU policy areas such as Common Agriculture policy, Common Fisheries policy, Foreign and Security policy or Justice and Home Affairs. In order to ensure equal conditions for business throughout the Internal Market, the EEA contains competition and state aid-rules. It also includes horizontal provisions relevant to the 4 freedoms, as well as cooperation outside the 4 freedoms through the participation of the EEA EFTA States in some EU programmes and agencies. EEA EFTA States promote social cohesion within the EEA by providing financial assistance to environment, transport, cultural heritage and education projects through the Financial Mechanism Office. Organizes EFTA Seminar (twice a year in the spring and fall, in Brussels) on the EEA. **Events** *Meeting* Prague (Czechia) 2017, *Meeting* Vaduz (Liechtenstein) 2016, *Meeting* Zagreb (Croatia) 2015, *Meeting* Oslo (Norway) 2014, *Meeting* Rovaniemi (Finland) 2013. **Publications** Annual Report; EEA Supplement.

Members Governments of 31 countries:

Austria, Belgium, Bulgaria, Croatia, Cyprus, Czechia, Denmark, Estonia, Finland, France, Germany, Greece, Hungary, Iceland, Ireland, Italy, Latvia, Liechtenstein, Lithuania, Luxembourg, Malta, Netherlands, Norway, Poland, Portugal, Romania, Slovakia, Slovenia, Spain, Sweden, UK.

IGO Relations *Council of the European Union (#04895)*. [2019/XF0847/**F***]

♦ European Economic Area Joint Parliamentary Committee / see EEA Joint Parliamentary Committee (#05382)

♦ European Economic Association (EEA) 06958

Association européenne d'économie

Gen Manager address not obtained.

URL: http://www.eeassoc.org/

History 1985. Founded on circulation of invitation to join as founding member, following meeting, Dec 1984. Statutes adopted 30 Aug 1986, Vienna (Austria), at 1st General Assembly. Registration: Belgium. **Aims** Contribute to development and application of economics as a science in Europe; improve communication and exchange between teachers, researchers and students in economics in different European countries; develop and sponsor cooperation between teaching institutions of university level and research institutions in Europe. **Structure** General Assembly (annual, at Congress); Council; Executive Committee. **Languages** English. **Staff** 1.00 FTE, paid. **Finance** Members' dues. Support of Institutional Members. **Activities** Events/meetings; awards/prizes/competitions. **Events** *Congress* Barcelona (Spain) 2023, *Congress* Milan (Italy) 2022, *Annual Congress* 2021, *Annual Congress* Rotterdam (Netherlands) 2020, *Annual Congress* Manchester (UK) 2019. **Publications** *Journal of the European Economic Association (JEEA)*. **Information Services** *Directory of Economists* – online database.

Members Individuals in 50 countries and territories:

Armenia, Australia, Austria, Belgium, Brazil, Bulgaria, Canada, Chile, China, Congo Brazzaville, Cyprus, Czechia, Denmark, Estonia, Finland, France, Germany, Greece, Hong Kong, Hungary, Iceland, Ireland, Israel, Italy, Japan, Korea Rep, Latvia, Lebanon, Lithuania, Luxembourg, Netherlands, Nigeria, Norway, Peru, Poland, Portugal, Romania, Russia, Serbia, Singapore, Slovenia, South Africa, Spain, Sweden, Switzerland, Taiwan, Türkiye, UK, Ukraine, USA.

IGO Relations *European Commission (EC, #06633).* **NGO Relations** Collaborates with a number of European associations specialized in the field of economics, including: *Econometric Society (ES, #05310).*

[2022/XD0483/v/**D**]

♦ European Economic Association for Foreign Trade (inactive)

♦ European Economic Chamber of Trade, Commerce and Industry . . . 06959

Chambre économique européenne de commerce, d'artisanat et d'industrie – Europäische Wirtschaftskammer für Handel, Gewerbe und Industrie

Chairman/CEO Square de Meeus 37, 1000 Brussels, Belgium. T. +3228921001. Fax +3228921002. E-mail: info@european-economic-chamber-eeig.eu.

URL: http://www.european-economic-chamber-eeig.eu/

History 1998. An organization of the type *European Economic Interest Grouping (EEIG, #06960).* Registration: EU Transparency Register, No/ID: 260330241843-67, Start date: 17 Mar 2021. **Aims** Support EU Eastern European integration; promote bridge-building of new markets globally; increase understanding and cooperation worldwide; promote and reward excellence in commerce, trade, industry, education, training, science and the arts. **Structure** Executive; Regional Branch Offices; Specialized Central Offices; Working Commissions (22). **Languages** English. **Staff** 200.00 FTE, voluntary. **Finance** Members' dues. Commission fees. **Activities** Advocacy/lobbying/activism; events/meetings. **Events** *Presidents conference* Vienna (Austria) 2008. **Publications** *EEIG Newsletter* (24 a year). Daily news; circular letters.

Members Functionaries in national and specialized offices in 45 countries:

Albania, Austria, Azerbaijan, Bangladesh, Belgium, Bhutan, Bosnia-Herzegovina, Bulgaria, China, Croatia, Cyprus, Czechia, Egypt, Eritrea, France, Ghana, Greece, Hungary, India, Iran Islamic Rep, Israel, Italy, Jordan, Kuwait, Liechtenstein, Moldova, Monaco, Montenegro, North Macedonia, Oman, Palestine, Qatar, Romania, Russia, Saudi Arabia, Serbia, Slovenia, South Africa, Sweden, Türkiye, UK, Ukraine, United Arab Emirates, USA, Uzbekistan. [2021/XM3330/t/**F**]

♦ European Economic and Customs Union (inactive)

♦ European Economic Interest Grouping (EEIG) 06960

Groupement européen d'intérêt économique (GEIE) – Europäische Wirtschaftliche Interessenvereinigung (EWIV) – Europese Economische Samenwerkingsverbanden (EESV)

Address not obtained.

History 25 Jul 1985. Founded by regulation 2137/85 of *Council of the European Union (#04895)*, effective from 1 Jul 1989. Not an organization itself but a legal device for companies, firms or natural persons to form an entity at European level, which may or may not have legal personality within individual EU or EEA states depending on the law of the state concerned. Administered within the framework of *European Commission (EC, #06633).* **Aims** Stimulate transnational economic cooperation, economic growth and integration of economies of European Union member countries; combine efforts of companies, notably SMEs, to facilitate or develop economic activity and to improve or increase the results of such activity, whether in marketing, research or some other area. **Structure** A Community law instrument at the disposal of enterprises, grouping to improve on individual efforts. Formalities for setting up and operation of an EEIG are very flexible and aim at simplicity with respect to location, cooperation, access, administration, financing, management standards, commercial and fiscal neutrality. Each grouping has 2 organs: the college of members; managers. **Finance** Funded equally by European Commission, member states and industry. Individual EEIGs may be formed without capital or assets; members' contributions may be in cash, in kind or in skill.

Activities An EEIG may: arrange sale of members' products; organize joint exploitation of partial licences in new technologies; coordinate members' production and delivery schedules; develop marketing for members; bid for and be awarded public works and public supplies contracts; implement joint research work; supply transport, purchasing, distribution or other services. An instrument for cooperation, not integration, an EEIG does not manage activities of its members but coordinates activities for whose execution it has been made responsible. Of over 800 EEIGs currently published in the Official Journal of the European Commission, the following are listed in this Yearbook:

- *A Soul for Europe (ASF, #19697);*
- *ACRISS EEIG (#00079);*
- *AGRINATURA (#00578);*
- *Association of Accountants and Auditors in Europe (AAAE, #02344);*
- *Association of Commercial Television in Europe (ACT, #02436);*
- *Association des constructeurs européens de motocycles (ACEM, #02450);*
- *Nuclear Medicine Europe (NMEU, #17619);*
- *Association méditerranéenne pour le développement local et la coopération transnationale (Meridiana, no recent information);*
- *Association Relative à la Télévision Européenne (ARTE G.E.I.E.);*
- *Association technique de l'industrie européenne des lubrifiants (ATIEL, #02950);*
- *Auditeurs consultants experts européens (ACEE, #03016);*
- *Baltic Organisations' Network for Funding Science EEIG (BONUS EEIG, inactive);*
- *CONSULEGIS – International Network of Law Firms (#04762);*
- *Coopération bancaire pour l'Europe (CBE);*
- *Coordination of European Picture Agencies, Press Stock Heritage (CEPIC, #04825);*
- *Crédit local d'Europe (no recent information);*
- *ECNC Group (no recent information);*
- *Ecomet (#05306);*
- *Euralliance Farma (no recent information);*
- *EUREC (#05619);*
- *Euro-Mediterranean Information System on Know-how in the Water Sector (EMWIS, #05722);*
- *Eurodéveloppement (no recent information);*
- *EUROJURIS International (#05696);*
- *EUROMAR (no recent information);*
- *Euronet Consulting (#05739);*
- *Europa Medica (#05764);*
- *European Acoustics Association (EAA, #05824);*
- *European Association of Authorised Representatives (EAAR, #05947);*
- *European Coalition on Homeopathic and Anthroposophic Medicinal Products (ECHAMP, #06595);*
- *European Committee on Romani Emancipation (ECRE);*
- *European Community Telework Forum (ECTF, no recent information);*
- *European Confederation of Tobacco Retailers (#06725);*
- *European Coordination of Film Festivals (no recent information);*
- *European Cosmetic Responsible Person Association (ERPA, #06800);*
- *European Council Union (ECU, no recent information);*
- *European Development Finance Institutions (EDFI, #06913);*
- *European Economic Chamber of Trade, Commerce and Industry (#06959);*
- *European Economic Research and Advisory Consortium (ERECO, no recent information);*
- *European Elevator Association (#06976);*
- *European Environmental Institute, Brussels (no recent information);*
- *European Environmental Network (EEN, no recent information);*
- *Méliès International Festivals Federation (MIFF, #16706);*
- *European Federation for Cosmetic Ingredients (EFfCI, #07092);*
- *European Foundation for Phytotherapy (EFP, no recent information);*
- *European Franchise Lawyers Association (EF LAW, #07355);*
- *European Fuel Cycle Consortium (EFCC, no recent information);*
- *European Group of Automotive Recycling Associations (EGARA, #07417);*
- *European Grouping of Societies of Authors and Composers (#07422);*
- *European Heat Pump Association (EHPA, #07469);*
- *European Internet Services Providers Association (EuroISPA, #07592);*
- *European Jewellery Technology Network (EJTN, no recent information);*
- *European Lift and Lift Component Association (ELCA, #07696);*
- *European Logistic Platforms Association (Europlatforms, #07709);*
- *European Materials Research Consortium (EMARC, no recent information);*
- *European Multiple Sclerosis Platform (EMSP, #07833);*
- *European Network of Business Schools (ENBS, no recent information);*
- *European Network for Communication and Information Perspectives (ENCIP, inactive);*
- *European Network for Economic Cooperation and Development (EUCED);*
- *European Network of Implementing Development Agencies (EUNIDA, #07926);*
- *European Payments Consulting Association (EPCA, #08174);*
- *European Power Supplies Manufacturer's Association (EPSMA, #08263);*
- *European Primate Resources Network (EUPREN, no recent information);*
- *European Property Federation (EPF, #08286);*
- *European Real Estate Valuers (Euroexperts, inactive);*
- *European Regions' Network for the Application of Communications Technology (ERNACT, #08348);*
- *European Research Consortium for Informatics and Mathematics (ERCIM, #08362);*
- *European Sound Directors' Association (ESDA, no recent information);*
- *European Union of Associations of Translation Companies (EUATC, #08977);*
- *European Vaccine Initiative (EVI, #09043);*
- *European Virtual Institute for Integrated Risk Management (EU-VRi, #09062);*
- *European Vision Institute (EVI, #09069);*
- *Eurovillages, association européenne (no recent information);*
- *European Vision Institute Clinical Research Network (EVICR.net, #09070);*
- *Federation of Harley-Davidson Clubs of Europe (FH-DCE, #09592);*
- *Firestop Europe (inactive);*
- *FLORNET (#09799);*
- *GEIE des associations des transporteurs internationaux de l'Europe du Sud (GATRIES, no recent information);*
- *Global Advertising Lawyers Alliance (GALA, #10171);*
- *Globaladvocaten (#10173);*
- *Greenovate! Europe (#10726);*
- *Groupement Européen pour la mise en oeuvre des Programmes de COoperation Transfrontalière, Transnationale, Interrégionale et d'autres Programmes Européens (GEIE GECOTTI-PE);*
- *Interlegal (#11517);*
- *International Centre for Alpine Environments (ICALPE, no recent information);*
- *International Florist Organisation (FLORINT, #13616);*
- *International Network for Information on Ventilation and Energy Performance (INIVE, #14288);*
- *International Port Community Systems Association (IPCSA, #14623);*
- *International Project Union (IPU, no recent information);*
- *MULTI-POLES (no recent information);*
- *Organization of European Cancer Institutes (OECI, #17865);*
- *PapiNet (#18192);*
- *Permanent Forum of European Civil Society (#18322);*
- *Pyramide Europe (#18585);*
- *Réseau européen d'arbitrage et de médiation (REAM, no recent information);*
- *Strategic and Economic Research Corporation (STRATECO, no recent information);*
- *SUBMARINER Network for Blue Growth EEIG (SUBMARINER Network, #20024);*
- *Top E – European Consulting Engineering Network (#20174);*
- *Ulixes European Union Training and Research EEIG (ULIXES, #20279);*
- *Underground Gasification Europe (no recent information);*
- *Université européenne de formation ouverte aux pays (no recent information);*
- *Vision 1250 (no recent information);*
- *Youth and European Social Work (YES Forum, #22015).*

Events *Annual General Assembly* Oslo (Norway) 2007. [2018/XE0630/y/**F***]

♦ European Economic and Monetary Union (EMU) 06961

Union économique et monétaire (UEM)

Contact c/o European Commission, DG Communication, 1049 Brussels, Belgium. T. +3222991111. Fax +3222950138 – +3222950140.

URL: https://ec.europa.eu/info/business-economy-euro/economic-and-fiscal-policy-coo rdination/economic-and-monetary-union_en

History 1 Jan 1999, when the *'euro'* became currency of 11 of the then 15 member states of *European Union (EU, #08967)* as laid down by *Treaty on European Union (Maastricht Treaty, 1992)*, signed 7 Feb 1992. Greece became the 12th member on 1 Jan 2001. Slovenia introduced the euro in 2007, Cyprus and Malta in 2008, Slovakia in 2009, Estonia in 2011, Latvia in 2014 and Lithuania in 2015. These countries are collectively referred to as *Euro Zone.* As from 1 Jan 2002, following a 3-year transition period to 31 Dec 2001, banks in these countries issue only euro notes and coins.

EMU was first proposed 1-2 Dec 1969, The Hague (Netherlands), at Summit Conference of Heads of Government and of State of the *European Communities (EC, inactive)*, within the framework of *Council of the European Union (#04895)*, as a long-term project to be achieved in stages. It was reconfirmed at subsequent meetings and in reports, notably the Werner report of 1971 and the Delors Report, 1989. The *Delors Committee – Comité Delors*, created Jun 1988, comprising presidents of the central banks of the then 12 EEC member states in their personal capacities and several independent personalities, was an *'ad hoc'* committee set up by *European Council (#06801)* to discuss EMU. The Delors Committee suggested 3 stages but without fixing a timetable. (1) From 1 Jul 1990, full liberalization of capital movement would come into effect, with all currencies being integrated in the *European Monetary System (EMS, inactive).* (2) EU member states would sign a treaty instituting EMU and aiming at setting up a European System of Central Banks as well as reinforcing convergence of economic policies. (3) Parities would be permanently fixed, and the European System of Central Banks established, thus opening the way to replacement of their national currencies by a single currency. *European Parliament (EP, #08146)* proposed a swifter timetable, installing EMU by 1 Jan 1995, with the complete disappearance of national currencies by 1 Jan 1998. A secretariat responding to *Committee of Governors of the Central Banks of the Member States of the European Economic Community (inactive)* monitored national financial economies and helped create the climate for progressive integration of the European economy. The overall design of a plan for economic and monetary union was agreed, Aug 1990, by *Council of Finance Ministers of the European Union (Ecofin)*; but several complex issues remained to be resolved. The European Council, meeting 27-28 Oct 1990, Rome (Italy), set out a timetable agreed by all members except the UK, which led to finalizing a first phase by 31 Dec 1993, a maximum of 3 years later for finalizing a second phase and the passage to a third phase occurring in a "reasonable" time. The process involved strengthening the ability of Community institutions to act towards economic union and creation of a new monetary institution, *European Central Bank (ECB, #06466)*, fully responsible for monetary policy and with the aim of maintaining price stability. Exchange rates would eventually be irrevocably fixed and the Community would have a single currency.

The Maastricht Treaty put the future establishment of the European Central Bank and *European System of Central Banks (ESCB, #08870)* on a firm footing. It formalized the setting up, 1 Jan 1994, of *European Monetary Institute (EMI, inactive)*, whose Council comprised the Governors of European central banks and which took over the tasks of their Committee and of the *European Monetary Cooperation Fund (EMCF, inactive).* The Institute functioned during the second stage of the run-up towards union, monitoring progress of the European Monetary System, The second stage was designed to ensure that differences in national economic indicators disappeared as inflation, interest rates, exchange fluctuations, budget and public sector deficits converged with those of the best performing economies, with Ecofin intervening if national budget policies were inconsistent with Maastricht Treaty provisions. A *Monetary Committee (inactive)* was set up to promote coordination of the policies of member states. This was superseded by an *Economic and Financial Committee (EFC)* at the beginning of the third stage, when the EMI was superseded by establishment of the European Central Bank. No date for the third stage had been fixed by 31 Dec 1997, so ESCB was established immediately after 1 Jul 1998 and Stage 3 followed on 1 Jan 1999, with establishment of the EMU as transition to the third stage occurred automatically on this date for those member states which had fulfilled the necessary conditions for the adoption of a single currency.

A Resolution of the European Council, 16 Jun 1997, Amsterdam (Netherlands), established an exchange-rate mechanism in the third stage of EMU; and agreement of 1 Sep 1998 between the European Central Bank and the National Central Banks of member states outside the euro area laid down operating procedures. Under the European Council resolution, a new *Exchange-Rate Mechanism (ERM II)* replaced the European Monetary System as from 1 Jan 1999, when Economic and Monetary Union became official and the EMS became obsolete. ERM II aims to maintain exchange-rate stability between the euro and participating national currencies so as to ensure that excessive exchange-rate fluctuations do not cause problems in the internal market.

Aims Coordinate economic policy-making between Member States; coordinate *fiscal* policies, notably through limits on government debt and deficit; promote the single *currency* and the euro area.

Activities Operation of EMU is governed by a framework of laws and institutions which oblige participating member states to strive for closely coordinated, stable and disciplined national economic policies and to maintain limits on budget deficits and public debts laid down by the Maastricht Treaty and by the *Stability and Growth Pact*, comprising:
– 1. Commitments set out in a resolution of the European Council, adopted Jun 1997, Amsterdam (Netherlands), aiming for budget balances close to or in surplus by 2002.
– 2. Surveillance of budgetary positions of member states and surveillance and coordination of their economic policies in accordance with regulations of the Council.
– 3. Early warning system to avoid an excessive budget deficit. Council may issue a recommendation to the member state concerned to take adjustment measures.
– 4. Council regulation on speeding up and clarifying implementation of excessive deficit procedures, including details of sanctions for failure to fulfil commitments on budgetary discipline.

The *euro*, replacing the *European Currency Unit (ECU)*, became a currency in its own right on 1 Jan 1999. In late 1998 these countries had already cut their interest rates to a uniformly low level so as to promote growth and prepare the way for a unified currency. Greece adopted the euro on 1 Jan 2001. Euro coins and notes were introduced into circulation in Jan 2002 and local currencies in the countries adopting the euro were withdrawn from circulation by Jul 2002.
Cohesion Fund (#04087), established under the Maastricht Treaty, worked with existing funds to smooth the way towards EMU for member states whose per capita GDP was less than 90% of the Community average.
Euro Interbank Offered Rate (Eurobor) is the benchmark interbank reference rate within the Economic and Monetary Union, the rate at which euro interbank term deposits are offered by one prime bank to another prime bank. It was first published on 30 Dec 1998 for value 4 Jan 1999, being the underlying rate of many derivatives transactions. The choice of banks quoting for Euribor is based on market criteria.
Publications *Euro Papers* – series. *Talking about the euro* – guide. *A Collection of Websites Dedicated to the Euro* – CD-ROM. Videos. **Members** All 27 EU Member States. **IGO Relations** *Integrated Programme in Favour of SMEs and the Craft Sector (CRAFT, no recent information)* is part of general economic policy in EMU framework. **NGO Relations** *Euro Institute (no recent information)* is concerned with macroeconomic aspects of EMU implementation. [2017/XF4335/**F***]

♦ European Economics and Finance Society (EEFS) 06962

Pres Dept of Economics, City, University of London, Northampton Square London EC1V 0HB, London, EC1V 0HB, UK. T. +442070400258.
SG address not obtained.
URL: http://www.eefs-eu.org/
History 2001. Founded as the European branch of *International Economics and Finance Society (IEFS)*. **Aims** Promote scientific research and scholarly work in the area of international economics broadly defined; encourage interdisciplinary communication among economists working in related fields; facilitate a wide dissemination of research output; foster the development of young economists, especially those undertaking PhD level research. **Structure** Officers: President; General Secretary; Treasurer. **Staff** 6.00 FTE, voluntary. **Activities** Events/meetings; research and development. **Events** *Annual Conference* Berlin (Germany) 2023, *Annual Meeting* Krakow (Poland) 2022, *Annual Meeting* London (UK) 2021, *Annual Meeting* Genoa (Italy) 2019, *Annual Meeting* London (UK) 2018. **Members** Individuals. Membership countries not specified. [2023.02.14/XM7973/**D**]

♦ European Economic and Social Committee (EESC) 06963

Comité économique et social européen – Comité Económico y Social Europeo – Europäischer Wirtschafts- und Sozialausschuss – Comité Económico e Social Europeu – Comitato Economico e Sociale Europeo – Europees Economisch en Sociaal Comité – Europeiska Ekonomiska och Sociala Kommittén – Det Europaeiske Økonomiske og Sociale Udvalg – Euroopan Talous-ja Sosiaalikomitea – Coiste Eacnamaíoch agus Sóisialta na hEorpa – Evropsky Hospodarsky a Socialni Vybor – Európsky Hospodarsky a Socialny Vybor – Európai Gazdasagi és Szocialis Bizottsag – Europejski Komitet Ekonomiczno-Spoleczny – Evropski Ekonomsko-Socialni Odbor – Euroopa Majandus- ja Sotsiaalkomitee – Eiropas Ekonomikas un Socialo Lietu Komiteja – Europos Ekonomikos ir Socialiniu Reikalu Komitetas – Europski Gospodarski i Socijalni Odbor – Comitetul Economic si Social Europea

Secretariat Rue Belliard 99, 1040 Brussels, Belgium. T. +3225469011 – +3225469022. Fax +3225134893.
URL: http://eesc.europa.eu/
History Jan 1958, Brussels (Belgium). Established by Article 193 of *Treaty on the Functioning of the European Union (TFEU, 1957)* and *Treaty Establishing the European Atomic Energy Community (Treaty of Rome, 1957)*, both signed 25 Mar 1957, Rome (Italy), to involve economic and social interest groups in the establishment of the common market, to provide institutional machinery for briefing the *European Commission (EC, #06633)* and the Council of Ministers on European Union issues, and to assist in decision-making of the Commissions set up for European Economic Community (EEC) and *European Atomic Energy Community (Euratom, inactive)*.
Since Jul 1967, on coming into force of the Treaty merging the executive of *European Coal and Steel Community (ECSC, inactive)* with those of the European Economic Community and Euratom, has maintained a similar role with respect to the European Commission. EESC's role has been reinforced by *Single European Act (SEA, 1986)* (1986), *Treaty on European Union (Maastricht Treaty, 1992)* (1992), *Treaty of Amsterdam (1997)* (1997) and *Nice Treaty (2001)* (2000).
Since *Treaty of Lisbon (2007)* came into force, 2009, functions as an advisory body of the *European Union (EU, #08967)*, for *European Parliament (EP, #08146)*, *Council of the European Union (#04895)* and the European Commission.
Name change followed the coming into effect of the *Maastricht Treaty*, when it became the Economic and Social Committee of the Union. Former names and other names: *Economic and Social Committee of the European Communities (ESC)* – former (1958); *Comité économique et social des Communautés européennes (CES)* – former (1958); *Comité Económico y Social de Comunidades Europeas* – former (1958); *Wirtschafts- und Sozialausschuss der Europäischen Gemeinschaften* – former (1958); *Comité Económico e Social dos Comunidades Européias* – former (1958); *Comitato Economico e Sociale delle Comunità Europee* – former (1958); *Economisch en Sociaal Comité van de Europese Gemeenschappen* – former (1958); *Økonomiske og Sociale Udvalg for de Europaeiske Faellesskaber* – former (1958); *Ikonomikis ke Kinonikis Epitropis ton Evropaikon Kinotiton* – former (1958); *Economic and Social Committee (ESC)* – former; *Comité économique et social européen (CES)* – former; *Comité Económico y Social* – former; *Wirtschafts- und Sozialausschuss* – former; *Comité Económico e Social* – former; *Comitato Economico e Sociale* – former; *Comité Económico e Social* – former; *Economisch en Sociaal Comité* – former; *Økonomiske og Sociale Udvalg* – former; *Talous-ja Sosiaalikomitea* – former; *Ikonomikis ke Kinonikis Epitropis* – former; *EcoSoc* – former.
Aims Contribute to strengthening the democratic legitimacy and effectiveness of the European Union by enabling civil society organizations from Member States to express their views at European level; help ensure that European policies and legislation tie in better with economic, social and civic circumstances on the ground, by assisting the European Parliament, Council and European Commission, making use of EESC members' experience and representativeness, dialogue and efforts to secure consensus serving the general interest; promote development of a more participatory European Union which is more in touch with popular opinion, by acting as an institutional forum representing, informing, expressing the views of and securing dialogue with organized civil society; promote the values on which European integration is founded and advance, in Europe and across the world, the cause of democracy and participatory democracy, as well as the role of civil society organizations. **Structure** Plenary of 350 members, subdivided into 6 Sections: Economic and Monetary Union and Economic and Social Cohesion (ECO); Single Market, Production and Consumption (INT); External Relations (REX); Agriculture, Rural Development and the Environment (NAT); Employment, Social Affairs and Citizenship; and the Consultative Commission on Industrial Change. Bureau Groups (3): Employers'; Workers'; Various Interests. Study Groups; Sub-committees. Secretariat. **Languages** EU languages. **Staff** 800.00 FTE, paid. Since 1 Jan 1995, the EESC and the *European Committee of the Regions (CoR, #06665)* have shared some services. **Finance** Budget (annual): about euro 120 million. **Activities** Cooperation with *European Parliament (EP, #08146)*, *Council of the European Union (#04895)* or *European Commission (EC, #06633)* is based on the *Treaty on the Functioning of the European Union (TFEU, 1957)* – Art 300, according to which, EESC is consulted on predefined policy areas. Additionally, the EESC may be consulted by these institutions in all cases in which they consider it appropriate. The EESC may, however, also adopt opinions on its own initiative. On average the EESC delivers 170 advisory documents and opinions a year (of which about 15% are issued on its own-initiative). Instrumental in setting up: *Community Charter of Fundamental Social Rights for Workers (European Social Charter, 1989)*. **Events** *European Migration Forum* Brussels (Belgium) 2022, *Plenary Session* Brussels (Belgium) 2022, *Plenary Session* Brussels (Belgium) 2022, *REPowering our EU Conference* Brussels (Belgium) 2022, *The role of legal professions in EU Anti Money Laundering* Brussels (Belgium) 2022. **Publications** *CESE Info* (12 a year) – newsletter. Annual Report; Opinions, bulletin.
Members Representatives of civil society (326) in all 27 EU member states:
Austria (12), Belgium (12), Bulgaria (12), Croatia (9), Cyprus (5), Czechia (12), Denmark (9), Estonia (6), Finland (9), France (24), Germany (24), Greece (12), Hungary (12), Ireland (9), Italy (24), Latvia (7), Lithuania (9), Luxembourg (5), Malta (5), Netherlands (12), Poland (21), Portugal (12), Romania (15), Slovakia (9), Slovenia (7), Spain (21), Sweden (12).
IGO Relations Cooperation agreement with: *European Committee of the Regions (CoR, #06665)*.
NGO Relations Each of EESC's 3 groups recognizes NGOs by giving "approved" status. Group I (Employers):
– *Association des chambres de commerce et d'industrie européennes (EUROCHAMBRES, #02423)*; *EuroCommerce (EC, #05665)*; *SGI Europe (#19253)*.

Group II (Workers' Group):
– *CEC European Managers (#03623)*;
– *European Confederation of Independent Trade Unions (CESI, #06705)*;
– *European Confederation of Police (EuroCOP, #06719)*;
– *European Federation of Building and Woodworkers (EFBWW, #07065)*;
– *European Federation of Food, Agriculture and Tourism Trade Unions (EFFAT, #07125)*;
– *European Federation of Journalists (EFJ, #07152)*;
– *European Federation of Public Service Unions (EPSU, #07202)*;
– *European Trade Union Committee for Education (ETUCE, #08926)*;
– *European Trade Union Federation for Textiles, Clothing and Leather (ETUF-TCL, inactive)*;
– *European Transport Workers' Federation (ETF, #08941)*;
– *Fédération européenne des retraités et des personnes âgées (FERPA, #09580)*;
– *UNI Global Union (#20338)* – MEI;
– *UNI Global Union – Europa (UNI Europa, #20342)*.

Group III (Various Interests):
– *Association des organisations nationales d'entreprises de pêche de l'UE (EUROPECHE, #02841)*;
– *Bureau Européen des Unions de Consommateurs (BEUC, #03360)*;
– *Confédération européenne des coopératives de travail associé, des coopératives sociales et des entreprises sociales et participatives (CECOP, #04541)*;
– *COPA – european farmers (COPA, #04829)*;
– *European Community of Consumer Cooperatives (EURO COOP, #06678)*;
– *European Council of Liberal Professions (#06828)*;
– *SMEunited (#19327)*;
– *Union of Finance Personnel in Europe (#20407)*.

Liaison Group with European Civil Society organizations and Networks, set up 2004:
– *AGE Platform Europe (#00557)*;
– *Architects Council of Europe (ACE, #01086)*;
– *Confédération européenne des ong d'urgence et de développement (CONCORD, #04547)*;
– *COFACE Families Europe (#04084)*;
– *Cooperatives Europe (#04801)*;
– *Culture Action Europe (CAE, #04981)*;
– *EURAG – European Federation of Older Persons (#05597)*;
– *Eurochild (#05657)*;
– *European Association for the Defence of Human Rights (AEDH, no recent information)*;
– *European Association of Institutes for Vocational Training (#06085)*;
– *European Citizen Action Service (ECAS, #06555)*;
– *European Civic Forum (ECF, #06562)*;
– *European College of Marketing and Marketing Research (ECMMR, inactive)*;
– *European Digital Rights (EDRi, #06924)*;
– *European Disability Forum (EDF, #06929)*;
– *European Environmental Bureau (EEB, #06996)*;
– *European Federation for Intercultural Learning (EFIL, #07146)*;
– *European Foundation Centre (EFC, inactive)*;
– *European Language Equality Network (ELEN, #07647)*;
– *European Movement International (EMI, #07825)*;
– *European Students' Union (ESU, #08848)*;
– *European Youth Forum (#09140)*;
– *Fédération Européenne d'Associations Nationales d'Ingénieurs (FEANI, #09558)*;
– *Front Line Defenders (FLD, #10008)*;
– *International Union of Property Owners (#15804)*;
– *International Union of Tenants (IUT, #15822)*;
– *Lifelong Learning Platform – European Civil Society for Education (LLLP, #16466)*;
– *Rurality – Environment – Development (RED, #19003)*;
– *SDG Watch Europe (#19162)*;
– *Social Economy Europe (SEE, #19335)*;
– *Social Platform (#19344)*;
– *Standing Committee of European Doctors (#19955)*;
– *Union of European Federalists, The (UEF, #20385)*;
– *Volonteurope (#20807)*. [2020/XE0669/**E***]

♦ European Economists for an Alternative Economic Policy in Europe (EuroMemo Group) 06964

Arbeitsgruppe Alternative Wirtschaftspolitik für Europa (EURO-MEMO-Gruppe)

Contact c/o AAW, Postfach 33 04 47, 28334 Bremen, Germany. E-mail: info@euromemo.eu.
URL: http://www.euromemo.eu/
History 1995. **Aims** Promote full employment with good work, social justice with an eradication of poverty and social exclusion, ecological sustainability, and international solidarity. **Structure** Steering Community of 11 members. **Activities** Organizes annual workshop. **Events** *Annual Workshop* London (UK) 2022, *Annual Workshop* Paris (France) 2019, *Annual Workshop* Helsinki (Finland) 2018, *Annual Workshop* Poznań (Poland) 2012, *Annual Meeting* Vienna (Austria) 2011. **Publications** *Memorandum* (annual). **NGO Relations** Signatory to: *Alter Summit*. [2013/XJ5461/**F**]

♦ European Ecumenical Youth Council / see Ecumenical Youth Council in Europe (#05352)

♦ European Educational Exchanges – Youth for Understanding (EEE-YFU) 06965

Echange éducatif européen – Youth for Understanding

Dir Av Ernest Cambier 161, 1030 Brussels, Belgium. T. +3226484790. E-mail: eee-yfu@yfu.world.
Training and Knowledge Manager address not obtained.
URL: https://about.yfu.org/eee-yfu
History Sep 1985. Founded as the European secretariat of *Youth for Understanding (YFU, #22027)*, set up in 1951. Registration: Banque-Carrefour des Entreprises, No/ID: 0428.158.097, Start date: 19 Dec 1985, Belgium; EU Transparency Register, No/ID: 85637203212-87, Start date: 12 Feb 2010. **Aims** Empower members to develop and retain strong networks of impactful youth workers, influence policy, position YFU as an expert and partner in intercultural learning, and develop and implement relevant and innovative responses to the challenges of an evolving society. **Structure** General Meeting (annual); Board. **Languages** English. **Staff** 3.00 FTE, paid. **Activities** Advocacy/lobbying/activism; capacity building; events/meetings; guidance/assistance/consulting; networking/liaising; projects/programmes; training/education. **Events** *European Conference and General Meeting* Brussels (Belgium) 2014, *General Meeting* Bucharest (Romania) 2013, *General Meeting* Rockville, MD (USA) 2012, *General Meeting* Vilnius (Lithuania) 2011, *General Meeting* Tallinn (Estonia) 2010. **Publications** *EEE-YFU Newsletter*, *Volunteer Updates*. Annual report; manuals.
Members Organizations in 28 countries:
Austria, Azerbaijan, Belgium, Bulgaria, Czechia, Denmark, Estonia, Finland, France, Georgia, Germany, Greece, Hungary, Italy, Latvia, Lithuania, Moldova, Netherlands, Norway, Poland, Romania, Serbia, Slovakia, Spain, Sweden, Switzerland, Türkiye, Ukraine.
Consultative Status Consultative status granted from: *Council of Europe (CE, #04881)* (Participatory Status).
NGO Relations Member of (3): *European Youth Forum (#09140)*; *Federation of European and International Associations Established in Belgium (FAIB, #09508)*; *Lifelong Learning Platform – European Civil Society for Education (LLLP, #16466)*. [2023.02.16/XF0584/**E**]

European Educational Publishers
06966
alphabetic sequence excludes
For the complete listing, see Yearbook Online at

♦ European Educational Publishers Group (EEPG) **06966**

Contact Wielandstr 33, 10629 Berlin, Germany. T. +49308816233.
Registered address c/o Advokat Søren Locher, Store Kongensgade 67C, 1264 Copenhagen K, Denmark.
URL: http://eepg.org/

History 1991. **Aims** Further development of quality educational materials in Europe. **Structure** Management Board. **Languages** English.
Members Full in 23 countries:
Austria, Bulgaria, Croatia, Czechia, Denmark, Estonia, Finland, Germany, Greece, Ireland, Israel, Latvia, Lithuania, Norway, Poland, Portugal, Romania, Serbia, Slovenia, Spain, Sweden, Switzerland, Ukraine.
NGO Relations Cooperates with (1): *International Association for Research on Textbooks and Educational Media (IARTEM, #12137)*. Associate member of: *European Association of History Educators (EUROCLIO, #06069)*. [2021/XJ6299/**D**]

♦ European Educational Research Association (EERA) **06967**
Association européenne de recherche en education

Office Manager Feurigstrasse 22, 10827 Berlin, Germany. T. +493085736220. Fax +493037719572. E-mail: office@eera.eu.
URL: http://www.eera.eu/

History Jun 1994, Strasbourg (France). Registration: EU Transparency Register, No/ID: 064412029735-61, Start date: 23 Jan 2018. **Aims** Encourage collaboration among educational researchers in Europe; promote communication between educational researchers and international governmental organizations; improve communication among educational research associations and institutes within Europe; disseminate findings of educational research and highlight their contribution to policy and practice. **Structure** Council; Executive Committee. Educational research networks (31). **Languages** English. **Staff** 2.50 FTE, paid. **Finance** Members' dues. Conference revenues. **Activities** Organizes annual European Conference on Educational Research and Network-led Seminars and Season Schools. **Events** *European Conference on Educational Research* Nicosia (Cyprus) 2024, *European Conference on Educational Research* Glasgow (UK) 2023, *European Conference on Educational Research* Yerevan (Armenia) 2022, *European Conference on Educational Research* Geneva (Switzerland) 2021, *European Conference on Educational Research* Glasgow (UK) 2020.
Members National associations in 28 countries:
Armenia, Austria, Belarus, Belgium, Cyprus, Czechia, Denmark, Estonia, Finland, France, Germany, Greece, Hungary, Iceland, Ireland, Italy, Lithuania, Netherlands, Norway, Poland, Portugal, Slovakia, Slovenia, Spain, Sweden, Switzerland, Türkiye, UK.
NGO Relations Member of: *European Alliance for the Social Sciences and Humanities (EASSH, #05885)*; *Initiative for Science in Europe (ISE, #11214)*. Founding member of: *World Education Research Association (WERA, #21372)*. Links with national educational research associations. [2021/XD4395/**D**]

♦ European Education Centre for Housing and Real Estate Economy / see Europäisches Bildungszentrum der Wohnungs- und Immobilienwirtschaft
♦ European Education and Meeting Centers / see Europäische Bildungs-und Begegnungszentren (#05750)

♦ European Educators' Christian Association (EurECA) **06968**

Exec Officer str Ciucea nr 1, bl P16 – sc 3 – ap 32, 032521 Bucharest, Romania. T. +40213459655. E-mail: sec@eureca-online.org.
Chairman 15 Lilac Ave, Worcester, WR4 9QU, UK.
URL: http://www.eureca-online.org/

History Founded 1990, following series of 'European Conference for Christian Educators', held 1985-1990 in Kandern (Germany FR). Registered in accordance with German law, 1993. **Aims** Encourage and equip Christian *teachers* to fulfil their calling and represent *Jesus*. **Structure** General Assembly; Governing Board. **Languages** English. Other European languages as required. **Staff** Voluntary. **Finance** Members' dues. Annual budget: euro 5,000. **Activities** Events/meetings; networking/liaising. **Events** *Conference* Toledo (Spain) 2019, *Conference* Sofia (Bulgaria) 2018, *Conference* Hurdal (Norway) 2017, *Conference* Lisbon (Portugal) 2016, *Support and encouragement in education* Warsaw (Poland) 2015. **Publications** *Catalogue of Materials* (2006); *Declaration of Education and Christian Belief* (1997). Articles.
Members Full in 32 countries:
Albania, Australia, Austria, Belgium, Bulgaria, Canada, Croatia, Czechia, Estonia, Finland, France, Germany, Greece, Hungary, Latvia, Netherlands, New Zealand, Norway, Poland, Portugal, Romania, Russia, Singapore, Slovakia, Slovenia, South Africa, Spain, Sweden, Switzerland, UK, Ukraine, USA.
NGO Relations Member of: *European Evangelical Alliance (EEA, #07010)*. [2019/XD7298/**D**]

♦ European Egg Packers and Traders Association (EEPTA) **06969**

SG Axelborg, Axeltorv 3, 1609 Copenhagen V, Denmark. T. +4527245691. E-mail: jnl@lf.dk.
URL: http://www.eepta.eu/

History 5 Jun 1997, Vienna (Austria). 5-6 Jun 1997, Vienna (Austria), at General Assembly of *European Union of Wholesale in Eggs, Egg-Products, Poultry and Game (EUWEP, #09021)*, as its independently-operating member in the field. Structure and rules of procedure covered by EUWEP rules adopted at the same meeting. **Aims** Protect and defend the rights, commercial functions and professional interests of members, by strengthening cooperation, studying common problems and representing the interest of members at the European Union; study trade-specific problems and present proposals in this regard to EUWEP Board. **Structure** Council. Board, comprising Chairman, Vice-Chairman, Treasurer and Secretary-General. **Languages** English. **Staff** 2.00 FTE, paid. **Finance** Members' dues. **Events** *Meeting* Paris (France) 1999.
Members National associations and companies of egg packers, traders, wholesalers and related processing industries in 12 countries:
Belgium, Denmark, Finland, France, Germany, Hungary, Ireland, Italy, Netherlands, Poland, Portugal, Romania, Spain, Sweden, UK.
NGO Relations Member of: EUWEP – Chairman, 2 nominees and (non-voting) Secretary-General are members of EUWEP Board. [2012.07.30/XD5938/t/**D**]

♦ European Egg Processors / see European Egg Processors Association (#06970)

♦ European Egg Processors Association (EEPA) **06970**

Administration Bilkske 93, 8000 Bruges, Belgium. T. +3250440070. Fax +3250440077. E-mail: info@eepa.info.
URL: http://www.eepa.info/

History Founded 1994, Brussels (Belgium), as *European Egg Processors (EEP)*. Structure and rules of procedure covered by EUWEP rules adopted 5-6 Jun 1997, Vienna (Austria), at General Assembly of *European Union of Wholesale in Eggs, Egg-Products, Poultry and Game (EUWEP, #09021)*. **Aims** Protect and promote the interests of European egg processors. **Structure** General Assembly; Committee; Permanent Secretariat in Bruges (Belgium). **Languages** Dutch, English, Finnish, French, German, Spanish, Swedish. **Finance** Members' dues. **Activities** Events/meetings. **Events** *Conference* Bruges (Belgium) 1996, *Conference* Brussels (Belgium) 1996.
Members Related processing industries in 14 countries:
Belgium, Denmark, Finland, France, Germany, Italy, Latvia, Lithuania, Netherlands, Poland, Portugal, Spain, Sweden, UK.
NGO Relations Member of: *European Union of Wholesale in Eggs, Egg-Products, Poultry and Game (EUWEP, #09021)*. [2018/XD4812/v/**D**]

♦ European E-Invoicing Service Providers Association (EESPA) **06971**

Secretariat Avenue Louise 149/24, 1050 Brussels, Belgium. T. +3216437415.
URL: http://eespa.eu/

History 2011. Registered in accordance with Belgian law. EU Transparency Register: 784493623035-87. **Aims** Promote interoperability and the creation of an interoperable eco-system for electronic invoicing; advocate and support the wide adoption of e-invoicing and its benefits; represent the industry, engage in the public policy debate and recommend best practices within appropriate European forums; provide services. **Structure** General Assembly (annual); Executive Committee. Working Groups. **Languages** English. **Finance** Members' dues. **Events** *Annual General Meeting* Brussels (Belgium) 2022, *Annual General Meeting* Brussels (Belgium) 2019, *Annual General Meeting* Brussels (Belgium) 2018, *Annual General Meeting* Brussels (Belgium) 2017, *General Assembly* Frankfurt-Main (Germany) 2017. **Publications** *Model Interoperability Agreement*.
Members Full; Associate. Members (over 70) in 21 countries:
Belgium, Denmark, Estonia, Finland, France, Germany, Greece, Italy, Mexico, Netherlands, Norway, Poland, Portugal, Romania, Spain, Sweden, Switzerland, Türkiye, UK, Ukraine, USA.
NGO Relations Liaison Organization of: *Comité européen de normalisation (CEN, #04162)*. [2020/XM4799/**D**]

♦ European Elasmobranch Association (EEA) **06972**

Contact c/o Shark Trust, Unit 4 Creykes Court, The Millfields, Plymouth, PL1 3JB, UK. E-mail: info@eulasmo.org.
URL: http://www.eulasmo.org/

History 1996, Birmingham (UK), as an umbrella organization. **Aims** Coordinate activities of European organizations dedicated to the study and conservation of *sharks*, skates, rays and chimaeras to advance research, sustainable management, conservation and education in the region. **Structure** Annual General Meeting; Board of Directors. **Languages** English. **Staff** All voluntary. **Finance** None. **Activities** Meeting activities. **Events** *EEA Meeting* Leiden (Netherlands) 2021, *EEA Meeting* Rende (Italy) 2019, *EEA Meeting* Peniche (Portugal) 2018, *EEA Meeting* Amsterdam (Netherlands) 2017, *EEA Meeting* Bristol (UK) 2016.
Members Organizations (11) in 11 countries:
France, Germany, Ireland, Italy, Malta, Netherlands, Norway, Portugal, Spain, Switzerland, UK.
IGO Relations Contact with: Elasmobranch Working Group of *International Council for the Exploration of the Sea (ICES, #13021)*; *International Commission for the Conservation of Atlantic Tunas (ICCAT, #12675)*. [2014/XD6768/**D**]

♦ European eLearning Industry Group / see European Learning Industry Group (#07674)
♦ European Electrical Products Certification Association / see European Testing Inspection Certification System (#08901)
♦ European Electrical Standards Coordinating Committee (inactive)
♦ European Electric Road Vehicle Association / see European Association for Electromobility (#06024)

♦ European Electronic Chips and Systems Design Initiative (ECSI) ... **06973**

Contact 47 chemin de la Croze, 38690 Belmont, France. T. +33469313854. Fax +33430650412.
URL: http://www.ecsi.org/

History Founded 1993, with initial support from *European Community Investment Partners (ECIP, inactive)*. **Aims** Help member companies create, improve and integrate new standards and design methodologies; disseminate system-on-chip design methodology and standards information. **Languages** English, French. **Activities** Standards/guidelines; research and development; events/meetings. **Events** *DASIP : Conference on Design and Architectures for Signal and Image Processing* Budapest (Hungary) 2022, *DASIP : Conference on Design and Architectures for Signal and Image Processing* Budapest (Hungary) 2021, *DASIP : Conference on Design and Architectures for Signal and Image Processing* Montréal, QC (Canada) 2019, *DASIP : Conference on Design and Architectures for Signal and Image Processing* Porto (Portugal) 2018, *Forum on Specification and Design Languages* Bremen (Germany) 2016. **Publications** *ECSI Letter*, *ECSI News Bulletin*. FDL Conference proceedings.
Members Industrial (large companies); Industrial Associate (SME companies); Associate (research institutes and universities). Members in 18 countries:
Austria, Belgium, Finland, France, Germany, Greece, Ireland, Italy, Netherlands, Poland, Portugal, Russia, Spain, Sweden, Switzerland, Türkiye, UK, USA. [2015/XF5608/**F**]

♦ European Electronic Component Manufacturers Association (EECA) **06974**
Association européenne des fabricants de composants électroniques – Verband der Europäischen Hersteller Elektronischer Bauelemente

Secretariat Rue de la Duchesse 11/13, 1150 Brussels, Belgium. T. +3222903660. Fax +3222903665. E-mail: secretariat@eusemiconductors.eu.
Pres address not obtained.
URL: https://www.eusemiconductors.eu/

History 1973. Statutes modified: 24 Sep 1992; 1 Jan 1997; 1 Jan 2001. Registration: Banque-Carrefour des Entreprises, No/ID: 0422.589.705, Start date: 31 Mar 1982; EU Transparency Register, No/ID: 22092908193-23, Start date: 28 Feb 2012. **Aims** Promote and defend the interests of the European electronic components industry; support its competitive position in the global marketplace. **Structure** General Assembly (annual); Secretariat in Brussels (Belgium). Industry Associations (2): *European Semiconductor Industry Association (ESIA, #08462)*; *European Passive Components Industry Association (EPCIA, #08164)*. **Languages** English. **Staff** 5.00 FTE, paid. **Finance** Members' dues. **Events** *Meeting* Berlin (Germany) 2016, *Joint meeting* Barcelona (Spain) 2010, *Half-yearly council meeting and general assembly* Brussels (Belgium) 2003, *Half-yearly council meeting and general assembly* Brussels (Belgium) 2002, *Half-yearly council meeting and general assembly* Brussels (Belgium) 2001. **Members** Component Manufactures Industries and national organizations. Membership countries not specified. **NGO Relations** Cooperates with: *European Committee for Electrotechnical Standardization (CENELEC, #06647)*. Member of: *Federation of European and International Associations Established in Belgium (FAIB, #09508)*. [2021/XD3741/**D**]

♦ European Electronic Mail Association / see European Association for e-Identity and Security (#06077)
♦ European Electronic Messaging Association / see European Association for e-Identity and Security (#06077)
♦ European Electronic Retailing Association / see ERA Global – Electronic Retailing Association (#05525)

♦ European Electronics Recyclers Association (EERA) **06975**

Address not obtained.
URL: http://www.eera-recyclers.com/

History 2004. Founded by 6 companies. Registration: EU Transparency Register, No/ID: 761037712721-72. **Aims** Promote the interests of recycling companies who are treating waste electrical and electronic equipment (WEEE) in Europe; aim for harmonization of national and international regulations for WEEE recycling in order to obtain a free market for demand and supply of services; call for environmentally sound operating practices for WEEE recycling activities and members who are signatories to the rules of conduct to safeguard protection of human health and the environment. **Structure** Board of Directors; Executive Secretary; Secretariat. **Languages** English. **Staff** 2.00 FTE, paid. **Finance** Sources: members' dues. **Activities** Advocacy/lobbying/activism; events/meetings; knowledge management/information dissemination; publishing activities.
Members European Electronics Recycling Companies that process and treat waste from electrical and electronic equipment (WEEE) in Europe. full (35) in 18 countries:
Austria, Belgium, Czechia, Denmark, Finland, France, Germany, Ireland, Italy, Netherlands, Norway, Poland, Portugal, Slovakia, Spain, Sweden, Switzerland, UK.
NGO Relations Technical Liaison Partner with: *European Committee for Electrotechnical Standardization (CENELEC, #06647)*. [2019/XJ3205/**D**]

♦ European Electrostatic Discharge Association (inactive)
♦ European Electrostimulation Group (inactive)
♦ European Elephant Keeper and Manager Association (inactive)

♦ European Elevator Association **06976**

SG Av Herrmann-Debroux 44, 1160 Brussels, Belgium. T. +3227721093. Fax +3227718661. E-mail: info@eea-eeig.org.
URL: http://www.eea-eeig.org/

History A grouping of the type *European Economic Interest Grouping (EEIG, #06960)*. Registration: EU Transparency Register, No/ID: 471970117739-42, Start date: 9 Jun 2015. **Aims** Make the built environment totally accessible, by promoting the quality and safety of equipment and services related to elevators, freight lifts, *escalators*, passenger conveyors and associated systems, manufactured, installed or maintained in the enlarged European Union and the European Free Trade Area. **Structure** General Assembly (annual); Management Committee. Committees (2): Budget; Legal. **Languages** English. **Staff** 3.00 FTE, paid.
Members Full in 26 countries:
Austria, Belgium, Bulgaria, Czechia, Denmark, Finland, France, Germany, Greece, Hungary, Ireland, Italy, Latvia, Lithuania, Luxembourg, Netherlands, Norway, Poland, Portugal, Romania, Slovakia, Slovenia, Spain, Sweden, Switzerland, UK.
NGO Relations Member of (3): *European Lift Association (ELA, #07695)*; *Industry4Europe (#11181)*; *World Elevator Federation*. [2019/XD5462/**D**]

♦ European Elite Athletes Association (EU Athletes) 06977

Gen Sec Rue Belliard 40, 1000 Brussels, Belgium. E-mail: info@euathletes.org.
Headquarters Michelangelostraat 55H, 1077 BT Amsterdam, Netherlands.
URL: http://www.euathletes.org/

History 2007. Registration: EU Transparency Register, No/ID: 638820912393-43, Start date: 6 Dec 2013. **Aims** Represent professional and elite level athletes at European and international level; promote good governance in sports organizations; educate athletes on the risks of match fixing; exchange good practices on dual career of athletes. **Structure** Executive Board. **Languages** English, French. **Staff** 3.00 FTE, paid. **Activities** Advocacy/lobbying/activism; knowledge management/information dissemination. **Publications** *Analyses of the Results of European NADO*; *EU Athletes Adverse Analyzing*; *SWAFE Guide*.
Members National players associations and athlete unions (over 35), representing 25,000 individual athletes, in 20 countries:
Belgium, Croatia, Cyprus, Czechia, Denmark, France, Greece, Iceland, Ireland, Italy, Lithuania, Malta, Netherlands, Norway, Poland, Slovenia, Spain, Sweden, Switzerland, UK.
International Beach Volleyball Players' Association (IBVPA, #12329); *The Cyclists' Alliance (TCA, #04990)*.
IGO Relations Member of Consultative Committee of: *Enlarged Partial Agreement on Sport (EPAS, #05487)*. Observer status with: *Council of Europe (CE, #04881)* T-DO; EU Expert Groups. **NGO Relations** Member of (2): *UNI Global Union (#20338)* (World Players Association); *UNI Global Union – Europa (UNI Europa, #20342)*. [2020/XJ5298/y/**D**]

♦ European Embryo Transfer Association (#02582)

♦ European Emergency Number Association (EENA) 06978

Association du Numéro d'Urgence Européen – Europese Noodnummer Associatie

Exec Dir Av de la Toison d'Or 79, 1060 Brussels, Belgium. T. +3225349789. E-mail: info@eena.org.
Communication Officer address not obtained.
URL: http://www.eena.org/

History 1999. Registration: Belgium; EU Transparency Register, No/ID: 68057486299-01. **Aims** Contribute to improving the functioning of emergency services for European citizens. **Structure** Board of Directors; Operations and Technical Committee. **Languages** English. **Staff** 9.00 FTE, paid. **Finance** Sources: fees for services; meeting proceeds; members' dues; revenue from activities/projects. **Activities** Advocacy/lobbying/activism; awards/prizes/competitions; certification/accreditation; events/meetings; projects/programmes; training/education. **Events** *Annual Conference* Marseille (France) 2022, *Annual Conference* Riga (Latvia) 2021, *Annual Conference* Riga (Latvia) 2020, *Annual Conference* Dubrovnik (Croatia) 2019, *Annual Conference* Ljubljana (Slovenia) 2018. **Publications** *Who-is-Who* (2 a year) – handbook; *Public Safety Answering Points* (annual) – global edition. Operations and Technical Committee documents; position papers; white papers. **Members** Emergency services representatives (over 1,500); solution providers (90); international organizations (12); MEPs (over 200); researchers (over 100); mobile network operators (14). Members in over 90 countries. Membership countries not specified. **NGO Relations** Member of (1): *European Telecommunications Standards Institute (ETSI, #08897)*. Supports (1): *European Citizens' Initiative Campaign (ECI Campaign, #06558)*. [2022.05.18/XJ3853/**E**]

♦ European EMES Network / see EMES International Research Network (#05440)
♦ European Employers' Network / see The Federation of International Employers (#09644)

♦ European Employment Lawyers Association (EELA) 06979

SG c/o Rechtsanwälte Gleiss Lutz, Lautenschlagerstr 21, 70173 Stuttgart, Germany. T. +497118997334 – +497118997334. Fax +49711855096. E-mail: info@eela.org.
Chair address not obtained.
URL: http://www.eela.org/

History 1998, London (UK). Registration: Germany. **Aims** Bring together practising employment lawyers across the European Union; exchange views and strengthen links between EU employment lawyers. **Structure** General Assembly (annual); Board; Conference Committee. **Languages** English. **Staff** 1.50 FTE, paid. **Finance** Sources: members' dues. **Activities** Events/meetings; networking/liaising. **Events** *Conference* Bucharest (Romania) 2023, *Annual Conference* Athens (Greece) 2022, *Annual Conference* Stuttgart (Germany) 2021, *Session* Hamburg (Germany) 2020, *Annual Conference* Tallinn (Estonia) 2019. **Publications** *European Employment Law Cases (EELC)* (24 a year).
Members Full in 33 countries and territories:
Austria, Belgium, Bulgaria, Croatia, Cyprus, Czechia, Denmark, Estonia, Finland, France, Germany, Greece, Hungary, Iceland, Ireland, Italy, Latvia, Liechtenstein, Lithuania, Luxembourg, Malta, Netherlands, Northern Ireland, Norway, Poland, Portugal, Romania, Slovakia, Slovenia, Spain, Sweden, Switzerland, UK. [2022/XD8695/**D**]

♦ European EMS Leadership Network 06980

Contact Emergency Medical Services Copenhagen, Telegrafvej 5, Ballerup, 2750 Copenhagen, Denmark. E-mail: ems2018@regionh.dk.
URL: https://emsleadershipnetwork.org/

History Founded 2016, during 1st European *Emergency Medical Services* Congress. **Aims** Create an overview of and establish cooperation between the EMS systems in Europe to explore each other's strengths, limitations and future challenges; describe a desired vision of the European emergency care system, and recommend strategies needed to reach our common and local goals; improve *patient* care and quality in EMS and ensure to benchmark patient outcome. **Activities** Events/meetings. **Events** *European Emergency Medical Services Congress* Glasgow (UK) 2022, *European Emergency Medical Services Congress* Glasgow (UK) 2021, *European Emergency Medical Services Congress* Glasgow (UK) 2020, *European Emergency Medical Services Congress* Madrid (Spain) 2019, *European Emergency Medical Services Congress* Copenhagen (Denmark) 2018.
Members Individual; organizational. Members in 6 countries:
Denmark, France, Germany, Norway, Spain, UK.
NGO Relations Part of: *Global Resuscitation Alliance (GRA)*. [2018/XM7548/**F**]

♦ European EMTP-ATP Users Group (EEUG) 06981

Chair O.S. Bragstadsplass 2E, 7491 Trondheim, Norway. E-mail: ask@eeug.org.
Sec address not obtained.
URL: http://www.eeug.org/

History 1994. Registration: Germany. **Aims** Act as a communication centre for ATP-EMTP users; coordinate programme distribution. **Structure** Members' Meeting. Executive Board, comprising Chairman, Deputy Chairman, Secretary, Treasurer and 3 members. **Finance** Sources: members' dues. **Activities** Events/meetings. **Events** *Conference* Grenoble (France) 2023, *Conference* Cagliari (Italy) 2014, *Conference* Dublin (Ireland) 2013, *Conference* Zwickau (Germany) 2012, *Conference* Ohrid (Macedonia) 2011. **Publications** *EEUG News*. **Members** Universities, research institutes, electric power utilities, manufacturers and consultants. Membership countries not specified. [2023/XJ1564/**E**]

♦ European Enamel Association (unconfirmed)
♦ European Enamel Authority (unconfirmed)

♦ European Endometriosis League (EEL) 06982

Europäische Endometriose Liga

Contact Habichtweg 7, 21244 Buchholz, Germany. T. +494181281075.
URL: http://www.endometriose-liga.eu/

History Sep 2005. Registered in accordance with German law. **Structure** Bureau, comprising President and 5 members. **Finance** Members' dues. **Events** *Congress* Prague (Czechia) 2019, *Congress* Vienna (Austria) 2018, *Congress* Paris (France) 2015, *European Congress / Congress* Berlin (Germany) 2013, *European Congress / Congress* Siena (Italy) 2012. [2015/XJ7423/**D**]

♦ European Endoscopy Study Group (inactive)

♦ European Endowment for Democracy (EED) 06983

Fonds Européen pour la Démocratie

Exec Dir Rue de la Loi 34, 1040 Brussels, Belgium. E-mail: secretariat@democracyendowment.eu.
URL: http://democracyendowment.eu/

History Set up Dec 2011, as an independent private law foundation, by Member States and European Union institutions, including *European External Action Service (EEAS, #07018)* and *Committee of Permanent Representatives to the European Union (#04278)*. Registered in accordance with Belgian law. EU Transparency Register: 986644617102-08. **Aims** Promote European values of freedom and democracy. **Structure** Board of Governors, consisting of a representative from each Ministry of Foreign Affairs of the Member States of *European Commission (EC, #06633)*, a member designated by the EC, a representative of the High Representative for the Union for Foreign Affairs and Security Policy, up to 9 representatives of within the framework of *European Parliament (EP, #08146)* and up to 3 persons selected from among people with major experience in the field of democracy support and/or democratic transition. Executive Committee. **Languages** Arabic, English, French, Russian. **Finance** Voluntary contributions; donations; grants. **Events** *Conference on No Democracy without Accountability* Brussels (Belgium) 2019.
Members Individuals in 29 countries:
Austria, Belgium, Bulgaria, Croatia, Cyprus, Czechia, Denmark, Estonia, Finland, France, Germany, Greece, Hungary, Ireland, Italy, Latvia, Lithuania, Luxembourg, Malta, Netherlands, Norway, Poland, Portugal, Romania, Slovakia, Slovenia, Spain, Sweden, UK. [2019.02.15/XJ7510/f/**E**]

♦ European Energy Association / see European Energy Forum (#06986)
♦ European Energy Centre (unconfirmed)

♦ European Energy Crops Inter-Network (EECI-Network) 06984

Coordinator Biomass Technology Group, PO Box 835, 7500 AV Enschede, Netherlands. T. +31534861186. Fax +31534861180. E-mail: office@btgworld.com.
URL: http://www.eeci.net/

Aims Provide information on energy crops in Europe.
Members Partners (19) in 14 countries:
Austria, Belgium, Denmark, Finland, France, Germany, Greece, Ireland, Italy, Netherlands, Portugal, Spain, Sweden, UK. [2012/XF7105/**F**]

♦ European Energy Efficiency Fund (eeef) 06985

Contact address not obtained. E-mail: info@eeef.eu.
URL: http://www.eeef.eu/

History 2011, Luxembourg. Set up as a public-private partnership. Initial capitalization provided by *European Commission (EC, #06633)*. Registration: Luxembourg. **Aims** Support the climate goals of the European Union; promote a sustainable energy environment; foster climate protection by enabling projects in European cities, regions and communities to build resilient infrastructure. **Structure** Board of Directors. **Languages** English. **Finance** Initial capitalization provided by *European Commission (EC, #06633)*; increased with contributions from *European Investment Bank (EIB, #07599)*, Cassa Depositi e Prestiti (Italy) and Investment manager Deutsche Bank (Germany). [2021.05.25/XM4094/f/**F**]

♦ European Energy Forum (EEF) 06986

Forum Européen de l'Energie

Dir Gen Square Eugène Plasky 92-94, bte 14, 1030 Brussels, Belgium. T. +3222270460. E-mail: assistant@europeanenergyforum.eu.
Registered Office 20 Place des Halles, 67000 Strasbourg, France.
URL: http://www.europeanenergyforum.eu/

History 1979. Founded by several members of the European Parliament. Statutes most recently modified, 18 Jun 2008. Former names and other names: *European Energy Association (EEA)* – former; *Association européenne de l'énergie* – former; *European Energy Foundation (EEF)* – former; *Fondation européenne de l'énergie* – former. Registration: Start date: 6 May 1981, France; Belgium; EU Transparency Register, No/ID: 45953576620-17. **Aims** Facilitate dialogue in the field of energy between members of the European Parliament, representatives from the European Commission, officials from the European Union and industries, organizations or research centres involved in the energy sector. **Structure** General Assembly (annual); Board of Directors; Bureau. **Languages** English, French. **Staff** 3.50 FTE, paid. **Finance** Sources: members' dues. **Activities** Events/meetings; networking/liaising. **Events** *Conference on Low Emission Mobility* Brussels (Belgium) 2018. **Publications** *EEF Newsletter* (12 a year). **Members** Active: members of European Parliament. Associate: companies; research organizations; associations; regulators. Membership countries not specified. **NGO Relations** Links with industry stakeholders (not specified). [2020.05.15/XD1026/y/**F**]

♦ European Energy Foundation / see European Energy Forum (#06986)

♦ European Energy Information Sharing and Analysis Centre (EE-ISAC) 06987

Contact Avenue Marnix 30 b14, 1000 Brussels, Belgium. E-mail: contact@ee-isac.eu.
Registered Address Avenue de la Toison d'Or 22 b1, 1050 Brussels, Belgium.
URL: https://www.ee-isac.eu/

History Registration: Banque-Carrefour des Entreprises, No/ID: 0643.937.072, Start date: 26 Nov 2015, Belgium; EU Transparency Register, No/ID: 089154834713-90, Start date: 1 May 2019. **Aims** Improve the resilience and security of the European energy infrastructure, by sharing trust-based information and enabling a joint effort for the analysis of threats, vulnerabilities, incidents, solutions and opportunities. **Structure** Plenary; Board of Directors. **Activities** Training/education; publishing activities; events/meetings. **Events** *Members Plenary* Brussels (Belgium) 2022, *Plenary Session* Porto (Portugal) 2022, *Plenary Meeting* Brussels (Belgium) 2021, *Plenary Meeting* Brussels (Belgium) 2021, *Plenary Meeting* Brussels (Belgium) 2020. **Publications** *EE-ISAC Newsletter*.
Members Utilities; technical and service providers; academia; research institutes; governmental and non-profit organizations. Membership countries not specified. Included in the above, 1 organization listed in this Yearbook:
Included in the above, 1 organization listed in this Yearbook:
European Union Agency for Network and Information Security (ENISA, #08971).
NGO Relations Memorandum of Understanding with (1): *European Utilities Telecom Council (EUTC, #09042)*. [2022/XM8785/**D**]

♦ European Energy Mediators Group (unconfirmed)

♦ European Energy Network (EnR) 06988

Sec c/o ADEME, 27 rue Louis Vicat, 75737 Paris CEDEX 15, France.
URL: http://www.enr-network.org/

History Former names and other names: *European Network of Energy Agencies* – former. Registration: EU Transparency Register, No/ID: 911689722889-60, Start date: 1 Aug 2016. **Aims** Increase Europe's energy *efficiency* and use of *renewable energy* sources by encouraging and facilitating exchange of information and expertise among members and by acting as a bridge between national activities and those of the European Community and other relevant international bodies; provide a channel for pan-European technical support to European organizations on matters of energy policy, strategy and programmes. **Structure** Administered by Presidency and Secretariat which rotate annually; task forces; working groups. **Languages** English. **Finance** No budget. Activities funded by national resources plus financial contributions from outside sources for specific projects within working groups and for major tasks involving members. **Events** *BEHAVE – European Conference on Behaviour and Energy Efficiency* Copenhagen (Denmark) 2021, *BEHAVE – European Conference on Behaviour and Energy Efficiency* Copenhagen (Denmark) 2020, *BEHAVE – European Conference on Behaviour and Energy Efficiency* Zurich (Switzerland) 2018, *BEHAVE – European Conference on Behaviour and Energy Efficiency* Coimbra (Portugal) 2016, *BEHAVE – European Conference on Behaviour and Energy Efficiency* Oxford (UK) 2014.
Members Organizations responsible for planning, management or review of national research, development, demonstration or dissemination programmes in the fields of energy efficiency and renewable energy in 23 countries:
Austria, Bulgaria, Croatia, Denmark, Finland, France, Germany, Greece, Ireland, Italy, Luxembourg, Netherlands, Norway, Poland, Portugal, Romania, Russia, Slovakia, Spain, Sweden, Switzerland, Türkiye, UK. [2021/XF6881/**F**]

♦ European Energy Research Alliance (EERA) 06989

Office Manager Rue de Namur 72, 1000 Brussels, Belgium. T. +3225111618. E-mail: secretariat@eera-set.eu.
URL: http://www.eera-set.eu/

History 27 Oct 2008, Paris (France). Founded by 10 European research institutes, in close collaboration and support of *European Commission (EC, #06633)*, in response to the 'European Energy Technology Plan (SET-plan)'. Registration: Start date: 2014, Belgium; EU Transparency Register, No/ID: 339037837173-73. **Aims** Strengthen, expand and optimize EU energy research capabilities through the sharing of world-class national facilities in Europe and the joint realization of pan-European research programmes. **Structure** General Assembly. Executive Committee. Secretariat. **Finance** Supported by: *European Commission (EC, #06633)* (DG General Research); participating organizations. **Activities** Events/meetings; projects/programmes; research and development. **Events** *Deep Sea Offshore Wind Conference* Trondheim (Norway) 2023, *Conference on Repowering Europe for a sustainable EU strategic autonomy* Brussels (Belgium) 2022, *Conference on Repowering Europe for a sustainable EU strategic autonomy* Brussels (Belgium) 2022, *Deep Sea Offshore Wind Conference* Trondheim (Norway) 2022, *Summer Strategy Meeting* Brussels (Belgium) 2021. **Publications** *EERA Newsletter*. Scientific publications.

Members Organizations (over 250) in 29 countries:
Austria, Belgium, Croatia, Cyprus, Czechia, Denmark, Estonia, Finland, France, Germany, Greece, Iceland, Ireland, Italy, Latvia, Lithuania, Malta, Netherlands, Norway, Poland, Portugal, Romania, Slovakia, Slovenia, Spain, Sweden, Switzerland, Türkiye, UK.
Included in the above, 2 organizations listed in this Yearbook:
Joint Research Centre (JRC, #16147); *SINTEF*. [2020.06.24/XJ2823/**D**]

♦ European Energy Retailers (EER) 06990

SG Rue d'Egmont 15, 1000 Brussels, Belgium. E-mail: tl@fortyeight.brussels.
URL: http://europeanenergyretailers.eu/

History Founded 2017. Full title: *European Energy Retailers – Network of Independent Energy and Solution Providers (EER)*. EU Transparency Register: 438257432313-42. **Aims** Achieve an active role of the retailer and other solution providers as a: promoter of competition; adviser to customers; enabler of customers' access to markets and provider of risk mitigation services; provider of new and innovative products and services. **Events** *Energy Data at your Fingertips?!* Brussels (Belgium) 2020.

Members Full in 5 countries:
France, Germany, Italy, Spain, Sweden. [2019/XM8786/**F**]

♦ European Energy Retailers – Network of Independent Energy and Solution Providers / see European Energy Retailers (#06990)
♦ European Energy Transition Conference (meeting series)
♦ European Engineered Construction Systems Association (inactive)

♦ European Engineering Industries Association (EUnited) 06991

Head of Office Bluepoint Bldg, Bvd A Reyers 80, 1030 Brussels, Belgium. T. +3227068209. E-mail: info@eu-nited.net.
URL: http://www.eu-nited.net/

History Registration: Banque-Carrefour des Entreprises, No/ID: 0874.269.908, Start date: 1 Jan 2005, Belgium; EU Transparency Register, No/ID: 0289344948-82, Start date: 12 Jan 2009. **Aims** Promote and support at an international level the European engineering industries, including tools and components, process, production, power transmission, automation engineering, manufacturing technology as well as software and product-related services and other related fields. **Structure** General Assembly (every 3 years); Board; Sectors (6). **Languages** English. **Staff** 2.00 FTE, paid. **Finance** Members' dues. **Events** *Plenary Meeting* Brussels (Belgium) 2020, *General Assembly* Brussels (Belgium) 2018, *Meeting* Brussels (Belgium) 2016, *General Assembly* Brussels (Belgium) 2015, *General Assembly* Brussels (Belgium) 2012. **IGO Relations** Registered with: *European Commission (EC, #06633)*. **NGO Relations** Member of: *International Association for Soaps, Detergents and Maintenance Products (#12166)*; *Industry4Europe (#11181)*. [2021/XJ5626/t/**D**]

♦ European Engineering and Management Association (inactive)
♦ European Engineering school of Chemistry, Polymers and Materials Science (internationally oriented national body)
♦ European Engine Power Plants Association (internationally oriented national body)

♦ European Enhanced Vehicle-Safety Committee (EEVC) 06992

Address not obtained.

History Founded Oct 1970, as *European Experimental Vehicles Committee (EEVC)*. **Aims** Provide impartial scientific advice to support the development of European vehicle safety standards and legislation; coordinate European research activities with regard to harmonized vehicle safety regulations. **Structure** Steering Committee. **Finance** Resources supplied by supporting governments.

Members Ministerial departments of 7 countries:
France, Germany, Italy, Netherlands, Poland, Spain, UK.
Regional entity:
European Commission (EC, #06633).

NGO Relations *Forum of European Road Safety Research Institutes (FERSI, #09913)*. [2017/XU3228/**D***]

♦ European Enterprise Institute (EEI) 06993

Contact address not obtained. T. +3222333837. Fax +3227421785.

History 27 Mar 2003, by *SME-UNION (inactive)*. **Aims** Preserve and strengthen foundations of freedom-limited governments, private entreprises, cultural and political institutions. **Events** *Seminar* Ljubljana (Slovenia) 2003.

Members in 6 countries:
Austria, Czechia, Hungary, Poland, Slovakia, Slovenia. [2010/XE4625/j/**E**]

♦ European Entertainment Alliance / see European Arts and Entertainment Alliance (#05918)

♦ European Entrepreneurs CEA-PME 06994

Confédération Européenne des Associations de Petites et Moyennes Entreprises (CEA-PME)

Managing Dir Av de la Renaissance 1, 1000 Brussels, Belgium. T. +3227396264. Fax +3227402032. E-mail: info@cea-pme.com.
URL: https://www.european-entrepreneurs.org/

History 1992, Germany. Former names and other names: *Europäische Vereinigung der Verbände kleiner und mittlerer Unternehmen* – alias. Registration: Start date: 2004, Belgium. **Aims** Represent the interests of SMEs *small and medium-sized entreprises* to the European institutions; contribute to Europe's economy with growth and jobs. **Structure** Board. **Languages** Dutch, English, French, German, Italian, Spanish. **Events** *EU-African SME Summit* Rome (Italy) 2020, *EU-African SME Summit* Brussels (Belgium) 2019, *Meeting on the Future of a Mobility Scheme for SMEs and their Employees in Europe* Brussels (Belgium) 2017.

Members in 24 countries:
Armenia, Austria, Belarus, Belgium, Bulgaria, Croatia, Estonia, France, Georgia, Germany, Greece, Hungary, Italy, Lithuania, Luxembourg, Netherlands, Poland, Portugal, Romania, Slovakia, Slovenia, Spain, Sweden, Türkiye.
International organizations (2):
European Association of Institutes for Vocational Training (#06085); *European Small Business Alliance of Small and Medium Independent Enterprises (ESBA, #08494)*. [2021.06.10/XM3459/y/**D**]

♦ European Entrepreneur Verlagsgesellschaft UG (unconfirmed)
♦ European Envelope Manufacturers Association (#09578)

♦ European Environment Agency (EEA) 06995

Agence européenne pour l'environnement – Agencia Europea de Medio Ambiente – Europäische Umweltagentur – Agência Europeia do Ambiente – Agenzia Europea dell'Ambiente – Europees Milieuagentschap – Europaeiske Miljøagentur – Europeiske Miljøbyrået

Exec Dir Kongens Nytorv 6, 1050 Copenhagen K, Denmark. T. +4533367100. Fax +4533367198.
URL: http://www.eea.europa.eu/

History 7 May 1990, Brussels (Belgium), on adoption of regulation by *Council of the European Union (#04895)*, following proposal, 12 Jul 1989, by *European Commission (EC, #06633)*. Regulation was amended: by Council Regulation (EC) No 933/1999 of 29 Apr 1999; by Regulation (EC) No 1641/2003 of *European Parliament (EP, #08146)* and of the Council of 22 Jul 2003. Original resolution was in force 30 Oct 1993, following decision to locate the Agency in Copenhagen (Denmark). Starting in 1993 with the then 12 EU Member States, EEA membership was broadened to include EFTA countries and EU membership of Austria, Finland and Sweden in 1995. Broadened again to include the 13 EU "candidate countries" – final acts of EEA membership ratified, Dec 2001, by 11 such countries, which joined EEA as member countries from 1 Jan 2002; Poland and Turkey ratified and joined later in 2002. Switzerland joined in 2006. Croatia joined in 2013. A decentralized agency of *European Union (EU, #08967)*. **Aims** As the EU body dedicated to providing sound, independent *information* on the environment, act as a major information source for those involved in developing, adopting, implementing and evaluating environmental *policy*, and also the general public; report on the effectiveness of environmental and sectoral policies and their implementation. **Structure** Management Board; Bureau (of the Board); Scientific Committee; Executive Director. *European Environment Information and Observation Network (EIONET, #07002)*, set up under the EEA regulation and coordinated by EEA, constituted by 6 European Topic Centres, National Focal Points (NFP) in each member country, plus in 6 cooperating countries (Albania, Bosnia-Herzegovina, North Macedonia, Serbia, Montenegro, Kosovo) under UN Security Council Resolution 1244/99; National Reference Centres (NRC) in all 39 countries, totalling about 1,000 experts in over 350 national environment agencies and other bodies dealing with environmental information. *'NFP/Eionet Group'*: national focal points in 39 countries; representatives from partners in the European Commission; European Topic Centres (6): *European Topic Centre for Air Pollution and Climate Change Mitigation (ETC/ACM)*; *European Topic Centre on Biological Diversity (ETC/BD)*; *European Topic Centre on Climate Change impacts, vulnerability and Adaptation (ETC/CCA)*; *European Topic Centre on Waste and Materials in a Green Economy (ETC/WMGE)*; *European Topic Centre on Inland, Coastal and Marine waters (ETC/ICM)*; *European Topic Centre on Urban, Land and Soil Systems (ETC/ULS)*. **Languages** Croatian, Czech, Danish, Dutch, English, Estonian, Finnish, French, German, Hungarian, Icelandic, Irish Gaelic, Italian, Latvian, Lithuanian, Maltese, Norwegian, Polish, Portuguese, Slovakian, Slovene, Spanish, Swedish, Turkish. **Staff** 218.00 FTE, paid. **Finance** Annual budget (2018): euro 43,100,000. **Activities** Knowledge management/information dissemination; advocacy/lobbying/activism. **Events** *ONE – Health Environment and Society Conference* Brussels (Belgium) 2022, *SOER 2020: Civil Society's Role for a Just (and Fast) Transition towards Sustainability* Brussels (Belgium) 2020, *WCEF : World Circular Economy Forum* Helsinki (Finland) 2019, *International Interdisciplinary Conference on Land Use and Water Quality* The Hague (Netherlands) 2013, *Eye on earth summit* Abu Dhabi (United Arab Emirates) 2011. **Publications** *EEA Signals* (annual) – report; *The European Environment: State and Outlook Report* (every 5 years). Briefings; reports and technical reports; data service; articles; corporate documents; brochures; videos; web services.

Members Governments of 32 countries (" indicates non-EU country):
Austria, Belgium, Bulgaria, Croatia, Cyprus, Czechia, Denmark, Estonia, Finland, France, Germany, Greece, Hungary, Iceland (*), Ireland, Italy, Latvia, Liechtenstein (*), Lithuania, Luxembourg, Malta, Netherlands, Norway (*), Poland, Portugal, Romania, Slovakia, Slovenia, Spain, Sweden, Switzerland (*), Türkiye (*).

IGO Relations Memorandum of Understanding signed with: *Commission on the Protection of the Black Sea Against Pollution (Black Sea Commission, #04237)*; *Secretariat of the Convention of Wetlands (#19200)*; *UNEP (#20299)*. Reports to: Council of Europe; European Commission; European Parliament; *European Court of Auditors (#06854)*. Participates without vote: *EFTA (#05391)*. Observer to: *Global Bioenergy Partnership (GBEP, #10251)*; *JPI Climate (#16156)*. According to Council Regulation 1210/90, close cooperation with: *Joint Research Centre (JRC, #16147)*; *Statistical Office of the European Union (Eurostat, #19974)*. According to Council Regulation 1210/90, active cooperation with: *Council of Europe (CE, #04881)*; *European Investment Bank (EIB, #07599)*; European Parliament; *European Space Agency (ESA, #08798)*; *International Atomic Energy Agency (IAEA, #12294)*; *International Energy Agency (IEA, #13270)*; *OECD (#17693)*; *United Nations Economic Commission for Europe (UNECE, #20555)*; *WHO (#20950)*; *World Meteorological Organization (WMO, #21649)*. Associate participant in: *Global Biodiversity Information Facility (GBIF, #10250)*. Member of: *Environmental Action Programme for Central and Eastern Europe (EAP, inactive)*. Participates in: *Group on Earth Observations (GEO, #10735)* and *EuroGEOSS (#05685)*. Active cooperation with:
- *Arctic Monitoring and Assessment Programme (AMAP, #01100)*;
- *Baltic Marine Environment Protection Commission – Helsinki Commission (HELCOM, #03126)*;
- *Committee on Environmental Policy (#04253)*;
- *Conference of European Statisticians (CES, #04600)*;
- *Cooperative Programme for Monitoring and Evaluation of the Long-range Transmission of Air Pollutants in Europe (EMEP, #04800)*;
- *International Council for the Exploration of the Sea (ICES, #13021)*;
- *International Rice Research Institute (IRRI, #14754)*;
- *Natura 2000 Network (see: #06633)*;
- *OSPAR Commission for the Protection of the Marine Environment of the North-East Atlantic (OSPAR Commission, #17905)*;
- *Conservation of Arctic Flora and Fauna (CAFF, #04728)*;
- *Secretariat of the Convention on Biological Diversity (SCBD, #19197)*;
- *Standing Committee to the Bern Convention on the Conservation of European Wildlife and Natural Habitats (#19949)*;
- *UN Environment Programme World Conservation Monitoring Centre (UNEP-WCMC, #20295)*;
- *WHO Regional Office for Europe (#20945)*.

NGO Relations Member of (3): *Biodiversity Indicators Partnership (BIP, #03242)*; *EU Agencies Network (EUAN, #05564)*; *Green Spider Network (GSN, #10728)*. Observer to: *European Umbrella Organization for Geographical Information (EUROGI, #08964)*. Supports: *European Food Sustainable Consumption and Production Round Table (European Food SCP Roundtable, #07289)*. Library is member of: *Eurolib (#05703)*. [2021/XF2419/**F***]

♦ European Environmental Advisory Councils / see European Environment and Sustainable Development Advisory Councils (#07003)

♦ European Environmental Bureau (EEB) 06996

SG Rue des Deux Eglises 14-16, 1000 Brussels, Belgium. T. +3222891090. E-mail: secretariat@eeb.org – eeb@eeb.org – secretarygeneral@eeb.org.
URL: https://eeb.org/

History 13 Dec 1974, Brussels (Belgium). 1 Jan 2014, took over *Northern Alliance for Sustainability (ANPED, inactive)*. Took over some of the activities of *Green Budget Europe (GBE, inactive)*. Former names and other names: *European Federation of Environmental NGOs* – alias; *Bureau européen de l'environnement (BEE)* – former; *Oficina Europea del Medio Ambiente* – former; *Ufficio Europeo dell' Ambiente* – former; *Secretariado Europeu do Ambiente* – former; *Europaeisk Miljøsekretariat* – former; *Evropaiko Grafio Perivallontos* – former; *Europees Milieubureau* – former; *Europäisches Umweltbüro* – former. Registration: Banque-Carrefour des Entreprises, No/ID: 0415.814.848, Start date: 9 Dec 1975, Belgium; EU Transparency Register, No/ID: 06798511314-27, Start date: 6 Mar 2009. **Aims** Promote environmental *sustainable* policies at European Union level; be effective in improving EU environmental policies and realizing sustainable development by integrating environmental objectives in horizontal and sectoral policies of the EU and by ensuring compliance with effective strategies to realize these objectives. **Structure** General Assembly (annual); Executive Committee; Working Groups. **Languages** English, French. **Staff** 85.00 FTE, paid. **Finance** Sources: contributions; grants; members' dues. **Activities** Events/meetings; politics/policy/regulatory. **Events** *Annual Conference* Stockholm (Sweden) 2023, *Annual Conference* Brussels (Belgium) 2022, *Conference* Paris (France) 2021, *Conference* Brussels (Belgium) 2020, *Circular Economy Working Group Meeting* Brussels (Belgium) 2019. **Information Services** *EEB Library*.

Members Full; Associate; Affiliate; Honoary. Civil sociey organizations (over 180) in 36 countries:
Austria, Belgium, Bulgaria, Croatia, Cyprus, Czechia, Denmark, Estonia, Finland, France, Georgia, Germany, Greece, Hungary, Ireland, Italy, Latvia, Lithuania, Luxembourg, Malta, Moldova, Netherlands, North Macedonia, Norway, Poland, Portugal, Romania, Serbia, Slovakia, Slovenia, Spain, Sweden, Switzerland, Türkiye, UK, Ukraine.
Health and Environment Justice Support (HEJSupport); *International Environmental Association of River Keepers (Eco-TIRAS)*; *MEDITERRANEAN SOS Network (MEDSOS)*; *Organization Earth*; *Stichting Mondiaal Alternatief (SMA, no recent information)*.
European Networks (25):
- *Air Pollution & Climate Secretariat (AirClim)*;
- *Association Justice and Environment, z.s. (J&E, #02774)*;
- *Bellona Europa*;
- *Carbon Market Watch (#03423)*;

- *CEEweb for Biodiversity (#03626)*;
- *CHEM Trust*;
- *ClientEarth (#03996)*;
- *Coastwatch Europe (CWE)*;
- *Compassion in World Farming (CIWF, #04414)*;
- *Eco-union*;
- *European Compost Network (ECN, #06694)*;
- *European Federation of City Farms (EFCF, #07078)*;
- *European Land and Soil Alliance (ELSA, #07645)*;
- *European Union of Mountaineering Associations (EUMA, #09002)*;
- *Fédération Spéléologique Européenne (FSE, #09705)*;
- *Fern (#09736)*;
- *IFLA Europe (#11103)*;
- *International Chemical Secretariat (ChemSec)*;
- *Internationals amis de la nature (IAN, #14780)*;
- *Pesticide Action Network (PAN, #18336)*;
- *Seas at Risk (SAR, #19189)*;
- *Stichting Changing Markets (#19984)*;
- *Union Européenne Contre les Nuisances des Avions (UECNA, #20395)*;
- *Women Engage for a Common Future (WECF, #20992)*;
- *Youth and Environment Europe (YEE, #22012)*.

Consultative Status Consultative status granted from: *ECOSOC (#05331)* (Ros A); *Council of Europe (CE, #04881)* (Participatory Status); *UNEP (#20299)*. [2023/XD5414/y/**E**]

♦ European Environmental Centre, Warsaw (internationally oriented national body)
♦ European Environmental Citizens' Organisation for Standardisation / see Environmental Coalition on Standards (#05499)

♦ European Environmental Communication Networks (EECN) 06997

Address not obtained.
URL: http://ec.europa.eu/environment/networks/index_en.htm

History 1995. **Aims** Support and stimulate communication and liaison between the European Union administration and national actors; work for coordination and continuous exchange of experience in the field of environmental communication and climate change. **Finance** Supported by *European Commission (EC, #06633)* (DG ENV). **Activities** Organizes annual meetings for each network. **Events** *Annual meeting* Copenhagen (Denmark) 2003, *Annual meeting* Helsinki (Finland) / Tallinn (Estonia) 2002, *Annual meeting* Nicosia (Cyprus) / Paphos (Cyprus) 2001. **NGO Relations** Member of: *Green Spider Network (GSN, #10728)*. Houses: *Climate Broadcasters Network – Europe (CBN-E, #04007)*. [2010/XF6323/**F**]

♦ European Environmental and Contact Dermatitis Research Group (EECDRG) 06998

Address not obtained.
URL: https://www.eecdrg.org/

History Founded 1984. UK Registered Charity: 328351. **Aims** Promote research in contact dermatitis and other skin-intolerance problems; standardize patch testing; organize meetings for dermatologists and other interested parties; perform group studies on specific projects; perform research on particular allergens; give advice to companies; help in consumer protection. **Structure** Chairperson; Secretary; Treasurer. **Languages** English. **Staff** Part-time, voluntary. **Finance** Through group studies and provision of advice. **Activities** Events/meetings; projects/programmes. **Events** *ESCD Congress* Amsterdam (Netherlands) 2021, *Meeting* Rome (Italy) 2002, *Meeting* Amsterdam (Netherlands) 2000, *Meeting* London (UK) 1998.
Members Individuals (21) in 12 countries:
Belgium, Denmark, Finland, France, Germany, Italy, Netherlands, Portugal, Spain, Sweden, UK, USA. [2019/XD6305/v/**D**]

♦ European Environmental Film Directors Society (internationally oriented national body)
♦ European Environmental Law Association (inactive)

♦ European Environmental Law Forum (EELF) 06999

Secretariat Helmholtz Ctr for Environmental Research, Permoserstr 15, 04318 Leipzig, Germany. E-mail: secretariat@eelf.info.
URL: http://www.eelf.info/

Aims Support intellectual exchange on the development and implementation of international, European and national environmental law in Europe. **Structure** Managing Board; Secretariat. **Activities** Events/meetings; networking/liaising. **Events** *Annual Conference* Utrecht (Netherlands) 2019, *Annual Conference* Copenhagen (Denmark) 2017, *Annual Conference* Wroclaw (Poland) 2016, *Annual Conference* Aix-en-Provence (France) 2015, *Annual Conference* Brussels (Belgium) 2014. **Members** Individuals. Membership countries not specified. **NGO Relations** Cooperates with: *Environmental Law Network International (ELNI, #05504)*; *European Union Forum of Judges for the Environment (EUFJE)*; *European Union Network for the Implementation and Enforcement of Environmental Law (IMPEL, #09005)*. [2016/XM5036/**F**]

♦ European Environmental Management Association (inactive)

♦ European Environmental Mutagenesis and Genomics Society (EEMGS) 07000

Sec address not obtained.
Pres address not obtained.
URL: https://www.eemgs.eu/

History 10 Jul 1970, Neuerburg (Germany). Former names and other names: *European Environmental Mutagen Society (EEMS)* – former (10 Jul 1970 to 2015). Registration: Switzerland. **Aims** Study and evaluate potential *genetic* and *carcinogenic hazards* to man due to exposure to the increasing number and variety of *chemicals* in the environment. **Structure** Council; Executive Committee; National Sections. **Languages** English. **Staff** Voluntary. **Finance** Members' dues (annual): euro 10 for members of regional societies; euro 20 for individual members. **Activities** Research; information dissemination; study; awards. **Events** *Annual General Meeting* 2021, *Annual Meeting* Porto (Portugal) 2020, *Annual Meeting* Rennes (France) 2019, *Annual Meeting* Potsdam (Germany) 2018, *Annual General Meeting* Leuven (Belgium) 2017. **Publications** *EEMS Newsletter*, *European Journal of Genetic Toxicology* – online.
Members Individuals (about 1,400) in 41 countries:
Argentina, Austria, Belarus, Belgium, Bulgaria, Canada, China, Croatia, Cuba, Czechia, Denmark, Estonia, Finland, France, Germany, Greece, Hungary, Iceland, Ireland, Israel, Italy, Japan, Latvia, Lithuania, Netherlands, New Zealand, Nigeria, Norway, Poland, Portugal, Qatar, Russia, Serbia, Slovenia, Spain, Sweden, Switzerland, UK, USA, Venezuela.
NGO Relations Member of: *International Association of Environmental Mutagenesis and Genomics Societies (IAEMGS, #11877)*. [2021/XD0444/v/**D**]

♦ European Environmental Mutagen Society / see European Environmental Mutagenesis and Genomics Society (#07000)
♦ European Environmental Research Organization (inactive)
♦ European Environment Campuses

♦ European Environment and Health Youth Coalition (EEHYC) 07001

Address not obtained.
URL: http://www.eehyc.org/

History Founded 2012. **Aims** Support, legitimize and give visibility to young people's participation in processes aimed at achieving a healthy and sustainable environment. **Structure** Executive Board; Advisory Board; National Youth Coordinators. **NGO Relations** Member of: *Global Climate and Health Alliance (GCHA, #10288)*. [2020/XM9001/**D**]

♦ European Environment Information and Observation Network (EIONET) 07002

Coordinator c/o European Environment Agency, Kongens Nytorv 6, 1050 Copenhagen K, Denmark. T. +4523683662.
URL: http://www.eionet.europa.eu/

History 7 May 1990, Brussels (Belgium), at the same time as *European Environment Agency (EEA, #06995)*, by Regulation 1210/90 of *Council of the European Union (#04895)*, which came into force 30 Oct 1993, on decision to locate the Agency in Copenhagen (Denmark). Regulation was amended: by Council Regulation (EC) No 933/1999 of 29 Apr 1999; by Regulation (EC) No 1641/2003 of the European Parliament and of the Council of 22 Jul 2003. **Aims** Together with the EEA, provide the *European Union* and its member states with objective, reliable and comparable information on environment at European level to enable them to take necessary measures to protect the environment, assess results of these measures and ensure that the public is properly informed about the state of the environment. **Structure** Coordinated by European Environment Agency (EEA). Eionet components: National Focal Points (NFP); National Reference Centres (NRC); European Topic Centres (6): *European Topic Centre for Air Pollution and Climate Change Mitigation (ETC/ACM)*; *European Topic Centre on Biological Diversity (ETC/BD)*; *European Topic Centre on Climate Change impacts, vulnerability and Adaptation (ETC/CCA)*; *European Topic Centre on Waste and Materials in a Green Economy (ETC/WMGE)*; *European Topic Centre on Inland, Coastal and Marine waters (ETC/ICM)*; *European Topic Centre on Urban, Land and Soil Systems (ETC/ULS)*. **Languages** English. **Staff** 209.00 FTE, paid. **Finance** Annual budget: euro 49,200,000. **Activities** Knowledge management/information dissemination. **Events** *Air Quality Management and Assessment Workshop* Prague (Czechia) 2018, *Air Quality Management and Assessment Workshop* Lisbon (Portugal) 2017, *Air Quality Management and Assessment Workshop* Stockholm (Sweden) 2016, *Air Quality Management and Assessment Workshop* Bern (Switzerland) 2014, *Noise Workshop* Bern (Switzerland) 2014. **Publications** *Eionet Connects* – brochure. **Information Services** *EIONET Information Technology Infrastructure* – is equipping NFPs with telematics capacity.
Members National Focal Points (NFPs) in 33 countries:
Austria, Belgium, Bulgaria, Croatia, Cyprus, Czechia, Denmark, Estonia, Finland, France, Germany, Greece, Hungary, Iceland, Ireland, Italy, Latvia, Liechtenstein, Lithuania, Luxembourg, Malta, Netherlands, Norway, Poland, Portugal, Romania, Slovakia, Slovenia, Spain, Sweden, Switzerland, Türkiye, UK.
National Focal Points in 6 cooperating countries:
Albania, Bosnia-Herzegovina, Kosovo, Montenegro, North Macedonia, Serbia.
IGO Relations Represented in the EIONET Group: *European Commission (EC, #06633)*; *Joint Research Centre (JRC, #16147)*; *Statistical Office of the European Union (Eurostat, #19974)*. [2018.08.28/XF5227/**F***]

♦ European Environment and Sustainable Development Advisory Councils (EEAC) 07003

Mailing Address PO 27, 2501 CA The Hague, Netherlands. E-mail: info@eeac.eu.
URL: http://www.eeac.eu/

History 1993. Former names and other names: *European Environmental Advisory Councils (EEAC)* – former (1993); *EEAC Network* – alias. **Aims** Bridge the gap between scientific knowledge and policymaking; enrich the advice that individual advisory bodies can give to their governments by encouraging exchange of experience among members. **Structure** Plenary Session (annual, at Conference); Steering Committee; Office (Secretariat). **Languages** English. **Staff** 0.50 FTE, paid. **Finance** Members' dues. **Activities** Events/meetings. **Events** *Annual Conference* Helsinki (Finland) 2022, *Annual Conference* Barcelona (Spain) 2021, *Annual Conference* Dublin (Ireland) 2020, *Annual Conference* Lisbon (Portugal) 2019, *Annual Conference* Berlin (Germany) 2018. **Publications** Newsletter. Summary documents; position papers.
Members National and regional European Advisory Councils or other advisory bodies for Environment and Sustainable Development in 12 countries:
Belgium, Czechia, France, Germany, Hungary, Ireland, Montenegro, Netherlands, Poland, Portugal, Spain, UK. [2022/XD8373/**D**]

♦ De Europeanen in de Wereld (#08839)

♦ European Equality Law Network 07004

General Coordinator address not obtained.
URL: https://www.equalitylaw.eu/

History Dec 2014. Founded on merger of European Network of Legal Experts in the Non-discrimination Field and European Network of Legal Experts in the field of Gender Equality. Former names and other names: *European network of legal experts in gender equality and non-discrimination* – full title. **Structure** Governed by Human European Consultancy, the School of Law of Utrecht University and *Migration Policy Group (MPG, #16801)*, on behalf of *European Commission (EC, #06633)*. Executive Committee of Senior Experts. **Activities** Events/meetings; knowledge management/information dissemination; research/documentation. [2020/AA2079/**F**]

♦ European Equestrian Federation (EEF) 07005

Fédération Equestre Européenne
SG Belgicastraat 9, Box 2, 1930 Zaventem, Belgium. E-mail: info@euroequestrian.eu.
URL: http://www.euroequestrian.eu/

History Sep 2009, Antwerp (Belgium). Statutes formally signed Feb 2010, Warendorf (Germany).. Registration: Banque-Carrefour des Entreprises, No/ID: 0828.245.287, Start date: 3 Aug 2010, Belgium; EU Transparency Register, No/ID: 497532043195-28, Start date: 16 Jun 2021. **Aims** Maximize the potential and development of equestrianism throughout the continent. **Structure** General Assembly; Board; Committees (5). **Languages** English. **Finance** Sources: members' dues. **Activities** Events/meetings. **Events** *General Assembly* 2020, *General Assembly* London (UK) 2011, *General Assembly* Istanbul (Turkey) 2010, *General Assembly* Warendorf (Germany) 2010, *Meeting* Tel Aviv (Israel) 1996.
Members National federations in 38 countries and territories:
Albania, Austria, Belgium, Bulgaria, Croatia, Cyprus, Czechia, Denmark, Estonia, Finland, France, Germany, Great Britain, Greece, Hungary, Ireland, Israel, Italy, Latvia, Liechtenstein, Lithuania, Luxembourg, Monaco, Netherlands, North Macedonia, Norway, Poland, Portugal, Romania, San Marino, Serbia, Slovakia, Slovenia, Spain, Sweden, Switzerland, Türkiye, Ukraine.
Associate members (8):
International Dressage Officials Club (IDOC, #13200); *International Dressage Riders Club (IDRC, #13201)*; *International Dressage Trainers Club (IDTC, #13202)*; *International Equestrian Organisers' Alliance (IEOA, #13289)*; *International Group for Equestrian Qualifications (IGEQ, #13744)*; *International Jumping Officials Club (IJOC, #13976)*; *International Jumping Riders Club (IJRC, #13977)*; Jumping Owners Club.
NGO Relations Member of (1): *European Horse Network (EHN, #07499)*. [2021/XJ5347/y/**D**]

♦ European Equine Health and Nutrition Association (internationally oriented national body)

♦ European Esperanto Union 07006

Union espérantiste européenne – Europa Esperanto-Unio (EEU)
Pres Av des Gémeaux 4, 1410 Waterloo, Belgium. T. +32498910516.
Vice-Pres Wapenplein 17 – 0201, 8400 Ostend, Belgium.
URL: http://seanoriain.eu/

History 1975. Registration: Banque-Carrefour des Entreprises, No/ID: 0880.712.884, Start date: 13 Apr 2006, Belgium; EU Transparency Register, No/ID: 640861131800-62, Start date: 15 Jun 2018. **Aims** Support linguistic justice and non-discrimination within the European Union by promoting the use of Esperanto so as to ensure equality, improve the learning of other languages and strengthen a European identity in harmony with national and regional identities. **Structure** Board; Committee. **Languages** Esperanto. **Staff** 2.00 FTE, voluntary. **Finance** Sources: members' dues. Supported by: *European Union (EU, #08967)*. Annual budget: 56,000 EUR. **Activities** Events/meetings. **Events** *Conference* Slubice (Poland) / Frankfurt-Oder (Germany) 2021, *Conference* Slubice (Poland) / Frankfurt-Oder (Germany) 2020, *Conference* Trieste (Italy) 2019, *Congress* Rijeka (Croatia) 2014, *Congress* Galway (Ireland) 2012. **Publications** *Europa Bulteno* (9 a year) – online.
Members National Associations in 27 countries:
Austria, Belgium, Bulgaria, Croatia, Cyprus, Czechia, Denmark, Estonia, Finland, France, Germany, Greece, Hungary, Ireland, Italy, Latvia, Lithuania, Luxembourg, Malta, Netherlands, Poland, Portugal, Romania, Slovakia, Slovenia, Spain, Sweden.
NGO Relations Member of (3): *European Civil Society Platform for Multilingualism (ECSPM, #06569)*; *Federation of European and International Associations Established in Belgium (FAIB, #09508)*; *Universal Esperanto Association (UEA, #20676)*. Supports (1): *European Alliance for the Statute of the European Association (EASEA, #05886)*. [2022.05.13/XD8216/**D**]

♦ European Esports Federation (EEF) 07007
Pres c/o Belgian Esports Federation, Boulevard de l'Empereur 14, 1000 Brussels, Belgium. E-mail: info@esportseurope.org.
URL: https://esportseurope.org/
History Founded Feb 2020. Popularly referred to as *Esports Europe*. **Aims** Represent esports players and organizations in European politics, media, sports and society; build a platform for its members and the esports movement to develop and promote esports as a conscious, responsible, sustainable, inclusive, healthy and value-based activity. **Publications** *Esports Europe Newsletter*. **Members** National esports organizations (23); stakeholders (3). Membership countries not specified. [2020/XM9013/**D**]

♦ European Esports Observatory (unconfirmed)

♦ European Ethylene Producers Committee (EEPC) 07008
Contact Rue Belliard 40, Box 15, 1040 Brussels, Belgium. T. +3224369481. E-mail: contact@eepc-eu.org.
URL: https://www.eepc-eu.org/
History 1996. Founded as part of the Lower Olefins Sector Group of *Petrochemicals Europe (#18342)*, within *Conseil européen de l'industrie chimique (CEFIC, #04687)*. **Structure** Executive Committee; Main Committee; Working Groups (2); Issue Groups (7). **Languages** English. **Events** *Ethylene Seminar* Brussels (Belgium) 2020. [2020.05.06/XM5417/**E**]

♦ European Evaluation Society (EES) 07009
Secretariat Combs Tannery, Tannery Road, Combs, Stowmarket, IP14 2EN, UK. T. +4407821520912. E-mail: secretariat@europeanevaluation.org.
URL: http://www.europeanevaluation.org/
History 1994, The Hague (Netherlands). Registration: Netherlands Chamber of Commerce, No/ID: 40413697, Netherlands, Europe. **Aims** Promote theory, practice and utilization of high quality evaluation, especially, but not exclusively, within the European countries. **Structure** Board. **Languages** English. **Staff** 1.00 FTE, paid. **Finance** Sources: members' dues. **Activities** Events/meetings; knowledge management/information dissemination; standards/guidelines. **Events** *Biennial Conference* Copenhagen (Denmark) 2022, *Biennial Conference* Copenhagen (Denmark) 2021, *Biennial Conference* Copenhagen (Denmark) 2020, *Biennial Conference* Thessaloniki (Greece) 2018, *Biennial Conference* Maastricht (Netherlands) 2016. **Publications** *Connections* (3-4 a year) – newsletter; *Evaluation – the International Journal of Theory, Research and Practice*. **Members** Individuals (450) and institutional (43) in 82 countries. Membership countries not specified. **NGO Relations** Member of (2): *DARA (#05009)*; *International Organisation for Cooperation in Evaluation (IOCE, #14426)*. Partner of (1): *EvalPartners (#09208)*. [2022.07.27/XD7014/**D**]

♦ European Evangelical Accrediting Association / see European Council for Theological Education (#06846)

♦ European Evangelical Alliance (EEA) 07010
Alliance évangélique européenne – Europäische Evangelische Allianz
Bonn Office Representation Reuterstr 116, 53129 Bonn, Germany. E-mail: info@europeanea.org.
Brussels Representation Office Rue Belliard 205/14, 1040 Brussels, Belgium.
URL: http://www.europeanea.org/
History 1953. Registration: EU Transparency Register, No/ID: 922173318516-97, Start date: 2 Sep 2015. **Aims** Foster unity and evangelical identity; provide a voice and platform to evangelical Christians. **Structure** General Assembly (annual); Council (annual); Executive Committee. **Languages** English, German. **Staff** 3.50 FTE, paid; 6.00 FTE, voluntary. **Finance** Sources: contributions. **Activities** Advocacy/lobbying/activism; events/meetings; networking/liaising. **Events** *General Assembly* Brussels (Belgium) 2020, *General Assembly* 2013, *General Assembly* Coma-ruga (Spain) 2012, *General Assembly* Comarruga (Spain) 2012, *General Assembly* Bad Liebenzell (Germany) 2011.
Members National alliances in 32 countries:
Albania, Austria, Azerbaijan, Belgium, Bosnia-Herzegovina, Bulgaria, Croatia, Cyprus, Czechia, Denmark, Estonia, Finland, France, Germany, Greece, Hungary, Ireland, Israel, Italy, Kazakhstan, Kosovo, Luxembourg, Netherlands, Norway, Portugal, Romania, Serbia, Spain, Sweden, Switzerland, Türkiye, UK.
Affiliate members (17):
Agape Europe; *Compass*; EA Arab Speaking Fellowship; *European Christian Mission (ECM International)*; *European Council for Theological Education (ECTE, #06846)*; *European Educators' Christian Association (EurECA, #06968)*; *International Fellowship of Evangelical Students (IFES, #13583)*; *International Teams*; *Jews for Jesus (JFJ)*; *Mission Without Borders International (MWBI, #16830)*; *OC International (OCI, #17688)*; *Operation Mobilisation (#17772)*; Reach Global; Scripture Union; *Trans World Radio (TWR)* (European section); World Without Orphans; *Youth for Christ International (YFCI, #22009)*.
NGO Relations Member of (2): *European Policy Centre (EPC, #08240)*; *World Evangelical Alliance (WEA, #21393)*. [2023.02.14/XD0712/y/**D**]

♦ European Evangelical Mission Association (EEMA) 07011
Sec c/o AEM, Johannes Daur Str 1, 70825 Korntal-Münchingen, Germany. E-mail: aem@aem.de.
URL: http://www.europeanema.org/
History 1989. **Aims** Bring together national mission networks and pan-European mission movements; promote partnership and good practice. **Structure** Members' Meeting (during Conference); Executive Committee. **Languages** Dutch, English, German. **Staff** None. **Finance** Sources: members' dues. **Activities** Events/meetings; networking/liaising. **Events** *Conference* Budapest (Hungary) 2019, *Conference* Malta 2017, *Conference* Romania 2016, *Revolutions in European mission* Bucharest (Romania) 2014, *Conference* Spain 2013. **Publications** *EEMA-Info*.
Members Full in 16 countries:
Austria, Denmark, Estonia, Finland, France, Germany, Hungary, Iceland, Ireland, Italy, Netherlands, Norway, Portugal, Sweden, Switzerland, UK.
Also pan-European associate members, not specified. [2020.07.17/XD7104/**D**]

♦ European Exchange on Archaeological Research and Communication / see EXARC (#09219)

♦ European Exhibition Industry Alliance (EEIA) 07012
SG Rue de l'Amazone 2, 1050 Brussels, Belgium. T. +3225357250.
URL: http://www.exhibition-alliance.eu/
History 2012. Founded by European members of *UFI – The Global Association of the Exhibition Industry (#20276)* and *European Major Exhibition Centres Association (EMECA, #07726)*. **Aims** Represent common interests of the European exhibition industry to European Union institutions and other relevant stakeholders in Brussels. **NGO Relations** Member of (1): *European Tourism Manifesto (#08921)*. [2019/XM6733/t/**D**]

♦ European Exo/Astrobiology Network Association / see European Astrobiology Network Association (#06286)

♦ European Expanded Clay Association (EXCA) 07013
SG Av Louise 480, IT Tower – 18th, 1050 Brussels, Belgium. T. +3228953110. E-mail: info@exca.eu.
URL: http://www.exca.eu/
History 12 Jan 2007. Registration: Banque Carrefour des Entreprises, No/ID: 0887.987.488, Start date: 15 Mar 2007, Belgium; EU Transparency Register, No/ID: 133772322651-41, Start date: 13 Jul 2016. **Aims** Promote the interests of the European expanded clay aggregates industry by representing its members on economic, technical, environmental, energy and promotional issues. **Structure** General Assembly; Board; Working Groups (2); Head Office, headed by Secretary General. **Languages** English. **Staff** 1.00 FTE, paid.
Members Companies (10) in 10 countries:
Belgium, Czechia, Denmark, Finland, Germany, Italy, Norway, Poland, Portugal, UK.
NGO Relations Member of (5): *Construction 2050 Alliance (#04760)*; *Construction Products Europe AISBL (#04761)* (Associate); *European Ceramic Industry Association (CERAME-UNIE, #06506)*; *European Network on Silica (NEPSI, #08001)*; *Industry4Europe (#11181)*. In liaison with technical committees of: *Comité européen de normalisation (CEN, #04162)*. [2023.02.14/XM7465/**D**]

♦ European Expedition Guild (internationally oriented national body)
♦ European Experimental Vehicles Committee / see European Enhanced Vehicle-Safety Committee (#06992)

♦ European Expert Group on the transition from institutional to community-based care (EEG) 07014
Coordinator address not obtained. E-mail: coordinator@deinstitutionalisation.com.
URL: https://deinstitutionalisation.com/
History Feb 2009. Convened by then Commissioner for Employment and Social Affairs Vladimir Špidla of *European Commission (EC, #06633)*. Former names and other names: *Ad Hoc Expert Group on the transition from institutional to community-based care* – former. **Aims** Advocate to replace institutionalization with family- and community-based support.
Members Full (12):
Autism-Europe (AE, #03040); *COFACE Families Europe (#04084)*; *Eurochild (#05657)*; *European Association of Service Providers for Persons with Disabilities (EASPD, #06204)*; *European Coalition for Community Living (ECCL, #06590)*; *European Disability Forum (EDF, #06929)*; *European Federation of National Organisations Working with the Homeless (#07174)*; *European Social Network (ESN, #08505)*; *Inclusion Europe – European Association of Societies of Persons with Intellectual Disability and their Families (Inclusion Europe, #11144)*; *Lumos Foundation*; *Mental Health Europe (MHE, #16715)*; *UNICEF (#20332)*.
Associate (2):
European Platform for Rehabilitation (EPR, #08230); *European Union Agency for Fundamental Rights (FRA, #08969)*. [2022/AA2737/y/**E**]

♦ European Expertise and Expert Institute (EEEI) 07015
Institut Européen de l'expertise et de l'expert (IEEE)
Hon Pres 38 rue de Villiers, 92532 Levallois-Perret CEDEX, France. T. +33141499601. Fax +33141490289. E-mail: contact@experts-institute.eu.
Registered Office 5 résidence petite place, 78000 Versailles, France.
URL: http://www.experts-institute.eu/
History Current statutes adopted 7 June 2019. Registration: EU Transparency Register, No/ID: 807004837808-45, Start date: 16 Apr 2020; France. **Aims** Set up a network of research and exchanges in *judicial* expertise across the EU; harmonize experts' practices and improve expertise. **Structure** General Assembly (annual); Executive Committee; Executive Office. Committees: Orientation; Scientific; Admission. Working Groups; Working Commissions. **Languages** English, French. **Staff** Mainly voluntary. **Finance** Sources: contributions; members' dues. Annual budget: 27,000 EUR (2013). **Events** *Congrès* Paris (France) 2008. **Members** Natural persons; Legal Persons; Institutions. Membership countries not specified. **IGO Relations** Member observer of: *Commission européenne pour l'efficacité de la justice (CEPEJ, #04213)*. [2020/XM2948/j/**D**]

♦ European Expert Network on Terrorism Issues (EENeT) 07016
Address not obtained.
URL: http://www.european-enet.org/
History 2007. In 2011, still in the process of being set up. **Aims** Promote multidisciplinary and multi-agency analysis and research which are considered prerequisites for providing comprehensive insights into the complexity of the phenomenon "terrorism". **Structure** Conference. Steering Committee. Administrative Office. **Events** *Annual Conference* Brussels (Belgium) 2010, *Annual Conference* Vienna (Austria) 2009, *Annual Conference* The Hague (Netherlands) 2008, *Annual Conference* The Hague (Netherlands) 2008, *Annual Conference* Wiesbaden (Germany) 2007. **Members** Full (about 70) in 17 European countries (countries not specified). [2012/XJ0153/**F**]

♦ European Express Association (EEA) 07017
Secretariat c/o Fleishman-Hillard, Square de Meeûs 35, 1000 Brussels, Belgium. T. +3222854604. Fax +3222305706. E-mail: info@euroexpress.org.
URL: http://www.euroexpress.org/
History 2000, on merger of *Association of European Express Carriers (AEEC, inactive)* with *European Express Organization (EEO, inactive)*. EU Transparency Register: 1894704851-83. **Aims** Regroup leading integrators, national express associations and small and medium-sized companies operating across Europe; represent members' interests at EU level; assist members to ensure time-definite, reliable express *transportation* services for documents, parcels and freight. **Structure** Board of Directors, comprising Chairman, Vice-Chairman, Treasurer, one Administrator from each member society, 4 representatives of member societies from the European Community countries. Secretary General. Working Groups (4): Competition and Market Reform; Customs; Security, Transport and Environment. **Languages** English. **Finance** Members' dues. **Activities** Assembles professional expertise; initiates and maintains constructive dialogue with relevant authorities at EU and national levels; offers EEA Hermes Award for contributions to development of the postal and express industry. **Publications** *Customs Expressed* (4 a year); *Express Newsletter* (4 a year).
Members Private carriers and national associations. Full members in 8 countries:
Belgium, Denmark, France, Germany, Netherlands, Spain, Switzerland, UK.
Subsidiary and partner members in 15 countries:
Belgium, Denmark, France, Germany, Hungary, Italy, Netherlands, Norway, Poland, Portugal, Spain, Sweden, Switzerland, Türkiye, UK.
IGO Relations Cooperates with: *European Aviation Security Training Institute (EASTI, #06304)*. **NGO Relations** Member of: *Council for Environmentally Friendly Aviation (CEFA, #04880)*; *Global Express Association (GEA, #10351)*. [2017/XD8583/**D**]

♦ European Expression (internationally oriented national body)

♦ European External Action Service (EEAS) 07018
Service européen pour l'action extérieure – Servicio Europeo de Acción Exterior – Europäischer Auswärtiger Dienst – Serviço para a Ação Externa – Servizio Europeo per l'Azione Esterna – Europese Dienst voor Extern Optreden – Europeiska Utrikestjänsten – Tjenesten for EU's Optraeden Udadtil – Euroopan Ulkosuhdehallinnon Sivustolle – tSeirbhis Eorpach Gniomhaiochta Eachtrai – Evropské Sluzby pro Vnejsi Cinnost – Európai Külügyi Szolgálat Honlapjan – Evropske Sluzbe za Zunanje Delovanje – Euroopa Välisteenistuse Veebisaidile – Eiropas Arejas Darbibas Dienesta – Ewropew Ghall-Azzjoni Esterna – Europsku Sluzbu za Vanjsko Djelovanje – Serviciului European de Actiune Externéa
Office EEAS Bldg, Rond Point Schuman 9A, 1046 Brussels, Belgium. T. +3225841111.
URL: http://www.eeas.europa.eu/
History Established by *Treaty of Lisbon (2007)*. Organization and functioning established by decision of *Council of the European Union (#04895)*, acting on proposal from *High Representative of Common Foreign and Security Policy (CFSP / PESC)* after consulting *European Parliament (EP, #08146)* and obtaining consent from *European Commission (EC, #06633)*. European Parliament passed resolution of approval, 8 Jul 2010. Council of European Union adopted decision confirming proposal, 26 Jul 2011. Launched 1 Jan 2011. A functionally autonomous body of *European Union (EU, #08967)*. **Aims** Help the EU's foreign affairs chief – the High Representative for Foreign Affairs and Security Policy – carry out the Union's Common Foreign and Security Policy (CFSP); run about 140 EU Delegations and Offices operating around the world, representing the EU and its citizens globally. **Structure** High Representative; Foreign Policy Instruments Service; *European Union Military Committee (EUMC)* and *European Union Military Staff*; 3 Deputy Secretaries General: Economic and Global Issues; Political Affairs; CSDP and Crisis Response. Also includes chair *Political and Security Committee (PSC / COPS)*. Operates around 140 delegations worldwide. Regional departments (5): Africa; Americas; Asia and Pacific; Europe and Central Asia; Middle East and North Africa. Departments (2): Budget and Administration; Human Rights, Global and Multilateral Issues. **Activities** Military operations include: *European Union Force in Bosnia and Herzegovina (EUFOR, #08990)*. **Events** *Meeting* Brussels (Belgium) 2019, *Meeting* Brussels (Belgium) 2019, *High-Level Meeting on Regional Cooperation in the North* Helsinki (Finland) 2019, *Conference* Madrid (Spain) 2019, *Joint Commission Meeting* Vienna (Austria) 2019. **IGO Relations** Cooperates with: *European Training Foundation (ETF, #08934)*. **NGO Relations** On Programme Board of: *Linear Collider Collaboration (LCC, #16481)*. Supports: *European Forum for International Mediation and Dialogue (mediatEUr)*. Member of: *Eurolib (#05703)*. Staff represented by: *Union syndicale du service public européen (#20486)*. [2018/XJ5453/**E***]

♦ **European Extruded Polystyrene Insulation Board Association (EXIBA)** **07019**

Contact Rue Belliard 40, Box 16, 1040 Brussels, Belgium. E-mail: info@styrenicsextranet.org.
URL: http://www.exiba.org/

History 1987. Founded as a sector group of *Conseil européen de l'industrie chimique (CEFIC, #04687)*. Currently operates as a Sector Group within *Association of Plastics Manufacturers in Europe (Plastics Europe, #02862)*. **Aims** Make known to authorities, industry and the general public the economic and social role of extruded polystyrene insulation board; study the use and applications of products covered, in particular from the viewpoint of protection of the *environment*, health and safety and product end-of-life; examine legislation which affects the *industry*, such as CFC phase out. **Structure** General Assembly; Steering Committee; Working Group.
Members Companies (9) in 9 countries:
Austria, Belgium, France, Germany, Hungary, Italy, Spain, Sweden, UK.
NGO Relations Member of (3): *Circular Plastics Alliance (#03936)*; *Modern Building Alliance (#16842)*; *Styrenics Circular Solutions (SCS, #20022)*. [2020/XE1508/**E**]

♦ **European Eye Bank Association (EEBA)** **07020**

Exec Officer Via Paccagnella 11, Padiglione Rama, 30174 Zelarino PD, Italy. T. +39419656422. Fax +39419656421. E-mail: admin@europeaneyebanks.org.
URL: https://www.eeba.eu/

History 1989, Aarhus (Denmark). Permanent Secretariat became operational in 2002. Registration: Start date: 2004, Italy; EU Transparency Register, No/ID: 840527028525-56. **Aims** Provide tissues and cells of optimum quality and safety for transplantation and the treatment of eye diseases, according to the highest medical and scientific standards. **Structure** General Assembly (annual); Committee. **Languages** English. **Staff** 0.20 FTE, paid. **Finance** Sources: members' dues. **Activities** Knowledge management/information dissemination; networking/liaising; research and development; standards/guidelines; training/education. **Events** *Annual Meeting* Heidelberg (Germany) 2026, *Annual Meeting* Rome (Italy) 2025, *Annual Meeting* Antwerp (Belgium) 2024, *Annual Meeting* Aachen (Germany) 2023, *Annual Meeting* Liverpool (UK) 2022. **Publications** *Directory of European Eye Banks*. Annual editions.
Members Full in 28 countries:
Australia, Austria, Belgium, Bulgaria, Croatia, Czechia, Denmark, Finland, France, Germany, Hungary, Ireland, Israel, Italy, Netherlands, New Zealand, Norway, Poland, Portugal, Russia, Slovakia, Slovenia, Spain, Sri Lanka, Sweden, Switzerland, UK, USA.
NGO Relations Member of (2): *European Alliance for Vision Research and Ophthalmology (EU-EYE, #05890)*; *Global Alliance of Eye Bank Associations (GAEBA, #10197)*. [2022.05.02/XD6081/**D**]

♦ European Facilities Management / see European Facility Management Network (#07021)

♦ **European Facility Management Network (EuroFM)** **07021**

Mailing Address PO Box 85612, 2508 CH The Hague, Netherlands. E-mail: mail@eurofm.org.
URL: http://www.eurofm.org/

History 22 Dec 1993. Former names and other names: *European Facilities Management* – alias. Registration: Netherlands. **Aims** Advance knowledge of facility management in *Europe*; improve education about, and practice of, facility management; initiate research and deliver "best practice". **Structure** Board; Secretariat; Network Groups; Project Teams. **Languages** English. **Staff** 0.50 FTE, paid. **Finance** Members' dues. Sponsoring. Annual budget: euro 80,000 – 90,000. **Activities** Knowledge management/information dissemination; training/education; networking/liaising; events/meetings. **Events** *European Facility Management Conference (EFMIC)* Barcelona (Spain) 2020, *European Facility Management Conference (EFMIC)* Barcelona (Spain) 2020, *European Facility Management Conference* Dublin (Ireland) 2019, *International Facility Management Congress* Vienna (Austria) 2019, *Members Meeting* Lisbon (Portugal) 2018. **Publications** *Facilities* (4 a year) – magazine; *Euro-FM Newsletter* (24 a year). Reports; research; proceedings.
Members Corporate Associates; Affiliates. National associations in 23 countries:
Austria, Belgium, Bulgaria, Czechia, Denmark, Finland, France, Germany, Hungary, Ireland, Italy, Latvia, Luxembourg, Netherlands, Norway, Poland, Portugal, Romania, Spain, Sweden, Switzerland, Türkiye, UK.
IFMA chapters in 14 countries:
Austria, Belgium, Czechia, Finland, France, Germany, Italy, Luxembourg, Netherlands, Poland, Spain, Sweden, Switzerland, UK.
Educational and research institutes in 12 countries:
Austria, Finland, Germany, Hungary, Ireland, Netherlands, Norway, Poland, Sweden, Switzerland, Türkiye, UK.
Research organizations in 7 countries:
Austria, Finland, Germany, Ireland, Netherlands, Sweden, UK. [2020/XF4374/**F**]

♦ **European Fact-checking Standards Network (EFCSN)** **07022**

Registered Address Boulevard Bischoffsheim 39, Bte 4, 1000 Brussels, Belgium.
URL: https://efcsn.com/

History Registration: Banque-Carrefour des Entreprises, No/ID: 0797.486.191, Start date: 23 Jan 2023, Belgium; EU Transparency Register, No/ID: 847550548807-30, Start date: 27 Jan 2023. **Aims** Uphold and promote the highest standards of fact-checking; promote media literacy for the public benefit. **Structure** Assembly; Governance Body. **Finance** Supported by: *European Union (EU, #08967)*.
Members Full in 5 countries:
France, Germany, Italy, Poland, Spain. [2023/AA3281/**F**]

♦ **European Factories of the Future Research Association (EFFRA)** **07023**

Exec Dir BluePoint Ctr, Boulevard Auguste Reyers 80, 1030 Brussels, Belgium. T. +3227068238. E-mail: info@effra.eu.
URL: http://www.effra.eu/

History Set up by MANUFUTURE technology platform and industrial associations. EU Transparency Register: 147908916864-59. **Aims** Promote pre-competitive research on production technologies within the European Research Area by engaging in a public-private partnership with the European Union called 'Factories of the Future'. **Structure** General Assembly; Board of Directors; Industrial Research Advisory Group (IRAG). Executive Director. **Activities** Research/documentation. **Events** *Factories of the Future Conference* Brussels (Belgium) 2016. **Publications** *Impact* – public newsletter.
Members Industry; Research; Association. Included in the above, 5 organizations listed in this Yearbook:
Conseil européen de l'industrie chimique (CEFIC, #04687); *European Association of the Machine tool Industries and related Manufacturing Technologies (CECIMO, #06113)*; *European Engineering Industries Association (EUnited, #06991)* (Robotics); *European Federation for Welding, Joining and Cutting (EWF, #07233)*; *Orgalim – Europe's Technology Industries (#17794)*.
IGO Relations *European Commission (EC, #06633)*. **NGO Relations** Member of: *European Technology Platform ALICE (ALICE, #08888)*. [2020/XJ8761/y/**E**]

♦ **European Factory Automation Committee (EFAC)** **07024**

Conference Organizer c/o Swissmem, Pfingstweidstrasse 102, 8005 Zurich ZH, Switzerland. T. +41443844811.
URL: http://www.efac.org/

History 15 Mar 2000. **Aims** Represent the manufacturers of assembly and handling technology. **Languages** English. **Activities** Main field of activity: Market surveys and statistics; Public relations; Marketing services; Trade fairs; Networking events and conferences. **Events** *Conference* Frankfurt-Main (Germany) 2015, *Conference* Davos (Switzerland) 2013, *International Precision Assembly Seminar* Chamonix (France) 2012, *Conference* Davos (Switzerland) 2011, *International precision assembly seminar* Chamonix (France) 2010.
Members Trade associations in 7 countries:
Finland, France, Germany, Italy, Netherlands, Spain, Switzerland.
NGO Relations *European Machine Vision Association (EMVA, #07721)*. [2017/XJ3164/**E**]

♦ European Faculty of Land Use and Development / see European Academy of Land Use and Development (#05797)

♦ **European Fair Play Movement (EFPM)** **07025**

Mouvement européen du fair play

Pres Maria Jacobi Gasse 1, 1030 Vienna, Austria.
URL: http://www.fairplayeur.com/

History May 28 1994, Zurich (Switzerland). **Aims** Promote fair play and tolerance in the broadest sense (in sports and everyday life) at European level. **Structure** General Assembly. Executive Committee, comprising President, 2 Vice-Presidents, General Secretary, Treasurer and 4 members. **Languages** English, French. **Staff** Voluntary. **Finance** Members' dues. Other sources: donations; sponsoring. Budget (annual): about euro 25,000. **Activities** Grants EFPM Fair Play Awards (annual). **Events** *European Fair Play Congress* Vienna (Austria) 2021, *European Fair Play Congress* Budapest (Hungary) 2019, *Sport, spirit of humanity* Brussels (Belgium) 2018, *Sports as a tool for reconciliation* Haifa (Israel) 2017, *Congress* Vienna (Austria) 2016. **Publications** *EFPM Newsletter* (4 a year); *Play Fair* (annual) – magazine.
Members National organizations in 39 countries:
Albania, Andorra, Armenia, Austria, Azerbaijan, Belarus, Bosnia-Herzegovina, Bulgaria, Croatia, Cyprus, Czechia, Denmark, Estonia, Finland, France, Georgia, Germany, Greece, Hungary, Ireland, Israel, Italy, Latvia, Lithuania, Luxembourg, Malta, Moldova, Netherlands, North Macedonia, Poland, Portugal, Romania, Russia, Serbia, Slovakia, Slovenia, Spain, Türkiye, Ukraine.
IGO Relations Represented on Board of: *Enlarged Partial Agreement on Sport (EPAS, #05487)*. **NGO Relations** Memorandum of Understanding with (1): *European Olympic Academies (EOA, #08082)*. Joint venture with: *European Olympic Committees (EOC, #08083)*; *International Sport and Culture Association (ISCA, #15587)*; *International Workers and Amateurs in Sports Confederation (#15905)*. Member of: *International Council of Sport Science and Physical Education (ICSSPE, #13077)*. *European Sports Press Union (AIPS Europe, #08822)* is member. [2020/XF3811/**F**]

♦ **European Fair Trade Association (EFTA)** **07026**

Association européenne pour un commerce équitable

Contact Via Francesco Crispi 9, 39100 Bolzano, Italy. E-mail: info@newefta.org.
Registered Office Godfried Bomansstraat 8/3, 4103 WR Culemborg, Netherlands.
URL: http://www.newefta.org/

History Oct 1987, a group of ATOs having been meeting regularly since 1978. Jointly funded secretariat set up Jan 1988. Registered in accordance with Dutch law, 15 Jan 1990. **Aims** Support member organizations in their work and encourage them to cooperate and coordinate; facilitate the exchange of information and network; create conditions for labour division; develop projects. **Structure** Board (meets at least annually). Executive Committee of a least 3 members, including Chairperson, Vice-Chairperson, Secretary and Treasurer (a member may hold more than one post). **Languages** English. **Staff** 1.00 FTE, paid. **Finance** Members' dues. Budget (annual): about euro 135,000. **Activities** Organizes meetings on food, handicrafts, monitoring, producer support and managers. Disseminates information. include: joint product design and development; project development assistance programme; coordinated activities in Europe, such as trading agreements, coordinated study and research and campaigning. **Publications** *Fair Trade Yearbook* (1998). Information Services: Database of suppliers and products.
Members Organizations (10) in 9 countries:
Austria, Belgium (2), France, Germany, Italy, Netherlands, Spain (1), Switzerland, UK.
Consultative Status Consultative status granted from: *UNCTAD (#20285)* (Special Category). **NGO Relations** Observer to: *World Fair Trade Organization (WFTO, #21396)*. Instrumental in setting up: *Fair Trade Advocacy Office (FTAO, #09238)*. [2018/XD2046/t/**D**]

♦ European Fairy Tale Association (#05755)

♦ **European Falcon Network** **07027**

Contact IFM-SEI, Rue Joseph II 120, 1000 Brussels, Belgium. T. +3222157927. E-mail: contact@ifm-sei.org.
URL: http://www.ifm-sei.org/

History within the framework of *International Falcon Movement – Socialist Educational International (IFM-SEI, #13327)*. **Aims** Empower *young people* in Europe by youth exchange, seminars and other ways of education; promote the participation of young people in decision making processes on all levels; lobby for children's *rights* in Europe. **Structure** Coordinated by Praesidium members of IFM-SEI. **Languages** English, French, Spanish. **Staff** 3.00 FTE, paid. **Finance** Sources: donations; members' dues. Other sources: subsidies. **Activities** Advocacy/lobbying/activism; events/meetings; training/education. **Events** *Meeting* Austria 2019, *Meeting* Norway 2017, *Seminar* Helsinki (Finland) / Stockholm (Sweden) 2016, *Meeting* Salzburg (Austria) 2013, *Meeting* Oer-Erkenschwick (Germany) 2012. **Publications** Handbooks; toolkits; videos.
Members Full in 19 countries:
Armenia, Austria, Belarus, Belgium, Czechia, Denmark, Finland, Georgia, Germany, Hungary, Lithuania, Norway, Slovakia, Slovenia, Spain, Sweden, Switzerland, Türkiye, UK. [2020.05.07/XF5815/**F**]

♦ European Familial ALS Association (no recent information)
♦ European Families in Business Conference (meeting series)

♦ **European Family Businesses (EFB)** **07028**

SG Square de Meeûs 35, 1000 Brussels, Belgium. T. +3228939710. Fax +3229839799. E-mail: info@europeanfamilybusinesses.eu.
URL: http://www.europeanfamilybusinesses.eu/

History 1997, as *European Group of Owner Managed and Family Enterprises (GEEF)*. Adopted the following title: *European Family Businesses-GEEF (EFB-GEEF)*, 2009. EU Transparency Register: 58849794266-75. **Aims** Press for policies that recognize the fundamental contribution of family businesses in Europe's economy and create a level playing field when compared to other types of companies. **Structure** General Assembly; Board; Management Committee. **Activities** Events/meetings. **Events** *Summit* Brussels (Belgium) 2018, *Summit* Amsterdam (Netherlands) 2017, *Summit* Lisbon (Portugal) 2016, *Summit* Paris (France) 2015, *Summit* Berlin (Germany) 2014. **Publications** *EFB News*.
Members Associations in 12 countries:
Andorra, Bulgaria, Finland, France, Germany, Malta, Netherlands, Portugal, Romania, Spain, UK.
Included in the above, 1 organzation listed in this Yearbook: [2017/XJ5057/y/**D**]

♦ European Family Businesses-GEEF / see European Family Businesses (#07028)
♦ European Family Institutes Network (#18653)

♦ **European Family Justice Center Alliance (EFJCA)** **07029**

Contact Boomkensdiep 27, 8032 XZ Zwolle, Netherlands. T. +31621292799. E-mail: info@efjca.eu.
URL: https://www.efjca.eu/

History Developed out of a project running 2013-2014. Registration: EU Transparency Register, No/ID: 140999342174-40, Start date: 7 Apr 2021. **Aims** Develop a safe place for victims of gender based, domestic violence, child abuse and sexual violence in all European countries and regions. **Structure** Supervisory Board; Advisory Board; Board; Team; Focal Points; Members. **Languages** Dutch, English, French, German, Italian. **Activities** Events/meetings; guidance/assistance/consulting; knowledge management/information dissemination; networking/liaising; training/education. Active in all member countries.
Members Members and partners in 32 countries and territories:
Albania, Armenia, Aruba, Belgium, Bonaire Is, Canada, Croatia, Cyprus, France, Georgia, Germany, Greece, Iceland, Ireland, Italy, Latvia, Lithuania, Luxembourg, Malta, Moldova, Netherlands, Norway, Poland, Portugal, Romania, Russia, Serbia, Slovenia, Spain, Sweden, UK, USA.
IGO Relations Cooperates with (2): *European Institute for Crime Prevention and Control affiliated with the United Nations (HEUNI, #07550)*; *OECD (#17693)*. **NGO Relations** Cooperates with (5): *European Forum for Restorative Justice (EFRJ, #07332)*; *European Network for the Work with Perpetrators of Domestic Violence (WWP EN, #08036)*; European Network of Female Genital Mutulation; *European Women's Lobby (EWL, #09102)*; *Soroptimist International (SI, #19686)*. Also cooperates with national organizations. [2022/AA0256/**E**]

♦ **European Family Support Network (EurofamNet)** **07030**

Administrative Officer address not obtained. E-mail: support@eurofamnet.eu.
URL: https://eurofamnet.eu/

History 14 Mar 2019. Functions within the *European Cooperation in Science and Technology (COST, #06784)* programme. Registration: EU Transparency Register, No/ID: 186778640602-42, Start date: 8 Dec 2020. **Aims** Inform family policies and practices towards the ultimate goal of ensuring children's rights and families' well-being. **Structure** Management Committee. Working Groups (5). **Activities** Events/meetings; research/documentation; training/education.
Members Full in 36 countries:
Albania, Austria, Belgium, Bosnia-Herzegovina, Bulgaria, Croatia, Cyprus, Czechia, Denmark, Estonia, France, Germany, Greece, Hungary, Ireland, Israel, Italy, Kosovo, Latvia, Lithuania, Malta, Moldova, Montenegro, Netherlands, North Macedonia, Norway, Poland, Portugal, Romania, Serbia, Slovenia, Spain, Sweden, Switzerland, Türkiye, UK. [2020/AA1270/**F**]

♦ European Family Therapy Association (EFTA) 07031

Association Européenne de Thérapie Familiale

Pres Rue de la Voie Cuivrée 26, 5503 Dinant, Belgium. T. +32496222296. E-mail: efta@scarlet.be.
URL: http://www.europeanfamilytherapy.eu/

History 1986. By-laws were adopted 1990, Paris (France). Former names and other names: *European Family Therapy Network* – former (1986 to 1990). Registration: Banque-Carrefour des Entreprises, Belgium. **Aims** Link and coordinate European national organizations, centres, institutes and individuals working or interested in the field of systemic approach and family therapy. **Structure** General Assembly (annual); Board; Executive Committee; Chambers (3); Committees (5). **Languages** English, French. **Staff** 0.50 FTE, paid. **Finance** Sources: members' dues. Annual budget: 100,000 EUR. **Activities** Events/meetings; networking/liaising. **Events** *Systemic Resonances and Interferences* Ljubljana (Slovenia) 2022, *Conference* Naples (Italy) 2019, *Congress* Toulouse (France) 2018, *Origins and originality in family therapy and systemic practice* Athens (Greece) 2016, *Scientific Meeting* Leuven (Belgium) 2015. **Publications** *EFTA Newsletter*. *EFTA Book Series*. **Members** Full; Honour; Candidate; Associate; Sponsor; Foreign. NFTO members in 29 countries:
Austria, Belgium, Bulgaria, Cyprus, Czechia, Denmark, Estonia, Finland, France, Germany, Greece, Hungary, Iceland, Ireland, Israel, Italy, Latvia, Malta, Netherlands, North Macedonia, Norway, Poland, Portugal, Serbia, Spain, Sweden, Switzerland, Türkiye, UK.
Individual members in 37 countries:
Austria, Belgium, Brazil, Bulgaria, Canada, Chile, China, Croatia, Cyprus, Czechia, Denmark, Estonia, Finland, France, Germany, Greece, Hungary, Iceland, Ireland, Israel, Italy, Luxembourg, Malta, Mexico, Netherlands, North Macedonia, Norway, Poland, Portugal, Senegal, Serbia, Spain, Sweden, Switzerland, Türkiye, UK, USA.
Training institutes in 29 countries:
Austria, Belgium, Bulgaria, Croatia, Cyprus, Denmark, Finland, France, Germany, Greece, Hungary, Ireland, Italy, Lebanon, Lithuania, Malta, Netherlands, North Macedonia, Norway, Poland, Portugal, Romania, Russia, Serbia, Slovenia, Spain, Switzerland, Türkiye, UK. [2021.09.01/XF0596/v/F]

♦ European Family Therapy Network / see European Family Therapy Association (#07031)
♦ European Fantastic Film Festivals Federation / see Méliès International Festivals Federation (#16706)
♦ European Farmers Coordination / see European Coordination Via Campesina (#06795)

♦ European FASD Alliance (EUFASD) 07032

Office c/o FAS-föreningen, Norra Långgatan 8, SE-261 32 Landskrona, Sweden. E-mail: info@eufasd.org.
URL: http://www.eufasd.org/

History 17 Feb 2011. Full title: *European Fetal Alcohol Spectrum Disorders Alliance.* Statutes adopted 17 Feb 2011. Registered in accordance with Swedish law, Landskrona (Sweden): 802459-2654. **Aims** Improve the quality of life for all people with FASD; increase awareness of the risks of drinking *alcohol* beverages during *pregnancy*. **Structure** General Assembly; Board; Scientific Advisory Council. **Languages** English. **Staff** None. **Finance** Members' dues. **Events** *European Conference on Fetal Alcohol Spectrum Disorders* Arendal (Norway) 2022, *European Conference on Fetal Alcohol Spectrum Disorders* Arendal (Norway) 2020, *Conference* Berlin (Germany) 2018, *Conference* London (UK) 2016, *Conference* Rome (Italy) 2014.
Members Full organizations (19) in 7 countries:
France, Germany, Italy, Netherlands, Poland, Sweden, UK.
Included in the above, 1 organization listed in this Yearbook:
European Birth Mother Support Network – FASD (eurobmsn, no recent information).
NGO Relations Member of: *European Alcohol Policy Alliance (Eurocare, #05856).* [2021/XJ6065/D]

♦ European Fashion Heritage Association (EFHA) 07033

Managing Dir Via di Brozzi 274, 50145 Florence FI, Italy. E-mail: info@fashionheritage.eu – communication@fashionheritage.eu.
URL: https://fashionheritage.eu/

History 2014. Founded following a successful project co-funded by *European Commission (EC, #06633).* Registration: EU Transparency Register, No/ID: 517552132110-52. **Aims** Help fashion galleries, libraries, archives and museums (GLAMs) and brands to get better value from their cultural heritage assets by opening them up and connecting with new audiences. **Languages** English, French, Italian. **Events** *International Symposium* 2022, *Symposium* Florence (Italy) 2020. [2022/XM8795/D]

♦ European Fastener Distributor Association (EFDA) 07034

SG Am Weidendamm 1A, 10117 Berlin, Germany. T. +4930590099581. Fax +4930590099481. E-mail: secretary@efda-fastenerdistributors.org.
URL: http://www.efda-fastenerdistributors.org/

History EU Transparency Register: 482340112795-80. **Aims** Defend *free trade* and international competitiveness. **Structure** Executive Board. **Events** *Triennial Conference* Rotterdam (Netherlands) 2018. [2018/XM6901/D]

♦ European Fast Reactor Associates (inactive)

♦ European Fat Processors and Renderers Association (EFPRA) 07035

SG Blvd Baudouin 18 bte 4, 1000 Brussels, Belgium. T. +3222035141. Fax +3222033244. E-mail: info@efpra.eu.
URL: http://www.efpra.eu/

History 1 Jan 2001, by merger of *European Renderers Association (EURA, inactive)* and *European Animal Fat Processors Association (UNEGA, inactive).* EU Transparency Register: 402216719647-87. **Structure** Officers. **Activities** Events/meetings. **Events** *Congress* Vilamoura (Portugal) 2022, *Congress* Naples (Italy) 2021, *Congress* Vilamoura (Portugal) 2020, *Congress* La Baule (France) 2019, *Congress* Barcelona (Spain) 2018.
Members Full: Manufacturers in 22 countries:
Austria, Belgium, Croatia, Czechia, Denmark, Finland, France, Germany, Greece, Hungary, Ireland, Italy, Lithuania, Netherlands, Poland, Portugal, Romania, Slovakia, Slovenia, Spain, Sweden, UK.
Associate: Manufacturers in 6 countries and territories:
Germany, Hong Kong, Iceland, Norway, Serbia, Switzerland.
IGO Relations Participates as observer in the activities of: *Codex Alimentarius Commission (CAC, #04081).*
NGO Relations In liaison with technical committees of: *International Organization for Standardization (ISO, #14473).* [2020/XD9089/D]

♦ European Federalist Party 07036

Parti Fédéraliste Européen

Contact BP 82204, 75122 Paris CEDEX 03, France. E-mail: contact-fede@lesfederalistes.eu.
URL: http://www.eurofederalistparty.eu/

History 2005, as *Europe United.* Current title adopted 2011, after merger with Parti Fédéraliste. **Aims** Advocate further integration of the EU and the establishment of a united Europe. **Structure** Board; National Chapters. **Languages** English, French, German. **Staff** 39.00 FTE, paid. **NGO Relations** Supports: *European Alliance for the Statute of the European Association (EASEA, #05886); Europeans for Fair Roaming (#08473).* [2017.06.01/XJ4972/F]

♦ European Federatioin of Professionists of Pedagogists (unconfirmed)
♦ European Federation of Academies of Sciences and Humanities / see ALLEA – ALL European Academies (#00647)
♦ European Federation of Accountants / see Accountancy Europe (#00061)

♦ European Federation of Accountants and Auditors for SMEs (EFAA) 07037

Head of Secretariat and Public Affairs Rue Jaques de Lalaing 4, 1040 Brussels, Belgium. T. +3227368886. Fax +3227362964. E-mail: secretariat@efaa.com.
URL: http://www.efaa.com/

History 1994, The Hague (Netherlands). Registration: EU Transparency Register, No/ID: 002077217226-17. **Aims** Serve as an umbrella organization for national accountants and auditors' organizations whose individual members provide professional services primarily to SMEs within the European Union and Europe as a whole. **Structure** Board. **Languages** English. **Staff** 1.20 FTE, paid. **Finance** Sources: members' dues. Annual budget: 300,000 EUR. **Activities** Advocacy/lobbying/activism; events/meetings; knowledge management/information dissemination. **Events** *International Conference* Brussels (Belgium) 2021, *International Conference* Berlin (Germany) 2020, *International Conference* Amsterdam (Netherlands) 2019, *International Conference* Brussels (Belgium) 2018, *International Conference* Berlin (Germany) 2017. **Publications** *Latest from Brussels* (22 a year). Articles; guides; statements; studies; survey reports.
Members Ordinary; Observer; Associate. Ordinary in 12 countries:
Albania, Austria, Azerbaijan, Belgium, Germany, Hungary, Kosovo, Netherlands, Portugal, Slovenia, Spain, UK.
IGO Relations *European Commission (EC, #06633).* **NGO Relations** Member of: *European Financial Reporting Advisory Group (EFRAG, #07254); SMEunited (#19327).* Memorandum of Understanding with: *Fédération des experts comptables méditerranéens (FCM, #09584); South Asian Federation of Accountants (SAFA, #19727).* [2020.06.24/XD6324/y/D]

♦ European Federation of Adapted Physical Activity (EUFAPA) 07038

Pres Univ of Coimbra, Pavilhão III – Estadio Universitario de Coimbra, 3040-156 Coimbra, Portugal.
URL: http://www.eufapa.eu/

History Founded as the European branch of *International Federation of Adapted Physical Activity (IFAPA, #13338).* Constitution adopted 4 Sep 1987. Reorganized, 2006. Former names and other names: *European Association for Research into Adapted Physical Activity (EARAPA)* – former (1987); *Association européenne de recherche en activité adaptée* – former (1987). Registration: Start date: Sep 1987, Belgium; Start date: 2006, Czech Rep. **Aims** Promote, stimulate and coordinate fundamental and applied research; encourage study and application of programmes in adapted physical activity; disseminate information on such programmes; encourage European cooperation in the field of physical activity. **Structure** Board. **Languages** English. **Staff** Voluntary. **Finance** EU subsidies. **Activities** Events/meetings; research/documentation. **Events** *European Congress of Adapted Physical Activity (EUCAPA)* Seville (Spain) 2024, *European Congress of Adapted Physical Activity* Seville (Spain) 2024, *European Congress of Adapted Physical Activity* Coimbra (Portugal) 2022, *European Congress of Adapted Physical Activity* Elche (Spain) 2020, *Open Day Symposium* Elche (Spain) 2020. **Publications** *European Journal of Adapted Physical Activity* – peer reviewed journal. Books; congress proceedings.
Members Individuals in 29 countries and territories:
Austria, Belgium, Bulgaria, Czechia, Denmark, Estonia, Finland, France, Germany, Greece, Hungary, Iceland, Ireland, Italy, Latvia, Netherlands, Northern Ireland, Norway, Poland, Portugal, Romania, Serbia, Slovakia, Spain, Sweden, Switzerland, Türkiye, UK, Ukraine. [2017.10.24/XE1105/v/E]

♦ European Federation of Addiction Societies (EUFAS) 07039

Pres Psychiatrisch Centrum Broeders Alexianen, Provinciesteenweg 408, 2530 Boechout, Belgium. T. +3232652902.
Gen Sec Innland Hospital Trust, PO Box 104, 2381 Brumunddal, Norway. T. +4748132975. E-mail: jgusta-b@online.no.
URL: http://www.eufas.net/

History Founded 2010, Paris (France). Constitution adopted 15 Sep 2010. **Aims** Promote education and advances in knowledge and understanding in the field of addiction in Europe for the non-profit protection of health. **Structure** General Assembly; Executive Committee; Advisory Board. **Languages** English. **Activities** Research and development; standards/guidelines; knowledge management/information dissemination; projects/programmes; events/meetings. **Events** *FENIQS-EU – Further enhancing the implementation of quality standards in DDR across Europe* Palma (Spain) 2022, *Meeting* Lisbon (Portugal) 2017, *Meeting* Alicante (Spain) 2016, *Meeting* Dundee (UK) 2015, *Meeting* Berlin (Germany) 2014. **Publications** *European Addiction Research.* Surveys; guidelines.
Members Societies in 23 countries:
Austria, Belgium, Croatia, Czechia, Denmark, Finland, France, Germany, Greece, Hungary, Ireland, Italy, Lithuania, Luxembourg, Netherlands, Norway, Poland, Portugal, Romania, Russia, Spain, Switzerland, UK.
Regional societies (2):
European Association for Substance Abuse Research (EASAR, #06238); European Society for Biomedical Research on Alcoholism (ESBRA, #08532).
IGO Relations *European Monitoring Centre for Drugs and Drug Addiction (EMCDDA, #07820).* [2019/XJ5152/y/D]

♦ European Federation for Additives in Animal Nutrition / see FEFANA – EU Association of Specialty Feed Ingredients and their Mixtures (#09720)

♦ European Federation for the Advancement of Anaesthesia in Dentistry (EFAAD) 07040

Association européenne de chirurgie buccale

Exec Sec Van Vredenburchalaan 37, 2661 HE Bergschenhoek, Netherlands.
Contact Andre and Milhe Dental Sedation Clinic, Route de Ferney 194, Le Grand-Saconnex, 1218 Geneva, Switzerland.
URL: http://www.efaadonline.org/

History 1974. New constitution adopted 1987. **Aims** Promote and further the science and technique of anaesthesia in dentistry. **Structure** Board. **Languages** English. **Staff** 5.00 FTE, voluntary. **Finance** Members' dues. **Events** *Congress* Padua (Italy) 2014, *Meeting* Moscow (Russia) 2010, *Meeting* Évian (France) 2010, *Meeting* Gold Coast, QLD (Australia) 2009, *Meeting* Padua (Italy) 2008.
Members Societies in 8 countries:
France, Germany, Israel, Italy, Netherlands, Russia, Sweden, UK.
NGO Relations Member of: *International Federation of Dental Anesthesiology Societies (IFDAS, #13403).* [2018/XD2695/D]

♦ European Federation Against High-Voltage Power Lines (no recent information)
♦ European Federation Against Hunting (inactive)
♦ European Federation Against Nuclear Arms (inactive)

♦ European Federation of Agencies and Regions for Energy and the Environment (FEDARENE) 07041

Fédération Européenne des Agences et des Régions pour l'Energie et l'Environnement

SG Rue de Stassart 131, 1050 Brussels, Belgium. T. +3226468210. E-mail: fedarene@fedarene.org.
URL: http://fedarene.org/

History 8 Jun 1990. Founded by 6 regional authorities: Rhône-Alpes; Provence-Alpes-Côte-d'Azur; Wallonia; Pais Vasco; Aquitaine; Nord-Pas-de-Calais. Brussels (Belgium) office created Nov 1991. Current statutes adopted 4 Nov 2020, Brussels (Belgium). Former names and other names: *Fédération européenne des agences régionales de l'énergie et de l'environnement* – former (8 Jun 1990); *European Federation of Regional Energy and Environment Agency* – former (8 Jun 1990). Registration: Banque-Carrefour des Entreprises, No/ID: 0454.606.831, Start date: 18 Oct 1994, Belgium; EU Transparency Register, No/ID: 579945334611-71. **Aims** Facilitate development of inter-regional partnerships in the fields of energy management, development of renewable energy and environment, thus encouraging exchange of experience and transfer of know-how and technology and enhancing energy efficiency; lobby European institutions on behalf of regional and local communities; promote regional dimension in energy and environment discussion, emphasizing demand, local supply and sustainable development; assist regions to develop capacity for action, especially in setting up energy and environment agencies. **Structure** Board of Administration; Office in Brussels (Belgium). **Languages** English, French. **Staff** 9.00 FTE, paid. Several voluntary. **Finance** Sources: grants; members' dues. Supported by: *European Union (EU, #08967).* Annual budget: 947,506 EUR. **Activities** Advocacy/lobbying/activism; events/meetings; guidance/assistance/consulting; knowledge management/information dissemination; networking/liaising; projects/programmes. **Events** *General Assembly* León (Spain) 2022, *General Assembly* Maribor (Slovenia) 2021, *General Assembly* Brussels (Belgium) 2020, *General Assembly* Paris (France) 2015, *General Assembly* Genoa (Italy) 2014. **Publications** *FEDARENE Info* (4 a year) – Magazine; *Internal Bulletin* (24 a year). Position papers – on European legislation and programmes; reports.
Members Active: regional and local agencies, ministries and departments working in the fields of energy and environment policy. Members in 25 countries:
Austria, Belgium, Bulgaria, Croatia, Cyprus, Czechia, Denmark, Estonia, Finland, France, Germany, Greece, Hungary, Ireland, Italy, Latvia, Lithuania, Malta, Netherlands, Poland, Portugal, Romania, Slovenia, Spain, Sweden.
NGO Relations Member of (1): *European Forum for Renewable Energy Sources (EUFORES, #07329).* Member of consortium managing: *Global Covenant of Mayors for Climate and Energy (GCoM, #10312).* [2022.10.24/XD3998/D]

♦ European Federation of Agents of Industry in Industrial Property .. 07042

Fédération européenne des mandataires de l'industrie en propriété industrielle (FEMIPI) – Europäischer Verband der Industrie-Patentingenieure

Pres c/o Siemens AG, Siemens Intellectual Property, Otto-Hahn-Ring 6, 81739 Munich, Germany. E-mail: anneliese.forster@siemens.com.

URL: http://www.femipi.org/

History 4 Mar 1971. Former names and other names: *European Federation of Industrial Property Representatives of Industry* – alias. **Aims** Study, develop and protect professional interests of agents of industry in industrial property. **Structure** General Assembly (annual); Board of Directors; Working Groups. **Languages** English, French, German. **Staff** Voluntary. **Finance** Sources: members' dues. **Activities** Networking/liaising. **Events** *Annual General Assembly* Vienna (Austria) 2022, *Annual General Assembly* Munich (Germany) 2021, *Annual General Assembly* Munich (Germany) 2020, *Annual general assembly* Basel (Switzerland) 2019, *Annual general assembly* Paris (France) 2018.

Members National associations, representing more than 3,000 individuals, and specific individuals granted membership by General Assembly, in 11 European countries:

Austria, Denmark, Finland, France, Germany, Luxembourg, Netherlands, Norway, Sweden, Switzerland, UK.

Consultative Status Consultative status granted from: *World Intellectual Property Organization (WIPO, #21593)* (Permanent Observer Status). **IGO Relations** Observer status with (1): *Union internationale pour la protection des obtentions végétales (UPOV, #20436)*. Cooperates with (1): *European Union Intellectual Property Office (EUIPO, #08996)*. [2022.05.23/XD0134/t/**D**]

♦ European Federation of Agricultural Exhibitions and Show Organizers (EURASCO) 07043

Société agricole européenne et Comité consultatif des organisateurs d'expositions

SG Veronafiere, Viale del Lavoro 8, 37135 Verona BL, Italy. T. +39458298240. E-mail: secretarygeneral@eurasco.org.

URL: http://www.eurasco.org/

History 1967. Current constitution approved 1972, Brussels (Belgium), and ratified 1973, Saragossa (Spain). Previously also known as *European Agricultural Society and Show Organizers Consultative Committee*. Present name adopted 1998. **Aims** Improve agricultural exhibitions internationally through exchange of information and experience, reciprocal advice and communicating information about European shows. **Structure** General Assembly (meets twice a year). **Languages** English. **Staff** 1.00 FTE, paid. **Finance** Members' dues. **Events** *General Meeting* Paris (France) 2019, *General Meeting* Rennes (France) 2019, *General Meeting* Bjärred (Sweden) 2018, *General Meeting* Bath (UK) 2017, *General Meeting* Hannover (Germany) 2017.

Members Organizations (34) in 23 countries and territories:

Belgium, Bulgaria, Croatia, Denmark, England, Estonia, France, Germany, Greece, Hungary, Ireland, Moldova, Netherlands, Poland, Portugal, Romania, Scotland, Serbia, Slovenia, Spain, Sweden, Switzerland, UK.

IGO Relations *European Commission (EC, #06633)* – DG Agriculture. **NGO Relations** Associate member of: *European Network of Agricultural Journalists (ENAJ, #07864)*. [2018/XF0415/**F**]

- ♦ European Federation for Agricultural Recycling (unconfirmed)
- ♦ European Federation of AIDS Research (inactive)

♦ European Federation of Airline Dispatchers Associations (EUFALDA) 07044

Pres Welzheimer Str 25, 63791 Karlstein, Germany.

Sec address not obtained.

URL: http://www.eufalda.org/

History 1991, Zurich (Switzerland). **Aims** Promote air transportation safety; work for development of a stronger aviation industry; sponsor and support air safety legislation; coordinate professional efforts and represent professional interest of aircraft dispatcher / flight operations officer member associations. **Structure** Annual General Meeting; Board. **Languages** English, French, German. **Staff** 4.00 FTE, paid. **Finance** Members' dues. **Events** *Annual General Meeting* 2021, *Annual General Meeting* Karlstein (Germany) 2020, *Annual General Meeting* Copenhagen (Denmark) 2019, *Annual General Meeting* Kuala Lumpur (Malaysia) 2006, *World airline flight dispatchers conference* Kuala Lumpur (Malaysia) 2006.

Members Full in 23 countries:

Austria, Belgium, Croatia, Denmark, Finland, France, Germany, Greece, Hungary, Iceland, Ireland, Italy, Luxembourg, Malta, Norway, Poland, Portugal, Serbia, Spain, Sweden, Switzerland, Türkiye, UK. [2020.03.10/XD5857/**D**]

♦ European Federation of Allergy and Airways Diseases Patients' Associations (EFA) 07045

Fédération européenne des associations des allergies et insuffisant respiratoires

Dir Rue du Congrès 35, 1000 Brussels, Belgium. T. +3222272712. Fax +3222183141. E-mail: info@efanet.org.

URL: http://www.efanet.org/

History Nov 1991, Stockholm (Sweden), as *European Federation of Asthma and Allergy Associations – Fédération européenne des associations de l'asthme et des allergies*. Registered in accordance with Swedish law. Incorporates activities of *European Network of COPD Patients Associations (ENCPA, inactive)*. EU Transparency Register: 28473847513-94. **Aims** Support patients of allergy, asthma and chronic obstructive pulmonary disease (COPD) by sharing information about their conditions and by advocating on their behalf in the European Parliament. **Structure** General Meeting (annual); Board; Secretariat. **Languages** English. **Staff** 3.50 FTE, voluntary. **Finance** Members' dues. Fundraising; *European Commission (EC, #06633)*. **Activities** Research and development; advocacy/lobbying/activism; capacity building. **Events** *Annual General Meeting and Extraordinary General Meeting* Reykjavik (Iceland) 2021, *Annual General Meeting* Reykjavik (Iceland) 2020, *Annual General Meeting* Brussels (Belgium) 2019, *Annual General Meeting* Lisbon (Portugal) 2018, *Annual General Meeting* Rome (Italy) 2013. **Publications** *EFA eZine Newsletter* (12 a year). *EFA Book on Respiratory Allergies: Raise Awareness, Relieve the Burden* (2011); *The Severity of Allergies, Asthma and COPD – The Patient's Perspective* (2004); *Indoor Air Pollution in Schools* (2001); *EFA Info Books* (2nd ed 1999); *Breathtaking Ideas* (1998); *Asthma in Europe, Report on Asthma Prevalence, Policy and Action in the European Union* (1997); *Fighting for Breath – A European Patient Perspectiveon Severe Asthma*; *Towards a Health Air in Dwellings in Europe (THADE)*. Abstract books; brochures.

Members National organizations (42) in 22 countries:

Austria, Belgium, Bulgaria, Croatia, Czechia, Denmark, Finland, France, Germany, Greece, Ireland, Italy, Latvia, Lithuania, Luxembourg, Netherlands, Poland, Portugal, Spain, Sweden, Switzerland, UK.

IGO Relations Accredited by: *United Nations Framework Convention on Climate Change – Secretariat (UNFCCC, #20564)*. **NGO Relations** Member of: *European Network for Smoking and Tobacco Prevention (ENSP, #08002)*; *European Patients' Forum (EPF, #08172)*; *Global Alliance Against Chronic Respiratory Diseases (GARD, #10182)*; *Global Allergy and Asthma European Network (GA2LEN, #10179)*; *Global Allergy and Airways Patient Platform (GAAPP, #10178)*; *Health and Environment Alliance (HEAL, #10879)*; *International COPD Coalition (ICC, #12961)*. Partner of: *Allergic Rhinitis and its Impact on Asthma Initiative (ARIA, #00648)*; *European Academy of Allergy and Clinical Immunology (EAACI, #05779)*; *European Lung Foundation (ELF, #07718)*; *European Respiratory Society (ERS, #08383)*; *Federation of European Heating, Ventilation and Air-Conditioning Associations (REHVA, #09507)*; *Global Initiative on Asthma (GINA, #10422)*; *Global Initiative for Chronic Obstructive Lung Disease (GOLD, #10423)*; *International Primary Care Respiratory Group (IPCRG, #14640)*. Endorses: *Steering Group on Influenza Vaccination (#19980)*. [2019/XD5645/**D**]

- ♦ European Federation for Alpha1 Antitrypsin Deficiency (inactive)
- ♦ European Federation of the Alpine System Bovine Breeds (#05752)
- ♦ European Federation of Amusement and Leisure Parks (inactive)
- ♦ European Federation of Anaesthesiologists (inactive)
- ♦ European Federation of Animal Feed Additive Manufacturers / see FEFANA – EU Association of Specialty Feed Ingredients and their Mixtures (#09720)
- ♦ European Federation of Animal Health (inactive)
- ♦ European Federation for Animal Health and Sanitary Security (#09581)
- ♦ European Federation of Animal Protein Importers and Traders (no recent information)

♦ European Federation of Animal Science (EAAP) 07046

Fédération européenne de zootechnie (FEZ) – Federación Europea de Zootecnia (FEZ) – Europäische Vereinigung für Tierproduktion (EVT)

SG Via G Tomassetti 3 – A/1, 00161 Rome RM, Italy. T. +39644202639. E-mail: eaap@eaap.org.

URL: http://www.eaap.org/

History 7 Nov 1949, Paris (France). International congresses held since 1910. Former names and other names: *European Association for Animal Production (EAAP)* – former. **Aims** Promote ever better economic and organizational conditions for animal production through active collaboration among members in the fields of scientific research, experimentation, animal husbandry and technical assistance. **Structure** General Assembly (annual); Council; Board; Secretariat, headed by Secretary-General. Joint meetings with: FAO; EU; WAAP; *International Dairy Federation (IDF, #13128)*; *CIHEAM – International Centre for Advanced Mediterranean Agronomic Studies (CIHEAM, #03927)*. **Languages** English, French, German. **Staff** 7.00 FTE, paid. **Finance** Sources: members' dues. **Activities** Events/meetings; research/documentation. **Events** *Annual General Assembly* Florence (Italy) 2024, *Joint International Congress on Animal Science* Lyon (France) 2023, *Annual General Assembly* Porto (Portugal) 2022, *Annual General Assembly* Davos (Switzerland) 2021, *Annual General Assembly* Rome (Italy) 2020. **Publications** *EAAP Newsletter* (weekly); *Animal* (10 a year); *Milk and Beef Yearly Enquiry* (every 2 years). EAAP series; proceedings of study groups and symposia. **Information Services** *EAAP-FAO Global Data Bank for Animal Genetic Resources*.

Members Representative national scientific, professional and administrative organizations in 35 countries:

Albania, Austria, Belgium, Croatia, Cyprus, Czechia, Denmark, Estonia, Finland, France, Germany, Greece, Hungary, Iceland, Ireland, Italy, Latvia, Lebanon, Lithuania, Luxembourg, Morocco, Netherlands, Norway, Poland, Portugal, Romania, Serbia, Slovakia, Slovenia, Spain, Sweden, Switzerland, Tunisia, Türkiye, UK.

Consultative Status Consultative status granted from: *ECOSOC (#05331)* (Ros C); *FAO (#09260)* (Special Status). **IGO Relations** Accredited by: *United Nations Office at Vienna (UNOV, #20604)*. **NGO Relations** Observer status with (1): *World Veterinary Association (WVA, #21901)*. Member of (2): *European Forum of Farm Animal Breeders (EFFAB, #07310)*; *World Association for Animal Production (WAAP, #21117)*. In liaison with technical committees of: *International Organization for Standardization (ISO, #14473)*. Working Group on Genetic Animal Resources cooperates with: *European Regional Focal Point for Animal Genetic Resources (ERFP, #08343)*. [2022/XD0546/**D**]

- ♦ European Federation of Animal Technologists (unconfirmed)
- ♦ European Federation of Aniridia Associations / see Aniridia Europe (#00845)
- ♦ European Federation of Anti-Leprosy Associations / see International Federation of Anti-Leprosy Associations (#13355)
- ♦ European Federation of Applied Optics (inactive)
- ♦ European Federation for Architectural Heritage Skills (#09576)

♦ European Federation of Art Therapy (EFAT) 07047

Europese Federatie van Beeldende Therapie

Gen Sec Tenboslaan 70, 1560 Hoeilaart, Belgium. E-mail: info@arttherapyfederation.eu.

URL: https://www.arttherapyfederation.eu/

History 12 Apr 2018, Brussels (Belgium). Registration: Banque-Carrefour des Entreprises, No/ID: 0700.958.028, Start date: 18 Aug 2018, Belgium. **Aims** Unite art therapists and professional art therapy associations in Europe. **Structure** General Assembly; Board. Committees. **Activities** Events/meetings. **Events** *Conference* Riga (Latvia) 2023. **NGO Relations** Member of (1): *Federation of European and International Associations Established in Belgium (FAIB, #09508)*. [2022/AA2153/**D**]

- ♦ European Federation of Associations of Beer and Beverages Wholesalers in European countries (#02555)
- ♦ European Federation of Associations of Business Economists (no recent information)

♦ European Federation of Associations and Centres of Irish Studies (EFACIS) 07048

Fédération européenne d'associations et centres d'etudes irlandaises

Coordinator Janseniusstraat 1, 3000 Leuven, Belgium. E-mail: efaciscoord@efacis.eu.

URL: https://www.efacis.eu/

History 1996. Registration: Belgium. **Aims** Promote interest in and support expansion of Irish studies throughout Europe. **Structure** General Meeting (annual). Steering Committee, composed of President, Treasurer, Secretary and 6 further members. **Finance** Sources: members' dues. **Events** *Conference* Prague (Czechia) 2021, *Conference* Ljubljana (Slovenia) 2019, *Conference* La Coruña (Spain) 2017, *Conference* Palermo (Italy) 2015, *Conference* Galway (Ireland) 2013. [2022.05.10/XD7530/**D**]

♦ European Federation of Associations of Certification Bodies (EFAC) 07049

Dir 52 Im Schlaun, 41189 Mönchengladbach, Germany.

Registered Address Dyke Yaxley, 1 Brassey Road, Shrewsbury, SY3 7FA, UK.

History 1998. Registration: Companies House, No/ID: 04369920, Start date: 8 Feb 2002, England and Wales. **Aims** Safeguard and represent the common interests of European associations of accredited certification bodies and individual European accredited certification bodies operating in the fields of product conformity, management system and personnel certification. **Structure** General Assembly (annual). Secretariat. **Languages** English. **Staff** 2.00 FTE, voluntary. **Finance** Members' dues. Budget (annual): pounds20,000.

Members Full; Associate. Organizations (14) in 12 countries:

Bulgaria, France, Greece, Ireland, Italy, Netherlands, Romania, Serbia, Spain, Sweden, UK.

NGO Relations Member of (1): *International Accreditation Forum (IAF, #11584)*. [2021/XM2706/**D**]

- ♦ European Federation of Associations for Certification of Specialised Waste Management Companies (#05763)
- ♦ European Federation of Associations of Coffee Roasters (inactive)

♦ European Federation of the Associations of Dietitians (EFAD) 07050

Fédération européenne des associations de diététiciens

Exec Dir Gooimeer 4-15, 1411 DC Naarden, Netherlands. E-mail: secretariat@efad.org.

Hon Pres address not obtained.

URL: http://www.efad.org/

History 3 Jun 1978, Oss (Netherlands). Founded to subsume activities of *Committee of Dietetic Associations in the European Community (CADEC, inactive)*, set up 27 Apr 1957 and dissolved 1982. Registration: EU Transparency Register, No/ID: 99138006725-91, Start date: 19 Sep 2011. **Aims** Promote development of the dietetic profession; develop dietetics on a scientific and professional level in the common interest of member associations; facilitate communication between national dietetic associations and other organizations – professional, education and governmental; encourage a better nutrition situation for the population of Europe. **Structure** General Meeting; Executive Committee. **Languages** English. **Staff** 1.40 FTE, paid; 8.00 FTE, voluntary. **Finance** Sources: members' dues; revenue from activities/projects. **Activities** Events/meetings; standards/guidelines. **Events** *General Meeting* Budapest (Hungary) 2022, *The Vital Link to Health* 2021, *General Meeting* Veldhoven (Netherlands) 2021, *General Meeting* Veldhoven (Netherlands) 2020, *Forum* Berlin (Germany) 2019. **Publications** *EFAD Standards*. Annual Report; brochure; reports; position papers; strategies.

Members Full; Affiliate. National associations (32) in 26 countries:

Austria, Belgium, Croatia, Cyprus, Denmark, Finland, France, Germany, Greece, Hungary, Iceland, Ireland, Israel, Italy, Luxembourg, Netherlands, Norway, Poland, Portugal, Romania, Slovenia, Spain, Sweden, Switzerland, Türkiye, UK.

Education Associate Members (39) in 17 countries:

Austria, Belgium, Croatia, Czechia, Denmark, Germany, Greece, Latvia, Lithuania, Netherlands, Portugal, Romania, Spain, Sweden, Switzerland, Türkiye, UK.

NGO Relations Member of (3): *EU Platform for Action on Diet, Physical Activity and Health (inactive)*; *European Forum for Primary Care (EFPC, #07326)*; *European Nutrition for Health Alliance, The (ENHA, #08069)*. [2023.02.14/XD6457/**D**]

- ♦ European Federation of Associations of Families of Mentally Ill People / see European Federation of Associations of Families of People with Mental Illness (#07051)

♦ European Federation of Associations of Families of People with Mental Illness (EUFAMI) 07051

Fédération européenne des associations de familles de malades psychiques – Europäische Föderation von Organisation der Angehörigen Psychisch Kranker – Europese Federatie van Verenigingen van Familieleden van de Psychisch Zieken

Exec Dir Martelarenplein 20E, 3000 Leuven, Belgium. T. +32468177148. E-mail: project.admin.office@eufami.org – executive.director@eufami.org.
Administration & Communications Officer address not obtained.
URL: http://www.eufami.org/

History Dec 1992. Founded following meeting 1990, De Haan (Belgium). Former names and other names: *European Federation of Associations of Families of Mentally Ill People (EUFAMI)* – former; *Fédération européenne des associations de familles de malades psychiques* – former; *Europäische Föderation von Organisation der Angehörigen Psychisch Kranker* – former; *Europese Federatie van Organisaties van Familieleden van Mensen met een Psychische Ziekte* – former; *Europese Federatie van Familieverenigingen van Psychisch Zieke Personen* – former; *Europese Federatie van Organisaties van Familieleden van Mensen met een Psychische Ziekte* – former; *Europäische Vereinigung der Angehörigen Psychisch Kranker* – former. Registration: Banque-Carrefour des Entreprises, No/ID: 0451.967.342, Start date: 1 Feb 1994, Belgium; EU Transparency Register, No/ID: 228054922076-85, Start date: 2 Jun 2016. **Aims** Achieve throughout Europe a continuous improvement in mental health, in quality of care and welfare of people with mental illness in society, and especially in support for their families, caring relatives and friends. **Structure** General Meeting; Board of Directors. **Languages** English. **Staff** 1.50 FTE, paid. **Finance** Annual budget varies. **Activities** Advocacy/lobbying/activism; research/documentation. **Events** *Congress* Helsinki (Finland) 2019, *When East meet West* Sofia (Bulgaria) 2015, *A perfect vision for mental health 2020* Dublin (Ireland) 2013, *Seminar* Helsinki (Finland) 2013, *Congress / European Congress* Basel (Switzerland) 2011. **Publications** *EUFAMI Bulletin* (12 a year). Annual Report; survey results.
Members National and regional organizations in 25 countries:
Austria, Belgium, Bulgaria, Cyprus, Czechia, Denmark, Estonia, Finland, France, Germany, Greece, Hungary, Ireland, Israel, Italy, Lithuania, Malta, Netherlands, Portugal, Russia, Slovenia, Spain, Sweden, Switzerland, UK.
IGO Relations Interacts with several EU bodies, including: *European Commission (EC, #06633)*; *European Parliament (EP, #08146)*; *WHO (#20950)*. **NGO Relations** Relationships with various European NGOs.
[2022.02.15/XD4320/D]

♦ European Federation of Associations of Health Food Manufacturers / see European Federation of Associations of Health Product Manufacturers (#07052)

♦ European Federation of Associations of Health Product Manufacturers (EHPM) 07052

Confédération Européenne d'associations de fabricants de produits de santé

Head of Policy and Admin Rue des Colonies 56, 1000 Brussels, Belgium. T. +3227216495. E-mail: info@ehpm.org.
URL: http://www.ehpm.org/

History 29 Aug 1975, Amsterdam (Netherlands), on signature of draft constitution by representatives of national associations of Germany and UK. Has also been referred to as *European Federation of Associations of Health Food Manufacturers*. EU Transparency Register: 65512466920-96. **Aims** Represent the interests of specialist health product manufacturers and distributors in Europe; develop an appropriate regulatory framework throughout the EU; promote industry best practices for product quality and safety. **Structure** Board; Working Groups. **Languages** Dutch, English, French, German, Italian, Spanish. **Staff** 2.00 FTE, paid. **Finance** Members' dues. Special funds. **Activities** Politics/policy/regulatory. **Events** *Joint conference* Berlin (Germany) 2005, *Annual General Meeting* Cape Town (South Africa) 2001, *Annual General Meeting* Naples (Italy) 2000, *Annual General Meeting* Geneva (Switzerland) 1999, *Annual General Meeting* Bologna (Italy) 1998.
Members National associations in 14 countries:
Belgium, Bulgaria, France, Germany, Greece, Hungary, Ireland, Italy, Lithuania, Netherlands, Poland, Portugal, Romania, UK.
Associate members (3) include the following organization listed in this Yearbook:
NSF International.
IGO Relations Recognized by: *European Commission (EC, #06633)*. Participates as observer in the activities of: *Codex Alimentarius Commission (CAC, #04081)*. **NGO Relations** Member of: *SMEunited (#19327)*.
[2019.10.23/XD1201/D]

♦ European Federation of Associations of Industrial and Technical Heritage (EFAITH) 07053

Fédération Européenne des Associations de Patrimoine Industriel et Technique – Federación Europea de Asociaciones de Patrimonio Industrial y Técnico – Europäisches Verband des Vereinigungen zum Erhalt des Industriellen und Technischen Erbes – Federação Europeia das Associações do Património Industrial e Técnico – Federazione Europea delle Associazioni per il Patrimonio Industriale e Tecnico – Europese Federatie van Verenigingen voor Industrieel en Technisch Erfgoed

Secretariat Vredelaan 72, 8500 Kortrijk, Belgium. E-mail: secretariat@e-faith.org.
URL: http://www.industrialheritage.eu/

History 14 Nov 1999, Belgium. Statutes adopted Nov 1999, Harelbeke (Belgium); new statutes signed, end 2017; statutes revised, 2019. Former names and other names: *E-FAITH* – former. Registration: Banque-Carrefour des Entreprises, No/ID: 0723.469.550, Start date: 22 Feb 2019, Belgium. **Aims** Promote study and research in recording, conservation, development, management and interpretation of industrial and technical heritage; promote the role of volunteers and associations; facilitate cooperation in the field. **Structure** Board of Directors. **Languages** Catalan, Dutch, English, French, German, Italian, Spanish. **Staff** Voluntary. **Finance** Members' dues; sponsorship. **Activities** Research/documentation; events/meetings. **Events** *Annual Meeting* Malaga (Spain) 2017, *Annual Meeting* Antwerp (Belgium) 2016, *Annual Meeting* Lyon (France) 2014, *Annual Meeting* Neuchâtel (Switzerland) / La Chaux-de-Fonds (Switzerland) 2013, *Annual Meeting* London (UK) 2012. **Publications** *EFAITH e-Newsletter*. **Members** Local and regional associations. Membership countries not specified. **NGO Relations** Member of (2): *Europa Nostra (#05767)*; *European Heritage Alliance 3.3 (#07477)*.
[2022/XD8242/t/D]

♦ European Federation of Associations of Insulation Contractors (#09582)

♦ European Federation of Associations of Locks and Builders Hardware Manufacturers (ARGE) 07054

Fédération Européenne des Associations de Fabricants de Serrures et de Ferrures – Federación Europea de Asociaciones de Fabricantes de Cerrajeros – Arbeitsgemeinschaft der Verbände der Europäischen Schloss- und Beschlagindustrie

Gen Sec Offerstrasse 12, 42551 Velbert, Germany. T. +492051950636. Fax +492051950625. E-mail: mail@arge.org.
URL: http://www.arge.org/

History 1959. Constitutional changes 1967-1977. Present Constitution adopted 2011. Former names and other names: *Community of European Lock and Fitting Industries* – former; *Communauté des industries européennes de la serrurerie et des ferrures* – former. Registration: EU Transparency Register, No/ID: 881365536049-72, Start date: 28 Sep 2019. **Aims** Provide an opportunity to meet colleagues and discuss common problems and interests; represent the interests of members on any international body, particularly in respect of matters of standardization; collect and disseminate information in the interests of members. **Structure** General Meeting; Executive Board; Permanent Working Groups. **Languages** English, French, German. **Staff** 2.00 FTE, paid. **Finance** Sources: members' dues. **Activities** Events/meetings; knowledge management/information dissemination; networking/liaising; standards/guidelines. **Events** *Annual Congress* Stockholm (Sweden) 2022, *Annual Congress* Stockholm (Sweden) 2021, *Members Meeting* Velbert (Germany) 2021, *Annual Congress* Stockholm (Sweden) 2020, *Members Meeting* Velbert (Germany) 2020.
Members National associations in 12 countries:
Austria, Czechia, Finland, France, Germany, Italy, Netherlands, Poland, Spain, Sweden, Switzerland, UK.
Regural members in 14 countries:
Austria, Czechia, Denmark, Finland, France, Germany, Italy, Netherlands, Poland, Spain, Sweden, Switzerland, Türkiye, UK.
IGO Relations Recognized by: *European Commission (EC, #06633)*. **NGO Relations** Member of (1): *Construction 2050 Alliance (#04760)*.
[2022/XD0387/t/D]

♦ European Federation of Associations of Manufacturers of Frozen Food Products (inactive)

♦ European Federation of Associations of Market Research Organizations (EFAMRO) 07055

Dir Bastion Tower level 20, Place du Champ de Mars 5, 1050 Brussels, Belgium. T. +3225503548. Fax +3225503584. E-mail: info@efamro.eu.
URL: http://www.efamro.eu/

History Apr 1992. EU Transparency Register: 90847842431-88. **Aims** Influence legislation and public opinion in favour of research; promote best practice; enforce compliance with the principles of international standards; advise the European research industry; publish information about the European research industry. **Languages** Dutch, English. **Staff** 2.00 FTE, paid. **Finance** Members' dues. **Publications** *EFAMRO Monitoring Report* (weekly); *EFAMRO Member Update* (4 a year); *EFAMRO Newsletter* (4 a year).
Members National associations in 15 countries:
Bulgaria, Cyprus, Finland, Germany, Ireland, Italy, Lithuania, Norway, Poland, Portugal, Russia, Spain, Sweden, Switzerland, UK.
NGO Relations *Americas Research Industry Alliance (ARIA)*; *Asia Pacific Research Committee (APRC, #02011)*; *Global Research Business Network (GRBN, #10572)*.
[2018.09.06/XD3188/D]

♦ European Federation of Associations of Open Systems Users (no recent information)
♦ European Federation of Associations of the Parquet Industry / see European Federation of the Parquet Industry (#07188)
♦ European Federation of Associations of Particleboard Manufacturers (inactive)

♦ European Federation of Associations of Patients with Haemochromatosis (EFAPH) 07056

Fédération Européenne des Associations de Patients de l'Hémochromatose (FEAPH)

Gen Sec 4 rue Paul Demange, 78290 Croissy-sur-Seine, France. E-mail: info@efaph.eu.
URL: http://www.efaph.eu/

History 4 Aug 2005, Rennes (France). Registration: France. **Aims** Federate all European associations concerned with Haemochromatosis through practical initiatives (prevention, screening, training and informing members and the public at large); heighten public awareness (notably among public services and authorities, as well as doctors) of the *genetic* Haemochromatosis condition. **Structure** General Assembly; Board of Directors. **Languages** English, French. **Staff** Voluntary. **Finance** Sources: fundraising; grants; members' dues. Annual budget: 17,500 EUR. **Activities** Awareness raising; events/meetings. **Events** *General Assembly* Oxford (UK) 2021, *General Assembly* Croissy-sur-Seine (France) 2020, *General Assembly* Heidelberg (Germany) 2019, *General Assembly* Zurich (Switzerland) 2018, *General Assembly* Münster (Germany) 2017. **Publications** *Hemo News* (annual). Workshop proceedings.
Members National Associations in 13 countries:
Belgium, Denmark, France, Germany, Hungary, Ireland, Italy, Netherlands, Norway, Portugal, Spain, Sweden, UK.
NGO Relations Member of (2): *EURORDIS – Rare Diseases Europe (#09175)*; *Health First Europe (HFE, #10881)*. Cooperates with (1): *European Hematology Association (EHA, #07473)*. Associate member of: *European Patients' Forum (EPF, #08172)*.
[2021.02.25/XM1556/D]

♦ European Federation of the Associations of Professional Congress Organisers (inactive)
♦ European Federation of Associations of Steel, Tube and Metal Merchants (#09559)
♦ European Federation of Associations of Teachers of the Deaf (inactive)
♦ European Federation of Associations for Teaching of Mother Tongues to Foreigners (no recent information)
♦ European Federation of the Associations of Tourism Journalists / see European Travel Press (#08944)
♦ European Federation of Asthma and Allergy Associations / see European Federation of Allergy and Airways Diseases Patients' Associations (#07045)

♦ European Federation of Auctioneers (EFA) 07057

Pres c/o Lempertz, Grote Hertstraat 6, 1000 Brussels, Belgium. E-mail: bruxelles@lempertz.com.

History 1973, as *Federation of Auctioneers of the EEC – Fédération des organisateurs de ventes publiques de la CEE*. Subsequently changed title to *European Federation of Auctioneers-Appraisers (EFAA) – Fédération européenne des commissaires-priseurs – Federación Europea de Subastadores – Europäischer Federation Auktionatoren – Federação Européia de Leiloeiros – Federazione Europea di Venditori all'Aste – Europese Federatie van Veilingmeesters-Taxateurs – Europaeiske Auktionsholder Forening – Evropaiki Omospondia Dimopraton Teksnis*. Current Statutes adopted 26 Apr 1993, Paris (France). **Structure** General Meeting (at least once a year); Board; Working Groups. **Languages** Czech, Danish, Dutch, English, Estonian, Finnish, French, German, Hungarian, Irish Gaelic, Italian, Latvian, Lithuanian, Maltese, Polish, Portuguese, Slovakian, Slovene, Spanish, Swedish. **Events** *General Assembly* Brussels (Belgium) 1996.
Members National organizations in 5 countries:
Belgium, France, Germany, Italy, UK.
Contacts in 2 countries:
Denmark, Netherlands.
IGO Relations Recognized by: *European Commission (EC, #06633)*.
[2019/XE2348/E]

♦ European Federation of Auctioneers-Appraisers / see European Federation of Auctioneers (#07057)

♦ European Federation of Audiology Societies (EFAS) 07058

SG Univ Oldenburg, Carl-von-Ossietzky-Str 9-11, 26111 Oldenburg, Germany. T. +494417985470. Fax +494417983902.
URL: http://www.efas.ws/

History Sep 1992, Cambridge (UK). Bylaws amended 1998. **Aims** Promote cooperation, exchange of experience and knowledge of audiology within Europe. **Structure** General Assembly (annual). Committee of Representatives, consisting of one voting representative per member nation and including Council: Chairman; Vice-Chairman; Secretary; Secretary; Treasurer; Past-President. **Languages** English. **Staff** Voluntary. **Finance** Members' dues. Sponsoring. **Activities** Events/meetings. **Events** *Congress* Vienna (Austria) 2025, *Congress* Sibenik (Croatia) 2023, *Congress* Germany 2021, *Congress* Sibenik (Croatia) 2021, *Congress* Lisbon (Portugal) 2019.
Members National societies in 34 countries:
Austria, Belgium, Bosnia-Herzegovina, Croatia, Czechia, Denmark, Estonia, Finland, France, Germany, Greece, Hungary, Iceland, Ireland, Israel, Italy, Latvia, Lithuania, Malta, Netherlands, Norway, Poland, Portugal, Romania, Russia, Serbia, Slovakia, Slovenia, Spain, Sweden, Switzerland, Türkiye, UK, Ukraine.
NGO Relations Member of: *Confederation of European Otorhinolaryngology – Head and Neck Surgery (Confederation of European ORL-HNS, #04528)*; *International Society of Audiology (ISA, #14948)*.
[2015/XD7409/D]

♦ European Federation of Autonomic Societies (EFAS) 07059

Sec c/o SEIN, Postbus 540, 2130 AM Hoofddorp, Netherlands.
URL: http://www.efasweb.com/

History Nov 1997, London (UK). **Aims** Advance development of research and clinical aspects within the field of the autonomic *nervous system*; stimulate, encourage and help develop European programmes of clinical and experimental autonomic research and pre- and post-graduate teaching; promote and cooperate in international exchange arrangements for all scientists involved in basic or clinical research on autonomic nervous system, especially those in training. **Structure** Council, comprising one representative elected by each associated National Autonomic Society and up to 4 co-opted members. Officers (elected by Council): Chairman; Secretary; Treasurer; Deputy Treasurer; Past President. **Languages** English. **Staff** 3-4 voluntary. **Finance** Members' dues. **Activities** Events/meetings. **Events** *Congress* Leiden (Netherlands) 2019, *Congress* Vienna (Austria) 2018, *Congress* Innsbruck (Austria) 2017, *Congress* Giesen (Germany) 2013, *Congress / Meeting* Stockholm (Sweden) 2012. **Publications** *Clinical Automatic Research* – official journal.
Members Ordinary, National Autonomic Societies; Individual; Honorary; Affiliated; Corporate. Members in 12 countries:
Austria, France, Germany, Greece, Italy, Netherlands, Portugal, Serbia, Slovenia, Spain, Switzerland, UK.
[2019/XD7699/D]

♦ European Federation of Bilateral Chambers of Commerce (EFBCC) . 07060

Fédération Européenne des Chambres de Commerce Bilatérales

Chairman 62 Obere Dorfstrasse, 3906 Saas Fee VS, Switzerland. T. +41767092865. E-mail: office@eurobilateralchambers.eu.

Hon Gen Sec Winchmore Hill, London, N21 1DL, UK. Fax +447459905196.

Acting Gen Dir Abdun, Amman 11183, Jordan. T. +972595933313.

URL: https://eurobilateralchambers.eu/

History 1 Apr 2017, Geneva (Switzerland). Registration: Swiss Civil Code, Switzerland. **Structure** General Assembly; Committee. **Languages** English, French. **Staff** 8.00 FTE, paid; 3.00 FTE, voluntary. **Finance** Sources: contributions; investments; members' dues. Annual budget: 2,000,000 CHF (2023). **Activities** Events/meetings.

Members Bilateral chambers of commerce in 14 countries:

Albania, Austria, Colombia, Czechia, Ireland, Israel, Nigeria, Portugal, Romania, Slovenia, Switzerland, Tanzania UR, Türkiye, UK. [2023.02.16/AA1419/**D**]

♦ European Federation for Bioenergetic Analysis Psychotherapy (EFBA-P) 07061

Pres Söhlwiese 15, 37081 Göttingen, Germany. T. +4915206930028.

URL: http://www.bioenergeticanalysis.net/

History May 1995, Frascati (Italy). **Aims** Strengthen the European identity and position within the world of Bioenergetic Analysis. **Structure** Board, comprising President, Secretary, Treasurer and 1 further member. **Languages** English. **Finance** Members' dues. **Activities** Events/meetings. **Publications** *Bioenergetic Analysis European Societies Information and Communication* – newsletter; *The European Journal of Bioenergetic Analysis and Psychotherapy*.

Members in 9 countries:

Austria, Belgium, France, Germany, Netherlands, Poland, Portugal, Spain, Switzerland.

NGO Relations Member of: *European Association for Body Psychotherapy (EABP, #05958)*; *European Association for Psychotherapy (EAP, #06176)*. [2017.10.11/XM2657/**D**]

♦ European Federation of Biotechnology (EFB) 07062

Fédération européenne de biotechnologie – Europäische Föderation Biotechnologie

Contact Gran Vía Carlos III 98, Torre Norte, Planta 10, 08028 Barcelona, Spain. T. +34934020599. Fax +34934020434. E-mail: info@efbiotechnology.org.

URL: https://www.efbiotechnology.org/

History 1978, Interlaken (Switzerland). **Aims** Promote cooperation, on scientific grounds, between national member societies, their individual members and scientists on a European level, for the general advancement of biotechnology as an interdisciplinary field of research and as a means of furthering scientific development and application of manufacturing processes in Europe. **Structure** General Assembly. Executive Committee of 32 members, including Chairman. Sections; Task Groups; Working Parties. **Languages** English, French, German. **Finance** No budget. **Activities** Initiates and organizes specialized meetings, including *'European Congress of Biotechnology (ECB)'* and *'European Symposium on Biochemical Engineering Science (EBES)'*. promotes education and training; promotes international cooperation in Europe and beyond; promotes public understanding of biotechnology; collaborates with European Commission in research funding. Sections (7): (1) Biochemical Engineering Science, including the following Working Groups: Measurement, Monitoring, Modelling and Control MSC; Downstream Processing and Recovery of Bioproducts; Bioreactor Performance; (2) (3) Microbial Physiology; (4) Applied Genome Research; (5) Agri-biotechnology; (6) Medical Biotechnology (under formation); (7) Applied Biocatalysis. Task Groups (2): Public Perceptions of Biotechnology; Education. Working Parties (2): Environmental Biotechnology; Safety in Biotechnology. **Events** *European Congress on Biotechnology* Maastricht (Netherlands) 2024, *European Congress on Biotechnology* Maastricht (Netherlands) 2022, *EFB 2021 Conference* 2021, *Designer Biology Meeting* Vienna (Austria) 2021, *European Congress on Biotechnology* Maastricht (Netherlands) 2020. **Publications** *EFB Newsletter* (4 a year). *Made by Genetic Engineering* – series; *Safe Biotechnology Series.* Opinion papers; review papers; briefing papers; books; proceedings.

Members Institutions, companies and other organizations (81) in 29 countries:

Albania, Austria, Belgium, Bulgaria, Croatia, Czechia, Denmark, Finland, France, Germany, Greece, Hungary, Ireland, Italy, Latvia, Lithuania, Netherlands, Norway, Poland, Portugal, Romania, Slovakia, Slovenia, Spain, Sweden, Switzerland, Türkiye, UK, Ukraine.

Included in the above, 1 organization listed in this Yearbook:

European Society for Animal Cell Technology (ESACT, #08520).

Corresponding societies in 5 countries:

Australia, India, Israel, Japan, USA.

IGO Relations *European Commission (EC, #06633).* **NGO Relations** Associate Member of: *Federation of Asian Biotech Associations (FABA, #09429).* [2022/XD6421/y/**D**]

♦ European Federation of Bottled Waters / see Natural Mineral Waters Europe (#16955)

♦ European Federation of Branches of the World's Poultry Science Association (EFWPSA) 07063

Fédération européenne des filiales de l'Association mondiale d'aviculture – Federación Europea de Ramas de la Asociación Mundial de Avicultura Científica – Europäische Föderation der Landesgruppen der Weltvereinigung für Geflügelwissenschaft

Pres Norwegian Univ of Life Sciences, 1432 Ås, Norway.

Sec-Treas Univ Hohenheim, WG Poultry Science, Dept Livestock Population Genomics – 460h, 70593 Stuttgart, Germany. T. +4971145922484.

URL: http://www.wpsa.com/

History Founded 15 Nov 1960, Utrecht (Netherlands), within the framework of *World's Poultry Science Association (WPSA, #21825)*, during 1st European Poultry Conference. **Aims** Promote extension of knowledge in the field of poultry science; facilitate exchange of knowledge and experience among persons in the *poultry industry*; institute regional conferences and assist in the promotion of the World Poultry Congresses. **Structure** Council; Executive Committee; Working Groups (12). **Languages** English. **Staff** None. **Finance** Members' dues. **Activities** Events/meetings. **Events** *European Symposium on the Quality of Poultry Meat* Krakow (Poland) 2023, *European Symposium on Poultry Nutrition (ESPN)* Rimini (Italy) 2023, *European Symposium on Poultry Nutrition* Rimini (Italy) 2022, *European Symposium on Poultry Nutrition* Rimini (Italy) 2021, *European Symposium on Poultry Nutrition* Gdansk (Poland) 2019. **Publications** Conference and symposia proceedings; working group reports.

Members Branches of WPSA, grouping over 3,000 members and affiliations in 28 countries:

Austria, Belgium, Croatia, Czechia, Denmark, Estonia, Finland, France, Germany, Greece, Hungary, Israel, Italy, Latvia, Lebanon, Lithuania, Netherlands, Norway, Poland, Romania, Russia, Serbia, Slovakia, Spain, Sweden, Switzerland, Türkiye, UK. [2017.10.29/XE0722/**E**]

♦ European Federation of Building Joinery Manufacturers (inactive)

♦ European Federation of Building Societies (EFBS) 07064

Fédération européenne d'épargne et de crédit pour le logement – Europäische Bausparkassenvereinigung

Managing Dir Rue Montoyer 25, 1000 Brussels, Belgium. T. +3222310371. Fax +3222308245. E-mail: info@efbs-bausparkassen.org.

URL: http://www.efbs.org/

History 29 Aug 1962, Brussels (Belgium). Former names and other names: *European Federation of Savings and Loan Institutions for Construction* – former; *Fédération européenne des institutions d'épargne et de crédit ou de crédit différé pour la construction* – former. Registration: EU Transparency Register, No/ID: 33192023937-30. **Aims** Promote the idea of home ownership; represent members' interests in the European Community; inform members on progress in European unification and measures to this end taken by EC bodies; support and intensify mutual information and exchange of experience among members in the fields of housing finance and policy. **Structure** General Assembly (annual); Council of Management; Technical Committees. **Languages** English, French, German. **Staff** None; administration through a member organization. **Finance** Sources: members' dues. **Events** *European Congress of the European Federation of Building Societies* Prague (Czechia) 2019, *Semi-Annual Meeting* Brussels (Belgium) 2017, *Annual Meeting* Bucharest (Romania) 2017, *Congress* Budapest (Hungary) 2016, *Annual Meeting* Prague (Czech Rep) 2015. **Publications** *EFBS Newsletter.* Annual report; directory of members; nomenclature; congress proceedings.

Members Participating; Corresponding. National associations or institutions in 10 countries:

Austria, Croatia, Cyprus, Czechia, Germany, Hungary, Luxembourg, Romania, Slovakia, Slovenia.

IGO Relations Recognized by: *European Commission (EC, #06633).* Working relations with: *United Nations Economic Commission for Europe (UNECE, #20555).* **NGO Relations** Member of (1): *International Union for Housing Finance (IUHF, #15780).* Instrumental in setting up (1): *European Banking Industry Committee (EBIC, #06314).* [2021.06.10/XD0751/**D**]

♦ European Federation of Building and Woodworkers (EFBWW) 07065

Fédération européenne des travailleurs du bâtiment et du bois (FETBB) – Federación Europea de los Trabajadores de la Construcción y la Madera (FETCM) – Europäische Föderation der Bau- und Holzarbeiter (EFBH) – Federazione Europea dei Lavoratori Edili e del Legno (FETBB) – Europese Federatie van Bouw- en Houtarbeiders (EFBH) – Europaeisk Federation af Bygnings- og Traeindustriarbejdere (EFBT)

Gen Sec Rue Royale 45, 1st Floor, 1000 Brussels, Belgium. T. +3222271040. Fax +3222198228. E-mail: info@efbww.eu.

URL: https://www.efbww.eu/

History 1958, Brussels (Belgium). Constitution revised at 1st General Assembly, 5 May 1974, Salerno (Italy), and ratified at General Assembly, Nov 1976, Luxembourg. Constitution amended and present name adopted during the General Assembly, 18 Nov 1983, Brussels. New statutes adopted at Congress, Dec 1991, Luxembourg. Former names and other names: *Joint Committee of Building and Woodworkers in the EEC* – former; *Commission commune des ouvriers du bâtiment et du bois dans la CEE* – former; *European Federation of Building and Woodworkers in the EEC (EFBWWC)* – former (1976 to 1983); *Fédération européenne des travailleurs du bâtiment et du bois dans la CEE* – former (1976 to 1983); *Europäische Föderation der Bau- und Holzarbeiter in der EWG* – former (1976 to 1983); *Federazione Europea dei Lavoratori Edili e del Legno nella CEE* – former (1976 to 1983); *Europese Bond van Bouw- en Houtarbeiders in de EEG* – former (1976 to 1983); *Europaeisk Federation af Bygnings- og Treindustriarbejdere ØEF* – former (1976 to 1983); *Europese Bond van Bouw- en Houtarbeiders (EBBH)* – alias. Registration: Banque Carrefour des Entreprises, No/ID: 0430.536.082, Start date: 6 Dec 1984, Belgium; EU Transparency Register, No/ID: 57745478360-42, Start date: 16 Mar 2012. **Aims** Represent affiliates in Europe and help them defend the rights and interests of workers in the construction industry, building materials industry, wood and furniture industry and forestry industry. **Structure** General Assembly (every 4 years); Executive Committee; Presidium; Standing Committees (2); Health and Safety Coordination Group; EWC Coordinators' Steering Group; Secretariat. **Languages** Danish, Dutch, English, French, German, Italian, Spanish. **Staff** 10.00 FTE, paid. **Finance** Sources: members' dues. **Activities** Events/meetings; knowledge management/information dissemination; projects/programmes; research/documentation; standards/guidelines. **Events** *General Assembly* 2023, *Quadrennial General Assembly* Vienna (Austria) 2019, *Quadrennial General Assembly* Warsaw (Poland) 2015, *Quadrennial General Assembly* Palermo (Italy) 2011, *Quadrennial General Assembly* Luxembourg (Luxembourg) 2007. **Publications** Newsletters; standards/guidelines; articles; brochures.

Members National organizations (76) in 36 countries:

Austria, Belgium, Bulgaria, Croatia, Cyprus, Czechia, Denmark, Estonia, Finland, France, Germany, Greece, Hungary, Iceland, Ireland, Italy, Latvia, Lithuania, Luxembourg, Malta, Monaco, Netherlands, North Macedonia, Norway, Poland, Portugal, Romania, Serbia, Slovakia, Slovenia, Spain, Sweden, Switzerland, Türkiye, UK, Ukraine.

NGO Relations Member of (2): *Construction 2050 Alliance (#04760)*; *Wood Sector Alliance for the New European Bauhaus (Wood4Bauhaus, #21046).* [2023.02.16/XE0299/t/**D**]

♦ European Federation of Building and Woodworkers in the EEC / see European Federation of Building and Woodworkers (#07065)

♦ European Federation of Business and Professional Women / see BPW Europe – European Region of BPW International (#03309)

♦ European Federation of Campingsite Organisations and Holiday Park Assocations (EFCO and HPA) 07066

Fédération européenne de l'hôtellerie de plein air (FEHPA)

SG EFCO Secretariat, 6 Pullman Court, Great Western Rd, Gloucester, GL1 3ND, UK. T. +441452526911. Fax +441452508508. E-mail: efco@bhhpa.org.uk.

Contact address not obtained.

URL: http://www.efcohpa.eu/

History 1978. Former names and other names: *European Federation of Camping Site Organizations (EFCO)* – former; *Verband Europäischer Campingplatzhalter (VECH)* – former. Registration: EU Transparency Register, No/ID: 25326099059-51, Start date: 28 Jun 2012. **Aims** Promote and protect the interests of owners of camping and caravanning sites; promote this form of *tourist* hospitality; seek to harmonize schemes for the sector to ensure a 'level playing field' for caravan and camping park business in Europe. **Structure** Governing Council (meets twice a year); Management Committee; Secretariat located in UK. **Languages** English, French. **Staff** 2.00 FTE, paid. **Finance** Sources: members' dues. **Activities** Advocacy/lobbying/activism; monitoring/evaluation. **Publications** Documents.

Members National representative professional bodies for the camping/caravanning park industry, including caravans, tents, motorhomes, chalets and all forms of park self-catering accommodation, in 23 countries:

Austria, Belgium, Croatia, Denmark, Estonia, Finland, France, Germany, Greece, Ireland, Italy, Latvia, Lithuania, Luxembourg, Netherlands, Norway, Portugal, Serbia, Slovenia, Spain, Sweden, Switzerland, UK.

IGO Relations Member of the Tourism Consultative Committee of: *European Commission (EC, #06633).* **NGO Relations** Member of (2): *European Tourism Manifesto (#08921)*; *Network for the European Private Sector in Tourism (NET, #17027).* Technical Liaison Partner with: *European Committee for Electrotechnical Standardization (CENELEC, #06647).* In liaison with technical committees of: *Comité européen de normalisation (CEN, #04162)*; *International Organization for Standardization (ISO, #14473).* [2021.09.09/XE0089/**D**]

♦ European Federation of Camping Site Organizations / see European Federation of Campingsite Organisations and Holiday Park Assocations (#07066)

♦ European Federation of Catalysis Societies (EFCATS) 07067

Sec Univ of Bucharest, Dep Organic Chemistry, Biochemistry, Catalysis, Bd Regina Elisabeta 4-12, 030018 Bucharest, Romania. T. +44214100241.

URL: http://www.efcats.org/

History 1990. **Aims** Unite catalysis societies; enhance visibility of catalysis in Europe. **Structure** 2 representatives of catalysis societies per European country. **Languages** English. **Finance** Conference levies. **Events** *EUROPACAT Congress* Aachen (Germany) 2019, *EUROPACAT Congress* Florence (Italy) 2017, *EUROPACAT Congress* Kazan (Russia) 2015, *EUROPACAT Congress* Lyon (France) 2013, *EUROPACAT Congress* Glasgow (UK) 2011.

Members Individuals in 25 countries:

Austria, Belgium, Bulgaria, Czechia, Denmark, Finland, France, Germany, Greece, Hungary, Ireland, Italy, Latvia, Netherlands, Norway, Poland, Portugal, Romania, Russia, Slovakia, Spain, Sweden, Switzerland, Türkiye, UK. [2013/XD4188/v/**D**]

♦ European Federation of Catering Equipment Manufacturers (EFCEM) 07068

Fédération européenne de constructeurs d'équipement de grandes cuisines – Europäischer Verband der Hersteller von Grosskochanlagen

General Secretariat APPLiA Italia, Via Matteo Bandello 5, 20123 Milan MI, Italy. T. +39243518826. E-mail: secretary.general@efcem.info.

URL: http://www.efcem.info/

History 23 Jun 1969, Düsseldorf (Germany FR). Registered in accordance with Belgian law: CF 97607900152. EU Transparency Register: 070284916886-11. Registration: No/ID: 97607900152, Belgium, Brussels. **Aims** Defend, promote and coordinate the interests of member associations. **Structure** General Assembly (annual) held by rotation in each member country. **Languages** English. **Finance** Members' dues. **Events** *Annual General Assembly* Brussels (Belgium) 2014, *Annual General Assembly* London (UK) 2013, *Annual General Assembly* Brussels (Belgium) 2012, *Annual General Assembly* Istanbul (Turkey) 2010, *Annual General Assembly* Berlin (Germany) 2009.

Members Associations in 9 countries:

Denmark, France, Germany, Ireland, Italy, Portugal, Sweden, Türkiye, UK.

IGO Relations Recognized by: *European Commission (EC, #06633).* **NGO Relations** Member of: *Industry4Europe (#11181).* [2019/XD3511/**D**]

European Federation Catholic
07069

alphabetic sequence excludes
For the complete listing, see Yearbook Online at

♦ European Federation of Catholic Married Priests (FE) 07069

Contact Hors-les-Murs, Rue Barbette 3, 1404 Nivelles, Belgium. T. +3267210285.
URL: http://www.pretresmaries.eu/

History Set up as one one of the federations descended from *International Federation of Married Catholic Priests (IFMCP, inactive)*. Also abbreviated as *Married Priests. Europe*. **Aims** Renew ministries with a view to the renewal of the church as it works towards a more just world. **Structure** Committee. **Events** *Annual Meeting* Brussels (Belgium) 2014, *Annual Meeting* Brussels (Belgium) 2013.
Members Full in 7 countries:
Austria, Belgium, France, Germany, Italy, Spain, UK. [2014.02.17/XJ7886/**D**]

♦ European Federation of Catholic Physicians Associations (no recent information)

♦ European Federation of Catholic Universities 07070

Fédération des universités catholiques européennes (FUCE) – Federación de Universidades Católicas de Europa

Sec 10 place des Archives, 69288 Lyon, France.
Pres address not obtained. E-mail: contact@fuce.eu.
URL: http://www.fuce.eu

History 18 Apr 1991, Warsaw (Poland). Founded during the 16th meeting of FIUC-Europe, as a network within the framework of *International Federation of Catholic Universities (IFCU, #13381)*. Statutes modified, May 2000, Milan (Italy) and May 2007, Namur (Belgium). Former names and other names: *Federation of European Catholic Universities* – former; *Fédération des Universités Catholiques d'Europe et du Liban* – alias. **Aims** Integrate Catholic universities to create new knowledge through research activities, transmit knowledge with consistently renewed pedagogical practices and serve society. **Structure** General Assembly (annual); Council; Bureau; International Relations Directors. **Languages** English, French, Spanish. **Staff** None. **Finance** Sources: members' dues. Members' dues. **Activities** Events/meetings. **Events** *General Assembly* Maynooth (Ireland) 2015, *Colloquium* Lyon (France) 2014, *Colloquium* Rome (Italy) 2013, *Colloquium* Lublin (Poland) 2012, *Colloquium* Beirut (Lebanon) 2011. **Publications** *Livre Blanc de la FUCE – La FUCE de 2004 à 2012: que de défis à relever.* Colloquium proceedings; documents.
Members Catholic universities in 17 countries:
Belgium, France, Georgia, Germany, Holy See, Hungary, Italy, Lebanon, Malta, Netherlands, Poland, Portugal, Romania, Slovakia, Spain, Switzerland, Ukraine.
NGO Relations Instrumental in setting up: *Plateforme Universitaire de Recherche sur L'Islam en Europe et au Liban (PLURIEL, #18396)*. Member of: *Global University Network for Innovation (GUNI, #10641)*. [2020.05.06/XD2826/**E**]

♦ European Federation of Centres for Positive Psychotherapy (EFCPP) 07071

Pres Luisenstrasse 28, 65185 Wiesbaden, Germany. T. +496114503440. Fax +496114503424. E-mail: wapp@positum.org.
URL: http://www.positum.org/

History 1997. Founded by *World Association for Positive and Transcultural Psychotherapy (WAPP, #21174)*, as the umbrella organization of national, regional and local centres of Positive Psychotherapy in Europe. **Aims** Train psychotherapists according to the standards of the European Certificate of Psychotherapy (ECP) of EAP; coordinate activities of centres of Positive Psychotherapy in Europe; represent interests of Positive Psychotherapy at continental level in Europe. **Structure** Board of Directors; Head Office in Wiesbaden (Germany). **Languages** English, German. **Staff** 5.00 FTE, paid. **Activities** Events/meetings; research/documentation; training/education. **Publications** Books.
Members Centres in 17 countries:
Armenia, Austria, Azerbaijan, Belarus, Bulgaria, Cyprus, Georgia, Germany, Kosovo, Latvia, North Macedonia, Poland, Romania, Russia, Türkiye, UK, Ukraine.
NGO Relations Accredited by (1): *European Association for Psychotherapy (EAP, #06176)*. Member of (1): *International Federation for Psychotherapy (IFP, #13523)*. [2022.05.04/XE2630/**E**]

♦ European Federation of Centres of Research and Information on Cults and Sects 07072

Fédération européenne des centres de recherche et d'information sur le sectarisme (FECRIS) – Europäische Föderation der Zentren für Forschung und Information über das Sektenwesen

Pres 26A rue Espérandieu, 13001 Marseille, France. E-mail: secretarygeneralfecris@gmail.com.
URL: http://www.fecris.org/

History 30 Jun 1994, Paris (France). Former names and other names: *European Federation for Research and Information on Sectarianism* – former. Registration: Start date: 30 Jun 1994, France. **Aims** Study and inform on the legal, medical, psychological, social, economic and scientific effect of *cults* on individuals, on their families and on democratic society and defend them against abuse carried out by such cults under the cover of protection afforded by states to philanthropic organizations; assist victims and represent them with civil and moral authorities so as to draw attention to and support their action; monitor activities of cults which may be contrary to the Universal Declaration of Human Rights, to human rights treaties and to European and national legislation. **Structure** General Assembly; Administrative Council. **Languages** English, French, German. **Staff** 2.50 FTE, voluntary. **Finance** Sources: members' dues. **Activities** Relevant treaties: *Convention for the Protection of Human Rights and Fundamental Freedoms (1950)*; *United Nations Convention on the Rights of the Child (CRC, 1989)*. Organizes conferences. **Events** *Conference* Brussels (Belgium) 2022, *Conference* Bordeaux (France) 2021, *European Virtual Conference* Marseille (France) 2020, *Conference* Paris (France) 2019, *Colloquium* Riga (Latvia) 2018.
Members Full in 14 countries:
Armenia, Austria, Belgium, France, Germany, Ireland, Italy, Poland, Russia, Spain, Sweden, Switzerland, UK, Ukraine.
Correspondants in 17 countries:
Belarus, Belgium, Bulgaria, Cyprus, Finland, France, Germany, Lithuania, Malta, Netherlands, Norway, Russia, Serbia, Slovakia, Sweden, UK, Ukraine.
Individuals in 1 country:
Estonia.
Non-European Correspondants in 4 countries:
Argentina, Australia, Israel, USA.
Consultative Status Consultative status granted from: *Council of Europe (CE, #04881)* (Participatory Status); *ECOSOC (#05331)* (Special). **IGO Relations** Participant in Fundamental Rights Platform of: *European Union Agency for Fundamental Rights (FRA, #08969)*. [2021/XD6234/**D**]

♦ European Federation of Ceramic Sanitaryware Manufacturers 07073

Fédération européenne des fabricants de céramiques sanitaires (FECS) – Federación Europea de Fabricantes de Ceramicas Sanitarias – Europäischer Verband der Fabrikanten von Sanitär-Keramik

Contact c/o Cerame-Unie, Rue Belliard 12, 1040 Brussels, Belgium. T. +3228083880. Fax +3225115174. E-mail: sec@cerameunie.eu.
URL: http://cerameunie.eu/members/sectors/

History 16 Dec 1954, Geneva (Switzerland). **Aims** Cooperate in studying technico-scientific, statistical and social problems facing European ceramic sanitary ware manufacturers. **Structure** General Assembly; Executive Committee; Committees (3). **Languages** English, French. **Staff** 3.00 FTE, paid. **Finance** Members' dues. **Activities** Knowledge management/information dissemination; events/meetings. **Events** *Annual meeting / Meeting* Istanbul (Turkey) 2007, *Annual meeting / Meeting* Berlin (Germany) 2006, *Annual meeting / Meeting* Prague (Czech Rep) 2005, *Annual meeting / Meeting* Copenhagen (Denmark) 2004, *Annual meeting / Meeting* Madrid (Spain) 2003. **Publications** Information Circulars.
Members National associations in 12 countries:
Austria, Belgium, France, Germany, Greece, Italy, Netherlands, Portugal, Spain, Switzerland, Türkiye, UK.
Also one association representing Scandinavian countries.
IGO Relations Recognized by: *European Commission (EC, #06633)*. **NGO Relations** Member of: *Industry4Europe (#11181)*. Associate member of: *European Ceramic Industry Association (CERAME-UNIE, #06506)*. [2018.09.10/XD0724/**D**]

♦ European Federation of Chemical Engineering (EFCE) 07074

Fédération européenne de génie chimique – Europäische Föderation für Chemie-Ingenieur-Wesen

Contact Inst of Chemical Engineers, Davis Bldg, 165-189 Railway Terrace, Rugby, CV21 3HQ, UK. T. +441788534411 – +441788578214. Fax +441788550904.
Contact c/o DECHEMA e v, Theodor-Heuss-Allee 25, 60486 Frankfurt-Main, Germany. T. +49697564143. Fax +49697564418.
URL: http://www.efce.info/

History 20 Jun 1953, Paris (France). Revised statutes approved 15 May 2009, Frankfurt-Main (Germany). New constitution as a Charitable Incorporated Organisation, approved 2015. Registration: Charities Commission, No/ID: 1159541, England and Wales; Companies House, No/ID: CE002439, England and Wales. **Aims** Promote cooperation in Europe between non-profit-making professional scientific and technical societies, for the general advancement of chemical engineering and as a means of furthering the scientific and economic development of chemical engineering. **Structure** General Assembly (biennial); Board of Trustees. **Languages** English, French, German. **Staff** Voluntary. **Finance** Sources: members' dues. **Activities** Events/meetings; training/education; knowledge management/information dissemination. Related conference series include: *European Congress of Chemical Engineering (ECCE)*; *Conférence internationale des industries de procédés (INTERCHIME)*; *European Conference on Mixing*; *European Symposium on Computer Aided Process Engineering (ESCAPE)*; *European Symposium on Electrochemical Engineering*; *International Conference on Electrostatics*; *International Conference on Gas-Liquid and Gas-Liquid-Solid Reactor Engineering (GLS)*; *International Congress of Chemical and Process Engineering (CHISA)*; *International Meeting on Chemical Engineering and Biotechnology (ACHEMA)*; *International Symposium Chemical Reaction Engineering (ISCRE)*; *World Congress of Chemical Engineering (WCCE)*; *World Filtration Congress*; *European Symposium on Comminution and Classification (ESCC)*; *European Process Intensification Conference (EPIC)*. **Events** *European Congress of Applied Biotechnology* Berlin (Germany) 2023, *European Congress of Chemical Engineering (ECCE)* Berlin (Germany) 2023, *International Symposium on Loss Prevention and Safety Promotion in Process Industries* Prague (Czechia) 2022, *European Congress of Chemical Engineering (ECCE)* Berlin (Germany) 2021, *European Symposium on Biochemical Engineering Sciences* Frankfurt-Main (Germany) 2021. **Publications** *Chemical Engineering Research and Design (ChERD)* – journal; *Education for Chemical Engineers* – journal; *Food and Bioproduct Processing* – journal; *Process Safety and Environmental Protection* – journal. Proceedings of symposia and congresses; reports.
Members Scientific and technical non-profit making societies in 28 European countries:
Austria, Belgium, Bulgaria, Croatia, Czechia, Denmark, Estonia, Finland, France, Germany, Greece, Hungary, Ireland, Italy, Netherlands, Norway, Poland, Portugal, Romania, Serbia, Slovakia, Slovenia, Spain, Sweden, Switzerland, Türkiye, UK, Ukraine.
European Membrane Society (EMS, #07777).
Corresponding members in 7 countries:
Brazil, Canada, India, Japan, Nigeria, South Africa, USA.
IGO Relations Cooperates with: *United Nations Economic Commission for Europe (UNECE, #20555)*. **NGO Relations** Cooperates with: *International Organization for Standardization (ISO, #14473)*. Member of: *Alliance for Chemical Sciences and Technologies in Europe (AllChemE, #00664)*; *World Chemical Engineering Council (WCEC, #21271)*. Set up: *European Desalination Society (EDS, #06908)*; *European Process Safety Centre (EPSC, #08279)*. [2021/XD0725/y/**D**]

♦ European Federation of Chemical General Workers Unions (inactive)
♦ European Federation of Chemical Trade / see Fédération européenne du commerce chimique (#09563)
♦ European Federation of Child Neurology Societies / see European Paediatric Neurology Society (#08126)
♦ European Federation of Chimney Sweepers / see Europäische Schornsteinfegermeister-Föderation (#05761)
♦ European Federation of Chimney Sweeps (#05761)
♦ European Federation of Chinese Tourism (unconfirmed)

♦ European Federation of Choirs of the Union 07075

Fédération européenne des choeurs de l'Union – Europäische Föderation der Chöre der Union

SG Torenstraat 13, 9160 Lokeren, Belgium. T. +3293484993. E-mail: fecujpva@telenet.be.
Registered Office 17 rue Rochechouart, 75009 Paris, France. T. +33144538686. Fax +33144538680.
URL: http://fecu-efcu.eu/

Aims Promote the European ideal in the context of choral music, in particular with regard to young people; further the recognition and development of the educational, social and cultural aspects of singing in choirs. **Structure** Council, including President. [2008/XM3682/**E**]

♦ European Federation of Christian Building and Woodworkers Unions (inactive)
♦ European Federation of Christian Miners' Trade Unions (inactive)

♦ European Federation of Christian Student Associations 07076

Fédération européenne d'associations d'étudiants chrétiens – Europäischer Kartellverband Christlicher Studentenverbände (EKV)

Pres Lerchenfelderstrasse 14, 1st Floor, 1080 Vienna, Austria. E-mail: president@ekv.info – praesident@ekv.info – office@ekv.info.
Gen Sec address not obtained. E-mail: social@ekv.info.
URL: http://www.ekv.info/

History 15 Oct 1975, Salzburg (Austria). Former names and other names: *Association of European Christian Fraternities (AECF)* – alias. Registration: Austria. **Aims** Develop, coordinate and promote platforms for cooperation, networking, culture, tradition and communication in Europe. **Structure** General Meeting; Chairmanship; Board of Trustees. *'Fürst Franz Josef II von und zu Liechtenstein'* – foundation. **Languages** English, French, German. **Staff** 4.00 FTE, paid. **Finance** Members' dues. **Activities** Networking/liaising; events/meetings. **Events** *General meeting* Aachen (Germany) 2000, *General meeting* Budapest (Hungary) 1996, *European study meeting* Vienna (Austria) 1993, *Studying in Europe* Brussels (Belgium) 1990, *Annual convention* Budapest (Hungary) 1990. **Publications** *European Academic Synopsis (EASY) – A Guide to Studying in Europe.*
Members Associations (14); Free Curia fraternities and sororities (19). Members in 16 countries:
Austria, Belgium, Cameroon, Czechia, France, Germany, Italy, Japan, Liechtenstein, Lithuania, Poland, Romania, Slovakia, Slovenia, Switzerland, Ukraine.
Consultative Status Consultative status granted from: *Council of Europe (CE, #04881)* (Participatory Status). **NGO Relations** Member of: *European Sunday Alliance (#08856)*. Supports: *European Citizens' Initiative Campaign (ECI Campaign, #06558)*. [2016.06.01/XD0440/**D**]

♦ European Federation of Cinematographers / see International Federation of Cinematographers (#13390)

♦ European Federation of Citizen Energy Cooperatives (REScoop.eu) . 07077

Coordinator Posthoflei 3, 2600 Berchem, Belgium. T. +32493400931. E-mail: info@rescoop.eu.
Brussels Office Av des Arts 7-8, 1210 Brussels, Belgium.
URL: http://www.rescoop.eu/

History Apr 2012. Former names and other names: *Renewable Energy Sources Cooperative (REScoop 20-20-20)* – former. Registration: Banque-Carrefour des Entreprises, No/ID: 0543.579.288, Start date: 5 Aug 2015, Belgium; EU Transparency Register, No/ID: 906602046269-23, Start date: 27 Apr 2022. **Aims** Empower citizens and cooperatives and wants to achieve energy democracy. **Languages** Dutch, French, German, Greek, Spanish. **Staff** 13.00 FTE, paid. **Finance** Sources: fees for services; international organizations; members' dues. Supported by: *European Climate Foundation (ECF, #06574)*; *Open Society Foundations (OSF, #17763)*; *Tides*. Annual budget: 1,300,000 EUR (2022). **Members** Individual and national/regional federations of citizen energy cooperatives. Membership countries not specified. **NGO Relations** Associate partner of: *Covenant of Mayors for Climate and Energy (#04939)*. Supports: *Global 100% RE (#10160)*. Sector federation of: *Cooperatives Europe (#04801)*. [2022.05.10/XJ7605/**D**]

♦ European Federation of City Farms (EFCF) 07078

Chairman Schapenstraat 14, 1750 Lennik, Belgium. T. +3225691445. Fax +3225692651. E-mail: info@cityfarms.org.
URL: http://www.cityfarms.org/

History 17 Oct 1990. Registered in accordance with Belgian law. **Aims** Promote interests and mutual cooperation of organizations that actively promote equal access and involvement of children, young people and adults through practical experience in a wide range of educational, environmental, recreational, social and economic activities focused around farming, empowering people to improve their own lives and environment in peaceful coexistence; promote the exchange of information, best practice and expertise of people engaged in the field; encourage organic management of land; promote education and training of members; promote transnational projects; promote and aid the organization of international conferences; commit to sustainable development principles and practices in all programmes and actions; promote a programme of European cooperation and integration. **Structure** General Meeting (annual). Board of Directors, consisting of Chairperson, Secretary, Treasurer and 3 members. Working Groups. Administrative Office located at office of Chairperson. **Languages** English. **Staff** None. **Finance** Members' dues (annual): Full euro 500; Associate euro 400. **Activities** Promotes work and image of city farms and raises the profile of EFCF, member federations and city farms; helps and facilitates member federations and city farms to deliver programmes, activities and research that benefit other federations and city farms; distributes information, in particular good practice, to member organisations; collaborates and networks with other like-minded organisations, particularly community-run land-based groups; helps further the aims and aspirations of member federations and their city farms; raises funding for operation of EFCF and participating member federations to deliver agreed programmes and action. Organizes youth exchange programmes; exchange of programmes; conferences; training courses; fund-raising for EFCF and for European cooperation programmes. Environmental Education Programme; fosters information exchange; publishing activity. **Events** *Annual Conference* Ghent (Belgium) 2015, *Annual Conference* Swansea (UK) 2014, *Annual Conference* Bodø (Norway) 2013, *Annual Conference* Lübeck (Germany) 2012, *Annual Conference* Kortrijk (Belgium) 2010. **Publications** *European Federation of City Farms Newsletter* (4 a year). Guidance papers.

Members Full organizations of city farms; Associate group of city farms working together to form an organization or independent city farms. Full members in 7 countries:
Belgium, France, Germany, Netherlands, Norway, Sweden, UK.
Associate members in 3 countries:
Italy, Portugal, Spain.
IGO Relations *European Commission (EC, #06633)* (DG XXIII). **NGO Relations** Member of: *European Environmental Bureau (EEB, #06996).* [2017/XF1689/F]

♦ European Federation of Clean Air and Environmental Protection Associations (EFCA) 07079

Admin Office c/o Fraunhofer Inst für Chemische Technologie, PO Box 1240, 76318 Pfinztal, Germany. T. +497214640391. Fax +497214640345. E-mail: info@efca.net.
URL: https://efca.net/

History Nov 1996. Registration: EU Transparency Register, No/ID: 66196446799-74. **Aims** Work at the interface between science and European policy on environmental problems, thus contributing to identification of solutions with a sound scientific basis, which are technologically feasible, cost-effective and politically acceptable. **Structure** Assembly; Executive Committee. **Languages** English. **Staff** None. **Finance** Members' dues. **Activities** Networking/liaising; events/meetings; politics/policy/regulatory. **Events** *International Symposium on Ultrafine Particles* Brussels (Belgium) 2022, *International Symposium on Non-CO2 Greenhouse Gases* Amsterdam (Netherlands) 2019, *International Symposium on Ultrafine Particles* Brussels (Belgium) 2019, *International Symposium on Ultrafine Particles* Brussels (Belgium) 2017, *Croatian Scientific and Professional Conference* Porec (Croatia) 2015. **Publications** *EFCA Electronic Newsletter* (3 a year); *EFCA Yearbook* (every 3 years). Conference proceedings; conference papers; articles.

Members Professional Associations (14, comprising over 10,000 professionals) active in the field of air pollution control and environmental protection in 11 countries:
Croatia, Finland, France, Germany (2), Italy, Netherlands, Poland, Sweden, Switzerland, Türkiye, UK (3).
Included in the above, 1 organization listed in this yearbook:
Commission on Air Pollution Prevention of VDI and DIN – Standards Committee (KRdL).
Associate members in 2 countries:
Norway, UK.
Observer association in 1 country:
Austria.
IGO Relations Observer status with: *Convention on Long-range Transboundary Air Pollution (#04787)*; *United Nations Framework Convention on Climate Change – Secretariat (UNFCCC, #20564).* **NGO Relations** Member of: *International Union of Air Pollution Prevention and Environmental Protection Associations (IUAPPA, #15753).* [2022/XD5727/y/D]

♦ European Federation of Cleaning Industries / see European Cleaning and Facility Services Industry (#06571)

♦ European Federation of Clinical Chemistry and Laboratory Medicine (EFLM) 07080

Office Via Carlo Farini 81, 20159 Milan MI, Italy. E-mail: eflm@eflm.eu.
URL: http://www.eflm.eu/

History 1993, Nice (France). Founded under the auspices of *International Federation of Clinical Chemistry and Laboratory Medicine (IFCC, #13392)*, when statutes were adopted and Board elected. Following merger with *European Communities Confederation of Clinical Chemistry and Laboratory Medicine (EC4, inactive)*, Jun 2007, Amsterdam (Netherlands), adopted current title. Represents IFCC in Europe. Former names and other names: *Forum of the European Societies of Clinical Chemistry and Laboratory Medicine (FESCC)* – former; *EFCC* – former (Jun 2007 to 23 Mar 2012). Registration: EU Transparency Register, No/ID: 400550533169-85, Start date: 13 Nov 2018. **Aims** Enhance *patient care* and improve outcomes by promoting and improving the scientific, professional and clinical aspects of clinical chemistry and laboratory medicine; ensure effective representation of laboratory medicine both at European Union level and to other pan-European and sub-regional bodies. **Structure** General Meeting (annual); Executive Board; Task Forces, Committees; Working Groups; Task Groups; Finish Groups. **Languages** English. **Activities** Certification/accreditation; events/meetings; research and development; training/education. **Events** *IFCC-EFLM EuroMedLab Congress* Rome (Italy) 2023, *Labquality Days – International Congress on Quality in Laboratory Medicine and Health Technology* Helsinki (Finland) 2022, *European Conference on Preanalytical Phase* Milan (Italy) 2022, *Strategic Conference* Milan (Italy) 2022, *EuroMedLab Congress* Munich (Germany) 2021. **Publications** *Clinical Chemistry and Laboratory Medicine (CCLM).* Papers; guidelines and recommendations; position and opinion papers; reviews and surveys.

Members National Societies in 41 countries:
Albania, Austria, Belgium, Bosnia-Herzegovina, Bulgaria, Croatia, Cyprus, Czechia, Denmark, Estonia, Finland, France, Georgia, Germany, Greece, Hungary, Iceland, Ireland, Israel, Italy, Kosovo, Latvia, Lithuania, Luxembourg, Montenegro, Netherlands, North Macedonia, Norway, Poland, Portugal, Romania, Russia, Serbia, Slovakia, Slovenia, Spain, Sweden, Switzerland, Türkiye, UK, Ukraine.
Affiliate members in 6 countries:
France, Ireland, Kazakhstan, Romania, Serbia, Spain.
Provisional in 1 country:
Slovakia.
NGO Relations Member of (1): *Biomedical Alliance in Europe (#03251).* Liaison Organization of: *Comité européen de normalisation (CEN, #04162). International Congress on Quality in Laboratory Medicine (LABQUALITY DAYS)* held under its auspices. [2022.05.05/XF3660/F]

♦ European Federation of Coin Machine Associations / see European Gaming and Amusement Federation (#07374)

♦ European Federation of Coin Operated Amusement Machine Associations / see European Gaming and Amusement Federation (#07374)

♦ European Federation for Colposcopy and Cervical Pathology / see European Federation for Colposcopy and Pathology of the Lower Genital Tract (#07081)

♦ European Federation for Colposcopy and Pathology of the Lower Genital Tract (EFC) 07081

Pres c/o Triumph Benelux, Rue de la Presse 4, 1000 Brussels, Belgium. T. +3222272730. E-mail: efcsecretariat@thetriumph.com.
URL: http://efcolposcopy.eu/

History 22 Sep 1998, Dublin (Ireland). Founded on the occasion of the First European Congress for Colposcopy. Former names and other names: *European Federation for Colposcopy and Cervical Pathology* – former. Registration: Banque-Carrefour des Entreprises, No/ID: 0700.641.985, Start date: 3 Aug 2018, Belgium; Companies House, No/ID: 06261383, Start date: 29 May 2007, End date: 25 Jun 2019, England and Wales. **Aims** Stimulate basic and applied research and the diffusion of knowledge in matters concerning uterine cervical pathology and colposcopy in Europe; contribute to the standardization and evaluation of diagnostic and therapeutic procedures in the field of cervical pathology among European clinicians and pathologists. **Structure** General Assembly; Executive Committee (meets annually); Scientific Committee for the Congress. **Languages** English. **Staff** 1.00 FTE, paid. **Finance** Sources: grants; members' dues. **Activities** Events/meetings. **Events** *European Congress* Krakow (Poland) 2024, *European Congress* Helsinki (Finland) 2022, *Triennial Congress* Rome (Italy) 2019, *Meeting* Brussels (Belgium) 2018, *Meeting* Brussels (Belgium) 2017. **Publications** Newsletter.

Members National societies or federations for colposcopy in Europe and the Mediterranean, in 34 countries:
Austria, Belgium, Croatia, Cyprus, Czechia, Estonia, Finland, France, Georgia, Germany, Greece, Hungary, Ireland, Israel, Italy, Kosovo, Latvia, Lithuania, Moldova, Netherlands, North Macedonia, Norway, Poland, Portugal, Romania, Russia, Serbia, Slovakia, Slovenia, Spain, Sweden, Switzerland, Türkiye, UK.
Associate members in 5 countries:
Albania, Bulgaria, Denmark, Malta, Montenegro.
IGO Relations Liaises with: *WHO (#20950)* International Network on Control of Gynaecological Cancer and Collaborating Centre for Research in Human Reproduction. **NGO Relations** Member of (2): *European Cancer Organisation (ECO, #06432)*; *Federation of European and International Associations Established in Belgium (FAIB, #09508).* Cooperates with (1): *European Board and College of Obstetrics and Gynaecology (EBCOG, #06357).* Liaises with: European Cervical Cancer Screening Network; *International Federation for Cervical Pathology and Colposcopy (IFCPC, #13385).* [2022/XJ4250/D]

♦ European Federation of Community Doctors / see European Federation of Salaried Doctors (#07209)

♦ European Federation of the Community of Sant'Egidio 07082

Fédération européenne des communautés de Sant'Egidio

Permanent Contact Rue des Riches Claires 26, 1000 Brussels, Belgium. T. +3225124546. E-mail: federation@santegidio.be.
SG Piazza S Egidio 3/a, 00153 Rome RM, Italy. T. +396585661. E-mail: info@santegidio.org.
URL: http://www.santegidio.org/

History Registration: Belgium; EU Transparency Register, No/ID: 045689014322-13. **Aims** Support activities for the poorest and excluded of society; contribute to culture in European cities; combat *racism.* **Languages** Dutch, English, French, German, Italian, Spanish. **Staff** 4.00 FTE, paid; 50.00 FTE, voluntary. **Activities** Runs after-schooling centres and camps. Organizes conferences, seminars and youth exchange programmes. Established small-scale housing and network of home-assistance for the elderly. Set up development and emergency aid programmes. Activities in the field of peace negotiation and conflict prevention. **Publications** *Where to East, Sleep and Wash* (annual). *Making Peace. The role played by the Community of Sant'Egidio in the international arena* (2010).

Members Individuals in 19 countries:
Argentina, Belgium, Cameroon, Côte d'Ivoire, El Salvador, France, Germany, Guatemala, Indonesia, Ireland, Italy, Mexico, Mozambique, Portugal, Romania, Russia, Spain, Ukraine, USA.
NGO Relations Member of: *Permanent Forum of European Civil Society (#18322).* Instrumental in setting up: *Solidarietà con il Terzo Mondo (no recent information).* [2020.05.06/XD7045/E]

♦ European Federation for Company Sport (EFCS) 07083

Fédération européenne des sports corporatifs – Europäische Föderation für Betriebssport

Gen Sec 28 rue Rosenwald, 75015 Paris, France. T. +33156640214. Fax +33147200450. E-mail: companysport@efcs.org.
URL: http://www.efcs.org/

History Founded 1962. Charter adopted at 7th Conference, 24 May 1974, Helsinki (Finland); amended at: 10 Conference, 31 May 1980, Oslo (Norway); 12th Conference, 19 May 1984, Herceg-Novi (Yugoslavia) 1984; 16th Conference, 23 May 1992. Also known as *Europäische Föderation für Firmen- und Betriebssport.* EU Transparency Register: 152811425024-40. **Aims** Promote and develop sport practice in the professional environment all across Europe. **Structure** Biennial European Congress (even years) forms the General Assembly; Executive Committee. **Languages** English, French, German. **Staff** 1.50 FTE, paid. **Finance** Annual ordinary members' dues. Contribution from participant at European Company Sport Games. Budget (annual): euro 25,500. **Activities** Sporting activities; events/meetings. **Events** *Biennial European Company Sport Summer Games* Prague (Czech Rep) 2013, *Biennial European Company Sport Winter Games* Falun (Sweden) 2012, *Biennial European Company Sport Summer Games* Hamburg (Germany) 2011, *Biennial European Company Sport Winter Games* Arêches-Beaufort (France) 2010, *Sport, marketing, health and sponsor management meeting* Eindhoven (Netherlands) 2009.

Members Ordinary in 34 countries:
Austria, Azerbaijan, Belarus, Belgium, Bosnia-Herzegovina, Bulgaria, Croatia, Czechia, Denmark, Estonia, France, Germany, Greece, Hungary, Iceland, Israel, Italy, Latvia, Lithuania, Malta, Moldova, Monaco, Montenegro, Netherlands, North Macedonia, Norway, Poland, Russia, San Marino, Slovakia, Slovenia, Spain, Sweden, Ukraine.
NGO Relations Partners include: *European Observatoire of Sport and Employment (EOSE, #08071)*; *European Platform for Sport Innovation (EPSI, #08232)*; *Sport and Citizenship.* [2019/XD7260/D]

♦ European Federation for Complementary and Alternative Medicine (EFCAM) 07084

Contact c/o EPHA, Rue de Trèves 49-51, 1040 Brussels, Belgium. T. +35318404021. E-mail: secretary@efcam.eu – contact@efcam.eu.
URL: http://www.efcam.eu/

History Dec 2001. Originally part of *European Public Health Alliance (EPHA, #08297).* Former names and other names: *European Forum for Complementary and Alternative Medicine (EFCAM)* – former; *Forum européen de la médecine complémentaire et alternative pour un service de santé intégré en Europe* – former; *Europäisches Forum für Komplementäre und Alternative Medizin Förderung der Integrierten Gesundheitsfürsorge* – former. Registration: Handelsregister, Netherlands; EU Transparency Register, No/ID: 390368027607-08. **Aims** Serve as a permanent forum for the exchange of views and information on complementary and alternative medicine; act as a point of reference for the European Union institutions on policy and regulatory issues of relevance. **Structure** Board. **Languages** English. **Activities** Healthcare; research/documentation.

Members National federation in 1 country:
Ireland.
Pan-European professional CAM organization:
European Shiatsu Federation (ESF, #08476). [2022.03.01/XM1686/y/F]

♦ European Federation of Concrete Admixtures Associations (EFCA) . 07085

Contact Rue d'Arlon 55, 1040 Brussels, Belgium. T. +3226455212. E-mail: info@efca.info.
URL: http://www.efca.info/

History 22 Jun 1984, Brussels (Belgium). Founded at inaugural meeting. Registration: Banque-Carrefour des Entreprises, No/ID: 0697.659.830, Start date: 6 Jun 2018, Belgium; Companies House, No/ID: 08454686, Start date: 21 Mar 2013, End date: 16 Apr 2019, England and Wales; EU Transparency Register, No/ID: 200215413337-34, Start date: 25 Mar 2014. **Aims** Act as the official representative of the admixture industry with approaching authorities, institutions or other competent bodies at European and international levels. **Structure** General Assembly; Executive Board, headed by President; Committees (2). **Languages** English. **Staff** 0.50 FTE, paid. **Finance** Sources: members' dues.

Members National associations in 11 countries:
Belgium, France, Germany, Italy, Netherlands, Norway, Spain, Sweden, Switzerland, Türkiye, UK.
IGO Relations Accredited by: *European Chemicals Agency (ECHA, #06523).* **NGO Relations** Member of (4): *Concrete Europe (#04433)* (Founding); *Construction 2050 Alliance (#04760)*; *Construction Products Europe AISBL (#04761)*; *Industry4Europe (#11181).* In liaison with technical committees of: *Comité européen de normalisation (CEN, #04162)*; *International Organization for Standardization (ISO, #14473).* [2020/XD2960/D]

♦ European Federation of Conference Towns (inactive)

♦ European Federation of Conflict Management and Treatment in Education and Care (EFeCT) 07086

Chairman OC Nieuwe Vaart, Jozelf Guislainstr 47-49, 9000 Ghent, Belgium.
URL: http://www.efect.be/

History 14 Nov 2007, Blankenberge (Belgium). Registration: Belgium. **Aims** Encourage strength-based practices in work and research concerning conflict management for vulnerable children and youth. **Structure** Founder/Chairman. **Languages** English. **Staff** Voluntary. **Finance** Sources: meeting proceeds. **Activities** Events/meetings; knowledge management/information dissemination; networking/liaising; research/documentation. **Events** *Conference* Leuven (Belgium) 2022, *Meeting* 2021, *Conference* Leuven (Belgium) 2020, *Conference* Ålesund (Norway) 2018, *Conference* Timisoara (Romania) 2016.
Members Full in 8 countries and territories:
Belgium, Germany, Hungary, Netherlands, Norway, Portugal, Romania, Scotland. [2022.05.30/XJ7649/**D**]

♦ European Federation of Connective Tissue Clubs / see European Matrix Biology (#07756)

♦ European Federation of Conservative Dentistry (EFCD) 07087

Admin Secretariat c/o Klinik für Zahnerhaltung, Freiburgstrasse 7, 3010 Bern, Switzerland. E-mail: contact@efcd.eu.
SG King's College London, Dental Inst, Denmark Hill Campus, Caldecot Road, London, SE5 9RW, UK. T. +442032993585. Fax +442032993826.
URL: http://www.efcd.eu/

History Registration: Switzerland. **Aims** Promote oral health by encouraging excellence in clinical practice, teaching and research in all aspects of conservative dentistry. **Structure** General Assembly (biannual); Executive Committee. **Languages** English. **Finance** Members' dues. **Activities** Events/meetings. **Events** *Congress with EFCD* Egmond aan Zee (Netherlands) 2023, *ConsEuro Meeting* Antalya (Turkey) 2022, *ConsEuro Meeting* Istanbul (Turkey) 2021, *ConsEuro Meeting* Berlin (Germany) 2019, *ConsEuro Meeting* Bologna (Italy) 2017. **Members** Membership countries not specified. [2022/XD9079/**D**]

♦ European Federation for Construction Chemicals (EFCC) 07088

Dir Gen Bvd du Triomphe 172, 4th Floor, 1160 Brussels, Belgium. T. +3228972039.
URL: http://www.efcc.eu/

History 2005. Registration: EU Transparency Register, No/ID: 126293811245-87; Start date: 3 Apr 2007, Belgium. **Aims** Represent construction chemical companies, both raw materials producers for construction chemicals and formulators of construction chemicals, and associations in Europe before the European Union institutions and other public authorities; communicate the industry's views on policy issues regarding product stewardship, including product safety and quality, health, sustainability and resource efficiency. **Structure** General Assembly; Executive Board. Task Forces. **Activities** Advocacy/lobbying/activism. **Events** *Joint Workshop on Use Maps* Brussels (Belgium) 2017. **NGO Relations** Member of: *Conseil européen de l'industrie chimique (CEFIC, #04687); Construction Products Europe AISBL (#04761); Downstream Users of Chemicals Co-ordination group (DUCC, #05127); Industry4Europe (#11181).* [2022/XM0688/**D**]

♦ European Federation of the Contact Lens Industry / see European Federation of the Contact Lens and IOL Industries (#07089)

♦ European Federation of the Contact Lens and IOL Industries (EFCLIN) 07089

Exec Dir Winkelbüel 2, 6043 Adligenswil LU, Switzerland. T. +41413721010. Fax +41413720683. E-mail: info@efclin.com.
URL: http://www.efclin.com/

History 1971. Former names and other names: *European Federation of the Contact Lens Industry* – former. **Aims** Expand the most prominent exhibition and meeting place for the global contact lens and IOL industry; initiate education; maintain the highest level of professional services and relevant information. **Structure** Board; Secretariat. **Languages** English. **Staff** 1.00 FTE, paid; 6.00 FTE, voluntary. **Finance** Sources: meeting proceeds; members' dues. Annual budget: 120,000 EUR. **Activities** Awards/prizes/competitions; events/meetings; knowledge management/information dissemination. **Events** *Annual Congress* The Hague (Netherlands) 2023, *Annual Congress* Sitges (Spain) 2022, *Annual Congress* Berlin (Germany) 2021, *Annual Congress* Berlin (Germany) 2020, *Annual Congress* Brussels (Belgium) 2019. **Members** Full (87) in 23 countries. Membership countries not specified. **NGO Relations** Member of (3): *European Academy of Optometry and Optics (EAOO, #05807); European Contact Lens Forum (ECLF, #06774); European Federation of National Associations and International Companies of Contact Lens and Contact Lens Care Product Manufacturers (EUROMCONTACT, #07167).* [2023.02.20/XD7033/t/**D**]

♦ European Federation of Contract Catering Organizations / see FoodServiceEurope (#09851)

♦ European Federation of Corrosion (EFC) 07090

Fédération européenne de la corrosion – Europäische Föderation Korrosion

Pres Av des Arts 56/4C, 1000 Brussels, Belgium. E-mail: offices@efcweb.org.
Honorary Treas Inst of Materials, Minerals and Mining (IoM3), 297 Euston Road, London, NW1 3AQ, UK. T. +442074517365. Fax +442078391702.
URL: http://www.efcweb.org/

History 1955, Frankfurt-Main (Germany). New statutes adopted 31 Oct 1994, Bournemouth (UK); revised Sep 2017. Registration: Banque-Carrefour des Entreprises, No/ID: 0425.591.656, Start date: 19 Apr 1984. **Aims** Promote European cooperation in research on corrosion, corrosion prevention and materials protection. **Structure** General Assembly (annual); Board of Administrators; Science and Technology Advisory Committee (STAC); Working Parties; Secretariats (3). **Languages** English, French, German. **Finance** Sources: members' dues. **Activities** Awards/prizes/competitions; events/meetings; training/education. **Events** *EUROCORR – European Corrosion Congress* Brussels (Belgium) 2023, *EUROCORR – European Corrosion Congress* Berlin (Germany) 2022, *EUROCORR – European Corrosion Conference* 2021, *EUROCORR – European Corrosion Conference* 2020, *EUROCORR: European Corrosion Conference* Seville (Spain) 2019. **Publications** *EFC Newsletter. EFC Publications* – produced by individual working parties. Reports; congress proceedings.
Members Honorary (individuals); Affiliate (universities and research organizations, companies); Effective, Associate and Founder (societies and associations). Technical and scientific societies in 24 countries:
Australia, Austria, Belgium, China, Croatia, Czechia, Denmark, Finland, France, Germany, Hungary, Italy, Netherlands, Norway, Poland, Portugal, Slovenia, Spain, Sweden, Switzerland, Türkiye, UK, Ukraine, USA.
NGO Relations Member of (2): *Federation of European and International Associations Established in Belgium (FAIB, #09508); World Corrosion Organization (WCO, #21316).* Cooperates with (1): *International Organization for Standardization (ISO, #14473).* [2022.05.18/XD0728/**D**]

♦ European Federation of Corrugated Board Manufacturers 07091

Fédération Européenne des Fabricants de Carton Ondulé (FEFCO) – Federación Europea de Fabricantes de Cartón Ondulado – Europäischer Verband der Wellpappenfabrikanten – Federazione Europea dei Fabbricanti di Cartone Ondulato

Office Manager Av Louise 250, 1050 Brussels, Belgium. T. +3226269831 – +3226464070. Fax +3226466460. E-mail: information@fefco.org – info@fefco.org.
URL: http://www.fefco.org/

History 17 Mar 1952, Santa Margherita (Italy). Registered by French Ministerial Decree, 28 Oct 1952. Also registered in accordance with Belgian law. Current by-laws approved 25 Oct 1996. **Aims** Promote the common interest of members across Europe; improve the image of the corrugated board industry. **Structure** General Assembly (annual); Board of Directors; Standing Committees (4). **Languages** Dutch, English, French, German. **Staff** 4.00 FTE, paid. **Finance** Members' dues. Fixed contributions from sympathizer members. Annual grants from industries. **Activities** Politics/policy/regulatory; research and development; networking/liaising; awareness raising; projects/programmes; events/meetings. **Events** *Technical Seminar* Geneva (Switzerland) 2019, *Summit* Stockholm (Sweden) 2018, *Technical Seminar* Vienna (Austria) 2017, *Summit* Berlin (Germany) 2016, *Technical Seminar* Barcelona (Spain) 2015. **Publications** *Annual Statistics. FEFCO/ESBO International Case Code.* Annual Report; manufacturing practices; guidelines; reports; address book; brochures; documents. **Information Services** *European Database for Corrugated Board Life Cycle Studies.*

Members Active national associations; Corresponding companies where there is no national association or whose national association is not a member; Sympathizers. Active members in 24 countries:
Austria, Belgium, Croatia, Czechia, Denmark, Finland, France, Germany, Greece, Hungary, Ireland, Italy, Netherlands, Norway, Poland, Portugal, Romania, Slovakia, Spain, Sweden, Switzerland, Türkiye, UK, Ukraine.
Corresponding members in 11 countries:
Argentina, Bulgaria, Egypt, Israel, Kazakhstan, Lebanon, Malta, Russia, Saudi Arabia, Slovenia, USA.
Sympathizer members (200) in 25 countries. Membership countries not specified.
NGO Relations Active Member of: *International Corrugated Case Association (ICCA, #12974)*, and its Offices in Chicago IL (USA) and at FEFCO in Brussels (Belgium). Extraordinary member of: *International Confederation of Paper and Board Converters in Europe (CITPA, #12866).* Member of: *The Consumer Goods Forum (CGF, #04772); Industry4Europe (#11181).* In liaison with technical committees of: *International Organization for Standardization (ISO, #14473).* Supports work of: Global Commerce Initiative; *GS1 (#10809)* (EAN International). [2022/XD0735/**D**]

♦ European Federation for Cosmetic Ingredients (EFfCI) 07092

SG Mainzer Landstrasse 55, 60329 Frankfurt-Main, Germany. T. +496925561341. Fax +496925561342. E-mail: contact@effci.com.
Head Office Av Louise 489, 1050 Brussels, Belgium. E-mail: info@effci.com.
URL: http://www.effci.com/

History 2000. Registration: Banque – Carrefour des Entreprises, No/ID: 0840 955 059, Belgium. **Aims** Represent and defend interests of chemical and natural ingredients manufacturing industry, suppliers and service providers. **Structure** General Assembly; Direct Members' Council; Board of Directors; Working Groups; General Secretariat. **Languages** English. **Finance** Sources: members' dues. **Activities** Events/meetings; knowledge management/information dissemination; networking/liaising; training/education. **Events** *Annual Conference* 2021, *Annual Conference* 2020, *Annual Conference* Edinburgh (UK) 2019, *Annual Conference* Barcelona (Spain) 2018, *Annual Conference* Nice (France) 2017. **Publications** *GMP Guide for Cosmetic Ingredients* (5th ed 2017).
Members Associate in 6 countries:
France, Germany, Italy, Spain, Switzerland, UK.
Direct companies in 8 countries:
Austria, Belgium, Czechia, France, Netherlands, Spain, Sweden, Switzerland.
NGO Relations In liaison with technical committees of: *Comité européen de normalisation (CEN, #04162).* [2022.05.04/XJ3281/**F**]

♦ European Federation of Cotton and Allied Textiles Industries 07093

Fédération européene de l'industrie textile du coton et des fibres connexes (EUROCOTON)

SG Rue Montoyer 24 – Bte 13, 1000 Brussels, Belgium. T. +3222303239. Fax +3222303622.

History Founded 1958, Brussels (Belgium), as *Committee of the Cotton and Allied Textile Industries of the EC – Comité des industries du coton et des fibres connexes de la CE – Comité de la Industria Algodonera y Fibras afines de la CE – Komitee der Baumwoll und Verwandten Textilindustriën der EG – Comitato delle Industrie del Cotone e delle Fibre Connesse della CE – Comité das Industrias de Algodão e Fibras afins da CE – Commissie van de Katoen-en Aanverwante Vezels Verwerkende Nijverheden van de EG – Komité for Bomulds- og Dermed Beslaegtede Textilindustrier i EF – Epitropi ton Viomihanion Vamvakos ke Sinafon Inon tis EK – Komitet ds Przemyslu Bawelniarskiego i Pokrewnych Przemyslow Wlokienniczych – Pamuklu Testil Sanaylieri Birligi.* Subsequently referred to as *Committee of the European Cotton Industry – Comité de l'industrie textile cotonnière européenne* and then *European Committee of the Cotton and Allied Textile Industries – Comité européen des industries textiles du coton et des fibres connexes.* Statutes accepted 1958; modified most recently 18 Jun 2010, Istanbul (Turkey). EU Transparency Register: 84723161705-62. **Aims** Represent the European cotton and allied textiles industry; defend the textile manufacturing pipeline's interests with the European and international authorities, directly and through Euratex. **Structure** General Assembly; Board of Directors; Working Groups on request. **Languages** English, French. **Finance** Members' dues. **Activities** Knowledge management/information dissemination; advocacy/lobbying/activism. **Events** *Annual General Assembly* Brussels (Belgium) 2014, *Annual General Assembly* Brussels (Belgium) 2013, *Annual General Assembly* Ronse (Belgium) 2012, *Annual General Assembly* Brussels (Belgium) 2011, *Annual General Assembly* Istanbul (Turkey) 2010. **Publications** *Economic Situation in the European Cotton Textile Industry.* Statistics; regular circulars.
Members Full (cotton spinners and weavers associations) in 7 countries:
Austria, Belgium, France, Germany, Greece, Poland, Türkiye.
Associate in 2 countries:
Greece, Spain.
Corporate associate in 3 countries:
Austria, Italy, Switzerland.
IGO Relations *European Commission (EC, #06633); International Cotton Advisory Committee (ICAC, #12979).*
NGO Relations Member of: *EURATEX – The European Apparel and Textile Confederation (EURATEX, #05616).* Observer status with: *International Textile Manufacturers Federation (ITMF, #15679).* [2016/XE0488/t/**E**]

♦ European Federation for the Creative Economy (unconfirmed)

♦ European Federation of Critical Care Nursing Associations (EfCCNa) 07094

Contact address not obtained. E-mail: info@efccna.org.
URL: http://www.efccna.org/

History 2 Oct 1999, Berlin (Germany). **Aims** Represent critical care nursing associations within Europe; strengthen the power of European critical care nurses associations; act as the collective voice of critical care nursing in Europe. **Structure** Council of Representatives (meets twice a year). Board of Officers. Committees (4): Exchange Programme; Education; Public Relations; Congress Planning. **Languages** English. **Staff** 0.50 FTE, paid. **Finance** Sources: members' dues. **Activities** Events/meetings; research/documentation; training/education. **Events** *Congress* Utrecht (Netherlands) 2022, *Congress* Utrecht (Netherlands) 2021, *Congress* Ljubljana (Slovenia) 2019, *Congress* Belfast (UK) 2017, *Congress* Valencia (Spain) 2015. **Publications** *Connect – The World of Critical Care Nursing* (4 a year) – online journal.
Members Organizations in 24 countries:
Austria, Belgium, Croatia, Cyprus, Denmark, Finland, France, Germany, Greece, Hungary, Iceland, Israel, Italy, Malta, Netherlands, Norway, Poland, Serbia, Slovenia, Spain, Sweden, Switzerland, Türkiye, UK.
NGO Relations Member of (1): *European Specialist Nurses Organisation (ESNO, #08808).* [2022/XD7833/**D**]

♦ European Federation of Crohn's and Ulcerative Colitis Associations (EFCCA) 07095

Fédération européenne des associations de malades de Crohn et rectocolite hémorragique – Federación de Asociaciones de Crohn y Colitis Ulcerosa – Europäische Föderation von Morbus Crohn und Colitis Ulcerosa Vereinigungen

CEO Rue des Chartreux 33-35, 1000 Brussels, Belgium. T. +3225408434. Fax +3225408434.
URL: http://www.efcca.org/

History 6 Sep 1993, Strasbourg (France), following meeting of national associations, Oct 1990, Freiburg (Germany). Registered in accordance with Belgian law, approved 20 Aug 1996, registered 23 Jan 1997. **Aims** Improve the wellbeing of inflammatory *bowel* disease sufferers; exchange information and promote cross-frontier activities; encourage scientific research into IBD causes, diagnosis and treatment. **Structure** General Assembly (annual); Board (meets annually); Executive Committee. **Languages** English. **Staff** None. **Finance** Members' dues. Other sources: donations; sponsoring by pharmaceutical companies. Budget (annual): about euro 40,000. **Activities** Organizes meetings and seminars. *'Social Security Project'* investigates national provisions for social security and other financial support in Europe, seeks to improve such provisions and intends to seek EC legislation as appropriate. *'Quality of Life Project'* canvasses sufferers on symptoms, complications and resultant social problems that they face. *'Guest Exchange Project'* facilitates exchange visits for IBD sufferers in different countries. *'Travellers' Brochure'* provides special information to allow and encourage patients to travel abroad. Issues 'Medical Passport' to provide the traveller with a portable, concise coverage of his condition and current treatment. New Millennium projects: Insurance in IBD; IBD in Childhood and Young People. **Events** *General Assembly* Helsinki (Finland) 2010, *General Assembly* Amsterdam (Netherlands) 2009, *Youth meeting* Amsterdam (Netherlands) 2009, *General Assembly* Seville (Spain) 2007,

General Assembly Birmingham (UK) 2005. **Publications** *EFCCA Newsletter* (2 a year). *Travellers' Brochure* – series, in several languages. *Medical Passport* – in several languages; *Travelling with IBD* – in several languages.
Members National Organizations in 22 countries:
Austria, Belgium, Croatia, Cyprus, Czechia, Denmark, Finland, France, Germany, Hungary, Iceland, Ireland, Italy, Luxembourg, Netherlands, Norway, Portugal, Slovakia, Spain, Sweden, Switzerland, UK.
NGO Relations Member of: *European Disability Forum (EDF, #06929)*; *European Patients' Forum (EPF, #08172)*; *Health First Europe (HFE, #10881)*; *International Alliance of Patients' Organizations (IAPO, #11633)*. [2018/XD5122/**D**]

♦ European Federation of Curiosities, Antiques and Folklore Collectors and Enthusiasts (inactive)

♦ European Federation of Cybersecurity Experts (EFCSE) 07096

Fédération Européenne des Experts en CyberSécurité (FEECS)

Contact Square de Meeus 37, 1000 Brussels, Belgium. T. +3227917554.
URL: https://www.efcse.eu/

History Founded 27 Jan 2016. Registered in accordance with Belgian law. EU Transparency Register: 071948526864-90. **Aims** Reinforce the regulation and European infrastructures for cybersecurity. **Structure** General Assembly; Board of Directors. **Members** Individuals. Membership countries not specified. [2020/XM8798/v/**D**]

♦ European Federation of Cytology Societies (EFCS) 07097

Fédération européenne des sociétés de cytologie – Vereinigung der Europäischen Gesellschaften für Zytologie

SG Dept of Pathology, Univ Paris Centre, Cochin Hosp, 27 rue du faubourg St Jacques, 75679 Paris CEDEX 14, France. T. +33158411577. E-mail: info@efcs.eu – efcs@adriacongrex.it.
Registered Office Onderbergen 63, 9000 Ghent, Belgium.
URL: http://www.efcs.eu/

History 1969, Sils-Maria (Switzerland). Statutes approved: 1991, Turku (Finland); 2007, Paris (France); 2009, Lisbon (Portugal). Registration: Belgium. **Aims** Encourage friendly relations between national societies, with exchange of knowledge and experience; promote unification of training and qualification in cytology. **Structure** Council; Board. **Languages** English, French, German. **Finance** Members' dues. **Events** *Annual congress* Wroclaw (Poland) 2021, *Annual congress* Wroclaw (Poland) 2020, *Annual Congress* Malmö (Sweden) 2019, *Annual Congress* Madrid (Spain) 2018, *Annual Congress* Liverpool (UK) 2016. **Publications** *EFCS Newsletter* (2 a year).
Members National Societies in 22 countries:
Albania, Austria, Belgium, Bulgaria, Croatia, Czechia, Denmark, Finland, France, Germany, Greece, Hungary, Italy, Netherlands, Norway, Poland, Russia, Slovenia, Spain, Sweden, Switzerland, UK.
Observers (2):
Portugal, Russia.
NGO Relations Affiliated to: *International Academy of Cytology (IAC, #11544)*. [2021/XD0056/**D**]

♦ European Federation of Dairy Retailers (inactive)

♦ European Federation of Data Protection Officers (EFDPO) 07098

Registered Address Rue de Namur 73A, 1000 Brussels, Belgium. T. +493020621441. E-mail: office@efdpo.eu.
URL: https://www.efdpo.eu/

History 7 Jun 2019, Berlin (Germany). Registration: Banque-Carrefour des Entreprises, No/ID: 0766.602.381, Start date: 12 Apr 2021, Belgium; EU Transparency Register, No/ID: 210439247792-47, Start date: 29 Sep 2022. **Aims** Represent the interests of data protection officers in Brussels, at the European Union. **Structure** Board of Directors. **Staff** 1.10 FTE, voluntary.
Members Associations in 9 countries:
Austria, Czechia, France, Germany, Greece, Liechtenstein, Portugal, Slovakia, Switzerland.
Associate members in 2 countries:
Brazil, Croatia. [2022/AA1372/**D**]

♦ European Federation of Defence Technology Associations / see Federation of European Defence Technology Associations (#09500)

♦ European Federation for Diaconia (Eurodiaconia) 07099

Fédération européenne de la diaconie – Europäischer Verband für Diakonie

SG 166 Rue Joseph II, 1000 Brussels, Belgium. T. +3222343861. Fax +3222343865. E-mail: office@eurodiaconia.org.
Office Manager address not obtained.
URL: http://www.eurodiaconia.org/

History Sep 1932. Present Statutes adopted 20 Oct 1954, Hannover (Germany FR), replacing those of 9 Jul 1932. Took over activities of Brussels-based *Association of Diaconal Organizations in Europe (Eurodiaconia, inactive)*, 1996, when new Statutes were adopted. Current Statutes adopted, Jun 2007. Former names and other names: *Kontinentaler Verband für Innere Mission und Diakonie* – former (Sep 1932 to 1947); *International Federation for Inner Mission and Christian Social Work* – former (1947); *Fédération internationale pour la mission intérieure et le service chrétien* – former (1947); *Internationaler Verband für Innere Mission und Diakonie* – former (1947). Registration: Banque-Carrefour des Entreprises, No/ID: 0809.444.709, Start date: 29 Jan 2009, Belgium; EU Transparency Register, No/ID: 4293010684-55, Start date: 27 Nov 2008. **Aims** Develop dialogue and partnership and influence and engage with the wider society, so as to enable inclusion, care and empowerment of the most vulnerable and excluded and ensure dignity for all. **Structure** Board; Secretariat, based in Brussels (Belgium). **Languages** English, French, German. **Staff** 7.00 FTE, paid. **Finance** Sources: members' dues. Supported by: *European Commission (EC, #06633)*. **Activities** Events/meetings. **Events** *Annual General Meeting and Conference* Edinburgh (UK) 2019, *Communications Network Meeting* Brussels (Belgium) 2018, *Regional Workshop of the ERASMUS+ Project Q-Europe* Brussels (Belgium) 2018, *Annual General Meeting and Conference* Wroclaw (Poland) 2018, *Annual General Meeting and Conference* Oslo (Norway) 2017. **Publications** Congress proceedings; position papers; newsletter; commentaries; reports.
Members Diaconal organizations (44) in 23 countries:
Armenia, Austria, Czechia, Denmark, Finland, France, Germany, Hungary, Iceland, Italy, Kosovo, Latvia, Lithuania, Netherlands, Norway, Poland, Romania, Serbia, Slovakia, Spain, Sweden, Switzerland, UK.
International organizations (2):
Europäischer Verband Freikirchlicher Diakoniewerke (evfdiakonie, #05759); Kaiserswerther Generalkonferenz; *Salvation Army (#19041)* (Europe).
IGO Relations *European Committee of the Regions (CoR, #06665)*; *European Commission (EC, #06633)*; *European Economic and Social Committee (EESC, #06963)*; *European Parliament (EP, #08146)*. **NGO Relations** Member of (6): *Conference of European Churches (CEC, #04593)*; *EU Alliance for a democratic, social and sustainable European Semester (EU Semester Alliance, #05565)*; *European Anti-Poverty Network (EAPN, #05908)*; *SDG Watch Europe (#19162)*; *Social Platform (#19344)*; *Social Services Europe (#19347)*. [2022/XD9470/y/**D**]

♦ European Federation for the Disappearance of Prostitution (no recent information)

♦ European Federation of DIY Manufacturers (FEDIYMA) 07100

Manager c/o HHG, Deutz-Mühlheimer Str 30, 50679 Cologne, Germany. T. +4922127980119. Fax +4922127980120. E-mail: info@fediyma.com.
Registered Office Raymond Delbekestr 373, 2980 Zoersel, Belgium.
URL: http://www.fediyma.com/

History Mar 2000. Registration: No/ID: 821.786.968, Belgium, Antwerp. **Aims** Promote the DIY industry in Europe by: tracking consumer trends; improving market knowledge; encouraging exports and international relationships; representing manufacturers and helping them grow. **Structure** Board, including President, 2 Vice-Presidents and Treasurer. **Events** *Global DIY Summit* Copenhagen (Denmark) 2022, *Virtual DIY Summit* 2021, *Global DIY Summit* Copenhagen (Denmark) 2021, *Global DIY Summit* Dublin (Ireland) 2019, *Global Summit* Barcelona (Spain) 2018.
Members National organizations in 6 countries:
Belgium, Denmark, France, Germany, Spain, UK. [2021/XM1208/**D**]

♦ European Federation of Doctors appointed to Corporate Institutions (inactive)
♦ European Federation of Drug Abuse Prevention Associations (no recent information)
♦ European Federation for the Education of the Children of the Occupational Travellers (inactive)
♦ European Federation for Education and Culture (inactive)

♦ European Federation of Education Employers (EFEE) 07101

Gen Sec Rue des Deux Eglises 26, 1000 Brussels, Belgium. E-mail: secretariat@educationemployers.eu.
URL: http://www.educationemployers.eu/

History Feb 2009. Registration: No/ID: 0823.099.933, Start date: 11 Feb 2010, Belgium; EU Transparency Register, No/ID: 009175623137-75, Start date: 5 Sep 2016. **Aims** Improve quality of teaching and school management through European cooperation and dialogue. **Structure** Executive Committee. **Events** *General Assembly* Brussels (Belgium) 2014, *General Assembly* Brussels (Belgium) 2012.
Members Full in 21 countries:
Belgium, Bulgaria, Croatia, Cyprus, Finland, Germany, Greece, Hungary, Ireland, Italy, Latvia, Malta, Montenegro, Netherlands, Norway, Portugal, Romania, Slovakia, Slovenia, Sweden, UK.
NGO Relations Member of: *SGI Europe (#19253)*; *European Policy Network on School Leadership (EPNoSL, #08245)*. [2019/XJ8298/**D**]

♦ European Federation of Educators in Nursing Sciences (FINE) 07102

Fédération européenne des enseignants en sciences infirmières

Pres address not obtained.
SG address not obtained.
URL: https://www.fine-europe.eu/

History 1992. Former names and other names: *Federation of International Nurse Education* – former (1992); *European Federation of Nurse Educators (FINE)* – former (2019). Registration: Belgium. **Aims** Promote excellence in nursing education, as well as nurse educators' skill acquisition and maintenance in the countries of the World Health Organization's European region, so as to better address their populations' constantly evolving health needs. **Structure** General Assembly (every 2 years); Executive Board; Advisory Board. **Languages** English, French. **Finance** Sources: members' dues. **Events** *Biennial Conference* Nancy (France) 2014, *Biennial Conference* Cardiff (UK) 2012, *Biennial conference* Lisbon (Portugal) 2010, *Biennial conference* Plovdiv (Bulgaria) 2008, *Biennial Conference* Paris (France) 2006. **Publications** *FINE Newsletter* (2 a year).
Members Categories Full – national delegations; Associate – organizations, institutes, bodies and individuals with an interest in nursing education; Candidate. Delegations from 15 countries:
Belgium, Bulgaria, Denmark, Finland, France, Greece, Ireland, Italy, Luxembourg, Netherlands, Portugal, Romania, Slovenia, Spain, UK.
NGO Relations Member of: *European Specialist Nurses Organisation (ESNO, #08808)*. [2021/XD6606/**D**]

♦ European Federation of the Electro-Ceramic Industry (inactive)

♦ European Federation of Electronic Retailers (EFER) 07103

Fédération européenne des commerçants en électronique domestique et électroménager

SG Nelectra, Stationlei 78 bus 1/1, 1800 Vilvoorde, Belgium. T. +3225501714. Fax +3225501729.

History Aug 1989. Registered in accordance with Belgian law. Statutes modified, 16 May 1999, Brussels (Belgium), at General Assembly. **Aims** Group national associations representing audiovisual and household electrical appliance trade and services in European countries; promote technical and commercial training of retailers; process and supply statistics so as to improve knowledge of the sector and its profile and maintain the highest standards of professional training; present a unified voice in the European context. **Structure** General Assembly (annual); Administrative Council; Bureau. **Languages** English, French. **Staff** 1.00 FTE, paid. **Finance** Members' dues. **Events** *Annual General Assembly* Brussels (Belgium) 2013, *Annual General Assembly* Brussels (Belgium) 2012, *Annual General Assembly* Brussels (Belgium) 2011, *Annual General Assembly* Brussels (Belgium) 2010, *Annual General Assembly* Brussels (Belgium) 2009. **Publications** *EFER Newsletter*.
Members Active; Associate. Organizations (15) in 12 countries:
Austria, Belgium (2), Denmark, Finland, France (2), Germany (2), Italy, Netherlands, Norway, Spain, Sweden, UK. [2018.06.01/XD3368/**D**]

♦ European Federation for Elevator Small and Medium-sized Enterprises (EFESME) 07104

Secretariat Rond-Point Schuman 6, 7th Floor – c/o Confartigianato Imprese, 1040 Brussels, Belgium. T. +3222307414. E-mail: secretariat@efesme.org – efesme@efesme.org.
URL: http://www.efesme.org/

History Apr 2005. Statutes changed into international non-profit association, 14 Nov 2008, Milan (Italy). Registration: Banque-Carrefour des Entreprises, No/ID: 0833.518.228, Start date: 7 Feb 2011, Belgium; EU Transparency Register, No/ID: 272211134200-17, Start date: 8 Mar 2019. **Aims** Represent and safeguard the interests of European small and medium-sized enterprises (SMEs) of the lift sector – such as installers, contractors, manufacturers and/or component producers – vis-à-vis the political, legislative, and normative institutions within the European Union. **Structure** General Assembly; Board of Directors. **Languages** English, French, German, Italian, Spanish. **Staff** 2.00 FTE, paid. **Activities** Advocacy/lobbying/activism; guidance/assistance/consulting. **Events** *Forum on Digitalisation in the Lift Sector* Brussels (Belgium) 2021, *Forum on Digitalisation in the Lift Sector* Brussels (Belgium) 2019, *SBS Lift Forum on Standardisation* Brussels (Belgium) 2018, *SBS Lift Forum on Standardisation* Brussels (Belgium) 2017. **Publications** *EFESME Newsletter*.
Members National Associations (15) belonging to all branches of the lift sector, in 14 countries:
Belgium, Bulgaria, Denmark, France, Germany, Greece, Hungary, Italy, Netherlands, Poland, Portugal, Romania, Slovakia, Spain.
NGO Relations Member of (3): *Small Business Standards (SBS, #19311)*; *SMEunited (#19327)*; *World Elevator Federation*. [2020/XJ4964/**D**]

♦ European Federation of Employed Shareholders for Employee Ownership and Participation / see European Federation of Employee Share Ownership (#07105)

♦ European Federation of Employee Share Ownership (EFES) 07105

Fédération européenne de l'actionnariat salarié (FEAS)

Main Office Ave Voltaire 135, 1030 Brussels, Belgium. T. +3222426430. Fax +3222426430. E-mail: efes@efesonline.org.
URL: http://www.efesonline.org/

History 7 May 1998, Brussels (Belgium). 7-8 May 1998, Brussels (Belgium), as *European Federation of Employed Shareholders for Employee Ownership and Participation – Fédération européenne des actionnaires salariés pour l'actionnariat salarié et la participation*, at 1st European meeting/constitutive General Assembly, on adoption of Charter. Registered in accordance with Belgian law. New name adopted, 2001. EU Transparency Register: 309808016043-82. **Aims** Act as the European umbrella organization of employee owners and all persons, companies, trade unions, experts, researchers, institutions and all those who are looking to promote employee ownership and participation in Europe. **Structure** General Assembly (annual); Board of Directors; Executive Bureau. Honorary Committee. **Activities** Program focuses on organizing European survey of employee ownership. **Events** *Conference* Brussels (Belgium) 2019, *Conference on ten years of public policies for employee ownership in Europe* Brussels (Belgium) 2010, *European conference on employee shareholders rights* Rome (Italy) 2010, *European meeting of employee ownership* Brussels (Belgium) 2009, *Colloquium on corporations and cities* Delft (Netherlands) 2008. **Publications** *EFES News*.
Members Statutory; Associate; Supporting; Honorary; Observing. Members in 28 countries:
Australia, Austria, Belgium, Canada, Chile, Croatia, Denmark, Egypt, Finland, France, Germany, Hungary, India, Ireland, Italy, Japan, Netherlands, North Macedonia, Norway, Poland, Portugal, Russia, Serbia, Slovenia, South Africa, Sweden, UK, USA.
NGO Relations Member of: *International Corporate Governance Network (ICGN, #12969)*. [2020/XD6584/**D**]

♦ European Federation of Employees in Public Services (EUROFEDOP) 07106

Fédération européenne du personnel des services publics – Federación Europea del Personal de los Servicios Públicos – Europäische Föderation der Öffentlich Bediensten – Europese Federatie van het Overheidspersoneel

SG Montoyerstraat 39, bus 20, 1000 Brussels, Belgium. T. +3222303865. E-mail: eurofedop@eurofedop.org – infedop@infedop.org.

European Federation Endocrine
07106

alphabetic sequence excludes
For the complete listing, see Yearbook Online at

URL: http://www.eurofedop.org/
History 1966, Vienna (Austria), as a regional organization of *International Federation of Employees in Public Services (INFEDOP, #13410)*. EU Transparency Register: 316613410489-78. **Aims** Defend and promote the economic and social interests of European *workers* in public services, taking into account their specific rights and duties. **Structure** Congress; Board; Executive Committee. Trade Councils (9). **Languages** Dutch, English, French, German, Spanish. **Staff** 45.00 FTE, paid. **Finance** Members' dues. **Activities** Advocacy/lobbying/activism; events/meetings; knowledge management/information dissemination. **Events** *Congress* Vienna (Austria) 2016, *Mobility and migration in the Public Service – better service for the public* Edinburgh (UK) 2014, *Responsibility has a future* Luxembourg (Luxembourg) 2013, *Responsibility has a future* Madrid (Spain) 2013, *What progress has social dialogue made in Eastern Europe and the Western Balkans* Vienna (Austria) 2013. **Publications** *EUROFEDOPINFO. Burnout in the Health Care Sector a European Perspective; High-Quality Public Services for the People of a Social Europe.* Reports of meetings, congresses.
Members Affiliated organizations (55) in 21 countries:
Albania, Austria, Belgium, Bulgaria, Czechia, Denmark, France, Germany, Hungary, Ireland, Italy, Kosovo, Lithuania, Luxembourg, Malta, Netherlands, North Macedonia, Portugal, Romania, Slovakia, Spain, Switzerland, UK.
Regional organization (1), listed in this Yearbook:
European Public Service Union (#08303).
Consultative Status Consultative status granted from: *Council of Europe (CE, #04881)* (Participatory Status). **NGO Relations** Full member of: *European Centre for Workers' Questions (#06505).* Member of: *Health First Europe (HFE, #10881).* [2020/XE9117/**E**]

♦ European Federation of Endocrine Societies (inactive)
♦ European Federation Energy – Chemistry – Miscellaneous Industries (inactive)

♦ European Federation of Energy Law Associations (EFELA) 07107

Contact 6 square de l'Opéra Louis Jouvet, 75009 Paris, France. E-mail: secretary@efela.eu.
URL: http://efela.eu/
History Registered in accordance with French law. EU Transparency Register: 111162132522-13. **Aims** Promote energy law and facilitate a better understanding of legal issues related to the energy sector; create a network of legal experts on energy law issues throughout Europe; provide institutions with a forum for discussion on topics related to EU and comparative energy law of high technicality. **Structure** General Assembly; Executive Committee; Scientific Committee. **Finance** Members' dues.
Members Full in 6 countries:
France, Greece, Italy, Portugal, Spain, UK.
Observing in 6 countries:
Germany, Ireland, Luxembourg, Norway, Serbia, Switzerland. [2019/XM8799/**D**]

♦ European Federation of Energy Management Associations (inactive)

♦ European Federation of Energy Traders (EFET) 07108

CEO Keizersgracht 62, 1015 CS Amsterdam, Netherlands. T. +31205207970. E-mail: secretariat@efet.org.
URL: http://www.efet.org/
History 22 Apr 1999, Amsterdam (Netherlands). Registration: Handelsregister, No/ID: KVK 34114458, Netherlands; EU Transparency Register, No/ID: 38589651649-14, Start date: 6 May 2009. **Aims** Improve conditions for energy trading in Europe; promote exchange of information in the field. **Structure** Board; Committees (3); Secretariat. **Languages** English. **Staff** 14.00 FTE, paid. **Finance** Sources: members' dues. **Activities** Advocacy/lobbying/activism; events/meetings; standards/guidelines. Active in all member countries. **Events** *Annual Congress* Paris (France) 2019, *Annual Congress* Vienna (Austria) 2018, *Annual Congress* Barcelona (Spain) 2017, *Annual Congress* Netherlands 2016, *Annual Cognress* Barcelona (Spain) 2015.
Members Companies in 28 countries:
Albania, Austria, Belgium, Bosnia-Herzegovina, Croatia, Czechia, Denmark, Finland, France, Germany, Greece, Hungary, Ireland, Italy, Liechtenstein, Netherlands, Norway, Poland, Portugal, Romania, Serbia, Slovakia, Slovenia, Spain, Sweden, Switzerland, UK, Ukraine.
IGO Relations *Agency for the Cooperation of Energy Regulators (ACER, #00552); European Commission (EC, #06633).* **NGO Relations** Member of (1): *European Association for the Streamlining of Energy Exchange-gas (EASEE-gas, #06224)* (Associate). Partner of (1): *RECS International (#18631).* Contacts with organizations active in European energy industry. [2022/XD7894/t/**D**]

♦ European Federation of Engineering Associations (inactive)

♦ European Federation of Engineering Consultancy Associations (EFCA) 07109

Dir-Gen Av des Arts 3/4/5, 1210 Brussels, Belgium. T. +3222090770. E-mail: efca@efca.be.
URL: http://www.efcanet.org/
History 22 May 1992, Amsterdam (Netherlands). Founded by merger of *European Committee of Consulting Firms (CEBI, inactive)* and *European Committee of the Consulting Engineers (inactive).* New statutes adopted 1996, amended Jan 2000. Statutes amended 2005; Dec 2010; May 2014; June 2017, June 2020, June 2021. Registration: Banque Carrefour des Entreprises, No/ID: 0449.175.326, Start date: 24 Nov 1992, Belgium; EU Transparency Register, No/ID: 45387205586-64, Start date: 31 Mar 2011. **Aims** Promote the engineering consulting industry in Europe and internationally; represent it to European institutions. **Structure** General Assembly; Board of Directors; Committees (8). **Languages** Dutch, English, French, German. **Staff** 3.50 FTE, paid. **Finance** Sources: members' dues. **Events** *General Assembly* Paris (France) 2022, *General Assembly and Conference* 2021, *General Assembly* 2020, *General Assembly and Conference* Dublin (Ireland) 2019, *General Assembly and Conference* Ghent (Belgium) 2018. **Publications** *EFCA Newsletter.* Guidelines; reports; surveys.
Members Effective: associations, societies or bodies, located in the EU or EFTA or in countries which are engaged in formal negotiations with regard to membership of the EU or EFTA. National associations in 28 countries:
Austria, Belgium, Bulgaria, Czechia, Denmark, Estonia, Finland, France, Germany, Greece, Hungary, Ireland, Italy, Latvia, Luxembourg, Netherlands, Norway, Poland, Portugal, Romania, Russia, Serbia, Slovenia, Spain, Sweden, Switzerland, Türkiye, Ukraine.
Russia temporarily suspended.
NGO Relations Member of (6): *Construction 2050 Alliance (#04760); European Business Services Alliance (EBSA, #06426); European Construction Forum (ECF, #06765); European Council for Construction Research, Development and Innovation (ECCREDI, #06813); European Services Forum (ESF, #08469); International Cost Management Standard Coalition (ICMS Coalition, #12978).* Cooperates with (1): *Comité européen de normalisation (CEN, #04162).* [2022.10.18/XD3327/**D**]

♦ European Federation of Environmental NGOs / see European Environmental Bureau (#06996)
♦ European Federation of Environmental Professionals (no recent information)

♦ European Federation of EPR Groups (EFEPR) 07110

Fédération européenne des groups RPE
Pres Campus Drie Eiken, Universiteitsplein 1, D N 216, 2610 Wilrijk, Belgium. T. +3232652461.
URL: http://efepr.uantwerpen.be/efepr/
History 1992. **Aims** Stimulate scientific development of electron paramagnetic resonance (EPR) *spectroscopy* in Europe. **Structure** General Assembly. President; 2 Vice-Presidents. **Events** *Triennial Conference* Turin (Italy) 2016, *Triennial Conference* Marseille (France) 2014, *Triennial Conference* Dublin (Ireland) 2012, *Triennial Conference* Frankfurt-Main (Germany) 2011, *Triennial Conference* Antwerp (Belgium) 2009.
Members National Groups (11) in 11 countries:
Bulgaria, France, Germany, Israel, Italy, Poland, Russia, Spain, UK.
Regional group:
NGO Relations *International EPR Society (IES, #13288).* [2016/XD8805/y/**D**]

♦ European Federation of Equipment Leasing Company Associations (LEASEUROPE) 07111

Fédération européenne des associations des établissements de crédit-bail – Europäische Vereinigung der Verbände von Leasing-Gesellschaften – Europese Federatie van Verenigingen van Leasing Ondernemingen
Dir-Gen Blvd Louis Schmidt 87, 1040 Brussels, Belgium. T. +3227780560. Fax +3227780578. E-mail: info@leaseurope.org.
Office Manager address not obtained.
URL: http://www.leaseurope.org/
History 3 May 1972, Brussels (Belgium). Registration: Banque-Carrefour des Entreprises, No/ID: 0413.032.334, Start date: 1 Mar 1973, Belgium; EU Transparency Register, No/ID: 430010622057-05, Start date: 8 Jun 2016. **Aims** Study at European level all questions of concern, directly or indirectly, to the business operations of leasing companies. **Structure** General Assembly (meeting at least annually); Board; Secretariat. Committees (3): Accounting and Taxation; Legal Affairs; Statistics and Marketing. Working Groups (2): PECOS; Basel II. European Auto-Forum. **Languages** English. **Staff** 4.00 FTE, paid. **Finance** Sources: members' dues. **Events** *Annual Convention* Cascais (Portugal) 2021, *Annual Conference* Lisbon (Portugal) 2015, *Annual Conference* Barcelona (Spain) 2014, *Annual Conference* Rome (Italy) 2013, *Annual Conference* Vienna (Austria) 2011. **Publications** Survey reports; meeting proceedings; statistics; studies on the impact of Basel II on the leasing industry; studies on international lease accounting debate, the impact of the revised directive on consumer credit and environmental liability issues.
Members National associations and correspondent members in 32 countries:
Austria, Belgium, Bulgaria, Croatia, Czechia, Denmark, Estonia, Finland, France, Georgia, Germany, Greece, Hungary, Ireland, Italy, Latvia, Lithuania, Luxembourg, Morocco, Netherlands, Norway, Poland, Portugal, Russia, Slovakia, Slovenia, Spain, Sweden, Switzerland, Türkiye, UK, Ukraine.
IGO Relations Recognized by: *European Commission (EC, #06633).* Links with EU Institutions. **NGO Relations** Member of (3): *European Banking Industry Committee (EBIC, #06314); European Tourism Manifesto (#08921); Federation of European and International Associations Established in Belgium (FAIB, #09508).* Special links with: *European Federation of Finance House Associations (EUROFINAS, #07121).* [2020/XD4565/**D**]

♦ European Federation of Essential Oils (EFEO) 07112

SG Sonninstr 28, 20097 Hamburg, Germany. T. +49402360160. E-mail: efeo@wga-hh.de.
URL: http://www.efeo-org.org/
History Apr 2002. Statutes approved 10 Jun 2002, Paris (France); amended: 16 Jun 2003, Barcelona (Spain); 15 Jun 2009, Grasse (France); 3 Jun 2013, Grasse (France); 3 Jun 2016, Grasse (France). **Aims** Represent, protect and promote the interest of production and trade of essential oils and related products within Europe; lobby for the defence of these products at relevant national, European and international institutions. **Structure** General Assembly; Board; Executive Committee. Standing Committees (2): Technical; Advocacy and Communication. **Languages** English. **Finance** Members' dues. **Activities** Advocacy/lobbying/activism. **Publications** *EFEO Newsletter.* **Members** Active; Associate. Membership countries not specified. [2017/XM5758/**D**]

♦ European Federation of Ethical and Alternative Banks and Financiers 07113

Fédération européenne de finances et banques éthiques et alternatives (FEBEA)
Main Office Square Ambiorix 32, PO box 47, 1000 Brussels, Belgium. E-mail: febea@febea.org.
URL: http://www.febea.org/
History 6 Jun 2001. Registration: Belgium. **Aims** Promote ethical, social and alternative banking and financing in Europe. **Structure** General Assembly; Board of Administration. Working Groups. **Languages** English, French. **Staff** Part-time. **Finance** Members' dues. Additional internal and external contributions. Budget (2011): about euro 110,000. **Events** *Conference* Barcelona (Spain) 2022, *Conference* Paris (France) 2016, *Annual General Assembly and Conference* Split (Croatia) 2016, *Annual General Assembly and Conference* Mons (Belgium) 2015, *Annual General Assembly and Conference* Freiburg (Germany) 2014. **Publications** *Atlas of Job Creation Good Practices for Social Inclusion* (2011). Annual Report.
Members Full (24) in 13 countries:
Belgium, Denmark, France, Germany, Italy, Malta, Norway, Poland, Slovakia, Spain, Sweden, Switzerland, UK.
IGO Relations Associated member of: Group III of *European Economic and Social Committee (EESC, #06963).* **NGO Relations** Member of: *European Inter-Network of Ethical and Responsible Initiatives (#07593).* [2021/XD8847/**D**]

♦ European Federation of European Coordination Networks of Scientific and Technical Cooperation 07114

Fédération européenne des réseaux de coopération scientifique et technique de coordination (FER)
Contact address not obtained. E-mail: europa.risk@coe.int.
History Also referred to as *European Federation of Scientific and Technical Networks of Cooperation.* **IGO Relations** *UNESCO (#20322).* **NGO Relations** Founding member of: *European Materials Forum (EMF, #07751).* [2008.06.01/XF2856/**F**]

♦ European Federation of Executives and Managerial Staff of the Insurance Sector / see Association Européenne des Cadres de l'Assurance (#02556)
♦ European Federation of Executives in the Sectors of Energy and Research (#09562)

♦ European Federation for Experimental Morphology (EFEM) 07115

SG Medicine Fac – Univ of Belgrade, Dr Subotica 8, Belgrade, PAK 11000, Serbia. T. +381113636368. Fax +381113636368. E-mail: teofilovski@med.bg.ac.rs – teofilovski@yahoo.com.
URL: http://www.efem.eu/
History Founded 1989. Current Statutes reviewed by EFEM Council, 11 Jul 2012, Edinburgh (UK); formally approved by next EFEM Council, 2 Mar 2013, Paris (France). Registered in accordance with Swiss Civil Code. **Aims** Advance science and education in the field of experimental morphology. **Structure** Council; Executive Board; Nominating Committee. **Languages** English, French, German. **Finance** Members' dues.
Members Constituent Societies; Associated Societies; Corporate Members. National and/or regional anatomical societies in 26 countries:
Austria, Belarus, Belgium, Bulgaria, Croatia, Czechia, Estonia, Finland, France, Germany, Greece, Hungary, Ireland, Italy, Netherlands, North Macedonia, Poland, Portugal, Russia, Serbia, Slovakia, Slovenia, Spain, Switzerland, UK, Ukraine.
NGO Relations Links with national societies in the field of anatomy. [2015.01.18/XD3744/**D**]

♦ European Federation for Exploratory Medicines Development (EUFEMED) 07116

Main Office Rue de l'Industrie 4, 1000 Brussels, Belgium. E-mail: info@eufemed.eu.
URL: https://www.eufemed.eu/
History 2015. Founded by national associations in Belgium, France, Germany – *Arbeitsgemeinschaft für Angewandte Humanpharmakologie (AGAH)* and UK. Registration: Banque-Carrefour des Entreprises, No/ID: 0629.959.669, Start date: 31 Mar 2015, Belgium. **Aims** Represent national and European federations, organizations or associations active in early clinical medicines development; promote the interest of early clinical medicines development in professional organizations, international organizations and public authorities; develop standards and promote guidance documents in early medicines development so as to improve European competitiveness. **Structure** Board. **Activities** Events/meetings; training/education. **Events** *Annual Conference* Brussels (Belgium) 2021, *Conference* Lyon (France) 2019. **Members** Full Associate. Membership countries not specified. **NGO Relations** Member of (1): *European Forum for Good Clinical Practice (EFGCP, #07313).* [2021.02.25/XM8760/**D**]

♦ European Federation of Explosives Engineers (EFEE) 07117

Fédération européenne des spécialistes du minage – Europäischer Sprengverband
SG Järngruvevägen 6, SE-618 92 Kolmården, Sweden. E-mail: info@efee.eu.
URL: http://efee.eu/
History 1988, Aachen (Germany). Registration: EU Transparency Register, No/ID: 156799113994-03. **Aims** Promote standardization and harmonization of explosives training in Europe; promote explosives technology in all fields related to this technology; issue European shotfirer's certificates regarding blasting work with explosives; promote safety, health, environment and security in the field of explosives technology; foster the image of the profession as well as good relations and cooperates with related associations; collaborate on development of laws and regulations within the EFEE field of activities. **Structure** General Assembly (annual); Council; Board. **Languages** English, French, German. **Staff** 1.00 FTE, voluntary. **Finance** Sources:

meeting proceeds; members' dues. Annual budget: 45,000 EUR (2022). **Activities** Certification/accreditation; events/meetings; politics/policy/regulatory; standards/guidelines. **Events** *World Conference on Explosives and Blasting Techniques* Dublin (Ireland) 2023, *World Conference on Explosives and Blasting Techniques* Maastricht (Netherlands) 2022, *World Conference on Explosives and Blasting Techniques* Helsinki (Finland) 2019, *World Conference on Explosives and Blasting Techniques* Stockholm (Sweden) 2017, *World Conference on Explosives and Blasting Techniques* Lyon (France) 2015. **Publications** *EFEE Newsletter* (4 a year).
Members National (25); Corporate (40); Individual (137). Members in 24 countries:
Austria, Belgium, Bulgaria, Czechia, Denmark, Estonia, Finland, France, Germany, Hungary, Ireland, Italy, Netherlands, Norway, Poland, Portugal, Romania, Slovakia, Spain, Sweden, Switzerland, Türkiye, UK, Ukraine.
NGO Relations Associate member of: *SAFEX International (#19030).* [2022.05.11/XM2754/**D**]

♦ European Federation for the Family (inactive)

♦ European Federation of Family Employment (EFFE) 07118

Fédération Européenne des Emplois de la Famille (FEEF) – Europäischer Verband der Dienstleistungen für Familien
Contact Square de Meeus 35, 1000 Brussels, Belgium.
URL: https://www.effe-homecare.eu/
History Founded 2012. EU Transparency Register: 716909919073-32. **Aims** Propose a social innovation model for the benefit of all fellow European citizens. **Structure** Bureau.
Members Organizations. Membership countries not specified. Included in the above, 1 organization listed in this Yearbook:
Included in the above, 1 organization listed in this Yearbook:
European Association of Service Providers for Persons with Disabilities (EASPD, #06204). [2019/XM8797/**D**]

♦ European Federation of Farriers Associations (EFFA) 07119

Sec Daltonstraat 3, 4904 KH Oosterhout, Netherlands. T. +31653747873.
URL: http://www.eurofarrier.org/
History Founded 14 Dec 1997, Paris (France), following preparatory meetings in Stoneleigh (UK) in 1995, and Utrecht (Netherlands) and Verona (Italy) in 1996. Original member countries: Belgium; Denmark; France; Ireland; Italy; Netherlands; Spain; Sweden; Switzerland; UK. **Aims** Improve the welfare of the horse by encouraging the highest standards of trimming and shoeing; provide a forum for the spread of knowledge and best practice amongst farriers throughout Europe. **Structure** Annual General Meeting; Executive Board; Accreditation Board; Official headquarters located at the headquarters of British Farriers and Blacksmiths Association at The Forge, Stoneleigh (UK). **Languages** English, French, German. **Staff** Voluntary. **Activities** Events/meetings; training/education; politics/policy/regulatory. **Events** *Annual General Meeting* Budapest (Hungary) 2014, *European Championships* UK 2014, *Educational Congress* Denmark 2013, *Annual General Meeting* Prague (Czech Rep) 2013, *Annual General Meeting / European Championships* Helsinki (Finland) 2012.
Members Full in 14 countries:
Austria, Czechia, Denmark, Finland, France, Germany, Hungary, Ireland, Netherlands, Norway, Spain, Sweden, Switzerland, UK.
Observers in 2 countries:
Iceland, Italy. [2014.06.19/XD8985/**D**]

♦ European Federation of Fibreboard Manufacturers (inactive)

♦ European Federation of Fibre-Cement Manufacturers (EFFCM) 07120

Fédération européenne des producteurs de fibres-ciment (FEPF)
Pres Kuiermanstraat 1, 1880 Kapelle-op-den-Bos, Belgium. T. +3215718270.
Registered Address Av de Tervueren 361, 1150 Brussels, Belgium. T. +3227781211. Fax +3227781212. E-mail: info@effcm.be.
History 1984. Registration: Crossroads Bank for Enterprises, No/ID: 0427.139.993, Start date: 1 Nov 1984, Belgium, Brussels; EU Transparency Register, No/ID: 267263048130-86, Start date: 16 Nov 2022. **Languages** English. **Staff** 0.7 FTE.
Members National organizations in 10 countries:
Austria, Belgium, Denmark, France, Germany, Ireland, Netherlands, Spain, Switzerland, UK.
IGO Relations Recognized by: *European Commission (EC, #06633).* **NGO Relations** In liaison with technical committees of: *International Organization for Standardization (ISO, #14473).* Member of: *Construction Products Europe AISBL (#04761).* [2022/XD6850/**D**]

♦ European Federation 'Pro Fide et Ecclesia' (inactive)

♦ European Federation of Finance House Associations (EUROFINAS) . 07121

Fédération européenne des associations des instituts de crédit – Europäische Vereinigung der Verbände von Finanzierungsbanken
Dir Gen Blvd Louis Schmidt 87, 1040 Brussels, Belgium. T. +3227780560. Fax +3227780578.
URL: http://www.eurofinas.org/
History 5 Nov 1959, Amsterdam (Netherlands). 5-6 Nov 1959, Amsterdam (Netherlands), when the Constitution was approved; reconstituted 22 Aug 1968, Brussels (Belgium). Registered in accordance with Belgian law. EU Transparency Register: 83211441580-56. **Aims** Study matters pertaining to legislation, official regulations, law, economics, finance and social welfare which are of concern to finance houses in each member country; consider problems relating to methods of conducting business, the internal structure of finance houses and other matters of concern to the profession; assemble statistical data and economic studies; study the above matters in cooperation with the competent European authorities and set up such non-profit-making organizations as may be deemed necessary for the achievement of these objectives. **Structure** General Assembly; Board of Directors; Technical Committees; Secretariat. **Languages** English. **Staff** 4.00 FTE, paid. **Finance** Members' dues. **Activities** Information dissemination. **Events** *Annual Conference* Cascais (Portugal) 2015, *Annual Conference* Hamburg (Germany) 2010, *Annual Conference* Prague (Czech Rep) 2009, *Annual Conference* Madrid (Spain) 2008, *Annual Conference* Edinburgh (UK) 2007. **Publications** *EUROFINAS Newsletter* (6 a year). Proceedings of Conferences; surveys and reports of Technical Committees.
Members National Associations in 17 countries:
Belgium, Czechia, Denmark, Finland, France, Germany, Italy, Lithuania, Morocco, Netherlands, Norway, Poland, Portugal, Spain, Sweden, Türkiye, UK.
IGO Relations Recognized by: *European Commission (EC, #06633).* **NGO Relations** Institutional member of: *Centre for European Policy Studies (CEPS, #03741).* Instrumental in setting up: *European Banking Industry Committee (EBIC, #06314).* Special links with: *European Federation of Equipment Leasing Company Associations (LEASEUROPE, #07111).* [2019/XD0731/**D**]

♦ European Federation of Financial Advisers and Financial Intermediaries 07122

Fédération européenne des conseils et intermédiaires financiers (FECIF) – Federación Europea de Asesores e Intermediarios Financieros – Federazione europea dei Consulenti e Intermediari Finanziari – Europäischer Dachverband der Unabhängigen Finanzberater und Finanzvermittler
SG Avenue Louise 143/4, 1050 Brussels, Belgium. T. +3225357622. E-mail: info@fecif.eu.
URL: https://www.fecif.eu/
History 30 Jun 1999. Registration: Banque-Carrefour des Entreprises, No/ID: 0473.662.579, Start date: 7 May 1999, Belgium; EU Transparency Register, No/ID: 22169245489-60, Start date: 14 Mar 2011. **Aims** Defend and promote the role of financial advisers and intermediaries in Europe. **Structure** General Assembly (annual); Board of Directors; FECIF European Pensions Institute (FEPI). **Languages** English, French. **Staff** 12.00 FTE, voluntary. **Finance** Sources: donations; members' dues; sponsorship. **Activities** Advocacy/lobbying/activism; events/meetings; knowledge management/information dissemination. **Events** *Conference* Brussels (Belgium) 2019, *Conference* Brussels (Belgium) 2018, *European Financial Conference* Brussels (Belgium) 2015, *General Assembly* Monte Carlo (Monaco) 2015, *General Assembly* Monte Carlo (Monaco) 2014. **Publications** *FECIF Newsletter* (12 a year).
Members Trade bodies or organizations (about 34) and individual corporate members in 15 countries:
Austria, Belgium, Cyprus, Czechia, France, Germany, Italy, Latvia, Luxembourg, Netherlands, Poland, Slovakia, Spain, Switzerland, UK.
European Financial Planning Association (EFPA, #07253); Federation of European Independent Financial Advisers (FEIFA).
NGO Relations Member of (2): *European Retail Financial Forum (ERFF); Federation of European and International Associations Established in Belgium (FAIB, #09508).* [2023.02.16/XD2133/**D**]

♦ European Federation of Financial Analysts Societies (EFFAS) 07123

Main Office Sophienstr 44, 60487 Frankfurt-Main, Germany. T. +496998959519. Fax +496998957529. E-mail: office@effas.com.
URL: http://effas.net/
History 25 May 1962, Paris (France). Registration: France; EU Transparency Register, No/ID: 222285223624-49. **Aims** Raise the standard of financial analysis; improve quality and quantity of information given to *investors*; unify methods of financial analysis in different countries. **Structure** General Assembly (annual); Board; Executive Management Committee; Secretariat; Permanent Commissions (5); Study Groups. **Languages** English. **Staff** 1.00 FTE, paid. **Finance** Members' dues. Grants. **Activities** Standards/guidelines; research/documentation; guidance/assistance/consulting; training/education; events/meeting. **Events** *Meeting* Paris (France) 2011, *Annual General Assembly* Stockholm (Sweden) 2003, *Meeting* Stockholm (Sweden) 2003, *Conference / Congress* Berlin (Germany) 2001, *Biennial Congress* Vienna (Austria) 2000. **Publications** Annual Report; congress proceedings; reports from standing groups.
Members National societies in 18 countries:
Austria, Belgium, Bosnia-Herzegovina, Bulgaria, Croatia, Finland, France, Germany, Greece, Hungary, Italy, Lithuania, Malta, Norway, Portugal, Romania, Spain, Sweden.
NGO Relations One Co-Chairman and 5 delegates to: *International Council of Investment Associations (ICIA, #13034).* Founding member of: *European Capital Markets Institute (ECMI, #06439).* Member of: *Association of Certified International Investment Analysts (ACIIA, #02422); European Financial Markets Federation (EFMF, #07252); European Financial Reporting Advisory Group (EFRAG, #07254).* [2020/XD0732/**D**]

♦ European Federation of Financial Executives Institutes (EFFEI) 07124

Fédération européenne des instituts de dirigeants financiers
Secretariat Avenue de Broqueville 116 Box 1, 1200 Brussels, Belgium. T. +3226761745. Fax +3227701724. E-mail: info@effei.eu.
URL: http://www.effei.eu/
History 1981, as *Committee of European Financial Executives Institutes (CEFEI).* Restructured under current title, 1991. Registered in accordance with Belgian law, 1992. **Aims** Promote European integration of Financial Executives – finance directors, CFOs, controllers – represent their interest beside the European institutions; promote information exchange between members. **Structure** General Assembly (annual); Board of Directors; Executive Committee; Advisory Board. **Languages** English. **Staff** 1.00 FTE, voluntary. **Finance** Members' dues. **Activities** Events/meetings; training/education; research/documentation. **Events** *Conference* Brussels (Belgium) 1991, *Conference* Dublin (Ireland) 1990.
Members Financial executives institutes. Founding in 9 countries:
Belgium, France, Germany, Ireland, Italy, Portugal, Spain, Switzerland, UK.
IGO Relations Recognized by: *European Commission (EC, #06633).* [2015.08.11/XE0631/**E**]

♦ European Federation of Financial Services Users / see BETTER FINANCE (#03219)
♦ European Federation of Fire Separating Element Producers (inactive)
♦ European Federation of Flat Glass Manufacturers / see Glass for Europe (#10157)
♦ European Federation for the Flexible Packaging Industry (inactive)
♦ European Federation of Foie Gras (#09569)

♦ European Federation of Food, Agriculture and Tourism Trade Unions (EFFAT) 07125

Fédération syndicale européenne pour les secteurs de l'agriculture, de l'alimentation et de l'hôtellerie – Europäische Gewerkschafts-Föderation für den Landwirtschafts-, Nahrungsmittel- und Tourismussektor
SG Av Louise 130A, Bte 3, 1050 Brussels, Belgium. T. +3222096263. Fax +3222183018. E-mail: effat@effat.org.
Office Manager address not obtained.
URL: http://www.effat.org/
History 1 Jan 2001. Founded on merger of *European Federation of Agricultural Workers' Unions (EFA, inactive)* and *European Federation of Food, Catering and Allied Workers' Unions within the IUF (ECF-IUF, inactive).* A regional organization within *International Union of Food, Agricultural, Hotel, Restaurant, Catering, Tobacco and Allied Workers Associations (IUF, #15772).* Former names and other names: *European Federation of Trade Unions in the Food, Agriculture and Tourism Sectors and allied branches* – former; *Fédération européenne des syndicats des secteurs de l'alimentation, de l'agriculture et du tourisme et des branches connexes* – former; *Europäische Föderation der Gewerkschaften des Lebens-, Genussmittel-, Landwirtschafts- und Tourismussektors und Verwandter Branchen* – former, Registration: No/ID: 0851.859.542, Start date: 1 Jan 2001, Belgium; EU Transparency Register, No/ID: 114904140054-91, Start date: 23 Oct 2020. **Aims** Support sustainable development of agrofood and tourism policy in which ethical, social and ecological aspects are considered; support member organizations to develop free and solid trade unions. **Structure** Congress (every 5 years); Executive Committee; Management Committee; Sectoral General Assemblies and Sectoral Boards; Secretariat; Committees (3). **Languages** English, French, German. **Staff** 12.00 FTE, paid. **Finance** Sources: members' dues. **Events** *EWC-TNC Conference* Brussels (Belgium) 2019, *General Assembly* Brussels (Belgium) 2019, *Congress* Zagreb (Croatia) 2019, *Congress* Vienna (Austria) 2014, *Conference on Ensuring Sustainable Employment and Competitiveness in the EU Food and Drink Industry* Brussels (Belgium) 2013. **Publications** *EFFAT Newsletter* (12 a year).
Members National trade unions (120) representing 22 million workers in 37 countries and territories:
Albania, Austria, Belgium, Bosnia-Herzegovina, Bulgaria, Croatia, Cyprus, Czechia, Denmark, Faeroe Is, Finland, France, Germany, Greece, Hungary, Iceland, Ireland, Italy, Kosovo, Latvia, Lithuania, Luxembourg, Malta, Montenegro, Netherlands, North Macedonia, Norway, Poland, Romania, Serbia, Slovakia, Slovenia, Spain, Sweden, Switzerland, Türkiye, UK.
NGO Relations Member of (2): *European Tourism Manifesto (#08921); European Trade Union Confederation (ETUC, #08927).* [2021.05.19/XF6035/t/**F**]

♦ European Federation of Food Banks / see European Food Banks Federation (#07280)
♦ European Federation of Food Retail (inactive)

♦ European Federation of Food Science and Technology (EFFoST) . . . 07126

Dir Agro Business Park 82, 6708 PW Wageningen, Netherlands. T. +31883663700. E-mail: info@effost.org.
URL: http://www.effost.org/
History 11 Mar 1984. Founded as a regional group within *International Union of Food Science and Technology (IUFoST, #15773).* **Aims** Provide a framework for cooperation among national, regional and global professional societies and their members; enhance Food Science and Technology competencies in Europe; improve public understanding of food science and technology. **Structure** General Assembly; Executive Committee. **Languages** English. **Staff** 2.50 FTE, paid; 7.50 FTE, voluntary. **Finance** Sources: meeting proceeds; members' dues; sponsorship. **Activities** Events/meetings; training/education. **Events** *EFFoST International Conference* Valencia (Spain) 2023, *EFFoST International Conference* Dublin (Ireland) 2022, *EFFoST International Conference* Lausanne (Switzerland) 2021, *EFFoST International Conference* 2020, *EFFoST International Conference* Rotterdam (Netherlands) 2019. **Publications** *Calendar of Food Science, Technology and Engineering Meetings in Europe and Major International Events* (4 a year). *EFFoST/IFIS/IUFoST Directory of Research and Education in Food Science, Technology and Engineering, Taste of Science.*
Members European IUFoST members in 34 countries:
Armenia, Austria, Belgium, Bulgaria, Croatia, Cyprus, Czechia, Denmark, Estonia, Finland, France, Germany, Greece, Hungary, Ireland, Italy, Lithuania, Montenegro, Netherlands, North Macedonia, Norway, Poland, Portugal, Romania, Russia, Serbia, Slovakia, Slovenia, Spain, Sweden, Switzerland, Türkiye, UK, Ukraine.
NGO Relations Cooperates with (1): *International Union of Food Science and Technology (IUFoST, #15773).* [2022.05.10/XE0424/**E**]

♦ European Federation of Fortified Sites (EFFORTS) 07127

Fédération européenne des sites fortifiés
Contact Rue de Trèves 67, 1000 Brussels, Belgium. E-mail: info@efforts-europe.eu.
URL: https://www.efforts-europe.eu/

European Federation Forum
07128

alphabetic sequence excludes
For the complete listing, see Yearbook Online at

History 2018, Venice (Italy). Registration: No/ID: 0695.436.451, Start date: 10 Nov 2017, Belgium. **Aims** Share expertise, promote cooperation and emphasize the significance of fortified heritage as a continuing connection to a common European history and as a condition for social, economic and spatial development. **Structure** Annual General Meeting; Board. **Finance** Sources: members' dues. **Activities** Events/meetings. **Events** *Congress* Antwerp (Belgium) 2019. **Publications** *EFFORTS Newsletter*. **NGO Relations** Member of (1): *European Heritage Alliance 3.3 (#07477)*. Partner of (2): *Architects Council of Europe (ACE, #01086)*; *Europa Nostra (#05767)*. [2020/AA0956/**D**]

♦ European Federation and Forum for Osteopathy (EFFO) 07128

Fédération et Forum Européens pour l'Ostéopathie

Gen Sec c/o MAI, Rue Washington 40, 1050 Brussels, Belgium. E-mail: hannaeffo@gmail.com.
Pres address not obtained.
URL: http://www.effo.eu/

History Founded Mar 2018, on merger of *European Federation of Osteopaths (inactive)* and *Forum for Osteopathic Regulation in Europe (FORE, inactive)*. Registration: Belgium. **Aims** Promote standards, regulation and recognition for osteopaths in Europe. **Languages** English. **Activities** Events/meetings. **Events** *Autumn Meeting* Madrid (Spain) 2019.
Members Effectif in 24 countries:
Austria, Belgium, Canada, Cyprus, Denmark, Estonia, Finland, France, Germany, Greece, Ireland, Israel, Italy, Luxembourg, Malta, Netherlands, Norway, Poland, Portugal, Slovenia, Spain, Sweden, Switzerland, UK.
NGO Relations Partner member of: *Osteopathic International Alliance (OIA, #17910)*. Affiliate of: *EUROCAM (#05653)*. [2020/XM7482/**D**]

♦ European Federation of Foundation Contractors (EFFC) 07129

Main Office 5 Jubilee Way, Forum Court Assoc – Office 205, Saphir House, Faversham, ME13 8GD, UK. E-mail: effc@effc.org.
URL: http://www.effc.org/

History 1989. **Aims** Promote members' common interests so as to improve standards of workmanship and maintain high standards of technical competence, safety and innovation; speed the development of technical execution codes in the European ground *engineering* sector. **Languages** English. **Finance** Subscriptions. **Events** *International Conference on Deep Foundations and Ground Improvement* Berlin (Germany) 2022, *International Conference on Piling and Deep Foundations* Stockholm (Sweden) 2014, *Annual General Assembly* Madrid (Spain) 2012, *Annual meeting* The Hague (Netherlands) 2007, *International conference on piling and foundations* Amsterdam (Netherlands) 2006. **Publications** *European Foundations* (4 a year).
Members Full in 16 countries:
Austria, Belgium, Czechia, Denmark, France, Germany, Hungary, Italy, Netherlands, Poland, Portugal, Romania, Spain, Sweden, Switzerland, UK. [2022/XD6064/**D**]

♦ European Federation for Freedom of Belief (internationally oriented national body)
♦ European Federation of Freelance Writers (no recent information)
♦ European Federation of Free Radios (inactive)

♦ European Federation for Freshwater Sciences (EFFS) 07130

Chairman address not obtained.
URL: http://www.freshwatersciences.eu/

History 2005, Krakow (Poland). Founded at 4th Symposium for European Freshwater Sciences. **Aims** Promote freshwater sciences throughout Europe. **Activities** Knowledge management/information dissemination; research/documentation; events/meetings; awards/prizes/competitions. **Events** *Symposium for European Freshwater Sciences (SEFS)* Newcastle upon Tyne (UK) 2023, *Symposium for European Freshwater Sciences (SEFS)* 2021, *Symposium for European Freshwater Sciences (SEFS)* Zagreb (Croatia) 2019, *Symposium for European Freshwater Sciences* Olomouc (Czechia) 2017, *Symposium for European Freshwater Sciences* Geneva (Switzerland) 2015.
Members Organizations in 15 countries:
Austria, Croatia, Czechia, Finland, France, Germany, Hungary, Italy, Poland, Romania, Slovakia, Spain, Switzerland, Türkiye, UK. [2022/XM7486/**D**]

♦ European Federation of Funeral Services (EFFS) 07131

Europäische Vereinigung für Bestattungsdienste

Exec Dir c/o Bundesverband Deutscher Bestatter eV, Cecilienallee 5, 40474 Düsseldorf, Germany. T. +492111600849.
URL: http://www.effs.eu/

History 16 Dec 1994. Replaces: *Association européenne de thanatologie (AET, inactive)*, set up 26 Mar 1966, Brussels (Belgium) and *Europäische Bestatter-Union (EBU, inactive)*, formed 16 Sep 1964. Registration: Austria. **Aims** Improve professionalism of the funeral services sector across Europe; engage in common research and joint study of legal, scientific and technical issues related to funeral services. **Structure** General Assembly (annual); Board; Arbitrators; Working Committees; Task Forces. **Languages** English. **Finance** Sources: members' dues. **Activities** Events/meetings; knowledge management/information dissemination; publishing activities. **Events** *General Assembly* Paris (France) 2019, *General Assembly* Saragossa (Spain) 2018, *General Assembly* Bologna (Italy) 2015, *General Assembly* Vienna (Austria) 2014, *General Assembly* Barcelona (Spain) 2013.
Members Associations of funeral directors, related organizations, corporate bodies and firms in 32 countries:
Australia, Austria, Belgium, Bosnia-Herzegovina, Croatia, Cyprus, Czechia, Denmark, Finland, France, Germany, Greece, Hungary, Iceland, Italy, Netherlands, Norway, Poland, Portugal, Romania, Russia, Serbia, Slovakia, Slovenia, Spain, Sweden, Switzerland, Tanzania UR, Türkiye, UK, Ukraine, USA.
NGO Relations *Comité européen de normalisation (CEN, #04162)*; *International Cremation Federation (ICF, #13104)*; *International Federation of Thanatologists Associations (IFTA, #13569)*. [2020.06.22/XD4608/**D**]

♦ European Federation of Furniture Retailers 07132

Fédération européenne du négoce de l'ameublement (FENA) – Europäischer Verband des Möbelhandels

Contact Hof-ter-Vleestdreef 5, 1070 Anderlecht, Belgium. T. +436645158275. E-mail: president@fena-furniture.com.
URL: http://www.fena-furniture.com/

History 30 Oct 1959, Paris (France). Founded when Statutes approved. Statutes modified: 1966; 1970; 1971; 2001. Registration: Banque-Carrefour des Entreprises, No/ID: 0475.028.301, Start date: 21 Jun 2001, Belgium; EU Transparency Register, No/ID: 821949742608-72, Start date: 4 May 2021. **Aims** Promote and preserve enduring contacts between the affiliated federations; determine and represent the general interests of the European furniture retail trade. **Structure** General Assembly; Board of Directors. **Languages** English, French, German. **Events** *Annual general meeting / Biennial General Meeting* Amsterdam (Netherlands) 1996. **Publications** Newsletter in English, German.
Members National associations of furniture retailers in 8 countries:
Austria, Belgium, France, Germany, Italy, Luxembourg, Netherlands, Switzerland.
NGO Relations In liaison with technical committees of: *International Organization for Standardization (ISO, #14473)*. [2021/XD3912/**D**]

♦ European Federation of Geologists (EFG) 07133

Fédération européenne des géologues (FEG) – Federación Europea de Geólogos (FEG)

Exec Dir c/o Service Géologique de Belgique, Rue Jenner 13, 1000 Brussels, Belgium. T. +3227887636. Fax +3226477359.
URL: http://www.eurogeologists.eu/

History Founded 1981, Paris (France). Registered in accordance with French law. EU Transparency Register: 97706556032-41. **Aims** Safeguard and promote present and future interests of the geological profession in Europe; promote best practice policies with regard to responsible use of the Earth's natural resources. **Structure** Council; Board; Office, headed by Executive Director. **Languages** English, French, Spanish. **Staff** 3.50 FTE, paid. **Finance** Subscription fees; European projects. **Activities** Standards/guidelines; awards/prizes/competitions; advocacy/lobbying/activism; events/meetings. **Events** *International Professional Geology Conference* Vancouver, BC (Canada) 2012, *International Professional Geology Conference* Vancouver, BC (Canada) 2012, *Workshop on geology at different education levels in Europe* Budapest (Hungary) 2011, *International Professional Geology Conference* Flagstaff, AZ (USA) 2008, *International professional geology conference* UK 2004. **Publications** *GeoNews* (12 a year) – newsletter; *European Geologist Magazine* (2 a year). Best practice codes and guidelines.
Members National associations in 26 countries:
Belgium, Bulgaria, Croatia, Cyprus, Czechia, Denmark, Finland, France, Germany, Greece, Hungary, Ireland, Italy, Luxembourg, Netherlands, Poland, Portugal, Russia, Serbia, Slovenia, Spain, Sweden, Switzerland, Türkiye, UK, Ukraine.
Associate in 2 countries:
Canada, USA.
NGO Relations Member of: *European Alliance of Subject-Specific and Professional Accreditation and Quality Assurance (EASPA, #05887)*. Cooperates with: *International Association for Promoting Geoethics (IAPG, #12107)*. [2022/XD6443/**D**]

♦ European Federation of Glass Recyclers 07134

Fédération Européenne des Recycleurs de Verre (FERVER)

SG Blvd Auguste Reyerslaan 80, 1030 Brussels, Belgium. T. +3227579170. E-mail: info@ferver.eu.
URL: http://www.ferver.eu/

History 3 Dec 2004. Registration: EU Transparency Register, No/ID: 912022335504-28; Belgium. **Aims** Unite the European glass recycling industry and represent its interests at the national and European levels. **Structure** General Assembly; Board of Directors. Steering Committee. **Events** *General Assembly* Naples (Italy) 2020, *Plenary Meeting* Brussels (Belgium) 2019, *General Assembly* Vienna (Austria) 2015.
Members Full in 20 countries:
Belgium, Denmark, Finland, France, Germany, Hungary, Ireland, Italy, Netherlands, North Macedonia, Norway, Poland, Portugal, Romania, Russia, Spain, Sweden, Türkiye, UK, Ukraine.
NGO Relations *European Recycling Industries' Confederation (EuRIC, #08335)*; *Fédération européenne du verre d'emballage (FEVE, #09583)*. [2021/XM8511/**D**]

♦ European Federation of Green Parties / see European Green Party (#07409)

♦ European Federation of Green Roof and Wall Associations (EFB) ... 07135

Main Office Favoritenstr 50, 1040 Vienna, Austria. E-mail: office@efb-greenroof.eu.
URL: http://www.efb-greenroof.eu/

History 1997. **Aims** Promote and encourage the uptake of green roofs and green walls to help address issues related to *climate change*, *ecosystem* services, green infrastructure and lack of green space in the built environment. **Structure** General Assembly (annual); Board; Office based in Vienna (Austria). **Languages** English, French, German. **Finance** Members' dues. In-kind and voluntary work. **Activities** Publishing activities; events/meetings; networking/liaising; advocacy/lobbying/activism; standards/guidelines; projects/programmes. **Events** *European Urban Green Infrastructure Conference (EUGIC)* Rotterdam (Netherlands) 2021, *European Urban Green Infrastructure Conference (EUGIC)* Rotterdam (Netherlands) 2020, *European Urban Green Infrastructure Conference* London (UK) 2019, *European Urban Green Infrastructure Conference* Budapest (Hungary) 2017, *European Urban Green Infrastructure Conference* Vienna (Austria) 2015. **Publications** *European Green Roof and Wall Market Report* (2015).
Members Full in 14 countries:
Austria, Belgium, Czechia, France, Germany, Hungary, Italy, Netherlands, Norway, Poland, Portugal, Sweden, Switzerland, UK.
Regional member (1):
Scandinavian Green Infrastructure Association (SGIA, #19088).
NGO Relations *European Landscape Contractors Association (ELCA, #07642)*; *International Federation of Landscape Architects (IFLA, #13467)*; *Local Governments for Sustainability (ICLEI, #16507)*; national associations. [2021/XM4311/**D**]

♦ European Federation of Hairdressers (inactive)
♦ European Federation of Handling Industries / see European Materials Handling Federation (#07752)

♦ European Federation of Hard of Hearing People (EFHOH) 07136

Gen Sec c/o NVVS, Randhoeve 221, 3995 GA Houten, Netherlands. E-mail: secretary@efhoh.org – office@efhoh.org.
Pres address not obtained.
URL: https://www.efhoh.org/

History 1992. Founded as the European organization of *International Federation of Hard of Hearing People (IFHOH, #13435)*. Former names and other names: *European Region – International Federation of Hard of Hearing People (IFHOH-Europe)* – former (1992 to 2002). Registration: Handelsregister, No/ID: 40482609, Start date: 1993, Netherlands; Charity, No/ID: 815 515 819, Netherlands; EU Transparency Register, No/ID: 2093041 18333-41. **Aims** Realize a Europe where hard of hearing people can live without barriers, and have the opportunity to participate on all levels in society. **Structure** Board. **Languages** English. **Staff** Voluntary. **Finance** Sources: members' dues. **Activities** Awareness raising; events/meetings; research and development. **Events** *Annual General Meeting* Budapest (Hungary) 2022, *Annual General Meeting* Houten (Netherlands) 2021, *European Conference of Speech to Text Reporters (ECOS)* Trondheim (Norway) 2020, *Annual General Meeting* Zagreb (Croatia) 2019, *European Conference of Speech to Text Reporters* Stockholm (Sweden) 2018. **Publications** *EFHOH Newsletter*.
Members National; Associate. National in 22 countries and territories:
Austria, Belgium, Croatia, Czechia, Denmark, Estonia, Faeroe Is, Finland, France, Germany, Hungary, Ireland, Netherlands, Norway, Poland, Portalegre, Slovakia, Slovenia, Sweden, Switzerland, Türkiye, UK.
Associate (3) in 3 countries:
Germany, Italy, Switzerland.
NGO Relations Member of (2): *European Disability Forum (EDF, #06929)*; *Federation of European and International Associations Established in Belgium (FAIB, #09508)*. [2022.10.19/XE1676/**E**]

♦ European Federation of Healthcare Clown Organizations (EFHCO) .. 07137

Secretariat Dreve du Pressoir 38, 1190 Brussels, Belgium. T. +32489247005. E-mail: info@efhco.eu.
URL: http://www.efhco.eu/

History 3 Mar 2011. Registration: EU transparency Register, No/ID: 897362334010-17, Start date: 19 Feb 2019. **Aims** Protect and support professional clown work in a healthcare environment on a European level. **Structure** General Assembly; Board of Directors. Working Groups (4): Artistic; Management; Research and Development, Fundraising. **Languages** English. Francais. **Staff** 0.50 FTE, paid. **Activities** Active in all member countries. **Members** Ordinary; Associate; Honorary. Membership countries not specified. [2022.11.02/XM8876/**D**]

♦ European Federation of Hereditary Ataxias (Euro-ATAXIA) 07138

Fédération européenne des ataxies héréditaires – Europese Federatie van Erfelijke Ataxieën

SG c/o Ataxia UK, 12 Broadbent Close, London, N6 5JW, UK. T. +442075821444.
Registered Address Av du Général Médicin Derache 36, 1050 Brussels, Belgium.
URL: https://www.euroataxia.org/

History 1 Oct 1989, Antwerp (Belgium). Registration: No/ID: 0446.777.050, Start date: 25 Feb 1992, Belgium; Charity, No/ID: 1149330, Start date: 16 Oct 2012, England and Wales. **Aims** Allow members to actively support each other and share information on the best way to help people with ataxia, and move forward towards finding a cure. **Structure** General Meeting (annual). Managing Council, comprising representatives of each national group. Board of Directors. **Languages** English. **Staff** Voluntary. **Finance** Members' dues. **Events** *Annual General Meeting* Nottwil (Switzerland) 2016, *Annual General Meeting* Windsor (UK) 2015, *Annual General Meeting* London (UK) 2012, *Annual General Meeting* Strasbourg (France) 2011, *Annual General Meeting* Dublin (Ireland) 2008. **Publications** *Euro-Ataxia Newsletter* (2 a year). Information leaflets.
Members Associations in 14 countries:
Belgium, Denmark, Finland, France, Germany, Ireland, Israel, Italy, Netherlands, Norway, Spain, Sweden, Switzerland, UK.
NGO Relations Member of: *European Disability Forum (EDF, #06929)*; *European Federation of Neurological Associations (EFNA, #07177)*; *EGAN – Patients Network for Medical Research and Health (EGAN, #05394)*; *EURORDIS – Rare Diseases Europe (#09175)*. [2020/XD3293/**D**]

♦ European Federation of High Tech SMEs (no recent information)
♦ European Federation Historic Aviation (internationally oriented national body)

♦ European Federation of Homeopathic Patients' Associations (EFHPA) 07139

Co-Pres c/o Homeopathy UK, Hamilton House, 13-18 Mabledon Place, London, WC1H 9BB, UK.

Registered Address p/a Vereniging Homeopathie Nederland, Teleportboulevard 110, 1043 EJ Amsterdam, Netherlands.
URL: http://www.efhpa.eu/

History Oct 2003, Marseille (France). Developed from Patient/Users Sub-Committee of *European Committee for Homeopathy (ECH, #06651)* to which it is still affiliated. Registration: Handelsregister, No/ID: KVK 81648642, Netherlands. **Aims** Defend patients' fundamental rights to patient-centred healthcare that respects their needs, preferences and values. **Structure** Board. **Languages** Dutch, English, French, German, Spanish. **Staff** 6.00 FTE, voluntary. **Finance** Sources: members' dues. **Activities** Advocacy/lobbying/activism; awareness raising; events/meetings; politics/policy/regulatory. **Events** *General Assembly* Barcelona (Spain) 2019, *General Assembly* Stuttgart (Germany) 2018, *General Assembly* Edinburgh (UK) 2017.

Members Organizations (20) in 14 countries:
Austria, Belgium, Bulgaria, France, Germany, Greece, Hungary, Iceland, Italy, Netherlands, Norway, Spain, Switzerland, UK.

NGO Relations Member of (6): *EUROCAM (#05653)*; *European Coalition on Homeopathic and Anthroposophic Medicinal Products (ECHAMP, #06595)*; *European Committee for Homeopathy (ECH, #06651)*; *European Patients' Forum (EPF, #08172)*; *European Public Health Alliance (EPHA, #08297)*; *World Patients Alliance (WPA)*. [2022/XM2536/D]

♦ European Federation of Honey Packers and Distributors 07140

Fédération européenne des emballeurs et distributeurs de miel (FEEDM)

SG c/o Waren-Verein der Hamburger Börse, Grosse Bäckerstrasse 4, 20095 Hamburg, Germany. T. +494037471913. Fax +494037471919. E-mail: feedm@waren-verein.de.
URL: http://www.feedm.com/

History Founded 1989, taking over activities of *Committee of the Associations of Honey Imports and Packers of Europe (CAHIPE, inactive)*. **Aims** Coordinate the interests of the European honey business; obtain relevant information with regard to honey.

Members Full in 15 countries:
Belgium, Denmark, Finland, France, Germany, Greece, Hungary, Italy, Netherlands, Poland, Portugal, Romania, Slovenia, Spain, UK.
Associated members in one country:
Switzerland.

IGO Relations Observer status with: *Codex Alimentarius Commission (CAC, #04081)*. **NGO Relations** Member of: *FoodDrinkEurope (#09841)*; *International Federation of Beekeepers' Associations (APIMONDIA, #13370)*. [2015.09.02/XD3552/D]

♦ European Federation of IASP Chapters / see European Pain Federation (#08131)
♦ European Federation of Illuminated Signs / see European Sign Federation (#08485)

♦ European Federation for Immunogenetics (EFI) 07141

Central Office EFI, Poortgebouw, Noordzijde, Room N00-002, Rijnsburgerweg 10, 2333 ZA Leiden, Netherlands.
Secretary Univ Hosp Dept of Clinical Immunology, The Rudbeck Laboratory, Dag Hammarskjölds v 20, SE-751 85 Uppsala, Sweden.
URL: http://www.efi-web.org/

History Mar 1985. Former names and other names: *European Foundation for Immunogenetics* – former (1985 to 1996). Registration: France. **Aims** Advance development of immunogenetics in Europe as a discipline of medicine and support research and training; provide a forum for exchange of scientific information and reinforce the skills and knowledge of young scientists and others working in the field. **Languages** English. **Activities** Awards/prizes/competitions; events/meetings; training/education. **Events** *European Immunogenetics and Histocompatibility Conference* Madrid (Spain) 2024, *European Immunogenetics and Histocompatibility Conference* Nantes (France) 2023, *European Immunogenetics and Histocompatibility Conference* Amsterdam (Netherlands) 2022, *European Immunogenetics and Histocompatibility Conference* Glasgow (UK) 2021, *European Immunogenetics and Histocompatibility Conference* Glasgow (UK) 2020. **Publications** *EFI Newsletter*, *HLA Journal*.

Members Individuals in 59 countries and territories:
Albania, Algeria, Armenia, Australia, Austria, Belgium, Brazil, Bulgaria, Canada, Croatia, Cuba, Cyprus, Czechia, Denmark, Estonia, Finland, France, Germany, Greece, Guadeloupe, Hong Kong, Hungary, Iceland, India, Iran Islamic Rep, Ireland, Israel, Italy, Japan, Lebanon, Lithuania, Luxembourg, Malaysia, Martinique, Mexico, Montenegro, Morocco, Netherlands, New Zealand, North Macedonia, Norway, Oman, Poland, Portugal, Romania, Russia, Saudi Arabia, Serbia, Slovenia, South Africa, Spain, Sweden, Switzerland, Syrian AR, Türkiye, UK, Ukraine, United Arab Emirates, USA.

NGO Relations Member of: *Alliance for Harmonisation of Cellular Therapy Accreditation (AHCTA, #00686)*; *Worldwide Network for Blood and Marrow Transplantation (WBMT, #21929)*. [2020.09.08/XF2547/v/F]

♦ European Federation of Immunological Societies (EFIS) 07142

Fédération européenne des sociétés d'immunologie

Coordinator Via N Fabrizi 14, 16148 Genoa GE, Italy. E-mail: office@efis.org.
Contact c/o DRFZ, Charitéplatz 1, 10117 Berlin, Germany.
URL: http://www.efis.org/

History 16 Sep 1975, Amsterdam (Netherlands). Founded as a regional federation of *International Union of Immunological Societies (IUIS, #15781)*. Constitution modified at a special General Assembly, 26 Sep 1981, Lucerne (Switzerland). Registration: Chamber of Commerce, Start date: 5 Apr 1995, Netherlands. **Aims** Support immunological research and education; strengthen scientific interaction among members. **Structure** General Assembly (triennial); Board. **Languages** English. **Staff** 1.50 FTE, voluntary. **Finance** Sources: sale of publications. **Activities** Awards/prizes/competitions; events/meetings; financial and/or material support. **Events** *European Congress of Immunology* Dublin (Ireland) 2024, *European Congress of Immunology* 2021, *European Congress of Immunology* Amsterdam (Netherlands) 2018, *European Congress of Immunology* Vienna (Austria) 2015, *European Congress of Immunology* Glasgow (UK) 2012. **Publications** *EFIS Newsletter*, *European Journal of Immunology*, *Immunology Letters* – journal.

Members Immunological societies (31), representing 38 countries:
Armenia, Austria, Belgium, Bosnia-Herzegovina, Bulgaria, Croatia, Czechia, Denmark, Estonia, Finland, France, Georgia, Germany, Greece, Hungary, Iceland, Ireland, Israel, Italy, Kosovo, Latvia, Lithuania, Montenegro, Netherlands, Norway, Poland, Portugal, Romania, Russia, Serbia, Slovakia, Slovenia, Spain, Sweden, Switzerland, Türkiye, UK, Ukraine.
Included in the above, 1 regional organizations:
Scandinavian Society for Immunology (SSI, #19110).

NGO Relations Member of (1): *Biomedical Alliance in Europe (#03251)*. [2022.05.10/XD8098/D]

♦ European Federation of Importers of Business Equipment (inactive)
♦ European Federation of Importers of Dried Fruits, Preserves, Spices and Honey / see European Federation of the Trade in Dried Fruit, Edible Nuts, Processed Fruit and Vegetables, Processed Fishery Products, Spices, Honey and Similar Foodstuffs (#07229)
♦ European Federation of Independent Air Transport (inactive)
♦ European Federation of Independent Electrical Wholesalers / see FEGIME (#09721)
♦ European Federation of Industrial Producers of Energy for Own Consumption (inactive)
♦ European Federation of Industrial Property Representatives of Industry / see European Federation of Agents of Industry in Industrial Property (#07042)
♦ European Federation of the Industries of Earthenware and China Tableware and Ornamental Ware (#09574)

♦ European Federation for Information Technology in Agriculture (EFITA) 07143

Pres address not obtained.
URL: http://www.efita.net/

History 17 Jun 1996, Wageningen (Netherlands). Founded at first General Assembly, when statutes were adopted. Former names and other names: *European Federation for Information Technology in Agriculture, Food and the Environment* – alias. **Aims** Facilitate exchange of information and experience and develop knowledge in the area of information and *communications* technology (ICT) developments and their application in agriculture. **Structure** General Assembly (every 2 years); Executive; General Secretariat. **Languages** English. **Staff** 0.50 FTE, voluntary. **Finance** Members' dues. Proceeds from associated activities and publications. **Activities** Events/meetings; knowledge management/information dissemination; research and development. **Events** *Conference* 2021, *World Congress on Computers in Agriculture* Rhodes Is (Greece) 2019, *World Congress on Computers in Agriculture* Montpellier (France) 2017, *Conference* Poznań (Poland) 2015, *Sustainable agriculture through ICT innovation* Turin (Italy) 2013. **Publications** *EFITA Newsletter*.

Members Full – national organizations; associate – individuals, institutions or companies in countries having no full member. Members in 16 countries:
Czechia, Denmark, Finland, France, Germany, Greece, Hungary, Ireland, Italy, Netherlands, Poland, Portugal, Spain, Sweden, Türkiye, UK.

NGO Relations Member of: *International Network for Information Technology in Agriculture (INFITA, #14287)*. [2021/XD5975/D]

♦ European Federation for Information Technology in Agriculture, Food and the Environment / see European Federation for Information Technology in Agriculture (#07143)

♦ European Federation of Inland Ports (EFIP) 07144

Fédération européenne des ports intérieurs (FEPI) – Europäischer Verband der Binnenhäfen (EVB)

Dir Treurenberg 6, 1000 Brussels, Belgium. T. +3222198207. Fax +3227366325. E-mail: director@inlandports.be – info@inlandports.be.
URL: http://www.inlandports.eu/

History 20 Apr 1994, Brussels (Belgium). Previously also referred to in Dutch as *Europese Vereniging van Binnenhavens*. Registered in accordance with Belgian law. EU Transparency Register: 41826153178-91. **Aims** Highlight and promote the role of European inland ports as real intermodal nodal points in the transport and logistic chain, combining inland waterway transport with rail, road and maritime *transport*. **Structure** General Assembly; Executive Committee; Presidency. **Languages** English, French, German. **Staff** 2.00 FTE, paid. **Finance** Members' dues. **Activities** Events/meeting; monitoring/evaluation. **Events** *Annual General Assembly* Galati (Romania) 2020, *Annual General Assembly* Aalborg (Denmark) 2019, *Annual General Assembly* Seville (Spain) 2018, *Annual General Assembly* Paris (France) 2017, *Annual General Assembly* La Louvière (Belgium) 2016. **Publications** Annual Report; strategy papers; brochures.

Members Inland ports and port authorities (about 200) in 18 countries:
Austria, Belgium, Bulgaria, Croatia, Czechia, Denmark, France, Germany, Italy, Luxembourg, Netherlands, Poland, Portugal, Romania, Slovakia, Spain, Sweden, Switzerland.
Observers in 3 countries:
Hungary, Serbia, Ukraine. [2020.01.09/XD4057/D]

♦ European Federation for Inland Water Transport / see Inland Navigation Europe (#11216)
♦ European Federation of Innovation Development Consultants (no recent information)

♦ European Federation of Intelligent Energy Efficiency Services (EFIEES) 07145

Fédération européenne des services en efficacité et intelligence énergétique

Main Office Rue Philippe le Bon 15, 1000 Brussels, Belgium. T. +3222306550. Fax +3222306550. E-mail: info@efiees.eu.
URL: http://www.efiees.eu/

History Registration: EU Transparency Register, No/ID: 25748484862-49. **Aims** Promote the activities of energy efficiency service companies in the European Union. **Events** *European Forum on Energy Efficiency / Forum* Bratislava (Slovakia) 2011, *European Forum on Energy Efficiency / Forum* Warsaw (Poland) 2009, *European Forum on Energy Efficiency / Forum* Madrid (Spain) 2008, *European Forum on Energy Efficiency / Forum* Vilnius (Lithuania) 2007. **NGO Relations** Member of: *Coalition for Energy Savings (#04056)*; *Energy Efficiency Industrial Forum (EEIF, #05470)*; *European PPP Operating Companies in Infrastructure and Services (E3PO, #08266)*. Liaison Organization of: *Comité européen de normalisation (CEN, #04162)*. [2021/XM1934/D]

♦ European Federation of Interconnection and Packaging (inactive)

♦ European Federation for Intercultural Learning (EFIL) 07146

Fédération européenne pour l'apprentissage interculturel

Secretariat Avenue des Arts 7-8, 1210 Brussels, Belgium. T. +3225145250. E-mail: efil@afs.org.
SG address not obtained.
URL: http://efil.afs.org/

History 1971. Founded as a result of contacts, from 1964, among European AFS national exchange organizations. Statutes amended 1983, 1994, 2005, 2010, 2015. Registration: Banque-Carrefour des Entreprises, No/ID: 0415.815.838, Start date: 9 Dec 1975, Belgium; EU Transparency Register, No/ID: 98470877752-88, Start date: 17 Jan 2012. **Aims** Contribute to peace and justice by promoting intercultural understanding and sensitivity among European and other countries. **Structure** General Assembly (every 2 years); Board of Directors; Permanent Secretariat. **Languages** English. **Staff** 3.00 FTE, paid; 3.00 FTE, voluntary. **Finance** Annual budget: 600,000 EUR. **Activities** Advocacy/lobbying/activism; events/meetings; networking/liaising; projects/programmes; training/education. **Events** *Biennial General Assembly* Krakow (Poland) 2019, *Biennial General Assembly* Prague (Czechia) 2017, *Biennial General Assembly* Budapest (Hungary) 2015, *Biennial General Assembly* Belgrade (Serbia) 2013, *Forum on Intercultural Learning and Exchange* Vienna (Austria) 2012. **Publications** Biennial Report; surveys; policy recommendations.

Members Organizations (27) in 26 countries:
Austria, Belgium, Bosnia-Herzegovina, Bulgaria, Czechia, Denmark, Egypt, Finland, France, Germany, Hungary, Iceland, Ireland, Italy, Latvia, Norway, Poland, Portugal, Russia, Serbia, Slovakia, Slovenia, Spain, Switzerland, Tunisia, Türkiye.

Consultative Status Consultative status granted from: *Council of Europe (CE, #04881)* (Participatory Status). **IGO Relations** Member of (1): *European Economic and Social Committee (EESC, #06963)* (Liaison Group). **NGO Relations** Member of (3): *European Youth Forum (#09140)*; *Federation of European and International Associations Established in Belgium (FAIB, #09508)*; *Lifelong Learning Platform – European Civil Society for Education (LLLP, #16466)*. Partner of (1): *AFS Intercultural Programs (AFS, #00541)*. [2021.08.18/XD4110/D]

♦ European Federation of Internal Medicine (EFIM) 07147

Fédération européenne de médecine interne

Secretariat Grensstraat 7, 1831 Diegem, Belgium. T. +3227259424. Fax +3226603821. E-mail: info@efim.org.
SG address not obtained.
URL: http://www.efim.org/

History 16 May 1969, Strasbourg (France). Statutes: adopted 1970, Brussels (Belgium); modified 1996, when AEMI dissolved, being replaced by a federation of national societies with the current title. New statutes adopted 21 Jun 2016 during Extraordinary General Assembly, Brussels (Belgium). Statutes amended during the General Assembly in 2020, Brussels (Belgium). Former names and other names: *Association européenne de médecine interne d'ensemble (AEMIE)* – former; *Europäische Gesellschaft der Gesamten Inneren Medizin* – former; *European Association of Internal Medicine* – former; *Association européenne de médecine interne (AEMI)* – former; *Europäische Gesellschaft für Innere Medizin* – former; *Associazione Europea di Medicina Interna* – former. Registration: Banque-Carrefour des Entreprises, No/ID: 0458.833.358, Start date: 19 Sep 1996, Belgium. **Aims** Promote internal medicine at ethical, scientific and professional levels; bring together European specialists and establish communication between them. **Structure** General Assembly; Executive Committee. **Languages** English. **Staff** 1.00 FTE, paid. **Finance** Sources: members' dues. **Activities** Events/meetings; training/education. **Events** *Joint European Congress of Internal Medicine (ECIM) & International Congress of Internal Medicine* Athens (Greece) 2023, *European Congress of Internal Medicine (ECIM)* Malaga (Spain) 2022, *European Congress of Internal Medicine* 2021, *EFIM Day Meeting* Diegem (Belgium) 2021, *EFIM Day Meeting* Krakow (Poland) 2020. **Publications** *European Journal of Case Reports in Internal Medicine (EJCRIM)*; *European Journal of Internal Medicine (EJIM)*.

Members National societies; individual internists where no society exists; institutions. Members in 35 countries:
Algeria, Argentina, Austria, Belgium, Cyprus, Czechia, Dominican Rep, Estonia, Finland, France, Germany, Greece, Iceland, Israel, Italy, Latvia, Lebanon, Malta, Morocco, Netherlands, North Macedonia, Norway, Poland, Portugal, Romania, Russia, Serbia, Slovakia, Slovenia, Spain, Sweden, Switzerland, Tunisia, Türkiye, UK.

NGO Relations Member of (1): *EU Health Coalition*. Maintains cooperative links with national and international societies for subspecialities related to internal medicine, including: *European Union of Medical Specialists (UEMS, #09001)*; *Foundation for the Development of Internal Medicine in Europe (FDIME, #09944)*; national societies. [2022.02.15/XD0569/D]

♦ European Federation of the International Association for the Study of Pain / see European Pain Federation (#08131)

♦ European Federation of the International College of Surgeons (see: #12650)

♦ European Federation – International Society for Digestive Surgery (EFISDS) 07148

Secretariat PO Box 2178, 5500 BD Veldhoven, Netherlands. T. +3165353640. E-mail: info@efisds.eu – info@esc-societycongress.com.
URL: http://efisds.eu/
History Set up 1990, on the initiative of *International Society for Digestive Surgery (ISDS, #15060)*. Registered in accordance with Dutch law. **Aims** Bring all European national representations together so as to stimulate growth, innovation and communications. **Structure** Executive Board. Committees (4): Education; Research; Public Affairs; International Affairs. **Activities** Training/education; networking/liaising; knowledge management/information dissemination; events/meetings. **Publications** *EFISDS Newsletter*. **NGO Relations** Member of: *United European Gastroenterology (UEG, #20506)*. [2018/XM6300/**D**]

♦ European Federation of International Trade Advisers (inactive)
♦ European Federation of Investment Funds and Companies / see European Fund and Asset Management Association (#07365)

♦ European Federation for Investment Law and Arbitration (EFILA) 07149

SG Rue Royale 97, 1000 Brussels, Belgium. T. +3222092200.
URL: http://efila.org/
History Jun 2014, Brussels (Belgium). Registration: EU Transparency Register, No/ID: 877607714842-74. **Aims** Promote knowledge of all aspects of EU and international investment law, including arbitration, at the European level. **Structure** Executive Board; Advisory Board; Secretariat. **Activities** Training/education; events/meetings. **Events** *Annual Conference* Madrid (Spain) 2023, *Annual Conference* Amsterdam (Netherlands) 2022, *Annual Conference* Brussels (Belgium) 2021, *Annual Conference* London (UK) 2020, *Annual Conference* London (UK) 2019. **Publications** *European Investment Law and Arbitration Review (EILA Review)*. [2022/XM6098/**D**]

♦ European Federation of Investors / see BETTER FINANCE (#03219)
♦ The European Federation of Investors and Financial Services Users / see BETTER FINANCE (#03219)

♦ European Federation of Jewellery (EFJ) 07150

Contact address not obtained. T. +3227200073.
Contact address not obtained.
URL: http://efjewellery.eu/
History Founded 2013. **Aims** Promote the European jewellery sector and defend its interest in the European Union. **Structure** General Assembly. **Activities** Networking/liaising; training/education.
Members Full in 4 countries:
Belgium, France, Italy, Portugal. [2022/XM8877/**D**]

♦ European Federation of Joint Management Societies of Producers for Private Audiovisual Copying (EUROCOPYA) 07151

Contact c/o PROCIREP, 11b Rue Jean Goujon, 75008 Paris, France. E-mail: contact@eurocopya.org.
URL: http://www.eurocopya.org/
History EU Transparency Register: 89874817197-02.
Members Organizations in 8 countries:
Austria, Belgium, Denmark, France, Germany, Netherlands, Spain, Sweden.
NGO Relations Member of: *Culture First Coalition (inactive)*. [2021/XM3285/**D**]

♦ European Federation of Journalists (EFJ) 07152

Fédération européenne des journalistes (FEJ)
Admin Résidence Palace – Bloc C, Rue de la Loi 155, 1040 Brussels, Belgium. T. +3222352208. Fax +3222352219. E-mail: secretariat@europeanjournalists.org.
Gen Sec address not obtained.
URL: http://europeanjournalists.org/
History 1988. Rules adopted by Annual General Meeting, 11-12 Jun 1994, Brussels (Belgium); revised Jun 1999, Brussels; May 2000, Nuremberg (Germany). A regional organization of *International Federation of Journalists (IFJ, #13462)*, created to deal with matters related to member unions' functions as trade unions and to the practice of professional journalism in Europe. Former names and other names: *European Group of Journalists* – former; *Groupe européen des journalistes (GEJ)* – former. Registration: Banque-Carrefour des Entreprises, No/ID: 0503.985.472, Start date: 11 Feb 2013, Belgium; EU Transparency Register, No/ID: 27471236588-39, Start date: 6 Sep 2011. **Aims** Develop and promote common interests in the field of social, economic, cultural and media policy; promote the status of the profession of journalism and media freedom; defend the material and moral working conditions of journalists in all media. **Structure** General Meeting (every 3 years); Steering Committee; Expert Groups (5); Headquarters in Brussels (Belgium). **Languages** English, French, German. **Staff** 6.00 FTE, paid. **Finance** Sources: contributions; members' dues; revenue from activities/projects. Supported by: *European Union (EU, #08967)*; *International Federation of Journalists (IFJ, #13462)*. **Activities** Advocacy/lobbying/activism; events/meetings. **Events** *Free European Media Conference* Gdansk (Poland) 2022, *Annual Meeting* 2020, *Annual Meeting* Tallinn (Estonia) 2019, *Annual Meeting* Lisbon (Portugal) 2018, *Meeting on Financial and Employment Models for Journalism* Vienna (Austria) 2014. **Publications** *EFJ Focus*. Professional studies; seminar reports; surveys on working conditions, gender, managing change, mapping, equal rights. **Members** Journalists (over 320,000) in 72 journalists' organizations across 45 countries. Membership countries not specified. **NGO Relations** Member of (2): *Ethical Journalism Network (EJN, #05554)*; *European Centre for Press and Media Freedom (ECPMF, #06497)*. [2023.02.14/XE1637/**D**]

♦ European Federation of Kickboxing / see WKF Europe (#20975)
♦ European Federation for Landscape Architecture / see IFLA Europe (#11103)
♦ European Federation of the Leather Glove Making Industry (no recent information)
♦ European Federation Lesch-Nyhan Disease (unconfirmed)
♦ European Federation of Liberal and Radical Youth (inactive)

♦ European Federation of Lighter Manufacturers (EFML) 07153

Fédération européenne des fabricants de briquets (FEFB)
Contact Rue Washington 40, 1050 Brussels, Belgium. T. +33145195381. E-mail: catherine.guillou@bicworld.com.
History 1990, Brussels (Belgium). Registration: No/ID: 0443.017.608, Start date: 21 Jun 1990, Belgium; EU Transparency Register, No/ID: 396781039168-43, Start date: 7 Aug 2020. **Aims** Group the European lighter manufacturers and lighter manufacturers' associations and organizations to discuss and jointly solve the problems which may arise within the profession. **Structure** General Assembly (annual); Board of Directors. **Languages** English. **Staff** None. **Finance** Members' dues. Other sources: grants; allocation; gifts; donations; legacies and other testamentary provisions; fundraising. **Members** Companies in 4 countries. Membership countries not specified. **NGO Relations** Member of: *Federation of European and International Associations Established in Belgium (FAIB, #09508)*. [2020/XD2235/v/**D**]

♦ European Federation of Light, Experimental and Vintage Aircraft (EFLEVA) 07154

Treas PO Box 2537, 3001 Bern, Switzerland.
URL: http://www.efleva.eu/
History Founded 2007. **Aims** Promote, support and represent members' interests at European level. **Structure** Executive Committee. **Publications** *EFLEVA Newsletter*.
Members Full in 15 countries:
Austria, Belgium, Czechia, Denmark, France, Germany, Ireland, Latvia, Netherlands, Norway, Portugal, Spain, Sweden, Switzerland, UK.
NGO Relations Member of: *Europe Air Sports (EAS, #05776)*. [2019.06.26/XM7571/**D**]

♦ European Federation for Living (EFL) 07155

Managing Dir Vijzelstraat 68, 1017 HL Amsterdam, Netherlands. E-mail: info@ef-l.eu.
URL: http://www.ef-l.eu/
History 2005. A *European Economic Interest Grouping (EEIG, #06960)*. Former names and other names: *Dutch-German Connection (NDC)* – former (2005). Registration: Handelsregister, No/ID: KVK 34318839, Netherlands. **Aims** Provide differentiated living and *working environments* for different target groups and income levels; realize high-quality design of built-up and vacant areas; realize suitable level of services for the environment; create sufficient employment and good conditions for setting up businesses for entrepreneurs; realize good, comfortable and affordable houses; contribute to Europe's environmental technological and energetic aims; share experience and knowledge. **Structure** General Meeting; Board; Executive Committee. **Activities** Events/meetings; projects/programmes; training/education. **Events** *Spring Conference* Berlin (Germany) 2022, *Autumn Conference* Glasgow (UK) 2022, *Spring Conference* 2021, *Autumn Conference* Stuttgart (Germany) 2021, *Autumn Conference* 2020. **Publications** *EFL Newsletter*.
Members Full in 9 countries:
Belgium, Denmark, Finland, France, Germany, Ireland, Italy, Netherlands, UK.
NGO Relations Partner of (1): *Initiative Wohnungswirtschaft Osteuropa (IWO)*. [2015/XJ2836/**D**]

♦ European Federation of Lobbying and Public Affairs / see Society of European Affairs Professionals (#19553)

♦ European Federation of Local Energy Companies (CEDEC) 07156

SG Galerie Ravenstein 4, Boîte 2, 1000 Brussels, Belgium. T. +3223000051. E-mail: info@cedec.com.
Events – Office and Event Manager address not obtained.
URL: http://www.cedec.com/
History 26 May 1992, Brussels (Belgium). Former names and other names: *European Confederation of Local Public Sector Energy Distribution Companies* – former; *Confédération européenne des distributeurs d'énergie publics communaux (CEDEC)* – former; *Confederazione Europea dei Distributori Comunali d'Energia* – former; *European Confederation of Public Sector Energy Distribution Companies* – former; *Confédération européenne des entreprises locales d'énergie* – former; *Europäischer Dachverband der Öffentlichen Kommunalen Energieversorgungsunternehmen* – former; *Confederazione Europea dei Distributori Comunali d'Energia* – former. Registration: Banque-Carrefour des Entreprises, No/ID: 0451.954.474, Start date: 26 May 1992, Belgium; EU Transparency Register, No/ID: 54829912208-85, Start date: 3 Sep 2009. **Aims** Represent the interests of local and regional energy companies – mostly in public hands – serving electricity and natural gas customers and connections in Europe. **Structure** General Assembly; Board of Directors; Coordinating Committee; Working Groups. **Languages** Dutch, English, French, German, Italian. **Activities** Advocacy/lobbying/activism; events/meetings; monitoring/evaluation; networking/liaising. **Events** *Congress* Brussels (Belgium) 2022, *Congress* Brussels (Belgium) 2021, *Local Integrated Energy Systems and an Inclusive Energy Transition* Brussels (Belgium) 2020, *Local Energy Transition – Mission possible* Brussels (Belgium) 2019, *Sustainability first! A central role for decentralised energy systems* Brussels (Belgium) 2018. **Publications** *CEDEC Brief News* (12 a year); *CEDEC Flash Reports* (every 15 days).
Members National associations representing about 1,500 local and regional energy companies serving 85 million electricity and gas customers, in 9 countries:
Austria, Belgium, France, Germany, Italy, Netherlands, Poland, Sweden, Switzerland.
NGO Relations Member of (2): *Centre international de recherches et d'information sur l'économie publique, sociale et coopérative (CIRIEC, #03764)*; *Federation of European and International Associations Established in Belgium (FAIB, #09508)*. Cooperates with (1): *Covenant of Mayors for Climate and Energy (#04939)*. . [2022.05.11/XD3835/**D**]

♦ European Federation of Local Forest Communities 07157

Fédération européenne des communes forestières (FECOF) – Europäische Vereinigung Gemeindlicher Waldbesitzervertretungen
Advisor c/o Gemeinde & Städtebund, Deutschhausplatz 1, 55116 Mainz, Germany. T. +49613123980. Fax +4961312398139.
National Office France Fédération nationale des Communes forestières, 13 rue du général Bertrand, 75007 Paris, France. T. +33145674798. E-mail: federation@communesforestieres.org.
URL: http://fecof.eu/
History 1990. Founded by Communes forestières de France (COFOR), currently FNCOFOR, and Deutscher Kommunalwald. Former names and other names: *European Federation of Municipal and Local Community Forests* – alias; *European Federation of Municipal Forest Owners* – alias; *Föderation der Europäischen Kommunalwälder* – alias. Registration: EU Transparency Register, No/ID: 22553705184-17. **Aims** Represent interests of European communal forests in European policy and legislation. **Structure** European Board. **Languages** English, French, German, Spanish. **Staff** Voluntary. **Finance** Members' dues. **Events** *General Assembly* Czechia 2019, *Forum* Brussels (Belgium) 2000.
Members in 7 countries:
Andorra, Bulgaria, Czechia, France, Germany, Italy, Spain (and Catalonia).
IGO Relations Observer status with: *Ministerial Conference on the Protection of Forests in Europe (FOREST EUROPE, #16817)*. Member of: Civil Dialogue Group on Forestry and Cork; EU Expert Group on Forest-based Industries and Sectorally Related Issues. [2021/XD3162/**D**]

♦ European Federation of Loss Adjusting Experts 07158

Fédération européenne des unions professionnelles d'experts en dommages après incendie et risques divers (FUEDI)
Exec Dir Boompjes 251, 3011 XZ Rotterdam, Netherlands. T. +31102428555. E-mail: fuedi@fuedi.eu.
URL: http://www.fuedi.eu/
History 1968, Paris (France). **Aims** Provide *insurers* throughout Europe with a professional adjusting service; ensure compliance with a strict code of conduct; promote the loss adjusting profession by establishing common high standards of training and examination and mutually recognized qualifications. **Structure** General Assembly (annual); Plenary Meeting (annual); Executive Committee; National Delegates; Treasurer; Secretariat managed by Executive Director. **Languages** English, French. **Staff** 1.00 FTE, paid. **Finance** Sources: members' dues. **Activities** Certification/accreditation; events/meetings. **Events** *General Assembly* Paris (France) 2022, *General Assembly* Netherlands 2021, *General Assembly* Netherlands 2020, *General Assembly* UK 2019, *Annual General Assembly* Brussels (Belgium) 2018.
Members Professional unions in 14 countries:
Austria, Belgium, Denmark, France, Germany, Ireland, Italy, Luxembourg, Netherlands, Poland, Portugal, Spain, Sweden, UK.
Provisional in 4 countries:
Czechia, Greece, Romania, Russia.
NGO Relations Member of (1): *International Federation of Adjusting Associations (IFAA, #13340)*. [2023.02.15/XD4512/t/**D**]

♦ European Federation of Management Consultancies Associations 07159

Fédération Européenne des Associations de Conseils en Organisation (FEACO) – Europäische Vereinigung der Verbände Beratender Organisatoren – Federazione Europea delle Associazioni di Consulenti in Materia Organizzativa – Europese Federatie van Verenigingen van Organisatiedeskundigen
Secretariat Av des Arts 3-5, 11th Floor, 1210 Brussels, Belgium. E-mail: feaco@feaco.org.
URL: http://www.feaco.org/
History Sep 1960, Paris (France). Founded following preliminary meetings having been held 25 Jun 1957, Paris, and 10-11 May 1958, Geneva (Switzerland). Originally headquartered in Paris; moved to Brussels (Belgium) Jan 1991. New constitution adopted May 2002. **Aims** Assist in promotion and development of the profession of Management Consultancy in Europe by providing support to constituent national association membership in those areas where a collective voice is stronger than the sum of its individual members. **Structure** General Assembly (annual); Executive Committee. **Languages** English, French. **Staff** 0.00 FTE, paid. **Finance** Sources: members' dues. **Activities** Awards/prizes/competitions; events/meetings; networking/liaising; research and development. **Events** *Annual Conference* London (UK) 2018, *Annual Conference* Brussels (Belgium) 2016, *Annual Conference* Athens (Greece) 2015, *Annual Conference* Madrid (Spain) 2014, *Annual Conference* Rome (Italy) 2013. **Publications** *FEACO Survey on the European Management Consultancy Market*.

Members National associations in 14 countries:
Austria, Denmark, Finland, France, Germany, Greece, Hungary, Italy, Portugal, Romania, Slovenia, Spain, Switzerland, UK.
Consultative Status Consultative status granted from: *ECOSOC (#05331)* (Ros C); *UNIDO (#20336)*. **IGO Relations** Recognized by: *European Commission (EC, #06633)*. **NGO Relations** Member of: *European Business Services Alliance (EBSA, #06426)*. [2022.02.22/XD0734/D]

♦ European Federation of the Managerial Staff of Agricultural and Food Production, Industry, Trade and Organizations (inactive)

♦ European Federation of Managerial Staff in the Chemical and Allied Industries (FECCIA) 07160

SG 33 Av de la République, 75011 Paris, France. T. +33142282805. E-mail: info@feccia.eu.
Pres address not obtained.
URL: http://www.feccia.org/

History 8 Jun 1956, Paris (France). Statutes modified: 22 Oct 1964; 20-22 Sep 1968. Current statutes adopted 29 Oct 1994 and modified 25 May 2012. Former names and other names: *International Federation of Management and Professional Staff in the Chemical and Related Industries* – former; *Fédération internationale des cadres de la chimie et des industries annexes (FICCIA)* – former; *International/European Federation of Management and Professional Staff in the Chemical and Related Industries* – former; *Fédération internationale/européenne des cadres de la chimie et des industries annexes (FICCIA/FECCIA)* – former. **Aims** Analyse and defend common professional interests of affiliated associations and their members by representation to international organizations. **Structure** General Assembly (every 3 years); Board. **Languages** English, French. **Staff** 10.00 FTE, voluntary. **Finance** Sources: members' dues. **Activities** Projects/programmes. **Events** *General Assembly* Mainz (Germany) 2021, *General Assembly* London (UK) 2018, *General Assembly* Edinburgh (UK) 2015, *Conference of the Social Partners in the European Chemical Industry* Copenhagen (Denmark) 2013, *General Assembly* Berlin (Germany) 2012.
Members National organizations in 7 countries:
France, Germany, Italy, Norway, Spain, Sweden, UK.
IGO Relations Acts as sectoral spokesman with: *European Commission (EC, #06633)*; *ILO (#11123)*. **NGO Relations** Supports (1): *European Chemical Society (EuCheMS, #06524)*. Professional federation member of: *CEC European Managers (#03623)*. [2022.10.19/XD5410/t/D]

♦ European Federation of Managerial Staff in Technologies of Information and Communication / see European Federation for Managers in Technologies of Information and Communication (#07163)

♦ European Federation of Managers in the Banking Sector 07161

Fédération européenne des cadres des établissements de crédit (FECEC) – Federación Europea de Cuadros de las Entidades de Crédito

Pres address not obtained.
SG address not obtained.
Communications Officer address not obtained.
URL: https://www.fecec.eu/

History as *Association européenne des cadres de banque (AECB)*, by 6 national organizations: Fédération des Cadres de Banque (Belgium); Fédération Nationale des Syndicats des Etablissements de Crédit – FNSEC – CFE/CGC, Federazione Nazionale Personale Direttivo Aziende di Credito e Finanziarie – FEDERDIRIGENTICREDITO (Italy), Federación de Asociaciones de Mandos Intermedios de Banca Ahorro y Entidades De Credito – FAMIBAC (Spain) and Beroepsorganisatie Banken en Verzekeringen – VKBV (Netherlands). Previously referred to in French as *Fédération européenne des cadres des établissements de crédit (FECEC)*. Statutes adopted 13 Oct 1989, Amsterdam (Netherlands); amended 18 May 1990, Lyon (France), 29 Sep 1992, Bruges (Belgium), 16 Nov 1995, Zeist (Netherlands). **Aims** Study, defend and represent European and international ethical, professional, economic and social interest of banking executives, credit institutions and/or any financial institution. **Structure** General Meeting (every 3 years). Management Committee (meets twice a year), comprising members designated by Adhering Organizations, including Chairman, one or more Deputy Chairmen, Secretary General, one or more Assistant Secretaries General, Treasurer and 2 Auditors. Each organization is entitled to: 2 representatives up to 5,000 members; 3 representatives 5,001 to 15,000 members and 4 representatives beyond 15,000 members. **Languages** English, French. **Finance** Members' dues. **Events** *General Assembly* Lisbon (Portugal) 2016, *Extraordinary General Assembly* Naples (Italy) 2010, *Extraordinary General Assembly* Zeist (Netherlands) 1995, *Extraordinary General Assembly* Bruges (Belgium) 1992, *Extraordinary General Assembly* Lyon (France) 1990.
Members European national trade union organizations in 7 countries:
Belgium, France, Germany, Italy, Netherlands, Spain, UK.
Also includes on regional organization, listed in this Yearbook:
Union Europäischer Bankpersonalverbände (UEB, no recent information).
NGO Relations Professional federation of: *CEC European Managers (#03623)*. [2022/XD2705/D]

♦ European Federation of Managers in the Steel Industry 07162

Fédération européenne de l'encadrement de la métallurgie (FEDEM)

Contact 33 av de la République 33, 75011 Paris, France. T. +496831964929.
URL: http://www.cec-managers.org/

History 1952, as *Internationale des cadres des industries métallurgiques (ICIM)* – *Internationaler Verband der Führunskräfte der Mettelindustrie*. Previously referred to as *Fédération internationale de l'encadrement des industries métallurgiques (FIEM)*. **Aims** Represent the interests of executives working in the fields of iron, steel, nonferrous materials, metallurgy and metal working. **Members** Associations in 7 European countries (membership countries not specified). **NGO Relations** Member of: *CEC European Managers (#03623)*. [2014/XD9507/t/D]

♦ European Federation for Managers in Technologies of Information and Communication (eTIC-CEC) 07163

SG rue du Faubourg Poissonnière 35, 75009 Paris, France. T. +33695975955 – +33682813009.
Pres Dir Führungskräfte, Office Hamburg, Grosse Bleichen 21, 20354 Hamburg, Germany. T. +4924882411. E-mail: mueller@die-fuehrungskraefte.de.
URL: http://www.etic-managers.eu/

History Founded Sep 1999, Brussels (Belgium), as *EUROPETEL*. Subsequently changed title to *European Federation of Managerial Staff in Technologies of Information and Communication (eTIC-CEC)*. Since Nov 1999 functions as a Europe-wide branch of the basically European Union body *CEC European Managers (#03623)*. Formerly known as *Media Managers*. Current name adopted, Sep 2006. Also referred to as *European Managers Federation of Technologies of Information and Communication*. EU Transparency Register: 551868910766-44. **Aims** Represent and defend interests of executives and managers in *telecommunications*, information, *media* and communications technology sector at the *European* level. **Staff** 0.50 FTE, paid. **Events** *General Assembly* Cologne (Germany) 2008.
Members Full in 17 countries:
Austria, Belgium, Croatia, Czechia, Denmark, France, Germany, Greece, Hungary, Italy, Norway, Poland, Portugal, Slovenia, Spain, Sweden, UK. [2019/XG6597/D]

♦ European Federation of the Manufacturers of Abrasive Products / see Federation of European Producers of Abrasives (#09532)
♦ European Federation of Manufacturers of Feed Additives / see FEFANA – EU Association of Specialty Feed Ingredients and their Mixtures (#09720)
♦ European Federation of Manufacturers of Refractory Products / see European Refractories Producers Federation (#08339)
♦ European Federation of Manufacturers of Waxed Packaging Materials / see EUROWAXPACK – European Association of Manufacturers of Waxed Packaging Materials (#09195)
♦ European Federation of Marine Science and Technology Societies (inactive)
♦ European Federation of Materials Handling / see European Materials Handling Federation (#07752)
♦ European Federation of Materials Handling, Lifting and Storage Equipment / see European Materials Handling Federation (#07752)
♦ European Federation of Mayors (inactive)

♦ European Federation for Medical Informatics (EFMI) 07164

Managing Dir Chemin de Maillefer 37, 1052 Le Mont-sur-Lausanne VD, Switzerland. T. +41792128885.
Sec Leipzig University, Inst. for Med. Informatics, Stats & Epidemiology, Haertelstrasse 16-18, 04107 Leipzig, Germany. T. +493419716107.
URL: http://www.efmi.org/

History Sep 1976, Copenhagen (Denmark). French title: *Fédération européenne d'informatique médicale*, no longer used. Registration: EU Transparency Register, No/ID: 210303222764-16, Start date: 21 Jul 2016. **Aims** Advance international cooperation and disseminate information in the field of information science and technology within health care, on a European basis; encourage high standards in the application of information systems and in educational activities in this field. **Structure** Governing Council; Executive Board; Working Groups. **Languages** English. **Staff** 17.00 FTE, voluntary. **Finance** Members' dues. **Activities** Events/meetings. **Events** *Medical Informatics Europe Conference* Gothenburg (Sweden) 2023, *Special Topic Conference* Cardiff (UK) 2022, *Medical Informatics Europe Conference* Nice (France) 2022, *Medical Informatics Europe Conference* 2021, *Special Topic Conference* 2021. **Publications** *European Journal of Biomedical Informatics* (periodical); *International Journal of Medical Informatics* (periodical); *Methods of Information in Medicine* (periodical). Studies in technoogy and health informatics.
Members Scientific Societies (one per country) in 30 countries:
Austria, Belgium, Bosnia-Herzegovina, Croatia, Cyprus, Czechia, Finland, France, Germany, Greece, Hungary, Iceland, Ireland, Israel, Italy, Moldova, Netherlands, Norway, Poland, Portugal, Romania, Russia, Serbia, Slovenia, Spain, Sweden, Switzerland, Türkiye, UK, Ukraine. [2022/XD0155/D]

♦ European Federation for Medicinal Chemistry (EFMC) 07165

Admin Sec LD Organisation sprl, Rue Michel de Ghelderode 33/2, 1348 Louvain-la-Neuve, Belgium. T. +3210454774. Fax +3210459719. E-mail: administration@efmc.info.
URL: http://www.efmc.info/

History Founded 19 Dec 1969, Paris (France); ratified 13 Sep 1972, Milan (Italy), on adoption of new regulation, replacing *European Committee on Medicinal Chemistry* which had been set up 1962, Florence (Italy), at 1st International Symposium on Medicinal Chemistry. Regulations established 24 Aug 1973, Munich (Germany) and modified: 1978, Brighton (UK); 6 Sep 1998, Edinburgh (UK); 18 Sep 2000, Bologna (Italy); 19 Oct 2003 (Krakow) Poland; 5 Sep 2010, Brussels (Belgium). **Aims** Advance the science of medicinal chemistry by promoting cooperation and encouraging strong links between national adhering organizations so as to promote contacts and exchanges between medicinal chemists in Europe and around the world. **Structure** Council; Executive Committee; Committees (3). **Languages** English. **Finance** Members' dues. **Activities** Events/meetings; awards/prizes/competitions. **Events** *International Symposium on Medicinal Chemistry* Rome (Italy) 2024, *International Symposium on Medicinal Chemistry* Nice (France) 2022, *International Symposium on Medicinal Chemistry* Basel (Switzerland) 2021, *International Symposium on Advances in Synthetic and Medicinal Chemistry* Zagreb (Croatia) 2021, *International Symposium on Medicinal Chemistry* Basel (Switzerland) 2020. **Publications** *MedChemComm* – official journal; *MedChemWatch* – official e-newsletter; *Medicinal Chemistry in Europe* – official yearbook.
Members Scientific organizations (25) in 23 countries:
Austria, Belgium, Croatia, Denmark, Finland, France, Germany, Greece, Hungary, Israel, Italy, Latvia, Netherlands, Poland, Portugal, Russia, Serbia, Slovenia, Spain, Sweden, Switzerland, Türkiye, UK. [2020.03.03/XD8490/D]

♦ European Federation of Medium Density Fibreboard Manufacturers (inactive)
♦ European Federation of Medium-size and Major Retail Distributors (inactive)
♦ European Federation of Metropolitan and Periurban Natural and Rural Spaces (inactive)
♦ European Federation of the Mining Timber Associations (inactive)

♦ European Federation for Missing and Sexually Exploited Children (Missing Children Europe) 07166

Fédération européenne pour enfants disparus et sexuellement exploités – Europese Federatie voor Vermiste en Seksueel Uitgebuite Kinderen

Main Office Rue de l'Industrie 10, 1000 Brussels, Belgium. T. +3228947484. E-mail: info@missingchildreneurope.eu.
URL: http://missingchildreneurope.eu/

History 4 May 2001, Brussels (Belgium). Also referred to as *Missing Children Europe*. Registration: No/ID: 0478.917.308, Start date: 5 Dec 2002, Belgium; EU Transparency Register, No/ID: 11823899666-63, Start date: 10 Oct 2012. **Aims** Develop and stimulate initiatives to improve the situation of children victims of disappearance or sexual exploitation. **Structure** General Assembly (annual, always in Brussels); Board of Directors. **Languages** English, French. **Finance** Members' dues: euro 100. Other sources: donations; sponsorship. **Events** *Conference on the phenomenon and reasons of children running away from care* Budapest (Hungary) 2011.
Members Organizations (30). Full in 22 countries:
Austria, Belgium, Bulgaria, Cyprus, Czechia, Denmark, Estonia, France, Germany, Greece, Hungary, Ireland, Italy, Lithuania, Netherlands, Poland, Portugal, Romania, Slovakia, Spain, Switzerland, UK.
Included in the above, 3 organizations listed in this Yearbook:
Centrum International Kinderontvoering (Centrum IKO); *European Centre for Missing and Sexually Exploited Children (Child Focus)*; *"Hope for Children" CRC Policy Center (HFC, #10943)*.
Associated in 3 countries:
Croatia, Czechia, Serbia.
IGO Relations Participant in Fundamental Rights Platform of: *European Union Agency for Fundamental Rights (FRA, #08969)*. **NGO Relations** Member of: *European Financial Coalition against Commercial Sexual Exploitation of Children Online (EFC, #07249)*; *Global Partnership to End Violence Against Children (End Violence Against Children, #10533)*. Partner: *King Baudouin Foundation (KBF)*. [2020/XD8315/D]

♦ European Federation of Multiwall Paper Sack Manufacturers / see EUROSAC (#09177)
♦ European Federation of Municipal Forest Owners / see European Federation of Local Forest Communities (#07157)
♦ European Federation of Municipal and Local Community Forests / see European Federation of Local Forest Communities (#07157)
♦ European Federation of the Nars (#09810)
♦ European Federation of National Associations of Contact Lens Manufacturers / see European Federation of National Associations and International Companies of Contact Lens and Contact Lens Care Product Manufacturers (#07167)

♦ European Federation of National Associations and International Companies of Contact Lens and Contact Lens Care Product Manufacturers (EUROMCONTACT) 07167

SG Rue de Tamines 10, 1060 Brussels, Belgium. T. +3225373711. Fax +3225373711. E-mail: info@euromcontact.org.
URL: http://www.euromcontact.org/

History Founded 7 Apr 1989, Paris (France), as *European Federation of National Associations of Contact Lens Manufacturers*. Subsequently referred to as *European Federation of National Associations and International Companies of Contact Lens Manufacturers*. EU Transparency Register: 97208951315-46. **Aims** Represent the European Manufacturers of contact lenses and lens care products to EU institutions, stakeholders and the trade press, providing expertise for policy-makers and helping shape the right regulatory environment. **Structure** Board. **Languages** English. **Staff** 1.00 FTE, paid. **Finance** Members' dues. **Publications** Position papers; stats reports.
Members National organizations; International companies; international organization. National organizations in 7 countries:
Finland, Germany, Italy, Netherlands, Spain, Switzerland, UK.
International member:
European Federation of the Contact Lens and IOL Industries (EFCLIN, #07089).
NGO Relations Member of: *European Coalition for Vision (ECV)*; *European Contact Lens Forum (ECLF, #06774)*. Cooperates with: *European Contact Lens Society of Ophthalmologists (ECLSO, #06775)*; *European Council of Optometry and Optics (ECOO, #06835)*; *International Organization for Standardization (ISO, #14473)*. [2019/XD6987/D]

♦ European Federation of National Associations and International Companies of Contact Lens Manufacturers / see European Federation of National Associations and International Companies of Contact Lens and Contact Lens Care Product Manufacturers (#07167)

♦ European Federation of National Associations of Measurement, Testing and Analytical Laboratories (EUROLAB) 07168

Gen Sec Rue du Commerce 20-22, 1000 Brussels, Belgium. T. +3222740712. E-mail: info@eurolab.org.
International Affairs Manager address not obtained.
URL: http://www.eurolab.org/

History 27 Apr 1990, Brussels (Belgium). Established on signature of a memorandum of understanding by delegations representing private and public testing and analytical laboratories in the countries comprising the European Community (currently European Union) and EFTA. Statutes adopted, Oct 1998. Former names and other names: *Organization for Testing in Europe* – former (27 Apr 1990). Registration: EU Transparency Register, No/ID: 93803793892-60. **Aims** Constitute a forum for exchange of opinion and experience; coordinate at the European level the interface between the testing and analytical laboratory community and all other parties concerned in their activities; provide an infrastructure for scientific and technical cooperation among European laboratories. **Structure** General Assembly; Board of Administrators; Technical Committees. **Languages** English. **Staff** 1.00 FTE, paid. **Finance** Sources: members' dues. **Activities** Events/meetings; monitoring/evaluation; standards/guidelines. **Events** *General Assembly* Brussels (Belgium) 2021, *Meeting* Brussels (Belgium) 2020, *General Assembly* Prague (Czechia) 2019, *National Members Meeting* Toledo (Spain) 2019, *Meeting* Brussels (Belgium) 2018. **Publications** *EUROLAB 25th Anniversary Book* (2020); *EUROLAB 30th Anniversary Video* (2020). Annual Report; report series; position paper series; newsbriefings; technical CookBooks; special briefings.

Members Active in 18 countries:
Austria, Belgium, Bulgaria, Croatia, Czechia, Denmark, Finland, France, Germany, Greece, Iceland, Italy, Netherlands, Poland, Portugal, Spain, Sweden, Switzerland.
Associated in 3 countries:
Lebanon, North Macedonia, Türkiye.
International Affiliates in 3 countries:
Congo DR, South Africa, USA.
10 organizations listed in this Yearbook:
Comité européen de normalisation (CEN, #04162); *EFTA (#05391)*; *Eurocer-Building (#05656)*; *European Association of Research and Technology Organizations (EARTO, #06197)*; *European Commission (EC, #06633)*; *European Committee for Electrotechnical Standardization (CENELEC, #06647)*; *European Cooperation for Accreditation (EA, #06782)*; *European Federation for Non-Destructive Testing (EFNDT, #07179)*; *European Group of Organisations for Fire Testing, Inspection and Certification (EGOLF, #07427)*; *NCSL International (NCSLI)*.

NGO Relations Member of (6): *EURACHEM (#05595)*; *European Accreditation Advisory Board (EAAB, see: #06782)*; *European Association of National Metrology Institutes (EURAMET, #06129)*; *International Laboratory Accreditation Cooperation (ILAC, #13995)*; *NCSL International (NCSLI)*; *TIC Council (#20160)*.
[2021.06.09/XD3123/y/**D**]

♦ European Federation of National Associations of Orthopaedic Sports Traumatology (inactive)

♦ European Federation of National Associations of Orthopaedics and Traumatology (EFORT) 07169

SG ZA La Pièce 2, 1180 Rolle VD, Switzerland. T. +41213434400. Fax +41213434411. E-mail: office@efort.org.
Corporate Governance/Membership Services Manager address not obtained.
URL: http://www.efort.org/

History 1991, Marentino (Italy), by national associations for orthopaedics and traumatology from 20 European countries. Statutes adopted at General Assembly, 11 Nov 1992, Paris (France); amended 19 Apr 1993, Paris; 19 Oct 1994, Vienna (Austria); 3 Jul 1995, Munich (Germany); 23 Apr 1997, Barcelona (Spain); 5 Jun 2001, Rhodes (Greece); 25 Sep 2004, Groningen (Netherlands); 21 Jun 2006, Geneva (Switzerland); 22 May 2012, Berlin (Germany); 3 Jun 2014, London (UK); 26 May 2015, Prague (Czech Rep); 31 May 2016. Registered in accordance with Swiss Civil Code. EU Transparency Register: 241995833892-89. **Aims** Promote exchange of scientific knowledge and experience in the field of prevention and the conservative and surgical treatment of diseases and injuries concerning the *musculo-skeletal* system. **Structure** General Assembly (annual); Executive Board; Head Office based in Rolle (Switzerland). **Languages** English. **Staff** 13.00 FTE, paid. **Finance** Members' dues. Other sources: congress and training programme payments; grants; donations. **Activities** Events/meetings; training/education. **Events** *Annual Congress* Lisbon (Portugal) 2022, *Annual Congress* 2021, *Annual Congress* 2020, *Annual Congress* Lisbon (Portugal) 2019, *Annual Congress* Barcelona (Spain) 2018. **Publications** *Orthopaedics Today Europe (OTE)* (12 a year) – newsletter; *EFORT Open Reviews (EOR)* (annual); *Instructional Lectures* (annual). *European Surgical Orthopaedics and Traumatology* – textbook.

Members European National Societies of orthopaedics, orthopaedic surgery and orthopaedic traumatology (41) in 39 countries:
Albania, Austria, Belarus, Belgium, Bosnia-Herzegovina, Bulgaria, Croatia, Cyprus, Czechia, Denmark, Estonia, Finland, France, Germany, Greece, Hungary, Iceland, Ireland, Italy, Kosovo, Lithuania, Luxembourg, Malta, Montenegro, Netherlands, North Macedonia, Norway, Poland, Portugal, Romania, Serbia, Slovakia, Slovenia, Spain, Sweden, Switzerland, Türkiye, UK, Ukraine.

NGO Relations Member of: *Associations and Conference Forum (AC Forum, #02909)*; *Biomedical Alliance in Europe (#03251)*; *Health First Europe (HFE, #10881)*. [2020/XD2647/**D**]

♦ European Federation of National Associations of Specialist Contractors and Material Suppliers to the Construction Industry / see Experts for Specialised Construction and Concrete Systems (#09226)

♦ European Federation of National Associations of Water and Waste Water Services 07170

Fédération européenne des associations nationales de services d'eau et assainissement (EurEau)

SG Rue du Luxembourg 47-51, 1050 Brussels, Belgium. T. +3227064080. Fax +3227064081. E-mail: secretariat@eureau.org – info@eureau.org.
URL: http://www.eureau.org/

History 21 Mar 1975, Brussels (Belgium). Founded as *Union of the Water Supply Associations from Countries of the European Communities – Union des associations des distributeurs d'eau de pays membres des Communautés européennes – Unión de las Asociaciones de Distribuidores de Agua de los Paises Miembros de las Comunidades Europeas – Union der Wasserversorgungsvereinigungen von Mitgliedländern der Europäischen Gemeinschaften – União das Associações de Distribuidores de Agua dos Paises Membros das Comunidades Européias – Unione delle Associazioni delle Aziende Distributrici d'Acqua dei Paesi Membri delle Comunità Europee – Unie der Verenigingen van Waterleidingbedrijven uit de Landen van de Europese Gemeenschap – Unionen af Vandforsyningsforeninger i de Europaeiske Faellesskabers Medlemslande*. Name subsequently changed to *European Union of National Associations of Water Suppliers – Union européenne des associations nationales des distributeurs d'eau (EUREAU) – Unión Europea de Asociaciones Nacionales de Distribuidores de Agua – Europäische Union der nationalen Vereinigungen der Wasserversorger – União Européia das Associações Nacionais dos Distribuidores de Agua – Unione Europea delle Associazioni Nazionali dei Distributori d'Acqua – Europese Unie van Nationale Verenigingen van Waterleidingbedrijven – Europaeiske Union af Nationale Vandforsyningsforeninger*. Subsequently referred as *Unión Europea de Asociaciones Nacionales de Distribuidores de Agua – Europäische Union der nationalen Vereinigungen der Wasserversorger – União Européia das Associações Nacionais dos Distribuidores de Agua – Unione Europea delle Associazioni Nazionali dei Distributori d'Acqua – Europese Unie van Nationale Verenigingen van Waterleidingbedrijven – Europaeske Union af Nationale Vandforsyningsforeninger*. Changed title again to: *European Union of National Associations of Water Suppliers and Waste Water Services – Union européenne des associations nationales des distributeurs d'eau et de services d'assainissement*. Previously a regional water supply organization of *International Water Services Association (IWSA, inactive)*, since 1999 active within *International Water Association (IWA, #15865)*. Registration: Banque-Carrefour des Entreprises, No/ID: 0416.415.357, Start date: 8 Mar 1976, Belgium; EU Transparency Register, No/ID: 39299129772-62, Start date: 8 Oct 2012. **Aims** Defend the quality and sustainability of water, water use and water management; promote and develop the study of scientific, technical, economic, administrative and legal problems concerning the catchment, treatment and supply of water in the member countries of the European Communities; identify, propose, encourage and implement solutions to these problems; represent the interests of members; make the European Communities aware of these problems. **Structure** General Assembly; Board of Managers. Executive Committee. Commissions (3): Drinking Water; Waste Water; Legislation and Economics. **Languages** English, French. **Staff** 3.00 FTE, paid. **Finance** Members' dues. Budget (annual): euro 500,000. **Events** *Conference* Vienna (Austria) 2014, *Conference* Malta 2012, *Workshop on Climate Changes Impact on Water Resources* Chania (Greece) 2008, *Conference* Vienna (Austria) 2008, *BULAQUA : international conference on water resources, technologies and services* Sofia (Bulgaria) 2007. **Publications** Newsletter – members only.

Members National organizations in 29 countries (refers to observer member):
Austria, Belgium, Bulgaria, Croatia (*), Cyprus, Czechia, Denmark, Estonia, Finland, France, Germany, Greece, Hungary, Iceland, Ireland, Italy, Lithuania, Luxembourg, Malta, Netherlands, Norway, Poland, Portugal, Romania, Slovakia, Spain, Sweden, Switzerland, UK.

IGO Relations Recognized by: *European Commission (EC, #06633)*. Observer to: *Baltic Marine Environment Protection Commission – Helsinki Commission (HELCOM, #03126)*. Partner of: *Global Alliances for Water and Climate (GAfWaC, #10230)*. **NGO Relations** In liaison with technical committees of: *International Organization for Standardization (ISO, #14473)*. Member of: *Federation of European and International Associations Established in Belgium (FAIB, #09508)*; *Water Europe (WE, #20828)*. Member of: *Global Water Operators' Partnerships Alliance (GWOPA, #10652)*. Observer to: *European Umbrella Organization for Geographical Information (EUROGI, #08964)*. Close contact with: *European Water Association (EWA, #09080)*; *World Wide Fund for Nature (WWF, #21922)*. [2021/XE3669/**D**]

♦ European Federation of National Engineering Associations (#09558)
♦ European Federation of National Foot and Ankle Societies (inactive)

♦ European Federation of National HSP Associations (EURO-HSP) . . . 07171

Sec Plateforme Maladies Rares, 99 rue Didot, 75014 Paris, France.
URL: http://www.eurohsp.eu/

History Jul 2010, Paris (France). HSP stands for *Hereditary Spastic Paraplegia*. Registration: RNA, No/ID: W751205920, Start date: Jul 2010, France. **Aims** Collaborate with scientists and researchers to better understand, discover treatments and find a cure for *Hereditary Spastic Paraplegia* (HSP); improve all social, political and cultural matters connected with the welfare of people affected by HSP; keep the broader society aware of the existence of HSP; expand international cooperation between patients, organizations and experts. **Structure** General Assembly; Board of Directors. **Languages** English, French. **Staff** None. **Finance** Sources: members' dues. **Activities** Awards/prizes/competitions; events/meetings. **Events** *Annual General Assembly* Klosterneuburg (Austria) 2019, *General Assembly and Annual Meeting* Alghero (Italy) 2017, *General Assembly and Annual Meeting* Paris (France) 2016, *General Assembly and Annual Meeting / General Assembly* Madrid (Spain) 2015, *General Assembly and Annual Meeting / General Assembly* Copenhagen (Denmark) 2014.

Members European associations in 8 countries:
Denmark, France, Italy, Netherlands, Norway, Spain, Sweden, Switzerland.

NGO Relations Member of (1): *EURORDIS – Rare Diseases Europe (#09175)*. [2021/XJ6566/**D**]

♦ European Federation of National Institutions for Language (EFNIL) . 07172

Gen Sec Nyelvtudomanyi Intézet, PO Box 360, Budapest 1394, Hungary. T. +3613429372. E-mail: efnil@nytud.hu.
Pres address not obtained.
URL: http://www.efnil.org/

History 14 Oct 2003, Stockholm (Sweden). Current constitution adopted 2016. Former names and other names: *Fédération européenne des institutions linguistiques nationales* – former; *Europäische Föderation Nationaler Sprachinstitutionen* – former; *Federazione Europea delle Istituzioni Linguistiche Nazionali (FEILN)* – former; *Europese Federatie van Nationale Taalinstellingen* – former; *Europeiska Samarbetsorganisationen för Nationella Språkinstitutioner* – former; *Europaeiske Samarbejdsorganisation for Nationale Sproginstitutioner* – former; *Euroopan Kansallisten Kielentutkimuslaitosten Yhteistyöelin* – former. Registration: Start date: 29 Sep 2016, Luxembourg. **Aims** Collect and exchange information about the officially recognized standard languages of the European Union; provide expert advice about language policy; preserve linguistic diversity within Europe; promote plurilingualism amongst the citizens of the European Union states. **Structure** General Assembly (annual); Executive Committee; Secretariat. **Languages** English. **Staff** Voluntary. **Finance** Sources: members' dues. Annual budget: 80,000 EUR. **Activities** Events/meetings. **Events** *EFNIL Webinar* 2021, *Seminar* Budapest (Hungary) 2020, *Annual Conference* Cavtat (Croatia) 2020, *Annual Conference* Tallinn (Estonia) 2019, *Annual Conference* Amsterdam (Netherlands) 2018. **Publications** Contributions to annual conferences are published as books (since 2007).

Members Full in 24 countries:
Austria, Belgium, Bulgaria, Croatia, Denmark, Estonia, Finland, France, Germany, Greece, Hungary, Ireland, Italy, Latvia, Lithuania, Luxembourg, Malta, Netherlands, Poland, Romania, Slovakia, Slovenia, Sweden, UK.
Associate in 5 countries:
Georgia, Iceland, Norway, Serbia, Switzerland.

NGO Relations Member of (3): *Cracking the Language Barrier (#04942)*; *European Civil Society Platform for Multilingualism (ECSPM, #06569)*; *Multilingual Europe Technology Alliance (META, #16892)*.
[2021.06.16/XJ3615/y/**D**]

♦ European Federation of National Maintenance Societies (EFNMS) . . 07173

Fédération européenne des sociétés nationales d'entretien

Chairman A Reyerlaan 80, Diamant 5th fl, 1030 Brussels, Belgium. T. +3227068715. E-mail: info@efnms.eu.
URL: http://www.efnms.eu/

History 12 Nov 1970, Duisburg (Germany). Constitution adopted by 5th Council meeting, 25 Nov 1971, Stockholm (Sweden); modified: by 31st Council Meeting, 21 May 1987, Weinfelden (Switzerland); by 49th Council Meeting, 4 Oct 1997, Dublin (Ireland). Registration: Start date: 18 Apr 2003, Belgium. **Aims** Stimulate study of improved maintenance techniques and practices, and publishing of scientific and practical studies in the field; initiate the organization of international congresses on maintenance; assist in efforts to develop maintenance in the developing countries, at their request and within the limit of available resources. **Structure** General Assembly; Board of Directors; Committees (5). **Languages** English. **Staff** Voluntary. **Finance** Expenses met by member societies. **Activities** Standards/guidelines; certification/accreditation; events/meetings. **Events** *EuroMaintenance Congress* Rotterdam (Netherlands) 2023, *EuroMaintenance Congress* Rotterdam (Netherlands) 2021, *EuroMaintenance Congress* Rotterdam (Netherlands) 2020, *EuroMaintenance Congress* Antwerp (Belgium) 2018, *EuroMaintenance Congress* Athens (Greece) 2016. **Publications** *EFNMS News Letter* (2 a year).

Members National maintenance associations in 23 countries:
Austria, Belgium, Croatia, Czechia, Denmark, Finland, France, Germany, Greece, Iceland, Italy, Lithuania, Netherlands, Norway, Poland, Portugal, Serbia, Slovakia, Slovenia, Spain, Sweden, Switzerland, UK.

Consultative Status Consultative status granted from: *ECOSOC (#05331)* (Ros C); *UNIDO (#20336)*. **NGO Relations** Member of: *A.SPIRE (#02311)*; *Global Forum on Maintenance and Asset Management (GFMAM, #10374)*. Cooperates with: *Federación Iberoamericana de Mantenimiento (FIM, #09315)*; *International Measurement Confederation (IMEKO, #14124)*. Links with national organizations. [2018/XD5390/**D**]

♦ European Federation of National Organisations Working with the Homeless 07174

Fédération européenne d'associations nationales travaillant avec les sans-abri (FEANTSA)

Dir Chée de Louvain 194, 1210 Brussels, Belgium. T. +3225386669. E-mail: information@feantsa.org.
URL: http://www.feantsa.org/

History 10 Jan 1989, Brussels (Belgium). Founded with the support of *European Commission (EC, #06633)*. Registration: Banque Carrefour des Entreprises, No/ID: 0440.718.312, Start date: 19 Oct 1989, Belgium; EU Transparency Register, No/ID: 42528706153-39, Start date: 6 Jul 2011. **Aims** Focus exclusively on the fight against homelessness. **Structure** General Assembly (annual); Administrative Council; Executive Committee. **Languages** English, French. **Staff** 14.00 FTE, paid. **Finance** Sources: contributions; members' dues. European funding. **Activities** Advocacy/lobbying/activism; events/meetings; networking/liaising; research/

documentation. **Events** *Annual Research Conference on Homelessness* Bergamo (Italy) 2022, *Motherhood and Homelessness* Brussels (Belgium) 2022, *Annual Research Conference on Homelessness* Bergamo (Italy) 2021, *Annual Research Conference on Homelessness* Bergamo (Italy) 2020, *Online Week Conference* Brussels (Belgium) 2020. **Publications** *Homeless in Europe* (3 a year) – magazine; *European Journal of Homelessness* (2 a year); *Comparative Studies on Homelessness* (annual); *FEANTSA Flash* (11 a year) – newsletter. Monographs; studies; research studies; policy reports; handbooks; toolkits.
Members Organizations in 28 countries:
Austria, Belgium, Czechia, Denmark, Estonia, Finland, France, Georgia, Germany, Greece, Hungary, Ireland, Italy, Lithuania, Luxembourg, Malta, Netherlands, Norway, Poland, Portugal, Romania, Russia, Slovakia, Slovenia, Spain, Sweden, Türkiye, UK.
Consultative Status Consultative status granted from: *Council of Europe (CE, #04881)* (Participatory Status).
IGO Relations Participant in Fundamental Rights Platform of: *European Union Agency for Fundamental Rights (FRA, #08969)*.
NGO Relations Member of (8): *EU Alliance for a democratic, social and sustainable European Semester (EU Semester Alliance, #05565)*; *EU Health Coalition*; *European Anti-Poverty Network (EAPN, #05908)*; *European Housing Forum (EHF, #07504)*; *European NGO Platform Asylum and Migration (EPAM, #08051)*; *European Public Health Alliance (EPHA, #08297)*; *SDG Watch Europe (#19162)*; *Social Services Europe (#19347)*.
Links with:.
- *Caritas Europa (#03579)*;
- *Emmaus International (#05445)*;
- *Eurochild (#05657)*;
- *EUROCITIES (#05662)*;
- *European Association of Service Providers for Persons with Disabilities (EASPD, #06204)*;
- *European Council for Non-Profit Organizations (#06834)*;
- *European Family Justice Center Alliance (EFJCA, #07029)*;
- *European Federation for Diaconia (Eurodiaconia, #07099)*;
- *European Network against Racism (ENAR, #07862)*;
- *European Trade Union Confederation (ETUC, #08927)*;
- *Global Network for Public Interest Law (PILnet)*;
- *Housing Europe – The European Federation for Public Cooperative and Social Housing (Housing Europe, #10956)*;
- *International Medical Assistance Foundation (AMI)*;
- *International Movement ATD Fourth World (#14193)*;
- *International Network of Street Papers (INSP, #14330)*;
- *International Union of Tenants (IUT, #15822)*;
- *Jesuit Refugee Service (JRS, #16106)*;
- *Mental Health Europe (MHE, #16715)*;
- *Observatoire social européen (OSE)*;
- *Platform for International Cooperation on Undocumented Migrants (PICUM, #18401)*;
- *Red Cross EU Office (#18643)*;
- *Réseaux ferroviaires Européens Développement social et Solidarité dans les Gares (Gare Européenne et Solidarité, #18910)*;
- *Santé mentale et exclusion sociale – Europa (SMES Europa, #19053)*;
- *SOLIDAR (#19680)*.

[2022.02.15/XD1711/**D**]

♦ European Federation of National Psoriasis Patients Associations (EUROPSO) 07175
Pres Glavni Trg 10, 3313 Polzela, Slovenia. E-mail: info@euro-pso.org.
URL: https://www.euro-pso.org/
History 19 Nov 1988, Rotterdam (Netherlands). Former names and other names: *EURO-PSO* – former. Registration: Netherlands. **Aims** Work for social and economic integration of psoriasis patients within the European Union by dispelling prejudice and other forms of discrimination; stimulate and coordinate scientific research into causes and consequences of psoriasis; combat the physical and psychological damage resulting from having to live with the complaint; foster and facilitate contacts and cooperation among psoriasis associations and similar organizations; work towards a better quality of life for psoriasis sufferers. **Structure** General Committee (meets every 2-3 years); Executive Board (meets at least twice a year). **Languages** English. **Staff** 0.50 FTE, paid; 1.00 FTE, voluntary. **Finance** Members' dues. Other sources: seed money; grants; donations; sponsorships. **Activities** Advocacy/lobbying/activism; events/meetings; research/documentation. **Events** *General Assembly* Dublin (Ireland) 2013, *Conferences* Düsseldorf (Germany) 2010, *Workshop to promote uniform international science-based standards to facilitate trade in agricultural commodities* Fort Collins, CO (USA) 2005, *Conference / Conferences* London (UK) 2005, *Patent conference / Plenary Meeting* Helsinki (Finland) 2004. **Publications** *EUROPSO Newsletter* (4 a year). Information Services: Databanks: Scientific research concerning psoriasis; Available treatment and acceptance of these treatments by national health and insurance bodies in EU member countries.
Members National psoriasis associations in 21 countries:
Austria, Belgium, Croatia, Czechia, Denmark, Estonia, Finland, France, Georgia, Germany, Greece, Italy, Netherlands, Norway, Portugal, Russia, Serbia, Slovakia, Slovenia, Spain, Switzerland.
NGO Relations Member of (1): *European Patients' Forum (EPF, #08172)* (Full).

[2020/XD2429/**D**]

♦ European Federation of National Theosophical Societies / see Theosophical Society in Europe (#20142)

♦ European Federation of National Youth Orchestras (EFNYO) 07176
Contact c/o Wiener Jeunesse Orchester, Vivenotweg 12, 3400 Klosterneuburg, Austria. T. +43224326626. Fax +43224333886. E-mail: info@efnyo.org.
URL: http://www.efnyo.org/
History 1994. Registration: Handelsregister, No/ID: 40538572, Start date: 9 Jun 1994, Netherlands, Amsterdam. **Aims** Provide a platform for exchange of expertise in music training, music performance, audience engagement, transnational mobility and intercultural dialogue between the leading national and international youth orchestras of Europe. **Structure** General Assembly and Annual Meeting; Board; Working Group. **Languages** Danish, English, French, German, Greek, Italian, Norwegian, Portuguese, Romanian, Spanish. **Staff** 2.00 FTE, paid. **Finance** Sources: members' dues. Supported by: *European Union (EU, #08967)*. **Activities** Events/meetings; networking/liaising; training/education. **Events** *General Assembly* Athens (Greece) 2022, *General Assembly* Bucharest (Romania) 2019, *General Assembly* Limassol (Cyprus) 2018, *General Assembly* Fiesole (Italy) 2017, *General Assembly* Paris (France) 2016. **Publications** Reports; articles; brochures; videos.
Members National youth orchestras in 20 countries and territories:
Austria, Denmark, Finland, France, Germany, Greece, Ireland, Italy, Netherlands, Norway, Poland, Portugal, Romania, Scotland, Slovakia, Slovenia, Spain, Türkiye, UK, Ukraine.
Associated members (international youth orchestras, music festivals, higher music education institutions) in 5 countries:
Canada, Colombia, Israel, Moldova, UK.
Included in the above, 5 organizations listed in this Yearbook:
Baltic Youth Philharmonic (BYP, #03157); *European Union Youth Orchestra (EUYO, #09024)*; *Gustav Mahler Youth Orchestra (GMJO)*; *Nordic Youth Orchestra (#17475)*; *Orchestre des Jeunes de la Méditerranée (OJM, #17788)*.
NGO Relations Also links with national associations.

[2022.10.24/XD5621/y/**D**]

♦ European Federation of Natural Medicine Users (no recent information)
♦ European Federation for Naturopathy (inactive)
♦ European Federation of Nautical Tourism Destinations (internationally oriented national body)

♦ European Federation of Neurological Associations (EFNA) 07177
Exec Dir Rue d'Egmont 11, 1000 Brussels, Belgium.
URL: http://www.efna.net/
History 16 Oct 2000, Copenhagen (Denmark). Registration: Banque-Carrefour des Entreprises, No/ID: 0543.319.269, Start date: 16 Dec 2013, Belgium; EU Transparency Register, No/ID: 321826714452-53, Start date: 7 Oct 2014. **Aims** Provide maximum opportunities for those people living with neurological conditions; work towards relieving the social and economic burden on patients, carers and society in general. **Structure** General Assembly (annual); Board of Directors. **Languages** English. **Staff** 0.50 FTE, paid. **Finance** Sources: members' dues. **Activities** Advocacy/lobbying/activism; events/meetings; networking/liaising; research/ documentation; training/education. **Events** *Meeting* Brussels (Belgium) 2018, *Meeting* Brussels (Belgium) 2015, *Beethoven the last master* Vienna (Austria) 2002. **Publications** *Common Neurological Symptoms and Conditions*; *Practical Handbook for Carers – Caring in the Comfort of Home*. Newsletters; directory of members; fact sheets; electronic media.
Members Voting: Founding; Pan-European patient support organizations. Non-Voting: national neurological patient organizations in European countries and others existing outside Europe, where no pan-European organization exists; Honorary members (individuals and organizations). Members: 20 organizations listed in this Yearbook:
ADHD-Europe (#00113); *Dystonia Europe (#05151)*; *European Alliance for Restless Legs Syndrome (EARLS, #05881)*; *European Alliance of Neuromuscular Disorders Associations (EAMDA, #05876)*; *European CMT Federation (ECMTF, #06586)*; *European Federation of Hereditary Ataxias (Euro-ATAXIA, #07138)*; *European Huntington Association (EHA, #07509)*; *European ME Alliance (EMEA, #07757)*; *European Migraine and Headache Alliance (EMHA, #07801)*; *European Multiple Sclerosis Platform (EMSP, #07833)*; *European Myasthenia Gravis Association (EuMGA, #07844)*; *European Parkinson's Disease Association (EPDA, #08145)*; *European Patient Organisation for Dysimmune and Inflammatory Neuropathies (EPODIN, #08169)*; *European Polio Union (EPU, #08246)*; *International Brain Tumour Alliance (IBTA, #12393)*; *International Bureau for Epilepsy (IBE, #12414)*; *Pain Alliance Europe (PAE, #18026)*; *Retina International (RI, #18926)*; *Stroke Alliance for Europe (SAFE, #20012)*; *Tics and Tourette Across the Globe (TTAG, #20161)* (provisional).
IGO Relations *European Commission (EC, #06633)*; *European Parliament (EP, #08146)*; *WHO (#20950)*.
NGO Relations Member of (6): *Alliance for Safe Online Pharmacy – EU (ASOP EU, #00720)*; *EU Health Coalition*; *European Alliance for Transformative Therapies (TRANSFORM, #05889)*; *European Brain Council (EBC, #06391)*; *European Patients' Forum (EPF, #08172)* (Associate); *Psychedelic Access and Research European Alliance (PAREA)* (Founding). Partner of (2): *European Alliance for Access to Safe Medicines (EAASM, #05859)*; *European Huntington Association (EHA, #07509)*.

[2022/XD8633/y/**D**]

♦ European Federation of Neurological Societies (inactive)
♦ European Federation of NeuroPsychiatry (no recent information)

♦ European Federation for NeuroRehabilitation Societies (EFNR) 07178
Secretariat Renngasse 12, 1010 Vienna, Austria. T. +4315055555. E-mail: front.desk@efnr.org.
URL: http://www.ecnr.org/
History 2009. Confirmed 2010, during world congress of NeuroRehabilitation. Registration: Austria. **Aims** Promote research, education, and scientific dialogue in the area of NeuroRehabilitation and related medical specialties. **Structure** Executive Board. **Activities** Advocacy/lobbying/activism; awards/prizes/competitions; events/meetings; research/documentation; standards/guidelines. **Events** *European Congress of NeuroRehabilitation 2021*, *European Congress* Vienna (Austria) 2015.
Members Societies in 7 countries:
Austria, Germany, Italy, Netherlands, Romania, Switzerland, UK.
NGO Relations Affiliated with (1): *International Society for Virtual Rehabilitation (ISVR, #15543)*.

[2022/XM4760/**D**]

♦ European Federation for Non-Destructive Testing (EFNDT) 07179
Fédération Européenne pour le Contrôle Non Destructif
Gen Sec c/o TIC Council, Rue du Commerce 20-22, 1000 Brussels, Belgium. E-mail: secretary@efndt.org.
URL: http://www.efndt.org/
History May 1998, Copenhagen (Denmark). Founded at 7th Conference of *European Council for Non-Destructive Testing (ECNDT, inactive)*, taking over activities of ECNDT. Registration: Banque-Carrefour des Entreprises, No/ID: 0468.647.481, Start date: 25 May 1998, Belgium. **Aims** Bring together resources of national societies and organizations involved in Nondestructive Testing (NDT) and related topics in Europe to create a more effective and more valuable voice for industry, the professions, users and the wider community. **Structure** General Assembly (annual); Board of Directors; Advisory Group; Certification Executive Committee; Working Groups; Secretariat. **Languages** English. **Activities** Certification/accreditation; events/meetings; networking/liaising. **Events** *Conference* Lisbon (Portugal) 2022, *Conference* Gothenburg (Sweden) 2018, *General Assembly* Vienna (Austria) 2017, *Conference* Prague (Czech Rep) 2014, *General Assembly* Vienna (Austria) 2013.
Members Full; Associate. Full member organizations in 31 countries:
Austria, Belarus, Belgium, Bulgaria, Croatia, Czechia, Denmark, Finland, France, Germany, Greece, Hungary, Italy, Latvia, Lithuania, Moldova, Netherlands, Norway, Poland, Portugal, Romania, Russia, Serbia, Slovakia, Slovenia, Spain, Sweden, Switzerland, Türkiye, UK, Ukraine.
Associate member organizations in 9 countries:
Australia, Brazil, China, India, Israel, Japan, Korea Rep, Singapore, South Africa.
NGO Relations Member of (2): *European Federation of National Associations of Measurement, Testing and Analytical Laboratories (EUROLAB, #07168)*; *International Committee on Non-Destructive Testing (ICNDT, #12793)*. In liaison with technical committees of: *Comité européen de normalisation (CEN, #04162)*.

[2021/XD7171/**D**]

♦ European Federation of Nurse Educators / see European Federation of Educators in Nursing Sciences (#07102)
♦ European Federation of Nurses / see European Federation of Nurses Associations (#07180)

♦ European Federation of Nurses Associations (EFN) 07180
Fédération Européenne des associations infirmières
Gen Sec Clos du Parnasse 11A, 1050 Brussels, Belgium. T. +3225127419. Fax +3225123550. E-mail: efn@efn.be.
URL: http://www.efnweb.eu/
History Founded 1971, Bern (Switzerland), as *Standing Committee of Nurses of the EC – Comité permanent des infirmiers/infirmières de la CE*. Previously also referred to as *Permanent Committee of Nurses in Liaison with EEC – Comité permanent des infirmières en liaison avec la CEE (PCN/CEE)*. Name changed to *Standing Committee of Nurses of the EU (PCN) – Comité permanent des infirmiers/infirmières de l'UE*. Subsequently changed title to *European Federation of Nurses*. Current title adopted, 1 Jan 2006. EU Transparency Register: 87872442953-08. **Aims** Strengthen the status and practice of the *profession* of nursing and the interests of nurses in the EU and Europe; ensure that nurses and nursing is central to the development of social and health policy and its implementation in the EU and Europe; support and facilitate a qualitative and equitable health service in the EU and Europe by a strategic contribution to the development of a sufficient, effective, competent and motivated workforce of nurses; strengthen EFN representation in the EU and Europe and develop EFN key role as a bridge between NNA and decision-makers in the EU institutions. **Structure** General Assembly; Executive Committee; Sub-Committees (3). **Languages** English. **Staff** 3.00 FTE, paid. **Finance** Annual contributions from member associations. **Activities** Advocacy/lobbying/activism. **Events** *General Assembly* Brussels (Belgium) 2022, *General Assembly* Brussels (Belgium) 2021, *General Assembly* Brussels (Belgium) 2021, *General Assembly* Estonia 2020, *General Assembly* Estonia 2020. **Publications** Position statements; activity reports; articles.
Members in 35 countries:
Albania, Austria, Belgium, Bulgaria, Croatia, Cyprus, Czechia, Denmark, Estonia, Finland, France, Germany, Greece, Hungary, Iceland, Ireland, Italy, Latvia, Lithuania, Luxembourg, Malta, Montenegro, Netherlands, North Macedonia, Norway, Poland, Portugal, Romania, Serbia, Slovakia, Slovenia, Spain, Sweden, Switzerland, UK.
IGO Relations Observers: *WHO (#20950)*. Participant in Fundamental Rights Platform of: *European Union Agency for Fundamental Rights (FRA, #08969)*. **NGO Relations** Instrumental in setting up: *European Nursing Research Foundation (ENRF, #08065)*. Observers: *European Forum of Nursing and Midwifery Associations (#07324)*; *European Nursing Students Association (ENSA, #08066)*; *International Council of Nurses (ICN, #13054)*. Participating organization of: *European Alliance for Personalised Medicine (EAPM, #05878)*. Observer to: *European Health professionals Competent Authorities (EurHeCA, #07460)*.

[2018.06.01/XE2450/**E**]

♦ European Federation of Older Students at Universities (EFOS) 07181
Fédération européenne des étudiants âgés aux universités – Europäische Vereinigung Älterer Studierender an den Universitäten
Gen Sec Cervenakova 19, 841 01 Bratislava, Slovakia. T. +421264361655.
Pres Univ Komenského, Centrum dalsieho vzdelavania, Ul Odbojarov 10/a, 831 04 Bratislava, Slovakia. T. +421250117700.
URL: http://www.efos-europa.eu/

European Federation Open
07181

alphabetic sequence excludes
For the complete listing, see Yearbook Online at

History 11 May 1990, Bressanone (Italy). Initially registered in accordance with Belgian law. Registration: Austria; EU Transparency Register, No/ID: 95665842136-67. **Aims** Protect the interests of older students in universities in Europe; foster joint projects; identify skills and expertise of older students for the benefit of science and society. **Structure** General Assembly (every 3 years); Board. **Languages** English, German. **Staff** None. **Finance** Sources: contributions; donations; members' dues; revenue from activities/projects. Supported by: *European Commission (EC, #06633)*. **Activities** Events/meetings; guidance/assistance/consulting; networking/liaising; projects/programmes; publishing activities. **Events** *Spring Meeting* Brno (Czechia) 2023, *Spring Meeting* Magdeburg (Germany) 2022, *Autumn Meeting* Wroclaw (Poland) 2022, *Winter Meeting* Alicante (Spain) 2021, *Autumn Meeting* Dresden (Germany) 2021. **Publications** *Education for Seniors in Europe*; *EFOS News* in English, German. Booklet; leaflets.
Members Full in 12 countries:
Austria, Czechia, France, Germany, Hungary, Netherlands, Poland, Slovakia, Spain, Sweden, Switzerland, UK.
Consultative Status Consultative status granted from: *ECOSOC (#05331)* (Special). **NGO Relations** Represented with: *Association internationale des universités du troisième âge (AIUTA, #02749)*.
[2023.02.23/XD3381/**D**]

♦ European Federation of Open and Digital Learning (no recent information)
♦ European Federation of Optometry / see European Society of Optometry (#08675)

♦ European Federation of Oral Surgery Societies (EFOSS) 07182

Europäischer Verband der Oralchirurgischen Gesellschaften
Gen Sec Rua do Carmo 11 sala8, 4700-309 Braga, Portugal. T. +351253610566. Fax +351253269649.
Pres Av Guerra Junqueiro 5 – 2 Esq, 1000 Lisbon, Portugal. T. +351218402992 – +351218402993. Fax +351218402992.
URL: http://www.efoss.eu/
History 10 Oct 1998, Barcelona (Spain). **Aims** Improve study, research and progress of the oral surgery in Europe. **Structure** Board of Directors, including President, Vice-President, Past-President, Treasurer and General Secretary. **Languages** English, French, German. **Events** *Congress* Berlin (Germany) 2014, *Congress* Milan (Italy) 2012, *Congress* Edinburgh (UK) 2010, *Congress* Porto (Portugal) 2008, *Congress* Paris (France) 2006.
Members National organizations in 6 countries:
France, Germany, Italy, Portugal, Spain, UK. [2012/XD8951/**D**]

♦ European Federation of Organisations for Medical Physics (EFOMP) 07183

Fédération européenne des organisations de physique médicale
SG Domus Medica, Mercatorlaan 1200, 3503 RA Utrecht, Netherlands.
URL: http://www.efomp.org/
History 7 May 1980, London (UK). Set up, jointly with *European Scientific Institute (ESI, #08448)*, *European Organization for Nuclear Research (CERN, #08108)* and CEA (Paris). Registration: Chamber of Commerce, No/ID: 81359691, Start date: 1 Jan 2021, Netherlands; Companies House, No/ID: 06480149, Start date: 22 Jan 2008, End date: 2021, England. **Aims** Foster and coordinate activities of member organizations in the field of medical physics and collaborate where appropriate with national and international organizations; encourage exchange between members and disseminate professional and scientific information through publications and meetings; encourage scholarships and exchange between countries; propose guidelines for education, training and accreditation programmes; make recommendations on the appropriate general responsibilities, organizational relationships and roles of workers in the field; encourage formation of organizations for medical physics where such organizations do not exist. **Structure** Council (meets annually); Board. Advisory Committees (6): Communications and Publications; Education and Training; European Matters; Professional Matters; Project; Scientific. **Languages** English. **Staff** 5.00 FTE, voluntary. **Finance** Sources: members' dues. **Activities** Events/meetings; politics/policy/regulatory; training/education. **Events** *European Congress of Medical Physics* Munich (Germany) 2024, *European Congress of Medical Physics* Dublin (Ireland) 2022, *European Congress of Medical Physics* Turin (Italy) 2021, *European Congress of Medical Physics* Turin (Italy) 2020, *European Congress of Medical Physics* Copenhagen (Denmark) 2018. **Publications** *European Journal of Medical Physics – Physica Medica*.
Members National organizations in 36 countries:
Albania, Austria, Belgium, Bosnia-Herzegovina, Bulgaria, Croatia, Cyprus, Czechia, Denmark, Estonia, Finland, France, Germany, Greece, Hungary, Ireland, Italy, Latvia, Lithuania, Malta, Moldova, Netherlands, North Macedonia, Norway, Poland, Portugal, Romania, Russia, Serbia, Slovakia, Slovenia, Spain, Sweden, Switzerland, UK, Ukraine.
IGO Relations Participates in the work of: *United Nations Economic Commission for Europe (UNECE, #20555)*. Recognized by: *European Commission (EC, #06633)*. **NGO Relations** Member of (1): *European Alliance for Medical Radiation Protection Research (EURAMED, #05874)*. Partner of (1): *Multidisciplinary European Low Dose Initiative Association (MELODI Association, #16882)*. Shareholder in: *European Institute for Biomedical Imaging Research (EIBIR, #07546)*. [2021.02.17/XD2603/**D**]

♦ European Federation of Origin Wines (EFOW) 07184

Contact Square Ambiorix 18, 1000 Brussels, Belgium. T. +3227335058 – +3227335060. E-mail: info@efow.eu.
URL: http://www.efow.eu/
History Evolved from cooperation started 2003. Registered in accordance with Belgian law. EU Transparency Register: 93296213494-75. **Aims** Promote the interests of European wines with an appellation of origin and/or a protected geographical indication towards EU and international institutions. **Structure** General Assembly; Executive Committee. Secretariat. **Events** *European Congress of Wine Appellation* Brussels (Belgium) 2017.
Members Full in 5 countries:
France, Hungary, Italy, Portugal, Spain. [2022/XJ8991/**D**]

♦ European Federation of Orthodontics (#09811)

♦ European Federation of Orthodontic Specialists Associations (EFOSA) 07185

Fédération européenne des associations de spécialistes en orthodontie
Pres Maxillofacial Unit – Kettering Hosp, Rothwell Road, Kettering, NN16 8UZ, UK. T. +441536492361. E-mail: julizone@yahoo.co.uk.
Sec Haaleitisbraut 1, 105 Reykjavik, Iceland. T. +3545343221.
URL: http://www.efosa.eu/
History Founded 1977, France. Registered in accordance with French law. **Aims** Play an active role in realizing the recognition of the speciality of orthodontics and the establishing of a specialists register in all European Union (EU) countries; promote high quality care provided by orthodontic specialists within the EU; promote high level training of these specialists; encourage evaluation of universities and other officially recognized institutions for the training of orthodontic specialists within the EU; present the interest of these specialists within the EU and to EU authorities and provide statements on political issues and economic matters; act in the same way upon request of a national association of orthodontic specialists in the country concerned. **Structure** General Assembly (annual); Council (meets twice a year) of 5 members; Working Committees. **Languages** English. **Staff** None. **Finance** Members' dues. Other sources: subsidies; donations; income from studies. **Events** *General Assembly* Dublin (Ireland) 2026, *General Assembly* Krakow (Poland) 2025, *General Assembly* Athens (Greece) 2024, *General Assembly* Oslo (Norway) 2023, *General Assembly* Limassol (Cyprus) 2022.
Members Active organizations in 25 countries:
Belgium, Bulgaria, Croatia, Cyprus, Czechia, Denmark, Estonia, Finland, France, Germany, Greece, Iceland, Ireland, Italy, Luxembourg, Malta, Netherlands, Norway, Poland, Portugal, Slovakia, Slovenia, Sweden, Switzerland, UK.
Provisional organizations in 2 countries:
Austria, Spain.
Affiliate organizations in 2 countries:
Serbia, Türkiye. [2015.06.25/XD7117/**D**]

♦ European Federation of Osteopaths / see European Federation and Forum for Osteopathy (#07128)
♦ European Federation of Otorhinolaryngological Societies (inactive)
♦ European Federation of Outdoor Advertising / see World Out of Home Organization (#21702)
♦ European Federation of Overseas Repatriates and East-European Refugee Organizations (inactive)
♦ European Federation of Paediatric Research Societies (inactive)

♦ European Federation of Parasitologists (EFP) 07186

Fédération européenne des parasitologistes
Sec Dept of Zoology, School of Natural Sciences, Trinity College, Dublin, CO. DUBLIN, Ireland. T. +35318961096. Fax +35316778094.
URL: http://www.eurofedpar.eu/
History 14 Nov 1966, Jablonna (Poland). **Aims** Promote exchange of knowledge and cooperation of scientific research in the field of parasitology in Europe. **Structure** Executive Board, comprising President, 2 Vice-Presidents, Treasurer, General Secretary and 4 members-at-large. **Languages** English. **Staff** Part-time, voluntary. **Finance** Members' dues. **Events** *Multicolloquium of Parasitology* Belgrade (Serbia) 2021, *Multicolloquium of Parasitology* Belgrade (Serbia) 2020, *Quadrennial Multicolloquium of Parasitology* Turku (Finland) 2016, *Quadrennial multicolloquium of parasitology / European Multicolloquium of Parasitology* Cluj-Napoca (Romania) 2012, *Quadrennial multicolloquium / European Multicolloquium of Parasitology* Paris (France) 2008.
Members National societies of 27 countries:
Armenia, Austria, Belarus, Belgium, Bulgaria, Czechia, Denmark, Estonia, France, Georgia, Germany, Greece, Hungary, Ireland, Israel, Italy, Netherlands, Poland, Romania, Russia, Serbia, Slovakia, Spain, Switzerland, Türkiye, UK, Ukraine.
Also members in Scandinavian, Baltic, South Eastern and Eastern European countries. Membership countries not specified.
Included in the above, 2 organizations listed in this Yearbook:
Scandinavian-Baltic Society for Parasitology (SBSP, #19081); *Southeastern and Eastern European Parasitologists (SEEEP, #19803)*.
Associate members in 4 countries:
Algeria, Egypt, Iran Islamic Rep, Pakistan.
NGO Relations Member of: *World Federation of Parasitologists (WFP, #21471)*. [2015.11.05/XD1140/y/**D**]

♦ European Federation of Parents and Carers at home (#09568)
♦ European Federation of Parents of Hearing Impaired Children (#09577)

♦ European Federation of Parquet Importers (EFPI) 07187

SG Rue du Luxembourg 22-24, 1000 Brussels, Belgium. T. +3222777 0518. Fax +3227770527.
History Jun 2005, by 8 founding members. **Aims** Facilitate discussion of ideas among parquet importers about the promotion of wood flooring in Europe; share information about EU legislation, standardization and issues concerning international trade for the parquet industry. **Activities** Defines, promotes and represents the industry of parquet importers in Europe; provides a European voice for the industry; works to increase awareness of legislative issues concerning parquet imports at European level and making it an issue of EU concern and action; encourages and develops common definitions and establishes guidelines and standards for the industry; encourages input in appropriate standard bodies and other relevant fora; provides a forum for discussion for issues of industry concern; collates and distributes statistical information and data on the industry.
Members Importers (7) of engineered and solid wood flooring in 5 countries:
Germany, Netherlands, Norway, Spain, UK.
Included in the above, 1 organization listed in this Yearbook:
Global Flooring Alliance (GFA, #10362).
NGO Relations Associate member of: *European Timber Trade Federation (ETTF, #08915)*.
[2011.06.24/XJ1109/y/**D**]

♦ European Federation of the Parquet Industry (FEP) 07188

Fédération Européenne de l'Industrie du Parquet – Föderation der Europäischen Parkett-Industrie
Managing Dir Rue Montoyer 24, box 20, 1000 Brussels, Belgium. T. +3222870877. E-mail: info@parquet.net.
URL: http://www.parquet.net/
History 13 Apr 1956, Wiesbaden (Germany). Former names and other names: *European Federation of Associations of the Parquet Industry (FEP)* – former (13 Apr 1956); *Fédération européenne des syndicats de fabricants de parquets* – former (13 Apr 1956); *Föderation der Europäischen Parkett-Industrie-Verbände* – former (13 Apr 1956). Registration: EU Transparency Register, No/ID: 294492727880-53. **Aims** Unite European parquet manufacturers, national parquet associations and suppliers to the industry; represent and defend their interests. **Structure** General Assembly; Board. **Languages** English. **Staff** 1.00 FTE, paid. **Finance** Sources: members' dues. **Activities** Events/meetings. **Events** *Congress* Hamburg (Germany) 2022, *General Assembly* 2021, *Congress* Athens (Greece) 2021, *General Assembly* 2020, *Congress* Lisbon (Portugal) 2019. **Publications** *FEP News* (6 a year) – for members only. *FEP Statistics*.
Members Parquet Manufacturers; national federations; supplying companies. Members in 21 countries:
Austria, Belgium, Canada, Croatia, Denmark, Estonia, Finland, France, Germany, Hungary, Italy, Latvia, Lithuania, Netherlands, Poland, Portugal, Russia, Spain, Sweden, Switzerland, Türkiye.
IGO Relations Accredited by (1): *European Commission (EC, #06633)*. **NGO Relations** In liaison with technical committees of: *International Organization for Standardization (ISO, #14473)*. [2022.05.11/XD5573/t/**D**]

♦ European Federation of Patients' Associations for Anthroposophic Medicine (EFPAM) 07189

Fédération européenne des associations de patients pour la médecine anthroposophique
Pres Sweelinckiaan 2, 6815 BH Leidschendam, Netherlands. E-mail: efpam.europe@gmail.com.
URL: http://www.efpam.eu/
History 3 Oct 2000, Dornach (Switzerland). Previously registered in Alsace (France). Registration: Kamer van Koophandel, No/ID: 76275841, Netherlands; EU Transparency Register, No/ID: 28735567576-83, Start date: 3 Jan 2012. **Aims** Represent views and interests of those using anthroposophic medicine, in particular in the light of the individual right to self-determination. **Structure** General Meeting (annual); Board. **Languages** English. **Staff** 1.50 FTE, voluntary. **Finance** Sources: contributions; gifts, legacies. Annual budget: 6,000 EUR (2020). **Activities** Awareness raising; knowledge management/information dissemination; projects/programmes; research/documentation. **Publications** *EFPAM Newsletter* (irregular).
Members Associations in 14 countries:
Austria, Belgium, Czechia, Finland, France, Germany, Iceland, Netherlands, Norway, Romania, Spain, Sweden, Switzerland, UK.
NGO Relations Member of (3): *Alliance ELIANT (#00672)*; *EUROCAM (#05653)*; *European Public Health Alliance (EPHA, #08297)*. [2021.09.06/XM0584/**D**]

♦ European Federation of Perfumery Retailers / see European Federation of Retail Perfumers (#07206)

♦ European Federation of Periodontology (EFP) 07190

Fédération européenne de parodontologie
Main Office Antonio Lopez Aguado 4, bajo dcha, 28029 Madrid, Spain. T. +34913142715. Fax +34913235745.
Pres address not obtained.
URL: http://www.efp.org/
History 1987, as a coordinating committee. Constitution: adopted 12 Dec 1991, when formally renamed; amended 7 Dec 1996. **Aims** Promote and monitor periodontal health in Europe; recommend and encourage adherence to minimum standards of theoretical and clinical professional periodontal education for dentists and dental hygienists; define a formal graduate specialty programme and a standardized European accreditation system, leading to quality standardization; promote and coordinate research on health and treatment needs in different countries and the impact on them of dental care systems; promote inter-professional relations in continuing education and research; establish guidelines for approval of relevant product safety and efficacy; advise governmental and nongovernmental bodies. **Structure** General Assembly (annual); Executive Committee. **Languages** English. **Staff** 1.50 FTE, paid. **Finance** Members' dues. **Activities** Events/meetings; knowledge management/information dissemination. **Events** *Triennial Congress* Copenhagen (Denmark) 2022, *Triennial Congress* Copenhagen (Denmark) 2021, *General Assembly* Pisa (Italy) 2020, *Triennial Congress* Amsterdam (Netherlands) 2018, *General Assembly* Vienna (Austria) 2018. **Publications** *EFP Newsletter* (2 a year); *Journal of Clinical Periodontology*.
Members Full; Associate. National societies in 29 countries:

Austria, Belgium, Croatia, Czechia, Denmark, Finland, France, Germany, Greece, Hungary, Ireland, Israel, Italy, Lithuania, Montenegro, Morocco, Netherlands, Norway, Poland, Portugal, Romania, Serbia, Slovenia, Spain, Sweden, Switzerland, Türkiye, UK, Ukraine.
NGO Relations Associate member of: *Platform for Better Oral Health in Europe (#18399).* [2020/XD4085/D]

♦ European Federation of Pharmaceutical Industries and Associations (EFPIA) 07191

Fédération européenne d'associations et d'industries pharmaceutiques

Dir Gen Leopold Plaza Bldg, Rue du Trône 108, 1050 Brussels, Belgium. T. +3226262555. Fax +3226262566. E-mail: reception@efpia.eu – communications@efpia.eu – info@efpia.eu.
Japan Office GSK Building, 6-15 Sendagaya 4-chome, Shibuyaku, Tokyo, 151-8566 Japan.
URL: http://www.efpia.eu/

History 1978. Includes activities of the previous *Pharmaceutical Industries' Association in the EFTA (PIA, inactive)*, set up 16 Oct 1959, Zurich (Switzerland). Most recent statutes adopted 20 Nov 1997. Registration: Banque-Carrefour des Entreprises, No/ID: 0418.762.559, Start date: 20 Sep 1978; EU Transparency Register, No/ID: 38526121292-88, Start date: 4 Mar 2009. **Aims** Promote pharmaceutical research and development in order to bring new medicines onto the market in the interest of patients and human health worldwide; foster a favourable policy climate that enables the pharmaceutical industry in Europe to meet growing high-quality health care expectations of present and future generations; contribute to the strength of EU economy and social well-being of its citizens. **Structure** General Assembly (annual); Board; Bureau; Policy Committees (4); Secretariat, headed by Director-General. Specialized group: *Vaccines Europe (VE, #20741).* **Languages** English, French. **Staff** 49.00 FTE, paid. **Finance** Sources: members' dues. **Activities** Events/meetings. Projects include: *Innovative Medicines Initiative (IMI, #11221).* **Events** *Enhancing Patient-Centric Outcome Measures and Clinical Trials with Digital Health Technologies* Brussels (Belgium) 2022, *European Health Summit* Brussels (Belgium) 2022, *From Unmet Medical Needs to Solutions* Brussels (Belgium) 2022, *From Crisis to Catalyst – Build Resilience, Back Innovation and Boost Access* Brussels (Belgium) 2022, *The Women's Brain Project* Brussels (Belgium) 2022. **Publications** *Pharmaceutical Industry in Figures* (2009); *Clinical Trials with Medicines in Europe.* Annual report; conference proceedings; economic surveys; press releases; position papers.
Members National associations (33); pharmaceutical companies (40). Full in 19 countries:
Austria, Belgium, Denmark, Finland, France, Germany, Greece, Ireland, Italy, Netherlands, Norway, Poland, Portugal, Russia, Spain, Sweden, Switzerland, Türkiye, UK.
Affiliate in 13 countries:
Bulgaria, Croatia, Cyprus, Czechia, Estonia, Hungary, Latvia, Lithuania, Malta, Romania, Serbia, Slovenia, Ukraine.
Consultative Status Consultative status granted from: *World Intellectual Property Organization (WIPO, #21593)* (Permanent Observer Status). **IGO Relations** Recognized by: *European Commission (EC, #06633).* Cooperates with: *European Union Intellectual Property Office (EUIPO, #08996).* **NGO Relations** Member of (5): *EU Health Coalition*; *European Alliance for Cardiovascular Health (EACH, #05863)*; *European Medicines Verification Organisation (EMVO, #07768)* (Founding); *Industry4Europe (#11181)*; *International Council on Harmonisation of Technical Requirements for Registration of Pharmaceuticals for Human Use (ICH, #13027).* [2022/XD6546/t/D]

♦ European Federation for Pharmaceutical Sciences (EUFEPS) 07192

Office and Promotion Manager Varrentrappstr 40-42, 60486 Frankfurt-Main, Germany. T. +4969719159620.
Pres address not obtained.
URL: http://www.eufeps.org/

History Founded 1991. **Aims** Support and advance pharmaceutical sciences and innovative drug research in Europe; represent scientific interests and scientists within academia, industry, government, private and public institutions engaged in drug research, development, regulation and policy making. **Structure** Council (meets annually); Executive Committee; Networks (7). **Languages** English. **Staff** 0.50 FTE, paid. **Finance** Members' dues. Income from meetings. **Activities** Advocacy/lobbying/activism; awards/prizes/competitions; events/meetings. **Events** *European Conference on Process Analytics and Control Technology* Copenhagen (Denmark) 2021, *European Conference on Process Analytics and Control Technology* Copenhagen (Denmark) 2020, *Annual Meeting* Frankfurt-Main (Germany) 2019, *Annual Meeting* Athens (Greece) 2018, *EuPAT : Pan-European Science Conference on QbD and PAT Sciences* Manchester (UK) 2018. **Publications** *European Journal of Pharmaceutical Sciences (EJPS)* (15 a year).
Members Societies; individuals. Societies (17) in 17 countries:
Austria, Croatia, Czechia, Denmark, Finland, Germany, Greece, Hungary, Kosovo, Netherlands, Poland, Romania, Slovenia, Spain, Sweden, Switzerland, Türkiye.
NGO Relations Liaison observers include: *'American Association of Pharmaceutical Scientists (AAPS)'*; *European Association for Clinical Pharmacology and Therapeutics (EACPT, #05977)*; *European Association of Faculties of Pharmacy (EAFP, #06036)*; *European Pharmaceutical Students' Association (EPSA, #08197).* Member of: *International Pharmaceutical Federation (#14566).* Associated with: *European Federation for Medicinal Chemistry (EFMC, #07165).* [2020/XD3989/D]

♦ European Federation of Pharmacologists / see Federation of European Pharmacological Societies (#09527)
♦ European Federation for Physical Medicine and Rehabilitation / see European Society of Physical and Rehabilitation Medicine (#08706)
♦ European Federation of Plastic Films Producers (inactive)
♦ European Federation of the Plywood Industry (inactive)
♦ European Federation for Precast Concrete / see Bureau international du béton manufacturé (#03363)

♦ European Federation of Precision Mechanical and Optical Industries (EUROM) 07193

Fédération européenne de l'industrie de l'optique et de la mécanique de précision – Federación Europea de la Industria Optica y de la Mecanica de Precisión – Europäische Industrievereinigung Feinmechanik und Optik – Federação Europeia da Indústria Optica e da Mecânica da Precisão – Federazione Europea dell'Industria dell'Ottica e della Meccanica di Precisione – Europese Federatie van Optische en Fijnmechanische Industrie – Europeiska Vörbundet av Industri Optik och Fin Mekanik – Sammenslutningen af Europaeiske Producenter af Optik og Finmekanik – Euroopan, Tarkkuus – ja Optiikkateollisuuden Yhdistys

SG c/o SPECTARIS eV, Werderscher Markt 15, 10117 Berlin, Germany. T. +4930414021 ext 67.
URL: http://www.eurom.org/

History 1958, Brussels (Belgium). Founded shortly after establishment of the European Community. Former names and other names: *European Photographic Manufacturers' Association* – former (1958). Registration: EU Transparency Register, No/ID: 585778511937-68. **Aims** Represent the interests of manufacturers in the European precision mechanical and optical industries in dealings with the EU Commission and other European, national and international institutions. **Structure** Active Branch Committees (3): EUROM I Optical Industries; EUROM II Optics, Laser & Laboratory Technology; EUROM VI Medical Technology. **Languages** English, German. **Activities** Advocacy/lobbying/activism; knowledge management/information dissemination; politics/policy/regulatory; research and development. **Events** *General Assembly Web Conference* Berlin (Germany) 2021, *General Assembly Web Conference* Berlin (Germany) 2020, *General Assembly* Berlin (Germany) 2019, *General Assembly* Barcelona (Spain) 2015, *Annual Meeting* Paris (France) 2015.
Members Professional organizations which represent the precision mechanical and optical industries in their respective countries and their member companies. European trade associations are responsible for determining, coordinating and representing the interests of their members dealings with third parties. Members in 11 countries:
Belgium, Denmark, France, Germany, Ireland, Italy, Luxembourg, Netherlands, Spain, Switzerland, UK. [2021/XD0367/t/D]

♦ European Federation of Press Clubs (EFPC) 07194

Fédération européenne des press clubs

Dir Press Club de France, Tour Sequana, 82 rue Henri Farman, 92130 Issy-les-Moulineaux, France. T. +33141337307.
URL: http://www.pressclub.fr/federation-europeenne/

History 1989, by the Press Club de France. Original title: *European Federation of Press Clubs and International Press Centres – Fédération européenne des press clubs et centres internationaux de presse.* **Aims** Foster dialogue, collaboration and experiences exchange between press clubs and international press centres; defend freedom of press. **Structure** General Assembly (annual); Bureau; Board of Directors; rotating Presidency. **Languages** English, French. **Finance** Members' dues. **Events** *General Assembly* Lille (France) 2018, *General Assembly* Milan (Italy) 2015, *General Assembly* Jerusalem (Israel) 2014, *Annual meeting* Antwerp (Belgium) 2005.
Members Clubs and centres in 22 countries:
Austria, Belarus, Belgium, France, Germany, India, Indonesia, Israel, Italy, Japan, Korea Rep, Malaysia, Mongolia, Nepal, New Zealand, Poland, Portugal, Singapore, Spain, Switzerland, Thailand, UK.
NGO Relations Member of: *International Association of Press Clubs (IAPC, #12099).* [2020.03.03/XJ4360/D]

♦ European Federation of Press Clubs and International Press Centres / see European Federation of Press Clubs (#07194)

♦ European Federation for Primatology (EFP) 07195

SG Inst Superiore di Sanità, Via le Regina Elena 299, 00161 Rome RM, Italy. Fax +3964957821.
URL: http://www.unipv.it/webbio/efp/efp.htm

History 17 Dec 1993, Strasbourg (France). EU Transparency Register: 675639823872-43. **Aims** Coordinate actions related to primatology between European societies; promote rational management of captive primates and make primate subjects and study sites available to a maximum of students and researchers; provide expertise on all issues related to primatology and participate in decisions relevant to primate trade and captive breeding; promote the establishment of national and European societies of primatologists. **Structure** Executive Council (meets annual). Officers: President; Secretary; Treasurer. **Languages** English. **Staff** None. **Finance** Members' dues. Gifts; donations; funds. Annual budget: about euro 16,000. **Activities** Organizes: annual workshop; international meetings. **Events** *Our primate heritage, our primate legacy* Oxford (UK) 2019, *Our primate heritage, our primate legacy* Strasbourg (France) 2017, *Congress* Rome (Italy) 2015, *Congress* Antwerp (Belgium) 2013, *Congress* Almada (Portugal) 2011. **Publications** *Folia Primatologica* – journal.
Members National societies and groups in 11 countries:
Belgium, Czechia, France, Germany, Italy, Netherlands, Portugal, Russia, Spain, Switzerland, UK.
IGO Relations Observer to: *European Convention for the Protection of Vertebrate Animals Used for Experimental and other Scientific Purposes (1986).* **NGO Relations** Member of: *International Primatological Society (IPS, #14642).* [2019/XD7016/D]

♦ European Federation for Print and Digital Communication / see Intergraf (#11505)
♦ European Federation of Private Schools / see Federation for EDucation in Europe (#09479)
♦ European Federation of Producers and Applicators of Specialist Products for Structures / see Experts for Specialised Construction and Concrete Systems (#09226)

♦ European Federation of Productivity Services (EFPS) 07196

Fédération européenne pour l'accroissement de la productivité – Europäischer Verband für Produktivitätsförderung – Federazione Europea dei Servizi di Produzione – Europese Federatie voor de Bevordering van de Produktiviteit – Európska Federacia pre Rozvoj Produktivity – Comhnascas Eorpach der Sheirbhisi Tairgióchta

Exec Sec c/o Deutsche MTM-Vereinigung e V, Elbchaussee 352, 22609 Hamburg, Germany. T. +4940822779-0.
URL: http://www.efps.ac/

History 16 Jun 1961, Heidelberg (Germany). Former names and other names: *European Work Study Federation (EWSF)* – former (1961 to 1970); *Fédération européenne pour l'étude du travail* – former (1961 to 1970); *Federación Europea para el Estudio del Trabajo* – former (1961 to 1970); *Europäischer Verband für Arbeitsstudien* – former (1961 to 1970). Registration: Germany, Hamburg; Start date: 1984, Switzerland; Netherlands. **Aims** Promote knowledge of productivity services applications throughout Europe; stimulate and support development of the practice and techniques of industrial and commercial productivity and efficiency as applied by members. **Structure** Board (elected). Functional Coordinators (appointed) for each of 5 functional areas: work and pay; work organization and job design; work measurement; productivity management; membership activities. *European Institute of Industrial Engineers (EIIE).* **Languages** English. **Staff** 3 part-time partly paid. **Finance** Members' dues. **Activities** Organizes seminars, experience exchanges, surveys, conferences. **Events** *International work and pay conference* 1991, *Conference* San Francisco, CA (USA) 1990, *Conference* The Hague (Netherlands) 1988, *International work and pay conference* The Hague (Netherlands) 1988, *Congress on productivity and the future of work* Munich (Germany FR) 1986. **Publications** *EFPS Newsletter* (2 a year). Surveys, study reports, conference proceedings.
Members Organizations in 11 countries:
Austria, Finland, Germany, Ireland, Italy, Netherlands, Norway, Poland, Sweden, Switzerland, UK.
Corresponding members (organizations) in 2 countries:
Japan, USA. [2019/XD0906/D]

♦ European Federation of Professional Circus Schools (#09565)
♦ European Federation of Professional Florists Associations / see International Florist Organisation (#13616)
♦ European Federation of Professional Psychologists Associations / see European Federation of Psychologists Associations (#07199)
♦ European Federation of the Professions of the Performing Arts (inactive)
♦ European Federation for the Promotion of Procurement Contracts – Textiles and Leather (inactive)
♦ European Federation for the Protection of Waters (inactive)

♦ European Federation of Psychiatric Trainees (EFPT) 07197

Pres EFPT Secretariat, Av de la Couronne 20, 1050 Brussels, Belgium. E-mail: president@efpt.eu.
SG address not obtained. E-mail: secretary@efpt.eu.
URL: http://www.efpt.eu/

History Jun 1992, London (UK). Formally set up Mar 1993, Utrecht (Netherlands). Constitution signed, 26 Feb 2010, Brussels (Belgium). Registered in accordance with Belgian law. **Aims** Enhance and harmonize standards of psychiatric education and training across Europe by working in partnership with relevant international and/or national bodies; promote creation of national trainee associations in all European countries. **Structure** General Assembly (annual); Board of Directors. **Activities** Events/meetings; awards/prizes/competitions; networking/liaising. **Events** *Forum* Brussels (Belgium) 2021, *Forum* Antwerp (Belgium) 2016, *Forum* Porto (Portugal) 2015, *Forum* London (UK) 2014, *Forum* Zurich (Switzerland) 2013. **Members** Full (37); Observer (5). Membership countries not specified. **NGO Relations** Affiliate member of: *World Psychiatric Association (WPA, #21741).* [2018.10.06/XJ7049/D]

♦ European Federation of Psychoanalysis and Psychoanalytical Schools of Strasbourg (internationally oriented national body)

♦ European Federation for Psychoanalytic Psychotherapy (EFPP) 07198

Sec address not obtained. E-mail: info@efpp.org.
URL: http://www.efpp.org/

History 1991, London (UK). Also referred to as *European Federation for Psychoanalytic Psychotherapy in the Public Sector.* Registered in UK. **Aims** Promote the development of adult, child, adolescent, couple, family and group psychoanalytic psychotherapy, especially in public sector mental health services. **Structure** General Meeting (every 2 years). Executive Committee, consisting of 9 members (3 delegates per section). Sections (3): Individual Adult Psychoanalytic Psychotherapy; Child and Adolescent Psychoanalytic Psychotherapy; Group Psychoanalytic Psychotherapy. **Languages** English. **Staff** 1.00 FTE, paid. **Finance** Members' subscriptions. **Activities** Meeting activities; research/documentation. **Events** *Conference* Copenhagen (Denmark) 2007, *International conference on child analysis* St Petersburg (Russia) 2007, *European conference* Lisbon (Portugal) 2004, *English-speaking conference* London (UK) 2004, *Meeting* Stockholm (Sweden) 2003. **Publications** Series of books on psychoanaltic psychotherapy.
Members National networks in 26 countries:
Austria, Belgium, Cyprus, Czechia, Denmark, Finland, France, Germany, Greece, Iceland, Ireland, Israel, Italy, Latvia, Lithuania, Luxembourg, Netherlands, Norway, Poland, Portugal, Romania, Russia, Spain, Sweden, Switzerland, UK.
NGO Relations Member of: *European Association for Psychotherapy (EAP, #06176).* [2020/XD3877/D]

♦ European Federation for Psychoanalytic Psychotherapy in the Public Sector / see European Federation for Psychoanalytic Psychotherapy (#07198)
♦ European Federation of Psychoanalytic Self-Psychology (no recent information)

♦ European Federation of Psychologists Associations (EFPA) 07199

Fédération européenne des associations de psychologues (FEAP) – Europäische Föderation der Psychologenverbände (EFP) – Europese Federatie van Psychologen Associaties

Dir Marché aux Herbes 105/39, 1000 Brussels, Belgium. T. +3225034953. Fax +3225033067. E-mail: headoffice@efpa.eu.
URL: http://www.efpa.eu/

History 12 Sep 1981, Heidelberg (Germany). Founded when statutes were adopted. Current statutes adopted Jul 1997. Former names and other names: *European Federation of Professional Psychologists Associations (EFPPA)* – former; *Europäische Föderation der Berufsverbände von Psychologen (EFBP)* – former. Registration: Banque-Carrefour des Entreprises, No/ID: 0478.487.736, Start date: 29 Mar 2002, Belgium; EU Transparency Register, No/ID: 513145143460-77, Start date: 27 Jul 2021. **Aims** Promote communication and cooperation between member associations and contribute to their development; further establishment of ethical codes of practice for psychologists; promote furtherance of psychology and its application; support member associations in promoting the interest of psychology within their own countries; facilitate contacts with international bodies of psychology; promote development of professional psychology. **Structure** General Assembly (every 2 years); Executive Council. President's Council, consisting of Presidents of member associations. Standing Committees (4); Task Forces (3); Working Groups (7). **Languages** English. **Staff** 1.50 FTE, paid. **Finance** Sources: members' dues. **Activities** Knowledge management/information dissemination; monitoring/evaluation; standards/guidelines; events/meetings; awards/prizes/committees. **Events** *European Congress of Psychology* Brighton (UK) 2023, *European Congress of Psychology* Ljubljana (Slovenia) 2022, *European Congress of Psychology* Ljubljana (Slovenia) 2021, *European Conference on Community Psychology* Oslo (Norway) 2021, *Biennial Congress* Moscow (Russia) 2019. **Publications** Online newsletter; booklets; reports of Standing Committees and Task Forces.
Members Associations of psychologists (representing about 200,000 psychologists) in 36 European countries:
Austria, Belgium, Bulgaria, Croatia, Cyprus, Czechia, Denmark, Estonia, Finland, France, Germany, Greece, Hungary, Iceland, Ireland, Italy, Latvia, Liechtenstein, Lithuania, Luxembourg, Malta, Netherlands, Norway, Poland, Portugal, Romania, Russia, San Marino, Serbia, Slovakia, Slovenia, Spain, Sweden, Switzerland, Türkiye, UK.
Associate members (11):
EMDR Europe Association (#05435); European Association for Aviation Psychology (EAAP, #05950); European Association of Developmental Psychology (EADP, #06010); European Association of Personality Psychology (EAPP, #06149); European Association of Psychological Assessment (EAPA, #06172); European Association of Work and Organizational Psychology (EAWOP, #06278); European Community Psychology Association (ECPA, #06682); European Federation of Sport Psychology (#07218); European Society for Traumatic Stress Studies (ESTSS, #08769); EUROPLAT – European Psychology leaning and teaching Network; *Federation of the European Societies of Neuropsychology (ESN, #09547).*
Affiliate members (2):
European Federation of Psychology Students' Associations (EFPSA, #07200); European Federation of Psychology Teachers' Association (EFPTA, #07201).
Consultative Status Consultative status granted from: *ECOSOC (#05331)* (Special). **IGO Relations** *WHO Regional Office for Europe (#20945).* **NGO Relations** Member of (2): *European Council of Liberal Professions (#06828); Federation of European and International Associations Established in Belgium (FAIB, #09508).* Instrumental in setting up (1): *European Society of Psychology Learning and Teaching (ESPLAT, #08717).*
[2021/XD0722/y/**D**]

♦ European Federation of Psychology Students' Associations (EFPSA) 07200

Fédération européenne des associations d'étudiants en psychologie (FEAEP)

SG address not obtained. E-mail: contact@efpsa.org – secretary@efpsa.org.
Pres address not obtained. E-mail: president@efpsa.org.
URL: http://www.efpsa.org/

History Apr 1987, Lisbon (Portugal). First statutes adopted, Apr 1988, Liège (Belgium). Registration: Start date: Jan 1989, Belgium. **Aims** Bring together psychology students on a European level to enrich their concept and application of psychology and encourage skill development to contribute to improvement in the field. **Structure** General Assembly (annual); Board of Management; Task Forces. **Languages** English, French. **Staff** Voluntary. **Finance** Sources: donations; grants; members' dues; sponsorship. **Activities** Projects/programmes; publishing activities; training/education. **Events** *Annual Congress* Amsterdam (Netherlands) 2021, *Annual Congress* Castlebar (Ireland) 2020, *Annual Congress* Grenaa (Denmark) 2019, *Annual Congress* Mellieha (Malta) 2018, *Overcoming divisions, broadening psychology* Sarajevo (Bosnia-Herzegovina) 2017. **Publications** *The Journal of European Psychology Students (JEPS).*
Members Organisations in 33 countries:
Albania, Austria, Azerbaijan, Belgium, Bosnia-Herzegovina, Croatia, Cyprus, Czechia, Denmark, Estonia, Finland, Germany, Greece, Hungary, Ireland, Kosovo, Lithuania, Luxembourg, Malta, Netherlands, North Macedonia, Norway, Poland, Portugal, Romania, Serbia, Slovakia, Slovenia, Spain, Sweden, Switzerland, Türkiye, UK.
Observer organization in 3 countries and territories:
Belgium/Flemish Region, France, Italy.
IGO Relations None. **NGO Relations** Member of (1): *The Right to Research Coalition (no recent information).* Partner of (3): *European Medical Students' Association (EMSA, #07764); Informal Forum of International Student Organizations (IFISO, #11193); International Association of Applied Psychology (IAAP, #11705).* Affiliated with (1): *European Federation of Psychologists Associations (EFPA, #07199).* [2021/XD1699/**D**]

♦ European Federation of Psychology Teachers' Association (EFPTA) . 07201

Sec address not obtained.
Pres address not obtained.
URL: http://www.efpta.org/

History Mar 2004, Helsinki (Finland). **Structure** Board, comprising President, Vice-President, Secretary, Treasurer, 2 Advisors, Newsletter Editor and 7 members. **Events** *Conference* Berlin (Germany) 2014, *Conference* Copenhagen (Denmark) 2012, *Conference* Bratislava (Slovakia) 2010, *Conference* Edinburgh (UK) 2009, *Conference* Cardiff (UK) 2008. **Publications** *EFPTA Newsletter.*
Members Associations in 6 countries and territories:
Denmark, England, Finland, Germany, Iceland, Scotland.
Individuals and Affiliate organizations in 4 countries:
Netherlands, Russia, Slovakia, Spain.
NGO Relations Affiliate of: *European Federation of Psychologists Associations (EFPA, #07199).*
[2015/XJ6130/**D**]

♦ European Federation of Psychosocial Oncology Societies (inactive)

♦ European Federation of Public Service Unions (EPSU) 07202

Fédération syndicale européenne des services publics (FSESP) – Federación Sindical Europea de Servicios Públicos – Europäischer Gewerkschaftsverband für den Öffentlichen Dienst (EGÖD) – Europeiska Federationen för Offentligaställdas Förbund

Gen Sec Rue Joseph II 40/5, 1000 Brussels, Belgium. T. +3222501080. Fax +3222501099. E-mail: epsu@epsu.org.
URL: http://www.epsu.org/

History 1978. Founded as *European Public Services Committee (EPSC) – Comité syndical européen des services publics (CSESP) – Comité Sindical Europeo de Servicios Públicos – Europäischer Gewerkschaftsausschuss Öffentlichen Dienst – Europeiska Kommittén för Offentliga Tjänster.* Current title adopted 1996. Current constitution adopted at 8th Congress, Jun 2009, Brussels (Belgium). Since 1 Jan 2010, merged with European branch of *Public Services International (PSI, #18572)*, and thus functions as its regional federation. Registration: EU Transparency Register, No/ID: 04902121531-04, Start date: 16 Apr 2009. **Aims** Coordinate activities of affiliated trade unions, work for attainment of equal rights and opportunities and promote representation of common interests in the fields of economic and social policy within European institutions; promote solidarity and understanding among all European public service trade union organizations; develop appropriate industrial relations systems for public service employees and negotiate agreements at a European level; assist trade unions in applicant countries in the EU enlargement process. **Structure** Congress (every 5 years); Executive Committee; Standing Committees (5); Secretariat. **Languages** English, French, German, Italian, Russian, Spanish, Swedish. **Staff** 20.00 FTE, paid. **Finance** Members' dues. **Activities** Advocacy/lobbying/activism; events/meetings. **Events** *Firefighters Network Meeting* Brussels (Belgium) 2022, *Health and Social Care Pan European Conference* Brussels (Belgium) 2022, *Joint Seminar on Digital Health Transformation of Integrated Care in Europe* Brussels (Belgium) 2022, *Joint Seminar on Preventing Damage to the Mental Heatlh if Health and Care Workers* Brussels (Belgium) 2022, *Pan-European Conference on Public Utilities* Brussels (Belgium) 2022. **Publications** *EPSU Directory.* Annual Report.
Members Public service trade unions in 49 countries:
Albania, Armenia, Austria, Azerbaijan, Belarus, Belgium, Bosnia-Herzegovina, Bulgaria, Croatia, Cyprus, Czechia, Denmark, Estonia, Finland, France, Georgia, Germany, Greece, Hungary, Iceland, Ireland, Israel, Italy, Kazakhstan, Kosovo, Kyrgyzstan, Latvia, Lithuania, Luxembourg, Malta, Moldova, Montenegro, Netherlands, North Macedonia, Norway, Poland, Portugal, Romania, Russia, Serbia, Slovakia, Slovenia, Spain, Sweden, Switzerland, Tajikistan, Türkiye, UK, Ukraine.
IGO Relations Member of: *European Economic and Social Committee (EESC, #06963).* Participant in Fundamental Rights Platform of: *European Union Agency for Fundamental Rights (FRA, #08969).* **NGO Relations** A trade union federation of: *European Trade Union Confederation (ETUC, #08927).* Signatory to Founding Statement of: *Alliance for Lobbying Transparency and Ethics Regulation (ALTER-EU, #00705).* Working relations with: *Union of the Electricity Industry – Eurelectric (#20379).* Member of: *EU Alliance for a democratic, social and sustainable European Semester (EU Semester Alliance, #05565); Spring Alliance (inactive); Public Services International (PSI, #18572).* Signatory to: *Alter Summit.* [2020/XE1598/y/**D**]

♦ European Federation of Purchasing (inactive)

♦ European Federation of Radiographer Societies (EFRS) 07203

Contact Rua Marechal Teixeira Rebelo 425, 5030-058 Cumieira, Portugal. E-mail: info@efrs.eu.
URL: http://www.efrs.eu/

History 2008. Founded by 26 Radiographer societies from 23 European countries. **Aims** Represent, promote and develop the profession of radiography in Europe, within the whole range of *medical* imaging, nuclear medicine and radiotherapy and moreover everything that is directly or indirectly related or beneficial to this role. **Structure** General Assembly; Executive Board; Advisory Committee; Expert Committees; Radiographer Expert Network; Project Groups. **Languages** English. **Staff** 2.00 FTE, voluntary. **Finance** Sources: members' dues; revenue from activities/projects. Annual budget: 80,000 EUR (2020). **Activities** Events/meetings. Active in all member countries. **Events** *Annual General Meeting* Helsinki (Finland) 2022, *Annual General Meeting* 2021, *Annual General Meeting* 2021, *Annual General Meeting* Riga (Latvia) 2019, *Annual General Meeting* Remscheid (Germany) 2018. **Publications** *Radiography.*
Members Professional societies (45) and universities of applied science (62) in 35 countries:
Austria, Belgium, Bosnia-Herzegovina, Bulgaria, Croatia, Cyprus, Czechia, Denmark, Estonia, Finland, France, Germany, Greece, Hungary, Iceland, Ireland, Italy, Latvia, Lithuania, Luxembourg, Malta, Netherlands, North Macedonia, Norway, Poland, Portugal, Russia, Serbia, Slovakia, Slovenia, Spain, Sweden, Switzerland, Türkiye, UK.
IGO Relations *European Commission (EC, #06633); International Atomic Energy Agency (IAEA, #12294); ILO (#11123); WHO (#20950).* **NGO Relations** Partner of (2): *European Alliance for Medical Radiation Protection Research (EURAMED, #05874); Multidisciplinary European Low Dose Initiative Association (MELODI Association, #16882). Cardiovascular and Interventional Radiological Society of Europe (CIRSE, #03427); European ALARA Network (EAN, #05855); European Association of Energy Service Companies (eu.ESCO, #06027); European Association of Nuclear Medicine (EANM, #06136); European Coordination Committee of the Radiological, Electromedical Healthcare IT Industry (COCIR, #06792); European Federation of Organisations for Medical Physics (EFOMP, #07183); European Society of Magnetic Resonance in Medicine and Biology (ESMRMB, #08644); European Society of Radiology (ESR, #08720); Heads of the European Radiological Protection Competent Authorities (HERCA, #10866); International Society of Radiographers and Radiological Technologists (ISRRT, #15410).* [2021/XM6524/**D**]

♦ European Federation of Radio Operated Model Automobiles (EFRA) 07204

Sec Herentalsesteenweg 20, 2220 Heist-op-den-Berg, Belgium. E-mail: secretary@efra.ws.
URL: http://www.efra.ws/

Aims Promote international friendship and cooperation through construction, competition and *sport* of radio-operated model automobiles. **Structure** Annual General Meeting; Board. **Languages** English. **Activities** Sporting activities.
Members Federations in 30 countries:
Austria, Belarus, Belgium, Bulgaria, Croatia, Czechia, Denmark, Estonia, Finland, France, Germany, Greece, Hungary, Ireland, Italy, Luxembourg, Monaco, Netherlands, Norway, Poland, Portugal, Romania, Russia, Slovakia, Slovenia, Spain, Sweden, Switzerland, Türkiye, UK.
NGO Relations Member of (1): *International Federation of Model Auto Racing (IFMAR, #13479).*
[2023.02.14/XM5259/**D**]

♦ European Federation of Railway Trackworks Contractors (EFRTC) . 07205

Fédération européenne des entreprises de travaux de voie

SG FNTP/SETVF, 9 rue de Berri, 75008 Paris, France. T. +33144133196.
Registered Office 2 rue Eucosider, L-4714 Pétange, Luxembourg.

History 1997. **Aims** Promote liberalization of European market for track construction, renewal and maintenance; support harmonization of rules and regulations in technology, safety and operation; achieve cross-acceptance of track machinery, staff and works as a key barrier for further market opening; support technical innovations and improvements in safety, quality and competency, contributing to increase of overall efficiency of rail sector. **Structure** General Meeting; Board; Committees; Working Groups; Task Force. **Languages** English. **Finance** Members' dues. **Events** *General Meeting* Madrid (Spain) 2016, *General Meeting* Madrid (Spain) 2016, *General Meeting* Poitiers (France) 2015, *General Meeting* Luxembourg (Luxembourg) 2014, *General Meeting* London (UK) 2013. **Publications** *EFRTC Newsletter* (2 a year); *EFRTC E-brief* (6-10 a year). Reports. **Members** National associations and individual construction companies. Membership countries not specified. **NGO Relations** Associate member of: *Comité européen de normalisation (CEN, #04162); Rail Forum Europe (RFE, #18607); Association of the European Rail Supply Industry (UNIFE, #02536).* In consultation with: *European Rail Research Advisory Council (ERRAC, #08325).* Cooperates with: *Community of European Railway and Infrastructure Companies (CER, #04396); European Rail Infrastructure Managers (EIM, #08324); International Union of Railways (#15813).* [2016.11.30/XD8458/**D**]

♦ European Federation of Regional Energy and Environment Agency / see European Federation of Agencies and Regions for Energy and the Environment (#07041)
♦ European Federation for Renewable Energy (inactive)
♦ European Federation for Research and Information on Sectarianism / see European Federation of Centres of Research and Information on Cults and Sects (#07072)
♦ European Federation for Research in Rehabilitation / see European Forum for Research in Rehabilitation (#07331)

♦ European Federation of Retail Perfumers 07206

Fédération Européenne des Parfumeurs Détaillants (FEPD) – Europäischer Parfümerieverband

Secretariat Kaiserstrasse 42a, 40479 Düsseldorf, Germany. T. +4921130181880. Fax +4921130181899. E-mail: contact@fepd.eu.
Registered Office 8 rue de la TErrasse, 75017 Paris, France. T. +33140547062.
URL: http://www.fepd.eu/

History 1960, Paris (France). Previously referred to in English as *European Federation of Perfumery Retailers.* Registered in accordance with French law. EU Transparency Register: 119462634240-74. **Aims** Promote the interests of national associations of perfumery retailers; represent the profession in the European market, as regards industry, consumers and European Community authorities. **Languages** French, German. **Events** *Annual Congress* Berlin (Germany) 1999, *Annual Congress* Évian (France) 1998, *Annual Congress* Rimini (Italy) 1997, *Annual Congress* New York, NY (USA) 1996, *Annual Congress* Bergen (Norway) 1995.
Members National organizations in 12 countries:
Austria, Belgium, Denmark, France, Germany, Italy, Luxembourg, Netherlands, Norway, Spain, Sweden, Switzerland.
IGO Relations Recognized by: *European Commission (EC, #06633).* [2019/XD0747/**D**]

♦ European Federation of Retired and Elderly Persons (#09580)
♦ European Federation for Retirement Provision / see PensionsEurope (#18291)

♦ European Federation of Right to Die Societies / see Right to Die Europe (#18941)
♦ European Federation for the Right to Voluntary Sterilisation (inactive)
♦ European Federation of Road Traffic Crash Victims / see European Federation of Road Traffic Victims (#07207)

♦ European Federation of Road Traffic Victims 07207

Fédération Européenne des Victimes de la Route (FEVR) – Europäische Vereinigung der Verkehrsunfallopfer Federazione Europea delle Vittime della Strada

Pres Chaussée de Haecht 1405, 1130 Brussels, Belgium. E-mail: president@fevr.org – info@fevr.org.
URL: http://www.fevr.org/

History 6 Jul 1991, Geneva (Switzerland). Founded following a number of informal meetings. An umbrella organizations of over 20 national organizations. Statutes are supported by bylaws. Former names and other names: *European Federation of Road Traffic Crash Victims* – alias. Registration: Swiss Civil Code, Switzerland; EU Transparency Register, No/ID: 47172565855-96. **Aims** Ensure provision of emotional and practical help and support to road crash victims, as well assistance with legal procedures; contribute to road safety by highlighting road danger and the causes of crashes in order to influence institutions and authorities to enforce road safety measures more effectively. **Structure** General Assembly (annual); Executive Board; Executive Committee; Committees for specific tasks. **Languages** English. **Staff** 8.00 FTE, paid. **Finance** Sources: donations; members' dues; revenue from activities/projects. **Activities** Advocacy/lobbying/activism; events/meetings; knowledge management/information dissemination; research/documentation; standards/guidelines. **Events** *General Assembly* Brussels (Belgium) 2021, *General Assembly* Münster (Germany) 2019, *General Assembly* Barcelona (Spain) 2018, *General Assembly* Leeuwarden (Netherlands) 2017, *General Assembly* Lisbon (Portugal) 2016. **Publications** *FEVR Newsletter* – e-mail. *Judicial Assistance for Road Users Who Had an Accident Outside their Home Country* (2003); *Impact of Road Death and Injury* (1995); *Study of the Physical, Psychological and Material Secondary Damage Inflicted on the Victims and their Families by Road Crashes.* Conference proceedings; Round Table conclusions; articles; papers; briefings; black boxes.
Members Road traffic victim organizations (over 20) in 17 countries:
Belgium, Croatia, France, Germany, Greece, Italy, Lebanon, Luxembourg, Netherlands, Poland, Portugal, Romania, Slovenia, Spain, Switzerland, Türkiye, UK.
Associated organizations in 4 countries:
Argentina, Poland, Spain, Türkiye.
Cooperating organizations in 5 countries:
Belgium, Greece, Italy, Netherlands, Portugal.
Consultative Status Consultative status granted from: *ECOSOC (#05331)* (Ros A). [2022.02.14/XD5053/**D**]

♦ European Federation of Rudolf Steiner Waldorf School Parents (inactive)

♦ European Federation of Rural Tourism (RuralTour) 07208

SG Sagunto 8-10-3, 04004 Almeria, Almería, Spain. T. +34656900371. E-mail: info@ruraltour.eu.
URL: https://www.ruraltour.eu/

History 29 Sep 1990, Tomar (Portugal). Founded based on a decision of a meeting, 6-7 July 1990, Oelde (Germany FR), following a colloquium, 10-11 Jan 1990, Strasbourg (France), organized by EUROTER and *Council of Europe (CE, #04881).* Former names and other names: *EUROGITES – European Federation of Farm and Village Tourism* – former; *EUROGITES – Fédération européenne pour l'accueil touristique chez l'habitant à la campagne, à la ferme et au village* – former; *Europäischer Verband für den Bauernhof und Land Tourismus* – former; *Europäischer Verband für Landtourismus* – former; *EUROGITES – Fédération européenne du tourisme rural* – former; *EUROGITES – European Federation of Rural Tourism* – former. Registration: EU Transparency Register, No/ID: 50751211239-57, Start date: 25 Feb 2009. **Aims** Promote knowledge and experience of the variety of European cultural, social, historical, natural, and environmental heritage through a concept of tourism that is based on direct contact and interaction with the local population, in the context of a sustainable rural and tourism development. **Structure** General Assembly; Executive Committee; Secretariat in Almeria (Spain). **Languages** English, French, German, Spanish. **Staff** 1.00 FTE, paid. **Finance** Sources: members' dues; revenue from activities/projects. Subventions. **Activities** Advocacy/lobbying/activism; events/meetings; guidance/assistance/consulting; research/documentation; training/education. **Events** *European Congress on Rural Tourism* Vierumäki (Finland) 2021, *European Congress on Rural Tourism* Vierumäki (Finland) 2020, *European Congress on Rural Tourism* Druskininkai (Lithuania) 2018, *Conference on Sustainable Tourism for Rural Development* Bergamo (Italy) 2017, *European Congress on Rural Tourism* Alpbach (Austria) 2014. **Publications** *Ruraltour Info* (3-4 a year). Annual Report for General Assembly; annual presentation in Powerpoint – online.
Members National and regional organizations in 27 countries and territories:
Austria, Belgium, Bosnia-Herzegovina, Bulgaria, Croatia, Cyprus, Estonia, Finland, Georgia, Germany, Greece, Hungary, Italy, Latvia, Lithuania, Luxembourg, Molise, Montenegro, North Macedonia, Norway, Poland, Romania, Serbia, Slovakia, Slovenia, Spain, Switzerland.
IGO Relations Member of: Rural Development Civil Dialogue Group of *European Commission (EC, #06633)* – DG Agriculture; European Rural Network (ERN). **NGO Relations** Member of (4): *European Council for the Village and Small Town (ECOVAST, #06848); European Tourism Manifesto (#08921); Network for the European Private Sector in Tourism (NET, #17027); World Tourism Network (WTN, #21860).* [2023.02.22/XD2540/**F**]

♦ European Federation of Salaried Doctors 07209

Fédération européenne des médecins salariés (FEMS) – Europäischer Verband der Angestellten Ärzte – Federación Europea de Médicos Asalariados – Federazione Europea dei Medici a Rapporto d'Impiego – Federação Européia dos Médicos Assalariados

Secretariat Rue Guimard 15, 1040 Brussels, Belgium. T. +3227366066. Fax +3227329972. E-mail: info@fems.net.
Pres address not obtained.
Registered Office 39 rue Victor Massé, 75009 Paris, France.
URL: http://www.fems.net/

History 29 Feb 1964, Paris (France). Former names and other names: *European Federation of Community Doctors* – former (29 Feb 1964 to 22 Nov 1981); *Fédération européenne des médecins de collectivité* – former (29 Feb 1964 to 22 Nov 1981). Registration: EU Transparency Register, No/ID: 736055610233-90; France. **Aims** Defend the legitimate interests of European salaried doctors in the following fields: working conditions; wages; medical liability; medical education; participation in clinical governance; health management and policy. **Structure** General Assembly; Board. **Languages** English, French. **Staff** 0.50 FTE, paid. **Finance** Members' dues. **Events** *Conference and General Assembly* Naples (Italy) 2019, *Conference on Inequalities in Doctors Working Conditions in the EU* Brussels (Belgium) 2018, *General Assembly* Strasbourg (France) 2012, *General Assembly* Varna (Bulgaria) 2012, *General Assembly* Catania (Italy) 2011. **Publications** *FEMS Newsletter.*
Members National organizations in 15 countries:
Austria, Belgium, Bulgaria, Croatia, Cyprus, Czechia, France, Italy, Netherlands, Poland, Portugal, Romania, Slovenia, Spain, Türkiye.
NGO Relations Member of: *European Forum of Medical Associations and WHO (EFMA, #07320); European Public Health Alliance (EPHA, #08297).* [2020.03.03/XD3158/**D**]

♦ European Federation of Sales Promotion / see Integrated Marketing Communications Council of Europe (#11369)
♦ European Federation of the Sanitary and Heating Wholesale Trade (#09570)
♦ European Federation of Savings and Loan Institutions for Construction / see European Federation of Building Societies (#07064)
♦ European Federation of Schools / see Federation for EDucation in Europe (#09479)

♦ European Federation for the Science and Technology of Lipids (Euro Fed Lipid) 07210

Contact PO Box 90 04 40, 60444 Frankfurt-Main, Germany. T. +496968604846. E-mail: info@eurofedlipid.org.
URL: http://www.eurofedlipid.org/

History 9 Oct 2000. Formal foundation 19 Sep 2001, Berlin (Germany). Registration: Vereinsregister, No/ID: VR 12887, Germany, Frankfurt-Main. **Aims** Promote the science and technology of lipids on a European level; promote cooperation and exchange between researchers and companies devoted to the lipids, *fats* and *oils* field in Europe. **Structure** General Assembly (annual); Council of Management; Divisions (11); Secretariat. **Languages** English. **Finance** Members' dues. **Activities** Events/meetings; training/education; awards/prizes/competitions. **Events** *Euro Fed Lipid Congress* Poznań (Poland) 2023, *Euro Fed Lipid Congress* Leipzig (Germany) 2021, *International Symposium on Lipid Oxidation and Antioxidants (ISOLA)* Frankfurt-Main (Germany) 2020, *International Symposium on Lipid Oxidation and Antioxidants (ISOLA)* Vigo (Spain) 2020, *Congress* Seville (Spain) 2019. **Publications** *European Journal of Lipid Science and Technology. Lipid Technology.* Scientific reports.
Members Individuals and organizations (2,000). Membership countries not specified. Included in the above, 1 regional organization listed in this Yearbook:
Included in the above, 1 regional organization listed in this Yearbook:
Nordic Forum for Lipid Research and Technology (Nordic Lipidforum, #17299).
NGO Relations Member of: *International Society for Fat Research (ISF, #15115).* [2022/XD8707/**D**]

♦ European Federation of the Scientific Image (no recent information)
♦ European Federation of Scientific and Technical Networks of Cooperation / see European Federation of European Coordination Networks of Scientific and Technical Cooperation (#07114)

♦ European Federation of Sea Anglers (EFSA) 07211

Sec 30 Dysart Ave, Kingston upon Thames, KT2 5RB, UK. T. +447715926050. E-mail: efsa@btinternet.com.
Pres Via S Gimignano 5, 00058 Santa Marinella RM, Italy. E-mail: hitrom@gmx.ch.
URL: http://www.efsafishing.org/

History Founded 1961, by a group of international anglers representing 7 countries and territories (England, Belgium, France, Netherlands, Denmark, Norway, Scotland) who were taking part in a fishing festival, Looe (UK). **Aims** Promote the *sport* of sea angling with rod and line worldwide. **Structure** General Meeting (annual); Standing Committee (meets twice a year); Executive. **Languages** English. **Staff** 2.50 FTE, voluntary. **Finance** Members' dues. Sponsorship. **Activities** Research/documentation; sporting events. **Publications** *EFSA Yearbook* (annual). *European List of Sea Fish Records.*
Members Sections (national organizations and clubs) in 21 countries and territories:
Albania, Austria, Belgium, Denmark, England, France, Germany, Gibraltar, Greece, Iceland, Ireland, Italy, Malta, Netherlands, Norway, Portugal, Russia, Scotland, Sweden, Switzerland, Wales.
Individuals in 2 countries:
Cuba, Spain.
Affiliates (2) in 1 country:
South Africa.
NGO Relations Observer status with: *European Anglers Alliance (EAA, #05900).* Member of: *International Game Fish Association (IGFA); Mediterranean Advisory Council (MEDAC, #16639).* [2018.10.04/XD0423/**D**]

♦ European Federation of Self-Employed and Executives (inactive)
♦ European Federation for the Self-Help of the Elderly / see EURAG – European Federation of Older Persons (#05597)

♦ European Federation for Services to Individuals (EFSI) 07212

Fédération européenne des Services à la personne

Manager Av du Port 86 – box 302, 1000 Brussels, Belgium. T. +3222040873. E-mail: info@efsi-europe.eu.
URL: http://www.efsi-europe.eu/

History 2006. Registration: EU Transparency Register, No/ID: 57795906755-89, Start date: 21 Sep 2011. **Aims** Shape a more favourable environment for the PHS – personal and household services – industry in Europe, especially by improving the image and perception of PHS sector and favouring adequate policy supporting its development; promote the development of domestic and care services in Europe thanks to a monitoring of national regulatory frameworks and markets and liasing the various stakeholders. **Structure** General Assembly; Board; Working groups. **Languages** English, French. **Staff** 1.50 FTE, paid. **Finance** Sources: members' dues. Annual budget: 150,000 EUR. **Activities** Advocacy/lobbying/activism; events/meetings; knowledge management/information dissemination; networking/liaising. trade show **Publications** *EFSI e-newsletter* (2 a year). Surveys; reports; statements.
Members Full in 22 countries:
Austria, Belgium, Bulgaria, Czechia, Denmark, Finland, France, Germany, Greece, Hungary, Ireland, Italy, Luxembourg, Netherlands, Poland, Portugal, Romania, Slovakia, Slovenia, Spain, Sweden, UK.
IGO Relations European institutions. [2022.10.19/XM5641/**D**]

♦ European Federation of Sexology (EFS) 07213

Gen Sec Naselje Marka Marulića 10 e, Karlovac, Croatia. E-mail: info@europeansexology.com.
URL: http://www.europeansexology.com/

History 1988. Regional continental federation of *World Association for Sexual Health (WAS, #21187).* Statutes modified: 2002; 2006; 2016. Registration: Switzerland. **Aims** Coordinate European associations working in the field of sexology by encouraging study, coordination and development of the teaching of sexology, including professional training programmes; encourage research projects at a European level. **Structure** General Assembly (every 2 years); Executive Committee. **Languages** English. **Staff** 2.00 FTE, paid. **Finance** Sources: members' dues. **Events** *Biennial Congress* Aalborg (Denmark) 2022, *Biennial Congress* Tilburg (Netherlands) 2021, *Biennial Congress* Albufeira (Portugal) 2018, *Biennial Congress* Dubrovnik (Croatia) 2016, *Biennial Congress* Istanbul (Turkey) 2014. **Publications** *Sexologies Journal* (4 a year).
Members Associations (52) in 24 countries:
Austria, Belgium, Bulgaria, Croatia, Czechia, Denmark, Estonia, Finland, France, Georgia, Germany, Greece, Hungary, Israel, Italy, Netherlands, Norway, Poland, Portugal, Spain, Sweden, Switzerland, Türkiye, UK.
Included in the above, 2 organizations listed in this Yearbook:
Centre international de formation et de recherche en sexualité (CIFRES); Istituto Internazionale di Sessuologia, Firenze (no recent information).
IGO Relations *WHO (#20950).* [2021/XD3699/y/**D**]

♦ European Federation of Sjögren's Disease Patient Association / see Sjögren Europe (#19302)
♦ European Federation of Sjögren's Syndrome Patient Associations / see Sjögren Europe (#19302)
♦ European Federation for Social Assistance and Integration through Housing Provision (inactive)

♦ European Federation of Social Employers 07214

Fédération européenne des employeurs sociaux (FEDES)

Address not obtained.

History 2007. **Aims** Promote and defend the interests of European organizations managing structures supporting vulnerable and disabled persons, in their mission as employers, in the framework of articles 138 and 139 of the Treaty of the European Union. **NGO Relations** Member of: *Social Economy Europe (SEE, #19335).* Partners with: *SGI Europe (#19253).* [2012/XM1489/y/**D**]

♦ European Federation of Social Sciences (no recent information)

♦ European Federation of Societies of Hand Therapy (EFSHT) 07215

Address not obtained.
URL: http://www.eurohandtherapy.org/

History 30 Nov 1989, Paris (France). Registration: Netherlands. **Aims** Increase interest in and exchange of knowledge about hand therapy; coordinate activities among European societies to promote the exchange and development of knowledge; share scientific experience and research with colleagues, and also with hand surgeons and allied professionals dealing with hand *patients*; expand the practice of hand therapy so that an increasing number of patients with hand injuries may receive hand rehabilitation. **Structure** Council, consisting of one delegate from each member nation. Executive Committee, comprising President, President-Elect, General Secretary, Treasurer, Immediate Past President. Committees (2): Permanent Scientific; Education. **Languages** English. **Staff** Voluntary. **Finance** Sources: members' dues. **Activities** Events/meetings; publishing activities. **Events** *Congress* Rimini (Italy) 2023, *Congress / Meeting* Oslo (Norway) 2011, *Congress* Lausanne (Switzerland) 2008, *Meeting* Ljubljana (Slovenia) 2007, *Meeting* Izmir (Turkey) 2006. **Publications** *Hand Therapy* (4 a year) – journal.

Members Full national organizations in 12 countries:
Belgium, France, Germany, Greece, Italy, Netherlands, Norway, Portugal, Slovenia, Sweden, Switzerland, UK.
Corresponding individuals from countries with no national organization. Membership countries not specified.
[2022/XD9360/**D**]

♦ European Federation of Societies for Microsurgery (EFSM) 07216
Fédération européenne des sociétés de microchirurgie
Pres Recovery Hospital, Viilor 46-50, 400347 Cluj-Napoca, Romania. T. +40722575963. Fax +40264438852.
SG address not obtained.
URL: http://www.efsm.eu/
History 10 Feb 1990. Former names and other names: *Federation of European Societies for Microsurgery (FESM)* – former. **Aims** Promote and rationalize training in microsurgery throughout Europe; develop microsurgical resources by advising national and European authorities concerning the requirements and quality of microsurgical technique. **Structure** General Assembly. Council, headed by Secretary-General. Standing Committees (4): Education; Informatics; International Relations; Historic. **Activities** Events/meetings; training/education. **Events** *Congress* Cluj-Napoca (Romania) 2020, *Congress* Antalya (Turkey) 2016, *Congress* Barcelona (Spain) 2014, *Congress* Paris (France) 2012, *Congress* Genoa (Italy) 2010. **Publications** *International Journal of Microsurgery*.
Members Full in 13 countries:
Austria, Denmark, France, Germany, Greece, Italy, Poland, Portugal, Romania, Spain, Sweden, Switzerland, Türkiye.
Associate in 3 countries:
Finland, Serbia, Slovenia.
Corresponding in 1 country:
Egypt. [2020/XD3551/**D**]

♦ European Federation of Societies for Ultrasound in Medicine and Biology (EFSUMB) 07217
Fédération européenne de sociétés pour la médecine et la biologie des ultra-sons
Pres PO Box 72718, London, SW19 9HD, UK. T. +447752589099. E-mail: admin@efsumb.org.
URL: http://www.efsumb.org/
History 1972, London (UK). Registration: Charity, No/ID: 1016118, England and Wales. **Aims** Promote research, teaching and development of all aspects of ultrasound related to medical diagnosis. **Structure** General Assembly; Board of Delegates; Executive Bureau; Committees (4); Secretariat. **Languages** English. **Staff** 0.50 FTE, paid. **Finance** Sources: members' dues. **Activities** Events/meetings; training/education. **Events** *Congress* Riga (Latvia) 2022, *Congress* Timisoara (Romania) 2021, *European Congress for Ultrasound in Medicine and Biology (EUROSON)* Bergen (Norway) 2020, *Congress* Granada (Spain) 2019, *Congress* Poznań (Poland) 2018. **Publications** *Ultraschall in der Medizin/European Journal of Ultrasound (EJU)* (6 a year) – including EFSUMB Newsletter.
Members National societies in 29 countries:
Austria, Bulgaria, Croatia, Czechia, Denmark, Georgia, Germany, Greece, Hungary, Israel, Italy, Kazakhstan, Latvia, Lithuania, Moldova, Netherlands, Norway, Poland, Portugal, Romania, Russia, Serbia, Slovakia, Slovenia, Spain, Sweden, Türkiye, UK, Ukraine. [2023.02.14/XD8856/**D**]

- ♦ European Federation for Soil Bioengineering (#05751)
- ♦ European Federation for Somato-Psychotherapy (no recent information)
- ♦ European Federation for Specialist Construction Chemicals and Concrete Systems / see Experts for Specialised Construction and Concrete Systems (#09226)
- ♦ European Federation of Special Waste Industries (inactive)

♦ European Federation of Sport Psychology 07218
Fédération européenne de psychologie des sports et des activités corporelles (FEPSAC) – Europäische Vereinigung für Sportpsychologie – Evropejskaja Federacija Psihologii Sporta
Pres German Sport Univ Cologne, Dept Performance Psychology, Am Sportpark Müngersdorf 6, 50933 Cologne, Germany. T. +4922149825491. Fax +4922149828320. E-mail: office@fepsac.com.
SG School of Applied Sciences, London South Bank Univ, 103 Borough Rd, London, SW1 0AA, UK. T. +4478157959.
URL: http://www.fepsac.com/
History 4 Jun 1969, Vittel (France). Founded on the initiative of *International Society of Sport Psychology (ISSP, #15455)*. Statutes adopted 1970; amended: 1975, Edinburgh (UK); 1977, Prague (Czechoslovakia); 1979, Varna (Bulgaria); 1991, Cologne (Germany); 1993, Prague (Czech Rep); 2003, Copenhagen (Denmark); 2007, Halkidiki (Greece); 2011, Madeira (Portugal); 2015 Bern (Switzerland); 2017 Nottingham (UK). **Aims** Promote scientific, educational and professional work in sport psychology; foster information dissemination, cooperation and collaboration in the field; encourage young scientists. **Structure** General Assembly (annual); Managing Council. **Languages** English. **Staff** 1.00 FTE, paid; 9.00 FTE, voluntary. **Finance** Sources: members' dues. **Activities** Awards/prizes/competitions; events/meetings; knowledge management/information dissemination; networking/liaising; research/documentation. **Events** *Quadrennial Congress* Padua (Italy) 2022, *Quadrennial Congress* Münster (Germany) 2019, *Conference* Nottingham (UK) 2017, *Quadrennial Congress* Bern (Switzerland) 2015, *Conference on the Development of Expertise and Excellence in Applied Sport Psychology* Paris (France) 2013. **Publications** *European Yearbook of Sport Psychology (1997-1999)*; *FEPSAC Newsletter*; *Psychology of Sport and Exercise*. Books; monographs.
Members National societies involved in sports psychology (19) in 18 countries:
Austria, Belgium, Croatia, Denmark, Finland, France, Germany, Greece, Italy, Netherlands, Poland, Slovakia, Slovenia, Spain, Sweden, Switzerland, Türkiye, UK.
Included in the above, 1 organization listed in this Yearbook:
European Network of Young Specialists in Sport Psychology (ENYSSP, #08038).
NGO Relations Associate member of: *European Federation of Psychologists Associations (EFPA, #07199)*.
[2022.05.25/XD1196/y/**D**]

- ♦ European Federation of Sports Medicine / see European Federation of Sports Medicine Associations (#07219)

♦ European Federation of Sports Medicine Associations (EFSMA) ... 07219
SG Baskent Univ School of Health Sciences, Dept of Sports Sciences, Eskisehir Yolu 20 km, 06590 Ankara/Ankara, Türkiye. T. +9031297455013467.
Pres Kieiwtstraat 141, 3500 Hasselt, Belgium. T. +3211265100. Fax +3211265101.
URL: http://www.efsma.eu/
History 26 Oct 1995, Granada (Spain), as a group of *International Federation of Sports Medicine (#13554)*. Original title: *European Federation of Sports Medicine (EFSM)*. Constitutive meeting 1 Jun 1996, Nice (France). Includes *North European Chapter of Sports and Exercise Medicine (NECSEM, inactive)*. **Aims** Have sports medicine recognized as a speciality in Europe; develop and harmonize education in sports medicine throughout Europe and get sports medicine included in the basic curricula at all medical schools and educational institutions; act as a pan-European forum for the improvement of communication between European organizations; coordinate European sports medicine actions and cooperate with sport science disciplines in Europe; increase understanding of the importance of physical activity and sport training for the whole European population and dissemination knowledge of the principles and methods for the prevention, treatment and rehabilitation of injuries and diseases; encourage the exchange of scientific results and experiences and encourage and engage in common research; establish common strength and propagate a sports medicine Code of Ethics throughout Europe. **Structure** General Assembly; Executive Committee. Scientific and Education Commission. **Activities** Training/education; events/meetings. **Events** *Biennial European Congress of Sports Medicine* Portoroz (Slovenia) 2019, *Biennial European Congress of Sports Medicine* Cascais (Portugal) 2017, *Biennial European Congress of Sports Medicine* Antwerp (Belgium) 2015, *Biennial European Congress of Sports Medicine* Strasbourg (France) 2013, *Biennial European Congress of Micro Surgery* Paris (France) 2012.
Members National associations in 41 countries:
Albania, Austria, Belarus, Belgium, Bosnia-Herzegovina, Bulgaria, Croatia, Cyprus, Czechia, Denmark, Estonia, Finland, France, Georgia, Germany, Great Britain, Greece, Hungary, Ireland, Israel, Italy, Latvia, Lithuania, Luxembourg, Malta, Netherlands, North Macedonia, Norway, Poland, Portugal, Romania, Russia, San Marino, Serbia, Slovakia, Slovenia, Spain, Sweden, Switzerland, Türkiye, Ukraine. [2017/XD7144/**D**]

- ♦ European Federation of Statisticians in the Pharmaceutical Industry / see European Federation of Statistics in the Pharmaceutical Industry (#07220)

♦ European Federation of Statistics in the Pharmaceutical Industry (EFSPI) 07220
Fédération européenne des statisticiens de l'industrie pharmaceutique
Main Office Ground Floor, 4 Victoria Square, St Albans, AL1 3TF, UK. E-mail: admin@efspi.org.
URL: http://www.efspi.org/
History Aug 1992. Former names and other names: *European Federation of Statisticians in the Pharmaceutical Industry* – former. Registration: EU Transparency Register, No/ID: 420759225344-39; No/ID: 39780909, Start date: Aug 2018, Denmark. **Aims** Promote professional standards of statistics and the standing of the statistical profession in matters pertinent to the European pharmaceutical industry; exchange information on and harmonize attitudes to the practice of statistics in the industry; offer a collective expert input on statistical matters to national and international authorities and organizations. **Structure** Council; Working Groups; Executive Office. **Languages** English. **Staff** None. **Finance** Annual contributions of national organizations. **Activities** Standards/guidelines; events/meetings. **Events** *Workshop on new ICH guidelines on choice of control group in clinical trials* Brussels (Belgium) 1999. **Publications** *EFSPI Newsletter*.
Members National biostatistical organizations representing biostatisticians in 10 countries:
Belgium, Denmark, Finland, France, Germany, Italy, Netherlands, Sweden, Switzerland, UK.
NGO Relations Agreement with: *European Federation of Pharmaceutical Industries and Associations (EFPIA, #07191)*. [2022/XD3557/t/**D**]

♦ European Federation of Steel Wire Rope Industries (EWRIS) 07221
SG Kaiserswerther Str 137, 40474 Düsseldorf, Germany.
URL: https://ewris.eu/
History 1962. Former names and other names: *European Wire Rope Information Service (EWRIS)* – former (1962); *Fédération européenne des industries de câbles d'acier* – former (1962). Registration: Commercial Register, Germany, Düsseldorf. **Aims** Promote the interests of European wire rope *manufacturers*; study technical aspects and provide relevant information. **Structure** General Assembly; Board; Committees; Technical Working Group (TWG); Ad Hoc Groups. **Languages** English. **Staff** 2.00 FTE, paid. **Finance** Members' dues. **Events** *Autumn Meeting* Düsseldorf (Germany) 2022, *Annual Meeting* Vienna (Austria) 2012.
Members Regular; Associate. National organizations and individuals. Members in 16 countries:
Argentina, Austria, Belgium, Czechia, Denmark, France, Germany, Italy, Japan, Poland, Portugal, Romania, Spain, Switzerland, Türkiye, UK.
NGO Relations Member of: *AEGIS Europe*; *Industry4Europe (#11181)*. Cooperates with: *International Organization for Standardization (ISO, #14473)*. [2022/XF6006/t/**F**]

♦ European Federation of Surgical Specialties (EFSS) 07222
Contact c/o UEMS, Rue de l'Industrie 24, 1040 Brussels, Belgium. T. +3226495164. Fax +3226403730. E-mail: uems@skynet.be.
URL: http://www.uems.net/
History by *European Union of Medical Specialists (UEMS, #09001)*. [2016/XM1868/**D**]

♦ European Federation of Tall People (EFTP) 07223
Chairman Schans 27, 1261 MJ Blaricum, Netherlands. T. +31355257893. E-mail: info@talleuro.nl.
URL: http://www.talleuro.nl/
History Previously referred to as *Tall Clubs International Europe – Europa Klub Langer Menschen (EKLM)*. **Aims** Improve *living conditions* for tall people. **Languages** Dutch, English, German. **Activities** Research/documentation. **Events** *European Conference* Tampere (Finland) 2012, *European conference* Paris (France) 2011, *European conference* Osnabrück (Germany) 2006, *European conference / Conference* Copenhagen (Denmark) 2002, *Conference* Vienna (Austria) 1992. **Members** in 14 countries (not specified).
[2015.09.02/XD3681/**D**]

♦ European Federation of Tank Cleaning Organizations (EFTCO) 07224
Europese Federatie van Tankreinigingsorganisaties
Sec Neue Grosse Bergstrasse 20, 22767 Hamburg, Germany. T. +494038616569. Fax +494038616529. E-mail: secretary@eftco.org.
Registered Office Common Lane, Knottingley, WF11 8BN, UK. E-mail: info@eftco.org.
URL: http://www.eftco.org/
History 1998, Brussels (Belgium). Registration: Companies House, No/ID: 3739660, Start date: 24 Mar 1999, England and Wales. **Aims** Distribute and promote the uniform European Cleaning Document (ECD) as the document par excellence in Europe; study, protect and develop the professional interest of EFTCO and members; seek and encourage development of relationships with other organizations having related activities and with regulatory bodies both nationally and internationally. **Structure** Board. **Languages** English. **Staff** 1.00 FTE, paid. **Finance** Sources: members' dues. Annual budget: 60,000 EUR. **Activities** Events/meetings; publishing activities; standards/guidelines. **Publications** *EFTCO Cleaning Codes*; *EFTCO Food Assessment*; *European Cleaning Document (ECD)*.
Members Full (" indicates founding) in 26 countries (Sweden acts for Nordic countries):
Austria, Belgium (*), Bulgaria, Croatia, Czechia, Denmark, Finland, France (*), Germany, Hungary, Ireland, Italy (*), Netherlands (*), Norway, Poland, Portugal, Romania, Russia, Slovakia, Slovenia, Spain (*), Sweden, Switzerland, Türkiye, UK (*), Ukraine.
NGO Relations *Conseil européen de l'industrie chimique (CEFIC, #04687)*; *European Chemical Transport Association (ECTA, #06525)*; *FoodDrinkEurope (#09841)*; *International Tank Container Organization (ITCO, #15654)*. [2020.06.22/XD7859/**D**]

- ♦ European Federation of Tax Advisers / see CFE Tax Advisers Europe (#03842)

♦ European Federation of Therapeutic Communities (EFTC) 07225
Sec-Treas c/o TG De Kiem, Vluchtenboerstraat 7a, 9890 Gavere, Belgium. T. +3293896666. Fax +3293848307.
URL: http://www.eftc-europe.com/
History Founded 1980. Registered in accordance with Belgian law. **Aims** Support the psychopedagogical approach helping *drug addicts* to return to a drug free life style and become contributing members of the wider community. **Structure** General Assembly (annual); Board; Secretariat. **Languages** English. **Staff** None. **Finance** Members' dues. **Activities** Events/meetings. **Events** *Conference* Thessaloniki (Greece) 2019, *International Symposium on Substance Abuse Treatment* Ghent (Belgium) 2018, *Conference* Dublin (Ireland) 2017, *Conference* Malaga (Spain) 2015, *Conference* Prague (Czech Rep) 2013.
Members Full; Associate; Individual; Corresponding; Honorary. Residential and non-residential facilities for youths and adults in 25 countries:
Austria, Belgium, Bulgaria, Cyprus, Czechia, Denmark, Finland, France, Germany, Greece, Hungary, Ireland, Italy, Latvia, Lithuania, Netherlands, Norway, Poland, Portugal, Russia, Slovenia, Spain, Sweden, Switzerland, UK.
NGO Relations *European Working Group on Drug Oriented Research (EWODOR, #09111)*; *Federation of Therapeutic Communities of Central and Eastern Europe (FTCCEE, #09707)*; *Vienna NGO Committee on Drugs (VNGOC, #20773)*; *World Federation of Therapeutic Communities (WFTC, #21491)*. [2015.07.31/XD1042/**D**]

♦ European Federation of Thoroughbred Breeders' Associations (EFTBA) 07226
Fédération Européenne des Associations déleveurs de Pur Sang Anglais
Contact 257 Avenue le Jour se Leve, 92655 Boulogne CEDEX, France. T. +33147610609. Fax +33147610474. E-mail: eftba.eu@gmail.com.
URL: http://www.eftba.eu/
History Founded 1994. **Aims** Provide a single focus for breeders to come together to discuss and formulate common policies; lobby at European level on issues which affect European breeders; promote the Thoroughbred breeding industry at European level including better access to EC Funding schemes. **Structure** General Meeting (annual). Board of 6 members. **Events** *Annual General Meeting* Paris (France) 2015, *Annual General Meeting* Paris (France) 2014, *Annual General Meeting* Paris (France) 2013, *Annual General Meeting* Paris (France) 2012, *Annual General Meeting* Paris (France) 2011. **Publications** *EFTBA Veterinary Newsletter*.
Members Full in 16 countries:

Austria, Cyprus, Czechia, Denmark, France, Germany, Hungary, Ireland, Italy, Norway, Poland, Spain, Sweden, Switzerland, Türkiye, UK.
Observer members in 3 countries:
Belgium, Finland, Netherlands.
NGO Relations Member of: *European Horse Network (EHN, #07499).* [2016.02.12/XJ5794/**D**]

- ♦ European Federation of Tile and Brick Manufacturers / see Tiles and Bricks Europe (#20163)
- ♦ European Federation of Timber Construction / see Timber Construction Europe (#20164)
- ♦ European Federation of Tinnitus Association (inactive)

♦ European Federation of Tobacco Processors 07227

Fédération européenne des transformateurs de tabac (FETRATAB) – Federazione Europea dei Trasformatori di Tabacco

SG c/o APTI, via Monte delle Gioie 1/C, 00199 Rome RM, Italy. T. +396482777. Fax +3964827767.
Legal Seat Rue de Tamines 10, 1060 Brussels, Belgium.

History EU Transparency Register: 835059415132-95. **NGO Relations** Member of: *European Liaison Committee for Agricultural and Agri-Food Trades (#07687).* [2019.05.10/XD3907/**D**]

- ♦ European Federation of Tobacco Retail Organizations / see European Confederation of Tobacco Retailers (#06725)

♦ European Federation of Tourist Guide Associations 07228

Fédération européenne des associations de guides touristiques (FEG)

Sec Avda da Liberdade 3, 3° Andar Sala 7, 1250-139 Lisbon, Portugal. E-mail: info@feg-touristguides.org – secretariat@feg-touristguides.org.
Pres address not obtained.
URL: http://www.feg-touristguides.org/

History 1986, Paris (France). Registration: RNA, No/ID: W922010960, France; EU Transparency Register, No/ID: 677743413396-10, Start date: 6 Apr 2014. **Aims** Publicise and improve the quality of Tourist Guiding services offered to all visitors to Europe; bring together and strengthen professional tourist guiding links across Europe. **Structure** General Meeting (once or twice a year); Executive Committee; Training Consultative Group. **Languages** English. **Staff** 4.00 FTE, voluntary. **Finance** Sources: members' dues. **Activities** Advocacy/lobbying/activism; networking/liaising; standards/guidelines; training/education. **Events** *Annual General Meeting* Las Palmas (Spain) 2021, *Annual General Assembly* 2020, *Convention* Faro (Portugal) 2019, *Convention* Crete (Greece) 2018, *Convention* Dublin (Ireland) 2017.
Members Associations of tourist guides in 32 countries and territories:
Armenia, Austria, Cyprus, Czechia, Denmark, England, Estonia, Finland, France, Germany, Greece, Hungary, Iceland, Ireland, Italy, Kosovo, Latvia, Malta, Montenegro, Netherlands, Northern Ireland, Poland, Portugal, Romania, Russia, Scotland, Serbia, Slovenia, Spain, Sweden, Ukraine, Wales.
IGO Relations Cooperates with (1): *Enlarged Partial Agreement on Cultural Routes (#05486).* **NGO Relations** Member of (4): *Comité européen de normalisation (CEN, #04162); Europa Nostra (#05767); European Council of Liberal Professions (#06828); European Tourism Manifesto (#08921).* [2022.05.10/XD1534/**D**]

- ♦ European Federation of Toy Distributors (inactive)
- ♦ European Federation of Toy Industries – Toys, Games and Childcare (inactive)
- ♦ European Federation of Toy Manufacturers' Associations (inactive)
- ♦ European Federation of Toy Retailers (inactive)
- ♦ European Federation of the Trade in Dried Fruit, Edible Nuts, Preserved Food, Spices, Honey and Similar Foodstuffs / see European Federation of the Trade in Dried Fruit, Edible Nuts, Processed Fruit and Vegetables, Processed Fishery Products, Spices, Honey and Similar Foodstuffs (#07229)

♦ European Federation of the Trade in Dried Fruit, Edible Nuts, Processed Fruit and Vegetables, Processed Fishery Products, Spices, Honey and Similar Foodstuffs (FRUCOM) 07229

SG Rue de Trèves 49-51, Box 14, 1040 Brussels, Belgium. T. +3222300333 – +3222310638. Fax +3227326766. E-mail: info@frucom.eu.
URL: http://www.frucom.eu/

History 30 Apr 1960, The Hague (Netherlands). Founded by five national organizations. Former names and other names: *European Federation of Importers of Dried Fruits, Preserves, Spices and Honey* – former (30 Apr 1960); *Fédération européenne des importateurs de fruits secs, conserves, épices et miel* – former (30 Apr 1960); *Europäische Föderation der Importeure von Getrockneten Früchten, Konserven, Gewürzen und Honig* – former (30 Apr 1960); *Federazione Europea degli Importatori di Frutta Secca, Conserve, Spezie e Miele* – former (30 Apr 1960); *Europese Federatie van Importeurs van Gedroogde Vruchten, Conserven, Specerijen en Honing* – former (30 Apr 1960); *Europaeiske Forbund for Importører af Tørrede Frugter, Konserves, Krydderier og Honning* – former (30 Apr 1960); *European Federation of the Trade in Dried Fruit, Edible Nuts, Preserved Food, Spices, Honey and Similar Foodstuffs* – former; *Fédération européenne du commerce en fruits secs, conserves, épices et miel (FRUCOM)* – former; *Europäische Vereinigung des Handels mit Trockenfrüchten, Konserven, Gewürzen, Honig und verwandten Waren* – former. Registration: Start date: 2008, Belgium; EU Transparency Register, No/ID: 40306802522-39. **Aims** Protect the interests of the trade in dried fruits, edible nuts, canned and preserved fish, fruit and vegetables and similar foodstuffs; promote the trade within the framework of the European Union, particularly with the authorities and bodies of the EC/EU. **Structure** General Assembly; Board; Steering Committee; Secretariat. Working Groups; Expert Groups. **Languages** English. **Staff** 24.00 FTE, paid. **Finance** Members' dues. **Activities** Monitoring/evaluation; advocacy/lobbying/activism; knowledge management/information dissemination; events/meetings. Annual General Assembly held in Brussels. **Events** *General Assembly* Brussels (Belgium) 2018.
Members Full – national trade associations in EU Member States; Affiliated – individual companies in EU countries. National trade associations in 7 countries:
Belgium, France, Germany, Italy, Netherlands, Spain, UK.
NGO Relations Member of: *Joint Secretariat of Agricultural Trade Associations (#16148).* [2021/XE0733/t/**D**]

- ♦ European Federation of Trade Unions in the Food, Agriculture and Tourism Sectors and allied branches / see European Federation of Food, Agriculture and Tourism Trade Unions (#07125)
- ♦ European Federation of Traditional Accommodation and Historic Houses / see Historic Hotels of Europe (#10930)

♦ European Federation for Transport and Environment (T and E) 07230

Fédération européenne pour le transport et l'environnement (T and E) – Europäischer Verband für Verkehr und Umwelt – Europese Federatie van Verkeer en Milieu

Exec Dir 2nd floor, Square de Meeus 18, 1050 Brussels, Belgium. T. +3228510221. Fax +3228930842. E-mail: info@transportenvironment.org – dale.chadwick@transportenvironment.org – zixin.li@transportenvironment.org.
URL: http://www.transportenvironment.org/

History 1989. Former names and other names: *Transport and Environment* – former. Registration: Banque-Carrefour des Entreprises, No/ID: 0443.549.326, Start date: 7 Mar 1991, Belgium; EU Transparency Register, No/ID: 58744833263-19, Start date: 22 Feb 2010. **Aims** Serve as Europe's principal environmental organization campaigning on sustainable transport. **Structure** General Assembly (annual, in Brussels – Belgium); Bureau; Secretariat in Brussels (Belgium). **Languages** English. **Staff** 26.00 FTE, paid. **Finance** Members' dues. Other sources: project work; European Commission grants. **Events** *Seminar on air pollution and greenhouse gas emission from maritime transport* Brussels (Belgium) 2007, *Conference on greening motorways of the sea* Stockholm (Sweden) 2005, *Conference on sustainable freight transport in sensitive areas* Vienna (Austria) 2004, *Annual General Assembly* Brussels (Belgium) 2001, *Conference on enlargement* Brussels (Belgium) 2000. **Publications** *The Bulletin* (10 a year) in English – newsletter. Frequently commissions studies and publishes reports in English on important issues in the field of transport and environment. Fact sheets; position papers. Information Services: Databases.
Members Full: national associations. Associate: international organizations. NGOs in 26 countries:
Austria, Belgium, Croatia, Czechia, Denmark, Estonia, Finland, France, Germany, Greece, Hungary, Ireland, Italy, Lithuania, Netherlands, Norway, Poland, Portugal, Romania, Russia, Slovenia, Spain, Sweden, Switzerland, UK, Ukraine.
Included in the above, 2 organizations listed in this Yearbook:
Alpen-Initiative; Eco-union.
Associate (7), listed in this Yearbook:
BirdLife International (#03266); Community of European Railway and Infrastructure Companies (CER, #04396); Environmental Coalition on Standards (ECOS, #05499); European Cyclists' Federation (ECF, #06877); International Association of Public Transport (#12118); International Union of Railways (#15813); World Wide Fund for Nature (WWF, #21922) (European Policy Office of).
IGO Relations Adviser to: *International Transport Forum (ITF, #15725).* Accredited by: *United Nations Framework Convention on Climate Change – Secretariat (UNFCCC, #20564).* **NGO Relations** Member of (7): *Clean Air Asia (#03983); Clean Air Initiative for Cities Around the World (CAI, #03984)* (Asia Programme); *Clean Shipping Coalition (CSC, #03989); European Road Transport Research Advisory Council (ERTRAC, #08396); Global Battery Alliance (GBA, #10249); NGO Shipbreaking Platform (#17126); The Green 10 (#10711).* Coordinates: *International Coalition for Sustainable Aviation (ICSA, #12623).* [2021/XD3649/y/**D**]

♦ European Federation of UNESCO Clubs, Centres and Associations (EFUCA) 07231

Fédération européenne des associations, clubs et centres UNESCO (FEACU)

Pres Strada Libertatii 93, 105500 Busteni, Romania. T. +40212313224. E-mail: efucaoffice@gmail.com.
URL: http://www.efuca.org/

History 2001. Founded as a regional branch of *World Federation of UNESCO Clubs, Centres and Associations (WFUCA, #21498).* **Aims** Promote collaboration among UNESCO national federations, associations and clubs in the European and North American region; promote the ideals, objectives and priority programmes of UNESCO. **Structure** General Assembly (meets once between two World Congresses of WFUCA); Executive Board; Secretariat. **Languages** English, French. **Staff** Paid; voluntary. **Finance** Sources: members' dues; revenue from activities/projects. **Activities** Advocacy/lobbying/activism; events/meetings; training/education. **Events** *Asia-Europe Forum on Education* Bucharest (Romania) 2015, *Asia-Europe Forum on Education* China 2013, *Asia-Europe Forum on Education* China 2012. **Publications** *AZURE* (annual) – magazine.
Members Full: clubs, centres, national federations and associations in 21 countries:
Armenia, Austria, Belarus, Belgium, Bulgaria, Croatia, Cyprus, Estonia, France, Greece, Italy, Malta, Moldova, Poland, Portugal, Romania, Russia, Serbia, Spain, Switzerland, USA.
Associate: Catalan Federation. [2022/XJ0793/**E**]

- ♦ European Federation of Unions of Honorary Consuls / see Fédération de l'Union Européenne des Consuls Honoraires (#09709)
- ♦ European Federation of Vending Associations / see European Vending and Coffee Service Association (#09049)
- ♦ European Federation for the Vitrified Clay Pipe Industry / see FEUGRES – European Clay Pipe Association (#09741)
- ♦ European Federation of Waste Management / see European Federation of Waste Management and Environmental Services (#07232)

♦ European Federation of Waste Management and Environmental Services 07232

Fédération européenne des activités de la dépollution et de l'environnement (FEAD) – Europäische Föderation der Entsorgungswirtschaft

Main Office Rue Philippe le Bon 15, 1000 Brussels, Belgium. T. +3227323213. Fax +3227349592. E-mail: info@fead.be.
URL: http://www.fead.be/

History 23 Jan 1981. Statutes modified 8 Aug 1996; 4 Apr 2007. Former names and other names: *European Federation of Waste Management* – former (1981); *Fédération européenne des activités du déchet (FEAD)* – former (1981); *Europäische Föderation der Abfallwirtschaft* – former (1981); *Federación Europea para las Actividades de Desecho* – former (1981); *Federazione Europea per la Gestione dei Rifiuti* – former (1981); *Europese Federatie van Milieudienstbedrijven* – former (1981); *Fédération européenne des activités du déchet et de l'environnement* – former. Registration: AISBL/IVZW, No/ID: 439.748.609, Belgium; EU Transparency Register, No/ID: 2157643512-49. **Aims** Promote waste management and protection of the environment in countries of the European Union; represent national associations and federations with the European Commission and the European Parliament; advise working committees of the EU on questions concerning treatment and disposal of all types of waste (household, industrial, hazardous), recycling and recovery; provide for exchange of know-how on these matters. **Structure** General Assembly (annual); Presidency; Administrative Council; Management Committee; General Secretariat. **Languages** English, French, German. **Finance** Members' dues. **Activities** Events/meetings; knowledge management/information dissemination. **Events** *Biennial Conference* Munich (Germany) 2022, *Biennial Conference* Paris (France) 2017, *Committee Meeting* Brussels (Belgium) 2015, *Biennial Conference* London (UK) 2015, *Biennial Conference* Ghent (Belgium) 2013. **Publications** *FEAD Bulletin* (6 a year).
Members Associations of waste management companies in 19 countries:
Austria, Belgium, Estonia, Finland, France, Germany, Greece, Ireland, Italy, Latvia, Luxembourg, Netherlands, Norway, Poland, Romania, Slovakia, Spain, Sweden, UK.
NGO Relations Member of: *Federation of European and International Associations Established in Belgium (FAIB, #09508); International Solid Waste Association (ISWA, #15567).* Cooperates with: *European Recovered Fuel Organisation (ERFO, #08334).* [2021/XD1098/**D**]

- ♦ European Federation for Water Treatment / see European Water and Wastewater Industry Association (#09087)

♦ European Federation for Welding, Joining and Cutting (EWF) 07233

Fédération européenne du soudage, de l'assemblage et du coupage – Europäische Verband für Schweisstechnik

Registered Address Av Antoon van Oss 1, BP 4, 1120 Brussels, Belgium. E-mail: ewf@ewf.be.
Management Team Av. Dr. Mário Soares 35, TagusPark, 2740-119 Porto Salvo, Portugal.
URL: http://www.ewf.be/

History 1 Jan 1992. Former names and other names: *European Welding Federation* – former (1 Jan 1992); *European Council for Cooperation in Welding (ECCW)* – former (1974 to 1992). Registration: Crossroads Bank for Enterprises, No/ID: 0451.889.445, Start date: 11 Mar 1994, Belgium; EU Transparency Register, No/ID: 450938813754-22. **Aims** Develop an international harmonized system for education, training and qualification in the field of welding technology. **Structure** General Assembly; Board of Directors; Technical Committee; Working Groups (5); Secretariat. **Languages** English. **Activities** Certification/accreditation; events/meetings; training/education. **Events** *International Additive Manufacturing Conference* Lisbon (Portugal) 2022, *International Workshop on Electromagnetic Nondestructive Evaluation* Lisbon (Portugal) 2016, *EUROJOIN : European Conference on Welding-Joining and Cutting* Bergen (Norway) 2015, *Nordic Laser Materials Processing Conference* Lappeenranta (Finland) 2015, *International congress on welding and joining* Vienna (Austria) 2010. **Publications** *EWF Newsletter* (2 a year). Guidelines; white papers; corporate profile.
Members Welding societies in 30 countries:
Austria, Belgium, Bulgaria, Croatia, Czechia, Denmark, Finland, France, Germany, Greece, Hungary, Iran Islamic Rep, Italy, Kazakhstan, Luxembourg, Netherlands, Norway, Poland, Portugal, Romania, Russia, Serbia, Slovakia, Slovenia, Spain, Sweden, Switzerland, Türkiye, UK, Ukraine.
NGO Relations Member of (1): *European Factories of the Future Research Association (EFFRA, #07023).* Agreement signed with: *International Institute of Welding (IIW, #13935).* Close relations with: *European Committee for Electrotechnical Standardization (CENELEC, #06647).* In liaison with technical committees of: *Comité européen de normalisation (CEN, #04162).* [2022/XF0058/**F**]

- ♦ European Federation for the Welfare of the Elderly / see EURAG – European Federation of Older Persons (#05597)
- ♦ European Federation for the Wholesale Watch Trade (inactive)

♦ **European Federation of Williams Syndrome (FEWS)** **07234**
Sec Tervuursesteenweg 30, 3001 Leuven, Belgium. T. +3216224232. E-mail: president@eurowilliams.org.
URL: http://www.eurowilliams.org/
History 1999. Officially founded 2001, when constitution was adopted. Former names and other names: *Federation of European Williams Syndrome (FEWS)* – former. Registration: Banque-Carrefour des Entreprises, No/ID: 0867.382.710, Start date: 30 Aug 2004, Belgium. **Aims** Improve the lives of all those who suffer from Williams Syndrome. **Structure** General Meeting (annual); Board. **Languages** English. **Staff** None. **Finance** Sources: members' dues. **Activities** Events/meetings. **Events** *General Meeting* Rome (Italy) 2022, *General Meeting* Dublin (Ireland) 2015, *European Conference on the Williams-Beuren Syndrome* Budapest (Hungary) 2014, *General Meeting* Madrid (Spain) 2014.
Members Full (16) in 16 countries:
Belgium, Bulgaria, Czechia, Denmark, France, Germany, Hungary, Ireland, Italy, Netherlands, Norway, Serbia, Slovakia, Spain, Sweden, UK.
NGO Relations Member of (1): *EURORDIS – Rare Diseases Europe (#09175).* [2022.05.21/XM1569/**D**]

♦ **European Federation of Wine and Spirit Importers and Distributors** **07235**
Groupement européen des importateurs et distributeurs des vins et spiritueux
Dir Rue de Livourne 13 – bte 5, 1060 Brussels, Belgium. T. +3225370051. Fax +3225378156. E-mail: efwsid@skynet.be.
History 1973, as *EEC Wine and Spirit Importers Group – Groupement des importateurs des vins et spiritueux de la CEE.* Present name adopted 1993. **Aims** Promote the interests of wine and spirits importers and distributors within national and European governments. **Structure** President; Director. **Finance** Members' dues.
Members National organizations in 11 countries:
Belgium, Finland, France, Germany, Hungary, Ireland, Netherlands, Norway, Sweden, Switzerland, UK.
IGO Relations Recognized by: *European Commission (EC, #06633).* [2011.07.27/XE3691/**E**]

♦ European Federation of Wooden Pallet and Packaging Manufacturers (#09567)
♦ European Federation of Workers in Food and Allied Industries – EO/WCL (inactive)
♦ European Federation of Youth Hostel Assoications / see European Union Federation of Youth Hostel Associations (#08988)
♦ European Federation of Youth Service Organizations (inactive)
♦ European Federation of Zoology (inactive)
♦ European Feed Additives and Premixtures Quality System European Association / see FAMI-QS (#09256)

♦ **European Feed and Food Ingredients Safety Certification (EFISC-GTP)** **07236**
Manager Av des Arts 43, 1040 Brussels, Belgium.
URL: http://www.efisc-gtp.eu/
History Founded within the framework of *European Feed Ingredients Platform (EFIP, #07237)*, as *European Feed Ingredients Safety Certification (EFISC).* 1 Jul 2017, merged with the *Good Trading Practice Code (GTP Code)* of *Committee of the Trade in Cereals, Oilseeds, Pulses, Olive Oil, Oils and Fats, Animal Feed and Agrosupply of the EU (COCERAL, #04289)*, assuming current name and updated legal structure. Registered in accordance with Belgian law. **Aims** Administer the Code and Certification and promote the scheme and its acceptance on the EU market. **Structure** Board of Directors; Technical Committee. **Languages** English.
Members Companies and associations, including the following 3 organizations listed in this Yearbook:
Committee of the Trade in Cereals, Oilseeds, Pulses, Olive Oil, Oils and Fats, Animal Feed and Agrosupply of the EU (COCERAL, #04289); FEDIOL – The EU Vegetable Oil and Proteinmeal Industry (#09718); Starch Europe (#19966). [2018.07.04/XJ5613/y/**E**]

♦ **European Feed Ingredients Platform (EFIP)** **07237**
Contact c/o FAMI QS, Level 21 Bastion Tower, Place du Champ de Mars 5, 1050 Brussels, Belgium. T. +3225503452. E-mail: fffs_info@fami-qs.org.
Aims Serve as a platform for cooperation, experience sharing, evaluation and guidance on the implementation of the Food Hygiene Regulation and relating safety schemes. **Structure** Includes: *European Feed and Food Ingredients Safety Certification (EFISC-GTP, #07236).*
Members International organizations (3):
Committee of the Trade in Cereals, Oilseeds, Pulses, Olive Oil, Oils and Fats, Animal Feed and Agrosupply of the EU (COCERAL, #04289); FEDIOL – The EU Vegetable Oil and Proteinmeal Industry (#09718); Starch Europe (#19966).
NGO Relations Hosted at: *FAMI-QS (#09256).* [2012/XM2145/y/**F**]

♦ European Feed Ingredients Safety Certification / see European Feed and Food Ingredients Safety Certification (#07236)
♦ European Feed Manufacturers' Federation (#09566)
♦ European Feed Technology Center (inactive)
♦ European Fellowship / see European Fellowship of Christian Youth (#07238)

♦ **European Fellowship of Christian Youth (EF)** **07238**
Chairperson 50 North Street, Newtownards, BT23 4DE, UK. E-mail: chair@europeanfellowship.com.
URL: https://www.europeanfellowship.com/
History 1964. Current constitution adopted 20 Feb 2021. Former names and other names: *European Fellowship (EF)* – former. **Aims** Unite organizations in Europe which are: an integral part of the Christian Church; ecumenical in membership and/or outlook; working with and for children and young people; organized on democratic principles. **Structure** General Meeting; Global Fellowship Council; Committee (annual); Secretariat. **Languages** English. **Staff** Voluntary. **Finance** Each member bears costs of its own representation and participation. Other costs shared by agreement. **Activities** Events/meetings; knowledge management/information dissemination; networking/liaising; training/education. **Events** *Annual Meeting* Belfast (UK) 2022, *Annual Meeting* 2021, *Annual Meeting* Helsinki (Finland) 2020, *Annual Meeting* Reykjavik (Iceland) 2019, *Development Meeting* Cluj-Napoca (Romania) 2018.
Members Full; Associate. Full in 6 countries:
Denmark, Finland, Iceland, Ireland, Romania, UK.
Associate in 10 countries:
Belgium, Estonia, Germany, Hungary, Iceland, Latvia, Lithuania, Malta, Sweden, Ukraine.
Included in the above, 1 organization listed in this Yearbook:
Boys' Brigade, The (BB, #03308). [2022.10.19/XD1359/**D**]

♦ European Fellowship of the Wholesale Bicycle Trade (inactive)

♦ **European Fencing Confederation (EFC)** **07239**
Confédération européenne d'escrime (CEE)
Main Office BP 797, L-2017 Luxembourg, Luxembourg. E-mail: info@fencing-efc.eu.
URL: http://www.eurofencing.com/
History 26 Oct 1991, Vienna (Austria). Former names and other names: *European Fencing Union* – former. Registration: Luxembourg. **Aims** Promote the *sport* of fencing in Europe. **Structure** General Assembly; Executive Committee; Commissions (8). **Languages** English, French. **Staff** 1.00 FTE, paid; 30.00 FTE, voluntary. **Finance** Sources: members' dues. Supported by: *Fédération internationale d'escrime (FIE, #09629).* **Activities** Events/meetings; sporting activities; training/education. **Events** *General Assembly* Torun (Poland) 2016, *General Assembly* Montreux (Switzerland) 2015, *General Assembly* Strasbourg (France) 2014, *General Assembly* Zagreb (Croatia) 2013, *General Assembly* Solbiate Olona (Italy) 2012.
Members National organizations in 45 countries:
Albania, Armenia, Austria, Azerbaijan, Belarus, Belgium, Bulgaria, Croatia, Cyprus, Czechia, Denmark, Estonia, Finland, France, Georgia, Germany, Greece, Hungary, Iceland, Ireland, Israel, Italy, Latvia, Lithuania, Luxembourg, Malta, Moldova, Monaco, Netherlands, North Macedonia, Norway, Poland, Portugal, Romania, Russia, San Marino, Serbia, Slovakia, Slovenia, Spain, Sweden, Switzerland, Türkiye, UK, Ukraine.
NGO Relations *Fédération internationale d'escrime (FIE, #09629).* [2020/XD9014/**D**]

♦ European Fencing Union / see European Fencing Confederation (#07239)

♦ **European Fermentation Group (EFG)** **07240**
SG c/o CEFIC, Rue Belliard 40, Box 15, 1040 Brussels, Belgium.
URL: http://efg.cefic.org/
History A sector group of *Conseil européen de l'industrie chimique (CEFIC, #04687).* Registration: European Transparency Register, No/ID: 64879142323-90.
Members Companies in 10 countries:
Austria, Belgium, France, Germany, Hungary, Italy, Netherlands, Slovakia, Slovenia, Spain. [2022.02.02/XJ5956/**E**]

♦ **European Fertiliser Blenders Association (EFBA)** **07241**
Gen Sec address not obtained.
Pres address not obtained.
URL: http://www.european-blenders.org/
History Jun 1993, by French and German associations. Registered in accordance with French law. EU Transparency Register: 078796523376-92. **Aims** Represent common interests of fertilizer blenders at government level; exchange knowledge and information; perform common actions to improve the quality of blended fertilizers. **Structure** General Assembly; Board. **Publications** *EFBA Newsletter.*
Members Full in 8 countries:
Belgium, France, Germany, Ireland, Italy, Netherlands, Switzerland, UK.
NGO Relations Liaison Organization of: *Comité européen de normalisation (CEN, #04162).* [2019/XM4800/**D**]

♦ European Fertilizer Import Association (inactive)
♦ European Fertilizer Manufacturers Association / see Fertilizers Europe (#09738)

♦ **European Festivals Association (EFA)** **07242**
SG European House for Culture, Sainctelettesquare 17, 1000 Brussels, Belgium. T. +3226444800. E-mail: info@efa-aef.eu.
URL: http://www.efa-aef.eu/
History 1952, Geneva (Switzerland). Founded with assistance from *European Centre for Culture (ECC, #06472).* Former names and other names: *European Association of Music Festivals (EAMF)* – former; *Association européenne des festivals de musique* – former; *Association européenne des festivals (AEF)* – former. Registration: EU Transparency Register, No/ID: 434027116304-07, Start date: 4 Mar 2015; No/ID: 0476.059.667, Start date: 29 Mar 2001, Belgium. **Aims** Unite and represent member festivals by contributing to the artistic life of Europe. **Structure** General Assembly (annual); Board. Membership is limited to regularly held international festivals. **Languages** English. **Staff** 6.00 FTE, paid. **Finance** Sources: members' dues. **Events** *General Assembly* Estoril (Portugal) 2019, *Annual General Assembly* Granada (Spain) 2013, *Annual General Assembly* Bergen (Norway) 2012, *Annual collective and affiliate members meeting* Budapest (Hungary) 2011, *Annual General Assembly* Varna (Bulgaria) 2011. **Publications** *FestFlash* – newsletter. *EFA BOOKS* – series.
Members National Festivals (86) in 40 countries:
Armenia, Austria, Belgium, Bosnia-Herzegovina, Bulgaria, Croatia, Czechia, France, Georgia, Germany, Greece, Hungary, Israel, Italy, Japan, Korea Rep, Latvia, Lebanon, Lithuania, Luxembourg, Malta, Mexico, Montenegro, Netherlands, North Macedonia, Norway, Poland, Portugal, Romania, Russia, Serbia, Slovakia, Slovenia, South Africa, Spain, Sweden, Switzerland, Türkiye, UK, United Arab Emirates.
National Festivals Associations (14) in 14 countries:
Belgium, Bulgaria, Czechia, Estonia, Finland, France, Ireland, Italy, Netherlands, Norway, Serbia, Spain, Sweden, UK.
European networks (2), listed in this Yearbook:
European Conference of Promoters of New Music (ECPNM, #06736); European Early Music Network (EEMN, #06953).
IGO Relations *UNESCO (#20322).* **NGO Relations** Member of (12): *Association of Asian and Pacific Arts Festivals (AAPAF, #02380); Audiences Europe Network (AEN, #03013); Culture Action Europe (CAE, #04981); European Alliance for Culture and the Arts (#05866); European Music Council (EMC, #07837); European Tourism Manifesto (#08921); Europe of Cultures Forum; IETM – International Network for Contemporary Performing Arts (#11098); International Music Council (IMC, #14199); International Society for the Performing Arts Foundation (ISPA, #15350); On the Move (OTM, #16868); Pearle – Live Performance Europe (#18284).* [2020.03.03/XD0572/y/**D**]

♦ European Fetal Alcohol Spectrum Disorders Alliance / see European FASD Alliance (#07032)
♦ **European FGC Network** European Network on Family Group Conference (#07907)

♦ **European FH Patient Network (FH Europe)** **07243**
Chief Exec c/o HEART UK, 7 North Road, Maidenhead, SL6 1PE, UK. E-mail: info@fheurope.org.
URL: https://fheurope.org/
History 2015. Registration: Charity Commission, No/ID: 1170731, England and Wales; EU Transparency Register, No/ID: 302460130801-47, Start date: 3 Apr 2018. **Aims** Actively work to secure early identification and diagnosis of Familial hypercholesterolaemia (FH) patients to prevent early *cardiovascular disease.* **Structure** Board of Trustees; Chief Executive. **Activities** Advocacy/lobbying/activism; events/meetings; knowledge management/information dissemination; networking/liaising. **Publications** *FH Europe Newsletter.*
Members Organizations in 27 countries:
Austria, Belgium, Bulgaria, Czechia, Finland, France, Germany, Greece, Hungary, Ireland, Israel, Italy, Latvia, Lithuania, Netherlands, Norway, Poland, Portugal, Romania, Russia, Slovakia, Slovenia, Spain, Sweden, Switzerland, Türkiye, UK.
NGO Relations Member of (3): *European Alliance for Cardiovascular Health (EACH, #05863); European Patients' Forum (EPF, #08172)* (Associate); *EURORDIS – Rare Diseases Europe (#09175).* [2021/XM8431/**F**]

♦ European FIBC Association / see European Flexible Intermediate Bulk Container Association (#07270)
♦ European FIB Network / see European Focused Ion Beam Network (#07276)
♦ European Fibrefill Association (inactive)

♦ **European Film Academy** **07244**
Communications Officer Kurfürstendamm 225, 10719 Berlin, Germany. T. +49308871670. Fax +493088716777. E-mail: contact@europeanfilmacademy.org – press@europeanfilmacademy.org.
URL: http://www.europeanfilmacademy.org/
History 1989. Founded on the initiative of a group of Europe's finest filmmakers brought together on the occasion of the first European Film Award's ceremony, Nov 1988. Former names and other names: *European Cinema Society* – former (1989). Registration: EU Transparency Register, No/ID: 758813517971-42. **Aims** Advance the interests of the European film industry; share knowledge and educate audiences of all ages about European cinema; strive to unite everyone who loves European cinema by positioning itself as a leading organization and facilitating crucial debates within the industry. **Structure** General Assembly; Board; Secretariat. **Languages** English. **Staff** 7.00 FTE, paid. **Activities** Awards/prizes/competitions; events/meetings; networking/liaising; training/education. European Film Awards. **Events** *European Film Awards* Riga (Latvia) 2014, *European Film Awards* Berlin (Germany) 2013, *European Film Awards* Malta 2012, *European Film Awards* Berlin (Germany) 2011, *European Film Awards* Tallinn (Estonia) 2010. **Publications** *European Film Awards – Programme.*
Members Voting, Honorary and Patrons, totalling 4,200 in 56 countries and territories:
Albania, Andorra, Armenia, Australia, Austria, Azerbaijan, Belarus, Belgium, Bosnia-Herzegovina, Bulgaria, Canada, Colombia, Croatia, Cyprus, Czechia, Denmark, Estonia, Finland, France, Georgia, Germany, Greece, Greenland, Hong Kong, Hungary, Iceland, Ireland, Israel, Italy, Kazakhstan, Kosovo, Kyrgyzstan, Latvia, Lithuania, Luxembourg, Malta, Moldova, Montenegro, Netherlands, North Macedonia, Norway, Palestine, Poland, Portugal, Romania, Russia, Serbia, Slovakia, Slovenia, Spain, Sweden, Switzerland, Türkiye, UK, Ukraine, USA. [2022.02.15/XF2772/v/**F**]

♦ European Film Agency Directors / see European Film Agency Directors Association (#07245)
♦ European Film Agency Directors Association / see European Film Agency Directors Association (#07245)

♦ **European Film Agency Directors Association (EFAD)** **07245**
Secretariat Bd Leopold II 44, 1080 Brussels, Belgium. T. +3222311299. E-mail: secretariat@europeanfilmagencies.eu.
URL: https://europeanfilmagencies.eu/

History 2001. Founded as an informal network for collaboration, coordination and exchange of ideas on issues of common interest with regard to European audiovisual policy. Became an international non-profit association (aisbl) established in Brussels (Belgium), Dec 9, 2014. Former names and other names: *European Film Agency Directors Group (EFAD)* – former; *European Film Agency Directors Association (EFAD)* – former; *European Film Agency Directors (EFADs)* – former. Registration: Banque-Carrefour des Entreprises, No/ID: 0599.781.484, Start date: 27 Feb 2015, Belgium; EU Transparency Register, No/ID: 430805515370-85, Start date: 22 Dec 2014. **Aims** Ensure the existence of an environment conducive to development of a European policy that supports audiovisual and cinematographic creativity in Europe, and which guarantees effective distribution of European works both in Europe and worldwide. **Structure** Board. **Languages** English. **Staff** 0.50 FTE, paid. **Finance** Sources: members' dues. **Activities** Advocacy/lobbying/activism; knowledge management/ information dissemination; politics/policy/regulatory. Active in all member countries.
Members National film agencies of 34 countries:
Austria, Belgium, Bulgaria, Croatia, Cyprus, Czechia, Denmark, Estonia, Finland, France, Germany, Greece, Hungary, Iceland, Ireland, Italy, Latvia, Lithuania, Luxembourg, Malta, Montenegro, Netherlands, North Macedonia, Norway, Poland, Portugal, Romania, Serbia, Slovakia, Slovenia, Spain, Sweden, Switzerland, UK.
NGO Relations Instrumental in setting up (1): *European Film Agency Research Network (EFARN, #07246).*
[2022.05.04/XJ5555/**F**]

♦ European Film Agency Directors Group / see European Film Agency Directors Association (#07245)

♦ European Film Agency Research Network (EFARN) 07246

Secretariat c/o European Audiovisual Observatory, 76 allée de la Robertsau, 67000 Strasbourg, France. T. +33390216000. Fax +33390216019. E-mail: obs@obs.coe.int.
History 2003, on the initiative of the UK Film Council, within the framework of *European Film Agency Directors Association (EFAD, #07245).* **Aims** Provide a forum for exchange of information and best practice; improve availability and harmonization of data on a pan-European level. **Structure** Coordinated by and housed at *European Audiovisual Observatory (#06294).* **Languages** English. **Staff** 0.50 FTE, paid. **Events** *Annual Meeting* Stockholm (Sweden) 2013, *Annual Meeting* Amsterdam (Netherlands) 2012, *Annual Meeting* Paris (France) 2011, *Annual Meeting* Wiesbaden (Germany) 2010, *Annual meeting* Prague (Czech Rep) 2009.
Members Mainly film agencies, and also organizations. Members (45) in 36 countries:
Albania, Armenia, Austria, Belgium, Bosnia-Herzegovina, Bulgaria, Croatia, Cyprus, Czechia, Denmark, Estonia, Finland, France, Germany, Greece, Hungary, Iceland, Ireland, Italy, Latvia, Lithuania, Luxembourg, Netherlands, North Macedonia, Norway, Poland, Portugal, Romania, Russia, Slovakia, Slovenia, Spain, Sweden, Switzerland, Türkiye, UK.
Organizations with Observer Status (3):
European Support Fund for the Co-Production and Distribution of Creative Cinematographic and Audiovisual Works (EURIMAGES, #08859); MEDIA Programme (MEDIA, inactive); MEDIA Salles (#16620).
[2018.06.01/XJ1180/**E**]

♦ European Film College (internationally oriented national body)

♦ European Film Promotion (EFP) 07247

Dir Friedensallee 14-16, 22765 Hamburg, Germany. T. +494039840311. E-mail: info@efp-online.com.
URL: http://www.efp-online.com/
History 1997. Registration: Germany. **Aims** Increase competitive opportunities for European films in, and improve access for European film professionals to the international marketplace; where possible, contribute to opening of new markets for European film and enhance distribution possibilities; share accumulated knowledge and experience via the Europe-wide network. **Structure** Board of Directors. **Languages** English. **Staff** 8.00 FTE, paid. 4 freelance. **Finance** Sources: members' dues. Other sources: national film funding organizations and private sponsors. Annual budget: 1,600,000 EUR. **Activities** Events/meetings; guidance/ assistance/consulting. **Publications** Information brochure; image brochure; individual project catalogues; E-blast; activities and promotion on all major social media platforms.
Members National organizations in 37 countries:
Albania, Austria, Belgium, Bosnia-Herzegovina, Bulgaria, Croatia, Cyprus, Czechia, Denmark, Estonia, Finland, France, Georgia, Germany, Greece, Hungary, Iceland, Ireland, Italy, Kosovo, Latvia, Lithuania, Luxembourg, Montenegro, Netherlands, North Macedonia, Norway, Poland, Portugal, Romania, Serbia, Slovakia, Slovenia, Spain, Sweden, Switzerland, UK.
Included in the above, 1 organization listed in this Yearbook:
British Council. [2023.01.05/XD9389/y/**D**]

♦ European Film and Television Workers' Union (inactive)
♦ European Film Union (inactive)

♦ European Finance Association (EFA) 07248

Exec Sec Rue Fossé aux Loups, 38, 1000 Brussels, Belgium. T. +32485729359. E-mail: info@european-finance.org.
URL: http://www.european-finance.org/
History May 1974, Brussels (Belgium). Former names and other names: *Association européenne de finance* – former. Registration: Crossroads Bank for Enterprises, No/ID: 0864639588, Start date: 1 Feb 2004. **Aims** Provide a professional member-based society for academics, practitioners, doctoral students and researchers with interest in the broad field of finance, including financial management, research, theoretical aspects and applications. **Structure** General Assembly (annual); Executive Committee. **Languages** English. **Activities** Events/meetings; training/education. **Events** *Annual Meeting* Bratislava (Slovakia) 2024, *Annual Meeting* Amsterdam (Netherlands) 2023, *Annual Meeting* Barcelona (Spain) 2022, *Annual Meeting* Milan (Italy) 2021, *Annual Meeting* Espoo (Finland) 2020. **Publications** *Review of Finance* – journal. **Members** Individuals (2,000-2,500) in 50 countries. Membership countries not specified. [2022.04.20/XD6072/**D**]

♦ European Finance Convention Foundation (internationally oriented national body)

♦ European Financial Coalition against Commercial Sexual Exploitation of Children Online (EFC) 07249

Contact c/o Missing Children Europe, Rue de l'Industrie 10, 1000 Brussels, Belgium. E-mail: secretariat@europeanfinancialcoalition.eu.
URL: http://www.europeanfinancialcoalition.eu/
History Pilot Project launched, 2009, under (UK) National Crime Agency – CEOP. Second phase launched Nov 2012, chaired by *European Cybercrime Centre (EC3)* at *European Police Office (Europol, #08239),* and coordinated by *European Federation for Missing and Sexually Exploited Children (Missing Children Europe, #07166).* **Aims** Contribute to the fight against the commercial online distribution of illegal content depicting the sexual abuse of children. **Structure** Steering Group. Working Packages (5). **Languages** English. **Staff** 1.50 FTE, paid; 1.00 FTE, voluntary. **Finance** Funding from: *European Commission (EC, #06633)* (90%); private sector members (10%). **Activities** Training/education; events/meetings; awareness raising. **Publications** *EFC Newsletter.* Assessments; leaflet.
Members Key actors from law enforcement, private sector and civil society in Europe. Organizations listed in this Yearbook (10):
End Child Prostitution, Child Pornography and Trafficking of Children for Sexual Purposes (ECPAT, #05456); Eurojust (#05698); European Federation for Missing and Sexually Exploited Children (Missing Children Europe, #07166); European Police Office (Europol, #08239) (European Cybercrime Centre EC3); *European Union Agency for Law Enforcement Training (CEPOL, #08970); GSM Association (GSMA, #10813); International Association of Internet Hotlines (INHOPE, #11970); International Centre for Missing and Exploited Children (ICMEC, #12505); Internet Watch Foundation (IWF); Terre des Hommes International Federation (TDHIF, #20133).*
IGO Relations *International Telecommunication Union (ITU, #15673).* **NGO Relations** *European NGO Alliance for Child Safety Online (eNACSO, #08049); Save the Children International (#19058).*
[2015.04.14/XJ9399/y/**D**]

♦ European Financial Inclusion Network (EFIN) 07250

Address not obtained.
History Registration: Banque-Carrefour des Entreprises, Start date: 28 Jan 2010, End date: 13 Jun 2018, Belgium. **Aims** Increase knowledge financial inclusion; be a forum and mutual learning place; ensure knowledge dissemination and financial inclusion promotion. **Structure** General Assembly; Management Committee; Steering Bureau. **Languages** English. **Staff** 1.00 FTE, paid. **Finance** Members' dues. **Activities** Research/documentation; advocacy/lobbying/activism; events/meetings. **Events** *Conference on Personal Indebtedness in the EU* Brussels (Belgium) 2016. **Publications** *EFIN Newsletter.* Position papers.
Members Organizations in 15 countries:
Austria, Belgium, Czechia, France, Greece, Hungary, Ireland, Luxembourg, Netherlands, Norway, Poland, Portugal, Romania, Spain, UK.
Included in the above, 3 organizations listed in this Yearbook:
Bureau Européen des Unions de Consommateurs (BEUC, #03360); COFACE Families Europe (#04084); European Savings and Retail Banking Group (ESBG, #08426).
Individuals in 7 countries:
Belgium, Bulgaria, Canada, Ireland, Poland, Sweden, UK. [2017/XJ8744/dy/**D**]

♦ European Financial Management Association (EFMA) 07251

Founder c/o Old Dominion Univ, College of Business, Constant Hall 2080, Norfolk VA 23529-0222, USA. T. +17576835521. Fax +17576835639.
URL: http://www.efmaefm.org/
History 1994. Founded on the initiative of John Doukas. **Aims** Encourage research and disseminate knowledge about financial decision making in all areas of finance as it relates to European corporations, financial institutions and capital markets. **Finance** Members' dues. **Activities** Research/documentation; knowledge management/information dissemination. **Events** *Annual Meeting* Leeds (UK) 2021, *Annual Meeting* Ponta Delgada (Portugal) 2019, *Retail Banking Summit in Asia* Singapore (Singapore) 2019, *Retail Banking Summit in Asia* Singapore (Singapore) 2018, *Annual Meeting* Basel (Switzerland) 2016. **Publications** *EFM Journal* (5 a year). **Members** Finance academics, PhD students and finance practitioners. Membership countries not specified. [2021/XD9026/**D**]

♦ European Financial Management and Marketing Association / see Efma (#05386)
♦ European Financial Marketing Association / see Efma (#05386)

♦ European Financial Markets Federation (EFMF) 07252

Contact address not obtained. T. +33156212718.
History Dec 2005. **Aims** Provide a forum for the exchange of ideas between participating associations concerning the global capital and financial markets; consider ways in which the participating associations can cooperate in areas of common interest to their members; consider other matters relevant to the global capital and financial markets that arise from time to time.
Members National and international organizations. National organizations in 4 countries:
Germany, Italy, Russia, UK.
International organizations (3):
Council for the Euro Debt Market (AMTE Council); *European Federation of Financial Analysts Societies (EFFAS, #07123);* European Securities Forum (ESF). [2010/XJ1646/y/**D**]

♦ European Financial Planning Association (EFPA) 07253

Contact BluePoint Brussels, Boulevard Auguste Reyers 80, 1030 Brussels, Belgium. T. +393423812699.
URL: http://www.efpa-eu.org/
History Founded 18 Dec 2000, Rotterdam (Netherlands), at a ceremony held at Erasmus University Rotterdam. Originally registered in accordance with Dutch law. Currently registered in accordance with Belgian law. EU Transparency Register: 254633518956-57. Registration: AISBL/IVZW, Belgium. **Aims** Foster the highest professional, educational and ethical standards in the field; bring together like-minded financial services practitioners to work for sustainable development of financial planning in Europe; cooperate with consumer advocacy groups and European policy making bodies to ensure consumer protection in financial services and ethical behaviour of financial planning and advising practitioners; as a body independent of commercial entreprises, become the standards setting and membership body for financial planners and advisers in Europe and oversee the proper development of the profession. **Structure** General Meeting; Board of Directors; Standards and Qualifications Committee. **Languages** English. **Staff** 1.00 FTE, paid. **Activities** Standards/ guidelines; certification/accreditation; training/education; events/meetings; research/documentation. **Events** *Annual Meeting* Giardini Naxos (Italy) 2016, *Conference on the Quality of Financial Advice* Paris (France) 2016, *Polish Club Annual Meeting of Certified Advisors* Poland 2016, *International Conference* Prague (Czechia) 2016, *Biennial Congress of Financial Advisors* Saragossa (Spain) 2016. **Publications** *EFPA Newsletter.*
Members Non-profit professional associations, national training institutes, and universities involved in banking, insurance or the financial services sector, in 12 countries:
Austria, Czechia, Estonia, France, Germany, Hungary, Ireland, Israel, Italy, Poland, Spain, UK.
NGO Relations Member of (1): *European Federation of Financial Advisers and Financial Intermediaries (#07122).* [2019/XD9469/**D**]

♦ European Financial Reporting Advisory Group (EFRAG) 07254

Groupe Consultatif Européen sur l'Information Financière
CEO Square de Meeûs 35, 5th floor, 1000 Brussels, Belgium. T. +3222079300. E-mail: info@efrag.org.
URL: http://www.efrag.org/
History 31 Mar 2001. Registration: Banque-Carrefour des Entreprises, No/ID: 0478.422.212, Start date: 3 Oct 2002, Belgium; Eu Transparency Register, No/ID: 411098519407-76, Start date: 3 Nov 2015. **Aims** Develop and promote European views in the field of financial reporting and ensure these views are properly considered in the IASB standard-setting process and in related international debates. **Structure** General Assembly; Secretariat. Expert Groups. **Languages** English. **Staff** 25.00 FTE, paid. **Finance** Sources: members' dues. Public sector funding. **Activities** Events/meetings; guidance/assistance/consulting; standards/guidelines. **Events** *Where is Corporate Reporting Heading?* Brussels (Belgium) 2022. **Publications** *Annual Review.*
Members National organizations in 8 countries:
Denmark, France, Germany, Italy, Luxembourg, Netherlands, Sweden, UK.
International organizations (8):
Accountancy Europe (#00061); BUSINESSEUROPE (#03381); European Association of Co-operative Banks (EACB, #05990); European Banking Federation (EBF, #06312); European Federation of Accountants and Auditors for SMEs (EFAA, #07037); European Federation of Financial Analysts Societies (EFFAS, #07123); European Savings and Retail Banking Group (ESBG, #08426); Insurance Europe (#11362).
[2022/XE4686/y/**E**]

♦ European Financial Services Round Table (EFR) 07255

SG 4th Floor, Rond Point Schuman 11, 1040 Brussels, Belgium. T. +3222567523. Fax +3222567570. E-mail: secretariat@efr.be.
URL: http://www.efr.be/
History 1 Mar 2001, by a group of leading European banks and insurers. Registered in accordance with Belgian law. EU Transparency Register: 27636291880-60. **Aims** Provide a strong industry voice concerning further integration of the European Union single market in financial services. **Activities** Research/ documentation. **Members** Chairmen or Chief Executives of leading European banks and insurance companies (20). **NGO Relations** Member of: *European Policy Centre (EPC, #08240).* [2017.06.08/XF6861/**F**]

♦ European Financial Society (inactive)

♦ European Fine Art Foundation 07256

General Manager Broekwal 64, 5268 HD Helvoirt, Netherlands. T. +31411645090. Fax +31411645091. E-mail: info@tefaf.com.
URL: http://www.tefaf.com/
History 1989, 's Hertogenbosch (Netherlands), by arts dealers and collectors as an educational and lobbying alliance. **Structure** Board of Trustees; Executive Committee, including Chairman. **Activities** Organizes 'The European Fine Art Fair' (TETAF Maastricht). **Events** *Conference* Maastricht (Netherlands) 2011. **Members** Exhibitors (about 260) in 18 countries. Membership countries not specified. [2014.11.06/XF7075/**f**/**F**]

European Fine Chemicals
07257

alphabetic sequence excludes
For the complete listing, see Yearbook Online at

♦ **European Fine Chemicals Group (EFCG)** **07257**
Dir CEFIC, Rue Belliard 40, Box 15, 1040 Brussels, Belgium. T. +3224369470. E-mail: efcg@cefic.be.
URL: https://efcg.cefic.org/

History as a sector group within *Conseil européen de l'industrie chimique (CEFIC, #04687)*. **Aims** Serve as the forum, focus and voice for European fine chemicals manufacturers. **Structure** Board; Pharmaceutical Activities Committee (PAC); Agrochemical Intermediates Manufacturers in Europe (AIME). **Events** *Chemspec Europe* Basel (Switzerland) 2023, *Chemspec Europe* Brussels (Belgium) 2022, *Chemspec Europe conference* Barcelona (Spain) 2009, *Pharma business conference* Lisbon (Portugal) 2008. **Members** Fine chemicals manufacturers (40). Membership countries not specified. [2023/XM3791/E]

♦ European FinTech Association (unconfirmed)
♦ European Fireplaces Association (internationally oriented national body)

♦ **European Fire Safety Alliance (EuroFSA)** **07258**
Secretariat p/a Postbus 7010, 3801 HA Arnhem, Netherlands. T. +31263552358. E-mail: info@eurofsa.org.
URL: http://www.europeanfiresafetyalliance.org/

History Set up as an independent alliance of fire professionals, not an organization on its own. Registration: EU Transparency Register, No/ID: 357212934460-62, Start date: 3 Apr 2019. **Aims** Reduce the risk from fire. **Structure** Secretariat. **Activities** Advocacy/lobbying/activism; knowledge management/information dissemination; guidance/assistance/support. **NGO Relations** Member of (1): *Forum for European Electrical Domestic Safety (FEEDS)*. *Bromine Science and Environmental Forum (BSEF, #03337)*; *Europacable (#05743)*; *European Fire Sprinkler Network (EFSN, #07262)*; *Federation of the European Union Fire Officer Associations (FEU, #09555)*; *Modern Building Alliance (#16842)*. [2019/XM7767/D]

♦ European Fire and Security Advisory Council (inactive)

♦ **European Fire and Security Group (EFSG)** **07259**
Secretariat c/o VdS Schadenverhütung GmbH, Amsterdamer Strasse 174, 50735 Cologne, Germany. T. +492217766375. Fax +492217766377. E-mail: gspaeth@vds.de – info@efsg.org.
URL: http://www.efsg.org/

History 20 Mar 1990. 20 March 1990, when EFSG Agreement was signed. Agreement group of *European Organisation for Conformity Assessment (EOTC, inactive)*. EU Transparency Register: 824156923815-12. **Aims** Establish a common approach to conformity certification to ensure that certification bodies and their associated testing laboratories operate on a common basis. **Structure** Board of Management. **Staff** 2.00 FTE, paid. **Finance** Members' dues. **Activities** Certification/accreditation. **Publications** Newsletter.
Members Certification bodies (8), specialists in the fire protection and security fields, in 6 countries:
Belgium, Denmark, France, Germany, Sweden, UK.
NGO Relations Cooperating bodies: *Association of European Manufacturers of Fire and Security Systems (EURALARM, #02520)*; *Confederation of Fire Protection Associations (CFPA Europe, #04552)*; *European Committee of the Manufacturers of Fire Protection Equipment and Fire Fighting Vehicles (#06659)*; *Eurosafe (#09178)*. [2019/XF5093/F]

♦ **European Fire Service Colleges' Association (EFSCA)** **07260**
Sec Police Academy "Alexandru Ioan Cuza" – Fire Officers Faculty (FOF), Soseaua Morarilor, Sector 2, 022451 Bucharest, Romania. T. +40212555668 – +40212555669. Fax +40212555663. E-mail: secretary@efsca.org.
URL: http://www.efsca.org/

History Founded 1988. **Aims** Provide a forum for formal working relationships among representatives of member countries of the European Union, who have the authority to present experiences, views and opinions of their colleges at national level; inform and influence the European Union and member governments in matters concerning education and vocational training, so as to more effectively meet the personal and organizational development needs of personnel engaged in European fire services and in civil safety; promote and assist research and development in the field. **Structure** General Assembly; Board. **Languages** English. **Staff** 6.00 FTE, voluntary. **Finance** Members' dues. **Activities** Research and development; training/education; networking/liaising. **Events** *Conference and General Assembly* Bucharest (Romania) 2016, *Conference and General Assembly* Vilnius (Lithuania) 2015, *Conference and General Assembly* Lviv (Ukraine) 2014, *Conference and General Assembly* Minsk (Belarus) 2013, *Conference and General Assembly* Jurmala (Latvia) 2012.
Members in 31 countries:
Andorra, Austria, Belarus, Belgium, Bulgaria, Cyprus, Czechia, Denmark, Estonia, Finland, France, Germany, Greece, Hungary, Iceland, Ireland, Italy, Latvia, Lithuania, Luxembourg, Malta, Netherlands, Poland, Portugal, Romania, Slovakia, Slovenia, Spain, Sweden, UK, Ukraine.
IGO Relations *European Commission (EC, #06633)*. **NGO Relations** *Federation of the European Union Fire Officer Associations (FEU, #09555)*. [2015.02.24/XD8263/D]

♦ **European Fire Service Sport Federation (ESF)** **07261**
Fédération sportive européenne des sapeurs pompiers – Europäischen Feuerwehr Sport Föderation
Pres Hellenic Athletic Firefighters Assoc, 22 Konstantinoupoleos Street, Piraeus, 185 40 Athens, Greece. T. +302122158402. Fax +302104190617. E-mail: info@aepe.gr.

History 19 Oct 1977, The Hague (Netherlands). Statutes adopted 1978. Statutes modified 1994. **Aims** Promote sport in the fire service; foster international cooperation. **Structure** General Assembly (annual); Board; Committees. **Languages** English, French. **Staff** Voluntary. **Finance** Members' dues. **Activities** Organizes: championships among firefighters; international sports events. Supports other parallel events.
Members National associations and federations representing sport in the fire service. Founding members in 6 countries:
Belgium, France, Germany, Ireland, Netherlands, UK.
Members in 18 countries. Membership countries not specified. [2015.03.09/XD7255/D]

♦ **European Fire Sprinkler Network (EFSN)** **07262**
Réseau européen du sprinkleur anti-incendie – Foro Europeo de Rociadores Automaticos
Chairman 70 Upper Richmond Road, London, SW15 2RP, UK. T. +442088772600. Fax +442088772642. E-mail: info@eurosprinkler.org.
URL: http://www.eurosprinkler.org/

History 2002. Registration: EU Transparency Register, No/ID: 54924446464-63; England and Wales. **Aims** Connect those in Europe who share the aim to improve fire safety through greater use of fire sprinklers. **Languages** Dutch, English, French, German, Polish, Spanish. **Staff** 3.00 FTE, paid. **Finance** Members' dues. Conference income. **Activities** Standards/guidelines; events/meetings. **Events** *Fire Sprinkler International Conference* Amsterdam (Netherlands) 2023, *Fire Sprinkler International Conference* London (UK) 2022, *Fire Sprinkler International Conference* Amsterdam (Netherlands) 2021, *Fire Sprinkler International Conference* Madrid (Spain) 2019, *Fire Sprinkler International Conference* Stockholm (Sweden) 2018. **Publications** *European Fire Sprinkler Network e-Newsletter*.
Members Companies and organizations (100) in 17 countries:
Belgium, China, Denmark, Finland, France, Germany, Ireland, Italy, Luxembourg, Malaysia, Norway, Poland, Spain, Sweden, Switzerland, UK, USA.
NGO Relations Cooperates with (1): *International Fire Suppression Alliance (IFSA, #13607)*. In liaison with technical committees of: *Comité européen de normalisation (CEN, #04162)*. [2022/XF7182/y/F]

♦ **European First Year Experience Network (EFYE)** **07263**
Contact Nottingham Trent Univ, Burton Street, Nottingham, NG1 4BU, UK. T. +441159418418. E-mail: efye2014@ntu.ac.uk.
URL: http://www.efye.eu/

Aims Create an environment where educators, researchers and other support staff from universities across Europe can meet and through the sessions, share new research results and innovative practices and experiences in the area. **Events** *Conference* Utrecht (Netherlands) 2018, *Institutional development – the student lifecycle* Bergen (Norway) 2015, *The student lifecycle – building a first year experience for international students* Nottingham (UK) 2014, *Conference* Helsinki (Finland) 2013, *Conference* Manchester (UK) 2011. [2019/XJ1464/E]

♦ European Fiscal Standards Association (unconfirmed)

♦ **European Fisheries Alliance (EUFA)** **07264**
Contact Rue Breydel 42, 1040 Brussels, Belgium. T. +32473803638.
URL: https://fisheriesalliance.eu/

History Registration: EU Transparency Register, No/ID: 203165138219-11, Start date: 19 May 2020. **Aims** Represent the interests of fishing fleets in the remaining Member States of the European Union who are traditionally also fishing in what are to become 'UK waters'.
Members Full in 9 countries:
Belgium, Denmark, France, Germany, Ireland, Netherlands, Poland, Spain, Sweden. [2021/XM8879/t/E]

♦ **European Fisheries and Aquaculture Research Organization (EFARO)** **07265**
Secretariat c/o IMARES, Postbus 68, 1970 AB Ijmuiden, Netherlands. E-mail: efaro@wur.nl.
URL: http://www.efaro.eu/

History 1989. **Aims** Stimulate cooperation on fisheries and aquaculture sciences; increase information exchange between European researchers. **Structure** General Meeting (annual); Board. **Languages** English. **Staff** 1.00 FTE, paid. **Finance** Members' dues. **Events** *Annual Seminar* Brussels (Belgium) 2019, *Annual Meeting* Bergen (Norway) 2015, *Annual Meeting* Ancona (Italy) 2014, *Annual Meeting* Tallinn (Estonia) 2013, *Annual Meeting* Copenhagen (Denmark) 2012.
Members Directors of research institutes (28) in 19 countries:
Belgium, Croatia, Denmark, Estonia, Finland, France, Germany, Greece, Iceland, Ireland, Italy, Latvia, Netherlands, Norway, Poland, Portugal, Spain, Sweden, UK.
IGO Relations *European Union (EU, #08967)*. **NGO Relations** *European Marine Board (EMB, #07738)*. [2016.12.15/XM2675/D]

♦ **European Fisheries Control Agency (EFCA)** **07266**
Exec Dir Av. García Barbón, 4, Edificio Odriozola, 36201 Vigo, La Coruña, Spain. T. +34986120610. E-mail: efca@efca.europa.eu.
URL: https://www.efca.europa.eu/

History Apr 2005. Agreement on establishment 2002. Formally set up through Council Regulation 768/2005, as a body of the *European Commission (EC, #06633)*. A decentralized agency of *European Union (EU, #08967)*. Regulation (EU) 2019/473 on the European Fisheries Control Agency. Former names and other names: *Community Fisheries Control Agency (CFCA)* – former (2005 to 1 Jan 2012). **Aims** Promote the highest common standards for control, inspection and surveillance under the Common Fisheries Policy (CFP). **Structure** Administrative Board, consisting of one representative of each Member State and 6 representatives of the *European Commission (EC, #06633)*; Advisory Board, comprising representatives of Regional Fisheries Councils; Executive Director. **Languages** English. **Staff** 100.00 FTE, paid. **Finance** Annual EU budget. Annual budget: 35,600,000 EUR (2022). **Activities** Events/meetings; knowledge management/information dissemination; standards/guidelines. **Publications** *Year in Review*. *Promoting Fisheries Compliance*. **IGO Relations** Cooperates with (2): *European Maritime Safety Agency (EMSA, #07744)*; *Frontex, the European Border and Coast Guard Agency (#10005)*. **NGO Relations** Member of (1): *EU Agencies Network (EUAN, #05564)*. Regional Advisory Councils (ACs); Regional Fisheries Management Organisations (RFMOs). [2022.10.13/XJ1778/E*]

♦ European Fisheries Fund (inactive)

♦ **European Fishing Tackle Trade Association (EFTTA)** **07267**
Communications Manager Rue de la Loi 81a, 1000 Brussels, Belgium. E-mail: info@eftta.com.
URL: https://www.eftta.com/

History 1981, London (UK). Former names and other names: *Verband der Europäischen Angelgerätehersteller* – former. Registration: Banque-Carrefour des Entreprises, No/ID: 0667.966.150, Start date: 30 Apr 1982, Belgium; EU Transparency Register, No/ID: 08955462188-48, Start date: 27 Aug 2009; SPF Economie, PME, Classes moyennes et Energie, No/ID: 0777.249.518, Start date: 29 Sep 2021, Belgium. **Aims** Promote the interests of the European sportfishing tackle sector – manufacturers and wholesalers, importers and exporters; promote and protect sportfishing activities, to grow the tackle business and influence policies and legislation of importance to the sector, recreational anglers and the environment. **Structure** General Assembly (annual); Board; CEO; Secretariat. **Languages** English. **Staff** 2.00 FTE, paid. **Finance** Sources: members' dues. **Activities** Advocacy/lobbying/activism; events/meetings; networking/liaising; politics/policy/regulatory. **Events** *Annual Meeting* Brussels (Belgium) 2019, *Annual Meeting* Amsterdam (Netherlands) 2018, *Annual Meeting* Budapest (Hungary) 2017, *Annual Meeting* Amsterdam (Netherlands) 2016, *Annual Meeting* Warsaw (Poland) 2015. **Publications** *EFTTA Newslines* (6 a year) in English. Updates on lobby activities; import and export statistics; general assembly minutes and finances. **Members** Individuals (over 250) in 37 countries and territories. Membership countries not specified. **NGO Relations** Member of (1): *Federation of European and International Associations Established in Belgium (FAIB, #09508)*. Partner of (1): *European Boating Industry (EBI, #06377)*. [2023/XD1083/tv/D]

♦ **European Fishmeal** European Fismeal and Fish Oil Producers (#07268)

♦ **European Fismeal and Fish Oil Producers (European Fishmeal)** **07268**
Managing Dir c/o Marine Ingredients Denmark, Axelborg, Axeltorv 6 – 6 sal, 1609 Copenhagen, Denmark. T. +4550477749. E-mail: mid@maring.org – effop@maring.org.
URL: https://effop.org/

History 1963. Former names and other names: *Union of Associations of Fishmeal Manufacturers in the European Economic Community* – former (1963); *Union des associations des fabricants de farine de poisson de la Communauté économique européenne* – former (1963); *Unión de Asociaciones de Fabricantes de Harinas de Pescado de la Comunidad Económica Europea* – former (1963); *Vereinigung der Verbände der Fischmehlhersteller in der Europäischen Wirtschaftsgemeinschaft* – former (1963); *Vereniging van Organisaties van Vismeelfabrikanten in de Europese Economische Gemeenschap* – former (1963); *Foreningen for Organisationen af Fiskemelproducenter i de Europaeiske Økonomiske Faelleskaber* – former (1963); *Union of Associations of Fish Meal Manufacturers in the EEC* – former; *Union of Fishmeal and Fishoil Manufacturers in the European Community* – former; *Union des fabricants de farine et huile de poisson de la Communauté européenne* – former; *Unión de Fabricantes de Harinas y Aceites de Pescado de la Comunidad Europea* – former; *Vereinigung der Fischmehl- und Fischölhersteller in der Europäischen Gemeinschaft* – former; *Vereniging van Vismeel- en Visoliefabrikanten in de Europese Gemeenschap* – former; *Foreningen af Fiskemel- og Fiskeolieproducenter i det Europaeiske Faelleskab* – former. Registration: EU Transparency Register, No/ID: 783980638121-41, Start date: 12 May 2020. **Aims** Represent and promote the European fishmeal and fish oil industry in the EU. **Languages** Danish, English. **Staff** 3.00 FTE, paid. **Activities** Advocacy/lobbying/activism; events/meetings; knowledge management/information dissemination; networking/liaising; politics/policy/regulatory.
Members National organizations and companies in 10 countries and territories:
Czechia, Denmark, Estonia, Faeroe Is, Iceland, Ireland, Norway, Spain, Sweden, UK.
IGO Relations Accredited by (1): *European Commission (EC, #06633)*. **NGO Relations** Member of (5): Aquaculture Advisory Council; *Baltic Sea Advisory Council (BSAC, #03139)*; *Market Advisory Council (MAC, #16584)*; *North Sea Advisory Council (NSAC, #17603)*; *Pelagic Advisory Council (Pelagic AC, #18289)*. Member of: Aquaculture Advisory Council. [2022.11.04/XE3346/t/E]

♦ European Fittings Manufacturers Association (inactive)
♦ European Flame Retardants Association / see Flame Retardants Europe (#09791)

♦ **European Flavour Association (EFFA)** **07269**
Exec Dir Ave des Arts 6, 1210 Brussels, Belgium. T. +3222142040. E-mail: info@effa.eu.
URL: http://www.effa.eu/

History 10 Mar 1961, Brussels (Belgium). Former names and other names: *Liaison Bureau of the European / EEC / Union of Aromatic Products* – former (1961 to 1991); *Bureau de liaison des syndicats européens – CEE / des produits aromatiques (BLA)* – former (1961 to 1991); *Verbindungsstelle der Europäischen Berufsverbände EWG / für Aromatische Erzeugnisse* – former (1961 to 1991); *European Flavour and Fragrance Association (EFFA)* – former (1991 to 2009). Registration: Banque-Carrefour des Entreprises, No/ID: 0828.835.108,

Start date: 30 Aug 2010, Belgium; EU Transparency Register, No/ID: 71022433397-11, Start date: 1 Apr 2010. **Aims** Promote and support a consistent European-wide strategy on flavour issues; monitor flavour-related EU legislation; stimulate, coordinate and monitor best practice in regulatory, safety, technical and scientific issues; create networks and alliances with other European associations; coordinate approved European work streams and projects; provide coordination and communication between members. **Structure** General Assembly; Pillars: Regulatory, Communication, Public Affairs. **Languages** English. **Staff** 4.00 FTE, paid. **Finance** Sources: members' dues. **Activities** Events/meetings; knowledge management/information dissemination; politics/policy/regulatory. **Events** *Annual General Assembly* Brussels (Belgium) 2005, *Annual General Assembly* Brussels (Belgium) 2004, *Annual General Assembly* Brussels (Belgium) 2003, *Annual General Assembly* Brussels (Belgium) 2002, *Annual General Assembly* Brussels (Belgium) 2001. **Publications** *EFFA Flavour Newsletter*.
Members National organizations in 12 countries:
Austria, Belgium, Denmark, France, Germany, Italy, Netherlands, Spain, Sweden, Switzerland, Türkiye, UK.
Companies (11). Membership countries not specified.
IGO Relations Recognized by: *European Commission (EC, #06633)*. **NGO Relations** Member of (3): *Federation of European and International Associations Established in Belgium (FAIB, #09508)*; *Industry4Europe (#11181)*; *International Organization of the Flavor Industry (IOFI, #14446)*. [2022.02.03/XE2912/**E**]

♦ European Flavour and Fragrance Association / see European Flavour Association (#07269)

♦ European Flexible Intermediate Bulk Container Association (EFIBCA) 07270

Secretariat c/o IK, Kaiser-Friedrich-Promenade 43, 61348 Bad Homburg, Germany. T. +496172926665. Fax +496172926670. E-mail: secretariat@efibca.com.
Pres address not obtained.
URL: http://www.efibca.com/

History Dec 1982, London (UK). Also referred to as *European FIBC Association*. **Aims** Represent interests of FIBC manufacturers, distributors and material suppliers towards authorities, regulatory bodies, the public and other institutions; offer a platform for exchange and cooperation on quality, safety and regulatory issues; provide guidance for the FIBC user. **Structure** General Meeting (annual); Council. **Languages** English. **Staff** 1.00 FTE, paid. **Finance** Members' dues. **Activities** Certification/accreditation; awareness raising. **Events** *World congress* Antwerp (Belgium) 2002, *Bulk bag meeting* Antwerp (Belgium) 2000, *World congress* Düsseldorf (Germany) 2000, *World congress* Amsterdam (Netherlands) 1998. **Publications** *FIBC Import Statistics* (annual); *EFIBCA Bulletin*; *EFIBCA Newsletter*. Brochure; booklet; pamphlet.
Members Companies operating in 40 countries and territories:
Austria, Azerbaijan, Bangladesh, Belgium, Bulgaria, China, Côte d'Ivoire, Czechia, Denmark, Egypt, Finland, France, Germany, Hungary, India, Indonesia, Iran Islamic Rep, Italy, Kazakhstan, Lithuania, Mexico, Morocco, Netherlands, Oman, Poland, Portugal, Romania, Russia, Saudi Arabia, Spain, Sweden, Switzerland, Taiwan, Thailand, Türkiye, UK, Ukraine, United Arab Emirates, USA, Vietnam.
NGO Relations Member of: *International Confederation of Plastics Packaging Manufacturers (ICPP)*. [2014.07.02/XD1621/**D**]

♦ European Flexographic Industry Association (internationally oriented national body)
♦ European Flexographic Technical Association / see European Flexographic Industry Association
♦ European Flexographic Technical Association Benelux (internationally oriented national body)
♦ European Flexpak Converters Federation (inactive)
♦ European Flight Engineers Organization (inactive)
♦ European Floorcovering Association / see European Floor Coverings Association (#07271)

♦ European Floor Coverings Association (EUFCA) 07271

Contact Rue Monteyer 24, 1000 Brussels, Belgium. T. +3222870873. E-mail: info@eufca.org.
URL: https://www.eufca.org/

History Former names and other names: *European Floorcovering Association* – alias. Registration: Banque Carrefour des Entreprises, No/ID: 0726.944.922, Start date: 21 May 2019, Belgium; EU Transparency Register, No/ID: 756958036725-89, Start date: 3 Dec 2019. **Aims** Represent the European floor coverings industry on a European and international level in ensuring the maintenance of high standards from a social, environmental, economic, ethical and technical or other point of view, in the broadest possible sense.
Members Organizations (4):
Association of European Producers of Laminate Flooring (EPLF, #02533); *European Carpet and Rug Association (ECRA, #06452)*; *European Resilient Flooring Manufacturers' Institute (ERFMI, #08380)*; *Multilayer Modular Flooring Association (MMFA)*.
NGO Relations Member of (2): *Construction 2050 Alliance (#04760)*; *Construction Products Europe AISBL (#04761)*. [2019/XM8880/y/**D**]

♦ European Flour Exporters Committee (inactive)

♦ European Flour Millers' Association 07272

SG Av de Tervuren 13A, 1040 Brussels, Belgium. T. +3227365354. Fax +3227323427. E-mail: secretariat@flourmillers.eu.
URL: https://www.flourmillers.eu/

History 16 Mar 1959, Paris (France). Took over activities of *International Milling Association (IMA, inactive)*. Former names and other names: *Flour Milling Associations Group of the EU Countries* – former; *Groupement des associations meunières des pays de la UE (GAM)* – former; *Gesamtverband der Mühlenbetriebe der EU-Länder* – former; *Gruppo delle Associazioni dei Mugnai dei Paesi della UE* – former; *Forbundet for Møllerisammenslutninger i det EU Lande* – former; *European Flour Milling Association* – former; *European Flour Milling Associations Group of the EU Countries* – former. Registration: EU Transparency Register, No/ID: 81318861355-20. **Aims** Facilitate development of a business environment in which all milling companies can meet the needs of consumers and society, while competing effectively for sustainable growth. **Structure** General Assembly (annual); Executive Committee; National Association Directors Committee; Tech & Regulatory Affairs/Wheat & Trade Policy Expert Committees. **Languages** English. **Staff** 1.50 FTE, paid. **Finance** Sources: contributions. **Activities** Advocacy/lobbying/activism; events/meetings; knowledge management/information dissemination; monitoring/evaluation; politics/policy/regulatory; research and development. **Events** *European Flour Millers' Congress* Munich (Germany) 2024, *European Flour Millers' Congress* Venice (Italy) 2022, *General Assembly and Congress* Paris (France) 2019, *European Flour Millers' Congress* Prague (Czechia) 2018, *General Assembly and Congress* Berlin (Germany) 2017. **Publications** *Manual on the European Flour Milling Industry* (every 2 years).
Members National associations in 26 countries:
Austria, Belgium, Bulgaria, Cyprus, Czechia, Denmark, Estonia, Finland, France, Germany, Greece, Iceland, Ireland, Italy, Latvia, Lithuania, Luxembourg, Netherlands, Poland, Portugal, Slovenia, Spain, Sweden, Switzerland, Türkiye, UK.
IGO Relations Recognized by: *European Commission (EC, #06633)*; *European Parliament (EP, #08146)*. Participates as observer in the activities of: *Codex Alimentarius Commission (CAC, #04081)*. **NGO Relations** Member of: *Industry4Europe (#11181)*; *Primary Food Processors (PFP, #18496)*. [2023.02.13/XE0969/**E**]

♦ European Flour Milling Association / see European Flour Millers' Association (#07272)
♦ European Flour Milling Associations Group of the EU Countries / see European Flour Millers' Association (#07272)

♦ European Fluid Power Committee (CETOP) 07273

Secretariat Lyoner Str 18, 60528 Frankfurt-Main, Germany. T. +496966031319. Fax +496966032658. E-mail: info@cetop.org.
URL: http://www.cetop.org/

History 15 Jun 1962, Stockholm (Sweden), as *Comité européen des transmissions oléohydrauliques et pneumatiques (CETOP) – European Oil Hydraulic and Pneumatic Committee – Europäisches Komitee Ölhydraulik und Pneumatik*. **Aims** Study issues raised by development and evolution in the oil hydraulic and pneumatic industries. **Structure** General Assembly (annual) elects (every 3 years) President Council composed of President, Technical Vice-President, Vice-President Economic; Vice-President Education; Vice-President Marketing and Communications; Secretary-General. **Languages** English, French, German. **Finance** Members' dues. Budget (annual): euro 42,000. **Events** *Annual General Assembly* Cesky Krumlov (Czechia) 2019, *Annual General Assembly* Barcelona (Spain) 2017, *Annual General Assembly* The Hague (Netherlands) 2013, *Annual General Assembly* Paris (France) 2012, *Annual General Assembly* Pris (France) 2012. **Publications** *CETOP Directory* (every 2 years).
Members National associations (18) of pneumatic and hydraulic equipment manufacturers in 17 countries:
Belgium, Czechia, Finland, France, Germany, Italy, Netherlands, Norway, Poland, Romania, Russia, Slovenia, Spain, Sweden, Switzerland (2), Türkiye, UK.
IGO Relations Recognized by: *European Commission (EC, #06633)*. **NGO Relations** In liaison with technical committees of: *International Organization for Standardization (ISO, #14473)*. [2018/XD0789/**D**]

♦ European Fluorocarbons Technical Committee (EFCTC) 07274

Contact c/o CEFIC, Rue Belliard 40, 1040 Brussels, Belgium. T. +3224369300. Fax +3226767241. E-mail: anc@cefic.be.
URL: https://www.fluorocarbons.org/

History Founded as a sector group and affiliate organization of *Conseil européen de l'industrie chimique (CEFIC, #04687)*. **Aims** Review EC and UNEP policies on CFC, HCFC, HFC, HFOs; represent European fluorocarbons *producers* in all aspects of the *ozone* layer issue; support implementation of Montréal Protocol and its amendments. **Languages** English.
Members Full in 7 countries:
Belgium, France, Germany, Italy, Netherlands, Switzerland, UK. [2022.05.04/XE5906/**E**]

♦ European Flying Disc Federation (EFDF) 07275

Sec Götgatan 31 III, SE-116 21 Stockholm, Sweden. T. +4686401445. Fax +4687012437.
Pres Brieger Strasse 8, 76139 Karlsruhe, Germany. T. +4972167698. Fax +497219683568.
URL: http://www.efdf.org/

History 1984. **Activities** Organizes championships.
Members National organizations (23) in 21 countries:
Austria, Belgium, Czechia, Denmark, Finland, France, Germany, Hungary, Ireland, Israel, Italy, Latvia, Netherlands, Norway, Portugal, Russia, Slovakia, Spain, Sweden, Switzerland, UK.
NGO Relations Instrumental in setting up: *World Flying Disc Federation (WFDF, #21509)*. •[2010/XD1061/**D**]

♦ European Focused Ion Beam Network (EuFN) 07276

Contact Minatec Campus, 17 avenue des Martyrs, 38054 Grenoble, France.
Contact address not obtained.
URL: https://www.eu-f-n.org/

History 2007. Former names and other names: *European FIB Network* – alias; *D-A-CH FIB Arbeitskreis* – former. **Aims** Promote Focused Ion Beam (FIB) processing and closely related technologies. **Structure** Steering Committee. **Activities** Events/meetings; knowledge management/information dissemination. **Events** *Workshop* Hamburg (Germany) 2022, *Workshop* Vienna (Austria) 2021, *Workshop* Dresden (Germany) 2019, *Workshop* Grenoble (France) 2018, *Workshop* Graz (Austria) 2017. [2022/AA2436/**F**]

♦ European Focused Ion Beam Users Group (EFUG) 07277

Contact IMEC, Kapeldreef 75, 3001 Leuven, Belgium. T. +3216281304. Fax +3216229400.
URL: http://efug.imec.be/

Aims Stimulate interaction and collaboration between focused ion beam users. **Languages** English. **Staff** 3.00 FTE, voluntary. **Finance** Supported by FIB manufacturers. **Activities** Events/meetings. **Events** *Annual Meeting* Bordeaux (France) 2017, *Annual Meeting* Halle (Saale) (Germany) 2016, *Annual Meeting* Toulouse (France) 2015, *Annual Meeting* Berlin (Germany) 2014, *Annual Meeting* Arcachon (France) 2013. **Members** Individuals (351). Membership countries not specified. [2019.02.19/XM2130/**F**]

♦ European Focused Ultrasound Charitable Society (EUFUS) 07278

Head Office Falkenweg 19, 65527 Niedernhausen, Germany. T. +4961288606800. Fax +4961288606801. E-mail: office@eufus.org.
URL: https://www.eufus.org/

History Registration: Hesse District court Wiesbaden, No/ID: VR 6768, Start date: 16 Jul 2013, Germany. **Aims** Serve as a philanthropic forum to establish research funding, sharing experiences, reviewing best practices and promoting cooperation in the field of Focused Ultrasound for better patient treatment. **Structure** General Assembly; Executive Board; International Board. **Activities** Awards/prizes/competitions; events/meetings; guidance/assistance/consulting; knowledge management/information dissemination; research/documentation. **Events** *Meeting* Barcelona (Spain) 2019, *Symposium* Leipzig (Germany) 2017. **Publications** *EUFUS Newsletter*. [2019/AA0638/**D**]

♦ European Folk Art and Craft Federation 07279

Fédération européenne pour l'art populaire et l'artisanat

Contact c/o Finnish Craft Organization, Kalevankatu 61, FI-00180 Helsinki, Finland.
URL: http://www.folkartandcraft.net/

History 1972, Switzerland. **Aims** Preserve and develop craft in a traditional and modern way; promote exchange of experiences. **Structure** General Meeting; Board. **Languages** English. **Staff** None. **Finance** Members' dues. **Activities** Knowledge management/information dissemination; research/documentation. **Events** *General Meeting* Bratislava (Slovakia) 2015, *General Meeting* Helsinki (Finland) 2013, *General Meeting* Stockholm (Sweden) 2012, *General Meeting* Tallinn (Estonia) 2011, *General Meeting* Jokkmokk (Sweden) 2010.
Members Full in 11 countries:
Austria, Denmark, Estonia, Finland, Hungary, Latvia, Norway, Poland, Serbia, Slovakia, Sweden.
Observer member in 1 country:
Serbia. [2014.06.23/XD6857/**D**]

♦ European Folklore Institute (internationally oriented national body)
♦ European Food Authority / see European Food Safety Authority (#07287)

♦ European Food Banks Federation (FEBA) 07280

SG Chaussée de Louvain 775, 1140 Brussels, Belgium. T. +3225389450. E-mail: info@eurofoodbank.org.
Pres address not obtained. E-mail: president@eurofoodbank.org.
URL: http://www.eurofoodbank.org/

History 23 Sep 1986. In 2018, moved from Bourg-la-Reine (Paris, France) to Brussels (Belgium). Headquarters officially opened 10 Oct 2018 in the presence of Bernard Dandrel, the founding father of FEBA, and Vytenis Andriukaitis, Commissioner for Health and Food Safety. Former names and other names: *Fédération européenne des banques alimentaires (FEBA)* – former; *European Federation of Food Banks* – former. Registration: Banque-Carrefour des Entreprises, No/ID: 0691.585.155, Start date: 28 Feb 2018, Belgium; EU Transparency Register, No/ID: 79355099508-47, Start date: 11 Sep 2012. **Aims** Contribute to reducing poverty and social exclusion through the recovery of edible and safe surplus food from the food supply chain and its redistribution of food in collaboration with charitable organisations that assist the most deprived in Europe. **Structure** General Assembly; Board of Directors; Secretariat. **Languages** English. **Staff** 7.00 FTE, paid. **Finance** Sources: donations; fundraising; members' dues. Annual budget: 739,781 EUR (2019). **Activities** Advocacy/lobbying/activism; awareness raising; capacity building; financial and/or material support; knowledge management/information dissemination; monitoring/evaluation; networking/liaising; training/education. **Events** *FEBA Annual Convention* Berlin (Germany) 2022, *FEBA Annual Convention* Prague (Czechia) 2021, *FEBA Annual Convention* Rome (Italy) 2019, *Annual Meeting* Budapest (Hungary) 2018, *Annual Meeting* Rotterdam (Netherlands) 2017.
Members Full Members: food banks in 23 countries that have accepted the 'Food Bank Charter':
Austria, Belgium, Bulgaria, Czechia, Denmark, Estonia, France, Germany, Greece, Hungary, Ireland, Italy, Lithuania, Luxembourg, Netherlands, Norway, Poland, Portugal, Serbia, Slovakia, Spain, Switzerland, UK.
Associate Members: food banks in 6 European countries:
Albania, Malta, North Macedonia, Romania, Slovenia, Ukraine.
NGO Relations Member of (1): *European Anti-Poverty Network (EAPN, #05908)*. Partner of (1): *Global FoodBanking Network (GFN, #10365)*. [2023.03.02/XD1072/**D**]

♦ European Food Brokers Association / see European Sales and Marketing Association (#08422)
♦ European Food Code Council (inactive)
♦ European Food Distributors Association (inactive)

European Food Emulsifier
07281

alphabetic sequence excludes
For the complete listing, see Yearbook Online at

♦ European Food Emulsifier Manufacturers' Association (EFEMA) . . . 07281
Association des fabricants européens d'émulsifiants alimentaires – Verband Europäischer Hersteller von Nahrungsmittel Emulgatoren – Associazione dei Fabbricanti Europei di Emulsionanti Alimentari – Vereniging van de Europese Fabrikanten van Levensmiddelenemulgatoren – Europaeiske Fabrikantforening for Fabrikanter af Levnedsmiddelemulgatorer
SG Av de Tervueren 13 A – Bte 7, 1040 Brussels, Belgium. T. +3227365354. Fax +3227323427. E-mail: efema@ecco-eu.com.
URL: http://www.emulsifiers.org/
History 13 Dec 1973. Registration: EU Transparency Register, No/ID: 61813266495-76. **Aims** Support and promote the general, scientific, economic and technical interest of European producers of food emulsifiers; promote a wider understanding of emulsifiers and their use. **Structure** General Assembly; Board; Technical Committee. Chairman; Secretary-General. **Languages** English. **Finance** Members' dues.
Members Producers of food emulsifiers (7) in 6 countries:
Belgium, Denmark, Germany, Ireland, Spain, UK.
IGO Relations Participates as observer in the activities of: *Codex Alimentarius Commission (CAC, #04081)*.
NGO Relations Member of: *EU Specialty Food Ingredients (#09200)*. [2019.10.14/XD4900/**D**]

♦ European Food and Feed Cultures Association (EFFCA) 07282
Association européenne des fabricants de ferments à usage agro-alimentaire
Main Office c/o Kellen, Av de Tervueren 188A, Box 4, 1150 Brussels, Belgium. T. +3227611671. Fax +3227611699. E-mail: effca@kellencompany.com.
URL: http://www.effca.org/
History Oct 1991. Statutes adopted 1 Jan 1992; most recently modified, 2016. **Aims** Enhance public knowledge of the contribution the use of microbial cultures make within the food chain while discouraging inappropriate promition or misuse. **Structure** General Assembly; Board; Working Groups (2). **Languages** English. **Staff** 1.00 FTE, paid. **Finance** Members' dues. **Activities** Events/meetings. **Events** *General Assembly* Amsterdam (Netherlands) 2012, *General Assembly* Sjöbo (Sweden) 2011, *General Assembly* Corsica (France) 2010, *General Assembly* Munich (Germany) 2009, *General Assembly* Krakow (Poland) 2008.
Members Manufacturers in 6 countries:
Denmark, Finland, France, Germany, Italy, Netherlands.
Affiliates in 2 countries:
Australia, USA.
IGO Relations Participates as observer in the activities of: *Codex Alimentarius Commission (CAC, #04081)*.
NGO Relations Member of: *EU Specialty Food Ingredients (#09200)*. [2020/XD3279/**D**]

♦ European Food Forum (EFF) 07283
Dir Rue Van Eick 22, 1000 Brussels, Belgium. E-mail: info@europeanfoodforum.eu.
URL: https://europeanfoodforum.eu/
History Nov 2019. Founded by 5 members of *European Parliament (EP, #08146)*. Registration: No/ID: 0737.616.011, Start date: 12 Nov 2019, Belgium; EU Transparency Register, No/ID: 793227839090-06, Start date: 28 Jul 2020. **Aims** Promote open dialogue on sustainable food systems among policymakers, food supply chain actors, civil society organizations, research and academia, and other public institutions. **Structure** General Assembly; Steering Committee; Board of Management; Programming Committee; Secretariat. **Activities** Events/meetings. [2021/AA1002/**F**]

♦ European Food Information Council (EUFIC) 07284
Conseil Européen de l'information sur l'alimentation – Consejo Europeo de Información sobre la Alimentación – Europäisches Informationszentrum für Lebensmittel
Main Office Rue des Deux Eglises 14, 3rd Fl, 1000 Brussels, Belgium. E-mail: eufic@eufic.org.
URL: http://www.eufic.org/
History 1995. Registration: Banque-Carrefour des Entreprises, No/ID: 0456.866.931, Start date: 21 Dec 1995, Belgium; EU Transparency Register, No/ID: 248894041414-94, Start date: 3 Mar 2021. **Aims** Communicate science-based information on *nutrition* and *health*, food *safety* and quality, to help *consumers* to be better informed when choosing a well-balanced, safe and healthful diet. **Structure** General Assembly (annual, since 2000 in Brussels, Belgium); Board of Directors; Technical Committees; Scientific Advisory Board; Editorial Board. **Languages** Czech, English, French, German, Hungarian, Irish Gaelic, Italian, Polish, Portuguese, Slovakian, Spanish. **Staff** 14.50 FTE, paid. **Finance** Members' dues. Other sources: support from: *European Commission (EC, #06633)*; funding from foundations and trade associations. **Activities** Knowledge management/information dissemination; events/meetings. **Events** *Biennial Savoury Snack Summit* Brussels (Belgium) 2012, *General Assembly* Rotterdam (Netherlands) 1999, *General Assembly* Paris (France) 1998, *Geneal assembly* Milan (Italy) 1997, *General Assembly* London (UK) 1996. **Publications** *Food Today* (5 a year) in Czech, English, French, German, Greek, Hungarian, Italian, Polish, Portuguese, Slovakian, Spanish, Turkish – newsletter; *EUFIC Review*. *EUFIC Forum*. Peer-reviewed scientific publications. **Members** Companies active in the European food and drink industries. Membership countries not specified. **NGO Relations** Member of: *EU Platform for Action on Diet, Physical Activity and Health (inactive)*. [2020/XD3887/**D**]

♦ European Food Information Resource (EuroFIR) 07285
Réseau européen de sources d'information sur les aliments – Europäischen Netzwerk für Lebensmittelinformation
Pres/Managing Dir Rue Washington 40, 1050 Brussels, Belgium. T. +3226262901. E-mail: secretariat@eurofir.org.
URL: http://www.eurofir.org/
History 2009. Founded as a members-based non-profit organization based in Brussels (Belgium). Registration: Banque-Carrefour des Entreprises, No/ID: 0811.804.183, Start date: 19 May 2009, Belgium; EU Transparency Register, No/ID: 490049114088-06, Start date: 31 Jul 2014. **Aims** Develop, publish and exploit food composition information; promote international cooperation and harmonization of standards to improve data quality, storage and access. **Structure** General Assembly; President; Executive Board; Office in Brussels (Belgium). **Languages** English, French, Italian, Polish, Serbian. **Staff** 7.00 FTE, paid. **Finance** Members' dues. Other sources: research and development projects; training; consultancies. **Activities** Research and development; training/education; guidance/assistance/consulting; events/meetings. **Events** *Food Forum* Brussels (Belgium) 2017, *DISH-RI Workshop* Brussels (Belgium) 2016, *Food Forum* Brussels (Belgium) 2016, *BACCHUS Seminar / Conference* Brussels (Belgium) 2014, *Nexus Project Meeting / Conference* Ljubljana (Slovenia) 2013. **Publications** *EuroFIR Newsletter* (2 a year). Annual Report; technical reports; scientific papers; oral communications.
Members Universities, research institutes, small and medium enterprises, and individuals. Members in 27 countries:
Australia, Austria, Belgium, Canada, Czechia, Denmark, Finland, France, Germany, Greece, Iceland, Ireland, Italy, Latvia, Lithuania, Netherlands, Norway, Poland, Portugal, Serbia, Slovakia, Slovenia, Spain, Sweden, Switzerland, Türkiye, UK.
NGO Relations Member of: *Federation of European and International Associations Established in Belgium (FAIB, #09508)*. [2020/XM3168/**F**]

♦ European Food Law Association (EFLA) 07286
Association Européenne pour le Droit de l'Alimentation (AEDA)
SG Ave de Tervueren 13 A – Bte 7, 1040 Brussels, Belgium. T. +3227365354. Fax +3227323427. E-mail: secretariat@efla-aeda.org.
URL: http://www.efla-aeda.org/
History 4 May 1973, Brussels (Belgium). Previously also referred to in Spanish as *Asociación Europea para el Derecho Alimentario*. Registered in accordance with Belgian law. **Aims** Study and promote food law; contribute to its development and international harmonization. **Structure** General Assembly; Council; Executive Committee. **Languages** English. **Staff** 1.00 FTE, paid. **Finance** Members' dues. Workshops/conferences/congresses. **Activities** Guidance/assistance/consulting; events/meetings; research and development. **Events** *Conference on the Management of a Food Crisis from the Food Law Perspective*. Brussels (Belgium) 2022, *Biennial Congress* Copenhagen (Denmark) 2021, *Conference on the Role of Trade Agreements in the Food Sector* Brussels (Belgium) 2019, *Workshop on Borderline Issues between Food Additives and Food Ingredients in the EU* Brussels (Belgium) 2019, *Biennial Congress* Hamburg (Germany) 2018. **Publications** *From Agricultural to Good Law* (2014); *Private Food Law* (2011).
Members Individuals; Corporate. Members in 16 countries:
Austria, Belgium, Denmark, France, Germany, Ireland, Italy, Netherlands, Norway, Poland, Spain, Sweden, Switzerland, Türkiye, UK, USA.
Consultative Status Consultative status granted from: *ECOSOC (#05331)* (Ros C); *FAO (#09260)* (Liaison Status). [2017.03.13/XD4409/**D**]

♦ European Food Safety Agency / see European Food Safety Authority (#07287)

♦ European Food Safety Authority (EFSA) 07287
Autorité européenne de sécurité des aliments – Europäische Behörde für Lebensmittelsicherheit – Autorità Europa di Sicurezza Alimentare
Exec Dir Via Carlo Magno 1-A, 43126 Parma PR, Italy. T. +39521036111. Fax +39521036110.
URL: http://www.efsa.europa.eu/
History 15 Dec 2001, Brussels (Belgium). Established by the Heads of State and Government of *European Union (EU, #08967)* meeting as *European Council (#06801)*. Legally established by European Parliament and Council Regulation No178-2002, adopted 28 Jan 2002. A decentralized agency of the European Union. Former names and other names: *European Food Safety Agency* – former; *Europees Agentschap voor Voedselveiligheid* – former; *European Food Authority (EFA)* – former; *Autorité alimentaire européenne (AAE)* – former; *Europese Voedselautoriteit* – former. **Aims** Provide an independent scientific source of advice, information and risk communication in the areas of food and feed safety; enable close collaboration with similar bodies in EU Member States. **Structure** Management Board; Departments (4); Scientific Panels; Management Team, headed by Executive Director. **Staff** 450.00 FTE, paid. **Finance** Funded by *European Commission (EC, #06633)*. **Activities** Networking/liaising. Knowledge management/information dissemination; networking/liaising; guidance/assistance/consulting; events/meetings. **Events** *Annual Meeting* Athens (Greece) 2022, *ONE – Health Environment and Society Conference* Brussels (Belgium) 2022, *Plenary Meeting* 2019, *Meeting* Parma (Italy) 2019, *Plenary Meeting* Parma (Italy) 2019. **Publications** Newsletters; opinions; press releases.
IGO Relations Audited by: *European Court of Auditors (#06854)*. Participant in: *Global Coalition for Regulatory Science Research (GCRSR, #10296)*. **NGO Relations** Member of (1): *EU Agencies Network (EUAN, #05564)*. [2020/XF6211/**F***]

♦ **European Food SCP Roundtable** European Food Sustainable Consumption and Production Round Table (#07289)
♦ European Foodservice Equipment Distributors Association (no recent information)
♦ European Food Service and Packaging Association / see Pack2Go Europe (#18014)

♦ European Food Sovereignty Movement (NYELENI) 07288
Contact c/o Via Campesina, Rue de la Sablonnière 18, 1000 Brussels, Belgium.
URL: https://nyeleni-eca.net/
History Proposed 1996, by *La Via Campesina (#20765)*. Framework reinforced by Nyeleni Forum, 2007, Mali. Former names and other names: *Nyéléni Europe* – alias. **NGO Relations** *European Coordination Via Campesina (ECVC, #06795)* is a member. [2020/XJ5556/**F**]

♦ European Food Sustainable Consumption and Production Round Table (European Food SCP Roundtable) 07289
Secretariat c/o Landmark Europe, Rue du Collège 27, 1050 Brussels, Belgium. T. +3228080644. Fax +3225028870.
History 2009. as an initiative co-chaired by *European Commission (EC, #06633)* and food supply chain, with the support of *UNEP (#20299)* and *European Environment Agency (EEA, #06995)*. **Aims** Promote a science-based, coherent approach to sustainable consumption and production in the food sector across Europe, while taking into account environmental interactions at all stages of the food chain. **Structure** Plenary Meeting. Steering Committee. Working Groups (4): Environmental Assessment Methodology; Environmental Information Tools; Continuous Environmental Improvement; International Initiatives and Non-Environmental Aspects of Sustainability. Secretariat. **Events** *Plenary Meeting* Brussels (Belgium) 2013, *Plenary Meeting* Brussels (Belgium) 2012, *Plenary Meeting* Brussels (Belgium) 2011, *Plenary Meeting* Brussels (Belgium) 2010.
Members Full: international and regional organizations (22) representing the European food supply chain ('*' indicates Founding Member):
- *Alliance for Beverage Cartons and the Environment (ACE, #00658)*;
- *AnimalhealthEurope (#00837)* (*);
- *Association de l'aviculture, de l'industrie et du commerce de volailles dans les pays de l'Union européenne (AVEC, #02390)*;
- *COPA – european farmers (COPA, #04829)*;
- *CropLife Europe (#04965)*;
- *European Association of Bioindustries (EuropaBio, #05956)*;
- *European Association of Producers of Steel for Packaging (#06167)*;
- *European Commission (EC, #06633)*;
- *European Community of Consumer Cooperatives (EURO COOP, #06678)* (*);
- *European Environment Agency (EEA, #06995)*;
- *European Liaison Committee for Agricultural and Agri-Food Trades (#07687)* (*);
- *European Organization for Packaging and the Environment (EUROPEN, #08110)* (*);
- *European Plastics Converters (EuPC, #08216)*;
- *Fédération européenne du verre d'emballage (FEVE, #09583)*;
- *FEFANA – EU Association of Specialty Feed Ingredients and their Mixtures (#09720)*;
- *Fertilizers Europe (#09738)* (*);
- *Flexible Packaging Europe (FPE, #09794)*;
- *FoodDrinkEurope (#09841)* (*);
- *General Confederation of Agricultural Cooperatives in the European Union (#10107)* (*);
- *Packaging Recovery Organization Europe (PRO-EUROPE, #18015)* (*);
- *Primary Food Processors (PFP, #18496)*;
- *Serving Europe (#19248)*.

Associate members (2):
Sustainability Consortium; *UNEP (#20299)*.
Observer: international, regional and national organizations (16). National organizations in 9 countries:
Canada, Denmark, France, Hungary, Netherlands, Spain, Sweden, UK, USA.
International and regional observer organizations (4):
Eurogroup for Animals (#05690); *FAO (#09260)*; *UNDP (#20292)*; *World Wide Fund for Nature (WWF, #21922)*.
Membership is also open to consumer representative organizations and environmental/nature conservation NGOs. [2013/XJ2068/y/**E**]

♦ European Foot and Ankle Society (EFAS) 07290
Secretariat MCO Congrès, Villa Gaby, 285 Corniche Kennedy, 13007 Marseille, France. E-mail: efassecretary@mcocongres.com.
URL: http://www.efas.net/
History 1999. Founded by merger of *European Federation of National Foot and Ankle Societies (EFFAS, inactive)* and *European Society of Foot and Ankle Surgeons (ESFAS, inactive)*. Regional organization of *International Federation of Foot and Ankle Societies (IFFAS, #13431)*. **Aims** Promote development of foot and ankle *surgery*; advance education, study and research in this speciality. **Structure** Council. **Languages** English. **Staff** 3.00 FTE, paid. **Finance** Sources: members' dues. **Activities** Events/meetings; training/education. **Events** *Congress* Edinburgh (UK) 2022, *Congress* Lyon (France) 2021, *Congress* Marseille (France) 2020, *Advanced Symposium* Helsinki (Finland) 2019, *Congress* Geneva (Switzerland) 2018. **Publications** *Foot and Ankle Journal* (4 a year).
Members Full in 35 countries:
Argentina, Australia, Austria, Belgium, Colombia, Czechia, Denmark, Estonia, Finland, France, Germany, Greece, Ireland, Israel, Italy, Latvia, Lithuania, Luxembourg, Mexico, Netherlands, Norway, Paraguay, Poland, Portugal, Russia, Slovakia, South Africa, Spain, Sweden, Switzerland, Türkiye, UK, United Arab Emirates, USA, Venezuela. [2022.10.18/XD7573/**D**]

♦ European Football for Development Network (EFDN) 07291
Contact Takkebijsters 9A 11, 4814 BL Breda, Netherlands. T. +31763690561. E-mail: info@efdn.org.
URL: https://www.efdn.org/
History 2014. Former names and other names: *Stichting European Football for Development Network (EFDN Foundation)* – legal name. Registration: Handelsregister, No/ID: KVK 60362391, Netherlands. **Aims** Inspire and support all professional football clubs, leagues and associations within the UEFA territory to become socially responsible and community-engaged organizations who use the social power of football to positively

change the lives of people in European society. **Structure** Management Board. **Activities** Awareness raising; capacity building; events/meetings; guidance/assistance/consulting; knowledge management/information dissemination; monitoring/evaluation; networking/liaising; projects/programmes; research and development; research/documentation; sporting activities; standards/guidelines; training/education. **Events** *Conference* Budapest (Hungary) 2022, *Conference* Liverpool (UK) 2022, *Conference* Breda (Netherlands) 2021, *Conference* Barcelona (Spain) 2019, *Conference* London (UK) 2019. **Members** Professional Football Clubs (136); Leagues and Football Associations (10). Members from 29 countries. Membership countries not specified.
[2022/XM6443/**F**]

♦ European Football Television Commentators Association (inactive)
♦ European Football Union / see Union of European Football Associations (#20386)

♦ European Forecasting Group for the Construction Industry (Euroconstruct) 07292

Contact c/o WIFO, Arsenal Objekt 20, 1030 Vienna, Austria.
URL: http://www.euroconstruct.org/

History 1975. **Aims** Provide decision makers in the construction sector and related markets and in ministries, agencies and national and international associations with information, analyses and forecasts to enable them to plan business more effectively. **Events** *Conference* London (UK) 2022, *Conference* Rome (Italy) 2019, *New challenges for European construction after 2020* Warsaw (Poland) 2019, *Conference* Helsinki (Finland) 2018, *Conference* Paris (France) 2018.
Members Institutes in 19 countries:
Austria, Belgium, Czechia, Denmark, Finland, France, Germany, Hungary, Ireland, Italy, Netherlands, Norway, Poland, Portugal, Slovakia, Spain, Sweden, Switzerland, UK. [2019/XU6512/t/**F**]

♦ European Forecasting Network (EFN) 07293

Coordinator c/o Robert Schuman Centre for Advanced Studies – European University Institute, Villa Raimondi VR 031, Via Boccaccio 121/111, 50133 Florence FI, Italy. T. +39554685550.
URL: http://www.eui.eu/Projects/EFN/Home.aspx

History 2001. **Aims** Provide: critical analysis of the economic situation in the Euro area; short-term forecasts of the main macroeconomic and financial variables; policy advice; study of topics of particular relevance for the working of the European Economic and Monetary Union. **Finance** *European Commission (EC, #06633)*. **Events** *Conference on Economic Policy issues in the European Union* Kiel (Germany) 2012, *Conference on Economic Policy Issues in the European Union* Helsinki (Finland) 2011. **Publications** Semi-annual report.
Members Participating institutions (7) in 5 countries:
France, Germany, Italy, Spain, UK.
Included in the above, 2 institutions listed in this Yearbook:
European University Institute (EUI, #09034); *French Leading Center for International Economic Studies, Paris (CEPII)*. [2017/XJ3735/**F**]

♦ European Forecasting Research Association for the Macro-Economy (EUROFRAME) 07294

Pres address not obtained.
URL: http://www.euroframe.org/

History 1998. Founded by 10 European research institutes. **Aims** Work towards more integrated forecasting and macroeconomic policy analysis in the European Union. **Structure** President; Coordinator; Treasurer. **Activities** Publishes the "Euro Growth Indicator". Organizes: November Conference Series – on Growth Prospects for the Euro Area; Jun Conference Series – on Economic Policy Issues in the European Union. **Events** *Conference on Economic Policy Issues in the European Union* Helsinki (Finland) 2022, *Conference on Economic Policy Issues in the European Union* 2021, *Conference on Economic Policy Issues in the European Union* 2020, *Conference on Economic Policy Issues in the European Union* Dublin (Ireland) 2019, *Conference on Economic Policy Issues in the European Union* Milan (Italy) 2018.
Members Research institutes in 9 countries:
Austria, Finland, France, Germany, Ireland, Italy, Netherlands, Poland, UK.
Included in the above, 1 organization listed in this Yearbook:
Kiel Institute for the World Economy (IfW). [2021/XJ5790/y/**D**]

♦ European Foresight Monitoring Network (EFMN) 07295

Project Coordinator AIT – Dept for Foresight and Policy Development, Tech Gate Vienna, Tower 7th Floor, Donau-City-Strasse 1, 1220 Vienna, Austria.
URL: http://www.foresight-platform.eu/

History 2004. **Aims** Provide support to policy professionals by monitoring and analysing foresight activities. **Finance** *European Commission (EC, #06633)* (DG for Research). **Activities** A network of correspondents write about their activities in Foresight Briefs, descriptions and/or analysis of foresight processes. Organizes annual workshop.
Members Partners (11) in 9 countries:
Austria, Belgium, Czechia, France, Germany, Greece, Malta, Netherlands, UK.
NGO Relations Member of: *The Millennium Project (MP, #16805)*. [2016/XM0871/**F**]

♦ European Forest Genetic Resources Programme (EUFORGEN) 07296

Programme européen pour les ressources génétiques forestières – Programma Europeo sobre Recursos Genéticos Forestales

Coordinator European Forest Inst (EFI) – Barcellona Office, Sant Pau Art Nouveau Site, Sant Leopold Pavilion, C/ Sant Antoni M Claret 167, 08025 Barcelona, Spain. T. +34673170501. E-mail: euforgen@efi.int.
URL: http://www.euforgen.org/

History Oct 1994. Established to implement Resolution S2 of 1st Ministerial Conference on the Protection of Forests in Europe, 1990, Strasbourg (France), and endorsed by 2nd Ministerial Conference, 1993, Helsinki (Finland). Second 5-year phase started on 1 Jan 2000. 3rd 5-year phase started on 1 Jan 2005, which continues implementation of S2 and also contributes to the implementation of Resolution V4 of 4th Ministerial Conference, 2003, Vienna (Austria). Phase IV (2010-2014) introduced small working groups of about 10 experts and larger workshops. Phase V (2015-2019) links the programme to the policy, strengthening communication and producing guidelines. **Aims** Collate, maintain and disseminate reliable information on forest genetic resources in Europe; coordinate and monitor the conservation of forest genetic resources in Europe; develop guidelines and analyses on topics and issues relevant for the use of forest genetic resources in Europe. **Structure** Steering Committee of National Coordinators nominated by participating countries; Secretariat hosted by European Forest Institute (EFI). **Languages** English. **Staff** 2.00 FTE, paid. **Finance** Sources: contributions of member/participating states. **Activities** Events/meetings; knowledge management/information dissemination; research/documentation. **Events** *Meeting* Luxembourg (Luxembourg) 2019, *Meeting* Bonn (Germany) 2018, *Meeting* Amsterdam (Netherlands) 2017, *Meeting* Dublin (Ireland) 2015, *Meeting* Edinburgh (UK) 2014. **Publications** Guidelines; network reports; conference proceedings.
Members Governments of 24 countries:
Austria, Belgium, Croatia, Czechia, Denmark, Estonia, Finland, France, Greece, Hungary, Iceland, Ireland, Italy, Lithuania, Luxembourg, Netherlands, Norway, Poland, Serbia, Slovakia, Slovenia, Sweden, Switzerland, UK.
IGO Relations Cooperates with (1): *Ministerial Conference on the Protection of Forests in Europe (FOREST EUROPE, #16817)* (Liaison Unit). **NGO Relations** Cooperates with (2): *International Union for Conservation of Nature and Natural Resources (IUCN, #15766)*; *International Union of Forest Research Organizations (IUFRO, #15774)*. [2021.03.02/XE2561/**E***]

♦ European Forest Institute (EFI) 07297

Dir Yliopistokatu 6B, FI-80100 Joensuu, Finland. T. +358107734300. E-mail: efisec@efi.int.
URL: http://www.efi.int/

History Jan 1993. Founded 1993 as an association. Restructured as an international organization, Sep 2005. Former names and other names: *Institut forestier européen (IFE)* – former. Registration: Finland; EU Transparency Register, No/ID: 38315289949-88. **Aims** Work for a world where the *sustainability* of forests and societies is secured by bringing together cross-boundary knowledge and expertise and contributing to ongoing dialogue on forests. **Structure** Annual Conference; Council; Scientific Advisory Board (SAB); Board; Facilities (6); Research Networks (4); Secretariat in Joensuu (Finland), headed by Director. Includes: *European Forest Institute Mediterranean Facility (EFIMED, #07298)*. **Languages** English. **Staff** 120.00 FTE, paid. **Finance** Annual budget: 15,000,000 EUR (2022). **Activities** Politics/policy/regulatory; research/documentation. **Events** *Annual Conference* Barcelona (Spain) 2022, *European Forum on Urban Forestry* Belgrade (Serbia) 2022, *Annual Conference* Joensuu (Finland) 2021, *European Forum on Urban Forestry* Manchester (UK) 2021, *Annual Conference* Joensuu (Finland) 2020. **Publications** *From Science to Policy*; *Knowledge to Action*; *What Science Can Tell Us*. Annual Report; policy briefs; technical reports; maps and models. **Information Services** *EFI Database*.
Members Countries that have ratified the EFI Convention (30):
Austria, Belgium, Bulgaria, Croatia, Czechia, Denmark, Estonia, Finland, France, Germany, Greece, Ireland, Italy, Latvia, Lithuania, Luxembourg, Netherlands, Norway, Poland, Portugal, Romania, Serbia, Slovakia, Slovenia, Spain, Sweden, Switzerland, Türkiye, UK, Ukraine.
Associate and Affiliate in 42 countries:
Austria, Belarus, Belgium, Bosnia-Herzegovina, Bulgaria, Canada, Chile, China, Croatia, Czechia, Denmark, Estonia, Finland, France, Georgia, Germany, Greece, Iceland, Ireland, Israel, Italy, Latvia, Lithuania, Netherlands, Norway, Pakistan, Poland, Portugal, Romania, Russia, Serbia, Sierra Leone, Slovakia, Slovenia, South Africa, Spain, Sweden, Switzerland, Türkiye, UK, Ukraine, USA.
Included in the above, 4 organizations listed in this Yearbook:
European State Forest Association (EUSTAFOR, #08832); *International Forestry Students' Association (IFSA, #13628)*; *Nordic Forest Research Cooperation Committee (#17296)*; *Unión de Silvicultores del Sur de Europa (USSE, #20478)*. [2022.12.07/XE1583/jy/**E***]

♦ European Forest Institute Mediterranean Facility (EFIMED) 07298

Head Sant Pau Historic Site, Sant Leopold Pavilion, St Antoni M Claret 167, 08025 Barcelona, Spain. T. +34935153211. E-mail: inazio.martinez@efi.int – efimed@efi.int.
URL: http://www.efimed.efi.int/

History Launched 2007, as the Mediterranean Regional Office of *European Forest Institute (EFI, #07297)*. Became its Mediterranean Facility, 2018. **Aims** Create sustainable value from Mediterranean forested landscapes through thematic research and networking. **Activities** Research/documentation; capacity building; networking/liaising. **Events** *Annual Meeting* Alghero (Italy) 2018, *Annual Meeting* Maierato (Italy) 2016, *Annual Meeting* Kavala (Greece) 2014.
Members Institutions in 18 countries:
Albania, Belgium, Bulgaria, Croatia, Cyprus, Finland, France, Greece, Israel, Italy, Lebanon, Morocco, Portugal, Romania, Slovenia, Spain, Syrian AR, Tunisia.
Included in the above, 11 organizations listed in this Yearbook:
AFWC/EFC/NEFC Committee on Mediterranean Forestry Questions – Silva Mediterranea (#00542); *ARCMED*; *Association internationale forêts méditerranéennes (AIFM, #02699)*; *CIHEAM – International Centre for Advanced Mediterranean Agronomic Studies (CIHEAM, #03927)*; *Deutsche Gesellschaft für Internationale Zusammenarbeit (GIZ)*; *FAO (#09260)* (Forestry); *International Center for Agricultural Research in the Dry Areas (ICARDA, #12466)*; *International Union for Conservation of Nature and Natural Resources (IUCN, #15766)* (Centre for Mediterranean Cooperation); *Mediterranean Model Forest Network (MMFN, #16662)*; *Plan Bleu pour l'environnement et le développement en Méditerranée (Plan Bleu, #18379)*; *World Wide Fund for Nature (WWF, #21922)* (Mediterranean Programme Office MEDPO). [2019.03.06/XM7149/y/**E**]

♦ European Forestry Commission (EFC) 07299

Commission européenne des forêts (CEF) – Comisión Forestal Europea (CFE)

Sec / Deputy Chief UNECE/FAO Forestry and Timber Section, Palais des Nations, 1211 Geneva 10, Switzerland. E-mail: info.timber@unece.org.
URL: http://www.fao.org/forestry/31095/en/

History Established 1947, Rome (Italy), as a commission of the *FAO (#09260)* (Article VI-1 of FAO Constitution), in pursuance of a recommendation of a FAO Conference, 1947, Marianské Lazne (Czechoslovakia). First session Jul 1948. Rules of procedure revised 1961 and 1977. Also referred to as *FAO European Forestry Commission*. **Aims** Advise on formulation of forestry policy; review and coordinate its implementation at a regional level; exchange information and, generally through special subsidiary bodies, advise on suitable practices and action in regard to technical and economic problems. **Structure** Working Party on the Management of Mountain Watersheds; FAO/ECE Working Party on Forest Statistics, Economics and Management; UNECE/FAO Teams of Specialists. **Languages** English, French, Russian, Spanish. **Staff** Serviced by joint UNECE/FAO Secretariat, based at UNECE: 8 FTE (UNECE) and 3 FTE (FAO); 1-2 interns. **Finance** Financed through UN and FAO regular budget: Economic Development for Europe – subprogramme 7 on timber and forestry. Also small share of extrabudgetary contributions. **Activities** Work programme according to the Strategic Plan, adopted 2008. **Events** *Session* San Marino (San Marino) 2023, *Session* Rome (Italy) 2021, *Session* Geneva (Switzerland) 2019, *European Forest Pedagogics Congress* Riga (Latvia) 2019, *Session* Warsaw (Poland) 2017. **Publications** *UNECE/FAO Forest Products Annual Market Review*. Resource assessments; outlook studies; profiles; study and discussion papers.
Members Open to FAO Member Nations and Associate Members whose territories are situated wholly or partly in Europe or who are responsible for the international relations of any non-self-governing territory in that region, and who desire to be considered members. Currently governments of 39 countries:
Albania, Austria, Belarus, Belgium, Bulgaria, Croatia, Cyprus, Czechia, Denmark, Estonia, Finland, France, Germany, Greece, Hungary, Iceland, Ireland, Israel, Italy, Latvia, Lithuania, Luxembourg, Malta, Netherlands, North Macedonia, Norway, Poland, Portugal, Romania, Russia, Slovakia, Slovenia, Spain, Sweden, Switzerland, Türkiye, UK, Ukraine, Uzbekistan.
IGO Relations Cooperates with: *Ministerial Conference on the Protection of Forests in Europe (FOREST EUROPE, #16817)*; *North American Forestry Commission (NAFC, #17565)*; *United Nations Economic Commission for Europe (UNECE, #20555)* Committee on Forests and the Forest Industry (COFFI). Instrumental within: *AFWC/EFC/NEFC Committee on Mediterranean Forestry Questions – Silva Mediterranea (#00542)*. Observer status with: *Intergovernmental Negotiating Committee for a Legally Binding Agreement on Forests in Europe (INC-Forests, inactive)*. **NGO Relations** Links with several private sector and civil society organizations.
[2016.01.21/XE6120/**E***]

♦ European Forest Science Academic Network (Silva Network) 07300

Pres Inst Forest Econ, TU Dresden, Dresden Dezernat 8, ServiceCenterStudium, 01062 Dresden, Germany.
SG University of Freiburg, Welcome Center, Erbprinzenstrasse 12, 79085 Freiburg, Germany. T. +497612035431.
URL: http://www.silva-network.eu/

History 1989, on the initiative of Pieter Schmidt. Standing Committee for Forestry of *Association for European Life Science Universities (ICA, #02519)*. **Aims** Stimulate and facilitate interuniversity cooperation in the field of *forestry education* in Europe. **Structure** General Assembly; Association Office, comprising President and Secretary General. **Finance** Members' dues. Other sources: *European Commission (EC, #06633)*; Ministry of Education of Finland; private companies. Budget (annual): euro 120,000. **Activities** Master programme in European Forestry; Virtual European Forestry Faculty (VIEFOR); Forestry in Changing Societies in Europe; Asia-Europe Forestry Exchange Programme ASEFOREP. **Events** *Annual Conference* Castelfranco Veneto (Italy) 2018, *Annual Conference* Prague (Czechia) 2017, *Annual Conference* Tartu (Estonia) 2016, *Annual Conference* Vienna (Austria) 2015, *Annual Conference* Bern (Switzerland) 2014. **Publications** *SILVA News* (2 a year). *Forestry in Changing Societies in Europe* (1999) by P Pelkonen et al – in 2 vols; *Forestry in Changing Societies in Europe – Teacher's Manual* (1999) by P Pelkonen et al; *New Requirements for University Education in Forestry* (1998) by P Schmidt et al. Books; proceedings.
Members Full in 22 countries:
Austria, Belarus, Belgium, Czechia, Denmark, Finland, France, Germany, Greece, Ireland, Italy, Netherlands, Norway, Poland, Portugal, Romania, Russia, Spain, Sweden, Switzerland, UK, Ukraine.
NGO Relations Memorandum of Understanding with: *International Forestry Students' Association (IFSA, #13628)*. [2017/XF5666/**F**]

♦ European Former Foodstuff Processors Association (EFFPA) 07301

Exec Dir Rue de la Loi 223/3, 1040 Brussels, Belgium. E-mail: info@effpa.eu.
URL: https://www.effpa.eu/

History 1 Jan 2014. **Aims** Represent, defend and promote the interests of the former foodstuffs processing industry towards the European Institutions. **Structure** General Assembly; Board; Secretariat.
Members National associations in 3 countries:
Germany, Netherlands, UK.

Companies in 3 countries:
Belgium, Italy, Spain.
Associate in 2 countries:
Canada, USA.
Observer in 3 countries:
Denmark, France, Greece. [2022/AA3245/t/D]

♦ European Formula Drivers' Association (inactive)
♦ European Forum for Advanced Business Communications / see European Association for e-Identity and Security (#06077)

♦ European Forum on Agricultural Research for Development (EFARD) 07302

Exec Sec c/o CTA, Agro Business Park 2, 6708 PW Wageningen, Netherlands. T. +31317467100.
Chairperson Ghent Univ, Fac of Bioscience Engineering, Coupure Links 653, 9000 Ghent, Belgium. T. +3292646087.
URL: http://www.efard.eu/

History 1997, Montpellier (France). **Aims** Provide a European multi-stakeholder platform of all Agricultural Research Development (ARD) stakeholders to promote more effective demand-driven and impact-focused ARD through building partnerships, particularly with developing countries. **Structure** Steering Committee; Management Team. **Languages** English. **Staff** None. **Finance** Sources: voluntary input from members; funding from GFAR; project funding. **Activities** Advocacy/lobbying/activism; networking/liaising; events/meetings. **Events** *Annual Technical and Business Meeting* Brussels (Belgium) 2017, *Annual Technical and Business Meeting* Prague (Czechia) 2016, *General Assembly* Brussels (Belgium) 2014, *European responses to changing global needs* Zurich (Switzerland) 2005, *Conference* Rome (Italy) 2002. **Publications** *InContact Newsletter*.
Members in 16 countries:
Austria, Belgium, Denmark, Finland, France, Germany, Greece, Ireland, Italy, Netherlands, Norway, Portugal, Spain, Sweden, Switzerland, UK.
International organizations involved:
AGRINATURA (#00578); European Commission (EC, #06633); Global Forum on Agricultural Research (GFAR, #10370).
NGO Relations Member of: *Global Forum on Agricultural Research (GFAR, #10370)*. Cooperates with: *Platform for African – European Partnership on Agricultural Research for Development (PAEPARD, #18398); Young Professionals for Agricultural Development (YPARD, #21996).* [2019/XF5965/F]

♦ European Forum for Agricultural and Rural Advisory Services (EUFRAS) 07303

Eiropas lauksaimniecibas un lauku konsultantu asociacija (ELLKA)
Secretariat Rigas iela 34, Ozolnieki, Ozolnieku pagasts, Ozolnieku novads, Riga LV-3018, Latvia.
URL: http://eufras.eu/

History 23 Sep 2013, Berlin (Germany). Launched by agricultural and rural advisory services from 20 European countries. Foundation prepared in a workshop 25-26 Feb 2013, Wroclaw (Poland), initiated and organized by the German extensionists' network IALB and inspired by the EU projects RENE and ProAkis. Representatives of European rural advisory institutions were invited to participate in the founding process and a second preparatory meeting in Dublin (Ireland). Affiliated to: *Global Forum for Rural Advisory Services (GFRAS, #10378)*. Registration: Start date: 13 Jan 2014, Latvia; EU Transparency Register, No/ID: 808043113459-74, Start date: 16 Apr 2014. **Aims** Improve quality, effectiveness and efficiency of agricultural and rural advisors' work aimed at supporting farming families, farmers local groups, agricultural organizations and individuals involved in agricultural and rural development and addressing the current and emerging problems (economic, environmental and social). **Structure** Members' Meeting (General Meeting, annual); Board. **Languages** English. **Finance** Sources: members' dues; revenue from activities/projects. **Activities** Advocacy/lobbying/activism; events/meetings; guidance/assistance/consulting; knowledge management/information dissemination; standards/guidelines; training/education. **Events** *General Assembly* Leuven (Belgium) 2022, *General Assembly* Lisbon (Portugal) 2019, *Conference* Mosonmagyaróvar (Hungary) 2018, *Conference* Münster (Germany) 2017, *Conference* Paris (France) 2016. **Members** Public and private advisory services and institutions whose work aims at supporting farming families, agricultural organizations, local groups and individuals involved in agriculture or rural development, and addresses current and emerging problems. Organizations (27) in 20 European countries. Membership countries not specified. **NGO Relations** Cooperates with (2): *Internationale Akademie land- und hauswirtschaftlicher Beraterinnen und Berater (IALB, #13212); South Eastern Europe Advisory Service Network (SEASN, #19805).* [2022/XJ8583/F]

♦ European Forum Alpbach 07304

Forum Européen d'Alpbach – Europäisches Forum Alpbach (EFA)
Pres Franz-Josefs-Kai 13/10, 1010 Vienna, Austria. T. +4317181711. Fax +4317181701. E-mail: forum@alpbach.org.
URL: http://www.alpbach.org/

History Founded 1945, as an Annual Conference organized by Austrian College. Integrated activities of *Club Alpbach for European Culture – International (inactive)*. Austrian College and the Forum merged activities and operate under current title, adopted in 2003. **Aims** Encourage *intellectual cooperation* with other nations in various fields such as science, culture, economy, politics and society across national and ideological frontiers, while preserving individual viewpoints and supporting all efforts to achieve a united Europe; establish contacts between international academic elite and young students from around the world. **Structure** Council. **Languages** English, German. **Finance** Congress fees; donations; sponsoring companies and public institutions. **Activities** Events/meetings; training/education; financial and/or material support. **Events** *Annual Conference* Alpbach (Austria) 2020, *Annual Conference* Alpbach (Austria) 2019, *Annual Conference* Alpbach (Austria) 2018, *Annual Conference* Alpbach (Austria) 2017, *Annual Conference* Alpbach (Austria) 2016. **Publications** *Alpbach Moments* (annual) – report; *Alpbach Panorama* (annual) – magazine.
Members Organizations; Individuals. Members in 32 countries and territories:
Albania, Armenia, Austria, Belgium, Bosnia-Herzegovina, Brazil, Bulgaria, Croatia, Czechia, Egypt, Ethiopia, France, Germany, Greece, Hungary, India, Italy, Kosovo, Liechtenstein, Moldova, Montenegro, Netherlands, North Macedonia, Poland, Romania, Serbia, Slovenia, Sweden, Switzerland, Türkiye, UK, Ukraine.
IGO Relations Project implementation in cooperation with: *Southeast European Cooperative Initiative (SECI, #19812)*. **NGO Relations** *A Soul for Europe (ASF, #19697)*. Links with national Alpbach committees worldwide. [2019.06.23/XF0347/c/F]

♦ European Forum for Animal Welfare Councils (EuroFAWC) 07305

Secretariat Koning Albert II-laan 20, PO Box 8, 1000 Brussels, Belgium. T. +3225531511.
URL: http://www.eurofawc.com/

History 2006. Registration: EU Transparency Register, No/ID: 815438326169-34. **Aims** Provide a platform for debate, for sharing information and views and a network for Animal Welfare advisory bodies throughout Europe. **Structure** Chair; Vice-Chair; Secretariat. **Languages** English. **Staff** 0.10 FTE, voluntary. **Activities** Events/meetings; knowledge management/information dissemination. **Events** *Meeting* Berlin (Germany) 2022, *Meeting* 2021, *Meeting* 2020, *Meeting* 2020, *Meeting* Uppsala (Sweden) 2019.
Members Animal welfare councils in 13 countries:
Austria, Belgium, Czechia, Denmark, Finland, Germany, Ireland, Netherlands, New Zealand, Norway, Sweden, Switzerland, UK. [2021.09.03/XM8915/F]

♦ European Forum on Antiphospholipid Antibodies (meeting series)
♦ European Forum of Applied Criminal Policy (internationally oriented national body)

♦ European Forum for Architectural Policies (EFAP) 07306

Forum européen des politiques architecturales
Acting Pres address not obtained.
URL: http://www.efap-fepa.eu/

History Jul 2000, Paris (France). Registered in accordance with Belgian law, 2007. **Aims** Foster and promote architectural policies in Europe while bridging public governance, profession and culture. **Structure** Forum; Steering Committee; Coordination Group; Secretariat. **Languages** English, French. **Staff** 1.50 FTE, paid. 1 intern. **Finance** Members' dues. Other sources: subsidies; donations. **Activities** Projects: UNDERCONSTRUCTIONS (Observatory of innovative architectural practice in Europe). **Events** *Conference* Dublin (Ireland) 2013, *Conference* Brussels (Belgium) 2012, *Conference* Budapest (Hungary) 2011, *Conference* Gdansk (Poland) 2011, *Conference* Brussels (Belgium) 2010. **Publications** *Survey on Architectural Policies in Europe* (2011).
Members National and regional governments and organizations in 31 countries:
Austria, Belgium, Bulgaria, Croatia, Cyprus, Czechia, Denmark, Estonia, Finland, France, Germany, Greece, Hungary, Ireland, Italy, Latvia, Lithuania, Luxembourg, Malta, Netherlands, Norway, Poland, Portugal, Romania, Slovakia, Slovenia, Spain, Sweden, Switzerland, Türkiye, UK.
International organizations (2), listed in this Yearbook:
Architects Council of Europe (ACE, #01086); European Commission (EC, #06633). [2013/XM2103/y/F]

♦ European Forum for the Arts and Heritage / see Culture Action Europe (#04981)
♦ European Forum for Complementary and Alternative Medicine / see European Federation for Complementary and Alternative Medicine (#07084)

♦ European Forum for Democracy and Solidarity (EFDS) 07307

Forum européen pour la démocratie et la solidarité
Mailing Address PO Box 30204, 2500 GE The Hague, Netherlands. T. +31705500567. E-mail: info@europeanforum.net.
Coordinator c/o Foundation Max van der Stoel, Leeghwaterplein 45, 11e verdieping, 2521 DB The Hague, Netherlands.
URL: http://www.europeanforum.net/

History 1993. Founded as an informal structure in the framework of *Socialist International (SI, #19340)*. Until Jan 2002, placed with secretary of *Party of European Socialists (PES, #18249)*. Between Jan 2003 and 2013, coordinated by *Alfred Mozer Foundation (AMF, inactive)*. Since 2013, coordinated by *Foundation Max van der Stoel (FMS)*. **Aims** Assist, with the help of *socialist* and *social-democratic* parties, the countries of *Central* and *Eastern Europe* in the process of transition. **Structure** Steering Committee, headed by President. Includes: *Central and Eastern European Network for Gender Issues (CEE Gender Network, #03695)*. **Languages** Armenian, Bosnian, Croatian, English, Russian, Serbian. **Staff** 4.00 FTE, paid. **Finance** Sources: members' dues; revenue from activities/projects. **Activities** Knowledge management/information dissemination. **Publications** *Newsflash*. Articles.
Members Parties and social democratic foundations in 7 countries:
Austria, Denmark, Germany, Netherlands, Norway, Sweden, UK.
Included in the above, 6 listed in this Yearbook:
Foundation Max van der Stoel (FMS); Friedrich-Ebert-Stiftung (FES); Jean-Jaurès Foundation (FJJ); Olof Palme International Center, Stockholm; Party of European Socialists (PES, #18249); Westminster Foundation for Democracy (WFD).
NGO Relations Partner of (1): *Progressive Alliance for Freedom, Justice and Solidarity (Progressive Alliance, #18530)*. Observer member of: *Foundation for European Progressive Studies (FEPS, #09954).* [2021/XK1316/y/F]

♦ European Forum of Deposit Insurers (EFDI) 07308

SG c/o House of Business, Room 113, Szechenyi Istvan ter 7-8, Budapest 1051, Hungary. E-mail: secretariat@efdi.eu.
Chairman FDGR, 65 rue de la Victoire, 75009 Paris, France. T. +33158183806.
Registered Office 4 Rue de La Presse, 1000 Brussels, Belgium.
URL: http://www.efdi.eu/

History 11 Oct 2002, Vienna (Austria). Statutes amended 2021. Former names and other names: *European Forum of Deposit Insurers – Association of European Deposit Guarantee Schemes and Investor Compensation Schemes* – legal name. Registration: Crossroads Bank for Enterprises, No/ID: 0892.945.871, Start date: 19 Oct 2007, Belgium; EU Transparency Register, No/ID: 497118818456-08, Start date: 6 Jan 2016. **Aims** Contribute to the stability of financial schemes by: promoting European cooperation in the field of deposit insurance, crisis resolution and investor compensation; facilitate exchange of expertise and information on issues of mutual interest and concern. **Structure** General Assembly (annual, at Conference); Board; Working Groups; Committees. **Languages** English. **Finance** Sources: members' dues. **Activities** Events/meetings. **Events** *Annual General Meeting* Rhodes (Greece) 2022, *Annual General Meeting* Sarajevo (Bosnia-Herzegovina) 2019, *Annual General Meeting* Vienna (Austria) 2018, *Annual Meeting* Oslo (Norway) 2017, *Annual General Assembly* Vilnius (Lithuania) 2016. **Publications** *EFDI Newsletter*.
Members Deposit Guarantee Schemes (68), representing 48 countries and territories:
Albania, Armenia, Austria, Azerbaijan, Belgium, Bosnia-Herzegovina, Bulgaria, Croatia, Cyprus, Czechia, Denmark, Estonia, Finland, France, Germany, Gibraltar, Greece, Guernsey, Hungary, Iceland, Ireland, Isle of Man, Italy, Jersey, Kosovo, Latvia, Liechtenstein, Lithuania, Luxembourg, Malta, Montenegro, Netherlands, North Macedonia, Norway, Poland, Portugal, Romania, Russia, San Marino, Serbia, Slovakia, Slovenia, Spain, Sweden, Switzerland, Türkiye, UK, Ukraine.
Investor Compensation Schemes in 11 countries:
Bulgaria, Croatia, Czechia, Finland, Germany, Hungary, Iceland, Italy, Norway, Romania, Türkiye.
IGO Relations Cooperates with (1): *European Commission (EC, #06633).* [2022.10.20/XM0192/F]

♦ European Forum of Deposit Insurers – Association of European Deposit Guarantee Schemes and Investor Compensation Schemes / see European Forum of Deposit Insurers (#07308)
♦ European FORUM on Development Service / see International Forum for Volunteering in Development (#13659)

♦ European Forum for Electroconvulsive Therapy (EFFECT) 07309

Contact Leuvensesteenweg 517, 3070 Kortenberg, Belgium. E-mail: info@theeffect.eu.
URL: http://www.theeffect.eu/

History Founding meeting Feb 2006, Leuven (Belgium). **Aims** Ensure that *patients* and service users across Europe have access to safe and effective ECT when appropriate. **Structure** Executive Board. **Activities** Advocacy/lobbying/activism; training/education; standards/guidelines; events/meetings. **Events** *Annual Meeting* Budapest (Hungary) 2019, *Annual Meeting* Rome (Italy) 2018. **Members** Individuals. Membership countries not specified. **NGO Relations** *Nordic Association for Convulsive Therapy (NACT, #17189).* [2018/XM6521/F]

♦ **European FORUM** European Forum of the insurance against accidents at work and occupational diseases (#07317)
♦ European Forum for External Trade, Excise and Customs (internationally oriented national body)

♦ European Forum of Farm Animal Breeders (EFFAB) 07310

Communications Officer Rue de Trèves 61, 1040 Brussels, Belgium. T. +32498254251. E-mail: effab@effab.info.
Dir Silkeborg 75, 2905 AT Capelle-aan-den-Ijssel, Netherlands.
Main: http://www.effab.info/

History Former names and other names: *Farm Animal Industrial Platform (FAIP)* – former (1995 to 2004). Registration: EU Transparency Register, No/ID: 065162648302-69, Start date: 6 Dec 2022. **Aims** Promote the political interest of the farm animal breeding and reproduction sector in Europe at EU and national level. **Structure** Annual General Meeting; Steering Committee; Working Groups; Contact Groups. **Languages** English. **Staff** 2.00 FTE, paid. **Finance** Sources: members' dues. **Activities** Advocacy/lobbying/activism; events/meetings; guidance/assistance/consulting; knowledge management/information dissemination. **Events** *Annual Meeting* Evora (Portugal) 2022, *Annual Meeting* Ås (Norway) 2015, *Annual Meeting* Brussels (Belgium) 2014, *Annual Meeting* Dummerstorf (Germany) 2013, *Annual Meeting* Edinburgh (UK) 2012. **Publications** *EFFAB News* (3-4 a year) – bulletin. Proposals; position papers; proceedings; reports. **Members** Farm animal breeding and reproduction organizations (over 30) in Europe. Membership countries not specified. **NGO Relations** Member of (2): *Agri-Food Chain Coalition (AFCC, #00577); European Platform for the Responsible Use of Medicines in Animals (EPRUMA, #08231)*. Cooperates with (1): *European Regional Focal Point for Animal Genetic Resources (ERFP, #08343)*. Links with other NGOs, not specified. [2022/XF4244/F]

♦ European Forum for Freedom in Education (EFFE) **07311**
Forum Européen pour la Liberté dans l'Education – Europäisches Forum für Freiheit im Bildungswesen
Registered address Dieburger Strasse 78, 64287 Darmstadt, Germany. E-mail: contact@effe-eu.org.
URL: http://www.effe-eu.org/
History 1990, Velence (Hungary). Registered in accordance with German law. EU Transparency Register: 542174334496-52. **Aims** Safeguard the dignity, worth and uniqueness of every *child*; ensure the *right* to education and freedom in education; protect within the context of education both ethnic *minorities* and minority educational approaches. **Structure** Council of National Representatives. Board of 5 members. Presidency, comprising President and 2 Vice-Presidents. International Secretariat. International Offices: Austria; Croatia; Finland; UK. **Languages** English, German. **Finance** Members' dues. **Activities** Events/meetings; financial and/or material supports; knowledge g management/information dissemination. **Events** *International Colloquium* Berlin (Germany) 2011, *International Colloquium* Vienna (Austria) 2011, *International colloquium* Witten (Germany) 2009, *International colloquium* Brussels (Belgium) 2008, *International colloquium* Ollerup (Denmark) 2007. **Publications** *effe Newsletter* (4 a year) in English, German. Book series; atlas.
Members Active; Campaign; Sponsor; Institutional. Individuals and organizations (about 3,000) in 34 countries:
Albania, Armenia, Austria, Belgium, Bulgaria, Croatia, Czechia, Denmark, Estonia, Finland, France, Georgia, Germany, Greece, Hungary, Ireland, Italy, Korea Rep, Latvia, Montenegro, Netherlands, Norway, Romania, Russia, Serbia, Slovakia, Slovenia, South Africa, Spain, Sweden, Switzerland, Türkiye, UK, Ukraine.
NGO Relations Member of: *EU Civil Society Contact Group (CSCG, #05572)*; *Lifelong Learning Platform – European Civil Society for Education (LLLP, #16466)*. Supports: *European Alliance for the Statute of the European Association (EASEA, #05886)*. [2019/XF3201/**F**]

♦ European Forum for Geography and Statistics (EFGS) **07312**
Sec Valhallavägen 145, c/o Backer Skaar, SE-115 31 Stockholm, Sweden.
URL: https://www.efgs.info/
History Originated in Nordic Forum for Geography and Statistics. Former names and other names: *European Forum for Geostatistics* – former. **Aims** Promote spatial statistics built on well integrated geography and statistics. **Structure** Steering Committee; Executive team. **Activities** Awards/prizes/competitions; events/meetings; training/education. **Events** *European Forum for Geography and Statistics* 2022, *European Forum for Geography and Statistics* Wiesbaden (Germany) 2021, *European Forum for Geography and Statistics* Warsaw (Poland) 2020, *Seminar* Warsaw (Poland) 2020, *European Forum for Geography and Statistics* Manchester (UK) 2019. [2021/AA2370/**F**]

♦ European Forum for Geostatistics / see European Forum for Geography and Statistics (#07312)
♦ European Forum for Golf and Environment (internationally oriented national body)

♦ European Forum for Good Clinical Practice (EFGCP) **07313**
Operations Manager Rue de l'Industrie 4, 1000 Brussels, Belgium. T. +3227328783. Fax +3225033108. E-mail: info@efgcp.eu.
Events Manager address not obtained.
Registered Office c/o MAI, Rue Washington 40, 1050 Brussels, Belgium.
URL: http://www.efgcp.eu/
History 1993. Registration: Banque-Carrefour des Entreprises, No/ID: 0457.666.685, Start date: 28 Mar 1996, Belgium; EU Transparency Register, No/ID: 620464443740-12, Start date: 30 Jul 2021. **Aims** Promote open discussion on critical issues in biomedical research and health; promote education and awareness leading to the application of ethical and scientific requirements in clinical research; facilitate the transfer of knowledge and skills across disciplines and sectors including training and advice; promote a renewed emphasis on human values in research involving human participants. **Structure** General Assembly; Elected Board; Science and Ethics Council. Current Working Parties (7): Audit; Children's Medicines; Education; Ethics; Geriatric Medicines; Medical Devices (jointly with MedTech Europe); Patient Roadmap to Treatment (jointly with EGAN). Bureau located in Brussels (Belgium). **Languages** English. **Staff** 3.00 FTE, paid. **Finance** Members' dues. Other sources: projects funded by EU and other governmental and non-governmental organizations; conference and workshop proceeds; training courses. **Activities** Networking/liaising; events/meetings; training/education; standards/guidelines. **Events** *Better Medicines for Children Conference* Brussels (Belgium) 2022, *Annual Conference* Brussels (Belgium) 2021, *Annual Conference* Brussels (Belgium) 2019, *Annual Conference* Brussels (Belgium) 2018, *Joint Better Medicines for Children Conference* Brussels (Belgium) 2018. **Publications** *The Procedure for the Ethical Review of Protocols for Clinical Research Projects in the European Union* (annual); *EFGCP Flash News*. Guidelines; position papers; reports.
Members Individual; Institutional; Corporate (Platinum, Gold, Silver, Bronze). Members in 30 countries:
Austria, Belgium, Canada, Cyprus, Czechia, Denmark, Estonia, Finland, France, Georgia, Germany, Greece, Hungary, India, Ireland, Italy, Japan, Kazakhstan, Luxembourg, Netherlands, Norway, Poland, Russia, Serbia, Slovakia, Spain, Sweden, Switzerland, UK, USA.
European AIDS Treatment Group (EATG, #05850); *European Clinical Research Infrastructure Network (ECRIN, #06577)*; *European CRO Federation (EUCROF, #06863)*; *European Federation for Exploratory Medicines Development (EUFEMED, #07116)*; *European Organisation for Research and Treatment of Cancer (EORTC, #08101)*; *European Society of Anaesthesiology and Intensive Care (ESAIC, #08518)*; *European Society of Oncology Pharmacy (ESOP, #08671)*; *MedTech Europe (#16692)*; *SIOP Europe (SIOPE, #19288)*.
NGO Relations Member of (2): *European Patients' Academy on Therapeutic Innovation (EUPATI, #08170)*; *Federation of European and International Associations Established in Belgium (FAIB, #09508)*. [2021/XF3049/**F**]

♦ European Forum of Heritage Associations (FORUM) **07314**
Forum européen des associations pour le patrimoine – Forum Europeo de Asociaciones Arqueológicas – Europäisches Forum der Altertums- und Denkmalschutzvereine – Forum Europeo delle Associazioni Archeologiche
Pres c/o Gruppi Archeologici del Veneto, Via Francesco Guardi 24 bis, 35134 Padua PD, Italy.
URL: http://www.heritageforum.org/
History 18 Apr 1990, Rome (Italy). **Aims** Raise public awareness of a common *history* in regional *diversity*; stimulate national *voluntary* movements for joint action on policy and management. **Structure** General Assembly. Executive Board, consisting of President, Secretary-General, Treasurer-General and one member of each of the National Committees of the member countries. **Finance** Members' dues: euro 60. **Activities** Organizes: Europe-wide international field work exchange programmes; summer camps for field work and conservation; educational programmes, including development of educational materials. **Events** *Annual General Assembly* Weimar (Germany) 2007, *Annual general assembly / Annual Conference* Hasselt (Belgium) 2006, *Annual general assembly / Annual Conference* Macau (Macau) 2005, *Annual Conference* Bulgaria 2004, *Annual General Assembly* Plovdiv (Bulgaria) 2004. **Publications** *FORUM Newsletter* (2 a year).
Members Full non-governmental, non-profit organizations active in the field of study or interpretation of archaeological and architectural heritage. Associate (semi) governmental and/or professional organizations. Members (31) in 15 European countries:
Austria, Belgium, Croatia, Czechia, Denmark, France, Germany, Italy, Netherlands, Portugal, Slovenia, Spain, Sweden, UK, Ukraine.
NGO Relations Member of: *Culture Action Europe (CAE, #04981)*. [2014/XF3643/**F**]

♦ European Forum for Hospital Sterile Supply / see World Federation for Hospital Sterilisation Sciences (#21438)

♦ European Forum for Human Rights and Family (EFFA) **07315**
Forum européen des droits de l'homme et de la famille (FEFA) – Europäisches Forum für die Menschenrechte und die Rechte der Familie (EFFA)
Gen Sec EP, Rue Wiertz 60, 1047 Brussels, Belgium.
Sec 22 Felbridge Av, Stanmore, HA7 2BH, UK.
Registered Seat Rue du Couvent 28, L-1363 Howald, Luxembourg.
History 18 Dec 1998. Registered in accordance with Luxembourg law. **Structure** General Assembly. **IGO Relations** Participant in Fundamental Rights Platform of: *European Union Agency for Fundamental Rights (FRA, #08969)*. [2010/XJ4959/**F**]

♦ European Forum for ICST **07316**
Pres address not obtained.
URL: http://www.eficst.eu/
History 7 Nov 2011, Milan (Italy). Subtitle: *The platform of the European Societies in Information and Communication Sciences and Technologies*. **Aims** Develop common viewpoints and strategies for ICST in Europe and, whenever appropriate or needed, a common representation of these viewpoints and strategies at the international level. **Structure** Coordinating Committee. Executive Board. **Activities** Meeting activities.
Members Organizations. National (2) in 2 countries:
France, Italy.
Regional organizations (7):
Association for Computing Machinery (ACM, #02447) (Europe); *European Association for Artificial Intelligence (EurAI, #05943)*; *European Association for Programming Languages and Systems (EAPLS, #06171)*; *European Association for Theoretical Computer Science (EATCS, #06253)*; *European Association of Software Science and Technology (EASST, #06213)*; *European Research Consortium for Informatics and Mathematics (ERCIM, #08362)*; *Informatics Europe (#11194)*. [2014/XJ7926/y/**F**]

♦ European Forum of Independent Professionals (unconfirmed)

♦ European Forum of the insurance against accidents at work and occupational diseases (European FORUM) **07317**
Forum européen de l'assurance accidents du travail et maladies professionnelles – Europäisches Forum der Versicherungen gegen Arbeitsunfälle und Berufskrankheiten – Forum Europeo dell'Assicurazione Contro gli Infortuni sul Lavoro e le Malattie Professionali
Permanent Office Maison Eur de la Protection Sociale, Rue d'Arlon 50, 1000 Brussels, Belgium. E-mail: info@europeanforum.org.
URL: http://www.europeanforum.org/
History 20 Jun 1992, Rome (Italy). Previously also referred to as *European Forum of Insurances Against Accidents at Work and Occupational Diseases*. **Aims** Promote and safeguard the principle of a specific insurance against accidents at work and occupational diseases; monitor actively the process of convergence between the systems in place in Europe against occupational accidents and occupational diseases. **Structure** Plenary Assembly; Enlarged Board; Bureau; Rotating Presidency (annual); Working Groups. **Languages** English, French, German, Italian. **Staff** None. **Activities** Events/meetings. **Events** *Accident insurance 4.0 – the impact of digitalisation* Lucerne (Switzerland) 2018, *Sustainable working life* Stockholm (Sweden) 2017, *Conference on Building Bridges* Vienna (Austria) 2015, *Conference on Building Bridges* Vienna (Austria) 2014, *Conference* Helsinki (Finland) 2013. **Publications** *FORUM News* (3 a year). Monographs; papers; conference proceedings.
Members National insurers against occupational injuries (24) in 21 countries:
Austria, Belgium, Croatia, Denmark, Finland, France, Germany, Greece, Italy, Latvia, Lithuania, Luxembourg, Malta, Norway, Poland, Portugal, Romania, Russia, Spain, Sweden, Switzerland. [2017.06.01/XF5578/**F**]

♦ European Forum of Insurances Against Accidents at Work and Occupational Diseases / see European Forum of the insurance against accidents at work and occupational diseases (#07317)
♦ European Forum for International Mediation and Dialogue (internationally oriented national body)

♦ European Forum of Lesbian, Gay, Bisexual and Transgender Christian Groups (Forum LGBT) **07318**
Forum européen des groupes chrétiens LGBT – Europees Forum van christelijke Lesbische, Homo, Biseksuele en Transgender groepen
Communications Coordinator Nieuwe Herengracht 49, 1011 RN Amsterdam, Netherlands. E-mail: presidents@lgbtchristians.eu – communications@lgbtchristians.eu – secretary@lgbtchristians.eu.
URL: https://www.lgbtchristians.eu/
History 1982, Paris (France). Registration: No/ID: KVK 40481053, Netherlands. **Aims** Work for equality for LGBT people within and through the Christian churches of Europe; stimulate *advocacy* work in political bodies, specifically to counteract *homophobic* religious voices; provide training and support for LGBT Christians where it is not easily available otherwise. **Structure** General Meeting of delegates (annual); Board; Working Groups. **Languages** English, French, Russian. **Staff** Voluntary. **Finance** Sources: donations; in-kind support; members' dues. **Events** *Annual Conference* Zurich (Switzerland) 2022, *Annual Conference* Venlo (Netherlands) 2021, *Annual Conference* Budapest (Hungary) 2020, *Annual Conference* London (UK) 2019, *Annual Conference* Gdansk (Poland) 2017.
Members Ecumenical groups (about 45) in 23 countries:
Armenia, Austria, Belgium, Croatia, Estonia, Finland, France, Germany, Hungary, Italy, Kyrgyzstan, Latvia, Malta, Moldova, Netherlands, Norway, Poland, Russia, Spain, Sweden, Switzerland, UK, Ukraine.
Consultative Status Consultative status granted from: *Council of Europe (CE, #04881)* (Participatory Status).
NGO Relations Member of (2): *ILGA-Europe (#11118)*; *ILGA World (International Lesbian, Gay, Bisexual, Trans and Intersex Association, #11120)*. [2022/XJ7040/**F**]

♦ European Forum of Logistics Education (unconfirmed)

♦ European Forum for Manufacturing (EFM) **07319**
SG Rue de la Science 14B, 1040 Brussels, Belgium. T. +3228086835.
URL: http://euromanuforum.com/
History EU Transparency Register: 113054111397-33. **Aims** Provide European political leadership for the development of multilateral public policies addressing the economic, social and environmental challenges facing manufacturing globally. **Structure** Board. **Activities** Events/meetings; knowledge management/information dissemination. [2020/XM8916/**F**]

♦ European Forum of Medical Associations and WHO (EFMA) **07320**
SG c/o Israel Medical Association, 2 Twin Towers, 35 Jabotinsky Street, PO Box 3566, 52136 Ramat Gan, Israel. T. +97236100444. Fax +97235750704.
URL: http://efma-forum.com
History 1991, Helsinki (Finland), by national medical associations and *WHO (#20950)*, meetings having taken place since 1984. **Aims** Improve the quality of *health care* in Europe; promote exchange of information and ideas between national medical associations and between the associations and WHO; integrate appropriate aspects of policies of Health For All into basic, postgraduate and continuing medical *education*; formulate consensus policy statements on health issues. **Structure** Not a formal organization but a series of joint annual meetings, governed by a Statement of Guiding Principles and orchestrated through a Liaison Committee. **Activities** Events/meetings; knowledge management/information dissemination; networking/liaising. **Events** *Annual meeting* Brussels (Belgium) 2011, *Meeting* Bratislava (Slovakia) 2009, *Annual meeting / Meeting* Lisbon (Portugal) 2007, *Annual meeting* Budapest (Hungary) 2006, *Meeting* Hungary 2006. **Publications** *Annual Handbook of National Medical Associations in Europe*. *Quality of Care Development – Why and How*. Annual report of national medical associations on specific areas of activity.
Members National associations in 45 countries:
Albania, Andorra, Armenia, Austria, Azerbaijan, Belarus, Belgium, Bosnia-Herzegovina, Bulgaria, Croatia, Czechia, Denmark, Estonia, Finland, France, Georgia, Germany, Greece, Hungary, Iceland, Ireland, Israel, Italy, Kazakhstan, Kyrgyzstan, Latvia, Lithuania, Luxembourg, Malta, Netherlands, North Macedonia, Norway, Poland, Portugal, Romania, Russia, Slovakia, Slovenia, Spain, Sweden, Switzerland, Türkiye, UK, Ukraine, Uzbekistan.
Organizations with observer status (10):
Association européenne des médecins des hôpitaux (AEMH, #02577); Canadian Medical Association; *EANA – European Working Group of Physicians in Private Practice (#05154)*; *European Federation of Salaried Doctors (#07209)*; *European Junior Doctors Association (EJD, #07620)*; *European Public Health Association (EUPHA, #08298)*; *European Union of General Practitioners / Family Physicians (#08993)*; *European Union of Medical Specialists (UEMS, #09001)*; *Standing Committee of European Doctors (#19955)*; *World Medical Association (WMA, #21646)*. [2015.12.16/XF3836/y/**F**]

♦ European Forum of Muslim Women (EFOMW) **07321**
Forum Européen des Femmes Musulmanes
Contact Rue Archimède 50, 1000 Brussels, Belgium. T. +32225123803. E-mail: info@efomw.eu.
URL: https://efomw.eu/

History Mar 2006, Brussels (Belgium). Registration: Banque-Carrefour des Entreprises, No/ID: 0897.257.027, Start date: 15 Apr 2008, Belgium. **Aims** Consolidate bonds and stimulate exchange of experience between members so as to support the involvement of Muslim women in society as a citizen, better respond to her needs, defend her interests and lobby with European and international authorities.
Members Full in 14 countries:
Belgium, Bosnia-Herzegovina, Denmark, France, Germany, Greece, Ireland, Italy, Romania, Spain, Sweden, Switzerland, UK, Ukraine.
Consultative Status Consultative status granted from: *ECOSOC (#05331)* (Special). **NGO Relations** Member of (2): *European Network against Racism (ENAR, #07862)*; *Social Platform (#19344)* (Associate).
[2022/XJ0509/**F**]

♦ European Forum of National Laity Committees 07322

Forum Européen des Comités Nationaux des Laïcs – Europäisches Forum der Nationalen Laienkomittees – Forum Europeo dei Comitati Nazionali dei Laici

Sec Grand-Rue 12-A, 1700 Fribourg, Switzerland. E-mail: info@europ-forum.org.
URL: http://www.europ-forum.org/

History 1970, Innsbruck (Austria), as an informal gathering of national committees for the apostolate of the laity in Europe. Also referred to as *European Lay Forum*. **Aims** Facilitate the exchange of experiences and information between members on questions of European importance, especially in relation to problems concerning the Church's mission in the world and pastoral work; maintain contacts and enhance cooperation with Church organizations on European and international levels; maintain contact with, cooperate with or address analyses or motions to the European, national or community authorities, civil and political organizations, and public opinion, for the promotion of christian values. **Structure** Study Assembly; Statutory Assembly; Study Assembly (every 2 years). President's Council; Steering Committee of 7. **Languages** English, French, German. **Staff** Voluntary. **Finance** Mainly from national committees' dues. **Events** *Biennial Assembly* Rome (Italy) 2014, *Biennial Assembly* Rome (Italy) 2014, *Biennial Assembly* Vienna (Austria) 2012, *Biennial Assembly* Birmingham (UK) 2010, *Biennial Assembly* Bratislava (Slovakia) 2008. **Publications** Conference proceedings.
Members National committees in 17 countries and territories:
Austria, Belarus, Belgium, Denmark, England, Germany, Ireland, Luxembourg, Netherlands, Poland, Portugal, Romania, Slovakia, Spain, Sweden, Switzerland, Wales. [2019/XD5484/**D**]

♦ European Forum of National Lift Associations / see European Lift Association (#07695)
♦ European Forum of National Nursing and Midwifery Associations / see European Forum of Nursing and Midwifery Associations (#07324)

♦ European Forum on Nature Conservation and Pastoralism (EFNCP) . 07323

Chief Exec Penygraig, Llanfair Clydogau, Lampeter, SA48 8LJ, UK. E-mail: info@efncp.org.
URL: http://www.efncp.org/

History Registration: Companies House, No/ID: 03150755, Start date: 24 Jan 1996; EU Transparency Register, No/ID: 851434349067-94, Start date: 14 Feb 2023. **Aims** Increase understanding of high nature conservation and cultural value of certain *farming* systems and inform work on their maintenance. **Structure** Board of Directors. **Languages** Bulgarian, English, French, Spanish. **Staff** 0.50 FTE, voluntary. **Finance** Sources: donations; fees for services; government support; grants. Supported by: *European Union (EU, #08967)*. Annual budget: 210,150 EUR (2021). **Activities** Events/meetings; guidance/assistance/consulting; politics/policy/regulatory; research/documentation. **Events** *Biennial Conference* Corofin (Ireland) 2015, *Biennial Conference* Bulgaria 2005, *Biennial Conference* Montpellier (France) 2003, *Biennial conference* Ennistymon (Ireland) 2000, *Biennial conference* Luhacovice (Czech Rep) 1998. **Publications** *La Cañada* (irregular). Reports; books.
Members Organizations in 23 countries:
Austria, Belgium, Bulgaria, Croatia, Estonia, France, Germany, Hungary, Ireland, Italy, Latvia, Lithuania, Netherlands, North Macedonia, Norway, Portugal, Romania, Slovakia, Spain, Sweden, Switzerland, UK, Ukraine.
Included in the above, one organization listed in this Yearbook:
ECNC – European Centre for Nature Conservation (#05289).
NGO Relations None. [2023/XF5634/**F**]

♦ European Forum of Nursing and Midwifery Associations 07324

Programme Manager Division of Health Systems and Public Health, WHO Regional Office for Europe, UN City, Marmorvej 51, 2100 Copenhagen, Denmark. T. +4545336809. E-mail: euronursingmidwifery@who.int.
Contact Ordem dos Enfermeiros, Avenida Almirante Gago Coutinho 75, 1700-028 Lisbon, Portugal. T. +351218455243 – +351218455233. Fax +351218455241. E-mail: gri@ordemenfermeiros.pt.
URL: http://www.euro.who.int/efnnma

History 6 Nov 1996, Madrid (Spain). Founded by national nursing and midwifery associations and *WHO Regional Office for Europe (#20945)*. Also referred to as *European Forum of National Nursing and Midwifery Associations (EFNNMA)*. **Aims** Contribute and inform the debate of improving health and quality of health care in Europe; promote exchange of information, ideas and policies between nursing/midwifery associations and WHO; support integration of appropriate policies for health for all into nursing practice as well as into basic, postgraduate and continuing nursing and midwifery education. **Languages** English, Russian. **Finance** Members' dues. **Events** *International Meeting* Copenhagen (Denmark) 2009, *International Meeting* Tashkent (Uzbekistan) 2008, *International Meeting* Copenhagen (Denmark) 2007, *International Meeting* St Petersburg (Russia) 2006, *International Meeting* Copenhagen (Denmark) 2005. **Publications** Meeting reports.
Members National nursing and midwifery organizations in 24 countries:
Albania, Andorra, Armenia, Austria, Bulgaria, Denmark, Finland, Germany, Ireland, Italy, Kyrgyzstan, Latvia, Moldova, Norway, Poland, Portugal, Romania, Russia, Serbia, Slovenia, Spain, Sweden, Switzerland, UK.
IGO Relations *WHO Regional Office for Europe (#20945)*. [2021/XF4807/**F**]

♦ European Forum of Official Gazettes (Forum) 07325

Secretariat Publications Office of the EU, Rue Mercier 2, MER 02/291, L-2985 Luxembourg, Luxembourg. T. +352292942768. E-mail: forum-official-gazettes@publications.europa.eu.
URL: http://circabc.europa.eu/webdav/CircaBC/OPOCE/ojf/Information/prod/htm l/index.htm

History 2004. **Aims** Exchange ideas and information on publication processes, technology and best practices between the official *publishers*. **Structure** Chair; Secretariat, provided by *Publications Office of the European Union (Publications Office, #18562)*. **Events** *The future of official publications* The Hague (Netherlands) 2019, *Meeting* Oslo (Norway) 2018, *Meeting* Sliema (Malta) 2017, *Meeting* Paris (France) 2015, *Meeting* Fribourg (Switzerland) 2014.
Members Gazettes in 38 countries:
Albania, Austria, Belgium, Bosnia-Herzegovina, Bulgaria, Croatia, Cyprus, Czechia, Denmark, Estonia, Finland, France, Germany, Greece, Hungary, Iceland, Ireland, Italy, Kosovo, Latvia, Liechtenstein, Lithuania, Luxembourg, Malta, Montenegro, Netherlands, North Macedonia, Poland, Portugal, Romania, Serbia, Slovakia, Slovenia, Spain, Sweden, Switzerland, Türkiye, UK.
Included in the above, 1 regional agency:
Publications Office of the European Union (Publications Office, #18562). [2017.06.21/XM4710/**F**]

♦ European Forum for Peace Researchers / see European Peace Research Association (#08177)

♦ European Forum for Primary Care (EFPC) 07326

Secretariat c/o Nivel, Otterstraat 118-124, 3513 CR Utrecht, Netherlands. T. +31629359635 – +31621966157. E-mail: info@euprimarycare.org.
URL: http://www.euprimarycare.org/

History 2005. Registration: EU Transparency Register, No/ID: 181778123351-61. **Aims** Improve health in Europe by promoting strong primary care. **Structure** Executive Board; Advisory Board; Secretariat. **Languages** English. **Staff** 1.50 FTE, paid. **Finance** Members' dues. Budget (annual): euro 150,000. **Activities** Research/documentation; events/meetings; training/education. **Events** *Conference* Bergen (Norway) 2021, *Empowering primary care through diversity* Ljubljana (Slovenia) 2020, *Primary care and local communities, health equity for everyone everywhere* Nanterre (France) 2019, *Vulnerability and compassion – the role of primary in Europe, how to overcome the austerity period* Heraklion (Greece) 2018, *Conference* Porto (Portugal) 2017. **Publications** Position papers.
Members National organizations; schools; universities; individuals. Institutional in 25 countries:
Austria, Belgium, Cyprus, Denmark, Estonia, France, Germany, Greece, Hungary, Italy, Kazakhstan, Latvia, Lithuania, Malta, Netherlands, Norway, Portugal, Slovakia, Slovenia, Spain, Sweden, Switzerland, Türkiye, UK, USA.
Included in the above, 4 organizations listed in this Yearbook:
AIDS Foundation East-West (AFEW); *European Federation of the Associations of Dietitians (EFAD, #07050)*; *Pharmaceutical Group of the European Union (PGEU, #18352)*; *WEMOS*.
Individuals. Membership countries not specified. Associated members include 31 organizations listed in this Yearbook:
Associated members include 31 organizations listed in this Yearbook:
- *Cancer and Primary Care Research International Network (Ca-PRI, #03415)*;
- *Council of Occupational Therapists for the European Countries (COTEC, #04912)*;
- *EuroHealthNet (#05693)*;
- *European Academy of Paediatrics (EAP, #05811)*;
- *European Association for Palliative Care (EAPC, #06141)*;
- *European Association Working for Carers (Eurocarers, #06277)*;
- *European General Practice Research Network (EGPRN, #07384)*;
- *European Health Futures Forum (EHFF, #07456)*;
- *European Health Management Association (EHMA, #07458)*;
- *European Men's Health Forum (EMHF, #07783)*;
- *European Network of Medical Residents in Public Health (Euronet MRPH, #07945)*;
- *European Network of Occupational Therapy in Higher Education (ENOTHE, #07956)*;
- *European Patients' Forum (EPF, #08172)*;
- *European Public Health Association (EUPHA, #08298)*;
- *European Rural and Isolated Practitioners Association (EURIPA, #08415)*;
- *European Society of General Practice/Family Medicine (WONCA Europe, #08609)*;
- *European Union of General Practitioners / Family Physicians (#08993)*;
- *Healthcare Information For All (HIFA, #10878)*;
- *International Association for Communication in Healthcare (EACH, #11792)*;
- *International Centre for Primary Health Care and Family Medicine (Primafamed-Ghent University)*;
- *International Collaboration for Community Health Nursing Research (ICCHNR)*;
- *International Foundation for Integrated Care (IFIC, #13672)*;
- *International Network for Health Workforce Education (INHWE, #14279)*;
- *International Primary Care Respiratory Group (IPCRG, #14640)*;
- *Northern Dimension Partnership in Public Health and Social Well-being (NDPHS, #17587)*;
- *Primary Care Diabetes Europe (PCDE, #18495)*;
- *The Network: Towards Unity for Health (The Network: TUFH, #17060)*;
- *WHO Regional Office for Europe (#20945)*;
- *World Confederation for Physical Therapy (WCPT, #21293)* (European Region);
- *World Federation of Public Health Associations (WFPHA, #21476)*.

IGO Relations *European Centre for Disease Prevention and Control (ECDC, #06476)*; *European Commission (EC, #06633)*; *WHO (#20950)*. **NGO Relations** Instrumental in setting up: *International Federation of Community Health Centres (IFCHC, #13395)*. Associate member of: *EuroHealthNet (#05693)*; *European Public Health Association (EUPHA, #08298)*; *World Organization of Family Doctors (WONCA, #21690)*. Endorses: *Steering Group on Influenza Vaccination (#19980)*. [2020/XM2296/y/**F**]

♦ European Forum of Psychomotor Activities / see European Forum of Psychomotricity (#07327)

♦ European Forum of Psychomotricity 07327

Forum Européen de la Psychomotricité – Europäisches Forum für Psychomotorik – Forum Europeo de Psicomotricidad

Sec address not obtained.
Pres address not obtained.
URL: http://www.psychomot.org/

History 18 Sep 1996, Marburg (Germany). Previously also referred to in English as *European Forum of Psychomotor Activities*. **Aims** Support psychomotor activities in the educational, re-educational and therapeutic practice, in the initial formation or continuing education, in the professionalization and the scientific research. **Structure** General Meeting (annual). Executive Committee, comprising President, 2 Vice-Presidents, Secretary, Treasurer and Delegates. **Activities** Committees (3): Training; Job; Science and Research. Organizes annual Student Academy. **Events** *Congress* Lucerne (Switzerland) 2016, *Annual General Meeting* Vienna (Austria) 2015, *Annual General Meeting* Dragør (Denmark) 2014, *Congress* Barcelona (Spain) 2013, *Annual General Meeting* Heidelberg (Germany) 2013.
Members Regular; extraordinary; associated. Partners in 15 countries:
Austria, Belgium, Czechia, Denmark, Finland, France, Germany, Italy, Luxembourg, Netherlands, Portugal, Slovenia, Spain, Sweden, Switzerland. [2014/XF5804/**F**]

♦ European Forum for Reciprocating Compressors (EFRC) 07328

Address not obtained.
URL: http://www.recip.org/

History Founded 1999. Registered in accordance with German law. Registration: Germany. **Aims** Support European users, manufacturers and scientists working in the field of reciprocating compressors in terms of technology, exchange of experience, formation and enforcement of standards and precompetitive research; facilitate the exchange of information between European operators, manufacturers and scientists working in the field. **Structure** General Assembly (annual); Board of 3 members. Working Groups (2): R and D; Standarisation. EFRC Office. **Languages** English, German. **Finance** Members' dues. **Activities** Events/meetings; training/education. **Events** *Conference* Warsaw (Poland) 2021, *Conference* Warsaw (Poland) 2020, *Conference* Madrid (Spain) 2018, *Conference* Madrid (Spain) 2016, *Conference* Düsseldorf (Germany) 2015.
Members Full in 12 countries:
Austria, Belgium, Czechia, Finland, France, Germany, Italy, Netherlands, Spain, Switzerland, UK, USA. [2020/XJ6685/**F**]

♦ European Forum for Religious Education in Schools (internationally oriented national body)

♦ European Forum for Renewable Energy Sources (EUFORES) 07329

SG Renewable Energy House, Rue d'Arlon 63-65, 1040 Brussels, Belgium. T. +3225461948. Fax +3225461934. E-mail: eufores@eufores.org.
URL: http://www.eufores.org/

History Founded Feb 1995. EU Transparency Register: 96507906043-80. **Aims** Promote the use of renewable energy in European institutions. **Structure** General Assembly; Board of Presidents; Extended Board; Advisory Committee. Secretariat. **Finance** Members' dues. Other sources: public funds through project development for the *European Commission (EC, #06633)*. **Activities** Organizes meetings and conferences. Through development of projects and initiatives, contributes to relevant EU documentation. **Events** *Inter-Parliamentary Meeting* Helsinki (Finland) 2019, *Inter-Parliamentary Meeting* Vienna (Austria) 2018, *Inter-Parliamentary Meeting* Valletta (Malta) 2017, *Inter-Parliamentary Meeting* Copenhagen (Denmark) 2016, *Inter-Parliamentary Meeting* Vienna (Austria) 2015. **Publications** *Renewables* – newsletter.
Members Members of parliament; Sponsoring Supporting; Supporting; Effective. Countries not specified but members include 12 organizations listed in this Yearbook:
Bioenergy Europe (#03247); *Euroheat and Power (EHP, #05694)*; *Europacable (#05743)*; *European Biogas Association (EBA, #06336)*; *European Copper Institute (ECI, #06796)*; *European Federation of Agencies and Regions for Energy and the Environment (FEDARENE, #07041)*; *European Geothermal Energy Council (EGEC, #07391)*; *European Small Hydropower Association (ESHA, #08495)*; *European Solar Shading Organization (ES-SO, #08794)*; *European Solar Thermal Electricity Association (ESTELA, #08795)*; *Solar Heat Europe (SHE, #19674)*; *SolarPower Europe (#19676)*; *WindEurope (#20965)*.
IGO Relations *European Parliament (EP, #08146)*; national parliaments. Proposed setting up of: *European Treaty on Renewable Energy (EURENEW)*. **NGO Relations** Supports: *Global 100% RE (#10160)*.
[2020/XF5775/y/**F**]

♦ European Forum for Research and Education in Allergy and Airway Diseases (EUFOREA) 07330

Main Office Bld Brand Whitlock 132, 1200 Sint-Lambrechts-Woluwe, Belgium. E-mail: contact@euforea.eu.
URL: http://www.euforea.eu/

History 2015, Belgium. Registration: Start date: 2015, Belgium. **Aims** Reduce the preventable and avoidable burden of morbidity and disability due to chronic airway diseases by means of a multidisciplinary practical approach with all stakeholders at national, regional and global levels, so that populations reach the highest attainable standards of health and productivity at every age and those diseases are no longer a barrier to well-being or socio-economic development. **Structure** Leadership; Scientific Advisory Board; Management Team. **Activities** Research/documentation; training/education; advocacy/lobbying/activism; events/meeting. **Events** *Forum* Sitges (Spain) 2019, *European Rhinology Research Forum* Brussels (Belgium) 2018, *European Rhinology Research Forum* Brussels (Belgium) 2017. **NGO Relations** Member of: *Biomedical Alliance in Europe (#03251)*. Partners include: *Alliance for Health Promotion (A4HP, #00687)*; *Global Alliance Against Chronic Respiratory Diseases (GARD, #10182)*; *Network of Universities from the Capitals of Europe (UNICA, #17061)*. [2020/XM6361/F]

♦ European Forum for Research in Rehabilitation (EFFR) 07331

Sec address not obtained.
URL: http://www.effr.org/

History 10 Jun 1988, Rotterdam (Netherlands), as *European Federation for Research in Rehabilitation* during the 3rd European Conference on Research in Rehabilitation. **Aims** Foster an interdisciplinary approach to research based on a biopsychosocial model of *health* and *disability*, thus focusing on rehabilitative research in the domains of impairments of body functions and structures, activity limitations and participation restrictions, as well as identification of environmental barriers and facilitators. **Structure** General Assembly; Council. **Languages** English. **Staff** None. **Finance** Members' dues. **Activities** Knowledge management/ information dissemination; projects/programmes; networking/liaising; events/meetings. **Events** *Congress* Berlin (Germany) 2019, *Congress* Glasgow (UK) 2017, *Congress* Espoo (Finland) 2015, *Congress* Istanbul (Turkey) 2013, *Perspectives and controversial issues for research in rehabilitation* Riva del Garda (Italy) 2011. **Publications** *International Journal of Rehabilitation Research* (4 a year). **IGO Relations** Global Rehabilitation Alliance; *WHO (#20950)* Call for Action Rehabilitation – Health Strategy 2030. **NGO Relations** Networking with scientific societies working in the field of rehabilitation, not specified. [2018.09.11/XD8719/D]

♦ European Forum for Restorative Justice (EFRJ) 07332

Exec Dir Hooverplein 10, 3000 Leuven, Belgium. T. +3216373598. Fax +3216325474. E-mail: info@ euforumrj.org.
Events and Communications Officer address not obtained.
URL: http://www.euforumrj.org/

History 8 Dec 2000. Former names and other names: *European Forum for Victim-Offender Mediation and Restorative Justice* – former. Registration: Banque-Carrefour des Entreprises, No/ID: 0474.656.137, Start date: 8 Dec 2000, Belgium; EU Transparency Register, No/ID: 987246143529-12, Start date: 14 Jul 2021. **Aims** Help establish and develop victim-offender mediation and other restorative justice practices throughout Europe; promote international exchange of information and mutual help; promote development of effective restorative justice policies, services and *legislation*; explore and develop the theoretical basis of restorative justice; stimulate research; assist development of principles, ethics, training and good practice. **Structure** General Meeting (annual); Board; Executive Committee; Secretariat. **Languages** English. **Staff** 4.40 FTE, paid; 1.00 FTE, voluntary. **Finance** Sources: members' dues. Supported by: *European Commission (EC, #06633)*. **Activities** Awareness raising; capacity building; conflict resolution; events/meetings; networking/liaising; politics/policy/regulatory; projects/programmes; standards/guidelines; training/education. **Events** *International Seminar* Pamplona (Spain) 2023, *International Conference* Sassari (Italy) 2022, *International Conference* Sassari (Italy) 2021, *International Conference* Sassari (Italy) 2020, *Biennial Conference* Tirana (Albania) 2018. **Publications** *Newsletter of the European Forum for Restorative Justice* (3 a year). Annual Report; Policy News; the Restorative Blog; newsflashes; research reports; books; thematic briefs; guidelines and manuals; conference resources; films and documentaries. **Information Services** *RJ Teaching Programmes Database*.
Members Individuals and organizations (about 450) in 46 countries:
Albania, Australia, Austria, Belarus, Belgium, Brazil, Bulgaria, Canada, Chile, China, Colombia, Croatia, Cyprus, Czechia, Denmark, Estonia, Finland, France, Georgia, Germany, Greece, Hungary, Iceland, Iran Islamic Rep, Ireland, Israel, Italy, Japan, Latvia, Luxembourg, Malta, Nepal, Netherlands, New Zealand, Norway, Poland, Portugal, Romania, Russia, Slovenia, Spain, Sweden, Switzerland, Tanzania UR, UK, USA.
IGO Relations Observer status with (1): *European Committee on Crime Problems (CDPC, #06645)*. Participant in Fundamental Rights Platform of: *European Union Agency for Fundamental Rights (FRA, #08969)*. [2023.02.16/XF6269/F]

♦ European Forum of Securities Associations (EFSA) 07333

BWF Contact Bundesverband der Wertpapierfirmen, Unterlindau 29, 60323 Frankfurt-Main, Germany. T. +496992101691. Fax +496992101692. E-mail: mail@efsa-securities.eu.
URL: https://www.efsa-securities.eu/

History Registration: EU Transparency Register, No/ID: 038014348035-13, Start date: 3 Nov 2022. **Aims** As a forum of European Securities Associations, help to deliver joint messages on policy issues in European securities markets to policy makers, regulators, industry representatives and the interested public. **Structure** A self-organising informal working-group. **Languages** English. **Staff** None paid. **Finance** No budget. **Events** *Meeting* Stockholm (Sweden) 2022, *Meeting* Paris (France) 2015, *Meeting* Copenhagen (Denmark) 2014, *Meeting* Madrid (Spain) 2014, *Meeting* Frankfurt-Main (Germany) 2013. **Publications** Policy statements; comment letters.
Members Organizations in 9 countries:
Belgium, Denmark, France, Germany, Italy, Poland, Spain, Sweden, UK.
IGO Relations No formal associations. **NGO Relations** No formal associations. [2022.02.09/XJ8430/F]

♦ European Forum of Sign Language Interpreters (efsli) 07334

Contact address not obtained. E-mail: admin@efsli.org – secretariat@efsli.org.
Admin Dir Rue de la Loi 26 / 15, 1040 Brussels, Belgium.
URL: http://www.efsli.org/

History 1992. Founded following a series of meetings beginning 1987. First Constitution ratified Aug 1993, Brussels (Belgium). Registration: Banque-Carrefour des Entreprises, No/ID: 0471.795.825, Start date: 16 Dec 1999, Belgium. **Aims** Encourage and promote deliberation and mutual exchange of information about the *profession* of interpreting and interpreting services within Europe; work to secure official recognition of the profession; encourage and promote scientific and *pedagogic* initiatives to improve standards of sign language interpreting and interpreter training. **Structure** General Meeting (annual); Board. **Languages** English, International Sign Language. **Staff** 2.00 FTE, paid. 4 voluntary Board members. **Finance** Sources: donations; grants; members' dues; sale of publications. **Activities** Events/meetings; knowledge management/information dissemination; projects/programmes; training/education. **Events** *Annual General Meeting and Conference* 2021, *Annual General Meeting and Conference* Cluj-Napoca (Romania) 2020, *Annual General Meeting and Conference* Malmö (Sweden) 2019, *Annual General Meeting and Conference* Dubrovnik (Croatia) 2018, *Annual general meeting and conference* Toulouse (France) 2017. **Publications** Conference proceedings; news bulletins; social media.
Members Full; Associate; Individual. Members in 31 countries and territories:
Austria, Belgium, Bulgaria, Croatia, Czechia, Denmark, Estonia, Finland, France, Germany, Greece, Hungary, Iceland, Ireland, Italy, Kosovo, Malta, Netherlands, Norway, Poland, Portugal, Romania, Russia, Scotland, Serbia, Slovakia, Slovenia, Spain, Sweden, Switzerland, UK.
NGO Relations Cooperates with (8): *Conférence internationale permanente d'instituts universitaires de traducteurs et interprètes (CIUTI, #04621)*; *European Deafblind Union (EDBU, #06891)*; *European Legal Interpreters and Translators Association (EULITA, #07678)*; *European Network of Sign Language Teachers (ENSLT, #08000)*; *European Union of Deaf Youth (EUDY, #08986)*; *European Union of the Deaf (EUD, #08985)*; *International Association of Conference Interpreters (#11807)*; *World Association of Sign Language Interpreters (WASLI, #21188)*. [2021.09.14/XF5339/F]

♦ European Forum, Stanford CA / see Forum on Contemporary Europe, Stanford CA

♦ European Forum for Studies of Policies for Research and Innovation (Eu-SPRI) 07335

Admin Dir Inst of Innovation Research, Manchester Business School, Booth Street West, Manchester, M15 6PB, UK. E-mail: info@euspri-forum.eu.
URL: http://www.euspri-forum.eu/

History Jun 2010, Paris (France). Registered in accordance with French law. **Aims** Strengthen the vibrant but dispersed interdisciplinary community of researchers focusing on interdisciplinary dimensions related to policy and governance in the field of knowledge creation and innovation. **Structure** General Assembly. Executive Committee. Secretariat. **Activities** Awards; meeting activities. **Events** *Conference* Utrecht (Netherlands) 2022, *Conference* Oslo (Norway) 2021, *Conference* Rome (Italy) 2019, *Conference* Paris (France) 2018, *Conference* Vienna (Austria) 2017.
Members Institutes in 11 countries:
Austria, Denmark, Finland, France, Germany, Italy, Netherlands, Norway, Spain, Sweden, UK. [2020/XJ7887/F]

♦ European Forum for the Study of Religion and the Environment 07336

Sec Löparegränden 3, SE-226 50 Lund, Sweden.
URL: https://www.religion-environment.com/

History 2005, Benediktbeuern (Germany). **Aims** Promote scholarly and critical inquiry into relationships between human beings and their diverse cultures, environments and religious beliefs and practices; foster interdisciplinary dialogues on human-environmental relationships and religion/nature/culture interactions. **Structure** Executive Committee. **Activities** Events/meetings; networking/liaising. **Events** *Myth, Ritual and Practice for the Age of Ecological Catastrophe* Potsdam (Germany) 2024, *Religion, Materialism and Ecology* 2021, *Religion, materialism and ecology* Manchester (UK) 2020, *Conference* Munich (Germany) 2015, *Conference* Sigtuna (Sweden) 2013. **Publications** *Studies in Religion and the Environment/Studien zur Religion und Umwelt* – book series, 13 vols to date. *Religion in the Anthropocene* (2017); *Technofutures, Nature and the Sacred: Transdisciplinary Perspectives* (2015); *Animals as Religious Subjects: Transdisciplinary Perspectives* (2014); *Religion and Ecology in the Public Sphere* (2011); *Nature, Space and the Sacred: Transdisciplinary Perspectives* (2009).
Members Individuals in 31 countries:
Australia, Austria, Brazil, Canada, Denmark, Estonia, Finland, France, Germany, Ghana, Greece, Hungary, Israel, Italy, Kenya, Korea Rep, Kyrgyzstan, Lebanon, New Zealand, Nigeria, Norway, Pakistan, Poland, Romania, Russia, South Africa, Sweden, Switzerland, Tanzania UR, UK, USA. [2021.05.21/XJ1414/F]

♦ European Forum for Sustainable Property Development (internationally oriented national body)

♦ European Forum for Teachers of Religious Education (EFTRE) 07337

Forum européen des professeurs d'éducation religieuse – Foro europeo para Maestros de la Educación Religiosa – Europäische Forum für Religionslehrer
Chair address not obtained.
URL: http://www.eftre.net/

History 1980, Helsinki (Finland). **Aims** Contribute to the international cooperation of teachers of religious education and religious studies in the theoretical and practical aspects of their work; strengthen and promote the position of religious education and religious studies in schools in Europe. **Structure** General Assembly (every 3 years during conference). Working Board, consisting of one representative from each member country, elects Executive Committee, comprising Chairperson, Secretary, Treasurer and 3 members. **Languages** Dutch, English, Finnish, French, German, Norwegian, Spanish. **Staff** Voluntary. **Finance** Members' dues (annual euro 100). **Activities** Organizes: triennial conference; teacher seminars. Offers consultancy services. **Events** *Conference* Rome (Italy) 2023, *Conference* Rome (Italy) 2022, *Conference* Dublin (Ireland) 2019, *Conference* Vienna (Austria) 2016, *Conference* Malmö (Sweden) 2013. **Publications** Newsletter (2 a year).
Members Associations of teachers of RE/RS in the school systems of Europe; Institutes or departments concerned with the training of RE/RS teachers and the support of RE/RS in schools in Europe. Members in 20 countries:
Austria, Belgium, Cyprus, Denmark, Estonia, Finland, France, Germany, Hungary, Italy, Latvia, Malta, Netherlands, Norway, Poland, Romania, Spain, Sweden, Switzerland, UK.
NGO Relations Member of: *Coordinating Group for Religion in Education (CoGREE, #04823)*. [2012.06.01/XD7417/D]

♦ European Forum of Technical and Vocational Education and Training (EfVET) 07338

Central Office Rue d'Arlon 40, 1000 Brussels, Belgium. T. +3222343763. Fax +3222350539. E-mail: vc@efvet.org.
URL: http://www.efvet.org/

History 1991, Amsterdam (Netherlands). EU Transparency Register: 147656111703-83. **Aims** Provide a transnational framework to support all cooperative actions aimed at enhancing and improving technical and vocational education and training. **Structure** Assembly General Meeting; Steering Committee; Executive Team. **Languages** English. **Staff** 1.00 FTE, paid; 5.00 FTE, voluntary. **Finance** Budget (annual): euro 220,000. **Activities** Projects/programmes; events/meetings. **Events** *Annual International Conference* Kuopio (Finland) 2022, *Annual International Conference* 2021, *Annual International Conference* 2020, *Annual International Conference* Ponta Delgada (Portugal) 2019, *Annual International Conference* Como (Italy) 2018. **Publications** *EFVET Newsletter*. Brochure; guides.
Members Organizations in 31 countries:
Belgium, Bosnia-Herzegovina, Bulgaria, Croatia, Cyprus, Czechia, Denmark, Estonia, Finland, France, Germany, Greece, Hungary, Iceland, Ireland, Italy, Lithuania, Malta, Netherlands, Norway, Poland, Portugal, Romania, Russia, Slovakia, Slovenia, Spain, Sweden, Switzerland, Türkiye, UK.
Associate in 3 countries and territories:
Hong Kong, Nigeria, USA.
IGO Relations *European Quality Assurance in Vocational Education and Training (EQAVET, #08312)*. **NGO Relations** Member of: *Lifelong Learning Platform – European Civil Society for Education (LLLP, #16466)*. [2020/XF2789/F]

♦ European Forum on Urban Forestry (EFUF) 07339

Contact address not obtained. E-mail: info@efuf.org.
URL: https://efuforg.wordpress.com/

Aims Disseminate the role of trees, woodlands and forests in urban areas. **Activities** Events/meetings. **Events** *European Forum on Urban Forestry* Cologne (Germany) 2019, *European Forum on Urban Forestry* Vantaa (Finland) 2018. [2019/XM7924/F]

♦ European Forum for Urban Safety / see European Forum for Urban Security (#07340)

♦ European Forum for Urban Security (Efus) 07340

Forum européen pour la sécurité urbaine
Exec Dir 10 rue des Montiboeufs, 75020 Paris, France. T. +33140644900. Fax +33140644910. E-mail: contact@efus.eu.
URL: https://efus.eu/

History Nov 1987, Barcelona (Spain). Former names and other names: *Forum of the Local and Regional Authorities of Europe for Urban Security* – former (Nov 1987 to 1992); *Forum des collectivités territoriales européennes pour la sécurité urbaine* – former (Nov 1987 to 1992); *European Forum for Urban Safety* – former (1992 to 1997); *FESU* – former alias; *Forum Europeo para la Seguridad Urbana* – former alias. **Aims** Build up a network of European local authorities – towns, provinces, regions – which implement actions and programmes to fight urban insecurity; prevent and treat delinquency; strengthen crime reduction policies; promote the role of local authorities in national and European policies. **Structure** General Assembly (annual); Executive Committee; National Forums for Urban Security (6). **Languages** English, French. **Staff** 10.00 FTE, paid. **Finance** Members' dues. Grants from governments. Programmes also financed by *European Commission (EC, #06633)*. **Activities** Knowledge management; networking/liaising; politics/policy/regulatory; guidance/assistance/consulting; training/education; events/meetings. **Events** *Public Spaces – PACTESUR Final Conference* Brussels (Belgium) 2022, *Conference on Security, Democracy and Cities* Nice (France) 2021, *Conference on Security, Democracy and Cities* Nice (France) 2020, *Workshop on Identifying Vulnerabilities and Mitigating the Risk of Terrorist Threats in Public Spaces* Brasov (Romania) 2019, *Workshop on the Security of Public Spaces* Brussels (Belgium) 2019. **Publications** *Efus Newsletter* (11 a year) – electronic. *Manifesto of Aubervilliers and Saint-Denis* (2012); *Manifesto of Saragossa* (2006); *Security, Democracy and Cities Manifestos: Manifesto of Naples* (2000). Conference papers and proceedings; studies.
Members Local authorities in 16 countries:
Austria, Belgium, Croatia, Czechia, France, Germany, Greece, Italy, Netherlands, Poland, Portugal, Romania, Spain, Sweden, Switzerland, UK.
National Forums in 6 countries:
Belgium, France, Germany, Italy, Portugal, Spain.

European Forum Victim 07340

alphabetic sequence excludes
For the complete listing, see Yearbook Online at

Consultative Status Consultative status granted from: *Council of Europe (CE, #04881)* (Participatory Status). **IGO Relations** Cooperates with: *Instituto Latinoamericano de las Naciones Unidas para la Prevención del Delito y Tratamiento del Delincuente (ILANUD, #11347)*; *International Bank for Reconstruction and Development (IBRD, #12317)* (World Bank); *United Nations Commission on Crime Prevention and Criminal Justice (CCPCJ, #20530)*; *United Nations Human Settlements Programme (UN-Habitat, #20572)*; *United Nations Office on Drugs and Crime (UNODC, #20596)*. *European Committee of the Regions (CoR, #06665)*; **NGO Relations** Member of: *Civil Society Forum on Drugs (CSFD, #03968)*. Cooperates with: *African Research Network for Urban Management (ARNUM, no recent information)*; *Council of European Municipalities and Regions (CEMR, #04891)*; *EUROCITIES (#05662)*; *International Association of Public Transport (#12118)*; *World Organization of United Cities and Local Governments (UCLG, #21695)*. Instrumental in setting up: *International Centre for the Prevention of Crime (ICPC, #12508)*. [2017.01.02/XF1808/F]

♦ European Forum for Victim-Offender Mediation and Restorative Justice / see European Forum for Restorative Justice (#07332)
♦ European Forum for Victim Services / see Victim Support Europe (#20767)
♦ European Forum of Worldwide Music Festivals / see Forum of Worldwide Music Festivals (#09933)

♦ European Foundation for the Accreditation of Hotel School Programmes (EFAP) 07341

Fondation européenne pour l'accréditation des écoles hôtelières – Europäische Stiftung für die Akkreditierung von Hotelschulen
Contact Av Theodore Flournoy 5, 1207 Geneva, Switzerland. T. +41217114283. E-mail: ihrapresident@gmail.com.
History Dec 1991. Registration: Banque-Carrefour des Entreprises, Belgium; Handelsregister, Netherlands. **Aims** Establish a system of *quality endorsement* for hotel school programmes across Europe; provide accreditation for those programmes that meet or exceed the quality standards set by the foundation. **Structure** Board of Governors; Council (meets annually); Advisory Committee. **Languages** English, French. **Staff** 10.00 FTE, paid; 22.00 FTE, voluntary. **Finance** Sources: donations; members' dues. Annual budget: 2,000,000 EUR (1999). **Activities** Certification/accreditation; events/meetings.
Members Full in 48 countries and territories:
Argentina, Austria, Bahamas, Bahrain, Belgium, Bosnia-Herzegovina, Brazil, Bulgaria, Canada, China, Côte d'Ivoire, Croatia, Cyprus, Czechia, Denmark, Dubai, Egypt, Estonia, Finland, France, Germany, Greece, Honduras, Hungary, Île-de-France, India, Ireland, Italy, Kenya, Korea DPR, Kuwait, Lebanon, Malta, Mexico, Montenegro, Netherlands, Norway, Peru, Portugal, Qatar, Serbia, Spain, Switzerland, Syrian AR, Tunisia, Türkiye, UK, USA.
IGO Relations *ECOSOC (#05331)*; *ILO (#11123)*; *International Air Transport Association (IATA, #11614)*; *UNEP (#20299)*; *World Tourism Organization (UNWTO, #21861)*. **NGO Relations** EFAP is a collective activity of: *International Hotel and Restaurant Association (IH&RA, #13813)*; *European Federation of Food, Agriculture and Tourism Trade Unions (EFFAT, #07125)*; *Institute of Hospitality (#11269)*; Also has consultative status through IH and RA. [2022.05.04/XF2574/f/F]

♦ European Foundation for Alcohol Research (ERAB) 07342

SG Rue Washington 40, 1050 Brussels, Belgium.
URL: http://www.erab.org/
History 2003, Brussels (Belgium). Former names and other names: *European Research Advisory Board (ERAB)* – former. Registration: Banque-Carrefour des Entreprises, No/ID: 0875.302.264, Start date: 1 Jul 2005. **Aims** Fund *biomedical* and *psychosocial* research into *beer* and other *alcoholic drinks*. **Structure** Board of Directors; Advisory Board; Secretary-General. **Languages** English. **Staff** 0.50 FTE, paid. **Events** *International Meeting on Alcohol and Global Health* Leuven (Belgium) 2018, *International Meeting on Alcohol and Global Health* Amsterdam (Netherlands) 2014. **Publications** Reports. **NGO Relations** Member of: *Federation of European and International Associations Established in Belgium (FAIB, #09508)*. [2019.12.11/XJ4004/f/F]

♦ European Foundation for Business Qualification (EFBQ) 07343

Contact PO Box 1, 3700 AA Zeist, Netherlands. T. +31306985500. Fax +31306985501.
Street Address Wagnerlaar 17, 3723 JT Bilthoven, Netherlands.
URL: http://www.efbq.nl/
Aims Promote, review and qualify strategic *entrepreneurship*.
Members in 3 countries:
Belgium, Germany, Netherlands.
IGO Relations Recognized by: *European Commission (EC, #06633)*. [2008/XF5661/f/F]

♦ European Foundation for the Care of Newborn Infants (EFCNI) 07344

Exec Assistant Hofmannstr 7A, 81379 Munich, Germany. T. +4989890832612. Fax +4989890832610. E-mail: info@efcni.org.
URL: http://www.efcni.org/
History Apr 2008. Registration: No/ID: 143/235/22619, Germany; EU Transparency Register, No/ID: 33597655264-22. **Aims** Represent the interests of preterm and newborn infants and their families; gather parents, families, adults born preterm and healthcare professional so as to improve long-term health of newborn and preterm children by ensuring the best possible prevention, treatment, care and support. **Structure** Board of Directors; Board of Trustees; Scientific Advisory Board; Parents' Advisory Board. **Languages** English, French, German, Spanish. **Staff** 20.00 FTE, paid. **Activities** Advocacy/lobbying/activism; awareness raising; capacity building; events/meetings; guidance/assistance/consulting; healthcare; knowledge management/information dissemination; networking/liaising; projects/programmes; research/documentation; standards/guidelines; training/education. **Events** *JENS : Congress of Joint European Neonatal Societies* 2021, *Stockholm Conference on Ultra-Early Intervention* Stockholm (Sweden) 2020, *Stockholm Conference on Ultra-Early Intervention* Stockholm (Sweden) 2020, *JENS : Congress of Joint European Neonatal Societies* Maastricht (Netherlands) 2019, *Stockholm Conference on Ultra-Early Intervention* Stockholm (Sweden) 2019. **Publications** *EFCNI Newsletter. Making Human Milk Matter – The need for regulation in the European Union* (2021) in English; *Zero Separation. Together for better care! Infant and family-centred developmental care in times of COVID-19 – A global survey of parents' experience* (2021) in English; *Born Too Soon – The Global Action Report on Preterm Birth* (2012); *Caring for Tomorrow – the EFCNI White Paper for Maternal and Newborn Health and Aftercare Services* (2011/2012); *EU Benchmarking Report – Too Little Too Late? Why Europe should do more for Preterm Infants – vol 99* (2011). Scientific publications; journal articles.
Members European national parents' associations. Membership countries not specified. **NGO Relations** Member of (1): *World Prematurity Network (#21736)*. Partner of (1): *International Council of Multiple Birth Organisations (ICOMBO, #13050)*. Supports (1): *Every Woman Every Child (EWEC, #09215)*. Instrumental in setting up (1): *Global Alliance for Newborn Care (GLANCE, #10215)*. Cooperates with: *COFACE Families Europe (#04084)*; *Council of International Neonatal Nurses (COINN, #04904)*; *European Board of Neonatology (EBN, #06363)*; *European Lung Foundation (ELF, #07718)*; *European Society for Paediatric Gastroenterology, Hepatology and Nutrition (ESPGHAN, #08680)*; *European Society of Paediatric and Neonatal Intensive Care (ESPNIC, #08683)*; *Fédération Internationale de Gynécologie et d'Obstétrique (FIGO, #09638)*; *Fetal Medicine Foundation (FMF)*; *Healthy Newborn Network (HNN, #10894)*; *International Federation for Spina Bifida and Hydrocephalus (IF SBH, #13552)*; *International Patient Organization for Primary Immunodeficiencies (IPOPI, #14533)*; *LittleBigSouls (LBS, #16494)*; national organizations; *NIDCAP Federation International (NFI)*; *Union of European Neonatal and Perinatal Societies (UENPS, #20389)*. [2022.02.09/XJ1789/f/F]

♦ European Foundation for Chinese Music Research (CHIME Foundation) 07345

Sec-Treas PO Box 11092, 2301 EB Leiden, Netherlands. T. +31715133974. Fax +31715133123. E-mail: chime@wxs.nl.
Secretariat Gerecht 1, 2311 TC Leiden, Netherlands.
URL: http://www.chimemusic.nl/
History Founded 1990, by scholars from 4 European countries. **Aims** Create a European network of scholars of Chinese music who meet regularly to discuss their work in progress. **Structure** Executive Board; Contemporary Music Section. **Languages** English. **Staff** 1.50 FTE, voluntary. **Finance** Sources: private donations; subscriptions; governmental funding for specific projects. **Activities** Networking/liaising; research/documentation; events/meetings. **Events** *Annual Conference* Prague (Czechia) 2021, *Annual Conference* Prague (Czechia) 2020, *Annual Conference* Beijing (China) 2019, *Annual Conference* Lisbon (Portugal) 2018, *Annual Conference* Los Angeles, CA (USA) 2017. **Publications** *CHIME Journal* (annual). *Chime Studies in East Asian Music – vols 1-2* – series. Compact discs. Information Services: Documentation centre/library; audio-visual archive.
Members Individuals in 33 countries and territories:
Australia, Austria, Belgium, Canada, China, Czechia, Denmark, Finland, France, Germany, Haiti, Hong Kong, Ireland, Italy, Japan, Korea Rep, Latvia, Lithuania, Luxembourg, Macau, Malaysia, Netherlands, New Zealand, Norway, Philippines, Russia, Singapore, Spain, Sweden, Switzerland, Taiwan, UK, USA. [2015/XF2667/fv/F]

♦ European Foundation for Clinical Nanomedicine (CLINAM) 07346

CEO Alemannengasse 12, PO Box, 4016 Basel BS, Switzerland. T. +41616959395. Fax +41616959390. E-mail: loeffler@clinam.org – clinam@clinam.org.
CSO address not obtained.
URL: http://www.clinam.org/
History Founded 2007, Basel (Switzerland). **Aims** Advance medicine to the benefit of individuals and society through the application of nanoscience in medicine, and translate the results to the benefit of patients. **Structure** Board of Trustees; Advisory Board. **Languages** Dutch, English, French, German, Italian. **Staff** 10.00 FTE, paid. **Finance** Sponsored and summits supported by Swiss Government to some level; income from projects. **Activities** Research/documentation; events/meetings. **Events** *European Summit on Clinical Nanomedicine and Targeted Medicine* Basel (Switzerland) 2017, *European Summit on Clinical Nanomedicine and Targeted Medicine* Basel (Switzerland) 2016, *European Summit on Clinical Nanomedicine / European Summit* Basel (Switzerland) 2015, *European Summit on Clinical Nanomedicine / European Summit* Basel (Switzerland) 2014, *European Summit on Clinical Nanomedicine / European Summit* Basel (Switzerland) 2013. **Publications** *European Journal of Nanomedicine*. **Members** in 47 countries. Membership countries not specified. [2017/XJ8718/f/F]

♦ European Foundation for Democracy (EDF) 07347

Pres Square de Meeûs 35, 1000 Brussels, Belgium. T. +3222130040. Fax +3222130049.
URL: http://www.europeandemocracy.eu/
History Nov 2005. Sub-title: *Supporting Freedom, Strengthening Europe*. Registration: EU Transparency Register, No/ID: 70156146692-35. **Aims** Support: universal human rights; *freedom* of conscience; individual liberty; pluralism of peaceful ideas. **Members** Membership countries not specified. **NGO Relations** Member of: *European Policy Centre (EPC, #08240)*. [2022/XJ0163/f/F]

♦ European Foundation of Drug Helplines (#09819)
♦ European Foundation For Financial Inclusion (unconfirmed)
♦ European Foundation for Human Rights and Tolerance (internationally oriented national body)
♦ European Foundation for Immunogenetics / see European Federation for Immunogenetics (#07141)

♦ European Foundation for the Improvement of Living and Working Conditions (Eurofound) 07348

Fondation européenne pour l'amélioration des conditions de vie et de travail – Fundación Europea para la Mejora de las Condiciones de Vida y de Trabajo – Europäische Stiftung zur Verbesserung der Lebens- und Arbeitsbedingungen – Europese Stichting tot verbetering van de levens- en arbeidsomstandigheden – Fondazione Europea per il Miglioramento delle Condizioni di Vita e di Lavoro
Exec Dir Wyattville Road, Loughlinstown, Dublin, CO. DUBLIN, D18 KP65, Ireland. T. +35312043100. Fax +35312826456. E-mail: information@eurofound.europa.eu.
Brussels Office Avenue d'Auderghem 18-20, 1040 Brussels, Belgium. T. +3222806476. Fax +3222806479. E-mail: eurofound.brusselsoffice@eurofound.europa.eu.
URL: https://www.eurofound.europa.eu/
History 26 May 1975, Dublin (Ireland). Established pursuant to a regulation of *Council of the European Union (#04895)*, the Council Regulation (EEC) No 1365/75, following a proposal of *European Commission (EC, #06633)* and taking into account earlier advice from *European Parliament (EP, #08146)* and *European Economic and Social Committee (EESC, #06963)*, as an autonomous European Community/European Union body. A decentralized agency of *European Union (EU, #08967)*. A new Founding Regulation was adopted on 20 Dec 2018 and took effect on 20 Feb 2019. Regulation (EU) 2019/127 of the European Parliament and of the Council of 16 Jan 2019 establishing the European Foundation for the improvement of living and working conditions (Eurofound), and repealing Council Regulation (EEC) No 1365/75. **Aims** Provide information, advice and expertise on working conditions and sustainable work, industrial relations, labour market change and quality and life and public services to support EU Institutions and bodies, Member States and Social Partners in shaping and implementing social and employment policies, as well as promoting social dialogue on the basis of comparative information, research and analysis. **Structure** Management Board (former Governing Board); Executive Director; Deputy Director; Brussels Liaison Office. **Staff** 100.00 FTE, paid. About 100 staff members drawn from a number of Member States; experts occasionally seconded from national administrations. **Finance** Comes under the general budget of the European Communities. **Activities** Events/meetings; politics/policy/regulatory; publishing activities; research and development; research/documentation. **Events** *Youth first! Employment, skills and social policies that work for young Europeans in times of uncertainty* Brussels (Belgium) 2022, *Foundation Forum* Dublin (Ireland) 2022, *Final Conference on the Future of Manufacturing Project* Brussels (Belgium) 2019, *Seminar on Economic and social convergence in the EU – Making it happen!* Brussels (Belgium) 2019, *Meeting on the Role of Survey Data for Evidence-Based Policymaking on Working Time in the EU* Brussels (Belgium) 2018. **Publications** Annual Work Programme; surveys; research reports; briefs; articles; blog posts; data resources; podcases; expert webinars. **Information Services** *European Foundation for the Improvement of Living and Working Conditions* – Eurofound provides information, advice and expertise on working conditions and sustainable work, industrial relations, labour market change and quality and life and public services, to support the EU Institutions and bodies, Member States and Social Partners in shaping and implementing social and employment policies, as well as promoting social dialogue on the basis of comparative information, research and analysis..
Members European Union Member States (27):
Austria, Belgium, Bulgaria, Croatia, Cyprus, Czechia, Denmark, Estonia, Finland, France, Germany, Greece, Hungary, Ireland, Italy, Latvia, Lithuania, Luxembourg, Malta, Netherlands, Poland, Portugal, Romania, Slovakia, Slovenia, Spain, Sweden.
European Commission (EC, #06633); *European Parliament (EP, #08146)*.
Active in 118 countries and territories:
Algeria, Angola, Antigua-Barbuda, Argentina, Australia, Austria, Bangladesh, Belgium, Bolivia, Botswana, Brazil, Brunei Darussalam, Bulgaria, Cameroon, Canada, Chile, China, Colombia, Congo DR, Costa Rica, Côte d'Ivoire, Croatia, Cuba, Cyprus, Czechia, Denmark, Egypt, El Salvador, Equatorial Guinea, Estonia, Eswatini, Ethiopia, Fiji, Finland, France, Gambia, Germany, Ghana, Greece, Grenada, Guatemala, Guinea, Guyana, Honduras, Hong Kong, Hungary, Iceland, India, Indonesia, Iran Islamic Rep, Iraq, Ireland, Israel, Italy, Jamaica, Japan, Jordan, Kenya, Korea DPR, Korea Rep, Kuwait, Lebanon, Lesotho, Liechtenstein, Lithuania, Luxembourg, Malawi, Malaysia, Mali, Malta, Mauritania, Mauritius, Mexico, Montenegro, Morocco, Netherlands, New Zealand, Niger, Nigeria, Norway, Oman, Pakistan, Panama, Papua New Guinea, Paraguay, Peru, Philippines, Poland, Portugal, Romania, Russia, Saudi Arabia, Serbia, Sierra Leone, Singapore, Slovakia, Slovenia, South Africa, Spain, Sri Lanka, Sudan, Suriname, Sweden, Switzerland, Taiwan, Tanzania UR, Thailand, Trinidad-Tobago, Tunisia, Türkiye, Uganda, UK, United Arab Emirates, Uruguay, USA, Venezuela, Zambia, Zimbabwe.
IGO Relations Memorandum of Understanding with (5): *European Agency for Safety and Health at Work (EU-OSHA, #05843)*; *European Centre for the Development of Vocational Training (Cedefop, #06474)*; *European Institute for Gender Equality (EIGE, #07557)*; *European Training Foundation (ETF, #08934)*; *European Union Agency for Fundamental Rights (FRA, #08969)*. Agreement with: *Council of Europe (CE, #04881)*. **NGO Relations** Member of (1): *EU Agencies Network (EUAN, #05564)*. [2023.03.02/XF9170/f/F*]

♦ European Foundation for Landscape Architecture / see IFLA Europe (#11103)
♦ European Foundation for Law and Economics / see European Association of Law and Economics (#06104)
♦ European Foundation for Management Development / see EFMD – The Management Development Network (#05387)
♦ European Foundation Il Nibbio (internationally oriented national body)
♦ European Foundation for Osteoporosis and Bone Disease / see International Osteoporosis Foundation (#14490)
♦ European Foundation for Philanthropy and Social Development (internationally oriented national body)

♦ European Foundation for Plant Pathology (EFPP) **07349**

Secretariat Wageningen Univ and Research/ Biointeractions/Plant Health, PO Box 16, 6700 AA Wageningen, Netherlands. T. +31317480629.

Street address Droevendaalsesteeg 1, Room WO Ec 011, NL-6708 PB, Wageningen, Netherlands.

URL: http://www.efpp.net/

History 1990. **Aims** Promote scientific and technical cooperation in the arena of plant health in Europe; facilitate exchange of scientific information between plant pathologists who are members of national or regional societies in the field of plant pathology or related fields. **Structure** Executive Committee; Secretariat. **Languages** English. **Staff** None. **Finance** Members' dues. **Activities** Events/meetings. **Events** *Triennial Conference* Birmingham (UK) 2021, *Triennial Conference* Birmingham (UK) 2020, *Triennial Conference* Dunkerque (France) 2017, *Biennial conference* Krakow (Poland) 2014, *Biennial conference* Wageningen (Netherlands) 2012. **Publications** *European Journal of Plant Pathology.*

Members National societies in 20 countries:

Belarus, Belgium, Czechia, Denmark, Finland, France, Greece, Ireland, Israel, Italy, Lithuania, Netherlands, Norway, Poland, Portugal, Romania, Spain, Sweden, Switzerland, UK.

IGO Relations *European and Mediterranean Plant Protection Organization (EPPO, #07773).* **NGO Relations** *European and Mediterranean Cereal Rusts Foundation (EMCRF, #07769); International Organisation for Biological Control (IOBC, #14424).* [2018.09.10/XF5320/f/**F**]

♦ European Foundation on Social Quality / see International Association on Social Quality (#12168)

♦ European Foundation Society and Education (internationally oriented national body)

♦ European Foundation for South Asian Studies (EFSAS) **07350**

Contact Rijnsburgstraat 54 – bg, 1059 AX Amsterdam, Netherlands. T. +31207373401. E-mail: y.barakova@efsas.org – info@efsas.org.

URL: http://www.efsas.org/

History Registration: Handelsregister, No/ID: 67033008, Netherlands; EU Transparency Register, No/ID: 730856826170-47. **Aims** Conduct in-depth research, research, statistical data, policy advice and forecasts related to developments in the fields of politics, international relations, conflict management, human rights, security, diplomacy, strategic affairs and conflict resolutions in South Asia; conceive new ideas so as to find sustainable solutions to conflicts and facilitate an atmosphere of reconciliation, peace and tranquility. **Finance** Sources: donations; fees for services; grants. Supported by: *European Commission (EC, #06633).* **Activities** Awards/prizes/competitions; events/meetings; guidance/assistance/consulting; knowledge management/ information dissemination; research/documentation. **Publications** Commentaries and Infographics; research papers; articles. [2022.02.09/XM6375/f/**F**]

♦ European Foundation for the Study of Diabetes (EFSD) **07351**

Acting Managing Dir Rheindorfer Weg 3, 40591 Düsseldorf, Germany. T. +492117584690. Fax +4921175846929. E-mail: foundation@easd.org.

URL: http://www.europeandiabetesfoundation.org/

History Created by *European Association for the Study of Diabetes (EASD, #06228).* **Aims** Encourage and support research in the field of diabetes; rapidly diffuse acquired knowledge; facilitate its application. **Structure** Board is same as that of *European Association for the Study of Diabetes (EASD, #06228).* Scientific Board. **Activities** Awards/prizes/competitions; research/documentation. **NGO Relations** Member of (1): *European Diabetes Forum (EUDF, #06916).* [2021/AA1363/**F**]

♦ European Foundation of Traditional Chinese Medicine (internationally oriented national body)

♦ European Foundation for Transplant Coordinators / see European Donation and Transplant Coordination Organisation (#06939)

♦ European Foundry Association, The (CAEF) **07352**

SG c/o Bundesverband der Deutschen, Giesserei-Industrie, Hansaallee 203, 40549 Düsseldorf, Germany. T. +492116871217. Fax +49211687140217. E-mail: info@caef.eu.

URL: http://www.caef.eu/

History 15 Jul 1953, Paris (France). Founded as *European Committee of Foundry Associations – Comité européen des associations de fonderies (CEAF)*, following the setting up, 1952, of a European liaison committee on foundry productivity. From 30 Apr 1970, referred to as *Committee of European Foundry Associations – Comité des associations européennes de fonderie – Vereinigung Europäischer Giessereiverbände.* Current title, adopted 9 Jun 1998, retains the previous French acronym 'CAEF'. Title changed to: *Committee of Associations of European Foundries.* New name adopted, 2003. Registration: Start date: 6 Jan 1956, France; EU Transparency Register, No/ID: 07813897843-74, Start date: 26 Jan 2012. **Aims** Bring together European foundry organizations, whatever *metals* or alloys they handle or techniques they employ; deal efficiently with foundry problems. **Structure** Plenary Assembly (annual); Council; General Secretariat; Commissions; Groups; Sections. **Languages** English. **Activities** Training/education; research/documentation; knowledge management/information dissemination; events/meetings. **Events** *Biennial International Foundry Forum* Amsterdam (Netherlands) 2018, *Biennial International Foundry Forum* Dresden (Germany) 2016, *Biennial International Foundry Forum* Venice (Italy) 2014, *Annual Plenary Assembly* Stockholm (Sweden) 2013, *Biennial International Foundry Forum* Prague (Czech Rep) 2012. **Publications** *The European Foundry Industry* (annual) – statistical reports.

Members National delegations (23) in 22 countries:

Austria, Belgium, Bulgaria, Croatia, Czechia, Denmark, Finland, France, Germany, Hungary, Italy, Lithuania, Netherlands (2), Norway, Poland, Portugal, Slovenia, Spain, Sweden, Switzerland, Türkiye, UK.

IGO Relations *European Commission (EC, #06633).* **NGO Relations** Member of: *European Network on Silica (NEPSI, #08001).* [2020/XD0640/**D**]

♦ European Foundry Equipment Suppliers Association, The (CEMAFON) **07353**

SG Lyoner Strasse 18, 60528 Frankfurt-Main, Germany. T. +496966031414. E-mail: info@cemafon.org.

URL: http://www.cemafon.org/

History 1972. Former names and other names: *European Committee for Materials and Products for Foundries* – former; *Comité européen des matériels et produits pour la fonderie (CEMAFON)* – former; *Europäisches Komitee der Hersteller von Giessereimaschinen und Giessereiausrüstungen* – former; *Comitato Europeo dei Materiali e Prodotti per la Fonderia* – former. **Aims** Act as the voice and lobby organization of the European manufacturers of foundry machinery and plants, furnaces and products for the foundry industry; represent its members' interests in economic as well as technical and trade issues. **Structure** General Assembly; Presidency; Directors; General Secretary; Commissions. **Languages** English. **Activities** Advocacy/lobbying/activism; events/meetings; knowledge management/information dissemination. **Events** *Biennial International Foundry Forum* Amsterdam (Netherlands) 2018, *Biennial International Foundry Forum* Dresden (Germany) 2016, *Biennial International Foundry Forum* Venice (Italy) 2014, *Biennial International Foundry Forum* Prague (Czech Rep) 2012, *World aluminium conference* Essen (Germany) 2010.

Members Associations of manufacturers of foundry machinery and equipment in 3 countries:

Germany, Italy, UK.

Individuals in 3 countries:

Denmark, Spain, Switzerland.

IGO Relations Recognized by: *European Commission (EC, #06633).* **NGO Relations** Joint publication with: *The European Committee of Industrial Furnace, Heating and Metallurgical Equipment Associations (CECOF, #06653).* [2021.06.21/XD9932/**D**]

♦ European Fragile X Network (unconfirmed)

♦ European Franchise Federation (EFF) **07354**

Exec Dir Rue Washington 40, 1050 Brussels, Belgium. T. +3225201607. E-mail: info@eff-franchise.com.

URL: http://www.eff-franchise.com/

History Takes over activities of *European Franchising Federation (EFF, inactive)*, founded 23 Sep 1972. Registration: Banque-Carrefour des Entreprises, No/ID: 0478.339.266, Start date: 19 Sep 2002, Belgium; EU Transparency Register, No/ID: 755515438089-04, Start date: 8 May 2020. **Aims** Promote, protect and contribute to development of franchising in Europe; be the single spokesbody for the franchise industry in Europe with regards to European institutions and other interests groups in Europe and Brussels. **Structure** General Assembly; Board of Directors; Executive Director. **Languages** English. **Staff** 1.00 FTE, paid. **Finance** Members' dues. **Activities** Advocacy/lobbying/activism; knowledge management/information dissemination. **Events** *European franchise conference* Brussels (Belgium) 2005, *Convention* London (UK) 1998, *Convention* Valencia (Spain) 1997. **Publications** *European Code of Ethics for Franchising* (2016).

Members National franchise associations or federations in 19 countries:

Belgium, Croatia, Czechia, Denmark, Finland, France, Greece, Hungary, Italy, Netherlands, Poland, Portugal, Slovakia, Slovenia, Spain, Sweden, Switzerland, Türkiye, UK.

IGO Relations *European Commission (EC, #06633); European Parliament (EP, #08146).* **NGO Relations** Member of: *Federation of European and International Associations Established in Belgium (FAIB, #09508).* Founding member of: *World Franchise Council (WFC, #21529).* [2020/XD5499/**D**]

♦ European Franchise Lawyers Association (EF LAW) **07355**

Contact c/o EF LAW Tübingen, Robert Gradmann Weg 1, 72076 Tübingen, Germany. T. +497071600630. Fax +497071600345.

URL: http://www.eflaw.de/

History 1992. A grouping of the type *European Economic Interest Grouping (EEIG, #06960).* **Aims** Offer the most comprehensive range of specialist international franchise experience and expertise available to exploit and expand international business opportunities in Western and Central Europe. **Languages** English, French. **Staff** 2.00 FTE, paid. **Finance** Sources: members' dues. **Activities** Events/meetings; networking/liaising. **Publications** *Jahrbuch Franchising* (annual). Biographical profiles.

Members Full in 9 countries:

Austria, Belgium, France, Germany, Italy, Spain, Switzerland, UK, USA. [2023.02.15/XD5524/**D**]

♦ European Franchising Federation (inactive)

♦ European Free Alliance / see European Free Alliance (#07356)

♦ European Free Alliance (EFA) **07356**

Alliance libre européenne (ALE) – Alleanza Libera Europea

Address not obtained.

URL: http://www.e-f-a.org/

History 7 Jul 1981, Brussels (Belgium). Founded on the initiative of a group of 8 independent members of *European Parliament (EP, #08146)*, and comprising 8 political parties. Was at one time a sub-group of the previous *Rainbow Group (inactive).* Officially founded as a federation of parties, 1994, in accordance with the provisions of Article 138 A of the Treaty of the Union. Founded as a political party under current title according to new EU regulation (EC 2004/2003), 26 Mar 2004, Barcelona (Spain). Officially recognized as a European Political Party, 13 Oct 2004. Former names and other names: *European Free Alliance (EFA)* – former (7 Jul 1981 to 2 Oct 1995); *Alliance libre européenne (ALE)* – former (7 Jul 1981 to 2 Oct 1995); *Alianza Libre Europea* – former (7 Jul 1981 to 2 Oct 1995); *Europäische Freie Allianz* – former (7 Jul 1981 to 2 Oct 1995); *Alleanza Libera Europea* – former (7 Jul 1981 to 2 Oct 1995); *Europese Vrije Alliantie* – former (7 Jul 1981 to 2 Oct 1995); *Democratic Party of the Peoples of Europe – European Free Alliance (DPPE-EFA)* – former (2 Oct 1995 to 26 Mar 2004); *Parti démocratique des peuples d'Europe – Alliance libre européenne (PDPE-ALE)* – former (2 Oct 1995 to 26 Mar 2004). **Aims** Defend the right to *self-determination* of peoples; promote European historic languages and cultures; activate cooperation among *democratic* and progressive nationalist and regionalist *political parties* in a European perspective; represent European stateless nations, regions and minorities, giving more competences and better representation to the European Union regions; voice the shared concerns of stateless nations, regions and minorities; defend the environment; promote subsidiarity, justice and equal chances and opportunities for all peoples of Europe. **Structure** General Assembly (annual); Board; Representatives in 17 EU member states. In European Parliament, EFA MEPs (12) sit within the Greens – European Free Alliance Group (7 MEPs), ECR Group (4 MEPs) and GUE-NGL Group (1 MEP). **Languages** Dutch, English, French, German, Italian, Spanish. **Staff** 2.00 FTE, paid. **Finance** Sources: contributions of member/ participating states. Supported by: *European Parliament (EP, #08146).* **Activities** Events/meetings; training/ education. **Events** *General Assembly* Santiago de Compostela (Spain) 2014, *General Assembly* Merano (Italy) 2013, *Unity and diversity – a democratic and decentralized Europe* Brussels (Belgium) 1997, *Half-yearly meeting* San Sebastian (Spain) 1989, *Half-yearly meeting* Brussels (Belgium) 1988. **Publications** *EFA Newsletter* (4 a year). *Manifesto for the European Elections; Who's Who.*

Members Political parties with over 300 elected representatives at European, state, national and regional levels. Full members (46 parties) in over 19 EU Member States (not specified).

Observers (4 parties) in 3 countries:

Italy, Latvia, Spain. [2020/XF1154/**F**]

♦ European Free Alliance Youth (EFAY) **07357**

Address not obtained.

URL: http://www.efay.eu/

History Registered in accordance with Belgian law. **Aims** Make young people more aware of the diversity of Europe; enable them to participate in activities that promote this diversity. **Structure** General Assembly (annual); Bureau. **Publications** *EFAY Newsletter.*

Members 31 youth organizations in 14 countries:

Austria, Belgium, Czechia, Finland, France, Greece, Italy, Lithuania, Netherlands, Poland, Romania, Slovakia, Spain, UK.

NGO Relations Observer member of: *European Youth Forum (#09140).* [2014.10.09/XM3533/**F**]

♦ European Free Newspaper Federation (inactive)

♦ European Free Trade Association (#05391)

♦ European Freight Forwarders Association (EFFA) **07358**

Pres Unit 17 Brook Industrial Estate, Hayes, UB4 0JZ, UK. T. +442087560500. Fax +442087560400.

URL: http://www.effa.com/

History 1994. **Aims** Provide a forum for good quality, independent freight forwarders; provide them with a global network of quality agents to make each member better able to compete in the growing global economy. **Structure** Officers: President; Vice-President; Secretary. **Languages** English. **Staff** 3.00 FTE, voluntary. **Activities** Networking/liaising. **Events** *Annual Conference* Hong Kong (Hong Kong) 2015, *Annual Conference* Milan (Italy) 2014, *Annual Conference* Chicago, IL (USA) 2013, *Annual Conference* Sydney, NSW (Australia) 2012, *Annual Conference* Lucerne (Switzerland) 2011. **Publications** *EFFA News.*

Members Individual agents (38) in 29 countries and territories:

Australia, Bangladesh, Bermuda, Canada, China, Denmark, France, Germany, Hong Kong, India, Indonesia, Ireland, Italy, Japan, Korea Rep, Malta, Mexico, Myanmar, Netherlands, Norway, Pakistan, Romania, Spain, Sweden, Switzerland, Taiwan, United Arab Emirates, USA, Vietnam.

Associate: companies in 14 countries and territories:

Bangladesh, China, India, Mexico, Netherlands, Nigeria, South Africa, Spain, Taiwan, Türkiye, UK, United Arab Emirates, USA, Vietnam. [2018.06.01/XD6884/**D**]

♦ European Freight and Logistics Leaders Club / see European Freight and Logistics Leaders Forum (#07359)

♦ European Freight and Logistics Leaders Forum (F and L) **07359**

Secretariat c/o Billiet, 146 Av Louise, 1050 Brussels, Belgium. T. +3223729168.

URL: http://www.europeanfreightleaders.eu/

History Founded 1994, as *European Freight and Logistics Leaders Club.* Registered under current title in accordance with Belgian law. **Aims** Promote closer integration of various methods of freight transport by any means; maximize exploitation and evolution of multimodal freight transport systems; improve quality of freight transport; enable exchange of experiences while conforming to EU competition rules. **Structure** General Meeting (twice a year); Board of Directors; Management Committee; Specialized Commissions; Working Groups (2); Secretariat. **Languages** English. **Staff** 3.00 FTE, paid. **Finance** Members' dues. **Activities** Events/meetings. **Events** *F&L Business Leaders Round Table* London (UK) 2022, *Half-Yearly General Meeting* Hamburg (Germany) 2019, *Half-Yearly General Meeting* Milan (Italy) 2019, *Half-Yearly General*

Meeting Gothenburg (Sweden) 2018, *Half-Yearly General Meeting* Madrid (Spain) 2018. **Publications** *F and L Newsletter*. Booklets; working group reports. **Members** Individuals or public and enterprises with activities closely related to that of F and L, with registered office or place of residence is Europe, as defined by membership to the Council of Europe. Membership countries not specified. **NGO Relations** Member of: *NewOpera (#17090)*. [2020/XD3938/F]

♦ European French Ethnic Association (inactive)

♦ European Frequency and Time Forum (EFTF) 07360

Forum européen fréquence et temps

Secretariat SFMC, 41bis av de l'Observatoire, 25000 Besançon, France. T. +33381666930. Fax +33381666944. E-mail: contact@sfmc.fr.
URL: http://www.eftf.org/

History 1987. **Aims** Provide information on recent advances and trends of scientific research and industrial development in the fields of frequency and time. **Structure** Executive Committee; Permanent Secretariat in Besançon (France). **Languages** English. **Activities** Events/meetings. **Events** *International Symposium on Frequency Control* Toyama City (Japan) 2023, *Annual Forum* Neuchâtel (Switzerland) 2014, *Annual Forum* Prague (Czech Rep) 2013, *Annual Forum* Gothenburg (Sweden) 2012, *Annual Forum* San Francisco, CA (USA) 2011. **Publications** Conference proceedings.
Members Full in 5 countries:
France, Germany, Italy, Switzerland, UK. [2017.06.01/XF7208/F]

♦ European Fresh Produce Association (FRESHFEL Europe) 07361

General Delegate Rue de Trèves 49-51 Bte 8, 1040 Brussels, Belgium. T. +3227771580. Fax +3227771581. E-mail: info@freshfel.org.
URL: http://www.freshfel.org/

History 1 Jan 2002. Founded by merger of *European Fresh Produce Importers Association (CIMO, inactive)* and *European Union of the Fruit and Vegetable Wholesale, Import and Export Trade (EUCOFEL, inactive)*. Since 2010, took over activities of *European Community Banana Trade Association (ECBTA, inactive)*. Registration: Banque-Carrefour des Entreprises, No/ID: 0413.638.088, Start date: 30 Oct 1973, Belgium; Eu Transparency Register, No/ID: 1637225479-02, Start date: 7 Oct 2008. **Aims** Represent the interests of small, medium and large companies in the fresh produce sector; study measures aiming at improving freedom of international trade and distribution of fresh produce; undertake research and set up educational programmes to improve the positioning and competitive performance of the fresh produce sector; provide a networking platform of common concern for the fresh produce sector. **Structure** General Meeting (annual). Board of Directors; Policy Bodies; Technical Ad Hoc Committees. Secretariat in Brussels (Belgium). **Languages** English. **Staff** 4.00 FTE, paid. **Events** *FRESH Annual Conference* Brussels (Belgium) 2022, *FRESH Annual Conference* Brussels (Belgium) 2021, *FRESH Annual Conference* London (UK) 2019, *FRESH Annual Conference* Hamburg (Germany) 2018, *FRESH Annual Conference* Brussels (Belgium) 2017.
Members Full in 22 countries:
Austria, Belgium, Croatia, Cyprus, Czechia, Denmark, Finland, France, Germany, Hungary, Ireland, Italy, Netherlands, Norway, Poland, Portugal, Slovenia, Spain, Sweden, Switzerland, Türkiye, UK.
IGO Relations *European Commission (EC, #06633)*; *European Parliament (EP, #08146)*; *Codex Alimentarius Commission (CAC, #04081)*; *United Nations Economic Commission for Europe (UNECE, #20555)*. **NGO Relations** Member of: *EU Platform for Action on Diet, Physical Activity and Health (inactive)*; *Federation of European and International Associations Established in Belgium (FAIB, #09508)*; *Global Alliance to Promote Fruits and Vegetable Consumption "5 a day" (AIAM5, #10221)*. [2021/XD8866/D]

♦ European Fresh Produce Importers Association (inactive)
♦ European Frontier Regions Joint Working Party / see Association of European Border Regions (#02499)

♦ European Fruit Juice Association (AIJN) 07362

SG Rue de la Loi 221 – Box 5, 1040 Brussels, Belgium. T. +3222350620. E-mail: aijn@aijn.eu.
URL: https://aijn.eu/en

History 23 Sep 1958, Strasbourg (France). Former names and other names: *Commission of the Fruit and Vegetable Juice Industry of the EEC* – former (23 Sep 1958 to 7 May 1987); *Commission de l'industrie des jus de fruits et de légumes de la CEE (CIJF)* – former (23 Sep 1958 to 7 May 1987); *Association of the Industry of Juices and Nectars from Fruits and Vegetables of the European Economic Community* – former (7 May 1987 to 1994); *Association de l'industrie des jus et nectars de fruits et de légumes de la Communauté économique européenne (AIJN)* – former (7 May 1987 to 1994); *Association of the Industry of Juices and Nectars from Fruits and Vegetables of the European Union* – former (1994); *Association de l'industrie des jus et nectars de fruits et de légumes de l'Union européenne* – former (1994); *European Association of Fruit Juice Industries* – alias. Registration: Belgium; EU Transparency Register, No/ID: 410052929385-59. **Aims** Represent the fruit juice *industry* in the *European Union*, from fruit processors to packers of consumer products; work for the best possible political, regulatory and economic framework at EU level in order to add value and promote the growth of the fruit juice industry. **Structure** General Assembly (twice a year); Executive Board; Committees and Expert Groups (6). **Activities** Events/meetings; guidance/assistance/consulting; politics/policy/regulatory. **Events** *Annual Juice Summit* Antwerp (Belgium) 2019, *Annual Juice Summit* Antwerp (Belgium) 2018, *Annual Juice Summit* Antwerp (Belgium) 2017, *Annual Juice Summit* Antwerp (Belgium) 2016, *Annual Juice Summit* Antwerp (Belgium) 2015. **Publications** *The Market Report*.
Members Full: national fruit juice associations in EU member states, currently 19 associations in 17 countries:
Austria, Belgium, Bulgaria, Cyprus, Denmark, Finland, France, Germany, Hungary, Ireland, Italy, Netherlands, Poland, Portugal, Spain, Sweden, UK.
Observer: national associations representing the fruit juice industry in European countries but not eligible to be full or associated members; companies from non-EU countries supplying raw materials to the EU juice industry and/or associations representing these suppliers; companies supplying packaging materials, equipment, ingredients or processing aids to the EU fruit and vegetable juices and nectars industry and/or associations who represent these companies; international associations active in field. Observers (25) in 12 countries:
Belgium, Brazil, France, Germany, Italy, Netherlands, Poland, Russia, Spain, Switzerland, UK, USA.
Affiliated members (2) in 2 countries:
Serbia, Türkiye.
IGO Relations Recognized by: *European Commission (EC, #06633)*, representing the industry in several committees and groups. **NGO Relations** Member of (2): *FoodDrinkEurope (#09841)*; *International Fruit and Vegetable Juice Association (IFU, #13687)*. [2020.11.17/XE0489/E]

♦ European Fruit Research Institute Network (EUFRIN) 07363

Chair c/o Laimburg Research Centre, Laimburg 6, 39040 Post Auer, Italy.
URL: https://eufrin.eu/

History 1993, Bonn (Germany). **Aims** Create a philosophy of fruit production through research; establish and improve cooperation between those involved in fruit R and D within Europe; prepare and submit joint bids for funding of R and D; enhance and facilitate coordinated research, development and technology transfer, focused on aiding sustainable production of quality fruit. **Structure** Board, including Chairperson, Secretary and Organizing Support Member. **Languages** English. **Staff** None. **Finance** Costs are covered by partners or sponsors. Budget: only for events. **Activities** Working Groups (11): Fruit quality; Fruit thinning; Soft fruit; Water relations; Stone fruit variety evaluation; Apple and pear variety evaluation; Plume and prune; Rootstocks for fruit trees; Improvement of fruit by biotechnology; Crop adapted spraying; Minimize residues. **Events** *Meeting* 2020, *Meeting* Brussels (Belgium) 2019, *Meeting* Paris (France) 2011, *Meeting* Bolzano (Italy) 2010, *Meeting* Bucharest (Romania) 2009. **Publications** *EUFRIN Newsletter*.
Members in 24 countries:
Austria, Belgium, Croatia, Czechia, Denmark, Estonia, France, Germany, Greece, Hungary, Italy, Latvia, Lithuania, Netherlands, Norway, Poland, Portugal, Romania, Slovenia, Spain, Sweden, Switzerland, Türkiye, UK. [2021/XF7025/F]

♦ European Fuel Association / see European Liquid Heating Fuels Association (#07701)

♦ European Fuel Cell Forum (EFCF) 07364

Main Office Obgardihalde 2, 6043 Adligenswil LU, Switzerland. E-mail: forum@efcf.com.
URL: http://www.efcf.com/

History 1994. Founded as a not-for-profit organization. Became a company, 2011. Registration: Commercial Register Office, No/ID: 100.3.791.835-0, Switzerland, Luzern. **Structure** Board of Advisors. **Activities** Events/meetings. **Events** *Fuel Cells, Electrolysers and H2 Processing Conference* Lucerne (Switzerland) 2023, *European Polymer Electrolyte Fuel Cells (PEFC) and Hydrogen/Electrolyser Forum* Lucerne (Switzerland) 2021, *European Grid Service Markets (GSM) Symposium* 2020, *European Solid Oxide Fuel Cell (SOFC) and Electrolyser (SOE) Forum* Lucerne (Switzerland) 2020, *European Solid Oxide Fuel Cell (SOFC) and Electrolyser (SOE) Forum* Lucerne (Switzerland) 2020. [2021/XQ0258/ce/F]

♦ European Fuel Information Centre (inactive)
♦ European Fuel Merchant's Union (inactive)
♦ European Fuel Oxygenates Association / see Sustainable Fuels (#20060)
♦ European Full-Scale Modelling Association (no recent information)

♦ European Fund and Asset Management Association (EFAMA) 07365

Dir Gen Rue Marie-Thérèse 11, 1000 Brussels, Belgium. T. +3225133969. E-mail: info@efama.org.
Head of Communications & Membership address not obtained.
URL: http://www.efama.org/

History 1974. Founded as *European Federation of Investment Funds and Companies – Fédération européenne des fonds et sociétés d'investissement (FEFSI) – Europäische Investment-Vereinigung*. Most recent statutes adopted 2004. Registration: Banque-Carrefour des Entreprises, No/ID: 0446.651.445, Start date: 11 Feb 1992, Belgium; EU Transparency Register, No/ID: 3373670692-24, Start date: 28 Nov 2008. **Aims** As the representative association for the European investment industry: support investor confidence in the asset management industry through promotion of governance standards, integrity, professionalism and performance throughout the industry; enhance smooth functioning of a European single market for investment management and a level playing field for saving and investment products; strengthen competitiveness of the industry in terms of cost and quality; promote the asset management industry and the UCITS brand on a worldwide level. **Structure** General Meeting (annual); Board of Directors; Secretariat in Brussels (Belgium). **Languages** English, French, German. **Staff** 15.00 FTE, paid. **Finance** Members' dues. **Activities** Standards/guidelines; networking/liaising; knowledge management/information dissemination; events/meetings. **Events** *Investment Management Forum* Brussels (Belgium) 2022, *Investment Management Forum* Brussels (Belgium) 2021, *Investment Management Forum* Brussels (Belgium) 2020, *Investment Management Forum* Brussels (Belgium) 2019, *Investment Management Forum* Brussels (Belgium) 2018. **Publications** Annual Report; Fact Book; position papers; reports.
Members Full; Corporate; Associate. Full: national associations in 28 countries:
Austria, Belgium, Bulgaria, Croatia, Cyprus, Czechia, Denmark, Finland, France, Germany, Greece, Hungary, Ireland, Italy, Liechtenstein, Luxembourg, Malta, Netherlands, Norway, Portugal, Romania, Slovakia, Slovenia, Spain, Sweden, Switzerland, Türkiye, UK.
Corporate (59); Associate (22). Membership countries not specified.
IGO Relations *Council of the European Union (#04895)*; *European Commission (EC, #06633)*; *European Economic and Social Committee (EESC, #06963)*; *European Parliament (EP, #08146)*. **NGO Relations** Member of: *Federation of European and International Associations Established in Belgium (FAIB, #09508)*. [2021/XD2259/D]

♦ European Fund for the Balkans (EFB) 07366

Exec Dir Resavska 35, Belgrade, PAK 11000, Serbia. E-mail: office@balkanfund.org.
URL: http://balkanfund.org

History 2007, as a multi-year joint initiative of *Robert Bosch Foundation, King Baudouin Foundation (KBF), Company of St Paul* and *ERSTE Foundation*. **Aims** Undertake and support initiatives aimed at bringing the Western Balkans closer to the European Union. **Structure** Steering Committee; Secretariat. **Activities** Financial and/or material support; capacity building; networking/liaising. Set up *Balkans in Europe Policy Advisory Group (BiEPAG)*. [2018/XM4327/f/F]

♦ European Fund for Engineering Education Development (unconfirmed)

♦ European Fundraising Association (EFA) 07367

Address not obtained.
URL: http://www.efa-net.eu/

History Feb 2002, Brussels (Belgium). Founded following a series of meetings which began in 1998. Registration: No/ID: 34212817, Netherlands. **Structure** General Assembly (annual). Board. **Activities** Certification/accreditation. **Events** *Skillshare* Berlin (Germany) 2008, *Summit* San Diego, CA (USA) 2008, *Meeting* Noordwijkerhout (Netherlands) 2007, *Summit* Noordwijkerhout (Netherlands) 2006, *Summit* London (UK) 2005. **Publications** *Fundraising Europe*.
Members Organizations in 16 countries:
Austria, Belgium, Denmark, Finland, France, Germany, Ireland, Italy, Netherlands, Norway, Poland, Spain, Sweden, Switzerland, UK, Ukraine.
NGO Relations Member of: *European Charities' Committee on Value-Added Tax (ECCVAT, #06519)*. [2014/XM3670/D]

♦ The European Fund for Southeast Europe (EFSE) 07368

Contact Finance in Motion, Carl-von-Noorden-Platz 5, 60596 Frankfurt-Main, Germany. T. +4969977876500. Fax +49699778765010. E-mail: investors@efse.lu.
URL: http://www.efse.lu/

History Dec 2005. Successor of various development finance initiatives known as the "European Funds for Bosnia and Herzegovina, Kosovo, Montenegro and Serbia". Started as a regional fund for Southeast Europe; expanded to European Eastern Neighbourhood region, 2010; expanded to include Turkey, 2011. **Aims** Foster economic development and prosperity in Southeast Europe and in the European Eastern Neighbourhood Region through the provision of sustainable additional development finance to micro and small enterprises and to private households through qualified financial institutions. **Structure** Board of Directors; Advisory Group; Committees. **Languages** English. **Staff** 100.00 FTE, paid. **Finance** Sources: donors; IFIs/DFIs; private investors. Donors include: *European Commission (EC, #06633)*; Governments of Germany, Denmark, Albania and Armenia; *Swiss Agency for Development and Cooperation (SDC)*; *Austrian Development Agency (ADA)*. IFIs/DFIs currently investing include: *European Bank for Reconstruction and Development (EBRD, #06315)*; *European Investment Bank (EIB, #07599)*; *International Finance Corporation (IFC, #13597)*; *Kreditanstalt für Wiederaufbau (KfW)*; *Nederlandse Financierings-Maatschappij voor Ontwikkelingslanden (FMO)*; Oesterreichische Entwicklungsbank (OeEB). Committed funding at Dec 2013: euro 962 million. **Activities** Financial support. Active in: Albania, Armenia, Azerbaijan, Belarus, Bosnia-Herzegovina, Bulgaria, Croatia, Georgia, Kosovo, Moldova, Montenegro, North Macedonia, Romania, Serbia, Türkiye, Ukraine. **Events** *Annual Meeting* Yerevan (Armenia) 2014, *Annual Meeting* Sarajevo (Bosnia-Herzegovina) 2013, *Annual Meeting* Tbilisi (Georgia) 2012, *Annual Meeting* Tirana (Albania) 2011, *Annual Meeting* Ohrid (Macedonia) 2010. **Publications** *Development Performance* (4 a year); *EFSE at a Glance* (4 a year); *Investment Portfolio Performance* (4 a year). Annual Report. **NGO Relations** Supports: *Microfinance Centre (MFC, #16745)*. [2021/XJ7019/f/F]

♦ European Funeral Directors' Association (inactive)
♦ European Fur Breeders Association (inactive)

♦ European Furniture Industries Confederation (EFIC) 07369

SG Rue Montoyer 24, 1000 Brussels, Belgium. E-mail: info@efic.eu.
URL: http://www.efic.eu/

History 2006. EU Transparency Register: 95910795422-52. **Aims** Represent furniture manufacturers, defend and promote their interests, by establishing and maintaining a constructive dialogue with European institutions, social partners and other stakeholders. **Structure** General Assembly; Board; Working Group (4); Secretariat. **Activities** Advocacy/lobbying/activism; networking/liaising; knowledge management/information dissemination. **Events** *Furniture Day Meeting* Brussels (Belgium) 2022, *Conference on Circular Economy and Furniture Sector* Brussels (Belgium) 2017.
Members Full in 12 countries:
Austria, Belgium, Denmark, France, Germany, Hungary, Italy, Netherlands, Norway, Portugal, Sweden, Türkiye.
NGO Relations Member of: *AEGIS Europe*; *Industry4Europe (#11181)*. [2020/XM4752/t/D]

♦ European Furniture Manufacturers Federation **07370**

Union européenne de l'ameublement (UEA) – Verband der Europäischen Möbelindustrie

SG c/o Asociace ceskych nabytkaru, Na Porici 12, 110 00 Prague 1, Czechia. T. +420777294404. E-mail: seceretary@ueanet.com.
URL: http://www.ueanet.com/

History 12 Oct 1950, Amsterdam (Netherlands), at 2nd *International Congress of Furniture Manufacturers.* EU Transparency Register: 815158223707-96. **Aims** Establish liaison among manufacturers' organizations and harmonize their interests; promote research on technical and economic problems; collect and distribute relevant documentation; support national and international exhibitions. **Structure** General Assembly (2 a year); Steering Committee. **Languages** English, French, German. **Staff** 4.00 FTE, paid. **Finance** Members' dues. Budget (annual): US$ 200,000. **Activities** Research/documentation. **Events** *International conference on wood science and engineering in the third millennium* Brasov (Romania) 2009, *World furniture congress* Palma (Spain) 2006, *Congress* Amsterdam (Netherlands) 2000, *Quality* Cannes (France) 1993, *Congress* Milan (Italy) 1991.
Members Full in 6 countries:
Czechia, Portugal, Romania, Spain, Türkiye, UK.
IGO Relations Recognized by: *European Commission (EC, #06633).* [2019/XD0769/t/**D**]

♦ European Fusarium Seminar (meeting series)
♦ European Fusion Development Agreement (inactive)

♦ European Futsal Association (EFA) **07371**

Union Europea de Futsal (UEFS)

Gen Sec 2nd Dinamovsky per 3-29, Moscow MOSKVA, Russia, 109044. T. +74956767715. E-mail: intercontinentalfutsalcup1@gmail.com.
Pres address not obtained.
URL: https://www.europeanfutsal.com/

History 1985, Spain. **Aims** Organize futsal and microfutsal competitions in Europe. **Structure** Congress; Executive Committee; Bureau. **Languages** English, Russian, Spanish. **Staff** 8.00 FTE, paid. **Finance** Sponsorship fees. Budget (annual): about euro 80,000. **Activities** Sporting events. **Events** *Congress* Spain 2010.
Members Full in 21 countries and territories:
Armenia, Basque Country, Belarus, Belgium, Bulgaria, Catalunya, Czechia, Estonia, France, Greece, Israel, Italy, Latvia, Lithuania, Moldova, Norway, Poland, Russia, Slovakia, Spain, Ukraine.
IGO Relations None. **NGO Relations** Founding member of: *World Futsal Association (#21532).* Cooperates with: *Pan American Indoor Football Confederation (#18112).* [2022/XJ8999/**D**]

♦ European Future Forum (unconfirmed)
♦ European Future Innovation System (unconfirmed)

♦ European Galactosaemia Society (EGS) **07372**

Chairman Zandoogjelaan 4, 5691 RJ Son en Breugel, Netherlands. T. +31499477509.
URL: http://www.galactosaemia.eu/

History 1997. **Aims** Share information, promote awareness of and stimulate research into Galactosaemia within Europe. **Structure** Board. **Activities** Events/meetings; research/documentation. **Events** *Joint Meeting* Amsterdam (Netherlands) 2021, *Joint Meeting* Amsterdam (Netherlands) 2019, *Meeting* Amsterdam (Netherlands) 2019, *Joint Meeting* Amsterdam (Netherlands) 2017, *Joint Meeting* Barcelona (Spain) 2015.
Members Full; Associate; Honorary. Members in 13 countries:
Austria, Belgium, Denmark, Estonia, France, Germany, Ireland, Netherlands, Norway, Portugal, Spain, Switzerland, UK.
NGO Relations Cooperates with (1): *Galactosemia Network (GalNet, #10063).* [2021/AA0790/**D**]

♦ European Games Developer Federation (EGDF) **07373**

COO Eteläranta 10, FI-00130 Helsinki, Finland. T. +358407163640.
Billing Address c/o Spelplan-ASGD, Box 22307, SE-104 22 Stockholm, Sweden.
URL: http://www.egdf.eu/

History EU Transparency Register: 57235487137-80. **Aims** Stimulate and develop a stable, vibrant and creative European games development sector that is competitive globally and recognized culturally. **Structure** General Assembly. **Events** *Annual General Assembly* 2021, *Annual General Assembly* Dubrovnik (Croatia) 2017, *Annual General Assembly* Berlin (Germany) 2013, *Annual General Assembly* Malmö (Sweden) 2009.
Members National members in 16 countries:
Austria, Belgium, Croatia, Denmark, Finland, France, Germany, Malta, Netherlands, Norway, Poland, Romania, Spain, Sweden, Türkiye, UK. [2019/XM5737/**D**]

♦ European Gaming and Amusement Federation (EUROMAT) **07374**

Secretariat Rue du Luxembourg 22-24, 1000 Brussels, Belgium. T. +3227616684. Fax +3222131363. E-mail: secretariat@euromat.org.
URL: http://www.euromat.org/

History 1979. Previously titles: *Federation of European Coin Machine Associations – Fédération des associations européennes de l'automatique – Vereinigung der Europäischen Verbände der Automatenwirtschaft; Federation of European Coin-Operated Amusement Machine Associations – Europäische Vereinigung der Verbände der Unterhaltungsautomatenwirtschaft; European Federation of Coin Operated Amusement Machine Associations; European Federation of Coin Machine Associations – Fédération européenne des associations de l'automatique – Europäische Vereinigung der Automaten-Verbände.* Current statutes approved 25 May 2007. Registered in accordance with Belgian law. EU Transparency Register: 87412665203-64. **Aims** Represent the gaming and amusement industry to increase overall competitiveness of the sector through engagement in policy and regulation formation at EU level. **Structure** General Assembly (annual); Executive Committee; Secretariat in Brussels (Belgium). **Languages** English, French. **Staff** 4.00 FTE, paid. **Finance** Members' dues. **Activities** Events/meetings. **Events** *European Gaming and Amusement Summit* Dublin (Ireland) 2022, *European Gaming and Amusement Summit* Dublin (Ireland) 2020, *European Gaming Summit* Monte Carlo (Monaco) 2018, *European Gaming Summit* Berlin (Germany) 2017, *European Gaming Summit* Barcelona (Spain) 2016. **Publications** Brochures.
Members National associations (18) in 12 countries:
Austria, Croatia, France, Germany, Ireland, Italy, Montenegro, Netherlands, Romania, Serbia, Spain, UK.
IGO Relations Recognized by: *European Commission (EC, #06633).* [2018.09.11/XD3698/**D**]

♦ European Gaming and Betting Association (EGBA) **07375**

SG Rue Gray 50, 1040 Brussels, Belgium. T. +3225540890. Fax +3225540895. E-mail: egba@egba.eu.
URL: http://www.egba.eu/

History by 7 online gaming operators. Registered in accordance with Belgian law. Previously also known as: *European Betting Association (EBA).* EU Transparency Register: 29508582413-52. **Aims** Promote fair competition for licensed EU operators and the possibility for consumers throughout Europe to access regulated, secured and safe gaming and betting services. **Structure** General Meeting; Executive Committee. **Languages** English. **Finance** Members' dues. **Events** *European Regulators Meeting* Brussels (Belgium) 2017, *Responsible Gaming Day Meeting* Brussels (Belgium) 2011. **Publications** *EGBA News.* **NGO Relations** Member of: *Anti-Money Laundering Europe (AME, #00857).* [2019/XM0361/**D**]

♦ European Gaming Organization (no recent information)

♦ European Gamma Knife Society (EGKS) **07376**

Scientific Secretariat Gamma Unit, Hôp de la Timone, 264 rue Saint Pierre, 13005 Marseille, France. T. +33491387058. Fax +33491387056.
URL: http://www.egksociety.org/

History 1989, as a forum. Registered as a society, Jun 1998. Previously also known as *European Leksell Gamma Knife Society.* **Aims** Further define and expand the role of Gamma Knife *Surgery* in the treatment of intracranial disorders. **Structure** Board. **Events** *Annual Meeting* Rabat (Morocco) 2019, *Annual Meeting* Marseille (France) 2015, *Annual Meeting* St Petersburg (Russia) 2014, *Annual Meeting* Madrid (Spain) 2013, *Annual Meeting* Amsterdam (Netherlands) 2012. [2015/XJ6897/**E**]

♦ European Garage Equipment Association (EGEA) **07377**

SG Silversquare Delta, Ave Arnaud Fraiteur 15-23, 1050 Brussels, Belgium. T. +32499390459. Fax +3227621255. E-mail: secretariat@egea-association.eu – sg@egea-association.eu.
URL: http://www.egea-association.eu/

History 1980. Registration: Banque-Carrefour des Entreprises, No/ID: 0883.057.910, Start date: 22 Aug 2006, Belgium; EU Transparency Register, No/ID: 42705074342-04, Start date: 13 Oct 2010. **Aims** Provide better information, international standards, best practices and an effective regulatory structure to the garage and test equipment industry. **Structure** General Assembly (2 a year); Board of Directors; Secretariat; Working Groups (9). **Languages** English. **Staff** 1.25 FTE, paid. **Finance** Sources: members' dues. **Activities** Knowledge management/information dissemination; politics/policy/regulatory; standards/guidelines.
Members National organizations in 13 countries:
Austria, Belgium, France, Germany, Italy, Netherlands, Norway, Poland, Serbia, Spain, Sweden, Switzerland, UK.
Consultative Status Consultative status granted from: *ECOSOC (#05331)* (Ros A). **NGO Relations** Accredited by (2): *Alliance for the Freedom of Car Repair in the EU (AFCAR, #00682); Industry4Europe (#11181).* In liaison with technical committees of: *Comité européen de normalisation (CEN, #04162).* [2022.05.20/XD7736/**D**]

♦ European Garden Heritage Network (EGHN) **07378**

Réseau Européen du Patrimoine des Jardins – Europäisches Gartennetzwerk – Europees Tuinennetwerk

Management c/o Stiftung Schloss Dyck, Zentrum für Gartenkunst und Landschaftskultur, 41363 Jüchen, Germany. T. +4921828240. Fax +492182824110. E-mail: info@eghn.eu – feedback@eghn.org.
URL: http://eghn.org/

History 2003. Founded as a Programme within INTERREG. Became a network, 2009. **Aims** Strengthen the profile of gardens; underline their central importance for politics, society, urban design, tourism and regional economic development. **Structure** Advisory Board; European Garden Award Jury. Managed by the Schloss Dyck Foundation as a non-profit unit. **Languages** English, German. **Staff** 1.00 FTE, paid; 1.00 FTE, voluntary. **Finance** Sources: members' dues; revenue from activities/projects; sponsorship. Supported by: Landschaftsverband Rheinland LVR; Landschaftsverband Westfalen-Lippe. **Activities** Awards/prizes/competitions; events/meetings; networking/liaising. **Publications** *EGHN Magazine.* European Garden Award Winners.
Members Gardens, municipalities, organizations and private owners owning, caring for or managing parks and gardens. Partners (about 200) in 15 countries:
Austria, Belgium, Denmark, France, Germany, Ireland, Italy, Netherlands, Poland, Portugal, Russia, Spain, Sweden, Switzerland, UK. [2022.10.19/XM4774/**F**]

♦ European Garden Machinery Industry Federation (EGMF) **07379**

Main Office BluePoint Brussels, Boulevard A Reyers 80, 1030 Brussels, Belgium. T. +3222066867. E-mail: secretariat@egmf.org.
URL: http://www.egmf.org/

History 1977. Former names and other names: *European Lawnmower Manufacturers' Federation (ELMF)* – former; *European Garden Machinery Manufacturers' Federation* – former. Registration: Banque-Carrefour des Entreprises, No/ID: 0477.280.679, Start date: 30 Apr 2002, Belgium; EU Trandsparency Register, No/ID: 82669082072-33, Start date: 28 Jul 2009. **Aims** Serve as a spokesman for the manufacturers of outdoor power equipment in Europe and internationally; provide expertise to stakeholders on technical, marketing, market data, and trends related to the garden and outdoor power equipment industry; provide an effective forum for exchange of information and knowledge about our sector and its equipment and services as well as looking towards new challenges and trends for the sector. **Structure** Technical Committee; Working Groups. **Languages** English. **Staff** 1.00 FTE, paid. **Finance** Sources: members' dues. **Activities** Knowledge management/information dissemination; standards/guidelines.
Members Companies; Associations. Associations in 7 countries:
Belgium, France, Germany, Italy, Netherlands, Spain, UK.
NGO Relations In liaison with technical committees of: *European Committee for Electrotechnical Standardization (CENELEC, #06647); Comité européen de normalisation (CEN, #04162); International Electrotechnical Commission (IEC, #13255); International Organization for Standardization (ISO, #14473).* [2021/XD2969/t/**D**]

♦ European Garden Machinery Manufacturers' Federation / see European Garden Machinery Industry Federation (#07379)
♦ European Gas Control Manufacturers' Association / see Association des fabricants européens d'appareils de contrôle et de régulation (#02592)
♦ European Gaseous Diffusion Uranium Enrichment Consortium / see EURODIF Corporation (#05676)

♦ European Gas Research Group **07380**

Groupe européen de recherches gazières (GERG) – Gruppe der Europäischen Gasforschung

SG Av Palmerston 4, 1000 Brussels, Belgium. T. +3222308017. Fax +3222306788. E-mail: contact@gerg.eu.
URL: http://www.gerg.eu/

History 1961. Registration: EU Transparency Register, No/ID: 329897622408-17, Start date: 22 Jun 2016; Banque-Carrefour des Entreprises, No/ID: 0847.566.501, Start date: 20 Jul 2012, Belgium. **Aims** Strengthen the gas industry in European Community countries by effective research and development; coordinate investigations and exchange experience to avoid duplication of effort. **Structure** Plenary (meets twice a year); Board (meets twice a year), chaired by President. Permanent Secretariat. Programme Committees. Ad hoc Expert Groups. **Languages** English. **Staff** 2.00 FTE, paid. **Finance** Sources: members' dues. External project funding where possible. **Activities** Awards/prizes/competitions; knowledge management/information dissemination; projects/programmes. **Events** *European Gas Technology Conference (EGATEC)* Hamburg (Germany) 2022, *Anniversary Conference* 2021, *European Gas Technology Conference* Groningen (Netherlands) 2019, *European Gas Technology Conference* Vienna (Austria) 2015, *European Gas Technology Conference* Paris (France) 2013.
Members European Gas Industry R and D organizations (22) in 13 countries:
Belgium, Denmark, France, Germany (2), Italy (2), Netherlands (3), Norway (2), Poland, Spain (3), Sweden, Switzerland, Türkiye, UK (3).
NGO Relations Member of (4): *Eurogas (#05682); European Energy Forum (EEF, #06986)* (Associate); *GasNaturally (#10074); Knowledge4Innovation (K4I, #16198).* [2022/XD2652/**E**]

♦ European Gastrointestinal Motility Society / see European Society of Neurogastroenterology and Motility (#08663)
♦ European Gaucher Alliance / see International Gaucher Alliance (#13701)

♦ European Gay and Lesbian Managers Association (egma) **07381**

Pres address not obtained. E-mail: info@egma.eu.
Vice-Pres address not obtained.
URL: http://www.egma.eu/

History 2005, Vienna (Austria), by associations in Austria, France, Germany, Italy and Switzerland. **Aims** Acts as a platform for national lesbian, gay, bisexual and transgender (LGBT) affiliated associations; provide de LGBT business community with easy access to local agendas and events as a base for European networking. **Structure** Board of Directors, comprising President, Vice-President, Treasurer, Communication Officer and one member. **Events** *Annual General Meeting* Vienna (Austria) 2010, *Annual General Meeting* Basel (Switzerland) 2009, *Annual General Meeting* Vienna (Austria) 2007, *Annual General Meeting* Bern (Switzerland) 2006.
Members Associations (8) in 6 countries:
Austria, Belgium, France, Germany, Netherlands, Switzerland.
NGO Relations European voice of: *International Gay and Lesbian Chamber of Commerce (IGLCC, no recent information).* [2014/XJ2196/**D**]

♦ European Gay and Lesbian Sport Federation (EGLSF) **07382**

Head Office c/o NCS, Asterweg 125, 1031 HM Amsterdam, Netherlands. E-mail: general.secretary@eglsf.info.

URL: http://www.eglsf.info/
History 1989, The Hague (Netherlands). Registration: No/ID: KVK 40413152, Netherlands. **Aims** Represent athletes in Europe regardless of their sexual orientation or gender identity. **Structure** General Assembly (annual); Board. **Languages** English. **Staff** Voluntary. **Finance** Sources: donations; members' dues. Other sources: national and international funding. **Activities** Advocacy/lobbying/activism; knowledge management/ information dissemination; sporting activities. **Events** *Annual General Assembly* Munich (Germany) 2023, *Annual General Assembly* Amsterdam (Netherlands) 2022, *Annual General Assembly* Bern (Switzerland) 2021, *Annual General Assembly* Stuttgart (Germany) 2020, *Annual General Assembly* Budapest (Hungary) 2019. **Publications** *EGLSF Newsletter. Invisible – Synopsis on Homophobia and Discrimination on Sexual Orientation in Sport* (2003); *Offside – European Document on Discrimination of Gays and Lesbians in Sport* (1999). Conference reports; brochures.
Members Individuals (22,000) and organizations (over 115) in 24 countries:
Albania, Austria, Belgium, Bulgaria, Croatia, Denmark, Finland, France, Germany, Greece, Hungary, Ireland, Italy, Netherlands, North Macedonia, Norway, Poland, Russia, Slovenia, Spain, Sweden, Switzerland, Türkiye, UK.
Consultative Status Consultative status granted from: *Council of Europe (CE, #04881)* (Participatory Status). **IGO Relations** Member of: Consultative Committee of *Enlarged Partial Agreement on Sport (EPAS, #05487)*. **NGO Relations** Member of (1): *ILGA World (International Lesbian, Gay, Bisexual, Trans and Intersex Association, #11120)*. [2021/XD6146/D]

♦ European Gay Police Association / see European LGBT Police Association (#07686)
♦ European Gendarmerie Force / see EUROGENDFOR (#05683)
♦ European Gender Institute / see European Institute for Gender Equality (#07557)

♦ European General Galvanizers Association (EGGA) 07383

Association européenne des industries de la galvanisation d'articles divers – Asociación General Europea de Galvanizadores – Europäische Vereinigung für Allgemeine Verzinkung – Associazione Europea di Zincatura Generale

Exec Dir 2nd Floor, 11 Emmanuel Court, 14-16 Reddicroft, Sutton, ColdfieldB73 6AZ, UK. T. +441213552119. Fax +441213544895. E-mail: mail@egga.com.
Events and Communications Manager address not obtained.
URL: http://www.egga.com/
History 1955, London (UK). Registered in accordance with UK law. Registration: EU Transparency Register, No/ID: 634416015579-93, Start date: 14 Jan 2015. **Aims** Improve the technique of galvanizing through exchange of technical information between European galvanizers; encourage and coordinate research; promote the use of galvanizing and galvanized products by disseminating information on their properties and uses. **Structure** Assembly; Board of Directors. Committees (3): Technical and Resaerch; Marketing; Environmental and Safety. **Languages** English. **Staff** 2.00 FTE, paid. **Finance** Members' dues. **Activities** Events/meetings; monitoring/evaluation. **Events** *International Galvanizing Conference (INTERGALVA)* Rome (Italy) 2022, *Assembly* Salzburg (Austria) 2021, *International Galvanizing Conference (INTERGALVA)* Verona (Italy) 2021, *Assembly* Antwerp (Belgium) 2019, *International Galvanizing Conference (INTERGALVA)* Berlin (Germany) 2018. **Publications** *EGGA Bulletin*. Conference proceedings.
Members Associations representing 22 countries:
Austria, Belgium, Bulgaria, Czechia, Denmark, Finland, France, Germany, Greece, Hungary, Ireland, Italy, Luxembourg, Netherlands, Norway, Poland, Romania, Slovakia, Spain, Sweden, Türkiye, UK.
Included in the above, 1 regional organization listed in this Yearbook:
Nordic Galvanizers (#17302).
Associate: companies. Membership countries not specified.
IGO Relations Recognized by: *European Commission (EC, #06633)*. **NGO Relations** Member of (5): *European Convention for Constructional Steelwork (ECCS, #06779)* (associate); *Industry4Europe (#11181)*; *International Zinc Association (IZA, #15942)*; *METALS FOR BUILDINGS (#16737)*; *ResponsibleSteel (#18921)* (Associate). In liaison with technical committees of: *Comité européen de normalisation (CEN, #04162)*. [2020/XD0771/t/D]

♦ European General Practice Research Network (EGPRN) 07384

Contact Dept General Practice, Univ Maastricht, Postbus 616, 6200 MD Maastricht, Netherlands. T. +31433882310. Fax +31433671458. E-mail: office@egprn.org.
URL: http://www.egprn.org/
History 1974. A network functioning within *European Society of General Practice/Family Medicine (WONCA Europe, #08609)*. Former names and other names: *European General Practice Research Workshop (EGPRW)* – former. **Aims** Provide a setting in which to discuss and develop research in primary care; foster and coordinate multinational studies; exchange experiences; develop a validated scientific basis for general practice. **Structure** National Representatives Board; Executive Board. **Languages** English. **Staff** 1.00 FTE, paid. **Finance** Sources: members' dues. **Activities** Events/meetings; networking/liaising; research/documentation; training/education. **Events** *Meeting* Istanbul (Turkey) 2022, *Spring Meeting* Tampere (Finland) 2019, *Spring Meeting* Vigo (Spain) 2019, *Spring Meeting* Lille (France) 2018, *Spring Meeting* Sarajevo (Bosnia-Herzegovina) 2018. **Publications** *EGPRN Abstracts* (2 a year).
Members Individual members and National Representatives in 40 countries and territories:
Andorra, Austria, Belgium, Bosnia-Herzegovina, Bulgaria, Canada, Croatia, Czechia, Denmark, Estonia, Finland, France, Germany, Greece, Hungary, Ireland, Italy, Kosovo, Latvia, Lithuania, Luxembourg, Malta, Monaco, Netherlands, North Macedonia, Norway, Poland, Portugal, Romania, Russia, Serbia, Slovakia, Slovenia, Spain, Sweden, Switzerland, Türkiye, UK, Ukraine, USA.
NGO Relations Collaborative relations with: *European Academy of Teachers in General Practice (EURACT, #05817)*; *European Forum for Primary Care (EFPC, #07326)*; *World Organization of Family Doctors (WONCA, #21690)*. Member of: *European Society of General Practice/Family Medicine (WONCA Europe, #08609)*. [2022/XF5311/v/F]

♦ European General Practice Research Workshop / see European General Practice Research Network (#07384)

♦ European Generating Set Association (EUROPGEN) 07385

SG 17 rue de l'Amiral Hamelin, 75783 Paris CEDEX 16, France.
URL: http://europgen.eu/
History 1989. Registration: RNA, No/ID: W751242917, Start date: 24 Jan 2018, France; EU Transparency Register, No/ID: 05847066277-30, Start date: 22 Jul 2011. **Aims** Promote the interests of the European generating set *industry*; facilitate publication of technical standards; facilitate exchange of ideas and information. **Structure** Council; Board. **Languages** English. **Finance** Sources: members' dues.
Members National organizations in 3 countries:
France, Italy, UK.
Also member companies outside EU, EEA, EFTA or UK. Membership countries not specified. [2023.02.14/XD6272/D]

♦ European Generic Medicines Association / see Medicines for Europe (#16633)
♦ European Generics Association / see Medicines for Europe (#16633)
♦ European Genetic Alliances' Network / see EGAN – Patients Network for Medical Research and Health (#05394)

♦ European Genetics Foundation (EGF) 07386

Contact address not obtained. T. +39512088426. Fax +39515870611. E-mail: egf@eurogene.org – serena.paterlini@eurogene.org.
URL: http://www.eurogene.org/
History 1995, with the support of *European Commission (EC, #06633)*, *European Molecular Biology Organization (EMBO, #07816)* and *WHO (#20950)*. **Aims** Promote the scientific and professional education of young European geneticists with particular attention to the applications of genetics in the field of preventive medicine; disseminate information; organize structures and programmes for the quality control of laboratory tests; coordinate and fund research activities in the field of genetics and *genomics*; raise public awareness of science. **Structure** Board; Scientific Council. **Languages** English, Italian. **Staff** 23.00 FTE, paid. **Finance** Grants, donations. Budget (annual): US$ 1.3 million. **Activities** Events/meetings; training/education; awards/ prizes/competitions; awareness raising; research and development.
Members Full in 3 countries:
Italy, UK, USA. [2012/XF5641/f/F]

♦ European Geographic Information Network (EGIN) 07387

Secretariat p/a CEKTRA, PO BOX 2316, 1001 Ljubljana, Slovenia.
History created following the *Pan European Associations Forum (PEAF)* and the 'Geographic Information Network in Europe (GINIE)' project. **Structure** Not a formal organization; host organization of each meeting acts as chair.
Members International organizations (6):
Association of Geographic Information Laboratories for Europe (AGILE, #02622); *EuroGeographics (#05684)*; *European Association of Remote Sensing Companies (EARSC, #06190)*; *European Umbrella Organization for Geographical Information (EUROGI, #08964)*; *Geographical Information Systems International Group (GISIG, #10133)*; *Urban Data Management Society (UDMS, #20730)*.
NGO Relations Secretariat provided by: EUROGI. [2011.06.01/XM2644/y/F]

♦ European Geography Association for Students and Young Geographers (EGEA) 07388

Contact EGEA European Office, Buys Ballotgebouw, Winthontlaan 30C, 3526 KV Utrecht, Netherlands. T. +31302539708. E-mail: egea@egea.eu.
URL: https://egea.eu/
History 1988, Utrecht (Netherlands). Founded by students of the universities of Barcelona (Spain), Utrecht (Netherlands) and Warsaw (Poland), when officially registered as a foundation. Legal status modified 2009, Heeg (Netherlands), during General Assembly, when changed into an association. Registration: Netherlands. **Aims** Bring together young geographers in an atmosphere of respect, inclusion and personal development, inspiring global understanding of environmental and social processes, bringing about a positive impact on society. **Structure** General Assembly; Board; Regions (4); Headquarters in Utrecht (Netherlands). **Languages** English. **Staff** Voluntary. **Finance** Grants from institutions, including: *European Union (EU, #08967)* Erasmus+; *European Youth Foundation (EYF, #09141)*. Sponsorship from: ESRI; University of Utrecht (Netherlands). **Activities** Events/meetings; knowledge management/information dissemination; training/education. **Events** *Western Regional Congress* Schalkau (Germany) 2023, *Annual Congress* Szentendre (Hungary) 2022, *Eastern Regional Congress* Gdansk (Poland) 2019, *Western Regional Congress* Salzburg (Austria) 2019, *Western Regional Congress* Brussels (Belgium) 2018. **Publications** *EGEA Newsletter* (12 a year); *The European Geographer Magazine*. Congress/Event reports. **Members** Universities (92) in 28 countries. Membership countries not specified. **NGO Relations** Member of (2): *European Youth Forum (#09140)* (Observer); *Informal Forum of International Student Organizations (IFISO, #11193)*. Partner of (6): *European Association of Geographers (EUROGEO, #06054)*; *International Association of Students in Agricultural and Related Sciences (IAAS, #12191)*; *International Forestry Students' Association (IFSA, #13628)*; *International Student One Health Alliance (ISOHA)*; *International Students of History Association (ISHA, #15613)*; *ThinkYoung (#20144)*. [2022.10.24/XD3717/D]

♦ European GeoMembranes Association (inactive)

♦ European Geoparks Network (EGN) 07389

Réseau des geoparks européens

Contact BP 156, 04005 Digne les Bains CEDEX, France. T. +334492367072. Fax +334492367070. E-mail: egnwebsite@hotmail.com.
Coordinator address not obtained. E-mail: nzour@aegean.gr.
URL: http://www.europeangeoparks.org/
History Jun 2000, Greece, by 4 Geoparks from France, Greece, Germany and Spain. **Aims** Protect *geological* heritage; promote sustainable development of geopark territories in Europe; share information and expertises, as well as definition of common tools; achieve sustainable economic growth in designated areas by making the most of cultural, geological and wider natural heritage, especially through geo-*tourism*. **Structure** Coordination Committee; Advisory Committee. **Languages** English. **Staff** None. **Finance** Members cover annual promotional fee. **Activities** Events/meetings; training/eduation. **Events** *Meeting* Croatia 2020, *Annual Conference* Seville (Spain) 2019, *Annual Conference* Ponta Delgada (Portugal) 2017, *GEOfood Meeting* Egersund (Norway) 2016, *Annual Conference* Oulu (Finland) 2015. **Publications** *EGN Magazine*. Leaflets; booklet; meeting proceedings.
Members Geoparks in 23 countries:
Austria, Croatia, Cyprus, Czechia, Denmark, Finland, France, Germany, Greece, Hungary, Iceland, Ireland, Italy, Netherlands, Norway, Poland, Portugal, Romania, Slovakia, Slovenia, Spain, Türkiye, UK.
IGO Relations Collaboration agreement with: *UNESCO (#20322)*. **NGO Relations** Regional network of: *Global Geoparks Network (GGN, #10389)*. Affiliated with: *International Union of Geological Sciences (IUGS, #15777)*. [2017.06.01/XM1612/F]

♦ European Geophysical Society (inactive)
♦ European Geopolitical Forum (unconfirmed)

♦ European Geosciences Union (EGU) 07390

Exec Sec Kastenbauerstr. 2, 81677 Munich, Germany. T. +4989205076300. Fax +4989205076399. E-mail: info@egu.eu.
URL: http://www.egu.eu/
History 7 Sep 2002, Munich (Germany). Founded by merger of *European Geophysical Society (EGS, inactive)* and *European Union of Geosciences (EUG, inactive)* with final stages of transition completed 31 Dec 2003. Registration: Bavaria District Court, No/ID: VR 206278, Start date: 13 Nov 2015, Germany, Munich; EU Transparency Register, No/ID: 941426139196-80, Start date: 28 Aug 2020. **Aims** Promote cooperation and discussion in Europe among scientists concerned with studies of the earth and its environment and of planetary and space sciences; promote and encourage development of any or all of the relevant sciences, within and outside Europe. **Structure** General Assembly (annual); Council; Scientific Divisions (22); Committees (8). **Languages** English. **Staff** 7.00 FTE, paid. **Activities** Awards/prizes/competitions; events/ meetings; networking/liaising; publishing activities; training/education. **Events** *General Assembly* Vienna (Austria) 2024, *Galileo Conference on Solid Earth and Geohazards in the Exascale Era* Barcelona (Spain) 2023, *Galileo Conference on A European Vision for Hydrological Observations and Experimentation* Naples (Italy) 2023, *General Assembly* Vienna (Austria) 2023, *General Assembly* Vienna (Austria) 2022. **Publications** Journals. **Members** Full (over 14,000). Membership countries not specified. **NGO Relations** Collaborates with: *American Geophysical Union (AGU)*; *Asia Oceania Geosciences Society (AOGS, #01799)*; *International Union of Forest Research Organizations (IUFRO, #15774)*; national societies. [2022/XD9190/D]

♦ European Geothermal Energy Council (EGEC) 07391

SG Place du Champs de Mars 2, 5th Floor, 1050 Brussels, Belgium. T. +3223184065. E-mail: com@ egec.org.
URL: http://www.egec.org/
History May 1998. Registration: No/ID: 0465.303.654, Start date: 10 Jan 1999, Belgium; EU Transparency Register, No/ID: 11458103335-07, Start date: 15 Mar 2010. **Aims** Promote the use of geothermal energy; consult on geothermal issues. **Structure** General Assembly (annual); Board. **Languages** English. **Staff** 5.00 FTE, paid. **Finance** Members' dues. **Activities** Events/meetings; knowledge management/information dissemination; guidance/assistance/consulting. **Events** *European Geothermal Congress* Zurich (Switzerland) 2025, *European Geothermal Congress* Berlin (Germany) 2022, *Geo-Energy Europe Seminar* Brussels (Belgium) 2022, *Geothermal Days* Brussels (Belgium) 2019, *European Geothermal Congress* The Hague (Netherlands) 2019. **Publications** Annual Geothermal Market Report. Brochures.
Members Full in 28 countries:
Austria, Belgium, Bulgaria, Czechia, Denmark, Estonia, France, Germany, Greece, Hungary, Iceland, Ireland, Israel, Italy, Luxembourg, Netherlands, North Macedonia, Norway, Poland, Portugal, Romania, Slovakia, Slovenia, Spain, Sweden, Switzerland, Türkiye, UK.
NGO Relations Member of: *European Forum for Renewable Energy Sources (EUFORES, #07329)*; *International Geothermal Association (IGA, #13717)*. Instrumental in setting up: *European Technology Platform on Renewable Heating and Cooling (RHC-Platform, #08891)*. Associate partner of: *Covenant of Mayors for Climate and Energy (#04939)*. [2020/XM0406/E]

♦ European Geriatric Medicine Society (EuGMS) 07392

Société de médecine gériatrique de l'Union européenne

Secretariat Via Roma 10, 16121 Genoa GE, Italy. T. +39105535937. E-mail: secretariat@eugms.org.
Registered Address Ecole de Santé Publique, Clos Chapelle aux Champs 30, Bte 3037, 1200 Brussels, Belgium.
URL: http://www.eugms.org/

History Jun 2000. Formally launched Aug 2001, Paris (France). Former names and other names: *European Union Geriatric Medicine Society (EUGMS)* – former; *Société de médecine gériatrique de l'Union européenne* – former. Registration: Banque Carrefour des Entreprises, No/ID: 0475.491.624, Start date: 13 Sep 2001, Belgium; EU Transparency Register, No/ID: 460052417196-83, Start date: 12 May 2015. **Aims** Develop geriatric medicine in members states of the EU as an independent speciality caring for all older people with age-related disease; support that geriatric services become available to all citizens of the EU; facilitate research and education; promote education and continuing professional development; represent the speciality of geriatric medicine in EU and national governments; liaise with other European bodies promoting the specialty in Europe; disseminate evidence-based guidelines for the most efficacious preventive and treatment strategies for older people in the EU. **Structure** Council; Full Board; Executive Board. Special Interest Groups; Policy Working Group. **Languages** Dutch, English, French, German. **Staff** None. **Finance** Members'dues. Sponsorship; *European Commission (EC, #06633)* projects. **Activities** Standards/guidelines; training/education; events/meetings; research/documentation. **Events** *Congress* Helsinki (Finland) 2023, *Congress* London (UK) 2022, *Congress* Athens (Greece) 2021, *COVID-19 – lessons and challenges for healthcare for older adults* Genoa (Italy) 2020, *Congress* Krakow (Poland) 2019. **Publications** *EuGMS Newsletter*; *European Geriatric Medicine* – official journal. Papers. **Information Services** *Geriatric Visit Bank*.

Members Full in 33 countries:
Armenia, Austria, Belarus, Belgium, Czechia, Denmark, Estonia, Finland, France, Germany, Greece, Hungary, Iceland, Ireland, Israel, Italy, Lithuania, Luxembourg, Malta, Netherlands, Norway, Poland, Portugal, Romania, Russia, Serbia, Slovakia, Slovenia, Spain, Sweden, Switzerland, Türkiye, UK.
Observer in 4 countries:
Albania, Bulgaria, Croatia, Cyprus.

IGO Relations Represented on the Executive Board of: *European Medicines Agency (EMA, #07767)*. **NGO Relations** Member of: *European Nutrition for Health Alliance, The (ENHA, #08069)*. [2020/XD8149/D]

- ♦ European Geriatric Surgery Society (no recent information)
- ♦ European Glass Container Manufacturers' Committee (inactive)
- ♦ European Glass Fibres Producers Association / see GlassFibreEurope (#10158)
- ♦ European Glass Weavers Association (no recent information)

♦ European Glaucoma Society (EGS) 07393

Pres Zeughausgasse 18, Postfach 1225, 6301 Zug, Switzerland. E-mail: egsexco@eugs.org – egssecretary@oic.it.
Gen Sec address not obtained.
URL: http://www.eugs.org/

History 1979, Ghent (Belgium). Founded 1979 at a meeting attended by representatives from many European countries, and following proposal by Erik Greve, 1978. Statutes most recently revised Jun 2014. Registration: Swiss Civil Code, Switzerland; EU Transparency Register, No/ID: 720911016370-40. **Aims** Establish personal contacts and promote sharing of knowledge among glaucoma specialists in Europe; stimulate, compare and register glaucoma research in Europe; promote dissemination of speciality knowledge to general ophthalmologists throughout Europe; liaise with glaucoma groups globally. **Structure** General Assembly; Executive Committee; Committees; Special Interest Groups. **Languages** English. **Staff** None. **Finance** Sources: donations. **Activities** Awards/prizes/competitions; events/meetings; training/education. **Events** *Congress* Dublin (Ireland) 2024, *Congress* Florence (Italy) 2022, *Congress* Brussels (Belgium) 2020, *Congress* Florence (Italy) 2018, *Meeting* London (UK) 2017. **Publications** *Exfoliation Syndrome and Exfoliative Glaucoma*; *Optic Nerve Head and Retinal Nerve Fibre Analysis*; *Terminology and Guidelines for Glaucoma* – 4th edition. **Members** Ordinary (European nationals) – practising ophthalmologists or research scientists specialized in glaucoma; Honorary – non practising ophthalmologists whose contributions to ophthalmology are fully recognized by the Society; Associate (non-European nationals) – practising ophthalmologists and research scientists specialized in glaucoma. Membership countries not specified. **NGO Relations** Member of (3): *European Alliance for Vision Research and Ophthalmology (EU-EYE, #05890)*; *European Coalition for Vision (ECV)*; *World Glaucoma Association (WGA, #21540)*. [2021/XD7943/v/D]

♦ European Glaziers Association 07394

Union européenne des miroitiers vitriers (UEMV)

Contact Glarmesterlauget, Gothersgade 160 2th, 1123 Copenhagen K, Denmark. E-mail: hgn@glarmesterlauget.dk.
URL: http://www.uemv.org/

History 21 Jan 1977, Germany FR. 21 Jan 1977, Bad Godesberg (Germany FR), as *International Union of Glaziers – Union internationale des miroitiers-vitriers (UIMV)*. **Aims** Speak with a single voice on behalf of the European glazing industry; be an active force for development and change in matters affecting the industry; investigate trade problems of general concern; identify and influence legislation and standards; promote international liaison with organizations with similar objectives; gather and make available statistics to the industry, official bodies and institutes. **Structure** Board of Directors; Officers Committee; Technical Committee; Training Committee; Specialist Groups. **Languages** English, French, German. **Activities** Advocacy/lobbying/activism; research and development; networking/liaising; knowledge management/information dissemination. **Publications** *Dictionary of Technical Glazier Terms* (1983) in English, French, German, Italian, Spanish.

Members Effective members in 11 countries:
Belgium, France, Germany, Greece, Italy, Netherlands, Norway, Spain, Sweden, Switzerland, UK.
Associated member in 1 country:
USA.

NGO Relations In liaison with technical committees of: *International Organization for Standardization (ISO, #14473)*. Cooperates with: *European Organisation for Technical Assessment (EOTA, #08103)*. [2015.01.06/XD1921/D]

♦ European Gliding Union (EGU) 07395

Secretariat EGU, c/o FFVV, 55 rue des Petites Ecuries, 75010 Paris, France. T. +33145440478. Fax +33145447093. E-mail: mika.mutru@gmail.com.
URL: http://www.egu-info.org/

History 14 Nov 1992, Paris (France). Statutes adopted at first Congress, 1 Oct 1993, Strasbourg (France); updated 2004; updated 2016. Registered in accordance with French law. **Aims** Support gliding sport in Europe; actively participate in the formulation of regulations and actions. **Structure** Congress (annual). Executive Board, comprising President, 1st and 2nd Vice-Presidents, General Secretary, Treasurer and 3 members. Technical Officers (4): Licensing and Medicals; Airspace, Transponders and Radio; Airworthiness and Maintenance; Operations. **Languages** English. **Finance** Members' dues. **Activities** cover: airspace; airworthiness and maintenance; environment; equipment; insurance; licensing; medicals and operations; transponders and radio. Organizes Annual Congress and workshops. **Events** *Annual Congress* Paris (France) 2018, *Annual Congress* London (UK) 2017, *Annual Congress* Graz (Austria) 2016, *Annual Congress* Berlin (Germany) 2015, *Annual Congress* Luxembourg (Luxembourg) 2014.

Members Full in 21 countries:
Austria, Belgium, Czechia, Denmark, Finland, France, Germany, Iceland, Ireland, Italy, Luxembourg, Netherlands, Norway, Poland, Serbia, Slovakia, Slovenia, Spain, Sweden, Switzerland, UK.
Affiliate in 2 countries:
New Zealand, USA.

NGO Relations Member of: *Europe Air Sports (EAS, #05776)*. Close cooperation with: *Organisation Scientifique et Technique Internationale de Vol à Voile (OSTIV, #17826)*. [2019/XD6205/D]

- ♦ European Global Navigation Satellite Systems Agency / see European Union Agency for the Space Programme (#08974)

♦ European Global Ocean Observing System (EuroGOOS) 07396

Dir Rue Vautier 29, 1000 Brussels, Belgium. T. +32027887666. E-mail: eurogoos@eurogoos.eu – info@eurogoos.eu.
URL: http://eurogoos.eu/

History Dec 1994. Founded to support the European component of *Global Ocean Observing System (GOOS, #10511)*. Former names and other names: *European Association of Agencies to Promote the Global Ocean Observing System (EuroGOOS)* – former (Dec 1994). Registration: Banque-Carrefour des Entreprises, No/ID: 0521.723.012, Start date: 4 Mar 2013, Belgium; EU Transparency Register, No/ID: 658215019572-89, Start date: 17 Nov 2015. **Aims** Act as the authoritative and competent expert voice of operational oceanography in all European activities; take the lead in representing and promoting operational marine services in Europe; improve the observing system for operational oceanography in Europe, and its contribution to global systems; encourage links between member state national systems and setting up of downstream services; contribute to further development of GOOS, in particular by taking the lead in advancing Coastal GOOS; promote EuroGOOS at a high level for members' countries and European organizations; promote and foster necessary research and technological developments for operational oceanography and their implementation in operational systems; work towards involving all European coastal states through their operational oceanographic institutions, in the work of EuroGOOS. **Structure** Task Teams (6): Atlantic; Arctic; Baltic; Mediterranean; North West Shelf; Biscay-Iberian Shelf. **Languages** English. **Staff** 2.00 FTE, paid. **Finance** Sources: members' dues. **Activities** Advocacy/lobbying/activism; events/meetings. **Events** *Triennial Conference* Galway (Ireland) 2023, *EOOS Technology Forum Workshop* Brussels (Belgium) 2022, *Workshop on Operational Measurements for Ocean Waves* Brussels (Belgium) 2022, *Triennial Conference* Brussels (Belgium) 2021, *Oceans of Knowledge: Ocean observations and emerging technologies enabling the blue economy* Brussels (Belgium) 2019. **Publications** *EuroGOOS Publication*. Annual Report; conference proceedings; workshop reports; other reports; surveys.

Members Governmental agencies (44) in 18 countries:
Belgium, Croatia, Cyprus, Denmark, Finland, France, Germany, Greece, Ireland, Italy, Netherlands, Norway, Poland, Portugal, Slovenia, Spain, Sweden, UK.

IGO Relations Partner of: *EuroGEOSS (#05685)*. [2023/XE2709/E]

- ♦ European Glued Laminated Timber Industries Association (no recent information)

♦ European GMO-Free Regions Network 07397

Pres c/o Hessian Ministry for Environment/Climate Protection/Agricultur/Consumer Protection, Mainzer Str 80, 65189 Wiesbaden, Germany. T. +496118151005. Fax +496118151958. E-mail: gmofree-hessen@umwelt.hessen.de.
URL: https://gmofree-eu-network.hessen.de/

History 2005. Founded when 20 regions signed the Charter of Florence. **Structure** Steering Committee. **Events** *GMO-Free Europe Conference* Berlin (Germany) 2018, *GMO-Free Europe Conference* Berlin (Germany) 2015, *GMO-Free Europe Conference* Brussels (Belgium) 2012, *GMO-Free Europe Conference* Brussels (Belgium) / Ghent (Belgium) 2010, *GMO-Free Europe Conference* Lucerne (Switzerland) 2009.

Members Regions (64) in 9 countries:
Austria, Belgium, Croatia, France, Germany, Greece, Italy, Spain, UK. [XM8371/F*]

- ♦ European GNSS Agency / see European Union Agency for the Space Programme (#08974)
- ♦ European GNSS Supervisory Authority / see European Union Agency for the Space Programme (#08974)

♦ European Go Federation (EGF) 07398

Pres Lissgattu 13, Hjulbäck 421, SE-792 97 Siljansnäs, Sweden. T. +4624722406. E-mail: egf-executive@eurogofed.org – president@eurogofed.org.
Sec address not obtained. E-mail: secretary@eurogofed.org.
URL: http://www.eurogofed.org/

History 1952. Registration: No/ID: KVK 34128382, Netherlands, Amsterdam. **Aims** Encourage, regulate, coordinate and disseminate the playing of Go in Europe; establish the rules of the *game*; establish regulations for tournaments and *championships*; ratify classifications of all European master players and the strongest players of each member nation; organize European Go Championships. **Structure** General Meeting (annual); Committee. **Languages** English. **Staff** 1.50 FTE, voluntary. **Finance** Sources: members' dues. **Activities** Events/meetings. **Events** *Annual Congress* Toulouse (France) 2024, *Annual Congress* Kamianets-Podilskyi (Ukraine) 2023, *Annual Congress* Vatra Dornei (Romania) 2022, *Annual Congress* Brussels (Belgium) 2019, *Annual Congress* Pisa (Italy) 2018.

Members National Go organizations in 36 countries:
Armenia, Austria, Azerbaijan, Belarus, Belgium, Bosnia-Herzegovina, Bulgaria, Croatia, Cyprus, Czechia, Denmark, Finland, France, Germany, Hungary, Ireland, Israel, Italy, Latvia, Lithuania, Luxembourg, Netherlands, Norway, Poland, Portugal, Romania, Russia, Serbia, Slovakia, Slovenia, Spain, Sweden, Switzerland, Türkiye, UK, Ukraine. [2022/XD7650/D]

- ♦ European Gold Manufacturers Association (no recent information)

♦ European Golf Association (EGA) 07399

Association européenne de golf – Europäischer Golf-Verband

SG Pl de la Croix-Blanche 19, Case Postale 110, 1066 Epalinges VD, Switzerland. T. +41217857060. E-mail: info@ega-golf.ch.
URL: http://www.ega-golf.ch/

History 20 Nov 1937, Luxembourg (Luxembourg). **Aims** Encourage international development of golf; strengthen bonds of friendship among members; encourage formation of new golf organizations. **Languages** English, French. **Finance** Sources: members' dues. **Activities** Events/meetings. **Events** *Annual General Meeting* France 2019.

Members European national amateur golf associations or unions (membership open to all European countries) in 49 countries and territories:
Albania, Andorra, Armenia, Austria, Azerbaijan, Belarus, Belgium, Bosnia-Herzegovina, Bulgaria, Croatia, Cyprus, Czechia, Denmark, England, Estonia, Finland, France, Georgia, Germany, Greece, Hungary, Iceland, Ireland, Israel, Italy, Kazakhstan, Latvia, Liechtenstein, Lithuania, Luxembourg, Malta, Netherlands, North Macedonia, Norway, Poland, Portugal, Romania, Russia, San Marino, Scotland, Serbia, Slovakia, Slovenia, Spain, Sweden, Switzerland, Türkiye, Ukraine, Wales.

NGO Relations Supports (1): *GEO Foundation (#10132)*. [2023.02.15/XD0773/D]

- ♦ European Golf Course Owners Association / see Golf Course Association Europe (#10677)

♦ European Golf and Travel Media Association (EGTMA) 07400

Chairman address not obtained. T. +35314429016. E-mail: info@egtma.com.
URL: http://www.egtma.com/

Aims Bring together all aspects of the modern golf media, writers, broadcasters, photographers, website editors, bloggers and others who contribute to some sort of media coverage for golf and travel. **Members** Full (104) in 18 countries. Membership countries not specified. [2016/XJ5150/D]

- ♦ European Goods Trains Timetable Conference (inactive)

♦ European Governmental LGBTI Focal Points Network (EFPN) 07401

Secretariat c/o SOGI, Council of Europe, Ave de l'Europe, 67075 Strasbourg CEDEX, France.
URL: https://www.coe.int/en/web/sogi/european-governmental-lgbti-focal-points-network

History 2004. Secretariat was initially hosted by Netherlands Ministry of Education, Culture and Science; as of 2020 Secretariat is at Council of Europe's SOGI Unit. **Aims** Share updated knowledge and discuss common challenges and possible measures to combat discrimination related to sexual orientation, gender identity, gender expression and sex characteristics. **Activities** Events/meetings. **Events** *Conference* Oslo (Norway) 2019.

Members European states (36).
Albania, Andorra, Austria, Belgium, Bosnia-Herzegovina, Bulgaria, Cyprus, Czechia, Denmark, Estonia, Finland, France, Georgia, Germany, Greece, Iceland, Ireland, Italy, Kosovo, Latvia, Lithuania, Luxembourg, Malta, Moldova, Montenegro, Netherlands, North Macedonia, Norway, Portugal, Serbia, Slovakia, Slovenia, Spain, Sweden, Switzerland, UK.
Partcipative Observers:

Council of Europe (CE, #04881); European Commission Against Racism and Intolerance (ECRI, see: #04881); European Forum of Lesbian, Gay, Bisexual and Transgender Christian Groups (Forum LGBT, #07318); European LGBT Police Association (EGPA, #07686); European Union Agency for Fundamental Rights (FRA, #08969); European Union (EU, #08967); ILGA-Europe (#11118); International Bank for Reconstruction and Development (IBRD, #12317); International Lesbian, Gay, Bisexual, Transgender, Queer and Intersex Youth and Student Organization (IGLYO, #14032); Joint United Nations Programme on HIV/AIDS (UNAIDS, #16149); OECD (#17693); Office of the United Nations High Commissioner for Human Rights (OHCHR, #17697); Organisation Intersex International Europe (OII Europe, #17812); Rainbow Cities Network (RCN, #18611); TGEU (#20138); United Nations (UN, #20515). [2021/AA0691/**F***]

♦ European GPR Association (EuroGPR) 07402

Chair c/o TRL, Crowthorne House, Nine Mile Ride, Wokingham, RG40 3GA, UK. E-mail: chairman@eurogpr.org – secretary@eurogpr.org.
URL: http://www.eurogpr.org/

History Jul 1997, deriving from the former *Impulse Radar Users' Association (IRUA)*. **Aims** Raise standards within the Ground Penetrating *Radar* (GPR) industry; look out for the rights of members, giving them voice at pan-European level on matters such as licensing, health and safety and market access. **Structure** Executive Committee. **Languages** English. **Events** *Annual General Meeting* Stockholm (Sweden) 2016, *Meeting* Brussels (Belgium) 2009, *Meeting* Pisa (Italy) 2007, *Meeting* Columbus, OH (USA) 2006, *Meeting* Delft (Netherlands) 2004. **Publications** *EuroGPR Quarterly Association Newsletter. EuroGPR Code of Practice.* Policy statements; guidelines. **Members** Membership countries not specified. **NGO Relations** Member of: *European Telecommunications Standards Institute (ETSI, #08897).* [2019.04.26/XJ0912/**E**]

♦ European Graduate School of Neuroscience (EURON) 07403

Dir School for Mental Health and Neuroscience, Fac of Health/Medicine/Life Sciences, Maastricht Univ, Universiteitssingel 40, 6229 ER Maastricht, Netherlands. T. +31433881021 – +31433884130. E-mail: secr.euron@maastrichtuniversity.nl – h.steinbusch@maastrichtuniversity.nl.
URL: http://www.euronschool.eu/

History 1995. **Aims** Share expertise, knowledge and infrastructure to offer Master and PhD students a chance to broaden their research competencies. **Structure** Governing Board; Management Board; Coordinating Office. **Languages** English. **Staff** 2.00 FTE, paid. **Finance** Financed by partners. **Activities** Training/education; reseach/documentation. **Events** *PhD student meeting* Liège (Belgium) 2005, *PhD student meeting* Homburg (Germany) 2004.
Members Universities (8) in 5 countries:
Belgium, France, Germany, Luxembourg, Netherlands. [2019/XM0466/**F**]

♦ European Graduate School for Training in Economic and Social Historical Research (ESTER) 07404

Scientific Dir NW Posthumus Inst, c/o Dept of History & Art History, Utrecht Univ, Drift 6, 3512 BS Utrecht, Netherlands. T. +31302536328. E-mail: posthumus@uu.nl.
URL: https://posthumusinstitute.org/ester-about/

History A European platform for postgraduate teaching. **Aims** Improve and internationalize education and training of young scholars in the field of economic and social history. **Structure** Board. **Activities** Events/meetings; training/education. **Events** *Seminar* Lund (Sweden) 2022, *Seminar* Lisbon (Portugal) 2021, *Seminar* Nijmegen (Netherlands) 2020, *Seminar* Lyon (France) 2019, *Seminar* Florence (Italy) 2018. **Members** Over 60 universities throughout Europe. Membership countries not specified. [2022.10.18/XM2031/**E**]

♦ European Graphic/Media Industry Network (EGIN) 07405

Sec Zomer 84, 8251 NN Dronten, Netherlands. T. +31321381636. E-mail: info@egin.nl.
URL: http://www.egin.nl/

History Founded 1990. Reorganized 1994. **Aims** Function as a network for education and for jointly developing education programmes; function as a centre of contacts, exchange of information, discussions and project creation. **Structure** Board, comprising Chairman, Secretary General, 6 members and 6 Observers (non-voting). Executive Committee. **Finance** Members' dues. **Activities** Organizes: annual conference; seminars. **Events** *Annual Meeting* Lisbon (Portugal) 2016, *Annual Conference* Madrid (Spain) 2013, *Annual Meeting / Annual Conference* Athens (Greece) 2012, *Annual Meeting / Annual Conference* Valencia (Spain) 2011, *Annual Conference* Venice (Italy) 2010. **Publications** *EGIN Newsletter.*
Members Organizations in 11 countries:
Denmark, Finland, Germany, Iceland, Italy, Netherlands, Norway, Spain, Sweden, Switzerland, UK. [2014/XJ5103/t/**F**]

♦ European Grassland Federation (EGF) 07406

Fédération européenne des herbages

Sec Schachenweg 6, 8908 Zurich ZH, Switzerland. T. +41793746230. E-mail: fedsecretary@europeangrassland.org.
URL: http://www.europeangrassland.org/

History 1963. **Aims** Facilitate and maintain close contact between European grassland organizations; promote exchange of scientific and practical experience between experts. **Structure** General Meeting (in even years); Symposia (in odd years); Executive Committee; Conference Organizing Committee; Federation Secretary. **Languages** English. **Staff** 0.50 FTE, voluntary. **Finance** No membership fees. **Activities** Events/meetings. **Events** *General Meeting* Caen (France) 2022, *Symposium* Kassel (Germany) 2021, *General Meeting* Helsinki (Finland) 2020, *Joint EGF/EUCARPIA Symposium* Zurich (Switzerland) 2019, *General Meeting* Cork (Ireland) 2018. **Publications** *Grass and Forage Science* – official journal of EGF, in cooperation with British Grassland Society. *Grassland Science in Europe* in English – 26 volumes to date – proceedings.
Members Full in 32 countries:
Austria, Belgium, Bosnia-Herzegovina, Bulgaria, Croatia, Czechia, Denmark, Estonia, Finland, France, Germany, Greece, Hungary, Iceland, Ireland, Italy, Lithuania, Luxembourg, Netherlands, Norway, Poland, Portugal, Romania, Russia, Serbia, Slovakia, Slovenia, Spain, Sweden, Switzerland, UK, Ukraine.
Corresponding in 3 countries:
Albania, Latvia, North Macedonia.
IGO Relations None. **NGO Relations** None. [2022.05.10/XD0775/**D**]

♦ European Grassroots Antiracist Movement (EGAM) 07407

Exec Dir 48 ter rue du Faubourg St Denis, 75010 Paris, France. T. +33683114645.
Facebook: https://www.facebook.com/EGAMOfficial/

History Nov 2010, Paris (France). **Aims** Answer the rise in racism, antisemitism and populism in Europe; structure civil society's commitment to equality and justice. **Structure** Board. **Activities** Advocacy/lobbying/activism. **Events** *Meeting* Vienna (Austria) 2015.
Members Full in 28 countries:
Albania, Austria, Bosnia-Herzegovina, Bulgaria, Croatia, Czechia, Denmark, Estonia, Finland, France, Germany, Greece, Hungary, Italy, Kosovo, Latvia, Moldova, Montenegro, Netherlands, Norway, Poland, Romania, Russia, Serbia, Slovakia, Slovenia, Sweden, Türkiye.
Consultative Status Consultative status granted from: *Council of Europe (CE, #04881)* (Participatory Status). **NGO Relations** *Armenian General Benevolent Union (AGBU, #01110); European Union of Jewish Students (EUJS, #08997); Phiren Amenca (#18362).* [2018/XJ9515/**F**]

♦ European Gravitational Observatory (internationally oriented national body)

♦ European Green Belt Association (EGBA) 07408

Contact c/o EuroNatur Foundation, Westendstr 3, 78315 Radolfzell, Germany. E-mail: info@europeangreenbelt.org.
URL: https://www.europeangreenbelt.org/

History Sep 2014, Czech Rep. Founded Sep 2014, Slavonice (Czech Rep), by 23 organizations. Registered in accordance with German law, Feb 2015: VR 33869 B. **Aims** Coordinate the transnational activities along the European Green Belt; ensure that the European Green Belt is efficiently protected and that its sustainable development is promoted by facilitating an on-going, coordinated transboundary cooperation at all levels and across all sectors of society. **Structure** General Assembly; Board. **Finance** Members' dues. **Publications** *European Green Belt Newsletter.* [2019/XM8921/**E**]

♦ European Green Party (EGP) 07409

SG Rue Wiertz 31, 1050 Brussels, Belgium. T. +3226260720. E-mail: mar.garcia@europeangreens.eu – info@europeangreens.eu.
Office Manager address not obtained.
URL: http://europeangreens.eu/

History Founded Mar 1984, Liège (Belgium), as *European Greens – Verts européens – Europa Verduloj*, subsequently *Green Coordination of Green Parties – Coordination verte des verts européens.* Previously referred to in French as *Alliance verte européenne.* Transformed coordination as *European Federation of Green Parties (EFGP)*, Jun 1993, Helsinki (Finland). Current title adopted, Feb 2004, Rome (Italy). Secretariat located in Brussels (Belgium). **Aims** Ensure a close and permanent cooperation among member *ecology* parties so as to accomplish a common policy; stimulate and organize initiatives and activities on a European scale; adopt an open, active, constructive and critical approach to the ongoing *integration* processes in Europe towards world-wide cooperation. **Structure** Congress (every 5 years); Council; Committee; Secretariat; Commissions and Working Groups; Financial Committee; Regional and Topical Networks. **Languages** English. **Staff** 18.00 FTE, paid. **Finance** Members' dues. Grant from: *European Parliament (EP, #08146).* **Activities** Politics/policy/regulatory. **Events** *Meeting* Tampere (Finland) 2019, *Meeting* Antwerp (Belgium) 2018, *Meeting* Berlin (Germany) 2018, *Meeting* Karlstad (Sweden) 2017, *Meeting* Liverpool (UK) 2017. **Publications** *EGP Newsletter* (26 a year).
Members Green political parties (42) in 31 countries:
Albania, Andorra, Austria, Belgium, Bulgaria, Cyprus, Czechia, Denmark, Estonia, Finland, France, Georgia, Germany, Greece, Hungary, Ireland, Italy, Luxembourg, Malta, Moldova, Netherlands, Norway, Poland, Portugal, Romania, Slovenia, Spain, Sweden, Switzerland, UK, Ukraine.
Associate members in 3 countries:
Azerbaijan, Belarus, Russia.
Youth wing:
Federation of Young European Greens (FYEG, #09715).
NGO Relations Member of: *Global Greens (#10394).* [2019.12.11/XF6464/y/**F**]

♦ European Greens / see European Green Party (#07409)

♦ European Green Vehicles Initiative Association (EGVIA) 07410

Office Head Avenue de Cortenbergh 66, 1000 Brussels, Belgium. T. +3227361265.
URL: http://www.egvia.eu/

History 2013, to engage in a contractual Public-Private Partnership on Green Vehicles in the framework of Horizon 2020. European Green Vehicles Initiative – public-private partnership *EGVI PPP* runs 2014-2020 and is successor to Successor to *European Green Cars Initiative* (2009-2013). **Aims** Gather industry and research members; deliver research topics recommendations for the Green Vehicles Initiative. **Structure** General Assembly. Executive Board. Industry Delegation. **Languages** English. **Staff** 1.00 FTE, paid. **Finance** Members' dues. **Activities** Research and development. **Events** *Energy4Transport Workshop* Brussels (Belgium) 2019, *European Conference on Results from Road Transport Research in H2020 Projects* Brussels (Belgium) 2019, *European Electric Vehicle Congress* Brussels (Belgium) 2014, *Joint Workshop* Brussels (Belgium) 2013, *Workshop* Brussels (Belgium) 2013.
Members Industry; Research; Associate. Research institutions in 12 countries:
Austria, Belgium, Czechia, France, Germany, Greece, Italy, Netherlands, Norway, Spain, Sweden, Türkiye.
Included in the above, 2 organizations listed in this Yearbook:
Oil Companies' European Association for Environment, Health and Safety in Refining and Distribution (CONCAWE, #17708); SINTEF.
Associate members include 6 organizations listed in this Yearbook:
Association des constructeurs européens de motocycles (ACEM, #02450); Association of European Automative and Industrial Battery Manufacturers (EUROBAT, #02498); European Association of Automotive Suppliers (CLEPA, #05948); European Council of Automotive Research and Development (EUCAR, #06806); Forum of European National Highway Research Laboratories (FEHRL, #09910); RECHARGE (#18627). [2020/XJ8333/y/**E**]

♦ European Green Vehicles Initiative Association for the 2Zero partnership (EGVIAfor2Zero) 07411

Dir Ave de de Cortenbergh 66, 1000 Brussels, Belgium. E-mail: info@2zeroemission.eu.
URL: https://www.2zeroemission.eu/

History 2021. Registration: Banque-Carrefour des Entreprises, No/ID: 0509.963.444, Start date: 19 Feb 2013, Belgium. **Structure** General Assembly; Executive Board. **Events** *European Conference on Results from Road Transport Research in H2020 Projects* Brussels (Belgium) 2023, *European Conference on Results from Road Transport Research in H2020 Projects* Brussels (Belgium) 2022, *European Conference on Results from Road Transport Research in H2020 Projects* Brussels (Belgium) 2020, *European Conference on Results from Road Transport Research in H2020 Projects* Brussels (Belgium) 2019.
Members Full Members (Industry Members and Research Members)
Associate Members (non-governmental organizations), including the following organizations listed in this Yearbook:
Association des constructeurs européens de motocycles (ACEM, #02450); Association of European Automative and Industrial Battery Manufacturers (EUROBAT, #02498); ERTICO ITS Europe (#05532); European Association of Automotive Suppliers (CLEPA, #05948); European Automotive Research Partners Association (EARPA, #06301); European Conference of Transport Research Institutes (ECTRI, #06737); European Council of Automotive Research and Development (EUCAR, #06806); Forum of European National Highway Research Laboratories (FEHRL, #09910); International Association of Public Transport (#12118); POLIS (#18419); RECHARGE (#18627).
IGO Relations Memorandum of Understanding with (1): *European Commission (EC, #06633).* **NGO Relations** Cooperates with (4): *ETIP Smart Networks for Energy Transition (ETIP SNET, #05558); European Road Transport Research Advisory Council (ERTRAC, #08396); European Technology Platform ALICE (ALICE, #08888); European Technology Platform on Smart Systems Integration (EPoSS, #08892).* [2023/AA3072/y/**E**]

♦ European Greenways Association (EGWA) 07412

Association Européenne des voies vertes (AEVV) – Asociación Europea de Vias Verdes (AEVV)

Dir C/ Santa Isabel 44, 28012 Madrid, Spain. T. +34911511098. Fax +34911511068. E-mail: info@aevv-egwa.org.
URL: http://www.aevv-egwa.org/

History 8 Jan 1998, Namur (Belgium). Founded at constituent assembly, following decision of 1st *European Conference on Soft Traffic and Railway Paths*, May 1997, Val-Dieu (Belgium). Statutes modified 19 Oct 2000; 13 Jun 2005. Registration: No/ID: 0465.074.319, Start date: 8 Jan 1998, Belgium. **Aims** Improve *communications* and non-motorized *local* itineraries in Europe; preserve *infrastructure* such as disused railway corridors, tow paths and historic routes and their use by the public as environmental facilities for open-air leisure, tourism and light transport; promote rural development, active tourism and local employment. **Structure** General Assembly (every 2 years, at conference); Board of Directors; Secretariat in Namur (Belgium), headed by Secretary-General. **Languages** English, French. **Staff** 1.00 FTE, paid. **Finance** Sources: members' dues. Secretariat location provided by the government of Wallonia (Belgium). **Activities** Awards/prizes/competitions; knowledge management/information dissemination; research and development. **Events** *European Greenways Conference* Vitoria-Gasteiz (Spain) 2019, *Eurovelo, Greenways and Cycling Tourism Conference* Vienna (Austria) 2016, *Eurovelo, Greenways and Cycling Tourism Conference* Basel (Switzerland) 2014, *Eurovelo, Greenways and Cycling Tourism Conference* Nantes (France) 2012, *International congress* Liège (Belgium) 2003.
Members Full and supporting. Founding institutes and associations in 18 countries:
Austria, Belgium, Czechia, Denmark, France, Hungary, Ireland, Italy, Latvia, Luxembourg, Norway, Poland, Portugal, Russia, Serbia, Spain, Sweden, UK.
Regional founding member (1), listed in this Yearbook:
European Cyclists' Federation (ECF, #06877).
NGO Relations Member of (1): *European Tourism Manifesto (#08921).* Cooperates with (1): *Rurality – Environment – Development (RED, #19003).* [2020/XD6221/**D**]

♦ European Grid Infrastructure / see EGI Foundation (#05395)
♦ European Grid Initiative / see EGI Foundation (#05395)

♦ European Group Analytic Training Institutions Network (EGATIN) .. 07413

Hon Sec c/o GASW, 12 Sydenham Road, Cotham, Bristol, BS6 5SH, UK.
International Liaison c/o GAS Belgrade, Palmotićeva 24, Belgrade, PAK 11000, Serbia.
URL: http://www.egatin.net/

History 1988, Heidelberg (Germany). **Events** *Study Days* Lisbon (Portugal) 2012, *Annual General Meeting* Athens (Greece) 2011, *Annual General Meeting* Vienna (Austria) 2010, *Study days* Vienna (Austria) 2010, *Meeting* Heidelberg (Germany) 2009. **NGO Relations** *European Association for Psychotherapy (EAP, #06176).* [2020/XF3556/**F**]

♦ European Group for the Ardennes and the Eifel 07414

Groupement Européen des Ardennes et de l'Eifel (GEAE) – Europäische Vereinigung für Eifel und Ardennen (EVEA)

Pres Herrenstrasse 8, 54673 Neuerburg, Germany. T. +496564930003. Fax +496564930005.
URL: http://www.evea.de/

History 10 May 1955, Namur (Belgium), having existed since 1950 as a national organization. **Aims** Promote development and recognition of a true European climate in the Belgian, French and Luxembourg Ardennes and in the German Eifel. **Structure** International Committee. National member sections (4). **Languages** French, German. **Finance** Members' dues. **Activities** International Commissions (6): Cultural Relations; Sport and Leisure; Youth Exchanges; Environment and Natural Resources; Equipment and Development Plan; Tourism. **Events** *Annual Congress* Bitburg (Germany) 2010, *Annual Congress* Sankt-Vith (Belgium) 2009, *Annual Congress* Vianden (Luxembourg) 2008, *Conference on EFTA-EU relations and enlargement* Oslo (Norway) 2001, *Annual Congress* Bogny sur Meuse (France) 1993.
Members Individuals adhering to national sections in 4 countries:
Belgium, France, Germany, Luxembourg. [2010.09.19/XD0776/**E**]

♦ European Group of Artists of the Ardennes and the Eifel 07415

Groupement européen des artistes des Ardennes et de l'Eifel – Europäische Vereinigung Bildender Künstler aus Eifel und Ardennen (EVBK)

Main Office Geschäftsstelle Prüm/Eifel, Hahnplatz 1, 54595 Prüm, Germany. T. +496551505. Fax +4965517640. E-mail: info@evbk.eu.
URL: https://www.evbk.eu/

History 1957. **Aims** Promote links, understanding and friendship between the Ardennes and Eifel regions; conserve the common cultural heritage of the two regions and enrich it for the benefit of future generations. **Languages** French, German. **Activities** Awards/prizes/competitions; events/meetings. **Events** *Meeting* Prüm (Germany) 1991, *Meeting* Prüm (Germany FR) 1988.
Members Sections (4) in 4 countries:
Belgium, France, Germany, Luxembourg. [2022.02.15/XD1382/**D**]

♦ European Group for Atomic Spectroscopy / see European Group on Atomic Systems (#07416)

♦ European Group on Atomic Systems (EGAS) 07416

Groupe européen des systèmes atomiques

Sec Dipto de Fisica e Astronomia, European Lab for Nonlinear Spectroscopy, Via Nello Carrara 1, 50019 Sesto Fiorentino FI, Italy.
URL: http://www.eps-egas.org/

History 1969. Currently functions as *Atomic Spectroscopy Section* within the Atomic and Molecular Physics Division of *European Physical Society (EPS, #08207).* Former names and other names: *European Group for Atomic Spectroscopy* – former (1969 to 2004). **Aims** Study all spectroscopic aspects of atoms, atomic systems, ions and small molecules as well as developments in instrumentation. **Structure** Annual meeting (every 3 years merged in ECAMP conference); Board. **Languages** English. **Activities** Events/meetings. **Events** *EGAS Conference* Zagreb (Croatia) 2021, *EGAS Conference* Zagreb (Croatia) 2020, *EGAS Conference & ECAMP* Florence (Italy) 2019, *Annual Conference* Krakow (Poland) 2018, *Annual Conference* Durham (UK) 2017. **Publications** Conference proceedings.
Members Individuals in 47 countries and territories:
Algeria, Argentina, Armenia, Austria, Belgium, Brazil, Bulgaria, Canada, Croatia, Cyprus, Denmark, Egypt, Finland, France, Germany, Ghana, Greece, India, Iran Islamic Rep, Iraq, Ireland, Israel, Italy, Japan, Korea Rep, Latvia, Lithuania, Malaysia, Mexico, Moldova, Morocco, Netherlands, New Zealand, Norway, Poland, Portugal, Russia, Serbia, Spain, Sweden, Switzerland, Taiwan, Türkiye, UK, Ukraine, USA, Uzbekistan. [2021/XD8362/v/**E**]

♦ European Group of Automotive Recycling Associations (EGARA) ... 07417

Secretariat Pompmolenlaan 10F, 3447 GK Woerden, Netherlands. T. +31885011090. E-mail: info@egaranet.org.
URL: http://www.egaranet.org/

History Nov 1991. A grouping of the type *European Economic Interest Grouping (EEIG, #06960).* EU Transparency Register: 678790929099-85. **Aims** Facilitate and develop economic activities of European automotive recyclers; stimulate development of environmentally justified working methods and product and material re-use. **Structure** Executive Committee. **Activities** Advocacy/lobbying/activism. **Events** *Nordic meeting* Tromsø (Norway) 2002, *Nordic meeting* Tromsø (Norway) 2000. **Publications** Position papers.
Members in 14 countries:
Denmark, Estonia, Finland, France, Hungary, Ireland, Italy, Netherlands, Norway, Poland, Spain, Sweden, Switzerland, UK. [2020/XF1507/**F**]

♦ European Group for Bone Marrow Transplantation / see European Society for Blood and Marrow Transplantation (#08533)

♦ European Group for the Certification of Constructional Steels (CONSCERT) 07418

Groupe européen pour la certification de l'acier de construction

Secretariat Rue Ravenstein 4, 1000 Brussels, Belgium. T. +3223720379. E-mail: ceqmas@skynet.be.
URL: http://www.conscert.eu/

History 14 Oct 1993, following a memorandum of understanding Dec 1991, London (UK). Registered in accordance with Belgian law. **Aims** In the interests of the consumer: coordinate certification of construction steel in accordance with European or national technical *standards*, regulations and norms; draw up common practical rules and methods to assist such certification; facilitate development of procedures for mutual recognition of the results of certification tests. **Structure** General Meeting (annual); Board of Directors; Consultative Group; Secretariat. **Languages** English. **Finance** Members' dues. Access fees. **Activities** Standards/guidelines; certification/accreditation. **Events** *International workshop* Brussels (Belgium) 1997, *International workshop* Brussels (Belgium) 1996. **Publications** Guidelines; check lists.
Members Full in 9 countries:
Belgium, France, Germany, Italy, Netherlands, Norway, Spain, Sweden, UK.
NGO Relations Member of: *Federation of European and International Associations Established in Belgium (FAIB, #09508).* Liaison with: *Fédération internationale du béton (FIB, #09615).* [2016.10.26/XE1843/**E**]

♦ European Group of Cryosurgery (inactive)
♦ European Group for the Development of Textile Research (unconfirmed)
♦ European Group for Ecological Policy (inactive)

♦ European Group of Emergency Nurses 07419

Contact 16 Gatacre St, Lower Gornal, Dudley, DY3 2NZ, UK.

History 6 Sep 2010, Pordenone (Italy). Inaugural meeting 6-7 Sep 2010, Pordenone (Italy). **Events** *Inaugural meeting* Pordenone (Italy) 2010. [2010/XJ2076/**D**]

♦ European Group for the Employment of Persons with Mental Disabilities (no recent information)
♦ European Group of Endoscopy Ultrasonography (inactive)

♦ European Group on Ethics in Science and New Technologies (EGE) . 07420

Groupe européen d'éthique des sciences et des nouvelles technologies – Europäische Gruppe für Ethik der Naturwissenschaften und der neuen Technologien

Head of Secretariat Frère Orban Square 8, 1049 Brussels, Belgium. E-mail: ec-ethics-group@ec.europa.eu.
URL: https://ec.europa.eu/research/ege/index.cfm?pg=home/

History 1992. Founded by Jacques Delors. Former names and other names: *Group of Advisers on the Ethical Implications of Biotechnology* – former; *European Group on Ethics in Sciences and New Technologies to the European Commission* – former; *Groupe européen d'éthique des sciences et des nouvelles technologies auprès de la Commission européenne* – former; *Europäische Gruppe für Ethik der Naturwissenschaften und der neuen Technologien bei der Europäischen Kommission* – former. **Aims** Advise the European Commission on ethical aspects of science and new technologies in connection with the preparation and implementation of Community *legislation* or *policies*. **Structure** Group of 15 members, appointed by President of European Commission; Secretariat. **Languages** English. **Staff** 4.00 FTE, paid. **Finance** Supported by: *European Commission (EC, #06633).* **Events** *Meeting* Brussels (Belgium) 2019, *Meeting* Brussels (Belgium) 2019, *Meeting* Brussels (Belgium) 2019, *Meeting* Brussels (Belgium) 2019, *Meeting* Brussels (Belgium) 2019. **Publications** Opinions; statements; reports; proceedings. **Members** Individuals (up to 15) serving in a personal capacity. [2021.05.25/XF4430/**F**]

♦ European Group on Ethics in Sciences and New Technologies to the European Commission / see European Group on Ethics in Science and New Technologies (#07420)
♦ **European Group** European Group for the Study of Deviance and Social Control (#07435)
♦ European Group of Expertise in Field Epidemiology (#10738)
♦ European Group for Eye Movement Research / see International Group for Eye Movement Research (#13747)
♦ European Group on Fracture / see European Structural Integrity Society (#08844)
♦ European Group for Generic Veterinary Products / see Access VetMed (#00054)

♦ European Group of Graves' Orbitopathy (EUGOGO) 07421

Pres Avenue Hippocrate 10, Cliniques Universitaires Saint Luc, Ophthalmology Dept, 1200 Brussels, Belgium.
Sec Clinic of Endocrinology, Clinical Centre of Serbia, Dr Subotića 13, Belgrade, 11000, PAK 112113, Serbia. E-mail: secretaryeugogo@gmail.com.
URL: http://www.eugogo.eu/

History 1999. Registration: No/ID: 93089300508, Italy. **Aims** Improve management and quality of life of patients with Graves' orbitopathy through standardized assessment, education and collaborative research. **Structure** Executive Committee. **Languages** English. **Staff** None paid. **Finance** Self-financing. **Activities** Events/meetings; training/education. Active in all member countries. **Events** *International Symposium on Graves' Orbitopathy – EUGOGO 20th Anniversary Meeting* Pisa (Italy) 2019, *Meeting* Essen (Germany) 2015, *Meeting* Newcastle upon Tyne (UK) 2014.
Members Centres in 15 countries:
Austria, Belgium, Croatia, Denmark, France, Germany, Greece, Italy, Poland, Serbia, Singapore, Spain, Switzerland, Türkiye, UK.
IGO Relations None. [2022.03.06/XJ8562/**D**]

♦ European Grouping of Film and Television Schools (see: #11771)

♦ European Grouping of Societies of Authors and Composers 07422

Groupement Européen des Sociétés d'Auteurs et Compositeurs (GESAC)

General Manager Rue Montoyer 23, 1000 Brussels, Belgium. T. +3225114454. E-mail: secretariat-general@gesac.org.
URL: http://www.authorsocieties.eu/

History Dec 1990. Establsihed as a grouping of the type *European Economic Interest Grouping (EEIG, #06960).* Registration: EU Transparency Register, No/ID: 36529354479-57. **Aims** Promote creators' rights and raise awareness about issues affecting the creative sector. **Languages** English, French. **Staff** 6.00 FTE, paid. **Finance** Sources: members' dues. **Activities** Advocacy/lobbying/activism. **Events** *Meeting* Brussels (Belgium) 2017, *Conference on collective management of copyright and related rights in Europe* Brussels (Belgium) 2008, *General Meeting* Brussels (Belgium) 2008, *Statutory annual general meeting* Brussels (Belgium) 2008, *Workshop on private copy remuneration* Brussels (Belgium) 2008.
Members National organizations (32) in 28 countries:
Austria, Belgium, Bulgaria, Croatia, Czechia, Denmark, Estonia, Finland, France, Germany, Greece, Hungary, Iceland, Ireland, Italy, Latvia, Lithuania, Luxembourg, Netherlands, Norway, Poland, Portugal, Romania, Slovakia, Spain, Sweden, Switzerland, UK.
International observers (2):
Confédération internationale des sociétés d'auteurs et compositeurs (CISAC, #04563); International Bureau of the Societies Administering the Rights of Mechanical Recording and Reproduction (#12416).
NGO Relations Associate member of: *Confédération internationale des sociétés d'auteurs et compositeurs (CISAC, #04563); European Movement International (EMI, #07825).* [2021.05.25/XF4043/y/**F**]

♦ European Grouping of Territorial Cooperation / see European Grouping of Territorial Cooperation – Twinned Cities and Areas in the Mediterranean (#07423)

♦ European Grouping of Territorial Cooperation – Twinned Cities and Areas in the Mediterranean (EGTC – AMPHICTYONY) 07423

Pres Vironos Str 29, Plaka, 105 58 Athens, Greece. T. +302103246139. Fax +302103243374.
URL: http://www.amphictyony.gr/

History Set up as a network 1986. Refounded 2008. Registered in the EGTC register, managed by *European Committee of the Regions (CoR, #06665). European Grouping of Territorial Cooperation.* Registered in accordance with Greek law. EU Transparency Register: 010922834782-77. **Aims** Work for the people of the Mediterranean so they can live in a continuously peaceful environment and one of constant development, financially effective, socially just and environmentally viable with cohesion and security. **Structure** General Assembly; Board of Directors (Presidium); Executive Committee. **Languages** English, Irish Gaelic. **Staff** 4.00 FTE, paid. **Finance** Members' dues. Annual budget: euro 150,000. **Activities** Projects/programmes; events/meetings.
Members Municipalities in 6 countries and territories:
Albania, Cyprus, France, Greece, Italy, Palestine.
IGO Relations Observer to: *Congress of Local and Regional Authorities of the Council of Europe (#04677).* [2019.02.14/XM2961/**E**]

♦ European Group of the Institutes of Navigation (EUGIN) 07424

Groupe Européen des Instituts de Navigation – Grupo Europeo de Institutos de Navegación

Exec Sec Veeweidestraat 9, 3300 Tienen, Belgium. E-mail: secretary@eugin.info.
URL: https://www.eugin.info/

History 22 Jan 1997. Former names and other names: *European Union Group of Institutes of Navigation* – former. Registration: Banque-Carrefour des Entreprises, No/ID: 0462.279.828, Start date: 15 Jan 1998, Belgium. **Aims** Initiate and support actions assisting in development of pan European policies and strategies in the fields of navigation and traffic management; participate in study works initiated by European authorities; foster co-operation and information exchange between members; provide information in its field of expertise by organising conferences and symposia, publishing papers and participating in various media methods of data dissemination; undertake other actions which are related to EUGIN's objectives and which should assist in their realisation. **Structure** General Assembly (annual); Council; Committees. **Languages** English. **Finance** Sources: grants; meeting proceeds; members' dues; subsidies. **Activities** Events/meetings; knowledge management/information dissemination; research/documentation. **Events** *European Navigation Conference (ENC)* Noordwijk (Netherlands) 2023, *European Navigation Conference (ENC)* Edinburgh (UK) 2021, *European Navigation Conference (ENC)* Dresden (Germany) 2020, *European Navigation Conference (ENC)* Warsaw (Poland) 2019, *European Navigation Conference (ENC)* Gothenburg (Sweden) 2018.
Members Full: national and regional associations; Honorary: individuals and associations. Institutes (Scandinavian countries * are grouped in one institute) in 12 countries:
Austria, Belgium, Denmark (*), France, Germany, Italy, Netherlands, Norway (*), Poland, Sweden (*), Switzerland, UK.

Regional institute:
Nordic Institute of Navigation (#17323).
IGO Relations Liaises with: *European Commission (EC, #06633).* [2022.11.10/XD5929/**D**]

♦ European Group for Intelligent Computing in Engineering (EG-ICE) . 07425

Sec Engineering School, Cardiff Univ, Cardiff, CF24 3AA, UK.
Chair Environmental Bldg Goup, Roland Levinsky Bldg room 301A, Drake Circus, Plymouth, PL4 8AA, UK. T. +441752586115. Fax +441752586003.
URL: http://www.eg-ice.org/

History as *European Group for Structural Engineering Applications of Artificial Intelligence (EG-SEA-AI).* **Aims** Promote advanced *informatics* research across Europe by improving contact between researchers; foster research collaboration and enhance awareness of latest developments; increase awareness of the industry of advanced informatics and the economic benefits that can be gained by implementing these techniques. **Structure** Committee. **Languages** English. **Staff** None. **Finance** Meeting proceeds. Annual budget: Swiss Fr 1,000. **Activities** Knowledge management/information dissemination; events/meetings; research/documentation. **Events** *Annual Workshop* Leuven (Belgium) 2019, *Annual Workshop* Lausanne (Switzerland) 2018, *Annual Workshop* Nottingham (UK) 2017, *Annual Workshop* Krakow (Poland) 2016, *Annual Workshop / International Workshop* Eindhoven (Netherlands) 2015. **Publications** Workshop proceedings.
Members Engineers, computer scientists, architects, psychologists and other interested people. Individuals in 24 countries and territories:
Australia, Austria, China, Croatia, Denmark, Finland, France, Germany, Greece, Hong Kong, Hungary, Ireland, Israel, Italy, Kuwait, Netherlands, Poland, Portugal, Slovenia, Spain, Sweden, Switzerland, UK, USA.
NGO Relations *Asian Group for Civil Engineering Informatics (AGCEI, #01497); International Association for Bridge and Structural Engineering (IABSE, #11737).* [2019.04.28/XF5899/v/**F**]

♦ European Group of International Accounting Networks and Associations (EGIAN) 07426

Exec Dir c/o DRT and Partners, Chaussee Romaine 1022, 1780 Wemmel, Belgium.
Sec address not obtained. E-mail: info@egian.eu.
URL: http://www.egian.eu/

History 1991. Founded as an informal group. Restructured 2011; 2016. Registration: EU Transparency Register, No/ID: 78403342288-89, Start date: 18 Sep 2009. **Aims** Provide a forum through which to collaborate so as to facilitate an exchange of ideas and information about key international professional developments affecting the accounting and auditing professions in Europe. **Structure** Non-executive Chairman; Executive Director; Expert Working Group Leaders. **Languages** English. **Finance** Sources: members' dues. **Activities** Advocacy/lobbying/activism; awareness raising; events/meetings; knowledge management/information dissemination; networking/liaising; politics/policy/regulatory.
Members Networks and associations (17) in 4 countries:
France, Germany, Switzerland, UK.
BKR International; GGI Global Alliance; HLB International; IAPA (#11005); INPACT International (#11227); International Association of Accountants, Auditors and Tax Consultants (IECnet, #11681); MGI Worldwide (#16740). [2021.05.20/XJ7552/y/**F**]

- ♦ European Group of Journalists / see European Federation of Journalists (#07152)
- ♦ European Group of Lymphology / see European Society of Lymphology (#08643)
- ♦ European Group for Metal Furniture (no recent information)
- ♦ European Group of National Human Rights Institutions / see European Network of National Human Rights Institutions (#07949)
- ♦ European Group of Official Laboratories for Fire Testing / see European Group of Organisations for Fire Testing, Inspection and Certification (#07427)

♦ European Group of Organisations for Fire Testing, Inspection and Certification (EGOLF) 07427

SG Laval Consulting, La Chavade, Quartier Laval, 07230 Planzolles, France.
Registered Office Ottergemsesteenweg 711, 9000 Ghent, Belgium. T. +3292437750. Fax +3292437751.
URL: http://www.egolf.global/

History 17 Dec 1988, Brussels (Belgium). 17-18 Dec 1988, Brussels (Belgium), as *European Group of Official Laboratories for Fire Testing (EGOLF).* Registered in accordance with Belgian law. **Aims** Be the main representative body for third party, independent and nationally recognized organizations involved at a European level in fire safety testing, inspection and certification activities. **Structure** Plenary; Executive Committee; Technical Committees (3). **Languages** English. **Staff** 0.50 FTE, paid. **Finance** Members' dues. **Activities** Research and development; networking/liaising; events/meetings; training/education. **Events** *Joint conference on fire safe products in construction* Luxembourg (Luxembourg) 2007, *The benefits of fire safety engineering within the European Union* Luxembourg (Luxembourg) 2002, *Joint conference on fire safe products in construction* Kirchberg (Luxembourg) 1999. **Publications** Annual Report; reports; position papers; recommendations; agreements.
Members Fire test laboratories in 30 countries:
Austria, Belarus, Belgium, Bulgaria, Czechia, Denmark, Estonia, Finland, France, Germany, Hungary, Israel, Italy, Latvia, Lithuania, Netherlands, Norway, Poland, Portugal, Romania, Russia, Slovakia, Slovenia, Spain, Sweden, Switzerland, Türkiye, UK, United Arab Emirates, USA.
NGO Relations Cooperates with: *Comité européen de normalisation (CEN, #04162); European Federation of National Associations of Measurement, Testing and Analytical Laboratories (EUROLAB, #07168); International Organization for Standardization (ISO, #14473).* [2019.12.11/XF2219/**F**]

♦ European Group for Organizational Studies (EGOS) 07428

Groupe européen pour les études organisationnelles

Exec Sec Chodowieckistr 31, 10405 Berlin, Germany. T. +493044354988. Fax +493044354989. E-mail: secretariat@egosnet.eu.
Registered Office Square de Meeûs 35, 1000 Brussels, Belgium.
URL: http://www.egosnet.org/

History 1973, as an informal network; formalized as an association, Jul 1997. Registered in accordance with Belgian law. **Aims** As a network of *professional* teachers and researchers: promote and carry out *interdisciplinary* research on organizational theory; provide a forum for presentation and discussion of such research; provide a platform to launch autonomous working groups; offer the possibility of publishing high quality research. **Structure** General Assembly (annual). Board, comprising Chairperson and 7 members. Executive Secretariat. **Languages** English, French, German. **Staff** 1.00 FTE, paid. **Finance** Members' dues: full – euro 125; PhD – euro 95. **Activities** Events/meetings; networking/liaising; training/education. **Events** *Annual Colloquium* Cagliari (Italy) 2023, *Annual Colloquium* Vienna (Austria) 2022, *Annual Colloquium* Amsterdam (Netherlands) 2021, *Annual Colloquium* Berlin (Germany) 2020, *Annual Colloquium* Edinburgh (UK) 2019. **Publications** *Organization Studies* (12 a year). **Members** Individual teachers and researchers (2,500) worldwide. Members in 60 countries. Membership countries not specified. [2017/XD5446/v/**E**]

- ♦ European Group of Owner Managed and Family Enterprises / see European Family Businesses (#07028)
- ♦ European Group for Pastoral Work / see Groupe européen de pastorale ouvrière (#10740)
- ♦ European Group for Prisoners Abroad (inactive)

♦ European Group for Private International Law 07429

Groupe européen de droit international privé (GEDIP)

Sec Rue Nicolas Adames 14, L-1114 Luxembourg, Luxembourg.
Pres Univ of Paris 2, 75006 Paris, France.
URL: http://www.gedip-egpil.eu/

History 3 Oct 1991, Louvain-la-Neuve (Belgium). Founded 3-5 Oct 1991, Louvain-la-Neuve (Belgium), at first meeting. Registered in accordance with the laws of Luxembourg. **Aims** Study theoretical and practical links between European Community/European Union law and private international law; exchange information on evolution of respective national legal systems; establish an academic network in European Union and EFTA countries. **Languages** English, French. **Staff** None. **Finance** Funded partly by member universities. **Activities** Research/documentation; events/meetings. **Events** *Meeting* Katowice (Poland) 2019, *Meeting* Antwerp (Belgium) 2018, *Meeting* Hamburg (Germany) 2017, *Meeting* Milan (Italy) 2016, *Meeting* Luxembourg (Luxembourg) 2015. **Publications** *Building European Private International Law* (2011).

Members Individual educators, lawyers, judges and civil servants, (who may also be members or observers of international institutions or European Union institutions), limited to 30 and coopted, in 18 countries:
Austria, Belgium, Cyprus, Czechia, Denmark, Finland, France, Germany, Greece, Italy, Luxembourg, Netherlands, Norway, Portugal, Spain, Sweden, Switzerland, UK. [2019.12.12/XF2163/v/**F**]

- ♦ European Group for the Protection of the Animal World (inactive)
- ♦ European Group of Public Administration / see European Group for Public Administration (#07430)

♦ European Group for Public Administration (EGPA) 07430

Groupe européen pour l'administration publique (GEAP)

Mailing Address c/o IIAS, Rue du Commerce 96, Block 6, 6th Floor, 1040 Brussels, Belgium. T. +3225360880. Fax +3225379702.
URL: https://egpa.iias-iisa.org/

History Founded Sep 1974, Speyer (Germany FR), having been proposed, 1971, at XVth International Congress of Administrative Sciences, as a section of *International Institute of Administrative Sciences (IIAS, #13859).* Officially set up, 1975. Now a regional group of IIAS. Original title: *European Group of Public Administration – Groupe européen d'administration publique.* Current title adopted, Mar/Jul 2009. **Aims** Organize and encourage exchange of information on developments in the theory and practice of public administration; foster comparative studies and development of public administrative theory within a European perspective; facilitate application of innovative ideas, methods and techniques in public administration; strengthen contacts between practitioners, teachers, researchers and civil servants. **Structure** General Assembly. Steering Committee, comprising Chairman, 10 members and the IIAS Director General (ex-officio). Study Groups (20), each managed by 3-4 Directors. Permanent Practitioners Group. **Languages** English, French. **Staff** 8.00 FTE, paid. **Finance** Members' dues. Individual: euro 75; Corporate: euro 375; Corporate plus Accreditation: euro 775. **Activities** Events/meetings; research/documentation. **Events** *Annual Conference* Zagreb (Croatia) 2023, *Annual Conference* Lisbon (Portugal) 2022, *Transatlantic Dialogue (TAD)* Røskilde (Denmark) 2022, *Annual Conference* Brussels (Belgium) 2021, *Annual Conference* Budapest (Hungary) 2020. **Publications** *International Review of Administrative Sciences* (4 a year) in Arabic, Chinese, English, French, Spanish. *EGPA (1975-2010): Perspectives for the Future* (2010). Scientific publications in Palgrave, Bruylant and IOS Series. **Members** Corporate (75); Individuals (160). Membership countries not specified. **NGO Relations** Member of: *European Alliance for the Social Sciences and Humanities (EASSH, #05885).* [2022/XE9257/**E**]

♦ European Group of Public Law (EGPL) 07431

Groupe européen de droit public

Contact c/o EPLO, 16 Achaiou Street, Kolonaki, 106 75 Athens, Greece. T. +302107258801 – +302107293103 – +30210(229206981011. Fax +302107258040 – +30210(2292069813.
URL: http://egpl.eplo.eu/

History Sep 1991, Spetses (Greece), following recommendations of a meeting of European public law professors, Sep 1989, Athens (Greece). **Aims** Organize research and specific study on themes of interest in the process of European *integration*; contribute to concepts and curricula in teaching of public law at European universities; respond with initiatives vis-à-vis new public law science in Central and Eastern Europe. **Structure** Reunion (annual, always in Spetses – Greece). Steering Committee of 2 members. Serves as scientific advisory body of *European Public Law Organization (EPLO, #08299).* **Languages** English, French. **Finance** Sources: donations; grants. **Activities** Events/meetings. **Events** *Annual meeting* Spetses (Greece) 1996, *Annual meeting* Spetses (Greece) 1995, *Annual meeting* Spetses (Greece) 1994, *Annual meeting* Spetses (Greece) 1993. **Publications** *European Review of Public Law* (4 a year) in English, French, German, Italian; *Central and Eastern European Legal Studies; European Papers. European Public Law Series.* **Members** Individuals (over 230). Membership countries not specified. **NGO Relations** *Academy of European Public Law (#00037).* [2015.11.04/XE3133/v/**E**]

- ♦ European Group for Rapid Laboratory Viral Diagnosis (inactive)

♦ European Group for Research into Elderly and Physical Activity (EGREPA) 07432

Pres Zinman College Physical Education and Sport Sciences, Wingate Inst, 42902 Netanya, Israel. T. +97298639314. Fax +97298639377.
Treas Inst für Sportwissenschaft, Univ of Münster, Horstmarer Landweg 62b, 48149 Münster, Germany. T. +492518338420. Fax +492518334862.
URL: http://www.egrepa.org/

History 1992, Jyväskylä (Finland). Founded during Third International Conference on Physical Activity, Aging and Sport. Previously registered in accordance with Swiss law. Registration: Germany, Cologne; EU Transparency Register, No/ID: 829670541151. **Aims** Promote physical activity and health in the elderly. **Structure** Board. **Languages** English. **Staff** Voluntary. **Finance** Members' dues. Other sources: fees; assessments; gifts; conference proceeds; publications and sales. **Activities** Research/documentation; publishing activities. **Events** *Conference* Krakow (Poland) 2021, *Conference* Israel 2014, *Conference* Glasgow (UK) 2012, *Conference* Prague (Czech Rep) 2010, *Conference* Pontevedra (Spain) 2007. **Publications** *European Review on Aging and Physical Activity* – journal. **Members** Membership countries not specified. **NGO Relations** Member of: *International Council of Sport Science and Physical Education (ICSSPE, #13077).* [2021/XD3946/**E**]

- ♦ European Group of Research into Norms (#10741)
- ♦ European Group for Research on Spatial Problems (inactive)
- ♦ European Group for Research and Training of Teachers Holding Christian and Other Beliefs and Convictions (#10759)
- ♦ European Group for the Rights of Prisoners (internationally oriented national body)

♦ European Group of Risk and Insurance Economists (EGRIE) 07433

Groupe européen d'économistes en matière de risque et d'assurance

Exec Sec c/o MRIC, Schackstr 4, 80539 Munich, Germany. T. +498921803883. Fax +49892180993883.
URL: http://www.egrie.org/

History 1973. Founded under the auspices of *Geneva Association (#10119).* Organizational structure formalized, Sep 2002 and on 16 Sep 2003 Statutes were ratified and Board of Directors elected during the founding assembly. Further institutionalized 2010. Registration: Germany. **Aims** Promote research on risk and insurance; stimulate contact between academics and professionals in the field of economics of risk and insurance. **Structure** General Assembly; Executive Board. **Languages** English. **Staff** Voluntary. **Finance** Sources: members' dues; sponsorship. **Activities** Awards/prizes/competitions; events/meetings; networking/liaising. **Events** *Annual Seminar* Munich (Germany) / Hohenheim (Germany) 2021, *World Risk and Insurance Economics Congress (WRIEC)* 2020, *Annual Seminar* Rome (Italy) 2019, *Annual Seminar* Nürburg (Germany) 2018, *Annual Seminar* London (UK) 2017. **Publications** *Geneva Risk and Insurance Review* – official journal.
Members Individuals – risk and insurance researchers. Members in 18 countries and territories:
Australia, Austria, Belgium, Canada, Chile, China, France, Germany, Hong Kong, Japan, New Zealand, Norway, Poland, Singapore, Switzerland, Taiwan, UK, USA.
NGO Relations Cooperates with (3): American Risk and Insurance Association; *Asia-Pacific Risk and Insurance Association (APRIA, #02016); Geneva Association (#10119).* [2022.02.01/XE5227/v/**E**]

♦ European Group for Rooflights and Smoke-Ventilation (EUROLUX) . 07434

Groupement européen de fabricants d'appareils d'éclairement zénithal et exutoires de fumées – Vereinigung der Europäischen Hersteller von Lichtkuppeln, Lichtbändern und RWA

SG Marx Van Ranst Vermeersch Partners, Avenue de Tervuren 270, 1150 Brussels, Belgium. T. +3222850100. Fax +3222303339.
Registered Office Rue Washington 40, 1050 Brussels, Belgium.
URL: https://www.eurolux-eu.com/

History 1990, Brussels (Belgium). Registration: Banque-Carrefour des Entreprises, No/ID: 0439.752.963, Start date: 18 Jan 1990, Brussels (Belgium). **Aims** Promote, on a European level, scientific studies on and knowledge of rooflights and smoke-ventilation. **Structure** General Assembly (once a year). Praesidium, consisting of President, immediate Past President, President-Elect and 2 Vice-Presidents. General Secretariat, headed by Secretary-General. **Languages** English, French, German. **Finance** Members' dues.

Members Associations in 6 countries:
Austria, Belgium, France, Germany, Italy, Netherlands.
NGO Relations Member of: *Construction Products Europe AISBL (#04761)*; *Federation of European and International Associations Established in Belgium (FAIB, #09508)*. In liaison with technical committees of: *Comité européen de normalisation (CEN, #04162)*. [2003.06.01/XF1628/F]

♦ European Group for Scientific Research on Stomato-Odontology / see International Group for Scientific Research on Stomato-Odontology (#13755)
♦ European Group for Social Work Education / see European Association of Schools of Social Work (#06200)
♦ European Group for Structural Engineering Applications of Artificial Intelligence / see European Group for Intelligent Computing in Engineering (#07425)
♦ European Group of Studies Against Sickness of the Esophagus / see European Society for Diseases of the Esophagus (#08585)

♦ European Group for the Study of Deviance and Social Control (European Group) 07435

Contact address not obtained. E-mail: europeangroupcoordinator@gmail.com.
URL: http://www.europeangroup.org/

History First proposed in 1970 by Stan Cohen, Mario Simondi and Karl Schumann of Berkeley University, California (USA). **Aims** Foster 'emancipatory knowledge' which has the explicit political and theoretical intention of not just understanding individual and social problems, but also challenging and transforming existing power relations. **Structure** Collective network based on support of members who contribute in various ways, linking members from different countries together and publicizing the Group as national representatives. **Languages** English, Spanish. **Staff** 1.00 FTE, voluntary. **Finance** Conference fees; donations; contributions from local organizing institutions. **Activities** Events/meetings; publishing activities. Active worldwide, although primarily in Europe. **Events** *Annual Conference* Tallinn (Estonia) 2015, *Annual Conference* Liverpool (UK) 2014, *Annual Conference* Oslo (Norway) 2013, *Annual Conference* Nicosia (Cyprus) 2012, *Annual Conference* Chambéry (France) 2011. **Publications** *Justice, Power and Resistance* – journal. Conference working papers; translations; monographs. **Members** Academics and activists in the field of social control. Membership countries not specified. **IGO Relations** None. **NGO Relations** None. [2020.01.14/XD5333/v/E]

♦ European Group of Surveyors (EGoS) 07436

SG 19 Church Street, Godalming, GU7 1EL, UK. T. +441483416411. Fax +441483419381.
Pres Sky Apartments Flat 13/16 – Block C, 177-179 Marina Sea Front, Tal-Pieta, MSD 08, Malta. T. +35621237914 – +35621251040.
Registered Office Rue du Nord 76, 1000 Brussels, Belgium.
URL: http://www.europeansurveyors.org/

History Founded 1989, Rome (Italy). **Aims** Create, promote and develop systems of mutual recognition of surveyor qualifications; facilitate free movement of professionally qualified surveyors; promote development of common curricula for education and training; encourage high standards of professionalism; promote members' services and represent their interests; develop and encourage dialogue between the surveying professions and European Union institutions. **Structure** General Assembly (twice a year); Board; Working Groups. **Languages** English. **Staff** All voluntary. **Finance** Budget: about euro 35,000. **Activities** Certification/accreditation; meeting activities; training/education. **Events** *General Assembly* Athens (Greece) 2014, *General Assembly* Malta 2014, *General Assembly* Berlin (Germany) 2013, *General Assembly* Skopje (Macedonia) 2013, *General Assembly* Tirana (Albania) 2012. **Publications** Reports; press releases.
Members Professional surveying organizations established in countries of the European Union. Full in 10 countries:
Belgium, Bulgaria, Cyprus, Germany, Greece, Ireland, Italy, Malta, Spain, UK.
Associate in 4 countries:
Albania, Kosovo, North Macedonia, Türkiye.
Included in the above, 1 organization listed in this Yearbook:
South-East European Research Institute on Geo Sciences (Geo-SEE Institute).
Observers in 4 countries:
Czechia, France, Hungary, Israel.
Included in the above, 1 organization listed in this Yearbook:
European Academy of Architecture (EAA). [2015.06.01/XF3290/y/F]

♦ European Group of Television Advertising / see egta – association of television and radio sales houses (#05397)

♦ European Group on Tort Law (EGTL) 07437

Contact c/o ECTIL, Reichsratsstrasse 17/2, 1010 Vienna, Austria. T. +431427729650. Fax +431427729670. E-mail: ectil@ectil.org.
URL: http://www.egtl.org/

History Former names and other names: *Tilburg Group* – former (1992). Registration: EU Transparency Register, No/ID: 008658631225-37. **Aims** Contribute to enhancement and harmonization of tort law in Europe through the field framework provided by its *Principles of European Tort Law (PETL)*. **Activities** Events/meetings; publishing activities; research/documentation. **Publications** *Principles of European Tort Law Series*; *Principles of European Tort Law – Text and Commentary*. *Prescription in Tort Law: Analytical and Comparative Perspectives* (2020) by Israel Gilead and Bjarte Askeland in English.
Members Individuals in 19 countries:
Austria, Belgium, Czechia, Denmark, France, Germany, Greece, Israel, Italy, Netherlands, Norway, Poland, Portugal, South Africa, Spain, Sweden, Switzerland, UK, USA.
NGO Relations Cooperates with: *European Centre of Tort and Insurance Law (ECTIL, #06502)*; *Institute for European Tort Law (ETL)*. [2019.11.12/XF5905/v/F]

♦ European Group on Tumour Markers (EGTM) 07438

Sec c/o Hospital Clinic, Escalera 9, Planta 1, Villarroel 170, 08036 Barcelona, Spain.
URL: http://www.egtm.eu/

History 15 Feb 1997. 15-16 Feb 1997, as an informal group with the title *Hamburg Symposia*. Formally set Feb 1997, Barcelona (Spain). Current constitution and by-laws adopted 16 Sep 2007, Prague (Czech Rep). **Aims** Publish guidelines for *clinicians* and other users of tumour markers; inform clinicians, laboratories and students about the proper use of tumour markers; give educational and scientific advice on the clinical and analytical evaluation of tumour markers. **Structure** Board, comprising Honorary Chairman, Chairman, Secretary, Treasurer and 3 members. **Events** *General Assembly* Prague (Czech Rep) 2007.
Members Individuals in 18 countries:
Austria, Belgium, Czechia, Denmark, Finland, France, Germany, Ireland, Israel, Italy, Netherlands, Norway, Poland, Slovakia, Spain, Sweden, Switzerland, UK. [2018/XJ2455/E]

♦ European Group of Valuers' Associations (TEGOVA) 07439

Managing Director Blvd Saint-Michel 45, 1040 Brussels, Belgium. T. +3225033234. Fax +3225033232. E-mail: info@tegova.org.
URL: http://www.tegova.org/

History 1997, by merger of *European Group of Valuers (TEGOVA, inactive)* and *European Property Valuers (EUROVAL, inactive)*. **Languages** English. **Staff** 3.00 FTE, paid. **Finance** Members' dues. **Events** *Spring General Meeting* Lisbon (Portugal) 2022, *Spring General Meeting* Berlin (Germany) 2015, *Spring General Meeting / Half-Yearly General Assembly* Oslo (Norway) 2014, *General Assembly* Riga (Latvia) 2014, *Half-Yearly General Assembly* Brussels (Belgium) 2009. **NGO Relations** Partner of: *Appraisal Institute (AI)*. [2018/XD5968/D]

♦ European Group for Worker Pastoral (#10740)
♦ European Growth Federation (no recent information)

♦ European Guide Dog Federation (EGDF) 07440

Exec Dir Marston Grange, Shuckburgh Road, Priors Marston, CV47 7RS, UK. T. +441327720027. E-mail: info@egdfed.org.
URL: http://www.egdfed.org/

History 2007. Registration: Charity Commission, No/ID: 1120553, England and Wales; Companies House, No/ID: 6302385, Start date: 4 Jul 2007, England and Wales; EU Transparency Register, No/ID: 425076230743-53, Start date: 9 Mar 2018. **Aims** Influence laws, policies and attitudes; ensure excellent facilities and access for guide dog users. **Structure** Board. **Events** *Annual Conference* Ljubljana (Slovenia) 2016, *Annual Conference* Bucharest (Romania) 2015, *Annual Conference* Brussels (Belgium) 2013, *Meeting* Amsterdam (Netherlands) 2012. **Publications** *EGDF Newsletter*.
Members Full in 25 countries:
Belgium, Bulgaria, Croatia, Czechia, Estonia, Finland, France, Germany, Greece, Hungary, Ireland, Italy, Luxembourg, Malta, Netherlands, Norway, Romania, Serbia, Slovakia, Slovenia, Spain, Sweden, Switzerland, Türkiye, UK.
NGO Relations Memorandum of Understanding with (2): *Assistance Dogs Europe (ADEu, #02322)*; *International Guide Dog Federation (IGDF, #13763)*. Member of (2): *European Coalition for Vision (ECV)*; *European Disability Forum (EDF, #06929)*. [2017.10.11/XM4350/D]

♦ European Guitar Builders (EGB) 07441

Contact Springer, Wirtschaftsweg 5, Ringenwalde, 15377 Märkische Höhe, Germany. T. +4318903915. E-mail: office@europeanguitarbuilders.com.
URL: http://www.europeanguitarbuilders.com/

History 2013. Registered in accordance with German law: DE294122534. **Aims** Support independent European luthiers by sharing knowledge, resources, and experience so as to preserve and innovate the art and craft of guitar building in Europe as a vital part of Europe's musical culture. **Structure** General Assembly; Board of Directors. **Finance** Members' dues. **Activities** Events/meetings. **Events** *Symposium* Berlin (Germany) 2016.
Members Individuals Full; Honorary; Support. Full in 20 countries:
Austria, Belgium, Bulgaria, Denmark, Estonia, Finland, France, Germany, Hungary, Iceland, Ireland, Italy, Netherlands, Norway, Portugal, Slovakia, Spain, Sweden, Switzerland, UK. [2016/XM4896/D]

♦ European Guitar Teachers Association (no recent information)

♦ European Gymnastics 07442

Gen Dir Av de la Gare 12, 1003 Lausanne VD, Switzerland. T. +41216131020. E-mail: info@europeangymnastics.com.
URL: https://www.europeangymnastics.com/

History 1982, Luxembourg. Former names and other names: *Union européenne de gymnastique (UEG)* – former; *European Union of Gymnastics* – former; *Europäische Turnunion* – former. **Aims** Promote gymnastics competitions and gymnastics for health, for adults and youth. **Structure** Executive Committee; Technical Commissions; Control Commission; Directorate (no voting right). Joint television commission with: *European Broadcasting Union (EBU, #06404)*. **Languages** English, French. **Staff** 5.00 FTE, paid. **Finance** Sources: members' dues; sponsorship. Other sources: media right sales; event hosting fees. **Activities** Events/meetings; sporting activities. **Events** *Congress* Albufeira (Portugal) 2022, *Congress* Albufeira (Portugal) 2021, *Congress* Sofia (Bulgaria) 2019, *Congress* Split (Croatia) 2017, *Congress* Bratislava (Slovakia) 2015. **Publications** *UEG Bulletin* (2-3 a year). *Yearbook*.
Members Affiliated federations in 50 countries:
Albania, Andorra, Armenia, Austria, Azerbaijan, Belarus, Belgium, Bosnia-Herzegovina, Bulgaria, Croatia, Cyprus, Czechia, Denmark, Estonia, Finland, France, Georgia, Germany, Greece, Hungary, Iceland, Ireland, Israel, Italy, Kosovo, Latvia, Liechtenstein, Lithuania, Luxembourg, Malta, Moldova, Monaco, Montenegro, Netherlands, North Macedonia, Norway, Poland, Portugal, Romania, Russia, San Marino, Serbia, Slovakia, Slovenia, Spain, Sweden, Switzerland, Türkiye, UK, Ukraine.
IGO Relations *European Commission (EC, #06633)*. [2023.02.14/XD1887/D]

♦ European Habitats Forum (EHF) 07443

Sec c/o IUCN EU Office, Bd Louis Schmidt 64, 1040 Brussels, Belgium. T. +3227390317. Fax +3227329499. E-mail: ehf_secretariat@iucn.org.
URL: https://www.iucn.org/regiona/europe/our-work/eu-biodiversity-policy/ european-habitats-forum/

History 1993, Brussels (Belgium). EU Transparency Register: 896045415778-75. **Aims** Represent the interests of civil society in *conserving* Europe's natural heritage, particularly implementation of EU Habitats and Birds Directives; positively influence *biodiversity* policy and legislation through discussion and partnership with relevant stakeholders. **Structure** Chair; Vice-Chairs; Secretariat provided by IUCN. **Languages** English. **Staff** 0.50 FTE, paid. **Finance** Members' dues. Annual budget: around euro 10,000. **Activities** Politics/policy/regulatory; awareness raising; knowledge management/information dissemination; training/education.
Members Nongovernmental organizations having a primary interest on an international level in conservation, rehabilitation and sustainable use of European habitats (22) of which 17 are listed in this Yearbook:
A Rocha International (#18965); *BirdLife International (#03266)*; *Butterfly Conservation Europe (BCE, #03388)*; *CEEweb for Biodiversity (#03626)*; *ClientEarth (#03996)*; *EuroNatur – European Nature Heritage Fund (#05738)*; *EUROPARC Federation (#05768)*; *European Environmental Bureau (EEB, #06996)*; *European Herpetological Society (#07481)*; *Eurosite (#09181)*; *Friends of the Earth Europe (FoEE, #10001)*; *International Mire Conservation Group (IMCG, #14169)*; *International Union for Conservation of Nature and Natural Resources (IUCN, #15766)*; *Rewilding Europe (#18933)*; *The Nature Conservancy (TNC)*; *Wetlands International (#20928)*; *World Wide Fund for Nature (WWF, #21922)*.
IGO Relations Observer to: *Standing Committee to the Bern Convention on the Conservation of European Wildlife and Natural Habitats (#19949)*. [2019.05.01/XF3289/y/F]

♦ European Haematology Association / see European Hematology Association (#07473)

♦ European Haemophilia Consortium (EHC) 07444

CEO Rue de l'Industrie 10, 1000 Brussels, Belgium. T. +3228932470. E-mail: office@ehc.eu.
Pres c/o Irish Haemophilia Society, First Floor, Cathedral Court, New Street 8, Dublin, CO. DUBLIN, Ireland. T. +35316579900.
URL: http://www.ehc.eu/

History Founded 1989, as a regional group of *World Federation of Hemophilia (WFH, #21437)*. Officially constituted 15 Nov 2006, Brussels (Belgium). Registered in accordance with Belgian law: No 887106966. EU Transparency Register: 786550013705-85. **Aims** Improve the quality of life of people with haemophilia in Europe. **Structure** General Assembly (annual, during Conference); Steering Committee; Office located in Brussels (Belgium). **Languages** English, Russian. **Staff** 6.00 FTE, paid. **Finance** Sources: membership contributions; pharmaceutical sponsorship. **Activities** Guidance/assistance/consulting; knowledge management/information dissemination; networking/liaising; events/meetings; advocacy/lobbying/activism. **Events** *Leadership Conference* Brussels (Belgium) 2022, *Annual General Meeting and Conference* Copenhagen (Denmark) 2022, *Annual General Meeting and Conference* Brussels (Belgium) 2021, *Inhibitor Summit* Brussels (Belgium) 2021, *Leadership Conference* Brussels (Belgium) 2021. **Publications** *EHC Newsletter* (3 a year). Annual report; monographs; articles.
Members NMOs (45) in 45 countries:
Albania, Armenia, Austria, Azerbaijan, Belarus, Belgium, Bosnia-Herzegovina, Bulgaria, Croatia, Cyprus, Czechia, Denmark, Estonia, Finland, France, Georgia, Germany, Greece, Hungary, Iceland, Ireland, Israel, Italy, Kyrgyzstan, Latvia, Lithuania, Luxembourg, Moldova, Montenegro, Netherlands, North Macedonia, Norway, Poland, Portugal, Romania, Russia, Serbia, Slovakia, Slovenia, Spain, Sweden, Switzerland, Türkiye, UK, Ukraine.
NGO Relations Member of: *EURORDIS – Rare Diseases Europe (#09175)*; *EGAN – Patients Network for Medical Research and Health (EGAN, #05394)*; *European Patients' Forum (EPF, #08172)*. Cooperates with: *European Association for Haemophilia and Allied Disorders (EAHAD, #06063)*; *World Federation of Hemophilia (WFH, #21437)*. [2020/XD4709/D]

♦ European Haemovigilance Network / see International Haemovigilance Network (#13768)

♦ European Hair Research Society (EHRS) 07445

Pres Dermatology Dept HHU, POB 12000, 9112001 Jerusalem, Israel. T. +97226777111. Fax +97226432883. E-mail: president@ehrs.org.
URL: http://www.ehrs.org/

History 11 Nov 1989, Brussels (Belgium). Founded following discussions in London (UK) in Apr 1989. **Aims** Promote research of hair biology and hair disease in Europe. **Structure** Board, comprising President, Secretary, Treasurer and 3 further members. **Languages** English. **Staff** Voluntary. **Finance** Members' dues. Conference fee. Administration budget (annual): euro 5,000. Conference budget (annual): euro 50,000. **Activities** Organizes annual conference for education on hair biology and hair disease research and research data dissemination; co-organizes *World Congress for Hair Research*. **Events** *Annual Meeting* Sheffield (UK)

European Haliaeetus Association
07445

alphabetic sequence excludes
For the complete listing, see Yearbook Online at

2023, *World Congress for Hair Research* Melbourne, VIC (Australia) 2022, *Conference* St Petersburg (Russia) 2022, *World Congress for Hair Research* Melbourne, VIC (Australia) 2021, *Annual Meeting* Sheffield (UK) 2020. **Publications** Conference abstracts.
Members Full in 24 countries and territories:
Australia, Austria, Belgium, Canada, Denmark, Egypt, France, Germany, Greece, Israel, Italy, Japan, Korea Rep, Lebanon, Netherlands, Serbia, Slovenia, South Africa, Spain, Sweden, Switzerland, Taiwan, UK, USA.
NGO Relations *Australasian Hair and Wool Research Society*; national organizations. [2016/XD8166/**D**]

♦ European Haliaeetus Association (inactive)

♦ European Handball Federation (EHF) 07446
Fédération européenne de handball – Europäische Handball Föderation
Main Office Hoffingergasse 18, 1120 Vienna, Austria. T. +431801510. E-mail: office@eurohandball.com.
URL: http://www.eurohandball.com/
History 17 Nov 1991, Berlin (Germany). Statutes most recently amended, 18 Nov 2016. **Aims** Strive for continued development and promotion of handball in Europe; organize European *competitions* for national teams and clubs. **Structure** Congress (every 2 years); Executive Committee; Technical Commissions; Office based in Vienna (Austria), headed by President and Secretary-General. **Languages** English, French, German. **Staff** 65.00 FTE, paid. **Finance** Sources: donations; members' dues; revenue from activities/projects; sponsorship. Other sources: television and advertising rights. **Activities** Events/meetings; sporting activities; training/education. **Events** *Extraordinary Congress* Luxembourg (Luxembourg) 2022, *Biennial Congress* Vienna (Austria) 2021, *Extraordinary Congress* Vienna (Austria) 2021, *Extraordinary Congress* Stockholm (Sweden) 2020, *Biennial Congress* Glasgow (UK) 2018. **Publications** *EHF News*. Annual Report; guides; bibliography; calendar of events; brochures; folders; documentation of EHF courses and seminars. **Information Services** *EHF Information System*.
Members National federations in 51 countries and territories:
Albania, Andorra, Armenia, Austria, Azerbaijan, Belarus, Belgium, Bosnia-Herzegovina, Bulgaria, Croatia, Cyprus, Czechia, Denmark, England, Estonia, Faeroe Is, Finland, France, Georgia, Germany, Greece, Hungary, Iceland, Ireland, Israel, Italy, Kosovo, Latvia, Liechtenstein, Lithuania, Luxembourg, Malta, Moldova, Monaco, Montenegro, Netherlands, North Macedonia, Norway, Poland, Portugal, Romania, Russia, Scotland, Serbia, Slovakia, Slovenia, Spain, Sweden, Switzerland, Türkiye, Ukraine.
NGO Relations Member of (1): *Association of European Team Sports (ETS, #02546)*. Supports (1): *Union sportive des polices d'Europe (USPE, #20482)*. Regional federation of: *International Handball Federation (IHF, #13771)*. [2022.10.19/XE3112/**E**]

♦ European Handbike Circuit / see European Handcycling Federation (#07447)

♦ European Handcycling Federation (EHF) 07447
Treas Heinrich Collin-Strasse 27/2/1, 1140 Vienna, Austria. T. +4319242737.
Head Office Via Ponchielli 19, 21052 Busto Arsizio MB, Italy.
URL: http://www.ehf-ehc.eu/
History Founded 2001, as *European Handbike Circuit (EHC)*. Current name adopted, 2006. Head office relocated from Belgium to Italy, 2009. **Aims** Further development of European handcycling; promote and support integration between able-bodied and *disabled athletes*; eliminate barriers by playing *sport* and give disabled and able-bodied athletes the chance to compete together with the same goal. **Structure** Executive Committee; registered office and secretariat located in Italy. **Languages** English. **Staff** All voluntary. **Finance** Members' dues. Sponsors. Budget (annual): about euro 12,000. **Activities** Events/meetings. *EHF European Championships* Details not obtained. *European Handbike Circuit* Details not obtained.
Members in 14 countries:
Austria, Belgium, Czechia, France, Germany, Ireland, Italy, Luxembourg, Netherlands, Poland, Spain, Switzerland, UK, United Arab Emirates. [2014.11.11/XF6333/**F**]

♦ European Hang Gliding and Paragliding Union (EHPU) 07448
SG Vagtelvej 15, 2000 Frederiksberg, Denmark. E-mail: ehpu@ehpu.org.
URL: http://www.ehpu.org/
History Founded 27 Jan 2001. **Aims** Promote and protect hang gliding and paragliding in Europe. **Structure** General Conference (annual). **Languages** English. **Finance** Members' dues. **Events** *Annual General Meeting* Taormina (Italy) 2013, *Annual General Meeting* Dublin (Ireland) 2012, *Annual General Meeting* Budapest (Hungary) 2011, *Annual General Meeting* Tegernsee (Germany) 2010, *Annual General Meeting* Nice (France) 2009.
Members National organizations in 18 countries:
Austria, Belgium, Czechia, Denmark, France, Germany, Hungary, Ireland, Italy, Netherlands, Norway, Portugal, Romania, Slovenia, Spain, Sweden, Switzerland, UK.
NGO Relations *Europe Air Sports (EAS, #05776)*; *European Gliding Union (EGU, #07395)*. [2013.08.20/XD9122/**D**]

♦ European Harbour Masters' Association / see European Harbour Masters' Committee (#07449)

♦ European Harbour Masters' Committee (EHMC) 07449
Contact PO Box 6622, 3002 AP Rotterdam, Netherlands. T. +31615822469.
URL: https://www.harbourmaster.org/about/ehmc
History Founded May 1985, Cork (Ireland), as *European Harbour Masters' Association (EHMA)*. Previously existed as an informal body, known from 1961 as *Harbour Masters of North Western Europe*. Instrumental in setting up *International Harbour Masters' Association (IHMA, #13774)*, 21 Jun 1996, when EHMA became an integral part of IHMA. Current title and form adopted May 2004, so as to make way for the formation of other regional groupings. EU Transparency Register: 50964709218-58. **Aims** Promote safe and efficient conduct of *marine* operations in port waters; develop and foster collaboration and good relations among harbour masters in Europe and represent their professional views; collect, collate and supply information of professional interest to members; focus on European issues; serve as a voice in European institutions; contribute as an expert group to European research projects. **Structure** Board. **Languages** English. **Staff** 1.00 FTE, paid. Staff shared with IHMA. **Finance** Integrated with budget of IHMA. **Activities** are integrated with those of IHMA. Events/meetings. **Events** *Seminar* Sillamäe (Estonia) 2021, *Seminar* Gothenburg (Sweden) 2019, *Seminar* Tangiers (Morocco) 2017, *Seminar* Marseille (France) 2015, *Seminar* Bremen (Germany) 2013. **Publications** Congress papers and proceedings.
Members Individuals, European members of IHMA, in 21 countries:
Belgium, Bulgaria, Cyprus, Denmark, Estonia, Finland, France, Germany, Iceland, Ireland, Latvia, Lithuania, Malta, Netherlands, Norway, Poland, Russia, Spain, Sweden, UK, Ukraine.
IGO Relations All contacts maintained through IHMA, including: *International Hydrographic Organization (IHO, #13825)*; *International Maritime Organization (IMO, #14102)*. [2022/XD3549/v/**E**]

♦ European Harmonisation Committee / see Federation of European Companion Animal Veterinary Associations (#09497)

♦ European Harm Reduction Network (EuroHRN) 07450
Deputy Dir c/o HRI, 61 Mansell Street, Aldgate, London, E1 8AN, UK.
URL: http://www.eurohrn.eu/
History Launched Apr 2010, Liverpool (UK). **Aims** Expand the knowledge base of harm reduction in Europe; raise awareness of drug-related harms; promote and support public health and human rights orientated responses to drug use across Europe. **Structure** Steering Group. Sub-regional networks (3): North Europe; South Europe; Eastern Europe. Coordinated by: *Harm Reduction International (HRI, #10861)*. **Events** *Conference* Amsterdam (Netherlands) 2014, *European Harm Reduction Conference* Basel (Switzerland) 2014, *Conference* Marseille (France) 2011.
Members Full in 27 countries:
Albania, Austria, Belgium, Bosnia-Herzegovina, Bulgaria, Czechia, Denmark, Estonia, Finland, France, Greece, Hungary, Ireland, Italy, Latvia, Luxembourg, North Macedonia, Norway, Poland, Romania, Serbia, Slovakia, Slovenia, Spain, Sweden, Switzerland, UK.
NGO Relations Partners include: *International Network of People who Use Drugs (INPUD, #14301)*. [2018/XJ9480/**F**]

♦ European HD Radio Alliance (inactive)
♦ European Headache Alliance / see European Migraine and Headache Alliance (#07801)

♦ European Headache Federation (EHF) 07451
Fédération européenne des céphalées
Main Office c/o Conventus, Carl-Pulfrich-Str 1, 07745 Jena, Germany. E-mail: ehf@conventus.de.
URL: http://www.ehf-headache.com
History 19 Apr 1991, Venice (Italy). By-laws adopted Jul 1992, Pavia (Italy). Registration: Companies House, No/ID: 04125594, Start date: 14 Dec 2000, England and Wales. **Aims** Widen and extend interest in and provide an understanding of headache in Europe; provide a forum for young researchers and scientists to present their work and get feedback from experienced workers in the field. **Structure** Board (meets annually); Executive Committee. Ad hoc Committees: Financial; Educational; Drug Information; Public Relations; Research. **Languages** English. **Staff** Voluntary. **Finance** Sources: in-kind support; meeting proceeds; revenue from activities/projects; sale of publications. **Activities** Events/meetings; guidance/assistance/consulting; networking/liaising; training/education. **Events** *International Headache Congress* Vienna (Austria) 2022, *International Headache Congress* 2021, *Conference* Jena (Germany) 2020, *Conference* Athens (Greece) 2019, *Conference* Florence (Italy) 2018. **Publications** *EHF News* (2 a year); *Journal of Headache and Pain*.
Members Individual graduates, either through member national societies or research groups. Research groups/national societies in 32 countries:
Albania, Austria, Belarus, Belgium, Bulgaria, Croatia, Denmark, Finland, France, Georgia, Germany, Greece, Hungary, Israel, Italy, Lithuania, Moldova, Netherlands, Norway, Poland, Portugal, Romania, Russia, Serbia, Slovakia, Slovenia, South Africa, Spain, Sweden, Switzerland, Türkiye, UK.
NGO Relations Cooperates with (1): *World Headache Alliance (WHA, #21555)*. Although independent, operates under auspices of: *International Headache Society (IHS, #13777)*. [2022.05.04/XD3594/**D**]

♦ European Head and Neck Society (EHNS) 07452
Société Européenne de Tête et Cou
Sec Seba Office Boulevard, Ayazaga Mah Mimar Sinan Sok No 21 Blok D44, Sariyer, 34485 Istanbul/Istanbul, Türkiye. E-mail: secretariat@ehns.org.
Contact Rue Héger-Bordet 1, 1000 Brussels, Belgium.
URL: http://www.ehns.org/
History 2006, Brussels (Belgium). Founded when official documents to set up EHNS were signed. Registration: Banque Carrefour des Entreprises, No/ID: 0881.171.358, Start date: 8 May 2006, Belgium. **Aims** Promote exchange of knowledge in all aspects of head and neck neoplastic diseases; promote the highest standards of research, education and training, disease prevention and patient care. **Structure** Board. **Languages** English. **Finance** Sources: members' dues. **Activities** Events/meetings; training/education. **Events** *Joint International Congress on Innovative Approaches in Head and Neck Oncology (ICHNO) and European Congress on Head and Neck Oncology (ECHNO)* Brussels (Belgium) 2022, *European Conference on Head and Neck Oncology* Brussels (Belgium) 2021, *European Head and Neck Robotic Conference* Paris (France) 2021, *European Conference on Head and Neck Oncology* Brussels (Belgium) 2020, *International Conference on Innovative Approaches in Head and Neck Oncology* Barcelona (Spain) 2019. **Publications** *EHNS Newsletter*.
Members Individuals; study groups. National societies in 20 countries:
Armenia, Austria, Belarus, Belgium, Croatia, Czechia, France, Germany, Greece, Hungary, Israel, Italy, Kazakhstan, Netherlands, Poland, Portugal, Romania, Russia, Serbia, Spain, Switzerland, Türkiye, UK.
Baltic States Head and Neck Oncology Association (BHNO Association); *Scandinavian Society for Head and Neck Oncology (SSHNO, #19109)*.
NGO Relations Member of (3): *Confederation of European Otorhinolaryngology – Head and Neck Surgery (Confederation of European ORL-HNS, #04528)*; *European Cancer Organisation (ECO, #06432)*; *International Federation of Head and Neck Oncologic Societies (IFHNOS, #13438)*. [2021.02.10/XM2052/**D**]

♦ European Healthcare Distribution Association (#10762)

♦ European Healthcare Fraud and Corruption Network (EHFCN) 07453
External Relations Officer Av de Tervuren 211, 1150 Brussels, Belgium. T. +31657274939. E-mail: office@ehfcn.org.
URL: http://www.ehfcn.org/
History 2005, following the first pan-European conference held in London (UK), Oct 2004. Foundation based on European Healthcare Fraud and Corruption Declaration. **Aims** Improve European healthcare systems by reducing loss to fraud, waste and corruption. **Structure** General Assembly (annual); Executive Committee; Standing Operational Committee; Working Groups. **Languages** English, French, German, Spanish. **Staff** 4.00 FTE, paid. **Finance** Members' dues. **Events** *Conference* Berlin (Germany) 2019, *Conference* Paris (France) 2017, *Annual Conference* The Hague (Netherlands) 2015, *Annual Conference* Windsor (UK) 2012, *Fighting fraud in healthcare and social security – how to maximise resources* Krakow (Poland) 2011.
Members Healthcare and counter-fraud associations (19) in 14 countries:
Belgium, Czechia, France, Germany, Greece, Italy, Luxembourg, Netherlands, Norway, Poland, Portugal, Serbia, Slovenia, UK.
NGO Relations Member of: *World Federation of Public Health Associations (WFPHA, #21476)*. [2021/XJ0565/**D**]

♦ European Healthcare Management Association / see European Health Management Association (#07458)
♦ European Health Chamber (unconfirmed)
♦ European Health Club / see European network for health promotion and economic development (#07920)
♦ European Health Committee (inactive)

♦ European Health Economics Association (EUHEA) 07454
Exec Sec Fac of Business and Economics, Peter Merian-Weg 6, 4002 Basel BS, Switzerland. T. +41612673226. E-mail: info@euhea.eu.
URL: http://www.euhea.eu/
History Registered in accordance with Swiss Civil Code. **Aims** Promote cooperation among all national health economics associations and groups in Europe; profile and foster health economics at European universities. **Structure** Assembly of Delegates; Executive Committee; Finance Committee. **Activities** Events/meetings. **Events** *Health economics for sustainable welfare systems* Oslo (Norway) 2022, *Conference* Oslo (Norway) 2020, *EUHEA PhD Student-supervisor Conference* Rotterdam (Netherlands) 2020, *Shaping the future – the role of health economics* Maastricht (Netherlands) 2018, *PhD Student- Supervisor Conference* Barcelona (Spain) 2016.
Members Associations and groups in 14 countries:
Austria, Belgium, Finland, France, Germany, Ireland, Italy, Norway, Poland, Portugal, Spain, Sweden, Switzerland, UK. [2021/XM5494/**D**]

♦ European Health and Fitness Association / see EuropeActive (#05772)

♦ European Health Forum Gastein (EHFG) 07455
Contact Tauernplatz 1, 5630 Bad Hofgastein, Austria. T. +4364323393270. Fax +4364323393271. E-mail: info@ehfg.org.
Vienna Office Biberstr 20, 1010 Vienna, Austria. T. +43151561510.
URL: http://www.ehfg.org/
History 1998, Bad Hofgastein (Austria). Registration: EU Transparency Register, No/ID: 022328713595-61, Start date: 28 May 2014. **Aims** Provide a platform for discussion for the various stakeholders in the field of public health and health care; facilitate establishment of a framework for advising and developing European health policy. **Structure** Board; Advisory Committee. **Activities** Events/meetings; networking/liaising; awards/prizes/competitions. **Events** *Annual Forum* Bad Hofgastein (Austria) 2019, *Annual Forum* Salzburg (Austria) 2018, *Annual Forum* Bad Hofgastein (Austria) 2017, *Annual Forum* Bad Hofgastein (Austria) 2016, *Annual Forum* Bad Hofgastein (Austria) 2015. **Publications** *Gastein Health Outcomes*. Conference reports.
Members Full in 6 countries:
Austria, Belgium, Germany, Netherlands, Poland, UK. [2020/XN7444/**F**]

♦ European Health Futures Forum (EHFF) 07456
Registered Address Edergole, Dromahair, CONNAUGHT, F91 W243, Ireland.
Dir Undercliff Cottage, Newport Road, Ventnor, PO38 1XA, UK.
URL: http://ehff.eu/

History Mar 2013. Founded following a period as the Lisbon Office of *European Society for Quality in Healthcare (ESQH, inactive)*. Registration: Charity, No/ID: 20160784, Ireland; EU Transparency Register, No/ID: 216585211114-86, Start date: 9 May 2013. **Aims** Improve the health of European citizens through a transformative collaborative process. **Structure** Board; Executive Directors (4); Non-executive Chair and Directors (5). **Languages** English. **Finance** Projects; donations. **Activities** Capacity building; projects/ programmes; events/meetings. **Members** Full in 20 countries. Membership countries not specified. **IGO Relations** *European Commission (EC, #06633)*. **NGO Relations** Member of (4): *EU Health Coalition*; *European Forum for Primary Care (EFPC, #07326)* (Associate); *Self-Care Initiative Europe (SCIE)*; *Wellbeing Economy Alliance (WEAll, #20856)*. [2020/XJ8942/**F**]

♦ European Health Industry Business Communications Council (EHIBCC) 07457

Contact Jozef Israelslaan 8, 2596 AS The Hague, Netherlands. T. +31703244754. Fax +31703242522. E-mail: info@ehibcc.com.
URL: http://www.ehibcc.com/

History Apr 1991, Brussels (Belgium). Reorganized 1994. Registered in accordance with Belgian law. **Aims** Develop and promote a uniform European *standard* for *bar coding* within health care. **Structure** General Assembly (annual); Board of Directors; Secretariat, headed by Secretary General. **Activities** Standards/ guidelines. **Events** *Logistics in health care – no bar-code, no business* Amsterdam (Netherlands) 1997. **Publications** *EHIBCC News* – internal; *EHIBCC Vision Lines* – public circulation. Information Services: Maintains database.
Members Full in 16 countries:
Austria, Belgium, Denmark, Finland, France, Germany, Ireland, Italy, Liechtenstein, Luxembourg, Netherlands, Norway, Portugal, Spain, Sweden, Switzerland.
NGO Relations In liaison with technical committees of: *Comité européen de normalisation (CEN, #04162)*; *European Hospital and Healthcare Federation (HOPE, #07501)*. [2019/XF2196/t/**F**]

♦ European Health Management Association (EHMA) 07458

Association européenne de gestion des systèmes de santé

Exec Dir Avenue de Cortenbergh 89, 1000 Brussels, Belgium. T. +3225026525. E-mail: communi-cations@ehma.org – info@ehma.org.
Events and Communications Assistant address not obtained.
URL: http://www.ehma.org/

History 14 May 1966, Leuven (Belgium). Most recent statutes adopted Jun 2002, Gdansk (Poland). Former names and other names: *European Association of Training Programmes in Hospital and Health Services Administration* – former (May 1966 to Oct 1977); *European Association of Programmes in Health Services Studies (EAPHSS)* – former (Oct 1977 to Jun 1999); *European Healthcare Management Association* – former. Registration: Banque Carrefour des Entreprises, No/ID: 0598.968.565, Start date: 26 Feb 2015, Belgium; EU Transparency Register, No/ID: 352972410521-12, Start date: 28 Jan 2013. **Aims** Improve health care in Europe by improving health management through: improving practice in healthcare delivery; influencing health policy, both nationally at at EU level; engaging in cutting-edge health services research. **Structure** General Assembly (annual); Board; Scientific Advisory Committee; Secretariat. Special Interest Groups. **Languages** English. **Staff** 5.50 FTE, paid. **Finance** Members' dues. Other sources: grants; revenue-generating activities. **Activities** Networking/liaising; events/meetings; knowledge management/information dissemination; financial and/or material support; training/education. **Events** *Annual Conference* Brussels (Belgium) 2022, *Annual Conference* Lisbon (Portugal) 2021, *Annual Conference* Rotterdam (Netherlands) 2020, *Annual Conference* Espoo (Finland) 2019, *Annual Conference* Budapest (Hungary) 2018. **Publications** *EHMA Newsletter* (12 a year); *Health Services Management Research* – offical journal.
Members Institutional; Individual. Institutions in 21 countries:
Austria, Belgium, Bulgaria, Croatia, Finland, France, Hungary, Italy, Latvia, Malta, Moldova, Netherlands, Norway, Peru, Portugal, Serbia, Spain, Sweden, Switzerland, UK, United Arab Emirates.
NGO Relations Member of (3): *EU Health Coalition*; *European Forum for Primary Care (EFPC, #07326)* (Associate); *Health First Europe (HFE, #10881)*. Instrumental in setting up (1): *Agency for Public Health Education Accreditation (APHEA, #00555)*. [2022/XD0585/y/**D**]

♦ European Health Managers Forum (no recent information)

♦ European Health Parliament (EHP) 07459

Contact Square de Meeûs 23, 1000 Brussels, Belgium. T. +3227463552. E-mail: contact@ healthparliament.eu.
URL: https://www.healthparliament.eu/

History Founded 2014. EU Transparency Register: 067711130762-48. **Aims** Provide the next generation of European leaders with the connections, knowledge and platform they need to build a healthier and more innovative Europe. **Activities** Events/meetings; networking/liaising.
Members Partners (7):
College of Europe (#04105); *EU40 (#05562)*; euronews; European Affairs Recruitment Specialists (EARS); *European Patients' Forum (EPF, #08172)*; Johnson&Johnson; Porter Novelli. [2020/XM8941/**F**]

♦ European Health professionals Competent Authorities (EurHeCA) 07460

Registered Office Henri Jaspar Avenue 94, 1060 Brussels, Belgium. T. +3225374267.
URL: http://www.eurheca.eu/

History Registered in accordance with Belgian law. EU Transparency Register: 357259233284-67. **Aims** Improve *patient* safety and well being by developing e-Health technologies, their applications and the corresponding tools (authentication, signature etc), and interoperability of systems and databases; coordinate work in Europe concerning healthcare professionals benefiting from the principle of automatic recognition; encourage continuous training for healthcare professionals; implement a platform so as to exchange all useful information between competent authorities representing health professions. **Structure** General Assembly; Administrative Board; Bureau. **Events** *General Assembly* Paris (France) 2022, *General Assembly* Paris (France) 2022, *General Assembly* Brussels (Belgium) 2020, *General Assembly* Sofia (Bulgaria) 2018, *General Assembly* Madrid (Spain) 2016.
Members Ordinary in 9 countries:
Belgium, Bulgaria, France, Ireland, Malta, Poland, Portugal, Romania, Spain.
Observer members include 3 organizations listed in this Yearbook:
European Council of Liberal Professions (#06828); *European Federation of Nurses Associations (EFN, #07180)*; *Pharmaceutical Group of the European Union (PGEU, #18352)*. [2018/XM5695/ty/**D**]

♦ European Health Professions Conference (meeting series)

♦ European Health Property Network (EuHPN) 07461

Address not obtained.
URL: http://www.euhpn.eu/

History 2000, Netherlands. **Aims** Promote excellence in health property provision and management. **Events** *Workshop* Madrid (Spain) 2016, *Workshop* Edinburgh (UK) 2014, *Annual Workshop* Budapest (Hungary) 2013, *Annual Workshop* Copenhagen (Denmark) 2012, *Annual Workshop* Bologna (Italy) 2011. **Publications** *EuHPN Newsletter*.
Members Organizations in 11 countries:
Belgium, Denmark, Hungary, Ireland, Italy, Malta, Netherlands, Norway, Poland, Sweden, UK.
Included in the above, 1 organization listed in this Yearbook:
European Investment Bank (EIB, #07599) (Human Capital Division).
NGO Relations Member of: *Nordic Center for Sustainable Healthcare (NCSH, #17229)*. [2014/XJ5861/**F**]

♦ European Health Psychology Society (EHPS) 07462

Admin address not obtained.
Sec c/o Psychology Dept, Bar Ilan University, 5290002 Ramat Gan, Israel.
URL: http://www.ehps.net/

History Jul 1986, Tilburg (Netherlands). Founded at 1st expert meeting. Statutes adopted 2-4 Jul 1990, Oxford (UK). Bylaws updated Aug 2014. Registration: Netherlands. **Aims** Promote and develop empirical and theoretical research in and applications of health psychology in Europe, in particular the study of behaviour, health, illness and health care; promote exchange of information with organizations throughout the world so as to achieve these aims internationally. **Structure** Members' Meeting (annual); Executive Committee; Interest Groups (2). **Languages** English. **Staff** 0.50 FTE, paid. **Finance** Members' dues. **Activities** Events/ meetings; networking/liaising. **Events** *Annual Conference* 2021, *Scientific Meeting* 2020, *Annual Conference* Bratislava (Slovakia) 2020, *Annual Conference* Dubrovnik (Croatia) 2019, *Annual Conference* Galway (Ireland) 2018. **Publications** *Psychology and Health* (12 a year) – journal; *The European Health Psychologist* (6 a year) – official bulletin; *Health Psychology Review* (4 a year); *Health Psychology and Behavioral Medicine*; *Health Psychology Bulletin*. **Members** Full qualified psychologists in the field; affiliate subscriber non-psychologists who are qualified professionals in complementary fields; post-graduate students. Members (539) in 50 countries. Membership countries not specified. **Consultative Status** Consultative status granted from: *ECOSOC (#05331)* (Special). **IGO Relations** Associated with Department of Global Communications of the United Nations. [2021/XD3303/v/**D**]

♦ European Health Telematics Association (EHTEL) 07463

SG Av de Tervuren 168, Box 2, 1150 Brussels, Belgium. T. +3222301534. Fax +3222308440. E-mail: info@ehtel.eu.
URL: http://www.ehtel.eu/

History Dec 1998, as a 2-year project funded by *European Commission (EC, #06633)*. Initial project completed Nov 2000. Obtained legal status as international not for profit association Jun 2000. Officially commenced activities as an association, Sep 2001, Erlangen (Germany). Registered in accordance with Belgian law. EU Transparency Register: 615038313868-42. **Aims** Provide a multi-stakeholder platform for information, representation, networking and cooperation to support implementation of information and communication technology – *ICT* – in health and social care in Europe: eHealth; Telehealth; Telemedicine; Integrated Care. **Structure** General Meeting (annual); Board of Directors; Executive Committee; Stakeholder Groups; Task Forces; Permanent Secretariat, headed by Secretary General. **Languages** English, French, German. **Staff** 4.00 FTE, paid. **Finance** Members' dues. Co-funded by European projects. **Activities** Knowledge management/information dissemination; events/meetings; awareness raising; healthcare. **Events** *Joining the Dots Conference* Brussels (Belgium) 2019, *Annual Symposium* Brussels (Belgium) 2018, *WoHIT : HIMSS Europe World of Health IT Conference* Barcelona (Spain) 2017, *Annual Symposium* Brussels (Belgium) 2017, *WoHIT : HIMSS Europe World of Health IT Conference* Barcelona (Spain) 2016. **Publications** *The Navigator* (2-4 a year) – newsletter. Conference proceedings; briefing papers; presentations; position papers; studies and reports.
Members All constituencies with an interest in ICTS in health and social care public authorities; health professionals; health institutions; social care organizations; patients and citizens; health insurers; implementation agencies; industrials; academics; innovation agencies; dissemination organizations. Members in 22 countries:
Austria, Belgium, Croatia, Czechia, Denmark, Estonia, Finland, France, Germany, Greece, Hungary, Israel, Italy, Latvia, Luxembourg, Netherlands, Norway, Spain, Sweden, Switzerland, UK, USA.
NGO Relations Member of: *Health First Europe (HFE, #10881)*. [2020/XD8508/**D**]

♦ European Healthy Stadia Network (Healthy Stadia) 07464

Coordinator c/o Health Equalities Network, 151 Dale Street, Liverpool, L2 2JH, UK. T. +441512372686.
URL: http://www.healthystadia.eu/

History Inaugural meeting, May 2010, Dublin (Ireland). **Aims** Act as a European-wide communications and expertise resource concerning public health policy and practice in relation to *sports* stadia. **Structure** Management Group. Working Groups. **Finance** Part-funded by *World Heart Federation (WHF, #21562)*. **Events** *International Conference* London (UK) 2017, *Conference* Geneva (Switzerland) 2014, *Conference* Manchester (UK) 2013, *Conference* Liverpool (UK) 2009. **Publications** *Health Stadia E-Bulletin*.
Members National networks (7) in 7 countries:
Belgium, France, Georgia, Italy, Latvia, Spain, UK. [2017/XJ4889/**F**]

♦ European Hearing Instrument Manufacturers Association (EHIMA) 07465

Secretariat Herriotstrasse 1, 60528 Frankfurt-Main, Germany.
URL: http://www.ehima.com/

History 1985. Founded following meetings of hearing aid manufacturers at European level beginning 1983. Registration: Belgium; EU Transparency Register, No/ID: 34590331316-73. **Aims** Increase cooperation between hearing instrument manufacturers; represent common interests before the bodies of the European Union; encourage research in the field of hearing instruments. **Languages** English. **Staff** 4.00 FTE, paid. **Finance** Sources: members' dues. **Activities** Events/meetings. **Events** *The world of hearing* Brussels (Belgium) 1999.
Members Companies in 6 countries:
Austria, Denmark, Italy, Singapore, Switzerland, USA.
NGO Relations Member of (2): *Federation of European and International Associations Established in Belgium (FAIB, #09508)*; World Hearing Forum (WHF). Also links with national organizations. [2022.05.11/XD6566/**D**]

♦ European Heart House (see: #08536)

♦ European Heart and Lung Transplant Federation (EHLTF) 07466

Fédération européenne des greffés du coeur et des poumons (FEGCP) – Europäischer Verband der Herz- und Lungentransplantierten

Mailing Address Hôpital Erasme, Route de Lennik 808, 1070 Brussels, Belgium. E-mail: info@ ehltf.org.
Pres address not obtained.
URL: https://ehltf.org/

History 3 Jul 1994, Helsinki (Finland). Former names and other names: *European Heart Transplant Federation (EHTF)* – former (3 Jul 1994 to 13 Oct 2005); *Fédération européenne des greffés du coeur (FEGC)* – former (3 Jul 1994 to 13 Oct 2005). Registration: Crossroads Bank for Enterprises, No/ID: 0461.644.378, Start date: 16 Oct 1997, Belgium. **Aims** Promote *organ donation* and cooperation among national European heart and lung transplant patient associations; advance the interests of all European heart and lung transplant recipients. **Structure** General Assembly (annual); Board. **Languages** English, French. **Staff** None. **Finance** Sources: donations; members' dues; revenue from activities/projects; sale of products; subsidies. **Activities** Events/ meetings; knowledge management/information dissemination.
Members National federations or associations in 21 countries:
Austria, Belgium, Croatia, Denmark, Finland, France, Greece, Hungary, Ireland, Israel, Italy, Netherlands, Norway, Poland, Romania, Slovakia, Slovenia, Spain, Sweden, Switzerland, UK.
Provisional members in 2 countries:
Bulgaria, Lithuania.
NGO Relations Member of (1): *European Patients' Forum (EPF, #08172)*. [2022/XD5939/**D**]

♦ European Heart Network (EHN) 07467

Réseau européen du coeur

CEO Rue Montoyer 31, 1000 Brussels, Belgium. T. +3225129174. E-mail: info@ehnheart.org.
URL: http://www.ehnheart.org/

History 1986. Statutes adopted and formally established under the present name in 1993. Former names and other names: *International Heart Network (IHN)* – former. Registration: Banque-Carrefour des Entreprises, Belgium; EU Transparency Register, No/ID: 3606882168-35. **Aims** Play a leading role in prevention and reduction of cardiovascular diseases, in particular heart disease and stroke, so that they are no longer a major cause of premature death and disability throughout Europe. **Structure** General Assembly; Board. **Languages** English. **Staff** 4.50 FTE, paid. **Finance** Sources: members' dues. Supported by: *European Union (EU, #08967)*. **Activities** Advocacy/lobbying/activism; capacity building; events/meetings; knowledge management/information dissemination; networking/liaising; politics/policy/regulatory; research and development; research/ documentation. **Events** *Annual Meeting* Madrid (Spain) 2022, *Annual Meeting* 2021, *Annual Meeting* 2020, *Annual Meeting* Savelettri (Italy) 2019, *Annual Meeting* Lucerne (Switzerland) 2018. **Publications** Annual Report; position papers; reports, scientific reviews.

European Heart Rhythm
07468
alphabetic sequence excludes
For the complete listing, see Yearbook Online at

Members An umbrella organization (alliance) of heart foundations, associations and other concerned non-governmental organizations, throughout Europe, who share a common commitment to the prevention of cardiovascular disease. Organizations in 24 countries and territories:
Belgium, Bosnia-Herzegovina, Croatia, Denmark, Faeroe Is, Finland, Germany, Greece, Hungary, Iceland, Ireland, Israel, Italy, Lithuania, Netherlands, Portugal, Romania, Serbia, Slovenia, Spain, Sweden, Switzerland, Türkiye, UK.
NGO Relations Member of (6): *European Alliance for Cardiovascular Health (EACH, #05863)*; *European Chronic Disease Alliance (ECDA, #06548)*; *Federation of European and International Associations Established in Belgium (FAIB, #09508)*; *Framework Convention Alliance (FCA, #09981)*; *The NCD Alliance (NCDA, #16963)*; *World Heart Federation (WHF, #21562)*. Partner of (2): *European Public Health Alliance (EPHA, #08297)*; *Smoke Free Partnership (SFP, #19329)*. Also links with national organizations. [2022.05.05/XF1506/**F**]

♦ European Heart Rhythm Association (EHRA) 07468

Main Office ESC European Heart House, 2035 route des Colles, 06903 Sophia Antipolis, France. T. +33492947600, Fax +33492947601. E-mail: ehra@escardio.org.
URL: http://www.escardio.org/EHRA/
History Founded 2003, by merger of ESC Working Group on Cardiac Pacing and ESC Working Group on Arrhythmias. Registered branch of *European Society of Cardiology (ESC, #08536)*. **Aims** Improve quality of life and reduce sudden cardiac death by limiting the impact of heart rhythm disturbances. **Structure** Board; Committees (13). **Languages** English. **Activities** Events/meetings; training/education; certification/accreditation. **Events** *EHRA Congress* Barcelona (Spain) 2023, *EHRA Congress* Copenhagen (Denmark) 2022, *EHRA Congress* Sophia Antipolis (France) 2021, *EHRA Congress* Vienna (Austria) 2020, *EHRA Congress* Lisbon (Portugal) 2019. **Publications** *EUROPACE Journal* (12 a year).
Members Open to members from any country, by invitation. Members in 56 countries and territories:
Albania, Algeria, Armenia, Austria, Azerbaijan, Belarus, Belgium, Bosnia-Herzegovina, Bulgaria, Croatia, Cyprus, Czechia, Denmark, Egypt, Estonia, Finland, France, Georgia, Germany, Greece, Hungary, Iceland, Ireland, Israel, Italy, Kazakhstan, Kosovo, Kyrgyzstan, Latvia, Lebanon, Libya, Lithuania, Luxembourg, Malta, Moldova, Montenegro, Morocco, Netherlands, North Macedonia, Norway, Poland, Portugal, Romania, Russia, San Marino, Serbia, Slovakia, Slovenia, Spain, Sweden, Switzerland, Tunisia, Türkiye, UK, Ukraine, Uzbekistan. [2022/XJ3392/**E**]

- ♦ European Heart Transplant Federation / see European Heart and Lung Transplant Federation (#07466)
- ♦ European Heating Boilers Association (inactive)
- ♦ European Heating Oil Association / see European Liquid Heating Fuels Association (#07701)

♦ European Heat Pump Association (EHPA) 07469

Office Manager Renewable Energy House, Rue d'Arlon 63-67, 1040 Brussels, Belgium. T. +3224001017. Fax +3224001018. E-mail: info@ehpa.org.
SG address not obtained.
URL: http://www.ehpa.org/
History Feb 2000. Founded as a *European Economic Interest Grouping (EEIG, #06960)*. Registration: Banque-Carrefour des Entreprises, No/ID: 0599.823.551, Start date: 2 Mar 2015, Belgium; EU Transparency Register, No/ID: 23643001178-02, Start date: 18 Feb 2009. **Aims** Promote awareness and proper deployment of heat pump technology in the European market place for residential, commercial and industrial applications. **Structure** General Assembly (annual); Board; Departments; Secretariat. Committees; Working Groups; Task Forces. **Languages** English. **Staff** 10.00 FTE, paid. **Finance** Sources: members' dues; revenue from activities/projects. **Activities** Certification/accreditation; events/meetings; politics/policy/regulatory; research and development; training/education. **Events** *European Heat Pump Forum* Brussels (Belgium) 2022, *Decarb Cities Conference* Vienna (Austria) 2022, *European Heat Pump Forum* Brussels (Belgium) 2021, *European Heat Pump Forum* Brussels (Belgium) 2020, *Decarb Cities Forum* Vienna (Austria) 2020. **Publications** *European Heat Pump Market and Statistics Report* (annual). **Information Services** *EHPA Quality Label* – database; *EUCERT Installer* – database; *Heat Pump Keymark* – database.
Members Full: commercial enterprises; research institutes, governmental organizations and universities; interest groups and national associations. Members in 26 countries:
Austria, Belgium, Bulgaria, Croatia, Czechia, Denmark, Estonia, Finland, France, Germany, Greece, Hungary, Ireland, Italy, Liechtenstein, Lithuania, Netherlands, Norway, Poland, Portugal, Slovakia, Slovenia, Spain, Sweden, Switzerland, UK.
Included in the above, 1 organization listed in this Yearbook:
European Partnership for Energy and the Environment (EPEE, #08157).
NGO Relations Member of (5): *European Partnership for Energy and the Environment (EPEE, #08157)*; *European Policy Centre (EPC, #08240)*; *Federation of European and International Associations Established in Belgium (FAIB, #09508)*; *Industry4Europe (#11181)*; *World Alliance for Efficient Solutions.*
[2022.02.23/XD8715/y/**D**]

♦ European Hedgehog Research Group (EHRG) 07470

Contact People's Trust for Endangered Species, 3 Cloister's House, 8 Battersea Park Road, London, SW8 4BG, UK.
History Apr 1996, Arendal (Norway), during the First International Hedgehog Workshop. **Aims** Provide a forum for scientists studying any aspect of European hedgehog biology or ecology, including those involved in research into the care and rehabilitation of injured or sick wild hedgehogs. **Structure** Informal network of hedgehog researchers and welfare workers. **Languages** English. **Staff** Voluntary. **Finance** Sponsorship and symposium fees cover meeting costs. **Events** *International Symposium* London (UK) 2019, *International symposium* Wageningen (Netherlands) 2008, *Symposium* Münster (Germany) 2004, *International symposium / Symposium* Rimini (Italy) 2002, *International symposium* Lund (Sweden) 2000. **Publications** Conference proceedings.
Members Full in 14 countries:
Austria, Denmark, Estonia, Germany, Italy, Latvia, Lithuania, Netherlands, New Zealand, Norway, Sweden, Switzerland, UK, USA. [2018.06.13/XE3807/**E**]

♦ European Helicobacter and Microbiota Study Group (EHMSG) 07471

Sec Hôpital Pellegrin, Place Amélie-Raba-Léon, 33076 Bordeaux CEDEX, France. T. +33556795977. Fax +33556796018.
URL: http://www.helicobacter.org/
History 1987, Copenhagen (Denmark). Former names and other names: *European Helicobacter Pylori Study Group (EHPSG)* – former; *European Helicobacter Study Group (EHSG)* – former. Registration: Start date: 1997, End date: 2018, France; Start date: 2019, Austria. **Aims** Promote research in the field of Helicobacter *bacteria* and *digestive* microbiota; disseminate medical, scientific and technical information in order to promote *health* and decrease the burden of digestive *diseases*. **Structure** Council; Bureau. **Languages** English. **Staff** No permanent staff. **Finance** Sources: sponsorship. Annual budget: 30,000 EUR. **Activities** Events/meetings; training/education. **Events** *Annual Workshop* Antwerp (Belgium) 2023, *Annual Workshop* Glasgow (UK) 2022, *International Workshop on Pathogenesis and Host Response in Helicobacter Infections* Helsingør (Denmark) 2022, *Annual Workshop* 2021, *International Workshop on Pathogenesis and Host Response in Helicobacter Infections* Helsingør (Denmark) 2021. **Publications** *Helicobacter*; *Microbiota in Health and Disease*; *The Year in Helicobacter* – special issue.
Members Individuals in 16 countries:
Austria, Belgium, Denmark, Finland, France, Germany, Greece, Ireland, Italy, Latvia, Netherlands, Portugal, Serbia, Spain, Sweden, UK.
Corresponding fellows in 9 countries and territories:
Brazil, China, India, Israel, Japan, Korea Rep, Russia, Taiwan, Thailand.
NGO Relations Member of (1): *United European Gastroenterology (UEG, #20506).* [2022.05.03/XF2802/v/**F**]

- ♦ European Helicobacter Pylori Study Group / see European Helicobacter and Microbiota Study Group (#07471)
- ♦ European Helicobacter Study Group / see European Helicobacter and Microbiota Study Group (#07471)

♦ European Helicopter Association (EHA) 07472

Association européenne des hélicoptères
Exec Dir Altenbergerstr 23, 50668 Cologne, Germany. T. +491794718406.
URL: http://www.eha-heli.eu/
History 1 Jan 1981. Founded following proposal, Sep 1980, London (UK), of a meeting of European helicopter operators. Registration: EU Transparency Register, No/ID: 154332612396-62. **Aims** Represent the problems and concerns of rotorcraft operators at EU institutions, giving priority to safety operations, reduction in bureaucracy, prohibitive rules and regulations. **Structure** General Assembly; Board of Governors; Executive Board; Working Groups and Workstreams. **Languages** English. **Staff** 2.00 FTE, paid. **Activities** Advocacy/lobbying/activism; events/meetings; networking/liaising; standards/guidelines. **Events** *European Rotors Safety Conference* Friedrichshafen (Germany) 2021, *European Rotors Safety Conference* Friedrichshafen (Germany) 2020, *Annual Conference* Barcelona (Spain) 2013, *Symposium / Annual Symposium* Bristol (UK) 2002, *Symposium* The Hague (Netherlands) 2000. **Publications** *The Social and Economic Value of European Helicopter Operations – Challenges Ahead* (2016).
Members National helicopter associations, operators, main leading OEMs, suppliers and service providers in 11 countries:
Austria, Belgium, France, Germany, Italy, Luxembourg, Norway, Spain, Sweden, Switzerland, UK.
IGO Relations Cooperates with (2): *European Union Aviation Safety Agency (EASA, #08978)*; *International Civil Aviation Organization (ICAO, #12581)*. **NGO Relations** Memorandum of Understanding with (1): *Helicopter Association International (HAI)*. Instrumental in setting up (1): *International Federation of Helicopter Associations (IFHA, #13444)*. Also links with helicopter representative bodies outside Europe. [2021.03.01/XD1110/**D**]

♦ European Hematology Association (EHA) 07473

Executive Office Koninginnegracht 12b, 2514 AA The Hague, Netherlands. T. +31703020099. E-mail: info@ehaweb.org – communication@ehaweb.org.
URL: http://www.ehaweb.org/
History Dec 1991, Brussels (Belgium). Originally registered in accordance with Belgian law. Former names and other names: *European Haematology Association* – former. Registration: Start date: 2006, Netherlands; EU Transparency Register, No/ID: 91666778136-14, Start date: 23 Feb 2012. **Aims** Promote excellence in patient care, research and education in hematology. **Structure** Board; Executive Board; Committees; Units. **Languages** English. **Finance** Members' dues. **Activities** Training/education; financial and/or material support; events/meetings; networking/liaising; advocacy/lobbying/activism. **Events** *Congress* Frankfurt-Main (Germany) 2023, *Joint European CAR T-cell Meeting* Rotterdam (Netherlands) 2023, *Congress* Vienna (Austria) 2022, *Congress* The Hague (Netherlands) 2021, *Scientific Meeting on Immunotherapy for Hematological Disorders* Rotterdam (Netherlands) 2020. **Publications** *HemaSphere* – journal.
Members Full; Junior; Health Care Affiliated Professional; Emeritus. Active members in 68 countries and territories:
Algeria, Argentina, Australia, Austria, Belarus, Belgium, Bulgaria, Canada, Chile, Costa Rica, Croatia, Cyprus, Czechia, Denmark, Egypt, Estonia, Finland, France, Germany, Greece, Guadeloupe, Hong Kong, Hungary, Iceland, India, Indonesia, Ireland, Israel, Italy, Japan, Kenya, Korea Rep, Kuwait, Lebanon, Lithuania, Luxembourg, Malaysia, Malta, Mexico, Morocco, Netherlands, Norway, Pakistan, Peru, Poland, Portugal, Puerto Rico, Romania, Russia, Saudi Arabia, Serbia, Singapore, Slovakia, South Africa, Spain, Sweden, Switzerland, Tanzania UR, Thailand, Togo, Trinidad-Tobago, Tunisia, Türkiye, UK, Ukraine, United Arab Emirates, Uruguay, USA.
IGO Relations Cooperates with: *European Medicines Agency (EMA, #07767)*. **NGO Relations** Member of (4): *Biomedical Alliance in Europe (#03251)*; *European Alliance for Personalised Medicine (EAPM, #05878)*; *European Cancer Organisation (ECO, #06432)*; *European Public Health Alliance (EPHA, #08297)*. Cooperates with (9): *CML Advocacy Network (#04040)*; *European Cancer Patient Coalition (ECPC, #06433)*; *European Federation of Associations of Patients with Haemochromatosis (EFAPH, #07056)*; *International Patient Organization for Primary Immunodeficiencies (IPOPI, #14533)*; ITP Association; *Lymphoma Coalition (LC, #16535)*; *MDS Alliance (#16608)*; *Myeloma Patients Europe (MPE, #16924)*; *Thalassaemia International Federation (#20139).* [2021/XD3631/v/**D**]

♦ European HEMS and Air Ambulance Committee (EHAC) 07474

Contact c/o DRF Luftrettung, Rita-Maiburg-Strasse 2, 70974 Filderstadt, Germany.
Contact Schillerstrasse 53, 80336 Munich, Germany. E-mail: contact@ehac.eu.
URL: http://www.ehac.eu/
History 25 Feb 2000, Munich (Germany). Statutes most recently revised, Jun 2018. Former names and other names: *European HEMS and Air Rescue Committee* – former. Registration: Bavaria District Court, No/ID: VR16806, Start date: 15 Mar 2000, Germany, Munich. **Aims** Promote education, science and research in the field of *life-saving* by *helicopter emergency* medical services (HEMS) and the international repatriation of *patients* by dedicated air ambulances. **Structure** General Assembly (annual); Board; Advisory Council; Permanent Expert Committees (4); ad hoc Expert Committees. **Languages** English, German. **Finance** Sources: members' dues. **Activities** Capacity building; events/meetings; humanitarian/emergency aid; training/education. **Events** *AirMed World Congress* Salzburg (Austria) 2022, *Annual General Meeting* Filderstadt (Germany) 2020, *EHAC Symposium and Annual General Meeting* Budapest (Hungary) 2019, *AIRMED World Congress* Warsaw (Poland) 2018, *EHAC Symposium and Annual General Meeting* Baden Baden (Germany) 2016.
Members Full; Associate. Members in 16 countries:
Austria, Canada, Denmark, Finland, Germany, Hungary, Ireland, Italy, Luxembourg, Netherlands, Norway, Poland, Slovakia, Sweden, Switzerland, UK.
IGO Relations Links with national civil aviation authorities in Europe. [2022.05.05/XE4667/**E**]

- ♦ European HEMS and Air Rescue Committee / see European HEMS and Air Ambulance Committee (#07474)
- ♦ European Hepato-Pancreato-Biliary Association / see European-African Hepato-Pancreato-Biliary Association (#05840)
- ♦ European Herbal Infusions Association (inactive)
- ♦ European Herbal Practitioners Association / see European Herbal and Traditional Medicine Practitioners Association (#07475)

♦ European Herbal and Traditional Medicine Practitioners Association (EHTPA) 07475

Contact c/o RCHM, Office 3, 47 St Giles Street, Norwich, NR2 1JR, UK. T. +447779414099.
URL: http://www.ehtpa.eu/
History 1993, UK, as a national association. Became a European association, 1994, when affiliated association formed *European Herbal Practitioners Association (EHPA)*. **Aims** Foster unity within the herbal profession; promote availability of professional herbal treatment; raise standards of training and practice within the profession. **Structure** Accreditation Board. **Languages** English. **Activities** Advocacy/lobbying/activism; certification/accreditation. **Publications** *Frankincense* (irregular) – newsletter.
Members Full organizations (registers of qualified herbal practitioners) in 1 country:
UK.
Associate members in 3 countries:
Denmark, Ireland, Italy.
NGO Relations *EUROCAM (#05653).* [2019.07.06/XD7204/**D**]

♦ European Hereditary Tumour Group (EHTG) 07476

Secretariat c/o Integrity Intl Events Ltd, The Coach House, 7 St Alban's Road, Edinburgh, EH9 2PA, UK. T. +441316246040. E-mail: ehtg@integrity-events.com.
URL: http://ehtg.org/
History Initiated 2006, as *Mallorca Group*. Transformed under current title 2016. **Aims** Conduct collaborative studies; establish guidelines; set up databases. **Finance** Members' dues. **Activities** Research/documentation; events/meetings; standards/guidelines. **Events** *Meeting* Vilnius (Lithuania) 2020, *Meeting* Barcelona (Spain) 2019, *Meeting* Nice (France) 2018, *Meeting* Florence (Italy) 2017, *Meeting* Palma (Spain) 2016. **NGO Relations** *European Cancer Organisation (ECO, #06432)*; *European Society of Coloproctology (ESCP, #08556).*
[2021/XM6721/**D**]

♦ European Heritage Alliance 3.3 07477

Contact Europa Nostra, Rue de Trèves 67, 1040 Brussels, Belgium. T. +3224007702. E-mail: bxl@europanostra.org.
URL: http://europeanheritagealliance.eu/
History Jun 2011, Amsterdam (Netherlands). Launched at European Heritage Congress, organized by *Europa Nostra (#05767)*. Name of organization refers to article 3.3 of the consolidated version of *Treaty of Lisbon (2007)* of *European Union (EU, #08967)*. **Aims** Promote the untapped potential of Europe's heritage, cultural and natural, immovable and movable. **Finance** Supported by: *European Commission (EC, #06633)* (Creative Europe).

Members European and international networks and organizations active in the field of cultural heritage (49):
- *Architects Council of Europe (ACE, #01086)*;
- *Blue Shield International (BSI, #03286)*;
- *Civilscape (#03966)*;
- *ENCATC (#05452)*;
- *EUROCITIES (#05662)*;
- *Europa Nostra (#05767)*;
- *Europeana Foundation (#05839)*;
- *European Association Architectural Heritage Restoration Firms (#05942)*;
- *European Association for Heritage Interpretation (Interpret Europe, #06067)*;
- *European Association of Archaeologists (EAA, #05940)*;
- *European Association of Historic Towns and Regions (Heritage Europe, #06068)*;
- *European Association of History Educators (EUROCLIO, #06069)*;
- *European Confederation of Conservator-Restorers' Organisations (ECCO, #06701)*;
- *European Council for the Village and Small Town (ECOVAST, #06848)*;
- *European Council of Spatial Planners (ECTP-CEU, #06843)*;
- *European Cultural Foundation (ECF, #06868)*;
- *European Cultural Tourism Network (ECTN, #06871)*;
- *European Federation of Associations of Industrial and Technical Heritage (EFAITH, #07053)*;
- *European Federation of Fortified Sites (EFFORTS, #07127)*;
- *European Historic Houses Association (EHH, #07491)*;
- *European Historic Thermal Towns Association (EHTTA, #07492)*;
- *European Landowners' Organization (ELO, #07639)*;
- *European Maritime Heritage (EMH, #07741)*;
- *European Museum Academy (EMA, #07835)*;
- *European Museum Forum (EMF, #07836)*;
- *European Network for Conservation/Restoration Education (ENCoRE, #07883)*;
- *European Network of Cultural Centres in Historic Monuments (ACCR)*;
- *European Route of Industrial Heritage (ERIH, #08409)*;
- *European Travel Commission (ETC, #08943)*;
- *European Walled Towns (EWT, #09079)*;
- *FEDECRAIL – European Federation of Museum and Tourist Railways (#09284)*;
- *Fédération Européenne pour les Métiers du Patrimoine Bâti (FEMP, #09576)*;
- *Future for Religious Heritage (FRH, #10051)*;
- *IFLA Europe (#11103)*;
- *International Committee for the Conservation of the Industrial Heritage (TICCIH, #12754)*;
- *International Council of Museums (ICOM, #13051)*;
- *International Council on Monuments and Sites (ICOMOS, #13049)*;
- *International National Trusts Organisation (INTO, #14214)*;
- *International Society of City and Regional Planners (ISOCARP, #15012)*;
- *Mad'in Europe*;
- *MICHAEL Culture Association (#16742)*;
- *Network of European Museum Organizations (NEMO, #17024)*;
- *Network of European Regions for a Sustainable and Competitive Tourism (NECSTouR, #17028)*;
- *Organization of World Heritage Cities (OWHC, #17891)*;
- *PERSPECTIV – Association of Historic Theatres in Europe (PERSPECTIV, #18335)*;
- *Réseau Art Nouveau Network (RANN, #18867)*;
- *South East European Heritage Network (SEE Heritage Network, #19814)*;
- *Trans Europe Halles – A Network of Independent Cultural Centres (TEH, #20211)*;
- *Union internationale des architectes (UIA, #20419)* (Workgroup Heritage Region 1). [2020/AA0955/y/**F**]

♦ European Heritage Association (internationally oriented national body)

♦ European Heritage Heads Forum (EHHF) 07478

Forum Européen des Directeurs du Patrimoine

Admin Sec/Editor Place Saint-Géry 23, 1000 Brussels, Belgium. T. +3225024424. E-mail: secretariat@ehhf.eu.
URL: http://www.ehhf.eu/

History 2006, London (UK). Founded as an informal network of heads of the European state heritage authorities. Registration: EU Transparency Register, No/ID: 045689014322-13, Start date: 2 Sep 2014. **Aims** Provide a forum for information and experience exchange about management of the historic environment in the 21st century. **Structure** Meeting of Heads (annual); Standing Committees; Permanent Secretariat, located in Brussels (Belgium). *European Heritage Legal Forum (EHLF, #07479)*. **Languages** English, French. **Staff** 1.00 FTE, paid. **Finance** Sources: meeting proceeds. **Activities** Events/meetings; research and development. **Events** *Annual Meeting* Edinburgh (UK) 2022, *Annual Meeting* Tallinn (Estonia) 2021, *Annual Meeting* Tallinn (Estonia) 2020, *Annual Meeting* Stockholm (Sweden) 2019, *Annual Meeting* Luxembourg (Luxembourg) 2018. **Publications** *EHHF E-Newsletter* (2 a year). News articles. **Members** Not a membership organization. [2022.10.19/XJ2316/**F**]

♦ European Heritage Legal Forum (EHLF) 07479

Chair c/o Bavarian State Monument Conservation Office (BLfD), Hofgraben 4, 80539 Munich, Germany. T. +49892114214.
URL: https://www.ehhf.eu/ehlf/

History Sep 2008, Brussels (Belgium). Established following annual meeting of *European Heritage Heads Forum (EHHF, #07478)*, Copenhagen (Denmark). Registration: EU Transparency Register, No/ID: 16807358674-96, Start date: 26 Apr 2012. **Aims** Ensure that relevant information on the development and potential consequences of proposed legislation developed by the European Union is circulated in a timely manner to heritage state authorities. **Structure** Chair; Secretariat. **Activities** Guidance/assistance/consulting; monitoring/evaluation. Active in all member countries. **Events** *Annual Meeting* Tallinn (Estonia) 2021. [2021.05.19/XM8942/**F**]

♦ European Hernia Society (EHS) 07480

Groupe de recherche européen sur la paroi abdominale (GREPA)

Main Office c/o Grupo Pacifico, Calle Castelló 128, 7o piso, 28006 Madrid, Spain. E-mail: secretariatehs@pacifico-meetings.com.
URL: https://www.europeanherniasociety.eu/

History 15 Jun 1979, Bobigny (France). Former names and other names: *Groupe de recherche et d'étude de la paroi abdominale* – former (15 Jun 1979 to Jun 1998); *Group for Research and Study of the Abdominal Wall* – former (15 Jun 1979 to Jun 1998). Registration: France. **Aims** Study all anatomic, physiologic, pathologic and therapeutic problems related to the *abdominal* wall. **Structure** Board (meets every 2 months); Advisory Boards (5). **Languages** English. **Staff** 2.00 FTE, paid. **Finance** Members' dues. Other sources: sponsorship; auspices for courses or events. **Activities** Research and development; publishing activities; liaising/networking; events/meetings; standards/guidelines. **Events** *Annual Congress* Manchester (UK) 2022, *Annual Meeting* Copenhagen (Denmark) 2021, *International Hernia Congress* Denmark 2021, *Annual Congress* Barcelona (Spain) 2020, *Annual Congress* Hamburg (Germany) 2019. **Publications** *Hernia* – journal.
Members Surgeons, intensive care specialists, anatomists, physiologists and scientific investigators engaged in the study of the abdominal wall. Members in 38 countries:
Australia, Austria, Belgium, Bosnia-Herzegovina, Bulgaria, Canada, Czechia, Denmark, Ecuador, Finland, France, Germany, Greece, Hungary, Iran Islamic Rep, Ireland, Israel, Italy, Japan, Lithuania, Netherlands, Norway, Poland, Portugal, Romania, Russia, Saudi Arabia, Serbia, Slovakia, Slovenia, South Africa, Spain, Sweden, Switzerland, Türkiye, UK, Ukraine, USA. [2021/XD6556/**D**]

♦ European Herpetological Society 07481

Société européenne d'herpétologie – Societas Europaea Herpetologica (SEH)

Gen Sec Ctr Studi Faunistica dei Vertebrati, Museo Civico di Storia Naturale, Corso Venezia 55, 20121 Milan MI, Italy. T. +393408229624. Fax +3929309734.
URL: http://www.seh-herpetology.org/

History 10 Sep 1979, Bonn (Germany). 10-11 Sep 1979, Bonn (Germany FR), by herpetologists from 8 European countries. Registered 20 May 1980, Bonn. **Aims** Conduct and promote scientific research and nature *conservation* in the field of herpetology; ensure close collaboration among herpetologists, especially those in Europe; support efforts directed towards the conservation of *amphibians* and *reptiles* and their habitats and mapping of Palaearctic species. **Structure** Ordinary General Meeting (every 2 years). Council (meets at least annually), consisting of President, Vice-President, General Secretary, Vice-Secretary, Treasurer, Vice Treasurer, 1st, 2nd and 3rd Co-Editors. Conservation Committee Chairman; Mapping Committee Chairman. **Languages** English. **Staff** Voluntary. **Finance** Members' dues. Sales of books. Budget (annual): euro 39,000. **Activities** Projects; meeting activities. **Events** *Biennial General Meeting* Milan (Italy) 2019, *Biennial General Meeting* Salzburg (Austria) 2017, *Biennial General Meeting* Luxembourg (Luxembourg) 2011, *Biennial general meeting / General Meeting* Kusadasi (Turkey) 2009, *Biennial general meeting / General Meeting* Porto (Portugal) 2007. **Publications** *Amphibia-Reptilia* (4 a year) – journal. *Atlas of Amphibians and Reptiles of Europe* (1997). Ordinary General Meeting proceedings; books.
Members Ordinary; Corporate; Affiliate; Lifetime; without journal; online subscribers; Honorary. Organizations and individuals (nearly 350) in 38 countries:
Argentina, Armenia, Austria, Belgium, Brazil, Bulgaria, Chile, Croatia, Czechia, Denmark, Estonia, Finland, France, Germany, Hungary, Iran Islamic Rep, Israel, Italy, Japan, Luxembourg, Morocco, Netherlands, Nigeria, North Macedonia, Poland, Portugal, Romania, Russia, Serbia, Singapore, Slovenia, Spain, Sweden, Switzerland, Türkiye, UK, Ukraine, USA.
IGO Relations Observer status at: *Standing Committee to the Bern Convention on the Conservation of European Wildlife and Natural Habitats (#19949)*. **NGO Relations** Member of: *European Habitats Forum (EHF, #07443)*; *International Union for Conservation of Nature and Natural Resources (IUCN, #15766)* and its Species Survival Commission (SSC). [2014/XD8170/**D**]

♦ European Hide Council (inactive)

♦ European Hidradenitis Suppurativa Foundation (EHSF) 07482

Pres Dept Dermatology, Dessau Medical Ctr, Auenweg 38, 06847 Dessau, Germany. T. +493405014000.
URL: http://www.ehsf.eu/

History 2012, Prague (Czechia). Founded as an independent sister-organization of the (USA) *Hidradenitis Suppurativa Foundation (HSF)*. Registration: Germany. **Aims** Raise funds for the promotion of research projects in the field of the disease hidradenitis suppurativa. **Structure** General Assembly; Executive Board. **Languages** English. **Staff** None paid. **Finance** Members' dues. Other sources: donations. **Activities** Events/meetings; research/documentation. **Events** *Conference* Florence (Italy) 2023, *Conference* 2022, *Conference* 2021, *Conference* Athens (Greece) 2020, *Conference* Wroclaw (Poland) 2019. **Publications** Abstracts.
Members Full in 31 countries:
Australia, Belgium, Brazil, Bulgaria, Canada, Chile, China, Denmark, France, Germany, Greece, Hungary, Iceland, Iran Islamic Rep, Ireland, Israel, Italy, Japan, Korea Rep, Lithuania, Malta, Netherlands, Norway, Poland, Portugal, Romania, Spain, Sweden, Switzerland, UK, USA.
IGO Relations None. **NGO Relations** *European Academy of Dermatology and Venereology (EADV, #05788)*. [2022/XM5613/f/**F**]

♦ European Higher Education Area (EHEA) 07483

Secretariat Bologna Follow-Up Group, Min éducation nat – enseignement – recherche, DG enseignement supérieur et insertion professionnelle, 1 rue Descartees, 75231 Paris CEDEX 5, France. T. +33155558090. E-mail: secretariat@ehea.info.
URL: http://www.ehea.info/

History Set up as a voluntary process, 1999, Bologna (Italy), following signature of the *Bologna Declaration*. Launched Mar 2010. **Aims** Through Bologna Process: strengthen competitiveness and attractiveness of European higher education; foster student mobility and employability through introduction of a system based on undergraduate and postgraduate studies with easily readable programmes and degrees. **Structure** Bologna Follow-Up Group (BFUG), consisting of representatives of all members and *European Commission (EC, #06633)*, with *UNESCO (#20322)*, *Council of Europe (CE, #04881)*, *European University Association (EUA, #09027)*, *European Association of Institutions of Higher Education (EURASHE, #06086)*, *European Students' Union (ESU, #08848)*, *Education International (EI, #05371)* and *BUSINESSEUROPE (#03381)* as consultative members, and co-chaired by country holding EU Presidency and a non-EU country (rotating every 6 months), with country organizing next Ministerial Conference as Vice-Chair. Board, comprising Chairs double Troika (outgoing, present and incoming Chairs), Vice-Chairs, EC and 4 consultative members. Secretariat, provided by country hosting next Ministerial Conference. **Languages** English. **Events** *Bologna Process Follow-Up Group meeting* Helsinki (Finland) 2019, *Bologna Process Ministerial Conference* Paris (France) 2018, *Bologna Process Ministerial Conference* Yerevan (Armenia) 2015, *Bologna Process Ministerial Conference* Bucharest (Romania) 2012, *Bologna Process Ministerial Conference* Budapest (Hungary) / Vienna (Austria) 2010.
Members States/Regions (49):
Albania, Andorra, Armenia, Austria, Azerbaijan, Belarus, Belgium/Flemish Region, Belgium/Wallonia Region, Bosnia-Herzegovina, Bulgaria, Croatia, Cyprus, Czechia, Denmark, Estonia, Finland, France, Georgia, Germany, Greece, Holy See, Hungary, Iceland, Ireland, Italy, Kazakhstan, Latvia, Liechtenstein, Lithuania, Luxembourg, Malta, Moldova, Montenegro, Netherlands, North Macedonia, Norway, Poland, Portugal, Romania, Russia, Serbia, Slovakia, Slovenia, Spain, Sweden, Switzerland, Türkiye, UK, Ukraine.
Regional entity:
European Commission (EC, #06633).
Consultative members (8):
BUSINESSEUROPE (#03381); *Council of Europe (CE, #04881)*; *Education International (EI, #05371)*; *European Association for Quality Assurance in Higher Education (ENQA, #06183)*; *European Association of Institutions of Higher Education (EURASHE, #06086)*; *European Students' Union (ESU, #08848)*; *European University Association (EUA, #09027)*; *UNESCO (#20322)*. [2018/XJ7531/y/**F***]

♦ European Higher Engineering and Technical Professionals Association (EurEta) 07484

Association européenne des professions supérieures d'ingénieurs et de la technique – Europäischer Verband Höherer Berufe des Ingenieurwesens und der Technik

SG 70 Coudenberg, 1000 Brussels, Belgium. T. +3225114439. Fax +3225110124. E-mail: info@eureta.org.
Pres c/o ABB Technikerschule, 5400 Baden AG, Switzerland. T. +41585854249. Fax +41585853668.
URL: http://www.eureta.org/

History 10 May 1993. Registered in accordance with Swiss Civil Code. **Aims** Set European qualification standards for higher engineering and technical professionals; represent these professionals and their official national organizations on European and worldwide levels; keep a European Register according to the level 4 set by the EU directives for those professionals who need registration. **Structure** General Assembly; Board; Registration Committee; Policy Committee; General Secretariat. **Languages** English. **Staff** Voluntary. **Finance** Members' dues. **Activities** Standards/guidelines; networking/liaising; knkowledge management/information dissemination. **Members** National organizations and representations in EU countries. Membership countries not specified. **IGO Relations** *European Commission (EC, #06633)*. **NGO Relations** Associate member of: *Société européenne pour la formation des ingénieurs (SEFI, #19462)*. [2016.07.27/XD5658/t/**D**]

♦ European High Level Group on Nuclear Safety and Waste Management / see European Nuclear Safety Regulators Group (#08058)

♦ European High Performance Computing Joint Undertaking (EuroHPC JU) 07485

Exec Dir Drosbach Bldg (DRB), Wing E – 1st floor, Rue Guillaume Kroll 12E, L-2920 Luxembourg, Luxembourg. T. +35228124500. E-mail: info@eurohpc-ju.europa.eu.
URL: https://eurohpc-ju.europa.eu/

History 2018. A Public-Private Partnership between *European Commission (EC, #06633)* and the industry. **Aims** Boost Europe's scientific excellence and industrial strength, supporting the digital transformation of the European economy while ensuring its technological sovereignty. **Structure** Governing Board; Industrial and Scientific Advisory Board. **Finance** Sources: contributions. EU long-term budget; Multiannual Financial Framework (MFF 2021-2027); contributions from participating countries and private members. Annual budget: 1,000,000,000 EUR.
Members Public members in 32 countries:
Austria, Belgium, Bulgaria, Croatia, Cyprus, Czechia, Denmark, Estonia, Finland, France, Germany, Greece, Hungary, Iceland, Ireland, Italy, Latvia, Lithuania, Luxembourg, Malta, Netherlands, North Macedonia, Norway, Poland, Portugal, Romania, Serbia, Slovakia, Slovenia, Spain, Sweden, Türkiye.
European Union (EU, #08967).
Private members include representatives of 3 organizations listed in this Yearbook:

Big Data Value Association (BDVA, #03232); European Quantum Industry Consortium (QuIC, #08315); European Technology Platform for High Performance Computing (ETP4HPC, #08889). **NGO Relations** Member of (1): *EU Agencies Network (EUAN, #05564).* [2022.07.05/AA1427/**E**]

♦ European High Pressure Research Group (EHPRG) 07486

Groupe européen de recherches sur les hautes pressions

Sec LENS – Euro Lab for Non-Linear Spectroscopy, Via Nello Carrara 1, 50019 Sesto Fiorentino FI, Italy. E-mail: secretary@ehprg.org.
Chairman Labo de Chimie Théorique (UPMC), Tour 12-13, Bureau 420, Univ P&M Curie, CC137 – 4 place Jussieu, 75252 Paris CEDEX 5, France. E-mail: chairman@ehprg.org.
URL: http://www.ehprg.org/

History May 1963, Harlow (UK). Registration: RNA, No/ID: W751231102, Start date: 15 Oct 2015, France. **Aims** Promote high pressure research in the fields of materials science and *physics*, technology, chemistry, mineralogy, biology, food science and astronomy. **Structure** General Assembly (annual); Organizing Committee. **Languages** English. **Staff** None. **Finance** Sources: members' dues. Annual budget: 1,500 GBP. **Activities** Events/meetings. **Events** *Annual Meeting* Thessaloniki (Greece) 2025, *Annual Meeting* Jerusalem (Israel) 2024, *Annual Meeting* Edinburgh (UK) 2023, *Annual Meeting* Uppsala (Sweden) 2022, *Annual Meeting* Edinburgh (UK) 2021.
Members Organizing Committee members in 23 countries:
Belgium, Czech Rep, Denmark, Estonia, Finland, France, Germany, Greece, Hungary, Ireland, Italy, Netherlands, Norway, Poland, Portugal, Russia, Slovenia, Spain, Sweden, Switzerland, Türkiye, UK, Ukraine.
NGO Relations Member of (1): *European Physical Society (EPS, #08207).* [2022.11.03/XD4281/v/**F**]

♦ European High Temperature Nuclear Power Stations Society (inactive)

♦ European High Temperature Reactor Technology Network (HTR-TN) 07487

Contact Joint Research Centre, European Commission, JRC Information and Public Relations Unit, SDME 10/78, Rue de la Loi 200, 1049 Brussels, Belgium. T. +3222957624. Fax +3222996322.
URL: https://odin.jrc.ec.europa.eu/htr-tn/

History 2000. **Structure** Steering Committee. **Activities** Organizes *International Conference on High Temperature Reactor Technology (HTR).* **Events** *International Topical Meeting on High Temperature Reactor Technology* Tokyo (Japan) 2012, *International topical meeting on high temperature reactor technology / Conference* Prague (Czech Rep) 2010, *Conference* Washington, DC (USA) 2008, *Conference* Johannesburg (South Africa) 2006, *International topical meeting on high-temperature reactor technology* Johannesburg (South Africa) 2006. **IGO Relations** *Joint Research Centre (JRC, #16147).* [2009/XF6556/**F**]

♦ European Hildegard Society (unconfirmed)

♦ European Hip Society (EHS) 07488

SG address not obtained.
URL: http://www.european-hip-society.org/

History 17 Oct 1992, Hamburg (Germany). Registration: Austria. **Aims** Provide a forum for the discussion of research, advances in clinical practice and the results of predominantly surgical procedures of all types relating to the hip joint. **Structure** General Assembly (annually); Executive Committee. **Languages** English. **Staff** 1.00 FTE, paid. **Finance** No official funding. **Events** *Congress* Lille (France) 2021, *Congress* Lille (France) 2020, *Congress* The Hague (Netherlands) 2018, *International Meeting of Hip Surgery in Young Adults* Madrid (Spain) 2017, *Meeting* Vienna (Austria) 2017. **Publications** *Hip International* – official publication. **Members** Full; International; Young; Emeritus; Honorary; Companion. Membership open to orthopaedic surgeons or other medical doctors interested in hip problems practising in Europe. Membership countries not specified. [2021.06.23/XD4780/**D**]

♦ European Histamine Research Society (EHRS) 07489

Pres Dept Pharmacology, Medical School, Natl and Kapodistrian Univ of Athens, M Asias 75, 115 27 Athens, Greece. T. +302107462575. Fax +302107462554. E-mail: ehrspresident@med.uoa.gr.
URL: http://www.ehrs.org.uk/

History Founded 1972, as *Histamine Club.* **Aims** Promote knowledge and research within all aspects of histamine and related fields. **Structure** Members meet once a year (in May); Council. **Languages** English. **Staff** Voluntary. **Finance** Meeting financed by delegates; voluntary donations. **Events** *Annual Congress* Hannover (Germany) 2021, *Annual Congress* Athens (Greece) 2020, *Annual Congress* Krakow (Poland) 2019, *Annual Congress* Dublin (Ireland) 2018, *Annual Congress* Amsterdam (Netherlands) 2017. **Publications** *Inflammation Research* – meeting proceedings.
Members Full in 30 countries and territories:
Argentina, Austria, Belgium, Brazil, Bulgaria, Canada, China, Czechia, Denmark, Finland, France, Germany, Greece, Hong Kong, Hungary, Iran Islamic Rep, Ireland, Italy, Japan, Mexico, Netherlands, Poland, Russia, Slovakia, Slovenia, Spain, Sweden, Switzerland, UK, USA. [2019.05.02/XD5246/**D**]

♦ European Historical Economics Society (EHES) 07490

SG address not obtained.
Pres address not obtained.
URL: http://www.ehes.org/

History 1991. Informal existence since the 2nd World Congress of Cliometrics conference, Santander (Spain) 1989. **Aims** Advance education in European economic history through study of European economies and comparative economic history. **Structure** Officers: President; Secretary; Treasurer; President Elect. **Languages** English. **Finance** Members' dues. **Activities** Meeting activities; education. **Events** *Biennial Conference* Paris (France) 2019, *Biennial Conference* Pisa (Italy) 2015, *Biennial Conference / Conference* London (UK) 2013, *Biennial Conference / Conference* Dublin (Ireland) 2011, *Biennial conference / Conference* Geneva (Switzerland) 2009. **Publications** *European Review of Economic History* (3 a year). **NGO Relations** Member of: *International Economic History Association (IEHA, #13224).* [2014/XD7337/**D**]

♦ European Historic Houses Association / see European Historic Houses Association (#07491)

♦ European Historic Houses Association (EHH) 07491

Association des demeures historiques européennes

Head of Office Rue de Trèves 67, 1040 Brussels, Belgium. T. +3227908863. Fax +3222343009. E-mail: info@europeanhistorichouses.eu.
Exec Pres address not obtained.
URL: http://www.europeanhistorichouses.eu/

History 1974. Former names and other names: *Union of European Historic Houses Associations (UEHHA)* – former; *Union d'associations européennes de demeures historiques* – former; *International Union of Historic House Associations (IUHHA)* – former; *Union internationale d'associations des demeures historiques* – former; *European Historic Houses Association* – former. Registration: Banque-Carrefour des Entreprises, No/ID: 0714.975.914, Start date: 30 Nov 2018, Belgium; EU Transparency Register, No/ID: 204022211093-63, Start date: 6 May 2013. **Aims** Raise awareness and advocates at a European level about private cultural heritage; defend the preservation, conservation and transmission of heritage houses and represent 50 000 of them throughout Europe. **Structure** General Assembly (annual); Executive Committee; Head Office in Brussels (Belgium). **Languages** English, French. **Staff** 2.00 FTE, paid. **Finance** Sources: members' dues; sponsorship. **Activities** Advocacy/lobbying/activism; awards/prizes/competitions; events/meetings; networking/liaising. **Events** *NextGen Conference* Co. Dublin (Ireland) 2022, *Extraordinary General Assembly* Brussels (Belgium) 2021, *General Assembly* Brussels (Belgium) 2021, *NextGen Conference* Dublin (Ireland) 2021, *Successful EU-funded Projects* Brussels (Belgium) 2020. **Publications** *Heritage Houses for Europe.*
Members National organizations, incorporating about 50,000 major classified private monuments and historic houses in 20 countries:
Austria, Belgium, Czechia, Denmark, Estonia, Finland, France, Germany, Greece, Ireland, Italy, Latvia, Netherlands, Norway, Portugal, Serbia, Spain, Sweden, Switzerland, UK.
Observers in 2 countries:
Germany, Romania.
IGO Relations European Union institutions. **NGO Relations** Member of (3): *European Heritage Alliance 3.3 (#07477); European Tourism Manifesto (#08921); Federation of European and International Associations Established in Belgium (FAIB, #09508).* Secretariat co-located with: *European Landowners' Organization (ELO, #07639).* [2022.02.17/XD0377/**D**]

♦ European Historic Thermal Towns Association (EHTTA) 07492

Registered Office Hôtel de Ville, Rue de l'Hôtel de Ville 44, 4900 Spa, Belgium. E-mail: contact@ehtta.eu.
URL: http://www.ehtta.eu/

History 2009, Brussels (Belgium). Founded by 6 founder members. Registration: No/ID: 0823.039.357, Start date: 10 Feb 2010, Belgium; EU Transparency Register, No/ID: 606724725263-31, Start date: 28 Dec 2016. **Aims** Create a strong network of partnerships between towns and *spas*, promoting exchanges of experience among the different cultural operators of the cities; promote the system at European level involving the institutions through support of European programmes, so as to create a European spa trail and complete the established programmes; encourage, promote and develop analytical research and statistics within the spa industry, focusing primarily on the history and artistic heritage, cultural, legal and legislative aspects linked to it. **Structure** General Assembly; Executive Council. **Activities** Created " European Route of Historical Thermal Towns". **Publications** *EHTTA Newsletter.* **Members** Founder (6); Active (50); Associate (17). Membership countries not specified. **IGO Relations** *Council of Europe (CE, #04881).* **NGO Relations** Member of (2): *European Heritage Alliance 3.3 (#07477); European Tourism Manifesto (#08921).* Partner of (1): *World Wellness Weekend (WWW). European Institute of Cultural Routes (EICR).* [2020/XJ5963/**D**]

♦ European HIV/AIDS Academy – European HIV/AIDS and Infectious Diseases Academy (internationally oriented national body)
♦ European HIV/AIDS and Infectious Diseases Academy (internationally oriented national body)
♦ European HIV/AIDS Surveillance Network / see European Network for HIV/AIDS Surveillance (#07923)

♦ European Hobbes Society (EHS) 07493

Pres address not obtained. E-mail: president@europeanhobbessociety.org.
URL: http://www.europeanhobbessociety.org/

History Originated 2011, as an informal network. **Aims** Promote scholarship on the thought of Thomas Hobbes by providing a platform for scholars from across the world to share ideas and exchange research. **Structure** General Meeting; Executive Committee; Advisory Board. **Finance** Members' dues. **Activities** Events/meetings; knowledge management/information dissemination. **Events** *Biennial Conference* Regensburg (Germany) 2023, *Biennial Conference* Dubrovnik (Croatia) 2021, *Biennial Conference* Amsterdam (Netherlands) 2018, *Biennial Conference* Leuven (Belgium) 2016. **Members** Individuals. Membership countries not specified. [2019/XM8019/**E**]

♦ European Hockey Federation (EHF) 07494

Fédération européenne de hockey (FEH)

Address not obtained.
URL: http://www.eurohockey.org/

History 1969. **Structure** Executive Board, comprising President, 2 Vice-Presidents, Honorary General Secretary, Honorary Treasurer, 7 members, Administration Officer, Competitions Manager and 1 additional member. Committees ( ): Appointment; Finance; Marketing; Competitions (including Clubs, Indoor and Nations); Development Coordination (including Coaches, Development and Umpires). **Languages** English, French. **Staff** 1.00 FTE, voluntary. **Finance** Members' dues. **Activities** Organizes and publishes results of European Championships and tournaments. **Events** *General Assembly* Brussels (Belgium) 2013, *General Assembly* Budapest (Hungary) 2007, *General Assembly* Cardiff (UK) 1997, *General Assembly* Dublin (Ireland) 1993, *General Assembly* 1991.
Members National hockey unions in 43 countries and territories:
Armenia, Austria, Azerbaijan, Belarus, Belgium, Bulgaria, Croatia, Cyprus, Czechia, Denmark, England, Finland, France, Georgia, Germany, Gibraltar, Great Britain, Greece, Hungary, Ireland, Israel, Italy, Latvia, Lithuania, Luxembourg, Malta, Moldova, Netherlands, Norway, Poland, Portugal, Romania, Russia, Scotland, Serbia, Slovakia, Slovenia, Spain, Sweden, Switzerland, Türkiye, Ukraine, Wales.
NGO Relations *International Olympic Committee (IOC, #14408).* Recognized by: *International Hockey Federation (#13802).* [2014/XD1125/**D**]

♦ European Holiday Adult Education Centers / see Europäische Bildungs-und Begegnungszentren (#05750)

♦ European Holiday Home Association (EHHA) 07495

SG Feriehusudlejernes Brancheforening, Amagertorv 9 – 2, 1160 Copenhagen, Denmark. T. +4531101090. E-mail: info@ehha.eu.
URL: https://ehha.eu/

History Founded 2013. EU Transparency Register: 748962812474-86. **Aims** Give a voice to short-term rental (STR) industry. **Activities** Awards/prizes/competitions.
Members Company members; trade associations; Affiliated members. Trade associations in 14 countries:
Belgium, Croatia, Czechia, Denmark, France, Germany, Ireland, Italy, Netherlands, Portugal, Spain, Switzerland, UK, USA. [2020/XM8943/**D**]

♦ European Holocaust Research Infrastructure (unconfirmed)
♦ European Holstein Federation / see European Holstein and Red-Holstein Confederation (#07496)

♦ European Holstein and Red-Holstein Confederation (EHRC) 07496

SG address not obtained. E-mail: euroholsteins@gmail.com.
URL: http://www.euholsteins.com/

History 7 Jul 1966, UK. Former names and other names: *European Holstein Federation* – former. **Aims** Improve, develop and promote the Holstein and Red Holstein breed by close cooperation of all officially recognized European Herdbooks. **Structure** General Assembly; Committee. **Languages** English. **Finance** Sources: members' dues. Members' dues calculated on the number of Holsteins registered in the country. **Activities** Advocacy/lobbying/activism; events/meetings; guidance/assistance/consulting; training/education. **Events** *Conference* Gijón (Spain) 2014, *Conference* Stockholm (Sweden) 2011, *Conference* Aarhus (Denmark) 2007, *Conference* Aarhus (Denmark) 2007, *Conference* Prague (Czech Rep) 2005.
Members Organizations in 28 countries:
Austria, Belgium, Croatia, Czechia, Denmark, Estonia, Finland, France, Germany, Greece, Hungary, Ireland, Italy, Latvia, Lithuania, Luxembourg, Netherlands, Poland, Portugal, Romania, Russia, Slovakia, Slovenia, Spain, Sweden, Switzerland, Türkiye, UK. [2021.05.26/XD8342/**E**]

♦ European Homeland Security Association (no recent information)
♦ European Home Study Council (inactive)
♦ European Home Systems Association (inactive)

♦ European Homeworking Group 07497

Groupe européen sur le travail à domicile – Grupo Europeu sobre o Trabalho no Domicilio

Contact c/o HomeWorkers Worldwide, Office 14, 30-38 Dock Street, Leeds, LS10 1JF, UK. T. +441133203214. E-mail: info@homeworkersww.org.uk.
URL: http://www.homeworkersww.org.uk/

History 1994, having previously existed as an ad-hoc group called *European Coordinating Group on Homeworking.* Currently part of *International Network for Homebased Workers (HomeNet, inactive).* **Aims** Link *homeworkers* and their organizations in different parts of Europe. **Finance** Equal Opportunities Unit of *European Commission (EC, #06633).* **Activities** Organizes meetings and exchange of experience and information; campaigns for improved pay and conditions for homeworkers; makes links with homeworking groups all over the world.
Members Full in 9 countries and territories:
Germany, Greece, Ireland, Italy, Madeira, Netherlands, Portugal, Spain, UK.
NGO Relations Supported by: *European Trade Union Confederation (ETUC, #08927); European Women's Lobby (EWL, #09102).* Coordinated by: *HomeWorkers Worldwide (HWW).* [2016/XE2179/**E**]

♦ European Homograft Bank (EHB) 07498

Main Office Tour Rosalind Franklin, Ave Mounier 49, Entrée F – Route 703 EHB, 1200 Brussels, Belgium. E-mail: ehb-saintluc@uclouvain.be.
URL: https://www.saintluc.be/fr/mch-presentation

History 1988. Commenced activities: 30 Jan 1989. Registration: Belgium. **Aims** Ensure the procurement, preparation, preservation, storage and distribution of the cryopreserved *aortic, pulmonary* and mitral valves as well as the large arterial allografts (since 1992); promote inter-bank cooperation and carry out basic research as well as clinical follow-up studies. **Structure** General Assembly (annual). Board of Directors (meets annually), consisting of Chairman, 2 Vice-Chairmen, Secretary and 7 Members. Medical Director of the Cardiovascular Tissue Bank. Scientific Committee of 6 members. **Languages** Dutch, English, French, German. **Staff** 6.00 FTE, paid. 4 external consultants. **Finance** Main Source: on basis of reimbursement of delivered allografts. **Activities** Runs research projects; stores and offers to surgeons a various sized aortic, pulmonary and mitral human valves; prepares and distributes large arteries, namely ascendens and descendens aortas, aortic bifurcation and superficial femoral arteries; organizes conferences and congresses. Works in accordance with EU requirements on the Tissue Banking as well as EATB General Standards as well as specific Standards for Cario-vascular Tissue Banking. **Events** *The mid- and longterm clinical results of EHB homgraft valves and arteries* Brussels (Belgium) 1998, *Cryopreserved arteries* Brussels (Belgium) 1995, *Annual symposium / Symposium* Brussels (Belgium) 1994, *Annual symposium / Symposium* Brussels (Belgium) 1992. **Publications** Activity report (annual); manual of procedures; articles. **Information Services** *EHB Databank.*
Members Individuals in 5 countries:
Belgium, France, Germany, Netherlands, Switzerland.
Procurement centres and associate members in 6 countries:
Belgium, France, Germany, Italy, Luxembourg, Switzerland. [2020/XF0023/**F**]

♦ European Hop Growers Convention / see International Hop Growers' Convention (#13807)
♦ European Horizons (internationally oriented national body)

♦ European Horse Network (EHN) 07499

Chairman Square de Meeus 40, 4th Floor, 1000 Brussels, Belgium. E-mail: info@europeanhorsenetwork.eu.
URL: http://www.europeanhorsenetwork.eu/
History Founded Oct 2009, Uppsala (Sweden), on a Swedish initiative during their EU presidency. EU Transparency Register: 157396313389-87. **Aims** Promote development of the equine sector in Europe. **Structure** Annual Meeting; Executive Board. **Languages** English. **Staff** None. **Finance** Members' dues. **Activities** Events/meetings. **Events** *Equine Conference* Brussels (Belgium) 2018. **Publications** *EHN Newsletter* (4 a year). Thematic leaflets.
Members Organizations (29), including 17 listed in this Yearbook:
Equestrian Educational Network (EEN, #05522); European and Mediterranean Horseracing Federation (EMHF, #07770); European Conference of Arab Horse Organizations (ECAHO, #06730); European Draught Horse Federation (#06944); European Equestrian Federation (EEF, #07005); European Equine Health and Nutrition Association (AAHNA); European Federation of Farriers Associations (EFFA, #07119); European Federation of Thoroughbred Breeders' Associations (EFTBA, #07226); European Pari Mutuel Association (EPMA, #08143); European State Studs Associations (ESSA, #08834); European Trainers Federation (ETF, #08932); European Trotting Union (#08952); Fédération Équestre Internationale (FEI, #09484); Federation of European Equine Veterinary Associations (FEEVA, #09503); International Federation of Icelandic Horse Associations (FEIF, #13454); World Breeding Federation for Sport Horses (WBFSH, #21245); World Horse Welfare. [2019.02.14/XJ5791/y/**D**]

♦ European Hospital and Healthcare Employers' Association (HOSPEEM) 07500

Manager Rue des Deux Eglises 26, Bte 5, 1000 Brussels, Belgium. T. +3222292157 – +3222292158. Fax +3222181213. E-mail: hospeem@hospeem.eu.
SG address not obtained.
URL: http://hospeem.org/
History Sep 2005. Founded by members of *SGI Europe (#19253).* Registration: EU Transparency Register, No/ID: 285977317289-74. **Aims** Establish a European autonomous frame so as to develop management and labour relations in the hospital and health care sector delivering services of general interest; act as the principal source of advice on social policies, including employment and industrial relations vis-à-vis the European Institutions. **Structure** General Assembly; Steering Committee; Financial Advisory Committee; Board; Secretariat. Expert Groups. **Staff** 4.00 FTE, paid. **Activities** Networking/liaising; events/meetings. **Events** *Joint Seminar on Digital Health Transformation of Integrated Care in Europe* Brussels (Belgium) 2022, *Plenary Meeting* Brussels (Belgium) 2021, *Plenary Meeting* Brussels (Belgium) 2020, *Plenary Meeting* Brussels (Belgium) 2019, *Joint Workshop on AMR and CPD* Brussels (Belgium) 2017. **Publications** *HOSPEEM Newsletter* (5 a year).
Members Full in 12 countries:
Denmark, Finland, France, Germany, Ireland, Italy, Latvia, Lithuania, Netherlands, Norway, Sweden, UK.
Observer in 1 country:
Netherlands.
IGO Relations Recognized by: *European Commission (EC, #06633).* **NGO Relations** *European Federation of Public Service Unions (EPSU, #07202).* [2022/XM5813/**D**]

♦ European Hospital and Healthcare Federation (HOPE) 07501

Fédération européenne des hôpitaux et des soins de santé
CEO Av Marnix 30, 3rd Floor, 1000 Brussels, Belgium. T. +3227421322. E-mail: sg@hope.be.
URL: http://www.hope.be/
History Oct 1966, Rome (Italy). New Constitution adopted in 1975. New Constitution adopted by 36th Plenary Assembly, 9 May 1995, Stockholm (Sweden). Current Constitution adopted 29 Nov 2004, Berlin (Germany). Former names and other names: *Study Committee of the Hospital Organizations in the Common Market* – former; *Hospital Committee of the Common Market* – former (1972); *Hospital Committee of the European Community (HCEC)* – former (1975); *Comité hospitalier de la Communauté européenne (CHCE)* – former (1975); *Comité Hospitalario de la Comunidad Europea* – former (1975); *Ausschuss der Krankenhäuser der Europäischen Gemeinschaft (AKEG)* – former (1975); *Standing Committee of the Hospitals of the European Union* – former (1995); *Comité permanent des hôpitaux de l'Union européenne* – former (1995); *Ständiger Ausschuss der Krankenhäuser der Europäischen Union* – former (1995). Registration: Start date: 2 Feb 1996, Belgium; EU Transparency Register, No/ID: 73872883198-91, Start date: 10 Feb 2010. **Aims** Promote a uniformly high standard of hospital care; foster efficiency, effectiveness and humanity in the organization and operation of hospital services; provide information; promote exchange programmes; maintain links with principal *health professions* in the European Union. **Structure** Board of Governors (meets twice a year); President's Committee; Working Parties. **Languages** English. **Staff** 4.20 FTE, paid. **Finance** Sources: members' dues; revenue from activities/projects. **Events** *Annual Agora* Brussels (Belgium) 2023, *Annual Agora* Brussels (Belgium) 2022, *Annual Agora* Brussels (Belgium) 2020, *Annual Agora* Ljubljana (Slovenia) 2019, *Annual Agora* Stockholm (Sweden) 2018. **Publications** *Hospital Healthcare Europe – the Official Hope Reference Book.* Discussion papers; monographs; brochures; articles.
Members National hospital organizations or national institutions responsible for the hospital sector in 30 countries:
Austria, Belgium, Bulgaria, Croatia, Cyprus, Czechia, Denmark, Estonia, Finland, France, Germany, Greece, Hungary, Ireland, Italy, Latvia, Lithuania, Luxembourg, Malta, Netherlands, Poland, Portugal, Romania, Serbia, Slovakia, Slovenia, Spain, Sweden, Switzerland, UK.
Observers in 2 countries:
Serbia, Switzerland.
NGO Relations Member of (1): *European Medicines Verification Organisation (EMVO, #07768).* Stakeholder in: *European Network for Health Technology Assessment (EUnetHTA, #07921).* [2022.10.19/XE3300/**E**]

♦ European Hotel Diploma / see EURHODIP (#05624)
♦ European Hotel Forum (unconfirmed)

♦ European Hotel Managers Association (EHMA) 07502

Association européenne des directeurs d'hôtels
Sec Via Cassiodoro 19, 00193 Rome RM, Italy. T. +39647824556. E-mail: secretariat.ehma@gmail.com.
URL: http://www.ehma.com/
History 1974, Rome (Italy). Present amended Statutes adopted by Extraordinary General Meeting, 18 Feb 1981, Monte Carlo (Monaco); modified 22 Feb 1986, Amsterdam (Netherlands); 21 Feb 1991, Cannes (France); 17 Feb 1994, Brussels (Belgium); 2 Apr 1998, Lugano (Switzerland); 22 May 1999, Stockholm (Sweden); 17 Feb 2001, Prague (Czech Rep); 24 Jan 2004, Athens (Greece); 27 Mar 2013, Milan (Italy). **Aims** Safeguard the ethics of the hotel profession; foster fellowship, respect and professional improvement to better serve the industry. **Structure** General Meeting (annual); Management Council; Board of Arbiters; Board of Auditors. **Languages** English. **Staff** 2.00 FTE, paid. **Finance** Sources: donations; gifts, legacies; members' dues. Other sources: surplus arising each year from the management. **Events** *Annual General Meeting* Lisbon (Portugal) 2023, *Annual General Meeting* Lugano (Switzerland) 2022, *Annual General Meeting* 2021, *Annual General Meeting* Lugano (Switzerland) 2020, *Annual General Meeting* Paris (France) 2019. **Members** Active (354); Meritorious (62); Honorary (6). Membership countries not specified. [2023.02.14/XD8943/v/**D**]

♦ European Housing Ecology Network (EHEN) 07503

Chairman Grote Markt 39, 2260 Westerlo, Belgium. T. +3214541941. E-mail: info@zonnigekempen.be.
History 1992, Copenhagen (Denmark). **Aims** Identify and develop good practice in all aspects of ecology involved in or affecting the provision, management and servicing of housing; lobby European and national authorities; develop a common base of knowledge on low energy housing; cooperate with European Union bodies on green issues, including energy conservation and the progressive orientation of human activity and development towards sustainable forms. **Structure** General Meeting (annual, in conjunction with a seminar); Executive Committee; Network Manager. **Finance** Members' dues. **Activities** Advocacy/lobbying/activism; knowledge management/information dissemination; publishing activities. **Events** *Conference* Cardiff (UK) 2006, *Sigulda – green and clean* Sigulda (Latvia) 2006, *Conference* Glasgow (UK) 2005, *Conference* Dublin (Ireland) 2004, *Conference* Lisbon (Portugal) 2004. **Publications** *Energy Guide – Energy Efficiency in the Public/Non-Profit Housing Sector in the European Community* (1997) by Erik Christiansen et al; *Environmental Checklist for Housing* (1995) by Martin Rowbottom et al.
Members Housing associations, housing departments of local authorities and consultants in 12 countries:
Denmark, Finland, France, Germany, Ireland, Italy, Netherlands, Norway, Portugal, Spain, Sweden, UK. [2014.10.06/XF3365/**F**]

♦ European Housing Forum (EHF) 07504

Forum européen du logement
Co-Chair RICS Europe, Rue Ducale 67, 1000 Brussels, Belgium. T. +3227394228. Fax +3227429748.
Co-Chair IUT-EU, Rue du Luxembourg 23, 5th floor, 1000 Brussels, Belgium. T. +3225130784. Fax +3225130955.
URL: http://www.europeanhousingforum.org/
History 1997. An informal organization. **Structure** No central office. Rotating Secretariat, currently *Royal Institution of Chartered Surveyors (RICS, #18991).* **Events** *International social housing summit* The Hague (Netherlands) 2010.
Members International organizations (12):
Architects Council of Europe (ACE, #01086); Build Europe (#03350); COFACE Families Europe (#04084); EUROCITIES (#05662); European Federation of National Organisations Working with the Homeless (#07174); European Network of Real Estate Owners and Managers (no recent information); European Social Housing Observatory (#08502); Housing Europe – The European Federation for Public Cooperative and Social Housing (Housing Europe, #10956); International Union of Tenants (IUT, #15822); Réseau habitat et francophonie (RHF, #18888); Royal Institution of Chartered Surveyors (RICS, #18991). [2010.06.24/XF4951/y/**F**]

♦ European Hovercraft Federation (EHF) 07505

Sec 29 Vale Road, Haywards Heath, RH16 4JF, UK. T. +441444414068. E-mail: hoverbod@aol.com.
URL: http://www.europeanhovercraftfederation.org/
History Statutes adopted 1994, 1998, 1999. **Aims** Promote the use of hovercraft for sport, competition and tourism; encourage construction of new prototype craft and scale models. **Structure** Board, comprising 2 representatives from each member country. Officers: President; Vice-President; Secretary; Treasurer. **Languages** English. **Finance** Members' dues. **Publications** *EHF News Letter.*
Members National organizations in 15 countries:
Belgium, Croatia, Czechia, Finland, France, Germany, Italy, Netherlands, Norway, Poland, Portugal, Slovakia, Spain, Sweden, UK. [2018/XD7529/**D**]

♦ European Human Behaviour and Evolution Association (EHBEA) ... 07506

Sec Dept of Anthropology, Univ of Oxford, 51-53 Banbury Road, Oxford, OX2 6PE, UK. T. +441865274688.
URL: https://ehbea.eu
History 2008, Montpellier (France). Founded following EHBE conferences starting in 2006. Registration: Charity Commission, No/ID: 1154585, England and Wales. **Aims** Support activities of European researchers with an interest in evolutionary accounts of human cognition, behaviour and society. **Structure** Steering Committee. **Languages** English. **Staff** None. **Finance** Members' dues. **Activities** Events/meetings; awards/prizes/competitions. **Events** *Annual Conference* London (UK) 2023, *EHBEA Conference* Oxford (UK) 2021, *Annual European Conference* Krakow (Poland) 2020, *Annual European Conference* Toulouse (France) 2019, *Annual European Conference* Pécs (Hungary) 2018. **Publications** *EHBEA Newsletter. EHBEA Book Series.*
Members Full; Associate; Student. Membership countries not specified. [2022/XM4666/**D**]

♦ European Humanist Federation (EHF) 07507

Fédération humaniste européenne (FHE)
Communications Dir c/o Campus de la Plaine ULB, Accès 2, CP 237, 1050 Brussels, Belgium. T. +3226276824. E-mail: admin@humanistfederation.eu.
URL: http://www.humanistfederation.eu/
History 13 Jul 1991, Prague (Czechia). Former names and other names: *EHF-FHE* – alias. Registration: EU Transparency Register, No/ID: 84310943110-81; Belgium. **Aims** Achieve separation between religion and the state throughout Europe; defend *freedom of religion* and belief; defend freedom of *thought* and *speech*; promote *non-discrimination* on all grounds; support *women's sexual* and *reproductive* health and *rights.* **Structure** General Assembly (annual, usually in conjunction with a conference); Board; Secretariat. **Languages** English, French. **Staff** 3.00 FTE, paid. **Finance** Members' dues. Budget (annual): euro 25,000. **Activities** Advocacy/lobbying/activism; politics/policy/regulatory; events/meetings. **Events** *Conference / General Assembly and Conference* Brussels (Belgium) 2014, *Conference* Bucharest (Romania) 2013, *General Assembly / General Assembly and Conference* Bucharest (Romania) 2013, *Conference / General Assembly and Conference* Utrecht (Netherlands) 2012, *General Assembly* Utrecht (Netherlands) 2012. **Publications** *A Key to Humanism in Europe* in English, French – series of pamphlets and booklets. *The European Dream* (2007) in English, French; *The EHF in Europe: 15th Anniversary* (2006) in English, French; *2500 Years (and More) of Free Thinking* (2003) – video. Conference proceedings in English/French; video.
Members Humanist and secularist associations, and individuals in 26 countries:
Austria, Belgium, Croatia, Cyprus, Denmark, Finland, France, Germany, Greece, Iceland, Ireland, Italy, Luxembourg, Malta, Moldova, Netherlands, Norway, Poland, Portugal, Romania, Russia, Slovakia, Spain, Sweden, Switzerland, UK.
Included in the above, 1 international organization listed in this Yearbook:
European Humanist Professionals (EHP, #07508).
Consultative Status Consultative status granted from: *Council of Europe (CE, #04881)* (Participatory Status); *ECOSOC (#05331)* (Special). **NGO Relations** Member of: *Civil Society Europe.* [2020/XD2738/**D**]

♦ European Humanist Professionals (EHP) 07508

Contact Jan Van Rijswijcklaan 96, 2018 Antwerp, Belgium. T. +3232591080. E-mail: info@humanistprofessionals.eu.
URL: http://www.humanistprofessionals.eu/
History 5 Mar 1994. Founded on adoption of constitution, deriving from the European section of *International Association of Humanist Educators, Counsellors and Leaders (IAHECL, inactive),* itself within the framework of *Humanists International (#10972).* **Aims** Support and connect humanist professionals and their organizations across Europe; develop quality and standards in humanist professional fields; inform the general public on humanism and humanist services. **Structure** Independent Board of representatives of European humanist organisations. **Languages** English. **Staff** 1.00 FTE, paid. **Finance** Sources: contributions. **Activities** Awareness

raising; events/meetings; training/education. **Events** *Building on secular Europe for all* Brussels (Belgium) 2014, *Conference* Berlin (Germany) 2009, *Annual European Seminar* Berlin (Germany) 2005, *Annual European Seminar* Oslo (Norway) 1995, *Annual European Seminar* Brussels (Belgium) 1994. **Members** Open to any humanist educator, counsellor or leader recognized as a humanist professional by a constituent organization of IHEU or the Board of EHP. Membership countries not specified. [2023.02.14/XE2253/**E**]

- ♦ European Humanities Research Centre, Oxford (internationally oriented national body)
- ♦ European Humanities University (internationally oriented national body)
- ♦ European Humanities University, Minsk / see European Humanities University
- ♦ European Human Rights Association (unconfirmed)
- ♦ European Human Rights Foundation (inactive)
- ♦ European Human Rights Funders Network / see Ariadne – European Funders for Social Change and Human Rights (#01103)

♦ European Huntington Association (EHA) 07509

Pres Vognsneset 30, 4643 Søgne, Norway. T. +4790202031.
URL: http://eurohuntington.org/

History Set up 1986, within the framework of *International Huntington Association (IHA, #13824)*. Current constitution adopted 22 may 2017, Riga (Latvia). EU Transparency Register: 322419733882-57. **Aims** Share information and connect people throughout Europe so as to improve the life of those affected by Huntington's *disease*. **Structure** Conference; Executive Board. **Activities** Events/meetings; awareness raising. **Events** *Meeting* Sofia (Bulgaria) 2017, *Meeting* Portugal 2008, *Meeting* UK 2008, *Meeting* Blankenberge (Belgium) 2006, *Meeting / European Meeting* Guadarrama (Spain) 2004. **Publications** *EHA Newsletter*.
Members Associations in 29 countries and territories:
Austria, Belgium, Bulgaria, Cyprus, Czechia, Denmark, England, Finland, France, Germany, Greece, Ireland, Israel, Italy, Lithuania, Malta, Netherlands, Northern Ireland, Norway, Poland, Portugal, Romania, Russia, Scotland, Slovenia, Spain, Sweden, Switzerland, Wales.
NGO Relations Member of: *EURORDIS – Rare Diseases Europe (#09175)*. Joint meeting with: *European Huntington's Disease Network (EHDN, #07510)*. Other partners: include: *European Federation of Neurological Associations (EFNA, #07177)*. [2019/XK1845/**E**]

♦ European Huntington's Disease Network (EHDN) 07510

COO Ulm Univ Hosp – Neurology, Oberer Eselsberg 45/1, 89081 Ulm, Germany. T. +4973150063107. Fax +4973150063082.
URL: http://www.ehdn.org/

History May 2003, Il Ciocco (Italy). Former names and other names: *Euro-HD Network* – former. **Aims** Provide a platform for professionals and people affected by Huntington's Disease and their relatives. **Structure** Executive Committee; Scientific and Bioethics Advisory Committee; EHDN Think Tank; Central Coordination. **Finance** Supported by (US) High-Q. **Activities** Events/meetings; research and development. **Events** *Plenary Meeting* Bologna (Italy) 2022, *Plenary Meeting* 2021, *Meeting* Ulm (Germany) 2020, *Annual Plenary Meeting* Vienna (Austria) 2018, *Annual Plenary Meeting* The Hague (Netherlands) 2016. **Publications** *EHDN Newsletter*.
Members Individuals Regular; Associate. Regular in 27 countries:
Austria, Belgium, Bulgaria, Canada, Croatia, Czechia, Denmark, Finland, France, Germany, Greece, Hungary, Ireland, Italy, Malta, Netherlands, Norway, Poland, Portugal, Romania, Russia, Slovakia, Spain, Sweden, Switzerland, UK, USA.
Associate in 22 countries and territories:
Argentina, Australia, Cameroon, Canada, China, Colombia, Cuba, Egypt, India, Israel, Japan, Korea Rep, Mexico, New Zealand, Singapore, South Africa, Sri Lanka, Sweden, Taiwan, Türkiye, USA, Venezuela.
NGO Relations Joint meeting with: *European Huntington Association (EHA, #07509)*. [2022/XM1815/**E**]

- ♦ European Hybrid Microelectronics Conference (meeting series)

♦ European Hydrogen Alliance (EHA) 07511

Secretariat Rue des Fiennes 77, 1070 Brussels, Belgium. T. +32471727491. Fax +3227725044. E-mail: ehasecretariat@h2euro.org.
Registered Address Avenue des Arts 3/4/5, 1210 Brussels, Belgium.
URL: http://www.h2euro.org/

History 25 Jan 2000, Brussels (Belgium). Former names and other names: *European Hydrogen Association (EHA)* – former (25 Jan 2000); *European Hydrogen and Fuel Cell Association (EHA)* – former. Registration: Banque-Carrefour des Entreprises, No/ID: 0474.503.115, Start date: 25 Jan 2000, Belgium; EU Transparency Register, No/ID: 48071001253-27, Start date: 26 Feb 2009. **Aims** Promote the use and development of hydrogen technology in Europe. **Structure** Board of Directors; Executive Committee. **Languages** English. **Finance** Members' dues. **Activities** Events/meeting. **Events** *EHEC: European Hydrogen Conference* Madrid (Spain) 2022, *EHEC: European Hydrogen Conference* Madrid (Spain) 2021, *EHEC: European Hydrogen Conference* Madrid (Spain) 2020, *EHEC: European Hydrogen Conference* Seville (Spain) 2014, *European electric vehicle congress* Brussels (Belgium) 2011. **Publications** *Monthly Updates*.
Members National associations; companies; individuals. National associations in 18 countries:
Bulgaria, Czechia, Finland, Hungary, Ireland, Italy, Latvia, North Macedonia, Norway, Poland, Portugal, Romania, Slovenia, Spain, Sweden, Türkiye, UK, Ukraine.
NGO Relations Member of: *Climate Technology Centre and Network (CTCN, #04023)*. [2020/XD8288/**D**]

- ♦ European Hydrogen Association / see European Hydrogen Alliance (#07511)
- ♦ European Hydrogen Energy Conference (meeting series)
- ♦ European Hydrogen and Fuel Cell Association / see European Hydrogen Alliance (#07511)

♦ European Hygienic Engineering Design Group (EHEDG) 07512

Operations Director Karspeldreef 8, 1101 CJ Amsterdam, Netherlands. T. +31610216958. E-mail: office@ehedg.org.
URL: http://www.ehedg.org/

History 1989, Netherlands. Former names and other names: *European Hygienic Equipment Design Group* – former. **Aims** Promote food safety and quality, as well as enhance productivity and sustainability through the application of hygienic engineering and design principles to all aspects of food manufacturing. **Structure** General Assembly; Foundation Board; Advisory Board; Executive Committee; Sub-Committees; Regional Sections; Working Groups (29+). **Languages** English. **Activities** Certification/accreditation; events/meetings; guidance/assistance/consulting; knowledge management/information dissemination; training/education. **Events** *EHEDG World Congress* Munich (Germany) 2022, *World Congress* Munich (Germany) 2022, *World Congress* Munich (Germany) 2020, *World Congress* London (UK) 2018, *World Congress* Herning (Denmark) 2016. **Publications** *EHEDG Newsletter* (6 a year); *EHEDG Journal on Hygienic Engineering and Design* (2 a year); *EHEDG Connects Magazine* (annual). Guidelines; position papers; reports; press articles.
Members Companies (56%); institutes (7%), individuals (37%). Members (1,000) in 48 countries and territories:
Argentina, Armenia, Australia, Austria, Belgium, Brazil, Bulgaria, Chile, China, Croatia, Cyprus, Czechia, Denmark, Finland, France, Germany, Greece, Hungary, India, Ireland, Israel, Italy, Japan, Latvia, Lithuania, Luxembourg, Malaysia, Mexico, Moldova, Netherlands, New Zealand, North Macedonia, Norway, Poland, Portugal, Romania, Russia, Serbia, Spain, Sweden, Switzerland, Taiwan, Thailand, Türkiye, UK, Ukraine, Uruguay, USA.
NGO Relations Also links with national organizations. [2023.02.14/XE3704/**E**]

- ♦ European Hygienic Equipment Design Group / see European Hygienic Engineering Design Group (#07512)
- ♦ European and Ibero-American Academy of Yuste Foundation (internationally oriented national body)

♦ European Ichthyological Society (EIS) 07513

Société européenne d'ichthyologie

Pres Hellenic Centre for Marine Research, Institute of Inland Waters, PO BOX 712, 190 13 Anavyssos, Greece. T. +302291076392. Fax +302291076419. E-mail: mstoum@ath.hcmr.gr.
URL: http://artedi.nrm.se/eis/

History 1976, Paris (France), as *European Ichthyological Union*. Name changed to *Societas Europaea Ichthyologorum* in 1991. Present name adopted 1997. **Aims** Coordinate research and promote international cooperation in the field of ichthyology. **Structure** General Assembly. Council of 15 members. Board, comprising President, Vice-President, Secretary, Treasurer, 2 members. Secretariat in Lisbon (Portugal). **Languages** English. **Staff** None. **Finance** Members' dues. **Events** *Triennial Congress* Porto (Portugal) 2015, *Biennial Congress / Triennial Congress* Liège (Belgium) 2012, *Biennial congress / Triennial Congress* Klaipeda (Lithuania) 2009, *Triennial Congress* Cavtat (Croatia) 2007, *Triennial Congress* Dubrovnik (Croatia) 2007. **Publications** Newsletter (irregular). Directory of European fish collections (1992). **Information Services** *EUROFISH-L* – electronic discussion forum. **Members** Individual scientists (150) – membership countries not specified. [2015/XD7150/**D**]

- ♦ European Ichthyological Union / see European Ichthyological Society (#07513)
- ♦ European ICT/CE Industry Association / see DIGITALEUROPE (#05073)

♦ European Ideas Network (EIN) 07514

Contact EPP Group, Rue Wiertz 60, 1047 Brussels, Belgium. T. +3222831456. Fax +3222831257.
URL: http://www.ein.eu/

History 2002. Founded with sponsorship of *Group of the European People's Party – Christian Democrats (EPP, #10775)*. **Aims** Engage and promote new thinking on key challenges facing the *EU* while involving as many different people and groups as possible in the *policy* discussions. **Structure** Board, comprising Chairman, 3 Vice-Chairmen, 3 Chairmen of National Delegations, 4 other members, President of *European People's Party (EPP, #08185)* and 3 members representing member foundations: *Robert Schuman Foundation*; Central for European Studies (CEP); *Konrad Adenauer Foundation (KAF)*. foundations. Secretariat. Working Groups (10). **Activities** Training/education; events/meetings. **Events** *Joint Seminar on Empowering European Innovators and Entrepreneurs* Brussels (Belgium) 2017, *Joint Seminar on Geopolitical Consequences of Brexit* Brussels (Belgium) 2017, *Seminar on Media, Political Correctness and Manipulation* Brussels (Belgium) 2017, *Seminar on The Future of Inter-Institutional/Constitutional Issues in Light of Brexit* Brussels (Belgium) 2017, *Seminar on the Transatlantic Relations after the US Presidential Elections* Brussels (Belgium) 2017. **Publications** Journals; articles. **Members** Policy-makers (around 600). Membership countries not specified. [2018/XJ4768/**E**]

♦ European Idiopathic Pulmonary Fibrosis and Related Disorders Federation (EU-IPFF) 07515

Sec Abstraat 127, 3090 Overijse, Belgium. E-mail: secretariat@eu-ipff.org.
URL: https://www.eu-ipff.org/

History Jul 2016. Registration: Banque-Carrefour des Entreprises, No/ID: 0662.459.817, Start date: 9 Sep 2016, Belgium; EU Transparency Register, No/ID: 098968923496-04, Start date: 20 Sep 2016. **Aims** Defend the rights of IPF *patients* at European level by supporting an immediate and sustainable improvement of the quality of life and survival time of IPF patients, and of patients suffering from other interstitial lung diseases. **Structure** General Assembly; Executive Board; Scientific Advisory Board; Secretariat. **Languages** English. **Events** *European PF Patient Summit* Gentbrugge (Belgium) 2021, *European IPF Patient Summit* Warsaw (Poland) 2020. **Publications** *EU-IPFF Newsletter*.
Members Organizations (21) in 15 countries:
Austria, Belgium, Bulgaria, France, Germany, Greece, Ireland, Italy, Netherlands, Norway, Poland, Portugal, Romania, Spain, UK.
Associated in 5 countries:
Australia, Canada, Italy, Türkiye, USA.
NGO Relations Member of (1): *EURORDIS – Rare Diseases Europe (#09175)* (Associate). [2021/XM8945/**D**]

♦ European IFYE Alumni Association 07516

Sec address not obtained. E-mail: ifye_europe@hotmail.com.
URL: http://www.ifye.org/pages/europe/

History 1958, by alumni of *International Four-H Youth Exchange (IFYE, inactive)*. Initially a forum for young Europeans returning from exchange visits to USA, gradually developed into an inter-Europe exchange. **Aims** Enhance *international understanding* through establishing and maintaining contacts among IFYE alumni. **Structure** General Assembly (annual); European Board; Executive Committee; National Contact Members. **Languages** English. **Finance** Members' dues. Development fund supports new programmes. **Events** *Annual European Meeting* Preston (UK) 2021, *Annual European Meeting* UK 2020, *Annual European Meeting* Hamar (Norway) 2019, *Annual European meeting* Rautavaara (Finland) 2011, *Annual European meeting* Salzburg (Austria) 2010. **Publications** *IFYE Newsletter* (4 a year). *Blue Booklet* (2016) – revised.
Members Open to all who have participated in long-term IFYE-exchange programmes or are members of national IFYE associations. Individuals in 22 countries and territories:
Austria, Belgium, Denmark, England, Estonia, Finland, France, Germany, Hungary, Iceland, Ireland, Italy, Latvia, Luxembourg, Netherlands, Northern Ireland, Norway, Poland, Scotland, Sweden, Switzerland, Wales. [2017.06.01/XE3497/v/**E**]

♦ European Illustrators Forum (EIF) 07517

Sec address not obtained.
URL: http://www.european-illustrators-forum.com/

Aims Defend the rights of illustrators; promote illustration within Europe. **Structure** General Assembly (every 2 years); Board. **Finance** Members' dues. **Events** *Congress* Oslo (Norway) 2014, *General Assembly* Frankfurt-Main (Germany) 2013.
Members Ordinary; Supportive; Associated/friends. Members in 13 countries:
Austria, Denmark, Finland, France, Germany, Ireland, Italy, Netherlands, Norway, Romania, Spain, Sweden, UK.
[2016/XJ9503/**F**]

♦ European Imaging and Sound Association (EISA) 07518

Pres R D Joao V, 6-R/C Esq, 1250-090 Lisbon, Portugal. T. +351213190654. Fax +351213190659. E-mail: contact@eisa.eu.
General Inquiries address not obtained.
Vice-Pres Hektoroviceva 1B / lokal 6, Belgrade, PAK 11050, Serbia. T. +381638866486.
URL: http://www.eisa.eu/

History 1989, having informally met since 1982. **Structure** Management, comprising President, Vice-President and 6 Panel Managers (Audio and Home Theatre; In-Car Electronics; Photo; Mobile Devices; Video; Event). **Activities** Grants the 'EISA Award'. [2016/XM2486/**D**]

- ♦ European Immunodermatology Society (inactive)

♦ European Immunogenicity Platform (EIP) 07519

Contact address not obtained. E-mail: info@e-i-p.eu.
URL: http://www.e-i-p.eu/

Aims Build know-how and expertise in the field of immunogenicity, driven by a close interaction between industry and scientific advisors. **Structure** Board; Working Groups. **Languages** English. **Activities** Events/meetings. **Events** *Symposium* Lisbon (Portugal) 2019, *Open Scientific Symposium* Lisbon (Portugal) 2017, *Symposium* Vilamoura (Portugal) 2016, *Symposium* Lisbon (Portugal) 2015, *Symposium* Lisbon (Portugal) 2014. [2019.02.20/XM6438/**F**]

♦ European Implementation Collaborative (EIC) 07520

Chair address not obtained. E-mail: info@implementation.eu.
URL: http://implementation.eu/

History Bylaws last revised 30 May 2018. **Aims** Improve the life of children, youth, adults, and families in Europe through effective evidence-informed implementation of evidence-informed human services. **Structure** General Assembly (annual); Board of Directors. **Activities** Awareness raising; knowledge management/information dissemination; networking/liaising; events/meetings. **Events** *European Implementation Event* Basel (Switzerland) 2023, *Meeting* Rotterdam (Netherlands) 2021, *Meeting* Rotterdam (Netherlands) 2020, *Nordic Implementation Conference* Copenhagen (Denmark) 2018. **Publications** *EIC Newsletter*.
Members Individuals in 28 countries:
Australia, Austria, Belgium, Burundi, Canada, Denmark, Finland, Germany, Iceland, India, Ireland, Italy, Japan, Malawi, Netherlands, Nigeria, Norway, Portugal, Singapore, South Africa, Spain, Sweden, Switzerland, Türkiye, UK, United Arab Emirates, USA, Zambia. [2021/XM7551/**F**]

♦ **European Implementation Network (EIN)** **07521**

Dir BP 80007, 67015 Strasbourg, France. E-mail: contact@einnetwork.org.
URL: https://www.einnetwork.org/

History Originally conceived as a project of *Judgment Watch (JW, no recent information)*, 2014. Registration: Start date: Jan 2017, France; EU Transparency Register, No/ID: 855541346280-45, Start date: 28 Apr 2022. **Aims** Champion implementation of judgments of the European Court of Human Rights. **Structure** Board; Bureau; Secretariat. **Activities** Advocacy/lobbying/activism. **Publications** *EIN Newsletter*.
Members Organizations in 25 countries and territories:
Albania, Armenia, Belgium, Bulgaria, Croatia, Czechia, Georgia, Germany, Greece, Hungary, Italy, Lithuania, Moldova, Netherlands, North Macedonia, Northern Ireland, Poland, Romania, Serbia, Spain, Switzerland, Türkiye, UK, Ukraine, USA.
Included in the above, 8 organizations listed in this Yearbook:
Advice on Individual Rights in Europe Centre (AIRE Centre); European Roma Rights Centre (ERRC, #08401); Fair Trials (#09242); International Commission of Jurists (ICJ, #12695); Judgment Watch (JW, no recent information); Open Society Fund, Prague (OSF); Stichting Justice Initiative (SJI, #19985); Validity Foundation (#20743).
Consultative Status Consultative status granted from: *Council of Europe (CE, #04881)* (Participatory Status).
IGO Relations *European Court of Human Rights (#06855).* [2022.10.19/XM5826/y/F]

♦ European Importers and Suppliers of Coal (inactive)

♦ **European Incoherent Scatter Scientific Association (EISCAT)** **07522**

Admin Dir Box 812, SE-981 28 Kiruna, Sweden. T. +4698079152 – +4698079150. Fax +4698079159.
URL: https://eiscat.se/

History 30 Dec 1975. Former names and other names: *EISCAT Scientific Association* – legal name. Registration: No/ID: 897300-2549, Sweden; No/ID: 971400536, Norway; No/ID: 3103178-2, Finland. **Aims** Study the high latitude *atmosphere*, the aurora and the coupling of the solar wind to the earth's polar ionosphere; investigate the relation between the solar wind, the magnetosphere, ionosphere, thermosphere and mesosphere. **Structure** Council, comprising members from each Associate country. Committees (2): Scientific Advisory (SAC); Administrative and Finance (AFC). Operational sites (4): Kiruna (Sweden); Sodankylä (Finland); Tromsø (Norway); Longyearbyen (Norway). Headquarters located at Kiruna (Sweden). **Finance** Investment and operational costs shared by member institutes. **Activities** Research/documentation. Global Incoherent Scatter Radars: at Longyearbyen (Norway) allows improved measurement of the ionosphere and atmosphere in the polar cap; 2 mainland radars at Tromsø (Norway) built around a VHF radar and a tri-static UHF radar (the world's only such facility able to measure full vector ionospheric plasma velocities without the need to integrate across wide spatial extents), with its transmitter at Tromsø (Norway) and additional receivers at Kiruna (Sweden) and Sodankylä (Finland). Ionospheric Heater and research ionosonde at Tromsø (Sweden). **Events** *International Symposium* Eskilstuna (Sweden) 2022, *International Symposium* Oulu (Finland) 2019, *International Symposium* Tokyo (Japan) 2017. **Publications** Annual Report; technical reports; books; journal articles.
Members National institutes in 7 countries:
Finland, France, Germany, Japan, Norway, Sweden, UK.
Included in the above, 1 organization listed in this Yearbook:
Max Planck Society for the Advancement of Science (MPG). [2022/XD6533/y/F]

♦ European Independent Business Confederation (inactive)
♦ European Independent Steelworks Association (inactive)

♦ **European Industrial & Beverage Ethanol Association (iEthanol)** ... **07523**

Registered Address Av Louise 523, 1050 Brussels, Belgium. T. +3226131686. E-mail: info@iethanol.eu.
URL: https://iethanol.eu/

History Registration: Banque-Carrefour des Entreprises, No/ID: 0894.308.920, Start date: 19 Dec 2007, Belgium; EU Transparency Register, No/ID: 482977343776-86, Start date: 3 Aug 2021. **Aims** Be the bridge between European, national and regional authorities and members acting as a source of information, data, experience and know- how for ethanol production, uses and social issues. [2022/AA2007/t/D]

♦ **European Industrial Fasteners Institute (EIFI)** **07524**

Institut européen des matériels industriels de fixation mécanique – Europäischer Schraubenverband

Secretariat Gianni Pezzoli, c/o UPIVEB, Piazza della Repubblica 10, 20121 Milan MI, Italy. T. +3926575295. Fax +3926572897. E-mail: info@eifi.org.
URL: http://www.eifi.org/

History 1 Jan 1978. Registered in accordance with Belgian law. EU Transparency Register: 317620816195-87. **Aims** Represent the economic, technical and scientific interests of members to government authorities, public bodies, customers and suppliers. **Structure** General Assembly. Board, comprising President, 2 Vice-Presidents, General Manager of the Executive Committee and 6 representatives. Executive Committee of 5 representatives. Secretariat, headed by Secretary. **Languages** English, French, German. **Staff** 1.00 FTE, paid. **Finance** Members' dues. **Activities** Fastener Groups (4): Aerospace; Automotive; Stainless; General. Collects statistical data; plans research and education programmes; disseminates technical know-how; provides up-to-date information. Organizes 3 meetings a year. **Events** *General Assembly* Stratford-upon-Avon (UK) 2013, *General Assembly* Venice (Italy) 2008.
Members Associations in 14 countries:
Belgium, Denmark, France, Germany, Ireland, Italy, Netherlands, Norway, Poland, Portugal, Spain, Sweden, Switzerland, UK.
IGO Relations Recognized by: *European Commission (EC, #06633).* **NGO Relations** A sector committee of: *Orgalim – Europe's Technology Industries (#17794).* Member of: *AEGIS Europe.* [2019/XD3544/jt/D]

♦ European Industrial Food Additives and Food Enzymes Liaison Committee / see EU Specialty Food Ingredients (#09200)

♦ **European Industrial Gases Association (EIGA)** **07525**

Association Européenne des Gaz Industriels

Gen Sec 30 Ave de l'Astronomie, 1210 Brussels, Belgium. T. +3222177098. Fax +3222198514. E-mail: info@eiga.eu.
URL: http://www.eiga.eu/

History 15 Dec 1923, Paris (France). Founded by 8th International Congress of Acetylene and Oxy-Acetylene Welding. 1989, merged with *European Carbon Dioxide Association (EDIA, inactive)*, which had been set up 29 May 1953, Bern (Switzerland). Moved to Brussels (Belgium), 1990. Former names and other names: *Permanent International Commission on Acetylene and Autogenous Welding* – former (15 Dec 1923); *Commission permanente internationale de l'acétylène, de la soudure autogène et des industries qui s'y rattachent* – former (15 Dec 1923); *Comisión Permanente Internacional del Acetileno, la Soldadura Autógena y las Industrias Afines* – former (15 Dec 1923); *Ständiger Internationaler Ausschuss für Acetylen, Autogen-Schweisstechnick und Verwandte Industriezweige* – former (15 Dec 1923); *Permanent International Committee on Acetylene, Oxy-Acetylene Welding and Allied Industries* – alias; *International European Permanent Commission of Industrial Gases and Calcium Carbide* – alias; *Commission permanente internationale européenne des gaz industriels et du carbure de calcium (CPI)* – alias. Registration: Banque-Carrefour des Entreprises, No/ID: 0439.385.452, Start date: 4 Dec 1989, Belgium; EU Transparency Register, No/ID: 04077716126-17, Start date: 30 Jun 2011. **Aims** Ensure harmonization, discussion and resolution of technical and safety aspects of production, distribution and use of industrial gases, medical gases and/or food gases. **Structure** General Assembly (annual); Administrative Board of Directors; Councils (4). **Languages** English. **Staff** 6.00 FTE, paid. **Finance** Sources: members' dues. **Activities** Awareness raising; research/documentation; standards/guidelines. **Events** *Winter Session* Brussels (Belgium) 2022, *Summer Session* Valencia (Spain) 2022, *Winter Session* Brussels (Belgium) 2021, *Summer Session* Valencia (Spain) 2021, *Winter Session* Brussels (Belgium) 2020. **Publications** *EIGAzette*; *Environmental Newsletter*; *Safety Newsletter*. Position papers; technical documents; technical bulletins. Over 450 publications available on the website. **Members** Manufacturers or distributors of industrial gases, medical gases, food gases and carbon dioxide in 43 countries. Membership countries not specified. **Consultative Status** Consultative status granted from: *ECOSOC (#05331)* (Ros A). **IGO Relations** Cooperates with: *United Nations Economic Commission for Europe (UNECE, #20555).* **NGO Relations** Member of (3): *Conseil européen de l'industrie chimique (CEFIC, #04687); Federation of European and International Associations Established in Belgium (FAIB, #09508); International Harmonization Council (IHC, #13775).* Cooperates with (2): *Comité européen de normalisation (CEN, #04162); International Organization for Standardization (ISO, #14473).* [2021/XD3126/t/D]

♦ **European Industrial Hemp Association (EIHA)** **07526**

Coordinator c/o nova-Institut GmbH, Chemiepark Knapsack, Industriestrasse 300, Gebäude 0611, 50354 Hürth, Germany. T. +492233481440. Fax +492233481450.
URL: http://www.eiha.org/

History Founded 14 Sep 2000, Wolfsburg (Germany). Officially founded as an association, 23 Nov 2005, Hürth (Germany). EU Transparency Register: 675176511033-32. **Aims** Support the cultivation, processing and use of industrial Hemp (Hemp strains that are allowed to be cultivated in accordance with EU law and the raw materials of which are processed industrially) and its products. **Languages** English. **Staff** None. **Finance** Members' dues. Annual budget: about euro 100,000. **Activities** Advocacy/lobbying/activism; events/meetings; knowledge management/information dissemination. **Events** *International Conference* Cologne (Germany) 2018, *International Conference* Cologne (Germany) 2017, *International Conference* Wesseling (Germany) 2016, *International Conference* Wesseling (Germany) 2015, *International Conference* Wesseling (Germany) 2012. **Publications** *European Industrial Hemp Industry: Cultivation, processing and product lines* (annual). Leaflets.
Members Regular (28) in 13 countries:
Austria, Canada, China, France, Germany, Ireland, Italy, Netherlands, Romania, Russia, Slovakia, UK, USA.
Associate (150). Membership countries not specified.
IGO Relations *European Commission (EC, #06633).* **NGO Relations** ASTM D37 Committee on Cannabis; Standing Committee on Agricultural Research (SCAR) – Sustainable Bioresources for a Growing Bioeconomy working group. [2018.09.06/XD8891/t/D]

♦ European Industrial Initiative Bioenergy / see European Technology and Innovation Platform Bioenergy (#08881)

♦ **European Industrial Insulation Foundation (EiiF)** **07527**

Dir Avenue du Mont-Blanc 33, 1196 Gland VD, Switzerland. T. +41229950070. Fax +41229950071. E-mail: info@eiif.org.
URL: http://www.eiif.org/

History Set up 2009, by *Fédération européenne des syndicats d'entreprises d'isolation (FESI, #09582)* and 11 other partners. Registered in accordance with Swiss Civil Code. EU Transparency Register: 658236415011-84. **Aims** Publicize the potential of sustainable insulation solutions with policy makers from the economic and political field and, through consultation as well as education and further training; initiate implementation of concrete projects. **Structure** General Assembly; Board. **Languages** English. **Finance** Members' dues. Training and application fees. **Activities** Training/education; events/meetings; knowledge management/information dissemination; advocacy/lobbying/activism. **Members** Companies. Membership countries not specified. [2019.12.11/XM5735/f/F]

♦ **European Industrial Nitrocellulose Association (EINA)** **07528**

SG c/o ARCO Association Management, Tödistr 42, 8002 Zurich ZH, Switzerland.

History Set up as *European Nitrators Association (ENA).* Previously also referred to as *European Nitrocellulose Producers Association.* Registered in accordance with Swiss Civil Code, 2018. **Aims** Further the use of industrial nitrocellulose; promote high standards for production, packaging, transport, storage, handling and safety of the product. **Structure** General Assembly (annual); Technical Committee. **Events** *Annual General Assembly* Rio de Janeiro (Brazil) 2007, *Annual General Assembly* Brussels (Belgium) 2000, *Annual General Assembly* Madrid (Spain) 1996, *Annual General Assembly* Avignon (France) 1995, *Annual General Assembly* Germany 1994. **Members** Nitrocellulose producing and marketing undertakings in Europe. Membership countries not specified. **NGO Relations** Member of: *Conseil européen de l'industrie chimique (CEFIC, #04687).* [2019.10.20/XE1222/t/D]

♦ **European Industrial Packaging Association (EIPA)** **07529**

Secretariat c/o Verband Metallverpackungen eV, Tersteegenstrasse 14, 40474 Düsseldorf, Germany. T. +492114546521. Fax +492114546530. E-mail: info@eipa-info.eu.
URL: http://eipa-info.org/

History Nov 2008. **Aims** Raise the visibility of industrial packaging and emphasizing its importance in the safe and reliable transport of goods throughout Europe and the world. **Structure** Board (meets twice a year). Transport and Regulatory Committee. **Languages** English. **Events** *Annual Meeting* Berlin (Germany) 2019, *Annual Meeting* Rome (Italy) 2015.
Members Regional organizations (3):
European Association of Fibre Drum Manufacturers (#06038); European Association of Steel Drum Manufacturers (#06222); European Reconditioners of Industrial Packaging (#08333). [2015/XM1092/ty/D]

♦ **European Industrial Pharmacist Group (EIPG)** **07530**

Groupement des pharmaciens de l'industrie en europe (GPIE)

Pres Ordre National des Pharmaciens, 4 avenue Ruysdaël, 75379 Paris CEDEX 08, France. T. +33156213434. Fax +33156213499. E-mail: president@eipg.eu – info@eipg.eu.
Exec Dir c/o Royal Pharmaceutical Society, 66-68 East Smithfield, London, E1W 1AW, UK. Fax +448452572570.
URL: http://eipg.eu/

History 1966. Former names and other names: *Professional Group of Industrial Pharmacists of Europe* – alias. Registration: EU Transparency Register, No/ID: 979567925318-36, Start date: 4 Jan 2017; France. **Aims** Represent national professional organizations of pharmacists employed in the pharmaceutical or allied industries of member states of the European Union, the European Economic Area, or European countries having a mutual recognition agreement with the European Union on compliance control of regulated medicines. **Structure** General Assembly (annual); Bureau. **Languages** English, French. **Staff** 6.00 FTE, voluntary. **Finance** Contributions from national industrial pharmacist organizations. **Activities** Research and development; standards/guidelines; guidance/assistance/consulting. **Events** *Symposium* Paris (France) 2016, *General Assembly* Edinburgh (UK) 2015, *General Assembly* Sofia (Bulgaria) 2014, *General Assembly* Brussels (Belgium) 2013, *General Assembly* Lisbon (Portugal) 2012. **Publications** *European Industrial Pharmacy Journal. Code of Practice for Qualified Persons; Code of Practice for Regulatory Affairs; Guidance on Continuing Professional Development for Qualified Persons.*
Members Represents about 10,000 pharmacists in Europe. Members in 16 countries:
Belgium, Bulgaria, Czechia, Finland, France, Greece, Hungary, Ireland, Italy, Latvia, Malta, Netherlands, Norway, Spain, Switzerland, UK. [2023/XD5993/t/D]

♦ European Industrial Regions Association (inactive)

♦ **European Industrial Research Management Association (EIRMA)** .. **07531**

Association européenne pour l'administration de la recherche industrielle – Europäische Vereinigung für das Management der Industrieforschung

SG Rue de la Loi 81-A, 1040 Brussels, Belgium. T. +3222331180. Fax +3222310835. E-mail: info@eirma.org.
Events – European Projects Manager address not obtained.
URL: http://www.eirma.org/

History 11 May 1966, Château de Ménars (France). Founded with the assistance of *OECD (#17693).* Registration: No/ID: 0847.677.159, Start date: 27 Jul 2012, Belgium; RNA, No/ID: W751009440, Start date: 8 Nov 2010, End date: 9 Mar 2015, France. **Aims** Help companies to improve the performance of their Research and Development and enhance innovation. **Structure** General Assembly (annual, at conference); Governing Board; Programme Planning Committee; Permanent Committees; Secretary-General. **Languages** English. **Staff** 4.00 FTE, paid. **Finance** Members' dues. **Activities** Events/meetings; knowledge management/information dissemination; networking/liaising. **Events** *Annual Conference* Prague (Czechia) 2021, *Annual Conference* Prague (Czechia) 2020, *Annual Conference* Gothenburg (Sweden) 2019, *Annual Conference* Lyon (France) 2018, *Annual Conference* Dublin (Ireland) 2017. **Publications** Newsletters – electronic. Annual Report; conference papers; working group reports; membership directory. **Members** Industrial firms (about 90) in 27 European countries. Membership countries not specified. **Consultative Status** Consultative status granted from: *World Intellectual Property Organization (WIPO, #21593)* (Permanent Observer Status). **NGO Relations** Close relations with *'Industrial Research Institute (IRI)'* in the USA. Associate expert of: *Business and Industry Advisory Committee to the OECD (BIAC, #03385)*. Member of, and instrumental in setting up: *World Federation of Industrial Research Associations (W-FIRA, #21442)*. Member of: *Federation of European and International Associations Established in Belgium (FAIB, #09508)*. Close links with national sister organizations. [2020/XD0783/t/**D**]

♦ European Industrial Space Study Group / see Association of European Space Industry (#02544)
♦ European Infertility Alliance / see Fertility Europe (#09737)

♦ European Influenza Surveillance Network (EISN) 07532

Contact c/o ECDC, SE-171 83 Stockholm, Sweden. T. +46858601000. E-mail: influenza@ecdc.europa.eu.
URL: https://www.ecdc.europa.eu/en/about-us/partnerships-and-networks/disease-and-laboratory-networks/eisn

History Originally a project under Netherlands Institute for Health Services Research (NIVEL), building on the *Eurosentinel* scheme (1987-1991) and the *ENS-CARE Influenza Early Warning Scheme* (1992-1995). Coordination taken over by *European Centre for Disease Prevention and Control (ECDC, #06476)*, Sep 2008. Former names and other names: *European Influenza Surveillance Scheme (EISS)* – former (1995 to 2008). **Aims** Facilitate rapid exchange of information on influenza activity in Europe; combine clinical and virological data in the same population; identify causal viruses in the population and recognize virological changes; provide standardized information of high quality. **Structure** Annual Meeting; Steering Committee. **Languages** English. **Staff** 4.50 FTE, paid. **Finance** Supported by: *European Centre for Disease Prevention and Control (ECDC, #06476)*. **Activities** include: weekly-based influenza surveillance in Europe; community network of sentinel networks; community network of national reference laboratories; contributing to influenza sequence/antiviral susceptibility databases; mapping project; clinical and virological quality control programmes; EU vaccination uptake assessment. **Events** *Annual Meeting* Stockholm (Sweden) 2015, *Annual Meeting* Warsaw (Poland) 2012, *Annual Meeting* Ljubljana (Slovenia) 2011, *Annual Meeting* Sofia (Bulgaria) 2010, *Annual Meeting* Torremolinos (Spain) 2007. **Publications** *EISN Weekly Electronic Bulletin*.
Members in the 27 European Union countries:
Austria, Belgium, Bulgaria, Cyprus, Czechia, Denmark, Estonia, Finland, France, Germany, Greece, Hungary, Ireland, Italy, Latvia, Lithuania, Luxembourg, Malta, Netherlands, Poland, Portugal, Romania, Slovakia, Slovenia, Spain, Sweden, UK.
Corresponding in 3 countries:
Croatia, Iceland, Norway.
IGO Relations *European Commission (EC, #06633)*; *WHO Regional Office for Europe (#20945)*; *WHO (#20950)*. [2023.02.20/XF6213/**F**]

♦ European Influenza Surveillance Scheme / see European Influenza Surveillance Network (#07532)
♦ European Informatics Market (internationally oriented national body)
♦ European Information Association (inactive)
♦ European Information Bureau for Animal Health Development / see Centre européen d'études pour la santé animale (#03745)
♦ European Information Centre for Complementary and Alternative Medicine (inactive)
♦ European Information Communications and Consumer Electronics Technology Industry Association / see DIGITALEUROPE (#05073)
♦ European Information and Communications Technology Industry Association / see DIGITALEUROPE (#05073)

♦ European Information Network on Cultural Heritage Policies (HEREIN Project) 07533

Réseau européen d'information sur les politiques du patrimoine culturel (Projet HEREIN)
Contact Council of Europe, Liaison Office to the EU, 85 avenue des Nerviens, 1040 Brussels, Belgium. T. +3222865002.
URL: http://www.coe.int/herein/

History Founded by *Council of Europe (CE, #04881)* at the request of member states to take stock of the changes in legislation and practices in the participating countries and provide a forum for pooling and sharing information on cultural heritage. In 1992, at the 3rd European Conference of Ministers Responsible for Cultural Heritage, Valletta (Malta), ministers supported the idea to "compile and manage a periodically updated European directory of heritage policies (Res No 3). In 1996, at the 4th European Conference, Helsinki (Finland), ministers asked for the creation of a permanent information system (Res No 1 and 2). In 2001, at the 5th European Conference, ministers requested to permanently establish HEREIN (Res No 2). In 2005, role and potential contribution was increased by *Council of Europe Framework Convention on the Value of Cultural Heritage for Society (2005)*. In 2014, the *'HEREIN System for the European Heritage Policies'* was launched. **Aims** Monitor implementation of the four Council of Europe Cultural Heritage Conventions; monitor current trends and challenges in the field of heritage for the benefit of the various competent institutions; facilitate cooperation between public administrations through exchanges, development an dissemination of good practices; enable the Council of Europe to fulfil its obligations regarding the monitoring of conventions and cooperation with its members states in the field of heritage; foster implementation of heritage projects which are able to improve citizen's quality of life and living environment. **Structure** Overseen by Steering Committee for Culture, Heritage and Landscape (CDCPP). Complemented by *International Association of the European Heritage Network (HEREIN Association, #11881)*. **Languages** English, French. **Staff** 3.00 FTE, paid. **Finance** *Council of Europe (CE, #04881)* budget; additional voluntary contributions from some Member States. 1998 funding by Fourth Framework Programme for Research and Technological Development of the European Commission. 2002 funding by the Fifth Framework Programme (FP5) of the European Commission. **Activities** Knowledge management/information dissemination; events/meetings. Management of treaties and agreements: *Convention for the Protection of the Architectural Heritage of Europe (1985)*; *European Convention on the Protection of the Archaeological Heritage, Revised (1992)*; *Council of Europe Framework Convention on the Value of Cultural Heritage for Society (2005)*; *European Landscape Convention (2000)*. **Events** *Annual Meeting* Mons (Belgium) 2014, *Meeting* Liège (Belgium) 2010, *Annual Meeting* Chaumont sur Loire (France) 2008, *Meeting* Strasbourg (France) 2003, *Meeting of the correspondents* Krakow (Poland) 2002. **Publications** Multilingual thesaurus on heritage terms in 15 European languages; brochures. Information Services: Database on European heritage policies and strategies; access to Internet resources including international actors, legislation, European public administrations.
Members National coordinators in 44 members states of the Council of Europe:
Andorra, Armenia, Austria, Azerbaijan, Belarus, Belgium, Bosnia-Herzegovina, Bulgaria, Croatia, Cyprus, Czechia, Denmark, Estonia, Finland, France, Georgia, Germany, Greece, Hungary, Iceland, Ireland, Italy, Latvia, Lithuania, Luxembourg, Malta, Moldova, Montenegro, Netherlands, North Macedonia, Norway, Poland, Portugal, Romania, Russia, Serbia, Slovakia, Slovenia, Spain, Sweden, Switzerland, Türkiye, UK, Ukraine. [2016.06.01/XK1920/**F**]

♦ European Information Network on International Relations and Area Studies (EINIRAS) 07534

Address not obtained.
History 1992, with support of *European Cooperation in Social Science Information and Documentation (ECSSID, inactive)*. **Aims** Expand practical cooperation and exchange of information, bibliographical data and publications on international relations in research and political practice; establish a common European database on international relations and area studies. **Structure** General Meeting (annual, at Conference); Steering Committee; Task Groups (4). **Languages** English. **Staff** None. **Finance** Member' dues. Voluntary contributions. **Activities** Organizes: annual conference. Task Groups (4): Standardization; Information and Communication Technology; Information Literacy; Funding. **Events** *Conference* Berlin (Germany) 2013, *Annual Conference* Paris (France) 2012, *Annual Conference* Strasbourg (France) 2011, *Annual Conference* Warsaw (Poland) 2010, *Annual conference* Madrid (Spain) 2009. **Publications** *EINIRAS Thesaurus on International Relations and Area Studies*.
Members International institutions (3), listed in this Yearbook:
Council of Europe (CE, #04881); *European Union Institute for Security Studies (EUISS, #08994)*; *United Nations Institute for Disarmament Research (UNIDIR, #20575)*.
National institutions in 27 countries:
Albania, Austria, Belgium, Bulgaria, Croatia, Czechia, Denmark, Estonia, Finland, France, Germany, Greece, Hungary, Italy, Kosovo, Netherlands, Norway, Poland, Portugal, Romania, Russia, Slovakia, Spain, Sweden, Switzerland, UK, USA.
Included in the above, 34 organizations listed in this Yearbook:
- *Austrian Institute for International Affairs (oiip)*;
- *Center for Comparative and International Studies (CIS)*;
- *Centre for International Information and Documentation, Barcelona (CIDOB Foundation)*;
- *Centro Español de Relaciones Internacionales (CERI)*;
- *Deutsche Gesellschaft für Auswärtige Politik (DGAP)*;
- *European Centre for Minority Issues (ECMI)*;
- *European Institute of Romania (IER)*;
- *Finnish Institute of International Affairs (FIIA)*;
- *GIGA – German Institute of Global and Area Studies*;
- *Groupe de recherche et d'information sur la paix et la sécurité (GRIP)*;
- *Hellenic Foundation for European and Foreign Policy (ELIAMEP)*;
- *Hungarian Institute of International Affairs (HIIA)*;
- *Institute for Development and International Relations (IRMO)*;
- *Institute for International Economic and Political Studies, Moscow (IIEPS)*;
- *Institute for Strategic and International Studies, Lisbon (IEEI)*;
- *Institute of Europe, Moscow*;
- *Institute of International Relations, Prague (IIR)*;
- *Institut français des relations internationales (IFRI)*;
- *Institut für Auslandsbeziehungen, Stuttgart (ifa)*;
- *Institut für den Donauraum und Mitteleuropa (IDM)*;
- *Institut Mirovoj Ekonomiki i Mezdunarodnyh Otnosenij Rossijskoj Akademii Nauk (IMEMO)*;
- *Institut of International Relations, Athens (IIR)*;
- *International Institute for Strategic Studies (IISS, #13927)*;
- *International Peace Information Service (IPIS)*;
- *International Relations and Security Network (ISN, inactive)*;
- *Netherlands Institute of International Relations – Clingendael*;
- *NIAS-Nordisk Institut for Asienstudier (NIAS, #17132)*;
- *Norwegian Institute of International Affairs (NUPI)*;
- *Polish Institute of International Affairs (PIIA)*;
- *Real Instituto Elcano de Estudios Internacionales y Estratégicos*;
- *Royal Institute of International Affairs (RIIA)*;
- *Stiftung Wissenschaft und Politik (SWP)*;
- *Stockholm International Peace Research Institute (SIPRI, #19994)*. [2014.06.24/XF3853/y/**F**]

♦ European Information Network on New and Emerging Health Technologies / see international HealthTechScan (#13784)
♦ European Information Providers' Association (inactive)

♦ European Information and Research Network on Parliamentary History (EuParl) 07535

Coordinator Montesquieu Inst, Lange Voorhout 86 – 32, 2514 EJ The Hague, Netherlands. T. +31703560238. E-mail: euparl@montesquieu-instituut.nl.
URL: http://euparl.net/

History Oct 2007. **Aims** Enhance international cooperation in the area of parliamentary history and development by creating a cluster, including all European research institutions and experts in parliamentary history. **Structure** Board of Directors. **Activities** Research/documentation; events/meetings. **Publications** *EuParl Newsletter* (2 a year).
Members Full in 16 countries:
Austria, Belgium, Czechia, Finland, France, Germany, Greece, Hungary, Italy, Luxembourg, Netherlands, Romania, Slovakia, Slovenia, Spain, UK. [2016/XM4684/**F**]

♦ European Infrastructure for Translational Medicine (EATRIS) 07536

Head Office De Boelelaan 1118, 1081 HZ Amsterdam, Netherlands. T. +31204442254. E-mail: info@eatris.eu.
URL: http://www.eatris.eu/

History Nov 2013, awarded status of *European Research Infrastructure Consortium (ERIC)*, following which it is also known as *European Advanced Translational Research Infrastructure in Medicine ERIC (EATRIS ERIC)*. Registration: Netherlands. **Aims** Make translation of scientific discoveries into medical products more effective to improve human health and quality of life. **Structure** Coordination and Supports (headquarters). Board of Governors. **Events** *Annual Meeting* Lisbon (Portugal) 2020, *Biennial Conference* Prague (Czechia) 2017, *Biennial Conference* Amsterdam (Netherlands) 2015, *Biennial Conference* Amsterdam (Netherlands) 2013. **Publications** *EATRIS Newsflash*.
Members Institutions in 9 countries:
Czechia, Denmark, Estonia, Finland, France, Italy, Luxembourg, Netherlands, Spain.
IGO Relations *European Commission (EC, #06633)*. **NGO Relations** *International Society for Cell & Gene Therapy (ISCT, #15000)*. [2020/XJ7870/**D**]

♦ European Initiative for Agricultural Research for Development (EIARD) 07537

Exec Sec European Commission, DG Research and Innovation, F3 – Agri Food Chain, COVE 08/105, 1049 Brussels, Belgium. T. +3222991790.
Chair address not obtained. T. +41313220305. Fax +41313259362.
URL: https://www.ard-europe.org/eiard/who-we-are/contact/

History Proposed at Research Council, 9 Sep 1994, and supported by French Presidency of *European Council (#06801)* at ministerial meeting Feb 1995, Lucerne (Switzerland). Working paper prepared by *European Commission (EC, #06633)*, suggesting set-up of European Coordination Group (ECG). EIARD launched at first meeting of ECG, Oct 1995. **Aims** Improve the impact of European investment in agricultural research for development (ARD) on food security, poverty elimination and environmental sustainability through enhanced coordination of policies and investments; promote coordination and research partnerships in Europe and between Europe and developing countries, based on equality and mutual respect. **Structure** European Coordination Group (ECG), comprising representatives of all 24 partners with national EIARD networks in each member country. Working Group; Task forces of experts. Executive Secretariat in Brussels (Belgium), headed by Executive Secretary and hosted by European Commission (DG Research and Innovation). **Languages** English. **Finance** No central budget, partners share cost of activities. **Activities** As a permanent informal donor coordination platform operating outside EU "comitology" procedures: developed institutional mechanisms to coordinate Agricultural Research for Development (ARD) policies and programmes between European states and the EC. **Events** *ECG Meeting* Brussels (Belgium) 2013, *Meeting* Brussels (Belgium) 2013, *ECG Meeting* Nyon (Switzerland) 2012, *ECG Meeting* Montpellier (France) 2011, *ECG Meeting* Uppsala (Sweden) 2010. **Publications** *Strategy for EIARD 2009-2013*. Papers; policy briefs; studies. **Information Services** *EARD-InfoSys*.
Members National partners – governments of 21 countries:
Austria, Belgium, Cyprus, Czechia, Denmark, Estonia, Finland, France, Germany, Hungary, Ireland, Italy, Lithuania, Netherlands, Norway, Portugal, Slovakia, Spain, Sweden, Switzerland, UK.
European partner:
European Commission.
IGO Relations Through the European Commission, recognized by and accountable to: *Council of the European Union (#04895)*; *European Parliament (EP, #08146)*. **NGO Relations** Facilitated founding of: *European Forum on Agricultural Research for Development (EFARD, #07302)*. Works with: *Young Professionals for Agricultural Development (YPARD, #21996)*. [2014/XF3870/**F***]

♦ European Initiative for Exercise in Medicine (EIEIM) 07538

Chair c/o Ulm Univ, Leimgrubenweg 14, 89075 Ulm, Germany. E-mail: exercise.medicine@uniklinik-ulm.de.
URL: https://www.exerciseismedicine.eu/

History 2015. The independent, European part of Exercise is Medicine (EIM), a global health initiative managed by the American College of Sports Medicine (ACSM). Registration: Baden-Württemberg District cour, No/ID: VR 720702, Start date: 21 Dec 2015, Germany, Ulm. **Aims** Make physical activity and exercise a standard part of a European disease prevention and treatment medical paradigm. **Structure** Board. **Languages** English, German. **Activities** Events/meetings. **Events** *Conference* Hamburg (Germany) 2023, *Sports, Medicine and Health Summit* Hamburg (Germany) 2023, *Conference* Padua (Italy) 2022, *Conference* Hamburg (Germany) 2021, *Conference* Amsterdam (Netherlands) 2019. [2022/AA2670/**E**]

♦ European Initiative for Human Rights and Democracy / see European Instrument for Democracy and for Human Rights (#07576)

♦ European Initiative for Security Studies (EISS) 07539

Registered Address 56 rue Jacob Ceri-Sciences Po, 75006 Paris, France. E-mail: eissnetwork@gmail.com.
URL: https://eiss-europa.com/

History Registration: RNA, No/ID: W751263001, Start date: 19 Nov 2021, France. **Aims** Develop and sustain a Europe-wide network in the field of security studies; establish a forum for the exchange of ideas so as to foster new joint research projects and develop international research partnerships. **Structure** Board. **Activities** Events/meetings. **Events** *Conference* Berlin (Germany) 2022, *Conference* Lisbon (Portugal) 2021, *Conference* Paris (France) 2019, *Conference* Paris (France) 2018, *Conference* Paris (France) 2017. [2022/AA2521/**F**]

♦ European Initiative for Sustainable Development in Agriculture (inactive)
♦ European Inland Fisheries Advisory Commission / see European Inland Fisheries and Aquaculture Advisory Commission (#07540)

♦ European Inland Fisheries and Aquaculture Advisory Commission (EIFAAC) 07540

Sec Fisheries and Aquaculture Policy and Resources Division, FAO, Viale delle Terme di Caracalla, 00153 Rome RM, Italy. T. +39657051604.
URL: http://www.fao.org/fishery/rfb/eifaac/

History Jun 1957, Madrid (Spain). Founded, as an Article VI body under *FAO (#09260)*, by FAO Council at its 26th Session. First session Apr 1960. Title and new statutes formally approved, May 2010. Former names and other names: *European Inland Fisheries Advisory Commission (EIFAC)* – former; *Commission européenne consultative pour les pêches dans les eaux intérieures (CECPI)* – former; *Comisión Asesora Europea sobre Pesca Continental* – former. Registration: EU Transparency Register, No/ID: 19920882621 7-90. **Aims** Promote long-term sustainable development, utilization, conservation, restoration and responsible management of European inland fisheries and aquaculture. **Structure** Management Committee; Technical and Scientific Committee. **Languages** English, French, German. **Activities** Capacity building; events/meetings; guidance/assistance/consulting; knowledge management/information dissemination; monitoring/evaluation; projects/programmes; research and development; standards/guidelines. **Events** *Biennial Session* Dresden (Germany) 2019, *Symposium on Food Safety and Conservation in Inland Fisheries* Dresden (Germany) 2019, *Biennial Session* Stare Joblanki (Poland) 2017, *International Symposium* Stare Joblanki (Poland) 2017, *Biennial Session* Lillehammer (Norway) 2015. **Publications** *EIFAC Series.* Technical papers.
Members Open to all FAO Member Nations in the European region. Currently governments of 33 countries:
Albania, Austria, Belgium, Bosnia-Herzegovina, Bulgaria, Croatia, Cyprus, Czechia, Denmark, Estonia, Finland, France, Germany, Greece, Hungary, Iceland, Ireland, Israel, Italy, Latvia, Lithuania, Luxembourg, Netherlands, Norway, Poland, Portugal, Romania, Slovakia, Spain, Sweden, Switzerland, Türkiye, UK.
Regional Entity:
European Union (EU, #08967).
IGO Relations Observer status with (1): *International Council for the Exploration of the Sea (ICES, #13021).* Collaborates on data collection with: *OIE – World Organisation for Animal Health (#17703).* [2021.09.07/XE1070/**E***]

♦ European Inland Transport Council (inactive)

♦ European Inland Waterway Transport Platform (European IWT Platform) 07541

Coordinator Avenue des Arts 53, 1000 Brussels, Belgium. T. +32494560707.
URL: http://inlandwaterwaytransport.eu/

History Activities started 2018; officially launched 21 Jan 2019. EU Transparency Register: 672000433672-15. **Aims** Achieve a stronger positioning of Inland Navigation in European and national transport policies. **Structure** Board of Directors; Executive Board; Coordinator; Committees.
Members Organizations in 11 countries:
Austria, Belgium, Czechia, France, Germany, Hungary, Luxembourg, Netherlands, Poland, Romania, Switzerland.
Regional associations (2):
European Barge Union (EBU, #06318); European Skippers Organisation (ESO-OEB, #08491). [2020/XM7441/y/**F**]

♦ European Inline Figure Skating Association / see World Inline Figure Skating Association (#21584)

♦ European Inorganic Coagulants Producers Association (INCOPA) . . 07542

Contact CEFIC, Rue Belliard 40, Box 15, 1040 Brussels, Belgium. T. +32024369408. E-mail: ppa@cefic.be – info@incopa.org.
URL: http://www.incopa.org/

History Apr 1999. Founded within the framework of *Conseil européen de l'industrie chimique (CEFIC, #04687)*, by merger of *Aluminium Sulphate Producers Association (ASUPA, inactive)* and CEFIC's *'Coagulants Water Treatment'* sector group. **Aims** Monitor and provide input on the regulatory developments on issues of importance to the industry; represent the industry with the regulatory bodies and trade associations active in the field; promote and defend the merits of the treatment of waste water with chemical coagulants by bringing forward evidence of their efficiency and cost effectiveness. **Structure** General Assembly (twice a year); Coordination Committee; Technical and Regulatory Affairs Committee; Strategy and Communications Committee. **Languages** English. **Members** Companies (30) in 14 countries. Membership countries not specified. **NGO Relations** Member of (1): *European Sustainable Phosphorus Platform (ESPP, #08866).* [2021.05.26/XK1875/**E**]

♦ European Insolvency Practitioners Association / see INSOL Europe (#11231)

♦ European Insolvency Practitioners Association (EIP) 07543

Contact Boulevard Edmond Machtens 180, 1080 Brussels, Belgium. E-mail: contact@eip-association.eu.
Contact 6 boulevard Capucines, 75009 Paris, France.
URL: https://eip-association.eu/

History 2016. Former names and other names: *Association Européenne des Organisations de Practiciens de l'Insolvabilité* – legal name; *European Association of Insolvency Practitioners Organizations* – legal name; *Europäischer Dachverband der Insolvenzpraktiker* – legal name. Registration: No/ID: 0671.830.908, Start date: 24 Feb 2017, Belgium; EU Transparency Register, No/ID: 497384739938-25, Start date: 15 Oct 2020. **Aims** Remain proactive and reactive in all insolvency processes. **Structure** Board of Directors; Committees.
Members Full in 12 countries:
Austria, Denmark, Estonia, France, Germany, Italy, Latvia, Lithuania, Poland, Slovenia, Spain, Sweden. [2020/AA1138/**D**]

♦ European Installation Bus Association (inactive)
♦ European Installation Bus Association / see KNX Association (#16202)
♦ European Institute / see Blinken European Institute, Columbia University, New York

♦ European Institute for Advanced Studies in Management (EIASM) . 07544

Institut européen de recherches et d'études supérieures en management

Main Office Passage du Nord 19, 1000 Brussels, Belgium. T. +3222266660. Fax +3225121929. E-mail: info@eiasm.be.
URL: https://www.eiasm.net/

History 9 Nov 1971, Brussels (Belgium). Started operation in 1972. Registration: Banque-Carrefour des Entreprises, No/ID: 0408.258.746, Start date: 13 Apr 1971, Belgium. **Aims** Enhance high quality in research and doctoral studies in management and related disciplines. **Structure** Board. **Languages** English. **Activities** Events/meetings; training/education; research and development; projects/programmes; awards/prizes/competitions. **Events** *Conference on Current Research in Taxation* Brussels (Belgium) 2022, *European Reward Management Conference* Brussels (Belgium) 2022, *RENT : Conference on Research in Entrepreneurship and Small Business* Naples (Italy) 2022, *Conference on Performance Measurement and Management Control* Brussels (Belgium) 2021, *RENT : Conference on Research in Entrepreneurship and Small Business* Turku (Finland) 2021. **Publications** *EIASM Newsletter.* Activity Reports. **Members** Universities, research institutes and business schools (75-90) in about 20 European countries. Membership countries not specified. **NGO Relations** Provides secretariat and legal seat of: *European Academy of Management (EURAM, #05800); European Accounting Association (EAA, #05820); European Association for Research in Industrial Economics (EARIE, #06193); European Finance Association (EFA, #07248); European International Business Academy (EIBA, #07585); European Marketing Academy (EMAC, #07745); European Operations Management Association (EurOMA, #08088).* Member of: *Federation of European and International Associations Established in Belgium (FAIB, #09508).* [2021/XF3945/j/**F**]

♦ European Institute for Asian Studies (EIAS) 07545

CEO Rue de la Loi 67, 1040 Brussels, Belgium. T. +3222308122. E-mail: eias@eias.org.
URL: http://www.eias.org/

History Founded Jul 1989, as *European Institute for South and South-East Asian Studies (EISSEAS).* Present name adopted Jun 1996. Registered in accordance with Belgian law. EU Transparency Register: 060904811513-73. **Aims** Promote understanding and cooperation between the EU and Asia while acting as a research and policy think tank on EU-Asia relations. **Structure** Administrative Board; Executive Committee; Working Committees. **Languages** English. **Staff** 6.00 FTE, paid. **Finance** Members' dues. Other sources: European institutions; sales of publications; expertise services. **Activities** Research/documentation; events/meetings; knowledge management/information dissemination. **Events** *Kazakhstan's Referendum on Constitutional Amendments – The future of Kazakhstan–EU relations* Brussels (Belgium) 2022, *Africa-EU-China: Avenues for a New Economic Partnership?* Brussels (Belgium) 2020, *Workshop on the future of ASEM* Singapore (Singapore) 2008, *Connecting civil societies of Asia and Europe conference* Helsinki (Finland) 2006, *Indonesia revival forum* Brussels (Belgium) 2000. **Publications** *EIAS Briefing Papers; EIAS Monthly Newsletter; EIAS Occasional Papers; EU-Asia at a Glance.* Event reports.
Members Individuals and organizations in 55 countries and territories:
Afghanistan, Austria, Bangladesh, Belgium, Bhutan, Brunei Darussalam, Bulgaria, Cambodia, China, Cyprus, Czechia, Denmark, Estonia, Finland, France, Germany, Greece, Hong Kong, Hungary, India, Indonesia, Ireland, Italy, Japan, Korea Rep, Laos, Latvia, Lithuania, Luxembourg, Macau, Malaysia, Maldives, Malta, Mongolia, Myanmar, Nepal, Netherlands, Norway, Pakistan, Philippines, Poland, Portugal, Romania, Singapore, Slovakia, Slovenia, Spain, Sri Lanka, Sweden, Switzerland, Taiwan, Thailand, Timor-Leste, UK, Vietnam.
NGO Relations Member of: *EFMD – The Management Development Network (#05387); European Alliance for Asian Studies (#05861); United Nations Global Compact (#20567).* [2020/XF1206/j/**F**]

♦ European Institute for the Best Interests of the Child (internationally oriented national body)
♦ European Institute of Bioethics (internationally oriented national body)
♦ European Institute for the Biology of Ageing (unconfirmed)

♦ European Institute for Biomedical Imaging Research (EIBIR) 07546

Dir c/o ESR Office, Neutorgasse 9, 1010 Vienna, Austria. T. +4315334064. Fax +4315357037. E-mail: mhierath@eibir.org.
URL: http://www.eibir.org/

History 2006, by *European Society of Radiology (ESR, #08720).* **Aims** Coordinate the development of biomedical imaging technologies within Europe; support the dissemination of knowledge within the ultimate goal of improving diagnosis, treatment and prevention of disease. **Structure** General Meeting; Shareholders; Scientific Advisory Board; Secretariat; ESR Research Committee. **Events** *Joint Scientific Symposium on Advances in Theranostics of Rare Cancer* Innsbruck (Austria) 2014.
Members Full in 36 countries:
Austria, Belgium, Bulgaria, Croatia, Cyprus, Czechia, Denmark, Egypt, Estonia, Finland, France, Germany, Greece, Hungary, India, Iran Islamic Rep, Ireland, Israel, Italy, Kazakhstan, Luxembourg, Netherlands, New Zealand, North Macedonia, Norway, Poland, Portugal, Romania, Russia, Slovakia, Slovenia, Spain, Sweden, Switzerland, Türkiye, UK.
NGO Relations Shareholder organizations: *Cardiovascular and Interventional Radiological Society of Europe (CIRSE, #03427), European Coordination Committee of the Radiological, Electromedical Healthcare IT Industry (COCIR, #06792); European Association of Nuclear Medicine (EANM, #06136); European Federation of Organisations for Medical Physics (EFOMP, #07183); European Organisation for Research and Treatment of Cancer (EORTC, #08101); European Society of Magnetic Resonance in Medicine and Biology (ESMRMB, #08644).* Office hosted by *European Society of Radiology (ESR, #08720).* [2010/XM3925/j/**D**]

♦ European Institute of Business Administration / see INSEAD (#11228)
♦ European Institute for Business Ethics (internationally oriented national body)
♦ European Institute of Communication and Culture (internationally oriented national body)

♦ European Institute for Comparative Cultural Research (ERICarts) . . 07547

Institut européen de recherche comparative sur la culture – Instituto Europeo de Investigación Cultural Comparativa – Europäisches Institut für vergleichende Kulturforschung

Exec Dir Ulmenallee 24a, 50999 Cologne, Germany. T. +4922365097972.
Pres c/o Univ of Barcelona, Gran Via de les Corts Catalanes, 585, 08007 Barcelona, Spain.
URL: http://www.ericarts-institute.org/

History 1993, Bonn (Germany). Former names and other names: *European Research Institute for Comparative Cultural Policy and the Arts – Scientific Council* – former (1993 to 2004); *ERICarts Institute* – alias. Registration: Court of Bonn Association Register, No/ID: VR 6877, Germany, Bonn; Court of Bonn Company Register, No/ID: HRB13623, Germany, Bonn. **Aims** Develop and execute comparative research focused on cultural/heritage policy and media developments, cultural education, culture industries and the status of various arts and media professions. **Structure** Board of Governors (ERICarts Network). **Languages** English, French, German. **Staff** 2.00 FTE, paid; 7.00 FTE, voluntary. Extra project staff: 26 paid (2021). **Finance** Sources: fees for services; revenue from activities/projects. Annual budget: 140,000 EUR (2022). **Activities** Events/meetings; guidance/assistance/consulting; projects/programmes. **Events** *Compendium Assembly* Paris (France) 2019, *Compendium Assembly* Prague (Czechia) 2017, *Compendium Assembly* St Julian's (Malta) 2016, *Compendium Assembly* Wroclaw (Poland) 2015, *Compendium Assembly* Brussels (Belgium) 2014. **Publications** Books; research agendas; project papers. **Information Services** *Compendium of Cultural Policies and Trends* – Founding member (with Council of Europe).
Members Experts and institutions (about 120) in 44 countries:
Argentina, Armenia, Australia, Austria, Azerbaijan, Belgium, Bulgaria, Canada, Chile, China, Croatia, Czechia, Denmark, Estonia, Finland, France, Georgia, Germany, Greece, Hungary, India, Ireland, Italy, Korea Rep, Lithuania, Malta, Moldova, Montenegro, Netherlands, North Macedonia, Norway, Poland, Portugal, Russia, Serbia, Slovakia, Slovenia, Spain, Sweden, Switzerland, Türkiye, UK, Ukraine, USA.
NGO Relations Member of (1): *International Network of Observatories in Cultural Policies (#14299).* Instrumental in setting up (1): *Association of the Compendium of Cultural Policies and Trends (CCPT Association, #02442).* Subsidiary of: *European Association of Cultural Researchers (ECURES, #06000).* [2022.05.04/XE3712/j/**E**]

♦ European Institute for Computer Anti-Virus Research (EICAR) 07548

Exec Sec c/o Data Business Services GmbH and Co KG, Hauptstrasse 4, 85579 Neubiberg, Germany. T. +491712440099. Fax +498966002036.
Office Obergasse 28A, 86943 Thaining, Germany. T. +498194998499. Fax +498194998501.
URL: http://www.eicar.org/

History 23 Sep 1991, Brussels (Belgium). Registered in accordance with German law. **Aims** Promote and support cooperation between *end-users*, researchers and manufacturers, so that all are better equipped to carry on the war against *malicious softwarecode.* **Structure** Board of Directors, including Chair and Executive Secretary. Task Forces. **Activities** Task Forces (3): Task Force on Critical Infrastructure Protection; Working Group 2 on Anti-Virus Practices; Task Force on European Cyber Crime Initiative. **Events** *Annual Conference* Frankfurt-Main (Germany) 2014, *Annual Conference* Cologne (Germany) 2013, *Annual Conference* Lisbon (Portugal) 2012, *Annual Conference* Krems (Austria) 2011, *Annual Conference* Paris (France) 2010.
Members Companies and individuals in 12 countries:
Australia, Austria, Belgium, Bulgaria, France, Germany, Netherlands, South Africa, Sweden, Switzerland, UK, USA. [2017/XE3106/j/**E**]

♦ European Institute for Construction Labour Research (CLR) 07549

Europees Instituut Onderzoek Arbeidsverhoudingen Bouw

Contact c/o EFBWW, Rue Royale 45, 1st fl, 1000 Brussels, Belgium. T. +3222271040. Fax +3222198228. E-mail: clr@efbh.be.

URL: http://www.clr-news.org/
History 1993, as *European Association for Construction Labour Research*. Founders (4): *European Federation of Building and Woodworkers (EFBWW, #07065)*; Technical University of Denmark; Fachhochschule Dortmund (Germany); University of Westminster (UK). Current name adopted 18 Dec 1996. Registered in accordance with Belgian law, 1996. **Aims** Initiate, coordinate and conduct labour research in the construction and *wood* industries; develop or support activities that are directly and indirectly connected with its objectives, including educational activities and the publication of research findings. **Structure** General Assembly; Management Committee; Administrator; Autonomous regional offices (3); Liaison with Thinknet-Swiss. **Languages** English. **Staff** No permanent staff. **Finance** Main source: income from publications. Participant's costs in activities paid by themselves or by their organization; research financed by one-off external funding. **Activities** Research and development; training/education; publishing activities; events/meetings. **Events** *Conference on migration research* 1999, *Annual meeting* Brussels (Belgium) 1998, *Annual meeting* Brussels (Belgium) 1997, *Annual meeting* Brussels (Belgium) 1996. **Publications** *CLR News* (4 a year) in English. Studies; reports.
Members Full in 5 countries:
Belgium, Denmark, Germany, Switzerland, UK.
Associate members in other European countries. Membership countries not specified.
IGO Relations Regularly consulted by several parts of: *European Commission (EC, #06633)*. National members have consultative status in several EU member states. **NGO Relations** Cooperation at European level is more or less permanent with social partners in the construction sector, including: *European Construction Industry Federation (#06766)*; *European Federation of Building and Woodworkers (EFBWW, #07065)*.
[2021/XE2682/j/E]

♦ European Institute for Cooperation and Development, Paris / see IECD

♦ European Institute for Crime Prevention and Control affiliated with the United Nations (HEUNI) 07550

Institut européen pour la prévention du crime et la lutte contre la délinquance affilié à l'Organisation des Nations Unies – Evropejskij Institut po Preduprezdeniju Prestupnosti i Borbe s nej svjazannyj s Organizaciej Obedinennyh Nacij – Europeiska institutet för kriminalpolitik verksamt i anslutning till Förenta Nationerna – Yhdistyneiden kansakuntien yhteydessä toimiva Euroopan Kriminaalipolitiikan instituutti
Dir Vilhonkatu 4 B19, FI-00100 Helsinki, Finland. T. +358295665287. E-mail: heuni@om.fi.
URL: http://www.heuni.fi/
History 23 Dec 1981. Established by an Agreement between the Finnish Government and *United Nations (UN, #20515)*. Commenced operations 1 Oct 1982. Agreement extended, 14 Apr 1987. Former names and other names: *Helsinki Institute for Crime Prevention and Control affiliated with the United Nations* – former; *Institut d'Helsinki pour la prévention du crime et la lutte contre la délinquance affilié à l'Organisation des Nations Unies* – former; *Helsinkskij Institut po Preduprezdeniju Prestupnosti i Borbe s nej svjazannyj s Organizaciej Obedinennyh Nacij* – former; *Helsingfors kriminalpolitiska institut verksamt i anslutning till Förenta Nationerna* – former; *Yhdistyneiden kansakuntien yhteydessä toimiva Helsingin kriminaalipoliittinen instituutti* – former. **Aims** Advance humane and rational criminal justice policies and systems in the European region, in line with the Sustainable Development Goals. **Structure** Operates under joint auspices of United Nations and Government of Finland. International Advisory Board. **Languages** English, Finnish, Swedish. **Staff** 9.00 FTE, paid. **Finance** Sources: government support. Government of Finland. **Activities** Events/meetings; financial and/or material support; guidance/assistance/consulting; knowledge management/information dissemination; research/documentation. **Publications** *HEUNI Reports Series*. Annual Report. All publications available electronically on website. **Members** Not a membership organization; services all European countries. **IGO Relations** Also links with national institutions. **NGO Relations** Member of (1): *World Criminal Justice Library Network (WCJLN, #21343)*.
[2022.10.11/XE0734/j/E*]

♦ European Institute of the Cultivated Forest (internationally oriented national body)
♦ European Institute of Cultural Itineraries / see European Institute of Cultural Routes
♦ European Institute of Cultural Routes (internationally oriented national body)
♦ European Institute for Democratic Participation (internationally oriented national body)
♦ European Institute of Design (internationally oriented national body)
♦ European Institute for Design and Disability / see EIDD – Design for All Europe (#05399)
♦ European Institute for Development of Human Resources, Willemstad (internationally oriented national body)
♦ European Institute of Diplomacy and International Relations (unconfirmed)

♦ European Institute of Education and Social Policy (EIESP) 07551

Institut européen d'éducation et de politique sociale (IEEPS)
Dir c/o ESCP Europe, 81 avenue de la République, 75543 Paris CEDEX 11, France. T. +33149235830 – +331(33638476819. E-mail: ieeps@eiesp.org.
URL: http://www.eiesp.org/
History Founded 1975, as *'Institute of Education'*, by *European Cultural Foundation (ECF, #06868)*, in cooperation with *International Council for Educational Development (ICED, inactive)*, to respond to a need of *European Commission (EC, #06633)* to develop cooperation in higher education. Current name adopted 1982. Previously also referred to in Dutch as *Europees Instituut voor Onderwijs en Sociale Politiek*. Registered in accordance with French law. EU Transparency Register: 76274494636-35. **Aims** Develop systems, approaches, tools and practices that place the learner at the centre of the learning process; create bridges among research, policy and practice; evaluate design, implementation and outcomes of polices at different decision-making levels; contribute to decision-making processes and exchange of good practice among countries, institutions or sectors. **Structure** General Assembly; Administrative Board. **Languages** English, French. **Staff** 2.50 FTE, paid. Voluntary; 6-10 consultants. **Finance** Self-funding. Projects funded through contracts with European Union and its agencies, governments, international organizations, foundations and private companies. **Activities** Training/education; research/documentation; monitoring/evaluation; guidance/assistance/consulting. **Events** *International symposium* Paris (France) 1986. **Publications** *European Journal of Education (EJE)* (4 a year) in English. Occasional papers; reports.
Members Individuals in 12 countries:
Belgium, Canada, Finland, France, Germany, Hungary, Italy, Netherlands, Spain, Switzerland, UK, USA.
[2015.09.01/XE5838/j/E]

♦ European Institute for E-Learning (EIfEL) 07552

CEO 1 rue Neuve, 89210 Champlost, France. T. +33386431343. Fax +33386431778.
URL: http://www.eife-l.org/eifel/
History Feb 2001. **Structure** Board, comprising President, Honorary President, 2 Vice-Presidents, Treasurer and 2 further members. **Events** *Annual international conference on interactive computer aided learning* Villach (Austria) 2009, *E-portfolio meeting* Maastricht (Netherlands) 2008, *Annual international conference on interactive computer aided learning* Villach (Austria) 2008, *e-portfolio meeting* Maastricht (Netherlands) 2007. **Members** National and international organizations (not specified). Included in the above, 3 organizations listed in this Yearbook:
Association of Language Testers in Europe (ALTE, #02779); *European Schoolnet (EUN, #08433)*; *IMS Global Learning Consortium (IMS)*.
NGO Relations Instrumental in setting up: *European Foundation for Quality in eLearning (EFQUEL, inactive)*.
[2016/XM1150/jy/E]

♦ European Institute Emmanuel Levinas (unconfirmed)
♦ European Institute for Environmental Education, Interpretation and Training (internationally oriented national body)
♦ European Institute for Environmental Education and Training / see European Institute for Environmental Education, Interpretation and Training

♦ European Institute for Export Compliance (EIFEC) 07553

EU Head Office Levels 5-6, European Quarter – Schuman, Schuman Roundabaout 2-4, 1040 Brussels, Belgium. T. +3228088660. Fax +3228088654. E-mail: info@eifec.eu.
Global website: http://www.eifec.org
History Registration: EU Transparency Register, No/ID: 93279557339-11. **Aims** Foster international security through promoting an effective international culture of compliance with the relevant export trade regulations within the financial, economic, industrial, academic and associative system of private and public sector. **Structure** Governors Council; Technical Committee; International Scientific Committee/Advisory Board. **Languages** English, French, German, Italian, Spanish. **Finance** Sources: international organizations; members' dues. **Activities** Awareness raising; capacity building; certification/accreditation; guidance/assistance/consulting; knowledge management/information dissemination; monitoring/evaluation; politics/policy/regulatory; publishing activities; research and development; standards/guidelines. **Publications** *EU Dual Use Regulation* (annual).
[2021.09.02/XM5221/E]

♦ European Institute for Family Life Education (EIFLE) 07554

Institut européen d'éducation familiale (IEEF)
Pres c/o PERLE eV, Birkenholz 27, 85567 Grafing, Germany. E-mail: board@ieef.eu.
1Registered Office 22 bd Maréchal Leclerc, 38000 Grenoble, France.
URL: http://www.eifle.org/
History 1992, Grenoble (France), as a European umbrella organization. Registered in accordance with French law, 1992; registered in accordance with Belgian law 1996. Statutes registered 28 Apr 1992; modified 28 Jun 1996, 18 Sep 1997. **Aims** Promote the values of family life and family life education, including in particular the study of *fertility* and its regulation by natural means. **Structure** General Assembly (annual); Council; Board of Directors. **Languages** English. **Staff** None. **Finance** Members' dues. Other sources: grants; publications. **Activities** Guidance/assistance/consulting; knowledge management/information dissemination. **Events** *Conference* Milan (Italy) 2015, *Conference* Rome (Italy) 2008, *Conference* Kaunas (Lithuania) 2004, *Conference* Milan (Italy) 2000.
Members Founding; Adhering. Associations in 16 countries:
Austria, Belgium, Czechia, France, Germany, Hungary, Italy, Lithuania, Malta, Poland, Portugal, Russia, Spain, Switzerland, UK, Ukraine.
Friends (individuals or organizations) in 7 countries:
Belgium, Denmark, Italy, Latvia, Netherlands, Sweden, UK.
[2022/XE2636/j/F]

♦ European Institute of Financial Directors (internationally oriented national body)

♦ European Institute for Fire Protection (EIFP) 07555

Dir Rüssenstr 5, 6340 Baar ZG, Switzerland. T. +41414440677.
URL: http://www.eifp.eu/
NGO Relations Liaison Organization of: *Comité européen de normalisation (CEN, #04162)*.
[2018/XM4801/D]

♦ European Institute of Food History / see Institut européen d'histoire et des cultures de l'alimentation (#11300)
♦ European Institute Foundation, Sofia (internationally oriented national body)

♦ European Institute for Futures Studies (EIFS) 07556

Address not obtained.
History Founded 1990, Røskilde (Denmark), as *Centre for European Regional Studies*, by *EURO-CHINA (#05658)*. Present name adopted 1995. **Aims** Provide a 'think-tank' and a forum to discuss *research* and disseminate knowledge of current and future factors concerning *welfare*, *security* and *quality of life* in Europe and elsewhere. **Structure** Chairman; Research Coordinator; European Advisory Board; Secretariat. **Finance** Self-financed through projects and studies commissioned by clients. **Activities** Geo-political and geo-economic future research, task-force discussions, meetings, workshops or symposia on critical issues that may affect the wellbeing and security of European Union's populations, in terms of socio-economic, technological, environmental, strategic, ethical, governance and cultural factors. Provides a context for global thinking on how European institutions and people could work together and with the rest of the world. Includes: *Centre for China and Asian Studies (inactive)*; *European Geopolitical Observatory (no recent information)*.
Members Individuals in 14 countries:
Canada, China, Denmark, Finland, France, Germany, Italy, Japan, Luxembourg, Monaco, Portugal, Sweden, Switzerland, UK.
IGO Relations Links with a large number of organizations, including: *European Bank for Reconstruction and Development (EBRD, #06315)*; *European Commission (EC, #06633)*; *European Parliament (EP, #08146)*; *International Bank for Reconstruction and Development (IBRD, #12317)*; *NATO (#16945)*; *Organization for Security and Cooperation in Europe (OSCE, #17887)*; *UNCTAD (#20285)*; *United Nations Economic Commission for Europe (UNECE, #20555)*; *United Nations Economic and Social Commission for Asia and the Pacific (ESCAP, #20557)*; *United Nations University (UNU, #20642)*.
[2012/XE2662/j/E]

♦ European Institute for Gender Equality (EIGE) 07557

Institut européen pour l'égalité entre les hommes et les femmes – Europäisches Institut für Gleichstellungsfragen
Dir Gedimino pr 16, LT-01103 Vilnius, Lithuania. T. +35052157400. E-mail: eige.sec@eige.europa.eu.
Communications/Media Officer address not obtained.
URL: http://www.eige.europa.eu/
History 20 Dec 2006. Founded by *Council of the European Union (#04895)* and *European Parliament (EP, #08146)*. Officially opened 16 Dec 2009, Vilnius (Lithuania). A decentralized agency of *European Union (EU, #08967)*. Former names and other names: *European Gender Institute (EGI)* – former. **Aims** Become the European knowledge centre on gender equality issues. **Structure** Management Board; Experts' Forum; Director. **Languages** English. **Activities** Research/documentation; monitoring/evaluation; knowledge management/information dissemination. **Events** *Gender Equality Forum* Brussels (Belgium) 2022, *Meeting on Gender Budgeting* Brussels (Belgium) 2018, *Experts Forum Meeting* Brussels (Belgium) 2017, *Gender Equality Index 2017 Conference* Brussels (Belgium) 2017, *High-Level Conference on Mainstreaming Gender Equality into Academic and Research Organisations* Brussels (Belgium) 2016. **IGO Relations** Supervised by: *European Ombudsman (#08084)*. Audited by: *European Court of Auditors (#06854)*. Cooperates with various EU agencies. **NGO Relations** Member of (2): *EU Agencies Network (EUAN, #05564)*; *Eurolib (#05703)*. Cooperates with (1): *Women Against Violence Europe (WAVE, #20986)*.
[2022/XJ0071/j/E*]

♦ European Institute of Golf Course Architects (EIGCA) 07558

Executive Officer Suite I, Windrush Court, Abingdon Business Park, Abingdon, OX14 1SY, UK. T. +441483891831. E-mail: info@eigca.org.
URL: http://www.eigca.org/
History 2000. Founded on merger of *European Society of Golf Course Architects (ESGA, inactive)* with other organizations. **Aims** Represent Europe's most qualified golf course architects; work to enhance the status of the golf course design profession and educate future golf course architects; increase opportunities for members to practice throughout the world. **Structure** General Meeting (annual); Council; Committees (9). **Languages** English. **Staff** 2.00 FTE, paid. **Activities** Awareness raising; events/meetings; knowledge management/information dissemination; projects/programmes; standards/guidelines; training/education. **Events** *Annual General Meeting* 2022, *Annual Meeting* Reykjavik (Iceland) 2022, *Annual General Meeting* Cardiff (UK) 2021, *Annual General Meeting* 2020, *Annual General Meeting* Paris (France) 2019. **Publications** *Fee Information Bulletin*. Handbooks.
Members Fellow; Member; Candidate for Membership. Individuals in 25 countries and territories:
Austria, Belgium, Canada, Czechia, Denmark, England, Finland, France, Germany, Iceland, Ireland, Italy, Mexico, Netherlands, Norway, Portugal, Scotland, Slovenia, Spain, Sweden, Switzerland, UK, United Arab Emirates, USA, Wales.
NGO Relations Supports (1): *GEO Foundation (#10132)*. Also links with national organizations.
[2022.05.13/XD8036/jv/F]

♦ European Institute for Health (EIH) 07559

Exec Dir Rue Abbé Cuypers 3, 1040 Brussels, Belgium. T. +33609130151.
URL: http://www.eih-eu.eu/
History Registered in accordance with Belgian law. EU Transparency Register: 916281517040-28. **Aims** Contribute to better health for the citizens of Europe by developing policy recommendations and guidelines on emerging health issues for European policy makers. **Structure** Board. **Finance** Sponsorship. **Activities** Events/meetings. **Events** *Symposium on Silver Economy and Habitat* Bordeaux (France) 2015, *Symposium on the Global Health* Brussels (Belgium) 2015, *Symposium on Silver Economy and Habitat* Bordeaux (France) 2014, *Symposium on Long Term Care* Brussels (Belgium) 2013, *Founding Symposium* Brussels (Belgium) 2010.
[2016/XM5310/D]

♦ European Institute for Health Records (EuroRec Institute) — 07560
Contact c/o Dept Medical Informatics and Statistics, Univ Hosp – Bldg 5Ks – 5th fl, entrance 42, C Heymanslaan 10, 9000 Ghent, Belgium. T. +3293324067. Fax +3293323439.
URL: http://www.eurorec.org
History Registration: Start date: 2003, France. **Aims** Facilitate international cooperation and dissemination of information on Electronic Health Record (EHR) at a European level; promote high quality standards in research, development and education regarding EHRs; facilitate implementations of EHR-systems. **Structure** General Assembly; Board. **Events** *EUROREC annual conference* Belgrade (Serbia) 2011, *eHealth week* Copenhagen (Denmark) 2011, *EUROREC annual conference* Tallinn (Estonia) 2010, *EUROREC annual conference* Sarajevo (Bosnia-Herzegovina) 2009, *WoHIT : World of health IT conference* Copenhagen (Denmark) 2008. **NGO Relations** Member of (1): *European Institute for Innovation through Health Data (i-HD, #07561).*
[2020/XE4488/j/E]

♦ European Institute for the History and Culture of Food (#11300)
♦ European Institute for Human Science (see: #09682)
♦ European Institute of Hunting and Sporting Weapons (#11299)
♦ European Institute for Industrial Leadership (internationally oriented national body)

♦ European Institute for Innovation through Health Data (i-HD) — 07561
Acting Managing Dir c/o Dept Medical Informatics & Statistics, Ghent Univ Hosp – Bldg 5K3, 5th Fl, Entrance 42, C. Heymanslaan 10, 9000 Ghent, Belgium.
Office Manager address not obtained.
Registered Address Oude Mechelsestraat 165, 1853 Strombeek-Bever, Belgium.
URL: https://www.i-hd.eu/
History 2016. Founded as the result of the Innovative Medicines Initiatives (IMI) sponsored project Electronic Health Records for Clinical Research (EHR4CR) and other European R&D projects supported by *European Commission (EC, #06633)*. Founded by *European Institute for Health Records (EuroRec Institute, #07560)*, RAMIT, empirica and TMF. Registration: Banque-Carrefour des Entreprises, No/ID: 0628.646.310, Start date: 24 Mar 2015, Belgium; EU Transparency Register, No/ID: 676053343264-27, Start date: 22 Jun 2021. **Aims** Promote, develop and share good practices, tools and quality assessments to maximize community value from health data for innovations in health, care and research. **Structure** General Assembly; Board of Directors; Executive Committee; Advisory Board; Office. Task Forces & Committees. **Activities** Knowledge management/ information dissemination; projects/programmes; research and development.
Members Full in 8 countries:
Austria, Belgium, Finland, France, Germany, Italy, Spain, UK.
Alzheimer Europe (AE, #00761); *European Clinical Research Infrastructure Network (ECRIN, #06577)*; *European Institute for Health Records (EuroRec Institute, #07560)*; *MedTech Europe (#16692).*
[2021/AA1889/y/D]

♦ European Institute of Innovation and Technology (EIT) — 07562
Dir Infopark 1/E, Neumann Janos utca, Budapest 1117, Hungary. T. +3614819300. E-mail: eit-director@eit.europa.eu.
URL: http://eit.europa.eu/
History 2005. Established by *European Commission (EC, #06633)*. Activities launched, 15 Sep 2008, Budapest (Hungary). A body within the *European Union (EU, #08967)*. Former names and other names: *European Institute of Technology (EIT)* – former; *Institut européen de technologie* – former; *Instituto Europeo de Tecnología* – former; *Europäisches Technologieinstitut* – former; *Istituto Europeo di Tecnologia* – former; *Europees Technologie-Instituut* – former; *Europeiskt Tekniskt Institut* – former; *Europaeisk Teknologisk Institut* – former; *Euroopan Teknologiainstituutin* – former; *Evropsky Technologicky Institut* – former; *Instituto Europeu de Tecnología* – former; *Európai Technológiai Intézet* – former; *Europejskiego Instytutu Technologii* – former; *Eiropas Tehnologijas Instituta* – former; *Istitut Ewropew Tat-Teknologija* – former. **Aims** Contribute to the competitiveness of Europe, its sustainable economic growth and job creation by promoting cooperation among businesses, education institutions and research organizations. **Structure** Governing Board; Executive Committee; Management Team. Innovation Communities (currently 9), each set up as a legal entity with its own CEO: *EIT Climate-KIC (#05403)*; *EIT Digital (#05404)*; *EIT Food (#05405)*; *EIT Health (#05406)*; *EIT InnoEnergy (#05407)*; *EIT Manufacturing (#05408)*; *EIT RawMaterials (#05409)*; *EIT Urban Mobility (EIT UM, #05410)*; *EIT Alumni*. **Languages** English. **Staff** 60.00 FTE, paid. **Finance** Financed by *European Commission (EC, #06633)*. **Activities** Networking/liaising; events/meetings. **Events** *Health Summit* 2020, *Conference on the Future of Food* Brussels (Belgium) 2019, *Final Conference* Brussels (Belgium) 2019, *Health Summit* Paris (France) 2019, *Innovation Forum* Budapest (Hungary) 2017. **Publications** *EIT Awards Yearbook 2016. Best of INNOVEIT 2016.* **IGO Relations** Audited by: *European Court of Auditors (#06854).* **NGO Relations** Member of (1): *EU Agencies Network (EUAN, #05564).*
[2021/XM2083/j/E*]

♦ European Institute of Interdisciplinary Research (EIIR) — 07563
Exec Dir 103 rue de Grenelle, 75007 Paris, France.
URL: http://www.eiir.org/
History 23 Jun 2003. Registered in accordance with French law. **Publications** Books; reports.
Members Universities (6) in 5 countries:
Bulgaria, France, Hungary, Italy, Lithuania.
[2013/XM0837/j/E]

♦ European Institute for International Economic Relations (internationally oriented national body)
♦ European Institute of International Management (internationally oriented national body)
♦ European Institute for International Studies (internationally oriented national body)

♦ European Institute for Intervention and Research on Burn Out (EIIRBO) — 07564
Dir Engelandstraat 353, 1180 Brussels, Belgium. T. +32475277830.
URL: http://www.burnout-institute.org/
Activities Training/education; research/documentation.
[2014/XJ8619/j/F]

♦ European Institute of Japanese Studies, Stockholm (internationally oriented national body)
♦ European Institute of Law, Science, and Technology (internationally oriented national body)

♦ European Institute for Local Development (EILD) — 07565
Contact address not obtained. E-mail: info@eurolocaldevelopment.org.
URL: http://eurolocaldevelopment.org/
History 2009, Greece. **Aims** Provide innovative tools for the sustainability of regions promoting experience sharing between members and partners for sustaining international cooperation, skillful networking and further progress and growth. **Structure** General Committee; Secretariat. **Languages** English, French, German, Irish Gaelic, Russian. **Staff** 9.00 FTE, paid. **Activities** Awareness raising; capacity building; events/meetings; guidance/assistance/consulting; knowledge management/information dissemination; networking/liaising; politics/policy/regulatory; projects/programmes; publishing activities; research and development; research/documentation; sporting activities; standards/guidelines; training/education.
Members Partners in 19 countries:
Belgium, Bulgaria, Croatia, Cyprus, Czechia, Denmark, Estonia, France, Germany, Greece, Hungary, Ireland, Italy, Latvia, Lithuania, Luxembourg, Malta, Netherlands, Spain.
[2021.06.09/XJ9947/D]

♦ European Institute, Lodz / see Foundation for European Studies – European Institute, Lodz
♦ European Institute, London School of Economics (internationally oriented national body)
♦ European Institute of the Mediterranean (internationally oriented national body)

♦ European Institute of Molecular Magnetism (EIMM) — 07566
Management Dir Dept of Chemistry, Univ of Florence, Polo Scientifico Universitario, Via della Lastruccia 3, 50019 Sesto Fiorentino Fl, Italy. T. +39554573285. Fax +39554573372.
Contact Consorzio INSTM, Via Giusti, 50121 Florence Fl, Italy. T. +39552338713. Fax +39552480111.
URL: http://www.eimm.eu/
History Set up 18 Mar 2008, as successor to the Network of excellence *MAGMANet*. Registered in accordance with Belgian law, 2014. **Aims** Provide provide organizational, technical and financial support to partners. **Structure** Management Board. **Activities** Research/documentation; training/education; guidance/assistance/consulting; advocacy/lobbying/activism; awards/prizes/competitions; events/meetings. **Events** *European Conference on Molecular Spintronics* Dortmund (Germany) 2022, *European Conference on Molecular Magnetism* Rennes (France) 2022, *European Conference on Molecular Magnetism* Florence (Italy) 2019, *European Conference on Molecular Magnetism* Bucharest (Romania) 2017, *European Conference on Molecular Spintronics* Bologna (Italy) 2016.
Members Institutions (6) in 6 countries:
Hungary, Italy, Poland, Portugal, Spain, UK.
[2017/XM6445/j/D]

♦ European Institute, New York / see Blinken European Institute, Columbia University, New York
♦ European Institute of Oncology, Milan (internationally oriented national body)
♦ European Institute for the PCB Community / see European Institute of Printed Circuits (#07568)

♦ European Institute of Peace (EIP) — 07567
Exec Dir Rue des Deux Églises 25, 1000 Brussels, Belgium. T. +3222800812. E-mail: info@eip.org.
URL: http://www.eip.org/
History 12 May 2014. Launched by foreign ministers of Belgium, Finland, Hungary, Italy, Luxembourg, Poland, Spain Sweden and Switzerland. Statutes created 18 Feb 2014. Registration: EU Transparency Register, No/ID: 272784617259-33; Start date: 10 Apr 2014, Belgium. **Aims** Contribute to and complement the global peace agenda of the European Union, primarily through mediation and informal dialogue; pursue multi-track diplomacy; promote best practice in conflict resolution. **Structure** Board of Governors; Advisory Council. **Languages** English, French. **Staff** 20-25. **Finance** Public and private funding. Budget (annual): about euro 3 million. **Activities** Capacity building; knowledge management/information dissemination.
Members Countries (9):
Belgium, Finland, Hungary, Italy, Luxembourg, Poland, Spain, Sweden, Switzerland.
IGO Relations Cooperates with: *European Commission (EC, #06633)*; *European Parliament (EP, #08146)*; External Action Service.
[2021/XJ8326/j/E]

♦ European Institute of the Pectin Industries (#11301)
♦ European Institute of Politics and Reforms (internationally oriented national body)

♦ European Institute of Printed Circuits (EIPC) — 07568
Exec Dir PO Box 610, 6160 AP Geleen, Netherlands. T. +31464264258. E-mail: eipc@eipc.org.
URL: http://www.eipc.org/
History 1968, Lugano (Switzerland). Former names and other names: *European Institute for the PCB Community* – alias. **Aims** Stimulate and encourage cooperation among organizations and individuals active in the field of printed circuits; promote exchange of technical and economic information in printed circuit business. **Structure** General Assembly. Board of Directors. Officers: President; Vice-Presidents; Treasurer; Executive Director; Technical Director. Committees. **Languages** English, French, German, Italian. **Staff** Secretariat run under contract. **Finance** Members' dues. Other sources: conference and training course fees; sales of publications. **Activities** Organizes: summer and winter conferences; training courses; technical conferences; local seminars; PCB World Convention. Offers technical consulting; EU related activities; provides '*IPC Standards*'; disseminates information. **Events** *Summer Conference* Örebro (Sweden) 2022, *Summer Conference* Leoben (Austria) 2019, *Winter Conference* Milan (Italy) 2019, *Summer Conference* Düsseldorf (Germany) 2018, *Winter Conference* Lyon (France) 2018. **Publications** *Speed News* (40 a year).
Members Regular; Allied; Associates. Companies (100) in 30 countries and territories:
Austria, Belgium, Bulgaria, China, Denmark, Finland, France, Germany, Hong Kong, India, Ireland, Israel, Italy, Japan, Korea Rep, Lithuania, Luxembourg, Moldova, Netherlands, Norway, Romania, Russia, Slovenia, Spain, Sweden, Switzerland, Taiwan, Türkiye, UK, Ukraine.
[2022/XE3100/j/E]

♦ European Institute for Progressive Cultural Policies (internationally oriented national body)

♦ European Institute of Public Administration (EIPA) — 07569
Institut européen d'administration publique (IEAP)
Dir-Gen PO Box 1229, 6201 BE Maastricht, Netherlands. T. +31433296222. Fax +31433296296. E-mail: info@eipa.eu.
URL: http://www.eipa.eu/
History 23 Mar 1981, Maastricht (Netherlands). Former names and other names: *Europäisches Institut für Öffentliche Verwaltung* – former; *Europees Instituut voor Bestuurskunde (EIB)* – former. Registration: Netherlands. **Aims** Support the European Union and its member states and countries associated with EIPA by providing relevant and high quality services to develop capacities of public officials in dealing with EU affairs. **Structure** Board of Governors, comprising representatives of the governments of EU member states, including Chairman and Vice-Chairman. Scientific Advisory Committee. Director-General. Antennae (2): *European Centre for Judges and Lawyers (#06488)* – legal activities addressed to judges and lawyers, Luxembourg (Luxembourg). **Languages** English, French. **Staff** 60.00 FTE, paid. **Finance** Sources: subsidies. Subsidies from the European Commission and EU member states represent about 40% of the annual budget. **Activities** Capacity building; events/meetings; guidance/assistance/consulting; knowledge management/information dissemination; research/documentation. **Events** *EU Law for Non-Lawyers* Luxembourg (Luxembourg) 2023, *Recent Trends in the Case Law of the Court of Justice of the European Union* Luxembourg (Luxembourg) 2022, *Competitive Dialogue and Negotiated Procedures Master Class* Maastricht (Netherlands) 2022, *Data Protection Certification* Maastricht (Netherlands) 2022, *Implementing the new EU Structural and Cohesion Funds Programmes Alongside the Recovery and Resilience Facility (RRF)* Maastricht (Netherlands) 2022. **Publications** Working papers; briefings; research and comparative studies, consultancy.
Members Statutory members: governments of 22 EU Member States plus Norway:
Austria, Belgium, Bulgaria, Cyprus, Czechia, Denmark, Finland, France, Germany, Greece, Hungary, Ireland, Italy, Lithuania, Luxembourg, Malta, Netherlands, Poland, Portugal, Slovakia, Spain, Sweden.
Supported by:
European Commission (EC, #06633).
Stakeholders (2):
Erasmus +; *European Commission (EC, #06633)*.
[2022.10.17/XD0275/j/E*]

♦ European Institute of Purchasing Management (internationally oriented national body)
♦ European Institute for Research and Information on Peace and Security / see Groupe de recherche et d'information sur la paix et la sécurité

♦ European Institute of Research on Water Policy — 07570
Institut européen de recherche sur la politique de l'eau (IERPE)
Secretariat Rue de La Poudrière 64, 1000 Brussels, Belgium. T. +3225025982. Fax +3225136106.
URL: http://ierpe.eu/
History 22 Sep 2007. Registered in accordance with Belgian law. **Aims** Promote recognition of the right to water as a *human right*, and the consideration of water as a common, public good; support participation of all *citizens* to the global management of water at all levels. **Structure** General Assembly (annual); Administration Council. **Languages** English, French, Spanish. **Finance** Members' dues (annual): organizations – euro 100; individuals – euro 50. **Members** Effective; Adherent. Organizations and individuals. Membership countries not specified.
[2014.07.08/XM3820/j/F]

♦ European Institute for Risk, Security and Communication Management (internationally oriented national body)
♦ European Institute of Romania (internationally oriented national body)

♦ European Institute of Social Security (EISS) — 07571
Institut européen de sécurité sociale – Instituto Europeo de Seguridad Social – Europäisches Institut für Soziale Sicherheit
SG Blijde Inkomstraat 17, Box 3409, 3000 Leuven, Belgium. T. +3216329433. Fax +3216325419. E-mail: thijs.keersmaekers@kuleuven.be.
URL: http://www.eiss.be/

History 5 Oct 1968, Leuven (Belgium). Registration: Banque-Carrefour des Entreprises, Belgium. **Aims** Gather people interested in the field of social security and social protection. **Structure** General Assembly (annual); Bureau; Praesidium. **Finance** Sources: members' dues; revenue from activities/projects; subscriptions. **Activities** Events/meetings; knowledge management/information dissemination; research/documentation; training/education. **Events** *Annual Conference* Leuven (Belgium) 2022, *Annual Conference* Zagreb (Croatia) 2021, *Online Event* 2020, *Annual Conference* Zurich (Switzerland) 2019, *Annual Conference* Venice (Italy) 2018. **Publications** *EISS-News*. Scientific reports.
Members National sections in countries of Western, Central and Eastern Europe. Individuals; institutions. Members in 25 countries:
Austria, Belgium, Brazil, Croatia, Cyprus, Czechia, Finland, Germany, Greece, Hungary, Italy, Luxembourg, Netherlands, Norway, Poland, Portugal, Saudi Arabia, Serbia, Slovenia, South Africa, Spain, Sweden, Switzerland, Türkiye, UK.
IGO Relations Official links with: *Council of Europe (CE, #04881)*. Recognized by: *European Commission (EC, #06633)*. [2022.02.02/XE9250/j/E]

♦ European Institute for Solidarity based Economy 07572
Institut européen de l'économie solidaire (INEES)
Contact 1 rue du Moulin, L-4251 Esch-sur-Alzette, Luxembourg. T. +3522726532670.
URL: http://www.inees.org/
History 1998. **Aims** Promote social and solidarity based economy in Luxembourg and in Europe. **Languages** English, French. **Staff** 2.00 FTE, paid. **Publications** *INEES Newsletter* (12 a year).
Members Individuals in 5 countries:
Belgium, France, Germany, Luxembourg, Switzerland.
NGO Relations Member of: *RIPESS Europe – Economy Solidarity Europe (RIPESS Europe, #18952)*. Cooperates with: *European Research Institute on Cooperative and Social Enterprises (EURICSE)*. [2018.08.28/XM1574/jv/E]

♦ European Institute for South and South-East Asian Studies / see European Institute for Asian Studies (#07545)
♦ European Institute for Statistics, Probability, Stochastic Operations Research and its Applications (internationally oriented national body)

♦ European Institute of Studies on Prevention (IREFREA) 07573
Pres Rambla 15 (2-3), 07003 Palma, Spain. T. +34971727434. Fax +34971213306. E-mail: info@irefrea.org.
URL: http://www.irefrea.org/
History 1988, Lyon (France). Former names and other names: *Irefrea Network* – alias. **Aims** Promote research, implementation and evaluation of interventions, covering questions like recreational *alcohol*, *drug* and family prevention as well as gender issues. **Structure** General Assembly; Board of Directors (meets annually); Board of Experts. **Languages** English, Spanish. **Staff** 20.00 FTE, paid. **Finance** Sources: government support; private foundations. Supported by: *European Commission (EC, #06633)*. **Activities** Events/meetings; knowledge management/information dissemination; projects/programmes; research/documentation; training/education. **Events** *FENIQS-EU – Further enhancing the implementation of quality standards in DDR across Europe* Palma (Spain) 2022, *Conference* Palma (Spain) 2019, *STAD in Europe Project Final Conference* Palma (Spain) 2019, *STOP-SV Project Final Conference* Palma (Spain) 2018, *International Conference on Nightlife, Substance Use and Related Health Issues* Lisbon (Portugal) 2015. **Publications** Books; project reports; prevention documents and resources; papers.
Members National offices; other institutions. National offices (6) in 6 countries:
Austria, Germany, Greece, Italy, Portugal, Spain.
Other national institutions (9) in 8 countries:
Belgium, Cyprus, Czechia, Germany, Netherlands, Slovenia, Sweden, UK.
IGO Relations Member of: *European Commission (EC, #06633)* – Civil Society Forum on Drugs (CSF). **NGO Relations** Member of: *Civil Society Forum on Drugs (CSFD, #03968)*; *European Society for Prevention Research (EUSPR, #08712)*. [2022.06.17/XM0152/j/F]

♦ European Institute for the Study of Industrial Fibres (inactive)
♦ European Institute for a Sustainable Information Society (internationally oriented national body)
♦ European Institute for Sustainable Transport (internationally oriented national body)
♦ European Institute of Technology / see European Institute of Innovation and Technology (#07562)
♦ European Institute of Telemedicine (internationally oriented national body)
♦ European Institute of Tele-Surgery (internationally oriented national body)
♦ European Institute for Theoretical Neuroscience (unconfirmed)
♦ European Institute for Transnational Legal Research, Maastricht (internationally oriented national body)
♦ European Institute of Urban Affairs, Liverpool (internationally oriented national body)
♦ European Institute for Vocational Training (inactive)

♦ European Institute of Women's Health (EIWH) 07574
Main Office 33 Pearse St, Dublin, CO. DUBLIN, Ireland. T. +35316715691. Fax +35316715662. E-mail: info@eurohealth.ie.
URL: http://www.eurohealth.ie/
History 1996, Ireland. Registered in accordance with Irish law. EU Transparency Register: 234045010359-36. **Aims** Ensure that women's health issues are on the European agenda. **Structure** Board. **Events** *Conference* Brussels (Belgium) 2017, *Meeting on promoting gender equity in public health in Europe* Dublin (Ireland) 2000. **Publications** *EuroWoman* (4 a year). **IGO Relations** Participant in Fundamental Rights Platform of: *European Union Agency for Fundamental Rights (FRA, #08969)*. **NGO Relations** Member of: *European Public Health Alliance (EPHA, #08297)*; *Health First Europe (HFE, #10881)*. Associate member of: *European Patients' Forum (EPF, #08172)*. Hosts: *European Advisory Council for Women's Health (EAC, #05831)*. [2019/XN7909/j/D]

♦ European Institute for Wood Preservation (WEI-IEO) 07575
Institut de l'Europe pour l'imprégnation du bois (WEI-IEO) – Europäisches Institut für Holzimprägnierung (WEI-IEO)
SG Rue Montoyer 24, Bte 20, 1000 Brussels, Belgium. T. +3225562586. Fax +3222870875. E-mail: info@wei-ieo.org.
URL: http://www.wei-ieo.org/
History 3 Jul 1951, The Hague (Netherlands). Former names and other names: *Western European Institute for Wood Preservation (WEI)* – former (3 Jul 1951); *Institut de l'Europe occidentale pour l'imprégnation du bois (IEO)* – former (3 Jul 1951); *West-Europäisches Institut für Holzimprägnierung (WEI)* – former (3 Jul 1951). Registration: EU Transparency Register, No/ID: 81739087951-41. **Aims** Disseminate and advance the knowledge of the possibilities and advantages of the preservation of wood and application of *preserved wood*; gather and elaborate knowledge and data relating to existing, improved and new methods for the preservation of wood; disseminate, exchange and unify the said knowledge. **Structure** General Assembly; Executive Committee. Working Commissions (3): Finished Products and Marketing; Wood Preservatives; Technical/Environmental Affairs. **Languages** English, French, German. **Staff** 3.00 FTE, paid. **Finance** Members' dues. **Activities** Guidance/assistance/consulting; standards/guidelines; research and development; events/meetings. **Events** *Congress* Milan (Italy) 2022, *Annual Congress* Stockholm (Sweden) 2011, *Annual Congress* Dresden (Germany) 2009, *Annual Congress* Lausanne (Switzerland) 2008, *Annual Congress* Seattle, WA (USA) 2007. **Publications** *WEI Newsletter* (6 a year) – for members only. Documents.
Members Full (impregnation plants); Associated (such as preservative products producers); Corresponding (such as laboratories). Members in 24 countries:
Austria, Belgium, Canada, Croatia, Denmark, Finland, France, Germany, Greece, Israel, Italy, Japan, Netherlands, Norway, Poland, Portugal, Slovenia, South Africa, Spain, Sweden, Switzerland, Türkiye, UK, USA.
NGO Relations Member of: *Confédération européenne des industries du bois (CEI Bois, #04545)*; *European Wood Preservative Manufacturers Group (EWPM, #09105)*. In liaison with technical committees of: *Comité européen de normalisation (CEN, #04162)*. [2022/XD6452/j/D]

♦ European Instrument for Democracy and for Human Rights (EIDHR) 07576
instrument européen pour la démocratie et les droits de l'Homme (IEDDH)
Contact c/o DG International Cooperation and Development, Rue de la Loi 41, 1049 Brussels, Belgium. T. +3222991111.
URL: https://www.eesc.europa.eu/en/documents/european-instrument-democracy-and-human-rights-eidhr
History Set up within the framework of *European Commission (EC, #06633)*. Replaced *European Initiative for Democracy and Human Rights outside EU* and originally managed through *Phare Programme (inactive)*. Includes the former *Phare and Tacis Democracy Programme (inactive)*. Previously also referred to as *European Initiative for Human Rights and Democracy*. Currently functions as a Thematic Instrument of EC DG Development and Cooperation – EuropeAid. Functions within the framework of *European Union (EU, #08967)*. **Aims** Help establish democracy, the rule of law and the protection of human rights and basic freedoms. **Finance** Budget (2014-2020): euro 1,332 million. **Activities** Provides funds to projects in line with the broad range of EU policy objectives in the field and on the basis of detailed provisions of the EIDHR Regulation. Priority issues: *'Promotion and Protection of Human Rights'* – Education, training and awareness raising; Racism, xenophobia, and protection of minorities; Freedom of opinion, expression and conscience and right to use own language; Rights of children; Abolition of death penalty. *'Democracy and Governance'* – Promotion of the rule of law, prison system; Promotion of pluralism, free press, independent media; Prevention of corruption; Participation in the decision-making process. **Events** *Conference* Brussels (Belgium) 2017, *Conference* Brussels (Belgium) 2017, *Brainstorming Meeting on Right to Development* Brussels (Belgium) 2015. **Publications** Thematic evaluation reports; Compendium. **IGO Relations** *Council of the European Union (#04895)*. **NGO Relations** Beneficiaries include over 500 NGOs worldwide. [2019/XK1926/E*]

♦ European Insulation Manufacturers Association (EURIMA) 07577
Association européenne des fabricants de matériaux isolants – Verband Europäischer Dämmstoffhersteller
Gen Dir Rue de Deux Eglises 29, 1000 Brussels, Belgium. T. +3226262090. E-mail: info@eurima.org.
Office Manager address not obtained.
Registered Office 7 Ave des Archiducs, L-1135 Luxembourg, Luxembourg.
URL: https://www.eurima.org/
History 26 Apr 1961, Petersberg (Germany). Statutes most recently modified, Jun 2000. Former names and other names: *EURISOL* – former. Registration: Start date: 1969, Luxembourg; Banque-Carrefour des Entreprises, No/ID: 0436.590.763, Start date: 1988, Belgium; EU Transparency Register, No/ID: 98345631631-22, Start date: 4 May 2009. **Aims** Create a favourable business environment for mineral wool insulation, by promoting common interests of the industry and working for positive regulations and standards. **Structure** General Assembly (annual). Management Board. Director General. Committee (3): Market Development; Technical; Health and Safety. **Languages** Dutch, English, French, German. **Staff** 6.00 FTE, paid. **Finance** Sources: members' dues. **Activities** Networking/liaising. **Events** *Annual Congress* Munich (Germany) 2012, *Annual Congress* Sitges (Spain) 2010, *Annual Congress* Athens (Greece) 2008, *Annual Congress* Budapest (Hungary) 2007, *Annual Congress* Cannes (France) 2006. **Publications** Case studies; conference proceedings; reports; corporate brochure; information booklet.
Members Associated; Affiliated. Companies in 8 countries:
Denmark, Finland, France, Germany, Greece, Norway, Spain, Switzerland.
National assoications in 18 countries:
Czechia, Denmark, Estonia, Finland, France, Germany, Italy, Latvia, Lithuania, Netherlands, Norway, Poland, Russia, Spain, Sweden, Switzerland, UK, Ukraine.
IGO Relations Accredited by (1): *United Nations Framework Convention on Climate Change – Secretariat (UNFCCC, #20564)*. **NGO Relations** Member of (11): *Coalition for Energy Savings (#04056)*; *Construction 2050 Alliance (#04760)*; *Energy Efficiency Industrial Forum (EEIF, #05470)*; *European Association for External Thermal Insulation Composite Systems (EAE, #06035)*; *European Business Council for a Sustainable Energy Future (e5, #06417)*; *European Construction Forum (ECF, #06765)*; *European Council for an Energy Efficient Economy (ECEEE, #06818)*; *European Network on Silica (NEPSI, #08001)*; *Federation of European and International Associations Established in Belgium (FAIB, #09508)*; *International Council for Research and Innovation in Building and Construction (CIB, #13069)*; *International Network for Sustainable Energy (INFORSE, #14331)*. In liaison with technical committees of: *Comité européen de normalisation (CEN, #04162)*; *International Organization for Standardization (ISO, #14473)*. Associate Expert Group of *Business and Industry Advisory Committee to the OECD (BIAC, #03385)*. In cooperation with Glass Fibres Producers' Group of *CIRFS – European Man-made Fibres Association (#03944)*, set up: *Joint European Medical Research Board (JEMRB, inactive)*. Associate partner of: *Covenant of Mayors for Climate and Energy (#04939)*. Supports: *Buildings Performance Institute Europe (BPIE, #03354)*. [2022/XD6769/t/D]

♦ European Insurance CFO Forum (unconfirmed)

♦ European Insurance and Occupational Pensions Authority (EIOPA) . 07578
Exec Dir Westhafenplatz 1, 60327 Frankfurt-Main, Germany. T. +496995111922. Fax +496995111919. E-mail: info@eiopa.europa.eu.
Chairman address not obtained.
URL: http://www.eiopa.europa.eu/
History 5 Nov 2003, Brussels (Belgium). Established by *European Commission (EC, #06633)* (Decision 2004/6/EC. Subsequently repealed and replaced by Decision 2009/79/EC), as a 'Level 3 Committee' following extension of the *'Lamfalussy Approach'* to the field of insurance, reinsurance and occupational pensions. Preceded by the Conference of the European Insurance Supervisory Authorities. Restructured as of 1 Jan 2011, when adopted current title and became part of *European System of Financial Supervision (ESFS)*, as an advisory body to *European Parliament (EP, #08146)*, *Council of the European Union (#04895)* and European Commission. A decentralized agency of *European Union (EU, #08967)*. Registered in accordance with German law, 28 May 2004. Former names and other names: *Committee of European Insurance and Occupational Pensions Supervisors (CEIOPS)* – former. **Aims** Better protect *consumers* and rebuild trust in the financial system; ensure a high, effective and consistent level of regulation and supervision, taking into account varying interests of member states and the different nature of financial institutions; obtain greater harmonization and coherent application of rules for financial institutions and markets across the European Union; strengthen oversight of cross-border groups; promote coordinated European Union supervisory response. **Structure** Board of Supervisors, composed of representatives of relevant supervisory authority in each European Member State and including Chairperson, representatives of *European Commission (EC, #06633)*, *European Systemic Risk Board (ESRB, #08872)*, *European Banking Authority (EBA, #06311)*, *European Securities and Markets Authority (ESMA, #08457)* and Observers. Management Board, comprising Chairperson, 6 representatives of national supervisory authorities and an EC representative. Board of Appeal, composed of 6 members and 6 alternates, and jointly shared with EBA and ESMA. Stakeholder Groups (2): Insurance and Reinsurance; Occupational Pensions. Working Groups. **Languages** English. **Staff** 160.00 FTE, paid. **Finance** Obligatory contributions from national supervisory authorities (60%); EU general budget (40%). **Activities** Politics/policy/regulatory; standards/guidelines; guidance/assistance/consulting; events/meetings. **Events** *Joint ESAs High-Level Conference on Financial Education and Literacy* Brussels (Belgium) 2022, *Annual Conference* Frankfurt-Main (Germany) 2022, *Annual Conference* Frankfurt-Main (Germany) 2021, *Annual Conference* Frankfurt-Main (Germany) 2019, *Annual Conference* Frankfurt-Main (Germany) 2018. **Publications** Annual Report; reports; guidelines; advice; opinions; work programmes.
Members National insurance and occupational pensions supervisory authorities in 27 EU member states:
Austria, Belgium, Bulgaria, Croatia, Cyprus, Czechia, Denmark, Estonia, Finland, France, Germany, Greece, Hungary, Ireland, Italy, Latvia, Lithuania, Luxembourg, Malta, Netherlands, Poland, Portugal, Romania, Slovakia, Slovenia, Spain, Sweden.
Observers: national insurance and occupational pensions supervisory authorities in 3 non-EU countries of the European Economic Area:
Iceland, Liechtenstein, Norway.
Regional (non-voting) organizations (4):
European Banking Authority (EBA, #06311); *European Commission (EC, #06633)* (DG Internal Market and Services); *European Securities and Markets Authority (ESMA, #08457)*; *European Systemic Risk Board (ESRB, #08872)*.
IGO Relations Audited by: *European Court of Auditors (#06854)*. **NGO Relations** Member of (1): *EU Agencies Network (EUAN, #05564)*. *International Association of Insurance Supervisors (IAIS, #11966)*. [2022/XJ4312/y/E*]

♦ European Integrated Center for the Development of new Metallic Alloys and Compounds (C-MAC) 07579
Contact Kasteelpark Arenberg 44, 3001 Leuven, Belgium.

URL: http://www.eucmac.eu/
History Set up as successor organization of 'European Network of Excellence Complex Metallic Alloys (NoE CMA)'. Registered in accordance with Belgian law. **Aims** Promote collaborative research in the field of metallic alloys and compounds at a European level. **Structure** C-MAC consortium (decision making body), comprising Governing Board and Science Board. C-MAC Network and Service Unit (C-MAC NSU), comprising Board of Directors. **Activities** Research and development; events/meetings; training/education. **Events** *International Conference on Quasicrystals* Bled (Slovenia) 2019, *International Conference on Quasicrystals* Kathmandu (Nepal) 2016.
Members Institutes and universities in 10 countries:
Austria, Belgium, France, Germany, Greece, Poland, Slovenia, Sweden, Switzerland, UK. [2017/XM6036/**D**]

♦ European Intellectual Property Institutes Network (EIPIN) 07580

Contact c/o MIPLC, Marstallstr 8, 80539 Munich, Germany.
URL: http://www.eipin.org/
History 1999. **Aims** Facilitate contacts and increase cooperation among intellectual property institutions and students in Europe. **Events** *Annual Congress* Strasbourg (France) 2016, *Annual Congress* Maastricht (Netherlands) 2015, *Annual Congress* Alicante (Spain) 2014, *Annual Congress* Maastricht (Netherlands) 2013, *Congress* Munich (Germany) 2012. **Publications** *EIPIN Series.* Team Reports.
Members Partners (5) in 5 countries:
France, Germany, Netherlands, Spain, UK. [2016/XJ6398/**F**]

- ♦ European Intelligence and Security Informatics Conference (meeting series)
- ♦ European Intelligent Building Group / see Intelligent Building Group (#11374)

♦ European Intelligent Cash Protection Association (EURICPA) 07581

Gen Sec Rue du Luxembourg 19-21, 1000 Brussels, Belgium. T. +3225068831. Fax +3225068825. E-mail: generalsecretary@euricpa.org.
URL: http://www.euricpa.org/
History 7 Apr 2005. **Aims** Promote technology as the best secure solution for cash in transit; represent the interests of European manufacturers. **Structure** General Assembly. Board, comprising Chairman, Vice-Chairman, Treasurer and 4 further members. **Languages** English, French.
Members Companies (6) in 6 countries:
Belgium, France, Germany, Sweden, Switzerland, UK.
NGO Relations Member of: *International Currency Association (ICA, #13123).* [2014/XM2553/**D**]

- ♦ European Interactive Advertising Association (inactive)

♦ European Interactive Digital Advertising Alliance (EDAA) 07582

Programme Development Dir Rue des Deux Eglises 26, 1000 Brussels, Belgium. E-mail: info@edaa.eu.
URL: http://www.edaa.eu/
History 2012. **Aims** Licence the 'OBA Icon' to companies involved in Online Behavioural Advertising across Europe. **Structure** Board; Secretariat based in Brussels (Belgium). **Languages** English. **Staff** 4.00 FTE, paid. **Finance** Licensing of the OBA Icon and integration on the YourOnlineChoices Consumer Choice Platform. **Activities** Awareness raising; events/meetings; training/education. **Events** *Summit* Brussels (Belgium) 2021, *Summit* London (UK) 2019, *Summit* Brussels (Belgium) 2016. **Publications** Activity reports; consumer research; campaigns; infographics; fact sheets.
Members Governing organizations (11):
Association of Commercial Television in Europe (ACT, #02436); Association of European Radios (AER, #02535); egta – association of television and radio sales houses (#05397); European Advertising Standards Alliance (EASA, #05829); European Association of Communications Agencies (EACA, #05983); European Magazine Media Association (EMMA, #07723); European Newspaper Publishers' Association (ENPA, #08048); European Publishers Council (EPC, #08304); Federation of European Data & Marketing (FEDMA, #09499); IAB Europe (#11002); World Federation of Advertisers (WFA, #21407). [2022.02.21/XJ7452/y/**D**]

- ♦ European Interagency Security Forum / see Global Interagency Security Forum (#10430)
- ♦ European Interdisciplinary Society for Haemapheresis and Haemotherapy / see European Society for Haemapheresis and Haemotherapy (#08614)

♦ European Interferometry Initiative (Eii) 07583

Science Council Pres Univ of Exeter, Astrophysics Group, Physics Building, Stocker Road, Exeter, EX4 4QL, UK. T. +441392724125.
Science Council Vice-Pres Max Planck Institute for Astronomy, Königstuhl 17, 69117 Heidelberg, Germany. T. +496221528202.
URL: https://european-interferometry.eu/
History 30 Jan 2002, Heidelberg (Germany). **Aims** Facilitate communications and collaborations between European scientists and institutes working on optical long-baseline interferometry for astronomy; exploit synergy within Europe in order to produce world leading science in the field of optical long-baseline interferometry; work toward integration of education activities on an European scale; work toward an European vision on the long term future of optical long-baseline interferometry. **Structure** Scientific Council; Board, comprising Chairman, 13 members and one observer member. **Events** *Workshop on perspectives in radiative transfer and interferometry* Saint-Jean-d'Ardières (France) 2007.
Members National representatives in 14 countries:
Austria, Belgium, Czechia, France, Germany, Hungary, Israel, Italy, Netherlands, Poland, Portugal, Spain, Switzerland, UK.
Also, 2 organizations listed in this Yearbook:
European Organization for Astronomical Research in the Southern hemisphere (ESO, #08106); European Space Agency (ESA, #08798). [2022/XM0655/**D**]

- ♦ European Interim Agreement on Social Security other Than Schemes for Old Age, Invalidity and Survivors (1953 treaty)
- ♦ European Interim Agreement on Social Security Schemes Relating to Old Age, Invalidity and Survivors (1953 treaty)
- ♦ European Intermodal Association (inactive)

♦ European and International Booksellers Federation (EIBF) 07584

Dir Square Marie-Louise 69, 1000 Brussels, Belgium. T. +3222234940. E-mail: info@europeanbooksellers.eu.
URL: http://www.europeanbooksellers.eu/
History Set up as *European Booksellers Federation (EBF)*, previously a separate branch along with *International Booksellers Federation (IBF).* Registration: EU Transparency Register, No/ID: 9031106115-62. **Aims** Give booksellers a strong voice in the public sphere; promote awareness of the beneficial role of bookshops among decision-makers at European level. **Structure** Co-Presidents (2); Executive Committee; Officers. **Languages** English. **Staff** 1.00 FTE, paid. **Activities** Advocacy/lobbying/activism; events/meetings. **Events** *RISE Bookselling Conference* Prague (Czechia) 2023, *Conference* Frankfurt-Main (Germany) 2022, *Conference* Frankfurt-Main (Germany) 2019, *Conference* Frankfurt-Main (Germany) 2018, *Creative and innovative solutions by bookshops and booksellers associations* Frankfurt-Main (Germany) 2017. **Publications** *EIBF Newsletter* (24 a year). Position papers.
Members Associations in 30 countries:
Australia, Austria, Belgium, Bulgaria, China, Cyprus, Czechia, Denmark, Estonia, Finland, France, Germany, Greece, Ireland, Italy, Latvia, Luxembourg, Netherlands, New Zealand, Norway, Poland, Portugal, Russia, Slovenia, South Africa, Spain, Sweden, Switzerland, UK, USA.
Consultative Status Consultative status granted from: *UNESCO (#20322)* (Consultative Status). [2020.06.24/XD6343/**D**]

♦ European International Business Academy (EIBA) 07585

Académie européenne de commerce international (EIBA)
Exec Sec c/o EIASM, Passage du Nord 19, 1000 Brussels, Belgium. T. +3222266660. Fax +3225121929. E-mail: info@eiba.org.
URL: https://www.eiba.org/
History 1974, Brussels (Belgium). Former names and other names: *European International Business Association (EIBA)* – former; *Association européenne de commerce international (EIBA)* – former. Registration: No/ID: 0896.648.994, Start date: 19 Mar 2008, Belgium. **Aims** Provide a professional society for members with an interest in the field of international business. **Languages** English. **Activities** Awards/prizes/competitions; events/meetings; research/documentation; training/education. **Events** *Annual Conference* Helsinki (Finland) 2024, *Annual Conference* Lisbon (Portugal) 2023, *Annual Conference* Oslo (Norway) 2022, *Annual Conference* Madrid (Spain) 2021, *Annual Conference* Vienna (Austria) 2020. **Members** Individuals (about 500) in about 50 countries. Membership countries not specified. **NGO Relations** Activities supported by: *European Institute for Advanced Studies in Management (EIASM, #07544).* [2021.07.27/XD5822/v/**D**]

- ♦ European International Business Association / see European International Business Academy (#07585)
- ♦ European International Consultants Association / see European Consultants Unit (#06769)

♦ European International Contractors (EIC) 07586

Dir Kurfürstenstrasse 129, 10785 Berlin, Germany. T. +493021286244. Fax +493021286285. E-mail: info@eic-federation.eu.
URL: http://www.eic-federation.eu/
History 1970. Former names and other names: *International Contractors' Group (ICG)* – former. Registration: Germany. **Aims** Represent and promote international interests of the European *construction* industry; encourage and organize exchange of views and experiences on international business aspects and international construction markets. **Structure** General Assembly (biannual); Board; Permanent Secretariat in Berlin (Germany), comprising Director and Assistant Director. **Languages** English. **Staff** 4.00 FTE, paid. **Activities** Events/meetings; knowledge management/information dissemination; politics/policy/regulatory. **Events** *General Assembly* Berlin (Germany) 2021, *General Assembly* Berlin (Germany) 2021, *General Assembly* Berlin (Germany) 2020, *Autumn Conference* Helsinki (Finland) 2019, *Spring Conference* Madrid (Spain) 2019. **Publications** *Mergers and Acquisitions in the European Construction Industry* (2 a year). *EIC Turnkey Contract* (1994); *List of Arbitrators* (3rd ed). List of members; books; reports; studies.
Members Construction industry federations in 14 countries:
Austria, Belgium, Denmark, Finland, France, Germany, Greece, Italy, Netherlands, Portugal, Spain, Sweden, Switzerland, Türkiye.
NGO Relations Protocol agreement signed, 1984, and amended 2002, with and represented on the Board of: *European Construction Industry Federation (#06766).* Associated with: *Confederation of International Contractors Associations (CICA, #04558).* [2022.03.11/XD2308/**D**]

♦ European and International Federation of Natural Stone Industries (EUROROC) 07587

Fédération européenne and internationale des industries de la pierre naturelle
SG Gluckstrasse 10, 65193 Wiesbaden, Germany. T. +496119771211. Fax +496119771248. E-mail: office@euroroc.net.
Pres c/o Marmi Ghirardi srl, 49 via S Croce, 25013 Brescia BS, Italy.
URL: http://www.euroroc.net/
History 13 Sep 1981, Italy. Founded 13 Sep 1981, Sant' Ambrogio di Valpolicella (Italy), when *Fédération de l'industrie marbrière de la Communauté économique européenne (FIMCEE, inactive)* and *Fédération de l'industrie granitière européenne (FIGE, inactive)* combined to form a single organization, originally with the title *Federation of the Marble Industry and the Granite Industry of the European Economic Community – Fédération de l'industrie marbrière et de l'industrie granitière de la Communauté économique européenne (FIMIGCEE).* **Aims** Promote, in a European cooperative framework, the development of national industries working with marble, granite, *onyx* and other ornamental natural stones, whether for scientific or technical research, cultural expansion, harmonization of human and social relations, economic promotion or safeguarding the environment. **Structure** Assembly of delegates of national associations (annual, always in Verona, Italy); Presidency; Congress – wider assembly of delegates – (every 2 years). Specialist Committees (8): Public Relations; Scientific and Technical Research; Financial and Tax Questions; Economic (including Statistics); Environment; Social Questions; Arbitration; Accounts. Secretariat Committee; Secretariat General. **Languages** English, French, German, Spanish. **Staff** 2.00 FTE, paid. **Finance** Members' dues. Other sources: sponsorship. **Events** *Annual General Meeting* Juuka (Finland) 2004, *Annual delegates assembly* Verona (Italy) 1999, *Annual delegates assembly* Verona (Italy) 1998, *Annual delegates assembly* Verona (Italy) 1997, *Annual delegates assembly* Verona (Italy) 1996. **Publications** Only for members.
Members Founding; Active; Associate (non-EC). National organizations in 14 countries:
Belgium, Finland, France, Germany, Greece, Ireland, Italy, Netherlands, Norway, Portugal, Slovakia, Spain, Sweden, UK.
NGO Relations Member of: *European Network on Silica (NEPSI, #08001).* [2014/XE1249/t/**D**]

- ♦ The European International Model United Nations (internationally oriented national body)
- ♦ European International Neuropsychology Society / see International Neuropsychological Society (#14358)

♦ European and International Research Group on Crime, Social Philosophy and Ethics (ERCES) 07588

Contact address not obtained. T. +3314018169.
URL: http://www.erces.com/
History within *European Society of Criminology (ESC, #08575).* **Events** *International conference* 2006, *Conference* Borovets (Bulgaria) 2006, *International conference / Conference* St Petersburg (Russia) 2005. **Publications** *ERCES Online Quarterly Review.* [2008/XM0197/**E**]

♦ European International Studies Association (EISA) 07589

Secretariat 5.kvetna 65, 170 00 Prague, Czechia. T. +420261174314. Fax +42027431550. E-mail: info@eisa-net.org.
URL: http://www.eisa-net.org/
History Constitution approved 10 Apr 2013. Registration: Swiss Civil Code, Switzerland. **Aims** Bring together academics and others working in the field and subfields of international studies in Europe and beyond. **Structure** General Assembly; Governing Board. **Languages** English, German. **Finance** Sources: members' dues. **Activities** Events/meetings; training/education. **Events** *EWIS : European Workshops in International Studies* Krakow (Poland) 2019, *Pan-European Conference on International Relations* Sofia (Bulgaria) 2019, *EWIS : European Workshops in International Studies* Groningen (Netherlands) 2018, *Pan-European Conference on International Relations* Prague (Czechia) 2018, *Pan-European Conference on International Relations* Barcelona (Spain) 2017. **Publications** *Global Affairs* – journal. *Palgrave Series on International Relations.* **Members** 1,100 in 53 countries. Membership countries not specified. **NGO Relations** Cooperates with (5): *Central and East European International Studies Association (CEEISA, #03700); European Consortium for Political Research (ECPR, #06762); European Standing Group on International Relations (SGIR, #08831); International Studies Association (ISA, #15615); World International Studies Committee (WISC, #21595).* Cooperates with: national organizations. [2020.06.25/XJ7449/**E**]

♦ European Internet Exchange Association (Euro-IX) 07590

SG PO Box 73533, London, E2 2DP, UK. E-mail: info@euro-ix.net – secretariat@euro-ix.net.
Events – Coordinator address not obtained.
URL: http://www.euro-ix.net/
History May 2001. **Aims** Further develop, strengthen and improve the Internet Exchange Point (IXP) community. **Languages** English. **Staff** 2.00 FTE, paid. **Activities** Events/meetings; networking/liaising; knowledge management/information dissemination; projects/programmes. **Events** *Euro-IX Forum* Tampere (Finland) 2022, *Euro-IX Forum* Toulouse (France) 2019, *Euro-IX Forum* Zaandam (Netherlands) 2019, *Euro-IX Forum* Venice (Italy) 2018, *Forum* Barcelona (Spain) 2017. **Publications** Annual Report; traffic statistics; benchmarking reports. **Members** Individual (81) in 49 countries. Membership countries not specified. [2021/XM3661/**D**]

♦ European Internet Forum (EIF) 07591

Dir Gen Av des Arts 56, 1000 Brussels, Belgium. T. +3228807880. E-mail: secretariat@internetforum.eu.
Dir Events & Operations address not obtained.
Main Website: https://www.internetforum.eu/

History Mar 2000. Founded by 3 members of *European Parliament (EP, #08146)*. Former names and other names: *European Internet Foundation* – former (2000 to 2014). Registration: Banque-Carrefour des Entreprises, No/ID: 0473.192.328, Start date: 28 Mar 2000, Belgium; EU Transparency Register, No/ID: 001968511387-52, Start date: 27 Jun 2013. **Aims** Support European political leadership for development of European and multilateral public policies responsive to the political, economic and social challenges of worldwide digital transformation, and to help MEPs ensure that European public policies are fit for the digital age. **Structure** General Assembly (annual); Steering Committee; Board of Management; Secretariat. **Languages** English. **Staff** 4.00 FTE, paid. **Finance** Sources: members' dues. **Activities** Events/meetings; networking/liaising; politics/policy/regulatory; projects/programmes. **Events** *The Limits of Self-Regulation in Tackling Harmful Content* Brussels (Belgium) 2021, *Meeting on the Future of Technology and its Implications for Society, the Economy and Regulation* Brussels (Belgium) 2013, *Workshop on The Digital World in 2030 Project* Brussels (Belgium) 2013, *Workshop on the Digital World in 2030* Brussels (Belgium) 2013, *General Assembly* Brussels (Belgium) 2003. **Publications** Reports.

Members Political: Members of the European Parliament; Business: companies; Associate: organizations. Included in the above, 50 organizations listed in the Yearbook:
- *ALL DIGITAL (#00646)*;
- *Association of Commercial Television in Europe (ACT, #02436)*;
- *Association of European Radios (AER, #02535)*;
- *BBC Media Action*;
- *Bertelsmann Foundation*;
- *Blockchain for Europe (#03281)*;
- *Business Software Alliance (BSA, #03387)*;
- *Computer and Communications Industry Association (CCIA)*;
- *Council of European National Top-Level Domain Registries (CENTR, #04892)*;
- *Council of European Professional Informatics Societies (CEPIS, #04893)*;
- *DIGITALEUROPE (#05073)*;
- *DOT Europe (#05125)*;
- *EGI Foundation (EGI.eu, #05395)*;
- *European Audiovisual Production (CEPI, #06295)*;
- *European Brands Association (#06397)*;
- *European Broadcasting Union (EBU, #06404)*;
- *European Competitive Telecommunications Association (ECTA, #06689)*;
- *European Digital SME Alliance (#06925)*;
- *European e-Skills Association (EeSA, #08489)*;
- *European Games Developer Federation (EGDF, #07373)*;
- *European Internet Services Providers Association (EuroISPA, #07592)*;
- *European Newspaper Publishers' Association (ENPA, #08048)*;
- *European Publishers Council (EPC, #08304)*;
- *European Registry of Internet Domain Names (EURid, #08351)*;
- *European Schoolnet (EUN, #08433)*;
- *European Telecommunications Network Operators' Association (ETNO, #08895)*;
- *European Telecommunications Standards Institute (ETSI, #08897)*;
- *Federation of European Publishers (FEP, #09536)*;
- *GÉANT Association (#10086)*;
- *GIGAEurope AISBL (#10151)*;
- *Global Satellite Operators' Association (GSOA, #10586)*;
- *GS1 (#10809)*;
- *GSM Association (GSMA, #10813)* (Europe);
- *IAB Europe (#11002)*;
- *Institut de l'audiovisuel et des télécommunications en Europe (IDATE)*;
- *Institute of Electrical and Electronics Engineers (IEEE, #11259)*;
- *Interactive Software Federation of Europe (ISFE, #11380)*;
- *International Confederation of Music Publishers (ICMP, #12864)*;
- *International Federation of the Phonographic Industry (IFPI, #13508)*;
- *International Video Federation (IVF, #15852)*;
- *Internet Corporation for Assigned Names and Numbers (ICANN, #15949)*;
- *Internet Society (ISOC, #15952)*;
- *Motion Picture Association (MPA)*;
- *MVNO Europe (#16920)*;
- *News Media Europe (NME, #17094)*;
- *Pearle – Live Performance Europe (#18284)*;
- *Research Data Alliance (RDA, #18853)*;
- *RIPE Network Coordination Centre (RIPE NCC, #18951)*;
- *Sports Rights Owners Coalition (SROC, #19929)*.

NGO Relations Member of (1): *European Society of Association Executives (ESAE, #08526)*. Also links with national organizations. [2022.08.01/XF5637/y/**F**]

♦ European Internet Foundation / see European Internet Forum (#07591)

♦ European Internet Services Providers Association (EuroISPA) 07592

Association européenne de fournisseurs de services Internet

Secretariat Rue de la Loi 38, Isabelle De Vinck, 1000 Brussels, Belgium. T. +3227896618. E-mail: secretariat@euroispa.org.
Registered Address Rue Montoyer 39 – Bte 3, 1000 Brussels, Belgium.
URL: http://www.euroispa.org/

History 12 Sep 1997, Brussels (Belgium), as a grouping of the type *European Economic Interest Grouping (EEIG, #06960)*. Registered in accordance with Belgian law: 0463 124 322. EU Transparency Register: 54437813115-56. **Aims** Act as principal spokesman for the Internet industry in Europe; encourage use of the Internet and interests of the industry; promote self-regulation and influence the regulatory process on behalf of the Internet industry; encourage development of a free and open telecommunications market; develop professional standards. **Structure** Council; Officers; Directorates; Secretariat, based in Brussels (Belgium). **Languages** English. **Staff** 1.00 FTE, paid. **Finance** Members' dues. **Activities** Events/meetings. **Events** *Annual European e-commerce conference* Brussels (Belgium) 2009, *Conference* Brussels (Belgium) 2001, *Conference* Brussels (Belgium) 1998. **Publications** *Eurolspa News*. Position papers; presentations; press releases.

Members Companies in 11 countries:
Austria, Belgium, Czechia, Finland, France, Germany, Ireland, Italy, Norway, Romania, UK.

NGO Relations Associate member of: *European Internet Forum (EIF, #07591)*. Member of: *Copyright for Creativity (C4C, #04832)*. [2019/XD6838/**D**]

♦ European Inter-Network of Ethical and Responsible Initiatives 07593

Inter-réseau européen des initiatives éthiques et solidaires (IRIS)

Gen Sec Espace Nord-Sud, 17 rue de Boston, 67000 Strasbourg, France. T. +33388450153. Fax +33388450153.

History Jan 2007. **Aims** Create synergies between the different networks in order to fight against poverty and social exclusion; promote sustainable social development with responsible economy. **Languages** English, French. **Activities** Groups (5): Ethical and solidarity-based finance; Fair trade; Responsible consumerism; Social responsibility of territories; Solidarity-based socio-economic integration. **Events** *EMES international conference on social enterprise* Trento (Italy) 2009. **Publications** *Iris Network Newsletter* (2 a year).

Members Members (8) include the following organizations listed in our Yearbook (5):
Alliance for Social and Ecological Consumer Organisations (ASECO, #00722); *Council of Europe (CE, #04881)*; *European Federation of Ethical and Alternative Banks and Financiers (#07113)*; *International Association of Investors in the Social Economy (INAISE, #11971)*; *World Fair Trade Organization (WFTO, #21396)*.

IGO Relations *Council of Europe (CE, #04881)*; *European Commission (EC, #06633)*. **NGO Relations** Member of: *RIPESS Europe – Economy Solidarity Europe (RIPESS Europe, #18952)*. [2013.06.27/XM3494/y/**D**]

♦ European Interoperability Testing Association (inactive)
♦ European Inter-Parliamentary Assembly on Orthodoxy / see Inter-Parliamentary Assembly on Orthodoxy (#15959)

♦ European Interparliamentary Space Conference (EISC) 07594

Contact c/o European Space Policy Inst, Schwarzenbergplatz 6, 1030 Vienna, Austria. T. +431718111878. E-mail: office@eisc-europa.eu.
URL: https://eisc-europa.eu/

History EISC Charter adopted 1999; amended 2006 and 2011. **Aims** Provide an interparliamentary forum for analysing and debating the European space policy and major issues at stake in the European space sector. **Structure** Rotating Presidency and Secretariat. **Activities** Awards/prizes/competitions; events/meetings. **Events** *Plenary Session* Norway 2021.

Members Full; Associate; Observer. Full – national parliaments of EU Member States or of the European Space Agency, in 13 countries:
Austria, Belgium, Czechia, Estonia, France, Germany, Italy, Luxembourg, Norway, Poland, Romania, Spain, UK.
Associate in 1 country:
Russia.

NGO Relations Cooperates with (1): *European Space Policy Institute (ESPI, #08801)*. [2021/AA1845/c/**F**]

♦ European Interprofessional Committee for the Intellectual Professions (inactive)

♦ European Interprofessional Education Network (EIPEN) 07595

Coordination Health Sciences and Practice Subject Ctr, Room 3-12 – Waterloo Bridge Wing, Franklin Wilkins Bldg, Kings College London, 150 Stamford Street, London, SE1 9NH, UK. T. +442078484220. Fax +442078483130. E-mail: info@eipen.eu.
URL: http://www.eipen.eu/

History 2004. **Aims** Develop and sustain a network in the EU to share and develop effective interprofessional training curricula, methods and materials for improving collaborative practice and multi agency working in health and social care. **Finance** Funding (75%) from *European Commission (EC, #06633)* through Lifelong Learning Programme. **Events** *Conference* Nijmegen (Netherlands) 2015, *Conference* Ljubljana (Slovenia) 2013, *Conference* Ghent (Belgium) 2011, *Conference* Oulu (Finland) 2009, *Conference* Krakow (Poland) 2007. **Publications** *E-Bulletin*.

Members Partners in 9 countries:
Belgium, Finland, Greece, Hungary, Ireland, Poland, Slovenia, Sweden, UK.

NGO Relations *International Association for Interprofessional Education and Collaborative Practice (InterEd, inactive)*; *Nordic Interprofessional Network (NIPNET, #17326)*. Member of: *Global Confederation for Interprofessional Education and Collaborative Practice (#10305)*. [2014/XJ2276/**F**]

♦ European Interregional Centre for Training Rescuers / see European Interregional Scientific and Educational Centre on Major Risk Management
♦ European Interregional Scientific and Educational Centre on Major Risk Management (internationally oriented national body)

♦ European Interreligious Forum for Religious Freedom (EIFRF) 07596

Contact 76 boulevard Diderot, 75012 Paris, France. E-mail: eiforumrf@gmail.com.
URL: http://www.eifrf-articles.org/

History Jan 2013. Approved by *United Religions Initiative (URI, #20658)*. Registration: RNA, No/ID: W751225102, Start date: 20 Jun 2014, France; EU Transparency Register, No/ID: 124201627781-58, Start date: 18 Jul 2017. **Aims** Promote: freedom of religion and belief; religious tolerance; interfaith dialogue; knowledge of religions. **Structure** Steering Committee. **Languages** English, French. **Staff** None paid. **Finance** Members' dues. Individual donations. Budget (annual): about euro 15,000. **Activities** Events/meetings; advocacy/lobbying/activism; knowledge management/information dissemination. **Publications** *EIFRF Newsletter*.

Members Full in 10 countries:
Belgium, Denmark, France, Germany, Israel, Italy, Netherlands, Spain, Switzerland, UK.

IGO Relations *Council of Europe (CE, #04881)*; *European Parliament (EP, #08146)*; *Organization for Security and Cooperation in Europe (OSCE, #17887)*. [2020/XM4871/**F**]

♦ European Interuniversity Association on Society, Science and Technology 07597

Association interuniversitaire européenne Société, science et technologie (ESST)

Intl Coordinator Univ Maastricht – Fac Arts and Social Sciences, Dept Technology and Society Studies, PO Box 616, 6200 MD Maastricht, Netherlands. T. +31433883339.
URL: http://www.esst.eu/

History 1991. Also referred to as *Association européenne EEST*. Registered in accordance with Belgian law. **Aims** Train future researchers, innovation consultants, research managers and policy-officers with a profound and critical understanding of the relation between research and innovation, and the specific socio-historical context from which they emerge and today's European socio-economical context in which they take place. **Structure** General Assembly (annual); Board of Directors; Bureau. **Languages** English. **Finance** Members' dues. **Activities** Training/education.

Members Universities (19) in 15 countries:
Austria, Belgium, Denmark, Estonia, Finland, France, Greece, Netherlands, Norway, Portugal, Spain, Sweden, Switzerland, Türkiye, UK.

IGO Relations Contacts with *European Commission (EC, #06633)* (DG Research). [2017.03.09/XF5423/**F**]

♦ European Inter-University Centre for Human Rights and Democratisation / see Global Campus of Human Rights (#10269)
♦ European Intraocular Implant Club / see European Society of Cataract and Refractive Surgeons (#08539)
♦ European Intraocular Implantlens Council / see European Society of Cataract and Refractive Surgeons (#08539)

♦ European Invasive Bacterial Diseases Surveillance Network (EU-IBD) 07598

Contact c/o ECDC, SE-169 73 Solna, Sweden. T. +46858601000. Fax +46858601001. E-mail: info@ecdc.europa.eu.
URL: https://www.ecdc.europa.eu/en/about-us/networks/disease-and-laboratory-networks/eu-ibd

History Taken over by *European Centre for Disease Prevention and Control (ECDC, #06476)*, 2007. Former names and other names: *Invasive Bacterial Infections Surveillance Network (EU-IBIS)* – former (2007). **Aims** Integrate surveillance of all invasive bacterial infections caused by N meningitidies, H influenzae and S pneumoniae from an epidemiological and laboratory point of view in order to contribute to reducing the burden of diseases associated with invasive bacterial infections. [2022.05.11/XJ2542/**F**]

♦ European Invertebrate Survey (inactive)

♦ European Investment Bank (EIB) 07599

Banque européenne d'investissement (BEI) – Banco Europeo de Inversiones (BEI) – Europäische Investitionsbank (EIB) – Banco Europeu de Investimento (BEI) – Banca Europea per gli Investimenti (BEI) – Europese Investeringsbank (EIB) – Europeiska Investeringsbanken (EIB) – Europaeiske Investeringsbank (EIB) – Euroopan Investointipankki (EIP) – Evropaiki Trapeza Ependiseon (ETE)

SG Bd Konrad Adenauer 98-100, L-2950 Luxembourg, Luxembourg. T. +35243791. Fax +352437704. E-mail: info@eib.org.
Main: http://www.eib.org/

History 25 Mar 1957, Rome (Italy). Established on signature of the *Treaty Establishing the European Economic Community (Treaty of Rome)*, which entered into force on 1 Jan 1958. The 6 founder states of the EEC were joined, 1 Jan 1973, by Denmark, Ireland and the United Kingdom, 1 Jan 1981, by Greece, 1 Jan 1986, by Portugal and Spain, 1 Jan 1995, by Austria, Finland and Sweden and 1 May 2004, by EU Accession States. The *Treaty on European Union (Maastricht Treaty, 1992)*, signed 7 Feb 1992, amended the Treaty of Rome, renaming the *'European Economic Community'* as the *European Community (inactive)*. An independent public body first of *European Communities (EC, inactive)* and subsequently, on signature of the Maastricht Treaty, of *European Union (EU, #08967)*, the EIB serves both as a Bank and a Community institution with the status of a public financial institution and having no organic links with other Community institutions. Since *Treaty of Lisbon (2007)* came into force, functions within the European Union. New function through *Treaty on the Functioning of the European Union (TFEU, 1957)*. Together with *European Investment Fund (EIF,*

#07601) and *EIB Institute (#05398)*, constitutes *EIB Group*. **Aims** Support projects that make a significant contribution to sustainable growth and employment in Europe and beyond. **Structure** Shareholders (27 Member States of the EU); Board of Governors; Board of Directors; Management Committee; Audit Committee; Directorates and Departments (11); General Secretariat. **Languages** English, French. **Staff** 3000.00 FTE, paid. **Finance** Operations funded by borrowing on capital markets. **Activities** Financial and/or material support; guidance/assistance/consulting. **Events** *Annual Meeting of the Initiative for Coal Regions in Transition in the Western Balkans and Ukraine* Brussels (Belgium) 2022, *CompNet-EIB-ENRI Annual Conference* Luxembourg (Luxembourg) 2022, *FI Campus Meetin* Brussels (Belgium) 2019, *FI Campus Meeting* Brussels (Belgium) 2019, *WCEF : World Circular Economy Forum* Helsinki (Finland) 2019.
Members The 27 Member States of the European Union:
Austria, Belgium, Bulgaria, Croatia, Cyprus, Czechia, Denmark, Estonia, Finland, France, Germany, Greece, Hungary, Ireland, Italy, Latvia, Lithuania, Luxembourg, Malta, Netherlands, Poland, Portugal, Romania, Slovakia, Slovenia, Spain, Sweden.
IGO Relations Partners with civil society organizations, the banking community, multilateral development banks and universities. [2020.09.04/XF0670/**F***]

♦ European Investment Casters' Association / see European Investment Casters' Federation (#07600)

♦ European Investment Casters' Federation (EICF) 07600

Fédération européenne de fondeurs à modèles perdus

Contact Holly Cottage, Gorcott Hill, Beoley, Redditch, B98 9EW, UK. T. +441564743077. Fax +441564742080.
Exec Dir Maison des Associations Internationales, Rue Washington 40, 1050 Brussels, Belgium.
URL: http://www.eicf.org/

History 1955, UK. Originally UK based. Relocated to Belgium, 2019, due to Brexit. Administration office maintained in UK. Former names and other names: *European Investment Casters' Association (EICA)* – former. Registration: Banque-Carrefour des Entreprises, No/ID: 0728.842.261, Start date: 25 Jun 2019, Belgium; Companies House, No/ID: 04694940, Start date: 12 Mar 2003, England and Wales; EU Transparency Register, No/ID: 966828336007-33, Start date: 25 Sep 2019. **Aims** Further the interests of the European investment casting industry; improve its working methods and practices; widen the markets for its products. **Structure** General Assembly; Board of Directors; Executive Committee. Working Groups. **Languages** English. **Staff** 1.00 FTE, paid. **Finance** Sources: meeting proceeds; members' dues. Annual budget: 400,000 EUR. **Activities** Advocacy/lobbying/activism; awards/prizes/competitions; awareness raising; events/meetings; guidance/assistance/consulting; knowledge management/information dissemination; networking/liaising; publishing activities; research and development; research/documentation; standards/guidelines; training/education. **Events** *International Conference* Bregenz (Austria) 2023, *International Conference* Santander (Spain) 2022, *International Conference* Bregenz (Austria) 2021, *International Conference* Bregenz (Austria) 2020, *Euro Seminar* Helsinki (Finland) 2019. **Publications** *INCAST Magazine* (12 a year). Annual Report; seminar and conference proceedings.
Members Full (around 112) in 24 countries and territories:
Belgium, Canada, China, Czechia, Finland, France, Germany, Hungary, India, Ireland, Italy, Netherlands, Poland, Portugal, Serbia, Slovakia, Spain, Sweden, Switzerland, Taiwan, Tunisia, Türkiye, UK, USA.
Individuals in 3 countries:
Belgium, Germany, UK.
NGO Relations Member of (2): *European Society of Association Executives (ESAE, #08526)*; *Federation of European and International Associations Established in Belgium (FAIB, #09508)*. Also links with national foundry associations. [2022.10.19/XD0791/**D**]

♦ European Investment Fund (EIF) 07601

Fonds européen d'investissement (FEI)

Chief Exec Av JF Kennedy 37B, L-2968 Luxembourg, Luxembourg. T. +35224851. Fax +352248581200. E-mail: info@eif.org.
URL: http://www.eif.org/

History 14 Jun 1994. Established at a meeting of shareholders, by *European Investment Bank (EIB, #07599)*, *European Commission (EC, #06633)* and several banks. Statutes amended, 19 Jun 2000, when EIB became the majority shareholder and operator. Together with EIB and *EIB Institute (#05398)*, constitutes the *EIB Group*. **Aims** Develop and deploy financial instruments (equity and debt financing) to ensure access to finance for Europe's small and medium-sized businesses (SMEs). **Structure** General Meeting (annual); Board of Directors; Audit Board; Chief Executive; Main Office, located in Luxembourg (Luxembourg). **Languages** English. **Staff** 600.00 FTE, paid. **Finance** The EIF has an authorised capital of €7 370m, divided into 7,370 shares with a nominal value of €1m each. On 31 December 2021, 7,300 shares were subscribed and the EIB held 59.4% (4,336) of the issued shares, the EU represented by the EC held 30% (2,190 shares) and 38 financial institutions held 10.6% (774 shares). **Activities** Financial and/or material support; guidance/assistance/consulting; publishing activities; research/documentation. European Union and associated countries. **Events** *Annual General Meeting* Luxembourg (Luxembourg) 2000, *Annual General Meeting* Copenhagen (Denmark) 1999, *Annual General Meeting* Brussels (Belgium) 1998, *Annual General Meeting* Luxembourg (Luxembourg) 1994. **Publications** Annual Report; country fact sheets; brochures; leaflets; research and market analysis papers.
Members Shareholders include 38 financial institutions as at 31 Dec 2021, in both public and private sectors in 20 countries:
Austria, Bulgaria, Croatia, Czechia, Denmark, France, Germany, Greece, Hungary, Ireland, Italy, Luxembourg, Malta, Netherlands, Poland, Portugal, Slovenia, Spain, Türkiye, UK.
International organizations (2):
European Investment Bank (EIB, #07599); *European Union (EU, #08967)*.
IGO Relations *Council of Europe Development Bank (CEB, #04897)*; *European Bank for Reconstruction and Development (EBRD, #06315)*; *European Investment Bank (EIB, #07599)*; *European Union (EU, #08967)*; *International Bank for Reconstruction and Development (IBRD, #12317)*; *International Monetary Fund (IMF, #14180)*; *UNDP (#20292)*; *The World Bank Group (#21218)*. **NGO Relations** Mainly European financial and non-financial associations and agencies, including: *European Association of Guarantee Institutions (#06061)*; *European Association of Long-Term Investors (ELTI, #06112)*; *European Trade Association for Business Angels, Seed Funds, and other Early Stage Market Players (EBAN, #08923)*; *Invest Europe – The Voice of Private Capital (Invest Europe, #15997)*. [2022.02.09/XF3054/f/**F***]

♦ European Investment Services Association (inactive)

♦ European Iron Club (EIC) 07602

Sec Weatherall Inst, Radcliffe Hospital, University of Oxford, Oxford, OX3 9DS, UK.
URL: http://ironmasterclass.eu/

History 1970. **Aims** Encourage research into biological inorganic chemistry of iron, specifically its metabolism, pathology and clinical relevance to man; promote discussion and interaction between biologists, biochemists, chemists, molecular biologists, nutritionists and clinicians in all aspects of iron metabolism in biological systems. **Structure** General Meeting (annual). Office, headed by Secretary. **Languages** English. **Staff** 1.00 FTE, paid. **Finance** Members' dues (annual): euro 15. **Events** *Annual Meeting* Oxford (UK) 2021, *Annual Meeting* Innsbruck (Austria) 2016, *Annual scientific meeting* St Gallen (Switzerland) 2008, *Annual scientific meeting* London (UK) 2007, *Annual scientific meeting* Barcelona (Spain) 2006. **Publications** Newsletter (annual).
Members Full (over 200) in 26 countries:
Austria, Belarus, Belgium, Czechia, Denmark, Finland, France, Germany, Greece, Hungary, Ireland, Israel, Italy, Latvia, Netherlands, Norway, Poland, Portugal, Romania, Russia, Serbia, Spain, Sweden, Switzerland, UK, Ukraine. [2018/XD7718/**D**]

♦ European Irrigation Association (EIA) 07603

Association européenne de l'irrigation

Gen Sec Diamant Bldg, Bd Auguste Reyers 80, 1030 Brussels, Belgium. E-mail: communication@irrigationeurope.eu – info@irrigationeurope.eu – secgen@irrigationeurope.eu.
Pres address not obtained.
URL: https://irrigationeurope.eu/

History 1991. Registration: Banque-Carrefour des Entreprises, No/ID: 0534.944.607, Start date: 5 Jun 2013, Belgium; EU Transparency Register, No/ID: 837818415965-04, Start date: 9 Feb 2015. **Aims** Promote and improve products, practices and services in managing water resources for urban and landscape irrigation. **Structure** General Assembly; Board of Directors; Committees; National Delegates. **Languages** English. **Staff** 1.00 FTE, paid. **Activities** Advocacy/lobbying/activism; certification/accreditation; events/meetings; knowledge management/information dissemination; standards/guidelines; training/education.
Members in 10 countries:
Belgium, France, Greece, India, Italy, Netherlands, Portugal, Spain, UK, USA.
NGO Relations Supports (1): *Farming First*. [2023/XD7969/**D**]

♦ European Isocyanate Producers Association / see European Diisocyanate and Polyol Producers Association (#06926)
♦ European Di-isocyanate Producers Association / see European Diisocyanate and Polyol Producers Association (#06926)

♦ European Isotopes Transport Association (EITA) 07604

Contact KVS and Partners, Nederokkerzeelstraat 6, 1910 Kampenhout, Belgium. T. +3216650812. Fax +3216898896.
Registered Office MAI, Rue Washington 40, 1050 Brussels, Belgium.
URL: http://www.eita.org/

History Founded 30 Oct 1997, at constituent assembly. Registered in accordance with Belgian law. **Aims** Promote, facilitate and contribute to: harmonization of policies, regulations and legislation affecting the sector at national, European and international levels; developing a favourable environment for the transport and handling of isotopes and/or radioactive and/or nuclear materials; improving communication and cooperation among members. **Structure** General Assembly (annual), founding members having 2 votes each and regular members 1 each. Council (meets at least 3 times a year) comprising 3 or more members (at least 1 representing a founder company) including President, plus (ex officio) Secretary-General. **Languages** English, French, German. **Finance** Members' dues. **Activities** Represents industries involved in transport and/or handling of isotopes and/or radioactive and/or nuclear materials with national and international institutions, including those of the European Union; establishes and maintains contacts with these institutions; provides members with the opportunity of representing their interests. **Members** Founder companies; regular (companies and individuals); honorary. Membership countries not specified. [2012.07.16/XD6582/**D**]

♦ EuropeanIssuers 07605

SG Rue Belliard 4-6 Bte 1, 1040 Brussels, Belgium. T. +3222892570. Fax +3225021560. E-mail: info@europeanissuers.eu.
URL: http://www.europeanissuers.eu/

History 6 Mar 2008. Founded on merger of *European Association of Listed Companies (EALIC, inactive)* and *Union of Issuers Quoted in Europe (UNIQUE, inactive)*. Registration: Belgium; EU Transparency Register, No/ID: 20935778703-23, Start date: 16 May 2012. **Aims** Represent the interests of publicly quoted companies from all sectors to the EU institutions; ensure that EU policy creates an environment in which companies of all sizes from emerging growth companies to the large blue chip companies can easily raise capital through the public markets and deliver growth over the longer term. **Structure** EuropeanIssuers Board; Secretariat; Committees (2); Working Groups (14); Annual General Assembly. **Languages** English. **Staff** 5.00 FTE, paid; 1.00 FTE, voluntary. **Finance** Sources: members' dues; revenue from activities/projects; sponsorship. **Activities** Awards/prizes/competitions; events/meetings; politics/policy/regulatory. **Events** *Audit and Compliance* 2021, *Digital Transformation, European Data Strategy* 2021, *Capital Markets Seminar* 2020, *Capital Markets Forum* Brussels (Belgium) 2018. **Publications** Annual Report; Press release; position papers; newsflash; press articles.
Members National associations; companies in 15 countries:
Belgium, Bulgaria, Finland, France, Germany, Greece, Italy, Luxembourg, Netherlands, Poland, Portugal, Romania, Spain, Switzerland, UK.
NGO Relations Member of (2): *Federation of European and International Associations Established in Belgium (FAIB, #09508)*; *International Organization of Securities Commissions (IOSCO, #14470)*. [2021.06.25/XJ5941/t/**D**]

♦ European IT Services Association (inactive)
♦ **European IWT Platform** European Inland Waterway Transport Platform (#07541)

♦ European Japan Experts Association (EJEA) 07606

Managing Dir Wurzerstr 136, 53175 Bonn, Germany. T. +492289562560. E-mail: ejea@ejea.eu.
URL: http://ejea.eu/

History 4 Nov 1995, Berlin (Germany). Established at founding meeting, when Standing Rules were adopted. Registration: Germany. **Aims** Establish a sustainable interdisciplinary network in order to provide a reliable foundation for European-Japanese relations. **Structure** Members' Meeting (every 1 to 3 years); Full Executive Committee; Advisory Board. **Languages** English. **Staff** 0.50 FTE, voluntary. **Finance** Sources: members' dues. **Activities** Events/meetings; networking/liaising; research/documentation. **Events** *Human-Centered Sustainability and Innovation for an AI-assisted Future* Kagawa (Japan) 2021, *Human-Centered Digitalization: How to Develop Next Generation of Humans and Robots for a Secure, Harmonic and Prosperous Future of Europe and Japan?* Graz (Austria) 2019, *Integration and Disintegration in the Japanese Vision of Society 5.0 – A Model for an Open Society in Europe?* Stockholm (Sweden) 2018, *Conference* Rhodes Is (Greece) 2014, *Conference* Graz (Austria) 2013. **Publications** Conference papers – series.
Members Individuals and organizations, mainly in Germany but in a total of 12 countries:
Austria, Belgium, Finland, France, Germany, Greece, Italy, Japan, Netherlands, Sweden, Switzerland, UK. [2021.07.05/XD6199/**E**]

♦ European Jazz Network / see Europe Jazz Network (#09160)

♦ European Jesuits in Social Sciences (EUROJESS) 07607

Jésuites européens en sciences sociales

Chairman Route de Morillons 4, 1211 Geneva 22, Switzerland. T. +41227996196.
URL: http://www.eurojess.net/

History 1949. **Aims** Ensure contact and periodic exchange of views and foster cooperation among Jesuits and institutions of the Society in Europe specialized in reflecting on social sciences within the framework of the social apostolate; foster relationships with other organizations of a similar nature in the Society of Jesus and with Jesuits dealing with the same problems in other parts of the world. **Structure** General Assembly. Steering Committee, comprising President and 4 elected members. Executive Secretariat. **Languages** English. **Finance** Members' contributions to cover general expenses. **Activities** Organizes plenary sessions and conferences. **Events** *Food and energy for all, Europe responsibilities for its inhabitants and for the planet* Milan (Italy) 2015, *Congress* Lviv (Ukraine) 2013, *Congress* Geneva (Switzerland) 2011, *Congress* Granada (Spain) 2009, *Congress* Piestany (Slovakia) 2007.
Members in 17 countries:
Austria, Belgium, Croatia, France, Germany, Greece, Ireland, Italy, Malta, Netherlands, Poland, Portugal, Slovenia, Spain, Switzerland, UK, Ukraine. [2015/XE4337/**E**]

♦ European Jewish Association (EJA) 07608

Contact Rue du Cornet 22, 1040 Brussels, Belgium. T. +3227211640. E-mail: info@ejassociation.eu.
URL: https://www.ejassociation.eu/

History EU Transparency Register: 707551412661-80. **Aims** Strengthen Jewish identity and expand Jewish activities in Europe; defend Jewish interests in Europe. **Structure** Advisory Board; Leadership. Financial arm is the *European Jewish Development Fund (EJDF)*. **Activities** Advocacy/lobbying/activism; events/meetings; knowledge management/information dissemination. **NGO Relations** Affiliated organizations include: *European Centre for Jewish Students (ECJS, #06487)*; *European Jewish Community Centre (EJCC)*; *Rabbinical Centre of Europe (RCE, #18598)*. [2020/XM8949/**E**]

♦ European Jewish Call for Reason (unconfirmed)
♦ European Jewish Community Centre (unconfirmed)

♦ **European Jewish Congress (EJC)** **07609**
Congrès juif européen (CJE)
Address not obtained.
URL: http://www.eurojewcong.org/
History 1986. Set up as an autonomous organization, affiliated to *World Jewish Congress (WJC, #21599)*. Registration: ASBL, Belgium; EU Transparency Register, No/ID: 36101356444-26. **Aims** Ensure survival of the Jewish people and strengthen its unity by coordinating the efforts of its affiliated organizations in political, economic, social and cultural fields, safeguarding the rights, status and interests of Jews and Jewish Communities, encouraging constructive development of Jewish social and cultural life in the world, and representing member organizations and the interests of the Jewish people as a whole with governmental, intergovernmental and international authorities. **Structure** General Assembly; Executive Committee; Council. **Activities** Advocacy/lobbying/activism. **Events** *Meeting* Brussels (Belgium) 2015, *General Assembly* Tel Aviv (Israel) 2015, *General Assembly* Brussels (Belgium) 2012, *Europe, against anti-semitism for a union of diversity* Brussels (Belgium) 2004, *Future of the Middle East* Brussels (Belgium) 2004.
Members Representatives of Jewish organizations in 38 countries:
Austria, Belarus, Belgium, Bosnia-Herzegovina, Bulgaria, Croatia, Cyprus, Czechia, Denmark, Estonia, Finland, France, Germany, Greece, Hungary, Ireland, Italy, Latvia, Lithuania, Luxembourg, Moldova, Monaco, Morocco, Netherlands, North Macedonia, Norway, Poland, Portugal, Romania, Russia, Serbia, Slovakia, Slovenia, Spain, Sweden, Switzerland, UK, Ukraine.
Observers in 1 country:
Türkiye.
Consultative Status Consultative status granted from: *Council of Europe (CE, #04881)* (Participatory Status). **IGO Relations** Participant in Fundamental Rights Platform of: *European Union Agency for Fundamental Rights (FRA, #08969)*. **NGO Relations** Member of: *World Jewish Restitution Organization (WJRO, #21601)*.
[2020/XE6303/**E**]

- ♦ European Jewish Fund (unconfirmed)
- ♦ European Jews for a Just Peace (unconfirmed)
- ♦ European Joint Airworthiness Requirements Body / see Joint Aviation Authorities Training Organisation (#16122)

♦ **European Joint Committee on Plasma and Ion Surface Engineering (EJC PISE)** **07610**
Chairman Fraunhofer Institut für Schicht und Oberflächentechnik, Bienroder Weg 54e, 38108 Braunschweig, Germany. T. +495312155501 – +4953100. Fax +495312155901. E-mail: gu-enter.braeuer@ist.fraunhofer.de.
Secretariat Europäische Forschungsgesellschaft Dünne Schichten – EFDS, Gostritzer Strasse 63, 01217 Dresden, Germany. T. +493518718370. Fax +493518718431.
URL: http://www.ejc-pise.org/
Events *AEPSE : Asian-European Conference on Plasma Surface Engineering* Busan (Korea Rep) 2023, *AEPSE : Asian-European Conference on Plasma Surface Engineering* Busan (Korea Rep) 2022, *AEPSE : Asian-European Conference on Plasma Surface Engineering* Busan (Korea Rep) 2021, *AEPSE : Asian-European Conference on Plasma Surface Engineering* Jeju (Korea Rep) 2019, *AEPSE : Asian-European Conference on Plasma Surface Engineering* Jeju (Korea Rep) 2017. **NGO Relations** *Asian Joint Committee on Plasma Surface Engineering (AJC PSE)*.
[2017.06.01/XM3565/**E**]

- ♦ European Joint Theoretical/Experimental Meeting on Membranes (meeting series)

♦ **European Joint Undertaking for ITER and the Development of Fusion Energy (Fusion for Energy)** **07611**
Dir c/ Josep Pla no 2, Torres Diagonal Litoral, Edificio B3, 08019 Barcelona, Spain.
URL: http://fusionforenergy.europa.eu/
History Created 19 Apr 2007, Barcelona (Spain), under the *Treaty Establishing the European Atomic Energy Community (Treaty of Rome, 1957)*, by a decision of the *Council of the European Union (#04895)* of *European Union (EU, #08967)*. Set up for a period of 35 years. **Aims** Provide Europe's contribution to ITER – a global scientific partnership aiming to demonstrate fusion as a viable and sustainable source of energy; support fusion research and development initiatives; contribute towards the construction of demonstration fusion reactors. **Structure** Governing Board; Bureau; Administration and Management Committee; Procurement and Contracts Committee; Technical Advisory Panel; Audit Committee. **Languages** English. **Staff** 460.00 FTE, paid. **Finance** Funded by EU and French government. Budget 2008-2020: euro 6,600,000,000. **Activities** Research and development. **Events** *Technical Coordination Meeting* Naka (Japan) 2019. **Publications** *F4E News* (4 a year) – newsletter; *Annual Highlights*. Annual Report; fact sheets; brochures.
Members Governments of 29 countries:
Austria, Belgium, Bulgaria, Croatia, Cyprus, Czechia, Denmark, Estonia, Finland, France, Germany, Greece, Hungary, Ireland, Italy, Latvia, Lithuania, Luxembourg, Malta, Netherlands, Poland, Portugal, Romania, Slovakia, Slovenia, Spain, Sweden, Switzerland, UK.
Regional entity:
European Commission (EC, #06633) (Euratom).
IGO Relations *European Union (EU, #08967)*; *ITER International Fusion Energy Organization (ITER Organization, #16072)*. **NGO Relations** Member of (1): *EU Agencies Network (EUAN, #05564)*.
[2021/XM5102/**E***]

♦ **European Journalism Centre (EJC)** **07612**
Centre européen du journalisme
Main Office Petrus Regoutplein 1F02, 6211 XX Maastricht, Netherlands. T. +31433254030. Fax +3224004220. E-mail: info@ejc.net.
Brussels Office Rue de la Loi 155, Block C Bureau 5/206, 1040 Brussels, Belgium. T. +3222352348.
URL: http://ejc.net/
History 30 Jun 1992. Founded by *European Journalism Training Association (EJTA, #07613)*. Registration: Handelsregister, No/ID: KVK 41078390, Netherlands. **Aims** Promote high quality journalism through professional *training*, particularly in a European context; train journalists in a European context and on European issues so as to create a European perspective; improve professional skills of journalists through training in subjects with an international and European perspective; provide a forum for discussion and exchanges of views and experience for journalists, *editors*, *media* executives and professionals; through training and networking, support high standards of journalism in transition and developing countries; via research, surveys and publications, monitor and reflect on present and future challenges facing the media; create and support networks among media professionals within Europe and other parts of the world. **Structure** Board of Directors; Board of Counsellors; Executive Committee. Activity staff consisting of Director, Director of Programmes, Editor and 2 Projects Managers. Supporting Staff. **Finance** Project work; service contracts; limited financial support from Dutch local and national authorities. **Activities** Standards/guidelines; guidance/assistance/consulting. **Events** *Conference on the role of media in the financial crisis* Brussels (Belgium) 2009, *Conference on regional media in Europe and the role of journalists* Chania (Greece) 1999. **Publications** Training manual; books. **Members** Not a membership organization. **NGO Relations** Member of (2): *Ethical Journalism Network (EJN, #05554)*; *Global Investigative Journalism Network (GIJN, #10433)*. Partner of (1): *Global Call for Climate Action (GCCA, inactive)*.
[2020/XE1745/**E**]

♦ **European Journalism Training Association (EJTA)** **07613**
Association européenne de formation au journalisme (AEFJ)
Office p/a Thomas More Mechelen, Zandpoortvest 13, 2800 Mechelen, Belgium. E-mail: info@ejta.eu.
Pres Hogeschool Windesheim, Campus 2-6, 8017 CA Zwolle, Netherlands.
URL: http://www.ejta.eu/
History Founded Nov 1990, Brussels (Belgium), superseding *Liaison Committee of the European Training Centres for Journalism – Comité de liaison des centres européens de formation au journalisme*, which had been set up Apr 1987, Brussels. **Aims** Enable journalism training centres and schools involved to collaborate regularly to encourage the emergence of a European consciousness and the development of journalism training. **Structure** General Meeting (annual); Executive Board. **Languages** English. **Staff** Part-time. **Finance** Members' entrance and annual fees. Other sources: funds raised from EJTA activities; European Commission programmes; various sponsors in private and public companies; foundations. **Activities** Events/meetings; publishing activities; research/documentation. **Events** *Annual General Meeting* Vienna (Austria) 2020, *Annual General Meeting* Paris (France) 2019, *Annual General Meeting* Barcelona (Spain) 2018, *Teachers Conference* Paris (France) 2016, *Annual Conference* Jyväskylä (Finland) 2014. **Publications** *EJTA Newsletter*.
Members Journalism schools and mid-career centres in 2' countries:
Albania, Austria, Belgium, Bulgaria, Czechia, Denmark, Estonia, Finland, France, Georgia, Germany, Ireland, Lithuania, Netherlands, Norway, Poland, Portugal, Romania, Russia, Slovakia, Spain, Sweden, Switzerland, UK.
Included in the above, 1 organization listed in this Yearbook:
European Journalism Centre (EJC, #07612).
NGO Relations Member of: *Global Forum for Media Development (GFMD, #10375)*; *World Journalism Education Council (WJEC, #21602)*. Instrumental in setting up: *European Journalism Centre (EJC, #07612)*.
[2020/XE1015/y/**D**]

- ♦ European Journals Group for Science and Technology (inactive)
- ♦ European Judges for Democracy and Liberties / see Magistrats européens pour la démocratie et les libertés (#16546)

♦ **European Judges and Prosecutors Association (EJPA)** **07614**
Association des Magistrats de l'Union Européenne (AMUE) – Asociación de los Juecez y Fiscales de la Union Europea – Associação dos Magistrados da União Europeia
SG address not obtained. E-mail: magistratsue@gmail.com.
Twitter: https://twitter.com/magistratsue
History Mar 2004. Registration: France. **Aims** Improve knowledge of the legal systems throughout the European Union; promote cooperation between magistrates in the region. **Structure** General Assembly (annual). Board of Directors of 15 members. Committee, comprising President, Vice-President, Secretary and Treasurer. **Activities** Organizes conferences, seminars and symposia. **Events** *Conference* Paris (France) 2011, *Conference* Paris (France) 2009, *Conference on creating an Area of criminal justice in the EU* Paris (France) 2007. **Publications** *La lettre des magistrats de l'Union européenne* – monthly electronic newsletter. **Members** Individuals in 9 countries:
Czechia, France, Germany, Hungary, Italy, Netherlands, Portugal, Romania, Spain.
[2017/XM3169/**D**]

♦ **European Judicial Network (EJN)** **07615**
Réseau judiciaire européen (RJE)
Coordinator Johan de Wittlaan 9, 2517 JR The Hague, Netherlands. Fax +31704125570. E-mail: ejn@eurojust.europa.eu.
URL: http://www.ejn-crimjust.europa.eu/
History 29 Jun 1998. Established on the basis of an Action Plan (recommendation no 2) on creation of a European Judicial Network (OJ L 191 of 07 Jun 1998, p4), adopted in 1997 by *European Council (#06801)* to combat organized crime, prepared by a High Level Group of experts from Member States. Several of the recommendations of this Action Plan aim at improving the standards of cooperation between judicial authorities in criminal matters. Officially inaugurated, 25 Sep 1998, by the Austrian Minister of Justice acting as the Presidency of the Council of the *European Union (EU, #08967)*. **Aims** Facilitate and speed-up judicial cooperation in criminal matters; give support to practitioners by means of information systems, facilitation of contacts and direct assistance in the preparation and execution of requests for assistance. **Structure** Composed of contact points of Member States, as well as in EU institutions and non-EU countries. The EJN Secretariat is part of *Eurojust (#05698)* , but functions as a separate and autonomous unit to support the functioning of the EJN. **Languages** English. **Activities** Events/meetings; knowledge management/information dissemination; networking/liaising. Carries out operational missions aimed at facilitating and speeding judicial cooperation; sets up and maintains information tools on judicial cooperation. **Events** *Plenary Meeting* Stockholm (Sweden) 2023, *Plenary meeting* Bordeaux (France) 2022, *Plenary Meeting* Czechia 2022, *Plenary meeting* Lisbon (Portugal) 2021, *Plenary meeting* Ljubljana (Slovenia) 2021. **Publications** Information Services: Internet-based information system on judicial cooperation in criminal matters in the European Union. **Members** EU member states. **NGO Relations** Cooperates with (1): *European Consumer Centres Network (ECC-Net, #06770)*.
[2022/XF6123/**F***]

♦ **European Judicial Network in Civil and Commercial Matters** **07616**
Réseau judiciaire européen en matière civile et commerciale – Red Judicial Europea en Materia Civil y Mercantil – Europäisches Justizielles Netz für Zivil- und Handelssachen – Rede Judiciaria Europeia em Matéria Civil e Comercial – Rete Giudiziaria Europea in Materia Civile e Commerciale – Europese Justitiële Netwerk in Burgerlijke en Handelszaken – Europeiskt Rättsligt Nätverk på Privaträttens Område – Europaeisk Retligt Netvaerk for Civil- og Handelssager – Euroopan Oikeudellinen Verkosto Sivilli- ja Kauppaoikeus – Evropska Soudni sit ve Vecech Obcanskych a Obchoichnich – Európska Justivcna siet v Civilnih in Gospodarskih Zadevah – Európai Igazsagügyi Halózat Polgari és Kereskedelmi Ügyekben – Europejska Siec Sadownicza w Sprawach Cywilnych i Handlowych – Evropska Pravosodna Mreza v Civilnih in gospodarskih Zadevah – Euroopa Justiitsvõrgustik Tsiviil- ja Kaubandusasjades – Eiropas Tiesiskas Sadarbības tikls Civillietas un Komerclietas – Europos Teisminiu Instituciju Nagrinejanciu Civilenes ir Komercines bylas, Tinklas – Network Gudizzjarju Ewropeu Fil-qasam Civili u Kummercjali
Contact EJTN, Rue du Commerce 123, 1000 Brussels, Belgium.
URL: https://e-justice.europa.eu/content_about_the_network-431-en.do/
History 28 May 2001, by *Council of the European Union (#04895)*, within the framework of *European Union (EU, #08967)*. Amended by Council Decision No 568/2009/EC, of 30 Jun 2009. **Aims** Improve and facilitate effective judicial cooperation between *European Union* member states in *civil* and *commercial* matters. **Structure** Work is carried out by contact points of the EU member states and representatives of central bodies and authorities. **Events** *Meeting* Helsinki (Finland) 2019.
Members Members States (26):
Austria, Belgium, Bulgaria, Cyprus, Czechia, Estonia, Finland, France, Germany, Greece, Hungary, Ireland, Italy, Latvia, Lithuania, Luxembourg, Malta, Netherlands, Poland, Portugal, Romania, Slovakia, Slovenia, Spain, Sweden, UK.
[2020/XM1082/**F***]

♦ **European Judicial Training Network (EJTN)** **07617**
Réseau européen de formation judiciaire (REFJ)
SG Rue du Commerce 123, 1000 Brussels, Belgium. T. +3222802242. Fax +3222802236. E-mail: ejtn@ejtn.eu.
URL: http://www.ejtn.eu/
History Founded 13 Oct 2000, Bordeaux (France). **Aims** Promote training and exchange of knowledge of the European judiciary. **Structure** General Assembly (annual); Steering Committee; Departments (5). **Languages** English, French. **Staff** 21.00 FTE, paid. **Finance** Members' dues. EU operating grant. **Activities** Standards/guidelines; training/education; networking/liaising; events/meetings. **Events** *Seminar on Legal Language Training* Barcelona (Spain) 2014, *Civil Law Conference* Vienna (Austria) 2013, *General Meeting* Budapest (Hungary) 2011, *General Meeting* Madrid (Spain) 2010, *Seminar on practical issues of cross-border mediation* Trier (Germany) 2009. **Publications** Catalogue of training activities open to European judges and prosecutors (annual). **Members** Organizations. Membership countries not specified. **IGO Relations** Observer status with: *Commission européenne pour l'efficacité de la justice (CEPEJ, #04213)*; *Consultative Council of European Judges (CCJE, #04767)*.
[2020/XF6405/y/**F**]

- ♦ European Judo Federation / see Union européenne de judo (#20399)
- ♦ European Judo Union (#20399)

♦ **European Juggling Association (EJA)** **07618**
Contact address not obtained. E-mail: directors@eja.net.
URL: http://www.eja.net/
History 1987, Saintes (France). Founded during European Juggling Convention (EJC), conventions having been held since 1948. **Aims** Promote juggling in Europe and beyond. **Structure** General Assembly (annual); Board of Directors; Executive Committee; Country Representatives. **Languages** Dutch, English, French, German. **Events** *Annual Convention* Punchestown (Ireland) 2023, *European Juggling Convention* Tres Cantos (Spain) 2022, *European Juggling Convention* Hanko (Finland) 2021, *European Juggling Convention* Hanko (Finland) 2020, *Annual Convention* Newark (UK) 2019.
Members Individuals in 29 countries:
Austria, Belgium, Czechia, Denmark, Finland, France, Germany, Greece, Hungary, Ireland, Israel, Italy, Japan, Luxembourg, Netherlands, New Zealand, Poland, Portugal, Romania, Slovakia, Slovenia, South Africa, Spain, Sweden, Switzerland, Thailand, Türkiye, UK, USA.
[2022.05.25/XD5987/**D**]

♦ European Ju-Jitsu Federation / see Ju-Jitsu European Union (#16163)
♦ European Ju-Jitsu Union / see Ju-Jitsu European Union (#16163)

♦ European Ju Jitsu Union (EJJU) 07619

Pres address not obtained. E-mail: kaizenryu_3@hotmail.com – oejju@hotmail.com.
URL: http://oejju.webs.com/

History Founded 16 Dec 1968, London (UK). Registered according to British law. Official constitution amended, 29-31 May 1982, Brussels (Belgium); 23 Jan 1999, Vienna (Austria); 25 May 2002, Vienna; 2005, Vienna. **Aims** Spread the pure traditional Japanese *martial art* of Jujitsu, also called Nippon Jujitsu including its values of self-defence, and its Japanese ethical and aesthetic backgrounds based on bushido. **Structure** Congress (annual). Committee, consisting of President, General Secretary, 1st Vice-President, Vice-Presidents (national President, Technical Director or Head Sensei of each member country). Technical Board, comprising all Vice-Presidents plus main delegates of member countries not represented in Vice-Presidents body, and headed by Chief Technical Director. Includes: *International Martial Arts Dan College*. **Languages** English, French, German. **Finance** Members' dues. **Activities** Sets out requirements for Dan examinations and awards diplomas. Several very big top level jujitsu courses and seminars every year all over Europe. **Events** *Annual european congress / Annual Eastern Europe Congress* Vienna (Austria) 2006, *Annual Eastern Europe Congress* Vienna (Austria) 2005, *Annual Eastern Europe congress* Jena (Germany) 2004, *Annual Eastern Europe Congress* Madrid (Spain) 2004, *Annual Eastern Europe congress* Vienna (Austria) 2003. **Publications** *Kanon des Nippon Jujitsu* (1993); *Edition Tyrolia*.
Members National jujitsu organizations, schools and federations and their blackbelt holders in 13 countries:
Austria, Belgium, France, Germany, Greece, Italy, Luxembourg, Poland, Portugal, Romania, Spain, Switzerland, UK.
IGO Relations *UNESCO (#20322)*. **NGO Relations** Affiliated to: *World Presidium of Bu Jitsu Arts (no recent information)*. [2014/XD2352/**D**]

♦ European Junior Doctors Association (EJD) 07620

Administration Officer Rue Guimard 15, 1040 Brussels, Belgium. E-mail: office@juniordoctors.eu.
URL: http://www.juniordoctors.eu/

History 1976, Bad Nauheim (Germany). Founded as *Permanent Working Group of European Junior Hospital Doctors – Groupe de travail permanent des jeunes médecins hospitaliers européens*. Subsequently changed title to *European Junior Doctors Permanent Working Group (EJD) – Groupe de travail permanent des jeunes médecins européens*. Registration: Banque-Carrefour des Entreprises, No/ID: 0834.556.821, Start date: 16 Mar 2011, Belgium; EU Transparency Register, No/ID: 540516714978-95, Start date: 21 Nov 2014. **Aims** Act as a liaison group linking national organizations which represent junior doctors in Europe; represent the professional interests of junior doctors at European level; improve conditions and organization of junior doctors' work and education; ensure that the voice of junior doctors is heard in international medical organizations. **Structure** Plenary Assembly; Executive Board; Secretariat. **Languages** English. **Staff** 5.00 FTE, paid. **Finance** Member organizations contributions. **Activities** Knowledge management/information dissemination; research/documentation; training/education; events/meetings. **Events** *Spring Meeting* Helsinki (Finland) 2022, *Autumn Meeting* Brussels (Belgium) 2020, *Spring Meeting* Brussels (Belgium) 2020, *Spring Meeting* Edinburgh (UK) 2019, *Autumn Meeting* Georgia 2019. **Publications** Policies and statements; reports; handbooks.
Members National organizations in 23 countries:
Austria, Croatia, Czechia, Denmark, Estonia, Finland, France, Germany, Greece, Hungary, Ireland, Italy, Latvia, Lithuania, Malta, Netherlands, Norway, Portugal, Slovenia, Spain, Sweden, Türkiye, UK. [2021/XD5441/**D**]

♦ European Junior Doctors Permanent Working Group / see European Junior Doctors Association (#07620)

♦ European Justice Forum (EJF) 07621

Exec Dir Marnixlaan 28, 1000 Brussels, Belgium. T. +3225480271. Fax +3222276189. E-mail: info@europeanjusticeforum.org.
URL: http://europeanjusticeforum.org/

History Registered in accordance with Belgian law. **Aims** Ensure that: the legal environment in Europe protects both consumers and businesses; those with a legitimate grievance have access to justice. **Publications** Position papers.
Members Corporate; Professional; Lawyers' Network. Lawyers' network in 17 countries:
Australia, Belgium, Denmark, Finland, France, Germany, Greece, Hungary, Ireland, Italy, Netherlands, Poland, Portugal, Spain, Sweden, Switzerland, UK.
Also members in the Baltics. Membership countries not specified. [2015/XJ0467/**F**]

♦ European Kansei Group (EKG) 07622

Sec Toyota Motor Europe R and D, Advanced Technology – Kansei, Hoge Wei 33, 1930 Zaventem, Belgium.
URL: http://www.kansei.eu/

History Founded Jun 2014, Linköping (Sweden). **Aims** Promote in European countries the use of Kansei engineering to develop or improve products and services by translating *customers' psychological* feelings and needs into *product design*; gather all interested in Kansei in Europe; promote use of Kansei engineering in both large corporations and SMEs; foster research to make Kansei more powerful, easier to use and more deeply adapted to European reality. **Structure** General Assembly; Council; Board. **Languages** English. **Staff** Voluntary. **Finance** Activities financed personally by members or their institutions. **Activities** Events/meetings; research and development. **Events** *Symposium* Eindhoven (Netherlands) 2017. [2018.03.12/XM6257/**E**]

♦ European Kaolin and Plastic Clay Association (inactive)

♦ European Kaolin and Plastic Clays Association (KPC Europe) 07623

SG c/o IMA Europe, Rue des Deux Eglises 26, 1000 Brussels, Belgium. T. +3222104410. E-mail: secretariat@ima-europe.eu.
URL: http://www.ima-europe.eu/about-ima-europe/associations/kpc-europe

History 1 Jan 2004, as a merger between *European Kaolin Association (EKA)* and *European Plastic Clays Association (EuroArgilla)*. Original title: *Kaolin and Plastic Clay Europe*. Registered in accordance with Belgian law. **Languages** English.
Members Full in 8 countries:
Austria, Czechia, France, Germany, Netherlands, Spain, Türkiye, UK.
NGO Relations Member of: *European Ceramic Industry Association (CERAME-UNIE, #06506)*; *Industrial Minerals Association – Europe (IMA Europe, #11179)*. Shares office staff with: *Calcium Carbonate Association – Europe (CCA-Europe, #03399)*; *European Association of Feldspar Producers (EUROFEL, #06037)*; *European Association of Industrial Silica Producers (EUROSIL, #06082)*; *European Bentonite Producers Association (EUBA, #06328)*; *European Borates Association (EBA, #06382)*; *European Lime Association (EuLA, #07699)*; *European Speciality Minerals Association (ESMA, #08811)*; *International Diatomite Producers Association (IDPA, #13172)*; *Scientific Association of European Talc Industry (Eurotalc, #19146)*. [2018.09.06/XJ3880/**D**]

♦ European Karate Federation (EKF) 07624

Pres C/Boix y Morer 15, Bo B, 28003 Madrid, Spain. T. +34915359632. Fax +34915359633. E-mail: ekf@ekf.com.es.
URL: http://www.ekf-karate.net/

History as *European Karate Union (EKU)*. A continental union of *World Karate Federation (WKF, #21608)*, previously of *World Union of Karatedo Organizations (WUKO, inactive)*. **Aims** Promote, organize, regulate and popularize the *sport* of karate. **Structure** Annual Congress and Referee Course (attended by all members). Executive Committee, consisting of President, Secretary General, 1st, 2nd and 3rd Vice Presidents, Assistant Secretary General, Treasurer, Assistant Treasurer, Sports Commissioner, Honorary President and 2 members. **Languages** English, French. **Staff** 2.00 FTE, paid. **Finance** Members' dues. Other sources: entrance fees for championships; sponsorship. **Activities** Holds: annual congress prior to Senior Championships; annual referee course and examination prior to Senior events. Organizes: Senior Championships (Male and Female); Junior and Cadet Championships; Regional Championships. Provides Referee Course. **Events** *Congress* Tampere (Finland) 2014, *Congress* Zurich (Switzerland) 2011, *Congress* Athens (Greece) 2010, *Congress* Zagreb (Croatia) 2009, *Congress* Tallinn (Estonia) 2008. **Publications** Newsletter (3 a year).
Members Regular; Provisional: Regular members in 52 countries and territories:
Albania, Andorra, Armenia, Austria, Azerbaijan, Belarus, Belgium, Bosnia-Herzegovina, Bulgaria, Croatia, Cyprus, Czechia, Denmark, England, Estonia, Finland, France, Georgia, Germany, Greece, Hungary, Iceland, Ireland, Israel, Italy, Latvia, Liechtenstein, Lithuania, Luxembourg, Malta, Monaco, Montenegro, Netherlands, North Macedonia, Northern Ireland, Norway, Poland, Portugal, Romania, Russia, San Marino, Scotland, Serbia, Slovakia, Slovenia, Spain, Sweden, Switzerland, Türkiye, Turkmenistan, Ukraine, Wales. [2016/XE3333/**E**]

♦ European Karate Union / see European Karate Federation (#07624)

♦ European Kendo Federation (EKF) 07625

SG Orisaarentie 2 G, FI-00840 Helsinki, Finland. T. +358505507544. E-mail: secretary@ekf-eu.com.
URL: http://www.ekf-eu.com/

History Founded 1969. Current statutes approved and adapted by General Assemblies of: 24 Apr 1987, Malmö (Sweden); 25 Mar 1989, Amsterdam (Netherlands); 26 Jun 1991, Toronto (Canada); 16 Apr 1992, Barcelona (Spain); 16 Apr 1993, Turku (Finland); 6 Apr 1994, Paris (France); 20 Apr 1995, Glasgow (UK); 25 Mar 1997, Kyoto (Japan); 9 Apr 1998, Basel (Switzerland); 22 Mar 2000, Santa Clara CA (USA); 12 Apr 2001, Bologna (Italy); 18 Apr 2002, Nantes (France); 2 Jul 2003, Glasgow (UK); 22 Apr 2004, Budapest (Hungary); 15 Apr 2005, Bern (Switzerland); 10 Feb 2006, Brussels (Belgium); Lisbon (Portugal) 2007; Helsinki (Finland) 2008; Sao Paulo (Brazil) 2009; Debrecen (Hungary) 2010. **Aims** Foster, develop and promote the practice and spirit of Kendo and related *martial arts* such as Iaido, Jodo and Naginata-do, along the traditional lines; promote the martial arts in countries which are not organized yet. **Structure** General Assembly (annual). Board of Officers, comprising President, Vice-President, Secretary-General, Treasurer and Technical Director. **Languages** English, Japanese. **Staff** Voluntary. **Finance** Members' dues. Other sources: exam inscription and registration fees; donations. **Activities** Organizes (principal activities): European Kendo Championships; European Iaido Championships; European Jodo Championships. Also organizes: seminars; referee seminars; grading examinations for all disciplines. **Events** *General Assembly* Novara (Italy) 2012, *General Assembly* Gdynia (Poland) 2011, *General Assembly* Debrecen (Hungary) 2010, *General Assembly* Sao Paulo (Brazil) 2009, *General Assembly* Helsinki (Finland) 2008.
Members National Associations. Full in 41 countries:
Andorra, Austria, Belgium, Bulgaria, Croatia, Czechia, Denmark, Estonia, Finland, France, Georgia, Germany, Greece, Hungary, Ireland, Israel, Italy, Jordan, Latvia, Lithuania, Luxembourg, Malta, Montenegro, Mozambique, Netherlands, North Macedonia, Norway, Poland, Portugal, Romania, Russia, Serbia, Slovakia, Slovenia, South Africa, Spain, Sweden, Switzerland, Türkiye, UK, Ukraine.
NGO Relations Through *International Kendo Federation (FIK, #13982)*, member of: *Global Association of International Sport Federations (GAISF, inactive)*. [2013.06.28/XD6244/**D**]

♦ European Kesterite Workshop (meeting series)

♦ European Kidney Health Alliance (EKHA) 07626

Secretariat Rue du Luxembourg 22-24, 1000 Brussels, Belgium. T. +3222131398 – +3222131305. E-mail: info@ekha.eu.
URL: https://ekha.eu/

History Mar 2007. Registration: Banque-Carrefour des Entreprises, No/ID: 0732.847.767, Start date: 26 Aug 2019, Belgium; EU Transparency Register, No/ID: 582565214754-24, Start date: 21 Nov 2014. **Aims** Work with kidney patients, renal nurses, nephrologists and kidney foundations to promote improved prevention and kidney care in Europe and increase access to transplantation. **Structure** Management Committee, headed by Chairman. **Activities** Events/meetings.
Members Full (5):
Dutch Kidney Foundation (DKF); *European Dialysis and Transplant Nurses Association – European Renal Care Association (EDTNA/ERCA, #06918)*; *European Kidney Patients' Federation (EKPF, #07627)*; *European Renal Association – European Dialysis and Transplant Association (ERA-EDTA, #08353)*; *International Federation of Kidney Foundations – World Kidney Alliance (IFKF-WKA, #13463)*.
Affiliate in 3 countries:
Belgium, Bosnia-Herzegovina, Croatia, Estonia, France, Georgia, Germany, Italy, Lithuania, Netherlands, Poland, Portugal, Russia, Slovenia, Spain, Türkiye, UK.
Federation of European Patient Groups Affected by Renal Genetic Diseases (FEDERG, #09526); *Société Francophone de Néphrologie Dialyse et Transplantation (SFNDT, #19470)*.
NGO Relations Member of (2): *European Alliance for Cardiovascular Health (EACH, #05863)*; *European Alliance for Personalised Medicine (EAPM, #05878)*. Head of: *European Chronic Disease Alliance (ECDA, #06548)*. [2022/XM2323/y/**F**]

♦ European Kidney Patients' Federation (EKPF) 07627

Pres c/o Federación Nacional Alcer, Calle Constancia 35, Local 2, 28002 Madrid, Spain. T. +34660285290. E-mail: info@ekpf.eu.
Head Office Hackhofergasse 8, 1190 Vienna, Austria.
URL: http://www.ekpf.eu/

History 1981, Paris (France). Former names and other names: *Europäischer Nierenpatientenverband* – alias. Registration: EU Transparency Register, No/ID: 619476249009-60, Start date: 13 Feb 2023. **Aims** Improve living conditions of patients with end stage kidney disease requiring dialysis and transplantation. **Languages** English. **Staff** 0.80 FTE, paid; 5.00 FTE, voluntary. **Finance** Sources: fees for services; grants; members' dues. Supported by: *European Union (EU, #08967)*. Annual budget: 203,946 EUR (2022). **Activities** Awareness raising; events/meetings; knowledge management/information dissemination; research and development. **Events** *Annual Summit and General Assembly* Cyprus 2023, *Annual Summit and General Assembly* Athens (Greece) 2022, *Annual Summit and General Assembly* Dublin (Ireland) 2021, *General Assembly* Vilnius (Lithuania) 2012, *Workshop on Aggressive Pituitary Tumors* Munich (Germany) 2011. **Publications** *European Renal Information* (3 a year); *Bulletin* – newsletter.
Members National kidney patients associations in 27 countries and territories:
Austria, Belgium, Bulgaria, Croatia, Cyprus, Denmark, Estonia, Finland, France, Germany, Greece, Hungary, Ireland, Italy, Latvia, Lithuania, Netherlands, Northern Ireland, Norway, Poland, Portugal, Slovenia, Spain, Sweden, Switzerland, UK, Ukraine.
NGO Relations Member of (2): *European Kidney Health Alliance (EKHA, #07626)*; *European Patients' Forum (EPF, #08172)*. Affiliated with (1): *International Kidney Cancer Coalition (IKCC, #13983)*. [2023/XD2141/**D**]

♦ European Kidney Research Association (inactive)

♦ European Knee Society (EKS) 07628

Secretariat Noorwegenstr 49, haven 8008X, 9940 Evergem, Belgium. T. +3292188585. Fax +3293444010. E-mail: eks@medicongress.com.
URL: http://www.europeankneesociety.com/

History Set up 2014. **Aims** Strengthen and consolidate European knowledge and expertise in the field of degenerative knee and knee arthroplasty. **Structure** General Assembly; Board. **Languages** Dutch, English, French, German. **Activities** Events/meetings; training/education; awards/prizes/competitions. **Events** *Arthroplasty Conference* Valencia (Spain) 2019, *Arthroplasty Conference* London (UK) 2017, *World Arthroplasty Congress* Paris (France) 2015.
Members Individuals in 12 countries:
Austria, Belgium, Denmark, France, Germany, India, Italy, Netherlands, Sweden, Switzerland, UK, USA. [2018.09.25/XM6498/**D**]

♦ European Knowledge Media Association (no recent information)

♦ European Knowledge and Technology Transfer Society (EuKTS) . . . 07629

Managing Dir Rue Abbé Cuypers 3, 1040 Brussels, Belgium.
URL: http://www.eukts.eu/

History Initial project ran 2008-2010 as *CERT-TT-M*. Set up as an organisation 2015. Registered in accordance with Belgian law. Registration: AISBL/IVZW, No/ID: 0847.777.228, Belgium. **Aims** Support development of knowledge transfer by increasing the standard, recognition, education, training and mobility of knowledge and technology transfer professionals across Europe and beyond. **Structure** General Assembly; Board of Directors. **Activities** Training/education; certification/accreditation.
Members Stakeholders in 10 countries:
Austria, Belgium, Czechia, Estonia, Finland, France, Luxembourg, Slovakia, Spain, Türkiye. [2017/XM6068/**E**]

♦ **European Kraft Paper Producers for the Flexible Packaging Industry (CEPI Eurokraft)** 07630
Mailing Address PO Box 5515, SE-114 85 Stockholm, Sweden. T. +4687838485. E-mail: info@cepi-eurokraft.org.
URL: http://www.cepi-eurokraft.org/
History as the legally autonomous industry sector of *Confederation of European Paper Industries (CEPI, #04529)*. Previously also referred to in German as *Verband der Europäischen Produzenten von Kraftsackpapieren*. **Aims** Promote paper as a *renewable* resource for packaging; study and inform on impact of packaging papers on the environment. **Structure** General Assembly. Board, comprising Chairman, Vice-Chairman and 5 members. Secretariat, headed by Secretary-General.
Members Companies (21) in 12 countries:
Austria, Bulgaria, Czechia, Estonia, Finland, France, Poland, Portugal, Slovakia, Spain, Sweden, UK.
NGO Relations Associate member of: *International Confederation of Paper and Board Converters in Europe (CITPA, #12866)*. [2020/XE3047/t/**E**]

♦ **European Kurash Confederation (EKC)** 07631
Contact 70A Usmon Yusupov Street, Tashkent, Uzbekistan, 100128. T. +998712447197 – +998712447198. E-mail: info@kurash-ika.org.
Pres Gençlik ve Spor Genel Müdürlügü, Ankara/Ankara, Türkiye.
URL: http://kurash-ika.org/en/evropejskaya-konfederatsiya-kurash/
History Continental federation of *International Kurash Association (IKA, #13993)*. **Activities** Events/meetings.
Members National federations in 27 countries:
Armenia, Austria, Azerbaijan, Belarus, Bulgaria, Cyprus, Czechia, France, Georgia, Germany, Great Britain, Greece, Hungary, Ireland, Israel, Italy, Latvia, Lithuania, Moldova, Monaco, Netherlands, North Macedonia, Poland, Russia, Serbia, Türkiye, Ukraine. [2015/XM0855/**D**]

♦ **European Kurdish Democratic Societies Congress** 07632
Contact 88-90 Rue de l'Etang Lodelinsart, 6042 Charleroi, Belgium. T. +3271318719. Fax +3271318719.
URL: http://www.kcde.eu/
History Founded 1 Oct 1993, at establishment congress, as *Confederation of Kurdish Associations in Europe – Confédération des associations kurdes en Europe – Konfederasyona Komalên Kurd li Ewrupa (KON-KURD)*. Statutes adopted 25 Nov 1994. Current name adopted, 2014. Registered in accordance with Belgian law. **Aims** Become the voice of Kurdish people in Europe; promote solidarity and friendship among Kurdish, other *immigrant* communities and European citizens; create greater understanding of social and cultural differences; inform Kurdish people, nongovernmental organizations and the media in Europe about developments in Kurdistan; lobby European governments and foreign policy-makers concerning *political* developments in Turkey, Kurdistan and Europe; improve relations among Kurdish organizations and coordinate activities of Kurdish community centres in Europe, bringing their concerns to European platforms; provide information on courses to meet the needs of the Kurdish community; conduct research on changes in political and social life of Kurdish people in Europe and publicize these changes; promote and find political solutions to their problems; assist students researching Kurdish history, language, culture and social and economic conditions; inform and assist *asylum* and *refugee* organizations; encourage Kurdish representation in decision-making bodies on asylum-seeking and refugee issues; create interest in Kurdish culture, language and identity and develop visual and written materials in this regard; provide financial and moral support for Kurdish people in need; inform newly-arrived Kurdish refugees of European culture, history, languages, social structure and legal and social *rights* and benefits; set up professionally staffed and coordinated advice centres for such immigrants. **Structure** General Assembly (annual), members having weighted (1 to 12) votes. Administrative Council of 3-20 members, including President, Secretary and Treasurer. **Languages** English, French. **Finance** Members' dues. Income from cultural activities. **Activities** Events/meetings; advocacy/lobbying/activism; training/education; research/documentation. **Events** *Congress* Genk (Belgium) 1996, *Congress* Schaffen (Belgium) 1995, *Congress* Overpelt (Belgium) 1993. **Publications** *Actualités du Kurdistan* (4 a year). Brochures.
Members Individuals, federations (11) and associations (165) in 19 countries:
Austria, Belgium, Canada, Cyprus, Denmark, Finland, France, Germany, Greece, Italy, Netherlands, Norway, Romania, Russia, Spain, Sweden, Switzerland, UK, USA.
IGO Relations Cooperates with: *Council of Europe (CE, #04881)*; *European Commission (EC, #06633)*; *European Parliament (EP, #08146)*. **NGO Relations** Contacts with a large number of human rights organizations, including: *Amnesty International (AI, #00801)*. [2016/XD3883/**D**]

♦ **European Kyudo Federation (EKF)** 07633
Pres Falkensteinerstrasse 43, 4053 Basel BS, Switzerland. T. +41613316517.
SG Naujakuriu 15-7, LT-10220 Vilnius, Lithuania.
URL: http://www.ekf-kyudo.org/
History Founded 1980. **Aims** Promote the art of the kyudo, the traditional Japanese *archery* bow. **Activities** Annual European seminar and examinations under the auspice of IKYF with ANKF. **Events** *Seminar* Montpellier (France) / Lilleshall (UK) 2013, *Seminar* Paris (France) 2012, *Seminar* Tokyo (Japan) 2010, *Seminar* Frankfurt-Main (Germany) 2009, *Seminar* Loughborough (UK) 2008.
Members Member countries are the governing bodies for ANKF style, which is the established style for kyudo worldwide. National organizations in 23 countries:
Austria, Belgium, Czechia, Denmark, Finland, France, Germany, Hungary, Iceland, Italy, Latvia, Lithuania, Luxembourg, Netherlands, Norway, Poland, Portugal, Romania, Russia, Spain, Sweden, Switzerland, UK.
NGO Relations Close cooperation with: All Nippon Kyudo Federation (ANKF); *International Kyudo Federation (IKYF, #13994)*. [2017.06.01/XD7527/**D**]

♦ European Laboratory for Industrial and Territorial Excellence (internationally oriented national body)
♦ European Laboratory Medicine (inactive)
♦ European Laboratory for Particle Physics / see European Organization for Nuclear Research (#08108)
♦ European Laboratory of Social Psychology (internationally oriented national body)

♦ **European Laboratory for Structural Assessment (ELSA)** 07634
Contact c/o JRC, Inst for the Protection and Security of the Citizen, Via Enrico Fermi 2749, 21027 Ispra MB, Italy. T. +39332789989 – +39332789562. Fax +39332789049.
URL: https://ec.europa.eu/jrc/en/research-facility/elsa
Aims Provide research and contribute to European standards harmonization in construction; perform vulnerability assessment of buildings and civil infrastructures for risk mitigation and develop appropriate methodologies through integrated use of experimental testing and numerical modelling in structural mechanics. [2020/XF4720/**F**]

♦ **European Labour Authority (ELA)** 07635
Exec Dir European Commission – DG EMPL, EMPL CAD – J27, 1049 Brussels, Belgium. E-mail: communication@ela.europa.eu – info@ela.europa.eu.
URL: https://www.ela.europa.eu/
History 31 Jul 2019. Created announced Sep 2017, by *European Commission (EC, #06633)* President Jean-Claude Juncker. Established by Regulation 2019/1149 of *European Parliament (EP, #08146)* and *Council of the European Union (#04895)*. Expected to reach full operational capacity by 2024. **Aims** Ensure that EU rules on labour mobility and social security coordination are enforced in a fair, simple, and effective way. **Structure** Management Board; Executive Director; Stakeholders Group. **Activities** Capacity building; guidance/assistance/consulting; knowledge management/information dissemination; research/documentation. **Events** *Youth first! Employment, skills and social policies that work for young Europeans in times of uncertainty* Brussels (Belgium) 2022. **IGO Relations** Represented on the Management Board: *European Centre for the Development of Vocational Training (Cedefop, #06474)*; *European Foundation for the Improvement of Living and Working Conditions (Eurofound, #07348)*; *European Commission (EC, #06633)*; *European Parliament (EP, #08146)*; *European Agency for Safety and Health at Work (EU-OSHA, #05843)*. **NGO Relations** Member of (1): *EU Agencies Network (EUAN, #05564)*. [2021/AA1426/**E***]

♦ **European Labour History Network (ELHN)** 07636
Contact c/o IISG, PO Box 2169, 1000 CD Amsterdam, Netherlands. E-mail: elhn@iisg.nl.
URL: https://socialhistoryportal.org/elhn/
History 12 Oct 2013, Amsterdam (Netherlands). **Structure** Committee. **Activities** Events/meetings; networking/liaising. **Events** *Conference* Vienna (Austria) 2021, *Conference* Amsterdam (Netherlands) 2019, *Conference* Paris (France) 2017, *Conference* Turin (Italy) 2015. [2022.10.13/AA0791/**F**]

♦ **European Lacrosse Federation (ELF)** 07637
Pres address not obtained. E-mail: president@europeanlacrosse.org.
Hon Sec address not obtained. E-mail: secretary@europeanlacrosse.org.
URL: http://www.europeanlacrosse.org/
History 1994, Prague (Czechia). **Aims** Promote the *sport* of lacrosse in Europe. **Structure** Committee. **Languages** English. **Staff** Voluntary. **Finance** Sources: members' dues. **Activities** Awards/prizes/competitions; sporting activities; training/education.
Members Organizations in 33 countries and territories:
Austria, Belgium, Bulgaria, Croatia, Czechia, Denmark, England, Estonia, Finland, France, Germany, Hungary, Ireland, Israel, Italy, Latvia, Lithuania, Luxembourg, Netherlands, Norway, Poland, Portugal, Russia, Scotland, Serbia, Slovakia, Slovenia, Spain, Sweden, Switzerland, Türkiye, Ukraine, Wales. [2021.06.09/XD7164/**D**]

♦ **European Lactation Consultants Alliance (ELACTA)** 07638
Alliance Européenne des Consultantes en Lactation – Europäische LaktationsberaterInnen Allianz
Contact address not obtained. E-mail: office@elacta.eu.
URL: http://www.elacta.eu/
History Set up as *Verband Europäischer Laktationsberaterinnen IBCLC (VELB)* Current title adopted Oct 2010. Registered in accordance with Austrian law: 708420941. **Structure** General Assembly. Bureau, comprising President, Vice-President, Secretary, Deputy Secretary, Treasurer and Deputy Treasurer. Includes *Europäisches Institut für Stillen und Laktation*. **Events** *Conference* Rotterdam (Netherlands) 2018, *an ancient art in a modern world* Athens (Greece) 2016, *Conference* Copenhagen (Denmark) 2014, *Conference* Basel (Switzerland) 2010. [2015/XJ6469/**D**]

♦ European LAM Federation (unconfirmed)
♦ European Lamp Companies Federation (inactive)

♦ **European Landowners' Organization (ELO)** 07639
Organisation européenne de la propriété rurale
SG Rue de Trèves 67, 1040 Brussels, Belgium. T. +3222343000. Fax +3222343009. E-mail: coordination@elo.org – elo@elo.org.
URL: https://www.europeanlandowners.org/
History 1971. Former names and other names: *European Landowning Organizations Group* – former; *Organisation européenne de la propriété agricole* – former. Registration: EU Transparency Register, No/ID: 36063991244-88; ASBL/VZW, Belgium. **Aims** Promote a prosperous and attractive countryside; ensure that private landowners can continue to make a positive contribution to the economy and to environment management; advise the European Commission on rural issues in the European Union. **Structure** Council, comprising Presidents of member organizations; Bureau, including President and Secretary General; Policy Group; technical committees; Communications Attaché; land-use analysts. **Languages** English, French. **Staff** 25.00 FTE, paid. **Finance** Members' dues. Other sources: subsidies from *European Commission (EC, #06633)*; sponsorship. **Activities** Events/meetings. **Events** *Forum for the Future of Agriculture* Brussels (Belgium) 2019, *Forum for the Future of Agriculture* Brussels (Belgium) 2018, *Forum for the Future of Agriculture* Brussels (Belgium) 2017, *Forum for the Future of Agriculture* Brussels (Belgium) 2016, *Forum for the Future of Agriculture* Brussels (Belgium) 2015. **Publications** *CountrySide Magazine* (6 a year) in English, French, German, Spanish.
Members Organizations and individuals in 27 European countries:
Austria, Belgium, Bulgaria, Cyprus, Czechia, Denmark, Estonia, Finland, France, Germany, Greece, Hungary, Ireland, Italy, Latvia, Lithuania, Luxembourg, Malta, Netherlands, Poland, Portugal, Romania, Slovakia, Slovenia, Spain, Sweden, UK.
Consultative Status Consultative status granted from: *ECOSOC (#05331)* (Ros A). **IGO Relations** Accredited by: *United Nations Framework Convention on Climate Change – Secretariat (UNFCCC, #20564)*. **NGO Relations** Member of (5): *Europa Nostra (#05767)*; *European Heritage Alliance 3.3 (#07477)*; *European Water Partnership (EWP, #09083)*; *PEFC Council (#18288)*; *TP Organics – European Technology Platform (TP Organics, #20180)*. Founding member of: *Rural Investment Support for Europe Foundation (RISE Foundation, #19002)*. Participant of: *United Nations Global Compact (#20567)*. Observer of: *European Plant Science Organization (EPSO, #08211)*. Links with a number of organizations interested in the field, including: *COPA – european farmers (COPA, #04829)*; *European Anglers Alliance (EAA, #05900)*; *European Family Businesses (EFB, #07028)*; *European Historic Houses Association (EHH, #07491)*; *Friends of the Countryside (FCS, #10000)*; *International Union of Property Owners (#15804)*; LIFE+ programme of the European Commission; *Young Friends of the Countryside (YFCS, #21991)*. [2021/XD6560/**D**]

♦ European Landowning Organizations Group / see European Landowners' Organization (#07639)

♦ **European Land Registry Association (ELRA)** 07640
Secretariat Av de Cortenbergh 66 – 2ème étage, 1000 Brussels, Belgium. T. +3222801445. Fax +3222801612. E-mail: secretariat@elra.eu.
SG address not obtained.
URL: http://www.elra.eu/
History Oct 2004. Registration: No/ID: 0877.958.480, Start date: 18 Oct 2005, Belgium; EU Transparency Register, No/ID: 992353838637-40, Start date: 18 Jun 2020. **Aims** Increase development and understanding of the role of land registration in real property and capital markets. **Structure** General Assembly (annual); Board. Includes: *European Land Registry Network (ELRN)*. **Events** *General Assembly* Rotterdam (Netherlands) 2019.
Members Organizations and administrations in 24 countries and territories:
Austria, Belgium, Bulgaria, Croatia, Cyprus, England and Wales, Estonia, Finland, France, Greece, Ireland, Italy, Latvia, Lithuania, Luxembourg, Malta, Netherlands, Northern Ireland, Poland, Portugal, Romania, Scotland, Spain, Sweden.
Observers in 4 countries:
Bosnia-Herzegovina, Estonia, Slovenia, Türkiye.
NGO Relations Institutional observer of: *International Association for Fire Protection (no recent information)*. [2020/XM3318/**D**]

♦ European Landscape Architecture Network / see European Landscape Architecture Students Association (#07641)

♦ **European Landscape Architecture Students Association (ELASA)** 07641
Contact address not obtained. E-mail: elasa@elasa.org.
URL: http://www.elasa.org/
History 1991, Hungary. Founded following inaugural conference, 1990, Portugal. Former names and other names: *European Landscape Architecture Network (eLAN)* – former. **Aims** Increase collaboration and exchange between students of landscape architecture throughout Europe. **Structure** Meeting (annual, always in Europe). An informal network coordinated through the Internet. **Languages** English. **Staff** Voluntary. **Finance** No members' dues. **Events** *Annual Meeting* Estonia / Finland 2019, *Annual Meeting* Belgium 2018, *Annual Meeting* Germany 2017, *Spring Meeting* Vienna (Austria) 2015, *Autumn Conference* Oslo (Norway) 2014. **Publications** Annual Report. **Information Services** *ELASA-L* – online mailing list.
Members Individuals (570) subscribing to the Network in 44 countries:
Argentina, Australia, Austria, Belgium, Bosnia-Herzegovina, Bulgaria, Canada, Croatia, Cyprus, Czechia, Denmark, Estonia, France, Germany, Greece, Hungary, Iceland, India, Indonesia, Ireland, Israel, Italy, Japan, Kuwait, Latvia, Lithuania, Malaysia, Netherlands, Nigeria, Norway, Poland, Portugal, Romania, Russia, Serbia, Slovakia, Slovenia, Spain, Sweden, Switzerland, Türkiye, UK, Ukraine, USA.
NGO Relations Located at: *IFLA Europe (#11103)*. [2020/XF4774/**F**]

♦ **European Landscape Contractors Association (ELCA)** 07642
Union européenne des entrepreneurs du paysage – Gemeinschaft des Europäischen Garten-Landschafts- und Sportplatzbaues
Contact Rond Point Robert Schuman 6, box 5, 1040 Brussels, Belgium. T. +32468351191. E-mail: contact@elca.info.

URL: http://www.elca.info/
History 1963, Hamburg (Germany). Former names and other names: *Association of European Landscape and Sports Ground Contractors (AELSC)* – former; *Union européenne des entreprises du paysage* – alias. Registration: EU Transparency Register, No/ID: 4535824354-95. **Aims** Promote mutual exchange of information and experience; look after interests of landscape contractors Europe-wide; support vocational training of young people and mutual exchange of young qualified landscape gardeners; promote cooperation with organizations with similar goals Europe-wide. **Structure** Presidium; Board; Committee of Firms. **Languages** English, French, German. **Staff** 1.00 FTE, paid. **Finance** Sources: members' dues. **Activities** Advocacy/lobbying/activism; events/meetings; standards/guidelines; training/education. **Events** *European Urban Green Congress / Jubilee Congress* Hamburg (Germany) 2013, *Biennial Congress* Paris (France) 2008, *Biennial congress* Nürburg (Germany) 1994, *Jubilee Congress* Paris (France) 1993, *Biennial Congress* Zeist (Netherlands) 1992. **Publications** Brochures; congress proceedings.
Members National associations (20) representing about 80,000 businesses in 20 countries:
Austria, Belgium, Czechia, Denmark, Finland, France, Germany, Greece, Hungary, Ireland, Italy, Luxembourg, Malta, Netherlands, Norway, Poland, Portugal, Spain, Sweden, Switzerland.
Associate members (3) in 3 countries:
Canada, Japan, UK. [2022.02.16/XD6490/y/**D**]

♦ European Landscape Convention (2000 treaty)

♦ European Landscape Education Exchanges (ELEE) 07643

Contact address not obtained. T. +442083319100. Fax +442083319105.
History 1985. **Languages** English. **Finance** Supported by: *SOCRATES Programme (inactive)*.
Members Schools and university department of landscape architecture (15) in 13 countries:
Belgium, Denmark, France, Germany, Hungary, Ireland, Italy, Latvia, Netherlands, Portugal, Spain, Sweden, UK.
NGO Relations *IFLA Europe (#11103)*. [2008/XF6275/**F**]

♦ European Landscape Network (Eurolandscape) 07644

Contact address not obtained. T. +39554221535. Fax +39554486511.
URL: http://www.eurolandscape.net/
History as an umbrella network in support of *European Landscape Convention (2000)*.
Members Organizations (3):
Civilscape (#03966); European Network of Local and Regional Authorities for the Implementation of the European Landscape Convention (RECEP-ENELC, #07939); European Network of Universities for the Implementation of the European Landscape Convention (UNISCAPE, #08030). [2010/XJ1805/y/**E**]

♦ European Land and Soil Alliance (ELSA) 07645

Dir European Office, c/o Stadt Osnabrück, Postfach 4460, 49034 Osnabrück, Germany. T. +495413237025. Fax +49541323157025. E-mail: mail@soil-alliance.org – bodenbuendnis@osnabrueck.de.
Registered Address Klaus-Strick-Weg 10, 49082 Osnabrück, Germany.
URL: http://www.bodenbuendnis.org/
History 24 Oct 2000, Bolzano (Italy). Established following the Manifesto of Bolzano. Registration: Germany; EU Transparency Register, No/ID: 131729047442-10, Start date: 26 Aug 2022. **Aims** Promote the *sustainable* use of all kinds of soils for the preservation and development of all soil functions, soil resources and natural and cultural heritage for current and future generations, as well as the socially fair use of soil and land. **Structure** General Meeting; Executive Committee. **Staff** 0.20 FTE, paid. **Finance** Sources: members' dues. Annual budget: 51,510 EUR.
Members Full; Associate. Full – European cities, municipalities or districts, or similar regional authorities, in 4 countries:
Austria, Czechia, Germany, Italy.
Associate – legal and natural entities, in 5 countries:
Austria, France, Germany, Italy, Switzerland.
NGO Relations Member of (1): *European Environmental Bureau (EEB, #06996).* [2022/XM8669/**D**]

♦ European Landworkers' Federation (inactive)

♦ European Language Council (ELC) 07646

Conseil Européen pour les Langues (CEL) – Consejo Europeo de Idiomas – Europäischer Sprachenrat – Consiglio Europeo delle Lingue
Manager c/o Servizio Linguistico, Università Cattolica, Largo Gemelli 1, 20123 Milan MI, Italy. E-mail: celelc@unicatt.it.
Registered Office c/o VUB, Fac Letteren en Wijsbegeerte, Av de la Plaine 2, 1050 Brussels, Belgium.
URL: https://www.celelc.org/
History 6 Jul 1996, Paris (France). Founded on the initiative of *Bilingual World (#03235)*. Officially launched, 1997, Lille (France). Registration: Banque-Carrefour des Entreprises, No/ID: 0462.316.252, Start date: 22 Jan 1998, Belgium. **Aims** Actively promote European cooperation between institutions of *higher education* in the area of languages. **Structure** General Assembly (annual); Board; Executive Committee. **Languages** English, French. **Staff** 4.00 FTE, paid. **Finance** Sources: members' dues. Support from Freie Universität Berlin. **Activities** Events/meetings; politics/policy/regulatory; projects/programmes. **Events** *Forum* Seville (Spain) 2022, *Conference* Antwerp (Belgium) 2021, *General Assembly* Berlin (Germany) 2015, *General Assembly* Brussels (Belgium) 2014, *General Assembly* Berlin (Germany) 2013. **Publications** *The European Journal of Language Policy/Revue européenne de politique linguistique* (2 a year).
Members Universities in 30 countries:
Armenia, Austria, Belgium, Bulgaria, Denmark, Finland, France, Germany, Greece, Hungary, Iceland, Ireland, Italy, Kazakhstan, Lithuania, Luxembourg, Malta, Moldova, Netherlands, Poland, Portugal, Romania, Russia, Serbia, Slovenia, Spain, Sweden, Switzerland, UK, Ukraine.
Organizations (7), including 2 organizations listed in this Yearbook:
Conférence internationale permanente d'instituts universitaires de traducteurs et interprètes (CIUTI, #04621); Universal Esperanto Association (UEA, #20676).
IGO Relations Cooperates with: *Council of Europe (CE, #04881); European Commission (EC, #06633).* **NGO Relations** Member of (1): *European Alliance for the Social Sciences and Humanities (EASSH, #05885).* Cooperates with (5): *Academic Cooperation Association (ACA, #00019); European Association of Institutions of Higher Education (EURASHE, #06086); European Students' Union (ESU, #08848); European University Association (EUA, #09027); Network of Universities from the Capitals of Europe (UNICA, #17061).* Signatory to agreement of *Coalition for Advancing Research Assessment (CoARA, #04045).* [2022/XE3298/y/**E**]

♦ European Language Equality Network (ELEN) 07647

Réseau Européen pour l'Égalité des Langues – Rouedad Europa evit Kevatalded ar Yezhoù
Secretariat 6 place des Droits de l'Homme, 29270 Carhaix-Plouguer, France. T. +33298732058. Fax +33298732058.
URL: https://elen.ngo/
History 2010. Registered in accordance with French law. **Aims** Promote and protect European lesser-used – i e regional, minority, endangered, indigenous, co-official and smaller national – languages; work towards linguistic equality for these languages, under the broader framework of human rights; be a voice for the speakers of these languages at local, regional, national, European and international level. **Structure** General Assembly; Steering Committee. **Members** Organizations (150) representing 45 languague groups in 23 countries. Membership countries not specified. **Consultative Status** Consultative status granted from: *ECOSOC (#05331)* (Special). **IGO Relations** *Council of Europe (CE, #04881); European Economic and Social Committee (EESC, #06963)* – Liaison Group; *European Parliament (EP, #08146); United Nations (UN, #20515); UNESCO (#20322).* [2020/XJ9103/**F**]

♦ European Language Industry Association (ELIA) 07648

Managing Dir Rue Washington 40, 1050 Brussels, Belgium. E-mail: info@elia-association.org.
Event Manager address not obtained.
URL: http://www.elia-association.org/
History Registration: Banque-Carrefour des Entreprises, No/ID: 0670.681.754, Start date: 2 Feb 2017, Belgium; Companies House, No/ID: 05454184, Start date: 17 Aug 2005, End date: 10 Jul 2018, England and Wales. **Aims** Represent and promote the interests of the language industry in Europe; forge relationships with companies across Europe including but not limited to, the EU, its new member states and those who have applied to join; develop relationships with colleagues and related bodies from other parts of the world to make our voice heard worldwide; share information and experience to develop the industry; provide a forum for members to network and exchange information; promote the concept of ethics and quality standards throughout the industry. **Structure** Board of Directors, comprising President, 2 Vice-Presidents, Treasurer, Deputy Treasurer, Past-President and 2 members. **Events** *Together Meeting* 2021, *Together Meeting* Barcelona (Spain) 2019, *Together Meeting* Berlin (Germany) 2017, *Together Meeting* Barcelona (Spain) 2016, *Networking Days* Brussels (Belgium) 2016.
Members Companies. Full in 29 countries:
Austria, Belgium, Bosnia-Herzegovina, Bulgaria, Croatia, Czechia, Finland, France, Germany, Greece, Hungary, Ireland, Italy, Latvia, Lithuania, Netherlands, Poland, Portugal, Romania, Russia, Serbia, Slovakia, Slovenia, Spain, Sweden, Türkiye, UK, Ukraine, USA.
Associate in 3 countries:
Germany, Hungary, UK.
NGO Relations Member of: *Federation of European and International Associations Established in Belgium (FAIB, #09508).* [2021/XJ2462/t/**D**]

♦ European Language Resource Coordination (ELRC) 07649

Secretariat address not obtained. T. +49681857755285. E-mail: info@lr-coordination.eu.
URL: http://www.lr-coordination.eu/
Aims Manage, maintain and coordinate the relevant language resources in all official languages of the EU and CEF associated countries. **Activities** Guidance/assistance/support; awareness raising; advocacy/lobbying/activism; events/meetings. **Events** *Meeting* Amsterdam (Netherlands) 2019, *Share your language data, shape Europe's multilingual future!* Helsinki (Finland) 2019, *Meeting* Nice (France) 2018, *Meeting* Paris (France) 2018, *Conference* Brussels (Belgium) 2017.
Members Full in 3 countries:
France, Germany, Greece.
IGO Relations *European Commission (EC, #06633).* [2019/XM8616/**E**]

♦ European Language Resources Association (ELRA) 07650

Association européenne pour les ressources linguistiques
Main Office c/o ELDA, 9 rue des Cordelières, 75013 Paris, France. T. +33143133333. Fax +33143133330. E-mail: info@elda.org.
URL: http://www.elra.info/
History Feb 1995, Luxembourg. Registration: No/ID: F3233, Luxembourg. **Structure** Operational body: *Evaluations and Language resources Distribution Agency (ELDA).* **Activities** International Standard Language Resource Number (ISLRN) schema. **Events** *International Conference on Language Resources and Evaluation (LREC)* Marseille (France) 2022, *Biennial International Conference on Language Resources and Evaluation* Marseille (France) 2020, *Biennial International Conference on Language Resources and Evaluation* Miyazaki (Japan) 2018, *Biennial International Conference on Language Resources and Evaluation* Portoroz (Slovenia) 2016, *Biennial Language Resources and Evaluation Conference* Reykjavik (Iceland) 2014. **Publications** *ELRA Newsletter* (4 a year). **NGO Relations** Member of: *centerNet; Cracking the Language Barrier (#04942).* [2021/XD6073/**D**]

♦ European Large Families Confederation (ELFAC) 07651

Contact Balmes 92 3-2, 08008 Barcelona, Spain. T. +34933511000. Fax +34934673298. E-mail: info@elfac.org.
URL: http://www.elfac.org/
History 27 Mar 2004, Lisbon (Portugal). Conceived at 1st European Large Families Conference Nov 2002, Madrid (Spain). Articles of Statute agreed Oct 2003, Brussels (Belgium). Founded at 2nd European Large Families Conference. Former names and other names: *Coordinadora Europea de Familias Numerosas* – alias. Registration: Ministerio del Interior, Registro Nacional de Asociaciones, No/ID: 586102, Spain; EU Transparency Register, No/ID: 92876453439-40. **Aims** Represent social and economic interests of families with children as the most appropriate environment for bringing up children, integrating them into society and providing mutual support and solidarity among generations; promote, develop and unify the movement of large family organizations. **Structure** Board of Directors; Secretary General; Executive Management. **Languages** English. **Staff** 3.00 FTE, paid; 23.00 FTE, voluntary. **Finance** Annual budget: 120,000 EUR. **Activities** Advocacy/lobbying/activism; events/meetings; knowledge management/information dissemination; publishing activities. **Events** *Biennial conference* Keszthely (Hungary) 2021, *European Convention of Family-Friendly Municipalities* Tallinn (Estonia) 2021, *European Congress of Family-Friendly Municipalities* 2020, *European Convention of Family-Friendly Municipalities* Brussels (Belgium) 2019, *Biennial Conference* Szczecin (Poland) 2018. **Publications** *ELFAC Newsletter* (12 a year); *ELFAC Papers* (6 a year) in English. Surveys; working papers.
Members Organizations (25) in 22 countries:
Andorra, Austria, Croatia, Cyprus, Czechia, Estonia, France, Germany, Greece, Hungary, Italy, Latvia, Lithuania, Netherlands, Poland, Portugal, Romania, Serbia, Slovakia, Spain, Switzerland, Ukraine.
NGO Relations Member of (1): *European Sunday Alliance (#08856).* [2021.06.15/XM0960/**D**]

♦ European Large Geotechnical Institutes Platform (ELGIP) 07652

Contact c/o Deltares, PO Box 177, 2600 MH Delft, Netherlands. T. +31883357200. Fax +31152610821.
URL: http://www.elgip.net/
History 2002. **Aims** Connect the scientific world (research) and construction industry; promote efficient continuity and quality of high-level disciplinary knowledge and innovation; support exchange, sharing and integration of research and development capabilities and skills. **Structure** Board of Directors; Secretariat. Includes *YELGIP*, set up Jan 2005, unites young geotechnical engineers from ELGIP members. **Activities** Research and development; knowmedge management/information dissemination. **Events** *Meeting* 2005, *Meeting* Brussels (Belgium) 2005, *Meeting* Darmstadt (Germany) 2005, *Meeting* Delft (Netherlands) 2005.
Members Organizations, institutes and companies (34) in 13 countries:
Belgium, Czechia, France, Germany, Italy, Netherlands, Norway, Poland, Portugal, Slovenia, Spain, Sweden, UK.
NGO Relations Member of: *European Council for Construction Research, Development and Innovation (ECCREDI, #06813).* [2020/XM0742/**F**]

♦ European Largest Textile and Apparel Companies (inactive)

♦ European Laryngological Society (ELS) 07653

Société européenne de laryngologie
Address not obtained.
URL: http://www.elsoc.org/
History 21 Jan 1995, Brussels (Belgium). Registration: Belgium. **Aims** Further scientific development in the field of laryngology, including anatomy, pathology, macro-surgery, head and neck surgery, research and associated specialties such as phoniatrics and radiotherapy; widen knowledge and assess practical implementation of technical and scientific developments in this field; encourage development of the discipline in regard to prevention, treatment and rehabilitation of diseases of the larynx; promote and foster professional skills of members; encourage continuing education of laryngologists. **Structure** General Assembly. Presidential Council consisting of President, President-Elect, Vice-President, Secretary and Treasurer. Scientific Council of 14, headed by President or President-Elect. **Languages** English. **Staff** Voluntary. **Finance** Members' dues. Sponsorship. **Activities** Organizes: biennial convention; scientific meetings; courses; workshops. **Events** *Congress* Milan (Italy) 2023, *Congress* 2021, *Highlights Virtual Meeting* 2020, *Congress* Stuttgart (Germany) 2020, *Workshop* Helsinki (Finland) 2019. **Publications** *European Archives of Otorhinolaryngology* – journal. Meeting reports.
Members Individual laryngologists (185). Ordinary members in 29 countries:
Austria, Belgium, Canada, Colombia, Croatia, Czechia, Denmark, Egypt, Finland, France, Germany, Greece, Hungary, Italy, Lithuania, Luxembourg, Morocco, Netherlands, Norway, Poland, Portugal, Romania, Slovenia, Spain, Sweden, Switzerland, Türkiye, UK, USA.

NGO Relations Member of: *Confederation of European Otorhinolaryngology – Head and Neck Surgery (Confederation of European ORL-HNS, #04528)*; *International Federation of Head and Neck Oncologic Societies (IFHNOS, #13438)*. [2021/XD5112/v/D]

♦ European Laser Association (ELA) 07654

Treas c/o DALA, Albrechtlaan 17, 1404 AJ Bussum, Netherlands. E-mail: enquiries@europeanlaserassociation.com.
SG c/o BMLA, Far Shirby, Upleatham, Redcar, TS11 8AG, UK.
URL: http://europeanlaserassociation.com/

History 1981, Cannes (France). **Aims** Provide a common platform for exchange of knowledge of laser, light and other energy-based technologies in medicine and biosciences; promote collaboration and understanding between clinical and scientific disciplines. **Structure** Trustees. **Languages** English. **Staff** None. **Finance** Members' dues. **Activities** Events/meetings; training/education. **Events** *Laser Europe Conference* Rotterdam (Netherlands) 2018, *Laser Europe Conference* Porto (Portugal) 2017, *Laser Europe Conference* Berlin (Germany) 2016, *Laser Europe Conference* Athens (Greece) 2015, *Laser Europe Conference* Amsterdam (Netherlands) 2014. **Publications** *Lasers in Medical Science* – journal.
Members Organizations, societies, associations, etc. Members in 6 countries:
France, Germany, Netherlands, Portugal, Spain, UK.
Included in the above, 1 organization listed in this Yearbook:
European Society for Laser Aesthetic Surgery (ESLAS, #08639).
NGO Relations Sister organization: *European Society for Laser Aesthetic Surgery (ESLAS, #08639)*. [2019/XD2618/y/D]

♦ European Laser Disc Association (inactive)

♦ European-Latin-American-Caribbean-Tuberculosis Consortium (EurolacTB) 07655

Exec Sec address not obtained. E-mail: eurolactb@gmail.com.
URL: http://www.eurolactb.org/

Aims Promote and strengthen research collaboration between European and Latin American scientists in the area of poverty-related and infectious diseases with initial emphasis on tuberculosis. **Structure** Steering Committee.
Members Individuals in 23 countries:
Argentina, Belgium, Bolivia, Brazil, Colombia, Cuba, Dominican Rep, Ecuador, France, Germany, Ireland, Italy, Mexico, Netherlands, Nicaragua, Peru, Portugal, Spain, Sweden, Switzerland, Trinidad-Tobago, UK, Venezuela. [2014/XJ8391/v/C]

♦ European-Latvian Institute (internationally oriented national body)
♦ European-Latvian Institute for Cultural and Scientific Exchange, Riga / see European-Latvian Institute
♦ European-Latvian Institute of LAS and EASA / see European-Latvian Institute
♦ European Laundry and Dry Cleaning Machinery Manufacturers Organization (no recent information)

♦ European Law Faculties Association (ELFA) 07656

Association des facultés de droit en Europe (AFDE) – Asociación de Facultades de Derecho en Europa – Europäische Vereinigung der Rechtsfakultäten

Contact Tiensestraat 41, 3000 Leuven, Belgium. E-mail: info@elfa-edu.org.
URL: https://elfa-edu.org/

History 15 Dec 1995, Leuven (Belgium). Founded at constitutive meeting. Registration: Netherlands. **Aims** Represent and promote members' interests in the field of *legal* education and research vis-à-vis EU institutions, international organizations as well as associations of legal professionals. **Structure** General Assembly (annual); Board of Directors. **Languages** English, French, German, Spanish. **Staff** 0.50 FTE, paid. **Finance** Sources: members' dues. **Activities** Awards/prizes/competitions; events/meetings; training/education. **Events** *Annual General Meeting* 2021, *Annual General Meeting and Conference* Warsaw (Poland) 2021, *Annual General Meeting* 2020, *Annual General Meeting and Conference* Warsaw (Poland) 2020, *Annual General Meeting and Conference* Turin (Italy) 2019. **Publications** *European Journal of Legal Education*.
Members Law faculties (over 150) in 45 countries and territories:
Armenia, Austria, Belgium, Bosnia-Herzegovina, Bulgaria, China, Croatia, Cyprus, Czechia, Denmark, Estonia, Finland, France, Georgia, Germany, Hungary, Ireland, Italy, Kazakhstan, Kosovo, Latvia, Lithuania, Luxembourg, Malta, Mexico, Netherlands, North Macedonia, Northern Cyprus, Norway, Poland, Portugal, Romania, Russia, Serbia, Slovakia, Slovenia, Spain, Sweden, Switzerland, Türkiye, UK, Ukraine, Uruguay, USA, Uzbekistan.
Included in the above, 2 institutes listed in this Yearbook:
Academy of European Law (#00035); *Eastern Mediterranean University*.
NGO Relations Instrumental in setting up (1): *Global Legal Education Associations Consortium (GLEAC, #10456)*. [2021.09.09/XD5102/D]

♦ European Law Firms Association – Avrio Advocati 07657

Chair c/o Caldwell and Robinson, Artillery Chambers, 10-12 Artillery Street, Londonderry, BT48 6RG, UK. T. +442871261334. E-mail: info@avrioadvocati.com.
URL: http://www.avrioadvocati.com/

History 1987, following merger of 2 groupings of law firms. Registered in accordance with Belgian law. **Aims** Facilitate international cooperation of lawyers; share expertise; foster international debate. **Structure** General Meeting (twice a year); Board; International Legal Teams (6). **Languages** English, French, German. **Staff** 9.00 FTE, paid. **Finance** Members' dues. **Activities** Legal Teams (6): AVRIO Eurolaw Assistance; Employment; Fraud; Real Estate; Sports Law; Mergers and Acquisitions. **Events** *Spring General Meeting* Zagreb (Croatia) 2022, *Annual General Meeting* London (UK) 2020, *Spring General Meeting* Zagreb (Croatia) 2020, *Spring General Meeting* Frankfurt-Main (Germany) 2019, *Autumn General Meeting* Québec, QC (Canada) 2019. **Publications** *Avrio Newsletter* (bi-weekly).
Members Law firms in 28 countries and territories Northern Ireland.
Northern Ireland.
Australia, Austria, Belgium, Brazil, China, Cyprus, Czechia, Denmark, England, Estonia, Finland, France, Germany, Greece, Hong Kong, Ireland, Italy, Liechtenstein, Netherlands, Northern Ireland, Norway, Poland, Portugal, Scotland, Slovenia, Sweden, Switzerland, Türkiye. [2019/XD9081/D]

♦ The European Law Group / see Globaladvocaten (#10173)

♦ European Law Institute (ELI) 07658

Secretariat Schottenring 16/175, 1010 Vienna, Austria. T. +431427722101. Fax +43142779221. E-mail: secretariat@europeanlawinstitute.eu.
URL: http://www.europeanlawinstitute.eu/

History 1 Jun 2011, Brussels (Belgium). Developed following two former initiatives: the *Association for a European Law Institute (ELIA)*, founded March 2010, and the Conference of the Robert Schuman Centre for Advanced Studies of the European University Institute (EUI), Apr 2010. Resulted in the Hamburg Memorandum, June 2010, according to which a joint project group was formed by the ELIA and EUI initiatives, and a first meeting was held, Vienna (Austria), 23-24 Nov 2010. Results of this meeting are summarized in the Vienna Memorandum. Meeting of the ELI Founding Committee, Athens (Greece), 15-16 Apr 2011, where statute and manifesto were adopted and first ELI Council appointed. A procedure for determining the place of the ELI Secretariat was agreed upon. Registration: No/ID: 0837.276.779, Start date: 1 Jun 2011, Belgium, Brussels. **Aims** Improve quality of European law; initiate, conduct and facilitate research, make recommendations, and provide practical guidance in the field of European legal development. **Structure** Membership; Council; Executive Committee; Senate; Arbitral Tribunal; Scientific Director; Secretariat, hosted by University of Vienna (Austria). **Languages** English. **Staff** 7.00 FTE, paid. **Finance** Sources: grants; members' dues; sponsorship. other sources: cooperation agreement with the University of Vienna, which hosts the Secretariat's seat, and runs until the end of 2023; project- specific funding with other partner organisations. Supported by: *European Union (EU, #08967)* (EU Operating Grants, 2018-2021 period). **Activities** Projects/programmes. The current list can be found here: https://europeanlawinstitute.eu/projects-publications/. **Events** *Annual Conference* Vienna (Austria) 2021, *Annual Conference* Vienna (Austria) 2020, *Annual Conference* Vienna (Austria) 2019, *General Assembly* Riga (Latvia) 2018, *General Assembly* Vienna (Austria) 2017. **Publications** *Innovation Papers*. *ELI-Unidroit Model European Rules of Civil Procedure* (2021) – Oxford University Press; *Rescue of Business in Europe* (2020) by Bob Wessels and Stephan Madaus – Oxford University Press; *Preventing and Resolving Conflicts of Jurisdiction in EU Criminal Law* (2018) by Katalin Ligeti and John Vervaele et al – Oxford University Press. *Project Results*. **Members** Institutional and Individuals Members from over 60 jurisdictions across the globe. **IGO Relations** Participant in Fundamental Rights Platform of *European Union Agency for Fundamental Rights (FRA, #08969)*. **NGO Relations** Supports (1): *Parliamentarians for Global Action (PGA, #18208)*. Instrumental in setting up (1): *Global Legal Education Associations Consortium (GLEAC, #10456)*. [2021.09.27/XJ7877/jy/D]

♦ European Law Moot Court Society (ELMC) 07659

Contact IDEE – Fac de Derecho, C/Julian Romea 22, 28003 Madrid, Spain. E-mail: organising.team.elmc@gmail.com.
URL: http://www.europeanlawmootcourt.eu/

History 1988. **Aims** As an annual international competition, get universities and law students involved, deepening their knowledge of EU law while offering a unique bilingual legal practice experience in written and oral form. **Structure** Board and President serve as governing bodies. Organising Team, composed of students serves as coordinating group. **Languages** English, French. **Staff** 15.00 FTE, voluntary. **Finance** Sponsoring from international law firms. Annual budget: euro 25,000. **Activities** Awards/prizes/competitions. **Publications** *Moot x25 – Celebrating 25 years of European Law Moot Court Competition*. **Members** Individuals (15). Membership countries not specified. [2017.03.13/XD3440/D]

♦ European Lawnmower Manufacturers' Federation / see European Garden Machinery Industry Federation (#07379)

♦ The European Law Students' Association (ELSA) 07660

SG Bd Général Jacques 239, 1050 Brussels, Belgium. T. +3226462626. Fax +3226462923. E-mail: secgen@elsa.org – elsa@elsa.org.
Pres address not obtained.
URL: http://www.elsa.org/

History 4 May 1981, Vienna (Austria). Founded by 5 students from Austria, Poland, Hungary and Germany. **Aims** Contribute to legal education; foster mutual understanding; promote social responsibility of law students and young lawyers. **Structure** International Council; International Board; National Groups; Local Groups. **Languages** English. **Staff** Voluntary. **Finance** Sources: fundraising; grants; meeting proceeds; revenue from activities/projects; sale of publications. **Activities** Capacity building; events/meetings; networking/liaising; projects/programmes; training/education. **Events** *Half-Yearly Meeting* 2021, *Strategy Meeting* 2021, *The European Project Beyond Corona – A Challenge For Law* Heidelberg (Germany) 2021, *Vienna Summit* Vienna (Austria) 2021, *Half-Yearly Meeting* 2020. **Publications** *ELSA Law Review* (2 a year) in English; *Synergy* (2 a year).
Members National groups representing over 65,000 individuals in over 430 law facilities in 43 countries:
Albania, Armenia, Austria, Azerbaijan, Belarus, Belgium, Bosnia-Herzegovina, Bulgaria, Croatia, Cyprus, Czechia, Denmark, Estonia, Finland, France, Georgia, Germany, Greece, Hungary, Iceland, Ireland, Italy, Latvia, Lithuania, Luxembourg, Malta, Moldova, Montenegro, Netherlands, North Macedonia, Norway, Poland, Portugal, Romania, Serbia, Slovakia, Slovenia, Spain, Sweden, Switzerland, Türkiye, UK, Ukraine.
Consultative Status Consultative status granted from: *UNESCO (#20322)* (Consultative Status); *ECOSOC (#05331)* (Special); *Council of Europe (CE, #04881)* (Participatory Status); *World Intellectual Property Organization (WIPO, #21593)* (Permanent Observer Status); *UNEP (#20299)*. **NGO Relations** Member of (1): *Informal Forum of International Student Organizations (IFISO, #11193)*. Cooperates with (2): *Hague Appeal for Peace (HAP, #10848)*; *International Trademark Association (INTA, #15706)*. [2022.05.18/XD1435/D]

♦ European Lawyers Association (ELA) 07661

Association européenne des avocats (AEA) – Europese Juristen Vereniging

Main Office Bloomz Bldg, Lambroekstraat 5-A, 1831 Diegem, Belgium.
URL: http://www.european-lawyers.org/

History 1985, Paris (France). Registration: Start date: 20 Feb 1992, Belgium. **Aims** Operate as an alumni association to promote contacts among lawyers involved in the 'British Council European Young Lawyers' Scheme (EYLS)' later known as the European Lawyers' Programme. **Structure** General Meeting (annual); Board. **Finance** Members' dues. **Events** *Annual Meeting* Chania (Greece) 2016, *Annual Meeting* Valencia (Spain) 2015, *Annual Meeting* Riga (Latvia) 2014, *Annual Meeting* Antwerp (Belgium) 2013, *Annual Meeting* Milan (Italy) 2012. **Publications** *ELA Newsletter* (periodical). *Law Profile of Finland* (1998); *Law Profile of Italy* (1995); *Survey of the Legal Profession in Europe (1997-1998)*.
Members Individuals in 23 countries:
Belgium, Bulgaria, Czechia, Denmark, Estonia, Finland, France, Germany, Greece, Hungary, Italy, Latvia, Liechtenstein, Lithuania, Luxembourg, Netherlands, Norway, Poland, Portugal, Spain, Sweden, Switzerland, UK. [2021/XF5298/v/E]

♦ European Lawyers Union (#20365)

♦ European Lawyers for Workers Network (ELW) 07662

Contact Chaussée de Haecht 55, 1210 Brussels, Belgium. E-mail: elw-office@elw-network.eu.
Contact address not obtained.
URL: https://elw-network.eu/

History 2013. **Aims** Support workers, workers' representatives and trade unions in advancing their interests. **Structure** Coordinating Committee. **Activities** Advocacy/lobbying/activism; events/meetings; knowledge management/information dissemination. **Events** *Conference on Labour rights and the Digital Transition* Brussels (Belgium) 2021, *Conference on Rethinking Labour Law in the Digitalisation Era* Brussels (Belgium) 2020, *European Labour Law Conference* Frankfurt-Main (Germany) 2019, *European Labour Law Conference* Florence (Italy) 2017, *Workshop on the Recent Development in Labour Law in Europe* Brussels (Belgium) 2016.
Members Full in 15 countries:
Belgium, France, Germany, Greece, Ireland, Italy, Luxembourg, Netherlands, Poland, Portugal, Russia, Spain, Sweden, Türkiye, UK.
NGO Relations Cooperates with (2): *European Trade Union Confederation (ETUC, #08927)*; *European Trade Union Institute (ETUI, #08928)*. [2021/AA2077/F]

♦ European Lay Forum / see European Forum of National Laity Committees (#07322)
♦ European Lead Development Committee (inactive)

♦ European LEADER Association for Rural Development (ELARD) 07663

Coordination Officer Luis Chaves, Rua Bartolomeu Dias, 172 D – 1o esq, 1400-031 Lisbon, Portugal. E-mail: lmchaves@minhaterra.pt – minhaterra@minhaterra.pt.
Pres address not obtained.
Brussels Office Boulevard Edmond Machtens 79/22, 1080 Brussels, Belgium.
URL: http://www.elard.eu/

History 1999, Belgium, by National LEADER Networks of Local Action Groups (LAGs) of France, Greece, Ireland, Italy and Spain. Current statutes adopted 7 May 2009. Registered in accordance with Belgian law. **Aims** Improve the quality of life in rural areas; maintain their population through sustainable, integrated local development. **Structure** General Assembly; Council; Rotating Presidency. **Events** *Conference on Renewing LEADER/CLLD for 2020* Tartu (Estonia) 2016, *General Assembly* Tartu (Estonia) 2016.
Members Active; Associated. Members in 22 countries:
Belgium, Croatia, Czechia, Denmark, Estonia, Finland, France, Greece, Hungary, Ireland, Italy, Latvia, Lithuania, North Macedonia, Poland, Portugal, Romania, Slovakia, Slovenia, Spain, Sweden, UK.
NGO Relations Cooperates with: *Rurality – Environment – Development (RED, #19003)*. [2018/XJ5618/D]

♦ European Leadership Centre (ELC) 07664

Contact c/o Bled School of Management, Presernova cesta 33, 4260 Bled, Slovenia. T. +38645792501. Fax +38645792500. E-mail: barbara.vilfan@iedc.si.
URL: http://www.iedc.si/elc/

History 2002. **Aims** Promote European leadership through conferences, workshops, round table discussions, and research. **Activities** Organizes annual conference, always at Bled (Slovenia). **Publications** Conference Proceedings. **NGO Relations** Based at: *IEDC – Bled School of Management*. [2012/XJ5740/E]

♦ European Leadership Forum 07665

Main Office 4699 Auvergne Ave, Lisle IL 60532, USA.
URL: http://www.euroleadership.org/

History founded on the initiative of Greg Pritchard, as *European Leadership Seminar.* **Aims** Unite, equip, and resource *evangelical* leaders to renew the *biblical church* and evangelize Europe. **Structure** Steering Committee. Networks (27) include: *European Apologetics Network*; *European Bible Teachers and Preachers Network*; *European Church Planters Network*; *European Disciple-Making Leaders Network*; *European Leaders of Christian Organisations Network*; *European Youth Ministry Leaders Network*; *European Counsellors Network*; *European Evangelism Network*; *European Mariage and Family Network*; *European Media Communicators Network*; *European Ministry to Muslims Network*; *European Mission Leaders Network*; *European Organisation Development and Fundraising Network*; *European Philosophers Network*; *European Politics and Society Network*; *European Scientists Network*; *European Theologians Network.* **Finance** Sponsored by (US) *Forum of Christian Leaders (FCOL).* **Activities** Events/meetings; training/education. **Events** *Annual Meeting* Wisla (Poland) 2018, *Annual Meeting* Wisla (Poland) 2015, *Annual Meeting* Sopron (Hungary) 2003.
[2018/XJ9264/**F**]

♦ European Leadership Network (ELNET) 07667

Exec Dir address not obtained. E-mail: info@elnetwork.eu.
URL: http://elnetwork.eu/

History 2007. **Aims** Pursue strategic partnerships between European countries and Israel, based on shared values of democracy, peace, freedom and prosperity, in building a brighter and safer tomorrow. **Structure** Leadership of 3. Offices in: Bonn (Germany); Paris (France): Brussels (Belgium); Warsaw (Poland); Tel Aviv (Israel). **Finance** Supported by private philanthropists and foundations in Europe, North America, Australia and Israel. **Events** *International Policy Conference* Paris (France) 2019. [2017/XM5709/**F**]

♦ European Leadership Network (ELN) 07666

Dir 8 St James's Square, London, SE1Y 4JU, UK. T. +442031762555. E-mail: secretariat@europeanleadershipnetwork.org.
Communications Officer address not obtained.
URL: http://www.europeanleadershipnetwork.org/

History 2011, London (UK). Registration: Companies House, No/ID: 07521896, UK; EU Transparency Register, No/ID: 713668418770-87. **Aims** Advance education in, undertake research about, and promote greater understanding of political, security, defence, economic and energy challenges in Europe, and related issues, in particular multilateral nuclear disarmament, non-proliferation and nuclear security; provide an independent platform for international dialogue and debate on such issues; advance national and international conflict resolution. **Structure** Executive Board. **Languages** English. **Staff** 18.00 FTE, paid. **Finance** Sources: grants; sponsorship. Other sources: philanthropy. **Activities** Advocacy/lobbying/activism; events/meetings; knowledge management/information dissemination; politics/policy/regulatory; research/documentation. **Events** *Meeting* Berlin (Germany) 2018, *Towards a More Stable NATO-Russia Relationship Seminar* Moscow (Russia) 2018, *Meeting* Minsk (Belarus) 2017, *Meeting* Vienna (Austria) 2017, *Meeting* Warsaw (Poland) 2017. **Publications** Commentaries; policy briefs; reports; group statements; speeches.
Members Participants (about 400) in 42 countries:
Albania, Armenia, Austria, Azerbaijan, Belarus, Belgium, Bosnia-Herzegovina, Bulgaria, Canada, Croatia, Czechia, Denmark, Estonia, Finland, France, Georgia, Germany, Greece, Hungary, Ireland, Italy, Kazakhstan, Kosovo, Latvia, Lithuania, Netherlands, North Macedonia, Norway, Poland, Portugal, Romania, Russia, Serbia, Slovakia, Slovenia, Spain, Sweden, Switzerland, Türkiye, UK, Ukraine, USA.
NGO Relations Member of (1): *European Network of Independent Non-Proliferation Think Tanks (EU Non-Proliferation Network, #07930).* Cooperates with (11): *Center for Security Studies (CSS)*; *Egmont Institute*; *Friedrich-Ebert-Stiftung (FES)*; *Istituto Affari Internazionali, Roma (IAI)*; *Latvian Institute of International Affairs (LIIA)*; *Nuclear Threat Initiative (NTI, #17622)*; *Polish Institute of International Affairs (PIIA)*; *Royal Institute of International Affairs (RIIA)*; *Royal United Services Institute for Defence and Security Studies (RUSI)*; *Russian International Affairs Council (RIAC)*; *Stockholm International Peace Research Institute (SIPRI, #19994).*
[2023.02.13/XJ6500/v/**F**]

- ♦ European Leadership Seminar / see European Leadership Forum (#07665)
- ♦ European Leading Association of High Intensity Gas Infrared Heater Manufacturers / see Europäischer Leit-Verband der Hersteller von Gas-Infrarot- Hellstrahlern (#05758)
- ♦ European Leading Association of Radiant Gas Heaters Manufacturers (#05758)
- ♦ European Lead Oxide Association (inactive)

♦ European Lead Sheet Industry Association (ELSIA) 07668

Technical Manager Bravington House, 2 Bravington Walk, London, N1 9AF, UK. T. +442078338090. Fax +442078331611.
URL: http://www.elsia-web.org/

Aims Represent the lead sheet industry; promote sustainability credentials of lead sheet; champion product stewardship; provide technical support. **Languages** English. **Staff** 1.00 FTE, paid.
Members Full in 6 countries:
France, Germany, Ireland, Netherlands, Spain, UK. [2018.08.16/XD2952/t/**D**]

- ♦ European Leaf Tobacco Interbranch (unconfirmed)
- ♦ European League Against Rheumatism / see European Alliance of Associations for Rheumatology (#05862)

♦ European League for Economic Cooperation (ELEC) 07669

Ligue européenne de coopération économique (LECE) – Liga Europea de Cooperación Económica – Europäische Liga für Wirtschaftliche Zusammenarbeit

Contact Rue d'Egmont 11, 1000 Brussels, Belgium. T. +32496867022. E-mail: info@elec-lece.eu.
URL: http://www.eleclece.eu/

History 1946, Brussels (Belgium). Founded under the presidency of Paul van Zeeland. Registration: Banque Carrefour des Entreprises, No/ID: 0408.289.628, Start date: 10 Nov 1948, Belgium; EU Transparency Register, No/ID: 213518813328-18, Start date: 24 Mar 2014. **Aims** Encourage *cultural* and economic rapprochement of the States which compose Europe, and develop between them a spirit of cooperation and collaboration. **Structure** Central Council, consisting of Presidents of National Sections and co-opted members; General Secretariat; Standing and ad hoc Commissions. Meetings closed. **Languages** English, French. **Staff** 1.00 FTE, paid. **Finance** Sources: members' dues. Annual budget: 79,400 EUR (2010). **Activities** Events/meetings; research/documentation. **Events** *Meeting* Barcelona (Spain) 2006, *Annual Conference* Morocco 2002, *Annual Conference* Berlin (Germany) 2000, *Annual conference* Barcelona (Spain) 1997, *Annual conference on the development of Economic and Monetary Union / Annual General Meeting* London (UK) 1996. **Publications** *Cahier Comte Boël* – series (15 up to 2011). *50th Anniversary of ELEC: 1946-1996 – In Remembrance of Joseph Retinger* (1996); *The Origins of the European League for Economic Co-operation* (1995); *Migration of Workers and Company Operations* (1990); *Other publications: What Future for European Agriculture ?* (1990); *Taxation in Europe* (1989); *Europe and the Case of Austria* (1988); *The European Dimension in Environmental Protection* (1987); *Financial Market for Europe* (1986); *The Reform of CAP and its Implications for International Trade* (1986); *Reorganizing Work* (1984); *Coexistence in the European Economy of Public and Private Enterprises* (1982); *Reports of colloquia in English/French: Europe in the Eighties – ELEC in Action* (1981). Annual Report. A number of other items published prior to 1980.
Members National Committees in 12 countries:
Andorra, Austria, Belgium, Bulgaria, France, Germany, Netherlands, Poland, Portugal, Romania, Spain, Switzerland.
IGO Relations Accredited by (1): *United Nations Office at Vienna (UNOV, #20604).* **NGO Relations** Supports (1): *European Alliance for the Statute of the European Association (EASEA, #05886).* Founder member of: *European Movement International (EMI, #07825).* [2021.04.28/XD0796/**D**]

- ♦ European League of Imams and Chaplains (inactive)

♦ European League of Institutes of the Arts (ELIA) 07670

Exec Dir Lab 106 – A Lab, Overhoeksplein 2, 1031 KS Amsterdam, Netherlands. T. +31203301116. E-mail: info@elia-artschools.org.
Pres Univ of Vienna, Dept Theater/Film/Media Studies, Althanstrasse 14, 1090 Vienna, Austria. T. +431427744301.
URL: http://www.elia-artschools.org/

History 3 Oct 1990, Amsterdam (Netherlands). **Aims** Represent Higher Arts Education; be an influential voice and advocate in promoting interests of members. **Structure** General Assembly (every 2 years); Board; Executive Committee. **Languages** English. **Staff** 6.50 FTE, paid. **Finance** Sources: members' dues; revenue from activities/projects; subsidies. **Activities** Advocacy/lobbying/activism; events/meetings; guidance/assistance/consulting; networking/liaising. **Events** *Biennial Conference* Helsinki (Finland) 2022, *Leadership Symposium* Tallinn (Estonia) 2022, *Multiplier Conference: Advancing Supervision for Artistic Research Doctorates & Beyond* Vienna (Austria) 2021, *Biennial Conference* Zurich (Switzerland) 2020, *Leadership Symposium* Hangzhou (China) 2019. **Publications** *ELIA Newsletter* (12 a year). *ArtFutures: Working with Contradictions in Higher Arts Education* (2014). Position papers; books; events documentation; videotapes; CD-ROMs. Information Services: Overview database of research in the arts in Europe. Documentation and archive material available to members.
Members Full; Associate; Non-European. Degree-granting institutions in the field of fine arts, crafts design, theatre design, architecture, industrial design, fashion, design and textile, film and video, communication arts, photography, music, drama, dance and training of teachers in the arts. Full members in 49 countries and territories:
Albania, Australia, Austria, Azerbaijan, Belgium, Bulgaria, Canada, China, Croatia, Cyprus, Czechia, Denmark, Estonia, Finland, France, Georgia, Germany, Hong Kong, Hungary, Iceland, India, Ireland, Italy, Japan, Korea Rep, Kosovo, Latvia, Lithuania, Malta, Monaco, Mongolia, Netherlands, New Zealand, Norway, Poland, Portugal, Qatar, Romania, Serbia, Singapore, Slovakia, Slovenia, Spain, Sweden, Switzerland, Taiwan, Türkiye, UK, USA.
Non-European members in 13 countries and territories:
Australia, Canada, China, Hong Kong, India, Kenya, Malaysia, Mongolia, New Zealand, Qatar, Taiwan, Türkiye, USA.
Associate members in 18 countries:
Belgium, Bulgaria, Canada, China, Finland, France, Iceland, India, Italy, Montenegro, Netherlands, Qatar, Romania, Serbia, Singapore, Spain, UK, USA.
NGO Relations Member of (1): *European Alliance for Culture and the Arts (#05866).* Cooperates with (9): *Association Européenne des Conservatoires, Académies de Musique et Musikhochschulen (AEC, #02560)*; *Culture Action Europe (CAE, #04981)*; *European Cultural Foundation (ECF, #06868)*; *European League of Institutes of the Arts (ELIA, #07670)*; *IETM – International Network for Contemporary Performing Arts (#11098)*; *International Association of Cinema, Audiovisual and Media Schools (#11771)*; *International Council of Fine Arts Deans (ICFAD)*; *International Federation of Arts Councils and Culture Agencies (IFACCA, #13358)*; *Network of European Foundations (NEF, #17019).* [2022.05.16/XD2378/y/**D**]

- ♦ European League for Mental Hygiene (inactive)

♦ European League for Middle Level Education (ELMLE) 07671

Sec address not obtained.
URL: http://www.elmle.org/

History 1986, Brussels (Belgium). **Aims** Promote unity among middle level educators in overseas schools; encourage implementation of middle level concepts to include staff development; provide leadership in planning and developing middle level education; serve as a clearing house resource body for the exchange of ideas. **Structure** Steering Committee of 10 members. **Languages** English. **Staff** 10.00 FTE, voluntary. **Finance** Members' dues. Conference proceeds. Budget: US$ 100,000. **Events** *Annual Conference* Budapest (Hungary) 2020, *Annual Conference* Valencia (Spain) 2019, *Annual Conference* Amsterdam (Netherlands) 2018, *Annual Conference* Vienna (Austria) 2017, *Annual Conference* Barcelona (Spain) 2016. **Publications** *A Bridge in the Middle* – journal; *ELME Newsletter.* **Members** Individuals in 33 countries. Membership countries not specified. [2017/XD7991/v/**D**]

♦ European Leagues 07672

Headquarters Chemin du Canal 1, 1260 Nyon VD, Switzerland. T. +41223085111. Fax +41223085101. E-mail: hq@europeanleagues.com.
URL: http://www.europeanleagues.com/

History 1997. Former names and other names: *Association of European Union Premier Professional Football Leagues (EUPPFL)* – former (1997 to 2005); *European Professional Football Leagues (EPFL)* – legal name (2005). Registration: Swiss Civil Code, Start date: 2005. **Aims** Enhance and protect the competitive balance of professional football competitions within European Football. **Structure** General Assembly (at least 3 times a year); Board of Directors; Administration; Strategic Committees. **Languages** English, French, Spanish. **Staff** 6.00 FTE, paid. **Activities** Events/meetings; training/education. **Events** *General Assembly* Istanbul (Turkey) 2022, *Club Advisory Platform (CAP) Convention* Madrid (Spain) 2021, *Club Advisory Platform (CAP) Annual Convention* Nyon (Switzerland) 2021, *General Assembly* Nyon (Switzerland) 2021, *General Assembly* Nyon (Switzerland) 2020.
Members Full in 27 countries and territories:
Austria, Azerbaijan, Belgium, Czechia, Denmark, England, Finland, France, Germany, Greece, Israel, Italy, Kazakhstan, Latvia, Lithuania, Netherlands, Norway, Poland, Portugal, Romania, Russia, Scotland, Serbia, Spain, Sweden, Switzerland, Ukraine.
Associate in 5 countries and territories:
France, Italy, Netherlands, Russia, Türkiye.
Development members in 4 countries and territories:
Latvia, Lithuania, Northern Ireland, Slovakia.
NGO Relations Member of (1): *Sports Rights Owners Coalition (SROC, #19929).* Cooperates with (2): *European Club Association (ECA, #06579)*; *Fédération internationale des footballeurs professionnels (FIFPRO, #09633).* [2021.06.09/XM3819/**D**]

- ♦ European League of Societies for the Mentally Handicapped / see Inclusion International (#11145)

♦ European League of Stuttering Associations (ELSA) 07673

Chair 31 Grosvenor Road, Jesmond, Newcastle upon Tyne, NE2 2RL, UK. T. +441912818003. Fax +441912818003. E-mail: elsa.europe@totalise.co.uk.
URL: http://www.elsa.info/

History Founded 22 Sep 1990, Darmstadt (Germany FR). Registered charity. Registration: Charity Commission, No/ID: 1074561, England and Wales. **Aims** Link together and further cooperation of Europe's national stuttering organizations; provide a forum for exchange of concepts and experiences in stuttering therapy and self-help; represent the interests of stutterers to European and international bodies; put stuttering onto the European agenda to ensure the needs and challenges faced by people who stutter are considered in a European context. **Structure** Executive Board; Committees. **Languages** English. **Staff** Voluntary. **Finance** Members' dues. Other sources: project funding; some funding from European Union and *Council of Europe (CE, #04881)* for conferences and meetings. **Activities** Events/meetings. **Events** *Annual Youth Meeting* 's Hertogenbosch (Netherlands) 2014, *World Congress* Netherlands 2013, *Annual Youth Meeting* Giggleswick (UK) 2011, *Annual Youth Meeting* Giggleswick (UK) 2009, *Annual Youth Meeting* Nijmegen (Netherlands) 2007. **Publications** *One Voice* – newsletter; *The Voice of Elsa* – newsletter. *International and European Disability Policy. Stuttering and Employment* – statement.
Members European national stuttering self-help associations in 23 countries:
Austria, Belgium, Bulgaria, Croatia, Denmark, Estonia, Finland, France, Germany, Hungary, Iceland, Ireland, Israel, Italy, Lithuania, Luxembourg, Netherlands, Norway, Poland, Portugal, Sweden, Switzerland, UK.
NGO Relations *European Speech and Language Therapy Association (ESLA, #08812)*; *European Disability Forum (EDF, #06929)*; *International Fluency Association (IFA, #13617)*; *International Stuttering Association (ISA, #15621).* [2021/XD2541/**D**]

- ♦ European Lean Educator Conference (meeting series)

♦ European Learning Industry Group (ELIG) 07674

SG 63 rue Rambuteau, 75004 Paris, France. T. +33140280947. Fax +33140280947.
URL: http://www.elig.org/

History 25 Apr 2002, as *European eLearning Industry Group*, in partnership with *European Commission (EC, #06633)* Commissioner Reding. **Aims** Promote innovation in learning, knowledge creation and dissemination throughout Europe. **Structure** General Meeting (annual). Executive Committee, comprising 2 Chairs, 6 members and (ex-officio) Secretary-General. **Events** *Learning Places of the future* Paris (France) 2016, *Annual General Meeting* Berlin (Germany) 2015, *Annual Meeting on Sustaining Markets for Learning in Europe* Espoo (Finland) 2011, *Annual international conference on interactive computer aided learning* Salzburg (Austria) 2011, *Annual international conference on interactive computer aided learning* Hasselt (Belgium) 2010. **Publications** *ELIG Newsletter.* **NGO Relations** Member of: *EFMD – The Management Development Network (#05387).* [2011/XJ0350/**E**]

♦ European Leather Association / see Confédération des associations nationales de tanneurs et mégissiers de la Communauté européenne (#04515)
♦ European Leather Fair Federation (unconfirmed)

♦ **European Lecithin Manufacturers Association (ELMA)** **07675**
Exec Sec Avenue de Tervueren 13 A – Bte 7, 1040 Brussels, Belgium. T. +3227365354. Fax +3227323427. E-mail: elma@ecco-eu.com.
URL: http://www.elma-eu.org/
History 1999, Brussels (Belgium). **Aims** Defend and represent members' interests at the level of the European Union and other European and international bodies; improve knowledge about lecithin's usefulness in different applications and provide factual information about lecithin to interested parties across Europe. **Structure** Committee of EU Members; Secretariat. **Languages** English. **Staff** 1.00 FTE, paid. **Finance** Members' dues. **NGO Relations** Member of: *EU Specialty Food Ingredients (#09200).* [2014/XD7959/**D**]

♦ **European Left (EL)** **07676**
Contact Square de Meeûs 25, 1000 Brussels, Belgium. T. +3225022606. Fax +3225020173. E-mail: info@european-left.org.
URL: http://www.european-left.org/
History May 2004, Rome (Italy). **Structure** Council of Chairpersons; Executive Board. **Events** *Congress* Madrid (Spain) 2013, *Meeting* Budapest (Hungary) 2011, *Congress* Prague (Czech Rep) 2007.
Members Political parties in 17 countries:
Austria, Belgium, Czechia, Estonia, France, Germany, Greece, Hungary, Italy, Luxembourg, Moldova, Portugal, Romania, San Marino, Spain, Switzerland, Türkiye.
Parties with observer status in 10 countries:
Belgium, Cyprus, Czechia, Denmark, Finland, Germany, Greece, Italy, Poland, Slovakia.
NGO Relations *transform! europe (transform, #20212).* [2015/XM2951/**F**]

♦ **European Legal English Teachers' Association (EULETA)** **07677**
Sec address not obtained. E-mail: secretary@euleta.org – euletasecretary@gmail.com.
URL: https://euleta.org/
History 2006, Greifswald (Germany). Registration: Hamburg District court, No/ID: VR 19362, Start date: 10 Apr 2007, Germany, Hamburg. **Aims** Promote the effective teaching of Legal English. **Structure** General Meeting; Board; Executive Board. **Activities** Events/meetings; knowledge management/information dissemination; publishing activities; training/education. **Events** *EULETA Legal English Conference* Paris (France) 2021, *EULETA Legal English Conference* Split (Croatia) 2018, *EULETA Legal English Conference* Zurich (Switzerland) 2016, *EULETA Legal English Conference* Warwick (UK) 2014. [2022/AA2712/v/**D**]

♦ **European Legal Interpreters and Translators Association (EULITA)** . **07678**
Secretariat Rue Glesener 11, L-1631 Luxembourg, Luxembourg. E-mail: info@eulita.eu.
URL: http://eulita.eu/
History 26 Nov 2009, Antwerp (Belgium). Set up under the Criminal Justice Programme of DG Justice, Freedom, Security of *European Commission (EC, #06633)*: JLS/2007/JPEN/249. Registration: Belgium. **Aims** Bring together professional associations and legal translators and spoken and sign-language legal interpreters in EU member states as well as general associations that include legal translators and spoken or *sign-language* legal interpreters among their membership. **Structure** General Assembly (annual); Executive Committee. **Languages** English, French. **Staff** 0.50 FTE, paid. **Finance** Sources: members' dues. Supported by: *European Commission (EC, #06633).* **Activities** Events/meetings. **Events** *Annual General Assembly* Luxembourg (Luxembourg) 2019, *Annual General Assembly* Sofia (Bulgaria) 2018, *Annual General Assembly* Vienna (Austria) 2017, *Annual General Assembly* Strasbourg (France) 2016, *Annual General Assembly* Opatija (Croatia) 2015.
Members Full; Associate. Full in 23 countries:
Austria, Belgium, Bulgaria, Croatia, Czechia, Denmark, Finland, France, Germany, Greece, Iceland, Ireland, Italy, Lithuania, Luxembourg, Netherlands, Norway, Poland, Slovakia, Slovenia, Spain, Sweden, UK.
Associate: institutions and associations in 20 countries:
Argentina, Austria, Belgium, China, Czechia, Denmark, Finland, France, Germany, Hungary, Italy, Luxembourg, Netherlands, Norway, Portugal, Serbia, Slovakia, Slovenia, Spain, Switzerland.
Included in the above, 3 organizations listed in this Yearbook:
Conférence internationale permanente d'instituts universitaires de traducteurs et interprètes (CIUTI, #04621); European Forum of Sign Language Interpreters (efsli, #07334); International Association of Conference Interpreters (#11807).
Associate: individuals in 15 countries:
Argentina, Brazil, China, Estonia, France, Germany, Hungary, Japan, Morocco, Russia, Switzerland, Türkiye, UK, Ukraine, USA. [2020.05.21/XJ4869/y/**E**]

♦ **European Legal Network on Asylum (ELENA)** **07679**
Senior Communication Coordinator ECRE, Rue Royale 146, 1st Floor, 1000 Brussels, Belgium. T. +3222120814 – +322(32472230041. Fax +3225145922. E-mail: ecre@ecre.org.
SG address not obtained.
URL: http://www.ecre.org/topics/elena/
History 1985, as a project of *European Council on Refugees and Exiles (ECRE, #06839).* **Aims** As a forum for legal practitioners, promote the highest human rights standards for the treatment of *refugees*, asylum seekers and other persons in need of international protection in their counselling and advocacy work. **Structure** Work is advised by ELENA national coordinators, comprising practising legal counsellors from a range of European countries. Work coordinated by Legal Officer – ECRE (Coordinator for ELENA). **Languages** English. **Staff** 2.50 FTE, paid; 0.50 FTE, voluntary. **Finance** Voluntary contributions from non-governmental agencies participating in ECRE. Special projects also funded by contributions from other institutions such as: *UNHCR (#20327); Council of Europe (CE, #04881).* **Activities** Provides and reinforces contact between practising lawyers and legal counsellors in different European countries who work on asylum cases; facilitates the exchange of information and experience; studies implementation of national and international law relating to refugees; organizes seminars; promotes the development of lawyers specializing in asylum law. **Events** *Annual General Assembly* Germany 2016, *Annual General Assembly* The Hague (Netherlands) 2015, *Annual General Conference* Brussels (Belgium) 2014, *Seminar* Lisbon (Portugal) 2013, *Seminar* Bologna (Italy) 2012. **Publications** *The ELENA Index.* Reports; research findings.
Members Lawyers and legal counsellors (about 1,500) in 27 countries:
Austria, Belgium, Bosnia-Herzegovina, Bulgaria, Czechia, Denmark, Finland, France, Germany, Greece, Hungary, Ireland, Italy, Lithuania, Luxembourg, Netherlands, Norway, Poland, Portugal, Romania, Russia, Slovakia, Slovenia, Spain, Sweden, Switzerland, UK. [2018/XF1059/**F**]

♦ European Legal Studies Institute (internationally oriented national body)

♦ **European Legal Technology Association (ELTA)** **07680**
Contact c/o Spielfeld Digital Hub GmbH, Skalitzer Str 85-86, 10997 Berlin, Germany. T. +494030706267. E-mail: info@lta-online.eu.
URL: https://europe-legaltech.org/
History Sep 2016. Registration: No/ID: VR 35460, Start date: 15 Dec 2016. **Aims** Promote public awareness of technology and software supported solutions and processes in the legal sector and of business enterprises, law firms, start-tups and other initiatives in this area. **Structure** General Meeting; Board. **Activities** Events/meetings; knowledge management/information dissemination. **Events** *Congress* Tel Aviv (Israel) 2021, *Congress* Tel Aviv (Israel) 2020, *Congress* Madrid (Spain) 2019, *Congress* Madrid (Spain) 2019. **Members** Corporate; Individuals. Membership countries not specified. [AA0552/**D**]

♦ **European Legionnaires' Disease Surveillance Network (ELDSNet)** . . **07681**
Address not obtained.
URL: http://ecdc.europa.eu/en/healthtopics/legionnaires_disease/ELDSNET/Pages/
History Founded 1987, as *European Surveillance Scheme for Travel Associated Legionnaires' Disease (EWGLINet) by European Working Group on Legionella Infections (EWGLI, inactive).* Subsequently known as *EWGLINET.* Scheme was coordinated by National Bacteriology Laboratory, Stockholm (Sweden) and funded by *WHO (#20950)* until 1993. Coordination then transferred to Public Health Laboratory Service Communicable Disease Surveillance Centre, London (UK), with *European Commission (EC, #06633)* as main sponsor. Between 2007-2010, funded by *European Centre for Disease Prevention and Control (ECDC, #06476).* Since 2010, also coordinated by ECDC, and adopted current title. **Aims** Carry out surveillance of Legionnaires' disease in order to identify relevant public health risks, enhance prevention of cases and monitor epidemiological trends. **Events** *Annual Meeting* Amsterdam (Netherlands) 2016, *Annual Meeting* London (UK) 2015, *Annual Meeting* Barcelona (Spain) 2014, *Annual Meeting* Athens (Greece) 2013, *Annual meeting* Dresden (Germany) 2012.
Members Epidemiologists or microbiologists nominated by national public health authorities. Members in 29 countries:
Austria, Belgium, Bulgaria, Croatia, Cyprus, Czechia, Denmark, Estonia, Finland, France, Germany, Greece, Hungary, Iceland, Ireland, Italy, Latvia, Lithuania, Malta, Netherlands, Norway, Poland, Portugal, Romania, Slovakia, Slovenia, Spain, Sweden, UK. [2016.10.28/XJ2543/**F**]

♦ European Leisure and Recreation Association (inactive)
♦ European Leksell Gamma Knife Society / see European Gamma Knife Society (#07376)

♦ **European Leptospirosis Society (ELS)** **07682**
Sec Vet Med – Univ of Zagreb, Dept of Microbiology, Heinzelova 55, HR-1000 Zagreb, Croatia. T. +38512390200. Fax +38512390207.
Pres address not obtained.
URL: http://eurolepto.ucd.ie/
History 2 Jun 2012, Dubrovnik (Croatia), at 1st Eurolepto Meeting. **Aims** Promote knowledge on leptospirosis and related haemorrhagic fevers through regional meetings, networking between European and African institutions and facilitating fundraising for research on the subject. **Structure** Board of Executive Officers. **Languages** English. **Finance** Members' dues. **Events** *Meeting on Leptospirosis and Other Rodent Borne Haemorrhagic Fevers* Alghero (Italy) 2018, *Meeting on Leptospirosis and Other Rodent Borne Haemorrhagic Fevers / Eurolepto Meeting* Amsterdam (Netherlands) 2015, *Eurolepto Meeting* Dubrovnik (Croatia) 2012.
Members Full in 15 countries:
Belgium, Croatia, France, Germany, Ireland, Italy, Netherlands, Portugal, Romania, Russia, Serbia, Slovenia, Sweden, Switzerland, UK.
NGO Relations *International Leptospirosis Society (ILS, #14031).* [2015.07.02/XJ8895/**D**]

♦ **European Letterbox Marketing Association (ELMA)** **07683**
Pres c/o Whistl (Doordrop Media) Ltd, Meridian House, Fieldhouse Lane, Marlow, SL7 1TB, UK. T. +441628816685.
URL: http://www.elma-europe.com/
History 1990, Birmingham (UK). **Aims** Be Europe's centre of excellence and innovation for letterbox marketing; provide clients with superior resources, experience and knowledge. **Structure** Board. **Languages** English. **Staff** 2.00 FTE, paid; 4.00 FTE, voluntary. **Finance** Sources: members' dues. Annual budget: 55,000 EUR. **Activities** Events/meetings; research and development. **Publications** Annual census.
Members Full in 17 countries:
Austria, Belgium, Cyprus, Denmark, Finland, France, Germany, Greece, Ireland, Italy, Netherlands, Portugal, Romania, Slovakia, Spain, Sweden, UK.
NGO Relations Member of (1): *Federation of European Data & Marketing (FEDMA, #09499).* [2022.11.03/XJ7978/**D**]

♦ **European Leucodystrophy Association (ELA)** **07684**
Association européenne contre les leucodystrophies
Secretariat 2 rue Mi-les-Vignes, CS 61024, 54521 Laxou CEDEX, France. T. +33383309334. Fax +33383300068. E-mail: ela@ela-asso.com.
URL: http://www.ela-asso.com/
History 1992. Registered in accordance with French law. **Aims** Increase public awareness of leukodystrophies; fund medical research; support families. **Structure** Board of Directors. **Languages** French. **Staff** 12.00 FTE, paid; 2.00 FTE, voluntary. **Finance** Public and private subsidies. Budget (annual): euro 3.39 million. **Events** *Scientific Congress* Paris (France) 2015, *Colloquium* Paris (France) 2010, *EUROGLIA : European Meeting on Glial Cells in Health and Disease / European Meeting on Glial Cells in Health and Disease* Paris (France) 2009, *EUROGLIA : European meeting on glial cell function in health and disease / European Meeting on Glial Cells in Health and Disease* Barcelona (Spain) 2000. **Publications** *ELA Info* (4 a year) – newsletter. *Livre de recettes diététiques pour régime ALD-AMN* (1993).
Members Associations in 12 countries:
Belgium, Brazil, France, Germany, Italy, Luxembourg, Netherlands, Spain, Switzerland, UK, United Arab Emirates, USA.
Individuals in 17 countries:
Algeria, Austria, Belgium, Brazil, Canada, Denmark, France, Germany, India, Italy, Luxembourg, Mauritius, Morocco, Spain, Switzerland, UK, USA. [2014/XD7325/**D**]

♦ **European LeukemiaNet (ELN)** **07685**
Contact ELN-Foundation, Im Langgewann 45, 69469 Weinheim, Germany. T. +496213836931. Fax +496213836932.
URL: http://www.leukemia-net.org/
History Set up 2004, as a project funded by *European Community (inactive)* – 6th Framework Programme. Subsequently funded by *European Science Foundation (ESF, #08441),* until Jun 2015. **Aims** Cure leukemia by cooperative research and spread of excellence. **Structure** Steering Committee. Includes *ELN Foundation* and *ELN Foundation Circle.* **Activities** Events/meetings; awards/prizes/competitions. **Events** *Annual Symposium* Mannheim (Germany) 2015, *Frontiers Meeting* Berlin (Germany) 2014, *Annual Symposium* Mannheim (Germany) 2014, *Meeting* Vienna (Austria) 2014, *Annual Symposium* Mannheim (Germany) 2013. **Publications** *E-Newsletter* (5 a year); *Information Letter* (annual). **NGO Relations** Member of: *Worldwide Network for Blood and Marrow Transplantation (WBMT, #21929).* Instrumental in setting up: *European Myelodysplastic Syndromes Cooperative Group (EMSCO, #07848).* [2018/XJ9570/**F**]

♦ **European LGBT Police Association (EGPA)** **07686**
Pres address not obtained. E-mail: contact@lgbtpolice.eu – president@lgbtpolice.eu.
URL: https://www.lgbtpolice.eu/
History 2005. Founded as an informal network of policemen and women. Former names and other names: *European Gay Police Association* – former; *Gay Police European Network* – former. **Aims** Optimize the position of Lesbian, Gay, Bi-sexual and Transgender (LGBT) police workers within European police organizations. **Structure** Executive Committee; General Board (meets 2-3 times a year, rotating between participating countries). **Languages** Czech, Danish, Dutch, English, Estonian, Finnish, French, German, Hungarian, Irish Gaelic, Italian, Latvian, Lithuanian, Maltese, Polish, Portuguese, Slovakian, Slovene, Spanish, Swedish. **Finance** Sources: contributions; fees for services; members' dues; revenue from activities/projects; sale of products; subscriptions. **Activities** Advocacy/lobbying/activism; events/meetings; knowledge management/information dissemination; networking/liaising; training/education. **Events** *Conference* Athens (Greece) 2022, *Conference* Thessaloniki (Greece) 2021, *Conference* Thessaloniki (Greece) 2020, *Conference* Paris (France) 2018, *Conference* Berlin (Germany) 2014.
Members Full in 16 countries and territories:
Austria, Belgium, Finland, France, Germany, Greece, Ireland, Italy, Netherlands, Norway, Scotland, Serbia, Spain, Sweden, Switzerland, UK.
IGO Relations Informal network of Governmental Focal Points Roundtable. **NGO Relations** Member of (2): *ILGA-Europe (#11118); ILGA World (International Lesbian, Gay, Bisexual, Trans and Intersex Association, #11120).* Links with NGOs across Europe. [2022.02.17/XM2672/**D**]

♦ European Liaison Committee / see EU Specialty Food Ingredients (#09200)

♦ **European Liaison Committee for Agricultural and Agri-Food Trades** **07687**
Comité européen de liaison des commerces agricoles et agro-alimentaires (CELCAA)
Contact Rue Gachard 80, 1050 Brussels, Belgium. E-mail: info@celcaa.eu.
URL: http://www.celcaa.eu/
History 3 Jan 1980, Brussels (Belgium). Founded to replace *Comité des organisations commerciales des pays de la CEE (COCCEE, inactive)*, which operated from 1957 to 1978. Former names and other names: *Comité européen de liaison des commerces agro-alimentaires* – former alias. Registration: Banque-Carrefour des Entreprises, No/ID: 0420.028.608, Start date: 3 Jan 1980, Belgium; EU Transparency Register, No/ID: 546282614966-51, Start date: 20 Nov 2014. **Aims** Promote scientific research and technical progress in the

field; defend and promote the interests of the agricultural and food trade, coordinate the actions of its members and represent them with European Union bodies. **Structure** General Assembly (annual); Board of Directors; Secretariat. **Languages** English. **Staff** 0.50 FTE, paid; 3.00 FTE, voluntary. **Finance** Sources: members' dues. **Events** *Conference* 2022, *Conference* 2021, *Conference* Brussels (Belgium) 2019, *Annual General Meeting* Brussels (Belgium) 1991.
Members International, regional and national associations (8):
Comité européen des entreprises vins (CEEV, #04157); Committee of the Trade in Cereals, Oilseeds, Pulses, Olive Oil, Oils and Fats, Animal Feed and Agrosupply of the EU (COCERAL, #04289); European Association of Dairy Trade (#06003); European Federation of Tobacco Processors (#07227); European Union of Wholesale in Eggs, Egg-Products, Poultry and Game (EUWEP, #09021); Grain and Feed Trade Association (GAFTA, #10692); International Butchers' Confederation (IBC, #12421); Union européenne du commerce du bétail et de la viande (UECBV, #20394).
NGO Relations Member of (1): *Federation of European and International Associations Established in Belgium (FAIB, #09508).* [2023/XD8919/ty/**E**]

- ♦ European Liaison Committee of Common Market Forwarders / see CLECAT (#03993)
- ♦ European Liaison Committee of Freight Forwarders / see CLECAT (#03993)
- ♦ European Liaison Committee of Machine Tools Importers (#04161)
- ♦ European Liaison Committee of Osteopaths (inactive)
- ♦ European Liaison Committee of Professional National Travel Agency Associations and Organizations (inactive)

♦ European Liaison Committee for Pulp and Paper (EUCEPA) 07688

Comité européen de liaison pour la cellulose et le papier (EUCEPA) – Comité Europeo de Enlace para la Pasta y el Papel – Europäischer Verband für Zellstoff und Papiertechnik
Main Office 23 rue d'Aumale, 75009 Paris, France. Fax +33145635309.
Pres address not obtained.
URL: http://www.eucepa.eu/

History Oct 1956, Paris (France). **Aims** Bring together European technical associations of chemists and engineers concerned with pulp and paper; establish relations with international organizations. **Structure** Assembly. Secretariat undertaken by the French Association. **Languages** English, French, German. **Finance** Members' dues. **Activities** Arranges special conferences and events. **Events** *International mechanical pulping conference* Oslo (Norway) 2005, *Sustainable development for the pulp and paper industry* Lisbon (Portugal) 2003, *Conference* Grenoble (France) 1999, *Symposium* Florence (Italy) 1998, *Conference* Baden Baden (Germany) 1997.
Members Pulp and paper technical associations in 17 countries:
Austria, Czechia, Denmark, Finland, France, Germany, Hungary, Italy, Netherlands, Norway, Poland, Portugal, Slovakia, Slovenia, Spain, Sweden, UK.
Consultative Status Consultative status granted from: *ECOSOC (#05331)* (Ros C); *FAO (#09260)* (Liaison Status). [2018/XD0798/**D**]

- ♦ European Liaison Committee on Services of General Interest (internationally oriented national body)
- ♦ European Liaison Committee for the Sewing Machine Industries (inactive)
- ♦ European Liaison Committee for Social Housing / see Housing Europe – The European Federation for Public Cooperative and Social Housing (#10956)
- ♦ European Liberal Democrat and Reform Party / see Renew Europe – Committee of the Regions (#18841)
- ♦ European Liberal, Democrat and Reform Party / see Alliance of Liberals and Democrats for Europe Party (#00703)

♦ European Liberal Forum (ELF) 07689

Forum Libéral Européen
Main Office Rue d'Idalie 11-13, boite 6, 1050 Brussels, Belgium. T. +3226691318. E-mail: info@liberalforum.eu.
URL: http://www.liberalforum.eu/

History 21 Sep 2007. Founded as the European political foundation of the liberal family. Registration: Belgium. **Aims** Bring together liberal think thanks, political foundations and institutes from around Europe to observe, analyse and contribute to the debate on European public policy issues and the process of European integration, through education, training, research and promotion of active citizenship within the EU. **Structure** General Assembly; Board of Directors; Secretariat, headed by Executive Director. **Languages** English, French, German. **Staff** 9.00 FTE, paid. **Finance** Funded by: *European Parliament (EP, #08146).* **Activities** Projects/programmes. **Publications** Annual Report.
Members Organizations in 21 countries:
Austria, Belgium, Bulgaria, Croatia, Czechia, Denmark, Estonia, Finland, Germany, Greece, Hungary, Italy, Latvia, Netherlands, Poland, Portugal, Romania, Slovakia, Slovenia, Spain, Sweden.
Included in the above, 1 organization listed in this Yearbook:
European Liberal Youth (LYMEC, #07690). [2021/XJ2754/fy/**F**]

♦ European Liberal Youth (LYMEC) 07690

SG Rue de d'Idalie 11, 6th floor, bt 2, 1050 Brussels, Belgium. T. +32484644068. E-mail: office@lymec.eu.
Pres address not obtained.
URL: https://action.lymec.eu/

History 2 Nov 1976, The Hague (Netherlands). Founded as successor to *Liberal European Youth.* Official youth organization of: *Alliance of Liberals and Democrats for Europe Party (ALDE Party, #00703); Renew Europe (#18840).* Former names and other names: *Liberal and Radical Youth Movement of the European Union* – former (2 Nov 1976); *Liberal European Youth* – former; *Mouvement des jeunesses libérales et radicales de l'Union européenne* – former. Registration: Start date: Feb 2004, Belgium. **Aims** Continue the political and educational understanding of young people throughout the European Union and its future members of liberal and radical parties; play a political role within the European Union as a youth organization in close cooperation with the ALDE Party and Renew Group in the European Parliament. **Structure** Congress; Executive Committee; Bureau. **Languages** English. **Staff** 1.00 FTE, paid. **Finance** Various sources. **Activities** Events/meetings; training/education; advocacy/lobbying/activism. **Events** *Young Leaders Meeting* Barcelona (Spain) 2015, *Autumn Congress / Congress* Helsinki (Finland) 2015, *Congress* Rotterdam (Netherlands) 2015, *Congress* Berlin (Germany) 2014, *Congress* Zagreb (Croatia) 2014. **Publications** *Libertas* (3 a year). Booklets; resolutions; reports; leaflets.
Members National organizations in 35 countries:
Albania, Andorra, Austria, Belarus, Belgium, Bosnia-Herzegovina, Bulgaria, Croatia, Denmark, Estonia, Finland, France, Germany, Greece, Hungary, Ireland, Italy, Latvia, Lithuania, Luxembourg, Moldova, Netherlands, North Macedonia, Norway, Poland, Portugal, Romania, Serbia, Slovakia, Slovenia, Spain, Sweden, Switzerland, Türkiye, UK.
NGO Relations Member of: *European Liberal Forum (ELF, #07689); European Youth Forum (#09140).* Cooperates with: Friedrich Neumann Foundation (FNF); *International Federation of Liberal Youth (IFLRY, #13469); Liberal International (LI, #16454).* Supports: *European Citizens' Initiative Campaign (ECI Campaign, #06558).* [2021/XE2933/**F**]

♦ European Librarians in African Studies (ELIAS) 07691

Contact c/o ASC, PO Box 9555, 2300 RB Leiden, Netherlands. T. +31715273376. Fax +31715273344.
URL: http://eliasnet.pbworks.com/w/page/25672398/FrontPage/

History 2005. **Events** *Annual Meeting* Vienna (Austria) 2018, *Annual Meeting* Basel (Switzerland) 2017, *Annual Meeting* Tervuren (Belgium) 2016, *Annual Meeting* Paris (France) 2015, *Annual Meeting* Frankfurt-Main (Germany) 2014.
Members Organizations, including:
African Studies Centre Leiden (ASCL); SCOLMA – UK Libraries and Archives Group on Africa. [2013.10.16/XJ7371/y/**F**]

♦ European Library Automation Group (ELAG) 07692

Chairperson c/o Wageningen UR, IT Informatie Systemen, Postbus 59, 6700 AB Wageningen, Netherlands.
URL: http://www.elag.org/

History 1979, Copenhagen (Denmark), as *Intermarc Software Group.* Present name adopted at 8th Seminar, Mar 1984, Florence (Italy). **Aims** Exchange information and experience between experts in the field of library automation; initiate informal cooperation in solving problems; promote library automation in Europe. **Structure** Board; Programme Committee. **Languages** English. **Staff** Voluntary. **Finance** Sponsorship of participating organizations and commercial organizations. **Activities** Events/meetings. **Events** *Library Systems Seminar* Riga (Latvia) 2020, *Library Systems Seminar* Berlin (Germany) 2019, *Library Systems Seminar* Prague (Czechia) 2018, *Library Systems Seminar* Copenhagen (Denmark) 2016, *Library Systems Seminar* Stockholm (Sweden) 2015. **Publications** ELAG library systems seminar reports.
Members Individuals in 36 countries:
Albania, Austria, Azerbaijan, Belgium, Bosnia-Herzegovina, Croatia, Czechia, Denmark, Finland, France, Georgia, Germany, Holy See, Hungary, Iceland, Israel, Italy, Latvia, Lithuania, Moldova, Montenegro, Netherlands, Norway, Poland, Romania, Russia, Serbia, Slovakia, Slovenia, Spain, Sweden, Switzerland, UK, Ukraine, USA, Uzbekistan.
NGO Relations *International Federation of Library Associations and Institutions (IFLA, #13470).* [2019.10.15/XE0547/v/**E**]

♦ European Life and Health Underwriters' Association (ELHUA) 07693

Pres address not obtained.
Sec address not obtained.
URL: http://www.elhua.eu/

Aims Raise the understanding and appreciation of life and health underwriting within the European insurance industry and beyond. **Structure** Committee. **Events** *Conference* Madrid (Spain) 2016, *Conference* Prague (Czech Rep) 2014, *Conference* Vienna (Austria) 2012, *Conference* Brussels (Belgium) 2010. [2019.02.14/XJ2049/**D**]

- ♦ European Life Network (internationally oriented national body)
- ♦ European Life Science Editors (inactive)
- ♦ European Life Scientist Organization (inactive)

♦ European Lifestyle Medicine Organization (ELMO) 07694

Pres c/o Erasmus Conferences SA, 6 Drosini Street, Voula, 166 73 Athens, Greece. T. +302107414700. E-mail: secretariat@eulm.org – info@eulm.org.
Registered Office Chemin des Mouilles 4, Petit-Lancy, 1213 Geneva, Switzerland.
URL: http://www.eulm.org/

History Registration: No/ID: CHE-245.611.678, Switzerland; EU Transparency Register, No/ID: 063949321631-11, Start date: 11 May 2016. **Aims** Provide leadership in research, prevention and treatment of chronic and lifestyle-related *diseases,* promoting evidence-based medicine. **Structure** Board; Advisory Board. **Languages** English. **Finance** Members' dues. **Activities** Research/documentation; training/education; awareness raising; events/meetings. **Events** *European Lifestyle Medicine Congress* Athens (Greece) 2022, *European Lifestyle Medicine Congress* Athens (Greece) 2021, *European Lifestyle Medicine Congress* Athens (Greece) 2020, *The European Lifestyle Medicine: Between Education and Practice* Athens (Greece) 2020, *European Lifestyle Medicine Congress* Rome (Italy) 2019.
Members Full (over 320) in 48 countries and territories:
Angola, Australia, Azerbaijan, Bahrain, Belgium, Brazil, Bulgaria, Croatia, Cyprus, Denmark, Ecuador, Egypt, France, Germany, Gibraltar, Greece, Hungary, Iceland, India, Ireland, Israel, Italy, Jordan, Kuwait, Lithuania, Netherlands, Nigeria, Norway, Pakistan, Poland, Portugal, Romania, Russia, Saudi Arabia, Singapore, Slovakia, Slovenia, South Africa, Spain, Sweden, Switzerland, Thailand, Türkiye, Uganda, UK, United Arab Emirates, USA, Zimbabwe.
NGO Relations Partners include: *Asian Society of Lifestyle Medicine (ASLM, #01727); Australasian Society of Lifestyle Medicine (ASLM); European College of Sport Science (ECSS, #06616); European Medical Association (EMA, #07761); European Medical Students' Association (EMSA, #07764); International Self-Care Foundation (ISF); Latin American Lifestyle Medicine Association (LALMA, #16347); World Obesity (#21678).* [2023/XM7828/**D**]

♦ European Lift Association (ELA) 07695

Association européenne des associations nationales de l'industrie de l'ascenseur
SG Avenue Herrman-Debroux 44/1, 1160 Brussels, Belgium. T. +3227795082. Fax +3227721685. E-mail: info@ela-aisbl.org.
URL: http://www.ela-aisbl.org/

History Former names and other names: *European Forum of National Lift Associations (EFLA)* – former; *Forum européen des associations nationales de l'industrie de l'ascenseur* – former. Registration: Banque-Carrefour des Entreprises, No/ID: 0465.901.292, Start date: 20 May 1999, Belgium; EU Transparency Register, No/ID: 32275624894-32, Start date: 4 Jan 2011. **Aims** Represent the lifts, *escalators* and moving walks associations active in the European Union or the European Free Trade Area, as well as represent their components manufacturers. **Structure** General Assembly (annual); Board. Committees (5): Codes and Standards; Communication; Statistical; Components; Quality, Safety, Environment and Education. **Languages** English. **Staff** 3.00 FTE, paid. **Events** *Annual General Assembly* London (UK) 2019, *Annual General Assembly* Stockholm (Sweden) 2018, *Annual General Assembly* Paris (France) 2015, *Annual General Assembly* Amsterdam (Netherlands) 2014, *Annual General Assembly* Berlin (Germany) 2010. **Publications** *ELA News* (2 a year).
Members Full in 21 countries:
Austria, Belgium, Cyprus, Czechia, Denmark, Finland, France, Germany, Greece, Hungary, Italy, Luxembourg, Netherlands, Norway, Poland, Portugal, Romania, Spain, Sweden, Switzerland, Türkiye, UK.
NGO Relations Member of (2): *Federation of European and International Associations Established in Belgium (FAIB, #09508); World Elevator Federation.* In liaison with technical committees of: *Comité européen de normalisation (CEN, #04162).* [2020/XF4407/t/**F**]

- ♦ European Lift Components Association / see European Lift and Lift Component Association (#07696)

♦ European Lift and Lift Component Association (ELCA) 07696

SG address not obtained. T. +32475455683. E-mail: elca@eustrategy.eu.

History 1998. Founded by 5 components producers from 5 European Union countries. A grouping of the type *European Economic Interest Grouping (EEIG, #06960).* Former names and other names: *European Lift Components Association (ELCA)* – former. Registration: Banque-Carrefour des Entreprises, No/ID: 0463.769.173, Start date: 8 Jul 1998, Belgium. **Aims** Represent European lift components manufacturers, vis-à-vis the European institutions, in order to be in a position to influence European Union policy for the benefit of the sector. **Structure** General Assembly (annual). Board, comprising President, Vice-President, Secretary General, Treasurer and a member. Committees (2): Political; Technical. Arbitration Tribunal. Central Office situated in Brussels (Belgium). **Staff** 1.00 FTE, paid. **Finance** Members' dues. **Publications** *ELCA Bulletin* (2 a year).
Members Full industrial or handicraft enterprises within the EEA; Adhering industrial or handicraft enterprises outside the EEA. Full members in 4 countries:
France, Germany, Italy, Spain, UK.
NGO Relations In liaison with technical committees of: *Comité européen de normalisation (CEN, #04162).* [2015/XD7971/**D**]

♦ European Ligand Assay Society (ELAS) 07697

Contact Via Libero Temolo 4, 20100 Milan MI, Italy. E-mail: info@elasitalia.it.
Registered Office 15 montée des Roches, 69340 Francheville, France.
URL: http://www.elasforum.org/

History 1992. Registered in accordance with French law. **Aims** Develop and promote using, develop scientific research on, and bring together European specialists of ligand assays. **Structure** Bureau, composed of 3 members per country. **Languages** English, French. **Staff** None. **Finance** Members' dues. **Activities** Organizes two meetings, one of which is annual, always in Bologna (Italy). **Events** *Annual Symposium* Bologna (Italy) 2013, *Meeting* Glasgow (UK) 2005, *Meeting* Barcelona (Spain) 2003, *Meeting* Edinburgh (UK) 1998, *Annual meeting / Meeting* Turin (Italy) 1997.
Members Societies in 3 countries:
France, Italy, Portugal. [2017/XD4168/**D**]

♦ **European Lighting Clusters Alliance (ELCA)** **07698**
SG Ca' Marcello, Via dei Marcello 13/11, Levada, 35017 Piombino Dese PD, Italy. T. +390499350457. E-mail: info@elcacluster.eu.
Project Manager address not obtained.
URL: http://elcacluster.eu/
History 2011. Previously registered in accordance with Danish law. Registration: Italy. **Aims** Gather forces on a European level so as to increase the competitiveness of the European lighting industries. **Structure** General Assembly; Executive Committee. **Finance** Sources: members' dues.
Members Full in 2 countries:
Belgium, France, Italy, Poland, Spain. [2020/XJ7438/**D**]

♦ European Light Steel Construction Association (no recent information)

♦ **European Lime Association (EuLA)** **07699**
Association européenne de la chaux – Europäischer Kalkverband
Contact c/o IMA Europe, Rue des Deux Eglises 26, Boîte 2, 1000 Brussels, Belgium. T. +3222104410. Fax +3222104429. E-mail: info@eula.eu.
URL: http://www.eula.eu/
History Mar 1990. Registered in accordance with Belgian law. **Aims** Promote the European lime industry. **Structure** General Assembly (annual); Board; Committee; Task Forces. **Languages** English, French, German. **Staff** 2.00 FTE, paid. **Finance** Members' dues. **Activities** Knowledge management/information dissemination. **Events** *European technical conference* Kuala Lumpur (Malaysia) 2007, *European Technical Conference* Prague (Czech Rep) 2006, *European Technical Conference* Seville (Spain) 2005, *European technical conference* Krakow (Poland) 2004, *European technical conference* Munich (Germany) 2000.
Members National organizations in 11 countries:
Austria, Belgium, Czechia, Finland, France, Germany, Italy, Poland, Spain, Sweden, UK.
Individuals in 8 countries:
Bulgaria, Denmark, Estonia, Hungary, Ireland, Norway, Portugal, Switzerland.
NGO Relations In liaison with technical committees of: *Comité européen de normalisation (CEN, #04162)*. Member of: *Construction Products Europe AISBL (#04761)*; *Industrial Minerals Association – Europe (IMA Europe, #11179)*; *International Lime Association (ILA, #14049)*. Shares office staff with: *Calcium Carbonate Association – Europe (CCA-Europe, #03399)*; *European Association of Feldspar Producers (EUROFEL, #06037)*; *European Association of Industrial Silica Producers (EUROSIL, #06082)*; *European Bentonite Producers Association (EUBA, #06328)*; *European Borates Association (EBA, #06382)*; *European Kaolin and Plastic Clays Association (KPC Europe, #07623)*; *European Speciality Minerals Association (ESMA, #08811)*; *International Diatomite Producers Association (IDPA, #13172)*; *Scientific Association of European Talc Industry (Eurotalc, #19146)*; IMA Europe. [2017/XD4821/**D**]

♦ **European Lipoprotein Club** **07700**
Chairman c/o European Atherosclerosis Society, PO Box 5243, SE-402 24 Gothenburg, Sweden. T. +46317602427. Fax +4631812022. E-mail: info@eas-elc.org – office@eas-society.org.
URL: http://www.eas-society.org/page/elc/
History 1977. **Aims** Support and promote active participation, collaboration and exchange of ideas concerning basic and clinical research on the structure, function and metabolism of lipoproteins in health and disease. **Structure** Organizing Committee. **Languages** English. **Staff** Voluntary. **Finance** Sponsoring from industry; grants from governmental organizations. **Activities** Events/meetings. **Events** *Annual Scientific Meeting* Tutzing (Germany) 2022, *Annual Meeting* Tutzing (Germany) 2021, *Annual Meeting* Tutzing (Germany) 2020, *Annual Meeting* Tutzing (Germany) 2019, *Annual Meeting* Tutzing (Germany) 2018. **Publications** Meeting reports.
Members Individuals in 39 countries:
Austria, Belgium, Bosnia-Herzegovina, Bulgaria, Canada, China, Croatia, Cyprus, Czechia, Denmark, Estonia, Finland, France, Germany, Greece, Hungary, Iceland, Ireland, Italy, Japan, Latvia, Malta, Netherlands, North Macedonia, Norway, Poland, Portugal, Romania, Russia, Serbia, Slovakia, Slovenia, Spain, Sweden, Switzerland, Türkiye, UK, USA, Venezuela. [2022/XF0743/**F**]

♦ European Liquefied Petroleum Gas Association / see Liquid Gas Europe (#16488)

♦ **European Liquid Heating Fuels Association (Eurofuel)** **07701**
SG Square de Meeûs 35, 1000 Brussels, Belgium. T. +3228939782.
URL: http://www.eurofuel.eu/
History Brussels (Belgium). Former names and other names: *European Fuel Association (Eurofuel)* – former; *European Heating Oil Association (Eurofuel)* – former. Registration: Banque-Carrefour des Entreprises, No/ID: 0472.611.516, Start date: 14 Jun 2001, Belgium; EU Transparency Register, No/ID: 31843397020-27, Start date: 25 Oct 2011. **Aims** Provide a platform for members to promote best practice in use of liquid heating fuel for domestic heating in a way which respects the environment. **Structure** General Assembly (annual); Board; Secretary-General; Technical Commission. **Languages** English. **Staff** 1.00 FTE, paid. **Finance** Sources: members' dues. Annual budget: 250,000 EUR. **Activities** Events/meetings; knowledge management/information dissemination; publishing activities. **Publications** *Eurofuel Newsletter* (6 a year).
Members National associations in 10 countries:
Austria, Belgium, Finland, France, Germany, Ireland, Italy, Luxembourg, Switzerland, UK. [2022.10.21/XD8625/**D**]

♦ **European Literacy Policy Network (ELINET)** **07702**
Coordinator Univ Köln – Philosophische Fak, Raum 0A 19, Richard-Strauss-Str 2, 50931 Cologne, Germany. T. +492214708850.
URL: http://www.eli-net.eu/
History Set up Feb 2014 Also referred to as *ELINET Association*. **Aims** Improve literacy policies; reduce the number of children, young people and adults with low literacy skills in Europe; help increase reading skills and *reading* for pleasure. **Finance** Funding from *European Commission (EC, #06633)*. **Activities** Research/documentation; advocacy/lobbying/activism; awareness raising; financial and/or material support; events/meetings. **Events** *Literacy in the 21st century – participation, inclusion, equity* Cologne (Germany) 2018, *Meeting* Madrid (Spain) 2017, *European Literacy Conference* Amsterdam (Netherlands) 2016, *Conference* Budapest (Hungary) 2015, *Conference* Vienna (Austria) 2014.
Members Partner organizations (77) in 28 countries:
Austria, Belgium, Bulgaria, Croatia, Cyprus, Czechia, Denmark, Estonia, Finland, France, Germany, Greece, Hungary, Iceland, Ireland, Italy, Lithuania, Malta, Netherlands, Norway, Portugal, Romania, Slovenia, Spain, Sweden, Switzerland, Türkiye, UK.
NGO Relations *Reading and Writing Foundation (RWF)*. [2018/XM6489/**F**]

♦ European Literature, Music and Poetry Association (inactive)

♦ **European Litter Prevention Association (ELPA)** **07703**
Secretariat Av Livingstone 13-15, 1000 Brussels, Belgium. T. +3222869493. E-mail: secretariat@cleaneuropenetwork.eu.
URL: http://www.cleaneuropenetwork.eu/
History Serves as legal vehicle for *Clean Europe Network*. Registration: Belgium. **Aims** Improve litter prevention across the EU. **Structure** General Assembly; Board; Secretariat.
Members Full in 11 countries:
Belgium, Denmark, Estonia, Finland, France, Netherlands, Norway, Spain, Sweden, Switzerland, UK.
NGO Relations Member of: *Federation of European and International Associations Established in Belgium (FAIB, #09508)*. [2020.06.26/XM4947/**D**]

♦ European Live Electronic Centre (internationally oriented national body)

♦ **European Live Music Association (ELMA)** **07704**
Contact Emile Feronstr 70, 1060 Brussels, Belgium. E-mail: info@elmnet.org.
URL: http://www.elmnet.org/
History 2015. Registration: Banque-Carrefour des Entreprises, No/ID: 0681.674.824, Start date: 22 Sep 2017, Belgium; EU Transparency Register, No/ID: 398910541960-11, Start date: 24 Mar 2021. **Aims** Federate and develop common interest initiatives in the live music sector; support members to anticipate cultural, economic, technologic, political and social changes, providing resources and tools so as to ensure complementarity and cooperation from local to international scale. **Activities** Knowledge management/information dissemination; networking/liaising; training/education. [2020/AA1508/**D**]

♦ European Live Poultry and Poultry Hatching Egg Association (unconfirmed)

♦ **European Liver and Intestine Transplant Association (ELITA)** **07705**
Sec Liver Unit, Queen Elizabeth Medical Centre, Edgbaston, Birmingham, B15 2TH, UK. E-mail: secretary@elita.org.
URL: http://www.esot.org/elita/
History 25 Oct 1993, as *European Liver Transplant Association (ELTA)*, within *European Society for Organ Transplantation (ESOT, #08676)*. Current title adopted at General Assembly, 18 Oct 2005, Geneva (Switzerland). **Aims** Provide a forum for those working in the field of liver and intestinal/multivisceral transplantation to exchange scientific information and views related primarily to providing best service for patients in Europe. **Structure** General Assembly. Board, comprising Chairman, Vice-Chairman, Secretary, Treasurer, Custodian of ELTR and 6 Councillors. **Languages** English. **Staff** ESOT executive. **Finance** Members' dues. Other sources: joint conferences; educational grants. **Activities** Organizes symposia and meetings. **Events** *Joint International Congress* Rotterdam (Netherlands) 2023, *Joint International Congress* Istanbul (Turkey) 2022, *Joint International Congress* Florence (Italy) 2021, *Joint International Congress* Istanbul (Turkey) 2020, *Joint International Congress* Lisbon (Portugal) 2018. **Publications** *Transplant International* – journal. **Information Services** *European Liver Transplant Registry (ELTR)*. **Members** Physicians and scientists (about 250). Membership countries not specified. **NGO Relations** Joint meeting with: *International Liver Transplantation Society (ILTS, #14061)*; *Liver Intensive Care Group of Europe (LICAGE, #16497)*. [2012.07.24/XD4177/**D**]

♦ **European Liver Patients 'Association (ELPA)** **07706**
Pres Rue de la Loi 235/27, 1040 Brussels, Belgium. E-mail: contact@elpa.eu.
URL: https://elpa.eu/
History 14 Apr 2005, Paris (France). Founded during annual conference of *European Association for the Study of the Liver (EASL, #06233)*. Statutes most recently amended Apr 2013. Registration: Banque-Carrefour des Entreprises, No/ID: 0875.568.916, Start date: 16 Aug 2005, Belgium; EU Transparency Register, No/ID: 89292219623-93, Start date: 13 Sep 2012. **Aims** Promote the interest of people with liver *disease*. **Structure** Annual General Meeting; Governing Board; Secretariat. **Finance** Sources: grants. **Activities** Projects/programmes; research/documentation. **Events** *International Workshop on HIV Pediatrics* Mexico City (Mexico) 2019, *International Workshop on HIV Pediatrics* Paris (France) 2017, *International Workshop on HIV Pediatrics* Durban (South Africa) 2016, *International Workshop on HIV Pediatrics* Vancouver, BC (Canada) 2015, *Meeting* Vienna (Austria) 2014.
Members Organizations in 23 countries:
Belgium, Bosnia-Herzegovina, Croatia, Cyprus, Denmark, Egypt, Finland, France, Georgia, Hungary, Ireland, Israel, North Macedonia, Portugal, Romania, Russia, Serbia, Slovakia, Slovenia, Spain, Sweden, Türkiye, UK.
NGO Relations Member of (3): *ACHIEVE (#00068)*; *European Cancer Organisation (ECO, #06432)* (Patient Advisory Committee); *European Patients' Forum (EPF, #08172)*. Partner of (4): *Association of European Cancer Leagues (ECL, #02500)*; *European Association for the Study of the Liver (EASL, #06233)*; *Viral Hepatitis Prevention Board (VHPB, #20782)*; *World Hepatitis Alliance (WHA, #21564)*. [2021/XJ1893/**D**]

♦ European Liver Transplant Association / see European Liver and Intestine Transplant Association (#07705)
♦ European Livestock Exporters and Producers Platform (unconfirmed)
♦ European Livestock and Meat Trades Union / see Union européenne du commerce du bétail et de la viande (#20394)
♦ European Livestock and Meat Trading Union (#20394)
♦ European Local Authorities Telematic Network (no recent information)

♦ **European Local Inclusion and Social Action Network (ELISAN)** **07707**
Réseau européen pour l'inclusion et l'action sociale locale
Address not obtained.
URL: http://www.elisan.eu/
History 28 Jan 2008, Brussels (Belgium). 28 jan 2008, Brussels (Belgium), at *European Committee of the Regions (CoR, #06665)*. **Aims** Raise awareness of local social action in Europe, the issues and players involved; promote local social innovation. **Structure** Board of Directors; Executive Board; Steering Committee. **Languages** English, French. **Finance** Members' dues. Project funding from: *European Union (EU, #08967)*. **Events** *European Conference on Prevention and Help with Addiction Disorders* Villach (Austria) 2019, *Annual General Assembly* Rotterdam (Netherlands) 2016, *Conference on Innovation in Care* Rotterdam (Netherlands) 2016, *European conference on social issues as a real investment against crisis* Brussels (Belgium) / Kortrijk (Belgium) 2010. **Consultative Status** Consultative status granted from: *Council of Europe (CE, #04881)* (Participatory Status). [2014.11.27/XJ0978/**E**]

♦ European Locksmith Association / see European Locksmith Federation (#07708)

♦ **European Locksmith Federation (ELF)** **07708**
Fédération européenne des industries de serrures de sécurité – Fachverband Europäischer Sicherheits- und Schlüsselfachgeschäfte
Sec c/o Turvaurakoitsijaliitto ry, Hitsaajankatu 22, FI-00810 Helsinki, Finland.
URL: http://www.eurolockfed.com/
History 27 Feb 1964, Frankfurt-Main (Germany). Former names and other names: *Gesellschaft Europäischer Schlüsseldienste* – alias; *European Locksmith Association* – alias. **Aims** Influence and develop the market; increase the total market and consequently increase market share, profitability and status; develop commercial packages of products and services; create community spirit and well-being within the international locksmith trade. **Structure** Board of Directors, comprising one officer of each association and including the Executive Committee. Executive Committee, comprising President and 2 Vice-Presidents. **Languages** English. **Finance** Members' dues. **Events** *Convention* Helsinki (Finland) 2023, *Convention* Bologna (Italy) 2022, *Convention* Helsinki (Finland) 2021, *Convention* Helsinki (Finland) 2020, *Annual Spring Convention* Bologna (Italy) 2019. **Publications** *Insight* – newsletter.
Members National locksmith associations in 11 countries:
Bulgaria, Denmark, Finland, Germany, Ireland, Italy, Netherlands, Norway, Spain, Sweden, UK.
Individual members in 2 countries:
Estonia, Russia. [2022/XD0084/**t/D**]

♦ **European Logistic Platforms Association (Europlatforms)** **07709**
Pres Ronda del Canal Imperial de Aragón 1, 50197 Saragossa, Spain. T. +34976203830. E-mail: president@europlatforms.eu – secretary@europlatforms.eu.
Registered Office Rue Washington 40, 1050 Brussels, Belgium.
URL: http://www.europlatforms.eu/
History A grouping of the type *European Economic Interest Grouping (EEIG, #06960)*. Former names and other names: *European Association of Freight Villages (Europlatforms)* – former. Registration: Banque-Carrefour des Entreprises, No/ID: 455 694 320, Start date: 28 Apr 1995, Belgium; EU Transparency Register, No/ID: 215690724573-35, Start date: 19 Nov 2016. **Aims** Promote and expand the concept of *logistic* platform in Europe and worldwide, by creating and developing relations among existing platform and by contributing at policy level to Pan-European and Cross-Mediterranean *transport* integration and partnership. **Structure** General Assembly; Board of Directors. **Events** *General Assembly* Parma (Italy) 2020, *General Assembly* Toledo (Spain) 2014, *Conference on climate change, green logistics, sustainable mobility* Valencia (Spain) 2008.
Members National associations in 7 countries:
Denmark, Finland, Germany, Greece, Italy, Portugal, Spain.
Consultative Status Consultative status granted from: *ECOSOC (#05331)* (Ros A). **IGO Relations** *European Commission (EC, #06633)* – CORDIS; *International Transport Forum (ITF, #15725)*; *United Nations Economic Commission for Europe (UNECE, #20555)*. **NGO Relations** Member of (1): *Federation of European and International Associations Established in Belgium (FAIB, #09508)*. [2020.03.03/XM0850/**D**]

♦ **European Logistics Association (ELA)** **07710**
Dir Rue du Commerce 77, 1040 Brussels, Belgium. T. +32471832989. E-mail: ela@elalog.org.
URL: http://www.elalog.eu/

History 1984. Incorporated *European Certification Board for Logistics (ECBL, inactive)*, 1 Jan 2021. Registration: Banque-Carrefour des Entreprises, No/ID: 0851.618.032, Start date: 1 Apr 1998, Belgium; EU Transparency Register, No/ID: 486101215470-41, Start date: 8 Jan 2015. **Aims** Provide an international forum for promotion and development of the logistics and supply chain professions. **Structure** General Meeting (annual); Board; Committees (6). **Languages** English. **Staff** 0.50 FTE, paid. **Finance** Sources: members' dues. **Activities** Awards/prizes/competitions; events/meetings; guidance/assistance/consulting; research/documentation. **Events** *EUROLOG Conference* Dublin (Ireland) 2023, *EUROLOG Conference* Laško (Slovenia) 2021, *EUROLOG Conference* Athens (Greece) 2019, *EUROLOG Conference* Marrakech (Morocco) 2018, *EUROLOG Conference* Bucharest (Romania) 2017. **Publications** *Logistics Europe*. *Success Factor People in Distribution Centres* (2004); *What Matters to Top Management* (2002); *Insight to Impact* (1999); *Some Occupational Profiles for Practitioners in Logistics* (1998); *Towards the 21ST Century* (1997); *Terminology in Logistics* (2nd ed 1994) in Dutch, English, French, German, Spanish; *Logistics Excellence in Europe* (1993); *Logistics Performance Measures, Requirements and Measuring*.
Members Full; Corporate; Fellow; Honorary. Associations (28) in 23 countries:
Austria, Czechia, Finland, France, Germany, Greece, Hungary, Ireland, Italy, Kazakhstan, Luxembourg, Morocco, Poland, Portugal, Romania, Russia, Slovenia, Spain, Sweden, Switzerland, UK, Ukraine.
Included in the above, 2 organizations listed in this Yearbook:
International Institute for the Management of Logistics and Supply Chain (IML, #13899); *International Society for Inventory Research (ISIR, #15216)*.
NGO Relations Member of (1): *European Technology Platform ALICE (ALICE, #08888)*. [2023/XD1106/y/**D**]

♦ European Logistics Platform (ELP) 07711

Secretariat c/o CLECAT, Rue du Commerce 77, 1000 Brussels, Belgium. E-mail: info@europeanlogisticsplatform.eu.
URL: http://www.european-logistics-platform.eu/
Aims Gather policy makers and industry stakeholders to collectively tackle the challenges of the logistics sector such as overstrained infrastructure, climate change, deployment of new technologies, risk management, trade barriers, customs processes and development of e-Commerce. **Structure** Steering Committee; Advisory Board; Secretariat. **Events** *Forum on Logistics in Transition* Brussels (Belgium) 2019, *Conference on Securing Safe and Secure Parking in the EU* Brussels (Belgium) 2018, *Conference on the Future of Multimodal Transport* Brussels (Belgium) 2018.
Members Actors involved in the industry. Included, 11 organizations listed in this Yearbook:
Association of European Vehicle Logistics (ECG, #02551); *CLECAT (#03993)*; *Community of European Railway and Infrastructure Companies (CER, #04396)*; *European Automobile Manufacturers' Association (ACEA, #06300)*; *European Cold Storage and Logistics Association (ECSLA, #06603)*; *European Rail Freight Association (ERFA, #08323)*; *European Shippers' Council (ESC, #08477)*; *Federation of European Private Port Companies and Terminals (FEPORT, #09531)*; *International Road Transport Union (IRU, #14761)*; *International Union for Combined Road – Rail Transport (UIRR, #15765)*; *Nordic Logistics Association (NLA, #17338)*.
NGO Relations *European Technology Platform ALICE (ALICE, #08888)*. [2020/XM6876/y/**F**]

♦ European Long-Term Ecosystem Research Network (LTER-Europe) . 07712

Secretariat c/o ERCE, c/o UNESCO Intl Inst of Polish Academy of Sciences, 3 Tylna St, 90-364 Lódz, Poland. T. +48426817007. Fax +48426813069. E-mail: secretariat@ltereurope.net – kingak@biol.uni.lodz.pl.
URL: http://www.lter-europe.net/
History Set up, 2007, Hungary, with the help of *Alternet (#00756)*. A section of *International Long-Term Ecological Research Network (ILTER, #14065)*. **Aims** Track and understand the effects of global, regional and local changes on socio-ecological systems and their feedbacks to environment and society; provide recommendations and support for solving current and future environmental problems. **Structure** Coordinating Committee; Executive Committee; Chair and Vice-Chair. **Events** *Global Workshop on Long-Term Observatories of Mountain Social-Ecological Systems* Reno, NV (USA) 2014, *Annual Conference* Rome (Italy) 2013, *Conference* Rome (Italy) 2013, *EnvEurope Final Conference* Rome (Italy) 2013, *Annual Conference / Conference* Sofia (Bulgaria) 2012.
Members National networks in 21 countries:
Austria, Bulgaria, Czechia, Finland, France, Germany, Hungary, Israel, Italy, Latvia, Lithuania, Poland, Portugal, Romania, Serbia, Slovakia, Slovenia, Spain, Sweden, Switzerland, UK.
NGO Relations Cooperates with: *International Cooperative Programme on Integrated Monitoring of Air Pollution Effects on Ecosystems (ICP-IM, #12951)*. [2014/XJ8587/**E**]

♦ European Long-Term Investors / see European Association of Long-Term Investors (#06112)
♦ European Lotteries / see European State Lotteries and Toto Association (#08833)
♦ European Lotteries Sports (inactive)
♦ European Lotto Betting Association (unconfirmed)

♦ European Low Fares Airline Association (ELFAA) 07713

SG 46 Av des Arts, 1000 Brussels, Belgium. T. +3225049005. Fax +3227327136.
URL: http://www.elfaa.com/
History Founded 2003. **Aims** Represent and protect the needs of low fare airlines and their customers; ensure that European policy and legislation promote free and equal competition to enable the continued growth and development of low fares into the future, allowing a greater number of people to travel by air. **Structure** General Meeting (annual); Executive Committee. Working Groups (6): Airports; Airspace; Consumer Affairs; Environment; Safety; Security. **Activities** Politics/policy/regulatory; advocacy/lobbying/activism. **Events** *World regional and low cost airports congress* Berlin (Germany) 2006, *Asia Pacific aviation summit* Brisbane, QLD (Australia) 2006, *World regional airports congress* Amsterdam (Netherlands) 2005.
Publications *York Aviation: Market Share of Low Fares Airlines in Europe* (2011); *Frontier Economics: Impact of emissions trading on pricing and profits in aviation: review of Vivid Economics reports* (2008); *Ernst and Young and York Aviation: Analysis of the EC Proposal to Include Aviation Activities in the Emissions Trading Scheme* (2007); *York Aviation: Social Benefits of Low Fares Airlines in Europe* (2007); *Frontier Economics: Economic consideration of extending the EU ETS to include aviation* (2006); *Liberalisation of European Air Transport: The Benefits of Low Fares Airlines to Consumers, Airports, Regions and the Environment* (2004). Position papers.
Members Airlines in 7 countries:
Hungary, Ireland, Netherlands, Norway, Spain, Sweden, UK.
NGO Relations Member of: *Council for Environmentally Friendly Aviation (CEFA, #04880)*.
[2015/XM0380/**D**]

♦ European Low Grade Glioma Network (ELGGN) 07714

Address not obtained.
History 2007. **Aims** Stimulate research and management of diffuse low grade gliomas. **Activities** Events/meetings. **Events** *European Low Grade Glioma Network Meeting* London (UK) 2019, *Meeting* Lisbon (Portugal) 2018. [2020/XM7957/c/**F**]

♦ European Low Gravity Research Association (ELGRA) 07715

Pres Microgravity Lab – Dept of Physics, Univ Politècnica de Catalunya-Barcelona Tech, c/E. Terradas 5, 08860 Barcelona, Spain. T. +34934134153. Fax +34934137007.
SG Science Services Div, Swedish Space Corporation, Torggatan 15, SE-171 04 Solna, Sweden. T. +4686276289. Fax +468987069.
URL: http://www.elgra.org/
History 9 Sep 1979, Munich (Germany). Founded under the auspices of *Council of Europe (CE, #04881)* and *European Space Agency (ESA, #08798)*. Registration: No/ID: VR9702, Germany. **Aims** Encourage and promote research in Europe using micro and hyper gravity condition for investigation of gravitational effects in various phenomena and technological processes. **Structure** General Assembly (every 2 years); Management Committee. **Languages** English. **Staff** None. **Finance** Sources: donations; fees for services; members' dues. Supported by: *European Space Agency (ESA, #08798)*. **Activities** Events/meetings; research and development; training/education. **Events** *Biennial Symposium* Granada (Spain) 2019, *Biennial Symposium* Juan-les-Pins (France) 2017, *Biennial Symposium* Corfu (Greece) 2015, *Biennial Symposium* Vatican City (Vatican) 2013, *Biennial Symposium* Antwerp (Belgium) 2011. **Publications** *ELGRA Newsletter* (every 2 years).

Members Full; Associate. Regular (individual) and corporate members in 29 countries:
Australia, Austria, Belgium, Brazil, Canada, China, Czechia, Denmark, France, Germany, Greece, Hungary, India, Ireland, Italy, Japan, Lithuania, Netherlands, Norway, Portugal, Romania, Russia, Slovakia, Spain, Sweden, Switzerland, UK, Ukraine, USA.
[2020.06.07/XD8539/**D**]

♦ European Lubricating Grease Institute (ELGI) 07716

Office Manager Hemonylaan 26, 1074 BJ Amsterdam, Netherlands. T. +31206716162. Fax +31206732760.
URL: http://www.elgi.org/
History Founded May 1989. **Aims** Promote understanding of all matters concerning lubricating grease and it associate products; facilitate the exchange of information concerning design, manufacture and use. **Structure** General Meeting (annual); Board of Directors; Working Groups (7). **Languages** English. **Staff** 1.00 FTE, paid. **Finance** Members' dues. **Activities** Standards/guidelines; events/meetings. **Events** *Meeting* Hamburg (Germany) 2020, *Annual General Meeting* Athens (Greece) 2019, *Annual General Meeting* London (UK) 2018, *Annual General Meeting* Helsinki (Finland) 2017, *Annual General Meeting* Venice (Italy) 2016. **Publications** *Eurogrease* (4 a year) – digital magazine. **Members** Full in 25 countries. Membership countries not specified.
[2019.12.11/XE4723/j/**E**]

♦ European Lumbar Spinal Centre (internationally oriented national body)

♦ European Lung Cancer Working Party (ELCWP) 07717

Pres Inst Jules Bordet – Serv de Cancérologie Pulmonaire, Rue Meylemmersch 90, 1070 Brussels, Belgium. T. +32025413191.
History 1989, Brussels (Belgium). Registration: Banque-Carrefour des Entreprises, No/ID: 0438.167.608, Start date: 17 Aug 1989, Belgium. **Aims** Encourage and develop European cooperation in the field of research on lung cancer; facilitate, in the framework of the European Union, by all appropriate means, cooperation between *physicians* and *scientists* in various fields related to the lung cancer research. **Structure** General Assembly (at least annually); Management Board; Executive Committee; Committees. **Languages** English, French. **Finance** Sources: members' dues. **Activities** Events/meetings; research/documentation. **Events** *World conference on clinical cooperative research* Brussels (Belgium) 2006, *General Assembly* Brussels (Belgium) 2004, *Workshop* Brussels (Belgium) 2004, *Workshop* Brussels (Belgium) 2004, *Workshop* Mons (Belgium) 2004.
Members Full; Adhering; Corresponding; Sponsoring. Members in 4 countries:
Belgium, France, Greece, Spain.
NGO Relations Member of (2): *European Thoracic Oncology Platform (ETOP, #08910)*; *Federation of European and International Associations Established in Belgium (FAIB, #09508)*. [2022.06.21/XF1068/**F**]

♦ European Lung Foundation (ELF) 07718

Head 442 Glossop Road, Sheffield, S10 2PX, UK. T. +441142672876. E-mail: info@europeanlung.org.
Brussels Office Rue de Trèves 49-51, 1040 Brussels, Belgium. T. +3222385360.
URL: http://www.europeanlung.org/
History 2000. Founded by *European Respiratory Society (ERS, #08383)*. Registration: Companies House, No/ID: 05718525, Start date: 22 Feb 2006, England and Wales; Charity Commission, No/ID: 1118930, England and Wales; Banque-Carrefour des Entreprises, No/ID: 0738.383.695, Start date: 25 Nov 2019, Belgium; EU Transparency Register, No/ID: 094039644810-79, Start date: 30 Nov 2021. **Aims** Share knowledge and expertise of the ERS with lung patients and the general public across Europe with the aim of bringing together patients, the public and respiratory professionals to positively influence respiratory medicine; ensure that people with lung diseases and the general public have the opportunity to influence respiratory research and guidelines at the European level. **Structure** Council. Advisory Committees (2): Professional; Patient. **Languages** English, French, German, Irish Gaelic, Italian, Polish, Portuguese, Russian, Spanish. **Staff** 7.00 FTE, paid. **Finance** Sources: donations. Supported by: *European Respiratory Society (ERS, #08383)*. **Activities** Advocacy/lobbying/activism; awards/prizes/competitions; research and development. **Events** *European PF Patient Summit* Gentbrugge (Belgium) 2021. **Publications** Patient fact sheets (currently 57) on lung health and disease topics. **Members** Not a membership organization. **NGO Relations** Member of (3): *EURORDIS – Rare Diseases Europe (#09175)* (Associate member); *Health and Environment Alliance (HEAL, #10879)*; *International Alliance of Patients' Organizations (IAPO, #11633)*. Cooperates with (1): *European Foundation for the Care of Newborn Infants (EFCNI, #07344)*. [2021.06.14/XM2069/f/**E**]

♦ European Lupus Erythematosus Federation / see LUPUS EUROPE (#16524)

♦ European Lupus Society (SLEuro) 07719

Pres Via Giuseppe Ripamonti 129, 20141 Milan MI, Italy. T. +392566011. Fax +39270048578. E-mail: sleurosecretariat@aimgroup.eu.
URL: https://sleuro.org/
History 30 Sep 2016, Venice (Italy). Founded a few days before the 10th European Lupus Meeting, in order to establish a solid infrastructure for European Lupus meetings and community with a social and philanthropic purposes. Registration: Italy. **Aims** Build up a community of clinicians and researchers interested in SLE at European and international levels, with special focus to engage younger physicians in the field; promote and coordinate the organization of research and educational meetings on SLE and related *syndromes*; promote equal access to best standard of care for SLE *patients* across Europe; facilitate research projects and clinical trials in SLE. **Structure** General Assembly; Executive Committee; Officers; Secretariat. **Languages** English. **Finance** Sources: meeting proceeds; sponsorship. **Activities** Events/meetings; research/documentation; training/education. **Events** *European Lupus Meeting* Lisbon (Portugal) 2026, *European Lupus Meeting* Bruges (Belgium) 2024, *European Lupus Meeting* Stockholm (Sweden) 2022, *European Lupus Meeting* Bruges (Belgium) 2020, *European Lupus Meeting* Düsseldorf (Germany) 2018. **Publications** *Sleuro Today*.
Members Worldwide membership, but mainly in 10 countries:
Croatia, Germany, India, Italy, Netherlands, Portugal, Spain, Sweden, UK, USA. [2023.01.13/XM7384/**D**]

♦ European Maccabi Confederation (EMC) 07720

Dir MWU Euro Desk, Kfar Maccabiah, 52105 Ramat Gan, Israel.
URL: http://www.maccabieurope.com/
History Founded in 1947, Switzerland.
Members Full in 27 countries and territories:
Austria, Belgium, Bulgaria, Croatia, Czechia, Denmark, Estonia, Finland, France, Germany, Gibraltar, Greece, Hungary, Ireland, Italy, Latvia, Lithuania, Netherlands, Norway, Poland, Romania, Serbia, Slovakia, Spain, Sweden, Switzerland, UK.
Also members in the Commonwealth of Independent States; membership countries not specified.
NGO Relations Member of: *Maccabi World Union (MWU, #16537)*. [2017/XD4820/**D**]

♦ European Machine Vision Association (EMVA) 07721

Main Office Gran Via de Carles III 84, 08028 Barcelona, Spain. T. +34931807060. Fax +34931807060. E-mail: info@emva.org.
URL: http://www.emva.org/
History 24 May 2003, Barcelona (Spain). **Aims** Ensure that imaging and machine vision technology is widely applied throughout all industry sectors, manufacturing and non-manufacturing. **Structure** Board. **Languages** English. **Staff** 2.50 FTE, paid. **Finance** Members' dues. **Activities** Knowledge management/information dissemination; standards/guidelines; liaising/networking; events/meetings. **Events** *Conference / Business Conference* Brussels (Belgium) 2022, *Conference* Copenhagen (Denmark) 2019, *Forum* Bologna (Italy) 2018, *Conference* Dubrovnik (Croatia) 2018, *Embedded Vision European Conference* Stuttgart (Germany) 2018.
Publications *Monthly EMVA Newsletter*.
Members Companies (105), national organizations (5) and research institutes (3). Members in 22 countries:
Belgium, Canada, China, Denmark, Finland, France, Germany, India, Ireland, Italy, Japan, Korea Rep, Netherlands, Norway, Russia, Slovenia, Spain, Sweden, Switzerland, Taiwan, UK, USA. [2021/XD9437/**D**]

♦ European Macrophage and Dendritic Cell Society (EMDS) 07722

Pres Internal Medicine VI, Medical Univ, Anichstr 35, 6020 Innsbruck, Austria. T. +4351250423251.
URL: http://www.macrophage.de/

History 1992, as *European Macrophage Study Group (EMSG)*. Name changed to *European Macrophage Society (EMS)*, 28 Apr 1999. Present name adopted 2000. **Aims** Promote studies in the field of macrophage and dendritic cell biology with respect to both basic and clinical research; provide a forum for interdisciplinary exchange of knowledge and concepts in the field of macrophages, dendritic cells and other myeloid cells; accelerate development and clinical application of new therapeutic strategies; improve and support training of young researchers; establish student exchange program. **Structure** Annual Meeting; Council; Advisory Board. **Languages** English. **Staff** None. **Finance** Members' dues. **Activities** Awards/prizes/competitions. **Events** *Annual Conference* Aarhus (Denmark) 2021, *Annual Conference* Aarhus (Denmark) 2020, *Annual Conference* Marseille (France) 2019, *Annual Conference* Verona (Italy) 2018, *Annual Conference* Madrid (Spain) 2017. **Publications** Abstract booklet of annual meeting (annual).
Members Corporate in 3 countries:
Belgium, France, Germany.
Individuals in 32 countries and territories:
Australia, Austria, Belgium, Brazil, Canada, Czechia, Denmark, France, Georgia, Germany, Hungary, India, Iran Islamic Rep, Israel, Italy, Japan, Korea Rep, Luxembourg, Montenegro, Netherlands, Norway, Poland, Russia, Serbia, Slovenia, Spain, Sweden, Switzerland, Türkiye, UK, Ukraine, USA. [2016/XE2632/v/**D**]

♦ European Macrophage Society / see European Macrophage and Dendritic Cell Society (#07722)
♦ European Macrophage Study Group / see European Macrophage and Dendritic Cell Society (#07722)

♦ European Magazine Media Association (EMMA) 07723

Exec Dir Rue de Namur 73-A, 1000 Brussels, Belgium. T. +3225360600. Fax +3225510199. E-mail: info@magazinemedia.eu.
URL: http://www.magazinemedia.eu/

History May 1975. Former names and other names: *Federation of Associations of Periodical Publishers in EC* – former (1975 to 1988); *Fédération des associations d'éditeurs de périodiques de la CE* – former (1975 to 1988); *European Magazine Publishers Federation* – former (1988 to 2012); *Fédération européenne d'éditeurs de périodiques (FAEP)* – former (1988 to 2012). Registration: Banque-Carrefour des Entreprises, No/ID: 0423.348.976, Start date: 29 Nov 1982, Belgium; EU Transparency Register, No/ID: 37937886834-69, Start date: 29 Sep 2011. **Aims** Represent periodical publishers' interests to the institutions of the *European Union*, specifically Council, Commission and Parliament, so that legislative measures enhance members' financial health, and do not damage it; provide to members a resource of information, guidance and expertise, so that they may create and implement more effective national representation for their own national members. **Structure** Board; Executive Committee; Secretariat, headed by Executive Director. **Languages** English. **Staff** 5.00 FTE, paid. **Finance** Sources: members' dues. **Activities** Monitoring/evaluation; research/documentation. **Events** *The future of content* Brussels (Belgium) 2014, *Conference* Brussels (Belgium) 2010, *Meeting* Brussels (Belgium) 2005.
Members National and International associations in 17 countries:
Austria, Belgium, Croatia, Czechia, Denmark, Finland, France, Germany, Greece, Ireland, Netherlands, Norway, Poland, Portugal, Spain, Sweden, UK.
Association for the Promotion of the International Circulation of the Press (DISTRIPRESS, #02876); *European Business Press (EBP, #06423)*; *FIPP (#09776)*.
IGO Relations Accredited by (2): *European Commission (EC, #06633)*; *European Parliament (EP, #08146)*. **NGO Relations** Member of (5): *Creative Media Business Alliance (CMBA, #04947)*; *Ethical Journalism Network (EJN, #05554)*; *European Advertising Standards Alliance (EASA, #05829)*; *European Interactive Digital Advertising Alliance (EDAA, #07582)*; *International Federation of Reproduction Rights Organizations (IFRRO, #13527)*. Partner of (1): *Advertising Information Group (AIG, #00137)*. Cooperates with (1): *Search and Information Industry Association (Siinda, #19188)*. [2021.06.09/XE5156/y/**E**]

♦ European Magazine Publishers Federation / see European Magazine Media Association (#07723)
♦ European Magistrates for Democracy and Liberties (#16546)

♦ European Magnetic Resonance Forum Foundation (EMRF Foundation) 07724

Pres address not obtained. E-mail: maindesk@emrf.org.
URL: http://www.trtf.eu/emrf.htm/

History 1982, as *European Workshop on Magnetic Resonance in Medicine*. Present name adopted 1991. Currently a chapter of *The Round Table Foundation (TRTF, #18981)*. **Aims** Promote continuing education, exchange of information, research, development and application in the field of magnetic resonance in *medicine*, *natural sciences* and *computer sciences*; support application of this technology to benefit environment and development of needy areas of the world. **Structure** Board; Humanitarian Branch directly supporting aid projects, at present in South America. **Languages** English. **Finance** Sponsorship fund raising. **Activities** Events/meetings; training/education; awards/prizes/competitions. **Events** *Biennial Conference* Valencia (Spain) 2013, *Meeting* Valencia (Spain) 2012, *Biennial conference / Meeting* Mons (Belgium) 2010, *Biennial conference / Meeting* Valencia (Spain) 2008, *Round table on appropriate use and ethics of medical imaging / Meeting* Berlin (Germany) / Potsdam (Germany) 2007. **Publications** *Rinckside*. *Magnetic Resonance in Medicine* – e-Learning textbook. **Members** Not a membership organization. [2019.12.11/XF5243/f/**F**]

♦ European Magnetism Association (EMA) 07725

Pres address not obtained. E-mail: ema@magnetism.eu.
URL: http://magnetism.eu/

History Aug 2016, Glasgow (UK). Based on 2 European collaborative actions: *Joint European Magnetic Symposium (JEMS)* and *European School of Magnetism (ESM)*. **Aims** Promote development of magnetism and magnetic materials in Europe through raising visibility and impact of research on fundamental and applied magnetism. **Structure** General Council; Executive Board; Focused Committees. **Languages** English. **Staff** 40.00 FTE, paid. **Finance** Sources: meeting proceeds; revenue from activities/projects. Annual budget: 100,000 EUR. **Activities** Events/meetings; knowledge management/information dissemination; networking/liaising; publishing activities. **Events** *JEMS : Joint European Magnetic Symposium* Warsaw (Poland) 2022, *JEMS : Joint European Magnetic Symposium* Lisbon (Portugal) 2020. **Publications** *EMA Newsletter*. Symposium proceedings.
Members National societies in 6 countries:
Denmark, Italy, Russia, Slovakia, Spain, UK.
NGO Relations Memorandum of Understanding with (3): *Asian Union of Magnetics Societies (AUMS, #01772)*; *European Physical Society (EPS, #08207)*; *IEEE Magnetics Society*. Cooperates with (1): *European Institute of Molecular Magnetism (EIMM, #07566)*. [2022.05.12/XM5161/**D**]

♦ European Mail and Express Services Users' Association (inactive)
♦ European Maize Milling Industry / see Euromaisiers (#05709)

♦ European Major Exhibition Centres Association (EMECA) 07726

Association des grands parcs d'expositions européens
SG Rue de l'Amazone 2, 1050 Brussels, Belgium. T. +3225357250. Fax +3225349696.
URL: http://www.emeca.eu/

History 30 Jan 1992, Paris (France). Founded on approval of Charter at Constituent General Assembly, following decision of a meeting, 19 Sep 1991, Madrid (Spain). Registration: Belgium; France. **Aims** Focus attention on the impact of the exhibition industry in Europe; highlight the role of trade fairs in the forefront of marketing activity; demonstrate how effective exhibition venues focus attention on newly developing market sectors; bring together and represent the views of European exhibition centres, share experience and carry out technical studies so as best to respond to clients' needs; improve technical and commercial information on fairs and exhibitions in Europe; dialogue with the European Union and with interested professional associations. **Structure** General Assembly (2 a year); Administration in Paris (France). **Languages** English, French, German. **Staff** 0.50 FTE, paid. **Finance** Members' dues. Budget (annual): euro 100,000. **Activities** Research/documentation. **Events** *General Assembly* Milan (Italy) 2015, *General Assembly* Lisbon (Portugal) 2014, *General Assembly* Moscow (Russia) 2014, *General Assembly* Brussels (Belgium) 2013, *General Assembly* Madrid (Spain) 2013. **Publications** *EMECA Dialogue* – newsletter. Annual report/review of business; members' directory.
Members Exhibition centres with an area of more than 100,000 sq metres, with a strong investment policy and a strong international orientation in their activities. Members (19) in 8 countries:
Belgium, France (3), Germany (3), Italy (4), Netherlands, Spain (3), Switzerland (2), UK.
NGO Relations Member of: *Joint Meetings Industry Council (JMIC, #16140)*; [2019/XD2564/**D**]

♦ European Malacological Union / see Unitas Malacologica (#20495)

♦ European Malignant Hyperthermia Group (EMHG) 07727

Sec Molecular Med Inst, St James's Univ Hosp, Leeds, LS9 7TF, UK.
URL: http://www.emhg.org/

History 1983. **Aims** Provide a forum for discussion among European malignant hyperthermia centres; improve, maintain and update the quality of diagnostic standards of malignant hyperthermia susceptibility in Europe. **Structure** Executive Committee, comprising President, Chairman, Secretary, Treasurer and 3 further members. **Finance** Members' dues. **Events** *Annual Meeting* Ulm (Germany) 2016, *Annual Meeting* Lille (France) 2015, *Annual Meeting* Würzburg (Germany) 2014, *Annual Meeting* Basel (Switzerland) 2013, *Annual Meeting* Leeds (UK) 2012.
Members Individuals and organizations in 17 countries:
Australia, Austria, Belgium, Brazil, Denmark, France, Germany, Iceland, Ireland, Italy, Netherlands, New Zealand, Norway, South Africa, Sweden, Switzerland, UK. [2014/XE4586/**E**]

♦ European Malt Extract Manufacturers Association / see European Malt Product Manufacturers Association (#07728)
♦ European Malt Product Association / see European Malt Product Manufacturers Association (#07728)

♦ European Malt Product Manufacturers Association 07728

Gen Sec 2a Newry Avenue, Felixstowe, IP11 7SA, UK. T. +441394271713. E-mail: reah.emma@btinternet.com.
URL: http://maltproductsassociationeurope.org/

History 1975, as *European Malt Extract Manufacturers Association*. Previously also referred to as *European Malt Product Association*.
Members Full in 4 countries:
Finland, Germany, Netherlands, UK. [2015/XD6045/**D**]

♦ European Managed Futures Association / see Alternative Investment Management Association (#00752)
♦ European Management Assistants / see International Management Assistants (#14081)

♦ European Management Association (EMA) 07729

Exec Sec c/o Hellenic Management Assn, 200 Ioniais Ave and Iakovaton St, 111 44 Athens, Greece. T. +302102112000 ext 405. Fax +3021021120201. E-mail: secretariat@europeanmanagement.org.
URL: https://europeanmanagement.org/

History 1956, as *European Council of Management (CECIOS)*, as one of the 5 Regional Councils of *World Council of Management (CIOS, inactive)*. New name adopted, 2001. Registered in accordance with Dutch law. **Aims** Promote excellence in management in Europe by stimulating business and mutual understanding. **Structure** Assembly (at least annual); Executive Committee; Secretariat. **Finance** Members' dues. **Activities** Research and development. **Events** *European Management Conference* Athens (Greece) 2014, *Annual Assembly* London (UK) 2014, *Annual Assembly* Eschborn (Germany) 2013, *Annual Assembly* Prague (Czech Rep) 2012, *Annual Assembly* London (UK) 2011. **Publications** Promotional leaflet; information packs; research reports.
Members National management organizations (representative of management of the country) in 14 countries:
Bulgaria, Czechia, France, Germany, Greece, Israel, Italy, Lithuania, Malta, Netherlands, Poland, Romania, Spain, UK.
Included in the above, 1 organization listed in this Yearbook:
Baltic Management Foundation (BMF, #03124). [2018.06.01/XE3560/y/**E**]

♦ European Management Development Centre, Huizen (internationally oriented national body)
♦ European Management Forum / see World Economic Forum (#21367)
♦ European Management Office for Veterinary Associations (internationally oriented national body)
♦ European Management Symposium / see World Economic Forum (#21367)
♦ European Manager Institute (internationally oriented national body)
♦ European Managers Federation of Technologies of Information and Communication / see European Federation for Managers in Technologies of Information and Communication (#07163)

♦ European Managers in the Transport Industry 07730

Fédération internationale des cadres des transports (FICT) – Internationaler Verband der Führungskrafte des Verkehrswesens
Contact 59-63 Rue du Rocher, 75008 Paris, France.
URL: http://fict.in/

History 29 Sep 1970, under the aegis of Transport Directorate of the Commission of the European Communities, currently European Commission. **Aims** Study problems referring to the transport and *tourism* sectors and their related activities; propose solutions to satisfy the needs for populations from the point of view of progress, by taking into account the economic, social, safety and environmental factors; promote the defence of professional interests of supervisory staff and search and proposal for any measure aiming at improving conditions of its existence. **Languages** English, French. **Staff** 8.00 FTE, paid. **Finance** Members' dues. **Publications** *Breves Transport* (10 a year); *FICT Newsletter* in English, French.
Members Organizations in 8 countries:
Belgium, Denmark, France, Italy, Spain, Sweden, Switzerland, UK.
NGO Relations Professional federation member of: *CEC European Managers (#03623)*. Liaison Organization of: *Comité européen de normalisation (CEN, #04162)*. [2017/XD9529/t/**D**]

♦ European Manufactured Marble Association (inactive)

♦ European Manufacturers of Autogenous Vaccines and Sera (EMAV) 07731

Acting Managing Dir Geyerspergerstr 27, 80689 Munich, Germany. E-mail: info@emav.be.
URL: https://www.emav.be/en/

History 1 Nov 2018, Hannover (Germany). Registration: No/ID: VR 207990, Start date: 6 Feb 2019, Germany, Munich; EU Transparency Register, No/ID: 224469535841-56, Start date: 9 Sep 2019. **Aims** Represent the common interests of officially recognized manufacturers of autogenous vaccines and antisera for animals. **Structure** General Assembly; Board; General Manager; Working Groups. **Languages** English. **Publications** Position papers.
Members in 12 countries:
Austria, Belgium, France, Germany, Greece, Hungary, Ireland, Italy, Netherlands, Poland, Spain, UK. [2022.04.12/AA1203/**D**]

♦ European Manufacturers of EPS / see European Manufacturers of Expanded Polystyrene (#07732)

♦ European Manufacturers of Expanded Polystyrene (EUMEPS) 07732

Acting Managing Dir Avenue Cortenbergh 71, 1000 Brussels, Belgium. E-mail: info@eumeps.org.
URL: http://www.eumeps.org/

History 1989. Former names and other names: *European Manufacturers of EPS* – alias. Registration: Banque Carrefour des Entreprises, No/ID: 0453.127.976, Start date: 19 Aug 1994, Belgium; EU Transparency Register, No/ID: 02100645398-66, Start date: 28 Feb 2011. **Aims** Represent the interests of Europe's leading manufacturers of expanded polystyrene (EPS); engage with policy and regulatory audiences on behalf of the entire EPS value chain. **Structure** General Assembly (annual); Administrative Council; Sections (3); Secretariat. **Languages** English. **Staff** 5.00 FTE, paid. **Finance** Members' dues. Industry commitment. **Activities** Events/meetings; knowledge management/information dissemination; networking/liaising. **Events** *Packaging conference* Pörtschach (Austria) 2002, *Conference* Barcelona (Spain) 1998, *Conference* Rome (Italy) 1996. **Publications** Documents available on website.
Members Effective: national associations. Associate: individuals and organizations. Members, whether of Construction and/or Packaging Sections, in 22 countries:
Austria, Belgium, Czechia, Denmark, Finland, France, Germany, Greece, Hungary, Ireland, Italy, Lithuania, Netherlands, Norway, Poland, Portugal, Romania, Slovakia, Spain, Sweden, Türkiye, UK.
IGO Relations Partner of (2): *European Chemicals Agency (ECHA, #06523)*; *European Food Safety Authority (EFSA, #07287)*. **NGO Relations** Member of (6): *Asian Manufacturers of Expanded Polystyrene (AMEPS, #01534)*; *Circular Plastics Alliance (#03936)*; *Construction Products Europe AISBL (#04761)* (Associate); *European Association for External Thermal Insulation Composite Systems (EAE, #06035)*; *Industry4Europe (#11181)*; *Modern Building Alliance (#16842)*. Partner of (4): *Association of Plastics Manufacturers in Europe (Plastics Europe, #02862)*; *European Plastics Converters (EuPC, #08216)*; *PolyStyreneLoop Cooperative (PS Loop)*; *Styrenics Circular Solutions (SCS, #20022)*. Environmental committee liaises with technical committees of: *Comité européen de normalisation (CEN, #04162)*; *European Organisation for Technical Assessment (EOTA, #08103)*; *International Organization for Standardization (ISO, #14473)*. [2022/XD2957/**D**]

♦ **European Manufacturers of Feed Minerals Association (EMFEMA)** . 07733

Association européenne des minéraux pour l'alimentation animale

SG Rue de la Loi 223/3, 1040 Brussels, Belgium. E-mail: info@emfema.org.
Pres address not obtained.
URL: http://www.emfema.org/

History Former names and other names: *International Association of the European Manufacturers of Major, Trace and Specific Feed Materials* – former (1996); *Association of the European Manufacturers of Feed Mineral Materials (EMFEMA)* – former (May 1996 to Apr 2013). Registration: Banque-Carrefour des Entreprises, Belgium. **Aims** Work for a continuous improvement of quality, safety and efficacy in animal feeding; be a platform for exchange and cooperation between companies producing and using mineral feed materials and additives. **Structure** General Assembly. **Languages** English. **Finance** Membership contributions. **NGO Relations** Member of (1): *Fédération européenne des fabricants d'aliments composés pour animaux (FEFAC, #09566)*. Liaison Organization of: *Comité européen de normalisation (CEN, #04162)*.
[2021.02.18/XD7571/**D**]

♦ European Manufacturers Paper Honeycomb Association (unconfirmed)

♦ **European Manufacturing and Innovation Research Association (EMIRAcle)** 07734

Admin Office 46 avenue Félix Viallet, 38031 Grenoble CEDEX 1, France. T. +33476574744. Fax +33476574695.
Head Office Chez Delegation General Rhône Alpes, Rue du Trône 62, Boite 6, 1050 Brussels, Belgium.

History Statutes adopted 14 Jan 2008. Registered in accordance with Belgian law. **Aims** Act as a collaboration partner for European product development enterprises in manufacturing and innovation research, so as to maintain and improve their leading positions worldwide by increasing productivity and innovation power. **Structure** General Assembly; Directory Board; Orientation Board. **Staff** 3.00 FTE, paid. **Finance** Members' dues. Grants for involvement in EU projects. **Activities** Training/education; Research and documentation. **Members** Full; Associated. Members in 14 countries:
France, Germany, Greece, Hungary, Israel, Italy, Netherlands, Poland, Romania, Slovenia, South Africa, Spain, Sweden, Thailand.
IGO Relations *European Commission (EC, #06633)* – DG Research. **NGO Relations** Member of: *European Certification and Qualification Association (ECQA, #06511)*. [2014.09.11/XJ8668/**F**]

♦ **European Marches Against Unemployment, Job Insecurity and Social Exclusions (Euromarches)** 07735

Marches européennes contre le chômage, la précarité et les exclusions – Marchas Europeas Contra el Paro, la Precariedad y la Exclusión – Euromärsche gegen Erwerbslosigkeit, Ungeschützte Beschäftigung und Ausgrenzung – Euromarsen Tegen Werkloosheid, Armoede en Sociale Uitsluiting – Europeiske Marche Imod Arbejdsløsighed Usikkre Jobs og Udstødelse

No fixed address address not obtained.
URL: http://www.euromarches.org/

History 1997. A network of organizations and trade unions. **Aims** Fight against unemployment, insecure jobs and other forms of discrimination as a result of globalization and deregulation. **Activities** Events/meetings. **NGO Relations** Member of: *World Social Forum (WSF, #21797)*. Signatory to: *Alter Summit*.
[2019/XJ4225/**F**]

♦ European Marfan Support Network / see Marfan Europe Network (#16573)

♦ **European Margarine Association (IMACE)** 07736

Acting Managing Dir Ave de Tervuren 168, Bte 12, 1150 Brussels, Belgium. T. +3227223353. Fax +3227714753. E-mail: info@imace.org.
URL: http://www.imace.org/

History 18 Sep 1958, Brussels (Belgium). Former names and other names: *Association of the Margarine Industry of the EC Countries* – former; *Association des industries margarinières des pays de la CE* – former; *Asociación de las Industrias de Margarina de los Paises de la CE* – former; *Vereinigung der Margarine-Industrie der EG-Länder* – former; *Associação da Indústria de Margarinas dos Paises da CE* – former; *Associazione della Industria Margariniera dei Paesi della CE* – former; *Vereniging van de Margarine-Industrie der EG Landen* – former; *Foreningen af Margarine-Industrier i EF-Landene* – former; *Sindesmos Viamihanion Margarinis Horon Evropaikis Kinonitas* – former; *International Margarine Association of the Countries of Europe (IMACE)* – former; *Association internationale des industries margarinières des pays d'Europe* – former. Registration: Banque-Carrefour des Entreprises, No/ID: 0465.823.001, Start date: 6 May 1999, Belgium; EU Transparency Register, No/ID: 580415127070-95, Start date: 5 May 2017. **Aims** Represent the interests of the European margarine industry with *European Union* institutions. **Structure** General Assembly; Executive Committee; Council of Experts. **Languages** English, French. **Staff** 2.50 FTE, paid. **Finance** Sources: members' dues. **Events** *Annual General Meeting* Brussels (Belgium) 2015, *Annual General Meeting* Brussels (Belgium) 2014, *Annual Congress* Stockholm (Sweden) 2002, *Congress* Vienna (Austria) 2001, *Annual Congress* Paris (France) 1994.
Members Associations in 22 countries:
Austria, Belgium, Czechia, Denmark, Finland, France, Germany, Greece, Hungary, Ireland, Italy, Netherlands, Norway, Poland, Portugal, Romania, Slovakia, Spain, Sweden, Switzerland, Türkiye, UK.
IGO Relations Recognized by: *European Commission (EC, #06633)*. **NGO Relations** Affiliated member of: *FoodDrinkEurope (#09841)*. [2020/XE0150/**D**]

♦ European Mariculture Society / see European Aquaculture Society (#05909)

♦ **European Marine Biological Resource Centre (EMBRC-ERIC)** 07737

Paris Headquarters 4 Place Jussieu, 75252 Paris, France. T. +33144276337. E-mail: secretariat@embrc.eu.
URL: http://www.embrc.eu/

History Preparatory phase: 2011-2014. Memorandum of Understanding came into effect Dec 2013. Implementation phase: Jan 2014-Dec 2017. Operational since 2018. Established as a legal structure in the form of a *European Research Infrastructure Consortium (ERIC)*, 20 Feb 2018. **Aims** Deliver services to the marine community and increasing numbers of scientists who have turned to marine model organisms to investigate fundamental questions in biology; provide key facilities, equipment and services to: access and study marine ecosystems and biodiversity; develop key enabling technologies; deliver training and joint development activities for staff and users to improve access to marine biological resources and marine models. **Structure** Implementation Board. **Finance** Sources: contributions of member/participating states. **Activities** Events/meetings; guidance/assistance/consulting; knowledge management/information dissemination; research and development; training/education. **Information Services** *E-Infrastructure and Data Services* – Datasets of sequences, metadata, historical time series and literature resources on marine research.
Members Governments having signed the Memorandum of Understanding (9):
Belgium, France, Greece, Israel, Italy, Norway, Portugal, Spain, UK.
Stations (13) in 9 countries:
Belgium, France, Greece, Israel, Italy, Norway, Portugal, Spain, UK. [2022/XJ8485/**E***]

♦ **European Marine Board (EMB)** 07738

Exec Dir Jacobsenstraat 1, 8400 Ostend, Belgium. T. +3259336924. E-mail: info@marineboard.eu.
URL: https://www.marineboard.eu/

History Oct 1995. Founded under the auspices of *European Science Foundation (ESF, #08441)*. Together with *European Polar Board (EPB, #08238)*, replaces *European Boards for Marine and Polar Science (EMaPS Boards, inactive)* and *European Secretariat for Marine and Polar Science (EMaPS, inactive)*. Since 2016, an independent organization. Became fully independent of ESF since 1 Jan 2017. Former names and other names: *Marine Board – ESF* – former; *EMB-IVZW* – alias. Registration: Banque-Carrefour des Entreprises, No/ID: 0650.608.890, Start date: 20 Jan 2016, Belgium; EU Transparency Register, No/ID: 571994418695-46, Start date: 8 Sep 2015. **Aims** Provide a pan-European platform for member organizations to develop common priorities, advance marine research and bridge the gap between science and policy, in order to meet future marine science challenges and opportunities. **Structure** Governing Board; Executive Committee; Secretariat. Expert Panels. **Languages** English. **Staff** 5.00 FTE, paid. **Finance** Members' contributions; special contributions; external contracts. **Activities** Events/meetings; monitoring/evaluation; research/documentation. **Events** *EUROCEAN : European Conference on Marine Science and Ocean Technology* Vigo (Spain) 2023, *Conference on Connecting Communities for End-to-End Solutions* Brussels (Belgium) 2018, *World Conference on Marine Biodiversity* Valencia (Spain) 2008. **Publications** Position papers; vision documents; science commentaries; policy briefs; science briefs.
Members National organizations involved in marine science, including both research funding organizations and research performing organizations. Organizations (35) in 18 countries:
Belgium, Croatia, Denmark, Estonia, France, Germany, Greece, Ireland, Italy, Netherlands, Norway, Poland, Portugal, Romania, Spain, Sweden, Türkiye, UK.
NGO Relations Links with by: *European Fisheries and Aquaculture Research Organization (EFARO, #07265)*; *European Ocean Observing System (EOOS, #08075)*; *Royal Netherlands Institute for Sea Research (NIOZ)*.
[2023/XK1977/**D**]

♦ European Marine Equipment Council (inactive)

♦ **European Marine Research Network (EUROMARINE)** 07739

Exec Dir Sorbonne Univ, EMBRC ERIC/EUROMARINE, BC 93, 4 place Jussieu, 75252 Paris CEDEX 05, France. E-mail: coordination@euromarinenetwork.eu – comm@euromarinenetwork.eu.
URL: https://euromarinenetwork.eu/

History 2014. Founded as a merger of 3 former European Networks of Excellence: EURO-OCEANS; Marine Genomics Europe; MarBEF. Registration: RNA, No/ID: W343022793, Start date: 30 Jul 2018, France. **Aims** Support the identification and initial development of important emerging scientific topics or issues and associated methodologies in marine sciences; foster new services relevant to the marine scientific community. **Structure** Uses a mixed legal model: EuroMarine Consortium, launched June 2014; contains General Assembly, Steering Committtee and 2 Co-Chairs; EuroMarine Association, created 2018 and operational since 2019 (Association is registered in France); contains General Assembly and Bureau; Secretariat. **Finance** Sources: members' dues. **Activities** Research/documentation; training/education. **Events** *General Assembly* Lisbon (Portugal) 2021. **Members** Organizations (over 50). Membership countries not specified.
[2022/AA2530/**F**]

♦ **European Marine Science Educators Association (EMSEA)** 07740

Chairperson Gentstraat 29, 9700 Oudenaarde, Belgium.
Pres c/o Ocean Conservation Trust, Rope Walk, Coxside, Plymouth, PL4 0LF, UK. E-mail: info@oceanconservationtrust.org.
URL: http://www.emsea.eu/

History 2011. Registration: Belgium. **Aims** Provide a platform for ocean education; promote ocean literacy within Europe. **Structure** Board of Directors. **Finance** Sources: members' dues. **Activities** Advocacy/lobbying/activism; awareness raising; events/meetings; knowledge management/information dissemination. **Events** *Conference* Gdynia (Poland) 2021, *Conference* 2020, *Conference* São Miguel (Portugal) 2019, *Conference* Newcastle upon Tyne (UK) 2018, *Conference* Valletta (Malta) 2017. [2020/XJ7729/**D**]

♦ European Marine Step Association (inactive)

♦ **European Maritime Heritage (EMH)** 07741

Sec Kuipersdijk 17, 1601 CL Enkhuizen, Netherlands.
URL: http://european-maritime-heritage.org/

History Registration: Netherlands. **Structure** General Assembly; General Board; Management Board. Councils (3): Safety; Inland Waterway; Cultural. **Languages** English.
Members National members in 9 countries:
Denmark, Germany, Greece, Lithuania, Netherlands, Norway, Portugal, Sweden, UK.
Regional in one territory:
Galicia.
Advisory members in 9 countries:
Belgium, Denmark, France, Germany, Lithuania, Netherlands, Norway, Portugal, Spain.
Associate in 9 countries and territories:
Basque Country, Canada, Denmark, Estonia, Iceland, Norway, Poland, Russia, UK.
Association of Mediterranean Maritime Museums (AMMM, #02801); *Baltic Sail*; *Sail Training International (#19036)*.
NGO Relations Member of (3): *Europa Nostra (#05767)*; *European Federation of Fortified Sites (EFFORTS, #07127)*; *Fédération Européenne pour les Métiers du Patrimoine Bâti (FEMP, #09576)*. [2018/AA0957/**F**]

♦ **European Maritime Law Organization (EMLO)** 07742

Treas c/o Mishcon de Reya, Africa House 70 Kingsway, London, WC2b 6AH, UK. E-mail: enquiries@emlo.org.
URL: http://www.emlo.org/

History 1991, UK, on the initiative of Philippe Ruttley. **Aims** Provide a neutral and independent forum for debate and research on issues of interest to those concerned with EU maritime affairs. **Structure** Council of Members; Chair. **Languages** English. **Staff** 1.00 FTE, paid. **Finance** Members' dues. **Activities** Events/meetings. **Events** *Annual Conference* Limassol (Cyprus) 2019, *Annual Conference* London (UK) 2018, *Annual Conference* Hamburg (Germany) 2017, *Annual Conference* London (UK) 2016, *Annual Conference* Copenhagen (Denmark) 2015.
Members Full in 27 countries:
Austria, Belgium, Brazil, China, Cyprus, Denmark, Finland, France, Germany, Greece, Ireland, Italy, Korea Rep, Latvia, Luxembourg, Malta, Netherlands, Norway, Poland, Russia, Singapore, Spain, Sweden, Türkiye, UK, Ukraine, USA.
[2018/XM3119/**D**]

♦ **European Maritime Pilots' Association (EMPA)** 07743

SG Regentlaan 43-44, 1000 Brussels, Belgium. T. +3224302578. E-mail: office@empa-pilots.eu.
URL: http://www.empa-pilots.eu/

History 28 Jan 1963, Antwerp (Belgium). Rules and Standing Orders adopted by 1st General Meeting, 22 Oct 1963, Hamburg (Germany FR). Rules amended by 5th General Meeting, 1967, Torremolinos (Spain); 20th General Meeting, 1982, Rotterdam (Netherlands). Current amended rules approved by 27th General Meeting, 1993, Copenhagen (Denmark). Registration: RPR Nederlandstalige Ondernemingsrechtbank Brussel, No/ID: 0864.611.379, Belgium; EU Transparency Register, No/ID: 642776135540-90. **Aims** Promote solidarity among pilots of various European countries; establish effective understanding between them through collating and exchange of information relating to professional, financial, legal and social aspects of pilotage; maintain and improve the status and conditions of employment of pilots; seek representation wherever matters relating to pilotage are discussed. **Structure** Annual General Meeting; Board; Secretary General. **Languages** English. **Staff** 1.00 FTE, paid; 7.00 FTE, voluntary. **Finance** Members' dues. **Activities** Knowledge management/information dissemination. **Events** *Annual General Meeting* Antwerp (Belgium) 2022, *Annual General Meeting* Brussels (Belgium) 2021, *Annual General Meeting* Antwerp (Belgium) 2020, *Annual General Meeting* Liverpool (UK) 2019, *Annual General Meeting* Antwerp (Belgium) 2018. **Publications** *EMPA Journal* (annual).
Members Associations in 24 countries:
Belgium, Bulgaria, Croatia, Denmark, Estonia, Finland, France, Georgia, Germany, Greece, Ireland, Italy, Malta, Netherlands, Norway, Poland, Portugal, Romania, Slovenia, Spain, Sweden, Türkiye, UK, Ukraine. [2019.10.18/XD5754/**D**]

♦ **European Maritime Safety Agency (EMSA)** 07744

Agence européenne pour la sécurité maritime (AESM) – Agencia Europea de la Seguridad Maritima – Europäische Agentur für die Sicherheit des Seeverkehrs – Agência Europeia para a Segurança Maritima – Agenzia Europea per la Sicurezza Marittima – Europees Agentschap voor de Maritieme Veiligheid – Europaeisk Sofartssikkerhedsagentur

Main Office Praça Europa 4, Cais Do Sodré, 1249-206 Lisbon, Portugal. T. +351211209200. Fax +351211209210. E-mail: information@emsa.europa.eu.
URL: http://www.emsa.europa.eu/

History Established by Regulation (EC) No 1406/2002, as a source of support to the *European Commission (EC, #06633)* and member states in the field of maritime safety prevention of pollution from ships. Concept of EMSA as a regulatory agency originated in the late 1990s along with a number of other major European maritime safety initiatives. Subsequent amendments have refined and enlarged its mandate. Became operational 2003. A decentralized agency of *European Union (EU, #08967)*. **Aims** Assist the EU in monitoring implementation of EU legislation relating, among others, to ship construction and planned maintenance, ship inspection and

reception of ship waste in EU ports, certification of marine equipment, ship security, training of seafarers in non-EU countries and Port State Control; operate, maintain and develop maritime information capabilities at EU level; contribute to an effective system for protecting EU coasts and waters from pollution by ships; provide technical and scientific advice to the EC in the field of maritime safety and prevention of pollution by ships. **Structure** Administrative Board; Units (11); Departments (4). **Languages** English. **Staff** As of end 2021, 252 FTE including temporary staff, SNEs and contract agents. **Finance** Sources: contributions. Supported by: *European Commission (EC, #06633)*. **Activities** Knowledge management/information dissemination; monitoring/evaluation; networking/liaising; training/education. **Publications** Annual Report; work programme; leaflets; inventories.
Members Full in 29 countries:
Austria, Belgium, Bulgaria, Croatia, Cyprus, Czechia, Denmark, Estonia, Finland, France, Germany, Greece, Hungary, Iceland, Ireland, Italy, Latvia, Lithuania, Luxembourg, Malta, Netherlands, Norway, Poland, Portugal, Romania, Slovakia, Slovenia, Spain, Sweden.
NGO Relations Member of (2): *EU Agencies Network (EUAN, #05564)*; *International Network for Autonomous Ships (INAS, #14232)*. [2022.10.13/XE4411/E*]

♦ European Marketing Academy (EMAC) 07745
Académie européenne de recherche en marketing
Secretariat c/o EIASM, Passagge du Nord 19, 1000 Brussels, Belgium. T. +3222266660. E-mail: emac@eiasm.be.
URL: http://www.emac-online.org/
History 1975, as *European Academy for Advanced Research in Marketing (EAARM)*, under the auspices of *EFMD – The Management Development Network (#05387)* and in close cooperation with *European Institute for Advanced Studies in Management (EIASM, #07544)*. **Aims** Serve as a centre of communications for better dissemination of information and promote international exchange in the field of marketing. **Languages** English. **Finance** Members' dues. **Activities** Meeting activities; advocacy/lobbying/activism; awards/prizes/competitions. **Events** *Annual Conference* Budapest (Hungary) 2022, *Annual Conference* Hamburg (Germany) 2019, *Regional Conference* St Petersburg (Russia) 2019, *Regional Conference* Prague (Czechia) 2018, *Global Marketing Conference* Tokyo (Japan) 2018. **Publications** *EMAC Chronicle*; *International Journal of Research in Marketing*. **Members** Individuals and institutions (over 1,000) in 57 countries. Membership countries not specified. **NGO Relations** Activities supported by EFMD and EIASM. Member of: *Global Alliance of Marketing and Management Associations (GAMMA, #10207)*. Cooperates with: *European Accounting Association (EAA, #05820)*; *European Finance Association (EFA, #07248)*; *European International Business Academy (EIBA, #07585)*. [2019/XD6099/v/D]

♦ European Marketing Association (EMA) 07746
Central Secretariat 18 St Peters Steps, Brixham, TQ5 9TE, UK.
History 1969, as *European Association for Industrial Marketing and Marketing Management*. Present name adopted 1973. Took over activities of *International Market Research Association (IMRA, inactive)*. **Aims** Become established as representative organization for industrial marketing in Europe; act in liaison with European official, professional or educational bodies or organizations and with European marketing organizations; promote national or industry-based marketing research study groups; encourage and improve contact between European marketing executives; establish ethical standards in industrial marketing research; improve technical standards and quality. **Structure** European Council for Industrial Marketing (CEMI), composed of national representatives. Committee. **Languages** English. **Staff** 5.00 FTE, paid; 16.00 FTE, voluntary. **Finance** Members' dues. **Activities** Organizes: study groups; working parties; conferences; seminars; symposia. **Events** *Seminar* London (UK) 2000, *International marketing and business to business research* Birmingham (UK) 1999, *Seminar* London (UK) 1999, *International marketing and business to business research* London (UK) 1998, *International marketing research seminar / Seminar* London (UK) 1998. **Publications** *Journal of International Marketing and Marketing Research* (3 a year); *Journal of International Selling and Sales Management* (2 a year); *EMA Newsletter*; *Journal of International Selling and Sales Management*. Conference proceedings; directories; textbooks.
Members Full in 28 European countries:
Belgium, Croatia, Czechia, Denmark, Finland, France, Germany, Greece, Hungary, Ireland, Italy, Latvia, Luxembourg, Netherlands, North Macedonia, Norway, Poland, Portugal, Romania, Russia, Serbia, Slovenia, Spain, Sweden, Switzerland, Türkiye, UK, Ukraine.
Also members in 22 other countries:
Argentina, Australia, Bahrain, Bolivia, Brazil, Canada, China, Egypt, India, Jamaica, Japan, Kenya, Korea Rep, Kuwait, Malaysia, Morocco, New Zealand, Pakistan, Saudi Arabia, Singapore, South Africa, USA.
NGO Relations Member of: *Commission internationale de marketing (#04224)*. [2010.06.01/XD0553/F]

♦ European Marketing Confederation (EMC) 07747
Confédération européen de marketing
Office Manager Square du Meeus 35, 1000 Brussels, Belgium. T. +3227421780. E-mail: info@emc.be.
URL: http://www.emc.be/
History Founded, replacing *European Marketing Council (EMC, inactive)*, following recommendations of EMC Congress, May 1992, Athens (Greece). Registration: Banque-Carrefour des Entreprises, Belgium. **Aims** Facilitate exchange of practical information about the practice of marketing, *sales* and *communication*; coordinate international activity related to marketing and, in particular, the governance and management of professional associations. **Structure** General Assembly; Board; Secretariat. **Languages** Dutch, English, French. **Staff** 4.00 FTE, paid. **Finance** Sources: fees for services; members' dues. **Activities** Certification/accreditation; events/meetings. **Events** *Annual Forum* 2021, *Annual Forum* 2020, *Annual Forum* Dublin (Ireland) 2019, *Annual Forum* Zurich (Switzerland) 2018, *Annual Forum* Hamburg (Germany) 2017.
Members Associations, institutes, branches of national organizations, professional or training bodies of the profession of marketing. Members in 7 countries:
Germany, Ireland, Lithuania, Netherlands, Russia, Switzerland, UK. [2021.06.25/XD3774/D]

♦ European Marketing Council (inactive)
♦ European Marketing Research Centre, Brussels (internationally oriented national body)
♦ European Market Research Centre, Brussels / see European Marketing Research Centre, Brussels
♦ European Martial Arts Association (internationally oriented national body)

♦ European Mast Cell and Basophil Research Network (EMBRN) 07748
Main Office c/o Stiftung ECARF, Robert-Koch-Platz 7, 10115 Berlin, Germany. E-mail: communication@embrn.eu.
Registered Office Wollgrasweg 49b, 70599 Stuttgart, Germany.
URL: http://www.embrn.eu/
History 2008, Stuttgart (Germany). Formalized 2009. Registration: Germany. **Structure** General Assembly; Extended Council; Council; Officers. **Languages** English, German. **Finance** Members' dues. **Activities** Training/education; events/meetings. **Events** *International Mast Cell and Basophil Meeting* Utrecht (Netherlands) 2022, *International Mast Cell and Basophil Meeting* Utrecht (Netherlands) 2021, *International Mast Cell and Basophil Meeting* Uppsala (Sweden) 2019, *International Mast Cell and Basophil Meeting* Prague (Czechia) 2017, *International Mast Cell and Basophil Meeting* Marseille (France) 2015. **IGO Relations** Cooperates with: *European Cooperation in Science and Technology (COST, #06784)*. **NGO Relations** Partners: *European Academy of Allergy and Clinical Immunology (EAACI, #05779)*; *European Competence Network on Mastocytosis (ECNM, #06687)*; *Global Allergy and Asthma European Network (GA2LEN, #10179)*; *European Centre for Allergy Research Foundation (ECARF)*; *European Histamine Research Society (EHRS, #07489)*. [2022/XJ9087/D]

♦ European Masterbatchers and Compounders (EuMBC) 07749
Contact Av de Cortenbergh 71, 1000 Brussels, Belgium. T. +3227324124. Fax +3227324218. E-mail: info@compounders.eu.
URL: https://www.compounders.eu/
History 26 Oct 2000. Sector group of *European Plastics Converters (EuPC, #08216)*. Former names and other names: *European Thermoplastic Independent Compounders (ETHIC)* – former. **Aims** Represent and defend the interests of European compounds and masterbatch producers vis-à-vis European institutions and other professional organizations. **Structure** Annual Meeting; Executive Committee; Working Groups. **Languages** English. **Activities** Events/meetings; guidance/assistance/consulting; politics/policy/regulatory; standards/guidelines. **Events** *Conference* Brussels (Belgium) 2021, *Conference* Brussels (Belgium) 2020, *Conference* Brussels (Belgium) 2019, *Conference* Brussels (Belgium) 2018. **Members** Companies (15) manufacturing polymeric masterbatches and/or compounds. Membership countries not specified. [2021.09.02/XM0256/D]

♦ European Masters Athletics (EMA) 07750
Pres Heckenweg 18, 33330 Gütersloh, Germany. T. +491739119540.
Office European Athletics Office, European Athletic Association, Av Louis-Ruchonnet 18, 1003 Lausanne VD, Switzerland. T. +41213134350. Fax +41213134351. E-mail: office@european-athletics.org.
URL: http://european-masters-athletics.org/
History Sep 1978, Viareggio (Italy). A regional body of *World Masters Athletics (WMA, #21640)*. Previously known as *European Veterans Athletic Association (EVAA)*. **Aims** Organize, regulate and administer athletics in Europe for masters. **Structure** General Assembly (every 2 years, during Stadia Championships); Council; Technical Board of Managers; EVAA Academy, set up 2007, Helsinki (Finland). **Languages** English, French, German, Italian, Spanish. **Staff** Voluntary. **Finance** Entry fees; grants. **Activities** Sporting activities; events/meetings. **Events** *EVAA Championships Non-Stadia* Regensburg (Germany) 2007, *EVAA Championships Stadia* Poznań (Poland) 2006, *EVAA Championships Indoors* Eskilstuna (Sweden) 2005.
Members Affiliates in 47 countries and territories:
Albania, Andorra, Armenia, Austria, Azerbaijan, Belarus, Belgium, Bulgaria, Cyprus, Czechia, Denmark, Estonia, Finland, France, Germany, Gibraltar, Great Britain, Greece, Hungary, Iceland, Ireland, Israel, Italy, Kosovo, Latvia, Liechtenstein, Lithuania, Luxembourg, Malta, Moldova, Monaco, Netherlands, Northern Ireland, Norway, Poland, Portugal, Romania, Russia, San Marino, Serbia, Slovakia, Slovenia, Spain, Sweden, Switzerland, Türkiye, Ukraine. [2019.06.26/XD7232/D]

♦ European Mastic Asphalt Association / see International Mastic Asphalt Association (#14119)

♦ European Materials Forum (EMF) 07751
Contact c/o E-MRS, BP 20, 67037 Strasbourg CEDEX 2, France. T. +33388106543. Fax +33388106293. E-mail: emrs@european-mrs.com.
URL: http://www.european-mrs.com/
History 28 Jun 2004, Cork (Ireland). Officially launched, 28-29 Jun 2004, Cork (Ireland). Registered in accordance with French law. **Aims** Stimulate, foster and promote education, research and innovation in materials science and technology; advance a European knowledge-based society. **Structure** General Assembly. President; Vice-President. **Languages** English. **Staff** 2.00 FTE, paid; 2.00 FTE, voluntary. **Finance** Members' dues. Donations. **Events** *Spring Meeting / World Materials Summit* Strasbourg (France) 2013, *Spring Meeting* Strasbourg (France) 2012, *Fall Meeting* Warsaw (Poland) 2012, *World Materials Summit* Washington, DC (USA) 2011, *World Materials Summit* Shanghai (China) 2009.
Members Founding members, including the following bodies listed in this Yearbook:
ALLEA – ALL European Academies (#00647); *European Academy of Sciences and Arts (EASA, #05814)*; *European Federation of European Coordination Networks of Scientific and Technical Cooperation (#07114)*; *European Materials Research Society (E-MRS, #07753)*; *European Neutron Scattering Association (ENSA, #08045)*; *European Physical Society (EPS, #08207)*; *European Science Foundation (ESF, #08441)*; *European Science-Industry Consortium for Biomaterials and Health Care (EUROBIOMATEX)*; *Federation of European Materials Societies (FEMS, #09515)*.
Members in 66 countries and territories:
Algeria, Argentina, Armenia, Australia, Austria, Azerbaijan, Belarus, Belgium, Brazil, Bulgaria, Canada, China, Colombia, Croatia, Cyprus, Czechia, Denmark, Estonia, Finland, France, Gambia, Germany, Greece, Hong Kong, Hungary, India, Iran Islamic Rep, Ireland, Israel, Italy, Japan, Jordan, Kazakhstan, Korea Rep, Kuwait, Latvia, Lebanon, Lithuania, Luxembourg, Mexico, Morocco, Netherlands, New Zealand, Nigeria, Norway, Poland, Portugal, Romania, Russia, Saudi Arabia, Serbia, Singapore, Slovenia, South Africa, Spain, Sweden, Switzerland, Taiwan, Thailand, Tunisia, Türkiye, UK, Ukraine, United Arab Emirates, USA, Uzbekistan. [2019.04.25/XM3392/y/F]

♦ European Materials Handling Federation 07752
Fédération Européenne de la Manutention (FEM) – Europäischen Vereinigung der Förder- und Lagertechnik
SG BluePoint Brussels, Bd A Reyers 80, 1030 Brussels, Belgium. T. +3227068237. Fax +3227068253. E-mail: info@fem-eur.com.
URL: http://www.fem-eur.com/
History 6 Nov 1953, Paris (France). Founded at 1st European Congress for Materials Handling, following recommendations of a study group set up in 1951 by the then *Organization for European Economic Cooperation (OEEC, inactive)*. Former names and other names: *European Federation of Handling Industries* – former; *Federación Europea de la Manutención* – former; *Europäische Vereinigung der Fördertechnik* – former; *European Federation of Materials Handling, Lifting and Storage Equipment* – former; *European Mechanical Handling Confederation* – former; *European Federation of Materials Handling* – former. Registration: Banque-Carrefour des Entreprises, No/ID: 0874.265.354, Start date: 1 May 2005, Belgium; EU Transparency Register, No/ID: 24068881115-97, Start date: 10 Feb 2009. **Aims** Represent and defend technical, economic and political interests of European manufacturers of materials handling, lifting and storage equipment; provide a platform for exchanges on market trends and technological developments; cooperate with other industrial sectors and international trade partners on issues of common interest. **Structure** General Assembly (every 2 years); Board; Executive Committee; General Secretariat. Product Groups. National Committee. **Languages** English, French, German. **Finance** Sources: members' dues. **Activities** Knowledge management/information dissemination; research/documentation; standards/guidelines. **Events** *Biennial Congress* York (UK) 2014, *Biennial Congress* Stresa (Italy) 2012, *Biennial Congress* Istanbul (Turkey) 2010, *Biennial Congress* Cannes (France) 2008, *Biennial Congress* Tampere (Finland) 2006. **Publications** Annual Statistics; Biennial Report.
Members National associations of manufacturers in 15 countries:
Belgium, Finland, France, Germany, Italy, Luxembourg, Netherlands, Poland, Portugal, Romania, Russia, Spain, Sweden, Türkiye, UK.
Consultative Status Consultative status granted from: *ECOSOC (#05331)* (Special). **IGO Relations** Recognized by: *European Commission (EC, #06633)*. **NGO Relations** In liaison with technical committees of: *Comité européen de normalisation (CEN, #04162)*; *International Organization for Standardization (ISO, #14473)*. [2021/XD0807/D]

♦ European Materials Research Society (E-MRS) 07753
Société européenne de recherche sur les matériaux
Main Office 23 rue du Loess, BP 20, 67037 Strasbourg CEDEX 02, France. E-mail: emrs@european-mrs.com.
URL: http://www.european-mrs.com/
History 1983, Strasbourg (France). Former names and other names: *MRS-Europe* – former. **Aims** Promote the efficiency of European efforts in materials science and new technologies through: exchange of information; close collaboration between research and industry and across national borders; specific training in advanced materials. **Structure** Senate; Executive Committee; Board of Delegates. **Languages** English. **Staff** 2.00 FTE, paid; 40.00 FTE, voluntary. **Finance** Sources: members' dues. **Activities** Awards/prizes/competitions; events/meetings; training/education. **Events** *Spring Conference* Strasbourg (France) 2021, *Fall Meeting* Warsaw (Poland) 2021, *Spring Conference* Strasbourg (France) 2020, *Fall Meeting* Warsaw (Poland) 2020, *Fall Meeting* Warsaw (Poland) 2019. **Publications** Scientific papers; symposia proceedings; monographs; reports.
Members National correspondents (over 4,000) from industry, government, academia and research laboratories, in 60 countries and territories:
Algeria, Armenia, Australia, Austria, Azerbaijan, Belarus, Belgium, Bosnia-Herzegovina, Brazil, Bulgaria, Canada, China, Colombia, Croatia, Czechia, Denmark, Egypt, Estonia, Finland, France, Georgia, Germany, Greece, Hong Kong, Hungary, Iceland, India, Indonesia, Ireland, Italy, Japan, Kazakhstan, Korea Rep, Latvia, Luxembourg, Mexico, Moldova, Morocco, Netherlands, New Zealand, Norway, Poland, Portugal, Romania, Russia, Saudi Arabia, Serbia, Singapore, Slovakia, Slovenia, South Africa, Spain, Sweden, Switzerland, Taiwan, Tunisia, Türkiye, UK, Ukraine, USA.
NGO Relations Member of (4): *Energy Materials Industrial Research Initiative (EMIRI, #05472)*; *EUREC (#05619)*; *European Materials Forum (EMF, #07751)*; *International Union of Materials Research Societies (IUMRS, #15790)*. [2021.02.17/XD1193/v/D]

♦ European Mathematical Psychology Group (EMPG) 07754
Groupe européen de psychologie mathématique
Contact VUB EXTO, Pleinlaan 2, 1050 Brussels, Belgium. T. +3226293948. Fax +3226292532.

History Apr 1971, Brussels (Belgium). **Aims** Promote research, discussion and cooperation in mathematical psychology throughout Europe. **Structure** Informal group with no statutes and no permanent secretariat. **Languages** English. **Activities** Annual scientific meeting. **Events** *Annual Congress* Copenhagen (Denmark) 2016, *Annual Congress* Pamplona (Spain) 2012, *Annual Congress* Jyväskylä (Finland) 2010, *Annual Congress* Amsterdam (Netherlands) 2009, *Annual Congress* Graz (Austria) 2008. **Publications** Congress proceedings.
Members Individuals in 17 countries:
Australia, Austria, Belgium, Canada, Denmark, Finland, France, Germany, Greece, Italy, Netherlands, Poland, Portugal, Spain, Sweden, UK, USA. [2012/XF8756/v/**F**]

♦ European Mathematical Society (EMS) 07755

Euroopan matemaattinen seura ry

Sec Univ of Helsinki, Dept of Mathematics and Statistics, PO Box 68, FI-00014 Helsinki, Finland. T. +358919151502. Fax +358919151400. E-mail: ems-office@helsinki.fi.
URL: http://www.euro-math-soc.eu/

History 28 Oct 1990, Madralin (Poland). Founded on the initiative of 30 national mathematical societies. Registration: No/ID: 1894243-4, Finland. **Aims** Further the development of all aspects of mathematics in the countries of Europe; promote research in mathematics and its applications. **Structure** Council (meets every 2 years); Executive Committee. Standing Committees (10): Applications and Interdisciplinary Relations; Developing Countries; Education; *European Research Centres of Mathematics (ERCOM, #08360)*; Ethics; European Solidarity; Meetings; Publications and Electronic Dissemination; Raising Public Awareness; Women in Mathematics. **Languages** English. **Staff** 0.50 FTE, paid. **Finance** Sources: members' dues. Annual budget: 100,000 EUR. **Activities** Awards/prizes/competitions; events/meetings; training/education. **Events** *European Congress of Mathematics* Seville (Spain) 2024, *European Congress of Mathematics* Portoroz (Slovenia) 2021, *Quadrennial Congress* Portoroz (Slovenia) 2020, *Quadrennial Congress* Berlin (Germany) 2016, *Quadrennial Congress* Krakow (Poland) 2012. **Publications** *EMS Magazine* (4 a year); *EMS Digest*; *Journal of the European Mathematical Society (JEMS)*. **Information Services** *European Mathematical Information Service (ELibEMS)* – electronic library on EMS Server (EMIS) contains: information on EMS, mathematical activities, institutions, events, other information services, software.
Members Corporate (109) in 44 countries:
Armenia, Australia, Austria, Belgium, Bosnia-Herzegovina, Bulgaria, Canada, Croatia, Cyprus, Czechia, Denmark, Estonia, Finland, France, Georgia, Germany, Greece, Hungary, Iceland, Israel, Italy, Japan, Kosovo, Latvia, Lithuania, Luxembourg, Moldova, Montenegro, Netherlands, Norway, Poland, Portugal, Romania, Russia, Serbia, Slovakia, Slovenia, Spain, Sweden, Switzerland, Türkiye, UK, Ukraine, USA.
Abdus Salam International Centre for Theoretical Physics (ICTP, #00005); *Centro Internacional de Matematica (CIM)*; *Erwin Schrödinger International Institute for Mathematical Physics (ESI)*; *European Institute for Statistics, Probability, Stochastic Operations Research and its Applications (EURANDOM)*; *European Set Theory Society (ESTS, #08470)*; *European Society for Mathematical and Theoretical Biology (ESMTB, #08646)*; *European Women in Mathematics (EWM, #09099)*; *International Center for Mathematical Meetings (CIRM)*; *International Centre for Mathematical Sciences (ICMS)*.
Individuals (about 3000). Membership countries not specified.
NGO Relations Member of (2): *International Council for Industrial and Applied Mathematics (ICIAM, #13032)* (Associate); *International Mathematical Union (IMU, #14121)* (Affiliate). Formal contacts with: *Unión Matematica de América Latina y el Caribe (UMALCA, #20456)*; *Centre international de mathématiques pures et appliquées (CIMPA, #03758)*; national organizations. Cooperates with: *Stefan Banach International Mathematical Center at the Institute of Mathematics of the Polish Academy of Sciences (#19981)*. [2022/XD2481/**D**]

♦ European Matrix Biology (EuMB) 07756

Contact UMCG Pathology, Hanzeplein 1, 9713 GZ Groningen, Netherlands.

History Jul 1968, Cambridge (UK). Former names and other names: *European Federation of Connective Tissue Clubs (EFCTC)* – former; *Fédération européenne des clubs du tissu conjonctif* – former; *Federation of European Connective Tissue Societies (FECTS)* – former; *Fédération des associations européennes du tissu conjonctif* – former. **Aims** Organize meetings for the discussion of all aspects of connective tissue research. **Structure** Meetings, organized locally, elect Federation representatives to maintain continuity. **Languages** English. **Finance** Registration fees; occasional sponsors. **Events** *Matrix Biology Europe (MBE) Conference* Florence (Italy) 2022, *Matrix Biology Europe (MBE) Conference* Manchester (UK) 2018, *Biennial Meeting* Athens (Greece) 2016, *European Matrix Biology Meeting* Rotterdam (Netherlands) 2014, *Biennial Meeting* Katowice (Poland) 2012. **Publications** Meeting Reports.
Members Individuals in 17 countries:
Austria, Belgium, Czechia, Denmark, Finland, France, Germany, Greece, Hungary, Italy, Netherlands, Norway, Poland, Russia, Sweden, Switzerland, UK. [2018/XD0937/v/**D**]

♦ European ME Alliance (EMEA) 07757

Contact Sinder Alle 5 – st 3, 9500 Hobro, Denmark. E-mail: info@euro-me.org.
URL: http://www.euro-me.org/

History Set up 2008. **Aims** Bring together a European lobby of groups to campaign for funding of biomedical research to establish an understanding of the aetiology, pathogenesis and *epidemiology* of *myalgic encephalomyelitis* (ME or ME/CFS). **Structure** General Meeting; Executive Committee. **Languages** English. **Finance** Members' dues.
Members Full in 14 countries:
Belgium, Denmark, Finland, France, Germany, Iceland, Ireland, Italy, Netherlands, Norway, Spain, Sweden, Switzerland, UK.
NGO Relations Member of: *European Federation of Neurological Associations (EFNA, #07177)*. [2018/XM6860/**D**]

- ♦ European Meat Association (inactive)
- ♦ European Mechanical Circulatory Support Summit (meeting series)
- ♦ European Mechanical Handling Confederation / see European Materials Handling Federation (#07752)
- ♦ European Mechanics Committee / see EUROMECH – European Mechanics Society (#05713)
- ♦ European Mechanics Council / see EUROMECH – European Mechanics Society (#05713)
- ♦ European Media Foundation / see Central and Eastern European Media Centre Foundation (#03694)

♦ European Media Management Education Association (emma) 07758

Sec Jönköping Univ, International Business School, Gjuterigatan 5, SE-553 18 Jönköping, Sweden.
URL: http://www.media-management.eu/

History 2003. **Aims** Provide a forum for the exchange of ideas between those teaching media; stimulate academic and intellectual interest in media management education and research; facilitate development of high quality teaching materials explicitly tailored to the field; build links between those teaching and researching in the field of the media arena and the media industry itself. **Structure** Board, comprising President, Deputy President, Secretary, Treasurer and 3 members. **Events** *Conference* Munich (Germany) 2022, *Conference* Jönköping (Sweden) 2021, *Conference* Jönköping (Sweden) 2020, *Conference* Cyprus 2019, *Conference* Warsaw (Poland) 2018.
Members Individual; Institutional. Members in 14 countries:
Belgium, Bulgaria, Cyprus, Finland, Germany, Hungary, Norway, Poland, Portugal, Russia, Spain, Sweden, Switzerland, UK. [2018/XJ5893/**D**]

- ♦ European Media Packaging Manufacturers (inactive)

♦ European Media Research Organizations (EMRO) 07759

Pres address not obtained.
URL: http://www.emro.org/

History 1960. Former names and other names: *Club Dubois* – alias. Registration: Switzerland. **Aims** Provide a forum for discussion of technical and administrative topics of mutual interest to non-profit organizations responsible for *measurement* of *mass media audiences*. **Structure** President; Programme Committee; Secretariat. **Staff** 0.50 FTE, paid. **Finance** Members' dues. **Events** *Annual Conference* Marrakech (Morocco) 2023, *Annual Conference* Cascais (Portugal) 2022, *Annual Conference* 2021, *Annual Conference* 2020, *Annual Conference* Bordeaux (France) 2019.
Members National delegations in 13 countries:
Austria, Belgium, Denmark, Finland, France, Germany, Italy, Netherlands, Norway, South Africa, Sweden, Switzerland, UK. [2022/XF0953/**F**]

♦ European Mediation Network Initiative (EMNI) 07760

Vice Chair Lammenschansweg 11, 2313 DH Leiden, Netherlands.
Sec FN 302661 s UID ATU63806279, Würzburggasse 33, 1130 Vienna, Austria. T. +4318763296.
URL: https://www.european-mediation.eu/

History Founded Sep 2007, Vienna (Austria). Registered in accordance with Austrian law. **Aims** Promote international exchange of information on alternative dispute resolution (ADR), mediation and conflict management; promote development of effective mediation policies, services and legislation; explore and develop the theoretical basis of mediation and promote research; promote development of principles, ethics, standards and good practice. **Structure** General Assembly; Board; Executive Committee; Country Coordinators. **Languages** English, French, German. **Activities** Networking/liaising; conflict resolution; politics/policy/regulatory; events/meetings. **Events** *Conference* Bratislava (Slovakia) 2013, *Conference* Bratislava (Slovakia) 2012, *Conference* Paris (France) 2010, *Conference* Belfast (UK) 2008, *Conference* Vienna (Austria) 2007. [2019.06.30/XJ2305/**F**]

♦ European Medical Association (EMA) 07761

Association médicale européenne – Asociación Médica Europea – Europäische Medizinische Assoziation – Associação Médica Europea – Associazione Medica Europea – Europese Medische Vereniging – Europaeiske Medisk Forening – Evropaiki Iatriki Enosi

Pres Place de Jamblinne de Meux 12, 1030 Brussels, Belgium. T. +3227351615. Fax +3227342135. E-mail: contact@emanet.org.
Head Office Av des Volontaires 19, 1160 Brussels, Belgium.
URL: http://www.emanet.org/

History 7 May 1990, Brussels (Belgium). Registration: Banque-Carrefour des Entreprises, No/ID: 0443.863.486, Start date: 28 Mar 1991, Belgium; EU Transparency Register, No/ID: 834080221070-18, Start date: 18 Aug 2022. **Aims** Improve the quality of health care and the working conditions of the medical professional in the Community's countries. **Structure** General Assembly (annual); Steering Committee; Executive Bureau. **Languages** Dutch, English, French, German, Italian, Spanish. **Staff** 1.00 FTE, voluntary. **Finance** Sources: members' dues; subsidies. **Activities** Events/meetings; knowledge management/information dissemination; projects/programmes. **Events** *Plenary Assembly and Annual Conference* Brussels (Belgium) 2020, *Acute and General Medicine Conference* London (UK) 2018, *Annual Conference* London (UK) 2018, *Annual Conference* London (UK) 2017, *Congress on Automation and Autoimmunity* Brussels (Belgium) 2012. **Publications** *EMA Journal*; *EMA News*. Directory; specialists' diary. Information Services: Databases: practitioners according to speciality; specialized medical centres; medical associations; medical journals; commonly used medical abbreviations and terminology.
Members Founder; Full (medical practitioners in the EU); Associate; Honorary; Adherent, Observant. Full and Associate (marked ") members in 17 countries:
Austria (*), Belgium, Bulgaria (*), Denmark, France, Germany, Greece, Hungary (*), Ireland, Italy, Luxembourg, Netherlands, Poland (*), Portugal, Spain, Switzerland, UK.
NGO Relations Member of (3): *European Health Chamber*; *Health First Europe (HFE, #10881)*; *Virtual Physiological Human Institute for Integrative Biomedical Research (VPH Institute, #20790)*. [2022.10.24/XD2656/**D**]

♦ European Medical Association on Smoking and Health (EMASH) . . . 07762

Association médicale européenne tabac ou santé (AMETOS)

Pres Rue de la Prulay 33, 1217 Meyrin GE, Switzerland. T. +41227820145.
URL: http://www.hon.ch/EMASH/

History 1986. Registration: Start date: 1988, France. **Aims** Promote non-smoking among doctors in Europe and smokefree policies in hospitals; train doctors on smoking cessation, including prescription of pharmacologic therapy for nicotine substitution; disseminate information on WHO tobacco-control activities to european experts. **Structure** Council; Executive Bureau. **Languages** English, French. **Staff** Voluntary. **Finance** None. **Events** *Conference* Coimbra (Portugal) 2013, *Conference* Coimbra (Portugal) 2012, *Conference* Coimbra (Portugal) 2011, *Conference* Coimbra (Portugal) 2010, *Conference* Coimbra (Portugal) 2009. **Publications** *European Medical Newsletter on Smoking and Health* (4 a year).
Members Physicians, biomedical scientists, pharmacists, nurses and other health professionals. Individuals (400) in 29 countries and territories:
Austria, Belgium, Brazil, Czechia, Denmark, Finland, France, Germany, Greece, Hong Kong, Hungary, Iceland, India, Ireland, Italy, Japan, Jordan, Luxembourg, Netherlands, Norway, Poland, Portugal, Romania, Russia, Spain, Sweden, Switzerland, Türkiye, UK.
IGO Relations *European Commission (EC, #06633)*; *WHO (#20950)*. **NGO Relations** Member of: *Framework Convention Alliance (FCA, #09981)*. [2018/XD2790/v/**D**]

- ♦ European Medical Imaging Film Manufacturers (no recent information)

♦ European Medical Laser Association (EMLA) 07763

Europäische Medizin Laser Gesellschaft

Pres Seefeldstrasse 128, 8008 Zurich ZH, Switzerland. E-mail: emla.office@gmail.com.
URL: http://www.emla-medical.com/

History Founded 1982, Locarno (Switzerland). Also referred to as *European Association for Research and Application of Laser and Related Technologies in Medicine, Surgery and Therapy*. Registered twice in accordance with German law, Stuttgart (Germany). **Aims** Enhance health care through the facilitation of high quality research (basic and clinical) and effective application of laser and related technologies in all fields of medicine (including veterinary medicine and rehabilitation), surgery and dentistry. **Structure** General Assembly (annual). Parliament (meets twice a year). Executive Committee, comprising President, Vice-President, Secretary, Treasurer and CEO, plus European National Branches. **Languages** English. **Finance** Members' dues. Other sources: donations; subscriptions. **Activities** Organizes courses and congresses. Sets up an international school on laser medicine and surgery. **Events** *International Laser Medical Congress / Congress* Sandvika (Norway) 2015, *Annual Congress / Congress* Opatija (Croatia) 2013, *Annual Congress* Helsinki (Finland) 2012, *Annual congress / Congress* Prague (Czech Rep) 2011, *LASER Helsinki international congress* Helsinki (Finland) 2010. **Publications** *EMLA Newsletter*; *Laser in Medicine* – official journal. *Millennium Laser Trilogy Books* – up until 2009.
Members Individuals (225) in 44 countries:
Algeria, Armenia, Australia, Austria, Bangladesh, Belarus, Brazil, Bulgaria, Canada, Croatia, Czechia, Denmark, Finland, France, Germany, Iran Islamic Rep, Iraq, Ireland, Israel, Italy, Korea DPR, Korea Rep, Latvia, Libya, Netherlands, New Zealand, North Macedonia, Norway, Peru, Poland, Portugal, Romania, Russia, Serbia, Slovakia, Slovenia, Sweden, Switzerland, Tunisia, Türkiye, UK, Ukraine, USA, Uzbekistan. [2015/XD7216/**D**]

♦ European Medical Students' Association (EMSA) 07764

Association européenne des étudiants en médecine – Europäische Medizinstudierenden Vereinigung

Main Office c/o CPME, Rue Guimard 15, 1040 Brussels, Belgium. E-mail: info@emsa-europe.eu.
URL: https://emsa-europe.eu/

History 1990, Leuven (Belgium). Former names and other names: *Europäische Vereinigung Junger Krankenhausverwalter* – former. Registration: Belgium. **Aims** Form a network between European medical students to facilitate European integration and develop a sense of European identity; represent and voice the opinions of the medical students of Europe; act as a forum for all medical students in Europe, to discuss topics related to the fields of medical education, medical ethics and medical research; promote the highest standards in European medical education and ensure the quality of healthcare in Europe; promote training, activities and projects related to health in Europe to the benefit of medical students and society; facilitate intercultural understanding by organizing social and cultural events; cooperate with other student organizations representing the medical profession. **Structure** GA- General Assembly (annual), comprising 2 representatives of each member faculty. NCM – National Coordinators' and Enthusiasts' Meeting (annual), comprising one representative of each country and EMSA enthusiasts. EEB – EMSA European Board, consisting of President, 2 Vice-Presidents (Internal Affairs, External Affairs), Secretary General, Treasurer and 5 Directors (Medical Science; Medical Education; Medical Ethics and Culture; European Integration; Public Health). Other officers: European Institution Liaison; Fundraising; Human Resources; Public Relation; Policy Making. **Languages** English. **Staff** 1.00 FTE, paid. Voluntary. **Finance** Sources: grants; members' dues. **Activities** Advocacy/lobbying/activism; events/meetings; training/education. **Events** *Autumn Assembly* Rotterdam (Netherlands) 2021, *Autumn Assembly* Rotterdam (Netherlands) 2020, *Autumn Assembly* Berlin

(Germany) 2015, *Spring Assembly* Warsaw (Poland) 2015, *Annual General Assembly and Congress* Plovdiv (Bulgaria) 2014. **Publications** *Euromeds* – newsletter; *JEMSA – Journal of EMSA on Medical and Scientific Affairs.* Information Services: Database on medical curricula; database on Teddybear Hospital activities; database on ethics / medical error; EMSA mailing-list.
Members Full: Faculty Member Organizations (FMOs) – medical faculties in Europe; Associate. Members in 23 countries:
Austria, Belgium, Bulgaria, Croatia, Georgia, Germany, Greece, Hungary, Italy, Kosovo, Lithuania, Malta, Moldova, Netherlands, North Macedonia, Poland, Portugal, Romania, Serbia, Slovenia, Türkiye, UK, Ukraine.
IGO Relations Member of (1): *European Youth Centres (EYCs, #09138).* **NGO Relations** Member of (6): *European Brain Council (EBC, #06391); European Public Health Alliance (EPHA, #08297); European Students' Union (ESU, #08848)* (Associate member); *Informal Forum of International Student Organizations (IFISO, #11193); International Youth Health Organization (YHO, #15933); The Right to Research Coalition (no recent information).* Associate organization of: *Standing Committee of European Doctors (#19955).* [2023.02.14/XD1919/v/**D**]

♦ European Medical Trade Association (no recent information)

♦ European Medical Writers Association (EMWA) 07765

Hon Sec EMWA HO, Chester House, 68 Chestergate, Macclesfield, SK11 6DY, UK. T. +441625664534. Fax +441625664510. E-mail: president@emwa.org – info@emwa.org.
Registered Address St James House, Vicar Lane, Sheffield, S1 2EX, UK.
URL: http://www.emwa.org/
History 1989. A non-profit organization. Registration: Companies House, No/ID: 03653609, England and Wales. **Aims** Represent, support and train medical communication professionals across Europe. **Structure** Executive Committee. **Languages** English. **Finance** Sources: members' dues; sponsorship. **Activities** Awards/prizes/competitions; events/meetings; training/education. **Events** *Conference* Prague (Czechia) 2023, *Conference* Riga (Latvia) 2022, *Autumn Meeting* Cascais (Portugal) 2021, *Annual Conference* Riga (Latvia) 2021, *Autumn Meeting* Macclesfield (UK) 2020. **Publications** *Medical Writing* (4 a year). **Members** Individuals (over 1200) in over 50 different countries. Membership countries not specified. [2020.07.13/XD6355/v/**D**]

♦ European Medicinal Cannabis Association (EUMCA) 07766

Gen Sec Immobilière du Noyer SA, Avenue Adolphe Lacomblé 69-71, 1030 Brussels, Belgium. T. +3223390281. E-mail: info@eumca.org.
URL: https://eumca.org/
History 14 Nov 2019, Malta. Registration: Banque Carrefour des Enterprises, No/ID: 0740.929.649, Start date: 8 Jan 2020, Belgium; EU Transparency Register, No/ID: 138219638308-52, Start date: 27 May 2020. **Aims** Advance patient access to medicinal cannabis treatment; improve the health outcomes of patients across Europe. **Structure** Executive Board. **Finance** Sources: members' dues. **Activities** Advocacy/lobbying/activism; events/meetings. **NGO Relations** Member of (1): *EU Health Coalition.* [2021/AA1366/**D**]

♦ European Medicines Agency (EMA) 07767

Agence européenne des médicaments
Exec Dir Domenico Scarlattilaan 6, 1083 HS Amsterdam, Netherlands. T. +31887816000.
URL: https://www.ema.europa.eu/
History 22 Jul 1993. Established by *Council of the European Union (#04895)* Regulation (EEC) No 2309/93. Became operational, Feb 1995, London (UK). A decentralized agency of *European Union (EU, #08967).* Former names and other names: *European Agency for the Evaluation of Medicinal Products (EMEA)* – former; *Agence européenne pour l'évaluation des médicaments* – former. **Aims** Protect and promote public and animal *health* through evaluation and supervision of medicines for human and veterinary use; support medicines development by giving scientific advice and providing guidance to developers of medicines; carry out robust scientific evaluations of medicines for human and veterinary use that are the basis of the European Commission's decision on whether a medicine can be authorized for marketing throughout the EU; monitor the safety of medicines in the EU after they have been authorized; provide information on medicines to healthcare professionals and patients. **Structure** Management Board. Executive Director. Scientific Committees. **Languages** English. **Staff** 908.00 FTE, paid. **Finance** Over 90% derived from fee revenue. Annual budget: 317,360,000 EUR (2017). **Activities** Knowledge management/information dissemination; monitoring/evaluation; politics/policy/regulatory. **Events** *ONE – Health Environment and Society Conference* Brussels (Belgium) 2022, *Joint Innovation Meeting* Helsinki (Finland) 2019, *Conference on Biosimilar Medicines* Brussels (Belgium) 2018, *Workshop on the Development of Antimicrobial Medicinal Products for Paediatric Patients* Brussels (Belgium) 2018, *Satellite Symposium* Vienna (Austria) 2017. **Publications** *European Public Assessment Reports.* Annual Report; work programmes; press releases; scientific guidelines on quality, safety and efficacy testing; regulatory guidelines; Committee and meeting agendas, minutes and reports; newsletters.
Members European Union member states (27) and EEA-EFTA states (3, marked *), comprising a network of over 4,500 European experts. Members in 30 countries:
Austria, Belgium, Bulgaria, Croatia, Cyprus, Czechia, Denmark, Estonia, Finland, France, Germany, Greece, Hungary, Iceland (*), Ireland, Italy, Latvia, Liechtenstein (*), Lithuania, Luxembourg, Malta, Netherlands, Norway (*), Poland, Portugal, Romania, Slovakia, Slovenia, Spain, Sweden.
NGO Relations Member of (1): *EU Agencies Network (EUAN, #05564).* Partner of (2): *European Network of Centres for Pharmacoepidemiology and Pharmacovigilance (ENCePP, #07875); European Network of Paediatric Research at the European Medicines Agency (Enpr-EMA, #07963).* [2023/XE2027/**E***]

♦ European Medicines Verification Organisation (EMVO) 07768

Gen Manager Rue du Commerce 123, 1000 Brussels, Belgium. T. +3226570008. E-mail: helpdesk@emvo-medicines.eu.
URL: http://emvo-medicines.eu/
History Set up by: *European Federation of Pharmaceutical Industries and Associations (EFPIA, #07191), Medicines for Europe (#16633), Pharmaceutical Group of the European Union (PGEU, #18352), Groupement International de la Répartition Pharmaceutique (GIRP, #10762)* and *Affordable Medicines Europe (#00150).* Registered in accordance with Belgian law. Registration: Belgium. **Aims** Advance the formation of the European Medicines Verification System (EMVS), to ensure implementation of a functioning, secure, interoperable and cost effective system across Europe. **Structure** Board of Directors; General Manager; Commercial and Partner Management; Operations; Quality Assurance. **Languages** English, French, German. **Publications** *EMVO Newsletter.* Guidelines; directives.
Members Organizations (6):
Affordable Medicines Europe (#00150); European Federation of Pharmaceutical Industries and Associations (EFPIA, #07191); European Hospital and Healthcare Federation (HOPE, #07501); Groupement International de la Répartition Pharmaceutique (GIRP, #10762); Medicines for Europe (#16633); Pharmaceutical Group of the European Union (PGEU, #18352). [2020/XM6760/y/**E**]

♦ European and Mediterranean Archery Union / see World Archery Europe (#21108)

♦ European and Mediterranean Cereal Rusts Foundation (EMCRF) . . . 07769

Chairman Aarhus Univ, Dept of Agroecology, Flakkebjerg, 4200 Slagelse, Denmark. E-mail: mogens.hovmoller@agro.au.dk.
URL: http://emcrf.au.dk/
History 18 Apr 1969. Founded after two international meetings having been held previously: 1964, UK; 1968, Portugal. **Aims** Promote international cooperation on study of cereal rusts and powdery mildew diseases of cereals in particular and, where necessary, of cereal diseases and pests in general; further practical application of scientific results. **Structure** Board. **Languages** English. **Staff** Voluntary. **Finance** No financial activities. **Events** *International Cereal Rusts and Powdery Mildews Conference* Cambridge (UK) 2022, *International Cereal Rusts and Powdery Mildews Conference* Kruger National Park (South Africa) 2018, *International Cereal Rusts and Powdery Mildews Conference* Helsingør (Denmark) 2015, *International Cereal Rusts and Powdery Mildews Conference* Beijing (China) 2012, *International Cereal Rusts and Powdery Mildews Conference* Antalya (Turkey) 2009. **Publications** *Cereal Rusts and Powdery Mildews Bulletin* (annual) – online. **Members** No formal membership. **NGO Relations** Member of: *International Society for Plant Pathology (ISPP, #15371).* [2022/XF0321/f/**F**]

♦ European and Mediterranean Coloproctology Association / see Mediterranean Society of Coloproctology (#16676)

♦ European Mediterranean Commission on Water Planning (no recent information)

♦ European and Mediterranean Horseracing Federation (EMHF) 07770

SG Chaussée de la Hulpe 61, 1170 Brussels, Belgium. T. +447860253910.
URL: http://www.euromedracing.eu/
History 2010, Stockholm (Sweden). Founding meeting 2010, building on achievements of *European Racing Development Conference (ERDC).* Registration: EU Transparency Register, No/ID: 109777918147-53, Start date: 14 Jul 2015. **Aims** Develop relations among European and Mediterranean Horseracing Authorities; identify best practice in horseracing administration and encourage its adoption across the membership; defend integrity and prestige of horseracing throughout the world; represent Europe and Mediterranean countries before IFHA; represent the Thoroughbred racing sector before political institutions. **Structure** General Assembly (annual); Executive Council; Chairman and 3 Vice-Chairmen; General Secretariat. **Finance** Sources: members' dues; sponsorship. Other sources: commercial concerns' attendance fees. **Events** *Annual General Assembly* Warsaw (Poland) 2023, *Annual General Assembly* Newbridge (Ireland) 2022, *Annual General Assembly* Warsaw (Poland) 2021, *Annual General Assembly* Brussels (Belgium) 2020, *Annual General Assembly* Oslo (Norway) 2019.
Members Full in 23 countries and territories:
Azerbaijan, Belgium, Channel Is, Cyprus, Czechia, Denmark, France, Germany, Hungary, Ireland, Italy, Libya, Morocco, Netherlands, Norway, Poland, Portugal, Slovakia, Spain, Sweden, Switzerland, Türkiye, UK.
Associate in 2 countries:
Lebanon, Romania.
NGO Relations Member of (2): *European Horse Network (EHN, #07499); International Federation of Horseracing Authorities (IFHA, #13449).* [2022.10.19/XM4186/**D**]

♦ European and Mediterranean League Against Thrombotic Diseases (EMLTD) 07771

Gen Sec Research Ctr – Univ Hosp "La Fe", Avda Campanar 21, 46009 Valencia, Spain.
Technical Secretariat Universidad 4, 46003 Valencia, Spain. T. +34963425889. Fax +34963942558. E-mail: mltd@geyseco.es.
Foundation Hosp de la Santa Creu i Sant Pau, Av Sant Antoni M Claret 167, 08025 Barcelona, Spain.
URL: http://www.medleague-thrombosis.org/
History Oct 1969, Bilbao (Spain). Also referred to as *Ligue méditerranéenne de thrombose.* **Aims** Promote the study, origin and causes of thromboembolic diseases, their diagnosis, prophylaxis and treatment; unite professional interest in thrombosis and *haemostasis* from basic to clinical sciences via multidisciplinary collaboration, in all countries considered geographically, culturally or historically part of the Mediterranean area; progressively incorporate all Mediterranean countries into the League. **Structure** General Assembly. Councillors Board, comprising President, General Secretary and 26 national councillors. Executive Board, President, Past-President, General Secretary and 3 members. Educational Board; Trustees Board; International Scientific Committee. Permanent General Secretariat. MLTD Foundation, founded 12 Feb 2008. **Languages** English. **Staff** None. **Finance** Members' dues. International Thrombosis Congress contributions. Budget (annual): euro 8,000. **Activities** Evaluates post-university education; standardizes diagnostic techniques. Organizes: biennial International Thrombosis Congress; biennial educational course in a Mediterranean country; epidemiological, pharmacological and therapeutic cooperative trials in multicentres in Mediterranean countries. **Events** *Biennial Congress* Lisbon (Portugal) 2021, *Biennial Congress* Athens (Greece) 2019, *Biennial Congress* Venice (Italy) 2018, *Biennial Congress* Valencia (Spain) 2014, *Biennial Congress* Nice (France) 2012. **Publications** *Journal of Pathophysiology of Hemostasis and Thrombosis* – official journal.
Members Full in 16 countries:
Bulgaria, Croatia, Cyprus, Egypt, France, Greece, Israel, Italy, Lebanon, Morocco, Portugal, Serbia, Slovenia, Spain, Tunisia, Türkiye.
NGO Relations Supports (1): *International Symposium on Women's Health Issues in Thrombosis and Haemostasis (WHITH).* [2020/XD8642/**D**]

♦ European/Mediterranean Planetarium Association (EMPA) 07772

Contact Eugenides Foundation 387 Syngrou Ave, Paliao Faliro, 175 64 Athens, Greece. Fax +302109417372. E-mail: mak@eef.edu.gr.
Members Membership countries not specified. **NGO Relations** Member of: *International Planetarium Society (IPS, #14588).* [2016.06.30/XD2102/**D**]

♦ European and Mediterranean Plant Protection Organization (EPPO) 07773

Organisation Européenne et Méditerranéenne pour la Protection des Plantes (OEPP)
Dir-Gen 21 blvd Richard Lenoir, 75011 Paris, France. T. +33145207794. Fax +33170766547. E-mail: hq@eppo.int.
URL: http://www.eppo.int/
History 18 Apr 1951. Established by convention signed in Paris (France), an *International Colorado Beetle Committee – Comité international de lutte contre le doryphore* having been set up in 1947, Brussels (Belgium), and expanded, Jan 1950, to become *European Plant Protection Organization – Organisation européenne pour la protection des plantes.* **Aims** Develop and international strategy against the introduction and spread of pests that damage cultivated and wild plants in natural and agricultural ecosystems, including invasive alien plants; encourage harmonization of phytosanitary regulations and all other areas of official plant protection action; promote the use of modern, safe and effective pest control methods; provide a documentation service on plant protection. **Structure** Council (meets annually); Executive Committee. Working Parties (2) open to officially appointed government representatives. International conferences are open. **Languages** English, French. **Staff** 15.00 FTE, paid. **Finance** Sources: contributions of member/participating states. **Activities** Events/meetings; knowledge management/information dissemination; networking/liaising; politics/policy/regulatory; standards/guidelines. **Events** *Annual Meeting* Athens (Greece) 2022, *Regional Plant Protection Organizations (RPPOs) Annual Technical Consultation* London (UK) 2022, *Regional Plant Protection Organizations (RPPOs) Annual Technical Consultation* Rome (Italy) 2021, *Regional Plant Protection Organizations (RPPOs) Annual Technical Consultation* Rome (Italy) 2020, *Regional Plant Protection Organizations (RPPOs) Annual Technical Consultation* Abuja (Nigeria) 2019. **Publications** *Bulletin OEPP/EPPO Bulletin* in English, French. *EPPO Standards; EPPO Technical Documents.* Scientific reports of conferences and on specific subjects. **Information Services** *EPPO Global Database; EPPO Reporting Service.*
Members Governments of 52 countries:
Albania, Algeria, Austria, Azerbaijan, Belarus, Belgium, Bosnia-Herzegovina, Bulgaria, Croatia, Cyprus, Czechia, Denmark, Estonia, Finland, France, Georgia, Germany, Greece, Guernsey, Hungary, Ireland, Israel, Italy, Jersey, Jordan, Kazakhstan, Kyrgyzstan, Latvia, Lithuania, Luxembourg, Malta, Moldova, Montenegro, Morocco, Netherlands, North Macedonia, Norway, Poland, Portugal, Romania, Russia, Serbia, Slovakia, Slovenia, Spain, Sweden, Switzerland, Tunisia, Türkiye, UK, Ukraine, Uzbekistan.
IGO Relations Observer status with (1): *Codex Alimentarius Commission (CAC, #04081).* Member of (1): *United Nations Joint Staff Pension Fund (UNJSPF, #20581).* Cooperates with (1): *FAO (#09260).* Serves as one of 10 Regional Plant Protection Organizations (RPPOs) of *International Plant Protection Convention, 1951 (IPPC, 1951).* **NGO Relations** In liaison with technical committees of: *International Organization for Standardization (ISO, #14473).* [2021/XD0544/**D***]

♦ European Mediterranean Regulators Groups (unconfirmed)

♦ European-Mediterranean Seismological Centre (EMSC) 07774

Centre sismologique euro-méditerranéen (CSEM)
SG c/o CEA – Bt Bard, Centre DAM Ile-de-France, Bruyères le Châtel, 91297 Arpajon CEDEX, France. T. +33169267814. Fax +33169267000.
URL: http://www.emsc-csem.org/
History Founded 1975, following a recommendation from the *European Seismological Commission (ESC, #08461)* based on the consideration that the European-Mediterranean region displayed a potentially dangerous seismic activity, which subsequently gained support of the International Association of Seismology and Physics of the Earth's Interior (IASPEI) and the International Union of Geodesy and Geophysics (IUGG). Began operations 1 Jan 1976, Strasbourg (France), at the Institut de Physique du Globe de Strasbourg (IPGS). Statutes adopted 1983; modified 1993 consecutively to an Extraordinary General Assembly 13 Dec 1993, Rome (Italy),

when the seat moved to the Laboratoire de Détection et de Géophysique (LDG) of the Commissariat à l'Energie Atomique (CEA) in Bruyères-le-Châtel (France). Charged by *Council of Europe (CE, #04881)*, 1987, to provide CoE with seismic warnings in the framework of the *Open Partial Agreement on the Prevention of, Protection against and Organization of Relief in Major Natural and Technological Disasters (EUR-OPA Major Hazards Agreement, #17762)*. Registered in accordance with French law, 1983. **Aims** Establish and operate a system for rapid determination of the European and Mediterranean *earthquake* epicentres, and transmit the results immediately to the appropriate international authorities and to members; determine the principal parameters (epicentre, depth, magnitude, focal mechanisms, etc) of major seismic events located within the European-Mediterranean region and dispatch widely the corresponding results; collect the data necessary for operations of the Centre and make them available to other international, regional or national data centres; encourage scientific cooperation among European and Mediterranean countries in the field of earthquake research, and develop studies of general interest; promote the exchange of seismological data between laboratories in the European-Mediterranean area; satisfy any request related to detailed studies of specific events; assure the functioning of an European seismological data bank; promote improvement of observational systems in the European-Mediterranean region. **Structure** Assembly (annual); Coordination Bureau of 3 members; Executive Council: EMSC-ORFEUS Scientific Advisory Board; ORFEUS-EMSC Coordinating Committee; Nodal Members carry out scientific activities; ad-hoc committees. **Languages** English, French. **Staff** 9.00 FTE, paid. **Finance** Members' dues. Grants. European research projects, including: MARsite; NERIES; NERA; REAKT; VERCE; IMPROVER; CARSIMAND. **Activities** Research and development; awareness raising; knowledge management/ information dissemination. **Events** *Annual Assembly* Prague (Czech Rep) 2015, *Annual Assembly* Istanbul (Turkey) 2014, *Annual Assembly* Gothenburg (Sweden) 2013, *Annual Assembly* Moscow (Russia) 2012, *Annual Assembly* Utrecht (Netherlands) 2011. **Publications** Articles; press releases; scientific papers. Information Services: Database of earthquake strong motion records, accessible to the scientific community for research purposes.
Members Key nodal members, active members and members by rights. Seismological institutions. Active in 54 countries and territories:
Albania, Algeria, Armenia, Austria, Azerbaijan, Belarus, Belgium, Bosnia-Herzegovina, Bulgaria, Croatia, Cyprus, Czechia, Denmark, Djibouti, Egypt, Finland, France, Georgia, Germany, Greece, Iceland, Ireland, Israel, Italy, Jordan, Kosovo, Lebanon, Libya, Luxembourg, Malta, Moldova, Monaco, Montenegro, Morocco, Netherlands, North Macedonia, Norway, Poland, Portugal, Romania, Russia, Saudi Arabia, Serbia, Slovakia, Slovenia, Spain, Sweden, Switzerland, Tunisia, Türkiye, UK, Ukraine, United Arab Emirates, Yemen.
Key Nodal members in 4 countries:
France, Germany, Italy, Spain.
Corporate member in 1 country:
Ireland.
Members by right (4), 3 of which are listed in this Yearbook:
European Seismological Commission (ESC, #08461); International Seismological Centre (ISC, #14830); Observatories and Research Facilities for European Seismology (ORFEUS, #17639); US Geological Survey.
[2015.08.27/XE4846/y/**E**]

- ♦ European Medium and Small Business Union (no recent information)
- ♦ European Meeting on Ancient Ceramics (meeting series)
- ♦ European Meeting on Cybernetics and Systems Research (meeting series)
- ♦ European Meeting on Fire Retardant Polymeric Materials (meeting series)
- ♦ European Meeting on Game Theory (meeting series)
- ♦ European Meeting of Teachers of Arabic / see European Association for Modern Arabic Literature (#06123)
- ♦ European Meeting of Young Ophthalmologists (meeting series)

♦ European Melamine Producers Association (EMPA) 07775

SG c/o CEFIC, Rue Belliard 40, Box 15, 1040 Brussels, Belgium. T. +3224369414. E-mail: eab@cefic.be.
URL: http://melamine.cefic.org/
History as a sector group of *Conseil européen de l'industrie chimique (CEFIC, #04687)*.
Members Melamine producers (5) in 5 countries:
Austria, France, Germany, Netherlands, Poland. [2019/XE2852/**E**]

♦ European Membrane House (EMH) 07776

Exec Dir CFCIB, Av des Arts 8, 1210 Brussels, Belgium.
URL: http://www.euromemhouse.com/
Aims Enhance industrial implementation of membrane-based technologies; help develop a coherent and structured European system for membrane research and technological innovation. **Structure** General Meeting; Governing Board; Departments (2). **Languages** English, French. **Staff** 3.00 FTE, paid. **Activities** Advocacy/ lobbying/activism; research and development. **Events** *ICCMR : International Conference on Catalysis in Membrane Reactors* Porto (Portugal) 2013.
Members Founding; Associate; Club of Interest. Founding in 10 countries:
Belgium, Czechia, Finland, France, Germany, Greece, Netherlands, Norway, Portugal, Spain.
Included in the above, 1 international organization:
European Membrane Society (EMS, #07777).
Associate in 2 countries:
Netherlands, Spain.
Club of Interest in 2 countries:
Czechia, France.
IGO Relations *UNESCO (#20322)*. **NGO Relations** Member of: *Water Europe (WE, #20828)*.
[2016.10.19/XJ1670/y/**F**]

♦ European Membrane Society (EMS) 07777

Sec address not obtained. E-mail: ems@chimie.ups-tlse.fr.
Pres address not obtained.
URL: http://www.emsoc.eu/
History 1982. Former names and other names: *European Society of Membrane Science and Technology (ESMST)* – former. Registration: France. **Aims** Promote research and development in the field of synthetic and artificial membranes and of membrane process; promote cooperation among European scientists and engineers in the field; contribute to the development of a common language among scientists of different disciplines involved (physical chemistry, chemical engineering, biology, bioengineering, medicine). **Structure** General Assembly (biennial); Council; Executive Committee; Committees (2); Industrial Applications. **Languages** English. **Staff** 0.50 FTE, paid. **Finance** Sources: grants; members' dues. **Activities** Awards/ prizes/competitions; events/meetings; training/education. **Events** *Euromembrane Conference* Copenhagen (Denmark) 2021, *ICOM – International Congress on Membranes and Membrane Processes* London (UK) 2020, *Euromembrane Conference* Valencia (Spain) 2018, *International Congress on Membrane and Membrane Processes* San Francisco, CA (USA) 2017, *Euromembrane Conference* Aachen (Germany) 2015. **Publications** *Membrane News* (periodical). Books; reports.
Members Individuals in 43 countries:
Algeria, Antigua-Barbuda, Argentina, Austria, Barbados, Belgium, Brazil, Bulgaria, Canada, China, Croatia, Cuba, Czechia, Denmark, Finland, France, Germany, Greece, Hungary, India, Indonesia, Ireland, Israel, Italy, Japan, Jordan, Mexico, Netherlands, Norway, Poland, Portugal, Romania, Russia, Serbia, Slovakia, Slovenia, South Africa, Spain, Sweden, Switzerland, Türkiye, UK, USA.
NGO Relations Member of (3): *European Federation of Chemical Engineering (EFCE, #07074); European Membrane House (EMH, #07776); World Association of Membrane Societies (WA-MS, #21165)* (Founding). Co-organizes *International Congress on Membranes and Membrane Processes (ICOM)*. [2021/XD5165/v/**D**]

♦ European Memory Clinics Association (EMCA) 07778

Secretariat c/o Bezirkskrankenhaus Günzburg, Ludwig-Heilmeyer-Str 2, 89312 Günzburg, Germany. E-mail: sekretariat.emca@memoryclinics-europe.eu.
URL: http://www.memoryclinics-Europe.eu/
History Registered in accordance with German law. **Aims** Promote the public health system as well as training in the area of multi-professional diagnosis and therapies of dementias. **Structure** General Assembly. Executive Board. **Finance** Members' dues. **Activities** Training; information dissemination. **Events** *Meeting* Vienna (Austria) 2013. [2014/XJ8284/**D**]

♦ European MEN Alliance (EMENA) 07779

Address not obtained.
URL: http://www.emena.eu/
History Founded 2013. Formally established as a German non-profit, 30 May 2016: VR 206832. Full title: *European Multiple Endocrine Neoplasia Alliance*. **Aims** Improve the *diagnosis*, care and lives of *patients* affected by MEN – multiple *endocrine neoplasia*. **Structure** General Assembly; Board; Medical and Scientific Advisory Committee. **Languages** English. **Finance** Members' dues.
Members Full; Affiliated; Sponsoring. Members in 5 countries:
Belgium, Germany, Italy, Netherlands, UK.
NGO Relations Associate member of: *EURORDIS – Rare Diseases Europe (#09175)*. [2018/XM7446/**D**]

♦ European Meningococcal Disease Society (EMGM) 07780

Sec Natl School of Public Health, Dept of Public Health, Natl Meningitis Reference Lab, 196 Alexandras Avenue, 115 21 Athens, Greece. T. +302132010267. Fax +302136423041.
URL: http://emgm.eu/
History Jun 2005. Registered in accordance with German law. **Aims** Support non-commercial national and international bodies working with meningococcal disease and/or meningococci. **Structure** General Assembly. Executive Board, comprising President, Vice-President, Secretary, Treasurer and members. Scientific Advisory Board. **Activities** Promotion of clinical microbiological laboratory work and epidemiology; research, teaching, training, quality assurance/control, study; Working Groups (7): European Meningococcal Epidemiology in Real Time (EMERT); Serology/Vaccines; Strain characterization; Carriage; Laboratory Safety; Public Health Management; Haemophilus influenza. **Events** *Congress* Lisbon (Portugal) 2019, *Congress* Amsterdam (Netherlands) 2015, *N Meningitidis, H influenzae* Loipersdorf (Austria) 2013, *Congress* Ljubljana (Slovenia) 2011, *Congress* Manchester (UK) 2009. **Members** Full; Student; Associate; Honorary. Membership countries not specified. [2013/XJ6923/**D**]

♦ European Meniscal Transplantation Group (EMTG) 07781

Coordinator Strandstraede 10, 2791 Dragør, Denmark. T. +4530119023.
Events *Meeting* Porto (Portugal) 2008, *Meeting* Innsbruck (Austria) 2006, *Meeting* Athens (Greece) 2004, *Meeting* Rome (Italy) 2002, *Meeting* London (UK) 2000. [2016.12.13/XM3327/**E**]

- ♦ European Mennonite Peace Committee (internationally oriented national body)

♦ European Menopause and Andropause Society (EMAS) 07782

Admin Office c/o KIT Group, Kurfürstendamm 71, 10709 Berlin, Germany. T. +4930246030. Fax +493024603200. E-mail: emas@kit-group.org – info@emas-online.org.
Registered Office Rue du Rhône 118, 1204 Geneva, Switzerland.
URL: http://www.emas-online.org/
History 12 Jun 1998, Switzerland. Registration: No/ID: CH-035.6.019.883-7, Switzerland, Geneva. **Aims** Advance midlife health and beyond in women and men by promoting the translation of science into clinical practice. **Structure** General Assembly; Board; Committees; Auditor. **Languages** English. **Staff** 1.00 FTE, paid. **Activities** Organizes, prepares and participates in international meetings and congresses on subjects related to climacteric. **Events** *European Congress on Menopause and Andropause* Florence (Italy) 2023, *European Congress on Menopause and Andropause* Florence (Italy) 2021, *European Congress on Menopause and Andropause* Berlin (Germany) 2019, *European Congress on Menopause and Andropause* Amsterdam (Netherlands) 2017, *European Congress on Menopause and Andropause* Madrid (Spain) 2015. **Publications** *Maturitas, The European Menopause Journal*.
Members Individuals in 47 countries:
Argentina, Australia, Austria, Belarus, Belgium, Bolivia, Brazil, Bulgaria, Canada, Chile, Croatia, Czechia, Denmark, Estonia, Finland, France, Germany, Greece, Hungary, Iceland, Ireland, Israel, Italy, Latvia, Lithuania, Luxembourg, Malta, Mexico, Netherlands, Norway, Poland, Portugal, Romania, Russia, Serbia, Slovakia, Slovenia, South Africa, Spain, Sweden, Switzerland, Thailand, Türkiye, UK, Ukraine, Uruguay, USA.
Affiliated societies in 21 countries:
Austria, Belgium, Croatia, Finland, France, Germany, Hungary, Israel, Luxembourg, Netherlands, Poland, Portugal, Romania, Russia, Serbia, Slovakia, Slovenia, Switzerland, Türkiye, UK, Ukraine.
Regional society:
Nordic Menopause Society (NOMS, no recent information). [2021/XD7227/y/**D**]

♦ European Men's Health Forum (EMHF) 07783

Dir Rue de l'Industrie 11, 1000 Brussels, Belgium. T. +3222343058. Fax +3222303300. E-mail: office@emhf.org.
URL: http://www.emhf.org/
History Jan 2002, Belgium. Registration: Banque-Carrefour des Entreprises, No/ID: 0478.167.933, Start date: 29 Aug 2002, Belgium. **Aims** Improve men's health in Europe by promoting collaboration on the development and application of health-related policies, research, education and prevention programmes. **Structure** General Assembly; Board. Network and Sponsors Committees. Secretariat, headed by Director. **Languages** English, German, Spanish. **Staff** 2.00 FTE, paid. **Finance** Annual budget: 100,000 GBP. **Activities** Events/meetings. **Events** *Conference / European Men's Health Conference* Dublin (Ireland) 2013, *Conference on Gender and Health through Life* Copenhagen (Denmark) 2012, *European conference / European Men's Health Conference* Vienna (Austria) 2005. **Publications** Manuals; reports.
Members Full in 15 countries:
Austria, Denmark, Finland, France, Germany, Hungary, Ireland, Italy, Netherlands, Norway, Portugal, Slovakia, Switzerland, UK, Ukraine.
International organization member (1):
International Society for Men's Health (ISMH, #15260).
NGO Relations Member of: *Alliance for Safe Online Pharmacy – EU (ASOP EU, #00720); European Coalition for Vision (ECV); Global Action on Men's Health (GAMH, #10167); Global Alliance of Mental Illness Advocacy Networks – Europe (GAMIAN Europe, #10211)*. Associate member of: *European Forum for Primary Care (EFPC, #07326)*. Link with: *European Cancer Patient Coalition (ECPC, #06433); European Union of General Practitioners / Family Physicians (#08993).* [2019/XF6804/y/**F**]

♦ European Mental Retardation Consortium (Euro-MRX Consortium) . 07784

Contact Dept of Human Genetics, Radboud Univ Nijmegen Medical Cntr, PO Box 9101, 6500 HB Nijmegen, Netherlands. T. +31243614017. Fax +31243668752.
URL: http://www.euromrx.com/
History 1996. **Aims** Identify (additional) genes involved in X-linked MR; understand their biological function.
Members Institutes (5) in 4 countries:
Belgium, France, Germany, Netherlands. [2013/XJ7508/**D**]

- ♦ European Mentoring and Coaching Council / see EMCC Global (#05434)
- ♦ European Mentoring Council / see EMCC Global (#05434)
- ♦ European Merit Foundation (internationally oriented national body)
- ♦ European Metabolic Group Meeting (meeting series)
- ♦ European Metallizers Association (inactive)
- ♦ European Metal Packaging (inactive)
- ♦ European metals alliance for recyclable and sustainable buildings – METALS FOR BUILDINGS / see METALS FOR BUILDINGS (#16737)

♦ European Metal Union (EMU) 07785

Union européenne du métal – Europäische Metall-Union – Europese Metaal-Unie
SG Anspachlaan 111, b13, 1000 Brussels, Belgium. T. +3222742207. Fax +3224007126. E-mail: office@emu-sme.eu.
URL: http://www.emu-sme.eu/
History 23 Aug 1954, Zurich (Switzerland). Statutes approved 22 Sep 1955, Luxembourg; most recently updated 23 Sep 2021, Graz (Austria). Former names and other names: *International Union of Blacksmithing and Forging* – former (1954 to 1972); *Union Internationale des forgerons-constructeurs* – former (1954 to 1972); *International Metal Union (IMU)* – former (1972 to 1993); *Union internationale du métal* – former (1972 to 1993); *Internationale Metall-Union (IMU)* – former (1972 to 1993). Registration: Banque-Carrefour des Entreprises, No/ID: 0820.688.690, Start date: 19 Nov 2009, Belgium; EU Transparency Register, No/ID:

457596413786-53, Start date: 12 Jun 2014. **Aims** Represent the interests of craft and small and medium-sized enterprises in the metal industry; provide a forum for discussion of training/educational affairs, promotion of the craft, branch-related problems and micro and macro-economic developments; represent interests of European members in European Union legislation and regulations. **Structure** General Assembly (annual); Board; Secretariat in Brussels (Belgium), headed by Secretary General. **Languages** English, German. **Activities** Advocacy/lobbying/activism; events/meetings; networking/liaising; standards/guidelines; training/education. **Events** *Annual Congress* Belgium 2000, *Annual Congress* Rotterdam (Netherlands) 1999, *Annual Congress* Switzerland 1998, *Annual Congress* Luxembourg (Luxembourg) 1997, *Annual Congress* Dresden (Germany) 1996.
Members National associations or committees of national associations of employers in the metal trade in 7 countries:
Belgium, Denmark, Germany, Hungary, Italy, Netherlands, Switzerland.
NGO Relations Member of (2): *Small Business Standards (SBS, #19311)*; *SMEunited (#19327)*.
[2022.05.10/XD2699/**D**]

♦ European Metalworkers' Federation (inactive)
♦ European Metalworking Plantmakers Association (inactive)

♦ European Meteorological Society (EMS) 07786
Société météorologique européenne – Europäische Meteorologische Gesellschaft
Exec Sec c/o FU Berlin – Meteorologie, Carl-Heinrich-Becker-Weg 6-10, 12165 Berlin, Germany. T. +493079708328. Fax +49307919002. E-mail: ems-sec@emetsoc.org.
URL: http://www.emetsoc.org/
History 14 Sep 1999, Norrköping (Sweden). **Aims** Advance meteorology at a European-wide level. **Structure** General Assembly (annual). Council, comprising Councillors from 3 permanent members (France, Germany, UK) and 6 non-permanent members for a period of 2 years, and comprising observers from associate members. Officers: President; 2 Vice-Presidents; Vice-President/Treasurer. Secretariat headed by Executive Secretary. **Languages** English. **Staff** 1.00 FTE, paid. **Finance** Members' dues. **Activities** Organizes meetings and conferences; provides meteorological education; carries out accreditation and quality control; organizes meteorology in the media; offers awards for young scientists. **Events** *Annual Meeting* Croatia 2025, *Annual Meeting* Barcelona (Spain) 2024, *Annual Meeting* Bratislava (Slovakia) 2023, *Annual Meeting* Bonn (Germany) 2022, *Annual Meeting* Barcelona (Spain) 2021. **Publications** *EMS Newsletter*. Books; series.
Members Full organizations (35) in 29 countries:
Andorra, Austria, Belgium, Bulgaria, Croatia, Cyprus, Czechia, Denmark, Finland, France, Germany, Greece, Hungary, Iceland, Ireland, Italy, Netherlands, North Macedonia, Norway, Poland, Portugal, Romania, Serbia, Slovakia, Slovenia, Spain, Sweden, Switzerland, UK.
Associate: weather services or companies (28). Membership countries not specified. Included in the above, 3 organizations listed in this Yearbook:
Included in the above, 3 organizations listed in this Yearbook:
European Centre for Medium-Range Weather Forecasts (ECMWF, #06490); *European Organisation for the Exploitation of Meteorological Satellites (EUMETSAT, #08096)*; *European Space Agency (ESA, #08798)*.
NGO Relations Member of: *International Forum of Meteorological Societies (IFMS, #13644)*.
[2021/XD7924/y/**D**]

♦ European Methadone Association / see European Opiate Addiction Treatment Association (#08090)

♦ European Methodist Council (EMC) 07787
Conseil européen des églises méthodistes – Europäischer Rat Methodistischer Kirchen
Support Officer address not obtained. E-mail: office@methodist.eu.
URL: http://www.methodist.eu/
History Founded 12 Sep 1993, Herrnhut (Germany), to replace *Consultative Conference of European Methodist Churches (inactive)* and the European Council of the United Methodist Church (UMC). **Aims** Enable member churches to consult together on matters of common concern; develop a stronger Methodist witness in Europe; enable member churches to share resources with one another. **Structure** Executive; Standing Committees; Ad-hoc Working Groups. **Languages** English, German. **Staff** 1.00 FTE, paid. **Finance** Members' contributions. **Activities** Events/meetings. **Events** *Annual Meeting* Porto (Portugal) 2016, *Annual Meeting* Ruse (Bulgaria) 2015, *Annual Meeting* Dublin (Ireland) 2014, *Annual Meeting* Wuppertal (Germany) 2013, *Annual Meeting* Krakow (Poland) 2012. **Members** A broad range of churches with links to Methodism. Membership countries not specified. [2019.05.01/XD4058/**D**]

♦ European Methodist Youth and Children's Council (EMYC) 07788
Methodistischer Rat für die Arbeit mit Kindern und Jugendlichen in Europa
Sec Roald Amundsensv 88, 1650 Fredrikstad, Norway. T. +4798606721.
Pres United Methodist Church, Ludolfusstr 2-4, 60487 Frankfurt-Main, Germany.
URL: http://www.methodistyouth.eu/
History Founded 1970, as *European Methodist Youth Council (EMYC) – Conseil européen de la jeunesse méthodiste – Europäischer Methodistischer Jugendrat*. **Aims** Create and strengthen links between those who work with *children* and young people in European Methodist Churches; consult on matters of common interest; initiate action to bring young people together. **Structure** Executive; Sub-committees. **Languages** English, German. **Finance** Contributions from different Methodist churches in Europe. Budget (annual): euro 30,000. **Activities** Events/meetings. **Events** *Meeting / Council Meeting* Dresden (Germany) 2015, *Meeting / Council Meeting* Velletri (Italy) 2014, *Meeting / Council Meeting* Stuttgart (Germany) 2013, *Meeting / Council Meeting* Varna (Bulgaria) 2012, *Meeting / Council Meeting* Vienna (Austria) 2011.
Members Full in 23 countries:
Austria, Belgium, Bulgaria, Czechia, Denmark, Estonia, Finland, France, Germany, Hungary, Ireland, Italy, Latvia, Lithuania, North Macedonia, Norway, Poland, Portugal, Russia, Serbia, Slovakia, Sweden, Switzerland, UK. [2019/XE1697/**E**]

♦ European Methodist Youth Council / see European Methodist Youth and Children's Council (#07788)

♦ European Metropolitan Transport Authorities (EMTA) 07789
SG 41 rue du Chateaudun, 75009 Paris, France. E-mail: contact@emta.com.
URL: http://www.emta.com/
History Apr 1998, Paris (France). **Aims** Serve as a forum for exchange of information, research and experience between public authorities responsible for planning, integrating and financing public transport services in the main European cities. **Structure** Board; Working Groups. **Languages** English. **Staff** 2.20 FTE, paid. **Finance** Sources: grants; members' dues; revenue from activities/projects. Annual budget: 250,000 EUR. **Activities** Events/meetings. **Events** *General Meeting* Barcelona (Spain) 2023, *General Meeting* Oslo (Norway) 2023, *General Meeting* Lisbon (Portugal) 2022, *General Meeting* Vienna (Austria) 2022, *General Meeting* Copenhagen (Denmark) 2021. **Publications** *EMTA News* (4 a year). *Barometer* – report. Directory.
Members Transport authorities in 32 metropolitan areas across 19 countries:
Austria, Belgium, Bulgaria, Czechia, Denmark, Finland, France, Germany, Greece, Hungary, Italy, Lithuania, Netherlands, Norway, Poland, Portugal, Spain, Sweden, UK. [2023.02.16/XD9353/**D**]

♦ European Mettray Organisation (EUROMET) 07790
Organisation européenne de Mettray
Sec address not obtained.
Treas address not obtained.
URL: http://www.euromet.in/
History Dating back to 1839. **Aims** Support and cooperate in joint comparative action research projects working *pedagogically* with seriously *disadvantaged children* and *youth* aged 4 to 25; share resources and expertise through contributing to exchange of knowledge, experience and information. **Structure** Board; Executive Board. **Languages** English, French. **Activities** Knowledge management/information dissemination; events/meetings. **Events** *Symposium* Kortrijk (Belgium) 2022, *Symposium* UK 2021, *Symposium* Tours (France) 2019, *Symposium* Ljubljana (Slovenia) 2018, *Symposium* Helsinki (Finland) 2017.
Members Full in 11 countries:
Belgium, Estonia, France, Germany, Hungary, Netherlands, Poland, Romania, Slovenia, Sweden, UK.
[2019.03.06/XM6530/**D**]

♦ European MHealth Alliance (inactive)

♦ European Microbeam Analysis Society (EMAS) 07791
Sec Labo Nacl de Energia e Geologia, Rua da Amieira, Aptdo 1089, 4466-901 São Mamede de Infesta e Senhora da Hora, Portugal. T. +351220400041. Fax +351229514040.
Pres AWE, Aldermaston, Reading, RG7 4PR, UK.
URL: http://www.microbeamanalysis.eu/
History 1987. Registered in accordance with German law. **Aims** Promote education, communication and innovation in *ultrastructural* analysis methodology; stimulate technical and scientific developments on a European scale; meet the growing needs and demands of users and scientists for further education, communication and counselling. **Structure** Executive Board. **Languages** English. **Staff** None. **Finance** Members' dues. **Activities** Training/education; networking/liaising; awards/prizes/competitions. **Events** *Biennial Workshop* Krakow (Poland) 2022, *Biennial Workshop* Trondheim (Norway) 2019, *Regional Workshop* Bristol (UK) 2018, *Biennial Workshop* Konstanz (Germany) 2017, *Regional Workshop* France 2016. **Publications** *EMAS News*; *Microscopy and Microanalysis (MiMi)* – journal.
Members Individuals in 30 countries:
Australia, Austria, Belgium, Brazil, Canada, Cyprus, Czechia, Denmark, Finland, France, Germany, Greece, Hungary, Italy, Japan, Korea Rep, Netherlands, Norway, Poland, Portugal, Singapore, Slovenia, South Africa, Spain, Sweden, Switzerland, Trinidad-Tobago, UK, Ukraine, USA.
NGO Relations Member of: *International Union of Microbeam Analysis Societies (IUMAS, #15793)*. In liaison with technical committees of: *International Organization for Standardization (ISO, #14473)*.
[2016.10.18/XD3985/v/**D**]

♦ European Microfilm Congress (meeting series)

♦ European Microfinance Network (EMN) 07792
Réseau Européen de la Microfinance (REM) – Red Europea de Microfinanzas (REM)
Mailing Address Av des Arts 7-8, 1210 Brussels, Belgium. T. +3223290030. E-mail: emn@european-microfinance.org.
Registered Office Rue de la Charité 22, 1210 Brussels, Belgium.
URL: http://www.european-microfinance.org/
History Apr 2003. Founding members: Association du Droit à l'Initiative Economique (ADIE), France; *New Economics Foundation (NEF, #17082)*, UK; EVERS and JUNG, Germany, and with support of the European Commission and French Caisse des Dépôts et Consignations (CDC). Registration: Banque-Carrefour des Entreprises, Start date: Dec 2012, Belgium; Start date: 23 May 2003, France, Paris. **Aims** Promote microfinance in the European Union as a tool to fight social and economic exclusion and unemployment through development of micro-entrepreneurship and self-employment. **Structure** Board. **Languages** Dutch, English, French, German, Italian, Spanish. **Staff** 8.00 FTE, paid. 1 trainee. **Finance** Sources: fees for services; members' dues; sponsorship. Supported by: *European Commission (EC, #06633)*. **Activities** Advocacy/lobbying/activism; awards/prizes/competitions; capacity building; events/meetings. **Events** *Annual Conference* Brussels (Belgium) 2022, *Annual Conference* Brussels (Belgium) 2021, *Annual Conference* Brussels (Belgium) 2020, *Conference* Helsinki (Finland) 2019, *Annual Conference* Vienna (Austria) 2019. **Publications** *Microfinance in Europe – Survey Report* (every 2 years); *EMN Newsletter*. *Good Practices Guide*. Thematic and sector studies; members' directory.
Members Active; Corporate; Partners. Members and partners (over 90) in 25 countries:
Albania, Armenia, Austria, Belgium, Bosnia-Herzegovina, Bulgaria, France, Germany, Greece, Hungary, Ireland, Italy, Kosovo, Luxembourg, Montenegro, Netherlands, Poland, Portugal, Romania, Serbia, Slovakia, Slovenia, Spain, Sweden, UK.
IGO Relations Links with EU institutions. [2022.02.09/XM4020/y/**E**]

♦ European Microfinance Platform (E-MFP) 07793
Exec Sec 39 rue Glesener, L-1631 Luxembourg, Luxembourg. T. +35226271382. Fax +35245686868. E-mail: contact@e-mfp.eu.
URL: http://www.e-mfp.eu/
History 2006. **Aims** Promote cooperation amongst European microfinance bodies working in developing countries, by facilitating communication and exchange of information. **Structure** Board of Directors; Executive Secretariat, headed by Executive Secretary. **Languages** English, French, German, Spanish. **Staff** 4.50 FTE, paid. **Activities** Knowledge management/information disseminationa. **Events** *European Research Conference on Microfinance* Paris (France) 2019, *European Research Conference on Microfinance* Geneva (Switzerland) 2015, *European Research Conference in Microfinance* Kristiansand (Norway) 2013, *European research conference on microfinance* Groningen (Netherlands) 2011. **Publications** *E-MFP Newsletter*, *European Dialogue*. Briefs; conference reports; directories; position and discussion papers; activity reports; fact sheets; workshop reports.
Members Organizations; individuals. Full (82) in 15 countries:
Belgium, Denmark, France, Germany, Ireland, Italy, Liechtenstein, Luxembourg, Netherlands, Norway, Poland, Spain, Sweden, Switzerland, UK.
Included in the above, 7 organizations listed in this Yearbook:
Catholic Organization for Relief and Development (Cordaid); *Concern Worldwide*; *ECLOF International (#05287)*; *Fondation RAFAD – Recherches et applications de financements alternatifs au développement (Fondation RAFAD, #09827)*; *International Solidarity for Development and Investment (SIDI)*; *Oikocredit International (Oikocredit, #17704)*; *TRIAS*.
Associate – Institutions (21) in 9 countries:
Bosnia-Herzegovina, France, Italy, Luxembourg, Netherlands, Russia, Spain, UK, USA.
Included in the above, 3 organizations listed in this Yearbook:
Consultative Group to Assist the Poor (CGAP, #04768); *FINCA International*; *Women's World Banking (WWB, #21037)*.
Associate – Individuals (23) in 14 countries:
Bangladesh, Belgium, Brazil, Denmark, France, Germany, Honduras, India, Italy, Luxembourg, Netherlands, Sweden, UK, USA.
NGO Relations Member of: *Microfinance Centre (MFC, #16745)*; *Social Performance Task Force (SPTF, #19343)*. [2015.08.31/XJ0381/y/**F**]

♦ European Microlight Federation (EMF) 07794
Gen Sec Ul Orla Bialego 12, 78-449 Borne Sulinowo, Poland. T. +420607789637.
Pres Asserbrink 54, 7812 Emmen, Netherlands. T. +31591610441.
URL: http://www.emf.aero/
History 17 Sep 2003, Maisons-Alfort (France). **Aims** Promote and protect microlight *aircraft* in Europe. **Structure** General Meeting (annual); Executive Committee. **Languages** English. **Staff** Voluntary. **Finance** Subscriptions. **Events** *General Conference / Annual General Conference* Prague (Czech Rep) 2015, *General Conference / Annual General Conference* St Julian's (Malta) 2014, *Annual General Conference* Portugal 2013, *Annual General Conference* St Julian's (Malta) 2012, *Annual General Conference* Ostend (Belgium) 2011.
Members National organizations in 24 countries:
Austria, Belgium, Croatia, Czechia, Denmark, Finland, France, Germany, Greece, Ireland, Italy, Lithuania, Luxembourg, Malta, Netherlands, Norway, Poland, Portugal, San Marino, Slovakia, Spain, Sweden, Switzerland, UK.
IGO Relations *Asian Federation of Osteoporosis Societies (AFOS, #01468)*; *European Commission (EC, #06633)*. **NGO Relations** *Europe Air Sports (EAS, #05776)*. [2018.09.05/XJ3282/**D**]

♦ European Microscopy Society (EMS) 07795
Sec UPR 8011, 29 rue Jeanne Marvig, BP 94347, 31055 Toulouse CEDEX 4, France. T. +3396257867. Fax +3396257999.
URL: http://www.eurmicsoc.org/
History Founded 1978, through 1980, Netherlands, as *Committee of European Societies for Electron Microscopy (CESEM)*, and subsequently as *Committee of European Societies for Microscopy (CESM)*, 1994. Previously sometimes also referred to as *Committee of European Electron Microscopy Societies*. Current title adopted 3 Sep 1998, when CESM was dissolved and its replacement by current society took place. Regional committee of: *International Federation of Societies for Microscopy (IFSM, #13550)*. **Aims** Promote the use and quality of microscopy in all its aspects in Europe, with particular reference to developments in instrumentation and methodology and novel applications of all types of microscopy. **Structure** General Assembly (at Congress); General Council (meeting with and directly following a General Assembly); Executive Board; Trade Committee. **Languages** English. **Finance** Members' dues. Contributions of EMC Congress participants. **Activities** Knowledge management/information dissemination; events/meetings. **Events** *EMC : European Microscopy Congress* Copenhagen (Denmark) 2024, *Early Career European Microscopy Congress*

2020, *EMC : European Microscopy Congress* Copenhagen (Denmark) 2020, *Multinational congress of the Croatian-Austrian-Czechish-Slovakian-Hungarian-Italian and Slovene societies for electron microscopy* Rovinj (Croatia) 2017, *EMC : European Microscopy Congress* Lyon (France) 2016. **Publications** *EMS Yearbook* (annual); *EMS Newsletter* (about 5 a year).
Members National societies in 52 countries and territories:
Armenia, Australia, Austria, Bangladesh, Belgium, Brazil, Canada, Chile, Croatia, Cuba, Czechia, Denmark, Egypt, Finland, France, Germany, Greece, Hong Kong, Hungary, Iceland, India, Iraq, Ireland, Israel, Italy, Japan, Lebanon, Luxembourg, Malta, Mexico, Netherlands, New Zealand, Norway, Philippines, Poland, Portugal, Romania, Russia, Saudi Arabia, Serbia, Singapore, Slovakia, Slovenia, South Africa, Spain, Sweden, Switzerland, Thailand, Türkiye, UK, USA, Venezuela.
NGO Relations Cooperates with: *International Federation of Societies for Microscopy (IFSM, #13550).*
[2020/XD3742/y/**D**]

♦ European Microwave Association (EuMA) 07796

Association européenne de micro-ondes

Secretariat Rue Louis de Geer 6, 1318 Louvain-la-Neuve, Belgium. T. +3210390068 – +3210390069. Fax +3210390001. E-mail: headquarters@eumwa.org.
URL: http://www.eumwa.org/

History 1998, Amsterdam (Netherlands). Founded during *European Microwave Week (EuMW, inactive).* Registration: Banque-Carrefour des Entreprises, No/ID: 0464.401.356, Start date: 29 Oct 1998, Belgium. **Aims** Develop interdisciplinary educational training and research activities; unite scientists and engineers in the field and act as their united voice; promote awareness and recognition of microwaves by the general public and their complete recognition by the European Union. **Structure** General Assembly (twice a year); Board of Directors. **Languages** English, French. **Staff** 1.50 FTE, paid; 5.00 FTE, voluntary. **Finance** Sources: fees for services; members' dues. Annual budget: 1,000,000 EUR (2022). **Activities** Events/meetings. **Events** *European Microwave Week* London (UK) 2021, *European Microwave Week* Utrecht (Netherlands) 2021, *European Microwave Week* Utrecht (Netherlands) 2020, *European Microwave Week* Paris (France) 2019, *European Microwave in Central Europe Conference* Prague (Czechia) 2019. **Publications** *International Journal on Microwave and Wireless Technologies.* **Members** Individuals. Membership countries not specified. **NGO Relations** Member of (1): *Federation of European and International Associations Established in Belgium (FAIB, #09508).*
[2022.10.11/XD6581/v/**D**]

♦ European Microwave Signature Laboratory (EMSL) 07797

Laboratoire européen de signatures micro-ondes

Head IPSC, DG-Joint Research Centre, 21020 Ispra MB, Italy. T. +39332789089. Fax +39332785469.

History Founded Apr 1992. A facility hosted by *Joint Research Centre (JRC, #16147).* **Aims** Serve as a unique and flexible facility for researchers and users of remote sensing in the field of earth observation; complement and help validate airborne and spaceborne observations of the earth's surface by providing stable and reproducible environmental conditions and operation modes for fully controlled experiments; measure and obtain signatures of natural objects and features on the earth's surface; provide realistic operation modes similar to those in use by aircraft and/or satellites; operate automatically and ensure real-time processing and analysis of measurement data. **Structure** Advisory Committee. Sub-groups: SAR Interferometric Techniques; Scattering Properties of Non Vegetated Terrain; Imaging Techniques; Vegetation Parameters; Scattering Properties of Individual Targets. **Activities** Acts as a European facility supporting also industrial applications, such as road condition monitoring, road control and obstacle avoidance. Serves also as key facility for the development of advanced techniques for the detection of anti-personnel landmines. Expected to provide quantitative information about radar signals while, for example, analysing observational data for studying deforestation or desertification. **Publications** *EMSL Newsletter.* Reports. Information Services: Data base which stores all measurement data resulting from the work in EMSL, and containing all relevant information such as object characteristics, optical documents, literature, etc. This data base has a remote lock-in capability with browsing options as well as with the potential to request data and experiments remotely.
[2016/XF5404/**F**]

♦ European, Middle East and Africa ORACLE User Group / see International Oracle Users Community (#14416)

♦ European, Middle Eastern and African Society for Biopreservation and Biobanking (ESBB) 07798

Exec Officer 20 boulevard du Roi René, 13100 Aix-en-Provence, France.
URL: http://www.esbb.org/

History Founded Aug 2010. Registered in accordance with French law. **Aims** Advance the field of biobanking in support of research relating to healthcare, education and the environment. **Structure** Council; Bureau. Working/Interest Groups: ESBBperanto (informatics); ESBBtranslate (pharma/academia/governmental links); Biobanking in Africa; Patient Outreach. **Staff** 1.00 FTE, paid. **Activities** Capacity building; events/meetings. **Events** *Europe Biobank Week Meeting* Aix-en-Provence (France) 2020, *Europe Biobank Week Meeting* Lübeck (Germany) 2019, *Europe Biobank Week Meeting* Antwerp (Belgium) 2018, *Global Biobank Week Meeting* Stockholm (Sweden) 2017, *Annual Conference* Vienna (Austria) 2016. **Members** Members worldwide, but particularly from Europe, Middle East and Africa. Membership countries not specified. **NGO Relations** Cooperates with: *Asian Network of Research Resource Centers (ANRRC, #01557)*; BEDO Record of Discussions; *European Association for Predictive, Preventive and Personalised Medicine (EPMA, #06163)*; *International Society for Biological and Environmental Repositories (ISBER, #14964)*; Korean National Research Resource Center (KNRRC).
[2015.01.06/XJ6428/**C**]

♦ European Middle East Project (EuMEP) 07799

Dir Rue des Tanneurs 165, 1000 Brussels, Belgium. E-mail: info@eumep.org.
URL: https://eumep.org/

History Registration: Banque-Carrefour des Entreprises, No/ID: 0630.865.135, Start date: 25 Apr 2015, Belgium; EU Transparency Register, No/ID: 733135223769-69, Start date: 19 Oct 2016. **Aims** Promote just, fact-based and effective policies towards both sides of the Israeli-Palestine conflict by the EU, European governments and the wider international community, based on respect for international law and equal human dignity of all Israelis and Palestinians. **Structure** Board. **Activities** Advocacy/lobbying/activism; research/documentation.
[2020/AA1204/**E**]

♦ European Midwives Association (EMA) 07800

Sec VBOV/EMA, Haantjeslei 185, 2018 Antwerp, Belgium. E-mail: board@europeanmidwives.com – secretary@europeanmidwives.com.
Pres address not obtained. E-mail: president@europeanmidwives.com.
URL: http://www.europeanmidwives.com/

History 1968. Founded as *EEC Liaison Committee of Midwives – Comité de liaison des sages-femmes des pays du Marché commun*, by *International Confederation of Midwives (ICM, #12863).* Subsequently changed title to *European Midwives Liaison Committee (EMLC) – Comité de liaison des sages-femmes européennes.* Statutes amended 26-27 Jun 1993, Amsterdam (Netherlands). Present name adopted with new constitution, and registered in accordance with Dutch law, 2004: 30200555. Office moved to Antwerp (Belgium) 2016, and new constitution notarised. Registration: Banque-Carrefour des Entreprises, No/ID: 0679.817.372, Start date: 3 Feb 2017, Belgium; EU Transparency Register, No/ID: 423054333046-19, Start date: 29 Oct 2018. **Aims** Promote high-quality midwifery *care.* **Structure** Committee (normally meets once a year); Executive Board. **Languages** English. **Finance** Members' dues. **Activities** Events/meetings; projects/programmes; guidance/assistance/consulting. **Events** *Education Conference* Athens (Greece) 2023, *Annual Meeting* 2021, *Annual Meeting* 2020, *Education Conference* Malmö (Sweden) 2019, *Annual Meeting* Prague (Czechia) 2019. **Publications** *Activities, Responsibilities and Independence of Midwives within the European Union* (1995) in English, French.
Members Full; Associate; Supporting. Members in 30 countries:
Austria, Belgium, Bulgaria, Croatia, Cyprus, Czechia, Denmark, Estonia, Finland, France, Germany, Greece, Iceland, Ireland, Italy, Latvia, Lithuania, Luxembourg, Malta, Netherlands, Norway, Portugal, Romania, Slovakia, Slovenia, Spain, Sweden, Switzerland, Türkiye, UK.
IGO Relations *WHO (#20950).* Recognized by: *European Commission (EC, #06633).* Informal links with: *WHO Regional Office for Europe (#20945).* **NGO Relations** Informal links with: *International Confederation of Midwives (ICM, #12863).*
[2022/XE3720/**E**]

♦ European Midwives Liaison Committee / see European Midwives Association (#07800)

♦ European Migraine and Headache Alliance (EMHA) 07801

Exec Dir Rue d'Egmont 11, 1000 Brussels, Belgium. T. +34639669965. E-mail: communications@emhalliance.org – info@emhalliance.org.
URL: https://www.emhalliance.org/

History Reconstituted in 2012 as ASBL. Former names and other names: *European Headache Alliance (EHA)* – former. Registration: Banque-Carrefour des Entreprises, No/ID: 0628.600.778, Start date: 28 Jan 2012, Belgium. **Aims** Promote awareness and understanding of migraine and any other headache disorders; improve access to appropriate diagnosis and treatment for people affected by a headache disorder. **Structure** General Assembly; Board. **Languages** English. **Staff** 3.00 FTE, paid. **Finance** Unrestricted educational grants from pharmaceutical companies for specific projects. **Activities** Events/meetings; advocacy/lobbying/activism; projects/programmes; research/documentation; capacity building; awareness raising. **Events** *Migraine and Headache International Patient Advocacy Summit* Amsterdam (Netherlands) 2018, *Congress* Valencia (Spain) 2015, *Congress* Copenhagen (Denmark) 2014, *Congress* London (UK) 2012, *Congress* Nice (France) 2010. **Publications** *EMHA Magazine.* Survey.
Members Organizations (29) in 19 countries:
Austria, Belgium, Denmark, Finland, France, Germany, Greece, Iceland, Ireland, Italy, Netherlands, Poland, Romania, Russia, Serbia, Spain, Sweden, Switzerland, UK.
NGO Relations Member of (2): *European Federation of Neurological Associations (EFNA, #07177)*; *European Patients' Forum (EPF, #08172).*
[2022/XM1137/**D**]

♦ European Migration Centre (internationally oriented national body)

♦ European Migration Network (EMN) 07802

Contact address not obtained. E-mail: home-emn@ec.europa.eu.
URL: http://ec.europa.eu/

History Set up by Council Decision 2008-381/EC, 14 May 2008, within *European Commission (EC, #06633)* – DG Home Affairs. **Aims** Provide up-to-date, objective, reliable and comparable information on migration and asylum to support policymaking in the EU. **Structure** Coordinated by European Commission DG Home Affairs, assisted by 2 Service Providers, in cooperation with National Contact Points (NCPs) in each Member State and in Norway. Steering Board. **Finance** Funded by *European Commission (EC, #06633).* **Activities** Knowledge management/information dissemination; research/documentation. **Events** *Annual Conference* Vienna (Austria) 2018, *Annual Conference* Tallinn (Estonia) 2017, *Annual Conference* Athens (Greece) 2014. **Publications** *EMN Bulletin. EMN Glossary and Thesaurus.* Reports; studies; factsheets.
Members National contact points in 29 countries:
Austria, Belgium, Bulgaria, Croatia, Cyprus, Czechia, Denmark, Estonia, Finland, France, Germany, Greece, Hungary, Ireland, Italy, Latvia, Lithuania, Luxembourg, Malta, Netherlands, Norway, Poland, Portugal, Romania, Slovakia, Slovenia, Spain, Sweden, UK.
[2015/XM4303/**F***]

♦ European Military Press Association (EMPA) 07803

Association Européenne de la presse militaire – Associazione Europea della Stampa Militare – Vereinigung der Militärpresse Europas

SG Per Albin Hansson Strasse 86, 1100 Vienna, Austria. T. +436764315840. E-mail: secgen.empa@gmail.com.
Pres Stiftgasse 2a, 1070 Vienna, Austria. T. +43150201 – +43128900. E-mail: red.oemz@bmlvs.gv.at.
URL: http://www.empa.media/

History 1977, Rome (Italy). First statutes passed 1980, Hamburg (Germany). Present Articles of Association approved by General Assembly, 17 Oct 1996, Warsaw (Poland); modified 20 Sep 2000, Spiez (Switzerland); 1 Oct 2002, Split (Croatia); 18 Oct 2017, Budapest (Hungary). Previously also referred to in French as *Association de la presse militaire de l'Europe.* Registered in accordance with Swiss Civil Code. **Aims** Act as a forum of the permanent exchange of ideas between military *journalists* and media representatives; contribute to strengthening peace in freedom, ensuring security and the defence readiness being inextricably linked therewith; promote understanding for security policy and general politics of other countries and knowledge of their armed forces. **Structure** General Meeting (annual); Board. **Languages** English, French, German. **Staff** None. **Finance** Members' dues. **Activities** Events/meetings. **Events** *Annual General Meeting* Zadar (Croatia) 2020, *Annual General Meeting* Vienna (Austria) 2019, *Annual General Meeting* Rotterdam (Netherlands) 2018, *Annual general meeting* Budapest (Hungary) 2017, *Annual General Meeting* Oslo (Norway) 2016. **Publications** *EMPA News.*
Members Full in 22 countries:
Austria, Belgium, Croatia, Czechia, Estonia, Finland, Germany, Hungary, Ireland, Italy, Latvia, Lithuania, Netherlands, Norway, Poland, Romania, Serbia, Slovakia, Slovenia, Spain, Sweden, Switzerland.
[2021/XD1032/**D**]

♦ European Milk Bank Association (EMBA) 07804

Sec c/o BIOMEDIA, Via Libero Temolo 4, 20126 Milan MI, Italy. E-mail: embamembership@biomedia.net.
URL: https://europeanmilkbanking.com/

History 15 Oct 2010. Founded when constitution was adopted. Registration: Italy. **Aims** Promote social and health related activities adhering to the principles of the International Agreement of Minors Rights and to the concepts of global and effective *perinatal* care. **Structure** Members' Assembly. Board of Directors. **Finance** Members' dues. **Activities** Relating to *United Nations Convention on the Rights of the Child (CRC, 1989).* **Events** *International Donor Milk Research Congress* Milan (Italy) 2022, *Congress* Warsaw (Poland) 2021, *International Congress* Glasgow (UK) 2017, *International Congress* Lyon (France) 2015, *International Congress* Istanbul (Turkey) 2013.
Members Milk banks in 25 countries:
Austria, Belgium, Bulgaria, Croatia, Czechia, Denmark, Estonia, Finland, France, Germany, Greece, Hungary, Italy, Netherlands, Norway, Poland, Portugal, Russia, Serbia, Slovenia, Spain, Sweden, Switzerland, Türkiye, UK.
[2021/XJ8519/**D**]

♦ European Milk Board (EMB) 07805

Contact Rue de la Loi 155, 1040 Brussels, Belgium. T. +3228081935. Fax +3228088265. E-mail: office@europeanmilkboard.org.
URL: http://www.europeanmilkboard.org/

History Founded as an umbrella organization of European dairy farmer associations. Registration: Banque-Carrefour des Entreprises, Belgium; EU Transârency Register, No/ID: 45338982456-46. **Aims** Unite European milk producers to put up a strong front against the highly concentrated *dairy* industry and food retail trade; explain to consumers the correlation between supermarket prices and food production in the future; introduce flexible control of volumes to adjust the volume of milk to market demand. **Structure** Executive Committee. **Languages** English, French, German. **Publications** *EMB Newsletter.*
Members Organizations (21) in 16 countries:
Belgium, Croatia, Denmark, France, Germany, Ireland, Italy, Latvia, Lithuania, Luxembourg, Netherlands, Norway, Portugal, Spain, Sweden, Switzerland.
[2022.02.15/XM3875/**D**]

♦ European Milk Forum (EMF) 07806

Communications Officer c/o NDC – The Studio, 55c Maple Avenue, Stillorgan, Dublin, CO. DUBLIN, A94 HY83, Ireland. E-mail: info@milkforum.org.
URL: http://www.milknutritiousbynature.eu/

History 2011. A grouping of the type *European Economic Interest Grouping (EEIG, #06960).* Registration: EU Transparency Register, No/ID: 231418743157-51, Start date: 15 Jun 2021. **Aims** Disseminate information based on scientific fact; establish a dialogue around the importance of milk and *dairy* products as part of a healthy, balanced *diet.* **Activities** Knowledge management/information dissemination; advocacy/lobbying/activism.
Members Full in 8 countries:
Austria, Belgium, Denmark, France, Ireland, Netherlands, Norway, UK.
IGO Relations *European Commission (EC, #06633).*
[2021/XM4357/f/**F**]

♦ European Mime Federation (inactive)
♦ European Mine, Chemical and Energy Workers' Federation (inactive)
♦ European Mineralogical Conference (meeting series)

♦ **European Mineralogical Union (EMU)** **07807**
Sec FSU Jena – Geowissenschaften, Carl-Zeiss-Promenade 10, 07745 Jena, Germany.
URL: http://www.eurominunion.org/
History 12 Apr 1987, Strasbourg (France), during constitutional meeting; formally set up 22 Jul 1987. **Aims** Advance cooperation in the mineralogical sciences, including *mineralogy, petrology* and *geochemistry*, and their applications. **Structure** Council (meets annually); Executive Committee. **Languages** English. **Staff** Voluntary. **Finance** Members' dues. Other sources: general and individual sponsors. **Activities** Advocacy/lobbying/activism; awards/prizes/competitions; financial and/or material support; events/meetings. **Events** *EMPG: Biennial International Conference on Experimental Mineralogy, Petrology and Geochemistry* Kiel (Germany) 2012, *European conference on mineralogy and spectroscopy* Potsdam (Germany) 2011, *International workshop on layered materials* Bochum (Germany) 2010, *EMPG: biennial international conference on experimental mineralogy, petrology and geochemistry* Toulouse (France) 2010, *EMPG : international conference on experimental mineralogy, petrology and geochemistry* Innsbruck (Austria) 2008. **Publications** *Notes in Mineralogy* (periodical). *EMU Notes in Mineralogy* – handbook series (20 vols).
Members National scientific societies representing mineral scientists (" indicates grouped in one society) in 28 countries:
Albania, Austria, Belgium, Bulgaria, Croatia, Czechia, Denmark, Finland, France, Germany, Greece, Hungary, Ireland (*), Italy, Montenegro, Netherlands, Norway, Poland, Romania, Russia, Serbia, Slovakia, Slovenia, Spain, Sweden, Switzerland, UK (*), Ukraine.
NGO Relations Member of: *International Union of Geological Sciences (IUGS, #15777)*. Cooperates with: *European Crystallographic Association (ECA, #06867); European Geosciences Union (EGU, #07390); International Mineralogical Association (IMA, #14165); International Union of Crystallography (IUCr, #15768).*
[2020.03.04/XD7498/**D**]

♦ European Mineral Resources Confederation / see EUMICON (#05587)

♦ **European Minifootball Federation (EMF)** **07808**
Contact Hvezdova 1716/2B, 140 78 Prague, Czechia. E-mail: kuzenkovaelizaveta@gmail.com.
URL: http://www.eurominifootball.com/
History 2012. Regional federation of *World Minifootball Federation (WMF, #21652)*. **Aims** Promote, supervise and direct minifootball in Europe, as a means to contribute to the positive development of society. **Structure** General Assembly; Executive Committee. Committees (11): CSR, Spirit Development and Student; Grants; History and Statistics; Health, Safety, Security and Environment (HSSE); Information Technology; Legislative; Marketing; Media and Public Relations; Referee; Strategic Development; Tournament. **Languages** English. **Finance** Members' dues. **Activities** Sporting events.
Members Federations in 30 countries and territories:
Armenia, Austria, Bulgaria, Croatia, Cyprus, Czechia, England, Germany, Greece, Ireland, Israel, Italy, Kazakhstan, Lithuania, Luxembourg, Moldova, Montenegro, Northern Ireland, Poland, Romania, Russia, Scotland, Serbia, Slovakia, Slovenia, Spain, Sweden, Switzerland, Türkiye, Wales.
NGO Relations *Asian Minifootball Confederation (AMC, #01541); Confederación Panamericana de Minifutbol (CPM, #04477); Oceania Mini Football Federation (OMF, #17666).* [2022/XJ9001/**D**]

♦ European Mint Directors' Conference / see Mint Directors Conference (#16822)

♦ **European Mitochondrial Disease Network (EMDN)** **07809**
Registered Office Mayfield House, 30 Heber Walk, Chester Way, Northwich, CW9 5JB, UK. T. +44160643946. Fax +44160643946. E-mail: info@cmdn.org.uk.
URL: http://www.cmdn.org.uk/
History Jul 1998. Also referred to under working name *Children's Mitochondrial Disease Network*. UK Registered Charity: 1070533. **Aims** Promote research into causes and treatment of mitochondrial *encephalomyopathies* and related mitochondrial disorders in children and adults, their pre-natal diagnosis and the publication of useful research results; advise, support and inform parents, carers and professionals; support, and assist financially, relevant professionals in attending European and overseas meetings. **Members** Membership countries not specified. [2017/XM0439/**F**]

♦ **European Mobile Seed Association (EMSA)** **07810**
SG Anspachlaan 111, b13, 1000 Brussels, Belgium. T. +3222742207. E-mail: info@emsa-seed.eu.
History 1983. Set up as the Seed Section of *European Organization of Agricultural and Rural Contractors (#08105)*. Since 15 Dec 2010, an autonomous legal entity. Statutes most recently updated 9 June 2021. Registration: Banque-Carrefour des Entreprises, Start date: Mar 2011, Belgium; EU Transparency Register, No/ID: 75964025885-59. **Aims** Advocate the interest of mobile seed processors at European level. **Structure** General Assembly; Board. [2023.02.14/XJ2974/**D**]

♦ European Mobility Group (unconfirmed)
♦ European Model Soldiers Societies Association (inactive)

♦ **European Modern Music Education Network (EMMEN)** **07811**
Coordinator De Vrièrestraat 17-19, 2000 Antwerp, Belgium. T. +3232482468. E-mail: info@jazzstudio.be.
URL: http://www.emmenet.org/
Structure General Assembly (annual). Council, elects President, 2 Vice-Presidents, Secretary-General and Treasurer. **Languages** English, French.
Members Schools in 7 countries:
Belgium, France, Germany, Greece, Italy, Spain, UK.
NGO Relations Member of: *International Music Council (IMC, #14199).* [2013/XF6656/**F**]

♦ European Modern Restaurant Association / see Serving Europe (#19248)

♦ **European Molecular Biology Conference (EMBC)** **07812**
Conférence européenne de biologie moléculaire – Europäische Konferenz für Molekularbiologie
Head Office Meyerhofstr 1, 69117 Heidelberg, Germany. E-mail: embc_office@embo.org – embc@embo.org.
URL: http://embc.embo.org/
History Established 13 Feb 1969, Geneva (Switzerland), at a conference convened by the Swiss government, with the dual aim of providing a secure source of funds for a generic programme which, in the first instance, includes the EMBO Fellowships, Courses, Workshops and administration, and to provide a framework to establish *European Molecular Biology Laboratory (EMBL, #07813)*. Registered in accordance with Swiss Civil Code, 7 May 1970. **Aims** Ensure cooperation between European states for basic research in molecular biology and allied fields, through the medium of the European Molecular Biology Organization (EMBO). **Structure** Officers: President; 2 Vice Presidents; Secretary General. **Languages** English. **Finance** Contributions by member Governments, based on net national income at factor cost. **Activities** Training/education; financial and/or material support.
Members Governments of 30 countries:
Austria, Belgium, Croatia, Czechia, Denmark, Estonia, Finland, France, Germany, Greece, Hungary, Iceland, Ireland, Israel, Italy, Lithuania, Luxembourg, Malta, Montenegro, Netherlands, Norway, Poland, Portugal, Slovakia, Slovenia, Spain, Sweden, Switzerland, Türkiye, UK.
Associate members (2):
India, Singapore.
NGO Relations Close cooperation with: *European Molecular Biology Organization (EMBO, #07816).*
[2021/XD3888/**F***]

♦ **European Molecular Biology Laboratory (EMBL)** **07813**
Laboratoire européen de biologie moléculaire – Europäisches Laboratorium für Molekularbiologie
Dir-Gen Meyerhofstrasse 1, 69117 Heidelberg, Germany. T. +4962213870. Fax +4962213878306. E-mail: info@embl.de – dg-office@embl.org.
URL: http://www.embl.org/
History 10 May 1973, Geneva (Switzerland). Established on signature of agreement by member states. Agreement ratified 4 Jul 1974, Heidelberg (Germany FR). Membership open only to members of *European Molecular Biology Conference (EMBC, #07812)*. **Aims** Promote molecular biology across Europe; create a centre of excellence for Europe's leading young molecular biologists. **Structure** Council; Finance Committee; Scientific Advisory Committee; Director General, supported by Directorate. Main laboratory: Heidelberg (Germany). Outstations (4): Grenoble (France); Hamburg (Germany); Monterotondo (Italy); *EMBL's European Bioinformatics Institute (EMBL-EBI, #05433)*, Hinxton (UK). **Languages** English, French, German. **Staff** 1800.00 FTE, paid. Staff negotiations through *European Molecular Biology Laboratory Staff Association (EMBL Staff Association, #07814). Administrative Tribunal of the International Labour Organization (ILO Tribunal, #00118)* is competent to settle disputes. **Finance** Sources: contributions of member/participating states. External funding. Annual budget: 230,837,000 EUR (2015). **Activities** Events/meetings; research and development; training/education. **Events** *Symposium on Innate Immunity in Host-Pathogen Interactions* Heidelberg (Germany) 2022, *Symposium on Plasticity across Scales : from Molecules to Phenotypes* Heidelberg (Germany) 2022, *Symposium on Reconstructing the Human Past : Using Ancient and Modern Genomics* Heidelberg (Germany) 2022, *Symposium on the Complex Life of RNA* Heidelberg (Germany) 2022, *Symposium on the Neurovascular Interface* Heidelberg (Germany) 2022. **Publications** *Research at a Glance* (annual). Annual Scientific Report; programme; brochures; press releases.
Members Governments of 27 countries:
Austria, Belgium, Croatia, Czechia, Denmark, Finland, France, Germany, Greece, Hungary, Iceland, Ireland, Israel, Italy, Lithuania, Luxembourg, Malta, Montenegro, Netherlands, Norway, Poland, Portugal, Slovakia, Spain, Sweden, Switzerland, UK.
Associate membership by 2 governments:
Argentina, Australia.
Prospect membership by 2 governments:
Estonia, Latvia.
IGO Relations Close relations with: *European Commission (EC, #06633).* [2021/XF7254/**F***]

♦ **European Molecular Biology Laboratory Staff Association (EMBL Staff Association)** **07814**
Administrative Officer Meyerhofstrasse 1, 69117 Heidelberg, Germany. T. +496221387541. Fax +496221387306. E-mail: staff@embl.de.
URL: http://www.embl-heidelberg.de/
History to represent staff of *European Molecular Biology Laboratory (EMBL, #07813)*. **Activities** Represents economic, professional, social and cultural interests of its members.
Members Full in 20 countries:
Austria, Belgium, Croatia, Denmark, Finland, France, Germany, Greece, Iceland, Ireland, Israel, Italy, Luxembourg, Netherlands, Norway, Portugal, Spain, Sweden, Switzerland, UK.
NGO Relations *Federation of International Civil Servants' Associations (FICSA, #09603).*
[2013.07.16/XE2806/**E**]

♦ **European Molecular Biology Network (EMBnet)** **07815**
Sec Centro Nacional de Biotecnologia – CSIC, Campus Univ Autónoma, Cantoblanco, 28049 Madrid, Spain. T. +34915854505. E-mail: jrvalverde@cnb.csic.es.
URL: http://www.embnet.org/
History Registered as a foundation in accordance with Dutch law. **Aims** Provide *databases* and *software* tools for molecular biology and *biotechnology* to the European scientific community. **Structure** General Meeting (annual). Executive Board, comprising Chairman, Treasurer and Secretary. Project Committees (3): Research and Development in EMBnet; Education and Training; Publicity and Public Relations, each comprising Chairman, Treasurer and Secretary. National nodes appointed by governmental authorities. **Activities** Services include: data and software accessibility to users; research; data distribution; networking; training; collaboration. Project Committees referee and fund grant applications. **Events** *Annual General Meeting* Valencia (Spain) 2013. **Publications** *EMBnet-News* (4 a year) – available through electronic mail. Communication maintained through electronic mail and Usenet News groups.
Members Collaborating nodes (38 biocomputing centres) in 29 countries:
Argentina, Australia, Brazil, Canada, Chile, China, Colombia, Costa Rica, Cuba, Finland, France, Greece, Hungary, India, Italy, Kenya, Mexico, Norway, Pakistan, Poland, Portugal, Russia, Slovakia, South Africa, Spain, Sri Lanka, Sweden, Switzerland, UK.
NGO Relations Affiliated organization of: *International Society for Computational Biology (ISCB, #15026).* Instrumental in setting up: *Global Organisation for Bioinformatics Learning, Education and Training (GOBLET, #10516).* [2010.06.23/XF3567/**F**]

♦ **European Molecular Biology Organization (EMBO)** **07816**
Organisation européenne de biologie moléculaire – Europäische Organisation für Molekularbiologie
Main Office Meyerhofstr 1, 69117 Heidelberg, Germany. E-mail: embo@embo.org.
Main: http://www.embo.org/
History Founded 4 Feb 1964, Geneva (Switzerland), following a meeting, Sep 1963, Ravello (Italy). **Aims** Promote excellence in the life sciences; enable the best science by supporting talented researchers, stimulating scientific exchange and advancing policies for a world-class European research environment. **Structure** *European Molecular Biology Conference (EMBC, #07812)*; EMBO Council. Committees (9): Fellowship; Course; Membership; Science and Society; Young Investigator Programme; Publications Advisory Board; Global Exchange; The EMBO Meeting; EMBO/EMBL Symposia. **Languages** English. **Staff** 50.00 FTE, paid. **Finance** Sources: *European Molecular Biology Conference (EMBC, #07812)*. **Activities** Awards/prizes/competitions; events/meetings; training/education. **Events** *Workshop on Trans-Scale Biology using exotic non-model organisms* Okazaki (Japan) 2023, *Workshop on Wnt* Awaji (Japan) 2022, *Symposium on Plasticity across Scales : from Molecules to Phenotypes* Heidelberg (Germany) 2022, *Symposium on the Complex Life of RNA* Heidelberg (Germany) 2022, *Symposium on the Neurovascular Interface* Heidelberg (Germany) 2022. **Publications** *Molecular Systems Biology* (weekly) – online; *The EMBO Journal* (24 a year); *Annual Facts and Figures*; *EMBO Molecular Medicine*. **Information Services** *EMBO Life Sciences Mobility Portal*.
Members Elected scientists (over 1,400) in the 27 EMBC countries:
Austria, Belgium, Croatia, Czechia, Denmark, Estonia, Finland, France, Germany, Greece, Hungary, Iceland, Ireland, Israel, Italy, Luxembourg, Netherlands, Norway, Poland, Portugal, Slovakia, Slovenia, Spain, Sweden, Switzerland, Türkiye, UK.
Associate scientists (over 100) worldwide. Membership countries not specified.
IGO Relations Cooperates with: *European Molecular Biology Laboratory (EMBL, #07813)*. **NGO Relations** Member of: *Initiative for Science in Europe (ISE, #11214); ORCID (#17790).* [2021/XD0811/**v/D**]

♦ **European Molecular Liquids Group (EMLG)** **07817**
Chair Institut of Chemistry, University of Rostock, Dr.-Lorenz-Weg 2, 18059 Rostock, Germany.
URL: http://139.30.122.11/EMLG/index.html
History 1981, Dublin (Ireland). Registration: Start date: 2015, Austria. **Aims** Study structure, dynamics and interactions of molecules in liquids by experimental, theoretical and simulation techniques. **Structure** Officers; Advisory Committee. **Languages** English. **Staff** Voluntary. **Finance** Sources: members' dues. **Activities** Events/meetings. **Events** *Annual Joint Meeting* Barcelona (Spain) 2022, *Annual Joint Meeting* Barcelona (Spain) 2021, *Annual Joint Meeting* Barcelona (Spain) 2020, *Annual Joint Meeting* Kutná Hora (Czechia) 2019, *Annual Joint Meeting* Nagoya (Japan) 2018. **Publications** *EMLG Newsletter*. **NGO Relations** Japanese Molecular Liquids Group (JMLG). [2022/XM3554/**E**]

♦ **European Mollusc Producers' Association (EMPA)** **07818**
Association européenne de producteurs de mollusques (AEPM) – Asociación Europea de Productores de Moluscos (AEPM) – Associazione Europea di Produttori di Molluschi (AEPM)
SG 122 rue de Javel, 75015 Paris, France. T. +33142974844. Fax +33142860824.
Chair address not obtained. E-mail: president@cnc-france.com.
History 1999, Brussels (Belgium). Previously also referred to in English as *European Association of Mollusc Producers (EAMP)*. Registration: Start date: 18 Apr 2005, France; EU Transparency Register, No/ID: 90987504898-26, Start date: 5 Jan 2011. **Languages** English, French, Italian, Spanish.
Members Full in 7 countries:
France, Ireland, Italy, Netherlands, Portugal, Spain, UK.
NGO Relations Member of: Advisory Aquaculture Council (AAC); *European Aquaculture Technology and Innovation Platform (EATiP, #05910)*. Cooperation agreement with: *Federation of European Aquaculture Producers (FEAP, #09491).* [2022/XM0360/**D**]

♦ European Monarchist Association (no recent information)
♦ European Monetary Agreement (1958 treaty)
♦ European Monetary Cooperation Fund (inactive)
♦ European Monetary Institute (inactive)

♦ European Money Markets Institute (EMMI) 07819

CEO Avenue des Arts 56, 1000 Brussels, Belgium. T. +3224315208. E-mail: info@emmi-benchmarks.eu.
Main Website: https://www.emmi-benchmarks.eu

History 1999. Former names and other names: *EURIBOR-EBF* – former (1999). Registration: Banque-Carrefour des Entreprises, No/ID: 0465.075.408, Start date: 4 Feb 1999, Belgium; EU Transparency Register, No/ID: 70092714192-21, Start date: 17 Sep 2010. **Aims** Facilitate the smooth functioning of euro money markets and foster their integration. As an Authorised Administrator under the Benchmarks Regulation of the European Union (BMR): develop and administer robust benchmarks – like Euribor – that are essential for financial markets and thus for the broader economy; promote labels, standards, and practices enabling harmonised access to the markets; explores initiatives to answer market's needs. **Structure** General Assembly; Board of Directors. Committees (5): Nomination; Audit & Risk; Conflict of Interest Oversight; Euribor – Efterm Oversight; STEP Market. Secretariat. **Languages** English. **Members** Full Members: national banking associations of the EU countries. Associate Members: EFTA countries. **NGO Relations** Member of (1): *Federation of European and International Associations Established in Belgium (FAIB, #09508)*.
[2023.02.14/XJ7588/**E**]

♦ European Monitoring Centre for Drugs and Drug Addiction (EMCDDA) 07820

Observatoire européen des drogues et des toxicomanies – Observatorio Europeo de las Drogas y las Toxicomanias – Europäische Beobachtungsstelle für Drogen und Drogensucht – Osservatorio Europeo delle Droghe e delle Tossicodipendenze – Observatório Europeu da Droga e da Toxicodependência – Europees Waarnemingscentrum voor Drugs en Drugsverslaving – Europeiska Centrumet för Kontroll av Narkotika och Narkotikamissbruk – Det Europaeiske Overvågningscenter for Narkotika og Narkotikamisbrug – Euroopan huumausaineiden ja niiden väärinkäytön seurantakeskus – Evropské Monitorovací Centrum pro Drogy a Drogovou Závislost – Európske Monitorovacie Centrum pre Drogy a Drogovú Závislosť – Kabítószer és Kabítószer-FüggOség Európai Megfigyelóközpontja – Europejskie Centrum Monitorowania Narkotyków i Narkomanii – Evropski Center za Spremljanje Drog in Zasvojensoti z Drogami – Euroopa Narkootikuminde ja Narkomaania Seirekeskus – Eiropas Narkotiku un Narkomānijas Uzraudzibas Centrs – Observatorul European pentru Droguri si Toxicomanie – Europeisk Overvåkingssenter for Narkotika og Narkotikamisbruk

Dir Praça Europa 1, Cais do Sodré, 1249-289 Lisbon, Portugal. T. +35121211210200. Fax +35121211210380. E-mail: info@emcdda.europa.eu.
Senior Policy Officer address not obtained.
URL: http://www.emcdda.europa.eu/

History 8 Feb 1993. Established on adoption by *Council of the European Union (#04895)* of Regulation (EEC) No 302/93; fully operational from early 1995. Set up following the initiative of French President François Mitterrand in Oct 1989 and in response to the *Plan européen de lutte contre la drogue*, which was adopted by *European Council (#06801)* in Nov 1992, Edinburgh (UK), having been coordinated by *Comité européen de lutte antidrogue (CELAD, inactive)*, set up in 1989. Based in Lisbon (Portugal), a decentralized agency of *European Union (EU, #08967)* under the terms of the *Treaty on European Union (Maastricht Treaty, 1992)*. Founding regulation was recast following an initiative of the EC, Aug 2005. After a co-decision procedure of Council and Parliament, it entered into force, 16 Jan 2007. Last amended by Regulation (EU) No 2017/2101 of Parliament and Council of 15 Nov 2017. Former names and other names: *OEDT* – former; *EBDD* – former; *EWDD* – former; *ECNN* – former; *EONN* – former. **Aims** Provide the Union and its Member States with factual, objective, reliable and comparable information at European level concerning drugs and drug addiction and their consequences; collect and analyse existing data; improve data-comparison methods; disseminate data; inform competent authorities of new developments and existing trends. **Structure** Management Board (meets at least annually), consisting of one representative from each EU Member State, 2 representatives of *European Commission (EC, #06633)* and 2 representatives designated by *European Parliament (EP, #08146)*, one representative from each country which has concluded an agreement pursuant to Article 21 of the EMCDDA recast Regulation (Norway and Turkey). Scientific Committee; Director and Executive Office; Scientific Director; Public Health and Risks to Public Safety and Security Units; other Units. **Staff** 109.00 FTE, paid. **Finance** Financed largely from the EU budget. Annual budget: 18,471,000 EUR (2023). **Activities** Knowledge management/information dissemination; politics/policy/regulatory. **Events** *Annual Meeting on Problem Drug Use Key Indicator* Lisbon (Portugal) 2019, *European Conference on Addictive Behaviours and Dependencies* Lisbon (Portugal) 2019, *Meeting on Drug-Related Infectious Diseases Key Indicator* Lisbon (Portugal) 2019, *Meeting on the Key Indicator Drug-Related Deaths* Lisbon (Portugal) 2019, *Meeting on the Treatment Demand Indicator* Lisbon (Portugal) 2019. **Publications** *DrugNet Europe* (4 a year) in English – newsletter. *Insights* in English – series; *Manuals* in English – series; *Risk Assessments* in English – series; *Scientific Monographs* in English – series. *EU Drug Market Report*; *European Drug Report: Trends and Developments*; *Health and Social Responses to Drug Problems: a European Guide*. General Report of Activities; policy briefings; brochures; flyers; catalogues; thematic papers; thematic data sheets. **Information Services** *Documentation and Information Centre (DIC)* – comprises a specialized library and electronic information service.

Members Member States of the European Union, Norway and Turkey (30):
Austria, Belgium, Bulgaria, Croatia, Cyprus, Czechia, Denmark, Estonia, Finland, France, Germany, Greece, Hungary, Ireland, Italy, Latvia, Lithuania, Luxembourg, Malta, Netherlands, Norway, Poland, Portugal, Romania, Slovakia, Slovenia, Spain, Sweden, Türkiye, UK.

IGO Relations Represented on the Management Board: *European Commission (EC, #06633)*; *European Parliament (EP, #08146)*. Observers to the Management Board: *Co-operation Group to Combat Drug Abuse and Illicit Trafficking in Drugs (Pompidou Group, #04796)*; spokesperson of national focal points of Réseau européen d'information sur les drogues et les toxicomanies (REITOX); *WHO (#20950)*. Other priority international partners: *European Police Office (Europol, #08239)*; *International Criminal Police Organization – INTERPOL (ICPO-INTERPOL, #13110)*; *World Customs Organization (WCO, #21350)*. Memorandum of Understanding with: Europol; *Inter-American Drug Abuse Control Commission (#11429)*; Interpol; Pompidou Group / Groupe Pompidou; *United Nations Office on Drugs and Crime (UNODC, #20596)*; WHO. Agreement with: *Council of Europe (CE, #04881)*. Cooperates with: *United Nations Office on Drugs and Crime (UNODC, #20596)*; other EU agencies. **NGO Relations** Member of (1): *EU Agencies Network (EUAN, #05564)*. Cooperates with international organizations competent in the sector of drugs (not specified).
[2023.02.15/XF2543/**E***]

♦ European Monoclonal Antibodies Network (EUROMABNET) 07821

Pres CNIO, Calle Melchor Fernández Almagro 3, 28029 Madrid, Spain. T. +34912246900.
URL: http://www.euromabnet.com/

History 2008. **Aims** Provide an arena in which people working in the field of monoclonal antibody production and technology can exchange knowledge, share the most up-to-date methodology and create common strategies to both standardize and improve the production of properly validated monoclonal antibodies; strengthen European leadership in mAb technology; improve education in the field internationally; actively engage with industrial partners to ensure optimum benefits from using mAb technology to improve human health. **Structure** Committee, includes President, Vice-President, Secretary and Advisory Board. **Languages** English. **Finance** Sources: members' dues. **Activities** Events/meetings; knowledge management/information dissemination. **Events** *Antibody Validation Workshop* Ghent (Belgium) 2018, *Meeting* Oxford (UK) 2018, *Workshop* Oxford (UK) 2018, *Antibody Validation Workshop* Pécs (Hungary) 2017, *Meeting* Pécs (Hungary) 2017. **Publications** Guide.

Members Individuals in 12 countries:
Belgium, Croatia, Denmark, France, Germany, Hungary, Italy, Lithuania, Russia, Slovenia, Spain, UK.
[2022.02.08/XM7888/**F**]

♦ European Mortar Industry Organization (EMO) 07822

Association de l'industrie européenne des mortiers – Europese Vereniging van Producten van Industriële Mortels

SG Boulevard du Souverain 68, Bte 1, 1170 Brussels, Belgium. T. +4924085996207. Fax +4924085996208. E-mail: info@euromortar.com.
URL: http://www.euromortar.com/

History 1991. Former names and other names: *Organisation européenne des producteurs de mortiers* – alias. Registration: Banque Carrefour des Entreprises, No/ID: 0543.605.915, Start date: 26 Dec 2013, Belgium; EU Transparency Register, No/ID: 775299618501-45, Start date: 18 Aug 2015. **Structure** General Assembly; Presidency; Executive Board; Technical Committee; General Secretary. **Languages** English. **Events** *European Mortar Summit* Lisbon (Portugal) 2015, *General Assembly* Amsterdam (Netherlands) 2014, *European Mortar summit* Barcelona (Spain) 2013, *European Mortar Summit* Paris (France) 2011, *General Assembly* Belgium 2002.

Members Organizations in 14 countries:
Austria, Belgium, Czechia, Denmark, Finland, France, Germany, Iceland, Ireland, Luxembourg, Netherlands, Portugal, Spain, UK.

NGO Relations Member of (3): *Construction 2050 Alliance (#04760)*; *European Network on Silica (NEPSI, #08001)*; *Industry4Europe (#11181)*. In liaison with technical committees of: *Comité européen de normalisation (CEN, #04162)*.
[2020/XD3526/t/**D**]

♦ European Mortgage Federation / see Covered Bond and Mortgage Council (#04940)
♦ European Mortgage Federation – European Covered Bond Council / see Covered Bond and Mortgage Council (#04940)

♦ European Mosquito Control Association (EMCA) 07823

Main Office c/o Ecodevelopment SA, PO BOX 2420, Filyro, 570 10 Thessaloniki, Greece. E-mail: office@emca-online.eu.
Headquarters 12 rue des Pucelles, 67000 Strasbourg, France.
Registered Office Cité Administrative Gaujot, 14 rue du Maréchal Juin, 67084 Strasbourg, France.
URL: http://www.emca-online.eu/

History Mar 2000, Waldsee (Germany). Current bylaws adopted 28 Mar 2000, Speyer (Germany). Registration: France. **Aims** Promote the effective and efficient control of mosquitoes and related subjects; disseminate affiliated information to members and others in Europe and neighbouring regions. **Structure** Board of Directors. Executive Committee, comprising President, Executive Director and Secretary/Treasurer. **Finance** Members' dues. **Events** *International Conference* Vienna (Austria) 2021, *Conference* La Rochelle (France) 2019, *Conference* Montenegro 2017, *Global change – impacts and strategies to fight against mosquitoes and mosquito-borne diseases* Valencia (Spain) 2015, *Workshop* Budapest (Hungary) 2011. **Publications** *European Mosquito Bulletin*. **Members** Regular; Sustaining; Honorary. Members (172) in 24 countries. Membership countries not specified.
[2022/XJ5376/**D**]

♦ European Motel Federation (inactive)
♦ European Motility Society / see European Society of Neurogastroenterology and Motility (#08663)
♦ European Motorcycle Union / see FIM Europe (#09760)
♦ European Moulded Fibre Association (unconfirmed)
♦ European Moulding Manufacturers Association (inactive)

♦ European Mountain Forum (EMF) 07824

Forum européen de la montagne – Foro Europeo de la Montaña – Evropské Horské Fórum – Forumul Montan European

Contact address not obtained. E-mail: christoph.maier@promonte-aem.net.
URL: http://archive.mtnforum.org/europe/

History 1998, within *Mountain Forum (MF, #16861)*. **Aims** Promote the idea, processes and best practices of *sustainable development* in the mountains of Europe; raise awareness of the importance of these mountains to Europeans. **Structure** Board of Directors, comprising Chair, Vice Chair, Treasurer and 4 members. Coordination Centre; contact offices in Georgia, Poland and Spain. **Staff** 5.00 FTE, paid. **Finance** Primary funder: *Swiss Agency for Development and Cooperation (SDC)*. Support also provided by: *European Union (EU, #08967)*; *FAO (#09260)*; *International Union for Conservation of Nature and Natural Resources (IUCN, #15766)*; *UNEP (#20299)*. **Activities** Operates an online permanent moderated discussion list; establishes different nodes in Europe in each mountain geographical massif. Organizes training sessions to use new technologies of information and communication for the benefit of mountain actors. Projects (2002): Training of Protected Areas Staff (TOPAS); Réseau alpestre francophone (RAF); South East of Europe Mountain Network (SEMNET). **Events** *Annual General Assembly* Les Planes de Son (Spain) 2002, *General Assembly* Spain 2002, *Annual general assembly / General Assembly* Liptovsky Mikulas (Slovakia) 1999. **Publications** *EMF Newsletter*. Membership directory online. Information Services: Online library with 3000 reference texts on mountain issues.

Members Individuals; organizations. Individuals in 59 countries and territories:
Albania, Andorra, Argentina, Armenia, Australia, Austria, Belgium, Bolivia, Bosnia-Herzegovina, Brazil, Bulgaria, Canada, China, Colombia, Croatia, Czechia, Denmark, Ecuador, Egypt, Fiji, Finland, France, Georgia, Germany, Greece, Hungary, India, Ireland, Italy, Japan, Kenya, Kyrgyzstan, Lesotho, Mexico, Morocco, Nepal, Netherlands, New Zealand, North Macedonia, Norway, Pakistan, Peru, Poland, Romania, Russia, Serbia, Singapore, Slovakia, Slovenia, South Africa, Spain, Sweden, Switzerland, Taiwan, Türkiye, UK, Ukraine, USA, Uzbekistan.

NGO Relations Founding organizations include: *Euromontana (#05737)*; European Programme of IUCN. Member of: *Mountain Partnership (MP, #16862)*.
[2009/XE3711/**E**]

♦ European Movement / see European Movement International (#07825)
♦ European Movement (internationally oriented national body)
♦ **European Movement for Detention Houses** RESCALED (#18849)

♦ European Movement International (EMI) 07825

Mouvement européen international

SG Place du Luxembourg 2, 1050 Brussels, Belgium. T. +3225083088. Fax +3225083089. E-mail: secretariat@europeanmovement.eu.
URL: https://europeanmovement.eu/

History Dec 1947, Paris (France). Founded by *Comité de coordination des mouvements militants pour l'unité européenne (inactive)*, a liaison committee consisting of representatives of: *Union of European Federalists, The (UEF, #20385)*; *European League for Economic Cooperation (ELEC, #07669)*; *Socialist Movement for the United States of Europe – Mouvement socialiste pour les Etats-Unis d'Europe (MSEUE)* – currently *European Socialist Movement (MSE, no recent information)*; *Mouvement libéral pour l'Europe unie (MLEU, inactive)*; *Association européenne des enseignants (AEDE, #02565)*; *Council of European Municipalities and Regions (CEMR, #04891)*; *Union of Resistance Veterans for a United Europe (URPE, inactive)*; and *Nouvelles équipes internationales (NEI)*, which in 1947, Chaudfontaine (Belgium), became *European Union of Christian Democrats (EUCD, inactive)*. Works as a permanent organization since *Congress of Europe*, which it convened May 1948, The Hague (Netherlands), and whose recommendations, inter alia, led to the creation of the Council of Europe, 5 May 1949, London (UK). Subsequent conferences led to the establishment of: *European Payments Union (EPU, inactive)*, 19 Sep 1950, replaced, 27 Dec 1958, by *European Monetary Agreement (1958)*; *European Centre for Culture (ECC, #06472)*, 7 Oct 1950, Geneva (Switzerland). Previously included *Parliamentary Council of the European Movement (no recent information)*, set up 1952, by merger of *European Parliamentary Union (EPU, inactive)*, formed Sep 1947, Gstaad (Switzerland), and *International Parliamentary Group of the European Movement (inactive)*. Registered in accordance with Belgian law. Former names and other names: *International Committee of the Movements for European Unity* – former; *Comité international des mouvements pour l'unité européenne* – former; *European Movement (EM)* – former; *Mouvement européen (ME)* – former; *Europäische Bewegung* – former; *Movimento Europeo* – former; *Europese Beweging* – former; *International European Movement (EM)* – former; *Mouvement européen international* – former; *Internationale Europäische Bewegung* – former. Registration: EU Transparency Register, No/ID: 35279857524-58, Start date: 21 Dec 2011. **Aims** Contribute to establishing a united, *federal* Europe founded on the principles of peace, democracy, liberty, solidarity and respect for basic human rights; provide a structure to encourage and facilitate active participation of *citizens* and *civil society* organizations in development of a united Europe. **Structure** Federal Assembly; Members Council; Board; Secretariat. Political Committees; Working Groups. **Languages** English, French. **Staff** 2.50 FTE, paid. **Finance** Contributions from national councils and member organizations; public funding. **Activities** Events/meetings; research/documentation; training/education; knowledge management/information dissemination. **Events** *Meeting on Investing in the Future of Ukraine in Europe* Brussels (Belgium) 2022, *Federal Assembly* Brussels (Belgium) 2020, *Federal Assembly* Helsinki (Finland) 2019, *Federal assembly* Vienna (Austria) 2018, *Meeting* Brussels (Belgium) 2017. **Publications** Reports of Congresses and meetings; brochures and studies on European problems.

European MS Platform
07825

alphabetic sequence excludes
For the complete listing, see Yearbook Online at

Members National councils in 34 countries:
Albania, Austria, Belgium, Bosnia-Herzegovina, Bulgaria, Croatia, Cyprus, Czechia, Denmark, Estonia, Finland, France, Germany, Greece, Hungary, Ireland, Italy, Latvia, Lithuania, Luxembourg, Malta, Montenegro, Netherlands, North Macedonia, Norway, Poland, Portugal, Romania, Serbia, Spain, Sweden, Switzerland, Türkiye, UK.
International associations (34):
- *Alliance of Liberals and Democrats for Europe Party (ALDE Party, #00703)*;
- *Association des états généraux des étudiants de l'Europe (AEGEE-Europe, #02495)*;
- *Association des femmes de l'Europe méridionale (AFEM, #02594)*;
- *Association européenne des enseignants (AEDE, #02565)*;
- *Association internationale des anciens de l'Union Européenne (AIACE, #02667)*;
- *CEC European Managers (#03623)*;
- *Centre international de formation européenne (CIFE, #03755)*;
- *Confédération Européenne des Anciens Combattants (CEAC, #04537)*;
- *Council of European Dentists (CED, #04886)*;
- *Council of European Municipalities and Regions (CEMR, #04891)*;
- *Democracy International (#05032)*;
- *Erasmus Student Network (ESN, #05529)*;
- *Europa Nostra (#05767)*;
- *European Association for Local Democracy (ALDA, #06110)*;
- *European Association of Institutes for Vocational Training (#06085)*;
- *European Centre for Culture (ECC, #06472)*;
- *European Confederation of Independent Trade Unions (CESI, #06705)*;
- *European Democratic Party (EDP, #06900)*;
- *European Environmental Bureau (EEB, #06996)*;
- European Friends of Armenia;
- *European Green Party (EGP, #07409)*;
- *European Grouping of Societies of Authors and Composers (#07422)*;
- *European League for Economic Cooperation (ELEC, #07669)*;
- *European Organisation of Military Associations and Trade Unions (EUROMIL, #08099)*;
- *European People's Party (EPP, #08185)*;
- *European Trade Union Confederation (ETUC, #08927)*;
- *European Women Lawyers' Association (EWLA, #09098)*;
- *European Youth Forum (#09140)*;
- *Eyes and Ears of Europe*;
- *New European Business Confederation (UNITEE)*;
- *Party of European Socialists (PES, #18249)*;
- *SGI Europe (#19253)*;
- *Union of European Federalists, The (UEF, #20385)*;
- *Young European Federalists (#21984)*.

Supporting Members (3):
College of Europe (#04105); *Fondation Euractiv PoliTech (#09818)*; Kosovar Civil Society Foundation.
Consultative Status Consultative status granted from: *Council of Europe (CE, #04881)* (Participatory Status).
IGO Relations Instrumental in setting up: *Parliamentary Council of the European Union (no recent information)*.
NGO Relations Member of (2): *Citizens for Europe (CFEU, #03956)*; *Eastern Partnership Civil Society Forum (EaP CSF, #05247)*. Instrumental in setting up (2): *Permanent Forum of European Civil Society (#18322)*; *Women of Europe Award (#20993)*. [2023/XD0814/y/**D**]

♦ European MS Platform / see European Multiple Sclerosis Platform (#07833)

♦ European Mucosal Immunology Group (EMIG) 07826

Contact address not obtained. T. +33437642167. Fax +33437642168.
URL: http://www.emig2014.com/
History 1998, by European members of *Society for Mucosal Immunology (SMI, #19601)*. **Aims** Unite European medical and scientific expertise on mucosal immunity. **Events** *Meeting* Copenhagen (Denmark) 2016, *Meeting* Glasgow (UK) 2014, *Meeting* Dublin (Ireland) 2012, *Meeting* Amsterdam (Netherlands) 2010, *Meeting* Milan (Italy) 2008. [2014/XJ3439/**E**]

♦ European Multicenter Study about Spinal Cord Injury (EMSCI) 07827

Head Uniklinik Balgrist, Zentrum für Paraplegie, Forchstr 340, 3800 Zurich ZH, Switzerland.
URL: http://www.emsci.org/
Aims Establish a multi-center basis for future *therapeutic* interventions in human *spinal* cord injury. **Activities** Events/meetings; training/education; research and development. **Events** *International Neurorehabilitation Symposium* Valencia (Spain) 2015.
Members Founding; Active; Passive; Associated. Institutions in 8 countries:
Canada, Czechia, Germany, Italy, Netherlands, Spain, Switzerland, UK. [2016/XM4424/**F**]

♦ European Multicentre Bronchiectasis Audit and Research Collaboration (EMBARC) 07828

Co-Chair College of Life Sciences – Univ of Dundee, Nethergate, Dundee, DD1 4HN, UK. E-mail: info@bronchiectasis.eu.
Co-Chair Respiratory Diseases Dept – Inst Clínic del Tòrax, Hosp Clinic i Provincial de Barcelona, Calle Villarroel 170, 08036 Barcelona, Spain.
URL: https://www.bronchiectasis.eu/
History 2012. Former names and other names: *EMBARC Network* – alias. **Aims** Facilitate multidisciplinary collaborative research in non-CF bronchiectasis. **Structure** Steering Committee; International Advisory Board. **Activities** Guidance/assistance/consulting; research/documentation. **Events** *World Bronchiectasis & NTM Workshop* 2020. **Publications** *EMBARC Newsletter*.
Members Centres (over 120) in 23 countries:
Austria, Belgium, Czechia, Denmark, France, Germany, Greece, Ireland, Israel, Italy, Lithuania, Malta, Netherlands, North Macedonia, Portugal, Romania, Russia, Serbia, Slovakia, Spain, Switzerland, Türkiye, UK. [2020/AA0597/**F**]

♦ European Multicentre Tics in Children Studies (EMTICS) 07829

Coordinator Univ Medical Ctr Groningen, Dept of Child and Adolescent Psychiatry, Hanzeplein 1, 9700 RB Groningen, Netherlands. T. +31503681122. Fax +31503681120.
Office Concentris Research Management, Ludwigstr 4, 82256 Fürstenfeldbruck, Germany. T. +49814162528573. Fax +49814162528577. E-mail: contact@concentris.de.
URL: http://www.emtics.eu/
History 1 Dec 2011 for a duration of 66 months. Also referred to as *European Multicentre Tics Study*. **Aims** Identify the genetic and environmental susceptibility factors of tic *disorders*; contribute to a better understanding of the underlying mechanisms, especially by elucidating the role of autoimmunity and infections. **Structure** General Assembly; External Advisory Board; Coordinator; Project Office. **Finance** Funded by *European Community (inactive)* – Seventh Framework Programme. **Events** *General Assembly* Budapest (Hungary) 2014. **Publications** *EMTICS Newsletter*.
Members Partners in 11 countries:
Belgium, Denmark, Germany, Greece, Hungary, Israel, Italy, Netherlands, Spain, Switzerland, UK. [2015/XJ9439/**F**]

♦ European Multicentre Tics Study / see European Multicentre Tics in Children Studies (#07829)

♦ European Multicultural Foundation (EMF) 07830

Chairman 51 Viking Way, Brentwood, CM15 9HY, UK. T. +441277263207. Fax +441277263207.
URL: http://www.emfoundation.eu/
History 1996. UK Registered Charity No 1083886. **Aims** Promote tolerance and understanding between all cultures in Europe. **Structure** Board of Management. **Languages** English. **Staff** 19.00 FTE, paid. **Finance** Supported by: Big Lottery Fund; *European Commission (EC, #06633)*; *Royal Commonwealth Society (RCS, #18990)*; *UNESCO (#20322)*. **Activities** Events/meetings. **Events** *Conference* Innsbruck (Austria) 2014, *Conference* Leicester (UK) 2014, *Conference* Madrid (Spain) 2014, *Conference* Leicester (UK) 2013, *Conference* London (UK) 2012. **Publications** *Third Way* in English, French – magazine.
Members Full in 17 countries:
Austria, Belgium, Croatia, Cyprus, Czechia, Finland, France, Germany, Greece, Ireland, Italy, Netherlands, Slovakia, Slovenia, Spain, Sweden, UK. [2015.09.10/XD8108/f/**D**]

♦ European Multidisciplinary Colorectal Cancer Congress (meeting series)

♦ European Multidisciplinary Seafloor and water-column Observatory (EMSO) 07831

Contact Via di Vigna Murata 605, 00143 Rome RM, Italy. T. +39651860428. Fax +39651860338. E-mail: interim.office@emso-eu.org.
URL: http://www.emso-eu.org/
History Officially awarded the status of *European Research Infrastructure Consortium (ERIC)*, 1 Oct 2016, a legal status designed to facilitate joint establishment and operation of research infrastructures of European interest, following which it is also referred to as *EMSO ERIC*. **Aims** Establish, coordinate, facilitate and optimize the use of pan-European facilities and sea operation resources so as to ensure maximum benefit to the ocean observation community. **Languages** English.
Members Full in 8 countries:
France, Greece, Ireland, Italy, Portugal, Romania, Spain, UK.
IGO Relations *European Commission (EC, #06633)*. [2016/XM5201/**E**]

♦ European Multidisciplinary Society for Modelling and Simulation Technology (EUROSIS) 07832

SG BlueBridge – Ostend Science Park, Wetenschapspark 1, Plassendale 1, 8400 Ostend, Belgium. T. +3259255330. Fax +3259255339.
URL: http://www.eurosis.org/
History Sep 2003. Registration: Banque-Carrefour des Entreprises, No/ID: 0873.715.028, Start date: 10 Aug 2005, Belgium. **Aims** Further European research activities in the field of *computer* simulation and related areas. **Structure** Boards (4). **Languages** English. **Staff** 1.00 FTE, paid. Voluntary. **Finance** Members' dues. Self-financing. **Activities** Events/meetings; knowledge management/information dissemination; projects/programmes; publishing activities. **Events** *Annual Industrial Simulation Conference* Dublin (Ireland) 2022, *Annual Industrial Simulation Conference* Valletta (Malta) 2021, *Annual Industrial Simulation Conference* Toulouse (France) 2020, *European Simulation and Modelling Conference* Toulouse (France) 2020, *MESM : Middle East Symposium on Simulation and Modeling* Dubai (United Arab Emirates) 2019. **Publications** Books; conference proceedings; catalogue. [2022/XD9372/**D**]

♦ European Multiple Endocrine Neoplasia Alliance / see European MEN Alliance (#07779)
♦ European Multiple Retailers' Association (inactive)

♦ European Multiple Sclerosis Platform (EMSP) 07833

CEO Rue Auguste Lambiotte 144, Boite 8, 1030 Brussels, Belgium. T. +3223045015. Fax +3223058011.
URL: http://www.emsp.org/
History 1989. Former names and other names: *European MS Platform* – alias. Registration: Banque Carrefour des Entreprises, No/ID: 0473.317.141, Start date: 30 Nov 2000, Belgium; EU Transparency Register, No/ID: 431655212354-82, Start date: 29 Nov 2013. **Aims** Exchange and disseminate information relating to Multiple Sclerosis (MS) considering all issues relevant for people affected by MS; encourage research of all kinds that is appropriate to MS through recognized medical and other organizations; promote development of join action programmes with the participation of national MS societies in Europe, aiming at improving the quality of their activities and services; act as a focal point for liaison with the institutions of the European Union and other European organizations in order to propose new measures to advance the rights of persons with disabilities and to ensure their full and effective participation in society. **Structure** Council; Executive Committee. **Languages** English. **Staff** 7.00 FTE, paid. **Finance** Members' dues. Other sources: funding from donations; sponsors. **Activities** Knowledge management/information dissemination; research and development; projects/programmes; networking/liaising; events/meetings. **Events** *Annual Conference* Madrid (Spain) 2022, *Spring Conference* Vilnius (Lithuania) 2019, *Spring Conference* Bratislava (Slovakia) 2018, *Spring Conference* Athens (Greece) 2017, *Spring Conference* Oslo (Norway) 2016. **Publications** *European Register for Multiple Sclerosis* (2011-2014); *European CODE of Good Practice in MS and the European Therapy Guidelines and Consensus Papers* (2003). Annual Report; studies; surveys; online training and campaigns.
Members MS Societies (40) representing 700,000 persons with multiple sclerosis in 36 countries:
Austria, Belarus, Belgium, Bosnia-Herzegovina, Bulgaria, Croatia, Czechia, Denmark, Estonia, Finland, France, Germany, Greece, Hungary, Iceland, Ireland, Italy, Latvia, Lithuania, Luxembourg, Malta, Moldova, Netherlands, Norway, Poland, Portugal, Romania, Russia, Serbia, Slovakia, Slovenia, Spain, Sweden, Switzerland, Türkiye, UK.
NGO Relations Member of (5): *EU Health Coalition*; *European Disability Forum (EDF, #06929)*; *European Federation of Neurological Associations (EFNA, #07177)*; *European Patients' Forum (EPF, #08172)*; *Multiple Sclerosis International Federation (MSIF, #16899)*. Stakeholder in: *European Network for Health Technology Assessment (EUnetHTA, #07921)*. Working relations with: *European Committee for Treatment and Research in Multiple Sclerosis (ECTRIMS, #06673)*; *Rehabilitation in Multiple Sclerosis (RIMS, #18826)*. [2022/XF3635/**F**]

♦ European Municipal Credit Community (inactive)
♦ European Muscle Club / see European Society for Muscle Research (#08657)

♦ European Musculo-Skeletal Oncology Society (EMSOS) 07834

Sec Klinik für Orthopädie, Auenbruggerplatz 5, 8036 Graz, Austria.
URL: http://www.emsos.org/
History 1987, Bologna (Italy). Former names and other names: *European Musculoskeletal Tumour Society (EMTS)* – alias; *European Skeletal Society* – alias. **Aims** Advance the science and practice of the diagnosis and treatment of bone and soft tissue tumours; promote basic and clinical research; disseminate knowledge in order to provide a common high standard of musculo-skeletal oncology. **Structure** Executive Committee, consisting of President, Vice President, Secretary, Treasurer, Past-President and 7 members. **Languages** English. **Finance** Members' dues. **Activities** Cooperative studies. **Events** *Annual Meeting* Brussels (Belgium) 2023, *Annual Meeting* London (UK) 2022, *Annual Meeting* Graz (Austria) 2021, *Annual Meeting* Graz (Austria) 2020, *Annual Meeting* Florence (Italy) 2019. **Publications** Meeting proceedings (annual).
Members Individuals full, honorary and corresponding in 24 countries:
Austria, Belgium, Bulgaria, Croatia, Czechia, Finland, France, Germany, Hungary, Ireland, Israel, Italy, Netherlands, Norway, Poland, Portugal, Russia, Slovenia, Spain, Sweden, Switzerland, Türkiye, UK, USA. [2021/XD2833/**D**]

♦ European Musculoskeletal Tumour Society / see European Musculo-Skeletal Oncology Society (#07834)

♦ European Museum Academy (EMA) 07835

Dir Fiskargränden 8b, SE-261 29 Landskrona, Sweden. T. +46702821168. E-mail: europeanmuseumacademy@gmail.com – communications@europeanmuseumacademy.eu – director@europeanmuseumacademy.eu.
Registered Office Kanaalweg 46, 2584 CL The Hague, Netherlands.
URL: http://www.europeanmuseumacademy.eu/
History 2009. Former names and other names: *European Museum Academy Foundation* – full title. Registration: No/ID: 27359130, Netherlands. **Aims** Preserve the legacy of museologist Kenneth Hudson; disseminate the values and pioneering intuitions and views of his museological thinking among new generations of museum professionals as well as cultural professionals active on a European scale. **Structure** Annual Meeting; Board. **Languages** English. **Activities** Awards/prizes/competitions; events/meetings. **Publications** *EMA Newsletter*. *Developing Exhibitions* (1st ed 2020) by Dirk Houtgraaf and Massimo Negri in English.
Members in 27 countries:
Austria, Belgium, Bulgaria, Cyprus, Czechia, Estonia, Finland, France, Georgia, Germany, Greece, Italy, Luxembourg, Moldova, Netherlands, North Macedonia, Portugal, Romania, Russia, Serbia, Slovenia, Spain, Sweden, Switzerland, Türkiye, UK, Ukraine.
Also members in the Middle East and Arab countries. Membership countries not specified. Founding Associate Partners (9) in 6 countries:
Founding Associate Partners (9) in 6 countries:
Germany, Portugal, Spain, Sweden, Türkiye, UK.
Associate Partners (2) in 2 countries:
Sweden, UK.
NGO Relations Member of (1): *European Heritage Alliance 3.3 (#07477)*. Partner of (3): *Europeana Foundation (#05839)*; *Network of European Museum Organizations (NEMO, #17024)*; *PASCAL International Observatory (#18251)*. Also links with national foundations. [2022.10.18/XJ6285/**D**]

♦ European Museum Academy Foundation / see European Museum Academy (#07835)

♦ European Museum Forum (EMF) 07836

Forum du musée européen

Admin c/o Museu de Portimo, Rua D Carlos I / Zona Ribeirinha, 8500-607 Portimão, Portugal. T. +351910278383 – +351282096016. E-mail: emf@europeanforum.museum.
URL: http://europeanforum.museum/

History 1977, Bristol (UK). Founded under the auspices of *Council of Europe (CE, #04881)* and under the patronage of Queen Fabiola of Belgium. Former names and other names: *European Museum of the Year Award Trust* – former. Registration: Companies House, No/ID: 07243034, Start date: 4 May 2010, England and Wales; Charity Commission, No/ID: 1136790, Start date: 8 Jul 2010, England and Wales. **Aims** Promote and recognize outstanding new achievements and ideas within the museum field throughout Europe, particularly in the area of public quality. **Structure** Judging Panel; Trustees; Chairman of Trustees acts as EMF Chairman. **Languages** English. **Staff** 1.00 FTE, paid. **Finance** Corporate, Institutional and Individual Partnership fees. Other sources: sponsorship; participation in EU projects; entry fees for EMYA competition. **Activities** Awards/prizes/competitions; events/meetings; knowledge management/information dissemination. **Events** *Annual Conference* Tartu (Estonia) 2022, *Annual Meeting* Glasgow (UK) 2015, *Annual Meeting* Tallinn (Estonia) 2014, *Annual Meeting* Tongeren (Belgium) 2013, *Annual Meeting* Penafiel (Portugal) 2012. **Publications** *Bulletin of the European Museum Forum*. Annual brochure on the awards.
Members Ordinary (individuals); Institutional; Corporate. Members in 32 countries:
Austria, Belgium, Croatia, Cyprus, Czechia, Denmark, Estonia, Finland, France, Germany, Greece, Hungary, Iceland, Ireland, Italy, Latvia, Luxembourg, Montenegro, Netherlands, Norway, Poland, Portugal, Romania, Russia, Serbia, Slovakia, Slovenia, Spain, Sweden, Switzerland, Türkiye, UK.
IGO Relations *Council of Europe (CE, #04881)*. **NGO Relations** Member of (2): *Culture Action Europe (CAE, #04981)*; *European Heritage Alliance 3.3 (#07477)*. Cooperates with: *Europeana Foundation (#05839)*; *International Council of Museums (ICOM, #13051)*; other EU programmes. [2022/XF4731/**F**]

♦ European Museum of the Year Award Trust / see European Museum Forum (#07836)
♦ European Mushroom Growers' Group (#10758)
♦ European Musical Press Association / see Presse musicale internationale (#18488)

♦ European Music Council (EMC) 07837

Conseil européen de la musique – Europäischer Musikrat

SG Haus der Kultur, Weberstr 59a, 53113 Bonn, Germany. T. +4922896699664. E-mail: info@emc-imc.org.
SG address not obtained.
URL: http://www.emc-imc.org/

History 1972, Strasbourg (France). Founded within *International Music Council (IMC, #14199)*. Former names and other names: *European Regional Group* – former (1972 to 1992); *Groupe régional européen* – former (1972 to 1992). Registration: North Rhine-Westphalia District court, No/ID: VR 8162, Start date: 4 Jul 2003, Germany, Bonn; EU Transparency Register, No/ID: 907167934846-43, Start date: 16 May 2019. **Aims** Promote the whole spectrum of musical life in Europe; encourage young *artists*; strengthen IMC functions within Europe by encouraging closer and more effective cooperation between European national committees and international organizations of IMC; enable treatment of multilateral problems in European National Committees and musical life; develop cooperation with other IMC regional groups and secretariats; observe the development of the European Union and Parliament. **Structure** Board. **Languages** English, French, German. **Staff** 6.00 FTE, paid. **Finance** Funded by: Federal Government Commissioner for Culture and the Media; *European Commission (EC, #06633)* Creative Europe Programme City of Bonn (Germany). **Activities** Events/meetings; networking/liaising. **Events** *Annual Meeting* Brussels (Belgium) 2022, *EMC Lab Forum* Brussels (Belgium) 2022, *European Forum on Music* 2021, *European Forum on Music* Paris (France) 2019, *European Forum on Music* Oslo (Norway) 2018. **Publications** *Sounds in Europe* (annual); *European Agenda for Music*.
Members National Music Councils; International and European Organizations; National Music Organizations. Members in 29 countries:
Armenia, Australia, Austria, Azerbaijan, Belgium, Croatia, Cyprus, Czechia, Estonia, Finland, France, Germany, Hungary, Israel, Italy, Latvia, Netherlands, Norway, Poland, Portugal, Russia, Spain, Sweden, Switzerland, UK, Ukraine, USA.
Included in the above, 34 organizations listed in this Yearbook:
- *Association Européenne des Conservatoires, Académies de Musique et Musikhochschulen (AEC, #02560)*;
- *Europäische Musikschul-Union (EMU, #05756)*;
- *European Association for Music in Schools (EAS, #06127)*;
- *European Broadcasting Union (EBU, #06404)*;
- *European Chamber Music Teachers' Association (ECMTA, #06516)*;
- *European Choral Association – Europa Cantat (#06541)*;
- *European Composer and Songwriter Alliance (ECSA, #06691)*;
- *European Conference of Promoters of New Music (ECPNM, #06736)*;
- *European Early Music Network (EEMN, #06953)*;
- *European Federation of National Youth Orchestras (EFNYO, #07176)*;
- *European Festivals Association (EFA, #07242)*;
- *European Orchestra Federation (EOFed, #08092)*;
- *European Society for Ethnomusicology (#08598)*;
- *European String Teachers Association (ESTA, #08842)*;
- *European Union of Music Competitions for Youth (EMCY, #09003)*;
- *European Voice Teachers Association (EVTA, #09076)*;
- *Europe Jazz Network (EJN, #09160)*;
- *IMZ International Music + Media Centre (#11139)*;
- *International Adkins Chiti: Women in Music Foundation (FACDIM)*;
- *International Association of Music Information Centres (IAMIC, #12041)*;
- *International Association of Music Libraries, Archives and Documentation Centres (IAML, #12042)*;
- *International Association of Schools of Jazz (IASJ, #12148)*;
- *International Confederation of Accordionists (ICA, #12841)*;
- *International Council of Organizations for Folklore Festivals and Folk Art (#13058)*;
- *International Federation for Choral Music (IFCM, #13388)*;
- *International Federation of Chopin Societies (IFCS, #13387)*;
- *International Federation of Musicians (#13486)*;
- *International Music Managers' Forum (IMMF, #14200)*;
- *International Music Products Association (NAMM)*;
- *International Society for Contemporary Music (ISCM, #15035)*;
- *International Society for Music Education (ISME, #15287)*;
- *Jeunesses Musicales International (JMI, #16110)*;
- *Live DMA European Network (#16495)*;
- *World Federation of International Music Competitions (WFIMC, #21445)*.

IGO Relations Cooperates with: *Council of Europe (CE, #04881)*; *UNESCO (#20322)*. Observes developments at: *European Commission (EC, #06633)*; *European Parliament (EP, #08146)*. **NGO Relations** Member of: *Culture Action Europe (CAE, #04981)*; *European Alliance for Culture and the Arts (#05866)*. Cooperates with: German Commission for UNESCO; German Culture Council; *International Music Council (IMC, #14199)*. [2023.03.02/XE2090/y/**E**]

♦ European Music Office (no recent information)
♦ European Music School Union (#05756)
♦ European Music Therapy Association / see European Music Therapy Confederation (#07838)

♦ European Music Therapy Confederation (EMTC) 07838

Confederazione Europea di Musicoterapia

Pres address not obtained. E-mail: emtc.publicrelations@gmail.com.
Registered Office Fiscamar SCRL, Klauwaartslaan 3, 1853 Bever, Belgium.
URL: http://emtc-eu.com/

History 1990. Statutes adopted May 2004, Brussels (Belgium). Former names and other names: *European Music Therapy Association (EMTA)* – former (1990 to 1998). Registration: Start date: 2004, Belgium. **Aims** Nurture mutual respect, understanding and exchange between music therapists in Europe. **Structure** General Assembly (annual). **Languages** English. **Staff** 6.00 FTE, voluntary. **Finance** Members' dues. **Activities** Working to set up the *'European Music Therapy Register (EMTR)'*, a qualified European music therapy registration, linked to the higher education standards of bachelor and master level qualifications. **Events** *European Music Therapy Conference* Hamburg (Germany) 2025, *European Music Therapy Conference* Edinburgh (UK) 2022, *European Music Therapy Conference* Aalborg (Denmark) 2019, *European Music Therapy Conference* Vienna (Austria) 2016, *European Music Therapy Conference* Oslo (Norway) 2013. **Publications** *EMTC Newsletter* (4 a year).
Members Full in 28 countries:
Austria, Belgium, Bulgaria, Cyprus, Czechia, Denmark, Estonia, Finland, France, Germany, Greece, Hungary, Iceland, Israel, Italy, Latvia, Lithuania, Luxembourg, Netherlands, Norway, Poland, Portugal, Serbia, Slovenia, Spain, Sweden, Switzerland, UK.
IGO Relations Recognized by: *WHO (#20950)*. [2022/XD7086/**D**]

♦ European Muslim Initiative for Social Cohesion (EMISCO) 07839

Coordinator 11 rue Horace, 67200 Strasbourg, France. T. +33689845227.
Facebook: https://fr-fr.facebook.com/pg/Emisco-European-Muslim-Initiative-for-Social-Cohesion-129883293733752/photos/

History Dec 2010, The Hague (Netherlands). **Aims** Promote mutual integration, reciprocal respect and full inclusion of ethnic and religious minorities. **Structure** Board; Executive Bureau. **Activities** Events/meetings. **Publications** *EMISCO Newsletter*.
Members Full in 14 countries:
Austria, Belgium, Bosnia-Herzegovina, Bulgaria, Denmark, France, Georgia, Germany, Greece, North Macedonia, Russia, Switzerland, Türkiye, UK.
Consultative Status Consultative status granted from: *Council of Europe (CE, #04881)* (Participatory Status).
IGO Relations Participates in: *European Union Agency for Fundamental Rights (FRA, #08969)*. [2020/XM6167/**F**]

♦ European Muslim Professionals Network (CEDAR) 07840

Address not obtained.
URL: http://www.thecedarnetwork.com/

History as a result of a series of trans-Atlantic workshops, 2008, organized by *Institute for Strategic Dialogue (ISD, #11296)* and *Salzburg Global Seminar (#19044)*. **Aims** Represent a growing generation of young successful Muslim professionals in Europe to bolster their influence within wider professional, political and social networks. **Structure** Advisory Board. Management Board. [2013/XJ4762/tv/**F**]

♦ European Muslims League (EML) 07841

Contact Via Faenza 24, 16127 Genoa GE, Italy. T. +39621126364. E-mail: european.muslims.league@gmail.com – secr.european.muslims.league@gmail.com – eml@eml.fm.
URL: http://www.eml.fm/

History Set up 10 May 2010. Registration: Italy; Switzerland. **Aims** Promote the very best of Islam in the EU community and beyond; support the interfaith dialogue and prevention of religion conflicts; help non-muslim communities understand Islamic religion. **Structure** International Council for Cooperation and Peace; International Academy of Diplomatic Action. **Languages** English, French, Italian, Portuguese, Spanish. **Staff** 45.00 FTE, voluntary. **Activities** Training/education; conflict resolution; certification/accreditation; guidance/assistance/consulting. **Publications** Brochure. **Members** in Africa, Asia, Europe, Latin America, New Zealand. Membership countries not specified. **IGO Relations** *Council of Europe (CE, #04881)*; *ECOSOC (#05331)*; *European Parliament (EP, #08146)*; *Islamic World Educational, Scientific and Cultural Organization (ICESCO, #16058)*; *Muslim World League (MWL, #16917)*; *Organisation of Islamic Cooperation (OIC, #17813)*. [2020.03.05/XM6892/**D**]

♦ European Muslim Union (unconfirmed)
♦ European Mustelid Colloquium (meeting series)

♦ European Mutual Association for Nuclear Insurance (EMANI) 07842

Accountant Avenue Jules Bordet 166, 1140 Brussels, Belgium. T. +3227029010. Fax +3227057292.
URL: http://www.emani.be/

History 20 Oct 1978. Statutes modified, 5 Dec 1985, Brussels (Belgium); 15 Jun 2000; 4 Mar 2006; 12 Dec 2010. Registration: Belgium. **Aims** Provide insurance for the nuclear industry. **Structure** Board of Directors. Administration and day-to-day management carried out by Executive Committee and General Manager. **Languages** English, French. **Staff** 10.50 FTE, paid. **Activities** Underwriting; claims handling. **Events** *Congress* Lisbon (Portugal) 2017. **Publications** Annual Report.
Members Full nuclear facilities in 16 countries:
Belgium, Canada, Czechia, Finland, France, Germany, Hungary, Italy, Netherlands, Romania, Slovakia, South Africa, Sweden, Switzerland, UK, USA. [2018/XD9639/**D**]

♦ European Mutual-Help Network for Alcohol-Related Problems (EMNA) 07843

Pres EMNA Secretariat, Rue Archimede 17, 1000 Brussels, Belgium. T. +3227360572.
Policy Officer address not obtained.

History Statutes adopted 5 Jun 2004, Brussels (Belgium); amended 2007, Hungary. **Aims** Promote mutual help-groups and community programmes as an important part of the treatment enabling people with alcohol related problems to overcome dependency, recover, reintegrate within their family and community and prevent relapse. **Structure** General Assembly (annual); Board; Executive Committee; Secretariat in Brussels (Belgium). **Languages** English, French. **Staff** 0.50 FTE, paid. **Finance** Members' dues. **Events** *Conference* London (UK) 2013, *Conference* Torremolinos (Spain) 2011. **Publications** *EMNA Newsletter*.
Members Full in 8 countries:
Denmark, France, Germany, Hungary, Italy, Netherlands, Spain, Sweden.
Associate in 1 country:
Norway.
International Associates (2):
International Blue Cross (IBC, #12364); *Movendi International (#16871)*.
NGO Relations Member of: *European Alcohol Policy Alliance (Eurocare, #05856)*. [2019/XJ2173/y/**D**]

♦ European Myasthenia Gravis Association (EuMGA) 07844

Pres c/o ABMM, Rue Achille Chavée 52/02, 7100 La Louvière, Belgium. E-mail: info@eumga.eu.
URL: http://www.eumga.eu/

History Former names and other names: *European Association of Myasthenia Gravis Patients' Associations* – alias. Registration: UBO register, No/ID: 0757.653.142, Start date: 30 Oct 2020, Belgium, Walloon; Charity Commission, Start date: 22 Jul 2009, End date: Sep 2019, England and Wales. **Aims** Promote the health and welfare of sufferers from Myasthenia Gravis, Lambert-Eaton Myasthenic Syndrome, Congenital Myasthenic Syndrome and other similar *diseases* of the human neuromuscular junction in Europe; assist and encourage the formation and development of organizations of patients suffering from these diseases, and their carers. **Structure** General Assembly; Board of Directors. **Events** *General Assembly* 2022, *General Assembly* 2021, *Annual General Meeting* Paris (France) 2018, *Annual General Meeting* Paris (France) 2017, *Annual General Meeting* Madrid (Spain) 2015.
Members Full in 11 countries:
Belgium, Croatia, Cyprus, Finland, France, Germany, Greece, Iceland, Italy, Romania, Spain.
Associate in 5 countries:
Denmark, Hungary, Kosovo, Netherlands, Sweden.
NGO Relations Member of (2): *European Federation of Neurological Associations (EFNA, #07177)*; *EURORDIS – Rare Diseases Europe (#09175)*. [2022.10.31/XJ2043/**D**]

♦ European Mycological Association (EMA) 07845

Pres address not obtained.
URL: http://www.euromould.org/

History Sep 2003, Yalta (Ukraine). Founded during 14th Congress of European Mycologists. Takes over functions of Congress of European Mycologists, organized since 1956. **Aims** Promote study and conservation of fungi; disseminate knowledge and information about fungi; establish and foster relations between those interested in mycology; improve infrastructure of mycology within Europe. **Structure** General Assembly (every 4 years); Council; Governing Committee. Conservation body: *European Council for the Conservation of Fungi (ECCF, #06811)*. **Languages** English. **Finance** Subscription fees. **Activities** *Congress of European Mycologists (CEM)*. **Events** *Congress of European Mycologists* Perugia (Italy) 2023, *Congress of European mycologists* Warsaw (Poland) / Bialowieza (Poland) 2019, *Meeting on Fungal Conservation in a Changing Europe* Ohrid (Macedonia) 2017, *Congress of European mycologists* Funchal (Portugal) 2015, *Congress of European mycologists* Porto Carras (Greece) 2011. **Publications** *EMA Electronic Newsletter*. **NGO Relations** Cooperates with: *International Mycological Association (IMA, #14203)*. [2021/XM2211/**D**]

♦ European Mycological Network (EMN) 07846
Chairperson Inst for Agricultural and Fisheries Research, Plant Sciences Unit – Crop Protection, Burg Van Gansberghelaan 95, 9820 Merelbeke, Belgium. T. +3292722474. Fax +3292722429.
Sec 30 Galtres Avenue, York, YO31 1JT, UK. T. +441904422165.
Events *Annual Meeting* Ghent (Belgium) 2016, *Annual Meeting* Budapest (Hungary) 2014, *Annual Meeting* Torun (Poland) 2012, *Annual Meeting* Ireland 2011, *Annual Meeting* Vienna (Austria) 2009. **IGO Relations** *European and Mediterranean Plant Protection Organization (EPPO, #07773)*. [2018/XJ1338/F]

♦ European Mycotoxins Awareness Network (EMAN) 07847
Scientific/Technical Coordinator c/o ATEKNEA Solutions Hungary, Tétényi út 84-86, Budapest 1119, Hungary. T. +3617874024. E-mail: mycohunt@ateknea.com.
URL: http://mycohunt.eu/
History 2000, as as project funded by *European Commission (EC, #06633)* (2000-2003). Currently a non-profit making consortium. **Aims** Provide high quality scientific information and news about mycotoxins to the food industry, consumers, legislators and the scientific community. **Finance** Funded through commercial sponsorship. **Publications** *Quarterly EMAN Bulletin*.
Members Consortium members in 6 countries:
Austria, Germany, Italy, Netherlands, Sweden, UK. [2018/XJ9091/F]

♦ European Myelodysplastic Syndromes Cooperative Group (EMSCO) . 07848
Project Management c/o GWT-TUD, Freiberger Str 33, 01067 Dresden, Germany. T. +493514584722. Fax +493514584367. E-mail: info@emsco.eu.
URL: http://www.emsco.eu/
History 2013. Founded on the initiative of *European LeukemiaNet (ELN, #07685)*. **Aims** Foster academic clinical research, education and consulting in the field of myelodysplastic syndromes (MDS). **Activities** Events/meetings; training/education. **Events** *Meeting* Nice (France) 2023, *Meeting* Leipzig (Germany) 2019, *Meeting* Amsterdam (Netherlands) 2018. **Publications** *EMSCO MDS Newsletter*. [2022/XM8018/D]

♦ European Myeloma Network (EMN) 07849
Contact Dr Molewaterplein 40, Kamer NA-822, 3015 GD Rotterdam, Netherlands. E-mail: info@emn.life – datacenter@emn.life.
Operating Office Via Donizetti 24, 10126 Turin TO, Italy. T. +391119037610. E-mail: amministrazione@emnresearch.it.
URL: https://www.myeloma-europe.org/
History 2003. Registration: No/ID: KVK 68523947, Netherlands, South Holland. **Aims** Support development of novel *diagnostics* and *therapies* for multiple myeloma. **Structure** Board, comprising Chairman, Secretary and 6 members. **Members** Membership countries not specified. [2022/XJ0468/F]

♦ European Myeloma Platform (inactive)

♦ European Nail Society (ENS) 07850
Société européenne de pathologie unguéale
Pres CHU Saint-Pierre, Rue Haute 322, 1000 Brussels, Belgium. T. +3225354381.
URL: http://www.euronailsociety.eu/
History Founded 31 May 1997, by a group of European dermatologists with special interest in the diseases and biology of the human nail. Registered in accordance with Belgian law. **Aims** Promote study of the nail and its normal and pathological states; evaluate *therapeutic* methods. **Structure** General Assembly (annual); Board. **Languages** English. **Staff** Voluntary. **Finance** Members' dues. **Activities** Events/meetings. **Events** *Meeting* Milan (Italy) 2022, *General Meeting* Vienna (Austria) 2016, *General Meeting* Copenhagen (Denmark) 2015, *General Meeting* Amsterdam (Netherlands) 2014, *General Meeting* Istanbul (Turkey) 2013. **Publications** *Skin Appendage Disorders*.
Members Individuals in 19 countries:
Australia, Belgium, Brazil, Canada, Chile, Finland, France, Germany, Hungary, Italy, Japan, Netherlands, Norway, Poland, Portugal, Spain, Switzerland, UK, USA.
NGO Relations Member of: *Federation of the European Dermatological and Surgical Societies (FEDSS, no recent information)*. Cooperates with: Council for Nail Disorders of North America. [2022/XD6774/v/D]

♦ European NanoBusiness Association (no recent information)
♦ European Nanoelectronics Initiative Advisory Council / see Association for European NanoElectronics ActivitieS (#02525)

♦ European Nanoporous Materials Institute of Excellence (ENMIX) ... 07851
CEO Inst of Chemical Technology, Univ of Stuttgart, Pfaffenwaldring 55, 70569 Stuttgart, Germany. T. +4971168565590. Fax +4971168564065.
Administrative Contact address not obtained.
URL: http://www.enmix.org/
Aims Stimulate sustainable development and strengthen the economic and societal fabric in Europe. **Structure** Board of Directors. **Activities** Events/meetings; awards/prizes/competitions. **Publications** *ENMIX Newsletter*.
Members Full in 8 countries:
Belgium, France, Germany, Greece, Netherlands, Norway, Slovenia, Spain.
Included in the above, 1 organization listed in this Yearbook:
SINTEF.
NGO Relations Member of: *A.SPIRE (#02311)*. [2016.06.01/XJ8756/j/F]

♦ European Nanoscience and Nanotechnology Association (unconfirmed)
♦ European Narcolepsy Association (no recent information)

♦ European Narcolepsy Network (EU-NN) 07852
Sec Leiden Univ Medical Centre, Dept Neurology, Albinusdraaf 2, 2300 RC Leiden, Netherlands. T. +31715262197.
URL: http://www.eu-nn.com/
History 9 Feb 2008, Zurich (Switzerland). Registration: Hesse District court, No/ID: VR 4620, Start date: 28 May 2008, Germany, Marburg. **Aims** Promote European scientific research in narcolepsy, hypersomnia, and related fields; optimize medical care for patients by improving diagnostic and therapeutic measures. **Structure** Assembly; Board; Committees. **Languages** English. **Finance** Sources: members' dues. **Activities** Events/meetings; knowledge management/information dissemination; research/documentation; standards/guidelines. **Events** *European Narcolepsy Meeting* Helsinki (Finland) 2016, *European Narcolepsy Meeting* Madrid (Spain) 2013. **Publications** Studies; guidelines. Maintains database.
Members Institutions in 17 countries:
Austria, Belgium, Czechia, Denmark, Finland, France, Germany, Hungary, Italy, Netherlands, Norway, Poland, Slovakia, Spain, Sweden, Switzerland, UK.
NGO Relations Cooperates with (2): *European Academy of Neurology (EAN, #05803)*; *European Sleep Research Society (ESRS, #08493)*. *Orphanet (#17898)*. Also links with national and international sleep societies, psychiatric, neurologic, paediatric and ENT societies. [2021/XJ3721/D]

♦ European Narratology Network (ENN) 07853
Chair Na Florenci 3/1420, 110 00 Prague 1, Czechia. E-mail: ennoffice01@gmail.com – huehn@uni-hamburg.de – v.tiupa@gmail.com.
URL: http://www.narratology.net/
History Current constitution adopted at founding meeting, 24 Jan 2009, Hamburg (Germany); amended 11 Mar 2011, Kolding (Denmark). Focus is predominantly, but not exclusively, European. **Aims** Promote study of narrative representation in literature, film, digital media, etc, across all European languages and cultures; promote narratology in research and teaching. **Structure** Steering Committee. **Events** *Modelling narrative across borders* Ghent (Belgium) 2015, *Emerging vectors of narratology – toward consolidation or diversification?* Paris (France) 2013, *Conference* Kolding (Denmark) 2011, *Conference* Hamburg (Germany) 2009. **Publications** *ENN Newsletter*. *Narratologia* – series. Meeting proceedings. **Members** Institutions and individuals. Membership countries not specified. **NGO Relations** *Nordic Network of Narrative Studies (#17360)*; national research institutes. [2019/XJ5145/D]

♦ European National Shippers' Councils / see European Shippers' Council (#08477)
♦ European Natural Casing Association / see European Natural Sausage Casings Association (#07854)
♦ European Natural Disasters Training Centre, Ankara (internationally oriented national body)
♦ European Natural Gas Vehicle Association / see NGVA Europe (#17130)
♦ European Natural Hygiene Society (inactive)

♦ European Natural Sausage Casings Association (ENSCA) 07854
Association européenne des industries et commerces de boyauderie
Secretariat c/o UECBV, Rue de la Loi 81-A, Bte 9, 1040 Brussels, Belgium. T. +3222304603. Fax +3222309400. E-mail: info@ensca.eu.
URL: https://ensca.org/
History 17 Mar 1967, France. Former names and other names: *European Association of the Casing-Dressing Industry and Trade* – alias; *European Natural Casing Association (ENCA)* – alias. **Aims** Represent national natural casings associations from 11 EU Member States and private companies. **Structure** General Assembly (annual); Board. **Languages** English. **Events** *General Assembly* Rome (Italy) 2013, *Meeting* Istanbul (Turkey) 1997, *Meeting* Barcelona (Spain) 1996, *Meeting* Berlin (Germany) 1996, *Meeting* Frankfurt-Main (Germany) 1995.
Members Full national associations in 11 countries:
Austria, Belgium, Denmark, France, Germany, Italy, Netherlands, Portugal, Spain, Sweden, UK.
Associate associations in 3 countries:
Switzerland, Türkiye, USA.
Included in the above, 1 organization listed in this Yearbook:
International Natural Sausage Casing Association (INSCA, #14216).
NGO Relations Member of: *Union européenne du commerce du bétail et de la viande (UECBV, #20394)*. [2022/XD3632/t/D]

♦ European Natural Sites Twinning Programme / see Eurosite (#09181)
♦ European Natural Soyfoods Manufacturers Association / see European Plant-Based Foods Association (#08210)
♦ European Natural Soy and Plant Based Foods Manufacturers Association / see European Plant-Based Foods Association (#08210)
♦ The European Nature Trust (internationally oriented national body)
♦ European Naturist Union (inactive)
♦ European Nazarene College (see: #12571)
♦ European Needlemakers' Association (inactive)

♦ European Neighbourhood Council (ENC) 07855
Managing Dir Rue Washington 40, 1050 Brussels, Belgium. T. +3226465139.
URL: http://www.encouncil.org/
History 2016. **Aims** Strengthen a common European neighbourhood; improve dialogue and neighbourhood coordination among EU Member States, Accession Countries, European Neighbourhood Policy (ENP) countries and Central Asia. **Structure** Academic Council. **Activities** Research/documentation; networking/liaising; knowledge management/information dissemination. **Publications** *ENC Newsletter*. **IGO Relations** *European Commission (EC, #06633)*; *European External Action Service (EEAS, #07018)*; *European Parliament (EP, #08146)*; *NATO (#16945)*. **NGO Relations** *Europe-Central Asia Monitoring (EUCAM, #09151)*; national academic institutions. [2018/XM5990/D]

♦ European Neonatal Network (inactive)
♦ European Neonatal Workshop (meeting series)

♦ European Network for Academic Integrity (ENAI) 07856
Main Office Zemedelska 1, 613 00 Brno, Czechia. T. +420545132725. E-mail: info@academicintegrity.eu.
URL: http://www.academicintegrity.eu/
History Registration: No/ID: 6273629, Czech Rep. **Aims** Support higher education institutions to work together in the field of academic integrity. **Structure** Annual General Meeting; Board; President; Executive Director; Working Groups. **Languages** English. **Finance** Sources: members' dues. **Activities** Guidance/assistance/consulting; networking/liaising; publishing activities. **Events** *European Conference on Academic Integrity and Plagiarism* Brno (Czechia) 2021, *International Conference on Plagiarism across Europe and Beyond (PAEB)* Dubai (United Arab Emirates) 2020, *International Conference on Plagiarism across Europe and Beyond (PAEB)* Vilnius (Lithuania) 2019, *International Conference on Plagiarism across Europe and Beyond (PAEB)* Gaziantep (Turkey) 2018, *International Conference on Plagiarism across Europe and Beyond (PAEB)* Brno (Czechia) 2017. **Publications** *ENAI Newsletter* (regular). Educational materials.
Members Institutions (35) in 26 countries:
Austria, Belgium, Bosnia-Herzegovina, Cyprus, Czechia, Estonia, Germany, Greece, Hungary, Ireland, Italy, Kazakhstan, Kosovo, Latvia, Lithuania, Montenegro, Portugal, Romania, Slovakia, Slovenia, Spain, Sweden, Türkiye, UK, Ukraine, United Arab Emirates. [2021.05.23/XM6646/F]

♦ European Network of Academic Sports Services (ENAS) 07857
Development Manager House of Sport, Av des Arts 43, 1040 Brussels, Belgium. E-mail: officer@enas-sport.net.
URL: http://www.enas-sport.net/
History 1997, Chambéry (France). **Aims** Foster development of *Sport for all* in universities. **Structure** General Assembly (annual); Executive Committee. **Languages** English. **Staff** 1.00 FTE, paid. **Activities** Knowledge management/information dissemination; networking/liaising; sporting activities; projects/programmes; politics/policy/regulatory; events/meetings. **Events** *Annual Conference* Trento (Italy) 2019, *Annual Conference* Nijmegen (Netherlands) 2018, *Annual Conference* Trondheim (Norway) 2017, *Annual Conference* Malta 2016, *Annual Conference* Berlin (Germany) 2015. **Publications** *ENAS News Letter*. **Members** Universities (126) in 20 countries. Membership countries not specified. **NGO Relations** Partner of (1): *European Esports Observatory (EEO)*. [2019/XF7123/F]

♦ European Network for Academic Steiner Teacher Education / see International Network for Academic Steiner Teacher Education (#14226)

♦ European Network for Accessible Tourism (ENAT) 07858
Managing Dir Rue du Commerce 72, 1040 Brussels, Belgium. E-mail: enat@accessibletourism.org.
URL: https://www.accessibletourism.org/
History Jan 2006. Set up as a project-bases initiative. Registration: No/ID: 0897.614.640, Start date: 8 May 2008, Belgium; EU Transparency Register, No/ID: 7964210133-55, Start date: 3 Jul 2008. **Aims** Make European tourism destinations, products and services accessible to all travellers; promote accessible tourism around the world. **Structure** General Assembly (annual); Board; Executive Board; Secretariat. **Languages** Dutch, English, French, Spanish. **Staff** 0.50 FTE, paid; 11.00 FTE, voluntary. **Finance** Sources: donations; members' dues. Annual budget: 20,000 EUR. **Activities** Advocacy/lobbying/activism; awareness raising; capacity building; certification/accreditation; events/meetings; guidance/assistance/consulting; knowledge management/information dissemination; monitoring/evaluation; networking/liaising; publishing activities; research/documentation; standards/guidelines; training/education. **Events** *Annual General Assembly* Brussels (Belgium) 2021, *World Summit on Destinations For All* Montréal, QC (Canada) 2014, *Biennial International Congress* Avila (Spain) 2013, *Congress* Vitoria-Gasteiz (Spain) 2013, *Biennial international congress* 2011. **Publications** Research reports; newsletters.
Members Organizations (170) in 42 countries:
Australia, Austria, Belgium, Bulgaria, Chile, Costa Rica, Cyprus, Czechia, Denmark, Ecuador, Egypt, Estonia, Finland, France, Georgia, Germany, Greece, Hungary, Iceland, Ireland, Israel, Italy, Jordan, Latvia, Libya, Lithuania, Luxembourg, Malta, Netherlands, Poland, Portugal, Romania, Russia, Serbia, Slovenia, South Africa, Spain, Sweden, Switzerland, Türkiye, UK, USA.
NGO Relations Member of (1): *European Tourism Manifesto (#08921)*. [2020.05.05/XJ8121/F]

♦ European Network for Accreditation of Engineering Education (ENAEE) 07859
Secretariat Maison des Associations Internationales, Rue Washington 40, 1050 Brussels, Belgium. T. +3222347878. E-mail: secretariat@enaee.eu.
SG address not obtained. E-mail: secretary.general@enaee.eu.

European Network Building

URL: http://www.enaee.eu/
History 9 Sep 2000. Founded as *European Standing Observatory for the Engineering Profession and Education (ESOEPE)*. Transformed into current structure and under current title, 8 Feb 2006. Current statutes approved Dec 2013. Registration: Banque-Carrefour des Entreprises, No/ID: 0882.389.895, Start date: 7 Jul 2006, Belgium; EU Transparency Register, No/ID: 69063914634-64, Start date: 30 Nov 2010. **Aims** Promote and run the EUR-ACE system of accreditation of Engineering Education. **Structure** General Assembly; Administrative Council; Permanent Secretariat. **Languages** English. **Finance** Members' dues. **Events** *Annual Conference* Florence (Italy) 2015, *World Engineering Education Forum* Florence (Italy) 2015, *Annual Conference* Brussels (Belgium) 2014, *Annual Conference* Leuven (Belgium) 2013, *Annual Conference* Porto (Portugal) 2012.
Members Associations (21) in 16 countries:
Denmark, Finland, France, Germany, Ireland, Italy, Kazakhstan, Poland, Portugal, Romania, Russia, Slovakia, Spain, Switzerland, Türkiye, UK.
Included in the above, 1 organization listed in this Yearbook:
Fédération Européenne d'Associations Nationales d'Ingénieurs (FEANI, #09558).
Associate (5) in 5 countries:
Austria, Belgium, France, Ukraine, USA.
Included in the above, 3 organizations listed in this Yearbook:
International Society for Engineering Pedagogy (#15089); Latin American and Caribbean Consortium of Engineering Institutions (LACCEI, #16270); Société européenne pour la formation des ingénieurs (SEFI, #19462).
NGO Relations Founding member of: *European Alliance of Subject-Specific and Professional Accreditation and Quality Assurance (EASPA, #05887)*. Member of: *International Federation of Engineering Education Societies (IFEES, #13412); International Network of Quality Assurance Agencies in Higher Education (INQAAHE, #14312)*.
[2021/XJ1444/y/E]

♦ **European Network for Action and Physical Activity (EUNAAPA)** 07860
Founder Inst for Biomedicine of Aging, Kobergerstr 60, 90408 Nuremberg, Germany. T. +49911530296162. Fax +49911530296151.
Twitter: https://twitter.com/EUNAAPA
History 2005. Registration: EU Transparency Register, No/ID: 11487521943-46, Start date: 1 Jul 2009. **Aims** Improve health, wellbeing and independence of older people throughout Europe through promotion of evidence based physical activity. **Structure** Steering Committee; Advisory Board; Office. **Languages** English. **Staff** 1.00 FTE, paid. **Finance** Financed by TNO (Netherlands) and *European Commission (EC, #06633)*. Annual budget: euro 150,000-200,000. No current funding. **Activities** Training/education; events/meetings; awareness raising; projects/programmes. **Publications** *EUNAAPA Newsletter*.
Members Individuals in 26 countries:
Australia, Austria, Brazil, Bulgaria, Canada, Czechia, Denmark, Finland, France, Germany, Greece, Ireland, Israel, Italy, Malta, Netherlands, New Zealand, North Macedonia, Norway, Poland, Portugal, Spain, Sweden, Switzerland, UK, USA.
IGO Relations *European Commission (EC, #06633)*; Prevention of Malnutrition in Senior Subjects in the EU (PROMISS); *WHO (#20950)*.
[2020/XJ8785/v/F]

♦ The European Network for Active Participation in Cultural Activities / see *Amateo (#00765)*
♦ European Network for the Advancement of Artificial Cognitive Systems / see *EUCognition – European Society for Cognitive Systems (#05577)*

♦ **European Network Against the Arms Trade (ENAAT)** 07861
Contact Quaker House, Square Ambiorix 50, 1000 Brussels, Belgium. T. +3222343060. Fax +3222306370.
URL: http://www.enaat.org/
History 1984, as *European Anti-Arms Trade Network*, by groups and individuals working against arms exports. EU Transparency Register: 198063521842-62. **Aims** Work against the arms trade at the European and national levels; monitor export of weapons and military equipment from Europe, particularly to countries using such arms against their own populations, to countries involved in armed conflicts and to countries whose population lack basic needs; monitor arms export legislation in member countries; monitor EU subsidies to the security and arms industry. **Structure** Meets annually. **Languages** English. **Staff** 1.00 FTE, paid. **Finance** Donations. **Activities** Monitoring/evaluation; training/education; politics/policy/regulatory; guidance/assistance/consulting; research/documentation. **Events** *Meeting* Antwerp (Belgium) 1994, *Meeting* Bremen (Germany) 1992, *Meeting* Utrecht (Netherlands) 1992.
Members Organizations (19) in 13 countries:
Belgium, Czechia, Denmark, Finland, France, Germany, Hungary, Italy, Netherlands, Spain, Sweden, Switzerland, UK.
Included in the above, 6 organizations listed in this Yearbook:
Campaign Against Arms Trade (CAAT); Norwegian Peace Association (NPA); Observatoire des armements / CDRPC; Peace Union of Finland; Swedish Peace and Arbitration Society (SPAS); Swiss Peace Council (SFR).
International organizations (2), listed in this Yearbook:
Group of the Greens – European Free Alliance (Greens/EFA, #10781); International Peace Bureau (IPB, #14535).
[2017.10.13/XF5265/y/F]

♦ **European Network against Racism (ENAR)** 07862
Réseau européen contre le racisme – Europäisches Netz gegen Rassismus
Secretariat Rue Ducale 67, 5th Floor, 1000 Brussels, Belgium. T. +3222293570. E-mail: info@enar-eu.org.
URL: http://www.enar-eu.org/
History 1998. Registration: No/ID: 0864.198.932, Start date: 30 Jun 2003, Belgium; Eu Transparency Register, No/ID: 09854512780-89, Start date: 14 Dec 2009. **Aims** Combat racism, racial discrimination, xenophobia and related intolerance. **Structure** General Assembly (annual); Board; Secretariat. **Languages** English. **Staff** 12.00 FTE, paid. **Finance** Funded by *European Commission (EC, #06633)* and various foundations. **Activities** Advocacy/lobbying/activism; capacity building; events/meetings. **Events** *General Assembly* Brussels (Belgium) 2022, *Equal@Work Platform Seminar* Brussels (Belgium) 2019, *General Assembly* Brussels (Belgium) 2019, *Symposium on Intersectionality* Brussels (Belgium) 2018, *Meeting* Brussels (Belgium) 2016. **Publications** *e-Newsletter*. Studies; reports; brochures.
Members in 30 countries:
Austria, Belgium, Bulgaria, Croatia, Cyprus, Czechia, Denmark, Estonia, Finland, France, Germany, Greece, Hungary, Ireland, Italy, Latvia, Lithuania, Luxembourg, Malta, Netherlands, North Macedonia, Poland, Portugal, Romania, Slovakia, Slovenia, Spain, Sweden, Türkiye, UK.
European organizations (9):
African Diaspora Youth Network in Europe (ADYNE, #00288); CEJI (#03628); Churches' Commission for Migrants in Europe (CCME, #03912); European Association of Lawyers for Democracy and World Human Rights (ELDH, #06105); European Coordination of Associations and Individuals for Freedom of Conscience (CAPLC); European Forum of Muslim Women (EFOMW, #07321); European Network on Religion and Belief (ENORB, #07985); Forum of European Muslim Youth and Student Organisations (FEMYSO, #09909); International Federation of Resistance Movements (#13529).
Consultative Status Consultative status granted from: *Council of Europe (CE, #04881)* (Participatory Status).
NGO Relations Member of: Alliance Against Antigypsyism; *European Anti-Poverty Network (EAPN, #05908); European NGO Platform Asylum and Migration (EPAM, #08051); Social Platform (#19344)*.
[2021/XF6017/y/F]

♦ European Network Against Trafficking in Women / see *European Network Against Trafficking in Women for Sexual Exploitation (#07863)*

♦ **European Network Against Trafficking in Women for Sexual Exploitation (ENATW)** 07863
Contact address not obtained. E-mail: info.aretusa@gmail.com – irene@irene.mi.it – progettazione@afpatronatosv.org.
URL: http://www.aretusa.net/
History 5 Jul 1991, Amsterdam (Netherlands), as *European Network Against Trafficking in Women*, at 1st European Working Conference on Trafficking in Women, organized by *Coördinatiecentrum Mensenhandel (CoMensha)* and *Group of the Greens – European Free Alliance (Greens/EFA, #10781)*. **NGO Relations** *Mediterranean Institute of Gender Studies (MIGS)* is a member.
[2008/XF1509/F]

♦ **European Network of Agricultural Journalists (ENAJ)** 07864
Chairman Karel Martelstraat 54, 1000 Brussels, Belgium. T. +32477488415.
SG address not obtained. T. +353876887960.
URL: http://www.enaj.eu/
History 6 Dec 2011, Brussels (Belgium), when Charter was drawn up; Charter approved 2012. **Aims** Establish closer working links between agricultural guilds throughout Europe. **Structure** General Assembly; Management Committee. **Staff** None. **Activities** Events/meetings; networking/liaising.
Members Full in 22 countries:
Austria, Belgium, Bulgaria, Croatia, Czechia, Denmark, Finland, France, Germany, Hungary, Ireland, Italy, Netherlands, Norway, Poland, Romania, Slovakia, Slovenia, Spain, Sweden, Switzerland, UK.
Observer in 5 countries:
Cyprus, Greece, Luxembourg, Malta, Portugal.
Also observer members in Baltic States. Associate members (10):
COPA – european farmers (COPA, #04829); CropLife Europe (#04965); European Agricultural Machinery Association (CEMA, #05846); European Federation of Agricultural Exhibitions and Show Organizers (EURASCO, #07043); Euroseeds (#09179); Fédération européenne des fabricants d'aliments composés pour animaux (FEFAC, #09566); FEFANA – EU Association of Specialty Feed Ingredients and their Mixtures (#09720); Fertilizers Europe (#09738); General Confederation of Agricultural Cooperatives in the European Union (#10107); Health for Animals (#10870).
[2017.11.27/XM4125/y/F]

♦ **European Network of Agricultural Social Protection Systems (ENASP)** 07865
Secretariat Weissensteinstr 70-72, 34131 Kassel, Germany. T. +4956178512142. E-mail: enasps-ecretariat@svlfg.de.
URL: http://www.enasp.eu/
History Registration: EU Transparency Register, No/ID: 100063234453-93, Start date: 3 Apr 2019. **Aims** Defend and strengthen the values and principles of agricultural social protection based on solidarity and territorial cohesion; defend and reinforce values and principles of welfare policy and social benefits; represent the interests of agricultural social security before Eu authorities. **Structure** Plenary Assembly; Secretariat. **Languages** English. **Staff** No staff. **Finance** Sources: members' dues. **Activities** Advocacy/lobbying/activism; events/meetings; guidance/assistance/consulting; knowledge management/information dissemination.
Members Full in 6 countries:
Austria, Finland, France, Germany, Greece, Poland.
[2022.02.14/XM6872/F]

♦ **European Network of Airport Law Enforcement Organisations (AIRPOL)** 07866
Réseau européen de police aéronautique et de service de sécurité frontalière
Permanent Office Federal Police Brussels Airport, Satellit, 1930 Zaventem, Belgium. T. +3227096601. Fax +3227096633. E-mail: airpol@airpoleuropa.eu.
URL: http://www.airpoleuropa.eu/
History Proposed during Belgian Presidency of *Council of the European Union (#04895)* (June-Dec 2010). **Aims** Enhance the overall security in the European Union airports and in the domain of civil aviation. **Structure** Project Manager; Deputy Project Manager. Permanent Office. **Finance** Supported by *European Commission (EC, #06633)* – DG Home Affairs. **Events** *Plenary Conference* Helsinki (Finland) 2018, *Airpol founding conference* Brussels (Belgium) 2010.
Members Core Group (police agencies) in 13 countries:
Belgium, Bulgaria, Cyprus, Denmark, Finland, France, Luxembourg, Netherlands, Portugal, Romania, Spain, Sweden, UK.
Included in the above, 1 regional organization:
Frontex, the European Border and Coast Guard Agency (#10005).
Airports in 29 countries:
Austria, Belgium, Bulgaria, Croatia, Cyprus, Czechia, Denmark, Estonia, Finland, France, Germany, Greece, Hungary, Ireland, Italy, Latvia, Lithuania, Luxembourg, Netherlands, Norway, Poland, Portugal, Romania, Slovakia, Slovenia, Spain, Sweden, Switzerland, UK.
IGO Relations Partners: *European Commission (EC, #06633); European Police Office (Europol, #08239); International Criminal Police Organization – INTERPOL (ICPO-INTERPOL, #13110)*.
[2015/XJ2445/E*]

♦ European Network of Analytical Sociologists / see *International Network of Analytical Sociologists (#14231)*

♦ **European Network for Avant-Garde and Modernism Studies (EAM)** . 07867
Chair Literary Theory and Cultural Studies – Fac of Arts, Blijde-Inkomstraat 21 – box 3311, 3000 Leuven, Belgium.
URL: http://www.eam-europe.be/
Aims Promote interdisciplinary and intermedial research on experimental *aesthetics* and *poetics*. **Structure** Steering Committee; Publication Commission; Conference Committee. **Languages** English, French, German. **Events** *International Conference* Lisbon (Portugal) 2022, *International Conference* Leuven (Belgium) 2020, *International Conference* Münster (Germany) 2018, *International Conference* Rennes (France) 2016, *International Conference* Helsinki (Finland) 2014. **Publications** *European Avant-Garde and Modernism Studies* in English, French, German.
Members Individuals in 33 countries:
Australia, Austria, Belgium, Bulgaria, Canada, Croatia, Czechia, Denmark, Estonia, Finland, France, Georgia, Germany, Greece, Hungary, Italy, Japan, Latvia, Netherlands, New Zealand, Norway, Poland, Portugal, Romania, Russia, Serbia, Slovenia, Spain, Sweden, Switzerland, UK, United Arab Emirates, USA.
[2020/XJ9244/F]

♦ European Network for Best Practice and Research / see *Rehabilitation in Multiple Sclerosis (#18826)*

♦ **European Network for Better Regulation (ENBR)** 07868
Coordinator CEPS, Place du Congrès 1, 1000 Brussels, Belgium. T. +3222293961. Fax +3222194151.
URL: http://www.enbr.org/
History 23 Jan 2006. Currently dormant. **Aims** Improve and disseminate knowledge on regulatory processes and the degree and mode of implementation of impact assessment procedures in European Union member states. **Finance** *European Commission (EC, #06633)*. **Publications** *ENBR Newsletter*. **NGO Relations** Coordinated by: *Centre for European Policy Studies (CEPS, #03741)*.
[2008/XM3411/d/F]

♦ European Network for Better Work Environment / see *European Work Hazards Network (#09106)*

♦ **European Network of Buddhist Christian Studies (ENBCS)** 07869
Sec Hohenbachern Str 37, 85354 Freising, Germany. T. +498161547806.
URL: http://www.buddhist-christian-studies.org/
History 1996, Hamburg (Germany). Former names and other names: *European Network for Christian Studies of Buddhism* – former (1996 to 1997). **Aims** Promote mutual understanding, practical cooperation, study at academic level, interchange and friendship between Christians and Buddhists in study and dialogue. **Structure** Officers: President; 3 Secretaries. **Finance** Conference fees. **Activities** Organizes biennial congress. **Events** *Conference* Salzburg (Austria) 2022, *Conference* St Ottilien (Germany) 2019, *Conference* Montserrat 2017, *Conference* St Ottilien (Germany) 2015, *Conference* Ghent (Belgium) 2013. **Publications** *NetworkInfo*.
Members Mainly in Europe. Membership countries not specified.
[2022/XF4882/F]

♦ **European Network of Building Research Institutes (ENBRI)** 07870
Exec Sec c/o WTCB/CSTC, Lozenberg 7, 1932 Sint-Stevens-Woluwe, Belgium. T. +3227164211 – +3226557711. Fax +3226530729.
URL: http://www.enbri.org/
History 1988. **Aims** Coordinate and promote research and technological development activities for the European construction industry, thus enabling members to contribute effectively together with all stakeholders of the European construction industry and European Commission to improve competitiveness, sustainability, quality and safety of the built environment. **Structure** Board of Directors comprising President, Vice-President, Executive Secretary and Directors of member institutes; Ad-hoc Working Groups. **Languages** English. **Activities** Research/documentation; advocacy/lobbying/activism.

Members Construction research organizations (one per country) in 21 countries:
Belgium, Croatia, Czechia, Denmark, Finland, France, Germany, Hungary, Iceland, Ireland, Norway, Poland, Portugal, Romania, Serbia, Slovakia, Slovenia, Spain, Sweden, Switzerland, UK.
IGO Relations Advises: *European Commission (EC, #06633)*. **NGO Relations** Member of: *European Council for Construction Research, Development and Innovation (ECCREDI, #06813).* [2017.03.09/XF3901/**F**]

♦ European Network for Business and Industrial Statistics (ENBIS) .. 07871

Dir address not obtained. E-mail: director@enbis.org.
URL: http://www.enbis.org/

History 11 Dec 2000, Amsterdam (Netherlands). **Aims** Foster and facilitate the application and understanding of statistical methods to the benefit of European business and industry; provide a forum for the exchange of ideas and facilitate networking among statistical practitioners. **Structure** General Assembly (annual); Council; Executive Committee; Permanent Secretariat in Amsterdam (Netherlands). **Finance** Members' dues. Income from meetings. **Activities** Awards/prizes/competitions; events/meetings. **Events** *Annual Conference* Budapest (Hungary) 2019, *Annual Conference* Linz (Austria) 2014, *Spring Meeting* Paris (France) 2014, *Annual Conference* Ankara (Turkey) 2013, *Annual Conference* Ljubljana (Slovenia) 2012. **Publications** *ENBIS Newsletter* (4 a year).
Members Individuals and organizations in 38 countries:
Australia, Austria, Belarus, Belgium, Bulgaria, Canada, Czechia, Denmark, Finland, France, Germany, Greece, Hungary, Iceland, India, Ireland, Israel, Italy, Korea Rep, Luxembourg, Netherlands, Norway, Poland, Portugal, Romania, Russia, Serbia, Singapore, Slovenia, Spain, Sweden, Switzerland, Türkiye, UK, Ukraine, USA, Venezuela, Zimbabwe. [2020/XF7031/t/**F**]

♦ European Network for Cancer Immunotherapy (ENCI) 07872

Contact c/o CIMT, Hölderlinstr 8, 55131 Mainz, Germany. T. +4961315547400. E-mail: office@cimt.eu.
URL: https://enci.network/

History A collaborative information and networking platform of *Association for Cancer Immunotherapy (CIMT, #02399), European Academy of Tumor Immunology (EATI)* and Italian Network for Tumor Biotherapy (NIBIT). **Aims** Harmonize activities of the European cancer immunotherapy community; foster collaboration across organizations and countries. **Structure** Council. **Events** *International Cancer Immunotherapy Conference* New York, NY (USA) 2022.
Members Organizations (3):
Italy.
Association for Cancer Immunotherapy (CIMT, #02399); European Academy of Tumor Immunology (EATI).
NGO Relations Co-organizes: *International Cancer Immunotherapy Conference (CICON).* [2021/AA1966/y/**F**]

♦ European Network of Cancer Registries (ENCR) 07873

Secretariat EC Joint Research Centre, F1 Health in Society Unit – Bldg 101, Via Enrico Fermi 2749 – TP 107, 21027 Ispra MB, Italy. E-mail: jrc-encr@ec.europa.eu.
URL: http://www.encr.eu/

History 1990. Established within the framework of *Europe Against Cancer Programme (EC, inactive).* Until 31 Mar 2004, supported by *European Commission (EC, #06633)* (SANCO). Subsequently supported by various EU projects until 2012. Co-funded by *International Agency for Research on Cancer (IARC, #11598)* until end 2012. Since Sep 2012, hosted by *Joint Research Centre (JRC, #16147).* **Aims** Improve the quality, comparability and availability of cancer incidence data; create a basis for monitoring cancer incidence and *mortality* in the European Union; provide regular information on the burden of cancer in Europe; promote use of cancer registry data for research and planning. **Structure** Steering Committee; Secretariat. **Languages** English. **Finance** Supported by: *European Commission (EC, #06633)* (DG SANTE); *Joint Research Centre (JRC, #16147).* **Activities** Awards/prizes/competitions; events/meetings; guidance/assistance/consulting; training/education. **Events** *Cancer Registration Saves Lives* 2021, *Meeting* Copenhagen (Denmark) 2018, *Meeting* Ispra (Italy) 2014, *Meeting* Cork (Ireland) 2012, *Meeting* London (UK) 2011. **Publications** Surveys; studies; monographs; factsheets. **Information Services** *European Cancer Information System (ECIS).* **Members** Full population-based cancer registries (about 160) operating in countries within the UN geographical definition of Europe, plus Cyprus. Associate non-population-based registries, networks of registries, cancer institutes and entities involved in cancer research, and organizations supporting cancer registration or cancer research and/or entities from countries belonging to the WHO European region. Membership countries not specified.
IGO Relations Cooperates with: *International Agency for Research on Cancer (IARC, #11598); Joint Research Centre (JRC, #16147).* **NGO Relations** Cooperates with: *Association of Nordic Cancer Registries (ANCR, #02826); Groupe de coordination pour l'épidémiologie et l'enregistrement du cancer dans les pays de langue latine (GRELL, #10737); International Association of Cancer Registries (IACR, #11753).* [2022.05.04/XF3002/**F**]

♦ European Network for Central Africa (EurAc) 07874

Réseau européen pour l'Afrique centrale

Exec Dir Rue Stevin 115, 1000 Brussels, Belgium. T. +3227254770. E-mail: info@eurac-network.org.
URL: http://www.eurac-network.org/

History 2003. Current title adopted on merger with *European NGO Network on Congo (inactive).* Former names and other names: *Great Lakes Advocacy Network (GLAN)* – former; *Concertation chrétienne pour l'Afrique centrale (CCAC) (CCAC)* – former. Registration: Banque Carrefour des Entreprises, No/ID: 0886.543.871, Start date: 28 Nov 2006, Belgium; EU Transparency Register, No/ID: 857297441342-86, Start date: 9 Feb 2021. **Aims** Bring together European development and *humanitarian organizations* active in Central Africa. **Structure** Board; Secretariat. **Finance** Sources: members' dues. **Activities** Knowledge management/information dissemination; advocacy/lobbying/activism; guidance/assistance/consultancy. **Events** *Conference on Elections 2023 in RD Congo* Brussels (Belgium) 2022, *Conference on Promoting Gender Equality in the DRC and in Rwanda* The Hague (Netherlands) 2019, *Conference on Burundi* Brussels (Belgium) 2018, *Conference on Civil Society on the Frontline* Brussels (Belgium) 2018, *Conference on the Criminalization of the Citizen Movement Lucha in the DR Congo* Brussels (Belgium) 2018.
Members Organizations (38) in 11 countries:
Belgium, France, Germany, Ireland, Italy, Netherlands, Norway, Spain, Sweden, Switzerland, UK.
Organizations:
- *Agir ensemble pour les droits humains;*
- *ALBOAN;*
- *Broederlijk Delen;*
- *Catholic Organization for Relief and Development (Cordaid);*
- *Christian Aid;*
- *CNCD Opération 11 11 11;*
- *Coalition of the Flemish North South Movement – 11 11 11;*
- *Comité Catholique contre la Faim et pour le Développement-Terre Solidaire (CCFD-Terre Solidaire);*
- *Commission justice et paix (CJP);*
- *Damien Foundation – Voluntary Organization for Leprosy and TB Control (AF);*
- *Diakonia;*
- *Entraide et fraternité;*
- Fastenopfer – Action de carême;
- FH Suisse;
- *Formation de cadres africains (FONCABA);*
- Forum Réfugiés/Cosi;
- *Franciscans International (FI, #09982);*
- Fundación Mainel;
- *International Peace Information Service (IPIS);*
- *Jesuit European Social Centre (JESC, #16103);*
- Lliga Dels Drets Dels Pobles;
- Maendeleo-Italia;
- *Médecins du Monde – International (MDM, #16613);*
- *MEMISA;*
- *Mensen met een Missie (Stichting CMC);*
- *Norwegian Church Aid;*
- *Ökumenisches Netz Zentralafrika (ÖNZ);*
- *PAX;*
- *Pax Christi – International Catholic Peace Movement (#18266);*
- *PMU Interlife;*
- *Protection International (PI, #18548);*
- *RCN Justice et Démocratie (RCN J&D);*
- Rete Pace per il Congo;
- *Save the People International (SAPI);*
- *Secours catholique – Caritas France;*
- *Solidarité socialiste – Fonds de coopération au développement (FCD);*
- *Swiss Interchurch Aid (EPER);*
- *Trocaire – Catholic Agency for World Development.*

[2022/XG9898/**F**]

♦ European Network of Centres for Pharmacoepidemiology and Pharmacovigilance (ENCePP) 07875

Secretariat c/o EMA, Domenico Scarlattilaan 6, 1083 HS Amsterdam, Netherlands. E-mail: enc-epp_secretariat@ema.europa.eu.
URL: https://www.encepp.eu/

Aims Strengthen the monitoring of the benefit-risk balance of medicinal products in Europe. **Structure** Plenary; Steering Group; Secretariat, provided by *European Medicines Agency (EMA, #07767).* Working Groups; Special Interest Groups. **Activities** Research/documentation; standards/guidelines. **IGO Relations** Partner of (1): *European Medicines Agency (EMA, #07767).* [2023/AA3233/**F**]

♦ European Network of Childbirth Associations (ENCA) 07876

Coordinator c/o GfG, Pohlstr 28, 10785 Berlin, Germany. T. +493045026920. Fax +493045026921.
URL: http://www.enca.info/

History 1993, Frankfurt-Main (Germany). **Aims** Improve perinatal care for *mothers* and *babies.* **Structure** Each country is represented by a contact person. **Languages** English, French, German. **Staff** Voluntary. **Finance** Members' dues. Donations. Each country is responsible for its own expenses. **Activities** Awareness raising; knowledge management/information dissemination; monitoring/evaluation; events/meetings. **Events** *Annual Meeting* Berlin (Germany) 2016, *Annual Meeting* Paris (France) 2015, *Annual Meeting* Prague (Czech Rep) 2014, *Annual Meeting* Bucharest (Romania) 2013, *Annual Meeting* Vienna (Austria) 2012.
Members Organizations in 19 countries:
Austria, Belgium, Bosnia-Herzegovina, Bulgaria, Czechia, France, Germany, Greece, Hungary, Italy, Lithuania, Luxembourg, Netherlands, Poland, Portugal, Slovakia, Spain, Switzerland, UK.
Associate members in 8 countries:
Bulgaria, Croatia, Estonia, Finland, Ireland, Latvia, Russia, USA.
IGO Relations Participates as observer in the activities of: *Codex Alimentarius Commission (CAC, #04081).* [2021/XF4764/**F**]

♦ European Network Child Friendly Cities (ENCFC) 07877

Pres St Jozefstraat 8, 2800 Mechelen, Belgium. T. +3215418289.
Secretariat c/o Assn of Netherlands Municipalities, PO Box 30435, 2500 GK The Hague, Netherlands. T. +31703738022.
Contact PO Box 822, 3700 AV Zeist, Netherlands. T. +31306981800. Fax +31306917394.
URL: http://www.childfriendlycities.eu/

History 2000. Previously also referred to as *European Child-Friendly-Cities Network (ECFCN) – Europees Netwerk Kindvriendelijke Steden.* **Aims** Promote the rights and interests of children and *youth* in local communities. **Structure** General Meeting. Board. **Languages** English. **Staff** Voluntary. **Finance** None. **Events** *Conference* Ghent (Belgium) 2016, *Conference* Odense (Denmark) 2014, *Conference* Zagreb (Croatia) 2012, *World Conference* Zagreb (Croatia) 2012, *World Conference* Florence (Italy) 2010. **Publications** *ENCFC Newsletter.*
Members Full in 15 countries:
Austria, Belgium, Bulgaria, Croatia, France, Germany, Greece, Ireland, Italy, Netherlands, Spain, Sweden, Switzerland, Türkiye, UK. [2016/XN9751/**F**]

♦ European Network for Christian Studies of Buddhism / see European Network of Buddhist Christian Studies (#07869)

♦ European Network Church-on-the-Move 07878

Réseau Européen Église et liberté – Europäisches Netzwerk Kirche im Aufbruch – Red Europea Iglesia por la Libertad

Contact Embajadores 106 7-C, 28012 Madrid, Spain. T. +34649332654.
URL: http://www.en-re.eu/

History Aug 1991, Eschborn (Germany). Statutes adopted 1996. **Aims** Foster contacts between organizations and individuals committed to the reform and renewal of the *Catholic* Church; work in favour of reform of the Catholic Church according to the spirit of Vatican II Council and develop initiatives related to the commitment of catholics in favour of a better world and a better Europe. **Structure** General Meeting (every two years). Includes *European Conference for Human Rights in the Church (inactive).* **Languages** English, French, German, Spanish. **Staff** 20.00 FTE, voluntary. **Finance** Sources: members' dues. **Activities** Events/meetings; publishing activities; religious activities. **Events** *Conference* 2021, *Annual Conference* Madrid (Spain) 2019, *Annual Conference* Rome (Italy) 2018, *Annual Conference* Strasbourg (France) 2017, *Annual Conference* Drongen (Belgium) 2014. **Publications** Reports; articles.
Members National organizations (26) in 10 countries:
Austria, Belgium, Denmark, France, Germany, Italy, Netherlands, Portugal, Spain, UK.
Regional organization:
Catholics for Choice (#03609) (Europe).
Consultative Status Consultative status granted from: *Council of Europe (CE, #04881)* (Participatory Status).
NGO Relations Member of (1): *European Parliament Platform for Secularism in Politics (EPPSP, #08152).* Cooperates with (1): *We Are Church International (WAC-I, #20841).* Also links with national organizations. [2022.05.17/XF6379/y/**F**]

♦ European Network for Cinema and Media Studies (NECS) 07879

Contact c/o Alexander Stark, Gabelsbergerstr 25, 35037 Marburg, Germany. E-mail: support@necs.org.
URL: http://www.necs.org/

History Feb 2006, Berlin (Germany). Registration: Germany. **Aims** Foster high-level and innovative research in film and media theory, history and practice; provide a forum for communication, exchange and scholarly debate; support young and early-career researchers; establish film and media studies as a dynamic and important part of the arts and humanities research in Europe. **Structure** General Meeting; Steering Committee; Committees (3); Advisory Board. **Languages** English. **Activities** Events/meetings. **Events** *Conference* Oslo (Norway) 2023, *Conference* Bucharest (Romania) 2022, *Conference* 2021, *Conference* Gdansk (Poland) 2019, *Conference* Amsterdam (Netherlands) 2018. **Publications** *European Journal of Media Studies (NECSUS).* [2022/XJ7642/**F**]

♦ European Network Cities for Children / see Cities for Children (#03951)
♦ European network of cities for local integration policies for migrants (inactive)
♦ European Network of Cities and Regions for the Social Economy (#18880)

♦ European Network for Civil Peace Services (EN.CPS) 07880

Treas address not obtained. E-mail: contact@en-cps.org.
URL: http://www.en-cps.org/

History May 1999. A loose network of organizations. **Aims** Support European expert organizations in civil conflict transformation and peace building. **Structure** Steering Committee. **Activities** Lobbies activities at European level. Participants: give training for non-violent civil peace work; send peace teams to conflict areas; lobby for recognition and support for violence prevention and conflict transformation. **Events** *Annual Meeting* Lillehammer (Norway) 2009, *Annual Meeting* Bratislava (Slovakia) 2008, *Annual Meeting* Berlin (Germany) 2007, *Annual Meeting* Barcelona (Spain) 2006, *Annual Meeting* Cluj-Napoca (Romania) 2005. **Publications** *Ziviler Friedensdienst, Fachleute für den Frieden* (2000).
Members Organizations in 12 countries:
Austria, Finland, France, Georgia, Germany, Italy, Moldova, Netherlands, Norway, Romania, Slovakia, UK.
Included in the above, 2 organizations listed in this Yearbook:

Forum Ziviler Friedensdienst (forumZFD); Norwegian Peace Association (NPA).
NGO Relations Close contacts with a number of peace organizations, including: *Centre for Peace, Non-Violence and Human Rights, Osijek; Danish Center for Conflict Resolution (DCCR); International Fellowship of Reconciliation (IFOR, #13586); Peace Brigades International (PBI, #18277); Stiftung Die Schwelle.* [2014/XF5959/y/**F**]

♦ European Network of Communities (enc) 07881
Europäisches Netzwerk der Gemeinschaften
Contact Servitengasse 9, 1090 Vienna, Austria. E-mail: info@e-n-c.org.
History 1997, London (UK). **Aims** Help each other in carrying out their calling; see new communities of the "Third Way" formed across Europe and beyond; see Europe "re-evangelized"; see God's people prepared for Jesus' Second Coming. **Structure** Council.
Members Communities in countries:
Austria, Bosnia-Herzegovina, Croatia, Germany, Israel, Lithuania, Poland, Romania, Slovakia, Spain, Switzerland, UK, Ukraine. [2021/AA2139/**F**]

♦ European Network for Community-Led Initiatives on Climate Change and Sustainability (ECOLISE) 07882
Exec Dir Mundo-B Building, Rue d'Edimbourg 26, 1050 Brussels, Belgium.
Pres address not obtained.
URL: http://www.ecolise.eu/
Aims Establish a common Europe-wide agenda and a platform for collective action. **Structure** Annual General Assembly.
Members European Networks; Local Initiatives; National Networks; Specialist Organizations. European Networks (4):
Baltic Ecovillage Network (BEN, #03114); Global Ecovillage Network – Europe (GEN Europe, #10332); Local Governments for Sustainability (ICLEI, #16507); Transition Network.
Local initiatives (4) in 2 countries:
France, Sweden.
National networks in 14 countries:
Belgium, Croatia, Denmark, Estonia, Germany, Ireland, Italy, Luxembourg, North Macedonia, Romania, Spain, Sweden, Switzerland, UK.
Specialist organizations in 4 countries:
Portugal, Romania, Slovenia, UK.
Included in the above, 1 organization listed in this Yearbook:
Global Ecovillage Network (GEN, #10331).
NGO Relations Member of: *SDG Watch Europe (#19162).* [2020/XM5115/y/**F**]

- ♦ European Network of Community Psychologists / see European Community Psychology Association (#06682)
- ♦ European Network for Comparative Analysis on Food and Eating (unconfirmed)
- ♦ European Network for Comparative Literary Studies / see European Society of Comparative Literature (#08561)
- ♦ European Network on Conflict, Gender and Violence / see European Network on Gender and Violence (#07913)

♦ European Network for Conservation/Restoration Education (ENCoRE) 07883
Contact School of Conservation, Esplanaden 34, 1263 Copenhagen K, Denmark. T. +4541701916. E-mail: encore@encore-edu.org.
URL: http://www.encore-edu.org/
History 9 Nov 1997, Dresden (Germany). Officially founded at first General Assembly, 23 May 1998, Copenhagen (Denmark). **Aims** Maintain and promote the education of the conservator-restorer on an *academic* level in Europe. **Structure** General Assembly. Board of 8 members. **Languages** English. **Staff** 0.50 FTE, paid. **Finance** Sources: members' dues. **Events** *General Assembly* Porto (Portugal) 2020, *General Assembly* Porto (Portugal) 2020, *General Assembly* Liège (Belgium) 2014, *General Assembly* Valencia (Spain) 2012, *General Assembly* Vienna (Austria) 2010. **Publications** *ENCORE e-Newsletter.*
Members Full in 19 countries:
Austria, Belgium, Czechia, Denmark, Finland, France, Germany, Greece, Hungary, Italy, Poland, Portugal, Slovakia, Spain, Sweden, Switzerland.
Associate in 5 countries:
Malta, Netherlands, Norway, Spain, UK.
Partners in 11 countries:
Austria, Belgium, Czechia, Denmark, France, Germany, Italy, Norway, Sweden, Türkiye, UK.
European Confederation of Conservator-Restorers' Organisations (ECCO, #06701); European Research Centre for Book and Paper Conservation-Restoration (ERC, #08359); International Institute for Conservation of Historic and Artistic Works (IIC, #13871).
NGO Relations Member of (1): *European Heritage Alliance 3.3 (#07477).* [2022/XF6764/**F**]

♦ European Network of Construction Companies for Research and Development (ENCORD) 07884
SG address not obtained. E-mail: dominik.mann@strabag.com.
Chairman address not obtained.
URL: http://www.encord.org/
History 1989. **Aims** Promote industry-led research, development and innovation in the construction sector. **Structure** Council. **Languages** English. **Finance** Sources: members' dues. **Activities** Events/meetings; knowledge management/information dissemination; networking/liaising.
Members Construction companies and suppliers in 9 countries:
Austria, Belgium, Finland, France, Germany, Greece, Liechtenstein, Netherlands, Portugal, Spain, Sweden, UK.
NGO Relations Member of (1): *European Council for Construction Research, Development and Innovation (ECCREDI, #06813).* [2021.06.09/XD5425/**D**]

♦ European Network for Copyright in support of Education and Science (ENCES) 07885
Contact c/o Prof Dr Rainer Kuhlen, Bogotastrasse 4, 14163 Berlin, Germany. T. +497731790895.
URL: http://www.ences.eu/
History 29 Jun 2010. Registration: No/ID: VR 29827 B, Germany. **Aims** Advocate an education- and research-friendly copyright; advocate access to knowledge and information produced in science, research, education, the arts and culture for the general public. **Structure** Executive Board. **Languages** English, German. **Staff** 1.50 FTE, voluntary. **Finance** Members' dues. Other sources: project funding. Budget (2013): euro 20,000. **Events** *Workshop* Berlin (Germany) 2012, *Workshop* London (UK) 2011, *Workshop* Amsterdam (Netherlands) 2010, *Workshop* Budapest (Hungary) 2010, *Workshop* Berlin (Germany) 2008. **Publications** Articles.
Members Individual; Institutional. Individual in 2 countries:
Austria, Germany.
Institutional in 6 countries:
Czechia, Estonia, Ireland, Latvia, Netherlands, UK.
Consultative Status Consultative status granted from: *World Intellectual Property Organization (WIPO, #21593)* (Observer Status). **IGO Relations** *European Union (EU, #08967).* **NGO Relations** Member of: *Copyright for Creativity (C4C, #04832).* Partner of: *Open Access Publishing in European Networks (OAPEN, #17746).* [2015.06.01/XJ6284/**F**]

♦ European Network of Councils for the Judiciary (ENCJ) 07886
Réseau européen des conseils de la justice (RECJ) – Red Europea de Consejos del Poder Judicial (RECPJ)
Secretariat Rue de la Croix de Fer 67, 1000 Brussels, Belgium. T. +3225351682. E-mail: office@encj.eu.
URL: http://www.encj.eu/
History 2004. Registration: EU Transparency Register, No/ID: 45444124056-57; Start date: Dec 2007, Belgium. **Aims** Improve cooperation between, and good mutual understanding among, Councils for the Judiciary and members of the judiciary of both the European Union Member States and of any European Union candidate Member States. **Structure** General Assembly (annual); Executive Board; Permanent Office. **Languages** English. **Staff** 1.40 FTE, paid. **Finance** Members' dues. Subvention from: *European Commission (EC, #06633).* **Events** *General Assembly* Brussels (Belgium) 2021, *General Assembly* Brussels (Belgium) 2020, *General Assembly* Bratislava (Slovakia) 2019, *General Assembly* Lisbon (Portugal) 2018, *General Assembly* Paris (France) 2017. **Publications** *ENCJ Guide* (annual). Annual Report; thematic reports.
Members Councils for the Judiciary or similar autonomous bodies in 23 countries and territories:
Belgium, Bulgaria, Croatia, Denmark, England, France, Greece, Hungary, Ireland, Italy, Latvia, Lithuania, Malta, Netherlands, Northern Ireland, Poland, Portugal, Romania, Scotland, Slovakia, Slovenia, Spain, Wales.
Observers Ministries of Justice or Councils for the Judiciary in 8 countries:
Austria, Cyprus, Czechia, Estonia, Finland, Germany, Luxembourg, Sweden.
IGO Relations Observer to: *Consultative Council of European Judges (CCJE, #04767).* **NGO Relations** Member of: *Global Forum on Law, Justice and Development (GFLJD, #10373).* [2021/XM3420/**D**]

- ♦ European Network for Countering Antisemitism through Education (unconfirmed)
- ♦ European Network of Creative Writing Programmes / see European Association of Creative Writing Programmes (#05996)
- ♦ European Network of Credit Unions (unconfirmed)

♦ European Network of Crystal Growth (ENCG) 07887
Coordinator Consiglio Naz delle Richerche, Piazzale Aldo Moro 7, 00185 Rome RM, Italy.
Sec Dept of Physics – Univ of Aveiro, Campus Universitário de Santiago, 3810-193 Aveiro, Portugal.
URL: https://encg.info/
History 21 Oct 2010, Berlin (Germany). **Structure** Council; Executive Committee. **Activities** Events/meetings; training/education. **Events** *ECCG: European Conference on Crystal Growth* Paris (France) 2022, *European Conference on Crystal Growth (ECCG-6)* Varna (Bulgaria) 2018, *European Conference on Crystal Growth (ECCG)* Bologna (Italy) 2015, *European Conference on Crystal Growth (ECCG)* Glasgow (UK) 2012.
Members National associations in 9 countries:
Czechia, France, Germany, Italy, Netherlands, Poland, Romania, Switzerland, USA.
NGO Relations Cooperates with (1): *International Organization for Crystal Growth (IOCG, #14443).* [2022/AA2713/**F**]

- ♦ European Network of Cultural Administration Training Centres / see ENCATC (#05452)
- ♦ European Network of Cultural Businesses and Institutions Located at Historical Sites / see European Network of Cultural Centres in Historic Monuments

♦ European Network of Cultural Centres (ENCC) 07888
Réseau européen des centres culturels – Europees Netwerk van Culturele Centra
Coordinator Rue Ravenstein 28, 1000 Brussels, Belgium. E-mail: office@encc.eu.
Legal address Av Van Overbeke 164, 1083 Brussels, Belgium.
URL: http://www.encc.eu/
History Jun 1994, Turnhout (Belgium). Registered in accordance with Belgian law. **Aims** Support and facilitate members to reach their goals by helping them to create networks, encouraging cooperation on all levels; represent cultural centres by placing the global importance of arts and culture in society on the political agenda. **Structure** General Assembly; Executive Committee. **Languages** English. **Staff** 6.00 FTE, paid. **Finance** Members' dues. Support from: *European Commission (EC, #06633)* Creative Europe. **Activities** Networking/liaising; events/meetings; capacity building; advocacy/lobbying/activism; training/education; publishing activities. **Events** *Cultural Impact Now! European Conference of Cultural and Creative Spaces* Ebeltoft (Denmark) 2021, *Conference on dealing with cultural differences on local, regional and European level* Germany 2006, *Annual General Meeting* Ljubljana (Slovenia) 1999, *Annual General Meeting* Helsinki (Finland) 1998, *Annual General Meeting* Krakow (Poland) 1997. **Members** Full; Associate. National, regional or local networks of cultural centers, as well as individual cultural centers. Membership countries not specified. **NGO Relations** Member of: *Culture Action Europe (CAE, #04981).* [2019.09.26/XF3781/**F**]

- ♦ European Network of Cultural Centres / Historical Monuments / see European Network of Cultural Centres in Historic Monuments
- ♦ European Network of Cultural Centres in Historical Places / see European Network of Cultural Centres in Historic Monuments
- ♦ European Network of Cultural Centres in Historic Monuments (internationally oriented national body)

♦ European Network for the Cure of ALS (ENCALS) 07889
Mailing Address PO Box 85500, 3508 GA Utrecht, Netherlands. T. +31887551221. E-mail: info@encals.eu.
URL: http://encals.eu/
History Former names and other names: *European ALS Consortium (EALSC)* – former. Registration: Netherlands. **Aims** Develop a European *Amyotrophic Lateral Sclerosis* (ALS) trial network and database/biobank. **Events** *ENCALS Meeting* Barcelona (Spain) 2023, *ENCALS Meeting* Edinburgh (UK) 2022, *ENCALS Meeting* 2021, *ENCALS Meeting* Edinburgh (UK) 2020, *ENCALS Meeting* Tours (France) 2019.
Members ALS centres in 14 countries:
Belgium, France, Germany, Ireland, Italy, Netherlands, Poland, Portugal, Slovenia, Spain, Sweden, Switzerland, Türkiye, UK.
NGO Relations *European Familial ALS Association (EFALS, no recent information).* [2021/XM2267/**F**]

♦ European Network for Cyber Security (ENCS) 07890
Acting Managing Dir Regulusweg 5, 2516 AC The Hague, Netherlands. T. +31882052678. E-mail: info@encs.eu.
URL: https://encs.eu/
History 2012. Registration: EU Transparency Register, No/ID: 876300220877-50, Start date: 11 Mar 2016. **Aims** Bring together critical infrastructure stake owners and security experts to deploy secure European critical energy grids and infrastructure. **Structure** General Assembly; Management Team. **Activities** Events/meetings; research and development; training/education. **Events** *Strategy Assembly* Amsterdam (Netherlands) 2022, *Seminar on Cybersecurity* Brussels (Belgium) 2022, *Roundtable* Lisbon (Portugal) 2022, *Seminar on Cybersecurity* Brussels (Belgium) 2021, *Workshop on Cybersecurity* Brussels (Belgium) 2020. **Publications** *ENCS Newsletter.* **NGO Relations** Partners include: *European Distribution System Operators' Association for Smart Grids (EDSO, #06931); European Network of Transmission System Operators for Electricity (ENTSO-E, #08026); European Utilities Telecom Council (EUTC, #09042).* [2022/XM7705/**F**]

♦ European Network on Debt and Development (EURODAD) 07891
Red Europea para Deuda y Desarrollo
Main Office Rue d'Edimbourg 18-26, Mundo B Bldg 3rd Floor, 1050 Brussels, Belgium. T. +3228944640. E-mail: assistant@eurodad.org.
URL: http://www.eurodad.org/
History 1990. Former names and other names: *European Campaign on Debt and Development* – former. Registration: EU Transparency Register, No/ID: 09136982496-09, Start date: 12 Oct 2009. **Aims** Push for development policies that support pro-poor and democratically-defined sustainable development strategies; support the empowerment of Southern peoples to chart their own path towards development and ending poverty; seek a lasting and sustainable solution to the debt crisis, appropriate development financing, and a stable international financial system conducive to development. **Structure** General Assembly (meets at least annually); Board of Directors. **Languages** English, French, Spanish. **Staff** 18.00 FTE, paid. **Finance** Sources: grants; members' dues. Supported by: *Bill and Melinda Gates Foundation (BMGF); Bread for the World, USA (BFW); Charles Stewart Mott Foundation; European Commission (EC, #06633); Financial Transparency Coalition (FTC, #09772); Norwegian Agency for Development Cooperation (Norad); Open Society Foundations (OSF, #17763).* **Activities** Advocacy/lobbying/activism; awareness raising; events/meetings; knowledge management/information dissemination; monitoring/evaluation; networking/liaising; projects/programmes. **Events** *International Conference* Brussels (Belgium) 2022, *Skilling-up on Climate Finance* Brussels (Belgium) 2022, *Skilling-up on Climate Finance* Brussels (Belgium) 2022, *The EU's Global Gateway: market creation or international development?* Brussels (Belgium) 2022, *Our Future is Public Conference* Santiago (Chile) 2022. **Publications** Reports; videos.

Members European NGOs (50) in 29 countries:
Austria, Belgium, Bulgaria, Croatia, Czechia, Denmark, Estonia, Finland, France, Germany, Hungary, Ireland, Latvia, Lithuania, Luxembourg, Malta, Netherlands, Norway, Poland, Portugal, Romania, Serbia, Slovakia, Slovenia, South Africa, Spain, Sweden, Switzerland, UK.
Included in the above, 38 organizations listed in this Yearbook:
- *ActionAid (#00087)*;
- *Alliance Sud, Swiss Alliance of Development Organisations Swissaid – Catholic Lenten Fund – Bread for All – Helvetas – Caritas – Interchurch Aid*;
- *Both ENDS (#03307)*;
- *Bretton Woods Project*;
- *Christian Aid*;
- *CNCD Opération 11 11 11*;
- *Coalition of the Flemish North South Movement – 11 11 11*;
- *Comité Catholique contre la Faim et pour le Développement-Terre Solidaire (CCFD-Terre Solidaire)*;
- *Diakonia*;
- *ForumCiv*;
- *Forum for Development and Environment (ForUM)*;
- *Global Justice Now*;
- *Global Policy Forum (GPF)*;
- *Globalt Fokus*;
- *Help for Children in Need (KNH)*;
- *Ibis – Denmark*;
- *Institute of Global Responsibility (IGO)*;
- *INTERMON OXFAM*;
- *Koordinierungstelle der Österreichischen Bischofskonferenz für Internationale Entwicklung und Mission (KOO)*;
- *Norwegian Church Aid*;
- *Observatori del Deute en la Globalització (ODG)*;
- *Oikos – Ecumenical Institute for Church and Development Cooperation*;
- *ONE (#17728)*;
- *Oxfam GB*;
- *Oxfam Novib*;
- *Public Eye*;
- *Recourse (#18630)*;
- *Save the Children Federation (SCF)*;
- *Save the Children Norway (Redd Barna)*;
- *Save the Children UK (SC UK)*;
- *Stichting Onderzoek Multinationale Ondernemingen (SOMO)*;
- *Suomalaiset Kehitysjärjestöt (Fingo)*;
- *Swedish NGO Centre for Development Cooperation (Forum Syd)*;
- *Trocaire – Catholic Agency for World Development*;
- *Urgewald*;
- *WaterAid (#20822)*;
- *WEMOS*;
- *World Economy, Ecology and Development (WEED)*.

Consultative Status Consultative status granted from: *UNCTAD (#20285)* (General); *ECOSOC (#05331)* (Special). **NGO Relations** On Coordinating Committee of: *Financial Transparency Coalition (FTC, #09772)*. Signatory to Founding Statement of: *Alliance for Lobbying Transparency and Ethics Regulation (ALTER-EU, #00705)*. Member of: *Transparency, Accountability and Participation Network (TAP Network, #20222)*. Working relations with: *African Forum and Network on Debt and Development (AFRODAD, #00321)*; *Bank Information Center (BIC)*; *Forum on Debt and Development (FONDAD, #09906)*; *Jubilee South (#16159)*; *Red Latinoamericana sobre Deuda, Desarrollo y Derechos (LATINDADD, #18711)*. Coordinates: *The Reality Of Aid (ROA, #18626)*. Together with: *African Network for Environment and Economic Justice (ANEEJ)*, instrumental in setting up: *ECOWAS Network on Debt and Development (ECONDAD, #05336)*. Supports: *Global Call for Action Against Poverty (GCAP, #10263)*. [2023.02.16/XF5518/y/**F**]

♦ European Network of Democratic Young Left (ENDYL) 07892

Contact 52 Themistokleous, 106 81 Athens, Greece. T. +302103809319. Fax +302103809318.
URL: http://www.endyl.jeunes-communistes.org/

History May 1994, Copenhagen (Denmark). **Events** *General Assembly* Istanbul (Turkey) 2006. [2010/XF4327/**F**]

♦ European Network of Digital Cities 07893

Réseau européen des villes numériques – Red Europea de Ciudades Digitales – Europäische Netz der Digitalen Städten – Rete Europea delle Città Digitali

SG 124 rue Saussure, 75017 Paris, France. T. +33143584573. Fax +33146368320. E-mail: fondation@villesnumeriques.org.
Contact address not obtained.
URL: http://www.villesnumeriques.org/

History 1997. Former names and other names: *Association des Villes Numériques* – former (1997 to 29 May 2001); *European Network of Numerical Cities* – former. Registration: Start date: 29 May 2001, France. **Structure** Council. **NGO Relations** Instrumental in setting up (1): *Association européen art éducation – nouvelles technologies (ARENOTECH, #02553)*. [2022/XM0651/**F**]

- ♦ European Network on Digital Labour (unconfirmed)
- ♦ European Network on Early Intervention / see Eurlyaid – European Association on Early Childhood Intervention (#05626)
- ♦ European Network for Economic Cooperation and Development (internationally oriented national body)

♦ European Network of Economic Policy Research Institutes (ENEPRI) 07894

Contact CEPS, Place du Congrès 1, 1000 Brussels, Belgium. T. +3222293949. Fax +3222194151. E-mail: info@ceps.eu.
URL: http://www.enepri.eu/

History 2000, at the initiative of *Centre for European Policy Studies (CEPS, #03741)*. **Activities** Organizes conferences and workshops. **Publications** *ENEPRI Newsletter*. Working papers; research papers; occasional papers.
Members Institutes (22) in 22 countries:
Austria, Belgium, Bulgaria, Cyprus, Czechia, Denmark, Estonia, Finland, France, Germany, Greece, Hungary, Ireland, Italy, Netherlands, Norway, Poland, Slovakia, Slovenia, Spain, Türkiye, UK.
Included in the above, 3 institutes listed in this Yearbook:
Centre for European Policy Studies (CEPS, #03741); *Cyprus Centre for European and International Affairs*; *French Leading Center for International Economic Studies, Paris (CEPII)*. [2016/XM3409/y/**F**]

♦ European Network for Economic Self-Help and Local Development 07895

Réseau européen de l'économie solidaire et du développement local – Europäisches Netzwerk für Ökonomische Selbsthilfe und Lokale Entwicklung

Contact Technologie-Netzwerk Berlin eV, Wiesenstrasse 29, 13357 Berlin, Germany. T. +493046609824 – +49304612409. Fax +49304612418. E-mail: k.birkhoelzer@technet-berlin.de.
URL: http://www.european-network.de/

History Sep 1994, Dessau (Germany), having existed as an informal network since the informal founding meeting in Nov 1992, Berlin (Germany). As of 2006, an informal 'network of friends' without formal membership. **Aims** Promote transnational cooperation by organizations and campaigns working for economic self-help and local development; enable joint project work and create a strong lobby in Europe. **Structure** General Meeting (every 2 years); Executive Committee; Regional Contact Offices. **Languages** English, French, German. **Staff** 2.00 FTE, voluntary. **Finance** Research contracts; small donations. **Activities** Networking/liaising; projects/programmes; advocacy/lobbying/activism. **Events** *Conference on solidarity economy* Berlin (Germany) 2006, *Conference on socialising the global economy / Biennial Congress* Liverpool (UK) 2004, *Biennial Congress* London (UK) 2003, *European conference* Carcassonne (France) / Mouthoumet (France) / Limoux (France) / Prades (France) / Florac (France) 2002, *Biennial Congress* Leipzig (Germany) 2002. **Publications** Learning Package; articles; series; proceedings. **Members** No formal membership. **IGO Relations** *European Commission (EC, #06633)*; *European Foundation for the Improvement of Living and Working Conditions (Eurofound, #07348)*. **NGO Relations** *Development Innovations and Networks (#05057)*; *EMES International Research Network (#05440)*; *European Community Development Network (EuCDN, #06679)*; *European Institute for Solidarity based Economy (#07572)*; *New Economics Foundation (NEF, #17082)*; *Positive Futures Network*; *Réseau Européen des Villes and Régions de l'Économie Sociale (REVES, #18880)*; *RIPESS Europe – Economy Solidarity Europe (RIPESS Europe, #18952)*. [2016.06.01/XF3560/**F**]

♦ European Network on the Economics of the Firm (ENEF) 07896

Contact address not obtained. E-mail: enef.mailing.list@gmail.com.
URL: https://sites.google.com/view/enef-webpage/home?authuser=0

History Jul 2004, Sheffield (UK). Founded at first Workshop. **Aims** Promote trans-European comparative work on the firm. **Structure** Informal network. **Activities** Events/meetings. **Events** *Workshop* Karlskrona (Sweden) 2022, *Workshop* 2021, *Workshop* Bergamo (Italy) 2021, *Global and regional value chains, industrial dynamics and enterprise strategies* Vienna (Austria) 2019, *Firm automation in the era of artificial intelligence – the future of organisation, employment and productivity* Brighton (UK) 2018. [2022/XJ1540/**E**]

♦ European Network for the Economics of Learning, Innovation, and Competence Building Systems (EUROLICS) 07897

Acting SG Aalborg Univ Business School, Fibigerstr 11, 9220 Aalborg Ø, Denmark. T. +4599408260. E-mail: bg@business.aau.dk.
URL: http://www.eurolics.org/

History 12 Sep 2014, Copenhagen (Denmark). A chapter of: *Global Network for Economics of Learning, Innovation and Competence Building Systems (GLOBELICS, #10488)*. **Aims** Develop and design activities that address the current problems of exclusion and increasing polarization in Europe on the basis of an assessment of the relative strength of European knowledge infrastructure. **Structure** Scientific Board; Secretary-General. **Languages** English. **Staff** All voluntary. **Finance** Funding through members, participants and ad hoc funding. No budget. **Activities** Events/meetings. **Events** *Workshop on University-Industry Interaction / Workshop* Ankara (Turkey) 2015.
Members Full in 10 countries:
Denmark, France, Hungary, Italy, Netherlands, Norway, Portugal, Sweden, Türkiye, UK. [2022.06.07/XJ9675/**F**]

♦ European Network of Education Councils (EUNEC) 07898

Réseau européen des conseils de l'éducation

Secretariat c/o Vlaamse Onderwijsraad, Koning Albert II-laan 37, 1030 Brussels, Belgium. T. +3222271370. E-mail: eunec@vlor.be.
URL: http://www.eunec.eu/

History 1999. Former names and other names: *European Network of National and Regional Education Councils* – former (1999). Registration: Start date: 18 Oct 2005, Belgium; EU Transparency Register, No/ID: 41228861912-38. **Aims** Discuss the findings and recommendations of all European projects in education and training; determine standpoints; formulate statements on these issues. **Structure** General Assembly (annual); Executive Committee; Secretariat. **Languages** English. **Staff** 4.00 FTE, voluntary. **Finance** Sources: members' dues. **Activities** Events/meetings. **Events** *General Assembly* Belgium 2021, *Seminar* Sèvres (France) 2019, *Seminar* Lisbon (Portugal) 2018, *Seminar* Bucharest (Romania) 2017, *Seminar* Amsterdam (Netherlands) 2016. **Publications** *EUNEC Newsletter* (4 a year). Reports.
Members Members of the general assembly and the executive committee in 7 countries and territories:
Belgium/Flemish Region, Belgium/Wallonia Region, Cyprus, France, Lithuania, Netherlands, Portugal.
Other members of the general assembly in 8 countries and territories:
Czechia, Estonia, Greece, Hungary, Ireland, Québec, Romania, Spain.
Network members in 2 countries and territories:
Northern Ireland, Wales.
Non-European members in 1 country:
Canada. [2021/XM0232/**D**]

- ♦ European Network of Education Departments in Opera Houses / see Réseau européen pour la sensibilisation à l'opéra et à la danse (#18878)
- ♦ European Network for Education in International Health / see TropEd (#20245)

♦ European Network for Education and Training (EUNET) 07899

Pres Weberstrasse 118, 53113 Bonn, Germany. T. +4922894930122. E-mail: info@european-net.org.
URL: http://www.european-net.org/

History Jul 2004, Brussels (Belgium). Registration: Nordrhein-Westphalia District court, No/ID: VR 8333, Start date: 16 Sep 2004, Germany, Bonn. **Aims** Intensify the experience-exchange; increase the quality of the offers; develop and distribute methodical-didactic materials as well as simulations; make member activities visible to a wider public; affiliate, coordinate and force different member efforts to advance the European integration and integrate the citizens into this process and make events more comprehensible on a European level. **Structure** General Assembly (annual); Supervisory Board; Committee for Content and Methodology; Council for Development and Cooperation; Youth Committee; Committee on Migration and Inter-Cultural Affairs. **Languages** English, French, German. **Staff** None. **Finance** Sources: members' dues. **Activities** Events/meetings; networking/liaising. Runs the *'EUNET Integration Network'*. **Events** *Annual Conference* Prague (Czech Rep) 2014, *Annual Conference and General Assembly / Annual Conference* Vukovar (Croatia) 2012, *Annual conference and general assembly / Annual Conference* Metz (France) 2011, *Annual Conference* Bad Marienberg (Germany) 2010, *Annual Conference* Marienheide (Germany) 2009. **Publications** *Europe in Your Pocket – Europa in der Tasche*; *Handbook of Best Practices for Integration*; *Picturing the Intergenerational Dialogue*; *REPERES*.
Members Institutions (61) in 20 countries:
Austria, Croatia, Cyprus, Czechia, Denmark, France, Germany, Greece, Italy, Malta, Netherlands, Norway, Poland, Portugal, Slovakia, Slovenia, Spain, Sweden, Türkiye, UK.
Included in the above, 11 organizations listed in this Yearbook:
Accademia Europeista del Friuli-Venezia Giulia; *Centre international de formation européenne (CIFE, #03755)*; *Centro Einstein di Studi Internazionali sul Federalismo, la Pace, la Politica del Territorio (CESI)*; *Europa-Haus Marienberg*; *Europäische Akademie Nordrhein-Westfalen*; *Europäische Akademie Otzenhausen (EAO)*; *Europäische Akademie, Schleswig Holstein (EASH)*; *Europäische Akademie Wien*; *European Robert Schuman Centre (CERS)*; *International Education Centre of Svendborg (IUC-Europe)*; *Maison de l'Europe de Paris*.
Consultative Status Consultative status granted from: *Council of Europe (CE, #04881)* (Participatory Status).
NGO Relations Supports (1): *European Alliance for the Statute of the European Association (EASEA, #05886)*. [2022.10.21/XM0771/y/**F**]

♦ European Network of Election Monitoring Organizations (ENEMO) . 07900

Main Office Bul Josipa Broza 23 A, Floor IV, Apartment 119, 81000 Podgorica, Montenegro. E-mail: info@enemo.eu.
URL: http://www.enemo.eu/

History 29 Sep 2001. **Aims** Support the international community's interest in and support for democracy in the post-communist countries of the OSCE region; assess electoral conditions and the political environment; offer accurate and impartial observation reports. **Structure** Assembly; Secretariat; Central Executive Office. **Languages** English. **Staff** 6.00 FTE, paid. **Finance** Support from: *European Union (EU, #08967)* Delegation to Ukraine; *Organization for Security and Cooperation in Europe (OSCE, #17887)*; *United States Agency for International Development (USAID)*; Black Sea Trust; National Endowment for Democracy; US State Department; Governments of Germany, Latvia, Luxembourg, Netherlands, Norway, Sweden, UK. **Activities** Monitoring/evaluation. **Publications** Reports.
Members Organizations (23) in 18 countries:
Albania, Armenia, Azerbaijan, Belarus, Bosnia-Herzegovina, Croatia, Georgia, Kazakhstan, Kosovo, Kyrgyzstan, Moldova, Montenegro, North Macedonia, Romania, Russia, Serbia, Slovakia, Ukraine.
Included in the above, 1 organization listed in this Yearbook:
International Society for Fair Elections and Democracy (ISFED).
IGO Relations *European Union (EU, #08967)* Network for Enhanced Electoral and Democratic Support (NEEDS). [2021/XJ7570/y/**F**]

- ♦ European Network of Energy Agencies / see European Energy Network (#06988)

◆ **European Network of Engineering for Agriculture and Environment (ENGAGE)** 07901

Gen Sec August Reyerslaan 80, 1030 Brussels, Belgium. E-mail: secgen@eurageng.eu.
Chairman Leibniz-Inst for Agricultural Engineering, Max-Eyth-Allee 100, 14469 Potsdam, Germany.
URL: http://www.eurageng.eu/engage/

History 1988. In 1998/99 became a strategic division of *European Society of Agricultural Engineers (EurAgEng, #08513)*. Former names and other names: *European Community Club of Advanced Engineering for Agriculture (ECCAEA)* – former; *European Union Club of Advanced Engineering for Agriculture (EUCAEA)* – former. **Aims** Identify and analyse opportunities for research and development in agricultural, biosystems and environmental engineering to advance agriculture and associated industries; encourage and facilitate cooperation between engineers and scientists within the EU and in countries with scientific agreements with the EU; make readily available expert advice in the areas of agriculture, biosystems and environmental engineering. **Structure** Network Meeting (annual); Chairmanship and Secretariat rotates every 4 years. Merged Secretariat with *European Society of Agricultural Engineers (EurAgEng, #08513)*. **Languages** English. **Finance** Organizations bear their own costs. **Activities** Events/meetings; knowledge management/information dissemination; research and development. **Publications** Technical reviews.

Members Organizations and individuals in 21 countries:
Austria, Belgium, Croatia, Denmark, Estonia, Finland, France, Germany, Greece, Hungary, Italy, Lithuania, Netherlands, Norway, Poland, Portugal, Romania, Spain, Sweden, Switzerland, UK. [2022.05.04/XF6080/F]

◆ European Network of Environmental Professionals (inactive)

◆ **European Network of Environmental Research Organizations (ENERO)** 07902

SG c/o ISSeP, Rue du Chéra 200, 4000 Liège, Belgium. T. +3242298369. Fax +3242524665.
Registered Office 60 rue d'Hauteville, 75010 Paris, France. T. +33145960956. Fax +33145960957.
URL: http://www.enero.eu/

History 1992. Registered in accordance with French law. Constitution amended, 24 Nov 2000, Ljubljana (Slovenia). **Aims** Exchange information and knowledge between European environmental institutes; be a leading actor in European Framework Programmes; coordinate research efforts between research institutes; build common European research and development projects; identify and focus on potential topics of interest to public authorities and industry in Europe. **Structure** General Assembly (2 a year); Board; General Secretariat. **Languages** English. **Finance** Members' dues. Grants. Budget (annual): euro 22,000. **Activities** Knowledge management/information dissemination; research and development; events/meetings. **Events** *Environment in horizon 2000* Brussels (Belgium) 2014, *Boosting and securing eco innovations through new partnerships* Brussels (Belgium) 2012, *Risk assessment and management of strategic energy technologies* Brussels (Belgium) 2010, *Interactions between atmospheric pollution and climate at regional scale* Brussels (Belgium) 2008, *Nanomaterials and nanoparticles risk management* Brussels (Belgium) 2006.

Members Full; Honorary. Full – bodies involved in supporting governmental institutions, community organizations or the European Commission and which belong to a country with the EU, to a country in pre-accession phase to the EU or to a country associated to the EU in the domain of research. Organizations totalling 5,000 research workers in 14 countries:
Austria, Belgium, Estonia, Finland, France, Germany, Greece, Italy, Netherlands, Norway, Poland, Slovenia, Spain, Sweden.
[2014.11.26/XF3212/F]

◆ **European Network of Equality Bodies (Equinet)** 07903

Exec Dir Rue Royale 138, 1000 Brussels, Belgium. T. +3222123182. Fax +3222123030.
URL: http://equineteurope.org/

History Registered in accordance with Belgian law, 2007. EU Transparency Register: 718971811339-46. **Aims** Promote equality in Europe through supporting and enabling the work of national equality bodies. **Structure** Annual General Meeting; Executive Board; Working Groups; Secretariat, headed by Executive Director. **Activities** Knowledge management/information dissemination; training/education; research/documentation. **Events** *Charting the charter – equality bodies and fundamental rights in the EU* Brussels (Belgium) 2015. **Publications** *Equinet Newsletter*.

Members Full in 33 countries:
Albania, Austria, Belgium, Bulgaria, Croatia, Cyprus, Czechia, Denmark, Estonia, Finland, France, Germany, Greece, Hungary, Ireland, Italy, Latvia, Lithuania, Luxembourg, Malta, Montenegro, Netherlands, North Macedonia, Norway, Poland, Portugal, Romania, Serbia, Slovakia, Slovenia, Spain, Sweden, UK. [2021/XM4973/F]

◆ European Network in European and Global History (internationally oriented national body)

◆ **European Network of Excellence on the Geological Storage of CO2 (CO2GeoNet)** 07904

Secretariat 3 av Claude Guillemin, BP 36009, 45058 Orléans, France. E-mail: info@co2geonet.com.
URL: http://www.co2geonet.com/

History Founded under *European Commission (EC, #06633)* 6th Framework Programme as a Network of Excellence (2004-2009). Launched as an association in Venice (Italy). Registration: Start date: 17 Apr 2008, France. **Aims** Enable safe and efficient deployment of CO2 Capture and Storage (CCS). **Structure** General Meeting; Executive Committee; Advisory Committee. **Languages** English. **Staff** No fixed staff. **Finance** Sources: donations; members' dues; revenue from activities/projects. **Activities** Capacity building; guidance/assistance/consulting; knowledge management/information dissemination; research/documentation; training/education. **Events** *CO2GeoNet Winter Seminar* 2020, *Conference* Madrid (Spain) 2019, *Open Forum* Venice (Italy) 2019, *Conference* Katowice (Poland) 2018, *Open Forum* Venice (Italy) 2018. **Publications** *CO2GeoNet Newsletter* (3 a year).

Members Partners (26) in 20 countries:
Austria, Belgium, Croatia, Czechia, Denmark, Estonia, France, Germany, Greece, Italy, Netherlands, Norway, Poland, Portugal, Romania, Slovenia, Spain, Switzerland, Türkiye, UK.
Included in the above, 1 organization listed in this Yearbook:
Middle East Technical University (METU). [2021.05.27/XJ2818/y/E]

◆ **European Network of Experimental and Representative Basins (ERB)** 07905

Réseau européen de bassins représentatifs et expérimentaux

Coordinator Inst of Hydrology, Slovak Academy of Sciences, Ondrasovecka 16, 031 05 Liptovsky Mikulas, Slovakia. T. +421445522522. Fax +421445522522.
URL: http://www.ih.savba.sk/ihp/friend5/erb7.htm

History 1986, under the name *Euro-Mediterranean Network of Experimental and Representative Basins – Réseau Euro-méditerranéen de bassins représentatifs et expérimentaux*. Currently also referred to as *ERB Network*. **Aims** Increase relationships among members, research teams and *hydrological* basin managers through regular conferences; enable joint operations and research of common interest; exchange data. **Structure** General Assembly (every 2 years). Steering Committee of National Correspondents (one or 2 per country) nominated by UNESCO-IHP National Committees. **Languages** English. **Finance** No central budget. Individual countries seek their own support for activities in the Network. Support of UNESCO – *International Hydrological Programme (IHP, #13826)* for organization of conferences and workshops. **Activities** Exchange of information and hydrological data; research collaboration and visits; biennial conferences and workshops. **Events** *Biennial international conference* Vienna (Austria) 2010, *Biennial international conference* Krakow (Poland) 2008, *Biennial international conference* Luxembourg (Luxembourg) 2006, *Biennial international conference* Turin (Italy) 2004, *Biennial international conference* Demänovska Dolina (Slovakia) 2002. **Publications** *ERB Newsletter* (annual). Conference proceedings; technical documents. **Information Services** *ERB Inventory (ICARE)* – database.

Members Countries having organizations with capacity to operate and manage basin studies, backed by a university-trained group and basins being operated on a long-term basis. National Correspondents in 20 countries:
Austria, Belgium, Bulgaria, Czechia, Finland, France, Germany, Italy, Lithuania, Luxembourg, Netherlands, Poland, Portugal, Romania, Russia, Slovakia, Slovenia, Spain, Switzerland, UK.

NGO Relations Cooperates with: *European Network of Catchments Organized for Research on Ecosystems (ENCORE, no recent information)*; *International Association of Hydrological Sciences (IAHS, #11954)*.
[2012/XF5164/F]

◆ **European Network of ex- Users and Survivors of Psychiatry (ENUSP)** 07906

Main Office Vesterbrogade 103, 1-sal, 1620 Copenhagen V, Denmark. E-mail: enusp.info@gmail.com.
URL: http://enusp.org/

History Founded 1991, Zandvoort (Netherlands), at first European Conference for Users and Ex-Users in Mental Health, following decision of survivors in the Netherlands in 1990 to form a European wide networking of organizations of (former) psychiatric patients. Former title: *European Network of Users and Ex-Users in Mental Health.* Received legal recognition in 1998. **Aims** Promote and improve human rights of users, ex-users and survivors of psychiatry / people with psychosocial disabilities; fight for equal rights, freedom of choice and users/survivor participation; promote self-help and user/survivor controlled alternatives to psychiatry and against abuse and coercion. **Structure** General Meeting (if possible, every 2 years at Conference); Board; Task Forces. **Languages** English. **Staff** Voluntary. **Finance** Members' dues (annual). **Activities** Politics/policy/regulatory. **Events** *European Conference* Hillerød (Denmark) 2014, *European conference* Thessaloniki (Greece) 2010, *European conference* Vejle (Denmark) 2004, *European Conference* Luxembourg (Luxembourg) 1999, *European conference* Berlin (Germany) 1998. **Publications** *Advocacy Updates*; *The European Newsletter of (ex-) Users and Survivors of Psychiatry*. Articles.

Members National and local associations (27) in 18 countries and territories:
Bosnia-Herzegovina, Czechia, Denmark, Finland, France, Georgia, Germany, Ireland, Italy, Lithuania, Moldova, Netherlands, Poland, Romania, Russia, Slovenia, Spain, UK.

NGO Relations Member of: *European Disability Forum (EDF, #06929)*; *European Patients' Forum (EPF, #08172)*; *World Network of Users and Survivors of Psychiatry (WNUSP, #21672).* [2018/XF3642/F]

◆ **European Network on Family Group Conference (European FGC Network)** 07907

Secretariat PO Box 753, 8000 AT Zwolle, Netherlands. T. +31384222526.
URL: https://fgcnetwork.eu/

History 2002. Initially an informal network. **Activities** Events/meetings. **Events** *Meeting* Spain 2021, *Meeting* 2020, *Meeting* Bratislava (Slovakia) 2019, *Meeting* Edinburgh (UK) 2018, *Meeting* Prague (Czechia) 2017.

Members Full in 17 countries:
Austria, Belgium, Bosnia-Herzegovina, Bulgaria, Czechia, France, Germany, Hungary, Italy, Netherlands, Norway, Russia, Serbia, Slovakia, Sweden, Switzerland, UK. [2021/AA2607/F]

◆ **European Network of Fibromyalgia Associations (ENFA)** 07908

Pres Impulsstraat 6c, 2220 Heist-op-den-Berg, Belgium. E-mail: president@enfa-europe.eu – contact@enfa-europe.eu.
Vice Chairman address not obtained.
URL: http://www.enfa-europe.eu/

History 16 Oct 2008, Belgium. Registration: Banque-Carrefour des Entreprises, No/ID: 0810.745.301, Start date: 16 Oct 2008, Belgium. **Aims** Champion increased awareness, research and support for people living with fibromyalgia across Europe. **Structure** Annual General Assembly; Board. **Languages** English. **Staff** None. **Finance** Sources: grants; members' dues.

Members Full in 16 countries:
Belgium, Bulgaria, Croatia, Cyprus, Denmark, Greece, Israel, Italy, Netherlands, Norway, Portugal, Serbia, Slovenia, Spain, Sweden, UK.

NGO Relations Member of: *Pain Alliance Europe (PAE, #18026)*. Associate member of: *European Patients' Forum (EPF, #08172)*. Co-opted member of: *European Alliance of Associations for Rheumatology (EULAR, #05862)* Standing Committee of People with Arthritis/Rheumatism in Europe (PARE).
[2021.09.08/XJ5994/D]

◆ **European Network of Filipino Diaspora (ENFiD)** 07909

Chairperson Vækerøeveien 148A, 0383 Oslo, Norway. T. +4791321968. E-mail: enfidsecretary@gmail.com.
URL: http://www.enfid.org/

History 2012, Rome (Italy). Registration: Start date: 31 Jan 2014, Malta. **Aims** Be the prime organization of Euro-Filipinos in Europe in promoting programs, projects and activities that will lead to character transformation and strengthen solidarity, sharing and principled volunteerism in the framework of respect for human rights. **Structure** General Assembly; Board of Directors; Advisory Council; Secretariat. **Staff** 14.00 FTE, voluntary. **Activities** Events/meetings. Active in all member countries. **Events** *General Assembly* 2021, *Annual General Meeting and Conference* London (UK) 2019.

Members Full in 18 countries:
Austria, Belgium, Cyprus, Czechia, Denmark, France, Germany, Iceland, Ireland, Israel, Italy, Malta, Netherlands, Norway, Romania, Sweden, Switzerland, UK. [2021.06.22/XM8435/F]

◆ **European Network of Forensic Science Institutes (ENFSI)** 07910

Sec c/o Bundeskriminalamt KT-AS, 65173 Wiesbaden, Germany. T. +496115516660. E-mail: secretariat@enfsi.eu.
URL: http://www.enfsi.eu/

History 20 Oct 1995, Rijswijk (Netherlands). Founded following a series of meetings since 1993. Former names and other names: *European Academy of Forensic Science (EAFS)* – alias. Registration: Germany. **Aims** Improve mutual exchange of information and the quality of forensic science delivery in Europe. **Structure** Board; Secretariat; Standing Committees (2); Working Groups (17). **Languages** English. **Finance** Sources: members' dues. Supported by: *European Union (EU, #08967)*. **Activities** Events/meetings; research and development; training/education. **Events** *Annual Meeting* Stockholm (Sweden) 2022, *European Academy of Forensic Science Conference (EAFS)* Stockholm (Sweden) 2022, *Annual Meeting* Athens (Greece) 2021, *European Academy of Forensic Science Conference* Stockholm (Sweden) 2021, *Annual Meeting* Madrid (Spain) 2020. **Publications** Annual Report; manuals; guidelines.

Members Forensic institutes (73) in 39 countries:
Armenia, Austria, Azerbaijan, Belgium, Bosnia-Herzegovina, Bulgaria, Croatia, Cyprus, Czechia, Denmark, Estonia, Finland, France, Georgia, Germany, Greece, Hungary, Ireland, Italy, Latvia, Lithuania, Malta, Montenegro, Netherlands, North Macedonia, Norway, Poland, Portugal, Romania, Russia, Serbia, Slovakia, Slovenia, Spain, Sweden, Switzerland, Türkiye, UK, Ukraine.

IGO Relations Cooperates with (2): *European Police Office (Europol, #08239)*; *International Criminal Police Organization – INTERPOL (ICPO-INTERPOL, #13110)*. **NGO Relations** Member of (1): *International Forensic Strategic Alliance (IFSA, #13626)*. Liaison Organization of: *Comité européen de normalisation (CEN, #04162)*.
[2022.02.09/XF3092/F]

◆ **European Network of Freshwater Research Organisations (EurAqua)** 07911

Chair Finnish Environment Inst, Latokartanonkaari 11, FI-00790 Helsinki, Finland. E-mail: chair@euraqua.org – secretariat@euraqua.org.
URL: http://www.euraqua.org/

History 1993. Former names and other names: *Forum of European Freshwater Research Organisations (EurAqua)* – former. **Aims** Contribute substantially to development of European freshwater science and technology and its dissemination on a European scale. **Structure** Network with rotating Chairmanship and Secretariat (every 2 years); Management Board. **Languages** English. **Staff** None. **Finance** Each member organization finances its participation or contribution with its own resources. **Activities** Events/meetings; knowledge management/information dissemination; research/documentation. **Events** *Connecting up land and sea – system thinking for Mission Starfish* 2021, *Human Health and Water in a Changing Environment Developing a European Response to Pandemics* 2020, *Water challenges in the European Green Deal* 2020, *Water-Related Ecosystem Services Workshop* Oslo (Norway) 2014, *Conference* Oslo (Norway) 2008. **Publications** *EurAqua Newsletter*. Leaflet.

Members Institutes in 26 countries:
Austria, Belgium, Croatia, Czechia, Denmark, Estonia, Finland, France, Germany, Greece, Iceland, Ireland, Italy, Latvia, Lithuania, Malta, Netherlands, Norway, Poland, Portugal, Romania, Slovakia, Slovenia, Spain, Sweden, UK.
[2022/XD7116/D]

♦ European Network of Gastrointestinal Pathology (ENGIP) 07912
Contact Medical Univ Graz, Neue Stiftungtalstraße 6, 8010 Graz, Austria. T. +433163850. E-mail: engip@medunigraz.at.
URL: https://www.medunigraz.at/en/engip
History Mar 2012. Founded by members of the Working Group of Digestive Diseases of *European Society of Pathology (ESP, #08689)*. **Structure** Steering Committee; Advisory Board. **Activities** Events/meetings; training/education. **Members** Individuals (about 570). [2022/AA2929/v/**D**]

♦ European Network on Gender and Violence (ENGV) 07913
Co-Coordinator Univ of Maine, 330A Merrill Hall, Orono ME 04469, USA. E-mail: info@engv.org.
Co-Coordinator Hochschule Ravensburg-Weingarten, Soziale Arbeit, Gesundheit und Pflege, Leibnizstr. 10, 88250 Weingarten, Germany.
URL: http://www.engv.org/
History 1996, Banff, AB (Canada). Former names and other names: *European Network on Conflict, Gender and Violence* – former (1996 to 2011). **Aims** Support exchange and collaboration among scholars and professionals who address violence, gender, prevention and related issues. **Structure** Informal network. **Languages** English. **Activities** Events/meetings; knowledge management/information dissemination. **Events** *Annual Conference* Copenhagen (Denmark) 2022, *Annual Conference* Freiburg-Breisgau (Germany) 2019, *Annual Conference* Bristol (UK) 2018, *Annual Conference* Milan (Italy) 2017, *Annual Conference* Istanbul (Turkey) 2016. **Publications** Conference proceedings; books.
Members Individuals (about 500) from 34 countries:
Australia, Austria, Belgium, Brazil, Bulgaria, Canada, Czechia, Denmark, Estonia, Finland, France, Germany, Iceland, India, Ireland, Israel, Italy, Lithuania, Luxembourg, Malta, Netherlands, New Zealand, Norway, Poland, Portugal, Romania, Slovakia, Slovenia, Spain, Sweden, Switzerland, Türkiye, UK, USA. [2022.05.04/XF6497/**F**]

♦ European Network of Geography Teachers' Associations / see European Association of Geographers (#06054)
♦ European Network for Global Desertification Research / see Association of the Network for International Research on Desertification (#02823)

♦ European Network of GMO Laboratories (ENGL) 07914
Chair European Commission, Joint Research Centre, Food and Feed Compliance Unit (F.5), TP331, 21027 Ispra MB, Italy. T. +39332785239. Fax +39332785483. E-mail: jrc-eurl-gmff@ec.europa.eu.
URL: https://gmo-crl.jrc.ec.europa.eu/ENGL/ENGL.html
History 4 Dec 2002, Brussels (Belgium). Founded by *European Commission (EC, #06633)*, through Regulation (EC) No 1829/2003 on GM Food Feed. **Aims** Contribute to the European harmonization and standardization of means and methods for sampling, detection, identification and quantification of *genetically modified* organisms or derived products in a wide variety of matrices, covering seed, grains, commodities, *food*, feed and environmental samples. **Structure** Plenary Meeting (annual); Steering Committee (twice a year); President; Secretariat; ad hoc Working Groups. **Languages** English. **Events** *Meeting* Ispra (Italy) 2022, *Meeting* Ispra (Italy) 2011, *Meeting* Ispra (Italy) 2010, *Meeting* Ispra (Italy) 2009, *Meeting* Ispra (Italy) 2008. **Publications** Activity reports; guidance documents.
Members As of Aug 2011, member laboratories (96) in 31 countries:
Austria, Belgium, Bulgaria, Croatia, Cyprus, Czechia, Denmark, Estonia, Finland, France, Germany, Greece, Hungary, Ireland, Italy, Latvia, Lithuania, Luxembourg, Malta, Netherlands, Norway, Poland, Portugal, Romania, Slovakia, Slovenia, Spain, Sweden, Switzerland, Türkiye, UK.
Observers in non-EU countries (not specified).
IGO Relations Chaired by: *Joint Research Centre (JRC, #16147)*. [2022.10.27/XF6919/**F**]

♦ European Network of Green Seniors (ENGS) 07915
Europäisches Netzwerk Grüner Senioren – Europees Netwerk van Groene Senioren
Chairperson Kerkelei 7, 2610 Wilrijk, Belgium. T. +3238304906.
Seat Rue Wiertz 31, 1050 Brussels, Belgium.
URL: http://www.greenseniors.eu/
History 7 Dec 2005, Brussels (Belgium). Registered in accordance with Belgian law. **Aims** Promote on a European level political consciousness of *elderly* people. **Structure** General Assembly; Board. **Languages** Dutch, English, German, Spanish. **Events** *General Assembly* Utrecht (Netherlands) 2008, *General Assembly* Vienna (Austria) 2007, *General Assembly* Germany 2006.
Members Individuals in 7 countries:
Austria, Belgium, Finland, Germany, Luxembourg, Netherlands, UK.
NGO Relations *European Green Party (EGP, #07409)*. [2016.06.22/XJ0105/**E**]

♦ European Network of Gynaecological Cancer Advocacy Groups (ENGAGe) 07916
Exec Dir Rue François-Versonnex 7, PO Box 6053, 1207 Geneva, Switzerland. E-mail: engage@esgo.org.
URL: https://engage.esgo.org/
History A network of *European Society of Gynaecological Oncology (ESGO, #08612)*. Registration: EU Transparency Register, No/ID: 758343826597-30, Start date: 3 Apr 2017. **Aims** Empower a patient-centric approach to gynaecological cancer care, research and prevention through awareness, advocacy and education. **Structure** Executive Group. Advocacy Groups. **Activities** Events/meetings; projects/programmes; research/documentation. [2022/AA2561/**F**]

♦ European Network of Heads of Nature Conservation Agencies (ENCA) 07917
Secretariat c/o, Environment Agency Austria, Spittelauer Laende 5, 1090 Vienna, Austria. T. +431313043260.
URL: http://www.encanetwork.eu/
History 2007. Also referred to as *Heads of European Nature Conservation Agencies*. EU Transparency Register: 206882037381-44. **Aims** Strengthen nature conservation in Europe by enhancing cooperation and collaboration between members. **Structure** Plenary; Troika; Secretariat. **Languages** English. **Staff** 1.00 FTE, paid. **Finance** Voluntary contributions. **Activities** Events/meetings; networking/liaising. **Events** *Plenary Meeting* Brussels (Belgium) 2016, *Plenary Meeting* Belgrade (Serbia) 2015, *European Conference on Biodiversity and Climate Change* Bonn (Germany) 2015, *Plenary Meeting / Plenary* Helsinki (Finland) 2015, *Plenary Meeting / Plenary* Peterborough (UK) 2014. **Publications** Proceedings; statements.
Members European agencies or bodies. Members in 16 countries:
Austria, Croatia, Czechia, Estonia, Finland, France, Germany, Italy, Latvia, Lithuania, Netherlands, Serbia, Slovenia, Sweden, Switzerland, UK.
Observer in 1 country:
Israel.
NGO Relations *International Union for Conservation of Nature and Natural Resources (IUCN, #15766)*. [2020/XJ9792/**F**]

♦ European Network of Heads of Schools of Architecture (ENHSA) . . . 07918
Réseau européen des directeurs d'écoles d'architecture
Coordinator c/o Aristotle Univ of Thessaloniki, University Campus, 541 24 Thessaloniki, Greece.
History 2001, Chania (Greece). Founded in collaboration with and with the support of *European Association for Architectural Education (EAAE, #05941)*, following a series of meetings since 1998. **Aims** Facilitate structuring of the European Higher Architectural Education Area in a way that renders it more active and more competitive with other intercontinental competitors, as well as more attractive to European and non-European learners. **Languages** English. **Staff** None. **Finance** *European Commission (EC, #06633)* through Lifelong Learning Erasmus Programme. **Activities** Research and development; knowledge management/information dissemination; monitoring/evaluation; events/meetings. **Events** *Meeting* Chania (Greece) 2013, *Meeting* Chania (Greece) 2008, *Meeting* Chania (Greece) 2007, *Meeting* Chania (Greece) 2005, *Meeting* Chania (Greece) 2003. **NGO Relations** *Architects Council of Europe (ACE, #01086)*; *European Association for Architectural Education (EAAE, #05941)*. [2018.01.25/XF6774/**F**]

♦ European Network of Health Care Chaplaincy (ENHCC) 07919
Coordinator address not obtained. E-mail: coordinator@enhcc.eu.
URL: http://www.enhcc.eu/
History Nov 2000, Crete (Greece). Founded during Sixth Consultation for Hospital Chaplaincy. **Aims** Enable participants serving in the multidisciplinary field of healthcare to: share and learn from one another; develop professional guidelines required to minister to existential and spiritual needs of patients, relatives and staff, drawing on personal, religious, cultural and community resources; promote a high quality standard of health care chaplaincy in Europe. **Events** *Consultation* Crete (Greece) 2022, *Consultation* Chania (Greece) 2021, *Consultation* Chania (Greece) 2020, *Consultation* Blankenberge (Belgium) 2018, *Consultation* Debrecen (Hungary) 2016.
Members Participants in countries:
Austria, Belgium, Bulgaria, Cyprus, Czechia, Denmark, Estonia, Finland, France, Germany, Greece, Hungary, Iceland, Ireland, Israel, Italy, Latvia, Luxembourg, Malta, Netherlands, Norway, Poland, Portugal, Romania, Russia, Slovakia, Spain, Sweden, Switzerland, UK, Ukraine.
Ecumenical Patriarchate of Constantinople (#05349).
NGO Relations Instrumental in setting up (1): *European Research Institute for Chaplains in Healthcare (ERICH, #08370)*. [2023.02.13/XF7126/**F**]

♦ European Network of Health Promoting Hospitals / see International Network of Health Promoting Hospitals and Health Services (#14277)
♦ European Network of Health Promoting Schools / see Schools for Health in Europe network foundation (#19133)

♦ European network for health promotion and economic development (Citizen@Work) 07920
Contact address not obtained. E-mail: info@citizenatwork.eu.
History 15 Apr 1970, Paris (France). Founded as *European Health Club – Club européen de la santé*. Subsequently changed title to *European Association for the Promotion of Health (EAPH) – Association européenne pour la promotion de la santé (AEPS)*. Current title adopted 2014. Registration: Banque-Carrefour des Entreprises, No/ID: 0867.383.007, Start date: 30 Aug 2004, Belgium. **Aims** Encourage and develop exchanges in the field of health promotion within Europe; facilitate adoption, implementation and evaluation of solutions to health problems; promote collaboration between organizations in the field of health. **Structure** General Assembly (annual). Board, comprising President, Vice-President and Treasurer. **Languages** English, French. **Staff** None. **Finance** Members' dues. **Events** *Colloquium* Vienna (Austria) 2002, *General Assembly* Paris (France) 2000, *La chute et les approches psychosociales du vieillissement* Paris (France) 1998, *General Assembly* Paris (France) 1993, *Congrès sur l'enfant et la sécurité en Europe* Paris (France) 1992.
Members Full in 4 countries:
Belgium, France, Luxembourg, Switzerland. [2016/XJ3404/**D**]

♦ European Network for Health Technology Assessment (EUnetHTA) . 07921
CEO c/o ZIN, Postbus 320, 1110 AH Diemen, Netherlands. E-mail: eunethta@zinl.nl.
URL: http://www.eunethta.eu/
History 2005. Founded on request of *European Commission (EC, #06633)* and Council of Ministers, by group of 35 organizations. Registration: EU Transparency Register, No/ID: 897835028069-13, Start date: 22 Aug 2017. **Aims** Support collaboration between European Health Technology Assessment (HTA) organizations bringing added value to healthcare systems at European, national and regional levels. **Structure** Plenary Assembly; Executive Committee; Stakeholder Forum; Secretariat. **Languages** English. **Staff** 6.00 FTE, paid. **Finance** Sources: members' dues. Co-financed by: *European Commission (EC, #06633)* – DG Sante. **Activities** Events/meetings; knowledge management/information dissemination; projects/programmes. Joint Actions (JA): JA1 (2010-2012); JA2 (2012-2015); JA3 (2016-2021). **Events** *Plenary Assembly and Forum* Amsterdam (Netherlands) 2019, *Joint Innovation Meeting* Helsinki (Finland) 2019, *Plenary Assembly* Amsterdam (Netherlands) 2017, *Plenary Assembly* Madrid (Spain) 2014, *HTA 2.0 – teaming up for value* Rome (Italy) 2014. **Publications** *EUnetHTA Magazine* (4 a year). Internal summaries.
Members Network made of organizations in 30 countries:
Austria, Belgium, Bulgaria, Croatia, Cyprus, Czechia, Denmark, Estonia, Finland, France, Germany, Greece, Hungary, Ireland, Italy, Latvia, Lithuania, Malta, Netherlands, Norway, Poland, Portugal, Romania, Slovakia, Slovenia, Spain, Sweden, Switzerland, UK, Ukraine.
Collaborating Partners in 11 countries:
Austria, Belgium, Bulgaria, Denmark, Germany, Ireland, Italy, Spain, Sweden, Switzerland, UK.
Stakeholders (16):
Association internationale de la mutualité (AIM, #02721); *Association of the European Self-Care Industry (#02543)*; *Bureau Européen des Unions de Consommateurs (BEUC, #03360)*; *European Association of Bioindustries (EuropaBio, #05956)*; *European Coordination Committee of the Radiological, Electromedical Healthcare IT Industry (COCIR, #06792)*; *European Federation of Pharmaceutical Industries and Associations (EFPIA, #07191)*; *European Hospital and Healthcare Federation (HOPE, #07501)*; *European Multiple Sclerosis Platform (EMSP, #07833)* (European Register for Multiple Sclerosis); *European Patients' Forum (EPF, #08172)*; *European Society for Medical Oncology (ESMO, #08648)*; *European Society of Cardiology (ESC, #08536)*; *EURORDIS – Rare Diseases Europe (#09175)*; Health Insurance Organisation (HIO); *Medicines for Europe (#16633)*; *Standing Committee of European Doctors (#19955)*; Weigth Watchers. [2022/XM2959/**E**]

♦ European Network on High-performance Embedded Architecture and Compilation (HiPEAC) 07922
Coordinator address not obtained. E-mail: info@hipeac.net.
URL: https://www.hipeac.net/
History 2004. **Aims** Advance computer architecture and computing systems research and development as a discipline in Europe. **Structure** Steering Committee. **Finance** Supported by: *European Union (EU, #08967)* (Horizon 2020). **Activities** Awards/prizes/competitions; events/meetings; projects/programmes; training/education. **Events** *HiPEAC : International Conference on High Performance Embedded Architectures and Compilers* Toulouse (France) 2023, *HiPEAC : International Conference on High Performance Embedded Architectures and Compilers* Budapest (Hungary) 2022, *HiPEAC : International Conference on High Performance Embedded Architectures and Compilers* Budapest (Hungary) 2021, *HiPEAC : International Conference on High Performance Embedded Architectures and Compilers* Bologna (Italy) 2020, *HiPEAC : International Conference on High Performance Embedded Architectures and Compilers* Valencia (Spain) 2019.
Members Individuals (over 800) from nearly 500 institutions in 50 countries:
Albania, Australia, Austria, Belgium, Bosnia-Herzegovina, Brazil, Bulgaria, Canada, China, Croatia, Cyprus, Czechia, Denmark, Egypt, Estonia, Finland, France, Germany, Greece, Hungary, India, Ireland, Israel, Italy, Latvia, Lithuania, Luxembourg, Malta, Montenegro, Netherlands, North Macedonia, Norway, Palestine, Poland, Portugal, Romania, Russia, Saudi Arabia, Serbia, Singapore, Slovakia, Slovenia, Spain, Sweden, Switzerland, Türkiye, UK, Ukraine, United Arab Emirates, USA. [2023/AA2156/**F**]

♦ European Network of Historical Cities and Territories / see Alliance de Villes Euro-méditerranéennes de Culture (#00726)
♦ European Network for Historic Places of Worship / see Future for Religious Heritage (#10051)

♦ European Network for HIV/AIDS Surveillance 07923
Address not obtained.
URL: http://www.eurohiv.org/
History as *EuroHIV – HIV/AIDS Surveillance in Europe – EuroHIV – Surveillance du VIH/SIDA en Europe* within the framework of *Centre européen pour la surveillance épidémiologique du SIDA (CESES, inactive)*. On 1 Nov 1999, activities were transferred to *'Institut de veille sanitaire (InVS)'*, the French National Institute for Public Health Surveillance. As of Jan 2008 joint coordination taken over by *European Centre for Disease Prevention and Control (ECDC, #06476)* and *WHO Regional Office for Europe (#20945)*. Also referred to as *European HIV/AIDS Surveillance Network*. **Aims** Describe and better understand the HIV *epidemic* and improve *prevention* and control through collection, analysis and dissemination of *epidemiological* data. **Languages** English, French, Russian. **Staff** 4.00 FTE, paid. **Finance** *European Commission (EC, #06633)* (DG SANCO). **Activities** Collects, analyzes, interprets and disseminates up-to-date standardized HIV and AIDS surveillance data for each EU member state and non-EU countries in the WHO European region. Other topics include: international comparisons; trend assessment; characterization of affected populations; analysis of

HIV-associated diseases; estimation of current and prediction of future disease burden through mathematical modelling; ongoing evaluation of surveillance methods. **Publications** Fact sheets on the epidemiology of HIV infection in each country (with UNAIDS); European and national studies. **Information Services** *Déclaration des cas d'infection à VIH* – database; *European HIV Prevalence Database* – aggregated data on HIV prevalence in specific population groups (eg pregnant women, injecting drug users); *European Non Aggregate AIDS Data Set (ENAADS)* – database of anonymous data on all AIDS cases reported in the WHO European Region since the beginning of the epidemic. [2011.06.01/XE4206/**E**]

♦ European Network for Housing Research (ENHR) 07924

Réseau européen pour la recherche sur le logement

Chair OTB TU-Delft, PO Box 5043, 2600 GA Delft, Netherlands. T. +31152781908. E-mail: enhr@tudelft.nl.
URL: http://www.enhr.net/

History 1988. **Aims** Promote contacts and communications between researchers and with practitioners within the housing field. **Structure** General Assembly; Coordination Committee; Head Office; Working Groups. **Languages** English. **Finance** Members' dues. **Activities** Networking/liaising; awards/prizes/competitions; events/meetings. **Events** *Conference* Belfast (UK) 2016, *Housing and cities in a time of change – are we focusing on people?* Lisbon (Portugal) 2015, *Beyond globalization – remaking housing policy in a complex world* Edinburgh (UK) 2014, *Conference / Research Conference* Tarragona (Spain) 2013, *Conference / Research Conference* Lillehammer (Norway) 2012. **Publications** *ENHR Newsletter* (4 a year). **Members** Membership countries not specified. **IGO Relations** Participates in the work of: *United Nations Economic Commission for Europe (UNECE, #20555).* [2018.02.05/XF2255/y/**F**]

♦ European Network for Housing and Urban Development (unconfirmed)
♦ European Network on Human Response to Environmental Stress (see: #05333)

♦ European Network for Hyperkinetic Disorders (EUNETHYDIS) 07925

Chairman address not obtained. T. +4962117034502. Fax +4962117034505.
URL: http://eunethydisconference.com/

History Registered in accordance with Dutch law. **Aims** Study *ADHD* from a clinical and fundamental research point of view. **Events** *International Conference* Edinburgh (UK) 2018, *International Conference* Berlin (Germany) 2016, *International Conference* Istanbul (Turkey) 2014, *International Conference* Barcelona (Spain) 2012, *Conference* Amsterdam (Netherlands) 2010. **NGO Relations** Member of: *European Network of Paediatric Research at the European Medicines Agency (Enpr-EMA, #07963).* [2019.02.16/XJ4538/**F**]

♦ European Network for Ichthyosis (unconfirmed)

♦ European Network of Implementing Development Agencies (EUNIDA) 07926

Coordinator Rue de la Charité 33, 1210 Brussels, Belgium. T. +3222292761.
Registered Address Rue Haute 147, 1000 Brussels, Belgium.

History 2000. Since Jun 2006, a grouping of the type *European Economic Interest Grouping (EEIG, #06960).* **Aims** Develop, manage and implement sustainable development programmes on behalf of the European Union. **Structure** General Assembly (annual); Board of Directors, headed by President (rotating function); Secretariat; Working Groups. **Languages** English, French. **Staff** 1.00 FTE, paid. **Finance** Members' dues. Project fees. **Events** *General Assembly* Brussels (Belgium) 2011, *General Assembly* Eschborn (Germany) 2010. **Members** Organizations (8):
Agency for European Integration and Economic Development (AEI); Crown Agents for Overseas Governments and Administrations; Deutsche Gesellschaft für Internationale Zusammenarbeit (GIZ); Enabel; European Public Law Organization (EPLO, #08299); France Expertise Internationale (FEI); Fundación Internacional y para Iberoamérica de Administración y Politicas Públicas (FIIAPP, #10030); SNV Netherlands Development Organisation (SNV).
Observers (8):
Agencia Española de Cooperación Internacional para el Desarrollo (AECID); Austrian Development Agency (ADA); Central Project Management Agency (CPMA); *Czech Development Agency (CzDA);* Instituto Português de Apoio ao Desenvolvimento; *International Agency of the Association of Netherlands Municipalities (VNG International);* Italian Directorate General for Cooperation; *Luxembourg Agency for Development Cooperation (LUXDEV).* [2016.06.01/XJ1771/y/**F**]

♦ European Network for Improving Research and Development in Educational Leadership and Management (ENIRDELM) 07927

Permanent Sec address not obtained.
URL: http://www.enirdelm.net/

History Founded 1991, Utrecht (Netherlands), as *European Network for Improving Research and Development in Educational Management (ENIRDEM),* following the opening up of the former Soviet bloc to the rest of Europe. **Aims** Improve the quality of educational leadership and management development and research across Europe; deepen and share understanding of the perspectives of multiple stakeholders in education and ultimately make an impact on learning at all levels of education systems. **Structure** Board; Secretariat. Chairperson changes each year and organizes the annual conference at their own institution. **Languages** English. **Staff** Voluntary. **Finance** Conference fees; supporting grants raised in the host country by the conference organizer. **Activities** Events/meetings; research and development; networking/liaising; projects/programmes. **Events** *Annual Conference* Halden (Norway) 2021, *Annual Conference* Fredrikstad (Norway) 2020, *Annual Conference* Ljubljana (Slovenia) 2019, *Annual Conference* Antwerp (Belgium) 2018, *Annual Conference* Krakow (Poland) 2017. **Publications** *ENIRDELM Newsletter* (2 a year). Conference proceedings. **NGO Relations** Member of: *European Policy Network on School Leadership (EPNoSL, #08245).* [2018/XF3122/**F**]

♦ European Network for Improving Research and Development in Educational Management / see European Network for Improving Research and Development in Educational Leadership and Management (#07927)

♦ European Network of Independent Film Distributors (Europa Distribution) 07928

General Manager Rue Royale 229, 1210 Brussels, Belgium. E-mail: communication@europa-distribution.org.
URL: http://www.europa-distribution.org/

History Created 2006. Registered in accordance with Belgian law. EU Transparency Register: 626116910064-95. **Aims** Strengthen existing ties to improve curation, promotion and distribution of independent films. **Structure** Board of Administration. **Languages** English, French. **Staff** 2.00 FTE, paid. **Activities** Networking/liaising; events/meetings; knowledge management/information dissemination. **Publications** *Europa Distribution Blog.*
Members Full (120) in 29 countries:
Australia, Austria, Belgium, Bulgaria, Croatia, Czechia, Denmark, Egypt, Finland, France, Germany, Greece, Hungary, Iceland, Israel, Italy, Lithuania, Netherlands, Norway, Poland, Portugal, Romania, Russia, Serbia, Slovakia, Spain, Sweden, Switzerland, UK.
IGO Relations *European Commission (EC, #06633).* [2018.09.05/XM5864/**F**]

♦ European Network on Independent Living (ENIL) 07929

Coordinator Rue de l'Industrie 10, 7th Floor- Mundo J, 1000 Brussels, Belgium. T. +3228932583. E-mail: secretariat@enil.eu.
URL: http://www.enil.eu/

History 1989, Strasbourg (France). Registration: Banque-Carrefour des Entreprises, No/ID: 0712.834.390, Start date: 5 Nov 2018, Belgium. **Aims** Provide a forum for *disabled* people, independent living organizations and other interested parties to campaign for independent living; raise the profile of the independent living movement; raise awareness of the independent living philosophy; promote development of, and facilitate interaction between, centres of independent living across Europe. **Structure** General Assembly; Board; Nominating Committee; Management Team; Secretariat, located in Brussels (Belgium). **Languages** English. **Staff** 8.00 FTE, paid. **Finance** Supported by: *European Union (EU, #08967).* **Activities** Events/meetings. **Events** *Freedom Drive Conference* Brussels (Belgium) 2022, *General Assembly* Brussels (Belgium) 2022, *Conference on The Present and Future of Personal Assistance in Europe* Brussels (Belgium) 2019, *Freedom Drive Conference* Brussels (Belgium) 2019, *General Assembly* Brussels (Belgium) 2019. **Publications** Manuals; reports; fact sheets; personal assistance; definitions.
Members Individuals and organizations (about 500) in 51 countries:
Albania, Argentina, Armenia, Austria, Azerbaijan, Belgium, Bosnia-Herzegovina, Bulgaria, Chile, Croatia, Cyprus, Estonia, Finland, France, Germany, Greece, Hungary, Iceland, India, Iraq, Ireland, Italy, Kosovo, Latvia, Lithuania, Luxembourg, Malta, Moldova, Montenegro, Morocco, Netherlands, North Macedonia, Norway, Pakistan, Poland, Portugal, Romania, Russia, San Marino, Serbia, Singapore, Slovakia, Slovenia, Spain, Sweden, Switzerland, Thailand, Türkiye, UK, Ukraine, USA.
Consultative Status Consultative status granted from: *Council of Europe (CE, #04881)* (Participatory Status); *ECOSOC (#05331)* (Special). **IGO Relations** Cooperates with: Fundamental Rights Platform of *European Union Agency for Fundamental Rights (FRA, #08969).* **NGO Relations** Instrumental in setting up and manages: *European Coalition for Community Living (ECCL, #06590).* Member of: *European Disability Forum (EDF, #06929).* [2022/XF5293/**F**]

♦ European Network of Independent Non-Proliferation Think Tanks (EU Non-Proliferation Network) 07930

Contact c/o Fondation pour la Recherche Stratégique (FRS), 4 bis rue des Pâtures, 75016 Paris, France. E-mail: b.hautecouverture@frstrategie.org.
URL: http://www.nonproliferation.eu/

History Jul 2010, by *Council of the European Union (#04895).* Activities commenced Jan 2011. **Aims** Encourage discussion of measures to combat proliferation of weapons of mass destruction and their delivery systems within civil society, particularly among experts, researchers and academics. **Structure** Jointly managed by *Fondation pour la recherche stratégique (FRS), Peace Research Institute Frankfurt (PRIF), International Institute for Strategic Studies (IISS, #13927)* and *Stockholm International Peace Research Institute (SIPRI, #19994);* close cooperation with representative of High Representative of the Union for Foreign Affairs and Security Policy.
Members Institutes in 18 countries:
Austria, Belgium, Denmark, Estonia, France, Germany, Greece, Hungary, Italy, Latvia, Luxembourg, Netherlands, Poland, Slovakia, Slovenia, Sweden, Switzerland, UK.
Included in the above, 33 institutes listed in this Yearbook:
- *Austrian Institute for International Affairs (oiip);*
- *British-American Security Information Council (BASIC);*
- *Carl Friedrich von Weizäcker Centre for Science and Peace Research (ZNF);*
- *Centre d'Etudes de Sécurité Internationale et de Maîtrise des Armements (CESIM);*
- *Centre for Transnational Relations, Foreign and Security Policy (ATASP);*
- *Danish Institute for International Studies (DIIS);*
- *Deutsche Gesellschaft für Auswärtige Politik (DGAP);*
- *Egmont Institute;*
- *European Centre for Space Law (ECSL, #06501);*
- *European Leadership Network (ELN, #07666);*
- *European Space Policy Institute (ESPI, #08801);*
- *European Union Institute for Security Studies (EUISS, #08994);*
- *Fondation pour la recherche stratégique (FRS);*
- *Geneva Centre for Security Policy (GCSP);*
- *Groupe de recherche et d'information sur la paix et la sécurité (GRIP);*
- *Hellenic Foundation for European and Foreign Policy (ELIAMEP);*
- *Hungarian Institute of International Affairs (HIIA);*
- *Institute for International Affairs and Foreign Policy, Madrid (INCIPE);*
- *Institute for Peace Research and Security Policy, Hamburg (IFSH);*
- *Institut français des relations internationales (IFRI);*
- *International Centre for Defence and Security (ICDS);*
- *International Institute for Strategic Studies (IISS, #13927);*
- *International Security Information Service (ISIS);*
- *Istituto di Studi Giuridici Internazionali (ISGI);*
- *Latvian Institute of International Affairs (LIIA);*
- *Luxembourg Institute for European and International Studies (LIEIS);*
- *Netherlands Institute of International Relations – Clingendael;*
- *Peace Research Institute Frankfurt (PRIF);*
- *Polish Institute of International Affairs (PIIA);*
- *Royal United Services Institute for Defence and Security Studies (RUSI);*
- *Stiftung Wissenschaft und Politik (SWP);*
- *Stockholm International Peace Research Institute (SIPRI, #19994);*
- *The Hague Centre for Strategic Studies (HCSS).*

[2014.10.30/XJ6501/y/**F**]

♦ European Network of Indicator Designers (ENID) 07931

Sec Kleine Präsidentenstr 1, 10178 Berlin, Germany. T. +4930206417724.
URL: https://enid-europe.eu/

History Founded as a project. Registration: France. **Aims** Facilitate and promote cooperation between institutions and individuals actively engaged in designing, constructing, producing as well as using and interpreting Science and Technology Indicators (S&T Indicators). **Activities** Events/meetings. **Events** *International Conference on Science, Technology and Innovation Indicators* Granada (Spain) 2022, *International Conference on Science, Technology and Innovation Indicators* Aarhus (Denmark) 2021, *STI Indicators Conference* Leiden (Netherlands) 2018, *STI Indicators Conference* Paris (France) 2017, *International Conference on Science and Technology Indicators* Valencia (Spain) 2016.
Members Full in 25 countries:
Austria, Belgium, Czechia, Denmark, Egypt, Estonia, Finland, France, Germany, Greece, Hungary, India, Iran Islamic Rep, Israel, Italy, Latvia, Lithuania, Netherlands, Norway, Poland, South Africa, Spain, Switzerland, Uganda, UK.
Regional organizations: [2023.02.14/XM3766/y/**E**]

♦ European Network for Indigenous Australian Rights (internationally oriented national body)

♦ European Network on Indigenous Peoples (ENIP) 07932

Contact c/o INFOE, Melchiorstr 3, 50670 Cologne, Germany. T. +492217392871. E-mail: infoe@infoe.de.
URL: http://www.enip.eu/

History 2013.
Members Organizations (4) include 2 organizations listed in this Yearbook:
Forest Peoples Programme (FPP, #09865); International Work Group for Indigenous Affairs (IWGIA, #15907). [2016/XM5200/y/**F**]

♦ European Network of Individuals and Campaigns for Humane Education / see International Network for Humane Education (#14285)

♦ European Network of Information Centres for the Performing Arts (ENICPA) 07933

Réseau européen de centres d'information du spectacle vivant

Main Office Ravensteingalerij 38, 1000 Brussels, Belgium. T. +3222741765. E-mail: catalina.gonzalez.m@juntadeandalucia.es – m.freundt@iti-germany.de.
URL: http://www.enicpa.info/

History Founded Sep 1989, Madrid (Spain). Formally registered as an international association, Feb 1990, Brussels (Belgium). Registered in accordance with Belgian law. **Aims** Distribute information on contemporary performing arts in Europe for the benefit of *professionals* in the field. **Structure** General Assembly (annual); Administrative Council; Bureau. **Languages** English, French. **Staff** None. **Finance** Members' dues. **Activities** Knowledge management/information dissemination. **Events** *Meeting* Warsaw (Poland) 2018, *Meeting* Bratislava (Slovakia) 2017, *Meeting* Berlin (Germany) 2016, *Meeting* Helsinki (Finland) 2015, *Meeting* Brussels (Belgium) 2014.
Members Organizations (19) in 14 countries:
Belgium, Czechia, Denmark, Finland, France, Germany, Ireland, Italy, Norway, Russia, Slovakia, Spain, Sweden, Switzerland. [2018/XF4078/**F**]

♦ European Network for Information and Documentation on Latin America (#18652)

♦ European Network for Information, Documentation and Research into Regional or Minority Languages in Education / see Mercator European Research Centre on Multilingualism and Language Learning (#16719)
♦ European Network and Information Security Agency / see European Union Agency for Network and Information Security (#08971)
♦ European Network for the Insertion of Disfavoured People (#18874)

♦ European Network on Intercultural Elderly Care (ENIEC) 07934

Chair Blauw Glidkruid 75, 2498 DB The Hague, Netherlands. E-mail: info@eniec.eu.
URL: http://www.eniec.eu/

History Founded Mar 2007, Copenhagen (Denmark). Registered in accordance with Dutch law. **Aims** Create an informal platform for exchanging ideas and experiences across borders in today's Europe; secure that European elderly with a foreign ethnic background can live in an environment of tolerance, intercultural understanding and respect for their needs and for their cultural background. **Structure** General Assembly (annual); Board functions as Secretariat; Working Groups. **Languages** English. **Staff** Voluntary. **Finance** Members' dues. Donations. **Events** *Annual Meeting* Bristol (UK) 2019, *Annual Meeting* Madrid (Spain) 2018, *Annual Meeting* Istanbul (Turkey) 2015, *Annual Meeting* Oslo (Norway) 2014, *Annual Meeting* Brussels (Belgium) 2013. **Publications** *From Home to Home*. Monthly newsletter.
Members Individuals (84) in 15 countries:
Austria, Belgium, Denmark, Finland, France, Germany, Hungary, Ireland, Italy, Netherlands, Norway, Spain, Sweden, Türkiye, UK. [2020.03.12/XJ6895/**D**]

♦ European Network of International Relations Officers at Higher Education Institutions for Agricultural and Related Sciences (IROICA) 07935

Gen Sec International Relations Office, Fac of Bioscience Engineering, Ghent Univ, Coupure Links 653, 9000 Ghent, Belgium. T. +3292645917. E-mail: iroica.vzw@gmail.com.
Registered Office Kasteelpark Arenberg 20, 3001 Leuven, Belgium.
URL: http://www.ica-iroica.eu/

History 1997, within Demeter Socrates Thematic Network. Became Standing Committee within *Association for European Life Science Universities (ICA, #02519)*, 1998. Registered under Belgian law. **Aims** Further and support the work of international relations officers. **Structure** Executive Committee, including President, Vice-President, Secretary General and Treasurer. **Staff** 8.00 FTE, paid. **Activities** Events/meetings. **Events** *Annual conference* Ghent (Belgium) 2021, *Annual conference* Ghent (Belgium) 2020, *Annual conference* Vic (Spain) 2019, *Annual conference* Wroclaw (Poland) 2018, *Halfway through the Erasmus+ adventure* Vienna (Austria) 2017. **Publications** *IROICA Newsletter* (4 a year) – online journal.
Members Partners institutions in 16 countries:
Austria, Belgium, Croatia, Czechia, Denmark, Estonia, Finland, France, Hungary, Ireland, Italy, Lithuania, Netherlands, Poland, Portugal, Romania. [2020.01.21/XF7145/**F**]

♦ European Network of Laboratories for Sequence Based Typing of Microbial Pathogens (SEQNET) 07936

Coordinator Dept of Medical Microbiology, Univ Medical Center Groningen, Hanzeplein 1, 9700 RB Groningen, Netherlands. E-mail: a.j.sabat@umcg.nl.
Coordinator Natl Reference Lab for Staphylococci and Enterococci, Robert Koch Inst, Wernigerode branch, Burgstr 36, 38855 Wernigerode, Germany.
URL: http://seqnet.org/

Aims Establish a European network of excellence for sequence based typing of microbial pathogens. **Structure** Advisory Board. Coordinators (2).
Members Participants in 33 countries:
Austria, Belgium, Bulgaria, Canada, China, Croatia, Czechia, Denmark, Finland, France, Germany, Greece, Hungary, Iceland, Ireland, Israel, Italy, Japan, Latvia, Lebanon, Luxembourg, Malta, Netherlands, Norway, Poland, Portugal, Romania, Slovenia, Spain, Sweden, Switzerland, Türkiye, UK.
NGO Relations Cooperates with: *International Nosocomial Infection Control Consortium (INICC, #14376).* [2014.11.04/XJ7433/**F**]

♦ European Network on Law and Society 07937

Réseau européen droit et société (REDS) – Red Europea Derecho y Sociedad – Rede Européia Direito e Sociedade – Rete Europea Diritto e Società

Co-Dir c/o Inst Sciences sociales du Politique, ENS Cachan – Bât Laplace – 4è étage, 61 avenue du Président Wilson, 94235 Cachan CEDEX, France. T. +33147405967. Fax +33147405956.
URL: http://ds.hypotheses.org/

History 1992. From 1979 until 1992 existed as a private scientific research group with the name *Cercle de sociologie et nomologie juridiques*. Registered in accordance with French law. **Aims** Promote research and education of the theory of law and legal sociology at national, European and international levels. **Structure** General Assembly (annually). Administrative Council of 6 members. Board, comprising President, Vice-President, Secretary and Treasurer. **Languages** English, French, German, Italian, Portuguese, Spanish. **Staff** None. **Finance** Members' dues. National and international research programmes. **Activities** Research/documentation; events/meetings; training/eduation. **Events** *Annual Seminar* Paris (France) 2010, *Annual Seminar* Rieux-Minervois (France) 2009, *Annual Seminar* Paris (France) 2008, *Annual Seminar* Bogota (Colombia) 2007, *Annual seminar* Paris (France) 2006. **Publications** *Droit et Société* – journal; *REDS News* – online. *Droit et Société* – series; *Droit et Société Classics* – series; *GEDIM/MOST-UNESCO* – series; *RED and S Travaux et recherches* – series; *Travaux et recherches on line* – series. Books; dictionnaries; legal documentation papers; online bibliographies.
Members Founder; Honorary; Benefactor; Active; Associate. Individuals in 40 countries:
Argentina, Australia, Belgium, Brazil, Bulgaria, Cameroon, Canada, Colombia, Congo Brazzaville, Costa Rica, Croatia, Czechia, Denmark, Egypt, France, Germany, Greece, Hungary, India, Israel, Italy, Japan, Mexico, Netherlands, Norway, Paraguay, Peru, Poland, Portugal, Romania, Russia, Senegal, Spain, Sweden, Switzerland, Tunisia, UK, Uruguay, USA, Venezuela.
Organizations in 3 countries:
Brazil, Canada, Spain. [2018/XF4821/**F**]

♦ European Network of Leading Institutes of Pharmacy/Departments of Pharmaceutics and Biopharmaceutics / see European Workshop on Particulate Systems (#09120)
♦ European network of legal experts in gender equality and non-discrimination / see European Equality Law Network (#07004)
♦ European Network of Literary Translation Centres (#18873)

♦ European Network of Living Labs (ENoLL) 07938

Contact Pleinlaan 9, 1050 Brussels, Belgium. T. +3226148547. Fax +3226291700. E-mail: info@enoll.org.
URL: http://www.enoll.org/

History 20 Nov 2006, Helsinki (Finland). Founded under the auspices of the Finnish European Presidency, as the international federation of benchmarked Living Labs in Europe and worldwide. To date, 11 Waves have been launched, the result showing a continuing reinforcement of ENoLL both in Europe and throughout the world, setting the stage for a strong role of the Living Lab movement in the context of EU 2020 Innovation Union and other relevant European Union policies. The Wave process, dating back to 2006, has up to today resulted in over 440 accredited ENoLL Living Labs, of which over 150 are active worldwide. Registration: Belgium. **Aims** Provide co-creation, user engagement, test and experimentation facilities targeting innovation in many different domains such as energy, media, mobility, healthcare and agrifood; act as a platform for best practice exchange, learning and support, and Living Lab international project development. **Structure** General Assembly; Council; Work Groups; Thematic Sub Groups; Headquarters in Brussels (Belgium). **Languages** English. **Staff** 9.00 FTE, paid. **Activities** Events/meetings; politics/policy/regulatory; research and development; training/education. **Events** *Conference* Brussels (Belgium) 2020, *Meeting* Thessaloniki (Greece) 2019, *Living labs and sustainable development goals – from theories to practice* Geneva (Switzerland) 2018, *Meeting* Krakow (Poland) 2017, *Meeting* Montréal, QC (Canada) 2016. **Publications** *ENoLL Newsletter*. *Citizen-Driven Innovation Handbook*; *Introducing ENoLL and its Living Lab Community*; *Living Lab Services for Business Support and Internationalisation*. Conference proceedings; white papers. **Members** Effective; Adherent. Over 440 recognized Living Labs and over 150 active members. Membership countries not specified. [2020.05.12/XM2355/**F**]

♦ European Network of Local and Regional Authorities for the Implementation of the European Landscape Convention (RECEP-ENELC) 07939

Address not obtained.
URL: http://www.recep-enelc.net/

History 30 May 2006, Strasbourg (France), under the aegis and following Resolution 178/2004 of *Congress of Local and Regional Authorities of the Council of Europe (#04677)*, in support of *European Landscape Convention (2000)*. **Aims** Support the interested local and regional authorities, at the scientific, technical, political and administrative levels, in their activities aimed at implementing the convention's principles within their territories. **Structure** General Assembly. Executive Board. President; 3 Vice-Presidents. Technical Coordination Board; Scientific Committee. **Languages** English, French, Italian, Spanish. **Staff** 3.00 FTE, paid. **Finance** Members' dues. Budget (2011): euro 200,000. **Events** *European Cold Chain Conference* Antwerp (Belgium) 2018, *Extraordinary General Assembly* Barcelona (Spain) 2012, *General Assembly* Strasbourg (France) 2011, *General Assembly* Strasbourg (France) 2010, *General Assembly* Strasbourg (France) 2009. **Publications** *We are the Landscape – Understanding the European Landscape Convention* (2010). Analyses.
Members Communities, provinces, regions, municipalities and areas in 6 countries:
Belgium, Italy, Romania, Slovakia, Spain, Sweden.
IGO Relations *Congress of Local and Regional Authorities of the Council of Europe (#04677)*. **NGO Relations** Together with *Civilscape (#03966)* and *European Network of Universities for the Implementation of the European Landscape Convention (UNISCAPE, #08030)*, constitutes *European Landscape Network (Eurolandscape, #07644)*. [2013/XJ1803/**E**]

♦ European Network of Logistics Competence Centres (Open ENLoCC) 07940

Pres Av Louise 146, 1050 Brussels, Belgium. E-mail: info@openenlocc.net.
URL: https://www.openenlocc.net/

History 2006, Turku (Finland). Founded as as follow-up of the "ENLoCC" project. Former names and other names: *European Network of Regional Logistics Competence Centers* – alias. Registration: Banque-Carrefour des Entreprises, No/ID: 0739.805.043, Start date: 19 Dec 2019, Belgium; EU Transparency Register, No/ID: 138828413651-57, Start date: 19 May 2014. **Aims** Promote the international exchange of experience and knowledge; promote a higher level of cooperation with European institutions. **Structure** General Assembly; Board of Directors. **Languages** English. **Staff** 15.00 FTE, voluntary. **Finance** Sources: members' dues. **Activities** Politics/policy/regulatory; publishing activities; research/documentation; training/education. Active in: Belgium/Wallonia Region, England, Finland, France, Germany, Greece, Italy, Luxembourg, Poland, Slovenia, Sweden, UK, Wallonia. **Publications** *European Regional Review*.
Members Full in 10 countries:
Belgium, France, Germany, Greece, Italy, Poland, Slovenia, Spain, Sweden, UK. [2022.05.03/AA2468/**F**]

♦ European Network of Marine Research Institutes and Stations (MARS Network) 07941

Pres c/o Marine Biological Assn, Citadel Hill, Plymouth, PL1 2PB, UK. E-mail: secretariat@marinestations.org.
URL: https://www.marinestations.org/

History 17 Mar 1995, Kapelle (Netherlands). **Aims** Create awareness of marine stations as an important part of Europe's scientific patrimony; contact, and lobby, with the managers of European research; identify relevant science priorities and strategic themes, and stimulate international interdisciplinary marine science programmes; be a meeting place for the heads of marine institutes and stations; create a critical mass and focus for European and global marine activities; call more attention for the unique function and location of marine research institutions. **Structure** Executive Board; Directors Meeting; Secretariat. **Languages** Dutch, English. **Staff** 0.40 FTE, paid. Voluntary. **Finance** Sources: members' dues. **Activities** Awards/prizes/competitions; events/meetings; knowledge management/information dissemination; networking/liaising. **Events** *European Conference on Scientific Diving (ECSD7)* Roscoff (France) 2023, *Directors Meeting* Amsterdam (Netherlands) 2014. **Publications** *MARS Newsletter*. Position papers; booklet.
Members Laboratories, institutes and university departments. Members in 21 countries:
Albania, Belgium, Denmark, Finland, France, Germany, Greece, Ireland, Italy, Latvia, Lithuania, Malta, Netherlands, Norway, Poland, Portugal, Russia, Slovenia, Spain, Sweden, UK.
IGO Relations Supports (1): *European Scientific Diving Panel (ESDP, #08446)*. *European Cooperation in Science and Technology (COST, #06784)*; *UNESCO (#20322)*. **NGO Relations** Member of (2): European Marine Biodiversity Observatory System (EMBOS); *World Association of Marine Stations (WAMS, #21161)*. Supports (1): *Committee for European Marine Biology Symposia (EMBS, #04255).* [2022/XJ9239/**F**]

♦ European Network of Maritime Clusters (ENMC) 07942

Contact c/o Luxembourg Maritime Cluster, Rue Erasme 14, L-1468 Luxembourg, Luxembourg. T. +352423939839. E-mail: contact@enmc.eu.
URL: http://enmc.eu/

History 2005. Registration: EU Transparency Register, No/ID: 458905915808-19. **Aims** Promote and reinforce the European maritime cluster. **Structure** Executive Board; Secretariat.
Members Full in 18 countries:
Belgium, Bulgaria, Denmark, Finland, France, Germany, Iceland, Ireland, Italy, Luxembourg, Malta, Netherlands, Norway, Poland, Portugal, Spain, Sweden, UK. [2023.02.15/XM5441/**F**]

♦ European Network of Masters in Children's Rights / see Children's Rights European Academic Network (#03878)

♦ European Network of Materials Research Centres (ENMat) 07943

Secretariat Ctr for Textile Science and Engineering Ghent Univ, Technologiepark 907, 9052 Zwijnaarde, Belgium. Fax +3292645846.
Pres Fraunhofer Inst for Ceramic Technologies and Systems (IKTS), Winterbergstrasse 28, 01277 Dresden, Germany.
URL: http://www.enmat.eu/

History Inaugurated, 4 Sep 2005, Prague (Czech Rep). **Aims** Encourage and strengthen the creation of knowledge, dissemination of results and beneficial use in materials science and technology; be the leading network for materials based innovation for students, researchers, engineers and industry in Europe. **Structure** President; Vice-President. **Languages** English. **Finance** Members' dues. **Activities** Research and development; knowledge management/information dissemination; events/meetings; training/education. **Events** *Meeting* Preston (UK) 2014, *Meeting* Warsaw (Poland) 2014, *Meeting* Krakow (Poland) 2013, *Meeting* London (UK) 2013, *Meeting* Espoo (Finland) 2012. **Publications** *ENMaT Newsletter*.
Members Full (14) in 11 countries:
Belgium, Czechia, France, Germany, Italy, Poland, Portugal, Romania, Spain, Switzerland, UK. [2017.03.08/XJ1170/**D**]

♦ European Network of Medical Competent Authorities (ENMCA) 07944

Réseau Européen des Autorités Compétentes Médicales – Europäisches Netzwerk für die Berufsanerkennung von Ärztinnen/Ärzten zuständigen Behörden

Contact address not obtained. E-mail: contact@enmca.eu.
URL: https://www.enmca.eu/

History 2010. Set up by *European Commission (EC, #06633)*. **Aims** Bring together European competent authorities responsible for the recognition of medical qualifications, in line with Directive 2005/36/EC on the recognition of professional qualifications.
Members Partners in 23 countries:
Austria, Belgium, Croatia, Cyprus, Denmark, Estonia, Finland, France, Germany, Hungary, Ireland, Latvia, Luxembourg, Malta, Netherlands, Norway, Poland, Portugal, Romania, Slovenia, Spain, Sweden, UK. [2022.06.17/XJ7719/**F**]

♦ European Network of Medical Residents in Public Health (Euronet MRPH) 07945

Sec address not obtained. E-mail: secretary@euronetmrph.org – mrphnet@gmail.com – president@euronetmrph.org.
URL: http://euronetmrph.org/

History Launched 30 Jun 2011, Paris (France). Registered in accordance with French law. **Aims** Promote professional excellence among medical residents in public health in Europe by exchanging scientific knowledge and training opportunities and organizing common activities. **Structure** Board; National Commissions. **Languages** English. **Activities** Events/meetings. **Events** *Spring Meeting* Murcia (Spain) 2020, *Spring Meeting* Turin (Italy) 2019, *Winter Meeting* Utrecht (Netherlands) 2019, *Meeting* Madrid (Spain) 2013. **Publications** Newsletter.
Members in 9 countries:
Croatia, France, Italy, Netherlands, Portugal, Slovenia, Spain, Türkiye, UK.
NGO Relations Member of: *European Public Health Alliance (EPHA, #08297)*. Associated member of: *European Forum for Primary Care (EFPC, #07326)*. [2019.03.06/XJ7892/F]

♦ European Network for Mental Health Promotion and Mental Disorder Prevention (inactive)

♦ European Network for Mental Health Service Evaluation (ENMESH) 07946

Chair Dept of Psychiatry II, Ulm Univ, Reisensburger Str 32, 89312 Günzburg, Germany. T. +498221962866. Fax +4982219628160.
URL: http://www.enmesh.eu/
History 1991, in collaboration with *WHO Regional Office for Europe (#20945)*. **Aims** Develop and maintain a network of active researchers in mental health service research in Europe; promote development and dissemination of study designs, research instruments, mental health outcome indicators and relevant forms of statistical indicators; function as a clearing house for mental health service evaluation information in Europe. **Structure** Executive Committee. **Languages** English. **Finance** No budget. **Activities** Events/meetings. **Events** *Conference* Lisbon (Portugal) 2019, *Biennial Conference* Groningen (Netherlands) 2017, *Conference* Malaga (Spain) 2015, *Biennial Conference* Verona (Italy) 2013, *Biennial conference / Conference* Ulm (Germany) 2011. [2019.04.26/XF6719/F]

♦ European Network of Migrant Women (ENoMW) 07947

Contact Rue Hydraulique 18, 1210 Brussels, Belgium. T. +3222179020.
URL: http://www.migrantwomennetwork.org/
Aims Promote equal treatment, equal rights and better integration for migrant women in Europe; provide regular input on all areas of EU policy development and implementation that have an impact on migrant women's lives; help shape social policies and design action programmes addressing migrant women's specific needs; represent members' organizations and lobby for and with migrant women to have a stronger voice at European level; support migrant women's organizations and movements through information and training. **Structure** General Assembly (annual). Board of Administration, comprising Chair, Vice-Chair, Treasurer, Secretary and 2 members. Working Groups. **NGO Relations** Member of: *European NGO Platform Asylum and Migration (EPAM, #08051)*; *Platform for International Cooperation on Undocumented Migrants (PICUM, #18401)*. Associate member of: *European Women's Lobby (EWL, #09102)*. [2012/XJ6252/F]

♦ European Network for Music Educators and Researchers of Young Children (EuNet MERYC) 07948

Address not obtained.
History Created 2003, Copenhagen (Denmark). **Aims** Provide a network for people sharing interests about music education and research in relation to young children. **Structure** Board. **Activities** Events/meetings; networking/liaising; knowledge management/information dissemination. **Events** *Biennial Conference* Ghent (Belgium) 2019, *Conference* Cambridge (UK) 2017, *Conference* Tallinn (Estonia) 2015, *Conference* The Hague (Netherlands) 2013, *Conference* Helsinki (Finland) 2011. [2020/XM8362/F]

♦ European Network of Music and Guided Imagery / see European Association of Music and Imagery (#06126)

♦ European Network of Myeloma Patient Groups (inactive)

♦ European Network of National Human Rights Institutions (ENNHRI) 07949

SG Place Victor Horta 40, Saint Gilles, 1060 Brussels, Belgium. T. +3222123158. E-mail: info@ennhri.org.
Communications Officer address not obtained.
URL: http://www.ennhri.org/
History 2003. Previously also referred to as *European Coordinating Group for National Institutions for the Promotion and Protection of Human Rights* and *European Group of National Human Rights Institutions*. Subsequently changed title to *European Network of National Institutions for the Promotion and Protection of Human Rights – Groupe de coordination européenne des institutions nationales pour la promotion et la protection des droits de l'homme*. One of 4 regional Groups of *Global Alliance of National Human Rights Institutions (GANHRI, #10214)*. **Structure** Bureau; Secretariat. **Languages** English, French. **Staff** 5.00 FTE, paid. **Events** *General Assembly* Brussels (Belgium) 2022, *Workshop on National Implementation of the EU Charter of Fundatmental Rights* Vienna (Austria) 2016.
Members National Human Rights Institutions (40) in 32 countries:
Albania, Armenia, Austria, Azerbaijan, Belgium, Bosnia-Herzegovina, Bulgaria, Croatia, Denmark, France, Georgia, Germany, Greece, Hungary, Ireland, Luxembourg, Moldova, Netherlands, North Macedonia, Norway, Poland, Portugal, Romania, Russia, Serbia, Slovakia, Slovenia, Spain, Sweden, Switzerland, UK, Ukraine.
IGO Relations Links with regional and international bodies including: *Council of Europe (CE, #04881)*; *European Union Agency for Fundamental Rights (FRA, #08969)*; *Office of the United Nations High Commissioner for Human Rights (OHCHR, #17697)*; *OSCE – Office for Democratic Institutions and Human Rights (OSCE/ODIHR, #17902)*; *UNDP (#20292)*. [2023/XE4423/E]

♦ European Network of National Information Centres on Academic Mobility and Equivalence / see European Network of National Information Centres on Academic Recognition and Mobility (#07950)

♦ European Network of National Information Centres on Academic Recognition and Mobility (ENIC) 07950

Réseau européen des centres nationaux d'information sur la reconnaissance et la mobilité académiques
Contact Administrateur, Div de l'enseignement supérieur et de la recherche, Conseil de l'Europe, 67075 Strasbourg CEDEX, France. T. +33388413217. Fax +33388412706.
URL: http://www.enic-naric.net/
History Established 1980, as *European Network of National Information Centres on Academic Mobility and Equivalence*, within the framework of *Council of Europe (CE, #04881)*, under activities developing from *European Cultural Convention (1954)*. Since 1994, a joint network with *UNESCO (#20322)*. **Aims** Bring together the national information centres of the states party to the European Cultural Convention and/or the Council of Europe/UNESCO Convention on Recognition of Qualifications concerning Higher Education in the European Region; implement the Convention for Recognition of Academic Qualifications (Lisbon Recognition Convention), and, in general, develop policy and practice for the recognition of qualifications. **Structure** Meeting (annual), in cooperation with NARIC; Bureau. **Languages** English, French. **Finance** Financed by state parties to European Cultural convention. Annual meeting financed by grants from *European Commission (EC, #06633)*. **Activities** Knowledge management/information dessmination. **Events** *Joint Meeting* Toledo (Spain) 2012, *Joint meeting* Valletta (Malta) 2008, *Joint meeting* Bucharest (Romania) 2007, *Joint meeting* Tallinn (Estonia) 2006, *Joint meeting* Strasbourg (France) 2004.
Members Governments of 55 countries:
Albania, Andorra, Armenia, Austria, Azerbaijan, Belarus, Belgium, Bosnia-Herzegovina, Bulgaria, Canada, Croatia, Cyprus, Czechia, Denmark, Estonia, Finland, France, Georgia, Germany, Greece, Holy See, Hungary, Iceland, Ireland, Israel, Italy, Kazakhstan, Latvia, Liechtenstein, Lithuania, Luxembourg, Malta, Moldova, Monaco, Montenegro, Netherlands, New Zealand, North Macedonia, Norway, Poland, Portugal, Romania, Russia, San Marino, Serbia, Slovakia, Slovenia, Spain, Sweden, Switzerland, Türkiye, UK, Ukraine, USA. [2013.10.18/XK0099/E*]

♦ European Network of National Institutions for the Promotion and Protection of Human Rights / see European Network of National Human Rights Institutions (#07949)

♦ European Network of National Observatories on Childhood (ChildONEurope) 07951

Secretariat c/o Office de la Naissance et de l'Enfance, Chaussée de Charleroi 95, 1060 Brussels, Belgium. T. +3225421200.
URL: http://www.childoneurope.org/
History 24 Jan 2003, Florence (Italy). Founded in the context of *L'Europe de l'enfance (#09152)*. **Aims** Increase the exchange of knowledge and information on laws, policies, programmes, statistics, studies, research and best practice regarding childhood and adolescence, and on methodology and indicators so as to obtain comparability of information; conduct analysis on specific subjects. **Structure** General Assembly (2 a year), always in Florence (Italy), comprising Network Members and Associated Members (institutions nominated by EU States which are not Network Members). Secretariat function assigned to the Italian National Childhood and Adolescence Documentation and Analysis Centre. **Languages** English, French. **Staff** 1.00 FTE, paid. Experts as collaborators for specific research. **Finance** Main source: Italian Ministry of Labour, Health and Social Policies and the Department of Family Policies – Italian Presidency of the Council of Ministries. Secondary source: voluntary contributions by competent Ministries of the French Community of Belgium, Denmark, France, Ireland, Luxembourg, Portugal and Spain. Budget (annual): euro 80,000. **Activities** Events/meetings. **Events** *Childhood policies and fight against poverty* Paris (France) 2015, *Assembly* Florence (Italy) 2014, *Assembly* Florence (Italy) 2013, *Public policies supporting positive parenthood – new policy perspectives* Florence (Italy) 2013, *Assembly* Florence (Italy) 2012. **Publications** *ChildONEurope Series*. *The On-Going Debate on the Assessment of Children's Conditions of Life* (2009); *Guidelines on Data Collection and Monitoring Systems on Child Abuse* (2009); *Early Childhood Education and Care Services in the European Union Countries*. Conference proceedings.
Members Governments of 8 countries and territories:
Belgium (French Community of), Denmark, France, Ireland, Italy, Luxembourg, Portugal, Spain.
Associate in 19 countries and territories:
Austria, Belgium/Flemish Region, Bulgaria, Cyprus, Czechia, Estonia, Finland, Germany, Greece, Hungary, Latvia, Lithuania, Malta, Netherlands, Poland, Slovakia, Slovenia, Sweden, UK. [2012.12.13/XM2620/F*]

♦ European Network of National and Regional Education Councils / see European Network of Education Councils (#07898)

♦ European Network of NGOs in Afghanistan (ENNA) 07952

Coordination address not obtained. T. +46854581736.
URL: http://www.ennanet.eu/
History Founded 2004. **Aims** Collaborate on matters of mutual interest to support the people in Afghanistan; maintain Afghanistan on the international political agenda; strengthen and improve humanitarian assistance and development efforts by means of evidence based advocacy. **Structure** Network. **Languages** English. **Activities** Advocacy/lobbying/activism; politics/policy/regulatory; humanitarian/emergency aid; events/meetings. **Events** *Peace for all Afghans?* Brussels (Belgium) 2013. **Publications** Reports; policy briefings; policy recommendations; position papers.
Members Full: organizations (20), including 9 listed in this Yearbook:
Action Against Hunger (#00086); *Catholic Agency for Overseas Development (CAFOD)*; *Catholic Organization for Relief and Development (Cordaid)*; *Global Witness (GW)*; *Humanity and Inclusion (HI, #10975)*; *Mission d'aide au développement des économies rurales afghanes (MADERA, #16828)*; *Norwegian Church Aid*; *Norwegian Refugee Council (NRC)*; *Oxfam Novib*.
NGO Relations *Agency Coordinating Body for Afghan Relief (ACBAR)*. [2019.02.13/XM0208/y/F]

♦ European Network of Numerical Cities / see European Network of Digital Cities (#07893)

♦ European Network of Nursing Academies (ENNA) 07953

Pres address not obtained. E-mail: info@en-na.eu.
URL: http://en-na.eu/
History 2008, by 8 European institutions. Registered in accordance with German law. **Aims** Act as a forum for exchange of expertise and ideas; advance nursing at national and international levels so as to improve heath care in general. **Structure** General Assembly; Board. **Activities** Training/education; research/documentation. **Events** *Meeting* Stockholm (Sweden) 2019, *Meeting* Halden (Norway) 2018, *Meeting* Hall in Tirol (Austria) 2018, *Meeting* Düsseldorf (Germany) 2014.
Members Institutions (8) in 4 countries:
Austria, Germany, Netherlands, Sweden. [2015/XM4226/F]

♦ European Network of Nursing in Higher Education (ENNE) 07954

Contact Satakunnan Ammattikorkeakoulu – Terveys, Maantiekatu 10, FI-28500 Pori, Finland.
URL: http://www.samk.fi/network_of_european_nursing/
Aims Bring together educational institutions of nursing education. **Structure** Flat structure with a general coordinator. **Activities** Training/education; knowledge management/information dissemination. **Events** *Coordinator Meeting* Estonia 2015, *Coordinator Meeting* Austria 2014, *Coordinator Meeting* Czech Rep 2014, *Coordinator Meeting* Croatia 2013, *Coordinator Meeting* Hungary 2013.
Members Schools in 13 countries:
Austria, Belgium, Croatia, Czechia, Estonia, Finland, Germany, Hungary, Netherlands, Spain, Sweden, Switzerland, UK. [2015/XM4224/F]

♦ European Network on Occupational Social Work (ENOS) 07955

Sec c/o Mensenwerk, Rozenlaan 35, 2771 DB Boskoop, Netherlands.
URL: http://www.enos-europe.com/
History Sep 1990, Loosdrecht (Netherlands) with the support of *European Centre for Social Welfare Policy and Research (European Centre, #06500)*. Articles adopted at 4th Conference, 10-13 May 1995, Athens (Greece). **Aims** Give occupational social workers (OSWs) in Europe an opportunity to exchange ideas, experiences, expertise, knowledge and skills. **Structure** Annual Plenary Meeting. Coordinating Group, consisting of one member from each represented country. European Secretariat. **Finance** Members' dues. Other sources: donations. **Activities** Serves as: a Transfer Point for the exchange of ideas, expertise and skills between individual occupational social work practitioners in Europe; an Information Point on relevant practice issues, e g the education of OSWs, forms of practice, special client issues, that is spreads via written or electronic mail and the publication of bulletins and newsletters; a Centre of Expertise that organize gatherings, meetings, lectures, workshops and excursions on subjects relevant to occupational social work practice. **Events** *Conference* The Hague (Netherlands) 2009, *Generations in organizations* The Hague (Netherlands) 2009, *Conference* Labourgade (France) 2006, *Corporate social responsibility* Toulouse (France) 2006, *The exercise of power in the work environment* Villars-sur-Ollon (Switzerland) 2004. **Publications** *ENOS Newsletter* (1-2 a year). *ENOS Vademecum for the Use of Members*. Books.
Members Individuals in 13 countries:
Austria, Belgium, France, Germany, Greece, Ireland, Israel, Netherlands, Norway, Portugal, Spain, Sweden, Switzerland. [2009/XF3899/v/F]

♦ European Network of Occupational Therapy in Higher Education (ENOTHE) 07956

Coordinator Holmeisergasse 7 – 9/2/1, 1210 Vienna, Austria. E-mail: info@enothe.eu.
URL: http://www.enothe.eu/
History 1995. Founded within the framework of *SOCRATES Programme (inactive)*. Registration: Start date: 2017, Austria. **Aims** Ensure a robust educational system for European occupational therapists, which demmonstrates comprability, high quality and flexibility to respond to changes in health and societal issues, policy and practice. **Structure** Executive Board; Office. **Languages** English. **Staff** Part-time. **Finance** Sources: members' dues. **Activities** Events/meetings; knowledge management/information dissemination; projects/programmes; training/education. **Events** *Annual Meeting* Leiria (Portugal) 2025, *Occupational Therapy Europe Congress* Krakow (Poland) 2024, *Annual Meeting* Oviedo (Spain) 2023, *Annual Meeting* Tbilisi (Georgia) 2022, *Joint Congress* Prague (Czechia) 2021.
Members Full in 27 countries:
Australia, Austria, Belgium, Canada, Croatia, Czechia, Denmark, Estonia, Finland, France, Germany, Greece, Ireland, Latvia, Lithuania, Malta, Netherlands, Norway, Poland, Portugal, Romania, Slovenia, Spain, Sweden, Switzerland, UK, USA.
NGO Relations Member of (2): *European Forum for Primary Care (EFPC, #07326)*; *Occupational Therapy Europe (OT-Europe, #17647)* (Founding). Set up by: *Council of Occupational Therapists for the European Countries (COTEC, #04912)*. [2023.03.03/XF6077/F]

European Network Official
07957
alphabetic sequence excludes
For the complete listing, see Yearbook Online at

♦ European Network of Official Medicines Control Laboratories (OMCL) 07957

Réseau européen des laboratoires officiels de contrôle des médicaments

Head Public Relations EDQM, 7 allée Kastner, CS 30026, 67081 Strasbourg, France. T. +33388413030. Fax +33388412771.
URL: http://www.edqm.eu/

History Established 1994, by *European Directorate for the Quality of Medicine and HealthCare (EDQM / DEQM)* within the wider framework of *Council of Europe (CE, #04881)* in cooperation with the *European Commission (EC, #06633)* – DG Enterprises and *European Medicines Agency (EMA, #07767)*. **Aims** Provide common quality standards to control the quality of medicines and of substances used in the manufacture of medicines (human and veterinary use). **Structure** Coordinated by EDQM – DBO Department, which serves as Secretariat. **Languages** English, French. **Finance** Sources: Member States contributions; partly funded by *European Commission (EC, #06633)*. **Activities** Monitoring/evaluation; training/education; knowledge management/ information dissemination; research/documentation; standards/guidelines. **Events** *Annual Meeting* Paris (France) 2016, *Annual Meeting* Brussels (Belgium) 2015, *Annual Meeting* Interlaken (Switzerland) 2014, *International Symposium on Active Pharmaceutical Ingredients from Bioprocesses* Amsterdam (Netherlands) 2013, *Meeting* Vienna (Austria) 2013. **Publications** *EDQM Newsletter* (12 a year). **Members** Over 40 European Member States. Membership countries not specified. **IGO Relations** Cooperates with: *European Commission (EC, #06633)*; *European Medicines Agency (EMA, #07767)*; *WHO (#20950)*. Relevant treaty: *Convention on the Elaboration of a European Pharmacopoeia (1964)*. [2018.10.31/XF6888/**F***]

♦ European Network of Older-Volunteer Organizations (internationally oriented national body)
♦ European Network of Older Volunteers / see European Network of Older-Volunteer Organizations
♦ European Network of Ombudsmen for Children / see European Network of Ombudspersons for Children (#07959)

♦ European Network for Ombudsmen in Higher Education (ENOHE) 07958

Cooordinator c/o BMBWF, Minoritenplatz 5, 1014 Vienna, Austria. T. +431531205533. E-mail: hello@enohe.net.
URL: http://www.enohe.net/

History 25 Feb 2003, Amsterdam (Netherlands). Previously known under the acronym *OEHE*. **Aims** Propagate and promote the ombudsman concept in higher education in general and within higher education institutions in particular. **Structure** General Assembly; Board; Secretariat. **Languages** English. **Finance** Members' dues. **Activities** Events/meetings; publishing activities. **Events** *Annual Conference* Athens (Greece) 2021, *Annual Conference* Athens (Greece) 2020, *Annual Conference* León (Spain) 2019, *Annual Conference* Edinburgh (UK) 2018, *Annual Conference* Strasbourg (France) 2017. **Publications** *ENOHE News*. *ENOHE Occasional Papers* – 12 vols to date. **Information Services** *ENOHE List Serv*.
Members Full in 18 countries:
Austria, Belgium, Canada, Denmark, France, Georgia, Germany, Greece, Italy, Mexico, Netherlands, Norway, Poland, Portugal, Spain, Switzerland, UK, USA.
IGO Relations Bologna Follow-Up Group; *European Commission (EC, #06633)*. [2020/XF7063/**F**]

♦ European Network of Ombudspersons for Children (ENOC) 07959

Secretariat c/o Council of Europe, Agora Bldg, Office no B5 07V, 67075 Strasbourg CEDEX, France. T. +33390215488. E-mail: secretariat@enoc.eu.
URL: http://enoc.eu/

History 9 Jun 1997, Trondheim (Norway). Former names and other names: *European Network of Ombudsmen for Children* – former. **Aims** Promote full implementation of the Convention on the Rights of the Child; support collective lobbying for children's rights; share information, approaches and strategies; promote development of effective independent offices for children. **Structure** General Assembly; Bureau; Secretariat. General Assembly usually held with annual meeting. **Languages** English. **Staff** 2.00 FTE, paid. **Finance** Sources: contributions; donations; grants; members' dues. **Activities** Events/meetings; knowledge management/ information dissemination. **Events** *Annual Conference* Reykjavik (Iceland) 2022, *Annual Meeting* Athens (Greece) 2021, *Annual Meeting* Edinburgh (UK) 2020, *Annual Meeting* Belfast (UK) 2019, *Annual Meeting* Paris (France) 2018. **Publications** Position papers; thematic reports; conference and seminar reports; members' reports; project outline.
Members Full (35) independent children's rights institutions (ICRIs) within Council of Europe member states, which fully meet membership criteria. Associate (8) institutions not meeting full membership criteria. Members in 33 countries:
Armenia, Azerbaijan, Belgium, Bosnia-Herzegovina, Bulgaria, Croatia, Cyprus, Denmark, Estonia, Finland, France, Georgia, Greece, Hungary, Iceland, Ireland, Italy, Latvia, Lithuania, Luxembourg, Malta, Moldova, Montenegro, Netherlands, Norway, Poland, Serbia, Slovakia, Slovenia, Spain, Sweden, UK, Ukraine.
Consultative Status Consultative status granted from: *Council of Europe (CE, #04881)* (Participatory Status). [2021.09.01/XF5064/**F**]

♦ European Network for Opera and Dance Education (#18878)

♦ European Network of Organizational and Work Psychologists (ENOP) 07960

Réseau européen de psychologie du travail et des organisations

Pres PO Box 616, 6200 MD Maastricht, Netherlands.
Hon Pres address not obtained.
URL: https://enop-psy.org/

History 1980. **Aims** Furnish specialists of work and organizational psychology teachers, researchers and practitioners with a European framework for cooperation in order to meet emerging societal and professional challenges from European integration. **Structure** Business Meeting (annual); Coordinating Committee (meets twice a year) of 7 members. **Languages** English. **Staff** 45.00 FTE, voluntary. **Finance** Administrative support structure provided by Université René Descartes, seed money and support for participants of East European countries provided by adhesion fees from members. Other sources: foundations; universities; individual contributions. **Activities** Events/meetings; training/education; research/documentation; networking/liaising. **Events** *Annual Symposium* Paris (France) 2022, *Annual Symposium* 2021, *Annual Symposium* Paris (France) 2019, *Annual Symposium* Paris (France) 2018, *Annual Symposium* Paris (France) 2017. **Publications** *ENOP Newsletter*. *ENOP Reports Series*. Books; reports; conference proceedings.
Members Professors in work and organizational psychology in 25 countries:
Austria, Belgium, Bulgaria, Croatia, Czechia, Denmark, Estonia, Finland, France, Germany, Greece, Hungary, Ireland, Italy, Netherlands, Norway, Poland, Portugal, Russia, Slovenia, Spain, Sweden, Switzerland, UK, Ukraine. [2023/XF1456/v/**F**]

♦ European Network of Outdoor Sports (ENOS) 07961

Secretariat House of Sport, Avenue des Arts 43, 1040 Brussels, Belgium. E-mail: enos@outdoor-sports-network.eu.
Sec address not obtained.
URL: http://www.outdoor-sports-network.eu/

History 2013, Liptovsky Mikulas (Slovakia). **Aims** Represent outdoor sports at a strategic level in Europe; promote the environmental, educative, social and economic benefits of outdoor sports to individuals, communities, regions and nations; encourage trans-national approaches to the recognition of leaders, instructors and coaches, to develop mobility and employment. **Structure** General Assembly; Board; Secretariat. **Finance** Sources: members' dues. **Events** *Outdoor Sports Euro'meet* Silkeborg (Denmark) 2021, *Outdoor Sports Euro'meet* Viana do Castelo (Portugal) 2019, *Nature & Sports Euro'meet* La Seu d'Urgell (Spain) 2017, *Nature & Sports Euro'meet* Newcastle upon Tyne (Northern Ireland) 2015, *Nature & Sports Euro'Meet* 2013.
Members Full in 8 countries:
Bulgaria, Finland, France, Germany, Ireland, Italy, Spain, UK.
Regional organizations (3):
European Outdoor Group (EOG, #08122); *Fédération Internationale de Tourisme Équestre (FITE, #09666)*; *International Mountain Bicycling Association Europe (IMBA Europe, #14189)*.
NGO Relations *EUROPARC Federation (#05768)*; *Rurality – Environment – Development (RED, #19003)*. [2021/XM6609/y/**F**]

♦ European Network for Oxysterol Research (ENOR) 07962

Founder Sapienza Univ of Rome, Dept of Medico-Surgical Sciences and Biotechnology, Vascular Biology and Mass Spectrometry Lab, Corso della Republica 79, 04100 Latina LT, Italy. T. +397731757231.
Founder Univ de Bourgogne INSERM, Biochimie du peroxysome/inflammation/métabolisme lipidique, Fac Sciences Gabriel, 6 bd Gabriel, 21000 Dijon, France. T. +33380396256. Fax +33380396250.
URL: http://www.oxysterols.net/

History 2010. Also referred to as *European Network on Oxysterols Research*. **Aims** Promote interaction between research groups; enrol young investigators in the field; stimulate novel research on the biological activities of oxysterols leading to *pharmacological* applications and innovative therapies. **Activities** Events/ meetings. **Events** *Symposium* Paris (France) 2016.
Members Full (about 80) in 17 countries:
Brazil, Czechia, Finland, France, Germany, Ireland, Israel, Italy, Netherlands, Poland, Portugal, Russia, Slovenia, Spain, Sweden, Switzerland, UK. [2017/XM5721/**F**]

♦ European Network on Oxysterols Research / see European Network for Oxysterol Research (#07962)

♦ European Network of Paediatric Research at the European Medicines Agency (Enpr-EMA) 07963

Contact c/o EMA, Domenico Scarlattilaan 6, 1083 HS Amsterdam, Netherlands. E-mail: enprema@ema.europa.eu.
URL: https://www.ema.europa.eu/

History Founded by *European Medicines Agency (EMA, #07767)* as a partner network. **Aims** Facilitate studies to increase the availability of medicines authorised for use the paediatric population. **Structure** Coordinating Group; Secretariat provided by *European Medicines Agency (EMA, #07767)*. **Activities** Events/meetings.
Members Category 1: full members; Category 2: network and centres undergoing clarification; Category 3: networks not currently qualifying. Category 1: national networks and centres in 7 countries:
Canada, Finland, France, Germany, Italy, Netherlands, UK.
Category 1 – international organizations (8):
European Cystic Fibrosis Society (ECFS, #06879); *European Network for Hyperkinetic Disorders (EUNETHYDIS, #07925)*; European Paediatric oncology Off-patent Medicines Consortium (EPOC); *European Society for Blood and Marrow Transplantation (EBMT, #08533)*; *Innovative Therapies for Children with Cancer Consortium (ITCC, #11222)*; *International BFM Study Group (I-BFM-SG, #12335)*; Paediatric European Network for the Treatment of AIDS; Pediatric Rheumatology International Trials Organisation (PRINTO).
IGO Relations Collaborates with: *WHO (#20950)*. [2015/XJ4539/y/**E**]

♦ European Network of Palm Scientists (EUNOPS) 07964

Contact Royal Botanic Gardens, Kew, Richmond, TW9 3AB, UK. E-mail: palms@kew.org.
URL: http://eunops.org/

History 2001, as an informal association. **Aims** Facilitate information exchange on palm research taking place in Europe; promote integration and collaboration. **Structure** Steering Group. **Finance** No funding. **Events** *Meeting* Paris (France) 2019, *Meeting* Las Palmas de Gran Canaria (Spain) 2016, *World Palm Symposium* Montenegro (Colombia) 2015, *Meeting / EUNOPS Meeting* Valencia (Spain) 2014, *Meeting / EUNOPS Meeting* Aarhus (Denmark) 2013. **Publications** No publications of its own.
Members Participants in 9 countries:
Denmark, France, Germany, Italy, Poland, Russia, Spain, Switzerland, UK. [2018.09.05/XJ9062/**F**]

♦ European Network on Patient Empowerment (ENOPE) 07965

Contact Danish Committee for Health Education, Classensgade 71 – 5th Fl, 2100 Copenhagen, Denmark. T. +4535265400. E-mail: kfs@sundkom.dk.
URL: http://enope.eu/

Aims Promote patient empowerment in Europe through evidence based programmes which focus on living with chronic disease. **Events** *Congress* Basel (Switzerland) 2014, *European Congress* Copenhagen (Denmark) 2012, *Congress* Denmark 2012.
Members Full in 3 countries:
Denmark, Switzerland, UK.
NGO Relations Member of: *Self-Care Initiative Europe (SCIE)*. [2014/XJ7093/**F**]

♦ European Network for the Philosophy of the Social Sciences (ENPOSS) 07966

Contact address not obtained. E-mail: info@enposs.eu.
URL: http://enposs.eu/

History 2011, Madrid (Spain). **Aims** Advocate an inclusive conception of the philosophy of the social sciences dealing with the whole range of multifarious philosophical issues raised by the social sciences; encourage and promote discussion of these issues by philosophers as well as social scientists. **Structure** Steering Committee. Occasional scientific committees. **Languages** English. **Staff** All voluntary. **Finance** Occasional grants for organization of events. **Activities** Events/meetings. **Events** *Conference* Helsinki (Finland) 2016, *Conference* Seattle, WA (USA) 2015, *Conference* Madrid (Spain) 2014, *Conference* Venice (Italy) 2013, *Conference* Copenhagen (Denmark) 2012. **Publications** *Philosophy of the Social Sciences* – official journal.
Members Individuals. Membership countries not specified. **NGO Relations** *European Network for Social Intelligence (ENSA, #08010)*; *European Philosophy of Science Association (EPSA, #08202)*; *International Network of Analytical Sociologists (INAS, #14231)*; *International Network for Economic Method (INEM, #14254)*; Philosophy of Social Science Roundtable. [2015.06.20/XJ9535/**F**]

♦ European Network of Physiotherapy in Higher Education (ENPHE) 07967

Contact Saxion Univ of Applied Sciences, School of Health, PO Box 70 000, 7500 Enschede, Netherlands. T. +31535376597. Fax +31534320373. E-mail: k.j.renkel@saxion.nl.
URL: http://www.enphe.org/

History 1995. **Aims** Bring together physiotherapy educational institutions in the European region. **Structure** General Assembly. Executive Board, comprising President, Vice-President, Treasurer and 2 Project Executives. **Events** *Conference* Vila Nova de Famalicão (Portugal) 2022, *European Congress – Physiotherapy Education* Brussels (Belgium) 2020, *Conference* Groningen (Netherlands) 2019, *Conference* Paris (France) 2018, *Conference* Graz (Austria) 2016. **Publications** *ENPHE Newsletter*.
Members Full in 30 countries:
Austria, Belgium, Bulgaria, Czechia, Denmark, Estonia, Finland, France, Germany, Greece, Hungary, Iceland, Ireland, Italy, Latvia, Lebanon, Lithuania, Malta, Netherlands, Norway, Poland, Portugal, Romania, Russia, Slovenia, Spain, Sweden, Switzerland, Türkiye, UK. [2020/XM2939/**D**]

♦ European Network of Picturebook Research (unconfirmed)

♦ European Network for Plant Endomembrane Research (ENPER) 07968

Address not obtained.

History Founded 1996. **Activities** Events/meetings. **Events** *Meeting* Valencia (Spain) 2019, *Meeting* Vienna (Austria) 2018. [2019/XM7997/c/**E**]

♦ European Network of Podiatry in Higher Education (ENPODHE) 07969

Sec address not obtained.
Sec address not obtained.
URL: http://enpodhe.com/

Aims Bring together and enhance collaboration between podiatry educational institutions in the European region. **Structure** Board. **Activities** Events/meetings. **Events** *Conference* Ghent (Belgium) 2022, *Conference* Malaga (Spain) 2020, *Conference* Brussels (Belgium) 2019, *Conference* Salford (UK) 2018, *Conference* Paris (France) 2017.
Members Partners in 8 countries:
Belgium, Finland, France, Malta, Netherlands, Portugal, Spain, UK. [2020/AA0076/**F**]

♦ **European Network of Policewomen (ENP)** **07970**
Réseau européen des femmes dans la police – Red Europea de Mujeres Policias – Europäische Verband von Polizistinnen – Associazione Europea delle Donne Poliziotto – Europees Netwerk van Politievrouwen
Pres Elisabets, 10, 2nd floor, PO Box 347, 08001 Barcelona, Spain. T. +34610229576. E-mail: president@enp.eu.
URL: http://www.enp.eu/
History 23 Mar 1989, Noordwijkerhout (Netherlands). Founded during the International Conference for Policewomen. Based on the United Nations Universal Declaration of Human Rights and on *Convention for the Protection of Human Rights and Fundamental Freedoms (1950)* of the Council of Europe. Registration: Start date: 14 Aug 1990, Netherlands. **Aims** Optimize the position of policewomen in European police forces through mutual support, exchange of know-how and experience, training, research and joint efforts to improve functioning. **Structure** Board; Head Office including Secretariat. **Languages** English. **Staff** 2.00 FTE, paid. **Activities** Events/meetings; guidance/assistance/consulting; research/documentation; training/education. **Events** *Police combating domestic violence* Madrid (Spain) 2002, *European career development seminar* Warnsveld (Netherlands) 2002, *European conference for female managers in the police* Mons (Belgium) 2001, *Gewaltige Verhältnisse* Marienheide (Germany) 2000, *Biennial conference / Bi-annual Conference* Stockholm (Sweden) 2000. **Publications** *ENP-News – newsletter* (4 a year) in English. *Facts, Figures and General Information* (2000). *Everything you Always Wanted to Know about Policewomen but were Afraid to Ask* – videofilm. Annual Report; pamphlets; reports; studies. Information Services: *International Equal Opportunities Information and Documentation Centre (no recent information).* Database of over 1,400 contact persons.
Members Open to individuals and organizations professionally concerned with the work of women in police forces. Members in 19 countries:
Albania, Andorra, Belgium, Bosnia-Herzegovina, Denmark, Estonia, France, Germany, Ireland, Kosovo, Lithuania, Luxembourg, Netherlands, Poland, Romania, Slovenia, Spain, Sweden, UK.
Consultative Status Consultative status granted from: *ECOSOC (#05331)* (Special).
[2021.09.07/XF2598/v/F]

♦ **European Network of Policy Makers for the Evaluation of Education Systems** **07971**
Réseau européen des responsables des politiques d'évaluation des systèmes éducatifs
Contact 61-65 rue Dutot, 75015 Paris, France. T. +33155557710.
URL: http://www.reva-education.eu/
History 1995, France, by *European Communities (EC, inactive).* **Aims** Facilitate and promote cooperation in the field of evaluation and monitoring. **Activities** Organizes 2 meetings per year. **Events** *Meeting* Prague (Czech Rep) 2009, *Meeting* Stockholm (Sweden) 2009, *Meeting* Helsinki (Finland) 2006. **Publications** *Evaluation* – newsletter.
Members in 24 countries:
Austria, Belgium, Czechia, Denmark, Estonia, Finland, France, Germany, Greece, Hungary, Iceland, Ireland, Italy, Latvia, Lithuania, Luxembourg, Malta, Netherlands, Norway, Portugal, Slovakia, Spain, Sweden, UK.
Observer (1):
Switzerland.
International organizations (2):
European Commission (EC, #06633); International Association for the Evaluation of Educational Achievement (IEA, #11882). [2008/XM2354/F]

♦ **European Network of Political Foundations (ENoP)** **07972**
Exec Dir Rue de l'Industrie 42, 1040 Brussels, Belgium. T. +322300029. E-mail: info@enop.eu.
URL: http://www.enop.eu/
History 2006. Registration: Banque-Carrefour des Entreprises, No/ID: 0730.925.880, Start date: 22 Jul 2019, Belgium; EU Transparency Register, No/ID: 029070342841-01, Start date: 1 Jun 2021. **Aims** Safeguard and enhance democracy; promote and strengthen the role of political foundations across the European Union; facilitate a debate on the legal framework for political foundations across the EU member states. **Structure** General Assembly; Coordination Board; Steering Committee; Political Board; Secretariat. Working Groups. **Events** *Forum on New Forms of Democratic Engagement* Brussels (Belgium) 2022, *EU-CSO steering group consultation on the joint Africa-EU strategy* Brussels (Belgium) 2010. **Publications** Policy papers.
Members Foundations (over 50) and political families (6) in 23 countries. Membership countries not specified.
Party families (6):
European Conservatives and Reformists Group (ECR, #06745); European People's Party (EPP, #08185); Group of the Greens – European Free Alliance (Greens/EFA, #10781); Group of the Progressive Alliance of Socialists and Democrats in the European Parliament (S and D, #10786); Renew Europe (#18840); The Left in the European Parliament (The Left, #16436). [2021/AA2086/F]

♦ **European Network for Positive Psychology (ENPP)** **07973**
Pres address not obtained. E-mail: info@enpp.eu.
URL: http://www.enpp.eu/
History Currently still an informal network. **Aims** Share knowledge and research on positive psychology with fellow researchers and all others who have an interest in the subject. **Structure** Executive Board. **Activities** Events/meetings. **Events** *European Conference on Positive Psychology* Reykjavik (Iceland) 2022, *European Conference on Positive Psychology* Reykjavik (Iceland) 2020, *European Conference on Positive Psychology* Budapest (Hungary) 2018, *European Conference on Positive Psychology* Angers (France) 2016, *European Conference on Positive Psychology* Amsterdam (Netherlands) 2014. **Publications** *ENPP Newsletter.* **Members** Membership countries not specified. [2017/XJ8074/F]

♦ **European Network for Prevention and Health Promotion in Family Medicine and General Practice (EUROPREV)** **07974**
Sec Inst for Development of Family Medicine, Poljanski nasip 58, 1000 Ljubljana, Slovenia. T. +38614386913. Fax +38614386910.
URL: https://europrev.woncaeurope.org/
History Jul 1996, Stockholm (Sweden). Establishment approved by *European Society of General Practice/Family Medicine (WONCA Europe, #08609).* Current title adopted when became a network organization of WONCA Europe. Former names and other names: *European Review Group on Health Promotion and Prevention in Family Medicine and General Practice (EUROPREV)* – former. **Aims** Review scientific evidence related to health promotion and prevention; create recommendations based on scientific evidence and their diffusion to general practice and family medicine associations in Europe; define the role of the primary care doctor in health promotion and prevention; promote and encourage multicentre research studies in health promotion and prevention throughout Europe. **Structure** General Council; Coordinating Group; International Advisory Committee. **Activities** Organizes workshops. **Events** *International conference on health promoting hospitals and health services* Hersonissos (Greece) 2009, *International workshop on tobacco and alcohol addiction* Barcelona (Spain) 2000, *European conference on health promotion in general practice and community pharmacy* Brussels (Belgium) 2000, *Workshop on helping problem drinkers* Vienna (Austria) 2000, *Workshop on helping smokers to quit* Vienna (Austria) 2000.
Members Individuals in 25 countries:
Austria, Belgium, Croatia, Cyprus, Estonia, Finland, Georgia, Germany, Greece, Hungary, Ireland, Israel, Italy, Lithuania, Malta, Netherlands, Poland, Portugal, Russia, Slovakia, Slovenia, Spain, Sweden, Switzerland, Türkiye. [2022/XE3731/v/E]

♦ European network for professional education in floristry – FLORNET / see FLORNET (#09799)

♦ **European Network to Promote Women's Entrepreneurship (WES)** . . **07975**
Coordinator Economic Development Manager, Municipal Exec Admin Dept for Economic Development, SE-631 86 Eskilstuna, Sweden. T. +46167102214.
URL: http://ec.europa.eu/enterprise/policies/sme/promoting-entrepreneurship/women/w es-network/
History by *European Commission (EC, #06633).* **Aims** Promote women's entrepreneurship by: raising the visibility of existing female entrepreneurs; creating a climate that is favourable to female entrepreneurs; increasing the number of new women entrepreneurs; increasing the size (scale) of existing women run businesses. **Activities** Advocacy/lobbying/activism; networking/liaising; knwoledge management/information dissemination. **Publications** Annual Report.
Members Delegates representing central national governments and institutions with the responsibility to promote female entrepreneurship in 30 countries:
Austria, Belgium, Bulgaria, Cyprus, Czechia, Denmark, Estonia, Finland, France, Germany, Greece, Hungary, Iceland, Ireland, Italy, Latvia, Lithuania, Luxembourg, Malta, Netherlands, Norway, Poland, Portugal, Romania, Slovakia, Slovenia, Spain, Sweden, Türkiye, UK. [2010/XJ2005/E]

♦ **European Network for the Promotion of Rights and Health among Migrant Sex Workers (TAMPEP)** **07976**
Contact c/o Pro-Tukipiste, Urho Kekkosen katu 4-6 B, FI-00100 Helsinki, Finland. T. +3582512730. E-mail: info@tampep.eu – coordinaor@tampep.eu.
URL: http://tampep.eu/
History 1993. Former names and other names: *Transnational AIDS/STD Prevention Among Migrant Prostitutes in Europe Project* – former; *TAMPEP International Foundation* – former. Registration: EU Transparency Register, No/ID: 903628623074-19, Start date: 19 Aug 2016. **Aims** Advance the rights and health of migrant and mobile sex workers across Europe, recognising their diversity as a crosscutting basis for empowerment. **Languages** English, French, German, Italian, Portuguese, Spanish. **Staff** 35.00 FTE, paid. **Finance** Sources: members' dues. Also support from local governments. Supported by: *European Commission (EC, #06633).* **Activities** Advocacy/lobbying/activism; events/meetings; research/documentation. **Publications** *TAMPEP NETWORK Newsletter.* Manuals; reports; guides; maps.
Members Organizations in 17 countries:
Austria, Belgium, Bulgaria, Estonia, Finland, Germany, Greece, Italy, Lithuania, Luxembourg, North Macedonia, Norway, Romania, Scotland, Spain, Switzerland, Türkiye.
NGO Relations Member of: *European Civil Society Forum on HIV/AIDS (CSF, #06568).* [2022/XF6305/t/F]

♦ **European Network for Psychological Anthropology (ENPA)** **07977**
Convenor address not obtained. E-mail: info@enpanthro.net.
URL: https://enpanthro.net/
History Jan 2018. Founded by Dr James Davies, Dr Keir Martin and Dr Thomas Stodulka. **Aims** Develop and support psychological anthropology. **Structure** Board. **Activities** Events/meetings. **Events** *Biennial Conference* 2023, *Biennial Conference* Helsinki (Finland) 2021. **NGO Relations** Affiliated with (1): *European Association of Social Anthropologists (EASA, #06209).* [2022/AA2621/F]

♦ European Network for Psychological Support / see European Network for Psychosocial Support (#07978)

♦ **European Network for Psychosocial Support (ENPS)** **07978**
Réseau européen pour le soutien psychosocial (RESP)
Chairperson Swedish Red Cross, Hornsatan 54, SE-118 21 Stockholm, Sweden. T. +4684524600. E-mail: enps@redcross.at.
Contact Austrian Red Cross, Wiedner Hauptstr 32, 1040 Vienna, Austria.
URL: http://enps.redcross.at/
History 2000, Lyon (France). Founded by national societies of *International Federation of Red Cross and Red Crescent Societies (#13526).* Former names and other names: *European Network for Psychological Support* – former; *Réseau européen de soutien psychologique* – former. **Aims** Offer Red Cross/Red Crescent National Societies, working in the domain of psychosocial support (PS), to exchange ideas, best practices, training and tactics. **Structure** Steering Committee; Coordinators (2); Guests (2). **Languages** English. **Staff** 5.00 FTE, voluntary. **Finance** Sources: donations; meeting proceeds. Annual forum paid by host Red Cross Society. **Activities** Events/meetings; networking/liaising; training/education. **Events** *Annual Forum* Stockholm (Sweden) 2020, *Annual Forum* Oslo (Norway) 2019, *Annual Forum* Sofia (Bulgaria) 2018, *Annual Forum* Helsinki (Finland) 2017, *Annual Forum* Lisbon (Portugal) 2016. **Publications** Forum proceedings. **Members** Red Cross and Red Crescent Societies (26). Membership countries not specified. [2020.10.15/XM1504/F]

♦ **European network of Public Employment Services (PES network)** . . **07979**
Secretariat Unit B1, 27 Rue Joseph II, 1049 Brussels, Belgium. E-mail: empl-pes-secretariat@ec.europa.eu – office@pesnetwork.eu.
URL: https://www.pesnetwork.eu/
History Established following Decision No 573/2014/EU of *European Parliament (EP, #08146)* and *Council of the European Union (#04895)*; amended 2020 by Decision (EU) 2020/1782 to extend the period of establishment until 31 Dec 2027. Former names and other names: *European PES Network* – alias. **Aims** Encourage cooperation between member states and support their action in the field of employment; modernize and strengthen public employment services (PES); develop and implement benchlearning among PES. **Structure** Board. **Finance** Through European Union Programme for Employment and Social Innovation (EaSI). Annual budget: 3,500,000 EUR. **Activities** Knowledge management/information dissemination. **Events** *Meeting of the Advisers for European PES Affairs* Brussels (Belgium) 2021, *Board Meeting* Lisbon (Portugal) 2021, *Board Meeting* 2020, *Meeting of the Advisers of European Affairs* Brussels (Belgium) 2020, *Board Meeting* Munich (Germany) 2020. **Publications** *PES Network Newsletter* (4 a year).
Members Public Employments Services by Governments (29):
Austria, Belgium, Bulgaria, Croatia, Cyprus, Czechia, Denmark, Estonia, Finland, France, Germany, Greece, Hungary, Iceland, Ireland, Italy, Latvia, Lithuania, Luxembourg, Malta, Netherlands, Norway, Poland, Portugal, Romania, Slovakia, Slovenia, Spain, Sweden.
Regional entity:
European Commission (EC, #06633). [2021.03.01/XM7787/F*]

♦ **European Network for Qualitative Inquiry (ENQI)** **07980**
Contact KU Leuven, Parkstraat 45, 3000 Leuven, Belgium. T. +3216326220. E-mail: enqi@kuleuven.be.
URL: https://www.europeannetworkqi.org/
History 6 Feb 2017, Belgium. **Aims** Stimulate collaboration and exchange between qualitative researchers; create opportunities for networking; enhance the visibility of qualitative research projects; strengthen the level of expertise in qualitative research; increase the quality of qualitative research projects. **Structure** Steering Group; Congress Chairs. **Languages** English. **Staff** 7.00 FTE, voluntary. **Finance** Sources: revenue from activities/projects; sponsorship. **Activities** Events/meetings; financial and/or material support. **Events** *European Congress of Qualitative Inquiry* Portsmouth (UK) 2023, *Qualitative Inquiry in the Online Technological Realm* Leuven (Belgium) 2022, *European Congress Qualitative Inquiry* Tromsø (Norway) 2021, *Qualitative Inquiry towards Sustainability* St Julian's (Malta) 2020, *Qualitative Inquiry as Activism* Edinburgh (UK) 2019. **NGO Relations** Affiliated with (1): *Arts-Based Research Global Consortium (ABR, #01126).* [2022.02.08/AA2068/F]

♦ European Network for Quality Assurance in Higher Education / see European Association for Quality Assurance in Higher Education (#06183)

♦ **European Network of Railway Police Forces (RAILPOL)** **07981**
Contact Beatrixpark 8E, 7101 BN Winterswijk, Netherlands. T. +31302912912.
URL: https://www.railpol.eu/
History EU Transparency Register: 706517722882-19. **Aims** Enhance and intensify international railway police cooperation in Europe; prevent threats and guarantee effectiveness of measures against cross-border crime. **Structure** Steering Group; Working Groups; Secretariat. **Languages** English. **Activities** Knowledge management/information dissemination; events/meetings. **Events** *Conference* Budapest (Hungary) 2019, *Conference* Lisbon (Portugal) 2017, *Conference* Riga (Latvia) 2017, *Conference* Breukelen (Netherlands) 2016, *Conference* Sofia (Bulgaria) 2015.
Members Participating countries and territories (15):
Belgium, Bulgaria, Czechia, France, Germany, Great Britain, Hungary, Italy, Latvia, Netherlands, Portugal, Romania, Slovakia, Spain, Switzerland.
Associate members (2) in 1 country:
USA. [2016.07.05/XJ2451/E*]

♦ **European Network for Rare and Congenital Anaemias (ENERCA)** . . . **07982**
Head of Project Ctra de Can Ruti, Cami de les escoles s/n, 08916 Badalona, Spain. T. +34935572816. E-mail: enerca@enerca.org.
URL: http://www.enerca.org/
History Oct 2002. **Aims** Provide patients and their relatives, family and care providers with clear and concise information, in their own language, about the different rare anaemias known; facilitate *physicians* with a rapid protocol for identification and diagnosis of rare anaemias as well as appropriate treatment by specialized centres/clinicians when referral or advice is needed. **Languages** English. **Finance** Co-funded by *European Commission (EC, #06633)* – DG SANCO. **Activities** Networking/liaising; projects/programmes; events/meetings; publishing activities. **Events** *European Symposium on Rare Anaemias* Amsterdam (Netherlands) 2015, *European symposium on rare anaemias* Madrid (Spain) 2010. **Publications** Articles.
Members Institutions (12) in 7 countries:
Belgium, Cyprus, France, Germany, Italy, Portugal, Spain.
NGO Relations Member of: *EURORDIS – Rare Diseases Europe (#09175).* [2020.03.04/XM1559/**D**]

♦ **European Network on Regional Labour Market Monitoring (EN RLMM)** **07983**
Coordinator c/o IWAK, Goethe Univ, Senckenberganlage 31, 60325 Frankfurt-Main, Germany. T. +496979822152.
URL: http://regionallabourmarketmonitoring.net/
History Mar 2006, Frankfurt-Main (Germany). **Aims** Develop further and diffuse the concepts and instruments used in regional labour market monitoring; diffuse common methods for the study, research and analysis of this issue. **Activities** Events/meetings; research/documentation. **Events** *Annual Meeting* Sardinia (Italy) 2022, *Transformations of local and regional labour markets across Europe in pandemic and post pandemic times.* Timisoara (Romania) 2021, *Annual Meeting* Frankfurt-Main (Germany) 2020, *Annual Meeting* Moscow (Russia) 2019, *Annual Meeting* Exeter (UK) 2018. **Publications** *EN RLMM Newsletter* (3 a year). **Members** Experts (over) 400 in 32 countries. Membership countries not specified. [2021.03.26/XM6875/**F**]

♦ European Network of Regional Logistics Competence Centers / see European Network of Logistics Competence Centres (#07940)
♦ European Network for Regional or Minority Languages and Education / see Mercator European Research Centre on Multilingualism and Language Learning (#16719)

♦ **European Network of Registers of Wills Association (ENRWA)** **07984**
Association du Réseau Européen des Registres Testamentaires (ARERT)
Address not obtained.
URL: http://www.arert.eu/
History Current statutes adopted Jun 2012. Registered in accordance with Belgian law: 0875.868.032. **Aims** Simplify the recognition of all dematerialized exchanges between European bodies of notaries or public authorities in order to, in particular, facilitate mutual recognition and execution of successions and, to that end, create a European network linking administrators of national registers of wills. **Structure** General Assembly (annual). Steering Committee of 2 to 5 members. **Languages** English, French. **Staff** 2.00 FTE, paid. **Finance** Members' dues. Inquiry costs. **Activities** Advocacy/lobbying/activism. **Events** *European wills closing conference* Brussels (Belgium) 2010.
Members Organizations. Full in 9 countries:
Austria, Belgium, Bulgaria, France, Hungary, Italy, Portugal, Romania, Slovenia.
Observer in 6 countries:
Croatia, Latvia, Luxembourg, Netherlands, Poland, Spain.
Associate in 2 countries:
Russia, Switzerland.
Partner in 2 countries:
Estonia, Lithuania. [2018/XJ7214/**F**]

♦ **European Network on Religion and Belief (ENORB)** **07985**
Dir Rue England 113, 1180 Brussels, Belgium. E-mail: enorb@enorb.eu.
URL: http://www.enorb.eu/
History 2011. Registered in accordance with Belgian law, May 2012. **Aims** Implement EU policies on equality and fundamental rights; combat discrimination and promote mutual understanding in the field of religion and belief. **Structure** General Assembly (annual); Board. **Languages** English, French, German, Spanish. **Staff** 2.00 FTE, paid; 3.00 FTE, voluntary. **Finance** Grants from foundations; commissioned projects. **Activities** Events/meetings; knowledge management/information dissemination; advocacy/lobbying/activism; projects/programmes; publishing activities. **Events** *General Assembly* Brussels (Belgium) 2017, *General Assembly* Brussels (Belgium) 2016, *General Assembly* Brussels (Belgium) 2015, *General Assembly* Brussels (Belgium) 2014, *General Assembly* Brussels (Belgium) 2013. **Publications** *ENORB Newsletter.* Reports; occasional papers.
Members Full: Organizations (45), including the following 5 listed in this Yearbook:
Conference of European Churches (CEC, #04593); Federation of Islamic Organisations in Europe (FIOE, #09682); Hindu Forum of Europe (HFE, #10920); Human Rights without Frontiers International (HRWF, #10983); Religions for Peace (RfP, #18831).
IGO Relations *Council of Europe (CE, #04881); European Commission (EC, #06633); European Parliament (EP, #08146).* **NGO Relations** Member of *European Network against Racism (ENAR, #07862).* Close working partnerships with other EU networks. [2018.09.05/XJ7390/y/**F**]

♦ **European Network Remembrance and Solidarity (ENRS)** **07986**
Dir ul Zielna 37, 00-108 Warsaw, Poland. T. +48223957600. Fax +48223957601. E-mail: office@enrs.eu.
URL: https://enrs.eu/
History 2 Feb 2005. Founded following discussions started in 2002 between culture ministers and historians from Austria, the Czech Republic, Germany, Hungary, Poland and Slovakia. **Aims** Support the development of a common European culture of remembrance. **Structure** Advisory Board; Academic Council; Steering Committee; Secretariat. **Activities** Events/meetings; knowledge management/information dissemination; research/documentation. **Events** *Symposium* Paris (France) 2019, *Symposium of European Institutions dealing with 20th Century History* Brussels (Belgium) 2017, *Symposium* Vienna (Austria) 2015. **Publications** *ENRS Newsletter* (12 a year).
Members Full in 5 countries:
Germany, Hungary, Poland, Romania, Slovakia.
Observer in 5 countries:
Albania, Austria, Czechia, Georgia, Latvia. [2020/AA0917/**F**]

♦ **European Network for Research on Alternating Hemiplegia (ENRAH)** **07987**
Sec Postbus 10009, Forest Altitude 100, 1190 Brussels, Belgium. T. +3223258694.
URL: http://www.enrah.net/
History Apr 2003, Vienna (Austria). Registration: Austria. **Aims** Forward research on Alternating Hemiplegia in Childhood (AHC) and other related rare pediatric neurological diseases by bringing together patients and their families with competent clinicians and relevant researchers. **Structure** Steering Committee. **Languages** English. **Staff** 1.00 FTE, voluntary. **Finance** Public funding – *European Commission (EC, #06633)* projects. **Activities** Projects/programmes. **Events** *Symposium on ATP1A3 in Disease* Stockholm (Sweden) 2021, *Symposium on ATP1A3 in Disease* Reykjavik (Iceland) 2019, *Workshop* London (UK) 2009, *Workshop* Leuven (Belgium) 2008, *Workshop* London (UK) 2007. **Publications** Online newsletter.
Members Full in 10 countries:
Austria, Belgium, Czechia, France, Germany, Italy, Netherlands, Slovenia, Spain, UK.
NGO Relations Member of (2): *EGAN – Patients Network for Medical Research and Health (EGAN, #05394); EURORDIS – Rare Diseases Europe (#09175).* [2021/XM1193/**D**]

♦ **European Network of Research Ethics Committees (EUREC)** **07988**
SG DRZE, Bonner Talweg 57, 53113 Bonn, Germany. T. +4922833641930.
URL: http://www.eurecnet.org/
History 2005. Registration: Vereinsregister, Germany, Bonn. **Aims** Promote capacity building and assistance for local RECs to cooperate in the *EU* European Research Area. **Structure** General Assembly; Board; Office. **Finance** Funding from *European Commission (EC, #06633).* **Activities** Training/education; events/meetings. **Events** *Joint Conference* Barcelona (Spain) 2017.
Members Full in 24 countries:
Austria, Belgium, Czechia, Denmark, Estonia, Finland, France, Germany, Greece, Hungary, Ireland, Italy, Latvia, Lithuania, Luxembourg, Netherlands, Norway, Poland, Portugal, Romania, Slovakia, Slovenia, Spain, Switzerland.
NGO Relations Collaborates with: *European Network of Paediatric Research at the European Medicines Agency (Enpr-EMA, #07963); European Network of Research Integrity Offices (ENRIO, #07990).* Instrumental in setting up: *European Network of Research Ethics and Research Integrity (ENERI).* [2021/XM6644/**F**]

♦ European Network of Research Ethics and Research Integrity (unconfirmed)

♦ **European Network for Research in Geo-Energy (ENeRG)** **07989**
Secretariat Univ of Zagreb, Fac of Mining/Geology/Petroleum Engineering, Pierottijeva 6, HR-10000 Zagreb, Croatia. T. +38515535708. Fax +38514836053.
Pres National Institute for Marine Geology and Geoecology – GeoEcoMar, 23-25 Dimitrie Onciul Str, 024053 Bucharest, Romania. T. +4072278643 – +40748222625. Fax +40213452056.
URL: http://www.energnet.eu/
History 1993. **Aims** Promote European RTD capability in the service of Europe's geo-energy exploration and production industry and its associated service and supply sector. **Publications** *GEO ENeRGY* – newsletter.
Members Organizations (60) in 30 countries:
Albania, Austria, Bosnia-Herzegovina, Bulgaria, Croatia, Czechia, Denmark, Estonia, Finland, France, Greece, Hungary, Italy, Latvia, Lithuania, Moldova, Montenegro, Netherlands, North Macedonia, Norway, Poland, Portugal, Romania, Russia, Serbia, Slovakia, Slovenia, Spain, Türkiye, UK.
NGO Relations Associate member of: *European Energy Forum (EEF, #06986).* [2015/XJ5839/**F**]

♦ European Network for Research and Innovation in Higher Education (#18877)

♦ **European Network of Research Integrity Offices (ENRIO)** **07990**
Chair c/o National Board on Research Integrity TENK, Snellmaninkatu 13, FI-00170 Helsinki, Finland. T. +358447750796. E-mail: chair@enrio.eu – office@enrio.eu.
URL: http://www.enrio.eu/
History 2008. Founded as an informal network. Terms of reference adopted 2009. Regulations adopted 16 Jun 2010, Bern (Switzerland); last updated Feb 2016. Registration: Federale Overheidsdients Justitie, No/ID: 0758.757.160, Start date: 25 Nov 2020, Belgium, Brussels. **Aims** Enhance research integrity within Europe. **Structure** General Meeting (twice a year); Board. **Languages** English. **Finance** Sources: members' dues. **Activities** Events/meetings. **Events** *Congress on Research Integrity Practice* Helsinki (Finland) 2021, *Midyear meeting* Helsinki (Finland) 2020, *Congress on Research Integrity Practice* Helsinki (Finland) / Espoo (Finland) 2020, *Midyear Meeting* Krakow (Poland) 2019, *Midyear Meeting* Prague (Czechia) 2019.
Members Organizations in 22 countries:
Austria, Belgium, Croatia, Czechia, Denmark, Estonia, Finland, France, Germany, Greece, Ireland, Italy, Luxembourg, Netherlands, Norway, Poland, Portugal, Slovenia, Spain, Sweden, Switzerland, UK.
NGO Relations Instrumental in setting up (1): *European Network of Research Ethics and Research Integrity (ENERI).* [2021.05.19/XM6645/**F**]

♦ **European Network for Research in Organisational and Accounting Change (ENROAC)** **07991**
Contact Univ of Exeter Business School, Streatham Court, Streatham Campus – Univ of Exeter, Exeter, EX4 4ST, UK.
URL: http://business-school.exeter.ac.uk/research/areas/topics/accounting/ enroac/
History 1999. An informal network of academics, practitioners and managers. **Activities** Organizes doctoral summer schools. **Events** *Conference* Jyväskylä (Finland) 2013, *Conference* Lisbon (Portugal) 2011, *Conference* Dundee (UK) 2009, *Conference* Paris (France) 2007, *Conference* Antwerp (Belgium) 2005. [2012/XJ6220/**F**]

♦ European Network on Research Programme Applied to the Protection of Tangible Cultural Heritage – NET-HERITAGE / see NET-HERITAGE (#16978)

♦ **European Network for REsearch on SERvices (RESER)** **07992**
Pres Dept of Human and Economic Geography, Univ of Gothenburg, Box 630, SE-405 30 Gothenburg, Sweden. T. +46317861404. Fax +46317861398.
Sec DINAMIA'CET-IUL, ISCTE – Univ Inst of Lisbon, Av Forças Armadas, 1649-026 Lisbon, Portugal. T. +351217903432.
URL: http://www.reser.net/
History 1989, France, as *European Network 'Services and Space' – Réseau européen 'Services et espace' (RESER).* Also referred to as *European Association for REsearch on SERvices.* **Aims** Carry out joint research on services within the European Union; promote service activities as a focus for research; raise awareness of the network's research teams and facilitate exchange of research and information; develop net methods for *statistical* analysis and measurement of services; provide policy and economic decision makers with reports and *analyses* related to the development of services and to their role and impact. **Structure** General Assembly (annual). Council of 11 members, including President and Secretary. **Languages** English, French. **Staff** Voluntary. **Finance** Members' dues. Additional private and public funding. **Activities** Events/meetings; research/documentation; guidance/assistance/consulting; awards/prizes/competitions. **Events** *Annual Conference* Copenhagen (Denmark) 2015, *Annual Conference* Helsinki (Finland) 2014, *Annual Conference* Aix-en-Provence (France) 2013, *Annual Conference* Bucharest (Romania) 2012, *Annual conference* Hamburg (Germany) 2011. **Publications** Research papers; reports; conference proceedings; annual reviews.
Members Institutes and individuals in 18 countries:
Belgium, Denmark, Finland, France, Germany, Hungary, Ireland, Italy, Lithuania, Norway, Poland, Portugal, Romania, Slovenia, Spain, Sweden, Switzerland, UK. [2015/XF5368/**F**]

♦ **European Network for Research on Supplementary Pensions (ENRSP)** **07993**
Chair Von-Ossietzky-Strasse 41, 48151 Münster, Germany. T. +49251798354. Fax +49251798364.
Sec Univ of Coimbra, Fac of Economics, Av Dias da Silva 165, 3004-512 Coimbra, Portugal.
Secretariat KU Leuven, Fac of Law, Inst for Social Law, Blijde Inkomststraat 19 box 3409, 3000 Leuven, Belgium. T. +3216325403.
URL: https://enrsp.org/
History Jan 1994, Paris (France). Founded at international conference. Launched 19 Nov 1995. **Aims** Enable members to exchange information and provide a forum of discussion as well as a framework for scientific cooperation. **Structure** Steering Committee. **Activities** Events/meetings. **Events** *International Seminar* Coimbra (Portugal) 2022, *International Seminar* Antwerp (Belgium) 2019, *Conference* Galway (Ireland) 2018, *Conference* Poznań (Poland) 2017, *Conference* Sopot (Poland) 2016. **Publications** *Supplementary Pensions* – newsletter. *The Evolution of Supplementary Pensions* (2022) by James Kolaczkowski and Michelle Maher et al in English; *Personal Provision of Retirement Income* (2009) by Prof Jim Stewart and Prof Gerald Hughes in English; *Reforming Pensions in Europe* (2004) by Prof Gerald Hughes and Prof Jim Stewart. Conference proceedings.
Members Individuals in 16 countries:
Chile, Denmark, Finland, France, Germany, Greece, Hungary, Ireland, Italy, Netherlands, Norway, Spain, Sweden, Switzerland, UK, USA. [2022.05.06/XF4076/**F**]

♦ **European Network for Responsible Consumption** **07994**
Réseau européen pour une consommation responsable (RECR)
Coordinator Chausée de Huy 215-3, 1325 Chaumont-Gistoux, Belgium. T. +3210881840.
URL: http://www.responsibleconsumption.eu/
History Founded 2001. **Aims** Become a major force in the development of responsible consumption at the European level. **Events** *Conference* Aalborg (Denmark) 2005, *Conference* Brussels (Belgium) 2003. **Members** Organizations in 13 countries. Membership countries not specified. [2014.10.03/XM3193/**F**]

♦ European Network for Ricoeur Studies (unconfirmed)

♦ European Network for Rural Development (ENRD) 07995
Réseau européen de développement rural (REDR) – Europäische Netzwerk für die Entwicklung des ländlichen Raums (ENLR) – Rete europea per lo sviluppo rurale (RESR) – Red Europea de Desarrollo Rural (REDR)
Main Office Rue de la Loi 38, 1040 Brussels, Belgium. T. +3228013800. E-mail: info@enrd.eu.
URL: http://enrd.ec.europa.eu/
History within *European Commission (EC, #06633)*. **Aims** Help bring rural communities closer together so as to improve the implementation of the Rural Development Policy. **Structure** Assembly; Steering Group; Subgroups. **Activities** Events/meetings. **Events** *The Rural Pact Conference* Brussels (Belgium) 2022, *Assembly* Brussels (Belgium) 2021, *Seminar on Improving Data Management and Information Systems for the Purpose of Evaluation* Brussels (Belgium) 2021, *Assembly* Brussels (Belgium) 2020, *Assembly* Brussels (Belgium) 2019. **Publications** *ENRD Newsletter*. **Members** Not a membership organizations. [2019/XJ0493/**E**]

♦ European Network of Safety and Health Professional Organisations (ENSHPO) 07996
Contact IOSH, The Grange, Highfield Drive, Wigston, LE18 1NN, UK. T. +441162573100. Fax +441162573101.
URL: http://www.enshpo.eu/
History 2001. **Aims** Serve as a platform for health and safety professional organizations in Europe. **Structure** Bureau, comprising Chairman, 2 Vice-Chairmen, Treasurer and Secretariat. **Events** *Annual Meeting* Madrid (Spain) 2018, *Opportunities and challenges for OSH practitioners in Europe* Brussels (Belgium) 2005. **Members** Organizations and individuals in 15 countries:
Austria, Belgium, Cyprus, Czechia, Denmark, Finland, Germany, Ireland, Italy, Malta, Netherlands, Portugal, Spain, Switzerland, UK. [2010/XM0154/ty/**F**]

♦ European Network of Sarcoma, GIST and Desmoid Patient Advocacy Groups / see Sarcoma Patients EuroNet (#19054)

♦ European Network of School-Age Childcare (ENSAC) 07997
Coordinator Hereweg 289, 9651 AH Meeden, Netherlands. T. +31598850541 – +3159(31653738911.
History Founded 1987. **Aims** Promote equality and improve quality of life for children and young people. **Structure** Open structure with each country organizing its own national ENSAC. **Languages** Dutch, English, French, German. **Staff** 3.00 FTE, voluntary. **Finance** Conferences financed by European and national funds. **Events** *Nature, exercise and cultural education as a part of the child's comprehensive well-being* Järvenpää (Finland) 2007, *Meaningful free time – every child's right* Copenhagen (Denmark) 2005, *Conference* London (UK) 2003, *Cultural differences, role of play, school-age childcare* Belfast (UK) 1999, *Conference* Edinburgh (UK) 1998. **Publications** *ENSAC Newsletter* (12 a year).
Members Individuals and organizations in 22 countries:
Austria, Belgium, Czechia, Denmark, Finland, France, Germany, Greece, Iceland, Ireland, Italy, Luxembourg, Netherlands, Norway, Poland, Portugal, Romania, Russia, Spain, Sweden, Switzerland, UK. [2019/XF6280/**F**]

♦ European Network of Science Centres and Museums (ECSITE) 07998
Exec Dir Av Louise 89/7, 1050 Brussels, Belgium. T. +3226497383. E-mail: info@ecsite.eu.
Admin Manager address not obtained.
URL: http://www.ecsite.eu/
History 1988, Paris (France). Founded on the initiative of the 'Cité des sciences' (Paris). Former names and other names: *European Collaborative for Science, Industry and Technology Exhibitions* – former; *Association européenne des expositions scientifiques, techniques et industrielles* – former. Registration: Banque-Carrefour des Entreprises, Belgium. **Aims** Promote public engagement of science and technology by facilitating cooperation among Europe's science centres, museums and related institutions. **Structure** General Assembly (annual); Board of Directors; Head Office. **Languages** English. **Staff** 10.00 FTE, paid. **Finance** Annual budget: 1,945,000 EUR. **Activities** Events/meetings; knowledge management/information dissemination; networking/liaising. **Events** *Annual Conference* Valletta (Malta) 2023, *Annual Directors Forum* Amsterdam (Netherlands) 2022, *Annual Conference* Heilbronn (Germany) 2022, *Annual Conference* Brussels (Belgium) 2021, *Annual Directors Forum* Paris (France) 2021. **Publications** *Spokes* (12 a year) – magazine.
Members Full: European-based museums, scientific and technical centres and other associations for the dissemination of scientific and technical culture (263) in 32 countries:
Austria, Belgium, Bulgaria, Croatia, Czechia, Denmark, Estonia, Finland, France, Germany, Greece, Hungary, Iceland, Ireland, Italy, Latvia, Luxembourg, Malta, Netherlands, Norway, Poland, Portugal, Romania, Russia, Serbia, Slovakia, Slovenia, Spain, Sweden, Switzerland, Türkiye, UK.
Included in the above, 1 organization listed in this Yearbook:
Blue World Institute of Marine Research and Conservation (Institut Plavi Svijet).
NGO Relations Instrumental in setting up (1): *Science Centre World Summit*. [2022.05.05/XF1578/y/**F**]

♦ European Network of Scientists for Social and Environmental Responsibility (ENSSER) 07999
Main Office Marienstr 19/20, 10117 Berlin, Germany. T. +493020654857. E-mail: office@ensser.org.
URL: http://ensser.org/
History 27 Aug 2009. Current statutes adopted Nov 2016. Registration: Germany. **Aims** Advance public-good science and research for the protection of the environmental, biological diversity and human health against adverse impacts of new technologies and their products. **Structure** Board. **Finance** Initial funding from: *Fondation Charles Léopold Mayer pour le progrès de l'homme (FPH, #09815)*; *Sciences Citoyennes*; national organizations in Germany. **Activities** Advocacy/lobbying/activism; research/documentation. **Events** *Annual Conference* Berlin (Germany) 2014. **Publications** *ENSSER Newsletter*. [2021/XM6459/**F**]

♦ European Network of Security Professionals, Research and Industry (internationally oriented national body)
♦ European Network 'Services and Space / see European Network for REsearch on SERvices (#07992)

♦ European Network of Sign Language Teachers (ENSLT) 08000
Contact Rue de la Loi 26 / 15, 1040 Brussels, Belgium. E-mail: info@enslt.eu.
URL: https://www.enslt.eu/
History 2018, Belgium. Proposed during a conference, Oct 2013, Prague (Czech Rep). Registration: Banque-Carrefour des Entreprises, No/ID: 0697.897.182, Start date: 14 Jun 2018, Belgium. **Aims** Promote knowledge and exchange of information and experience in professional Sign Language teaching, learning and assessment; provide advice, training and support to Sign Language Teachers/Instructors; ensure for Deaf people the protection of their profession. **Structure** General Assembly; Board. **Languages** International Sign Language. **Activities** Events/meetings; guidance/assistance/consulting; knowledge management/information dissemination; training/education. **Events** *LESICO – Sign Language Teachers Conference* Edinburgh (UK) 2023, *LESICO – Sign Language Teachers Conference* Warsaw (Poland) 2021, *LESICO – Sign Language Teachers Conference* Warsaw (Poland) 2020, *LESICO – Sign Language Teachers Conference* Basel (Switzerland) 2017, *LESICO – Sign Language Teachers Conference* Paris (France) 2015. [2021.06.04/AA1624/**F**]

♦ European Network on Silica (NEPSI) 08001
Noyau Européen pour la Silice – Europäisches Netzwerk für Quarz
Secretariat c/o IMA-Europe, Twin Gardens – 6th Floor, Rue des Deux Eglises 26, 1000 Brussels, Belgium. T. +3222104410. Fax +3222104429.
URL: http://www.nepsi.eu/
History 25 apr 2006, by the Employee and Employer European sectoral associations on signing the Social Dialogue "Agreement on Workers' Health Protection Through the Good Handling and Use of Crystalline Silica and Products Containing it". **Structure** Council; Secretariat.
Members Signatories (16):
Aggregates Europe (UEPG, #00558); *Bureau international du béton manufacturé (BIBM, #03363)*; *CEMBUREAU – The European Cement Association (CEMBUREAU, #03634)*; *Council of European Employers of the Metal, Engineering and Technology-Based Industries (CEEMET, #04887)*; *European and International Federation of Natural Stone Industries (EUROROC, #07587)*; *European Association of Mining Industries, Metal Ores and Industrial Minerals (EUROMINES, #06122)*; *European Ceramic Industry Association (CERAME-UNIE, #06506)*; *European Expanded Clay Association (EXCA, #07013)*; *European Foundry Association, The (CAEF, #07352)*; *European Insulation Manufacturers Association (EURIMA, #07577)*; *European Mortar Industry Organization (EMO, #07822)*; *Fédération européenne du verre d'emballage (FEVE, #09583)*; *GlassFibreEurope (#10158)*; *Glass for Europe (#10157)*; *IndustriALL Global Union (IndustriALL, #11177)*; *Industrial Minerals Association – Europe (IMA Europe, #11179)*. [2016.02.04/XJ9099/y/**F**]

♦ European Network of Site Management Organizations / see Eurosite (#09181)
♦ European Network for SME Research / see European Network for Social and Economic Research (#08005)
♦ European Network for Smoke-Free Hospitals / see ENSH-Global Network for Tobacco Free Health Care Services (#05490)
♦ European Network for Smoke/Tobacco-Free Healthcare Services / see ENSH-Global Network for Tobacco Free Health Care Services (#05490)
♦ European Network for Smoking Prevention / see European Network for Smoking and Tobacco Prevention (#08002)

♦ European Network for Smoking and Tobacco Prevention (ENSP) ... 08002
SG Chée d'Ixelles 144, 1050 Brussels, Belgium. T. +3222306515. Fax +3222307507.
URL: http://www.ensp.org/
History Nov 1996, Brussels (Belgium), as *European Network for Smoking Prevention (ENSP) – Réseau européen pour la prévention du tabagisme (REPT)*. Registered in accordance with Belgian law: 16377/97. EU Transparency Register: 17882036839-35. **Aims** Develop a strategy for coordinated action among organizations active in tobacco control in Europe. **Structure** General Assembly (annual), comprising 1-2 representatives of each member organization. Board, consisting of President, Vice-President, Treasurer and 4 Directors. **Languages** Danish, English, French, Romanian, Spanish. **Staff** 3.00 FTE, paid. **Finance** Members' dues. Funding from *European Commission (EC, #06633)*. **Activities** Knowledge management/information dissemination; projects/programmes; advocacy/lobbying/activism; research/documentation; events/meetings; training/education. **Events** *International Conference on Tobacco Control* Bucharest (Romania) 2019, *International Conference on Tobacco Control* Madrid (Spain) 2018, *International Conference on Tobacco Control* Athens (Greece) 2017, *International Conference on Tobacco Control* Brussels (Belgium) 2016, *Annual Conference* Cascais (Portugal) 2007. **Publications** *The Network* (12 a year) – newsletter.
Members Full anti-smoking organizations in 34 countries:
Austria, Belgium, Bulgaria, Cyprus, Czechia, Denmark, Estonia, Finland, France, Georgia, Germany, Greece, Hungary, Iceland, Ireland, Israel, Italy, Latvia, Lithuania, Luxembourg, Moldova, Netherlands, Norway, Poland, Portugal, Romania, Slovakia, Slovenia, Spain, Sweden, Switzerland, Türkiye, UK, Ukraine.
Specialized networks (4):
ENSH-Global Network for Tobacco Free Health Care Services (ENSH-Global, #05490); *European Federation of Allergy and Airways Diseases Patients' Associations (EFA, #07045)*; *European Union of Nonsmokers (#09006)*; *International Network of Women Against Tobacco (INWAT, #14343)*.
IGO Relations *UNICEF (#20332)*; *WHO (#20950)*. **NGO Relations** Member of: *European Public Health Alliance (EPHA, #08297)*; *Framework Convention Alliance (FCA, #09981)*. [2016.06.17/XD5996/y/**F**]

♦ European Network for Social Action (ENSACT) 08003
Contact address not obtained. T. +4563184706. Fax +4563113232.
History Sep 2007. **Aims** Foster social professionals, teachers, lecturers, trainers and social services in innovating and strengthening their practices, concepts and theories. **Activities** Voices members on the European level; brings members together in joint conferences and expert meetings. **Events** *European Conference / Conference* Istanbul (Turkey) 2013, *European conference / Conference* Brussels (Belgium) 2011, *European conference / Conference* Dubrovnik (Croatia) 2009.
Members Organizations (7):
European Association of Schools of Social Work (EASSW, #06200); *Fédération internationale des communautés éducatives (FICE-International, #09622)*; *Formation d'éducateurs sociaux européens (FESET, #09873)*; *IFSW Europe (#11106)*; *International Association of Social Educators (#12167)*; *International Council on Social Welfare (ICSW, #13076)* (European Region); *International Federation of Social Workers (IFSW, #13544)*. [2013/XM2918/y/**E**]

♦ European Network of Social Authorities (ENSA) 08004
Social Policy Officer Av de Tervuren 67, 1040 Brussels, Belgium. T. +3227437010. Fax +3227437019.
Communications Officer address not obtained.
URL: http://www.ensa-network.eu/
History 1999, Italy, as a network of cities and European regions. **Aims** Promote international cooperation in the social field. **Structure** General Assembly; General Coordinator. **Languages** English. **Activities** Events/meetings. **Events** *Annual General Assembly* Villach (Austria) 2019, *European Conference on Prevention and Help with Addiction Disorders* Villach (Austria) 2019, *Annual General Assembly* Vänersborg (Sweden) 2018, *Annual General Assembly* Valencia (Spain) 2017, *Conference on Innovation in Care* Rotterdam (Netherlands) 2016.
Members Partners in 16 countries:
Austria, Belgium, Bulgaria, Croatia, Finland, France, Germany, Greece, Italy, Latvia, Netherlands, Norway, Romania, Spain, Sweden, UK. [2022/XJ4465/**F***]

♦ European Network for Social and Economic Research (ENSR) 08005
Réseau européen de recherche social et économique
Acting Managing Dir Panteia, PO Box 7001, 2701 AA Zoetermeer, Netherlands. T. +31793430200. E-mail: secretariat@ensr.eu.
URL: http://www.ensr.eu/
History 1990. Founded at the initiative of EIM Business and Policy Research (currently Panteia), as a network of institutes specialized in social and economic research, with a special emphasis on small and medium-sized enterprises (SMEs). Former names and other names: *European Network for SME Research (ENSR)* – former; *Réseau européen de recherche pour les PME* – former. **Aims** Carry out economic and social research for clients who are interested in policy-oriented international studies; apply sound scientific principles in rendering these services; increase the revenue of their members from international research activities; execute common international research activities that have no commercial basis, thus strengthening the academic and scientific basis of the network. **Structure** General Meeting; Executive Committee; Executive Director; Secretariat. **Languages** English. **Staff** 500.00 FTE, paid. **Finance** Sources: members' dues; revenue from activities/projects. **Activities** Knowledge management/information dissemination; networking/liaising; research/documentation. **Publications** Clients decide on publication of study reports. Most studies conducted for the European Commission published on the Commission's website.
Members Partners – national institutes specialized in social and economic research in 33 countries:
Austria, Belgium, Bulgaria, Croatia, Cyprus, Czechia, Denmark, Estonia, Finland, France, Germany, Greece, Hungary, Iceland, Ireland, Italy, Latvia, Liechtenstein, Lithuania, Luxembourg, Malta, Netherlands, Norway, Poland, Portugal, Romania, Slovakia, Slovenia, Spain, Sweden, Switzerland, Türkiye, UK. [2020.09.01/XF2798/**F**]

♦ European Network for Social and Emotional Competence (ENSEC) .. 08006
Co-Chair Univ of Rijeka, Fac of Teacher Education, Sveučilišna avenija 6, HR-51000 Rijeka, Croatia. T. +38551265830. Fax +38551584999. E-mail: ensec.europe@gmail.com.
Founding Chair Ctr for Resilience and Socio-Emotional Health, Univ of Malta, Old Humanities Bldg – Room 241, Msida, MSD 2080, Malta.
URL: http://www.enseceurope.com/
History Dec 2007. Founded following First European Conference on Social, Emotional and Behaviour Competence and Difficulties in Children and Young People, 13-15 Sep 2007, Malta. **Aims** Develop and promote evidence-based practice in social and emotional competence among school students across Europe. **Structure** Joint Chairs (2); Founding Chairs(2). *Centre for Resilience and Socio-Emotional Health (#03783)* serves as regional base. **Languages** English. **Staff** 4.00 FTE, voluntary. **Finance** Activities funded by members or through funding for projects from public bodies. **Activities** Events/meetings; knowledge management/information dissemination; networking/liaising; publishing activities; research/documentation. N **Events** *Social Emotional Learning and Positive Development* Suceava (Romania) 2022, *Well-being and social, emotional development* Budapest (Hungary) 2019, *Conference* Stockholm (Sweden) 2017, *Social and*

emotional learning and culture Lisbon (Portugal) 2015, *Social and emotional competence in a changing world* Zagreb (Croatia) 2013. **Publications** *ENSEC Newsletter*, *International Journal of Emotional Education*. Special issues in various university journals.
Members Full (over 291) in 32 countries and territories:
Austria, Belgium, Bulgaria, Croatia, Cyprus, Czechia, Denmark, Estonia, Finland, France, Georgia, Germany, Greece, Hungary, Ireland, Italy, Kosovo, Latvia, Lithuania, Malta, Netherlands, Norway, Poland, Portugal, Romania, Russia, Slovenia, Spain, Sweden, Switzerland, Türkiye, UK.
Associate (88) in 18 countries and territories:
Argentina, Australia, Barbados, Canada, Cayman Is, Egypt, Hong Kong, India, Israel, Japan, Kuwait, Lebanon, Mexico, New Zealand, Philippines, Singapore, South Africa, USA.
NGO Relations *Centre for Resilience and Socio-Emotional Health (#03783)*; national organizations.
[2022.11.09/XJ0659/**D**]

♦ European Network on Social Inclusion and Roma under the Structural Funds (EURoma) 08007

Technical Secretariat c/o Fundacion Secretariado Gitano (FSG), c/Ahijones s/n, 28018 Madrid, Spain. T. +34914220968. Fax +34914220961. E-mail: info@euromanet.eu.
URL: http://www.euromanet.eu/
History Set up following a working seminar, Jun 2007, Madrid (Spain). **Aims** Promote use of Structural Funds (SF) for inclusion of the Roma population and enhance effectiveness of policies targeting the Roma community. **Structure** Management Committee; Technical Secretariat. **Languages** English, Spanish. **Finance** Technical Assistance from Spanish European Social Fund. **Activities** Knowledge management/information dissemination; events/meetings; research/documentation; publishing activities; awareness raising. **Events** *Autumn Meeting* Madrid (Spain) 2014, *Conference* Rome (Italy) 2014, *Conference* Vienna (Austria) 2014, *Conference* Budapest (Hungary) 2009, *Conference* Stockholm (Sweden) 2009. **Publications** Analysis; guides; information and guidance mateials; position papers; recommendations; reports.
Members ESF Managing Authorities or delegated Intermediate Bodies/Implementing Authorities in 15 countries:
Austria, Belgium, Bulgaria, Croatia, Czechia, Finland, Greece, Hungary, Italy, Poland, Portugal, Romania, Slovakia, Spain, Sweden.
IGO Relations European institutions. [2016.09.27/XJ9483/**F**]

♦ European Network for Social Innovation and Solidarity (ENSIS) ... 08008

Chair ENSIS, Moorweg 28, 21337 Lüneburg, Germany. T. +4941317570495. E-mail: contact@ensis.eu.
URL: https://ensis.network
History 2014, Germany. Registration: No/ID: VR 201145, Germany; EU Transparency Register, No/ID: 523465116221-96. **Aims** Bring together local, regional, national and Europe-wide organizations within the social sector as well as not for profit initiatives, committed to a collective solidarity and wishing to develop a social Europe through programmes of social innovation. **Structure** Board; President; Regional Committees. **Languages** English, Finnish, French, German, Italian, Portuguese. **Staff** 12.00 FTE, voluntary. **Finance** Sources: members' dues. **Activities** Advocacy/lobbying/activism; capacity building; events/meetings; guidance/assistance/consulting; knowledge management/information dissemination; networking/liaising. **Publications** *ENSIS Newsletter*.
Members Organizations in 5 countries:
Belgium, France, Germany, Portugal, UK. [2021.09.02/XJ9692/**F**]

♦ European Network of Social Integration Enterprises (ENSIE) 08009

Dir Rue du Commerce 72, 1040 Brussels, Belgium. E-mail: ensie@ensie.org.
URL: http://www.ensie.org/
History 11 May 2001, Bruges (Belgium). Registration: EU Transparency Register, No/ID: 56663585277-75, Start date: 10 Feb 2011. **Aims** Strive for more inclusive and integrated forms of employment at European level; represent the interests of national and regional networks of 'Work Integration Social Enterprises' (WISEs), which are defined by three identifying pillars: promote social and professional integration of disadvantaged people; be at the core of the economic system; present a strong pedagogical dimension. **Structure** General Assembly (annual); Board of Directors; Steering Committee. **Languages** English, French. **Staff** 5.00 FTE, paid. **Finance** Annual budget: 250,000 EUR. **Activities** Advocacy/lobbying/activism; events/meetings; networking/liaising; projects/programmes. Active in EU member states, Western Balkans and EU Neighbourhood countries. **Events** *Being a WISE in 2022!* Brussels (Belgium) 2022, *General Assembly* Katowice (Poland) 2022, *Supporting Inclusive Labour Markets ? #WISEs #BuyResponsible* Brussels (Belgium) 2021, *European Conference on Political Recommendations for Fighting and Exclusion through Work Integration* Bucharest (Romania) 2019, *Conference on WISE Exchange of Good Practices* Budapest (Hungary) 2019.
Members National and regional networks (31) in 25 countries:
Austria, Azerbaijan, Belgium, Croatia, Czechia, Denmark, France, Germany, Greece, Hungary, Ireland, Italy, Latvia, Lithuania, Luxembourg, Moldova, Netherlands, Poland, Portugal, Romania, Serbia, Slovakia, Slovenia, Spain, Ukraine.
NGO Relations Member of (2): *Social Economy Europe (SEE, #19335)*; *Social Platform (#19344)*.
[2022.10.19/XF6332/**F**]

♦ European Network for Social Intelligence (ENSA) 08010

Coordination address not obtained.
Coordination address not obtained.
URL: http://www.sintelnet.eu/
Aims Examine IT-enabled domains as a means for the critical examination of basic concepts of philosophy, humanities and social sciences; propose new approaches to understand and develop future IT-enabled social situations, by adapting and applying traditional concepts. **Activities** Events/meetings; training/education. **Events** *European Conference on Social Intelligence* Barcelona (Spain) 2014.
Members Institutions (145); individuals. Institutions in 25 countries:
Belgium, Brazil, China, Colombia, Croatia, Denmark, Finland, France, Germany, Greece, Hungary, India, Ireland, Italy, Luxembourg, Malaysia, Mexico, Netherlands, Poland, Portugal, Romania, Spain, Sweden, UK, USA.
Included in the above, 2 institutions listed in this Yearbook:
Central European University (CEU, #03717); *International Islamic University Malaysia (IIUM, #13961)*.
NGO Relations *European Network for the Philosophy of the Social Sciences (ENPOSS, #07966)*.
[2015/XJ9536/y/**F**]

♦ European Network for the Sociological and Demographic Study of Divorce 08011

Address not obtained.
URL: http://www.eui.eu/Personal/Dronkers/NetworkDivorce.htm
History 2002, Florence (Italy), at 1st conference. **Aims** Bring together scholars who work empirically on this topic; form a European network for empirical and comparative research on the sociological aspects of divorce. **Structure** Informal structure. **Staff** None. **Finance** Funded by conference participants and their universities. **Events** *Conference* Tel Aviv (Israel) 2018, *Conference* Antwerp (Belgium) 2017, *Conference* Stockholm (Sweden) 2016, *Conference* Vilnius (Lithuania) 2015, *Conference* Paris (France) 2014. **Publications** Presentations. **Members** Not a membership organization. [2016/XJ6582/c/**F**]

- ♦ European Network of Specialist Centres / see European Centre of Technological Safety
- ♦ European Network of Specialist Centres / see Euro-Mediterranean Centre on Insular Coastal Dynamics (#05718)

♦ European Network of Sport Education (ENSE) 08012

Europäisches Netzwerk für Sportausbildung
Exec Dir Auf der Schmelz 6, USZ 1, 1150 Vienna, Austria. T. +431427748862. E-mail: info@sporteducation.eu.
URL: http://sporteducation.eu/
History Founded 1989, Luxembourg, as *European Network of Sport Sciences in Higher Education (ENSSHE)* – *Réseau européen des instituts de sciences du sport (REISS)*. Previously also referred to as *Réseau universitaire européen en sciences du sport*. Statutes changed and approved by General Assembly, 15 Sep 1997, London (UK); 1 Sep 2001, Budapest (Hungary); 21 Sep 2007, Rio Maior (Portugal). Subsequently changed title to *European Network of Sport Science, Education and Employment (ENSSEE)* – *Réseau européen des institutions en sciences du sport pour l'éducation et pour l'emploi (REISSE)*, 1 Sep 2001. Current statutes changed and approved, Sep 2015, when current title was also adopted. **Aims** Develop sport education in Europe. **Structure** General Assembly (every 2 years); Executive Board. **Languages** English, French, German. **Staff** Voluntary. **Finance** Members' dues. Project funding. **Activities** Research and development; events/meetings; projects/programmes; training/education. Maintains database. **Events** *Biennial Forum* Guimarães (Portugal) 2022, *Biennial Forum* Guimarães (Portugal) 2021, *Biennial Forum* Vienna (Austria) 2019, *Biennial Forum* Aarhus (Denmark) 2017, *Biennial Forum* Rome (Italy) 2015. **Publications** *Network News*. *Curriculum Development for European Physical Education Teachers*; *Mountain Guides*; *Physical Education Teachers for Secondary Schools in the EU*; *Sport Management Occupations in Europe*. Directories; reports. Information Services: Computerized database contains essential information on the Network (Luxembourg).
Members Full (18) in 7 countries:
Austria, Belgium, Czechia, Denmark, Germany, Italy, Lithuania.
Included in the above, 1 organization listed in this Yearbook:
International Council for Coaching Excellence (ICCE, #13008).
Associate members and project partners in 21 countries:
Albania, Bosnia-Herzegovina, Bulgaria, Croatia, Czechia, Denmark, Finland, France, Germany, Greece, Hungary, Ireland, Israel, Italy, Kosovo, Malta, Netherlands, Poland, Portugal, Sweden, UK.
IGO Relations Member of: *Enlarged Partial Agreement on Sport (EPAS, #05487)*; European Commission Expert Group on Human Resources abd Skills Development in Sport. [2019.06.25/XF5255/y/**F**]

- ♦ European Network of Sport Science, Education and Employment / see European Network of Sport Education (#08012)
- ♦ European Network of Sport Sciences in Higher Education / see European Network of Sport Education (#08012)
- ♦ European Network on Staff Development in Higher Education (inactive)

♦ European Network on Statelessness (ENS) 08013

Dir 16 Preston Avenue, London, E4 9NL, UK. T. +447522525673. E-mail: info@statelessness.eu.
URL: http://www.statelessness.eu/
History Registration: Charity, No/ID: 1158414, England and Wales; EU Transparency Register, No/ID: 846912240133-43, Start date: 4 Nov 2020. **Aims** Strengthen the voice of stateless persons in Europe; advocate for full respect of their human rights. **Structure** Board of Trustees; Advisory Comittee; Secretariat. **Activities** Capacity building; training/education.
Members Membership open to NGOs, academic initiatives, and individual experts (Associate). Membership countries not specified. Organizations include 3 listed in this Yearbook:
Churches' Commission for Migrants in Europe (CCME, #03912); *Equal Rights Trust (#05520)*; *European Roma Rights Centre (ERRC, #08401)*.
Consultative Status Consultative status granted from: *Council of Europe (CE, #04881)* (Participatory Status).
NGO Relations *Institute on Statelessness and Inclusion (ISI, #11295)*. [2020/XM4203/y/**F**]

♦ European Network of Steiner Waldorf Parents (ENSWaP) 08014

Contact address not obtained. E-mail: enswap@enswap.org.
URL: https://enswap.org/
History 2007. Former names and other names: *International Network of Steiner Waldorf Parents (INSWaP)* – former (2014). **Aims** Develop solidarity and understanding for a more harmonious world through Steiner Waldorf education and school communities. **Structure** Coordinating Core Group. **Activities** Events/meetings; networking/liaising. **Events** *Conference* Berlin (Germany) 2019, *Conference* Bologna (Italy) 2018.
[2020/AA0737/**F**]

♦ European Network for STI Surveillance 08015

Contact c/o ECDC, SE-171 83 Stockholm, Sweden. T. +46858601000. Fax +46858601001. E-mail: stihiv@ecdc.europa.eu – info@ecdc.europa.eu.
URL: http://ecdc.europa.eu/en/healthtopics/sti/sti-network/Pages/index.aspx
History Set up as a surveillance network of *European Centre for Disease Prevention and Control (ECDC, #06476)*. **Aims** Improve collaboration, build capacity and facilitate robust dissemination of information on *sexually transmitted* infections (STI) to inform public health policy and planning across Europe.
[2016.07.27/XJ2547/**F**]

♦ European Network for the Study of Adrenal Tumours (ENS@T) 08016

Chairperson Endocrinology UKW-ZIM, Oberdürrbacherstr 6, 97080 Würzburg, Germany. E-mail: ensatweb@gmail.com.
Sec Div of Endocrinology – Dept of Internal Medicine, Radboud Univ Medical Ctr, Geert Grooteplein Zuid 8, 6525 GA Nijmegen, Netherlands.
URL: http://www.ensat.org/
History 2002. Founded on merger of national organizations in France, Germany and Italy and teams from UK. Since 2009, a membership-based society. **Aims** Improve understanding of genetics, tumourigenesis and hypersecretion in patients with adrenal tumours and associated familial syndromes; improve prediction of recurrence and management of malignant adrenal tumours. **Structure** Steering Committee. **Languages** English. **Finance** Sources: members' dues. Supported by: *European Science Foundation (ESF, #08441)*; *European Society of Endocrinology (ESE, #08594)*; HRA Pharma; 7th Framework Programme of *European Commission (EC, #06633)*. **Activities** Awards/prizes/competitions; events/meetings; research and development; research/documentation. **Events** *Scientific Meeting* Zurich (Switzerland) 2020, *Scientific Meeting* Uppsala (Sweden) 2019, *Scientific Meeting* Florence (Italy) 2018, *Scientific Meeting* Paris (France) 2017, *Scientific Meeting* Birmingham (UK) 2016.
Members Centres in 13 countries:
Belgium, Croatia, France, Germany, Hungary, Italy, Netherlands, Poland, Portugal, Slovenia, Spain, Sweden, UK.
[2021/XJ6596/**F**]

♦ European Network for the Study of Islam and Esotericism (ENSIE) .. 08017

Coordinator Aarhus Univ, School of Culture and Society, Arab and Islam Studies, Jens Chr Skous Vej 3 – Bldg 1451 – 522, 8000 Aarhus C, Denmark. E-mail: mjrs@cas.au.dk.
URL: http://www.ensie.site/
History 2016, as a thematic network of *European Society for the Study of Western Esotericism (ESSWE, #08749)*. **Aims** Bridge the gap between the study of Islamic esotericism and mysticism and the study of Western Esotericism. **Activities** Events/meetings. **Events** *Conference* Aarhus (Denmark) 2021, *Conference* Louvain-la-Neuve (Belgium) 2020, *Conference* Venice (Italy) 2018.
Members Individuals in 7 countries:
Denmark, France, Germany, Morocco, Sweden, Türkiye, UK. [2018/XM6370/**F**]

♦ European Network for Sustainable Tourism Development (ECOTRANS) 08018

Pres Hedwig-Dohm-Str 22, 66117 Saarbrücken, Germany. T. +491755724849. E-mail: contact@ecotrans.de.
Secretariat: http://www.ecotrans.org/
History 1993, Berlin (Germany). **Aims** Advance *environmentally* and socially responsible forms of *tourism*. **Structure** Executive Committee. National working groups. **Finance** Members' dues. **Activities** Events/meetings; research/documentation. Together with *European Centre for Ecological and Agricultural Tourism (ECEAT International, inactive)* and 2 regional organizations, powers the *'European VISIT Initiative'* – for the promotion of Ecolabels and sustainable development. **Events** *Seminar on sustainable tourism in protected areas* Lisbon (Portugal) 1999. **Information Services** *ECO-TIP* – online database.
Members Active; associate. Individuals and organizations in 12 countries:
Austria, Belgium, Denmark, France, Germany, Greece, Italy, Netherlands, Portugal, Spain, Switzerland, UK.
Included in the above, 6 organizations listed in this Yearbook:
Coastal and Marine Union – EUCC (#04072); *European Travel Commission (ETC, #08943)*; *European Union Federation of Youth Hostel Associations (EUFED, #08988)*; *Global Nature Fund (GNF, #10479)*; *International Institute for Industrial Environmental Economics (IIIEE)*; *The International Ecotourism Society (TIES, #13225)*.
NGO Relations Member of: *Global Sustainable Tourism Council (GSTC, #10619)*. [2021/XF3828/y/**F**]

◆ **European Network on Teacher Education Policies (ENTEP)** 08019
Coordinator Hessische Lehrkräfteakademie, Stuttgarter Str 18-24, 60329 Frankfurt-Main, Germany. T. +6938989 ext 350.
URL: http://www.entep.eu/
History Established 23 May 2000, Loulé (Portugal), at the initiative of the Portuguese Minister of Education. **Aims** Promote cooperation among *European Union* member states regarding their teacher education policies in relation to initial, in-service and continuous professional development programmes. **Structure** Comprises one representative of the minister of education from each member state. Coordinator (elected for 4-year period) organizes ongoing work with support of Coordination Group, consisting of 5 members of ENTEP. **Languages** English. **Staff** 6.00 FTE, voluntary. **Finance** No budget. Meetings financed by hosting governments and partly by participating members' home institutions. **Activities** Events/meetings; politics/policy/regulatory. **Events** *Meeting* Ljubljana (Slovenia) 2015, *Meeting* Budapest (Hungary) 2014, *Meeting* Essen (Germany) 2014, *Meeting* Galway (Ireland) 2013, *Meeting* Wroclaw (Poland) 2012. **Publications** *Teacher Education: the Bologna Process and the Future of Teaching* (2020); *Teacher Education for Multilingual and Multicultural Settings* (2016); *The Changing Role of Teachers* (2014); *The First Ten Years after Bologna* (2010); *Strategies of Change in Teacher Education – European Views* (2002); *The Role of Graduate and Postgraduate Studies and Research in Teacher Education Reform Policies in the European Union* (2001). **Members** Representatives of the Ministers of Education of 24 countries:
Austria, Belgium, Bulgaria, Croatia, Cyprus, Czechia, Denmark, Estonia, Finland, France, Germany, Greece, Hungary, Ireland, Latvia, Lithuania, Luxembourg, Malta, Poland, Portugal, Romania, Slovakia, Slovenia, UK.
Regional organization (1), listed in this Yearbook:
European Commission (EC, #06633). [2020.02.27/XF6316/**F***]

◆ European network of teacher training institutes (#18875)

◆ **European Network of Teratology Information Services (ENTIS)** 08020
Sec Swiss Teratogen Info Service, Div de pharmacologie clinique, Centre Hosp Univ Vaudois, Rue du Bugnon 17/01/14, 1011 Lausanne VD, Switzerland. T. +41213144275.
URL: http://www.entis-org.eu/
History May 1990, Milan (Italy). **Aims** Recognize and detect risk factors so as to prevent *birth defects*; increase the efficiency of each Teratology Information Service (TIS) and contribute to the primary prevention of birth defects and developmental disorders. **Structure** Teratology Information Services. **Languages** English. **Finance** Members' dues. Annual budget: about euro 9,000. **Events** *Annual Conference* Oslo (Norway) 2019, *Annual Conference* Newcastle upon Tyne (UK) 2018, *Annual Conference* Budapest (Hungary) 2017, *Annual Conference* Berlin (Germany) 2016, *Conference* Jerusalem (Israel) 2011.
Members Centres (about 30) in 18 countries:
Argentina, Austria, Brazil, Croatia, Czechia, Denmark, Finland, Germany, Greece, Israel, Italy, Japan, Netherlands, Russia, Spain, Switzerland, Türkiye, UK. [2019.12.11/XF6983/**F**]

◆ European Network for Textile Research Organizations / see TEXTRANET (#20137)
◆ European Network Of Tissue Establishments (unconfirmed)

◆ **European Network of Trainees in Obstetrics and Gynaecology** 08021
(ENTOG)
Main Office c/o UEMS, Rue de l'Industrie 24, 1040 Brussels, Belgium. E-mail: info@entog.eu – secretariat@uems.eu.
URL: http://www.entog.eu/
History 1996, Barcelona (Spain). Founded by *European Board and College of Obstetrics and Gynaecology (EBCOG, #06357)*. A series of meetings having been organized since 1992. Registration: Belgium. **Aims** Serve as a forum for exchange of information between trainees in obstetrics and gynaecology. **Structure** Council; Executive Committee. **Languages** English. **Finance** *European Board and College of Obstetrics and Gynaecology (EBCOG, #06357)*. **Activities** Events/meetings; networking/liaising. **Events** *Meeting* Athens (Greece) 2021, *Meeting* Bergen (Norway) 2020, *Meeting* Warsaw (Poland) 2019, *Meeting* Paris (France) 2018, *Meeting* Ljubljana (Slovenia) 2017.
Members Full in 30 countries:
Austria, Belgium, Bosnia-Herzegovina, Bulgaria, Croatia, Cyprus, Czechia, Denmark, Estonia, Finland, France, Germany, Greece, Hungary, Iceland, Ireland, Italy, Latvia, Lithuania, Malta, Netherlands, Norway, Poland, Portugal, Romania, Slovakia, Slovenia, Spain, Sweden, Türkiye, UK, Ukraine. [2021/XF5735/**F**]

◆ European Network of Training Centres / see European Network of Training Organizations for Local and Regional Authorities (#08023)

◆ **European Network on Training, Evaluation and Research in Mental** 08022
Health (ENTER)
Sec Ac of Special Education, Maria Grzegorzewska Univ, Szczesliwicka Street 40, 02-353 Warsaw, Poland. T. +4775501618. Fax +4775501224. E-mail: entermentalhealth@gmail.com – ida@nlsh.no.
URL: http://www.entermentalhealth.net/
History 2000, London (UK). **Aims** Promote and defend the highest standards of mental health prevention and care in Europe. **Structure** General Meeting (annual); Steering Group. **Languages** English. **Finance** Members finance own activities. **Activities** Projects/programmes; training/education; standards/guidelines; capacity building. **Events** *Annual General Meeting* Bodø (Norway) 2019, *Conference* Bodø (Norway) 2019, *Annual General Meeting* Athens (Greece) 2018, *Annual General Meeting* St Andrews (UK) 2016, *Annual General Meeting* Dublin (Ireland) 2015.
Members Individual institutions (17) in 14 countries:
Bosnia-Herzegovina, Denmark, Finland, France, Germany, Greece, Ireland, Italy, Lithuania, Norway, Poland, Slovenia, Spain, UK. [2018.06.14/XJ3080/**F**]

◆ European Network of Training in the Management of Aggression (unconfirmed)
◆ European Network of Training Organizations / see European Network of Training Organizations for Local and Regional Authorities (#08023)

◆ **European Network of Training Organizations for Local and** 08023
Regional Authorities (ENTO)
Réseau européen des institutions de formation pour les collectivités territoriales
Pres Maison des Associations, 1a Place des Orphelins, 67000 Strasbourg, France.
URL: http://www.ento.org/
History Sep 1994. Initiated, 1988, by *Standing Conference of Local and Regional Authorities of Europe*, currently *Congress of Local and Regional Authorities of the Council of Europe (#04677)*. Current constitution adopted, 25-26 June 2002, Paris (France). Former names and other names: *European Network of Training Organizations* – former (1994); *European Network of Training Centres* – former. **Aims** Develop capacity of local and regional authorities to fulfil their roles by ensuring staff and political representatives are well trained and qualified to undertake their duties in a democratic, legal, professional and efficient manner. **Structure** General Assembly (annual); Bureau. **Languages** English, French. **Finance** Sources: members' dues; sponsorship. Supported by: *Council of Europe (CE, #04881)*. **Activities** Knowledge management/information dissemination; training/education. **Events** *ENTO Study Lab* Strasbourg (France) / *Tbilisi* (Georgia) 2019, *ENTO Study Lab* Kiev (Ukraine) 2018, *Annual Seminar and General Assembly* Liège (Belgium) 2014, *Annual Seminar and General Assembly* Seville (Spain) 2010, *Annual Seminar and General Assembly* / *Annual General Assembly and Seminar* Strasbourg (France) 2009. **Publications** *ENTO Newsletter* in English, French.
Members Organizations (22) in 12 countries:
Armenia, Belgium, Croatia, Czechia, France, Georgia, Germany, Italy, Lithuania, Poland, Switzerland, Ukraine.
NGO Relations Member of (1): *European Association for Local Democracy (ALDA, #06110)*.
[2021/XK0137/**E**]

◆ European Network for Transfer and Exploitation of EU Project Results (internationally oriented national body)

◆ **European Network of Transfusion Medicine Societies (EuroNet-** 08024
TMS) ....
Réseau européen de la transfusion sanguine
Contact address not obtained.
URL: http://www.ints.fr/EN/EuroNet_TMS.aspx
History 2002. **Aims** Allow emergence of a medical and scientific Europe in matters of blood transfusion; coordinated activities of professionals in the European Union so as to improve practices and decision-making; promote interactive exchanges of information between participants. **Structure** Coordinator; Scientific Director; Responsible International Missions; Responsible CEO Mission; representatives of each member state. **Finance** Supported by French National Institute of Blood Transfusion (INTS). **Activities** Organizes meetings. **Events** *Euro SAT : seminar for advances in transfusion* Paris (France) 2006.
Members Full in 31 countries:
Austria, Belgium, Bulgaria, Cyprus, Czechia, Denmark, Estonia, Finland, France, Germany, Greece, Hungary, Iceland, Ireland, Italy, Latvia, Lithuania, Luxembourg, Malta, Netherlands, Norway, Poland, Portugal, Romania, Slovakia, Slovenia, Spain, Sweden, Switzerland, Türkiye, UK. [2010/XM2702/**F**]

◆ **European Network for Translational Research in Ovarian Cancer** 08025
(EUTROC)
Pres Inst of Reproductive and Developmental Biology, ICL Hammersmith Campus, Du Cane Road, London, W12 0NN, UK.
Contact address not obtained.
Aims Improve the current and future management of ovarian cancer. **Structure** Steering Committee. **Activities** Research and development. **Events** *Meeting* Berlin (Germany) 2015, *Meeting* London (UK) 2014, *Symposium* / *Meeting* Liverpool (UK) 2012, *Symposium* / *Meeting* Berlin (Germany) 2011, *Meeting* Valencia (Spain) 2011. [2016.06.23/XJ5268/**D**]

◆ European Network of Transmission System Operators / see European Network of Transmission System Operators for Electricity (#08026)

◆ **European Network of Transmission System Operators for** 08026
Electricity (ENTSO-E)
Secretariat Ave de Cortenbergh 100, 1000 Brussels, Belgium. T. +3227410950. Fax +3227410951.
E-mail: info@entsoe.eu.
URL: http://www.entsoe.eu/
History Founded 1 Jul 1999, Frankfurt-Main (Germany), as *European Transmission System Operators (ETSO) – Gestionnaires européen de réseaux de transport*. Subsequently known as *European Network of Transmission System Operators (ENTSO)*. Became an international organization on 29 Jun 2001, Brussels (Belgium). Merged with 5 other TSO associations in Europe, 19 Dec 2008, namely *'Association of the Transmission System Operators of Ireland (ATSOI)', Organization of Estonian, Latvian and Lithuanian Transmission System Operators (BALTSO, inactive), Organization of the Nordic Transmission System Operators (Nordel, inactive), Union for the Coordination of Transmission of Electricity (UCTE, inactive)* and UKTSOA. Became fully operation 1 Jul 2009. Registered in accordance with Belgian law. **Aims** Set up the internal *energy* market and ensure its optimal functioning; support the European energy and climate agenda; promote the integration of a high degree of Renewables in Europe's energy system, the development of consecutive flexibility, and a much more customer centric approach; develop the most suitable responses to the challenge of a changing power system while maintening security of supply; promote regional cooperation. **Structure** Assembly; Board; Committees (4). **Languages** English. **Staff** 100.00 FTE, paid. **Finance** Members' dues. **Activities** Research/documentation. **Events** *InnoGrid Session* Brussels (Belgium) 2022, *Seminar on Cybersecurity* Brussels (Belgium) 2022, *Living the Transition Conference* Brussels (Belgium) 2021, *Seminar on Cybersecurity* Brussels (Belgium) 2021, *Workshop on Cybersecurity* Brussels (Belgium) 2020. **Publications** *Summer/Winter Outlook*. Plans; network codes; forecasts; retrospects; statistics; yearbooks.
Members Transmission System Operators (43) in 36 countries:
Albania, Austria, Belgium, Bosnia-Herzegovina, Bulgaria, Croatia, Cyprus, Czechia, Denmark, Estonia, Finland, France, Germany, Greece, Hungary, Iceland, Ireland, Italy, Latvia, Lithuania, Luxembourg, Montenegro, Netherlands, North Macedonia, Norway, Poland, Portugal, Romania, Serbia, Slovakia, Slovenia, Spain, Sweden, Switzerland, Türkiye, UK.
IGO Relations EU institutions. [2018.09.20/XD7234/y/**D**]

◆ **European Network of Transmission System Operators for Gas** 08027
(ENTSOG)
Gen Dir Av de Cortenbergh 100 – 2nd floor, 1000 Brussels, Belgium. T. +3228945100. E-mail: info@entsog.eu.
External Communication address not obtained.
Main Website: http://www.entsog.eu/
History 1 Dec 2009. Registration: EU Transparency Register, No/ID: 565032821273-72, Start date: 13 Apr 2016. **Aims** Facilitate and enhance cooperation between national gas transmission system operators (TSOs) across Europe in order to ensure the development of a pan-European transmission system in line with European Union energy goals. **Structure** General Assembly; Management Board; Working and Regional Groups. **Languages** English. **Staff** 41.00 FTE, paid. **Finance** Financial statement published in Annual Report. **Activities** Events/meetings. **Events** *Communication Protocol Workshop* Brussels (Belgium) 2014, *Refinement Workshop for the Tariff Network Code Development* Brussels (Belgium) 2014, *Tariff Network Code Kick-Off Meeting* Brussels (Belgium) 2014, *Tariff network Code Development* Brussels (Belgium) 2014, *Transparency Workshop* Brussels (Belgium) 2014. **Publications** Annual Report and Workplan; maps.
Members Full: Transmission System Operators (45) in 25 countries:
Austria, Belgium, Bulgaria, Croatia, Czechia, Denmark, Finland, France, Germany, Greece, Hungary, Ireland, Italy, Latvia, Lithuania, Luxembourg, Netherlands, Poland, Portugal, Romania, Slovakia, Slovenia, Spain, Sweden, UK.
Associate Partners (2) in 2 countries:
Estonia, Switzerland.
Observers (9) in 7 countries:
Albania, Bosnia-Herzegovina, Moldova, North Macedonia, Norway, Switzerland, Ukraine.
NGO Relations Member of (1): *European Energy Forum (EEF, #06986)*. [2022/XJ4631/**D**]

◆ **European Network for Traveller Education (ENTE)** 08028
Pres Gerresheimer Str 74, 40721 Hilden, Germany. T. +492103299994. E-mail: ente@ente.education.
Treas Balken 9, 42799 Leichlingen, Germany.
URL: http://ente.education/
History 1 Dec 2006. Registration: EU Transparency Register, No/ID: 330003938599-30, Start date: 17 Jun 2020. **Aims** Develop and coordinate the cooperation of all those concerned to guarantee the right to education of the children of travellers in Europe. **Structure** Member Assembly; Excutive Committee. **Languages** English, German. **Staff** Voluntary. **Finance** Sources: members' dues. **Activities** Training/education. **Events** *Conference* Wiesbaden (Germany) 2014, *Conference* Wiesbaden (Germany) 2012, *Conference* Wiesbaden (Germany) 2010. **Publications** *ENTE Newsletter* (2 a year).
Members Full in 4 countries:
France, Germany, Netherlands, UK. [2020/XM1260/**D**]

◆ European Network of Unesco Sites (internationally oriented national body)

◆ **European Network in Universal and Global History (ENIUGH)** 08029
Main Office Univ of Leipzig, c/o ReCentGlobe, IPF 348001, 04081 Leipzig, Germany. E-mail: headquarters@eniugh.org.
URL: https://research.uni-leipzig.de/~eniugh/
History 2002. **Aims** Foster and promote research and teaching through establishment of platforms of communication and exchange for scholars working in the field of world and global history all over Europe. **Structure** Steering Committee. **Activities** Events/meetings; publishing activities; networking/liaising. **Events** *European Congress on World and Global History* The Hague (Netherlands) 2023, *European Congress on World and Global History* Turku (Finland) 2021, *European Congress on World and Global History* Budapest (Hungary) 2017, *European Congress on World and Global History* Paris (France) 2014, *European Congress on World and Global History* London (UK) 2011. **Publications** *Comparativ* (6 a year) – journal; *Connections* – journal. *Global History and International Studies* – series. **NGO Relations** Member of: *Network of Global and World History Organizations (NOGWHISTO, #17033)*. [2021/XJ5063/**D**]

♦ European Network for Universities of Applied Sciences / see Universities of Applied Sciences Network (#20693)
♦ European Network of Universities and Companies in Information and Communication Technology / see EUNICE Network (#05590)

♦ European Network of Universities for the Implementation of the European Landscape Convention (UNISCAPE) 08030

Contact Villa Medicea di Careggi, Viale G Pieraccini 15, 50139 Florence FI, Italy. T. +39554221535. Fax +39554486511. E-mail: info@uniscape.eu.
URL: http://www.uniscape.eu/

History Jan 2008, Florence (Italy) to promote the principles and objectives of *European Landscape Convention (2000)*. **Aims** Support and reinforce interdisciplinary cooperation within and among European universities regarding landscape issues, especially in the areas of research and education. **Structure** General Assembly (annual). Executive Board, comprising President, 2 Vice-Presidents, Director and 7 members. **Events** *Joint Conference* Ås (Norway) 2019, *General Assembly* Oslo (Norway) 2015, *International Conference on Defining Landscape Democracy* Oslo (Norway) 2015, *International Conference on Landscape and Imagination* Paris (France) 2013, *Careggi Seminar on the Role of Soundscapes in a Biocultural Perspectives* Florence (Italy) 2012.
Members Universities (50) in 8 countries:
Belgium, France, Italy, Netherlands, Portugal, Slovakia, Slovenia, Spain.
Consultative Status Consultative status granted from: *Council of Europe (CE, #04881)* (Participatory Status).
NGO Relations Together with *Civilscape (#03966)* and *European Network of Local and Regional Authorities for the Implementation of the European Landscape Convention (RECEP-ENELC, #07939)*, constitutes *European Landscape Network (Eurolandscape, #07644)*. [2010/XJ1802/**E**]

♦ European Network of Users and Ex-Users in Mental Health / see European Network of ex- Users and Survivors of Psychiatry (#07906)
♦ European Network of Utilitarian Scholars (internationally oriented national body)
♦ European Network of Victims of Terrorism / see Network of Associations of Victims of Terrorism (#16998)

♦ European Network for Visual Literacy (ENViL) 08031

Chairman address not obtained.
URL: http://envil.eu/

History 2010. Founded as a network of European curriculum developers, researchers and teachers trainers for all school subjects related to visual art / visual literacy. **Aims** Provide a platform for all persons interested in research and curriculum development in the domain of visual literacy/art education in European education. **Structure** Governing Board; Working Groups. **Languages** English. **Staff** None. **Finance** No structural financial support. **Activities** Events/meetings; knowledge management/information dissemination; publishing activities; research and development. **Events** *Meeting* Salzburg (Austria) 2019, *Meeting* Paris (France) 2018, *Meeting* Budapest (Hungary) 2016, *Meeting* Leuven (Belgium) 2016. **Publications** *Newsletter. Common European Framework of Reference for Visual Literacy – Prototype* (2016) by E Wagner and D Schönau.
Members Individuals (180) in 23 countries:
Austria, Belgium, China, Cyprus, Czechia, Denmark, Finland, France, Germany, Greece, Hungary, Ireland, Japan, Latvia, Malta, Netherlands, Portugal, Slovenia, Spain, Sweden, Switzerland, UK, USA. [2022/XJ9649/**F**]

♦ European Network on Volunteer Development (ENDOV) 08032

Dir Volunteer Mobilisation c/o British Red Cross, 44 Moorfields, London, EC2Y 9AL, UK. T. +442078777000.
URL: http://www.rcvolunteering.org/

History Founded by *International Federation of Red Cross and Red Crescent Societies (#13526)*, as *Western European Network on Volunteer Development (WENDOV)*. **Aims** Share knowledge and discuss trends on volunteering in Europe. **Languages** English. **Staff** None. **Finance** Self-financing. **Activities** Networking/ liaising; events/meetings. **Events** *Meeting* Budapest (Hungary) 2009.
Members National Red Cross Societies in 32 countries:
Andorra, Armenia, Austria, Belgium, Bulgaria, Denmark, Estonia, Finland, France, Germany, Greece, Hungary, Iceland, Ireland, Italy, Latvia, Liechtenstein, Lithuania, Luxembourg, Malta, Monaco, Netherlands, North Macedonia, Norway, Poland, Portugal, Russia, Slovenia, Spain, Sweden, Switzerland, UK.
NGO Relations *Red Cross EU Office (#18643)*. [2019.06.28/XM1507/**F**]

♦ European Network of Wine Cities (#18881)
♦ European Network of Wine Growing Towns / see Réseau Européen des Villes du Vin (#18881)

♦ European Network of Women with Disabilities 08033

Contact Weibernetz, Samuel Beckett Anlage 6, 34119 Kassel, Germany. T. +4956172885310. Fax +49561728852310. E-mail: info@weibernetz.de.
URL: http://www.weibernetz.de/english.html

History 4 May 2007, Berlin (Germany). [2015/XM8270/**D**]

♦ European Network for Women in Leadership (WIL) 08034

Gen Manager 163 bd Malesherbes, 75017 Paris, France. T. +33183648325. E-mail: contact@ wileurope.org.
URL: http://www.wileurope.org/

History 2008, as an informal network at the initiative of Microsoft, *INSEAD (#11228)* and Women's Forum gathering high level women from EU countries. Registered in accordance with French law, 2010. **Aims** Promote and advance the professional and social interests of women in leadership positions across Europe. **Structure** Board of Directors; Executive Committee. **Languages** English. **Activities** Events/meetings; research/documentation; networking/liaising. **Events** *Meeting* Athens (Greece) 2015, *Half-Yearly Meeting* Madrid (Spain) 2014. **Publications** *WIL Newsletter* (9 a year). [2017.12.11/XJ9539/**F**]

♦ European Network of Women's Organisations in Fisheries and Aquaculture (AKTEA) 08035

Réseau européen des organisations de femmes de la pêche et de l'aquaculture
Chairperson address not obtained. E-mail: contact@akteaplatform.eu.
URL: http://akteaplatform.eu/

History 'AKTEA' derives from the name of the Nereid in Greek mythology which symbolizes the shore. **Structure** Board, comprising President, Vice-President, Secretary, Treasurer and 1 member. **Languages** English, French.
Members Full in 8 countries:
France, Greece, Ireland, Italy, Netherlands, Portugal, Spain, UK.
NGO Relations Cooperates with (1): *Low Impact Fishers of Europe (LIFE, #16517)*. [2021/XM8269/**D**]

♦ European Network for the Work with Perpetrators of Domestic Violence (WWP EN) 08036

Exec Dir Leunaer Str 7, 12681 Berlin, Germany.
URL: https://www.work-with-perpetrators.eu/

History 2014. Registration: No/ID: VR 6150, Germany; EU Transparency Register, No/ID: 792079038216-17, Start date: 19 May 2020. **Aims** Prevent violence in close relationships as a gender-based phenomenon; foster gender equality. **Structure** Annual General Assembly; Board. **Activities** Advocacy/lobbying/activism; awareness raising; capacity building; events/meetings; knowledge management/information dissemination; standards/guidelines; training/education.
Members Full (about 65) in 31 countries:
Albania, Austria, Belgium, Bosnia-Herzegovina, Bulgaria, Croatia, Cyprus, Czechia, Estonia, Finland, France, Georgia, Germany, Greece, Ireland, Italy, Kosovo, Malta, Moldova, Netherlands, Norway, Poland, Romania, Russia, Serbia, Slovakia, Slovenia, Spain, Sweden, Switzerland, UK.
European Family Justice Center Alliance (EFJCA, #07029). [2022.02.09/AA0255/**F**]

♦ European Network for Workplace Health Promotion (ENWHP) 08037

Pres Westfeld 68, 58730 Fröndenberg, Germany. T. +492378866549. E-mail: info@enwhp.net.
Contact Univ of Perugia, Piazza Lucio Severi 1, Edificio D Piano 0, 06129 Perugia PG, Italy.
URL: http://enwhp.net

History 1995. Registration: Start date: 2016, Italy. **Aims** Promote health in the workplace in Europe. **Structure** Advisory Committee; Secretariat; National Contact Office (NCO) in each member state. **Languages** English. **Finance** 70% funded by *European Commission (EC, #06633)*. Annual budget: euro 250,000. **Activities** Politics/policy/regulatory; monitoring/evaluation; networking/liaising; events/meetings. **Events** *Conference* Brussels (Belgium) 2013, *European Conference* Berlin (Germany) 2011, *Annual European employment week* Brussels (Belgium) 2009, *International conference on health promoting hospitals and health services* Hersonissos (Greece) 2009, *Conference / European Conference* Perugia (Italy) 2009. **Publications** *WHP-NET-NEWS* (2 a year). Annual Report; meeting reports; project reports; policy documents and declarations.
Members Organizations in 28 countries:
Austria, Belgium, Bulgaria, Cyprus, Czechia, Denmark, Estonia, Finland, France, Germany, Greece, Hungary, Iceland, Ireland, Italy, Latvia, Lithuania, Luxembourg, Netherlands, Norway, Poland, Portugal, Romania, Slovakia, Slovenia, Spain, Sweden, UK.
IGO Relations Cooperates with: *European Agency for Safety and Health at Work (EU-OSHA, #05843)*; *European Foundation for the Improvement of Living and Working Conditions (Eurofound, #07348)*; *ILO (#11123)*; *WHO (#20950)*. **NGO Relations** Cooperates with: *EuroHealthNet (#05693)*; *European Network for Mental Health Promotion (ENMHP, inactive)*. [2020.01.14/XF5793/**F**]

♦ European Network of Young Opera Friends / see European Association of Young Opera Friends (#06282)

♦ European Network of Young Specialists in Sport Psychology (ENYSSP) 08038

Pres address not obtained.
URL: https://www.enyssp.com/

History Jul 2003, Copenhagen (Denmark), at 1st General Assembly at the XIth European Congress for Sport Psychology. **Aims** Promote and disseminate knowledge in the field of sport and exercise psychology in the areas of research, education and applied work. **Structure** General Assembly. Managing Council, comprising President, Secretary-General, Treasurer and Past Coordinator. Departments (3): Research; Applied; Education. **Languages** English. **Activities** Collaborates with other governing bodies interested in Sport and Exercise Psychology; coordinates European links between young researchers, educators and professional practitioners; promotes and facilitates a cross-national cooperation for research, education and applied work in the field; encourages young researchers and professionals in the field to enhance the quality of their work; disseminates information; supports the development and standardization of official degrees in Sport and Exercise Psychology within Europe; promotes Sport and Exercise Psychology in sport and exercise governing bodies, sport federations and clubs, health and rehabilitation centres, etc; promotes Sport and Exercise Psychology as an independent branch of study, which intercepts sport science and psychology but is not dependent of any of them. Organizes: meeting (every 4 years, at FEPSAC Congress); workshops. **Events** *Conference* Ghent (Belgium) 2021, *Conference* Ghent (Belgium) 2020, *Conference* Zagreb (Croatia) 2018, *Conference* Bratislava (Slovakia) 2017, *Annual Workshop* Girona (Spain) 2015.
Members Full in 20 countries:
Belgium, Czechia, Denmark, Finland, Germany, Greece, Hungary, Ireland, Italy, Latvia, Lithuania, Netherlands, Portugal, Russia, Slovakia, Spain, Sweden, Switzerland, UK, Ukraine.
NGO Relations Member of: *European Federation of Sport Psychology (#07218)*. [2020/XJ0897/**F**]

♦ European Neural Network Society (ENNS) 08039

Treas Univ of Lausanne, Internef 138-2, Quartier UNIL Chamberonne, 1015 Lausanne VD, Switzerland. T. +41216923587. E-mail: secretary@e-nns.org.
URL: http://www.e-nns.org/

History 1991, Helsinki (Finland). Founded at 1st International Conference on Artificial Neural Networks. **Aims** Provide an interdisciplinary network for researchers coming from different disciplinary backgrounds with a common interest in the study of artificial and biological neural networks. **Structure** General Assembly; Executive Committee. **Languages** English. **Staff** 7.50 FTE, voluntary. **Finance** Sources: members' dues. **Activities** Awards/prizes/competitions; events/meetings. **Events** *International Conference on Industrial, Engineering and Other Applications of Applied Intelligent Systems* Kitakyushu (Japan) 2022, *ICANN: International Conference on Artificial Neural Networks* Bratislava (Slovakia) 2021, *ICANN: International Conference on Artificial Neural Networks* Bratislava (Slovakia) 2020, *ICANN : Annual International Conference on Artificial Neural Networks* Munich (Germany) 2019, *ICANN : Annual International Conference on Artificial Neural Networks* Rhodes Is (Greece) 2018. **Publications** *ENNS Newsletter*, *Neural Networks*.
Members Individuals in 26 countries:
Austria, Belgium, Canada, Croatia, Denmark, Finland, France, Germany, Greece, Israel, Italy, Japan, Netherlands, New Zealand, Norway, Poland, Romania, Serbia, Slovakia, Slovenia, Spain, Sweden, Switzerland, Türkiye, UK, USA.
NGO Relations Journal co-published with: jointly with *International Neural Network Society (INNS)* and Japanese national society. [2020/XD3441/v/**D**]

♦ European Neuroendocrine Association (ENEA) 08040

Association européenne de neuroendocrinologie (AENE)
Contact EndoScience Service, Hopfengartenweg 18, 90518 Altdorf, Germany. T. +4991879742411. Fax +4991879742471. E-mail: then@endoscience.de.
URL: http://www.eneassoc.org/

History 1984. **Aims** Promote development of basic research and clinical investigation in the field of neuroendocrinology; disseminate knowledge of neuroendocrine physiology, pathophysiology and therapeutics. **Structure** Executive Committee, comprising President, Secretary, Treasurer and 10 members. **Languages** English. **Staff** 0.50 FTE, paid. **Finance** Members' dues. **Activities** Organizes Scientific Meeting (every 2 years). Awards prizes. **Events** *Congress* Lyon (France) 2022, *Congress* Porto (Portugal) 2020, *Congress* Wroclaw (Poland) 2018, *Congress* Milan (Italy) 2016, *Congress* Sofia (Bulgaria) 2014. **Publications** Conference proceedings.
Members Ordinary; Associate; Affiliate; Honorary. Members in 36 countries:
Australia, Austria, Azerbaijan, Belgium, Brazil, Bulgaria, Canada, Croatia, Czechia, Denmark, Finland, France, Germany, Greece, Hungary, Ireland, Israel, Italy, Malta, Mexico, Netherlands, Norway, Pakistan, Poland, Portugal, Romania, Russia, Saudi Arabia, Serbia, Slovenia, Spain, Sweden, Switzerland, Türkiye, UK, USA.
NGO Relations Member of: *European Society of Endocrinology (ESE, #08594)*. Working relations with national groups/societies and with major drug companies. [2014/XD2151/v/**D**]

♦ European Neuroendocrine Tumor Society (ENETS) 08041

Coordinating Office Langenbeck-Virchow-Haus, Luisenstr 58/59, 10117 Berlin, Germany. T. +4930994045340. Fax +4930994045349. E-mail: office@enets.org – info@enets.org.
URL: http://www.enets.org/

History 11 Mar 2004, Frankfurt-Main (Germany). Registration: Amtsgericht, No/ID: VR 23838 B, Germany, Charlottenburg. **Aims** Promote research in the field of diagnosis and therapy of neuroendocrine tumour disease. **Structure** General Assembly (annual). Executive Committee, comprising Chairman, Vice-Chairman, Chairman-Elect, Treasurer, Scientific Secretary and 4 members. Advisory Board. Task Forces. Coordinating Office, based in Berlin (Germany). **Languages** English. **Staff** 5.00 FTE, paid. **Finance** Members' dues. Support from pharmaceutical industry. **Activities** Develops diagnosis and treatment guidelines. Organizes annual conference and expert consensus meetings. Established Centres of Excellence. Currently developing patient registry and matrix for international clinical trials. **Events** *Annual Conference* Barcelona (Spain) 2022, *Annual Conference* Berlin (Germany) 2021, *ENETS Conference for the Diagnosis and Treatment of Neuroendocrine Tumor Disease* Berlin (Germany) 2020, *Annual Conference* Barcelona (Spain) 2019, *Annual Conference* Barcelona (Spain) 2018. **Publications** *ENETS Newsletter*, *Neuroendocrinology* – official journal. *Virchows Archiv*. **Members** Physicians and researchers (about 2,000). Membership countries not specified.
NGO Relations Member of: *European Society of Endocrinology (ESE, #08594)*. [2021/XM2746/**D**]

♦ European Neurological Society (inactive)

♦ European Neuromuscular Centre (ENMC) 08042

Centre neuromusculaire européen
Man Dir Lt Gen van Heutszlaan 6, 3743 JN Baarn, Netherlands. T. +31355480481. Fax +31355480499. E-mail: enmc@enmc.org.

URL: http://www.enmc.org/
History 1989, Paris (France), with the name *European Neuromuscular Centre for the Coordination of Medical and Scientific Affairs*, as a joint venture of *European Alliance of Neuromuscular Disorders Associations (EAMDA, #05876)* and the 'Association française contre les myopathies (AFM)'. Became an independent foundation in Nov 1992. **Aims** Promote scientific research on causes, *prevention* and treatment of neuromuscular *diseases*; stimulate and facilitate top-level scientific collaboration; collect and circulate information. **Structure** Executive Committee; Research Committee; Secretariat in Baarn (Netherlands); Research Manager. **Staff** 4.00 FTE, paid. **Activities** Financial and/or material support; knowledge management/information dissemination; research/documentation. **Events** European workshop on Emery-Dreifuss muscular dystrophy Baarn (Netherlands) 1991, *European workshop on the genetics of hereditary motor and sensory neuropathies* Baarn (Netherlands) 1991, *European workshop on new mutations and germline mosaicism in Duchenne muscular dystrophy* Groningen (Netherlands) 1991. **Publications** *Diagnostic Criteria for Neuromuscular Disorders* by Alan E H Emery; *Neuromuscular Disorders: Clinical and Molecular Genetics* by Alan E H Emery; *Who's Who in Neuromuscular Disorders in ENMC*. Annual Report; workshop reports. **Information Services** *Databank of Epidemiological Information*.
Members Full in 8 countries:
Denmark, Finland, France, Germany, Italy, Netherlands, Switzerland, UK.
NGO Relations Member of: *TREAT-NMD Neuromuscular Network (TREAT-NMD, #20231).* [2016/XE1359/**E**]

♦ European Neuromuscular Centre for the Coordination of Medical and Scientific Affairs / see European Neuromuscular Centre (#08042)

♦ European Neuro-Ophthalmological Society (EUNOS) 08043
Treas UniversitätsSpital Zürich, Frauenklinikstr 24, 8091 Zurich ZH, Switzerland. T. +41442554900. Fax +41442554349. E-mail: synapse@eunosweb.eu.
Pres Dept of Neuro-Ophthalmology, National Hosp for Neurology and Neurosurgery, Queen Square, London, WC1N 3BG, UK.
URL: http://www.eunosweb.eu/
History 1993. Founded by Professors Huber and Neetens. An informal organization. Former names and other names: *European Neuro-Ophthalmologists Society (EUNOS)* – former. **Aims** Extend knowledge and promote collaboration between neuro-ophthalmologists and *vision* scientists in Europe and elsewhere. **Structure** Council; Executive Board. **Languages** English. **Staff** 5.00 FTE, voluntary. **Finance** Sources: contributions. **Activities** Events/meetings; training/education. **Events** *Meeting* Porto (Portugal) 2019, *Meeting* Budapest (Hungary) 2017, *Meeting* Ljubljana (Slovenia) 2015, *Practical Neuro-Ophthalmology Meeting* Zurich (Switzerland) 2014, *Meeting* Oxford (UK) 2013. **Members** Physicians and researchers interested in neuro-ophthalmology. Membership countries not specified. [2023.02.14/XD4362/**D**]

♦ European Neuro-Ophthalmologists Society / see European Neuro-Ophthalmological Society (#08043)

♦ European Neuropeptide Club (ENC) 08044
SG TAU Sackler School of Med, Sackler Bldg Rm 727, Ramat Aviv, Israel.
Pres address not obtained.
URL: http://www.tau.ac.il/~igozes/enc/
History 1989. **Aims** Improve neuropeptide research in Europe. **Structure** Committee, comprising Chair, Vice-Chair, Secretary and Treasurer. **Finance** Meeting benefits. **Activities** Annual meeting; winter conference; training courses for young scientists. **Events** *Annual Meeting / Annual Conference* London (UK) 2012, *Annual Meeting / Annual Conference* Cambridge, MA (USA) 2011, *Annual Meeting* Cambridge, MA (USA) 2011, *Annual meeting / Annual Conference* Pécs (Hungary) 2010, *Annual Conference* Salzburg (Austria) 2009. **Publications** *ENC Newsletter*.
Members Individuals (over 500) in 30 countries and territories:
Australia, Austria, Belarus, Belgium, Bulgaria, Croatia, Denmark, Estonia, Finland, France, Germany, Greece, Hong Kong, Hungary, Israel, Italy, Japan, Latvia, Netherlands, New Zealand, Norway, Poland, Russia, Serbia, Spain, Sweden, Switzerland, UK, Ukraine, USA.
NGO Relations Member of: *International Neuropeptide Society (INPS, #14355).* [2012.08.02/XF1592/v/**F**]

♦ European Neuroscience Association (inactive)

♦ European Neutron Scattering Association (ENSA) 08045
Chairman EPFL SB IPHYS LQM, PH D2 435 – Bât PH, Station 3, 1015 Lausanne VD, Switzerland. T. +41216930329. E-mail: henrik.ronnow@epfl.ch.
Registered Office Gupfenstr 18A, 8166 Niederweningen ZH, Switzerland.
URL: http://www.neutrons-ensa.eu/
History 13 Dec 1994, Madrid (Spain). Registered in accordance with Swiss Civil Code, 21 Feb 2007. **Aims** Provide a platform for discussion and a focus for action in neutron scattering and related topics in Europe. **Structure** Committee; Board. **Languages** English. **Finance** No regular financial allocations. Costs associated with a delegate participating in an ENSA Committee meeting usually met by the delegate or his/her nominating body. **Activities** Awards/prizes/competitions; events/meetings. **Events** *ECNS : European Conference on Neutron Scattering* St Petersburg (Russia) 2019, *ECNS : European Conference on Neutron Scattering* Saragossa (Spain) 2015, *Meeting* Berlin (Germany) 2012, *Meeting* Dubna, Tula (Russia) 2012, *Meeting* Athens (Greece) 2011. **Publications** Surveys.
Members National societies and committees (" indicates observers) in 22 countries:
Austria, Belgium, Czechia, Denmark, France, Germany, Greece, Hungary, Italy, Latvia (*), Netherlands, Norway, Poland, Portugal (*), Romania, Russia, Slovakia, Spain, Sweden, Switzerland, UK, Ukraine (*).
NGO Relations Founding member of: *European Materials Forum (EMF, #07751).* [2019/XD6110/**D**]

♦ European New Car Assessment Programme (EURO NCAP) 08046
SG Mgr Ladeuzeplein 10, 3000 Leuven, Belgium. T. +3224007740. Fax +3224007741. E-mail: info@euroncap.com.
URL: http://www.euroncap.com/
History Formal inauguration, Dec 1996. Previous French title *Programme européen pour l'évaluation d'automobiles neuves*. Registered in accordance with Belgian law. Also referred to as *EuroNCAP*. **Aims** Assess new car *safety*. **Structure** General Assembly (annual); Council. **Languages** English. **Staff** 12.00 FTE, paid. **Events** Press conference Paris (France) 2000.
Members Government departments and consumer groups in 7 countries:
France, Germany, Luxembourg, Netherlands, Spain, Sweden, UK.
International consumer groups (2):
Fédération Internationale de l'Automobile (FIA, #09613); *International Consumer Research and Testing (ICRT, #12931).*
NGO Relations Affiliated to: *Global New Car Assessment Programme (Global NCAP, #10506).* Sister programme: *European Road Assessment Programme (EuroRAP, #08392).* Member of: *eSafetyAware (#05533).* [2019.06.19/XD6943/**F**]

♦ European News Exchange (ENEX) 08047
Managing Dir Bd Pierre Frieden 43, L-1543 Luxembourg, Luxembourg. T. +352421423101. E-mail: administration@enex.tv.
URL: http://www.enex.tv/
History 1994. Merged 1996 with the *NEWS Consortium*. **Aims** Exchange news footage between *television broadcasters* worldwide; organize pool operations for coverage of big events. **Structure** General Assembly; Executive Committee. **Languages** English. **Staff** 14.00 FTE, paid. **Finance** Sources: members' dues. **Activities** Networking/liaising. **Events** *General Assembly* Abu Dhabi (United Arab Emirates) 2022, *General Assembly* Willemstad (Curaçao) 2021, *General Assembly* 2020, *General Assembly* Lisbon (Portugal) 2019, *General Assembly* Berlin (Germany) 2014.
Members Television channels in 51 countries and territories:
Argentina, Aruba, Australia, Austria, Belgium, Bolivia, Bosnia-Herzegovina, Bulgaria, China, Colombia, Croatia, Curaçao, Czechia, Denmark, Dominican Rep, Ecuador, England, Finland, France, Germany, Greece, Honduras, Hungary, Iraq, Ireland, Israel, Italy, Japan, Jordan, Luxembourg, Mexico, Netherlands, Norway, Panama, Paraguay, Poland, Portugal, Puerto Rico, Romania, Russia, Serbia, Slovakia, Slovenia, Spain, Sweden, Türkiye, UK, Ukraine, United Arab Emirates, Uruguay, USA. [2022.10.20/XF6798/**F**]

♦ European Newspaper Publishers' Association (ENPA) 08048
Association européenne des éditeurs de journaux
Main Office Rue de Namur 73A, 1000 Brussels, Belgium. T. +3225360600. Fax +3225510199. E-mail: enpa@enpa.eu.
URL: http://www.enpa.eu/
History 1960, Garmisch-Partenkirchen (Germany). Former names and other names: *EEC Community of Associations of Newspaper Publishers* – former; *Communauté des associations d'éditeurs de journaux de la CEE* – former; *Gemeinschaft der Zeitungsverlegerverbände der EWG* – former; *Comunità delle Federazioni di Editori di Giornali della CEE* – former; *Gemeenschap van Verenigingen van Krantenuitgevers in de EEG* – former. Registration: Banque-Carrefour des Entreprises, No/ID: 0442.953.666, Start date: 18 Oct 1991; EU Transparency Register, No/ID: 5950962136-12, Start date: 4 Jul 2008. **Aims** Advocate the interests of the European newspaper publishing sector towards European and international institutions, on all platforms, from printed editions to the digital environment; ensure a legislative environment in which the newspaper industry can develop a successful and sustainable future. **Structure** General Assembly (twice a year); Board; Committees; Secretariat, headed by Executive Director. **Languages** English, French. **Staff** 5.00 FTE, paid. **Finance** Sources: members' dues. **Activities** Events/meetings. **Events** *Conference on Press Freedom in a Digital World* Brussels (Belgium) 2016, *General Assembly* Brussels (Belgium) 2016, *General Assembly* Amsterdam (Netherlands) 2015, *General Assembly* Brussels (Belgium) 2015, *The Future of Press in Europe Congress* Brussels (Belgium) 2011. **Publications** *Copyright in the EU Digital Single Market*; *ENPA 10 Action oint for a Free, Independent and Sustainable Press in Europe*.
Members Associations of newspaper publishers in 14 countries:
Austria, Belgium, Bulgaria, Croatia, Czechia, France, Germany, Greece, Italy, Luxembourg, Poland, Serbia, Slovakia, Switzerland.
Associate member:
Association for the Promotion of the International Circulation of the Press (DISTRIPRESS, #02876).
Consultative Status Consultative status granted from: *World Intellectual Property Organization (WIPO, #21593)* (Permanent Observer Status). **NGO Relations** Member of (6): *Creative Media Business Alliance (CMBA, #04947)*; *European Advertising Standards Alliance (EASA, #05829)*; *European Interactive Digital Advertising Alliance (EDAA, #07582)*; *International Federation of Reproduction Rights Organizations (IFRRO, #13527)*; *News Media Coalition (NMC, #17093)*; *World Association of Newspapers and News Publishers (WAN-IFRA, #21166).* Cooperates with (1): *Search and Information Industry Association (Siinda, #19188).* [2023.02.20/XE0496/y/**D**]

♦ European NF Meeting (meeting series)

♦ European NGO Alliance for Child Safety Online (eNACSO) 08049
Coordinator Save the Children Italy Onlus, Via Volturno 58, 00185 Rome RM, Italy.
Twitter: https://twitter.com/enacso
Aims Promote and support actions at national, European and international level to protect children and promote their rights in relation to the Internet and new technologies.
Members Full in 18 countries:
Belgium, Czechia, Denmark, Estonia, Finland, France, Germany, Greece, Hungary, Ireland, Lithuania, Luxembourg, Netherlands, Norway, Poland, Portugal, Romania, Spain.
Associate in 6 countries:
Armenia, Czechia, Germany, Russia, Switzerland, Türkiye, Ukraine.
IGO Relations Participant in Fundamental Rights Platform of: *European Union Agency for Fundamental Rights (FRA, #08969).* [2016/XJ6208/**D**]

♦ European NGO Confederation for Relief and Development (#04547)
♦ European NGO Council on Drugs / see European Coalition for Just and Effective Drug Policies (#06596)
♦ European NGO Council on Drugs and Development / see European Coalition for Just and Effective Drug Policies (#06596)

♦ European NGO Network on Genetic Engineering (GENET) 08050
Contact address not obtained. E-mail: coordination@genet-info.org.
URL: http://www.genet-info.org/
History 1995. Current statutes adopted, 24 Oct 1999, Madrid (Spain). Registration: Swiss Civil Code, Start date: 1999, Switzerland. **Aims** Provide information on genetic engineering; coordinate members' activities. **Structure** Assembly (at least annual). Board of 5 to 6 members. **Languages** English. **Staff** 1.00 FTE, paid. **Finance** Sources: grants; members' dues. **Activities** Events/meetings. **Events** *Conference* Brussels (Belgium) 2012, *Conference* Brussels (Belgium) / Ghent (Belgium) 2010, *Conference* Lucerne (Switzerland) 2009, *Planet Diversity : world congress on the future of food and agriculture* Bonn (Germany) 2008, *GMO-Free Europe Conference* Brussels (Belgium) 2007. **Publications** *GENET-News*.
Members Organizations (40) in 21 countries:
Albania, Austria, Belgium, Bulgaria, Estonia, France, Georgia, Germany, Greece, Hungary, Italy, Luxembourg, Netherlands, North Macedonia, Norway, Portugal, Slovenia, Spain, Sweden, Switzerland, UK.
Included in the above, 3 organizations listed in this Yearbook:
Friends of the Earth International (FoEI, #10002); *Greenpeace International (#10727)*; *IFOAM – Organics International (IFOAM, #11105).*
NGO Relations Partner of (2): *Friends of the Earth Europe (FoEE, #10001)*; *IFOAM Organics Europe (#11104).* [2013.09.19/XM3419/y/**D**]

♦ European NGO Platform Asylum and Migration (EPAM) 08051
Contact c/o CCME, Rue Joseph II 174, 1000 Brussels, Belgium.
Contact c/o MPG, Rue Belliard 205, Box 1, 1040 Brussels, Belgium.
Contact c/o ECRE, Rue Royal 146, 1st Floor, 1000 Brussels, Belgium.
URL: http://www.ngo-platform-asylum-migration.eu/
History Has been running on a voluntary basis since 1994. **Aims** Contribute to the development of asylum and migration policy in the European Union. **Structure** No Permanent Secretariat. **Languages** English. **Activities** Networking/liaising; knowledge management/information dissemination.
Members Organizations (28):
– *Amnesty International – European Institutions Office (#00802)*;
– *Caritas Europa (#03579)*;
– *Churches' Commission for Migrants in Europe (CCME, #03912)*;
– *COFACE Families Europe (#04084)*;
– *Commission justice et paix (CJP)*;
– *Commission of the Bishops' Conferences of the European Union (COMECE, #04205)*;
– EKD – Protestant Church of Germany – Brussels Office;
– *European Association for the Defence of Human Rights (AEDH, no recent information)*;
– *European Council on Refugees and Exiles (ECRE, #06839)*;
– *European Federation of National Organisations Working with the Homeless (#07174)*;
– *European Network against Racism (ENAR, #07862)*;
– *European Network of Migrant Women (ENoMW, #07947)*;
– *European Women's Lobby (EWL, #09102)*;
– *Human Rights Watch (HRW, #10990)*;
– *ILGA-Europe (#11118)*;
– *International Catholic Migration Commission (ICMC, #12459)*;
– *International Detention Coalition (IDC, #13154)*;
– *International Federation for Human Rights (#13452)*;
– *International Rehabilitation Council for Torture Victims (IRCT, #14712)*;
– *International Rescue Committee (IRC, #14717)*;
– *Jesuit Refugee Service Europe (JRS Europe, #16107)*;
– *Médecins du Monde – International (MDM, #16613)*;
– *Migration Policy Group (MPG, #16801)*;
– *Pax Christi – International Catholic Peace Movement (#18266)*;
– *Platform for International Cooperation on Undocumented Migrants (PICUM, #18401)*;
– *Quaker Council for European Affairs (QCEA, #18587)*;
– *Save the Children International (#19058)* (European Office);
– *Social Platform (#19344)*;
– *SOLIDAR (#19680).*
Observers (4):

European Nickel Industry
08051

alphabetic sequence excludes
For the complete listing, see Yearbook Online at

Bureau international des Médecins sans frontières (MSF International, #03366); Odysseus Network; *Red Cross EU Office (#18643)*; *UNHCR (#20327)*.
IGO Relations *UNHCR (#20327)*. [2017.03.09/XJ9954/y/**F**]

♦ European Nickel Industry Association (inactive)
♦ European Nightlife Association (unconfirmed)
♦ European Nitrators Association / see European Industrial Nitrocellulose Association (#07528)
♦ European Nitrocellulose Producers Association / see European Industrial Nitrocellulose Association (#07528)
♦ European Nitrogen Cycle Meeting (meeting series)
♦ European Nitrogen Fixation Conference (meeting series)
♦ European Nitrogen Producers' Association (inactive)

♦ European Noise Barrier Federation (ENBF) 08052

Secretariat Place Stéphanie 6, 1050 Brussels, Belgium. T. +3226445877.
URL: http://www.enbf.org/

History Set up 2009, as *European Noise Federation*. EU Transparency Register: 273528411049-03. **Aims** Support R and D activities to develop more innovative systems and products; promote qualification standards to facilitate quality solutions increasing competitiveness; provide strategic advise to professionals and raise-awareness actions towards citizens; represent private stakeholders and promote dialogue with public administrations. **Structure** Officers. **Languages** English. **Finance** Members' dues. **Activities** Standards/guidelines; guidance/assistance/consulting; events/meetings; monitoring/evaluation; networking/liaising; knowledge management/information dissemination. **Events** *Meeting* Bratislava (Slovakia) 2016, *Meeting* Bratislava (Slovakia) 2016, *Meeting* Belgrade (Serbia) 2015, *Noise barriers European standards – CE marking* Belgrade (Serbia) 2015, *Noise barriers European standards – CE marking* Sarajevo (Bosnia-Herzegovina) 2015. **Publications** Guidelines and recommendations.
Members Effective in 4 countries:
France, Germany, Italy, Spain.
Associated in 8 countries:
Austria, Belgium, Germany, Italy, Netherlands, Poland, Slovenia, Türkiye.
IGO Relations *European Commission (EC, #06633)* – DG ENVI; *European Parliament (EP, #08146)*. **NGO Relations** Member of: *European Union Road Federation (ERF, #09014)*. [2017.10.12/XM5340/**D**]

♦ European Noise Federation / see European Noise Barrier Federation (#08052)

♦ European Non-GMO Industry Association (ENGA) 08053

SG Rue du Monastère 10-12, 1000 Brussels, Belgium. T. +3249333591. E-mail: info@enga.org.
URL: https://www.enga.org/

History Registration: Banque-Carrefour des Entreprises, No/ID: 0751.800.478, Start date: 5 Aug 2020, Belgium; EU Transparency Register, No/ID: 069365444306-89, Start date: 6 Oct 2021. **Aims** Advocate for EU legislation and policies that secure non-GMO production in the long term. **Structure** General Assembly; Board of Directors. **Publications** Position Papers. **Members** Regular; Supporting. Membership countries not specified. [2021/AA2117/**D**]

♦ European Non-Governmental Organizations for Sexual and Reproductive Health and Rights, Population and Development / see Inspire – the European Partnership for Sexual and Reproductive Health and Rights (#11232)

♦ European Non-Governmental Sports Organization (ENGSO) 08054

Office Director House of Sports, Box 110 16, SE-100 61 Stockholm, Sweden. E-mail: secretariat@engso.eu.
SG Avenue de Cortenbergh 71, 1000 Brussels, Belgium. T. +32475343640.
URL: http://www.engso.eu/

History 1968. Registered within the National Olympic and Sports Committee of France, 1 Jul 2006. Former names and other names: *NGO Club* – former (1968 to 1990). Registration: EU Transparency Register, No/ID: 114500024887-83, Start date: 2 Dec 2016. **Aims** Promote the broad spectrum of sport in Europe, raise its status and credibility and defend its common interests, independence and autonomy; increase cooperation within European sport and assist in improving sports development in member countries; support amateurism; develop democracy and promote equality between men and women in sport; promote sport as a factor of integration, a learning field for democratic principles and a preparation for personal discipline, performance and excellence. **Structure** General Assembly (annual). Executive Committee, comprising President, Vice-President, Secretary-General, Treasurer, 4-6 members and ex officio Chairperson of ENGSO Youth. ENGSO-Youth, set up 2003, represents the interests of people under the age of 35 dealing with sport in Europe. Youth Committee. **Languages** English. **Finance** Sources: members' dues. **Events** *European Sport Platform – Sport Coaching for Mental Well-Being Conference* Arnhem (Netherlands) 2022, *Annual General Assembly* Thórshavn (Faeroe Is) 2022, *Annual General Assembly* Thórshavn (Faeroe Is) 2021, *Annual General Assembly* Thórshavn (Faeroe Is) 2020, *Annual General Assembly* Rome (Italy) 2019. **Publications** *Sports in Europe* – newsletter.
Members National sport confederations and national Olympic committees in 40 countries and territories:
Albania, Andorra, Austria, Belarus, Belgium, Bosnia-Herzegovina, Bulgaria, Croatia, Czechia, Denmark, Estonia, Faeroe Is, Finland, France, Georgia, Germany, Greenland, Hungary, Iceland, Ireland, Israel, Italy, Lithuania, Luxembourg, Malta, Netherlands, North Macedonia, Norway, Poland, Portugal, Russia, Serbia, Slovakia, Slovenia, Spain, Sweden, Switzerland, Türkiye, UK.
IGO Relations Member of: *European Youth Centres (EYCs, #09138)*. Represented on Board of: *Enlarged Partial Agreement on Sport (EPAS, #05487)*. **NGO Relations** Recognized by: *International Olympic Committee (IOC, #14408)*. Member of: *EU Platform for Action on Diet, Physical Activity and Health (inactive)*; *European Sports Workforce Development Alliance (ESWDA, #08823)*. ENGSO Youth is member of: *Eurochild (#05657)*; *European Youth Forum (#09140)*. *European Women and Sport Network (EWS, #09104)* is a member. Supports: *European Alliance for the Statute of the European Association (EASEA, #05886)*. [2022.10.18/XD6349/**D**]

♦ European Non-Integrated Wire Rod Processors Association (EUNIRPA) 08055

SG c/o Van Bael and Bellis, Terhulpensteenweg 166, 1170 Brussels, Belgium. T. +3252338667. Fax +3252203020. E-mail: contact@eunirpa.eu.
URL: http://www.eunirpa.eu/

History 11 Jul 2016, Brussels (Belgium). **Aims** Protect interests of European non-integrated processors of wire rod and other long steel products in all EU trade, customs and anti-trust matters affecting their business activities, whether at national or European Community level. **Structure** Board of Directors. [2020/XM8527/**D**]

♦ European NORM Association (ENA) 08056

Contact address not obtained. E-mail: secretary@ena-norm.eu.
URL: https://ena-norm.eu/

History Founded on merger of *European ALARA Network for Naturally Occurring Radioactive Materials (EAN NORM, inactive)* and *EU-NORM*. Registration: Banque-Carrefour des Entreprises, No/ID: 0694.699.152, Start date: 12 Apr 2018, Belgium. **Aims** Promote and advance *radiation* protection in the context of exposure to *naturally occurring radioactive material* (NORM). **Structure** Board. **Finance** Members' dues. **Activities** Events/meetings; knowledge management/information dissemination; training/education; research/documentation. **Members** Individuals; organizations. Membership countries not specified. **NGO Relations** *European ALARA Network (EAN, #05855)*. [2021/XM8758/**D**]

♦ European Nuclear Disarmament (inactive)

♦ European Nuclear Education Network (ENEN) 08057

Réseau européen pour l'enseignement des sciences nucléaires
Head Office Rue d'Egmont 11, 1000 Brussels, Belgium. T. +32485868037. E-mail: secretariat@enen.eu.
URL: http://www.enen.eu/

History 22 Sep 2003. Registration: France; Start date: 2018, Belgium. **Aims** Preserve and further develop expertise in the nuclear fields through higher education and training. **Languages** English. **Activities** Events/meetings; training/education. **Events** *General Assembly* Brussels (Belgium) 2022, *General Assembly* Brussels (Belgium) 2021, *General Assembly* Espoo (Finland) 2015, *International seminar on dismantling experience of nuclear facilities* Gif-sur-Yvette (France) 2006. **Publications** *Nuclear Education and Training: Cause for Concern?* (2000); *World Energy Outlook 2007*. Educational and training materials; articles; reports. **Members** Members (87) include universities, research centres, TSO and international organizations. Membership countries not specified. **NGO Relations** Member of (1): *Sustainable Nuclear Energy Technology Platform (SNETP, #20063)*. [2022.04.21/XM2264/**F**]

♦ European Nuclear Medicine Society (inactive)

♦ European Nuclear Safety Regulators Group (ENSREG) 08058

Address not obtained.
URL: http://www.ensreg.eu/

History 2007, following a decision of *European Commission (EC, #06633)*, as *European High Level Group on Nuclear Safety and Waste Management*. Endorsed by *European Council (#06801)*. **Aims** Help establish conditions for continuous improvement; reach a common understanding in the areas of nuclear safety and *radioactive* waste management. **Structure** Chair; 2 Vice-Chairpersons. Working Groups (3): Nuclear Safety; Waste Spent Fuel Decommissioning; Transparency Arrangements. **Events** *Conference* Brussels (Belgium) 2017, *Conference* Brussels (Belgium) 2015, *Conference* Brussels (Belgium) 2013, *Conference* Brussels (Belgium) 2011. **Publications** *ENSREG Newsletter*.
Members National regulators in 28 countries:
Austria, Belgium, Bulgaria, Croatia, Cyprus, Czechia, Denmark, Estonia, Finland, France, Germany, Greece, Hungary, Ireland, Italy, Latvia, Lithuania, Luxembourg, Malta, Netherlands, Poland, Portugal, Romania, Slovakia, Slovenia, Spain, Sweden, UK.
Observer states (2):
Norway, Switzerland.
Observer organizations (2):
Council of the European Union (#04895); *International Atomic Energy Agency (IAEA, #12294)*.
IGO Relations *Global Nuclear Safety and Security Network (GNSSN, #10509)*. [2018/XM6491/**E***]

♦ European Nuclear Society (ENS) 08059

Société européenne de l'énergie nucléaire – Europäische Kernenergie-Gesellschaft
SG Av des Arts 56, 1000 Brussels, Belgium. T. +3225053050. Fax +3225023902. E-mail: info@euronuclear.org – ens@euronuclear.org.
URL: https://www.euronuclear.org/

History 20 Apr 1975, Paris (France). Transferred to Brussels (Belgium), 2002. Registration: No/ID: 0478.307.097, Start date: 17 Sep 2002, Belgium; EU Transparency Register, No/ID: 083308125409-83, Start date: 12 Jan 2017. **Aims** Promote and contribute to advancement of science and engineering in the field of peaceful uses of *nuclear energy* by all suitable means. **Structure** General Assembly; Board of Directors; High Scientific Council; Programme Committee; Nuclear Information Committee Europe (NICE); Young Generation Network; Secretariat in Brussels (Belgium). **Languages** English. **Finance** Sources: meeting proceeds; members' dues. **Activities** Events/meetings; knowledge management/information dissemination; training/education. **Events** *European Research Rector Conference* Antwerp (Belgium) 2023, *ENYGF : European Nuclear Young Generation Forum* Krakow (Poland) 2023, *RRFM : European Research Reactor Conference* Budapest (Hungary) 2022, *NEST-et Conference* Brussels (Belgium) 2021, *RRFM : European Research Reactor Conference* Helsinki (Finland) 2021. **Publications** *ENS NEWS* – online bulletin. Position papers; statements.
Members Organizations in 22 countries:
Austria, Belgium, Bulgaria, Croatia, Czechia, Finland, France, Germany, Hungary, Israel, Italy, Lithuania, Netherlands, Poland, Romania, Slovakia, Slovenia, Spain, Sweden, Switzerland, UK, Ukraine.
IGO Relations Accredited by (1): *United Nations Framework Convention on Climate Change – Secretariat (UNFCCC, #20564)*. Affiliated with (1): *International Atomic Energy Agency (IAEA, #12294)*. **NGO Relations** Member of (1): *Sustainable Nuclear Energy Technology Platform (SNETP, #20063)*. Instrumental in setting up (2): *NucNet (#17623)*; *Women in Nuclear (WIN, #21009)*. [2023/XD5330/**D**]

♦ European Nuclear Steelmaking Club (inactive)
♦ European Nuclear Young Generation Forum (meeting series)
♦ European Numismatic Alliance (internationally oriented national body)

♦ European Nurse Directors Association (ENDA) 08060

Pres Medical School Hannover, OE 3010, Carl-Neuberg-Str 1, 30625 Hannover, Germany. T. +495115322624. Fax +495115322551.
URL: https://enda-europe.com/

History 1992, Geneva (Switzerland). Registration: Germany. **Aims** Strengthen the nursing contribution to policy making in the context of healthcare management in Europe; establish formal links between Nurse Directors and Nurse Leaders across Europe to support a communication network of experts; promote further development of the art and science of nursing leadership and management. **Structure** General Meeting (annual); Board. **Languages** English. **Finance** Sources: members' dues. **Activities** Networking/liaising; events/meetings; standards/guidelines. **Events** *Congress* Selfoss (Iceland) 2022, *Congress* Helsinki (Finland) 2019, *Build it, live it, share it* Opatija (Croatia) 2017, *Congress* Hannover (Germany) 2015, *Congress* Zurich (Switzerland) 2013. **Publications** Annual Report; research reports; posts. **Members** Nurse leaders. Membership countries not specified. [2020.03.12/XD6238/**D**]

♦ European Nursery Products Confederation (ENPC) 08061

Coordinator Square de Meeus, 1000 Brussels, Belgium. T. +3224016167. E-mail: info@enpc.eu.
URL: http://enpc.eu/

History 2011. **Aims** Represent *childcare* industries in Europe to create a united voice to EU institutions and national administration; participate actively in relevant European policy for the sector. **Structure** General Assembly (annual); Board of Directors; Secretariat. **Languages** English. **Staff** 1.00 FTE, paid. **Finance** Members' dues. **Activities** Events/meetings; politics/policy/regulatory.
Members National associations in 8 countries:
Austria, Belgium, France, Germany, Italy, Netherlands, Spain, UK.
NGO Relations Liaison Organization of: *Comité européen de normalisation (CEN, #04162)*; ISO PC 310. [2018.09.06/XM4803/**D**]

♦ European Nurserystock Association (ENA) 08062

Secretariat Kortrijksesteenweg 1144J, 9051 Sint-Denijs-Westrem, Belgium. E-mail: ena@enaplants.eu.
URL: https://www.enaplants.eu/

History Statutes renewed 2013. Registration: Banque-Carrefour des Entreprises, No/ID: 0536.747.223, Start date: 24 Jan 2013, Belgium; EU Transparency Register, No/ID: 248993414712-40, Start date: 17 Oct 2014. **Aims** Represent, at an international level, the common interests of growers and traders of hardy nursery stock products, including perennials. **Structure** General Assembly; Board; Working Groups. **Languages** English. **Activities** Advocacy/lobbying/activism; knowledge management/information dissemination. **Events** *Summer Meeting* Bavaria (Germany) 2021.
Members Full in 22 countries:
Belgium, Bulgaria, Czechia, Denmark, Finland, France, Germany, Greece, Hungary, Ireland, Italy, Netherlands, Norway, Poland, Portugal, Serbia, Spain, Sweden, Switzerland, Türkiye, UK, Ukraine. [2021/AA2558/t/**D**]

♦ European Nursing Council (ENC) 08063

Contact Coudenberg 70, 1000 Brussels, Belgium. T. +3225114439. Fax +3225110124. E-mail: secretary-enc@enc-eu.org.
URL: https://enc-eu.org/

History 2004. Former names and other names: *European Council of Nursing Regulators (FEPI)* – former; *Consiglio Europeo degli Enti Regolatori delle Professioni Infermieristiche* – former. **Aims** Protect European citizens by securing excellence in: nursing competence and practice; professional standards; continuous education and training; codes of conduct. **Structure** General Assembly; Executive Board; General Secretary. **Languages** English. **Staff** 4.00 FTE, paid. **Finance** Sources: members' dues. **Activities** Advocacy/lobbying/activism; knowledge management/information dissemination; networking/liaising. **Events** *General Assembly*

Dublin (Ireland) 2015, *General Assembly* Budapest (Hungary) 2014, *Conference* Zagreb (Croatia) 2013, *Conference* Split (Croatia) 2012, *Conference* Thessaloniki (Greece) 2008. **Publications** *ENC Newsletter* (12 a year).
Members Full in 5 countries:
Albania, Croatia, Greece, Hungary, Romania.
Observer in 3 countries:
Canada, Ireland, USA.
IGO Relations *European Commission (EC, #06633)*; *European Economic and Social Committee (EESC, #06963)*; *European Parliament (EP, #08146)*; *WHO (#20950)*. **NGO Relations** Partner of (1): *European Council of Liberal Professions (#06828)*. [2022/XM3651/**D**]

♦ European Nursing Education Information Technology Association (inactive)
♦ European Nursing Group (inactive)

♦ European Nursing Module Network (ENM) 08064

Coordinator c/o School of Healthcare, Baines Wing, Univ of Leeds, Leeds, LS2 9JT, UK.
URL: https://www.enm-network.com/

History 1994, Lewes (UK). **Aims** Provide a structured framework for international student exchange in nursing education. **Structure** General Meeting (annual). Steering Group. **Languages** English. **Staff** 3.00 FTE, voluntary. **Finance** Members'dues. **Activities** Organizes: annual conference; 2-week exchange of students. **Events** *Annual Conference* Plovdiv (Bulgaria) 2010, *Annual Conference* Biel (Switzerland) 2009, *Annual Conference* Taganrog (Russia) 2008, *Annual Conference* Póvoa de Lanhoso (Portugal) 2007, *Meeting* Stockholm (Sweden) 2006.
Members Institutions (28) in 13 countries:
Bulgaria, Denmark, Germany, Netherlands, Norway, Portugal, Romania, Russia, Serbia, Spain, Sweden, Switzerland, UK.
[2018/XJ3081/**F**]

♦ European Nursing Research Foundation (ENRF) 08065

SG Clos du Parnasse 11B, 1050 Brussels, Belgium. T. +3225113484. E-mail: enrf@enrf.eu.
URL: http://www.enrf.eu/

History May 2013. Founded by *European Federation of Nurses Associations (EFN, #07180)*. Registration: No/ID: 0533.978.961, Start date: 8 May 2013, Belgium; Eu Transparency Register, No/ID: 067386320464-72, Start date: 28 Jan 2016. **Aims** Pursue and enhance nursing research as an element of professional excellence to benefit the health of citizens in the *EU* and Europe; use nursing research to influence EU *policies*; promote evidence-based decision-making. **Structure** Board of Directors. **Languages** English. **Staff** 2.00 FTE, paid. **Finance** Sources: members' dues. **Activities** Research and development. **Publications** *ENRF Briefing Notes*; *ENRF Newsletter*; *ENRF Policy Briefs*. **Members** Not a membership organization. [2021.08.31/XM6612/f/**F**]

♦ European Nursing Student Group / see European Nursing Students Association (#08066)

♦ European Nursing Students Association (ENSA) 08066

Contact address not obtained. E-mail: ensaagm@gmail.com – ensa.president@gmail.com – info@ensanetwork.eu.
URL: http://www.ensanetwork.eu/

History Founded 1970 as *European Nursing Student Group (ENSG)*. Part of: *European Healthcare Students Association (EHSAS)*. Registered under Belgian law, 4 Oct 2014. **Aims** Increase cooperation between national nursing student organizations and nursing colleges in Europe; promote the best standard of education for nursing students. **Structure** Annual General Meeting; Board; Executive Committee. **Languages** English. **Staff** 5.00 FTE, paid. **Finance** Funding. **Activities** Events/meetings; networking/liaising. **Events** *Annual Meeting* Athens (Greece) 2019, *Annual Meeting* Madrid (Spain) 2016, *Annual Meeting* London (UK) 2015, *Annual Meeting* Dublin (Ireland) 2014, *Annual Meeting* Istanbul (Turkey) 2013. **Publications** *ENSA Update*.
Members National organizations representing nursing students in 9 countries:
Croatia, Denmark, Finland, France, Ireland, Norway, Portugal, Spain, Sweden.
NGO Relations Observer status with: *European Federation of Nurses Associations (EFN, #07180)*. Associate member of: *European Students' Union (ESU, #08848)*. [2019.05.11/XM1930/**D**]

♦ European Nutraceutical Association (ENA) 08067

CEO c/o Ist KURZ, Via Golfo dei Poeti 1/A, 43126 Parma PR, Italy. E-mail: office@enaonline.eu.
URL: http://www.enaonline.eu/

History Registered in accordance with Swiss Civil Code. **Aims** Provide a scientific platform for nutraceuticals. **Structure** Board, comprising President, Secretary and 3 members. Advisory Board of Scientists. **Languages** English, German. **Finance** Members' dues. **Events** *Meeting* Dresden (Germany) 2012, *Conference on nutraceuticals and obesity* Vienna (Austria) 2010. **Publications** *Annals of Nutrition and Metabolism* – official journal; *ENA Newsletter* – electronic. [2019/XJ4787/**D**]

♦ European Nutrigenomics Organisation (NuGO) 08068

Dir PO Box 17, 6703 AA Wageningen, Netherlands. T. +31317486108.
URL: http://www.nugo.org/

History Jan 2004, as a project to be funded by *European Commission (EC, #06633)* until Dec 2009. **Aims** Train European scientists to use post-genomic technologies in nutrition research; develop and integrate genomic technologies for the benefit of European nutritional science; facilitate the application of these technologies in nutritional research worldwide; create the world-leading virtual centre of excellence in nutrigenomics. Overcome the fragmentation of research, giving researchers from across Europe the chance to work together, share facilities and their expertise. **Finance** Funded by *European Commission (EC, #06633)* – Research DG. **Events** *Annual Conference* Copenhagen (Denmark) 2016, *Annual Conference* Barcelona (Spain) 2015, *Annual Conference* Castellammare di Stabia (Italy) 2014, *Annual Conference* Weihenstephan (Germany) 2013, *Annual Conference* Helsinki (Finland) 2012. **Publications** *NuGO E-zine*.
Members Partner universities and institutions in 10 countries:
France, Germany, Ireland, Italy, Netherlands, Norway, Poland, Spain, Sweden, UK. [2018/XM0359/**E**]

♦ European Nutrition for Health Alliance, The (ENHA) 08069

Exec Dir 308 High Street, Croydon, CR0 1NG, UK. T. +442073440440. E-mail: secretariat@european-nutrition.org.
Co-Chair School of Medical Sciences, Örebro Univ, SE-701 82 Örebro, Sweden. T. +4619303000.
URL: https://european-nutrition.org/enha/

History Registration: Registered Charity, No/ID: 1123711, England and Wales. **Aims** Improve nutritional care across Europe. **Structure** Board of Trustees of at least 3, including representatives from *European Geriatric Medicine Society (EuGMS, #07392)* and *European Society for Clinical Nutrition and Metabolism (ESPEN, #08550)*, who act as Co-Chairs. **Finance** Members' dues. **Events** *Optimal Nutritional Care for All Conference* Copenhagen (Denmark) 2021, *Optimal Nutritional Care for All Conference* Cambridge (UK) 2019, *Optimal Nutritional Care for All Conference* Sintra (Portugal) 2018, *Optimal Nutritional Care for All Conference* Bled (Slovenia) 2017, *Optimal Nutritional Care for All Conference* Madrid (Spain) 2016.
Members Partners (9):
Association internationale de la mutualité (AIM, #02721); *European Federation of the Associations of Dietitians (EFAD, #07050)*; *European Geriatric Medicine Society (EuGMS, #07392)*; *European Nurse Directors Association (ENDA, #08060)*; *European Society for Clinical Nutrition and Metabolism (ESPEN, #08550)*; *International Association of Gerontology and Geriatrics (IAGG, #11920)*; International Longevity Centre – UK; *Medical Nutrition International Industry (MNI, #16626)*; *Pharmaceutical Group of the European Union (PGEU, #18352)*.
NGO Relations Memorandum of Understanding with (2): *EGAN – Patients Network for Medical Research and Health (EGAN, #05394)*; *European Patients' Forum (EPF, #08172)*. [2020/XJ0422/y/**D**]

♦ European Observation Network on Territorial Development and Cohesion (ESPON) 08070

Contact ESPON EGTC, Rue Erasme 4, L-1468 Kirchberg, Luxembourg. T. +35220600280. E-mail: info@espon.eu.
URL: http://www.espon.eu/

History Set up 2002, by *European Community (inactive)*, following a proposal Dec 1997, Echternach (Luxembourg). Previously also referred to as *European Spatial Planning Observatory Network* and subsequently as *European Spatial Planning Observation Network*. Current title adopted 7 Nov 2007, when ESPON 2013 Programme was adopted by *European Commission (EC, #06633)*. As part of a renewal and upgrade of ESPON for the period 2014-2020 and beyond, an European Grouping on Territorial Cooperation – EGTC has been established according to European law to act as Single Beneficiary and deliver the content envisaged by the ESPON 2020 Cooperation Programme. Since then, also referred to as *ESON EGTC*. **Aims** Promote and foster a European territorial dimension in development and cooperation by providing evidence, knowledge transfer and policy learning to public authorities and other policy actors at all levels. **Structure** Monitoring Committee; Managing Authority; Certifying Authority; ESPON EGTC; Contact Points. **Languages** English. **Staff** 18.00 FTE, paid. **Finance** Programme budget of euro 47 million is financed for 75% by *European Regional Development Fund (ERDF, #08342)* under Objective 3 for European Territorial Cooperation – *INTERREG V (#15966)*. Remainder financed by participating Member States. ESPON 2020 Cooperation budget: euro 48,678,841. **Activities** Research and development; projects/programmes; knowledge management/information dissemination; politics/policy/regulatory. **Events** *Seminar on eHealth* Oulu (Finland) 2019, *Conference* Brussels (Belgium) 2011, *Database 2013 workshop* Esch-sur-Alzette (Luxembourg) 2010, *Database 2013 seminar* Prague (Czech Rep) 2009, *Seminar* Espoo (Finland) 2006. **Publications** Newsletter. activities reports; policy briefs; working papers; maps; posters; territorial review.
Members Full in 32 countries:
Austria, Belgium, Bulgaria, Croatia, Cyprus, Czechia, Denmark, Estonia, Finland, France, Germany, Greece, Hungary, Iceland, Ireland, Italy, Latvia, Liechtenstein, Lithuania, Luxembourg, Malta, Netherlands, Norway, Poland, Portugal, Romania, Slovakia, Slovenia, Spain, Sweden, Switzerland, UK. [2017.03.09/XF6547/**F***]

♦ European Observatoire of Sport and Employment (EOSE) 08071

Secretariat 1 grande rue des Feuillants, 69001 Lyon, France. T. +33437431939. Fax +33437430988. E-mail: eosesec@eose.org.
URL: http://www.eose.org/

Aims Promtoe a dialogue and a strong link between employment, education and training at national and European levels between all key stakeholders of the sport and active leisure sectors. **Structure** Management Board. Executive Board, comprising President, Vice-President, General Secretary and Treasurer. Secretariat.
Members Full in 6 countries:
Belgium, France, Italy, Malta, Portugal, UK.
NGO Relations Member of: *European Sports Workforce Development Alliance (ESWDA, #08823)*. Cooperates with: *European Tennis Federation (#08898)*. [2014/XM2663/**E**]

♦ European Observatory on Health Care Systems / see European Observatory on Health Systems and Policies (#08072)
♦ European Observatory on Health Care Systems and Policies / see European Observatory on Health Systems and Policies (#08072)

♦ European Observatory on Health Systems and Policies 08072

Observatoire européen des systèmes et des politiques de santé – Europäisches Observatorium für Gesundheitssysteme und Gesundheitspolitik

Dir WHO ECHP, Eurostation – Office 07C020, Place Victor Horta, 40/10, 1060 Brussels, Belgium. T. +3225249240.
URL: http://www.euro.who.int/observatory

History Jun 1998, as *European Observatory on Health Care Systems (EOHCS)*, a partnership between *WHO Regional Office for Europe (#20945)*, Government of Norway, Government of Spain, *European Investment Bank (EIB, #07599)*, *International Bank for Reconstruction and Development (IBRD, #12317)*, *'London School of Economics and Political Science'* and *London School of Hygiene and Tropical Medicine (LSHTM)* in association with *'Open Society Institute'*. Subsequently known as *European Observatory on Health Care Systems and Policies*. Secretariat based at *European Centre for Health Policy (ECHP, see: #20945)*. **Aims** Monitor, analyse and evaluate reform initiatives in WHO member states. **Structure** Steering Committee; Core Management Team; Research Policy Group; Secretariat. **Activities** Guidance/assistance/consulting; knowledge manegement/information dissemination; training/education. **Events** *Annual Meeting* Vienna (Austria) 2017. **Publications** *Eurohealth* (4 a year) – journal. *Health Care Systems in Transition (HiT)* – series; *Observatory Studies* – series; *Policy Briefs* – series. Country profiles.
Members Full in 51 countries:
Albania, Andorra, Armenia, Austria, Azerbaijan, Belarus, Belgium, Bosnia-Herzegovina, Bulgaria, Croatia, Cyprus, Czechia, Denmark, Estonia, Finland, France, Georgia, Germany, Greece, Hungary, Iceland, Ireland, Israel, Italy, Kyrgyzstan, Latvia, Lithuania, Luxembourg, Malta, Moldova, Monaco, Netherlands, North Macedonia, Norway, Poland, Portugal, Romania, Russia, San Marino, Serbia, Slovakia, Slovenia, Spain, Sweden, Switzerland, Tajikistan, Türkiye, Turkmenistan, UK, Ukraine, Uzbekistan.
NGO Relations Partner of: *European Network for Health Technology Assessment (EUnetHTA, #07921)*.
[2020/XF4975/**F**]

♦ European Observatory on Memories (unconfirmed)

♦ European Observatory of Mountain Forests (EOMF) 08073

l'Observatoire européen des forêts de montagne (OEFM)

Contact Maison des Parcs et de la Montagne, 256 rue de la République, 7300 Chambéry, France. T. +33479334952. Fax +33479333895.

Aims Promote regular exchanges and meetings among forest owners, managers, scientists, decision makers; foster experiences and implementations to strengthen communication, transfer and exchange; maintain a platform of all measures supporting mountain forest development in view of a more efficient use of existing tools and a more effective proposal of new measures. **Events** *Quadrennial international congress of integrated management in high watersheds* Megève (France) 2006, *Integrated watershed management conference* Porto Cervo (Italy) 2003, *Quadrennial congress of integrated management in high watersheds* Megève (France) 2002, *Conference* Spain 2002. **Publications** *White Book 2000 on Moutain Forest in Europe*.
Members in 6 countries:
Andorra, Austria, France, Germany, Greece, Spain.
IGO Relations Observer to *Ministerial Conference on the Protection of Forests in Europe (FOREST EUROPE, #16817)*. [2008/XF6396/**F**]

♦ European Observatory for Non-Discrimination and Fundamental Rights (unconfirmed)
♦ European Observatory for Plurilingualism (internationally oriented national body)
♦ European Observatory of Religions and Secularism (internationally oriented national body)
♦ European Observatory of Violence in Schools / see International Observatory of Violence in the School Environment (#14389)

♦ European Occupational Safety and Health Network (EUROSHNET) . . 08074

Secretariat c/o KAN – Kommission Arbeitsschutz und Normung, Alte Heerstrasse 111, 53757 St Augustin, Germany. T. +4922412313463. E-mail: info@euroshnet.eu.
URL: http://www.euroshnet.eu/

Aims Facilitate contact between individual Occupational Safety and Health (OSH) experts; promote discussion of issues of common interest; disseminate information. **Structure** Steering Committee. **Events** *Be smart, stay safe together – innovative products and workplaces* Dresden (Germany) 2019, *Improving the quality of working life – a challenge for standardization, testing and certification* Seville (Spain) 2015, *Conference* Espoo (Finland) 2012, *Conference* Krakow (Poland) 2008, *Conference* Paris (France) 2005.
Members Participating institutions (7) in 5 countries:
Finland, France, Germany, Poland, Spain. [2019/XJ6576/**F**]

♦ European Ocean Energy Association / see Ocean Energy Europe (#17649)
♦ European Oceanic Association (inactive)

♦ European Ocean Observing System (EOOS) 08075

SG c/o EuroGOOS, Rue Vautier 29, 1000 Brussels, Belgium.
Exec Dir Jacobsenstraat 1, 8400 Ostend, Belgium.
URL: http://www.eoos-ocean.eu/

History Steering Group convened by *European Global Ocean Observing System (EuroGOOS, #07396)* and *European Marine Board (EMB, #07738)*, 2016. **Aims** Provide a framework within which European marine observations can be sustained and made available on a continuous basis for applications ranging from real-time services, through ocean health to climate services. **Structure** Steering Group. **Events** *Conference on Connecting Communities for End-to-End Solutions* Brussels (Belgium) 2018. [2022/XM7704/F]

♦ European Oenogastronomic Brotherhoods Council 08076

Conseil Européen des Confréries Enogastronomiques (CEUCO) – Consejo Europeo de Cofradias Enogastronómicas – Europäischer Rat der Wein- und Gastronomie-Bruderschaften – Conselho Europeu de Confrarias Enogastronômicas – Consiglio Europeo di Confraternite Enogastronomiche – Európai Bor és Gasztronómiai Egyesületek Szövetse

Pres Calle Carlos Dinnbier 13 puerta 6, 46015 Valencia, Spain. T. +34629693386. Fax +34963480709. E-mail: ceuco@ceuco.com – president@ceuco.com.
URL: http://www.ceuco.com/

History 29 May 2005, Bayonne (France). **Structure** General Assembly. Board of Directors. **Events** *Congress* Lisbon (Portugal) 2016, *Congress* Liège (Belgium) 2014, *Congress* Pécs (Hungary) 2013, *General Assembly* Susegana (Italy) 2013, *Congress* Tartu (Estonia) 2012. [2013/XJ7000/D]

♦ European Offender Employment Forum (EOEF) 08077

Contact c/o Inclusion, Camelford House, 3rd Floor, 89 Albert Embankment, London, SE1 7TP, UK. T. +442075827221. Fax +442075826391.
URL: http://www.eoef.net/

History Former names and other names: *European Offender Employment Group* – former. **Aims** Contribute to a reduction in offending by promoting *social integration* and reintegration of offenders through employment and training. **Structure** Managed by Inclusion, London (UK). Director. **Languages** English. **Finance** Sources: members' dues; revenue from activities/projects. **Activities** Events/meetings; guidance/assistance/consulting. **Events** *Conference* Spain 2010, *Conference* Valencia (Spain) 2010, *Conference* Lisbon (Portugal) 2009, *Conference* Sofia (Bulgaria) 2008, *Annual international conference / Conference* Prague (Czech Rep) 2005. **Publications** *EOEF Newsletter*. E-bulletins.

Members Full; Associate. Organizations (over 700) in 25 countries:
Austria, Belgium, Cyprus, Czechia, Denmark, Estonia, Finland, France, Germany, Greece, Hungary, Ireland, Italy, Latvia, Lithuania, Luxembourg, Malta, Netherlands, Poland, Portugal, Slovakia, Slovenia, Spain, Sweden, UK. [2013.07.17/XF5945/F]

♦ European Offender Employment Group / see European Offender Employment Forum (#08077)
♦ European Office of Consumer Unions / see Bureau Européen des Unions de Consommateurs (#03360)
♦ European Office of Processors and Distributors of Organic Products (no recent information)

♦ European Oilfield Speciality Chemicals Association (EOSCA) 08078

Exec Sec c/o NIKAM Consulting Ltd, North Standryford, Newmachar, AB21 7PW, UK. T. +441224959185. E-mail: secretary@eosca.eu.
URL: http://www.eosca.eu/

History 1990. Registered in accordance with Scottish law. **Aims** Provide a forum for oilfield speciality chemical companies and their support organizations to address health, safety and environmental issues relating to the industry. **Structure** General Meeting (annual); Board; Management Committee, including Executive Secretary. **Languages** English. **Finance** Members' dues. **Activities** Events/meetings. **Publications** Position statements. **Members** Full (37); associate (4). Membership countries not specified. **IGO Relations** Observer to: *OSPAR Commission for the Protection of the Marine Environment of the North-East Atlantic (OSPAR Commission, #17905).* [2015.01.28/XD8606/D]

♦ European Oil and Gas Archives Network (EOGAN) 08079

Contact address not obtained. E-mail: eogan.network@gmail.com.
URL: http://www.eogan.org/

History Oct 2009, Stavanger (Norway). Statutes adopted 2012. **Aims** Promote the preservation and usage of relevant archives; share skills and experience. **Structure** Board; Chairman. **Events** *Conference* Rotterdam (Netherlands) 2014, *Conference* Aberdeen (UK) 2013, *Conference* Rome (Italy) 2012, *Conference* Stavanger (Norway) 2011, *Conference* Stavanger (Norway) 2009. [2015/XJ9235/F]

♦ European Oil Hydraulic and Pneumatic Committee / see European Fluid Power Committee (#07273)

♦ European Oilseed Alliance (EOA) 08080

Contact 11 rue de Monceau, CS 60003, 75378 Paris CEDEX 08, France. E-mail: sg@euoilseed.org.
URL: http://www.euoilseed.org/

History Apr 2002. Registration: EU Transparency Register, No/ID: 265299815747-31, Start date: 23 Jan 2015. **Aims** Represent the EU oilseed sector; make its voice heard at the EU level.

Members Organizations in 8 countries:
Belgium, Czechia, Finland, France, Germany, Poland, Sweden, UK.

Associate members (3):
European Biodiesel Board (EBB, #06333); Euroseeds (#09179); FEDIOL – The EU Vegetable Oil and Proteinmeal Industry (#09718).

NGO Relations Cooperates with (2): *COPA – european farmers (COPA, #04829); General Confederation of Agricultural Cooperatives in the European Union (#10107).* [2021/AA2557/ty/D]

♦ European Oleochemicals and Allied Products Group (APAG) 08081

Groupement européen des produits oléochimiques et associés

Contact c/o CEFIC, Rue Belliard 40 – bte 15, 1040 Brussels, Belgium. T. +3224369452. E-mail: oleosurfactant@cefic.be – cdc@cefic.be.
URL: http://www.apag.org/

History 1976, Brussels (Belgium), as *European Association of Fatty Acid Producing Companies – Association européenne des producteurs d'acides gras (APAG)*, as a sector group of *Conseil européen de l'industrie chimique (CEFIC, #04687).* Present adopted Aug 1993. Registered in accordance with Belgian law, 7 Oct 1977. **Aims** Represent and promote the European oleochemicals and allied products *industry* effectively without restricting free competition between companies; examine all matters relating to the oleochemicals production, supply and use; promote common interests and knowledge of members; seek collective solutions to technical problems of common concern; collect, exchange and distribute information of relevance to these objectives. **Structure** General Assembly (annual); Steering Committee. Secretariat, headed by Secretary General. **Languages** English, French. **Staff** Provided by CEFIC. **Activities** Major concerns are: international agreements on trade; harmonized system of nomenclature; protection of the environment and any relevant legislative proposals. **Events** *Annual General Assembly* Munich (Germany) 2013, *Annual General Assembly* Sitges (Spain) 2011, *Annual General Assembly* Malmö (Sweden) 2010, *Annual General Assembly* Netherlands 2009, *Annual General Assembly* Czech Rep 2008. **Publications** *Fatty Acids and their Raw Materials – Compendium on Test Methods* (2nd ed); *Glycerol – Compendium of Test Methods.*

Members Companies with production and sales organizations in Europe in 12 countries:
Belgium, Czechia, Denmark, France, Germany, Italy, Netherlands, Spain, Sweden, Switzerland, Türkiye, UK. [2019.07.04/XD7696/E]

♦ European Olympic Academies (EOA) 08082

Europäische Olympische Akademien

Exec Dir Otto-Fleck-Schneise 12, 60528 Frankfurt-Main, Germany. E-mail: info@eoaolympic.org.
Gen Sec address not obtained.
URL: https://www.eoaolympic.org/

History 20 Sep 2018, Ljubljana (Slovenia). Founded on the initiative of the National Academies in concert with the IOA and the EOC, following discussions initiated in 2012. Statutes adopted at Founding Assembly. Registration: Hessen District court, No/ID: VR 16567, Start date: 14 Nov 2019, Germany. **Aims** Gather the National Olympic Academies of the European continent so as to promote the Olympic Values, Philosophy and Ideals. **Structure** General Assembly; Executive Board; Commissions. **Languages** English. **Activities** Events/meetings. **Events** *EOA Congress Frankfurt* Frankfurt-Main (Germany) 2022.

Members National Olympic Academies from 29 countries:
Albania, Armenia, Austria, Azerbaijan, Belarus, Belgium, Bulgaria, Croatia, Cyprus, Czechia, Estonia, France, Germany, Greece, Hungary, Israel, Italy, Kosovo, Latvia, Lithuania, Netherlands, Portugal, Romania, Russia, Serbia, Slovakia, Slovenia, Spain, Ukraine.

NGO Relations Memorandum of Understanding with (2): *European Fair Play Movement (EFPM, #07025); European Olympic Committees (EOC, #08083).* Partner of (2): *International Council of Sport Science and Physical Education (ICSSPE, #13077); International Olympic Academy (IOA, #14406).* [2022.11.01/AA2979/F]

♦ European Olympic Committees (EOC) 08083

Les comités olympiques européens (COE)

Secretariat Palazzina CONI Villino G Onesti, Via delle Pallacanestro 19, 00194 Rome RM, Italy. T. +39636857828. Fax +39636857666.
URL: http://www.eurolympic.org/

History 17 Oct 1975, Lisbon (Portugal). Statutes amended 1978, 1995 and 2001; reshaped 2006. Former names and other names: *Association of the European National Olympic Committees (AENOC)* – former (Oct 1975 to Nov 1995); *Association des comités nationaux olympiques européens (ACNOE)* – former (Oct 1975 to Nov 1995). **Aims** Spread throughout Europe the Olympic ideals as defined in IOC's Olympic Charter, in close cooperation with International Olympic Committee (IOC), Association of National Olympic Committees (ANOC) and the Olympic Associations in other continents; educate young people through sport in a spirit of better understanding and friendship, thereby contributing towards building a better and peaceful world; promote cooperation between European NOCs through research, the study of issues of common interest, exchange of information and standing for common positions; develop IOC Olympic Solidarity programmes in Europe. **Structure** General Assembly (annual). Executive Committee, comprising President, Vice President, Secretary General and 14 members (2 of which are ex-officio). Commissions (6): Technical Cooperation and Sport Development; Preparation of the Olympic Games; European Youth Olympic Festival; Medical and Scientific; European Union; Athletes. Working Groups. **Languages** English, French. **Finance** Members' dues. Grants from IOC through: *Olympic Solidarity (OS, #17721).* **Activities** Organizes meetings, seminars, festivals and colloquia. **Events** *General Assembly* Istanbul (Turkey) 2020, *General Assembly* Warsaw (Poland) 2019, *Annual General Assembly* Rome (Italy) 2013, *Annual General Assembly* Lisbon (Portugal) 2009, *Annual General Assembly* Istanbul (Turkey) 2008. **Publications** *EOC Newsletter* (12 a year) in English, French; *Sport Europe* (annual).

Members National Olympic Committees in 49 countries:
Albania, Andorra, Armenia, Austria, Azerbaijan, Belarus, Belgium, Bosnia-Herzegovina, Bulgaria, Croatia, Cyprus, Czechia, Denmark, Estonia, Finland, France, Georgia, Germany, Greece, Hungary, Iceland, Ireland, Israel, Italy, Latvia, Liechtenstein, Lithuania, Luxembourg, Malta, Moldova, Monaco, Montenegro, Netherlands, North Macedonia, Norway, Poland, Portugal, Romania, Russia, San Marino, Serbia, Slovakia, Slovenia, Spain, Sweden, Switzerland, Türkiye, UK, Ukraine.

IGO Relations *Council of Europe (CE, #04881); European Commission (EC, #06633).* Represented on Board of: *Enlarged Partial Agreement on Sport (EPAS, #05487).* **NGO Relations** Memorandum of Understanding with (1): *European Olympic Academies (EOA, #08082).* Member of (1): *European Sports Workforce Development Alliance (ESWDA, #08823).* Cooperates with (2): *European Tennis Federation (#08898); International Testing Agency (ITA, #15678).* Continental Association of: *Association of National Olympic Committees (ANOC, #02819).* Recognized by: *International Olympic Committee (IOC, #14408).* [2021/XD3358/D]

♦ European Ombudsman 08084

Médiateur européen – Defensor del Pueblo Europeo – Europäische Ombudsstelle – Provedor de Justiça Europeu – Mediatore Europeo – Europese Ombudsman – Europeiska Ombudsmannen – Europaeiske Ombudsmand – Euroopan Oikeusasiamies – Ombudsman Eorpach – Evropsky ve Ejny Ochrance Prav – Európsky Ombudsman – Európai Ombudsman – Europejski Rzecznik Praw Obywatelskich – Evropski varuh Clovekovih Pravic – Euroopa Ombudsman – Eiropas Ombuds – Europos Ombudsmenas – Ombudsman Ewropew – Europski Ombudsman – Ombudsmanul European

European Ombudsman 1 av du Président Robert Schuman, CS 30403, 67001 Strasbourg CEDEX, France. T. +33388172313. Fax +33388179062. E-mail: eo@ombudsman.europa.eu.
Communication Unit Rue Froissart 87, 1000 Brussels, Belgium.
URL: https://www.ombudsman.europa.eu/

History 9 Mar 1994. Established on adoption by *European Parliament (EP, #08146)* of *'Statute of the European Ombudsman'* covering regulations and general conditions governing performance of the Ombudsman's duties. Set up under the terms of *Treaty on European Union (Maastricht Treaty, 1992)* and within the framework of *European Union (EU, #08967).* First European Ombudsman was elected by the European Parliament on 12 Jul 1995. Former names and other names: *Office of the European Ombudsman* – former. **Aims** Work to promote good administrative practice and transparency at EU level; investigate complaints about maladministration by EU institutions, bodies, offices and agencies, as well as proactively looking into broader systemic issues. **Structure** Ombudsman elected by the European Parliament after each parliamentary election for the duration of a parliamentary term. Team includes Cabinet, Secretariat-General, Units and Data Protection Officer. **Languages** EU languages. **Staff** 95.00 FTE, paid. **Finance** Annual budget: 12,222,108 EUR (2022). **Activities** Events/meetings. **Events** *The evolving role of the European Ombudsman* Florence (Italy) 2022, *The role of Ombudsmen in times of crisis – European Network of Ombudsmen* Strasbourg (France) 2022, *Access to EU documents: what next?* Brussels (Belgium) 2021, *Seminar for investigators and liaison colleagues* Brussels (Belgium) 2021, *Transparency and Democracy in the EU of tomorrow?* Strasbourg (France) 2021. **Publications** *Network in Focus. Good administration in practice: the European Ombudsman's decisions; Problems with the EU? – Who can help you?; The European Code of Good Administrative Behaviour – Public Service Principles; The European Ombudsman – Good for business; The European Ombudsman – Origins, Establishment, Evolution; The European Ombudsman's Guide to Complaints.* Annual Report.

Members The 27 EU countries:
Austria, Belgium, Bulgaria, Croatia, Cyprus, Czechia, Denmark, Estonia, Finland, France, Germany, Greece, Hungary, Ireland, Italy, Latvia, Lithuania, Luxembourg, Malta, Netherlands, Poland, Portugal, Romania, Slovakia, Slovenia, Spain, Sweden.

IGO Relations Required to swear impartiality before: *Court of Justice of the European Union (CJEU, #04938).* Supervises operations of all EU institutions, bodies, offices and agencies with the exception of the CJEU acting in its judicial role. Close working relations with European national and regional ombudsmen offices and committees on petitions. [2022.12.15/XK1266/E*]

♦ European Ombudsman Academy / see European Ombudsman Institute (#08085)

♦ European Ombudsman Institute 08085

Institut européen de l'ombudsman – Europäisches Ombudsman Institut (EOI) – Instituto Europeo del Ombudsman – Istituto Europeo dell' Ombudsman

SG Meraner Strasse 5/V, 6020 Innsbruck, Austria. T. +43512566910. Fax +43512575971. E-mail: eoi@tirol.com.
URL: http://www.eoi.at/

History 22 Jan 1988, Gnadenwald (Austria). Founded following conference, Oct 1982, Innsbruck (Austria). Current statutes adopted Feb 2000, amended May 2002, Sep 2005, Oct 2013 and Sep 2017. Former names and other names: *European Ombudsman Academy* – former (22 Jan 1988). **Aims** Propagate and promote the ombudsman concept. **Structure** General Assembly; Presidium; Board of Directors; Executive Board; General Board. **Languages** English, French, German, Italian, Russian. **Finance** Sources: donations; gifts, legacies; members' dues; subsidies. **Activities** Events/meetings. Entitled to lodge collective complaints according to the Renewed European Social Charter with *Council of Europe (CE, #04881).* **Events** *European Ombudsman Conference* Innsbruck (Austria) 2013, *European Ombudsman Conference* Novi Sad (Serbia) 2011, *European ombudsman Conference* Innsbruck (Austria) 2007, *European ombudsman conference* Innsbruck (Austria) 2006, *European ombudsman conference* Innsbruck (Austria) 2003. **Publications** *European Ombudsman Institute Series* – occasional. Reports; conference proceedings; open letters; draft laws; papers; membership lists. Published in some or all of the following languages: English, French, German, Italian, Russian, Spanish.

Members Institutions (114) and individuals (81) in 60 countries and territories:
Albania, Armenia, Austria, Azerbaijan, Belgium, Bosnia-Herzegovina, Bulgaria, Burkina Faso, China, Croatia, Cyprus, Czechia, Dagestan, Denmark, Egypt, Estonia, Finland, France, Georgia, Germany, Gibraltar, Greenland, Hungary, Iceland, India, Ireland, Israel, Italy, Japan, Kosovo, Kyrgyzstan, Latvia, Liechtenstein, Lithuania, Luxembourg, Malta, Mexico, Moldova, Montenegro, Nagorno-Karabakh, Netherlands, North Macedonia, Norway, Palestine, Poland, Portugal, Romania, Russia, Serbia, Slovakia, Slovenia, Spain, Sweden, Switzerland, Transnistria, Türkiye, UK, Ukraine, USA, Uzbekistan.

Also members in Latin America. Membership countries not specified.

Consultative Status Consultative status granted from: *Council of Europe (CE, #04881)* (Participatory Status). [2021.06.02/XE3491/j/E]

♦ European Oncology Nursing Society (EONS) 08086

Secretariat c/o BLSI, Bte 1.30.30, Clos Chapelle au Champs 30, 1200 Brussels, Belgium. E-mail: eons.secretariat@cancernurse.eu.
URL: http://www.cancernurse.eu/

History Founded by Rosette Poletti. Originally headquartered in London (UK); relocated to Brussels (Belgium), 1997. Former names and other names: *Fellowship of European Oncology Nursing Societies* – former (1984); *European Organization for Cancer Nursing (EOCN)* – former. Registration: Charity Commission, No/ID: 802484, Start date: 17 Jan 1990, End date: 11 Jul 2019, England and Wales; EU Transparency Register, No/ID: 43916872639-25, Start date: 19 Nov 2009. **Aims** Promote and develop the practice of cancer nursing in European countries, thus improving the quality of care that cancer patients receive; develop educational resources for nurses engaged in caring for patients with cancer, promote educational programmes and identify and build on a body of knowledge specific to cancer nursing; encourage development of and participation in collaborative research and the publication of results; encourage exchange programmes; provide a means of communication between oncology nursing groups and individuals engaged in cancer nursing. **Structure** General Meeting; Executive Board; Advisory Council. Working Groups (5): Communication; Advocacy; Education; Research; Young Cancer Nurses. **Languages** English. **Staff** 7.00 FTE, paid. **Finance** Sources: members' dues; sponsorship. **Activities** Advocacy/lobbying/activism; awards/prizes/competitions; awareness raising; capacity building; certification/accreditation; events/meetings; networking/liaising; research and development; research/documentation; training/education. **Events** *Annual Congress* Paris (France) 2022, *Annual Congress* 2021, *Annual Congress* 2020, *Annual Congress* Barcelona (Spain) 2019, *Biennial Congress* Munich (Germany) 2018. **Publications** *EONS Newsletter* (12 a year) – electronic. *EONS Magazine Archive*.

Members National (33); Associate (13); Individual (140). National members in 30 countries:
Austria, Belgium, Bulgaria, Croatia, Cyprus, Czechia, Denmark, Estonia, Finland, France, Germany, Greece, Hungary, Iceland, Ireland, Israel, Italy, Lithuania, Malta, Netherlands, Norway, Poland, Portugal, Serbia, Slovenia, Spain, Sweden, Switzerland, Türkiye, UK.
International member:
International Society of Paediatric Oncology (#15339).
Associate in 9 countries:
Albania, Austria, Belgium, Cyprus, Germany, Ireland, Italy, Switzerland, UK.
NGO Relations Member of (3): *European Alliance for Personalised Medicine (EAPM, #05878)*; *European Specialist Nurses Organisation (ESNO, #08808)*; *Rare Cancers Europe (RCE, #18620)*.
[2022.02.16/XD1548/D]

♦ European Open Partial Agreement on Prevention of and Protection Against Major Natural and Technological Disasters / see Open Partial Agreement on the Prevention of, Protection against and Organization of Relief in Major Natural and Technological Disasters (#17762)
♦ European Opera Centre Trust (internationally oriented national body)

♦ European Operating Room Nurses Association (EORNA) 08087

Sec address not obtained. E-mail: secretariat@eorna.eu.
URL: http://www.eorna.eu/

History 1980. Formalized, 1992. Registration: Crossroads Bank for Enterprises, No/ID: 0459.260.455, Start date: 28 Nov 1996, Belgium, Brussels. **Aims** Create a forum to promote discussion and exchange of ideas between European Operating Nurses and operating assistants; promote and maintain a high standard of nursing of patients within the operating area by operating nurses and their colleagues; define and defend the ethics of operation nursing; promote research applications for operation nursing; recognize the level of education and professional recognition of operation nursing throughout Europe; collaborate with other professional bodies with similar objectives. **Structure** Board of Directors (meets twice a year); Executive Committee; Committees (3); Work Groups (5). Includes *'European Operating Room Nurses Association Congress (EORNACONGRESS)'*. **Languages** English. **Staff** Voluntary. **Finance** Sources: members' dues. Meeting attendance by representatives financed by individual associations. **Activities** Events/meetings; projects/programmes; research/documentation; training/education. **Events** *Congress* Stavanger (Norway) 2022, *Congress* 2021, *Congress* The Hague (Netherlands) 2019, *Asia Pacific Global Summit on Healthcare* Singapore (Singapore) 2018, *Congress* Rhodes Is (Greece) 2017. **Publications** *EORNA e-journal*; *EORNA News e-letter*. *Position Statements and Guidelines for Perioperative Nursing Practice, Part I*. Competency document; e-learning documents; core curriculum; position statements.

Members Associations (28) in 27 countries:
Belgium, Croatia, Cyprus, Czechia, Denmark, Estonia, Finland, France, Germany, Greece, Hungary, Iceland, Ireland, Israel, Italy, Netherlands, Norway, Poland, Portugal, Russia, Serbia, Slovenia, Spain, Sweden, Switzerland, Türkiye, UK.
NGO Relations Member of (1): *European Specialist Nurses Organisation (ESNO, #08808)* (as Active member of). In liaison with technical committees of: *Comité européen de normalisation (CEN, #04162)*. Adviser to: *EDANA, the voice of nonwovens (EDANA, #05353)*. [2023.02.14/XD5683/D]

♦ European Operations Management Association (EurOMA) 08088

Exec Sec Place de Brouckère 31, 1000 Brussels, Belgium. T. +3222266669. E-mail: euroma@eiasm.be.
URL: http://www.euroma-online.org/

History Oct 1993, deriving from a UK group set up in 1984. Registered in accordance with Belgian law. **Aims** Develop operations management in both manufacturing and service industries through research, education and practice. **Structure** General Assembly (annual); Board. **Languages** English. **Activities** Events/meetings. **Events** *Annual International Conference* Berlin (Germany) 2021, *Annual International Conference* Coventry (UK) 2020, *Annual International Conference* Helsinki (Finland) 2019, *Annual International Conference* Budapest (Hungary) 2018, *Annual International Conference* Edinburgh (UK) 2017. **Publications** *International Journal of Operations and Production Management (IJOPM)*.

Members Teachers and researchers in 49 countries and territories:
Argentina, Australia, Austria, Belgium, Brazil, Canada, China, Colombia, Croatia, Cyprus, Denmark, Finland, France, Germany, Greece, Hong Kong, Hungary, India, Indonesia, Iran Islamic Rep, Ireland, Israel, Italy, Japan, Latvia, Malaysia, Malta, Netherlands, New Zealand, Nigeria, Norway, Oman, Poland, Portugal, Saudi Arabia, Serbia, Slovenia, South Africa, Spain, Sweden, Switzerland, Taiwan, Thailand, Türkiye, UK, United Arab Emirates, Uruguay, USA, Venezuela.
[2018.09.24/XD6022/D]

♦ European Ophthalmic Pathology Club / see European Ophthalmic Pathology Society (#08089)

♦ European Ophthalmic Pathology Society (EOPS) 08089

Sec Univ Hospitals Leuven, Herestraat 49, Gasthuisberg, 3290 Leuven, Belgium.
URL: http://eopsonline.org/

History 10 Apr 1962, London (UK). Former names and other names: *European Ophthalmic Pathology Club* – former (10 Apr 1962). **Aims** Advance knowledge in clinical and experimental ophthalmic pathology. **Structure** Steering Committee. **Languages** English. **Events** *Meeting* Valencia (Spain) 2022, *Meeting* Helsinki (Finland) 2021, *Meeting* Lausanne (Switzerland) 2019, *Meeting* Glasgow (UK) 2018, *Meeting* Leuven (Belgium) 2017.
Members Full in 19 countries:
Austria, Belgium, Czechia, Denmark, Finland, France, Germany, Hungary, Ireland, Italy, Montenegro, Netherlands, Poland, Portugal, Serbia, Spain, Sweden, Switzerland, UK.
NGO Relations Close collaboration with (US) Verhoeff Society. [2022.02.15/XD6288/D]

♦ European Opiate Addiction Treatment Association (EUROPAD) 08090

Office c/o AU-CNS, Via XX Settembre 83, 55045 Pietrasanta LU, Italy. E-mail: info@europad.org.
SG Cntr for Treatment of Drug Addiction – Univ Psychiatric Clinic Ljubljana, Studenec 48, 1260 Ljubljana, Slovenia.
URL: http://www.europad.org/

History 26 Sep 1994, Geneva (Switzerland), as *European Methadone Association (EUMA)*. Current name adopted, 1998. **Aims** Improve the lives of opiate misusers and their families; reduce the impact of illicit *drug* use on society as a whole; develop opiate addiction treatment in Europe; make a major contribution to the knowledge of, and attitudes to, addiction treatment worldwide. **Structure** Board of Directors; Secretariat activities carried out by Association for the Application of Neuroscientific Knowledge to Social Aims (AU-CNS). **Languages** English. **Staff** All voluntary. **Finance** Educational grants from international companies; journal subscriptions; minor sponsorships. Annual budget: about euro 10,000-20,000; about euro 100,000 when conference is organized. **Activities** Events/meetings; awards/prizes/competitions. **Events** *European Congress on Heroin Addiction and Related Clinical Problems* Lisbon (Portugal) 2024, *European Congress on Heroin Addiction and Related Clinical Problems* Pisa (Italy) 2022, *European Congress on Heroin Addiction and Related Clinical Problems* Grenoble (France) 2021, *European Congress on Heroin Addiction and Related Clinical Problems* Grenoble (France) 2020, *European Congress on Heroin Addiction and Related Clinical Problems* Krakow (Poland) 2018. **Publications** *Heroin Addiction and Related Clinical Problems* (6 a year) – official journal. **Members** Full (around 1,000). Membership countries not specified. **IGO Relations** Consultative status with: *ECOSOC (#05331)*. **NGO Relations** Collaborates with: American Association for the Treatment of Opioid Dependence (AATOD). In collaboration with AATOD, set up: *World Federation for the Treatment of Opioid Dependence (WFTOD, #21495)*. [2019.09.27/XD5203/D]

♦ European Optical Society (EOS) 08091

Exec Dir Länsikatu 15, FI-80110 Joensuu, Finland. T. +358505954348. Fax +358132637111. E-mail: eosam@europeanoptics.org.
Events – Conference Manager address not obtained.
URL: http://www.myeos.org/

History Founded 24 May 1991, The Hague (Netherlands), by the Optics Division of *European Physical Society (EPS, #08207)* – which had been independent of EOS up to 1984 as *European Optical Committee (EOC, inactive)* – replacing *European Federation of Applied Optics (EUROPTICA, inactive)* and part of the Optics Division, the optical physics part of that Division then coming within the Quantum Electronics Division of EPS. Registered in accordance with French law. **Aims** Contribute to the progress of optics and related sciences; promote their applications in Europe and worldwide, by bringing together individual persons and legal bodies involved in these disciplines and their applications; promote optics in cooperation with industry and research; approach essential optics-related matters; establish an open coordination of international conferences in Europe. **Structure** General Meeting (annual); Board of Directors; Executive Committee; Advisory Committee. **Languages** English. **Activities** Events/meetings; advocacy/lobbying/activism. **Events** *Annual Scientific Meeting* Porto (Portugal) 2022, *Annual Scientific Meeting* Paris (France) 2021, *Annual Scientific Meeting* Joensuu (Finland) 2020, *Topical Meeting on Terahertz Science and Technology* Berlin (Germany) 2018, *Conference on Laser Ablation and Nanoparticle Generation in Liquids* Lyon (France) 2018. **Publications** *EOS Newsletter*; *Journal of the European Optical Society – Part A: Pure and Applied Optics*; *Online Journal of the European Optical Society*.

Members Individual; Corporate; Learned Societies. National optical societies in 21 countries:
Belgium, Czechia, Denmark, Finland, France, Germany, Hungary, Ireland, Italy, Latvia, Netherlands, Norway, Poland, Romania, Russia, Slovakia, Spain, Sweden, Switzerland, UK, Ukraine.
Individual and Student in 58 countries and territories:
Algeria, Argentina, Australia, Austria, Belarus, Belgium, Brazil, Bulgaria, Canada, Chile, China, Colombia, Czechia, Denmark, Egypt, Estonia, Finland, France, Georgia, Germany, Greece, Hungary, India, Ireland, Israel, Italy, Japan, Korea DPR, Korea Rep, Latvia, Liechtenstein, Lithuania, Mexico, Morocco, Netherlands, New Zealand, Nigeria, Norway, Pakistan, Poland, Portugal, Puerto Rico, Romania, Russia, Saudi Arabia, Senegal, Singapore, Spain, Sweden, Switzerland, Syrian AR, Taiwan, Trinidad-Tobago, Türkiye, UK, Ukraine, USA, Uzbekistan.
Corporate in 13 countries:
Australia, China, Finland, France, Germany, Greece, Italy, Netherlands, Norway, Russia, Switzerland, UK, USA.
NGO Relations Member of: *International Commission for Optics (ICO, #12710)*. [2022/XD3320/D]

♦ European Oral Microbiology Workshop (meeting series)

♦ European Orchestra Federation (EOFed) 08092

Pres PO Box 56, 9477 Trübbach SG, Switzerland. T. +41817831027.
URL: http://www.eofed.org/

History Founded 21 May 2009, Dalfsen (Netherlands), on merger of *European Association of Amateur Orchestras (EAAO, inactive)* and *European Association of Youth Orchestras (EAYO, inactive)*. **Aims** Promote *music* making as a free time voluntary activity in amateur orchestras and ensembles; support adult and youth ensembles in joining forces for joint projects; run musical libraries. **Structure** Board of 9. **Languages** English. **Staff** None; voluntary for projects. **Finance** Members' dues. **Activities** Events/meetings. **Events** *General assembly / Assembly / European Orchestra Festival* Tallinn (Estonia) 2012, *Assembly* Dalfsen (Netherlands) 2009, *Biennial General Assembly* Hoogeveen (Netherlands) 2009.
Members Full in 17 countries:
Austria, Bulgaria, Czechia, Estonia, Finland, France, Germany, Hungary, Ireland, Italy, Latvia, Liechtenstein, Luxembourg, Netherlands, Norway, Slovenia, Switzerland.
NGO Relations Member of: *European Music Council (EMC, #07837)*; *International Music Council (IMC, #14199)*; *World Federation of Amateur Orchestras (WFAO, #21409)*. [2015.06.25/XJ0164/D]

♦ European Orchid Committee / see European Orchid Council (#08093)

♦ European Orchid Council (EOC) 08093

Treas address not obtained.
URL: http://www.europeanorchidcouncil.eu/

History Former names and other names: *European Orchid Committee* – former; *Comité européen orchidées* – former; *Europäische Orchideen-Kommission* – former. Registration: Switzerland. **Aims** Help member organisations and their individual members to exchange experiences and ideas in order to facilitate a common realisation of all activities concerning orchids. **Structure** General Assembly (annual). Board of Directors of 7 members. **Languages** English. **Staff** Voluntary. **Finance** Sources: members' dues. **Activities** Events/meetings; knowledge management/information dissemination; networking/liaising. **Events** *Triennial Congress* Florence (Italy) 2027, *Triennial Congress* Dresden (Germany) 2024, *Triennial Congress* Copenhagen (Denmark) 2021, *Triennial Congress* Paris (France) 2018, *Triennial Congress* Vienna (Austria) 2015. **Publications** *CAESIANA* – scientific journal; *Orchid Review*.
Members Organizations in 14 countries:
Belgium, Denmark, Finland, France, Germany, Hungary, Ireland, Italy, Netherlands, Poland, Portugal, Spain, Switzerland, UK.
[2023.02.13/XE3303/E]

♦ European Organic Certifiers Council (EOCC) 08094

SG Rue d'Arlon 63-67, 1040 Brussels, Belgium. E-mail: representative@eocc.nu.
URL: http://www.eocc.nu/

History Registration: Banque Carrefour des Entreprises, No/ID: 0824.026.282, Start date: 17 Mar 2010, Belgium; EU Transparency Register, No/ID: 755639413555-75, Start date: 28 Apr 2014. **Aims** Increase reliability of control and certification activities and decisions in relation to European legislation with regard to organic production and labelling of organic *products*. **Structure** General Assembly (annual); Board of Directors; Working Groups; Task Forces. **Languages** English. **Staff** 0.50 FTE, paid. **Finance** Sources: members' dues. **Activities** Certification/accreditation; knowledge management/information dissemination; politics/policy/regulatory. **Events** *General Assembly* Esslingen (Germany) 2015, *General Assembly* Barcelona (Spain) 2014, *General Assembly* Amsterdam (Netherlands) 2013, *General Assembly* Nürburg (Germany) 2012, *General Assembly* Nürburg (Germany) 2011.
Members Organic control bodies (50). Full in 24 countries:
Austria, Belgium, Denmark, Finland, France, Germany, Greece, India, Italy, Netherlands, Norway, Poland, Portugal, Romania, Serbia, Slovakia, Slovenia, Spain, Sweden, Switzerland, Türkiye, UK, Ukraine, USA.
NGO Relations Member of: *TP Organics – European Technology Platform (TP Organics, #20180)*. Partner of: *European Cooperation for Accreditation (EA, #06782)*; *IFOAM Organics Europe (#11104)*. [2020/XJ0892/D]

♦ European Organic Fertilizers Manufacturers Association (EUROFEMA) 08095

Sec p/a Bannerlaan 79, 2280 Grobbendonk, Belgium. T. +3214861655. E-mail: info@eurofema.eu.
URL: http://www.eurofema.eu/

History 2007. Registration: EU Transparency Register, No/ID: 952946917159-89, Start date: 19 May 2015. **Aims** Act as the contact point for the regulatory and supervisory authorities in the European Union; defende the quality of organic fertilizers in the European Union so as to safeguard the interests of both consumers and crops; promote organic fertilizers for the advancement of sustainable agri-and horticulture and a healthy environment. **Structure** Executive Committee. **Activities** Advocacy/lobbying/activism; knowledge management/information dissemination. **Events** *Summit of the Organic and organo-mineral Fertilisers Industries in Europe (SOFIE)* Brussels (Belgium) 2023.

Members Full in 5 countries:
Belgium, France, Germany, Netherlands, Spain. [2023.02.16/AA2559/t/D]

- ♦ European Organisation of Airline Pilots Associations (inactive)
- ♦ European Organisation for Conformity Assessment (inactive)

♦ European Organisation for the Exploitation of Meteorological Satellites (EUMETSAT) 08096

Organisation Européenne pour l'Exploitation de Satellites Météorologiques – Europäische Organisation zur Nutzung von Wettersatelliten

Contact EUMETSAT-Allee 1, 64295 Darmstadt, Germany. T. +4961518077. Fax +496151807555. E-mail: press@eumetsat.int.
URL: http://www.eumetsat.int/

History 19 Jun 1986. Established on entry into force of the EUMETSAT Convention, and following the success of the ESA pre-operational METEOSAT programme. **Aims** Establish, maintain and exploit European Systems of operational meteorological satellites; contribute to operational monitoring of the *climate* and detection of global *climatic changes*. **Structure** Council; Director General; Directors (4); Divisions. **Languages** English, French. **Staff** 520.00 FTE, paid. Social dialogue through *European Organisation for the Exploitation of Meteorological Satellites Staff Association Committee (EUMETSAT Staff Association Committee, #08097)*. **Finance** Sources: contributions of member/participating states. Marginal revenue from sale of EUMETSAT satellite data. **Activities** Monitoring/evaluation. **Events** *Meteorological Satellite Conference* Tokyo (Japan) 2023, *Meteorological Satellite Conference* Bucharest (Romania) 2021, *Meteorological Satellite Conference* Würzburg (Germany) 2020, *Joint Conference* Boston, MA (USA) 2019, *Meeting* Stockholm (Sweden) 2019. **Publications** Annual Report; brochures; technical and scientific documentation; conference and workshop proceedings.
Members Governments of 30 countries:
Austria, Belgium, Bulgaria, Croatia, Czechia, Denmark, Estonia, Finland, France, Germany, Greece, Hungary, Iceland, Ireland, Italy, Latvia, Lithuania, Luxembourg, Netherlands, Norway, Poland, Portugal, Romania, Slovakia, Slovenia, Spain, Sweden, Switzerland, Türkiye, UK.
Cooperating State:
Serbia.
IGO Relations Member of (2): *EuroGEOSS (#05685)*; *Group on Earth Observations (GEO, #10735)*. Cooperates with (6): *European Centre for Medium-Range Weather Forecasts (ECMWF, #06490)*; *European Commission (EC, #06633)*; *European Space Agency (ESA, #08798)*; *European Union (EU, #08967)*; *United Nations Office for Outer Space Affairs (UNOOSA, #20601)*; *World Meteorological Organization (WMO, #21649)*. Accepts: *Convention on Registration of Objects Launched into Outer Space (1974)*. **NGO Relations** Member of (5): *Committee on Earth Observation Satellites (CEOS, #04249)*; *European Meteorological Society (EMS, #07786)*; *International Charter "Space and Major Disasters" (#12538)*; *International Committee on Technical Interchange for Space Mission Operations (SpaceOps, #12808)*; *International Space University (ISU, #15575)*. [2022.02.15/XD7305/E*]

♦ European Organisation for the Exploitation of Meteorological Satellites Staff Association Committee (EUMETSAT Staff Association Committee) 08097

Contact Eumetsat-Allee 1, 64295 Darmstadt, Germany. E-mail: sac@eumetsat.int.

History 19 Jun 1986. Established to represent staff of *European Organisation for the Exploitation of Meteorological Satellites (EUMETSAT, #08096)*. **Aims** Protect professional and social interests of staff members. **Structure** Staff Assembly (2 a year); Rotating Chairmanship (annual); Committee Members elected for 3-year mandate, renewable. **Languages** English, French. **Staff** 572.00 FTE, paid. Dec 2021 **Finance** Funds and infrastructure provided by EUMETSAT. **Activities** Events/meetings; guidance/assistance/consulting. **NGO Relations** Member of (1): *Federation of International Civil Servants' Associations (FICSA, #09603)*. [2022.10.31/XE2808/E]

- ♦ European Organisation for External Quality Assessment Programmes in Laboratory Medicine / see European Organisation for External Quality Assurance Providers in Laboratory Medicine (#08098)

♦ European Organisation for External Quality Assurance Providers in Laboratory Medicine (EQALM) 08098

Contact Centre Suisse de Contrôle de Qualité, 2 Ch du Petit Bel-Air, 1225 Chêne Bourg GE, Switzerland. E-mail: office@eqalm.org.
URL: http://www.eqalm.org/

History Founded 1997, as *European Committee for External Quality Assessment Programmes in Laboratory Medicine*. Previously also referred to as *European Organisation for External Quality Assessment Programmes in Laboratory Medicine*. Registered in accordance with Swiss Civil Code. **Aims** Provide a forum for cooperation and knowledge exchange on quality-related matters especially with regard to external quality assessment/assurance programmes in Europe. **Structure** General Assembly (annual); Executive Board; Working Groups (6). Sub-Committees (5): EU and CEN; Co-operation with Industry; Non-EU Countries; Nordic Countries; International Organizations. **Languages** English. **Finance** Members' dues. **Activities** Events/meetings; publishing activity; advocacy/lobbying/activism. **Events** *Annual General Assembly* Barcelona (Spain) 2016, *Symposium* Barcelona (Spain) 2016, *Annual General Assembly* Bergen (Norway) 2015, *Symposium* Bergen (Norway) 2015, *Symposium* Toulouse (France) 2014. **Publications** *EQALM Newsletter*; *EQA News*. Books.
Members Full; Associate; Individual. Members in 36 countries:
Argentina, Austria, Belgium, Bulgaria, Canada, Croatia, Cuba, Czechia, Denmark, Estonia, Finland, France, Germany, Greece, Hungary, India, Iran Islamic Rep, Ireland, Italy, Mexico, Netherlands, Norway, Oman, Poland, Portugal, Romania, Russia, Saudi Arabia, Serbia, Slovakia, Slovenia, South Africa, Spain, Sweden, Switzerland, UK.
NGO Relations Stakeholder of: *Joint Committee for Traceability in Laboratory Medicine (JCTLM, #16127)*. [2015.01.05/XE3335/E]

- ♦ European Organisation of Fish Immunology / see International Society of Fish and Shellfish Immunology (#15122)
- ♦ European Organisation of Military Associations / see European Organisation of Military Associations and Trade Unions (#08099)

♦ European Organisation of Military Associations and Trade Unions (EUROMIL) 08099

Pres Bd du Roi Albert II 5, B1, 1210 Brussels, Belgium. T. +32480660933. E-mail: euromil@euromil.org.
URL: https://euromil.org/

History 1972. Secretariat moved from Bonn (Germany) to Brussels (Belgium) in autumn 1995. Charter adopted by Congress, Apr 2013. New Charter adopted 21 Oct 2021. Former names and other names: *Organisation européenne des associations militaires* – former; *Organización Europea de Asociaciones Militares* – former; *Europäische Organisation der Militärverbände* – former; *Europese Organisatie van Militaire Verenigingen* – former; *European Organisation of Military Associations (EUROMIL)* – former. Registration: Banque-Carrefour des Entreprises, No/ID: 0538.809.759, Start date: 23 Sep 2013, Belgium; EU Transparency Register, No/ID: 14575766603-44, Start date: 7 Sep 2011. **Aims** Promote and protect professional and social interests as well as fundamental rights and freedoms of military personnel. **Structure** General Assembly (twice a year); Extraordinary GA (every four years), Brussels (Belgium) Office. **Languages** English. **Staff** 3.00 FTE, paid. **Finance** Sources: members' dues. **Activities** Advocacy/lobbying/activism; events/meetings; knowledge management/information dissemination; monitoring/evaluation. **Events** *General Assembly* Trencin (Slovakia) 2022, *Meeting* Brussels (Belgium) 2020, *Conference on the Climate-Security Nexus* Brussels (Belgium) 2019, *Meeting* Brussels (Belgium) 2019, *The Climate-Security Nexus: Implications for the Military* Brussels (Belgium) 2019. **Publications** Newsletters; reports.
Members Military associations and trade unions (32) in 21 countries.
Belgium, Bulgaria, Cyprus, Denmark, Germany, Greece, Hungary, Ireland, Italy, Latvia, Malta, Montenegro, Netherlands, North Macedonia, Poland, Portugal, Romania, Serbia, Slovakia, Spain, Sweden.
Consultative Status Consultative status granted from: *Council of Europe (CE, #04881)* (Participatory Status); *ECOSOC (#05331)* (Special). [2022.05.10/XD6448/t/D]

♦ European Organisation of Prison and Correctional Services (EuroPris) 08100

Exec Dir PO Box 13635, 2501 EP The Hague, Netherlands. T. +31625055692.
URL: http://www.europris.org/

History Set up 2011. Registered in accordance with Dutch law, Dec 2011. EU Transparency Register: 972634836901-11. **Aims** Promote ethical and rights-based imprisonment; exchange information; provide expert assistance; improve cooperation among European prison and correctional services, so as to enhance public safety and security, reduce re-offending, improve detention standards and advance professionalism in the corrections field. **Structure** Board; Executive Committee. **Languages** English. **Staff** 4.50 FTE, paid. **Finance** Members' dues. Support from *European Union (EU, #08967)* – Justice Programme. **Activities** Events/meetings; knowledge management/information dissemination. Collects and disseminates: information on the refugee problem in Latin America; information to achieve peace; systematization of torture victims' experience of treatment and care. **Events** *International Correctional Research Symposium (CRS)* Porto (Portugal) 2021, *Global Technology in Corrections Conference* Lisbon (Portugal) 2019, *ICT in Prisons Workshop* Stockholm (Sweden) 2018, *Conference and Annual General Meeting* Lillestrøm (Norway) 2017, *Conference and Annual General Meeting* Helsinki (Finland) 2014. **Publications** *EuroPris Newsletter* (6 a year). Expert Group reports.
Members Prison services in 30 countries and territories (England and Wales a joint service):
Austria, Belgium, Bulgaria, Croatia, Cyprus, Czechia, Denmark, England, Estonia, Finland, Georgia, Germany, Hungary, Ireland, Italy, Latvia, Lithuania, Luxembourg, Netherlands, Northern Ireland, Norway, Portugal, Romania, Scotland, Slovakia, Slovenia, Spain, Sweden, Türkiye, Wales. [2020/XJ7138/D]

- ♦ European Organisation for Probation / see Confederation of European Probation (#04530)
- ♦ European Organisation for Rare Diseases / see EURORDIS – Rare Diseases Europe (#09175)

♦ European Organisation for Research and Treatment of Cancer (EORTC) 08101

Organisation européenne pour la recherche et le traitement du cancer (OERTC) – Europäische Organisation zur Erforschung und Behandlung von Krebs – Organizzazione Europea per la Ricerca e il Trattamento del Cancro – Europese Organisatie voor Onderzoek en Kankerbehandeling

Dir-Gen Av E Mounier 83/11, 1200 Brussels, Belgium. T. +3227741641.
URL: http://www.eortc.org/

History 1962. Statutes recognized, Jul 1963, Brussels (Belgium). Current title adopted in 1968. Current statutes adopted by Council 20 Jun 1980; modified 12 Oct 1984, 20 Nov 1986, 22 Jun 2005, 25 Jul 2011, 4 Apr 2013. Former names and other names: *Groupe européen de chimiothérapie anticancéreuse (GECA)* – former. Registration: Banque-Carrefour des Entreprises, No/ID: 0408.292.992, Start date: 18 Jun 1963, Belgium; EU Transparency Register, No/ID: 70539554035-46, Start date: 20 Aug 2010. **Aims** Develop, conduct, coordinate and stimulate clinical research in Europe to improve the management of cancer and related problems by increasing survival and also patients' quality of life. **Structure** General Assembly; Board; Executive Committee; Committees (8); Groups (18); Task Forces (3). **Languages** English. **Staff** 183.00 FTE, paid. **Finance** *EORTC Cancer Research Fund*. Support from US National Cancer Institute. Core grants from: national cancer organizations; Belgian Lottery; *European Commission (EC, #06633)*; pharmaceutical industry (for projects). **Activities** Events/meetings; networking/liaising; research and development; training/education. **Events** *European Breast Cancer Conference (EBCC)* Milan (Italy) 2024, *European Breast Cancer Conference (EBCC)* Barcelona (Spain) 2022, *EORTC 60th Anniversary Meeting* Brussels (Belgium) 2022, *Gastrointestinal Tract Cancer Group Autumn Meeting* Brussels (Belgium) 2022, *Pharmacology and Molecular Mechanisms Group Meeting* Florence (Italy) 2022. **Publications** *European Journal of Cancer*. Annual Report; national journals; leaflets. **Information Services** *CDISC – Clinical Data Interchange Standards Consortium*; *DICOM Data* – online platform for medical imaging review; *ORTA-system (Online Randomized Trials Access)*; *RDC – Remote Data Capture*; *VISTA System* – clinical trial management system. **Members** Individuals in 55 countries. Membership countries not specified. **NGO Relations** Member of (2): *Associations and Conference Forum (AC Forum, #02909)*; *Biomedical Alliance in Europe (#03251)*. [2022/XD0822/v/D]

- ♦ European Organisation for the Safety of Air Navigation / see EUROCONTROL (#05667)

♦ European Organisation for Security (EOS) 08102

Contact Rue Montoyer 10, 1000 Brussels, Belgium. T. +3227770257. E-mail: info@eos-eu.com.
URL: http://www.eos-eu.com/

History Jul 2007, by European private sector providers of technology solutions and services, as a Cooperative Company with Limited Responsibility. Registered in accordance with Belgian law. EU Transparency Register: 32134385519-64. Registration: EU Transparency Register, No/ID: 32134385519-64. **Aims** Develop a harmonized European security market satisfying political, societal and economic needs through the efficient use of budgets and implementation of available solutions in priority areas, in particular with the creation of relevant EU security programmes. **Structure** Board of Directors; Working Groups (7); Sub-working Groups (4). **Languages** English. **Staff** 10.00 FTE, paid. **Finance** Members' dues. Other sources: in-kind contributions; study contracts; other services. Projects also funded by: *European Commission (EC, #06633)*. **Activities** Politics/policy/regulatory. **Events** *Security Mission Information and Innovation Group (SMI2G) Meeting* Brussels (Belgium) 2019, *Conference on a New Partnership for European Security* Brussels (Belgium) 2011, *Meeting on Securing Europe's Energy Infrastructure* Brussels (Belgium) 2011. **Publications** Position papers; white papers.
Members Companies and organizations (39). International organizations (2):
Aerospace and Defence Industries Association of Europe (ASD, #00146); *Confederation of Organizations in Road Transport Enforcement (CORTE, #04574)*.
Companies in 13 countries:
Belgium, France, Germany, Greece, Ireland, Italy, Netherlands, Portugal, Spain, Sweden, Switzerland, Türkiye, UK. [2020/XM1714/y/D]

- ♦ European Organisation for Technical Approvals / see European Organisation for Technical Assessment (#08103)

♦ European Organisation for Technical Assessment (EOTA) 08103

Organisation Européenne pour l'évaluation technique

SG Av des Arts 40, 1040 Brussels, Belgium. T. +3225026900. Fax +3225023814. E-mail: info@eota.eu.
URL: http://www.eota.eu/

History 10 Oct 1990, Brussels (Belgium). Founded under provisions of *Internationale Franz Lehar Gesellschaft (#13235)* – Council Directive, 21 Dec 1988 (89/106/EEC). Registered in accordance with Belgian law, 23 Mar 1993. New statutes adopted 1995; amended 2000, 2004, 2013 and 2014. Former names and other names: *European Organisation for Technical Approvals* – former; *Organisation européenne pour l'agrément technique* – former; *Europäische Organisation für Technische Zulassungen* – former. Registration: Banque-Carrefour des Entreprises, No/ID: 0449.719.714, Start date: 23 Mar 1993, Belgium; EU Transparency Register, No/ID: 208852948297-25, Start date: 6 Dec 2022. **Aims** Develop and adopt European Assessment Documents (EADs) by using scientific and technological expertise of its members. **Structure** General Assembly; Executive Board; Technical Board. **Languages** English, French, German. **Staff** 2.00 FTE, paid. **Finance** Sources: members' dues. Mandates from European Commission and EFTA. **Activities** Certification/accreditation; standards/guidelines. **Events** *Conference* Brussels (Belgium) 2016.
Members Organizations in 28 countries:
Austria, Belgium, Cyprus, Czechia, Denmark, Finland, France, Germany, Hungary, Ireland, Italy, Latvia, Lithuania, Luxembourg, Netherlands, Norway, Poland, Portugal, Romania, Slovakia, Slovenia, Spain, Sweden, Switzerland, Türkiye.
Observers in 4 countries:
Luxembourg, Netherlands, UK, USA.
IGO Relations European Commission Enterprise Directorate-General.
NGO Relations Member of (1): *Federation of European and International Associations Established in Belgium (FAIB, #09508)*.
Formal links with: *European Group of Organisations for Fire Testing, Inspection and Certification (EGOLF, #07427)*; *Union européenne pour l'agrément technique dans la construction (UEAtc, #20393)*.
Industrial organizations involved in the Technical Board: *Association of European Experts in Building and Construction (The) (AEEBC, #02510)*; *Construction Products Europe AISBL (#04761)*; *European Builders Confederation (EBC, #06408)*; *European Construction Industry Federation (#06766)*; *European Federation of Building and Woodworkers (EFBWW, #07065)*; *Build Europe (#03350)*.

Industrial associations involved:
- *QUALICOAT (#18590)*;
- *Comité européen de l'outillage (CEO, #04163)*;
- *Confédération européenne des industries du bois (CEI Bois, #04545)*;
- *Conseil européen de l'industrie des peintures, des encres d'imprimerie et des couleurs d'art (CEPE, #04688)*;
- *European Association for Panels and Profiles (PPA-Europe, #06142)*;
- *European Association for Passive Fire Protection (EAPFP, #06143)*;
- *European Association of Plaster and Plaster Product Manufacturers (EUROGYPSUM, #06152)*;
- *European Bearing and Joint Manufacture Association (EBJA, no recent information)*;
- *European Consortium of Anchors Producers (ECAP, #06749)*;
- *European Extruded Polystyrene Insulation Board Association (EXIBA, #07019)*;
- *European Federation of Fibre-Cement Manufacturers (EFFCM, #07120)*;
- *European Glaziers Association (#07394)*;
- *European Group for Rooflights and Smoke-Ventilation (EUROLUX, #07434)*;
- *European Insulation Manufacturers Association (EURIMA, #07577)*;
- *European Manufacturers of Expanded Polystyrene (EUMEPS, #07732)*;
- *European Mortar Industry Organization (EMO, #07822)*;
- *European Plastics Converters (EuPC, #08216)*;
- *European Single Ply Waterproofing Association (ESWA, #08488)*;
- *European Waterproofing Association (EWA, #09084)*;
- *Fédération des associations européennes des constructeurs de fenêtres et de façades (FAECF, #09456)*;
- *Flame Retardants Europe (FRE, #09791)*;
- *Glass for Europe (#10157)*;
- *International Federation for the Roofing Trade (#13534)*;
- *PAN and PRO EUROPE (inactive)*;
- *QUALANOD (#18589)*. [2022/XD2256/**D**]

♦ European Organisation of Tomato Industries (TomatoEurope) 08104

Organisation européenne des industries de la tomate

Contact c/o KELLEN, Av de Tervuren 188A box 4, 1150 Brussels, Belgium. T. +3227611657. Fax +3227611699. E-mail: tomatoeurope@kellencompany.com.
URL: http://www.tomatoeurope.eu/

History 14 May 1963, as *Association of European Tomato Processing Industries – Organisation européenne des industries de la conserve de tomates (OEICT) – Organización Europea de las Industrias de la Conserva de Tomates – Europäische Organisation der Tomatenkonserven-Industrie – Organizzazione Europea delle Industrie delle Conserve di Pomodoro – Organização Europeia da Industria de Conserva do Tomate – Europese Organisatie der Tomatenconserves-industrieën – Evropaiki Organosi Viomihanion Metapiisis Tomatas*. Restructured 26 Apr 1977. Subsequently known under the French acronym *OEIT*. EU Transparency Register: 35628678901-76. **Aims** Represent the tomato processing industry from France, Greece, Italy, Portugal and Spain. **Structure** General Assembly; Association Bureau; Commissions; Working Groups. **Languages** English, French.
Members National organizations in 5 countries:
France, Greece, Italy, Portugal, Spain.
IGO Relations Recognized by: *European Commission (EC, #06633)*. [2020.03.03/XD0826/t/**D**]

♦ European Organization of Agricultural and Rural Contractors 08105

Confédération européenne des entrepreneurs de travaux techniques agricoles, ruraux et forestiers (CEETTAR) – Europäischer Zentralverband der land- und forstwirtschaftlichen Lohnunternehmer und ländlichen Dienstleistungsunternehmern

Main Office Bd Anspach 111, bte 13, 1000 Brussels, Belgium. T. +3222742206. Fax +3224007126. E-mail: ceettar@ceettar.eu.
URL: http://www.ceettar.eu/

History 31 May 1961. *European Network of Forest Entrepreneurs (ENFE, inactive)* merged into CEETTAR, 2016. Former names and other names: *Comité des organisations des entrepreneurs de travaux agricoles de la CEE* – former; *Confédération européenne des organisations des entrepreneurs de travaux techniques agricoles et ruraux* – former; *Confédération européenne des entrepreneurs de travaux techniques agricoles et ruraux* – former. Registration: No/ID: 0851.826.977, Start date: 2 Jan 2001, Belgium; EU Transparency Register, No/ID: 15086733813-03, Start date: 1 Jul 2010. **Aims** Represent the interests of land-based contractors in Europe. **Structure** General Assembly; Management Committee; Board. **Languages** English, French. **Staff** 2.00 FTE, paid. **Finance** Sources: members' dues.
Members Organizations in 19 countries:
Austria, Belgium, Denmark, Finland, France, Germany, Ireland, Italy, Lithuania, Luxembourg, Netherlands, Norway, Poland, Portugal, Romania, Spain, Sweden, Switzerland, UK.
IGO Relations Observer status with (1): *Union internationale pour la protection des obtentions végétales (UPOV, #20436)*. **NGO Relations** Member of (1): *PEFC Council (#18288)*. Cooperates with (1): *European Federation of Food, Agriculture and Tourism Trade Unions (EFFAT, #07125)*. [2022.05.04/XE0492/**E**]

♦ European Organization for Astronomical Research in the Southern hemisphere (ESO) 08106

Organisation européenne pour des recherches astronomiques dans l'hémisphère austral – Europäische Organisation für Astronomische Forschung in der Südlichen Hemisphäre

Dir Gen Karl-Schwarzschild-Str 2, 85748 Garching, Germany. T. +498932006226. Fax +498932006366. E-mail: information@eso.org.
Santiago Office Alonso de Córdova 3107, Vitacura, Casilla 19001, 19 Santiago, Santiago Metropolitan, Chile. T. +5624633000. Fax +5624633101. E-mail: contacto@eso.org.
Main Website: http://www.eso.org/

History 5 Oct 1962, Paris (France). Statutes registered in *'UNTS 1/14697'*. Former names and other names: *European Southern Observatory* – former (1962). **Aims** Establish and operate astronomical observatories in the southern hemisphere, furthering and organizing collaboration in *astronomy*, covering a wide spectrum of activities, including design and construction of world-class ground-based observational facilities for member-state scientists, large telescope projects, design of innovative scientific instruments, developing new and advanced technologies, furthering European cooperation in astronomy and carrying out European educational programmes. **Structure** Council; Visiting Committee of distinguished scientists. Other Committees (4): Scientific-Technical (STC); Finance (FC); Observing Programmes (OPC); Users (UC). Headquarters (Scientific, Technical and Administrative Centre) in Garching (Germany) comprises 5 Directorates (Science, Programmes, Operations, Engineering, Administration). Cabinet of the Director General. Offices and facilities: Santiago (Chile); La Silla Paranal Observatory in Chile on 2 sites – Cerro La Silla (IV Region) and Cerro Paranal (II Region). Participates in ALMA Millimeter/Submillimeter Observatory on Llano Chajnantor with North America and East Asia, Cerro Amazones (II Region), in Chile. **Languages** English, French, German, Spanish. **Staff** 700.00 FTE, paid. As of Feb 2020: staff from more than 30 different countries. Staff representation through *European Southern Observatory Staff Association (ESO Staff Association, #08797)*. Staff benefits through *Association coopérative financière des fonctionnaires internationaux (AMFIE, #02455)*. *Administrative Tribunal of the International Labour Organization (ILO Tribunal, #00118)* is competent to settle disputes. **Finance** Sources: contributions of member/participating states. Annual budget: 214,000,000 EUR (2021). **Activities** Events/meetings; knowledge management/information dissemination; monitoring/evaluation; networking/liaising; projects/programmes; research and development. **Events** *European Big Science Business Forum* Granada (Spain) 2022, *European Big Science Business Forum* Granada (Spain) 2021, *European Big Science Business Forum* Granada (Spain) 2020, *European Big Science Business Forum* Copenhagen (Denmark) 2018, *Deconstructing Galaxies Workshop* Santiago (Chile) 2013. **Publications** *ESO Messenger* (4 a year). Annual Report; scientific and technical reports; proceedings of meetings; press releases; video news reels. **Information Services** *ESO Science Archive Facility*; *VizieR System for Accessing Astronomical Data* – with Strasbourg (France) Astronomical Data Centre (CDS).
Members Governments of 18 countries, including 1 strategic partner (*) and 1 host State (**):
Australia (*), Austria, Belgium, Chile (**), Czechia, Denmark, Finland, France, Germany, Ireland, Italy, Netherlands, Poland, Portugal, Spain, Sweden, Switzerland, UK.
IGO Relations Joint projects with: *European Space Agency (ESA, #08798)*. Permanent Observer to: *Committee on the Peaceful Uses of Outer Space (COPUOS, #04277)*. Observer or participant in various EU-funded astronomy-related networks. **NGO Relations** Member of (2): *Cryogenics Society of Europe (CSE, #04975)*; *European Interferometry Initiative (Eii, #07583)*. Founding member of: *EIROforum (#05401)* with CERN, ESA, EFDA JET, EMBL, ESRF, ILL and XFEL. [2022.10.11/XD3947/**D***]

♦ European Organization for Cancer Nursing / see European Oncology Nursing Society (#08086)

♦ European Organization for Caries Research (ORCA) 08107

Organisme européen de recherches sur la carie – Europäische Arbeitsgemeinschaft für Kariesforschung

SG ACTA – Prev Dentistry, Gustav Mahlerlaan 3004, 1081 LA Amsterdam, Netherlands. T. +31205980437.
URL: http://www.orca-caries-research.org/

History 1953, Germany FR. Constitution amended 24 May 1975, Vienna (Austria). Former names and other names: *European Organization for Research on Fluorine and Dental Caries Prevention* – former (1953 to 1966); *Organisme européen de coordination des recherches sur le fluor et la prophylaxie de la carie dentaire* – former (1953 to 1966); *Europäische Arbeitsgemeinschaft für Fluorforschung und Kariesprophylaxe* – former (1953 to 1966). Registration: Switzerland. **Aims** Promote and undertake research on dental caries and related matters; evaluate the findings of research, encourage their practical application and prevent their abuse; make the public aware of the importance of care of the teeth. **Structure** General Assembly (annual). Board, consisting of Executive Council (9 members) and Advisory Council (10 members). **Languages** English. **Finance** Members' dues. Grants from official and private bodies. **Activities** Training/education; research/documentation. **Events** *Congress* Zagreb (Croatia) 2026, *Congress* Leeds (UK) 2025, *Congress* Crete (Greece) 2024, *Congress with EFCD* Egmond aan Zee (Netherlands) 2023, *Annual Congress* Cartagena de Indias (Colombia) 2019. **Publications** *Caries Research* (6 a year). Reports.
Members Individuals (Senior, Introductory, Honorary) in 39 countries and territories:
Australia, Austria, Belgium, Brazil, Bulgaria, Canada, Chile, Colombia, Croatia, Denmark, Finland, France, Germany, Greece, Hong Kong, Hungary, Iceland, Ireland, Israel, Italy, Japan, Jordan, Liechtenstein, Lithuania, Netherlands, New Zealand, Norway, Peru, Poland, Romania, Slovenia, South Africa, Spain, Sweden, Switzerland, Türkiye, UK, Ukraine, USA.
Corporate members in 9 countries and territories:
Belgium, France, Germany, Japan, Liechtenstein, Netherlands, Switzerland, UK, USA.
NGO Relations Associate member of: *Platform for Better Oral Health in Europe (#18399)*. [2022/XD0818/**D**]

♦ European Organization for Civil Aviation Electronics / see EUROCAE (#05652)
♦ European Organization for Civil Aviation Equipment / see EUROCAE (#05652)
♦ European Organization for the Control of Circulatory Diseases (no recent information)
♦ European Organization for Cooperation in Cancer Prevention Studies / see European Cancer Prevention Organization (#06434)
♦ European Organization of Cosmetic Ingredients Industries and Services (internationally oriented national body)
♦ European Organization for Experimental Photogrammetric Research / see European Spatial Data Research (#08806)
♦ European Organization of Homes and Services for Young Workers (inactive)
♦ European Organization for Home Textiles, Laces and Embroideries (no recent information)

♦ European Organization for Nuclear Research (CERN) 08108

Organisation européenne pour la recherche nucléaire – Centro Europeo para la Investigación Nuclear – Europäische Organisation für Kernforschung

Contact CERN, 1211 Geneva 23, Switzerland. T. +41227678484 – +41227677676. Fax +41227676555. E-mail: cern.reception@cern.ch – alexander.kohls@cern.ch.
URL: http://home.cern/

History 29 Sep 1954, Paris (France). Established on ratification by 9 of the 12 original member countries of a Convention drawn up 1 Jul 1953, Paris, following a resolution, 1950, Florence (Italy), of General Conference of UNESCO and an inter-governmental conference convened by UNESCO, Dec 1951. Replaced *European Council for Nuclear Research (CERN, inactive)* which had come into being on 15 Feb 1952 and by whose acronym the organization is still known. On 13 Sep 1965, an agreement was made with France for the lease of a further 40 hectares of land adjacent to the existing 40 hectares in Switzerland. On 17 Jan 1971 a revised Convention came into force under which an area of 480 hectares (412 in France and 68 in Switzerland) was made available for a proton synchrotron of 450 GeV (the SPS) now installed there. Present site: 112 hectares in Switzerland and 490 hectares in France.
Original aims, according to the Convention: Provide for collaboration among European states in (sub-) nuclear research of a pure scientific and fundamental character and in research essentially related thereto. The Organization shall have no concern with work for military requirements and the results of its experimental and theoretical work shall be published or otherwise made generally available. Since the signing of the Convention in 1954 'nuclear research' has de facto been replaced by 'particle physics research'. In practice, tasks are to: ensure construction and operation of *particle accelerators* and their necessary ancillary apparatus; define a programme of activities and submit it to the Council; organize and sponsor international cooperation in this field of research, particularly with and among member state laboratories. Former names and other names: *European Laboratory for Particle Physics* – alias; *Laboratoire européen pour la physique des particules* – alias. **Aims** Play a leading role in fundamental research in *particle physics* by constructing and operating experimental apparatus – mainly accelerators and detectors; educate Europe's *youth* in fundamental particle physics and techniques; transfer technology to member states' industry; bring nations together through research. **Structure** Council; Scientific Policy Committee; Finance Committee; Director General; Directors (4); Departments (10); Staff Association; Pension Fund; Research Board; Advisory Committee of CERN users. **Languages** English, French. **Staff** 2600.00 FTE, paid. *Administrative Tribunal of the International Labour Organization (ILO Tribunal, #00118)* is competent to settle disputes. **Finance** Member states' contributions.
Activities International laboratory, constructed for the study of fundamental particles and forces. Operates with a large accelerator complex: 3 linear accelerators, Linac-2 and Linac-3 (started in 1978 and 1993), and Linac-4 (will be connected to CERN's accelerator complex during the upcoming long technical shut down in 2019)20. Linac-4 will replace Linac-2. The 28 GeV Proton Synchrotron (PS) began operations in 1959. The 450 GeV Super-Proton Synchroton (SPS) with 6.9 Km circumference has operated since 1977. In 2000, the SPS's heavy ion programme began compelling evidence for a new state of matter in which the quarks and gluons, which are usually bound in the protons and neutrons roam freely. The largest accelerator, the 7+7 TeV Large Hadron Collider (LHC) started operation in 2008. By colliding high-energy particles with each other, the LHC will recreate conditions of the early Universe. It is installed in a tunnel 27 Km in circumference which previously housed the Large Electron-Positron Collider (LEP), operating from 1989 until 2000. Designed for 100 GeV per beam the LEP was used to test the Standard Model of Particle Physics. The Isotope Separator Online DEvice (ISOLDE) located at the PS Booster has been producing radioactive nuclei since 1967 for a number of applications. The 100 MeV Antiproton Decelerator (AD) has been used since 2000 to study antihydrogen atoms.
Discovered W and Z bosons at the SPS in 1983, which is the most accurate testing to date of the Standard Model at LEP (1989 to 2000) and the invention of the World Wide Web in 1992.
Research is largely carried out by visiting teams from member state institutes, with an increasing participation from non-member states such as China, Japan, USA, Canada, Russia and Latin American countries. Total of 494 institutes and universities in member states and 468 in non-member states participate in the experimental programme, which amounts to 12,372 experimental physicists, of which 6,971 are from member states.
Training/education. Instrumental in setting up: *European Committee for Future Accelerators (ECFA, #06650)*; *World Wide Web Consortium (W3C, #21935)*. Set up *European School of Medical Physics*, jointly with *European Scientific Institute (ESI, #08448)*, *European Federation of Organisations for Medical Physics (EFOMP, #07183)* and CEA (Paris); *European School of Particle Physics*; *'CERN-CLAF School of High Energy Physics'*.
Events *European Big Science Business Forum* Granada (Spain) 2022, *Triennial Vienna Conference on Instrumentation* Vienna (Austria) 2022, *DIS : Annual International Workshop on Deep Inelastic Scattering and Related Subjects* Brooklyn, NY (USA) 2021, *European Big Science Business Forum* Granada (Spain) 2021, *LHCP : Annual Large Hadron Collider Physics Conference* Paris (France) 2021. **Publications** *CERN Bulletin* (bi-weekly) – online and print; *CERN Courier* (10 a year) – paper and online. Annual report (since 1955); scientific reports; general and technical publications; web updates; brochures (online and print); press releases. Information Services: Library of over 500,000 electronic documents, over 110,000 books, 1,000 current periodicals (mostly electronic) and 500,000 scientific reports.
Members Governments of 22 countries:
Austria, Belgium, Bulgaria, Czechia, Denmark, Finland, France, Germany, Greece, Hungary, Israel, Italy, Netherlands, Norway, Poland, Portugal, Romania, Serbia, Slovakia, Spain, Sweden, Switzerland, UK.

Associate Member States in Pre-Stage to Membership (3):
Cyprus, Estonia, Slovenia.
Associate Members (6):
Croatia, India, Lithuania, Pakistan, Türkiye, Ukraine.
Observers (non-contributing), governments of 3 countries:
Japan, Russia, USA.
Observer intergovernmental bodies (non-contributing) (3):
European Union (EU, #08967); Joint Institute for Nuclear Research (JINR, #16134); UNESCO (#20322).
IGO Relations Observer status with (1): *United Nations (UN, #20515)* (General Assembly). Member of (2): *Committee of Legal Advisers on Public International Law (CAHDI, #04267); International Nuclear Information System (INIS, #14378).* Cooperates with (2): *United Nations Economic Commission for Europe (UNECE, #20555); United Nations Institute for Training and Research (UNITAR, #20576).* Agreements with: *European Commission (EC, #06633); European Organization for Astronomical Research in the Southern hemisphere (ESO, #08106); International Association for the Promotion of Cooperation with Scientists from the New Independent States of the former Soviet Union (INTAS, inactive); Joint Institute for Nuclear Research (JINR, #16134);* UNESCO. **NGO Relations** Member of (10): *Alliance for Permanent Access (#00712); Association for Human Resources Management in International Organizations (AHRMIO, #02634); Cryogenics Society of Europe (CSE, #04975); DataCite (#05011); EIROforum (#05401)* (Associate); *EUDAT Collaborative Data Infrastructure (EUDAT CDI, #05580); European Physical Society (EPS, #08207)* (Associate); *GÉANT Association (#10086)* (Associate); *High Energy Physics Technology Transfer Network (HEPTech, #10914)* (Founding); *ORCID (#17790).* Partner of (2): *Confederation of Open Access Repositories (COAR, #04573); International Communications Volunteers (ICVolunteers, #12817).* Instrumental in setting up (1): *European Centre for AstroParticle Theory (EuCAPT, #06470).* Member states represented on: *International Committee for Future Accelerators (ICFA, #12774).* Participates in: *EGI Foundation (EGI.eu, #05395).* In liaison with technical committees of: *International Organization for Standardization (ISO, #14473).* [2022/XD0820/F*]

♦ European Organization of Office Furniture Manufacturers 08109

Fédération européenne du mobilier de bureau (FEMB) – Vereinigung der Europäischen Büromöbel Hersteller

Secretariat Bierstradter Str 39, 65189 Wiesbaden, Germany. T. +4961117360. Fax +49611173620. E-mail: info@femb.org.
URL: http://www.femb.org/

History Founded 1966. **Aims** Stand as a catalyst and an enabler offering both protection and fraternity to the office furniture industry in Europe and throughout the world. **Events** *Annual Summer Meeting* Rotterdam (Netherlands) 2005, *Winter Meeting* Düsseldorf (Germany) 2004, *Annual Summer Meeting* Sirmione (Italy) 2004, *Annual summer meeting* Germany 2003, *Annual summer meeting* Germany 2003.
Members National associations in 9 countries:
Belgium, Estonia, Finland, France, Germany, Italy, Netherlands, Norway, UK. [2013.12.16/XD0913/D]

♦ European Organization for Packaging and the Environment (EUROPEN) 08110

Organisation européenne pour l'emballage et l'environnement – Europäische Vereinigung für Verpackung und Umwelt

SG c/o WeWork, Rue du Commerce 31, 1000 Brussels, Belgium. E-mail: packaging@europen-packaging.eu.
Registered Office Le Royal Tervuren, Av de l'Armée 6, 1040 Brussels, Belgium. T. +3227363600. Fax +3227363521. E-mail: packaging@europen-packaging.eu.
URL: http://www.europen-packaging.eu/

History 1992. Current statutes adopted 1997; modified: 4 Mar 2003; 23 Nov 2005; 14 Oct 2013. Registration: Banque-Carrefour des Entreprises, No/ID: 0450.413.857, Start date: 3 Jul 1993, Belgium; EU Transparency Register, No/ID: 0001976677-12, Start date: 26 Nov 2008. **Aims** Achieve a fully accessible European market for packaging used for packaged products, whereby best use is made of the role, benefits and functions of packaging in society, such as protection of products and the environment and supplying information to, and meeting the needs of, consumers and customers. **Structure** General Assembly/Council of Members (at least annual); Executive Committee; Managing Director. **Languages** English, French. **Staff** 3.00 FTE, paid. **Finance** Sources: members' dues. **Activities** Advocacy/lobbying/activism; events/meetings; knowledge management/information dissemination. **Events** *Annual Packaging Waste and Sustainability Forum* Brussels (Belgium) 2016, *Comparative costs of packaging waste management organizations* Brussels (Belgium) 1996, *Workshop* Vienna (Austria) 1995. **Publications** *Economic Instruments in Packaging and Packaging Waste Policy* (2015); *Packaging in the Sustainability Agenda* (2009); *Essential Requirements for Packaging in Europe: A Practical Guide to Using the CEN Standards* (2005); *Packaging and the Environment – European and National Legislation* (2004, revised 2007 and 2012). Seminar proceedings; discussion and briefing papers; brochures. **Members** Corporate – businesses, including multinationals; national organization; associate. Members in 28 countries. Membership countries not specified. **NGO Relations** Member of (2): *Circular Plastics Alliance (#03936); European Policy Centre (EPC, #08240).* In liaison with technical committees of: *Comité européen de normalisation (CEN, #04162).* Also liaises with trade and industry organizations representing individual sectors of the packaging chain (not specified). Founding Member of: *European Food Sustainable Consumption and Production Round Table (European Food SCP Roundtable, #07289).* [2023/XD3685/D]

- ♦ European Organization of Pakistani Minorities (internationally oriented national body)
- ♦ European Organization of Petrol and Service Stations (inactive)
- ♦ European Organization of Plastic Technical Parts Producers (inactive)
- ♦ European Organization of Preserved and Tinned Fruit Industries (inactive)

♦ European Organization for Professionals and Patients with ALS (EUpALS) 08111

Chairwoman Vaartkom 17, 3000 Leuven, Belgium. T. +3216239582. E-mail: info@als.eu.
URL: https://als.eu/

History Registration: Banque-Carrefour des Entreprises, No/ID: 0684.923.631, Start date: 22 Nov 2017, Belgium. **Aims** Create equal rights for all the European ALS patients and provide better access to research and information about it. **Structure** Board of Directors. [2022.05.11/AA0494/t/D]

- ♦ European Organization for the Promotion of Equestrian Tourism (inactive)
- ♦ European Organization for the Promotion of New Techniques and Methods in Building (inactive)
- ♦ European Organization for the Protection of Textile Credit (inactive)

♦ European Organization for Quality (EOQ) 08112

Organisation européenne pour la qualité (OEQ)

Coordinator Arduinkaai 29, 1000 Brussels, Belgium. T. +32471648927.
URL: http://www.eoq.org/

History 1956, Paris (France). Founded following 1st European Conference on Quality Control organized by *European Productivity Agency (EPA, inactive).* Initials adopted 1989. Former names and other names: *European Organization for Quality Control (EOQC)* – former; *Europäische Organisation für Qualität* – former; *OECQ* – former. Registration: Banque-Carrefour des Entreprises, No/ID: 0472.150.468, Start date: 14 Dec 1999, Belgium. **Aims** Improve European society through promotion of quality in its broadest sense. **Structure** General Assembly (twice a year); Executive Board; General Secretariat. **Languages** English. **Finance** Sources: members' dues. **Activities** Awards/prizes/competitions; certification/accreditation; events/meetings; networking/liaising; training/education. **Events** *Annual Congress* Lisbon (Portugal) 2019, *Annual Congress* Paris (France) 2018, *Annual Congress* Bled (Slovenia) 2017, *Annual Congress* Helsinki (Finland) 2016, *Annual Congress* Athens (Greece) 2015. **Publications** E-newsletter. Congress proceedings; register of certificate holders; promotional leaflets and cards. **Information Services** *European Voluntary Registration System (EVROS)* – database.
Members Full: national quality organizations in Europe, represented in the General Assembly. Associate: national quality organizations in Europe approved by Executive Board. Affiliate: Individuals and organizations in or outside Europe having direct links with EOQ. Full members in 33 countries and territories:
Austria, Belgium, Bosnia-Herzegovina, Bulgaria, Croatia, Cyprus, Czechia, Denmark, Estonia, Finland, France, Georgia, Germany, Greece, Hungary, Kazakhstan, Kosovo, Malta, Moldova, Netherlands, Norway, Poland, Portugal, Romania, Russia, Serbia, Slovakia, Slovenia, Spain, Sweden, Switzerland, Türkiye, Ukraine.
Associate and Affiliate members in 9 countries:
Croatia, Finland, Kazakhstan, Kosovo, Morocco, North Macedonia, Norway, Russia, Saudi Arabia.
Partners in 9 countries and territories:
Ireland, Japan, Korea Rep, Mexico, Russia, Singapore, Taiwan, Ukraine, USA.
Consultative Status Consultative status granted from: *ECOSOC (#05331)* (Ros A); *UNIDO (#20336).* **NGO Relations** Cooperates with (8): *Association des chambres de commerce et d'industrie européennes (EUROCHAMBRES, #02423); BUSINESSEUROPE (#03381); Comité européen de normalisation (CEN, #04162); EFQM – European Foundation for Quality Management (EFQM, #05388); European Cooperation for Accreditation (EA, #06782); International Accreditation Forum (IAF, #11584); International Organization for Standardization (ISO, #14473); International Personnel Certification Association (IPC, #14560).* [2022.05.17/XD0821/D]

- ♦ European Organization for Quality Control / see European Organization for Quality (#08112)
- ♦ European Organization for Rare Disorders / see EURORDIS – Rare Diseases Europe (#09175)

♦ European Organization of Regional External Public Audit Finance Institutions (EURORAI) 08113

Secretariat Sindicatura de Comptes de Comunitat Valenciana, c/ San Vicente 4, 46002 Valencia, Spain. T. +34673412328 – +34673411805. Fax +34963869653. E-mail: eurorai@gva.es.
SG address not obtained.
URL: https://www.eurorai.org/

History Oct 1992. **Aims** Provide exchange of experiences and make progress in the common field of regional and local public sector financial control in order to guarantee a better use of public finances. **Structure** Management Committee; Working Groups. **Languages** English, French, German, Russian, Spanish. **Staff** 2.00 FTE, paid. **Finance** Sources: members' dues. Supported by: *European Commission (EC, #06633).* **Activities** Events/meetings; knowledge management/information dissemination; networking/liaising; research/documentation; training/education. **Events** *Public Sector Audit in Times of Digital Changes* Frankfurt-Main (Germany) 2022, *Congress* Palma (Spain) 2022, *Seminar* Sarajevo (Bosnia-Herzegovina) 2021, *Congress* Linz (Austria) 2019, *Audit of public debt* Warsaw (Poland) 2019. **Publications** Meeting reports, booklet; good practice; guidelines; studies.
Members Institutions. Full in 10 countries:
Austria, France, Germany, Ireland, Netherlands, Poland, Russia (cooperation suspended), Spain, Switzerland, UK.
Associate in 11 countries:
Argentina, Bosnia-Herzegovina, Brazil, Canada, Cyprus, Hungary, Lithuania, Norway, Portugal, Slovakia, Slovenia. [2023.02.28/XD6839/D]

- ♦ European Organization of Reinforced Plastic Associations – Composite Materials / see European Composites Industry Association (#06692)
- ♦ European Organization for Re-insertion and Housing of Young Workers (no recent information)
- ♦ European Organization for Research on Fluorine and Dental Caries Prevention / see European Organization for Caries Research (#08107)

♦ European Organization of the Sawmill Industry (EOS) 08114

Organisation européenne des scieries (OES) – Europäische Organisation der Sägewerke (EOS) – Europese Organisatie der Zagerijen (EOZ)

SG Rue Montoyer 24, Bte 20, 1000 Brussels, Belgium. T. +3222870876. E-mail: info@eos-oes.eu.
URL: http://www.eos-oes.eu/

History 1958. Includes activities of the previous *Groupement des scieries des pays de la CEE (inactive).* Former names and other names: *Groupement des fédérations des scieries européennes* – former (1958); *Organization of European Saw-Mills* – alias. Registration: Banque-Carrefour des Entreprises, No/ID: 0875.570.993, Start date: 16 Aug 2005, Belgium; EU Transparency Register, No/ID: 024776016336-52, Start date: 4 Mar 2015. **Aims** Influence EU policy-making in order to further the interests of the European sawmilling sector. **Structure** General Assembly (twice a year); Board of Directors; General Secretariat in Brussels (Belgium). **Languages** English, French. **Staff** 2.00 FTE, paid. **Finance** Sources: members' dues. **Activities** Knowledge management/information dissemination; events/meetings; advocacy/lobbying/activism. **Events** *International Softwood Conference* Copenhagen (Denmark) 2022, *International Hardwood Conference* Lyon (France) 2022, *International Softwood Conference* Helsinki (Finland) 2021, *International Softwood Conference* Brussels (Belgium) 2020, *International Hardwood Conference* Berlin (Germany) 2019. **Publications** Annual Report.
Members National organizations in 11 countries:
Austria, Belgium, Denmark, Finland, France, Germany, Latvia, Norway, Romania, Sweden, Switzerland.
Associate members in 2 countries:
Croatia, Romania.
IGO Relations Recognized by: *European Commission (EC, #06633).* **NGO Relations** Member of (3): *Confédération européenne des industries du bois (CEI Bois, #04545); Woodrise Alliance (#21045); Wood Sector Alliance for the New European Bauhaus (Wood4Bauhaus, #21046)* (Founding). Cooperates with (1): *European Timber Trade Federation (ETTF, #08915).* [2022/XD0505/t/D]

- ♦ European Organization of Scientific Anti-Aging Medicine (inactive)

♦ European Organization of Supreme Audit Institutions (EUROSAI) .. 08115

Organisation des Institutions Supérieures de contrôle des finances publiques d'Europe – Organización de Entidades Fiscalizadoras Superiores de Europa – Europäische Organisation der Obersten Rechnungskontrollbehörden – Evropejskaja Organizacija Vyssih Kontrolnyh Organov

SG Tribunal de Cuentas de España, Fuencarral 81, 28004 Madrid, Spain. T. +34914460466. E-mail: eurosai@tcu.es.
URL: http://www.eurosai.org/

History 12 Nov 1990, Madrid (Spain). Founded when statutes were adopted, following a series of meetings after preliminary initiatives, 1989, Berlin West (Germany FR), at meeting of INTOSAI. **Aims** Promote professional cooperation among SAI members; encourage exchange of information and documentation; advance the study of public sector audit; work towards harmonization of terminology in the field of public audit. **Structure** Congress; Governing Board; headed by President; Secretariat, headed by Secretary General. **Languages** English, French, German, Russian, Spanish. **Staff** 3.00 FTE, paid. Paid by Spanish Court of Audit. **Finance** Sources: members' dues. **Activities** Events/meetings; knowledge management/information dissemination; research/documentation; standards/guidelines; training/education. Active in all member countries. **Events** *Post-Congress Get-Together* Prague (Czechia) 2022, *Triennial Congress* Prague (Czechia) 2021, *Triennial Congress* Prague (Czechia) 2020, *Young EUROSAI Conference* London (UK) 2019, *Triennial Congress* Istanbul (Turkey) 2017. **Publications** *EUROSAI Magazine* (annual). Information Services: Maintains database. **Information Services** *EUROSAI Database.*
Members Supreme Audit Institutions in 49 countries:
Albania, Andorra, Armenia, Austria, Azerbaijan, Belarus, Belgium, Bosnia-Herzegovina, Bulgaria, Croatia, Cyprus, Czechia, Denmark, Estonia, Finland, France, Georgia, Germany, Greece, Hungary, Iceland, Ireland, Israel, Italy, Kazakhstan, Latvia, Liechtenstein, Lithuania, Luxembourg, Malta, Moldova, Monaco, Montenegro, Netherlands, North Macedonia, Norway, Poland, Portugal, Romania, Russia, Serbia, Slovakia, Slovenia, Spain, Sweden, Switzerland, Türkiye, UK, Ukraine.
European Union entity:
European Court of Auditors (#06854). [2022/XD2555/D]

- ♦ European Organization of Territorial State Representatives (no recent information)
- ♦ European Organization for Testing New Flowerseeds / see International Association of Breeders and Distributors of Ornamental Plant Varieties (#11735)
- ♦ European Organization for the Textile Wholesale Trade (inactive)
- ♦ European Organization of the World Federation of Clerical Workers / see European Organization of the World Organization of Workers (#08116)

♦ European Organization of the World Organization of Workers (EO/WOW) 08116

Organisation européenne de l'organisation mondiale des travailleurs – Organización Europea de l'Organización Mundial de Trabajadores – Europäische Organisation der Weltorganisation der Arbeitnehmer

Exec Sec c/o WOW, Rue Montoyer 39 I, 1000 Brussels, Belgium. T. +3225027276. Fax +3225027276.

Pres address not obtained.
URL: http://www.wownetwork.be/

History within the framework of *World Organization of Workers (WOW, #21697)*, as *European Organization of the World Federation of Clerical Workers (EO/WFCW) – Organisation européenne de la Fédération mondiale des employés – Organización Europea de la Federación Mundial de Empleados*. Statutes most recently amended 21-22 Jan 1993, Innsbruck (Austria). Previously also referred to as *Organization européenne de la FME – Organización Europea de la FME*. Current title adopted 1 Nov 2006. Statutes are currently in preparation and adapted from the statutes of the former WFCW. **Aims** Coordinate the activities of affiliated national organizations in the framework of international institutions dealing with European questions, among others, those of the *European Union*; inform these organizations of problems linked to economic and social development of Europe as they concern their members and *employees* in general; represent these organizations with executive authorities and other official European institutions. **Structure** European Council (meets every 4 years), comprising one or more representatives of each affiliate; European Bureau, comprising the Secretary-General of WOW (who has a right to vote only if he/she represents an organization registered and active in Europe) plus at least 5 members of WOW Executive Bureau who represent organizations whose headquarters and area of activities are in Europe. Officers: President; one or more Vice-Presidents; Treasurer. Permanent Secretariat at European office of WOW. [2017.03.09/XE2258/**E**]

♦ European Oriental Federation (inactive)

♦ European Ornithologists' Union (EOU) 08117

Sec c/o Swiss Ornithological Institute, Seerose 1, 6204 Sempach LU, Switzerland. T. +414629761.
Pres address not obtained.
URL: https://eounion.org/

History Aug 2000, Zurich (Switzerland). A series of meetings having been organized in Bologna (Italy) 1997, Gdansk (Poland) 1999 and Groningen (Netherlands) 2001. Registration: Swiss Civil Code, Switzerland. **Aims** Advance ornithology; promote scientific study of birds among ornithologists within Europe. **Structure** General Meeting (at Conference); Council. **Languages** English. **Staff** None. **Finance** Sources: donations; gifts, legacies; members' dues; revenue from activities/projects. **Activities** Events/meetings. **Events** *Biennial Conference* Lund (Sweden) 2023, *Biennial Conference* Giessen (Germany) 2022, *Biennial Conference* Giesen (Germany) 2021, *Biennial Conference* Cluj-Napoca (Romania) 2019, *Biennial Conference* Turku (Finland) 2017. **Publications** *Avian Science* – journal.
Members Full in 38 countries:
Australia, Austria, Belgium, Bulgaria, Canada, Chile, Croatia, Czechia, Denmark, Estonia, Finland, France, Germany, Greece, Hungary, Ireland, Israel, Italy, Japan, Latvia, Lithuania, Luxembourg, Netherlands, Norway, Poland, Portugal, Romania, Russia, Slovakia, Slovenia, South Africa, Spain, Sweden, Switzerland, Tunisia, UK, Ukraine, USA. [2022/XD7561/**D**]

♦ European Orthodontia Society / see European Orthodontic Society (#08118)
♦ European Orthodontics College (#04106)

♦ European Orthodontic Society (EOS) 08118

Secretariat Flat 20, 49 Hallam Street, London, W1W 6JN, UK. T. +442076370367. Fax +442073230410. E-mail: admin@eoseurope.org.
URL: http://www.eoseurope.org/

History 27 Sep 1907, Berlin (Germany). Former names and other names: *European Orthodontia Society* – former (27 Sep 1907 to 1935). Registration: Charity Commission, No/ID: 1095190, England and Wales; Companies House, No/ID: 04539916, England and Wales. **Aims** Advance science of orthodontics and its relations with the collateral arts and sciences; further orthodontics amongst all branches of the dental profession working in private practice, hospitals and universities throughout Europe; maintain standards of orthodontic care and orthodontic training of both undergraduates and postgraduates. **Structure** Congress and Final Business Meeting (annual); Council. Membership by election. Meetings closed. **Languages** English. **Staff** 1.00 FTE, paid. **Finance** Sources: members' dues. **Activities** Events/meetings. **Events** *Annual Congress* Innsbruck (Austria) 2027, *Annual Congress* Dublin (Ireland) 2026, *Annual Congress* Krakow (Poland) 2025, *Annual Congress* Athens (Greece) 2024, *Annual Congress* Oslo (Norway) 2023. **Publications** *European Journal of Orthodontics* (6 a year). **Members** Individuals Active; Associate; Honorary; Life; Post-graduate. Members (3075) in 84 countries and territories. Membership countries not specified. **NGO Relations** Cooperates with (1): *European Federation of Orthodontic Specialists Associations (EFOSA, #07185)*. Affiliated with (1): *World Federation of Orthodontists (#21469)*. [2022.11.01/XD0829/v/**D**]

♦ European Orthopaedic Research Society (EORS) 08119

Secretariat c/o hph Halmburger and Kampf, Partnerschaft mbB, Sapporobogen 6-8, 80637 Munich, Germany. E-mail: eors@eors.info.
Sec Gen AO Research Institute Davos, Clavadelerstrasse 8, 7270 Davos GR, Switzerland.
URL: http://www.eors.info/

History 1991, Munich (Germany). Current bylaws adopted Jan 2011. Registration: No/ID: VR 13564, Germany. **Aims** Provide a platform for clinicians and researchers to discuss orthopaedic research, issues and innovations. **Structure** General Assembly; Executive Committee; Committees. **Languages** English, German. **Finance** Members' dues. Congress proceeds. **Activities** Events/meetings; awards/prizes/competitions. **Events** *Annual Conference* Porto (Portugal) 2023, *Annual Conference* Edinburgh (UK) 2022, *World Orthopaedic Research Congress (WORC)* Edinburgh (UK) 2022, *Annual Conference* Rome (Italy) 2021, *Annual Conference* Izmir (Turkey) 2020. **Publications** *Journal of Bone and Joint Surgery*. **Members** Individuals (498). Membership countries not specified. **NGO Relations** Member of: *International Combined Orthopaedic Research Societies (I-CORS, #12657)*. Cooperates with: *European Federation of National Associations of Orthopaedics and Traumatology (EFORT, #07169)*. [2022/XD4052/**D**]

♦ European Ostomy Association (EOA) 08120

Pres Thomas-Mann-Str 40, 53111 Bonn, Germany. E-mail: president@ostomyeurope.org.
URL: http://www.ostomyeurope.org/

History 1979, Königswinter (Germany FR), as a regional organization of *International Ostomy Association (IOA, #14491)*. **Aims** Represent the viewpoint and interests of ostomates on European level; encourage the highest possible standards of surgery, medical attention and ostomate patient after-care. **Structure** Executive Council; Executive Committee. **Languages** English. **Staff** No staff. **Finance** Members' dues. **Activities** Events/meetings; monitoring/evaluation; knowledge management/information dissemination; standards/guidelines; healthcare. **Events** *Congress* Garda (Italy) 2021, *Congress* Garda (Italy) 2020, *Congress* Taastrup (Denmark) 2017, *Congress* Krakow (Poland) 2014, *Congress* Lviv (Ukraine) 2011.
Members National organizations (31) in 28 countries:
Austria, Belgium, Bulgaria, Croatia, Czechia, Denmark, Finland, Germany, Hungary, Iceland, Israel, Italy, Kenya, Lebanon, Luxembourg, Netherlands, Norway, Poland, Portugal, Romania, Russia, Slovakia, Slovenia, Sweden, Switzerland, UK, Ukraine, Zimbabwe.
Associate members (12) in 12 countries and territories:
Belgium, Bosnia-Herzegovina, Egypt, Estonia, France, Kosovo, Latvia, Lithuania, Moldova, Palestine, Serbia, Spain.
NGO Relations Member of: *European Disability Forum (EDF, #06929)*. [2018.06.01/XD4907/**D**]

♦ European Ostrich Association (no recent information)

♦ European Outdoor Conservation Association (EOCA) 08121

Gen Sec Gartenstrasse 2, Postfach 7142, 6302 Zug, Switzerland. T. +441539727255. E-mail: info@eocaconservation.org – catherine@eocaconservation.org.
URL: http://www.eocaconservation.org

History Jun 2006. Former names and other names: *EOG Association for Conservation* – former. Registration: Swiss Civil Code, No/ID: CH-170.6.000.188-3, Switzerland. **Aims** Harness the collective power of the industry to put money directly into grassroots projects and make a tangible difference to threatened wild areas, species and habitats. **Structure** Board. **Languages** English. **Staff** 2.00 FTE, paid. **Finance** Sources: fundraising; members' dues. **Activities** Advocacy/lobbying/activism; awards/prizes/competitions; events/meetings; financial and/or material support. Conservation project funding. **Publications** *Members and Friends of EOCA Newsletter* (4 a year). **Members** Companies, trade association partners and media partners (160) involved in the European outdoor industry. Membership countries not specified. **NGO Relations** Member of (2): *1% for the Planet*; *International Union for Conservation of Nature and Natural Resources (IUCN, #15766)*. [2022.05.16/XJ9183/**D**]

♦ European Outdoor Group (EOG) 08122

Gen Sec Gartenstr 2, Postfach 7142, 6302 Zug, Switzerland. T. +441539727255. Fax +441539733225. E-mail: info@europeanoutdoorgroup.com.
URL: http://www.europeanoutdoorgroup.com/

History 2003. Registration: EU Transparency Register, No/ID: 904895640207-33, Start date: 5 Nov 2020. **Aims** Represent the common interests of the European outdoor industry. **Structure** Board; Executive Team. **Activities** Knowledge management/information dissemination; research/documentation; networking/liaising; advocacy/lobbying/activism; events/meetings. **Publications** *EOG Newsletter*. **Members** Outdoor brands and retailers. Membership countries not specified. **NGO Relations** Member of (1): *ResponsibleSteel (#18921)* (associate). *Aluminium Stewardship Initiative (ASI, #00758)*; *European Outdoor Conservation Association (EOCA, #08121)*; *European Network of Outdoor Sports (ENOS, #07961)*. [2020/XM6207/**D**]

♦ European Outline Convention on Transfrontier Cooperation between Territorial Communities or Authorities (1980 treaty)
♦ European Outsourcing Association / see Global Sourcing Association
♦ European Ozone Research Coordinating Unit (internationally oriented national body)
♦ European Ozone Trade Association (unconfirmed)
♦ European Packaging Design Association / see European Brand and Packaging Design Association (#06396)
♦ European Packaging Institute Consortium / see European Packaging Institutes Consortium (#08123)

♦ European Packaging Institutes Consortium (EPIC) 08123

Gen Sec c/o Obalovy Inst SYBA, Sezemická 2757/2, 193 00 Prague, Czechia. T. +420730173101. E-mail: info@epic-packaging.org.
URL: http://www.epic-packaging.org/

History 26 Apr 2002. Former names and other names: *European Packaging Institute Consortium (EPIC)* – former. Registration: EU Transparency Register, No/ID: 678570313778-23, Start date: 11 Jun 2014. **Aims** Identify areas where regional or pan-European cooperation might best be initiated or concentrated for the future development of the entire packaging chain in a sustainable manner. **Structure** Secretariat based at NVC Netherlands Packaging Centre. Specific activities hosted by other member institutes in different European countries. **Languages** English.
Members Institutes (17) in 17 countries:
Austria, Belgium, Croatia, Czechia, Denmark, Finland, France, Germany, Hungary, Italy, Lithuania, Netherlands, Norway, Spain, Sweden, Switzerland, UK.
NGO Relations Cooperates with (1): *International Organization for Standardization (ISO, #14473)*. [2022/XF6927/**F**]

♦ European Packaging Machinery Association (no recent information)
♦ European Packaging Statistics Group (inactive)

♦ European Paediatric Association (EPA/UNEPSA) 08124

Pres ALT.Office, Wandlitzstraße 10, 10318, 10318 Berlin, Germany. E-mail: info@epa-unepsa.org – administration@epa-unepsa.org.
Treas EPA-UNEPSA Chemin de Chamblandes, 37, 1009 Pully, 1009 Lausanne VD, Switzerland. E-mail: secretarygeneral@epa-unepsa.org – ekose@epa-unepsa.org.
URL: http://www.epa-unepsa.org/

History 1975, Montreux (Switzerland). Former names and other names: *Union of National European Paediatric Societies and Associations (UNEPSA)* – former (1976 to 2007); *Union des sociétés et des associations nationales européennes de pédiatrie* – former. **Aims** Encourage cooperation between organizations and paediatricians working in primary, secondary and tertiary paediatric care in Europe, so as to promote child health and comprehensive paediatric care; stimulate collaborative research; improve the quality of care in Europe; promote exchange of national experiences in various fields of patient care and make national practices known to others; cooperate with paediatric associations worldwide. **Structure** General Assembly; Executive Board/Council. **Languages** English. **Finance** Sources: contributions; fees for services; grants; meeting proceeds; members' dues; revenue from activities/projects; sponsorship. **Activities** Events/meetings; projects/programmes; publishing activities; training/education. **Events** *Europaediatrics Congress* Istanbul (Türkiye) 2022, *Europaediatrics Congress* Zagreb (Croatia) 2021, *Europaediatrics Congress* Dublin (Ireland) 2019, *Europaediatrics Congress* Bucharest (Romania) 2017, *Europaediatrics Congress* Florence (Italy) 2015. **Publications** *EPA/UNEPSA Newsletter* (12 a year) in English; *Journal of Pediatrics Affiliation* (12 a year) in English. Articles.
Members Full: National European Pediatric Societies and Associations in 43 countries:
Albania, Armenia, Azerbaijan, Belgium, Bosnia-Herzegovina, Bulgaria, Croatia, Cyprus, Czechia, Denmark, Estonia, Finland, France, Georgia, Greece, Holy See, Hungary, India, Iraq, Ireland, Israel, Italy, Kazakhstan, Kyrgyzstan, Latvia, Lithuania, Luxembourg, Norway, Poland, Portugal, Romania, Russia, Serbia, Slovakia, Slovenia, Spain, Sweden, Tajikistan, Türkiye, Turkmenistan, UK, Ukraine, Uzbekistan.
Affiliate: Doctors certified as paediatricians in non-European countries. Membership countries not specified.
IGO Relations Accredited by (1): *European Union (EU, #08967)*. **NGO Relations** Member of (1): *International Pediatric Association (IPA, #14541)*. Formal contacts with: *Association for Paediatric Education in Europe (APEE, #02847)*; *International Pediatric Nephrology Association (IPNA, #14543)*; *International Society for Social Pediatrics and Child Health (ISSOP, #15448)*; *Union of National African Paediatric Societies and Associations (UNAPSA, #20465)*. [2022.02.14/XD6852/**D**]

♦ European Paediatric Formulation Initiative (EuPFI) 08125

Contact Univ College London School of Pharmacy, 29-39 Brunswick Square, London, WC1N 1AX, UK. T. +442077535846. Fax +442077535942. E-mail: s.salunke@ucl.ac.uk – admin@eupfi.org.
URL: http://www.eupfi.org/

History Founded 2007. **Aims** Identify and scope issues and challenges in paediatric formulation development so as to raise awareness and facilitate preparation of better and safer *medicines* for children. **Structure** Core Group; Subgroups (5): Pharmaceutical Excipients; Taste Masking and Testing; Administration Devices; Extemporaneous Preparations and Dispensing; Age Appropriateness of Formulation. **Events** *Annual Conference* London (UK) 2020, *Annual Conference* Malmö (Sweden) 2019, *Annual Conference* London (UK) 2018, *Annual Conference* Lisbon (Portugal) 2016, *Annual Conference* Barcelona (Spain) 2013.
Members Academia; Associations; companies. Academics from 2 countries:
Germany, UK.
Associations (2), including one international organization listed in this Yearbook:
International Pharmaceutical Excipients Council Europe (IPEC Europe, #14565). [2020.10.13/XJ5003/y/**F**]

♦ European Paediatric Neurology Society (EPNS) 08126

Membership Secretary The Coach House, Rear of 22 Chorley New Road, Bolton, BL1 4AP, UK. E-mail: info@epns.info.
Pres Fraser of Allander Neurosciences Unit, Royal Hosp for Children, Glasgow, G51 4TF, UK.
URL: http://www.epns.info/

History 1970, Oxford (UK). Former names and other names: *European Federation of Child Neurology Societies (EFCNS)* – former. **Aims** Promote training, clinical care and scientific research in the field of paediatric neurology. **Structure** Board; Committees (4); Secretariat. **Languages** English. **Staff** 1.00 FTE, paid. **Finance** Meetings financed by host country. **Activities** Events/meetings; research/documentation; training/education. **Events** *Congress* Munich (Germany) 2025, *Congress* Prague (Czechia) 2023, *Congress* Glasgow (UK) 2022, *Congress* 2021, *Biennial Congress* Athens (Greece) 2019. **Publications** *European Journal of Paediatric Neurology (EJPN)*. **Members** Full (over 1,500). Membership countries not specified. **NGO Relations** Also links with national European associations. [2022/XD1229/**D**]

♦ European Paediatric Ophthalmological Society (EPOS) 08127

Sec Ophthalmology Dept, Semmelweis University, Maria Str 39, Budapest 1805, Hungary.
URL: http://www.epos-focus.org/

History 1973. Initially founded as an informal grouping; formally structured under current name in 2001. Statutes adopted by Constitutional Session at Geneva, 27 Oct 2001; statutes amended: Leuven, 2008; Bad Nauheim, 2010. Former names and other names: *European Paediatric Ophthalmology Group (EPOG)* – former (1973 to 2001). Registration: Switzerland. **Aims** Serve as a forum for researchers in the field of paediatric ophthalmology, including genetic diseases of the eye. **Structure** General Assembly (annual).

Board, comprising President, Secretary, Treasurer and 4 members. **Languages** English. **Staff** 1.00 FTE, paid. **Finance** Members' dues: Full – euro 75; Training – euro 20, including one online subscription to the 'European Journal of Ophthalmology. **Activities** Meeting activities; awards/prizes/competitions. **Events** *Annual Meeting* Leuven (Belgium) 2023, *Annual Meeting* Munich (Germany) 2022, *Annual Meeting* Copenhagen (Denmark) 2021, *Annual Meeting* Copenhagen (Denmark) 2020, *Annual Meeting* Riga (Latvia) 2019.
Members Individuals in 31 countries:
Austria, Belgium, Bulgaria, Denmark, Egypt, Finland, France, Germany, Greece, Hungary, India, Ireland, Italy, Kuwait, Latvia, Lithuania, Netherlands, Norway, Oman, Pakistan, Poland, Portugal, Romania, Russia, Slovenia, Spain, Sweden, Switzerland, Türkiye, UK, USA.
NGO Relations Member of (2): *International Pediatric Ophthalmology and Strabismus Council (IPOSC, #14544)*; *World Society of Paediatric Ophthalmology and Strabismus (WSPOS, #21807)*.
[2021/XD9398/v/D]

♦ European Paediatric Ophthalmology Group / see European Paediatric Ophthalmological Society (#08127)

♦ European Paediatric Orthopaedic Society (EPOS) 08128
Société d'orthopédie pédiatrique européenne
Secretariat ZA La Pièce 2, 1180 Rolle VD, Switzerland. E-mail: secretariat@epos.org.
URL: http://www.epos.org/
History 13 Mar 1982, France. Founded on the initiative of Henri Bensahel (1928-2009). Former names and other names: *European Society for Paediatric Orthopaedics* – alias. **Aims** Promote the advancement of paediatric orthopaedics in all its aspects, particularly in the practice, scientific research and teaching of effects on the *locomotor system* during growth, and of understanding of the bone pathology of the child; improve public health; intensify European and international exchanges. **Structure** General Assembly (annual); Executive Committee. **Languages** English. **Staff** Voluntary. **Finance** Sources: meeting proceeds; members' dues. **Activities** International congresses. **Events** *Combined EPOS/POSNA Meeting* Washington, DC (USA) 2024, *Annual Meeting* Krakow (Poland) 2023, *Annual Meeting* Copenhagen (Denmark) 2022, *Annual Meeting* Rolle (Switzerland) 2021, *Annual Meeting* Tel Aviv (Israel) 2019. **Publications** *EPOS News*; *Journal of Paediatric Orthopaedics*.
Members Individuals. Full (197), Corresponding (35) and Emeritus (20), in 40 countries:
Argentina, Australia, Austria, Belgium, Brazil, Bulgaria, Canada, Chile, Croatia, Czechia, Denmark, Egypt, Finland, France, Germany, Greece, Hungary, Ireland, Israel, Italy, Japan, Latvia, Lebanon, Netherlands, North Macedonia (former Yugoslav Rep of), Norway, Poland, Portugal, Romania, Serbia, Slovakia, Slovenia, Spain, Sweden, Switzerland, Thailand, Türkiye, UK, USA, Venezuela.
NGO Relations Member of (1): *International Federation of Paediatric Orthopaedic Societies (IFPOS, #13497)*. Cooperates with (1): *Pediatric Orthopaedic Society of North America (POSNA)*. [2021/XD1427/v/D]

♦ European Paediatric Pathological Society / see Paediatric Pathology Society (#18018)
♦ European Paediatric Pathology Society / see Paediatric Pathology Society (#18018)
♦ European Paediatric Psychology Network (unconfirmed)
♦ European Paediatric Respiratory Society (inactive)

♦ European paediatric Soft tissue sarcoma Study Group (EpSSG) 08129
Contact Haematology/Oncology Div, Dept of Paediatrics, Via Giustiniani 3, 35128 Padua PD, Italy. E-mail: info@epssgassociation.it.
URL: http://www.epssgassociation.it/
Aims Improve the quality of care offered to children, teenagers and young adults with soft tissue sarcoma (STS). **Structure** Assembly; Board; Coordinating Group. Trial Management Committees (TMC); Sub Committees. **Activities** Events/meetings. **Events** *Spring Meeting* Prague (Czechia) 2019, *Spring Meeting* Utrecht (Netherlands) 2018. **NGO Relations** *SIOP Europe (SIOPE, #19288)*. [2019/XM7808/D]

♦ European Paediatric Surgeons' Association (EUPSA) 08130
Secretariat c/o T+R AG, Sägeweg 11, 3073 Gümligen, Switzerland. T. +393457878729. Fax +39409870136. E-mail: office@eupsa.info.
Pres Kinderchirurgische Klinik – Zentrum Chirurgie, E 6760 – Gebäude K10, Medizinische Hochschule Hannover, Carl Neuberg Strasse 1, 30625 Hannover, Germany. T. +495115329260. Fax +495115329059.
URL: http://www.eupsa.info/
History 1972, Graz (Austria), as *European Union of Paediatric Surgical Associations (EUPSA)*. Reconstituted 2003, Tours (France). **Aims** Coordinate paediatric surgery in Europe. **Structure** General Assembly. Council, consisting of representatives of each national association. **Languages** English. **Staff** None. **Finance** Annual members' dues: pounds15. **Events** *Congress* Vienna (Austria) 2020, *Congress* Belgrade (Serbia) 2019, *Congress* Paris (France) 2018, *Paediatric Colorectal Club International Meeting* Tokyo (Japan) 2018, *Strategies and Trends in European Pediatric Surgery Seminar* Madrid (Spain) 2017.
Members Paediatric surgical associations in 26 countries and territories:
Armenia, Austria, Belgium, Bulgaria, Croatia, Denmark, Finland, France, Germany, Great Britain, Greece, Hungary, Ireland, Italy, Luxembourg, Netherlands, Norway, Poland, Portugal, Romania, Russia, Slovakia, Spain, Sweden, Switzerland, Türkiye.
Also in Baltic countries. [2018/XD2134/D]

♦ European Paediatric Translational Research Infrastructure (unconfirmed)

♦ European Pain Federation (EFIC) 08131
Exec Sec Rue de Londres 18, 1050 Brussels, Belgium. T. +3222515510. E-mail: secretary@efic.org.
URL: http://www.efic.org/
History Aug 1993, Paris (France). Founded within *International Association for the Study of Pain (IASP, #12206)*. Officially registered 1995. Current statutes amended: Dec 2012. Former names and other names: *European Federation of IASP Chapters (EFIC)* – former (Aug 1993); *European Federation of the International Association for the Study of Pain* – alias. Registration: EU Transparency Register, No/ID: 35010244568-04; Belgium. **Aims** Promote multidisciplinary research, education and management of pain; create a forum for European collaboration on pain issues; encourage communication at a European level in the field of pain research and *therapy*. **Structure** General Assembly (annual); Council; Executive Board; Committees (11). **Languages** English. **Staff** Contractual: 4. **Activities** Events/meetings; awards/prizes/competitions; advocacy/lobbying/activism; training/education. **Events** *Congress* Budapest (Hungary) 2023, *Congress* Dublin (Ireland) 2022, *Biennial Congress* Valencia (Spain) 2019, *Biennial Congress* Copenhagen (Denmark) 2017, *Societal Impact of Pain Focus Groups Meeting* Brussels (Belgium) 2016. **Publications** *EFIC Newsletter* (4 a year); *European Journal of Pain (EJP)*. Annual Report; core curricula for chronic pain specialists; pamphlets; booklets.
Members Ordinary; Contributing; Individual; Honorary. IASP Chapters (37) representing 37 countries:
Albania, Austria, Belgium, Bosnia-Herzegovina, Bulgaria, Croatia, Czechia, Denmark, Estonia, Finland, France, Germany, Greece, Hungary, Ireland, Israel, Italy, Kosovo, Latvia, Lithuania, Moldova, Netherlands, Norway, Poland, Portugal, Romania, Russia, San Marino, Serbia, Slovakia, Slovenia, Spain, Sweden, Switzerland, Türkiye, UK, Ukraine.
NGO Relations Member of (1): *European Cancer Organisation (ECO, #06432)*. [2021/XD7293/D]

♦ European Paintball Federation (EPBF) 08132
Sec 1 route de la Liberation, 94510 La Queue-en-Brie, France. T. +33145761871.
Pres address not obtained.
URL: https://www.epbf.net/
Activities Sporting activities. **NGO Relations** Member of (1): *United Paintball Federation (UPBF, #20654)*.
[2021/AA1941/D]

♦ European Palaeontological Association (inactive)

♦ European Pallet Association (EPAL) 08133
Secretariat Wahlerstr 28, 40472 Düsseldorf, Germany. T. +4921198480480. Fax +49211984804889. E-mail: info@epal-pallets.org.
URL: http://www.epal-pallets.org/
History Founded 1991. **Aims** As the umbrella association of licensed producers and repairers of EPAL/EUR-pallets and box pallets: ensure the consistent quality of the EPAL load carriers; grant exclusive licenses for production and repair of euro pallets with the "EPAL in oval" branded marking. **Structure** General Assembly; Board; Working Groups. **Languages** English, French, German. **Members** National committees (14) representing over 30 countries (not specified). [2015.01.05/XD8929/D]

♦ European Palm Oil Alliance (EPOA) 08134
Contact Louis Braillelaan 80, 2719 EK Zoetermeer, Netherlands. E-mail: info@palmoilalliance.eu.
URL: http://www.palmoilandfood.eu/
History Registration: EU Transparency Register, No/ID: 675799233923-17, Start date: 11 Feb 2019. **Aims** Engage with and educate stakeholders on the full palm oil story. **Structure** Steering Committee; Scientific Advisory Panel. **Events** *Conference* Madrid (Spain) 2018, *Conference* Brussels (Belgium) 2017.
[2019/XM6938/D]

♦ European Palm Society (internationally oriented national body)

♦ European Pancreas and Islet Transplant Association (EPITA) 08135
Sec Rm S3316 Transplant Unit, Royal Infirmary, Little France Crescent, Edinburgh, EH16 5SA, UK. E-mail: secretariat@esot.org.
URL: http://www.esot.org/
History 2007, Prague (Czech Rep), as a section of *European Society for Organ Transplantation (ESOT, #08676)*. **Aims** Provide a forum for the pancreas and islet transplantation community in Europe; contribute to the development of this field and of alternate forms of beta-cell replacement therapy for the benefit of patients suffering from diabetes. **Events** *Joint Winter Symposium* Innsbruck (Austria) 2020, *EPITA Symposium* Innsbruck (Austria) 2019, *EPITA Symposium* Innsbruck (Austria) 2018, *Joint Winter Symposium* Innsbruck (Austria) 2017, *Joint Winter Symposium* Innsbruck (Austria) / Igls (Austria) 2016. [2010/XM2927/D]

♦ European Pancreatic Club (EPC) 08136
Club pancréatique européen
Sec c/o First Dept of Medicine, University of Szeged, Koranyi alley 8-10, Szeged 6720, Hungary. T. +3662545200. Fax +3662545185. E-mail: secretariat.epc@gmail.com.
Assistant Sec address not obtained. E-mail: secretariat.epc@gmail.com.
URL: http://www.e-p-c.org/
History 1962. Statutes revised and adopted: 30 Jun 2000, Kiel (Germany); 15 Jun 2001, Toulouse (France); 28 Jun 2013, Zurich (Switzerland). Registered in accordance with Swiss Civil Code. **Aims** Promote communication between basic and clinical scientists in Europe interested in the pancreas and its disorders; promote scientific, epidemiological and clinical research into pancreatic function and into the prevention, diagnosis and therapy of pancreatic diseases; establish scholarships and promote postgraduate education and training. **Structure** General Assembly. Executive Council. **Languages** English. **Staff** 0.50 FTE, paid. **Finance** Members' dues. Budget (annual): about euro 100,000. **Activities** Active in: Eastern Europe, European Union, Russia, Switzerland, Ukraine. **Events** *Annual Meeting* 2022, *Annual Meeting* Verona (Italy) 2021, *Annual Meeting* Paris (France) 2020, *Annual Meeting* Bergen (Norway) 2019, *Annual Meeting* Berlin (Germany) 2018. **Publications** *European Pancreatic Club Newsletter*; *Pancreatology* – official journal.
Members Basic and clinical pancreatic researchers (400 to 500) in 44 countries:
Argentina, Armenia, Australia, Austria, Belgium, Brazil, Bulgaria, Canada, Chile, China, Croatia, Czechia, Denmark, Finland, France, Germany, Greece, Hungary, Ireland, Israel, Italy, Japan, Kazakhstan, Korea Rep, Latvia, Lithuania, Mexico, Netherlands, Norway, Peru, Poland, Portugal, Romania, Russia, Serbia-Montenegro, Singapore, Spain, Sweden, Switzerland, UK, Ukraine, USA, Uzbekistan, Venezuela.
NGO Relations Member of (1): *European Cancer Organisation (ECO, #06432)*. Through: *United European Gastroenterology (UEG, #20506)*, a consortium of 7 European associations, organizes an annual scientific meeting in the field (the first in Sep 1992, Athens, Greece). The other 5 associations are: *International Society for Digestive Surgery (ISDS, #15060)* (European chapter); *European Association for Gastroenterology, Endoscopy and Nutrition (EAGEN, #06051)*; *European Association for the Study of the Liver (EASL, #06233)*; *European Society of Gastrointestinal Endoscopy (ESGE, #08606)*; *European Society for Paediatric Gastroenterology, Hepatology and Nutrition (ESPGHAN, #08680)*. Special links with: *International Association of Pancreatology (IAP, #12065)*. [2016/XF2331/v/F]

♦ European Panel Federation (EPF) 08137
Fédération européenne de panneaux à base de bois – Europäischer Holzwerkstoffverband
Acting Managing Dir Rue Montoyer 24, Box 20, 1000 Brussels, Belgium. T. +3225562589. Fax +3222870875. E-mail: info@europanels.org.
URL: http://www.europanels.org/
History 1 Jan 1999. Founded when it took over activities of *Fédération européenne des syndicats de fabricants de panneaux de particules (FESYP, inactive)* and *European Federation of Medium Density Fibreboard Manufacturers (Euro MDF Board, inactive)*. Took over activities of *European Federation of Fibreboard Manufacturers (FEROPA, inactive)*, 2012. Former names and other names: *European Wood-Based Panels Federation* – former; *Europäische Holzwerkstoff-Platten Föderation* – former. Registration: Banque Carrefour des Entreprises, No/ID: 0464.722.149, Start date: 18 Sep 1998, Belgium; EU Transparency Register, No/ID: 572064811767-22, Start date: 29 Aug 2013. **Aims** Represent the European manufacturers of particleboard, MDF and OSB. **Structure** Annual General Meeting; Managing Board; Secretariat. Working Groups. **Languages** English. **Finance** Sources: members' dues. **Events** *European Wood-based Panel Symposium* Hamburg (Germany) 2022, *European Wood-based Panel Symposium* Hamburg (Germany) 2020, *Annual General Meeting* Vienna (Austria) 2015, *Annual General Meeting* Bruges (Belgium) 2014, *Annual General Meeting* Dublin (Ireland) 2013. **Publications** Annual Report.
Members Full in 23 countries:
Austria, Belgium, Czechia, Denmark, Estonia, Finland, France, Germany, Greece, Ireland, Italy, Latvia, Lithuania, Luxembourg, Norway, Portugal, Romania, Slovenia, Spain, Sweden, Switzerland, Türkiye, UK.
NGO Relations Member of (4): *Construction 2050 Alliance (#04760)*; *Construction Products Europe AISBL (#04761)*; *Industry4Europe (#11181)*; *Wood Sector Alliance for the New European Bauhaus (Wood4Bauhaus, #21046)* (Founding). Partner of (1): *Conseil européen de l'industrie chimique (CEFIC, #04687)*. Cooperates with (1): *International Association for Technical Issues Related to Wood (iVTH)*. In liaison with technical committees of: *International Organization for Standardization (ISO, #14473)*. Stakeholder member of: *PEFC Council (#18288)*. [2022/XD7558/D]

♦ European Pan-Keltic League (inactive)
♦ European Paper Forum (inactive)
♦ European Paper Institute (inactive)

♦ European Paper Merchants Association (Eugropa) 08138
Contact c/o IGEPA group Gmbh & Co KG, Heidenkampweg 74-76, 20097 Hamburg, Germany. T. +491702244415.
SG Biezenwei 16, 4004 MB Tiel, Netherlands.
URL: http://www.eugropa.com/
History 1971. Founded by merger of *Union of Paper and Carton Distributors in the European Economic Community (inactive)*, set up 31 May 1957, with *European Liaison Committee for the Paper and Board Wholesale Trade (inactive)*, formed 19 Oct 1967. A Participating Industry Sector of *Confederation of European Paper Industries (CEPI, #04529)*. Former names and other names: *Union européenne des commerces de gros en papiers, cartons et emballages (EUGROPA)* – former; *European Union of Paper, Board and Packaging Wholesalers* – former; *Unión Europea de Almacenistas de Papel, Cartón y Embalajes* – former; *Europäische Vereinigung des Grosshandels für Papier, Pappe und Verpackung* – former; *União Européia do Comércio por Grosso em Papel, Cartão e Embalagens* – former; *Unione Europea dei Grossisti in Carte, Cartoni e Imballaggi* – former; *Federatie van Papier-, Karton- en Verpakkings-Groothandelaren in Europa* – former; *Europeiska Federationen för Grossister i Papper, Papp och Emballage* – former; *Europeiske Sammenslutning av Papir- Kartong- og Emballasjegrossister* – former; *Europaeiske Sammenslutning af Papir-Karton- og Emballogegrossister* – former; *Eurooppalaisten Paperipukkqliikkeiden Yhdistysten Liitto* – former. Registration: Handelsregister, No/ID: KVK 11046603, Netherlands. **Aims** Develop and promote merchant distribution as the channel of choice of customers and suppliers; provide a necessary forum for national merchants associations to work together to decide a common position; foster and enhance communication among all members of the paper chain; promote interests of merchant distribution through lobbying and consultation. **Languages** English. **Activities** Advocacy/lobbying/activism; networking/liaising. **Events** *Annual Congress* Prague (Czech Rep) 2007, *Annual Congress* Rome (Italy) 2005, *Annual Congress* Rome (Italy) 2005, *Annual Congress* Dublin (Ireland) 2003, *Annual Congress* Montreux (Switzerland) 2002.
Members European paper Merchants/Distributors in 23 countries:
Austria, Belgium, Czechia, Denmark, Estonia, Finland, France, Germany, Greece, Hungary, Italy, Latvia, Lithuania, Netherlands, Norway, Poland, Portugal, Russia, Spain, Sweden, Switzerland, Türkiye, UK. [2014.06.01/XD3361/E]

♦ European Paper Packaging Alliance (unconfirmed)

♦ **European Paper Recycling Council (EPRC)** **08139**

Secretariat c/o CEPI, Av Louise 250, Box 80, 1050 Brussels, Belgium. T. +3226274923. Fax +3226468137. E-mail: erpc@cepi.org.
URL: http://www.paperforrecycling.eu/

History Nov 2000 as *European Recovered Paper Council (ERPC)* after the launch of the European Declaration on Paper Recovery. **Aims** Monitor the progress made towards meeting the targets set out in the European Declaration. **Activities** Monitoring/evaluation; advocacy/lobbying/activism; knowledge management/information dissemination; awards/prizes/competitions.
Members Signatories to the Declaration (7):
Alliance for Beverage Cartons and the Environment (ACE, #00658); Confederation of European Paper Industries (CEPI, #04529); European Moulded Fibre Association (EMFA); European Tissue Symposium (ETS, #08917); Fédération européenne des producteurs d'enveloppes (FEPE, #09578); Intergraf (#11505); International Confederation of Paper and Board Converters in Europe (CITPA, #12866); Internationale Forschungsgemeinschaft Deinking-Technik (INGEDE, #13233).
Supporters (5):
European Adhesive Tape Association (AFERA, #05826); European Printing Ink Association (EuPIA, #08275); Fédération européenne des industries de colles et adhésifs (FEICA, #09572); FINAT (#09773); RadTech Europe (RTE, #18606). [2018/XJ0039/y/**E**]

♦ European Paper Tube Manufacturers Association (no recent information)

♦ **European Paralympic Committee (EPC)** **08140**

Head of Office Untere Donaustr 47, Top B8b, 1020 Vienna, Austria. T. +431890067610. Fax +431890067690.
URL: http://www.europaralympic.org/

History Nov 1991. Founded within *International Paralympic Committee (IPC, #14512).* Former names and other names: *IPC European Committee* – former (1991 to 1999). Registration: EU Transparency Register, No/ID: 102411438593-51, Start date: 16 Jun 2020; Austria, Vienna. **Aims** Promote *sports* for the *disabled* in Europe. **Structure** General Assembly; Executive Committee; Permanent Office and Headquarters in Vienna (Austria). **Languages** English. **Staff** 1.00 FTE, paid. **Events** *Biennial General Assembly* Lisbon (Portugal) 2015, *Conference on Empowering Women for Leadership* Vienna (Austria) 2014, *General Assembly* Dublin (Ireland) 2013, *Biennial General Assembly / General Assembly* Moscow (Russia) 2011, *General Assembly* Vienna (Austria) 2009.
Members National Paralympic Committees (44) and International Federations (9) in 50 countries and territories:
Albania, Andorra, Armenia, Austria, Azerbaijan, Belarus, Belgium, Bosnia-Herzegovina, Bulgaria, Croatia, Cyprus, Czechia, Denmark, Estonia, Faeroe Is, Finland, France, Georgia, Germany, Greece, Hungary, Iceland, Ireland, Israel, Italy, Kazakhstan, Latvia, Liechtenstein, Lithuania, Luxembourg, Malta, Moldova, Netherlands, North Macedonia, Norway, Poland, Portugal, Romania, Russia, San Marino, Serbia, Slovakia, Slovenia, Spain, Sweden, Switzerland, Turkmenistan, UK, Ukraine, Uzbekistan.
Consultative Status Consultative status granted from: *Council of Europe (CE, #04881)* (Participatory Status). **IGO Relations** Austrian Ministry of Sport; *Enlarged Partial Agreement on Sport (EPAS, #05487); European Union (EU, #08967).* **NGO Relations** Member of: *European Disability Forum (EDF, #06929).* [2020/XE4312/**E**]

♦ **European Paratroopers Association** **08141**

Sec address not obtained. E-mail: info@europeanparatroopers.org.
URL: http://www.europeanparatroopers.org/

History Aug 2001, as *Association of European Military Parachutists.* Current title adopted, Sep 2004. **Structure** Board of Directors. **Activities** Offers training courses. **Publications** *ParatrooperNews.* [2012/XJ0018/v/**D**]

♦ **European Parents' Association (EPA)** **08142**

Project Coordinator c/o LLLPlatform, Rue de l'Industrie 10, 1000 Brussels, Belgium. T. +436507004448. E-mail: office@europarents.eu.
Pres address not obtained.
URL: https://europarents.eu/

History 1983, Luxembourg. Former names and other names: *Association européenne des parents d'élèves* – former; *Asociación Europea de Padres* – former; *Europäische Eltern Organisation* – former; *Associazione Genitori d'Europa* – former; *Europese Ouderverenigingе* – former. Registration: Banque-Carrefour des Entreprises, No/ID: 0431.341.380, Start date: 16 Jun 1987, Belgium; EU Transparency Register, No/ID: 604634342917-26, Start date: 27 May 2021. **Aims** Promote collaboration between schools and parents' associations, enhancing the partnership between *families* and schools; support recognition for parents as primary educators of their children and the need for their active involvement at all stages of their children's education; advance parents' associations in the different countries; share good practices between parents' associations; coordinate various organizations of parents' associations; represent parents at the European level primarily in educational matters. **Structure** General Assembly (twice a year); Board; Working Group on Early School Leaving and Early Childhood Education. **Languages** English. **Staff** 0.50 FTE, paid. **Finance** Sources: members' dues. **Activities** Events/meetings. **Events** *General Assembly* Bilbao (Spain) 2021, *General Assembly* Brussels (Belgium) 2020, *General Assembly and Conference* Kolding (Denmark) 2019, *General Assembly and Conference* Vienna (Austria) 2019, *General Assembly and Conference* Bilbao (Spain) 2018. **Publications** *EPA Newsletter.* **Members** Full parents associations concerned with education of children at school; Associate other organizations concerned with similar purposes. Associations (49). Membership countries not specified. **Consultative Status** Consultative status granted from: *Council of Europe (CE, #04881)* (Participatory Status). **IGO Relations** Consultative status with: *European Commission (EC, #06633)* DG Education, Culture and Sport. **NGO Relations** Member of: *Alliance for Childhood European Network Group (AFC-ENG, #00666); Lifelong Learning Platform – European Civil Society for Education (LLLP, #16466); European Policy Network on School Leadership (EPNoSL, #08245); SIRIUS – Policy Network on Migrant Education (SIRIUS, #19291); Social Platform (#19344).* [2021.09.02/XD1000/**D**]

♦ **European Pari Mutuel Association (EPMA)** **08143**

Contact Square de Meeus 38-40, 1000 Brussels, Belgium. T. +3224016165. E-mail: contact@parimutuel-europe.org.
URL: http://www.parimutuel-europe.org/

History Also referred to as *Pari Mutuel Europe.* **Aims** Promote pari mutuel *betting* on *horseracing* and its business model. **Structure** General Assembly; Board of Directors; Chairman; Working Groups (3). **Languages** English. **Finance** Members' dues. **Activities** Events/meetings. **Members** Full (14) in Europe; Associate (8) outside Europe. Membership countries not specified. **NGO Relations** Founding member of: *European Horse Network (EHN, #07499).* Cooperates with: *European Trotting Union (#08952); International Federation of Horseracing Authorities (IFHA, #13449).* [2019.02.13/XJ5796/**D**]

♦ **European Parking Association (EPA)** **08144**

SG Richartzstr 10, 50667 Cologne, Germany. T. +492212571018. Fax +492212571019. E-mail: epa@europeanparking.eu.
URL: http://www.europeanparking.eu/

History 1983, Madrid (Spain). Founded by 9 European parking associations. Registration: Germany. **Aims** Facilitate cooperation between professional parking organizations of different European countries; facilitate exchange and mutual support of professional experience among members; exert influence on measures and resolutions of the European Commission and other relevant international bodies relating to parking and urban mobility. **Structure** General Assembly (annual); Board. **Languages** English. **Staff** 1.00 FTE, paid. **Finance** Sources: members' dues. **Activities** Events/meetings; monitoring/evaluation; research/documentation. **Events** *EPA Congress* Brussels (Belgium) 2022, *Biennial Congress* Malaga (Spain) 2019, *Biennial Congress* Rotterdam (Netherlands) 2017, *Biennial Congress* Berlin (Germany) 2015, *Biennial Congress* Dublin (Ireland) 2013. **Publications** *Parking Trend International Magazine* (4 a year).
Members Full; Associate; Institutional; International Affiliate; Honorary. National Parking Associations (23) in 22 countries:
Austria, Belgium, Bulgaria, Croatia, Cyprus, Czechia, Finland (2), France, Germany, Ireland, Italy, Luxembourg, Netherlands, Norway, Poland, Serbia, Slovakia, Spain, Sweden, Switzerland, Türkiye, UK.
Associate in 11 countries:
Austria, Belgium, France, Germany, Italy, Netherlands, Portugal, Spain, Switzerland, Türkiye, UK. [2022.05.10/XD0468/**D**]

♦ **European Parkinson's Disease Association (EPDA)** **08145**

Association européenne pour la maladie de Parkinson

Address not obtained.
URL: http://www.epda.eu.com/

History 1992, Munich (Germany). Registration: EU Transparency Register, No/ID: 073833319732-61, Start date: 1 Dec 2015. **Aims** Work for the health and welfare of people with Parkinson's and their families; partner with European patient and neurological organizations. **Structure** House of Delegates (General Assembly, annual); Administration Board; Professional Advisory Boards. **Languages** English. **Staff** 4 freelance. **Finance** Members' dues. Other sources: sponsorship; foundation grants. **Activities** Awareness raising; capacity building; knowledge management/information dissemination. Maintains information and documentation centre and library. **Events** *General Assembly* London (UK) 2015, *General Assembly* Luxembourg (Luxembourg) 2014, *General Assembly* Amsterdam (Netherlands) 2012, *General Assembly* Glasgow (UK) 2010, *Multidisciplinary conference* Budapest (Hungary) 2009. **Publications** *EPDA Plus* – magazine. Annual Report. Supplements; booklets, DVDs.
Members Full; Associate. Organizations (43) in 36 countries and territories:
Austria, Belgium, Bulgaria, Croatia, Cyprus, Czechia, Denmark, Estonia, Faeroe Is, Finland, France, Georgia, Germany, Greece, Hungary, Iceland, Ireland, Israel, Italy, Lithuania, Luxembourg, Malta, Netherlands, Norway, Poland, Portugal, Romania, Russia, Serbia, Slovenia, Spain, Sweden, Switzerland, Türkiye, UK, Ukraine.
Associate members in 7 countries:
Austria, Bulgaria, Italy, Luxembourg, UK, USA.
Included in the above, 3 organizations listed in this Yearbook:
European Federation of Neurological Associations (EFNA, #07177); European Federation of Neurological Societies (EFNS, inactive); International Parkinson and Movement Disorder Society (MDS, #14515).
NGO Relations Member of: *Alliance for Safe Online Pharmacy – EU (ASOP EU, #00720); European Alliance for Personalised Medicine (EAPM, #05878); European Patients' Forum (EPF, #08172).* Partner of: *European Alliance for Access to Safe Medicines (EAASM, #05859).* [2020/XD4713/y/**D**]

♦ **European Parliament (EP)** **08146**

Parlement européen (PE) – Parlamento Europeo (PE) – Europäisches Parlament (EP) – Parlamento Europeu (PE) – Europees Parlement (EP) – Europaparlamentet (EP) – Europa-Parlamentet (EP) – Euroopan Parlamentti – Evropaiko Kinovulio (EK) – Parlaimint na hEorpa – Evropsky Parlament – Európsky Parlament – Európai Parlament – Parlament Europejski – Evropski Parlament – Euroopa Parlament – Eiropas Parlaments – Europos Parlamentas – Parlament Ewropew – Europski Parlament – Parlamentul European

SG Rue Wiertz 60, 1047 Brussels, Belgium. T. +3222842111.
Luxembourg Plateau du Kirchberg, BP 1601, L-2929 Luxembourg, Luxembourg. T. +35243001.
Strasbourg 1 av du Président Robert, Schuman – CS 91024, 67070 Strasbourg CEDEX, France. T. +3222842111.
URL: http://www.europarl.europa.eu/

History 19 Mar 1958, Strasbourg (France). Established at 1st meeting, replacing and extending the *Common Assembly of the European Coal and Steel Community – Assemblée commune de la Communauté européenne du charbon et de l'acier*, which had held its first session 10 Sep 1952, Strasbourg.
Treaty Establishing the European Economic Community (Treaty of Rome) and *Treaty Establishing the European Atomic Energy Community (Treaty of Rome, 1957)* stipulated that the European Parliament would eventually be elected by direct universal suffrage. The draft *'Convention on Direct Elections'*, which was prepared by Parliament in 1960, was never adopted by the Council but Heads of Government agreed in principle to direct elections in Dec 1974, Rome (Italy), and in Jan 1975 the *European Council (#06801)* confirmed that first direct elections would take place in 1978 (later postponed until 1979). In Jul 1976, Council decided on the number and allocation of seats in the elected Parliament and on 20 Sep 1976, Council approved and signed the *'Act concerning the election of the representatives of the Assembly by direct universal suffrage'* which entered into force 1 Jul 1978, after ratification by all member states. On 7 and 10 Jun 1979 the citizens of the Community elected their representatives to the European Parliament for the first time; prior to this date, members were appointed by national parliaments from among their own members. The new Parliament met on 17 Jul 1979 in Strasbourg. Elections held in Greece, Oct 1981. Direct elections held in all member countries, 14-17 Jun 1984, and every 5 years since.
The *Single European Act (SEA, 1986)* made the name "European Parliament" official. Until 2009, Parliament was an institution of *European Communities (EC, inactive).* Since *Treaty of Lisbon (2007)* came into force, 2009, the Parliament is an institution of *European Union (EU, #08967).* The EP adopted a draft treaty on the European Union, 14 Feb 1984. The Union itself came to fruition under the *Treaty on European Union (Maastricht Treaty, 1992)*, signed 7 Feb 1992 and into force 1 Nov 1993. The Maastricht Treaty introduced the co-decision procedure giving Parliament an equal say with the *Council of the European Union (#04895)* in some areas of legislation and gave Parliament the power to approve the *European Commission (EC, #06633)* as a whole. The *Treaty of Amsterdam (1997)*, 1 May 1999, simplified and broadened the application of the co-decision law-making procedure and gave Parliament the right to approve the Commission president. With active involvement of MEPS, the *Charter of Fundamental Rights of the European Union (2000)* was proclaimed, 7 Dec 2000. Parliament played an active role in the *Convention on the Future of Europe (inactive)*, which produced a draft Constitution for Europe, Europe 2003. The *Nice Treaty (2001)* of Feb 2003 further reformed EU institutions and extended application of co-decision. The Lisbon Treaty completed reform of the EU, made Charter of Fundamental Rights binding and put Parliament on an equal decision-making footing with EU governments in most legal areas through *Treaty on the Functioning of the European Union (TFEU, 1957).* Former names and other names: *European Parliamentary Assembly* – former; *Assemblée parlementaire européenne* – former.
Aims Serve as a forum for political debate and decision-making at the EU level; promote *democratic* decision-making in Europe; support the fight for democracy, freedom of speech and fair elections in Europe and worldwide; act as a co-legislator, sharing with the Council the power to adopt and amend *legislative* proposals, and decide on the EU budget; supervise the work of the Commission and other EU bodies; cooperate with national parliaments of EU countries to get their input.
Structure Seat located in Strasbourg (France) where the 12 monthly plenary part-sessions are held, including the session at which the decision on the annual EU budget is taken. *European Commission (EC, #06633)* and *Council of the European Union (#04895)* take part in the sittings so as to facilitate collaboration between institutions in the decision-making process. Additional part-sessions, and parliamentary committee meetings held in Brussels (Belgium). Secretariat and back-up departments located in Luxembourg (Luxembourg).
'Political bodies': Bureau, comprising President and 14 Vice-Presidents; Conference of Presidents, composed of President and the political group chairs; Quaestors (5), responsible for members' administrative and financial business; Conference of Committee Chairs; Conference of Delegation Chairs. Terms of office of President, Vice-Presidents, Quaestors and committee and delegations chairs is 2.5 years.
'Committees' (20), consisting of 25 to 71 MEPS, including a chair, bureau and secretariat: AFET – Foreign Affairs, including 2 sub-committees (DROI – Human Rights, SEDE – Security and Defence); DEVE – Development; INTA – International Trade; BUDG – Budgets; CONT – Budgetary Control; ECON – Economic and Monetary Affairs; EMPL – Employment and Social Affairs; ENVI – Environment, Public Health and Food Safety; ITRE – Industry, Research and Energy; IMCO – Internal Market and Consumer Protection; TRAN – Transport and Tourism; REGI – Regional Development; AGRI – Agriculture and Rural Development; PECH – Fisheries; CULT – Culture and Education; JURI – Legal Affairs; LIBE – Civil Liberties, Justice and Home Affairs; AFCO – Constitutional Affairs; FEMM – Women's Rights and Gender Equality; PETI – Petitions.
'Delegations' (39) – interparliamentary delegations and delegations to joint parliamentary committees, parliamentary cooperation committees and multilateral parliamentary assemblies. Parliament also sends a delegation to *ACP-EU Joint Parliamentary Assembly (#00077).*
'Political groups' (currently 7) – members sit according to their political affinities in transnational group, not by nationality: *Group of the European People's Party – Christian Democrats (EPP, #10775)* – Christian Democrats; *Group of the Progressive Alliance of Socialists and Democrats in the European Parliament (S and D, #10786); European Conservatives and Reformists Group (ECR, #06745);* Group of the *Renew Europe (#18840); The Left in the European Parliament (The Left, #16436); Group of the Greens – European Free Alliance (Greens/EFA, #10781); Europe of Nations and Freedom Group (ENF, #09163).*

'Intergroups' can be formed by members from any political group and any committee, with a view to holding informal exchanges of views on particular subjects and promoting contact between members and civil society. *'European political parties'*: European People's Party; Party of European Socialists; Alliance of Liberals and Democrats for Europe; European Green Party; Alliance of European Conservatives and Reformists; Party of the European Left; Movement for a Europe of Liberties and Democracy; European Democratic Party; European Free Alliance; European Alliance for Freedom; Alliance of European National Movements; European Christian Political Movement; EU Democrats. These supranational parties work in close cooperation with the corresponding political groups in the European Parliament.
'Secretariat': comprises: Office of the Secretary-General; Directorates-General (12) – Presidency; Internal Policies of the Union; External Policies of the Union; Parliamentary Research Services; Communication; Personnel; Infrastructure and Logistics; Translation; Interpretation and Conferences; Finance; Innovation and Technological Support; Security; Legal Service.
Languages EU languages. **Staff** About 4,600 officials and other employees, of which half in Luxembourg (Luxembourg), almost half in Brussels (Belgium), and the rest in Strasbourg (France). Staff representation through staff committee. **Finance** Part of general budget of *European Union (EU, #08967)*, of which it makes up of about 1%. Annual budget: 1,756,000,000 EUR (2014). **Activities** *'Legislative powers'*: Ordinary legislative procedure gives the same weight to the European Parliament and the Council of the European Union on a wide range of areas. The vast majority of European laws are adopted jointly by the Parliament and the Council. *'Budgetary powers'*: Following the entry into force of the Lisbon Treaty, Parliament now shares the power to decide on the entire annual budget of the EU with the Council and it has the final say. Decisions about annual expenditure and revenue must fall within the annual spending limits laid down in the EU's long-term financial plan, the Multiannual Financial Framework, negotiated once every seven years. Once the EU budget is adopted, the European Commission is responsible for its implementation (other institutions are in charge of their own administrative budgets). As a directly-elected institution representing EU taxpayers, Parliament exercises democratic oversight to make sure that the Commission and the other institutions deal properly with European funds. *'Supervisory powers'*: Parliament has a range of supervisory and control powers allowing it to exercise oversight over other institutions, to monitor the proper use of the EU budget and to ensure the correct implementation of EU law. Any EU citizen, resident, company or organization can submit a petition to Parliament about EU law. **Events** *Inter-Parliamentary Committee Meeting on the Rights of Ukrainian Women Fleeing the War* Brussels (Belgium) 2022, *Meeting on Enlargement* Brussels (Belgium) 2022, *Conference on the Future of Europe Plenary Session* Strasbourg (France) 2022, *Conference on the Future of Europe Plenary Session* Strasbourg (France) 2022, *Conference on the Future of Europe Plenary Session* Strasbourg (France) 2022. **Publications** All publication go through *Publications Office of the European Union (Publications Office, #18562)*.
Members Currently comprises 705 Parliamentarians directly elected by nationals of the 27 member countries of the European Union:
Austria, Belgium, Bulgaria, Croatia, Cyprus, Czechia, Denmark, Estonia, Finland, France, Germany, Greece, Hungary, Ireland, Italy, Latvia, Lithuania, Luxembourg, Malta, Netherlands, Poland, Portugal, Romania, Slovakia, Slovenia, Spain, Sweden.
IGO Relations Special links with: *Committee of Members of Parliament of the EFTA States Party to the EEA (EFTA MPS, #04270)*; *European Court of Auditors (#06854)*; *European Monitoring Centre for Drugs and Drug Addiction (EMCDDA, #07820)*. Cooperates with: *Parliamentary Assembly of the Council of Europe (PACE, #18211)*. Member of: *Parliamentary Assembly of the Organization of the Black Sea Economic Cooperation (PABSEC, #18213)*. Instrumental in: *European Declaration Against Racism and Xenophobia (1986)*; *Résolution sur les Minorités Linguistiques et Culturelles dans la Communauté Européenne (1994)*. Approves EU legislation in regard to: *EU Customs Union (#05579)*. Through Interparliamentary Delegations, relations with: *Arab Maghreb Union (AMU, #01004)*; *ASEAN (#01141)*; *South Asian Association for Regional Cooperation (SAARC, #19721)*; *NATO (#16945)*. Exercises supervisory oversight of other institutions, including: *European Council (#06801)*; *Council of the European Union (#04895)*; *European Commission (EC, #06633)*; *Court of Justice of the European Union (CJEU, #04938)*; *European Central Bank (ECB, #06466)*; *European Court of Auditors (#06854)*; *European Ombudsman (#08084)*. Instrumental in setting up: *European Centre for Parliamentary Research and Documentation (ECPRD, #06495)*; *European Food Safety Authority (EFSA, #07287)*; *European Institute for Gender Equality (EIGE, #07557)*. **NGO Relations** No official links with international NGOs. Through Interparliamentary Delegations, relations with: *ASEAN Inter-Parliamentary Assembly (AIPA, #01205)*; *NATO Parliamentary Assembly (NATO PA, #16946)*. Cooperates with: *European Parliament Financial Services Forum (EPFSF, #08148)*. Instrumental in setting up: *European Parliament Internet Group (E-PING, no recent information)*. [2022/XF0667/F*]

♦ European Parliamentarians and Industrialists Council (EPIC) 08147

Contact address not obtained. T. +3222847710. Fax +3222849710.
History 1983. **Aims** Provide a forum for bringing together industrialists and members of the European Parliament with a view to increasing understanding between them and for discussing relevant subjects of mutual interest. **Finance** Members' dues. **Activities** Work organized around conferences and luncheons which normally take place during plenary sessions (in Strasbourg) of the European Parliament. In addition, one or two major events are organized each year, focusing on the most important issues of the day. **Events** *Conference on the European central bank* Madrid (Spain) 1992, *Work and social policies in the new Europe* Brussels (Belgium) 1990. **Publications** Conference proceedings.
Members Industrial members in 10 countries:
Belgium, Denmark, France, Germany, Italy, Netherlands, Spain, Türkiye, UK, USA. [2009.06.01/XF1669/tv/F]

♦ European Parliamentary Assembly / see European Parliament (#08146)
♦ European Parliamentary Association (internationally oriented national body)

♦ European Parliamentary Financial Services Forum (EPFSF) 08148

Dir Rond-Point Schuman 2-4, 1040 Brussels, Belgium. T. +3225146800. E-mail: secretariat@epfsf.org.
Office Manager address not obtained. T. +32473657867.
URL: http://www.epfsf.org/
History Founded May 2000. Registered in accordance with Belgian law. EU Transparency Register: 77823123416-69. **Aims** Promote integration of a single European market for financial services across national borders; provide a focal point and resources for members of the European Parliament; deploy the joint expertise of financial industry members to spread information about financial markets and services to the European Parliament. **Structure** General Assembly; Administrative Committee; Steering Committee; Secretariat in Brussels (Belgium). **Languages** English. **Staff** 2.00 FTE, paid. **Finance** Members' dues. **Activities** Events/meetings; training/education. **Events** *Meeting* Brussels (Belgium) 2016, *Annual Conference* Brussels (Belgium) 2007. **Publications** Briefing paper compendium on financial services issues (annual).
Members Financial institutions in 9 countries:
Austria, Belgium, Denmark, Finland, France, Germany, Sweden, Switzerland, UK.
International organizations (13):
Accountancy Europe (#00061); *Association for Financial Markets in Europe (AFME, #02596)*; *Covered Bond and Mortgage Council (CBMC, #04940)*; *European Association of Public Banks (EAPB, #06178)*; *European Banking Federation (EBF, #06312)*; *European Central Securities Depositories Association (ECSDA, #06468)*; *European Fund and Asset Management Association (EFAMA, #07365)*; *European Savings and Retail Banking Group (ESBG, #08426)*; *European Structured Investment Products Association (EUSIPA, #08845)*; *Federation of European Securities Exchanges (FESE, #09542)*; *Futures and Options Association (FOA)*; *International Swaps and Derivatives Association (ISDA, #15638)*; *PensionsEurope (#18291)*. [2017/XM3347/y/F]

♦ European Parliamentary Forum for Sexual & Reproductive Rights (EPF) 08149

Sec Rue Montoyer 23, 1000 Brussels, Belgium. T. +3225008650. Fax +3225116762. E-mail: secretariat@epfweb.org.
URL: http://www.epfweb.org/
History Dec 2000, Paris (France). Founded as a project of *International Planned Parenthood Federation (IPPF, #14589)* European Network. Became independent in 2004. Former names and other names: *Inter-European Parliamentary Forum on Population and Development (IEPFPD)* – former; *Forum parlementaire inter-européen sur la population et le développement* – former. Registration: Banque Carrefour des Entreprises, No/ID: 2.230.047.024, Start date: 1 Jan 2008, Belgium. **Aims** Protect the sexual and reproductive rights (SRHR) of all people, both at home and overseas. **Structure** Council; Executive Committee; Secretariat. **Languages** English, French, German, Italian, Russian, Spanish. **Staff** 10.00 FTE, paid. **Finance** Supported by: *Bill and Melinda Gates Foundation (BMGF)*; *United Nations Population Fund (UNFPA, #20612)*. **Activities** Awareness raising; events/meetings; research/documentation; training/education. **Events** *Meeting / Council Meeting* Berlin (Germany) 2015, *International Parliamentarians Conference on the Implementation of the ICPD Programme of Action / Council Meeting* Stockholm (Sweden) 2014, *Meeting / Council Meeting* London (UK) 2013, *Council Meeting* Istanbul (Turkey) 2012, *Council Meeting* London (UK) 2011. **Publications** *EPF Newsletter* (12 a year); *Contraception Policy Atlas Europe* (annual) in English – The Contraception Policy Atlas Europe is a research project led by the European Parliamentary Forum for Sexual and Reproductive Rights, which investigates how European public authorities perform across: access to contraception, counselling, and online information.; *European Atlas of Fertility Treatment Policies* (annual) in English – Each year, Fertility Europe in conjunction with the European Parliamentary Forum for Sexual and Reproductive rights come together to launch the European Atlas of Fertility Treatment. The document offers a detailed look into the state of fertility policy across 43 European countries.; *SRHR Funding Atlas 2022: A Guide to SRHR Donor Country Funding* (annual) in English – The Sexual and Reproductive Health and Rights Funding Atlas 2022: A Guide to SRHR Donor Country Funding was launched on 16th November 2022 at the International Conference on Family Planning 2022 in Pattaya City, Thailand. This Atlas presents, in an accessible format, the most recent data on how the world's most affluent countries are performing in meeting their commitments to provide funding for sexual and reproductive health and rights (SRHR) programmes in the world's Low- and Middle-Income Countries (LMICs).. *Contraceptive use and awareness among young people in the European region – results from a cross-sectional survey* (2022) in English – Young people are a particular group when it comes to contraceptive use. The median age of first sexual intercourse among young people in Europe is around 17–18 years, while the mean age at first birth among women in the European Union has been gradually increasing over the years and stood at 29.4 years in 2019. This means that there is a substantial period of time during which the vast majority of young people are sexually active and do not yet aspire to have children.; *Tip of the Iceberg: Religious extremist – Funders against Human Rights for Sexuality & Reproductive Health in Europe* (2021) in French, German, Polish – This report examines the funding system which supports the anti-gender actors' efforts to roll back human rights in Europe.; *Modern-day Crusaders in Europe* (2020) in Croatian, English, French, Italian, Lithuanian, Polish – Three recent events affecting human rights in sexuality and reproduction (a proposed ban on abortion in Poland, blocking support for She Decides in Croatia and halting a civil union law in Estonia) were spearheaded by organisations which appear to be the national antennae of the transnational, socially conservative network called Tradition, Family and Property (TFP). TFP refers to a set of interrelated conservative, Catholic-inspired organisations which share a common world view inspired by the TFP founder, Plinio Corrêa de Oliveira.; *"Restoring the Natural Order": The religious extremists' vision to mobilize European societies against human rights on sexuality and reproduction* (2018) – campaigners from the US and Europe have been strategizing 'achievable goals' to roll back human rights in Europe since 2013. Documents have recently emerged showing a detailed, extremist strategy called Restoring the Natural Order: an Agenda for Europe, which seeks to overturn existing laws on basic human rights related to sexuality and reproduction. The book examines that strategy document and the workings of the Vatican-inspired professional advocacy network, going by the name Agenda Europe, aiming for its implementation.. Annual Report; brochure; handbook; articles.
Members Parliamentary groups of 26 countries:
Albania, Armenia, Austria, Azerbaijan, Belgium, Bosnia-Herzegovina, Croatia, Denmark, Finland, France, Germany, Ireland, Italy, Latvia, Lithuania, Netherlands, North Macedonia, Norway, Poland, Portugal, Serbia, Spain, Sweden, Switzerland, Türkiye, UK.
European Parliament (EP, #08146).
Consultative Status Consultative status granted from: *Council of Europe (CE, #04881)* (Participatory Status); *ECOSOC (#05331)* (Special). **IGO Relations** Cooperates with (3): *Commonwealth of Independent States (CIS, #04341)* (Inter-Parliamentary Assembly); *European Parliament (EP, #08146)*; *Parliamentary Assembly of the Council of Europe (PACE, #18211)*. **NGO Relations** Member of (2): *Action for Global Health (AfGH, #00090)*; *Reproductive Health Supplies Coalition (RHSC, #18847)*. Partner of (1): *Every Woman Every Child (EWEC, #09215)*. [2023.02.28/XD2817/F]

♦ European Parliamentary Technology Assessment (EPTA) 08150

Contact Office of Technology Assessment at the German Bundestag, 10178 Berlin, Germany. E-mail: webmaster@eptanetwork.org.
URL: http://www.eptanetwork.org/
History 1990. Founded under the patronage of the then President of *European Parliament (EP, #08146)*. **Aims** Advise parliaments on the social, economic and environmental impact of new sciences and technologies. **Structure** Conference (annual). Council (meets annually), comprising members of Parliament or representatives of the advisory boards for the respective EPTA organization. Rotating Presidency (annual); Directors' Meeting (annual); Practitioners' Meeting (twice a year). **Languages** English. **Staff** None. **Activities** Events/meetings; knowledge management/information dissemination. **Events** *European Technology Assessment Conference* Cork (Ireland) 2017, *Annual Conference* Vienna (Austria) 2016, *Annual Conference* Barcelona (Spain) 2012, *Annual Conference* Germany 2011, *Annual Conference* Denmark 2010. **Publications** Policy briefs; project reports.
Members Full: European organizations carrying out TA activities on behalf of parliaments, in 11 countries and territories:
Austria, Finland, France, Germany, Greece, Netherlands, Norway, Spain (Catalonia), Sweden, Switzerland, UK.
Full regional member (1):
European Parliament (EP, #08146) (STOA Panel).
Associates: organizations in 9 countries and territories:
Belgium (Wallonia), Chile, Denmark, Japan, Mexico, Poland, Portugal, Russia, USA.
Associate regional organization:
Council of Europe (CE, #04881). [2022.04.21/XM0654/y/F]

♦ European Parliamentary Union (inactive)
♦ European Parliament – European Liberal, Democrat and Reform Party Group / see Renew Europe (#18840)

♦ European Parliament Former Members Association (FMA) 08151

Association des anciens députés au Parlement européen (AAD)
SG European Parliament, Bât József Antall 02Q073, Rue Wiertz, 1047 Brussels, Belgium. T. +3222840703. Fax +3222840989. E-mail: formermembers@europarl.europa.eu.
URL: http://www.formermembers.eu/
History Nov 2001, by former members of *European Parliament (EP, #08146)*. Registered in accordance with Belgian law, 25 Oct 2001. **Aims** Bring former members together and provide a forum for meetings, discussions and cultural, scientific and social events; facilitate exchange of information and news between former members of the European Parliament; foster relations between former and current members of the European Parliament by establishing and using an information network; use the experience of former members to strengthen parliamentary democracy and to serve European unity; promote contacts between similar organizations in Europe and elsewhere, including former members' associations of national parliaments; promote debate on development of the European Union in the political field as well as in public opinion and to study its consequences for institutions, local authorities and citizens. **Structure** General Assembly (annual). Board of 10 members, including President, Vice-President, Treasurer and Secretary. *Foundation for Parliamentary Democracy* is a registered charitable organization which raises funds for FMA activities. **Languages** English, French. **Finance** Members' dues. **Activities** Organizes: EP to Campus; seminars and conferences; annual study visits; election observation missions; technical assistance missions; annual dinner; dinner-debates. **Publications** *FMA Bulletin* (4 a year) in English, French. Members' directory.
Members Individuals in 26 countries:
Austria, Belgium, Bulgaria, Cyprus, Czechia, Denmark, Estonia, Finland, France, Germany, Greece, Hungary, Ireland, Italy, Latvia, Lithuania, Luxembourg, Netherlands, Poland, Portugal, Romania, Slovakia, Slovenia, Spain, Sweden, UK.
NGO Relations Member of: *European Association of Former Parliamentarians (FP-AP, #06047)*. [2020/XE4259/v/E]

♦ European Parliament Liberal, Democratic and Reform Group / see Renew Europe (#18840)

♦ European Parliament Platform for Secularism in Politics (EPPSP) .. 08152

Chair c/o EP, Bât Altiero Spinelli, 10G317, Rue Wiertz 60, 1047 Brussels, Belgium. E-mail: leonhard.denhertog@ep.europa.eu.
URL: http://www.politicsreligion.eu/

History 2004, as *All Party Working Group on the Separation of Religion and Politics (WGSRP)*. Current title adopted 2009. **Aims** Identify and raise awareness about issues pertaining to the intersection of religion and politics in which the political values and principles of the European Union (EU) are at stake; promote knowledge, understanding and acceptance of freedom of religion and non-religion, and the impartiality of the EU regarding organizations of faith and conviction; take action, where appropriate, to counter any attempts to undermine democracy, human rights and in particular women's rights and minority rights, sexual and reproductive health and rights, pluralism and the rule of law. **Structure** Board, comprising Chair and 4 Vice-Chairs. Advisory Board, consisting of NGOs based in Europe. **Activities** Panel debates; expert meetings.
NGO Relations Advisory Board members include: *European Association of the Free Thought (EAFT, #06048); European Humanist Federation (EHF, #07507); European Network Church-on-the-Move (#07878); Human Rights without Frontiers International (HRWF, #10983).* [2017/XJ1782/**F**]

♦ European Parquet Alliance / see Global Flooring Alliance (#10362)

♦ European Partners against Corruption (EPAC) 08153

Pres c/o Federal Ministry of the Interior of the Republic of Austria, Federal Bureau of Anti-Corruption, Herrengasse 7, 1010 Vienna, Austria. E-mail: secretariat@epac-eacn.org.
URL: http://www.epac-eacn.org/

History Set up 2004, as an independent, informal, non-political network of operational Police Oversight Bodies (POB) and operational Anti-Corruption Authorities (ACA) from *European Commission (EC, #06633)* Member States, and since 2009, also from Member States of *Council of Europe (CE, #04881)*. **Aims** Contribute to prevention of, and fight against, corruption within Europe and beyond; provide a platform for dialogue, exchange of information and experiences on a practical and professional level; support development of common standards and best practices and promote instruments for improving anti-corruption measures; facilitate establishment and active maintenance of contact between members; offer a medium for practitioners to share experiences, identify opportunities and cooperate across national borders in developing common strategies and high professional standards. **Structure** General Assembly. President; 2 Vice-Presidents; 2 Deputy Vice-Presidents. Working Groups; Secretariat. Includes: *European Contact-point Network against Corruption (EACN, #06776)*. **Languages** English. **Finance** Voluntary contributions. **Activities** Events/meetings; networking/liaising; standards/guidelines; knowledge management/information dissemination. **Events** *Annual Professional Conference and General Assembly* Stockholm (Sweden) 2019, *Annual Conference* Paris (France) 2015, *Annual Conference* Sofia (Bulgaria) 2014, *Annual Conference* Krakow (Poland) 2013, *Annual Conference* Barcelona (Spain) 2012. **Publications** *Setting Standards for Europe Handbook – Anti-Corruption Authority Standards and Police Oversight Principles* (2012).
Members Organizations of national remit and/or broad jurisdiction within EU and Council of Europe Member States; European organizations and networks. POBs and ACAs (over 70) in 34 countries:
Albania, Austria, Azerbaijan, Belgium, Bulgaria, Croatia, Cyprus, Czechia, Denmark, Estonia, Finland, France, Georgia, Germany, Greece, Hungary, Italy, Latvia, Lithuania, Luxembourg, Malta, Moldova, Montenegro, Netherlands, North Macedonia, Norway, Poland, Romania, Serbia, Slovakia, Slovenia, Spain, UK, Ukraine.
Included in the above, one organization listed in this Yearbook:
European Anti-Fraud Office (#05906).
Observer:
Kosovo.
IGO Relations Memorandum of Understanding with: *International Anti-Corruption Academy (IACA, #11654); The World Bank Group (#21218)* – Integrity Vice Presidency (INT). [2018.06.01/XJ0293/**F***]

♦ European Partners for Blindness Prevention (inactive)

♦ European Partners for the Environment (EPE) 08154

Partenaires européens pour l'environnement (PEE) – Europartner Umwelt (EPU)
Main Office 160-A Avenue Louise, Bte 22, 1050 Brussels, Belgium.
URL: https://www.the-epe.org/

History Jan 1993, Brussels (Belgium). Registration: Start date: 2004, Belgium. **Aims** Bring together a wide range of players applying the concept of "Leadership through Partnership" to advance system change towards *resource* efficiency and *sustainable development*. **Structure** General Assembly (annual), usually in Brussels (Belgium); Council; Executive Director; Secretariat located in Brussels (Belgium). **Languages** English, French. **Staff** 1.00 FTE, voluntary. **Finance** Members' dues. **Events** *Workshop on Sustainable Mobility and Integrated Planning in Urban Areas* Brussels (Belgium) 2013, *Annual General Assembly* Brussels (Belgium) 2002, *European Rio plus 10 coalition annual progress conference* Brussels (Belgium) 2002, *Extraordinary general assembly* Brussels (Belgium) 2002, *European Rio Plus 10 Coalition annual progress conference* Brussels (Belgium) 2001.
Members Active; Associate; Honorary: public authorities, businesses, trade unions, environmental NGOs, social partners and professionals. Members in 15 countries:
Belgium, Croatia, Denmark, France, Germany, Greece, Hungary, Ireland, Italy, Netherlands, Poland, Portugal, Spain, Sweden, UK.
Included in the above, 7 organizations listed in this Yearbook:
European Alliance for Innovation (EAI, #05872); European Committee of Environmental Technology Suppliers Associations (EUCETSA, #06648); European Environmental Bureau (EEB, #06996); European Trade Union Confederation (ETUC, #08927); Local Governments for Sustainability (ICLEI, #16507) (European Section); *Regional Environmental Centre for Central and Eastern Europe (REC, #18782).*
IGO Relations Partners include: *European Commission (EC, #06633)* and EU Member States; *United Nations (UN, #20515).* [2021/XF2822/y/**E**]

♦ European Partnership for Alternative Approaches to Animal Testing (EPAA) 08155

Advisor c/o European Commission, DG Internal Market – Industry – Entrepreneurship and SMEs Communication, Access to Documents and Document Management Unit A1, BREY 07/045, 1049 Brussels, Belgium. E-mail: grow-epaa@ec.europa.eu.
URL: https://single-market-economy.ec.europa.eu/sectors/chemicals/european-partnership-alternative-approaches-animal-testing_en

History 7 Nov 2005. Founded by *European Commission (EC, #06633)* and companies, together with their European trade associations, from 8 industrial sectors. **Aims** Promote replacement, reduction and refinement (3Rs) of animal use for meeting regulatory requirements through better and more predictive science. **Structure** Conference (annual); Steering Committee; Mirror Group; Project Platform. **Languages** English. **Staff** 3.00 FTE, paid. **Finance** Members' dues. Support from *European Commission (EC, #06633)*. **Activities** Events/meetings; projects/programmes. **Events** *Annual Conference* Brussels (Belgium) 2022, *Annual Conference* Brussels (Belgium) 2020, *Annual Conference* Brussels (Belgium) 2019, *Annual Conference* Brussels (Belgium) 2018, *Annual Conference* Brussels (Belgium) 2016. **Publications** *EPAA Newsletter.*
Members Companies (37); Industry Associations (7):
AnimalhealthEurope (#00837); Conseil européen de l'industrie chimique (CEFIC, #04687); Cosmetics Europe – The Personal Care Association (#04852); CropLife Europe (#04965); European Federation of Pharmaceutical Industries and Associations (EFPIA, #07191); International Association for Soaps, Detergents and Maintenance Products (#12166); International Fragrance Association (IFRA, #13680).
Services of European Commission (6):
DG Environment; DG GROW; DG Health and Consumer Protection; DG Research and Innovation; EURL ECVAM; *Joint Research Centre (JRC, #16147)* (DG). [2019.07.05/XM2909/y/**E**]

♦ European Partnership for a Circular Bio-based Europe (unconfirmed)
♦ European Partnership for Clean Aviation (unconfirmed)

♦ European Partnership for Democracy (EPD) 08156

Exec Dir Rue Froissart 123-133, 1040 Brussels, Belgium. T. +3227332282. E-mail: info@epd.eu.
URL: http://www.epd.eu/

History Registered in accordance with Dutch law. Registered in Belgium as a branch office. **Aims** Support democracy outside the European Union. **Structure** General Assembly; Board of Directors; Secretariat. **Activities** Advocacy/lobbying/activism; knowledge management/information dissemination. **Events** *Transatlantic Dialogue on Strengthening Cooperation on Democracy Support* Brussels (Belgium) 2011.
Members Conceived as "Community of practice". Members (14) include 8 organizations listed in this Yearbook:
Eastern Europe Studies Centre (EESC); European Association for Local Democracy (ALDA, #06110); Netherlands Institute for Multiparty Democracy (IMD); OneWorld International Foundation (OWIF, #17738); People in Need (PIN); Westminster Foundation for Democracy (WFD); World Leadership Alliance – Club de Madrid (WLA-CdM, #21619).
NGO Relations Full member of: *Human Rights and Democracy Network (HRDN, #10980).* Member of: *SDG Watch Europe (#19162).* Partners include: *Crisis Management Initiative (CMI); European Centre for Development Policy Management (ECDPM, #06473); People in Peril.* [2018/XJ1689/**F**]

♦ European Partnership for Energy and the Environment (EPEE) 08157

Dir Gen Av des Arts 46, 1000 Brussels, Belgium. T. +3227327040. Fax +3227327176. E-mail: secretariat@epeeglobal.org.
URL: http://www.epeeglobal.org/

History Sep 2000. Takes over activities of *European Consortium for the Responsible Application of Refrigerants (EUCRAR, inactive)*. Registered in accordance with Belgian law. EU Transparency Register: 22276738915-67. **Aims** Promote a better understanding of the *heating, ventilation*, air-conditioning and *refrigeration* (HVACR) sector in the EU. **Structure** General Assembly (annual); Leadership; Working Groups; Secretariat. **Languages** English. **Staff** 2.00 FTE, paid. **Finance** Members' dues. **Activities** Events/meetings. **Events** *International Symposium on Alternative Refrigerants and Environmental Technology* Kobe (Japan) 2012. **Publications** *EPEE Newsletter.* Press releases.
Members Companies and associations (48) in 9 countries:
Belgium, Denmark, France, Germany, Italy, Netherlands, Spain, UK, USA.
Included in the above, 4 international organizations:
Air Conditioning and Refrigeration European Association (AREA, #00601); Association of European Refrigeration Component Manufacturers (ASERCOM, #02537); European Fluorocarbons Technical Committee (EFCTC, #07274); European Heat Pump Association (EHPA, #07469).
IGO Relations Accredited by: *United Nations Framework Convention on Climate Change – Secretariat (UNFCCC, #20564).* **NGO Relations** Member of: *Coalition for Energy Savings (#04056); Energy Efficiency Industrial Forum (EEIF, #05470); European Heat Pump Association (EHPA, #07469); Industry4Europe (#11181).* In liaison with technical committees of: *Comité européen de normalisation (CEN, #04162).* [2020/XF6728/y/**F**]

♦ European Partnership for Key Digital Technologies (KDT) 08158

Acting Exec Dir TO 56 5/5, 1049 Brussels, Belgium. T. +3222218102. E-mail: enquiries@kdt-ju.europa.eu – executive-director@kdt-ju.europa.eu.
Street Addresss White Atrium Bldg, Av de la Toison d'Or 56-60, 1060 Brussels, Belgium.
URL: https://www.kdt-ju.europa.eu/

History 30 Nov 2021. Proposed 23 Feb 2021. Established through *Council of the European Union (#04895)* Council Regulation (EU) 2021/2085. Succeeded *ECSEL Joint Undertaking (ECSEL JU, inactive)*. **Structure** Governing Board; Public Authorities Board; Private Members Board.
Members Representatives from 27 countries and from 4 organizations:
Austria, Belgium, Cyprus, Czechia, Denmark, Estonia, Finland, France, Germany, Greece, Hungary, Ireland, Israel, Italy, Latvia, Luxembourg, Malta, Netherlands, Norway, Poland, Portugal, Romania, Slovakia, Slovenia, Spain, Sweden, Türkiye.
Association for European NanoElectronics ActivitieS (AENEAS, #02525); European Commission (EC, #06633); European Technology Platform on Smart Systems Integration (EPoSS, #08892); Inside Industry Association (Inside, #11230). [2023/AA1425/y/**E**]

♦ European Partnership on Rail Research and Innovation (unconfirmed)

♦ European Partnership for Responsible Minerals (EPRM) 08159

Secretariat Prinses Beatrixlaan 2, 2595 AL The Hague, Netherlands. T. +31703798000. E-mail: eprm@rvo.nl.
URL: https://europeanpartnership-responsibleminerals.eu/

History Launched 2016. **Aims** Create better social and economic conditions for mine *workers* and local *mining* communities, by increasing the number of mines that adopt responsible mining practices in Conflict and High Risk Areas (CAHRAs). **Structure** Board; Secretariat. Represented pillars: Supply Chain Actors; Civil Society; Governments and Institutions. **Languages** English. **Staff** 2.50 FTE, paid. **Finance** Members' dues. Other sources: government donors and DG DEVCO – *European Commission (EC, #06633)*. **Activities** Advocacy/lobbying/activism; awareness raising; capacity building; certification/accreditation; events/meetings; guidance/assistance/consulting; knowledge management/information dissemination; networking/liaising; politics/policy/regulatory; standards/guidelines; training/education. **Publications** *EPRM Newsletter.*
Members Strategic; Regular; Basic; Civil Society Actors; Governments and Institutions; Observers. Membership countries not specified. Included in the above, 7 organizations listed in this Yearbook:
Included in the above, 7 organizations listed in this Yearbook:
Catholic Organization for Relief and Development (Cordaid); Diakonia; International Peace Information Service (IPIS); Pact (#18016); Responsible Minerals Initiative (RMI); SOLIDARIDAD Network (#19681); Tantalum-Niobium International Study Center (T.I.C., #20095).
Governments of 3 countries:
Germany, Netherlands, UK.
Observers (3):
European Commission (EC, #06633) (DG for International Cooperation and Development DG DEVCO); *OECD (#17693); UNEP (#20299).*
NGO Relations Member of: *IMPACT (#11136).* [2018.09.18/XM6941/y/**F**]

♦ European Partnership of Supervisory Organisations in Health Services and Social Care (EPSO) 08160

Secretariat Benoordenhoutseweg 21, 2596 BA The Hague, Netherlands. E-mail: info@epsonet.eu.
URL: http://www.epsonet.eu/

History 1996, as *European Platform for Supervisory Organisations (EPSO)*. **Aims** Improve quality of health care and social care in Europe; connect between supervisory organizations and their individual members to improve exchange of ideas, outcome of research, information and good practice; promote cooperation on topics such as education and dissemination of knowledge. **Structure** Board; Secretariat. **Languages** English. **Staff** 2.00 FTE, paid. **Finance** Contributions. **Activities** Events/meetings; training/education; knowledge management/information dissemination; networking/liaising. **Events** *Conference* Copenhagen (Denmark) 2018, *Conference* Sofia (Bulgaria) 2018, *Conference* Reykjavik (Iceland) 2017, *Conference* Saaremaa (Estonia) 2017, *Conference* Stockholm (Sweden) 2016.
Members Agencies in 19 countries and territories:
Bulgaria, Denmark, England, Estonia, Finland, France, Iceland, Ireland, Italy, Kosovo, Latvia, Malta, Netherlands, Northern Ireland, Norway, Portugal, Scotland, Sweden, Wales.
Participating agencies without membership in 2 countries:
Germany, Slovenia. [2017.03.09/XJ7726/**F***]

♦ European Party Caterer Association (EPCAS) 08161

Secretariat Jeruzalemweg 2, 6222 NG Maastricht, Netherlands. T. +31433561091. E-mail: office@epcas.eu.
URL: http://epcas.eu/

History Founded 23 Jan 2007. **Aims** Offer European party caterers a platform in which networking and knowledge sharing on mutual and current subjects are key issues; connect party caterers with a current and reputable source for news, information, products, services and networking opportunities relevant to the industry. **Structure** Board; Advisory Council; Secretariat. **Languages** English. **Activities** Events/meetings; networking/liaising. **Events** *General Assembly* Vienna (Austria) 2019. **Members** National associations; party caterers; suppliers to the catering branch operating in more than one European country. Membership countries not specified. [2019/XJ7943/**D**]

European Passengers
08162

alphabetic sequence excludes
For the complete listing, see Yearbook Online at

♦ European Passengers' Federation (EPF) 08162

Fédération européenne des voyageurs – Europäischer Fahrgastverband – Europese Reizigersfederatie

Contact Kortrijksesteenweg 304, 9000 Ghent, Belgium. T. +3292239729. E-mail: secretariat@epf.eu.
URL: http://www.epf.eu/

History 18 Oct 2002, Ghent (Belgium). Registration: Banque-Carrefour des Entreprises, Belgium. **Aims** Represent the end-users of all transport modes at European level; improve standards on public transport; achieve comprehensive passenger rights throughout Europe; promote effective and seamless multi-modal travel. **Structure** General Meeting (annual); Management Board; Secretariat. **Languages** Dutch, English, French, German. **Staff** 3.00 FTE, paid; 10.00 FTE, voluntary. **Events** *Annual Conference* Stockholm (Sweden) 2019, *Annual Conference* Aachen (Germany) 2018, *Annual Conference* Rotterdam (Netherlands) 2017, *Annual Conference* Berlin (Germany) 2016, *Annual Conference* Budapest (Hungary) 2015. **Publications** *EPF Newsletter*.

Members Full in 21 countries:
Austria, Belgium, Bulgaria, Czechia, Denmark, Finland, France, Germany, Greece, Hungary, Ireland, Italy, Luxembourg, Netherlands, Norway, Poland, Russia, Spain, Sweden, Switzerland, UK.

NGO Relations Associate member of: *Rail Forum Europe (RFE, #18607)*. [2021.02.21/XJ0253/**D**]

♦ European Passenger Train Timetable Conference (inactive)

♦ European Passenger Transport Operators (EPTO) 08163

SG Lacon House 6th Fl, 84 Theobalds Road, London, WC1X 8NL, UK. E-mail: admin@jgtransportconsulting.co.uk – enquiries@jgtransportconsulting.co.uk.
Brussels Office Rue Sainte Marie 6, 1080 Brussels, Belgium. E-mail: info@epto.net.
URL: https://www.epto.net/

History 2007. EU Transparency Register: 91337303018-28. **Aims** Serve as the trade association of the passenger transport operators in Europe. **Structure** Board. **Activities** Advocacy/lobbying/activism. **Publications** Briefings; position papers. **Members** Passenger transport operators (7). Membership countries not specified. **NGO Relations** Represented in: *European Citizens' Mobility Forum (ECMF, #06559)*. [2022/XJ1115/**D**]

♦ European Passive Components Industry Association (EPCIA) 08164

Sec Rue de la Duchesse 11/13, 1150 Brussels, Belgium. E-mail: epcia@t-online.de – secretariat@eusemiconductors.eu.
Pres TDK Electronics AG, Rosenheimer Strasse 141 e, 81671 Munich, Germany. T. +491622664928.
URL: https://www.eusemiconductors.eu/

History Founded as an industry association within *European Electronic Component Manufacturers Association (EECA, #06974)*. Registration: EU Transparency Register, No/ID: 22092908193-23. **Aims** Represent and promote the common interests of the Passive Components Manufacturers active in Europe; ensure an open and transparent market for Passive Components in Europe as part of the global market place. **Activities** Events/meetings; monitoring/evaluation; networking/liaising; research/documentation; standards/guidelines. **Events** *Passive Components Networking Symposium* Milan (Italy) 2021. **Publications** *EPCIA Newsletter*. [2021/XK2147/t/**E**]

♦ European patent convention – Convention on the Grant of European Patents (1973 treaty)
♦ European Patent Institute / see Institute of Professional Representatives before the European Patent Office (#11288)

♦ European Patent Lawyers Association (EPLAW) 08165

Association européenne d'avocats spécialisés dans le contentieux des brevets d'invention – Europäische Vereinigung der Patentrechtsanwälte

Sec c/ Simont Braun, Avenue Louise 149/20, 1050 Brussels, Belgium. E-mail: eplaw@danubialegal.hu.
URL: http://www.eplaw.org/

History 2001. Founded to work towards a harmonized European patent litigation system. Registered in accordance with Belgian law. Registration: Banque-Carrefour des Entreprises, No/ID: 0476.673.737, Start date: 23 Jul 2001, Belgium. **Aims** Promote the equitable and efficacious handling of patent disputes across Europe; assist in the development of proposals for a new pan-European patent court system, involving members in preparation of draft Rules of Procedure for the Unified Patents Court (UPC); strengthen the links between lawyers having relevant litigious experience in patent *law* in Europe. **Structure** General Assembly (annual in December, at Congress) always in Brussels (Belgium); Board; Advisory Board. **Languages** English, French, German. **Finance** Sources: members' dues. **Activities** Events/meetings; training/education. **Events** *Congress* 2020, *General Assembly* Brussels (Belgium) 2015, *Congress and General Assembly* Brussels (Belgium) 2014, *Young Congress / General Assembly* Brussels (Belgium) 2014, *Congress and General Assembly* Brussels (Belgium) 2012. **Publications** EPLAW Blog.

Members Lawyers admitted to a bar or similar law society in a country in the European Economic Area (and also including Switzerland), and must have substantial experience in the conduct of patient litigation cases to trial. Individuals in 18 countries:
Austria, Belgium, Denmark, Finland, France, Germany, Greece, Hungary, Ireland, Italy, Netherlands, Norway, Poland, Spain, Sweden, Switzerland, UK, USA.

IGO Relations Cooperates with: *European Patent Office (EPO, #08166)* on organization of annual Venice Patent Judges' Forum. [2021/XD8457/v/**D**]

♦ European Patent Office (EPO) 08166

Office européen des brevets (OEB) – Europäisches Patentamt (EPA)

Headquarters Bob-van-Benthem-Platz 1, 80469 Munich, Germany. T. +49892399-0. Fax +498923994465. E-mail: info@epo.org.
URL: http://www.epo.org/

History Established 7 Oct 1977, based on adoption of *Convention on the Grant of European Patents (European patent convention, 1973)* at a diplomatic conference on 5 Oct 1973, Munich (Germany FR). The convention was signed by 16 European States in 1973 and entered into force on 7 Oct 1977. On 1 Jan 1978, EPO took over the functions of *International Patent Institute (IIB, inactive)*, set up 6 Jun 1947, The Hague (Netherlands). First patent applications accepted 1 Jun 1978; first European patents granted 9 Jan 1980. **Aims** Support innovation, competitiveness and economic growth for the benefit of the citizens of Europe; grant European patents for inventions, on the basis of a centralized procedure. **Structure** European Patent Office is executive organ of *European Patent Organisation (#08167)* and consists of President and 5 Directorates General, headed by a Vice-President each: Operations; Operational Support; Appeals; Administration; Legal/International Affairs. **Languages** English, French, German. **Staff** 7000.00 FTE, paid. Staff from over 35 different nationalities. **Finance** Self-financing from procedural fees and renewal fees. Annual budget (2019): euro 2,400,000. **Activities** Any person or legal entity, regardless of nationality and place of business or residence, can apply for a European patent through a 2-phase (sometimes 3-phase) grant procedure: *'first phase'* (Munich – Germany; The Hague – Netherlands; Berlin – Germany) – Filing the application, examination on filing and formalities examination, search, publication of application and search report; *'second phase'* (Munich; The Hague; Berlin) – Substantive examination (grant of patent or refusal of application); *'third phase'* (Munich) – in some cases; Opposition, appeal. Organizes Patent Information Conference. Offer European Inventor Award. **Events** *International Trilateral Symposium on IP and Environmental Issues* Tokyo (Japan) 2022, *East meets West Forum* Munich (Germany) 2020, *Patent Information Conference* Munich (Germany) 2020, *IP5 Deputy Heads of Office Meeting* Seoul (Korea Rep) 2019, *East meets West Forum* Vienna (Austria) 2019. **Publications** *Official Journal of the European Patent Office* (12 a year); *Patent Information News* (4 a year); *EPO Newsletter* (24 a year) – online; *European Patent Bulletin* – online. *Case Law of the EPO Boards of Appeal* (7th ed 2013); *European Patent Convention* (15th ed 2013); *Guidelines for Examination in the EPO* (2013); *Ancillary Regulations implementing the European Patent Convention* (2010); *Directory of Professional Representatives*. Reports; brochures; DVDs. **Information Services** *Common Citation Document*, *espacenet*, *European Patent Register*, *INPADOC*, *IPScore*, *Patent Translate*.

Members Contracting States (38):
Albania, Austria, Belgium, Bulgaria, Croatia, Cyprus, Czechia, Denmark, Estonia, Finland, France, Germany, Greece, Hungary, Iceland, Ireland, Italy, Latvia, Liechtenstein, Lithuania, Luxembourg, Malta, Monaco, Netherlands, North Macedonia, Norway, Poland, Portugal, Romania, San Marino, Serbia, Slovakia, Slovenia, Spain, Sweden, Switzerland, Türkiye, UK.
Extension States (2):
Bosnia-Herzegovina, Montenegro.

IGO Relations Organisation has permanent observer status with: *United Nations Framework Convention on Climate Change (UNFCCC, 1992)*; *World Intellectual Property Organization (WIPO, #21593)*. Recognized as an International Deposit Authority (IDA) by WIPO, for patent deposits under the terms of *Budapest Treaty on the International Recognition of the Deposit of Microorganisms for the Purposes of Patent Procedure (Budapest Treaty of 1977, 1977)*. Relationship agreement with: *International Telecommunication Union (ITU, #15673)*; *European Union Intellectual Property Office (EUIPO, #08996)*; *UNEP (#20299)*; *UNIDO (#20336)*. **NGO Relations** Relationship agreement with: *IEEE Standards Association (IEEE-SA)*; *International Electrotechnical Commission (IEC, #13255)*; *European Telecommunications Standards Institute (ETSI, #08897)*; *International Centre for Trade and Sustainable Development, Geneva (ICTSD, #12524)*. [2020/XD4489/**D***]

♦ European Patent Organisation 08167

Organisation européenne des brevets – Europäische Patentorganisation

Address not obtained.
URL: http://www.epo.org/

History by *Convention on the Grant of European Patents (European patent convention, 1973)*, signed 5 Oct 1973, Munich (Germany FR). The convention was signed by 16 European States in 1973 and 1974 and entered into force on 7 Oct 1977. **Structure** Administrative Council is legislative body and includes Chairman and Deputy Chairman. *European Patent Office (EPO, #08166)* is executive body. Budget and Finance Committee. Secretariat. **Languages** English, French, German.

Members Contracting States (32):
Austria, Belgium, Bulgaria, Cyprus, Czechia, Denmark, Estonia, Finland, France, Germany, Greece, Hungary, Iceland, Ireland, Italy, Latvia, Liechtenstein, Lithuania, Luxembourg, Malta, Monaco, Netherlands, Poland, Portugal, Romania, Slovakia, Slovenia, Spain, Sweden, Switzerland, Türkiye, UK.
Extension States (5):
Albania, Bosnia-Herzegovina, Croatia, North Macedonia, Serbia.

IGO Relations Permanent observer status with: *World Intellectual Property Organization (WIPO, #21593)*. *Nordic Patent Institute (NPI, #17381)* has observer status to Administrative Council. **NGO Relations** Member of (1): *European Telecommunications Standards Institute (ETSI, #08897)*. *Institute of Professional Representatives before the European Patent Office (epi, #11288)* has observer status to Administrative Council. [2022/XJ3725/**D***]

♦ European Pathogenesis and Immunology Study Group / see European Study Group on Pathogenesis and Immunology in Helicobacter Infections (#08851)

♦ European Pathway Association (E-P-A) 08168

Office Manager Kapucijnenvoer 35 / 4, 3000 Leuven, Belgium. T. +3216376573. Fax +3216336970.
URL: http://e-p-a.org/

History Sep 2004, Jesi (Italy). Registration: Belgium. **Aims** Conduct international research into the quality and efficiency of organizing *healthcare* and methods for the coordination of primary healthcare and care pathways (aka clinical pathways, integrated care pathways (ICPs) or critical pathways); set up an international network for pooling know-how and international training initiatives; foster international cooperation between healthcare researchers, managers and healthcare providers from European countries and the wider international community; advise policymakers within the area of healthcare management. **Structure** Council; Bureau. **Activities** Research/documentation; networking/liaising; guidance/assistance/consulting; training/education. **Events** *Conference* Reggio Emilia (Italy) 2015, *Conference* Glasgow (UK) 2013, *Conference* Amsterdam (Netherlands) 2012. **Publications** *E-P-A Newsletter*.

Members National sections in 11 countries and territories:
Belgium, Canada, England, Ireland, Italy, Mongolia, Netherlands, Norway, Scotland, Spain, Wales. [2019/XM4461/**D**]

♦ European Patient Organisation for Dysimmune and Inflammatory Neuropathies (EPODIN) 08169

Contact 7 rue du Centre, 44510 Le Pouliguen, France.
URL: https://www.epodin.org/

History Registration: RNA, No/ID: W443009472, Start date: 25 Mar 2019, France; EU Transparency Register, No/ID: 551594935772-82, Start date: 2 Sep 2019. **Aims** Mobilize and strengthen the patient's voice to give each European citizen living with a rare immune-mediated peripheral neuropathy the opportunity to reduce the burden and inequities due to the disease.

Members Full in 4 countries:
France, Italy, Romania, Spain.

NGO Relations Member of (2): *European Federation of Neurological Associations (EFNA, #07177)*; *EURORDIS – Rare Diseases Europe (#09175)* (Associate). [2023/AA2338/**D**]

♦ European Patients' Academy on Therapeutic Innovation (EUPATI) .. 08170

Dir Am Rothenanger 1b, 85521 Riemerling, Germany. T. +498966086968.
Project Coordinator c/o EPF, Rue du Commerce 31, 1000 Brussels, Belgium.
URL: http://www.patientsacademy.eu/

History Set up as a consortium under Innovative Medicines Initiative (IMI) with *European Patients' Forum (EPF, #08172)* as leader. **Aims** Address health education issues to make available more patient-friendly and user-friendly information. **Structure** Coordinated by: *European Patients' Forum (EPF, #08172)*. **Languages** English, French, German, Italian, Polish, Russian, Spanish. **Staff** Voluntary. **Finance** Support from *European Commission (EC, #06633)* through Innovative Medicines Initiative and *European Federation of Pharmaceutical Industries and Associations (EFPIA, #07191)* companies. Budget (annual): about euro 2 million. **Activities** Meeting activities; training; information dissemination. **Events** *Conference on All Aboard to a Better Health Future* Brussels (Belgium) 2016, *Annual General Meeting* Rome (Italy) 2013. **Publications** *EUPATI Email Newsletter*, *EUPATI Platform Newsletter*.

Members Patient advocacy groups; Academic partners; Not-for-Profit organisations; Industry. Patient advocacy groups (4):
EGAN – Patients Network for Medical Research and Health (EGAN, #05394); *European AIDS Treatment Group (EATG, #05850)*; *European Patients' Forum (EPF, #08172)*; *EURORDIS – Rare Diseases Europe (#09175)*.
Academic partners (3) in 3 countries:
Denmark, Ireland, UK.
Not-for-Profit organizations (5):
Drug Information Association (DIA, #05135); *European Forum for Good Clinical Practice (EFGCP, #07313)*; *European Organisation for Research and Treatment of Cancer (EORTC, #08101)*; *International Society for Pharmacoeconomics and Outcomes Research (ISPOR, #15354)*; Irish Platform for Patients' Organisations, Science and Industry (IPPOSI).
Industry: 17 pharmaceutical companies. [2016/XJ7867/y/**D**]

♦ European Patient Safety Foundation (EUPSF) 08171

General Manager Domus Medica Europea, Rue de l'Industrie 24, 1040 Brussels, Belgium. E-mail: contact@eupsf.org – membership@eupsf.org.
Main Website: https://www.eupsf.org

History Launched end 2013, by *European Society of Anaesthesiology and Intensive Care (ESAIC, #08518)*. Currently independent. **Aims** Empower people for patient safety; develop innovative, meaningful, sustainable and replicable patient safety projects; create a European multidisciplinary platform for exchanging knowledge and best practices; promote and stimulate application of best practices that lead to long-lasting changes in safety culture in healthcare. **Structure** Board (maximum 10 members proposed by Non-profit Organization Affiliates and Industry Affiliates); Advisory Board (international experts in the field of patient safety and quality of care); Council of Affiliates; Council of Affairs (Non-profit Affiliates, Industry Affiliates and Individual Affiliates). **Languages** English. **Finance** Sources: donations; members' dues; revenue from activities/projects. **Activities** Europe. **Members** Individuals; Non-profit Organizations; Industry. National organizations (6). **NGO Relations** Memorandum of Understanding with (1): *Active Citizenship Network (ACN)*. [2021.10.20/XM5591/f/**F**]

♦ European Patients Empowerment for Customised Solutions (internationally oriented national body)

♦ **European Patients' Forum (EPF)** **08172**
SG Chaussée d'Etterbeek 180, 1040 Brussels, Belgium. T. +3222802334. Fax +3222311447. E-mail: info@eu-patient.eu.
URL: http://www.eu-patient.eu/
History 31 Jan 2003, Brussels (Belgium). Registration: Banque Carrefour des Entreprises, No/ID: 0807.605.667, Start date: 1 Jan 2008, Belgium; ASBL, No/ID: F 448, Belgium; EU Transparency Register, No/ID: 61911227368-75, Start date: 7 Dec 2011. **Aims** Ensure the patient community drives policies and programmes that affect patients' lives to bring changes empowering them to be equal citizens in the EU. **Structure** General Meeting (annual); Council; Executive Committee; Secretariat in Brussels (Belgium). **Languages** English, French. **Staff** 20.00 FTE, paid. **Finance** Sources: members' dues; sponsorship. Supported by: *European Union (EU, #08967)*. **Activities** Events/meetings; politics/policy/regulatory. **Events** *Congress* Brussels (Belgium) 2022, *Congress* 2021, *Advancing meaningful patient involvement* Brussels (Belgium) 2019, *Roadmap to Achieving Universal Health Coverage for All Patients by 2030 Meeting* Brussels (Belgium) 2017, *Round Table on Cross-Border Healthcare* Brussels (Belgium) 2017. **Publications** *EPF Newsletter* (11 a year). Annual Report; leaflet.
Members Full (58) include the following 39 organizations listed in this Yearbook:
– *Alzheimer Europe (AE, #00761)*;
– *Association of European Coeliac Societies (AOECS, #02504)*;
– *Cystic Fibrosis Europe (CF Europe, #04991)*;
– *Digestive Cancers Europe (DiCE, #05070)*;
– *Dystonia Europe (#05151)*;
– *EGAN – Patients Network for Medical Research and Health (EGAN, #05394)*;
– *Europa Donna – The European Breast Cancer Coalition (#05745)*;
– *Europa Uomo (#05770)*;
– *European AIDS Treatment Group (EATG, #05850)*;
– *European Alliance of Neuromuscular Disorders Associations (EAMDA, #05876)*;
– *European Congenital Heart Disease Organisation (ECHDO, #06738)*;
– *European Federation of Allergy and Airways Diseases Patients' Associations (EFA, #07045)*;
– *European Federation of Associations of Families of People with Mental Illness (EUFAMI, #07051)*;
– *European Federation of Associations of Patients with Haemochromatosis (EFAPH, #07056)*;
– *European Federation of Crohn's and Ulcerative Colitis Associations (EFCCA, #07095)*;
– *European Federation of Homeopathic Patients' Associations (EFHPA, #07139)*;
– *European Federation of National Psoriasis Patients Associations (EUROPSO, #07175)*;
– *European Haemophilia Consortium (EHC, #07444)*;
– *European Heart and Lung Transplant Federation (EHLTF, #07466)*;
– *European Kidney Patients' Federation (EKPF, #07627)*;
– *European Liver Patients 'Association (ELPA, #07706)*;
– *European Migraine and Headache Alliance (EMHA, #07801)*;
– *European Multiple Sclerosis Platform (EMSP, #07833)*;
– *European Network of ex- Users and Survivors of Psychiatry (ENUSP, #07906)*;
– *European Parkinson's Disease Association (EPDA, #08145)*;
– *EURORDIS – Rare Diseases Europe (#09175)*;
– *Federation of European Scleroderma Associations (FESCA, #09540)*;
– *Fertility Europe (FE, #09737)*;
– *Global Alliance of Mental Illness Advocacy Networks – Europe (GAMIAN Europe, #10211)*;
– *Global Heart Hub (#10407)*;
– *International Diabetes Federation Europe (IDF Europe, #13165)*;
– *International Federation for Spina Bifida and Hydrocephalus (IF SBH, #13552)*;
– *International Osteoporosis Foundation (IOF, #14490)*;
– *International Patient Organization for Primary Immunodeficiencies (IPOPI, #14533)*;
– *Lung Cancer Europe (LuCE, #16523)*;
– *LUPUS EUROPE (#16524)*;
– *Pulmonary Hypertension Association Europe (PHA Europe, #18575)*;
– *Retina International (RI, #18926)*;
– *World Duchenne Organization (WDO, #21366)*.
Associate (18) include the following 11 organizations listed in this Yearbook:
DEBRA International (#05021); *European Cleft Organisation (ECO, #06572)*; *European Federation of Neurological Associations (EFNA, #07177)*; *European FH Patient Network (FH Europe, #07243)*; *European Institute of Women's Health (EIWH, #07574)*; *European Network of Fibromyalgia Associations (ENFA, #07908)*; *International Alliance of Dermatology Patient Organizations (IAPDO, #11626)*; *International Bureau for Epilepsy (IBE, #12414)*; *Mental Health Europe (MHE, #16715)*; *Stroke Alliance for Europe (SAFE, #20012)*; *World Federation for Incontinence and Pelvic Problems (WFIPP, #21440)*.
IGO Relations Participant in Fundamental Rights Platform of: *European Union Agency for Fundamental Rights (FRA, #08969)*. **NGO Relations** Member of (6): *Alliance for Safe Online Pharmacy – EU (ASOP EU, #00720)*; *EU Health Coalition*; *European Alliance for Personalised Medicine (EAPM, #05878)*; *European Forum for Primary Care (EFPC, #07326)* (Associated); *European Patients' Academy on Therapeutic Innovation (EUPATI, #08170)*; *SDG Watch Europe (#19162)*. Stakeholder in: *European Network for Health Technology Assessment (EUnetHTA, #07921)*. Partner in: *European Health Parliament (EHP, #07459)*. Endorses: *Steering Group on Influenza Vaccination (#19980)*. [2022.02.23/XF6989/y/**F**]

♦ **European Payment Institutions Federation (EPIF)** **08173**
Contact Rue du Trône 100, 1050 Brussels, Belgium. T. +32475760158. E-mail: info@paymentinstitutions.eu.
Registered Address Chaussée d'Alsemberg 999, 1180 Brussels, Belgium.
URL: https://paymentinstitutions.eu/
History Jun 2011. Founded in response to the adoption of the Payment Services Directive (PSD). Registration: Banque-Carrefour des Entreprises, No/ID: 0841.649.501, Start date: 8 Dec 2011, Belgium; EU Transparency Register, No/ID: 461826311486-83, Start date: 1 Jul 2013. **Aims** Act as a forum to exchange views, form common positions, exchange best practice and provide information to its members and a wider audience. **Structure** General Meeting; Executive Board; Executive Steering Committee. Working Group; Task Forces. **Events** *Annual Conference* 2021, *Annual Conference* 2020, *Annual Conference* Brussels (Belgium) 2019.
Members Full; Associate; Corporate; Observer. Membership countries not specified.
European Association of Payment Service Providers for Merchants (EPSM, #06145) (Observer).
[2021/AA2560/t/**D**]

♦ **European Payments Consulting Association (EPCA)** **08174**
Contact Im Uhrig 7 D, 60433 Frankfurt-Main, Germany. T. +49699511770. Fax +4969521090. E-mail: ewanner@paysys.de.
URL: https://europeanpaymentadvisors.com/
History 1998. An organization of the type *European Economic Interest Grouping (EEIG, #06960)* since 2000. Registration: Germany. **Aims** Stimulate synergies in Europe-wide consulting business; promote Europe-wide networking. **Structure** Central Administration and Office in Frankfurt-Main (Germany). **Languages** English. **Finance** Sources: members' dues. **Activities** Events/meetings; guidance/assistance/consulting. **Events** *Summit* Brussels (Belgium) 2014, *Conference* Brussels (Belgium) 2013.
Members Consultancy firms in 11 countries:
Denmark, Finland, France, Germany, Hungary, Italy, Latvia, Netherlands, Norway, Russia, UK. [2021.09.09/XJ8328/**D**]

♦ **European Payments Council (EPC)** **08175**
Contact SECUREX Building – Main Entrance, Cours Saint-Michel 30, 1040 Brussels, Belgium. T. +3227333533. Fax +3227364988. E-mail: secretariat@epc-cep.eu.
URL: http://www.epc-cep.eu/
History 17 Jun 2002, Brussels (Belgium). Founded by the European banking industry. From 2006, took over activities of the former *European Committee for Banking Standards (ECBS, inactive)*. Registration: Belgium. **Aims** Contribute to safe, reliable, efficient, convenient, economically balanced and sustainable payments, which meet the needs of payment service users and support the goals of competitiveness and innovation in an integrated European economy. **Structure** General Assembly; Board. Scheme Management Board; Committees, Groups and Forums (13); Secretariat. **Languages** English. **Staff** 12.00 FTE, paid. **Finance** Sources: members' dues. Payment service providers. **Publications** *Rep(l)ay* (12 a year). SEPA scheme rulebooks; white papers; clarification papers.
Members Full (77) and Associate (2), representing payment service providers, banking communities and payment institutions. Members in 29 countries:
Austria, Belgium, Bulgaria, Croatia, Cyprus, Czechia, Denmark, Estonia, Finland, France, Germany, Greece, Hungary, Iceland, Ireland, Italy, Liechtenstein, Luxembourg, Malta, Netherlands, Norway, Poland, Portugal, Romania, Slovakia, Slovenia, Spain, Sweden, Switzerland.
Included in the above, 4 organizations listed in this Yearbook:
Euro Banking Association (EBA, #05647); *European Association of Co-operative Banks (EACB, #05990)*; *European Banking Federation (EBF, #06312)*; *European Savings and Retail Banking Group (ESBG, #08426)*.
IGO Relations Cooperates with (2): *European Central Bank (ECB, #06466)*; *European Commission (EC, #06633)*. **NGO Relations** Cooperates with organizations representing end-users of EPC payment schemes. [2022.10.20/XJ3808/y/**E**]

♦ European Payments Union (inactive)
♦ European Peace Action (internationally oriented national body)

♦ **European Peacebuilding Liaison Office (EPLO)** **08176**
Exec Dir Av de Tervueren 12, 1040 Brussels, Belgium. T. +3222333732. E-mail: office@eplo.org.
URL: http://www.eplo.org/
History 28 Feb 2002. Registration: No/ID: 0476.721.544, Start date: 28 Feb 2002, Belgium; EU Transparency Register, No/ID: 0878397912-17, Start date: 2 Jan 2009. **Aims** Influence the EU so that it promotes and implements measures which lead to sustainable peace between states and within states and peoples, and which transform and resolve conflicts non-violently; encourage recognition by the EU of the crucial connection between peacebuilding, the eradication of poverty, and sustainable development worldwide, and the crucial role NGOs have to play in sustainable EU efforts for peacebuilding, conflict prevention and crisis management. **Structure** General Assembly (annual); Steering Committee; Secretariat, based in Brussels (Belgium). **Languages** English. **Staff** 8.20 FTE, paid. **Finance** Sources: grants; members' dues. Supported by: *European Commission (EC, #06633)*. **Activities** Advocacy/lobbying/activism; awareness raising; knowledge management/information dissemination; networking/liaising; politics/policy/regulatory; projects/programmes. **Events** *Meeting on the UN Guidance for Effective Mediation* Brussels (Belgium) 2013, *Conference on enhancing the EU's response to violent conflict* Brussels (Belgium) 2000. **Publications** *EPLO Newsletter* (12 a year). Policy papers; briefing papers; statements; meeting reports; letters.
Members Organizations (41):
– Agency for Peacebuilding;
– *Berghof Foundation*;
– *Budapest Centre for the International Prevention of Genocide and Mass Atrocities*;
– *Catholic Organization for Relief and Development (Cordaid)*;
– *Center for Civilians in Conflict (CIVIC)*;
– Centre for Feminist Foreign Policy;
– *Centre for Humanitarian Dialogue (The HD Centre)*;
– Christian Aid Ireland;
– *Community of Sant'Egidio*;
– *Conciliation Resources (CR)*;
– *Concordis International*;
– Conducive Space for Peace;
– *Crisis Management Initiative (CMI)*;
– CSSP – Berlin Center for Integrative Mediation;
– *Democratic Progress Institute (DPI)*;
– ESSEC IRENE;
– *European Centre for Electoral Support (ECES, #06478)*;
– European Institute of Peace;
– German Platform for Peaceful Conflict Management;
– *Guerrand-Hermès Foundation for Peace (#10815)*;
– Independent Diplomat;
– Institute for Integrated Transitions;
– *International Alert (#11615)*;
– International Catalan Institute for Peace;
– *International Center for Transitional Justice (ICTJ)*;
– *International Crisis Group (Crisis Group, #13111)*;
– *Interpeace (#15962)*;
– Kosovar Center for Security Studies (KCSS);
– Kulturanova;
– *Kvinna till Kvinna Foundation*;
– *Life and Peace Institute (LPI, #16467)*;
– Mercy Corps Netherlands;
– Nansen Center for Peace and Dialogue;
– *Nonviolent Peaceforce (NP, #17153)*;
– *Oxfam International (#17922)*;
– Partners Bulgaria;
– *Pax Christi – International Catholic Peace Movement (#18266)*;
– *Peace Action, Training and Research Institute of Romania (PATRIR)*;
– *Peace Direct*;
– Peaceful Change initiative;
– *Quaker Council for European Affairs (QCEA, #18587)*;
– SaferGlobe;
– *Saferworld*;
– *Search for Common Ground (SFCG)*;
– *Swisspeace*;
– Un Ponte Per;
– Wider Security Network (WISE);
– *World Vision International (WVI, #21904)*.
NGO Relations Member of (1): *Human Rights and Democracy Network (HRDN, #10980)*.
[2022.05.11/XE4106/y/**E**]

♦ **European Peace Research Association (EUPRA)** **08177**
Pres Kalevantie 5, Linna 6077, Tampere Univ, FI-33100 Tampere, Finland. T. +358451646526. E-mail: secretary@euprapeace.org – euprapeace@gmail.com.
URL: https://www.euprapeace.org
History 1 Dec 1990, Bonn (Germany). Founded following decision 5 Jul 1990, Groningen (Netherlands), of general conference of International Peace Research Association (IPRA), having been initiated at a meeting on 16 Dec 1988, Groningen (Netherlands). Former names and other names: *European Forum for Peace Researchers* – alias. Registration: Germany. **Aims** Advance interdisciplinary research into the causes of war and conditions of peace by: providing a European Forum for Peace Researchers; stimulating national and international research and education related to the pursuit of peace; facilitating contact between scholars; encouraging dissemination of information on peace research and its results; assisting coordination of peace research in different countries, including exchange of lecturers and researchers. **Structure** General Conference (every 2 years); Board. **Languages** English, French, German. **Staff** Voluntary. **Finance** Sources: fees for services; members' dues; subscriptions. **Activities** Events/meetings; financial and/or material support; networking/liaising; publishing activities. **Events** *General Conference* Tampere (Finland) 2022, *General Conference* Tampere (Finland) 2021, *General Conference* Catania (Italy) 2019, *General Conference* Schwerte (Germany) 2017, *General Conference* Tromsø (Norway) 2015. **Publications** *Changes, Chances, and Challenges – Europe 2000* (1995); *Peace Research for the 1990s* (1993).
Members Individuals (250) and organizations in 31 countries:
Austria, Belgium, Bulgaria, Croatia, Czechia, Denmark, Finland, France, Germany, Greece, Hungary, Ireland, Italy, Latvia, Malta, Netherlands, North Macedonia, Norway, Poland, Portugal, Romania, Russia, Serbia, Slovakia, Slovenia, Spain, Sweden, Switzerland, Türkiye, UK, Ukraine.
NGO Relations Regional Association of: *International Peace Research Association (IPRA, #14537)*.
[2023/XD1902/**D**]

♦ European Peace Treaty (1814 treaty)
♦ European Peat and Growing Media Association (inactive)

♦ **European Pediatrics Thematic Network (EUROPET)** **08178**
Contact Univ of Oulu, Fac of Medicine, PO Box 5000, FI-90014 Oulu, Finland.
Aims Address educational, professional and regional issues in European paediatric education so as to harmonize educational schemes using tuning principles for provision of a uniformly high level European paediatric service. **Structure** General Assembly (annual). Board. **Events** *Annual meeting / General Assembly* Oulu (Finland) 2008, *General Assembly* Gelsenkirchen (Germany) 2007.

Members Partners in 29 countries:
Austria, Belgium, Bulgaria, Czechia, Denmark, Estonia, Finland, France, Germany, Greece, Hungary, Iceland, Ireland, Italy, Latvia, Lithuania, Luxembourg, Malta, Netherlands, Norway, Poland, Portugal, Romania, Slovakia, Slovenia, Spain, Sweden, Türkiye, UK.
Included in the above, 2 organizations listed in this Yearbook:
European Academy of Paediatrics (EAP, #05811); European Medical Association (EMA, #07761).
[2009/XJ0095/y/**F**]

- ♦ European Peering Forum (meeting series)
- ♦ European Peer Training Organization (internationally oriented national body)

♦ European Pellet Council (EPC) 08179
Contact c/o Bioenergy Europe, Place du Champ de Mars 2, 1050 Brussels, Belgium. T. +3223184035.
URL: http://www.pelletcouncil.eu/

History Part of *Bioenergy Europe (#03247)* group. **Aims** Represent the interests of the European *wood pellet* sector. **Activities** Networking/liaising; events/meetings; certification/accreditation. **Events** *European Pellet Forum* Graz (Austria) 2023, *International Workshop on Pellet Safety* Fügen (Austria) 2014, *International Workshop on Pellet Safety* Fügen (Austria) 2013.
Members Full in 18 countries:
Austria, Belgium, Canada, Czechia, Denmark, Finland, France, Germany, Hungary, Italy, Latvia, Lithuania, Portugal, Spain, Sweden, Switzerland, UK, Ukraine.
Observer in 3 countries:
Belgium, Japan, USA. [2019/XJ9289/**E**]

- ♦ European Pencil Manufacturer's Association (inactive)

♦ European Penitentiary Training Academies Network (EPTA) 08180
Exec Dir c/o EuroPris, PO Box 13635, 2501 EP The Hague, Netherlands. E-mail: secretariat@europris.org – secretariat@epta.info.
URL: https://www.epta.info/

History Proposed Nov 2008. Joint declaration drafted Jun 2009, Rome (Italy). Declaration and protocol signed Apr 2010. Former names and other names: *European Penitentiary Training Network (EPTA)* – former. **Aims** Promote the exchange of knowledge, contents, programmes and good practices; facilitate an exchange of professionals and trainers in favour of mutual enrichment; development communication. **Structure** Conference; Steering Committee; Secretariat. **Languages** English. **Activities** Events/meetings; training/education. **Events** *Annual Conference* Târgu Ocna (Romania) 2019, *Annual Conference* Toulouse (France) 2018, *Annual Conference* Murten (Switzerland) 2017, *Annual Conference* Kalisz (Poland) 2016, *Annual Conference* Rome (Italy) 2015.
Members Founding members (11) in 10 countries:
Andorra, Belgium, Croatia, France, Italy, Norway, Romania, Spain, Sweden, Switzerland.
Members currently in 23 countries:
Andorra, Armenia, Austria, Belgium, Croatia, Czechia, Denmark, Estonia, Finland, France, Georgia, Germany, Ireland, Italy, Moldova, Norway, Poland, Portugal, Romania, Spain, Sweden, Switzerland, UK.
NGO Relations *European Organisation of Prison and Correctional Services (EuroPris, #08100).*
[2020/XM5788/**F**]

- ♦ European Penitentiary Training Network / see European Penitentiary Training Academies Network (#08180)

♦ European Pension Fund Investment Forum (EPFIF) 08181
Membership Manager Fulling Mill Barn, Welwyn, AL6 9NP, UK. T. +441438712345. E-mail: enquiries@epfif.com.
Co-Founder and Exec Dir address not obtained.
Co-Founder and Exec Dir address not obtained.
URL: http://www.epfif.com/

History 1994. Registration: Companies House, No/ID: 3058079, Start date: 18 May 1995, England. **Aims** Improve quality of information available to pension fund managers. **Structure** Divisions (5): Benelux; Nordic; Southern African; Swiss; UK. **Languages** English. **Staff** 11.00 FTE, paid. **Finance** Sources: members' dues. **Events** *International Seminar* Antwerp (Belgium) 2021, *International Seminar* Antwerp (Belgium) 2020, *International seminar* Cambridge (UK) 2019, *International seminar* Noordwijk (Netherlands) 2009.
[2021/XM0102/f/**D**]

♦ European Pentecostal and Charismatic Research Association (EPCRA) 08182
Chairman Teufibalm 6, 6354 Vitznau LU, Switzerland. E-mail: contact@epcra.ch.
URL: http://www.epcra.ch/

Aims Facilitate contacts and exchange among researchers and academicians with interests in the study of Pentecostal and Charismatic movements. **Events** *Conference* Sarnen (Switzerland) 2014, *Conference* Riga (Latvia) 2011, *Conference* Oxford (UK) 2009, *Conference* Uppsala (Sweden) 2007, *Conference* Rheinfelden (Switzerland) 2005. [2014.09.01/XD7898/**D**]

♦ European Pentecostal Fellowship (PEF) 08183
Exec Dir Chaussée de Waterloo 45, 1640 St-Genesius-Rode, Belgium. T. +3223800885. Fax +3223586758. E-mail: headoffice@pef.eu.
URL: http://www.pef.eu/

History 1958, Sweden. **Aims** Through fellowship and conferences, work together in mission, media and other matters. **Structure** Presidium; Chairman; Executive Team; Executive Director. Branches: *Pentecostal European Mission (PEM, #18294); Pentecostal European Forum for Youth Ministries (PEFY, #18293); Pentecostal European Fellowship – Women (PEF-W); European Pentecostal Theological Association (EPTA, #08184); PEF-Kids.* **Languages** English. **Staff** 20.00 FTE, paid; 10.00 FTE, voluntary. **Finance** Donations. **Activities** Events/meetings; training/education. **Events** *Church planting in today's Europe* Zagreb (Croatia) 2016, *Conference* Zagreb (Croatia) 2016, *Conference* Budapest (Hungary) 2011, *Conference* Stockholm (Sweden) 2011, *Conference* Stockholm (Sweden) 2010. **Members** Pentecostal movements (55) in Europe. Membership countries not specified. **IGO Relations** *European Parliament (EP, #08146).* **NGO Relations** Member of: *Pentecostal World Fellowship (#18295).* [2016/XF1284/**F**]

- ♦ European Pentecostal Relief Organization (inactive)

♦ European Pentecostal Theological Association (EPTA) 08184
Chair London School of Theology, Green Lane, Northwood, HA6 2UW, UK. T. +441923456000.
URL: http://www.eptaonline.com/

History Founded 1979, Vienna (Austria). A branch of *European Pentecostal Fellowship (PEF, #08183).* **Aims** Promote excellence and effectiveness in Pentecostal scholarship, ministerial education and theological literature; foster exchange, fellowship and cooperation between member institutions and individuals; foster exchange and fellowship between the Association and other associations with similar objectives and commitments; strengthen the testimony of Jesus Christ and His Church in Europe; bring glory to God in all actions and concerns. **Structure** Executive Committee; Editorial Board. **Languages** English. **Staff** 1.00 FTE, voluntary. **Finance** Members' dues. Non-member subscriptions. **Activities** Events/meetings; networking/liaising; training/education; religious activities. **Events** *Annual Conference* Kolding (Denmark) 2019, *Annual Conference* Sint-Pieters-Leeuw (Belgium) 2018, *Annual Conference* Malvern (UK) 2017, *Annual Conference* Florence (Italy) 2015, *Annual Conference* St Niklausen (Switzerland) 2014. **Publications** *Journal of the European Pentecostal Theological Assocaition (JEPTA)* (2 a year).
Members Active Institutes (14) in 9 countries:
Finland, Germany, Hungary, Netherlands, Norway, Portugal, Russia, Sweden, UK.
Individuals (about 135) worldwide. Membership countries not specified.
NGO Relations Member of: *World Alliance for Pentecostal Theological Education (WAPTE, #21086).*
[2017.10.16/XD2054/**D**]

- ♦ European People (internationally oriented national body)
- ♦ European People's Party / see Group of the European People's Party – Christian Democrats (#10775)

♦ European People's Party (EPP) 08185
Parti populaire européen (PPE) – Partido Popular Europeo (PPE) – Europäische Volkspartei (EVP) – Partito Popolare Europeo (PPE) – Partido Popular Europeu (PPE) – Europese Volkspartij (EVP) – Evropaiko Laiko Komma
Headquarters Rue du Commerce 10, 1000 Brussels, Belgium. T. +3222854140. Fax +3222854141. E-mail: connect@epp.eu.
URL: http://www.epp.eu/

History 8 Jul 1976. Statutes modified, Feb 1999, when absorbed *European Union of Christian Democrats (EUCD, inactive).* In 2002, absorbed *European Democrat Union (EDU, inactive).* Constitutes a European political party as envisaged under Article 138A of *Treaty on European Union (Maastricht Treaty, 1992).* Recognized by *European Union (EU, #08967)* as an official European level (transnational) political party, according to the EU Regulation No 2004/2003 of the European Parliament and of the Council of 4 Nov 2004, and amended 18 Dec 2007. Statutes modified Dec 2009 and Dec 2011, and Internal Regulations modified, Dec 2009. Former names and other names: *European People's Party – Federation of Christian Democratic Parties of the European Community* – former (8 Jul 1976); *Parti populaire européen – Fédération des partis démocrates chrétiens de la Communauté européenne* – former (8 Jul 1976); *Partido Popular Europeo – Federación de los Partidos Demócratas Cristianos de la Comunidad Europea* – former (8 Jul 1976); *Europäische Volkspartei – Föderation der Christlich-Demokratischen Parteien der Europäischen Gemeinschaft* – former (8 Jul 1976); *Partito Popolare Europeo – Federazione dei Partiti Democratici Cristiani della Comunità Europea* – former (8 Jul 1976). Registration: Belgium. **Aims** Ensure close permanent collaboration among centre-right political parties of Europe in order to achieve their common policies; promote and organize common action at European level; work to achieve a free and *pluralist democracy*; promote a Europe-wide social market economy; pursue the process of integration in Europe as a constituent element of the European Union; promote and consolidate democracy in transition countries; promote transatlantic and international relations. **Structure** Congress; Political Assembly; Presidency; Secretariat. Working Groups. Foundations (3): *Wilfried Martens Centre for European Studies (Martens Centre, #20962); European Ideas Network (EIN, #07514); Robert Schuman Institute for Developing Democracy in Central and Eastern Europe (RSI, #18958).* **Languages** English, French, German. **Staff** 31.74 FTE, paid. Plus auxiliary staff and interns. **Finance** 75% by the European Parliament and 25% by contributions from member parties, based on number of votes from last European Parliament election. **Activities** Events/meetings; knowledge management/information dissemination; networking/liaising. **Events** *Congress* Rotterdam (Netherlands) 2022, *Congress* Zagreb (Croatia) 2019, *Biennial Congress* Helsinki (Finland) 2018, *Congress* St Julian's (Malta) 2017, *Congress* Madrid (Spain) 2015.
Members Full, Associate; Observer. Full: political parties in 26 countries:
Austria, Belgium, Bulgaria, Croatia, Cyprus, Czechia, Denmark, Estonia, Finland, France, Germany, Hungary, Ireland, Italy, Latvia, Lithuania, Luxembourg, Malta, Netherlands, Poland, Portugal, Romania, Slovakia, Slovenia, Spain, Sweden.
Associate in 5 countries:
Albania, North Macedonia, Norway, Serbia, Switzerland.
Observer in 11 countries:
Armenia, Belarus, Bosnia-Herzegovina, Finland, Georgia, Italy, Kosovo, Moldova, Norway, San Marino, Ukraine.
Partners in 1 country:
Lebanon.
Specialized organizations (6), listed in this Yearbook:
EPP Women (#05516); European Democrat Students (EDS, #06901); European Seniors' Union (ESU, #08466); European Union of Christian Democratic Workers (EUCDW, #08981); Small and Medium Entrepreneurs Europe (SME Europe, #19316); Youth of the European People's Party (YEPP, #22014).
IGO Relations EPP members and Groups associated with: *European Committee of the Regions (CoR, #06665); Council of Europe (CE, #04881); European Commission (EC, #06633); European Council (#06801); European Parliament (EP, #08146); Parliamentary Assembly of the Council of Europe (PACE, #18211); Parliamentary Assembly of the Organization for Security and Cooperation in Europe (OSCE PA, #18214).* **NGO Relations** Member of (4): *Centrist Democrat International (CDI, #03792); European Energy Forum (EEF, #06986); European Movement International (EMI, #07825); International Democrat Union (IDU, #13147).* Relations with the European Parliament through: *Group of the European People's Party – Christian Democrats (EPP, #10775).* Relations with Council of Europe through: *Group of the European People's Party (#10774).* Relations with Committee of the Regions through: *Group of the European People's Party in the Committee of the Regions (EPP-CoR, #10776).* Foundations/Think-tanks cooperating with EPP include: *Eduardo Frei Foundation; Hanns Seidel Foundation; Jarl Hjalmarson Foundation; International Republican Institute (IRI); Konrad Adenauer Foundation (KAF).* [2022.11.21/XF6414/y/**F**]

- ♦ European People's Party – Federation of Christian Democratic Parties of the European Community / see European People's Party (#08185)
- ♦ European Pepinieres of Creation (internationally oriented national body)
- ♦ European Pépinières for Young Artists / see Pépinières Européenes de Création

♦ European Peptide Society (EPS) 08186
Sec Univ of Porto – Fac of Sciences, Chemistry and Biochemistry Dept, Rua do Campo Alegre s/n, 4169-007 Porto, Portugal. T. +351220402563.
Communication Officer Univ of Gdansk – Fac of Chemistry, Wita Stwosza 63, 80-308 Gdansk, Poland. T. +48585235088. Fax +48585235012.
URL: http://www.eurpepsoc.com/

History 1989. Constituted under Italian law, Mar 2012. **Aims** Coordinate, promote and represent to other similar entities and/or institutional organisms at international level, so as to promote advancement of research and training in the peptide sciences in Europe and in other extra-European countries. **Structure** General Assembly; Council; Executive Committee. **Languages** English. **Staff** None. **Finance** Sponsors; income from symposia; subscriptions. **Activities** Events/meetings; knowledge management/information dissemination; networking/liaising; training/education. **Events** *European Peptide Symposium* Sitges (Spain) 2022, *European Peptide Symposium* Sitges (Spain) 2021, *European Peptide Symposium* Sitges (Spain) 2020, *Chemical Biology Group Meeting* Barcelona (Spain) 2018, *Symposium* Dublin (Ireland) 2018. **Publications** *EPS Newsletter, Journal of Peptide Science.*
Members Ordinary; Honorary; Effective. Members in 32 countries:
Australia, Austria, Belarus, Belgium, Bulgaria, Canada, China, Croatia, Czechia, Finland, France, Germany, Greece, Hungary, Iceland, India, Ireland, Israel, Italy, Japan, Netherlands, Norway, Poland, Portugal, Russia, Slovakia, Slovenia, Spain, Sweden, Switzerland, UK, USA. [2021/XD4435/**D**]

♦ European Perforators Association (EUROPERF) 08187
SG Diamant Bldg 5th Floor, Bd A Reyers 80, 1030 Brussels, Belgium. T. +14142761667. Fax +14142767704.
Pres Graepel Perforators and Weavers, Barrack Green, Kinsale, CO. CORK, Ireland.
URL: http://www.europerf.org/

History 1962. **Aims** Establish perforating as an industry; provide industry statistics on production and sales; establish standards and promote standardization; promote perforated *metal* and its applications. **Structure** General Assembly; Board; Working Groups. **Languages** English, French, German, Italian, Spanish. **Staff** 1.00 FTE, paid. **Finance** Members' dues. **Activities** Events/meetings; standards/guidelines; knowledge management/information dissemination. **Events** *World Perforating Conference* Barcelona (Spain) 2014, *World Perforating Conference* Baltimore, MD (USA) 2011, *Triennial world conference* Naples, FL (USA) 2005, *World conference* Orlando, FL (USA) 1999, *World conference* Rome (Italy) 1996.
Members Full; Supplier; Associate. Member companies in 16 countries:
Belgium, Bulgaria, Denmark, France, Germany, Hungary, Ireland, Italy, Norway, Poland, South Africa, Spain, Sweden, Switzerland, Türkiye, UK. [2017/XD8850/**D**]

♦ European Performance Co-Extruders (EPEX) 08188
Managing Dir EuPC Head Office, Avenue de Cortenbergh 71, Box 4, 1000 Brussels, Belgium. T. +3227324124. Fax +3227324218. E-mail: info@eupc.org.
Pres address not obtained.
URL: http://www.plasticsconverters.eu/

History Founded in 1989, as a sector group of *European Plastics Converters (EuPC, #08216).* **Aims** Defend and promote the interests of the European plastics converting industry. [2016/XM3513/**D**]

♦ **European Perlite Association (EPA)** **08189**
Contact c/o Perlite Institute, 2207 Forest Hills Drive, Harrisburg PA 17112, USA. T. +17172389723. Fax +17172389985. E-mail: admin@perlite.org – info@perlite.org – office@perlite.org.
URL: https://www.perlite.org/support/about-perlite-institute.html
Events *Meeting* Nashville, TN (USA) 2022, *Meeting* Harrisburg, PA (USA) 2021, *Meeting* Harrisburg, PA (USA) 2020, *Meeting* Barcelona (Spain) 2006. [2016/XD7441/**D**]

♦ European Permanent Committee for Experimental Mechanics / see European Association for Experimental Mechanics (#06034)

♦ **European Personal Construct Association (EPCA)** **08190**
Contact Psychology Dept, Univ of Hertfordshire, Hatfield, AL10 9AB, UK.
URL: http://www.kellysociety.org/epca/
History 1990. **Aims** Raise awareness among Europeans of personal construct *psychology* (PCP) and its applications; promote exchange of ideas, information and training. **Events** *Biennial Conference* Barcelona (Spain) 2020, *Biennial Conference* Edinburgh (UK) 2018, *Biennial Conference* Padua (Italy) 2016, *Biennial Conference* Prague (Czech Rep) / Brno (Czech Rep) 2014, *Biennial Conference* Dublin (Ireland) 2012. **Publications** *EPCA Newsletter* (2 a year). [2017/XD6287/**D**]

♦ European Personalised Medicine Association (no recent information)
♦ European Perspective (internationally oriented national body)
♦ European PES Network / see European network of Public Employment Services (#07979)
♦ European Pesticide Residue Workshop (meeting series)
♦ European PET film and sheet producers / see PET Sheet Europe (#18344)
♦ European Petfood Industry Federation (#09571)
♦ European Pet Network (unconfirmed)

♦ **European Pet Organization (EPO)** **08191**
Head office Postbus 94, 3800 AB Amersfoort, Netherlands. T. +31620411601. E-mail: secretariat@europets.org.
URL: http://www.europets.org/
History Founded 1990, Vienna (Austria). **Aims** Protect and promote the interests of the European pet industry. **Languages** English. **Activities** Networking/liaising. **Events** *Meeting* Nürburg (Germany) 1998. **Publications** Documents.
Members in 10 countries:
Austria, France, Germany, Italy, Netherlands, Norway, Spain, Sweden, Switzerland, UK. [2020.03.03/XD8592/**D**]

♦ **European Petrochemical Association, The (EPCA)** **08192**
CEO Av de Tervueren 270, 1150 Brussels, Belgium. T. +3227418660. Fax +3227418680. E-mail: communication@epca.eu – admin@epca.eu.
Main Website: http://www.epca.eu/
History 1968, Brussels (Belgium). Former names and other names: *Association Européenne de la Pétrochimie* – former. Registration: Banque-Carrefour des Entreprises, No/ID: 0408.299.922, Start date: 27 Dec 1968, Belgium. **Aims** Be the primary European business network for the global petrochemical business community. **Structure** General Meeting; Board of Directors; Executive Committee; Working Groups. **Languages** English. **Staff** 8.00 FTE, paid. **Finance** Sources: meeting proceeds; members' dues. **Activities** Events/meetings; knowledge management/information dissemination; networking/liaising; projects/programmes. **Events** *Annual Meeting* Berlin (Germany) 2022, *Annual Meeting* Brussels (Belgium) 2021, *Annual Meeting* Brussels (Belgium) 2020, *Annual Meeting* Berlin (Germany) 2019, *Annual Meeting* Vienna (Austria) 2018. **Publications** *Do and Don't – Checklists for Meetings – Compliance with National and European Competition Laws.* Annual Report; brochure; reports; case studies; videos.
Members Full; Associate. Members (over 550) in 58 countries and territories:
Argentina, Austria, Bahrain, Belgium, Bosnia-Herzegovina, Brazil, Canada, China, Cyprus, Czechia, Denmark, Ecuador, Egypt, Estonia, Finland, France, Germany, Greece, Hong Kong, Hungary, India, Iran Islamic Rep, Ireland, Israel, Italy, Japan, Korea Rep, Kuwait, Lebanon, Lithuania, Luxembourg, Mexico, Monaco, Morocco, Netherlands, Norway, Pakistan, Poland, Portugal, Qatar, Romania, Russia, Saudi Arabia, Scotland, Serbia, Singapore, South Africa, Spain, Sweden, Switzerland, Taiwan, Tatarstan, Türkiye, UK, Ukraine, United Arab Emirates, USA, Venezuela. [2022.05.02/XD4671/**D**]

♦ European Petrochemical Luncheon / see European Petrochemical Luncheon International Association (#08193)

♦ **European Petrochemical Luncheon International Association (EPL)** **08193**
SG Avenue Louise 143/4, 1050 Brussels, Belgium. E-mail: epl@e-p-l.eu.
Events Manager Bredabaan 859/12, 2930 Brasschaat, Belgium.
URL: http://www.e-p-l.eu/
History 27 Feb 1981, Brussels (Belgium). Former names and other names: *European Petrochemical Luncheon* – former. Registration: Banque-Carrefour des Entreprises, No/ID: 0421.501.325, Start date: 17 Apr 1981, Belgium. **Aims** Contribute to exchange of ideas and dissemination of information on the petrochemical industry and related activities; encourage activities dealing with problems and achievements related to the processing of raw materials extracted from *petroleum*, *coal tar* and *oil shales* and their derivatives. **Structure** General Assembly (annual); Executive Committee. **Languages** English. **Staff** 1.00 FTE, paid. **Finance** Sources: members' dues. Annual budget: 125,000 EUR. **Activities** Events/meetings; knowledge management/information dissemination; research/documentation. **Events** *Conference* Marseille (France) 2022, *Conference* Rotterdam (Netherlands) 2022, *Meeting* Lisbon (Portugal) 2019, *Conference* Rome (Italy) 2019, *Meeting* Brussels (Belgium) 2010. **Information Services** *European Conciliation and Advisory Services (ECAS).*
Members Active (companies); Honorary (individuals and companies). Members in 30 countries:
Austria, Belgium, Bulgaria, Cyprus, Czechia, Denmark, Estonia, Finland, France, Germany, Greece, Hungary, Ireland, Italy, Latvia, Lithuania, Luxembourg, Malta, Netherlands, Norway, Poland, Portugal, Romania, Slovakia, Slovenia, Spain, Sweden, Switzerland, Türkiye, UK. [2022.10.25/XF0205/**F**]

♦ European Petroleum Industry Association / see FuelsEurope (#10014)

♦ **European Petroleum Refiners Association** **08194**
Dir Gen Bd du Souverain 165, 1160 Brussels, Belgium. T. +3225669160 – +3225669110. Fax +3225669181. E-mail: info@concawe.org – info@fuelseurope.eu.
URL: http://www.concawe.eu/
History Registration: Banque-Carrefour des Entreprises, No/ID: 0440.441.663, Start date: 25 Apr 1990, Belgium. **Aims** Be the voice of European petroleum refining and distribution and highlight its value to the EU economy and its citizens. **Structure** Divisions (2): *FuelsEurope (#10014); Oil Companies' European Association for Environment, Health and Safety in Refining and Distribution (CONCAWE, #17708).* **Members** Companies (41) operating petroleum refineries in the European Economic Area Membership countries not specified. **NGO Relations** Member of: *Federation of European and International Associations Established in Belgium (FAIB, #09508).* [2021/XJ9526/**D**]

♦ **European Pharmaceutical Aerosol Group (EPAG)** **08195**
Contact Unit Q, Troon Way Business Centre, Humberstone Lane, Thurmaston, Leicester, LE4 9HA, UK. T. +441477538878. Fax +441477537121.
URL: http://www.epag.co.uk/
History 1999, Loughborough (UK). **Aims** Focus on pharmaceutical issues relevant to pulmonary and nasal products, including clinical aspects as appropriate; establish scientifically based best practices; provide consensus comment to industry and government agencies to promote safety and quality standards; recommend harmonized standards and methodology; work with regulatory agencies to develop evidence based guidance. **Structure** Plenary Committee; Chairperson; Organizational Team; Technical Sub-teams. **Languages** English. **Finance** Members' dues.
Members Companies in 11 countries:
Canada, Finland, France, Germany, Italy, Netherlands, Portugal, Spain, Sweden, Switzerland, UK.
NGO Relations *International Pharmaceutical Aerosol Consortium on Regulation and Science (IPAC-RS).* [2015/XJ3128/**D**]

♦ European Pharmaceutical Congress Advisory Association / see International Pharmaceutical Congress Advisory Association (#14564)

♦ **European Pharmaceutical Market Research Association (EphMRA)** **08196**
Association européenne pour l'étude du marché pharmaceutique – Europäische Vereinigung für Pharmazeutische Marktforschung – Associazione Europea per lo Studio del Mercato Farmaceutico
Gen Manager c/o Streicher und Brotschin Treuhand, Gartenstrasse 101, 4052 Basel BS, Switzerland. T. +443333661024. E-mail: generalmanager@ephmra.org.
Main Website: http://www.ephmra.org/
History 5 May 1961, Geneva (Switzerland). Registration: Swiss Civil Code, Switzerland. **Aims** Create excellence in professional standards and practices to enable *healthcare* market researchers to become highly valued business partners. **Structure** Meeting (annual); Board; General Manager. **Languages** English. **Staff** 1.00 FTE, paid. **Finance** Sources: members' dues. **Activities** Guidance/assistance/consulting; training/education. **Events** *Conference* Antwerp (Belgium) 2023, *Annual Conference* 2022, *Asia Pacific Conference* 2022, *Annual Conference* London (UK) 2021, *Annual Conference* Warsaw (Poland) 2019. **Publications** *EPhMRA Newsletter* (4 a year). **Members** Industry: globally oriented research-based companies operating in healthcare, OTC, diagnostics and medical devices arenas; Agency: suppliers, agencies. Membership countries not specified. **IGO Relations** None **NGO Relations** Also links with national associations. [2022.06.07/XD0028/**D**]

♦ **European Pharmaceutical Students' Association (EPSA)** **08197**
Contact Rue du Luxembourg 19 bte 6, 1000 Brussels, Belgium. E-mail: info@epsa-online.org.
URL: http://www.epsa-online.org/
History 1978, Edinburgh (UK). Initially founded as a committee of the *International Pharmaceutical Students' Federation (IPSF, #14568)*; became independent, 1982. Terms of Reference approved 12 Apr 1985, Illkirch (France). Former names and other names: *European Sub-Committee of the International Pharmaceutical Students' Federation* – former (1978 to 1982); *European Pharmaceutical Students' Committee (ESC)* – former (1982 to 1993). Registration: France; EU Transparency Register, No/ID: 94017012777-69. **Aims** Actively engage at student and professional level, bringing pharmacy, knowledge and students together while promoting personal development. **Structure** General Assembly (biannual); Team; Subcommittees. **Languages** English. **Finance** Members' dues. Other sources: sponsorship; grants. **Activities** Events/meetings; knowledge management/information dissemination; networking/liaising; advocacy/lobbying/activism; capacity building. **Events** *Annual Congress and General Assembly* Lyon (France) 2021, *Autumn Meeting* Brussels (Belgium) 2019, *Autumn Assembly* Porec (Croatia) 2019, *Annual Congress and General Assembly* Sofia (Bulgaria) 2019, *Autumn Assembly* Belgrade (Serbia) 2018. **Publications** *EPSA Monthly Dose* (12 a year); *EPSA Newsletter* (3 a year); *EPSA Students'Science Publication* (3 a year). *Research in European Schools of Pharmacy; Studying Pharmacy in Europe* – in 2 vols. Booklets; reports; press releases; circular; information letter. **Information Services** *EPSA Students' Guide* – a guide to students participating in Erasmus+ exchanges.
Members Ordinary: associations (45), representing over 100,000 European pharmaceutical students in 29 countries:
Austria, Belgium, Bosnia-Herzegovina, Bulgaria, Croatia, Cyprus, Czechia, Denmark, Estonia, Finland, France, Germany, Latvia, Lithuania, Malta, Netherlands, North Macedonia, Norway, Poland, Portugal, Romania, Serbia, Slovakia, Slovenia, Spain, Sweden, Switzerland, Türkiye, UK.
Associate in 12 countries:
Albania, Armenia, Cyprus, Czechia, Greece, Hungary, Ireland, Moldova, Montenegro, Portugal, Romania, Ukraine.
IGO Relations *European Commission (EC, #06633).* **NGO Relations** Member of: *European Public Health Alliance (EPHA, #08297).* Associate member of: *European Students' Union (ESU, #08848); International Youth Health Organization (YHO, #15933).* Partner of: *Informal Forum of International Student Organizations (IFISO, #11193).* Endorses: *Steering Group on Influenza Vaccination (#19980).* [2018.09.20/XE2664/y/**D**]

♦ European Pharmaceutical Students' Committee / see European Pharmaceutical Students' Association (#08197)
♦ European Pharmacies Conference (meeting series)

♦ **European Pharmacopoeia Commission** **08198**
Commission européenne de pharmacopée
Dir c/o EDQM, 7 allée Kastner, CS 30026, 67081 Strasbourg, France. T. +33388414031. Fax +33388412771.
URL: https://www.edqm.eu/en/european-pharmacopoeia-commission/
History Established 1964, Strasbourg (France), by *Council of Europe (CE, #04881)*, under *Convention on the Elaboration of a European Pharmacopoeia (1964).* Also known as *Ph Eur Commission.* **Aims** Produce a European Pharmacopoeia which serves as a single reference work for the quality control of *medicines* in the signatory states of the Convention, provides official standards including a legal and scientific basis for quality control during development, production and marketing processes. **Structure** European Pharmacopoeia Commission Session (3 a year). Commission comprises 38 member states and the European Union which are signatories to the Convention on the Elaboration of a European Pharmacopoeia. European Directorate for the Quality of Medicine and HealthCare (EDQM / DEQM). **Languages** English, French. **Activities** Standards/guidelines; monitoring/evaluation; events/meetings. **Events** *International symposium on herbal drugs and herbal drug preparations* Vienna (Austria) 2009, *International conference on new frontiers in the quality of medicines* Strasbourg (France) 2007, *International conference on certification* Istanbul (Turkey) 2005, *International conference on quality on the move* Budapest (Hungary) 2004, *Meeting* Strasbourg (France) 2004. **Publications** *European Pharmeuropa* (9th ed) in English, French; *Pharmeuropa; Pharmeuropa Bio and Scientific Notes.* List of standard terms; blood transfusion guide; organs, tissues and cells transplanation guides; cosmetics and food contact material guides; pharmaceutical care reports.
Members Member States (38):
Austria, Belgium, Bosnia-Herzegovina, Bulgaria, Croatia, Cyprus, Czechia, Denmark, Estonia, Finland, France, Germany, Greece, Hungary, Iceland, Ireland, Italy, Latvia, Lithuania, Luxembourg, Malta, Moldova, Montenegro, Netherlands, North Macedonia, Norway, Poland, Portugal, Romania, Serbia, Slovakia, Slovenia, Spain, Sweden, Switzerland, Türkiye, UK, Ukraine.
Regional member, listed in this Yearbook:
European Union (EU, #08967).
Observer countries (28):
Albania, Algeria, Argentina, Armenia, Australia, Azerbaijan, Belarus, Brazil, Canada, China, Georgia, Guinea, India, Israel, Japan, Kazakhstan, Korea Rep, Madagascar, Malaysia, Morocco, Russia, Senegal, Singapore, South Africa, Syrian AR, Tunisia, USA, Uzbekistan.
Observer organizations (2):
Taiwan Food and Drug Administration; *WHO (#20950).*
IGO Relations Cooperates with: *European Union (EU, #08967)*; European Commission – DG SANTE; *WHO (#20950).* [2018.06.25/XE7159/**E***]

♦ European Pharmacovigilance Research Group (inactive)
♦ European Phase Change and Ovonics Symposium (meeting series)

♦ **European Phenolic Foam Association (EPFA)** **08199**
Sec BASE Bordon Innovation Ctr, Broxhead House, 60 Barbados Road, Bordon, GU35 0FX, UK. T. +441420471617. E-mail: admin@epfa.org.
Events Manager address not obtained.
URL: http://www.epfa.org.uk/
History 1990. Supersedes the (UK) Phenolic Foam Manufacturers Association (PFMA). Registration: Companies House, No/ID: 04146502, Start date: 24 Jan 2001, England; EU Transparency Register, No/ID: 971823440634-76, Start date: 9 Dec 2020. **Aims** Promote benefits of the use of phenolic foam in *insulation* applications. **Structure** Committee. **Languages** English. **Staff** 7.00 FTE, paid. **Finance** Subscription income. **Activities** Standards/guidelines. **Publications** Brochure; fact sheets.
Members Full companies who are producers of phenolic foam insulation products or companies closely linked with the industry. Members in 8 countries:
Belgium, France, Germany, Ireland, Italy, Netherlands, Sweden, UK.
NGO Relations Member of: *Construction Products Europe AISBL (#04761); European Association for External Thermal Insulation Composite Systems (EAE, #06035).* Liaison Organization of: *Comité européen de normalisation (CEN, #04162).* [2020/XD6062/**D**]

European Phenolic Resins
08200
alphabetic sequence excludes
For the complete listing, see Yearbook Online at

♦ European Phenolic Resins Association (EPRA) **08200**
Sec DNU Treuhandbüro, Hallbergstrasse 5, 40239 Düsseldorf, Germany. T. +492116878940. Fax +492116878935. E-mail: epra.treuhandbuero@dnu.eu.
URL: http://www.epra.eu/
Structure General Assembly; Regulatory and Safety Committee. **Languages** English.
Members Phenolic Resins producers (13) in 12 countries:
Austria, Belgium, Finland, France, Germany, Italy, Poland, Russia, Slovenia, Spain, Sweden, Switzerland.
NGO Relations Affiliated member and industry group of: *Conseil européen de l'industrie chimique (CEFIC, #04687).* [2018.07.31/XD5115/**E**]

♦ European Pherology Organizations Confederation (inactive)
♦ European Philosophers for Peace (internationally oriented national body)

♦ European Philosophical Society for the Study of Emotions (EPSSE) . **08201**
Contact address not obtained. E-mail: the.epsse@gmail.com.
URL: http://www.epsse.org/
History Statutes in force Oct 2013. Inaugural conference Jul 2014, Lisbon (Portugal). Registered in accordance with Swiss Civil Code. **Aims** Foster the philosophical study of emotions by providing a forum for exchanging views, so as to increase interaction or collaboration among its members. **Structure** General Assembly; Executive Committee. **Finance** Members' dues. **Activities** Events/meetings. **Events** *Annual Conference* Graz (Austria) 2021, *Annual Conference* Graz (Austria) 2020, *Annual Conference* Pisa (Italy) 2019, *Annual Conference* Tallinn (Estonia) 2018, *Annual Conference* Madrid (Spain) 2017. **Members** Individuals. Membership countries not specified. [2017/XM6527/**D**]

♦ European Philosophy of Science Association (EPSA) **08202**
Pres Dept of Philosophy – Cotham House, Univ of Bristol, Bristol, BS6 6JL, UK. E-mail: phil-epsa@bristol.ac.uk.
URL: http://philsci.eu/
History Registration: No/ID: 376455747, Austria. **Aims** Promote and advance philosophy of science in Europe. **Structure** General Assembly; Steering Committee. **Languages** English. **Staff** None paid. **Events** *Conference* Turin (Italy) 2021, *Conference* Geneva (Switzerland) 2019, *Conference* Exeter (UK) 2017, *Conference* Düsseldorf (Germany) 2015, *Conference* Helsinki (Finland) 2013. **Publications** *European Journal for Philosophy of Science* (3 a year); *EPSA Newsletter.* Conference proceedings. **IGO Relations** None. **NGO Relations** Member of (1): *International Union of History and Philosophy of Science and Technology (IUHPST, #15779)* (Division of Logic, Methodology and Philosophy of Science and Technology (DLMPST)). [2020/XJ1541/**D**]

♦ European Photocatalysis Federation (EPF) **08203**
Fédération Européenne de Photocatalyse
Pres c/o OTECI, 10 rue du Havre, 75009 Paris, France. E-mail: president@efp-fep.com – contact@efp-fep.com.
URL: http://www.photocatalysis-federation.eu/
History Set up as *'Fédération française de la photocatalyse'*. Restructured under current title, May 2009. Registered in accordance with French law. **Aims** Further national and international recognition for photocatalysis by federating all parties participating in development of this technology. **Structure** Steering Committee. **Languages** English. **Staff** 5.00 FTE, voluntary. **Finance** Members' dues: Company – euro 750 – 2,000 – 4,000; Association – euro 200; Retired/Student/Independent – euro 200; Associated Members – case by case. **Activities** Meeting activities. **Events** *European Symposium on Photocatalysis* Paris (France) 2015, *European Symposium on Photocatalysis* Portoroz (Slovenia) 2013, *European Symposium on Photocatalysis* Bordeaux (France) 2011, *European Symposium on Photocatalysis* Bordeaux (France) 2009. **Publications** *EPF Newsletter.*
Members Organizations in 4 countries:
France, Germany, Spain, UK.
Universities, research laboratories and technical centres in 16 countries:
Belgium, Czechia, Denmark, France, Germany, Greece, Ireland, Italy, Netherlands, Poland, Portugal, Russia, Slovenia, Spain, Sweden, Switzerland.
IGO Relations French Ministry of Industry. **NGO Relations** Affiliate member of: *Conseil européen de l'industrie chimique (CEFIC, #04687).* [2014.06.19/XJ6847/**D**]

♦ European Photochemical Association / see European Photochemistry Association (#08204)

♦ European Photochemistry Association (EPA) **08204**
Association européenne de photochimie
Pres CISQO, Univ de Huelva, 21007 Huelva, Spain.
Sec Dept Inorganic and Analytical Chemistry, Univ of Geneva, Quai Ernset-Anermet 30, 1211 Geneva 4, Switzerland. E-mail: treasurer@photochemistry.eu.
URL: http://www.photochemistry.eu/
History 1963. Former names and other names: *European Photochemical Association* – alias. **Aims** Ensure that science related to light induced processes is flourishing and continues developing. **Structure** General Assembly; Executive Committee. **Languages** English. **Staff** Voluntary. **Finance** Sources: contributions; government support; members' dues; sale of publications. **Activities** Awards/prizes/competitions; events/meetings. **Events** *CECP : Central European Conference on Photochemistry* Bad Hofgastein (Austria) 2022, *CECP : Central European Conference on Photochemistry* Bad Hofgastein (Austria) 2020, *CECP : Central European Conference on Photochemistry* Bad Hofgastein (Austria) 2018, *CECP : Central European Conference on Photochemistry* Bad Hofgastein (Austria) 2016, *CECP : Central European Conference on Photochemistry* Bad Hofgastein (Austria) 2014. **Publications** *Photochemical and Photobiological Sciences* (12 a year); *EPA Newsletter.* **Members** Individuals in 40 countries. Membership countries not specified. [2021.06.08/XD2805/v/**D**]

♦ European Photographic Manufacturers' Association / see European Federation of Precision Mechanical and Optical Industries (#07193)

♦ European Photonics Industry Consortium (EPIC) **08205**
Dir-Gen 17 rue Hamelin, 75016 Paris, France. T. +33623391013.
Events Manager address not obtained.
URL: http://www.epic-assoc.com/
History 10 Dec 2003. Registration: Start date: Dec 2003, France. **Aims** Promote sustainable growth for the European photonics industry. **Structure** Board, including General Secretary. **Languages** English. **Staff** 2.00 FTE, paid. **Finance** Sources: members' dues. Contracts. Annual budget: 300,000 EUR. **Activities** Events/meetings; guidance/assistance/consulting; networking/liaising. **Events** *EPIC Annual General Meeting* Helsinki (Finland) 2023, *EPIC Annual General Meeting* Vilnius (Lithuania) 2022, *World Photonics Technology Summit* Berlin (Germany) 2019, *Annual General Assembly* Geneva (Switzerland) 2016, *Annual General Assembly* Paris (France) 2015. **Publications** *EPIC Quarterly Update.* **NGO Relations** Member of (3): *Association for Vertical Farming (AVF); Industry4Europe (#11181); Skillman Network (#19306).* [2022/XM0374/t/**F**]

♦ European Photovoltaic Industry Association / see SolarPower Europe (#19676)
♦ European Photovoltaic Solar Energy Conference (meeting series)
♦ European Phycological Society (inactive)

♦ European Physical Education Association (EUPEA) **08206**
SG 11 Portse des Sciences, L-4366 Esch-sur-Alzette, Luxembourg. T. +3524666449233. E-mail: info@eupea.com.
Pres address not obtained.
URL: http://www.eupea.com/
History 1991, Brussels (Belgium). Founded at meeting of Presidents/representatives of national physical education associations. Formal *'Declaration of Madrid'* agreed 27 Oct 1991, Madrid; amended 2009, Madrid (Spain), and 2011, Amsterdam (Netherlands). Formal structure and procedures adopted 1994, Coimbra (Portugal). **Aims** Promote physical education and school sport in Europe. **Structure** Forum Meeting (annual); Board; Executive Committee. **Languages** English. **Staff** None. **Finance** Sources: members' dues. **Activities** Events/meetings; training/education. **Events** *Forum* Glasgow (UK) 2016, *Forum / Annual Forum* Budapest (Hungary) 2015, *Forum / Annual Forum* Milan (Italy) 2014, *Forum / Annual Forum* Magglingen (Switzerland) 2013, *Forum / Annual Forum* Helsinki (Finland) 2012. **Publications** *EUPEA Newsletter. Code of Ethics and Good Practice Guide for Physical Education* (2002). Articles; proceedings.
Members National associations in 37 countries and territories:
Albania, Austria, Belgium, Bosnia-Herzegovina, Croatia, Czechia, Denmark, Estonia, Faeroe Is, Finland, France, Germany, Greece, Hungary, Iceland, Ireland, Italy, Liechtenstein, Lithuania, Luxembourg, Malta, Montenegro, Netherlands, North Macedonia, Norway, Poland, Portugal, Romania, Russia, Serbia, Slovakia, Slovenia, Spain, Sweden, Switzerland, Türkiye, UK.
IGO Relations Cooperates with (1): *Enlarged Partial Agreement on Sport (EPAS, #05487).* **NGO Relations** Member of (4): *European Network of Sport Education (ENSE, #08012); European Non-Governmental Sports Organization (ENGSO, #08054); International Council of Sport Science and Physical Education (ICSSPE, #13077); International Federation of Physical and Sport Education (#13510).* [2021.03.22/XD5183/**D**]

♦ European Physical Society (EPS) **08207**
Société européenne de physique
SG 6 rue des Frères Lumière, 68200 Mulhouse, France. T. +33389329440.
Conference Manager address not obtained.
URL: http://www.eps.org/
History 26 Sep 1968, Geneva (Switzerland). Constitution revised; latest amendments date from 28 Mar 1998. Registration: EU Transparency Register, No/ID: 32601792674-69, Start date: 27 Nov 2009. **Aims** Contribute to and encourage the advancement of *physics* in Europe and its neighbouring countries; foster high standards in physics research. **Structure** General Meeting (every 3 years); Council (meets annually); Executive Committee. Secretariat: Mulhouse (France). Committees. Divisions: Atomic, Molecular and Optical Physics, including *European Group on Atomic Systems (EGAS, #07416)*; Condensed Matter; Physics Education; Environmental Physics; High Energy and Particle Physics; Nuclear Physics; Physics in Life Sciences; Plasma Physics; Quantum Electronics and Optics, Solar Physics; Statistical and Nonlinear Physics. **Languages** English. **Staff** 11.00 FTE, paid. **Finance** Sources: donations; grants; meeting proceeds; members' dues; subscriptions. **Activities** Awards/prizes/competitions; events/meetings; knowledge management/information dissemination; research and development; training/education. **Events** *International Conference on Hyperfine Interactions and their Applications* Nara (Japan) 2023, *Europhoton Conference* Hannover (Germany) 2022, *Biennial International Conference on Ultrafast Phenomena* Montréal, QC (Canada) 2022, *ESCAMPIG : European Conference on Atomic and Molecular Physics of Ionized Gases* Paris (France) 2022, *ECAMP: European Conference on Atoms Molecules and Photons* Vilnius (Lithuania) 2022. **Publications** *Europhysics News* (6 a year); *European Journal of Physics* (4 a year); *Europhysics Letters* (24 a year). *Europhysics Conference Abstracts.* Booklets; proceedings.
Members Ordinary: individuals (4,000), national societies, laboratories and academies; Associate: industry, research organizations, companies. National societies in 41 countries:
Albania, Armenia, Austria, Belarus, Belgium, Bulgaria, Croatia, Czechia, Denmark, Estonia, Finland, France, Georgia, Germany, Greece, Hungary, Iceland, Ireland, Israel, Italy, Latvia, Liechtenstein, Lithuania, Luxembourg, Moldova, Netherlands, North Macedonia, Norway, Poland, Portugal, Romania, Russia, Serbia, Slovakia, Slovenia, Spain, Sweden, Switzerland, Türkiye, UK, Ukraine.
Collaborating societies (25) in Africa and the following 12 countries:
Australia, Belgium, Canada, China, France, Germany, Japan, Korea Rep, Netherlands, Spain, Switzerland, USA.
International Society for Theoretical Chemical Physics (ISTCP, #15506).
Associate members – international or internationally-oriented organizations and scientific contacts (37) in 14 countries:
Belgium, Denmark, France, Germany, Italy, Netherlands, Norway, Poland, Portugal, Russia, Spain, Sweden, Switzerland, UK.
European Organization for Nuclear Research (CERN, #08108); European Space Agency (ESA, #08798); European Synchrotron Radiation Facility (ESRF, #08868); Joint Institute for Nuclear Research (JINR, #16134); Nordic Institute for Theoretical Physics (NORDITA, #17324).
IGO Relations Member of (1): *Abdus Salam International Centre for Theoretical Physics (ICTP, #00005).* Affiliated with (1): *International Atomic Energy Agency (IAEA, #12294).* Supports (1): *Central European Exchange Programme for University Students (CEEPUS).* **NGO Relations** Member of (1): *Initiative for Science in Europe (ISE, #11214).* Instrumental in setting up (1): *Europhysics Letters Association (EPL Association, #09169).* [2022/XD0834/y/**D**]

♦ European Piano Teachers' Association (EPTA) **08208**
Organizing Sec 34 Carver Road, London, SE24 9LT, UK. T. +442072746821.
URL: http://www.epta-europe.org/
History Mar 1978. **Aims** Bring together piano teachers from European countries and from other parts of the world. **Structure** Executive Council. **Languages** English, French, German. **Staff** Mostly voluntary. **Finance** Sources: members' dues. **Activities** Events/meetings. **Events** *International EPTA Conference* Guimarães (Portugal) 2022, *International EPTA Conference* Madrid (Spain) 2021, *Annual Conference* Fulda (Germany) 2020, *Annual Conference* Vienna (Austria) 2019, *Annual Conference* Valletta (Malta) 2018. **Publications** *Piano Journal* (3 a year).
Members Full: National associations in 39 countries:
Albania, Austria, Belarus, Belgium, Bosnia-Herzegovina, Bulgaria, Croatia, Cyprus, Czechia, Denmark, Estonia, Finland, France, Georgia, Germany, Greece, Hungary, Iceland, Ireland, Italy, Latvia, Lithuania, Malta, Montenegro, Netherlands, North Macedonia, Norway, Poland, Portugal, Romania, Russia, Serbia, Slovakia, Slovenia, Spain, Sweden, Switzerland, UK, Ukraine.
Associate in 17 countries and territories:
Argentina, Australia, Brazil, Canada, China, Hong Kong, India, Israel, Korea Rep, Malaysia, Mexico, New Zealand, Pakistan, Singapore, Sri Lanka, Taiwan, USA. [2022.05.19/XD8090/**D**]

♦ European Picture Union (inactive)
♦ European Pineal and Biological Rhythms Society / see European Biological Rhythms Society (#06337)
♦ European Pineal Society / see European Biological Rhythms Society (#06337)
♦ European Pineal Study Group / see European Biological Rhythms Society (#06337)

♦ European Placenta Group (EPG) **08209**
Contact Clinica Ostetrico-Ginecologica, Ospedale San Paolo, Via A Di Rudint 8, 20142 Milan MI, Italy. Fax +3928135662.
History 1984. **Events** *Meeting* Jouy-en-Josas (France) 2022, *Meeting* Paris (France) 2014, *Placenta – the key to pregnancy success* Adelaide, SA (Australia) 2009, *Meeting* Seggauberg (Austria) 2008, *Meeting* Budapest (Hungary) 2007. **Members** Covers Europe and the Middle East. Membership countries not specified. **NGO Relations** Instrumental in setting up and member of: *International Federation of Placenta Associations (IFPA, #13513).* [2010/XF2819/**E**]

♦ European Plan Science Retreat (meeting series)

♦ European Plant-Based Foods Association (ENSA) **08210**
Main Office Rue du Luxembourg 22-24, 1000 Brussels, Belgium. T. +3227616672. E-mail: secretariat@ensa-eu.org.
URL: http://www.ensa-eu.org/
History Jan 2003. Founded by European manufacturers producing plant-based alternatives to dairy and meat products. Former names and other names: *European Natural Soyfoods Manufacturers Association (ENSA)* – former (2003); *European Natural Soy and Plant Based Foods Manufacturers Association (ENSA)* – former. Registration: Banque-Carrefour des Entreprises, No/ID: 0862.348.113, Start date: 22 Dec 2003, Belgium; EU Transparency Register, No/ID: 689045810852-79, Start date: 20 Mar 2013. **Aims** Ensure development of an appropriate and balanced regulatory framework for plant-based food products in Europe. **Languages** English. **Finance** Sources: members' dues.
Members Companies (8) in 6 countries:
Belgium, France, Italy, Spain, Sweden, UK.
Supporting members (2) in 2 countries:
Germany, Portugal.
IGO Relations Participates as observer in the activities of: *Codex Alimentarius Commission (CAC, #04081).* **NGO Relations** Member of (1): *FoodDrinkEurope (#09841).* Partner of (1): *European Alliance for Plant-based Foods (EAPF).* Affiliated with (1): *International Plant Based Foods Working Group (IPBFWG).* [2023.02.16/XJ3403/**D**]

♦ European Plantmakers' Committee (no recent information)

♦ European Plant Science Organization (EPSO) 08211

Europese Organisatie voor Wetenschappelijk Plantenonderzoek

Exec Dir Rue de l'Industrie 4, 1000 Brussels, Belgium. T. +3222136260. Fax +3222136269. E-mail: epso@epsomail.org.

Publications Officer address not obtained.

URL: http://www.epsoweb.org/

History 15 Dec 2000. Registration: Banque-Carrefour des Entreprises, No/ID: 0477.802.204, Start date: 4 Jul 2002, Belgium; EU Transparency Register, No/ID: 38511867304-09, Start date: 30 Nov 2011. **Aims** Increase visibility and impact of the European plant science community; articulate its vision for the future and advise on decisions of funding agencies at European and national level on long term strategies to support plant science; ensure independent dissemination of plant science information; improve public perception of plant science and prepare for a permanent and effective engagement with public opinion at several levels; encourage plant scientists to respect and understand a broad spectrum of views on the role of modern plant science in food production and the environment; promote the inclusion research relevant to interests and needs of European and developing nations into basic, applied and strategic research in Europe; contribute to development of *agriculture, horticulture, forestry* and biodiversity. **Structure** General Meeting; Board of Directors. **Languages** English. **Staff** 3.00 FTE, paid. **Finance** Sources: members' dues. Annual budget: 450,000 EUR. **Activities** Events/meetings; knowledge management/information dissemination; networking/liaising; research and development. **Events** *Plant Biology Europe Conference* Marseille (France) 2023, *Fascination of Plants Day 2021* 2021, *Plant Biology Europe Conference* Turin (Italy) 2021, *Plant Biology Europe Conference* Turin (Italy) 2020, *Fascination of Plants Day 2019* 2019. **Publications** *EPSO News*. Science-Policy Recommendation Papers; articles; video in English, French German, Italian, Spanish; brochures.

Members Institutions (200) in 32 countries.
Australia, Austria, Belgium, Bulgaria, Cyprus, Czechia, Denmark, Estonia, Finland, France, Germany, Greece, Hungary, Ireland, Israel, Italy, Latvia, Lithuania, Netherlands, New Zealand, Norway, Poland, Portugal, Romania, Serbia, Slovakia, Slovenia, Spain, Sweden, Switzerland, UK, Ukraine.
Observers representing the industry (16) not specified.

NGO Relations Member of (4): *European Technology Platform 'Plants for the Future' (Plant ETP, #08890); Federation of European and International Associations Established in Belgium (FAIB, #09508); Global Plant Council (#10550); Initiative for Science in Europe (ISE, #11214).* [2022/XD8289/y/**D**]

- ♦ European Plasma Fractionation Association / see International Plasma and Fractionation Association (#14597)
- ♦ European Plastic Automotive Fuel Systems Manufacturers / see European Plastic Energy Storage Systems Association (#08212)

♦ European Plastic Energy Storage Systems Association (PlasEnSys) 08212

Contact EuPC Head Office, Avenue de Cortenbergh 71, 1000 Brussels, Belgium. T. +3227324124. Fax +3227324218. E-mail: info@eupc.org.

URL: https://www.plasensys.org/

History Sector Group of *European Plastics Converters (EuPC, #08216)*. Former names and other names: *European Plastic Automotive Fuel Systems Manufacturers (PlasFuelSys)* – former. **Aims** Represent and promote the interest of the Automotive Energy Storage Systems providing a common voice to the market and its institutions. **Structure** Executive Committee.

Members Companies (5) in 4 countries:
Belgium, France, Germany, Italy. [2019/XM0257/t/**D**]

- ♦ European Plastic Film, Membrane and Covering Manufacturers' Association (inactive)

♦ European Plastic Films (EuPF) 08213

Registered Office Avenue de Cortenbergh 71, PO Box 4, 1000 Brussels, Belgium. T. +3227324124. Fax +3227324218. E-mail: info@europeanplasticfilms.eu.

URL: http://www.europeanplasticfilms.eu/

History 20 Oct 2006, under the umbrella of *European Plastics Converters (EuPC, #08216)*. **Structure** Plenary Session (annually). Executive Committee, headed by President. Product Technical Working Groups (3): Bags and Sacks; Agri; Construct and Industrial. Horizontal Technical Working Groups (2): Quality Measurement; Printing. [2018/XM3512/**E**]

♦ European Plasticisers 08214

Secretariat CEFIC, Avenue E van Nieuwenhuyse 4 – Bte 2, 1160 Brussels, Belgium. T. +3227927363. Fax +3226767216. E-mail: info@europeanplasticisers.eu.

URL: http://www.europeanplasticisers.eu/

History 26 May 1992, as *European Council for Plasticisers and Intermediates (ECPI)*, a sector group of *Conseil européen de l'industrie chimique (CEFIC, #04687)*, on merging of the previous *'Plasticiser Sector Group', 'Plasticiser Range Alcohols Sector Group', 'Phthalic Anhydride Sector Group'* and *'Technical Committee for Plasticisers and Related Products'*. **Aims** Provide clear and concise information about the many applications of plasticisers and its safe use, supported by robust scientific research. **Structure** General Assembly; Scientific Working Groups; Task Forces. **Languages** English. **Activities** Provides input to legislative and regulatory authorities, non-government organizations, consumer groups and other stakeholders; encourage open dialogue and actively supports research programmes. **Events** *Plasticisers Conference* Brussels (Belgium) 2014.

Members Companies (6) in 5 countries:
Belgium, Czechia, Germany, Poland, Sweden.

NGO Relations Instrumental in setting up: *VinylPlus (#20780).* [2017/XE3113/**E**]

♦ The European Plastic Pipes and Fittings Association (TEPPFA) 08215

Gen Manager Av de Cortenbergh 71, 1000 Brussels, Belgium. T. +3227362406. E-mail: contact@teppfa.eu – info@teppfa.eu.

URL: http://www.teppfa.eu/

History 8 Jun 1992. Former names and other names: *The European Plastics Pipe and Fitting Association* – former. Registration: No/ID: 0448.654.791, Start date: 19 Nov 1992, Belgium; EU Transparency Register, No/ID: 82117319399-44, Start date: 23 Aug 2012. **Aims** Promote plastic pipe systems as a durable, sustainable and high performance solution for critical infrastructure and essential services to society. **Structure** General Assembly (annual); Executive Committee; Permanent Working Groups (4); Application Groups (2), Advisory Groups (3). **Languages** English. **Staff** 3.00 FTE, paid. **Finance** Sources: members' dues. **Activities** Advocacy/lobbying/activism; knowledge management/information dissemination; networking/liaising; politics/policy/regulatory; research and development; standards/guidelines. **Events** *Forum* Brussels (Belgium) 2018, *Forum* Brussels (Belgium) 2016, *Forum* Brussels (Belgium) 2015, *Forum* Brussels (Belgium) 2014, *Biennial plastics pipes conference* Budapest (Hungary) 2008. **Publications** *TEPPFA Newsletter*. Social media; press releases; position papers; manuals; EPDs; videos.

Members Open to national and supranational trade associations and to companies based in countries covered by CEN. Company members (14) in 10 countries:
Austria, Belgium, Finland, Germany, Italy, Netherlands, Romania, Spain, Sweden, Switzerland, UK.
National association members (15) in 15 countries:
Austria, Belgium, Czechia, Denmark, Finland, France, Germany, Hungary, Ireland, Italy, Netherlands, Poland, Spain, Sweden, UK.
Associated members in 3 countries:
Austria, Belgium, Germany.
Supporting members in 1 country:
Netherlands.

NGO Relations Member of (6): *Circular Plastics Alliance (#03936); Construction Products Europe AISBL (#04761); European Composites, Plastics and Polymer Processing Platform (ECP4, #06693);* European Drinking Water Consortium; *European Plastics Converters (EuPC, #08216); Plastic Pipes Conference Association (PPCA, #18393).* [2021.06.10/XD3140/**D**]

♦ European Plastics Converters (EuPC) 08216

Confédération européenne de la plasturgie – Verband Europäischer Kunststoffverarbeiter

Acting Managing Dir Av de Cortenbergh 71, 1000 Brussels, Belgium. T. +3227324124. Fax +3227324218. E-mail: info@eupc.org.

URL: http://www.plasticsconverters.eu/

History 30 Sep 1989, Brussels (Belgium). Founded by merger of *Committee of Plastic Converters Associations of Western Europe (EUTRAPLAST, inactive)* and *European Plastic Film, Membrane and Covering Manufacturers' Association (AEC, inactive).* Although EUTRAPLAST still exists its activities are carried out through EuPC. Former names and other names: *EPC* – alias. Registration: No/ID: 0441.556.668, Start date: 27 Sep 1990, Belgium; EU Transparency Register, No/ID: 93255296152-29, Start date: 6 Jul 2011. **Aims** Create a good trading environment for plastics converters in Europe. **Structure** General Assembly; Steering Committee; Market divisions (3); Horizontal Committees (4); Office in Brussels (Belgium), headed by Director. **Languages** Dutch, English, French, German, Italian. **Staff** 8.00 FTE, paid. **Finance** Sources: members' dues. Annual budget: 250,000 EUR. **Activities** Advocacy/lobbying/activism; projects/programmes; events/meetings; networking/liaising; standards/guidelines. **Events** *Annual Conference* Lyon (France) 2023, *A Circular Future with Plastics* Brussels (Belgium) 2022, *Annual Meeting* Brussels (Belgium) 2021, *Annual Meeting* Brussels (Belgium) 2020, *Annual Meeting* Berlin (Germany) 2019. **Publications** *EuPC Focus* (12 a year) – newsletter – internal. *European Recycling Directory*. Monographs; statistical leaflet (annual).

Members National Plastics Associations in 21 countries:
Austria, Belgium, Bulgaria, Croatia, Czechia, Denmark, France, Germany, Greece, Ireland, Italy, Lithuania, Netherlands, Norway, Poland, Portugal, Spain, Sweden, Switzerland, Türkiye, UK.
Sector Organizations (19):
CEFEP – European Interest Group for FEF and PEF Insulation (CEFEP, #03627); Engineering Polymer Shapes for Machining (EPSM); *European Association of Flexible Polyurethane Foam Blocks Manufacturers (EUROPUR, #06042); European Carpet and Rug Association (ECRA, #06452); European Manufacturers of Expanded Polystyrene (EUMEPS, #07732); European Masterbatchers and Compounders (EuMBC, #07749); European Performance Co-Extruders (EPEX, #08188); European Plastic Energy Storage Systems Association (PlasEnSys, #08212); European Plastic Films (EuPF, #08213); European Polycarbonate Sheet Extruders (EPSE, #08249); European Resilient Flooring Manufacturers' Institute (ERFMI, #08380); European Single Ply Waterproofing Association (ESWA, #08488); European Trade Association of PVC Window System Supplies (EPPA, #08924); Industrieverband Kunststoffbahnen (IVK Europe); MedPharmPlast Europe (MPPE, #16690); PET Sheet Europe (#18344); Plastics Recyclers Europe (PRE, #18394); The European Plastic Pipes and Fittings Association (TEPPFA, #08215); Vinyl Films and Sheets Europe (VFSE, #20779).*

IGO Relations *European Commission (EC, #06633).* **NGO Relations** Member of (6): *Circular Plastics Alliance (#03936); Construction Products Europe AISBL (#04761); European Composites, Plastics and Polymer Processing Platform (ECP4, #06693); European Food Sustainable Consumption and Production Round Table (European Food SCP Roundtable, #07289); PET Container Recycling Europe (Petcore Europe, #18339); Styrenics Circular Solutions (SCS, #20022).* Instrumental in setting up (1): *VinylPlus (#20780).* In liaison with technical committees of: *Comité européen de normalisation (CEN, #04162).* Close relations with: *Association of Plastics Manufacturers in Europe (Plastics Europe, #02862); European Committee of Machinery Manufacturers for the Plastics and Rubber Industries (EUROMAP, #06656); European Council of Vinyl Manufacturers (ECVM, #06849).* [2022/XD2231/y/**D**]

♦ European Plastics Distributors Association (EPDA) 08217

Contact c/o SAS Event Management, The Old George Brewery, Rollerstone Street, Salisbury, SP1 1DX, UK. T. +441722339811. Fax +441722331313. E-mail: info@epda.com.

URL: http://www.epda.com/

History Jun 1975. Founded as *European Plastics Distributors Club (EPDC)*. Present name adopted 1982. Registration: Companies House, No/ID: 11409257, Start date: 11 Jun 2018, England and Wales. **Aims** Safeguard and improve the level of distribution and quality of plastic semifinished products; ensure that cross-fertilization of ideas are shared; increase prestige of the plastics distribution industry; promote members as superior sources of distribution; establish a communications network between distributor and manufacturer members. **Structure** Executive Board; Committees (2). **Languages** English. **Staff** 0.50 FTE, paid. **Finance** Members' dues. **Activities** Knowledge management/information dissemination; events/meetings; monitoring/evaluation. **Events** *Annual Conference* London (UK) 2023, *Annual Conference* Nice (France) 2022, *Annual Conference* 2021, *Annual Conference* Nice (France) 2020, *Annual Conference* Salzburg (Austria) 2019. **Publications** *EPDA Newsletter* (4 a year). Information Services: Directory and product data of members.

Members Companies engaged in distribution and manufacture of plastic sheet, rod, tube, pipe, valves, fittings, film and related products. Independent distributors (45) and manufacturers (34) in 20 countries:
Austria, Denmark, Estonia, Finland, France, Germany, Greece, Ireland, Israel, Italy, Lithuania, Netherlands, Portugal, Romania, Russia, Spain, Sweden, Switzerland, UK, Ukraine.

NGO Relations Associate member of: *International Association of Plastics Distribution (IAPD).* [2022/XD2275/**D**]

- ♦ European Plastics Distributors Club / see European Plastics Distributors Association (#08217)
- ♦ The European Plastics Pipe and Fitting Association / see The European Plastic Pipes and Fittings Association (#08215)
- ♦ European Plastics Recyclers / see Plastics Recyclers Europe (#18394)

♦ European Plastic Surgery Research Council (EPSRC) 08218

Contact c/o Technische Univ München, Ismaninger Str 22, 81675 Munich, Germany. E-mail: info@epsrc.eu.

Pres c/o Medical Univ of Vienna, Dept Plastic and Reconstructive Survery, Universitätsring 1, 1010 Vienna, Austria.

URL: http://www.epsrc.eu/

History 2009. **Aims** Promote research in the field of plastic and reconstructive surgery. **Languages** English. **Events** *Meeting* Turku (Finland) 2021, *Meeting* Hamburg (Germany) 2013, *Meeting* Hamburg (Germany) 2012, *Meeting* Hamburg (Germany) 2011, *Meeting* Hamburg (Germany) 2010. **Members** Resident; Active; Associate; Senior; Senior Emeritus. Membership countries not specified. [2019.02.13/XJ0594/**D**]

- ♦ European Plastic Window Association (inactive)

♦ European Platelet Network (EUPLAN) 08219

Contact Univ of Pavia, Dept of Biochemistry, via Bassi 21, 27100 Pavia PV, Italy.

Contact address not obtained.

URL: http://www.euplan.eu/

History 2010. **Aims** Promote and facilitate collaboration between basic science and clinical research groups. **Events** *Conference* Germany 2025, *Conference* UK 2023, *Conference* Milan (Italy) 2022, *Conference* Milan (Italy) 2021, *Conference* Bruges (Belgium) 2018.

Members Laboratories in 9 countries:
Austria, Belgium, Finland, France, Germany, Italy, Netherlands, Sweden, UK. [2021/XJ5632/**F**]

♦ European Plate Observing System (EPOS) 08220

Address not obtained.

URL: http://www.epos-ip.org/

History Conceived 2002; approved Dec 2008. Preparatory phase ran 2010-2014. Implementation phase 2014-2019, resulting in establishment of EPOS as a *European Research Infrastructure Consortium (ERIC)*, with legal seat in Italy. Operational phase as of 2020. **Aims** Facilitate integrated use of data, data products, and facilities from distributed research infrastructures for solid Earth science in Europe. **Structure** General Assembly; Coordination Office, headed by Executive Director. Services Coordination Board. **Activities** Research and development; research/documentation; networking/liaising; events/meetings. **Events** *Nordic EPOS meeting* Helsinki (Finland) 2022, *Meeting* Copenhagen (Denmark) 2018, *Meeting* Lisbon (Portugal) 2018, *Antropogenic Hazard Workshop* Oulu (Finland) 2018. **Publications** *EPOS Newsletter*.

Members Partners (46) in 22 countries:
Belgium, Czechia, Denmark, Finland, France, Germany, Greece, Hungary, Iceland, Ireland, Italy, Netherlands, Norway, Poland, Portugal, Romania, Slovenia, Spain, Sweden, Switzerland, Türkiye, UK.

IGO Relations Partner of: *Group on Earth Observations (GEO, #10735).* **NGO Relations** Member of: *euroCRIS (#05672).* [2018/XM6843/**E**]

♦ European Platform Against Windfarms (EPAW) 08221

Contact Drumsallagh, Kingscourt, CO. CAVAN, Ireland. E-mail: contact@epaw.org.

URL: http://www.epaw.org/

History 4 Oct 2008. Registration: EU Transparency Register, No/ID: 66046067830-67. **Aims** Obtain a moratorium on European wind energy projects. **Activities** Advocacy/lobbying/activism. [2020.10.19/XM5731/**F**]

♦ **European Platform for Biodiversity Research Strategy (EPBRS) 08222**
Contact c/o Belgian Biodiversity Platform, Inst of Natural Sciences, Rue Vautier 29, 1000 Brussels, Belgium. T. +3226274318. Fax +3226274113.
Chair address not obtained.
URL: http://www.epbrs.org/
History 1999. **Aims** Promote knowledge for sustainability. **Structure** Steering Committee. **Languages** EU languages. **Activities** Events/meetings; guidance/assistance/consulting. **Events** *Meeting* Dublin (Ireland) 2013, *Meeting* Copenhagen (Denmark) 2012, *Meeting* Budapest (Hungary) 2011, *Meeting* Brussels (Belgium) 2010, *Meeting* Visby (Sweden) 2009.
Members Scientists and policy-makers from 31 countries:
Austria, Belgium, Bulgaria, Cyprus, Czechia, Denmark, Estonia, Finland, France, Germany, Greece, Hungary, Iceland, Ireland, Italy, Latvia, Lithuania, Luxembourg, Montenegro, Netherlands, Norway, Poland, Portugal, Romania, Slovakia, Slovenia, Spain, Sweden, Switzerland, Türkiye, UK.
Also included in the above, delegates from one organization listed in this Yearbook:
European Commission (EC, #06633).
IGO Relations Close connections with relevant international bodies, national governments and research organizations, EU institutions and EU projects in the field of biodiversity research. [2017.11.17/XM0670/F]

♦ **European Platform for Chemicals Using Manufacturing Industries (CheMI) 08223**
Contact Intergraf, Avenue Louise 130A, 1050 Brussels, Belgium. T. +3222308646.
URL: http://www.intergraf.eu/
History 2003. EU Transparency Register: 744688015518-46. **Aims** Work as a channel for the downstream users in article producing industries to represent their interests; contribute to the successful implementation of REACH. **Languages** English. **Activities** Advocacy/lobbying/activism; knowledge management/information dissemination.
Members Organizations (13):
Confédération des associations nationales de tanneurs et mégissiers de la Communauté européenne (COTANCE, #04515); Confédération européenne des industries du bois (CEI Bois, #04545); EDANA, the voice of nonwovens (EDANA, #05353); EURATEX – The European Apparel and Textile Confederation (EURATEX, #05616); European Adhesive Tape Association (AFERA, #05826); European Carton Makers Association (ECMA, #06453); European Ceramic Industry Association (CERAME-UNIE, #06506); European Tyre and Rubber Manufacturers' Association (ETRMA, #08963); FINAT (#09773); Flexible Packaging Europe (FPE, #09794); Intergraf (#11505); International Confederation of Paper and Board Converters in Europe (CITPA, #12866).
[2017.03.09/XJ8483/ty/F]

♦ European Platform for Conflict Prevention / see Global Partnership for the Prevention of Armed Conflict (#10538)

♦ **European Platform for Democratic Elections (EPDE) 08224**
Coordinator Europäischer Austausch gmbH, Erkelenzdamm 59, 10999 Berlin, Germany. T. +4930616714640. Fax +4930616714643.
URL: http://www.epde.org/
History 12 Dec 2012, Warsaw (Poland). **Aims** Assist citizens' election observation in countries of the Eastern Partnership and in the Russian Federation; contribute to democratic election processes throughout Europe. **Structure** Coordination Council; Secretariat. **Languages** English, Russian. **Finance** Funding from: *Council of Europe (CE, #04881); European Commission (EC, #06633)*; national organizations. **Activities** Training/education; advocacy/lobbying/activism; monitoring/evaluation. **Publications** *EPDE Newsletter*. Election observation reports.
Members Organizations in 11 countries:
Armenia, Azerbaijan, Belarus, Georgia, Germany, Moldova, Norway, Poland, Russia, Sweden, Ukraine.
Included in the above, 1 organization listed in this Yearbook:
International Society for Fair Elections and Democracy (ISFED). [2018.09.06/XJ7572/y/F]

♦ European Platform for Dutch Education / see European Platform – internationalising education
♦ European Platform – internationalising education (internationally oriented national body)

♦ **European Platform for Migrant Workers' Rights (EPMWR) 08225**
Contact c/o December 18, Kapellestraat 157, 9600 Ronse, Belgium.
History 1 Oct 2004, Brussels (Belgium). **Aims** Promote and protect the human rights of all migrant workers and their families; support implementation of the UN migrant workers' convention across Europe.
Members Organizations (18) in 9 countries:
Belgium, Denmark, France, Ireland, Italy, Netherlands, Spain, Sweden, UK.
Included in the above, 6 organizations listed in this Yearbook:
European Association for the Defence of Human Rights (AEDH, no recent information); European Coordination for Foreigners' Right to Family Life (COORDEUROP, #06794); Joint Council for the Welfare of Immigrants (JCWI); Multiethnic Interaction on Xenophobia in Europe (MixEurope); Platform for International Cooperation on Undocumented Migrants (PICUM, #18401); WSM. [2012/XM1273/y/F]

♦ **European Platform on Mobility Management (EPOMM) 08226**
Main Office c/o Mobiel 21, Vital Decosterstraat 67 A 0101, 3000 Leuven, Belgium.
Pres Stubenbastei 5, 1010 Vienna, Austria.
URL: https://epomm.eu/
History Apr 1999, Münster (Germany). Founded during 3rd European Conference on Mobility Management. **Aims** Promote and further develop mobility management in Europe; fine tune the implementation of mobility management in the European Union. **Structure** Board; Management; Secretariat. National Focal Points (4): France; Sweden; Netherlands; Switzerland. **Finance** Supported by the Governments of France, The Netherlands, Sweden and Switzerland. **Activities** Organizes *European Conference on Mobility Management (ECOMM)*. **Events** *ECOMM : European Conference on Mobility Management* Turku (Finland) 2022, *ECOMM : European Conference on Mobility Management* Cascais (Portugal) 2021, *ECOMM : European Conference on Mobility Management* Cascais (Portugal) 2020, *ECOMM : European Conference on Mobility Management* Uppsala (Sweden) 2018, *ECOMM : European Conference on Mobility Management* Maastricht (Netherlands) 2017. **Publications** *EPOMM Newsletter*. Activity Report.
Members in 11 countries or regions:
Austria, Belgium, Finland, France, Germany, Italy, Netherlands, Norway, Portugal, Sweden, UK.
NGO Relations Coordinated by: *EUROCITIES (#05662)* Mobility Forum. [2018/XJ3076/F]

♦ European Platform of Notified Bodies working in legal Metrology / see NoBoMet (#17145)
♦ European Platform for Patients' Organizations, Science and Industry / see DigitalHealthEurope (#05078)

♦ **European Platform for Photodynamic Medicine (EPPM) 08227**
Contact School of Chemical Sciences, Univ of East Anglia, Norwich, NR4 7TJ, UK. T. +441603593012. Fax +441603593012.
URL: http://www.eppm-photomedicine.org/
History 18 Sep 2006, Geneva (Switzerland). Registered in England. **Aims** Promote photodiagnosis and photodynamic *therapy*. **Structure** Board. **Events** *Conference* Ustron (Poland) 2013, *Conference / Congress* Wroclaw (Poland) 2009, *Congress* Dubrovnik (Croatia) 2008. **Publications** *Photodiagnosis and Photodynamic Therapy* – journal. **Members** Full (over 60). Membership countries not specified. [2014.10.28/XJ0446/F]

♦ **European Platform on preparedness for nuclear and radiological emergency response and recovery (NERIS) 08228**
Contact c/o CEPN, 28 rue de la Redoute, 92260 Fontenay-aux-Roses, France. T. +33155521920. E-mail: sec@eu-neris.net.
URL: http://www.eu-neris.net/
History Nov 2009, building on the EURANOS Project. Current statutes approved, 15 May 2012, Glasgow (UK). Registered in accordance with French law. **Aims** Establish a forum for dialogue and methodological development between all European organizations and associations taking part in decision making of protective actions in nuclear and radiological emergencies and recovery in Europe. **Structure** General Assembly. Management Board. R and D Committee. Secretariat. **Events** *General Assembly* 2021, *Workshop* 2021, *Workshop* Røskilde (Denmark) 2019, *Workshop* Dublin (Ireland) 2018, *Workshop* Lisbon (Portugal) 2017. **Publications** *NERIS Newsletter*. Annual Report.
Members Organizations (49) Supporting and Full. Members in 23 countries and territories:
Austria, Belarus, Belgium, Croatia, Denmark, Finland, France, Germany, Greece, Ireland, Italy, Netherlands, Norway, Poland, Portugal, Romania, Slovakia, Slovenia, Spain, Switzerland, Taiwan, UK, Ukraine. [2014/XJ7889/F]

♦ **European Platform of Regulatory Authorities (EPRA) 08229**
Plate-forme européenne des instances de régulation de l'audiovisuel
Head of Secretariat 76 allée de la Robertsau, 67000 Strasbourg, France. T. +33388413963. Fax +33390216019. E-mail: info@epra.org.
URL: http://www.epra.org/
History Apr 1995, Malta. **Aims** Serve as a forum for: informal discussion and exchange of views between regulatory authorities in the field of media; exchange of information about common issues of national and European media regulation; discussion of practical solutions to legal problems regarding interpretation and application of media regulation. **Structure** Board; Permanent Secretariat in Strasbourg (France), hosted by *European Audiovisual Observatory (#06294)*. **Languages** English, French. **Staff** 1.50 FTE, paid. **Finance** Members dues. **Events** *EPRA Meeting* Istanbul (Turkey) 2021, *EPRA Meeting* Strasbourg (France) 2021, *EPRA Meeting* Antwerp (Belgium) 2020, *EPRA Meeting* Rotterdam (Netherlands) 2020, *EPRA Meeting* Athens (Greece) 2019.
Members Regulatory authorities (53) in 47 countries and territories:
Albania, Andorra, Armenia, Austria, Azerbaijan, Belgium (3), Bosnia-Herzegovina, Bulgaria, Croatia, Cyprus, Czechia, Denmark, Estonia, Finland, France, Georgia, Germany, Gibraltar, Greece, Hungary, Ireland, Isle of Man, Israel (2), Italy, Kosovo (under UNSCR 1244), Latvia, Liechtenstein, Lithuania, Luxembourg, Malta, Moldova, Montenegro, Netherlands, North Macedonia, Norway, Poland, Portugal, Romania, Serbia, Slovakia, Slovenia, Spain (3), Sweden, Switzerland (2), Türkiye, UK, Ukraine.
[2021/XF5166/F]

♦ **European Platform for Rehabilitation (EPR) 08230**
Gen Sec Ave des Arts 8, c/o CCI, 1210 Brussels, Belgium. T. +3227365444. Fax +3227368622. E-mail: epr@epr.eu.
Pres Heliomare, Relweg 51, 1949 EC Wijk aan Zee, Netherlands.
URL: http://www.epr.eu/
History 1993. Former names and other names: *European Platform for Vocational Rehabilitation (EPVR)* – former. Registration: Banque-Carrefour des Entreprises, No/ID: 0864.922.670, Start date: 23 Apr 2004, Belgium; EU Transparency Register, No/ID: 45696998939-63, Start date: 11 Jun 2012. **Aims** Build capacity of members to provide sustainable, high quality services through mutual learning and training. **Structure** General Assembly; Board of Directors; Centre Coordinators. **Languages** English. **Staff** 4.00 FTE, paid. **Finance** Sources: fees for services; members' dues; revenue from activities/projects. **Activities** Events/meetings; guidance/assistance/consulting; knowledge management/information dissemination; training/education. **Events** *Annual Conference* Dublin (Ireland) 2022, *EQUASS Conference* Lisbon (Portugal) 2018, *Annual Conference* Utrecht (Netherlands) 2018, *Annual Conference* Lisbon (Portugal) 2016, *Annual Conference* Valencia (Spain) 2015. **Publications** Annual Report; reports; studies; position papers; analytical papers; recommendations; booklets; brochures; leaflets; newsletter.
Members Organizations (25) in 18 countries:
Belgium, Denmark, Estonia, France, Germany, Greece, Hungary, Ireland, Italy, Latvia, Lithuania, Netherlands, Norway, Poland, Portugal, Slovenia, Spain, UK.
Consultative Status Consultative status granted from: *Council of Europe (CE, #04881)* (Participatory Status).
NGO Relations Member of (2): *European Alliance for Mental Health – Employment & Work (EUMH Alliance, #05875); Social Services Europe (#19347).* [2022/XF6760/F]

♦ **European Platform for the Responsible Use of Medicines in Animals (EPRUMA) 08231**
Chairman Av de Tervueren 168, Box 8 – 5th Floor, 1150 Brussels, Belgium. T. +3225437564. E-mail: info@epruma.eu.
URL: http://www.epruma.eu/
History 2005. **Aims** Ensure best practice through responsible use of medicines in the prevention and control of animal diseases. **Structure** Core Group; Chair. **Activities** Events/meetings.
Members Partners (9):
AccessVetMed (Access VetMed); *AnimalhealthEurope (#00837); COPA – european farmers (COPA, #04829); Diagnostics For Animals (#05062); European Forum of Farm Animal Breeders (EFFAB, #07310); Fédération européenne des fabricants d'aliments composés pour animaux (FEFAC, #09566); Fédération européenne pour la santé animale et la sécurité sanitaire (FESASS, #09581); Federation of European Companion Animal Veterinary Associations (FECAVA, #09497); Federation of Veterinarians of Europe (#09713); General Confederation of Agricultural Cooperatives in the European Union (#10107).* [2023.02.14/XJ8487/y/F]

♦ **European Platform for Sport Innovation (EPSI) 08232**
Exec Dir Avenue des Arts 43, 1040 Brussels, Belgium. E-mail: info@epsi.eu.
Exec Dir address not obtained.
URL: http://epsi.eu/
History Registered in accordance with Belgian law. **Aims** Achieve a more innovation-friendly environment for the sports industry in the EU so as to stimulate technological innovation and establish businesses based on innovation technology. **Activities** Advocacy/lobbying/activism; financial and/or material support; networking/liaising; events/meetings. **Events** *Conference* Brussels (Belgium) 2019, *Sports Tech Transfer and R and D Summit* Ghent (Belgium) 2018.
Members Full in 16 countries:
Austria, Belgium, Denmark, Finland, France, Germany, Hungary, Ireland, Italy, Netherlands, Romania, Serbia, Spain, Sweden, Switzerland, UK. [2019/XM7894/F]

♦ **European Platform & Stairlift Association (EPSA) 08233**
Secretariat Unit 19 Omega Business Village, Thurston Road, Northallerton, DL6 2NJ, UK. T. +442082534503. Fax +442082534510. E-mail: epsa@admin.co.uk.
URL: http://www.epsa.eu.com/
History 17 Nov 1999, London (UK). Registration: EU Transparency Register, No/ID: 172039636517-45, Start date: 8 Nov 2019. **Aims** Provide information, advice and guidance on accessibility to authorities and organisations, so as to promote easier, safe and affordable access to different levels of private, public and commercial buildings for people with impaired mobility. **Structure** General Assembly; Board; Secretariat. Working Groups.
Members Companies in 11 countries:
Austria, Belgium, Denmark, France, Germany, Italy, Norway, Spain, Sweden, Switzerland, UK.
NGO Relations Member of (1): *World Elevator Federation.* [2018/AA1226/D]

♦ European Platform for Supervisory Organisations / see European Partnership of Supervisory Organisations in Health Services and Social Care (#08160)

♦ **European Platform of Transport Sciences (EPTS Foundation) 08234**
SG PO Box 110129, 42301 Wuppertal, Germany. E-mail: office@epts.eu.
Registered Address Bessie-Coleman-Strasse 7, 60549 Frankfurt-Main, Germany.
URL: https://www.epts.eu/
History 2001, Vienna (Austria). Registration: Hesse District court, No/ID: VR 16293, Start date: 23 Aug 2018, Germany, Frankfurt-Main; EU Transparency Register, No/ID: 154300233791-83, Start date: 29 Jan 2019. **Aims** Enhance dialogue between politicians, policymakers, scientists and researchers in the field of European transport. **Structure** Executive Board. Young Forum of European Transport Sciences (YFE). **Activities** Awards/prizes/competitions; events/meetings; knowledge management/information dissemination; networking/liaising; research/documentation. **Events** *European Transport Congress* Györ (Hungary) 2022, *European Transport Congress* Maribor (Slovenia) 2021, *European Transport Congress* Rostock (Germany) 2020, *European Transport Congress* Bratislava (Slovakia) 2019, *European Transport Congress* Warsaw (Poland) 2018.

Members Institutional in 12 countries:
Austria, Bosnia-Herzegovina, Croatia, Czechia, France, Germany, Greece, Hungary, North Macedonia, Slovakia, Slovenia, Switzerland. [2022.10.19/AA2563/f/**F**]

♦ European Platform for Vocational Rehabilitation / see European Platform for Rehabilitation (#08230)

♦ European Platform of Women Scientists (EPWS) 08235
Plateforme européenne des femmes scientifiques
Pres M.A.I., Rue Washington 40, 1050 Brussels, Belgium. E-mail: contact@epws.org.
Vice-Pres Lab d'Analyse et de Mathématiques Appliquées, UPEC- bureau P3 411, 61 avenue du Général de Gaulle, Bât P, 94010 Créteil, France.
URL: https://www.epws.org/
History 2005, Brussels (Belgium). Launched 28 Mar 2006. Registration: Banque-Carrefour des Entreprises, No/ID: 0877.239.987, Start date: 14 Nov 2005, Belgium. **Aims** Promote women scientists and integration of the gender dimension in science. **Structure** General Assembly (annual); Board of Administration; Executive Committee. **Languages** English, French. **Staff** None. **Finance** Sources: members' dues. Several supporting organizations, not specified. Annual budget: 16,000 EUR (2018). **Activities** Events/meetings; politics/policy/regulatory. **Events** *Annual Conference* Brussels (Belgium) 2022, *Annual Conference* Brussels (Belgium) 2019, *General Assembly* Pisa (Italy) 2018, *General Assembly* Brussels (Belgium) 2017, *General Assembly* Paris (France) 2016. **Publications** *EPWS Updates* (6 a year); *Interview of the Month*. Science policy position papers; articles.
Members Full; Associate; Individual Supporting; Supporting Organizations. Members in 33 countries:
Armenia, Austria, Belarus, Belgium, Bulgaria, Cyprus, Czechia, Denmark, Finland, France, Germany, Greece, Hungary, Ireland, Israel, Italy, Kazakhstan, Latvia, Lithuania, Netherlands, North Macedonia, Norway, Pakistan, Poland, Portugal, Romania, Russia, Spain, Sweden, Switzerland, Türkiye, UK, USA.
Included in the above, 1 organization listed in this Yearbook:
Women in Nuclear (WIN, #21009).
NGO Relations Member of (1): *Federation of European and International Associations Established in Belgium (FAIB, #09508).* [2022/XJ4267/**F**]

♦ European Play Equipment Manufacturers Association (inactive)
♦ European Playleaders Association / see european playwork association (#08236)

♦ european playwork association (epa) 08236
Contact Palmaille 102, 22767 Hamburg, Germany. T. +4940433190. E-mail: contact@epa-network.org.
Main Website: https://epa-network.org
History 1976, Hamburg (Germany). Former names and other names: *European Playleaders Association* – former (1976); *European Playworkers Association* – former; *Association européenne des animateurs* – former. Registration: Germany. **Aims** Join with children, young people, women and men who want to get playfully involved for a life in dignity and enjoy worldwide friendship. **Languages** English, Finnish, French, German, Italian, Portuguese, Spanish. **Staff** 2.80 FTE, paid. **Finance** Sources: contributions. Supported by: City of Hamburg; *European Commission (EC, #06633); European Youth Foundation (EYF, #09141).* **Activities** Advocacy/lobbying/activism; events/meetings; guidance/assistance/consulting; knowledge management/information dissemination; networking/liaising; training/education. **Events** *Congress* Liverpool (UK) 2014, *Congress* Malaga (Spain) 2014, *Congress* Malta 2014, *Congress* Tirana (Albania) 2014, *Congress* Sfax (Tunisia) / Gabes (Tunisia) 2013.
Members Associations in 39 countries:
Albania, Algeria, Argentina, Austria, Belarus, Belgium, Bosnia-Herzegovina, Brazil, Bulgaria, Colombia, Dominican Rep, France, Germany, Ghana, Greece, Ireland, Italy, Jamaica, Lebanon, Liberia, Malta, Montenegro, Morocco, Netherlands, Nigeria, North Macedonia, Peru, Portugal, Romania, Russia, Serbia, Slovakia, Slovenia, Spain, Switzerland, Tunisia, Türkiye, UK, Ukraine. [2021.10.20/XD1102/**D**]

♦ European Playworkers Association / see european playwork association (#08236)

♦ European Pocket Billiard Federation (EPBF) 08237
Main Office Clercstraat 2, 6441 CT Brunssum, Netherlands. E-mail: gre.leenders@planet.nl.
URL: http://www.epbf.com/
History Founded 1978. **Aims** Gather national pool-billiard associations in Europe; support development of all pool-billiard disciplines; represent the European sport of pool-billiard; support youth; spread the sport; determine uniform rules and regulations for the realization of the sport in Europe; arrange education of coaches and referees; approve and assign international tournaments; create regulations for the realization of European Championships; assign the organization of European Championships. **Structure** General Assembly (every 2 years); Board of 6 members; Honorary Board; Court of Arbitration. **Languages** English. **Activities** Sporting activities.
Members National organizations in 35 countries and territories:
Albania, Austria, Belarus, Belgium, Bosnia-Herzegovina, Croatia, Cyprus, Czechia, Denmark, England, Estonia, Finland, France, Germany, Greece, Hungary, Italy, Latvia, Liechtenstein, Lithuania, Luxembourg, Netherlands, Northern Cyprus, Norway, Poland, Portugal, Romania, Russia, Slovakia, Slovenia, Spain, Sweden, Switzerland, Türkiye, Ukraine.
NGO Relations Member of: *World Pool-Billiard Association (WPA, #21733),* through which links with *World Confederation of Billiards Sports (WCBS, #21291).* [2016.02.12/XD4618/**D**]

♦ European Point-of-Use Drinking Water Association / see European Drinking Water Cooler Association
♦ European Poker Players' Association (no recent information)

♦ European Polar Board (EPB) 08238
Exec Sec NWO, Laan van Nieuw Oost-Indië 300, 2593 CE The Hague, Netherlands. E-mail: epb@nwo.nl.
URL: http://www.europeanpolarboard.org/
History Oct 1995. Founded under the auspices of *European Science Foundation (ESF, #08441).* Together with *European Marine Board (EMB, #07738),* replaces *European Boards for Marine and Polar Science (EMaPS Boards, inactive)* and *European Secretariat for Marine and Polar Science (EMaPS, inactive).* Became an independent body in 2015. **Aims** Improve European coordination in Arctic and Antarctic research through improved information sharing, optimised infrastructure use and joint initiatives between members; promote multilateral collaborative activities between Members and provide a single contact point for to the European Polar research community as a whole for international partners; advance the collective knowledge of Polar issues, particularly in the context of European societal relevance. **Structure** Executive Committee, comprising Chairperson, 5 Vice-Chairpersons and up to 2 delegates from each member country. **Activities** Politics/policy/regulatory; publishing activities; research/documentation. **Events** *Annual Arctic Science Summit* Arkhangelsk (Russia) 2019, *Annual Arctic Science Summit* Davos (Switzerland) 2018, *Annual Arctic Science Summit* Prague (Czechia) 2017, *ISAR : International Symposium on the Arctic Research* Prague (Czechia) 2017, *Annual Arctic Science Summit* Fairbanks, AK (USA) 2016. **Publications** *EPB Newsletter*. Annual Report; policy papers.
Members Polar research organizations (29) in 21 countries:
Austria, Belgium, Bulgaria, Denmark, Estonia, Finland, France, Germany, Iceland, Italy, Luxembourg, Netherlands, Norway, Poland, Portugal, Spain, Sweden, Switzerland, Türkiye, UK, Ukraine. [2023.02.14/XE3932/**E**]

♦ European Police Chiefs Operational Task Force (no recent information)
♦ European Police College / see European Union Agency for Law Enforcement Training (#08970)

♦ European Police Office (Europol) 08239
Office central européen de police criminelle
Dir PO Box 90850, 2509 LW The Hague, Netherlands. T. +31703025000. Fax +31703455896. E-mail: corporate.communications@europol.europa.eu – g41@europol.europa.eu.
Street Address Eisenhowerlaan 73, 2517 KK The Hague, Netherlands.
URL: http://www.europol.europa.eu/
History 3 Jan 1994. Commenced limited operations fighting against drugs with first unit *Europol Drugs Unit (EDU)* following work of Europol project development team, Sep 1992-Dec 1993 and covered under the interior policy protocol to *Treaty on European Union (Maastricht Treaty, 1992),* signed 7 Feb 1992, Maastricht (Netherlands), in the progress towards the *European Union (EU, #08967).* Legal basis: Ministerial Agreement signed by the ministers of *Trevi Group (inactive),* 2 Jun 1993, Copenhagen (Denmark), and entered into force 30 Oct 1993, following decision of *European Council (#06801)* on the location of Europol. Europol Convention, signed 26 Jul 1995, ratified by all member states in Jun 1998 and entered into force on 1 Oct 1998, extended the mandate (20 Mar 1995 and further extended 16 Dec 1996) to deal with all serious forms of international crime as listed in the Annex to the Europol Convention. Commenced full activities 1 Jul 1999. Legal status: until end 2009 – Europol Convention; from Jan 2010 – EU Council decision, it a EU decentralized agency. **Aims** Act as a support centre for *law* enforcement operations, a hub for *criminal* information, and a centre for law enforcement expertise; support and strengthen action by the competent authorities of Member States and their mutual cooperation in preventing and combating organized crime, *terrorism* and other forms of serious crime affecting 2 or more Member States. **Structure** Management Board, composed of one representative from each Member State and one representative from *European Commission (EC, #06633).* Director and Deputy Directors, appointed by *Council of the European Union (#04895).* Data Protection Officer, appointed by Management Board. Departments (3): Governance; Operations; Capabilities. Includes: *European Cybercrime Centre (EC3); European Counter Terrorism Centre (ectc, #06851).* **Languages** Bulgarian, Czech, Danish, Dutch, English, Estonian, Finnish, French, German, Hungarian, Irish Gaelic, Italian, Latvian, Lithuanian, Maltese, Polish, Portuguese, Romanian, Slovakian, Slovene, Spanish, Swedish. **Staff** 1323.00 FTE, paid. **Finance** As of 1 Jan 2010, funded from general budget of *European Commission (EC, #06633),* and subject to budgetary authority of *European Parliament (EP, #08146)* and *Council of Europe (CE, #04881).* Annual budget: 172,964,254 EUR (2021). **Activities** Competence covers organized crime, terrorism and other forms of serious crime affecting 2 or more Member States. In particular supports law enforcement activities of Member States against: illicit drug trafficking; illicit immigration networks; terrorism; illicit vehicle trafficking; trafficking in human being including child sexual abuse material; forgery of money (counterfeiting of the euro) and other means of payment; money-laundering. Additional priorities: crimes against persons; financial crime; cybercrime. Provides support to Member States by: information exchange; analysis; strategic reports; expertise and technical support for investigations and operations carried out with the EU. Organizes conferences and training. Functions as a non-operational unit (without executive authority) in support of law enforcement authorities within and between EU Member States. '*Europol National Units (ENUs)*' are the interface between Europol and the National Units. *Europol Drugs Unit (EDU),* set up 3 Jan 1994, The Hague (Netherlands), was the first unit of Europol to become operational. **Events** *Criminals Leverage AI for Malicious Use – And It's Not Just Deep Fakes* Dallas, GA (USA) 2020, *Meeting* Vienna (Austria) 2018, *European Conference on Fighting Organized Crime and Terrorism* Brussels (Belgium) 2017, *Cybercrime Conference* The Hague (Netherlands) 2017, *Cybercrime Conference* Singapore (Singapore) 2016. **Publications** *EUROPOL Review* – Fact sheets. Fact sheets; analyses; brochures, articles. **Information Services** *Analysis Work Files (AWFs); Europol Information System (EIS); SCanning, Analysis and Notification (SCAN) System; Secure Information Exchange Network Application (SIENA).*
Members Member States of the European Union (27):
Austria, Belgium, Bulgaria, Croatia, Cyprus, Czechia, Denmark, Estonia, Finland, France, Germany, Greece, Hungary, Ireland, Italy, Latvia, Lithuania, Luxembourg, Malta, Netherlands, Poland, Portugal, Romania, Slovakia, Slovenia, Spain, Sweden.
IGO Relations Member of: *Virtual Global Taskforce (VGT, #20788).* Disputes normally adjudicated by *Court of Justice of the European Union (CJEU, #04938).* Audited by: *European Court of Auditors (#06854).* Plays an important role in assisting: *European Police Chiefs Operational Task Force (no recent information).* Agreement with: *Eurojust (#05698); Frontex, the European Border and Coast Guard Agency (#10005); European Anti-Fraud Office (#05906); European Central Bank (ECB, #06466); European Monitoring Centre for Drugs and Drug Addiction (EMCDDA, #07820); International Criminal Police Organization – INTERPOL (ICPO-INTERPOL, #13110); United Nations Office on Drugs and Crime (UNODC, #20596); World Customs Organization (WCO, #21350).* Observer to the Governing Board of: *European Union Agency for Law Enforcement Training (CEPOL, #08970).* Close liaison with: *European Institute for Crime Prevention and Control affiliated with the United Nations (HEUNI, #07550); Financial Action Task Force (FATF, #09765); Maritime Analysis and Operations Centre – Narcotics (MAOC-N, #16581); Task Force on Organized Crime in the Baltic Sea Region (#20099); United Nations Interregional Crime and Justice Research Institute (UNICRI, #20580).* Cooperates in: *Budapest Process (#03344).* Cooperates with: *European Union Agency for the Operational Management of Large-Scale IT Systems in the Area of Freedom, Security and Justice (eu-LISA, #08972).* **NGO Relations** Member of (2): *EU Agencies Network (EUAN, #05564); Eurolib (#05703).* [2021/XE1915/**E***]

♦ European Police Sports Association (#20482)
♦ European Policies Research Centre, University of Strathclyde (internationally oriented national body)

♦ European Policy Centre (EPC) 08240
Chief Executive Rue du Trône 14-16, 1000 Brussels, Belgium. T. +3222310340. E-mail: info@epc.eu.
COO address not obtained.
URL: http://www.epc.eu/
History Jan 1997. Registration: No/ID: 0452.525.487, Start date: 12 Apr 1994, Belgium; EU Transparency Register, No/ID: 89632641000-47, Start date: 22 Jan 2009. **Aims** Promote European *integration* by working at the cutting-edge of European and global policy-making to provide members and the wider public with rapid, high-quality information and analysis on the EU and global policy agenda; promote a balanced dialogue between the different constituencies of membership, spanning all aspects of economic and social life. **Structure** Governing Board; Strategic Council; Management Team, including Chief Executive. **Languages** English. **Finance** Members' dues. Other sources: grants; contributions. **Activities** Knowledge management/information dissemination; research/documentation; events/meetings; monitoring/evaluation. **Events** *Conference on the Future of Europe* Brussels (Belgium) 2022, *Meeting on Digital Enlargement* Brussels (Belgium) 2017, *Meeting* Brussels (Belgium) 2014, *Meeting* Brussels (Belgium) 2014, *Meeting* Brussels (Belgium) 2014. **Publications** *Challenge Europe* – journal. *EU@60 – Countering a regressive and illiberal Europe* (2016) by Janis A Emmanouilidis and Fabian Zuleeg. Annual Report; commentaries; working papers; policy briefs; issue papers; post-summit analyses.
Members Platinum (3); Corporate (58); Professional and business associations (73); Diplomatic (61); Foundations (23); Governmental organizations (4); Intergovernmental organizations (13); Platform of non-governmental organizations (1); Non-governmental organizations (49); Regional bodies and local authorities (34); Religious organizations (6); Academic (2); Others (2); Individual (8). Professional business associations include the following 45 organizations listed in this Yearbook:
– *Alliance for Beverage Cartons and the Environment (ACE, #00658);*
– *American Chamber of Commerce to the European Union (AmCham EU);*
– *Association des chambres de commerce et d'industrie européennes (EUROCHAMBRES, #02423);*
– *Association européenne des métaux (EUROMETAUX, #02578);*
– *Association of Chartered Certified Accountants (ACCA);*
– *BUSINESSEUROPE (#03381);*
– *Computer and Communications Industry Association (CCIA);*
– *Confederation of European Community Cigarette Manufacturers (CECCM, #04521);*
– *Confederation of European Paper Industries (CEPI, #04529);*
– *Conseil européen de l'industrie chimique (CEFIC, #04687);*
– *Cosmetics Europe – The Personal Care Association (#04852);*
– *CropLife Europe (#04965);*
– *DIGITALEUROPE (#05073);*
– *EFMD – The Management Development Network (#05387);*
– *EU-Japan Centre for Industrial Cooperation;*
– *European Aluminium (#05893);*
– *European Association of Bioindustries (EuropaBio, #05956);*
– *European Association of the Machine tool Industries and related Manufacturing Technologies (CECIMO, #06113);*
– *European Automobile Manufacturers' Association (ACEA, #06300);*
– *European Bioplastics (#06342);*
– *European Confederation of Independent Trade Unions (CESI, #06705);*
– *European Financial Services Round Table (EFR, #07255);*
– *European Heat Pump Association (EHPA, #07469);*
– *European Organization for Packaging and the Environment (EUROPEN, #08110);*
– *European Telecommunications Network Operators' Association (ETNO, #08895);*
– *European Trade Union Confederation (ETUC, #08927);*
– *Euroseeds (#09179);*
– *Fertilizers Europe (#09738);*
– *Gas Infrastructure Europe (GIE, #10073);*
– *GSMA Europe (#10811);*
– *Industrial Minerals Association – Europe (IMA Europe, #11179);*

- *International Association of Oil and Gas Producers (IOGP, #12053)*;
- *International Federation of Reproduction Rights Organizations (IFRRO, #13527)*;
- *International Fur Federation (IFF, #13696)*;
- *Japan External Trade Organization (JETRO)*;
- *Korea International Trade Association (KITA)*;
- *Liquid Gas Europe (#16488)*;
- *MedTech Europe (#16692)*;
- *Oil Companies' European Association for Environment, Health and Safety in Refining and Distribution (CONCAWE, #17708)*;
- *Orgalim – Europe's Technology Industries (#17794)*;
- *Pack2Go Europe (#18014)*;
- *Starch Europe (#19966)*;
- *The Brewers of Europe (#03324)*;
- *UNESDA Soft Drinks Europe (UNESDA, #20323)*;
- *World Employment Federation Europe (#21377)*.

Diplomatic in 65 countries and territories:
Albania, Andorra, Angola, Australia, Austria, Azerbaijan, Bosnia-Herzegovina, Brazil, Brunei Darussalam, Canada (Québec), Chile, China, Cyprus, Czechia, Denmark, Estonia, Faeroe Is, Finland, France, Georgia, Germany, Greece, Hong Kong, Hungary, Iceland, Indonesia, Iran Islamic Rep, Ireland, Israel, Italy, Japan, Korea Rep, Kosovo, Kuwait, Lithuania, Luxembourg, Macau, Malta, Mexico, Moldova, Montenegro, Morocco, Netherlands, New Zealand, North Macedonia, Norway, Philippines, Poland, Romania, Russia, Saudi Arabia, Serbia, Singapore, Slovakia, South Africa, Sweden, Switzerland, Taiwan, Thailand, Türkiye, UK, Ukraine, Uruguay, USA, Uzbekistan.
Foundations include 20 organizations listed in this Yearbook:
Bertelsmann Foundation; *British Council* (Brussels); *Calouste Gulbenkian Foundation*; *Company of St Paul*; *Egmont Institute*; *European Climate Foundation (ECF, #06574)*; *European Cultural Foundation (ECF, #06868)*; *European Foundation Centre (EFC, inactive)*; *European Foundation for Democracy (EDF, #07347)*; *Friedrich-Ebert-Stiftung (FES)*; *Friedrich Naumann Foundation for Freedom*; *Hanns Seidel Foundation*; *Institute of International European Affairs, Dublin (IIEA)*; *ISMU Foundation – Foundation for Initiatives and Studies on Multi-ethnicity*; *King Baudouin Foundation (KBF)*; *Konrad Adenauer Foundation (KAF)*; *Stiftung Mercator*; *Stiftung Wissenschaft und Politik (SWP)*; *Transatlantic Policy Network (TPN, #20204)*; *Wilfried Martens Centre for European Studies (Martens Centre, #20962)*.
Intergovernmental include 15 organizations listed in this Yearbook:
Council of Europe (CE, #04881); *EFTA (#05391)*; *EFTA Surveillance Authority (ESA, #05392)*; *Energy Charter Conference (#05466)*; *European Bank for Reconstruction and Development (EBRD, #06315)*; *European Investment Bank (EIB, #07599)*; *International Bank for Reconstruction and Development (IBRD, #12317)* (World Bank EU Office); *International Centre for Migration Policy Development (ICMPD, #12503)*; *International Monetary Fund (IMF, #14180)*; *International Organization for Migration (IOM, #14454)*; *Japan Bank for International Cooperation (JBIC)*; *NATO Parliamentary Assembly (NATO PA, #16946)*; *Regional Cooperation Council (RCC, #18773)*; *UNDP (#20292)*; *WHO (#20950)*.
Non-governmental include 34 organizations listed in this Yearbook:
- *Amnesty International (AI, #00801)*;
- *Association européenne pour la coordination de la représentation des consommateurs pour la normalisation (ANEC, #02561)*;
- *Carbon Market Watch (#03423)*;
- *Caritas Europa (#03579)*;
- *Central Europe Energy Partners (CEEP)*;
- *Confederation of European Community Cigarette Manufacturers (CECCM, #04521)*;
- *Confrontations for a European Participative Democracy (Confrontations Europe)*;
- *Crisis Management Initiative (CMI)*;
- *European Academy of Sciences and Arts (EASA, #05814)*;
- *European Armenian Federation for Justice and Democracy (EAFJD)*;
- *European Council on Refugees and Exiles (ECRE, #06839)*;
- *European Disability Forum (EDF, #06929)*;
- *European Stability Initiative (ESI, #08828)*;
- *European Youth Forum (#09140)*;
- *Foster Europe*;
- *German Marshall Fund of the United States (GMF)*;
- *International Catholic Migration Commission (ICMC, #12459)*;
- *International Crisis Group (Crisis Group, #13111)*;
- *International Foundation for Sustainable Peace and Development (IFSPD, #13678)*;
- *International Partnership for Human Rights (IPHR)*;
- *International Rescue Committee (IRC, #14717)*;
- *International Security Information Service (ISIS)*;
- *Internet Society (ISOC, #15952)*;
- *Junior Enterprises Europe (JE Europe, #16169)*;
- *Network of European Foundations (NEF, #17019)*;
- *Norwegian Refugee Council (NRC)* (NRC Europe of);
- *ONE (#17728)*;
- *Oxfam International (#17922)* (EU Advocacy Office);
- *Social Platform (#19344)*;
- *Social Progress Imperative (#19345)*;
- *Sustainable Digital Infrastructure Alliance (SDIA)*;
- *VoteWatch Europe (#20811)*;
- *World Vision International (WVI, #21904)*;
- *World Wide Fund for Nature (WWF, #21922)* (European Policy Office).

Regional bodies and local authorities include 2 organizations listed in this Yearbook:
Conference of Peripheral Maritime Regions of Europe (CPMR, #04638); *EUROCITIES (#05662)*.
Religious include 4 organizations listed in this Yearbook:
Commission of the Bishops' Conferences of the European Union (COMECE, #04205); *European Evangelical Alliance (EEA, #07010)*; *Jesuit European Social Centre (JESC, #16103)*; *Jesuit Refugee Service Europe (JRS Europe, #16107)*.
Other includes 1 organization listed in this Yearbook:
International Committee of the Red Cross (ICRC, #12799).
NGO Relations Member of: Brussels Think Tank Dialogue; *DARA (#05009)*; *Euro-Mediterranean Study Commission (EuroMeSCo, #05727)*; Euromed Migration II; European Economic Governance Monitor; European Global Strategy; New Atlantic Capitalism; Odysseus Network; Think Global Act European project of *Institut Jacques Delors (IJD)*; *Transatlantic Policy Network (TPN, #20204)*. [2022/XN4518/y/**F**]

♦ European Policy Forum (internationally oriented national body)

♦ European Policy Information Center (EPICENTER) 08241

Dir The Library Ambiorix, Square Ambiorix 10, 1000 Brussels, Belgium. T. +442077998922. E-mail: info@epicenternetwork.eu.
URL: https://www.epicenternetwork.eu/
History Oct 2014. Registration: Banque-Carrefour des Entreprises, No/ID: 0736.964.824, Start date: 31 Oct 2019, Belgium; EU Transparency Register, No/ID: 080362721653-38, Start date: 4 May 2016. **Activities** Events/meetings; knowledge management/information dissemination.
Members Think tanks (8) in 8 countries:
Denmark, France, Greece, Italy, Lithuania, Poland, Sweden, UK. [2022/AA2990/**D**]

♦ European Policy Institutes Network (EPIN) 08242

Coordinator c/o CEPS, Place du Congrès 1, 1000 Brussels, Belgium. T. +3222293961. E-mail: info@ceps.eu.
URL: http://www.epin.org/
History 2002, Brussels (Belgium). Founded by *Centre for European Policy Studies (CEPS, #03741)*. **Aims** Expand and deepen knowledge on EU affairs; develop valuable insights into the future of European integration; provide a platform for researchers and policy analysts to develop professional links, exchange knowledge and collaborate on EU-related projects; bring an European dimension in national debates on Europe. **Structure** Coordinated by CEPS. **Languages** English. **Staff** 2.00 FTE, paid. **Finance** Project funding. Supported by: *Centre for European Policy Studies (CEPS, #03741)*. **Activities** Events/meetings; projects/programmes. **Publications** *Deliberative Democracy in the EU. Countering Populism with Participation and Debate.* (2020) by Steven Blockmans and Sophia Russack; *Representative Democracy in the EU – Recovering Legitimacy* (2019) by Steven Blockmans and Sophia Russack; *Direct Democracy in the EU – The Myth of a Citizens' Union* (2018) by Steven Blockmans and Sophia Russack.
Members Institutes (38) in 25 countries:
Austria, Belgium, Bulgaria, Cyprus, Czechia, Denmark, Estonia, Finland, France, Germany, Greece, Iceland, Ireland, Italy, Latvia, Lithuania, Netherlands, North Macedonia, Poland, Romania, Slovakia, Spain, Sweden, Türkiye, UK. [2020.05.20/XJ3216/y/**F**]

♦ European Policy for Intellectual Property (EPIP) 08243

SG Dept Economics/Management/Statistics, Univ of Milano Bicocca, Piazza dell'Ateneo Nuovo, 20126 Milan MI, Italy.
URL: http://www.epip.eu/
History Founded 7 Oct 2005, Santiago de Compostela (Spain), developing out of a network financed by *European Commission (EC, #06633)* (2003-2005). Registered in accordance with Danish law. **Aims** Be a leading European platform for analysis and discussion of intellectual property systems and intangible assets; encourage research regarding economic, legal, social, political and historical aspects of intellectual property rights at national, European and international levels; contribute ideas, concepts and discussions that will promote innovation, productivity and growth in Europe and beyond; inform and encourage policy-oriented discussion involving political and administrative bodies and stakeholders in Europe; cooperate with other associations with similar objectives. **Structure** General Assembly (annual, at Conference); Board; Executive Committee. **Languages** English. **Staff** 2.00 FTE, voluntary. **Finance** Members' dues. **Activities** Events/meetings; training/education; networking/liaising. **Events** *Annual Conference* Berlin (Germany) 2018, *Annual Conference* Bordeaux (France) 2017, *Annual Conference* Oxford (UK) 2016, *Annual Conference* Glasgow (UK) 2015, *Annual Conference* Brussels (Belgium) 2014.
Members Full in 24 countries and territories:
Australia, Austria, Azerbaijan, Belgium, Canada, Denmark, France, Germany, Israel, Italy, Japan, Korea Rep, Luxembourg, Netherlands, Norway, Poland, Portugal, Russia, Spain, Sweden, Switzerland, Taiwan, UK, USA.
IGO Relations None. **NGO Relations** None. [2018.09.29/XJ4154/**E**]

♦ European Policy Management Authority for Grid Authentication in e-Science (EUGridPMA) 08244

Contact address not obtained. E-mail: concerns@eugridpma.org.
URL: http://www.eugridpma.org/
Aims Coordinate the trust fabric for e-Science authentication in Europe. **NGO Relations** Member of: *International Grid Trust Federation (IGTF, #13738)*. Collaborates with: *Asia Pacific Grid Policy Management Authority (APGrid PMA, no recent information)*; *EGI Foundation (EGI.eu, #05395)*. [2011/XJ3975/**F**]

♦ European Policy Network on the Education of Children and Young People with a Migrant Background / see SIRIUS – Policy Network on Migrant Education (#19291)

♦ European Policy Network on School Leadership (EPNoSL) 08245

Coordinator Foundation for Research and Technology – Hellas, N Plastira 100, Vassilika Vouton, 700 13 Heraklion, Greece. T. +302810391584. Fax +302810391801.
URL: http://www.schoolleadership.eu/
History 2011. **Aims** Promote knowledge and experience sharing, collaboration, and planning of policies, enabling school leadership to address challenges of equity and learning in Europe's schools. **Structure** Project Management Committee (PMC). Advisory Board; Scientific Advisory Group. Coordinated by Foundation for Research and Technology, Greece. **Languages** English. **Staff** Paid. **Finance** Funding from *European Commission (EC, #06633)* – DG Education and Culture, in the framework of Lifelong Learning Programme. **Activities** Events/meeting; research/documentation; politics/policy/regulatory. Active in: Austria, Belgium, Cyprus, Denmark, Estonia, Finland, France, Germany, Greece, Hungary, Ireland, Italy, Latvia, Lithuania, Malta, Netherlands, Poland, Portugal, Slovenia, Spain, Sweden, UK. **Publications** *EPNoSL Newsletter* (3 a year).
Members Academies; associations; capacity building organizations; ministries; experts. Academies in 10 countries:
Austria, Bulgaria, Denmark, Estonia, Finland, Lithuania, Netherlands, Slovenia, Sweden, UK.
Associations (7):
Association for Teacher Education in Europe (ATEE, #02949); *European Federation of Education Employers (EFEE, #07101)*; *European Network for Improving Research and Development in Educational Leadership and Management (ENIRDELM, #07927)*; *European Parents' Association (EPA, #08142)*; *European Providers of Vocational Education and Training (EUproVET, #08289)*; *European School Heads Association (ESHA, #08431)*; *European Trade Union Committee for Education (ETUCE, #08926)*.
Capacity building organizations in 9 countries:
Austria, Belgium, Bulgaria, Greece, Hungary, Lithuania, Portugal, Slovenia, UK.
Ministries of 11 countries:
Belgium, Cyprus, Estonia, France, Germany, Greece, Italy, Latvia, Poland, Spain, Sweden. [2016.10.24/XJ8297/y/**F**]

♦ European Polio Union (EPU) 08246

Pres Polio Denmark, Fjeldhammervej 8, 2610 Rødovre, Denmark.
Registered Address c/o Assn Belge des Paralysés, Chaussée de Gand 1434, 1082 Brussels, Belgium.
URL: http://www.europeanpolio.eu/
History Registered in accordance with Belgian law: 0817 863 022. **Aims** Work across all countries in Europe to strive for greater recognition of the issues facing those affected by polio and Post Polio Syndrome. **Structure** Board, comprising President, Treasurer, Secretary and four members. **Languages** English, French, German, Italian, Spanish. **Staff** 2.00 FTE, voluntary. **Finance** Members' dues. Voluntary contributions. **Activities** Events/meetings. **Events** *Annual General Meeting* Rheinsberg (Germany) 2018, *Conference* Stockholm (Sweden) 2017, *Annual General Meeting* Bratislava (Slovakia) 2016, *Australasia Pacific Post-Polio Conference* Sydney, NSW (Australia) 2016, *Annual General Meetings* London (UK) 2015. **Publications** *EPU Newsletter* (2 a year).
Members Full in 16 countries:
Belgium, Czechia, Denmark, France, Georgia, Germany, Hungary, Ireland, Italy, Netherlands, Norway, Portugal, Slovakia, Spain, Sweden, UK.
Affiliate in 4 countries. Membership countries not specified.
NGO Relations Member of: *European Federation of Neurological Associations (EFNA, #07177)*. Associate member of: *European Disability Forum (EDF, #06929)*. [2017.09.21/XJ0183/**D**]

♦ European Political Science Association (EPSA) 08247

Admin Office c/o EPS Academic, Nirvana Roscath, Glenealy, CO. WICKLOW, Ireland. T. +353868619632. E-mail: ken.benoit@epsanet.org – info@epsanet.org.
URL: http://epsanet.org/
History 2010. **Aims** Represent and promote political science in Europe; foster development in postgraduate training of political scientists in Europe; promote undergraduate teaching of political scientists in Europe; facilitate networking by political scientists worldwide. **Structure** Executive Committee, including President and President-Elect. **Events** *Annual Conference* Prague (Czechia) 2022, *Annual Conference* 2021, *Annual Conference* 2020, *Annual Conference* Belfast (UK) 2019, *Annual Conference* Vienna (Austria) 2018. **Members** Individuals. Membership countries not specified. [2019.06.04/XJ6392/**D**]

♦ European Political Science Network / see ECPR European Political Science Network (#05339)

♦ European Political Strategy Centre (EPSC) 08248

Head European Commission, 1049 Brussels, Belgium. T. +3222962328.
URL: http://ec.europa.eu/epsc/
History 1989, as the Forward Studies Unit, by *European Commission (EC, #06633)*, to function as a small think thank staffed with EU officials reporting directly to the EC President. Developed into the *Group of Policy Advisers (GOPA)*, May 2000, under the direct authority of the EC President. Restructured 2004, when changed title to *Bureau of European Policy Advisers (BEPA)*. Restructured under current title, Nov 2014, by EC President Jean-Claude Juncker. **Aims** Provide the EC President, his College of Commissioners and the Commission Directorates General with strategic thinking and policy advice. **Structure** Head; Deputy Head. Coordination Unit. **Activities** Politics/policy/regulatory. **Events** *Conference on Challenges and Choices for Europe* Brussels (Belgium) 2019, *Conference on Global Trends to 2030* Brussels (Belgium) 2018, *Conference on Shaping the Future in a Fast-Changing World* Brussels (Belgium) 2018, *High-Level Conference on Shaping our Future* Brussels (Belgium) 2018, *Meeting on Global Europe as an Investment Destination* Brussels (Belgium) 2018. **Publications** *BEPA Monthly*. [2019/XJ4911/**E**]

♦ **European Polycarbonate Sheet Extruders (EPSE)** **08249**
Contact c/o EuPC, Avenue de Cortenbergh 71, 1000 Brussels, Belgium. T. +3227324124. Fax +3227324218. E-mail: info@epse.org.
URL: http://www.epse.org/
History 2003. Sector group of *European Plastics Converters (EuPC, #08216)*. Merged activities of *European Association of Manufacturers of Polycarbonate Sheet (EAMPCS, inactive)*, Feb 2005. **Aims** Promote polycarbonate sheets in all its applications; carry out data collection; develop quality and technical standards. **Structure** General Assembly. Executive Committee; Technical Committee.
Members Full; associate. Companies (10) in 7 countries:
Austria, Belgium, France, Germany, Israel, Italy, Sweden. [2020/XM0255/D]

♦ European Polyester Terephthalate Film Manufacturers Association (inactive)

♦ **European Polymer Dispersions and Latex Association (EPDLA)** **08250**
Manager c/o CEFIC, Rue Belliard 40, Bte 15, 1040 Brussels, Belgium. T. +3224369323.
Assistant address not obtained.
URL: http://specialty-chemicals.eu/epdla/
History 1991. A sector group of *Conseil européen de l'industrie chimique (CEFIC, #04687)*. **Structure** General Assembly; Steering Committee; Task Forces (6).
Members Western European manufacturers of polymer dispersions and lattices (25) in 9 countries:
Belgium, Czechia, Finland, France, Germany, Italy, Netherlands, Switzerland, UK. [2020/XE3101/E]

♦ **European Polymer Federation (EPF)** **08251**
Chairperson Heyrovskeho nam 2, 162 06 Prague 6, Czechia.
Gen Sec viale T Michel 11, Dipto di Scienze, 15121 Alessandria AL, Italy.
URL: https://www.epfwebsite.org/
History Mar 1986. **Aims** Coordinate and stimulate the activities of European countries in the areas of science, technology and applications of synthetic and natural macromolecules; facilitate exchange of information between members; encourage dissemination of scientific and technical knowledge; promote exchange of young researchers within European countries. **Structure** General Assembly; Committee; Executive Board. **Languages** English. **Staff** None. **Finance** No fees. **Activities** Events/meetings; networking/liaising; research and development. **Events** *European Polymer Conference (EUPOC 2022)* Bertinoro (Italy) 2022, *European Polymer Congress* Prague (Czechia) 2022, *European Polymer Congress* Prague (Czechia) 2021, *Biennial Congress* Heraklion (Greece) 2019, *Biennial Congress* Lyon (France) 2017. **Publications** *e-Polymers* – online journal.
Members National academic and industrial organizations (23 full and 5 associate members) in 26 countries:
Austria, Belgium, Bulgaria, Croatia, Czechia, Denmark, Estonia, Finland, France, Germany, Greece, Israel, Italy, Latvia, Netherlands, Poland, Portugal, Russia, Slovakia, Slovenia, Spain, Sweden, Switzerland, Türkiye, UK, Ukraine.
NGO Relations Affiliated with (1): *European Science Foundation (ESF, #08441)* (seat of registered office).
[2022/XD1154/D]

♦ European Polyol Association / see European Association of Polyol Producers (#06157)
♦ European Polyolefin Clingfilm Association (inactive)

♦ **European Polysaccharide Network of Excellence (EPNOE)** **08252**
Pres Centre de Mise en Forme des Matériaux, Mines ParisTech, 1 rue Claude Daunesse, BP207, 06904 Sophia Antipolis CEDEX, France. T. +33493957466. Fax +33492389752.
URL: http://www.epnoe.eu/
Aims Ensure effective cooperation to enhance polysaccharide innovation within the *EU*; perform multidisciplinary *research* on polysaccharides; develop strong links with industry to invent new materials; educate young scientists; disseminate polysaccharide knowledge at all levels of society. **Structure** Board, including President and 2 Vice-Presidents (Research; Education). **Events** *International Polysaccharide Conference* Nantes (France) 2021, *International Polysaccharide Conference* Aveiro (Portugal) 2019, *International Polysaccharide Conference* Jena (Germany) 2017, *International Polysaccharide Conference* Warsaw (Poland) 2015, *International Polysaccharide Conference* Nice (France) 2013. **Publications** *EPNOE Newsletter*.
Members Laboratories (16) in 9 countries:
Austria, Finland, France, Germany, Netherlands, Poland, Romania, Slovenia, UK. [2013/XJ0373/E]

♦ European Polyvinyl Film Manufacturers Association (inactive)

♦ **European Pond Conservation Network (EPCN)** **08253**
Contact c/o Pond Conservation, School of Life Sciences, Oxford Brookes Univ, Gipsy Lane, Headington, Oxford, OX3 0BP, UK. T. +441865483694. E-mail: serrano@us.es.
URL: http://www.europeanponds.org/
History 30 Oct 2004, Geneva (Switzerland), deriving from 1st European Pond Workshop. Registered in accordance with Swiss law. **Aims** Promote conservation of ponds and their biodiversity in a changing European landscape. **Structure** Steering Committee of 9 members. **Staff** Voluntary. **Activities** Knowledge management/information dissemination; research and development; politics/policy/regulatory. **Events** *Workshop* Huesca (Spain) 2014, *Workshop* Luxembourg 2012, *European pond workshop / Workshop* Berlin (Germany) 2010, *International conference on Mediterranean temporary ponds* Mahón (Spain) 2009, *European pond workshop / Workshop* Valencia (Spain) 2008. **Publications** *EPCN Newsletter*. *The Pond Manifesto* (2008) in English, French, German, Italian, Serbian, Spanish. **Members** Participants in 35 countries. Membership countries not specified. **IGO Relations** *Secretariat of the Convention of Wetlands (#19200)*.
[2016.06.01/XM2954/F]

♦ **European Popular Culture Association (EPCA)** **08254**
Pres IIPC, Cultural History, Univ of Turku, FI-20014 Turku, Finland.
URL: http://epcablog.wordpress.com/
History 2011. **Aims** Promote popular cultures studies in the European region. **Languages** English. **Staff** 6.00 FTE, paid. **Finance** Sources: meeting proceeds; members' dues. **Activities** Events/meetings. **Events** *Annual Conference* Krakow (Poland) 2022, *Annual Conference* Limerick (Ireland) 2019, *Annual Conference* Prague (Czechia) 2018, *Annual Conference* London (UK) 2017, *Annual Conference* Nanterre (France) 2016. **Publications** *Journal of European Popular Culture*. [2021.02.17/XJ9583/D]

♦ **European Portable Battery Association (EPBA)** **08255**
SG c/o Kellen, Av de Tervuren 188A, Box 4, 1150 Brussels, Belgium. T. +3227611602. E-mail: epba@kellencompany.com.
URL: http://www.epbaeurope.net/
History 1957, as *Association of European Dry Battery Manufacturers – Association des fabricants européens de piles électriques (EUROPILE) – Vereinigung Europäischer Trockenbatterie-Hersteller*. Present name adopted 1993. EU Transparency Register: 71549072613-57. **Aims** Support the common interests of members regarding portable batteries and *battery chargers* with European institutions and other leading international bodies to provide consumers with complete *power* solutions which are sustainable across their life-cycle. **Structure** Annual General Meeting; Board of Directors; Working Groups (2). **Languages** English. **Staff** 1.50 FTE, paid. **Finance** Members' dues. **Activities** Knowledge management/information dissemination; politics/policy/regulatory; standards/guidelines. **Events** *Annual General Meeting* Brussels (Belgium) 2014, *Annual General Meeting* Brussels (Belgium) 2013, *Annual General Meeting* Brussels (Belgium) 2012, *Annual General Meeting* Brussels (Belgium) 2011, *Annual General Meeting* Brussels (Belgium) 2010. **Publications** Reports; studies.
Members Regular (8) manufacturers in 8 countries. Membership countries not specified. Associate (1) manufacturers. Membership country not specified.
Associate (1) manufacturers. Membership country not specified.
IGO Relations Recognized by: *European Commission (EC, #06633)*. Involved in the work of: *United Nations Committee of Experts on the Transport of Dangerous Goods and on the Globally Harmonized System of Classification and Labelling of Chemicals (Committee of Experts on TDG and GHS, #20543)*.
[2019.12.17/XD2953/D]

♦ European Portable Electric Power Tool Manufacturers' Association / see European Power Tool Association (#08264)

♦ European Port Community Systems Association / see International Port Community Systems Association (#14623)
♦ European Port Data Processing Association (inactive)

♦ **European Position Determination System (EUPOS)** **08256**
Chairman Geodetic and Cartographic Inst Bratislava, Chlumeckeho 4, 827 45 Bratislava, Slovakia.
Vice-Chairman Univ of Latvia, Jelgavas street 3-718, Riga LV-1004, Latvia.
URL: http://www.eupos.org/
History Founded 2002, Berlin (Germany) by representatives of national-level policy makers and scientific institutions in the field of geodesy in Central and Eastern Europe. Organization structure changes and membership revised, 2014, Warsaw (Poland). **Aims** Establish a uniform Differential Global *Navigation Satellite* System (DGNSS) basis infrastructure in Europe; act as a European-wide DGNSS service providers branch organization. **Structure** Council; Executive Board. **Languages** English. **Staff** 2 FTE, voluntary or paid by a member institution and part of their duties delegated to EUPOS. **Finance** All activities financed directly by members. **Activities** Guidance/assistance/consulting; advocacy/lobbying/activism; research and development; events/meetings. **Events** *International Symposium* Berlin (Germany) 2011, *International Symposium* Brussels (Belgium) 2010, *International Symposium* Berlin (Germany) 2009, *International Symposium* Berlin (Germany) 2008.
Members Full: Public authorities of 13 countries:
Bulgaria, Czechia, Estonia, Germany, Hungary, Latvia, Lithuania, Moldova, North Macedonia, Poland, Romania, Slovakia, Slovenia.
Associate: Public authorities of 2 countries:
Albania, Uzbekistan.
Observer: Public authority of 1 country:
Germany.
IGO Relations Member of: *International Committee on Global Navigation Satellite Systems (ICG, #12775)*. Cooperates with: *European Union Agency for the Space Programme (EUSPA, #08974)*. **NGO Relations** Cooperates with: *Council of European Geodetic Surveyors (#04890)*; *EuroGeographics (#05684)*; *European Reference Organization for Quality Assured Breast Screening and Diagnostic Services (EUREF, #08338)*.
[2019.12.12/XJ2492/F*]

♦ European Postal Financial Services Commission (inactive)
♦ European Post Giro Directors Group / see EUROGIRO – Giro, Postbank, Commercial Bank Payment Institutions Organizations Worldwide (#05687)
♦ European Post-Graduate Training Institute in Health Care / see Groupe pluri-professionnelle européen de reflexion et de formation en santé (#10766)
♦ European Potash Producers Association (#02872)

♦ **European Potato Trade Association (EUROPATAT)** **08257**
Association européenne du commerce des pommes de terre – Asociación Europea del Comercio de Patatas – Europäische Union des Kartoffelshandels
SG Rue de Trèves 49-51, Bte 8, 1040 Brussels, Belgium. T. +3227771585. Fax +3227771586. E-mail: secretariat@europatat.eu.
URL: http://www.europatat.eu/
History 12 Jan 1952, Paris (France). Founded following preliminary meeting, 1951, Assmannshausen (Germany FR). Statutes modified, 1 Sep 1952, Moorslede (Belgium). New statutes adopted, 5 Jun 2003, Ostend (Belgium). Current statutes adopted, 2010, Edinburgh (UK). Former names and other names: *European Union of the Wholesale Potato Trade* – former (1952 to 2003); *Union européenne du commerce de gros des pommes de terre (UECGPT)* – former (1952 to 2003); *Europäische Union des Kartoffelgrosshandels* – former (1952 to 2003); *European Union of the Wholesale Potato Merchants* – former (1952 to 2005); *Union européenne du commerce des pommes de terre (EUROPATAT)* – former (2003); *European Union of the Potato Trade* – former (2003); *Unión Europea del Comercio de Patatas* – former (2003); *Europäische Union des Kartoffelshandels* – former (2003). Registration: Banque-Carrefour des Entreprises, Start date: 2010, Belgium; EU Transparency Register, No/ID: 16057181340-75. **Aims** Protect the interests of wholesale potato merchants, in particular: develop international commercial activity in wholesale potato trading; protect professional and commercial interests on both European and international levels; represent the profession within official and international organizations; define common policy to further technical and commercial advancement of all traders and with particular emphasis on maintaining free trade in potatoes. **Structure** General Assembly; Board; Commissions; Working Groups. Includes: *European Committee on the Rules and Usages of Inter-European Trade in Potatoes (European RUCIP Committee, #06666)*. **Languages** English. **Staff** 2.00 FTE, paid. **Activities** Standards/guidelines. **Events** *Congress* Dublin (Ireland) 2022, *Congress* 2021, *Congress* Brussels (Belgium) 2020, *Congress* Oslo (Norway) 2019, *Congress* Brussels (Belgium) 2018. **Information Services** *Rules and Usages for the Inter-European Trade in Potatoes*.
Members National associations in 16 countries:
Austria, Belgium, Czechia, France, Germany, Hungary, Ireland, Italy, Netherlands, Norway, Poland, Portugal, Slovakia, Spain, Switzerland, UK.
Companies (40); associate members (7). Membership countries not specified.
IGO Relations Observer status with (1): *Codex Alimentarius Commission (CAC, #04081)*. Cooperates with (1): *United Nations Economic Commission for Europe (UNECE, #20555)*. **NGO Relations** Member of (1): *Federation of European and International Associations Established in Belgium (FAIB, #09508)*. [2021.02.17/XD5990/t/D]

♦ **European Poultry, Egg and Game Association (EPEGA)** **08258**
Association européenne du commerce des oeufs, de la volaille et du gibier – Europäischer Vereiniging der Eier-, Wild- und Geflügel-, Wirtschaft
Gen Manager Konrad-Zuse Platz 5, 53227 Bonn, Germany. T. +4922895960-15. Fax +4922895969-50. E-mail: info@epega.org.
President address not obtained.
URL: http://www.epega.org/
History 19 Mar 1970, as *Confédération des détaillants en volaille et gibier des pays de la CEE – Verband der Wild- und Geflügeleinzelhändler der EWG-Länder – Confederazione dei Rivenditori di Pollame e Selvaggina dei Paesi della CEE – Confederatie van Kleinhandelaren in Wild en Gevogelte in de EEG Landen – Samorganisationen af Detailhandlere inden for Vildt- og Fjerkraesektoren i EØF-Landene*. Took over activities of *EUWEP Committee on Poultry and Game (inactive)*. Subsequently changed German title to *Europäischer Verband des Wild- und Geflügel-, Gross- und Aussenhandels* and, in 2001, changed English title to *European Poultry and Game Association (EPGA)*. EU Transparency Register: 98538474751-91. **Aims** Support and defend the professions of poultry and game retailer and wholesaler. **Structure** Officers: President; Secretary. **Finance** Members' dues.
Members National federations in 5 countries:
Austria, Belgium, France, Germany, Netherlands.
Included in the above, 1 organization listed in this Yearbook:
European Poultry and Game Association (EPG, #08259).
Individuals in 3 countries:
Luxembourg, Poland, UK.
IGO Relations Recognized by: *European Commission (EC, #06633)*. [2017.06.26/XE5601/E]

♦ European Poultry and Game Association / see European Poultry, Egg and Game Association (#08258)

♦ **European Poultry and Game Association (EPG)** **08259**
Europäischer Verband des Wild- und Geflügel- Gross- und Aussenhandels
Contact c/o EPEGA, Konrad-Zuse Platz 5, 53227 Bonn, Germany. T. +4922895960-15. Fax +4922895969-50. E-mail: info@epega.org.
URL: http://epg.epega.org/
History Previously also known under the acronym *EPGA*. **Aims** Promote and represent members' interests through regular information and advice, representing common interests in relation to authorities and institutions, and promoting cooperation between members and with external parties. **Events** *Symposium* Berlin (Germany) 2015. **Publications** *EPG Newsletter*. **Members** Companies; national associations; individuals. Membership countries not specified. **NGO Relations** Member of: *European Poultry, Egg and Game Association (EPEGA, #08258)*. Took over activities of: *EUWEP Committee on Poultry and Game (inactive)*.
[2015/XD7836/D]

♦ **European Powder Metallurgy Association (EPMA)** **08260**
Association européenne de la métallurgie des poudres
Exec Dir 1 ave du Général de Gaulle, 60500 Chantilly, France. T. +33344581524. E-mail: info@epma.com.
Registered Office Maison des Assoc Internationales, Rue Washington 40, 1050 Brussels, Belgium.
URL: http://www.epma.com/
History 26 Apr 1984. Former names and other names: *European Powder Metallurgy Federation (EPMF)* – former (1984 to 1988); *Fédération européenne de la métallurgie des poudres* – former (1984 to 1988); *Europäische Vereinigung für Pulvermetallurgie* – former (1984 to 1988). Registration: Start date: 6 Jul 1989, France; Banque-Carrefour des Entreprises, No/ID: 0442.396.412, Start date: 2 Jan 1991, Belgium. **Aims** Promote and develop Powder Metallurgy (PM) in Europe; represent the European PM industry within Europe and internationally; develop the future of PM. **Structure** General Assembly; Council; Executive Board; Committees (7). **Languages** English. **Staff** 10.80 FTE, paid. **Finance** Members' dues. Other sources: congress fees; European projects; industrial projects. **Activities** Awareness raising; training/education; knowledge management/information dissemination; research and development; standards/guidelines; awards/prizes/competitions; events/meetings. **Events** *European Powder Metallurgy Congress* Glasgow (UK) 2025, *European Powder Metallurgy Congress* Malmö (Sweden) 2024, *European Powder Metallurgy Congress* Lisbon (Portugal) 2023, *World Powder Metallurgy Congress* Lyon (France) 2022, *European Powder Metallurgy Congress* Lisbon (Portugal) 2021. **Publications** *EPMA News* (4 a year). Membership Directory; Annual Report.
Members Full; Affiliate; Associate; Individual; Junior membership. Full (90) in 16 countries:
Austria, Belgium, Denmark, Finland, France, Germany, Italy, Liechtenstein, Poland, Portugal, Romania, Serbia, Spain, Sweden, Switzerland, UK.
Affiliate members (24) and consultants (4) in 11 countries:
Austria, Brazil, France, Germany, India, Italy, Luxembourg, Slovakia, Spain, Sweden, UK.
Associate (54) (non-voting) in 17 countries and territories:
Australia, Belgium, Brazil, Canada, France, Germany, India, Israel, Italy, Japan, Singapore, Spain, Sweden, Switzerland, Taiwan, UK, USA.
Individuals (97) in 26 countries:
Australia, Austria, Belgium, Canada, Czechia, Denmark, Estonia, France, Germany, Greece, Iran Islamic Rep, Ireland, Israel, Italy, Malaysia, Netherlands, Poland, Russia, Slovakia, Slovenia, Spain, Sweden, Switzerland, Thailand, UK, USA.
NGO Relations Member of: *Industry4Europe (#11181)*. Associate member of: *Association européenne des métaux (EUROMETAUX, #02578)*. [2022/XD0895/**D**]

♦ European Powder Metallurgy Federation / see European Powder Metallurgy Association (#08260)
♦ European Powered Flying Union (unconfirmed)

♦ **European Power Electronics and Drives Association (EPE)** **08261**
Association européenne en électronique de puissance et entraînements électriques
Mailing Address c/o VUB-IrW-ETEC, Pleinlaan 2, 1050 Brussels, Belgium. T. +3226292819. Fax +3226293620.
Registered Office c/o Tractebel, Simon Bolivarlaan 34-36, 1000 Brussels, Belgium.
URL: http://www.epe-association.org/
History 16 Nov 1983. Registration: Start date: 9 Jan 1989, Belgium. **Aims** Promote and coordinate exchange and publication of technical, scientific and economic information in the fields of power electronics and electrical drives in the countries of the European Union and the rest of the world. **Structure** General Assembly (annual). Executive Council, comprising 15 members. Bureau, consisting of President, Vice Presidents, Secretary and Treasurer. Permanent Secretariat, managed by Secretary-General. **Languages** English. **Staff** 1.00 FTE, paid. **Finance** Members' dues. **Activities** Chapters: Electric Drive Design and Applications; Components; Control; Wind Energy; Education. Publishing activity. Organizes Conferences (every 2 years); sponsors conferences. **Events** *European Conference on Power Electronics and Applications* Aalborg (Denmark) 2023, *European Conference on Power Electronics and Applications* Hannover (Germany) 2022, *European Conference on Power Electronics and Applications* Brussels (Belgium) 2021, *European Conference on Power Electronics and Applications* Lyon (France) 2020, *European Conference on Power Electronics and Applications* Genoa (Italy) 2019. **Publications** *EPE Journal* (4 a year).
Members Individuals (700) in 66 countries and territories:
Albania, Australia, Austria, Belarus, Belgium, Bosnia-Herzegovina, Brazil, Bulgaria, Canada, Chile, China, Croatia, Cyprus, Czechia, Denmark, Egypt, Estonia, Finland, France, Georgia, Germany, Greece, Hong Kong, Hungary, Iceland, India, Indonesia, Iraq, Ireland, Israel, Italy, Japan, Korea DPR, Korea Rep, Latvia, Lebanon, Lithuania, Luxembourg, Malta, Mexico, Netherlands, New Zealand, North Macedonia, Norway, Poland, Portugal, Romania, Russia, Saudi Arabia, Serbia, Singapore, Slovakia, Slovenia, South Africa, Spain, Sri Lanka, Sweden, Switzerland, Taiwan, Thailand, Türkiye, UK, Ukraine, USA, Venezuela, Vietnam.
NGO Relations Conference activity with constituent societies of *Institute of Electrical and Electronics Engineers (IEEE, #11259)*. [2023/XD4514/v/**D**]

♦ **European Powerlifting Federation (EPF)** **08262**
Gen Sec Calle Galena 5, Casa 44, Villapiedra, 03189 Orihuela, Castellón, Spain. T. +34650041559.
URL: http://www.europowerlifting.org/
History 1977. Current by laws adopted 20 May 1987, most recently amended 1998. A regional federation of *International Powerlifting Federation (IPF, #14630)*. **Aims** Group all eligible amateur athletic clubs, organizations and groups in Europe active in powerlifting; develop standardized competitive rules according to the IPF rules; establish and enforce rules which govern international amateur powerlifting; establish and maintain a system for recognizing and approving records. **Structure** Congress (annual meeting, prior to Men's European Powerlifting Championship); Executive Committee. **Languages** English. **Staff** 1.00 FTE, voluntary. **Finance** Sources: smaller international contracts. Budget (annual): euro 60,000. **Activities** Sporting activities. **Publications** *EPF Newsletter*.
Members National affiliates representing amateur athletic clubs, organizations and other groups in Europe active in the field. Full in 36 countries:
Armenia, Austria, Belarus, Belgium, Bulgaria, Croatia, Czechia, Denmark, Estonia, Finland, France, Georgia, Germany, Greece, Hungary, Iceland, Ireland, Israel, Italy, Latvia, Lithuania, Luxembourg, Netherlands, Norway, Poland, Portugal, Romania, Russia, Serbia, Slovakia, Slovenia, Spain, Sweden, Switzerland, UK, Ukraine.
Provisional in 2 countries:
Bosnia-Herzegovina, Malta. [2016.03.07/XD5989/**D**]

♦ European Power Plant Suppliers Association / see Energy Technologies Europe (#05477)

♦ **European Power Supplies Manufacturer's Association (EPSMA)** ... **08263**
Secretariat 20 Little Haseley, Oxford, OX44 7LH, UK. T. +447712134294. E-mail: secretariat@epsma.org.
URL: http://www.epsma.org/
History 1995. Founded as a grouping of the type *European Economic Interest Grouping (EEIG, #06960)*. Withdrew from EEIG status, 31st Dec 2020, and converted to UKEEIG. **Aims** Provide a forum for discussing and progressing issues of common concern to the power supply industry, for the benefit of power supply manufacturers and users alike. **Structure** Management Committee; Technical Committee. **Languages** English. **Staff** 0.50 FTE, paid. **Finance** Sources: members' dues. Annual budget: 40,000 GBP. **Activities** Networking/liaising; politics/policy/regulatory; standards/guidelines; training/education. **Publications** Technical guidelines on regulatory and other issues relating to the power conversion industry (about 2 a year).
Members Full; associate. Companies (23) in 10 countries:
Belgium, Finland, France, Germany, Ireland, Italy, Netherlands, Sweden, Switzerland, UK.
Supplier members (3) in 2 members:
Germany, UK.
Affiliate members (5) in 5 countries:
Ireland, Netherlands, Spain, Switzerland, UK.
NGO Relations Cooperates with (1): *European Committee for Electrotechnical Standardization (CENELEC, #06647)* (Liaison Organization). [2022.05.10/XD8954/**D**]

♦ **European Power Tool Association (EPTA)** **08264**
Association européenne de l'outillage électrique – Verband der Europäischen Elektrowerkzeug-Hersteller
Main Office Rue Marie de Bourgogne 58, 1000 Brussels, Belgium. E-mail: eich@epta.eu.
URL: http://www.epta.eu/
History Sep 1952, on an informal basis, as *European Portable Electric Power Tool Manufacturers' Association – Association des constructeurs européens de machines électro-portatives – Vereinigung der Europäischen Elektrowerkzeug-Hersteller*. Current name and Constitution adopted 31 Jan 1984, Milan (Italy). Registration: AISBL/IVZW, Belgium; EU Transparency Register, No/ID: 460603337124-71. **Aims** Preserve free and fair competition; ensure exchange of technical, economic and environmental data among members; foster cooperation with European authorities and other entities; seek dialogue with professional and economic organizations whose members do not belong to the Association. **Structure** General Assembly; Board. **Languages** English. **Staff** 1.50 FTE, paid. **Finance** Members' dues. **Activities** Politics/policy/regulatory. **Events** *Biennial General Assembly* Milan (Italy) 2016, *Biennial General Assembly* London (UK) 2014, *Biennial General Assembly* Moscow (Russia) 2012, *Biennial General Assembly* Germany 2010, *Biennial General Assembly* Sofia (Bulgaria) 2008. **Publications** *EPTA Newsflash* (4 a year).
Members Full (27): manufacturing companies. Associate (2): national associations. Members in 12 countries and territories:
Bulgaria, Finland, Germany, Hong Kong, Ireland, Italy, Japan, Liechtenstein, Russia, Sweden, UK, USA.
IGO Relations Recognized by: *European Commission (EC, #06633)*. **NGO Relations** Member of: *Industry4Europe (#11181); RECHARGE (#18627)*. [2020/XD3653/**D**]

♦ **European Power Transmission Distributors Association (EPTDA)** ... **08265**
Main Office Grensstraat 7, bus 3, 1831 Diegem, Belgium. T. +3226600501. Fax +3226603821. E-mail: info@eptda.org.
URL: http://www.eptda.org/
History May 1998. Initially founded as an affiliated organization of (USA) *Power Transmission Distributors Association (PTDA)*. Former names and other names: *EMEA Power Transmission Distributors Association* – alias. Registration: No/ID: BE0866898896, Belgium. **Aims** Provide information, education and business tools required to profitably meet the needs of the industrial market place; advance distribution and strengthen members to become more successful, profitable and competitive in a changing market environment. **Structure** General Assembly; Board of Directors; Executive Committee; Advisory Council; Committees (4); Manufacturer Council. **Languages** English. **Activities** Networking/liaising; research and development; training/education; knowledge management/information dissemination; events/meetings. **Events** *Annual Convention* Warsaw (Poland) 2022, *Annual Convention* Warsaw (Poland) 2021, *Annual Convention* Warsaw (Poland) 2020, *Annual Convention* Santa Cruz de Tenerife (Spain) 2019, *Annual Convention* London (UK) 2018. **Publications** *e-Motion* (6 a year) – electronic newsletter; *Manufacturer Focus* (4 a year) – newsletter. *Blue Book* – print and online. Reports; guidelines; recommendations. Information Services: Maintains a virtual library of industry and economic reports and sources of information. **Information Services** *EPTDA Member Locator, EPTDA Product Locator*.
Members Organizations (over 250) in 28 countries:
Austria, Belgium, Canada, Denmark, Egypt, Finland, France, Germany, Greece, Hungary, Iceland, Ireland, Italy, Netherlands, Nigeria, Norway, Poland, Portugal, Russia, Slovenia, South Africa, Spain, Sweden, Switzerland, Türkiye, UK, United Arab Emirates, USA. [2021/XD8613/**D**]

♦ **European PPP Operating Companies in Infrastructure and Services (E3PO)** **08266**
Secretariat Rue Philippe le Bon 15, 1000 Brussels, Belgium. T. +3222306550.
URL: http://www.e3po.org/
History Founded 17 Dec 2008. PPP stands for *Public Private Partnership*. Registered in accordance with Belgian law. EU Transparency Register: 424726117325-78. **Aims** Promote the benefits that public authorities and users of public services can derive from the management of SGEI in partnerships with the private sector. **Structure** General Assembly; Board of Directors; Bureau; Secretariat.
Members National, European and international federations. Full in 3 countries:
France, Italy, Spain.
Included in the above, 2 organizations listed in this Yearbook:
European Federation of Intelligent Energy Efficiency Services (EFIEES, #07145); International Federation of Private Water Operators (AquaFed, #13517). [2019/XM8681/y/**D**]

♦ European Pragmatism Association (unconfirmed)

♦ **European Precious Metals Federation (EPMF)** **08267**
Main Office Ave de Tervueren 168, Box 6, 1150 Brussels, Belgium. T. +3227756323. E-mail: info@epmf.be.
URL: http://www.epmf.be/
History 2006. Registration: No/ID: BE0821614645, Belgium. **Aims** Represent and defend the interests of members; represent the European Precious Metals industry sector vis-à-vis European authorities on topics such as safety of chemicals and end-of-life/waste management, access to raw materials, resource efficiency, recycling and sustainability, energy and climate change, transparency, trade, customs, tax and competitiveness. **Structure** General Assembly; Board; Committees (4); Trade and Competitiveness Network. **Languages** Dutch, English, French, Spanish. **Staff** 2.00 FTE, paid. **Events** *Plenary Meeting* Milan (Italy) 2015, *Plenary Meeting* Bern (Switzerland) 2014, *Plenary Meeting* Stockholm (Sweden) 2013, *Plenary Meeting* Antwerp (Belgium) 2012, *Plenary Meeting* Cambridge (UK) 2011. **NGO Relations** Member of: *Association européenne des métaux (EUROMETAUX, #02578); Industry4Europe (#11181)*. Partners/Network: *International Platinum Group Metals Association (IPA, #14602); International Precious Metals Institute (IPMI); Silver Institute (SI, #19282); World Gold Council (WGC, #21541)*; national associations. [2020/XM2771/**D**]

♦ European Pressphoto Union (inactive)

♦ **European Pressure Die Casting Committee (EPDCC)** **08268**
Comité européen pour le moulage sous pression
Manager address not obtained. T. +492116871215.
Administration address not obtained. T. +492116871163.
URL: http://www.gdm-metallguss.de/GDM/deutsch/EPDCC.htm
History 1953. Rules defined and agreed, 1955; new rules and guidelines adopted 29 Sep 1975, Stockholm (Sweden). **Aims** Further cooperation among die casters in Europe by encouraging exchange of technical information, undertaking joint promotional work, exchanging works visits. **Structure** Full Committee (meeting at least once a year). Conference (every 3 years). Secretariat, supplied jointly by *'British Metal Casting Association'* in collaboration with other main European associations. **Languages** English. **Staff** 0.50 FTE, paid. **Finance** Members' dues. **Events** *Conference / Triennial Conference* Germany 2000, *Triennial Conference* Montreux (Switzerland) 1996, *Triennial Conference* Solihull (UK) 1993, *Triennial conference* Munich (Germany FR) 1990, *Triennial conference* Florence (Italy) 1987. **Publications** *Die Casting Glossary* in English, French, German, Italian, Spanish. Conference proceedings.
Members Die casting associations or firms in 13 countries:
Austria, Belgium, Finland, France, Germany, Italy, Netherlands, Norway, Portugal, Spain, Sweden, Switzerland, UK.
IGO Relations Recognized by: *European Commission (EC, #06633)*. **NGO Relations** *International Organization for Standardization (ISO, #14473)*. [2018/XD0836/**D**]

♦ **European Pressure Equipment Research Council (EPERC)** **08269**
Conseil européen de la recherche en équipements sous pression – Europäischer Rat für Druckgeräte Forschung
Contact Sant'Ambrogio Servizi Industriali srl, Piazza Carlo Donegani 8, 20124 Milan MI, Italy. T. +39335380634. E-mail: info@eperc-aisbl.eu.
Registered Office Blue Point Brussels, Bd Auguste Reyers 80, 1030 Brussels, Belgium. T. +3226161304.
URL: http://www.eperc-aisbl.eu/
History 20 Oct 1995, Paris (France). Founded by *International Council for Pressure Vessel Technology (ICPVT, #13064)*. Registration: 3ème Bureau de l'Enregistrement d'Ixelles, No/ID: 0842668296, Start date: 29 Apr 2011, Belgium, Bruxelles. **Aims** Serve as a network in support of the non-nuclear pressure equipment industry and Small and Medium Enterprises (SMEs) in particular. **Structure** General Assembly; Board; Task Groups (12). **Languages** English, French. **Finance** Annual budget: 12,000 EUR (2021). **Activities** Research/documentation. **Events** *Annual General Assembly* Milan (Italy) 2021, *Annual General Assembly* Milan (Italy) 2020, *International Conference* Rome (Italy) 2019, *Annual General Meeting* Brussels (Belgium) 2005, *Annual General Meeting* Ghent (Belgium) 2003.
Members Companies; SMEs; Individuals. Members in 7 countries:
Austria, Belgium, France, Germany, Italy, Netherlands, UK. [2021.10.05/XD6915/v/**D**]

♦ European Pressure Sensitive Manufacturers Association (inactive)

♦ European Pressure Ulcer Advisory Panel (EPUAP) 08270

Contact EPUAP Business office, Provaznická 11, 110 00 Prague, Czechia. T. +420251019379. E-mail: office@epuap.org.
URL: http://www.epuap.org/

History Dec 1996, London (UK). **Aims** Provide a platform for clinicians, researchers, educators, policy makers, industry and the public to collaboratively work on improved *health* outcomes for those at risk or suffering from pressure ulcers; provide relief for persons suffering from, or at risk of, pressure ulcers, through research and education of the public and by influencing pressure ulcer policy in all European countries towards an adequate patient-centered and cost effective pressure ulcer care. **Structure** Executive Board; Trustees; Committees (4). **Languages** English. **Staff** 7.00 FTE, paid. **Finance** Sources: members' dues; sponsorship. **Activities** Events/meetings; training/education. **Events** *Annual Meeting* Leeds (UK) 2023, *Pressure Ulcer* Porto (Portugal) 2022, *Annual Meeting* Prague (Czechia) 2022, *Meeting* Prague (Czechia) 2021, *Focus Meeting* Sønderborg (Denmark) 2021. **Publications** *EPUAP Review. Prevention and Treatment of Pressure Ulcers/Injuries: Clinical Practice Guideline* (3rd ed 2019); *Science and Practice of Pressure Ulcer Management.*
Members Individuals in 21 countries:
Austria, Belgium, Czechia, Denmark, Finland, France, Germany, Greece, Hungary, Israel, Italy, Japan, Netherlands, Norway, Portugal, Slovakia, Spain, Sweden, Switzerland, UK, USA. [2023.02.17/XE3736/v/E]

♦ European Prevention of Alzheimer's Dementia Consortium (EPAD) . . 08271

Project Coordinator address not obtained. E-mail: info@ep-ad.org.
Project Coordinator address not obtained.
URL: http://ep-ad.org/

Aims Conduct collaborative research to better understand the early stages of Alzheimer's disease and prevent dementia before symptoms occur. **Structure** General Assembly; Steering Committee; Executive Committee. **Activities** Research/documentation. **Events** *Conference* Geneva (Switzerland) 2019, *General Assembly* Amsterdam (Netherlands) 2018, *General Assembly* Stockholm (Sweden) 2017.
Members Universities, pharmaceutical companies and patient organizations. Membership countries not specified. Partners include 1 organization listed in this Yearbook:
Partners include 1 organization listed in this Yearbook:
IGO Relations *European Commission (EC, #06633).* **NGO Relations** *European Federation of Pharmaceutical Industries and Associations (EFPIA, #07191).* [2018/XM6502/F]

♦ European Pride Organizers Association (EPOA) 08272

Pres Rue du Marché au Charbon 42, 1000 Brussels, Belgium. E-mail: president@europride.info – info@europride.info – secretary@europride.info.
Events Manager address not obtained.
URL: http://www.europride.info/

History London (UK). Registration: Banque-Carrefour des Entreprises, No/ID: 0836.217.697, Start date: 21 May 2011, Belgium. **Aims** Promote *lesbian, gay,* bisexual and transgender pride on a pan-European level; empower and support local and national pride organizations in planning and promoting pride celebrations. **Structure** Board of Directors, including President, Secretary and Treasurer. **Activities** Awards/prizes/ competitions; events/meetings. **Events** *Annual General Meeting* Turin (Italy) 2022, *Annual General Meeting* 2021, *Annual General Meeting* 2020, *Annual General Meeting* Bilbao (Spain) 2019, *Annual General Meeting* Vienna (Austria) 2018.
Members Full; Associate. Members in 36 countries:
Australia, Austria, Belgium, Bosnia-Herzegovina, Bulgaria, Canada, Czechia, Denmark, France, Georgia, Germany, Greece, Hungary, Iceland, Ireland, Italy, Latvia, Lithuania, Luxembourg, Malta, Moldova, Montenegro, Netherlands, North Macedonia, Norway, Poland, Portugal, Romania, Serbia, Slovakia, Spain, Sweden, Switzerland, Türkiye, UK, Ukraine.
NGO Relations Member of (1): *ILGA World (International Lesbian, Gay, Bisexual, Trans and Intersex Association, #11120). InterPride (#15965)*; national associations. [2020/XD9119/D]

♦ European Primary Aluminium Association (inactive)

♦ European Primary Care Cardiovascular Society (EPCCS) 08273

Chair Dept Primary Care Health Sciences, 2nd Floor, 23-38 Hythe Bridge Street, Oxford, OX1 2ET, UK.
Sec address not obtained.
URL: http://www.epccs.eu/

History 2000. **Aims** Provide a focus of support, education, research, and policy on issues relating to cardiovascular disease within primary care settings. **Structure** Board, comprising Chairman and 7 members. **Events** *Annual Scientific Meeting* Lisbon (Portugal) 2019, *Annual Scientific Meeting* Barcelona (Spain) 2018, *Annual Scientific Meeting* Prague (Czech Rep) 2015, *Annual Scientific Meeting / Scientific Meeting* Brussels (Belgium) 2014, *Annual Scientific Meeting / Scientific Meeting* London (UK) 2013. **Publications** *E-EPCCS Journal.* **NGO Relations** Affiliated with (1): *World Organization of Family Doctors (WONCA, #21690).* [2020/XJ5261/D]

♦ European Primary Schools Association (inactive)

♦ European Primate Veterinarians (EPV) 08274

Registered Office c/o Ctr de Primatologie, Louis Pasteur Univ, Fort Foch, 67207 Niederhausbergen, France. E-mail: epvassociation@gmail.com.
URL: https://www.epvassociation.org/

History 29 Sep 2007, Tortosa (Spain), at constituent Assembly. Registered in accordance with French law. **Aims** Promote fellowship among private veterinarians to facilitate data exchange, research in primatology and education; provide a European interface to promote the dissemination of information, advice, expertise and recommendations relating to the health, care and welfare of non-human primates (NHPs), plus all circumstantial measures to protect professionals working with NHPs. **Structure** General Assembly (annual). Board, comprising President, Vice-President, Treasurer, Secretary and 3 trustees. **Languages** English. **Staff** Voluntary. **Finance** Members' dues. **Activities** Events/meetings. **Events** *Conference* Barcelona (Spain) 2022, *Symposium* Toulouse (France) 2016, *Symposium* Marseille (France) 2010, *Symposium* London (UK) 2009, *Symposium* Leipzig (Germany) 2008.
Members Individuals in 11 countries:
Belgium, France, Germany, Israel, Italy, Mauritius, Netherlands, Spain, Sweden, Switzerland, UK.
NGO Relations Member of: *European Animal Research Association (EARA, #05903).* [2022/XM3235/D]

♦ European Printer Manufacturers and Importers (no recent information)

♦ European Printing Ink Association (EuPIA) 08275

Exec Manager Boulevard du Triomphe 172, 4th Floor, 1160 Brussels, Belgium. T. +3228972020. E-mail: eupia@cepe.org.
URL: http://www.eupia.org/

History 2003. Founded as a group within *Conseil européen de l'industrie des peintures, des encres d'imprimerie et des couleurs d'art (CEPE, #04688).* **Aims** Promote the image of the printing ink industry along the supply chain, the public and the media. **Structure** Council; Management Team; Technical Committee. **Events** *Annual Conference* Budapest (Hungary) 2021, *Conference* Budapest (Hungary) 2021, *Annual Conference* London (UK) 2019, *Annual Conference* Lisbon (Portugal) 2014, *Meeting* Vienna (Austria) 2011.
Members National associations in 14 countries:
Austria, Belgium, Denmark, Finland, France, Germany, Greece, Italy, Netherlands, Portugal, Spain, Sweden, Switzerland, UK.
NGO Relations Supporter of Declaration of on Paper Recovery, maintained by: *European Paper Recycling Council (EPRC, #08139).* [2020/XJ1252/E]

♦ European Prison Education Association (EPEA) 08276

Association européenne pour l'éducation en milieu pénitentiaire
Chair c/o PI Nieuwegein, De Liesbosch 100, 3439 LC Nieuwegein, Netherlands. E-mail: chair@epea.org – secretary@epea.org.
URL: http://www.epea.org/

History 1991. Constitution adopted 1993. **Aims** Support and assist professional development of those involved in prison education through European cooperation; work with related professional organizations; support research in the field of education in prisons. **Structure** General Council (every 2 years, usually in combination with Conference); Steering Committee. **Languages** English. **Staff** Voluntary. **Finance** Members' dues. Conference proceeds. **Activities** Training/education; events/meetings. **Events** *International Conference* Dublin (Ireland) 2019, *International Conference* Vienna (Austria) 2017, *International Conference* Antwerp (Belgium) 2015, *International Conference / Conference* Hveragerdi (Iceland) 2013, *International conference* Paralimni (Cyprus) 2009. **Publications** *EPEA Newsletter.*
Members Branches in 7 countries and territories:
Belgium, Greece, Ireland, Netherlands, Norway, Portugal, Switzerland.
Organizational members in 6 countries:
Belgium, Cyprus, Czechia, Portugal, Sweden, UK.
Consultative Status Consultative status granted from: *Council of Europe (CE, #04881)* (Participatory Status).
NGO Relations Member of: *Conference of INGOs of the Council of Europe (#04607).* [2020.03.04/XD1913/D]

♦ European Prison Litigation Network (EPLN) 08277

Head Office 21 Ter rue Voltaire, 75011 Paris, France. E-mail: hugues.de-suremain@prisonlitigation.org – julia.krikorian@prisonlitigation.org.
URL: http://www.prisonlitigation.org/

History 2013. Previously also known as *Réseau Contentieux Pénitentiaire (RCP) – Prison Litigation Network (PLN).* Registration: No/ID: SIRET 800 075 806 00011, France. **Aims** Heighten the judicial protection of prisoners' fundamental rights in Member States of the Council of Europe. **Structure** Board; Scientific Council; Secretariat. **Activities** Networking/liaising; capacity building; research/documentation. **Consultative Status** Consultative status granted from: *Council of Europe (CE, #04881)* (Participatory Status). [2020/XM6168/F]

♦ European Privacy Association (EPA) 08278

Address not obtained.
URL: http://europeanprivacyassociation.eu/

Aims Provide a 'space' for bringing together experts across Europe, engaging with them so as to seek new policies to enhance privacy, e-security and *data protection.* **Structure** Executive Board, comprising Chair, Vice-Chair, Treasurer, Executive Officer and 3 members. **IGO Relations** Participant in Fundamental Rights Platform of: *European Union Agency for Fundamental Rights (FRA, #08969).* [2017/XJ6190/D]

♦ European Privacy Institute (no recent information)
♦ European Private Equity and Venture Capital Association / see Invest Europe – The Voice of Private Capital (#15997)
♦ European Probiotic Association (inactive)
♦ European Process Intensification Conference (meeting series)

♦ European Process Safety Centre (EPSC) 08279

Main Office c/o DECHEMA, Theodor-Heuss-Allee 25, 60486 Frankfurt-Main, Germany.
URL: http://www.epsc.org/

History 1992, by *European Federation of Chemical Engineering (EFCE, #07074).* Previously also referred to in French and German as *Centre européen de sécurité des procédés – Europäisches Zentrum für Anlagensicherheit.* Registered in accordance with the law of England and Wales. **Aims** Provide objective information on process safety matters; encourage development and use of *best practice* to prevent process incidents associated with processing and storing of *hazardous* materials and to mitigate the consequences of any such event; serve as an independent technical focus for process safety in Europe; advise on specific issues of general industry concern; provide a single source of technical and scientific background information in connection with European safety *legislation.* **Structure** Management Board; Subcommittees; Working Parties; Secretariat at IChemE, Rugby (UK). **Languages** English. **Staff** 3.50 FTE, paid. **Finance** Industry subscriptions; European Commission Project funding; income from public events. **Activities** Commissions research work in process safety. Subcommittees (4): Major Accident Prevention Policies and Management Systems (including auditing); Safety Reports; Inspection; Land-Use Planning. Working party on incident and near-miss data. Contact groups (3): Fire Protection of Pressurized LPG Storage and Prevention of BLEVEs; Safety-Related Failure Frequencies; Mitigation of Gas Dispersion. Offers annual EPSC Award. Assists access to safety information and process safety databases; provides independent safety information to legislators and standards bodies and information on training materials. **Events** *International Conference on Safety* Ahmedabad (India) 2014, *Conference* Antwerp (Belgium) 2008, *Conference* Schiphol (Netherlands) 2006, *Conference* Frankfurt-Main (Germany) 2002, *Safety integrity – the implications of IEC 61508 and other standards for the process industries* Paris (France) 1999. **Publications** *Hazard Identification Methods* (2003); *Safety Health and Environment Management Systems for Small to Medium Sized Enterprises* (2000); *Safety Issues in a Dynamic Business Environment* (2000); *HAZOP: Guide to Best Practice* (1999); *Safety Integrity: Implications of IEC 61508 and Other Standards for the Process Industries* (1999); *Atmospheric Dispersion* (1998); *Safety Performance Measurement* (1995); *Safety Management Systems* (1994). Annual Report; research reports.
Members Full; Associate companies and organizations in 10 countries:
Austria, Belgium, France, Germany, Italy, Netherlands, Spain, Sweden, Switzerland, UK.
IGO Relations Represented at: *OECD (#17693).* Participates in working groups of: *European Commission (EC, #06633)* (DGs Research and Environment). **NGO Relations** Acts as process safety advisor on technical matters to: *Conseil européen de l'industrie chimique (CEFIC, #04687).* Also acts as an industry representative to various Technical Working Groups at European level on Seveso implementation. [2019/XE3257/E]

♦ European PRO Committee (EUROPRO) 08280

Secretariat 24 rue Chauchat, 75009 Paris, France. T. +33155347680. E-mail: contact@europrocommittee.org.
URL: http://europrocommittee.org/

History Originally a more formally constituted organization; currently a loose association. Original title: *Association of Committees of Simplified Procedures for International Trade within the European Community and the European Free Trade Association (EUROPRO) – Association des comités de simplification des procédures du commerce international au sein de l'Union européenne et de l'Association européenne de libre-échange.* Registration: EU Transparency Register, No/ID: 075062722939-38, Start date: 4 Aug 2016. **Aims** Remove red tape in international *trade*; ensure that regulatory burden does not frustrate *business* competitiveness. **Structure** General Meeting (annual); Council; Secretariat. **Finance** Members' dues: maximum euro 1,250. **Activities** Working groups (3): Official Procedures; Payments; Trade Facilitation in Eastern- and Mid-European Countries.
Members Active in 4 countries:
Croatia, France, Germany, Netherlands.
Included in the above, 1 organization listed in this Yearbook:
Europäisches Forum für Aussenwirtschaft, Verbrauchssteuern und Zoll (EFA).
Other members in 13 countries:
Belgium, Bulgaria, Czechia, Finland, Greece, Hungary, Iceland, Ireland, Italy, Norway, Poland, Spain, Sweden.
Included in the above, 2 organizations listed in this Yearbook:
EFTA (#05391) (Secretariat); *European Sea Ports Organisation (ESPO, #08453).*
IGO Relations *United Nations Economic Commission for Europe (UNECE, #20555).* **NGO Relations** *European Association for e-Identity and Security (EEMA, #06077); Simpler Trade Procedures Board (SITPRO, inactive).* [1998.06.01/XE3269/y/F]

♦ European Producers Club (EPC) 08281

Contact 42 rue du Fbg du Temple, 75011 Paris, France. T. +33144900613. Fax +33144900319. E-mail: info@europeanproducersclub.org.
URL: https://www.europeanproducersclub.org/

History 1993. Founded within the framework of the *General Agreement on Trade in Services (GATS, 1994)* negotiations. **Aims** Keep members up-to-date with the latest developments in the film industry in Europe and across the world. **Structure** Board of Directors; Executive Committee. **Activities** Advocacy/lobbying/activism.
Members Producers and production companies (over 130) in 35 countries:
Austria, Belgium, Bulgaria, Canada, Croatia, Cyprus, Denmark, Finland, France, Germany, Greece, Hungary, Iceland, Ireland, Italy, Latvia, Lithuania, Luxembourg, Moldova, Netherlands, North Macedonia, Norway, Poland, Portugal, Romania, Russia, Serbia, Slovakia, Slovenia, Spain, Sweden, Switzerland, Türkiye, UK, Ukraine. [2022/AA2991/D]

♦ **European Producers of Specialty Aluminas (EPSA)** **08282**
Contact CEFIC, Rue Belliard, Box 15, 1040 Brussels, Belgium. T. +3224369458. E-mail: caj@cefic.be.
URL: http://specialty-chemicals.eu/epsa/
History 2012, as a Sector group of *Conseil européen de l'industrie chimique (CEFIC, #04687)*. Replaced *European Producers of Electrofused Minerals (EPEM, inactive)*. **Languages** English, French. **Staff** 0.20 FTE, paid.
Members Companies (6) in 6 countries:
Austria, Belgium, France, Germany, Hungary, UK. [2020/XJ5953/**E**]

♦ European Producers Union of Renewable Ethanol / see ePURE (#05517)

♦ **European Professional Association for Transgender Health (EPATH)** **08283**
Registered Address Succalaan 26, 9070 Destelbergen, Belgium. E-mail: contact@epath.eu.
URL: https://epath.eu/
History Dec 2013. Officially launched 14 Feb 2014, Bangkok (Thailand), at conference of *World Professional Association For Transgender Health (WPATH, #21739)*. Registration: Banque-Carrefour des Entreprises, No/ID: 0720.495.808, Start date: 10 Sep 2018, Belgium; EU Transparency Register, No/ID: 351523847997-63, Start date: 27 Oct 2022. **Aims** Promote mental, physical and social health of transgender people in Europe; increase the quality of life among transgender people in Europe; ensure transgender people's rights for healthy development and well-being. **Structure** Board of Directors; Scientific Committee. Divisions (3): Academic; Clinical; Policy. **Activities** Events/meetings. **Events** *Conference* Killarney (Ireland) 2023, *Conference* Gothenburg (Sweden) 2021, *Conference* Rome (Italy) 2019, *Conference* Belgrade (Serbia) 2017, *Conference* Ghent (Belgium) 2015. **Members** European WPATH members. Membership countries not specified. **NGO Relations** Cooperates with (1): *World Professional Association For Transgender Health (WPATH, #21739)*.
[2022/XM4242/**E**]

♦ **European Professional Beekeepers Association (EPBA)** **08284**
Association européenne des apiculteurs professionnels – Europäischer Berufsimkerverband
Managing Dir KOCH Imkerei-Technik eK, Hauptstrasse 67, 77728 Oppenau, Germany. T. +497804910810. E-mail: epba@imkerei-technik.de.
URL: http://www.professional-beekeepers.eu/
History Oct 1997. Officially launched Jan 1998. Reincorporated as European Economic Interest Grouping (EEIG), Mar 2011. Registration: EU Transparency Register, No/ID: 897117717544-36. **Aims** Represent the interests of beekeepers, with a focus on commercial and professional beekeepers, as well as related environmental interests towards all relevant authorities, institutions, politicians, media and the public, at international European, members states, regional and local levels; encourage Europe wide and international cooperation of members; coordinate activities. **Structure** General Assembly. Officers: President; 3 Vice-Presidents; Secretary; Treasurer. **Staff** Voluntary. **Finance** Members' dues (annual). **Events** *European Beekeeping Congress BEECOME* Krakow (Poland) 2021, *Symposium on Collecting and Sharing Data on Bee Health* Brussels (Belgium) 2017.
Members Organizations (14) representing professional and semi-professional beekeepers in Europe, in 15 countries:
Austria, Cyprus, Czechia, Estonia, Finland, France, Germany, Greece, Hungary, Ireland, Malta, Poland, Slovakia, Sweden, Switzerland.
NGO Relations Member of: *International Federation of Beekeepers' Associations (APIMONDIA, #13370)*. Cooperates with: *European Agricultural Machinery Association (CEMA, #05846)*. [2021/XD7142/t/**D**]

♦ European Professional Club Rugby (unconfirmed)
♦ European Professional Drivers Association (unconfirmed)
♦ European Professional Football Leagues / see European Leagues (#07672)
♦ European Professionals Network (unconfirmed)
♦ European Professional Women's Network / see PWN Global – Professional Women's Network (#18584)
♦ European Profiles and Panels Producers Federation (inactive)

♦ **European Programme for Integration and Migration (EPIM)** **08285**
Main Office Rue Royale 94, 1000 Brussels, Belgium. T. +3222352419. E-mail: contact@epim.info.
URL: http://www.epim.info/
History 2005, as an initiative of *Network of European Foundations (NEF, #17019)*. Currently in its 4th phase. **Aims** Strengthen he role played by civil society in influencing EU policy developments; advocate for constructive approaches to migration in Europe. **Structure** Steering Committee; Executive Committee; Working Groups. Secretariat.
Members Partner organizations (11) in 8 countries:
Belgium, France, Germany, Italy, Netherlands, Portugal, Spain, UK.
Included in the above, 8 organizations listed in this Yearbook:
Barrow Cadbury Trust; Calouste Gulbenkian Foundation; Company of St Paul; Joseph Rowntree Charitable Trust; King Baudouin Foundation (KBF); Oak Foundation; Open Society Foundations (OSF, #17763); Robert Bosch Foundation.
NGO Relations *European Citizen Action Service (ECAS, #06555)*. [2021/XM4431/y/**E**]

♦ European Project on Clean Clothes / see Clean Clothes Campaign (#03986)
♦ European Project for Digital Video Broadcasting / see DVB Project (#05147)
♦ European Projects Association (unconfirmed)
♦ European Promotion Association for Composite Tanks and Tubulars (inactive)

♦ **European Property Federation (EPF)** **08286**
Fédération européenne de la propriété immobilière (FEPI)
Deputy Dir Gen Bd Saint Michel 45, 1040 Brussels, Belgium. T. +3225144229. Fax +3225116721. E-mail: info@epf-fepi.com.
URL: http://www.epf-fepi.com/
History May 1997, Brussels (Belgium). A grouping of the type *European Economic Interest Grouping (EEIG, #06960)*. Registered in accordance with Belgian law. EU Transparency Register: 36120303854-92. **Aims** Represent all aspects of private property ownership and investment. **Structure** General Assembly. Managing Committee, including President and Chairman. Secretariat in Brussels (Belgium).
Members National organizations (16) in 12 countries:
Bulgaria, Denmark, Finland, Ireland, Italy, Netherlands, Norway, Portugal, Romania, Spain, Sweden, UK. [2014/XM2551/**D**]

♦ European Proprietary Medicines Manufacturers' Association / see Association of the European Self-Care Industry (#02543)
♦ European Prosthetics Association / see European Prosthodontic Association (#08287)

♦ **European Prosthodontic Association (EPA)** **08287**
Hon Sec Div Dental Biomaterials, Centre for Oral and Dental Medicine, Plattenstrasse 11, 8032 Zurich ZH, Switzerland.
URL: http://www.epadental.org/
History 6 Apr 1977, London (UK). Founded at Inaugural Conference. Former names and other names: *European Prosthetics Association* – alias; *European Prosthodontic Trust* – alias. **Aims** Further knowledge and promote the teaching and practice of prosthodontics in Europe. **Structure** Business Meeting (annual, at Conference); Council; Executive Committee; Board of Trustees. **Languages** English. **Staff** None. **Finance** Members' dues. **Activities** Training/education; certification/accreditation. **Events** *Annual Conference* Siena (Italy) 2022, *Annual Conference* Athens (Greece) 2021, *Annual Conference* Amsterdam (Netherlands) 2019, *Annual Conference* Madrid (Spain) 2018, *Annual Conference* Bucharest (Romania) 2017. **Publications** *European Prosthodontic Association eNewsletter* (annual).
Members Ordinary (individual doctors, dentists and scientists); Honorary. Members in 48 countries and territories:
Australia, Austria, Belgium, Bosnia-Herzegovina, Bulgaria, Canada, Croatia, Czechia, Denmark, Estonia, Finland, France, Georgia, Germany, Greece, Hong Kong, Hungary, India, Iran Islamic Rep, Ireland, Israel, Italy, Japan, Jordan, Korea Rep, Kosovo, Kuwait, Latvia, Lebanon, Lithuania, Netherlands, Nigeria, North Macedonia, Norway, Oman, Poland, Portugal, Qatar, Romania, Serbia, Slovakia, Spain, Sweden, Switzerland, Türkiye, UK, Ukraine, USA. [2022/XD2840/v/**D**]

♦ European Prosthodontic Trust / see European Prosthodontic Association (#08287)

♦ **European Proteomics Association (EuPA)** **08288**
Sec c/o Life Sci Service, Burggasse 12/11, 8010 Graz, Austria. T. +43316831439.
URL: http://www.eupa.org/
Aims Strengthen and promote fundamental research and applications, education and training in all areas of proteomics throughout Europe. **Structure** Executive Committee, including President. **Events** *Conference* Leipzig (Germany) 2022, *Conference* Potsdam (Germany) 2019, *Conference* Santiago de Compostela (Spain) 2018, *Conference* Dublin (Ireland) 2017, *Conference* Istanbul (Turkey) 2016.
Members National organizations in 8 countries:
Italy, Netherlands, Norway, Portugal, Spain, Sweden, Switzerland, UK. [2015/XM3663/**D**]

♦ **European Providers of Vocational Education and Training (EUproVET)** **08289**
Sec MBO Raad, Houttuinlaan 6, 3447 GM Woerden, Netherlands. T. +31348753552.
URL: http://www.euprovet.eu/
History 14 Jul 2009, Utrecht (Netherlands). EU Transparency Register: 69105262717-09. **Aims** Voice the interests of providers of vocational education and training and adult education within the European Union; reach common European goals on European policy level, in member states of the European Union and European countries which do not form part of the European Union. **Structure** Chairman; Secretary; Treasurer. **Languages** English. **Staff** None. **Finance** Members' dues. Budget (annual): about euro 5,000. **Activities** Training/education; events/meetings. **Events** *Conference* Nova Gorica (Slovenia) 2017.
Members Full in 6 countries:
Finland, Ireland, Lithuania, Netherlands, Slovenia, UK.
IGO Relations *European Quality Assurance in Vocational Education and Training (EQAVET, #08312)*. **NGO Relations** Member of: *European Policy Network on School Leadership (EPNoSL, #08245)*. Collaborates with: *European Association of Institutions of Higher Education (EURASHE, #06086); European Forum of Technical and Vocational Education and Training (EfVET, #07338); European Vocational Training Association (EVTA, #09075)*. [2017/XJ6859/**F**]

♦ **European Psychiatric Association (EPA)** **08290**
Association européenne de psychiatrie (AEP)
SG 15 av de la Liberté, 67000 Strasbourg, France. T. +33388239930. Fax +33388352973. E-mail: epa.assistant@europsy.net.
Main: http://www.europsy.net/
History 1983, Strasbourg (France). Founded by 12 French and German university psychiatrists. Former names and other names: *Association of European Psychiatrists* – former. **Aims** Improve psychiatry and mental health care in Europe. **Structure** Board and Executive Committee; Sections (23); Administrative Office in Strasbourg (France); also has office in Brussels (Belgium). **Languages** English, French. **Staff** 9.80 FTE, paid. **Finance** Sources: grants; meeting proceeds; members' dues. **Activities** Awards/prizes/competitions; events/meetings; financial and/or material support; publishing activities; research/documentation; training/education. **Events** *European Congress of Psychiatry* Paris (France) 2023, *European Congress of Psychiatry* 2022, *European Congress of Psychiatry* 2021, *European Congress of Psychiatry* 2020, *European Congress of Psychiatry* Warsaw (Poland) 2019. **Publications** *European Psychiatry* in English.
Members National societies/associations (43), representing over 80,000 European psychiatrists, in 40 countries:
Armenia, Austria, Azerbaijan, Belarus, Belgium, Bosnia-Herzegovina, Bulgaria, Croatia, Czechia, Denmark, Estonia, Finland, France, Georgia, Germany, Greece, Hungary, Iceland, Ireland, Israel, Italy, Latvia, Lithuania, Malta, Moldova, Netherlands, Norway, Poland, Portugal, Romania, Russia, Serbia, Slovakia, Slovenia, Spain, Sweden, Switzerland, Türkiye, UK, Ukraine.
Active individuals in 88 countries. Membership countries not specified.
Consultative Status Consultative status granted from: *Council of Europe (CE, #04881)* (Participatory Status).
NGO Relations Member of (1): *European Brain Council (EBC, #06391)*. Cooperates with (6): *European College of Neuropsychopharmacology (ECNP, #06612); European Federation of Associations of Families of People with Mental Illness (EUFAMI, #07051); European Federation of Psychiatric Trainees (EFPT, #07197); European Union of Medical Specialists (UEMS, #09001); Global Alliance of Mental Illness Advocacy Networks – Europe (GAMIAN Europe, #10211); World Psychiatric Association (WPA, #21741)*. [2022.05.11/XD5700/**D**]

♦ **European Psychiatric Nurses (HORATIO)** **08291**
Gen Sec address not obtained. E-mail: info@horatio-web.eu.
URL: http://www.horatio-web.eu/
History Apr 2006. **Aims** Represent interests of psychiatric nurses in Europe; increase cooperation with nursing organizations; advance the art and science of psychiatric nursing in Europe. **Structure** General Assembly (annual); Board; Expert Panel. **Languages** English. **Staff** Voluntary. **Finance** Contributions from members. **Events** *Congress* Berlin (Germany) 2020, *Congress* Copenhagen (Denmark) 2019, *Congress* Lisbon (Portugal) 2015, *Congress* Istanbul (Turkey) 2013, *Congress* Stockholm (Sweden) 2012.
Members Full national organizations and specialist sections in 10 countries:
Croatia, Cyprus, Czechia, Finland, Greece, Ireland, Malta, Netherlands, Norway, Sweden.
NGO Relations Member of: *Mental Health Europe (MHE, #16715)*. [2020/XM3035/**D**]

♦ **European Psychoanalytical Federation (EPF)** **08292**
Fédération européenne de psychanalyse (FEP) – Europäische Psychoanalytische Föderation
Contact Rue Gérard 35, 1040 Brussels, Belgium. T. +32476806497.
Gen Sec Ul Zeromskiego 9, 05-806 Komorów, Poland.
URL: https://www.epf-fep.eu/
History 1966, Geneva (Switzerland). **Aims** Facilitate *scientific* exchanges and communications between psychoanalytic societies. **Structure** Council, composed of the Presidents of the European societies. Executive Committee. **Languages** English, French, German. **Staff** 6.00 FTE, voluntary. **Finance** Members' dues. Budget (annual): Swiss Fr 250,000. **Activities** Organizes conferences, symposia and seminars on psychoanalytic theory practice and technique of adults and children. **Events** *Annual Conference* Cannes (France) 2023, *Annual Conference* Vienna (Austria) 2022, *Annual Conference* 2021, *Annual Conference* Vienna (Austria) 2020, *Annual Conference* Madrid (Spain) 2019. **Publications** *Bulletin intérieur* (annual) in English.
Members Psychoanalytical societies and study groups, in 22 countries:
Australia, Belgium, Czechia, Denmark, Finland, France, Germany, Greece, Hungary, Israel, Italy, Netherlands, Norway, Poland, Portugal, Romania, Serbia, Spain, Sweden, Switzerland, UK. [2021/XD0837/**D**]

♦ European Psycholinguistics Association (inactive)

♦ **European Public Administration Network (EUPAN)** **08293**
Contact c/o Fed Min-Civil Service, Hohenstaufengasse 3, 1010 Vienna, Austria. E-mail: eupan@bmoeds.gv.at.
URL: http://www.eupan.eu/
History Founded as an informal network. Former names and other names: *EPAN* – alias. Registration: Netherlands. **Aims** Stimulate and promote Europeanization in teaching public administration; provide a platform for exchange of information concerning Europeanization; facilitate dialogue among public administration teaching institutions in Europe. **Structure** Board, including Chairman. Advisory Board. **Languages** Dutch, English. **Activities** Common Assessment Framework (CAF). **Events** *Directors General Meeting* Helsinki (Finland) 2019, *Meeting* Helsinki (Finland) 2019, *Meeting* Copenhagen (Denmark) 2012, *Meeting* Stockholm (Sweden) 2009, *International quality conference for public administration in the European Union* Paris (France) 2008.
[2022/XF5872/**F**]

♦ **European Public Affairs Consultancies' Association (EPACA)** **08294**
Chairwoman Rue de la Loi 38, 1000 Brussels, Belgium. T. +3222300814. Fax +3227376940. E-mail: info@epaca.org.
URL: https://epaca.org/
History 28 Jan 2005. Registration: EU Transparency Register, No/ID: 8828523562-52, Start date: 28 Oct 2008. **Aims** Act as the representative *trade* body for public affairs consultancies working with EU institutions. **Structure** General Assembly; Management Committee; Secretariat. **Languages** English. **Finance** Sources: members' dues. **Activities** Advocacy/lobbying/activism; networking/liaising; training/education. **Events** *EPACA Charter Launch Meeting* Brussels (Belgium) 2014, *General Assembly* Brussels (Belgium) 2014.
Members Companies (34). Membership countries not specified. **NGO Relations** Member of (1): *Federation of European and International Associations Established in Belgium (FAIB, #09508)*. Cooperates with (1): *Society of European Affairs Professionals (SEAP, #19553)*. [2021/XM8119/**D**]

♦ European Public Choice Society (EPCS) 08295

Pres address not obtained. E-mail: contact@epcs-home.org.
URL: http://www.epcs-home.org/

History 1974, Basel (Switzerland). **Aims** Promote research and exchange ideas about the area of public choice, public finance and economics. **Structure** President; Board of 8 members. **Languages** English. **Staff** None. **Finance** Conferences are financed by sponsoring and contributions of members. **Events** *Meeting* Braga (Portugal) 2022, *Meeting* Lille (France) 2021, *Meeting* Lucerne (Switzerland) 2020, *Meeting* Jerusalem (Israel) 2019, *Meeting* Rome (Italy) 2018. **Publications** *European Journal of Political Economy*; *Public Choice*.
Members Scientists (200) from 26 countries:
Albania, Austria, Belgium, Canada, Czechia, Denmark, Estonia, Finland, France, Germany, Greece, Hungary, Ireland, Israel, Italy, Netherlands, Norway, Poland, Portugal, Slovakia, Slovenia, Spain, Sweden, Switzerland, Türkiye, USA.
NGO Relations *European Association of Law and Economics (EALE, #06104).* [2020/XD2611/v/D]

♦ European Public Health and Agriculture Consortium (EPHAC) 08296

Manager Rue de Trèves 49 – 51, 1040 Brussels, Belgium. T. +3222333875. Fax +3222333880.
URL: http://www.healthyagriculture.eu/

Aims Advocate for a healthier, more sustainable Common Agriculture Policy (CAP).
Members National and international organizations (7), including:
EuroHealthNet (#05693); *European Alcohol Policy Alliance (Eurocare, #05856)*; *European Public Health Alliance (EPHA, #08297).* [2014/XJ5559/y/D]

♦ European Public Health Alliance (EPHA) 08297

Alliance européenne pour la santé publique
SG Rue de Trèves 49-51 – boite 6, 1040 Brussels, Belgium. T. +3222303056. Fax +3222333880. E-mail: epha@epha.org.
URL: http://www.epha.org/

History Mar 1993, Brussels (Belgium). Registration: Banque Carrefour des Entreprises, No/ID: 0451.133.736, Start date: 12 Oct 1993, Belgium; EU Transparency Register, No/ID: 18941013532-08, Start date: 3 May 2010. **Aims** Promote and protect health interests of all people living in Europe; strengthen dialogue between EU institutions, citizens and NGOs in support of healthy public *policies*. **Structure** General Assembly; Executive Committee; Secretariat in Brussels (Belgium). **Languages** English. **Staff** 10.00 FTE, paid. **Finance** Members' dues. Other sources: projects partially funded by the *European Commission (EC, #06633)*; grants; fees from conferences; charitable donations. **Activities** Politics/policy/regulatory; awareness raising. **Events** *Annual Conference* Brussels (Belgium) 2017, *Annual Conference* Brussels (Belgium) 2016, *Conference on Healthy Innovation for All* Brussels (Belgium) 2016, *Annual Conference* Brussels (Belgium) 2014, *Annual Conference* Brussels (Belgium) 2013. **Publications** Electronic newsletter (12 a year). Annual Report; media manual for NGOs; platform manual for NGOs.
Members Full and Associate organizations in 31 countries:
Albania, Armenia, Austria, Azerbaijan, Belgium, Bulgaria, Croatia, Cyprus, Finland, France, Georgia, Germany, Ireland, Israel, Italy, Lithuania, Malta, Netherlands, North Macedonia, Norway, Poland, Portugal, Romania, Russia, Serbia, Slovenia, Spain, Switzerland, Türkiye, UK, Ukraine.
Included in the above, 46 organizations listed in this Yearbook:
- *AGE Platform Europe (#00557)*;
- *Association européenne des médecins des hôpitaux (AEMH, #02577)*;
- *Association of European Cancer Leagues (ECL, #02500)*;
- *Association of Natural Medicine in Europe (ANME)*;
- *Association of Schools of Public Health in the European Region (ASPHER, #02904)*;
- *EUROCAM (#05653)*;
- *Eurochild (#05657)*;
- *European Academy of Paediatrics (EAP, #05811)*;
- *European AIDS Treatment Group (EATG, #05850)*;
- *European Alcohol Policy Alliance (Eurocare, #05856)*;
- *European Association for the Study of the Liver (EASL, #06233)*;
- *European Association of Hospital Pharmacists (EAHP, #06074)*;
- *European Cancer Organisation (ECO, #06432)*;
- *European Central Council of Homeopaths (ECCH, #06467)*;
- *European Chiropractors' Union (ECU, #06538)*;
- *European Committee for Homeopathy (ECH, #06651)*;
- *European Council of Doctors for Plurality in Medicine (ECPM, #06816)*;
- *European Council of Optometry and Optics (ECOO, #06835)*;
- *European Federation of Homeopathic Patients' Associations (EFHPA, #07139)*;
- *European Federation of National Organisations Working with the Homeless (#07174)*;
- *European Federation of Patients' Associations for Anthroposophic Medicine (EFPAM, #07189)*;
- *European Federation of Salaried Doctors (#07209)*;
- *European Heart Network (EHN, #07467)*;
- *European Hematology Association (EHA, #07473)*;
- *European Institute of Women's Health (EIWH, #07574)*;
- *European Medical Students' Association (EMSA, #07764)*;
- *European Network for Smoking and Tobacco Prevention (ENSP, #08002)*;
- *European Network of Medical Residents in Public Health (Euronet MRPH, #07945)*;
- *European Pharmaceutical Students' Association (EPSA, #08197)*;
- *European Respiratory Society (ERS, #08383)*;
- *European Scientific Working Group on Influenza (ESWI, #08450)*;
- *European Shiatsu Federation (ESF, #08476)*;
- *European Society of Intensive Care Medicine (ESICM, #08632)*;
- *European Specialist Nurses Organisation (ESNO, #08808)*;
- *Health Action International (HAI, #10868)* (Europe);
- *International Council of Medical Acupuncture and Related Techniques (ICMART, #13046)*;
- *International Diabetes Federation Europe (IDF Europe, #13168)*;
- *Internationale Vereinigung Anthroposophischer Ärztegesellschaften (IVAA, #13314)*;
- *International Federation of Medical Students' Associations (IFMSA, #13478)*;
- *Médecins du Monde – International (MDM, #16613)*;
- *Mental Health Europe (MHE, #16715)*;
- *Pulmonary Hypertension Association Europe (PHA Europe, #18575)*;
- *Safe Food Advocacy Europe (SAFE, #19026)*;
- *Smoke Free Partnership (SFP, #19329)*;
- *VAS-European Independent Foundation in Angiology/Vascular Medicine (VAS, #20748)*;
- *World Confederation for Physical Therapy (WCPT, #21293)*.

NGO Relations Member of (4): *EU Alliance for a democratic, social and sustainable European Semester (EU Semester Alliance, #05565)*; *EU Civil Society Contact Group (CSCG, #05572)*; *European Public Health and Agriculture Consortium (EPHAC, #08296)*; *SDG Watch Europe (#19162)*. Supports (1): *European Alliance for the Statute of the European Association (EASEA, #05886).* [2021/XF1777/y/F]

♦ European Public Health Association (EUPHA) 08298

Exec Dir Postbox 1568, 3500 BN Utrecht, Netherlands. T. +31302729709. Fax +31302729729. E-mail: office@eupha.org.
Street Address Otterstraat 118-124, 3513 CR Utrecht, Netherlands.
Brussels Office Rue Belliard 15-17, 1040 Brussels, Belgium.
URL: http://eupha.org/

History Founded at a meeting of national public health associations. **Aims** Build capacity and knowledge in the field of public health; support practice and policy decisions through scientific evidence and producing and sharing knowledge with members and partners in Europe. **Structure** Governing Board; Executive Council. **Languages** English. **Staff** 3.50 FTE, paid. **Finance** Sources: meeting proceeds; members' dues; revenue from activities/projects; sale of publications. **Activities** Capacity building; events/meetings; knowledge management/information dissemination; publishing activities. **Events** *European Public Health Conference* Berlin (Germany) 2022, *European Public Health Conference* Dublin (Ireland) 2021, *European Public Heath Conference* Utrecht (Netherlands) 2020, *European Public Health Conference* Marseille (France) 2019, *European Public Health Conference* Ljubljana (Slovenia) 2018. **Publications** *EUPHA Newsletter* (12 a year); *European Journal of Public Health* (6 a year); *EUPHActs* (42 a year). Annual Report; statements.
Members National scientific associations (41); Institutional (24); Individual (7). Members in 46 countries:
Albania, Andorra, Armenia, Austria, Azerbaijan, Belgium, Bosnia-Herzegovina, Bulgaria, Croatia, Cyprus, Czechia, Denmark, Estonia, Finland, France, Georgia, Germany, Greece, Hungary, Ireland, Israel, Italy, Kazakhstan, Kosovo, Latvia, Lithuania, Luxembourg, Malta, Moldova, Nepal, Netherlands, North Macedonia, Norway, Poland, Portugal, Romania, Russia, Serbia, Slovakia, Slovenia, Spain, Sweden, Switzerland, Türkiye, UK, Ukraine.
Associate members, 8 organizations listed in this Yearbook:
Association of Schools of Public Health in the European Region (ASPHER, #02904); *European Association of Dental Public Health (EADPH, #06007)*; *European Forum for Primary Care (EFPC, #07326)*; *European Health Management Association (EHMA, #07458)*; *European Society for Prevention Research (EUSPR, #08712)*; *European Union of Medical Specialists (UEMS, #09001)* (Public Health section); *International Association for Communication in Healthcare (EACH, #11792)*; *International Union for Health Promotion and Education (IUHPE, #15778)*.
NGO Relations Member of: *World Federation of Public Health Associations (WFPHA, #21476)*. Observer to: *European Forum of Medical Associations and WHO (EFMA, #07320)*. Instrumental in setting up: *Agency for Public Health Education Accreditation (APHEA, #00555).* [2020.03.23/XD4046/y/D]

♦ European Public Health Students Association (inactive)

♦ European Public Law Organization (EPLO) 08299

Contact 2 Polygnotou and Dioskouron St, Plaka, 105 55 Athens, Greece. T. +302113110671. Fax +302292069813. E-mail: iskrapa@eplo.int – info@eplo.int.
URL: http://www.eplo.int/

History 27 Oct 2004, upon the initiative of the Hellenic Republic, on signing of "Agreement for the Establishment and Statute of the European Public Law Organization". Creation effective as of 10 Sep 2007, upon receipt by Depositary of notifications by 3 parties: Hellenic Republic; Republic of Italy; Republic of Cyprus. Initiatives for setting up EPLO proposed by *European Group of Public Law (EGPL, #07431)*. Acts as continuation of *European Public Law Centre (EPLC, inactive)*, which title it may continue to use, especially acting as a Greek institution. **Aims** Create and disseminate knowledge in the area of Public Law lato sensu and Governance, including but not limited to, inter alia, national, comparative and European public law, human rights law and environmental law and promotion of European values for a better generation of lawyers and democratic institutions worldwide. **Structure** Board of Directors. European Scientific Council – *European Group of Public Law (EGPL, #07431)*. Administrative Court; Board of Auditors; Executive Committee; Director/President. Includes: *Academy of European Public Law (#00037)*. **Languages** English, French, Irish Gaelic. **Staff** 25.00 FTE, paid. **Finance** Members' dues. Other sources: donations; educational activity; EU funded projects. **Activities** Training/education; guidance/assistance/consulting; awareness raising; research/documentation; publishing activities; events/meetings; capacity building. **Publications** *European Review of Public Law* (4 a year); *Central and Eastern European Legal Studies* (2 a year); *European Politeia* (2 a year). *Academy of European Public Law Series*; *European Environmental Law Series*; *European Papers* – series; *European Public Law Series*; *Stand Alone Editions*.
Members Signatory governments to the Agreement (17):
Albania, Armenia, Azerbaijan, Bosnia-Herzegovina, Bulgaria, Cyprus, Estonia, France, Georgia, Greece, Hungary, Italy, Moldova, Poland, Romania, Serbia, Ukraine.
Public Authorities (7); Universities (71). Membership countries not specified.
IGO Relations Observer status with (4): *ILO (#11123)*; *International Organization for Migration (IOM, #14454)*; *United Nations (UN, #20515)* (General Assembly); *World Intellectual Property Organization (WIPO, #21593)*.
NGO Relations Member of: *European Network of Implementing Development Agencies (EUNIDA, #07926)*. Partner of: *Global Forum on Law, Justice and Development (GFLJD, #10373)*. Memorandum of Understanding with: *Geneva Centre for Human Rights Advancement and Global Dialogue (GCHRAGD, #10120).* [2019.02.14/XJ1767/E*]

♦ European Public Prosecutor's Office (EPPO) 08300

Admin Dir Avenue John F Kennedy 11, L-1855 Luxembourg, Luxembourg. E-mail: info@eppo.europa.eu.
URL: https://www.eppo.europa.eu/

History Established through *Council of the European Union (#04895)* Regulation 2017/1939, 12 Oct 2017. Initially proposed by the Council, 2013. Functions as a decentralized agency of *European Union (EU, #08967)*. Operations officially commenced 1 June 2021. **Aims** Investigate and prosecute EU-fraud and other *crimes* affecting the Union's financial interests. **Structure** Central level with European Public Prosecutor and European Prosecutors (one per participating EU country). Decentralized level: European Delegated Prosecutors.
Members Participating Member States (22):
Austria, Belgium, Bulgaria, Croatia, Cyprus, Czechia, Estonia, Finland, France, Germany, Greece, Italy, Latvia, Lithuania, Luxembourg, Malta, Netherlands, Portugal, Romania, Slovakia, Slovenia, Spain.
IGO Relations Cooperates with (1): *Eurojust (#05698)*. **NGO Relations** Member of (1): *EU Agencies Network (EUAN, #05564).* [2021/XM4609/E*]

♦ European Public Real Estate Association (EPRA) 08301

Office Manager Square de Meeus 23, 9th fl, 1000 Brussels, Belgium. T. +3227391010. E-mail: info@epra.com.
CEO address not obtained.
URL: http://www.epra.com/

History Oct 1999. Registration: Banque-Carrefour des Entreprises, No/ID: 0811.738.560, Start date: 14 May 2009, Belgium; EU Transparency Register, No/ID: 09307393718-06, Start date: 9 Jun 2010. **Aims** Promote, develop and represent the European public real estate sector through provision of information to investors and stakeholders, active involvement in the public and political debate, improvement of the general operating environment, encouragement of best practices and cohesion, and strengthening of the industry; encourage greater investment in listed real estate companies in Europe. **Structure** Board of Directors; Working Committees. **Languages** Chinese, Dutch, English, French. **Staff** 19.00 FTE, paid. **Activities** Advocacy/lobbying/activism; capacity building; events/meetings; knowledge management/information dissemination; networking/liaising; research/documentation; standards/guidelines. **Events** *Conference* Paris (France) 2022, *Annual Conference* Brussels (Belgium) 2021, *Virtual Sustainability Summit* Brussels (Belgium) 2021, *Annual Conference* Brussels (Belgium) 2020, *Virtual Sustainability Summit* Brussels (Belgium) 2020. **Publications** *Chart Book* (12 a year); *Emerging Markets Review* (12 a year); *Monthly Market Review* (12 a year); *NAV Bulletin* (12 a year); *Statistical Bulletin* (12 a year); *Transactions Report* (12 a year); *EPRA Newsletter* (4 a year); *Global REIT Survey* (annual). Research reports; Index Ground-rules; EPRA Financial BPR and Sustainability sBPR; Industry Calendar.
Members Companies, investors and suppliers of the listed real estate industry representing over 450 billion euros of real estate assets and 94% of the market capitalization of the FTSE EPRA Nareit Europe Index. Members in 27 countries and territories:
Australia, Austria, Belgium, Canada, Finland, France, Germany, Greece, Hong Kong, Ireland, Israel, Italy, Japan, Luxembourg, Mauritius, Netherlands, Norway, Romania, Singapore, South Africa, Spain, Sweden, Switzerland, UK, United Arab Emirates, USA, Virgin Is UK.
IGO Relations Links with EU bodies and national regulators in Europe. **NGO Relations** Member of: *Cross Border Benefits Alliance-Europe (CBBA-Europe, #04969)*; *European Real Estate Forum (#08331).* [2022/XM1669/D]

♦ European Public Relations Confederation (inactive)

♦ European Public Relations Education and Research Association (EUPRERA) 08302

Admin Dir Bd du Jubilé 71 bte 3, 1080 Brussels, Belgium. E-mail: dpra@euprera.org – info@euprera.org.
URL: http://www.euprera.org/

History 1959. Originally set up within *Confédération européenne des relations publiques (CERP, inactive)*, as *European Association for Education and Research in Public Relations (CERP EDUCATION AND RESEARCH, inactive)*. Became an autonomous organization under current title, 2000. Registration: Banque-Carrefour des Entreprises, No/ID: 0478.953.039, Start date: 7 Jul 2002, Belgium. **Aims** Stimulate and promote innovative knowledge and practices of public relations education and research in Europe. **Structure** General Assembly; Board of Directors. **Languages** English. **Staff** Mainly voluntary. **Finance** Sources: members' dues; sponsorship. **Activities** Awards/prizes/competitions; events/meetings; knowledge management/information dissemination; networking/liaising; projects/programmes; publishing activities; research/documentation; training/education. Mainly Europe. **Events** *Annual Congress* Prague (Czechia) 2023, *Annual Congress* Vienna (Austria) 2022, *Annual Congress* Pamplona (Spain) 2021, *Annual Congress* Pamplona (Spain) 2020, *Annual*

Congress Zagreb (Croatia) 2019. **Publications** *Journal of Communication Management. Advances in Public Relations and Communication Management.* **Members** Individual; Institutional. About 500 members in 40 countries. Membership countries not specified. **NGO Relations** Partner of (7): *European Communication Research and Education Association (ECREA, #06675); Fundacom (#10039); Global Alliance for Public Relations and Communication Management (GA, #10223); Institute of Public Relations, London (IPR, no recent information); International Communication Association (ICA, #12814); International Public Relations Association (IPRA, #14671); MARPE Network (#16587).* Also partner of other international and national organizations. [2023.02.14/XD8996/**D**]

♦ European Public Services Committee / see European Federation of Public Service Unions (#07202)

♦ European Public Service Union 08303

Syndicat de la fonction publique européenne

Sec SFE, Rue Joseph II, Bâtiment J70, 01/200 Bloc A, 1049 Brussels, Belgium. T. +3222963127. Fax +3222964328. E-mail: osp-sfe@ec.europa.eu.
Pres address not obtained. T. +3222954357.
URL: http://www.conf-sfe.org/

History 1963, Brussels (Belgium), as *Union of International and European Civil Servants (UIECS) – Syndicat des fonctionnaires internationaux et européens (SFIE) – Verband der Internationalen und Europäischen Beamtem – Sindicato dei Funzionari Internazionali ed Europei – Bond van Internationale en Europese Ambtenaren*, to unite organizations in the European Communities, later extended to cover other international organizations. Present name adopted 1988. Previously also referred to in English as *Union of European Officials.* Subsequently changed name to *Union of European Civil Servants – Syndicat des fonctionnaires européens (SFE) – Sindicato de los Funcionarios Europeos – Verband der Europäischen Beamtem – Sindicato dos Funcionarios Europeus – Sindacato dei Funzionari Europei – Bond van Europese Ambtenaren – Europeiska Tjänstemäns Fackförening – Europaeiske Tjenestemaends Fagforening – Euroopan Virkamiesliitto – Sindikato Ipallilon Evropaikon Organismon.* SFE stems in its history and fundamental values from a movement which found its origin in the Christian inspired trade union movement. Also referred to as *Conf-SFE.* **Aims** Defend the individual and collective interests of all staff. **Structure** Organs: (1) Annual General Meeting. (2) Executive Committee, comprising 16 members. (3) Bureau, consisting of Chairperson, 3 Vice-Chairpersons, Secretary-General, Political Secretary, Treasurer and Delegate for organizational matters. (4) Audit Committee, made up of 3 members. (5) Litigation Committee made up of 3 members. *'Staff Representatives'* Local Staff Committee (CLP): 27 full members and 27 substitute members; Central Staff Committee: 41 full members and 41 substitute members. Editorial Board. Secretariat. **Languages** Dutch, English, French, German, Italian. **Finance** Members' dues. Funded by European officials and agents working mainly in the European Union. **Activities** Gives legal advice, information and replies to all questions concerning staff regulations, rights privileges, statutory obligations and tax matters; intervenes with the host country, the administration and/or line management at members' request; defends staff regulations by taking union action. Organizes union training days and courses. **Events** *Union day* Brussels (Belgium) 1999. **Publications** *Le panoptique* – review. *250 Questions about Europe* – in several languages.

Members Individuals employed by an institution or other body, governed by public or private law, working in the European field. International civil servants based in Brussels, Florence, Luxembourg, Paris, Strasbourg, i e in 4 countries:
Belgium, France, Italy, Luxembourg.

IGO Relations Staff representatives to: *European Commission (EC, #06633); European Parliament (EP, #08146).* **NGO Relations** Member of: *Confédération syndicale européenne (CSE, no recent information).* [2019/XE2748/v/**E**]

♦ European Public Service Union (#20486)
♦ European Public Support Group (internationally oriented national body)

♦ European Publishers Council (EPC) 08304

Exec Dir Av des Arts 43, 1040 Brussels, Belgium. T. +322311299. E-mail: info@epceurope.eu.
URL: http://www.epceurope.eu/

History Jan 1991, Amsterdam (Netherlands). Registration: EU Transparency Register, No/ID: 4456380381-30, Start date: 9 Sep 2008. **Aims** Promote freedom of expression, including commercial free speech; ensure freedom for journalists to report and inform readers; to earn essential funding from advertising and licensing; to manage copyright both in print and online; to adopt businesses in the media environment; to compete fairly with publicly funded broadcasters; to regulate own industry where tried, tested and appropriate. **Structure** Council. **Languages** English, French. **Staff** 2.00 FTE, paid. **Finance** Sources: members' dues. Annual budget: 450,000 EUR. **Activities** Advocacy/lobbying/activism; knowledge management/information dissemination. **Publications** *The Answer to the Machine is in the Machine* (2010); *What's the Problem ? Booklet on Advertising* (2000); *Don't Tax Reading* (1998); *Copyright and the Publishers* (1996); *Media Ownership Regulation in the UK: The Facts, the History and the Anomalies* (1994); *Strategic Study on the Emergence of a Multimedia Industry* (1993); *Safeguarding the Future of the European Audiovisual Market. 2025 Policy Vision with Key Recommendations* in English; *Report on the Impact of the GDPR* in English.

Members Companies in 16 countries:
Austria, Belgium, Denmark, Finland, France, Germany, Greece, Ireland, Italy, Netherlands, Norway, Poland, Spain, Sweden, Switzerland, UK.

Consultative Status Consultative status granted from: *World Intellectual Property Organization (WIPO, #21593)* (Permanent Observer Status). **NGO Relations** Member of (6): *Coalition for APP Fairness* (Founding); *Creative Media Business Alliance (CMBA, #04947); Ethical Journalism Network (EJN, #05554); European Interactive Digital Advertising Alliance (EDAA, #07582); International Council for Advertising Self-Regulation (ICAS, #12984); News Media Coalition (NMC, #17093)* (Founding). [2021.06.08/XD2575/**D**]

♦ European Pulp Group / see European Pulp Industry Sector Association (#08305)
♦ European Pulp Industry Sector / see European Pulp Industry Sector Association (#08305)

♦ European Pulp Industry Sector Association (EPIS) 08305

SG c/o Sustinendo Oy, Tunturikatu 4 A 9, FI-00100 Helsinki, Finland. T. +358505724200.
URL: http://www.epis.org/

History A legally autonomous industry sector of *Confederation of European Paper Industries (CEPI, #04529).* Previously referred to as *European Pulp Group (EPG)* and *European Pulp Industry Sector.* **Aims** Collect, process and distribute statistics regarding chemical market pulps in compliance with applicable antitrust laws. **Structure** General Assembly; Steering Committee; Secretariat. **Languages** English. **Staff** 0.50 FTE, paid. **Finance** Members' dues. **Activities** Knowledge management/information dissemination; networking/liaising; research/documentation; standards/guidelines.

Members Companies (21) in 10 countries:
Austria, Belgium, Brazil, Canada, Chile, Finland, Germany, Portugal, Spain, Sweden.

NGO Relations Stakeholder in: *Forest Stewardship Council (FSC, #09869); PEFC Council (#18288).* [2019.12.11/XE2985/t/**E**]

♦ European Pulp and Paper Chemicals Group (EPCG) 08306

SG Mainzer Landstr 55, 60329 Frankfurt-Main, Germany. E-mail: info@epcg.eu – otterbein@vci.de.
Head Office Reception Steptoe, Avenue Louise 489, 1050 Brussels, Belgium.
URL: http://www.epcg.eu/

History 2002. Registration: Banque-Carrefour des Entreprises, No/ID: 0893.758.097, Start date: 4 Jul 2007, Belgium; EU Transparency Register, No/ID: 907610511640-90, Start date: 25 Jul 2013. **Aims** Promote the safe use and benefits of papermaking chemicals to society. **Activities** Advocacy/lobbying/activism; networking/liaising. **Members** Companies (13). Membership countries not specified. [2022/AA2994/**D**]

♦ European Pultrusion Technology Association (EPTA) 08307

Association européenne de technologie en pultrusion – Europäischer Verband für Pultrusions Technik

Secretariat Am Hauptbahnhof 10, 60329 Frankfurt-Main, Germany. T. +49692710770. Fax +496927107710.
URL: https://pultruders.com/

History Dec 1989, Netherlands. **Aims** Promote: responsible use of fibre reinforced pultruded composite materials and pultruded products; better understanding of advantages of pultrusion. **Structure** Secretariat. **Languages** English. **Staff** 1.50 FTE, paid. **Finance** Members' dues. **Activities** Organizes: meetings; seminars; conferences; *'World Pultrusion Conference'* (every 2 years); exchange of knowledge and data among members. **Events** *World Pultrusion Conference* Paris (France) 2022, *World Conference* Antwerp (Belgium) 2020, *World Conference* Vienna (Austria) 2018, *World Conference* Prague (Czech Rep) 2016, *Meeting* Tokyo (Japan) 2016. **Publications** *Composite Profile* (bi-weekly) – newsletter. Conference and seminar proceedings; information on standardization; market information.

Members Companies, universities, academic and research institutes. Full in 16 countries:
Belgium, Czechia, Finland, France, Germany, Italy, Netherlands, Norway, Pakistan, Russia, Slovenia, South Africa, Spain, Sweden, UK, USA.

Associate in 14 countries and territories:
Belgium, Brazil, Canada, Chile, France, Germany, India, Italy, Netherlands, Russia, Switzerland, Taiwan, UK, USA.

Sponsor members (11) in 5 countries:
Belgium, Finland, Germany, Netherlands, UK.

NGO Relations Sectorial member of: *European Composites Industry Association (EuCIA, #06692).* [2021/XD2164/**D**]

♦ European PVC Window Profile and Related Building Products Association / see European Trade Association of PVC Window System Supplies (#08924)
♦ European PWN / see PWN Global – Professional Women's Network (#18584)
♦ European Pyrotechnic Association (inactive)

♦ European QP Association 08308

Contact c/o ECA Foundation, PO Box 102168, 69011 Heidelberg, Germany.
URL: http://www.qp-association.eu/

History Founded 7 Jul 2006, at annual meeting of ECA Foundation Advisory Board. **Aims** Provide qualified persons (QPs) with a platform allowing them to exchange their experience, discuss the latest regulatory requirements, identify and address difficulties and challenges and support a harmonized European approach. **Structure** Authority Advisory Board; Board of Directors. **Activities** Events/meetings; training/education. **Events** *Forum* Prague (Czechia) 2018. **Publications** *QP Association News.* [2019/XM7950/**D**]

♦ European Quadricycle League (EQUAL) 08309

Association européenne de promotion des quadricycles

Gen Sec 17 rue de Miromesnil, 75008 Paris, France. T. +33156885210. Fax +33156885211.
URL: http://www.equal-mobility.com/

History 1996, as *Association européenne des fabricants de quadricycles (AFQUAD).* Current title adopted Apr 2007. EU Transparency Register: 77903441267-16. **Structure** President.

Members Full in 4 countries:
France, Germany, Italy, Netherlands. [2017/XD6571/**D**]

♦ European Quality Alliance (inactive)
♦ European Quality Association for Candles (internationally oriented national body)
♦ European Quality Assurance Association of Expanded Polystyrene Foam Manufacturers for Food Packaging (inactive)
♦ European Quality Assurance Association for Panels and Profiles / see European Association for Panels and Profiles (#06142)

♦ European Quality Assurance Network for Informatics Education (EQANIE) 08310

SG c/o ASIIN, PO Box 10 11 39, 40002 Düsseldorf, Germany. T. +4925159081552. E-mail: secretariat@eqanie.eu.
Pres address not obtained.
URL: https://eqanie.eu/

History 9 Jan 2009, Düsseldorf (Germany). **Aims** Enhance evaluation and quality assurance of informatics study programmes and education in Europe. **Structure** General Assembly (annual); Executive Board; Permanent Secretariat. Board of Appeals; Accreditation Committee; Audit Team; Expert Pool. **Activities** Certification/accreditation; projects/programmes; standards/guidelines. **Events** *Conference on Learning Outcomes and Quality Management in Information Education* Vienna (Austria) 2011.

Members Organizations (7) in 3 countries:
Germany, Spain, UK.

NGO Relations Member of (1): *European Alliance of Subject-Specific and Professional Accreditation and Quality Assurance (EASPA, #05887)* (Founding). [2022.02.22/XJ4577/**F**]

♦ European Quality Assurance Register for Higher Education (EQAR) . 08311

Dir Aarlenstraat 22, 1050 Brussels, Belgium. T. +3222343911. Fax +3222303347. E-mail: info@eqar.eu.
Events – Events and Communications Officer address not obtained. T. +3222343912.
URL: http://www.eqar.eu/

History 4 Mar 2008. Founded as *European Quality Assurance Register for Higher Education Association (EQAR Association)*, by *European Association for Quality Assurance in Higher Education (ENQA, #06183), European Students' Union (ESU, #08848), European University Association (EUA, #09027)* and *European Association of Institutions of Higher Education (EURASHE, #06086)*, at the request of European ministers of higher education (London Summit 2007). Registration: Banque-Carrefour des Entreprises, No/ID: 0897.690.557, Start date: 5 May 2008, Belgium; EU Transparency Register, No/ID: 672204711627-29, Start date: 12 Aug 2013. **Aims** Further the development of the European Higher Education Area by enhancing confidence in higher education and by facilitating the mutual recognition of quality assurance decisions; serve as a register of European higher education institutions and study programmes which are subject to regular external review by a quality assurance agency, and that have demonstrated their substantial compliance with a common set of principles for quality assurance in Europe, the European Standard and Guidelines (ESG). **Structure** General Assembly, comprising founders, stakeholder organizations and representatives from 37 European governments. Executive Board. Committees (2): Register; Appeals. Secretariat. **Languages** English. **Staff** 2.00 FTE, paid. **Finance** Budget (annual): euro 300,000. **Activities** Certification/accreditation; knowledge management/information dissemination. **Events** *DEQAR Conference* Madrid (Spain) 2019.

Members Categories: Founding; Social Partner; Governmental. Founding (4):
European Association for Quality Assurance in Higher Education (ENQA, #06183); European Association of Institutions of Higher Education (EURASHE, #06086); European Students' Union (ESU, #08848); European University Association (EUA, #09027).

Social Partner Members (2):
BUSINESSEUROPE (#03381); Education International (EI, #05371).

Governmental members (37):
Armenia, Austria, Azerbaijan, Belgium (Flemish community and French-speaking community), Bosnia-Herzegovina, Bulgaria, Central African Rep, Croatia, Cyprus, Denmark, Estonia, Finland, France, Georgia, Germany, Ireland, Kazakhstan, Latvia, Liechtenstein, Lithuania, Luxembourg, Malta, Moldova, Montenegro, Netherlands, North Macedonia, Norway, Poland, Portugal, Romania, Slovenia, Spain, Switzerland, Türkiye, UK, Ukraine.

IGO Relations Observer status with: *Council of Europe (CE, #04881); European Commission (EC, #06633); UNESCO (#20322).*

NGO Relations Member of: *Federation of European and International Associations Established in Belgium (FAIB, #09508).*

Quality Assurance Agencies that are listed on the Register:
- Accreditation Agency in Health and Social Sciences (AHPGS), Germany;
- Accreditation, Certification and Quality Assurance Institute (ACQUIN), Germany;
- Accreditation Organisation of the Netherlands and Flanders (NVAO);
- Agence pour l'Evaluation de la Qualité de l'Enseignement Supérieur (AEQES), Belgium;
- Agency for Evaluation and Accreditation of Higher Education (A3ES), Portugal;
- Agency for Quality Assurance and Accreditation Austria (AQ Austria);
- Agency for Quality Assurance through Accreditation of Study Programmes (AQAS), Germany;
- Agency for Quality Assurance in the Galician University System (ACSG), Spain;
- Agency for Quality of the Basque University System (UNIBASQ), Spain;

- Agency for Science and Higher Education (QSHE), Croatia;
- Andalusian Agency of Knowledge, Department of Evaluation and Accreditation (AAC-DEVA), Spain;
- ASIN, Germany;
- British Accreditation Council for Independent Further and Higher Education (BAC), UK;
- Catalan University Quality Assurance Agency (AQU), Spain;
- Central Evaluation and Accreditation Agency (ZEVA), Germany;
- Centre for Quality Assessment in Higher Education (SKVC), Lithuania;
- Commission for Accreditation and Quality Assurance (CAQA), Serbia;
- The Danish Accreditation Institution;
- Engineering Degree Commission (CTI), France;
- Estonian Higher Education Quality Agency (EKKA);
- *European Association for Public Administration Accreditation (EAPAA, #06177)*;
- Evaluation Agency Baden-Württemberg (EVALAG), Germany;
- Finnish Education Evaluation Centre (FINEEC);
- *Foundation for International Business Administration Accreditation (FIBAA, #09961)*;
- Fundación para el Conocimiento Madrimasd (FMID), Spain;
- High Council for Evaluation of Research and Higher Education (HCERES), France;
- Institutional Evaluation Programme (IEP), Switzerland;
- Kosovo Accreditation Agency (KAA);
- National Agency for the Quality Assessment and Accreditation of Spain (QNECA), Spain;
- Norwegian Agency for Quality Assurance in Education (NOKUT);
- Polish Accreditation Committee (PKA);
- Quality Assurance Agency for Higher Education (QAA), UK;
- The Quality Assurance Agency for the University System in Castilla y León (ACSUCYL), Spain;
- Quality Assurance Netherlands Universities (QANU);
- Quality Assurance Unit of the Flemish University and University Colleges Council (VLUHR QAU), Belgium;
- Quality and Qualifications Ireland (QQI);
- Romanian Agency for Quality Assurance in Higher Education (ARACIS);
- Slovenian Quality Assurance Agency (SQAA);
- Swiss Center of Accreditation and Quality Assurance in Higher Education (OAQ). [2021/XJ5508/y/**D**]

♦ European Quality Assurance Register for Higher Education Association / see European Quality Assurance Register for Higher Education (#08311)

♦ European Quality Assurance in Vocational Education and Training (EQAVET) 08312

Dir EQAVET Secretariat, Quality and Qualifications Ireland (QQI), 10 Lower Mount Str, Dublin, CO. DUBLIN, Ireland. T. +35319058144.
URL: http://www.eqavet.eu/

History Launched Jan 2010, following adoption of Recommendations of *European Parliament (EP, #08146)* and *European Council (#06801)* on establishment of European Quality Assurance Reference Framework. **Aims** Develop and improve quality assurance in European VET (Vocation Education and Training) systems within the context of the implementation of the European Quality Assurance Reference Framework. **Structure** European Network, comprising 2 representatives per member state, Social Partners, *European Commission (EC, #06633)* (Chair) and *European Centre for the Development of Vocational Training (Cedefop, #06474)* and *European Training Foundation (ETF, #08934)* as Scientific Advisors. Steering Committee, comprising 3 members representing countries from EU Team-Presidency, 4 elected members and 2 representatives of Social Partners, chaired by European Commission. Secretariat; Working Groups. **Languages** English. **Staff** 2.50 FTE, paid. Several experts. **Finance** Funded by: *European Commission (EC, #06633)*. Budget (annual): about euro 600,000. **Activities** Training/education; research/documentation. **Events** *Forum on Quality Assurance of the Continuing Professional Development (CPD) of Teachers and Trainers in Continuous Vocational Education and Training* Lille (France) 2017, *Annual Forum* Jurmala (Latvia) 2015, *Annual Forum* Athens (Greece) 2014, *Annual Forum* Dublin (Ireland) 2013, *Seminar* Paris (France) 2012. **Publications** Newsletters; policy briefs; reports; international material.
Members Member States (33):
Austria, Belgium, Bulgaria, Croatia, Cyprus, Czechia, Denmark, Estonia, Finland, France, Germany, Greece, Hungary, Ireland, Italy, Latvia, Liechtenstein, Lithuania, Luxembourg, Malta, Netherlands, North Macedonia, Norway, Poland, Portugal, Romania, Slovakia, Slovenia, Spain, Sweden, Switzerland, Türkiye, UK.
Full: Social Partners (4):
BUSINESSEUROPE (#03381); *European Trade Union Confederation (ETUC, #08927)*; *SGI Europe (#19253)*; *SMEunited (#19327)*.
IGO Relations Cooperates with: *European Centre for the Development of Vocational Training (Cedefop, #06474)*; *European Commission (EC, #06633)*; *European Training Foundation (ETF, #08934)*.
[2015.09.17/XJ6829/y/**F***]

♦ European Quality Control System (EQCS) 08313

Registered Office Rue de la Loi 221, 1040 Brussels, Belgium.
URL: http://www.eqcs.org/

History Set up 1994, by *European Fruit Juice Association (AIJN, #07362)* and national organizations. Full official title: *European Quality Control System of the European Fruit Juice Industry*. Alternative full title: *European Quality Control System for Juice and Necatrs from Fruits and Vegetals*. Registered in accordance with Belgian law. Dissolved 31 Dec 2018. **Aims** Harmonize within the European Economic Area and EU candidate country markets the work and control activities of market and packer control systems; support fruit juice manufacturers in complying with legal and industrial standards for due diligence. **Structure** General Assembly; Board of Directors. **Languages** English, French.
Members Ordinary; Observer; Supporting. Members in 5 countries:
Belgium, France, Germany, Spain, UK.
Included in the above, 2 organizations listed in this Yearbook:
European Fruit Juice Association (AIJN, #07362); *SGF International (#19252)*. [2019.06.13/XM6017/y/**F**]

♦ European Quality Control System of the European Fruit Juice Industry / see European Quality Control System (#08313)
♦ European Quality Control System for Juice and Necatrs from Fruits and Vegetals / see European Quality Control System (#08313)

♦ European Quality Link (EQUAL) 08314

Secretariat c/o EFMD, Rue Gachard 88 box 3, 1050 Brussels, Belgium. T. +3226290810. Fax +3226290811.
URL: http://www.efmd.org/index.php/business-schools/equal/

History Jun 1996, by *EFMD – The Management Development Network (#05387)*. **Aims** Act as a think tank and policy development organization primarily in Europe for international business and management education, training, research and development for the benefit of member schools, students, end users and society at large. **Languages** English. **Finance** Members' dues. **Activities** Promotes continuous improvement of quality in business and management education training, research and development institutions; promotes convergence of quality assurance processes; participates in the development and facilitation of quality assurance and accreditation systems; support development of quality assurance; disseminates information; cooperates with international bodies; undertakes and shares results of research and projects.
Members Organizations in 17 countries:
Belgium, Canada, Czechia, Denmark, Finland, France, Italy, Lithuania, Netherlands, Norway, Poland, Russia, Slovenia, Spain, Sweden, UK, USA.
Included in the above, 3 organizations listed in this Yearbook:
AACSB International – Association to Advance Collegiate Schools of Business; *CEEMAN – International Association for Management Development in Dynamic Societies (CEEMAN, #03625)*; EFMD.
[2012.06.25/XE4416/y/**E**]

♦ European Quantitative Structure-Activity Relationships (meeting series)

♦ European Quantum Industry Consortium (QuIC) 08315

Exec Dir Leo-Brandt-Str, 52428 Jülich, Germany. E-mail: info@euroquic.org.
Pres address not obtained.
URL: https://www.euroquic.org/

History 2021. Registration: North Rhine-Westphalia District court, No/ID: VR 2852, Start date: 15 Jun 2021, Germany, Düren; EU Transparency Register, No/ID: 968437243335-49, Start date: 28 Jun 2021. **Aims** Boost European industry competitiveness in quantum technologies; foster economic growth and value creation for business and citizens. **Structure** General Assembly; Board. **Events** *Plenary Meeting* Lisbon (Portugal) 2022, *Plenary Meeting* Paris (France) 2022. **Members** Full; Asscociate. Companies. Membership countries not specified. [2023/AA1909/**D**]

♦ European Quaternary Mammal Research Association (inactive)

♦ European Quilt Association (EQA) 08316

Address not obtained.
URL: http://www.e-q-a.eu/

History 1989. **Aims** Promote the knowledge of quilting in Europe.
Members Full in 18 countries:
Austria, Belgium, Denmark, Finland, France, Germany, Hungary, Iceland, Ireland, Italy, Latvia, Luxembourg, Netherlands, Norway, Spain, Sweden, Switzerland, UK. [2021/AA2389/**D**]

♦ European Racquetball Federation (ERF) 08317

Technical Dir 8 Cashel Park, Castlebar, CO. MAYO, Ireland.
URL: http://www.european-racquetball.org/

History May 1982, Zoetermeer (Netherlands). **Aims** Develop and promote the *sport* of racquetball within Europe. **Structure** Executive Committee, comprising President, Vice-President, General Secretary, Treasurer, Technical Director and Media Officer. **Languages** English. **Staff** 100.00 FTE, voluntary. **Finance** Members' dues. Other sources: competition fees; sponsorship. **Activities** Events/meetings; awards/prizes/competitions. **Publications** *ERF News*.
Members Full members in 11 countries and territories:
Belgium, England, France, Germany, Ireland, Italy, Netherlands, Poland, Spain, Sweden, Türkiye.
NGO Relations Affiliated with: *International Racquetball Federation (IRF, #14683)*. [2014.09.09/XD7135/**D**]

♦ European Radiant Floor Heating Association / see European Association of Surface Heating and Cooling (#06241)

♦ European Radiation Dosimetry Group (EURADOS) 08318

Contact Postfach 1129, 85758 Neuherberg, Germany. T. +498931873107. E-mail: office@eurados.org.
General: http://www.eurados.org/

History 1981. Registration: Germany. **Aims** Foster European collaboration in research on and development of radiation dosimetry. **Structure** Council; Working Groups. **Languages** English. **Staff** None. **Finance** Budget (annual): about euro 150,000. **Activities** Research and development; monitoring/evaluation; training/education. **Events** *Annual Meeting* Belgrade (Serbia) 2021, *Annual Meeting* Florence (Italy) 2020, *Annual Meeting* Łódź (Poland) 2019, *Annual Meeting* Lisbon (Portugal) 2018, *Annual Meeting* Karlsruhe (Germany) 2017. **Publications** *EURADOS Newsletter* (2 a year).
Members Individual membership: Associate; Honorary; Corresponding. Institutional membership: Voting (laboratories carrying out or promoting scientific research and development in radiation dosimetry). Laboratories and individuals in 32 countries:
Austria, Belgium, Bulgaria, Canada, Croatia, Czechia, Denmark, Finland, France, Germany, Greece, Hungary, Ireland, Italy, Latvia, Lithuania, Netherlands, North Macedonia, Poland, Portugal, Romania, Russia, Serbia, Slovakia, Slovenia, South Africa, Spain, Sweden, Switzerland, UK, Ukraine, USA. [2020/XF3342/**F**]

♦ European Radiation Protection Week (meeting series)

♦ European Radiation Research Society (ERRS) 08319

Sec-Treas Molecular and Cellular Biology, Inst for Environment Health and Safety, Belgian Nuclear Research Centre, Boeretang 200, 2400 Mol, Belgium. T. +3214332730. Fax +3214314793. E-mail: err_secretariat@sckcen.be.
URL: http://www.errs.eu/

History Founded 1959, Brussels (Belgium), as *Association of Radiobiologists of Euratom Countries – Association des radiobiologistes des pays de l'Euratom*. Constitution amended and name changed to *European Society for Radiation Biology – Société européenne de radiobiologie*, Jun 1964. Present name adopted, 2005. Registered in accordance with Belgian law. **Aims** Promote scientific research, information exchange and collaboration in the physical, chemical, biochemical, biological and medical aspects of research on radiation, between radiobiologists of European and non European countries. **Structure** Council. **Languages** English, French. **Staff** No less than 9. **Finance** Members' dues. Budget (annual): about euro 2,500. **Activities** Annual scientific meeting, superseded every 4 years by IARR congress. Grants Bacq and Alexander Award (annual). **Events** *Annual Meeting* Catania (Italy) 2022, *Annual Meeting* Caen (France) 2021, *Annual Meeting* Lund (Sweden) 2020, *Annual Meeting* Pécs (Hungary) 2018, *Annual Meeting* Essen (Germany) 2017. **Publications** *International Journal of Radiation Biology*.
Members Full (individual scientists who have contributed to the advancement of radiation biology); Associate; Honorary, in 26 countries:
Austria, Belgium, Canada, Czechia, Finland, France, Germany, Hungary, India, Ireland, Israel, Italy, Japan, Montenegro, Netherlands, Poland, Portugal, Romania, Russia, Serbia, Slovakia, Slovenia, Sweden, UK, Ukraine, USA.
NGO Relations Member of: *International Association for Radiation Research (IARR, #12119)*.
[2013/XD0856/v/**D**]

♦ European Radio Amateurs' Organization (EURAO) 08320

Organisation Européenne des Radioamateurs
Contact PO Box 3050, 08200 Sabadell, Barcelona, Spain. T. +3228080796. E-mail: eurao@eurao.org.
URL: https://www.eurao.org/

History Proposed 2005. First statutes adopted 29 Jun 2013, Friedrichshafen (Germany). Registration: Start date: 2014, France; EU Transparency Register, No/ID: 79718451904-90. **Aims** Be a meeting point for independent radio amateurs' associations around the world, mainly from Europe, interested in sharing activities and experiences, making up common services, working together in new projects and lobbying Public Administrations. **Structure** General Assembly; Board of Directors. **Languages** English. **Finance** Sources: members' dues. Annual budget: 3,000 EUR (2020). **Activities** Events/meetings. Human Rights International Online Program. **Publications** *European Radio Amateurs' Organization Newsletter*. **Information Services** *EuroBureauQSL*. **Members** Associations; individuals; clubs and groups. Members in 80 countries. Membership countries not specified. **Consultative Status** Consultative status granted from: *ECOSOC (#05331)* (Special). **IGO Relations** Observer status with (1): *Conférence européenne des administrations des postes et des télécommunications (CEPT, #04602)*. Member of (1): *International Telecommunication Union (ITU, #15673)* (Radiocommunications Sector). [2021.06.08/XM5322/**D**]

♦ European Radiocommunications Office / see European Communications Office (#06676)
♦ European Radio Data Association (no recent information)

♦ European Radioecology Alliance (ERA) 08321

Head Office c/o IRSN, 31 avenue de la Division Leclerc, BP 17, 92262 Fontenay-aux-Roses CEDEX, France.
URL: http://www.er-alliance.org/

History Founded when Memorandum of Understanding signed Jun 2009. Registered in accordance with French law. **Aims** Coordinate and promote European research on radioecology. **Structure** General Assembly; Board of Directors; Bureau. **Finance** Members' dues. **Activities** Research/documentation; knowledge management/information dissemination.
Members Founding; Subscribing; Honorary. Founding in 8 countries:
Belgium, Finland, France, Germany, Norway, Spain, Sweden, UK.
Subscribing in 7 countries:
Greece, Hungary, Ireland, Japan, Kazakhstan, Poland, Portugal. [2019.07.30/XM7376/**D**]

♦ European Radio Taxi Association (unconfirmed)

♦ **European Radon Association (ERA)** **08322**

Registered Address Rue Ravenstein 36, 1000 Brussels, Belgium. E-mail: secretary@radoneurope.org – radoneurope@radoneurope.org.
URL: https://radoneurope.org/

History May 2013, Bouillon (Belgium). Registration: Banque-Carrefour des Entreprises, No/ID: 0549.923.484, Start date: 2 Apr 2014, Belgium. **Aims** Improve awareness and reduce risk of radon exposure across Europe. **Structure** General Assembly; Executive Committee. **Finance** Sources: members' dues.
Members Companies and organizations in 9 countries:
Finland, Germany, Hungary, Italy, Romania, Spain, Sweden, UK, USA.
Individuals in 24 countries:
Australia, Austria, Belgium, Bulgaria, Croatia, Czechia, France, Germany, Ireland, Italy, Luxembourg, Netherlands, Nigeria, Poland, Portugal, Qatar, Romania, Serbia, Slovenia, Spain, Sweden, Switzerland, Türkiye, UK. [2020/AA1211/**D**]

♦ European Rail Circle (inactive)

♦ **European Rail Freight Association (ERFA)** **08323**

SG Rue Montoyer 23, 1000 Brussels, Belgium. T. +3225136087. Fax +3226728114. E-mail: info@erfarail.eu.
URL: http://www.erfarail.eu/

History 23 Jul 2002, Brussels (Belgium). Registration: Belgium; EU Transparency Register, No/ID: 215618129516-28. **Aims** Promote European rail freight transport and rail transport enterprises active in that area. **Structure** President; Vice-President; Secretary General. **Events** *Annual Meeting* Brussels (Belgium) 2020, *General Assembly* Brussels (Belgium) 2014, *General Assembly* Como (Italy) 2007, *General Assembly* Rotterdam (Netherlands) 2004.
Members Railway companies in 14 countries:
Austria, Belgium, Bulgaria, France, Germany, Hungary, Italy, Lithuania, Netherlands, Norway, Poland, Spain, UK, Ukraine.
NGO Relations Member of (3): *European Logistics Platform (ELP, #07711)*; *International Rail Freight Business Association (IBS)*; *Rail Forum Europe (RFE, #18607)* (Associate). Instrumental in setting up (1): *Alliance of Rail New Entrants (ALLRAIL, #00714).* [2020/XD9144/**D**]

♦ **European Rail Infrastructure Managers (EIM)** **08324**

Exec Dir Square de Meeus 1, 1000 Brussels, Belgium. T. +3222343770. Fax +3222343779. E-mail: direction@eimrail.org.
URL: http://www.eimrail.org/

History Founded 11 Dec 2001, Brussels (Belgium). Registered in accordance with Belgian law. **Aims** Represent the interests of the rail infrastructure management sector in relation to European Union legislative developments. **Structure** General Assembly (2 a year). **Languages** English. **Staff** 5.00 FTE, paid. 2 secondments. **Finance** Members' dues. **Activities** Advocacy/lobbying/activism; networking/liaising; standards/guidelines. **Events** *HIGHSPEED : World Congress on High Speed Rail* Tokyo (Japan) 2015, *Towards Zero Conference* Stockholm (Sweden) 2013, *Conference on structuring the future of Europe's railways* Brussels (Belgium) 2009, *High level infrastructure meeting* Brussels (Belgium) 2008, *Conference on employability* Potsdam (Germany) 2008. **Publications** Position papers (4-6 a year); press releases (4 a year); newsletter.
Members Rail infrastructure managers (15) in 11 countries:
Belgium, Denmark, Finland, France, Netherlands, Norway, Poland, Portugal, Spain, Sweden, UK.
[2018.06.20/XD8848/y/**D**]

♦ **European Rail Research Advisory Council (ERRAC)** **08325**

Conseil consultatif de la recherche ferroviaire européenne

Secretariat c/o UNIFE, Avenue Louise 221, bte 11, 1050 Brussels, Belgium. T. +3226261260. Fax +3226261261.
URL: http://www.errac.org/

History 26 Nov 2001, Cologne (Germany), by *Community of European Railway and Infrastructure Companies (CER, #04396)*, *International Association of Public Transport (#12118)*, *International Union of Railways (#15813)* and *Association of the European Rail Supply Industry (UNIFE, #02536).* **Aims** Create a coordinated rail research strategy for Europe. **Structure** Plenary (2 or 3 times a year). Support Group; Working groups; working teams. Project Management; Secretariat. Officers: Chairman; 2 Vice-Chairmen. **Events** *Transport Research Arena (TRA) Conference* Lisbon (Portugal) 2022, *TRA – European Transport Research Arena Conference* Helsinki (Finland) 2020, *TRA – European Transport Research Arena Conference* Vienna (Austria) 2018, *TRA – European Transport Research Arena Conference* Warsaw (Poland) 2016, *TRA European Transport Research Arena Conference* Paris (France) 2014. **Publications** *Strategic Rail Research Agenda.*
Members in 16 countries:
Austria, Belgium, Czechia, Finland, France, Germany, Greece, Ireland, Italy, Luxembourg, Netherlands, Portugal, Slovakia, Spain, Sweden, UK.
Included in the above, one organization listed in this Yearbook:
European Transport Safety Council (ETSC, #08940).
IGO Relations *European Commission (EC, #06633).* [2014/XE4490/**E**]

♦ **EUropean rail Research Network of EXcellence (EURNEX)** **08326**

Main Office Hardenbergstr 12, 10623 Berlin, Germany. T. +493031997020. E-mail: info@eurnex.eu.
URL: http://www.eurnex.org/

History 30 Oct 2007, Germany. Originally set up with EU support, 2004. Former names and other names: *EURNEX Association* – alias. Registration: Germany. **Aims** Integrate the fragmented rail research landscape in Europe; contribute to a more competitive future European rail system by providing excellent research and education; achieve sustainability for the NoE through a sound business model, providing durable added value for members and rail system stakeholders. **Structure** Council.
Members Scientific institutes (37) in 20 countries:
Austria, China, Czechia, Estonia, France, Germany, Greece, Hungary, Italy, Latvia, Lithuania, Poland, Russia, Serbia, Slovakia, Slovenia, Spain, Sweden, UK, Ukraine.
NGO Relations Member of: *European Transport Research Alliance (ETRA, #08939).* [2021/XJ6210/**F**]

♦ **European Rail Traffic Management System (ERTMS)** **08327**

Project Manager c/o UNIFE, Ave Louise 221, 1050 Brussels, Belgium. T. +3226437081. E-mail: jonathan.cutuli@unife.org.
Contact ERA, 120 rue Marc Lefrancq, BP 20392, 59300 Valenciennes, France. T. +33327096500. Fax +33327334065. E-mail: communication@era.europa.eu.
URL: http://www.ertms.net/

History Developed by 8 members of *Association of the European Rail Supply Industry (UNIFE, #02536).* Memorandum of Understanding signed, 2005, by *European Commission (EC, #06633)* and rail industry manufacturers, infrastructure managers and undertakings, covers deployment of ERTMS on a key part of the European network with an emphasis on 6 freight corridors. A 2nd MoU, signed Jul 2008, includes new partners and sets objectives for the deployment of the European Train Control System across key freight corridors and high speed lines so as to improve competitiveness of European railways. 22 Jul 2009, European Deployment Plan for ERTMS adopted by the Commission, provides for progressive deployment of ERTMS along the main European rail routes. *European Union Agency for Railways (#08973)* is responsible for ERTMS specifications. **Aims** Attain rail *interoperability*, so that trains can cross *borders* without stopping; make rail transport *safer* and more *competitive*. **Structure** Includes *European Train Control System (ETCS, see: #08327)*, which guarantees a common standard that enables trains to cross national borders and enhances safety. **Activities** Provides in-cab signalling and automatic train protection which, under EC law, must be implemented for upgrades of nationally defined interoperable *Trans-European Transport Network (TEN-T, inactive).* **Events** *Control Command and Railway Communication Conference* Lille (France) 2015. **Members** Membership countries not specified. [2019/XJ7734/**F**]

♦ European Railway Agency / see European Union Agency for Railways (#08973)
♦ European Rainforest Movement / see Forest Movement Europe (#09864)

♦ **European Ramblers' Association (ERA)** **08328**

Fédération Européenne de la Randonnée Pédestre (FERP) – Europäische Wandervereinigung (EWV)

Secretariat Prusikova 2577/16, 155 00 Prague 5, Czechia. E-mail: secretariat@era-ewv-ferp.com.
Official seat c/o Deutscher Wanderverband, Kleine Rosenstr 1-3, 34117 Kassel, Germany. T. +49561938730. Fax +495619378310.
URL: http://www.era-ewv-ferp.com/

History 19 Oct 1969, Nägelehaus (Germany FR). Former names and other names: *Association européenne de tourisme pédestre* – alias. Registration: EU Transparency Register, No/ID: 069944637849-40, Start date: 15 Apr 2020. **Aims** Encourage and promote *walking* and *mountaineering* activities; help protect the environment; facilitate frontier crossings for members; encourage and improve friendship and understanding among the peoples of Europe by walking and mountaineering together. **Languages** English, French, German. **Staff** 1.00 FTE, paid. **Activities** Events/meetings; knowledge management/information dissemination. **Events** *Annual conference* Helsingør (Denmark) 2022, *Annual conference* Sibiu (Romania) 2021, *Annual conference* Prague (Czechia) 2020, *Annual conference* Bad Urach (Germany) 2019, *Annual conference* Echternach (Luxembourg) 2018. **Publications** *ERA Newsletter. 50 years of ERA commemorative book* (1st ed 2019); *E-Paths Map.*
Members European walking and mountaineering organizations (65) representing 3 million members in 35 countries:
Albania, Austria, Belgium, Bosnia-Herzegovina, Bulgaria, Croatia, Cyprus, Czechia, Denmark, Estonia, France, Germany, Greece, Hungary, Ireland, Italy, Latvia, Lithuania, Luxembourg, Malta, Montenegro, Netherlands, North Macedonia, Norway, Poland, Portugal, Romania, Russia, Serbia, Slovakia, Slovenia, Spain, Sweden, Switzerland, UK.
NGO Relations Member of (1): *European Tourism Manifesto (#08921).* Partner of (1): *European Union of Mountaineering Associations (EUMA, #09002).* [2021.03.03/XD4537/**D**]

♦ **European Rare-Earth and Actinide Society (ERES)** **08329**

Pres Swiss Fed'l Inst of Technology, Lausanne, Inst of Chemical Sciences and Engineering, CH H3 605 – Station 6, 1015 Lausanne VD, Switzerland. T. +41216939821.
URL: http://ereswww.epfl.ch/

History 1989, Lausanne (Switzerland). Commenced activities 1990. Registration: Swiss Civil Code, Switzerland. **Aims** Encourage development of scientific and technical activities in the field of f-elements; encourage exchange of professional, technical, industrial and economic information; coordinates international interdisciplinary conferences on f-elements. **Structure** General Council (at least every 3 years); Executive Committee. **Languages** English. **Staff** 0.10 FTE, voluntary. **Finance** Sources: sponsorship. Annual budget: 3,000 CHF (2019). **Activities** Events/meetings. **Events** *International Conference on f Elements* Hong Kong (Hong Kong) 2022, *International Conference on f Elements* Lausanne (Switzerland) 2018, *International Conference on f-Elements* Oxford (UK) 2015, *International Conference on f-Elements* Udine (Italy) 2012, *International conference of f-Elements* Cologne (Germany) 2009.
Members Individuals (650) in 38 countries:
Austria, Belarus, Belgium, Brazil, Bulgaria, Canada, China, Czechia, Denmark, Finland, France, Germany, Greece, Hungary, India, Israel, Italy, Japan, Korea Rep, Latvia, Mexico, Moldova, Netherlands, New Zealand, Poland, Portugal, Romania, Russia, South Africa, Spain, Sweden, Switzerland, Thailand, Tunisia, Ukraine, Uruguay, USA, Vietnam. [2020.06.24/XD2594/v/**D**]

♦ **European Ready Mixed Concrete Organization (ERMCO)** **08330**

Association européenne du béton prêt à l'emploi – Europäischer Transportbetonverband

SG Bd du Souverain 68, 1170 Brussels, Belgium. T. +3226455212. E-mail: secretariat@ermco.eu.
URL: http://www.ermco.eu/

History 27 Oct 1967, Munich (Germany). Registration: Banque-Carrefour des Entreprises, No/ID: 0864.250.204, Start date: 24 Mar 2004, Belgium; EU Transparency Register, No/ID: 15077947344-66, Start date: 8 Dec 2011. **Aims** Promote and develop ready-mixed concrete cast-on site solutions. **Structure** Board; Strategy and Development Committee; Sustainability Committee; Technical Committee. **Languages** English. **Staff** 1.50 FTE, paid. **Finance** Members' dues. **Activities** Standards/guidelines; politics/policy/regulatory. **Events** *Triennial Congress* Oslo (Norway) 2018, *Meeting of Representatives* Berlin (Germany) 2016, *Triennial Congress* Istanbul (Turkey) 2015, *Meeting / Triennial Congress* Cascais (Portugal) 2013, *Triennial Congress* Verona (Italy) 2012. **Publications** National statistics; guidelines.
Members Full associations in 20 countries:
Austria, Belgium, Czechia, Denmark, Finland, France, Germany, Ireland, Israel, Italy, Netherlands, Norway, Poland, Portugal, Romania, Slovakia, Sweden, Switzerland, Türkiye, UK.
Associate members in 4 countries:
India, Japan, New Zealand, USA.
Associated organization:
Federación Iberoamericana del Hormigón Premezclado (FIHP, #09312).
Corresponding members in 1 country:
Russia.
NGO Relations Founding member of: *Concrete Europe (#04433).* Member of: *European Concrete Paving Association (EUPAVE, #06697)*; *Federation of European and International Associations Established in Belgium (FAIB, #09508)*; *Industry4Europe (#11181).* Friendly liaison with: *Bureau international du béton manufacturé (BIBM, #03363)*; *CEMBUREAU – The European Cement Association (CEMBUREAU, #03634)* (including joint working committee); *European Construction Industry Federation (#06766)*; *European Federation of Concrete Admixtures Associations (EFCA, #07085).* In liaison with technical committees of: *Comité européen de normalisation (CEN, #04162).* [2020/XD4707/**D**]

♦ **European Real Estate Forum** **08331**

Contact INREV, Square de Meeûs 23, 1000 Brussels, Belgium. T. +3222138160. E-mail: info@europeanrealestateforum.eu.
URL: http://www.europeanrealestateforum.eu/

History Set up as an informal alliance. EU Transparence Register: 724956214484-76. **Aims** Improve the public awareness about institutional investment in real estate and increase understanding of its social and economic value; support the policy making process affecting institutional real estate investment in Europe by improving knowledge and understanding of the sector. **Staff** None permanent.
Members International organizations (7):
CREFC Europe; *European Association for Investors in Non-listed Real Estate Vehicles (INREV, #06093)*; *European Council of Shopping Places (ECSP)*; *European Public Real Estate Association (EPRA, #08301)*; Global Real Estate Sustainability Benchmark (GRESB); *Royal Institution of Chartered Surveyors (RICS, #18991)*; *Urban Land Institute (ULI).*
National organisations in 8 countries:
Belgium, Finland, France, Italy, Luxembourg, Netherlands, Sweden, UK. [2019.03.12/XM6880/**F**]

♦ **European Real Estate Society (ERES)** **08332**

Exec Dir Plantage Muidergracht 12, 1018 TV Amsterdam, Netherlands. E-mail: info@eres.org.
URL: http://www.eres.org/

History 1994. **Aims** Encourage research and promote education, development and research in real estate and closely allied areas, especially in European countries; improve communication and exchange information in real estate and allied matters among college/university/faculty members and practitioners in research in property, real estate and land use; facilitate the association of academic, professional and research persons in the field; encourage professionalism in practices related to the field. **Structure** Board. **Languages** English. **Activities** Events/meetings; networking/liaising. **Events** *Conference* Kaiserslautern (Germany) 2021, *Industry Seminar* London (UK) 2020, *Conference* Tallinn (Estonia) 2020, *Conference* Cergy-Pontoise (France) 2019, *Industry Seminar* Lisbon (Portugal) 2019. **Publications** *Journal of European Real Estate Research* (3 a year); *ERES Newsletter* (2 a year). **NGO Relations** Observer status with (1): *European Umbrella Organization for Geographical Information (EUROGI, #08964).* [2023.02.16/XD5504/**D**]

♦ European Real Estate Valuers (inactive)

♦ **European Reconditioners of Industrial Packaging** **08333**

Syndicat européen des récupérateurs et rénovateurs de drums (SERRED)

Secretariat Boval House, 24 Mount Parade, Harrogate, HG1 1BX, UK. T. +447770633320. E-mail: info@serred.org.
URL: http://www.serred.org/

History 1975, France. In English also referred to as *European Association of Industrial Container Reconditioners.* **Aims** Promote safe, efficient and environmentally responsible design, manufacturing, collection, reconditioning, remanufacturing and reuse of reusable industrial packaging, including preparation for recycling at the end of its useful life. **Structure** Officers: President; 2 Vice-Presidents; Treasurer; Secretary. **Languages** English. **Staff** 0.50 FTE, paid. **Finance** Annual budget: Swiss Fr 90,000. **Activities** Guidance/assistance/consulting. **Events** *Conference* Tokyo (Japan) 2018, *Conference* Vancouver, BC (Canada) 2015, *Conference* Bangkok (Thailand) 2011, *International conference on industrial packaging* San Francisco, CA (USA) 2006, *Conference* Istanbul (Turkey) 2005.

Members in 15 countries:
Austria, Belgium, Denmark, Finland, France, Germany, Italy, Netherlands, Norway, Poland, Portugal, Spain, Switzerland, Türkiye, UK.
NGO Relations Member of: *European Industrial Packaging Association (EIPA, #07529)*; *International Confederation of Container Reconditioners (ICCR, #12854)*; *Reloop Platform (Reloop, #18835)*. [2018.08.06/XD2125/t/**D**]

♦ European Recovered Fuel Organisation (ERFO) 08334

SG Rue d'Arlon 21, 1050 Brussels, Belgium. T. +31657598835.
URL: https://erfo.info/
History 2001, Brussels (Belgium). Registration: Banque-Carrefour des Entreprises, No/ID: 0474.749.573, Start date: 17 May 2001, Belgium; EU Transparency Register, No/ID: 908165525166-03, Start date: 19 Dec 2016. **Aims** Promote the use of fuels from non hazardous waste in Europe. **Structure** General Assembly (twice a year). Executive Committee of 5 members. **Languages** English. **Finance** Sources: members' dues.
Members Companies (15) in 9 countries:
Belgium, Finland, France, Germany, Greece, Italy, Spain, Sweden, UK.
NGO Relations In liaison with technical committees of: *Comité européen de normalisation (CEN, #04162)*. Cooperates with: *Association of Plastics Manufacturers in Europe (Plastics Europe, #02862)*; *CEMBUREAU – The European Cement Association (CEMBUREAU, #03634)*; *Confederation of European Waste-to-Energy Plants (CEWEP, #04535)*; *European Association for Co-Processing (EUCOPRO, #05991)*; *European Federation of Waste Management and Environmental Services (#07232)*. [2021/XD8303/**D**]

♦ European Recovered Paper Council / see European Paper Recycling Council (#08139)
♦ European Recovery and Recycling Association (inactive)
♦ European Recycling Coalition (inactive)

♦ European Recycling Industries' Confederation (EuRIC) 08335

SG Bd Auguste Reyers 80, 1030 Brussels, Belgium. T. +3227068723 – +3227068720. E-mail: euric@euric-aisbl.eu.
Registered Seat Franklin Roosevelt 24, 1050 Brussels, Belgium.
URL: http://www.euric-aisbl.eu/
History 2014. Founded by *European Ferrous Recovery and Recycling Federation (EFR, inactive)*, *European Recovered Paper Association (ERPA, inactive)* and *European Metal Trade and Recycling Association (EUROMETREC, inactive)*, which currently serve as branches. Registration: Banque-Carrefour des Entreprises, No/ID: 0598.755.363, Start date: 13 Jan 2015, Belgium; EU Transparency Register, No/ID: 764633015511-42, Start date: 11 Jan 2015. **Aims** Represent the interests of the European recycling industries. **Structure** General Assembly; Board; Secretariat, based in Brussels (Belgium). **Languages** English, French, German, Spanish. **Staff** 7.00 FTE, paid. **Activities** Advocacy/lobbying/activism; events/meetings; guidance/assistance/consulting; knowledge management/information dissemination; monitoring/evaluation; networking/liaising. **Events** *European Recycling Conference* Madrid (Spain) 2021, *Conference* Madrid (Spain) 2020, *Conference on Implementing Circular Value Chains* Brussels (Belgium) 2019, *Conference* Paris (France) 2019, *Conference* Berlin (Germany) 2018. **Publications** Position papers; Press releases.
Members Affiliated members in 17 countries:
Belgium, Bulgaria, Czechia, Finland, France, Germany, Greece, Hungary, Italy, Netherlands, Norway, Portugal, Slovakia, Spain, Sweden, Switzerland, UK.
Branches (3):
European Ferrous Recovery and Recycling Federation (EFR); European Metal Trade and Recycling Association (EUROMETREC); European Recovered Paper Association (ERPA).
IGO Relations Accredited by (1): *European Chemicals Agency (ECHA, #06523)*. **NGO Relations** Member of (4): *Bureau of International Recycling (BIR, #03368)*; *Circular Plastics Alliance (#03936)*; *Comité européen de normalisation (CEN, #04162)*; *European Committee for Electrotechnical Standardization (CENELEC, #06647)*. Associate Expert Group of *Business and Industry Advisory Committee to the OECD (BIAC, #03385)*. [2023/XM5382/ty/**D**]

♦ European Recycling Platform (ERP) 08336

Coordination Office c/o ERP Italia srl, Viale Assunta 101, 20063 Cernusco sul Naviglio MI, Italy. T. +39292147479. E-mail: info@erp-recycling.org.
URL: http://erp-recycling.org/
History 2002. **Aims** Implement the European Union's regulations on the recycling of *electrical* and *electronic waste* (WEEE Directive).
Members Full in 18 countries:
Austria, China, Denmark, Finland, France, Germany, Ireland, Israel, Italy, Netherlands, Norway, Poland, Portugal, Slovakia, Spain, Sweden, Türkiye, UK.
NGO Relations Member of: *WEEELABEX Organisation (#20851)*. Technical Liaison Partner with: *European Committee for Electrotechnical Standardization (CENELEC, #06647)*. [2015/XM4097/**F**]

♦ European Red Cell Society (unconfirmed)
♦ European Reference Centre for First Aid Education (internationally oriented national body)

♦ European Reference Networks (ERN) 08337

Address not obtained.
URL: https://ec.europa.eu/health/ern_en/
History First ERNs launched Mar 2017, as virtual networks involving healthcare providers across Europe. Process and criteria for establishing an ERN set in *European Union (EU, #08967)* legislation. **Aims** Facilitate discussion on complex or rare *diseases* and conditions that require highly specialised treatment, and concentrated knowledge and resources.
Structure Initiative mainly driven by EU countries. Formal body: Board of Member States. Current ERNs (24):
- *European Reference Network on bone disorders (ERN BOND)*;
- *European Reference Network on craniofacial anomalies and ear, nose and throat (ENT) disorders (ERN CRANIO)*;
- *European Reference Network on endocrine conditions (Endo-ERN)*;
- *European Reference Network on epilepsies (ERN EpiCARE)*;
- *European Reference Network on kidney diseases (ERKNet)*;
- *European Reference Network on neurological diseases (ERN-RND)*;
- *European Reference Network on inherited and congenital anomalies (ERNICA)*;
- *European Reference Network on respiratory diseases (ERN LUNG)*;
- *European Reference Network on skin disorders (ERN Skin)*;
- *European Reference Network on adult cancers (solid tumours) (ERN EURACAN)*;
- *European Reference Network on haematological diseases (ERN EuroBloodNet)*;
- *European Reference Network on urogenital diseases and conditions (ERN eUROGEN)*;
- *European Reference Network on neuromuscular diseases (ERN EURO-NMD)*;
- *European Reference Network on eye diseases (ERN EYE)*;
- *European Reference Network on genetic tumour risk syndromes (ERN GENTURIS)*;
- *European Reference Network on diseases of the heart (ERN GUARD-HEART)*;
- *European Reference Network on congenital malformations and rare intellectual disability (ERN ITHACA)*;
- *European Reference Network on hereditary metabolic disorders (MetabERN)*;
- *European Reference Network on paediatric cancer (haemato-oncology) (ERN PaedCan)*;
- *European Reference Network on hepatological diseases (ERN RARE-LIVER)*;
- *European Reference Network on connective tissue and musculoskeletal diseases (ERN ReCONNET)*;
- *European Reference Network on immunodeficiency, autoinflammatory and autoimmune diseases (ERN RITA)*;
- *European Reference Network on Transplantation in Children (ERN TRANSPLANT-CHILD)*;
- *European Reference Network on Rare Multisystemic Vascular Diseases (VASCERN)*.

Events *World Congress on Rare Skin Disorders* Paris (France) 2022, *European PF Patient Summit* Gentbrugge (Belgium) 2021, *European IPF Patient Summit* Warsaw (Poland) 2020. [2022/XM8759/**F**]

♦ European Reference Organization for Quality Assured Breast Screening and Diagnostic Services (EUREF) 08338

Main Office Radboud Univ Medical Centre, Radiology/DIAG loc 766, PO Box 9101, 6500 HB Nijmegen, Netherlands. E-mail: info@euref.org.
URL: http://www.euref.org/
Structure Council; Management Board; Affiliated Experts; Administrative Office. **IGO Relations** Cooperates with: *European Position Determination System (EUPOS, #08256)*. [2016/XD9434/**D**]

♦ European Refractive Surgery Society / see European Society of Cataract and Refractive Surgeons (#08539)

♦ European Refractories Producers Federation 08339

Fédération européenne des fabricants de produits réfractaires (PRE) – Europäische Vereinigung der Hersteller Feuerfester Erzeugnisse – Federazione Europea dei Fabbricanti di Prodotti Refrattari
SG Rue Belliard 12, 1040 Brussels, Belgium. T. +3225113012 – +3225117025. Fax +3225115174. E-mail: sec@cerameunie.eu.
URL: http://www.pre.eu/
History 27 Apr 1953, Geneva (Switzerland). Former names and other names: *European Federation of Manufacturers of Refractory Products* – alias. Registration: EU Transparency Register, No/ID: 09090633680-90. **Aims** Promote the interests of European Refractory Producers. **Structure** General Assembly; Executive Committee; Technical Committee. President; Secretary-General. **Languages** English, French, German. **Staff** 6.00 FTE, paid. **Activities** Knowledge management/information dissemination. **Events** *PRE Congress* 2021, *PRE Congress* Madrid (Spain) 2020, *Annual General Assembly* Istanbul (Turkey) 2015, *Annual General Assembly* Portoroz (Slovenia) 2014, *Annual General Assembly* Berlin (Germany) 2013.
Members Organizations in 16 countries:
Austria, Czechia, Denmark, Finland, France, Germany, Italy, Norway, Poland, Portugal, Slovakia, Slovenia, Spain, Sweden, Türkiye, UK.
IGO Relations Recognized by: *European Commission (EC, #06633)*. **NGO Relations** Member of: *European Ceramic Industry Association (CERAME-UNIE, #06506)*; *Industry4Europe (#11181)*. Principal member of: *UNITECR International Executive Board (UNITECR IEB, #20496)*. In liaison with technical committees of: *International Organization for Standardization (ISO, #14473)*. [2019/XD0738/**D**]

♦ European Refugee Fund (inactive)

♦ European Refurbishment Association (EUREFAS) 08340

Registered Address Rue Montoyer 25, 1000 Brussels, Belgium. E-mail: contact@eurefas.com.
URL: https://www.eurefas.com/
History Registration: Banque-Carrefour des Enterprises, No/ID: 0764.678.318, Start date: 5 Mar 2021, Belgium; EU Transparency Register, No/ID: 332404341982-26, Start date: 31 Mar 2021. **Aims** Represent the EU refurbished smartphone market; ensure and define quality standards for the interests of end customers and contribute to a greener world. **Languages** English. **Members** Organizations (17). Membership countries not specified. [2022.05.10/AA1524/**D**]

♦ European Region of the Airports Council International / see Airports Council International – European Region (#00612)
♦ European Regional Aerodromes Community (unconfirmed)
♦ European Regional Airlines Organisation / see European Regions Airline Association (#08347)
♦ European Regional Branch of the International Council on Archives (see: #12996)
♦ European Regional Centre for Ecohydrology, Lodz / see European Regional Centre for Ecohydrology of the Polish Academy of Sciences, Lodz (#08341)

♦ European Regional Centre for Ecohydrology of the Polish Academy of Sciences, Lodz (ERCE PAS) 08341

Centre régional européen d'écohydrologie, Lodz
Dir 3 Tylna St, 90-364 Lódz, Poland. T. +48426817007. Fax +48426813069. E-mail: erce@erce.unesco.lodz.pl.
URL: http://www.erce.unesco.lodz.pl/
History 31 May 2006, Lódz (Poland). Established 31 May 2006, Lodz (Poland), as *European Regional Centre for Ecohydrology, Lodz (ERCE)*, under the auspices of *UNESCO (#20322)*, following an agreement with the Government of Poland, signed 8 Mar 2006, Paris (France). Grew out of the International Centre for Ecology (ICE) of the Polish Academy of Sciences, whose profile was based on ecological bioenergetics developed in the 1970s through the International Biological Programme (IBP). The background of "aquatic ecohydrology" was established in the framework of the UNESCO MAB "Ecotone" Programme. The concept of integrating hydrology and ecology was formulated and developed in the framework of the UNESCO International Hydrological Programme IHP V and VI. During the development of the framework of UNESCO IHP phases V and VI, ecohydrology has become a transdisciplinary science. One of the achievements of the IBP programme was the reduction of ecological processes to physics, providing fundamentals for dialogue between ecologists and hydrologists in the 1990s. The theoretical and empirical background for formulation of ecohydrological principles was developed in the 1980s and 1990s at the Department of Applied Ecology, University of Lodz. By agreement between the President of the Academy of Science and the Rector of the University of Lodz, cooperation between these institutions was formalized in 2004. Comes within the framework of *International Hydrological Programme (IHP, #13826)*. Registered in accordance with Polish law. **Aims** Develop ecohydrological science and its implementation for restoring freshwater resources in the framework of the UNESCO International Hydrological Programme; deliver tools for implementing the European Water Framework Directive ad part of Poland's national cooperation. **Structure** Research Council; Headed by Director; Personnel and Accounting Team, headed by Chief Accountant; Research Units (2), headed by Deputy Director: Fluvial Ecosystems and Urban Areas Ecohydrology; Molecular Ecohydrology. Editorial Office; Secretariat. **Languages** English. **Staff** 32.00 FTE, paid. **Activities** Events/meetings; training/education. **Events** *International conference on ecohydrological processes and sustainable foodplain management* Lódz (Poland) 2008. **Publications** *Ecohydrology and Hydrobiology Journal*. Papers; articles. **IGO Relations** Partner of (1): *Global Alliances for Water and Climate (GAfWaC, #10230)*. **NGO Relations** Member of (2): *Alternet (#00756)*; *International Centre for Coast Ecohydrology (ICCE, #12481)*. Links with universities. [2019.10.04/XM1322/**E***]

♦ European Regional Convention for the Maritime Mobile Radio Service (1948 treaty)
♦ European Regional Council of WFMH / see Mental Health Europe (#16715)
♦ European Regional Council of the World Federation for Mental Health / see Mental Health Europe (#16715)

♦ European Regional Development Fund (ERDF) 08342

Fonds européen de développement régional (FEDER) – Europees Fonds voor Regionale Ontwikkeling (EFRO)
Contact DG REGIO/02 – Communication, European Commission – BU1 0/10, 1049 Brussels, Belgium. T. +3222953258.
URL: http://ec.europa.eu/regional_policy/thefunds/cohesion/index_en.cfm/
History Established 18 Mar 1975, Brussels (Belgium), by Resolution 725/75 of *Council of the European Union (#04895)*. Reorganized: Jan 1985; Dec 1988. Current specific provisions laid down in Regulation (EC) No 1080/2006 of *European Parliament (EP, #08146)* and of the Council of 5 Jul 2006 on ERDF and repealing Regulation (EC) 1783/1999. An integral part of *European Communities (EC, inactive)* and, following signature of *Treaty on European Union (Maastricht Treaty, 1992)*, of *European Union (EU, #08967)*. **Aims** Reduce structural disparities and help the least prosperous regions catch up with those that are more developed to improve the overall 'cohesion' of the EU; foster conditions necessary for increased growth and jobs, with priority financing aimed at research, innovation, environmental upgrading and risk prevention, renewable energies and energy efficiency and improving accessibility to transport and telecommunications services. **Structure** Fund managed by all EU members states and supervised by *European Commission (EC, #06633)*, DG Regional Policy (DG REGIO). **Staff** 650.00 FTE, paid. **Finance** Budget assessed by *European Parliament (EP, #08146)*. **Activities** Financial and/or material support; events/meetings. Finances: direct aid to investments in companies (particularly SMEs) to create sustainable jobs; infrastructure linked notably to research and innovation, telecommunications, environment, energy and transport; financial instruments (capital risk funds, local development funds, etc) to support regional and local development and to foster cooperation between towns and regions. **Events** *Interactive Water Management Project Final Conference* Finland 2019, *Interreg 2 Seas Midterm Review Meeting* Ghent (Belgium) 2019, *FEMINA Convention* Grimstad (Norway) 2019, *Interact Meeting* Amsterdam (Netherlands) 2016, *North Sea Conference* Billund (Denmark) 2016. **Publications** *Regio Flash* (12 a year) – electronic newsletter; *Panorama* (4 a year) – brochure. **Members** Not a membership organization. **IGO Relations** Works jointly on specific objectives with *European Social Fund (ESF, #08501)*, *European Agricultural Guarantee Fund (EAGF)*. [2018/XF5543/f/**F***]

♦ European Regional Focal Point for Animal Genetic Resources (ERFP) 08343

Secretariat Institut de l'Elevage, 149 rue de Bercy, 75595 Paris Cedex 12, France. T. +33140045314.
URL: https://www.animalgeneticresources.net/

History Aug 2001. Founded under the auspices of *FAO (#09260)*, to serve as the European implementation organization for the global strategy for the management of farm animal genetic resources. **Aims** Support the *'in situ'* and *'ex situ' conservation* and sustainable use of Animal Genetic Resources (AnGR); facilitate implementation of FAO's Global Plan of Action for AnGR in Europe. **Structure** Assembly of National Coordinators for AnGR (Annual Meeting); Steering Committee; Working Groups (3); Task Forces (2). **Languages** English. **Staff** Voluntary. National Coordinators paid by home countries. **Finance** Sources: contributions. **Activities** Projects/programmes; research/documentation. **Events** *Annual Meeting* Ghent (Belgium) 2019, *Annual Meeting* Zagreb (Croatia) 2018, *Annual Meeting* Tallinn (Estonia) 2017, *Annual Meeting* Belfast (UK) 2016, *Annual Meeting* Krakow (Poland) 2015. **Publications** *ERFP Newsletter*. Project reports.
Members National Focal Points in 44 countries:
Albania, Austria, Azerbaijan, Belarus, Belgium, Bosnia-Herzegovina, Bulgaria, Croatia, Cyprus, Czechia, Denmark, Estonia, Finland, France, Georgia, Germany, Greece, Hungary, Iceland, Ireland, Israel, Italy, Latvia, Lithuania, Luxembourg, Malta, Moldova, Montenegro, Netherlands, North Macedonia, Norway, Poland, Portugal, Romania, Russia, Serbia, Slovakia, Slovenia, Spain, Sweden, Switzerland, Türkiye, UK, Ukraine.
IGO Relations *European Cooperative Programme for Plant Genetic Resources (ECPGR, #06787)*; *European Forest Genetic Resources Programme (EUFORGEN, #07296)*; *FAO (#09260)*. **NGO Relations** Cooperates with: *Dunamenti Állatfajták Génmegőrző Nemzetközi Egyesülete (DAGENE, #05146)*; *European Federation of Animal Science (EAAP, #07046)* – Working Group on Animal Genetic Resources; *European Forum of Farm Animal Breeders (EFFAB, #07310)*; ProSpecieRara; *Rare Breeds International (RBI, inactive)*; *Safeguard for Agricultural Varieties in Europe (SAVE Foundation, #19027)*. [2020.05.12/XJ0883/**E**]

- ♦ European Regional Group / see European Music Council (#07837)
- ♦ European Regional Group for Social Work Education / see European Association of Schools of Social Work (#06200)
- ♦ European Regional Industrial Development Organization (inactive)
- ♦ European Regional Information Society Association (no recent information)

♦ European Regional and Local Health Authorities (EUREGHA) 08344

Secretariat Rond Point Schuman 11, 1040 Brussels, Belgium. T. +32484759828. E-mail: secretariat@euregha.net – info@euregha.net.
URL: http://www.euregha.net/

History 2012. Proposed 30 Jan 2006, according to an opinion of *European Committee of the Regions (CoR, #06665)*. Registration: Banque Carrefour des Entreprises, No/ID: 0843.942.560, Start date: 24 Feb 2012, Belgium; EU Transparency Register, No/ID: 117410219881-21, Start date: 25 Jan 2016. **Aims** Bring regional and local health authorities together as a means to improve health policy in Europe. **Structure** General Assembly; Executive Board; Secretariat. **Activities** Healthcare; networking/liaising; politics/policy/regulatory; projects/programmes. **Events** *European Value-Based Procurement Conference* Brussels (Belgium) 2019, *EHTEL Annual Symposium* Brussels (Belgium) 2010.
Members States (10):
Austria, Belgium, Czechia, Italy, Netherlands, Norway, Poland, Spain, Sweden, UK.
NGO Relations Member of (1): *EU Health Coalition*. [2020.09.01/XJ2050/**E***]

♦ European Regional Organization of the Fédération dentaire internationale (ERO) 08345

Organisation régionale européenne de la FDI (ORE) – Europäische Regionale Organisation der FDI
Contact c/o SSO, Münzgraben 2, PO Box, 3001 Bern 7, Switzerland. T. +41313133161. Fax +41313133140. E-mail: ero-sekretariat@sso.ch.
URL: http://www.erodental.org/

History 30 Jan 1965, Liège (Belgium). Founded as a regional organization of *FDI – World Dental Federation (#09281)*, following activities initiated in 1955 with the creation of the Special Commission for European Cooperation of the FDI which was renamed in 1958 to the Regional Commission for Europe. Former names and other names: *Organisation régionale de la FDI pour l'Europe (ORE)* – former alias; *Regionale Organisation der FDI für Europa* – former alias. **Aims** Establish closer cooperation between member associations or national committees of FDI in Europe in the fields of research, education and *public health* in order to improve the *dental* and general health of all peoples and safeguard the interests of the *profession*; increase information exchange in the region in the interest of all members. **Structure** Delegate Plenary Session (2 a year). **Languages** English, French, German. **Finance** Members' dues. **Events** *Plenary Session* Istanbul (Türkiye) 2023, *Plenary Session* Bucharest (Romania) 2022, *Plenary Session* Frankfurt-Main (Germany) 2019, *Plenary Session* Buenos Aires (Argentina) 2018, *Plenary Session* Salzburg (Austria) 2018. **Publications** Information circulars/presidential letters (at least 4 a year).
Members Affiliate; Associate. Associations and national committees of FDI in 36 countries:
Albania, Armenia, Austria, Azerbaijan, Belarus, Belgium, Bosnia-Herzegovina, Bulgaria, Croatia, Cyprus, Czechia, Denmark, Estonia, France, Georgia, Germany, Greece, Iceland, Israel, Italy, Kazakhstan, Kyrgyzstan, Latvia, Lithuania, Luxembourg, Netherlands, North Macedonia, Poland, Portugal, Romania, Slovakia, Slovenia, Spain, Switzerland, Türkiye, UK, Ukraine.
Included in the above, 1 organization listed in this Yearbook:
European Society of Dental Ergonomics (ESDE, #08577). [2022/XE0842/y/**E**]

- ♦ European Regional Red Cross and Red Crescent Conference (meeting series)

♦ European Regional Science Association (ERSA) 08346

Association européenne de science régionale
Exec Dir c/o CORE-UCL, Voie du Roman Pays 34, L1-03-01, 1348 Louvain-la-Neuve, Belgium. T. +3210474362. E-mail: info@ersa.org – office@ersa.org.
URL: http://www.ersa.org/

History 1950. Founded within *Regional Science Association International (RSAI, #18813)*. Registration: Belgium. **Aims** Advance regional analysis and related spatial and areal studies; foster exchange of ideas at the European level. **Structure** European Regional Science Association Council (ERSAC), including ERSAC Board; European Organizing Committee. Working Committees (2): Conference; Communications. **Languages** English. **Staff** 1.00 FTE, paid. **Finance** Members' dues; conference's fees. **Activities** Events/meetings; training/education; awards/prizes/competitions. **Events** *Annual Congress* Pécs (Hungary) 2022, *Annual Congress* 2021, *Annual Congress* Bolzano (Italy) 2020, *Conference* Louvain-la-Neuve (Belgium) 2020, *Annual Congress* Lyon (France) 2019. **Publications** *REGION* – online journal. Section journals.
Members Organizations in 26 countries:
Austria, Belgium, Croatia, Denmark, Finland, France, Germany, Greece, Hungary, Ireland, Israel, Italy, Luxembourg, Netherlands, Norway, Poland, Portugal, Russia, Slovakia, Slovenia, Spain, Sweden, Switzerland, Türkiye, UK, Ukraine.
IGO Relations *EIB Institute (#05398)*. **NGO Relations** Member of: *European Alliance for the Social Sciences and Humanities (EASSH, #05885)*. Cooperates with: *Association of European Schools of Planning (AESOP, #02542)*. [2022/XD6736/**D**]

- ♦ European Regional/spatial Planning Charter (1983 treaty)
- ♦ European Region – International Federation of Hard of Hearing People / see European Federation of Hard of Hearing People (#07136)

♦ European Regions Airline Association (ERA) 08347

Association des compagnies d'aviation des régions d'Europe – Asociación de las Compañias de Aviación de las Regiones de Europa – Verband Europäischer Regionen der Fluglinien
Dir Gen Park House, 127 Guildford Road, Lightwater, GU18 5RA, UK. T. +441276856495. Fax +441276857038. E-mail: info@eraa.org.
Brussels Office Office 50-710, Eurocontrol, Rue de la Fusée 96, 1130 Brussels, Belgium.
URL: http://www.eraa.org/

History 24 Jan 1981, Zurich (Switzerland), as *European Regional Airlines Organisation – Organisation européenne des compagnies d'aviation régionales – Organización Europea de las Compañias Regionales de Aviación – Organisation Europäischer Regional-Luftverkehrsgesellschaften*. Present name adopted Oct 1996. EU Transparency Register: 73491621553-11. **Aims** Act as principal body representing interests of organizations involved in air transport in Europe's regions by: influencing regulatory and environmental conditions; facilitating technical cooperation and advancement; gaining public and political support. **Structure** General Assembly (annual); Board; Work Groups; Directorate, comprising Director General and staff. **Languages** English. **Staff** 14.00 FTE, paid. **Finance** Members' dues. Contributions. **Activities** Politics/policy/regulatory; research and development; awareness raising; networking/liaising; advocacy/lobbying/activism. **Events** *Annual Safety Forum* Brussels (Belgium) 2022, *Annual Safety Forum* Brussels (Belgium) 2021, *Annual Safety Forum* Brussels (Belgium) 2020, *Annual Safety Forum* Brussels (Belgium) 2019, *Annual General Assembly and Conference* Juan-les-Pins (France) 2019. **Publications** *ERA Regional International* (6 a year); *ERA Yearbook* (annual). Documents on relevant issues; reports of meetings; circulars; ad hoc press releases.
Members Airlines (50), airports (21) and other bodies (over 100). Members in 38 countries and territories:
Austria, Belgium, Brazil, Canada, Channel Is, Croatia, Denmark, Faeroe Is, Finland, France, Germany, Greece, Iceland, Ireland, Italy, Japan, Latvia, Lithuania, Luxembourg, Morocco, Netherlands, North Macedonia, Norway, Palestine, Poland, Portugal, Romania, Russia, Serbia, Singapore, Slovenia, Spain, Sweden, Switzerland, Türkiye, UK, Ukraine, USA.
IGO Relations Represented on External Committees and participates in the work of: *European Union Aviation Safety Agency (EASA, #08978)*; *European Civil Aviation Conference (ECAC, #06564)*; *European Commission (EC, #06633)*. **NGO Relations** Instrumental in setting up: *Council for Environmentally Friendly Aviation (CEFA, #04880)*; *International Federation of Regional Airlines Associations (IFRAA, inactive)*. [2019/XD6504/**D**]

- ♦ European Regions and Municipalities Partnership for Hydrogen and Fuel Cells / see European Association for Hydrogen and fuel cells and Electro-mobility in European Regions (#06076)

♦ European Regions' Network for the Application of Communications Technology (ERNACT) 08348

General Manager Unit 271 – CoLab, LYIT Campus, Port Road, Letterkenny, CO. DONEGAL, Ireland. T. +353749168212. E-mail: info@ernact.eu.
URL: http://www.ernact.eu/

History Set up, originally within the framework of *Regions and Cities of Europe (RECITE Programme, inactive)*. An organization of the type *European Economic Interest Grouping (EEIG, #06960)*. **Aims** Develop and transfer practical e-services for citizens and business, broadband and innovation strategies and applications. **Structure** International Management Committee; Office. **Languages** English. **Staff** 7.00 FTE, paid. **Activities** Projects/programmes.
Members Local and regional authorities (8) in 8 countries:
Canada, Finland, Ireland, Romania, Slovenia, Spain, Sweden, UK. [2022.02.08/XU4294/**F**]

♦ European Regions Research and Innovation Network (ERRIN) 08349

Dir Rue du Luxembourg 3, Floor 2, 1000 Brussels, Belgium. T. +3225033554.
URL: http://www.errinnetwork.eu/

History Apr 2004, as a *European Commission (EC, #06633)* funded project. Relaunched Dec 2006 as an independent organization, registered under Belgian law. **Aims** Strengthen regional research and innovation capacities by exchanging information, sharing best practices, supporting European project development, policy shaping and profile raising by working together with a partnership approach. **Structure** Management Board; Thematic Working Groups; Secretariat. **Languages** English. **Staff** 6.00 FTE, paid. **Finance** Members' dues. **Events** *Annual General Meeting* Brussels (Belgium) 2019, *Circular Economy Conference* Brussels (Belgium) 2018, *Conference on Shaping the Mobility of the Future* Brussels (Belgium) 2011, *Conference* Brussels (Belgium) 2010. **Publications** *ERRIN Newsletter* (weekly).
Members Full; Associate. Members in 24 countries:
Austria, Belgium, Croatia, Cyprus, Czechia, Denmark, Finland, France, Germany, Greece, Hungary, Ireland, Italy, Luxembourg, Malta, Netherlands, Norway, Poland, Portugal, Slovenia, Spain, Sweden, Türkiye, UK. [2019/XM3299/**F**]

- ♦ European Region of the World Union for Progressive Judaism / see European Union for Progressive Judaism (#09010)

♦ European Register for Osteopathic Physicians (EROP) 08350

Pres c/o Ak für Gesundheitsfachberufe am Diakoniekrankenhaus, Belchenstr 1-5, 68163 Mannheim, Germany. T. +4962143626692. Fax +4962143626691. E-mail: kontakt@dgom.info.
URL: http://www.erop.org/

History Current articles adopted Feb 2003. Registered in accordance with German law. **Aims** Define the conception and significance of Osteopathic Medicine within health care systems in Europe. **Structure** Membership Assembly; Executive Committee; Scientific Advisory Council. **Finance** Members' dues. **Activities** Standards/guidelines; training/education.
Members Ordinary; Supporting. Members in 5 countries:
Austria, France, Germany, Italy, Switzerland.
NGO Relations Partner member of: *Osteopathic International Alliance (OIA, #17910)*. [2018/XM7481/**F**]

- ♦ European Registrars Conference (meeting series)
- ♦ European Registration of Congenital Anomalies / see EUROCAT – European Surveillance of Congenital Anomalies (#05655)
- ♦ European Registration Plate Association / see Europlate (#09171)
- ♦ European Registry of Hereditary Pancreatitis and Familial Pancreatic Cancer (internationally oriented national body)

♦ European Registry of Internet Domain Names (EURid) 08351

Gen Manager Telecomlaan 9, 1831 Diegem, Belgium. T. +3224012750.
URL: http://www.eurid.eu/

History 2003. Registration: No/ID: 0864.240.405, Start date: 27 Jun 2003, Belgium; EU Transparency Register, No/ID: 486684937120-73, Start date: 28 Jan 2020. **Aims** Organize and manage the 'dot'eu top-level domain on the Internet. **Structure** General Assembly (annual); Board of Directors; Strategic Committee; Registrar Advisory Board. Management Team. Regional Offices (3): Prague (Czech Rep); Pisa (Italy); Stockholm (Sweden). **Languages** Czech, Danish, Dutch, English, Estonian, Finnish, French, German, Hungarian, Irish Gaelic, Italian, Latvian, Lithuanian, Maltese, Polish, Portuguese, Slovakian, Slovene, Spanish, Swedish. **Staff** 57.00 FTE, paid. **Finance** Annual domain fees. **Events** *European business summit* Brussels (Belgium) 2009. **Publications** *Registrar Newsletter* (12 a year) – online; *dot eu Identity Magazine* (2 a year). Brochures.
Members Individuals representing national or international organizations in 4 countries:
Belgium, Czechia, Italy, Slovenia.
BUSINESSEUROPE (#03381); *Council of European Professional Informatics Societies (CEPIS, #04893)*; *Ecommerce Europe (#05307)*; *Euroconsumers (#05666)*; *European Competitive Telecommunications Association (ECTA, #06689)*; *IAB Europe (#11002)*; *SMEunited (#19327)*.
IGO Relations *European Commission (EC, #06633)*. **NGO Relations** Member of: *Council of European National Top-Level Domain Registries (CENTR, #04892)*; *European Internet Forum (EIF, #07591)*. Cooperates with: *Internet Corporation for Assigned Names and Numbers (ICANN, #15949)*. [2020/XJ3145/**F**]

- ♦ European Regulators Group / see Body of European Regulators for Electronic Communications (#03299)

♦ European Relocation Association (EuRA) 08352

CEO Meadowside, Pottery Hill, Wattisfield, Diss, IP22 1NH, UK. T. +441379640883. E-mail: enquiries@eura-relocation.com.
Events – Coordinator address not obtained.
URL: http://www.eura-relocation.com/

History May 1998, Brussels (Belgium). Registration: Companies House, No/ID: 03690726, Start date: 31 Dec 1998, England and Wales, Norfolk. **Aims** Spread knowledge and understanding of issues surrounding *corporate mobility*; enhance industry performance standards by communication and education. **Structure** Council. **Languages** English. **Staff** 3.50 FTE, paid. **Finance** Sources: subscriptions. Annual budget: 625 EUR. **Activities** Certification/accreditation; training/education. **Events** *Annual Conference* Seville (Spain) 2022, *Annual Conference* Seville (Spain) 2021, *Annual Conference* Seville (Spain) 2020, *Annual Conference* Munich (Germany) 2019, *Annual Conference* Dubrovnik (Croatia) 2018. **Publications** *The EuRAPEAN* (3 a year); *e-EuRA Newsletter* – online.

Members Full; associate; affiliate; corporate; worldwide. Individuals in 88 countries and territories:
Albania, Argentina, Armenia, Australia, Austria, Azerbaijan, Bahrain, Belgium, Bolivia, Bosnia-Herzegovina, Brazil, Bulgaria, Canada, Chile, China, Colombia, Costa Rica, Côte d'Ivoire, Croatia, Czechia, Denmark, Dominican Rep, Ecuador, Egypt, El Salvador, Estonia, Finland, France, Georgia, Germany, Greece, Guatemala, Guernsey, Hong Kong, Hungary, India, Ireland, Israel, Italy, Jersey, Kazakhstan, Korea Rep, Kuwait, Latvia, Lithuania, Luxembourg, Malaysia, Mexico, Moldova, Morocco, Mozambique, Netherlands, New Zealand, Nigeria, North Macedonia, Norway, Oman, Panama, Paraguay, Peru, Philippines, Poland, Portugal, Puerto Rico, Qatar, Romania, Russia, Saudi Arabia, Serbia, Singapore, Slovakia, Slovenia, South Africa, Spain, Sudan, Sweden, Switzerland, Taiwan, Thailand, Trinidad-Tobago, Tunisia, Türkiye, UK, Ukraine, United Arab Emirates, Uruguay, USA, Venezuela. [2022.05.10/XD8567/v/**D**]

♦ European Renal Association – European Dialysis and Transplant Association (ERA-EDTA) 08353

Association européenne de maladies rénales – Association européenne de dialyse et de transplantation

Address not obtained.

Registered Address c/o PKF Littlejohn, 15 Westferry Circus, Canary Wharf, London, E14 4HD, UK.

General: https://www.era-online.org/

History Sep 1964, Amsterdam (Netherlands). Present Constitution adopted by the General Assembly of 33rd Congress, 20 Jun 1996, Amsterdam. Former names and other names: *European Dialysis and Transplant Association – European Renal Association (EDTA-ERA)* – former; *Association européenne de dialyse et de transplantation – Association européenne de maladies rénales* – former. Registration: Charity, No/ID: 1060134, Start date: 1997, England and Wales; EU Transparency Register, No/ID: 388620435175-53. **Aims** Encourage and report advances of medical science by promoting fundamental and clinical advances in the field of nephrology, dialysis, renal transplantation, hypertension and related subjects. **Structure** General Assembly (annual); Council. **Languages** English. **Finance** Sources: members' dues. **Activities** Awards/prizes/competitions; events/meetings; knowledge management/information dissemination. **Events** *Congress* Milan (Italy) 2023, *Congress* Paris (France) 2022, *Annual Congress* Berlin (Germany) 2021, *Annual Congress* Parma (Italy) 2020, *Annual Congress* Budapest (Hungary) 2019. **Publications** *Nephrology, Dialysis, Transplantation* (12 a year); *Clinicl Kidney Journal (ckj)* (6 a year) – online; *NDT-Educational* – electronic journal.

Members Full individuals within Europe and adjacent countries (defined as the countries bordering Europe and the Mediterranean countries); Associate individuals living outside Europe or adjacent countries. Full in 51 countries and territories:
Albania, Algeria, Austria, Belarus, Belgium, Bosnia-Herzegovina, Bulgaria, Croatia, Cyprus, Czechia, Denmark, Egypt, Estonia, Finland, France, Germany, Greece, Hungary, Iceland, Ireland, Israel, Italy, Latvia, Lebanon, Libya, Lithuania, Luxembourg, Malta, Moldova, Monaco, Morocco, Netherlands, North Macedonia, Norway, Poland, Polynesia Fr, Portugal, Réunion, Romania, Russia, Serbia, Slovakia, Slovenia, Spain, Sweden, Switzerland, Syrian AR, Tunisia, Türkiye, UK, Ukraine.
Associate in 57 countries and territories:
Argentina, Armenia, Australia, Azerbaijan, Bahamas, Bahrain, Bangladesh, Bermuda, Brazil, Canada, Chile, China, Colombia, Costa Rica, Côte d'Ivoire, Dominican Rep, Ecuador, Gabon, Georgia, Hong Kong, India, Indonesia, Iran Islamic Rep, Iraq, Jamaica, Japan, Jordan, Kazakhstan, Kenya, Korea Rep, Kuwait, Kyrgyzstan, Malaysia, Mexico, New Caledonia, New Zealand, Nigeria, Pakistan, Panama, Paraguay, Peru, Philippines, Puerto Rico, Qatar, Saudi Arabia, Singapore, South Africa, Sudan, Taiwan, Thailand, United Arab Emirates, Uruguay, USA, Venezuela, Vietnam, Yemen.

IGO Relations *WHO (#20950).* **NGO Relations** Member of (3): *Biomedical Alliance in Europe (#03251); European Kidney Health Alliance (EKHA, #07626); International Society of Nephrology (ISN, #15294).* Endorses: *International Renal Conference.* [2022/XD0706/v/**D**]

♦ European Renal Cell Study Group (ERCSG) 08354

Contact UMR-S 1155 Hôpital Tenon, 4 rue de la Chine, 75020 Paris, France.

Events *Meeting* Paris (France) 2016, *Meeting* Carlingford (Ireland) 2015, *Meeting* Kelkheim (Germany) 2014, *Meeting* Greece 2009, *Meeting* UK 2008. [2016/XJ0092/**E**]

♦ European Renderers Association (inactive)

♦ European Renewable Energies Federation (EREF) 08355

Fédération européenne des énergies renouvelables

Contact Avenue Marnix 28, 1000 Brussels, Belgium. T. +3222044400. Fax +3222044499. E-mail: info@eref-europe.org.

URL: http://www.eref-europe.org/

History 1999. Registration: EU Transparency Register, No/ID: 48677174683-66. **Aims** As the voice of independent producers of *electricity* and fuels from all renewable energy sources (except large hydro): create an operational network of renewable energy power producers; raise awareness in the public and European institutions and other stakeholders about the sector as it develops; acts as a watchdog of the energy sector for independent power producers in Europe on aspects such as fair access to the market, strong investment, abatement of barriers and security policies. **Structure** Board; Advisory Council. **Languages** Danish, Dutch, English, Estonian, French, German, Irish Gaelic, Italian, Polish, Portuguese, Slovakian, Spanish, Swedish. **Staff** 1.50 FTE, voluntary. **Finance** Sources: members' dues; revenue from activities/projects; sponsorship. **Activities** Events/meetings. **Events** *European Photovoltaic Solar Energy Conference* Hamburg (Germany) 2015, *European Photovoltaic Solar Energy Conference* Amsterdam (Netherlands) 2014, *European Photovoltaic Solar Energy Conference* Paris (France) 2013, *European Photovoltaic Solar Energy Conference* Frankfurt-Main (Germany) 2012, *European photovoltaic solar energy conference* Hamburg (Germany) 2011. **Publications** Price Report.

Members Full (30) in 14 countries:
Austria, Belgium, Bulgaria, Denmark, Estonia, France, Germany, Greece, Netherlands, Poland, Portugal, Spain, Sweden, UK.

NGO Relations Member of (1): *World Alliance for Efficient Solutions.* Supports (1): *Global 100% RE (#10160).* [2022.02.15/XD8452/**D**]

♦ European Renewable Energy Centres Agency / see EUREC (#05619)
♦ European Renewable Energy Council (inactive)

♦ European Renewable Gas Registry (ERGaR) 08356

Secretariat Rue d'Arlon 63-67, 1040 Brussels, Belgium. T. +3224001082.

SG address not obtained.

URL: http://www.ergar.org/

History Registered in accordance with Belgian law. **Aims** Enable cross-border trade of renewable gases. **Structure** General Assembly; Executive Board; Secretariat. **Activities** Events/meetings; knowledge management/information dissemination. **Events** *Power-to-Methane Joint Workshop* Brussels (Belgium) 2017.

Members Full; Associate. Members in 8 countries:
Austria, Denmark, France, Germany, Italy, Netherlands, Switzerland, UK.
Included in the above, 1 organization listed in this Yearbook: [2017/XM6062/**D**]

♦ European Renewable Raw Materials Association (ERRMA) 08357

Gen Sec Südliche Ringstr 111, 63225 Langen, Germany. T. +4961032020309.

Pres c/o NNFCC, York Science Park, Innovation Way, Heslington, YO10 5DG, UK.

URL: http://www.errma.com/

Aims Promote the market-led use of renewable raw materials; advise in the setting up of appropriate regulatory frameworks; establish contacts with major players in the production, use and regulation of renewable raw materials worldwide. **Structure** Officers: President, Vice-President, General Secretary. **Activities** Projects/programmes.

Members National organizations in 5 countries:
Belgium, France, Germany, Netherlands, UK.

IGO Relations *Committee of the Regions (CoR, #06665); European Commission (EC, #06633); European Parliament (EP, #08146).* **NGO Relations** *COPA – european farmers (COPA, #04829); European Association of Bioindustries (EuropaBio, #05956); Conseil européen de l'industrie chimique (CEFIC, #04687).* [2015/XD6899/**D**]

♦ European Rental Association (ERA) 08358

SG Av de Tervuren 188A, 4th Floor, Postbox 4, 1150 Brussels, Belgium. T. +3227611604. Fax +3227611699. E-mail: era@erarental.org.

URL: http://www.erarental.org/

History 2006. **Aims** Act as the representative association of the equipment rental sector at European level. **Structure** Board; Committees (5). **Languages** English. **Events** *Annual Convention* Maastricht (Netherlands) 2021, *Annual Convention* Maastricht (Netherlands) 2020, *Annual Convention* Madrid (Spain) 2019, *Annual Convention* Vienna (Austria) 2018, *Annual Convention* Amsterdam (Netherlands) 2017.

Members National rental associations in 24 countries:
Austria, Belgium, Bulgaria, China, Czechia, Denmark, Finland, France, Georgia, Germany, Italy, Liechtenstein, Luxembourg, Netherlands, Norway, Portugal, Romania, Russia, Spain, Sweden, Switzerland, Türkiye, UK, USA.
Included in the above, 1 international association:
Hire Association Europe (HAE, #10922). [2019.06.26/XM3322/**D**]

♦ European Re-refining Industry Section / see GEIR (#10088)
♦ European Re-refining Industry Section of UEIL / see GEIR (#10088)
♦ European Research Advisory Board / see European Foundation for Alcohol Research (#07342)
♦ European Research Advisory Board (inactive)
♦ European Research Area in Diabetes / see European Alliance for Diabetes Research (#05868)
♦ European Research Center for Information Systems (unconfirmed)

♦ European Research Centre for Book and Paper Conservation-Restoration (ERC) 08359

Exec Officer University for Continuing Education, Center for Cultural Property Protection, Dr.-Karl-Dorrek-Strasse 30, 3500 Krems, Austria.

URL: https://www.restauratorenohnegrenzen.eu/erc/

History 2010. Registration: No/ID: 286234, Austria. **Aims** Execute, initiate and support research in the field of book and paper conservation-restoration; communicate and disseminate research results to those who can apply them to heritage. **Structure** Board; Executive. **Languages** English. **Activities** Events/meetings; research/documentation; training/education. **Events** *IPH Congress* Krems (Austria) 2022, *Conference* Horn (Austria) 2012, *Conference* Horn (Austria) 2011. **Publications** *Conservation Update* (2 a year). Studies; reports. **Members** Individuals; Institutions. Membership countries not specified. **NGO Relations** Member of (1): *International Centre for Archival Research (ICARUS, #12477).* Partner of (1): *European Network for Conservation/Restoration Education (ENCoRE, #07883).* [2022.05.17/XJ5266/**D**]

♦ European Research Centre on Information in the Event of Disaster Situations / see European Centre for Research into Techniques for Informing the Population in Emergency Situations
♦ European Research Centre for Information to the Public in the Event of Disaster / see European Centre for Research into Techniques for Informing the Population in Emergency Situations
♦ European Research Centre on Migration and Ethnic Relations (internationally oriented national body)

♦ European Research Centres of Mathematics (ERCOM) 08360

Chair address not obtained.

URL: http://www.ercom.org/

History A committee of *European Mathematical Society (EMS, #07755).* **Aims** Serve as a forum for communications and exchange of information between the centres and EMS; foster advanced research training on a European level. **Structure** Committee (meets once a year). Chairman appointed by EMS; Vice Chairman; Scientific Secretary. **Languages** English. **Events** *Annual Members Meeting* Linz (Austria) 2017, *Annual Members Meeting* St Petersburg (Russia) 2016, *Annual Members Meeting* Zurich (Switzerland) 2015, *Annual Members Meeting* Rome (Italy) 2014, *Annual Members Meeting* Luminy (France) 2013.

Members International organizations (27), including the following 5 listed in this Yearbook:
Abdus Salam International Centre for Theoretical Physics (ICTP, #00005); Centro Internacional de Matematica (CIM); European Institute for Statistics, Probability, Stochastic Operations Research and its Applications (EURANDOM); International Center for Mathematical Meetings (CIRM); Stefan Banach International Mathematical Center at the Institute of Mathematics of the Polish Academy of Sciences (#19981). [2022/XJ4204/y/**E**]

♦ European Research Community on Flow, Turbulence and Combustion (ERCOFTAC) 08361

Communauté européenne de recherche en matière d'écoulement, de turbulence et de combustion

Address not obtained.

URL: http://www.ercoftac.org/

History 3 Jun 1988, Paris (France). Registration: Belgium. **Aims** Define a strategy for research, education and information exchange in flow, turbulence and combustion, in order to improve quality of life and the generation of wealth; strengthen the research base and improve the quality and relevance of its output to industry and government; provide members with access to all sources of useful information on flow, turbulence and combustion; influence funding agencies, governments and the European Commission and Parliament; act as a focus for contact with non-European groups. **Structure** General Assembly (annual). Managing Board, consisting of Executive Committee (Chairman, 2 Deputy Chairmen, Treasurer, Deputy Treasurer and 5 members), Secretary and 28 members. Central Administration and Development Office (CADO). Pilot Centres; Special Interest Groups (24). **Finance** Members' dues. **Activities** Training/education; events/meetings. **Events** *European Drag Reduction and Flow Control Meeting* Bad Herrenalb (Germany) 2019, *Workshop on Direct and Large-Eddy Simulation* Madrid (Spain) 2019, *Workshop on Turbulent Cascades* Lyon (France) 2017, *Seminar on Oil and Gas* Kongsberg (Norway) 2016, *International Workshop on Uncertainty Quantification in Computational Fluid Dynamics* Paris (France) 2015. **Publications** *ERCOFTAC Bulletin* (4 a year). Guidelines books.

Members Voting; Associate; Honorary. European (EC and EFTA) research groups from academic, governmental or industrial institutions and industry, engaged in the advancement of knowledge and application of flow, turbulence and combustion. Members in 19 countries:
Austria, Belgium, Czechia, Denmark, Finland, France, Germany, Greece, Hungary, Italy, Netherlands, Norway, Poland, Portugal, Slovenia, Spain, Sweden, Switzerland, UK.
Pilots Centres in 13 countries:
Austria, Belgium, Czechia, France (3), Germany (3), Greece, Italy, Netherlands, Poland, Spain, Sweden, Switzerland, UK.

NGO Relations Member of: *European Committee on Computational Methods in Applied Sciences (ECCOMAS, #06644).* Cooperates with: *International Smoothed Particle Hydrodynamics European Research Interest Community (SPHERIC, #14878).* [2020/XF0718/**F**]

♦ European Research Conference on Hypertension and Cardiovascular Disease (meeting series)

♦ European Research Consortium for Informatics and Mathematics (ERCIM) 08362

Manager 2004 Route des Lucioles, BP93, 06902 Sophia Antipolis CEDEX, France. T. +33492385010. Fax +33492385011. E-mail: contact@ercim.eu.

URL: http://www.ercim.eu/

History 13 Apr 1989, St Augustin (Germany). A grouping of the type *European Economic Interest Grouping (EEIG, #06960)* since 1992. **Aims** Foster collaborative work within the European research community; increase cooperation with European industry. **Structure** Board of Directors; Executive Committee; Manager; Working Groups; Task Groups. **Finance** Source: partner institutes. Some projects funded by *European Commission (EC, #06633).* **Activities** Awards/prizes/competitions; guidance/assistance/consulting; knowledge management/information dissemination; projects/programmes; research/documentation. mobility programme **Events** *Spring Meeting* Berlin (Germany) 2022, *Forum on Digital Ethics in Research* Paris (France) 2022, *Spring Meeting* Paris (France) 2022, *Joint Workshop* Rocquencourt (France) 2022, *Joint Workshop* Kyoto (Japan) 2021. **Publications** *ERCIM News* (4 a year). Annual Report; workshop proceedings; policy documents. **Information Services** *Digital Library Initiative.*

Members Research centres in 15 countries:
Austria, Cyprus, Finland, France, Germany, Greece, Hungary, Italy, Luxembourg, Norway, Poland, Portugal, Spain, Sweden, Switzerland.

NGO Relations Member of: *European Forum for ICST (#07316).* Participates in programmes of: *World Wide Web Consortium (W3C, #21935).* [2023.02.13/XF1803/**F**]

♦ **European Research into Consumer Affairs (ERICA)** **08363**
Institut européen de recherches pour les problèmes de consommation
Contact The Burrows, Peregrine Way, Bicester, OX26 6XB, UK.
URL: http://www.net-consumers.org/
History 1973, London (UK). UK registered charity: 281678. **Aims** Improve life for Europe's consumers, especially the disadvantaged and vulnerable, through research leading to action and through consumer education. **Structure** Directors (8). **Languages** English. **Staff** Freelance. **Finance** Funds for individual research projects obtained from private and public sources. **Activities** Investigates problems important to all European consumers: Food safety; Health issues; EU citizenship; Environment; Biodiversity; Plain Language. Provides online consumer education and information. **Publications** Books.
Members Full in 4 countries:
Greece, Ireland, Spain, UK.
NGO Relations Member of: *Consumers International (CI, #04773).* [2008.06.01/XF0515/**F**]

♦ **European Research Council (ERC)** **08364**
Dir c/o European Commission, ERC Executive Agency – COV2, 1049 Brussels, Belgium. T. +3222994145. Fax +3222979629. E-mail: erc-info@ec.europa.eu.
Street address ERC Executive Agency, Covent Garden, Place Charles Rogier 16, Saint-Josse-ten-Noode, 1210 Brussels, Belgium.
URL: http://erc.europa.eu/
History Established Feb 2007, by *European Commission (EC, #06633)*, under 7th Framework Programme for Research of *European Union (EU, #08967).* **Aims** Encourage the highest quality research in Europe through competitive funding; support investigator-driven frontier research across all fields, on the basis of scientific excellence. **Structure** Scientific Council (governing body); Executive Agency (EA); Standing Committees; Working Groups. **Languages** English. **Staff** 494.00 FTE, paid. **Finance** On Horizon Europe Budget. Total budget (2020-2027): euro 16,000,000. **Activities** Financial and/or material support; projects/programmes. **Events** *International Expert Group Meeting on Measuring Population Ageing* Bangkok (Thailand) 2019, *Seminar on Grants in Practice* Singapore (Singapore) 2019, *Conference on the Cultures of Security in the Nineteenth Century* Utrecht (Netherlands) 2019, *Conference on Frontier Research and Artificial Intelligence* Brussels (Belgium) 2018, *Joint Workshop on Cosmological Frontiers in Fundamental Physics* Brussels (Belgium) 2018. **Publications** *ERC Magazine.* Annual Report; Work Programme (annual); leaflets; brochures.
Members EU Member States and 16 associated countries. Membership countries not specified.
[2021.10.27/XM0450/**E***]

♦ **European Research and Development Service for the Social Economy (DIESIS)** **08365**
Exec Pres Boulevard Charlemagne 74, 1000 Brussels, Belgium. T. +3225431043. E-mail: diesis@diesis.coop.
Exec Dir address not obtained.
URL: http://www.diesis.coop/
History 1997. Registration: EU Transparency Register, No/ID: 210387343357-01, Start date: 30 Jun 2021. **Aims** Support the development of the *social economy.* **Structure** Board of Directors. **Activities** Awareness raising; guidance/assistance/consulting; networking/liaising; research/documentation; training/education. **Members** Organizations in 20 countries. Membership countries not specified. **IGO Relations** Member of: *OECD (#17693)* Local Economic and Employment Development Programme. **NGO Relations** Member of (3): *European Alliance for Innovation (EAI, #05872); European Alliance of Responsible Tourism and Hospitality (EARTH, #05880); International Organisation of Industrial and Service Cooperatives (CICOPA, #14429)* (Associate). Cooperates with (7): *Confédération européenne des coopératives de travail associé, des coopératives sociales et des entreprises sociales et participatives (CECOP, #04541); EMES International Research Network (#05440); European Anti-Poverty Network (EAPN, #05908); European Citizen Action Service (ECAS, #06555); Housing Europe – The European Federation for Public Cooperative and Social Housing (Housing Europe, #10956); Réseau Européen des Villes and Régions de l'Économie Sociale (REVES, #18880); Social Economy Europe (SEE, #19335).* [2021/XJ2465/**F**]

♦ **European Researchers in Didactics of Biology (ERIDOB)** **08366**
Contact address not obtained. E-mail: rtal@technion.ac.il – anat.yarden@weizmann.ac.il – kerenk@technion.ac.il.
URL: http://eridob.net.technion.ac.il/
History An informal group of researchers. Takes over activities of *Association européenne de didactique de la biologie (inactive).* Previously referred to as *European Researchers in Didaktik of Biology.* **Structure** Academic Committee of 7 members, including Secretary. **Events** *Conference* Karlstad (Sweden) 2016, *Conference / Biennial Conference* Haifa (Israel) 2014, *Conference / Biennial Conference* Berlin (Germany) 2012, *Conference / Biennial Conference* Braga (Portugal) 2010, *Biennial Conference* Utrecht (Netherlands) 2008. **Members** Membership countries not specified. **NGO Relations** *European Science Education Research Association (ESERA, #08438).* [2015.02.24/XD9348/**D**]

♦ European Researchers in Didaktik of Biology / see European Researchers in Didactics of Biology (#08366)

♦ **European Research Group on Experimental Contact Dermatitis (ERGECD)** **08367**
Contact Office of Professional Development, Univ of Maryland, School of Medicine, 655 W Balrimore St, Baltimore MD 21201, USA. T. +14107068633. Fax +14107063103.
Events *Meeting* Gothenburg (Sweden) 2011, *Meeting* Amsterdam (Netherlands) 2009, *Meeting* Lyon (France) 2006, *Meeting* Flörsheim am Main (Germany) 2005, *Meeting* Germany 2005. [2012/XD6304/**E**]

♦ **European Research Group on Military and Society (ERGOMAS)** **08368**
SG Defense Research and Development, 400 Cumberland St, Postbus 20701, Ottawa ON K1N 1J8, Canada.
Pres Institute of Social Studies, Univ of Tartu, Lossi 36, 51003 Tartu, Estonia.
URL: http://www.ergomas.ch/
History 1988. Registration: Germany. **Events** *Biennial Conference* Tartu (Estonia) 2021, *Biennial Conference* Lisbon (Portugal) 2019, *Biennial Conference* Athens (Greece) 2017, *Biennial Conference* Ra'anana (Israel) 2015, *Biennial Conference* Madrid (Spain) 2013.
Members Individuals in 23 countries:
Austria, Belgium, Bulgaria, Czechoslovakia, Denmark, Finland, France, Germany, Greece, Hungary, Ireland, Italy, Netherlands, Norway, Poland, Portugal, Russia, Slovenia, Spain, Sweden, Switzerland, Türkiye, UK. [2021/XF0833/v/**E**]

♦ European Research Infrastructure Consortium / see Joint Institute for VLBI in Europe (#16135)
♦ European Research Infrastructure Consortium / see European Infrastructure for Translational Medicine (#07536)
♦ European Research Infrastructure Consortium / see European Plate Observing System (#08220)
♦ European Research Infrastructure Consortium / see European Marine Biological Resource Centre (#07737)
♦ European Research Infrastructure Consortium / see European Carbon Dioxide Capture and Storage Laboratory Infrastructure (#06446)

♦ **European Research Institute of Catalysis (ERIC)** **08369**
CEO Operational Office, INSTM, Via G Giusti 9, 50121 Florence FI, Italy. T. +39552338713. Fax +39552480111.
Registered Office Rond-Point Schuman 14 – 5th floor, 1040 Brussels, Belgium.
URL: http://www.eric-aisbl.eu/
History 13 Nov 2008. Registered in accordance with Belgian law. **Aims** Be a knowledge-based, market oriented network designed to facilitate rapid exploitation of research and development results and know-how. **Structure** General Assembly. Board of Directors. Technical Scientific Committee. CEO.
Members Partners in 10 countries:
Belgium, Czechia, Finland, France, Germany, Italy, Netherlands, Poland, Sweden, UK.
ERIC plus partners in 3 countries:
France, Germany, Italy.
Included in the above, 1 organization listed in this Yearbook:
Max Planck Society for the Advancement of Science (MPG). [2012/XJ5615/jy/**D**]

♦ **European Research Institute for Chaplains in Healthcare (ERICH)** . . **08370**
Dir address not obtained. E-mail: erich@enhcc.eu.
Coordinator address not obtained.
URL: https://www.pastoralezorg.be/page/erich/
History 2016, Debrecen (Hungary). Founded on the instigation of *European Network of Health Care Chaplaincy (ENHCC, #07919).* **Aims** Promote research by chaplains into chaplaincy practice and in doing so encourage reflection on its theoretical underpinning. **Structure** Board. **Activities** Events/meetings; research/documentation. [2020/AA1233/**E**]

♦ European Research Institute for Comparative Cultural Policy and the Arts – Scientific Council / see European Institute for Comparative Cultural Research (#07547)
♦ European Research Institute on Cooperative and Social Enterprises (internationally oriented national body)

♦ **European Research Institute for Gas and Energy Innovation (ERIG)** . **08371**
Sec Josef-Wirmer-Str 1-3, 53123 Bonn, Germany. T. +4922891885. Fax +492289188990. E-mail: info@dvgw.de.
URL: http://www.erig.eu/
History 2 Jun 2015, Paris (France). Registration: AISBL, Belgium. **Aims** Foster the role of gas and innovative gas technologies in the future energy system. **Activities** Advocacy/lobbying/activism; knowledge management/information dissemination; research and development. **Events** *Workgroup Summit* Brussels (Belgium) 2019.
Members Full in 5 countries:
Austria, Denmark, Germany, Netherlands, Switzerland. [2019/AA0060/j/**D**]

♦ European Research Institute for Regional and Urban Planning (inactive)

♦ **European Research Network for Evaluation and Improvement of Screening, Diagnosis and Treatment of Inherited Disorders of Metabolism (ERNDIM)** **08372**
Exec Administrator Genomic Medicine, 6th Fl St Mary's Hospital, Oxford Road, Manchester, M13 9WL, UK. T. +441612766741. Fax +441618501145.
Chair Clinical Genetics Ee2422, Erasmus MC, PO Box 1738, 3000 DR Rotterdam, Netherlands. T. +31107044592. Fax +31107047200.
URL: http://www.erndim.org/
History 5 Sep 1994. A series of meetings having been held since 1992. Registered in accordance with Dutch law. **Finance** Participant subscriptions. Supported by: *European Commission (EC, #06633).* **Events** *Meeting* Basel (Switzerland) 2009, *The role of QA in the diagnosis and dietary managment of IEM – the European perspectives* Prague (Czech Rep) 2006. **Publications** *ERNDIM Newsletter. PF6 Eurogentest.*
[2020/XF4655/**F**]

♦ **European Research Network on Global Pentecostalism (GloPent)** . . **08373**
Coordinator Univ of Cambridge, Fac of Divinity, West Road, Cambridge, CB3 9BS, UK.
URL: http://www.glopent.net/
History Founded 2004, by representatives of: Centre for Pentecostal and Charismatic Studies, Birmingham (UK); Hollenweger-Center, Amsterdam (Netherlands); Department of History of Religion and Missions Studies Heidelberg (Germany). **Aims** Promote international and interdisciplinary research on Pentecostal and *Charismatic* movements by networking researchers and research institutes across the world. **Structure** Steering Group; network of researchers. **Languages** English. **Staff** 6.00 FTE, paid. **Activities** Research/documentation; events/meetings; networking/liaising. **Events** *International conference* Uppsala (Sweden) 2011, *International conference* Amsterdam (Netherlands) 2010, *International conference* Birmingham (UK) 2009. **Publications** *PentecoStudies: An Interdisciplinary Journal for Research on the Pentecostal and Charismatic Movements.*
Members Full in 48 countries and territories:
Algeria, Australia, Austria, Belgium, Bolivia, Brazil, Cameroon, Canada, Chile, Croatia, Czechia, Denmark, Ecuador, Finland, France, Germany, Ghana, Hong Kong, Hungary, India, Ireland, Israel, Italy, Japan, Kenya, Luxembourg, Malawi, Netherlands, New Zealand, Nigeria, Norway, Peru, Philippines, Poland, Portugal, Russia, Singapore, South Africa, Sweden, Switzerland, Taiwan, Tanzania UR, Türkiye, Uganda, UK, USA, Venezuela, Zimbabwe. [2019.07.20/XM8148/**F**]

♦ European Research Network on Men in Europe / see Critical Research on Men in Europe (#04960)

♦ **European Research Network About Parents in Education (ERNAPE)** **08374**
Pres Dipto di Psicologia di Milano-Bicocca, ed U6 Piazza dell'Ateneo Nuovo 1, 20126 Milan MI, Italy. E-mail: ernape@ernape.org – conference@ernape.org.
URL: https://www.ernape.org/
History Oct 1993, Glasgow (UK). **Structure** Core Group. **Events** *Biennial Conference* Nijmegen (Netherlands) 2022, *Biennial Conference* Nijmegen (Netherlands) 2021, *Bienial Conference* Gdansk (Poland) 2019, *Biennial Conference* London (UK) 2017, *Biennial Conference* Tromsø (Norway) 2015. **Publications** *International Journal about Parents in Education (IJPE).* [2022/XM4435/**F**]

♦ **European Research Network on Philanthropy (ERNOP)** **08375**
Exec Dir VU Univ Amsterdam, Fac of Social Sciences, Dept of Philanthropic Studies, De Boelelaan 1081, 1081 HV Amsterdam, Netherlands. E-mail: info@ernop.eu.
URL: http://www.ernop.eu/
History Jan 2008. **Aims** Advance, coordinate and promote excellence in philanthropic research in Europe. **Structure** Board. **Languages** English. **Staff** 0.50 FTE, paid. **Finance** Members' dues. Other sources: conference proceeds; donations. Annual budget: euro 20,000. **Activities** Research/documentation; events/meetings. **Events** *International Research Conference* Zagreb (Croatia) 2023, *ERNOP International Conference* Dublin (Ireland) 2021, *International Conference* Basel (Switzerland) 2019, *International Conference* Copenhagen (Denmark) 2017, *International Conference* Paris (France) 2015. **Publications** *ERNOP Newsletter* (4 a year). *Giving in Europe.*
Members Researchers (about 200) in 27 countries:
Australia, Austria, Belgium, Canada, Croatia, Czechia, Denmark, Finland, France, Germany, Hungary, Ireland, Israel, Italy, Latvia, Lithuania, Netherlands, Norway, Poland, Portugal, Russia, Singapore, Spain, Sweden, Switzerland, UK, USA.
NGO Relations Cooperates with: *Association for Research on Nonprofit Organizations and Voluntary Action (ARNOVA); EMES International Research Network (#05440); European Foundation Centre (EFC, inactive); European Fundraising Association (EFA, #07367); European Venture Philanthropy Association (EVPA, #09053); International Committee on Fundraising Organizations (ICFO, #12773); International Society for Third-Sector Research (ISTR, #15510).* [2021/XJ6400/**F**]

♦ European Research Network on Sheep and Goat Production / see Inter-regional FAO-CIHEAM Network for Research and Development in Sheep and Goats (#15970)

♦ **European Research Network System Identification (ERNSI)** **08376**
Coordinator Dept of Automatic Control, KTH Royal Inst of Technology, SE-100 44 Stockholm, Sweden.
URL: https://people.kth.se/~bo/ERNSI/
History Launched 1992, by *European Commission (EC, #06633)*, as a science project. **Aims** Carry out joint research on selected topics of system identification; advance *modelling* and identification procedures. **Activities** Research/documentation; events/meetings. **Events** *Workshop* Lyon (France) 2017.
[2018/XM6387/**F**]

♦ **European Research Network on Transitions in Youth (TIY)** **08377**
Réseau européen de recherche sur l'insertion des jeunes
Chairman Radboud Univ, Fac of Social Sciences, Dept of Sociology, PO Box 9104, 6500 HE Nijmegen, Netherlands. T. +31243612920.
URL: http://www.socsci.ru.nl/~maartenw/tiy/

History Apr 1992, Paris (France). Supported 1993-1996 as a Scientific Network of *European Science Foundation (ESF, #08441)*. Independent constitution drawn up in Dec 1996, adopted at Network meeting, Sep 1997, Dublin (Ireland). **Aims** Promote comparative research on transitions in youth by: providing a forum for contact among European scholars in the field; promoting theoretical and methodological development; encouraging the development and analysis of cross-national datasets (a particular interest focuses on promoting the use of regular and longitudinal surveys of young people for comparative analysis). **Structure** Committee. **Finance** No membership fee. No general budget, but may seek funding for specific activities. Members may be required to obtain part of all of the funding to support their own participation at workshops or in other Network activities. **Activities** Events/meetings; knowledge management/information dissemination. **Events** *Annual Workshop* Maastricht (Netherlands) 2019, *Annual Workshop* Mannheim (Germany) 2018, *Annual Workshop* Brussels (Belgium) 2017, *Annual Workshop* Brno (Czech Rep) 2015, *Annual Workshop* Barcelona (Spain) 2014. **Publications** Proceedings of workshops. Information Services: E-mail communications among membership. **Members** Individual researchers and others interested in research in transitions in youth. Membership countries not specified. **NGO Relations** Special links with: European Science Foundation (ESF).
[2016.02.18/XF2823/**F**]

♦ European Research Organization on Genital Infection and Neoplasia (EUROGIN) 08378

Exec Sec 174 rue de Courcelles, 75017 Paris, France. T. +33144400120. Fax +33147667470. E-mail: admin@eurogin.com.
URL: http://www.eurogin.com/

Aims Promote research in the field of genital infections, pre-cancers and cancers. **Structure** Executive Committee. **Activities** Organizes conferences, congresses and symposia. **Events** *International Multidisciplinary HPV Congress* 2021, *International Multidisciplinary HPV Congress* Monaco (Monaco) 2019, *International Multidisciplinary Congress* Lisbon (Portugal) 2018, *International Multidisciplinary HPV Congress* Amsterdam (Netherlands) 2017, *International Multidisciplinary Congress* Salzburg (Austria) 2016. **NGO Relations** *Women Against Cervical Cancer (WACC, #20985)*.
[2021/XD5964/**D**]

♦ European Research and Study Group for the Training of Christian Educators / see Groupement Européen pour la Recherche et la Formation des Enseignants Chrétiens, Croyants et de toutes Convictions (#10759)

♦ European Research Vessel Operators (ERVO) 08379

Chair address not obtained.
Vice-Chair address not obtained.
URL: https://www.ervo-group.eu/

History 1999. Initiated by *European Science Foundation (ESF, #08441)* – Marine Board. Terms of Reference adopted 2011; updated 2016. **Aims** Create and maintain a forum for European research vessel operators, with special focus on research vessels and associated equipment and/or instruments. **Structure** Executive Committee. **Activities** Events/meetings. **Events** *Meeting* 2021, *Meeting* Bucharest (Romania) 2020, *Meeting* Hamburg (Germany) 2019, *Meeting* Valletta (Malta) 2018, *Meeting* Helsinki (Finland) 2017.
Members Full in 20 countries and territories:
Belgium, Denmark, Faeroe Is, Finland, France, Germany, Greece, Iceland, Ireland, Italy, Malta, Netherlands, Norway, Poland, Portugal, Romania, Spain, Sweden, Türkiye, UK.
NGO Relations Memorandum of Understanding with (1): *European Centre for Information on Marine Science and Technology (EurOcean)*.
[2022/AA2728/**F**]

♦ European Resilient Flooring Manufacturers' Institute (ERFMI) 08380

Technical Manager Rue Montoyer 24, 1000 Brussels, Belgium. T. +3222870872. E-mail: info@erfmi.com.
URL: http://www.erfmi.com/

Aims Represent interests of the resilient flooring industry in ensuring maintenance of high ethical standards within the industry. **Members** Companies (17). Membership countries not specified. **NGO Relations** Member of (3): *Circular Plastics Alliance (#03936)*; *European Composites, Plastics and Polymer Processing Platform (ECP4, #06693)*; *European Floor Coverings Association (EUFCA, #07271)*. Cooperates with (1): *International Organization for Standardization (ISO, #14473)*.
[2022.10.19/XF2221/j/**F**]

♦ European Resin Manufacturers' Association (ERMA) 08381

Admin Office Orrest Business Solutions, 250 Bury New Road, Whitefield, Manchester, M45 8QN, UK. E-mail: info@erma.org.uk.
URL: http://www.erma.org.uk/

History Founded Oct 1990. **Aims** Promote the interests of the European resins industry; provide the services to the members. **Structure** General Assembly (annual); Management Board; Technical Committee. **Languages** English. **Staff** 3.00 FTE, paid. **Finance** Members' dues. **Activities** Organizes symposia, seminars and meetings.
Members Companies (25) in 8 countries:
Belgium, Estonia, France, Germany, Italy, Netherlands, Poland, UK.
IGO Relations *European Commission (EC, #06633)*. **NGO Relations** *Conseil européen de l'industrie chimique (CEFIC, #04687)*.
[2014/XD6057/**D**]

♦ European Resource Bank Meeting (meeting series)
♦ European Resource Centre on Education for Intercultural Understanding, Human Rights and Democratic Citizenship / see European Wergeland Centre (#09092)

♦ European Respiratory Care Association (ERCA) 08382

Secretariat Haukeland Univ Hosp, Jonas Lies vei 65, 5021 Bergen, Norway.
Pres CHUV, Rue du Bugnon 21, 1011 Lausanne VD, Switzerland.
Registered Address Hippokrateslaan 10, 1200 Sint-Lambrechts-Woluwe, Belgium.
URL: https://europeanrespiratorycareassociation.org/

History 25 May 2002, Brussels (Belgium). Registration: Banquel-Carrefour des Entreprises, No/ID: 0860.463.145, Start date: 12 Sep 2003, Belgium. **Structure** General Assembly. **Activities** Events/meetings. **Events** *Congress* Lyon (France) 2022, *Congress* Lyon (France) 2018, *Congress* Lyon (France) 2015, *Congress* Barcelona (Spain) 2012, *Congress* Stresa (Italy) 2009. **NGO Relations** Cooperates with (1): *JIVD-AER*.
[2021/XD9007/**D**]

♦ European Respiratory Nurses Association (no recent information)

♦ European Respiratory Society (ERS) 08383

Exec Dir Ave Ste-Luce 4, 1003 Lausanne VD, Switzerland. T. +41212130101. Fax +41212130100. E-mail: info@ersnet.org.
Advocacy Office 49-51 Rue de Trèves, 1040 Brussels, Belgium. T. +3222385360. Fax +3222385361.
Communications Office 442 Glossop Road, Sheffield, S10 2PX, UK.
URL: http://www.ersnet.org/

History Sep 1990, on merger of *European Society of Pneumology (SEP, inactive)* / Societas Europaea Pneumologiae and *Societas Europaea Physiologiae Clinicae Respiratoriae (SEPCR, inactive)* / Societas Europaea Physiologiae Clinicae Repiratoriae. Registered in accordance with Swiss Civil Code. EU Transparency Register: 38091528151-27. **Aims** Alleviate suffering from respiratory diseases; promote lung health through research, knowledge sharing, medical and public education. **Structure** General Assembly (annual, at Congress); Council; Executive Committee; National Delegates; Scientific Assemblies; Special Committees. Includes: *European Lung Foundation (ELF, #07718)*. **Languages** English. **Staff** 80.00 FTE, paid. Staff based in 3 offices in Lausanne (Switzerland), Brussels (Belgium) and Sheffield (UK). **Finance** Members' dues. Congress proceeds. **Activities** Training/education; knowledge management/information dissemination; research/documentation; events/meetings. **Events** *ERS International Congress* Milan (Italy) 2023, *ERS International Congress* Barcelona (Spain) 2022, *ERS International Congress* Lausanne (Switzerland) 2021, *International Sleep and Breathing Conference* Lausanne (Switzerland) 2021, *Annual Congress* Lausanne (Switzerland) 2020. **Publications** *European Respiratory Journal* (12 a year); *ERS Newsletter* (6 a year); *Breathe – Continuing Medical Education for Respiratory Professionals* (4 a year); *European Respiratory Review* (4-6 a year). *ERS Monograph Series* (4 a year). **Members** Individuals (over 36,500) in 181 countries. Partnership agreements (96) mainly in Europe. Membership countries not specified.

NGO Relations Member of:
– *Biomedical Alliance in Europe (#03251)*; *Association of Learned and Professional Society Publishers (ALPSP, #02786)*; *Associations and Conference Forum (AC Forum, #02909)*; *European Alliance for Personalised Medicine (EAPM, #05878)*; *European Cancer Organisation (ECO, #06432)*; *European Chronic Disease Alliance (ECDA, #06548)*; *European Public Health Alliance (EPHA, #08297)*; *Global Climate and Health Alliance (GCHA, #10288)*; *Health and Environment Alliance (HEAL, #10879)*; *International Non Governmental Coalition Against Tobacco (INGCAT, no recent information)*; *ORCID (#17790)*.
Supports: *Pan-African Thoracic Society (PATS, #18070)*. Cooperates with: *European Sleep Research Society (ESRS, #08493)*
[2020.03.03/XD2606/v/**D**]

♦ European Responsible Investment Network (unconfirmed)
♦ European Responsible Nutrition Alliance / see Food Supplements Europe (#09852)

♦ European Restless Legs Syndrome Study Group (EURLSSG) 08384

Office Kirchstetten 14a, 87754 Kammlach, Germany. Fax +498261759114. E-mail: office@eurlssg.org.
URL: http://www.eurlssg.org/

History 15 Oct 2005, Berlin (Germany). Registration: Germany. **Aims** Promote scientific research in the field of Restless Legs Syndrome (RLS); optimize medical care for *patients* by improving diagnostic and therapeutic measures; contribute to and improve the European information and communication structures; support establishment of standardized patient data banks. **Structure** Executive Committee. **Languages** English. **Staff** 1.00 FTE, paid. Several voluntary. **Finance** Sources: members' dues. **Activities** Events/meetings; training/education. **Events** *Annual Meeting* Munich (Germany) 2021, *Annual Meeting* 2020, *Annual Meeting* Munich (Germany) 2019, *Annual Meeting* Munich (Germany) 2018, *Annual Meeting* Munich (Germany) 2017. **Publications** Reports; studies.
Members Full in 23 countries:
Armenia, Austria, Canada, Cyprus, Czechia, Finland, France, Georgia, Germany, Greece, Ireland, Italy, Japan, Netherlands, Norway, Poland, Romania, Russia, Spain, Sweden, Switzerland, UK, USA.
IGO Relations None. **NGO Relations** Associate member of: *World Sleep Society (#21793)*.
[2021.09.09/XM8469/**D**]

♦ European Resuscitation Council (ERC) 08385

Main Office Emile Vanderveldelaan 35, 1845 Niel, Belgium. T. +3232464666. Fax +3235010015. E-mail: ceo@erc.edu.
URL: http://www.erc.edu/

History 1989. Registration: VZW/ASBL, Belgium. **Aims** Preserve human life by making high quality resuscitation available to all. **Structure** General Assembly; Board; General Purpose Committee; International Course Committees; Task Forces; Working Groups (4); Office. **Languages** English. **Staff** 6.8 FTE. **Activities** Training/education; events/meetings; knowledge management/information dissemination. **Events** *Congress* Antwerp (Belgium) 2022, *Congress* Manchester (UK) 2020, *Congress* Ljubljana (Slovenia) 2019, *Congress* Bologna (Italy) 2018, *Congress* Freiburg-Breisgau (Germany) 2017. **Publications** *Resuscitation* – official journal. *European Resuscitation Guidelines* (2010). Manuals; posters; presentations.
Members Organizations and individuals in 33 countries:
Austria, Belgium, Bosnia-Herzegovina, Croatia, Cyprus, Czechia, Denmark, Egypt, Finland, France, Germany, Hungary, Iceland, Italy, Luxembourg, Malta, Netherlands, Norway, Poland, Portugal, Romania, Russia, Serbia, Slovakia, Slovenia, Spain, Sudan, Sweden, Switzerland, Tunisia, Türkiye, UK, United Arab Emirates.
Representatives of 5 regional organizations:
European Society for Emergency Medicine (EuSEM, #08590); *European Society of Anaesthesiology and Intensive Care (ESAIC, #08518)*; *European Society of Cardiology (ESC, #08536)*; *European Society of Intensive Care Medicine (ESICM, #08632)*; *Red Cross EU Office (#18643)*.
NGO Relations Member of: *International Liaison Committee on Resuscitation (ILCOR, #14036)*.
[2021/XD3444/y/**D**]

♦ European Retail Academy (ERA) 08386

Managing Dir Veilchenweg 8, 51503 Rösrath, Germany. T. +49220584442.
URL: http://www.european-retail-academy.org/

History 17 Feb 2005. Registered in accordance with German law. **Aims** Promote international retail transfer know-how between businesses and universities. **Structure** Board of Trustees. **Languages** English. **Staff** 1.00 FTE, paid; 160.00 FTE, voluntary. **Finance** Sponsorship. **Events** *Annual Meeting* Düsseldorf (Germany) 2014, *Annual meeting* Düsseldorf (Germany) 2011, *Annual Meeting* Mumbai (India) 2009, *Annual meeting* Düsseldorf (Germany) 2008, *Annual meeting* Moscow (Russia) 2007.
Members Institutions (225) in 54 countries and territories:
Armenia, Australia, Austria, Belarus, Belgium, Brazil, Bulgaria, Canada, China, Croatia, Cyprus, Czechia, Egypt, Estonia, Finland, France, Germany, Greece, Hungary, India, Ireland, Israel, Italy, Japan, Kazakhstan, Kenya, Korea Rep, Lithuania, Malaysia, Mexico, Moldova, Mongolia, Montenegro, Netherlands, New Zealand, Norway, Poland, Portugal, Romania, Russia, Serbia, Singapore, Slovakia, South Africa, Spain, Sweden, Switzerland, Taiwan, Tajikistan, Türkiye, UK, Ukraine, United Arab Emirates, USA.
NGO Relations Exchange member of: *CEEMAN – International Association for Management Development in Dynamic Societies (CEEMAN, #03625)*.
[2019.12.12/XM2736/**E**]

♦ European Retail Alliance (inactive)
♦ European Retail Financial Forum (unconfirmed)
♦ European Reticulo-Endothelial Society (inactive)
♦ European Retina Meeting (meeting series)
♦ European Reusable Packaging and Reverse Logistics Consortium (unconfirmed)
♦ European Review Group on Health Promotion and Prevention in Family Medicine and General Practice / see European Network for Prevention and Health Promotion in Family Medicine and General Practice (#07974)

♦ European Rheumatism and Arthritis Surgical Society (ERASS) 08387

Société européenne de chirurgie orthopédique de la polyarthrite chronique évolutive – Europäische Gesellschaft für Rheumaorthopädie

Hon Sec Rheinisches Rheuma-Zentrum, Hauptstr 74, 40668 Meerbusch, Germany. T. +492150917145. E-mail: erass@lumc.nl.
URL: http://www.erass.org/

History 4 Sep 1979, Wiesbaden (Germany). Founded following the activities of a EULAR subgroup initiated in 1977. Former names and other names: *European Rheumatoid Arthritis Surgical Society* – former; *Association européenne de chirurgie de l'arthrose rhumatoïde* – former. **Aims** Further scientific and clinical work in rheumatoid arthritis surgery on a European level; promote training and continuing education of doctors interested in this field; encourage interdisciplinary collaboration. **Structure** General Assembly; Executive Committee. Expertise Network. **Languages** English. **Staff** 0.50 FTE, paid. **Finance** Sources: members' dues. **Activities** Awards/prizes/competitions; events/meetings; training/education. **Events** *ERASS Master Class* Amsterdam (Netherlands) / Leiden (Netherlands) 2012, *Biennial Congress* Florence (Italy) 2012, *Biennial Congress* Leiden (Netherlands) 2010, *Biennial Congress* Barcelona (Spain) 2008, *Biennial Congress* Zurich (Switzerland) 2006. **Publications** *ERASS Information Bulletin*. *ERASS Handbook*. Information Services: Documentation centre.
Members Individuals in 26 countries (" indicates overseas members):
Australia (*), Austria, Belgium, Canada (*), Czechia, Denmark, Finland, France, Germany, Greece, Hungary, Ireland, Italy, Japan (*), Netherlands, Norway, Poland, Slovakia, Slovenia, South Africa (*), Spain, Sweden, Switzerland, UK, USA (*), Venezuela (*).
Associate members in 1 country:
UK.
NGO Relations Cooperates closely with the Standing Committee of: *European Alliance of Associations for Rheumatology (EULAR, #05862)*.
[2020/XD2279/v/**D**]

♦ European Rheumatoid Arthritis Surgical Society / see European Rheumatism and Arthritis Surgical Society (#08387)

♦ European Rhinologic Society (ERS) 08388

Association européenne de rhinologie

Admin Otorhinolaryngology Room A2-234, Meibergdreef 9, 1105 AZ Amsterdam, Netherlands. E-mail: secretary@rhinologicsociety.eu.

European Rifle Association
08388

alphabetic sequence excludes
For the complete listing, see Yearbook Online at

URL: http://www.europeanrhinologicsociety.org/
History Jul 1963, Leiden (Netherlands). Founded on the initiative of Van Dishoeck. **Aims** Provide a forum for exchange of experience among accredited rhinologists and other specialists interested in rhinology, allergology, related facial plastic surgery, immunology and other fields. **Structure** General Assembly (every 2 years); Executive Committee; Advisory Board; Secretariat. **Languages** English. **Finance** Sources: donations; members' dues. **Activities** Awards/prizes/competitions; events/meetings; training/education. **Events** *Congress* Sofia (Bulgaria) 2023, *Biennial Congress* Thessaloniki (Greece) 2021, *Biennial Congress* Thessaloniki (Greece) 2020, *Biennial Congress* London (UK) 2018, *Biennial Congress* Stockholm (Sweden) 2016. **Publications** *Rhinology* (6 a year). Annual Report; reports. **Members** Regular; Junior; Senior; Honorary. Individuals (2,783) in 87 countries and territories. Membership countries not specified. [2022.10.20/XD0843/v/**D**]

♦ European Rifle Association (inactive)

♦ European Rigid PVC-Film Association (ERPA) 08389

Europäischer PVC-Hartfolien-Verband

Exec Dir Industriepark Höchst, Geb F-821, 65926 Frankfurt-Main, Germany. T. +49693057148. Fax +496930516039.
ERPA Belgium Operating Office, Avenue de Cortenbergh 71, Box 4, 1000 Brussels, Belgium. T. +3227324124. Fax +3227324218.
URL: http://www.pvc-films.org/
History 1992. **Languages** English, German.
Members Full in 4 countries:
France, Germany, Italy, Poland, Switzerland, UK. [2017/XD4806/**D**]

♦ European Risk Forum (unconfirmed)
♦ European Risk Management Association / see Federation of European Risk Management Associations (#09539)
♦ European Risk & Resilience Institute / see European Virtual Institute for Integrated Risk Management (#09062)

♦ European River/Sea Transport Union (ERSTU) 08390

Europäische Fluss-See-Transport Union

Pres ERSTU e V bei Rhenus Port Logistics, August-Hirsch-Str 3, 47119 Duisburg, Germany. T. +493039802662. Fax +493039802663. E-mail: erstu-ev@t-online.de.
URL: http://www.erstu.com/
History Current statutes adopted, 20 Jan 2001. Registered in accordance with German law. **Aims** Promote East-West integration in the area of sea and inland navigation, in order to create alternative, highly efficient transport links for the intra-European trade, featuring a high ecological, technological and technical safety standard. **Structure** General Assembly (annual). Praesidium, comprising President and a Vice-President respectively from each member state. Secretariat, headed by General Secretary. **Languages** English, German, Russian. **Staff** 1.00 FTE, paid. **Finance** Members' dues. **Events** *Pan European conference* 2005, *Plenary meeting / General Assembly* Berlin (Germany) 2003, *Plenary Meeting* 2002. **Publications** *ERSTU-Navigator* (2 a year); *ERSTU Bulletin*.
Members Ordinary; Honorary. Members in 12 countries:
Austria, Bulgaria, Czechia, Denmark, Germany, Hungary, Netherlands, Poland, Russia, Slovakia, UK, Ukraine.
NGO Relations Instrumental in setting up: *European Small Business Alliance of Small and Medium Independent Enterprises (ESBA, #08494)*. Corresponding member of: *European Barge Union (EBU, #06318)*. [2019/XD4109/**D**]

♦ European Rivers Network (ERN) 08391

Exec Dir 8 rue Crozatier, 43000 Le Puy, France. T. +33471020814. Fax +33471026099. E-mail: infos@ern.org – contact@erninfo.net – ern.info@ern.org.
URL: http://www.ern.org/
History 1994. **Aims** Link groups, organizations and individuals working for the protection of rivers; improve communication; promote the sustainable wise management of living rivers in opposition to exploitation, pollution and degradation. **Languages** English, French, German. **Staff** 8.00 FTE, paid. Many voluntary. **Finance** Members' dues. Other sources: donations; sponsoring; national government subventions; EU funds. Budget (annual): US$ 450,000. **Activities** Projects/programmes. **Publications** *RIVERNEWS* – by e-mail. Information Services: Geographical Information System on European River Basins (under development). **Information Services** *RIVERNET* – server. **IGO Relations** *European Commission (EC, #06633)*; *International Commission for the Protection of the Rhine (ICPR, #12721)*; *International Network of Basin Organizations (INBO, #14235)*; *UNESCO (#20322)*. **NGO Relations** Partner of: *1% for the Planet*. [2022/XF4699/**F**]

♦ European Road Assessment Programme (EuroRAP) 08392

Chairman Worting House, Basingstoke, RG23 8PX, UK. T. +441256345598. E-mail: icanhelp@eurorap.net.
URL: http://www.eurorap.org/
History Registered in accordance with Belgian law. **Aims** Reduce death and serious injury on European roads through a programme of systematic testing of risk that identifies major *safety* shortcomings which can be addressed by practical road improvement measures; ensure assessment of risk lies at the heart of strategic decisions on route improvements, crash protection and standards of route management; forge partnerships between those responsible for a safe roads system. **Finance** Supported by: *European Commission (EC, #06633)*; *Fédération Internationale de l'Automobile (FIA, #09613)*. **Events** *Meeting* The Hague (Netherlands) 2006.
Members Automobile clubs in 17 countries:
Austria, Belgium, Croatia, Czechia, Finland, France, Germany, Ireland, Italy, Netherlands, Norway, Slovakia, Slovenia, Spain, Sweden, Switzerland, UK.
NGO Relations Sister programme: *European New Car Assessment Programme (EURO NCAP, #08046)*. Member of: Fédération internationale de l'automobile; *FIA Foundation (#09742)*. [2017/XM2846/**F**]

♦ European Road Hauliers Association (UETR) 08393

SG Rue Washington 40, 1050 Brussels, Belgium. T. +32477973816. E-mail: info@uetr.eu.
URL: https://uetr.eu/
History 1998. Former names and other names: *Union européenne des transporteurs routiers (UETR)* – former (4 Feb 1999). Registration: Banque-Carrefour des Entreprises, No/ID: 0465.078.871, Start date: 4 Feb 1999, Belgium; EU Transparency Register, No/ID: 647912812046-35, Start date: 8 Oct 2013. **Aims** Defend the interests of small and medium sized enterprises (SMEs) in the road transport sector (road hauliers). **Structure** General Assembly; Board of Directors; Secretariat General. **Languages** English, French. **Staff** 3.00 FTE, paid. **Finance** Fully independent and self-financed. **Activities** Events/meetings. **Events** *Parking Areas Meeting COVID-19 Challenges for Road Haulers* 2021, *Congress* Brussels (Belgium) 2007.
Members Professional organizations (14) in 9 countries:
Belgium, Croatia, France, Germany, Hungary, Italy, Portugal, Serbia, Spain.
NGO Relations Member of (2): *Federation of European and International Associations Established in Belgium (FAIB, #09508)*; *SMEunited (#19327)*. [2023.02.14/XM2638/**D**]

♦ European Road Profile Users' Group (ERPUG) 08394

Contact address not obtained.
URL: http://www.erpug.org/
History Founded 2012. **Aims** Act as a source for knowledge and information on functional characteristics of trevelled surfaces; act as a forum for information exchange between equipment and data providers, road owners researchers and other stakeholders. **Structure** Steering Committee. **Activities** Events/meetings. **Events** *Annual Conference* Vienna (Austria) 2021, *Annual Conference* Vilnius (Lithuania) 2019, *Annual Conference* Madrid (Spain) 2018. [2019/XM7682/**F**]

♦ European Road Safety Equipment Federation (inactive)
♦ European Road Safety Federation (inactive)

♦ European Roads Policing Network (ROADPOL) 08395

Gen Sec Zum Roten Berge 18-24, 48165 Münster, Germany. T. +491716833977. E-mail: roadpol@roadpol.eu.
URL: https://www.roadpol.eu/
History Succeeds *European Traffic Police Organisation (TISPOL, inactive)*. Registration: North Rhine-Westphalia District court, No/ID: VR 5947, Start date: 27 Mar 2020, Germany, Münster. **Aims** Reduce the number of deaths and serious injuries on European roads. **Structure** Council; Executive Committee. Working Groups.
Members Traffic police forces of 28 countries:
Austria, Belgium, Bulgaria, Croatia, Cyprus, Czechia, Denmark, Estonia, Finland, France, Germany, Hungary, Italy, Latvia, Lithuania, Luxembourg, Malta, Netherlands, Norway, Poland, Romania, Serbia, Slovenia, Spain, Sweden, Switzerland, Türkiye, United Arab Emirates.
IGO Relations Cooperates with (4): *Euro Contrôle Route (ECR, #05668)*; *European Commission (EC, #06633)*; *European Network of Airport Law Enforcement Organisations (AIRPOL, #07866)*; *European Network of Railway Police Forces (RAILPOL, #07981)*. [2021/AA2185/**F**]

♦ European Road Transport Research Advisory Council (ERTRAC) 08396

Dir Avenue de Cortenbergh 66, 1000 Brussels, Belgium. T. +3227361221. E-mail: info@ertrac.org.
URL: https://www.ertrac.org/
Aims Provide a strategic vision for the road transport sector with respect to research and development; define strategies and road maps; stimulate public and private investment in road transport; improve coordination between European, national, regional and private research and development actions on road transport; enhance networking and clustering of Europe's research and development capacity; promote European commitment to research and technological development. **Structure** Plenary (meets 3 times a year); Steering Group; Executive Group. Working Groups. Secretariat. Supporting Institutions Group. **Events** *Conference on Results from Road Transport Research (RTR Conference)* Brussels (Belgium) 2023, *European Conference on Results from Road Transport Research in H2020 Projects* Brussels (Belgium) 2023, *European Conference on Results from Road Transport Research in H2020 Projects* Brussels (Belgium) 2022, *Transport Research Arena (TRA) Conference* Lisbon (Portugal) 2022, *Annual Conference* Brussels (Belgium) 2021.
Members Governments of 34 countries:
Austria, Belgium, Bulgaria, Croatia, Cyprus, Czechia, Denmark, Estonia, Finland, France, Germany, Greece, Hungary, Iceland, Ireland, Israel, Italy, Latvia, Liechtenstein, Lithuania, Luxembourg, Malta, Netherlands, Norway, Poland, Portugal, Romania, Slovakia, Slovenia, Spain, Sweden, Switzerland, Türkiye, UK.
Organizations, academia and companies (27), including 17 organizations listed in this Yearbook:
Association Européenne des Concessionnaires d'Autoroutes et d'Ouvrages à Péage (ASECAP, #02559); *Comité européen de normalisation (CEN, #04162)*; *ERTICO ITS Europe (#05532)*; *European Asphalt Pavement Association (EAPA, #05920)*; *European Association of Automotive Suppliers (CLEPA, #05948)*; *European Automotive Research Partners Association (EARPA, #06301)*; *European Commission (EC, #06633)*; *European Conference of Transport Research Institutes (ECTRI, #06737)*; *European Council of Automotive Research and Development (EUCAR, #06806)*; *European Federation for Transport and Environment (T and E, #07230)*; *European Union Road Federation (ERF, #09014)*; *Fédération Internationale de l'Automobile (FIA, #09613)*; *Forum of European National Highway Research Laboratories (FEHRL, #09910)*; *International Association of Public Transport (#12118)*; *International Road Transport Union (IRU, #14761)*; *Oil Companies' European Association for Environment, Health and Safety in Refining and Distribution (CONCAWE, #17708)*; *POLIS (#18419)*. [2023/XM0719/y/**E**]

♦ European Road Transport Telematics Implementation Coordination Organization / see ERTICO ITS Europe (#05532)
♦ European Robert Schuman Centre (internationally oriented national body)
♦ European Robotic Urology Society (inactive)

♦ European Rohingya Council (ERC) 08397

Contact Geldershoofd 905, 1103 BG Amsterdam, Netherlands. E-mail: info@theerc.eu.
URL: https://www.theerc.eu/
History Oct 2012, Esbjerg (Denmark). Registered in accordance with Dutch law: KVK-56454791. **Aims** Promote the cause of Rohingya *minority* that is on the verge of *extermination* from the Arakan State, Burma (Myanmar). **Structure** Council; Executive Body; Secretariat. **Languages** Burmese, English. **Finance** Members' dues. **Activities** Advocacy/lobbying/activism. **Events** *Annual Conference* Drøbak (Norway) 2015.
Members Full in 12 countries:
Austria, Belgium, Denmark, France, Germany, Ireland, Italy, Netherlands, Norway, Sweden, Switzerland, UK. [2022/XJ9990/**E**]

♦ European Rolfing Association (ERA) 08398

Office Saarstr 5, 80797 Munich, Germany. T. +498954370940. Fax +498954370942. E-mail: info@rolfing.org.
URL: http://www.rolfing.org/
History 1991. Registration: Verein, No/ID: VR 135 22, Germany FR. **Aims** Group all certified Rolfers practising in Europe, for the benefit of them all. **Structure** General Assembly; Board of Directors; Executive Director; Committees (8). **Languages** English, German. **Staff** 4.00 FTE, paid. **Activities** Events/meetings; training/education. **Events** *Conference* Berlin (Germany) 2018, *Conference* Switzerland 2011, *Biennial Conference* Catania (Italy) 2009.
Members Rolfing practitioners (561) in 18 countries:
Austria, Czechia, Denmark, France, Germany, Hungary, Iceland, Ireland, Italy, Luxembourg, Netherlands, Norway, Portugal, Slovenia, Spain, Sweden, Switzerland, UK.
NGO Relations *Rolf Institute of Structural Integration*. [2020/XD6319/v/**D**]

♦ European Rolling Paper Association (ERPA) 08399

Managing Dir Chausseestrasse 22, 10115 Berlin, Germany. T. +4915164973458. E-mail: info@erpa-online.com.
URL: http://www.erpa-online.com/
History 1995, as *Association of the European Cigarette Paper Converting Industry (ECPCI) – Association européenne de l'industrie de transformation du papier à cigarettes – Verband der Europäischen Zigaretten Papier Verarbeitenden Industrie*. Current title adopted, 2003. EU Transparency Register: 804211322967-55. **Staff** 3.00 FTE, paid. **Members** European companies (22). Membership countries not specified. **NGO Relations** In liaison with technical committees of: *International Organization for Standardization (ISO, #14473)*. [2018/XD9088/**D**]

♦ European Roma Equality Network (EREN) 08400

Contact Rue Washington 40, 1050 Brussels, Belgium. T. +3226401665. E-mail: rromaequality@gmail.com.
URL: https://www.eren-eu.org/
History Registration: Banque-Carrefour des Entreprises, No/ID: 0763.685.849, Start date: 16 Feb 2021, Belgium. **Aims** Become a credible voice of Roma ethnic minority, key stakeholder and partner in the international scene and a respected empowering force of Roma leadership structures.
Members Organizations in 7 countries:
Albania, Bosnia-Herzegovina, Kosovo, Montenegro, North Macedonia, Serbia, Türkiye.
NGO Relations Member of (1): *Federation of European and International Associations Established in Belgium (FAIB, #09508)*. [2021/AA1259/**F**]

♦ European Roma Grassroots Organisations Network / see ERGO Network (#05531)
♦ European Roma Information Office (internationally oriented national body)

♦ European Roma Rights Centre (ERRC) 08401

Europäisches Roma Rechtszentrum – Europako Rromano Cacipasko Centro

Main Office Kéthly Anna Tér 1, Greenpoint 7, 1st Floor, Budapest 1077, Hungary.
Brussels Rond-point Schuman 2-4, 1000 Brussels, Belgium. E-mail: office@errc.org.
URL: http://www.errc.org/

History 11 Mar 1996, Budapest (Hungary). EU Transparency Register: 201496333876-92. **Aims** Monitor *human rights* situation of Roma and provide legal defence in cases of human rights abuse. **Structure** Board of Directors; President; Managing Director. **Languages** English. **Staff** 21.50 FTE, paid. **Finance** Sponsors: *European Commission (EC, #06633)*; Open Society Institute; *Swedish International Development Cooperation Agency (Sida)*. **Activities** Advocacy/lobbying/activism; research and development; training/education; publishing activities. **Publications** *ERRC News* (4 a year); *Roma Rights* (1-2 a year) – journal. Thematic reports. **Members** Not a membership organization. **Consultative Status** Consultative status granted from: *Council of Europe (CE, #04881)* (Participatory Status). **IGO Relations** Participant in Fundamental Rights Platform of: *European Union Agency for Fundamental Rights (FRA, #08969)*. **NGO Relations** *Open Society Foundations (OSF, #17763)* (Open Society Institute) is founding funder. Associated member of: *European Network against Racism (ENAR, #07862)*. Member of: *European Implementation Network (EIN, #07521)*; *European Network on Statelessness (ENS, #08013)*; *European Roma Policy Coalition (ERPC, no recent information)*. [2019/XK1294/**E**]

♦ European Roma and Travellers Forum (ERTF) 08402

Forum européen des Roms et des gens du voyage (FERV) – Evropako Forumo e Romango thaj e Phirutnengo (EFRP)

Contact CoE AGORA Bât, 1 quai Jacoutot, 67075 Strasbourg, France. T. +33390214331. Fax +33390215658.

URL: http://www.ertf.org/

History 2004. Registration: France. **Aims** Oversee the effective exercise by Roma, Sinti, Travellers and related groups of all human rights and fundamental freedoms as protected by the legal instruments of the Council of Europe and other international legal instruments where applicable; promote the fight against racism and discrimination and facilitate the integration of these population groups into the European societies and their participation in public life and decision-making process. **Structure** Plenary Assembly (meets at least annually) of up to 75 delegates, including one delegate and 3 substitutes of each International and National member. Executive Committee, comprising President, 2 Vice-Presidents, Treasurer, Secretary and 5 members. Secretariat. **Languages** English, French, Romany. **Staff** 3.00 FTE, paid. **Finance** Main donors: Council of Europe; Finnish government. **Activities** Advocacy/lobbying/activism; networking/liaising. Entitled to lodge complaints of violations of *European Social Charter (1961)* with *European Committee of Social Rights (ECSR, #06668)*. **Events** *Plenary Session* Strasbourg (France) 2005.

Members International; National; Honorary: organizations in 35 countries:
Albania, Austria, Belarus, Belgium, Bosnia-Herzegovina, Bulgaria, Croatia, Czechia, Denmark, Finland, France, Germany, Greece, Hungary, Ireland, Latvia, Lithuania, Moldova, Montenegro, Netherlands, North Macedonia, Norway, Poland, Portugal, Romania, Russia, Serbia, Slovakia, Slovenia, Spain, Sweden, Switzerland, Türkiye, UK, Ukraine.
Observer in 1 country:
Greece.

Consultative Status Consultative status granted from: *Council of Europe (CE, #04881)* (Participatory Status); *ECOSOC (#05331)* (Special). **IGO Relations** Observer to: *Congress of Local and Regional Authorities of the Council of Europe (#04677)*; several working and expert groups. [2021/XM0307/**F**]

♦ European Rope Skipping Organization (ERSO) 08403

SG Gaussstr 3, 8010 Graz, Austria. E-mail: erso.secretariat@gmail.com.

URL: http://www.erso.info/

History 1989. Registered in accordance with Austrian law: 1434805976. **Aims** Expand and promote rope skipping as a sport, as well as a recreational activity. **Structure** General Assembly (annual); Board of Directors. **Languages** English. **Staff** 8.00 FTE, voluntary. **Finance** Members' dues. Competition fees. Budget (annual): euro 3,500. **Activities** Sporting events. **Events** *General Assembly* Loughborough (UK) 2001.

Members National in 12 countries:
Austria, Belgium, Czechia, Denmark, Finland, Germany, Hungary, Italy, Russia, Slovakia, Sweden, Switzerland.
Club members in 2 countries:
Estonia, Netherlands. [2019/XD2175/**D**]

♦ European Rorschach Association for the Comprehensive System / see Comprehensive System International Rorschach Association (#04421)

♦ European Rotogravure Association (ERA) 08404

Association européenne de rotogravure

SG Swakopmunder Str 3, 81827 Munich, Germany. T. +49894395051. Fax +49894394107. E-mail: info@era-eu.org.

URL: https://era-eu.org/

History 1956. **Aims** Promote and further develop the gravure *printing* process. **Structure** General Assembly; Board; Secretariat. Technical Commissions. Divisions (2): Packaging; Decorative Printing. **Languages** English. **Staff** 3.50 FTE, paid. **Finance** Sources: members' dues. **Activities** Awards/prizes/competitions; events/meetings; research/documentation. **Events** *Annual & Packaging/Decorative Conference* Baveno (Italy) 2022, *Annual & Packaging/Decorative Conference* Thessaloniki (Greece) 2021, *Annual Conference* Hamburg (Germany) 2020, *Packaging and Decorative Conference* Kiel (Germany) 2019, *Annual Meeting* Munich (Germany) 2019. **Publications** *ERA Newsletter* (2 a year). Guidelines; standardization manuals. Information Services: Lists of press installations (publication gravure, packaging gravure, heatset offset).

Members Active; Associate; Affiliate; Overseas; Packaging; Decorative. Individuals in 17 countries:
Austria, Belgium, Brazil, Denmark, Finland, France, Germany, Italy, Japan, Netherlands, South Africa, Spain, Sweden, Switzerland, UK, Ukraine, USA.

NGO Relations Cooperates with (1): *International Organization for Standardization (ISO, #14473)*. [2022/XD1302/**D**]

♦ European Rotorcraft Forum (ERF) 08405

Contact Polish Soc of Aeronautics and Astronautics, ul Nowowiejska 24, 00-665 Warsaw, Poland. E-mail: psaa@meil.pw.edu.pl.

URL: https://rotorcraft-forum.eu/

History 1975. **Aims** Exchange scientific and technical information in the field of rotary wing *aircraft*. **Structure** International Committee; Secretariat revolves yearly to country organization in charge of annual forum. **Languages** English. **Activities** Events/meetings. **Events** *Annual Meeting* Warsaw (Poland) 2019, *Annual Meeting* Delft (Netherlands) 2018, *Annual Meeting* Milan (Italy) 2017, *Annual Meeting* Lille (France) 2016, *Annual Meeting* Munich (Germany) 2015.

Members Covers 7 countries:
France, Germany, Italy, Netherlands, Poland, Russia, UK. [2019/XF0684/**F**]

♦ European Round Table / see European Round Table for Industry (#08407)

♦ European Roundtable on Cleaner Production / see European Roundtable on Sustainable Consumption and Production Society (#08408)

♦ European Roundtable on Climate Change and Sustainable Transition (ERCST) 08406

Exec Dir Rue Archimède 61, 1000 Brussels, Belgium.

URL: https://ercst.org/

History Sep 2016. Launched under the umbrella of *International Centre for Trade and Sustainable Development, Geneva (ICTSD, #12524)*. Independent since Nov 2018. Registration: Banque-Carrefour des Entreprises, No/ID: 0713.761.335, Start date: 21 Nov 2018, Belgium; EU Transparency Register, No/ID: 971029940352-73, Start date: 17 Nov 2020. **Aims** Provide a neutral space where policy-makers and regulators can meet stakeholders to discuss climate change policy and how to manage the transition to a low GHG-economy in a sustainable way. **Structure** Board; Scientific Committee. **Events** *Informal Forum on Implementation of Article 6 of the Paris Agreement* Tokyo (Japan) 2022. **Members** Corporate; Associate. [2020/AA1221/**F**]

♦ European Round Table of Industrialists / see European Round Table for Industry (#08407)

♦ European Round Table for Industry (ERT) 08407

SG Bd Brand Whitlock 165, 1200 Brussels, Belgium. T. +3225343100. E-mail: contact@ert.eu.

URL: http://www.ert.eu/

History Founded 1983, by 17 leading European industrialists. Also referred to as *European Round Table*. Registration: Belgium; EU Transparency Register, No/ID: 25487567824-45. **Aims** Strive for a strong, open and competitive Europe, with the EU, including its Single Market, as a driver for inclusive growth and sustainable prosperity. **Structure** Plenary Session (2 a year); Associates; Working Groups. **Languages** English. **Staff** 9.00 FTE, paid. **Finance** Members' dues. **Activities** Events/meetings. **Events** *Environmental watchdog meeting* Szentendre (Hungary) 1997, *Conference on a strategy for European competitiveness* Brussels (Belgium) 1994, *Talking to the EC conference* Brussels (Belgium) 1993, *Joint US-ERT education forum* Brussels (Belgium) 1992, *Conference* Lisbon (Portugal) 1992. **Publications** Reports; case studies; position papers; press releases. **Members** Chief Executives and Chairs (about 50) of major multinational companies covering a wide range of industrial and technological sectors. Membership by invitation only. Membership countries not specified. **IGO Relations** *European Commission (EC, #06633)*; *European Economic and Social Committee (EESC, #06963)*; *European Parliament (EP, #08146)*; *European Schoolnet (EUN, #08433)*; *OECD (#17693)*; *United Nations Framework Convention on Climate Change – Secretariat (UNFCCC, #20564)*. **NGO Relations** AmCham EU; Business Roundtable; *BUSINESSEUROPE (#03381)*; *European Climate Foundation (ECF, #06574)*; *International Chamber of Commerce (ICC, #12534)*; *JA Europe (#16085)*; national organizations and roundtables. [2019.12.11/XF1009/tv/**F**]

♦ European Round Table of Senior Administrators / see Heads of University Management and Administration Network in Europe (#10867)

♦ European Roundtable on Sustainable Consumption and Production / see European Roundtable on Sustainable Consumption and Production Society (#08408)

♦ European Roundtable on Sustainable Consumption and Production Society (ERSCP Society) 08408

Coordinator address not obtained. E-mail: info@erscp.org.

URL: https://erscp.eu/

History 1994, Graz (Austria). Founded as a roundtable, organized in an informal way. Proposed as a society in 2010 and officially established in 2012. Former names and other names: *European Roundtable on Cleaner Production (ERCP)* – former (1994 to 2002); *European Roundtable on Sustainable Consumption and Production (ERSCP)* – former (2004 to 2012). **Aims** Motivate and encourage all stakeholders to work on new ideas of Sustainable Consumption and Production in order to promote transition to sustainable societies by knowledge, research, action and engagement. **Structure** General Assembly; Board. **Activities** Events/meetings. **Events** *European Roundtable for Sustainable Consumption and Production* Wageningen (Netherlands) 2023, *European Roundtable for Sustainable Consumption and Production* Graz (Austria) 2021, *European Roundtable for Sustainable Consumption and Production* Barcelona (Spain) 2019, *European Roundtable on Sustainable Consumption and Production* Skiathos Is (Greece) 2017, *European Roundtable on Sustainable Consumption and Production* Portoroz (Slovenia) 2014. **Publications** *ERSCP Newsletter*. **NGO Relations** Partner of (1): *PREPARE Network (#18483)*. Cooperates with (2): *SCORAI Europe (#19157)*; *Sustainable Consumption Research and Action Initiative (SCORAI, #20053)*. [2021.05.25/XS0260/c/**E**]

♦ European Route of Industrial Heritage (ERIH) 08409

SG Am Striebruch 42, 40668 Meerbusch, Germany. T. +492150756496. Fax +492150756497. E-mail: info@erih.net.

URL: http://www.erih.net/

History 1999. Initially a project funded by *INTERREG V (#15966)*. Registration: No/ID: VR 5224, Start date: 2 Oct 2013, Germany; EU Transparency Register, No/ID: 891246734849-49, Start date: 4 Jun 2019. **Aims** Support the establishment of industrial heritage as kind of a *tourism* brand. **Structure** General Assembly; Board of Management. **Activities** Events/meetings; knowledge management/information dissemination. **Events** *Conference* Berlin (Germany) 2019. **Publications** *ERIH Newsletter*.

Members Full (over 250) in 23 countries:
Austria, Belgium, Croatia, Czechia, Denmark, Finland, France, Germany, Greece, Ireland, Italy, Luxembourg, Netherlands, Norway, Poland, Portugal, Serbia, Spain, Sweden, Switzerland, Türkiye, UK, Ukraine.

IGO Relations Member of (1): *European Commission (EC, #06633)* (Expert Group on Cultural Heritage). **NGO Relations** Member of (1): *European Heritage Alliance 3.3 (#07477)*. [2020/XM6279/**F**]

♦ European Rubber Chemicals Association (ERCA) 08410

Manager c/o CEFIC, Rue Belliard 40, Box 15, 1040 Brussels, Belgium. T. +3224369300. E-mail: ova@cefic.be.

URL: https://specialty-chemicals.eu/erca/

History 1999. A sector group of *Conseil européen de l'industrie chimique (CEFIC, #04687)*, since 2007. **Aims** Represent the rubber chemicals industry in Europe; address legislative and regulatory issues; promote policy initiatives to contribute to competitiveness, growth and development of the sector. **Languages** English. **Activities** Politics/policy/regulatory.

Members Companies (7) in 5 countries:
France, Germany, Netherlands, Spain, UK. [2021.09.01/XE4339/**E**]

♦ European Rubber Reclaimers' Association (no recent information)

♦ European Ruby Conference (meeting series)

♦ **European RUCIP Committee** European Committee on the Rules and Usages of Inter-European Trade in Potatoes (#06666)

♦ European Rugby League (ERL) 08411

General Manager 10 Queen Street Place, London, EC4R 1AG, UK. E-mail: info@europeanrugbyleague.com.

URL: https://europeanrugbyleague.com/

History Jan 2003, Paris (France). Former names and other names: *Rugby League European Federation (RLEF)* – former (2003 to 2021). Registration: Companies House, No/ID: 7508065, Start date: 27 Jan 2011, England and Wales. **Aims** Develop the rugby league practice in Europe and the Northern Hemisphere; spread the ethos of and increase participation in the sport of rugby league for all ages, genders, social groupings and ability levels. **Structure** General Meeting (annual); Board of Directors. **Languages** English, French. **Staff** 7.00 FTE, paid; 14.00 FTE, voluntary. **Finance** Sources: government support; grants; members' dues; sponsorship. Supported by: *International Rugby League (IRL, #14773)*. **Activities** Awards/prizes/competitions; sporting activities; training/education. **Publications** Annual Report.

Members Rugby leagues Full; Affiliate; Observer. Full in 10 countries and territories:
England, France, Ireland, Italy, Jamaica, Lebanon, Russia, Serbia, Ukraine, Wales.
Affiliate in 15 countries and territories:
Cameroon, Canada, Czechia, Germany, Ghana, Greece, Malta, Morocco, Netherlands, Nigeria, Norway, Scotland, Spain, Türkiye, USA.
Observer in 17 countries and territories:
Albania, Belgium, Bosnia-Herzegovina, Bulgaria, Burundi, Congo DR, Denmark, Ethiopia, Hungary, Latvia, Libya, Montenegro, Palestine, Poland, Saudi Arabia, Sierra Leone, Sweden.

NGO Relations Member of (1): *International Rugby League (IRL, #14773)* (Associate). [2022.05.10/XJ3280/**D**]

♦ European Rum Association (no recent information)

♦ European Rural Alliance (inactive)

♦ European Rural Community Alliance (ERCA) 08412

Coordinator address not obtained.

URL: http://www.ruralcommunities.eu/

History Set up 2004, as an informal network with the title *European Rural Community Association*. Became an organization 2009. Merged with *European Rural Alliance (ERA, inactive)*, 2013, when current title was adopted. **Aims** Support the rural communities of Europe, through their national and regional rural movements; develop connections; share experience and mutual learning; take collective action to strengthen their position. **Structure** Directors. [2015/XJ9648/**D**]

♦ European Rural Community Association / see European Rural Community Alliance (#08412)

♦ European Rural Development Network (ERDN) 08413

Coordinator Szkolna 2/4 room 207, 00-006 Warsaw, Poland. T. +48225054774. E-mail: erdn@erdn.eu.
URL: http://www.erdn.eu/
History 2002. Registration: National Court Register, No/ID: 0000755777, Poland. **Aims** Integrate the efforts and competences of various European research institutions in their joint work on the state and paths of transformation of rural areas, in particular farming, with the view to extension of the *EU* and its future policies. **Structure** Presidency; Audit Committee. **Languages** Bulgarian, Czech, English, German, Hungarian, Italian, Lithuanian, Polish, Romanian, Slovakian. **Staff** 4.00 FTE, paid; 25.00 FTE, voluntary. **Finance** Supported by: *Research Executive Agency (REA)*. **Activities** Events/meetings; knowledge management/information dissemination; research and development. **Events** *Conference* Velké Bílovice (Czechia) 2019, *Conference* Cluj-Napoca (Romania) 2018, *Conference* Eisenstadt (Austria) 2017, *Conference* Budapest (Hungary) 2016, *Conference* Zakopane (Poland) 2015. **Publications** *ERDN Yearbook*. Conference proceedings.
Members Research Institutions in 14 Central Eastern and Southern European countries:
Austria, Bosnia-Herzegovina, Bulgaria, Czechia, Hungary, Italy, Latvia, Lithuania, Moldova, Poland, Romania, Serbia, Slovakia, Ukraine. [2022.02.09/XM6642/**F**]

♦ European Rural History Organisation (EURHO) 08414

Address not obtained.
URL: http://www.ruralhistory.eu/
History 2010, Brighton (UK) at the the Rural History conference. **Aims** Promote the study of all aspects of rural history in Europe and beyond. **Structure** Management Committee. **Languages** English. **Staff** 0.10 FTE, paid; 0.40 FTE, voluntary. **Finance** Members' dues. Annual budget: euro 5,000. **Activities** Events/meetings. **Events** *Conference* Uppsala (Sweden) 2021, *Conference* Paris (France) 2019, *Conference* Leuven (Belgium) 2017, *Conference* Girona (Spain) 2015, *Conference* Bern (Switzerland) 2013. **Publications** *EURHO Newsletter*.
Members Scientific institutions in 13 countries:
Austria, Belgium, France, Germany, Greece, Hungary, Italy, Netherlands, Portugal, Spain, Sweden, Switzerland, UK.
Conference participants become individual members for the following 2 years. [2020/XJ8652/**D**]

♦ European Rural and Isolated Practitioners Association (EURIPA) ... 08415

Exec Sec address not obtained.
URL: http://www.euripa.org/
History 1995, as *Group for Rural And Isolated Practitioners in Europe (GRAIPE)*. Present name adopted 1997. A network of *European Society of General Practice/Family Medicine (WONCA Europe, #08609)*. Constitution revised 2012 and 2017. **Aims** Address the *health* needs of rural communities and the professional needs of those serving them. **Structure** International Advisory Board. Executive Committee. **Languages** English. **Staff** 0.50 FTE, paid. **Finance** Funding through *World Organization of Family Doctors (WONCA, #21690)* – Europe; additional project funding possible. **Activities** Advocacy/lobbying/activism; standards/guidelines; knowledge management/information dissemination; networking/liaising; events/meetings; research/documentation. **Events** *Rural Health Forum* Siedlce (Poland) 2020, *Rural Health Forum* Ponta Delgada (Portugal) 2019, *Rural Health Forum* Maale HaHamisha (Israel) 2018, *Rural Health Forum* Panormos (Greece) 2017, *Rural Health Forum* Marseille (France) 2016. **Publications** *Grapevine* (4 a year) – newsletter; *European Journal of Rural and Remote Health* – electronic. **Members** Rural practitioners from across Europe. Membership countries not specified. [2021/XD7071/**D**]

♦ European Rural Poultry Association (ERPA) 08416

Association Européenne des Volailles Rurales – Asociación Europea de Aves Rurales – Associazione Europea di Volatili Rurali
Gen Sec 7 rue du Faubourg, Poissonnière, 75009 Paris, France. E-mail: contact@erpa-ruralpoultry.eu.
URL: http://www.erpa-ruralpoultry.eu/
History May 2007. Registered in accordance with French law. EU Transparency Register: 5235485727-61. **Aims** Help and promote European rural poultry. **Structure** General Assembly (annual). **Activities** Research/documentation; advocacy/lobbying/activism. **Events** *General Assembly* Namur (Belgium) 2019, *General Assembly* Madrid (Spain) 2018, *General Assembly* Brussels (Belgium) 2017, *General Assembly* Bucharest (Romania) 2015, *General Assembly* Saragossa (Spain) 2014.
Members Full; Associate. Members in 4 countries:
Belgium, France, Italy, Spain. [2017/XM5222/**D**]

♦ European Rural University / see Association for European Rural Universities (#02541)

♦ European Safeguards Research and Development Association (ESARDA) 08417

Sec c/o EC JRC Bldg 42A, Via E Fermi 2749, 21027 Ispra MB, Italy. T. +39332789603. Fax +39332789185. E-mail: jrc-esarda@ec.europa.eu – ec-esarda-connector@ec.europa.eu.
URL: https://esarda.jrc.ec.europa.eu/index_en
History 1969. Established by Agreement. Control of civil nuclear material is mandatory within *European Union (EU, #08967)* territory in line with the Treaty establishing the *European Atomic Energy Community (Euratom, inactive)*. Former names and other names: *European Association for Safeguards Research and Development* – former. **Aims** Advance and harmonize research and development of safeguards; provide a forum for exchange of information and ideas between nuclear facility operators and safeguarding authorities. **Structure** Steering Committee; Executive Board; annually rotating Chairmanship. Permanent secretariat assured by *Joint Research Centre (JRC, #16147)*. **Languages** English. **Staff** Voluntary. **Activities** Events/meetings; research and development; training/education. **Events** *Annual Meeting* Luxembourg (Luxembourg) 2022, *Annual Meeting* Vienna (Austria) 2021, *Annual Meeting* Manchester (UK) 2015, *Annual Meeting* Luxembourg (Luxembourg) 2014, *Annual Meeting* Bruges (Belgium) 2013. **Publications** *ESARDA Bulletin* (2 a year); *The Connector* – newsletter.
Members National regulatory authorities; operators of nuclear facilities; research centres and universities. Parties to the Agreement (32) in 14 countries:
Austria, Belgium, Czechia, Finland, France, Germany, Hungary, Italy, Lithuania, Netherlands, Poland, Romania, Spain, Sweden.
European Commission (EC, #06633) (DG Energy); *Joint Research Centre (JRC, #16147)*.
Associated Parties in 5 countries:
Japan, Norway, Switzerland, UK, USA.
Individual members in7 countries:
Belgium, France, Germany, Portugal, Sweden, Switzerland, UK.
IGO Relations Cooperates with (3): *African Commission on Nuclear Energy (AFCONE, #00256)*; *Asia-Pacific Safeguards Network (APSN, #02020)*; *International Atomic Energy Agency (IAEA, #12294)*. **NGO Relations** Cooperates with (2): *European Nuclear Education Network (ENEN, #08057)*; Institute of Nuclear Materials Management. [2022/XD4726/**E***]

♦ European Safety Federation (ESF) 08418

Fédération européenne des fabricants et distributeurs d'équipements de protection individuelle – Federación Europea de Fabricantes y Distribuidores de Equipos de Protección Individual – Europäische Vereinigung von Herstellern und Distributeuren von Persönlichen Schutzausrüstungen – Federazione Europea dei Fabbricanti e Distributori di Dispositivi di Protezione Individuali – Europese Federatie van Fabrikanten en Distributeuren van Persoonlijke Beschermingsmiddelen
SG ESF Secretariat, Bavikhoofsestraat 190, 8531 Harelbeke, Belgium. T. +3256701103. E-mail: info@eu-esf.org.
Pres address not obtained.
URL: http://www.eu-esf.org/
History 7 Jun 1992. Statutes modified: 26 Oct 1993; 25 Sep 2019. Registration: Banque-Carrefour des Entreprises, Belgium; EU Transparency Register, No/ID: 91447653655-65. **Aims** Support development and promotion of Health and Safety in the workplace; create awareness of occupational accident prevention and protection at all levels, emphasizing the importance of proper selection and use of Personal Protective Equipment; support members in further development of the sector. **Structure** General Assembly (annual); Board; Daily Management Team; Permanent Secretariat. **Languages** English. **Staff** 0.50 FTE, paid. **Finance** Sources: members' dues. **Activities** Events/meetings; guidance/assistance/consulting; knowledge management/information dissemination. **Events** *European Seminar on Personal Protective Equipment* Rovaniemi (Finland) 2014.
Members National federations of personal protection equipment manufacturers and distributors in 13 countries:
Belgium, Denmark, Finland, France, Germany, Iceland, Italy, Netherlands, Norway, Spain, Sweden, Türkiye, UK.
Cooperative: individual companies. Membership countries not specified.
Admitted members (2) include 1 listed in this Yearbook:
European Textile Services Association (ETSA, #08904).
NGO Relations Member of (1): *Federation of European and International Associations Established in Belgium (FAIB, #09508)*. Cooperates with (7): *Confédération Européenne de l'Industrie de la Chaussure (CEC, #04544)*; *EDANA, the voice of nonwovens (EDANA, #05353)*; *EURATEX – The European Apparel and Textile Confederation (EURATEX, #05616)*; *European Society of Protective Clothing (ESPC, #08716)*; *European Solvents Industry Group (ESIG, #08796)*; *European Textile Services Association (ETSA, #08904)*; *Federation of the European Sporting Goods Industry (FESI, #09552)*. [2022.05.10/XD4847/**D**]

♦ European Safety and Reliability Association (ESRA) 08419

Chairperson Univ of Stavanger, Ullandhaug, 4036 Stavanger, Norway. Fax +4751831750.
Gen Sec address not obtained.
URL: http://www.esrahomepage.org/
History 1986, on the initiative of the European Commission. **Aims** Work toward advancement and application of safety and reliability technology in all areas of human endeavour. **Structure** Management Committee, comprising Chairman, Vice-Chairman, General Secretary, Treasurer, 2 Newsletter editors and 1 member from each country. Standing Committees (3); Technical Committees (7); Working Groups (2). **Activities** Standing Committees (3): Conference; Education and Training; Publications. Technical Committees (7): Offshore Safety; Reliability of Mechanical Components; Uncertainty and Sensitivity Analysis; Human Factors; Risk Management; Monte-Carlo Simulation; Dependability Modelling. Working Groups (2): Quantified Risk Assessment; Structural Reliability. **Events** *ESREL : European Safety and Reliability Conference* Venice (Italy) 2020, *ESREL : European Safety and Reliability Conference* Hannover (Germany) 2019, *ESREL : European Safety and Reliability Conference* Trondheim (Norway) 2018, *ESREL : European Safety and Reliability Conference* Glasgow (UK) 2016, *ESREL : European Safety and Reliability Conference* Zurich (Switzerland) 2015. **Publications** *ESRA Newsletter*.
Members Professional associations; companies; institutions. Members (93) in 22 countries:
Austria, Belgium, Bulgaria, Czechia, Denmark, Estonia, Finland, France, Germany, Greece, Hungary, Italy, Netherlands, Norway, Poland, Portugal, Romania, Slovakia, Slovenia, Spain, Sweden, UK.
Regional organization (1), listed in this Yearbook:
European Safety, Reliability and Data Association (ESReDA, #08420). [2015/XF0803/**F**]

♦ European Safety, Reliability and Data Association (ESReDA) 08420

Association européenne pour la sûreté, la fiabilité et les données
Gen Sec Breslaujos g 3, LT-44403 Kaunas, Lithuania. T. +37037401948.
URL: http://www.esreda.org/
History 1992, on merger of *European Reliability Data Bank Association (EuReData, inactive)* with *European Safety and Reliability Research and Development Association (ESRRDA)*. Registered in accordance with Belgian law. **Aims** Focus the European experience in the fields of security, safety, reliability, maintainability, lifetime and management of technological and human risk; harmonize and facilitate European Research and Development on these techniques; promote the setting up, development, operation and maintenance of data banks concerning these techniques; provide expert opinion in these fields to the European Commission and other national, European or international organisms; improve the communication between researchers, industry, university, databank owners and users and government bodies; contribute to safety and reliability education, its integration with engineering disciplines and in arriving at international definitions, methods and norms; contribute to national, European and international efforts in field of standardization and methodological guides elaboration. **Structure** General Assembly (once a year); Board of Directors (twice a year). **Languages** English. **Finance** Members' dues. **Activities** Projects/programmes; events/meetings; standards/guidelines. **Events** *Critical services continuity – resilience and security* Linz (Austria) 2019, *Accident investigation and learning to improve safety management in complex system – remaining challenges* Bucharest (Romania) 2018, *Risk, reliability and safety of energy systems in coastal and marine environment* Nantes (France) 2018, *Critical infrastructures – enhancing safety, the challenge of foresight* Ispra (Italy) 2017, *Critical infrastructures – enhancing preparedness and resilience for the security of citizens and services supply continuity* Kaunas (Lithuania) 2017. **Publications** Seminar proceedings; books; guidelines.
Members Effective organizations, private and governmental institutes, industry researchers and consultants. Sponsoring sponsoring organizations. Honorary individuals. Members in 19 countries:
Belgium, Czechia, Denmark, Finland, France, Germany, Italy, Lithuania, Netherlands, Norway, Poland, Portugal, Romania, Slovakia, Spain, Sweden, Switzerland, UK, USA.
NGO Relations Member of: *European Safety and Reliability Association (ESRA, #08419)*.
[2017.03.13/XD4167/**D**]

♦ European Sailing Federation (EUROSAF) 08421

SG Seestrasse 17B, 7100 Neusiedl am See, Austria. T. +4366087100247.
Pres address not obtained.
Registered Address c/o Swiss Sailing, Haus des Sportes, Postfach 606, 3000 Bern, Switzerland.
URL: http://www.eurosaf.org/
History Founded 1998. Registered in accordance with Swiss Civil Code. **Aims** Coordinate and develop the sport of sailing in the region. **Structure** General Assembly (annual); Executive Committee; Board. **Languages** English. **Staff** 0.50 FTE, paid. Voluntary. **Finance** Members' dues; income from events and educational developments. **Activities** Events/meetings. **Events** *Annual Meeting* Istanbul (Turkey) 2019, *Annual Meeting* Limassol (Cyprus) 2018, *Annual Meeting* Sofia (Bulgaria) 2017, *Annual Meeting* Minsk (Belarus) 2016, *Annual Meeting* Gdansk (Poland) 2015.
Members National organizations in 42 countries:
Andorra, Armenia, Austria, Azerbaijan, Belarus, Belgium, Bulgaria, Croatia, Cyprus, Czechia, Denmark, Estonia, Finland, France, Germany, Greece, Hungary, Iceland, Ireland, Israel, Italy, Latvia, Lithuania, Malta, Monaco, Montenegro, Netherlands, Norway, Poland, Portugal, Romania, Russia, San Marino, Serbia, Slovakia, Slovenia, Spain, Sweden, Switzerland, Türkiye, UK, Ukraine.
Observers (3):
European Boating Association (EBA, #06376); *European Boating Industry (EBI, #06377)*; *International Association for Disabled Sailing (IFDS, #11849)*.
NGO Relations Member of: *World Sailing (#21760)*. [2017.03.10/XM2788/y/**D**]

♦ European Sales and Marketing Association (ESMA) 08422

CEO Brookfield House, Butterstream, Clane, W91 Y066, CO. KILDARE, Ireland. T. +353874442121.
URL: http://www.esma.org/
History Founded 1977, UK, as *European Food Brokers Association (EFBA)*. Relaunched under current title, 1988. **Aims** Promote discussion of trade between manufacturers and distributors across Europe and the rest of the world; ensure members gain a global understanding of the value chain. **Languages** English. **Staff** 1.50 FTE, paid. **Finance** Members' dues. Sponsorship. **Activities** Guidance/assistance/consulting; events/meetings. **Events** *Annual Conference* Frankfurt-Main (Germany) 2019, *Annual Conference* Madrid (Spain) 2018, *Annual Conference* Brussels (Belgium) 2016, *Annual Conference* Krakow (Poland) 2016, *Annual Conference* Krakow (Poland) 2015. **Publications** *ESMA News*; *ESMA News and Views* – newsletter; *E-Watch* – briefing.
Members Marketing, selling and distributing organizations in 37 countries and territories:
Australia, Austria, Belgium, Bulgaria, Croatia, Czechia, Denmark, Estonia, Finland, France, Germany, Greece, Hong Kong, Hungary, Iceland, Ireland, Italy, Korea Rep, Lithuania, Luxembourg, Moldova, Netherlands, New Zealand, Norway, Poland, Portugal, Romania, Russia, Slovakia, South Africa, Spain, Sweden, Switzerland, Türkiye, UK, Ukraine, USA.
NGO Relations *The Consumer Goods Forum (CGF, #04772)*; *Internationally United Commercial Agents and Brokers (IUCAB, #14072)*. [2020.03.03/XD1191/**D**]

♦ European Salivary Gland Society (ESGS) 08423

Gen Sec Cours de Rive 16, 1204 Geneva, Switzerland. T. +41227357373. Fax +41227357058.
URL: http://www.esgs.ch/
History 2002, Geneva (Switzerland). Branch of *International Salivary Gland Society (ISGS, #14778)*. **Aims** Increase exchange and dissemination of knowledge and information about basic and clinical science pertinent to saliva, salivary glands and related disorders. **Structure** Board, including President, General Secretary and Treasurer. **Events** *International congress on salivary gland diseases* Geneva (Switzerland) 2012, *Sialendoscopy conference* Geneva (Switzerland) 2012. [2010/XM3221/**D**]

- European Salmon Breeding Federation / see Federation of European Aquaculture Producers (#09491)
- European Salmonid Producers Federation / see Federation of European Aquaculture Producers (#09491)

♦ European Salmon Smokers Association (ESSA) 08424
SG c/o Kellen, Avenue de Tervueren 188A, Box 4, 1150 Brussels, Belgium. T. +3227611674. Fax +3227611699. E-mail: essa@kellencompany.com.
URL: http://www.essa-salmon.org/
History EU Transparency Register: 874084216961-91. **Aims** Serve as the European salmon and trout smokers association. **Structure** General Assembly; Management Committee; Working Groups. **Staff** 2.00 FTE, paid. **Activities** Knowledge management/information dissemination.
Members Full: companies (16) in 7 countries:
Finland, France, Greece, Netherlands, Poland, Spain, UK.
Associated members (3) include 2 organizations listed in this Yearbook:
Comité des organisations nationales des importateurs et exportateurs de poisson de l'UE (CEP, #04194); European Union Fish Processors Association (#08989).
IGO Relations Cooperates with: *Codex Alimentarius Commission (CAC, #04081); European Commission (EC, #06633); World Trade Organization (WTO, #21864).*
[2019/XM3983/**D**]

♦ European Salt Producers Association (EUsalt) 08425
Managing Director Avenue de Tervueren 188A, Box 4, 1150 Brussels, Belgium. T. +3227611678. E-mail: eusalt@kellencompany.com.
URL: http://www.eusalt.com/
History 1958, Paris (France). Former names and other names: *European Committee for the Study of Salt (ECSS)* – former; *Comité européen d'étude du sel (CEES)* – former; *Europäischer Salzstudienausschuss (ESSA)* – former. Registration: No/ID: 0871.009.817, Start date: 1 Dec 2004, Belgium; EU Transparency Register, No/ID: 03451096957-77, Start date: 17 Oct 2011. **Aims** Represent salt producers across Europe; provide information to salt producers as well as interested parties outside the salt industry; act as a platform of exchange for the different actors involved on both European and international scenes and represent the interests of the salt industry accordingly. **Structure** Plenary Assembly (annual); Board; Technical Committees; Working Groups; Secretariat. **Languages** English. **Staff** Paid. **Finance** Annual budget: 500,000 EUR. **Activities** Events/meetings; politics/policy/regulatory; research/documentation; standards/guidelines. **Events** *EUsalt Conference* Berchtesgaden (Germany) 2022, *Annual General Assembly* Berchtesgaden (Germany) 2021, *Annual General Assembly* Rotterdam (Netherlands) 2019, *World Salt Symposium* Park City, UT (USA) 2018, *Safety Working Group Meeting* Brussels (Belgium) 2017. **Publications** *A Grain of Salt* (4 a year).
Members Salt producers (25). Full in 9 countries:
France, Germany, Greece, Italy, Netherlands, Poland, Spain, Switzerland, UK.
Associate in 6 countries:
Armenia, China, Egypt, Israel, Tunisia, Türkiye.
IGO Relations Observer status with (1): *Codex Alimentarius Commission (CAC, #04081).* **NGO Relations** Observer status with (1): *Comité européen de normalisation (CEN, #04162).* Member of (1): *World Iodine Association (WIA, #21596)* (Associate member of).
[2023.02.24/XD4851/**D**]

- European Sand Sculptors Association (inactive)
- European Sarcoidosis Foundation (unconfirmed)
- European Satellite Operators Association / see Global Satellite Operators' Association (#10586)
- European Savings Banks Group / see European Savings and Retail Banking Group (#08426)
- European Savings Institute (internationally oriented national body)

♦ European Savings and Retail Banking Group (ESBG) 08426
Groupement européen des caisses d'épargne et banques de détail (GECE) – Agrupación Europea de Cajas de Ahorros – Europäische Sparkassenvereinigung (ESV)
Acting Managing Dir Rue Marie-Thérèse 11, 1000 Brussels, Belgium. T. +3222111111. Fax +3222111199. E-mail: info@wsbi-esbg.org.
URL: https://www.wsbi-esbg.org/
History 23 Apr 1963, Brussels (Belgium). Reorganized in 1994, when activities began being jointly organized under a common structure with *World Savings Banks Institute (WSBI, #21764).* Statutes modified Nov 2004. Former names and other names: *Savings Banks Group of the European Economic Community* – former (1963 to 1988); *Groupement des caisses d'épargne de la Communauté économique européenne (GCECEE)* – former (1963 to 1988); *European Savings Banks Group (ESBG)* – former (1988 to 2013); *Groupement européen des caisses d'épargne (GECE)* – former (1988 to 2013); *Agrupación Europea de Cajas de Ahorros* – former (1988 to 2013); *Europäische Sparkassenvereinigung (ESV)* – former (1988 to 2013); *Grupo Europeu das Caixas Económicas* – former (1988 to 2013); *Gruppo Europeo delle Casse di Risparmio* – former (1988 to 2013); *Europese Spaarbankenvereniging* – former (1988 to 2013); *Europaeiske Sparekasseforening* – former (1988 to 2013); *Enosi Evropaikon Tamievtirion* – former (1988 to 2013). Registration: Banque-Carrefour des Entreprises, No/ID: 0407.146.216, Start date: 25 May 1967, Belgium; EU Transparency Register, No/ID: 8765978796-80, Start date: 16 Dec 2008. **Aims** Represent the interests of savings and retail banks at European level; make the position of savings and retail banks known to European policy makers, particularly the institutions of the European Union. **Structure** Brussels-based Joint Office operates common structure with WSBI; Departments (3). **Languages** English, French, German, Spanish. **Staff** 33.00 FTE, paid. **Finance** Sources: members' dues. **Activities** Events/meetings; guidance/assistance/consulting; monitoring/evaluation; training/education. **Events** *ESG Financing Summit* Brussels (Belgium) 2022, *Financial Education Conference* Brussels (Belgium) 2019, *Retail Banking Conference* Brussels (Belgium) 2019, *World Congress* Delhi (India) 2018, *World Saving Day Kick-Off Meeting* Brussels (Belgium) 2017. **Publications** *WSBI/ESBG Newsletter* in English, French, German, Italian, Spanish. **Perspectives** – series of brochures on savings and retail bank issues. Activity reports; corporate brochures; position papers; directory.
Members Savings and retail banks (24). Members in 20 countries:
Albania, Austria, Belgium, Czechia, Denmark, Finland, France, Germany, Hungary, Iceland, Italy, Luxembourg, Malta, Netherlands, Norway, Portugal, Slovakia, Spain, Sweden, UK.
NGO Relations Member of (4): *Centre for European Policy Studies (CEPS, #03741); European Financial Reporting Advisory Group (EFRAG, #07254); European Services Forum (ESF, #08469); Federation of European and International Associations Established in Belgium (FAIB, #09508).* Cooperates with (2): *European Association of Co-operative Banks (EACB, #05990); European Banking Federation (EBF, #06312).* Instrumental in setting up (3): *European Banking Industry Committee (EBIC, #06314); European Committee for Banking Standards (ECBS, inactive); European Payments Council (EPC, #08175).* Associate Expert Group of *Business and Industry Advisory Committee to the OECD (BIAC, #03385).* Also links with all European trade unions active in the international services field.
[2023/XE0511/**E**]

♦ European School of Administration (EUSA) 08427
Dir Rue De Mot 24, 1049 Brussels, Belgium. T. +3222968323.
URL: http://europa.eu/eas/index.en.htm
History 10 Feb 2005, Brussels (Belgium), as *European Administrative School (EAS).* An interinstitutional body of *European Union (EU, #08967).* **Aims** Promote cooperation between the institutions of the European Union in the area of training; support the spread of common values and harmonized professional practices; create synergies in the use of human and financial resources. **Staff** 26.00 FTE, paid. **Finance** Budget (2012): euro 3.5 million. **IGO Relations** Participating organizations: *European Committee of the Regions (CoR, #06665); Council of the European Union (#04895); Court of Justice of the European Union (CJEU, #04938); European Commission (EC, #06633); European Court of Auditors (#06854); European Economic and Social Committee (EESC, #06963); European Parliament (EP, #08146); European Ombudsman (#08084).*
[2017/XM1289/**E**]

♦ European School for Advanced Studies in Ophthalmology (ESASO) . 08428
Head Office Manager Villa Saroli, Viale Stefano Franscini 9, PO Box 5269, 6901 Lugano TI, Switzerland. T. +41919211154. E-mail: info@esaso.org.
URL: http://www.esaso.org/
History 2008, Lugano (Switzerland). **Aims** Facilitate dissemination of new and effective ophthalmological learning and expertise through in-depth exposition of topics and face-to-face training. **Structure** Foundation Board. **Languages** English. **Staff** 5.00 FTE, paid. **Finance** Members' dues. Donations. **Activities** Training/education; events/meetings. **Events** *International AMD and Retina Congress* Lisbon (Portugal) 2011. **Publications** *ESASO Course Series.* **Members** Individuals (280). Membership countries not specified. **NGO Relations** *European Accreditation Council for Continuing Medical Education (EACCME, #05823); Eyes of the World Foundation;* national societies; scientific associations; publishers; professional communities.
[2022/XJ5515/**D**]

♦ European School of Advanced Veterinary Studies (ESAVS) 08429
Contact Schadtengasse 2, 55765 Birkenfeld, Germany. T. +4967822329 – +496782(491607114450. Fax +4967824314. E-mail: info@esavs.org.
URL: http://www.esavs.org/
History 1991, as a COMETT II pilot-project of the European Union. Comes within *European Association for Veterinary Specialization (EAVS, no recent information).* **Aims** Provide committed veterinarians appropriate continued *professional* development courses. **Structure** Board of 3 members; Office Manager and 2 Secretaries; Advisory Committee. **Languages** English, French, German. **Finance** Supported by: Vetcontact.
Activities Organizes: training programmes and seminars covering over 20 veterinary disciplines; residential courses in Austria, Czech Rep, Luxembourg, Poland, Spain, Switzerland, Italy, France and UK; Continuing Professional Development (CPD). Courses: *'Branch A – Advanced Veterinary Studies'* – Behavioural Medicine; Cardiology; Dentistry; Dermatology; Diagnostic Ultrasound; Emergency Care; Endoscopy; Exotic Pets; Feline Medicine and Surgery; Internal Medicine; Neurology; Ophthalmology; Small Animal Reproduction; Surgery; *'Branch B – Excellence in Veterinary Therapy'* – Small Animal Therapy; Optimizing the Management of Clinical Disorders in Companion Animals. **Publications** *ESAVS Statistics 2005/2006.* Brochures.
[2010/XE3327/**E**]

- European School of Cardio-Thoracic Surgery (internationally oriented national body)

♦ European School of Haematology (ESH) 08430
Ecole européenne d'hématologie
Exec Dir ESH-IUH Centre Hayem, Hôp Saint Louis, 1 av Claude Vellefaux, 75475 Paris CEDEX 10, France. T. +33157276739. Fax +33142060587.
URL: http://www.esh.org/
History 1986. **Aims** Promote and facilitate access to state of the art and cutting-edge knowledge in haematology and related disciplines at the European level. **Languages** English. **Staff** 7.00 FTE, paid. **Activities** Events/meetings; training/education; certification/accreditation. **Events** *International Conference on Myelodysplastic Syndromes* Estoril (Portugal) 2016, *International Conference on Myeloproliferative Neoplasms* Estoril (Portugal) 2016, *International Conference on Myelodysplastic Syndromes* Estoril (Portugal) 2014, *International Conference on Haematological Disorders in the Elderly* Barcelona (Spain) 2013, *International Conference on Multiple Myeloma* Dublin (Ireland) 2013. **Publications** *Clinical Handbook on Haemopoietic Stem Cell Transplantation* – jointly with EBMT; *Handbook on Disorders of Iron Homeostasis, Erythrocytes, Erythropoisis* – jointly with Club du Globule Rouge et du Fer. **IGO Relations** Many activities supported by: *European Commission (EC, #06633).* **NGO Relations** Member of: *Worldwide Network for Blood and Marrow Transplantation (WBMT, #21929).* Coorganizes events with: *International Chronic Myeloid Leukemia Foundation (iCMLf, #12569).*
[2016.02.18/XG6156/**D**]

♦ European School Heads Association (ESHA) 08431
Association européenne des chefs d'établissements – Europäische Schulleitervereinigung
Dir PO Box 1003, 3500 BA Utrecht, Netherlands. T. +31302361010. Fax +31302361036.
SG Ovre Vollgt 11, 0104 Oslo, Norway. T. +4724101911.
URL: http://www.esha.org/
History Nov 1988, as *European Secondary Heads Association – Association européenne des chefs d'établissements du secondaire – Europäische Schulleitervereinigung im Sekundarbereich II,* at a conference on 'Educating Tomorrow's Europeans', Maastricht (Netherlands). Revised constitution adopted: Nov 1993, Seville (Spain); Feb 1997, Colle Val d'Elsa (Italy); Nov 2003, Toulon (France). Registered as a foundation in accordance with Dutch law. **Aims** Promote development of quality education throughout Europe; improve *management* skills of heads and deputy heads in an international context; facilitate links between school leaders and their schools; extend knowledge about educational programmes within and outside the European Union; initiate educational programmes and competitions with a European dimension; influence European educational policy. **Structure** General Board (meeting twice a year), comprising one representative of each member countries. Executive Board, comprising President, President Elect or Past President (alternatively), General Secretary, Treasurer and one annual member. **Languages** English, French. **Staff** None. **Finance** Members' dues. **Activities** Education; networking/liaising; meeting activities. **Events** *Biennial Conference* Limassol (Cyprus) 2022, *Biennial Conference* Limassol (Cyprus) 2020, *Biennial Conference* Tallinn (Estonia) 2018, *Biennial Conference* Maastricht (Netherlands) 2016, *Biennial Conference* Dubrovnik (Croatia) 2014. **Publications** *ESHA Vademecum for School Heads* (1994); *DEEP – Project 1992-1998.* Conference reports. **Information Services** *European School Exchange Databank (ESED).*
Members Full: organizations of school heads (both primary and secondary) and deputy heads (about 65,000) in 30 countries:
Austria, Belarus, Belgium, Bulgaria, Czechia, Denmark, Estonia, Finland, France, Germany, Greece, Hungary, Iceland, Ireland, Israel, Italy, Latvia, Lithuania, Luxembourg, Netherlands, North Macedonia, Norway, Poland, Portugal, Romania, Slovakia, Spain, Switzerland, UK, Ukraine.
IGO Relations *Council of Europe (CE, #04881); European Parliament (EP, #08146).* EU programmes: *SOCRATES Programme (inactive).* **NGO Relations** Member of: *Lifelong Learning Platform – European Civil Society for Education (LLLP, #16466); International Confederation of Principals (ICP, #12868).*
[2014/XD1338/**D**]

- European School Magazine Association (inactive)
- European School of Management and Technology / see ESMT Berlin
- European School of Molecular Medicine (internationally oriented national body)

♦ European School of Multimodality Imaging & Therapy (ESMIT) 08432
Education Chair Schmalzhofgasse 26, 1060 Vienna, Austria. T. +4318904427. Fax +43189044279. E-mail: esmit@eanm.org.
URL: https://www.eanm.org/esmit/
History 2015. Founded by *European Association of Nuclear Medicine (EANM, #06136).* **Structure** Education Chair; Representatives. Project Groups. **Activities** Training/education.
[AA1617/**E**]

♦ European Schoolnet (EUN) 08433
Contact Rue de Trèves 61, 1040 Brussels, Belgium. T. +3227907575. Fax +3227907585. E-mail: info@eun.org.
URL: http://www.eun.org/
History 1997. Registration: Banque-Carrefour des Entreprises, Belgium; EU Transparency Register, No/ID: 977907115068-02. **Aims** Promote use of *information technology* and *communications technology* among *schools* in Europe, in particular by: supporting professional development of teachers; fostering and supporting collaboration and cooperation among schools in Europe; making available to schools in Europe pedagogical and information services with a European added value. **Structure** Steering Committee; Board of Director;. Policy and Innovation Committee; Learning Resource Exchange Subcommittee; Working Groups. **Activities** Events/meetings; knowledge management/information dissemination; standards/guidelines; training/education. **Events** *School Innovation Forum* Brussels (Belgium) 2022, *EMINENT : Expert Meeting in Education Networking* Brussels (Belgium) 2021, *EMINENT : Expert Meeting in Education Networking* Warsaw (Poland) 2019, *EMINENT : Expert Meeting in Education Networking* Lisbon (Portugal) 2018, *EMINENT : Expert Meeting in Education Networking* Lisbon (Portugal) 2018. **Publications** *European Schoolnet Policy Newsletter, European Schoolnet Policy Newsletter.* Books.
Members Ministries of education and agencies responsible for ICT in education. Full in 24 countries:
Austria, Belgium, Czechia, Denmark, Estonia, Finland, France, Greece, Hungary, Ireland, Israel, Italy, Lithuania, Luxembourg, Malta, Netherlands, Norway, Poland, Portugal, Slovakia, Spain, Sweden, Switzerland, Türkiye.
Observer in 9 countries:
Bulgaria, Croatia, Georgia, Germany, Iceland, Kosovo, Latvia, Romania, Slovenia.
NGO Relations Member of (1): *European Institute for E-Learning (EIfEL, #07552).* Cooperates with (1): *CSR Europe (#04977).* .
[2021/XF5621/**F***]

European School Oncology
08434

alphabetic sequence excludes
For the complete listing, see Yearbook Online at

♦ European School of Oncology (ESO) 08434

Ecole européenne d'oncologie – Escuela Europea de Oncologia – Europäische Onkologie-Schule – Scuola Europea di Oncologia

CEO Via Turati 29, 20121 Milan MI, Italy. T. +3928546451. Fax +39285464545. E-mail: eso@eso.net.
URL: http://www.eso.net/

History 1982, Milan (Italy). Founded by leading oncologists worldwide. Registration: EU Transparency Register, No/ID: 476238443185-54, Start date: 16 Jun 2021. **Aims** Contribute to the reduction of deaths from *cancer* due to late diagnosis and/or inadequate treatment; function as an educational tool in order to improve the general level of oncologists and to disseminate in Europe the results of *clinical* research: organize and conduct theoretical and practical *teaching* courses and fellowships in different fields of oncology for graduates; produce and disseminate teaching material; organize workshops in oncology. **Structure** Board of Directors; Scientific Committee. Offices: Milan (Italy); Bellinzona (Switzerland). **Languages** English, Italian. **Staff** 12.00 FTE, paid. **Finance** Registration fees; donations; industry support (less than 25%). **Activities** Awards/prizes/competitions; events/meetings; financial and/or material support; training/education. **Events** *Familial Cancer Conference* Madrid (Spain) 2018, *Familial Cancer Conference* Madrid (Spain) 2016, *Conference on Cachexia and Nutrition in Advanced Cancer Patients* Barcelona (Spain) 2015, *Meeting on Prostate Cancer Observatory* Madrid (Spain) 2015, *Breast Cancer in Young Women Conference* Tel Aviv (Israel) 2014. **Publications** *Cancer World* (6 a year) – magazine; *CROH – Critical Reviews in Oncology/Hematology* – official journal.
Members Membership covers 129 countries and territories:
Albania, Algeria, Argentina, Armenia, Australia, Austria, Azerbaijan, Bahrain, Bangladesh, Barbados, Belarus, Belgium, Belize, Bolivia, Bosnia-Herzegovina, Brazil, Bulgaria, Burkina Faso, Cameroon, Canada, Chile, China, Colombia, Costa Rica, Côte d'Ivoire, Croatia, Cuba, Cyprus, Czechia, Denmark, Dominica, Ecuador, Egypt, El Salvador, Estonia, Ethiopia, Finland, France, Georgia, Germany, Ghana, Greece, Guatemala, Honduras, Hong Kong, Hungary, Iceland, India, Indonesia, Iran Islamic Rep, Iraq, Ireland, Israel, Italy, Japan, Jordan, Kazakhstan, Kenya, Korea DPR, Korea Rep, Kosovo, Kuwait, Kyrgyzstan, Latvia, Lebanon, Libya, Liechtenstein, Lithuania, Luxembourg, Malaysia, Mali, Malta, Martinique, Mexico, Moldova, Monaco, Montenegro, Morocco, Myanmar, Nepal, Netherlands, New Zealand, Nicaragua, Nigeria, North Macedonia, Norway, Oman, Pakistan, Palestine, Panama, Paraguay, Peru, Philippines, Poland, Portugal, Puerto Rico, Romania, Russia, San Marino, Saudi Arabia, Senegal, Serbia, Sierra Leone, Singapore, Slovakia, Slovenia, South Africa, Spain, Sri Lanka, Sudan, Sweden, Switzerland, Syrian AR, Taiwan, Tajikistan, Thailand, Tunisia, Türkiye, Turkmenistan, UK, Ukraine, United Arab Emirates, Uruguay, USA, Uzbekistan, Venezuela, Vietnam, Yemen, Zimbabwe.
NGO Relations Member of (6): *Accreditation Council for Oncology in Europe (ACOE, #00063)*; *European Society for Medical Oncology (ESMO, #08648)*; *Lung Cancer Europe (LuCE, #16523)*; *Rare Cancers Europe (RCE, #18620)*; *The NCD Alliance (NCDA, #16963)*; *Union for International Cancer Control (UICC, #20415)*. Cooperates with (4): *European Institute of Oncology, Milan (EIO)*; *European Oncology Nursing Society (EONS, #08086)*; *European Organisation for Research and Treatment of Cancer (EORTC, #08101)*; *European SocieTy for Radiotherapy and Oncology (ESTRO, #08721)*. Instrumental in setting up (8): *ABC Global Alliance (#00004)*; *Breast Centres Network (BCN, #03317)*; *Europa Donna – The European Breast Cancer Coalition (#05745)*; *Europa Uomo (#05770)*; *European Cancer Organisation (ECO, #06432)*; *European School of Oncology Foundation (ESOF, no recent information)*; *International Society of Cancer Prevention (ISCaP, #14992)*; *Sharing Progress in Cancer Care (SPCC)*. [2021/XF1916/F]

♦ European School of Oral Rehabilitation, Implantology and Biomaterials (ESORIB) 08435

Dir Plaza de España 5-10e, 46007 Valencia, Spain. T. +34963803245. Fax +34963803465. E-mail: esorib@esorib.com.
Registered Office Rue Washington 40, 1050 Brussels, Belgium.
URL: http://www.esorib.com/

History 1990, Brussels (Belgium). Registered in accordance with Belgian law. **Aims** Group *professionals* concerned by the implantable systems; promote the knowledge in the field; facilitate the information of professionals, the planning of research and the exchange of information between all *practitioners* involved. **Structure** General Assembly (annual). Council, comprising not less than 3 and not more than 7 members, including President, Secretary and Treasurer. **Events** *Annual Meeting* Valencia (Spain) 2013, *Annual meeting* Marbella (Spain) 2005. **Members** Individuals. Membership countries not specified. [2016/XF2444/F]

♦ European School of Osteopathy (internationally oriented national body)

♦ European Schools Project Association (ESP) 08436

Main Office Kantershof 423, ZUIDOOST, 1104 GX Amsterdam, Netherlands. E-mail: karenthomsen@versanet.de.
URL: http://www.espnet.eu/

History Founded 1988, Amsterdam (Netherlands). Formally registered as an Association, 2005. **Aims** Improve learning and teaching by supporting pupils and teachers in using the Internet. **Structure** Board. **Events** *Conference* Bolzano (Italy) 2014, *Conference* Gouda (Netherlands) 2013, *Conference* Haugesund (Norway) 2012, *Conference* Helsingør (Denmark) 2011, *Conference* London (UK) 2010.
Members Schools (over 300) in 24 countries:
Belgium, Bosnia-Herzegovina, Chile, Czechia, Denmark, Estonia, Finland, France, Germany, Italy, Japan, Lithuania, Netherlands, Norway, Poland, Portugal, Russia, Slovakia, Slovenia, Spain, Sweden, Türkiye, UK, USA. [2013.12.22/XM0354/D]

♦ European School of Theosophy (meeting series)

♦ European School of Transfusion Medicine (ESTM) 08437

Sec c/o Viale Beatrice d'Este 5, 20122 Milan MI, Italy. T. +39258316515. Fax +39258308111. E-mail: estm.secretariat@estm.info.
Pres address not obtained.
URL: http://www.estm.info/

History 30 Mar 1992, Milan (Italy). Registered in accordance with Italian law. **Aims** Raise transfusion medicine practice to a common level of excellence in all European countries. **Structure** Assembly; Council of Administration; Executive Committee; Scientific Committee; Operational Centres (4). **Languages** English, French, German, Italian, Portuguese, Spanish. **Staff** Varies according to needs. **Finance** Members' dues. Grants; additional funding. **Activities** Training/education; networking/liaising. **Publications** Course proceedings; journal articles.
Members Course participants in 34 countries:
Albania, Argentina, Armenia, Austria, Belgium, Bosnia-Herzegovina, Brazil, Bulgaria, Croatia, Czechia, Estonia, France, Germany, Greece, Israel, Italy, Latvia, Netherlands, North Macedonia, Norway, Peru, Poland, Portugal, Romania, Russia, Senegal, Serbia, Slovakia, Slovenia, Spain, Switzerland, Türkiye, UK, Ukraine. [2018.09.06/XJ8840/D]

♦ European School of Urology (see: #06264)

♦ European Science Education Research Association (ESERA) 08438

Sec address not obtained.
URL: http://www.esera.org/

History Apr 1995, Leeds (UK). **Aims** Enhance the range and quality of research and research training in science education in Europe; provide a forum for collaboration in science education research between European countries; represent the professional interests of science education researchers in Europe; seek to relate research to the policy and practice of science education in Europe; foster links between science education researchers in Europe and similar communities elsewhere in the world. **Structure** General Assembly. Executive Committee, including President, Secretary and Treasurer. **Languages** English. **Finance** Members' dues. **Activities** Organizes: conference (every 2 years); summer school for PhD student (every 2 years, alternating with conference). **Events** *Conference* Nevsehir (Türkiye) 2023, *Conference* Braga (Portugal) 2021, *Biennial Conference* Bologna (Italy) 2019, *Biennial Conference* Dublin (Ireland) 2017, *Biennial Conference* Helsinki (Finland) 2015. **Publications** *ESERA eNews* (4 a year). *ESERA Science Education Research Series*. Conference proceedings.
Members Individuals in 58 countries and territories:
Argentina, Australia, Austria, Belgium, Brazil, Bulgaria, Canada, Chile, China, Colombia, Croatia, Cyprus, Czechia, Denmark, Estonia, Finland, France, Georgia, Germany, Ghana, Greece, Hong Kong, India, Iran Islamic Rep, Ireland, Israel, Italy, Japan, Kazakhstan, Kenya, Korea Rep, Lebanon, Luxembourg, Malaysia, Malta, Mexico, Netherlands, New Zealand, Norway, Palestine, Poland, Portugal, Romania, Russia, Saudi Arabia, Singapore, Slovakia, Slovenia, South Africa, Spain, Sweden, Switzerland, Taiwan, Türkiye, UK, United Arab Emirates, USA, Uzbekistan. [2022/XD9349/D]

♦ European Science Engagement Association (EUSEA) 08439

Exec Dir c/o Verein ScienceCenter, Landstraßer Hauptstr 71/1/309, 1030 Vienna, Austria. E-mail: info@eusea.info.
URL: http://www.eusea.info/

History Apr 2001, as *European Science Events Association (EUSCEA)*. Also known by the acronym *EUSEA*. Present name adopted, 2017. **Structure** General Assembly. Executive Committee, comprising President, Vice President, General Secretary, Vice General Secretary, Treasurer and Vice Treasurer. **Events** *Annual Conference* Vienna (Austria) 2019, *Annual Conference* Madrid (Spain) 2018, *Annual Conference* Jerusalem (Israel) 2013, *Annual Conference* Dublin (Ireland) 2012, *Annual Conference* Gothenburg (Sweden) 2011.
Members National organizations in 25 countries:
Austria, Belgium, Cyprus, Denmark, Finland, France, Germany, Hungary, Iceland, Ireland, Israel, Italy, Latvia, Luxembourg, Malta, Netherlands, Norway, Poland, Portugal, Slovakia, Slovenia, Spain, Sweden, Switzerland, UK. [2018/XM0372/D]

♦ European Science Events Association / see European Science Engagement Association (#08439)

♦ European Science Fiction Society (ESFS) 08440

Société européenne de science fiction

Sec 562 Forest Road, Walthamstow, E17 3ED, UK. E-mail: bjw@cix.co.uk.
Registered Office 64 Richborne Terrace, London, SW8 1AX, UK.
URL: http://www.esfs.info/

History Founded 1972, Trieste (Italy), at first European Science Fiction Convention, Eurocon. **Aims** Find means of establishing contact between science fiction professionals and fans; ensure better mutual knowledge of science fiction literature and arts in European countries; promote knowledge European science fiction in the rest of the world. **Structure** General Meeting (meets at least every 2 years). Committee, consisting of Chairman; Elected Vice-Chairman; Nominated Vice-Chairman; Secretary; Treasurer; Honorary Members of ESFS; National Delegates for each country. **Languages** English, French, German, Russian. **Finance** Members' dues. Other sources: grants; gifts. **Activities** Makes 'European Science Fiction Awards'. **Events** *Eurocon Convention* Rotterdam (Netherlands) 2024, *Eurocon Convention* Uppsala (Sweden) 2023, *Eurocon Convention* Dudelange (Luxembourg) 2022, *Eurocon Convention* Fiuggi (Italy) 2021, *Eurocon Convention* Rijeka (Croatia) 2020. **Publications** *ESFS Newsletter*. *European Science Fiction Guide*. Directory.
Members Full in 27 countries:
Andorra, Austria, Belgium, Bulgaria, Croatia, Czechia, Denmark, Finland, France, Germany, Hungary, Ireland, Italy, Lithuania, Netherlands, Norway, Poland, Portugal, Romania, Russia, Slovakia, Spain, Sweden, Switzerland, Türkiye, UK, Ukraine. [2019/XD6369/D]

♦ European Science Foundation (ESF) 08441

Fondation européenne de la science – Europäische Wissenschaftsstiftung

Pres 1 quai Lezay Marnésia, BP 90015, 67080 Strasbourg CEDEX, France. T. +33388767100. Fax +33388370532. E-mail: elegoux@esf.org.
CEO address not obtained.
URL: http://www.esf.org/

History 18 Nov 1974, Strasbourg (France). **Aims** Promote high quality science in Europe to drive progress in research and innovation. **Structure** General Assembly (annual); Executive Board; Expert Boards, Committees and Societies: *ESF Committee on Radio Astronomy Frequencies (CRAF, see: #08441)*; *European Space Sciences Committee (ESSC, see: #08441)*; *Nuclear Physics European Collaboration Committee (NuPECC, #17620)*; *Europlanet Society (#09170)*; *European Astrobiology Institute (EAI, #06285)*; cOAlition S Executive Office; Core Technologies for Life Sciences (CTLS). **Languages** Croatian, Dutch, English, Estonian, Finnish, French, Greek, Hungarian, Italian, Polish, Romanian, Russian, Spanish. **Staff** 35.00 FTE, paid. **Finance** Sources: members' dues. Provision of science-support services on a not-for-profit basis. **Activities** Monitoring/evaluation; politics/policy/regulatory; projects/programmes; research/documentation; training/education. **Events** *Workshop on Symplectic Geometry, Contact Geometry and Interactions* Berlin (Germany) 2019, *International Conference on the Fundamental Science of Graphene and Applications of Graphene-Based Devices* Helsinki (Finland) 2019, *EUROCEAN : European Conference on Marine Science and Ocean Technology* Paris (France) 2019, *Workshop on Symplectic Geometry, Contact Geometry and Interactions* Lyon (France) 2015, *Workshop on new Research on the Migration of Peoples in the 12th Century BCE* Vienna (Austria) 2014. **Publications** Guides; scientific and evaluation reports; research studies; research career surveys.
Members Research councils, academies, scientific associations and learned societies in 8 countries:
Belgium, Bulgaria, France, Hungary, Luxembourg, Romania, Serbia, Türkiye.
IGO Relations Member of (1): *Standing Committee to the Bern Convention on the Conservation of European Wildlife and Natural Habitats (#19949)*. **NGO Relations** Close relations with: *Academia Europaea (#00011)*. Instrumental in setting up: *ALLEA – ALL European Academies (#00647)*; *Baha'i International Community (#03062)*; *ESF Committee for the World Ocean Circulation Experiment (WOCE, no recent information)*; *Network on European Communications and Transport Activity Research (NECTAR, #17016)*. Founding member of: *European Materials Forum (EMF, #07751)*. Member of: *European Alliance for Personalised Medicine (EAPM, #05878)*; *European Alliance for the Social Sciences and Humanities (EASSH, #05885)*; *European Committee for Future Accelerators (ECFA, #06650)*. [2022.05.10/XF2152/f/F]

♦ European Science-Industry Consortium for Biomaterials and Health Care (unconfirmed)
♦ European Science Teachers Association (inactive)
♦ European Scientific Association of Applied Economics (no recent information)

♦ European Scientific Association for Material Forming (ESAFORM) . . 08442

Mailing Address c/o CEMEF – Mines ParisTech, CS10, 207 Rue Claude Daunesse, 06904 Sophia Antipolis CEDEX, France.
URL: http://www.esaform.org/

History Jan 1997. **Aims** Propagate interest for all types of materials and all topics connected to material forming; stimulate and diffuse applied research in academic laboratories, public organizations and industrial companies; spread scientific information on material forming; link industry and public research; teach material forming sciences in Europe; promote the image of material forming. **Structure** Board of Directors, comprising President, Vice-President, Treasurer, Secretary, Deputy-Secretary and 19 members. Scientific Committee. **Languages** English. **Finance** Members' dues. **Activities** Awards scientific prize and PhD prize for Industrial Research during annual scientific conference. Organizes courses and tutorial seminars. Creates European networks on general topics. Favours training periods. **Events** *Annual Conference* Toulouse (France) 2024, *International ESAFORM Conference on Material Forming* Krakow (Poland) 2023, *Annual Conference* Braga (Portugal) 2022, *Annual Conference* Liège (Belgium) 2021, *Annual Conference* Cottbus (Germany) 2020. **Publications** *International Journal of Material Forming* (4 a year); *ESAFORM Bulletin* (annual). *ESAFORM Bookseries on Material Forming*.
Members Individuals in 38 countries:
Argentina, Austria, Belgium, Brazil, Bulgaria, Canada, Chile, China, Croatia, Czechia, Denmark, Finland, France, Germany, Greece, Hungary, India, Israel, Italy, Japan, Jordan, Korea Rep, Mexico, Netherlands, Norway, Pakistan, Poland, Portugal, Romania, Russia, Serbia, Slovenia, Spain, Sweden, Switzerland, Türkiye, UK, USA. [2022/XD7803/v/D]

♦ European Scientific Association for Residential and Foster Care of Children and Adolescents (inactive)

♦ European Scientific Association on Schizophrenia and other Psychoses (ESAS) 08443

Pres c/o Dept of Psychiatry and Psychotherapy, Heinrich-Heine-Univ Düsseldorf, LVR-Klinikum Düsseldorf, Bergische Landstr 2, 40629 Düsseldorf, Germany. T. +492119222773. E-mail: info@esasnet.eu.
Registered Office c/ Wartmann and Merker, Kirchgasse 48, 8024 Zurich ZH, Switzerland.
URL: http://www.esasnet.eu/

History Set up Sep 2011, at 3rd European Conference on Schizophrenia Research. Articles adopted, 26 Sep 2011, Düsseldorf (Germany). Registered in accordance with Swiss Civil Code. **Aims** Stimulate cross-border science cooperation and networking; stimulate scientific exchange; advance research; shape science and research policy with regard to psychoses. **Structure** General Assembly (every 2 years); Executive Committee. **Languages** English. **Events** *European Conference on Schizophrenia Research* Berlin (Germany) 2021, *European Conference on Schizophrenia Research* Berlin (Germany) 2019, *European Conference on Schizophrenia Research* Berlin (Germany) 2017, *European Conference on Schizophrenia Research / European Conference on Schizophrenia Research – ECSR* Berlin (Germany) 2015, *European Conference on Schizophrenia Research* Berlin (Germany) 2013. **Members** Full; Corporate; Supporting. Membership countries not specified. [2016.06.23/XJ6262/D]

♦ **European Scientific Cooperative on Phytotherapy (ESCOP)** **08444**
Secretariat Notaris House, Chapel Street, Exeter, EX1 1EZ, UK. T. +441392424626. E-mail: secretariat@escop.com.
URL: http://www.escop.com/
History 18 Jun 1989, Cologne (Germany). Founded following decision of a convention, 18 May 1989, Netherlands. Research Committee took over activities of *European Phytotherapy Research Group (inactive)*. **Aims** Advance the scientific status of *herbal medicinal* products and assist with harmonization of their regulatory status at European level. **Structure** Board; Committees (2); Secretariat (Administration). **Languages** English. **Staff** 0.50 FTE, paid; 1.00 FTE, voluntary. **Finance** Sources: members' dues. Annual budget: 30,000 GBP. **Activities** Events/meetings; politics/policy/regulatory; research and development. **Events** *New Insights on the Pharmacological Potential of Echinacea sp* Graz (Austria) 2022, *International Phytotherapy Meeting* Winterthur (Switzerland) 2014, *Biennial International Symposium* Cologne (Germany) 2009, *Biennial international symposium* 2004, *Biennial international symposium* Bonn (Germany) 2001. **Publications** *European Phyto Journal. Summaries of Product Characteristics*; *The Scientific Foundation for Herbal Medicinal Products*. Monographs; position papers; articles. Publications on the quality, safety and efficacy of herbal medicines and their clinical use in Europe.
Members Full in 11 countries:
Austria, Germany, Hungary, Italy, Netherlands, Poland, Portugal, Spain, Switzerland, Türkiye, UK. [2022.11.18/XF2287/**F**]

♦ **European Scientific Counsel Companion Animal Parasites (ESCCAP)** **08445**
Secretariat Malvern Hills Science Park, Geraldine Road, Malvern, WR14 3SZ, UK. T. +441684585135. E-mail: info@esccap.org.
Registered Office Granta Lodge, 71 Graham Road, Malvern, WR14 2JS, UK.
URL: http://www.esccap.org/
History 2005. Registration: No/ID: 5821601, England and Wales. **Aims** Provide veterinary professionals with free expert information in the form of guidelines derived from independent and soundly-based investigation and research. **Languages** Dutch, English, French, German, Greek, Hungarian, Italian, Polish, Portuguese, Spanish, Ukrainian. **Activities** Events/meetings; knowledge management/information dissemination; standards/guidelines. **Events** *Vector-borne Diseases Meeting* Granada (Spain) 2016, *Echinococcus Meeting* Vilnius (Lithuania) 2014, *Toxocara Meeting* Budapest (Hungary) 2012, *European Science Forum* Lisbon (Portugal) 2012. **Publications** Guidelines; modular guide series; fact sheets.
Members National associations in 17 countries:
Austria, Belgium, Denmark, France, Germany, Greece, Hungary, Ireland, Italy, Luxembourg, Netherlands, Poland, Portugal, Spain, Switzerland, UK, Ukraine.
Austria/Germany, Belgium/Luxembourg/Netherlands, UK/Ireland each forming 1 group.
NGO Relations Also links with national associations. [2022.02.09/XJ5775/**F**]

♦ European Scientific Diving Committee / see European Scientific Diving Panel (#08446)

♦ **European Scientific Diving Panel (ESDP)** **08446**
Contact c/o IMBE, Ave Escadrille Normandie Niémen, Service 421 Fac Sci, 13397 Marseille CEDEX 20, France.
URL: https://www.esdpanel.eu/
History 2007. Became an approved Panel of the *European Marine Board (EMB, #07738)* of *European Science Foundation (ESF, #08441)*, Oct 2008. Since 2017, under the umbrella of *European Network of Marine Research Institutes and Stations (MARS Network, #07941)*. Former names and other names: *European Scientific Diving Committee (ESDC)* – former. **Aims** Advance underwater scientific excellence; promote and provide a practical support framework for scientific diving at a European scale. **Structure** Annual Meeting. **Activities** Capacity building; events/meetings; knowledge management/information dissemination; standards/guidelines. The *European Conference on Scientific Diving (ECSD)* was created by the Panel in order to to combine the "*International Symposium on Occupational Scientific Diving* (ISOSD)" and the international workshop "*Research in Shallow Marine Water Systems*" into one annual meeting. **Events** *European Conference on Scientific Diving (ECSD7)* Roscoff (France) 2023, *ECSD: European Conference on Scientific Diving* Roscoff (France) 2022, *European Conference on Scientific Diving (ECSD)* Freiburg (Germany) 2021, *European Conference on Scientific Diving (ECSD)* Sopot (Poland) 2019, *European Conference on Scientific Diving (ECSD)* Orkney (UK) 2018.
Members Membership is at nation level with an identified representative. Current national representatives from 16 countries and territories:
Belgium, Bulgaria, Cyprus, Finland, France, Germany, Gibraltar, Greece, Italy, Netherlands, Norway, Poland, Portugal, Slovenia, Sweden, UK.
NGO Relations Cooperates with (1): *World Underwater Federation (#21873)*. [2023/AA3132/**F***]

♦ **European Scientific foundation for Laboratory Hemato Oncology (ESLHO)** **08447**
Registered Address c/o Dept of IHB, Bldg 1, Postal zone E3-Q, Room L01-71G, Albinusdreef 2, 2333 ZA Leiden, Netherlands. E-mail: info@eslho.org.
URL: http://www.eslho.org/
History Registration: No/ID: 24457776, Netherlands. **Activities** Certification/accreditation; events/meetings; standards/guidelines. **Events** *Symposium* Leiden (Netherlands) 2021, *Symposium* Leiden (Netherlands) 2020, *Symposium* Ghent (Belgium) 2019. [2020/AA0275/f/**F**]

♦ **European Scientific Institute (ESI)** **08448**
Main Office Mont-Blanc 1, 61 rue Antoine Redier, Archamps Technopole, 74160 Archamps, France. T. +33456448140. E-mail: logistics@esi-archamps.eu.
URL: http://www.esi-archamps.eu/
History 1994, on the initiative of CERN-based scientists and a group of universities. Registered in accordance with French law. **Aims** Provide Master/PhD students and early career scientists and engineers with specialist knowledge and skills enabling them to pursue international careers in research, industry and innovative entrepreneurship. **Structure** Board. **Languages** English, French. **Staff** 6.00 FTE, paid. **Finance** Annual budget: euro 300,000. **Activities** Training/education; events/meetings.
Members Universities and research and industry partners in 8 countries:
France, Germany, Italy, Japan, Norway, Spain, Switzerland, UK. [2022/XE2825/j/**E**]

♦ **European Scientific Institute (ESI)** **08449**
Pres 203 No 1, 2300 Kocani, North Macedonia. T. +38970223631. E-mail: contact@euinstitute.com – contact@eujournal.org.
Contact Rua da Cruz No 55-1 andar, S José, 9500-051 Ponta Delgada, Portugal.
URL: http://euinstitute.net/
History Set up 2010, Macedonia. **Aims** Cooperate in the field of education; create a global multidisciplinary *academic* platform. **Structure** General Assembly; Board; President. **Languages** English. **Staff** 5.00 FTE, paid; 7.00 FTE, voluntary. **Finance** Self-financing. **Activities** Capacity building; knowledge management/information dissemination; publishing activities; training/education; events/meetings. Active in: Albania, Argentina, India, Jordan, Lithuania, North Macedonia, Portugal, Spain, USA. **Events** *Eurasian Multidisciplinary Forum* Vienna (Austria) 2017, *Mediterranean Interdisciplinary Forum on Social Sciences and Humanities* Barcelona (Spain) 2016, *Annual International Interdisciplinary Conference* Pamukkale (Turkey) 2016, *Eurasian Multidisciplinary Forum* Tbilisi (Georgia) 2016, *International Scientific Forum* Tokyo (Japan) 2016. **Publications** *European Journal of Economics, Law and Politics (ELP)*; *European Journal of Educational Sciences (EJES)*; *International Journal of Linguistics, Literature and Culture (LLC)*.
Members Individuals in 10 countries:
Australia, Canada, Denmark, Finland, Georgia, Malta, North Macedonia, Portugal, Spain, USA.
IGO Relations *UNESCO (#20322)*. **NGO Relations** Member of: *International Community for Open Research and Education (ICORE)*. [2022/XJ9124/j/**D**]

♦ **European Scientific Working Group on Influenza (ESWI)** **08450**
Events Manager ADS Insight, Résidence Palace, Rue de la Loi 155, BTE 97, 1040 Brussels, Belgium.
Dir address not obtained.
URL: http://www.eswi.org/
History 1993. Registration: Banque-Carrefour des Entreprises, No/ID: 0474.316.835, Start date: 7 Oct 1998, Belgium; EU Transparency Register, No/ID: 135580544504-13, Start date: 15 Nov 2021. **Aims** Improve public health protection against influenza. **Structure** General Assembly (annual); Board of Directors; Executive Committee. **Languages** English. **Finance** Supported by pharmaceutical companies. **Activities** Events/meetings; knowledge management/information dissemination; networking/liaising; research and development; training/education. **Events** *ESWI Influenza Conference* Valencia (Spain) 2023, *ESWI Influenza Conference* Salzburg (Austria) 2021, *European Influenza Conference* Valencia (Spain) 2020, *European Influenza Conference* Riga (Latvia) 2017, *Science Policy Flu Summit* Brussels (Belgium) 2016. **Publications** *Influenza Bulletin* (2 a year) – for scientists; *Influenza Newsletter* (2 a year) – for policy-makers. Annual Report.
Members Individuals (12) from 8 countries:
Czechia, Finland, France, Germany, Netherlands, Türkiye, UK, USA.
NGO Relations Member of (1): *European Public Health Alliance (EPHA, #08297)*. Endorses: *Steering Group on Influenza Vaccination (#19980)*. [2022.10.19/XD7228/v/**E**]

♦ **European Scout Foundation** **08451**
Fondation européenne du Scoutisme
Chair PO Box 327, 1211 Geneva 4, Switzerland. T. +41227051100. Fax +41227051109. E-mail: europefoundation@scout.org.
Office Rue Henri-Christiné 5, 1205 Geneva, Switzerland.
URL: http://www.europeanscoutfoundation.com/
History 1974. Former names and other names: *Friends of Scouting in Europe* – alias. **Aims** Provide financial support for development of scouting in Europe, emphasizing national scout organizations in Central and Eastern Europe; develop Friends of Scouting in Europe (FOSE) as a means of raising money to support scout projects; increase endowment capital so as to provide financial support to Scouting in Europe. **Structure** Includes: *Friends of Scouting in Europe (FOSE)*. **Languages** English, French. **Staff** Voluntary. **Finance** Sources: donations. **Activities** Events/meetings. **Events** *Annual Gathering* Bratislava (Slovakia) 2021, *Annual Gathering* Sibiu (Romania) 2019, *Annual Gathering* Jagodina (Serbia) 2017, *Annual Gathering* Sarajevo (Bosnia-Herzegovina) 2012, *Annual Gathering* Tallinn (Estonia) 2011. **Members** Membership countries not specified. [2021.09.05/XF7059/f/**F**]

♦ European Scout Office / see World Scout Bureau – European Regional Office (#21771)
♦ European Screen Printing Manufacturers Associations / see European Specialist Printing Manufacturers Associations (#08809)

♦ **European Sealing Association (ESA)** **08452**
Association européenne de l'étanchéité – Asociación Europea de Estanqueidad
SG 310 Route de la Plagne Morzine, 74110 Morzine, France. T. +33631941600.
URL: http://www.europeansealing.com/
History Founded 1992. Registered in accordance with German law. **Aims** Act as a forum in which issues of common interest can be discussed and actions formulated; raise the credibility of the sealing industry; work towards harmonization of standards and legislation, development of sealing technology, and safety, efficiency and environmental protection. **Structure** General Meeting (twice a year); Executive Committee. Divisions (3); Working Groups (2). Environmental Charter accepted at General Meeting, Apr 1994. **Languages** English. **Staff** 1.00 FTE, paid. **Finance** Members' dues. **Events** *Annual General Meeting* Vienna (Austria) 2022, *Annual General Meeting* 2021, *Annual General Meeting* Vienna (Austria) 2021, *Annual General Meeting* Vienna (Austria) 2020, *Annual General Meeting* Lisbon (Portugal) 2019. **Publications** *ESA Environmental News* (4 a year). Technical reports.
Members Companies (49) in 16 countries and territories:
Austria, Bulgaria, Denmark, France, Germany, Ireland, Italy, Netherlands, Poland, Slovenia, Spain, Sweden, Taiwan, Türkiye, UK, USA.
NGO Relations Formal contacts with a number of national organizations interested in the field. [2020/XD3623/**D**]

♦ European Seals and Gaskets Association (unconfirmed)

♦ **European Sea Ports Organisation (ESPO)** **08453**
Organisation des ports maritimes européens – Organisatie van de Europese Zeehavens
SG Treurenberg 6, 1000 Brussels, Belgium. T. +3227363463. E-mail: mail@espo.be.
Personal Assistant address not obtained.
URL: http://www.espo.be/
History 26 Jan 1993, Brussels (Belgium). Founded as an ad hoc *Port Working Group (inactive)* having previously existed for a number of years, meeting twice a year. Took over activities of *Europese Vereniging voor Haveninformatica (EVHA, inactive)* when the latter ceased to exist. Former names and other names: *European Community Sea Ports Organisation* – former; *Organisation européenne des ports maritimes communautaires* – former; *Organisatie van de Zeehavens van de Europese Gemeenschap (OZEG)* – former. Registration: No/ID: 0449.925.986, Start date: 26 Jan 1993, Belgium; EU Transparency Register, No/ID: 01554483175-08, Start date: 4 Feb 2010. **Aims** Influence public policy in the European Union so as to achieve a safe, efficient and environmentally sustainable European port sector, operating as a key element of a transport industry where free and undistorted market conditions prevail, as far as practicable. **Structure** General Assembly (twice a year); Executive Committee; Secretariat. Technical Committees (9). **Languages** English. **Staff** 7.00 FTE, paid. **Finance** Members' dues. **Activities** Politics/policy/regulatory; knowledge management/information dissemination; standards/guidelines; awards/prizes/competitions; events/meetings. **Events** *Conference* Valencia (Spain) 2022, *Conference* Oslo (Norway) 2021, *Conference* Oslo (Norway) 2020, *Conference* Rotterdam (Netherlands) 2018, *Conference* Barcelona (Spain) 2017. **Publications** *ESPO News*. Annual Report.
Members Representatives, on a national scale, of port authorities, administrations or associations. Members in 21 countries:
Bulgaria, Croatia, Cyprus, Denmark, Estonia, Finland, France, Germany, Greece, Ireland, Italy, Latvia, Lithuania, Malta, Netherlands, Norway, Poland, Portugal, Slovenia, Sweden, UK.
Observers in 2 countries:
Iceland, Israel.
Consultative Status Consultative status granted from: *UNCTAD (#20285)* (Special Category). **NGO Relations** Participant in: *WATERBORNE (#20823)*. Member of: *European PRO Committee (EUROPRO, #08280)*. [2020/XE1845/**D**]

♦ **European Search and Matching Network (SaM)** **08454**
Contact address not obtained. E-mail: searchandmatching@gmail.com.
URL: http://www.searchandmatching.org/
History Former names and other names: *Search and Matching research group* – alias. **Aims** Support and encourage the pursuit of high quality theoretical and applied research in search and matching models. **Structure** Executive and Scientific Committee. **Activities** Events/meetings; networking/liaising; training/education. **Events** *Annual Conference* Copenhagen (Denmark) 2021, *Annual Conference* Copenhagen (Denmark) 2020, *Annual Conference* Oslo (Norway) 2019, *Annual Conference* UK 2018, *Annual Conference* Barcelona (Spain) 2017. [2020/AA0690/v/**F**]

♦ **European Sea Scouting** **08455**
Scouts marins en Europe
Eurosea coordinator address not obtained. E-mail: odysseus@seascouts.eu.
URL: http://seascouts.eu/
Activities Events/meetings. **Events** *Seminar* Athens (Greece) 2022, *Seminar* Athens (Greece) 2021, *Seminar* Athens (Greece) 2020, *Seminar* Barcelona (Spain) 2018, *Seminar* Puck (Poland) 2016. **Publications** *Euronaut* (irregular) – newsletter.
Members in 41 countries:
Albania, Austria, Belgium, Bosnia-Herzegovina, Bulgaria, Croatia, Cyprus, Czechia, Denmark, Estonia, Finland, France, Germany, Greece, Hungary, Iceland, Ireland, Israel, Italy, Latvia, Liechtenstein, Lithuania, Luxembourg, Malta, Monaco, Montenegro, Netherlands, North Macedonia, Norway, Poland, Portugal, Romania, San Marino, Serbia, Slovakia, Slovenia, Spain, Sweden, Switzerland, Türkiye, UK. [2022.06.17/XM3090/**F**]

♦ European Secondary Heads Association / see European School Heads Association (#08431)

♦ European Second Language Association (EUROSLA) 08456

Contact Dept of Education, University of York, York, YO10 5DD, UK.
URL: http://eurosla.org/

History 1989, Colchester (UK). **Aims** Promote and disseminate second language acquisition research; bring European researchers together. **Structure** Committee. **Staff** None. **Finance** Members' dues (annual): Full euro 40; Student euro 25. Budget (annual): about euro 7,000. **Activities** Events/meetings. **Events** *Annual Conference* Barcelona (Spain) 2021, *Annual Conference* Barcelona (Spain) 2020, *Annual Conference* Lund (Sweden) 2019, *Annual Conference* Münster (Germany) 2018, *Annual Conference* Reading (UK) 2017. **Publications** *The Clarion* (2 a year) – online. *EuroSla Yearbook* – series. Papers taken from Annual Conference.
Members Individuals in 34 countries:
Australia, Austria, Belgium, Canada, Croatia, Czechia, Denmark, Finland, France, Germany, Greece, Hungary, Iceland, India, Iran Islamic Rep, Ireland, Israel, Italy, Japan, Latvia, Malta, Mexico, Netherlands, New Zealand, Norway, Poland, Romania, Singapore, South Africa, Spain, Sweden, Switzerland, Türkiye, USA. [2022/XD9057/v/**D**]

- ♦ European Secretariat of Cultural NGOs in Germany (internationally oriented national body)
- ♦ European Secretariat of the Liberal, Independent and Social Professions / see European Council of Liberal Professions (#06828)
- ♦ European Secretariat for the Liberal Professions / see European Council of Liberal Professions (#06828)
- ♦ European Secretariat of Manufacturers of Light Metal Packages (inactive)
- ♦ European Secretariat for Scientific Publications (internationally oriented national body)
- ♦ European Secretariat of Social Independent Professions / see Confédération internationale des travailleurs intellectuels (#04564)
- ♦ European Secretariat of the Steel Drums Industry / see European Association of Steel Drum Manufacturers (#06222)
- ♦ European Secretariat of the United Agricultural Trade Associations / see Joint Secretariat of Agricultural Trade Associations (#16148)
- ♦ European Secretary for Toll Motorway Concessionaires / see Association Européenne des Concessionnaires d'Autoroutes et d'Ouvrages à Péage (#02559)
- ♦ European Secure Parking Organisation (unconfirmed)

♦ European Securities and Markets Authority (ESMA) 08457

Exec Dir CS 60747, 103 rue de Grenelle, 75345 Paris CEDEX 07, France. T. +33158364321. Fax +33158364330. E-mail: info@esma.europa.eu.
Street address 201-203 rue de Bercy, 75012 Paris, France.
URL: http://www.esma.europa.eu/

History 8 Dec 1997, Paris (France). New organizational charter adopted 11 Sep 2001 by Decision of *European Commission (EC, #06633)*, following the Resolution of the Stockholm (Sweden) European Council of Heads of State and Government, Mar 2001. Developed into a decentralized agency of *European Union (EU, #08967)*, 1 Jan 2011, by amending Decision No 716/2009/EC of *Council of the European Union (#04895)* and *European Parliament (EP, #08146)* and repealing European Commission Decision 2009/77/EC. Part of *European System of Financial Supervision (ESFS)*. Former names and other names: *Forum of European Securities Commissions (FESCO)* – former (8 Dec 1997 to 11 Sep 2001); *Committee of European Securities Regulators (CESR)* – former (11 Sep 2001). **Aims** Enhance investor protection; promote stable and orderly financial markets. **Structure** Board of Supervisors, composed of 31 national authorities, including non-voting members from Iceland, Liechtenstein and Norway, and representatives from: *European Commission (EC, #06633)*; *European Banking Authority (EBA, #06311)*; *European Insurance and Occupational Pensions Authority (EIOPA, #07578)*; *European Systemic Risk Board (ESRB, #08872)*; Management Board; Joint Board of Appeal, with EIOPA and EBA; Standing Committees; Securities Markets Stakeholders Group (SMSG). **Languages** English. **Staff** 230.00 FTE, paid. **Finance** Sources: contributions of member/participating states; fees for services. Supported by: *European Union (EU, #08967)*. **Activities** Events/meetings; knowledge management/information dissemination; monitoring/evaluation. **Events** *Joint ESAs High-Level Conference on Financial Education and Literacy* Brussels (Belgium) 2022, *Asia-Pacific Forum on Financial Regulation* Tokyo (Japan) 2019, *Conference* Paris (France) 2017. **Publications** News items; press releases; speeches; consultation papers; reports; risk dashboards; guidelines; Q and As. **Information Services** *Registers and Data*.
Members National Authorities of 31 countries (indicates non-voting members):
Austria, Belgium, Bulgaria, Croatia, Cyprus, Czechia, Denmark, Estonia, Finland, France, Germany, Greece, Hungary, Iceland (*), Ireland, Italy, Latvia, Liechtenstein (*), Lithuania, Luxembourg, Malta, Netherlands, Norway (*), Poland, Portugal, Romania, Slovakia, Slovenia, Spain, Sweden, UK.
International Observers (4):
European Banking Authority (EBA, #06311); *European Commission (EC, #06633)*; *European Insurance and Occupational Pensions Authority (EIOPA, #07578)*; *European Systemic Risk Board (ESRB, #08872)*.
IGO Relations Audited by: *European Court of Auditors (#06854)*. **NGO Relations** Member of (2): *EU Agencies Network (EUAN, #05564)*; *International Organization of Securities Commissions (IOSCO, #14470)*. [2020/XJ2854/y/**E***]

- ♦ European Security Advocacy Group (internationally oriented national body)
- ♦ European Security and Defence College (#04107)
- ♦ European Security Forum / see Information Security Forum (#11198)
- ♦ European Security Systems Association / see ESSA – The International Security Association (#05547)

♦ European Security Transport Association (ESTA) 08458

Association européenne du transport et convoyage de valeurs – Europäische Vereinigung für Geldtransporte und- Begleitung

Secretariat Rue de la Loi 223, 1040 Brussels, Belgium. T. +3222347820. E-mail: contact@esta-cash.eu.
Registered Office address not obtained.
URL: http://www.esta-cash.eu/

History 1975, Brussels (Belgium). Also referred to as *European Cash Management Companies Association*. Registered in accordance with Belgian law, 31 Mar 1976 and 1 Sep 2004. **Aims** Represent the interests of members, who provide transportation and cash logistic services in Europe; define and promote joint positions of members with regard to European policy concerning their sector of activity; increase the quality level of the entire industry. **Structure** General Assembly (annual). Board of Directors. Officers: President; 2 Vice-Presidents; Secretary-General. **Languages** English, French. **Finance** Members' dues. **Events** *Conference* Dublin (Ireland) 2022, *Conference* Dublin (Ireland) 2021, *Conference* Dublin (Ireland) 2020, *Conference* Vienna (Austria) 2019, *Conference* Budapest (Hungary) 2018. **Publications** *ESTA Bulletin* (4 a year) in English, French, Italian. Reports.
Members Effective European cash carriers; Associate non-European cash carriers; Adherent suppliers of security equipment and services. Effective members in 34 countries:
Andorra, Austria, Belgium, Bulgaria, Croatia, Cyprus, Czechia, Denmark, Estonia, Finland, France, Germany, Greece, Guadeloupe, Hungary, Ireland, Italy, Latvia, Lithuania, Luxembourg, Malta, Netherlands, Norway, Poland, Portugal, Réunion, Romania, Serbia, Slovakia, Slovenia, Spain, Sweden, Switzerland, UK.
Associate members in 4 countries:
Russia, Singapore, South Africa, Türkiye.
Adherent members in 13 countries:
Belgium, Canada, Croatia, Czechia, Denmark, France, Germany, Italy, Netherlands, Sweden, Switzerland, UK, USA.
NGO Relations Member of: *Confederation of European Security Services (CoESS, #04532)*; *Federation of European and International Associations Established in Belgium (FAIB, #09508)*. [2021/XD5426/**D**]

♦ European Sediment Network (SedNet) 08459

Secretariat DSBP BV, Hofplein 20, 3032 AC Rotterdam, Netherlands. E-mail: secretariat@sednet.org.
URL: http://www.sednet.org/

History 2002, as a Thematic Network under the 5th RTD Framework Programme, funded by *European Commission (EC, #06633)* DG Research. **Aims** Incorporate sediment issues and knowledge into European strategies to support the achievement of a good environmental status and to develop new tools for sediment management. **Structure** Steering Group, headed by Chairman. Secretariat. **Languages** English. **Staff** Voluntary. **Finance** Contributions of steering group members. Budget (annual): euro 80,000. **Events** *International SedNet Conference* 2021, *International SedNet Conference* Dubrovnik (Croatia) 2019, *International Conference* Krakow (Poland) 2015, *International Conference* Lisbon (Portugal) 2013, *International conference / Conference* Venice (Italy) 2011. **Publications** Round Table Document; reports; books; booklet. **IGO Relations** Partner of: *UNESCO (#20322)*. Also cooperates with: *International Commission for the Protection of the Rhine (ICPR, #12721)*; *Internationale Kommission zum Schutz der Elbe (IKSE, #13249)*; *Internationale Kommission zum Schutz der Oder gegen Verunreinigung (IKSOgV, #13250)*. **NGO Relations** Cooperates with: *Central Dredging Association (CEDA, #03688)*; *European Network of Freshwater Research Organisations (EurAqua, #07911)*; *European Sea Ports Organisation (ESPO, #08453)*; *International Sediment Initiative (ISI, #14827)*; *Future Earth Coasts (#10049)*; *PIANC (#18371)*; *Society of Environmental Toxicology and Chemistry (SETAC, #19551)*. [2022/XJ2255/**E**]

- ♦ European Seed Association / see Euroseeds (#09179)

♦ European Seed Certification Agencies Association (ESCAA) 08460

Contact c/o GNIS, 44 rue du Louvre, 75001 Paris, France. E-mail: escaa@gnis.fr.
URL: http://www.escaa.org/

Aims Allow the contact between European seed certification agencies; exchange experiences of national seed certification systems; harmonize implementation of EU legislation. **Structure** General Meeting (annual). Board. **Events** *Annual Meeting* Austria 2016, *Annual Meeting* Riga (Latvia) 2015, *Annual Meeting* Belgium 2014, *Annual Meeting* Bruges (Belgium) 2014, *Annual Meeting* Longyearbyen (Norway) 2013.
Members Agencies in 32 countries:
Austria, Belgium, Bulgaria, Croatia, Cyprus, Czechia, Denmark, Estonia, Finland, France, Germany, Greece, Hungary, Iceland, Ireland, Italy, Latvia, Lithuania, Luxembourg, Malta, Netherlands, Norway, Poland, Portugal, Romania, Serbia, Slovakia, Slovenia, Spain, Sweden, Switzerland, UK. [2014/XJ8357/**D**]

- ♦ European Seed Testing Association / see International Seed Testing Association (#14829)

♦ European Seismological Commission (ESC) 08461

Commission Séismologique Européenne (CSE)

SG c/o ECGS, Rue Josy Welter 19, L-7256 Walferdange, Luxembourg. T. +35233148735.
URL: http://www.esc-web.org/

History Founded 1951, Brussels (Belgium). Restructured: at General Assembly, 28 Sep 1976, Krakow (Poland); Sep 2006, Geneva (Switzerland). Bylaws amended and adopted Sep 2006, Geneva. Part of *International Association of Seismology and Physics of the Earth's Interior (IASPEI, #12157)*, which in its turn is a constituent association of *International Union of Geodesy and Geophysics (IUGG, #15776)*. **Aims** Promote seismological studies and projects in Europe, countries bordering the Mediterranean and immediate neighbours – from the Mid-Atlantic Ridge to the Urals and the Arctic Ocean to northern Africa. **Structure** General Assembly (every 2 years); Council; Executive Committee; Resolution Committee; Nominating Committee; Working Groups. **Languages** English. **Staff** Voluntary. **Finance** *International Association of Seismology and Physics of the Earth's Interior (IASPEI, #12157)* contributes every 2 years for training courses. No annual budget. **Activities** Research/documentation. Active in: Europe; Mediterranean. **Events** *European Conference on Earthquake Engineering and Seismology* Bucharest (Romania) 2022, *General Assembly* Bucharest (Romania) 2022, *General Assembly* Corfu (Greece) 2021, *General Assembly* Corfu (Greece) 2020, *Biennial General Assembly* Valletta (Malta) 2018. **Publications** Activity reports; proceedings; special publications.
Members Titular (one per country which adheres to IUGG and is situated within the ESC region) in 34 countries:
Austria, Azerbaijan, Belgium, Bulgaria, Croatia, Czechia, Denmark, Egypt, Estonia, Finland, France, Germany, Greece, Hungary, Iceland, Ireland, Israel, Italy, Jordan, Luxembourg, Netherlands, North Macedonia, Norway, Poland, Portugal, Romania, Russia, Slovakia, Slovenia, Spain, Sweden, Switzerland, Türkiye, UK.
Observers in 10 countries:
Albania, Algeria, Armenia, Georgia, Lebanon, Libya, Malta, Monaco, Morocco, Tunisia. [2022/XD8301/**E**]

- ♦ European Self Adhesive Tapes Manufacturers Association / see European Adhesive Tape Association (#05826)

♦ European Semiconductor Industry Association (ESIA) 08462

Dir Gen c/o EECA, Rue de la Duchesse 11/13, 1150 Brussels, Belgium. T. +3222903660. Fax +3222903665. E-mail: secretariat@eusemiconductors.eu.
URL: https://www.eusemiconductors.eu/

History Founded as an industry association within *European Electronic Component Manufacturers Association (EECA, #06974)*. **Aims** Represent, promote and defend the interests of the European-based semiconductor industry; ensure competitiveness of the industry in the global market. **Structure** Board; Committees (5). **Languages** English. **Staff** 4.50 FTE, paid. **Finance** Annual budget: 700,000 EUR. **NGO Relations** Member of (2): *Industry4Europe (#11181)*; *World Semiconductor Council (WSC, #21776)*. [2021.06.09/XK2145/t/**E**]

- ♦ European Seminar of Applied Thermodynamics (meeting series)

♦ European Seminar in Ethnomusicology (ESEM) 08463

Séminaire européen d'ethnomusicologie (SEEM)

SG Music Dept, Durham Univ, Palace Green, Durham, DH1 3RL, UK.
Pres Inst für Musikwissenschaft, Hallerstr 5, 3013 Bern, Switzerland.
URL: http://www.esem-music.eu/

History Founded 1981, Belfast (UK). No fixed organizational postal address. **Aims** Cultivate every aspect of the professional discipline of ethnomusicology. **Structure** Coordinating Committee (CORD); Secretariat. **Languages** English, French, German. **Staff** None. **Finance** Members' dues. **Activities** Events/meetings. **Events** *Annual Seminar* Bern (Switzerland) 2013, *Annual Seminar* Ljubljana (Slovenia) 2012, *Annual seminar* Aberdeen (UK) 2011, *Annual seminar* Budapest (Hungary) 2010, *Annual seminar* Milton Keynes (UK) 2009. **Publications** *ESEMpoint* (annual).
Members in 40 countries and territories:
Albania, Armenia, Australia, Austria, Belarus, Bulgaria, Canada, Denmark, Estonia, Finland, France, Georgia, Germany, Greece, Hungary, India, Iran Islamic Rep, Ireland, Israel, Italy, Japan, Korea Rep, Latvia, Lithuania, Morocco, Netherlands, Norway, Poland, Portugal, Romania, Russia, Serbia, Slovakia, Spain, Sweden, Switzerland, Taiwan, Türkiye, UK, USA.
NGO Relations Member of: *International Music Council (IMC, #14199)*. [2016.10.26/XF6295/**F**]

- ♦ European Senior Citizens' Union / see European Seniors' Union (#08466)

♦ European Senior Golf Association (ESGA) 08464

Association européenne de seniors golfeurs

Gen Sec pa Gold club Grand-Ducal, Rue de Trêves 1, L-2633 Senningerberg, Luxembourg. E-mail: gs@esgagolf.com.
URL: https://www.esgagolf.com/

History 1995. Former names and other names: *Union of European Seniors Golf Associations (ESGA)* – former; *Union des associations européennes de seniors golfeurs* – former; *Union of European Senior Amateur Golf Associations* – former; *Union des Associations Européennes de Seniors Golfeurs Amateurs* – former. **Aims** Promote golf competitions and friendship among senior golfers in Europe. **Structure** General Assembly (annual); Board. **Languages** English. **Finance** Sources: members' dues. **Activities** Sporting activities. **Events** *International meeting* Nyborg (Denmark) 1992.
Members Full in 24 countries:
Austria, Belgium, Bulgaria, Croatia, Czechia, Denmark, Finland, France, Germany, Greece, Hungary, Iceland, Italy, Luxembourg, Netherlands, Norway, Poland, Portugal, Slovakia, Slovenia, Spain, Sweden, Switzerland, UK. [2021.08.31/XD2321/**D**]

♦ European Senior Organization (ESO) 08465

Europäische Senioren Organisation

SG Guimardstraat 10, 1000 Brussels, Belgium. T. +3225150206. E-mail: eso@socialistseniors.eu.
Street address De Brouckèretoren, Anspachlaan 1, 1000 Brussels, Belgium.
URL: http://socialistseniors.eu/

History 19 Oct 2001, Vienna (Austria). Sub-title: *Federation of Retired People of the PES*. Registration: Banque-Carrefour des Entreprises, No/ID: 0834.308.084, Start date: 7 Mar 2011, Belgium. **Aims** Promote and safeguard the social, cultural and economic interests of senior citizens in Europe. **Structure** General Assembly; Board of Directors. **Languages** English. **Finance** Members' dues. **Activities** Awareness raising; events/meetings; knowledge management/information dissemination; networking/liaising; politics/policy/regulatory. **Events** *Congress and General Assembly* Brussels (Belgium) 2017, *Congress and General Assembly* Brussels (Belgium) 2016, *Congress and General Assembly* Brussels (Belgium) 2016, *Congress and General Assembly* Brussels (Belgium) 2015, *Congress and General Assembly* Budapest (Hungary) 2015. **Members** Organizations (19) in 16 countries. Membership countries not specified. **NGO Relations** Recognized by: *Party of European Socialists (PES, #18249)*. Member of: *AGE Platform Europe (#00557)*. [2023/XD8751/**D**]

♦ European Senior Service Network (inactive)
♦ European Seniors Union / see European Seniors' Union (#08466)

♦ European Seniors' Union (ESU) 08466

Union européenne des seniors – Europäische Senioren Union

Pres Handelsstraat 10, 1000 Brussels, Belgium. T. +3223092866 – +322(32476705853. E-mail: esu@epp.eu.
SG address not obtained. T. +32475780960. E-mail: esu@epp.eu.
URL: http://esu-epp.eu/

History Founded 1995, within the framework of *European Union of Christian Democrats (EUCD, inactive)*, at first consultative congress, 7 Nov 1995, Madrid (Spain). Original English title: *European Senior Citizens' Union (ESCU)*. Also referred to as *European Union of Elderly Christian Democrats* and *European Seniors Union*. Current statutes adopted, 18 Apr 2014, Brussels (Belgium). Registered in accordance with Belgian law. **Aims** Contribute to dissemination of the idea of a united Europe in the *Christian democratic* parties in particular and in the public in general; defend interests of seniors all over Europe; advance rights of European senior citizens and their engagement in society. **Structure** Congress (every 3 years); Executive Committee; Board; General Secretariat. **Languages** English, French, German. **Staff** Voluntary. **Finance** Members' dues. Other sources: sponsoring; income from services; donations and subsidies. **Activities** Events/meetings. **Events** *Congress* Brussels (Belgium) 2013, *Congress* Bad Honnef (Germany) 2010, *Congress* Pulheim (Germany) 2007, *Congress* Bonn (Germany) / Königswinter (Germany) / Bad Godesberg (Germany) 2004, *Congress* Brussels (Belgium) 2001. **Publications** Yearbook.

Members National organizations (35) in 25 countries:
Austria, Belgium, Bulgaria, Croatia, Cyprus, Czechia, Estonia, Finland, Germany, Greece, Hungary, Italy, Latvia, Lithuania, Luxembourg, Malta, Netherlands, Norway, Poland, Romania, Slovakia, Slovenia, Spain, Sweden, UK.
Observers (3), including the following international organization listed in this Yearbook:
NGO Relations Member of: *AGE Platform Europe (#00557)*; *European People's Party (EPP, #08185)*; *Robert Schuman Institute for Developing Democracy in Central and Eastern Europe (RSI, #18958)*.
[2017.10.11/XE2492/y/**E**]

♦ European Senior Volunteer Network / see European Network of Older-Volunteer Organizations

♦ European Sensory Network (ESN) 08467

Chair c/o DFST, Muthgasse 18, 1190 Vienna, Austria.
Sec c/o ACCE, 2575-B Dunwin Dr, Mississauga ON L5L 3N9, Canada.
URL: http://www.esn-network.com/

History Jan 1989, Oslo (Norway), as a basis for collaboration and cooperation between major food and consumer research centres in European countries and worldwide. **Aims** Further the development and application of sensory science in Europe; improve sensory and *consumer* testing methodology for the benefit of the European food and non-food industry; promote the application of sensory analysis in the industry; work towards standard methodologies; exchange ideas and collaborate in joint research programmes in sensory analysis and consumer acceptance. **Structure** Chair; Treasurer/Vice-Chair; Secretary; Strategy/Pr Chair; Research Chair; Industry Partner Representative; ESN Advisor. **Languages** English. **Staff** Voluntary. **Finance** Members' dues. **Activities** Provides consultancy services; cooperates on research programmes and publishes results; develops and tests new methods; creates guidelines; offers grant programmes for young scientists. Organizes: internal meetings; international seminars and conferences; tailored courses for users. **Events** *Seminar* Vienna (Austria) 2016, *Seminar* Budapest (Hungary) 2014, *Conference* Pretoria (South Africa) 2008, *Systematic approach to planning and performing sensory tests* Porto (Portugal) 2007, *Sensory evaluation – more than just food* Madrid (Spain) 2005.

Members Associations (24) in 20 countries:
Australia, Austria, Belgium, Canada, Denmark (2), Finland, France (2), Germany (2), Hungary, Iceland, Israel, Italy (2), Netherlands, Norway, Poland, Portugal, South Africa, Spain, Sweden, UK.
International member organization listed in this Yearbook:
Commonwealth Scientific and Industrial Research Organization (CSIRO). [2014/XF1196/y/**F**]

♦ European Sensory Science Society (E3S) 08468

Sec Via della Cernaia 21, 50129 Florence FI, Italy. E-mail: secretary@e3sensory.eu.
URL: http://www.e3sensory.eu/

History 12 May 2011. **Aims** Promote cooperation, shared goals, integration of activities, knowledge and information exchange among national sensory science organizations across Europe. **Structure** General Assembly; Board. **Activities** Events/meetings; training/education. **Events** *EUROSENSE : European Conference on Sensory and Consumer Research* Turku (Finland) 2022, *EUROSENSE : European Conference on Sensory and Consumer Research* Rotterdam (Netherlands) 2020, *EUROSENSE : European Conference on Sensory and Consumer Research* Verona (Italy) 2018, *EUROSENSE : European Conference on Sensory and Consumer Research* Dijon (France) 2016, *General Assembly* Oslo (Norway) 2015. **Publications** *Food Quality and Preference* – journal.

Members Full in 12 countries:
Austria, Denmark, Finland, France, Germany, Italy, Netherlands, Norway, Spain, Sweden, Switzerland, UK.
[2022/XJ9587/**D**]

♦ European Service-Learning Association (inactive)

♦ European Services Forum (ESF) 08469

Managing Dir Av de Cortenbergh 168, 1000 Brussels, Belgium. T. +3222307514. Fax +3222306168. E-mail: esf@esf.be.
URL: http://www.esf.be/

History Founded 26 Jan 1999, as *European Services Network (ESN)*, with the political support of Sir Leon Brittan, Vice-President of *European Commission (EC, #06633)* and EU Trade Commissioner, within the framework of negotiations relating to *General Agreement on Trade in Services (GATS, 1994)*. Replaces *European Tradeable Services' Network (inactive)*. Current name adopted in 2001. Original Memorandum of Understanding adopted 21 Oct 1998, updated Oct 2008. EU Transparency Register: 91447653655-65. **Aims** Actively promote liberalization of international trade and investment in services. **Structure** Policy Committee; Executive Bureau; Secretariat. **Languages** English. **Staff** 1.00 FTE, paid. **Finance** Members' dues. Annual budget: about euro 250,000. **Activities** Monitoring/evaluation; advocacy/lobbying/activism; events/meetings. **Events** *Seminar on the Role of Services in Chinese Reforms* Brussels (Belgium) 2014, *Conference* 2000. **Publications** Series of papers covering: trade negotiations; emergency safeguards; public procurement; regulation; scheduling commitments; e-commerce; trade and investment; subsidies; movement of business personnel.

Members European service companies and national associations, in 12 countries:
Austria, Belgium, Denmark, Finland, France, Germany, Ireland, Italy, Netherlands, Spain, Sweden, UK.
European service federations including 18 organizations listed in this Yearbook:
Accountancy Europe (#00061); *amfori (#00797)*; *Architects Council of Europe (ACE, #01086)*; *Association of European Public Postal Operators (PostEurop, #02534)*; *BIPAR – European Federation of Insurance Intermediaries (#03263)*; *BUSINESSEUROPE (#03381)*; *Council of Bars and Law Societies of Europe (CCBE, #04871)*; *EuroCommerce (EC, #05665)*; *European Banking Federation (EBF, #06312)*; *European Broadcasting Union (EBU, #06404)*; *European Community Shipowners' Associations (ECSA, #06683)*; *European Construction Industry Federation (#06766)*; *European Express Association (EEA, #07017)*; *European Federation of Engineering Consultancy Associations (EFCA, #07109)*; *European Savings and Retail Banking Group (ESBG, #08426)*; *European Telecommunications Network Operators' Association (ETNO, #08895)*; *Global Satellite Operators' Association (GSOA, #10586)*; *Insurance Europe (#11362)*. [2019/XF4766/y/**F**]

♦ European Services Network / see European Services Forum (#08469)
♦ European Services Strategy Unit (internationally oriented national body)

♦ European Set Theory Society (ESTS) 08470

Treas Dept of Mathematics and Statistics, PO Box 68, Univ of Helsinki, FI-00014 Helsinki, Finland.
Sec address not obtained.
URL: http://ests.wordpress.com/

Aims Strengthen set-theoretical research and scholarship in Europe. **Structure** Trustees. **Activities** Awards/prizes/competitions; events/meetings. **Events** *European Set Theory Conference* Turin (Italy) 2022, *Conference* Vienna (Austria) 2019, *Conference* Edinburgh (UK) 2011. **NGO Relations** Member of (1): *European Mathematical Society (EMS, #07755)*. [2022/XJ2340/**D**]

♦ European Severe Storms Laboratory (ESSL) 08471

Dir c/o DLR, Münchner Str 20, Geb 126, 82234 Wessling, Germany. T. +496221516281. Fax +498151965999911. E-mail: inflow@essl.org.
URL: http://www.essl.org/

History 2002, as an informal network. Formally founded, 28 Sep 2006. Registered in accordance with German law. Registration: Start date: 2006, Germany. **Aims** Advance meteorology and related sciences in the field of research on severe convective storms and extreme weather events on a European level. **Structure** Executive Board, comprising Director, Deputy Director, Technical Director and Treasurer. Advisory Council. Subsidiary body: *European Severe Storms Laboratory – Science and Training*. **Finance** Members' dues. **Activities** Grants awards. **Events** *European Conference on Severe Storms* Bucharest (Romania) 2023, *European Conference on Severe Storms* Krakow (Poland) 2019, *European Conference on Severe Storms* Pula (Croatia) 2017, *European Conference on Severe Storms* Wiener Neustadt (Austria) 2015, *European Conference on Severe Storms* Helsinki (Finland) 2013. **Publications** Reports; proceedings. **Information Services** *European Severe Weather Database*. **Members** Individual; Institutional. **IGO Relations** Partner of: *Group on Earth Observations (GEO, #10735)*. [2018/XM1126/**F**]

♦ European Sexual Health Alliance (inactive)

♦ European Sex Workers' Rights Alliance (ESWA) 08472

Coordinator Eerste Helmersstraat 17 D, 1054 CX Amsterdam, Netherlands. T. +31447460060506. E-mail: info@sexworkeurope.org.
URL: https://www.eswalliance.org/

History 2004, Netherlands. Former names and other names: *International Committee on the Rights of Sex Workers (ICRSW)* – alias; *International Committee on the Rights of Sex Workers in Europe (ICRSE)* – former (2002 to Sep 2021). Registration: Chamber of Commerce, No/ID: 34216253, Netherlands. **Aims** Ensure that the voices of sex workers in the region are heard, listened to and respected; raise awareness about the social exclusion of cis and trans female, male, and non-binary sex workers in Europe and Central Asia; promote the human, health and labour rights of all sex workers at community, national and regional level. **Structure** Steering Committee; Board. Advisory Groups. **Consultative Status** Consultative status granted from: *Council of Europe (CE, #04881)* (Participatory Status). **NGO Relations** Member of (2): *Conference of INGOs of the Council of Europe (#04607)*; *ILGA World (International Lesbian, Gay, Bisexual, Trans and Intersex Association, #11120)*. [2022/XM4562/**D**]

♦ Europeans for Fair Roaming 08473

Address not obtained.
URL: http://fairroaming.org/

History 1 May 2010, Salzburg (Austria), at the Convention of *European Federalist Party (#07036)*. **Aims** Make *mobile phone* roaming across Europe as cheap as domestic phone calls already are as soon as possible; further the creation of a single market for *telecommunication* services. **Structure** Management Team of 4 and chaired by Coordinator. **Languages** English, German. **Staff** 4.00 FTE, paid. **Activities** Advice and lobbying at European institutions. **IGO Relations** *European Commission (EC, #06633)*; *Council of Europe (CE, #04881)*; *European Parliament (EP, #08146)*. **NGO Relations** Supported by: *Austrian Institute for European Law and Policy*; *European Federalist Party (#07036)*; *Federation of Young European Greens (FYEG, #09715)*; *Young European Federalists (#21984)*; national organizations. [2015/XJ5113/**F**]

♦ European Shadow Financial Regulatory Committee (ESFRC) 08474

Chairman Tilburg Univ, PO Box 90153, 5000 LE Tilburg, Netherlands.

NGO Relations *Centre for European Policy Studies (CEPS, #03741)*; *Latin American Committee on Macroeconomic and Financial Issues (#16300)*. [2010/XE4589/**E**]

♦ European Shakespeare Research Association (ESRA) 08475

Sec address not obtained.
URL: https://www.um.es/shakespeare/esra/

History 1998. **Aims** Encourage and support research into Shakespeare as a cultural presence in Europe and the relationship between this presence and the construction of European culture and identity. **Structure** Board. **Activities** Events/meetings; knowledge management/information dissemination; research/documentation. **Events** *Conference* Budapest (Hungary) 2023, *Conference* Athens (Greece) 2021, *Conference* Rome (Italy) 2019, *Conference* Gdansk (Poland) 2017, *Conference* Worcester (UK) 2015. [2021/AA2066/**E**]

♦ European shareholders associations / see BETTER FINANCE (#03219)
♦ European Sheep Committee (inactive)

♦ European Shiatsu Federation (ESF) 08476

Pres AlternativAkademin, Rundelsgränd 2B, SE-753 12 Uppsala, Sweden. E-mail: info@europeanshiatsufederation.eu.
URL: http://www.europeanshiatsufederation.eu/

History 1990. Registration: No/ID: 817605-3521, Sweden. **Aims** Realize the official recognition of Shiatsu practice as an independent profession throughout Europe. **Structure** Annual General Meeting (AGM); Board. **Languages** English, German, Italian, Spanish. **Staff** Voluntary. **Finance** Members' dues. **Events** *Congress* Amsterdam (Netherlands) 2020, *Congress* Vienna (Austria) 2017, *Congress* Madrid (Spain) 2014.

Members National organizations in 9 countries:
Austria, Belgium, Czechia, Greece, Hungary, Ireland, Italy, Spain, Sweden.
IGO Relations *European Commission (EC, #06633)*; *European Parliament (EP, #08146)*; *European Union (EU, #08967)* – Health Policy Platform (HPP). **NGO Relations** Member of: *European Federation for Complementary and Alternative Medicine (EFCAM, #07084)*; *European Public Health Alliance (EPHA, #08297)*.
[2021/XM0583/**D**]

♦ European Shippers' Council (ESC) 08477

SG Bvd Auguste Reyers 80, Bluepoint Bldg, 1030 Brussels, Belgium. T. +3227068186. E-mail: info@europeanshippers.eu.
URL: https://europeanshippers.eu/

History 1963. 1996 included activities of the previous *European Inland Transport Council (EITC, inactive)*. *European Rail Freight Customers' Platform (ERFCP, inactive)* merged into the organization, May 2009. Former names and other names: *European National Shippers' Councils* – former (1963); *European Shippers' Councils* – former (1996). Registration: EU Transparency Register, No/ID: 805519124034-79. **Aims** Represent the interests of cargo owners and transport users/shippers in logistics and transportation vis-à-vis European institutions and other stakeholders; promote efficient and competitive freight transport services by sea, road, rail and inland waterways to enhance competitiveness of companies conducting business in Europe. **Structure** General Assembly (meets twice a year); ESC Executive. **Languages** English. **Activities** Politics/policy/regulatory; knowledge management/information dissemination; guidance/assistance/consulting; research and development. **Events** *Forum* Rotterdam (Netherlands) 2011, *European shipper forum / Conference* Oslo (Norway) 2008, *Conference* Athens (Greece) 2002, *Conference* Antwerp (Belgium) 1996.

Members National shippers' councils representing 9 countries:
Austria, Belgium, France, Israel, Netherlands, Portugal, Spain, Sweden, UK.
Sectoral associations (4):
Confederation of European Paper Industries (CEPI, #04529); *Conseil européen de l'industrie chimique (CEFIC, #04687)*; *European Brands Association (#06397)*; *European Steel Association (EUROFER, #08835)*.
Corporate members in countries not covered by national shippers' councils.
NGO Relations Founding member of: *Global Shippers' Forum (GSF, #10596)*. Member of: *European Logistics Platform (ELP, #07711)*; *European Technology Platform ALICE (ALICE, #08888)*; Global Logistics Emissions Council (GLEC); *Global Shippers' Alliance (GSA, #10595)*. [2022/XD4002/y/**D**]

♦ European Shippers' Councils / see European Shippers' Council (#08477)
♦ European Ships and Maritime Equipment Association / see European Shipyards' and Maritime Equipment Association (#08479)
♦ European Shipsuppliers Organization / see European Ship Suppliers Organization (#08478)

♦ European Ship Suppliers Organization (OCEAN) 08478

SG c/o UECBV, Rue de la Loi 81A, 4th Floor, 1040 Brussels, Belgium. E-mail: info@shipsupply.eu.
Admin Sec The Baltic Exchange, St Mary Axe, London, EC3A 8BH, UK. T. +442076266236. Fax +442076266234. E-mail: secretariat@shipsupply.eu.
URL: https://www.shipsupply.eu/

History 29 Jun 1976, Hamburg (Germany). A committee of *Union européenne du commerce du bétail et de la viande (UECBV, #20394)*. Former names and other names: *Organization of Shipsuppliers in EC-Countries* – former; *Organisation de la Communauté Européenne des ravitailleurs de navires (OCEAN)* – former; *Schiffsausrüster-Verband der EG-Länder* – former; *Organization of European Shipsuppliers* – former; *European Shipsuppliers Organization* – former. Registration: EU Transparency Register, No/ID: 52916966911-90, Start date: 8 Oct 2011. **Aims** Represent the interests of all European ship suppliers in European Union matters relating to the shipping industry, including customs, maritime transport, trade and veterinary affairs. **Structure** Board. Working Groups (2): Victualling and Veterinary Affairs; Customs and Taxation. Secretariats – London (UK); Brussels (Belgium).
Members National organizations of ship suppliers in 17 countries:
Belgium, Bulgaria, Cyprus, Denmark, Estonia, Finland, France, Germany, Greece, Italy, Latvia, Malta, Netherlands, Portugal, Spain, Sweden, Türkiye.
NGO Relations *International Ship Suppliers and Services Association (ISSA, #14850).* [2022/XE2829/**D**]

♦ European Shipyards' and Maritime Equipment Association (SEA Europe) 08479

SG Rue de la Loi 67, 4th Floor, 1000 Brussels, Belgium. T. +3222302791. E-mail: info@seaeurope.eu.
URL: http://www.seaeurope.eu/

History Founded Feb 2012, on merger of *Community of European Shipyards Associations (CESA, inactive)* and *European Marine Equipment Council (EMEC, inactive)*. Registered in accordance with Belgian law. Previously known as *European Ships and Maritime Equipment Association*. Registration: ASBL/VZW, Belgium. **Aims** Provide a wide range of services and activities for the benefit of maritime civil and naval industries, including European shipyards and maritime equipment manufacturers. **Structure** General Assembly; Directors' Committee; Working Groups (10); Secretariat. **Languages** English. **Staff** 8.00 FTE, paid. **Finance** Members' dues. **Activities** Knowledge management/information dissemination. **Events** *Europe Workshop on EU Financing and Funding Tools for the European Maritime Technology Sector* Brussels (Belgium) 2019, *Europort Maritime Conference* Rotterdam (Netherlands) 2019, *Triennial International Ship and Offshore Structures Congress* Liège (Belgium) / Amsterdam (Netherlands) 2018, *Seminar on Sharing Cases of Safety/Crisis Management* Seoul (Korea Rep) 2018, *Europe Maritime Conference* Brussels (Belgium) 2017. **Publications** *Market Developments Report*. Brochures.
Members Associations in 16 countries:
Belgium, Bulgaria, Croatia, Denmark, Finland, France, Germany, Greece, Italy, Netherlands, Norway, Poland, Portugal, Romania, Spain, Türkiye.
Consultative Status Consultative status granted from: *UNCTAD (#20285)* (General Category). **NGO Relations** Member of: *Industry4Europe (#11181)*. Participates in: *WATERBORNE (#20823)*. [2019.02.15/XJ5945/**D**]

♦ European Shock Absorbers Manufacturers Association (inactive)

♦ European Shock Society, The (ESS) 08480

Gen Sec Institute of Surgical Research, University of Szeged, Pulz utca 1, Szeged 6724, Hungary.
Pres 4th Dept of Internal Medicine, ATTIKON Univ Hospital, Rimini St 1, 124 62 Athens, Greece.
URL: http://www.europeanshocksociety.org/

History 1983, Malmö (Sweden). **Aims** Advance the study of shock, *trauma* and sepsis, or of an allied discipline experimentally and clinically. **Structure** Executive Committee. **Languages** English. **Finance** Sources: members' dues. **Activities** Events/meetings. **Events** *Congress* Vienna (Austria) 2023, *Biennial Congress* 2021, *Biennial Congress* Chania (Greece) 2019, *Biennial Congress* Paris (France) 2017, *Biennial Congress* Cologne (Germany) 2015. **Publications** *ESS Newsletter*.
Members Societies in 37 countries:
Australia, Austria, Belgium, Brazil, Bulgaria, Canada, China, Croatia, Czechia, Finland, France, Germany, Greece, Hungary, India, Indonesia, Ireland, Israel, Italy, Japan, Korea Rep, Netherlands, Norway, Portugal, Romania, Russia, Saudi Arabia, Serbia, Slovakia, South Africa, Spain, Sweden, Switzerland, Türkiye, UK, Ukraine, USA.
NGO Relations Member of (1): *International Federation of Shock Societies (#13540)*. Cooperates with (8): *European Donation and Transplant Coordination Organisation (EDTCO, #06939)*; *European Society for Microcirculation (ESM, #08651)*; *European Society for Surgical Research (ESSR, #08754)*; *European Society for Trauma and Emergency Surgery (ESTES, #08768)*; *European Society of Intensive Care Medicine (ESICM, #08632)*; *European Society of Paediatric and Neonatal Intensive Care (ESPNIC, #08683)*; *Society for Complexity in Acute Illness (SCAI, #19532)*; *Surgical Infection Society – Europe (SIS-E, #20043)*. [2023/XD0564/**D**]

♦ European Shoe Press Association (no recent information)

♦ European Shooting Confederation (ESC) 08481

SG Voie du Chariot 3, 1003 Lausanne VD, Switzerland. T. +41215605574. E-mail: esc@escsport.eu.
Gen Sec Luzhnetskaya nab 8, Moscow MOSKVA, Russia, 119991. T. +74956379232. Fax +74956379431.
URL: http://www.esc-shooting.org/

History 18 Aug 1969, Pilsen (Czechia). Founded at European Shooting Championships, when statutes were adopted. Acknowledged, Oct 1969, Wiesbaden (Germany FR), as the continental confederation of *International Shooting Sport Federation (ISSF, #14852)*. Statutes most recently updated 17 May 2013, Moscow (Russia). **Aims** Maintain, strengthen and develop the sport of shooting in Europe in accordance with the Constitution and General Regulations of International Shooting Sport Federation; strengthen bonds of friendship and good relations among national member federations without political, religious or racial discrimination; ensure the common interest of members. **Structure** General Assembly (every 2 years); Praesidium; Permanent Committees (3); Sub-Committees (3); Secretariat located in Moscow (Russia). **Languages** English, French, German, Russian, Spanish. **Staff** Voluntary. **Finance** Members' dues. Other sources: entry fees from European Championships; sponsorship. **Activities** Sporting activities; events/meetings. **Events** *Biennial General Assembly* Moscow (Russia) 2013, *Biennial General Assembly* Belgrade (Serbia) 2011, *Biennial General Assembly* Osijek (Croatia) 2009, *Biennial General Assembly* Granada (Spain) 2007, *Biennial General Assembly* Belgrade (Serbia-Montenegro) 2005. **Publications** *ECS Newsletter* (12 a year); *ESC News* (annual). General regulations.
Members Shooting federations (56) in 49 countries:
Albania, Andorra, Armenia, Austria (2), Azerbaijan, Belarus, Belgium (2), Bosnia-Herzegovina, Bulgaria (2), Croatia, Cyprus, Czechia, Denmark, Estonia, Finland, France, Georgia, Germany, Greece, Hungary, Iceland, Ireland (2), Israel, Italy (2), Latvia, Liechtenstein, Lithuania, Luxembourg, Malta, Moldova, Monaco, Montenegro, Netherlands, North Macedonia, Norway, Poland, Portugal (2), Romania, Russia, San Marino (2), Serbia, Slovakia, Slovenia, Spain, Sweden, Switzerland, Türkiye, UK, Ukraine.
NGO Relations Partner of (1): *Association of European Manufacturers of Sporting Firearms (ESFAM, #02523)*. *European Olympic Committees (EOC, #08083)*; *International Shooting Sport Federation (ISSF, #14852)*; *World Forum on Shooting Activities (WFSA, #21523)*. [2022/XD0815/**D**]

♦ European Shooting Sport Council (unconfirmed)
♦ European Shortsea Network (unconfirmed)

♦ European Shotokan Karate-do Association (ESKA) 08482

Contact Teichwiese 18, 56743 Mendig, Germany. E-mail: eska-office-mendig@online.de.
URL: http://www.eska-karate.com/

History Founded 8 Feb 1986, Ghent (Belgium). Takes over activities of *European Amateur Karate Federation (EAKF, inactive)*. **Aims** Develop shotokan karate in Europe. **Structure** Board of Officials. **Languages** English. **Staff** None. **Finance** Members' dues; fees. **Events** *Annual Congress* Zurich (Switzerland) 2014, *Annual Congress and Championship* Póvoa de Varzim (Portugal) 2013, *Annual Congress and Championship* Belgrade (Serbia) 2012, *Annual Congress and Championship* Bielsko-Biala (Poland) 2011, *Annual Congress and Championship* Koblenz (Germany) 2010.
Members National organizations in 20 countries:
Austria, Belarus, Belgium, Cyprus, Czechia, Germany, Hungary, Ireland, Israel, Italy, Lithuania, Monaco, Poland, Portugal, Russia, Spain, Sweden, Switzerland, UK, Ukraine.
NGO Relations *World Shotokan Karate Association (WSKA, #21783).* [2013.10.21/XD9302/**D**]

♦ European Showmen's Ladies Union (see: #08483)

♦ European Showmen's Union (ESU) 08483

Union foraine européenne (UFE) – Europäische Schausteller-Union
Pres Schnieringshof 8, 45329 Essen, Germany.
Registered Office Conf du Commerce, Forains, 31 Rue Alcide de Gasperie, L-1615 Luxembourg, Luxembourg.
URL: http://esu-ufe.eu/

History 1954, Amsterdam (Netherlands). Registration: Start date: 13 Apr 1992, Luxembourg. **Aims** Promote friendly cooperation, international understanding and amicable exchange; act as a voluntary international European trade congregation in negotiations on economics, traffic, culture and trade with European bodies; further technical harmonization of mobile buildings in Europe. **Structure** Congress (every 2 years) of 4 delegates per member country. Board of Directors (meets at least once a year), consisting of Presidents of national member countries and associated European organizations. Executive Board, comprising President and 3 Executive Vice-Presidents, General Secretary and 2 Deputy General Secretaries. Divisions (4): *European Showmen's Ladies Union (see: #08483)*; *International Group of Priests for Circus and Showmen of All Confessions (#13752)*; *European Showmen Youth Union (see: #08483)*. **Languages** English, French, German. **Staff** 3.00 FTE, paid. **Finance** Members' dues. **Activities** Convention (every 2 years); Presidential meetings (twice a year). **Events** *Biennial Congress* Lisbon (Portugal) 2016, *Congress* Stuttgart (Germany) 2008, *Meeting* Berlin (Germany) 1999, *Biennial Congress* Budapest (Hungary) 1999, *Meeting* Athens (Greece) 1998. **Publications** *ESU Newsletter* (4 a year).
Members National organizations (19) representing 25 countries:
Andorra, Austria, Belgium, Czechia, Denmark, Finland, France, Germany, Greece, Holy See, Hungary, Iceland, Ireland, Italy, Liechtenstein, Luxembourg, Monaco, Netherlands, Norway, Portugal, San Marino, Spain, Sweden, Switzerland, UK.
IGO Relations Recognized by: *European Commission (EC, #06633)*. **NGO Relations** Member of: *European Movement International (EMI, #07825)*. [2018/XD2290/**D**]

♦ European Showmen Youth Union (see: #08483)
♦ European Shredder Group (no recent information)
♦ European Sialendoscopy Training Centre (internationally oriented national body)

♦ European Sickle Cell Federation (ESCF) 08484

Address not obtained.
URL: https://escfederation.eu/

History 5 Jun 2020. Proposed Oct 2019, Hamburg (Germany). Registration: Start date: 5 Jun 2020, Ireland. **Aims** Engage in a united, unique and strong voice for Sickle Cell patients, family members, carers, and all national patient organisations of people with Sickle Cell Disease and related conditions in Europe by promoting, enabling, enhancing and fostering of their ability to improve the quality of health, life, and services for all patients. **Structure** Management Committee; Medical Advisory Board.
Members Organizations in 4 countries:
Belgium, France, Ireland, UK.
NGO Relations Member of (1): *EURORDIS – Rare Diseases Europe (#09175)* (Associate). [2021/AA2342/**D**]

♦ European Sign Federation (ESF) 08485

Fédération européenne de l'enseigne et de la signalétique – Europäischer Verband der Lichtwerbung
Office Maurice Herbettelaan 38a, 1070 Brussels, Belgium. E-mail: mail@eusigns.org.
General Manager Kirchstr 12a, 47918 Tönisvorst, Germany. T. +492151796224. E-mail: post@eusignco.com.
URL: http://esf.d-s-g.eu/

History 1966. In English previously referred to as *European Federation of Illuminated Signs* and in French as *Fédération européenne de la publicité lumineuse*. Previously used the German acronym *EVL*. Registration: No/ID: 0566.926.396, Start date: 16 Oct 2014, Belgium; EU Transparency Register, No/ID: 063377615456-10, Start date: 7 Jan 2015. **Aims** Promote and enhance appreciation of signs and the image of signmakers throughout Europe; promote technical, environmental and economic improvements; represent interests of the European sign industry worldwide; protect and develop mutual legal and economic interests of members; encourage creation of national sign associations; create harmonized technical regulations to reduce barriers to international trade; encourage friendly links between members. **Structure** General Assembly (annual); Board of Directors. **Languages** English. **Staff** Voluntary. **Finance** Members' dues. **Activities** Advocacy/lobbying/activism; events/meetings. **Events** *General Assembly* Porto (Portugal) 2019, *General Assembly* Catania (Italy) 2018, *General Assembly* Stockholm (Sweden) 2014, *Meeting* Utrecht (Netherlands) 1994.
Members Full; Associate; Individual. Full in 24 countries:
Austria, Belgium, Bulgaria, Croatia, Denmark, Finland, France, Germany, Greece, Hungary, Italy, Latvia, Lithuania, Netherlands, Portugal, Romania, Serbia, Spain, Sweden, Switzerland, Türkiye, UK, Ukraine, USA. [2020/XD1456/**D**]

♦ European Silica Fume Committee 08486

SG address not obtained.
URL: http://www.microsilicafume.eu/

History Founded by *Euroalliages (#05629)*. **Aims** Represent the interests of the European silica fume producers; promote the use of Silica Fume by making the technical and environmental benefits of using Silica Fume known to users and public authorities.
Members Full in 7 countries:
Bosnia-Herzegovina, Germany, North Macedonia, Norway, Poland, Slovakia, UK. [2021.02.15/AA1306/**E**]

♦ European Silicates Centre (#03746)
♦ European Silicones Centre / see CES – Silicones Europe (#03838)

♦ European Simmental Federation (ESF) 08487

Fédération européenne des éleveurs de la race pie rouge – Europäische Vereinigung der Fleckviehzüchter (EVF)
Sec Senator-Gerauer-Str 23a, 85586 Poing, Germany. T. +498920603120. Fax +4989206031211. E-mail: rinderzucht@t-online.de.
URL: http://www.evf-esf.info/

History 1961, Munich (Germany FR). **Aims** Promote cooperation among associations of Simmental *cattle breeders* in Europe for improvement in breeding, joint promotions and publications. **Structure** Meeting of members (every 2 years); Council (meets annually); Sub-Committees. **Languages** English, French, German. **Staff** 2.00 FTE, voluntary. **Finance** Members' dues. **Events** *Biennial Meeting* Udine (Italy) 2011, *Biennial Meeting* Siófok (Hungary) 2009, *Biennial Meeting* Zagreb (Croatia) 2007, *Biennial Meeting* Vienna (Austria) 2005, *Congress / Biennial Meeting* Belgrade (Serbia-Montenegro) 2003.
Members National associations in 16 countries:
Austria, Croatia, Czechia, Denmark, France, Germany, Hungary, Ireland, Italy, Poland, Serbia, Slovakia, Slovenia, Sweden, Switzerland, UK.
Observers in 7 countries:
Bosnia-Herzegovina, Netherlands, Norway, Romania, Spain, Türkiye, Ukraine. [2020/XD0070/**E**]

♦ European Simulation Council / see European Council for Modelling and Simulation (#06831)

♦ European Single Ply Waterproofing Association (ESWA) 08488

Main Office c/o EuPC, Av de Cortenbergh 71, 1000 Brussels, Belgium. T. +3227396383. Fax +3227324218. E-mail: info@eswa-synthetics.org.
URL: https://www.eswa-synthetics.org/

History 19 Mar 1997. Former names and other names: *European Synthetic Waterproofing Association* – alias; *Association européenne de l'étanchéité au moyen de matières synthétiques* – alias. Registration: Belgium. **Aims** Represent and promote the interests of the industry and be its voice vis-à-vis the European institutions; promote innovative and safer solutions from manufacture to application; provide optimum economic and ecological benefits to the specifiers of its products. **Structure** General Assembly; Executive Committee; Working Groups (4). **Activities** Politics/policy/regulatory; certification/accreditation; research and development; guidance/assistance/consulting.
Members Founding members (9) in 7 countries:
Belgium, France, Germany, Italy, Netherlands, Norway, Switzerland.
Company Members (7) in 5 countries:
Belgium, Germany, Italy, Norway, Switzerland.
Association Members (2) in 2 countries:
France, Germany. [2021/XD5949/**D**]

♦ European Single Service Association / see Pack2Go Europe (#18014)
♦ European Skeletal Society / see European Musculo-Skeletal Oncology Society (#07834)

♦ European e-Skills Association (EeSA) 08489

General Manager Boulevard Charlemagne 1, 1041 Brussels, Belgium. T. +3222317131. Fax +3222317139.
URL: http://www.eskillsassociation.eu/

History Jun 2007. Registered in accordance with Belgian law. EU Transparency Register: 416562915447-63. **Aims** Act as the reference European platform to develop ICT skills and competences for professionals, practitioners, citizens, and users across all sectors and society to build a more inclusive, efficient, competitive and innovative Europe. **Structure** General Assembly; Board of Directors; Executive Committee; Secretariat, headed by General Manager. **Activities** Awareness raising; training/education; research/documentation.
Members Organizations and companies. Included in the above, 2 organizations listed in this Yearbook:
Council of European Professional Informatics Societies (CEPIS, #04893); European CIO Association (EuroCIO, #06550).
NGO Relations Liaison Organization of: *Comité européen de normalisation (CEN, #04162).*
[2019/XJ4578/y/**D**]

♦ European Skin Cancer Foundation (internationally oriented national body)

♦ European Skin Research Foundation (ESRF) 08490

Administrative Dir Rue Cingria 7, 1205 Geneva, Switzerland. T. +41223214890. Fax +41223214892.
URL: http://www.euroskinresearch.org/

History 5 Sep 2007, Zurich (Switzerland), originally suggested by members of *European Society for Dermatological Research (ESDR, #08578).* **Aims** Broadly promote research and development so as to establish the highest possible quality of care to *patients* who suffer from *diseases* of the skin or from sexually transmitted diseases. **Structure** Board of Trustees. Benefactors' Board; Scientific Board. Administrative Office. **Finance** Support from: *European Academy of Dermatology and Venereology (EADV, #05788); European Society for Dermatological Research (ESDR, #08578).* **Activities** Grants the "ESRF New Investigator Awards".
[2011/XJ2329/f/**F**]

♦ European Skippers Organisation (ESO-OEB) 08491

Association européenne des bateliers (OEB) – Europäische Schiffer Organisation (ESO) – Europese Schippersorganisatie – Europejska Organizacja Armatorów Sródladowych

SG St Pieterskaai 74, 8000 Bruges, Belgium. T. +3250470720 – +3250335337. E-mail: secretariat@eso-oeb.org.
Registered Address Avenue des Arts 56, 1000 Brussels, Belgium.
URL: https://www.eso-oeb.org/

History 1975, Brussels (Belgium). Registration: No/ID: 0690.929.119, Start date: 26 Feb 2018, Belgium; EU Transparency Register, No/ID: 63974235880-21, Start date: 20 May 2011. **Aims** Represent, in the widest sense of the word, the socio-economic and professional interests of members of affiliated organizations in inland shipping, dry cargo as well as tanker shipping, enabling optimal professional transportation on Europe's waterways. **Structure** General Assembly; Governing Body; Policy Commissions; Secretariat. **Languages** Dutch, English, French, German. **Staff** 1.50 FTE, voluntary. **Finance** Sources: members' dues. **Activities** Advocacy/lobbying/activism; events/meetings. **Events** *Congress* Antwerp (Belgium) 2000, *L'avenir de la navigation intérieure* Maasbracht (Netherlands) 1994. **Publications** *Juridisch Memorandum omtrent de Toerbeurt* (1992) by Hans Van Houtte. *Inland Navigation – The Market Regulation the Year 1992.*
Members Organizations representing independent entrepreneurs in inland shipping (whether tankers or dry holds). Members in 6 countries:
Belgium, France, Germany, Netherlands, Poland, UK.
IGO Relations Cooperates with (3): *Central Commission for the Navigation of the Rhine (CCNR, #03687);* EEC committees; *European Commission (EC, #06633)* (DG MOVE Dept of Inland Shipping). **NGO Relations** Member of (1): *European Inland Waterway Transport Platform (European IWT Platform, #07541).*
[2022.05.12/XD0899/**D**]

♦ European Skull Base Society (ESBS) 08492

Sec-Treas c/o Events, Radboudumc Health Ac, Postbus 9101, 6500 HB Nijmegen, Netherlands. E-mail: europeanskullbasesociety.rha@radboudumc.nl.
URL: http://www.esbs.eu/

History 1992, Italy. Founded at first congress, dating back to 1985. Registration: No/ID: 53010/8419, Start date: 16 Apr 1992, Italy, Bergamo. **Aims** Evaluate and systematize current advances made by skull base disciplines to benefit patients with skull base disease; promote research in diseases of the skull base. **Structure** Executive Committee. **Languages** English. **Staff** 0.50 FTE, paid. **Events** *Congress* Maastricht (Netherlands) 2024, *Congress* Riva del Garda (Italy) 2022, *Congress* Riva del Garda (Italy) 2021, *Mutual learning – overcoming limitations* Prague (Czechia) 2018, *Congress* Berlin (Germany) 2016. **Publications** *Skull Base* – journal.
Members in 33 countries:
Austria, Belgium, Bosnia-Herzegovina, Bulgaria, Croatia, Czechia, Denmark, Estonia, Finland, France, Germany, Greece, Hungary, Ireland, Italy, Lithuania, Netherlands, North Macedonia, Norway, Poland, Portugal, Romania, Russia, Serbia, Slovakia, Slovenia, Spain, Sweden, Switzerland, Türkiye, UK, Ukraine.
NGO Relations Member of (1): *Confederation of European Otorhinolaryngology – Head and Neck Surgery (Confederation of European ORL-HNS, #04528).* Also links with national organizations.
[2022.11.04/XD8304/**D**]

♦ European Sled Dog Racing Association (inactive)

♦ European Sleep Research Society (ESRS) 08493

Société européenne de recherche sur le sommeil

Main Office Andreasstr 4, 93053 Regensburg, Germany. T. +4994129091271. Fax +4994129080975. E-mail: maria.wiechmann@esrs.eu.
Contact Günzstr 4, 93059 Regensburg, Germany. T. +4994189939875. Fax +4994189939877. E-mail: esrs@esrs.eu.
URL: http://www.esrs.eu/

History 1972, Basel (Switzerland). Registration: Bavaria District court, No/ID: VR 1646, Start date: 7 Jun 1999, Germany, Regensburg. **Aims** Support the research on all aspects of sleep and sleep-wake cycle; promote basic research and clinical applications. **Structure** Board of Officers; Scientific Committee. **Languages** English. **Staff** 0.50 FTE, paid. **Finance** Sources: members' dues. **Activities** Events/meetings; research/documentation; training/education. **Events** *Congress* Seville (Spain) 2024, *Congress* Athens (Greece) 2022, *International Sleep and Breathing Conference* Lausanne (Switzerland) 2021, *Biennial Congress* Regensburg (Germany) 2020, *Meeting* St Petersburg (Russia) 2019. **Publications** *European Sleep Research Society Newsletter* (4 a year); *Journal of Sleep Research.* Congress proceedings.
Members Individuals (822) in 51 countries and territories:
Argentina, Australia, Austria, Belgium, Brazil, Bulgaria, Canada, Chile, China, Croatia, Czechia, Denmark, Egypt, Estonia, Finland, France, Georgia, Germany, Greece, Hong Kong, Hungary, Iceland, India, Ireland, Israel, Italy, Japan, Lithuania, Luxembourg, Netherlands, Nigeria, Norway, Poland, Portugal, Romania, Russia, Serbia, Slovakia, Slovenia, South Africa, Spain, Sweden, Switzerland, Syrian AR, Tunisia, Türkiye, UK, Ukraine, Uruguay, USA, Venezuela.
NGO Relations Member of (2): *Federation of European Neuroscience Societies (FENS, #09522); World Sleep Society (#21793).* Cooperates with (2): *European Narcolepsy Network (EU-NN, #07852); European Respiratory Society (ERS, #08383).*
[2021/XD6214/v/**D**]

♦ European Small Business Alliance of Small and Medium Independent Enterprises / see European Small Business Alliance of Small and Medium Independent Enterprises (#08494)

♦ European Small Business Alliance of Small and Medium Independent Enterprises (ESBA) 08494

Alliance européenne des PMI/PME – Alianza Europea de la Pequeña y Mediana Empresa – Europäische Allianz der Kleinen und Mittleren Unternehmen – Alleanza Europea dell Piccole e Medie Imprese Indipendenti – Europeiska Smaföåretagarealliansen av Oberoende Små- och Medelstora Företag

Pres Avenue de la Renaissance 1, 1000 Brussels, Belgium. T. +322496775334. E-mail: secretariat@esba-europe.org.
Contact UK Federation of Small Businesses, 2 Catherine Place, London, SW1E 6HF, UK.
URL: http://www.esba-europe.org/

History 1998. Previously also listed under full title: *European Small Business Alliance of Small and Medium Independent Enterprises (ESBA).* Previously also referred to as *EUROGROUP.* Registration: Banque-Carrefour des Entreprises, No/ID: 0474.121.053, Start date: 22 Feb 2001, Belgium; EU Transparency Register, No/ID: 741179426673-35, Start date: 7 Apr 2017. **Aims** Care for small business entrepreneurs and self-employed; represent them through targeted EU advocacy activities; work towards the development of strong independent lobby and benefits groups in European countries. **Structure** General Assembly (annual). Management Committee; Executive Committee. **Languages** English. **Staff** 4.00 FTE, paid. **Finance** Members' dues. **Activities** Knowledge management/information dissemination; training/education; events/meetings. **Publications** *ESBA Bulletin* (bi-weekly).
Members Full in 9 countries and territories:
Belgium, Croatia, Germany, Gibraltar, Netherlands, Northern Cyprus, Poland, Slovenia, Sweden.
Included in the above, 1 organization listed in this Yearbook:
Flock Association of Europe.
IGO Relations *European Commission (EC, #06633); OECD (#17693); World Intellectual Property Organization (WIPO, #21593).* **NGO Relations** Member of: *European Entrepreneurs CEA-PME (#06994).*
[2021/XF4106/y/**F**]

♦ European Small Hydropower Association (ESHA) 08495

Association européenne pour la petite hydraulique – Asociación Europea de Energia Mini-hidraulica – Verband Europäischer Kleinwasserkraftwerke – Associação Européia de Energia Mini-Hidrica – Associazione Europea per il Piccolo Idroelettrico

Contact Ms Christine Lins, Renewable Energy House, Rue d'Arlon 63-65, 1040 Brussels, Belgium. T. +3225461945. E-mail: info@esha.be.
URL: http://www.esha.be/

History 1989, at the initiative of *European Commission (EC, #06633).* Registered in accordance with Belgian law. New statutes adopted 2010. **Aims** Promote the use of hydropower to generate electrical energy on a small scale; represent the interests of small hydropower industry in Europe; encourage exchange of technology; study and analyse environmental, legislative, technical and economic problems. **Structure** General Assembly (annual). Governing Board, consisting of up to 34 persons, including national representatives and elected members. Executive Board, comprising President, 2 Vice-Presidents, Treasurer and elected Governing Board members. **Languages** English, French, German. **Staff** 5.50 FTE, paid. **Finance** Members' dues. Project funding from the European Commission. **Activities** Advocacy/lobbying/activism; events/meetings; training/education. **Events** *Biennial Hidroenergia Conference* Verona (Italy) 2016, *Biennial Hidroenergia Conference / Biennial Hidroenergia Conference* Istanbul (Turkey) 2014, *European Hydropower Summit* Bucharest (Romania) 2012, *European Hydropower Generation and Pumped Storage Forum* Vienna (Austria) 2012, *Biennial Hidroenergia Conference / Biennial Hidroenergia Conference* Wroclaw (Poland) 2012. **Publications** *BlueAGE: Blue Energy for Europe, SHP Situation in the New European Member States and Candidate Countries; Guidebook on How to Develop a Small Hydropower Plant; Proposals for a European R and D Strategy for the SHP Sector.* Brochures. **Members** Full individuals and organizations in European countries. Associate individuals and organizations in other countries. Membership countries not specified. **NGO Relations** Member of: *European Forum for Renewable Energy Sources (EUFORES, #07329); European Water Partnership (EWP, #09083); International Network on Small Hydro Power (IN-SHP, #14324).* Instrumental in setting up: *Alliance for Rural Electrification (ARE, #00719).* Associate partner of: *Covenant of Mayors for Climate and Energy (#04939).*
[2014/XD3737/**D**]

♦ European Small Islands Federation (ESIN) 08496

Sec Inishlyre, Kilmeena, Westport, CO. MAYO, F28 Y208, Ireland. T. +4562513993. E-mail: secretary@europeansmallislands.com.
Chair Bere Island Projects Group, Bere Island, Bantry, CO. CORK, P75 W660, Ireland.
URL: http://europeansmallislands.com/

History 23 May 2001, Stockholm (Sweden). Former names and other names: *European Small Islands Network (E-SIN)* – former (23 May 2001). **Aims** Promote sustainable social, cultural and economic development of small islands. **Activities** Events/meetings. **Events** *Annual General Meeting* 2020, *Annual General Meeting* Ven Is (Sweden) 2019, *Annual General Meeting* Brussels (Belgium) 2018, *Annual General Meeting* Kirkwall (UK) 2017, *Annual General Meeting* Brussels (Belgium) 2016.
Members Island organizations in 11 countries and territories:
Åland, Croatia, Denmark, Estonia, Finland, France, Greece, Ireland, Italy, Scotland, Sweden.
NGO Relations Member of (1): *Global Islands Network (GIN, #10437).*
[2022/XF7161/**F**]

♦ European Small Islands Network / see European Small Islands Federation (#08496)
♦ European Small Volume Car Manufacturers Alliance (unconfirmed)
♦ European Smart Card Group / see EUROSMART (#09182)
♦ European Smart Card Industry Association / see EUROSMART (#09182)
♦ European Smart Metering Industry Group / see ESMIG (#05539)

♦ European Smoking Tobacco Association (ESTA) 08497

SG Rond-Point R Schuman 9, Box 1, 1040 Brussels, Belgium. T. +3222308092. Fax +3222308214. E-mail: info@esta.be.
URL: http://www.esta.be/

History 1990, Brussels (Belgium). Founded by German and Dutch associations. Registration: EU Transparency Register, No/ID: 0138855852-93, Start date: 22 Dec 2008. **Aims** Represent the interests of European manufacturers, distributors and importers of fine-cut (rolling) tobacco, pipe tobacco, chewing tobacco and nasal snuff tobacco. **Structure** Board; Executive Committee; Secretariat. **Languages** English. **Staff** 4.00 FTE, paid. **Events** *Meeting* Milan (Italy) 2010, *Meeting* Budapest (Hungary) 2009, *Meeting* Cologne (Germany) 2008, *Meeting* Svendborg (Denmark) 2008, *Meeting* Paris (France) 2007.
Members Full in 18 countries:
Belgium, Denmark, Finland, France, Germany, Greece, Hungary, Italy, Luxembourg, Malta, Netherlands, Norway, Poland, Slovakia, Spain, Sweden, Switzerland, UK.
NGO Relations In liaison with technical committees of: *International Organization for Standardization (ISO, #14473).*
[2020/XD5463/**D**]

♦ European Snacks Association (ESA) 08498

Association européenne des fabricants de snacks

Address not obtained.
URL: http://www.esasnacks.eu/

History 1965, London (UK). Current By-laws adopted 1 Jun 2010, Brussels (Belgium). Former names and other names: *European Chips and Snacks Association (ECSA)* – former (1965). Registration: No/ID: 0848.381.301, Start date: 3 Sep 2012, Belgium; EU Transparency Register, No/ID: 00849042167-65, Start date: 20 Aug 2009. **Aims** Advance the savoury snacks industry on behalf of member snack manufacturers and suppliers; work to create an operating environment that helps promote members' interests and increase consumer confidence, leading to category growth. **Structure** Board of Directors; Executive Committee. Integrated *International Peanut Forum (IPF, inactive)* into the SNAKEX Exhibition and Conference. **Languages** English. **Staff** 5.00 FTE, paid. **Finance** Sources: members' dues. Annual budget: 600,000 GBP. **Activities** Networking/liaising; Politics/policy/regulatory; events/meetings. **Events** *SNACKEX Biennial Conference* Hamburg (Germany) 2022, *SNACKEX Biennial Conference* Hamburg (Germany) 2021, *SNACKEX Biennial Conference* Barcelona (Spain) 2019, *SNACKEX Biennial Conference* Vienna (Austria) 2017, *Biennial Savoury Snack Summit* Brussels (Belgium) 2015. **Publications** *The Snack Magazine* (4 a year).
Members Business; Associate; Trade Associate. National organizations in 4 countries:
Germany, Netherlands, Spain, UK.
Associates in 11 countries:
Canada, Denmark, France, Germany, Japan, Netherlands, Spain, Sweden, Switzerland, UK, USA.
Business links in 37 countries:

Australia, Austria, Belgium, Canada, Cyprus, Czechia, Denmark, Egypt, Finland, France, Germany, Greece, India, Ireland, Israel, Italy, Japan, Jordan, Kuwait, Malta, Mexico, Netherlands, New Zealand, Norway, Pakistan, Poland, Russia, Saudi Arabia, South Africa, Spain, Sri Lanka, Sweden, Switzerland, Türkiye, UK, United Arab Emirates, USA.
IGO Relations Recognized by: *European Commission (EC, #06633).* **NGO Relations** Member of (2): *Circular Plastics Alliance (#03936); FoodDrinkEurope (#09841)* (Affiliate). [2021/XD9815/**D**]

♦ European Sobudo Rengokai (inactive)

♦ European Social Action Network (ESAN) 08499

Réseau européen d'action sociale – Red Europea de Acción Social – Europäisches Netzwerk für Soziales Handeln – Rete Europea d'Azione Sociale – Rede Européia de Ação Social – Europees Netwerk voor Sociale Actie

Main Office Rue du Luxembourg 19-21, 1000 Brussels, Belgium. T. +3228889920.
URL: http://esan-aisbl.eu/

History Founded 5 Nov 1991, Brussels (Belgium), by a number of social welfare and social development agencies, a Steering Committee having been set up in Jun 1989. Registered in accordance with Belgian law. Registration: AISBL/IVZW, Belgium. **Structure** General Meeting (annual); Board; Work Committees (3). A network of existing local, national and European agencies. **Staff** None. **Finance** Members' dues. Other sources: donations, grants. **Activities** Knowledge managamant/information dissemination; advocacy/lobbying/activism; projects/programmes; awards/prizes/competitions. **Events** *General Assembly* Brussels (Belgium) 2016, *General Assembly* Brussels (Belgium) 2012, *General Assembly* Brussels (Belgium) 2002, *Social forum* Brussels (Belgium) 2001, *Droits de tous les résidents en Europe* Paris (France) 2000.
Members Non-governmental social welfare and social development agencies (26) in 12 countries:
Belgium, Bulgaria, France, Germany, Greece, Italy, Portugal, Russia, Slovakia, Spain, Türkiye, UK.
Included in the above, 3 organizations listed in this Yearbook:
Fédération des Agences Internationales pour le Développement (AIDE Fédération, #09414); International Federation of Social Workers (IFSW, #13544); World Organization for Early Childhood Education (OMEP, #21689).
Consultative Status Consultative status granted from: *Council of Europe (CE, #04881)* (Participatory Status).
IGO Relations *European Commission (EC, #06633).* **NGO Relations** *Comité pour les Partenariats avec l'Europe Continentale (Comité PECO); Forum international développement démocratie (FIDDEM, no recent information); People from Here and Elsewhere Federation (#18298); Social Platform (#19344); Spring Alliance (inactive).* [2020/XF2158/y/**F**]

♦ European Social Charter (1961 treaty)
♦ European Social Charter – Community Charter of Fundamental Social Rights for Workers (1989 treaty)
♦ European Social Charter – Revised (1996 treaty)
♦ European Social Dance Council / see European Dance Council (#06886)
♦ European Social Educator Training (#09873)

♦ European Social Franchising Network (ESFN) 08500

Contact Coompanion, Packhusplatsen 2, SE-411 13 Gothenburg, Sweden.
URL: http://www.socialfranchising.coop/

History EU Transparency Register: 561214416503-76. **Aims** Promote the concept of social franchising and the social franchise offer of members; facilitate development of best practice in social franchising; create a positive environment for the development of social franchising. **Activities** Events/meetings. [2017/XM5643/**F**]

♦ European Social Fund (ESF) 08501

Fonds social européen (FSE) – Fondo Social Europeo – Europäischer Sozialfonds – Fundo Social Europeu – Fondo Sociale Europeo – Europees Sociaal Fonds – Europaeiske Socialfond – Europeiska Socialfonden – Euroopan Sosiaalirahasto – Evropaiko Kinoniko Tamio

Contact European Commission, DG Employment/Social Affairs/Inclusion, 1049 Brussels, Belgium. T. +3222951883. Fax +3222969429. E-mail: isabelle.mordelle@ec.europa.eu – christian.wigand@ec.europa.eu.
URL: http://ec.europa.eu/esf/

History 25 May 1957, under the provisions of the *Treaty on the Functioning of the European Union (TFEU, 1957)*, modified by the Council Regulation (EEC) 2084/93 of 20 Jul 1993, in force 1994. New regulations in force 1 Jan 2014 until end 2020. Comes under Directorate-General Employment and Social Affairs of *European Commission (EC, #06633)*, and now also of *European Union (EU, #08967)*, being the main tool by which the European Union translates employment policy aims into action. **Aims** As part of *European Union* policy of economic and social cohesion and European social policy: support European *employment* policy and national action plans for employment linked to it; promote high employment equality between men and women, sustainable development and economic and social cohesion by supporting measures to prevent and combat unemployment and to develop human resources and social integration into the labour market, and in particular, contribute to actions undertaken in pursuance of 'European Employment Strategy' and 'Annual Guidelines on Employment'. **Structure** Implemented by Managing Authorities at national or regional level. **Finance** European Community. Budget (2014-2020): euro 86,400,000. **Activities** Advocacy/lobbying/activism; financial and/or material support. **Events** *Conference on Bringing the Long-Term Unemployed Back into Work* Brussels (Belgium) 2019, *ESF Transnational Platform Annual Conference* Brussels (Belgium) 2019, *Migrants Thematic Network Meeting* Helsinki (Finland) 2018, *Conference* Dijon (France) 2009, *Joint conference on quality of work, quality of life* Riga (Latvia) 2008. **Publications** Annual implementation reports; evaluation reports; project examples; information leaflets. **Members** EU member states (27). **IGO Relations** Works jointly on specific objectives with *European Agricultural Guarantee Fund (EAGF)*, previously *European Agricultural Guidance and Guarantee Fund (EAGGF, inactive)* – Guidance Section *European Regional Development Fund (ERDF, #08342)* and, from 2007, *European Fisheries Fund (EFF, inactive)*. Budget assessed by: *European Parliament (EP, #08146).* [2019/XF5544/f/**F***]

♦ European Social Housing Observation Unit / see European Social Housing Observatory (#08502)

♦ European Social Housing Observatory 08502

Observatoire européen du logement social (OELS)

Research Dir c/o CECODHAS Housing Europe, Square de Meeûs 18, 1050 Brussels, Belgium. T. +3225410564. Fax +3225410569.
URL: http://www.housingeurope.eu/about/observatory/

History Oct 1993, Athens (Greece). Research branch of *Housing Europe – The European Federation for Public Cooperative and Social Housing (Housing Europe, #10956)*. Previously also referred to as *European Social Housing Observation Unit.* **Aims** Monitor trends in housing and social housing policies and markets; carry out thematic studies on strategic issues in this field; participate in expert groups and task forces. **Activities** Monitors trends in national social housing policies in the member countries of European Union plus Norway and Switzerland. Identifies and compares innovative European practices in social housing. Analyses the effects of European integration on the social housing sector. Keeps statistical record of social housing in Europe. Organizes European seminars. **Publications** *Research Briefings* – series. *Housing Europe Review* (2012).
Members National correspondents (34) covering 17 countries:
Austria, Belgium, Denmark, Finland, France, Germany, Greece, Ireland, Italy, Luxembourg, Netherlands, Norway, Portugal, Spain, Sweden, Switzerland, UK.
NGO Relations Member of: *European Housing Forum (EHF, #07504).* [2013/XF4214/**F**]

♦ European Social Insurance Partners / see European Social Insurance Platform (#08503)

♦ European Social Insurance Platform (ESIP) 08503

Dir c/o Maison européenne de la protection sociale, Rue d'Arlon 50, 1000 Brussels, Belgium. T. +3222820560. Fax +3222820598. E-mail: esip@esip.eu.
URL: http://www.esip.eu/

History Founded 1996, as *European Social Insurance Partners.* Registered in accordance with Belgian law: 808072950. **Aims** Preserve high-profile social security for Europe; reinforce solidarity-based social insurance systems; maintain European social protection quality. **Structure** General Assembly; Board of Governors; Standing Committees (4). **Languages** English. **Staff** 2.50 FTE, paid. **Finance** Members' dues. Annual budget (2019): euro 212,000. **Activities** Events/meetings. **Events** *Meeting* Brussels (Belgium) 2019, *Conference* Brussels (Belgium) 2015, *Conference* Brussels (Belgium) 2013, *Conference* Brussels (Belgium) 2012, *Conference* Brussels (Belgium) 2010.
Members Organizations in 17 countries:
Austria, Belgium, Bulgaria, Croatia, Czechia, Finland, France, Germany, Greece, Italy, Luxembourg, Netherlands, Poland, Slovakia, Slovenia, Spain, Switzerland. [2019.02.13/XD9011/**D**]

♦ European Social Investment Forum / see European Sustainable Investment Forum (#08865)
♦ European Socialist Movement (no recent information)

♦ European Social Marketing Association (ESMA) 08504

Contact Strategic Social Marketing Ltd, Attabara, Conford, Liphook, GU30 7QW, UK. T. +441428751475. E-mail: info@europeansocialmarketing.org.
Registered Address Unit 2-3 Abotts Quay, Monksferry, Wirral, CH41 5LH, UK.
URL: https://europeansocialmarketing.org/

History Nov 2012, Lisbon (Portugal). Registration: Companies House, No/ID: 08767830, Start date: 8 Nov 2013, England and Wales. **Aims** Connect social marketing people, research and practice at European level. **Structure** Board. **Languages** English. **Staff** 0.20 FTE, paid. **Finance** Sources: members' dues. **Events** *European Social Marketing Conference* Antwerp (Belgium) 2018, *European Obesity Forum* Amsterdam (Netherlands) 2016, *European Social Marketing Conference* Espoo (Finland) 2016, *European Social Marketing Conference* Rotterdam (Netherlands) 2014, *European Social Marketing Conference* Lisbon (Portugal) 2012.
Members Full in 19 countries:
Belgium, Congo DR, Egypt, Estonia, Finland, France, Kuwait, Netherlands, New Zealand, Norway, Philippines, Portugal, Romania, Slovakia, Slovenia, Spain, Switzerland, UK, USA.
NGO Relations Cooperates with (2): *International Social Marketing Association (iSMA, #14882); World Social Marketing.* [2022/XJ9234/**D**]

♦ European Social Network (ESN) 08505

Réseau social européen – Europäisches Soziales Netzwerk

Chief Exec Av des Arts 3-4-5, 8th Floor, 1210 Brussels, Belgium. T. +3225111093.
URL: http://www.esn-eu.org/

History 1998, as *European Association of Directors of Social Services.* UK Registered Charity: 1079394. **Aims** Facilitate good practice exchange among directors of social services, senior care professionals and other stakeholders; bridge the gap between European policy-making and local social care practice and management; deliver social policy and social work and care practice knowledge to members and other stakeholders; advocate empowerment of service users, joint working across service boundaries and quality assurance in service management. **Structure** General Meeting; Board (meets 3 times a year); Business Committee; Secretariat, headed by Chief Executive, located in Brighton (UK). **Languages** English, French, German, Italian, Polish, Spanish. **Staff** 11.00 FTE, paid. **Finance** Members' dues. Co-funded by *European Commission (EC, #06633)* through 'Progress'. Other sources: conference sponsorship. **Activities** Politics/policy/regulatory; advocacy/lobbying/activism; knowledge management/information dissemination; events/meetings. Active inclusion; Children and families – breaking the cycle of deprivation. **Events** *Seminar* Lisbon (Portugal) 2019, *Annual Conference* Milan (Italy) 2019, *Annual Conference* Seville (Spain) 2018, *Seminar on Inclusive Activation* Vienna (Austria) 2018, *Seminar on Migrant Children and Young People* Stockholm (Sweden) 2017. **Publications** Policy statements; EU consultation responses.
Members National directors associations in 34 countries and territories:
Austria, Azerbaijan, Belgium, Bulgaria, Croatia, Czechia, Denmark, Estonia, Faeroe Is, Finland, France, Georgia, Germany, Greece, Hungary, Iceland, Ireland, Israel, Italy, Kosovo, Latvia, Lithuania, Malta, Netherlands, Norway, Poland, Portugal, Romania, Serbia, Slovenia, Spain, Sweden, Switzerland, UK.
Consultative Status Consultative status granted from: *Council of Europe (CE, #04881)* (Participatory Status). [2018/XD5696/**D**]

♦ European Social Observatory (internationally oriented national body)

♦ European Social Simulation Association (ESSA) 08506

Pres Johannes Gutenberg Uni Mainz -Fac 02, Inst of Sociology, Jakob-Welder-Weg 20, 55128 Mainz, Germany. E-mail: info@essa.eu.org.
URL: http://www.essa.eu.org/

History 2003. **Aims** Encourage development of social simulation in Europe and more widely; promote international cooperation among those working in the field while recognizing the distinctiveness of European social simulation research; promote and support development of European post-graduate courses and qualifications in social simulation; liaise with other groups to reduce unnecessary clashes in scheduling of events relating to social simulation. **Structure** Management Committee. **Languages** English. **Finance** Sources: members' dues. **Activities** Awards/prizes/competitions; events/meetings; training/education. **Events** *Social Simulation Conference* Krakow (Poland) 2021, *Conference* Mainz (Germany) 2019, *Conference* Stockholm (Sweden) 2018, *Conference* Groningen (Netherlands) 2015, *Conference* Barcelona (Spain) 2014. **Publications** *ESSA Newsletter.* **NGO Relations** Cooperates with: Computational Social Science Society of America (CSSSA); *Pacific Asian Association for Agent-based Approach in Social Systems Sciences (PAAA).* [2022/XM3574/**D**]

♦ European Social Survey (ESS) 08507

Dir City – Univ of London, Northampton Square, London, EC1V 0HB, UK. T. +442070404901. E-mail: ess@city.ac.uk.
URL: http://www.europeansocialsurvey.org/

History Set up 2001, as an academically driven cross-national survey. Since 30 Nov 2013, awarded *European Research Infrastructure Consortium (ERIC)* status, following which it is also referred to as *ESS ERIC.* **Aims** Measure attitudes, beliefs and behaviour patterns of diverse populations. **Structure** General Assembly; Scientific Advisory Board; Methods Advisory Board; Finance Committee; Core Scientific Team; Headquarters hosted by City, University of London (UK). **Languages** English. **Activities** Research/documentation; research and development; knowledge management/information dissemination; capacity building; events/meetings. **Events** *International ESS Conference* Lausanne (Switzerland) 2016. **Publications** *ESS Country Specific Topline Results Series; ESS Topline Results Series.*
Members States (25):
Austria, Belgium, Bulgaria, Croatia, Cyprus, Czechia, Estonia, Finland, France, Germany, Hungary, Iceland, Ireland, Israel, Italy, Latvia, Lithuania, Netherlands, Norway, Poland, Portugal, Slovakia, Slovenia, Sweden, UK.
Observer State (1):
Switzerland.
IGO Relations *European Commission (EC, #06633).* [2020.02.05/XM5205/**E***]

♦ European Social Work Research Association (ESWRA) 08508

Exec Administrator address not obtained. E-mail: info@eswra.org.
URL: http://www.eswra.org/

History 2014, to create a hub for social work research development, collaboration and exchange across Europe. **Aims** Take forward the development, practice and utilization of social work research to enhance knowledge about individual and social problems; promote just and equitable societies. **Structure** Board; Special Interest Groups. **Languages** English. **Staff** 1.00 FTE, paid. **Finance** Members' dues. **Activities** Events/meetings; knowledge management/information dissemination. **Events** *European Conference for Social Work Research* Milan (Italy) 2023, *European Conference for Social Work Research* Amsterdam (Netherlands) 2022, *European Conference for Social Work Research* Amsterdam (Netherlands) 2021, *European Conference for Social Work Research* Bucharest (Romania) 2021, *European Conference for Social Work Research* Bucharest (Romania) 2020. **Publications** *Research in Social Work* – series. **Members** Full; Student; Associate; Emeritus. Members (over 600) in 33 countries. Membership countries not specified. **NGO Relations** Member of: *European Alliance for the Social Sciences and Humanities (EASSH, #05885).* [2018.09.13/XM4421/v/**D**]

♦ European Society of Aerospace Medicine (ESAM) 08509

Contact address not obtained. E-mail: esam.assistant@gmail.com.
URL: http://www.esam.aero/

History 18 Nov 2006, Brussels (Belgium). Founded during 1st General Assembly. Current statutes revised 2011. Registration: Germany. **Aims** Work for the health and safety of all persons involved in *aviation* and space operations, including passengers. **Structure** General Assembly; Executive Committee; Scientific Advisory Board; Working Groups. **Languages** English. **Finance** Sources: members' dues. **Events** *Conference* Paris (France) 2021, *Conference* Paris (France) 2020, *Conference* Prague (Czechia) 2018, *Pushing the limits of aerospace medicine together* Oslo (Norway) 2016, *Conference* Bucharest (Romania) 2014.

Members Regular in 35 countries:
Austria, Belgium, Bulgaria, Croatia, Cyprus, Czechia, Estonia, Finland, France, Georgia, Germany, Greece, Hungary, Ireland, Italy, Kazakhstan, Malta, Moldova, Montenegro, Netherlands, North Macedonia, Norway, Poland, Portugal, Romania, Russia, Serbia, Slovakia, Slovenia, Spain, Sweden, Switzerland, Türkiye, UK, Ukraine.
Associate in 2 countries:
Belgium, France.
Included in the above, 2 organizations listed in this Yearbook:
Aerospace Medical Association (ASMA); EUROCONTROL (#05667) (Medical Board).
NGO Relations Liaison Organization of: *Comité européen de normalisation (CEN, #04162).* [2021.06.29/XM8217/**D**]

♦ European Society of Aesthetic Gynecology (unconfirmed)

♦ European Society of Aesthetic Plastic Surgery (ESAPS) 08510

Acting Sec Rue de Grand-Bigard 14, 1080 Sint-Agatha-Berchem, Belgium. E-mail: info@esaps.eu – office@esaps.eu.
URL: https://www.esaps.eu/

History 23 May 2019, Bruges (Belgium). Founded by *European Association of Societies of Aesthetic Plastic Surgery (EASAPS, #06211).* Current by-laws adopted May 2019. Registration: Banque Carrefour des Entreprises, No/ID: 0734.792.420, Start date: 24 Sep 2019, Belgium. **Aims** Serve individual European plastic surgeons with an interest in Aesthetic Plastic Surgery; protect the safety of all patients and the public at large where Aesthetic procedures are concerned; uphold and maintain the highest ethical standards of personal and professional conduct among members; promote aesthetic plastic surgery by all channels and methods available. **Structure** General Assembly; Board of Directors; Executive Committee; Committees. **Languages** English. **Staff** 1.00 FTE, paid. Support from AOS management agency. [2023.02.14/AA1405/**D**]

♦ European Society for Aesthetics (ESA) 08511

Sec Dept of Philosophy – Univ of Fribourg, Avenue de l'Europe 20, 1700 Fribourg, Switzerland. E-mail: secretary@eurosa.org.
Events Manager address not obtained.
URL: http://www.eurosa.org/

History 2008, Fribourg (Switzerland). Registration: Swiss Civil Code, Switzerland. **Aims** Promote philosophical and other academic research and teaching in aesthetics and the theory of art; encourage exchange between those pursuing these activities in different parts of Europe, and in the diverse traditions that European aesthetics involves. **Structure** General Assembly; Executive Committee. **Activities** Awards/prizes/competitions; events/meetings; knowledge management/information dissemination; research/documentation. **Events** *Conference* Fribourg (Switzerland) 2021, *Conference* Tallinn (Estonia) 2020, *Conference* Warsaw (Poland) 2019. **Publications** *ESA Newsletter.* **Members** Institutional; Individual. [2021/AA1406/**D**]

♦ European Society of Aesthetic Surgery (ESAS) 08512

Head Office Pear Tree Cottage, 43 Cambridge Road, Wimpole, SG8 5QD, UK. T. +441223208268. Fax +441223207131.

History Previously also referred to as *European Society of Cosmetic Surgery (ESCS).* **Aims** Foster, promote, support, augment, develop and encourage the science, art and practice of aesthetic, cosmetic surgery. **Structure** General Meeting. Management Board, including Chairman, Vice-Chairman, Treasurer and General Secretary. **Finance** Members' dues. **Events** *International European congress* Bucharest (Romania) 2007. **Members** Membership countries not specified. [2011/XM0013/**D**]

♦ European Society Against Virus Diseases (inactive)

♦ European Society of Agricultural Engineers (EurAgEng) 08513

SG August Reyerslaan 80, 1030 Brussels, Belgium. T. +3227068173. E-mail: secgen@eurageng.eu.
URL: http://www.eurageng.eu/

History Founded 1984. **Aims** Promote the profession of agricultural and *biosystems* engineering in Europe and the people who serve it. **Structure** Council including Executive; Secretariat; Working Groups; Strategic Division – *European Network of Engineering for Agriculture and Environment (ENGAGE, #07901).* **Languages** English. **Staff** 0.50 FTE, paid. **Finance** Members' dues. Conference revenue. **Activities** Events/meetings; networking/liaising; advocacy/lobbying/activism. **Events** *Joint AgEng Biennial Conference* Evora (Portugal) 2021, *Joint AgEng Biennial Conference* Evora (Portugal) 2020, *Joint AgEng Biennial Conference* Wageningen (Netherlands) 2018, *Joint AgEng Biennial Conference* Aarhus (Denmark) 2016, *Joint AgEng Biennial Conference* Zurich (Switzerland) 2014. **Publications** *Biosystems Engineering* (12 a year) – journal; *EurAgEng Newsletter* (2 a year).

Members En bloc (through membership of accepted national society); Student; Affiliate (companies and institutions). Individuals and life members in 25 countries:
Austria, Belgium, Bulgaria, Croatia, Denmark, Finland, France, Germany, Greece, Hungary, Israel, Italy, Lithuania, Netherlands, Norway, Poland, Portugal, Romania, Slovakia, Slovenia, Spain, Sweden, Switzerland, UK, Ukraine. [2019.04.25/XD4290/**D**]

♦ European Society for Agricultural and Food Ethics (EurSafe) 08514

Secretariat Wageningen Univ, Dept of Social Sciences/Philosophy, PO Box 8130, 6700 EW Wageningen, Netherlands.
URL: http://www.eursafe.org/

History Aug 2000, following a series of activities since 1999. First statutes written 2000; amended 2007. Registered in accordance with Dutch law. **Aims** Encourage academic education, research and international debate on the ethical issues involved in agriculture and food supply. **Structure** General Assembly (annual); Executive Committee. **Languages** English. **Staff** None. **Finance** Members' dues: euro 30. **Activities** Events/meetings. **Events** *Justice and Food Security in a Changing Climate* Fribourg (Switzerland) 2021, *Congress* Tampere (Finland) 2019, *Congress* Vienna (Austria) 2018, *Know your food, food ethics and innovation* Cluj-Napoca (Romania) 2015, *The ethics of consumption – the citizen, the market, and the law* Uppsala (Sweden) 2013. **Publications** *EurSafe Newsletter* (4 a year). Annual report. Conference proceedings.
Members Individual; Institutional. Full in 18 countries:
Belgium, Canada, Denmark, Finland, France, Germany, Greece, Hungary, Ireland, Netherlands, Norway, Poland, Portugal, Spain, Sweden, Switzerland, UK, USA. [2019/XD8331/**D**]

♦ European Society for Agronomy (ESA) 08515

Société européenne d'agronomie

Contact c/o Agroscope, Route des Eterpys 18, 1964 Conthey VS, Switzerland. T. +41584813511. E-mail: info@european-agronomy.org.
URL: http://www.european-agronomy.org/

History 5 Dec 1990, Paris (France). Founded at 1st Congress. **Aims** Stimulate further integration of knowledge on crop physiology, ecophysiology, plant/soil relationships, cropping systems and environment; develop indicators, models, methods, tools and knowledge to assess and design cropping and *farming* systems in a multi-scale and multi-criteria approach. **Structure** General Assembly (at Congress); Steering Committee. **Languages** English. **Staff** None. **Activities** Events/meetings; knowledge management/information dissemination. **Events** *Biennial Congress* Rennes (France) 2024, *Biennial Congress* Potsdam (Germany) 2022, *Biennial Congress* Seville (Spain) 2020, *Biennial Congress* Geneva (Switzerland) 2018, *Biennial Congress* Edinburgh (UK) 2016. **Publications** *European Journal of Agronomy (EJA).* Congress proceedings. **Members** Scientists involved in agronomic research and development. Membership countries not specified. [2021/XD2312/v/**D**]

♦ European Society of Air Safety Investigators (ESASI) 08516

Pres Farnborough House, Berkshire Copse Road, Aldershot, GU11 2HH, UK.

History within *International Society of Air Safety Investigators (ISASI, #14914).* **Events** *Seminar* Budapest (Hungary) 2022, *Seminar* Budapest (Hungary) 2021, *Annual General Meeting* Aldershot (UK) 2020, *Annual Conference* Milan (Italy) 2014, *Seminar / Annual Conference* Madrid (Spain) 2013. [2016/XD9442/**D**]

♦ European Society for Alternatives to Animal Testing (EUSAAT) 08517

SG Apostelgasse 13/10, 1030 Vienna, Austria. E-mail: secretary.general@eusaat.eu – contact@eusaat.eu.
URL: http://www.eusaat.org/

History 1991, Linz (Austria). Former names and other names: *MittelEuropäische Gesellschaft für Alternativmethoden zu Tierversuchen (MEGAT)* – former (1 Jan 1991). Registration: Austria. **Aims** Promote protection of experimental animals. **Structure** General Assembly (annual); Board. **Languages** English, German. **Staff** Voluntary. **Finance** Sources: members' dues. **Events** *European Congress on Alternatives to Animal Testing* Linz (Austria) 2022, *Annual Congress* Linz (Austria) 2019, *Annual Congress* Linz (Austria) 2018, *Annual Congress* Linz (Austria) 2016, *Annual Congress* Linz (Austria) 2015. **Publications** *ALTEX – Alternatives to Animal Experimentation* (4 a year). **Members** Membership countries not specified. **NGO Relations** Japanese Society for Alternatives to Animal Experiments (JaSAAE). [2022/XJ1745/**D**]

♦ European Society of Ambulatory Pediatrics (inactive)

♦ European Society of Anaesthesiologists / see European Society of Anaesthesiology and Intensive Care (#08518)

♦ European Society of Anaesthesiology and Intensive Care (ESAIC) .. 08518

Exec Manager Rue des Comédiens 24, 1000 Brussels, Belgium. T. +3227433290. Fax +3227433298. E-mail: info@esaic.org – communication@esaic.org.
External Relations Manager address not obtained.
URL: https://www.esaic.org/

History 10 Apr 1992, Brussels (Belgium). Signed Amalgamation Agreement with *European Academy of Anaesthesiology (EAA, inactive)* and *Confederation of European National Societies of Anaesthesiologists (CENSA, inactive),* 19 Apr 2004, which prepared for EAA and CENSA to liquidate and transfer assets to ESA by 31 Dec 2004. New by-laws were adopted, 1 Jan 2005. Integrated *Fondation européenne d'enseignement en anesthésiologie (FEEA, inactive),* which became CEEA within ESA, 2008. Regional section of *World Federation of Societies of Anaesthesiologists (WFSA, #21482).* Former names and other names: *European Society of Anaesthesiologists (ESA)* – former (1992 to 31 Dec 2004). Registration: Banque Carrefour des Entreprises, No/ID: 0447.289.368, Start date: 10 Apr 1992, Belgium; EU Transparency Register, No/ID: 405138432409-56, Start date: 26 Aug 2018. **Aims** Contribute to growth and innovation found in the field of anaesthesiology and intensive care. **Structure** General Assembly (annual); Council (biannual); Board of Directors; Scientific Committees (17); National Anaesthesiology Societies Committee (NASC). **Languages** English. **Staff** 38.00 FTE, paid. **Finance** Sources: members' dues. Other sources: industry partners. **Activities** Advocacy/lobbying/activism; awards/prizes/competitions; events/meetings; knowledge management/information dissemination; research/documentation; standards/guidelines; training/education. **Events** *Euroanaesthesia Annual Meeting* Munich (Germany) 2024, *Euroanaesthesia Annual Meeting* Glasgow (UK) 2023, *Focus Meeting on Perioperative Medicine* Barcelona (Spain) 2022, *Euroanaesthesia Annual Meeting* Milan (Italy) 2022, *Euroanaesthesia Annual Meeting* Munich (Germany) 2021. **Publications** *ESAIC e-Newsletter* (12 a year); *European Journal of Anaesthesiology and Intensive Care (EJAIC)* (12 a year); *European Journal of Anaesthesiology (EJA)* (12 a year).
Members Individuals: Active; Affiliate; Trainee; Retired; Honorary. Societies: national societies of anaesthesiologists (39); European anaesthesiology sub-speciality societies (10). Individuals in 83 countries and territories:
Albania, Argentina, Australia, Austria, Belarus, Belgium, Bosnia-Herzegovina, Brazil, Bulgaria, Cameroon, Canada, Chile, China, Croatia, Cyprus, Czechia, Denmark, Egypt, Estonia, Finland, France, Georgia, Germany, Greece, Hungary, Iceland, India, Indonesia, Iran Islamic Rep, Iraq, Ireland, Israel, Italy, Japan, Jordan, Korea DPR, Korea Rep, Kuwait, Latvia, Lebanon, Lithuania, Luxembourg, Malawi, Malaysia, Malta, Mexico, Morocco, Netherlands, New Caledonia, New Zealand, Nigeria, North Macedonia, Norway, Pakistan, Peru, Poland, Portugal, Qatar, Romania, Russia, Saudi Arabia, Serbia, Singapore, Slovakia, Slovenia, South Africa, Spain, Sudan, Suriname, Sweden, Switzerland, Syrian AR, Taiwan, Thailand, Tunisia, Türkiye, Uganda, UK, Ukraine, United Arab Emirates, USA, Uzbekistan, Venezuela.
National societies in 43 countries:
Albania, Armenia, Austria, Belarus, Belgium, Bulgaria, Croatia, Cyprus, Czechia, Denmark, Estonia, Finland, France, Georgia, Germany, Greece, Hungary, Iceland, Israel, Italy, Kazakhstan, Kosovo, Latvia, Lithuania, Malta, Moldova, Montenegro, Netherlands, North Macedonia, Norway, Poland, Portugal, Romania, Russia, Serbia, Slovakia, Slovenia, Spain, Sweden, Switzerland, Türkiye, UK, Ukraine.
Specialist societies (13):
ERAS Society (#05530); European Airway Management Society (EAMS, #05854); European Association of Cardiothoracic Anaesthesiology and Intensive Care (EACTAIC, #05963); European Malignant Hyperthermia Group (EMHG, #07727); European Society for Computing and Technology in Anaesthesia and Intensive Care (ESCTAIC, #08564); European Society for Paediatric Anaesthesiology (ESPA, #08677); European Society for Perioperative Care of the Obese Patient (ESPCOP, #08694); European Society of Intravenous Anaesthesia (EuroSIVA, #08635); International Fluid Academy (iFA); International Suspected Perioperative Allergic Reaction Group (ISPAR, #15633); Liver Intensive Care Group of Europe (LICAGE, #16497); Society for Ultrasound in Anaesthesia (SUA); *WSACS – the Abdominal Compartment Society (#21963).*
NGO Relations Member of (3): *Biomedical Alliance in Europe (#03251); European Forum for Good Clinical Practice (EFGCP, #07313); Federation of European and International Associations Established in Belgium (FAIB, #09508).* [2022.11.23/XD3312/y/**D**]

♦ European Society for Analytical Cellular Pathology (inactive)

♦ European Society for Analytic Philosophy (ESAP) 08519

President c/o Central European Univ, Dept of Philosophy, Quellenstrasse 51, 1030 Vienna, Austria. T. +431252307111. E-mail: ecap10@uu.nl.
URL: http://analyticphilosophy.eu/

History Jun 1990. **Aims** Promote analytic philosophy in Europe and contacts among analytic philosophers. **Structure** General Assembly; Steering Committee; Board of National Representatives. **Languages** English. **Staff** None paid. **Events** *Triennial Congress* 2020, *Triennial Congress* Munich (Germany) 2017, *Triennial Congress* Bucharest (Romania) 2014, *Triennial Congress* Milan (Italy) 2011, *Triennial Congress* Krakow (Poland) 2008. **Publications** *Dialectica* (4 a year) – journal; *ESAP Newsletter* (3 a year). **IGO Relations** None. [2021.02.22/XD7392/**D**]

♦ European Society for Animal Blood Group Research / see International Society for Animal Genetics (#14921)

♦ European Society for Animal Cell Technology (ESACT) 08520

Société européenne de technologie cellulaire animale

Office c/o SK Frankfurt, Zeilweg 42, 60430 Frankfurt-Main, Germany. E-mail: office@esact.org.
URL: http://esact.org/

History 1976. **Aims** Bring together scientists, engineers and other specialists working with animal cells in order to promote communication of experiences between European and international investigators and progress the development of cell systems and productions derived from them. **Structure** General Meeting (every 2 years). Executive Committee, consisting of Officers (Chairman, Vice-Chairman, Secretary, Treasurer, Meeting Secretary) and 4 elected members. **Languages** English. **Staff** 0.50 FTE, paid. **Finance** Members' dues (annual): euro 20. Other sources: donations; grants. **Activities** focus on the entire animal cell production process from the initial genetic studies of the cells through the stages of process development and validation, production, purification, regulatory issues for product release, to the efficacy, safety, testing and application of the final product. Interests include: derivation, characterization, acceptance and validation of cell lines; optimization and enhancement of the biochemical and physiological behaviour of cells; process design, optimization, scale-up and technology transfer (upstream and downstream); biosynthesis and processing of cell products; cells and vectors for genetic medicine/therapy; tissue engineering and biomedical devices; cells as tools for product discovery and testing; replacement of animals in testing and research. Runs a free career center for jobs in the field of animal cell technology; organizes Scientific Meeting (every 2 years); awards bursaries to young scientists to attend the Scientific Meetings; offers financial and administrative support to selected training courses, additional specialist meetings and publications in the field; awards medals to outstanding contributors to animal cell technology and/or ESACT. **Events** *Scientific Meeting* Lisbon (Portugal) 2022, *Scientific Meeting* Lisbon (Portugal) 2021, *Scientific Meeting* Copenhagen (Denmark) 2019, *Scientific Meeting* Lausanne (Switzerland) 2017, *Scientific Meeting* Barcelona (Spain) 2015. **Publications** *ESACT Newsletter* (3 a year). Meeting proceedings.
Members Scientists and engineers in academic, medical and industrial R and D and Production at applied science institutions and universities. Ordinary; Honorary; Associate; Associated national societies (3, marked "). Members in 35 countries:
Australia, Austria, Belgium (*), Brazil, Canada, China, Croatia, Denmark, Finland, France, Germany (*), Greece, India, Ireland, Israel, Italy, Japan, Luxembourg, Netherlands, New Zealand, Norway, Pakistan, Portugal, Russia, Singapore, Slovenia, Spain, Sweden, Switzerland, Taiwan, Tunisia, Türkiye, UK (*), Ukraine, USA.
IGO Relations Working relationship with *European Commission (EC, #06633)* (DGXII). [2022/XD2768/v/**D**]

♦ European Society of Anti-Aging Medicine / see European Society of Preventive, Regenerative and Anti-Aging Medicine (#08714)

♦ European Society for Applied Mathematics (EUROSAM) 08521

Address not obtained.
URL: http://www.eurosam.org/

Structure Scientific Committee, comprising Honorary Chairman and 40 members. **Events** *EURO-SIAM Conference* Heraklion (Greece) 2014, *EURO-SIAM Conference* Montreux (Switzerland) 2011, *EURO-SIAM Conference* Athens (Greece) 2010. **Publications** *Journal of the European Society for Applied Mathematics.* Books; scientific publications; conference proceedings. **NGO Relations** Collaborates with: *Association for Computing Machinery (ACM, #02447); Society for Industrial and Applied Mathematics (SIAM).* [2014/XJ2030/**D**]

♦ European Society for Applied Superconductivity (ESAS) 08522

Sec CERN, Esplanade des Particules 1, 1211 Meyrin GE, Switzerland. E-mail: secretary@esas.org – office@esas.org.
Registered address Drienerlolaan 5, 7522 NB Enschede, Netherlands.
URL: http://www.esas.org/

History 4 Sep 1998, Frankfurt-Main (Germany). Registration: No/ID: 06090962, Netherlands. **Aims** Strengthen the international position of applied superconductivity, to represent it in social, scientific, industrial and political forums; promote communication in the area of applied superconductivity. **Structure** General Assembly; Board. **Languages** English, German. **Staff** 3.00 FTE, paid. **Finance** Sources: members' dues. **Activities** Events/meetings. **Events** *EUCAS : European Conference on Applied Superconductivity* Glasgow (UK) 2019, *EUCAS : European Conference on Applied Superconductivity* Geneva (Switzerland) 2017, *EUCAS : European Conference on Applied Superconductivity* Lyon (France) 2015, *EUCAS : European Conference on Applied Superconductivity / EUCAS* Genoa (Italy) 2013, *EUCAS : European conference on applied superconductivity* The Hague (Netherlands) 2011.
Members in 9 countries:
France, Germany, Hungary, Italy, Japan, Netherlands, Poland, UK, USA.
NGO Relations *Consortium of European Companies Determined to Use Superconductivity (CONECTUS, #04740).* [2020.03.07/XD8156/**D**]

♦ European Society of Arachnology 08523

Société européenne d'arachnologie (SEA)

Sec Dep Molecular Biology and Genetics, Democritus Univ of Thrace, Dimitras 19, 681 00 Alexandroupoli, Greece.
URL: http://www.european-arachnology.org/

History 1980. **Aims** Support study and development of arachnology; facilitate exchanges between researchers and institutes. **Structure** Council, including President, Vice-President, Secretary and Treasurer. **Languages** English. **Finance** Members' dues. **Events** *European Congress of Arachnology* Saint-Malo (France) 2025, *European Congress of Arachnology* Dublin (Ireland) 2024, *European Congress of Arachnology* Greifswald (Germany) 2022, *European Congress of Arachnology* 2021, *European Congress of Arachnology* Vác (Hungary) 2018. **Publications** Colloqium proceedings. **Members** Membership countries not specified. **NGO Relations** *International Society of Arachnology (ISA, #14935).* [2014/XM3158/**D**]

♦ European Society for Artificial Intelligence in Medicine (AIME) 08524

Chair Dept of Computer Science, Room 89, 1st Floor, Univ of Verona, Ca' Vignal 2, Strada le Grazie 15, 37134 Verona BL, Italy. T. +39458027985. Fax +39458027068.
Secretariat 73 bis Grande Rue, 38700 La Tronche, France. T. +3376010054. Fax +3376631636.
URL: http://aimedicine.info/

History 1986. **Aims** Foster research in the application of artificial intelligence techniques to medical care and medical research; provide a forum for reporting significant results achieved at biennial conferences. **Structure** Board, chaired by local organizer of the previous conference. **Events** *Conference* Porto (Portugal) 2021, *Biennial Conference* Poznań (Poland) 2019, *Biennial Conference* Vienna (Austria) 2017, *Biennial Conference* Pavia (Italy) 2015, *Biennial Conference* Murcia (Spain) 2013. [2019/XD7867/**D**]

♦ European Society for Artificial Internal Organs / see European Society for Artificial Organs (#08525)

♦ European Society for Artificial Organs (ESAO) 08525

Société européenne pour les organes artificiels

Office Ctr for Biomedical Technology, Danube-Univ Krems, Dr Karl Dorrekstr 30, 3500 Krems, Austria. T. +4327328932633. Fax +4327328934600.
URL: http://www.esao.org/

History Founded 1974, Berlin West (Germany FR), as *European Society for Artificial Internal Organs.* New statutes adopted 1981. **Aims** Encourage and report advances in the field of artificial and bio-artificial organs and related subjects; coordinate and develop research in artificial organs in Europe and represent research in this field to scientific institutions concerned. **Structure** General Assembly; Board of Governors; Executive Office; Working Groups. **Languages** English. **Staff** 3.00 FTE, voluntary. **Finance** Members' dues. Other sources: gifts and legacies; proceeds from activities (particularly sale of publications). **Activities** Events/meetings; training/education. **Events** *Annual Congress* Bergamo (Italy) 2023, *Annual Congress* Krems (Austria) 2022, *Annual Congress* London (UK) 2021, *Annual Congress* Hannover (Germany) 2019, *Annual Congress* Madrid (Spain) 2018. **Publications** *International Journal of Artificial Organs* (12 a year). Proceedings and abstracts of annual meetings.
Members Full: persons pursuing a scientific activity in Europe involving research, development or application of artificial organs; Honorary: persons who have particularly distinguished themselves in the field or have contributed to ESAO development; Affiliated Societies: national associations concerned with artificial organs or with similar aims. Members in 39 countries and territories:
Australia, Austria, Belgium, Brazil, Bulgaria, Canada, China, Croatia, Czechia, Denmark, Finland, France, Georgia, Germany, Greece, Hungary, Iran Islamic Rep, Israel, Italy, Japan, Korea DPR, Netherlands, North Macedonia, Norway, Poland, Russia, Saudi Arabia, Serbia, Slovakia, Slovenia, Spain, Sweden, Switzerland, Taiwan, Türkiye, UK, Ukraine, USA, Zimbabwe.
NGO Relations Member of: *European Alliance for Medical and Biological Engineering and Science (EAMBES, #05873); International Federation for Artificial Organs (IFAO, #13357); World Apheresis Association (WAA, #21097).* Cooperates with: *International Organization for Standardization (ISO, #14473).* [2021/XD5277/**D**]

♦ European Society of Association Executives (ESAE) 08526

Head Office Square de Meeûs 38-40, 1000 Brussels, Belgium. T. +32465224439. E-mail: info@esae.eu.
URL: https://www.esae.eu/

History 1979. Former names and other names: *Société européenne des dirigeants d'associations* – former; *Gesellschaft Europäischer Verbandsleiter* – former. **Aims** Promote and facilitate promotion of the profession and professional standing of managers of international and national associations; educate members and the public in areas that affect development and improvement of associations or similar international organizations. **Structure** General Assembly (annual); Board of Directors. **Languages** English, French, Italian. **Staff** 2.00 FTE, paid. **Finance** Sources: members' dues; sponsorship. **Activities** Advocacy/lobbying/activism; events/meetings; knowledge management/information dissemination; networking/liaising; training/education. **Events** *EAS : European Association Summit* Brussels (Belgium) 2021, *EAS : European Association Summit* Brussels (Belgium) 2020, *From strategic priorities to policy manifestos* Brussels (Belgium) 2020, *Annual General Assembly* Brussels (Belgium) 2019, *Companies and associations code* Brussels (Belgium) 2019. **Publications** *Headquarters* (6 a year) – magazine; *Boardroom Magazine*; *Journal of Association Leadership.*
Members Full: individual association executives in Europe; Partners: associations; service providers. Members in 19 countries:
Austria, Belgium, Denmark, Finland, France, Germany, Greece, Ireland, Italy, Luxembourg, Netherlands, Norway, Poland, Portugal, Spain, Sweden, Switzerland, UK, Ukraine. [2022.10.19/XD3190/v/**D**]

♦ European Society for Astronomy in Culture (#19461)

♦ European Society for Automatic Alarm Systems (EUSAS) 08527

Vice-Chairman c/o Uni Duisburg-Essen, Dept Nachrichtentechnische Systeme, Bismarckstr 81, 47057 Duisburg, Germany. E-mail: eusas@uni-duisburg-essen.de.
URL: https://eusas.org

History 11 Dec 1989. 2007-2008 restructured under German law. Registration: Start date: 2004, Germany; Start date: 11 Dec 1989, End date: 2004, Switzerland. **Aims** Promote experience sharing, exchange of views among professionals and know-how consolidation. **Structure** General Meeting. Executive Committee, including Chairman, Vice-Chairman and Secretary. Working Groups. **Events** *Fire detection in challenging environments* Garston (UK) 2013, *Conference on Industrial Fire Protection in Power Production and Storage / Conference* Lübeck (Germany) 2012, *Conference on the Future of Gas Sensors for Fire Detection and Safety Techniques* Saarbrücken (Germany) 2012, *Conference on Fire Safety in High-Rise Buildings* Vienna (Austria) 2011. **Publications** *EUSAS Journal*; *EUSAS Newsletter.* Conference proceedings. **Members** Ordinary; Associated; Junior; Honorary; Academic. Membership countries not specified. **NGO Relations** Supports (1): *International Conference on Automatic Fire Detection (AUBE).* [2021/XJ5434/**D**]

♦ European Society for Ballistocardiographic Research / see European Society for Noninvasive and Preventive Cardiology (#08668)

♦ European Society for Ballistocardiography and Cardiovascular Dynamics / see European Society for Noninvasive and Preventive Cardiology (#08668)

♦ European Society of Bassists (BASSEUROPE) 08528

Sec Amselstrasse 13a, 13125 Berlin, Germany.

History Registration: Germany. **Aims** Unify players, institutions and industries to share, discuss and develop to multiply and spread the *double bass* culture. **Structure** Board; Artistic Advisory Board; Industrial Advisory Board; National Contacts. **Languages** English, German. **Finance** Members' dues. **Activities** Events/meetings; networking/liaising; financial and/or material support. **Events** *Biennial Congress* Lucca (Italy) 2018, *Biennial Congress* Prague (Czechia) 2016, *Biennial Congress* Amsterdam (Netherlands) 2014, *Biennial Congress* Copenhagen (Denmark) 2012, *Biennial Congress* Berlin (Germany) 2010. [2016.06.27/XJ7092/**E**]

♦ European Society of Biochemical Engineering Sciences (ESBES) .. 08529

Main Office c/o DECHEMA eV, Theodor-Heuss-Allee 25, 60486 Frankfurt-Main, Germany. E-mail: office@esbesweb.org.
URL: http://www.esbesweb.org/

Aims Stimulate scientific advances in the field of biochemical engineering provide a platform for communication, education and interdisciplinary exchange. **Structure** Committee. Sections (9): Biocatalysis; Bioenergy and Bioeconomy (BEE); Bioreactor Performance (BRP); Downstream Processing (DSP); Food Bioprocess; Metabolic Engineering and System Bioloy (MESB); Microalgae Bioengineering (MAB); Modelling, Monitoring, Measurement and Control (M3C); Regenerative Medicine Manufacturing (RMM). **Activities** Awards/prizes/competitions; events/meetings; training/education. **Events** *European Congress of Applied Biotechnology* Berlin (Germany) 2023, *European Congress of Applied Biotechnology* Frankfurt-Main (Germany) 2021, *European Symposium on Biochemical Engineering Sciences* Frankfurt-Main (Germany) 2021, *European Symposium on Biochemical Engineering Sciences* Frankfurt-Main (Germany) 2020, *European Congress of Applied Biotechnology* Florence (Italy) 2019. **NGO Relations** Cooperates with (1): *International Society for Molecular Recognition (ISMR, #15278).* [2023.02.23/XJ7716/**D**]

♦ European Society of Biochemical Pharmacology (inactive)

♦ European Society for Biomaterials (ESB) 08530

Sec INEB – i3S, Rua Alfredo Allen 208, 4200-135 Porto, Portugal. T. +351220408800. E-mail: secretary@esbiomaterials.eu.
Pres MERLN Inst for Technology-Inspired Regenerative Medicine, Dept of Instructive Biomaterials Engineering, PO Box 616, 6200 MD Maastricht, Netherlands. T. +31612186343. E-mail: president@esbiomaterials.eu.
URL: http://www.esbiomaterials.eu/

History 1976. Registration: France. **Aims** Promote and develop research in biomaterials; encourage communication, information exchange and scientific collaboration among scientists, clinicians, industrials and regulatory affair experts to maximize R and D and commercial opportunities to the benefit of patients. **Structure** General Assembly (at least every 2 years); Council. **Languages** English. **Staff** None. **Finance** Sources: members' dues. **Activities** Events/meetings; knowledge management/information dissemination; research and development. **Events** *Conference* Ghent (Belgium) 2026, *Conference* Bordeaux (France) 2022, *Conference* Porto (Portugal) 2021, *Conference* Dresden (Germany) 2019, *Conference* Maastricht (Netherlands) 2018. **Publications** *Biomaterials Science* (12 a year) – journal. Annual Report; conference proceedings; text; journals.
Members Scientists (over 900) in around 30 countries. Membership countries not specified. Affiliated societies in 12 countries:
Affiliated societies in 12 countries:
Finland, France, Germany, Greece, Italy, Netherlands, Poland, Romania, Spain, Switzerland, Türkiye, UK.
Included in the above, 2 organizations listed in this Yearbook:
Australasian Society for Biomaterials and Tissue Engineering (ASBTE); Scandinavian Society for Biomaterials (ScSB, #19103).
NGO Relations Member of (1): *International Union of Societies for Biomaterials Science and Engineering (IUSBSE, #15816).* [2021.06.08/XD5627/**D**]

♦ European Society of Biomechanics (ESB) 08531

SG Insigneo Institute for in silico medicine, University of Sheffield, Western Bank, Sheffield, S10 2TN, UK.
Pres LBMC, Univ Lyon – Univ Eiffel, 25 av François Mitterand, Case 24, Cité des mobilités, 69675 Bron CEDEX, France.
URL: http://www.esbiomech.org/

History May 1976, Brussels (Belgium). Former names and other names: *Association européenne de biomécanique* – former; *Société européenne de biomécanique* – former. Registration: France. **Aims** Promote research and development of biomechanics and its applications including orthopaedic, cardiovascular and sport. **Structure** General Assembly; Council of 10; Executive Board, comprising President, Vice-President, Secretary-General and Treasurer. Conference; Executive Committee. **Languages** English. **Finance** Sources: donations; members' dues; sponsorship. **Activities** Events/meetings. **Events** *Conference* Edinburgh (UK) 2024, *Conference* Maastricht (Netherlands) 2023, *Conference* Porto (Portugal) 2022, *Conference* Milan (Italy) 2021, *Conference* Milan (Italy) 2020.
Members Individuals in 38 countries:
Australia, Austria, Belgium, Bulgaria, Canada, China, Croatia, Czechia, Denmark, Finland, France, Germany, Greece, Hungary, Ireland, Israel, Italy, Japan, Latvia, Lithuania, Montenegro, Netherlands, Poland, Portugal, Romania, Russia, Saudi Arabia, Serbia, Singapore, Slovakia, Slovenia, Spain, Sweden, Switzerland, Türkiye, UK, Ukraine, USA. [2022/XD2582/v/**D**]

♦ European Society for Biomedical Research on Alcoholism (ESBRA) . 08532

Société européenne de recherches biomédicales sur l'alcoolisme

Sec Wimbergergasse 21/22, 1070 Vienna, Austria. T. +436766430320. E-mail: office@esbra.com.
URL: https://www.esbra.com/

History 28 May 1987. Registered in accordance with Belgian law. **Aims** Promote biomedical research on alcoholism in European countries; disseminate information related to biomedical problems arising from use and abuse of alcohol; assist in prevention and education in matters related to alcoholism. **Structure** Board of Directors, comprising President, Vice-President, Secretary, Treasurer, Past-President, Founder-President and 5 members. **Languages** English, French, German. **Finance** Members' dues. **Activities** Organizes: congress (every 2 years); ESBRA Nordmann Award meeting (every other year). Members cooperate in organizing meetings, lectures, seminars, symposia and congresses. **Events** *World Congress on Alcohol and Alcoholism* Krakow (Poland) 2022, *Congress* Timisoara (Romania) 2021, *Congress* Lille (France) 2019, *Congress* Heraklion (Greece) 2017, *Congress* Valencia (Spain) 2015. **Publications** *Alcohol and Alcoholism* – journal. Congress proceedings.
Members Active; Student; Honorary; Associate; Corresponding. Members in 30 countries:
Australia, Austria, Belarus, Belgium, Cameroon, China, Czechia, Denmark, Estonia, Finland, France, Germany, Greece, Iceland, Ireland, Israel, Italy, Japan, Netherlands, Norway, Poland, Portugal, Russia, Spain, Sweden, Switzerland, Türkiye, UK, Ukraine, USA.
NGO Relations Member of: *European Federation of Addiction Societies (EUFAS, #07039).* Close contacts with: *International Society for Biomedical Research on Alcoholism (ISBRA, #14968).* [2020/XD1023/**D**]

♦ **European Society for Blood and Marrow Transplantation (EBMT)** .. **08533**
Main Office Passeig Taulat 116, Edif Dr F Duran i Jordà, 08005 Barcelona, Spain. T. +34934538750. E-mail: info@ebmt.org – secretariat@ebmt.org.
URL: http://www.ebmt.org/
History 1974. Founded by *'European Group for Immunodeficiencies (EGID)'*, currently *European Society for Immunodeficiencies (ESID, #08630)*. Former names and other names: *European Bone Marrow Transplant Group* – former (1974); *European Group for Bone Marrow Transplantation* – alias. Registration: Netherlands. **Aims** Focus on innovation, research and the advancement of cellular and stem cell-based therapies to save and improve the lives of patients with blood-related disorders; be the connection between patients, scientific community and other stakeholders to anticipate the future of the field. **Structure** General Assembly; Board of Association; Executive Committee; Scientific Council (10 Working Parties plus Nurses Group); Committees; Offices (3). **Languages** English. **Staff** 75.00 FTE, paid. **Finance** Sources: meeting proceeds; members' dues; sponsorship. **Activities** Advocacy/lobbying/activism; certification/accreditation; events/meetings; healthcare; knowledge management/information dissemination; publishing activities; research/documentation; training/education. **Events** *Annual Meeting* Paris (France) 2023, *Joint European CAR T-cell Meeting* Rotterdam (Netherlands) 2023, *Annual Meeting (EBMT2022)* Prague (Czechia) 2022, *Annual Meeting* Barcelona (Spain) 2021, *Annual Meeting* Barcelona (Spain) 2020. **Publications** *EBMT Newsletter* (12 a year); *Transplant Activity Survey* (annual); *Bone Marrow Transplantation Journal* – official journal. *The EBMT Handbook* (2019); *The European Blood and Marrow Transplantation Textbook for Nurses* (2018). **Members** Centres and individuals active in the field of hematopoietic stem cell transplantation and cellular and gene therapy research, or any other organisation involved in the care of donors and recipients of haematopoietic stem cells. Over 6,000 members in over 70 countries. Membership countries not specified. **NGO Relations** Member of (4): *Alliance for Harmonisation of Cellular Therapy Accreditation (AHCTA, #00686)*; *Associations and Conference Forum (AC Forum, #02909)*; *European Network of Paediatric Research at the European Medicines Agency (Enpr-EMA, #07963)*; *Worldwide Network for Blood and Marrow Transplantation (WBMT, #21929)*. Cooperates with (1): *EUROCORD (no recent information)*. [2023.02.14/XD1161/F]

♦ **European Society of Breast Cancer Specialists (EUSOMA)** **08534**
Secretariat Viale Belfiore 10, 50144 Florence FI, Italy. T. +3955576260. Fax +39555530281. E-mail: information@eusoma.org.
URL: http://www.eusoma.org/
History 25 Aug 1986, Budapest (Hungary). Former names and other names: *European Society of Mastology* – former. Registration: EU Transparency Register, No/ID: 979906240060-02, Start date: 26 Oct 2020. **Aims** Foster scientific research and increase contacts between scientists interested in cancer and other diseases of the breast; harmonize the quality of patient care in Europe by identifying widely accepted guidelines for diagnosis and treatment of breast cancer; elaborate proposals to European health authorities for the improvement in the control of breast cancer; foster postgraduate educational programmes in mastology at the national and international levels. **Structure** General Assembly; Executive Committee. **Languages** English. **Finance** Sources: donations; members' dues. Annual budget: 50,000 USD. **Activities** Certification/accreditation; events/meetings; knowledge management/information dissemination. **Events** *European Breast Cancer Conference (EBCC)* Barcelona (Spain) 2022, *IMPAKT Breast Cancer Conference* Brussels (Belgium) 2014, *European Breast Cancer Conference* Glasgow (UK) 2014, *IMPAKT Breast Cancer Conference* Brussels (Belgium) 2013, *IMPAKT breast cancer conference* Brussels (Belgium) 2012. **Publications** *European Journal of Cancer*. Information Services: Database containing personal and professional information of all registered members.
Members Experts interested in breast cancer care. Individuals in 51 countries and territories:
Argentina, Australia, Austria, Belgium, Brazil, Canada, Croatia, Cuba, Cyprus, Czechia, Denmark, Finland, France, Germany, Greece, Hong Kong, Hungary, Iceland, Iran Islamic Rep, Ireland, Italy, Japan, Lebanon, Malta, Netherlands, Norway, Poland, Portugal, Romania, Russia, Serbia, Slovakia, Slovenia, South Africa, Spain, Sweden, Switzerland, Türkiye, UK, USA.
NGO Relations Member of (1): *European Breast Cancer Council (EBCC, #06400)*. Cooperates with (5): *Europa Donna – The European Breast Cancer Coalition (#05745)*; *European Cancer Organisation (ECO, #06432)*; *European Organisation for Research and Treatment of Cancer (EORTC, #08101)* (Breast Cancer Group); *European School of Oncology (ESO, #08434)*; *European Society of Surgical Oncology (ESSO, #08753)*. [2020/XD2239/v/D]

♦ **European Society of Breast Imaging (EUSOBI)** **08535**
Secretariat Am Gestade 1, 1010 Vienna, Austria. T. +4315334064912. E-mail: office@eusobi.org.
URL: http://www.eusobi.org/
History Registration: No/ID: 841807386, Austria. **Aims** Promote high quality and the setting of standards, interest in the advancement of breast imaging as well as the teaching and furtherance of the study of the normal and abnormal breast, with emphasis on the integration of *roentgenology*, *ultrasonography*, magnetic resonance, computed tomography, nuclear medicine and any new imaging techniques as well as research on contrast media; further European research and education within the field of breast imaging; represent European breast imaging interests with public authorities, both nationally and internationally. **Structure** General Assembly (annual); Executive Board. Committees (4): Educational; Scientific; International Relations; EUSOBI Young Club. Secretariat in Vienna (Austria). **Finance** Members' dues (annual): euro 40. Other sources: proceeds from scientific meetings, workshops and enterprises owned by the society; donations; legacies. **Activities** Training/education; events/meetings; knowledge management/information dissemination. **Events** *Congress* Valencia (Spain) 2023, *Congress* Malmö (Sweden) 2022, *Congress* Vienna (Austria) 2021, *Congress* Malmö (Sweden) 2020, *Congress* Budapest (Hungary) 2019.
Members Active European radiologists; Associate; Corporate; Fellows; Honorary. Members in 33 countries and territories:
Austria, Belgium, Bosnia-Herzegovina, Brazil, Croatia, Czechia, Denmark, Estonia, Finland, France, Germany, Greece, Hong Kong, Ireland, Israel, Italy, Lebanon, Lithuania, Luxembourg, Montenegro, Netherlands, Norway, Poland, Portugal, Serbia, Slovenia, Spain, Sweden, Switzerland, Syrian AR, Türkiye, Ukraine, USA.
NGO Relations Member of: *European Cancer Organisation (ECO, #06432)*; *European Society of Radiology (ESR, #08720)*. [2020/XD7431/D]

♦ European Society of Cardiac Imaging / see European Society of Cardiovascular Radiology (#08538)
♦ European Society of Cardiac Radiology / see European Society of Cardiovascular Radiology (#08538)

♦ **European Society of Cardiology (ESC)** **08536**
Société Européenne de Cardiologie (SEC)
CEO 2035 route des Colles, CS 80179 Biot, Les Templiers, 06903 Sophia Antipolis CEDEX, France. T. +33492947600. Fax +33492947601. E-mail: mxímeris@escardio.org – escboard@escardio.org.
European Heart Agency 29 square de Meeus, 4th Floor, 1000 Brussels, Belgium.
URL: http://www.escardio.org/
History 2 Sep 1950, Paris (France). Registration: EU Transparency Register, No/ID: 01150446981-34, Start date: 20 Oct 2011. **Aims** Foster the development of cardiology; further scientific exchanges; encourage personal contacts; establish standards of training for cardiologists and those who work in the field of cardiovascular disease; improve the quality of life of the European population by reducing the impact of cardiovascular disease. **Structure** General Assembly (annual); Board; Management Group. Associations (6): Acute Cardiovascular Care Association (ACCA); *European Association of Cardiovascular Imaging (EACVI, see: #08536)*; *European Association of Preventive Cardiology (EAPC, #06164)*; *Heart Failure Association of the ESC (#10898)*; *European Association of Percutaneous Cardiovascular Interventions (EAPCI, #06147)*; *European Heart Rhythm Association (EHRA, #07468)*. Councils (5); Working Groups (15); ESC Fellowship; Offices located at *European Heart House (see: #08536)*, which acts as ESC headquarters. **Languages** English. **Staff** 122.00 FTE, paid. **Finance** Members' dues. Returns on activities. **Activities** Advocacy/lobbying/activism; events/meetings; research/documentation; standards/guidelines; training/education. **Events** *Annual Congress* Madrid (Spain) 2025, *Annual Congress* London (UK) 2024, *Annual Congress* Amsterdam (Netherlands) 2023, *Congress* Barcelona (Spain) 2022, *EuroThrombosis and EuroVessels Summit* Lisbon (Portugal) 2022. **Publications** *EP Europace* (12 a year); *European Heart Journal – Cardiovascular Imaging* (12 a year); *European Journal of Heart Failure* (12 a year); *European Journal of Cardiovascular Prevention and Rehabilitation* (6 a year); *European Journal of Cardiovascular Nursing* (4 a year); *Cardiovascular Research* (14 a year) – journal; *European Heart Journal* (24 a year).
Members National societies (56); Individuals: members of Associations, Working Groups, Councils, Fellows (around 70,000) in 56 countries:
Albania, Algeria, Armenia, Austria, Azerbaijan, Belarus, Belgium, Bosnia-Herzegovina, Bulgaria, Croatia, Cyprus, Czechia, Denmark, Egypt, Estonia, Finland, France, Georgia, Germany, Greece, Hungary, Iceland, Ireland, Israel, Italy, Kazakhstan, Kosovo, Kyrgyzstan, Latvia, Lebanon, Libya, Lithuania, Luxembourg, Malta, Moldova, Montenegro, Morocco, Netherlands, North Macedonia, Norway, Poland, Portugal, Romania, Russia, San Marino, Serbia, Slovakia, Slovenia, Spain, Sweden, Switzerland, Syrian AR, Tunisia, Türkiye, UK, Ukraine.
Affiliated organizations (39) in 38 countries and territories:
Argentina, Australia, Bangladesh, Brazil, Canada, Chile, China, Colombia, Costa Rica, Cuba, Ecuador, Guatemala, Hong Kong, India, Indonesia, Iran Islamic Rep, Iraq, Japan, Jordan, Korea Rep, Macau, Malaysia, Mexico, New Zealand, Oman, Pakistan, Panama, Paraguay, Peru, Saudi Arabia, Singapore, South Africa, Sudan, Taiwan, Thailand, Uruguay, Venezuela, Vietnam.
Regional affiliates (2):
Caribbean Cardiac Society (CCS, #03467); *Gulf Heart Association (GHA, #10831)*.
IGO Relations *WHO Regional Office for Europe (#20945)*. **NGO Relations** Member of (9): *Association of Learned and Professional Society Publishers (ALPSP, #02786)*; *Associations and Conference Forum (AC Forum, #02909)* (Founding); *Biomedical Alliance in Europe (#03251)*; *Council for International Organizations of Medical Sciences (CIOMS, #04905)* (Associate); *European Alliance for Cardiovascular Health (EACH, #05863)*; *European Alliance for Personalised Medicine (EAPM, #05878)*; *European Chronic Disease Alliance (ECDA, #06548)*; *The NCD Alliance (NCDA, #16963)*; *World Heart Federation (WHF, #21562)*. Stakeholder in: *European Network for Health Technology Assessment (EUnetHTA, #07921)*. Represented on: *European Board for Accreditation in Cardiology (EBAC, #06353)*; *European Resuscitation Council (ERC, #08385)*. Together with *European Association of Nuclear Medicine (EANM, #06136)*, set up: *European Council of Nuclear Cardiology (ECNC, inactive)*. Together with: *European Union of Medical Specialists (UEMS, #09001)*, created *European Board for the Specialty of Cardiology (EBSC, inactive)*. [2022/XD0859/D]

♦ **European Society for Cardiovascular and Endovascular Surgery (ESCVS)** **08537**
Société européenne de chirurgie cardiovasculaire et endovasculaire – Europäische Vereinigung für Kardiovaskuläre und Endovaskuläre Chirurgie
Gen Sec Hufelandstrasse 55, 45147 Essen, Germany. T. +4920172384927. Fax +4920172236800. E-mail: secretary@escvs.com.
Registered Office Bonin Uffer Rechtsanwälte, Dufourstrasse 32, 8008 Zurich ZH, Switzerland.
URL: http://www.escvs.com/
History 31 May 1951, Turin (Italy). Founded by René Leriche, as European Chapter of *International Society for Vascular Specialists (ISVS, inactive)*. Former names and other names: *European Society for Cardiovascular Surgery (ESCVS)* – former (1951); *Société européenne de chirurgie cardiovasculaire* – former (1951); *Europäische Vereinigung für Herz- und Gefässchirurgie* – former (1951). **Aims** Promote investigation and study of the art, science and therapy of cardiovascular diseases, coordinate this knowledge and disseminate it; facilitate exchange of ideas in the field of cardiovascular diseases through meetings and by personal contacts among cardiovascular specialists. **Structure** General Assembly (annual); Executive Committee; National Delegates' Committee; Cardiac and Vascular Programme Committees. **Languages** English. **Staff** Voluntary. **Finance** Individual subscriptions. Annual budget: US$ 30,000. **Activities** Events/meetings. **Events** *ESCVS International Congress* Liège (Belgium) 2022, *ESCVS International Congress* Essen (Germany) 2021, *Annual European Congress* Groningen (Netherlands) 2019, *Annual European Congress* Strasbourg (France) 2018, *Annual European Congress* Thessaloniki (Greece) 2017. **Publications** *Cardiovascular Surgery* (1993) – journal (1993); *Journal of Cardiovascular Surgery* – journal (to Dec 1992).
Members National Delegates in 27 countries. Individuals: Active; Senior (over 65 years old); Junior; Honorary. Members in 38 countries:
Austria, Belgium, Bosnia-Herzegovina, Bulgaria, Croatia, Cyprus, Czechia, Denmark, Estonia, Finland, France, Germany, Greece, Hungary, Ireland, Italy, Korea Rep, Latvia, Lebanon, Lithuania, Luxembourg, Monaco, Netherlands, North Macedonia, Norway, Peru, Poland, Portugal, Romania, Russia, Serbia, Slovenia, Spain, Sweden, Switzerland, Türkiye, UK, Ukraine.
NGO Relations Together with: *European Association for Cardio-Thoracic Surgery (EACTS, #05964)* and *European Society of Thoracic Surgeons (ESTS, #08760)*, set up: *European Board of Cardiothoracic Surgery (EBCTS, #06355)*; *European Cardiovascular and Thoracic Surgery Institute of Accreditation (ECTSIA, #06450)*; *European School of Cardio-Thoracic Surgery (ESCTS)*. [2021/XD0860/D]

♦ **European Society of Cardiovascular Radiology (ESCR)** **08538**
Pres Am Gestade 1, 1010 Vienna, Austria. T. +43153340664909. E-mail: office@escr.org.
URL: http://www.escr.org/
History Founded 1999 as *European Society of Cardiac Radiology (ESCR)* – *European Society of Cardiac Imaging*. **Aims** Promote and coordinate scientific, philanthropic, intellectual and professional activities of cardiac radiology. **Structure** Annual Scientific Meeting. **Languages** English. **Activities** Events/meetings. **Events** *Annual Scientific Meeting on Cardiac Imaging* Antwerp (Belgium) 2019, *Annual Scientific Meeting on Cardiac Imaging* Geneva (Switzerland) 2018, *Joint Congress* Geneva (Switzerland) 2018, *Annual Scientific Meeting on Cardiac Imaging* Milan (Italy) 2017, *Annual Scientific Meeting on Cardiac Imaging* Krakow (Poland) 2016. **Members** Full; Full – Nuclear Medicine; Corresponding; Associate; Resident; Corporate; Honorary. Members in 82 countries. Membership countries not specified. **NGO Relations** Member of: *European Society of Radiology (ESR, #08720)*. [2019.07.02/XD1628/v/D]

♦ European Society of Cardio-Vascular Radiology and Interventional Radiology (inactive)
♦ European Society for Cardiovascular Surgery / see European Society for Cardiovascular and Endovascular Surgery (#08537)

♦ **European Society of Cataract and Refractive Surgeons (ESCRS)** ... **08539**
Société européenne de la cataracte et chirurgie réfractive
Dir Temple House, Temple Road, Blackrock, Dublin, CO. DUBLIN, A94 Y5W5, Ireland. T. +35312091100. Fax +35312091112. E-mail: escrs@escrs.org.
URL: http://www.escrs.org/
History 1981. Formal society created in 1987. Former names and other names: *European Intraocular Implantlens Council (EIIC)* – former (1981 to 1987); *European Refractive Surgery Society (ERSS)* – alias; *European Intraocular Implant Club* – former. **Aims** Promote education and research in the field of implant and refractive surgery; advance and promote the study and practice of ophthalmology. **Structure** Board. **Languages** English. **Staff** 25.00 FTE, paid. **Finance** Members' dues. **Activities** Events/meetings. **Events** *Annual Congress* Milan (Italy) 2022, *Annual Congress* Amsterdam (Netherlands) 2021, *Winter Meeting* Krakow (Poland) 2021, *Annual Congress* Dublin (Ireland) 2020, *Winter Meeting* Marrakech (Morocco) 2020. **Publications** *Journal of Cataract and Refractive Surgery* (12 a year); *Euro Times* (11 a year). **Members** Full; Trainee. Members in over 124 countries and territories. Membership countries not specified. **NGO Relations** Member of (1): *European Alliance for Vision Research and Ophthalmology (EU-EYE, #05890)*. Instrumental in setting up (1): *European Society of Ophthalmic Nurses and Technicians (ESONT, #08672)*. [2021/XF1225/D]

♦ **European Society for Catholic Theology (ET)** **08540**
Association européenne de théologie catholique (AETC) – Asociación Europea de Teología Católica – Europäische Gesellschaft für Katholische Theologie
SG KU Leuven, Sint-Michielsstraat 6, Box 3101, 3000 Leuven, Belgium. T. +3216324557.
URL: http://www.eurotheo.eu/
History 1 Dec 1989, Tübingen (Germany FR). **Aims** Promote theology and theological research in Europe; strengthen communication between European theologians; reflect on the meaning of Christian faith and faith communities. **Structure** General Assembly. Executive Committee, comprising President, 2 Vice-Presidents, Secretary, Treasurer and Coordinator. **Languages** English, French, German, Italian. **Staff** 1050.00 FTE, paid. **Finance** Members' dues. Donations. **Activities** Organizes congresses and seminars. **Events** *Congress* Osnabrück (Germany) 2021, *Symposium* Vienna (Austria) 2020, *International Congress* Bratislava (Slovakia) 2019, *International Congress* Bressanone (Italy) 2013, *Congress* Vienna (Austria) 2011. **Publications** *European Society for Catholic Theology Bulletin* (2 a year); *Bulletin ET*.
Members Individuals in 25 countries:
Australia, Austria, Belgium, Bosnia-Herzegovina, Croatia, Czechia, France, Germany, Hungary, Ireland, Italy, Malta, Netherlands, Norway, Poland, Portugal, Romania, Russia, Serbia, Slovakia, Slovenia, Spain, Switzerland, UK, USA.
NGO Relations Member of: *International Network of Societies for Catholic Theology (INSeCT, #14328)*. [2022/XD6197/v/D]

♦ European Society for Central Asian Studies (ESCAS) 08541

Permanent Secretariat c/o TCMO Leiden Univ, Witte Singel 25, PO Box 9515, 2300 RA Leiden, Netherlands.
Sec address not obtained.
URL: http://www.escas.org/

History 1985, Utrecht (Netherlands). **Aims** Give Central Asian studies status as a research field in its own right; promote joint research and interdisciplinary studies among European scholars of Central Asia; re-establish research links with disciplines working in adjacent areas; create opportunities for direct cooperation between scholars of the former Soviet Central Asia and those in adjacent areas. **Activities** Initiates and coordinates: research, workshops and conferences; data bases; library facilities; fund raising. Set up: *Anthropological Network on Central Asia (no recent information)*. **Events** *Biennial Conference* Exeter (UK) 2019, *Conference* Zurich (Switzerland) 2015, *Biennial Conference / Conference* Astana (Kazakhstan) 2013, *Conference* Cambridge (UK) 2011, *Conference* Budapest (Hungary) 2009.
Members Full in 29 countries:
Azerbaijan, Belgium, China, Denmark, Finland, France, Germany, Hungary, India, Indonesia, Iran Islamic Rep, Israel, Italy, Japan, Kazakhstan, Kyrgyzstan, Mongolia, Netherlands, Norway, Pakistan, Poland, Russia, Sweden, Tajikistan, Türkiye, Turkmenistan, UK, USA, Uzbekistan. [2020/XD5097/**D**]

♦ European Society of Chartered Surveyors / see RICS Europe (#18939)

♦ European Society of Chemotherapy – Infectious Diseases (ESC) 08542

SG Dept of Infectious Diseases and Chemotherapy, Univ of Vienna, Währinger Gürtel 18-20, 1090 Vienna, Austria. T. +431404005139. Fax +431404005167.

History 1992, Vienna (Austria). **Aims** Represent a European Forum for all researchers, scientists and clinicians to exchange ideas, innovative projects and results of all disciplines related to the field of chemotherapy and infectious diseases. **Structure** Board of Directors, comprising President, Past-President, Secretary-General, Treasurer and 17 members. **Languages** English. **Events** *Scientific meeting* Vienna (Austria) 2010, *Scientific meeting* Vienna (Austria) 2008, *Scientific meeting* Aachen (Germany) 2006, *Scientific meeting* Moscow (Russia) 2004, *Scientific meeting* Vienna (Austria) 2003. **Publications** *Infection* – journal. [2012.06.01/XM3859/**D**]

♦ European Society of Child and Adolescent Psychiatry (ESCAP) 08543

Société européenne de psychiatrie de l'enfant et de l'adolescent – Europäische Gesellschaft für Kinder- und Jugendpsychiatrie
Secretariat 24 Kerasountos str, 157 71 Zografou, Greece. E-mail: info@hscap.gr – info@escap.eu.
URL: http://www.escap.eu/

History First meeting Oct 1954, Magglingen (Switzerland). Several conferences held until officially founded in 1960, Paris (France), during the first congress 16-19 Sep 1960. Former names and other names: *Union of European Paedopsychiatrists* – former (1954 to 1982); *Union européenne de pédopsychiatres (UEP)* – former (1954 to 1982); *Union Europäischer Kinderpsychiater* – former (1954 to 1982); *European Association for Child and Adolescent Psychiatry* – former (1982 to 1983). Registration: Switzerland. **Aims** Promote mental health of children and adolescents in Europe; increase quality of life among children and families; ensure children's right for healthy development and wellbeing. **Structure** Assembly; Board; Divisions (3); Bylaws Working Group. **Languages** English. **Staff** None. **Finance** Members' dues. Congresses proceedings. **Activities** Events/meetings; training/education; knowledge management/information dissemination; politics/policy/regulatory. **Events** *International Congress* Copenhagen (Denmark) 2023, *International Congress* Maastricht (Netherlands) 2022, *International Congress* Maastricht (Netherlands) 2021, *International Congress* Vienna (Austria) 2019, *International Congress* Geneva (Switzerland) 2017. **Publications** *ECAP – European Child and Adolescent Psychiatry* (12 a year).
Members National organizations; individuals. Members in 30 countries:
Austria, Belgium, Bulgaria, Croatia, Cyprus, Denmark, Estonia, Finland, France, Germany, Greece, Hungary, Iceland, Ireland, Italy, Lithuania, Netherlands, Norway, Poland, Portugal, Romania, Russia, Serbia, Slovenia, Spain, Sweden, Switzerland, Türkiye, UK, Ukraine.
IGO Relations *UNCTAD (#20285)*. [2021/XD0881/**D**]

♦ European Society for Children's Radiology / see European Society of Paediatric Radiology (#08686)
♦ European Society of Chlamydia Research (no recent information)
♦ European Society for Chromatophonics (inactive)
♦ European Society of Chronobiology (no recent information)
♦ European Society for Classical Natural Medicine (no recent information)
♦ European Society of Climatotherapy (inactive)

♦ European Society for Clinical Cell Analysis (ESCCA) 08544

Pres c/o EEKX, Alopeki 47, 1 Stock, 106 76 Athens, Greece.
Sec UniMi – Immunology, Via Festa del Perdono 7, 20122 Milan MI, Italy.
URL: http://www.escca.eu/

History Founded 1996, as *European Working Group on Clinical Cell Analysis (EWGCCA)*. Current title adopted, 2007. **Aims** Foster development, standardization and implementation of clinical applications of cell analysis in the diagnosis and management of human pathologic conditions. **Structure** Annual Meeting (in September), in conjunction with EuroCourse and Euroconference; Board; Committees (6). **Languages** English. **Staff** None. **Finance** Members' dues. Other sources: local authorities and industrial sponsors; proceeds from meeting organization. **Activities** Events/meetings; training/education; standards/guidelines. **Events** *Conference* Vilnius (Lithuania) 2023, *Conference* Belfast (UK) 2022, *Conference* Athens (Greece) 2021, *Conference* Vilnius (Lithuania) 2020, *Conference* Bergen (Norway) 2019. **Publications** *Clinical Cytometry Part B* (6 a year).
Members in Europe, South America, Africa, Middle East. Membership countries not specified. International organizations (3):
International organizations (3):
European Cytometry Network; *International Clinical Cytometry Society (ICCS)*; *International Society for Advancement of Cytometry (ISAC, #14900)*. [2019/XJ0748/y/**D**]

♦ European Society for Clinical and Economic Aspects of Osteoporosis and Osteoarthritis / see European Society for Clinical and Economic Aspects of Osteoporosis, Osteoarthritis and Musculoskeletal Diseases (#08545)

♦ European Society for Clinical and Economic Aspects of Osteoporosis, Osteoarthritis and Musculoskeletal Diseases (ESCEO) 08545

Pres Quai Godefroid Kurth 13B, 4020 Liège, Belgium. T. +3243443769. Fax +3243412314. E-mail: esceoasbl@skynet.be.
URL: http://www.esceo.org/

History Former names and other names: *European Society for Clinical and Economic Aspects of Osteoporosis and Osteoarthritis (ESCEO)* – former. **Aims** Provide practitioners with the latest clinical and economic information in the field. **Languages** English, French. **Activities** Events/meetings. **Events** *World Congress on Osteoporosis, Osteoarthritis and Musculoskeletal Diseases* London (UK) 2024, *World Congress on Osteoporosis, Osteoarthritis and Musculoskeletal Diseases* Barcelona (Spain) 2023, *World Congress on Osteoporosis, Osteoarthritis and Musculoskeletal Diseases* 2022, *World Congress on Osteoporosis, Osteoarthritis and Musculoskeletal Diseases* 2021, *World Congress on Osteoporosis, Osteoarthritis and Musculoskeletal Diseases* Barcelona (Spain) 2020. [2022.05.12/XM2603/**D**]

♦ European Society of Clinical Hemorheology / see European Society for Clinical Hemorheology and Microcirculation (#08546)

♦ European Society for Clinical Hemorheology and Microcirculation (ESCHM) 08546

Pres 2 Meidzinische Klinik, Universitätsmedizin Mainz, Langenbeckstrasse 1, 55131 Mainz, Germany. T. +496131176903. Fax +496131176428.
URL: http://www.unisi.it/ricerca/asso/esch/

History Founded 1993, Frankfurt-Main (Germany), as *European Society of Clinical Hemorheology (ESCH)*. Succeeds *European Coordinating Committee for Clinical Haemorheology (ECCCH)*, founded 1979. **Aims** Advance the science and art of clinical haemorheology and clinical micro- and macro-circulation through research, education and nurturing haemorheological knowledge into clinical practice. **Structure** Council; Advisory Committee. **Languages** English. **Staff** None. **Finance** No funds of its own. Meeting expenses sustained by each national society or group. **Activities** Events/meetings; training/education. **Events** *Biennial Conference* Lisbon (Portugal) 2016, *Biennial Conference* Pécs (Hungary) 2013, *Biennial Conference* Munich (Germany) 2011, *Biennial Conference* Pontresina (Switzerland) 2009, *Biennial Conference* St Moritz (Switzerland) 2009. **Publications** *Clinical Hemorheology and Microcirculation* (12 a year) – official journal. Conference proceedings.
Members Organizations in 21 countries:
Austria, Bulgaria, Cyprus, Czechia, Denmark, Finland, France, Georgia, Greece, Hungary, Ireland, Italy, Netherlands, Poland, Portugal, Romania, Russia, Spain, Sweden, Türkiye, UK. [2016/XD9115/**D**]

♦ European Society for Clinical Investigation (ESCI) 08547

Manager Bolognalaan 34, 3584 CJ Utrecht, Netherlands. T. +31887558787. Fax +31302515724. E-mail: esci@umcutrecht.nl.
URL: http://www.esci.eu.com/

History Founded Feb 1967, Noordwijk (Netherlands). **Aims** Integrate clinicians and scientists with a genuine interest in uncovering the mechanism of *disease*; provide a forum for discussion, debate and meeting colleagues in order to further the science of clinical investigation. **Structure** Annual Scientific Meeting; Council. **Languages** English. **Staff** 1.00 FTE, paid. **Finance** Members' dues. **Activities** Events/meetings; financial and/or material support; awards/prizes/competitions; training/education. **Events** *Annual Scientific Meeting* Coimbra (Portugal) 2019, *Annual Scientific Meeting* Barcelona (Spain) 2018, *Annual Scientific Meeting* Genoa (Italy) 2017, *Annual Scientific Meeting* Paris (France) 2016, *Annual Scientific Meeting* Cluj-Napoca (Romania) 2015. **Publications** *European Journal of Clinical Investigation* (12 a year).
Members Corporate; individual. Individuals (about 300) in 33 countries and territories:
Austria, Belarus, Belgium, Brazil, Canada, Croatia, Czechia, Denmark, Finland, France, Germany, Greece, Hungary, Iceland, Ireland, Israel, Italy, Japan, Luxembourg, Netherlands, Poland, Portugal, Romania, Russia, Serbia, Slovakia, Spain, Sweden, Switzerland, Taiwan, UK, Ukraine, United Arab Emirates, USA. [2019.06.26/XD0851/**D**]

♦ European Society of Clinical Microbiology / see European Society of Clinical Microbiology and Infectious Diseases (#08548)

♦ European Society of Clinical Microbiology and Infectious Diseases (ESCMID) 08548

Société européenne de microbiologie clinique et des maladies infectieuses
Main Office PO Box 214, 4010 Basel BS, Switzerland. T. +41615080153. Fax +41615080151. E-mail: info@escmid.org.
Street address Streitgasse 20, 4051 Basel BS, Switzerland.
URL: http://www.escmid.org/

History 1983. Former names and other names: *European Society of Clinical Microbiology (ESCM)* – former. Registration: Civil Code, Switzerland. **Aims** Promote and support research, education, training and good medical practice to improve diagnosis, treatment and prevention of infection-related diseases. **Structure** General Assembly of Members (annual); Executive Committee; Ad-hoc Executive Committee; Executive Office; Study Groups; Subcommittees. **Languages** English. **Staff** 7.00 FTE, paid. **Finance** Sources: meeting proceeds; members' dues. **Activities** Awards/prizes/competitions; events/meetings; financial and/or material support; training/education. **Events** *European Congress of Clinical Microbiology and Infectious Diseases* Barcelona (Spain) 2024, *European Congress of Clinical Microbiology and Infectious Diseases* Copenhagen (Denmark) 2023, *International Meeting on Microbial Epidemiological Markers* Bath (UK) 2022, *European Congress of Clinical Microbiology and Infectious Diseases* Lisbon (Portugal) 2022, *European Congress of Clinical Microbiology and Infectious Diseases* Vienna (Austria) 2021. **Publications** *Clinical Microbiology and Infection* (12 a year); *ESCMID Newsletter*; *ESCMID Yearbook*; *European Manual of Clinical Microbiology*.
Members Full; Affiliated; Associate; Corporate; Honorary. Individuals (6,000) in over 100 countries and territories. Membership countries not specified. **IGO Relations** *European Centre for Disease Prevention and Control (ECDC, #06476)*. **NGO Relations** Member of (1): *Biomedical Alliance in Europe (#03251)*. Instrumental in setting up (1): *European Committee on Antimicrobial Susceptibility Testing (EUCAST, #06642)*. [2020/XD1672/**D**]

♦ European Society for Clinical Neuropharmacology (ESCNP) 08549

Pres Dept of Neurosciences, Faculty of Medicine, Iuliu Hatieganu University of Medicine and Pharmacy, Strada Victor Babes 43, 400347 Cluj-Napoca, Romania. E-mail: office@escnp.org.
SG Dept of Pharmacology, toxicology and clinical pharmacology, Iuliu Haieganu University of Medicine and Pharmacy, Strada Gheorghe Marinescu 23, 400394 Cluj-Napoca, Romania.
URL: https://escnp.org/

History Mar 1983, Vienna (Austria). Former names and other names: *European Association for Clinical Neuropharmacology* – former (1983 to 1994). **Aims** Contribute to progress in the field of clinical neuropharmacology, at the scientific and educational levels, with full independence from industrial and pharmaceutical influences. **Structure** Board. **Languages** English. **Staff** 1.00 FTE, paid. 1. **Activities** Events/meetings; standards/guidelines. **Events** *Congress* Madrid (Spain) 2019, *Congress* Warsaw (Poland) 2018, *Congress* Athens (Greece) 2017, *Congress* Cluj-Napoca (Romania) 2015, *Congress* Athens (Greece) 2014. **Publications** *Journal of Neural Transmission*.
Members Individuals in 17 countries:
Austria, Croatia, Czechia, Germany, Hungary, Israel, Italy, Netherlands, Norway, Poland, Romania, Russia, Slovakia, Sweden, Switzerland, Türkiye, UK. [2019/XD7655/v/**D**]

♦ European Society for Clinical Nutrition and Metabolism (ESPEN) 08550

Secretariat Rue de Muhlenbach 121, L-2168 Luxembourg, Luxembourg. E-mail: gen.secretary@espen.org.
URL: http://www.espen.org/

History 1980, Newcastle upon Tyne (UK). Foundations laid at first ESPEN meeting, 1979 Stockholm (Sweden). Former names and other names: *European Society of Parenteral Nutrition (ESPN)* – former (1980); *European Society of Parenteral and Enteral Nutrition* – former; *Société européenne d'alimentation parentérale et entérale* – former. Registration: No/ID: F.8909, Luxembourg. **Aims** Study metabolic problems associated with acute diseases and their nutritional implications and management. **Structure** Council; Executive Committee; Committees (2). **Languages** English. **Staff** 1.00 FTE, paid. **Finance** Sources: meeting proceeds; members' dues. Annual budget: 800,000 EUR. **Activities** Events/meetings; publishing activities; research/documentation; standards/guidelines; training/education. **Events** *Symposium* Luxembourg (Luxembourg) 2021, *Congress* Milan (Italy) 2021, *Congress* Lyon (France) 2020, *Congress* Krakow (Poland) 2019, *Symposium on How to Best Assess Energy Requirements* Vienna (Austria) 2019. **Publications** *Clinical Nutrition* (6 a year) – with supplement; *e-SPEN* (6 a year); *Clinical Nutrition Experimental* – e-journal. Blue Book. Clinical guidelines.
Members Individuals (approx 3,500) in 65 countries and territories:
Argentina, Australia, Austria, Belgium, Bosnia-Herzegovina, Brazil, Bulgaria, Canada, Chile, China, Colombia, Costa Rica, Croatia, Cyprus, Czechia, Denmark, Dominican Rep, Ecuador, Egypt, Estonia, Finland, France, Germany, Greece, Hong Kong, Hungary, India, Indonesia, Iran Islamic Rep, Ireland, Israel, Italy, Japan, Korea Rep, Kyrgyzstan, Latvia, Lithuania, Malaysia, Mexico, Netherlands, New Zealand, North Macedonia, Norway, Peru, Philippines, Poland, Portugal, Romania, Russia, Saudi Arabia, Serbia, Singapore, Slovakia (Slovak Republic), Slovenia, South Africa, Spain, Sri Lanka, Sweden, Switzerland, Thailand, Türkiye, UK, Ukraine, Uruguay, USA.
NGO Relations Member of (3): *European Cancer Organisation (ECO, #06432)*; *European Nutrition for Health Alliance, The (ENHA, #08069)*; *United European Gastroenterology (UEG, #20506)*. Cooperates with (1): *Medical Nutrition International Industry (MNI, #16626)*. [2021.08.23/XD5624/v/**D**]

♦ European Society of Clinical Pharmacy (ESCP) 08551

Main Office Theda Mansholtstraat 5b, 2331 JE Leiden, Netherlands. T. +31715766157. Fax +31715722431. E-mail: international.office@escpweb.org.
URL: http://www.escpweb.org/

History 1979, Lyon (France). Founded during European Pharmacy Symposium. Statutes most recently revised 2009. Former names and other names: *European Clinical Pharmacists Association (ECPA)* – former alias. Registration: Chamber of Commerce, No/ID: 40532427, Netherlands. **Aims** Develop and promote rational and appropriate use of *drugs* and medical devices by individuals and by society; provide a forum for communication of new knowledge and developments in clinical pharmacy. **Structure** General Assembly (annual); General Committee; Executive Committee; Special Interest Groups (12). **Languages** English. **Staff** 1.00 FTE, paid. **Finance** Members' dues. Other sources: conference fees; sponsorship. **Activities** Events/meetings; certification/accreditation. **Events** *Annual Symposium* Aberdeen (UK) 2023, *Annual Symposium* Prague (Czechia) 2022, *Annual Symposium* Lisbon (Portugal) 2021, *International Workshop* Antwerp (Belgium) 2019, *Annual Symposium* Ljubljana (Slovenia) 2019. **Publications** *International Journal of Clinical Pharmacy (IJCP)* (6 a year); *ESCP Newsletter* (4 a year).
Members Ordinary; Honorary; Patron; Student. Members in 52 countries:
Australia, Austria, Belgium, Bosnia-Herzegovina, Canada, Chile, China, Croatia, Cyprus, Czechia, Denmark, Egypt, Estonia, Finland, France, Germany, Greece, Hungary, Iceland, India, Indonesia, Ireland, Israel, Italy, Japan, Latvia, Libya, Luxembourg, Malaysia, Malta, Netherlands, New Zealand, Nigeria, Norway, Philippines, Poland, Portugal, Qatar, Romania, Saudi Arabia, Singapore, Slovakia, Slovenia, South Africa, Spain, Sweden, Switzerland, Türkiye, UK, Ukraine, United Arab Emirates, USA.
[2022/XD2221/v/D]

♦ European Society for Clinical Respiratory Physiology (inactive)

♦ European Society for Clinical Virology (ESCV) 08552

Secretariat Calle Eraso 36 – 2°, 28028 Madrid, Spain. T. +34913612600. E-mail: secretariat.escv@kenes.com.
Sec Manchester Royal Infirmary, Virology – 3rd floor – CSB, MRI, Oxford Road, Manchester, M13 9WL, UK.
URL: http://www.escv.org/
History 1 Jan 1997. Founded on merger of *European Society Against Virus Diseases (inactive)* and *European Group for Rapid Laboratory Viral Diagnosis (inactive).* **Aims** Act as a forum for clinical and diagnostic virology in Europe; work on laboratory standards and quality control; promote knowledge of viruses, particularly as it relates to the clinical diagnosis and management of viral diseases, their pathogenesis, natural history, treatment and prevention; gather and distribute information on methods and other relevant problems. **Structure** Council (meets annually); Executive. **Languages** English. **Staff** Voluntary. **Finance** Sources: members' dues. **Activities** Awards/prizes/competitions; events/meetings; projects/programmes. **Events** *Annual Conference* Manchester (UK) 2021, *Annual Conference* Manchester (UK) 2020, *Annual World Meeting* Copenhagen (Denmark) 2019, *Annual World Meeting* Athens (Greece) 2018, *Annual World Meeting* Stresa (Italy) 2017. **Publications** *ESCV Newsletter* (2 a year) – online; *Journal of Clinical Virology.*
Members Individuals in 47 countries and territories:
Algeria, Argentina, Australia, Austria, Belarus, Belgium, Brazil, Bulgaria, Canada, Colombia, Croatia, Czechia, Denmark, Egypt, Estonia, Finland, France, Germany, Greece, Hong Kong, Hungary, Iceland, India, Ireland, Israel, Italy, Japan, Latvia, Lithuania, Luxembourg, Netherlands, Norway, Poland, Portugal, Romania, Russia, Serbia, Slovakia, Slovenia, South Africa, Spain, Sweden, Switzerland, Türkiye, UK, Ukraine, USA.
NGO Relations Associate member of: *International Union of Microbiological Societies (IUMS, #15794).* Member of: *Federation of European Microbiological Societies (FEMS, #09516).* [2021/XD5653/v/D]

♦ European Society for Cognitive and Affective Neuroscience (ESCAN) 08553

Sec address not obtained. E-mail: escan@escaneurosci.eu.
URL: https://escaneurosci.eu/
History 9 Jul 2010, Amsterdam (Netherlands). Registration: Netherlands. **Aims** Promote scientific enquiry within the field of human cognitive, affective and social neuroscience, particularly with respect to collaboration and exchange of information between researchers in different European countries. **Structure** Board. **Activities** Awards/prizes/competitions; events/meetings; training/education. **Events** *Meeting* Vienna (Austria) 2022, *International Conference* Budapest (Hungary) 2021, *International Conference* Budapest (Hungary) 2020, *International Conference* Leiden (Netherlands) 2018, *International Conference* Porto (Portugal) 2016.
[2022/AA2479/D]

♦ European Society for Cognitive Psychology (ESCoP) 08554

Sec Univ of Geneva, Fac of Psychology and Educational Sciences, Bd du Pont d'Arve 40, 1205 Geneva, Switzerland.
URL: http://www.escop.eu/
History Founded Sep 1985, Nijmegen (Netherlands). Registered in accordance with Dutch law as a foundation. **Aims** Promote cognitive psychology within Europe and foster working relationships between European scientists in the field. **Languages** English. **Staff** 2.00 FTE, voluntary. **Finance** Members' dues. **Activities** Events/meetings. **Events** *Conference* Porto (Portugal) 2023, *Conference* Lille (France) 2022, *Conference* Santa Cruz de Tenerife (Spain) 2019, *Conference* Potsdam (Germany) 2017, *Conference* Paphos (Cyprus) 2015. **Publications** *European Society for Cognitive Psychology Newsletter*; *Journal of Cognitive Psychology.* Conference Book of Abstracts.
Members Individuals in 26 countries and territories:
Australia, Belgium, Bulgaria, Canada, Colombia, Cyprus, Denmark, Finland, France, Germany, Greece, Hungary, Israel, Italy, Netherlands, Poland, Portugal, Russia, Spain, Sweden, Switzerland, Taiwan, Türkiye, UK, Ukraine, USA.
[2018.04.24/XF0759/v/E]

♦ European Society for the Cognitive Sciences of Music (ESCOM) 08555

Association européenne pour les sciences cognitives de la musique
Pres c/o Ctr for Systematic Musicology, Glacisstr 27, 8010 Graz, Austria. E-mail: escom@escom.org.
Gen Sec c/o AIAS, Høegh-Guldbergs Gade 6B, 8000 Aarhus C, Denmark.
URL: https://www.escomsociety.org/
History 18 Dec 1990, Liège (Belgium). Statues modified: 17 Dec 1994; 12 Sep 2003; 23 Oct 2004. Registration: Banque-Carrefour des Entreprises, No/ID: 0447.525.138, Start date: 15 May 1992, Belgium. **Aims** Promote theoretical, experimental and applied research and education in perception and mental processes underlying musical experience and activity; develop and disseminate knowledge of musical perception and cognition and promote its practical application; encourage European communication and cooperation in musicology, theory of music, psychology, acoustics, neurophysiology, mathematics, artificial intelligence and other related domains. **Structure** General Assembly; Executive Council; Executive Committee. **Languages** English, French. **Staff** Voluntary. **Finance** Sources: members' dues. **Activities** Events/meetings. **Events** *Triennial Conference* Sheffield (UK) 2021, *Triennial Conference* Montréal, QC (Canada) 2018, *Expressive interaction with music* Ghent (Belgium) 2017, *Triennial Conference* Manchester (UK) 2015, *Conference on Interdisciplinary Musicology* Berlin (Germany) 2014. **Publications** *Musicae Scientiae* (2 a year). Special issues.
Members Individuals in 28 countries:
Australia, Austria, Belgium, Denmark, Estonia, Finland, France, Germany, Greece, Hungary, Ireland, Israel, Italy, Japan, Korea Rep, Lithuania, Netherlands, Norway, Poland, Portugal, Russia, Serbia, Slovakia, Spain, Sweden, Switzerland, Türkiye, UK.
NGO Relations Participating organization in: *International Conference on Music Perception and Cognition (ICMPC).* [2022/XD3226/v/D]

♦ European Society of Coloproctology (ESCP) 08556

Secretariat c/o Integrity Intl Events, The Coach House, 7 St Alban's Road, Edinburgh, EH9 2PA, UK. T. +441316246040. E-mail: info@escp.eu.com.
URL: http://www.escp.eu.com/
History 1 Jan 2006 by merger of *European Association of Coloproctology (EACP, inactive)* and *European Council of Coloproctology (ECCP, inactive).* Regional federation of *International Council of Coloproctology (ICCP, #13009).* **Aims** Further prevention, treatment, education and research into colorectal disease. **Structure** Council; Executive; Committee; Trustees; Secretariat based in Edinburgh (UK). **Languages** English. **Activities** Events/meetings; training/education; financial and/or material support. **Events** *Tripartite Colorectal Meeting* Auckland (New Zealand) 2022, *Annual Meeting* Dublin (Ireland) 2022, *Annual Meeting* 2021, *Tripartite Colorectal Meeting* Auckland (New Zealand) 2020, *Annual Meeting* Vilnius (Lithuania) 2020. **Publications** *European Manual of Medicine: Coloproctology.* **Members** Full in 80 countries. Membership countries not specified. **NGO Relations** Policy partner of: *Digestive Cancers Europe (DiCE, #05070).* Member of: *European Cancer Organisation (ECO, #06432)*; [2020/XJ4189/D]

♦ European Society for Communicative Psychotherapy (ESCP) 08557

Chair 106 Oaklands Avenue, Oxhey, Watford, WD19 4LW, UK.
History 1990, London (UK). **Aims** Further development of the communicative approach to psychotherapy and explore its wider implementation; encourage individuals to join who are interested in unconscious communication, concerns about the imbalance of power within the therapeutic relationship, as well as boundary issues in psychotherapy and other contexts. **Structure** Committee; Chair. **Languages** English. **Finance** Members' dues. Conference proceeds. **Activities** Organizes: annual conference; fora; meetings; training. **Events** *Annual Conference* London (UK) 2005. **Publications** Books; articles; essays.
Members Full in 10 countries:
Germany, Greece, Israel, Italy, Japan, Netherlands, Portugal, Spain, UK, USA.
NGO Relations Accredited by: *European Association for Psychotherapy (EAP, #06176).* [2010/XD4722/D]

♦ European Society for Comparative Endocrinology (ESCE) 08558

Société européenne d'endocrinologie comparée
Pres Ctr of Marine Sciences – Comparative Molecular Endocrinology, Univ of Algarve – Campus de Gambelas, 8005-139 Faro, Portugal.
SG Fac of Biology, Univ of Barcelona, Gran Via de les Corts Catalanes 585, 08007 Barcelona, Spain.
URL: http://www.escendo.info/
History 5 Aug 1965, Copenhagen (Denmark). **Aims** Promote interdisciplinary knowledge in all fields concerned with comparative endocrinology. **Structure** Business Meeting (every 2 years); Council; Officers. **Languages** English, French, German. **Staff** 0.50 FTE, voluntary. **Finance** Members' dues. **Activities** Financial and/or material support; awards/prizes/competitions. **Events** *Conference of European Comparative Endocrinologists (CECE) & International Symposium of Fish Endocrinology* Faro (Portugal) 2022, *Conference of European Comparative Endocrinologists (CECE)* Faro (Portugal) 2020, *Biennial Conference* Glasgow (UK) 2018, *Biennial Conference* Leuven (Belgium) 2016, *Biennial Conference* Rennes (France) 2014. **Publications** Conference papers.
Members Full; Honorary qualified investigators in comparative endocrinology and related fields. Individuals in 54 countries and territories:
Argentina, Australia, Austria, Belgium, Brazil, Bulgaria, Cameroon, Canada, Chile, China, Côte d'Ivoire, Czechia, Denmark, Egypt, Finland, France, Germany, Greece, Hong Kong, Hungary, India, Iran Islamic Rep, Ireland, Israel, Italy, Japan, Mexico, Montenegro, Morocco, Netherlands, Nigeria, Norway, Pakistan, Poland, Portugal, Romania, Russia, Serbia, Slovakia, South Africa, Spain, Sri Lanka, Sweden, Switzerland, Syrian AR, Tanzania UR, Tunisia, Türkiye, UK, Ukraine, Uruguay, USA, Uzbekistan, Venezuela.
NGO Relations Member of (2): *International Federation of Comparative Endocrinological Societies (IFCES, #13396)* (Scientific); *International Union of Biological Sciences (IUBS, #15760)* (Scientific). Cooperates with (1): *International Society for Fish Endocrinology (ISFE, #15121).* [2021/XD0852/v/D]

♦ European Society of Comparative Gastroenterology (ESCG) 08559

Address not obtained.
URL: http://www.escg.org.uk/
Events *Joint meeting on gastrointestinal tumours* Ghent (Belgium) 2008, *European endoscopic surgery week* Glasgow (UK) 2003. **Publications** *European Journal of Comparative Gastroenterology.* [2010/XD6908/D]

♦ European Society for Comparative Legal History (ESCLH) 08560

SG address not obtained. E-mail: esclhblog@gmail.com.
Registered Office c/ D'En Llop No 2, 4th floor, 10th door, 46002 Valencia, Spain.
URL: http://esclh.blogspot.com/
History 5 Dec 2009, The Hague (Netherlands). Registration: Spain. **Aims** Promote comparative legal history; seek affiliation with individuals and organizations with complementary aims. **Structure** Executive Council; Advisory Board. **Languages** English. **Staff** 5.00 FTE, voluntary. **Finance** Members' dues. Annual budget: about euro 3,000. **Events** *Conference* Augsburg (Germany) 2023, *Biennial Conference* Lisbon (Portugal) 2022, *Biennial Conference* Lisbon (Portugal) 2021, *Biennial Conference* Lisbon (Portugal) 2020, *Biennial Conference* Paris (France) 2018. **Publications** *Comparative Legal History: An International and Comparative Review of Law and History.*
Members Full in 18 countries:
Australia, Belgium, Denmark, Finland, France, Germany, Ireland, Italy, Latvia, Lithuania, Netherlands, Norway, Romania, Russia, Spain, Sweden, UK, USA.
NGO Relations Member of: *European Alliance for the Social Sciences and Humanities (EASSH, #05885).*
[2022/XJ2452/D]

♦ European Society of Comparative Literature (ESCL) 08561

Société Européenne de Littérature Comparée (SELC)
Coordinator Fac de Filologia, Univ Complutense Madrid, Plaza Menéndez Pelayo s/n, 28040 Madrid, Spain.
Office Bib Georges Ascoli, Univ Sorbonne, 1 rue Victor-Cousin, 75005 Paris, France.
URL: http://escl-selc.eu/
History 2001. Current statutes adopted 2017. Former names and other names: *European Network for Comparative Literary Studies (ENCLS)* – former; *Réseau Européen d'Etudes Littéraires Comparées (REELC)* – former. Registration: France. **Aims** Provide a European space for *interdisciplinary* dialogue on culture, literature and literary studies; facilitate exchange of ideas and information among scholars, promoting international collaborative research and teaching, generating relevant debates, enabling circulation of students and staff, and generally supporting and internationalizing the work of regional, national, cross-national associations of comparative literature. **Structure** General Assembly; Executive Committee. **Languages** English, French, Spanish. **Staff** 17.00 FTE, voluntary. **Finance** Sources: members' dues. Annual budget: 10,000 EUR (2020). **Activities** Events/meetings; networking/liaising. **Events** *Congress* Paris (France) 2024, *Biennial Congress* Rome (Italy) 2022, *Biennial Congress* Rome (Italy) 2021, *Biennial Congress* Lille (France) 2019, *Biennial Congress* Helsinki (Finland) 2017. **Publications** *ESCL Newsletter*; *Journal of the European Society of Comparative Literature (JESC).*
Members Full (over 650) in 45 countries and territories:
Algeria, Argentina, Austria, Bangladesh, Belgium, Bosnia-Herzegovina, Brazil, Bulgaria, Canada, Croatia, Denmark, Egypt, Finland, France, Germany, Greece, Hong Kong, Hungary, India, Ireland, Italy, Japan, Lithuania, Mexico, Netherlands, North Macedonia, Norway, Pakistan, Philippines, Poland, Portugal, Romania, Saudi Arabia, Serbia, Slovenia, Spain, Sweden, Switzerland, Taiwan, Thailand, Tunisia, Türkiye, UK, Ukraine, USA.
NGO Relations Member of (1): *European Alliance for the Social Sciences and Humanities (EASSH, #05885).*
[2021.06.10/XM6531/D]

♦ European Society for Comparative Physiology and Biochemistry (ESCPB) 08562

Société européenne de physiologie et de biochimie comparées
Contact IDAEA-CSIC, C Jordi Girona 18-26, 08034 Barcelona, Spain. T. +34934006100. Fax +34932045904.
Facebook: https://www.facebook.com/ESCPB-European-Society-for-Comparative-Biochemistry-and-Physiology-469263480270015/
History 1978, Liège (Belgium), by Professor R Gilles and M Florkin. Constitution adopted Mar 1978; modified 22 Jun 1979. Statutes registered in accordance with Belgian law. **Aims** Advance and promote research topics and concepts of biological studies using the comparative approach and the techniques of physiology, biochemistry and/or biophysics, including fundamental and applied aspects such as adaptations, environmental fitness, evolution, ecology, ethology, cell biology, marine biology, pharmacology, toxicology, parasitology and disease. **Structure** General Meeting (annual). Board, consisting of up to 16 members, including President, Vice-President and Secretary-General/Treasurer. Executive Office comprises Director, General Secretary-Treasurer and Coordinating Editor. **Languages** English. **Staff** 2.50 FTE, voluntary. **Finance** Members' dues: Active – euro 30; Student – euro 15; Family – euro 45; Retired – euro 15. **Activities** Events/meetings; awards/prizes/competitions. **Events** *Congress* Naples (Italy) 2022, *Shifting Biological Landscapes* Porto (Portugal) 2018, *Unraveling complexity – from molecules to ecosystems* Barcelona (Spain) 2016, *Congress* Glasgow (UK) 2014, *Congress* Bilbao (Spain) 2012. **Publications** *ESCPB News* (2 a year). Conference proceedings.
Members Research scientists (about 400) in 25 countries:
Australia, Austria, Belgium, Canada, Denmark, Estonia, Finland, France, Germany, Greece, India, Israel, Italy, Japan, Latvia, Netherlands, Norway, Portugal, South Africa, Spain, Sweden, Switzerland, Thailand, UK, USA.
NGO Relations Member of: *International Union of Biological Sciences (IUBS, #15760).* [2020/XD6660/v/D]

European Society Comparative
08562

alphabetic sequence excludes
For the complete listing, see Yearbook Online at

♦ European Society for Comparative Skin Biology (inactive)

♦ **European Society for Composite Materials (ESCM)** **08563**
SG Tech Univ of Munich, Boltzmannstr 15, 85748 Garching, Germany. E-mail: drechsler@lcc.mw.tum.de.
URL: http://www.escm.eu.org/
History Founded Jun 1998, Naples (Italy). Took over activities of *European Association for Composite Materials (EACM)*, founded in 1984. **Aims** Encourage free interchange of information on all those aspects related to composite materials which are of interest to the scientific and engineering community; provide a Europe-wide forum for discussion of such topics; guide and foster understanding and utilization of the science and technology of composite materials; promote European cooperation in the field; promote liaison with engineering and scientific bodies throughout Europe with similar aims and serve as a facilitator for communication between such bodies; foster an environment for timely and cost-effective research, development and implementation of advanced technology in composites; encourage the education of young specialists in the disciplines supporting composite materials science and technology; recognize individuals of outstanding achievement in the science, technology, engineering and application of composite materials. **Structure** General Assembly (during ECCM Conference); Council; Executive Committee; Conference Organizing Committee. **Languages** English, French. **Finance** Members' dues. **Activities** Events/meetings. **Events** *European Conference on Composite Materials* Nantes (France) 2020, *European Conference on Composite Materials* Athens (Greece) 2018, *European Conference on Composite Materials* Munich (Germany) 2016, *European Conference on Composite Materials* Seville (Spain) 2014, *European conference on composite materials* Venice (Italy) 2012. **Publications** Proceedings.
Members Individuals from European countries; Honorary; Associated from non-European countries. Members in 17 countries:
Belgium, Canada, Denmark, France, Germany, Israel, Italy, Japan, Netherlands, Norway, Portugal, Russia, Spain, Sweden, Switzerland, UK, USA. [2018.06.01/XD3286/**D**]

♦ **European Society for Computing and Technology in Anaesthesia and Intensive Care (ESCTAIC)** **08564**
Treas Blanckstr 33, 23564 Lübeck, Germany. E-mail: info@esctaic.org.
URL: http://www.esctaic.org/
History 1989, Glasgow (UK). Registration: Schleswig-Holstein District court, No/ID: VR 3742 HL, Start date: 17 Dec 1992, Germany, Lübeck. **Aims** Facilitate exchange of ideas in the area of computing and technology in anaesthesia and intensive care medicine by providing a forum where members can present their developments and take part in discussions with others involved in similar fields and with similar interests. **Structure** Executive Committee. **Languages** English. **Staff** 5.00 FTE, voluntary. **Finance** Sources: members' dues. **Events** *Annual Meeting* Zurich (Switzerland) 2023, *Symposium* Vienna (Austria) 2019, *Annual Meeting* Chisinau (Moldova) 2018, *Symposium* Copenhagen (Denmark) 2018, *Symposium* Geneva (Switzerland) 2017. **Publications** *International Journal of Clinical Monitoring and Computing.*
Members Individuals in 34 countries:
Australia, Austria, Belgium, Canada, Croatia, Czechia, Denmark, Egypt, Estonia, Finland, France, Germany, Greece, Hungary, Ireland, Israel, Italy, Japan, Jordan, Kuwait, Netherlands, New Zealand, Norway, Poland, Portugal, Romania, Russia, Serbia, South Africa, Spain, Sweden, Switzerland, UK, USA.
NGO Relations Cooperates with (2): *European Society of Anaesthesiology and Intensive Care (ESAIC, #08518); Pediatric Anesthesia and Intensive Care Society and Applied Technologies (PAICSAT, #18285).* [2022/XD6429/v/**D**]

♦ European Society of Concurrent Enterprising / see European Society of Concurrent Enterprising Network (#08565)

♦ **European Society of Concurrent Enterprising Network (ESoCE-NET)** **08565**
Contact Via Cortina d'Ampezzo 164, 00135 Rome RM, Italy. T. +396335470121. Fax +3963310252. E-mail: info@esoce.net.
URL: http://www.esoce.net/
History Nov 1991. Former names and other names: *European Society of Concurrent Enterprising (ESoCE)* – former (Nov 1991). Registration: Italy. **Aims** Provide members with support in achieving competitiveness through the Concurrent Enterprising (CE) paradigm and with professional opportunities to exploit their expertise; promote and enact the sharing and exchange of latest developments in the field; act as catalyst for CE adoption in industry; promote initiatives to widen knowledge on CE and to complete the methodological framework for industrial deployment of CE Concepts. **Structure** General Assembly. **Activities** Coordinates the 'Concurrent Enterprising NETwork of Excellence (CE-NET)'. **Events** *Net Industry Forum* Rome (Italy) 2013, *International Conference of Concurrent Enterprising* The Hague (Netherlands) 2013, *Conference* Rome (Italy) 2010, *International conference on concurrent enterprising* Leiden (Netherlands) 2009, *Conference* Paris (France) 2009. [2018/XD4298/**D**]

♦ **European Society for Construction Law (ESCL)** **08566**
Europäische Gesellschaft für Baurecht – Europese Vereniging voor Bouwrecht (EVBR)
SG IBR, Anna van Buerenplein 47, 2595 DA The Hague, Netherlands. T. +31703245544. E-mail: info@ibr.nl.
URL: http://www.escl.org/
History 23 Oct 1981, Milan (Italy). Founded by 4 national societies. **Aims** Promote education, study and research in the field of construction law and related subjects primarily within Europe. **Structure** Council. **Languages** English. **Finance** Sources: members' dues. **Activities** Awards/prizes/competitions; events/meetings; publishing activities. **Events** *Annual Meeting* Sofia (Bulgaria) 2021, *Annual Meeting* Sofia (Bulgaria) 2020, *Annual Meeting* Delft (Netherlands) 2019, *Annual Meeting* Bucharest (Romania) 2018, *Annual Meeting* Fribourg (Switzerland) 2017. **Publications** *Studies in European Construction Law, The Hague: IBR 2015.*
Members National societies in 18 countries:
Austria, Belgium, Bulgaria, Czechia, Denmark, France, Germany, Greece, Hungary, Italy, Netherlands, Romania, Slovakia, Spain, Sweden, Switzerland, UK, Ukraine.
NGO Relations Sister organization: *SCL International (#19155).* [2022.05.10/XD4823/**D**]

♦ **European Society of Contact Dermatitis (ESCD)** **08567**
Société européenne sur les dermatoses de contact
Sec address not obtained.
URL: http://www.escd.org/
History 1988, Heidelberg (Germany FR). Also referred to by acronym as *ESCD.* **Aims** Promote interest, stimulate research and disseminate information on all aspects of contact dermatitis and other environmental and occupational skin diseases. **Structure** Council; Executive Committee. **Languages** English. **Staff** None. **Finance** Members' dues. **Activities** Awareness raising; research/documentation; knowledge management/information dissemination. **Events** *Congress* Amsterdam (Netherlands) 2022, *Congress* Amsterdam (Netherlands) 2021, *EAACI-ESCD Skin Allergy Meeting* Copenhagen (Denmark) 2021, *Congress* Amsterdam (Netherlands) 2020, *Congress* Milan (Italy) 2018. **Publications** *Contact Dermatitis* (12 a year).
Members Full in 36 countries and territories:
Australia, Belgium, Brazil, Canada, Cape Verde, China, Denmark, Finland, France, Germany, Greece, Hong Kong, Hungary, Iran Islamic Rep, Ireland, Israel, Italy, Japan, Luxembourg, Mexico, Netherlands, New Zealand, Norway, Poland, Portugal, Romania, Saudi Arabia, Singapore, South Africa, Spain, Sweden, Switzerland, Türkiye, UK, United Arab Emirates, USA. [2018.09.06/XD0764/**D**]

♦ European Society of Contraception / see European Society of Contraception and Reproductive Health (#08568)

♦ **European Society of Contraception and Reproductive Health (ESC)** . **08568**
Central Office Opalfeneweg 3, 1740 Ternat, Belgium. T. +3225820852. Fax +3225825515. E-mail: info@escrh.eu.
URL: http://www.escrh.eu/
History 16 Dec 1988, Paris (France). Former names and other names: *European Society of Contraception (ESC)* – former; *Société européenne de la contraception (SEC)* – former. **Aims** Work collaboratively in Europe and beyond to champion evidence-based education and research in sexual and reproductive health and rights including facilitating people's informed decisions in choosing and using contraception. **Structure** General Assembly; Board of Directors; Executive Committee; Science and Education Committee; Website & Multimedia Committee; Editorial Team. **Languages** English. **Staff** 3.00 FTE, paid. **Finance** Sources: members' dues. **Activities** Events/meetings; research/documentation. **Events** *ESC Virtual Seminar* 2023, *ESC Congress* Ghent (Belgium) 2022, *ESC Congress* Dublin (Ireland) 2020, *Biennial Congress* Budapest (Hungary) 2018, *Biennial Seminar* St Petersburg (Russia) 2017. **Publications** *European Journal of Contraception and Reproductive Health Care* (6 a year). **Information Services** *Training improvement programme* – This self-study concept allows everybody to use the programme for self-training and update their knowledge around contraceptive methods; *Weblibrary on abortion* – Books, guidelines, e-learning sources; *Weblibrary on sexuality education* – educational tools; downloads; presentations. **Members** Full in 56 countries. Membership countries not specified. [2023.02.22/XD1291/**E**]

♦ **European Society of Cornea and Ocular Surface Disease Specialists (EuCornea)** **08569**
Main Office Temple House, Temple Road, Blackrock, Dublin, 18, CO. DUBLIN, D18 H6K2, Ireland. T. +35312883674. Fax +35312091112. E-mail: eucornea@eucornea.org.
URL: http://www.eucornea.org/
History Sep 2009. Registered in accordance with Irish law. **Aims** Promote personal relationships and exchange of scientific knowledge and practical skills among corneal specialists in Europe; encourage, support and register scientific research in the field of cornea and ocular surface disease in Europe; promote dissemination of the highest level of knowledge in the field of ophthalmology and specifically in cornea and ocular surface disease among ophthalmologists and the public; promote an efficient collaboration with similar organizations worldwide which contribute to progress. **Structure** Board. **Languages** English. **Finance** Members' dues. Other sources: congress proceeds; other revenue. **Activities** Organizes: annual scientific congress; annual members meeting; special and regional meetings. **Events** *EuCornea Congress* Barcelona (Spain) 2023, *EuCornea Congress* Athens (Greece) 2022, *Eucornea Congress* 2021, *Congress* Amsterdam (Netherlands) 2020, *Congress* Paris (France) 2019. **Members** Full; Trainee; International; Honorary. Membership countries not specified. **NGO Relations** Member of: *European Alliance for Vision Research and Ophthalmology (EU-EYE, #05890).* [2020/XJ5109/**D**]

♦ **European Society for Cosmetic and Aesthetic Dermatology (ESCAD)** **08570**
SG The office, via san Nicolo 14, 34121 Trieste TS, Italy. T. +3940368343. Fax +3940368808. E-mail: escadsecretariat@theoffice.it.
Registered Address 57 Rue de l'Université, 75007 Paris, France.
URL: http://www.escad.org/
History 1997. **Aims** Improve patient care in cosmetic dermatology by: promoting education, teaching and research in cosmetic dermatology; fostering the link between biological/scientific cosmetic dermatology and interventional dermatology. **Structure** Executive Board. **Languages** English. **Staff** Part-time. **Finance** Unrestricted educational grants. Annual budget: 10,000 GBP. **Activities** Events/meetings; training/education. **Events** *Cosmoderm Congress* Madrid (Spain) 2012, *Cosmoderm congress* Beirut (Lebanon) 2008, *Cosmoderm congress* Crete (Greece) 2008, *Annual meeting* Paris (France) 2008, *Cosmoderm congress* Istanbul (Turkey) 2007. **Publications** *Journal of Cosmetic Dermatology* (4 a year). *Cosmetic Medicine.* **Members** Individuals. Membership countries not specified. **NGO Relations** Member of: *Federation of the European Dermatological and Surgical Societies (FEDSS, no recent information); International League of Dermatological Societies (ILDS, #14018).* Sister organization of: *European Academy of Dermatology and Venereology (EADV, #05788); International Peeling Society (IPS, #14550)* [2021/XD7902/**D**]

♦ **European Society of Cosmetic Dentistry (ESCD)** **08571**
Pres Dr Pasteur Street No 1A, Bucharest, Romania. E-mail: andreea@sser.ro.
Gen Sec address not obtained.
URL: http://www.escdonline.eu/
History 24 May 2003, Capri (Italy), as *European Society of Esthetic Dentistry (ESED).* **Aims** Promote research and continuing education in the area of aesthetic procedures of dentistry and dental laboratory techniques. **Structure** General Assembly (annual); Executive Committee. **Languages** English. **Finance** Members' dues. **Events** *Annual Meeting* Bucharest (Romania) 2020, *Annual Meeting* St Petersburg (Russia) 2019, *Annual Meeting* Lisbon (Portugal) 2018, *Annual Meeting* Zagreb (Croatia) 2017, *Annual Meeting* Krakow (Poland) 2016. **Publications** *ESED Newsletter.* **Members** Individuals (600) in 58 countries. Membership countries not specified. [2018.09.06/XM2048/**D**]

♦ **European Society of Cosmetic and Reconstructive Gynecology (ESCORG)** **08572**
Contact Mithatpasa Caddesi No 49/8 Yenisehir, 06420 Ankara/Ankara, Türkiye. T. +903124354594. Fax +903124350357. E-mail: feritsaracoglu@gmail.com.
History 2011, Moscow (Russia). **Structure** Board, comprising President, President-Elect, Vice-President and Secretary General. **Languages** English. **Finance** Members' dues. **Activities** Sections (9): Reconstructive Gynecology; Cosmetology; Laser Surgery; Urogynecology; Cosmetic Gynecology; Ethics and Law; Education; Congresses; Industry Relations. **Members** Active; Senior; Associate. Membership countries not specified. [2019/XJ7627/**D**]

♦ European Society of Cosmetic Surgery / see European Society of Aesthetic Surgery (#08512)

♦ **European Society Coudenhove-Kalergi (ES-CK)** **08573**
SG Neulinggasse 37, 1030 Vienna, Austria. T. +4315051593. E-mail: europa@coudenhove-kalergi-society.eu.
Pres address not obtained.
URL: http://www.coudenhove-kalergi-society.eu/
History 15 Sep 1978. Founded by Vittorio Pons, Gérard Bauer, Otto von Habsburg, Alfred Maleta, Edmond Giscard d'Estaing and Marco Pons, being linked to *International Paneuropean Union (#14509).* Together with *European Centre for Culture (ECC, #06472)* and *European Institute of the University of Geneva (inactive)*, set up, 1984, *European Archives Centre (inactive).* Former names and other names: *Coudenhove-Kalergi Foundation (CKF)* – former (15 Sep 1978 to 20 Feb 2008); *Fondation Coudenhove-Kalergi* – former (15 Sep 1978 to 20 Feb 2008). Registration: Swiss Civil Code, Switzerland; Start date: 2008, Austria. **Aims** Promote a united Europe by extending awards to European celebrities and financing projects that serve the Pan-Europa idea, using the Europe *archives* from the Coudenhove-Kalergi estate. **Structure** Council; Executive Committee; Honorary Council; Consultative Scientific Commission. **Languages** English, French, German. **Staff** Voluntary. **Finance** Sources: donations; gifts, legacies. **Activities** Awards/prizes/competitions. **Publications** *European Letters.*
Members Individuals in 17 countries:
Austria, Belgium, Bosnia-Herzegovina, Estonia, France, Germany, Italy, Latvia, Liechtenstein, Portugal, Romania, Slovakia, Spain, Sweden, Switzerland, Ukraine, USA. [2022.05.06/XF4984/v/**F**]

♦ **European Society of Craniofacial Surgery (ESCFS)** **08574**
SG c/o Velthuis Kliniek, Jan Leentvaarlaan 14-24, 1213 RH Rotterdam, Netherlands. E-mail: info@velthuiskliniek.nl.
Pres c/o The Westbourne Centre Ltd, 53 Church Road, Edgbaston, Birmingham, B15 3SJ, UK.
URL: http://www.escfs.org/
History Jan 1984, Paris (France). Acts as European branch of *International Society of Craniofacial Surgery (ISCFS, #15037).* **Aims** Promote and foster the best multidisciplinary surgical treatment to the facially deformed. **Structure** Council. **Events** *Meeting* Birmingham (UK) 2016, *Meeting* Paris (France) 2014, *Biennial Meeting* Gothenburg (Sweden) 2012, *Biennial Meeting* Rotterdam (Netherlands) 2010, *Biennial Meeting* Lille (France) 2008.
Members Individuals in 14 countries:
Austria, Bulgaria, Denmark, France, Germany, Greece, Italy, Netherlands, Poland, South Africa, Sweden, Switzerland, Türkiye, UK. [2015/XJ9145/v/**D**]

♦ **European Society of Criminology (ESC)** **08575**
Exec Sec Univ of Lausanne, ESC – ICDP, Sorge – BCH, 1015 Lausanne VD, Switzerland. T. +41216924638. Fax +41216924645. E-mail: secretariat@esc-eurocrim.org.
URL: http://www.esc-eurocrim.org/
History Sep 2000. Registration: England and Wales. **Aims** Bring together, in one multi-disciplinary society on a European level, persons actively engaged in research, teaching and/or practice in the field of criminology; foster scholarly, scientific and practical exchange and cooperation among those engaged in criminology, particularly at the European and international levels; serve as a forum for the dissemination of criminological knowledge at the European level. **Structure** Executive Board. Executive Secretariat. **Languages** English. **Activities** Events/meetings; awards/prizes/competitions. **Events** *Annual Conference* Athens (Greece) 2025, *Annual Conference* Bucharest (Romania) 2024, *Annual Conference* Florence (Italy) 2023, *Annual Conference* Malaga (Spain) 2022, *Annual Conference* Bucharest (Romania) 2021. **Publications** *ESC Newsletter*, *European Journal of Criminology.*
Members Individuals in 50 countries:
Albania, Armenia, Australia, Austria, Belarus, Belgium, Bosnia-Herzegovina, Brazil, Canada, Croatia, Cyprus, Czechia, Denmark, Estonia, Finland, France, Georgia, Germany, Greece, Hong Kong, Hungary, Iceland, Iran Islamic Rep, Ireland, Israel, Italy, Japan, Lithuania, Luxembourg, Malta, Moldova, Montenegro, Netherlands, New Zealand, Norway, Poland, Portugal, Russia, Serbia, Slovakia, Slovenia, South Africa, Spain, Sweden, Switzerland, Trinidad-Tobago, Türkiye, UK, Ukraine, USA.
Also members in West Indies. Membership countries not specified. [2022/XD8750/**D**]

♦ European Society of Cryosurgery (inactive)

♦ **European Society of Culture** **08576**
Société européenne de culture – Sociedad Europea de Cultura (SEC) – Europäische Kulturgesellschaft – Società Europea di Cultura – Evropejskoe Obscestvo Kultury
Int SG via Benvenuto Pasquinelli 6, 51012 Collodi PI, Italy. T. +39572429613. E-mail: info@societaeuropeacultura.it.
URL: http://www.societaeuropeacultura.it/
History Founded 31 May 1950, Venice, when statutes were adopted; statutes last amended 28 May 2010, Florence (Italy). Registered in accordance with Italian law. **Aims** Promote cooperation and friendship among those involved in cultural activities, regardless of origin and creed; develop theory and practice to safeguard and improve the conditions required for the affirmation of culture; develop a 'politics of culture' in keeping with evolving times. **Structure** General Assembly (every 2 years); Executive Council; Bureau. Meetings closed. **Languages** English, French, Italian. **Staff** Voluntary. **Finance** Members' dues. Occasional grants. **Activities** Events/meetings. **Events** *Biennial General Assembly* Venice (Italy) 2013, *Biennial General Assembly* Innsbruck (Austria) 2009, *Biennial general assembly* Montecatini Terme (Italy) 2007, *Biennial General Assembly* Venice (Italy) 2005, *Biennial General Assembly* Bucharest (Romania) 2003. **Publications** *Comprendre* (irregular) – review. Brochures. Information Services: Maintains a library, holding some 6,000 volumes.
Members Individuals in 53 countries and territories:
Argentina, Armenia, Austria, Belgium, Brazil, Bulgaria, Canada, Chile, China, Colombia, Croatia, Cuba, Czechia, Denmark, Ecuador, Estonia, Finland, France, Georgia, Germany, Greece, Holy See, Hungary, Iceland, India, Ireland, Israel, Italy, Kazakhstan, Luxembourg, Mexico, Netherlands, North Macedonia, Norway, Peru, Poland, Portugal, Puerto Rico, Romania, Russia, San Marino, Senegal, Serbia, Slovakia, Spain, Sweden, Switzerland, Türkiye, UK, Ukraine, Uruguay, USA, Venezuela.
National centres in 8 countries:
France, Greece, Italy, Netherlands, Poland, Romania, Russia, Switzerland.
IGO Relations *UNESCO (#20322).* [2018.10.10/XD0861/v/**D**]

♦ European Society for Cystic Fibrosis / see European Cystic Fibrosis Society (#06879)

♦ **European Society of Dental Ergonomics (ESDE)** **08577**
Pres c/o ZZMK Carolinum, Theodor-Stern-Kai 7, 60596 Frankfurt-Main, Germany. E-mail: president@esde.org.
SG address not obtained.
URL: http://www.esde.org/
History 1987, Kirchen (Germany). Previously also referred to as: *Société européenne d'ergonomie dentaire (SEED) – Europäische Gesellschaft für Zahnärztliche Ergonomie (EGZE) – Società Europea Ergonomia Dentale – Europese Vereniging voor Tandheelkundige Ergonomie.* Registration: France. **Aims** Collect, analyse, follow up, publish and archive scientific knowledge concerning dental ergonomics and dental practice (organization, hygiene, psychology, etc) and all included and/or related activities. **Structure** General Assembly; Executive Committee. **Languages** English. **Staff** None. **Finance** Members' dues. Sponsorships of dental industry. **Events** *Annual Congress* Chia (Italy) 2019, *Annual Congress* Wroclaw (Poland) 2016, *Annual Congress* Vilnius (Lithuania) 2014, *Annual Congress* Sofia (Bulgaria) 2013, *Annual Congress* Biberach an der Riss (Germany) 2011.
Members Full; Associate. Individuals in 15 countries:
Belgium, Brazil, Czechia, Denmark, Finland, France, Germany, Israel, Italy, Netherlands, Poland, Romania, Russia, Slovakia, Switzerland.
NGO Relations *European Regional Organization of the Fédération dentaire internationale (ERO, #08345).* [2020.03.03/XD5529/v/**D**]

♦ **European Society for Dermatological Research (ESDR)** **08578**
Société européenne de recherche en dermatologie
Admin Dir Rue Cingria 7, 1205 Geneva, Switzerland. T. +41223214890. Fax +41223214892. E-mail: office@esdr.org.
Admin Dir address not obtained.
URL: http://www.esdr.org/
History 1971. **Aims** Facilitate communication of ideas and formation of contacts within the field of dermatological research in Europe. **Structure** General Assembly. Board of Directors, comprising President, Secretary-Treasurer and at least 12 members. **Languages** English. **Staff** 1.00 FTE, paid. **Finance** Members's dues. Support from industrial membership. **Activities** Events/meetings; awards/prizes/competitions; training/education. **Events** *Annual Meeting* Amsterdam (Netherlands) 2021, *Annual Meeting* Amsterdam (Netherlands) 2020, *Annual Meeting* Bordeaux (France) 2019, *IID : International Investigative Dermatology Joint Quinquennial Meeting* Orlando, FL (USA) 2018, *Annual Meeting* Salzburg (Austria) 2017. **Publications** *ESDR Newsletter*, *Journal of Investigative Dermatology.*
Members Full in 18 countries:
Austria, Belgium, Czechia, Denmark, Finland, France, Germany, Hungary, Italy, Netherlands, Norway, Poland, Russia, Spain, Sweden, Switzerland, UK, USA.
NGO Relations Member of: *International League of Dermatological Societies (ILDS, #14018).* Supports: *European Skin Research Foundation (ESRF, #08490).* [2016/XD5593/**D**]

♦ European Society for Dermatological Surgery (inactive)

♦ **European Society for Dermatology and Psychiatry (ESDaP)** **08579**
Contact Dept Dermatology, Royal London Hosp, Whitechapel, London, E1 1BB, UK.
URL: http://www.psychodermatology.net/
History 1990, Vienna (Austria). **Aims** Provide a forum for European physicians and psychologists working in *psychodermatology, psychosomatic dermatology* and *dermatopsychiatry.* **Structure** Executive Committee. **Languages** English. **Staff** 3.00 FTE, voluntary. **Finance** Members' dues. **Activities** Training/education; events/meetings. **Events** *Congress* Giesen (Germany) 2019, *Congress* Brest (France) 2017, *Congress* St Petersburg (Russia) 2015, *Congress* Røskilde (Denmark) 2013, *Congress* Saragossa (Spain) 2011. **Publications** *Acta Dermato-Venereologica Scandinava* (annual).
Members Full in 23 countries:
Austria, Belgium, Croatia, Czechia, Denmark, Estonia, Finland, France, Georgia, Germany, Iceland, Italy, Netherlands, North Macedonia, Norway, Poland, Portugal, Romania, Russia, Spain, Switzerland, Türkiye, UK.
Associate in 9 countries:
Argentina, Australia, Brazil, Canada, Iceland, Israel, Japan, Philippines, USA.
IGO Relations None. [2018.09.09/XD8184/**D**]

♦ **European Society for Dermatopathology (ESDP)** **08580**
Admin Dir Rue Cingria 7, 1205 Geneva, Switzerland. T. +41223214890. Fax +41223214892.
URL: http://www.esdp.net/
History Founded Jun 1996, Zurich (Switzerland). **Aims** Educate by organizing meetings, creating slide sets and providing opportunities for trainees in pathology and dermatology to spend time in centres of dermatopathology of their choice; establish a European Diploma of Dermatopathology accessible to both pathologists and dermatologists. **Structure** Board, comprising President, Past President, Secretary, Treasurer and 10 members. **Languages** English. **Staff** None. **Finance** Members' dues (annual): euro 25. Currently no budget. **Activities** Organizes symposia. **Events** *Meeting* Paris (France) 2008, *Meeting* Vienna (Austria) 2007, *Meeting* Zurich (Switzerland) 2007, *Meeting* Paris (France) 2006, *Meeting* Rhodes Is (Greece) 2006. **Members** Membership countries not specified. **NGO Relations** *European Academy of Dermatology and Venereology (EADV, #05788).* [2014/XD9084/**D**]

♦ **European Society for Developmental Perinatal and Paediatric Pharmacology (ESDPPP)** **08581**
Contact Heinrich-Heins-Univ Düsseldorf, Universitätsstrasse 1, 40225 Düsseldorf, Germany. E-mail: stephanie.laeer@uni-duesseldorf.de.
Main: http://www.esdppp.org/
History 23 Apr 1988, Les Diablerets (Switzerland), as *European Society for Developmental Pharmacology (ESDP).* **Aims** Promote developmental pharmacology whether foetal, perinatal or paediatric; publish scientific articles that improve the understanding of the relationship between medicines and young patients. **Structure** Council, consisting of President, Past President, President-Elect, General Secretary, Treasurer and 4 Councillors. **Languages** English. **Staff** None. **Finance** Members' dues: euro 85. **Activities** Accepts manuscripts via the journal website. **Events** *Congress* Liverpool (UK) 2021, *Congress* Basel (Switzerland) 2019, *Congress* Leuven (Belgium) 2017, *Congress* Belgrade (Serbia) 2015, *Congress* Salzburg (Austria) 2013. **Publications** *Archives of Disease in Childhood* – official journal.
Members Full in 21 countries:
Austria, Belgium, Egypt, Estonia, Finland, France, Germany, Hungary, Israel, Italy, Netherlands, Nigeria, Norway, Portugal, Romania, Serbia, Spain, Sweden, Switzerland, Türkiye, UK.
Associate in 5 countries:
Australia, Canada, Japan, New Zealand, USA.
NGO Relations Member of: *International Union of Basic and Clinical Pharmacology (IUPHAR, #15758).* [2012.06.01/XD2560/**D**]

♦ European Society for Developmental Pharmacology / see European Society for Developmental Perinatal and Paediatric Pharmacology (#08581)
♦ European Society for Developmental Psychology / see European Association of Developmental Psychology (#06010)
♦ European Society of Digestive Endoscopy / see European Society of Gastrointestinal Endoscopy (#08606)

♦ **European Society of Digestive Oncology (ESDO)** **08582**
Office Alser Strasse 4, 1090 Vienna, Austria. E-mail: info@esdo.eu.
URL: http://www.esdo.eu/
History Inaugural meeting, 13 Jun 2008, Prague (Czech Rep). **Aims** Improve and propagate medical treatment of GI-tract *tumours*, particularly in a multidisciplinary evidence-based approach; enhance and promote the screening, early detection, primary prevention and management of pre-malignant and/or malignant diseases of the GI-tract. **Structure** General Assembly; Advisory Council; Governing Board. European chapter of: *International Digestive Cancer Alliance (IDCA, #13174).* **Activities** Research/documentation; training/education; standards/guidelines. **Events** *Symposium on Upper GI Endoscopy and Neoplasia Quality in Endoscopy* Berlin (Germany) 2016. **Publications** *ESDO Newsletter* (12 a year). Documents; guidelines. **Members** Individual; National Societies; Honorary. Membership countries not specified. **NGO Relations** Member of: *European Cancer Organisation (ECO, #06432); United European Gastroenterology (UEG, #20506).* Policy partner of: *Digestive Cancers Europe (DiCE, #05070).* [2017/XJ1860/**D**]

♦ **European Society of Digital and Integrative Pathology (ESDIP)** **08583**
Address not obtained.
URL: https://digitalpathologysociety.org/
History Announced May 2016, Berlin (Germany) at 13th European Congress on Digital Pathology, which had been organized since 1994. **Aims** Support the key role of the pathologist by integrative digital pathology initiatives. **Structure** Board. **Activities** Events/meetings. **Events** *European Congress on Digital Pathology* Helsinki (Finland) 2018, *European Congress on Digital Pathology* Berlin (Germany) 2016, *International Congress on Digital Pathology* Paris (France) 2014. [2019/XM7928/c/**E**]

♦ **European Society of Dirofilariosis and Angiostrongylosis (ESDA)** . . **08584**
Pres address not obtained.
Sec address not obtained. E-mail: rmorgar@usal.es.
URL: http://esda.usal.es/
History 2009, Salamanca (Spain), as *European Dirofilaria Society (EDiS).* Current title adopted 2012, Parma (Italy). **Aims** Be an European resource for the prevention, diagnosis and treatment of both D immitis and D repens *infection* in humans and animals and of Angiostrongylus vasorum in *dogs.* **Structure** Executive Board. **Events** *Meeting* Vienna (Austria) 2016, *Meeting / European Dirofilaria Days* Budapest (Hungary) 2014, *European Dirofilaria Days* Parma (Italy) 2012, *European Dirofilaria Days* Salamanca (Spain) 2009, *European Dirofilaria Days* Zagreb (Croatia) 2007. [2014/XJ8471/**D**]

♦ **European Society for Diseases of the Esophagus (ESDE)** **08585**
Pres Div of Surgery, Karolinska Inst, SE-171 77 Stockholm, Sweden.
URL: http://www.esdeesophagus.org/
History Also known as *European Group of Studies Against Sickness of the Esophagus.* Registered in accordance with Belgian law. **Aims** Contribute to the knowledge of esophageal pathophysiology in its largest sense, optimal diagnosis and treatment of esophageal disorders and establishment of scientific connections between experts in this field. **Activities** Knowledge management/information dissemination; awards/prizes/competitions; events/meetings; training/education. **Events** *Congress* Athens (Greece) 2019, *Congress* Vienna (Austria) 2018, *Congress* Utrecht (Netherlands) 2017, *Congress* Munich (Germany) 2016, *Congress / Meeting* Stockholm (Sweden) 2015. [2018/XE3435/**E**]

♦ **European Society of Domestic Animal Reproduction (ESDAR)** **08586**
Pres UGent Veterinary Med, Salisburylaan 133, 9820 Merelbeke, Belgium. E-mail: info@esdar.org.
Sec Veterinary Faculty, Gerbiceva 60, 1000 Ljubljana, Slovenia.
URL: https://www.esdar.org/
History Statutes adopted 27 Oct 1997. **Aims** Stimulate education and research in the field of domestic and wild animal reproduction, especially for clinical aspects, biotechnology and physiology of reproduction. **Structure** General Meeting (annual). Board, comprising President, Vice-President, Secretary, Program Secretary, Treasurer and 4 members. **Languages** English. **Staff** Voluntary. **Finance** Members' dues. **Activities** Includes *'College of Theriogenology'*; organizes scientific meetings and workshops; provides post academic (professional and post-graduate) education either by ESDAR itself or in collaboration with other national and international organizations. **Events** *European Symposium on Animal Reproduction* Nantes (France) 2023, *Annual Conference* St Petersburg (Russia) 2019, *Annual Conference* Córdoba (Spain) 2018, *Annual Conference* Bern (Switzerland) 2017, *Annual Conference* Lisbon (Portugal) 2016. **Publications** *Reproduction in Domestic Animals* – journal.
Members Researchers with a PhD, DVSc or Habilitation in animal reproduction; post-graduates / students with a university degree in veterinary medicine, animal science or related science. Individuals in 39 countries:
Albania, Austria, Belarus, Belgium, Bosnia-Herzegovina, Bulgaria, Croatia, Czechia, Denmark, Estonia, Finland, France, Georgia, Germany, Greece, Hungary, Ireland, Italy, Latvia, Lithuania, Moldova, Montenegro, Netherlands, North Macedonia, Norway, Poland, Portugal, Romania, Russia, Serbia, Slovakia, Slovenia, Spain, Sweden, Switzerland, Türkiye, UK, Ukraine, USA.
NGO Relations Cooperates with (1): *European Veterinary Society for Small Animal Reproduction (EVSSAR, #09059).* Instrumental in setting up (1): *European College of Animal Reproduction (ECAR, #06605).* [2023/XD7777/v/**D**]

European Society Ecological
08587

alphabetic sequence excludes
For the complete listing, see Yearbook Online at

♦ European Society for Ecological Economics (ESEE) 08587

Société européenne d'économie écologique

Pres Dept Intl Environment and Development Studies, Norwegian Univ of Life Sciences, PO Box 5003, 1432 Ås, Norway. E-mail: erik.gomez@nmbu.no.
URL: http://www.euroecolecon.org/

History 24 May 1996, Guyancourt (France), at inaugural General Meeting, when statement of aims was adopted. A branch of *International Society for Ecological Economics (ISEE, #15069)*. Registered initially in accordance with French law. Now registered in accordance with the law on England and Wales. **Aims** Foster transdisciplinary discourse and research among the social and natural sciences regarding problems of nature and the environment; provide a European network for activities in ecological economics; produce and disseminate information on sustainability policies; promote education, graduate research and research funding in the field; assist in building links between European members and other regions, notably through other regional networks. **Structure** General Meeting; Board; Executive Committee; Secretariat. **Languages** English. **Staff** Voluntary. **Finance** Members' dues. Other sources: grants; interest; revenue from goods and assets. **Activities** Events/meetings; training/education; networking/liaising; knowledge management/ information dissemination; publishing activities. **Events** *Biennial Conference* Turku (Finland) 2019, *Biennial Conference* Budapest (Hungary) 2017, *Biennial Conference* Leeds (UK) 2015, *Biennial Conference* Lille (France) 2013, *Biennial Conference* Istanbul (Turkey) 2011. **Publications** *ESEE Newsletter* (4 a year) in English. Books; series; journals. **Members** Individual. Open to all persons and institutions with an interest in the field. Individual members automatically become members of ISEE. Membership countries not specified.
[2019.02.15/XD6127/**D**]

♦ European Society for Electro Analytical Chemistry / see European Society for Electroanalytical Chemistry (#08588)

♦ European Society for Electroanalytical Chemistry (ESEAC) 08588

Pres School of Chemical Sciences, Dublin City Univ, Glasnevin, Dublin, CO. DUBLIN, Ireland.

History Also referred to as *European Society for Electro Analytical Chemistry*. **Events** *International Conference on Electroanalysis* Malmö (Sweden) 2014, *International Conference on Electroanalysis / Congress* Portoroz (Slovenia) 2012, *International conference on electroanalysis / Congress* Gijón (Spain) 2010, *International conference on electroanalysis / Congress* Prague (Czech Rep) 2008, *International conference on electroanalysis / Congress* Bordeaux (France) 2006. **Members** Membership countries not specified.
[2011.10.20/XD2906/**D**]

♦ European Society for Electromechanically Active Polymer Transducers and Artificial Muscles (EuroEAP Society) 08589

Headquarters c/o Empa, Überlandstr 129, 8600 Dübendorf ZH, Switzerland. E-mail: info@ euroeap.eu.
URL: http://www.euroeap.eu/

History 11 Dec 2012, London (UK), when bylaws were adopted. Registered in accordance with Swiss Civil Code. **Aims** Contribute to and promote the scientific and technological advancement and the diffusion of Transducers and Artificial Muscles based on Electromechanically Active Polymers (EAP). **Structure** General Assembly; Executive Committee. Committees (4): Scientific; Conference; Scientific Missions Grants; Dissemination and Outreach. **Activities** Events/meetings; networking/liaising; standards/guidelines. **Events** *Conference* Dresden (Germany) 2019, *Conference* Lyon (France) 2018, *Conference* Copenhagen (Denmark) 2016.
[2017/XM5450/**D**]

♦ European Society for Emergency Medicine (EuSEM) 08590

Société Européenne pour la Médecine d'Urgence

CEO Antwerpsesteenweg 124, B-27, 2630 Aartselaar, Belgium. T. +3238704616. E-mail: info@ eusem.org.
Registered office Rue de l'Industrie 24, 1050 Brussels, Belgium.
URL: http://www.eusem.org/

History May 1994, London (UK). Founded by a multidisciplinary group of experts in emergency medicine which became known as the *Club of Leuven*. **Aims** Ensure: the highest quality of emergency care for all patients; delivery of such care by specialists trained in emergency medicine; a comparable standard of clinical care in emergency departments across Europe. **Structure** General Assembly; Council; Executive Committee. **Languages** English. **Staff** 3.00 FTE, paid. **Finance** Sources: members' dues. **Activities** Events/meetings; knowledge management/information dissemination; training/education. **Events** *European Emergency Medicine Congress (EUSEM 2022)* Berlin (Germany) 2022, *Congress* Lisbon (Portugal) 2021, *Congress* Aartselaar (Belgium) 2020, *Congress* Prague (Czechia) 2019, *Congress* Glasgow (UK) 2018. **Publications** *European Journal for Emergency Medicine*.

Members Individuals who's main professional activity is within a structure providing pre-, inter- and/or in-hospital emergency medical care in and outside Europe, or who is interested in the practice of emergency medicine. National Societies for Emergency Medicine in 35 countries:
Albania, Austria, Belgium, Bulgaria, Croatia, Czechia, Denmark, Estonia, Finland, France, Georgia, Germany, Greece, Hungary, Iceland, Ireland, Israel, Italy, Latvia, Lithuania, Malta, Moldova, Netherlands, Norway, Poland, Portugal, Romania, Serbia, Slovakia, Slovenia, Spain, Sweden, Switzerland, Türkiye, UK.

NGO Relations Member of (1): *International Federation for Emergency Medicine (IFEM, #13409)*.
[2020.06.23/XD5461/v/**D**]

♦ European Society for Emergency Nursing (EuSEN) 08591

Pres Bd de la Constitution 139, 4020 Liège, Belgium. E-mail: president@eusen.org.
URL: http://eusen.org/

History Registration: Banque-Carrefour des Entreprises, No/ID: 0764.948.532, Start date: 11 Mar 2021, Belgium. **Structure** General Assembly; Executive Board. **Languages** English. **Publications** *Eusen E-Newsletter*.
Members Organizations in 14 countries:
Belgium, Croatia, Cyprus, Denmark, Germany, Iceland, Italy, Malta, Netherlands, Norway, Poland, Spain, Sweden, Türkiye.
[2021.06.08/AA1829/**D**]

♦ European Society of Emergency Radiology (ESER) 08592

Europäische Gesellschaft für Notfallradiologie (ESER)

Office Am Gestade 1, 1010 Vienna, Austria. T. +4315334064927. E-mail: office@eser-society.org.
URL: http://www.eser-society.org/

History Registration: Austria. **Aims** Serve the health care needs of the general public through support of science, teaching and research and the quality of service in the field of Emergency Radiology. **Structure** General Assembly; Executive Board. **Languages** English. **Finance** Sources: members' dues. **Publications** *ESER Newsletter* in English. Books: https://www.eser-society.org/er-books/. **Members** Full; Corresponding; Associate; Junior. Membership countries not specified.
[2021.02.17/XJ7152/**D**]

♦ European Society for Emerging Infections (no recent information)

♦ European Society of Endocrine Surgeons (ESES) 08593

Contact Vienna Medical Ac, Alser Strasse 4, 1090 Vienna, Austria. T. +4314051383 – +4314051337. E-mail: eses@medacad.org.
URL: http://www.eses.cc/

History 4 May 2003, Vienna (Austria). Took over activities of *European Study Group on Endocrine Surgery (ESGES, inactive)*. **Aims** Advance knowledge and techniques in endocrine surgery; promote and maintain high standards in the clinical practice of endocrine surgery, education and research. **Structure** Executive Council. **Languages** English. **Finance** Sources: members' dues. **Activities** Financial and/or material support. **Events** *Biennial Congress* Athens (Greece) 2022, *Biennial Congress* Athens (Greece) 2021, *Biennial Congress* Athens (Greece) 2020, *Volume, outcomes and quality standards in endocrine surgery* Granada (Spain) 2019, *Biennial Congress* Amsterdam (Netherlands) 2018.
Members Individuals in 35 countries and territories:
Austria, Belgium, Bulgaria, Canaries, Croatia, Cyprus, Denmark, France, Germany, Greece, Ireland, Italy, Japan, Latvia, Lithuania, Mexico, Montenegro, Netherlands, Norway, Poland, Portugal, Romania, Russia, Saudi Arabia, Serbia, Slovakia, Slovenia, Spain, Sweden, Switzerland, Türkiye, UK, Ukraine, United Arab Emirates, USA.
[2022.02.15/XM2734/**D**]

♦ European Society of Endocrinology (ESE) 08594

CEO Starling House, 1600 Bristol Parkway North, Bristol, BS34 8YU, UK. T. +441454642247. E-mail: info@euro-endo.org.
Brussels Office Avenue des Arts 56, 1000 Brussels, Belgium. T. +3228011365.
URL: http://www.ese-hormones.org/

History 1 Jan 2006. Replaces *European Federation of Endocrine Societies (EFES, inactive)*. Registration: Registered Charity, No/ID: 1123492, England and Wales; EU Transparency Register, No/ID: 524404430464-42, Start date: 1 Mar 2018. **Aims** Promote research, education and clinical practice in endocrinology. **Structure** Council. **Languages** English. **Activities** Events/meetings; training/education. **Events** *European Congress of Endocrinology (ECE)* Stockholm (Sweden) 2024, *European Congress of Endocrinology (ECE)* Istanbul (Türkiye) 2023, *European Congress of Endocrinology (ECE)* Milan (Italy) 2022, *Congress* Prague (Czechia) 2021, *Congress* Bristol (UK) 2020. **Publications** *Endocrine-Related Cancer*, *European Journal of Endocrinology*, *Journal of Endocrinology*, *Journal of Molecular Endocrinology*.

Members Ordinary; Affiliate; Corporate. National organizations in 44 countries and territories:
Albania, Austria, Belarus, Belgium, Bosnia-Herzegovina, Bulgaria, Croatia, Cyprus, Czechia, Denmark, Egypt, Estonia, Finland, France, Georgia, Germany, Greece, Hungary, Iceland, Ireland, Israel, Italy, Latvia, Libya, Lithuania, Montenegro, Netherlands, North Macedonia, Norway, Poland, Portugal, Romania, Russia, Serbia, Slovakia, Slovenia, Spain, Srpska, Sweden, Switzerland, Tunisia, Türkiye, UK, Ukraine.
Regional organizations (10):
European Academy of Andrology (EAA, #05780); *European Biological Rhythms Society (EBRS, #06337)*; *European Calcified Tissue Society (ECTS, #06429)*; *European Neuroendocrine Association (ENEA, #08040)*; *European Neuroendocrine Tumor Society (ENETS, #08041)*; *European Society for Paediatric Endocrinology (ESPE, #08678)*; *European Society for Paediatric Urology (ESPU, #08688)*; *European Society of Gynecology (ESG, #08613)*; *European Thyroid Association (ETA, #08913)*; *International Society for IGF Research (IGF Society, #15191)*.

NGO Relations Member of: *European Cancer Organisation (ECO, #06432)*. Supports: *European Network for the Study of Adrenal Tumours (ENS@T, #08016)*. Nurses' Group is member of: *European Specialist Nurses Organisation (ESNO, #08808)*.
[2022/XM1470/y/**D**]

♦ European Society of Endodontology (ESE) 08595

Administrator Postboks 1237 Vika, 0110 Oslo, Norway.
President address not obtained.
URL: http://www.e-s-e.eu/

History 1982. New constitution adopted, Jun 2001. Registration: No/ID: 984 150 806, Norway. **Aims** Enhance development of endodontology for the benefit of patients, general *dentists*, endodontists, educators, researchers and those in training; represent endodontology and endodontists within Europe and beyond. **Structure** General Assembly; Executive Board; Standing Committees (5). **Languages** English. **Staff** 1.00 FTE, paid. **Finance** Sources: meeting proceeds; members' dues. **Activities** Advocacy/lobbying/activism; awards/ prizes/competitions; events/meetings; research and development; standards/guidelines; training/education. **Events** *Biennial Congress* Helsinki (Finland) 2022, *World Congress on Dental Traumatology* Lisbon (Portugal) 2022, *Biennial Congress* Helsinki (Finland) 2021, *World Congress on Dental Traumatology* Lisbon (Portugal) 2021, *Biennial Congress* Vienna (Austria) 2019. **Publications** *International Endodontic Journal*. Position statements; guidelines.

Members Individual (431); Honorary (3); Specialist (30); Certified (300); Guest (35); Postgraduate (150). Full: National endodontic societies (37) in 33 countries:
Albania, Austria, Belgium, Croatia, Cyprus, Czechia, Denmark, Estonia, Finland, France, Germany, Greece, Hungary, Ireland, Israel, Italy, Kosovo, Latvia, Lebanon, Lithuania, Norway, Poland, Portugal, Romania, Russia, Serbia, Slovakia, Slovenia, Spain, Sweden, Switzerland, Türkiye, UK.
[2020.06.23/XD5910/**D**]

♦ European Society of Endosonography in Gynecology and Obstetrics (inactive)
♦ European Society for Engineering Education (#19462)
♦ European Society for Engineering and Medicine / see Educating Students in Engineering and Medicine (#05364)
♦ European Society for Engineers and Industrialists (internationally oriented national body)

♦ European Society for Environmental History (ESEH) 08596

Sec c/o Planck Inst, Boltzmannstr 22, 14195 Berlin, Germany. E-mail: secretary@eseh.org.
URL: http://eseh.org/

History 1999. **Aims** Encourage and support research, teaching and publications in environmental history in Europe; stimulate dialogue between humanistic scholarship, environmental science and other disciplines. **Structure** Board; Council of Regional Representatives; Specialist Committees. **Languages** English. **Staff** None. **Finance** Members' dues. **Activities** Research/documentation. **Events** *Conference* Bern (Switzerland) 2023, *Conference* Bristol (UK) 2022, *Conference* Tallinn (Estonia) 2019, *Conference* Zagreb (Croatia) 2017, *Biennial Conference* Paris (France) 2015. **Publications** *ESEH Notepad* (4 a year).
Members in 36 countries and territories:
Armenia, Australia, Austria, Belgium, Canada, Czechia, Denmark, Finland, France, Germany, Greenland, Hungary, Iceland, India, Ireland, Israel, Italy, Japan, Moldova, Netherlands, Norway, Poland, Portugal, Russia, Slovakia, Slovenia, South Africa, Spain, Sri Lanka, Sweden, Switzerland, Türkiye, UK, Ukraine, USA, Vietnam.

NGO Relations Founding member of: *International Consortium of Environmental History Organizations (ICEHO, #12912)*. Member of: *European Alliance for the Social Sciences and Humanities (EASSH, #05885)*. Collaborates with national organizations.
[2019/XD9104/**D**]

♦ European Society for Environmental and Occupational Medicine (EOM) 08597

Europäische Fachgesellschaft für Umweltmedizin und Arbeitsmedizin

Registered Office PO Box 370514, 14135 Berlin, Germany. T. +493055570238. Fax +493020847505. E-mail: info@eomsociety.org.
Registered Office Am Waldhaus 41, 14129 Berlin, Germany.
URL: http://www.eomsociety.org/

History 2011. Registration: No/ID: VR 21579, SOM, Germany. **Aims** Protect European workers and citizens from new health hazards: initiate independent interdisciplinary research; lobby for joint fund rising on EU level; gain influence in political advisory groups in Europe. **Structure** Board; Working Groups. **Languages** English. **Staff** None paid. **Finance** Sources: donations; members' dues. **Activities** Standards/guidelines; training/ education. **Publications** Articles. **Members** Individual; Supporting; Honorary; Institutional. Membership countries not specified. **NGO Relations** Associate member of: *International Network for Epidemiology in Policy (INEP, #14264)*.
[2021.09.07/XM7264/**D**]

♦ European Society for Environment and Development (inactive)
♦ European Society of Esthetic Dentistry / see European Society of Cosmetic Dentistry (#08571)

♦ European Society for Ethnomusicology 08598

Société européenne d'ethnomusicologie

Address not obtained.

NGO Relations Member of: *European Music Council (EMC, #07837)*; *International Music Council (IMC, #14199)*.
[2016/XD7267/**D**]

♦ European Society of Ethnopharmacology 08599

Pres Inst d'Histoire des Sciences, Univ Louis Pasteur, 7 rue de l'université, 67000 Strasbourg, France.
Pres Univ de Metz, Société Française d'Ethnopharmacologie, 1 rue des Récollets, 57000 Metz, France. T. +33387748889.
URL: http://www.ethnopharma.free.fr/

History 23 Mar 1990, Metz (France), during 1st European Colloquium on Ethnopharmacology. **Aims** Promote cooperation within Europe in the field of ethnopharmacology. **Structure** General Assembly. Council, including President, Honorary President, 3 Vice-Presidents, Secretary-General and Treasurer. **Languages** English, French. **Staff** Voluntary. **Finance** Members' dues. **Activities** Organizes training courses. **Events** *Colloquium* Gosier (Guadeloupe) 2014, *Colloquium* Grasse (France) 2010, *Colloquium* Leipzig (Germany) 2007, *Colloquium* Valencia (Spain) 2003, *Colloquium* Metz (France) 2000. **Publications** *Ethnopharmacologia* – bulletin. **Members** Membership countries not specified.
[2011/XD9447/**D**]

♦ European Society for Evolutionary Biology (ESEB) 08600

Office Manager Postfach 910225, 90260 Nuremberg, Germany. E-mail: office@eseb.org.
Registered Address Molenstraat 156, 6712 CW Ede, Netherlands.
URL: https://www.eseb.org/

History 30 Aug 1987, Basel (Switzerland). Set up at founding congress. Registration: ANBI, No/ID: 8080.77.223, Netherlands; EU Transparency Register, No/ID: 369395530506-80, Start date: 2 Mar 2018. **Aims** Support the study of organic evolution. **Structure** Steering Committee; Council. **Languages** English. **Staff** 0.75 FTE, paid. **Finance** Sources: members' dues; sale of publications. **Activities** Awards/prizes/competitions; events/meetings; publishing activities. **Events** *ESEB Congress* Prague (Czech Rep) 2022, *Symposium on Genomic Signatures and Consequences of Sex and Asexuality* 2021, *Symposium on Tandem Repeats* 2021, *ESEB Congress* Turku (Finland) 2019, *Joint Congress on Evolutionary Biology* Montpellier (France) 2018. **Publications** *Journal of Evolutionary Biology (JEB)* (12 a year) in English; *Evolution Letters (EL)* (6 a year) in English.

Members Ordinary and Student in 44 countries:
Argentina, Australia, Austria, Belgium, Brazil, Canada, Chile, China, Colombia, Croatia, Czechia, Denmark, Estonia, Finland, France, Germany, Greece, Hungary, Iceland, India, Iran Islamic Rep, Ireland, Israel, Italy, Japan, Latvia, Mexico, Netherlands, New Zealand, Norway, Panama, Poland, Portugal, Russia, Serbia, Slovenia, South Africa, Spain, Sweden, Switzerland, Thailand, Türkiye, UK, USA.

NGO Relations Member of (1): *Dryad (#05139).* [2022.11.01/XD3402/**D**]

♦ European Society for Evolutionary Developmental Biology (EED) . . . 08601

Sec Univ College Dublin, School of Biology and Environmental Science, Science Centre West, Belfield, Dublin, 4, CO. DUBLIN, Ireland. T. +35317162290. E-mail: eed.soc@gmail.com.
Pres Univ of Vienna, Fac of Life Sciences, Dept of Theoretical Biology, Althanstrasse 14, 1090 Vienna, Austria. T. +431427756700. E-mail: gerhard.mueller@univie.ac.at.
URL: https://evodevo.eu/

History Founded 2006. Registered in accordance with Dutch law. Former names and other names: *EuroEvoDevo* – alias. **Aims** Promote evolutionary developmental biology. **Structure** Council; Executive Committee. **Languages** English. **Staff** Voluntary. **Finance** Members' dues. Meetings. **Activities** Events/meetings. **Events** *Euro Evo Devo Conference* Naples (Italy) 2022, *Conference* Naples (Italy) 2021, *Conference* Naples (Italy) 2020, *Conference* Galway (Ireland) 2018, *Conference* Uppsala (Sweden) 2016. **Members** Student; Regular. Membership countries not specified. [2022/XM3418/**D**]

♦ European Society of Extracorporeal Technology (inactive)

♦ European Society on Family Relations (ESFR) 08602

Sec address not obtained.
Pres address not obtained.
URL: http://www.esfr.org/

History 2 Nov 2002, Nijmegen (Netherlands). Founded during 1st inaugural conference. **Aims** Promote excellence in the scientific study of family relations; advance theoretical and empirically-oriented research; foster excellence in the training of family researchers; encourage cooperation and information exchange between family scientists from European countries; serve as a platform for expert knowledge concerning family relations. **Structure** Board, comprising President, Secretary, Treasurer and 5 further members. Scientific Committee. **Finance** Members's dues. **Events** *Sustainable relationships? Families, personal lives and global change* Oxford (UK) 2021, *Sustainable relationships? Families, personal lives and global change* Oxford (UK) 2020, *Families through the lens of diversity* Porto (Portugal) 2018, *Congress* Dortmund (Germany) 2016, *Families in the context of economic crisis, recent trends in multidisciplinary perspective* Madrid (Spain) 2014. [2022/XM1218/**D**]

♦ European Society of Feline Medicine / see International Society of Feline Medicine (#15116)
♦ European Society of Foot and Ankle Surgeons (inactive)

♦ European Society for Fuzzy Logic and Technology (EUSFLAT) 08603

Pres Faculty of Sciences, 33007 Oviedo, Asturias, Spain. T. +34985103358. E-mail: president@eusflat.org.
Secretary address not obtained.
URL: http://www.eusflat.org/

History 1998, Spain. **Aims** Promote and disseminate fuzzy logic and technologies; encourage scientific communication and collaboration in this field; advise on subjects regarding fuzzy logic and related matters. **Structure** Assembly; Board. **Languages** English. **Staff** None. **Finance** Sources: members' dues. **Activities** Awards/prizes/competitions; events/meetings; training/education. **Events** *Conference* Bratislava (Slovakia) 2021, *Conference* Prague (Czechia) 2019, *Conference* Warsaw (Poland) 2017, *Conference* Gijón (Spain) 2015, *Assembly* Montpellier (France) 2014. **Publications** *International Journal of Computational Intelligence Systems* – official journal; *Mathware and Soft Computing* – magazine. Conference proceedings.

Members Regular; Student; Institutional. Members in 30 countries and territories:
Argentina, Australia, Austria, Belgium, Brazil, Bulgaria, Canada, Czechia, Denmark, Egypt, Finland, France, Germany, Greece, Hungary, Ireland, Israel, Italy, Japan, Lebanon, Poland, Russia, Serbia, Slovakia, Slovenia, Spain, Sweden, Taiwan, UK, Vietnam.

NGO Relations Member of (1): *International Fuzzy Systems Association (IFSA, #13697).* Also links with national associations. [2023.02.24/XD2253/**D**]

♦ European Society for Gastrocamera Diagnosis and Endoscopy / see European Association for Gastroenterology, Endoscopy and Nutrition (#06051)

♦ European Society of Gastroenterology and Endoscopy Nurses and Associates (ESGENA) 08604

Secretariat Am Kastell 2, 85077 Manching, Germany. T. +498459323941. Fax +498459323942. E-mail: info@esgena.org.
URL: http://www.esgena.org/

History Registered in accordance with Austrian law. **Aims** Promote endoscopy and gastroenterology nursing. **Events** *Annual Conference* Barcelona (Spain) 2019, *Annual Conference* Vienna (Austria) 2018, *Annual Conference* Barcelona (Spain) 2017, *Annual Conference* Vienna (Austria) 2016, *Annual Conference* Barcelona (Spain) 2015. **Publications** *ESGENA Newsletter.*

Members Societies and individuals. Membres in 38 countries and territories:
Australia, Austria, Belgium, Bosnia-Herzegovina, Bulgaria, Canada, Croatia, Czechia, Denmark, Estonia, Finland, France, Germany, Hong Kong, Hungary, Iceland, India, Ireland, Israel, Italy, Jordan, Luxembourg, Malta, Monaco, Montenegro, Netherlands, Norway, Poland, Portugal, Romania, Serbia, Slovenia, Spain, Sweden, Switzerland, Thailand, UK, USA.

NGO Relations Member of: *European Specialist Nurses Organisation (ESNO, #08808).* [2018/XD8643/**D**]

♦ European Society of Gastrointestinal and Abdominal Radiology (ESGAR) 08605

Exec Dir ESGAR Central Office, Esslinggasse 2/3, 1010 Vienna, Austria. T. +4315358927. Fax +4315357037. E-mail: office@esgar.org.
URL: http://www.esgar.org/

History 1990, as *European Society of Gastrointestinal Radiologists (ESGR).* Present name adopted, 1994. **Aims** Advance gastrointestinal and abdominal radiology and its associated diseases. **Structure** General Assembly (annual); Executive Committee; Executive Board; Central Office. **Languages** English. **Staff** 6.00 FTE, paid. **Finance** Members' dues. Other sources: surplus from annual meetings and workshops; donations; sponsorship from industry. **Activities** Knowledge management/information dissemination; research/documentation; networking/liaising; training/education; events/meetings. **Events** *Annual Meeting* Gothenburg (Sweden) 2024, *Annual Meeting* Valencia (Spain) 2023, *Annual Meeting* Lisbon (Portugal) 2022, *Annual Meeting* Lisbon (Portugal) 2021, *Annual Meeting* Vienna (Austria) 2020. **Publications** Annual Report; brochures; meeting programme. **Members** Ordinary (Active, Corresponding, Fellows, Corresponding Fellows, Junior), Extraordinary (Corporate) and Honorary (Honorary Fellows, Emeritus Fellows). Individuals (2,343) in 79 countries. Membership countries not specified. **NGO Relations** Member of: *European Society of Radiology (ESR, #08720).* Associate member of: *United European Gastroenterology (UEG, #20506).* [2020.03.03/XD2661/v/**D**]

♦ European Society of Gastrointestinal Endoscopy (ESGE) 08606

Secretariat c/o Hamilton Services, Landwehr Str 9, 80336 Munich, Germany. T. +4989907793611. Fax +4989907793620. E-mail: secretariat@esge.com.
URL: http://www.esge.com/

History 1964, Brussels (Belgium). Founded at 7th Congress of *Association of National European and Mediterranean Societies of Gastroenterology (ASNEMGE, inactive),* when statutes were also adopted. New statutes ratified, 13 Jun 1991, Munich (Germany); modified, 29 Sep 1992, Munich and 3 Oct 1994, Los Angeles CA (USA); reprinted 17 Aug 1998, Munich; modified Jul 2001, Amsterdam (Netherlands); modified Oct 2006, Berlin (Germany). Former names and other names: *European Society of Digestive Endoscopy* – alias. **Aims** Promote Quality in endoscopy and good endoscopic practice. **Structure** Assembly of Delegates (at Congress); Board. **Languages** English. **Finance** Sources: members' dues. Other sources: contributions; grants; bequests; income from activities. **Activities** Training/education; standards/guidelines; financial and/or material support; publishing activities. **Events** *ESGE Days* Dublin (Ireland) 2023, *ESGE Days* Prague (Czechia) 2022, *Gastroenterology and Endotherapy European Workshop* Brussels (Belgium) 2019, *Days* Prague (Czechia) 2019, *Gastroenterology and Endotherapy European Workshop* Brussels (Belgium) 2018. **Publications** *Endoscopy* – journal.

Members National organizations in 49 countries and territories:
Austria, Belgium, Bosnia-Herzegovina, Bulgaria, Croatia, Cyprus, Czechia, Denmark, Egypt, Estonia, Finland, France, Germany, Greece, Hungary, Iraq, Ireland, Israel, Italy, Jordan, Latvia, Lebanon, Libya, Lithuania, Luxembourg, Montenegro, Morocco, Netherlands, North Macedonia, Norway, Palestine, Poland, Portugal, Romania, Russia, Serbia, Slovakia, Slovenia, Spain, Sudan, Sweden, Switzerland, Syrian AR, Tunisia, Türkiye, UK, Ukraine, United Arab Emirates, Yemen.

NGO Relations Member of (2): *United European Gastroenterology (UEG, #20506); World Endoscopy Organization (WEO, #21380).* Partner of (1): *European Society of Gastroenterology and Endoscopy Nurses and Associates (ESGENA, #08604).* [2022/XD2679/**D**]

♦ European Society of Gastrointestinal Motility / see European Society of Neurogastroenterology and Motility (#08663)
♦ European Society of Gastrointestinal Radiologists / see European Society of Gastrointestinal and Abdominal Radiology (#08605)

♦ European Society of Gender Health and Medicine (ESGHM) 08607

Contact Viale Piave 35, 20129 Milan MI, Italy. T. +39229006267. Fax +39229007018. E-mail: info@gendermedicine.org.
URL: http://www.gendermedicine.org/

Events *International symposium on multiple risk factors in cardiovascular diseases* Lido Is (Italy) 2008. [2012/XM2420/**D**]

♦ European Society of Gene and Cell Therapy (ESGCT) 08608

Contact WATS.ON, 1 Abbey Street, Eynsham, OX29 4TB, UK. E-mail: office@esgct.eu.
Gen Sec address not obtained.
Events Manager address not obtained.
URL: http://www.esgct.eu/

History Jan 1992. Founded with support of *European Hematology Association (EHA, #07473).* Former names and other names: *European Working Group on Human Gene Transfer and Gene Therapy (EWGGT)* – former; *European Society of Gene Therapy (ESGT)* – former (1998). **Aims** Promote basic and clinical research in gene therapy; facilitate education and exchange of information and technologies related to gene therapy; serve as a professional adviser to the community and to regulatory bodies in Europe. **Structure** General Assembly; Board. Scientific sub-committees. **Finance** Sources: members' dues; sponsorship. **Activities** Advocacy/lobbying/activism; awards/prizes/competitions; events/meetings; knowledge management/information dissemination; networking/liaising. **Events** *Annual Congress* Brussels (Belgium) 2023, *Annual Congress* Edinburgh (UK) 2022, *Annual Congress* Brussels (Belgium) 2021, *Annual Congress* Barcelona (Spain) 2019, *Annual Congress* Lausanne (Switzerland) 2018. **Publications** *Journal of Gene Medicine* (12 a year) – official journal. **Members** Individuals (700) in 14 European countries, including Israel. Associate members in countries outside Europe. Membership countries not specified. **IGO Relations** Consultative status with: *European Medicines Agency (EMA, #07767); European Commission (EC, #06633).* **NGO Relations** Member of (1): *Alliance for Regenerative Medicine (ARM).* [2021/XK0751/**D**]

♦ European Society of General Practice/Family Medicine (WONCA Europe) 08609

Sociedad Europea de Medicina de Familia

Admin Sec Inst for Development of Family Medicine, Poljanski nasip 58, 1000 Ljubljana, Slovenia. T. +38614386913. Fax +38614386910. E-mail: secretariateurope@wonca.net.
URL: http://www.woncaeurope.org/

History Founded within *World Organization of Family Doctors (WONCA, #21690).* Also referred to as *WONCA Region Europe.* Bylaws approved Jun 1995; most recently amended Oct 2015, Istanbul (Turkey). Stichting WONCA Europe founded 2007, as a legal entity registered in accordance with Dutch law. **Aims** Improve quality of life through fostering and maintaining high standards of care in general practice/family medicine. **Structure** Council; Executive Board; Statutory Committees (4); Committees (4) includes *European Association for Quality in General Practice/Family Medicine (EQuiP, #06184);* Working Parties. Networks (6): *European Academy of Teachers in General Practice (EURACT, #05817); European General Practice Research Network (EGPRN, #07384); European Network for Prevention and Health Promotion in Family Medicine and General Practice (EUROPREV, #07974); European Rural and Isolated Practitioners Association (EURIPA, #08415); European Society for Quality and Safety in Family Practice (EQUIP, #08718);* The Vasco Da Gama Movement (VdGM). Special Interest Groups (6): *European Primary Care Cardiovascular Society (EPCCS, #08273);* General Practice Infectious diseases Network (GRIN); *International Primary Care Respiratory Group (IPCRG, #14640);* Primary Care Allergy Interest Group (PCAIG); *Primary Care Diabetes Europe (PCDE, #18495); European Society of Primary Care Gastroenterology (ESPCG, #08715).* **Languages** English. **Staff** 1.00 FTE, paid. **Finance** Members' dues. **Activities** Events/meetings; awards/prizes/competitions; training/education; financial and/or material support. **Events** *WONCA Europe Conference* Brussels (Belgium) 2023, *Europe Regional Conference* London (UK) 2022, *Europe Regional Conference* Amsterdam (Netherlands) 2021, *Europe Regional Conference* Bangkok (Thailand) 2020, *European Regional Conference* Bratislava (Slovakia) 2019. **Publications** *European Journal of General Practice (EJGP).* Position papers.

Members Organizations (47) in 45 countries:
Andorra, Armenia, Austria, Belarus, Belgium, Bosnia-Herzegovina, Bulgaria, Croatia, Czechia, Denmark, Estonia, Finland, France, Georgia, Germany, Greece, Hungary, Iceland, Ireland, Israel, Italy, Kazakhstan, Kosovo, Kyrgyzstan, Latvia, Lithuania, Luxembourg, Malta, Netherlands, North Macedonia, Norway, Poland, Portugal, Romania, Russia, Serbia, Slovakia, Slovenia, Spain, Sweden, Switzerland, Tajikistan, Türkiye, UK, Ukraine.

NGO Relations Associated member of: *European Forum for Primary Care (EFPC, #07326).* [2022/XD7183/**D**]

♦ European Society for General Semantics (no recent information)
♦ European Society of Gene Therapy / see European Society of Gene and Cell Therapy (#08608)
♦ European Society for Geography / see Association of European Geographical Societies (#02512)

♦ European Society of Glass Science and Technology (ESG) 08610

Contact Deutsche Glastechnische Gesellschaft eV, Siemensstr 45, 63071 Offenbach, Germany. T. +49699758610. Fax +496997586199. E-mail: info@hvg-dgg.de.

History 23 Oct 1990, Düsseldorf (Germany). **Aims** Advance the science, technology, applications and art of glass, glass ceramics and related materials. **Structure** Rotating Presidency. **Languages** English. **Staff** Voluntary. **Activities** Events/meetings. **Events** *Biennial Conference* Montpellier (France) 2018, *Biennial Conference* Sheffield (UK) 2016, *Biennial Conference* Parma (Italy) 2014, *Biennial Conference* Maastricht (Netherlands) 2012, *Biennial conference* Magdeburg (Germany) 2010.

Members Founding members and European glass technical societies in 3 countries:
Belgium, Germany, UK. [2021.09.07/XD3554/**D**]

♦ European Society of Golf Course Architects (inactive)

European Society Gynaecological
08611

alphabetic sequence excludes
For the complete listing, see Yearbook Online at

♦ European Society for Gynaecological Endoscopy (ESGE) 08611
Central Office Manager Diestsevest 43/0001, 3000 Leuven, Belgium. T. +3216629629. Fax +3216629639. E-mail: centraloffice@esge.org.
URL: http://www.esge.org/
History 1994. Took over activities of *European Society of Hysteroscopy (inactive)*. Registration: Belgium. **Aims** Promote study of gynaecological surgical techniques using endoscopy; encourage exchange of clinical and scientific experience, research and evaluation; recommend standards of training in gynaecological endoscopy. **Structure** Board of Directors; Executive Board; Advisory Board; Special Interest Groups; Working Groups. **Languages** English. **Finance** Members' dues. **Activities** Events/meetings; training/education. **Events** *Annual Congress* Lisbon (Portugal) 2022, *Annual Congress* Rome (Italy) 2021, *Annual Congress* Lisbon (Portugal) 2020, *Regional Meeting* Manila (Philippines) 2019, *Annual Congress* Thessaloniki (Greece) 2019. **Publications** *Gynecological Surgery* (4 a year) – journal.
Members Individuals (800) in 43 countries:
Albania, Argentina, Australia, Austria, Belgium, Brazil, Chile, Croatia, Czechia, Denmark, Egypt, Estonia, Finland, France, Georgia, Germany, Greece, Guatemala, Hungary, Iceland, Indonesia, Ireland, Israel, Italy, Lebanon, Netherlands, Norway, Poland, Portugal, Romania, Russia, Saudi Arabia, Serbia, Slovakia, Slovenia, Spain, Sweden, Switzerland, Tunisia, Türkiye, UK, United Arab Emirates, USA.
NGO Relations Instrumental in setting up: *European Academy of Gynaecological Surgery (EAGS, #05795)*.
[2021/XD5717/v/**D**]

♦ European Society of Gynaecological Oncology (ESGO) 08612
Exec Dir ESGO Office, YMCA Palace, Na Porici 12/1041, 110 00 Prague, Czechia. T. +420725537730. E-mail: adminoffice@esgo.org.
Events Manager address not obtained.
Registered Office 7 Rue François-Versonnex, 1207 Geneva, Switzerland.
URL: https://esgo.org/
History 1983, Venice (Italy). Registration: Switzerland. **Aims** Create an open European platform of individual professionals dedicated to the care of women with gynaecological cancer; be the authority responsible for recognition of gynaecological oncology in Europe; lead Europe in clinical and scientific education in gynaecological oncology and provide standards and supervision for certified training; independently set multi-professional standards of care for women with gynaecological cancer; integrate clinical and basic research into the educational, training and collaborative activities of the Society; promote communication with scientific and professional organizations within Europe and worldwide. **Structure** General Assembly (every 2 years); Executive Council. Committees. Networks: Pan-European Network of Gynaecological Oncological Trial groups (ENGOT); European Network of Young Gynaecological Oncologists (ENYGO); European Network of Translational Research in Gynaecological Oncology (ENTRIGO); European Network of Individualized Treatment in Endometrial Cancer (ENITEC); *European Network of Gynaecological Cancer Advocacy Groups (ENGAGe, #07916)*; International Network on Cancer, Infertility and Pregnancy (INCIP). **Languages** English. **Staff** None. **Finance** Sources: members' dues. **Activities** Certification/accreditation; events/meetings; financial and/or material support; research/documentation; training/education. **Events** *European Congress on Gynaecological Oncology* Berlin (Germany) 2022, *International Meeting* Prague (Czechia) 2021, *State of the Art Conference* Prague (Czechia) 2020, *International Meeting* Athens (Greece) 2019, *Conference on new Insights in Rare Gynaecological Cancers* Lyon (France) 2018. **Publications** *International Journal of Gynaecological Cancer*.
Members Active; Associate; Senior; Honorary: currently about 1,000. Members in 66 countries and territories:
Albania, Algeria, Argentina, Australia, Austria, Belarus, Belgium, Bosnia-Herzegovina, Brazil, Bulgaria, Canada, Chile, China, Croatia, Cyprus, Czechia, Denmark, Egypt, Estonia, Finland, France, Germany, Greece, Guatemala, Hungary, India, Iran Islamic Rep, Ireland, Israel, Italy, Japan, Jordan, Kazakhstan, Korea Rep, Latvia, Lebanon, Lithuania, Mexico, Montenegro, Netherlands, North Macedonia, Norway, Pakistan, Peru, Philippines, Poland, Portugal, Romania, Russia, Saudi Arabia, Serbia, Singapore, Slovakia, Slovenia, South Africa, Spain, Sweden, Switzerland, Taiwan, Tunisia, Türkiye, UK, Ukraine, USA, Uzbekistan, Venezuela.
Members also in the West Indies. Membership countries not specified.
NGO Relations Member of (1): *European Cancer Organisation (ECO, #06432)* (affiliate). Cooperates with (3): *European Board and College of Obstetrics and Gynaecology (EBCOG, #06357)*; *Fédération Internationale de Gynécologie et d'Obstétrique (FIGO, #09638)*; *International Gynecologic Cancer Society (IGCS, #13767)*.
[2022/XD0406/v/**D**]

♦ European Society for Gynaecologic and Obstetric Investigation (internationally oriented national body)

♦ European Society of Gynecology (ESG) 08613
Société Européenne de Gynécologie (SEG)
SG Dipto di Medicina Clinica e Sperimentale, Univ di Pisa, Via Roma 67, 56126 Pisa PI, Italy. E-mail: members@esgynecology.org.
URL: http://www.esgynecology.org/
History Current Articles approved 20 Oct 2017. Registered in accordance with Swiss Civil Code. **Aims** Study and promote the advances in the *gynaecology*, obstetrics and reproductive organs *medicine* fields. **Structure** General Assembly; Board of Directors; Executive Committee. **Activities** Events/meetings; training/education; awards/prizes/competitions. **Events** *Congress* Venice (Italy) 2021, *Congress* Vienna (Austria) 2019, *Congress* Barcelona (Spain) 2017, *Congress* Prague (Czech Rep) 2015, *Congress* Brussels (Belgium) 2013. **Publications** *Seg-Weg* (12 a year) – electronic newsletter. **Members** Founding; Ordinary; Honorary; Supporting. Membership countries not specified. **NGO Relations** Member of: *European Society of Endocrinology (ESE, #08594)*.
[2018/XD7724/**D**]

♦ European Society for Haemapheresis / see European Society for Haemapheresis and Haemotherapy (#08614)

♦ European Society for Haemapheresis and Haemotherapy (ESFH) .. 08614
Pres Dept of Hemotherapy and Hemostasis, Clinic Univ Hosp, Villarroel 170, 08036 Barcelona, Spain.
Admin Assistant Bertegasse 8, 1230 Vienna, Austria. T. +4318895001. Fax +4318895001.
URL: http://www.esfh.eu./
History Current bylaws approved May 2014. Previously also known as: *European Interdisciplinary Society for Haemapheresis and Haemotherapy*; *European Society for Haemapheresis (ESFH)*. **Aims** Function as a European society for all professionals involved and interested in apheresis. **Structure** General Assembly (every 2 years); Executive Board; Industrial Liaison Committee. **Languages** English. **Staff** Voluntary. **Finance** Members' dues. **Activities** Events/meetings; training/education. **Events** *Congress* Vienna (Austria) 2021, *Congress* Vienna (Austria) 2020, *Congress* Valencia (Spain) 2018, *Congress* Florence (Italy) 2014, *Congress* The Hague (Netherlands) 2012. **Publications** *Transfusion and Apheresis Science*. Meeting proceedings.
Members Individuals in 15 countries:
Australia, Austria, Belgium, Canada, Czechia, Hungary, Israel, Italy, Netherlands, Norway, Spain, Sweden, Switzerland, UK, USA.
[2020/XD4444/v/**D**]

♦ European Society of Hair Restoration Surgery (ESHRS) 08615
Admin 46 avenue Foch, 75116 Paris, France.
URL: http://www.eshrs.com/
History 1998. **Events** *Annual Congress* Berlin (Germany) 2011, *Annual Congress* Vienna (Austria) 2010, *Annual Congress* Lisbon (Portugal) 2009, *Annual Congress* Madrid (Spain) 2008, *Annual Congress* Paris (France) 2007.
[2010/XM3738/**D**]

♦ European Society of Handwriting Psychology (ESHP) 08616
Société européenne de graphologie (SEG) – Sociedad Europea de las Ciencias del Grafismo (SEG) – Europäische Gesellschaft für Schriftpsychologie und Schriftexpertise (EGS) – Società Europea di Psicologia della Scrittura (SEPS) – Europees Verbond voor Schriftpsychologie (EVS) – Europeiska Grafologförbundet (EGF) – Europaeisk Selskab for Skriftpsykologi (ESS)
Pres Martha-Ringier-Str 11, 5600 Lenzburg AG, Switzerland.
URL: http://www.egs-graphologie.org/
History Founded 1972. Also referred to as *Europäische Gesellschaft für Schriftpsychologie und Schriftexpertise – European Society of Handwriting Psychology and Handwriting Expertise*. Statutes adopted 14 May 1972; modified 16 May 1973; 15 May 1980; 31 May 1984; 12 May 1988; 24 May 1990. **Aims** As an umbrella organization: coordinate and support international scientific cooperation; provide information and publications for members and the general public; improve the quality of the handwriting psychology discipline; support single organizations and members; carry out public relation work. **Structure** General Assembly; Board of Directors; Scientific Committee; Court of Arbitration; Auditors. **Languages** Dutch, English, French, German. **Finance** Members' dues. Other sources: fees for participation in seminars and congresses; donations. **Activities** Events/meetings. **Events** *Congress* Lindau (Germany) 2021, *Ist Intelligenz das Geheimnis des Erfolgs?* Lindau (Germany) 2016, *Congress* Lindau (Germany) 2014, *Congress* Lindau (Germany) 2012, *Congress* Lindau (Germany) 2010. **Publications** *GraphologyNews*. *GraphoLogisches – Serie 1: Diagnostik & Beratung*.
Members Societies (9), in 11 countries:
Argentina, Austria, Belgium, Denmark, Germany, Israel, Italy, Netherlands, Sweden, Switzerland, USA.
[2021/XD7830/**D**]

♦ European Society of Handwriting Psychology and Handwriting Expertise / see European Society of Handwriting Psychology (#08616)

♦ European Society of Head and Neck Radiology (ESHNR) 08617
Société européenne de radiologie de la tête et du cou – Sociedad Europea de Radiologia de la Cabeza y del Cuello
Office Am Gestade 1, 1010 Vienna, Austria. T. +4315334064-918. E-mail: office@eshnr.eu.
URL: https://eshnr.eu/
History 21 Jan 1987, Antwerp (Belgium). Registration: Zentrales Vereinsregister, No/ID: 421925549, Austria, Vienna. **Aims** Advance knowledge in the field of head and neck diagnostic radiology, interventional radiology and diagnostic imaging. **Structure** Executive Committee. **Languages** English. **Finance** Members' dues. **Activities** Research/documentation; training/education; events/meetings; awards/prizes/competitions. **Events** *Annual Congress* Tallinn (Estonia) 2022, *Annual Congress* Vienna (Austria) 2021, *Annual Congress* Salzburg (Austria) 2020, *Annual Congress* Palermo (Italy) 2019, *Annual Congress* London (UK) 2018. **Publications** *European Radiology* (6 a year) – journal.
Members Societies in 32 countries:
Australia, Austria, Belgium, Canada, Chile, China, Croatia, Czechia, Finland, France, Germany, Greece, Hungary, Ireland, Italy, Mexico, Netherlands, Norway, Poland, Portugal, Romania, Serbia, Singapore, Slovakia, Slovenia, South Africa, Spain, Sweden, Switzerland, Tunisia, UK, USA.
NGO Relations Member of: *European Society of Radiology (ESR, #08720)*.
[2021/XD1710/**D**]

♦ European Society of Head and Neck Reconstructive Surgeons (inactive)

♦ European Society of Health and Medical Sociology (ESHMS) 08618
Chair Korte Meer, 5, 9000 Ghent, Belgium. T. +3292646803.
URL: http://www.eshms.eu/
History 1983, Edinburgh, under the auspices of *WHO Regional Office for Europe (#20945)*, as *European Society of Medical Sociology (ESMS)*. Provisional constitution accepted 3 Jun 1986, Groningen (Netherlands). Constitution accepted 25 Sep 1988, Zagreb (Yugoslavia). **Aims** Create a forum for discussion of health issues by scientists in the field of sociology and public health; collate and synthesize knowledge and experience; create opportunities for research and for participation in international cooperation and planning. **Structure** General Assembly (every 2 years). Executive Committee of 9, including President, Secretary/Treasurer and Editor. **Languages** English. **Staff** Part-time, voluntary. **Finance** Members' dues: euro 25. **Activities** Standing working groups for specific research topics; biennial scientific meetings and summer schools. **Events** *Imagining beyond crisis – health, society, medicine* Uppsala (Sweden) 2020, *Congress* Lisbon (Portugal) 2018, *Congress* Geneva (Switzerland) 2016, *Health and welfare challenges in Europe – East, West, North and South* Helsinki (Finland) 2014, *Congress / Scientific Congress* Hannover (Germany) 2012. **Publications** *ESHMS Newsletter* (3 a year).
Members Individuals (200) in 25 countries:
Austria, Belgium, Croatia, Czechia, Denmark, Estonia, Finland, France, Germany, Greece, Hungary, Ireland, Italy, Latvia, Lithuania, Netherlands, Norway, Poland, Portugal, Romania, Slovakia, Spain, Sweden, Switzerland, UK.
[2012.06.01/XD0999/v/**D**]

♦ European Society for Heart and Lung Transplantation (ESHLT) 08619
Hon Pres Mater Hosp, Eccles St, Dublin, CO. DUBLIN, Ireland.
Hon Sec address not obtained.
URL: http://www.eshlt.org/
Events *Annual Meeting* Wengen (Switzerland) 2022, *Annual Meeting* Wengen (Switzerland) 2019, *Annual Meeting* Wengen (Switzerland) 2018, *Annual Meeting* Wengen (Switzerland) 2017, *Annual Meeting* Wengen (Switzerland) 2016.
Members Full in 13 countries:
Austria, Belgium, Denmark, Finland, Germany, Israel, Italy, Netherlands, Norway, Spain, Sweden, Switzerland, UK.
NGO Relations Close links with: *European Society for Organ Transplantation (ESOT, #08676)*.
[2019/XD9313/**D**]

♦ European Society for Hemapheresis / see European Society for Haemapheresis and Haemotherapy (#08614)
♦ European Society of Hematology (inactive)
♦ European Society for the History of Dermatology and Venerology (no recent information)

♦ European Society for the History of Economic Thought (ESHET) ... 08620
Gen Sec c/o Univ Haute-Alsace, 61 ave de la Forêt Noire, 67085 Strasbourg CEDEX, France.
URL: http://www.eshet.net/
History 1995. **Aims** Promote: teaching and research in the history of economic thought in Europe, taking account of different traditions and languages; cooperation with European national economic societies and organizations in the field; communications and the exchange of ideas amongst European teachers and researchers in the field; establishment of links with national economic societies and organizations in the field; innovative methods in the teaching of the subject; collaborative research on a European basis. **Structure** Executive Committee, comprising President, Vice-President, Secretary, Treasurer, Chair of the Council and 3 members. Council, comprising Chair, Vice-Chair and 14 members. **Languages** English. **Events** *Annual Conference* Padua (Italy) 2022, *Annual Conference* Sofia (Bulgaria) 2021, *Annual Conference* Sofia (Bulgaria) 2020, *Annual Conference* Lille (France) 2019, *Annual Conference* Madrid (Spain) 2018. **Publications** Conference papers.
Members in 28 countries:
Argentina, Australia, Austria, Belgium, Brazil, Canada, Colombia, Czechia, Denmark, France, Germany, Greece, Hungary, Ireland, Italy, Japan, Korea Rep, Mexico, Netherlands, Norway, Poland, Portugal, Russia, Spain, Sweden, Switzerland, UK, USA.
[2022/XD6605/**D**]

♦ European Society for the History of the Human Sciences (ESHHS) .. 08621
Sec address not obtained.
Pres address not obtained.
URL: http://www.eshhs.eu/
History 1982, Amsterdam (Netherlands), as *Cheiron-Europe*. **Aims** Promote international, multidisciplinary cooperation in scholarly activity and research in the history of the human sciences. **Structure** Executive Board, comprising President, Treasurer and Secretary. **Languages** English, French, German. **Staff** None. **Finance** Members' dues. **Events** *Annual Conference* Budapest (Hungary) 2019, *Annual Conference* Groningen (Netherlands) 2018, *Annual Conference* Bari (Italy) 2017, *Annual Conference* Barcelona (Spain) 2016, *Annual Conference* Angers (France) 2015.
Members Individuals in 28 countries:
Argentina, Australia, Austria, Belgium, Brazil, Bulgaria, Canada, Finland, France, Germany, Greece, Hungary, Ireland, Israel, Italy, Japan, Netherlands, Norway, Romania, Russia, Serbia, South Africa, Spain, Sweden, Switzerland, Türkiye, UK, USA.
[2015/XD8325/v/**D**]

♦ European Society for History of Law (unconfirmed)

♦ European Society for the History of Photography (ESHPh) 08622
Association européenne pour l'histoire de la photographie – Europäische Gesellschaft für die Geschichte der Photographie
Pres Komoediengasse 1-1-17, 1020 Vienna, Austria. T. +436764303365. E-mail: office@eshph.org.
URL: http://www.eshph.org/

History 19 Nov 1978, Leverkusen (Germany). Founded after Resolution had been passed, 15-16 Dec 1978, Deurne, Antwerp (Belgium). Moved to London (UK), 1989, and to Vienna (Austria), 2001. Registration: Start date: 3 Mar 2004, Austria. **Aims** Further interest in the history of photography; promote extension of knowledge in the field, including establishment and maintenance of a system for exchange of information; organize and coordinate international meetings. **Structure** General Assembly (annual); Executive Committee; International Advisory Board; Secretariat in Vienna (Austria). **Languages** English, German. **Finance** Sources: donations; members' dues. **Activities** Events/meetings; research and development. **Events** *Symposium* Toronto, ON (Canada) 2022, *Symposium* Vienna (Austria) 2019, *Round Table on Cairo* Cairo (Egypt) 2018, *Symposium* Vienna (Austria) 2016, *Symposium* Vienna (Austria) 2012. **Publications** *ESHPh The International Letter – ESHPh La lettre internationale* (3 a year) – newsletter; *PhotoResearcher* (2 a year). Symposium proceedings (regular).
Members Institutional; Personal; Student. Institutional (125) in 21 countries:
Australia, Austria, Belgium, Canada, Czechia, Denmark, Finland, France, Germany, Hungary, Italy, Japan, Lithuania, Netherlands, Norway, Romania, Spain, Sweden, Switzerland, UK, USA. [2022.10.31/XD6559/**D**]

♦ European Society for the History of Science (ESHS) 08623

Sec c/o CHSTM, Univ of Manchester, Oxford Rd, Manchester, M13 9PL, UK.
URL: http://www.eshs.org/

History 2003. Registration: France. **Aims** Promote European cooperation in the field of the history of science understood in the broadest sense. **Structure** Steering Committee, comprising President, Vice-President, President Elect, Treasurer, Secretary and 4 members. **Languages** English. **Events** *International Conference* Brussels (Belgium) 2022, *International Conference* Bologna (Italy) 2020, *International Conference* London (UK) 2018, *International Conference* Prague (Czechia) 2016, *International Conference* Lisbon (Portugal) 2014. **Publications** *Centaurus* – journal.
Members Full in 25 countries:
Austria, Belgium, Czechia, Denmark, Egypt, France, Germany, Greece, Hungary, Italy, Netherlands, Norway, Poland, Portugal, Romania, Russia, Slovakia, Slovenia, Spain, Sweden, Switzerland, Türkiye, UK, Ukraine, USA. [2021/XJ0159/**D**]

♦ European Society for Histotechnology (inactive)
♦ European Society for Hospital Sterile Supply (inactive)

♦ European Society of Human Genetics (ESHG) 08624

Exec Officer c/o WMA GmbH, Alserstrasse 4, 1090 Vienna, Austria. T. +431405138335. Fax +4314078274. E-mail: office@eshg.org – eo@eshg.org.
URL: http://www.eshg.org/

History 1967. Registration: Banque-Carrefour des Entreprises, Start date: 15 Jul 1991, Belgium; Start date: 14 Jan 2020, Austria. **Aims** Promote research in basic and applied human and medical genetics; facilitate contact between all persons who share these aims. **Structure** Membership Meeting; Board; Executive Board; Committees. **Languages** English. **Finance** Sources: contributions; meeting proceeds; members' dues. **Activities** Advocacy/lobbying/activism; awards/prizes/competitions; awareness raising; events/meetings; networking/liaising; publishing activities; standards/guidelines; training/education. **Events** *Annual Congress* Gothenburg (Sweden) 2026, *Annual Congress* Vienna (Austria) 2025, *Annual Congress* Berlin (Germany) 2024, *Annual Congress* Glasgow (UK) 2023, *Annual Congress* Vienna (Austria) 2022. **Publications** *European Journal of Human Genetics (IJHG).*
Members Categories: Regular; Student; Senior; Honorary. Individuals in 77 countries and territories:
Albania, Angola, Argentina, Armenia, Australia, Austria, Bahrain, Belarus, Belgium, Bosnia-Herzegovina, Brazil, Bulgaria, Canada, Chile, China, Colombia, Croatia, Cyprus, Czechia, Denmark, Dominica, Ecuador, Egypt, Estonia, Finland, France, Germany, Greece, Hong Kong, Hungary, Iceland, India, Indonesia, Iran Islamic Rep, Iraq, Ireland, Israel, Italy, Japan, Korea Rep, Kuwait, Latvia, Lebanon, Libya, Lithuania, Malta, Mexico, Netherlands, New Zealand, North Macedonia, Norway, Philippines, Poland, Portugal, Qatar, Romania, Russia, Saudi Arabia, Serbia, Singapore, Slovakia, Slovenia, South Africa, Spain, Sweden, Switzerland, Syrian AR, Taiwan, Tanzania UR, Thailand, Tunisia, Türkiye, UK, Ukraine, United Arab Emirates, USA, Venezuela.
NGO Relations Member of (2): *Biomedical Alliance in Europe (#03251); Global Alliance for Genomics and Health (GA4GH, #10199).* Affiliated with (1): *European Board of Medical Genetics (EBMG, #06361).* Instrumental in setting up (3): *EGAN – Patients Network for Medical Research and Health (EGAN, #05394); International Federation of Human Genetics Societies (IFHGS, #13451); World Alliance of Organizations for the Prevention and Treatment of Genetic and Congenital Conditions (WAO, #21085).* [2022.02.18/XD8510/v/**D**]

♦ European Society of Human Reproduction and Embryology (ESHRE) 08625

Société européenne de reproduction humaine et d'embryologie – Europese Vereniging voor Humane Reproductie en Embryologie

Managing Dir Meerstraat 60, 1852 Grimbergen, Belgium. E-mail: info@eshre.eu.
Communications Assistant address not obtained.
Chair Human Reproduction Unit, Dept of Ob/Gyn – CHLN, Hosp de Santa Maria, Av Prof Egas Moniz MB, 1649-028 Lisbon, Portugal.
URL: http://www.eshre.eu/

History 1985, Bonn (Germany). Founded at first Annual Meeting. Registration: Banque-Carrefour des Entreprises, No/ID: 0430.069.888, Start date: 30 Dec 1986, Belgium. **Aims** Promote interest in, and understanding of, reproductive biology and medicine. **Structure** General Assembly (annual, at Annual Meeting); Executive Committee; Advisory Committee. Sub-Committees (3): Publications; Finance; Annual Meeting. Special Interest Groups (12). Central Office located in Grimbergen (Belgium). International Scientific Committee appointed by Executive Committee for each Annual Meeting. ESHRE Paramedical Group. **Languages** English. **Staff** 11.00 FTE, paid. **Finance** Sources: meeting proceeds; members' dues. Other sources: funds from pharmaceutical companies. **Activities** Certification/accreditation; events/meetings; knowledge management/information dissemination; research/documentation. **Events** *Annual Meeting* Copenhagen (Denmark) 2023, *Annual Meeting* Milan (Italy) 2022, *Joint Meeting* Lisbon (Portugal) 2021, *FUSION : International Conference on Reproductive Medicine and ART* Mumbai (India) 2021, *Annual Meeting* Paris (France) 2021. **Publications** *ESHRE Update* (12 a year) – electronic newsletter; *Human Reproduction* (12 a year) – journal; *Molecular Human Reproduction* (12 a year); *Human Reproduction Update* (6 a year); *Focus on Reproduction* (3 a year) – magazine.
Members Individuals active in the field in 105 countries and territories:
Albania, Algeria, Argentina, Armenia, Australia, Austria, Azerbaijan, Bahrain, Bangladesh, Barbados, Belarus, Belgium, Bolivia, Bosnia-Herzegovina, Brazil, Bulgaria, Canada, Chile, China, Colombia, Comoros, Costa Rica, Croatia, Cyprus, Czechia, Denmark, Ecuador, Egypt, Estonia, Finland, France, Georgia, Germany, Ghana, Greece, Guatemala, Hong Kong, Hungary, Iceland, India, Indonesia, Iran Islamic Rep, Iraq, Ireland, Israel, Italy, Jamaica, Japan, Jordan, Kazakhstan, Korea Rep, Kuwait, Latvia, Lebanon, Libya, Liechtenstein, Lithuania, Luxembourg, Malaysia, Malta, Mexico, Moldova, Morocco, Netherlands, New Zealand, Nigeria, North Macedonia, Norway, Oman, Pakistan, Palestine, Panama, Peru, Philippines, Poland, Portugal, Qatar, Romania, Russia, San Marino, Saudi Arabia, Serbia, Singapore, Slovakia, Slovenia, South Africa, Spain, Sri Lanka, Sudan, Sweden, Switzerland, Syrian AR, Taiwan, Thailand, Tunisia, Türkiye, Uganda, UK, Ukraine, United Arab Emirates, Uruguay, USA, Uzbekistan, Venezuela, Yemen.
NGO Relations Member of (3): *Associations and Conference Forum (AC Forum, #02909); Biomedical Alliance in Europe (#03251); International Infertility Counseling Organization (IICO, #13843).* Instrumental in setting up (1): *World Endometriosis Research Foundation (WERF).* [2021/XD0497/v/**D**]

♦ European Society for Hybrid, Molecular and Translational Imaging (ESHIMT) 08626

Europäische Gesellschaft für hybride, molekulare und translationale Bildgebung

Contact Am Gestade 1, 1010 Vienna, Austria. T. +4315334064903. Fax +4315334064445. E-mail: office@eshi-society.org.
URL: http://www.eshi-society.org/

History Current statutes approved Mar 2018. Registered in accordance with Austrian law: ZVR 703077733. **Aims** Develop clinically relevant imaging probes and technologies and translate them from bench to bedside to help improve *patient* care. **Structure** General Assembly; Executive Committee. **Languages** English. **Finance** Members' dues. **Activities** Events/meetings; knowledge management/information dissemination; networking/liaising; awareness raising. **Members** Full; Corresponding; Training; Honorary; Retired; Associate; Supporting. Membership countries not specified. **NGO Relations** Member of: *European Cancer Organisation (ECO, #06432).* [2020/XM8708/**D**]

♦ European Society of Hypertension (ESH) 08627

Società Europea dell'Ipertensione

Pres First Cardiology Clinic, Hippokration Hosp, Univ of Athens, 114 Vassilisis Sofias Ave, 115 27 Athens, Greece.
Sec Inst für Klinische Pharmakologie und Toxikologie, Charité-Univ Berlin, Charitéplatz 1, 10117 Berlin, Germany. T. +4930450525112. Fax +4930450752511 2.
URL: http://www.eshonline.org/

History Founded 1989, following a series of European Hypertension Meetings in Milan (Italy), when the need for support from a scientific society was demonstrated. **Aims** Provide a stable and organized European platform for scientific exchange in hypertension. **Structure** Scientific Council. **Languages** English. **Staff** 3.00 FTE, voluntary. **Finance** Members' dues. Meeting proceeds. Annual budget: about Swiss Fr 500,000. **Activities** Events/meetings; training/education; projects/programmes; awards/prizes/competitions; knowledge management/information dissemination. **Events** *Annual Meeting* Athens (Greece) 2022, *Annual Meeting* 2021, *Annual Meeting* Milan (Italy) 2021, *Annual Meeting* Glasgow (UK) 2020, *Annual Meeting* Milan (Italy) 2019. **Publications** *Blood Pressure* – journal; *ESH Clinical Newsletter*; *Journal of Hypertension.*
Members Full in 52 countries and territories:
Algeria, Argentina, Australia, Bahrain, Bangladesh, Brazil, Cambodia, Cameroon, Canada, Chile, China, Colombia, Cuba, Dominican Rep, Egypt, Ethiopia, Guadeloupe, Guatemala, Hong Kong, India, Indonesia, Iraq, Israel, Japan, Jordan, Kenya, Korea Rep, Kuwait, Lebanon, Libya, Malaysia, Mexico, Mozambique, New Zealand, Nigeria, Oman, Pakistan, Paraguay, Peru, Puerto Rico, Saudi Arabia, Singapore, South Africa, Syrian AR, Taiwan, Thailand, Tunisia, United Arab Emirates, Uruguay, USA, Venezuela, Yemen.
IGO Relations *European Commission (EC, #06633).* **NGO Relations** Represented on Board of: *European Board for Accreditation in Cardiology (EBAC, #06353).* [2019.02.13/XD2396/**D**]

♦ European Society for Hyperthermic Oncology (ESHO) 08628

Office c/o Conventus Congressmanagement & Marketing GmbH, Kristin Geist, Carl-Pulfrich-Strasse 1, 07745 Jena, Germany. T. +4936413116163. Fax +4936413116244. E-mail: esho-society@conventus.de.
Sec Amsterdam UMC, Cancer Center Amsterdam Institute, De Boelelaan 1118, 1081 HV Amsterdam, Netherlands.
URL: http://www.esho.info/

History 6 Feb 1987, Cardiff (UK). Registration: Start date: 16 Sep 1990, Germany. **Aims** Promote fundamental and applied research in physics, engineering, biological and clinical sciences relating to the use of hyperthermia in *cancer* therapy; facilitate integration and exchange of information between different disciplines in the study of biological effects of heat in treatment of cancer. **Structure** Council; Committees (3). **Languages** English. **Finance** Annual budget: euro 20,000. **Activities** Events/meetings. **Events** *Annual Meeting* Gothenburg (Sweden) 2022, *International Congress of Hyperthermic Oncology (ICHO)* Rotterdam (Netherlands) 2021, *ICHO : Quadrennial International Congress of Hyperthermic Oncology* Rotterdam (Netherlands) 2020, *Annual Conference* Warsaw (Poland) 2019, *ESHO Annual Conference* Berlin (Germany) 2018. **Publications** *International Journal of Hyperthermia.*
Members Individuals in 31 countries and territories:
Austria, Belarus, Canada, Czechia, Denmark, France, Germany, Greece, Hong Kong, Hungary, India, Iran Islamic Rep, Ireland, Israel, Italy, Japan, Jordan, Korea Rep, Netherlands, Norway, Poland, Portugal, Russia, Saudi Arabia, Spain, Sweden, Switzerland, Türkiye, UK, Ukraine, USA.
NGO Relations Cooperates with (2): *Asian Society for Hyperthermic Oncology (ASHO)*; Society for Thermal Medicine. [2022/XD0366/v/**D**]

♦ European Society of Hypnosis (ESH) 08629

Main Office Suite 2/8, Waterloo Chambers, 19 Waterloo St, Glasgow, G2 6AY, UK. E-mail: info@esh-hypnosis.eu – mail@esh-hypnosis.eu.
URL: http://www.esh-hypnosis.eu/

History Aug 1980, Malmö (Sweden). Initally set up informally. Formal establishment, 20 Aug 1990, Konstanz (Germany FR), during 5th European Congress of Hypnosis, when constitution was ratified. **Aims** Develop experimental and clinical hypnosis in Europe; encourage closer cooperation between both Western and Eastern European societies in the field of hypnosis, psychosomatic medicine and related disciplines and schools. **Structure** Board of Directors. **Languages** English. **Staff** Voluntary. **Finance** Sources: members' dues. **Activities** Awards/prizes/competitions; events/meetings; research/documentation. **Events** *Congress* Türkiye 2023, *Congress* Basel (Switzerland) 2020, *Congress* Manchester (UK) 2017, *Triennial Congress* Sorrento (Italy) 2014, *Triennial Congress* Istanbul (Turkey) 2011. **Publications** *Contemporary Hypnosis and Integrative Medicine* – official journal.
Members National European societies (48), representing 14,000 members, in 24 countries:
Austria, Belgium, Bulgaria, Czechia, Denmark, Finland, France, Germany, Hungary, Iceland, Israel, Italy, Latvia, Luxembourg, Netherlands, Norway, Russia, Slovenia, Spain, Sweden, Switzerland, Türkiye, UK, Ukraine.
Confédération Francophone d'Hypnose et Thérapies brèves (CFHTB).
NGO Relations Cooperates with (1): *International Society of Hypnosis (ISH, #15190).* [2021/XD2431/**D**]

♦ European Society for Immunodeficiencies (ESID) 08630

Groupe européen sur les immunodéficiences

Admin Office address not obtained. E-mail: info@esid.org.
Sec Anna Meyer Children's Hospital, Viale Gaetano Pieraccini 24, 50139 Florence FI, Italy.
URL: http://www.esid.org/

History 1994. Developing from an informal group *European Group for Immunodeficiencies (EGID),* which had existed since 1983. **Aims** Facilitate exchange of ideas and information among doctors, nurses, biomedical investigators, patients and their families concerned with primary immunodeficiency diseases; promote research on causes, mechanisms and treatment of these disorders. **Languages** English. **Finance** Sources: sponsorship; subscriptions. **Activities** Events/meetings; research and development; training/education. **Events** *Biennial Meeting* Gothenburg (Sweden) 2022, *Biennial Meeting* Amsterdam (Netherlands) 2020, *Biennial Meeting* Lisbon (Portugal) 2018, *Biennial Meeting* Barcelona (Spain) 2016, *Biennial Meeting* Prague (Czech Rep) 2014. **Publications** *ESID Newsletter* (4 a year). Information Services: password-protected access for registered users in documenting centres. **Information Services** *Online Patient and Research Database for PID.*
Members Full in 51 countries:
Australia, Austria, Belgium, Brazil, Bulgaria, Canada, Costa Rica, Croatia, Cyprus, Czechia, Denmark, Egypt, Estonia, Finland, France, Germany, Greece, Hungary, Iceland, India, Iran Islamic Rep, Ireland, Israel, Italy, Japan, Korea Rep, Kuwait, Lithuania, Malaysia, Mexico, Montenegro, Netherlands, New Zealand, Norway, Oman, Poland, Portugal, Romania, Russia, Saudi Arabia, Serbia, Slovakia, Slovenia, South Africa, Spain, Sweden, Switzerland, Türkiye, UK, Ukraine, USA.
Associate members in 3 countries:
Australia, India, USA.
NGO Relations Instrumental in setting up (1): *European Society for Blood and Marrow Transplantation (EBMT, #08533)* (as EGID). Joint meetings with: *International Nursing Group for Immunodeficiencies (INGID, #14386).* [2022/XD3264/**D**]

♦ European Society for Impotence Research / see European Society for Sexual Medicine (#08733)
♦ European Society for Infectious Diseases in Obstetrics and Gynaecology (no recent information)

♦ European Society of Integrative Medicine (ESIM) 08631

Pres Luisenstr 57, 10117 Berlin, Germany. T. +4930450529002. Fax +4930450529902. E-mail: esim@charite.de.
Sec address not obtained.
URL: https://www.european-society-integrative-medicine.org/

History Jul 2011, Berlin (Germany). Registration: Germany. **Aims** Advance science, research, education and further training; support medical care; provide advice on policy in the realm of integrative medicine. **Structure** General Assembly; Expanded Executive Board; Executive Board. **Languages** English. **Staff** Voluntary. **Finance** Sources: members' dues. **Activities** Awards/prizes/competitions; events/meetings; politics/policy/regulatory. **Events** *World Congress on Integrative Medicine and Health (WCIMH)* Rome (Italy) 2023, *European Congress for Integrative Medicine* Porto (Portugal) 2022, *European Congress for Integrative Medicine* London (UK) 2021, *European Congress for Integrative Medicine* Barcelona (Spain) 2019, *European Congress for Integrative Medicine* Ljubljana (Slovenia) 2018. **Publications** None. **Members** Full; Sponsoring; Honorary. Membership countries not specified. **IGO Relations** None. **NGO Relations** Also links with national organizations. [2023.02.14/XJ9127/**D**]

♦ **European Society of Intensive Care Medicine (ESICM)** **08632**
CEO Rue Belliard 19, 1040 Brussels, Belgium. T. +3225590350. Fax +3225590379. E-mail: dominique.deboom@esicm.org – administration@esicm.org.
URL: http://www.esicm.org/
History 1982, Geneva (Switzerland). Registration: Banque-Carrefour des Entreprises, No/ID: 0467.040.944, Start date: 21 Oct 1999, Belgium; EU Transparency Register, No/ID: 872244238453-63, Start date: 8 Jun 2020. **Aims** Promote the highest standards of multidisciplinary care of critically ill patients through education, research and professional development. **Structure** General Assembly; Council; Executive Committee. **Languages** English. **Staff** 12.50 FTE, paid. **Finance** Sources: meeting proceeds; members' dues. **Activities** Awards/prizes/competitions; awareness raising; events/meetings; standards/guidelines; training/education. **Events** *LIVES 40 Conference* Madrid (Spain) 2022, *LIVES Annual Congress* Paris (France) 2022, *LIVES Annual Congress* Copenhagen (Denmark) 2021, *LIVES Annual Congress* Madrid (Spain) 2020, *EuroAsia Conference* Taipei (Taiwan) 2020. **Publications** *Intensive Care Medicine* (12 a year) – journal; *Intensive Care Experimental Journal*.
Members National societies in 56 countries and territories:
Argentina, Australia, Austria, Belgium, Brazil, Bulgaria, Canada, Chile, China, Colombia, Croatia, Cyprus, Czechia, Denmark, Egypt, Estonia, Finland, France, Georgia, Germany, Greece, Hungary, Iceland, India, Ireland, Israel, Italy, Japan, Korea Rep, Lebanon, Libya, Lithuania, Moldova, Netherlands, New Zealand, North Macedonia, Norway, Panama, Peru, Poland, Portugal, Russia, Saudi Arabia, Scotland, Serbia, Singapore, Slovenia, Spain, Sweden, Switzerland, Taiwan, Türkiye, UK, United Arab Emirates, USA, Vietnam.
Included in the above, 1 regional society:
Consorcio Centroamericano y del Caribe de Terapia Intensiva.
Individuals (9,000) in 122 countries and territories. Membership countries not specified.
NGO Relations Represented on: *European Resuscitation Council (ERC, #08385)*. Member of: *Biomedical Alliance in Europe (#03251)*; *European Public Health Alliance (EPHA, #08297)*; *Federation of European and International Associations Established in Belgium (FAIB, #09508)*. [2022.05.10/XD0801/v/**D**]

♦ **European Society for Intercultural Theology and Interreligious Studies (ESITIS)** **08633**
Pres c/o Uppsala University, Teologiska institutionen, PO Box 511, SE-751 20 Uppsala, Sweden. T. +46184712197.
URL: http://www.esitis.org/
History 19 Mar 2005, Amsterdam (Netherlands). **Aims** Stimulate and coordinate research and education in intercultural and interreligious studies in theology, science of religion, anthropology and philosophy at graduate and post-graduate level. **Structure** Board of 6 members, including Chairman and Secretary. Secretariat rotates. **Languages** English. **Events** *Resurgence of religion in Europe – exploring the implications of religious pluralism in Europe* Birmingham (UK) 2007. **Publications** *Studies in Interreligious Dialogue. Currents of Encounter* – series; *Studies in World Christianity and Interreligious Relations* – series. **Members** Membership countries not specified. [2015/XM3331/**D**]

♦ European Society for Intermediate Filament Biology (inactive)

♦ **European Society of International Law (ESIL)** **08634**
Société européenne de droit international (SEDI)
Secretariat c/o Ac of European Law EUI, Villa Salviati, Via Bolognese 156, 50139 Florence FI, Italy. T. +39554685512. Fax +39554685517. E-mail: esil.secretariat@eui.eu.
URL: http://www.esil-sedi.eu/
History 27 May 2001, Florence (Italy). **Aims** Encourage study of international law to foster inquiry, discussion and innovation; promote greater understanding of the role of international law in the world today. **Structure** General Assembly (annual); Board; Interest groups (16); Secretariat based at Academy of European Law at the European University Institute, Florence (Italy). **Languages** English, French. **Staff** 2.00 FTE, paid. **Finance** Members' dues. Supported by: *Academy of European Law, Florence (see: #09034)*. **Activities** Networking/liaising; events/meetings; training/education; awareness raising. **Events** *Annual Conference* Vilnius (Lithuania) 2024, *Annual Conference* Aix-en-Provence (France) 2023, *Annual Conference* Utrecht (Netherlands) 2022, *Annual Conference* Stockholm (Sweden) 2021, *Annual Conference* Stockholm (Sweden) 2020. **Publications** *Conference Paper Series*; *ESIL Book Series (OUP)*. Conference proceedings. **Members** Membership open to all those with an interest in international law who are interested in contributing to the realization of the goals of the Society; no limitations of nationality or qualification. Categories: Lifetime; Honorary; Institutional; Regular; Student; Retired; Reduced regular; Reduced student. Membership countries not specified. [2021/XD9371/**D**]

♦ **European Society of Intravenous Anaesthesia (EuroSIVA)** **08635**
Scientific Secretariat Univ Dept of Anaesthesia, Level 2 – Queen Elizabeth Bldg, Glasgow Royal Infirmary, 10 Alexandra Parade, Glasgow, G4 0SF, UK. T. +441412114625. Fax +441412111191. E-mail: secretariat@eurosiva.eu.
Registration Secretariat Dept of Anaesthesiology and Intensive Care, Orthopaedic Univ Clinic Balgrist, Forchstrasse 340, 8008 Zurich ZH, Switzerland. T. +4113863101. Fax +4113861609. E-mail: registration@eurosiva.eu.
URL: http://www.eurosiva.eu/
History 1998. **Structure** Board of 9 members. **Events** *Annual Meeting / Meeting* Berlin (Germany) 2015, *Annual Meeting / Meeting* Stockholm (Sweden) 2014, *Winter Meeting* Crans-Montana (Switzerland) 2012, *Annual Meeting / Meeting* Paris (France) 2012, *Annual Meeting / Meeting* Amsterdam (Netherlands) 2011. **NGO Relations** *Asian and Oceanic Society for Intravenous Anaesthesia (AOSIVA, no recent information)*; *World Society of Intravenous Anaesthesia (World SIVA ONLUS, #21803)*. Speciality organization of: *European Society of Anaesthesiology and Intensive Care (ESAIC, #08518)*. [2013/XD7702/**D**]

♦ **European Society for Isotope Research (ESIR)** **08636**
Contact address not obtained.
Pres pl Marii Curie-Sklodowskiej 1, 20-031 Lublin, Poland.
URL: https://www.esir.org.pl/
History 1992. Founded during Isotope Workshop I. **Structure** General Assembly; Advisory Board; Revision Committee. **Finance** Sources: members' dues. **Events** *Isotope Workshop* Graz (Austria) 2023, *Isotope Workshop* Lublin (Poland) 2019, *Isotope Workshop* Băile Govora (Romania) 2017, *Isotope Workshop* Zadar (Croatia) 2015, *Isotope Workshop* Freiberg (Germany) 2013. **Members** Membership countries not specified. [2023/XJ8084/**D**]

♦ **European Society for Jet Ventilation (ESJV)** **08637**
Pres Dept of Anesthesiology, Univ Clinics Heidelberg, Im Neuenheimer Feld 110, 69121 Heidelberg, Germany. T. +496221566351. Fax +496221565234.
URL: http://www.esjv.org/
History 21 Sep 2000, Paris (France). **Aims** Promote exchange of information among european medical doctors and engineers who use, develop, investigate or are interested in jet ventilation; raise the standards of jet ventilation by fostering and encouraging education, research, scientific programmes and exchange of knowledge and information; promote improvements in safety and quality of care of patients undergoing jet ventilation and related techniques; promote and protect the interests of its members. **Structure** General Assembly (every 2 years). Board, comprising President, Vice-President and Treasurer. **Languages** English. **Staff** Voluntary. **Finance** Members' dues: euro 30. **Activities** Organizes symposia and workshops. **Events** *Biennial meeting and general assembly* Tampere (Finland) 2010, *Biennial meeting and general assembly* Heidelberg (Germany) 2008, *Biennial meeting and general assembly* London (UK) 2006, *Biennial meeting and general assembly* Vienna (Austria) 2004, *Biennial meeting and general assembly* Jena (Germany) 2002. [2009.06.01/XJ4172/**D**]

♦ European Society of Knee Surgery and Arthroscopy / see European Society of Sports Traumatology, Knee Surgery and Arthroscopy (#08741)

♦ **European Society for Laboratory Animal Veterinarians (ESLAV)** . . . **08638**
Pres address not obtained. E-mail: president@eslav.org.
Pres-Elect address not obtained. E-mail: president.elect@eslav.org.
Registered Office c/o Pfizer Research Center, Pocé sur Cisse, BP 109, 37401 Amboise CEDEX, France.
URL: https://www.eslav.org/
History Jun 1996, Basel (Switzerland). Founded at the 6th symposium of *Federation of European Laboratory Animal Science Associations (FELASA, #09509)*. Registration: France; EU Transparency Register, No/ID: 877221923440-53. **Aims** Provide a forum for veterinarians to discuss common issues of concern in the field of laboratory animal science and pool resources where appropriate, in general and in Europe specifically; promote and disseminate expert veterinary knowledge in the field of laboratory animal science; serve as a contact point for other organisations seeking advice from veterinary specialists in the humane care and use of animals in research. **Structure** General Meeting (annual); Governing Board; Ad hoc committees. **Languages** English. **Finance** Sources: grants; members' dues; sponsorship. **Activities** Events/meetings. **Events** *Joint Scientific Meeting* Barcelona (Spain) 2018, *Joint Scientific Meeting* Lyon (France) 2016, *Joint Scientific Meeting* Hannover (Germany) 2015, *Joint Scientific Meeting* Athens (Greece) 2014, *Joint Scientific Meeting* Cambridge (UK) 2013. **Publications** *Briefing* – newsletter.
Members Ordinary; Student; Honorary. Members in 24 countries:
Austria, Belgium, China, Croatia, Czechia, Denmark, Finland, France, Germany, Greece, Hungary, Ireland, Israel, Italy, Netherlands, Norway, Poland, Portugal, Slovenia, Spain, Sweden, Switzerland, UK, USA.
NGO Relations Member of (2): *AAALAC International*; *European Animal Research Association (EARA, #05903)*. Instrumental in setting up (1): *European College of Laboratory Animal Medicine (ECLAM, #06611)*. [2020/XD7781/**D**]

♦ **European Society for Laser Aesthetic Surgery (ESLAS)** **08639**
Hon Treas – Membership Sec address not obtained. T. +306944291975.
History Founded Mar 1997, Tarragona (Spain). Registration: Charity, No/ID: 1087852, England and Wales. **Aims** Serve as a medium for practical instruction in the use of light and lasers for application in Plastic and Aesthetic Surgery; encourage and support research and exchange of scientific knowledge related to the above applications of phototherapy; offer an open forum for questions and answers, comments on, and discussion of, results, ideas, practical tips and hints and any problems related to phototherapy in aesthetic surgery. **Structure** Annual Meeting; Executive Committee. **Languages** English. **Finance** Members' dues (annual): Full – euro 180. **Activities** Organizes Laser Europe congress. **Events** *Laser Europe Conference* Amsterdam (Netherlands) 2014, *Congress* Mykonos (Greece) 2011, *Annual Congress* Prague (Czech Rep) 2011, *Annual Congress* Tarragona (Spain) 2010, *Laser Europe conference* Tarragona (Spain) 2010. **Publications** *Wavelengths* (2-3 a year) – newsletter; *Cosmetic Laser Therapy* – journal. **Members** Individuals accredited in Plastic, Reconstructive and Aesthetic Surgery, Ophthalmic and Oculo-plastic Surgery, Maxillofacial and Facial Plastic Surgery, ENT Surgery, Dermatology and Laser Scientists. Membership countries not specified. **NGO Relations** *European Laser Association (ELA, #07654)*. [2014/XD7245/v/**D**]

♦ European Society for Laser Dermatology / see European Society for Lasers and Energy Based Devices (#08640)

♦ European Society for Lasers and EBD Dermatology / see European Society for Lasers and Energy Based Devices (#08640)

♦ **European Society for Lasers and Energy Based Devices (ESLD)** . . . **08640**
Main Office c/o the office srl, via San Nicolò 14, 34121 Trieste TS, Italy. E-mail: theoffice@esld.eu.
Registered Office 34 Rue Fortuny, 75017 Paris, France.
URL: https://www.esld.eu/
History Former names and other names: *European Society for Laser Dermatology (ESLD)* – former; *European Society for Lasers and EBD Dermatology (ELSD)* – former. Registration: Start date: 22 Aug 1998, France. **Aims** Teach excellence in standards of techniques. **Structure** Board; Executive Committee. **Activities** Events/meetings; standards/guidelines; training/education. **Events** *Abu Dhabi International Conference on Dermatology and Aesthetics* Abu Dhabi (United Arab Emirates) 2022, *5CC – 5 Continent Congress* Barcelona (Spain) 2022, *5CC – 5 Continent Congress* Trieste (Italy) 2021, *Abu Dhabi International Conference on Dermatology and Aesthetics* Abu Dhabi (United Arab Emirates) 2020, *5CC – 5 Continent Congress* Barcelona (Spain) 2020. **NGO Relations** Member of (1): *International League of Dermatological Societies (ILDS, #14018)*. Member of: *Federation of the European Dermatological and Surgical Societies (FEDSS, no recent information)*. Sister organization: *Afro-Asian Society for Cosmetic Dermatology and Laser (ASCDL, no recent information)*. [2021/XD7701/**D**]

♦ **European Society of Lingual Orthodontics (ESLO)** **08641**
Pres address not obtained.
URL: http://www.eslo-info.org/
Events *World Congress* Sorrento (Italy) 2022, *World Congress* Sorrento (Italy) 2020, *World Congress* Cascais (Portugal) 2018, *World Congress* Athens (Greece) 2016, *World Congress* Como (Italy) 2014. [2014/XD8688/**D**]

♦ **European Society for Literature, Science and the Arts (SLSAeu)** . . . **08642**
Exec Dir Dept of English, Univ of Basel, Nadelberg 6, 4051 Basel BS, Switzerland.
URL: http://www.slsa-eu.org/
History Current constitution adopted 16 Aug 2013. Registration: Switzerland. **Aims** Promote the inter- and transdisciplinary exchange between literature, the arts, the natural sciences, medicine and technology; foster dialogue and collaboration between researchers, practitioners and activists. **Structure** General Assembly; Executive Board; Ambassadors. **Languages** English. **Finance** Members' dues. Conference fees. **Activities** Events/meetings; publishing activities. **Events** *Conference* Erlangen (Germany) 2023, *Conference* Erlangen (Germany) 2022, *Conference* 2021, *Conference* Katowice (Poland) 2020, *Conference* Athens (Greece) 2019. **Publications** *Journal of Literature and Science* (2 a year); *Configurations* – official journal. *Experimental Practices Monographs* – series; *Experimental Practices Yearbook* – series. Books. **NGO Relations** Sister organization of: *Society for Literature, Science and the Arts (SLSA)*. [2021/XM4967/**D**]

♦ **European Society of Lymphology** **08643**
Gen Sec Lab de physiologie, Ave Charles Schaller 91, 1160 Brussels, Belgium.
URL: http://www.eurolymphology.org/
History May 1980, Brussels (Belgium), as *Groupement pour l'étude des lymphatiques*. Changed title to *European Group of Lymphology – Groupement européen de lymphologie (GEL)*, May 1982. Current title adopted in 2006. Registered in accordance with Belgian law. **Aims** Study the anatomy, physiology and pathology of the lymphatics. **Structure** General Assembly. Board of Trustees. **Languages** English, French. **Staff** Voluntary. **Finance** Members' dues. **Events** *Meeting* Assisi (Italy) 2021, *Meeting* Assisi (Italy) 2020, *Meeting* Brussels (Belgium) 2019, *Meeting* Prague (Czechia) 2018, *Meeting* Stuttgart (Germany) 2017. **Publications** *European Journal of Lymphology and Related Problems* (4 a year).
Members Individuals (100) in 19 countries:
Argentina, Austria, Belgium, China, Czechia, France, Germany, Greece, Italy, Japan, Netherlands, Norway, Poland, Portugal, Spain, Sweden, Switzerland, UK, USA.
NGO Relations Affiliated to: *International Society of Lymphology (ISL, #15238)*. [2018/XD4234/**D**]

♦ **European Society of Magnetic Resonance in Medicine and Biology (ESMRMB)** **08644**
Main Office Am Gestade 1, 1010 Vienna, Austria. E-mail: office@esmrmb.org.
URL: http://www.esmrmb.org/
History Founded following the First Symposium on NMR, 14-15 Oct 1983, Geneva, when it was decided to found a European NMR society. In 1984, and informal group of radiologists and physicists was organized with the common interest of founding the Society. Statutes prepared and ratified during first congress, autumn 1984, Geneva; amended continuously during following years. New statutes adopted in 1995 and 2003. Registration: No/ID: 865933126, Austria. **Aims** Support educational activities and research in the widest sense in the field of magnetic resonance in medicine and biology. **Structure** General Assembly (held annually at Annual Congress); Council; Executive Committee. **Languages** English, German. **Staff** 4.00 FTE, paid. **Finance** Sources: meeting proceeds; members' dues. **Activities** Events/meetings; research and development; training/education. **Events** *Annual Scientific Meeting* London (UK) 2022, *Annual Scientific Meeting* Vienna (Austria) 2021, *Annual Scientific Meeting* Barcelona (Spain) 2020, *Annual Congress and General Assembly* Rotterdam (Netherlands) 2019, *Annual Congress and General Assembly* Paris (France) 2018. **Publications** *Magnetic Resonance Materials in Physics, Biology and Medicine MAGMA* (6 a year) – official journal.

Members Individuals: Ordinary; Associate; Emeritus; Honorary. Open to physicians, engineers, scientists and other individuals interested in the development of introduction of magnetic resonance techniques in the fields of medicine and biology. Members in 79 countries and territories:
Albania, Antigua-Barbuda, Argentina, Armenia, Australia, Austria, Azerbaijan, Belarus, Belgium, Benin, Bosnia-Herzegovina, Brazil, Bulgaria, Cambodia, Canada, Chile, China, Colombia, Croatia, Cyprus, Czechia, Denmark, Egypt, Estonia, Finland, France, Germany, Greece, Hong Kong, Hungary, Iceland, India, Indonesia, Iran Islamic Rep, Iraq, Ireland, Israel, Italy, Japan, Kazakhstan, Korea Rep, Kuwait, Lebanon, Luxembourg, Malaysia, Malta, Mexico, Moldova, Netherlands, New Zealand, Nigeria, North Macedonia, Norway, Pakistan, Panama, Philippines, Poland, Portugal, Qatar, Romania, Russia, Saudi Arabia, Serbia, Singapore, Slovakia, Slovenia, South Africa, Spain, Sri Lanka, Sweden, Switzerland, Taiwan, Thailand, Türkiye, UK, Ukraine, United Arab Emirates, USA, Venezuela.
NGO Relations Cooperates with (1): *International Society for Magnetic Resonance in Medicine (ISMRM, #15241)*. Shareholder in: *European Institute for Biomedical Imaging Research (EIBIR, #07546)*.
[2021/XD6150/v/**D**]

- ♦ European Society of Magnetic Resonance in Neuropaediatrics (inactive)
- ♦ European Society for Male Genital Surgery (no recent information)

♦ European Society for Marine Biotechnology (ESMB) 08645

Sec GEOMAR Helmholtz Centre for Ocean Research Kiel, Am Kiel-Kanal 44, 24106 Kiel, Germany.
History 26 Apr 1995, France. **Aims** Promote marine biotechnology in Europe; increase research collaboration between marine biotechnologists. **Structure** Council, including President, General Secretary and Treasurer. Advisory Board. **Activities** Events/meetings. **Publications** *ESMB Journal*; *ESMB Newsletter*.
[2019/XM3027/**D**]

- ♦ European Society for Mass Spectrometry (inactive)
- ♦ European Society of Mastology / see European Society of Breast Cancer Specialists (#08534)
- ♦ European Society of Mathematical Physics (inactive)

♦ European Society for Mathematical and Theoretical Biology (ESMTB) 08646

Pres Fac of Technology, Bielefeld Univ, Universitätsstr 25, 33615 Bielefeld, Germany. T. +495211064896. Fax +495211066481.
Sec Dept de Matemàtiques, Fac de Ciències, Univ Autònoma de Barcelona, 08193 Cerdanyola del Vallès, Barcelona, Spain. T. +34935868568. Fax +34935812790. E-mail: info@esmtb.org.
URL: http://www.esmtb.org/
History 1991, Alpe d'Huez (France). **Aims** Promote theoretical approaches and mathematical tools in biology and medicine in a European and wider context. **Structure** General Assembly; Board. **Languages** English. **Staff** None. **Finance** Sources: members' dues. **Activities** Awards/prizes/competitions; events/meetings; guidance/assistance/consulting; knowledge management/information dissemination; training/education. **Events** *Conference* Heidelberg (Germany) 2022, *Conference* Heidelberg (Germany) 2021, *Conference* Heidelberg (Germany) 2020, *Conference* Lisbon (Portugal) 2018, *Conference* Nottingham (UK) 2016. **Publications** *ESMTB Infoletter*; *European Communications in Mathematical and Theoretical Biology*; *Journal of Mathematical Biology*; *Perspectives in Mathematical Biology*. **Members** Full in 34 countries. Membership countries not specified. **NGO Relations** Member of (2): *European Mathematical Society (EMS, #07755)*; *International Council for Industrial and Applied Mathematics (ICIAM, #13032)*.
[2022/XD8855/**D**]

- ♦ European Society for Mathematics and the Arts (internationally oriented national body)
- ♦ European Society of Medical Hypnosis (no recent information)

♦ European Society of Medical Imaging Informatics (EuSoMII) 08647

Pres Am Gestade 1, 1010 Vienna, Austria. T. +393287228688. E-mail: info@eusomii.org.
Admin Support address not obtained.
URL: https://www.eusomii.org/
History 1984. Registered in accordance with Dutch law, 1 Mar 1989, Leiden (Netherlands). Registered in accordance with Austrian law, 17 Jun 2005, Vienna (Austria), by full title: *EuroPACS – European Society for the Promotion of Picture Archiving and Communication Systems in Medicine – Europäische Gesellschaft zur Förderung von Bildarchivierungs und Kommunikationssystemen in der Medizin*. Present name adopted, 2013. **Aims** Foster the transition from research to clinical application and education. **Structure** Board, including of President, Past President, Secretary and Treasurer. **Finance** Members' dues. Budget (annual): about euro 10,000. **Activities** Events/meetings. **Events** *Annual Conference* Valencia (Spain) 2019, *Annual Conference* Rotterdam (Netherlands) 2018, *Annual Conference* Rotterdam (Netherlands) 2017, *Annual Conference* Valencia (Spain) 2016, *Annual Conference* Barcelona (Spain) 2015. **Publications** *EuroPACS Newsletter*. **Members** Individuals and corporate. Membership countries not specified. **NGO Relations** Cooperates with: Computer Assister Radiology and Surgery (CARS). Institutional member of: *European Society of Radiology (ESR, #08720)*.
[2020/XF0939/**F**]

♦ European Society for Medical Oncology (ESMO) 08648

Main Office Via Ginevra 4, 6900 Lugano TI, Switzerland. T. +41919731900. Fax +41919731902. E-mail: administration@esmo.org – esmo@esmo.org.
URL: http://www.esmo.org/
History 1975, Nice (France). Former names and other names: *Société européenne de médecine interne cancérologique* – former (1975 to 1980). Registration: Switzerland. **Aims** Improve quality of prevention, diagnosis, treatment, supportive and palliative care, as well as follow-up of patients with malignant disorders; foster and facilitate research; advance the art, science, recognition and practice of oncology; generate and disseminate knowledge to cancer patients and the public; educate and train persons involved in clinical cancer care and research; promote education in oncology so as to ensure a high standard of qualification of medical oncologists within the multidisciplinary team; promote equal access to optimal cancer care of all cancer patients; maintain liaisons with other key oncology stakeholders. **Structure** General Assembly (annual); Executive Board; Permanent Committees (12); Working Groups (13); Faculty Groups (21). **Languages** English. **Staff** 60.00 FTE, paid. **Finance** Members' dues. Other sources: donations; sponsorship of publications; advertisements; congresses, meetings and courses. **Activities** Advocacy/lobbying/activism; events/meetings; standards/guidelines; training/education; awards/prizes/competitions. **Events** *Summit Africa* Cape Town (South Africa) 2023, *Annual Congress* Madrid (Spain) 2023, *European Multidisciplinary Congress on Urological Cancers (EMUC)* Marseille (France) 2023, *Molecular Analysis for Precision Oncology Congress* Paris (France) 2023, *Asia Congress* Singapore (Singapore) 2022. **Publications** *Annals of Oncology* (12 a year); *ESMO Newsletter*. *ESMO Education and Abstract Book*. Annual Report.
Members Full (medical, radiation and surgical oncologists); Honorary; Associate (related professions); Junior (in training). Individuals (about 6,000) in 118 countries and territories:
Afghanistan, Albania, Algeria, Antigua-Barbuda, Argentina, Armenia, Australia, Austria, Azerbaijan, Bangladesh, Belarus, Belgium, Bolivia, Bosnia-Herzegovina, Brazil, Bulgaria, Canada, Chile, China, Colombia, Costa Rica, Croatia, Cuba, Cyprus, Czechia, Denmark, Dominican Rep, Ecuador, Egypt, El Salvador, Estonia, Finland, France, Gambia, Georgia, Germany, Ghana, Greece, Guatemala, Guyana, Honduras, Hungary, Iceland, India, Indonesia, Iran Islamic Rep, Iraq, Ireland, Israel, Italy, Japan, Jordan, Kazakhstan, Kenya, Korea Rep, Kosovo, Kuwait, Kyrgyzstan, Latvia, Lebanon, Libya, Lithuania, Luxembourg, Malaysia, Malta, Mauritius, Mexico, Moldova, Mongolia, Montenegro, Morocco, Mozambique, Myanmar, Netherlands, New Zealand, Nigeria, North Macedonia, Norway, Oman, Pakistan, Panama, Paraguay, Peru, Philippines, Poland, Portugal, Puerto Rico, Qatar, Romania, Russia, Saudi Arabia, Senegal, Serbia, Singapore, Slovakia, Slovenia, South Africa, Spain, Sudan, Sweden, Switzerland, Syrian AR, Taiwan, Thailand, Trinidad-Tobago, Tunisia, Türkiye, UK, Ukraine, United Arab Emirates, Uruguay, USA, Uzbekistan, Venezuela, Vietnam, Yemen, Zambia.
Consultative Status Consultative status granted from: *WHO (#20950)* (Official).
NGO Relations Member of: *European Alliance for Personalised Medicine (EAPM, #05878)*; *European Chronic Disease Alliance (ECDA, #06548)*; *The NCD Alliance (NCDA, #16963)*; *Rare Cancers Europe (RCE, #18620)*; *Union for International Cancer Control (UICC, #20415)*. Founding member of: *Associations and Conference Forum (AC Forum, #02909)*. Stakeholder in: *European Network for Health Technology Assessment (EUnetHTA, #07921)*. Cooperates with: *Lymphoma Coalition (LC, #16535)*.
Also links with national societies.
[2020/XD5771/v/**D**]

- ♦ European Society of Medical Sociology / see European Society of Health and Medical Sociology (#08618)
- ♦ European Society of Membrane Science and Technology / see European Membrane Society (#07777)

♦ European Society for Mental Health and Deafness (ESMHD) 08649

Société européenne de santé mentale et surdité – Sociedad Europea Para La Sordera y La Salud Mental – Europäische Gesellschaft für seelische Gesundheit und Taubheit – Società Europea per l'Igiene Mentale e Sordità – Europese Vereniging voor Geestelijke Gezondheid en Doofheid
Dir C/ Miguel Hernandez 11, 28150 Valdetorres de Jarama, Madrid, Spain. T. +34647573679.
URL: http://www.esmhd.org/
History Aug 1986, Ghent (Belgium). Registration: Start date: 20 Nov 1987, Netherlands. **Aims** Develop and promote standards and methodologies of professional practice in the field of mental health and deafness which will enable the continuing inclusion and personal development of all deaf people within their communities. **Structure** General Assembly (annual). Council. Executive Committee, consisting of President, Honorary Treasurer, Honorary Secretary and Co-opted Member. Advisory Committee; Special Interest Groups. **Languages** English, French, International Sign Language. **Staff** 1.00 FTE, paid. **Finance** Members' dues. **Activities** Events/meetings; networking/liasing. **Events** *World Congress on Mental Health and Deafness* London (UK) 2018, *World Congress on Mental Health and Deafness* Belfast (UK) 2014, *International Symposium on Diagnosis and Treatment in Mental Health and Deafness* Madrid (Spain) 2013, *World conference on mental health and deafness* Monterrey (Mexico) 2012, *World conference on mental health and deafness* Brisbane, QLD (Australia) 2009. **Publications** Congress proceedings; booklets.
Members Full; Sponsoring; Honorary; Affiliate; Observer. Members in 18 countries:
Argentina, Australia, Austria, Belgium, Cyprus, Denmark, Finland, France, Germany, Ireland, Italy, Netherlands, Norway, Poland, Spain, Sweden, Switzerland, UK.
IGO Relations *European Commission (EC, #06633)*; *WHO Regional Office for Europe (#20945)*.
[2021/XD2635/**D**]

♦ European Society of Microalgal Biotechnology 08650

Contact Fac of Agricultural and Food Sciences, Univ of West Hungary, Kolbai K Str 8, Mosonmagyaróvar 9200, Hungary. T. +3696566631. Fax +3696566620.
History 1992. **Aims** Promote microalgae, *algae* and other phototrophic organisms and their use in commercial applications and areas. **Languages** English, German, Hungarian. **Finance** Symposia and workshops are financed by sponsorship and fees. **Activities** Research and development; events/meetings. **Events** *Symposium on Microalgae and Seaweed Products in Plant/Soil Systems* Mosonmagyaróvar (Hungary) 2015, *European workshop on microalgal biotechnology* Nuthetal (Germany) 2012, *International algae congress* Berlin (Germany) 2011, *European workshop on microalgal biotechnology* Potsdam (Germany) 2010, *European workshop on microalgal biotechnology* Nuthetal (Germany) 2007.
Members Full in 10 countries:
France, Germany, Hungary, Israel, Italy, Portugal, Russia, Spain, UK, Ukraine.
[2015/XJ0218/**D**]

♦ European Society for Microcirculation (ESM) 08651

Société européenne de microcirculation
SG Univ of Physical Education, Alkotas Street 44, Budapest 1123, Hungary. T. +3614879200.
URL: http://www.esmicrocirculation.eu/
History 1960, Hamburg (Germany). Created following a first meeting of interested scientists in Lund (Sweden), 1959. **Aims** Advance integrative understanding of physiology and pathophysiology of terminal vascular beds; support classical microcirculation as well as vascular biology; use basic as well as clinical studies. **Structure** General Meeting (every 2 years, at conference); Executive Committee; Sub-Committees. **Languages** English. **Staff** Voluntary. **Finance** Sources: meeting proceeds; members' dues. **Activities** Awards/prizes/competitions; events/meetings. **Events** *Conference* Aarhus (Denmark) 2023, *World Congress for Microcirculation* Beijing (China) 2022, *Biennial Conference* Maastricht (Netherlands) 2019, *World Congress for Microcirculation* Vancouver, BC (Canada) 2018, *Biennial Conference* Geneva (Switzerland) 2017. **Publications** *ESM Newsletter*; *Journal of Vascular Research (JVR)*.
Members Ordinary; Honorary individuals (600), in 25 countries:
Australia, Austria, Belgium, Brazil, Canada, China, Czechia, Denmark, France, Germany, Israel, Italy, Japan, Jordan, Netherlands, Norway, Poland, Portugal, Russia, Spain, Sweden, Switzerland, UK, United Arab Emirates, USA.
NGO Relations Joint meetings with: *European Shock Society, The (ESS, #08480)*. Represented in: *International Liaison Committee for Microcirculation (#14035)*.
[2023/XD4192/v/**D**]

♦ European Society for Micrographic Surgery (ESMS) 08652

Contact Dermatology dept, Catharina-Ziekenhuis, Postbox 1350, 5602 ZA Eindhoven, Netherlands. T. +31402397277.
URL: http://www.esms-mohs.eu/
History 1990, Brussels (Belgium). Registered in accordance with Belgian law. **Aims** Promote, support and encourage research in the field of micrographic surgery; contribute to the establishment of the highest possible professional standards in the field of micrographic surgery, cutaneous oncology and related fields; contribute to the improvement of the training and act as a forum for discussions, exchange of ideas and innovations. **Structure** General Assembly (annual). Management Board. Executive Council, consisting of President, Vice-President, Secretary, and Treasurer. **Languages** Dutch, English. **Staff** 4.00 FTE, paid. **Members** Individuals Full; Correspondent; Honorary; Members in Training. Membership countries not specified. **NGO Relations** Member of: *Federation of the European Dermatological and Surgical Societies (FEDSS, no recent information)*.
[2012.08.20/XD3052/**D**]

♦ European Society of Microscope Dentistry (ESMD) 08653

Exec Manager address not obtained. T. +37062027485. E-mail: info@esmd.info.
Pres address not obtained.
URL: http://www.esmd.info/
History 2007. **Aims** Offer the opportunity to exchange experiences, discuss possibilities and enhance skills to individual dentists, and to national or regional organizations interested in or devoted to Microscope Dentistry; introduce the use of microscope magnification to all dental disciplines. **Structure** Board, comprising President, Treasurer, Secretary and 2 members. **Languages** English. **Activities** Meeting activities; education; training. **Events** *Congress* Barcelona (Spain) 2014, *Congress* Berlin (Germany) 2012, *Congress* Vilnius (Lithuania) 2010, *Congress* Amsterdam (Netherlands) 2008. **Publications** *Why Worry Now?* by Philippe Van Audenhove. Journal and magazine articles.
[2013.08.20/XM8230/**D**]

♦ European Society of Minimally Invasive Neurological Therapy (ESMINT) 08654

Central Office Seefeldstr 88, 8008 Zurich ZH, Switzerland. T. +41443884083. Fax +41443884089. E-mail: office@esmint.eu.
URL: http://www.esmint.eu/
History Jun 2009, Paris (France). **Aims** Organize training and education for neuroradiologists, neurosurgeons, and neurologists involved in the field of Interventional Neuroradiology. **Structure** Includes *European Foundation of Minimally Invasive Neurological Therapy*. **Languages** English. **Staff** 2.00 FTE, paid. **Events** *Congress* Nice (France) 2019, *Congress* Nice (France) 2018, *Congress* Nice (France) 2017, *Congress* Nice (France) 2016, *Congress* Nice (France) 2015.
[2018.06.01/XJ0512/**D**]

♦ European Society for Molecular Imaging (ESMI) 08655

Exec Dir Berrenrather Str 188c, 50937 Cologne, Germany. T. +4922178966180. E-mail: office@e-smi.eu.
Pres Univ of Manchester, Div Neuroscience & Experimental Psychology, Oxford Rd, Manchester, M13 9PL, UK.
URL: http://www.e-smi.eu/
History 2005. Extends actions initiated in the scope of the EC 6th Framework Programme by the European Molecular Imaging Laboratories (EMIL) (ended 2009), Diagnostic Molecular Imaging (DiMI) (ended 2010), and the European Integrated Project for In-vivo Imaging (MI) (ended in 2009). **Aims** Represent an academic community developing and validating imaging technologies and multimodality imaging biomarkers in the life sciences, and use of innovative imaging methods to support basic and clinical research. **Structure** Council; Executive Committee; Management. **Languages** English. **Staff** 2.00 FTE, paid. **Activities** Awards/prizes/competitions; events/meetings; knowledge management/information dissemination; training/education. **Events** *European Molecular Imaging Meeting* Salzburg (Austria) 2023, *Iceland Summer Conference* Iceland 2022, *European Molecular Imaging Meeting* Thessaloniki (Greece) 2022, *European Molecular Imaging*

Meeting Göttingen (Germany) 2021, *European Molecular Imaging Meeting* Cologne (Germany) 2020. **Publications** *Molecular Imaging and Biology (MIB)* (6 a year); *ESMI Newsletter* (4 a year). Conference proceedings. **Members** Scientists working in the field of Imaging Science and interested companies. Membership countries not specified. **NGO Relations** Organizes joint congresses with: *Federation of Asian Societies for Molecular Imaging (FASMI, #09450)*; *World Molecular Imaging Society (WMIS, #21656)*. [2022.05.25/XM2678/**D**]

♦ European Society for Movement Analysis in Adults and Children (ESMAC) 08656

Chairman 5 kvetna 65, 140 21 Prague 4, Czechia. T. +420261174301. E-mail: info@esmac.org.
URL: http://www.esmac.org/

History Founded 31 Oct 1992, Oswestry (UK). Also referred to as *European Society for Movement Analysis in Children*. **Aims** Stimulate and advance scientific knowledge, professional interaction and exchange of ideas among society members relating to movement analysis in adults and children in clinical and research setting. **Structure** General Meeting (annual); Committee. **Languages** English. **Staff** 0.50 FTE, paid; 9.00 FTE, voluntary. **Finance** Members' dues. **Activities** Training/education; events/meetings. **Events** *Annual Conference* Odense (Denmark) 2021, *Annual Conference* Prague (Czechia) 2020, *Annual Conference* Amsterdam (Netherlands) 2019, *Annual Conference* Prague (Czechia) 2018, *Annual Conference* Trondheim (Norway) 2017. **Publications** *Gait and Posture* (4 a year).
Members Individuals in 25 countries:
Australia, Austria, Belgium, Cyprus, Denmark, Finland, France, Germany, Greece, Hungary, Ireland, Israel, Italy, Latvia, Luxembourg, Netherlands, Norway, Poland, Portugal, Spain, Sweden, Switzerland, Türkiye, UK, USA.
[2020.03.06/XD5812/v/**D**]

♦ European Society for Movement Analysis in Children / see European Society for Movement Analysis in Adults and Children (#08656)

♦ European Society for Muscle Research (ESMR) 08657

Chair Dept of Cardiovascular Physiology, Ruhr University Bochum, MA 3/56, 44780 Bochum, Germany. T. +492343229100. Fax +492343214040.
URL: http://www.esmr.org/

History 1971, as *European Muscle Club (EMC)*. New name adopted 1991. **Aims** Bring into contact scientists doing mainly basic and applied research in the field of muscle biology from different laboratories in Europe – the field of muscle biology is characteristically interdisciplinary, involving biochemistry, physiology, cell biology, genetics and biophysics, and these must have a platform to come together. **Structure** Board, comprising Chairman and 6 members. **Languages** English. **Staff** 0.50 FTE, voluntary. **Finance** Budget (for annual meetings): US$ 120,000-150,000. **Events** *European Muscle Conference* Prague (Czechia) 2022, *European Muscle Conference* Warsaw (Poland) 2021, *European Muscle Conference* Cambridge (UK) 2019, *European Muscle Conference* Budapest (Hungary) 2018, *European Muscle Conference* Potsdam (Germany) 2017. **Publications** Monographs; meeting abstracts.
Members Individuals (920) in 36 countries:
Australia, Austria, Belgium, Bosnia-Herzegovina, Canada, Croatia, Czechia, Denmark, Estonia, Finland, France, Georgia, Germany, Greece, Hungary, Iceland, Ireland, Israel, Italy, Latvia, Lithuania, Netherlands, North Macedonia (former Yugoslav Rep of), Norway, Poland, Romania, Russia, Serbia, Slovakia, Slovenia, Spain, Sweden, Switzerland, UK, Ukraine, USA.
[2018/XF1824/v/**D**]

♦ European Society of Musculoskeletal Radiology (ESSR) 08658

Society and Congress Management Am Gestade 1, 1010 Vienna, Austria. T. +4315334064-906. E-mail: office@essr.org.
URL: http://www.essr.org/

History Founded 20 Mar 1993, Bonn (Germany), as *European Society of Skeletal Radiology (ESSR)*. **Aims** Promote musculoskeletal radiology in Europe with particular emphasis on education and research. **Structure** Executive Committee; Subcommittees. **Languages** English. **Activities** Events/meetings; training/education; research/documentation. **Events** *Annual Meeting* Rostock (Germany) 2022, *Annual Meeting* Krakow (Poland) 2021, *Annual Meeting* Vienna (Austria) 2020, *Annual Meeting* Lisbon (Portugal) 2019, *Annual Meeting* Amsterdam (Netherlands) 2018. **Publications** *ESSR Newsletter*. Guidelines; protocols.
Members Individuals in 30 countries:
Austria, Belgium, Bulgaria, Croatia, Cyprus, Czechia, Denmark, Finland, France, Germany, Greece, Hungary, Ireland, Italy, Latvia, Lithuania, Montenegro, Netherlands, North Macedonia, Norway, Poland, Portugal, Romania, Russia, Serbia, Slovenia, Sweden, Switzerland, Türkiye, UK.
Corresponding members in 7 countries:
Australia, Brazil, Egypt, Israel, Korea Rep, Singapore, USA.
NGO Relations *Asian Musculoskeletal Society (AMS, #01543)*; *European Society of Radiology (ESR, #08720)*; *International Skeletal Society (ISS, #14867)*. [2019.12.12/XD4106/v/**D**]

♦ European Society for Musculoskeletal Shockwave Therapy / see International Society for Medical Shockwave Therapy (#15258)

♦ European Society for Mycobacteriology (ESM) 08659

Contact c/o Treasurer, Parkallee 1, 23845 Borstel, Germany. E-mail: office@esmycobacteriology.eu.
URL: http://www.esmycobacteriology.eu/

History 5 Jun 1980, Borstel (Germany FR). **Aims** Promote a better understanding of mycobacteriology through information dissemination and collaboration between scientists; eradicate tuberculosis and other mycobacterial diseases. **Structure** General Assembly; Steering Committee; President; General Secretary, heading Office. **Languages** English. **Staff** Voluntary. **Finance** Budget: none. Annual congress financed by inscription fees and some grants. **Activities** Database of suppliers and products. **Events** *Annual Congress* 2021, *Annual Congress* Tirana (Albania) 2020, *Annual Congress* Valencia (Spain) 2019, *Annual Congress* Dresden (Germany) 2018, *Annual Congress* Sibenik (Croatia) 2017. **Publications** *Mycobacteriology* (1998). Annual abstract book.
Members Individuals (318) in 42 countries:
Albania, Argentina, Austria, Bangladesh, Belarus, Belgium, Brazil, Bulgaria, Canada, Colombia, Croatia, Czechia, Denmark, Finland, France, Germany, Greece, Guadeloupe, Hungary, Iran Islamic Rep, Ireland, Italy, Japan, Kuwait, Latvia, Lebanon, Mexico, Netherlands, Peru, Portugal, Qatar, Romania, Russia, Saudi Arabia, Slovakia, Spain, Sweden, Switzerland, Türkiye, UK, USA, Zambia. [2020.03.10/XD5078/v/**D**]

♦ European Society for Nanomedicine (ESNAM) 08660

Gen Sec c/o CLINAM, Alemannengasse 12, PO Box, 4016 Basel BS, Switzerland. T. +41616959395. Fax +41616959390. E-mail: loeffler@loeffler.ch – esnam@esnam.org.
URL: http://www.esnam.org/

History Set up Apr 2007. Registered in accordance with Swiss Civil Code. **Aims** Promote research and application of nanomedicine and its implication for humanity and for the environment, always keeping in view the welfare of individuals and society. **NGO Relations** *European Foundation for Clinical Nanomedicine (CLINAM, #07346)*. [2014/XJ8719/**D**]

♦ European Society of Nematologists (ESN) 08661

Pres Centre for Plant Science, Univ of Leeds, Leeds, LS2 9JT, UK.
Sec INRA UMR IGEPP, BP 35327, 35653 Le Rheu CEDEX, France.
URL: http://www.esn-online.org/

History 1955, Wageningen (Netherlands). **Aims** Advance the science of nematology; foster communication and collaboration between nematologists; represent the views of nematologists to other bodies, organizations and governments. **Structure** General Meeting; Governing Board. **Languages** English. **Finance** Sources: members' dues. **Activities** Events/meetings. **Events** *Biennal Symposium* Córdoba (Spain) 2024, *International Congress of Nematology* Juan-les-Pins (France) 2022, *International Congress* Antibes (France) 2020, *Biennial Symposium* Ghent (Belgium) 2018, *Biennial Symposium* Braga (Portugal) 2016. **Publications** *Nematology News* (2 a year). **Members** Individuals (390) in 47 countries. Membership countries not specified. **NGO Relations** Member of (3): *International Federation of Nematology Societies (IFNS, #13488)*; *International Society for Plant Pathology (ISPP, #15371)*; *International Union of Biological Sciences (IUBS, #15760)*.
[2022.05.31/XD0863/v/**D**]

♦ European Society of Neonatology / see European Board of Neonatology (#06363)

♦ European Society for Neurochemistry (ESN) 08662

Société européenne de neurochimie

Pres School of Biomedical Sciences, Fac of Biological Sciences, Univ of Leeds, Leeds, LS2 9JT, UK.
Sec Dept Human Molecular Genetics and Biochemistry, Sackler Fac of Medicine, Tel Aviv Univ, Yafo, Tel Aviv, Israel.
URL: http://www.neurochemsoc.eu/

History Sep 1976, Bath (UK). Founded at inaugural meeting. Constitution adopted by 2nd meeting, Aug 1978, Göttingen (Germany FR). Registration: Charity Commission, No/ID: 1098662, Start date: 21 Jul 2003, England and Wales. **Aims** Promote development of neurochemistry in Europe and facilitate exchange of ideas and interests amongst members; foster interaction between clinical and basic neurochemistry for public benefit. **Structure** Council; Officers: President, Secretary, Treasurer. **Languages** English. **Staff** Voluntary. **Finance** Members' dues, which also provides membership in ISN and FENS. All meetings self financed. **Activities** Events/meetings; training/education. **Events** *Joint Meeting* Porto (Portugal) 2023, *Biennial Meeting* St Petersburg (Russia) 2022, *Future Perspectives for European Neurochemistry* 2021, *Biennial Meeting* St Petersburg (Russia) 2021, *Biennial Meeting* Milan (Italy) 2019.
Members Individuals in 30 countries:
Australia, Belgium, Brazil, Canada, Czechia, Denmark, Estonia, Finland, France, Germany, Greece, Hungary, India, Israel, Italy, Latvia, Malta, Norway, Pakistan, Poland, Portugal, Russia, Serbia, Slovakia, Slovenia, Spain, Sweden, UK, Ukraine, USA.
NGO Relations Member of (1): *Federation of European Neuroscience Societies (FENS, #09522)*.
[2022.10.19/XD8327/v/**D**]

♦ European Society of Neurogastroenterology and Gastrointestinal Motility / see European Society of Neurogastroenterology and Motility (#08663)

♦ European Society of Neurogastroenterology and Motility (ESNM) .. 08663

Office c/o WMA Gmbh, Alser Str 4, 1090 Vienna, Austria. T. +431405138331. E-mail: info@esnm.eu.
URL: http://www.esnm.eu/

History 1981, Leuven (Belgium). Former names and other names: *European Motility Society* – former (1981 to 1996); *European Society of Gastrointestinal Motility* – alias; *European Gastrointestinal Motility Society* – alias; *Société européenne pour l'étude de la motilité gastro-intestinale* – alias; *European Society of Neurogastroenterology and Gastrointestinal Motility (ESNM)* – former. Registration: Belgium. **Aims** Expand knowledge and interest, and encourage basic and clinical research, in the field of neurogastroenterology and motility; establish standards for good clinical practice and patient care. **Structure** General Assembly; Steering Committee; Office. Gut Microbiota and Health Section. **Languages** English. **Staff** 14.00 FTE, voluntary. **Activities** Events/meetings; training/education. **Events** *Meeting* Bangkok (Thailand) 2024, *NeuroGASTRO Meeting* Bucharest (Romania) 2023, *Biennial Neurogastro Meeting* 2021, *Biennial Neurogastro Meeting* Lisbon (Portugal) 2019, *Joint International Neurogastroenterology and Motility Meeting* Amsterdam (Netherlands) 2018. **Publications** *Neurogastroenterology and Motility* (6 a year) – journal.
Members Individuals (about 3,200) in Europe. Membership countries not specified. National groups and societies in 18 countries:
National groups and societies in 18 countries:
Belgium, Croatia, Denmark, France, Germany, Ireland, Israel, Italy, Netherlands, Norway, Portugal, Romania, Russia, Spain, Sweden, Switzerland, Türkiye, UK.
NGO Relations Member of: *United European Gastroenterology (UEG, #20506)*. Founding member of: *Federation of Neurogastroenterology and Motility (FNM, #09696)*. [2021/XD2150/**D**]

♦ European Society of Neuroradiology (ESNR) 08664

Société européenne de neuroradiologie

Central office Althardstrasse 70, 8105 Regensdorf ZH, Switzerland. E-mail: info@esnr.org.
Main Website: http://www.esnr.org/

History 5 Sep 1969, Colmar (France). Incorporated in Strasbourg (France), 8 Sep 1970. Constitution revised 10 Oct 1991, Zurich (Switzerland). Constitution amended, Sep 2000, Oslo (Norway), Sep 2007, Genoa (Italy), Oct 2010, Bologna (Italy), Antwerp (Belgium), 17 Dec 2011. Re-founded, 29 Dec 2008, Zurich (Switzerland). **Aims** Promote the specialty of neuroradiology in Europe. **Structure** General Assembly (annual, at scientific meeting); International Council of National Delegates; Executive Committee; Central Office; Standing Committees; Subspecialty Committees. **Languages** English. **Staff** 5.00 FTE, paid. **Finance** Sources: members' dues. **Activities** Awards/prizes/competitions; certification/accreditation; events/meetings; knowledge management/information dissemination; research and development; standards/guidelines; training/education. **Events** *Annual Meeting* Vienna (Austria) 2023, *Annual Meeting* Lisbon (Portugal) 2022, *Annual Meeting* Geneva (Switzerland) 2021, *Annual Congress* Regensdorf (Switzerland) 2020, *Annual Congress* Oslo (Norway) 2019. **Publications** *European Radiology* (12 a year); *Neuroradiology* (8 a year).
Members Full; Associate; Institutional; Emeritus; Honorary; Junior; Corporate. Individuals in 32 countries and territories:
Australia, Austria, Belgium, Bosnia-Herzegovina, Bulgaria, Croatia, Denmark, Finland, France, Germany, Greece, Hungary, Iceland, Ireland, Italy, Latvia, Luxembourg, Netherlands, New Zealand, Norway, Poland, Portugal, Romania, Russia, Serbia, Slovenia, South Africa, Spain, Sweden, Switzerland, Türkiye, UK.
NGO Relations Member of (3): *European Society of Radiology (ESR, #08720)*; *European Union of Medical Specialists (UEMS, #09001)*; *World Federation of Neuroradiological Societies (WFNRS, #21463)*. Also links with national societies. [2023.02.16/XD4775/**D**]

♦ European Society of Neurosonology and Cerebral Hemodynamics (ESNCH) 08665

Sec Dept Neuroscience, Univ of Padua School of Medicine, Via Giustiniani 5, 35128 Padua PD, Italy.
Pres Dept Neurology Stroke Unit, Tel Aviv Sourasky Medical Center, 6 Weizman St, 64239 Tel Aviv, Israel.
URL: http://www.esnch.org/

History Founded 1997, Utrecht (Netherlands). **Aims** Define neurovascular standards in Europe and beyond; promote scientific research, education and training in the field of neurosonology. **Structure** General Assembly (annual); Executive Committee; Administrative Secretariat. **Languages** English. **Staff** None. **Finance** Grants from governmental and nongovernmental agencies and industry; private donations. **Activities** Organizes scientific meetings and symposia. **Events** *Meeting* Linz (Austria) 2019, *Meeting* Prague (Czechia) 2018, *Meeting* Berlin (Germany) 2017, *Meeting* Budapest (Hungary) 2016, *Meeting* Zadar (Croatia) 2015. **Publications** *ESNCH Newsletter*. **Members** Active; Honorary. Membership countries not specified. [2020/XD5198/**D**]

♦ European Society for New Methods in Agricultural Research (ESNA) 08666

Sec Mendel Univ, Zemědělská 1, 613 00 Brno, Czechia. T. +420545133294. Fax +420545133295.
Pres Univ della Tuscia, Via S C De Lellis, 01100 Viterbo VITERBO, Italy.
URL: http://web2.mendelu.cz/esna/

History 1969, Wageningen (Netherlands). **Aims** Promote the advancement of agricultural science through exchange of ideas and techniques; study aspects of agricultural and environmental protection and the application of nuclear techniques, new methods and biotechnology in agricultural research. **Structure** Committee, comprising President, Vice-President and 9 members. Secretariat, headed by Secretary General. **Languages** English. **Staff** 12.00 FTE, voluntary. **Finance** Members' dues; euro 25. Other sources: grants; registration fees. **Activities** Organizes: annual meetings in various European countries; scientific programmes. Working Groups (6): WG1 – Food preservation and safety; WG2 – Advanced methods in animal sciences; WG3 – Soil-plant relationships; WG4 – Plant Science and Biotechnology; WG5 – Quality of agro-ecosystem; WG6 – Plant Crop Protection and Biotechnology. **Events** *Annual meeting* Craiova (Romania) 2011, *Annual meeting* Brno (Czech Rep) 2009, *Annual meeting* Krakow (Poland) 2008, *Annual meeting* Dubna, Tula (Russia) 2007, *Annual meeting* Iasi (Romania) 2006. **Publications** *ESNA Book of Abstracts* (annual).
Members Individuals in 33 countries:
Armenia, Australia, Austria, Belarus, Belgium, Bulgaria, Croatia, Czechia, Denmark, Egypt, France, Germany, Greece, Hungary, India, Israel, Italy, Libya, Moldova, Netherlands, Norway, Poland, Romania, Russia, Serbia, Slovakia, Slovenia, Spain, Sweden, Türkiye, UK, Ukraine, USA.
NGO Relations *International Union of Radioecology (IUR, #15812)*. [2017/XD3060/**D**]

♦ European Society for Nineteenth-Century Art (unconfirmed)

♦ **European Society for Noninvasive Cardiology** **08667**

Sec Cardiology Dept, UZ Gasthuisberg O/N1 704, Herestraat 49, 3000 Leuven, Belgium. T. +3216345840. Fax +3216345844.

History 1978. **Aims** Promote study and use of noninvasive cardiology; stimulate scientific research and discuss results. **Structure** Board of Directors of 5 members. Officers: President; Secretary-General. Managing Director. **Languages** English. **Staff** 2.00 FTE, voluntary. **Finance** Members' dues. Meeting registration. **Activities** Organizes: annual European conference under the auspices of ISCN; national meetings. Cooperative research projects: phonocardiogram; ECG; echo-Doppler; seismocardiography; nuclear imaging. **Events** *Annual European Conference* Amsterdam (Netherlands) 2013, *Annual European Conference* Buenos Aires (Argentina) 2012, *Annual European Conference* Paris (France) 2011, *Annual European Conference* Berlin (Germany) 2010, *Annual European Conference* Barcelona (Spain) 2009. **Publications** Scientific papers on research projects; presentations.

Members Societies in 50 countries and territories:
Argentina, Australia, Austria, Belgium, Brazil, Canada, China, Congo DR, Cuba, Czechia, Denmark, Egypt, Finland, France, Germany, Greece, Hong Kong, Hungary, India, Indonesia, Israel, Italy, Jamaica, Japan, Kenya, Korea Rep, Luxembourg, Mexico, Montenegro, Morocco, Netherlands, New Zealand, Nigeria, Peru, Philippines, Poland, Portugal, Puerto Rico, Romania, Russia, Serbia, South Africa, Spain, Sweden, Switzerland, Tanzania UR, Türkiye, UK, USA, Vietnam.

IGO Relations *European Commission (EC, #06633)* – DG Health; *WHO (#20950).* [2013.06.28/XD3094/**D**]

♦ European Society for Noninvasive Cardiovascular Dynamics / see European Society for Noninvasive and Preventive Cardiology (#08668)

♦ **European Society for Noninvasive and Preventive Cardiology (ESNIPC)** **08668**

Pres School of Cardiology, Dept of Experimental and Applied Medicine, Univ of Brescia, 25121 Brescia BS, Italy.

Sec-Treas Dept of Experimental and Applied Medicine, Univ of Brescia, P le Spedali Civili 1, 25100 Brescia BS, Italy.

History 1960, Zeist (Netherlands), as *European Society for Ballistocardiographic Research.* Subsequent name changes: to *European Society for Ballistocardiography and Cardiovascular Dynamics*, 1971; *European Society for Noninvasive Cardiovascular Dynamics (ESNICVD)*, 1978. Current name adopted, 2009. Also referred to as *BCG Society.* Current by-laws adopted 22 Sep 1986, Purmerend (Netherlands). Registered in accordance with Netherlands Civil Code. **Aims** Unite scientists and professionals whose common interest is to promote understanding of cardiovascular physiology, pathophysiology and imaging with non-invasive methods, in both research and medical practice, with major commitment in prevention of the most common forms of cardiovascular disease in adults and in prevention of sudden death in athletes. **Structure** General Assembly. Executive Council, consisting of President, Vice-President, Secretary-Treasurer and 2 members (5-year terms, one retiring each year). **Languages** English. **Staff** Voluntary. **Finance** Members' dues. Other sources: Congress proceeds; gifts. **Activities** Knowledge management/information dissemination; networking/liaising; events/meetings; awards/prizes/competitions. **Events** *Pan American conference for non-destructive testing* Cancún (Mexico) 2011, *Cardiovascular medicine in the era of advanced technology* Brescia (Italy) 2009, *Congress* Portoroz (Slovenia) 2004, *Congress* Budapest (Hungary) 2002, *Congress* Venice (Italy) 2000. **Publications** *Bibliotheca Cardiologica*; *Cardiovascular Newsletter*; *Journal of Cardiovascular Diagnosis and Procedures. LV Diastolic Function, Dysfunction and Failure* (2004).

Members Individuals active in human and veterinary medicine: clinicians, surgeons, physiologists, pharmacologists, biophysicists, specialists in hydrodynamics, mechanical and electrical engineering. Members in 20 countries:
Belgium, Bosnia-Herzegovina, Bulgaria, Canada, Croatia, Czechia, Germany, Greece, Hungary, Italy, Japan, Lithuania, Netherlands, North Macedonia, Poland, Russia, Slovenia, South Africa, Spain, USA. [2019/XD4712/v/**D**]

♦ European Society of Nuclear Methods in Agriculture (inactive)
♦ European Society of Obstetric Anaesthesiology (no recent information)

♦ **European Society for Oceanists (ESfO)** **08669**

Chair Radboud Univ Nijmegen, PO Box 9104, 6500 HE Nijmegen, Netherlands. T. +31243615579.
Deputy Chair address not obtained. T. +31243616113.
URL: http://www.esfo-org.eu/

History 1992, Nijmegen (Netherlands), during the First European Colloquium on Pacific Studies. **Aims** Enhance exchange and cooperation between researchers and institutions with an interest in Oceania. **Structure** Board. **Languages** English. **Finance** Conference fees. **Events** *Biennial Conference* Ajaccio (France) 2022, *Biennial Conference* Ajaccio (France) 2020, *Biennial Conference* Cambridge (UK) 2018, *Biennial Conference* Munich (Germany) 2017, *Biennial Conference* Brussels (Belgium) 2015. **Publications** Conference proceedings.

Members Individuals in 37 countries and territories:
Australia, Austria, Belgium, Canada, Chile, Cook Is, Denmark, Fiji, Finland, France, Germany, Iceland, India, Ireland, Italy, Japan, Marshall Is, Namibia, Netherlands, New Caledonia, New Zealand, Norway, Pakistan, Papua New Guinea, Poland, Romania, Russia, Samoa, Slovenia, Spain, Sweden, Switzerland, Taiwan, Türkiye, UK, USA, Vanuatu.

NGO Relations *Austrian-South Pacific Society (no recent information).* [2015/XD6885/v/**D**]

♦ **European Society of Oncologic Imaging (ESOI)** **08670**

Office Am Gestade 1, 1010 Vienna, Austria. T. +4315334064924. E-mail: office@esoi-society.org.
URL: http://www.esoi-society.org/

History Registered in accordance with Austrian law: 897953653. **Aims** Promote and coordinate the scientific, philanthropic, intellectual and professional activities of oncologic imaging. **Structure** Executive Board; Committees (4). **Languages** English. **Activities** Training/education. **Members** Active (over 1,100) in 88 countries. Membership countries not specified. **NGO Relations** Member of (2): *European Cancer Organisation (ECO, #06432)*; *European Society of Radiology (ESR, #08720).* [2021.02.17/XM4124/**D**]

♦ **European Society of Oncology Pharmacy (ESOP)** **08671**

Treas Rue des Arquebusiers 7, L-1138 Luxembourg, Luxembourg. T. +49404665000. E-mail: km@esop.li – membershipservice@esop.li.
Sec address not obtained. E-mail: ff@esop.li.
URL: http://www.esop.eu/

History Apr 2000, Prague (Czechia). Current constitution adopted, 27 Jan 2006, Hamburg (Germany). Registration: EU Transparency Register, No/ID: 112006128054-87. **Aims** Support optimal treatment for cancer patients. **Structure** Delegate Assembly (every 3 years); Board of Directors; Executive Board. **Languages** English. **Events** *Conference* Dubrovnik (Croatia) 2016. **Publications** *European Journal of Oncology Pharmacy (EJOP)* (2 a year). **Members** Individuals (3,319) in 63 countries. Membership countries not specified. **NGO Relations** Member of (2): *European Cancer Organisation (ECO, #06432)* (Associate); *European Forum for Good Clinical Practice (EFGCP, #07313).* [2020/XM3404/**D**]

♦ **European Society of Ophthalmic Nurses and Technicians (ESONT)** . **08672**

Programme Manager Temple House, Temple Road, Blackrock, Dublin, CO. DUBLIN, Ireland. T. +35312091100. Fax +35312091112. E-mail: niall.slowey@escrs.org.
URL: http://www.esont.org/

History Founded 2002, as a division of *European Society of Cataract and Refractive Surgeons (ESCRS, #08539).* **Aims** Offer a European support network for ophthalmic nurses and technicians; enhance and improve the care of the ophthalmic patient. **Structure** Annual Meeting (during Annual Congress of ESCRS); Organizing Committee, reports to ESCRS Board. **Languages** English. **Activities** Provides of a forum for communication and ongoing education. **Events** *Meeting* Paris (France) 2019, *Meeting* Vienna (Austria) 2018, *Meeting* Lisbon (Portugal) 2017, *Meeting* Copenhagen (Denmark) 2016, *Meeting* Barcelona (Spain) 2015. [2016.10.20/XD9145/**D**]

♦ **European Society of Ophthalmic Plastic and Reconstructive Surgery (ESOPRS)** **08673**

Europäische Gesellschaft für Oculoplastische Chirurgie

Sec Rotterdam Eye Hosp, Schiedamsevest 180, 3011 BH Rotterdam, Netherlands. T. +31104017777. E-mail: secretary@esoprs.eu.
URL: http://www.esoprs.eu/

History 1981. Founded under the auspices of *European Society of Ophthalmology (SOE, #08674)* but as an independent body. Former names and other names: *European Society for Orbital Plastic and Reconstructive Surgery (ESOPRS)* – former. **Aims** Promote teaching and exchange of new ideas of ophthalmic plastic and reconstructive surgery. **Structure** General Meeting (annual); Committee. **Languages** English. **Staff** 3.00 FTE, voluntary. **Finance** Sources: meeting proceeds; members' dues. **Activities** Awards/prizes/competitions; events/meetings. **Events** *Annual General Meeting* Naples (Italy) 2023, *Annual General Meeting* Nice (France) 2022, *Annual General Meeting* 2021, *Annual General Meeting* Naples (Italy) 2020, *Annual General Meeting* Hamburg (Germany) 2019. **Publications** Scientific papers are published in the journal *Orbit.*

Members Individuals in 41 countries:
Australia, Austria, Belarus, Belgium, Brazil, Canada, Colombia, Croatia, Denmark, Egypt, Estonia, Finland, France, Germany, Greece, Hungary, Iceland, India, Ireland, Israel, Italy, Japan, Jordan, Korea Rep, Kosovo, Kuwait, Lebanon, Morocco, Netherlands, New Zealand, Norway, Russia, Saudi Arabia, Slovenia, Spain, Sweden, Switzerland, Tunisia, Türkiye, UK, USA. [2022.02.14/XD1615/v/**D**]

♦ **European Society of Ophthalmology (SOE)** **08674**

Société européenne d'ophtalmologie – Societas Ophthalmologica Europaea (SOE)

Pres address not obtained. E-mail: secretariat@soevision.org.
URL: http://www.soevision.org/

History 1958. **Aims** Promote ophthalmology in Europe; stimulate cooperation between European ophthalmologists and between their national organizations, as well as execute all that is directly or indirectly connected with or may attribute to the aforementioned, in the widest sense. **Structure** Executive Committee; Board; Scientific Committee; Scientific Advisory Board. **Languages** English. **Finance** Congress revenue. **Activities** Awards/prizes/competitions; events/meetings. **Events** *Congress* Prague (Czechia) 2021, *Congress* Nice (France) 2019, *WOC : World Ophthalmology congress* Barcelona (Spain) 2018, *Congress* Barcelona (Spain) 2017, *Congress* Vienna (Austria) 2015. **Publications** Congress proceedings.

Members European national ophthalmological societies in 39 countries:
Austria, Belarus, Belgium, Bosnia-Herzegovina, Bulgaria, Croatia, Czechia, Denmark, Estonia, Finland, France, Georgia, Germany, Greece, Hungary, Iceland, Ireland, Italy, Latvia, Lithuania, Malta, Moldova, Montenegro, Netherlands, North Macedonia, Norway, Poland, Portugal, Romania, Russia, Serbia, Slovakia, Slovenia, Spain, Sweden, Switzerland, Türkiye, UK, Ukraine.

Associate in 3 countries:
Egypt, Israel, Jordan. [2017.10.12/XD0817/**D**]

♦ European Society of Ophthalmology and Traditional Medicine (no recent information)
♦ European Society for Opinion and Marketing Research / see World Association of Research Professionals (#21182)

♦ **European Society of Optometry** **08675**

Société d'optométrie d'Europe (SOE) – Sociedad Europea de Optometria – Europäische Gesellschaft für Optometrie – Società d'Optometria d'Europa – Sociedade de Optometria de Europa – Europese Optometrie Vereniging

Dir Av Georges Henri 308, 1200 Brussels, Belgium. E-mail: info@soe-optometry.eu.
URL: http://www.soe-optometry.eu/

History 1967. Statutes revised 1979. Former names and other names: *European Federation of Optometry* – former. **Aims** Develop the concept of vision as part of the total psychosomatic activity of the human being; strive for: professional education for optometrists at the university level throughout Europe, the right for optometrists to carry out complete eye examinations by both objective and subjective methods, the establishment of optometry as an independent profession and the awarding of a European-wide diploma allowing optometrists to operate in any country of Europe. **Structure** General Council (meets twice a year); Executive Committee. Works through linguistic but not through national groupings. Includes *American Colleagues of the European Society of Optometry (ACEOS)* for members not living or practising in Europe. **Languages** Dutch, English, French, German, Italian, Portuguese, Spanish. **Staff** Voluntary. **Finance** Sources: members' dues. **Activities** Takes part in EC negotiations; operates programme of *'Continuing Education Courses in Optometry (CECO)'*; organizes congresses; develops professional code of conduct. **Events** *Annual World Congress* USA 1993, *Annual World Congress* Monte Carlo (Monaco) 1990, *International congress on behavioral optometry* Monte Carlo (Monaco) 1990, *Annual world congress* USA 1988, *Scientific congress / Annual World Congress* Brussels (Belgium) 1987. **Publications** *SOE Communications* (regular) in Dutch, English, French, German, Italian, Portuguese, Spanish. **Members** Individuals. Membership languages or individual membership registered by language and not by country. [2018/XD5690/**D**]

♦ European Society for Oral Laser Applications / see International Society for Oral Laser Applications (#15326)
♦ European Society for Orbital Plastic and Reconstructive Surgery / see European Society of Ophthalmic Plastic and Reconstructive Surgery (#08673)

♦ **European Society for Organ Transplantation (ESOT)** **08676**

CEO 8/24 Riviera dei Mugnai, 35137 Padua PD, Italy. T. +39498597652. Fax +39492106306. E-mail: askme@esot.org.
URL: http://www.esot.org/

History 1982, Zurich (Switzerland). Registered seat in Amsterdam (Netherlands). Registration: No/ID: KVK 34329686, Netherlands, Amsterdam; EU Transparency Register, No/ID: 344914634803-90, Start date: 12 May 2019. **Aims** Promote and encourage education and research relevant to organ transplantation. **Structure** Congress (every 2 years); Council. Sections (7): Ethical, Legal and Psychosocial Aspects of Organ Transplantation (ELPAT); European Cardio-Thoracic Transplant Association; *European Donation and Transplant Coordination Organisation (EDTCO, #06939)*; European Kidney Transplant Association (EKITA); *European Liver and Intestine Transplant Association (ELITA, #07705)*; *European Pancreas and Islet Transplant Association (EPITA, #08135)*; Vascularized Composite Allotransplantation (VCA). Committees (4); Working Group. **Languages** English. **Staff** 5.00 FTE, paid. **Finance** Members' dues. Other sources: sponsorship; events. **Activities** Awards/prizes/competitions; events/meetings; training/education. **Events** *Biennial Congress* Athens (Greece) 2023, *Biennial Congress* Milan (Italy) 2021, *Joint Winter Symposium* Innsbruck (Austria) 2020, *Biennial Congress* Copenhagen (Denmark) 2019, *EPITA Symposium* Innsbruck (Austria) 2019. **Publications** *Transplant International* (12 a year) – newsletter.

Members Regular; International; Joint; Trainee; Non Medical. Members in 78 countries and territories:
Afghanistan, Albania, Algeria, Argentina, Australia, Austria, Azerbaijan, Bangladesh, Belarus, Belgium, Bosnia-Herzegovina, Brazil, Bulgaria, Canada, Chile, China, Colombia, Croatia, Cyprus, Czechia, Denmark, Ecuador, Egypt, Estonia, Finland, France, Georgia, Germany, Greece, Haiti, Hong Kong, Hungary, India, Iran Islamic Rep, Iraq, Ireland, Israel, Italy, Japan, Kazakhstan, Korea Rep, Latvia, Libya, Lithuania, Malta, Mexico, Moldova, Morocco, Netherlands, North Macedonia, Norway, Pakistan, Peru, Philippines, Poland, Portugal, Qatar, Romania, Russia, Saudi Arabia, Serbia, Singapore, Slovakia, Slovenia, South Africa, Spain, Sri Lanka, Sweden, Switzerland, Syrian AR, Taiwan, Tunisia, Türkiye, UK, Ukraine, United Arab Emirates, USA, Vietnam.

NGO Relations Member of: *Associations and Conference Forum (AC Forum, #02909).* Cooperates with transplantation related organizations in and outside Europe, including with: *European Society for Heart and Lung Transplantation (ESHLT, #08619)*; *The Transplantation Society (TTS, #20224).* [2022/XD1115/v/**D**]

♦ European Society of Osteoarthrology (inactive)
♦ European Society for Out-Patient Eye Surgery (no recent information)
♦ European Society of Paediatric Allergy and Clinical Immunology (inactive)
♦ European Society for Paediatric Anaesthesia / see European Society for Paediatric Anaesthesiology (#08677)

♦ **European Society for Paediatric Anaesthesiology (ESPA)** **08677**

Secretariat Českomoravská 19, 190 00 Prague 4, Czechia. T. +420284001444. E-mail: info@euroespa.com.
Registered Address Dept Anaesthesia, The Royal Hospital for Sick Children, Dalnair Street, Glasgow, G3 8SJ, UK.
URL: http://www.euroespa.com/

History 10 May 1989, Rotterdam (Netherlands). Relaunched, Sep 2009, Warsaw (Poland), when assets transferred to new organization. Old structure of FEAPA only officially dissolved 1 June 2010. Former names and other names: *Federation of European Associations of Paediatric Anaesthesia (FEAPA)* – former; *European Society for Paediatric Anaesthesia* – former. Registration: Netherlands. **Aims** Promote safety and quality

European Society Paediatric
08678

alphabetic sequence excludes
For the complete listing, see Yearbook Online at

of care in paediatric anaesthesiology. **Structure** General Assembly (annual); Executive Board; Advisory Council; Committees (7). **Languages** English. **Staff** 5.00 FTE, voluntary. **Finance** Sources: donations; meeting proceeds; members' dues; subsidies. Other sources: income from capital. **Activities** Knowledge management/information dissemination; networking/liaising; standards/guidelines. **Events** *Annual Congress* Lisbon (Portugal) 2022, *Annual Congress* Porto (Portugal) 2020, *Seminar* Prague (Czechia) 2020, *Annual Congress* Rotterdam (Netherlands) 2019, *Annual Congress* Brussels (Belgium) 2018. **Publications** *ESPA Newsletter*.
Members Individuals Active; Affiliate; Trainee; Retired; Honorary. National representatives in 33 countries:
Austria, Belgium, Bulgaria, Croatia, Czechia, Denmark, Estonia, Finland, France, Germany, Greece, Hungary, Iceland, Ireland, Israel, Italy, Latvia, Lithuania, Malta, Netherlands, Norway, Poland, Portugal, Romania, Russia, Serbia, Slovakia, Slovenia, Spain, Sweden, Switzerland, Türkiye, UK. [2021.09.15/XD2318/**D**]

♦ European Society for Paediatric Endocrinology (ESPE) 08678

Secretariat c/o BioScientifica, Starling House, 1600 Bristol Parkway North, Bristol, BS34 8YU, UK. T. +441454642246. Fax +441454642222. E-mail: espe@eurospe.org.
URL: http://www.eurospe.org/

History 10 Jul 1962, Zurich (Switzerland). Constitution adopted 10 Aug 1965, Copenhagen (Denmark). Covers Europe and Mediterranean countries. Registration: Charity Commission, No/ID: 1122484, England and Wales. **Aims** Promote knowledge of and research on paediatric endocrinology in the widest sense, including: metabolism; haematology; immunology; molecular biology; growth and development; nephrology; electrolyte and water metabolism; and any other subjects, insofar as they concern hormones. **Structure** General Meeting (annual); Council. Council Committees (7): Communications; Corporate Liaison Board; Clinical Practice; Education and Training; Programme Organising; Science; Strategic and Finance. Other Committees (10): Andrea Prader; Caucasus and Central Asia Steering; Clinical Fellowship; Diabetes, Obesity and Metabolism School Steering; Maghreb School Steering; Newsletter Editorial Board; Online Learning; Summer School Steering; Travel Grant Steering; Winter School Steering. Working Groups. **Languages** English. **Staff** None. **Finance** Members' dues. Proceedings from events. **Activities** Training/education; awards/prizes/competitions; events/meetings; research/documentation. **Events** *Annual Meeting* Marseille (France) 2026, *Annual Meeting* Copenhagen (Denmark) 2025, *Annual Meeting* Liverpool (UK) 2024, *Annual Meeting* The Hague (Netherlands) 2023, *Science Symposium* Utrecht (Netherlands) 2022. **Publications** *Hormone Research in Paediatrics* – journal. **Members** Ordinary; Basic Scientists; Middle Income; Low Income; Fellow in Training; Retired. Individuals (940) in over 70 countries. Membership countries not specified. **NGO Relations** Member of: *European Alliance for Diabetes Research (EURADIA, #05868); European Society of Endocrinology (ESE, #08594); Global Pediatric Endocrinology and Diabetes (GPED, #10545).* [2020/XD0854/v/**D**]

♦ European Society of Paediatric Endoscopic Surgeons (ESPES) 08679

Hon Sec address not obtained. E-mail: espes.secretary@gmail.com.
CEO address not obtained.
URL: http://www.espes.eu/

History Sep 2004. **Structure** General Assembly; Executive Board. **Finance** Members' dues. **Events** *Annual Congress* Sorrento (Italy) 2023, *Annual Congress* Barcelona (Spain) 2022, *Annual Congress* Lugano (Switzerland) 2021, *Annual Congress* 2020, *Annual Congress* Vienna (Austria) 2020. [2023/XJ9663/**D**]

♦ European Society for Paediatric Gastroenterology, Hepatology and Nutrition (ESPGHAN) 08680

Société Européenne pour la gastro-entérologie, d'hépatologie et de nutrition pédiatriques

Contact Rue Pellegrino Rossi 16, 1201 Geneva, Switzerland. E-mail: office@espghan.org.
URL: http://www.espghan.org/

History 1968, Paris (France). Constitution adopted 1968; amended: 2007, Barcelona (Spain); 2014, Jerusalem (Israel). Current version adopted 2021, Vienna (Austria). One of 7 associations comprising *United European Gastroenterology (UEG, #20506)*. Former names and other names: *European Society for Paediatric Gastroenterology and Nutrition (ESPGAN)* – former. Registration: France. **Aims** Further the science of Paediatric Gastroenterology, Hepatology and Nutrition. **Structure** General Meeting (annual); Council; Executive Committee. **Languages** English. **Staff** 3.00 FTE, paid. **Finance** Sources: members' dues; revenue from activities/projects; sale of publications. Supported by: *United European Gastroenterology (UEG, #20506)*. Annual budget: 300,000 EUR. **Activities** Awards/prizes/competitions; events/meetings; research/documentation; training/education. **Events** *Annual Meeting* Vienna (Austria) 2023, *Annual Meeting* Copenhagen (Denmark) 2022, *Quadrennial World Congress of Pediatric Gastroenterology, Hepatology and Nutrition* Vienna (Austria) 2021, *Annual Meeting* Copenhagen (Denmark) 2020, *Quadrennial World Congress of Pediatric Gastroenterology, Hepatology and Nutrition* Copenhagen (Denmark) 2020. **Publications** *Journal of Pediatric Gastroenterology and Nutrition*.
Members National Societies in 42 countries:
Albania, Armenia, Austria, Belarus, Belgium, Bosnia-Herzegovina, Bulgaria, Croatia, Cyprus, Czechia, Denmark, Estonia, Finland, France, Georgia, Germany, Greece, Hungary, Ireland, Israel, Italy, Kosovo, Latvia, Lithuania, Moldova, Montenegro, Netherlands, North Macedonia, Norway, Poland, Portugal, Romania, Russia, Serbia, Slovakia, Slovenia, Spain, Sweden, Switzerland, Türkiye, UK, Ukraine.
IGO Relations Observer status with (1): *Codex Alimentarius Commission (CAC, #04081)*. **NGO Relations** Member of (2): *Biomedical Alliance in Europe (#03251); Federation of International Societies for Pediatric Gastroenterology, Hepatology and Nutrition (FISPGHAN, #09678)* (Founding). Cooperates with (6): *European Association for Gastroenterology, Endoscopy and Nutrition (EAGEN, #06051); European Association for the Study of the Liver (EASL, #06233); European Foundation for the Care of Newborn Infants (EFCNI, #07344); European Pancreatic Club (EPC, #08136); European Society of Gastrointestinal Endoscopy (ESGE, #08606); International Society for Digestive Surgery (ISDS, #15060)* (European Chapter). [2022/XD1679/**D**]

♦ European Society for Paediatric Gastroenterology and Nutrition / see European Society for Paediatric Gastroenterology, Hepatology and Nutrition (#08680)

♦ European Society for Paediatric Haematology and Immunology (ESPHI) 08681

Société européenne d'hématologie et d'immunologie pédiatriques

Sec address not obtained.
Pres Charité – Univ Berlin, Charitéplatz 1, 10117 Berlin, Germany.
URL: http://esphi.info/

History 1969, Interlaken (Switzerland). **Aims** Advance research in paediatric haematology and immunology. Promote: interchange of ideas and information; proposals by clinical and laboratory investigators from European countries on common research fields; establishment of new registries on rare and rarer diseases; intergroup communication. **Structure** Board of 6 members. **Languages** English. **Staff** Voluntary. **Finance** Members' dues. Budget (biennial): about Dutch Fl 20,000. **Events** *Biennial Meeting* Berlin (Germany) 2016, *Biennial Meeting* Kiel (Germany) 2013, *Biennial Meeting* Barcelona (Spain) 2011, *Annual meeting / Biennial Meeting* Lecce (Italy) 2009, *Biennial Meeting* Athens (Greece) 2007.
Members Individuals in 24 countries:
Afghanistan, Belgium, Denmark, Finland, France, Germany, Greece, Hungary, Iran Islamic Rep, Israel, Italy, Kazakhstan, Netherlands, Norway, Pakistan, Russia, South Africa, Spain, Sweden, Switzerland, Türkiye, UK, USA, Uzbekistan. [2011.06.11/XD5483/v/**D**]

♦ European Society for Paediatric Infectious Diseases (ESPID) 08682

Société européenne des maladies infectieuses pédiatriques

Main Office c/o Fitwise Management, Blackburn House, Redhouse Road, Seafield, Bathgate, EH47 7AQ, UK. T. +441506639619. Fax +441506811477. E-mail: admin@espid.org.
URL: https://www.espid.org/

History 1981, Munich (Germany). **Aims** Promote science and research, education and public health in the field of paediatric infectious diseases. **Structure** Board; Executive Committee; Committees (3). **Languages** English. **Staff** 8.00 FTE, voluntary. **Finance** Sources: donations; meeting proceeds; members' dues; sponsorship. **Activities** Awards/prizes/competitions; events/meetings; research and development; training/education. **Events** *Annual Congress* Athens (Greece) 2022, *Annual Congress* Geneva (Switzerland) 2021, *Annual Congress* Rotterdam (Netherlands) 2020, *Annual Congress* Ljubljana (Slovenia) 2019, *Annual Congress* Malmö (Sweden) 2018. **Publications** *Pediatric Infectious Diseases Journal* (12 a year).
Members Organizations and individuals in 60 countries:
Albania, Angola, Armenia, Australia, Austria, Belgium, Brazil, Bulgaria, Canada, Chile, Costa Rica, Croatia, Cyprus, Czechia, Denmark, Egypt, Estonia, Finland, France, Gambia, Georgia, Germany, Greece, Hungary, Iceland, Indonesia, Iran Islamic Rep, Ireland, Israel, Italy, Japan, Kenya, Latvia, Lithuania, Malawi, Malta, Namibia, Netherlands, New Zealand, Norway, Pakistan, Paraguay, Poland, Portugal, Romania, Russia, Serbia, Slovenia, South Africa, Spain, Sweden, Switzerland, Syrian AR, Türkiye, Uganda, UK, Ukraine, USA, Vietnam, Zambia.
NGO Relations Member of (2): *Federation of European Societies for Chemotherapy and for Infections (FESCI, #09546); World Society of Pediatric Infectious Diseases (WSPID, #21810).* [2022/XD0742/v/**D**]

♦ European Society of Paediatric Intensive Care / see European Society of Paediatric and Neonatal Intensive Care (#08683)

♦ European Society of Paediatric and Neonatal Intensive Care (ESPNIC) 08683

Société européenne de soins intensifs pédiatriques et neonataux

Communications Manager c/o Kenes Intl, Rue François-Versonnex 7, 1200 Geneva, Switzerland. T. +41229069178. E-mail: membership@espnic.eu.
URL: https://www.espnic.eu/

History 1980, Barcelona (Spain). Former names and other names: *European Club on Paediatric Intensive Care (ECPIC)* – former; *European Society of Paediatric Intensive Care (ESPIC)* – former; *Société européenne de soins intensifs pédiatriques* – former. Registration: Chamber of Commerce Geneva, Switzerland; Start date: 17 Aug 2004, Netherlands. **Aims** Promote paediatric and neonatal intensive care in Europe; encourage development of new treatments and technologies; promote multidisciplinary collaboration among paediatric and neonatal intensivists, nurses and healthcare providers in Europe; encourage research and education into all aspects of paediatric and neonatal intensive care. **Structure** General Meeting (annual); Executive Committee; Scientific Committee; Educational Committee. **Languages** English. **Staff** None. **Finance** Sources: contributions; meeting proceeds; members' dues; sponsorship. **Activities** Events/meetings; healthcare; networking/liaising; projects/programmes; training/education. **Events** *Congress* 2023, *Annual Congress* Salzburg (Austria) 2019, *Annual Meeting* Salzburg (Austria) 2019, *Annual Congress* Paris (France) 2018, *European Conference on Paediatric and Neonatal Cardiac Intensive Care* Marbella (Spain) 2017. **Publications** *ESPNIC Newsletter*; *Intensive Care Medicine*.
Members Full: Corporate; Medical; Honorary. Individuals in 61 countries and territories:
Albania, Argentina, Australia, Austria, Belgium, Bosnia-Herzegovina, Brazil, Canada, Chile, China, Croatia, Cyprus, Czechia, Denmark, Egypt, Finland, France, Georgia, Germany, Greece, Hong Kong, Hungary, India, Indonesia, Iran Islamic Rep, Iraq, Ireland, Israel, Italy, Japan, Kuwait, Latvia, Libya, Lithuania, Malta, Martinique, Mauritius, Mexico, Netherlands, New Zealand, Norway, Poland, Portugal, Qatar, Romania, Russia, Saudi Arabia, Serbia, Singapore, Slovakia, Slovenia, South Africa, Spain, Sweden, Switzerland, Tunisia, Türkiye, UK, United Arab Emirates, USA, Vietnam.
NGO Relations Together with *European Academy of Paediatrics (EAP, #05811)* and *European Society for Paediatric Research (ESPR, #08687)*, instrumental in setting up: *European Academy of Paediatrics Societies (EAPS)*. Collaborates with: *Council of International Neonatal Nurses (COINN, #04904); European Federation of Critical Care Nursing Associations (EfCCNa, #07094); European Society for Paediatric Anaesthesiology (ESPA, #08677); Global Sepsis Alliance (GSA, #10590); World Federation of Pediatric Intensive and Critical Care Societies (WFPICCS, #21473).* [2020.06.23/XD0608/v/**D**]

♦ European Society for Paediatric Nephrology (ESPN) 08684

Société européenne de néphrologie pédiatrique

SG Univ Hosp Leuven, Herestraat 49, 3000 Leuven, Belgium.
Secretariat Podgoritsa Caddesi No 1, 06610 Ankara/Ankara, Türkiye. T. +903124540000. Fax +903124540001.
URL: http://espn-online.org/

History 1967, Glasgow (UK). Statutes amended 1999, Prague (Czech Rep); 2004, Adelaide (Australia). **Aims** Promote research knowledge of paediatric nephrology through teaching, scientific meetings and other methods for the benefit of children with *renal* disease. **Structure** General Meeting (annual); Council. Meetings closed. **Languages** English. **Staff** 11.00 FTE, paid. **Finance** Members' dues. Company grants and support. **Activities** Events/meetings; training/education. **Events** *Annual General Meeting* Ljubljana (Slovenia) 2022, *Annual General Meeting* Amsterdam (Netherlands) 2021, *Annual General Meeting* Leuven (Belgium) 2020, *Annual General Meeting* Ljubljana (Slovenia) 2020, *Annual General Meeting* Belek (Turkey) 2018. **Publications** *ESPN Newsletter*. Congress books; abstracts.
Members Full – specialists in paediatric nephrology residing in Europe; also open to eligible doctors who work in countries which border the Mediterranean Sea as well as those to the north which fall within the conventional definition of Europe. Honorary; Associate – specialists outside Europe. Individuals (500) in 39 countries:
Armenia, Austria, Belgium, Bosnia-Herzegovina, Bulgaria, Canada, Croatia, Czechia, Egypt, Finland, France, Germany, Greece, Hungary, Ireland, Israel, Italy, Lebanon, Libya, Lithuania, Morocco, Netherlands, North Macedonia, Norway, Poland, Portugal, Romania, Russia, Saudi Arabia, Serbia, Slovakia, Slovenia, Spain, Sweden, Switzerland, Türkiye, UK, Ukraine, USA.
Associate in 4 countries:
Canada, Saudi Arabia, South Africa, USA.
NGO Relations Affiliate member of: *International Pediatric Association (IPA, #14541).* [2018.09.24/XD0855/v/**D**]

♦ European Society for Paediatric Neurosurgery (ESPN) 08685

Société européenne de neurochirurgie pédiatrique – Europäische Gesellschaft für Kinderneurochirurgie

Sec Erasmus University Medical Center, PO BOX 2040, 3000 CA Rotterdam, Netherlands. E-mail: secretariat@espnsociety.org.
Legal Seat Chemin de la Gravière 6, Case postale 71, 1211 Geneva, Switzerland.
URL: http://www.espneurosurgery.org/

History 1967. Registration: IDE/UID, No/ID: 334.882.819, Switzerland. **Aims** Promote paediatric neurosurgery and carry out research in the field. **Structure** Membership Meeting; Executive Board; Executive Committee; Committees (5). **Languages** English. **Staff** None. **Finance** Sources: members' dues. **Activities** Training/education. **Events** *Biennial Congress* Rome (Italy) 2023, *Consensus Conference* Athens (Greece) 2022, *Biennial Congress* 2021, *Biennial Congress* Athens (Greece) 2020, *Consensus Conference* Paris (France) 2019. **Publications** *Child's Nervous System* (12 a year) – journal.
Members Full in 28 countries:
Austria, Belgium, Bosnia-Herzegovina, Croatia, Czechia, Denmark, Finland, France, Germany, Greece, Hungary, Ireland, Israel, Italy, Netherlands, North Macedonia, Norway, Poland, Portugal, Romania, Russia, Serbia, Slovenia, Spain, Sweden, Switzerland, Türkiye, UK.
Corresponding in 9 countries:
Argentina, Brazil, Canada, Egypt, India, Japan, Korea Rep, Saudi Arabia, USA.
NGO Relations Affiliated with (1): *European Association of Neurosurgical Societies (EANS, #06134).* [2022/XD8726/**D**]

♦ European Society for Paediatric Oncology / see SIOP Europe (#19288)
♦ European Society for Paediatric Orthopaedics / see European Paediatric Orthopaedic Society (#08128)

♦ European Society of Paediatric Radiology (ESPR) 08686

Société européenne de radiologie pédiatrique – Europäische Gesellschaft für Kinderradiologie

Office Am Gestade 1, 1010 Vienna, Austria. T. +4315334064. E-mail: office@espr.org.
Registered Office Bicêtre Hospital, Paediatric Radiology Dept, 78 rue du General Leclerc, 94270 Le Kremlin-Bicêtre, France.
URL: http://www.espr.org/

History 1963. Former names and other names: *European Society for Children's Radiology* – former. Registration: Law of 1901, France. **Aims** Organize and bring together paediatric radiologists; contribute to progress of paediatric radiology in European countries in conjunction with other branches of radiology and paediatrics, both in clinical and scientific fields and in education and teaching. **Structure** General Assembly; Board; Committees; Taskforces. **Languages** English. **Finance** Members' dues. **Activities** Events/meetings; awards/prizes/competitions. *International Pediatric Radiology Congress (IPR)* held every five years, alternating between Europe and North America. *European Course in Paediatric Radiology (ECPR)*. **Events** *Annual Congress* Harrogate (UK) 2027, *International Pediatric Radiology Congress (IPR)* 2026, *Annual Congress* Bucharest (Romania) 2025, *Annual Congress* Seville (Spain) 2024, *Annual Congress* Belgrade (Serbia) 2023. **Publications** *Paediatric Radiology* (annual).

Members Active; Associate; Affiliate; Honorary. Individuals in 48 countries and territories:
Algeria, Australia, Austria, Belgium, Brazil, Canada, China, Côte d'Ivoire, Czechia, Denmark, Finland, France, Germany, Greece, Hungary, Indonesia, Iran Islamic Rep, Ireland, Israel, Italy, Japan, Jordan, Kenya, Kuwait, Lebanon, Morocco, Netherlands, New Zealand, Norway, Poland, Portugal, Qatar, Romania, Russia, Saudi Arabia, Serbia, Slovakia, South Africa, Spain, Sweden, Switzerland, Taiwan, Tunisia, Türkiye, UK, Ukraine, Uruguay, USA.
NGO Relations Member of: *European Society of Radiology (ESR, #08720).* Founding member of: *World Federation of Pediatric Imaging (WFPI, #21472).* [2021/XD7965/v/**D**]

♦ European Society for Paediatric Research (ESPR) 08687

Société européenne de recherche en pédiatrie – Europäische Gesellschaft für Pädiatrische Forschung

Secretariat Rue de Sablieres 5, 1242 Satigny GE, Switzerland. Fax +4117657992196. E-mail: office@espr.eu.
URL: https://espr.eu/

History 26 Aug 1968. Took over the activities of *European Club for Paediatric Research (inactive).* Constitution amended Jun 1971. Registration: Swiss Civil Code, Switzerland. **Aims** Advance paediatric research in Europe; promote interchange of ideas and information among investigators in relevant subjects, with particular emphasis on the contribution of young research workers. **Structure** Annual Meeting; Council. Sections (6): *European Board of Neonatology (EBN, #06363),* responsible for accreditations and educational programme in neonatology and member of CESP; Brain and Development; Haematology; Oxygen Transport and Microcirculation; Nutrition and Mineral Metabolism; Epidemiology. **Languages** English. **Finance** Members' dues. **Events** *JENS : Congress of Joint European Neonatal Societies* 2021, *Annual Meeting* Maastricht (Netherlands) 2019, *JENS : Congress of Joint European Neonatal Societies* Maastricht (Netherlands) 2019, *Annual Meeting* Paris (France) 2018, *JENS : Congress of Joint European Neonatal Societies* Venice (Italy) 2017.
Members Individuals Active; Senior (over the age of 60). Members in 26 countries:
Australia, Austria, Belgium, Czechia, Denmark, Estonia, Finland, France, Germany, Greece, Hungary, Iceland, Ireland, Israel, Italy, Lebanon, Lithuania, Netherlands, Norway, Poland, Russia, Spain, Sweden, Switzerland, Türkiye, UK.
Affiliates in 2 countries:
Canada, USA.
NGO Relations Member of: *Biomedical Alliance in Europe (#03251).* Together with ESPNIC and EAP, instrumental in setting up: *European Academy of Paediatrics Societies (EAPS).* [2020/XD3890/v/**D**]

♦ European Society for Paediatric Urology (ESPU) 08688

Société européenne d'urologie de l'enfant

Admin Coordinator Herestraat 49, 3000 Leuven, Belgium. T. +32494631046. E-mail: administrative.coordinator@espu.org.
Sec Erasmus MC – Sophia Children's Hospital, 3015 GD Rotterdam, Netherlands. E-mail: secretary@espu.org.
URL: http://www.espu.org/

History 1989, Rotterdam (Netherlands). Registration: Handelsregister, Netherlands. **Aims** Promote paediatric urological science and practice; contribute to training and postgraduate courses for paediatric urologists; stimulate international cooperation; set standards for the practice of paediatric urology in Europe. **Structure** General Assembly; Board. **Languages** English. **Staff** Voluntary. **Finance** Sources: meeting proceeds; members' dues. **Activities** Events/meetings; training/education. **Events** *Annual Congress* Lisbon (Portugal) 2023, *Annual Congress* Ghent (Belgium) 2022, *ESPU-SPU Joint Meeting* Lisbon (Portugal) 2021, *Annual Congress* Lyon (France) 2019, *Seminar on Urethral Reconstruction* Lyon (France) 2019. **Publications** *Journal of Pediatric Urology* (6 a year).
Members Individuals in 44 countries and territories:
Argentina, Australia, Austria, Belgium, Brazil, Canada, China, Czechia, Denmark, Egypt, Finland, France, Germany, Greece, Hungary, India, Iran Islamic Rep, Ireland, Israel, Italy, Korea Rep, Latvia, Lithuania, Mexico, Montenegro, Netherlands, New Zealand, Norway, Pakistan, Poland, Romania, Russia, Saudi Arabia, Serbia, Slovakia, South Africa, Spain, Sweden, Switzerland, Taiwan, Tunisia, Türkiye, UK, USA.
NGO Relations Together with: *European Board of Paediatric Surgery (EBPS, #06369); European Board of Urology (EBU, #06374); European Union of Medical Specialists (UEMS, #09001),* set up: *Multidisciplinary Joint Committee on Paediatric Urology (JCPU, #16883).* Member of: *European Society of Endocrinology (ESE, #08594).* [2022.10.19/XD2852/v/**D**]

- ♦ European Society of Parametrology (inactive)
- ♦ European Society of Parenteral and Enteral Nutrition / see European Society for Clinical Nutrition and Metabolism (#08550)
- ♦ European Society of Parenteral Nutrition / see European Society for Clinical Nutrition and Metabolism (#08550)

♦ European Society of Pathology (ESP) 08689

Société européenne de pathologie – Societas Pathologorum Europae

Dir Gen Rue Bara 6, 1070 Brussels, Belgium. T. +3225208036. E-mail: admin@esp-pathology.org.
URL: http://esp-pathology.org/

History 7 Nov 1964, Salzburg (Austria). Also referred to as *European Congress of Pathology.* Registration: Banque-Carrefour des Entreprises, No/ID: 0871.010.114, Start date: 1 Dec 2004, Belgium. **Aims** Promote high quality diagnostic practice, applied and translational research, and under- and postgraduate education in the field of human pathology. **Structure** Annual General Assembly; Council; Executive Committee; Working Groups; Advisory Board. **Languages** English. **Staff** 0.50 FTE, paid. **Finance** Members' dues. **Activities** Events/meetings; training/education; awards/prizes/competitions. **Events** *European Congress of Pathology* Basel (Switzerland) 2022, *Compass for Optimal Patient Therapy* 2021, *Congress* Glasgow (UK) 2020, *Congress* Nice (France) 2019, *Congress* Bilbao (Spain) 2018. **Publications** *Virchows Archiv* (12 a year); *EESP Newsletter* (4 a year). **Members** Individuals (4,400) in 85 countries. Membership countries not specified. **NGO Relations** Member of: *Biomedical Alliance in Europe (#03251); European Alliance for Personalised Medicine (EAPM, #05878); European Cancer Organisation (ECO, #06432); International Collaboration on Cancer Reporting (ICCR, #12637); Rare Cancers Europe (RCE, #18620).* Liaison Organization of: *Comité européen de normalisation (CEN, #04162).* [2022/XD0864/v/**D**]

♦ European Society for Patient Adherence, COMpliance and Persistence (ESPACOMP) 08690

Managing Dir Rue des Cyclistes Frontière 24, 4600 Visé, Belgium. E-mail: info@espacomp.eu.
URL: http://www.espacomp.eu/

History 2009. **Aims** Promote the science concerned with the quantitative assessment of what patients do with *medicines* they have been prescribed. **Structure** Board of Trustees. **Activities** Organizes annual symposium. **Events** *Annual Symposium* Lisbon (Portugal) 2016, *Annual Symposium* Prague (Czech Rep) 2015, *Annual Symposium* Lausanne (Switzerland) 2014, *Annual Symposium* Budapest (Hungary) 2013, *Annual Symposium* Ghent (Belgium) 2012. [2015/XJ5252/**D**]

♦ European Society for Pediatric Dermatology (ESPD) 08691

Société européenne de dermatologie pédiatrique

ESPD Office c/o C-IN, Prague Congress Centre, 5 kvetna 65, 140 21 Prague 4, Czechia. E-mail: office@espd.info.
URL: http://www.espd.info/

History Set up 4 Jun 1983, Brussels (Belgium), with 1st congress organized 1984, Munster (Germany FR). **Aims** Promote clinical care, interdisciplinary research, education and training; serve as a platform favouring international contacts within Europe and worldwide in the field of pediatric dermatology. **Structure** General Assembly; Board of Directors; Executive Board. **Languages** English. **Finance** Members' dues. Industry partners. **Activities** Training/education; events/meetings; awards/prizes/competitions. **Events** *Annual Meeting* Malaga (Spain) 2023, *Annual Meeting* Munich (Germany) 2022, *Annual Meeting* Vienna (Austria) 2021, *Annual Meeting* Vienna (Austria) 2020, *Annual Meeting* Dubrovnik (Croatia) 2019. **Publications** *European Journal of Pediatric Dermatology; Pediatric Dermatology* – official journal. **Members** Mostly European member base. Membership countries not specified. **NGO Relations** Member of: *International League of Dermatological Societies (ILDS, #14018).* Affiliated with: *International Society of Pediatric Dermatology (ISPD, #15345).* [2020/XD1722/v/**D**]

♦ European Society of Pediatric Otorhinolaryngology (ESPO) 08692

Secretariat c/o Abbey Conference & Events, City Gate, 22 Bridge Street Lower, Dublin, CO. DUBLIN, D08 DW30, Ireland. T. +35316486276 – +35316486130. Fax +35316486197. E-mail: espo@abbey.ie.
SG address not obtained.
URL: https://www.espo.eu.com/

History 1977. Former names and other names: *European Working Group in Pediatric Otorhinolaryngology (EWGPO)* – former. **Aims** Promote high quality care of children with otorhinolaryngologic disorders within Europe. **Structure** General Assembly; Council; Executive Board; Members' Committee. **Languages** English. **Staff** Paid. **Finance** Sources: meeting proceeds; members' dues. **Activities** Advocacy/lobbying/activism; events/meetings; knowledge management/information dissemination; networking/liaising; research/documentation; standards/guidelines; training/education. Europe. **Events** *Congress* Liverpool (UK) 2023, *Congress* Marseille (France) 2021, *Congress* Marseille (France) 2020, *Congress* Stockholm (Sweden) 2018, *Congress* Lisbon (Portugal) 2016. **Publications** *International Journal of Pediatric ORL.* **Members** Individuals (400) in 53 countries. Membership countries not specified. **NGO Relations** Member of (1): *Confederation of European Otorhinolaryngology – Head and Neck Surgery (Confederation of European ORL-HNS, #04528).* Also links with national ENT societies. [2022.05.17/XE1197/v/**E**]

♦ European Society of Periodical Research (ESPRit) 08693

Chair Örebro Univ, Fakultetsgatan 1, SE-702 81 Örebro, Sweden.
URL: http://www.ru.nl/esprit/

History 2009. Became a formal Society, 2018. **Aims** Unite the resources of individual scholars from various disciplines who work with periodicals. **Structure** Executive Board; Committee. **Languages** English, French, German. **Activities** Events/meetings. **Events** *Conference* Paris (France) 2018, *Conference* Nijmegen (Netherlands) 2014, *Conference* Ghent (Belgium) 2012, *Conference* Salford (UK) 2011. **Publications** *Journal of European Periodical Studies (JEPS).* **Members** Individuals (about 400). Membership countries not specified. **NGO Relations** Also links with national organizations. [2021.02.17/XJ7884/**D**]

♦ European Society for Perioperative Care of the Obese Patient (ESPCOP) 08694

Sec Dept of Anaesthesiology, UZGent, De Pintelaan 185, 9000 Ghent, Belgium. E-mail: luc.debaerdemaeker@ugent.be – daniela.godoroja@reginamaria.ro.
Vice-Pres St Richards Hosp, Spitalfield Ln, Chichester, PO19 6SE, UK.
Treas Sint Jan Brugge-Oostende, Ruddershove 10, 8000 Bruges, Belgium.
URL: http://www.espcop.org/

History Feb 2009, Bruges (Belgium). **Aims** Affiliate into one organization, all anesthetists, intensivists and non physicians who are engaged in the clinical care, education and research of the obese surgical patient. **Structure** Representative Council; Board. **Events** *Scientific Meeting* Bruges (Belgium) 2019, *Scientific Meeting* Bruges (Belgium) 2013, *Scientific Meeting* Chichester (UK) 2011, *Scientific Meeting* Pordenone (Italy) 2010, *Scientific Meeting* Ostend (Belgium) 2009. **NGO Relations** Specialty organization of: *European Society of Anaesthesiology and Intensive Care (ESAIC, #08518).* [2022/XJ6883/**D**]

♦ European Society for Person Centered Healthcare (ESPCH) 08695

Contact c/o 77 Victoria Street, Westminster, London, SW1H 0HW, UK. E-mail: info@pchealthcare.org.uk.
Senior Vice-Pres/SG/CEO address not obtained.
URL: http://www.pchealthcare.org.uk/

History Created late 2013, but became fully functional Jan 2014. **Aims** Address the challenges that clinicians and *healthcare* systems face in terms of the increasing depersonalization of *clinical* care and the current – and growing – epidemic of long term chronic *illness.* **Structure** Council; Officers; Special Interest Groups; Academic Council. **Events** *Annual Conference* Madrid (Spain) 2015, *Annual Conference* Madrid (Spain) 2014. [2019/XJ9454/**D**]

- ♦ European Society for Phako- and Laser Surgery (inactive)
- ♦ European Society for Pharmaceutical Cooperation (#19359)

♦ European Society of Pharmacogenomics and Personalised Therapy (ESPT) 08696

Société Européenne de Pharmacogénomique et Thérapie Personalisée

Office Via Carlo Farini 81, 20159 Milan MI, Italy. E-mail: office@esptsociety.eu.
URL: https://www.esptsociety.eu/

History Founded 2010, as *European Society of Pharmacogenomics and Theranostics (ESPT) – Société Européenne de Pharmacogénomique et Théranostique.* Full legal name: *European Society of Pharmacogenomics and Personalised Therapy; A Scientific Society for Individualised Medicine.* Registered in accordance with French law. **Aims** Bring together people interested in all aspects of pharmacogenetics, pharmacogenomics and all approaches focused on improving delivery of medicines to the right patient at the right dose and at the right time; facilitate networking and encourage teamwork among members. **Structure** General Assembly; Board; Steering Committee. Divisions (4): Scientific and Clinical Implementation; Education and Course; Communication and External Relations; Congress and Meetings. **Languages** English. **Events** *Conference* Seville (Spain) 2019, *Conference* Catania (Italy) 2017, *Santorini Conference* Santorini Is (Greece) 2016, *Integration of pharmacogenomics in clinical decision support* Budapest (Hungary) 2015, *Santorini Conference / Conference* Santorini Is (Greece) 2014. **Publications** *Drug Metabolism and Personalized Therapy (DMPT)* – journal.
Members Individual; Industrial; National; Institutional; Foreign Associate; Emeritus; Honorary. Institutional members (15):
European Alliance for Personalised Medicine (EAPM, #05878); European Diagnostic Manufacturers Association (EDMA, inactive); European Federation for Pharmaceutical Sciences (EUFEPS, #07192); European Federation of Clinical Chemistry and Laboratory Medicine (EFLM, #07080); European Science Foundation (ESF, #08441); European Society of Human Genetics (ESHG, #08624); European Society of Predictive Medicine (EUSPM, #08711); Federation of European Pharmacological Societies (EPHAR, #09527); International Association for Therapeutic Drug Monitoring and Clinical Toxicology (IATDMCT, #12227); International Federation of Clinical Chemistry and Laboratory Medicine (IFCC, #13392); International Pharmaceutical Federation (#14566); International Society for Translational Medicine (ISTM, #15517); International Society of Nutrigenetics / Nutrigenomics (ISNN, #15314); International Society of Pharmacogenomics (ISP); *International Union of Basic and Clinical Pharmacology (IUPHAR, #15758).* [2021/XJ6425/y/**D**]

- ♦ European Society of Pharmacogenomics and Personalised Therapy; A Scientific Society for Individualised Medicine / see European Society of Pharmacogenomics and Personalised Therapy (#08696)
- ♦ European Society of Pharmacogenomics and Theranostics / see European Society of Pharmacogenomics and Personalised Therapy (#08696)
- ♦ European Society of Pharmacovigilance / see International Society of Pharmacovigilance (#15356)

♦ European Society for Phenylketonuria and Allied Disorders (ESPKU) 08697

Sec Wilhelm-Mellies-Str 10, 32120 Hiddenhausen, Germany. T. +495221122066. Fax +495221699014. E-mail: info@espku.org – espku@espku.org.
Registered Office Woestijne 16, 9880 Aalter, Belgium.
URL: http://www.espku.org/

History 1987. Registration: Banque-Carrefour des Entreprsies, No/ID: 0445.489.227, Start date: 11 May 1991, Belgium. **Aims** Promote educational and social welfare of persons affected by phenylketonuria (PKU) and allied disorders treated as PKU; stimulate scientific and medical research in PKU. **Structure** General Assembly; Executive Board. Scientific Advisory Committee. **Languages** English. **Staff** 9.00 FTE, voluntary. **Finance** Sources: members' dues; sponsorship. **Activities** Healthcare; research and development; networking/liaising; advocacy/lobbying/activism; awards/prizes/competitions; events/meetings. **Events** *Conference* Seville (Spain) 2022, *Conference* Hiddenhausen (Germany) 2021, *Conference* Hiddenhausen (Germany) 2020, *Conference* Izmir (Turkey) 2019, *Conference* Venice (Italy) 2018. **Publications** *Living with PKU* (2010) in Dutch, French, German, Italian, Spanish, Turkish – jointly with Merck Serono. Reports; brochure; articles.

Members National and regional organizations (40) in 32 countries:
Austria, Belarus, Belgium, Croatia, Czechia, Denmark, Estonia, France, Georgia, Germany, Hungary, Iceland, Ireland, Israel, Italy, Latvia, Lithuania, Moldova, Norway, Palestine, Poland, Portugal, Romania, Serbia, Slovakia, Slovenia, Spain, Sweden, Switzerland, Türkiye, UK, Ukraine.
NGO Relations Member of (1): *EURORDIS – Rare Diseases Europe (#09175)* (Associate). [2021/XD2921/**D**]

♦ European Society for Philosophy of Medicine and Health Care (ESPMH) 08698

Société européenne pour la philosophie de la médecine et de la santé

Sec Inst of Ethics, Dublin City Univ, All Hallows Campus, Senior House S212, Dublin, 9, CO. DUBLIN, Ireland. T. +35317006140. Fax +35317006142.
Pres address not obtained.
URL: http://www.espmh.org/

History Aug 1987. **Aims** Stimulate and promote development and methodology in the field of philosophy of medicine and health care; be a center of contact for European scholars in this field; promote international contact between members in and outside Europe. **Structure** General Assembly (annual); Board; Executive Committee. **Languages** English. **Staff** Voluntary. **Finance** Sources: members' dues. **Activities** Events/meetings. Europe. **Events** *Annual Conference* Frankfurt-Main (Germany) 2024, *Annual Conference* Riga (Latvia) 2023, *Annual Conference* Warsaw (Poland) 2022, *Annual Conference* Warsaw (Poland) 2021, *Annual Conference* Warsaw (Poland) 2020. **Publications** *Medicine, Health Care and Philosophy: A European Journal* (4 a year).
Members Ordinary, Institutional and Honorary in 50 countries and territories:
Albania, Argentina, Australia, Austria, Belgium, Brazil, Bulgaria, Canada, Chile, China, Croatia, Czechia, Denmark, Estonia, Finland, France, Germany, Greece, Hong Kong, Hungary, Iceland, Iraq, Ireland, Israel, Italy, Japan, Korea Rep, Latvia, Lithuania, Malta, Netherlands, Norway, Oman, Pakistan, Philippines, Poland, Portugal, Romania, Russia, Serbia, Slovakia, South Africa, Spain, Sweden, Switzerland, Taiwan, Türkiye, UK, Ukraine, USA. [2020.07.03/XD4096/**D**]

♦ European Society for Philosophy and Psychology (ESPP) 08699

Exec Sec Kulturwissenschaftliches Inst, Goethestrasse 31, 45128 Essen, Germany. T. +492017204209. Fax +492017204111. E-mail: executive_secretary@eurospp.org.
Information Officer Universität Duisburg-Essen, Fakultät für Geisteswissenschaften, Universitätsstrasse 12, 45117 Essen, Germany. T. +492011833368. Fax +492011834118. E-mail: bernhard.schroeder@uni-due.de.
URL: http://www.eurospp.org/

History 1992, Leuven (Belgium). **Aims** Promote interaction between philosophers, psychologists and linguists on issues of common concern. **Structure** Committee; Programme Chairs; Advisory Board. **Events** *Annual Meeting* Athens (Greece) 2019, *Annual Meeting* Rijeka (Croatia) 2018, *Annual Meeting* Hatfield (UK) 2017, *Annual Meeting* St Andrews (UK) 2016, *Annual Meeting* Tartu (Estonia) 2015. [2016.06.14/XD7661/**D**]

♦ European Society for Philosophy of Religion (ESPR) 08700

Pres Seminar für Systematische Theologie, Raum 424, Universitätstrasse 13-17, 48143 Münster, Germany. T. +492518322575.
URL: http://www.philosophy-of-religion.org/

History 1976. Registration: Netherlands. **Aims** Promote study of the philosophy of religion in Europe. **Structure** General Meeting (every 2 years); Board. **Languages** English, German. **Staff** None. **Finance** Sources: members' dues. **Events** *Biennial Conference* Oxford (UK) 2022, *Biennial Conference* Prague (Czechia) 2018, *Biennial Conference* Uppsala (Sweden) 2016, *Biennial Conference* Münster (Germany) 2014, *Biennial Conference* Soesterberg (Netherlands) 2012.
Members Full in 33 countries and territories:
Austria, Belgium, Bosnia-Herzegovina, Bulgaria, Croatia, Czechia, Denmark, England, Finland, France, Germany, Greece, Hungary, Ireland, Israel, Italy, Latvia, Liechtenstein, Netherlands, Norway, Poland, Portugal, Romania, Russia, Scotland, Serbia, Slovakia, Slovenia, Spain, Sweden, Switzerland, UK, Wales.
NGO Relations Accredited by (1): *International Philosophy of Religion Association (IPRA).* [2021.02.16/XD8314/**D**]

♦ European Society of Phlebectomy 08701

Société européenne de phlébectomie (SEP)

Secretariat 37 rue de Chaillot, 75116 Paris, France.
Pres address not obtained.
Registered Office 44 Avenue de Versailles, 75016 Paris, France.
URL: http://www.phlebectomy.org/

History 1987, Paris (France). **Aims** Improve venous treatments. **Languages** English, French. **Staff** 11.50 FTE, voluntary. **Finance** Members' dues. **Events** *Congress* Paris (France) 2020, *Congress* Brussels (Belgium) 2019, *Congress* Barcelona (Spain) 2018, *Congress* Roscoff (France) 2018, *Congress* Milan (Italy) 2017.
Members Full in 15 countries:
Austria, Belgium, Czechia, France, Germany, Italy, Luxembourg, Poland, Portugal, Slovakia, Spain, Sweden, Switzerland, Ukraine, USA.
NGO Relations Member of: *International Union of Phlebology (#15797)*; *Sociedad Panamericana de Flebologia y Linfologia (#19433)*. Links with national organizations. [2020/XD7247/**D**]

♦ European Society for Photobiology (ESP) 08702

Sec School of Pharmacy and Biomolecular Sciences, Liverpool John Moores Univ, Liverpool, L3 2AJ, UK.
Pres Dept of Chemistry, Univ of Aveiro, 3810-193 Aveiro, Portugal.
Treas Dept Pharmaceutical and Pharmacological Sciences, Univ of Padova, Via Marzolo 5, 35131 Padua PD, Italy.
URL: http://www.photobiology.eu/

History 1986. Registration: No/ID: 1359916974, Start date: 2 Sep 2021, Austria. **Aims** Coordinate and promote all aspects of photobiology in Europe so as to optimize achievements of European photobiology across a range of scientific, technological and medical arenas. **Structure** General Assembly (normally meets at biennial meeting); Executive Committee. **Languages** English. **Finance** Sources: contributions; donations; gifts, legacies; government support; grants; members' dues. **Activities** Events/meetings; training/education. **Events** *Biennial Congress* Lyon (France) 2023, *Biennial Congress* Salzburg (Austria) 2021, *Biennial Congress* Barcelona (Spain) 2019, *Biennial Congress* Pisa (Italy) 2017, *Biennial Congress* Aveiro (Portugal) 2015. **Publications** *Photochemical and Photobiological Sciences (PPS). Comprehensive Series in Photochemical and Photobiological Sciences.*
Members Full in 53 countries:
Argentina, Australia, Austria, Belgium, Brazil, Bulgaria, Canada, Chile, China, Croatia, Czechia, Denmark, Egypt, Estonia, Finland, France, Germany, Greece, Hungary, India, Indonesia, Ireland, Israel, Italy, Japan, Jordan, Korea Rep, Kuwait, Libya, Lithuania, Mali, Netherlands, New Zealand, Nigeria, Norway, Oman, Poland, Portugal, Russia, Singapore, Slovakia, South Africa, Spain, Sudan, Sweden, Switzerland, Syrian AR, Türkiye, UK, Ukraine, United Arab Emirates, USA, Venezuela. [2022.05.20/XD4558/**D**]

♦ European Society for Photodermatology (ESPD) 08703

Contact Service de Dermatologie, Hôpital Larrey, 24 chemin de Pouvourville TSA 30030, 31059 Toulouse CEDEX, France. E-mail: info@espd.eu.com.
URL: http://www.espd.eu.com/

History 1999. **Aims** Promote photodermatology in all its aspects. **Structure** Board of 7 members. **Languages** English. **Finance** Members' dues. **Activities** Annual Photodermatology Day. **Publications** *ESPD Newsletter.*
Members Full in 18 countries:
Austria, Belgium, Czechia, Denmark, Egypt, France, Germany, Greece, Hungary, Ireland, Israel, Italy, Netherlands, Portugal, Spain, Sweden, UK, USA.
NGO Relations *European Academy of Dermatology and Venereology (EADV, #05788).* [2013.09.23/XD8179/**D**]

♦ European Society for Photodynamic Therapy (EURO-PDT) 08704

Vice-Pres c/o Klinik für Umweltkrankungen, Knappschaftskrankenhaus, Dorstener Str 151, 45657 Recklinghausen, Germany. E-mail: webmaster@euro-pdt.org.
Sec Dermatology Dept, Stirling Royal Infirmary, Stirling, FK8 2AU, UK. T. +44178634096. E-mail: info@euro-pdt.com.
URL: http://euro-pdt.org/

Aims Serve as a communications platform between researchers working with fluorescence diagnosis and photodynamic therapy; promote international cooperation in this field in Europe. **Structure** Board, comprising President, Vice-President, Treasurer and Secretary. **Events** *EURO-PDT Annual Congress* 2022, *EURO-PDT Annual Congress* 2021, *Annual Congress* Seville (Spain) 2020, *Annual Congress* Brussels (Belgium) 2019, *Annual Congress* Nice (France) 2018. [2022/XD9390/**D**]

♦ European Society of Phraseology (EUROPHRAS) 08705

Société européenne de phraséologie – Europäische Gesellschaft für Phraseologie

Chairwoman Inst für Deutsche Sprache, Postfach 10 16 21, 68016 Mannheim, Germany. T. +496211581414. Fax +496211581200.
URL: http://www.europhras.org/

History Founded Jan 1999, Bielefeld (Germany). Registered in accordance with Swiss law. **Aims** Advance and support research projects in the field of phraseology among scholars; encourage worldwide cooperation in the field. **Structure** General Meeting (every 2-3 years); Board; Advisory Council. **Languages** English, French, German, Spanish. **Staff** 1.00 FTE, paid. **Finance** Members' dues. **Activities** Events/meetings. **Events** *International Conference* Milan (Italy) 2023, *International Conference* Malaga (Spain) 2022, *International Conference* Louvain-la-Neuve (Belgium) 2021, *International Conference* Louvain-la-Neuve (Belgium) 2020, *International Conference* Malaga (Spain) 2019. **Publications** *Yearbook of Phraseology.*
Members Individuals in 33 countries:
Armenia, Austria, Belgium, Bulgaria, Canada, Croatia, Czechia, Denmark, Estonia, Finland, France, Germany, Greece, Hungary, Iceland, Italy, Latvia, Lithuania, Luxembourg, New Zealand, North Macedonia, Poland, Romania, Russia, Serbia, Slovenia, Sweden, Switzerland, Tunisia, UK, Ukraine, USA. [2018.08.28/XM1424/v/**D**]

♦ European Society of Physical and Rehabilitation Medicine (ESPRM) 08706

Pres ESPRM Central Office, 1st km Paianias-Markopoulou Avenue, 190 02 PO Box 126, Paiania, 190 02 Athens, Greece. T. +302103274570. Fax +302103311021.

History 29 Mar 1963, Brussels (Belgium). Former names and other names: *European Federation for Physical Medicine and Rehabilitation* – former; *Fédération européenne de médecine physique et réadaptation* – former; *Europäische Vereinigung für Physikalische Medizin und Funktionelle Neuerziehung* – former. Registration: Banque Carrefour des Entreprises, No/ID: 0409.559.635, Start date: 25 Apr 1963, Belgium. **Aims** Organize at scientific level all bodies in Europe aimed at development of *physical medicine* and rehabilitation; harmonize specialist research work and standards of professional qualification. **Structure** General Assembly (annual); Executive Committee. **Languages** English, French. **Staff** Voluntary. **Finance** Sources: members' dues. **Events** *Congress* Ljubljana (Slovenia) 2022, *Congress* Belgrade (Serbia) 2020, *Baltic and North Sea Conference on Physical and Rehabilitation Medicine* Stockholm (Sweden) 2018, *Congress* Vilnius (Lithuania) 2018, *Congress* Estoril (Portugal) 2016. **Publications** *European Journal of Physical and Rehabilitation Medicine. Europa Medicophysica.*
Members National societies in 34 countries:
Austria, Belgium, Bulgaria, Croatia, Cyprus, Denmark, Estonia, Finland, France, Georgia, Germany, Greece, Hungary, Ireland, Italy, Latvia, Lithuania, Luxembourg, Montenegro, Netherlands, North Macedonia, Norway, Poland, Portugal, Romania, Russia, Serbia, Slovakia, Slovenia, Spain, Sweden, Switzerland, Türkiye, Ukraine. [2021/XD0714/**D**]

♦ European Society for Pigment Cell Research (ESPCR) 08707

Pres Rue Héger-Bordet 7, 1000 Brussels, Belgium. T. +34915854844. Fax +34915854506. E-mail: espcr@espcr.org.
Sec-Treas address not obtained.
URL: http://www.espcr.org/

History 1985. Current constitution adopted 2000. **Aims** Promote interdisciplinary knowledge in the field of physics, chemistry, biology and medicine concerned with pigment cells, pigmentation and associated processes in man and other living organisms. **Structure** General Assembly (at annual Scientific Meeting). Council of 11 members. Officers: President, Secretary, Treasurer. **Languages** English. **Staff** Voluntary. **Finance** Members' dues. **Activities** Provides a forum for interactive discussions by bringing together basic researchers and clinicians from various disciplines, including: development biology; biochemistry; cell and molecular biology; immunology; pharmacology; toxicology; chemistry; physics; dermatology. **Events** *Meeting* 2022, *A bridge between the pathology and physiology of the melanocyte* Brussels (Belgium) 2019, *Meeting* Rennes (France) 2018, *Meeting* Milan (Italy) 2016, *Meeting* Edinburgh (UK) 2015. **Publications** *ESPCR Bulletin.*
Members Organizations in 19 countries and territories:
Australia, Austria, Belgium, Czechia, Denmark, France, Germany, Italy, Japan, Netherlands, Norway, Poland, Romania, Spain, Sweden, Switzerland, Taiwan, UK, USA.
NGO Relations Founding member of: *International Federation of Pigment Cell Societies (IFPCS, #13512).* [2022/XD2267/**D**]

♦ European Society of Plastic, Reconstructive and Aesthetic Surgery (ESPRAS) 08708

Pres Avenija G Suska 6, HR-10000 Zagreb, Croatia. E-mail: office@espras.org – treasurer@espras.org.
URL: http://www.espras.org/

History Jul 1990. Founded as the new denomination of the European section of *International Confederation for Plastic, Reconstructive and Aesthetic Surgery (IPRAS, inactive).* Currently independent. Registration: Switzerland. **Aims** Increase connections among the different European National Societies. **Structure** Executive Committee. **Activities** Events/meetings; training/education. **Events** *Quadrennial Congress* Porto (Portugal) 2022, *Quadrennial Congress* Limassol (Cyprus) 2018, *Quadrennial Congress* Edinburgh (UK) 2014, *Chinese European Congress of Plastic, Reconstructive and Aesthetic Surgery* Beijing (China) 2011, *Quadrennial Congress* Rhodes Is (Greece) 2009. **NGO Relations** In liaison with technical committees of: *Comité européen de normalisation (CEN, #04162).* [2022/XM2934/**E**]

♦ European Society of Pneumology (inactive)

♦ European Society for Population Economics (ESPE) 08709

Sec address not obtained. E-mail: info@espe.org.
URL: http://www.espe.org/

History 30 Sep 1986, Hagen (Germany). Founded at inaugural meeting when statutes were adopted. **Aims** Further theoretical and empirical research on population economics; disseminate results of such research; organize communication and exchange between researchers in different European countries and with scientists from other parts of the world; give equal emphasis to theoretical and applied research dealing with broadly defined relationships between economic and demographic variables. **Structure** General Assembly (annual). Executive Committee, consisting of President, President-Elect, Treasurer and Secretary. Council of 9 to 18 members. **Languages** English. **Staff** About 500, mostly academics, that do research in population and labour economics. **Finance** Members' dues (annual), determined by Executive Committee. **Events** *Annual Conference* Rotterdam (Netherlands) 2024, *Annual Conference* Belgrade (Serbia) 2023, *Annual Conference* Rende (Italy) 2022, *Annual Conference* Barcelona (Spain) 2021, *Annual Conference* Bath (UK) 2019. **Publications** *Journal of Population Economics* (4 a year); *ESPE Newsletter.*
Members Individuals in 26 countries:
Austria, Belgium, Bulgaria, Canada, Cyprus, Czechia, Denmark, Estonia, Finland, France, Germany, Greece, Hungary, Iceland, Ireland, Italy, Netherlands, Norway, Poland, Portugal, Spain, Sweden, Switzerland, Türkiye, UK, USA. [2022/XD1982/v/**D**]

♦ European Society for Precision Engineering and Nanotechnology (EUSPEN) 08710

Associazione Europea di Ingegneria di Precisione

Business Development Manager Bldg 90, Cranfield Univ, Cranfield, MK43 0AL, UK. T. +441234754023. Fax +441234754080. E-mail: info@euspen.eu.
URL: http://www.euspen.eu/

History 1 Oct 1998. Founded with initial funding from the European Commission. Registration: Charity, No/ID: 1091120, England and Wales; Company, No/ID: 4132591, England and Wales. **Aims** Promote awareness, skills, research and development of ultra-precision technologies and nanotechnology; promote dissemination through education and training; facilitate exploitation by science and industry. **Structure** General Meeting (annual); Council (Board of Directors); Executive Board; Directors (13); Standing Committees (4); Headquarters

in Cranfield (UK). **Languages** English. **Staff** 3.50 FTE, paid. **Finance** Members' dues. **Activities** Events/meetings; research and development; knowledge management/information dissemination; training/education. Special Interest Group (SIG) meetings in addition to major annual event with exhibition. **Events** *International Conference* Geneva (Switzerland) 2022, *International Conference* Copenhagen (Denmark) 2021, *International Conference* 2020, *International Conference* Bilbao (Spain) 2019, *International Conference* Venice (Italy) 2018. **Publications** *Precision Engineering – Journal of the International Societies for Precision Engineering and Nanotechnology* – in conjunction with American and Japanese Precision Engineering Societies. Conference and seminar proceedings.
Members Corporate industrial organizations, universities and research institutes; Individual; Sponsoring. Members in 33 countries and territories:
Australia, Austria, Belgium, Brazil, Canada, China, Croatia, Denmark, Finland, France, Germany, Greece, Hong Kong, India, Ireland, Israel, Italy, Japan, Korea Rep, Latvia, Malaysia, Netherlands, Poland, Russia, Singapore, South Africa, Spain, Sweden, Switzerland, Taiwan, UK, Ukraine, USA. [2020/XD2636/D]

♦ European Society of Predictive Medicine (EUSPM) 08711

Sec Medical Fac – Univ of Milan, Via Luigi Mangiagalli 31, 20133 Milan MI, Italy. T. +39250315341. Fax +39250315338.
Pres Univ Vita-Salute San Raffaele, Clinicla Molecular Biology/Cytogenetics Lab, Diagnostica/Ricerca San Raffaelel, Via Olgettina 60, 20132 Milan MI, Italy. T. +39226432303. Fax +39226434351.
URL: http://www.euspm.org/
Aims Promote public airing of points of dissension between medical experts in the field of predictive medicine; promote plurality in respect to predictive medicine; monitor quality control in health care. **Structure** Executive Board, comprising President, Vice-President, Secretary, Treasurer and 2 members. **Events** *Congress* Riolo Terme (Italy) 2013, *Congress* Berlin (Germany) 2011, *Congress* Innsbruck (Austria) 2009. **NGO Relations** Member of: *European Society of Pharmacogenomics and Personalised Therapy (ESPT, #08696).* Memorandum of Understanding with: *European Association for Predictive, Preventive and Personalised Medicine (EPMA, #06163).* [2013/XJ6424/D]

♦ European Society for Prevention Research (EUSPR) 08712

Contact Rambla 15, 2-3, 07003 Palma, Spain. T. +34971727434. E-mail: office@euspr.org.
URL: http://www.euspr.org/
History 18 Nov 2009. Formally approved 30 Dec 2010. Registration: Spain. **Aims** Promote development of prevention science and its application to practice so as to promote human health and well-being through high quality research, evidence-based interventions, policies and practices. **Structure** Board of Directors. **Finance** Sources: grants; members' dues. **Activities** Awareness raising; events/meetings; knowledge management/information dissemination; networking/liaising; publishing activities; research and development. **Events** *Prevention – Between Ethics and Effectiveness* Tallinn (Estonia) 2022, *Prevention in a COVID Recovery Society* Palma (Spain) 2021, *Conference* Palma (Spain) 2020, *Conference* Ghent (Belgium) 2019, *Conference* Lisbon (Portugal) 2018.
Members Individuals (about 100) in 22 countries:
Australia, Austria, Belgium, Bosnia-Herzegovina, Brazil, Croatia, Czechia, Ecuador, Estonia, France, Germany, Greece, Ireland, Italy, Latvia, Luxembourg, Poland, Portugal, Spain, Sweden, UK, USA.
NGO Relations Member of (1): *European Public Health Association (EUPHA, #08298).* [2022.05.29/XJ1662/D]

♦ European Society of Preventive Medicine (ESPREVMED) 08713

Contact 37A South Parade, Oxford, OX2 7JN, UK.
URL: http://www.esprevmed.org/
History Registration: EU Transparency Register, No/ID: 175336931620-56. **Aims** Promote preventive medicine with a focus on preventive approaches for chronic *diseases.* **Structure** Stakeholder Council. **Publications** *Progress in Preventive Mediicne* – journal. [2019/XM5651/D]

♦ European Society of Preventive, Regenerative and Anti-Aging Medicine (ESAAM) 08714

Exec Sec address not obtained.
Vice-Pres Tree of Life, 13B Petrozavodskaya Street, St Petersburg SANKT-PETERBURG, Russia. T. +78124100011. E-mail: drevo.med@gmail.com.
URL: https://esaam.global/
History Mar 2003, Paris (France). Originally came within *World Academy of Anti-Aging Medicine (WAAAM, inactive).* Former names and other names: *European Society of Anti-Aging Medicine (ESAAM)* – former. **Aims** As an umbrella organization to national and European clinical and research associations for preventive, regenerative and anti-aging medicine: intensify contacts between, and cooperation among, these associations, as well as with non-European associations and other international medical societies; promote education and support research in the field in Europe. **Structure** General Assembly (annual); Board; Executive Committees; Committees; Main Office based in Paris (France). **Languages** English. **Staff** 0.50 FTE, voluntary. **Finance** Sources: members' dues. **Activities** Events/meetings; training/education. **Events** *Mediterranean Congress of Anti-Aging Medicine* Larnaca (Cyprus) 2022, *European Congress for Preventive, Regenerative and Anti-Aging Medicine (ECOPRAM)* Gelendzhik (Russia) 2019, *Mediterranean Congress of Anti-aging Medicine* Larnaca (Cyprus) 2019, *Conference* Corfu (Greece) 2016, *ECOPRAM : European Congress on Preventative Regenerative and Aging Medicine* St Petersburg (Russia) 2016. **Publications** *Rejuvenation Research* (12 a year) – offical journal; *ESAAM Bulletin.*
Members National societies (24) in 16 countries:
Armenia, Austria, Cyprus, Czechia, France, Georgia, Greece, Italy, Poland, Romania, Russia, Spain, Switzerland, Türkiye, UK, Ukraine.
Individuals in 10 countries and territories:
Bulgaria, France, Germany, Greece, Hungary, Italy, Sweden, Taiwan, Thailand, USA. [2022/XM2042/D]

♦ European Society of Primary Care Gastroenterology (ESPCG) 08715

Secretariat c/o Satellite PR, 154-158 Shoreditch High Street, London, E1 6HU, UK. T. +442038724901. E-mail: kirsty@satellitepr.com.
URL: http://www.espcg.eu/
History Mar 1996, London (UK). **Aims** Promote high standards in management of gastrointestinal problems in primary care in Europe through research, education and exchange and dissemination of ideas. **Structure** Officers: Chairman, Secretary, Treasurer; Steering Group; Communication Officer. **Languages** English. **Staff** 4.00 FTE, voluntary. **Activities** Research/documentation; training/education; knowledge management/information dissemination; events/meetings. **Events** *Annual General Meeting* Istanbul (Turkey) 2015, *Annual General Meeting* Istanbul (Turkey) 2008, *Annual General Meeting* London (UK) 2002. **Publications** *EuroDigest* – journal.
Members Individuals in 24 countries:
Australia, Belgium, Croatia, Czechia, Denmark, Estonia, France, Germany, Greece, Hungary, Ireland, Israel, Italy, Libya, Netherlands, Norway, Poland, Portugal, Russia, Spain, Sweden, Türkiye, UK, USA.
National groups in 13 countries:
Belgium, Czechia, Denmark, Estonia, Greece, Italy, Netherlands, Norway, Poland, Spain, Sweden, Türkiye, UK.
NGO Relations Member of: *United European Gastroenterology (UEG, #20506).* [2016.10.18/XD7098/D]

♦ European Society of Professionals Working with Drug Dependences / see European Association of Professionals Working in the Drug Field (#06169)

♦ European Society of Protective Clothing (ESPC) 08716

Chair c/o CITEVE, Technological Textile Centre of Portugal, Rua Fernando Mesquita nº 2785, 4760-034 Vila Nova de Famalicão, Portugal. E-mail: info@es-pc.org.
URL: http://www.es-pc.org/
History 1997, Denmark. **Aims** Act as a forum for discussions and knowledge exchange for persons working in the area of protective clothing including gloves and footwear. **Structure** Board. **Languages** English. **Staff** None. **Activities** Events/meetings. **Events** *European Conference of Protective Clothing* Arnhem (Netherlands) 2023, *European Conference of Protective Clothing* Bönnigheim (Germany) 2021, *European Conference of Protective Clothing* Porto (Portugal) 2018, *European Conference on Protective Clothing* Cesme (Turkey) 2016, *European Conference on Protective Clothing* Bruges (Belgium) 2014. **Publications** Conference proceedings; news updates. [2022.03.10/XJ6415/D]

♦ European Society of Psychology Learning and Teaching (ESPLAT) 08717

Pres c/o EFPA, Marché aux Herbes 105/39, Rue Washington 40, 1000 Brussels, Belgium.
URL: https://www.esplat.org/
History Sep 2017, Salzburg (Austria). Developed out of the European Psychology Learning and Teaching (EuroPLAT) network, set up by *European Commission (EC, #06633).* Founded with the support of *European Federation of Psychologists Associations (EFPA, #07199).* Registration: Banque-Carrefour des Entreprises, No/ID: 0720.794.726, Start date: 15 Feb 2019, Belgium. **Aims** Advance the learning and teaching of scientific psychology at all educational levels on the basis of scientific evidence, within Europe and beyond. **Structure** General Assembly; Executive Committee. **Finance** Sources: members' dues. **Events** *Conference* Heidelberg (Germany) 2021, *Conference* Utrecht (Netherlands) 2019. **Publications** *ESPLAT Newsletter*, *Psychology Learning and Teaching* – academic journal. [2021/AA1894/D]

♦ European Society for Psychosocial Oncology (inactive)
♦ European Society of Public Health Ophthalmology (no recent information)
♦ European Society for Quality in Healthcare (inactive)
♦ European Society for Quality Research (unconfirmed)

♦ European Society for Quality and Safety in Family Practice (EQUIP) 08718

Manager Store Molle Vej 19, 1 tv, 2300 Copenhagen S, Denmark. T. +4528864863. E-mail: equip@woncaeurope.org.
URL: http://equip.woncaeurope.org/
History Set up 1989, as Improvement of Quality Working Party. A network of: *European Society of General Practice/Family Medicine (WONCA Europe, #08609).* Current constitution adopted Apr 2013, Paris (France). **Aims** Contribute to achievement of high levels of quality and safety of care for patients in general practice in all European countries. **Structure** Assembly; Executive Board. **Languages** Croatian, Czech, Danish, Dutch, English, Estonian, French, German, Hungarian, Irish Gaelic, Italian, Norwegian, Slovene, Swedish, Turkish. **Staff** 1.00 FTE, paid. **Finance** Funding from: *European Society of General Practice/Family Medicine (WONCA Europe, #08609)*; EU project funding. **Activities** Knowledge management/information dissemination; events/meetings. **Events** *EQUIP Conference* 2022, *Assembly* Prague (Czech Rep) 2016, *Assembly* Fischingen (Switzerland) 2015, *Assembly* Zagreb (Croatia) 2015, *Assembly* Tallinn (Estonia) 2014. **Publications** *EQuiP Newsletter* (irregular). Studies; protocols.
Members National medical societies in 7 countries:
Belgium, Croatia, Finland, Norway, Portugal, Slovenia, Spain.
Individuals (about 50) from 23 European countries. Membership countries not specified. [2022/XJ7226/E]

♦ European Society for Quantum Solar Energy Conversion 08719

Pres University of Luxembourg, 41, rue du Brill, L-4422 Belvaux, Luxembourg.
Gen Sec Anzengrubergasse 50, 3400 Klosterneuburg, Austria. E-mail: secretary.general@quantsol.org.
URL: http://www.quantsol.org/
History 1994, Interlaken (Switzerland). Founded at 10th International Conference on Photochemical Storage of Solar Energy; Executive Board elected at 1st General Assembly, Mar 1996, Rauris (Austria). **Aims** Advance basic research in quantum solar energy conversion. **Structure** General Assembly; Executive Board; Scientific Advisory Board. **Languages** English, French, German. **Finance** Sources: members' dues. **Activities** Awards/prizes/competitions; events/meetings; guidance/assistance/consulting; knowledge management/information dissemination; training/education. **Events** *QUANTSOL : Workshop on Quantum Solar Energy Conversion* Rauris (Austria) 2023, *QUANTSOL : Workshop on Quantum Solar Energy Conversion* Rauris (Austria) 2022, *QUANTSOL : Workshop on Quantum Solar Energy Conversion* Rauris (Austria) 2019, *QUANTSOL : Workshop on Quantum Solar Energy Conversion* Rauris (Austria) 2018, *QUANTSOL : Workshop on Quantum Solar Energy Conversion* Rauris (Austria) 2017. **Publications** Conference proceedings.
Members Individuals in 24 countries:
Argentina, Australia, Austria, Belarus, Belgium, Brazil, Canada, China, Czechia, Egypt, Estonia, France, Germany, Israel, Italy, Japan, Netherlands, Russia, Spain, Sweden, Switzerland, UK, Ukraine, USA. [2022.10.23/XD7607/D]

♦ European Society for Radiation Biology / see European Radiation Research Society (#08319)

♦ European Society of Radiology (ESR) 08720

Main Office Am Gestade 1, 1010 Vienna, Austria. E-mail: communications@myesr.org.
URL: http://www.myesr.org/
History 10 Dec 2005, Vienna (Austria). Founded on merger of the *European Congress of Radiology (ECR)* and *European Association of Radiology (EAR, inactive).* Launched Mar 2006, Vienna. Registration: EU Transparency Register, No/ID: 478131313572-40; ZVR, No/ID: 083757049, Austria. **Aims** Primary aim: organize the leading meeting in radiology by maintaining and increasing the excellence of the annual European Congress of Radiology. In addition: maximize the efficiency of both institutions to avoid duplication of effort, to create synergies, as well as to optimize the resources necessary for the tasks ahead; pursue joint initiatives. **Structure** General Assembly; Board; Executive Council. **Languages** English. **Finance** Sources: members' dues. **Activities** Training/education; research/documentation; standards/guidelines; events/meetings. **Events** *European Congress of Radiology* Vienna (Austria) 2023, *European Congress of Radiology* Vienna (Austria) 2022, *European Congress of Radiology* Vienna (Austria) 2021, *European Congress of Radiology* Vienna (Austria) 2020, *European Congress of Radiology* Vienna (Austria) 2019. **Publications** *ESR Newsletter* – electronic and paper; *European Radiology* – journal.
Members (22,500). Categories: Institutional – national societies of radiology of European countries, and European Subspecialty Societies of Radiology; Associate – national societies of radiology of countries not eligible for Institutional Membership, and qualified professionals. Institutional member societies in 40 countries:
Albania, Austria, Belarus, Belgium, Bosnia-Herzegovina, Bulgaria, Croatia, Cyprus, Czechia, Denmark, Estonia, Finland, France, Georgia, Germany, Greece, Hungary, Iceland, Ireland, Italy, Latvia, Luxembourg, Malta, Montenegro, Netherlands, North Macedonia, Norway, Poland, Portugal, Romania, Russia, Serbia, Slovakia, Slovenia, Spain, Sweden, Switzerland, Türkiye, UK, Ukraine.
Included in the above, 10 organizations listed in this Yearbook:
European Society of Breast Imaging (EUSOBI, #08535); European Society of Cardiovascular Radiology (ESCR, #08538); European Society of Gastrointestinal and Abdominal Radiology (ESGAR, #08605); European Society of Head and Neck Radiology (ESHNR, #08617); European Society of Musculoskeletal Radiology (ESSR, #08658); European Society of Neuroradiology (ESNR, #08664); European Society of Oncologic Imaging (ESOI, #08670); European Society of Paediatric Radiology (ESPR, #08686); European Society of Thoracic Imaging (ESTI, #08759); European Society of Urogenital Radiology (ESUR, #08770).
Associate member societies in 6 countries:
Australia, China, Israel, Japan, New Zealand, Saudi Arabia.
NGO Relations Memorandum of Understanding with (1): *European Association for Predictive, Preventive and Personalised Medicine (EPMA, #06163).* Member of (5): *Biomedical Alliance in Europe (#03251); European Alliance for Medical Radiation Protection Research (EURAMED, #05874); European Alliance for Personalised Medicine (EAPM, #05878); European Cancer Organisation (ECO, #06432); Integrating Healthcare Enterprise International (IHE International, #11372).* Partner of (1): *Multidisciplinary European Low Dose Initiative Association (MELODI Association, #16882).* Instrumental in setting up and hosts office of: *European Institute for Biomedical Imaging Research (EIBIR, #07546).* Instrumental in setting up: *International Society for the History of Radiology (ISHRAD, #15176).* Founding member of: *Associations and Conference Forum (AC Forum, #02909).* [2021/XM1543/y/D]

♦ European SocieTy for Radiotherapy and Oncology (ESTRO) 08721

CEO Av Marnix 17, 1000 Brussels, Belgium. T. +3227759340. Fax +3227795494. E-mail: info@estro.org – events@estro.org.
URL: http://www.estro.org/
History Sep 1980, Milan (Italy). Former names and other names: *European Society for Therapeutic Radiology and Oncology* – former (1980). Registration: No/ID: 0432.894.370, Start date: 4 Jan 1988, Belgium; EU Transparency Register, No/ID: 114144232470-50, Start date: 21 Sep 2018. **Aims** Foster, in all its aspects, radiotherapy (also known as radiation oncology), clinical oncology and related subjects, including physics as applied to radiotherapy, radiation technology and radiobiology. **Structure** General Assembly; Board; Councils (4); Committees (9); Task Forces: *European Particle Therapy Network (EPTN), Health Economics in Radiation Oncology (HERO).* **Languages** English. **Staff** 30.00 FTE, paid. **Finance** Sources: grants; members'

European Society Regional
08721

alphabetic sequence excludes
For the complete listing, see Yearbook Online at

dues; revenue from activities/projects; sponsorship. **Activities** Awards/prizes/competitions; events/meetings; financial and/or material support; training/education. **Events** *ESTRO Meets Asia Conference* 2024, *European Multidisciplinary Congress on Urological Cancers (EMUC)* Marseille (France) 2023, *Annual Congress* Vienna (Austria) 2023, *European Multidisciplinary Congress on Urological Cancers (EMUC)* Budapest (Hungary) 2022, *Annual Congress* Copenhagen (Denmark) 2022. **Publications** *Radiotherapy and Oncology* (12 a year); *ESTRO Newsletter* (6 a year); *Clinical and Translational Radiation Oncology (ctRO)* – journal; *Physics and Imaging in Radiation Oncology (phiRO)* – journal; *Technical Innovations and Patient Support in Radiatin Oncology (tipsRO)* – journal. Educational material. **Members** Individual; Institutional. Members in 97 countries and territories. Membership countries not specified. **NGO Relations** Member of: *Accreditation Council for Oncology in Europe (ACOE, #00063)*; *Associations and Conference Forum (AC Forum, #02909)*; *European Cancer Organisation (ECO, #06432)*; *Federation of European and International Associations Established in Belgium (FAIB, #09508)*; *The NCD Alliance (NCDA, #16963)*; *Union for International Cancer Control (UICC, #20415)*. Cooperates with: American Brachytherapy Society (ABS). Also links with a large number of national organizations interested in the field. [2022.05.12/XD2617/v/**D**]

♦ European Society of Regional Anaesthesia / see European Society of Regional Anaesthesia and Pain Therapy (#08722)

♦ European Society of Regional Anaesthesia and Pain Therapy (ESRA) 08722

Admin Manager Rue de Chantepoulet 10, 1201 Geneva, Switzerland. T. +41225105610. Fax +41225105614. E-mail: office@esraeurope.org.
Events Manager Clinique Médipôle Garonne, 45 rue de Gironis, 31000 Toulouse, France.
URL: http://esraeurope.org/

History 31 Jan 1980, Overijse (Belgium). Former names and other names: *Society of Regional Anaesthesia* – former; *European Society of Regional Anaesthesia (ESRA)* – former; *Société européenne d'anesthésie régionale* – former. Registration: Swiss Civil Code, Switzerland. **Aims** Carry out study, promotion, education and training of local and regional anaesthesia and acute or chronic pain management; encourage scientific research and dissemination of information. **Structure** Council of Representatives; Executive Board; Board; Office. Committees (6): Abstract; Education; Grants; Scientific; e-ESRA; European Day. **Languages** English. **Staff** 2.00 FTE, paid. **Finance** Members' dues. Other sources: congress proceeds; educational support. **Activities** Awards/prizes/competitions; events/meetings; training/education. **Events** *Winter Week Conference* Längenfeld (Austria) 2023, *Annual Congress* Paris (France) 2023, *Congress* Thessaloniki (Greece) 2022, *Annual Congress* 2021, *ESRA Scandinavia Meeting* Oslo (Norway) 2020. **Publications** *Regional Anesthesia & Pain Medicine (RAPM)*.
Members Administrators in 33 countries:
Austria, Belgium, Bulgaria, Croatia, Cyprus, Czechia, Denmark, Estonia, Finland, France, Germany, Greece, Hungary, Iceland, Ireland, Italy, Latvia, Lithuania, Luxembourg, Malta, Netherlands, Norway, Poland, Portugal, Romania, Serbia, Slovakia, Slovenia, Spain, Sweden, Switzerland, Türkiye, UK. [2021/XD9048/v/**D**]

♦ European Society of Regulatory Affairs / see The Organization for Professionals in Regulatory Affairs (#17885)
♦ European Society for Religion Literature and Arts / see International Society for Religion, Literature and Culture (#15417)
♦ European Society for Religion Literature and Culture / see International Society for Religion, Literature and Culture (#15417)
♦ European Society of Reproductive and Developmental Immunology (inactive)

♦ European Society for Reproductive Immunology (ESRI) 08723

SG Largo Brambilla 3, 50134 Florence FI, Italy.
URL: http://www.esri.org.hu/

History 2007, by merger of *Alps Adria Society for Immunology of Reproduction (AASIR, inactive)* and *European Society of Reproductive and Developmental Immunology (ESRADI, inactive)*. **Aims** Encourage, develop and promote fundamental and applied research concerning immunological processes in reproductive physiology, pathology, therapeutics and biotechnology in human and animals. **Structure** General Assembly. Executive Council, including Board Officers: Past-President, President, President-Elect, General Secretary and Treasurer. **Languages** English. **Finance** Members' dues. **Activities** Workshops; colloquia; conferences; congresses. **Events** *European Congress of Reproductive Immunology* Aalborg (Denmark) 2018, *European Congress of Reproductive Immunology* Budapest (Hungary) 2014, *Joint International Congress* Hamburg (Germany) 2012, *European Congress of Reproductive Immunology* Copenhagen (Denmark) 2011, *European congress of reproductive immunology* Munich (Germany) 2010. **Publications** Congress abstracts. **Members** Over 140. Membership countries not specified. [2017/XM2126/**D**]

♦ European Society for Research in Adult Development (ESRAD) 08724

Vice-Pres address not obtained. E-mail: esradinfo@gmail.com – kristian.stalne@mah.se.
URL: http://www.europeadultdevelopment.org/

History 2011, Lund (Sweden). **Aims** Support the interests of adult developmentalists working in Europe. **Structure** Officers. **Finance** Members' dues. **Events** *Conference* Jönköping (Sweden) 2021, *Conference* Jönköping (Sweden) 2020, *Conference* London (UK) 2018, *Conference* The Hague (Netherlands) 2016, *Conference* Helsinki (Finland) 2014. [2016/XJ9292/**D**]

♦ European Society for Research on the Education of Adults (ESREA) 08725

Société Européenne pour la recherche en formation des adultes (SERFA) – Sociedad europeo para investigación de la educación de adultos – Europäische Gesellschaft zur Forschung in der Erwachsenenbildung – Associazione Europea per la ricerca dell' educazione degli adulti

Sec c/o DIE, Heinemannstr 12-14, 53175 Bonn, Germany.
URL: http://www.esrea.org/

History 1991. Registration: Germany. **Aims** Encourage and support the advancement of high quality research on the education of adults in European countries. **Structure** General Assembly (annual). Steering Committee of 12 members. Secretariat. Research Networks (11). **Languages** English. **Staff** 0.50 FTE, paid. **Finance** Members' dues. **Activities** Organizes conferences and seminars. **Events** *Policy Studies in Adult Education (PSAE) Network Conference* Lisbon (Portugal) 2023, *Triennial Conference* Milan (Italy) 2022, *Triennial Conference* Belgrade (Serbia) 2019, *Network on Policy Studies in Adult Education Triennial Conference* Prague (Czechia) 2019, *Triennial Conference* Maynooth (Ireland) 2016. **Publications** *European Journal for Research on the Education and Learning of Adults (RELA)* – open access journal. Book series. **Members** in most European countries. Membership countries not specified. [2022/XD4065/**D**]

♦ European Society for Research in Ethics (Societas Ethica) 08726

Societé européenne de recherche en éthique – Europäische Forschungsgesellschaft für Ethik

Pres Lutheran Univ for Applied Science/Anthropology/Ethics for Health Care Professionals, Baerenschanzstr 4, 90429 Nürburg, Germany.
URL: http://www.societasethica.info/

History Founded 1964, Basel (Switzerland), on the initiative of the theologian Hendrik von Oyen. **Aims** Serve as a platform for exchange of scholarly work, ideas and experiences stemming from different philosophical and theological traditions; stimulate contacts between scholars in different countries, promotion of young academics, surpassing political, ideological and religious curtains. **Structure** Executive Committee; Presidency. **Languages** English, French, German. **Staff** Voluntary. **Finance** Members' dues. Registration fees. **Activities** Events/meetings. **Events** *Annual Conference* Tutzing (Germany) 2019, *Annual Conference* Louvain-la-Neuve (Belgium) 2018, *Annual Conference* Volos (Greece) 2017, *Annual Conference* Bad Boll (Germany) 2016, *Annual Conference* Linköping (Sweden) 2015. **Publications** *De Ethica* – journal. *Societas Ethica* – series. Conference proceedings. **Members** Moral theologians, moral philosophers and scholars interested in ethics (over 300) in about 25 countries. Membership countries not specified. [2020.03.04/XM0429/**D**]

♦ European Society for Research on Internet Interventions (esrii) . . . 08727

Contact Psykologiska Inst, Stockholm Univ, S-106 91, Stockholm, Sweden.
URL: http://esrii.org/

History 2012. **Aims** Advance the scientific approach to studying eHealth interventions. **Structure** Board of Directors. **Activities** Events/meetings. Conferences alternate periodically with the *Swedish Congress on Internet Interventions (SWEsrii)*. **Events** *Conference* Copenhagen (Denmark) 2019, *Conference* Dublin (Ireland) 2018, *Conference* Bergen (Norway) 2016, *Conference* Warsaw (Poland) 2015, *Conference* Linköping (Sweden) 2013. **Publications** *Internet Interventions* – journal. **NGO Relations** *International Society for Research on Internet Interventions (ISRII, #15423)*. [2021/XM5539/**D**]

♦ European Society for Research in Mathematics Education (ERME) . 08728

Société Européenne pour les Recherches en Education Mathématique

Pres address not obtained.
URL: http://erme.site/

History 1999, Osnabrück (Germany). Founded following meeting 2-4 May 1997. Current constitution adopted, 25 Feb 2007. Registration: End date: 2017, UK; Start date: 2017, France. **Aims** Promote communication, cooperation and collaboration in research in mathematics education in Europe. **Structure** General Meeting; Board; Executive Committee. Includes: *Young European Researchers in Mathematics Education (YERME, #21987)*. **Finance** Sources: members' dues. **Activities** Events/meetings; training/education. **Events** *Congress of the European Society for Research in Mathematics Education (CERME)* Budapest (Hungary) 2023, *Congress of the European Society for Research in Mathematics Education (CERME)* Bolzano (Italy) 2022, *Conference* Utrecht (Netherlands) 2019, *Conference on Mathematics Education in the Digital Age* Copenhagen (Denmark) 2018, *Conference* Dublin (Ireland) 2017. **NGO Relations** Affiliated with (1): *International Commission on Mathematical Instruction (ICMI, #12700)*. [2022.10.11/XM0685/**D**]

♦ European Society of Residents in Urology (ESRU) 08729

Chairman address not obtained.
Sec address not obtained. E-mail: juangomezr@gmail.com.
URL: http://www.esru.eu/

History 1991, as *European Board of Urologists in Training (EBUT)*. **Aims** Encourage improvement of training in urology across Europe; promote communication between urological trainees; provide a forum for discussion. **Structure** Executive Committee, comprising Chairman, Treasurer, Secretary. **Finance** Grants; meetings proceeds. **Events** *Copenhagen Symposium on Endoscopic Urological Surgery* Copenhagen (Denmark) 2015, *Meeting* Barcelona (Spain) 2010, *Meeting* Paris (France) 2006, *Meeting* Madrid (Spain) 2005, *Scientific meeting / Meeting* Madrid (Spain) 2003.
Members in 36 countries:
Armenia, Austria, Belarus, Belgium, Bulgaria, Croatia, Czechia, Denmark, Estonia, Finland, France, Georgia, Germany, Greece, Hungary, Ireland, Italy, Latvia, Lithuania, Moldova, Netherlands, North Macedonia, Norway, Poland, Portugal, Romania, Russia, Slovakia, Slovenia, Spain, Sweden, Switzerland, Türkiye, UK, Ukraine, Uzbekistan. [2016/XD6406/**D**]

♦ European Society for Respiratory and Cardiovascular Kinesitherapy (inactive)

♦ European Society of Rheology (ESR) 08730

Pres SIK, Chalmers Univ of Technology/Structure and Material Design, PO Box 5401, SE-402 29 Gothenburg, Sweden. T. +46105166637 – +46105166600. Fax +4631833782.
URL: http://rheology-esr.org/

History Founded 26 Jun 1996, Cambridge (UK). Inaugural meeting 4 Mar 1997, Leuven (Belgium). UK Registered Charity: 1065904. **Aims** Encourage cooperation in all aspects of rheology; promote rheology and be active at national and international level in seeking funds for rheological research, education and training. **Structure** Committee. **Languages** Bulgarian, Czech, Danish, Dutch, English, Finnish, French, German, Irish Gaelic, Italian, Norwegian, Polish, Portuguese, Russian, Serbo-Croatian, Slovakian, Slovene, Spanish, Swedish. **Staff** None. **Finance** Members' dues. **Activities** Events/meetings; knowledge management/information dissemination; awards/prizes/competitions. **Events** *Annual European Rheology Conference* 2021, *AERC Annual Conference* Portoroz (Slovenia) 2019, *AERC Annual Conference* Sorrento (Italy) 2018, *AERC Annual Conference* Copenhagen (Denmark) 2017, *AERC Annual Conference* Nantes (France) 2015. **Publications** *Applied Rheology*; *European Rheology Newsletter*; *Rheologica Acta* – official journal. *Rheological Phenomena*. Abstracts.
Members National societies and groups; Observers. Members in 23 countries:
Austria, Belgium, Bulgaria, Czechia, Denmark, Finland, France, Germany, Greece, Iceland, Italy, Netherlands, Norway, Poland, Portugal, Romania, Russia, Slovenia, South Africa, Spain, Sweden, Switzerland, UK.
Regional member (1):
Nordic Rheology Society (NRS, #17400). [2016/XD6204/y/**D**]

♦ European Society for Rural Sociology (ESRS) 08731

Société européenne de sociologie rurale – Sociedad Europea de Sociologia Rural – Europäische Gesellschaft für Ländliche Soziologie

Pres Dept of Agricultural Economics, Fac of Bioscience Engineering, Ghent Univ, Coupure Links 653, 9000 Ghent, Belgium. T. +3292645927.
Sec Postboks 1490, 8049 Bodø, Norway. T. +4775411827. E-mail: ksv@nforsk.no.
URL: http://www.ruralsociology.eu/

History Founded 29 Nov 1957, Wageningen (Netherlands). **Aims** Represent scientists involved in the study of agriculture and fisheries, food production and consumption, rural development and change, rurality and cultural heritage, equality and inequality in rural society, and nature and environmental care. **Structure** General Assembly; Council; Executive Committee. **Languages** English, French, German. **Staff** 0.50 FTE, voluntary. **Finance** Members' dues. **Activities** Events/meetings; training/education. **Events** *Congress* Aveiro (Portugal) 2022, *Biennial Congress* Trondheim (Norway) 2019, *Biennial Congress* Krakow (Poland) 2017, *Biennial Congress* Aberdeen (UK) 2015, *Biennial Congress* Florence (Italy) 2013. **Publications** *Sociologia Ruralis* (3 a year) – scholarly journal; *ESRS Newsletter*.
Members Individuals in 47 countries:
Albania, Argentina, Austria, Belgium, Benin, Brazil, Bulgaria, Cameroon, Canada, Côte d'Ivoire, Croatia, Czechia, Denmark, Estonia, Finland, France, Germany, Ghana, Greece, Hungary, Iceland, India, Iran Islamic Rep, Ireland, Israel, Italy, Japan, Latvia, Lithuania, Netherlands, Norway, Poland, Portugal, Romania, Russia, Serbia, Slovakia, Slovenia, Spain, Sweden, Switzerland, Thailand, Türkiye, UK, USA, Venezuela, Yemen.
NGO Relations Member of: *International Rural Sociology Association (IRSA, #14774)*. [2020.03.03/XD0857/v/**D**]

♦ European Society for Separation Science (EuSSS) 08732

Pres Ecole Supérieure de Physique et Chimie Industrielles (ESPCI), Lab Sciences Analytiques/Bioanalytiques/Miniaturisation, 10 rue Vauquelin, 75231 Paris CEDEX 05, France.
URL: http://www.eusss.org/

History 2003, during *International Symposium on Chromatography (ISC)*. Registered in accordance with German law. **Aims** Advance and harmonize Separation Science. **Structure** Assembly (annual); Steering Committee. **Events** *International Symposium on Chromatography* Salzburg (Austria) 2014, *International Symposium on Separation Science, New Achievements in Chromatography* Porec (Croatia) 2013, *International Symposium on Chromatography* Torun (Poland) 2012, *International symposium on chromatography* Valencia (Spain) 2010, *International symposium on chromatography* Paris (France) 2004.
Members Full in 18 countries:
Austria, Croatia, Czechia, Denmark, France, Germany, Hungary, Italy, Netherlands, Norway, Poland, Romania, Russia, Slovakia, Slovenia, Spain, UK, Ukraine. [2017.11.27/XJ3598/**D**]

♦ European Society for Sexual and Impotence Research / see European Society for Sexual Medicine (#08733)

♦ European Society for Sexual Medicine (ESSM) 08733

Exec Officer Via Ripamonti 129, 20141 Milan MI, Italy. T. +39256601625. Fax +39270048577. E-mail: admin@essm.org.
Registered Office Waterloosesteenweg 1151, 1180 Brussels, Belgium.
URL: http://www.essm.org/

History European chapter of *International Society for Sexual Medicine (ISSM, #15441)*. Former names and other names: *European Society for Impotence Research (ESIR)* – former; *European Society for Sexual and Impotence Research (ESSIR)* – former. Registration: Banque-Carrefour des Entreprises, No/ID: 0737-408-648, Belgium; EU Transparency Register, No/ID: 750686733699-08. **Aims** Establish a scientific society to benefit the public by encouraging the highest standards of practice, education and research in the field of sexual medicine; promote cooperation and improve interaction between Europeans working in the field. **Structure** Executive Committee. **Languages** English. **Staff** 2.00 FTE, paid. **Finance** Sources: members' dues. **Activities** Events/meetings; guidance/assistance/consulting; research/documentation; training/education. **Events** *Congress* Rotterdam (Netherlands) 2023, *Congress* Milan (Italy) 2022, *ESSM Virtual Meeting* Milan (Italy) 2021, *Congress* Prague (Czechia) 2020, *Congress* Ljubljana (Slovenia) 2019. **Publications** *ESSM Today Newsletter* (3 a year). Clinical and research papers; congress reports. **Members** Full; Associate. Membership countries not specified. **NGO Relations** Member of (2): *Alliance for Safe Online Pharmacy – EU (ASOP EU, #00720)*; *European Cancer Organisation (ECO, #06432)*. [2022.02.02/XE3371/E]

♦ European Society for Shoulder and Elbow Rehabilitation (EUSSER) . 08734

Contact Route de Frontenex 86bis, 1208 Geneva, Switzerland. E-mail: info@eusser.org.
URL: http://www.eusser.org/

History Founded 2008. Bylaws agreed Sep 2008, Bruges (Belgium); last reviewed Sep 2017. Registered in accordance with Swiss Civil Code. **Aims** Promote the importance of high quality in rehabilitation; promote communication between various medical professionals in the field of should and elbow rehabilitation to enhance *patient* care; promote high quality research and education in the field throughout Europe; promote work towards a standardized terminology in the field; promote communication with and spread information to other organizations active in the field of trauma and diseases in the shoulder and elbow. **Structure** General Assembly; Board; Executive Committee. Committees (3): Website; Education; Scientific. **Languages** English. **Finance** Members' dues. Other sources: public or private grants; subsidies. **Activities** Events/meetings; training/education; knowledge management/information dissemination. **Publications** *EdComm Newsletter*. **Members** Individuals. Membership countries not specified. **NGO Relations** *European Society for Surgery of Shoulder and Elbow (ESSSE, #08752)*. [2019/XM7534/v/D]

♦ European Society of Skeletal Radiology / see European Society of Musculoskeletal Radiology (#08658)

♦ European Society of Skin Cancer Prevention (EUROSKIN) 08735

Contact c/o Elbekliniken, Am Krankenhaus 1, 21614 Buxtehude, Germany. E-mail: info@euroskin.eu.
URL: http://www.euroskin.eu/

History 18 Jun 1999, Frankfurt-Main (Germany). Registration: Hamburg District court, No/ID: VR 16583, Start date: 3 Jul 2000, Germany, Hamburg. **Aims** Reduce skin cancer incidence and mortality; promote and coordinate collaboration between European and international professionals active in the fields of prevention of skin cancer. **Structure** Council; Board of Directors. **Languages** English. **Finance** Members' dues. **Events** *International UV and Skin Cancer Prevention Conference* Mechelen (Belgium) 2021, *International UV and Skin Cancer Prevention Conference* Mechelen (Belgium) 2020, *Conference* Bergen (Norway) 2016, *Conference* Milan (Italy) 2014, *Conference* Berlin (Germany) 2012. **Publications** *European Journal of Cancer Prevention*. *EUROSKIN: Towards the promotion and harmonization of skin cancer prevention in Europe – Recommendations* (2001) by EW Breitbart et al and Angel Maldonado; *Informa healthcare: Skin Cancer Prevention*. Articles.
Members Individuals in 22 countries:
Australia, Austria, Croatia, Finland, France, Germany, Iceland, Ireland, Israel, Italy, Lithuania, Luxembourg, Monaco, Netherlands, Norway, Poland, Portugal, Romania, Sweden, Switzerland, UK, USA. [2021/XD8153/D]

♦ European Society for Social Drug Research (ESSD) 08736

Secretariat c/o ISD, Ghent Univ, Universiteitstraat 4, 9000 Ghent, Belgium. T. +3292646962. E-mail: essd.research@ugent.be.
Pres Univ Amsterdam, Fac der Rechtsgeleerdheid, Oudemanhuispoort 4-6, 1012 CN Amsterdam, Netherlands. T. +31205253930.
URL: http://www.essd-research.eu/en/

History Founded in 1990. **Aims** Promote social science approaches to drug research, with special reference to the situation in Europe. **Structure** Board, including Chair and organizers of past 3 conferences. **Finance** Supported by: *Co-operation Group to Combat Drug Abuse and Illicit Trafficking in Drugs (Pompidou Group, #04796)*. **Activities** Organizes annual conference. **Events** *Annual Conference* Vienna (Austria) 2020, *Annual Conference* Riga (Latvia) 2019, *Annual Conference* Budapest (Hungary) 2018, *Annual Conference* Lisbon (Portugal) 2017, *Annual Conference* Frankfurt-Main (Germany) 2016. **Publications** Books.
Members Full (about 250) in 25 countries:
Austria, Belgium, Canada, Denmark, Estonia, Finland, France, Germany, Greece, Hungary, Iceland, Ireland, Italy, Luxembourg, Netherlands, Norway, Poland, Portugal, Romania, Russia, Spain, Sweden, Switzerland, UK, USA. [2020/XD8535/D]

♦ European Society of Socially Embedded Technologies (EUSSET) ... 08737

Chair c/o UTT, 2 rue Marie Curie, CS 42060, 10004 Troyes CEDEX, France. E-mail: coreteam@eusset.eu.
Chair University Siegen, Unteres Schloss 3, 57072 Siegen, Germany. T. +492717402910.
URL: http://www.eusset.eu/

History Founded as an institute of "*Social Computing e.V.*" which is registered in Germany. **Aims** Develop technological tools and infrastructures that incorporate a human-centred design perspective. **Activities** Events/meetings. European Conference on Computer-Supported Cooperative Work (ECSCW); infraHEALTH – International Conference on Infrastructures in Healthcare. **Events** *European Conference on Computer Supported Cooperative Work (ECSCW)* Trondheim (Norway) 2023, *International Conference on Infrastructures in Healthcare (infraHEALTH)* Kristiansand (Norway) 2021, *Biennial International Conference on Communities and Technologies* Seattle, WA (USA) 2021, *European Conference on Computer Supported Cooperative Work* Zurich (Switzerland) 2021, *European Conference on Computer Supported Cooperative Work* Siegen (Germany) 2020.
Members Individuals in 10 countries:
Austria, Denmark, Finland, France, Germany, Ireland, Italy, Netherlands, Sweden, UK.
NGO Relations Affiliated conference: *European Conference on Computer Supported Cooperative Work (ECSCW)*. [2022/XJ1833/D]

♦ European Society for Social Paediatrics / see International Society for Social Pediatrics and Child Health (#15448)

♦ European Society of Social Psychiatry (ESSP) 08738

Secretariat address not obtained. T. +33155999933. E-mail: esspsy@kuoni-congress.com.
URL: http://www.esspsy.org/

Aims Promote greater understanding of the interactions between individuals and their physical and human environment, and the impact of these interactions on the clinical expression, treatment of mental and behavioural problems and disorders and their prevention; promote mental health; promote national and international collaboration. **Structure** General Assembly; Council; Executive Committee. **Languages** English. **Finance** Members' dues. **Activities** Events/meetings; training/education; research/documentation; networking/liaising. **Events** *Congress* Geneva (Switzerland) 2018. [2018/XM6628/D]

♦ European Society for Soil Conservation (ESSC) 08739

Association européenne pour la conservation du sol – Sociedad Europea de Conservación de Suelos – Europäische Gesellschaft für den Schutz des Bodens

Pres SAAF-Dipto Scienze Agrarie, Alimentarie Forestali, Viale Delle Scienze Ed 4, 90128 Palermo PA, Italy.
Sec CREA-AA Centro di ricerca Agricoltura e Ambiente, via Lanciola 12/A, 50125 Florence FI, Italy.
URL: http://www.soilconservation.eu/

History Founded 4 Nov 1988, Leuven (Belgium). **Aims** Promote soundly based policies of soil conservation in its broadest sense throughout the countries of Europe. **Structure** Council; Executive Committee; Editorial Board. **Languages** English, French, German, Spanish. **Finance** Members' dues. **Activities** Research/documentation; networking/liaising; knowledge management/information dissemination; publishing activities; guidance/assistance/consulting; events/meetings; awards/prizes/competitions; politics/policy/regulatory; financial and/or material support. **Events** *International Congress* Tirana (Albania) 2019, *International Conference on Soil and Water Security* Imola (Italy) 2018, *CONSOWA : World Conference on Soil and Water Conservation under Global Change* Lleida (Spain) 2017, *International Congress* Lleida (Spain) 2017, *International Conference* Cluj-Napoca (Romania) 2016. **Publications** *ESSC Newsletter* (2 a year) in English. Meeting proceedings (irregular).
Members Researchers, teachers, students, farmers, planners and policy makers with interests in agriculture, soil science, geographical sciences, economics, forestry and ecology. Individuals (585) in 47 countries and territories:
Albania, Argentina, Australia, Austria, Belarus, Belgium, Bosnia-Herzegovina, Bulgaria, Canada, China, Croatia, Cuba, Czechia, Denmark, Estonia, France, Georgia, Germany, Greece, Hungary, Iceland, India, Israel, Italy, Japan, Latvia, Lithuania, Luxembourg, Moldova, Netherlands, Norway, Poland, Romania, Russia, Serbia, Slovakia, Slovenia, Spain, Sweden, Switzerland, Taiwan, Thailand, Türkiye, UK, Ukraine, USA.
IGO Relations Cooperates with: *Global Soil Partnership (GSP, #10608)*. [2018.10.30/XD2166/v/D]

♦ European Society for Sonochemistry (ESS) 08740

Sec Dept Physical Chemistry, Via Golgi 19, 20133 Milan MI, Italy. T. +39250314253. Fax +39250314300.
Pres Univ di Torino, Via Pietro Giuria 9, 10125 Turin TO, Italy. T. +39116707684. Fax +39112367684.
URL: http://www.europeansocietyofsonochemistry.eu/

History 1990. Registered in accordance with French law. **Aims** Foster research into applications of *ultrasound* in academia and industry; act as an information centre and link for those interested in sonochemistry in its many different forms. **Structure** General Meeting; Executive Committee; Committee; President. **Languages** English. **Staff** Voluntary. **Finance** Members' dues. **Activities** Events/meetings; training/education. **Events** *Meeting* Jena (Germany) 2020, *Meeting* Besançon (France) 2018, *Meeting* Istanbul (Turkey) 2016, *Meeting* Avignon (France) 2014, *Meeting* Lviv (Ukraine) 2012. **Members** Individuals (150) in 30 countries. Membership countries not specified. **IGO Relations** *European Cooperation in Science and Technology (COST, #06784)*. [2020.03.03/XD7676/D]

♦ European Society of Sports Traumatology, Knee Surgery and Arthroscopy (ESSKA) 08741

Exec Dir Cntr médical, Fondation Norbert Metz, Rue d'Eich 76, L-1460 Luxembourg, Luxembourg. T. +35244117019. Fax +35244117678. E-mail: info@esska.org.
Events Manager address not obtained.
URL: http://www.esska.org/

History 1986, Berlin (Germany). Former names and other names: *European Society of Knee Surgery and Arthroscopy (ESKA)* – former; *ESSKA 2000* – former. **Aims** Represent Europe in the fields of degenerative *joint disease* and sports medicine. **Structure** Board; Sections (4); Committees (10); Executive Office. **Languages** English. **Staff** 9.00 FTE, paid. **Finance** Sources: meeting proceeds; members' dues; sale of publications. **Activities** Events/meetings; knowledge management/information dissemination; projects/programmes; publishing activities; standards/guidelines; training/education. **Events** *Congress* Milan (Italy) 2024, *Congress* Paris (France) 2022, *Congress* 2021, *Congress* Milan (Italy) 2020, *Congress* Glasgow (UK) 2018. **Publications** *Knee Surgery, Sports Traumatology and Arthroscopy (KSSTA)* (12 a year) – journal; *ESSKA Newsletter* (4 a year); *Journal of Experimental Orthopaedics (JEO)*. Books. **Information Services** *ESSKA Academy* – online. **Members** Individuals in 109 countries and territories over 5 continents. Membership countries not specified. [2022.02.15/XD2229/v/D]

♦ European Society for Stereotactic and Functional Neurosurgery (ESSFN) 08742

Société européenne de neurochirurgie stéréotaxique et fonctionnelle

Sec Service de Neurochirurgie Fonctionelle, Hop d'Adultes de la TImone, 264 rue Saint-Pierre, 13385 Marseille, France. T. +33491387060. Fax +33491387056.
Pres Dept of Neurosurgery, Evangelismos Hosp, 4 Marasli Street, 10676 Athens, Greece. T. +302107201705. Fax +302132041701.
URL: http://www.essfn.org/

History 1970, Freiburg (Germany FR). Regional chapter of *World Society for Stereotactic and Functional Neurosurgery (WSSFN, #21812)*. **Aims** Encourage research and regulation of practice of stereotactic and functional neurosurgery; study and teach methods of introducing guided electrodes and other instruments into the human nervous system, as well as promote scientific investigations in connection with these endeavours; investigate the genesis and causes of diseases of the nervous system and their treatment; teach and promote investigation on the functioning of the nervous system and its parts; establish scholarships for educational training in these fields. **Structure** General Meeting (every 2 years) of active members. Council, comprising President, Vice-President, Secretary, Second Secretary and Treasurer. Executive Committee (meets every 2 years, during General Meeting), consisting of Council and 19 national representatives from European countries. Committees. Registered office in Toulouse (France). **Languages** English. **Finance** Members' dues. Other sources: donations; profits from events. **Activities** Events/meetings; training/education; awards/prizes/competitions. **Events** *Congress* Marseille (France) 2021, *Congress* Edinburgh (UK) 2018, *Congress* Madrid (Spain) 2016, *Biennial Congress / Congress* Maastricht (Netherlands) 2014, *Biennial congress / Congress* Cascais (Portugal) 2012. **Publications** Meeting proceedings.
Members Active; Associate; Corresponding; Honorary. Individuals in 32 countries:
Argentina, Austria, Belgium, Bolivia, Brazil, Czechia, Denmark, Egypt, Finland, France, Georgia, Germany, Greece, Hungary, Iceland, Ireland, Israel, Italy, Japan, Korea Rep, Mexico, Norway, Poland, Portugal, Russia, Slovakia, South Africa, Spain, Sweden, Switzerland, Türkiye, UK.
NGO Relations American Society for Stereotactic and Functional Neurosurgery; *Asian-Australasian Society for Stereotactic and Functional Neurosurgery (AASSFN, #01354)*; *European Association of Neurosurgical Societies (EANS, #06134)*; *Latin American Society for Stereotactic and Functional Neurosurgery (LSSFN, #16386)*. [2016/XD6015/v/D]

♦ European Society for Study of Coeliac Disease (unconfirmed)
♦ European Society for the Study of Cognitive Systems (inactive)
♦ European Society for the Study of Drug Toxicity / see EUROTOX (#09191)

♦ European Society for the Study of English (ESSE) 08743

Chairman Univ of Zurich, English Dept, Plattenstrasse 47, 8032 Zurich ZH, Switzerland. T. +41446343550. E-mail: esse.president@outlook.com.
URL: http://www.essenglish.org/

History Jan 1990, Rome (Italy). Inaugural conference held 1991, Norwich (UK). Constitution adopted 7 Sep 1995, Glasgow (UK). Registration: Swiss Civil Code, Switzerland. **Aims** Advance education of the public by promoting European study and understanding of English languages, literatures and cultures; encourage recognition of British, Irish, Scottish and Welsh cultures as aspects of European cultural history. **Structure** Board (meets annually); Executive Committee; National Representatives. **Languages** English. **Staff** Voluntary. **Finance** Sources: donations; members' dues. **Activities** Events/meetings; financial and/or material support; knowledge management/information dissemination; training/education. **Events** *ESSE Conference* Lausanne (Switzerland) 2024, *ESSE Conference* Mainz (Germany) 2022, *ESSE Conference* Lyon (France) 2021, *ESSE Conference* Lyon (France) 2020, *Biennial Conference* Brno (Czechia) 2018. **Publications** *European Journal of English Studies* (3 a year); *European English Messenger* (2 a year). Conference proceedings.
Members National or regional higher constituent associations, grouping about 7,600 individual members, in 34 countries:
Albania, Armenia, Austria, Belgium, Bulgaria, Croatia, Cyprus, Czechia, Denmark, Finland, France, Germany, Greece, Hungary, Ireland, Italy, Latvia, Lithuania, Malta, North Macedonia, Norway, Poland, Portugal, Romania, Russia, Serbia, Slovakia, Slovenia, Spain, Sweden, Switzerland, Türkiye, UK, Ukraine.
Included in the above, one regional organization listed in this Yearbook:
Nordic Association of English Studies (NAES, #17192).
NGO Relations Member of (1): *International Federation for Modern Languages and Literatures (#13480)*. [2020.07.25/XD3428/D]

♦ European Society for the study of Human Evolution (ESHE) 08744

Europäische Gesellschaft zur Erforschung der menschlichen Evolution

Contact address not obtained. E-mail: info@eshe.eu.
URL: http://www.eshe.eu/

History Registered in accordance with German law. **Aims** Promote research into human biological and cultural evolution, by stimulating communication and cooperation between scientists and raising public awareness and understanding. **Structure** General Assembly (annual); Board. **Languages** English, German. **Finance** Members' dues. **Activities** Events/meetings; awareness raising. **Events** *Annual Meeting* Tübingen (Germany) 2022, *Annual Meeting* 2021, *Annual Meeting* 2020, *Annual Meeting* Liège (Belgium) 2019, *Annual Meeting* Faro (Portugal) 2018. **Publications** Proceedings. [2017.10.26/XJ7367/D]

European Society Study
08744

alphabetic sequence excludes
For the complete listing, see Yearbook Online at

- ♦ European Society for Study and Integration of Space Systems (inactive)
- ♦ European Society for the Study of International Relations (inactive)
- ♦ European Society for the Study of Interstitial Cystitis – Bladder Pain Syndrome / see International Society for the Study of Bladder Pain Syndrome (#15466)
- ♦ European Society for the Study of Interstitial Cystitis – Painful Bladder Syndrome / see International Society for the Study of Bladder Pain Syndrome (#15466)

♦ European Society for the Study of Peripheral Nerve Repair and Regeneration (ESPNR) 08745

Pres address not obtained. E-mail: info.espnr@gmail.com.
URL: https://sites.google.com/site/espnreu/

History 27 May 2014, Brussels (Belgium). **Aims** Bring together basic and clinical scientists so as to promote the study on peripheral nerve repair and regeneration both in the pre-clinical and clinical level. **Activities** Events/meetings. **Events** *International Symposium on Peripheral Nerve Regeneration* Milan (Italy) 2024, *International Symposium on Peripheral Nerve Regeneration* London (UK) 2022, *International Symposium on Peripheral Nerve Regeneration* Porto (Portugal) 2019, *International Symposium on Peripheral Nerve Regeneration* Barcelona (Spain) 2017, *International Symposium on Peripheral Nerve Regeneration* Hannover (Germany) 2015. [2022.05.17/AA1888/**D**]

♦ European Society for the Study of Personality Disorders (ESSPD) .. 08746

Main Office c/o Kenniscentrum Persoonlijkheidsstoornissen, Postbox 725, 3500 AS Utrecht, Netherlands. E-mail: info@esspd.eu.
URL: http://www.esspd.eu/

History Registration: Netherlands. **Aims** Address the specific needs of the European personality disorder field; actively expand it to the countries in which it is less developed. **Structure** General Meeting; Board; Advisory Board. **Languages** English. **Finance** Members' dues. **Activities** Events/meetings; awards/prizes/competitions; training/education. **Events** *International Congress on Borderline Personality Disorder and Allied Disorders* 2022, *International Congress on Borderline Personality Disorder and Allied Disorders* Antwerp (Belgium) 2020, *International Congress on Borderline Personality Disorder and Allied Disorders* Sitges (Spain) 2018, *International Congress on Borderline Personality Disorder and Allied Disorders* Vienna (Austria) 2016, *International Congress on Borderline Personality Disorder and Allied Disorders* Rome (Italy) 2014. **Publications** *ESSPD Newsletter*. **NGO Relations** Closely cooperates with: *International Society for the Study of Personality Disorders (ISSPD, #15482)*. Affiliated with: *European Society for Traumatic Stress Studies (ESTSS, #08769)*. [2020/XJ5007/**D**]

- ♦ European Society for the Study and Prevention of Infant Death (inactive)
- ♦ European Society for the Study of Purine and Pyrimidine Metabolism in Man / see Purine and Pyrimidine Society (#18579)

♦ European Society for the Study of Science and Theology (ESSSAT) . 08747

Pres c/o Inst für Systematische Theologie und Praktische Theologie und Religionswissenschaft, Franckeplatz 1/26 – 2 0G, 06099 Halle (Saale), Germany. T. +493455523012. E-mail: secretariat@esssat.eu – esssatsec@gmail.com.
Sec address not obtained.
URL: http://www.esssat.net/

History 1990, Geneva (Switzerland). **Aims** Promote the study of relationships between natural sciences and theological views. **Structure** General Assembly (every 2 years, during Conference); Council. **Languages** English. **Staff** Voluntary. **Finance** Sources: members' dues. **Activities** Awards/prizes/competitions. **Events** *Conference* Ålesund (Norway) 2022, *Conference* Madrid (Spain) 2021, *Nature and Beyond – Immanence and Transcendence in Science and Religion* Lyon (France) 2018, *Are we special? Science and theology questioning human uniqueness* Warsaw (Poland) 2016, *Do emotions shape the world? Perspectives from science and theology* Assisi (Italy) 2014. **Publications** *Issues in Science and Religion (ISR)* (every 2 years); *Studies in Science and Theology (SSTh)* (every 2 years).
Members Personal; Student; Eastern European; Member of a voluntary society; Member of a public or international institution. Members in 34 countries:
Australia, Austria, Belgium, Canada, Croatia, Czechia, Denmark, Estonia, Finland, France, Germany, Greece, Hungary, Ireland, Italy, Latvia, Lithuania, Netherlands, Norway, Philippines, Poland, Portugal, Romania, Russia, Slovakia, Slovenia, South Africa, Spain, Sweden, Switzerland, Türkiye, UK, Ukraine, USA. [2022.02.16/XD6931/**D**]

♦ European Society for Study of Tourette Syndrome (ESSTS) 08748

Chair Democritus Univ – Thrace, University Campus, 691 00 Komotini, Greece.
URL: http://tourette-eu.org/

History Nov 2000, Copenhagen (Denmark), as *European Society for Tourette Syndrome (ESTS)*. **Aims** Educate professionals about and treating patients with the Gilles de la Tourette Syndrome; promote collaboration in research in Tourette Syndrome. **Structure** Chair; Secretary; Treasurer; Meeting Coordinator. **Languages** English. **Staff** None. **Finance** None. **Activities** Produces guidelines for management of TS; collaborates on research projects; coordinates training events. **Events** *European Conference on Tourette Syndrome and Tic Disorders* Hannover (Germany) 2019, *European Conference on Tourette Syndrome and Tic Disorders* Copenhagen (Denmark) 2018, *European Conference on Tourette Syndrome and Tic Disorders* Seville (Spain) 2017, *European Conference on Tourette Syndrome and Tic Disorders* Warsaw (Poland) 2016, *World Congress on Tourette Syndrome and Tic Disorders* London (UK) 2015. **Members** Membership countries not specified. [2014/XD9278/**D**]

♦ European Society for the Study of Western Esotericism (ESSWE) .. 08749

Sec Dept of Literature/History of Ideas and Religion, Univ of Gothenburgh, Box 200, SE-405 30 Gothenburg, Sweden. E-mail: secretary@esswe.org.
URL: http://www.esswe.org/

History 2005. Registered in accordance with Dutch law, 21 apr 2005. **Aims** Advance the academic study of the various manifestations of Western esotericism from late antiquity to the present; secure the future development of the field. **Structure** Board. Regional subgroups (4): *Central and Eastern European Network for the Academic Study of Western Esotericism (CEENASWE)*; INASWE – Israel; INSEP – Irish; *Scandinavian Network for the Academic Study of Western Esotericism (SNASWE, #19091)*. Thematic Networks (5): Contemporary Esotericism Research Network (ContERN); ESSWE Network for the Study of Esotericism in Antiquity; *European Network for the Study of Islam and Esotericism (ENSIE, #08017)*; Western Esotericism in modern Art and Visual Culture (WEAVE); ESSWE Student Network. **Finance** Members' dues. **Activities** Events/meetings; advocacy/lobbying/activism; networking/liaising; knowledge management/information dissemination; awards/prizes/competitions. **Events** *Biennial Conference* Cork (Ireland) 2022, *Biennial Conference* Cork (Ireland) 2021, *Biennial Conference* Amsterdam (Netherlands) 2019, *Biennial Conference* Erfurt (Germany) 2017. **Publications** *ARIES – Journal for the Study of Western Esotericism*. *The Aries Book Series: Texts and Studies in Western Esotericism*. **Members** Full; Associate; Honorary; Student. Membership countries not specified. **NGO Relations** Affiliate member of: *International Association for the History of Religions (IAHR, #11936)*. Affiliated with: *Centro de Estudios sobre el Esoterismo Occidental de la Unión de Naciones Suramericanas (CEEO-UNASUR, #03798)*; *Centro Studi sulle Nuove Religioni (CESNUR International, #03820)*. [2018/XM6367/**D**]

♦ European Society for Sugar Technology (ESST) 08750

Sec c/o Verlag Dr Albert Bartens KG, Lückhoffstr 16, 14129 Berlin, Germany. T. +49308035678. Fax +49308032049. E-mail: mail@esst-sugar.org.
URL: http://www.esst-sugar.org/

History Founded 12 Sep 2007, Berlin (Germany). Took over functions of *Commission internationale technique de sucrerie (CITS, inactive)*. **Aims** Promote scientific work in the sugar industry and related industries and facilitate exchange of scientific findings; give young scientists and technicians in practice the opportunity to report on their work; support exchange of scientific reflections at an international level; further pursue the formation and development of the next generation. **Structure** Board; Conference Programme Committee. **Languages** English. **Staff** 1.00 FTE, paid. **Finance** Members' dues. **Events** *Conference* Poznań (Poland) 2019, *Conference* Dresden (Germany) 2017, *Conference* Reims (France) 2015, *Conference* Warsaw (Poland) 2013, *Conference* Bratislava (Slovakia) 2011. **Publications** Proceedings.
Members Full in 10 countries:
Austria, France, Germany, India, Italy, Netherlands, Poland, Switzerland, UK, USA. [2018.09.13/XM2699/**D**]

♦ European Society of Surgery (ESS) 08751

SG Dept of General and GI Surgery, Medical College, Jagiellonian Univ, 40 Kopernika St, 31-501 Krakow, Poland. T. +48124248007. Fax +48124248007. E-mail: info@essurg.org.
URL: http://www.essurg.org/

History 1996. Registered in accordance with Luxembourg law, 3 Dec 1999. **Aims** Advance the art and science of surgery by promoting exchange of clinical and scientific ideas, by establishing controlled studies and by encouraging original clinical and laboratory investigation. **Structure** General meeting (annual); Board of Directors. **Languages** English, French. **Staff** Voluntary. **Finance** Members' dues. **Activities** Events/meetings; training/education. **Events** *Annual Congress* Varna (Bulgaria) 2019, *Annual Congress* Yerevan (Armenia) 2018, *Annual Congress* Krakow (Poland) 2017, *Annual Congress* Naples (Italy) 2016, *Annual Congress* Beijing (China) 2015. **Publications** *ESS Newsletter*.
Members Active; Associate; Correspondant; Honorary. Members in 40 countries:
Austria, Azerbaijan, Belarus, Belgium, Bosnia-Herzegovina, Bulgaria, Croatia, Cyprus, Czechia, Denmark, Estonia, Finland, France, Georgia, Germany, Greece, Hungary, Ireland, Italy, Latvia, Lithuania, Luxembourg, Malta, Moldova, Netherlands, North Macedonia, Norway, Poland, Portugal, Romania, Russia, Serbia, Slovakia, Slovenia, Spain, Sweden, Switzerland, Türkiye, UK, Ukraine. [2017/XD6675/**D**]

♦ European Society for Surgery of Shoulder and Elbow (ESSSE) 08752

Société européenne pour la chirurgie de l'épaule et du coude (SECEC)

Sec 69 Bld des Canuts, 69004 Lyon, France. T. +33683178613. E-mail: sececoffice@gmail.com.
URL: https://www.secec-essse.org/

History Nov 1987, Melun (France). **Structure** Executive Committee, comprising President, Treasurer, General Secretary, Secretary and 6 members. Committees (7): Education; Website; Membership; Research and Development; Eastern European; Programme; Qualification. **Staff** 1.00 FTE, paid. **Events** *Congress* Dublin (Ireland) 2022, *International Congress on Surgery of the Shoulder* Poznań (Poland) 2021, *International Congress on Surgery of the Shoulder* Poznań (Poland) 2020, *International Congress on Surgery of the Shoulder* Geneva (Switzerland) 2018, *International Congress on Surgery of the Shoulder* Berlin (Germany) 2017. **Publications** *Journal of Shoulder and Elbow Surgery*.
Members Individuals in 22 countries:
Austria, Croatia, Czechia, Denmark, Finland, France, Germany, Greece, Hungary, Iceland, Ireland, Italy, Netherlands, Norway, Poland, Portugal, Russia, Spain, Sweden, Switzerland, Türkiye, UK. [2020/XD2559/v/**D**]

♦ European Society of Surgical Oncology (ESSO) 08753

Société européenne d'oncologie chirurgicale – Europäische Gesellschaft für chirurgische Onkologie – Europese Gemeenschap voor Chirurgische Oncologie

Chief Officer Clos Chapelle-aux-Champs 30, bte 1.30.30, 1200 Brussels, Belgium. E-mail: info@essoweb.org.
URL: http://www.essoweb.org/

History 29 Oct 1981, Lausanne (Switzerland). Registration: Belgium; EU Transparency Register, No/ID: 435865219097-86. **Aims** Advance the art, science and practice of surgery for the treatment of cancer; improve methods of surgical treatment used either alone or jointly with other therapies; encourage and promote education and training in surgical oncology at all levels, especially through Training Fellowships to support trainees in surgical oncology; promote and encourage collaboration between specialists in all branches of oncology. **Structure** General Assembly (annual); Executive Committee; Committees (6); Permanent Secretariat in Brussels (Belgium). **Languages** English. **Staff** 3.50 FTE, paid. **Finance** Members 'dues. Other sources: congress fees; sponsorship. **Activities** Events/meetings; training/education; awards/prizes/competitions; financial and/or material support; standards/guidelines. **Events** *Congress* Bordeaux (France) 2022, *Congress* Lisbon (Portugal) 2021, *Congress* Rotterdam (Netherlands) 2019, *Congress* Budapest (Hungary) 2018, *Congress* Amsterdam (Netherlands) 2017. **Publications** *EJSO – Journal of Cancer Surgery* (12 a year).
Members Surgeons, who may join individually or through their national society, in 110 countries and territories:
Afghanistan, Albania, Algeria, Andorra, Argentina, Armenia, Australia, Austria, Azerbaijan, Bangladesh, Barbados, Belarus, Belgium, Bosnia-Herzegovina, Brazil, Bulgaria, Cameroon, Canada, Chile, China, Colombia, Congo DR, Costa Rica, Croatia, Curaçao, Cyprus, Czechia, Denmark, Dominican Rep, Egypt, Estonia, Finland, France, Georgia, Germany, Gibraltar, Greece, Honduras, Hong Kong, Hungary, Iceland, India, Indonesia, Iran Islamic Rep, Iraq, Ireland, Israel, Italy, Japan, Jordan, Kazakhstan, Kenya, Korea Rep, Kuwait, Latvia, Lebanon, Libya, Lithuania, Luxembourg, Madagascar, Malaysia, Malta, Mauritius, Mexico, Moldova, Morocco, Myanmar, Nepal, Netherlands, New Zealand, Nicaragua, Nigeria, Norway, Oman, Pakistan, Palestine, Panama, Peru, Philippines, Poland, Portugal, Puerto Rico, Qatar, Romania, Russia, Saudi Arabia, Senegal, Serbia, Singapore, Slovakia, Slovenia, South Africa, Spain, Sri Lanka, Sudan, Sweden, Switzerland, Syrian AR, Taiwan, Tanzania UR, Thailand, Tunisia, Türkiye, UK, Ukraine, United Arab Emirates, USA, Uzbekistan, Venezuela, Yemen.
NGO Relations Founding and executive member of: *European Cancer Organisation (ECO, #06432)*. Member of: *Accreditation Council for Oncology in Europe (ACOE, #00063)*; *Rare Cancers Europe (RCE, #18620)*. Joint meetings/courses/projects with: *European Oncology Nursing Society (EONS, #08086)*; *European School of Oncology (ESO, #08434)*; *European Society of Breast Cancer Specialists (EUSOMA, #08534)*; *European Society for Medical Oncology (ESMO, #08648)*; *European SocieTy for Radiotherapy and Oncology (ESTRO, #08721)*; *SIOP Europe (SIOPE, #19288)*. [2021/XD1580/v/**D**]

♦ European Society for Surgical Research (ESSR) 08754

Société européenne de recherches chirurgicales – Europäische Gesellschaft für Chirurgische Forschung

SG Univ Hosp – Fac of Medicine, 1 place de Verdun, 59045 Lille, France.
Pres Inst for Lab Animal Science and Experimental Surgery, RWTH Aachen Univ, Templergraben 55, 52062 Aachen, Germany.
URL: http://www.essr.info/

History 11 Feb 1966, Nancy (France). Registered in accordance with French law. **Aims** Encourage scientific meetings and contacts between research workers on experimental surgery in Europe. **Languages** English. **Finance** Members' dues. Gifts. **Events** *Annual Congress* Geneva (Switzerland) 2019, *Annual Congress* Madrid (Spain) 2018, *Annual Congress* Amsterdam (Netherlands) 2017, *Annual Congress* Prague (Czech Rep) 2016, *Annual Congress* Liverpool (UK) 2015. **Publications** *European Surgical Research* – official journal.
Members Individuals; National sections. Members in 26 countries and territories:
Austria, Belgium, Brazil, China, Czechia, Denmark, Finland, France, Germany, Greece, Hong Kong, Hungary, India, Ireland, Italy, Japan, Netherlands, Norway, Poland, Slovakia, Spain, Sweden, Switzerland, Türkiye, UK, USA. [2016.07.06/XD0862/**D**]

♦ European Society for Swallowing Disorders (ESSD) 08755

Exec Officer Carrer Major de Can Caralleu 1-7, 08017 Barcelona, Spain. E-mail: info@essd.org.
URL: https://essd.org/

History 2011. Evolved out of *European Study Group for Dysphagia and Globus (EGDG, inactive)*. **Aims** Promote care, education and research in swallowing physiology and swallowing disorders. **Structure** Board. **Languages** English. **Staff** 3.00 FTE, paid. **Finance** Sources: members' dues. **Activities** Events/meetings; training/education. **Events** *World Dysphagia Summit* San Francisco, CA (USA) 2023, *Congress* Leuven (Belgium) 2022, *World Dysphagia Summit* Aichi (Japan) 2021, *World Dysphagia Summit* 2020, *Congress* Vienna (Austria) 2019. **Publications** *Dysphagia* (6 a year) – journal. **Members** Individuals. Membership countries not specified. [2022.02.15/XJ5257/v/**D**]

♦ European Society on Tattoo and Pigment research (ESTP) 08756

Secretariat c/o CAP Partner, Nordre Fasanvej 113, 2nd Floor, 2000 Frederiksberg, Denmark. T. +4570200305. Fax +4570200315. E-mail: info@cap-partner.eu.
URL: http://www.estpresearch.org/

History Nov 2013, Copenhagen (Denmark). **Aims** Advance academic research on tattoos; deliver independent expert advice; educate the medical community and other groups of professionals in all aspects of tattoos; advance manufacturing, distribution and sales of safer tattoo ink; develop and support research projects, guidelines and publications. **Structure** General Meeting; Board; Executive Committee. **Languages** English. **Finance** Members' dues. **Activities** Events/meetings. **Events** *World Congress on Tattoo and Pigment Research* Amsterdam (Netherlands) 2021, *European Congress on Tattoo and Pigment Research* Bern (Switzerland) 2019, *European Congress on Tattoo and Pigment Research* Regensburg (Germany) 2017, *European Congress on Tattoo and Pigment Research* Bruges (Belgium) 2015, *European Congress on Tattoo and Pigment Research* Copenhagen (Denmark) 2013. **Publications** *Dermatology* – official journal. **Members** Ordinary; Specialist; Junior; International; Supporting; Honorary. Membership countries not specified. **NGO Relations** Liaison Organization of: *Comité européen de normalisation (CEN, #04162)*. [2020/XM4807/**D**]

♦ European Society for Technical Education / see European Society for Technology Education (#08757)

♦ European Society for Technology Education 08757

Association européenne pour l'éducation technologique (AEET) – Europäische Gesellschaft für Technische Bildung (EGTB)

Secretariat 20 rue des Groux, 92140 Clamart, France. T. +33146448859.
Registered office AFDET, 178 rue du Temple, 75003 Paris, France. T. +33142740064.
URL: http://www.aeet.fr/

History Previously also referred to in English as *European Society for Technical Education*. Registered in accordance with French law. Registration: Start date: 3 Jul 1989, France. **Aims** Promote establishment of technology in general education curriculum. **Structure** General Assembly; Executive Committee. **Languages** French. **Finance** Members' dues. Subventions. **Activities** Colloquium. **NGO Relations** Member of: *World Council of Associations for Technology Education (WOCATE, no recent information).* [2018/XD5002/**D**]

♦ The European Society of Telemetry (internationally oriented national body)

♦ European Society for Textual Scholarship (ESTS) 08758

Sec Fac of Librarianship, Information, Education and IT, University of Borås, Högskolan, SE-501 90 Borås, Sweden.
Pres Loughborough Univ, Martin Hall, Epinal Way, Loughborough, LE11 3TS, UK.
URL: http://www.textualscholarship.eu/

History Nov 2001, Leicester (UK). Bylaws approved Dec 2005; updated Mar 2012. **Aims** Provide an international and interdisciplinary forum for the theory and practice of textual scholarship in Europe. **Structure** Board. **Languages** English. **Staff** Voluntary. **Finance** Sources: members' dues. **Events** *Textual scholarship in the 21st century* Malaga (Spain) 2019, *Conference* Prague (Czechia) 2018, *Editorial degrees of intervention* Alcala de Henares (Spain) 2017, *Conference* Madrid (Spain) 2017, *Conference* Antwerp (Belgium) 2016. **Publications** *Variants: Journal of the European Society for Textual Scholarship. Lexicon for Scholarly Editing.*
Members Full in 17 countries:
Australia, Belgium, Canada, Denmark, Finland, France, Germany, Italy, Lithuania, Netherlands, Portugal, South Africa, Spain, Sweden, Switzerland, UK, USA. [2022.02.15/XJ6366/**D**]

♦ European Society for Therapeutic Education (#19459)
♦ European Society for Therapeutic Radiology and Oncology / see European SocieTy for Radiotherapy and Oncology (#08721)

♦ European Society of Thoracic Imaging (ESTI) 08759

Société européenne d'imagerie thoracique

Address not obtained.
URL: http://www.esti-society.org/

History 13 Jun 1993. **Aims** Promote training and research in this *radiology* sub-specialty. **Structure** Bureau, comprising President, President-Elect, Secretary, Treasurer, 2 Vice-Presidents, 2 Councillors. Committees (7); By Law and Financial; Jury and Financial; Program and Financial; Training Educational; Eurorad; Strategic Planning and International Relation; Electronic Media. **Languages** English. **Finance** Members' dues. Donations. **Activities** Annual congress provides post-university training to both members and non-members. **Events** *Annual Scientific Meeting* Oxford (UK) 2022, *Annual Scientific Meeting* Oxford (UK) 2021, *Annual Scientific Meeting* Oxford (UK) 2020, *Joint Meeting* Paris (France) 2019, *Joint Congress* Geneva (Switzerland) 2018. **Publications** *European Radiology* – official journal.
Members Individual radiologists in 16 countries:
Austria, Belgium, Czechia, Finland, France, Germany, Greece, Hungary, Italy, Luxembourg, Netherlands, Russia, Spain, Sweden, Switzerland, USA.
NGO Relations Member of: *European Society of Radiology (ESR, #08720).* [2014/XD4311/v/**D**]

♦ European Society of Thoracic Surgeons (ESTS) 08760

Exec Dir 1 The Quadrant, Wonford Road, Exeter, EX2 4LE, UK. T. +441392430671. Fax +441392430671.
Sec Vice-Dir Div of Thoracic Surgery, Ospedali Riuniti, 60020 Ancona AN, Italy. E-mail: secretary.general@ests.org.uk.
URL: http://www.ests.org/

History Founded 18 Nov 1993, Heidelberg (Germany). UK Registered Charity: 1094888. **Aims** Improve quality in all aspects of thoracic surgery, from clinical and surgical management of patients to education, training and credentialing of thoracic surgeons in Europe and worldwide. **Structure** General Assembly (annual). Executive Committee, including President, President Elect, Past-President, General Secretary and Treasurer. **Languages** English. **Staff** 3.00 FTE, paid. **Finance** Members' dues, since 2007 related to average per capita income of the country in which they practice. These are defined each year by the World Bank and are used to create 3 categories: low middle-income countries; high middle-income countries; high income countries. **Activities** Includes: ESTS School of Thoracic Surgery, which offers theoretical and practical courses. **Events** *Annual Conference* Barcelona (Spain) 2024, *Annual Conference* Milan (Italy) 2023, *Annual Conference* The Hague (Netherlands) 2022, *Annual Conference* The Hague (Netherlands) 2021, *Annual Conference* The Hague (Netherlands) 2020. **Publications** *European Journal of Cardiothoracic Surgery.*
Members Individuals in 65 countries and territories:
Albania, Argentina, Armenia, Australia, Austria, Azerbaijan, Belgium, Bosnia-Herzegovina, Brazil, Bulgaria, Canada, China, Croatia, Cyprus, Czechia, Denmark, Egypt, Estonia, France, Georgia, Germany, Greece, Hungary, India, Iran Islamic Rep, Ireland, Israel, Italy, Japan, Jordan, Korea Rep, Kosovo, Latvia, Libya, Lithuania, Luxembourg, Mexico, Montenegro, Morocco, Netherlands, Nigeria, North Macedonia, Norway, Pakistan, Poland, Portugal, Romania, Russia, Saudi Arabia, Serbia, Slovakia, Slovenia, South Africa, Spain, Sri Lanka, Sweden, Switzerland, Syrian AR, Tajikistan, Türkiye, UK, Ukraine, United Arab Emirates, Uruguay, USA. [2013.06.27/XD8349/v/**D**]

♦ European Society of Tissue Regeneration in Orthopaedics and Traumatology (ESTROT) 08761

Secretariat Keep Intl, Via Giuseppe Vigoni 11, 20122 Milan MI, Italy. T. +390254122579. Fax +390254124871. E-mail: estrot@keepinternational.net.
URL: http://www.estrot.org/

Aims Relieve sickness in particular by advancing and promoting education and research in the treatment of musculoskeletal disorders. **Structure** Board. **Activities** Events/meetings; training/education. **Events** *Congress* Maastricht (Netherlands) 2022, *Congress* Maastricht (Netherlands) 2021, *Congress* Maastricht (Netherlands) 2020, *Congress* Malaga (Spain) 2019, *Congress* Heidelberg (Germany) 2018.
Members Affiliates in 24 countries:
Albania, Belgium, Bosnia-Herzegovina, Cyprus, Estonia, Finland, France, Germany, Greece, Ireland, Italy, Malta, Netherlands, North Macedonia, Norway, Portugal, Romania, Serbia, Slovenia, Spain, Sweden, Switzerland, Türkiye, UK. [2020/AA0979/**D**]

♦ European Society for Tourette Syndrome / see European Society for Study of Tourette Syndrome (#08748)

♦ European Society of Toxicologic Pathology (ESTP) 08762

Address not obtained.
URL: http://www.eurotoxpath.org/

History Founded 28 Nov 1986, Frankfurt-Main (Germany FR), as Gesellschaft für Toxikologische Pathologie. Present name adopted 2002. Current constitution adopted 23 Sep 2015, Guildford (UK). **Aims** Protect man against harmful effects that may result from intended use of active ingredients or additives, or which may be due to toxins at the workplace or in the environment; support scientific interests of toxicologic pathology; aid in research of spontaneous and toxic changes which manifest themselves morphologically; further promote importance of toxicologic pathology as an independent, specialized area. **Structure** General Assembly (annual); Executive Committee. Committees (7). **Languages** English. **Staff** Voluntary. **Finance** Members' dues. **Activities** Events/meetings; awards/prizes/competitions. **Events** *Congress* Maastricht (Netherlands) 2022, *Congress* 2021, *Congress* Turin (Italy) 2020, *Digitalization meets pathology* Cologne (Germany) 2019, *Congress* Copenhagen (Denmark) 2018. **Publications** *ESTP Newsletter*, *Experimental and Toxicologic Pathology* – journal.
Members Full (300) in 27 countries:
Belgium, Brazil, Canada, China, Czechia, Denmark, Finland, France, Germany, Hungary, India, Ireland, Israel, Italy, Japan, Jordan, Malaysia, Netherlands, New Zealand, Nigeria, Romania, Spain, Sweden, Switzerland, UK, USA, Yemen.
NGO Relations Member of: *International Federation of Societies of Toxicologic Pathologists (IFSTP, no recent information).* Joint activities with: *European College of Veterinary Pathologists (ECVP, #06627); European Society of Veterinary Pathology (ESVP, #08785).* [2017/XD9430/**D**]

♦ European Society of Toxicology (inactive)

♦ European Society for Toxicology In Vitro (ESTIV) 08763

Sec Regentenlaan 35, 3994 TZ Houten, Netherlands. E-mail: secretariat@estiv.org.
Admin Sec address not obtained.
URL: http://www.estiv.org/

History Previously registered in accordance with French law, Oct 1994, Paris (France). Registration: Handelsregister, No/ID: KVK 17171302, Start date: Nov 2004, Netherlands; EU Transparency Register, No/ID: 279517211643-71, Start date: 26 Jul 2013. **Aims** Promote in vitro toxicology, both scientifically and educationally, in Europe; stimulate exchange of knowledge between young and senior scientists. **Structure** General Meeting (every 2 years, during Workshop); Executive Board; Scientific Committee. **Languages** English. **Staff** Voluntary. **Finance** Sources: members' dues; sponsorship. **Activities** Events/meetings; knowledge management/information dissemination; networking/liaising; research/documentation; training/education. **Events** *International Congress on in Vitro Toxicology* Sitges (Spain) 2022, *International Congress on in Vitro Toxicology* Sitges (Spain) 2021, *International Congress on in Vitro Toxicology* Sitges (Spain) 2020, *International Congress on in Vitro Toxicology* Berlin (Germany) 2018, *International Congress on in Vitro Toxicology* Juan-les-Pins (France) 2016. **Publications** *ESTIV Newsletter* (2 a year); *Toxicology in Vitro* (8 a year).
Members Corporate; Affiliate; Individual. Individuals in 25 countries:
Australia, Belgium, Cuba, Czechia, Denmark, Estonia, Finland, France, Germany, India, Ireland, Italy, Korea Rep, Malaysia, Montenegro, Netherlands, Poland, Portugal, Serbia, Slovakia, Slovenia, Spain, Sweden, UK, USA. [2022/XD7264/**D**]

♦ European Society for translational Antiviral Research (ESAR) 08764

Exec Officer Univ Medical Ctr Utrecht, Dept of Medical Microbiology, Heidelberglaan 100, G 04-614, 3584 CX Utrecht, Netherlands. T. +31887556526. Fax +31887555426. E-mail: info@esar-society.eu.
URL: http://www.esar-society.eu/

Aims Unite scientists and clinicians throughout Europe to expand knowledge on resistant viruses and investigate the molecular epidemiology of drug-resistant viruses in Europe from public health and scientific perspectives. **Structure** Board. **Finance** Members' dues. **Activities** Training/education; events/meetings; research/documentation; standards/guidelines; knowledge management/information dissemination. **Events** *International Workshop on HIV Pediatrics* Mexico City (Mexico) 2019, *International Workshop on HIV Pediatrics* Paris (France) 2017, *International Workshop on HIV Pediatrics* Durban (South Africa) 2016, *International Workshop on HIV Pediatrics* Vancouver, BC (Canada) 2015. **Members** Individuals. Membership countries not specified. **NGO Relations** *Baltic Network against Life-Threatening Viral Infections (Baltic Antiviral Network, #03130); European Virus Archive goes Global (EVAg, #09067).* [2016/XM4935/v/**D**]

♦ European Society for Translational Medicine (EUSTM) 08765

Europäische Gesellschaft für Translationale Medizin

Pres Schwindgasse 4/7, 1040 Vienna, Austria. T. +4318923562. Fax +4318923562. E-mail: info@eutranslationalmedicine.org.
URL: http://eutranslationalmedicine.org/

Aims Enhance research and development of novel and affordable diagnostic tools and treatments for clinical disorders affecting global population; educate the clinicians, scientists and patients. **Structure** General Assembly; Executive Board; CEO. **Finance** Sources: members' dues. **Activities** Events/meetings; training/education. **Events** *Annual Congress* Venice (Italy) 2022, *Annual Congress* 2021, *Annual Congress* Austria 2020, *Annual Congress* Vienna (Austria) 2019, *European Congress of Clinical Case Reports* Vienna (Austria) 2018. **Publications** *New Horizons in Translational Medicine* – journal. **Members** Regular; Extraordinary; Honorary. Membership countries not specified. [2021/XJ9594/**D**]

♦ European Society for Translation Studies (EST) 08766

SG address not obtained. E-mail: secretary-generalest@gmail.com.
Pres address not obtained.
URL: http://www.est-translationstudies.org/

History Sep 1992, Vienna (Austria). **Aims** Stimulate and coordinate research in translation and interpreting; act as a forum for exchange and dissemination of new ideas and insights in translation studies. **Structure** General Meeting (every 3 years); Executive Board. **Languages** English. **Staff** None. **Finance** Sources: members' dues. **Activities** Events/meetings; financial and/or material support; knowledge management/information dissemination; research/documentation. **Events** *Triennial Congress* Leeds (UK) 2025, *Triennial Congress* Oslo (Norway) 2022, *Triennial Congress* Stellenbosch (South Africa) 2019, *Triennial Congress* Aarhus (Denmark) 2016, *Triennial Congress* Germersheim (Germany) 2013. **Publications** *EST Newsletter* (2 a year).
Members Individuals (almost 600) in 45 countries and territories:
Albania, Argentina, Austria, Belgium, Brazil, Bulgaria, Canada, Croatia, Cyprus, Czechia, Denmark, Egypt, Finland, France, Germany, Greece, Hungary, India, Iran Islamic Rep, Ireland, Israel, Italy, Kazakhstan, Kuwait, Latvia, Lebanon, Luxembourg, Netherlands, New Zealand, Norway, Oman, Poland, Portugal, Romania, Russia, Slovakia, Slovenia, South Africa, Spain, Sweden, Switzerland, Taiwan, Türkiye, UK, USA.
NGO Relations Member of (1): *International Network of Translation and Interpreting Studies Associations (INTISA, #14335).* [2022.10.12/XD6315/**D**]

♦ European Society of Transport Institutes (inactive)

♦ European Society for Trauma and Dissociation (ESTD) 08767

Secretariat 1ste Hogeweg 16-A, 3701 HK Zeist, Netherlands. T. +31306977841. Fax +31306977841. E-mail: info@estd.org.
URL: http://www.estd.org/

History Apr 2006. **Aims** Promote an increase in the knowledge of Trauma, Dissociation and all disorders related to chronic traumatization; provide professional and public education; support communication and cooperation among clinicians and other professionals in the field; stimulate national and international research projects; provide knowledge and education specifically to those countries in Europe who do not have easy access in this field. **Structure** Executive Board, comprising President, Secretary, Treasurer and 7 members. **Languages** English, French, German, Italian, Spanish. **Events** *International Trauma, Dissociation and Psychosis Conference* Kristiansand (Norway) 2019, *International Conference* Kristiansand (Norway) 2017, *Biennial Conference* Amsterdam (Netherlands) 2016, *Biennial Conference / Conference* Copenhagen (Denmark) 2014, *Biennial Conference / Conference* Berlin (Germany) 2012. **Members** Full; Student. Membership countries not specified. [2014/XM4634/**D**]

♦ European Society for Trauma and Emergency Surgery (ESTES) 08768

Europäische Gesellschaft für Trauma- und Akutchirurgie

Main Office Franz-Käfer-Str 8, 3100 St Pölten, Austria. E-mail: office@estesonline.org – association@estesonline.org.
URL: http://www.estesonline.org/

History 25 May 2007, Graz (Austria). Founded on merger of *European Association for Trauma and Emergency Surgery (EATES, inactive)* and *European Trauma Society (ETS, inactive)*, following a series of discussions since 2004 between the Boards of the 2 societies in connection to the EATES Congress, Rotterdam (Netherlands). Discussions continued at: ETS congress, 2006, Ljubljana (Slovenia); EATES congress, 2006, Malmö (Sweden); joint Board meeting, Jan 2007, Graz; 1st Joint Congress of EATES and ETS, 23-26 May 2007, Graz. **Aims** Promote trauma and emergency surgery in general; disseminate interest, knowledge and quality in these fields. **Events** *European Congress of Trauma and Emergency Surgery (ECTES)* Oslo (Norway) 2022, *European Congress on Trauma and Emergency Surgery* Oslo (Norway) 2021, *European Congress on Trauma and Emergency Surgery* Oslo (Norway) 2020, *European Congress on Trauma and Emergency Surgery* Prague (Czechia) 2019, *European Congress on Trauma and Emergency Surgery* Valencia (Spain) 2018. **Publications** *European Journal of Trauma and Emergency.* **Members** Individuals in 55 countries and territories (not specified). **NGO Relations** Member of (1): *World Coalition for Trauma Care (WCTC, #21282).* Cooperates with (1): *European Shock Society, The (ESS, #08480).* [2020/XM3200/**D**]

♦ **European Society for Traumatic Stress Studies (ESTSS)** **08769**
Exec Sec Univ of Rijeka, Dept for Psychiatry, Brace Branchetta 20, HR-51000 Rijeka, Croatia. T. +38551311057. Fax +38551311062. E-mail: secretariat@estss.org.
Registered Address Bedrijvenweg 4, 1619 BK Andijk, Netherlands.
URL: http://www.estss.org/

History Jun 1993, Bergen (Norway). **Aims** Ensure continued prominence is given to all aspects of traumatic stress and its many repercussions; promote networking between individuals and organizations within the field of psychotraumatology. **Structure** Board; Executive Committee. **Languages** English. **Finance** Members' dues. **Events** *European Conference on Traumatic Stress* Belfast (UK) 2023, *European Conference on Traumatic Stress* Belfast (UK) 2022, *European Conference on Traumatic Stress* Belfast (UK) 2021, *European Conference on Traumatic Stress* Rotterdam (Netherlands) 2019, *European Conference on Traumatic Stress* Odense (Denmark) 2017. **Publications** *ESTSS Bulletin* (2 a year).
Members Full; Associate; Student. Individuals in 37 countries:
Australia, Austria, Belgium, Canada, Colombia, Croatia, Denmark, Egypt, Finland, France, Georgia, Germany, Greece, Hungary, Iceland, India, Ireland, Israel, Italy, Kenya, Lithuania, Netherlands, Nigeria, Norway, Pakistan, Poland, Portugal, Russia, Saudi Arabia, Serbia, Spain, Sweden, Switzerland, Türkiye, UK, Ukraine, USA.
NGO Relations Associate member of: *European Federation of Psychologists Associations (EFPA, #07199).*
[2022/XD4748/v/**D**]

♦ **European Society of Urogenital Radiology (ESUR)** **08770**
Main Office Am Gestade 1, 1010 Vienna, Austria. T. +4315334064929. E-mail: esursecretary@esur.org.
URL: http://www.esur.org/

History 26 Aug 1990, Copenhagen (Denmark), as *European Society of Uroradiology*. By-laws agreed after postal ballot, Mar-Apr 1991; most recent by-laws approved after postal ballot, Jan 2006. Registered in accordance with Austrian law. **Aims** Promote interest in advancement of urogenital imaging and intervention; stimulate study of normal and abnormal kidney, urinary tract and genital organs. **Structure** General Assembly (every 2 years, preferable in even years); Board; Committees (3); Working groups (2). **Languages** English. **Staff** None. **Finance** Members' dues. Sponsors. **Activities** Events/meetings; training/education. **Events** *Symposium* Athens (Greece) 2022, *Symposium* Lisbon (Portugal) 2021, *Symposium* Lisbon (Portugal) 2020, *Symposium* Dublin (Ireland) 2019, *Symposium* Barcelona (Spain) 2018. **Publications** *European Uroradiology* (every 2 years); *European Radiology* – journal.
Members Full Fellows; Emeritus; Honorary individual physicians and other scientists in the uroradiology field, in 26 countries:
Austria, Belgium, Bulgaria, Cyprus, Denmark, Egypt, Finland, France, Germany, Greece, Hungary, Iceland, Ireland, Israel, Italy, Netherlands, Norway, Poland, Portugal, Russia, Sweden, Switzerland, Türkiye, UK, Ukraine, USA.
NGO Relations Member of: *European Society of Radiology (ESR, #08720).* [2020/XD2863/v/**D**]

♦ European Society of Urological Oncology (inactive)
♦ European Society for Urological Research (inactive)
♦ European Society of Uroradiology / see European Society of Urogenital Radiology (#08770)

♦ **European Society for Vascular Medicine (ESVM)** **08771**
Exec Officer address not obtained. T. +393282705284. E-mail: adm@vascular-medicine.org.
SG address not obtained. E-mail: secretary@vascular-medicine.org.
Registered Office Maison de l'Angiologie, 18 rue de l'Université, 75007 Paris, France.
URL: http://vascular-medicine.org/

History 2014. Registered in accordance with French law. **Aims** Promote scientific exchange, education, cooperative research, and high quality of practice in the field of vascular medicine. **Structure** General Assembly; Council; Executive Board. **Languages** English. **Finance** Members' dues. Other sources: donations; publication proceeds; income from activities; grants. **Activities** Events/meetings. **Events** *Annual Congress* Naples (Italy) 2024, *Annual Congress* Saint-Malo (France) 2023, *Annual Congress* Stockholm (Sweden) 2022, *Annual Congress* London (UK) 2021, *Annual Congress* Torremolinos (Spain) 2020. **Publications** *European Journal of Vascular Medicine (VASA).*
Members Full in 16 countries:
Austria, Belgium, Czechia, France, Germany, Hungary, Ireland, Italy, Romania, Serbia, Slovakia, Slovenia, Sweden, Switzerland, UK, Ukraine. [2018/XM4825/**D**]

♦ **European Society for Vascular Surgery (ESVS)** **08772**
Main Office 244 bd Albert 1er, 33800 Bordeaux, France. T. +33556490307. E-mail: info@esvs.org.
URL: http://www.esvs.org/

History 6 May 1987, London (UK). Constitution and By-laws approved Sep 1990. **Aims** Improve vascular health for the public benefit. **Structure** General Assembly (annual); Council; Committees; Secretariat, headed by Secretary General. **Languages** English. **Staff** 6.00 FTE, paid. **Finance** Sources: members' dues; sponsorship. **Activities** Events/meetings; financial and/or material support; publishing activities; standards/guidelines; training/education. **Events** *Annual Meeting* Krakow (Poland) 2024, *Annual Meeting* Belfast (UK) 2023, *Annual Meeting* Rome (Italy) 2022, *Annual Meeting* Rotterdam (Netherlands) 2021, *Annual Meeting* Krakow (Poland) 2020. **Publications** *European Journal of Vascular and Endovascular Surgery* (12 a year) in English; *EJVES Vascular Forum* (4 a year) in English. Annual Report; conference proceedings; text; journals.
Members Honorary; Senior; European; Non-European; Trainee; Associate; Industrial. Members (about 1,900) in 73 countries and territories:
Albania, Argentina, Armenia, Australia, Austria, Belarus, Belgium, Bosnia-Herzegovina, Brazil, Bulgaria, Canada, Chile, China, Colombia, Costa Rica, Croatia, Curaçao, Cyprus, Czechia, Denmark, Egypt, Estonia, Finland, France, Germany, Greece, Hungary, Iceland, India, Indonesia, Iraq, Ireland, Israel, Italy, Japan, Jordan, Korea Rep, Kosovo, Latvia, Liechtenstein, Lithuania, Luxembourg, Malta, Mexico, Netherlands, New Zealand, North Macedonia, Norway, Pakistan, Poland, Portugal, Réunion, Romania, Russia, Saudi Arabia, Serbia, Singapore, Slovakia, Slovenia, South Africa, Spain, Sweden, Switzerland, Tajikistan, Thailand, Tunisia, Türkiye, UK, Ukraine, United Arab Emirates, USA, Uzbekistan, Vietnam.
NGO Relations Member of (1): *World Federation of Vascular Societies (WFVS, #21500).* Instrumental in setting up (1): *European Vascular Surgeons in Training (EVST, #09045).* Close relations with: *European Association of Vascular Surgeons in Training (EAVST, inactive).* [2021.06.09/XD3038/v/**D**]

♦ **European Society of Veterinary Cardiology (ESVC)** **08773**
Sec Dept of Veterinary Sciences, Univ degli Studi di Parma – Parma Univ, Via del Taglio 10, 43126 Parma PR, Italy.
Pres c/o ACAPULCO, Masta 11, 4970 Stavelot, Belgium.
URL: http://esvcardio.com/

Aims Promote and increase knowledge in veterinary cardiology. **Structure** Executive Committee. **Languages** English. **Staff** 8.00 FTE, voluntary. **Events** *Annual Meeting* Lisbon (Portugal) 2015, *Annual Meeting* Liverpool (UK) 2013, *Annual Meeting* Maastricht (Netherlands) 2012, *Annual Meeting* Porto (Portugal) 2009, *Annual Meeting* Budapest (Hungary) 2007. **Publications** *Journal Veterinary Cardiology.*
Members Individuals in 23 countries and territories:
Argentina, Austria, Belgium, Brazil, Canada, Denmark, Finland, France, Germany, Ireland, Italy, Luxembourg, Netherlands, Norway, Scotland, Slovakia, Slovenia, Spain, Sweden, Switzerland, UK, USA, Venezuela.
NGO Relations Member of: *European Society of Veterinary Internal Medicine (ESVIM, #08779).*
[2016/XD6109/v/**D**]

♦ **European Society of Veterinary Clinical Ethology (ESVCE)** **08774**
Pres Hohensasel 16, 22395 Hamburg, Germany. E-mail: president@esvce.org – secretary@esvce.org.
URL: http://www.esvce.org/

History 1994. **Aims** Further scientific progress in veterinary and comparative clinical ethology by: providing an organization for recognized specialists and for individuals who take an interest in research, teaching or the practice of clinical ethology in animals; establish a specialized organization for veterinary clinical ethology; further education in veterinary clinical ethology; facilitate exchange of information. **Structure** Board. Officers: President, Vice-President, Treasurer, Secretary, Membership Secretary; Communications Officer. **Languages** English. **Staff** None. **Finance** Members' dues. **Activities** Sponsors the 'Blue Dog Project' for prevention of dog bites on children; promotes veterinary behavioural medicine in Europe. **Events** *European Veterinary Congress of Behavioural Medicine and Animal Welfare* Palma (Spain) 2022, *European Veterinary Congress of Behavioural Medicine and Animal Welfare* Ghent (Belgium) 2021, *Annual General Meeting* Germany 2020, *European Veterinary Congress of Behavioural Medicine and Animal Welfare* Eindhoven (Netherlands) 2019, *Annual Meeting* Berlin (Germany) 2018. **Publications** *ESVCE Newsletter* (2 a year).
Members Individuals and organizations. Members in 26 countries:
Argentina, Australia, Austria, Belgium, Brazil, Denmark, Estonia, Finland, France, Germany, Greece, Ireland, Israel, Italy, Mexico, Netherlands, New Zealand, Norway, Poland, Portugal, South Africa, Spain, Sweden, Switzerland, UK, USA.
[2022/XD6139/**D**]

♦ **European Society of Veterinary Clinical Pathology (ESVCP)** **08775**
Pres School of Veterinary Medicine and Science, Room C33 Gateway Building, Sutton Bonington Campus, Sutton Bonington, LE12 5RD, UK. T. +441159516430.
Secretariat address not obtained. E-mail: secretariat@ecvcp.org.
URL: http://www.esvcp.org/

History 26 Sep 1998. Registered in accordance with German law. **Structure** General Meeting (annual). Board, comprising President, Vice-President, Secretary, Treasurer and 2 Councillors. **Languages** English, French, Italian, Spanish. **Staff** Voluntary. **Finance** Members' dues. **Activities** Set up: *European College of Veterinary Clinical Pathology (ECVCP, #06620).* **Events** *Joint Congress* Vienna (Austria) 2020, *Joint Congress* Arnhem (Netherlands) 2019, *Congress* Athens (Greece) 2018, *Congress* London (UK) 2017, *Congress / Joint Meeting ESVONC – ESVCP* Nantes (France) 2016. **Publications** *Veterinary Clinical Pathology* (4-5 a year) – journal.
Members Individuals and societies. Members in 35 countries:
Australia, Austria, Belgium, Bosnia-Herzegovina, Bulgaria, Canada, Chile, Croatia, Cyprus, Czechia, Denmark, France, Germany, Grenada, Hungary, Ireland, Israel, Italy, Luxembourg, Moldova, Netherlands, New Zealand, Norway, Poland, Portugal, Romania, Russia, Slovenia, South Africa, Spain, St Kitts-Nevis, Sweden, Switzerland, UK, USA. [2019/XD9125/**D**]

♦ **European Society of Veterinary and Comparative Nutrition (ESVCN)** . **08776**
Address not obtained.
URL: http://www.esvcn.eu/

History Founded 1991, Vienna (Austria). **Aims** Increase interaction of European veterinary nutritionists; compare and harmonize veterinary nutrition education; advance applied and scientific veterinary nutrition. **Structure** Board. **Languages** English. **Staff** 2.50 FTE, voluntary. **Finance** Members' dues: euro 40. **Events** *Annual Conference* Basel (Switzerland) 2022, *Annual Conference* Vila Real (Portugal) 2021, *Annual Conference* Munich (Germany) 2020, *Annual Conference* Turin (Italy) 2019, *Annual Conference* Munich (Germany) 2018.
Members Individuals in 22 countries:
Austria, Belgium, Canada, Denmark, Egypt, France, Germany, Hungary, Ireland, Italy, Netherlands, Norway, Poland, Portugal, Romania, Serbia, Slovenia, Spain, Sweden, Switzerland, UK, USA. [2022/XD5564/**D**]

♦ **European Society of Veterinary Dermatology (ESVD)** **08777**
Main Office Av Ceramique 222, 6221 KX Maastricht, Netherlands. E-mail: secretariat@esvd.org – secretary@esvd.org.
URL: http://www.esvd.org/

History Sep 1984, Hamburg (Germany). Founded when 1st meeting was held as part of 9th World Congress of the *World Small Animal Veterinary Association (WSAVA, #21795).* Registration: Charity Commission, UK. **Aims** Further scientific progress in veterinary and comparative dermatology. **Structure** Executive Board. **Languages** English. **Staff** 6.00 FTE, voluntary. **Finance** Sources: meeting proceeds; members' dues; sponsorship. **Activities** Events/meetings; training/education. **Events** *World Congress of Veterinary Dermatology* Boston, MA (USA) 2024, *European Veterinary Dermatology Congress* Gothenburg (Sweden) 2023, *Annual Congress* Porto (Portugal) 2022, *Annual Congress* 2021, *World Congress of Veterinary Dermatology* Sydney, NSW (Australia) 2020. **Publications** *Veterinary Dermatology* (6 a year); *ESVD Bulletin* (2 a year); *ESVD Newsletter*. Annual Report; Membership Directory.
Members Honorary; Founder; Full; Associate. Members in 41 countries and territories:
Argentina, Australia, Austria, Belgium, Brazil, Canada, Croatia, Czechia, Denmark, Estonia, Finland, France, Germany, Greece, Hong Kong, Hungary, India, Ireland, Israel, Italy, Japan, Lithuania, Luxembourg, Malta, Mexico, Netherlands, Norway, Poland, Portugal, Romania, Russia, Serbia, Slovakia, Slovenia, South Africa, Spain, Sweden, Switzerland, Taiwan, UK, USA.
NGO Relations Member of (1): *World Association for Veterinary Dermatology (WAVD, #21203).*
[2021/XD7160/v/**D**]

♦ **European Society of Veterinary Endocrinology (ESVE)** **08778**
Sec Dept of Clinical Veterinary Science, Vetsuisse Faculty – Bern University, Läanggasstrasse 124, 3001 Bern, Switzerland.
URL: https://www.esve-payments.org/default.aspx/

History 2001. **Structure** Board. **Finance** Members' dues. **Activities** Events/meetings; awards/prizes/competitions; training/education; standards/guidelines. **Events** *Annual Conference* Milan (Italy) 2019, *Annual Conference* Rotterdam (Netherlands) 2018, *Annual Conference* Lisbon (Portugal) 2015, *Annual Conference* Mainz (Germany) 2014, *Annual Conference* Liverpool (UK) 2013. **NGO Relations** Affiliated with: *European College of Veterinary Internal Medicine – Companion Animals (ECVIM – CA, #06624).* [2019/XM4178/**D**]

♦ **European Society of Veterinary Internal Medicine (ESVIM)** **08779**
Pres LMU Small Animal Med Clinic, Veterinaerstr 13, 80539 Munich, Germany. T. +498921802653. Fax +498921816501.
URL: http://www.ecvimcongress.org/

Aims Advance companion animal internal medicine in Europe. **Structure** Board. **Languages** English. **Events** *Congress* Lyon (France) 2024, *Congress* Barcelona (Spain) 2023, *Congress* Gothenburg (Sweden) 2022, *Congress* Munich (Germany) 2021, *Congress* Munich (Germany) 2020. **NGO Relations** Instrumental in setting up: *European College of Veterinary Internal Medicine – Companion Animals (ECVIM – CA, #06624).*
[2013/XD3630/**D**]

♦ **European Society of Veterinary Nephrology and Urology (ESVNU)** .. **08780**
Pres Vetsuisse Faculty, Univ of Zurich, Winterthurstrasse, 2608 Zurich ZH 57, Switzerland.
URL: http://esvnu.eu/

Aims Increase the quality of life of dogs and cats by enhancing veterinary care in renal and urinary tract disease. **Structure** General Meeting (annually, at Congress). Board, comprising President, Treasurer, Secretary and Information Officer. **Finance** Members' dues. **Activities** Organizes annual scientific congress.
Members Individuals in 16 countries:
Australia, Austria, Belgium, France, Germany, Italy, Netherlands, Norway, Slovakia, South Africa, Spain, Sweden, Switzerland, Türkiye, UK, USA.
NGO Relations Affiliated with: *European College of Veterinary Internal Medicine – Companion Animals (ECVIM – CA, #06624).* [2015/XD5561/**D**]

♦ **European Society of Veterinary Neurology (ESVN)** **08781**
Sec Aúna Especialidades Veterinarias, Algepser 22-1, Parque Empresarial Tactica, Paterna, 46980 Valencia, Spain. E-mail: secretary@ecvn.org – admin@ecvn.org.
Pres Small Animal Med, University of Leipzig, An den Tierkliniken 23, 04107 Leipzig, Germany. E-mail: president@ecvn.org.
URL: http://www.esvn.org/

History 1988, Bern (Switzerland). **Aims** Advance veterinary neurology in Europe and increase the competency of those who practice in this field by: (a) establishing guidelines for post-graduate education and experience as a prerequisite to becoming a specialist in the discipline of veterinary neurology through the academic college 'European College of Veterinary Neurology (ECVN)'; (b) examining and authenticating veterinarians as specialists in veterinary neurology through the ECVN to serve the veterinary patients, their owners and the public in general, by providing expert care for animals with neurological disease; (c) encouraging research and other contributions to knowledge relating to the pathogenesis, diagnosis, therapy, prevention and the control of diseases directly or indirectly affecting the nervous system of animals, and promoting communication and dissemination of this knowledge; (d) remaining a non-profit making organization that does not pursue commercial interests. **Structure** General Meeting (annual); Board. Academic college: *European College of Veterinary Neurology (ECVN, #06626).* **Languages** English. **Finance** Members' dues. Other sources: meeting organization; sponsors. **Events** *Annual Symposium* Venice (Italy) 2021, *Annual Symposium* Venice (Italy) 2020, *Annual Symposium* Wroclaw (Poland) 2019, *Annual Symposium* Copenhagen (Denmark) 2018, *Annual Symposium* Helsinki (Finland) 2017. **Publications** *ESVN/ECVN Annual Newsletter.*
Members Individuals in 25 countries and territories:
Australia, Austria, Belgium, Canada, China, Czechia, Denmark, Finland, France, Germany, Greece, Ireland, Israel, Italy, Netherlands, New Zealand, Poland, Portugal, Spain, Sweden, Switzerland, Taiwan, Türkiye, UK, USA. [2017/XD2697/v/**D**]

♦ **European Society of Veterinary Oncology (ESVONC)** **08782**
Main Office Ave Ceramique 222, 6221 KX Maastricht, Netherlands. T. +31433250521. E-mail: office@esvonc.com.
URL: http://www.esvonc.com/
History 1993, Utrecht (Netherlands). Former names and other names: *Vereniging European Society of Veterinary Oncology (ESVONC)* – full title. Registration: Kamer van Koophandel, No/ID: 40482509, Netherlands. **Aims** Encourage and facilitate coordination of research and other contributions to the knowledge related to pathogenesis, diagnosis, therapy, prevention and control of animal tumour diseases; provide an organization for recognized specialists in veterinary oncology and for individuals who take interest in research, teaching or the practice of veterinary and comparative oncology; further education in veterinary oncology. **Structure** Members' Scientific Congress and Annual Business Meeting (in Spring); General Meeting (in Autumn, usually in conjunction with annual congress of ECVIM-CA). Executive Committee of 5 Officers. **Languages** English. **Staff** 1.00 FTE, paid. **Finance** Members' dues (annual): euro 100. **Activities** Organizes scientific congress. **Events** *ESVONC Congress* Maastricht (Netherlands) 2021, *ESVONC Congress* Siracusa (Italy) 2020, *World Veterinary Cancer Congress* Tokyo (Japan) 2020, *Congress* Frankfurt-Main (Germany) 2019, *Congress* Las Palmas de Gran Canaria (Spain) 2018. **Publications** Congress proceedings.
Members Individuals in 24 countries:
Australia, Austria, Belgium, Denmark, Finland, France, Germany, Hungary, Ireland, Israel, Italy, Netherlands, Norway, Poland, Portugal, Romania, Slovakia, Slovenia, South Africa, Spain, Sweden, Switzerland, UK, USA.
NGO Relations Member of: *Federation of European Companion Animal Veterinary Associations (FECAVA, #09497)*. Associated with: *European Society of Veterinary Internal Medicine (ESVIM, #08779)*.
[2020/XD5556/v/**D**]

♦ **European Society of Veterinary Ophthalmology (ESVO)** **08783**
Sec ARVO, Bargaului 5, 13233 Bucharest, Romania. E-mail: admin@esvo.org.
URL: http://www.esvo.org/
History 1985, at the BSAVA meeting. **Aims** Promote veterinary ophthalmology by a yearly event in Europe. **Structure** Academic college: *European College of Veterinary Ophthalmologists (ECVO, see: #08783)*. Officers: President, Secretary and Treasurer and 5 other Members. **Languages** English. **Staff** Voluntary. **Finance** Members' dues. **Events** *Annual ECVO Conference* Antwerp (Belgium) 2019, *Annual ECVO Conference* Florence (Italy) 2018, *Meeting* Prague (Czechia) 2018, *Annual ECVO Conference* Estoril (Portugal) 2017, *Meeting* Toulouse (France) 2016.
Members Veterinarians and veterinary students interested in ophthalmology (currently 160) in 19 countries:
Austria, Belgium, Denmark, Finland, France, Germany, Greece, Ireland, Israel, Italy, Luxembourg, Netherlands, Norway, Poland, Slovenia, Spain, Sweden, Switzerland, UK. [2015/XD5558/**D**]

♦ **European Society of Veterinary Orthopaedics and Traumatology (ESVOT)** **08784**
Main Office EMOVA – Trecchi Palace, Via Trecchi 20, 26100 Cremona CR, Italy. T. +39372403509. Fax +39372403558. E-mail: info@emova.it.
URL: http://www.esvot.org/
Aims Disseminate basic principles and advances in veterinary orthopaedics by means of continuing education. **Languages** English. **Events** *Congress* Nice (France) 2022, *Congress* Barcelona (Spain) 2018, *Congress* London (UK) 2016, *Congress* Venice (Italy) 2014, *Congress* Bologna (Italy) 2012. **Publications** *ESVOT Newsletter*. **Members** Accredited European veterinarians (about 350). Membership countries not specified. **NGO Relations** Housed at: *European Management Office for Veterinary Associations (EMOVA)*.
[2016.06.01/XD6108/**D**]

♦ **European Society of Veterinary Pathology (ESVP)** **08785**
Société européenne de pathologie vétérinaire – Europäische Gesellschaft für Veterinärpathologie
Hon Sec Inst of Veterinary Science, Univ of Liverpool, Leahurst, Chester High Road, Neston, CH64 7TE, UK. T. +441517946003. E-mail: secretary@esvp.eu.
Pres Dept of Pathology, Univ of Veterinary Medicine, Buenteweg 17, 30559 Hannover, Germany. E-mail: president@esvp.eu.
URL: http://www.esvp.eu/
History 1951, as *Arbeitsgemeinschaft fur Veterinärpathologen*. Name changed, 1968, to *Europäische Arbeitsgemeinschaft für Veterinärpathologen*. Name changed, 1974, to *Europäische Gesellschaft für Veterinärpathologie*. Since 1994, only known in English title, when French and German titles were abandoned: *Société européenne de pathologie vétérinaire – Europäische Gesellschaft für Veterinärpathologie*. **Aims** Promote scientific work of veterinary surgeons and physicians active in the areas of functional and morphological pathology of animals, as well as that of other interested biological scientists. **Structure** Annual Meeting; Board. **Languages** English. **Staff** Voluntary. **Finance** Members' dues. **Activities** Training/education; events/meetings. **Events** *Annual Meeting* Athens (Greece) 2022, *Annual Meeting* 2021, *Annual Meeting* Turin (Italy) 2020, *Annual Meeting* Cluj-Napoca (Romania) 2018, *Annual Meeting* Lyon (France) 2017. **Publications** *ESVP Newsletter*.
Members Individuals (over 600) in 48 countries:
Andorra, Argentina, Australia, Austria, Bangladesh, Belgium, Bosnia-Herzegovina, Brazil, Bulgaria, Canada, Costa Rica, Croatia, Czechia, Denmark, Egypt, Estonia, Finland, France, Germany, Greece, Hungary, Iran Islamic Rep, Ireland, Israel, Italy, Latvia, Lithuania, Namibia, Netherlands, North Macedonia, Norway, Poland, Portugal, Romania, Russia, Serbia, Slovakia, Slovenia, South Africa, Spain, Sweden, Switzerland, Thailand, Türkiye, Uganda, UK, United Arab Emirates, USA.
NGO Relations Joint activities with: *European College of Veterinary Pathologists (ECVP, #06627)*; *European Society of Toxicologic Pathology (ESTP, #08762)*. [2019.12.13/XD2731/v/**D**]

♦ **European Society for Veterinary Virology (ESVV)** **08786**
Sec INIA-CISA, Valdeolmos, 28130 Madrid, Spain. T. +34916202300.
Pres CIRAD, Domaine Duclos, F-97117 Petit-Bourg Guadeloupe, France. T. +590590255431.
URL: http://esvv.eu/
History 1988, Belgium. **Aims** Further progress in veterinary virology; provide an organization for individuals who devote a significant portion of their professional activities to research, teaching or the practical application of veterinary virology; encourage and promote improved methods of diagnosis, prevention and treatment of animal viral diseases; further veterinary virological education; promote exchange of information in the field of veterinary virology. **Structure** General Assembly (at Scientific Congress); Executive Board; National Coordinators. **Languages** English. **Staff** 6.00 FTE, voluntary. **Finance** Members' dues. Sponsorship for specific activities such as meetings and publications. **Activities** Events/meetings. **Events** *Congress* Ghent (Belgium) 2022, *Congress* Vienna (Austria) 2018, *Congress* Montpellier (France) 2015, *Congress* Madrid (Spain) 2012, *Congress / Scientific Congress* Budapest (Hungary) 2009. **Publications** *ESVV Newsletter*, *ESVV Technical Newsletters* – only for members. Scientific meeting proceedings.
Members Full; Associate; Honorary. Individuals in 31 countries:
Australia, Austria, Belgium, Bosnia-Herzegovina, Bulgaria, Croatia, Czechia, Denmark, Finland, France, Germany, Greece, Hungary, Iceland, Indonesia, Ireland, Italy, Latvia, Netherlands, Nigeria, Norway, Poland, Portugal, Serbia, Slovakia, Spain, Sweden, Switzerland, UK, USA, Zimbabwe.
NGO Relations Associate member of: *International Union of Microbiological Societies (IUMS, #15794)*.
[2018.06.01/XD1556/v/**D**]

♦ **European Society for Virology (ESV)** **08787**
SG address not obtained.
Pres address not obtained.
URL: http://www.eusv.eu/
History 30 Oct 2008. **Aims** Promote and stimulate the exchange of information and collaboration among individual scientists as well as among national and international associations of Virology throughout Europe. **Structure** Assembly; Executive Board; Advisory Council. Committees (3): Award; Meeting; Relationships with Virology Societies and Institutes. **Finance** Sources: members' dues. **Activities** Awards/prizes/competitions; events/meetings; training/education. **Events** *European Congress of Virology* Gdansk (Poland) 2023, *European Congress of Virology* Gdansk (Poland) 2022, *European Virology Congress* Rotterdam (Netherlands) 2019, *European Congress on Virology* Hamburg (Germany) 2016, *European Congress on Virology* Lyon (France) 2013. **Publications** *ESV News*. **Members** Full; Student; Corporate; Associate; Affiliate. Membership countries not specified. [2020/AA0536/**D**]

♦ **European Society for Vocational Designing and Career Counseling (ESVDC)** **08788**
Admin Office c/o Univ of Bern, Dept of Psychology, Fabrikstrasse 8, 3012 Bern, Switzerland. T. +41316314045.
Pres Univ of Padova, Via Belzoni 84, 35121 Padua PD, Italy.
URL: http://www.esvdc.org/
History 2011, Padua (Italy). Statutes adopted, 11 Sep 2011. Registered in accordance with Swiss Civil Code. **Aims** Stimulate and promote European and international collaboration in research and development in the fields of life-designing, vocational guidance and career counselling. **Structure** General Assembly; Executive Board. **Languages** English. **Staff** Voluntary. **Finance** Members' dues. Funding for European projects. Budget (annual): euro 2,500-3,000. **Activities** Networking/liaising; awards/prizes/competitions; knowledge management/information dissemination. **Events** *General Assembly* Bratislava (Slovakia) 2015, *General Assembly* Paris (France) 2014, *General Assembly* Padua (Italy) 2013, *General Assembly* Heidelberg (Germany) 2012. **Publications** *ESVDC Newsletter*. **Members** Full; Associate: Membership countries not specified. **IGO Relations** *European Commission (EC, #06633)*. **NGO Relations** Partner of: European Doctoral Programme in Career Guidance and Counselling (ECADOC); *Network for Innovation in Career Guidance and Counselling in Europe (NICE, #17038)*; national associations or corporations in career guidance.
[2015.09.26/XJ9319/**D**]

♦ **European Society of Women in Theological Research (ESWTR)** **08789**
Association européenne des femmes pour la recherche théologique (AFERT) – Europäische Gesellschaft für Theologische Forschung von Frauen – Asociación europea de mujeres pra la investigación teológica
Pres Inst für Systematische Theologie, Karl-Rahner-Platz 1, 6020 Innsbruck, Austria.
URL: http://www.eswtr.org/
History 1986, Boldern (Switzerland). Former names and other names: *Association oecuménique des femmes européennes en recherche théologique* – alias. **Aims** Build and maintain a network of European women who conduct research in theology and religious studies; support development of feminist theology and religious studies. **Structure** Board. **Languages** English, German, Spanish. **Staff** 7.00 FTE, voluntary. **Finance** Sources: fundraising; members' dues. **Activities** Events/meetings; networking/liaising; research/documentation. **Events** *Biennial International Conference* Oslo (Norway) 2022, *Central and Eastern European Conference* Ljubljana (Slovenia) 2021, *Biennial International Conference* Oslo (Norway) 2021, *Central and Eastern European Conference* Ljubljana (Slovenia) 2020, *Symposium* Vienna (Austria) 2020. **Publications** *Journal of the European Society of Women in Theological Research*.
Members Individuals in 32 countries:
Austria, Belgium, Bosnia-Herzegovina, Bulgaria, Canada, Croatia, Czechia, Denmark, Estonia, Finland, France, Georgia, Germany, Greece, Hungary, Iceland, Ireland, Italy, Latvia, Lithuania, Netherlands, Norway, Poland, Portugal, Romania, Russia, Spain, Sweden, Switzerland, UK, Ukraine, USA. [2021.09.02/XD2691/v/**D**]

♦ European Society for Wood Mechanics (inactive)
♦ European Sociobiological Society (inactive)

♦ **European Sociological Association (ESA)** **08790**
Main Office c/o FMSH, 54 blvd Raspail, Bureau P1-04, 75270 Paris CEDEX 06, France. E-mail: esa@europeansociology.org.
URL: http://www.europeansociology.org/
History 1995, Budapest (Hungary). Founded at 2nd conference, when statutes were adopted; a Steering Committee having been set up at 1st conference, 1992, Vienna (Austria). Registration: SIRET, No/ID: 484 990 825 00024, France. **Aims** Facilitate sociological research, teaching and communication on European issues; give sociology a voice in European affairs. **Structure** General Assembly (every 2 years); Executive Committee; Council of National Associations; Council of Research Networks; Research Networks (37). **Languages** English. **Staff** 2.00 FTE, paid. **Finance** Members' dues. **Activities** Research/documentation; training/education; advocacy/lobbying/activism; events/meetings; publishing activities. **Events** *Conference* 2023, *Midterm Conference* Tampere (Finland) 2022, *Conference* Barcelona (Spain) 2021, *Midterm Conference* Jyväskylä (Finland) 2021, *Midterm Conference* Tampere (Finland) 2021. **Publications** *ESA Monthly Bulletin* (12 a year); *European Societies* (5 a year) – journal; *European Journal of Cultural and Political Sociology* (4 a year); *European Sociologist* (2 a year) – newsletter. *Studies in European Societies* – book series. Conference papers. Information Services: E-mail discussion list. **Members** Regular; Student; Institutions; National Associations in 58 countries. Membership countries not specified. **NGO Relations** Member of: *Asian Thermal Spray Society (ATSS, #01768)*. Instrumental in setting up: *Regional Network on Southern European Societies (see: #08790)*. [2021/XD5607/v/**D**]

♦ European Sociology Students' Association (inactive)

♦ **European Soda Ash Producers Association (ESAPA)** **08791**
Contact c/o CEFIC, Rue Belliard 40, Box 15, 1040 Brussels, Belgium. E-mail: pvd@cefic.be – mail@cefic.be.
URL: http://www.esapa.eu/
History as a sector group of *Conseil européen de l'industrie chimique (CEFIC, #04687)*. **Events** *World Conference* Cannes (France) 2019.
Members Soda ash producers in 7 countries:
Belgium, France, Germany, Poland, Romania, Türkiye, UK. [2019/XE2172/**E**]

♦ **European Softball Federation (ESF)** **08792**
SG Pardess 229, 38830 Maor, Israel. E-mail: office@wbsceurope.org.
Communications Dir address not obtained.
URL: http://www.europeansoftball.org/
History 1976, Rome (Italy). Founded by representatives of national baseball and softball federations of Belgium, France, Italy, Germany, Netherlands and Spain. Since 2019, a judicial organization within *World Baseball Softball Confederation Europe (WBSC Europe, #21223)*. **Aims** Promote and develop softball in Europe. **Structure** General Congress; Executive Council. **Languages** English. **Staff** 1.00 FTE, paid; 9.00 FTE, voluntary. **Finance** Members' dues. Competition fees. **Activities** Sporting activities; training/education. **Events** *Joint Congress* Vilnius (Lithuania) 2020, *Joint Congress* Athens (Greece) 2019, *Joint Congress* Paris (France) 2018, *Joint Congress* Belgrade (Serbia) 2017, *Joint Congress* Hoofddorp (Netherlands) 2016. **Publications** *ESF Newsletter* (6 a year).
Members Affiliated national associations in 33 countries and territories:
Austria, Belgium, Bulgaria, Croatia, Czechia, Denmark, Finland, France, Germany, Great Britain, Greece, Guernsey, Hungary, Ireland, Israel, Italy, Jersey, Lithuania, Malta, Netherlands, Norway, Poland, Romania, Russia, San Marino, Serbia, Slovakia, Slovenia, Spain, Sweden, Switzerland, Türkiye, Ukraine.
IGO Relations None. [2022/XD7532/**E**]

♦ European Software Association (inactive)
♦ European Software Engineering Conference (meeting series)
♦ European Software Institute / see Tecnalia Research and Innovation Foundation
♦ European Software Institute / see ESI Center Eastern Europe
♦ European Softwood Federation (inactive)

♦ **European Soil Bureau (ESB)** **08793**
Head TP122, JRC, Via E Fermi, 21020 Ispra MB, Italy. T. +39332785349. Fax +39332789936.
URL: http://eusoils.jrc.ec.europa.eu/
History 1996, as as a network of national soil science institutions, managed through a permanent Secretariat. Also known as *European Soil Bureau Network (ESBN)*. **Events** *International meeting on soil with Mediterranean type of climate* Valenzano (Italy) 2001. [2019.10.17/XD6662/**D**]

♦ European Soil Bureau Network / see European Soil Bureau (#08793)
♦ European Solar Energy Organization / see EUROSOLAR – European Association for Renewable Energy (#09183)
♦ European Solar Industry Federation / see Solar Heat Europe (#19674)

♦ **European Solar Shading Organization (ES-SO)** **08794**
SG Vilvoordelaan 126, 1930 Zaventem, Belgium. T. +3223139944. E-mail: info@es-so.com.
URL: http://www.es-so.com/
History 2005. Registration: Belgium; EU Transparency Register, No/ID: 744314031180-93. **Aims** Defend, promote and support the interests of the European solar shading and roller shutter industry; promote contacts between members and European authorities. **Structure** General Assembly; Board of Directors.
Members Full National organizations in 12 countries:
Austria, Belgium, Czechia, Finland, France, Germany, Italy, Netherlands, Norway, Sweden, Switzerland, UK.
Associate in 5 countries:
Cyprus, Denmark, Ireland, Norway, Spain.
Supporting in 3 countries:
Greece, UK, USA.
NGO Relations Member of (2): *Active House Alliance (#00100); European Forum for Renewable Energy Sources (EUFORES, #07329).* Supporting member of: *Federation of European Heating, Ventilation and Air-Conditioning Associations (REHVA, #09507).* [2016/XM2552/**D**]

♦ **European Solar Thermal Electricity Association (ESTELA)** **08795**
SG Rue de l'Industrie 10, 1000 Brussels, Belgium. T. +3228932596. E-mail: contact@estelasolar.org.
URL: http://www.estelasolar.org/
History 1 Jun 2007. Registration: Belgium; EU Transparency Register, No/ID: 347776811076-78. **Aims** Support the European solar thermal electricity industry for the generation of green power in Europe. **Structure** General Assembly (annual); Executive Committee. **Languages** English. **Staff** 3.00 FTE, paid; 1.00 FTE, voluntary. **Finance** Sources: members' dues. **Activities** Events/meetings; research/documentation. **Events** *General Assembly* Brussels (Belgium) 2022, *General Assembly* Brussels (Belgium) 2021, *General Assembly* Brussels (Belgium) 2020, *General Assembly* Brussels (Belgium) 2019, *General Assembly* Brussels (Belgium) 2018. **Publications** Leaflet.
Members Full; Associate National. Companies and organizations in 7 countries:
Belgium, Cyprus, France, Germany, Italy, Spain, UK.
NGO Relations Member of (1): *European Forum for Renewable Energy Sources (EUFORES, #07329).* Instrumental in setting up (1): *World Solar Thermal Electricity Association (STELA-World, #21817).* [2022.05.16/XM3430/**D**]

♦ European Solar Thermal Industry Federation / see Solar Heat Europe (#19674)
♦ European Solidarity towards Equal Participation of People / see Europe External Programme with Africa (#09155)
♦ European Solid Board Organization (inactive)
♦ European Solid Fuels' Association / see European Association for Coal and Lignite (#05978)
♦ European Solid-State Circuits Conference / see ESSDERC/ESSCIRC Steering Committee (#05548)
♦ European Solid-State Device Research Conference / see ESSDERC/ESSCIRC Steering Committee (#05548)
♦ European Solid State Device Research Conference (meeting series)

♦ **European Solvents Industry Group (ESIG)** **08796**
SG c/o CEFIC, Rue Belliard 40, Bte 15, 1040 Brussels, Belgium. E-mail: esig@cefic.be.
Assistant address not obtained.
URL: https://www.esig.org/
History 1996, Brussels (Belgium). **Aims** Promote safe and sustainable use of oxygenated and hydrocarbon solvents in Europe; ensure the regulatory framework relevant to the manufacture, storage, distribution and application of these solvents is based on sound science and best practice. **Structure** Steering Committee; Task Forces (4). **Languages** English. **Staff** 4.00 FTE, paid. **Finance** Sources: members' dues. **Activities** Advocacy/lobbying/activism; awards/prizes/competitions; guidance/assistance/consulting; politics/policy/regulatory; projects/programmes; training/education. **Publications** *Solutions Newsletter* (2 a year) in English. Fact sheets; best practice guidelines; brochures; posters; videos; news; contacts
Members Companies (24) in 12 countries:
Belgium, Finland, France, Germany, Greece, Italy, Netherlands, South Africa, Spain, Sweden, Switzerland, UK.
NGO Relations Close links with: *Conseil européen de l'industrie chimique (CEFIC, #04687)* through *Hydrocarbon Solvents Producers Association (HSPA, #10997)* and *Oxygenated Solvents Producers Association (OSPA, #17923).* [2022.05.04/XE4122/t/**E**]

♦ European Sound Directors' Association (no recent information)
♦ European Southern Observatory / see European Organization for Astronomical Research in the Southern hemisphere (#08106)

♦ **European Southern Observatory Staff Association (ESO Staff Association)** **08797**
Pres Karl-Scharzschil Str 2, 85748 Garching, Germany. T. +4989320060. Fax +49893202362. E-mail: information@eso.org – isce@eso.org.
Santiago Office Alonso de Córdova 3107, Vitacura, Casilla 19001, Santiago, Santiago Metropolitan, Chile. E-mail: contacto@eso.org.
URL: http://www.eso.org/
History to represent staff of *European Organization for Astronomical Research in the Southern hemisphere (ESO, #08106).* **NGO Relations** Associate status with: *Federation of International Civil Servants' Associations (FICSA, #09603).* [2022.02.10/XE2807/**E**]

♦ **European Space Agency (ESA)** **08798**
Agence spatiale européenne – Organismo Espacial Europeo
Dir Gen c/o ESA HQ Bertrand, 24 rue du Général Bertrand, CS 30798, 75345 Paris CEDEX 7, France. T. +33153697654. Fax +33153697560. E-mail: media@esa.int – contactesa@esa.int.
Headquarters / Communications c/o ESA HQ Dauemsnil, 52 rue Jacques Hillairet, 75012 Paris, France.
URL: http://www.esa.int/
History 31 May 1975. Established when came into 'de facto' operation on signature of the ESA Convention, following meeting of ministers of 10 European countries, Jul 1973, Brussels (Belgium). Came into existence 'de jure' on ratification of the ESA Convention, 30 Oct 1980, by 11 European countries: Belgium; Denmark; France; Germany FR; Ireland; Italy; Netherlands; Spain; Sweden; Switzerland; UK. Austria and Norway subsequently became associate member states, becoming full members on 1 Jan 1987. Finland became an associate member on 1 Jan 1987, and a full member from 1 Jan 1995. Portugal joined later. Ties exist with Canada under an agreement signed Dec 1981 and renewed in May 1989.
/Preceding organizations/: *European Space Vehicle Launcher Development Organization (ELDO, inactive)* – also referred to as *'Centre européen pour la mise au point et la construction des lanceurs d'engins spatiaux (CECLES)'* – whose Convention entered into force on 28 Feb 1964, and *European Space Research Organization (ESRO, inactive)* – also referred to as *'Centre européen de recherches spatiales (CERS)'* – whose Convention entered into force on 20 Mar 1964. ELDO and ESRO were provided for under a Convention signed 14 Jun 1962, Paris (France), which also came into force 20 Mar 1964. The ESA Convention resulted in the termination of the ELDO and ESRO Conventions. Prior to ELDO/ESRO, a *European Preparatory Commission for Space Research – Commission préparatoire européenne pour la recherche spatiale (COPERS),* had been set up at an Intergovernmental Conference, 1 Dec 1960, Meyrin (Switzerland). *European Space Conference (ECS, inactive)* was formed in 1966. *European Conference on Satellite Communications (CETS, inactive),* convened for the first time in May 1963, ceased activity in 1970.
Statutes registered in *'UNTS 1/215241'.*
Aims Shape the development of Europe's space capability and ensure that investment in space continues to deliver benefits to the citizens of Europe and the world. **Structure** Council (policy-making body) comprises representatives of member states, each state having 1 vote (only states participating in an optional programme may vote on that programme). Council may also meet at ministerial level. Committees (5): Science Programme; Administrative and Finance; International Relations; Industrial Policy; Security. Specialized Boards oversee management of specific ESA programmes. Council appoints Director General for 4-year term as chief executive and legal representative of the Agency, who is assisted by: 10 Directors – Earth Observation (EOP); Technical and Quality Management (TEC); Launcher (LAU); Human Spaceflight; Resources Management (RES); Legal Affairs and External Relations; Science and Robotic Exploration; Telecommunications and Integrated Applications; Galileo Programme and Navigation-related Activities; Operations and Infrastructure. Programme Boards (6): Satellite Communications; Earth Observation; Launchers; Human Spaceflight, Microgravity and Exploration; Navigation; Space Situational Awareness. Head of Cabinet. Headquarters in Paris (France). Establishments and sites: *European Space Research and Technology Centre (ESTEC, #08802); European Space Operations Centre (ESOC, #08800); ESRIN (#05546); European Space Security and Education Centre (ESEC); European Centre for Space Applications and Telecommunications (ECSAT).* Offices: Brussels (Belgium); Moscow (Russia); Washington DC (USA). **Languages** English, French, German. **Staff** About 2,200 from all Member States. **Finance** Mandatory activities (space science programmes and general budget) are financed by a financial contribution from all Member States, calculated in accordance with each country's gross national product. In addition, ESA conducts a number of optional programmes. Each Member State decides in which optional programme they with to participate and the amount they wish to contribute. ESA operates on the basis of geographical return – it invests in each Member State, through industrial contracts for space programmes, an amount more or less equivalent to each country's contribution.
Activities ESA activities are defined in 'Article II, Purpose, Convention of establishment of a European Space Agency, SP-1271(E), 2003' which states:
– ESA's purpose shall be to provide for, and to promote, for exclusively peaceful purposes, cooperation among European States in space research and technology and their space applications, with a view to their being used for scientific purposes and for operational space applications systems: by elaborating and implementing a long-term European space policy, by recommending space objectives to the Member States, and by concerting the policies of the Member States with respect to other national and international organisations and institutions; by elaborating and implementing activities and programmes in the space field; by coordinating the European space programme and national programmes, and by integrating the latter progressively and as completely as possible into the European space programme, in particular as regards the development of applications satellites; by elaborating and implementing the industrial policy appropriate to its programme and by recommending a coherent industrial policy to the Member States.
Events *Joint Hinode 16 and IRIS 13 Meeting* Niigata (Japan) 2023, *Symposium on Space Educational Activities (SSEA)* Barcelona (Spain) 2022, *HiSST – International Conference on High-Speed Vehicle Science and Technology* Bruges (Belgium) 2022, *European Big Science Business Forum* Granada (Spain) 2022, *Joint Hinode 15 and IRIS 12 Meeting* Prague (Czech Rep) 2022. **Publications** *On Station* (4 a year) – newsletter; *ESA Bulletin* (4 a year); *Preparing for the Future* (4 a year) – newsletter; *Reaching for the Skies* (4 a year) – newsletter; *ECSL News.* Monographs; scientific and technical reports; proceedings of symposia, conferences and workshops.
Members Member States (22):
Austria, Belgium, Czechia, Denmark, Estonia, Finland, France, Germany, Greece, Hungary, Ireland, Italy, Luxembourg, Netherlands, Norway, Poland, Portugal, Romania, Spain, Sweden, Switzerland, UK.
Associate Member:
Slovenia.
Cooperation agreements (7):
Bulgaria, Croatia, Cyprus, Latvia, Lithuania, Malta, Slovakia.
Cooperation agreement for some projects:
Canada.
IGO Relations Accredited to the Conference of the Parties of: *Secretariat of the United Nations Convention to Combat Desertification (Secretariat of the UNCCD, #19208).* Cooperation agreement with: *International Maritime Organization (IMO, #14102).* Accredited by: *United Nations Framework Convention on Climate Change – Secretariat (UNFCCC, #20564).* Cooperates with: *Committee on the Peaceful Uses of Outer Space (COPUOS, #04277); European Commission (EC, #06633); European Parliament (EP, #08146); European Telecommunications Satellite Organization (EUTELSAT IGO, #08896); International Telecommunication Union (ITU, #15673); Joint Research Centre (JRC, #16147); Statistical Office of the European Union (Eurostat, #19974); UNESCO (#20322); United Nations Institute for Training and Research (UNITAR, #20576).*
NGO Relations Observer to: *European Umbrella Organization for Geographical Information (EUROGI, #08964).* Cooperates with: *Committee on Earth Observation Satellites (CEOS, #04249); Earth Observation International Coordination Working Group (EO-ICWG, no recent information); Inter-Agency Space Debris Coordination Committee (IADC, #11392); Space Agency Forum (SAF, no recent information); Strasbourg Astronomical Data Centre (#20003).* Sponsors: *International Space University (ISU, #15575).* Founding member of: *European Space Policy Institute (ESPI, #08801).*
Member of:
– *Alliance for Permanent Access (#00712);*
– *Asia-Pacific Regional Space Agency Forum (APRSAF, #02010);*
– *Association for Human Resources Management in International Organizations (AHRMIO, #02634);*
– *DVB Project (#05147);*
– *EIROforum (#05401);*
– *Eurisy (#05625);*
– *European Meteorological Society (EMS, #07786);*
– *European Telecommunications Standards Institute (ETSI, #08897);*
– *International Committee on Technical Interchange for Space Mission Operations (SpaceOps, #12808);*
– *International Council for Film, Television and Audiovisual Communication (IFTC, #13022).*
Associate member of: *GÉANT Association (#10086).* Memorandum of Understanding with: *Association of European Space Industry (EUROSPACE, #02544); Global Satellite Operators' Association (GSOA, #10586).* [2021/XD0868/**D***]

♦ European Space Association (inactive)

♦ **European Space Astronomy Centre (ESAC)** **08799**
Contact PO Box 78, Villanueva de la Cañada, 28691 Madrid, Spain. T. +34918131100. Fax +34918131139.
Street Address ESA, Camino bajo del Castillo s/n, Urbanizacion Villafranca del Castillo, Villanueva de la Cañada, 28692 Madrid, Spain.
URL: http://www.esa.int/esaMI/ESAC/
History Founded as a Telemetry, Tracking and Commanding (TT and C) station of *European Space Agency (ESA, #08798).* Subsequently became an ESA Centre. **Aims** Act as the centre of ESA's space-telescope and planetary missions, the place from where science operations are conducted, and where all of the scientific data produced are archived and made publically accessible. **Events** *Data Analysis and Statistics Workshop* Madrid (Spain) 2019, *XMM-NEWTON Science Workshop* Madrid (Spain) 2019, *Data Analysis and Statistics Workshop* Madrid (Spain) 2017, *XMM-NEWTON Science Workshop* Madrid (Spain) 2016, *XMM-NEWTON Science Workshop* Madrid (Spain) 2015. [2011/XJ4714/**E***]

♦ **European Space Operations Centre (ESOC)** **08800**
Centre européen d'opérations spatiales – Europäisches Satelittenkontrollzentrum
Communication Office Robert-Bosch-Strasse 5, 64293 Darmstadt, Germany. T. +496151902000. E-mail: esoc.communication@esa.int.
Main Website: http://www.esa.int/SPECIALS/ESOC/
History 8 Sep 1967, Germany FR. One of 5 establishments of *European Space Agency (ESA, #08798),* being part of ESA's Directorate of Operations and Infrastructure. Former names and other names: *Europäisches Weltraum-Operationszentrum* – former. **Aims** Serve as the satellite control centre for ESA, with responsibility for the operation of all ESA satellites missions, as well as for development and maintenance of worldwide ground stations and communication network. **Structure** *'Directorate of Human Spaceflight and Operations';* ISS Exploitation Programme; Departments (6). **Languages** English, French, German. **Staff** 270.00 FTE, paid. Contractors – 600. **Finance** Governments of Member States within ESA budget. **Activities** Advocacy/lobbying/activism; monitoring/evaluation. **Events** *European Conference on Space Debris* Darmstadt (Germany) 2013, *International Conference on Space Operations / SpaceOps Conference* Stockholm (Sweden) 2012, *European conference on space debris* Darmstadt (Germany) 2009, *SpaceOps Conference* Heidelberg (Germany) 2007, *International symposium on space flight dynamics* Darmstadt (Germany) 1997. **Publications** None.
Members Member States of the European Space Agency (ESA) (22):
Austria, Belgium, Czechia, Denmark, Estonia, Finland, France, Germany, Greece, Hungary, Ireland, Italy, Luxembourg, Netherlands, Norway, Poland, Portugal, Romania, Spain, Sweden, Switzerland, UK.
Cooperation agreement with ESA (7):
Bulgaria, Canada, Croatia, Cyprus, Lithuania, Malta, Slovakia.
Associate Members (2):
Latvia, Slovenia.
NGO Relations Member of (1): *Consultative Committee for Space Data Systems (CCSDS, #04764).* [2022.10.11/XE7412/**E***]

♦ **European Space Policy Institute (ESPI)** **08801**

Dir Schwarzenbergplatz 6, 1030 Vienna, Austria. T. +43171811180. Fax +431718111899. E-mail: office@espi.or.at.
Treas address not obtained.
URL: http://www.espi.or.at/

History Registration: Austria; EU Transparency Register, No/ID: 036412124178-16. **Aims** Carry out studies and research to provide decision-makers with an independent view on mid- to long-term issues relevant to the governance of space. **Structure** General Assembly; Advisory Council; Secretariat, with Director leading the Institute and Treasurer responsible for administration and finance. **Languages** English. **Staff** 16.00 FTE, paid. **Finance** Sources: government support. Supported by: *European Space Agency (ESA, #08798)*. **Activities** Events/meetings; research/documentation. **Events** *Autumn Conference* Vienna (Austria) 2022, *Autumn Conference* Vienna (Austria) 2021, *Autumn Conference* Vienna (Austria) 2020, *Autumn Conference* Vienna (Austria) 2019, *Autumn Conference* Vienna (Austria) 2018. **Publications** *ESPI Perspectives*; *ESPI Reports*. Book series; studies; specials and memoranda; presentations; articles by staff.
Members Space agencies, space industry and space operators (15) in 7 countries:
Austria, Belgium, France, Germany, Italy, Norway, Romania.
Regional member:
Consultative Status Consultative status granted from: *ECOSOC (#05331)* (Special). **IGO Relations** Observer status with: *Committee on the Peaceful Uses of Outer Space (COPUOS, #04277)* of the United Nations. Observer member of: *International Committee on Global Navigation Satellite Systems (ICG, #12775)*. **NGO Relations** Member of (1): *European Network of Independent Non-Proliferation Think Tanks (EU Non-Proliferation Network, #07930)*. Partner of (1): *Eurisy (#05625)*. [2022/XM2800/j/**E**]

♦ European Space Research Institute / see ESRIN (#05546)
♦ European Space Research Organization / see European Space Research and Technology Centre (#08802)
♦ European Space Research Organization (inactive)

♦ **European Space Research and Technology Centre (ESTEC)** **08802**

Centre européen de recherche et de technologie spatiales

Communications Office PO Box 299, 2200 AG Noordwijk, Netherlands. T. +31715656565. Fax +31715656040. E-mail: estecpr@esa.int.
Street Address Keplerlaan 1, 2200 AG Noordwijk, Netherlands.
URL: http://www.esa.int/

History 1967, as *European Space Technology Centre – Centre européen de technologie spatiale*, on the entry into force of convention establishing the *European Space Research Organization (ESRO) – Organisation européenne de recherches spatiales (OERS)*, and pursuant to a resolution adopted at the Conference of Plenipotentiaries, 14 Jun 1962, Paris (France), and amended by ESRO Council on 22 Oct 1964. Agreement for establishment of the Centre in the Netherlands signed 2 Feb 1967, The Hague (Netherlands), confirmed 1 Jul 1967, Paris. A new convention, signed 31 May 1975, setting up *European Space Agency (ESA, #08798)*, resulted in the termination of the ESRO convention. ESTEC is therefore currently not an autonomous entity but the largest establishment of ESA. **Aims** Develop and manage all types of ESA missions; provide all managerial and technical competences and facilities needed to initiate and manage development of space systems and technologies; operate an environmental test centre for spacecraft, with supporting engineering laboratories specialized in systems engineering, components and materials; support European space industry.
Structure Reporting to Directors based at ESTEC:
'Directorate of Technical and Quality Management' Inspector General and 4 Departments: Mechanical Engineering; Electrical Engineering; Product Assurance and Safety; Systems, Software and Technology. *'Directorate of Human Spaceflight and Operations'*, containing *European Astronaut Centre (EAC, #06287)* and 4 Departments: Transportation and Human Exploration; ISS Programme; ISS Utilization; ATV Production. *'Directorate of Telecommunications and Integrated Applications'*, containing 3 departments: Integrated and Telecom Related Applications; Telecom Satellite Programmes; Telecommunication Technologies Product and System.
Reporting to Directors not based at ESTEC:
'Directorate of Operations and Infrastructure', containing ESTEC Informatics and Facilities Division and 2 departments: Ground Systems Engineering; Human Spaceflight Operations. *'Directorate of Science and Robotic Exploration'*, containing 3 departments: Science Operations; Science and Robotic Explorations Projects; Research and Scientific Support. *'Directorate of Earth Observation Programmes'*, containing Earth Observation Projects Department. *'Directorate of Legal Affairs and External Relations'*, containing Education and Knowledge Management Office. *'Directorate of the Galileo Programme and Navigation Related Activities'*, containing Galileo Operations and Evolution Department.
Staff 1250.00 FTE, paid. **Activities** Projects/programmes. **Events** *ESLAB : European Space Research Laboratory Symposium* Leiden (Netherlands) 2016, *Asteroids, Comets and Meteors Conferennce* Helsinki (Finland) 2014, *ESLAB : European Space Research Laboratory Symposium* Noordwijkerhout (Netherlands) 2014, *Workshop on Star Formation across Space and Time* Noordwijkerhout (Netherlands) 2014, *European Space Cryogenics Workshop* Noordwijk (Netherlands) 2013. **Members** Member States of the European Space Agency (ESA). **IGO Relations** *Joint Research Centre (JRC, #16147)*. **NGO Relations** Together with Joint Research Centre, proposes setting up: *European Network for Large Microwave Measurement Facilities (no recent information)*. Member of: *Asia-Pacific Regional Space Agency Forum (APRSAF, #02010)*. [2019.10.17/XE7353/**E***]

♦ European Space Sciences Committee (see: #08441)
♦ European Space Technology Centre / see European Space Research and Technology Centre (#08802)

♦ **European Space Tribology Laboratory (ESTL)** **08803**

Contact ESR Technology, 202 Cavendish Place, Birchwood Park, Warrington, WA3 6WU, UK. T. +441925843400. Fax +441925843500. E-mail: estl@esrtechnology.com.
URL: http://www.esrtechnology.com/

History 1972. **Aims** Provide solutions to friction, wear and lubrication issues in precision mechanisms for operation in the vacuum environment of space and terrestrial systems. **Activities** Training/education. [2017/XF2161/**F**]

♦ European Space Vehicle Launcher Development Organization (inactive)
♦ European Spaceward Association (unconfirmed)

♦ **European Spallation Source ERIC (ESS)** **08804**

Dir Gen PO Box 176, SE-221 00 Lund, Sweden. T. +46468883000. E-mail: info@ess.eu.
Communications Manager Partikelgatan 2, SE-224 84 Lund, Sweden.
URL: http://ess.eu

History Founded when ESS Council was formed. Decision to build ESS in Lund (Sweden), 28 May 2009. Construction on site began 2 Sep 2014. Since 1 Oct 2015, a *European Research Infrastructure Consortium (ERIC)*. The project entered Initial Operations in 2019, and expects to be fully operational in 2027. Former names and other names: *European Spallation Source Project* – former (1993). Registration: EU Transparency Register, No/ID: 976366017165-64. **Aims** Become a multi-scientific facility for advanced research and industrial development using neutrons by operating the world's most powerful spallation source. **Structure** Council; Committees (4). **Languages** English. **Staff** 520.00 FTE, paid. **Activities** Active in: Denmark, Sweden. **Events** *European Big Science Business Forum* Granada (Spain) 2022, *European Big Science Business Forum* Granada (Spain) 2021, *European Big Science Business Forum* Granada (Spain) 2020, *In-Kind Contributions Meeting for Neutron Science* Paris (France) 2018, *IPAC : International Particle Accelerator Conference* Copenhagen (Denmark) 2017.
Members 13 countries:
Czechia, Denmark, Estonia, France, Germany, Hungary, Italy, Norway, Poland, Spain, Sweden, Switzerland, UK.
NGO Relations Member of (1): *High Energy Physics Technology Transfer Network (HEPTech, #10914)*. [2022.05.10/XE4582/**E**]

♦ European Spallation Source Project / see European Spallation Source ERIC (#08804)

♦ **European Spas Association (ESPA)** **08805**

Association européenne du thermalisme et du climatisme (AETC) – Asociación Europea de Estaciones Termales (AEDET) – Europäischer Heilbäderverband (EHV) – Associazione Europea del Termalismo e Climatismo (AETC) – Europese Vereniging van het Kuurwezen (EVK)

Pres c/o DELFINE SA, Rue de Crayer 7, 1000 Brussels, Belgium. E-mail: office@europeanspas.eu.
SG address not obtained.
URL: http://www.europeanspas.eu/

History Nov 1995, Brussels (Belgium). Registration: No/ID: 0463.412.055, Start date: 4 Jun 1998, Belgium; EU Transparency Register, No/ID: 719955636256-02, Start date: 17 Oct 2019. **Aims** Promote spa *medicine* as a curative and preventive approach. **Structure** Board. **Languages** English, German. **Staff** 1.00 FTE, paid. **Finance** Sources: members' dues. **Activities** Monitoring/evaluation; knowledge management/information dissemination; advocacy/lobbying/activism; networking/liaising; training/education; awards/prizes/competitions; events/meetings. **Events** *Annual Congress* Piestany (Slovakia) 2022, *Think Green – Be Active – Stay Healthy* Moravske Toplice (Slovenia) 2021, *Annual Congress* Tuheljske Toplice (Croatia) 2019, *Annual Congress* Sopot (Poland) 2015, *Annual Congress* Vejle (Denmark) 2014. **Publications** *ESPA e-Newsletter*. *Epidemiological Survey on Balneotherapy (2017-2020)*. Information Services: E-library about research in balneology.
Members Full: national spas and balneology associations in 19 countries:
Bulgaria, Croatia, Czechia, Denmark, Estonia, France, Germany, Hungary, Iceland, Italy, Latvia, Lithuania, Luxembourg, Netherlands, Romania, Serbia, Slovakia, Slovenia, Spain.
Advisory members in 4 countries:
China, France, Germany, USA.
NGO Relations Member of (1): *European Tourism Manifesto (#08921)*. [2022/XD6665/**D**]

♦ **European Spatial Data Research (EuroSDR)** **08806**

SG KU Leuven Public Governance Inst, Parkstraat 45 box 3609, 3000 Leuven, Belgium. T. +3216323134. E-mail: eurosdr@kuleuven.be.
URL: http://www.eurosdr.net/

History 12 Oct 1953, Paris (France). Founded in accordance with recommendations of the Council of the then *Organization for European Economic Cooperation (OEEC, inactive)*, currently *OECD (#17693)*. Statutes amended 27 Oct 1994, at 85th meeting of OEEPE Steering Committee. Former names and other names: *European Organization for Experimental Photogrammetric Research (OEEPE)* – former. Registration: Start date: 17 Jun 2005, Ireland. **Aims** Link national mapping and cadastral agencies with research institutes and universities in Europe for the purpose of applied research in spatial data provision, management and delivery. **Structure** General Assembly; Board of Delegates; Executive Management Team; Commissions; Secretariat. **Languages** English. **Finance** Sources: members' dues. **Activities** Events/meetings; knowledge management/information dissemination; monitoring/evaluation; research/documentation; standards/guidelines; training/education. **Publications** Annual Report; research reports; workshop reports.
Members Full in 19 countries:
Austria, Belgium, Croatia, Cyprus, Denmark, Estonia, Finland, France, Germany, Ireland, Netherlands, Norway, Poland, Portugal, Slovenia, Spain, Sweden, Switzerland, UK.
NGO Relations Partner of (4): *Association of Geographic Information Laboratories for Europe (AGILE, #02622)*; *EuroGeographics (#05684)*; *Open Geospatial Consortium (OGC, #17752)*; *Unmanned Vehicle Systems International (UVS International, #20708)*. Regional member of: *International Society for Photogrammetry and Remote Sensing (ISPRS, #15362)*. [2022.02.18/XD1410/**D**]

♦ European Spatial Planning Observation Network / see European Observation Network on Territorial Development and Cohesion (#08070)
♦ European Spatial Planning Observatory Network / see European Observation Network on Territorial Development and Cohesion (#08070)

♦ **European Special Glass Association (ESGA)** **08807**

Regulatory Advisor Av Louise 89 – Bte 5, 1050 Brussels, Belgium. T. +3225384446. Fax +3225378469.
Pres address not obtained.

History 1999. Registration: No/ID: 0474.161.140, Start date: 15 Jan 1999, Belgium; EU Transparency Register, No/ID: 053892115799-18, Start date: 28 Jan 2015. **Aims** Act as a forum to discuss specific problems to special glass manufacturing regarding EU legislation. **Languages** English, French, German. **Staff** 0.50 FTE, paid.
Members Special glass manufacturers in 3 countries:
France, Germany, Italy.
NGO Relations Member of (2): *Glass Alliance Europe (#10156)*; *Industry4Europe (#11181)*. [2019/XD7446/**D**]

♦ **European Specialist Nurses Organisation (ESNO)** **08808**

Exec Dir Rue Belliard 15-17, 6th floor, 1040 Brussels, Belgium. E-mail: secretariat@esno.org.
URL: http://www.esno.org/

History Former names and other names: *European Specialist Nurses Organization* – former; *European Specialist Nursing Organization* – former. Registration: Netherlands; EU Transparency Register, No/ID: 70183498905-52. **Aims** Strengthen the status and practice of the profession of nursing and the interests of nurses in Europe. **Languages** English. **Finance** Members' dues. **Events** *Congress* Brussels (Belgium) 2023, *Congress* Brussels (Belgium) 2022, *Congress* Brussels (Belgium) 2021, *Congress* Brussels (Belgium) 2020, *Congress* Brussels (Belgium) 2019.
Members National organizations. Membership countries not specified. International organizations (13):
International organizations (13):
Association for Common European Nursing Diagnoses, Interventions and Outcomes (ACENDIO, #02437); *European Alliance of Associations for Rheumatology (EULAR, #05862)* (Nurses Section); *European Association of Urology Nurses (EAUN, #06265)*; *European Dialysis and Transplant Nurses Association – European Renal Care Association (EDTNA/ERCA, #06918)*; *European Federation of Critical Care Nursing Associations (EfCCNa, #07094)*; *European Federation of Educators in Nursing Sciences (FINE, #07102)*; *European Nurse Directors Association (ENDA, #08060)*; *European Oncology Nursing Society (EONS, #08086)*; *European Operating Room Nurses Association (EORNA, #08087)*; *European Respiratory Nurses Association (ERNA, no recent information)*; *European Society of Endocrinology (ESE, #08594)* (Nurses' Group); *European Society of Gastroenterology and Endoscopy Nurses and Associates (ESGENA, #08604)*; *International Federation of Nurse Anesthetists (IFNA, #13492)*.
IGO Relations Partner of: *European Medicines Agency (EMA, #07767)*. **NGO Relations** Member of: *European Public Health Alliance (EPHA, #08297)*; *Health First Europe (HFE, #10881)*. Endorses: *Steering Group on Influenza Vaccination (#19980)*. [2020/XM1042/y/**D**]

♦ European Specialist Nurses Organization / see European Specialist Nurses Organisation (#08808)
♦ European Specialist Nursing Organization / see European Specialist Nurses Organisation (#08808)

♦ **European Specialist Printing Manufacturers Associations (ESMA)** . **08809**

CEO Kraasbeekstraat 3, 3390 Tielt-Winge, Belgium. T. +3216894353. E-mail: info@esma.com.
URL: http://www.esma.com/

History 29 May 1990, Frankfurt-Main (Germany). Former names and other names: *European Screen Printing Manufacturers Associations (ESMA)* – former; *Association des fabricants européens pour la sérigraphie* – former; *Europäische Siebdruck-Herstellerverband* – former. Registration: Banque-Carrefour des Entreprises, No/ID: 0887.979.075, Start date: 14 Mar 2007, Belgium; EU Transparency Register, No/ID: 647034848426-96, Start date: 16 Dec 2022. **Aims** Promote adoption and correct use of various specialist printing processes. **Structure** General Assembly; Board; Working Committees. **Languages** Dutch, English, French, German. **Staff** 4.00 FTE, paid. **Finance** Sources: members' dues. Annual budget: 190,000 EUR. **Activities** Events/meetings; guidance/assistance/consulting; training/education. **Events** *GlassPrint Conference* Düsseldorf (Germany) 2023, *Industrial Print Integration Conference* Neuss (Germany) 2023, *Textile Printing and Sustainability Conference* Neuss (Germany) 2022, *Inkjet Conference* Düsseldorf (Germany) 2020, *Inkjet Conference* Düsseldorf (Germany) 2019.
Members Companies engaged in manufacturing machinery and consumables for the specialist printing industry, including screen, digital and pad printing processes. Members in 9 countries:

Austria, Belgium, France, Germany, Italy, Netherlands, Spain, Switzerland, UK.
NGO Relations Member of (1): *Federation of European and International Associations Established in Belgium (FAIB, #09508).* [2022.10.24/XD3508/**D**]

♦ European Specialist Sports Nutrition Alliance (ESSNA) **08810**
Contact Square de Meeûs 35, 1000 Brussels, Belgium. T. +3228953679.
URL: http://www.essna.com/
History Created 2003. EU Transparency Register: 507122115709-49. **Aims** Campaign for appropriate European legislation on sports nutrition products. **Structure** Officers; Secretariat. **Activities** Advocacy/lobbying/activism. **IGO Relations** Observer to: *Codex Alimentarius Commission (CAC, #04081).* [2018/XM6915/**D**]

♦ European Speciality Minerals Association (ESMA) **08811**
SG c/o IMA-Europe aisbl, Rue des Deux Eglises 26, Box 2, 1000 Brussels, Belgium. T. +3222104410. E-mail: secretariat@ima-europe.eu.
URL: http://www.ima-europe.eu/
Languages English. **Finance** Members' dues. **NGO Relations** Member of: *Industrial Minerals Association – Europe (IMA Europe, #11179).* Cooperates with: *Calcium Carbonate Association – Europe (CCA-Europe, #03399); European Association of Feldspar Producers (EUROFEL, #06037); European Association of Industrial Silica Producers (EUROSIL, #06082); European Bentonite Producers Association (EUBA, #06328); European Borates Association (EBA, #06382); European Kaolin and Plastic Clays Association (KPC Europe, #07623); European Lime Association (EuLA, #07699); International Diatomite Producers Association (IDPA, #13172); Scientific Association of European Talc Industry (Eurotalc, #19146);* IMA-Europe. [2018.09.06/XM1743/**D**]

♦ European Speech Communication Association / see International Speech Communication Association (#15578)

♦ European Speech and Language Therapy Association (ESLA) **08812**
Chairperson Square Charles-Maurice Wiser 13, 1040 Brussels, Belgium. E-mail: esla@eslaeurope.eu – president@eslaeurope.eu.
Gen Sec address not obtained. E-mail: gen.sec@eslaeurope.eu.
URL: https://eslaeurope.eu/
History 6 Mar 1988, France. Former names and other names: *Standing Liaison Committee of Speech and Language Therapists /Logopedists of the European Union (LCSTL)* – former; *Permanent Liaison Committee of EU Speech and Language Therapists and Logopedists* – former (2021); *Comité permanent de liaison des orthophonistes-logopèdes de l'Union européenne (CPLOL)* – former (2021). Registration: Banque-Carrefour des Entreprises, No/ID: 0770.260.172, Start date: 24 Jun 2021, Belgium; EU Transparency Register, No/ID: 860047243984-52, Start date: 2 Sep 2021. **Aims** Represent member professional organizations to the European and international political, parliamentary and administrative authorities; promote coordination of conditions for the practice of speech and language therapy-logopedics; stimulate exchange of scientific knowledge and research; promote and develop harmonization of standards and quality of education; provide expert advice. **Structure** General Assembly (every 3 years); Board; Strategic Task Forces. **Languages** English, French. **Staff** 0.20 FTE, paid. Voluntary. **Finance** Sources: members' dues. **Activities** Events/meetings; guidance/assistance/consulting; knowledge management/information dissemination; politics/policy/regulatory; standards/guidelines. Active in all member countries. **Events** *Congress* Salzburg (Austria) 2022, *Congress* Bilbao (Spain) 2021, *Congress* Estoril (Portugal) 2018, *Congress* Florence (Italy) 2015, *Congress* The Hague (Netherlands) 2012. **Publications** *CPLOL Newsletter* in English, French. Newsletters; reports; congress proceedings; book; folders; leaflets; position statements; web based information; guidelines.
Members National associations (30), representing over 50,000 speech and language therapists in 27 countries:
Austria, Belgium, Bulgaria, Croatia, Cyprus, Denmark, Estonia, Finland, Greece, Hungary, Iceland, Ireland, Italy, Latvia, Lithuania, Luxembourg, Malta, Netherlands, Norway, Portugal, Romania, Slovakia, Slovenia, Sweden, Switzerland, Türkiye, UK.
NGO Relations Member of (1): *European Council of Liberal Professions (#06828)* (as Observer member). [2022/XD3904/**E**]

♦ European Speechwriter Network (ESN) **08813**
Contact 159 Windham Road, Bournemouth, BH1 4RG, UK. T. +447545232980. E-mail: info@europeanspeechwriters.org.
URL: http://www.europeanspeechwriters.org/
Aims Bring together international *communicators* to promote the profession of speechwriting. **Languages** English. **Staff** 1.00 FTE, paid. **Finance** Members' dues. **Activities** Events/meetings; training/education. **Events** *Conference* Cambridge (UK) 2022, *Conference* Cambridge (UK) 2020, *Conference* Oxford (UK) 2019, *Conference* Paris (France) 2019, *Conference* Helsinki (Finland) 2018. **Publications** *The Speechwriter* – electronic magazine. **Members** Individuals (over 400). Membership countries not specified. [2020.02.28/XM4595/**F**]

♦ European Speleological Federation (#09705)

♦ European Spice Association (ESA) **08814**
Contact Reuterstrasse 151, 53113 Bonn, Germany. T. +49228216162. Fax +49228229460. E-mail: esa@verbaendebuero.de.
URL: http://www.esa-spices.org/
History 1984. Registration: North Rhine-Westphalia District court, No/ID: VR 9162, Start date: 25 Feb 2010, Germany, Bonn; EU Transparency Register, No/ID: 404593641312-23, Start date: 8 Feb 2021. **Aims** Promote and protect the interest of members; ensure members are fully aware of all current and future legislation; act as a central medium of communication with the European Commission, European Parliament and the Confederation of the Food and Drink Industries of the EU. strengthen links with worldwide spice trade associations and non-governmental organizations. **Structure** General Assembly; Board; Technical Commission. **Languages** English. **Events** *General Assembly* Malmö (Sweden) 2021, *General Assembly* Malmö (Sweden) 2020, *General Assembly* Rotterdam (Netherlands) 2019, *Conference* Helsinki (Finland) 1999.
Members Full Organizations in 12 countries:
Austria, Belgium, Finland, France, Germany, Italy, Netherlands, Spain, Sweden, Switzerland, Türkiye, UK.
Full spice companies in 16 countries:
Belgium, Bulgaria, Denmark, Finland, France, Germany, Greece, Italy, Netherlands, Norway, Poland, Slovakia, Spain, Sweden, Türkiye, UK.
Associate associations in 2 countries:
Grenada, India.
Associate companies in 8 countries:
Egypt, Indonesia, Israel, Morocco, Switzerland, Uganda, USA, Vietnam.
NGO Relations Cooperates with: *International Organization for Standardization (ISO, #14473).* Member of: *FoodDrinkEurope (#09841); International Organization for Spice Trade Associations (IOSTA).* [2021/XD0667/**D**]

♦ European Spinal Cord Injury Federation (ESCIF) **08815**
Sec c/o Swiss Paraplegics Assn, Kantonstrasse 40, 6207 Nottwil LU, Switzerland. E-mail: info@escif.org.
URL: http://www.escif.org/
History 2006, Nottwil (Switzerland). **Aims** Improve the quality of life of people in all parts of Europe who are living with a spinal cord injury. **Structure** Assembly of Delegates; Executive Board. **Languages** English. **Staff** Voluntary. **Finance** Sources: meeting proceeds; members' dues; sponsorship. **Events** *Congress and Assembly of Delegates* Samorin (Slovakia) 2022, *Congress* Nottwil (Switzerland) 2021, *Congress and Assembly of Delegates* Gothenburg (Sweden) 2019, *Congress and Assembly of Delegates* Prague (Czechia) 2018, *Congress and Assembly of Delegates* Piran (Slovenia) 2017.
Members National organizations in 24 countries and territories:
Austria, Belgium, Bosnia-Herzegovina, Croatia, Czechia, Denmark, England, Finland, France, Germany, Ireland, Italy, Lithuania, Netherlands, Norway, Portugal, Romania, Scotland, Slovenia, Spain, Sweden, Switzerland, Türkiye, Ukraine.
NGO Relations Member of (1): *European Disability Forum (EDF, #06929).* [2022.02.15/XJ1355/**D**]

♦ European Spinal Deformities Society (inactive)
♦ European Spinal Muscular Atrophy Task Force / see SMA Europe (#19310)

♦ European Spinal Psychologists Association (ESPA) **08816**
Administration Office NSIC Dept of Clinical Psychology – Natl Spinal Injuries Ctr, Stoke Mandeville Hosp – Buckinghamshire Healthcare NHS Trust, Mandeville Road, Aylesbury, HP21 8AL, UK.
Sec address not obtained.
URL: https://www.espaspinal.org/
History 2005. **Aims** Provide the latest updates from international colleagues in the field of spinal cord injury. **Activities** Events/meetings. **Events** *Conference* Dublin (Ireland) 2022, *Decision Making About Living with SCI Complications: Pre-Post COVID-19 Clinical and Research Implications* 2021, *Conference* Zurich (Switzerland) 2019, *Conference* Oxford (UK) 2017, *Conference* Vienna (Austria) 2015. [2022/AA1884/**D**]

♦ European Spine Society (inactive)

♦ European Spirits Companies Liaison Group (ESCLG) **08817**
Groupe de liaison des entreprises européennes de spiritueux
Dir Communications Rue Belliard 12, Boîte 5, 1040 Brussels, Belgium. T. +3227792423. E-mail: info@spirits.eu.
History EU Transparency Register: 64926487056-58. **Structure** General Assembly (annual); Board of Administration. **Finance** Members' dues. **Members** Multinational spirits producers (8), which are also members of spiritsEUROPE. **NGO Relations** *spiritsEUROPE (#19921).* [2017.10.10/XE4267/**E**]

♦ European Spirits Organization / see spiritsEUROPE (#19921)

♦ European Sponsorship Association (ESA) **08818**
Gen Manager Ste 130 – 61 Victoria Road, Surbiton, KT6 4JX, UK. T. +442083903311. E-mail: office@sponsorship.org.
URL: https://sponsorship.org/
History Founded by merger of *European Sponsorship Consultants Association (ESCA, inactive)* and (UK) Institute of Sports Sponsorship. Registration: EU Transparency Register, No/ID: 327568117807-24. **Aims** Inspire, unite and grow a welcoming and diverse sponsorship industry. **Structure** Board. **Languages** English. **Staff** 4.00 FTE, paid. **Finance** Sources: members' dues. **Activities** Awards/prizes/competitions; events/meetings; knowledge management/information dissemination; networking/liaising; politics/policy/regulatory; training/education. **Events** *Annual Congress* Brussels (Belgium) 2008, *Annual Congress* Brussels (Belgium) 2007, *Annual Congress* Brussels (Belgium) 2006, *Annual Congress* Rome (Italy) 2005, *Annual Congress* Lisbon (Portugal) 2004. **Publications** *ESA Bulletin* – Guides. Guides; press releases.
Members Full in 23 countries and territories:
Belgium, Canada, China, Denmark, Finland, France, Germany, Greece, Ireland, Italy, Netherlands, New Zealand, Nigeria, Norway, Slovenia, South Africa, Spain, Sweden, Switzerland, UK, USA, Vietnam, Virgin Is UK. [2022.10.20/XD9392/**D**]

♦ European Sponsorship Consultants Association (inactive)

♦ European Sport for All Federation (UESpT) **08819**
Union Européenne Sport pour Tous (UESpT)
President Bari, 70123 Bari BA, Italy. E-mail: fispteurope@gmail.com – uespt@outlook.com.
URL: http://www.uespt.org/
History Set up as the continental section of *Fédération internationale Sport pour tous (FISpT, #09661)* Statutes adopted Feb 1984 Commissioned Federation from FISpT from FISpT AGM of October 2022 **Aims** Promote sport for all. **Structure** General Assembly; Board of Directors. **Languages** English, French. **Activities** Advocacy/lobbying/activism; events/meetings; training/education. **Publications** *Newsletter of UESpT.* [2022.11.21/XM6819/**E**]

♦ European Sport for All Network / see TAFISA Europe (#20087)

♦ European Sport Economics Association (ESEA) **08820**
Gen Sec c/o Bielefeld Univ, Sport und Wirtschaft, Postfach 10 01 31, 33501 Bielefeld, Germany.
URL: http://sporteconomics.eu/
History 4 Oct 2010, Cologne (Germany). Registration: Germany. **Aims** Promote communication between scientists as well as scientists and practitioners working in the field of sports economics; demonstrate to the fields of science, day-to-day practice, politics and the general public the benefits derived from appropriate research and academic education in Europe. **Structure** Members' Assembly; Board. **Languages** English. **Staff** No paid staff. **Finance** Members' dues. **Activities** Events/meetings; awards/prizes/competitions. **Events** *ESEA Conference on Sport Economics* Rotterdam (Netherlands) 2024, *ESEA Conference on Sport Economics* Cork (Ireland) 2023, *Annual Conference* Helsinki (Finland) 2022, *Annual Conference* Bielefeld (Germany) 2021, *Annual Conference* Helsinki (Finland) 2021. **Publications** *International Journal of Sport Finance* – official journal. [2022/XM4402/**D**]

♦ European Sport Jiu Jitsu Federation (unconfirmed)
♦ European Sport Nutrition Society (unconfirmed)
♦ European Sports Academy (unconfirmed)

♦ European Sports Conference (ESC) **08821**
Sec American School of Valencia, Urbanización Los Monasterios, Av Sierra Calderona 29, Puzol, 46530 Valencia, Spain.
URL: http://www.eurosportconference.eu/
History Inauguration Sep 2013, Geneva (Switzerland). **Aims** Provide opportunities for Varsity teams in international *schools* located in Europe to meet in specified *tournament* activities on a competitive basis. **Languages** English. **Staff** Voluntary. **Finance** Members' dues. **Activities** Sporting activities; awards/prizes/competitions.
Members Schools (12) in 6 countries:
France, Germany, Italy, Portugal, Spain, Switzerland. [2018.03.20/XM6563/**D**]

♦ European Sport Security Association / see Internatioanl Betting Integrity Association (#11527)

♦ European Sports Press Union (AIPS Europe) **08822**
Union européenne de la presse sportive (UEPS)
SG 22 Altamarea, Claire Engel Street, St Julian's, Malta. T. +35699493753.
URL: http://aipseurope.eu/
History 1977. A continental section of *Association internationale de la presse sportive (AIPS, #02729).* **Aims** Unite national associations of sports *journalists* in Europe; promote association of sports writers on a national basis; defend moral and professional interests of members and obtain their best possible working conditions; promote a spirit of mutual aid and solidarity among sports writers in Europe. **Structure** Congress (annual, usually at Annual Congress of AIPS); Committee; Bureau; Specialist Commissions (2). President represents UEPS on Executive Committee of AIPS. **Languages** English, French. **Staff** 1.00 FTE, voluntary. **Finance** Members' dues. Grants. **Events** *Annual Congress* Marrakech (Morocco) 2005, *Annual Congress* Porto (Portugal) 2003, *Annual Congress* Istanbul (Turkey) 1993, *Annual Congress* Budapest (Hungary) 1992, *Annual Congress* Nicosia (Cyprus) 1991. **Publications** *AIPS Magazine* (4 a year).
Members National journalists sports' associations in 47 countries:
Albania, Armenia, Austria, Azerbaijan, Belarus, Belgium, Bosnia-Herzegovina, Bulgaria, Croatia, Cyprus, Czechia, Denmark, Estonia, Finland, France, Georgia, Germany, Greece, Hungary, Iceland, Ireland, Israel, Italy, Kosovo, Latvia, Lithuania, Luxembourg, Malta, Moldova, Monaco, Netherlands, North Macedonia, Norway, Poland, Portugal, Romania, Russia, San Marino, Serbia, Slovakia, Slovenia, Spain, Sweden, Switzerland, Türkiye, UK, Ukraine.
NGO Relations Recognized by: *International Olympic Committee (IOC, #14408).* Memorandum of Understanding with: *European Taekwondo Union (ETU, #08874); European University Sports Association (EUSA, #09036).* Member of: *European Fair Play Movement (EFPM, #07025).* [2016.06.23/XD3385/**D**]

♦ European Sports Workforce Development Alliance (ESWDA) **08823**
Contact c/o EOSE, 1 grande rue des Feuillants, 69001 Lyon, France. T. +33437431939. Fax +33437430988. E-mail: eosesec@eose.org.
Members Organizations (5):
European Association of Sport Employers (EASE, #06218); European Non-Governmental Sports Organization (ENGSO, #08054); European Observatoire of Sport and Employment (EOSE, #08071); European Olympic Committees (EOC, #08083); UNI Global Union – Europa (UNI Europa, #20342). [2008/XM2668/y/**E**]

♦ European Sports Youth Conference (inactive)

♦ European Spreadsheet Risks Interest Group (EuSpRIG) 08824

Chair Systems Modelling Ltd, Tara Hill, Gorey, CO. WEXFORD, Ireland. T. +353868352233. E-mail: contact@eusprig.org.
Alternating Chair address not obtained.
URL: http://eusprig.org/

History Founded Mar 1999. **Aims** Introduce into organizations processes and methods to inventory, test, correct, document, backup, archive, compare and control the legions of spread sheets that support critical corporate infrastructure. **Structure** Management Committee. Sub – Committees (3): Conference Organizing; Conference Programme; Marketing. **Languages** English. **Staff** Voluntary. **Finance** Conference is self-financing. **Activities** Events/meetings; knowledge management/information dissemination. **Events** *Annual Conference* London (UK) 2018, *Annual Conference* London (UK) 2017, *Annual Conference* London (UK) 2016, *Annual Conference* Greenwich (UK) 2015, *Annual Conference* Delft (Netherlands) 2014. **Publications** Conference papers.
Members in 13 countries:
Australia, Austria, Belgium, France, Germany, Ireland, Italy, Netherlands, Portugal, Slovenia, Spain, UK, USA.
[2019/XJ1274/**D**]

♦ European Spring Federation (ESF) 08825

Gen Sec Goldene Pforte 1, 58093 Hagen, Germany. T. +492331958851. Fax +492331587484. E-mail: contact@esf-springs.org.
URL: http://www.esf-springs.com/

History 1989. **Aims** Act as a forum for exchange of marketing information on manufacturers, buyers and suppliers in the spring *industry*; provide statistics on the industry in Europe; monitor imports of springs from outside Europe and export of springs from Europe; provide information on sector growth, technology and market opportunities in the industry; obtain early information on and influence any EU decision affecting the industry; promote and participate in standardization relating to springs and spring materials by coordinating members' efforts in this area. **Activities** Negotiates research contracts from the EU on behalf of EU members; organizes exhibitions, seminars, fact finding missions, conferences and other events, joint research and technical development.
Members Ordinary (National associations of spring manufacturers); Associate (individuals). Ordinary in 7 countries:
Austria, Finland, France, Germany, Italy, Spain, UK.
Associate in 3 countries:
Denmark, Russia, Sweden.
[2012.09.06/XD5056/**D**]

♦ European Squash Federation (ESF) 08826

Sec c/o Arden Club, Sharmans Cross Road, Solihull, B91 1RG, UK. E-mail: info@europeansquash.com.
URL: http://www.europeansquash.com/

History Apr 1973. Founded as the European Committee of *World Squash Federation (WSF, #21826)*. Former names and other names: *European Squash Rackets Federation (ESRF)* – former. Registration: Companies House, No/ID: 4628339, Start date: 3 Jan 2003, England and Wales. **Aims** Promote the *game* of squash rackets in Europe; uphold the rules of the *game* (playing rules of the Federation are those of WSF); coordinate international *matches* between member countries. **Structure** Annual General Meeting; Officials. **Languages** English. **Staff** 2.00 FTE, paid. **Finance** Sources: members' dues. **Activities** Sporting activities. **Events** *Annual General Meeting* 2021, *Annual General Meeting* 2020, *Annual General Meeting* Monaco 2020, *Annual General Meeting* Birmingham (UK) 2019, *Annual General Meeting* Espoo (Finland) 2011.
Members National associations in 46 countries and territories:
Armenia, Austria, Belarus, Belgium, Bulgaria, Croatia, Cyprus, Czechia, Denmark, England, Estonia, Finland, France, Germany, Gibraltar, Greece, Guernsey, Hungary, Iceland, Ireland, Isle of Man, Israel, Italy, Jersey, Latvia, Liechtenstein, Lithuania, Luxembourg, Malta, Monaco, Netherlands, Norway, Poland, Portugal, Romania, Russia, Scotland, Serbia, Slovakia, Slovenia, Spain, Sweden, Switzerland, Türkiye, Ukraine, Wales.
NGO Relations Regional federation of: *World Squash Federation (WSF, #21826)*.
[2021/XE1440/**E**]

♦ European Squash Rackets Federation / see European Squash Federation (#08826)
♦ European Squirrel Initiative (internationally oriented national body)

♦ European Stabiliser Producers Association (ESPA) 08827

SG CEFIC, Rue Belliard 40, Box 15, 1040 Brussels, Belgium. T. +3224369460. Fax +3224369550. E-mail: espa@cefic.be.
URL: http://www.stabilisers.eu/

History Set up as a sector group of *Conseil européen de l'industrie chimique (CEFIC, #04687)*. Previously also referred to as *European Stabilizers Producers Association*. **Aims** Promote the use of stabilizer additives for PVC and other applications; provide a forum for the study and discussion of matters of scientific, technical, and environmental interest. **Staff** 1.00 FTE, paid. **Activities** Research/documentation; knowledge management/information dissemination.
Members European manufacturers of stabiliser systems in 7 countries:
Austria, Germany, Italy, Netherlands, Spain, Türkiye, UK.
NGO Relations Instrumental in setting up: *VinylPlus (#20780)*.
[2017.11.17/XE3721/y/**E**]

♦ European Stability Initiative (ESI) 08828

Chairman Grossbeerenstr 83, 10963 Berlin, Germany. T. +493053214455. Fax +493053214457. E-mail: info@esiweb.org.
URL: http://www.esiweb.org/

History Jul 1999. Registered in accordance with German law. EU Transparency Register: 545618415097-69. **Aims** Contribute to development of a stable, prosperous and peaceful Europe by providing timely and relevant analyses of *political* and *economic* trends in South Eastern Europe and Turkey. **Structure** Executive Board; Financial Board; Advisory Board. **Languages** English, French, German, Turkish. **Staff** Researchers, analysts and support staff: 15. **Finance** Grants from governments, international organizations and private foundations, including: Governments of Sweden, Netherlands, UK, Norway, Ireland, Switzerland, Slovenia, USA, Germany and Canada; *Charles Stewart Mott Foundation*; *ERSTE Foundation*; *European Commission (EC, #06633)*; *German Marshall Fund of the United States (GMF)*; *NATO (#16945)*; *Open Society Foundations (OSF, #17763)*; *Robert Bosch Foundation*; *Rockefeller Brothers Fund (RBF)*; Stiftung Mercator; *United States Institute of Peace (USIP)*. **Activities** Knowledge management/information dissemination. **Publications** *ESI Newsletter*. Reports and discussion papers; presentations and background briefings; documentaries. **Members** Full (9); Friends (15). Membership countries not specified. **NGO Relations** Member of: *European Policy Centre (EPC, #08240)*; *Network of Democracy Research Institutes (NDRI, #17003)*; *A Soul for Europe (ASF, #19697)*.
[2017.10.11/XF7124/**F**]

♦ European Stability Mechanism (ESM) 08829

Main Office Circuit de la Foire Int 6a, L-1347 Luxembourg, Luxembourg. T. +3522609620. E-mail: info@esm.europa.eu.
URL: http://www.esm.europa.eu/

History Founded as a successor to the *European Financial Stability Facility (EFSF)*. Set up through *European Stability Mechanism Treaty (ESM Treaty, 2011)*, signed Jul 2011, by Member States of the *Euro Zone*. Membership open to other Member States of the *European Union (EU, #08967)* as from entry into force of decision of *Council of the European Union (#04895)* taken in accordance with Art 140(2) TFEU to abrogate their derogation from adoption the euro. Operational following entry into force of treaty, after Member States representing 90% of the capital commitments have ratified it. Inaugurated 8 Oct 2012. Based in Luxembourg. **Aims** Ensure *financial* stability of the euro area; mobilize funding and provide financial assistance, under strict economic policy conditionally, to the benefit of ESM Members which are experiencing or are threatened by severe financing problems, if indispensable to safeguard the financial stability of the euro area as a whole. **Structure** Board of Governors, consisting of a Governor and alternate Governor of each Member State, with Member of *European Commission (EC, #06633)* in charge of economic and monetary affairs, President of *European Central Bank (ECB, #06466)* and President of *Eurogroup (#05689)* as observers. Board of Directors, comprising one Director and one alternate Director per Governor. Managing Director. Voting rights are equal to the number of shares allocated to it in the authorized capital stock. **Staff** 140.00 FTE, paid. **Finance** Authorized capital stock: euro 704,800 million. **Activities** Financial and/or material support; politics/policy/regulatory. **Events** *Annual Meeting* Luxembourg (Luxembourg) 2015.
Members Member States (19):
Austria, Belgium, Cyprus, Estonia, Finland, France, Germany, Greece, Ireland, Italy, Latvia, Lithuania, Luxembourg, Malta, Netherlands, Portugal, Slovakia, Slovenia, Spain.
IGO Relations Cooperation agreement signed with: *Council of Europe Development Bank (CEB, #04897)*.
[2021/XJ4958/**F***]

♦ European Stability Mechanism Treaty (2011 treaty)
♦ European Stabilizers Producers Association / see European Stabiliser Producers Association (#08827)
♦ European Stadium Management Association / see European Stadium and Safety Management Association (#08830)
♦ European Stadium Managers Association / see European Stadium and Safety Management Association (#08830)

♦ European Stadium and Safety Management Association (ESSMA) . 08830

Managing Dir Tiensesteenweg 168, 3800 Sint-Truiden, Belgium. E-mail: contact@essma.eu.
Pres Highbury House, 75 Drayton Park, London, N5 1BU, UK. T. +442077044030. Fax +442077044031.
URL: http://www.essma.eu/

History 1995, Paris (France). Currently based in Brussels (Belgium). Former names and other names: *European Stadium Management Association (ESMA)* – former; *European Stadium Managers Association* – former. Registration: Charity Commission, No/ID: 235825, England and Wales. **Aims** Create a European network of legal persons responsible for stadium administration and management in order to represent and promote interests of this profession; exchange ideas, information and experiences and study ways of optimizing stadium management and making it profitable. **Structure** General Meeting (annual); Board; Expert Groups (3): Head Ground Managers, Safety, Sustainability. **Languages** English, French, German, Portuguese, Russian, Spanish. **Staff** 7.00 FTE, paid. **Finance** Sources: members' dues; sponsorship. **Activities** Events/meetings; knowledge management/information dissemination. **Events** *Summit* Turin (Italy) 2021, *Summit* Budapest (Hungary) 2020, *Summit* Porto (Portugal) 2019, *Summit* Dublin (Ireland) 2018, *Summit* Lyon (France) 2017.
Members Active; Honorary. Members (270) in 24 countries:
Austria, Belgium, Brazil, Cyprus, Denmark, France, Germany, Israel, Italy, Montenegro, Netherlands, New Zealand, Norway, Poland, Portugal, Russia, Serbia, Singapore, Spain, Sweden, Switzerland, UK, Ukraine, USA.
[2023.02.14/XD5901/**D**]

♦ European stakeholder group for Complementary and Alternative Medicine / see EUROCAM (#05653)
♦ European Stamp Dealers Association (inactive)
♦ European STAMP Workshop and Conference (meeting series)
♦ European Standard International Association (unconfirmed)
♦ European Standards Coordinating Committee / see Comité européen de normalisation (#04162)
♦ European Standing Conference of European National Ethics Committees / see European Conference of National Ethics Committees (#06734)
♦ European Standing Conference of Geography Teachers' Associations / see European Association of Geographers (#06054)
♦ European Standing Conference of History Teachers' Associations / see European Association of History Educators (#06069)

♦ European Standing Group on International Relations (SGIR) 08831

Chairperson Aarhus Univ, Bartholins Allé 7, Bygning 1332, 8000 Aarhus C, Denmark.
URL: http://standinggroups.ecpr.eu/sgir/

History Founded 1990, after a series of meetings in the late 1980s. Affiliated with *European Consortium for Political Research (ECPR, #06762)*. **Aims** Facilitate research and teaching about international relations on a Pan-European basis. **Structure** Steering Committee. **Finance** Support in kind from home institutions of the Group; journal royalties. **Activities** Events/meetings; knowledge management/information dissemination; training/education. **Events** *Pan-European Conference on International Relations* Warsaw (Poland) 2013, *Pan-European conference / Conference* Stockholm (Sweden) 2010, *Pan-European Conference / Conference* Turin (Italy) 2007, *Conference* The Hague (Netherlands) 2004, *Pan-European conference on international relations* The Hague (Netherlands) 2004. **Publications** *European Journal of International Relations* (4 a year); *SGIR – Palgrave Studies in International Relations*. Book series.
Members Not a membership organization. Serves individuals in mainly European countries (24):
Austria, Belgium, Czechia, Denmark, Estonia, Finland, France, Germany, Ireland, Italy, Netherlands, Norway, Poland, Portugal, Russia, Serbia, Slovakia, Slovenia, Spain, Sweden, Switzerland, Türkiye, UK, Ukraine.
[2018.07.31/XF5427/v/**F**]

♦ European Standing Observatory for the Engineering Profession and Education / see European Network for Accreditation of Engineering Education (#07859)
♦ European Starch Industry Association / see Starch Europe (#19966)

♦ European State Forest Association (EUSTAFOR) 08832

Exec Dir European Forestry House, Rue du Luxembourg 66, 1000 Brussels, Belgium. T. +3222392300. Fax +3222192191. E-mail: office@eustafor.eu – kathleen.begemann@eustafor.eu.
URL: http://www.eustafor.eu/

History 2006, by state forest management agencies from Finland, France, Latvia and Austria. Registered in accordance with Belgian law. EU Transparency Register: 99982273034-52. **Aims** Support and strengthen State Forest Management Organizations (SFMOs) throughout Europe, helping them maintain and enhance economically viable, socially beneficial, culturally valuable and ecologically responsible sustainable forest management. **Structure** General Assembly; Executive Committee; Executive Office, headed by Executive Director. **Languages** English. **Staff** 3.00 FTE, paid. **Finance** Members' dues. **Activities** Events/meetings. **Events** *Conference* Maynooth (Ireland) 2014.
Members State forest companies, enterprises and agencies (34) in 24 European countries and territories:
Austria, Belgium, Bosnia-Herzegovina, Bulgaria, Croatia, Czechia, England, Estonia, Finland, France, Germany, Hungary, Ireland, Italy, Latvia, Lithuania, Norway, Poland, Romania, Scotland, Slovakia, Slovenia, Spain, Sweden.
IGO Relations Observer status with: *Intergovernmental Negotiating Committee for a Legally Binding Agreement on Forests in Europe (INC-Forests, inactive)*; *Ministerial Conference on the Protection of Forests in Europe (FOREST EUROPE, #16817)*. **NGO Relations** Stakeholder: *Forest-Based Sector Technology Platform (FTP, #09861)*. Member of: *European Forest Institute (EFI, #07297)*.
[2019.12.12/XJ7564/**D***]

♦ European State Lotteries and Toto Association 08833

Association Européenne des Loteries et Totos d'Etat – Asociación Europea de Loterias y Apuestas Deportivas de Estado – Europäische Vereinigung der Staatlichen Lotterien und Totogesellschaften

SG Av des Nerviens 9-31, 1040 Brussels, Belgium. T. +3222343821. E-mail: info@european-lotteries.org.
Main Office Av de Provence 14, CP 6744, 1002 Lausanne VD, Switzerland.
URL: http://www.european-lotteries.org/

History Nov 1983, Montreux (Switzerland). As of May 2012, includes the former *European Lotteries Sports (ELS, inactive)*. Former names and other names: *European Association of State Lotteries* – former (1983 to 1999); *Association européenne des loteries d'Etat (AELE)* – former (1983 to 1999); *European Association of State Lotteries and Lottos* – former (1989 to 1999); *European Lotteries (EL)* – alias. Registration: EU Transparency Register, No/ID: 97609783845-15, Start date: 20 Jun 2017; No/ID: 0888.001.247, Belgium; Switzerland. **Aims** Offer experience, expertise and best practice in the fields of gaming and gambling, especially lotteries, and thereby drive innovation in this field. **Structure** General Assembly (annual); Executive Committee; Working Committees and Working Groups; Lausanne Office (statutory office); Brussels Office. **Languages** English, French, German, Spanish. **Staff** 8.00 FTE, paid. **Finance** Sources: members' dues. **Activities** Events/meetings; guidance/assistance/consulting. **Events** *Biennial Congress* Sibenik (Croatia) 2023, *Lotteries in the Digital Age Meeting* Brussels (Belgium) 2022, *Industry Days* Wiesbaden (Germany) 2022, *Data and Research Seminar* Brussels (Belgium) 2021, *Data and Research Seminar* Brussels (Belgium) 2021. **Publications** Factsheets.
Members Regular: European State Lotteries and Lottos in 41 countries:
Albania, Austria, Azerbaijan, Belarus, Belgium, Bosnia-Herzegovina, Bulgaria, Croatia, Cyprus, Czechia, Denmark, Estonia, Finland, France, Germany, Greece, Hungary, Iceland, Ireland, Israel, Italy, Latvia, Lithuania, Luxembourg, Malta, Netherlands, North Macedonia, Norway, Poland, Portugal, Romania, Russia, Serbia, Slovakia, Slovenia, Spain, Sweden, Switzerland, Türkiye, UK, Ukraine.
Associate: companies in lottery industry in 17 countries:

European State Studs
08834
alphabetic sequence excludes
For the complete listing, see Yearbook Online at

Austria, Bulgaria, Canada, Cyprus, France, Germany, Greece, India, Israel, Italy, Malta, Netherlands, Slovenia, Spain, Sweden, UK, USA.
Observer: State Lottery and Lotto, in 2 countries:
Kazakhstan, Morocco.
NGO Relations Regional association of: *World Lottery Association (WLA, #21628).* [2021.09.07/XD1406/**D**]

♦ European State Studs Associations (ESSA) 08834

Office c/o Haupt- und Landgestüt Marbach, Gestütshof 2, 72532 Gomadingen, Germany. T. +4973965717. Fax +4973965738. E-mail: info@europeanstatestuds.org.
URL: http://www.europeanstatestuds.org/
History 2008. Registration: Start date: 2009, Germany. **Aims** Campaign for preservation of the European state studs' *heritage.* **Structure** General Assembly (annual); Board, comprising President, Vice-President, Treasurer and Assessor. **Languages** English, French, German. **Staff** Voluntary. **Finance** Members' dues. **Activities** Events/meetings; publishing activities. **Events** *Conference and General Assembly* Kladruby (Czech Rep) 2018, *Conference and General Assembly* Ypäjä (Finland) 2017. **Publications** Leaflet and brochure.
Members Full in 16 countries:
Austria, Bulgaria, Croatia, Czechia, Finland, France, Germany, Hungary, Ireland, Poland, Portugal, Romania, Slovakia, Slovenia, Sweden, Switzerland.
NGO Relations Member of: *European Horse Network (EHN, #07499).* Partner with: *Europa Nostra (#05767).* [2022/XJ5797/**D**]

♦ European Steel Association (EUROFER) 08835

Association européenne de la sidérurgie – Asociación Europea de Siderurgia Associação Européia da Siderurgia – Associazione Europea della Siderurgia
Dir Gen Av Cortenbergh 172, 1000 Brussels, Belgium. T. +3227387920. Fax +3227387955. E-mail: mail@eurofer.be.
URL: http://www.eurofer.eu/
History 1 Sep 1956, as *EEC Steel Manufacturers Club.* Changed title to *European Confederation of Iron and Steel Industries (EUROFER) – Association européenne de la sidérurgie – Asociación Europea de Siderurgia – Europäische Wirtschaftsvereinigung der Eisen- und Stahlindustrie – Associação Européia da Siderurgia – Associazione Europea della Siderurgia – Europese Vereniging van Ijzer- en Staalproducerende Industrieën – Foreningen af Europaeiske Staalproducenter,* when new constitution was adopted 9 Dec 1976, Amsterdam (Netherlands). Current title adopted, 2011. 2002, integrated activities of *European Independent Steelworks Association (EISA, inactive).* Registration: AISBL/IVZW, Belgium. **Aims** Promote cooperation among national federations and companies for advancement of steel as a product and as an industry on European level. **Structure** General Meeting (annual); Board. **Languages** English. **Finance** Members' dues. **Activities** Events/meetings. **Events** *Annual European Steel Day Meeting* Brussels (Belgium) 2020, *Annual European Steel Day Meeting* Brussels (Belgium) 2019, *State of the EU Ssteel Market Seminar* Brussels (Belgium) 2019, *Annual European Steel Day Meeting* Brussels (Belgium) 2018, *European Steel Day Event* Brussels (Belgium) 2016. **Publications** *EUROFER Newsletter.* Annual report; directory of members; nomenclature; congress proceedings.
Members National federations and companies (61 in total) in 22 countries:
Austria, Belgium, Bulgaria, Czechia, Denmark, Finland, France, Germany, Greece, Hungary, Italy, Latvia, Luxembourg, Netherlands, Poland, Portugal, Romania, Slovakia, Slovenia, Spain, Sweden, UK.
NGO Relations In liaison with technical committees of: *Comité européen de normalisation (CEN, #04162).* Member of: *AEGIS Europe; European Steel Technology Platform (ESTEP, #08836); Industry4Europe (#11181); METALS FOR BUILDINGS (#16737).* Affiliate member of: *world stainless association (worldstainless, #21828).* Institutional member of: [2020/XD0515/**D**]

♦ European Steel Cartel (inactive)
♦ European Steel Industry Confederation (inactive)
♦ European Steel Technology and Application Days (meeting series)

♦ European Steel Technology Platform (ESTEP) 08836

SG c/o EUROFER, Av de Cortenbergh 172, 1000 Brussels, Belgium. T. +3227387947. E-mail: secretariat@steelresearch-estep.eu.
URL: http://www.estep.eu/
History 2003. EU Transparency Register: 71063945715-33. **Aims** Maintain and reinforce the global leadership of the EU steel industry. **Structure** Steering Committee; Support Group; Working Groups. **Publications** *ESTEP Newsletter.* Annual Report.
Members Steel producers. Membership countries not specified. Regional organization:
Regional organization:
European Steel Association (EUROFER, #08835).
NGO Relations Member of: *European Technology Platform on Sustainable Mineral Resources (ETP SMR, #08894).* [2015/XM5521/y/**F**]

♦ European Steel Tube Association (ESTA) 08837

Association européenne du tube d'acier
SG 16 rue de Solferino, 92100 Boulogne-Billancourt, France. T. +33141315640. Fax +33141310024.
History 2000. Registration: EU Transparency Register, No/ID: 244351340524-30, Start date: 1 Dec 2020. **Aims** Represent the interests of national steel piper associations and consequently of most producers of steel pipes in the EU.
Members Organizations in 9 countries:
Czechia, France, Germany, Italy, Poland, Romania, Spain, Sweden, UK.
NGO Relations Member of (2): *AEGIS Europe; Industry4Europe (#11181).* [2020/XM4625/t/**D**]

♦ European Sterilization Packaging Association / see Sterile Barrier Association (#19983)

♦ European Stevia Association (EUSTAS) 08838

Asociación Europea de la Estevia
Office Calle Maladeta 20, 22300 Barbastro, Huesca, Spain. T. +34974311478. E-mail: office@eustas.org – info@eustas.org.
URL: http://www.eustas.org/
History 2006. Registered in accordance with Spanish law. **Aims** Promote and coordinate all activities focusing on research and health in relation to Stevia rebaudiana and related compounds. **Structure** General Assembly; Executive Board. **Activities** Events/meetings; advocacy/lobbying/activism; knowledge management/information dissemination; certification/accreditation. [2016/XM5286/**D**]

♦ Europeans throughout the World (ETTW) 08839

Les Européens dans le monde – Los Europeos en el Mundo – Die Europeer in der Welt – Os Europeus no Mundo – Gli Europei nel Mondo – De Europeanen in de Wereld – Europarne i Verden
SG c/o Fondation Universitaire, Rue d'Egmont 11, 1000 Brussels, Belgium. T. +3225450456.
URL: http://www.euromonde.eu/
History 2 Apr 1982. Previously known as *League of the Societies of the Citizens of the European Community Living Abroad – Confédération des associations de résidents à l'étranger de la Communauté européenne (CARECE) – Bund der Vereinigungen der im Ausland Lebenden Bürger der Europäischen Gemeinschaft – Confederazione delle Associazioni dei Cittadini all'Estero della Comunità Europea – Verbond van Verenigingen van in het Buitenland Woonachtige Landgenoten uit de Europese Gemeenschap – Forbundet af Foreninger for i Udland Bosiddende EF Borgere.* Current name adopted 15 Jun 1983. Registration: No/ID: 0425.411.118, Start date: 9 Feb 1983, Belgium; EU Transparency Register, No/ID: 055088121896-37, Start date: 13 Jun 2016. **Aims** Promote international cooperation among associations of Europeans living *abroad,* in another country of their origin, either within th EU or around the world; improve assistance to European citizens; ensure democratic rights for European Union citizens; promote European values in diaspora communities. **Structure** General Assembly (annual); Board of Directors; Executive Bureau. **Languages** Dutch, English, French. **Staff** 2.50 FTE, voluntary. **Finance** Annual budget: euro 15,000. **Activities** Advocacy/lobbying/activism; knowledge management/information dissemination; research and documentation; events/meetings. **Events** *Latvian EU Presidency High-Level Conference on how to improve Intra-European Mobility and Circular Migration* Riga (Latvia) 2015, *Conference* Copenhagen (Denmark) 2012, *Conference* Bratislava (Slovakia) 2010, *Conference* Rome (Italy) 2010, *Conference* Stockholm (Sweden) 2009. **Publications** *ETTW News Service. Europeans Throughout the World* in English, French. Documents; reports; studies.
Members Associate; Correspondent. Member Associations in 16 countries:
Belgium, Denmark, Estonia, Finland, France, Greece, Ireland, Italy, Latvia, Malta, Norway, Romania, Slovakia, Spain, Sweden, UK.
NGO Relations Sponsors: *European Union Cross Identity Network (EUxIN, #08983).* Supports: *European Citizens' Initiative Campaign (ECI Campaign, #06558).* [2020/XE2661/**F**]

♦ European Strabismological Association (ESA) 08840

Association strabismologique européenne
Sec-Treas Studio Oculistico, Via Verdi 22, 36022 Cassola VICENZA, Italy.
URL: http://www.esa-strabismology.com/
History 1962, as *European Council for Research on Strabismus – Société européenne d'études du strabisme – Consilium Europaeum Strabismi Studio Deditum (CESSD).* Present name adopted 1981. **Aims** Promote studies and research in the field of strabismology. **Structure** Executive Committee. **Languages** English, French, German. **Finance** Members' dues. **Events** *Annual Congress* Paris (France) 2021, *Annual Congress* Helsinki (Finland) 2019, *Annual Congress* Porto (Portugal) 2017, *Annual Congress* Budapest (Hungary) 2016, *Annual Congress* Venice (Italy) 2015. **Publications** Congress transactions.
Members Strabologists (185) in 30 countries:
Algeria, Austria, Belgium, Denmark, Egypt, Finland, France, Germany, Greece, Hungary, Ireland, Israel, Italy, Japan, Luxembourg, Netherlands, Norway, Poland, Portugal, Romania, Russia, Saudi Arabia, Serbia, Spain, Sweden, Switzerland, Türkiye, Ukraine, United Arab Emirates, USA.
NGO Relations Member of: *International Pediatric Ophthalmology and Strabismus Council (IPOSC, #14544).* [2018.06.15/XD0701/v/**D**]

♦ European Straight Wire Society (unconfirmed)
♦ European Strategic Intelligence and Security Centre (internationally oriented national body)
♦ European Strategic Planning Federation (no recent information)

♦ European Street Rod Association (ESRA) 08841

Contact BSRA, Passendalestraat 14, 2600 Berchem, Belgium. E-mail: luc@bsra.be.
URL: http://www.esra-rod.eu/
History Founded Jun 1995, France. **Aims** Promote the hobby of hotrod *cars.* **Languages** English. **Activities** Organizes annual European Street Rod Nationals.
Members National organizations in 9 countries:
Belgium, Denmark, Finland, France, Germany, Norway, Sweden, Switzerland, UK. [2013.08.20/XD9307/**D**]

♦ European Stress Wave Emission Working Group / see European Working Group on Acoustic Emission (#09108)

♦ European String Teachers Association (ESTA) 08842

Association européenne de professeurs d'instruments à cordes
Sec c/o Musikschule Konservatorium, Kramgasse 36, 3011 Bern, Switzerland. T. +41313513894 – +41314107955777. E-mail: info@estastrings.org.
URL: http://www.estastrings.org/
History 1972, Graz (Austria). Most recent statutes adopted 18 Oct 2002. Registration: Switzerland. **Aims** Improve the standard of string teaching, professional training of string-players and general interest in string playing; foster international relations through conferences, workshops and youth *orchestra* performances. **Structure** Delegates Assembly (annual); Central Committee; Central Secretariat; National Boards. **Languages** English, French, German. **Staff** 0.50 FTE, paid. **Finance** Members' dues. **Activities** Events/meetings; knowledge management/information dissemination; networking/liaising. **Events** *Conference* Finland 2026, *Conference* Netherlands 2025, *Conference* Porto (Portugal) 2024, *Conference* Cardiff (UK) 2023, *International ESTA Conference* Graz (Austria) 2022. **Publications** National branch magazines. Information Services: Database of members by country and by instrument.
Members European national groups in 26 countries and territories:
Austria, Belgium, Croatia, Denmark, Estonia, Finland, France, Germany, Greece, Hungary, Iceland, Italy, Kosovo, Malta, Netherlands, Norway, Poland, Portugal, Romania, Serbia, Slovenia, Sweden, Switzerland, Tatarstan, UK, Ukraine.
Consultative Status Consultative status granted from: *Council of Europe (CE, #04881)* (Participatory Status).
NGO Relations Associate member of: *International Music Council (IMC, #14199).* [2022/XD5890/**D**]

♦ European Stroke Conference (inactive)

♦ European Stroke Organisation (ESO) 08843

Exec Manager Reinacherstr 131, 4053 Basel BS, Switzerland. T. +41616867776. Fax +41616909421. E-mail: esoinfo@eso-stroke.org.
URL: https://eso-stroke.org/
History 17 Dec 2007, Heidelberg (Germany). Founded on merger of *European Stroke Council (ESC)* and *European Stroke Initiative (EUSI),* a joint initiative of *European Federation of Neurological Societies (EFNS, inactive), European Neurological Society (ENS, inactive)* and *European Stroke Conference (inactive).* Registration: EU Transparancy Register, No/ID: 991191345510-16, Start date: 14 Feb 2022. **Aims** Improve stroke care in Europe by providing medical education to healthcare professionals and the lay public. **Structure** General Assembly; Board of Directors; Executive Committee; Head Office. **Languages** English. **Activities** Certification/accreditation; events/meetings; research/documentation; training/education. **Events** *European Stroke Conference* Munich (Germany) 2023, *European Stroke Conference* Lyon (France) 2022, *European Stroke Conference* 2021, *Joint Stroke Conference* Vienna (Austria) 2020, *European Stroke Conference* Milan (Italy) 2019. **Publications** *ESO Newsletter; European Stroke Journal.* Articles; guidelines. **Members** Stroke researchers, national and regional stroke societies and others with an interest in stroke. Membership countries not specified. **IGO Relations** Accredited by (1): *WHO Regional Office for Europe (#20945).* **NGO Relations** Member of (4): *European Alliance for Cardiovascular Health (EACH, #05863); European Brain Council (EBC, #06391); Stroke Alliance for Europe (SAFE, #20012); World Stroke Organization (WSO, #21831).* [2023/XE4520/**E**]

♦ European Stroke Research Foundation (internationally oriented national body)

♦ European Structural Integrity Society (ESIS) 08844

Pres Univ di Cassino e del Lazio Meridionale, via G Di Biasio 43, 03043 Cassino FR, Italy. Fax +397762993671.
Sec Dept Mechanical Engineering, Imperial College London, South Kensington Campus, London, SW7 2BZ, UK.
URL: http://www.structuralintegrity.eu/
History 1978, Darmstadt (Germany). Founded as a regional organization of *International Congress on Fracture (ICF, #12894).* Former names and other names: *European Group on Fracture (EGF)* – former; *Groupe européen d'études sur la rupture* – former. **Aims** Develop and extend knowledge in all aspects of structural integrity and disseminate that knowledge to improve safety and performance of *engineering* equipment, individual components and structures. **Structure** Council; (meets every 2 years); Executive Committee. **Languages** English, French, German. **Staff** None. Executive Committee voluntary. **Finance** Members' dues. **Activities** Research and development; knowledge management/information dissemination; events/meetings. **Events** *European Conference on Fracture* Dubrovnik (Croatia) 2024, *European Conference on Fracture* Funchal (Portugal) 2022, *European Conference on Fracture* Funchal (Portugal) 2020, *European Conference on Structural Integrity of Additively Manufactured Materials* Trondheim (Norway) 2019, *Biennial European Conference on Fracture* Belgrade (Serbia) 2018. **Publications** *ESIS Newsletter* (annual). *ESIS Procedures.* Proceedings of conferences and other meetings.
Members Associations and individuals in 27 countries:
Austria, Brazil, Bulgaria, Canada, Croatia, Czechia, Denmark, Finland, France, Germany, Greece, Israel, Italy, Netherlands, Norway, Poland, Portugal, Romania, Russia, Serbia, Slovenia, Spain, Sweden, Switzerland, UK, Ukraine, USA.
IGO Relations *Commonwealth Secretariat (#04362).* **NGO Relations** Associate member of: *Federation of European Materials Societies (FEMS, #09515).* Cooperates with: *Far East Oceanic Fracture Society (FEOFS, #09271).* [2020.03.03/XD2335/**D**]

♦ European Structured Investment Products Association (EUSIPA) ... 08845

Association Européenne des Produits d'Investissement Structurés
SG Bastion Tower – Level 20, Place du Champs de Mars 5, 1050 Brussels, Belgium. T. +3225503415. Fax +3225503416. E-mail: secretariat@eusipa.org.

URL: http://www.eusipa.org/
History 2 Jul 2008. Articles registered 6 Nov 2011. Registered in accordance with Belgian law: 0150272. EU Transparency Register: 37488345650-13. **Aims** Promote the interests of the structured retail investment products market; coordinate transparency initiatives at the European level; support uniform market standards. **Structure** General Assembly (annual); Board of Directors. Committees (3): Legal; Principles; Categorisation. **Members** Full/Ordinary; Associate. Full in 6 countries:
Austria, France, Germany, Italy, Sweden, Switzerland.
Associate in 1 country:
UK.
NGO Relations Member of: *European Parliamentary Financial Services Forum (EPFSF, #08148)*.
[2017/XJ7398/**D**]

♦ European Student Conference on Behaviour and Cognition (meeting series)
♦ European Student Information Bureau / see European Students' Union (#08848)
♦ European Student Relief / see World University Service (#21892)
♦ European Students' Forum (#02495)

♦ European Students of Industrial Engineering and Management (ESTIEM) 08846
Contact Paviljoen B-6, PO Box 513, 5600 MB Eindhoven, Netherlands. E-mail: board@estiem.org – vp-pr@estiem.org – info@estiem.org.
URL: http://www.estiem.org
History 1990, Berlin (Germany). Registration: Handelsregister, No/ID: 40240535, Netherlands. **Aims** Connect and support the growth and sustainability of European associations of IEM students, foster relations and develop IEM students, personally and professionally. **Structure** Council of Members (meets twice a year); International Board; Committees. **Languages** English. **Staff** 6.00 FTE, voluntary. **Finance** Sources: corporate and academic partnerships; donations. **Activities** Advocacy/lobbying/activism; awards/prizes/competitions; capacity building; certification/accreditation; events/meetings; networking/liaising; projects/programmes; publishing activities; research/documentation; training/education. **Events** *Council Meeting* 2021, *IEM Conference* 2021, *Council Meeting* 2020, *Meeting* Barcelona (Spain) 2018, *Meeting* Helsinki (Finland) 2016. **Publications** *ESTIEM Magazine* (2 a year) in English.
Members Student groups (77) in 26 countries:
Austria, Belarus, Belgium, Bulgaria, Croatia, Estonia, Finland, France, Germany, Greece, Hungary, Italy, Netherlands, North Macedonia, Northern Cyprus, Norway, Poland, Portugal, Romania, Russia, Serbia, Spain, Sweden, Switzerland, Türkiye, Ukraine.
NGO Relations Partner of (5): *Board of European Students of Technology (BEST, #03294)*; *Electrical Engineering STudents' European assoCiation (EESTEC, #05416)*; *European Institute for Industrial Leadership (EIIL)*; *Informal Forum of International Student Organizations (IFISO, #11193)*; *Société européenne pour la formation des ingénieurs (SEFI, #19462)*.
[2022.12.10/XD4782/t/**D**]

♦ European Students For Liberty (ESFL) 08847
Office c/o Students For Liberty, 1101 17th St NW, Ste 810, Washington DC 20036, USA. E-mail: europe@studentsforliberty.org.
URL: http://www.studentsforliberty.org/europe/
History Set up by the US Students for Liberty (SFL). **Aims** Provide support for pro-liberty students and student groups in Europe; empower the next generation of leaders in the global liberty movement. **Structure** Executive Board. **Staff** 3.00 FTE, paid. **Events** *European Regional Conference* Madrid (Spain) 2016, *Conference* Berlin (Germany) 2015, *Regional Conference* Bergen (Norway) 2014.
[2017/XJ9438/**F**]

♦ European Students' Union (ESU) 08848
Pres Mundo-Madou, Avenue des Arts 7/8, 1210 Brussels, Belgium. T. +3228932545. E-mail: secretariat@esu-online.org.
Main Website: http://www.esu-online.org
History 17 Oct 1982, Stockholm (Sweden). Former names and other names: *West European Student Information Bureau (WESIB)* – former (17 Oct 1982 to 1990); *Bureau d'information des étudiants ouest-européens* – former (17 Oct 1982 to 1990); *European Student Information Bureau* – former (9 Feb 1990 to May 1993); *Bureau d'information des étudiants européens* – former (9 Feb 1990 to May 1993); *ESIB – National Unions of Students in Europe (ESIB)* – former (May 1993 to May 2007). Registration: Banque-Carrefour des Entreprises, No/ID: 0896.361.756, Start date: 11 Mar 2008, Belgium; EU Transparency Register, No/ID: 947001511571-77, Start date: 12 Jul 2013. **Aims** Represent the views of students to all stakeholders in the field of education and of student life in general. **Structure** Board (meets at least twice a year); Executive Committee; Coordinators; Secretariat based in Brussels (Belgium). **Languages** English, French. **Staff** 6.00 FTE, paid. **Finance** Sources: grants; members' dues. **Activities** Events/meetings; knowledge management/information dissemination; networking/liaising. **Events** *European Quality Assurance Forum* Aveiro (Portugal) 2023, *European Quality Assurance Forum* Timisoara (Romania) 2022, *European Quality Assurance Forum* Brussels (Belgium) 2021, *European Students Convention* Brussels (Belgium) 2020, *European Quality Assurance Forum* Espoo (Finland) 2020. **Publications** *The Student Voice* (12 a year) – electronic newsletter; *European Student Handbook* (every 2 years); *Bologna with Students' Eyes* (6th ed 2018); *Lisbon Handbook* (2nd ed 2006). Reports of seminars; booklets; research documents; various policy papers; handbooks.
Members Full; Associate; Candidate. National unions of students (45) representing about 20 million students. Full in 40 countries and territories:
Armenia, Austria, Belarus, Belgium, Bosnia-Herzegovina, Bulgaria, Croatia, Cyprus, Czechia, Denmark, Estonia, Faeroe Is, Finland, France, Georgia, Germany, Hungary, Iceland, Ireland, Israel, Italy, Latvia, Lithuania, Luxembourg, Malta, Moldova, Montenegro, Netherlands, Norway, Poland, Portugal, Romania, Serbia, Slovakia, Slovenia, Spain, Sweden, Switzerland, UK, Ukraine.
Associate organizations (13):
Association of Norwegian Students Abroad (ANSA); *European Deaf Students' Union (EDSU, #06893)*; *European Dental Students Association (EDSA, #06904)*; *European Medical Students' Association (EMSA, #07764)*; *European Nursing Students Association (ENSA, #08066)*; *European Pharmaceutical Students' Association (EPSA, #08197)*; *European Union of Jewish Students (EUJS, #08997)*; Forum of European Muslim Youth and Student Organisations (FEMYSO, #09909); *International Association for Political Science Students (IAPSS, #12095)*; *International Federation of Medical Students' Associations (IFMSA, #13478)*; International Lesbian, Gay, Bisexual, Transgender, Queer and Intersex Youth and Student Organization (IGLYO, #14032); *International Students of History Association (ISHA, #15613)*; Organising Bureau of European School Student Unions (OBESSU, #17829).
Consultative Status Consultative status granted from: UNESCO (#20322) (Consultative Status); *Council of Europe (CE, #04881)*. **IGO Relations** Consultative member of: *European Higher Education Area (EHEA, #07483)*. Member of: *European Economic and Social Committee (EESC, #06963)* Liaison Group. Works with: *European Commission (EC, #06633)*; *European Parliament (EP, #08146)*; *European Youth Foundation (EYF, #09141)*; Information Network on Education in Europe (EURYDICE, inactive); OECD (#17693).
NGO Relations Member of (9): *Euro-Mediterranean University (EMUNI, #05728)*; EuroMed Permanent University Forum (EPUF, #05731); *European Quality Assurance Register for Higher Education (EQAR, #08311)* (Founding); *European Youth Forum (#09140)*; Federation of European and International Associations Established in Belgium (FAIB, #09508); Generation Climate Europe (GCE, #10114); Global Student Forum (GSF, #10614); Lifelong Learning Platform – European Civil Society for Education (LLLP, #16466); SIRIUS – Policy Network on Migrant Education (SIRIUS, #19291). Partner of (2): *100 Million (#22042)*; Central European Student Network (CSN, no recent information). Cooperates with (1): International Lesbian, Gay, Bisexual, Transgender, Queer and Intersex Youth and Student Organization (IGLYO, #14032).
Works with:
– All-Africa Students Union (AASU, #00644);
– Asia Students Association (ASA, no recent information);
– Asian Students Information Centre (ASIC, no recent information);
– Board of European Students of Technology (BEST, #03294);
– Education International (EI, #05371);
– EUROCADRES – Council of European Professional and Managerial Staff (#05651);
– European Association of Institutions of Higher Education (EURASHE, #06086);
– European Association for International Education (EAIE, #06092);
– European Association for Quality Assurance in Higher Education (ENQA, #06183);
– European Democrat Students (EDS, #06901);
– EDEN Digital Learning Europe (EDEN, #05356);
– European Language Council (ELC, #07646);
– The European Law Students' Association (ELSA, #07660);
– European Trade Union Committee for Education (ETUCE, #08926);
– European University Association (EUA, #09027);
– General European Study of Philosophy Assembly (GESPA, no recent information);
– General Union of Arab Students (GUAS, no recent information);
– Informal Consultative Meeting of Regional and International Students Structures;
– International Association for the Exchange of Students for Technical Experience (IAESTE, #11885);
– International Association of Students in Agricultural and Related Sciences (IAAS, #12191);
– International Association of Universities (IAU, #12246);
– International Union of Socialist Youth (IUSY, #15815);
– Meeting of Students Aiming at the Integration of the Coimbra Group (MOSAIC, inactive);
– Network for Foreign Students and Student Mobility in Europe and North America (NFSSM, no recent information);
– Organización Continental Latinoamericana y Caribeña de Estudiantes (OCLAE, #17834);
– World Student Christian Federation (WSCF, #21833);
– World University Service (WUS, #21892);
– World Youth Student and Educational Travel Confederation (WYSE Travel Confederation, #21959);
– Youth for Development and Cooperation (YDC, inactive).
[2023.02.14/XE0066/y/**D**]

♦ European Studies Alliance, Madison WI (internationally oriented national body)
♦ European Studies Center, Pittsburgh PA (internationally oriented national body)
♦ European Studies Centre, Lisbon / see Instituto de Estudos Europeus, Lisboa
♦ European Studies Centre, Oxford (internationally oriented national body)
♦ European Studies Centre, Sydney (internationally oriented national body)
♦ European Studies Institute, Lisbon (internationally oriented national body)
♦ European Studies Research Institute, Salford (internationally oriented national body)
♦ European Study Conference on Low Energy Molecular Collisions (meeting series)

♦ European Study Group on Cardiovascular Oscillations (ESGCO) 08849
Chair Univ degli Studi di Milano, Dipto di Scienze Biomediche per la Salute, Ist Ortopedico Galeazzi, Via R Galeazzi 4, 20161 Milan MI, Italy. T. +39250319976.
URL: http://events.unitn.it/en/esgco2014/
History 1998. **Aims** Foster *interdisciplinary* discussions among engineers, physicists, computer scientists, biologists, physiologists and clinicians about *physiological* states and transitions, regulatory mechanisms and clinical implications of cardiovascular oscillations in all their forms. **Structure** Board. **Languages** English. **Staff** Voluntary. **Finance** No official budget. **Activities** Training/education; knowledge management/information dissemination. **Events** *Conference* Vienna (Austria) 2018, *Conference* Trento (Italy) 2014, *Conference* Kazimierz Dolny (Poland) 2012, *Conference* Berlin (Germany) 2010, *Conference* Parma (Italy) 2008.
Members Full in 25 countries:
Australia, Austria, Belgium, Brazil, Canada, Denmark, Finland, France, Germany, Greece, Israel, Italy, Japan, Netherlands, Norway, Poland, Russia, Serbia, Slovakia, Slovenia, South Africa, Spain, Sweden, UK, USA.
IGO Relations None. **NGO Relations** None.
[2015.06.01/XJ8835/**E**]

♦ European Study Group for Cell Proliferation / see European Cell Proliferation Society (#06459)

♦ European Study Group on Lysosomal Diseases (ESGLD) 08850
Groupe européen pour l'étude des lysosomes
Sec Inst of Inherited Metabolic Disorders, 1 st Fac of Medicine, Charles Univ in Prague, Ke Karlovu 2, 120 00 Prague 2, Czechia. T. +420224967208.
Chairman address not obtained.
URL: http://www.esgld.org/
History Founded May 1978, Windsor (UK). Registered in accordance with Dutch law in Rotterdam (Netherlands): 24352201. **Aims** Encourage contact and collaboration between European research groups by exchange of information and materials, and promote other activities to facilitate personal contacts. **Structure** Committee of 8 scientists (elected by Pan-European ballot). Sub Group, set up in 1994: European Working Group on Gaucher's Disease. **Languages** English. **Staff** Voluntary. **Finance** Members' dues (annual). **Activities** Events/meetings; networking/liaising. **Events** *Biennial Workshop* Barcelona (Spain) 2019, *Biennial Workshop* Lyon (France) 2017, *Biennial Workshop* Pozzuoli (Italy) 2015, *Biennial Workshop* Graz (Austria) 2013, *Biennial Workshop* Kirkkonummi (Finland) 2011. **Publications** *Lysosome Newsletter* (every 2 years).
Members Research groups and laboratories (about 160) in 22 countries:
Austria, Belarus, Belgium, Cyprus, Czechia, Denmark, Finland, France, Germany, Greece, Israel, Italy, Netherlands, Norway, Poland, Portugal, Russia, Spain, Sweden, Switzerland, UK, Ukraine.
[2018/XD0777/**D**]

♦ European Study Group on the Molecular Biology of Picornaviruses (meeting series)

♦ European Study Group on Pathogenesis and Immunology in Helicobacter Infections (ESGPIHI) 08851
Sec Div of Bacteriology, Lund Univ, Sölvegatan 23, SE-223 62 Lund, Sweden. T. +4646173240. Fax +4646152564.
URL: http://www.helicobacter-helsingor.eu/
History 1992, as *European Pathogenesis and Immunology Study Group*. **Structure** Executive Committee, including 2 Chairmen. **Activities** Organizes workshops. **Events** *International Workshop on Pathogenesis and Host Response in Helicobacter Infections* Helsingør (Denmark) 2022, *International Workshop on Pathogenesis and Host Response in Helicobacter Infections* Helsingør (Denmark) 2021, *International Workshop on Pathogenesis and Host Response in Helicobacter Infections* Helsingør (Denmark) 2020, *International Workshop on Pathogenesis and Host Response in Helicobacter Infections* Helsingør (Denmark) 2018, *International Workshop on Pathogenesis and Host Response in Helicobacter Infections* Helsingør (Denmark) 2016. **NGO Relations** Affiliated with: *European Helicobacter and Microbiota Study Group (EHMSG, #07471)*.
[2022/XJ4301/**E**]

♦ European Study Group for Rehabilitation and Functional Surgery Following Laryngectomy (EGFL) 08852
Address not obtained.
URL: http://www.ceorlhns.org/index.php?id=104
History 1991, formalizing a group which had organized conferences in the field since 1986, Würzburg (Germany). **Aims** Disseminate information so as to reinforce potential of European research in the field; encourage European research and clinical networks; promote cultural and scientific exchange of researchers at European level; cooperate with organizations concerned with research on treatment of laryngeal *cancer* and rehabilitation strategies. **Structure** Board of 10 members including President and Secretary General. **Activities** Organizes biennial *International Congress on Surgical and Prosthetic Rehabilitation after Laryngectomy*. Creates European research networks, leading to a number of European projects. **Events** *Biennial Congress* London (UK) 2011, *Biennial Congress* Lisbon (Portugal) 2009, *Biennial Congress* Rome (Italy) 2007, *Congress* Rome (Italy) 2007, *International EGFL workshop on high tech rehabilitation after laryngectomy* Groningen (Netherlands) 2005.
Members Individuals (10) in 8 countries:
Belgium, France, Germany, Italy, Netherlands, Portugal, Spain, UK.
NGO Relations Member of: *Confederation of European Otorhinolaryngology – Head and Neck Surgery (Confederation of European ORL-HNS, #04528)*. Cooperates with: *Educating Students in Engineering and Medicine (ESEM, #05364)*.
[2014/XJ3646/**E**]

♦ European Sub-Committee of the International Pharmaceutical Students' Federation / see European Pharmaceutical Students' Association (#08197)

♦ European Sugar Refineries Association (ESRA) 08853
Main Office Place Poelaert 6, 1000 Brussels, Belgium. T. +3228999394. E-mail: secretariat@sugarrefineries.eu.
URL: https://sugarrefineries.eu
History 2011. Registration: Start date: 2012, Belgium; EU Transparency Register, No/ID: 153540811905-01. **Aims** Establish a constructive dialogue between European sugar refineries and decision-makers at European and national levels, as well as with other parties involved in the development of the sugar industry. **Structure** General Assembly (annual); Board of Directors. **Publications** Position Papers. **Members** Cane sugar refineries (26) in 9 countries. Membership countries not specified.
[2021/XJ5890/**D**]

♦ European Sugar Users / see CIUS – European Sugar Users (#03961)

♦ European Sulphuric Acid Association (ESA) **08854**
Contact CEFIC, Rue Belliard 40, Bte 15, 1040 Brussels, Belgium. T. +3226767372. Fax +3226767241. E-mail: for@cefic.be.
URL: http://www.sulphuric-acid.eu/
History 1954, as *European Centre for Studies of Sulphuric Acid – Centre européen d'études de l'acide sulfurique (CEAAS)*. Currently a sector group of *Conseil européen de l'industrie chimique (CEFIC, #04687)*. **Aims** Represent and defend the interests of the sulphuric acid, oleum, sulphur dioxide and sulphur trioxide sector at national and international levels; provide a forum for issues of general and technical interest. **Structure** General Assembly; Plenary Committee; Management Committee; Technical Committee; Statistics. **Languages** English, French. **Staff** 0.35 FTE, paid. **Activities** Advocacy/lobbying/activism; awareness raising; certification/accreditation; events/meetings; guidance/assistance/consulting; knowledge management/information dissemination; networking/liaising; politics/policy/regulatory. **Publications** *Sulphuric Acid* (1994); *CESAS Recommendation for the Safe Handling of Liquid Sulphur Dioxide* (1993). CESAS Presentation.
Members Sulphuric acid producers in 16 countries:
Austria, Belgium, Bulgaria, Czechia, Finland, France, Germany, Italy, Netherlands, Norway, Poland, Slovenia, Spain, Sweden, Switzerland, UK. [2017.11.08/XE3957/**E**]

♦ European Summit / see European Council (#06801)

♦ European Sumo Federation (ESF) **08855**
Pres Maly Rynek Street 13, 63-700 Krotoszyn, Poland. T. +48601983698.
URL: http://www.europeansumofederation.com/
Activities Sporting activities.
Members Full in 32 countries:
Armenia, Austria, Azerbaijan, Belarus, Belgium, Bulgaria, Czechia, Denmark, Estonia, Finland, Georgia, Germany, Great Britain, Hungary, Ireland, Israel, Italy, Latvia, Lithuania, Moldova, Netherlands, North Macedonia, Norway, Poland, Portugal, Romania, Russia, Serbia, Slovakia, Switzerland, Türkiye, Ukraine.
NGO Relations Continental federation of: *International Sumo Federation (IFS, #15624)*. [2020/XM7593/**D**]

♦ European Sumo Union (no recent information)

♦ European Sunday Alliance **08856**
Secretariat c/o CEC, Ecumenical Centre, Rue Joseph II 174, 1000 Brussels, Belgium. T. +3222301732. E-mail: contact@europeansundayalliance.eu – press@europeansundayalliance.eu.
URL: http://www.europeansundayalliance.eu/
History 20 Jun 2011, Brussels (Belgium). **Aims** Raise awareness of the unique value of synchronized free time for European societies.
Members National Sunday alliances; trade unions; civil society organizations; religious communities. Members in 16 countries:
Austria, Belgium, Czechia, Estonia, France, Germany, Hungary, Italy, Luxembourg, Netherlands, Norway, Poland, Romania, Slovakia, Spain, Switzerland.
Included in the above, 8 organizations listed in this Yearbook:
Conference of European Churches (CEC, #04593); *European Alliance of Catholic Women's Organisations (ANDANTE, #05864)*; *European Christian Workers Movement (ECWM, #06546)*; *European Federation of Christian Student Associations (#07076)*; *European Large Families Confederation (ELFAC, #07651)*; *Federation of Catholic Family Associations in Europe (#09468)*; *International Christian Union of Business Executives (#12566)*; *UNI Global Union – Europa (UNI Europa, #20342)*.
NGO Relations Supporting organizations: *Commission of the Bishops' Conferences of the European Union (COMECE, #04205)*; *European Trade Union Confederation (ETUC, #08927)*; *Jesuit European Social Centre (JESC, #16103)*. [2021/XJ2873/y/**D**]

♦ European Sunglass Association (inactive)

♦ European Sunlight Association (ESA) **08857**
Sec Boulevard Saint-Michel 65, 1040 Brussels, Belgium. T. +3228810925. E-mail: info@europeansunlight.eu.
URL: http://www.europeansunlight.eu/
History Re-founded 28 Jan 2009. Registration: Banque-Carrefour des Entreprises, No/ID: 0809.133.418, Start date: 5 Dec 2008, Belgium; EU Transparency Register, No/ID: 725088918731-87, Start date: 15 Sep 2015. **Aims** Offer objective and balanced information about responsible tanning. **Structure** General Meeting; Board. Technical Working Group. **Events** *General Meeting* Frankfurt-Main (Germany) 2011.
Members National members in 14 countries:
Austria, Belgium, Czechia, Denmark, Estonia, France, Germany, Hungary, Netherlands, Norway, Poland, Sweden, Switzerland, UK.
Company members in 4 countries:
Germany, Hungary, Netherlands, USA. [2023/XJ4961/**D**]

♦ European Supercentenarian Organisation (unconfirmed)

♦ European Suppliers of Waste to Energy Technology (ESWET) **08858**
SG Av Adolphe Lacomblé 59, 1030 Brussels, Belgium. T. +3227432988. Fax +3227432990. E-mail: info@eswet.eu.
URL: http://www.eswet.eu/
History Founded 2004. EU Transparency Register: 56047551356-84. **Aims** Foster the development and dissemination of Waste-to-Energy technology; raise awareness of the positive implications of the technology in terms of better waste management, energy and for the environment. **Structure** General Assembly. Committees (2). **Languages** English. **Staff** 2.00 FTE, paid. **Finance** Members' dues. **Activities** Meeting activities; presentations. **Events** *South East European conference on waste management, recycling and environment* Sofia (Bulgaria) 2012.
Members Full in 7 countries:
Belgium, Denmark, France, Germany, Italy, Sweden, Switzerland.
NGO Relations Member of: *Industry4Europe (#11181)*. [2020/XJ4890/**D**]

♦ European Support Fund for the Co-Production and Distribution of Creative Cinematographic and Audiovisual Works (EURIMAGES) **08859**
Fonds Européen de Soutien à la Coproduction et la Diffusion des Oeuvres de Création Cinématographiques et Audiovisuelles
Exec Dir c/o Council of Europe, Agora Bldg, Allée des Droits de l'Homme, 67075 Strasbourg CEDEX, France. T. +33388412640. Fax +33388412760. E-mail: eurimages@coe.int.
URL: http://www.coe.int/Eurimages/
History 1988, by Resolution (88) 15, on the basis of a partial agreement of *Council of Europe (CE, #04881)*, regrouping 12 Member States. Also referred to as *Eurimages Support Fund – Fonds de soutien "Eurimages"* and *European Cinema Support Fund – Fonds de Soutien au Cinéma Européen*. Operational from 1 Jan 1989. **Aims** Promote the international *film* industry. **Structure** Board of Management; Secretariat. **Languages** English, French. **Staff** 25.00 FTE, paid. **Finance** Annual budget: euro 26,000,000. **Activities** Financial and/or material support; awards/prizes/competitions. **Events** *Meeting* Helsinki (Finland) 2011. **Publications** *Support for the Co-production* (2016).
Members Open to Member States of the Council of Europe, with possibility of any non-Member State of acceding, either as a Associate Member. Currently 38 countries:
Albania, Armenia, Austria, Belgium, Bosnia-Herzegovina, Bulgaria, Croatia, Cyprus, Czechia, Denmark, Estonia, Finland, France, Georgia, Germany, Greece, Hungary, Iceland, Ireland, Italy, Latvia, Lithuania, Luxembourg, Montenegro, Netherlands, North Macedonia, Norway, Poland, Portugal, Romania, Russia, Serbia, Slovakia, Slovenia, Spain, Sweden, Switzerland, Türkiye.
Associate members in 2 countries:
Argentina, Canada. [2019.12.12/XF0932/f/**F***]

♦ European Surfing Association / see European Surfing Federation (#08860)

♦ European Surfing Federation (ESF) **08860**
Fédération européenne de surf
SG 16 Beacon Estate Sancreed, Penzance, TR20 8QR, UK. T. +447534983046.
URL: http://www.eurosurfing.org/
History 1970. Constitution adopted at Annual General Meeting, 5 May 1979, Jersey; revised at Annual General Meetings: 21 Nov 1982, London (UK); 31 Oct 1983, Jersey; 8 Dec 1984, Paris (France); 3 Oct 1985, Ireland. New constitution adopted 27 Aug 1989, France; revised at Annual General Meetings: 29 Dec 1991, Portugal; 23 Aug 2000, Jersey. Former names and other names: *European Surfing Association* – former. Registration: Companies House, No/ID: 5290754, Start date: 18 Nov 2004, England and Wales. **Aims** Establish and maintain a European federation to promote the interests of surfing in all its forms throughout all countries of Europe to which all recognized national surfing associations/bodies concerned with the sport of surf riding, surfing or its related activities may gain affiliation; encourage the formation of national surfing associations/bodies in the individual countries to promote, coordinate and control activities of organized surfing within their own countries. **Structure** Annual General Meeting; Executive Committee. **Languages** English. **Staff** Voluntary. **Finance** Sources: members' dues. **Activities** Events/meetings; training/education. **Events** *Annual General Meeting* Jersey (UK) 2010, *Annual General Meeting* Jersey (UK) 2009, *Annual General Meeting* Jersey (UK) 2008, *Annual General Meeting* Ferrol (Spain) 2006, *Annual General Meeting* Jersey (UK) 2000. **Publications** *ESF Newsletter* (2 a year).
Members National federations or associations; Persons federated in one of the ESF member countries; Honorary Members. Members in 23 countries and territories:
Austria, Belgium, Channel Is, Denmark, England, Finland, France, Germany, Greece, Hungary, Ireland, Italy, Morocco, Netherlands, Norway, Portugal, Russia, Scotland, Spain, Sweden, Switzerland, Türkiye, Wales. [2021/XD6550/**D**]

♦ European Surgical Association (ESA) **08861**
Admin Office c/o Hopscotch Congrès, 23/25 rue Notre Dame des Victoires, 75002 Paris, France. E-mail: esa@hopscotchcongres.com.
URL: http://europeansurgicalassociation.org/
History 1993. **Events** *Annual Meeting* Madrid (Spain) 2019, *Annual Meeting* Edinburgh (UK) 2016, *Annual Meeting* Warsaw (Poland) 2015, *Annual Meeting* Athens (Greece) 2014, *Annual Meeting* Beaune (France) 2013. **Publications** *Annals of Surgery*. [2021/XD8529/**D**]

♦ European Surgical Dressings Manufacturers' Association (inactive)
♦ European Surveillance Scheme for Travel Associated Legionnaires' Disease / see European Legionnaires' Disease Surveillance Network (#07681)
♦ European Surveyors' Liaison Committee / see Council of European Geodetic Surveyors (#04890)

♦ European Survey Research Association (ESRA) **08862**
Contact Division of Social Statistics, School of Social Science, Southampton, SO17 1BJ, UK. E-mail: info@europeansurveyresearch.org.
URL: http://www.europeansurveyresearch.org/
History 22 Jul 2005, Barcelona (Spain), as *European Association for Survey Research (EASR)*. **Aims** Provide coordination in the field of survey research in Europe; encourage communication between researchers. **Languages** English. **Staff** 4.00 FTE, paid. **Finance** Budget (annual): less than euro 10,000. **Events** *Biennial Conference* Zagreb (Croatia) 2019, *Big Data Meets Survey Science Conference* Barcelona (Spain) 2018, *Biennial Conference* Lisbon (Portugal) 2017, *Biennial Conference* Reykjavik (Iceland) 2015, *Biennial Conference* Ljubljana (Slovenia) 2013. **Publications** *Survey Research Methods* – online journal.
Members Institutional members in 5 countries:
Germany, Spain, Switzerland, UK, USA.
NGO Relations *European Association of Methodology (EAM, #06119)*. [2014/XM0557/**D**]

♦ European Sustainable Agriculture through Genome Editing (unconfirmed)

♦ European Sustainable Cities and Towns Campaign **08863**
Campagne des villes européennes durables
Contact address not obtained. E-mail: info@sustainablecities.eu.
URL: http://www.sustainable-cities.eu/
History 27 May 1994, Ålborg (Denmark), on signature of the *'Ålborg Charter'* by over 80 European local authorities and 253 representatives of international organizations, national governments, scientific institutes, consultants and individuals. **Aims** Encourage and support European local authorities in drawing up long-term *strategic* plans for sustainable development and *local Agenda 21* programmes. **Structure** Campaign Coordinating Committee of major European networks of local authorities. **Finance** Campaign Office sponsored by: cities of Hannover (Germany), Barcelona (Spain) and Malmö (Sweden); Coordinamento Italiano Agenda 21 Locali (Italy); *European Commission (EC, #06633)* (DG Environment). **Activities** Disseminates information on urban sustainability; organizes thematic working session; supports regional initiatives; organizes and grants European Sustainable Award; organizes an Open Platform for Sustainable Development (OPUS). **Events** *European conference on sustainable cities and towns* Dunkerque (France) 2010, *European conference on sustainable cities and towns* Seville (Spain) 2007, *Conference* Aalborg (Denmark) 2004, *European conference on sustainable cities and towns* Aalborg (Denmark) 2004, *Conference* Hannover (Germany) 2002. **Publications** *Campaign Newsletter* (4 a year) in Catalan, English, French, German, Italian, Spanish. *The Lisbon Action Plan: From Charter to Action* (1996); *Charter of European Cities and Towns Towards Sustainability (The Aalborg Charter)* (1994); *The Hannover Call of European Municipal Leaders at the Turn of the 21st Century*. Reports; conference proceedings; leaflets; guidelines; action plans.
Members Local authorities (1,537) in 39 countries and territories:
Albania, Austria, Belgium, Bulgaria, Croatia, Cyprus, Czechia, Denmark, Estonia, Finland, France, Germany, Greece, Hungary, Iceland, Ireland, Italy, Latvia, Lebanon, Lithuania, Luxembourg, Moldova, Montenegro, Morocco, Netherlands, Norway, Poland, Portugal, Romania, Russia, Serbia, Slovakia, Slovenia, Spain, Sweden, Switzerland, Türkiye, UK, Ukraine.
NGO Relations Coordinated by: *Climate Alliance (#04005)*; *Council of European Municipalities and Regions (CEMR, #04891)*; *WHO European Healthy Cities Network (WHO Healthy Cities, #20936)*; *MEDCITIES Network (#16610)*; *Union of the Baltic Cities (UBC, #20366)*; *World Organization of United Cities and Local Governments (UCLG, #21695)*. [2007/XK0950/**F**]

♦ European Sustainable Development Network (ESDN) **08864**
Managing Dir WU RIMAS, Welthandelsplatz 1, Building D1, 1020 Vienna, Austria. T. +43431313366044. E-mail: office@esdn.eu.
URL: https://www.esdn.eu/
History Founded as an informal network of public administrators and other experts. Since early 2006, supported by ESDN Office. Registration: EU Transparency Register, No/ID: 770141548146-23, Start date: 17 Nov 2022. **Aims** Exchange experiences, knowledge and good practices regarding the key features of SD strategy processes at EU, national and regional levels, including the 2030 Agenda for Sustainable Development and SDGs. **Structure** Steering Group. **Languages** English. **Staff** 1.00 FTE, paid. **Finance** Contributions from Steering Group countries. **Activities** Events/meetings. **Events** *Conference* Bucharest (Romania) 2022, *Conference* Austria 2021, *Conference* Germany 2020, *Conference* Helsinki (Finland) 2019, *Annual Conference* Vienna (Austria) 2018. **Publications** Quarterly Report; policy briefs; discussion papers; event reports. [2022/XM2935/**E**]

♦ European Sustainable Investment Forum (EUROSIF) **08865**
Communications Officer Rue Belliard 40, 1040 Brussels, Belgium. T. +3227863092. E-mail: contact@eurosif.org.
URL: http://www.eurosif.org/
History 28 Nov 2001. Former names and other names: *European Sustainable and Responsible Investment Forum* – former (28 Nov 2001); *European Social Investment Forum (Eurosif)* – former. Registration: No/ID: W751164129, Start date: 28 Jun 2012, France, Paris; EU Transparency Register, No/ID: 480715239269-75, Start date: 31 Aug 2020. **Aims** Promote *sustainability* through European *financial* markets. **Structure** Advisory Council Meeting (annual). Governed by national sustainable investment forums (SIFs). **Languages** English, French, Italian. **Staff** 4.00 FTE, paid. **Finance** Sources: members' dues. **Activities** Advocacy/lobbying/activism; awareness raising; events/meetings; knowledge management/information dissemination; projects/programmes; research and development. **Events** *Annual Conference* Brussels (Belgium) 2011, *Annual Advisory Council Meeting* Amsterdam (Netherlands) 2010, *Annual Advisory Council Meeting* Paris

(France) 2009, *Annual Advisory Council Meeting* Paris (France) 2007, *Meeting / Annual Advisory Council Meeting* Paris (France) 2006. **Publications** *European SRI Market Study* (every 2 years); *Eurosif InFocus*; *Eurosif InSight*; *Eurosif Newsletter/SRI Headlines*. Policy positions; reports.
Members National Sustainable Investment Forums (SIFs) in 9 countries:
Finland, France, Germany, Ireland, Italy, Spain, Sweden, Switzerland, UK.
Observers in 3 countries:
Czechia, Luxembourg, Norway.
Supporters (2):
European Climate Foundation (ECF, #06574); *King Baudouin Foundation (KBF)*.
IGO Relations Member of (1): *European Commission (EC, #06633)* (High Level Expert Group on Sustainable Finance). **NGO Relations** Founding member of: Global Sustainable Investment Alliance (GSIA). [2022.03.04/XF7053/y/**F**]

♦ European Sustainable Phosphorus Platform (ESPP) 08866
SG 67 rue de Trèves, 1040 Brussels, Belgium. E-mail: info@phosphorusplatform.eu.
URL: http://www.phosphorusplatform.eu/
History Mar 2013. Formally established 2 Dec 2014, Brussels (Belgium). Registration: EU Transparency Register, No/ID: 260483415852-40; No/ID: 0568 830 863, Start date: 2 Dec 2014, Belgium. **Aims** Promote, facilitate, contribute to and/or implement phosphorus sustainability in Europe. **Structure** General Assembly (annual); Board of Directors. **Languages** English. **Staff** 1.00 FTE, paid. **Finance** Members' dues. **Activities** Knowledge management/information dissemination; networking/liaising; advocacy/lobbying/activism; events/meetings. **Events** *Summit of the Organic and organo-mineral Fertilisers Industries in Europe (SOFIE)* Brussels (Belgium) 2023, *European Sustainable Phosphorus Conference (ESPC4)* Vienna (Austria) 2022, *European Sustainable Phosphorus Conference (ESPC4)* Vienna (Austria) 2020, *European Sustainable Phosphorus Conference* Helsinki (Finland) 2018, *European Sustainable Phosphorus Conference (ESPC2)* Berlin (Germany) 2015.
Members Full; Partners. Members in 11 countries:
Austria, Belgium, Finland, France, Germany, Ireland, Italy, Netherlands, Spain, Switzerland, UK.
Included in the above, 2 organizations listed in this Yearbook:
Fertilizers Europe (#09738); *Foundation for a Living Baltic Sea*. [2022/XM6904/y/**F**]

- ♦ European Sustainable and Responsible Investment Forum / see European Sustainable Investment Forum (#08865)
- ♦ European Sustainable Tropical Timber Coalition (unconfirmed)

♦ European Suzuki Association (ESA) 08867
Chair 45 Main Upper Benefield, Peterborough, PE8 5AN, UK. E-mail: esa@europeansuzuki.org – chair@europeansuzuki.org.
URL: http://www.europeansuzuki.org/
History 1980. **Aims** Further Dr Shinichi Suzuki's approach to education through the provision of a Suzuki Teacher Training Program which maintains the quality of Suzuki teaching throughout the region. **Structure** Board of Directors. **Languages** English. **Finance** Sources: members' dues. A proportion of membership fees collected by National Suzuki Associations is paid to the ESA, who in turn pays an annual membership fee on behalf of all Suzuki teacher members to the ISA. **Events** *European Suzuki Children's Convention* Cuneo (Italy) 2022, *European Online Conference* 2021, *International Teacher Trainer's Conference* Madrid (Spain) 2019, *European Teacher Conference* Reykjavik (Iceland) 2018, *European Teacher Trainer's Conference* London (UK) 2017. **Publications** *European Suzuki Teachers' Newsletter*.
Members Associations in 26 countries and territories:
Austria, Belgium, Czechia, Denmark, Estonia, Faeroe Is, Finland, France, Germany, Iceland, Ireland, Italy, Latvia, Lithuania, Netherlands, Norway, Poland, Russia, South Africa, Spain, Sweden, Switzerland, Türkiye, UK, Ukraine, Zimbabwe.
NGO Relations Member of (1): *International Suzuki Association (ISA, #15637)*. [2023.02.13/XE3155/**E**]

- ♦ European Swimming Federation (#16477)
- ♦ European Symposium on Algorithms (meeting series)
- ♦ European Symposium on Ambulatory Anesthesia and Analgesia (meeting series)
- ♦ European Symposium on Artificial Neural Networks, Computational Intelligence and Machine Learning (meeting series)
- ♦ European Symposium on Atomic Spectrometry (meeting series)
- ♦ European Symposium on Comminution and Classification (meeting series)
- ♦ European Symposium on Computer Aided Process Engineering (meeting series)
- ♦ European Symposium on Computer and Communications (meeting series)
- ♦ European Symposium on Electrochemical Engineering (meeting series)
- ♦ European Symposium on Fluorine Chemistry (meeting series)
- ♦ European Symposium on Late Complications After Childhood Cancer (meeting series)
- ♦ European Symposium on Organic Chemistry (meeting series)
- ♦ European Symposium on Organic Reactivity (meeting series)
- ♦ European Symposium on Paediatric Cochlear Implantation (meeting series)
- ♦ European Symposium on Pediatric Hand Surgery and Rehabilitation (meeting series)
- ♦ European Symposium on Polymer Blends (meeting series)
- ♦ European Symposium on Research in Architecture and Urban Design (meeting series)
- ♦ European Symposium on Suicide and Suicidal Behaviour (meeting series)
- ♦ European Symposium on Thermal Analysis and Calorimetry (meeting series)
- ♦ European Symposium on Ultrasonic Characterization of Bone (meeting series)

♦ European Synchrotron Radiation Facility (ESRF) 08868
Dir Gen 71 av des Martyrs – CS 40220, 38043 Grenoble CEDEX 9, France. T. +33476882000. Fax +33476882020. E-mail: communication@esrf.fr.
URL: http://www.esrf.eu/
History 10 Dec 1985. Established with the signing of a Memorandum of Understanding (MoU) by France, Germany FR, Italy, Spain and UK, the conceptual phase covering the period 1975-1980 and the pre-foundation phase 1980-1985. The construction period started on 1 Jan 1988, based on a protocol, signed on 22 Dec 1987, by the 5 countries mentioned above, plus Switzerland and the 4 Nordic countries, Denmark, Finland, Norway and Sweden. A 'Convention concerning the construction and operation of a European Synchrotron Radiation Facility' signed 16 Dec 1988, Paris (France), by research ministers of France, Germany, Italy, Spain, UK, Switzerland, Denmark, Finland, Norway, Sweden and Belgium. ESRF company (société civile) established 12 Jan 1989, according to French law. Representatives of the above mentioned 11 countries and of the Netherlands signed, 9 Dec 1991, a Protocol of accession by the latter to the ESRF Convention. First operation 1992. Official inauguration 30 Sep 1994. Former names and other names: *Source européenne de rayonnement synchrotron* – former; *Installation européenne de rayonnement synchrotron* – former. **Aims** Design, build, operate and develop a synchrotron radiation source and associated equipment for the use of scientific communities of contracting parties, and promote the use of this facility. **Structure** Council; Board of Directors; Committees (2). **Languages** English. **Staff** 70.00 FTE, paid. **Finance** Sources: members' dues. Annual budget: 115,000 EUR (2020). **Activities** Events/meetings; research and development. **Events** *European Big Science Business Forum* Granada (Spain) 2022, *International Conference on Tomography of Materials and Structures* Grenoble (France) 2022, *European Big Science Business Forum* Granada (Spain) 2021, *IPAC : International Particle Accelerator Conference* Caen (France) 2020, *European Big Science Business Forum* Granada (Spain) 2020. **Publications** *ESRFnews* (3 a year); *Scientific Highlights* (annual).
Members Member states (13):
Belgium, Denmark, Finland, France, Germany, Italy, Netherlands, Norway, Russia, Spain, Sweden, Switzerland, UK.
Associate countries (9):
Austria, Czechia, Hungary, India, Israel, Poland, Portugal, Slovakia, South Africa.
IGO Relations Nordic governments represented by: *NORDSYNC (#17550)*. Belgium and Dutch governments represented by BENESYNC. **NGO Relations** Member of (1): *EIROforum (#05401)*. [2021.09.03/XF2355/**F***]

- ♦ European Synchrotron Radiation Society (no recent information)
- ♦ European Syndicate on Steel Drums / see European Association of Steel Drum Manufacturers (#06222)

♦ European Synthetic Biology Society (EUSynBioS) 08869
Main Office 128 Rue La Boétie, 75008 Paris, France. E-mail: sc@eusynbios.org.
URL: http://www.eusynbios.org/
History 2014, Cambridge (UK). Former names and other names: *European Association of Synthetic Biology Students and Postdocs (EUSynBioS)* – former (2014 to 2019). Registration: France. **Aims** Shape and foster a community of young researchers active in the scientific discipline of synthetic biology within Europe by means of providing an integrative central resource for interaction and professional development. **Structure** Steering Committee; Advisory Board. **Activities** Events/meetings; networking/liaising. **Events** *Symposium* Brno (Czech Rep) 2019, *Symposium* Madrid (Spain) 2017, *Symposium* London (UK) 2016. [2022/XM6528/**D**]

- ♦ European Synthetic Rubber Association (no recent information)
- ♦ European Synthetic Turf Organisation / see EMEA Synthetic Turf Council (#05436)
- ♦ European Synthetic Waterproofing Association / see European Single Ply Waterproofing Association (#08488)
- ♦ European Syrian Civil Society Exchange (unconfirmed)

♦ European System of Central Banks (ESCB) 08870
Système européen des banques centrales (SEBC)
Main Office c/o ECB, Sonnemannstr 20, 60314 Frankfurt-Main, Germany. T. +496913440. Fax +496913446000. E-mail: info@ecb.europa.eu.
URL: http://www.ecb.europa.eu/
History Established as an integral part of *European Union (EU, #08967)*. Establishment was envisaged in the *Treaty on European Union (Maastricht Treaty, 1992)*, 7 Feb 1992, together with that of the European Central Bank, under the 3rd stage of *European Economic and Monetary Union (EMU, #06961)*. The *Committee of Governors of the Central Banks of the Member States of the European Economic Community (inactive)* was closely involved in drawing up the ESCB statute, which is laid down in a protocol to the Maastricht Treaty. *European Monetary Institute (EMI, inactive)*, set up 1 Jan 1994, under the second stage of EMU, prepared the regulatory, organizational and logistic framework necessary for the ESCB to perform its tasks; its work was completed 31 May 1998 and succeeded on 1 Jun 1998 by establishment of ECB and ESCB. The 3rd stage of EMU was launched following decision of *Council of the European Union (#04895)*, that the majority of member states had met convergence criteria and fulfilled conditions for adoption of a single currency. This 3rd stage commenced on 1 Jan 1999, with the irrevocable fixing of the exchange rates of the currencies of the participating Member States and when the new European currency – the *'euro'* – became effective, and was finalized on 31 Dec 2001. From 1 Jan 2002, banks of countries of the *Euro Area* (Eurosystem) issue only euro notes and coins. Legal framework for the single monetary policy is the *Treaty on the Functioning of the European Union (TFEU, 1957)* and the Statute of the European System of Central Banks and of the European Central Bank. **Aims** Primary objective: maintain price stability. Without prejudice to objective price stability: support general economic policies in the European Community; act in accordance with the principle of an open market economy, with free competition, favouring efficient allocation of resources. Basic tasks: define and implement the monetary policy of the Community; conduct foreign exchange operations; hold and manage official foreign reserves of euro area Member States; promote smooth operation of payment systems; contribute to smooth conduct of policies pursued by the competent authorities relating to the prudential supervision of credit institutions and the stability of the financial system. **Structure** ESCB comprises *European Central Bank (ECB, #06466)* and the National Central Banks (NCBs) of European Union countries. Since the ESCB is an independent system, neither the ECB, nor a NCB, nor any member of their decision-making bodies, may seek or take instructions from any external body when performing ESCB-related tasks. **Languages** EU languages.
Members NCBs in 28 countries:
Austria, Belgium, Bulgaria, Croatia, Cyprus, Czechia, Denmark, Estonia, Finland, France, Germany, Greece, Hungary, Ireland, Italy, Latvia, Lithuania, Luxembourg, Malta, Netherlands, Poland, Portugal, Romania, Slovakia, Slovenia, Spain, Sweden, UK. [2022.11.10/XF2712/**F***]

♦ European System of Cooperative Research Networks in Agriculture (ESCORENA) 08871
Système européen de réseaux coopératifs de recherche en agriculture – Sistema Europeo de Redes Cooperativas de Investigación Agricola
Focal Point Coordinator c/o Taylor and Francis, 530 Walnut St, Ste 850, Philadelphia PA 19106, USA. T. +48602239255. E-mail: rkscience.biuro@gmail.com.
Secretariat Inst of Natural Fibres and Medicinal Plants, Wjoska Polskiego 71b, 60-630 Poznań, Poland. T. +48604169115. Fax +488417830.
Main: http://www.agrowebcee.net/
History 1973. Established at Regional Conference for Europe of *FAO (#09260)*, as a programme within *European Commission on Agriculture (ECA)*. Commenced operations 1974. **Aims** Promote the voluntary exchange of information and experimental data; support joint research projects; facilitate the sharing of expertise, germplasm and technologies, especially from the more advanced nations to developing countries. **Structure** Serves as an umbrella for 22 networks working on issues of global interest:
- *Recycling of Agricultural, Municipal and Industrial Residues in Agriculture (RAMIRAN)*;
- *European Cooperative Research Network on Flax and other Bast Plants (see: #08871)*;
- *European Cooperative Research Network on Sunflower (see: #08871)*;
- *European Cooperative Research Network on Sustainable Rural Environmental and Energy (SREN, see: #08871)*;
- *FAO/CIHEAM Inter-Regional Cooperative Research Network on Nuts (NUCIS, #09258)*;
- *FAO/CIHEAM International Network for the Research and Development of Pasture and Forage Crops (#09257)*;
- *Inter-regional FAO-CIHEAM Network for Research and Development in Sheep and Goats (#15970)*;
- *Inter-Regional Cooperative Research Network on Buffalo (Buffalo Network, #15967)*;
- *Inter-Regional Cooperative Research Network on Cotton for the Mediterranean and Middle East Regions (#15968)*;
- *Inter-Regional Cooperative Research Network on Olives (#15969)*;
- *FAO Inter-Regional Cooperative Research Network on Rice in the Mediterranean Climate Areas (MedRice Network, #09263)*;
- *Agromarketing Network*;
- *Apricot Network*;
- *Biomedical Technology, Epidemiology and Food Safety Global Network (CENTAUR Network)*;
- Farm Animal Welfare Network (FAW);
- Legumes and Pulses Knowledge Thematic Network;
- MAP – Medicinal and Aromatic Plants Network;
- Rye Thematic Knowledge Network;
- *Network of Aquaculture Centres in Central-Eastern Europe (NACEE, #16992)*;
- *Capacity Development Network in Nutrition in Central and Eastern Europe (CAPNUTRA, #03418)*;
- *Association internationale des musées d'agriculture (AIMA, #02720)*;
- OrganicEdunet Network;
- Legumes and Pulses Knowledge Thematic Network;
- MAP – Medicinal and Aromatic Plants Network;
- Rye Thematic Knowledge Network;
- Sericulture Network.

Languages English, Russian. **Staff** Voluntary. **Finance** Each participating institution defrays expenses covering its own contribution to the joint programme. Limited financial support from FAO and CIHEAM. **Activities** Research/documentation; knowledge management/information dissemination; guidance/assistance/consulting; events/meetings; networking/liaising. **Events** *Quadrennial coordinators meeting* Grignon (France) 2000, *Meeting on legumes for Mediterranean forage crops, pastures and alternative uses* Sassari (Italy) 2000, *Quadrennial coordinators meeting* Bella (Italy) 1996, *Workshop on environmental aspects of production and conversion of biomass for energy* Freising (Germany) 1994, *Special workshop on the management and breeding of perennial lucerne for diversified purposes* Lusignan (France) 1994. **Publications** *Scientific Bulletin of ESCORENA*. *REU Technical Series*. Progress reports; reports of consultations. Information Services: Website; Wikipedia; Networks' Newsletters, databases. **Members** A global network of networks. Membership countries not specified. **IGO Relations** *UNICEF (#20332)*; *WHO (#20950)*. [2021/XF5077/**F***]

♦ European Systemic Risk Board (ESRB) 08872
Secretariat c/o ECB, Kaiserstrasse 29, 60311 Frankfurt-Main, Germany. E-mail: info@esrb.europa.eu.
URL: http://www.esrb.europa.eu/

History Established 16 Dec 2010, when legislation establishing ESRB entered into force: Regulation (EU) No 1092/2010 of *Council of the European Union (#04895)* and *European Parliament (EP, #08146)* of 24 Nov 2010; Council Regulation (EU) No 1096/2010 of 17 Nov 2010. Part of *European System of Financial Supervision (ESFS)*. **Aims** Be the responsible body for the macro-prudential oversight of the financial system within the Union in order to contribute to the prevention or mitigation of systemic risks to financial stability in the Union that arise from developments within the financial system and taking into account macro-economic developments, so as to avoid periods of widespread financial distress. **Structure** General Board, comprising President and Vice-President of *European Central Bank (ECB, #06466)*, Governors of national central banks of Member States, one member of *European Commission (EC, #06633)*, Chairpersons of *European Banking Authority (EBA, #06311)*, *European Insurance and Occupational Pensions Authority (EIOPA, #07578)*, *European Securities and Markets Authority (ESMA, #08457)*, Chair and 2 Vice-Chairs of Advisory Scientific Committee (ASC), Chair of Advisory Technical Committee (ATC), and non-voting: one high-level representative per Member State of the competent national supervisory authorities and President of *Economic and Financial Committee (EFC)*. Steering Committee. Secretariat, ensured by ECB. Advisory Technical Committee; Advisory Scientific Committee. **Languages** English. **Staff** 61.80 FTE, paid. **Finance** Provided by ECB. Annual budget (2016): euro 9,500,000. **Activities** Knowledge management/information dissemination; research/documentation; guidance/assistance/consulting; monitoring/evaluation; publishing activities; events/meetings; politics/policy/regulatory. **Events** *Conference on Systemic Risk Analytics* Helsinki (Finland) 2021, *Conference on Systemic Risk Analytics* Helsinki (Finland) 2018, *Conference on Systemic Risk Analysis* Helsinki (Finland) 2017, *Conference on Systemic Risk Analysis* Helsinki (Finland) 2016, *Conference on Systemic Risk Analysis* Helsinki (Finland) 2015. **Publications** Reports; occasional and working papers; commentaries.
Members National authorities of 28 countries:
Austria, Belgium, Bulgaria, Croatia, Cyprus, Czechia, Denmark, Estonia, Finland, France, Germany, Greece, Hungary, Ireland, Italy, Latvia, Lithuania, Luxembourg, Malta, Netherlands, Poland, Portugal, Romania, Slovakia, Slovenia, Spain, Sweden, UK.
Regional institutions (6):
European Banking Authority (EBA, #06311); *European Central Bank (ECB, #06466)*; *European Commission (EC, #06633)*; *European Insurance and Occupational Pensions Authority (EIOPA, #07578)*; *European Securities and Markets Authority (ESMA, #08457)*.
Participate in General Board without voting rights (3):
Iceland, Liechtenstein, Norway.
IGO Relations *Financial Stability Board (FSB, #09770)*; *International Monetary Fund (IMF, #14180)*; various EU institutions and agencies. [2017.10.23/XJ2857/y/**E***]

♦ European Table Soccer Association (no recent information)

♦ European Table Tennis Union (ETTU) 08873

Union européenne de tennis de table – Europäische Tisch-Tennis Union
Secretariat 73 rue Adolphe Fischer, L-1520 Luxembourg, Luxembourg. T. +352223030. E-mail: office@ettu.org.
URL: http://www.ettu.org/
History Founded 13 Mar 1957, Budapest (Hungary). Continental federation of: *International Table Tennis Federation (ITTF, #15650)*. **Aims** Promote any event – *championships* and tournaments – which is in the interests of table tennis; coordinate dates and conditions for international events, in consultation with ITTF and the associations concerned; develop and advance coaching, umpiring and refereeing in Europe; uphold the principles, rules and policies of ITTF. **Structure** General Meeting; Congress (every year during European or World Championships); Extraordinary General Meeting; Executive Board; Sub-committees (6). **Languages** English, French, German. **Staff** 3.00 FTE, paid. **Finance** Members' dues. **Activities** Events/meetings. **Events** *Ordinary Congress* Lisbon (Portugal) 2014, *Extraordinary Congress* Tokyo (Japan) 2014, *Extraordinary Congress* Paris (France) 2013, *Congress / Ordinary Congress* Schwechat (Austria) 2013, *Extraordinary Congress* Dortmund (Germany) 2012.
Members Associations in 58 countries and territories:
Albania, Andorra, Armenia, Austria, Azerbaijan, Belarus, Belgium, Bosnia-Herzegovina, Bulgaria, Croatia, Cyprus, Czechia, Denmark, England, Estonia, Faeroe Is, Finland, France, Georgia, Germany, Gibraltar, Greece, Greenland, Guernsey, Hungary, Iceland, Ireland, Isle of Man, Israel, Italy, Jersey, Kosovo, Latvia, Liechtenstein, Lithuania, Luxembourg, Malta, Moldova, Monaco, Montenegro, Netherlands, North Macedonia, Norway, Poland, Portugal, Romania, Russia, San Marino, Scotland, Serbia, Slovakia, Slovenia, Spain, Sweden, Switzerland, Türkiye, Ukraine, Wales. [2020/XD0872/**D**]

♦ European Taekwondo Union (ETU) 08874

SG Hofestatt 13, 57439 Attendorn Eichen, Germany. T. +4927226346340.
URL: https://europeantaekwondounion.org/
History 25 May 1976. Founded as a regional union of *World Taekwondo (#21844)*. Former names and other names: *Taekwondo Europe* – alias. **Aims** Promote and develop Taekwondo in Europe. **Structure** General Assembly; Council; Executive Council; Committees. **Languages** English, French, German, Italian. **Staff** Full-time, paid. **Finance** Members' dues. Other sources: sponsors; profit from activities. **Activities** Awards/prizes/competitions; sporting activities. **Events** *General Assembly* Bucharest (Romania) 2013, *General Assembly* Paphos (Cyprus) 2011, *General Assembly* Vigo (Spain) 2009, *General Assembly* Düsseldorf (Germany) 2006, *General Assembly* Baku (Azerbaijan) 2005. **Publications** *Taekwondo Europe Magazine*.
Members National organizations in 49 countries:
Albania, Andorra, Armenia, Austria, Azerbaijan, Belarus, Belgium, Bosnia-Herzegovina, Bulgaria, Croatia, Cyprus, Czechia, Denmark, Estonia, Finland, France, Georgia, Germany, Great Britain, Greece, Hungary, Iceland, Ireland, Israel, Italy, Kosovo, Latvia, Lithuania, Luxembourg, Malta, Moldova, Monaco, Montenegro, Netherlands, North Macedonia, Norway, Poland, Portugal, Romania, Russia, San Marino, Serbia, Slovakia, Slovenia, Spain, Sweden, Switzerland, Türkiye, Ukraine.
Associate member in 1 territory:
Isle of Man.
NGO Relations Memorandum of Understanding with: *European Sports Press Union (AIPS Europe, #08822)*. [2022/XD0400/**D**]

♦ European Tax Adviser Federation (ETAF) 08875

Registered Office Rue des Deux Eglises 35, 1000 Brussels, Belgium. T. +3222350105. E-mail: info@etaf.tax.
URL: http://www.etaf.tax/
History Launched 15 Dec 2015. Registered in accordance with Belgian law. EU Transparency Register: 760084520382-92. **Aims** Represent the tax profession at European level in liaising closely with European policy makers so as to promote good legislation in tax and professional matters, contribute to fight abuse and illegal acts and enhance certainty and transparency. **Structure** General Assembly; Board; Working Committees. **Languages** English. **Activities** Networking/liaising; events/meetings. **Events** *Conference* Brussels (Belgium) 2022, *Conference* Brussels (Belgium) 2022, *Conference* Brussels (Belgium) 2021, *Conference* Brussels (Belgium) 2020, *Conference* Brussels (Belgium) 2020. **Publications** *ETAF Newsletter*.
Members Ordinary; Observers. Members in 4 countries:
Belgium, France, Germany, Italy. [2020/XM6078/**D**]

♦ European Tax Confederation / see CFE Tax Advisers Europe (#03842)
♦ European Taxi Confederation (inactive)
♦ European Taxidermy Federation (inactive)
♦ European Taxpayers Association / see Taxpayers Association of Europe (#20102)

♦ European Teacher Education Network (ETEN) 08876

Sec University College UCC, Social Education Copenhagen, Ejbyvej 35, 2740 Skovlunde, Denmark. T. +4541897808. Fax +4543446996. E-mail: hsc@ucc.dk.
URL: http://www.eten-online.org/
History 1988. **Aims** Promote cooperation and exchanges between institutions in higher professional education. **Finance** Members' dues. **Events** *Annual Conference* Barcelona (Spain) 2019, *Annual Conference* Rotterdam (Netherlands) 2018, *Annual Conference* Lisbon (Portugal) 2016, *Annual Conference* Amsterdam (Netherlands) 2011, *Annual Conference* Helsinki (Finland) 2010. [2014/XJ3333/**F**]

♦ European Teachers Trade Union Committee (inactive)
♦ European Tea Committee (inactive)
♦ European Technical Association for Protective Coatings (inactive)

♦ European Technical Caramel Association (EUTECA) 08877

Association européenne des fabricants de caramel
Contact Av de Tervueren 13 A – Bte 7, 1040 Brussels, Belgium. T. +3227365354. Fax +3227323427. E-mail: euteca@ecco-eu.com.
URL: http://www.euteca.org/
History 14 Sep 1978. Registration: EU Transparency Register, No/ID: 32106266349-71. **Aims** Improve general knowledge about caramel colour and its benefits; deliver factual information about caramel colour to European authorities and the general public. **Structure** Officers: President; Vice-President. Secretariat. **Languages** English. **Staff** Part-time. **Finance** Sources: members' dues. **Activities** Knowledge management/information dissemination.
Members National associations and companies in 6 countries:
Belgium, France, Germany, Ireland, Italy, Netherlands.
IGO Relations Recognized by: *European Commission (EC, #06633)*. **NGO Relations** Member of (1): *EU Specialty Food Ingredients (#09200)*. [2020/XD3792/**D**]

♦ European Technical Ceramics Federation (EuTeCer) 08878

Dir Gen Rue Belliard 12, 1040 Brussels, Belgium. T. +3228083880. Fax +3225115174. E-mail: sec@cerameunie.eu.
URL: http://cerameunie.eu/members/sectors/
History 9 Nov 1967, as *EEC Group of Producers of Mineral Insulating Material for Electrotechnical Use – Groupement des producteurs d'isolateurs et de pièces isolantes minérales à usage électro-technique de la CEE*. Name changed, 1985, to *Association of the EEC Manufacturers of Technical Ceramics for Electronic, Electrical, Mechanical and Other Applications – Groupement des producteurs de la CEE de céramiques techniques pour applications électroniques, électriques, mécaniques et autres – Vereinigung der Hersteller von Technischer Keramik in der EWG für Elektronische, Elektrische, Mechanische und andere Anwendungen*. Took over, 1989, the relevant activities of *European Ceramic Association (AEC, inactive)*, on suspension of the latter's activities, together with *European Ceramic Society (ECerS, #06507)*. Name changed, 1991 to: *Association of the European Manufacturers of Technical Ceramics for Electronic, Electrical, Mechanical and Other Applications – Groupement des producteurs européens de céramiques techniques pour applications électroniques, électriques, mécaniques et autres (GROUPISOL) – Vereinigung der Europäischen Hersteller von Technischer Keramik für Elektronische, Elektrische, Mechanische und andere Anwendungen*. New name adopted, 2000. **Aims** Represent the common interest of its members to the European Community institutions; study all problems of general interest to members in order to promote full cooperation in conformity with the Treaty of Rome (Italy); encourage the solution of problems in the common interest of the sector. **Structure** General Assembly. Secretariat; Technical Committee. **Languages** English. **Finance** Members' dues. **Activities** Events/meetings; knowledge management/information dissemination. **Events** *Meeting* Lyon (France) 2013, *General Assembly* Brussels (Belgium) 2006, *General Assembly* Paris (France) 2004, *General Assembly* Munich (Germany) 2003, *General Assembly* Birmingham (UK) 2002.
Members National organizations in 4 countries:
France, Germany, Türkiye, UK.
IGO Relations Recognized by: *European Commission (EC, #06633)*. **NGO Relations** Member of: *European Ceramic Industry Association (CERAME-UNIE, #06506)*; *Industry4Europe (#11181)*. [2020/XE0503/**E**]

♦ European Technical Committee for Fluorine / see EUROFLUOR (#05681)

♦ European Technical Contractors Committee for the Construction Industry 08879

Comité européen des équipements techniques du bâtiment (CEETB)
Contact UNETO-VNI, Postbus 188, 2700 AD Zoetermeer, Netherlands. T. +31793250650.
History 1976, as successor to *Committee for the Common Market Countries of the International Union of Associations of Heating, Ventilation and Air Conditioning Equipment Contractors (inactive)*. Registered in accordance with Belgian law, 1998. **Aims** Promote technical contractors, especially in the field of energy efficiency services represented by member associations at an international, particularly European, level and ensure their *professional* representation with European Community bodies; consider contractual rules and regulations in the interest of the professions represented and propose them to Community authorities and other partners; reach agreement with bodies representing other professions in the industry so as to ensure equitable contractual arrangements and good relations among the parties concerned. **Structure** Council, comprising 3 delegates of each international professional member association. Permanent representative to the EC; Secretary-General. **Languages** English, French, German. **Finance** Members' dues. **Activities** Participates in work of various commissions; makes proposals concerning work and payment procedures for the building industry. Particularly concerned with work undertaken by the European Commission and elaboration of European regulations on: procurement procedures; responsibilities, guarantees and insurance; engineering services; free circulation and access to markets; pre-qualification; subcontracting. **Events** *Congress* Valencia (Spain) 2011, *Congress* Stockholm (Sweden) 2010, *Congress* Bern (Switzerland) 2009, *Congress* Prague (Czech Rep) 2008, *Congress* Rome (Italy) 2007. **Publications** Annual Report.
Members National organizations representing 450,000 companies (including numerous SMEs) in 26 countries:
Austria, Belgium, Bulgaria, Canada, Cyprus, Czechia, Denmark, Finland, France, Germany, Hungary, Ireland, Italy, Luxembourg, Netherlands, Norway, Poland, Portugal, Slovenia, South Africa, Spain, Sweden, Switzerland, UK, Ukraine, USA.
IGO Relations Recognized by: *European Commission (EC, #06633)*. [2013.06.20/XD3064/t/**E**]

♦ European Technical Institute for Wood Energy / see Bioenergy Institute

♦ European Technical Safety Organisations Network (ETSON) 08880

Pres GRS, Boltzmannstr 14, 85748 Garching, Germany. T. +498932004100 – +491754396464. Fax +49893200410100.
Sec IRSN, BP 17, 92262 Fontenay-aux-Roses CEDEX, France. T. +33158357179.
URL: http://www.etson.eu/
History 2006. Registration: RNA, No/ID: W921001929, Start date: 2011, France. **Aims** Develop and promote best practices in *nuclear* safety assessment. **Structure** General Assembly (at least twice a year); Board. **Languages** English. **Staff** Voluntary. **Finance** Sources: members' dues. Annual budget: 32,000 EUR. **Activities** Advocacy/lobbying/activism; awards/prizes/competitions; capacity building; conflict resolution; events/meetings; guidance/assistance/consulting; knowledge management/information dissemination; research and development; research/documentation. **Events** *EUROSAFE* Paris (France) 2021, *EUROSAFE* Cologne (Germany) 2019, *Conference* Brussels (Belgium) 2018, *EUROSAFE : International Forum on Nuclear Safety* Paris (France) 2017, *EUROSAFE : International Forum on Nuclear Safety* Brussels (Belgium) 2015. **Publications** Annual Progress Report. Position papers; guides.
Members Full; Associate. Full in 12 countries:
Belgium, Czechia, Finland, France, Germany, Hungary, Italy, Lithuania, Romania, Slovakia, Slovenia, Switzerland.
Associate in 4 countries:
Japan, Russia, UK, Ukraine.
IGO Relations Memorandum of Understanding with (1): *Foro Iberoamericano de Organismos Reguladores Radiológicos y Nucleares (FORO, #09878)*. Cooperates with (6): *Asian Nuclear Safety Network (ANSN, #01572)*; *European Commission (EC, #06633)*; *Global Nuclear Safety and Security Network (GNSSN, #10509)*; *International Atomic Energy Agency (IAEA, #12294)*; *Joint Research Centre (JRC, #16147)*; *Nuclear Energy Agency (NEA, #17615)*. **NGO Relations** Cooperates with (4): *International Commission on Radiological Protection (ICRP, #12724)*; *Nuclear Generation II and III Association (NUGENIA, #17618)*; *Sustainable Nuclear Energy Technology Platform (SNETP, #20063)*; *Western European Nuclear Regulators Association (WENRA, #20914)*. [2021.07.02/XJ8976/**F**]

♦ European Technological Forecasting Association (inactive)
♦ European Technological Platform for Economic, Ecologic Extraction of Underground Earth Energy (unconfirmed)
♦ European Technology Chamber (unconfirmed)
♦ European Technology and Innovation Platform / see ETIP Smart Networks for Energy Transition (#05558)

♦ European Technology and Innovation Platform Bioenergy (ETIP Bioenergy) 08881

Secretariat c/o Fachagentur Nachwachsende Rohstoffe, Hofplatz 1, 18276 Gülzow, Germany. E-mail: secretariat@etipbioenergy.eu.
Secretariat address not obtained.
URL: http://etipbioenergy.eu/

History Launched by fusion of European Biofuels Technology Platform (EBTP) and European Industrial Initiative Bioenergy (EIBI). Recognized by *European Commission (EC, #06633)*. Registration: EU Transparency Register, No/ID: 448796725018-54, Start date: 13 Dec 2016. **Aims** Contribute to: development of cost-competitive, innovative world-class bio-energy and bio-fuels value chains; creation and strengthening of a healthy European bio-energy industry; acceleration of sustainable deployment of bio-energy in the EU through a process of guidance, prioritization and promotion of research, technology development and demonstration. **Structure** Steering Committee; Advisory Board; Coordination Group; Working Groups (4); Task Forces; Stakeholder Plenary Meeting; Secretariat, with EC as active observer. Supported by the ETIP Bioenergy-SABS 2 Project, which is funded under the Horizon 2020, the EU Framework Programme for Research and Innovation. **Languages** English. **Finance** Supported by: *European Commission (EC, #06633)*. **Activities** Events/meetings; guidance/assistance/consulting; research and development; standards/guidelines. **Events** *Stakeholder Plenary Meeting* Brussels (Belgium) 2021, *Innovation Fund Stakeholder Workshop* Brussels (Belgium) 2019, *Stakeholder Plenary Meeting* Brussels (Belgium) 2019, *Stakeholder Plenary Meeting* Brussels (Belgium) 2018, *Stakeholder Plenary Meeting* Brussels (Belgium) 2014. **Publications** *Biogas through Anaerobic Digestion from Waste Streams as a Renewable Transportation Fuel – A Brief Review of Technology* (2021); *Biomass to liquids (BtL) via Fischer-Tropsch – a brief review* (2021); *Current Status of Advanced Biofuels Demonstrations in Europe*; *ETIP Bioenergy Working Group 3 Distribution & End-use – Orientation and Action Plan 2021*; *Opportunities and Challenges for Broadening Biomass Feedstock in Europe*; *Strategic Research and Innovation Agenda 2018*; *The Importance of Bioenergy in Achieving the European Energy Transition*. **Members** Membership countries not specified. [2021.09.01/XJ0782/F]

♦ European Technology & Innovation Platform on Deep Geothermal (ETIP-DG) 08882

Secretariat address not obtained. E-mail: info@etip-dg.eu.
URL: https://www.etip-dg.eu/

History Mar 2016. Governance and procedures adopted June 2016. officially recognized by *European Commission (EC, #06633)* , July 2016. **Aims** Accelerate the development of deep geothermal technology in Europe. **Structure** Steering Committee; Secretariat; Working Groups. **Finance** Supported by: *European Union (EU, #08967)* (Horizon 2020 Research and Innovation Programme). **Activities** Advocacy/lobbying/activism; events/meetings; guidance/assistance/consulting; research/documentation. **Publications** *ETIP-DG Newsletter*. [2020/AA0061/F]

♦ European Technology and Innovation Platform for Photovoltaics (ETIP PV) 08883

Contact c/o WIP Renewable Energies, Sylvensteinstr 2, 81369 Munich, Germany. T. +498972012722. Fax +498972012791. E-mail: info@etip-pv.eu.
URL: http://www.eupvplatform.org/

Aims Be the recognized point of reference for key decision and policy makers; develop a strategy and corresponding implementation plan for education, research and technology development, innovation and market deployment of photovoltaic solar energy. **Structure** Steering Committee, composed of 20 members representing the Industry, Research and Development, and Policy and Instruments, and including Chairman and 2 Vice-Chairmen. Working Groups (4): Policy and instruments; Market deployment; Science, Technology and Applications Group; Developing countries. **Events** *Annual Conference* Brussels (Belgium) 2017, *General Assembly* Brussels (Belgium) 2014, *General Assembly* Amsterdam (Netherlands) 2012, *General Assembly* Brussels (Belgium) 2011, *General Assembly* Toledo (Spain) 2010. **NGO Relations** *SolarPower Europe (#19676)*; *EUREC (#05619)*. [2022/XJ6898/F]

♦ European Technology and Innovation Platform Photovoltaics (ETIP PV) 08884

Secretariat c/o WIP – Renewable Energies, Sylvensteinstr 2, 81369 Munich, Germany. T. +498972012722. Fax +498972012791. E-mail: info@etip-pv.eu.
URL: http://www.etip-pv.eu/

History A continuation of *European PV Technology Platform (EU PVTP)* and *Solar European Industry Initiative (SEII)*. **Aims** Provide consensus-based strategic advice on all issues relevant to progressing research and innovation (R&I) efforts in the photovoltaics sector. **Structure** Steering Committee; Secretariat. **Activities** Events/meetings. **Events** *Annual Conference* Munich (Germany) 2021, *Annual Conference* Brussels (Belgium) 2020, *Annual Conference* Brussels (Belgium) 2019, *Annual Conference* Brussels (Belgium) 2018, *Annual Conference* Brussels (Belgium) 2016. **Publications** Reports.
Members Full (3):
Asia-Pacific Lawyers Association (APLA, no recent information); *SOLARUNITED (#19677)*; WIP – Renewable Energies.
IGO Relations *European Commission (EC, #06633)*. [2017/XM5691/y/F]

♦ European Technology and Innovation Platform on Wind Energy (ETIPWind) 08885

Project Coordinator c/o WindEurope, Rue Belliard 40, 1040 Brussels, Belgium. E-mail: secretariat@etipwind.eu.
URL: https://etipwind.eu/

History 2016. Founded by *WindEurope (#20965)*. Combines 2 prior initiatives: *European Wind Energy Technology Platform (TPWind, inactive)* and European Wind Industry Initiative. **Aims** Define and agree on concrete research and innovation (R&I) priorities and communicate these to the European institutions and other decision making bodies in order to support the EU's ambition of a decarbonized economy by 2050. **Structure** Executive Committee; Secretariat; Advisory Group. **Finance** Supported by: *European Commission (EC, #06633)*. **Publications** Reports. [2021/AA1213/F]

♦ European Technology Platform in Additive Manufacturing (AM Platform) 08886

Coordinator PO Box 513, 5600 MB Eindhoven, Netherlands.
URL: http://www.rm-platform.com/

History Founded as *Rapid Manufacturing Platform (RM Platform)*. Also referred to as *Additive Manufacturing Platform (AM Platform)*. **Structure** General Assembly. Management Board, including Chairman and Coordinator. **Activities** Meetings. **Events** *Meeting* Brussels (Belgium) 2013, *Meeting* Brussels (Belgium) 2013, *Meeting* Leiria (Portugal) 2011, *Meeting* Paris (France) 2011, *Meeting* Brussels (Belgium) 2010. **Publications** Newsletter. [2019/XJ5377/F]

♦ European Technology Platform on Advanced Engineering Materials and Technologies (EuMaT) 08887

Co-Secretary IK4 TEKNIKER, Ignacio Goenaga 5, 20600 Eibar, Guipúzcoa, Spain. T. +34680656085.
Chair APRE, Via Cavour 71, 00184 Rome RM, Italy. T. +39648939993. E-mail: direzione@apre.it.
URL: http://www.eumat.eu/

History Founding meeting held 30 Aug 2004, Stuttgart (Germany). Officially launched 27 Jun 2006, Brussels (Belgium). **Aims** Ensure optimal involvement of industry and other important stakeholders in the process of establishing of R and D priorities in the area of advanced engineering materials and technologies. **Structure** Steering Committee; Working Groups. **Languages** English. **Staff** All voluntary. **Finance** No direct financing. **Activities** Networking/liaising; knowledge management/information dissemination; advocacy/lobbying/activism. **Publications** *EuMaT Strategic Research Agenda*. **Members** Full in European countries. Membership countries not specified. **NGO Relations** Member of: *Energy Materials Industrial Research Initiative (EMIRI, #05472)*. [2022/XJ0045/F]

♦ European Technology Platform ALICE (ALICE) 08888

SG address not obtained. E-mail: info@etp-alice.eu.
URL: http://www.etp-logistics.eu/

History Officially recognized as an European Technology Platform by *European Commission (EC, #06633)*, Jul 2013. Former names and other names: *Alliance for Logistics Innovation through Collaboration in Europe (ALICE)* – full title. **Aims** Develop new logistics and supply chain concepts and innovation for a more competitive and sustainable industry. **Structure** General Assembly; Executive Group; Steering Group; Secretariat. Working Groups. **Activities** Research and development. **Publications** *ALICE Newsletter*.
Members Organizations, including 11 listed in this Yearbook:
Association of European Vehicle Logistics (ECG, #02551); *CLECAT (#03993)*; *Conseil européen de l'industrie chimique (CEFIC, #04687)*; *European Association for Logistics and Transportation in Healthcare (EALTH, #06111)*; *European Conference of Transport Research Institutes (ECTRI, #06737)*; *European Council of Automotive Research and Development (EUCAR, #06806)*; *European Factories of the Future Research Association (EFFRA, #07023)*; *European Logistics Association (ELA, #07710)*; *European Shippers' Council (ESC, #08477)*; *International Union for Combined Road – Rail Transport (UIRR, #15765)*; *Manufuture (#16567)*.
NGO Relations *European Logistics Platform (ELP, #07711)*. [2018/XM7510/y/F]

♦ European Technology Platform for High Performance Computing (ETP4HPC) 08889

Contact Abtspoelhof 7, 2341 NS Oegstgeest, Netherlands. T. +33130803204. E-mail: office@etp4hpc.eu.
URL: https://www.etp4hpc.eu/

History Jun 2012. Registration: Start date: Dec 2012, Netherlands; EU Transparency Register, No/ID: 585772227148-18. **Aims** Promote European high performance computing (HPC) research and innovation to support Europe's competitiveness. **Structure** Steering Board. Offices in France, Germany, Hungary, Netherlands and Spain. **Languages** English. **Staff** 3.50 FTE, paid. **Finance** Sources: members' dues. Annual budget: 300,000 EUR. **Activities** Events/meetings; monitoring/evaluation; networking/liaising; research and development; standards/guidelines. **Events** *General Assembly* 2022, *General Assembly* 2021, *General Assembly* 2020, *General Assembly* Sassenheim (Netherlands) 2019, *General Assembly* Leixlip (Ireland) 2018. **Publications** *ETP4HPC White Paper – Federated HPC, Cloud and Data Infrastructures* (2022); *ETP4HPC White Paper – Heterogeneous High Performance Computing* (2022); *ETP4HPC White Paper – HPC for Urgent Decision-Making* (2022); *ETP4HPC White Paper – Quantum for HPC* (2022); *ETP4HPC White Paper – Task-Based Performance Portability in HPC* (2022); *ETP4HPC White Paper – Unconventional HPC Architectures* (2022); *ETP4HPC White Paper – Processing in Memory: the Tipping Point* (2021); *ETP4HPC White Paper – Towards Integrated Hardware/Software Ecosystems for the Edge-Cloud-HPC Continuum* (2021); *Strategic Research Agenda* (2020).
Members Over 100 in 23 countries:
Canada, China, Croatia, Czechia, Denmark, Finland, France, Germany, Greece, Hungary, Ireland, Israel, Italy, Japan, Luxembourg, Netherlands, Norway, Poland, Slovenia, Spain, Sweden, UK, USA.
NGO Relations Memorandum of Understanding with (1): *Alliance for Internet of Things Innovation (AIOTI, #00697)*. Member of (1): *European High Performance Computing Joint Undertaking (EuroHPC JU, #07485)*. [2022.05.04/XJ9329/F]

♦ European Technology Platform Manufuture / see Manufuture (#16567)
♦ European Technology Platform for Nanoelectronics / see Association for European NanoElectronics ActivitieS (#02525)

♦ European Technology Platform 'Plants for the Future' (Plant ETP) . . 08890

Exec Manager Av des Arts 52, 1000 Brussels, Belgium. T. +3227432865. Fax +3227432869. E-mail: secretariat@plantetp.eu.
URL: http://www.plantetp.org/

History Set up via a Specific Support Action under FP6 of *European Commission (EC, #06633)*, until Jul 2007. Transformed into a membership-based ETP, May 2008. Current statutes adopted, Mar 2009. Registration: Belgium; EU Transparency Register, No/ID: 167413627983-49. **Aims** Strengthen the European *Plant Research* and Innovation Area, mobilizing both public and private support at European, national and regional levels. **Structure** General Assembly; Board of Directors; Executive Manager. **Finance** Sources: members' dues. **Events** *Meeting on Stimulating Innovation in Plant Genetic Resources* Brussels (Belgium) 2013.
Members Individual companies; European associations. Membership countries not specified.
COPA – european farmers (COPA, #04829); *European Plant Science Organization (EPSO, #08211)*; *Euroseeds (#09179)*; *General Confederation of Agricultural Cooperatives in the European Union (#10107)*. [2022/XJ8327/y/F]

♦ European Technology Platform on Renewable Heating and Cooling (RHC-Platform) 08891

Secretariat c/o EUREC Agency, Place du Champs de Mars 2, 1050 Brussels, Belgium. T. +3223181051. E-mail: info@rhc-platform.org.
URL: http://www.rhc-platform.org/

History Set up as successor to *European Technology Platform on Renewable Heating and Cooling (RHC-Platform, inactive)* by: *EUREC (#05619)*; *Bioenergy Europe (#03247)*; *European Geothermal Energy Council (EGEC, #07391)*; *Solar Heat Europe (SHE, #19674)*. Officially endorsed by *European Commission (EC, #06633)*, 27 Oct 2008. **Aims** Consolidate Europe's leading position in the renewable heating and cooling sector by maximizing synergy and strengthening efforts towards research, development and technical innovation. **Structure** Board, headed by President; Secretariat. **Events** *Challenges and Solutions for a 100% Renewable Heating and Cooling Sector in Germany* Brussels (Belgium) 2022, *How to Empower Women in the RHC Sector* Brussels (Belgium) 2022, *Overcoming the Invisible Barrier: Gender Dimensions of the RHC Sector* Brussels (Belgium) 2022, *Renewable heating and cooling in Croatia* Brussels (Belgium) 2022, *The Belgian Heat Transition* Brussels (Belgium) 2022. [2016.01.29/XM7431/F]

♦ European Technology Platform on Smart Systems Integration (EPoSS) 08892

Contact c/o VDI/VDE Innovation + Technik GmbH, Steinplatz 1, 10623 Berlin, Germany. T. +4930310078155. Fax +4930310078225. E-mail: contact@smart-systems-integration.org.
URL: http://www.smart-systems-integration.org/

History Status adopted 18 Sep 2013. Registration: Germany; EU Transparency Register, No/ID: 583500530587-70. **Aims** Bring together European private and public stakeholders in order to create an enduring basis for structuring initiatives, co-ordinating and bundling efforts, setting up sustainable structures of a European Research Area on Smart Systems Integration. **Structure** General Assembly; Board; Executive Committee; Working Groups/Task Forces (10). Office located in Berlin (Germany). **Languages** English. **Staff** 4.00 FTE, paid. **Finance** Sources: members' dues. **Activities** Events/meetings; projects/programmes; research and development. **Events** *Smart Systems Integration (SSI) Conference* Bruges (Belgium) 2023, *Electronic Components and Systems Brokerage Event* Brussels (Belgium) 2022, *Annual Forum* Turin (Italy) 2022, *Annual Forum* Freiburg-Breisgau (Germany) 2021, *European Forum for Electronic Components and Systems (EFECS)* Netherlands 2021. **Publications** *ECS-SRA Update* (annual); *EPoSS Newsletter*. *Strategic Research Agenda*. Position papers; scientific publications. **Members** Industrial companies and research organizations from more than 20 European Member States. Membership countries not specified. **NGO Relations** Partner of (2): *European Partnership for Key Digital Technologies (KDT, #08158)*; *Inside Industry Association (Inside, #11230)*. [2023/XM3847/F]

♦ European Technology Platform for Sustainable Chemistry (SusChem) 08893

Communications Officer c/o Cefic, Avenue E van Nieuwenhuyse 4- box 1, 1160 Brussels, Belgium. T. +3226767461. Fax +3226767433. E-mail: eab@cefic.be – suschem@suschem.org.
URL: http://www.suschem.org/

History 2004, as joint initiative between *Conseil européen de l'industrie chimique (CEFIC, #04687), European Association of Bioindustries (EuropaBio, #05956), European Federation of Biotechnology (EFB, #07062)* – Section on Applied Biocatalysis (ESAB) and national organizations in Germany and the UK. **Aims** Initiate and inspire European chemical and biochemical innovation to respond effectively to society's challenges by providing sustainable solutions. **Structure** Board; Management Team; Secretariat, based at *Conseil européen de l'industrie chimique (CEFIC, #04687)*. **Activities** Research/documentation; knowledge management/information dissemination; financial and/or material support. **Events** *Stakeholder Event* Brussels (Belgium) 2015, *Stakeholder Meeting / Stakeholder Event* Brussels (Belgium) 2014, *Stakeholder Event* Brussels (Belgium) 2013, *Stakeholder Event* Brussels (Belgium) 2012. **IGO Relations** *European Commission (EC, #06633).* [2021/XJ9523/**F**]

♦ European Technology Platform on Sustainable Mineral Resources (ETP SMR) 08894

Secretariat c/o EuroGeoSurveys, Rue Joseph II 36-38, b7, 1000 Brussels, Belgium. T. +3228887553. E-mail: info@eurogeosurveys.org.
URL: http://www.etpsmr.org/
History Mar 2005. Registration: Banque-Carrefour des Entreprises, No/ID: 0525 643 394, Start date: 8 Apr 2013, Belgium; EU Transparency Register, No/ID: 899865419498-82. **Aims** Develop long-term European raw materials research and innovation agendas and roadmaps for action at EU and national level. **Structure** General Assembly; Executive Committee; Executive Secretariat. Housed at: *EuroGeoSurveys (#05686).* **Activities** Advocacy/lobbying/activism. **Publications** *Raw Materials Research and Innovation to achieve the European Green Deal* (2022); *ETP SMR Strategic Research and Innovation Agenda*; *VERAM Research and Innovation Roadmap 2050: A Sustainable and Competitive Future for European Raw Materials.*
Members Full (25) in 11 countries:
Austria, Belgium, Finland, Germany, Ireland, Netherlands, Norway, Poland, Slovakia, Spain, Sweden.
Associate (1) in 1 country:
South Africa.
IGO Relations Recognized by: *European Commission (EC, #06633).* [2023.02.14/XM5520/**F**]

- ♦ European Technology Platform for Zero Emission Fossil Fuel Power Plants / see Zero Emissions Platform (#22032)
- ♦ European Technology and Travel Services Association / see eu travel tech (#09205)
- ♦ European Telecommunication Services Association (inactive)
- ♦ European Telecommunications Informatics Services / see ETIS – Global IT Association for Telecommunications (#05559)
- ♦ European Telecommunications Network Operators' Association / see European Telecommunications Network Operators' Association (#08895)

♦ European Telecommunications Network Operators' Association (ETNO) 08895

Dir of Strategy & Communications Blvd du Régent 43-44, 1000 Brussels, Belgium. T. +3222193242. Fax +3222196412. E-mail: info@etno.eu.
URL: http://www.etno.eu/
History 12 May 1992, Madrid (Spain). Activities commenced 1 Jan 1993; official inauguration 17 May 1993, Brussels (Belgium). Originally referred to as *European Telecommunications Network Operators' Association.* Registration: Banque-Carrefour des Entreprises, No/ID: 0448.199.881, Start date: 17 Sep 1992, Belgium; EU U Transparency Register, No/ID: 08957111909-85, Start date: 26 Jun 2009. **Aims** Be the voice of Europe's telecommunications network operators and the principal policy group for European electronic communications network operators. **Structure** General Assembly (once a year); Executive Board; Administrative Committee; Working Groups; Special Rapporteurs; ETNO Office in Brussels (Belgium), headed by Director. **Languages** English. **Staff** 8.00 FTE, paid. **Finance** Members' dues. **Activities** Politics/policy/regulatory; knowledge management/information dissemination; events/meetings. **Events** *Europe's Internet Ecosystem: Is Everybody Contributing Their Fair Share?* Brussels (Belgium) 2022, *Setting the WACC in Low Interest Environments: Bridging Theory and Practice* Brussels (Belgium) 2022, *Summit* Brussels (Belgium) 2019, *Summit* Brussels (Belgium) 2016, *Summit* Brussels (Belgium) 2015. **Publications** *ETNO Update* – newsletter. Annual Report; reports; agendas.
Members Full: companies providing public voice telephony service; Associate: those providing other public telecoms networks and services. Members in 35 countries:
Albania, Austria, Belgium, Bosnia-Herzegovina, Bulgaria, Croatia, Cyprus, Czechia, Denmark, Estonia, Finland, France, Germany, Greece, Hungary, Iceland, Ireland, Italy, Latvia, Lithuania, Luxembourg, Malta, Netherlands, North Macedonia, Norway, Poland, Portugal, Romania, Slovakia, Slovenia, Spain, Sweden, Switzerland, Türkiye, UK.
NGO Relations Member of: *European Policy Centre (EPC, #08240); Internet Society (ISOC, #15952).* Links with a large number of organizations active in the field. [2020/XD3382/**D**]

♦ European Telecommunications Satellite Organization (EUTELSAT IGO) 08896

Organisation européenne de télécommunications par satellite
Exec Sec EUTELSAT IGO Secretariat, Tour Maine Montparnasse, 33 av du Maine, 75755 Paris CEDEX 15, France. T. +33140648285. Fax +33143278646. E-mail: secigo@eutelsatigo.int.
URL: http://www.eutelsatigo.int/
History 30 Jun 1977, Paris (France). Established on a provisional basis by 17 European telecommunications entities, members of *Conférence européenne des administrations des postes et des télécommunications (CEPT, #04602).* Intergovernmental Convention (Convention and Operating Agreement) adopted, May 1982, by 26 European States establishing the definitive Organization, opened for signature 15 Jul 1982 and entered into force 1 Sep 1985 (date of formal establishment). Following decision of the Assembly of Parties, May 1999, Cardiff (UK), all assets, operational activities and related liabilities of EUTELSAT were transferred to a limited company, Eutelsat SA, under French law on 2 Jul 2001. Amended Convention entered info force, 28 Nov 2002. Former names and other names: *Provisional European Telecommunications Satellite Organization* – former (1977 to 1985); *Organisation européenne provisoire de télécommunications par satellite* – former (1977 to 1985); *Eutelsat intérimaire* – former (1977 to 1985). Registration: France, 2001-07-02. **Aims** Maintain the rights to use radiofrequencies and orbital locations which were assigned collectively to the Member States and the Organization by the ITU; Ensure that Eutelsat SA continues to observe the Basic Principles set forth in EUTELSAT Amended Convention on pan-European coverage, universal service, non-discrimination and fair competition; monitor the developments within the global telecommunications and space sectors; play an active role in the European and global regulatory environment. **Structure** Assembly of Parties consisting of representatives of Member States. Secretariat, headed by Executive Secretary. **Languages** English, French. **Staff** 3.00 FTE, paid. **Activities** Monitoring/evaluation; networking/liaising; politics/policy/regulatory. **Events** *Assembly of parties* Paris (France) 2023, *Assembly of parties* Paris (France) 2021, *Assembly of Parties* Paris (France) 2019, *Assembly of Parties* Paris (France) 2017, *Assembly of Parties* Paris (France) 2015. **Publications** Annual Report.
Members Signatories of international Convention: Governments of 49 countries (Parties):
Albania, Andorra, Armenia, Austria, Azerbaijan, Belarus, Belgium, Bosnia-Herzegovina, Bulgaria, Croatia, Cyprus, Czechia, Denmark, Finland, France, Georgia, Germany, Greece, Holy See, Hungary, Iceland, Ireland, Italy, Kazakhstan, Latvia, Liechtenstein, Lithuania, Luxembourg, Malta, Moldova, Monaco, Montenegro, Netherlands, North Macedonia, Norway, Poland, Portugal, Romania, Russia, San Marino, Serbia, Slovakia, Slovenia, Spain, Sweden, Switzerland, Türkiye, UK, Ukraine.
IGO Relations Cooperates with: *International Telecommunication Union (ITU, #15673).* Observer status with: *Committee on the Peaceful Uses of Outer Space (COPUOS, #04277); Regional Commonwealth in the Field of Communications (RCC, #18767).* Relevant treaties: Convention establishing the European Telecommunications Satellite Organization EUTELSAT; EUTELSAT Amended Convention; *Convention on the International Liability for Damage Caused by Space Objects (1972); Convention on Registration of Objects Launched into Outer Space (1974); European Convention on Transfrontier Television (1989); Treaty on Principles Governing the Activities of States in the Exploration and Use of Outer Space, Including the Moon and other Celestial Bodies (1967).* [2023/XD6538/**F***]

♦ European Telecommunications Standards Institute (ETSI) 08897

Institut européen des normes de télécommunication – Europäisches Institut für Telekommunikationsnormen
Secretariat 650 route des Lucioles, 06921 Sophia Antipolis CEDEX, France. T. +33492944200. Fax +33493654716. E-mail: info@etsi.org.
URL: http://www.etsi.org/
History Set up on the initiative of *Conférence européenne des administrations des postes et des télécommunications (CEPT, #04602)* and in response to the Green Paper on development of telecommunications in Europe published by the *European Commission (EC, #06633).* Most recent Statutes adopted, by General Assembly, 22 Nov 2000. Most recent Rules of Procedure adopted by General Assembly, 18 Apr 2002. Former names and other names: *European Telecom Standard Institute* – alias. Registration: France; EU Transparency Register, No/ID: 474710916419-15. **Aims** Provide platforms for interested parties to work together to produce standards for ICT systems and services that are used globally. **Structure** General Assembly (twice a year) always in Nice, (France); Board; Secretariat, headed by Director General. Committees. **Languages** English, French, German. **Staff** Secretariat: about 120; more than 2,500 voluntary experts. **Finance** Sources: grants; members' dues. Other sources: revenue from assets; sums received in return for services provided by the Institute. Annual budget: 25,000,000 EUR. **Activities** Standardization. **Events** *Cybersecurity Standardisation Conference* Brussels (Belgium) 2022, *Third Generation Partnership Project Ran Access Network Plenary Meeting* Budapest (Hungary) 2022, *Third Generation Partnership Project Ran Access Network Plenary Meeting* Jeju (Korea Rep) 2020, *Zero Touch Automation Congress* Madrid (Spain) 2019, *3GPP Submission towards IMT-2020 Workshop* Brussels (Belgium) 2018. **Publications** *Bulletin of the European Standards Organizations CEN/CENELEC/ETSI* – jointly with CENELEC and CEN; *ETSI News* – electronic. Annual Report; Activity Report. DVD-ROM containing complete library of ETSI standards (4 a year). Information Services: ETSI Documentation Library.
Members Full; Observers; Associate. Members (over 850) in 63 countries and territories:
Albania, Andorra, Australia, Austria, Belgium, Bosnia-Herzegovina, Botswana, Bulgaria, Canada, China, Croatia, Cyprus, Czechia, Denmark, Estonia, Finland, France, Georgia, Germany, Greece, Hungary, Iceland, India, Indonesia, Ireland, Israel, Italy, Japan, Korea Rep, Kosovo, Latvia, Lebanon, Lesotho, Liechtenstein, Lithuania, Luxembourg, Malaysia, Malta, Mexico, Moldova, Montenegro, Netherlands, North Macedonia, Norway, Poland, Portugal, Qatar, Romania, Russia, Serbia, Slovakia, Slovenia, South Africa, Spain, Sweden, Switzerland, Taiwan, Tunisia, Türkiye, UK, United Arab Emirates, USA, Uzbekistan.
International organizations listed in this Yearbook include:
Ecma International (#05288); Environmental Coalition on Standards (ECOS, #05499); EUROCONTROL (#05667); European Broadcasting Union (EBU, #06404); European Communications Office (ECO, #06676); European Disability Forum (EDF, #06929); European Emergency Number Association (EENA, #06978); European GPR Association (EuroGPR, #07402); European Patent Organisation (#08167); European Trade Union Confederation (ETUC, #08927); European Union Agency for Railways (#08973); European Utilities Telecom Council (EUTC, #09042); GIGAEurope AISBL (#10151); GS1 (#10809); International Amateur Radio Club (IARC); International Mobile Satellite Organization (IMSO, #14174); International Union of Railways (#15813); Low Power Radio Association (LPRA, #16518).
IGO Relations Working relations with: European Commission; CEPT; *EFTA (#05391); Eureka Association (Eureka, #05621); European Telecommunications Satellite Organization (EUTELSAT IGO, #08896); International Telecommunication Union (ITU, #15673)* – Radiocommunication and Telecommunication Standardization Sectors. Cooperates with: *Electronic Communications Committee (ECC, see: #04602).* Formal agreement with: *International Telecommunications Satellite Organization (ITSO, #15670).* Agreement with: *European Patent Office (EPO, #08166).* **NGO Relations** Member of (3): *Alliance for Internet of Things Innovation (AIOTI, #00697); oneM2M (#17732); WorldDAB (#21351).* Cooperation agreement with: *International Electrotechnical Commission (IEC, #13255); International Multimedia Telecommunications Consortium (IMTC, inactive).* Cooperates with: *CAR 2 CAR Communication Consortium (CAR 2 CAR, #03421); Comité européen de normalisation (CEN, #04162); European Committee for Electrotechnical Standardization (CENELEC, #06647).* In liaison with technical committees of: *International Organization for Standardization (ISO, #14473).* Associated member of: *EFQM – European Foundation for Quality Management (EFQM, #05388); European Internet Forum (EIF, #07591).* Organizational partner of: *Third Generation Partnership Project (3GPP, #20145).* [2020/XE5922/jy/**D**]

- ♦ European Telecom Standard Institute / see European Telecommunications Standards Institute (#08897)
- ♦ European Teleconferencing Federation (inactive)
- ♦ European Telemarketing Federation (inactive)
- ♦ European Telemetering Standardisation Committee / see European Telemetry Standardisation Committee
- ♦ European Telemetry Standardisation Committee (internationally oriented national body)
- ♦ European Television Magazines Association (no recent information)
- ♦ European Tennis Association / see European Tennis Federation (#08898)

♦ European Tennis Federation 08898

CEO Zur Gempenfluh 36, 4059 Basel BS, Switzerland. T. +41613359040. Fax +41613317253. E-mail: contactus@tenniseurope.org.
URL: http://www.tenniseurope.org/
History Founded 31 May 1975, Rome (Italy), as *European Tennis Association (ETA)*, at meeting of delegates of 19 European countries. Recognized by *International Tennis Federation (ITF, #15676)*, 29 Sep 1976. Brand is *Tennis Europe.* Current name adopted May 2003. **Aims** Cooperate with constituent national federations to sanction, manage and support international tennis tournaments. **Structure** General Meeting (annual); Board of Management; Committees (4); General Secretariat at headquarters in Basel (Switzerland). **Languages** English. **Staff** 15.00 FTE, paid. **Finance** Members' dues. Other sources: tournament sanction/services; European Championships entry fees; ITF/Tennis Europe development grants; commercial income; ITF grants; bank interest. **Activities** Events/meetings. **Events** *Annual General Meeting* Esch-sur-Alzette (Luxembourg) 2021, *Annual General Meeting* Hersonissos (Greece) 2020, *Annual General Meeting* Valletta (Malta) 2019, *Annual General Meeting* Budapest (Hungary) 2018, *Annual General Meeting* Sochi (Russia) 2017. **Publications** *25 Years of the Tennis Europe Junior Tour* (2016); *European Tennis Report* (2015).
Members National organizations in 50 countries and territories:
Albania, Andorra, Armenia, Austria, Azerbaijan, Belarus, Belgium, Bosnia-Herzegovina, Bulgaria, Croatia, Cyprus, Czechia, Denmark, Estonia, Finland, France, Georgia, Germany, Greece, Hungary, Iceland, Ireland, Israel, Italy, Kosovo, Latvia, Liechtenstein, Lithuania, Luxembourg, Malta, Moldova, Monaco, Montenegro, Netherlands, North Macedonia, Norway, Poland, Portugal, Romania, Russia, San Marino, Serbia, Slovakia, Slovenia, Spain, Sweden, Switzerland, Türkiye, UK, Ukraine.
NGO Relations Cooperates with: *ATP World Tour (#03011); European Observatoire of Sport and Employment (EOSE, #08071); European Olympic Committees (EOC, #08083); International Olympic Committee (IOC, #14408); International Tennis Federation (ITF, #15676)* committees; *Women's Tennis Association (WTA).* [2021/XD6630/**D**]

♦ European Tenpin Bowling Federation (ETBF) 08899

SG address not obtained.
URL: http://www.etbf.eu/
History Founded as the European geographical zone of *World Tenpin Bowling Association (WTBA, inactive).* Statutes originally adopted on 31 Mar 1979, 's Hertogenbosch (Netherlands). Currently a zone of *International Bowling Federation (IBF, #12384).* **Aims** Encourage the development of tenpin bowling throughout the ETBF geographical area; support and encourage national organizations in their efforts to develop and promote tenpin bowling; conduct European tenpin bowling championships for adult and youth members; promote international competition; contribute to the development of tenpin bowling worldwide; support the efforts to get tenpin bowling accepted as a fully recognized athletic competition in the Olympic Games. **Structure** Congress (every 2 years); Presidium. Committees (3): Tournament; Technical; Education. **Languages** English. **Staff** None. **Finance** Members' dues. Budget (annual): euro 60,000. **Activities** Events/meetings; training/education; certification/accreditation. **Events** *Congress* Aalborg (Denmark) 2009, *Congress* Vienna (Austria) 2007, *Congress* Moscow (Russia) 2005, *Congress* Poznań (Poland) 2003.
Members National federations (46) in 45 countries and territories:
Austria, Azerbaijan, Belarus, Belgium, Bulgaria, Croatia, Cyprus, Czechia, Denmark, England, Estonia, Finland, France, Germany, Gibraltar, Greece, Hungary, Iceland, Ireland, Israel, Italy, Jersey, Latvia, Lithuania, Luxembourg, Malta, Moldova, Netherlands, Northern Ireland, Norway, Poland, Romania, Russia, San Marino, Scotland, Serbia, Slovakia, Slovenia, South Africa, Spain (2), Sweden, Switzerland, Türkiye, Ukraine, Wales. [2021/XM1788/**D**]

♦ **European Teratology Society (ETS)** **08900**
Société européenne de tératologie
Sec Sequani Ltd, Bromyard Road, Ledbury, HR8 1LH, UK. E-mail: secretary@etsoc.com.
Treas School of Medicine and Medical Science, Health Sciences Bldg, UCD Belfield, Donnybrook, Dublin, CO. DUBLIN, Ireland. E-mail: treasurer@etsoc.com.
URL: http://www.etsoc.com/
History 1971. Sometimes referred to in French as *Société européenne d'études de monstres.* **Aims** Stimulate scientific interest in and promote the exchange of ideas and information about actiology prevention and treatment of *congenital* malformations. **Structure** General Assembly (usually annual). Council, consisting of Officers (President, President-elect/Past President, Secretary, Treasurer) and 12 members. **Languages** English. **Staff** None. **Finance** Members' dues. Financial support for scientific activities. **Activities** Conferences (held annually); workshops and seminars. **Events** *Annual Conference* Antwerp (Belgium) 2022, *Annual Conference* Madrid (Spain) 2021, *Annual Conference* 2020, *Annual Conference* Cologne (Germany) 2019, *Annual Conference* Berlin (Germany) 2018. **Publications** *ETS Newsletter* (2 a year).
Members Individuals (over 450) in 32 countries:
Australia, Belgium, Brazil, Bulgaria, Canada, Czechia, Denmark, Egypt, Finland, France, Germany, Grenada, Hungary, Ireland, Israel, Italy, Japan, Netherlands, Norway, Poland, Portugal, Romania, Serbia, South Africa, Spain, Sweden, Switzerland, Tunisia, UK, United Arab Emirates, USA, Venezuela.
Members also in the former USSR; countries not specified.
NGO Relations Full member of: *International Federation of Teratology Societies (IFTS, inactive).*
[2015/XD2966/v/**D**]

♦ European Territorial Cooperation / see INTERREG V (#15966)
♦ European Testing Conference (meeting series)

♦ **European Testing Inspection Certification System (ETICS)** **08901**
SG Rue des deux églises 29, 1000 Brussels, Belgium. E-mail: secretariat@etics.org – info@etics.org.
URL: http://www.etics.org/
History Originally registered in accordance with French law. Former names and other names: *European Electrical Products Certification Association (EEPCA)* – former (1998). Registration: Start date: 2016, Belgium; EU Transparency Register, No/ID: 535644220179-18. **Aims** Administer evaluation systems for third party compliance carried out within the electrotechnical sector, and also in other areas that are associated with inspection, testing and product certification, as well as certifying personnel. **Structure** General Assembly; Board of Directors; Secretariat. **Languages** English. **Activities** Certification/accreditation; events/meetings; knowledge management/information dissemination; monitoring/evaluation; training/education. **Events** *Annual General Meeting* Budapest (Hungary) 2019, *Annual General Meeting* Brussels (Belgium) 2018, *Annual General Meeting* Prague (Czech Rep) 2016.
Members Full in 21 countries:
Austria, Belgium, Czechia, Denmark, Finland, France, Germany, Greece, Hungary, Italy, Netherlands, Norway, Poland, Portugal, Slovakia, Slovenia, Spain, Sweden, Switzerland, Türkiye, UK.
NGO Relations Member of (1): *European Accreditation Advisory Board (EAAB, see: #06782).* Technical Liaison Partner with: *European Committee for Electrotechnical Standardization (CENELEC, #06647).*
[2020.06.26/XD8952/**D**]

♦ **European Test Publishers Group (ETPG)** **08902**
Exec Dir c/o Only Connect Ltd, 23 Church Street, Hampton, TW12 2EB, UK. T. +447966509390.
URL: http://www.etpg.org/
History 1991. Registration: Switzerland. **Aims** Create, maintain and improve a *psychological* test publishing community in Europe. **Structure** General Assembly; Board; Secretariat. **Languages** English. **Staff** 1.00 FTE, paid. **Finance** Members' dues. **Activities** Events/meetings; research/documentation. **Events** *Conference* Ukraine 2020, *Conference* Ljubljana (Slovenia) 2019, *Conference* Bucharest (Romania) 2018, *Conference* Vienna (Austria) 2017, *Conference* Krakow (Poland) 2016.
Members Full; Associate. Full in 12 countries:
Austria, Croatia, France, Germany, Italy, Poland, Portugal, Slovenia, Spain, Sweden, Switzerland, UK.
Associate in 12 countries:
Bulgaria, Czechia, Denmark, Finland, France, Hungary, Italy, Netherlands, Romania, Sweden, UK, Ukraine.
[2021/XM6653/**D**]

♦ European Textile Association / see Association des collectivités textiles européennes (#02435)
♦ European Textile Collectivities Association (#02435)

♦ **European Textile Network (ETN)** **08903**
Réseau européen du textile (RET) – Europäisches Textil-Netzwerk (ETN)
Sec Stahlmühle 4, 4170 Haslach an der Mühl, Austria. E-mail: info@etn-net.org.
URL: http://www.etn-net.org/
History Founded under the auspices of *Council of Europe (CE, #04881)*, as its cultural itineraries carrier network for textiles. Initiated Feb 1990. Statutes adopted 4 Apr 1993, Strasbourg (France). Former names and other names: *Europäisches Netzwerk für Textil (ENT)* – former. **Aims** Develop European cooperation to intensify textile cultural interchanges, accentuate regional identities and strengthen the idea of Europe; promote East-West integration within all fields of activities; develop common interests and cooperating experiences for the cooperation with partners outside Europe by: interlacing existing local and regional activities in order to make their supra-regionally relevant significance accessible; developing joint European projects focusing on themes, methods and publicity; completing a central documentation and information service with decentralized basic data registers to improve *professional* cooperation of member institutions. **Structure** General Assembly; Administrative Council; Executive Bureau; consisting of President, Secretary-General and Treasurer; Working Groups include: *Textile Education and Research in Europe (TEXERE, see: #08903).* **Languages** English, French, German. **Finance** Sources: donations; grants; members' dues; revenue from activities/projects. **Activities** Events/meetings; financial and/or material support; knowledge management/information dissemination; research/documentation. **Events** *Conference* Lódz (Poland) 2022, *Biennial Conference* Leiden (Netherlands) 2015, *Biennial Conference* Berlin (Germany) 2009, *Biennial Conference* Haslach an der Mühl (Austria) 2009, *Biennial conference* London (UK) 2007. **Publications** *ETN Newsletter* (4 a year).
Members Organizations in 45 countries:
Armenia, Austria, Azerbaijan, Belgium, Brazil, Bulgaria, Canada, Croatia, Cyprus, Denmark, Estonia, Finland, France, Georgia, Germany, Greece, Hungary, Iceland, India, Indonesia, Ireland, Italy, Japan, Latvia, Lithuania, Luxembourg, Nepal, Netherlands, Norway, Poland, Portugal, Romania, Russia, Saudi Arabia, Serbia, Slovakia, Slovenia, Spain, Sweden, Switzerland, Türkiye, UK, Ukraine, USA, Vietnam.
Individuals in 38 countries:
Argentina, Austria, Belgium, Brazil, China, Colombia, Czechia, Denmark, Finland, France, Georgia, Germany, Greece, Hungary, Iceland, India, Israel, Italy, Japan, Korea Rep, Latvia, Lithuania, Moldova, Netherlands, New Zealand, Norway, Portugal, Romania, Russia, Serbia, Slovenia, South Africa, Spain, Sweden, Switzerland, UK, Ukraine, USA.
NGO Relations Member of (1): *Textile Education and Research in Europe (TEXERE, see: #08903).*
[2023.02.14/XF3970/**F**]

♦ European Textile Rental Association (inactive)

♦ **European Textile Services Association (ETSA)** **08904**
SG Rue Montoyer 24 – Bte 7, 1000 Brussels, Belgium. T. +3222820990. E-mail: etsa@etsa-europe.org.
URL: http://www.textile-services.eu/
History 1994. Registration: Banque-Carrefour des Entreprises, No/ID: 0476.091.935, Start date: 11 Jun 2001, Belgium; EU Transparency Register, No/ID: 042969910219-77, Start date: 30 Nov 2012. **Aims** Represent and promote the textile rental services sector in Europe. **Structure** Members' Conference (every 2 years); General Meeting (annual); Board of Directors; Steering Committees; Project Groups and Working Groups. **Languages** English. **Staff** 2.50 FTE, paid. **Finance** Sources: members' dues. **Activities** Events/meetings; research/documentation. **Events** *Biennial Conference* Dublin (Ireland) 2019, *Biennial Conference* Paris (France) 2017, *Biennial Conference* Vienna (Austria) 2015, *Members conference* Copenhagen (Denmark) 2001, *Meeting* Amsterdam (Netherlands) 2000. **Publications** Market and scientific studies.
Members Textile rental/service companies; suppliers of detergents, machinery and fabric; textile rental national associations; research institutes and testing houses. Members (37) in 22 countries:
Austria, Belgium, Czechia, Denmark, Finland, France, Germany, Hungary, Ireland, Italy, Netherlands, Norway, Poland, Portugal, Russia, Slovakia, Slovenia, Spain, Sweden, Switzerland, UK, USA.
IGO Relations *European Commission (EC, #06633).* **NGO Relations** Member of (3): *European Business Services Alliance (EBSA, #06426); European Safety Federation (ESF, #08418); Federation of European and International Associations Established in Belgium (FAIB, #09508).* Instrumental in setting up and member of: *International Textile Services Alliance (ITSA, #15681).* In liaison with technical committees of: *Comité européen de normalisation (CEN, #04162); International Organization for Standardization (ISO, #14473).*
[2021/XD5422/**D**]

♦ European Thanatological Association (inactive)

♦ **European Theatre Convention (ETC)** **08905**
Project & Network Manager c/o Deutsches Theater Berlin, Schumannstr 13A, 10117 Berlin, Germany. T. +493028441460. E-mail: convention@europeantheatre.eu.
URL: https://www.europeantheatre.eu/
History 1988. Registration: France; EU Transparency Register, No/ID: 721873432604-06. **Aims** Promote European theatre as a vital platform for dialogue, democracy and interaction that responds to, reflects and engages with today's diverse audiences and changing societies; foster an inclusive and sustainable notion of theatre that brings Europe's social, linguistic and cultural heritage to audiences and communities in Europe and beyond. **Structure** General Assembly (2 a year); Board of Directors. **Languages** English. **Staff** 4.00 FTE, paid. **Finance** Sources: members' dues. Subsidized by: Creative Europe. **Activities** Advocacy/lobbying/activism; events/meetings; networking/liaising; publishing activities. **Events** *The Week of New European Drama* Graz (Austria) 2021, *ETC International Theatre Conference* Valletta (Malta) 2021, *ETC International Theatre Conference* 2020, *ETC International Theatre Conference* 2020, *ETC International Theatre Conference* Amsterdam (Netherlands) 2019. **Publications** *ETC Journal.*
Members Theatres (44) subsidized by public authorities and associates in 25 countries:
Albania, Austria, Belgium, Bulgaria, Croatia, Cyprus, Czechia, France, Georgia, Germany, Hungary, Italy, Luxembourg, Malta, Netherlands, Norway, Poland, Portugal, Romania, Serbia, Slovakia, Slovenia, Sweden, UK, Ukraine.
NGO Relations Member of (2): *Culture Action Europe (CAE, #04981); European Alliance for Culture and the Arts (#05866).* Affiliated to: *International Theatre Institute (ITI, #15683).* Associate member of: *Pearle – Live Performance Europe (#18284).*
[2021.09.06/XF5231/**F**]

♦ **European Theological Libraries** **08906**
Bibliothèques européennes de théologie (BETH) – Europäische Bibliotheken für Theologie
Exec Sec address not obtained.
URL: http://www.beth.be/
History Founded 18 Oct 1961, Frankfurt-Main (Germany FR), as *Comité international de coordination des associations de bibliothèques de théologie catholique (CIC)*, following *Projet de collaboration internationale entre bibliothèques théologiques*, Sep 1960, and uniting associations of Germany FR, Netherlands and France. Name changed to *International Council of Theological Library Associations – Conseil international des associations de bibliothèques de théologie – Internationaler Rat der Vereinigungen theologischer Bibliotheken.* Current name adopted 2000. Most recent statutes adopted 1980; most recently amended, Sept 2002. Registered under Dutch law. **Aims** Promote cooperation among theological and ecclesiastical libraries in Europe; stimulate the development of theological libraries through shared knowledge and experience and through training theological librarians; serve the interest of those libraries in the scientific/academic sphere and on an international level; preserve the rich cultural patrimony found in those libraries. **Structure** General Assembly (annual); Executive Bureau. **Languages** English, French, German, Italian, Spanish. **Staff** Voluntary. **Finance** Member' dues. Other sources: grants from foundations; charitable donations from publishers and other related industries. **Events** *General Assembly* Helsinki (Finland) 2016, *General Assembly* Wroclaw (Poland) 2014, *General Assembly* Paris (France) 2013, *General Assembly* Belfast (UK) 2012, *General Assembly* Amsterdam (Netherlands) 2011. **Publications** *BETH Newsletter* – online. *Conseil international des associations de bibliothèques de théologie 1961-1990.*
Members Ordinary (12); Extraordinary (17); Personal (8), representing over 1,200 libraries, with more than 60 millions of volumes. Ordinary in 13 countries:
Belgium, Finland, France, Germany, Hungary, Ireland, Italy, Netherlands, Norway, Poland, Spain, Switzerland, UK.
Extraordinary in 11 countries:
Austria, Belgium, Croatia, Czechia, Denmark, France, Germany, Hungary, Italy, Netherlands, Switzerland.
Personal in 6 countries:
Belgium, Germany, Hungary, Italy, Spain, USA.
International associates (5), including the following organization listed in this Yearbook:
Red Latinoamericana de Información Teologica (RLIT, #18713).
IGO Relations *European Commission (EC, #06633)* (DG XIII).
[2019.03.01/XD3640/y/**D**]

♦ **European Theoretical Spectroscopy Facility (ETSF)** **08907**
Chair CESAM and Dept of Physics, Bât B5a, Univ de Liège, Allée de 6 août 19, Sart-Tilman, 4000 Liège, Belgium. T. +3243669017.
URL: http://www.etsf.eu/
History Formalized within the Nanoquanta Network of Excellence, in EU Framework Programme 6 (FP6). Fully established, 2007. Expanded under FP7. **Aims** Serve as a global leader in the scientific field of spectroscopy, developing new approaches, theories and software; serve external users (industrial, experimental and theoreticians) in areas such as materials science, energy, biology and nanoelectronics, and enable revolutionary technologies of the future; provide tools for training in the theory and practice of calculating spectroscopic observables. **Structure** Steering Committee; Research Teams; Collaboration Teams; Workshop Teams. **Languages** English. **Staff** 2.5-5 FTE, paid; several voluntary. **Finance** Funding from: participating institutions; regional and national sources; industrial consulting. Most Research Teams have EU funding and active collaborations with industry and private foundations. **Activities** Research and development; training/education; events/meetings. **Events** *Workshop on Electronic Excitations* Lund (Sweden) 2016, *Workshop on Electronic Excitations* Paris (France) 2015, *Young Researchers Meeting* Paris (France) 2015, *Workshop on Electronic Excitations* Saragossa (Spain) 2014, *Workshop on Electronic Excitations* Luxembourg (Luxembourg) 2013.
Members Research teams in 14 countries:
Austria, Belgium, Denmark, Finland, France, Germany, Italy, Luxembourg, Portugal, Slovakia, Spain, Sweden, UK, USA.
[2019.12.11/XM4708/**F**]

♦ **European Thermal Spray Association (ETSA)** **08908**
Association Européenne de la Projection Thermique
Pres c/o SPCTS – CEC, Univ of Limoges, 12 rue Atlantis, 87068 Limoges, France.
Sec Thermal Spray Enter, Univ of Barcelona, Carrer de Marti i Franqùes 1, 08028 Barcelona, Spain.
VZU Dept Thermal Spray Tylova 1581/46, 301 00 Pilsen, Czechia. E-mail: houdkova@vzuplzen.cz.
URL: http://etsa-thermal-spray.org/
History Registration: Start date: Dec 2009, France. **Aims** Organize information exchange on thermal spraying at European level. **Structure** College of Members; General Assembly; Board of Delegates; Executive Committee. **Languages** English. **Finance** Sources: members' dues. **Activities** Events/meetings; standards/guidelines; training/education. **Events** *Rencontres Internationales de la Projection Thermique* Jülich (Germany) 2022, *Biennial Meeting on Cold Spray* Barcelona (Spain) 2021, *Bioapplication Meeting* Pilsen (Czechia) 2021, *Meeting on Suspension and Solution Thermal Spraying* Trollhättan (Sweden) 2021, *Workshop on High-Kinetic Thermal Spray Coating* Tampere (Finland) 2017. **Publications** *Surface and Coatings Technology.* Conference papers. **Members** about 150 in mainly European countries. Membership countries not specified.
[2022.05.11/XM6523/**D**]

♦ **European Thermoelectric Society (ETS)** **08909**
Pres c/o Inst for Materials Sci, Heisenbergstr 3, 70569 Stuttgart, Germany. E-mail: contact@thermoelectricity.eu.
URL: http://www.thermoelectricity.eu/
History 1995. Founded as a regional organization of *International Thermoelectric Society (ITS, #15686).* Registration: Germany. **Languages** English. **Activities** Organizes workshops. **Events** *European Conference on Thermoelectrics (ECT)* Barcelona (Spain) 2022, *European Conference on Thermoelectrics (ECT)* Barcelona (Spain) 2020, *European Conference on Thermoelectrics (ECT)* Limassol (Cyprus) 2019, *European Conference on Thermoelectrics* Padua (Italy) 2017, *European Conference on Thermoelectrics* Lisbon (Portugal) 2016.
Members Membership countries not specified.
[2021/XD7185/**E**]

- ♦ European Thermographic Association (inactive)
- ♦ European Thermoplastic Independent Compounders / see European Masterbatchers and Compounders (#07749)
- ♦ European Third Party Providers Association (unconfirmed)

♦ European Thoracic Oncology Platform (ETOP) 08910

Contact Effingerstrasse 40, 3008 Bern, Switzerland. E-mail: etop@etop-eu.org.
URL: http://www.etop-eu.org/

History 2009. Registered under Swiss law. **Aims** Promote the exchange of ideas and research in the field of thoracic malignancies; sponsor and manage translational research projects and clinical trials with an emphasis on advancing the knowledge in thoracic malignancies. **Structure** Foundation Council; Scientific Committee. **Languages** English. **Activities** Events/meetings; projects/programmes; training/education. **Events** *Annual Meeting* Barcelona (Spain) 2021, *ELCC : European Lung Cancer Conference* Lugano (Switzerland) 2021, *ELCC : European Lung Cancer Conference* Geneva (Switzerland) 2020, *Annual Meeting* Zurich (Switzerland) 2020, *Annual Meeting* Amsterdam (Netherlands) 2019. **Publications** Annual Report; papers; meeting abstracts.
Members Full in 23 countries:
Australia, Austria, Belgium, China, Czechia, Denmark, Finland, France, Germany, Greece, Hungary, Ireland, Israel, Italy, Netherlands, Norway, Poland, Portugal, Spain, Sweden, Switzerland, UK, USA.
Included in the above, 2 organizations listed in this Yearbook:
Central European Cooperative Oncology Group (CECOG, #03706); European Lung Cancer Working Party (ELCWP, #07717).
NGO Relations Member of (1): *Lung Cancer Europe (LuCE, #16523).* [2020/XJ8527/y/**F**]

♦ European Thrombosis and Haemostasis Alliance (ETHA) 08911

Contact Rue Montoyer 47, 1000 Brussels, Belgium. T. +3226459862.
URL: https://etha.eu/

History 27 Mar 2018, Brussels (Belgium). Registration: EU Transparency Register, No/ID: 603220130426-56, Start date: 27 Feb 2018. **Aims** Give the thrombosis and haemostasis community a voice and drive prioritization of thrombosis and haemostasis in European Union patient safety and research programmes. **Activities** Advocacy/lobbying/activism.
Members Organizations in 19 countries:
Austria, Belgium, Czechia, Denmark, France, Germany, Greece, Hungary, Ireland, Italy, Netherlands, Norway, Poland, Russia, Serbia, Slovakia, Spain, Sweden, UK.
Included in the above, 3 organizations listed in this Yearbook:
Danubian League Against Thrombosis and Haemorrhagic Disorders (#05007); Gesellschaft für Thrombose- und Hämostaseforschung (GTH, #10146); International Society on Thrombosis and Haemostasis (ISTH, #15511).
NGO Relations Member of (1): *World Patients Alliance (WPA).* [2022/XM7022/y/**D**]

♦ European Thrombosis Research Organization (ETRO) 08912

Exec Officer KULAK, Lab for Thrombosis Research, E Sabbelaan 53, 8500 Kortrijk, Belgium. T. +3256246422. Fax +3256246997.
SG Dept of Medicine, Jageliellonian Univ Medical College, Skawinska 8, 31-066 Krakow, Poland. T. +48124305314. Fax +48124305314. E-mail: mmmusia@cyf-kr.edu.pl.

History Founded 1972. Also referred to in Italian as *Organizzazione Europea per la Ricerca sulla Trombosi.* 2006, reformed and registered in accordance with Belgian law. **Aims** Stimulate fundamental research in the field of thrombosis and *haemostasis*; facilitate scientific exchange between participating institutions; coordinate specific research activities. **Structure** General Assembly (every 2 years); Council; Executive Committee. **Languages** English. **Staff** None. **Finance** Members' dues. Budget (annual): euro 130,000. **Activities** Research/documentation; training/education; events/meetings. **Events** *Teaching Course* Krakow (Poland) 2013, *International Factor XIII Workshop* Debrecen (Hungary) 2012, *Teaching Course* Campobasso (Italy) 2011, *Teaching Course* Krakow (Poland) 2009, *Teaching Course* Blankenberge (Belgium) 2003. **Publications** *Thrombosis Research* – official journal.
Members European laboratories and institutions doing research in the field (124) in 23 countries:
Austria, Belgium, Czechia, Denmark, Finland, France, Germany, Greece, Hungary, Ireland, Israel, Italy, Luxembourg, Netherlands, Norway, Poland, Portugal, Slovakia, Slovenia, Spain, Sweden, Switzerland, UK.
IGO Relations *Council of Europe (CE, #04881); European Commission (EC, #06633).*
[2014.12.04/XD3420/**D**]

- ♦ European Throwsters' Association (inactive)

♦ European Thyroid Association (ETA) 08913

Standing Office EndoScience Endokrinologie Service GmbH, Hopfengartenweg 19, 90518 Altdorf bei Nürnberg, Germany. T. +4991879742415. Fax +4991879742475. E-mail: euro-thyroid-assoc@endoscience.de.
Sec Evgenideion Hosp, Unit of Endocrinology/Diabetes/Metabolism, Papadiamantopoulou 20, 115 28 Athens, Greece. T. +302106748878.
URL: http://www.eurothyroid.com/

History Jun 1967, Leuven (Belgium). Founded following initiative taken at 5th International Thyroid Congress, 24 May 1965, Rome (Italy). Former names and other names: *Association européenne de recherches sur la glande thyroïde* – former; *Association européenne thyroïde (AET)* – former. Registration: Registry Regensburg, No/ID: VR200481, Start date: 13 Sep 2009, Germany. **Aims** Promote knowledge in the thyroid field; improve knowledge on the thyroid gland and its diseases. **Structure** Executive Committee. **Languages** English. **Staff** Voluntary. **Finance** Sources: members' dues. **Activities** Events/meetings; training/education. **Events** *Annual Meeting* Milan (Italy) 2023, *Annual Meeting* Brussels (Belgium) 2022, *Annual Meeting* 2021, *International Thyroid Congress* 2020, *Annual Meeting* Budapest (Hungary) 2019. **Publications** *ETA Newsletter*; *European Thyroid Journal (ETJ)*; *Thyroidologist.* **Members** Specialist and research workers in over 50 countries and territories. Membership countries not specified. [2022.05.25/XD0877/v/**D**]

♦ European Timber Council (ETC) 08914

Contact address not obtained. E-mail: jan.soderlind@skogsindustrierna.org.
Events *Meeting* Copenhagen (Denmark) 2003.
Members Timber councils in 11 countries:
Austria, Belgium, Denmark, Estonia, Finland, France, Netherlands, Norway, Sweden, Switzerland, UK. [2007/XJ3486/**E**]

- ♦ European Timber Exporters' Convention (inactive)
- ♦ European Timber Trade Association (inactive)

♦ European Timber Trade Federation (ETTF) 08915

SG Am Weidendamm 1A, 10117 Berlin, Germany. T. +493072625800.
Communications Officer address not obtained.
URL: http://www.ettf.info/

History Founded at members' meeting of *European Hardwood Federation (inactive), Union pour le commerce des bois résineux dans l'UE (UCBR, inactive), Union for the Imported Softwood Trade of the EEC (inactive)* and *Fédération européenne du négoce de bois (FEBO, inactive).* Founding of ETTF resulted in simultaneous termination of above-mentioned associations. Registration: EU Transparency Register, No/ID: 808658823757-40, Start date: 6 Oct 2016. **Aims** Represent trade interests at European level. **Structure** General Assembly (2 a year); Board; Management team. **Activities** Events/meetings. **Events** *International Softwood Conference* Copenhagen (Denmark) 2022, *International Hardwood Conference* Lyon (France) 2022, *International Softwood Conference* Helsinki (Finland) 2021, *International Softwood Conference* Helsinki (Finland) 2021, *International Softwood Conference* Brussels (Belgium) 2020.
Members National importer associations in 12 countries:
Belgium, Denmark, France, Germany, Greece, Italy, Netherlands, Norway, Portugal, Spain, Sweden, UK.
Associate members:
Morocco, Norway, Sweden.
European Federation of Parquet Importers (EFPI, #07187); International Technical Tropical Timber Association (ITTTA, #15668).
NGO Relations Cooperates with (3): *Confédération européenne des industries du bois (CEI Bois, #04545); European Organization of the Sawmill Industry (EOS, #08114); European Sustainable Tropical Timber Coalition (STTC).* Stakeholder in: *PEFC Council (#18288).* [2021/XJ1060/t/**D**]

- ♦ European Timeshare Federation / see Resort Development Organisation (#18913)
- ♦ European Tissue Culture Society (inactive)
- ♦ European Tissue Engineering Society (inactive)

♦ European Tissue Repair Society (ETRS) 08916

Business Office Manager Rue Cingria 7, 1205 Geneva, Switzerland. T. +41223214890. Fax +41223214892. E-mail: office@etrs.org.
Registered Office Avenue de l'Hôpital 13, Bte 23-3, Sart-Tilman, 4000 Liège, Belgium.
URL: http://www.etrs.org/

History 30 Sep 1988. Statutes modified 16 Apr 1992. Registration: Belgium. **Aims** Motivated by scientific progress related to biology, pharmacology and clinical application of such new concepts as growth factors, artificial organs, biologically directed healing and related new products applicable to pathological conditions: promote knowledge and improve contact between scientists in biology, pharmacology and clinical care interested in the healing and related reaction of any organ resulting from any pathomechanism; provide a forum for interactive discussion among physicians and other practitioners, academic and industrial scientists and governmental agencies; close the gap of information between disciplines; transfer knowledge of clinicians and basic science researchers to developmental agencies and industries. **Structure** General Assembly (annual). International Board of Directors, consisting of 3 to 11 persons. Officers: President; Vice-President; Secretary-Treasurer. **Languages** English. **Staff** 2.00 FTE, paid; 1.00 FTE, voluntary. **Finance** Members' dues: Active, euro 85; Associate, euro 40. **Events** *Annual Meeting* Lyon (France) 2022, *Annual Meeting* Lyon (France) 2020, *Annual Meeting* Munich (Germany) 2019, *Annual Meeting* Amsterdam (Netherlands) 2018, *Annual Meeting* Brussels (Belgium) 2017. **Publications** *ETRS Bulletin* (annual) – inhouse journal; *Wound Repair and Regeneration* – journal jointly with American Wound Healing Society.
Members Clinical and scientific investigators in 28 countries:
Argentina, Australia, Austria, Belgium, Canada, China, Czechia, Denmark, Finland, France, Germany, India, Israel, Italy, Japan, Korea Rep, Kuwait, Netherlands, Norway, Poland, Portugal, Russia, Spain, Sweden, Switzerland, UK, USA, Zimbabwe.
[2021/XD3244/v/**D**]

♦ European Tissue Symposium (ETS) 08917

Chairman Manhattan Center, Avenue du Boulevard 21, 1210 Brussels, Belgium. T. +3225495230. Fax +3225021598. E-mail: info@europeantissue.com.
URL: http://www.europeantissue.com/

History 1971. Registration: Banque-Carrefour des Entreprises, No/ID: 0453.161.036, Start date: 14 Jun 1994; EU Transparency Register, No/ID: 28542716181-43, Start date: 11 Jul 2011. **Aims** Offer members the opportunity to exchange views on issues which are of importance to the European *tissue paper* industry; research and develop issues and policies which have an impact on the industry; develop a greater understanding of the sector and its products; liaise with other non-governmental associations, including industry trade associations; represent, on an ancillary basis, the industry towards authorities and stakeholders. **Structure** General Assembly (twice a year); Advisory Board; Project Stewardship Committee; Away from Home Project Group. **Languages** English. **Staff** Paid. **Finance** Members' dues. Special activity fees. **Activities** Research/documentation; events/meetings. **Events** *Members Summer Meeting* Lucca (Italy) 2022, *Members Winter Meeting* Brussels (Belgium) 2021, *Members winter meeting* Graz (Austria) 2006, *Members summer meeting* Vienna (Austria) 2006, *Members Winter Meeting* Brussels (Belgium) 2001. **Members** Tissue paper producing companies in Western Europe. Membership countries not specified. **NGO Relations** Member of: *Federation of European and International Associations Established in Belgium (FAIB, #09508); PEFC Council (#18288).*
[2022/XF3181/**F**]

♦ European Tobacco Harm Reduction Advocates (ETHRA) 08918

Contact NNA Ireland, Milltown, Convoy, Convoy, CO. DONEGAL, F93 YW9R, Ireland. E-mail: europethra@gmail.com.
URL: https://ethra.co/

History 2019. Set up as an advocacy group. Registration: EU Transparency Register, No/ID: 354946837243-73. **Aims** Promote public health by means of tobacco harm reduction, promotion of discussions and exchange of information and potential actions to reduce exposure to tobacco-related harms. **Activities** Advocacy/lobbying/activism. [2022.05.24/XM8835/**F**]

- ♦ European Tobacco Products Wholesalers' Union / see European Tobacco Wholesalers Association (#08919)

♦ European Tobacco Wholesalers Association 08919

Association européenne des grossistes en produits du tabac – Europäischer Tabakwaren-Grosshandelsverband (ETV)

Admin Konrad-Zuse-Ring 4, 41179 Mönchengladbach, Germany. T. +492161462440. E-mail: info@etv-online.eu.
URL: http://www.etv-online.eu/

History 1973. Former names and other names: *European Tobacco Products Wholesalers' Union* – former; *Union européenne des grossistes en produits de tabac* – former. Registration: EU Transparency Register, No/ID: 79170323734-59. **Aims** Defend the interests of the tobacco wholesale and vending sector in Europe. **Languages** English, German. **Finance** Sources: members' dues. **Events** *Annual Meeting* Zurich (Switzerland) 2019, *Annual Meeting* Krems (Austria) 2018, *Annual Meeting* Hamburg (Germany) 2017, *Annual Meeting* Lecce (Italy) 2016, *Annual Meeting* Berlin (Germany) 2015.
Members National organizations in 6 countries:
Austria, Belgium, Germany, Italy, Portugal, Switzerland. [2023.02.14/XD0327/**D**]

♦ European Toner and Inkjet Remanufacturers Association (ETIRA) . . 08920

SG Grieglaan 7, 4837 CB Breda, Netherlands. T. +31641461463. Fax +31765640451. E-mail: info@etira.org.
URL: http://www.etira.org/

History 2003. Registered in accordance with Belgian law. EU Transparency Register: 66749712601-11. **Aims** Represent the interests of remanufacturers in the European Union; act as the recognized industry body for all matters regarding the inkjet and toner remanufacturing industry. **Structure** General Assembly (annual). Board of Directors, comprising President, Vice-President, Treasurer and 4 members. Secretary-General. President and Vice-President. Working Groups; Committees; Secretariat in Breda (Netherlands). **Languages** English. **Staff** 1.00 FTE, paid. **Finance** Members' dues. **Activities** Developed a Code of Conduct. Organizes seminars and workshops. **Events** *Annual General Meeting* Brussels (Belgium) 2019, *General Assembly* Düsseldorf (Germany) 2009, *General Assembly* Barcelona (Spain) 2004. **Publications** Annual Report; Flyers.
Members Full; Associate. Members in 20 countries:
Austria, Belgium, Bosnia-Herzegovina, Bulgaria, Croatia, Czechia, France, Germany, Greece, Hungary, Italy, Netherlands, Poland, Portugal, Romania, Serbia, Spain, Sweden, Switzerland, UK. [2017/XM1399/**D**]

- ♦ European Tool Committee (#04163)
- ♦ European Tourism Action Group / see European Travel and Tourism Advisory Group (#08946)
- ♦ European Tourism Association AISBL / see European Tour Operators Association (#08922)
- ♦ European Tourism Liaison Committee / see European Trade Union Liaison Committee on Tourism (#08929)

♦ European Tourism Manifesto 08921

Sec c/o European Travel Commission, Rue du Marché aux Herbes 61, 1000 Brussels, Belgium.
Chairman address not obtained.
URL: https://tourismmanifesto.eu/

History Feb 2016. **Aims** Allow for tourism in Europe to continue being a key driver for sustainable growth and job creation, fostering and promoting European values, cultural divesity, European way of life and EU citizenship on a global scale. **Activities** Advocacy/lobbying/activism; guidance/assistance/consulting.
Members Public and private organizations (over 60), including 50 listed in this Yearbook:
- *Airline Catering Association (ACA, #00604);*
- *Airlines for Europe (A4E, #00607);*
- *Airports Council International – European Region (ACI EUROPE, #00612);*
- *Airport Services Association (ASA, #00613);*
- *CLIA Europe (#03995);*

- *Confederation of National Associations of Hotels, Restaurants, Cafés and Similar Establishments in the European Union and European Economic Area (HOTREC, #04569);*
- *Europa Nostra (#05767);*
- *European Alliance of Responsible Tourism and Hospitality (EARTH, #05880);*
- *European Association for Aquatic Mammals (EAAM, #05938);*
- *European Boating Industry (EBI, #06377);*
- *European Cultural Tourism Network (ECTN, #06871);*
- *European Cyclists' Federation (ECF, #06877);*
- *European Exhibition Industry Alliance (EEIA, #07012);*
- *European Federation of Campingsite Organisations and Holiday Park Associations (EFCO and HPA, #07066);*
- *European Federation of Equipment Leasing Company Associations (LEASEUROPE, #07111);*
- *European Federation of Food, Agriculture and Tourism Trade Unions (EFFAT, #07125);*
- *European Federation of Rural Tourism (RuralTour, #07208);*
- *European Federation of Tourist Guide Associations (#07228);*
- *European Festivals Association (EFA, #07242);*
- *European Greenways Association (EGWA, #07412);*
- *European Historic Houses Association (EHH, #07491);*
- *European Historic Thermal Towns Association (EHTTA, #07492);*
- *European Hotel Forum (EHF);*
- *European Network for Accessible Tourism (ENAT, #07858);*
- *European Network of Unesco Sites (MIRABILIA Network);*
- *European Ramblers' Association (ERA, #08328);*
- *European Spas Association (ESPA, #08805);*
- *European Tour Operators Association (ETOA, #08922);*
- *European Trade Union Liaison Committee on Tourism (ETLC, #08929);*
- *European Transport Workers' Federation (ETF, #08941);*
- *European Travel Commission (ETC, #08943);*
- *European Union Federation of Youth Hostel Associations (EUFED, #08988);*
- *European Union Road Federation (ERF, #09014);*
- *eu travel tech (#09205);*
- *Global Business Travel Association (GBTA);*
- *International Association of Amusement Parks and Attractions (IAAPA, #11699);*
- *International Association of Tour Managers (IATM, #12231);*
- *International Committee of Tourism Film Festivals (CIFFT);*
- *International Institute of Gastronomy, Culture, Arts and Tourism (IGCAT, #13883);*
- *International Road Transport Union (IRU, #14761);*
- *International Social Tourism Organisation (ISTO, #14889);*
- *Mad'in Europe;*
- *Network of European Regions for a Sustainable and Competitive Tourism (NECSTouR, #17028);*
- *Nordic Tourism Collective (#17450);*
- *Observatory on Tourism in the European Islands (OTIE, #17645);*
- *Pearle – Live Performance Europe (#18284);*
- *spiritsEUROPE (#19921);*
- *The European Travel Agents' and Tour Operators' Associations (ECTAA, #08942);*
- *UNI Global Union – Europa (UNI Europa, #20342);*
- *World Travel and Tourism Council (WTTC, #21871).* [2020/AA0992/y/**F**]

♦ European Tourism Research Institute (internationally oriented national body)

♦ European Tourism Trade Fairs Association / see International Tourism Trade Fairs Association (#15697)

♦ European Tour Operators Association Ltd / see European Tour Operators Association (#08922)

♦ European Tour Operators Association (ETOA) 08922

Contact 4th Floor, Grays Inn House, 127 Clerkenwell Road, London, EC1R 5DB, UK. T. +442074994412. E-mail: info@etoa.org.
Brussels Office Rue du Marché aux Herbes 61, 1000 Brussels, Belgium.
URL: http://www.etoa.org/

History 1989, London (UK). Former names and other names: *European Tourism Association AISBL* – legal name; *European Tour Operators Association Ltd* – legal name. Registration: EU Transparency Register, No/ID: 700500614404-28, Start date: 6 Mar 2018; No/ID: 0525.647.552, Start date: 2 Apr 2013, Belgium; Private company limited by guarantee, No/ID: 04950752, Start date: 3 Nov 2003, England and Wales. **Aims** Represent international inbound tour operators based in Europe. **Structure** Board; Advisory Council. Working Groups (5); Secretariat. **Languages** English, French, German, Italian, Polish, Spanish. **Staff** 12.00 FTE, paid. **Finance** Sources: meeting proceeds; members' dues. Funds on ad hoc basis from the Tourism Unit of *European Commission (EC, #06633)* (DG XXIII) for specific projects. **Activities** Advocacy/lobbying/activism; standards/guidelines; networking/liaising; projects/programmes; training/education; events/meetings. **Events** *GEM : Global European Marketplace Workshop* London (UK) 2020, *HEM : Hoteliers European Marketplace Workshop* Seville (Spain) 2020, *HEM : Hoteliers European Marketplace Workshop* Florence (Italy) 2018, *GEM : Global European Marketplace Conference and Workshop* London (UK) 2017, *Annual Tourism Summit in the Alps* Lucerne (Switzerland) 2017. **Publications** *ETOA Newsletter and Briefing* (12 a year); *ETOA Yearbook and Directory* (annual).

Members Full tour operators (over 100) selling tours outside the EC and operating tours in Europe, based in 20 countries:
Austria, Bulgaria, Croatia, Czechia, France, Germany, Greece, Israel, Italy, Latvia, Netherlands, Norway, Poland, Portugal, Romania, Spain, Sweden, Switzerland, UK, USA.
Associate (250) canal/lake/river cruises; coach operators; consultancies; cruise/ferry operations; folklore shows/cabarets/restaurants; concerts and events; ground handlers; hotels; mountain railways; shops and cultural demonstrations; tourist board; tourism services, in 25 countries:
Andorra, Austria, Belgium, Croatia, Czechia, Denmark, Finland, France, Germany, Greece, Ireland, Israel, Italy, Latvia, Morocco, Netherlands, Norway, Poland, Portugal, Romania, Spain, Switzerland, Türkiye, UK, USA.
Nordic Tourism Collective (#17450).

NGO Relations Member of (2): *European Tourism Manifesto (#08921); Network for the European Private Sector in Tourism (NET, #17027).* Close links with: *International Hotel and Restaurant Association (IH&RA, #13813); World Travel and Tourism Council (WTTC, #21871).* [2021/XD3674/**D**]

♦ European Toy Confederation (inactive)

♦ European Track and Field Coaches Association / see European Athletics Coaches Association (#06292)

♦ European Trade Association for Business Angels, Seed Funds, and other Early Stage Market Players (EBAN) 08923

Main Office Ave des Arts 56, 1000 Brussels, Belgium. E-mail: info@eban.org.
URL: http://www.eban.org/

History 1999. Founded by *European Business Angels Network.* Registration: No/ID: 0474.621.394, Start date: 13 Feb 2001, Belgium; EU Transparency Register, No/ID: 117463229970-40, Start date: 2 Feb 2018. **Aims** Represent the early stage *investor* community. **Structure** Board of Directors; Secretariat. **Languages** English. **Staff** 4.00 FTE, paid. **Finance** Members' dues. Other sources: sponsorship; events; publications; training. **Activities** Certification/accreditation; training/education; research/documentation; networking/liaising; advocacy/lobbying/activism; awareness raising; capacity building. **Events** *Annual Congress* Athens (Greece) 2023, *Annual Congress* Cork (Ireland) 2022, *Annual Congress* 2021, *Annual Congress* Helsinki (Finland) 2019, *Annual Congress* Sofia (Bulgaria) 2018. **Publications** *Statistics Compendium* (annual). Activity Report (annual); Directory of networks (annual); compendiums; statements.

Members in 53 countries:
Albania, Andorra, Australia, Austria, Belarus, Belgium, Brazil, Bulgaria, Canada, Chile, Colombia, Croatia, Cyprus, Czechia, Denmark, Egypt, Estonia, Finland, France, Germany, Greece, Hungary, Ireland, Italy, Jordan, Latvia, Lebanon, Lithuania, Luxembourg, Malaysia, Malta, Monaco, Netherlands, New Zealand, Nigeria, North Macedonia, Norway, Oman, Poland, Portugal, Russia, Serbia, Slovakia, Slovenia, South Africa, Spain, Sweden, Switzerland, Tunisia, Türkiye, UK, Ukraine, USA.

NGO Relations Member of: *ANIMA Investment Network (#00833); EFMD – The Management Development Network (#05387); Multilingual Europe Technology Alliance (META, #16892).* [2022/XF5996/t/**F**]

♦ European Trade Association of PVC Window System Supplies (EPPA) 08924

Managing Dir Avenue de Cortenbergh 71, 1000 Brussels, Belgium. T. +3227396381. Fax +3227324218. E-mail: info@eppa-profiles.eu.
URL: https://www.eppa-profiles.eu/

History Mar 2000. A sectorial organization of *European Plastics Converters (EuPC, #08216).* Former names and other names: *European PVC Window Profile and Related Building Products Association (EPPA)* – former. Registration: Banque Carrefour des Entreprises, No/ID: 0848.567.579, Start date: 10 Sep 2012, Belgium; EU Transparency Register, No/ID: 847748313670-41, Start date: 22 May 2014. **Aims** Set up projects based on the VinylPlus Voluntary Commitment; represent the PVC window profile industry. **Structure** General Assembly; Board. **Languages** English, French, German. **Staff** 3.00 FTE, paid. **Members** Company Members; Association Members; Associated Members. Membership countries not specified. **NGO Relations** Member of (3): *Circular Plastics Alliance (#03936); Construction 2050 Alliance (#04760); Construction Products Europe AISBL (#04761).* [2022/XD8215/**D**]

♦ European Trade Law Association (no recent information)

♦ European Trade Promotion Organization (no recent information)

♦ European Trade Promotion Organizations Association / see Trade Promotion Europe (#20184)

♦ European Trade Study Group (ETSG) 08925

Co-Dir Dept of Economics, Strathclyde Business School, 199 Cathedral Street, Glasgow, G4 0QU, UK. T. +441415483580.
Co-Dir World Trade Inst, Univ of Bern, Hallerstrasse 6, 3012 Bern, Switzerland. T. +41316313270.
Co-Dir School of Economics, Univ of Surrey, Elizabeth Fry Bldg, Guildford, GU2 7XH, UK. T. +441483689380.
URL: http://www.etsg.org/

History 1999. Founded with initial funding from *European Science Foundation (ESF, #08441).* **Aims** Serve as a forum for academic discussion and research on international trade among European universities and research institutes. **Structure** Scientific Committee (meets annually); Managing Board. **Languages** English. **Staff** Voluntary. **Finance** Sources: meeting proceeds. **Events** *Annual Conference* Groningen (Netherlands) 2022, *Annual Conference* Ghent (Belgium) 2021, *Annual Conference* Ghent (Belgium) 2020, *Annual Conference* Bern (Switzerland) 2019, *Annual Conference* Warsaw (Poland) 2018. [2022.05.04/XE3779/t/**E**]

♦ European Trade Union Committee for Education (ETUCE) 08926

Comité syndical européen de l'éducation (CSEE) – Europäisches Gewerkschaftskomitee für Bildung und Wissenschaft

European Dir Bd Bischoffsheim 15, 6eme étage, 1000 Brussels, Belgium. T. +3222240691 – +3222240692. E-mail: secretariat@csee-etuce.org.
URL: http://www.csee-etuce.org/

History 13 Oct 1981, Brussels (Belgium). Founded within the framework of *European Trade Union Confederation (ETUC, #08927)*, superseding *European Teachers Trade Union Committee (ETTUC, inactive)*, which was dissolved at that time. Statutes modified 4-5 Jun 1996, Luxembourg. Current By-laws adopted Dec 2010. Registration: EU Transparency Register, No/ID: 72197913011-06. **Aims** Be the teachers' social partner at European level and a defender of teachers' interests to the European Commission. **Structure** Conference (every 4 years); Committee; Bureau; Secretariat, headed by European Director. **Languages** English, French, German, Russian, Spanish. **Staff** 8.00 FTE, paid. **Finance** Sources: members' dues. **Activities** Events/meetings; training/education. **Events** *Special Conference* Vienna (Austria) 2014, *Conference* Budapest (Hungary) 2012, *Launching conference of the project on Roma children* Budapest (Hungary) 2005, *Regional seminar* Vilnius (Lithuania) 2005, *Biennial Congress* Luxembourg (Luxembourg) 2001. **Publications** *ETUCE Newsletter* (4 a year) in English, French, Russian.

Members Full: trade unions (132) representing about 11 million teachers in 48 countries:
Albania, Armenia, Austria, Azerbaijan, Belarus, Belgium, Bosnia-Herzegovina, Bulgaria, Croatia, Cyprus, Czechia, Denmark, Estonia, Finland, France, Georgia, Germany, Greece, Hungary, Iceland, Ireland, Israel, Italy, Kazakhstan, Kyrgyzstan, Latvia, Lithuania, Luxembourg, Malta, Moldova, Montenegro, Netherlands, North Macedonia, Norway, Poland, Portugal, Romania, Russia, Serbia, Slovakia, Slovenia, Spain, Sweden, Switzerland, Tajikistan, Türkiye, UK, Ukraine.

IGO Relations Recognized by: *European Commission (EC, #06633).* Participant in Fundamental Rights Platform of *European Union Agency for Fundamental Rights (FRA, #08969).*

NGO Relations Secretariat at: *International Trade Union House, Brussels (ITUH).* Members are member organizations of: *Education International (EI, #05371).* EI is represented on the ETUCE Committee. Signatory to: *Alter Summit.* Member of: *European Policy Network on School Leadership (EPNoSL, #08245); SIRIUS – Policy Network on Migrant Education (SIRIUS, #19291).*
- *Association des chambres de commerce et d'industrie européennes (EUROCHAMBRES, #02423);*
- *Association des états généraux des étudiants de l'Europe (AEGEE-Europe, #02495);*
- *BUSINESSEUROPE (#03381);*
- *European Association of Institutions of Higher Education (EURASHE, #06086);*
- *SGI Europe (#19253);*
- *European Federation of Education Employers (EFEE, #07101);*
- *European Federation of Public Service Unions (EPSU, #07202);*
- *European Institute for Gender Equality (EIGE, #07557);*
- *European School Heads Association (ESHA, #08431);*
- *ILGA-Europe (#11118);*
- *Lifelong Learning Platform – European Civil Society for Education (LLLP, #16466);*
- *Nordic Teachers' Council (#17444);*
- *Organising Bureau of European School Student Unions (OBESSU, #17829);*
- *SMEunited (#19327);*
- *SOLIDAR (#19680);*
- *UNI Global Union – Europa (UNI Europa, #20342).* [2022.05.05/XE0787/t/**E**]

♦ European Trade Union Confederation (ETUC) 08927

Confédération européenne des syndicats (CES) – Confederación Europea de Sindicatos (CES) – Europäischer Gewerkschaftsbund (EGB) – Confederazione Europea dei Sindacati (CES) – Den Europeiske Faglige Samorganisasjon (DEFS)

SG International Trade Union House, Boulevard du Roi Albert II 5, 1210 Brussels, Belgium. E-mail: generalsecretary@etuc.org – etuc@etuc.org.
Main Office Silversquare, Boulevard Roi Albert II 4, 1210 Brussels, Belgium.
URL: http://www.etuc.org/

History 9 Feb 1973, Brussels (Belgium). Constituent Assembly and Founding Congress, Brussels (Belgium), 8-9 Feb 1973. Current constitution approved by 14th Statutory Congress, May 2019, Vienna (Austria). Former names and other names: *European Confederation of Free Trade Unions in the Community (ECFTU)* – former; *Confédération européenne des syndicats libres dans la Communauté (CESL)* – former. Registration: EU Transparency Register, No/ID: 06698681039-26, Start date: 2 Feb 2009. **Aims** Promote the European Social Model and work for development of a united Europe of peace and stability where working people and their families can enjoy full human and civil rights and high living standards; speak with a single voice, on behalf of the common interests of workers, at European level. **Structure** Congress (every 4 years); Executive Committee; Steering Committee; Secretariat, headed by General Secretary. European Industry Federations comprise organizations of trade unions within one or more public or private economic sector. Secretary-General also heads Secretariat of *Pan-European Regional Council (PERC, #18180).* **Languages** English, French. **Staff** 58.00 FTE, paid. **Finance** Sources: members' dues. **Activities** Advocacy/lobbying/activism; events/meetings; networking/liaising; politics/policy/regulatory. **Events** *European Works Councils Conference* Brussels (Belgium) 2022, *Midterm Conference* Lisbon (Portugal) 2021, *Conference on Rethinking Labour Law in the Digitalisation Era* Brussels (Belgium) 2020, *Quadrennial Congress* Vienna (Austria) 2019, *Seminar on the Future of Trade Unions in Europe, Young, Digital and Organized* Vienna (Austria) 2019. **Publications** *ETUC Newsletter* (10 a year) in English, French; *National UPdates* (4 a year); *European Trade Union News.* Press releases in English, French.

Members National trade union confederations (93) in 41 countries. Membership countries not specified.
European industry federations (9), listed in this Yearbook:
European Arts and Entertainment Alliance (EAEA, #05918); European Confederation of Police (EuroCOP, #06719); European Federation of Building and Woodworkers (EFBWW, #07065); European Federation of Food, Agriculture and Tourism Trade Unions (EFFAT, #07125); European Federation of Journalists (EFJ, #07152); European Federation of Public Service Unions (EPSU, #07202); European Trade Union Committee for Education (ETUCE, #08926); European Transport Workers' Federation (ETF, #08941); industriAll European Trade Union (industriALL Europe, #11176).

Consultative Status Consultative status granted from: *ILO (#11123)* (Regional); *Council of Europe (CE, #04881)* (Participatory Status). **IGO Relations** Accredited by (1): *United Nations Framework Convention on Climate Change – Secretariat (UNFCCC, #20564).* Partner of (2): *European Commission (EC, #06633)* (as European Social Partner); *European Quality Assurance in Vocational Education and Training (EQAVET, #08312)* (as Social Partner). Regular relations with: *European Economic and Social Committee (EESC, #06963)*; *European Youth Centres (EYCs, #09138).* Participant in Fundamental Rights Platform of: *European Union Agency for Fundamental Rights (FRA, #08969).* **NGO Relations** Member of (5): *Comité européen de normalisation (CEN, #04162)* (as Associate member); *Eastern Partnership Civil Society Forum (EaP CSF, #05247)*; *European Youth Forum (#09140)*; *Finance Watch (#09764)*; *Spring Alliance (inactive)* (as Founding member of). Partner of (2): *European Disability Forum (EDF, #06929)*; *IGLOO Europe (no recent information)* (as Founding partner). Cooperates with (2): *International Federation of ACLI (#13336)*; *OITS/ European Commission for Social Tourism (CETS, #17713)* (Cooperation agreement). Instrumental in setting up (2): *Baltic Sea Trade Union Network (BASTUN, #03151)*; *EUROCADRES – Council of European Professional and Managerial Staff (#05651).* Set up: *European Trade Union Institute (ETUI, #08928)*; *Fédération européenne des retraités et des personnes âgées (FERPA, #09580).* [2023.02.14/XD0688/y/**D**]

- ♦ European Trade Union Federation of Diamond and Precious Stone Workers (no recent information)
- ♦ European Trade Union Federation for Textiles, Clothing and Leather (inactive)

♦ European Trade Union Institute (ETUI) 08928

Institut syndical européen (ISE) – Europäisches Gewerkschaftsinstitut (EGI) – Europees Vakbondsinstituut (EVI) – Europeiske Fagforeningsinstitut (DEFI)

Communications Dir Bd du Roi Albert II 5, Box 4, 1210 Brussels, Belgium. T. +3222240556. E-mail: etui@etui.org.

Gen Dir address not obtained.

URL: http://www.etui.org/

History Founded within *European Trade Union Confederation (ETUC, #08927)*, by merger of *European Trade Union College (ETUCO, inactive)*, *European Trade Union Institute (ETUI, inactive)* and *European Trade Union Technical Bureau for Health and Safety (TUTB, inactive).* Former names and other names: *European Trade Union Institute for Research, Education and Health and Safety (ETUI-REHS)* – former (Apr 2005 to Oct 2008). Registration: Banque-Carrefour des Entreprises, No/ID: 0418.812.841, Start date: 22 Sep 1978, Belgium; EU Transparency Register, No/ID: 521878025223-22, Start date: 22 Dec 2016. **Aims** Conduct studies on socio-economic topics and industrial relations; monitor European policy development of importance for the world of labour; create bridges between the academic sphere; the world of research and the trade union movement to encourage independent research relevant to the world of labour; encourage training and learning activities for the ETUC and its affiliates with programmes and exchanges that strengthen the European trade union identity; provide technical assistance in the field of health and safety with a view to achieving a high level of occupational health and safety protection for workers throughout Europe. **Structure** General Assembly; Management Committee; Directors' Committee; Advisory Group. **Languages** English, French. **Staff** 60.00 FTE, paid. **Activities** Events/meetings; guidance/assistance/consulting; monitoring/evaluation; networking/liaising; projects/programmes; publishing activities; research/documentation; training/education. **Events** *A Blueprint for Equality* Brussels (Belgium) 2022, *European Network for the Fair Sharing of Working Time Conference* Brussels (Belgium) 2022, *Joint Seminar on Preventing Damage to the Mental Health if Health and Care Workers* Brussels (Belgium) 2022, *Psychosocial Risks in (Un)expected Places* Brussels (Belgium) 2022, *Conference on Labour rights and the Digital Transition* Brussels (Belgium) 2021. **Publications** *Collective Bargaining* (12 a year) – electronic only; *etui.hesamail* (12 a year) – electronic only; *etui.news* (12 a year) – electronic only; *etui.greennewdeal* (10 a year) in English – electronic only; *Transfer* (4 a year) in English – European review of labour and research; *HesaMag* (2 a year) in English, French – The health and safety magazine with a European view; *SEER* (2 a year) in English – Journal for labour and social affairs in Eastern Europe. *Betwixt and between: Integrating refugees into the EU labour market* (2021) by Dr Béla Galgóczi; *Social policy in the European Union: state of play 2020* (2021) by Dr Bart Vanhercke and Dr Slavina Spasova et al; *Benchmarking Working Europe 2020* (2020) by Dr Nicola Countouris and Romuald Jagodzinski – Covid-19 and the world of work: the impact of a pandemic; *The challenge of digital transformation in the automotive industry* (2020) by Dr Jan Drahokoupil – Jobs, upgrading and the prospects for development; *Collective bargaining in Europe: towards an endgame* (2019) by Dr Torsten Müller and Dr Kurt Vandaele et al. Information Services: ETUI-REHS Education Resource Centre; ETUI-REHS Documentation Centre. **Members** Not a membership organization. **IGO Relations** Member of (1): *European Agency for Safety and Health at Work (EU-OSHA, #05843).* Recognized by: *European Commission (EC, #06633).* **NGO Relations** Member of (1): *Global Labour University (GLU, #10448).* Based at: *International Trade Union House, Brussels (ITUH).* Associate member of: *Comité européen de normalisation (CEN, #04162).* [2022.05.20/XM0854/jty/**E**]

- ♦ European Trade Union Institute for Research, Education and Health and Safety / see European Trade Union Institute (#08928)

♦ European Trade Union Liaison Committee on Tourism (ETLC) 08929

Coordinator c/o EFFAT, Av Louise 130A – Bte 3, 1050 Brussels, Belgium. T. +3222187730. Fax +3222183018.

URL: https://www.etlc-network.eu/

History Mar 1995, Brussels (Belgium). A cooperation of: *European Federation of Food, Agriculture and Tourism Trade Unions (EFFAT, #07125)*; *UNI Global Union – Europa (UNI Europa, #20342)*; *European Transport Workers' Federation (ETF, #08941)*; *International Union of Food, Agricultural, Hotel, Restaurant, Catering, Tobacco and Allied Workers Associations (IUF, #15772)*; *UNI Global Union (#20338)*; *International Transport Workers' Federation (ITF, #15726).* Former names and other names: *European Tourism Liaison Committee* – alias. **Aims** Promote the creation of sustainable development in tourism; improve working conditions for tourism workers; promote basic and continuing training in the tourism industry; promote social dialogue in the tourism sector; strengthen cross-border cooperation between trade union organizations representing employees in the tourism sector. **Structure** Committee. **Languages** English, French. **Staff** None. **Finance** Funded by participating organizations. **Activities** Events/meetings. **Events** *European Trade Union Conference* Palma (Spain) 2010, *European Trade Union Conference* Portimão (Portugal) 2007, *European Trade Union Conference* Limassol (Cyprus) 2006, *European Trade Union Conference* Malta 2005, *European Trade Union Conference* Budapest (Hungary) 2004. **Publications** Position papers; policy documents.

Members Organizations in 31 countries:
Austria, Belgium, Bosnia-Herzegovina, Croatia, Cyprus, Czechia, Denmark, Estonia, Finland, France, Germany, Greece, Iceland, Ireland, Italy, Latvia, Lithuania, Luxembourg, Malta, Netherlands, Norway, Poland, Portugal, Romania, Slovakia, Slovenia, Spain, Sweden, Switzerland, Türkiye, UK.

NGO Relations Member of (1): *European Tourism Manifesto (#08921).* [2013.06.24/XE4333/t/**E**]

♦ European Traditional Chinese Medicine Association (ETCMA) 08930

Vice-Pres Parkzichtlaan 336E, 3544 MN Utrecht, Netherlands. E-mail: vice-president@etcma.org – president@etcma.org.

Honorary Sec address not obtained. E-mail: secretary@etcma.org.

URL: http://www.etcma.org/

History 2002. **Aims** See Chinese Medicine equally accepted and integrated into *healthcare* systems for the citizens of Europe. **Structure** General Assembly; Executive Committee. **Languages** English. **Staff** 9.00 FTE, paid. **Finance** Members' dues. **Activities** Events/meetings. **Events** *World Scientific and Cultural Dialogue on Acupuncture* Paris (France) 2018, *General Assembly* Prague (Czech Rep) 2014.

Members Full in 18 countries:
Austria, Belgium, Denmark, Finland, France, Germany, Greece, Iceland, Ireland, Italy, Netherlands, Norway, Poland, Portugal, Romania, Sweden, Switzerland, UK.

Affiliate in 1 country:
Israel.

NGO Relations Member of: *EUROCAM (#05653)*; *World Federation of Acupuncture-Moxibustion Societies (WFAS, #21405).* [2020.03.09/XJ0358/**D**]

♦ European Traditional Sports and Games Association (ETSGA) 08931

Association européenne des jeux et sports traditionnels (AEJeST) – Asociación Europea de Juegos y Deportes Tradicionales (AEJDT)

Contact address not obtained. E-mail: info@aejest.com.

URL: http://aejest.com

History 28 Apr 2001, Lesneven (France). **Aims** Encourage and support development and practice of traditional sports and games, as well as recognition of the values contained by traditional sports and games in general. **Structure** General Assembly (annual); Council; Executive Committee. **Languages** English, French, Spanish. **Staff** Voluntary. **Finance** Sources: members' dues. **Activities** Events/meetings; research/documentation. **Events** *Conference* Angers (France) 2014, *Conference* L'Hospitalet de l'Infant (Spain) 2014, *Conference* Spain 2014, *General Assembly* Civitanova Marche (Italy) 2013, *Conference* Ourense (Spain) 2013.

Members Organizations (75) and individuals (11) in 16 countries:
Belgium, Bosnia-Herzegovina, Croatia, Cyprus, Czechia, France, Hungary, Italy, North Macedonia, Poland, Portugal, Romania, Russia, Serbia, Spain, Switzerland.

Included in the above, one international organization listed in this Yearbook:
International Federation of Celtic Wrestling (IFCW, #13383). [2022.05.11/XD8761/y/**D**]

- ♦ European Traffic Police Organisation (inactive)
- ♦ European Train Control System (see: #08327)

♦ European Trainers Federation (ETF) 08932

Contact Assn des Entraineurs de Galop, 18 bis Avenue du General Leclerc, 60501 Chantilly, France. T. +33344572539. Fax +33344575885.

URL: http://trainersfederation.eu/

Aims Provide a network of contacts to assist each member to develop its policy and services to member trainers; liaise with political and administrative bodies on behalf of European trainers. **Events** *Annual General Meeting* Newbridge (Ireland) 2015. **Publications** *European Trainer* (4 a year) – magazine.

Members Full in 12 countries:
Belgium, Czechia, France, Germany, Hungary, Ireland, Netherlands, Norway, Slovakia, Spain, Sweden, UK.

NGO Relations Member of: *European Horse Network (EHN, #07499).* [2015/XM4184/**D**]

- ♦ European Training Association for Farming and Rural Affairs (inactive)
- ♦ European Training Centre for Railways (internationally oriented national body)

♦ European Training and Development Federation (ETDF) 08933

Fédération européenne pour la formation et le développement (FEFD)

Contact c/o AFFEN, 253 rue Saint Honoré, 75001 Paris, France.

History following several meetings starting 11 Mar 1993. Current title adopted, 20 Nov 1994, Brussels (Belgium), with first constituent office set up, 18 Nov 1995, Paris (France). Registered in accordance with French law. **Structure** General Assembly; Executive Committee. **Events** *General Assembly* Bologna (Italy) 2006, *General Assembly* Stuttgart (Germany) 2005.

Members Full in 10 countries:
Belgium, France, Germany, Ireland, Italy, Netherlands, Portugal, Spain, Switzerland, UK. [2008/XM0234/**D**]

♦ European Training Foundation (ETF) 08934

Fondation européenne pour la formation – Europäische Stiftung für Berufsbildung

Dir Villa Gualino, Viale Settimio Severo 65, 10133 Turin TO, Italy. T. +39116302222. Fax +39116302200. E-mail: information_service@etf.europa.eu – info@etf.europa.eu.

URL: http://www.etf.europa.eu/

History May 1990. Established by Council Regulation EC 1360/90; amended Jul 1994 (Regulation EC 2063/94) and Jul 1998 (Regulation EC 1572/98); recast in 2008 (Regulation EC 1339/2008). A decentralized agency of *European Union (EU, #08967)*, set up under *Treaty on European Union (Maastricht Treaty, 1992).* Became operational in 1994. Located at Villa Gualino, Turin (Italy). **Aims** Contribute to the lifelong development of individuals' skills and competences through improvement of vocational education and training systems in partner countries; help transition and developing countries in the context of the EU's external relations policy. **Structure** Governing Board (meets twice a year), comprises representatives of all EU Member States, chaired by the European Commission (DG EMPL). **Languages** Arabic, English, French, German, Italian, Russian, Spanish. **Staff** 130.00 FTE, paid. **Finance** On the European Union budget. **Activities** Guidance/assistance/consulting. **Events** *Youth first! Employment, skills and social policies that work for young Europeans in times of uncertainty* Brussels (Belgium) 2022, *Workshop on the first draft of the operation programme for human resources development in Serbia* Belgrade (Serbia) 2011, *Meeting on advancements, challenges and priorities* Brussels (Belgium) 2011, *Conference on promoting social inclusion and combating poverty through cooperation in education, training and work in EU neighbouring countries* Brussels (Belgium) 2010, *Conference on women and work* Turin (Italy) 2010. **Publications** Work Programme; thematic analyses; statistical reports; general information materials; periodicals.

Members Governments of EU member countries (27):
Austria, Belgium, Bulgaria, Croatia, Cyprus, Czechia, Denmark, Estonia, Finland, France, Germany, Greece, Hungary, Ireland, Italy, Latvia, Lithuania, Luxembourg, Malta, Netherlands, Poland, Portugal, Romania, Slovakia, Slovenia, Spain, Sweden.

Partner countries and territories (29) (not specified). Candidate countries (5):

Candidate countries (5):
Albania, Montenegro, North Macedonia, Serbia, Türkiye.

South European countries and territories (2):
Bosnia-Herzegovina, Kosovo.

EU Neighbourhood South countries and territories (9):
Algeria, Egypt, Israel, Jordan, Lebanon, Morocco, Palestine, Syrian AR, Tunisia.

EU Neighbourhood East countries (7):
Armenia, Azerbaijan, Belarus, Georgia, Moldova, Russia, Ukraine.

Central Asia countries (5):
Kazakhstan, Kyrgyzstan, Tajikistan, Turkmenistan, Uzbekistan.

IGO Relations Scientific Advisor to: *European Quality Assurance in Vocational Education and Training (EQAVET, #08312).* Cooperates with:

- *African Development Bank (ADB, #00283)*;
- *Asian Development Bank (ADB, #01422)*;
- *Assemblée Régionale et Locale Euro-Méditerranéenne (ARLEM, #02313)*;
- *European Committee of the Regions (CoR, #06665)*;
- *Council of the European Union (#04895)*;
- *European Bank for Reconstruction and Development (EBRD, #06315)*;
- *European Centre for the Development of Vocational Training (Cedefop, #06474)*;
- *European Court of Auditors (#06854)*;
- *European Economic and Social Committee (EESC, #06963)*;
- *European External Action Service (EEAS, #07018)*;
- *European Foundation for the Improvement of Living and Working Conditions (Eurofound, #07348)*;
- *European Investment Bank (EIB, #07599)*;
- *European Parliament (EP, #08146)*;
- *ILO (#11123)*;
- *International Bank for Reconstruction and Development (IBRD, #12317)* (World Bank);
- *International Finance Corporation (IFC, #13597)*;
- *OECD (#17693)*;
- several European Commission DGs (EMPL, NEAR, DEVO, EAC, HOME);
- *Statistical Office of the European Union (Eurostat, #19974)*;
- *UNESCO International Centre for Technical and Vocational Education and Training (UNESCO-UNEVOC, #20307).*

NGO Relations Member of (1): *EU Agencies Network (EUAN, #05564).* Library is member of: *Eurolib (#05703).* Supports: *International Centre for Career Development and Public Policy (ICCDPP, #12479).* [2021/XF1462/f/**F***]

- ♦ European Training Information Centre / see European Centre on Training and Formation of Local and Regional Authorities and Population in the Field of Natural and Technological Disasters
- ♦ European Training- and Research Centre for Human Rights and Democracy (internationally oriented national body)

♦ European Training and Simulation Association (ETSA) 08935

Dir 14 Madison Ave, Bispham, Blackpool, FY2 9HE, UK. T. +4407578205873. E-mail: admin@etsa.eu.

URL: https://www.etsa.eu

History 12 Nov 2003, Paris (France). Registration: Community Interest Company (CIC), No/ID: 07287729, Start date: 16 Jun 2010, UK. **Aims** Represent the European training and simulation community; provide an environment for users and suppliers to exchange opportunities, ideas, information and strategies on training and simulation technology and methodology. **Structure** Governing Board. **Languages** English. **Staff** 3.00 FTE, voluntary. **Finance** Sources: members' dues. Self-funding exhibition. **Activities** Events/meetings; knowledge management/information dissemination; training/education. **Events** *IT2EC : International Training Technology Exhibition and Conference* London (UK) 2022, *ITEC : International Training Exhibition and Conference* London (UK) 2020, *ITEC : Annual Defence Training, Education and Simulation Conference* Stockholm (Sweden) 2019, *ITEC : Annual Defence Training, Education and Simulation Conference* Stuttgart (Germany) 2018, *I/ITSEC : Interservice/ Industry Training, Simulation and Education Conference* Orlando, FL (USA) 2017. **Publications** *ETSA Newsletter* (4 a year).

Members Full in 29 countries:
Austria, Belgium, Bulgaria, Cyprus, Czechia, Estonia, Finland, France, Germany, Greece, Hungary, Ireland, Italy, Latvia, Lithuania, Luxembourg, Netherlands, Norway, Poland, Portugal, Romania, Slovakia, Slovenia, Spain, Sweden, Switzerland, Türkiye, UK, Ukraine.
Associate members in 5 countries:
Australia, Canada, China, Korea Rep, USA.

IGO Relations Member of (1): *European Defence Agency (EDA, #06895)* (Cap Tech group). **NGO Relations** Member of (1): *International Training and Simulation Alliance (ITSA, #15718)*. Partner of (1): *Augmented Reality for Enterprise Alliance (AREA)*. Cooperates with national organizations. [2023.02.14/XM1909/**D**]

♦ European Transcultural Nurses' Association (ETNA) 08936

Pres Dept Mental Health and Social Work, Middlesex Univ, The Burroughs, London, NW4 4BT, UK. T. +442084114014.
Contact address not obtained.
URL: http://www.europeantransculturalnurses.eu/

History Feb 2005, Modena (Italy). **Aims** Promote research and knowledge development on principles of equitable quality care, human rights and culturally competent care within a holistic framework, with particular focus on the socio-cultural diversity of people living in an increasingly global community. **Structure** Board. Officers: President; Honorary President; Vice-President; Secretary; Treasurer; Webmaster. **Languages** English. **Staff** 6.00 FTE, voluntary. **Activities** Events/meetings. **Events** *Conference* 2022, *Conference* Fuerteventura Is (Spain) 2020, *Conference* Ceské Budejovice (Czechia) 2019, *Conference* Odense (Denmark) 2017, *Conference* Budapest (Hungary) 2015. [2022.05.10/XM0379/**D**]

- ♦ European Transgender – Network and Council / see TGEU (#20138)
- ♦ European Translation Centre / see Centre de traduction des organes de l'Union européenne (#03790)
- ♦ European Translators' College (internationally oriented national body)
- ♦ European Transmission System Operators / see European Network of Transmission System Operators for Electricity (#08026)

♦ European Transpersonal Association (EUROTAS- Global Transpersonal Network) 08937

Exec Dir Maskavas Street 222E-1B, Riga LV-1019, Latvia. T. +37129528591. E-mail: office@eurotas.world – artterapija@gmail.com.
Pres 44 rue de la chapelle, 95310 Saint-Ouen, France. T. +33130371731. Fax +33130375333.
URL: https://eurotas.world

History 1987. A first conference having been held 1984, Brussels (Belgium). Registration: Austria. **Aims** Promote transpersonal research and activities; create a network of European organizations active in the transpersonal field. **Structure** Meeting (annual); Delegate Council of national association representatives; Executive Board. **Languages** English. **Staff** Voluntary. **Finance** Sources: members' dues. **Activities** Certification/accreditation; events/meetings; networking/liaising. **Events** *Gathering* France 2022, *Conference* Tallinn (Estonia) 2021, *Conference* Tallinn (Estonia) 2020, *Being human in a world in transition* Paris (France) 2019, *Conference* St Petersburg (Russia) 2018. **Publications** *EUROTAS Newsletter* (3 a year); *Integral Transpersonal Journal of Arts, Science and Technologies* (2 a year). *Forgiveness and Reconciliation: Towards an Enlightened World Culture* (2007); *Ways Through the Wall* (2004).

Members National associations in 27 countries (and also in Catalonia):
Austria, Belgium, Brazil, Bulgaria, Croatia, Estonia, France, Germany, Greece, Hungary, India, Israel, Italy, Latvia, Mexico, Moldova, Netherlands, Poland, Portugal, Romania, Russia, Sweden, Switzerland, Türkiye, UK, Ukraine, USA.
Accredited institutes in 9 countries:
Austria, Estonia, France, Germany, Israel, Italy, Latvia, Russia, Spain.
Professional and individual members from Europe, Australia, USA and Canada.

NGO Relations Also links with national institutes and associations. [2023.02.26/XD1437/**D**]

♦ European Transpersonal Psychology Association (ETPA) 08938

Association Européenne de Psychologie Transpersonnelle

Contact address not obtained. E-mail: office@etpa.eu.com.
URL: https://etpa.eu.com/

Aims Develop a spiritual psychology, as already intended by A Maslow, focused on the needs of whole humanity rather than egocentric needs, able to love all human beings and to respect life, bringing values and hope to mankind. **Structure** Board. **Finance** Sources: members' dues. **Activities** Events/meetings.

Members Active; Associate. Members in 7 countries:
Estonia, France, Italy, Portugal, Romania, Spain, Sweden. [2020/AA1215/**D**]

- ♦ European Transplant Coordinators Organization / see European Donation and Transplant Coordination Organisation (#06939)
- ♦ European Transport Forum (meeting series)
- ♦ European Transport Maintenance Council (inactive)

♦ European Transport Research Alliance (ETRA) 08939

SG EURNEX, Hardenbergstrasse 12, 10623 Berlin, Germany. T. +493031997021. E-mail: info@eurnex.eu.
Chairman Federal Highway Research Inst (BASt), Bruederstrassse 53, 51427 Bergisch-Gladbach, Germany. T. +49220443439. Fax +49220443682.
URL: http://www.etralliance.eu/

History 20 Sep 2012, Brussels (Belgium). Founded by 5 European research associations. Not a legal entity. **Aims** Foster cooperation and synergies between different European transport research stakeholders; enhance the integration process in the field of European transport research necessary for materialization of a "unified" research space across the whole of Europe, known as the European Research Area – ERA. **Structure** Plenary of the Partners; Officers: Chair, Vice-Chair, Secretary. **Languages** English. **Staff** Voluntary. **Finance** Anual contribution and in-kind services provided by partners. **Activities** Events/meetings. **Events** *Transport Research Arena (TRA) Conference* Lisbon (Portugal) 2022, *Workshop on Academia and Job Market* Warsaw (Poland) 2016, *Workshop on Transport and Climate Change* Paris (France) 2015, *Conference* Paris (France) 2014, *Conference* Brussels (Belgium) 2013. **Publications** Position papers; reports.

Members Partners (5):
European Conference of Transport Research Institutes (ECTRI, #06737); EUropean rail Research Network of EXcellence (EURNEX, #08326); Forum of European National Highway Research Laboratories (FEHRL, #09910); Forum of European Road Safety Research Institutes (FERSI, #09913); Humanist (#10970).
Observer:
World Conference on Transport Research Society (WCTRS, #21301).

IGO Relations *European Union (EU, #08967).* [2022.02.15/XJ8640/y/**D**]

♦ European Transport Safety Council (ETSC) 08940

Conseil européen pour la sécurité des transports – Europäischer Verkehrssicherheitsrat

Exec Dir Ave des Celtes 20, 1040 Brussels, Belgium. T. +3222304106. Fax +3222304215. E-mail: information@etsc.eu.
URL: http://www.etsc.eu/

History 1993. Registration: EU Transparency Register, No/ID: 78891371297-34; Belgium. **Aims** Provide impartial advice on transport safety matters to the European Commission, the European Parliament and to national governments and associated organizations as appropriate; identify and promote science-based solutions to transport collisions and casualties, with due consideration to practicality, cost and acceptability; encourage common measures to provide genuine safety benefits and lead to adoption of best practice; encourage wider awareness of causes, effects and solutions to transport collisions and casualties and publicize best practice. **Structure** Main Council (meets twice a year); Board of Directors; Pool of Experts; Secretariat. **Languages** English. **Staff** 8.00 FTE, paid. **Finance** Members' dues. Other sources: *European Commission (EC, #06633)*; public and private sector sponsorship. **Activities** Research/documentation; events/meetings. **Events** *International Road Safety Conference* Bucharest (Romania) 2019, *Preventing Road Accidents and Injuries for the Safety of Employees Conference* Brussels (Belgium) 2018, *Meeting* Vienna (Austria) 2017, *Meeting on Alcohol Interlocks and the Fight against Drink-Driving* Vienna (Austria) 2015, *Meeting* Brussels (Belgium) 2010. **Publications** *The Performance Index Report* (annual); *The Drink Driving Monitor*, *The Safety Monitor*, *The Speed Monitor*. Road Safety PIN Flashes; reviews; fact sheets; briefings; policy papers.

Members National and international organizations (46) in 21 countries:
Austria, Belgium, Czechia, Denmark, Finland, France, Germany, Greece, Ireland, Italy, Lithuania, Netherlands, Norway, Poland, Portugal, Serbia, Slovenia, Spain, Sweden, Switzerland, UK.
International members (5), listed in this Yearbook:
Confederation of Organizations in Road Transport Enforcement (CORTE, #04574); European Federation of Road Traffic Victims (#07207); Fédération Internationale de Motocyclisme (FIM, #09643); Global Road Safety Partnership (GRSP, #10581); MOVING International Road Safety Association (MOVING, #16874).

Consultative Status Consultative status granted from: *ECOSOC (#05331)* (Special). **IGO Relations** *International Transport Forum (ITF, #15725)*; UN Road Safety Collaboration (UNRSC). **NGO Relations** *European Federation of Road Traffic Victims (#07207)*; European Level Crossing Forum (ELCF); *European Rail Research Advisory Council (ERRAC, #08325)*; European Strategic Safety Initiative (ESSI); Parliamentary Advisory Council for Transport Safety (PACTS). [2019/XD3727/y/**D**]

- ♦ European Transport Training Association (#02571)

♦ European Transport Workers' Federation (ETF) 08941

Fédération Européenne des Travailleurs des Transports – Federación Europea de los Trabajadores del Transporte – Europäische Transportarbeiter-Föderation

Gen Sec Galerie AGORA, Rue du Marché aux Herbes 105/11b, 1000 Brussels, Belgium. T. +3222854660. E-mail: etf@etf-europe.org.
Pres address not obtained.
URL: http://www.etf-europe.org/

History 1958. Former names and other names: *Committee of Transport Workers' Unions in the European Community (CTWU)* – former (1958 to 1996); *Comité syndical des transports dans la Communauté européenne (CSTCE)* – former (1958 to 1996); *Gewerkschaftlicher Verkehrsausschuss in der Europäischen Gemeinschaft (GVG)* – former (1958 to 1996); *Federation of Transport Worker's Unions in the European Union (FST)* – former (1996 to 1999); *Fédération des syndicats des transports dans l'Union européenne* – former (1996 to 1999); *Verband der Verkehrsgewerkschaften in der Europäischen Union* – former (1996 to 1999). Registration: No/ID: 0858.363.391, Start date: 1 Jul 1999, Belgium; EU Transparency Register, No/ID: 92545571128-74, Start date: 12 Feb 2009. **Aims** As a Pan-European trade union organization, represent and defend the interests of transport, logistics and *fisheries* workers; set workers' priorities in the European Social Dialogue; formulate and coordinate trade union transport and social policies. **Structure** Congress (every 5 years); Executive Committee; Management Committee; Sections (8); Urban Public Transport Committee; Women's Committee; Youth Committee; Secretariat in Brussels (Belgium). **Languages** English, French, German. **Staff** 23.00 FTE, paid. **Finance** Sources: members' dues. Annual contribution from ITF. **Activities** Advocacy/lobbying/activism; research/documentation; training/education. **Events** *Congress* Budapest (Hungary) 2022, *Congress* Barcelona (Spain) 2017, *Congress* Berlin (Germany) 2013, *Meeting* Berlin (Germany) 2012, *Congress* Ponta Delgada (Portugal) 2009.

Members Organizations (representing about 5 million transport workers from more than 230 transport unions) in 41 European countries:
Albania, Austria, Belarus, Belgium, Bosnia-Herzegovina, Bulgaria, Croatia, Cyprus, Czechia, Denmark, Estonia, Finland, France, Georgia, Germany, Greece, Hungary, Iceland, Ireland, Italy, Latvia, Lithuania, Luxembourg, Malta, Montenegro, Netherlands, North Macedonia, Norway, Poland, Portugal, Romania, Russia, Serbia, Slovakia, Slovenia, Spain, Sweden, Switzerland, Türkiye, UK, Ukraine.

NGO Relations Member of (10): *Baltic Sea Advisory Council (BSAC, #03139); Confederation of Organizations in Road Transport Enforcement (CORTE, #04574); European Tourism Manifesto (#08921); European Trade Union Confederation (ETUC, #08927); International Transport Workers' Federation (ITF, #15726); Long Distance Advisory Council (LDAC, #16511); Maritime Industries Forum (MIF, no recent information); Mediterranean Advisory Council (MEDAC, #16639); North Sea Advisory Council (NSAC, #17603); North Western Waters Advisory Council (NWWAC, #17607).* Liaison Organization of: *Comité européen de normalisation (CEN, #04162).* Signatory to: *Alter Summit.* Active in: *European Trade Union Liaison Committee on Tourism (ETLC, #08929).* [2023.02.14/XE0317/**E**]

- ♦ European Trauma Society (inactive)

♦ The European Travel Agents' and Tour Operators' Associations (ECTAA) 08942

SG Rue Dautzenberg 36, Boîte 6, 1050 Brussels, Belgium. T. +3226443450. E-mail: secretariat@ectaa.eu.
URL: http://www.ectaa.eu/

History Oct 1961, Bad Kreuznach (Germany). Founded by national associations of travel agents and tour operators of the 6 founding member states of the Common Market. Former names and other names: *Group of National Travel Agents' Associations within the EEC* – former; *Groupement des unions nationales des agences de voyages de la CEE* – former; *Group of National Travel Agents' and Tour Operators' Associations within the EEC* – former; *Groupement des unions nationales des agences et organisateurs de voyages de la CEE* – former; *Group of National Travel Agents' and Tour Operators' Associations within the EU (ECTAA)* – former; *Groupement des unions nationales des agences et organisateurs de voyages de l'UE* – former. Registration: No/ID: 0439.839.966, Start date: 28 Sep 1989, Belgium; EU Transparency Register, No/ID: 88072891086-36, Start date: 6 Feb 2009. **Aims** Promote the interests of *tourism* and the tourist industry in general and of travel agents and tour operators in particular; cooperate with *European Union* institutions and international organizations to ensure that these interests and special requirements are taken into consideration. **Structure** General Assembly; Board of Directors; Executive Board. Committees (6): Air Matters; Legal; Fiscal; Technology; Tour Operators; Incoming, Destinations & Sustainability. **Finance** Sources: members' dues. **Activities** Advocacy/lobbying/activism; events/meetings. **Events** *Seminar* Brussels (Belgium) 2014, *Half-Yearly Meeting* Stockholm (Sweden) 2011, *Half-yearly meeting* Budapest (Hungary) 2009, *European bus and coach forum* Kortrijk (Belgium) 2009, *Half-yearly meeting* Valencia (Spain) 2008. **Publications** *ECTAA Report of the EU Policies Affecting the Tourism Industry*. Annual Activity Report.

Members Associations of travel agents. Full in 31 countries:
Austria, Belgium, Bulgaria, Croatia, Cyprus, Czechia, Denmark, Estonia, Finland, France, Germany, Greece, Hungary, Ireland, Italy, Latvia, Lithuania, Malta, Netherlands, Norway, Poland, Portugal, Romania, Slovakia, Slovenia, Spain, Sweden, Switzerland, UK.
International members in 4 countries:
Israel, Malaysia, Morocco, Tunisia.

NGO Relations Member of (3): *European Tourism Manifesto (#08921); Federation of European and International Associations Established in Belgium (FAIB, #09508); Network for the European Private Sector in Tourism (NET, #17027).* [2021/XE0502/**E**]

♦ European Travel Commission (ETC) 08943

Commission européenne du tourisme (CET)

Exec Dir Rue du Marché aux Herbes 61, 1000 Brussels, Belgium. T. +3225489000. Fax +3225141843. E-mail: info@visiteurope.com.
URL: https://etc-corporate.org/

History 18 Jun 1948, Stalheim (Norway). Registration: Banque-Carrefour des Entreprises, No/ID: 0408.138.386, Start date: 21 Mar 1959, Belgium; EU Transparency Register, No/ID: 778717116759-86, Start date: 26 Mar 2015. **Aims** Promote Europe as an attractive tourist destination, particularly in overseas markets; assist members to exchange knowledge and work collaboratively; provide industry partners and other interested parties with easy access to material and statistics regarding inbound tourism to Europe. **Structure** Board of Directors; Executive Unit; Operations Groups (4); Working Groups (2). **Languages** English. **Staff** 11.00 FTE, paid. **Finance** Sources: grants; members' dues. Supported by: *European Commission (EC, #06633)*. **Activities** Advocacy/lobbying/activism; events/meetings; knowledge management/information dissemination; research/documentation. **Events** *TourMIS Users Workshop and International Seminar* Vienna (Austria) 2022, *General Meeting* Algarve (Portugal) 2021, *General Meeting* Brussels (Belgium) 2021, *TourMIS Users Workshop and International Seminar* Vienna (Austria) 2021, *General Meeting* Luxembourg (Luxembourg) 2020. **Publications** *ETC Bulletin* (4 a year). Annual Report; market research studies; survey reports.
Members National Tourism Organizations (whether governmental, non-governmental or semi-governmental bodies) in 32 countries:
Austria, Belgium, Bulgaria, Croatia, Cyprus, Czechia, Denmark, Estonia, Finland, Germany, Greece, Hungary, Iceland, Ireland, Italy, Latvia, Lithuania, Luxembourg, Malta, Monaco, Montenegro, Netherlands, Norway, Poland, Portugal, Romania, San Marino, Serbia, Slovakia, Slovenia, Spain, Switzerland.
IGO Relations Member of (1): *World Tourism Organization (UNWTO, #21861)*. Cooperates with (1): *OECD (#17693)*. **NGO Relations** Member of (3): *Adventure Travel Trade Association (ATTA, #00135)*; *European Heritage Alliance 3.3 (#07477)*; *European Tourism Manifesto (#08921)*. Cooperates with (4): *Airports Council International – European Region (ACI EUROPE, #00612)*; *European Tour Operators Association (ETOA, #08922)*; Foundation for European Sustainable Development (FEST); *World Travel and Tourism Council (WTTC, #21871)*. [2022/XD4394/**D**]

♦ European Travel Insurance Group / see International Travel Insurance Alliance e.V. (#15728)

♦ European Travel Press (ETP) 08944

Contact address not obtained. T. +3225040217. Fax +3225136950. E-mail: salvadordias@gmail.com.
History 1993, as *European Federation of the Associations of Tourism Journalists – Fédération européenne des associations de journalistes du tourisme (FEDAJT)*. Current name adopted 2003. Registered in accordance with Belgian law. **Aims** Promote practical cooperation among national associations of professional travel writers; highlight the importance of travel information and the profession of *tourism journalist*; strengthen professional links and assist exchange of information and a common approach to European and national authorities. **Structure** General Assembly. Administrative Council, comprising one representative of each member association (normally the president). Officers: President; Vice-President; Secretary-General; Treasurer. **Languages** English. **Staff** 0.50 FTE, paid; 1.00 FTE, voluntary. **Finance** Members' dues. **Activities** Awards; meeting activities. **Publications** *European Press Card*.
Members National associations in 7 countries:
Belgium, Germany, Italy, Portugal, Sweden, Switzerland, UK.
IGO Relations *European Commission (EC, #06633)*; *World Tourism Organization (UNWTO, #21861)*. [2013.06.01/XD4606/**D**]

♦ European Travel Retail Confederation (ETRC) 08945

SG Rue de la Science 41, 1040 Brussels, Belgium.
Registered Address 1 Paper Mews, 330 High Street, Dorking, RH4 2TU, UK.
URL: http://www.etrc.org/
History Jun 1988, as *International Duty Free Confederation (IDFC)*. Subsequently changed name to *International Travel Retail Confederation (ITRC)*, May 2000. Subsequently changed title to: *European Travel Retail Council (ETRC)*, Jul 2004. Registered in accordance with UK law. EU Transparency Register: 90905271757-87. **Aims** Represent the travel retail and duty free industry, covering all sectors of the trade – airports, airlines, ferry operators – and including all major brand owners, their distributors and agents, so as to secure the most favourable operating environment for the industry. **Structure** Supervisory Board; Managing Board; Secretariat. **Languages** English, French. **Staff** 2.00 FTE, paid. **Finance** Members' dues. Donations. **Activities** Networking/liaising; events/meetings; research/documentation; knowledge management/information dissemination. **Events** *Business Forum* Amsterdam (Netherlands) 2023, *Business Forum* Brussels (Belgium) 2016, *Business Forum* Brussels (Belgium) 2015, *Business Forum* Brussels (Belgium) 2013, *Business forum* Brussels (Belgium) 2009.
Members National associations in 10 countries:
Cyprus, France, Germany, Greece, Ireland, Italy, Portugal, Spain, Türkiye, UK.
Regional associations (4):
BeNeLux Travel Retail Association (BTRA, #03206); *Central and Eastern European Travel Retail Association (CEETRA, #03699)*; *Nordic Travel Retail Group (NTRG, #17453)*; *Tax Free World Association (TFWA)*. [2019.05.22/XD2089/**D**]

♦ European Travel Retail Council / see European Travel Retail Confederation (#08945)
♦ European Travel and Tourism Action Group / see European Travel and Tourism Advisory Group (#08946)

♦ European Travel and Tourism Advisory Group (ETAG) 08946

Groupe d'action du tourisme européen
Headquarters c/o ETC, Rue du Marché aux Herbes 61, 1000 Brussels, Belgium. T. +3225489000. Fax +3225141843.
Secretariat 14 Bushwood Road, Richmond, TW9 3BQ, UK. T. +442089481153.
Vice Chairman c/o World Youth Student and Educational Travel Confederation, Keizersgracht 174, 1016 DW Amsterdam, Netherlands.
History Jul 1981, under the name *European Tourism Action Group*, on the initiative of *European Travel Commission (ETC, #08943)*, as a technical liaison group between the different industry sectors in its member countries. Subsequently changed title to *European Travel and Tourism Action Group – Groupe d'action du tourisme européen*. Registered in accordance with Belgian law, Apr 2013. **Aims** Encourage cooperation between public and private sectors of European tourism; exchange information and joint action between the different sectors of tourism and travel *industry* in Europe. **Structure** Liaison group of leading international and European tourism associations. **Finance** Secretariat financed by members. **Events** *Joint seminar* Prague (Czech Rep) 1999, *Seminar* Brussels (Belgium) 1998, *Marketing intelligence, planning the future* London (UK) 1998, *Seminar* Brussels (Belgium) 1997, *Seminar* Glasgow (UK) 1997. **Publications** *Megatrends in European Tourism* (2006); *Marketing Intelligence for Planning the Future* (1998); *Collect Action for the Successful Development of Europe's Tourism* (1994); *Tourism and Environment* (1993); *Tourism Policy for Europe in the 1990s*. Brochure.
Members International and European organizations (8):
Association for Tourism and Leisure Education and Research (ATLAS, #02956); *European Travel Commission (ETC, #08943)*; *European Union Federation of Youth Hostel Associations (EUFED, #08988)*; *Fédération Internationale de l'Automobile (FIA, #09613)* (Brussels Belgium Bureau); *International Air Transport Association (IATA, #11614)*; *International Association of Tour Managers (IATM, #12231)*; *International Road Transport Union (IRU, #14761)*.
IGO Relations Negotiates with and represented in WTO and European Union bodies concerned with tourism. Observers: *European Commission (EC, #06633)*, Tourism Division; *OECD (#17693)*, Tourism Committee; *World Tourism Organization (UNWTO, #21861)*. **NGO Relations** Observers: *International Chamber of Commerce (ICC, #12534)*. In liaison with technical committees of: *Comité européen de normalisation (CEN, #04162)*. [2013/XE6695/y/**E**]

♦ European Treatment Centers for Drug Addiction (EURO-TC) 08947

Operational office Beatrixgasse 6/20, 1030 Vienna, Austria. T. +4317153515. E-mail: info@euro-tc.org.
URL: http://www.euro-tc.org/
History 1980. Former names and other names: *Federation of Drugfree Treatment Centres in Europe* – former; *Fédération des aides aux toxicomanes en Europe* – former; *Föderation der Drogenhilfen in Europa* – former. Registration: EU Transparency Register, No/ID: 974577624872-43; Germany. **Aims** Further steady progress in optimizing treatment programmes towards the needs of clients. **Structure** General Assembly (twice a year); Board. **Languages** English. **Staff** Voluntary. **Finance** Sources: members' dues. Annual budget: 10,000 EUR. **Activities** Events/meetings; guidance/assistance/consulting; knowledge management/information dissemination; networking/liaising; training/education. **Events** *FENIQS-EU – Further enhancing the implementation of quality standards in DDR across Europe* Palma (Spain) 2022, *Conference* Madeira (Portugal) 2019, *Conference* Toledo (Spain) 2017, *Assembly* Berlin (Germany) 2015, *Conference* Parma (Italy) 2002.
Members Full (26) in 13 countries:
Austria, Bosnia-Herzegovina, Croatia, Cyprus, France, Germany, Hungary, Italy, Poland, Portugal, Spain, UK, Ukraine.
NGO Relations Member of (2): *Civil Society Forum on Drugs (CSFD, #03968)*; *International Council on Alcohol and Addictions (ICAA, #12989)*. [2022.03.22/XD5105/**D**]

♦ European Treaty on Renewable Energy (unconfirmed)

♦ European Triathlon Union (ETU) 08948

Union européenne de triathlon – Europäische Triathlon Union
SG Kroonstraat 72, 3581 Beringen, Belgium. T. +3211744728. E-mail: etu_hq@etu.triathlon.org – office@europe.triathlon.org.
Registered Office 13a Avenue Guillaume, L-1651 Luxembourg, Luxembourg.
URL: https://europe.triathlon.org/
History 1984. Ceased to exist as an independent body, 5 Jul 2002. Currently a regional union of *World Triathlon (#21872)*. Former names and other names: *Europe Triathlon* – alias. Registration: ASBL, Luxembourg. **Aims** Develop, regulate and safeguard the interests of triathlon, *duathlon*, winter triathlon and related multisports for the benefit of member associations; initiate and coordinate education programmes for children and coordinate research programmes. **Structure** Executive Board, consisting of President, Vice-President, Secretary-General, Treasurer, Athletes Representative and 3 members. Committees (4): Technical; Development; Medical and Research; Audit. Athletes Commission. Jury of Appeal. **Languages** English. **Staff** 0.50 FTE, paid. **Finance** Members' dues. Other sources: event fees; sponsorship. **Activities** Organizes and coordinates European Championships in triathlon, duathlon, long distance triathlon, cross triathlon and winter triathlon, European Cup series for triathlon, duathlon and winter triathlon, Eurokids training camps, education programmes for technical officials. Works on specific women programmes. Editing of specific publications. **Events** *Summer congress* Athlone (Ireland) 2010, *Summer congress* Holten (Netherlands) 2009, *Summer Congress* Lisbon (Portugal) 2008, *Summer Congress* Copenhagen (Denmark) 2007, *Summer Congress* Autun (France) 2006. **Publications** *ETU Newsletter*. Athletes and media guides; books; brochure; congress proceedings.
Members Full in 42 countries and territories:
Andorra, Austria, Belarus, Bosnia-Herzegovina, Bulgaria, Croatia, Cyprus, Czechia, Denmark, Estonia, Finland, France, Germany, Gibraltar, Greece, Hungary, Ireland, Israel, Italy, Latvia, Liechtenstein, Lithuania, Luxembourg, Malta, Moldova, Monaco, Netherlands, North Macedonia, Norway, Poland, Portugal, Romania, Russia, Serbia, Slovakia, Slovenia, Spain, Sweden, Switzerland, Türkiye, UK, Ukraine.
NGO Relations *International Olympic Committee (IOC, #14408)*. [2020/XD0730/**D**]

♦ European TRIZ Association (ETRIA) 08949

Administrative Management Kaiser-Joseph-Str. 254, 79098 Freiburg, Germany. Fax +49761216095169. E-mail: info@etria.eu.
Pres address not obtained.
URL: http://www.etria.eu/
History 2001. Former names and other names: *Theory of Inventive Problem Solving* – full title. Registration: No/ID: VR 8197, Germany. **Aims** Promote professional training, research and development in the area of *knowledge*-based *innovation* methods; support inventive and creative techniques in particular on the conceptual approaches of the theory of inventive *problem solving* TRIZ; encourage international exchange of information and experience between academics, practitioners, industrial companies, universities and other organizations in the area of innovation and knowledge management. **Structure** Executive Board. **Languages** English. **Staff** N/A. **Finance** Sources: members' dues. **Activities** Knowledge management/information dissemination; research and development; training/education. **Events** *World Conference* Bolzano (Italy) 2021, *World Conference* Cluj-Napoca (Romania) 2020, *World Conference* Marrakech (Morocco) 2019, *World Conference* Strasbourg (France) 2018, *World Conference* Lappeenranta (Finland) 2017. **Publications** Conference proceedings. **IGO Relations** None. **NGO Relations** None. [2021.02.16/XJ9475/**D**]

♦ European Tropical Forest Research Network (ETFRN) 08950

Réseau européen de recherche forestière tropicale (RERFT)
Main Office c/o Tropenbos, PO Box 232, 6700 AE Wageningen, Netherlands. E-mail: tropenbos@tropenbos.org.
URL: http://www.etfrn.org/
History Sep 1991. Founded by *European Commission (EC, #06633)*. Phase 1 (1992 – 1996); Phase 2 (1997 – 1999); Phase 3 (2000 – 2003). **Aims** Ensure that European research contributes to *conservation* and *sustainable* use of forest and tree resources in tropical and subtropical countries; promote dialogue between researchers, policy-makers and forest users, increased coherence of European tropical forest research, and increased collaboration with researchers in developing countries. **Structure** General Assembly (every 3 years). Steering Committee of National Focal Points (meets annually). Executive Committee (meets twice a year), consisting of Steering Committee Chair, Vice-Chair, and one or 2 elected members of the Steering Committee. One observer from the European Commission. Coordination Unit, hosted by Tropenbos International. National Focal Points (15). **Finance** European Commission. **Activities** Research exchange Question and Answer Service. Organizes workshops. Main activities: dialogue and information exchange on forest research in the tropics, subtropics and Mediterranean; increase collaboration with developing country researchers; improve dialogue between researchers, policy makers and forest managers and others influencing the forest environment. *'Research Information Market'* – tool for users of research results to address the European tropical forest research community and others, to ask for existing knowledge on specific technical problems. Organizes meetings, workshops. **Events** *Globalisation, localisation and tropical forest management in the 21st century* Amsterdam (Netherlands) 2003, *Rehabilitation of degraded lands in Sub-Saharan Africa* Hyytiälä (Finland) 2003, *Participatory monitoring and evaluation of biodiversity* Oxford (UK) 2002, *Innovative financing mechanisms for conservation and sustainable management of tropical forests* The Hague (Netherlands) 2002, *Cultivating in tropical forests – the evolution and sustainability of intermediate systems between extractivism and plantations* Lofoten Is (Norway) 2000. **Publications** *ETFRN News* (3 a year). *ETFRN Series*. *Developing Needs-Based Inventory Methods for Non-Timber Forest Products*; *Directory of European Tropical Forest Research Organizations*; *Forestry, Forest Users and Research: New Ways of Learning*; *FORNESSA and IUFRO-SPDC Initiative on Rehabilitation of Degraded Lands in Sub-Saharan Africa*; *Prunings* – compilation of one-sheet human interest stories taken from project outputs. CD-Roms. Information Services: Information on European tropical forest research institutions and projects via on-line directory, newsletter, international calendar of meetings, Question and Answer Service and annotated tropical forestry links via World Wide Web.
Members National Focal Points (15) in 16 countries:
Austria, Belgium, Denmark, Finland, France, Germany, Ireland, Italy, Norway, Portugal, Spain, Sweden, UK.
Included in the above, 2 organizations listed in this Yearbook:
European Commission (EC, #06633); *International Institute for Environment and Development (IIED, #13877)*.
NGO Relations Member of: *International Society of Tropical Foresters (ISTF, #15522)*. Office space and general support for Coordination Unit provided by: *Tropenbos International (TBI)*. [2021/XF3719/y/**F**]

♦ European Tropical Tuna Fishing and Processing Committee / see European Tropical Tuna Trade and Industry Committee (#08951)

♦ European Tropical Tuna Trade and Industry Committee (EUROTHON) 08951

Comité Européen Interprofessionnel du Thon Tropical
Registered Office 44 Rue d'Alésia, 75682 Paris CEDEX 14, France. T. +33153914540. E-mail: adepale@adepale.org – contacto@anfaco.es.
URL: http://eurothon.eu/

History Nov 2004. Also referred to as *European Tropical Tuna Fishing and Processing Committee*. Registered under French law, Nov 2014. EU Transparency Register: 46018232355-49. **Aims** Represent the interests of European Tropical Tuna Fishing and Processing companies, through their national organizations in EU member states. Also covers tuna canning activities of European countries located in African ACP countries and Latin American countries. **Languages** English, French, Italian, Spanish.
Members Full in 4 countries:
France, Italy, Portugal, Spain.
NGO Relations Member of: *Long Distance Advisory Council (LDAC, #16511)*; *Market Advisory Council (MAC, #16584)*. [2015.11.04/XM3984/t/D]

♦ European Trotting Union 08952
Union européenne du trot (UET)
Exec Sec 7 rue d'Astorg, 75008 Paris, France. T. +33149771403. Fax +33149771704. E-mail: uet@letrot.com.
Gen Sec address not obtained.
URL: http://www.uet-trot.eu/
History 1973. Constitution adopted, 9 May 1973; amended 9 Oct 1978, 30 Jun 1979, 10 Oct 1987 and 25 Oct 1997. **Aims** Promote trotting *races* and *horse* breeding in Europe as well as their integrity and prestige in the world. **Structure** General Assembly (annual); Board; Committees. **Activities** Sporting events.
Members National organizations in 20 countries:
Austria, Belgium, Czechia, Denmark, Estonia, Finland, France, Germany, Hungary, Italy, Lithuania, Malta, Netherlands, Norway, Russia, Serbia, Slovenia, Spain, Sweden, Switzerland.
NGO Relations Founding member of: *European Horse Network (EHN, #07499)*. Associate member of: *International Trotting Association (ITA, #15738)*. [2015/XD8482/D]

♦ European Tube Association / see european tube manufacturers association (#08953)

♦ european tube manufacturers association (etma) 08953
Sec Haus der Metalle – 2nd Floor, Am Bonneshof 5, 40474 Düsseldorf, Germany. T. +492114796144. Fax +49211479625141. E-mail: info@etma-online.org.
URL: http://www.etma-online.org/
History Founded 25 Apr 1959, as *European Tube Association (ETA)* – *European Tube Association (ETA)* – *Association européenne des fabricants de tubes souples* – *Europäische Tuben-Vereinigung*. **Aims** Enter into an open dialogue with public and other stakeholders in order to promote tubes as packaging and the products of members. **Languages** English, French, German. **Activities** focus on: representation of the European tube industry to third parties; supply of statistics and packaging market information for members; supply of packaging and raw material market information; monitoring of the European packaging, food contact and environmental legislation; creation of European collapsible tube standards; public relations; cooperation with other packaging and flexible tube associations. Organizes "Tube of the Year" contest (annual) which reflects the innovative power of the industry. **Events** *General Assembly and Annual Conference* Copenhagen (Denmark) 2019, *Annual Assembly* Milan (Italy) 2014, *Annual Assembly* Budapest (Hungary) 2013, *Annual Assembly* Brussels (Belgium) 2012, *Annual Assembly* Scotland (UK) 2011. **Publications** *Tubes and TRENDS* (2 a year, May and October).
Members Manufacturers (52) in 19 countries:
Austria, Czechia, Finland, France, Germany, Greece, Hungary, Italy, Norway, Poland, Portugal, Russia, Slovakia, Slovenia, Spain, Sweden, Switzerland, Türkiye, UK.
IGO Relations Recognized by: *European Commission (EC, #06633)*. [2013.06.27/XD6920/D]

♦ European Tuberculosis Surveillance Network 08954
Contact ECDC, SE-171 83 Stockholm, Sweden. T. +46858601345. E-mail: tuberculosis@ecdc.europa.eu.
URL: http://www.ecdc.europa.eu/
History as *EuroTB – Surveillance of Tuberculosis in Europe – Euro TB – Surveillance de la tuberculose dans les pays de la région Europe de l'OMS* within the framework of *Centre européen pour la surveillance épidémiologique du SIDA (CESES, inactive)*. On 1 Nov 1999, activities transferred to *'Institut de veille sanitaire (InVS)'*, the French National Institute for Public Health Surveillance. Original title in English: *EuroTB – Tuberculosis Cases Notified in Europe*. Current name adopted Jan 2008 when because jointly coordinated by *European Centre for Disease Prevention and Control (ECDC, #06476)* and WHO/EURO. **Aims** Improve the contribution of surveillance to TB control in Europe. **Structure** EuroTB Team; Advisory Committee; National Contact Points. **Staff** 4.00 FTE, paid. **Finance** *European Commission (EC, #06633)* (50%); Institut de Veille Sanitaire – France (30%); RIVM – Netherlands (7%); national contributions, in kind (13%). **Activities** National Contact Points in the 53 countries of WHO European region provide computerized individual or grouped data conforming to an agreed format. These data are analysed, interpreted and disseminated. Partner with RIVM – Netherlands on: Molecular Surveillance of Multi-Drug Resistance in Europe; *Tuberculosis Surveillance Research Unit (TSRU, #20256)*; Technical Advisory Group for Europe (WHO). **Events** *Annual General Meeting* Vilnius (Lithuania) 2006. **Publications** *EuroTB Newsletter* (4 a year) – online; *Surveillance of Tuberculosis in Europe* (annual) – report. Scientific communications; congress communications; slides.
Members Based in France with Advisory Committee members from 9 countries:
Austria, Denmark, Finland, Germany, Ireland, Netherlands, Poland, Romania, UK.
Project participants – organizations in 52 countries:
Albania, Andorra, Armenia, Austria, Azerbaijan, Belarus, Belgium, Bosnia-Herzegovina, Bulgaria, Croatia, Cyprus, Czechia, Denmark, Estonia, Finland, France, Georgia, Germany, Greece, Hungary, Iceland, Ireland, Israel, Italy, Kazakhstan, Kyrgyzstan, Latvia, Lithuania, Luxembourg, Malta, Moldova, Monaco, Montenegro, Netherlands, North Macedonia, Norway, Poland, Portugal, Romania, Russia, San Marino, Serbia, Slovakia, Slovenia, Spain, Sweden, Switzerland, Tajikistan, Türkiye, Turkmenistan, UK, Ukraine, Uzbekistan.
IGO Relations Collaborating Centre of: *WHO (#20950)*. Partnership with: *European Centre for Disease Prevention and Control (ECDC, #06476)*. **NGO Relations** *International Union Against Tuberculosis and Lung Disease (The Union, #15752)*; national organizations. [2010.07.02/XE4207/E]

♦ European Tuberous Sclerosis Complex Association (ETSC) 08955
Contact In den Birken 30, 45711 Datteln, Germany. E-mail: info@e-tsc.eu.
URL: http://www.e-tsc.eu/
History Founded 2012. **Aims** Increase knowledge and awareness on tuberous sclerosis complex (TSC); promote implementation of European and international diagnostic criteria, surveillance and treatment guidelines; stimulate research; exchange information.
Members Full in 23 countries:
Austria, Belgium, Denmark, Finland, France, Germany, Greece, Ireland, Israel, Italy, Netherlands, North Macedonia, Norway, Poland, Portugal, Russia, Serbia, Slovenia, Spain, Sweden, Switzerland, UK, Ukraine.
NGO Relations Member of: *EURORDIS – Rare Diseases Europe (#09175)*. [2018/XM7425/D]

♦ European Tugowners Association (ETA) 08956
Association européenne de propriétaires de remorqueurs – Asociación Europea de Propietarios de Remolques
SG Rue de Colonies 11, 1000 Brussels, Belgium. T. +3222516026. E-mail: info@eurotugowners.com.
URL: http://www.eurotugowners.com/
History Jan 1963. Registration: EU Transparency Register, No/ID: 808295611738-96. **Aims** Bring together European owners/operators of *tugs* and tenders serving vessels using the *ports* of Europe; provide members with information and guidance on any matter affecting the common interests of members. **Structure** Executive Committee. **Languages** English. **Staff** 2.00 FTE, paid. **Events** *General Meeting and Conference* Turku (Finland) 2021, *General Meeting and Conference* Cork (Ireland) 2020, *General Meeting and Conference* Limassol (Cyprus) 2019, *General Meeting and Conference* Antwerp (Belgium) 2018, *General Meeting and Conference* Edinburgh (UK) 2016.
Members Companies (over 80) engaged port towage in Europe, in 21 countries:
Belgium, Bulgaria, Croatia, Denmark, Finland, France, Germany, Greece, Ireland, Italy, Lithuania, Malta, Netherlands, Norway, Poland, Portugal, Romania, Spain, Sweden, Türkiye, UK.
Associate membership open to all persons, companies, authorities or associations related to towage or other maritime-related industry and which contribute to the goals of the Association. Members in 4 countries:
Belgium, Germany, Netherlands, UK.
NGO Relations Affiliate member of: *International Salvage Union (ISU, #14779)*. [2017.10.27/XD0879/D]

♦ European Turbine Network (ETN) 08957
Managing Dir Chausee de Charleroi 146-148/20, 1060 Brussels, Belgium. T. +3226461577. E-mail: info@etn.global.
URL: https://etn.global/
History Jan 2005, Brussels (Belgium). Registration: No/ID: 0875.462.018, Start date: 2005, Belgium; EU Transparency Register, No/ID: 03589906592-68, Start date: 6 Sep 2011. **Aims** Bring together the entire value chain of turbomachinery technology worldwide; develop safe, secure, affordable and dispatchable carbon-neutral energy solutions. **Structure** Board; Project Board; Committees; Working Groups; Office. **Languages** English. **Staff** 7.00 FTE, paid. **Finance** Sources: members' dues. **Events** *LM2500 User Group Meeting* Aberdeen (UK) 2022, *Conference* Berlin (Germany) 2022, *Annual General Meeting and Workshop* Brussels (Belgium) 2022, *Meeting* Brussels (Belgium) 2022, *Meeting* Stavanger (Norway) 2022. **Publications** *ETN Newsletter* (4 a year). **Members** OEMs; oil and gas companies; utilities; third-party suppliers and service providers; consultancies; research institutes; universities. Members (111) in 22 countries. Membership countries not specified. **NGO Relations** Member of (1): *European Energy Forum (EEF, #06986)*. [2022.10.21/XM0666/F]

♦ European Turbomachinery Committee / see European Turbomachinery Society (#08958)

♦ European Turbomachinery Society (EUROTURBO) 08958
Main Office c/o Dept of Industrial Engineering, via Santa Marta 3, 50139 Florence FI, Italy.
URL: http://www.euroturbo.eu/
History Formally constituted 22 Feb 2012, Italy, as *European Turbomachinery Committee*. Previously existed as a conference series managed by an informal committee. Registered in accordance with Italian law. **Aims** Provide and facilitate European and worldwide dissemination and harmonization of information, knowledge and technology in the field of turbomachinery and turbomachinery based power systems. **Structure** General Assembly/Committee; Executive Board; Officers. **Finance** Members' dues. **Activities** Events/meetings. **Events** *Biennial European Turbomachinery Conference* Lausanne (Switzerland) 2019, *Biennial European Turbomachinery Conference* Stockholm (Sweden) 2017, *Biennial European Turbomachinery Conference* Madrid (Spain) 2015, *Biennial European Turbomachinery Conference* Lappeenranta (Finland) 2013, *Biennial European Turbomachinery Conference* Istanbul (Turkey) 2011.
Members Individuals in 19 countries:
Austria, Belgium, Czechia, Finland, France, Germany, Greece, Hungary, Israel, Italy, Netherlands, Norway, Poland, Portugal, Spain, Sweden, Switzerland, UK, Ukraine. [2017/XJ1593/cv/D]

♦ European Turfgrass Society (ETS) 08959
Sec/Treas Landlab Studio Associato, Via Quintarello 12/A, 36050 Quinto Vicentino VICENZA, Italy. T. +39444357929. Fax +39444357937. E-mail: info@landlab.net.
URL: http://www.turfgrasssociety.eu/
History 6 Jul 2007, Pisa (Italy). **Aims** Work towards the spread of innovative applications and encouragement of a holistic view of *turf*, particularly with respect to its influence on urban and environmental quality. **Structure** General Assembly (at least annually). Directive Committee (Board), of 5 to 9 members, including President, Secretary and Treasurer. **Events** *Meeting* Amsterdam (Netherlands) 2020, *Meeting* Manchester (UK) 2018, *Meeting* Albufeira (Portugal) 2016, *Sustainability Copenhagen* (Denmark) 2015, *Conference* Osnabrück (Germany) 2014. **Members** Golden (14); Silver (10); Ordinary (101); Student (2). [2014/XM1778/D]

♦ European Two-Phase Flow Group (ETPFG) 08960
Hon Chair c/o ENEA, CR Casaccia, Via Anguillarese 301, SM di Galeria, 00060 Rome RM, Italy.
URL: http://termserv.casaccia.enea.it/etpfgm/
History 4 Oct 1963, Stockholm (Sweden). **Events** *Meeting* Dresden (Germany) 2014, *Meeting* Lyon (France) 2013, *Meeting* Udine (Italy) 2012, *Meeting* Tel Aviv (Israel) 2011, *Meeting* London (UK) 2010. **Members** Membership countries not specified. [2014/XE4474/E]

♦ European Twowheel Retailers Association (inactive)

♦ European Tyre Recycling Association (ETRA) 08961
Pres Av de Tervuren 16, BTE-3, 1040 Brussels, Belgium. T. +3227343727. Fax +3227340727. E-mail: etra@wanadoo.fr – info@etra-eu.org.
URL: http://www.etra-eu.org/
History 23 Sep 1994. Registration: France. **Aims** Represent the independent tyre and recycling sector in Europe. **Structure** General Assembly (annual); Board; Secretariat; Committees (7). **Languages** English. **Staff** 2.00 FTE, paid. Several voluntary. **Finance** Sources: contributions; members' dues; revenue from activities/projects. EU and national funding for projects and research; contributions by individual members/companies for specific projects and/or programmes. **Activities** Events/meetings; projects/programmes; research/documentation; training/education. **Events** *ETRA Conference on Tyre Recycling* Brussels (Belgium) 2023, *Annual Conference* Brussels (Belgium) 2022, *Annual Conference* Brussels (Belgium) 2020, *Annual Conference* Brussels (Belgium) 2019, *Annual Conference* Brussels (Belgium) 2018. **Publications** *ETRA Newsnotes* (12 a year); *Introduction to Tyre Recycling* (every 2 years). Conference proceedings; periodic topical reports; e-books.
Members Individuals and organizations in 47 countries:
Australia, Austria, Belgium, Bulgaria, Canada, China, Croatia, Cyprus, Czechia, Denmark, Egypt, Estonia, Finland, France, Germany, Greece, Hungary, India, Ireland, Israel, Italy, Japan, Korea Rep, Kuwait, Latvia, Lithuania, Malaysia, Mexico, Netherlands, Norway, Poland, Portugal, Qatar, Romania, Russia, Saudi Arabia, Slovakia, South Africa, Spain, Sweden, Switzerland, Thailand, Türkiye, UK, Ukraine, United Arab Emirates, USA.
NGO Relations Affiliated with (1): *EMEA Synthetic Turf Council (ESTC, #05436)*. [2022.05.10/XD7093/D]

♦ European Tyre and Rim Technical Organisation (ETRTO) 08962
Organisation technique européenne du pneumatique et de la jante – Technische Organisation der Europäischen Reifen- und Felgenhersteller
SG Rue Defacqz 78, 1060 Brussels, Belgium. T. +3223444059. Fax +3223440084. E-mail: info@etrto.org.
URL: http://www.etrto.org/
History Founded Oct 1964, the *European Tyre and Wheel Technical Conference (ETWTC)* having existed between 1956-1964. Current constitution adopted Oct 2012. EU Transparency Register: 527634222457-60. **Aims** Further alignment of national standards and ultimately achieve interchangeability of pneumatic tyres, rims and valves in Europe as far as fitting and use are concerned; establish common engineering dimensions, load/pressure characteristics and operational guidelines; promote free exchange of technical information appertaining to pneumatic tyres, rims and valves. **Structure** General Meeting (annual); Board; Executive Committee; Technical Committees. **Languages** English, French, German. **Staff** 4.00 FTE, paid. **Finance** Members' dues. **Activities** Standards/guidelines. **Events** *Annual General Meeting* Turin (Italy) 2014, *Annual General Meeting* Porto (Portugal) 2013, *Annual General Meeting* Windsor (UK) 2012, *Annual General Meeting* Utrecht (Netherlands) 2011, *Annual General Meeting* Stockholm (Sweden) 2010. **Publications** *Engineering Design Information* (annual); *Recommendations (Care and Maintenance of Tyres)* (annual) in English, French, German; *Standards Manual* (annual). Dictionary in English, French, German, Spanish; manuals; PDF downloads.
Members Full; Affiliated; Corresponding; Associate. Members in 45 countries and territories:
Australia, Austria, Belarus, Belgium, Brazil, Bulgaria, Canada, China, Croatia, Czechia, Egypt, Finland, France, Germany, Hong Kong, Hungary, India, Iran Islamic Rep, Israel, Italy, Japan, Jordan, Korea Rep, Luxembourg, Montenegro, Morocco, Netherlands, Norway, Philippines, Poland, Portugal, Romania, Russia, Saudi Arabia, Serbia, Slovenia, Spain, Sweden, Taiwan, Thailand, Türkiye, UK, Ukraine, United Arab Emirates, USA.
Included in the above, 1 organization listed in this Yearbook:
Scandinavian Tire and Rim Organization (STRO, #19124).
Consultative Status Consultative status granted from: *ECOSOC (#05331)* (Special). **IGO Relations** Cooperates with: *United Nations Economic Commission for Europe (UNECE, #20555)*. **NGO Relations** Cooperates with: *International Organization for Standardization (ISO, #14473)*. [2019.02.15/XD9892/y/D]

♦ European Tyre and Rubber Manufacturers' Association (ETRMA) .. 08963
Office Manager Avenue d'Auderghem 22-28, Box 9, 1040 Brussels, Belgium. T. +3222184940. E-mail: info@etrma.org.
SG address not obtained.

European Tyre Wheel
08963

alphabetic sequence excludes
For the complete listing, see Yearbook Online at

URL: http://www.etrma.org/

History 1959, Brussels (Belgium). Structure and identity modernized 2006. Former names and other names: *Liaison Office of the Rubber Industries of the European Common Market* – former (1959); *Bureau de liaison des industries du caoutchouc du Marché commun européen* – former (1959); *Liaison Office of the Rubber Industries of the European Communities* – former; *Bureau de liaison des industries du caoutchouc de la Communauté économique européenne* – former; *Verbindungsbüro der Kautschukindustrien der Europäischen Wirtschaftsgemeinschaft* – former; *Liaison Office of the Rubber Industries of the European Union* – former (2001); *Bureau de liaison des industries du caoutchouc de l'Union européenne (BLIC)* – former (2001); *Verbindungsbüro der Kautschukindustrien der Europäischen Union* – former (2001); *European Association of the Rubber Industry* – former (2001 to 2006). Registration: Banque-Carrefour des Entreprises, No/ID: 0881.606.175, Start date: 16 Feb 2006, Belgium; EU Transparency Register, No/ID: 6025320863-10, Start date: 23 Dec 2008. **Aims** Act in 4 interdependent areas: representation, coordination, information and promotion, at international and European levels at the interests of the European tyre and rubber manufacturers. **Structure** General Assembly; Board of Directors; Secretariat. Policy Committees; Sector Groups; Working Groups. **Languages** English. **Staff** 7.00 FTE, paid. **Finance** Sources: members' dues. **Activities** Advocacy/lobbying/activism; politics/policy/regulatory. **Events** *Meeting on European competitiveness* Brussels (Belgium) 1994, *Meeting* Brussels (Belgium) 1990, *Meeting* Brussels (Belgium) 1989, *Meeting* Brussels (Belgium) 1988. **Publications** Annual Activity Report; Statistics; ELT Management Report.

Members Tyre Companies (11); National Rubber Manufacturers' Associations (10); Affiliate Corporate members (3). Members in 18 countries:

Belgium, Czechia, Finland, France, Germany, Hungary, Italy, Luxembourg, Netherlands, Poland, Portugal, Romania, Serbia, Slovakia, Slovenia, Spain, Türkiye, UK.

Consultative Status Consultative status granted from: *ECOSOC (#05331)* (Ros C); *UNCTAD (#20285)* (Special Category). **IGO Relations** *European Commission (EC, #06633)*; *European Parliament (EP, #08146)*; *International Rubber Study Group (IRSG, #14772)* (Industry Member); *OECD (#17693)*; *United Nations Economic Commission for Europe (UNECE, #20555)* (Industry Member). **NGO Relations** Member of (3): *European Platform for Chemicals Using Manufacturing Industries (CheMI, #08223)*; *Industry4Europe (#11181)*; *Mobility for Prosperity in Europe (MPE, #16839)*. Affiliate member of: *Global Platform for Sustainable Natural Rubber (GPSNR, #10552)*. Liaison Organization of: *Comité européen de normalisation (CEN, #04162)*.

[2023/XE3168/**E**]

♦ European Tyre and Wheel Technical Conference / see European Tyre and Rim Technical Organisation (#08962)

♦ European Umbrella Organization for Geographical Information (EUROGI) 08964

Organisation européenne pour l'information géographique – Europäische Organisation für Geoinformation – Europese Organisatie voor Geografische Informatie

Mailing Address House of the European Surveyor and GeoInformation, Rue du Nord 76, 1000 Brussels, Belgium. T. +3222196281.

Registered Office Soerenseweg 15, 7314 CA Apeldoorn, Netherlands.

URL: https://eurogi.org/

History 26 Nov 1993, Luxembourg. Founded as the result of a study commissioned by DG XIII of the *European Commission (EC, #06633)* to develop a unified European approach to the use of geographic technologies (GT). Former names and other names: *Stichting EUROGI* – legal name. Registration: Handelsregister, No/ID: KVK 41190235, Netherlands; EU Transparency Register, No/ID: 564096343432-21, Start date: 6 Jul 2021. **Aims** Maximize the use of geographic information (GI) for the benefit of citizens, good *governance* and *commerce* in Europe; encourage greater use of GI in Europe; raise awareness of the value of and its associated technologies; work towards development of strong national associations in all European countries; facilitate development of a European Spatial Data Infrastructure; represent European interests in the Global Spatial Data infrastructure. **Structure** General Meeting (annual); General Board; Executive Committee; Secretariat, headed by Secretary General. **Staff** 3.00 FTE, paid. **Finance** Sources: members' dues. **Activities** Advocacy/lobbying/activism; knowledge management/information dissemination. **Events** *Meeting* Brussels (Belgium) 2019, *Members Meeting* Dublin (Ireland) 2019, *Members Meeting* Fisciano (Italy) 2018, *Members Meeting* Brussels (Belgium) 2017, *Members Meeting* Saint-Mandé (France) 2017. **Publications** Annual Report; directories.

Members National Geographic Information Representatives (A-members); Corporate Members (B-members); Other Organizations (C-members). Members (25) in 16 countries and territories:

Austria, Belgium, Croatia, Denmark, Estonia, France, Germany, Hungary, Iceland, Ireland, Italy, Latvia, Portugal, Slovenia, Spain, Switzerland.

European Association of Aerial Surveying Industries (EAASI, #05929); *European Association of Remote Sensing Companies (EARSC, #06190)*.

IGO Relations Partner of (1): *United Nations Committee of Experts on Global Geospatial Information Management (UN-GGIM, #20540)*. Cooperates with (2): *International Hydrographic Organization (IHO, #13825)*; *Regional Committee of United Nations Global Geospatial Information Management for Asia and the Pacific (UN-GGIM-AP, #18766)*. **NGO Relations** Memorandum of Understanding with (1): *EuroGeographics (#05684)*. Member of (1): *European Geographic Information Network (EGIN, #07387)*. Cooperates with (3): *International Federation of Surveyors (FIG, #13561)*; *International Society for Photogrammetry and Remote Sensing (ISPRS, #15362)*; *Union of the Electricity Industry – Eurelectric (#20379)*. [2023/XE2097/y/**E**]

♦ European Underseas Bio-Medical Society / see European Underwater and Baromedical Society (#08965)

♦ European Underwater and Baromedical Society (EUBS) 08965

Sec 35 Sutherland Crescent, Abernethy, Perth, PH2 9GA, UK. E-mail: secretary@eubs.org.

Hon Sec address not obtained.

URL: http://www.eubs.org/

History 30 Sep 1971. Former names and other names: *European Underseas Bio-Medical Society* – former; *Société européenne de bio-médecine sous-marine* – former. Registration: Charities Commission, No/ID: 264970, England and Wales. **Aims** Study and promote *diving* and *hyperbaric medicine*. **Structure** Executive Committee; Presidents; Committees (6). **Languages** English. **Staff** 1.00 FTE, voluntary. **Finance** Sources: members' dues. **Activities** Events/meetings. **Events** *Annual Scientific Meeting* Prague (Czechia) 2022, *Annual Scientific Meeting* Prague (Czechia) 2021, *Annual Scientific Meeting* Prague (Czechia) 2020, *Annual Scientific Meeting* Tel Aviv (Israel) 2019, *Tri-Continental Annual Scientific Meeting* Durban (South Africa) 2018. **Publications** *Diving and Hyperbaric Medicine* (4 a year).

Members Individuals (290): Undergraduate (4); Full (272); Corporate (6); Associate (8). Members in 42 countries and territories:

Argentina, Australia, Austria, Barbados, Belgium, Brazil, Canada, Cyprus, Denmark, Egypt, Finland, France, Germany, Greece, Hong Kong, Iceland, India, Ireland, Israel, Italy, Japan, Latvia, Malaysia, Malta, Mexico, Netherlands, Nigeria, Norway, Philippines, Poland, Portugal, Russia, Saudi Arabia, Serbia, Slovenia, Spain, Sweden, Switzerland, Taiwan, Türkiye, UK, USA.

[2022.05.11/XD4049/v/**D**]

♦ European Underwater Federation (EUF) 08966

SG 150 Impasse de la Vielle Ecole, Frontenex, 74210 Faverges, France. T. +33450444046. E-mail: dje735@me.com – secgen@euf.eu – info@euf.eu.

URL: http://www.euf.eu/

History Registration: Companies House, No/ID: 4329764, Start date: 27 Nov 2001, England and Wales. **Aims** Serve as a platform for recreational *diving* activities; act as the consultative body for all matters concerning safety, regulation or legislation in areas affecting the sector; ensure no discrimination because of race, nationality or creed in the field. **Structure** Elected Executive Board. **Languages** English. **Activities** Accreditation/certification; events/meetings.

Members Full in 17 countries:

Austria, Belgium, Denmark, Estonia, Finland, France, Germany, Iceland, Ireland, Israel, Italy, Luxembourg, Netherlands, Norway, Russia, Switzerland, UK.

NGO Relations Observer and Corresponding member of: *European Diving Technology Committee (EDTC, #06932)*. [2021/XD7105/**D**]

♦ European Union (inactive)

♦ European Union (EU) 08967

Union européenne (UE) – Unión Europea (UE) – Europäische Union (EU) – União Européia (UE) – Unione Europea (UE) – Europese Unie (EU) – Europeiska Unionen (EU) – Europaeiske Union (EU) – Euroopan Unioni (EU) – Evropaiki Enosi (EE) – tAontas Eorpach – Evropska Unie – Európska Unia – Európai Unió – Unia Europejska – Evropska Unija – Euroopa Liit – Eiropas Savieniba – Europos Sajunga – Unjoni Ewropea – Europska Unija – Uniunea Europeana

Headquarters c/o European Commission, Rue de la Loi 170, 1049 Brussels, Belgium. T. +3222991111. Fax +3222950138 – +3222950140.

URL: http://europa.eu/

History Established 1 Nov 1993, on entry into force of *Treaty on European Union (Maastricht Treaty, 1992)*, signed 7 Feb 1992. Received full legal personality, 2 Oct 1997, on signature of *Treaty of Amsterdam (1997)*, following agreement among the Heads of State and Government meeting as the *European Council (#06801)*, 16-17 Jun 1997, Amsterdam (Netherlands). The Amsterdam treaty allows the Union to negotiate as one entity. Means of operation of the Union were revised by the *Nice Treaty (2001)*, signed 26 Feb 2001, Nice, which came into effect 1 Feb 2003. Further revisions, especially regarding enlargement, were formalized in the *Treaty of Accession*, also known as *Treaty of Athens*, signed 16 Apr 2003, Athens, which entered into force with the accession of 10 new member states on 1 May 2004. Further modified by *Treaty of Lisbon (2007)*, signed Dec 2007, which added further responsibilities to the Union previously held by the European Communities.

The European Union is the culmination of the process of integration initiated by the European Community Treaties:

- *Treaty Establishing the European Coal and Steel Community (Treaty of Paris, 1951)*;
- *Treaty Establishing the European Economic Community (Treaty of Rome)*; and
- *Treaty Establishing the European Atomic Energy Community (Treaty of Rome, 1957)*.

These treaties set up what was collectively referred to as *European Communities (EC, inactive)*:

- *European Coal and Steel Community (ECSC, inactive)*, which ceased to exist in Jul 2002, following expiration of the Paris Treaty, leaving the European Community responsible for the steel sector;
- *'European Economic Community (EEC)'*, known since the Maastricht Treaty as *European Community (inactive)*, which ceased to exist, 1 Dec 2009, when Treaty of Lisbon entered into force, original Treaty of Rome amended to become *Treaty on the Functioning of the European Union (TFEU, 1957)*, and European Union replaced the Community;
- *European Atomic Energy Community (Euratom, inactive)*, which ceased to exist as a community, 1 Dec 2009, when Treaty of Lisbon entered into force, and European Commission took over its responsabilities.

The preamble to the EEC Treaty speaks of 'an ever closer union'. Meeting on 29 Oct 1972, Paris (France), the Heads of State and Government declared that the aim should be to establish the European Union by 1980.Several initiatives, proposals and projects existed prior to and after this meeting, among which may be quoted: a proposed European Defence Community (EDC), 1952-1954; an abandoned project of political union contained in Fouchet plans, 1961-1962; Leo Tindemans' report, 1975; the 'Three Wise Men' report, 1979; *Crocodile Club (inactive)* activities 1980 to 1984; Genscher-Colombo project of the European Act. Meanwhile, the European Council passed a series of resolutions on what was to become the European Union: 1973, Copenhagen (Denmark); Dec 1974, Paris; Dec 1978, Brussels (Belgium). In Jun 1983, Stuttgart (Germany FR), the Heads of State and Government, in the Solemn Declaration on the European Union, reaffirmed their intention of continuing to work towards it. The European Parliament adopted, 14 Feb 1984, the Treaty establishing the European Union; a resolution of Feb 1989 called for cooperation between the Community and national institutions to facilitate ratification of the Treaty.

The *Single European Act (SEA, 1986)*, signed Feb 1986 and ratified by member parliaments by 31 Mar 1987, came into force on 1 Jul 1987. It amended the EEC Treaty and paved the way for completing the single market. The Maastricht Treaty aimed to prepare for a European Monetary Union and introduce elements of a political union (citizenship, common foreign and internal affairs policy). Apart from establishing the European Union, it introduced the co-decision procedure, giving Parliament more say in union decision-making.

Treaty on Stability, Coordination and Governance in the Economic and Monetary Union (TSCG, 2012) is an intergovernmental treaty, signed 2012 by all EU Member States except Czech Rep and UK. It is not an EU treaty but an intergovernmental treaty, but with with the intention to bring it into EU law.

The European Union was awarded the Nobel Peace Prize in 2012.

Aims According to Article 3 of the Treaty of Lisbon: (1) promote peace, its values and the well-being of its peoples; (2) offer its citizens an area of freedom, security and justice without internal *frontiers*, in which the free movement of persons is ensured in conjunction with appropriate measures with respect to external *border* controls, *asylum*, immigration and the prevention and combating of crime; (3) establish an *internal market*; work for the sustainable development of Europe based on balanced economic growth and price stability, a highly competitive social market economy, aiming at full employment and social progress, and a high of protection and improvement of the quality of the environment; promote scientific and technological advance; combat social exclusion and discrimination, and promote social justice and protection, *equality* between women and men, solidarity between generations and protection of the rights of the child; promote economic, social and territorial cohesion, and solidarity among Member States; respect its rich *cultural* and *linguistic* diversity, and ensure that Europe's cultural *heritage* is safeguarded and enhanced; (4) establish an economic and *monetary* union whose currency is the euro; (5) in its relations with the wider world, uphold and promote its values and interests and contribute to the protection of its citizens; contribute to peace, security, the sustainable development of the Earth, solidarity and mutual respect among peoples, free and faire trade, eradication of poverty and the protection of human rights, in particular the rights of the child, as well as to the strict observance and the development of international law, including respect for the principles of the United Nations Charter.

Structure The Union is based on the rule of law and founded on treaties that have been approved voluntarily and democratically by all EU countries. Competences not conferred upon the Union in the Treaties remain with the States. The EU's 7 main institions are:

European Council (#06801), consisting of Heads of State or Government of the EU Member States and headed by President, sets EU's overall political direction, but has no powers to pass laws.

Three institutions involved in EU legislation produce through the "Ordinary Legislative Procedure" policies and laws that apply throughout the EU:

- *European Parliament (EP, #08146)*, which represents EU citizens and is directly elected by them;
- *Council of the European Union (#04895)*, which represents the governments of the individual member countries and with rotating Presidency;
- *European Commission (EC, #06633)*, which represents the interests of the EU as a whole.

Three other key institutions:

- *Court of Justice of the European Union (CJEU, #04938)*, upholds the rule of European law;
- *European Court of Auditors (#06854)*, which checks financing of the EU's activities.
- *European Central Bank (ECB, #06466)*, which is responsible for European monetary policy.

Advisory bodies that must be consulted when proposed legislation involves their area of interest:

- *European Economic and Social Committee (EESC, #06963)*, representing civil society groups;
- *European Committee of the Regions (CoR, #06665)*, which represents local and regional governments.

Other institutions that play specialized roles:

- *European External Action Service (EEAS, #07018)*, which assists the *High Representative of the Union for Foreign Affairs and Security Policy*;
- *European Investment Bank (EIB, #07599)*, which finances EU investment projects and helps small businesses through the *European Investment Fund (EIF, #07601)*;
- *European Ombudsman (#08084)*, who investigates complaints about maladministration by EU institutions and bodies;
- *European Data Protection Supervisor (EDPS)*, who safeguards the privacy of people's personal data.

Interinstitutional bodies:

- *Computer Emergency Response Team (CERT)*, which helps to manage threats to EU institutions' computer systems;
- *European School of Administration (EUSA, #08427)*, which provides training in specific areas for members of EU staff;
- *European Personnel Selection Office (EPSO)*, which sets competitive examinations for recruiting staff to work in all EU institution;
- *Publications Office of the European Union (Publications Office, #18562)*, which publishes information about the EU.

EU agencies are distinct from EU institutions, as they have separate legal entities set up to perform specific tasks under EU law. Separated into 5 categories:

'Decentralized Agencies' – contribute to the implementation of EU policies and support cooperation between the EU and national governments. Set up for an indefinite period and located across the EU:

- *Agency for the Cooperation of Energy Regulators (ACER, #00552)*;
- *Body of European Regulators for Electronic Communications (BEREC, #03299)*;
- *Community Plant Variety Office (CPVO, #04404)*;
- *European Agency for Safety and Health at Work (EU-OSHA, #05843)*;
- *Frontex, the European Border and Coast Guard Agency (#10005)*;

- *European Union Agency for the Operational Management of Large-Scale IT Systems in the Area of Freedom, Security and Justice (eu-LISA, #08972)*;
- *European Union Agency for Asylum (EUAA, #08968)*;
- *European Union Aviation Safety Agency (EASA, #08978)*;
- *European Banking Authority (EBA, #06311)*;
- *European Centre for Disease Prevention and Control (ECDC, #06476)*;
- *European Centre for the Development of Vocational Training (Cedefop, #06474)*;
- *European Chemicals Agency (ECHA, #06523)*;
- *European Environment Agency (EEA, #06995)*;
- *European Fisheries Control Agency (EFCA, #07266)*;
- *European Food Safety Authority (EFSA, #07287)*;
- *European Foundation for the Improvement of Living and Working Conditions (Eurofound, #07348)*;
- *European Union Agency for the Space Programme (EUSPA, #08974)*;
- *European Institute for Gender Equality (EIGE, #07557)*;
- *European Insurance and Occupational Pensions Authority (EIOPA, #07578)*;
- *European Maritime Safety Agency (EMSA, #07744)*;
- *European Medicines Agency (EMA, #07767)*;
- *European Monitoring Centre for Drugs and Drug Addiction (EMCDDA, #07820)*;
- *European Union Agency for Network and Information Security (ENISA, #08971)*;
- *European Union Agency for Law Enforcement Training (CEPOL, #08970)*;
- *European Police Office (Europol, #08239)*;
- *European Public Prosecutor's Office (EPPO, #08300)* (in preparation);
- *European Union Agency for Railways (#08973)*;
- *European Securities and Markets Authority (ESMA, #08457)*;
- *European Training Foundation (ETF, #08934)*;
- *European Union Agency for Fundamental Rights (FRA, #08969)*;
- *European Union Intellectual Property Office (EUIPO, #08996)*;
- *Single Resolution Board (SRB, #19287)*;
- *Eurojust (#05698)*;
- *Centre de traduction des organes de l'Union européenne (CdT, #03790)*.

'Agencies under Common Security and Defence Policy' – set up to carry out very specific technical, scientific and management tasks:
- *European Defence Agency (EDA, #06895)*;
- *European Union Institute for Security Studies (EUISS, #08994)*;
- *European Union Satellite Centre (SatCen, #09015)*.

'Executive Agencies' – set up for a limited period to manage specific tasks related to EU programmes:
- *Education, Audiovisual and Culture Executive Agency (EACEA)*;
- *Executive Agency for Small and Medium-sized Enterprises (EASME)*;
- *European Research Council Executive Agency (ERC Executive Agency)*;
- *Consumers, Health, Agriculture and Food Executive Agency (CHAFEA)*;
- *Research Executive Agency (REA)*;
- *Innovation and Networks Executive Agency (INEA)*.

'EURATOM Agencies and Bodies' – support the aims of *Treaty Establishing the European Atomic Energy Community (Treaty of Rome, 1957)* – EURATOM:
- *Euratom Supply Agency (ESA, #05617)*;
- *European Joint Undertaking for ITER and the Development of Fusion Energy (Fusion for Energy, #07611)*.

'Other Organizations' – include bodies set up as part of EU programmes and public-private partnerships:
- *European Institute of Innovation and Technology (EIT, #07562)*;
- Bio-based Industries Joint Undertaking;
- Clean Sky 2 Joint Undertaking;
- ECSEL Joint Undertaking;
- Fuel Cells and Hydrogen 2 Joint Undertaking;
- *Innovative Medicines Initiative (IMI, #11221)* 2 Joint Undertaking;
- SESAR Joint Joint Undertaking;
- Shift2Rail Joint Undertaking.

Languages Bulgarian, Croatian, Czech, Danish, Dutch, English, Estonian, Finnish, French, German, Hungarian, Irish Gaelic, Italian, Latvian, Lithuanian, Maltese, Polish, Portuguese, Romanian, Slovakian, Slovene, Spanish, Swedish. **Finance** Budget (2015): euro 145,000 million – constitutes about 1% of the wealth generated by EU economies every year. Budget is subject to limits established by the multiannual financial framework. *European Commission (EC, #06633)* proposes budget and national governments – acting through *European Council (#06801)* – and *European Parliament (EP, #08146)* approve proposal.
Activities Among its greatest achievements, the European Union lists: peace, stability and prosperity, raised living standards and the single European currency – the euro; creation of the *Schengen Area*; the single or 'internal' market as the main economic engine. The Union is active in various topics for which organizations, funds, institutions and/or programmes are created, usually functioning within one of the main EU institutions:
- Agriculture;
- Audiovisual and media;
- Budget;
- Climate action;
- Competition;
- Consumers;
- Culture;
- Customs – *EU Customs Union (#05579)*;
- Development and Cooperation;
- Digital economy and society;
- Economic and monetary affairs – *European Economic and Monetary Union (EMU, #06961)*;
- Education, training and youth;
- Employment and social affairs;
- Energy – *Energy Union* planned;
- Enlargement;
- Enterprise;
- Environment;
- EU citizenship;
- Food safety;
- Foreign and security policy;
- Fraud prevention;
- Health;
- Humanitarian aid and Civil Protection;
- Human rights – *Charter of Fundamental Rights of the European Union (2000)*;
- Institutional affairs;
- Justice and Home Affairs;
- Maritime affairs and fisheries;
- Multilingualism;
- Regional policy;
- Research and innovation – towards a *European Research Area*;
- Single market;
- Space;
- Sport;
- Taxation;
- Trade;
- Transport.

Events *Economic and Financial Affairs Council Meeting* Brussels (Belgium) 2022, *Eurogroup Meeting* Brussels (Belgium) 2022, *One Health EJP Annual Scientific Meeting – OHEJPASM* Copenhagen (Denmark) 2021, *The Role of Responsible Business Conduct in Building Resilience* Tokyo (Japan) 2021, *International Solidarity Conference on the Venezuelan Refugee and Migrant Crisis* Brussels (Belgium) 2019. **Publications** *Publications Office of the European Union (Publications Office, #18562)* is the official publisher of all EU institutions.
Members Any European state may apply to the Council to become a member of the Union. The Council acts unanimously after consulting the Commission and after receiving the assent of the European Parliament. Current member countries (27):
Austria, Belgium, Bulgaria, Croatia, Cyprus, Czechia, Denmark, Estonia, Finland, France, Germany, Greece, Hungary, Ireland, Italy, Latvia, Lithuania, Luxembourg, Malta, Netherlands, Poland, Portugal, Romania, Slovakia, Slovenia, Spain, Sweden.
Enlargement: Bosnia-Herzegovina and Kosovo were promised the prospect of joining when they are ready; Albania, North Macedonia, Montenegro, Serbia and Turkey are negotiating – or waiting to start.
IGO Relations Institutional relations with: *NATO (#16945)*. Special relationship with: *Council of Europe (CE, #04881)*. Cooperates with: *European Organisation for the Exploitation of Meteorological Satellites (EUMETSAT, #08096)*; *European Space Agency (ESA, #08798)*; *International Civil Aviation Organization (ICAO, #12581)*; *International Maritime Organization (IMO, #14102)*; *Union of African Shippers' Councils (UASC, #20348)*. International cooperation outside the EU – *INCO*: Individual, tailor-made Stabilization and Association Agreements are being offered to the Balkan countries: Albania, Bosnia-Herzegovina, North Macedonia and Serbia. Cooperation with Mediterranean partnership countries – *INCO-MED* – covers Algeria, Cyprus, Egypt, Israel, Jordan, Lebanon, Malta, Morocco, Palestine Authority, Syria, Tunisia and Turkey. Bilateral *'Science and Technology'* agreements with: Argentina; Australia; Canada; China; Russia; South Africa; USA (Argentina, China and Russia not yet in force). Institutionalized cooperation with the countries of: *EFTA (#05391)*, through *European Economic Area (EEA, #06957)*; *Organisation of African, Caribbean and Pacific States (OACPS, #17796)*, through *ACP-EEC Convention (Lomé convention, 1975)*, *Second ACP-EEC Convention (Lomé II, 1979)*, *Third ACP-EEC Convention (Lomé III, 1984)*, *Fourth ACP-EEC Convention (Lomé IV, 1989)* and *ACP-EU Partnership Agreement (Cotonou agreement, 2000)*. Participates in the activities of: *UNCTAD (#20285)*. Observer to: *OAS (#17629)*. Signatory to: *Agreement on the Conservation of Small Cetaceans of the Baltic, North East Atlantic, Irish and North Seas (ASCOBANS, 1992)*; *United Nations Convention to Combat Desertification (UNCCD, 1994)*.
[2020/XF2147/**F***]

♦ European Union of Abattoir Veterinarians (inactive)
♦ European Union Against Aircraft Nuisance (#20395)

♦ European Union Agency for Asylum (EUAA) 08968

Exec Dir MTC Block A, Winemakers Wharf, Grand Harbour, Valletta, MRS 1917, Malta. T. +35622487500. E-mail: info@euaa.europa.eu.
URL: https://euaa.europa.eu/

History 2012, Malta. Proposed by *European Commission (EC, #06633)*, 18 Feb 2009, and set up by EC and *European Parliament (EP, #08146)* following Regulation (EU) 439/2010, coming into force, 19 June 2010. Operational since 1 Feb 2011. Officially inaugurated in Malta, 19 June 2011. A decentralized agency of *European Union (EU, #08967)*. Current name adopted following entry into force of Regulation (EU) 2021/2303 on 19 Jan 2022. Former names and other names: *European Asylum Support Office (EASO)* – former. **Aims** Enhance practical cooperation on asylum matters; help Member States fulfill their European and international obligations to give protection to people in need. **Structure** Management Board; Executive Office. **Staff** 516.00 FTE, paid. **Finance** Sources: international organizations. Supported by: *European Union (EU, #08967)*. Annual budget: 172,000,000 EUR (2023). URL: https://commission.europa.eu/strategy-and-policy/eu-budget_en **Activities** Knowledge management/information dissemination; politics/policy/regulatory; training/education. Active in: Austria, Belgium, Bulgaria, Cyprus, Czechia, Greece, Italy, Lithuania, Malta, Moldova, Netherlands, Romania, Slovenia, Spain. **Events** *Meeting* Vienna (Austria) 2018, *Journalist Network Meeting* Brussels (Belgium) 2016, *Meeting* Brussels (Belgium) 2016, *Plenary Meeting* Brussels (Belgium) 2014. **Publications** *EUAA Daily Press Bulletin* (daily) in English – Request from press@euaa.europa.eu; *EUAA Quarterly Newsletter* (4 a year) in English.
Members Governments (25):
Austria, Belgium, Bulgaria, Croatia, Cyprus, Czechia, Estonia, Finland, France, Germany, Greece, Hungary, Italy, Latvia, Lithuania, Luxembourg, Malta, Netherlands, Poland, Portugal, Romania, Slovakia, Slovenia, Spain, Sweden.
Institutions (2):
European Commission (EC, #06633); *UNHCR (#20327)*.
Observer States (4):
Iceland, Liechtenstein, Norway, Switzerland.
IGO Relations Cooperates with (1): *European Union Agency for the Operational Management of Large-Scale IT Systems in the Area of Freedom, Security and Justice (eu-LISA, #08972)*. Member of Consultative Forum of *Frontex, the European Border and Coast Guard Agency (#10005)*. **NGO Relations** Member of (1): *EU Agencies Network (EUAN, #05564)*.
[2023.02.16/XJ8472/**E***]

♦ European Union Agency for Fundamental Rights (FRA) 08969

Agence des droits fondamentaux de l'Union européenne – Agencia de los Derechos Fundamentales de la Unión Europea – Agentur der Europäischen Union für Gründrechte – Bureau van de Europese Unie voor de Grondrechten

Headquarters Schwarzenbergplatz 11, 1040 Vienna, Austria.
URL: https://fra.europa.eu/

History 15 Feb 2007. Established by Council Regulation (EC) No 168/2007 of *Council of the European Union (#04895)*. Inaugurated 1 Mar 2007. Successor to *European Monitoring Centre on Racism and Xenophobia (EUMC, inactive)*. A decentralized agency of *European Union (EU, #08967)*. Former names and other names: *Agencia de los Derechos Fundamentales de la Unión Europea* – alias; *Bureau van de Europese Unie voor de Grondrechten* – alias. **Aims** Provide assistance and expertise relating to fundamental rights to EU institutions and Member States, when implementing European Union law; engage in data collection, improving comparability and reliability of data, research and analysis; cooperate with international organizations, national specialized bodies and civil society; raise public awareness of fundamental rights; formulate conclusions and opinions to policy makers, partner organizations and those who implement policy and take action on the ground. **Structure** Management Board, consisting of one independent person from each Member State, one independent person appointed by Council of Europe and 2 representatives of *European Commission (EC, #06633)*. Executive Board; Scientific Committee; Director. Units (5): Research and Data; Technical Assistance and Capacity Building; Communications and Events; Institutional Cooperation and Networks; Corporate Services. **Languages** English. **Staff** 105 TAs and CAs; 9 SNEs; 20 trainees. **Finance** Annual budget (2018): euro 22,350,000. **Activities** Research/documentation; events/meetings; training/education; knowledge management/information dissemination. **Events** *Meeting* Vienna (Austria) 2021, *National Liaison Officers Meeting* Vienna (Austria) 2021, *Finnish Presidency Conference on the Charter of Fundamental Rights of the European Union* Brussels (Belgium) 2019, *Human Rights Workshop* Vienna (Austria) 2019, *National Liaison Officers Meeting* Vienna (Austria) 2019. **Publications** *Fundamental Rights Report* (annual). Thematic reports; papers; legal opinions; general information products. **Information Services** *Charterpedia*.
Members in 27 countries:
Austria, Belgium, Bulgaria, Croatia, Cyprus, Czechia, Denmark, Estonia, Finland, France, Germany, Greece, Hungary, Ireland, Italy, Latvia, Lithuania, Luxembourg, Malta, Netherlands, Poland, Portugal, Romania, Slovakia, Slovenia, Spain, Sweden.
IGO Relations Links with various EU agencies and UN bodies, including:
- *European Committee of the Regions (CoR, #06665)*;
- *Council of Europe (CE, #04881)*;
- *Council of the European Union (#04895)*;
- *Court of Justice of the European Union (CJEU, #04938)*;
- *Eurojust (#05698)*;
- *Frontex, the European Border and Coast Guard Agency (#10005)*;
- *European Union Agency for the Operational Management of Large-Scale IT Systems in the Area of Freedom, Security and Justice (eu-LISA, #08972)*;
- *European Commission (EC, #06633)*;
- *European Crime Prevention Network (EUCPN, #06858)*;
- European Data Protection Supervisor (EDPS);
- *European Economic and Social Committee (EESC, #06963)*;
- *European Ombudsman (#08084)*;
- *European Parliament (EP, #08146)*;
- *Office of the United Nations High Commissioner for Human Rights (OHCHR, #17697)*;
- *OSCE High Commissioner on National Minorities (HCNM, #17901)*;
- *OSCE – Office for Democratic Institutions and Human Rights (OSCE/ODIHR, #17902)*;
- *UNESCO (#20322)*;
- *UNHCR (#20327)*.

NGO Relations Member of (1): *EU Agencies Network (EUAN, #05564)*.
Through *Fundamental Rights Platform (FRP)*, cooperates with some 370 civil society organization, including:
- *Access Info Europe*;
- *ADF International (#00112)*;
- *Centre d'études des discriminations, du racisme et de l'antisémitisme (CEDRA, inactive)*;
- *Centre for Science, Society and Citizenship (CSSC)*;
- *Council of Bars and Law Societies of Europe (CCBE, #04871)*;
- *Don Bosco International (DBI, #05117)*;
- *Equal Rights Trust (#05520)*;
- *Academy of European Law (#00035)*;
- *Europe Against Drugs (EURAD, #05774)*;
- *European AIDS Treatment Group (EATG, #05850)*;

European Union Agency
08970

alphabetic sequence excludes
For the complete listing, see Yearbook Online at

- European Alternatives (EA, #05891);
- European Association of Service Providers for Persons with Disabilities (EASPD, #06204);
- European Centre for Research and Training in Human Rights and Humanitarian Law;
- European Coordination of Associations and Individuals for Freedom of Conscience (CAPLC);
- european forum for migration studies (efms, inactive);
- European Human Rights Association (EHRA);
- Global Campus of Human Rights (#10269);
- European Law Institute (ELI, #07658);
- European Muslim Initiative for Social Cohesion (EMISCO, #07839);
- European Ombudsman Institute (#08085);
- European Public Health Alliance (EPHA, #08297);
- European Trade Union Committee for Education (ETUCE, #08926);
- Federal Union of European Nationalities (FUEN, #09396);
- Federation of Catholic Family Associations in Europe (#09468);
- Global Network for Public Interest Law (PILnet);
- Instituto Internacional de Estudios sobre la Familia (Family Watch);
- Humanists International (#10972);
- Ludwig Boltzmann Institut für Grund- und Menschenrechte (LBI);
- Österreichische Liga für Menschenrechte (LIGA);
- Scandinavian Human Rights Lawyers (SHRL);
- Standing Committee of European Doctors (#19955). [2020/XM3280/**D***]

♦ European Union Agency for Law Enforcement Training (CEPOL) 08970

Contact Pf 314, Budapest 1903, Hungary. E-mail: info@cepol.europa.eu.
Street address Ó utca 27, Budapest 1066, Hungary.
URL: http://www.cepol.europa.eu/

History Founded following agreement of *European Council (#06801)* at a meeting, 15-16 Oct 1999, Tampere (Finland), by Council Decision 2000/820/JHA. Became operational 1 Jan 2001. Seat of Secretariat was temporarily based in Copenhagen (Denmark). Decision amended, Jul 2004, by: Council Decision 2004/566/JHA, stating that CEPOL shall have legal personality; 2004/567/JHA, stating that the seat shall be in Bramshill (UK), and the Governing Board shall set up a permanent secretariat. Established as a decentralized agency of *European Union (EU, #08967)* by Council Decision 2005/681/JHA – amended by Regulation (EU) No 543-2014 of *European Parliament (EP, #08146)* and the Council. Relocated to Budapest (Hungary), 1 Oct 2014. Current title adopted when received new legal mandate (Regulation EU 2015/2219) of European Parliament and of European Council. Former names and other names: *Collège européen de police (CEPOL)* – former; *European Police College* – former; *Europese Politie-Akademie* – former. **Aims** Make Europe a safer place through law enforcement training and learning. **Structure** Management Board (meets at least twice a year); CEPOL National Units (CNUs); Executive Director. **Languages** English. **Finance** Supported by: *European Commission (EC, #06633)*. Annual budget: 10,845,030 EUR (2022). **Activities** Capacity building; events/meetings; financial and/or material support; networking/liaising; research/documentation; training/education. **Events** *Research and Science Conference* Vilnius (Lithuania) 2022, *Research and Science Conference* 2021, *Conference on Policing the Pandemic* Budapest (Hungary) 2020, *Research and Science Conference* Budapest (Hungary) 2017, *Research and Science Conference* Lisbon (Portugal) 2015. **Publications** *European Law Enforcement Research Bulletin* (2 a year). *European Union Strategic Training Needs Assessment 2022-2025 (EU-STNA 2022-2025)* (2021). Annual Report; Operational Training Needs Analysis reports; training catalogue; brochures; posters; factsheets. **Members** National law enforcement training institutions from EU Member States and associated countries. Membership countries not specified. **NGO Relations** Member of (1): *EU Agencies Network (EUAN, #05564)*. [2022.10.27/XF6502/**F***]

♦ European Union Agency for Network and Information Security (ENISA) 08971

Agence européenne de cyber-sécurité – Europäischen Agentur für Netz- und Informationssicherheit

Exec Dir PO Box 1309, 710 01 Heraklion, Greece. T. +302814409710. Fax +302810391410. E-mail: info@enisa.europa.eu.
URL: http://www.enisa.europa.eu/

History 14 Mar 2004. Established following adopted of Regulation (EC) No 460/2004 of the *European Parliament (EP, #08146)* and of *Council of Europe (CE, #04881)*, as a decentralized agency of the *European Union (EU, #08967)*. Mandate amended Jun 2011 by Regulation (EU) No 580/2011. Operations started, Sep 2005, Crete (Greece). New mandate since 2013 (526/2013). Former names and other names: *European Network and Information Security Agency* – former. **Aims** Develop a culture of network and information security for the benefit of citizens, consumers, business and public sector organizations in the European Union; help the European Commission, Member States and the business community to address, respond to and especially prevent network and information security problems. **Structure** Management Board; Executive Director. Permanent Stakeholders Group (PSG); National Liaison Officers (NLOs). **Finance** Annual budget: 10,000,000 EUR (2015). **Activities** Guidance/assistance/consulting; knowledge management/information dissemination; awareness raising; events/meetings. **Events** *Cybersecurity Market Analysis Conference* Brussels (Belgium) 2022, *Cybersecurity Standardisation Conference* Brussels (Belgium) 2022, *Telecom Security Forum* Brussels (Belgium) 2022, *Annual Privacy Forum* Oslo (Norway) 2021, *Joint Workshop on 5G Cybersecurity Toolbox Developments and Way(s) Forward* Riga (Latvia) 2020. **Publications** Expert reports; studies; position papers. **IGO Relations** Audited by: *European Court of Auditors (#06854)*. **NGO Relations** Member of (2): *EU Agencies Network (EUAN, #05564)*; *European Energy Information Sharing and Analysis Centre (EE-ISAC, #06987)*. Part of Programme Board of: *Linear Collider Collaboration (LCC, #16481)*. [2021/XJ1550/**F***]

♦ European Union Agency for the Operational Management of Large-Scale IT Systems in the Area of Freedom, Security and Justice (eu-LISA) 08972

Exec Dir Vesilennuki 5, 10415 Tallinn, Estonia. E-mail: info@eulisa.europa.eu.
Operational Centre 18 rue de la Faisanderie, 67100 Strasbourg, France.
Main Website: https://www.eulisa.europa.eu/

History Established by Regulation (EU) No 1077/2011 of *European Parliament (EP, #08146)* and *Council of the European Union (#04895)*. Activities started 1 Dec 2012. Mandate expanded through Regulation (EU) 201/1726, in 2018. A decentralized agency of *European Union (EU, #08967)*. **Aims** Provide a long-term solution for the operational management of large-scale IT systems, which are essential instruments in the implementation of the asylum, border management and migration policies of the EU. **Structure** Management Board; Executive Director; Advisory Groups. Headquarters based in Tallinn (Estonia); operational centre in Strasbourg (France). **Languages** EU languages. **Staff** 274.00 FTE, paid. **Finance** Funded by: subsidy from general budget of *European Union (EU, #08967)*; contribution from countries associated with the implementation, application and development of the Schengen aquis and Eurodac-related measures; other financial contributions from Member States. Annual budget: 229,900,000 EUR (2021). **Activities** Knowledge management/information dissemination; monitoring/evaluation; research and development; training/education. **Events** *Joint Meeting* Brussels (Belgium) 2016. **Publications** None.
Members EU Member States (27):
Austria, Belgium, Bulgaria, Croatia, Cyprus, Czechia, Denmark, Estonia, Finland, France, Germany, Greece, Hungary, Ireland, Italy, Latvia, Lithuania, Luxembourg, Malta, Netherlands, Poland, Portugal, Romania, Slovakia, Slovenia, Spain, Sweden.
IGO Relations Partner of (5): *European Commission (EC, #06633)*; *European Council (#06801)*; *European Court of Auditors (#06854)*; European Data Protection Supervisor; *European Parliament (EP, #08146)*. Cooperates with (6): *Eurojust (#05698)*; *European Police Office (Europol, #08239)*; *European Union Agency for Asylum (EUAA, #08968)*; *European Union Agency for Fundamental Rights (FRA, #08969)*; *European Union Agency for Law Enforcement Training (CEPOL, #08970)*; *Frontex, the European Border and Coast Guard Agency (#10005)*. **NGO Relations** Member of (1): *EU Agencies Network (EUAN, #05564)*. [2021.03.01/XM4608/**E***]

♦ European Union Agency for Railways 08973

Exec Dir 120 rue Marc Lefrancq, BP 20392, 59300 Valenciennes, France. T. +33327096500. E-mail: helene.senechal@era.europa.eu.
URL: http://www.era.europa.eu/

History Established by Council resolution 881/2004 of *European Parliament (EP, #08146)*. Took over activities of *European Association for Railway Interoperability (AEIF, inactive)*. A decentralized agency of *European Union (EU, #08967)*. Restructured 15 Jun 2016, following Regulation 2016/796. Former names and other names: *European Railway Agency (ERA)* – former (2004 to 2016). **Aims** Issue single safety certificates and vehicle (type) authorisations valid in multiple European countries; ensure an interoperable European Rail Traffic Management System, in development and implementation of the Single European Railway Area. **Structure** Management Board; Executive Board; Management Team, including Executive Director. **Languages** English. **Staff** 200.00 FTE, paid. **Finance** On *European Union (EU, #08967)* budget. **Activities** Certification/accreditation; guidance/assistance/consulting; knowledge management/information dissemination; monitoring/evaluation; networking/liaising; standards/guidelines. **Events** *ERTMS Conference* Valenciennes (France) 2022, *Multimodal Freight Conference* Brussels (Belgium) 2018, *Leadership Forum* Amsterdam (Netherlands) 2017, *Single European Railway Area North Sea Regional Conference* Amsterdam (Netherlands) 2017, *Seminar on Safety Culture, Automation of Railway Tasks and ERTMS* Brussels (Belgium) 2017. **Publications** *ERA News*. **IGO Relations** Cooperates with (1): *Organisation intergouvernementale pour les transports internationaux ferroviaires (OTIF, #17807)*. **NGO Relations** Member of (2): *EU Agencies Network (EUAN, #05564)*; *European Telecommunications Standards Institute (ETSI, #08897)*. *FEDECRAIL – European Federation of Museum and Tourist Railways (#09284)* is member of Group of Representative Bodies (GRB). [2022.11.30/XM2732/**F***]

♦ European Union Agency for the Space Programme (EUSPA) 08974

Exec Dir Janovského 438/2, Holesovice, 170 00 Prague 7, Czechia. T. +420234766000. E-mail: com@euspa.europa.eu – news@euspa.europa.eu.
France Office GSMC, 8 av de Président Kennedy, 78102 Saint-Germain-en-Laye, France.
URL: http://www.euspa.europa.eu/

History 12 Jul 2004. Set up as a *European Community (inactive)* Agency, by *European Council (#06801)* Regulation (EC) 1321/2004. Status amended, 2006, by Council Regulation (EC) No 1942/2006. Successor to *GALILEO Joint Undertaking (GJU)*, set up May 2002; took over GJU tasks, 1 Jan 2007. Restructured into a decentralized agency of the *European Union (EU, #08967)* following Regulation (EU) No 912/2010 and Regulation (EU) No 512/2014. Former names and other names: *European GNSS Supervisory Authority (GSA)* – former; *European Global Navigation Satellite Systems Agency* – former; *European GNSS Agency* – former. **Aims** Manage all public interests related to, promote use of, and ensure security of European Space Programmes (EGNOS and Galileo); achieve a fully operational Galileo system and make it the world's leading *satellite navigation* system for civilian applications. **Structure** Administrative Board; Management Team; Security Accreditation Board; Executive Director; Departments (9). Manages: *European Geostationary Navigation Overlay Service (EGNOS)*; *Galileo Satellite Navigation Project*. **Languages** English. **Staff** 250.00 FTE, paid. **Events** *European Space Week Meeting* Prague (Czechia) 2022, *European Space Week Meeting* 2020, *Munich Satellite Navigation Summit* Munich (Germany) 2019, *European Space Week Meeting* Marseille (France) 2018, *Munich Satellite Navigation Summit* Munich (Germany) 2018.
Members Governments (28):
Austria, Belgium, Bulgaria, Croatia, Cyprus, Czechia, Denmark, Estonia, Finland, France, Germany, Greece, Hungary, Ireland, Italy, Latvia, Lithuania, Luxembourg, Malta, Netherlands, Poland, Portugal, Romania, Slovakia, Slovenia, Spain, Sweden, UK.
Regional entity:
European Commission (EC, #06633).
Observer member:
European Space Agency (ESA, #08798).
Non-voting government (1):
Norway.
Non-voting entity:
European Parliament (EP, #08146).
IGO Relations Partners: *European Commission (EC, #06633)* – DG Growth. Agreement with: *European Investment Bank (EIB, #07599)*; *EUROCONTROL (#05667)*. Cooperates with: *European Position Determination System (EUPOS, #08256)*. Audited by: *European Court of Auditors (#06854)*. **NGO Relations** Member of (1): *EU Agencies Network (EUAN, #05564)*. [2022.10.26/XM3145/**E***]

♦ European Union of Agrément (#20393)
♦ European Union of Alysh (unconfirmed)

♦ European Union of Aquarium Curators (EUAC) 08975

Registered Office Alcobendas, Calle del Helecho 4, 28109 Madrid, Spain. E-mail: info@euac.org.
URL: http://www.euac.org/

History 1972, Basel (Switzerland). Registration: Start date: 2000, Spain, Catalonia. **Aims** Promote professional improvement between specialists in the public aquarium field. **Structure** Executive Committee. **Languages** Dutch, English, French, German. **Staff** Voluntary. **Finance** Sources: members' dues. **Events** *Annual Conference* Boulogne-sur-Mer (France) 2019, *Annual Conference* Hull (UK) 2018, *Annual Conference* Genoa (Italy) 2014, *Annual Conference* Billund (Denmark) 2013, *Annual Conference* Cape Town (South Africa) 2012. **Publications** Proceedings; DVDs.
Members European aquarium curators in 24 countries:
Austria, Belgium, Denmark, Finland, France, Germany, Greece, Hungary, Ireland, Italy, Lithuania, Monaco, Netherlands, Norway, Poland, Portugal, Romania, Russia, Spain, Sweden, Switzerland, Türkiye, UK, Ukraine. [2022.02.21/XD9269/v/**D**]

♦ European Union of Arab and Islamic Studies / see European Union of Arabists and Islamicists (#08976)

♦ European Union of Arabists and Islamicists 08976

Union européenne des arabisants et islamisants (UEAI)

Deputy SG address not obtained.
Pres address not obtained.
URL: http://www.ueai.info/

History 1962, Córdoba (Spain). Founded on adoption of Constitution, following initial steps taken at 20th International Congress of Orientalists, 1960, Moscow (USSR). Former names and other names: *Congress of Arabic and Islamic Studies (CAIS)* – former; *European Union of Arab and Islamic Studies* – alias. **Aims** Facilitate meetings and exchange of ideas and information among Arabists and Islamicists. **Structure** Congress (every 2 years). Council, meeting every 2 years, consists of national representatives (who are also members of UEAI and have already taken part in at least 2 congresses), elects from its members the Executive Committee (meets every 2 years), comprising President, Vice-President, Secretary General, Deputy Secretary General and Treasurer. Sub-Committees. **Languages** English, French. **Staff** Voluntary. **Finance** Members' dues (annual): euro 20. **Events** *Congress* Granada (Spain) 2024, *Congress* Utrecht (Netherlands) 2022, *Congress* Münster (Germany) 2018, *Congress* Palermo (Italy) 2016, *Congress* Helsinki (Finland) 2014. **Publications** Congress proceedings.
Members Individuals: scholars holding the degree of doctor or similar appropriate status in 30 countries:
Austria, Belgium, Bulgaria, Canada, Denmark, Egypt, Finland, France, Germany, Hungary, Indonesia, Israel, Italy, Lebanon, Netherlands, Nigeria, North Macedonia, Norway, Poland, Portugal, Romania, Russia, Spain, Sweden, Switzerland, Tajikistan, Tunisia, Türkiye, UK, USA. [2022/XD0410/v/**D**]

♦ European Union of Artists (inactive)
♦ European Union Association (internationally oriented national body)
♦ European Union of Associations of Science Journalists / see European Union of Science Journalists' Associations (#09017)

♦ European Union of Associations of Translation Companies (EUATC) 08977

Contact Rue de la Presse 4, 1000 Brussels, Belgium. T. +3222291900. Fax +3222183141.
Pres BQTA, Bloemendallaan 54, 1853 Grimbergen, Belgium. E-mail: info@bqta.be.
URL: http://www.euatc.org/

History 1994, as an organization of the type *European Economic Interest Grouping (EEIG, #06960)*. **Events** *International Conference* Porto (Portugal) 2021, *International Conference* Porto (Portugal) 2020, *International Conference* Tallinn (Estonia) 2019, *International Conference* Madrid (Spain) 2018, *International Conference* Berlin (Germany) 2017. [2015/XM4626/**D**]

♦ European Union Aviation Safety Agency (EASA) 08978

Agence européenne de la sécurité aérienne – Agencia Europea de Seguridad Aérea – Europäische Agentur für Flugsicherheit – Agência Europeia para a Segurança da Aviação – Agenzia Europea per la Sicurezza Aerea – Europees Agentschap voor de Veiligheid van de Luchtvaart – Europeiska Byrån för Luftfartssäkerhet – Det Europaeske Luftfartssikkerhedsagentur – Euroopan Lentoturvallisuusvirasto – Evropska Agentura pro Bezpecnost Letectvi – Európska Agentúra pre Bezpecnost' Letectva – Európai Repülésbiztonsagi Ügynökség – Europejska Agencja Bezpiecsenstwa Lotniczego – Evropska Agencija za Varnost v Letalstvu – Euroopa Lennundusohutusamet – Eiropas Aviacijas Drosibas Agentura – Europos Aviacijos Saugos Agentura – L-Agenzija Ewropea tas-Sigurtà ta' l-Avjazzjoni

Head of Communication Dept Konrad-Adenauer-Ufer 3, 50668 Cologne, Germany. T. +49221899900000. Fax +492218999099. E-mail: communications@easa.europa.eu.
URL: http://www.easa.europa.eu/

History 15 Jul 2002. Established by Council and Parliament regulation (Regulation 1592/2002), repealed by Regulation 216/2008. Operational since 28 Sep 2003. Headquarters in Cologne (Germany) since 2004. Took over all responsiblities of *Joint Aviation Authorities (JAA)*, 19 Mar 2008. A decentralized agency of *European Union (EU, #08967)*. **Aims** Ensure the highest common level of safety protection for EU citizens; ensure the highest common level of environmental protection; maintain a single regulatory and certification process among Member States; facilitate the internal aviation single market and create a level playing field; work with other international aviation organizations and regulators. **Structure** EU Agency; Management Board; Advisory Board; Board of Appeal; Directorates (5); International Permanent Representations (4): Canada (Montréal QC); China (Beijing); Singapore (Singapore); USA (Washington DC). **Languages** Czech, Danish, Dutch, English, Estonian, Finnish, French, German, Hungarian, Irish Gaelic, Italian, Latvian, Lithuanian, Maltese, Polish, Portuguese, Slovakian, Slovene, Spanish, Swedish. **Staff** 800.00 FTE, paid. **Finance** EU Industry (64%); EU Budget (23%); third country contributions (2%), earmarked funds (11%). Annual budget: 161,000,000 EUR. **Activities** Certification/accreditation; events/meetings; guidance/assistance/consulting; networking/liaising; standards/guidelines. **Events** *International Aviation Safety Conference* Washington, DC (USA) 2022, *European Rotors Conference* Cologne (Germany) 2021, *European Rotors Safety Conference* Friedrichshafen (Germany) 2021, *International Aviation Safety Conference* Washington, DC (USA) 2021, *European Rotors Conference* Cologne (Germany) 2020. **Publications** *European Plan for Aviation Safety (EPAS)*. Annual Activity Report; Annual Safety Review; regulations; certification specifications; airworthiness directives; safety information bulleting; agreements; reviews; leaflets/safety promotion.

Members Governments of 31 countries:
Austria, Belgium, Bulgaria, Croatia, Cyprus, Czechia, Denmark, Estonia, Finland, France, Germany, Greece, Hungary, Iceland, Ireland, Italy, Latvia, Liechtenstein, Lithuania, Luxembourg, Malta, Netherlands, Norway, Poland, Portugal, Romania, Slovakia, Slovenia, Spain, Sweden, Switzerland.

IGO Relations Audited by: *European Court of Auditors (#06854)*; *International Civil Aviation Organization (ICAO, #12581)*. **NGO Relations** Member of (1): *EU Agencies Network (EUAN, #05564)*. [2022.02.15/XJ7382/**D***]

♦ European Union of Basketball Coaches' Associations (#20383)

♦ European Union for Bird Ringing (EURING) 08979

Gen Sec Ringing Centre, Finnish Museum of Natural History, PO Box 17, FI-00014 Helsinki, Finland. T. +358505820572. E-mail: enquiries@euring.org.
URL: http://www.euring.org/

History 1963. **Aims** Promote international collaboration on all aspects of scientific bird ringing, particularly in Europe and along the Eurasian African flyway. **Structure** General Assembly; Board; Committees (3). **Languages** English. **Staff** None. **Finance** Sources: donations; members' dues. **Activities** Research/documentation. **Events** *General Assembly* 2021, *Analytical Meeting* Québec, QC (Canada) 2021, *General Assembly* Zrenjanin (Serbia) 2019, *Analytical Meeting* Barcelona (Spain) 2017, *General Assembly* Copenhagen (Denmark) 2017. **Publications** *EDB Newsletter*, *EURING Newsletter*. **Information Services** *EURING Data Bank*.

Members Full in 38 countries:
Albania, Austria, Belarus, Belgium, Bulgaria, Croatia, Cyprus, Czechia, Denmark, Estonia, Finland, France, Germany, Greece, Hungary, Iceland, Ireland, Italy, Latvia, Lithuania, Malta, Montenegro, Netherlands, North Macedonia, Norway, Poland, Portugal, Romania, Russia, Serbia, Slovakia, Slovenia, Spain, Sweden, Switzerland, Türkiye, UK, Ukraine. [2022/XD6992/**D**]

♦ European Union for Blind Workers (inactive)
♦ European Union Center of Excellence / European Studies Center, Pittsburgh PA / see European Studies Center, Pittsburgh PA
♦ European Union Center of Excellence, Madison WI (internationally oriented national body)
♦ European Union Center, Madison WI / see European Union Center of Excellence, Madison WI

♦ European Union Choir 08980

Choeurs de l'Union européenne – Koor van de Europese Unie

Chairwoman Av de la Gazelle 63, 1180 Brussels, Belgium. T. +3223754929. E-mail: chantezavecnous.cue@gmail.com.
Musical Dir Rue Paul Hankar 25, 1180 Brussels, Belgium. T. +3223744067.
URL: http://eusing.eu/

History Oct 1958. Former names and other names: *European Communities Choir* – former; *Choeurs des Communautés européennes* – former; *Coros de las Comunidades Europeas* – former; *Chor der Europäischen Gemeinschaften* – former; *Coro das Comunidades Européias* – former; *Coro delle Comunità Europee* – former; *Koor van de Europese Gemeenschappen* – former; *Europaeiske Faellesskabers Kor* – former; *Horodia ton Evropaikon Kinotiton* – former; *Coros de la Unión Europea* – former; *Chor der Europäischen Union* – former; *Coro da União Europeia* – former; *Coro dell'Unione Europea* – former; *Europaeiske Unions Kor* – former; *Europeiska Unionens Kör* – former; *Euroopan Unionin Kuoro* – former; *Horodia tis Evropaikis Enosis* – former. Registration: Banque-Carrefour des Entreprises, Start date: 11 Sep 1961, Belgium. **Aims** Promote the construction of Europe through classical vocal *music*. **Structure** International Non-profit Organization **Languages** English, French. **Staff** 80.00 FTE, voluntary. **Finance** Sources: government support; members' dues; subsidies. Annual budget: 65,200 EUR (2018). **Activities** Events/meetings.

Members Membership covers all European Union countries and some countries outside of Europe. Members in 31 countries:
Austria, Belgium, Bulgaria, Cameroon, Croatia, Cyprus, Czechia, Denmark, Egypt, Estonia, Finland, France, Germany, Greece, Hungary, Ireland, Italy, Latvia, Lithuania, Luxembourg, Malta, Netherlands, Poland, Portugal, Romania, Slovakia, Slovenia, Spain, Sweden, UK, Uzbekistan. [2022.10.19/XF7939/**F**]

♦ European Union of Christian-Democratic and Conservative Students / see European Democrat Students (#06901)
♦ European Union of Christian Democratic Women / see EPP Women (#05516)

♦ European Union of Christian Democratic Workers (EUCDW) 08981

Union européenne des travailleurs démocrates-chrétiens (UETDC) – Europäische Union Christlich Demokratischer Arbeitnehmer (EUCDA) – Unione Europea dei Lavoratori Democratici Cristiani (UELDC) – Europese Unie van Christen Demokratische Werknemers (EUCDW)

SG c/o EPP, Rue du Commerce 10, 1000 Brussels, Belgium. T. +3222854164. Fax +3222854141. E-mail: eucdw@epp.eu.
Pres c/o European Parliament, Rue Wiertz ASP-10E132, 1047 Brussels, Belgium.
URL: http://www.eucdw.org/

History 1977. **Aims** Unite Christian *social workers* and press for the political unification of a democratic Europe based on common values and fundamental rights; promote the development of the EPP in form and content on the basis of Christian-social teaching; represent and defend worker interests within the EPP, the European institutions, especially the European Parliament, together with other social, political and trade union organizations on European level; work for the achievement of Christian-social principles and policies in the European workers' mouvements; step up cooperation with the workers and their organizations, particularly those, in Europe and elsewhere, with a Christian outlook; spread Christian-social ideas; promote the establishment of national and regional associations of Christian-social workers. **Structure** Officers: President; Vice-Presidents; Treasurer; Secretary-General. **Languages** English, French, German. **Finance** Members' dues. **Activities** Organizes: seminars; colloquia; meetings; working groups. **Events** *Congress* Zagreb (Croatia) 2019, *Congress* Vienna (Austria) 2018, *Congress* Bled (Slovenia) 2009, *For a Europe of social market economy* Vienna (Austria) 2005, *Congress* Brussels (Belgium) 2001.

Members Full trade unions, political and social organizations (23), in 13 countries:
Austria, Belgium, Germany, Greece, Italy, Luxembourg, Malta, Netherlands, Portugal, Romania, Slovenia, Spain, Switzerland.
Observers in 6 countries:
Belgium, Czechia, France, Ireland, Italy, Moldova.

NGO Relations Specialized organization of: *European People's Party (EPP, #08185)*. Member of: *Christian Democratic Workers International (CDWI, no recent information)*; *Robert Schuman Institute for Developing Democracy in Central and Eastern Europe (RSI, #18958)*. Special relations with: Workers Group of the *Group of the European People's Party – Christian Democrats (EPP, #10775)*. [2020/XD1966/**D**]

♦ European Union of Christian Democrats (inactive)
♦ European Union of Clinicians in Implant Dentistry (inactive)
♦ European Union Club of Advanced Engineering for Agriculture / see European Network of Engineering for Agriculture and Environment (#07901)
♦ European Union of Coachbuilders (inactive)
♦ European Union for Coastal Conservation / see Coastal and Marine Union – EUCC (#04072)
♦ European Union Conference (meeting series)
♦ European Union of Contractors of Plastering, Dry Lining, Stucco and Related Activities (inactive)

♦ European Union Control Association (EUCA) 08982

Sec Dept of Engineering Science, Univ of Oxford, Parks Road, Oxford, OX1 3PJ, UK. T. +441865273105. E-mail: emma.tegling@control.lth.se.
URL: https://euca-ecc.org/

History 1990. **Aims** Promote EU initiatives aiming at enhancing scientific exchange, disseminating information, coordinating research networks and technology transfer in the field of systems and control. **Structure** General Assembly; Council. **Languages** English. **Staff** None. **Finance** Budget (annual): about euro 15,000. **Activities** Events/meetings. **Events** *European Control Conference (ECC)* London (UK) 2022, *European Control Conference* Rotterdam (Netherlands) 2021, *European Control Conference* St Petersburg (Russia) 2020, *European Control Conference* Naples (Italy) 2019, *European Control Conference* Limassol (Cyprus) 2018. **Publications** *European Journal of Control* (4 a year). Vade Mecum.

Members Individuals in 28 countries:
Austria, Belgium, Croatia, Cyprus, Czechia, Denmark, Finland, France, Germany, Greece, Hungary, Ireland, Italy, Malta, Netherlands, Norway, Poland, Portugal, Romania, Russia, Serbia, Slovakia, Slovenia, Spain, Sweden, Switzerland, Türkiye, UK.

NGO Relations *Institute of Electrical and Electronics Engineers (IEEE, #11259)*; *International Federation of Automatic Control (IFAC, #13367)*. [2021/XD6176/v/**D**]

♦ European Union Cross Identity Network (EUxIN) 08983

Contact c/o Fondation Universitaire, Rue d'Egmont 11, 1000 Brussels, Belgium. T. +3225029901. Fax +3225029901.

History Registration: No/ID: 0475.575.459, Belgium. **Aims** Promote research, illustration, dissemination and defence of the European *culture*. **Structure** General Assembly (annual); Board of Directors. **Finance** Members' dues. Sponsored by: *European Commission (EC, #06633)*; *Europeans throughout the World (ETTW, #08839)*. **Events** *Seminar on science and cultural frontiers* Bologna (Italy) 2003, *Seminar on urban structures and European identity* Heidelberg (Germany) 2003, *Seminar on visions of Europe* Louvain-la-Neuve (Belgium) 2003, *Seminar on the university and the city* Montpellier (France) 2003, *Seminar on European cultural identity in the multicultural Europe* Salamanca (Spain) 2003. **NGO Relations** Affiliated with: *Coimbra Group (#04089)*. [2011.06.01/XF5903/**F**]

♦ European Union of Cycle Tourism (#20396)

♦ European Union Cyclists' Group (EUCG) 08984

Association des cyclistes de l'UE

Contact address not obtained. E-mail: helpdesk@eucg.eu.
URL: http://www.eucg.eu/

History Also referred to as *EU Cyclists' Group*. **Aims** Encourage the daily use of bicycles by all staff of the Institutions of the European Union in Brussels and promote their interests. **Structure** Committee of 21 members. [2015/XG9192/v/**E**]

♦ European Union of the Deaf (EUD) 08985

Exec Dir Rue de la Loi 26/15, 1000 Brussels, Belgium. T. +3222824600 – +3222824600. Fax +3222824609. E-mail: info@edf-feph.org.
URL: http://www.eud.eu/

History 1985. Founded on the initiative of the British Deaf Association. Inaugural meeting Sep 1986, London (UK). Continues to function as European Union secretariat of *World Federation of the Deaf (WFD, #21425)*. Former names and other names: *European Community Regional Secretariat of the World Federation of the Deaf (ECRS)* – former. Registration: Banque-Carrefour des Entreprises, No/ID: 0462.071.871, Start date: 18 May 1997, Belgium; EU Transparency Register, No/ID: 69368065472-71, Start date: 10 Mar 2011. **Aims** Promote, advance and protect the interests, needs and challenges of deaf people within the European Union; achieve an equal position in society for deaf people and their recognition as full citizens though application of equal opportunities. **Structure** General Assembly; Board; Executive Committee. Includes: *European Union of Deaf Youth (EUDY, #08986)*. **Languages** English, International Sign Language. **Staff** 1.50 FTE, paid. **Finance** Funded by: *European Commission (EC, #06633)*. **Activities** Events/meetings; training/education; research/documentation; advocacy/lobbying/activism. **Events** *General Assembly* Bucharest (Romania) 2019, *General Assembly* Vienna (Austria) 2018, *Joint Seminar* Vienna (Austria) 2018, *General Assembly* Valletta (Malta) 2017, *General Assembly* The Hague (Netherlands) 2016. **Publications** Reports; surveys; seminar and conference proceedings.

Members National associations of deaf people in 31 countries:
Austria, Belgium, Bulgaria, Croatia, Cyprus, Czechia, Denmark, Estonia, Finland, France, Germany, Greece, Hungary, Iceland, Ireland, Italy, Latvia, Lithuania, Luxembourg, Malta, Netherlands, Norway, Poland, Portugal, Romania, Serbia, Slovakia, Slovenia, Spain, Sweden, UK.
Affiliate in 3 countries:
Israel, North Macedonia, Serbia.

Consultative Status Consultative status granted from: *Council of Europe (CE, #04881)* (Participatory Status); *ECOSOC (#05331)* (Special). **NGO Relations** Member of (1): *European Disability Forum (EDF, #06929)*. Partner of (5): *European Deafblind Network (EDbN, #06890)*; *European Federation of Hard of Hearing People (EFHOH, #07136)*; *European Forum of Sign Language Interpreters (efsli, #07334)*; *European Society for Mental Health and Deafness (ESMHD, #08649)*; *World Federation of the Deaf (WFD, #21425)*. [2021/XD4984/**D**]

♦ European Union of Deaf Youth (EUDY) 08986

Contact Rue de la Loi 26/15, 1040 Brussels, Belgium. E-mail: info@eudy.info.
URL: http://www.eudy.info/

History Dissolved 1992, and later became Youth Section of European Community Regional Secretariat of the World Federation of the Deaf (ECRS). Became a Youth Commission of *European Union of the Deaf (EUD, #08985)*, 1995, at conference in Helsinki (Finland). Former names and other names: *EuroAction* – former (1984 to 1987); *European Youth Deaf Council (EYDC)* – former (1987 to 1992); *Conseil euro-jeunes sourds* – former (1987 to 1992); *Youth Section of European Community Regional Secretariat of the World Federation of the Deaf (ECRS)* – former; *Youth Commission of ECRS (YC-ECRS)* – former (1993 to 1995); *EUD Youth Commission* – former (1995 to 1996); *EUYD* – former (1996 to 2002). Registration: EU Transparency Register, No/ID: 599841812260-74. **Aims** Improve cooperation and social life between European deaf youth; provide non-formal education for deaf youth. **Structure** General Assembly; Board. **Languages** English, International Sign Language. **Staff** 2.00 FTE, paid. **Finance** Board activities financed by respective member's association. **Activities** Events/meetings. **Events** *General Assembly* Ghent (Belgium) 2019, *General Assembly* Berlin (Germany) 2013, *General Assembly* Madrid (Spain) 2011, *General Assembly* Lausanne (Switzerland) 2010, *General Assembly* Amsterdam (Netherlands) 2009. **Publications** *EUDY Newsletter* (12 a year); *EUDY OFC! Magazine* (annual).

Members Full; Associate; Honorary. Associations in 28 countries:
Albania, Austria, Belgium, Bosnia-Herzegovina, Bulgaria, Czechia, Denmark, Estonia, Finland, France, Germany, Iceland, Ireland, Italy, Kosovo, Latvia, Lithuania, Netherlands, Norway, Portugal, Romania, Serbia, Slovakia, Spain, Sweden, Switzerland, Türkiye, UK.

Consultative Status Consultative status granted from: *Council of Europe (CE, #04881)* (Participatory Status). **NGO Relations** Member of (1): *European Youth Forum (#09140)*. Cooperates with a number of youth organizations and disability organizations, including *European Disability Forum (EDF, #06929)* and *European Deaf Students' Union (EDSU, #06893)*, and with deaf associations and youth sections in Europe and the European Union of the Deaf (EUD). [2017.03.21/XF2372/**E**]

- ♦ European Union of Dentists (inactive)
- ♦ European Union of Developers and House Builders / see Build Europe (#03350)
- ♦ European Union for Dune Conservation and Coastal Management / see Coastal and Marine Union – EUCC (#04072)
- ♦ European Union of Elderly Christian Democrats / see European Seniors' Union (#08466)

♦ European Union of Electrical Wholesalers (EUEW) 08987

Union européenne des grossistes en matériel électrique – Union Europäischer Elektro-Grosshändler

Main Office 17 rue de l'Amiral Hamelin, 75783 Paris CEDEX 16, France. E-mail: info@euew.org.
Gen Sec Grensstraat 7, 1831 Diegem, Belgium. T. +3226600501. Fax +3226603821.
URL: http://www.euew.org/

History 1955, Paris (France). Registration: EU Transparency Register, No/ID: 252567334220-94; Start date: 6 Dec 1956, France. **Aims** Represent the distribution channel of electrical products for domestic and industrial equipment, lamps, lighting fittings, electric cables, household appliances and electronics. **Structure** General Assembly; Board of Director; General Secretary; Secretariat in Zaventem (Belgium). **Languages** English, French, German. **Finance** Members' dues. **Events** *Annual General Assembly* Barcelona (Spain) 2021, *Annual General Assembly* Barcelona (Spain) 2021, *Annual General Assembly* Barcelona (Spain) 2020, *Annual General Assembly* Brussels (Belgium) 2019, *Annual General Assembly* Bonn (Germany) 2018. **Publications** *Vademecum*. Statistics (annual).

Members National federations representing over 1,000 wholesalers in 15 countries:
Belgium, Denmark, Finland, France, Germany, Hungary, Italy, Netherlands, Norway, Poland, Portugal, Spain, Sweden, Switzerland, UK.

NGO Relations Affiliate member of: *EuroCommerce (EC, #05665)*. [2021/XD1205/**D**]

- ♦ European Union Employers' Network / see The Federation of International Employers (#09644)
- ♦ European Union of Environmental Journalists (no recent information)
- ♦ European Union of Ethanol Producers (inactive)

♦ European Union Federation of Youth Hostel Associations (EUFED) .. 08988

Fédération des auberges de jeunesse de l'Union européenne

Pres Place des Martyrs 10, 1000 Brussels, Belgium. T. +3225028066. Fax +3225025578. E-mail: info@eufed.org.
URL: http://www.eufed.org/

History 19 May 1987. Replaces *Standing Consultative Committee of Youth Hostel Associations within the EEC (inactive)*. Former names and other names: *European Community Federation of Youth Hostel Associations (ECFED)* – former; *Fédération des auberges de jeunesse des Communautés européennes* – former; *Federation of European Youth Hostels in the EC* – alias; *European Federation of Youth Hostel Assoications* – alias. Registration: No/ID: 0866.881.575, Start date: 23 Aug 2004, Belgium; EU Transparency Register, No/ID: 461803612062-11, Start date: 10 Oct 2013. **Aims** Represent the views of youth hostels at European political level; promote education, intercultural change, mutual understanding and dialogue between young people. **Structure** General Assembly; Executive Committee; Youth Committee; Secretariat, based in Brussels (Belgium). **Languages** English, French, German. **Staff** No paid staff. **Finance** Members' dues. Some funding. **Activities** Networking/liaising; projects/programmes. **Events** *General Assembly* Rouen (France) 2011, *General Assembly* Manchester (UK) 2010, *General Assembly* Düsseldorf (Germany) 2009, *General Assembly* Namur (Belgium) 2008, *General Assembly* Zurich (Switzerland) 2007. **Publications** *EUFED E-bulletin*. Annual Report; surveys; press releases; leaflets.

Members Associations (17) in 14 countries:
Austria, Belgium, Croatia, France, Germany, Hungary, Israel, North Macedonia, Poland, Romania, Serbia, Slovenia, Spain, UK.

NGO Relations Member of (3): *European Tourism Manifesto (#08921)*; *European Travel and Tourism Advisory Group (ETAG, #08946)*; *Spring Alliance (inactive)*. Close cooperation with: *Hostelling International (#10950)*. In liaison with technical committees of: *Comité européen de normalisation (CEN, #04162)*. Supports: *European Citizens' Initiative Campaign (ECI Campaign, #06558)*. [2019/XE1111/**E**]

- ♦ European Union of Film and Television Technicians (inactive)

♦ European Union Fish Processors Association 08989

Association des industries du poisson de l'Union Européenne (AIPCE) – Vereinigung der Fischindustrie in der Europäischen Union – Associazione delle Industrie Conserviere Ittiche della Commissione Europea – Verbond van Organisaties uit de Europese Unie op het Gebied van het Verduurzamen van Vis

Gen Secretariat c/o Kellen, Av de Tervuren 188A, Box 4, 1150 Brussels, Belgium. T. +3227611649. Fax +3227611699. E-mail: aipce@kellencompany.com.
URL: http://www.aipce-cep.org/

History 9 Apr 1959. New Statutes adopted: 21 Feb 1964, Brussels (Belgium); Apr 2019, Brussels (Belgium). Former names and other names: *EEC Fish Processors Association* – former; *Association des industries du poisson de la CEE* – former; *Vereinigung der Fischindustrie in der EWG* – former; *Vereinigung der Fischindustrie in der Europäischen Gemeinschaft* – former; *Associazione delle Industrie Conserviere Ittiche della CEE* – former; *Verbond van Organisaties uit de EEG-Landen op het Gebied van het Verduurzamen van Vis* – former. **Aims** Study problems raised by EU Treaties in the field; coordinate actions of national federations of fish industries; ensure a link with official institutions of EU. **Structure** General Assembly (annual); Board of Directors; Working Groups. **Languages** English, French. **Staff** 1.50 FTE, paid. **Finance** Sources: members' dues. **Activities** Events/meetings. **Events** *International Conference* Utrecht (Netherlands) 2022, *General Assembly* Brussels (Belgium) 2020, *General Assembly* Bergen (Norway) 2015, *General Assembly* Bruges (Belgium) 1987.

Members National organizations in 15 countries:
Belgium, Denmark, Finland, France, Germany, Ireland, Italy, Morocco, Netherlands, Norway, Poland, Portugal, Spain, Sweden, UK.

IGO Relations Observer status with (1): *Codex Alimentarius Commission (CAC, #04081)*. **NGO Relations** Observer status with (1): *European Salmon Smokers Association (ESSA, #08424)*. Member of (8): Aquaculture Advisory Council; *Baltic Sea Advisory Council (BSAC, #03139)*; *Long Distance Advisory Council (LDAC, #16511)*; *Market Advisory Council (MAC, #16584)*; *Mediterranean Advisory Council (MEDAC, #16639)*; *North Western Waters Advisory Council (NWWAC, #17607)*; *Pelagic Advisory Council (Pelagic AC, #18289)*; South Advisory Council (CCS). Shares secretariat with: *Comité des organisations nationales des importateurs et exportateurs de poisson de l'UE (CEP, #04194)*. [2020.11.18/XE0131/t/**E**]

♦ European Union Force in Bosnia and Herzegovina (EUFOR) 08990

Commander Camp Butmir, 71000 Sarajevo, Bosnia-Herzegovina. T. +38733495214. E-mail: elma.robovic@eufor.europa.eu.
URL: http://www.euforbih.org/

History Established 2 Dec 2004, by *European Union (EU, #08967)*, following a decision at Summit of *NATO (#16945)*, Jun 2004, Istanbul (Turkey), to complete the mission of *NATO-led Stabilization Force in Bosnia and Herzegovina (SFOR, inactive)*. Mandate is being reviewed every 6 months. Part of a wider European Security and Defence Policy (ESDP) mission. **Aims** Conduct the EU-led operation in Bosnia-Herzegovina, under the political control and strategic direction of the EU Political and Security Committee (PSC), under the authority of the EU Council, and in line with its mandate, in order to monitor and ensure continued compliance with the responsibility to fulfil the role specified in Annexes 1A and 2 of the General Framework Agreement for Peace (Dayton Agreement) and contribute to the safe and secure environment required to support the core tasks of other EU and international organizations. Main objectives of EUFOR Operation Althea are: support Bosnia-Herzegovina efforts to maintain a safe and secure environment; provide support to the overall EU comprehensive approach in Bosnia-Herzegovina; provide support for combined and collective training and exercises for the Armed Forces of Bosnia-Herzegovina (AFBiH); provide support for AFBiH demining and weapon/ammunition management and disposal. **Structure** Basic decisions taken by *Council of the European Union (#04895)*. EU *Political and Security Committee (PSC)* exercises political and strategic direction of the operation. *EU Military Committee (EUMC)* – within *European External Action Service (EEAS, #07018)* – monitors proper execution. Initial deployment: just over 6,000 troops. As of Sep 2017, 600 troops. **Languages** English. **Staff** 600 military staff from 20 troop contributing countries (15 EEU, 5 non-EU). **Finance** Financed by EU member and troop contributing states. **Activities** Training/education; guidance/assistance/consulting; events/meetings.

Members EU contributing countries (15):
Austria, Bulgaria, Czechia, France, Greece, Hungary, Ireland, Italy, Poland, Portugal, Romania, Slovakia, Slovenia, Spain, UK.
Non-EU contributing countries (5):
Albania, Chile, North Macedonia, Switzerland, Türkiye.

IGO Relations Cooperates with: *European Union Monitoring Commission (EUMM, inactive)*; *Organization for Security and Cooperation in Europe (OSCE, #17887)*. [2022/XJ3881/**F***]

♦ European Union Foreign Affairs Spouses' Associations (EUFASA) .. 08991

Contact address not obtained. E-mail: info@eufasa.org.
URL: http://www.eufasa.org/

History Established following a series of meetings by diplomat spouses' associations within the European Community. Former names and other names: *European Community Foreign Affairs Spouses' Association (ECFASA)* – former (1985 to 1994). **Activities** Events/meetings. **Events** *Annual EUFASA Conference* Madrid (Spain) 2023, *Annual EUFASA Conference* Paris (France) 2022, *Annual EUFASA Conference* Lisbon (Portugal) 2021, *Annual Conference* Berlin (Germany) 2020, *Annual Conference* London (UK) 2019. **Publications** *EUFASA Newsletter*.

Members National organizations in 19 countries:
Austria, Belgium, Czechia, Estonia, Finland, France, Germany, Iceland, Ireland, Italy, Latvia, Lithuania, Luxembourg, Netherlands, Portugal, Slovenia, Spain, Sweden, UK.
Included in the above, 1 organization listed in this Yearbook:
Organization of Spouses of the European Commission (ACSEC).
Observers in 1 country:
Iceland. [2022.06.16/XF6723/c/**F**]

♦ European Union of Former Pupils of Catholic Education 08992

Union européenne des anciens et anciennes élèves de l'enseignement catholique (UNAEC-Europe) – Unión Europea de Antiguos Alumnos y Antiguas Alumnas de la Enseñanza Católica

Contact c/o COFAEC, 48 rue de Richelieu, 75001 Paris, France. T. +33142608903. E-mail: contact@cofaec.fr – secretary@unaec-europe.eu.
URL: https://www.unaec-europe.eu/

History 7 Dec 1980, Rome (Italy). Statutes entered into force 31 May 1984. Registration: Banque-Carrefour des Entreprises, Start date: 27 Jul 1982, Belgium. **Aims** Promote union between all groups, associations and federations of European Catholic past pupils. **Structure** General Assembly (annual); Direction Committee; Executive Board. A continental confederation of *Organisation mondiale des anciens élèves de l'enseignement catholique (OMAEC, #17816)*. **Languages** English, French, Spanish. **Staff** Voluntary. **Events** *General assembly and congress / General Assembly* Strasbourg (France) 2010, *General Assembly* Rome (Italy) 2007, *General Assembly* Strasbourg (France) 2004, *General Assembly* Paris (France) 2001, *General assembly and congress* 1998.

Members National organizations (15) in 6 countries:
France, Italy, Malta, Portugal, Spain, Türkiye.
European Federation of Jesuit Alumni.
Individuals in 9 countries:
Austria, Belgium, Czechia, Germany, Greece, Ireland, Netherlands, Poland, Switzerland.

Consultative Status Consultative status granted from: *Council of Europe (CE, #04881)* (Participatory Status). **NGO Relations** Associate member of: *Comité Européen pour l'Enseignement Catholique (CEEC, #04156)*. [2022/XD1477/**D**]

- ♦ European Union Forum of Judges for the Environment (unconfirmed)
- ♦ European Union of the Fruit and Vegetable Wholesale, Import and Export Trade (inactive)
- ♦ European Union of General Practitioners / see European Union of General Practitioners / Family Physicians (#08993)

♦ European Union of General Practitioners / Family Physicians 08993

Union européenne des médecins omnipraticiens / médecins de famille (UEMO)

Pres c/o RCP, Pictor Alexandru Romano Street 14, 023965 Bucharest, Romania. E-mail: secretariat@uemo.eu.
Policy Officer Rue de Deux Eglises 39, 1000 Brussels, Belgium.
URL: http://www.uemo.eu/

History 1967, Paris (France). Established by the national medical associations of 5 countries. Former names and other names: *European Union of General Practitioners* – former (1967 to 2009); *Union européenne des médecins omnipraticiens (UEMO)* – former (1967 to 2009); *Europäische Vereinigung der Allgemeinärzte* – former (1967 to 2009); *Unión Europea de Médicos Generalistas* – former (1967 to 2009); *Unione Europea dei Medici Generali* – former (1967 to 2009); *União Europêia de Clinicos Gerais* – former (1967 to 2009); *Europese Huisartsen Vereniging* – former (1967 to 2009); *Alment Praktiserende Laegers Europaeiske Organisation* – former (1967 to 2009). Registration: Banque-Carrefour des Entreprises, No/ID: 0810.431.535, Start date: 16 Mar 2009, Belgium; EU Transparency Register, No/ID: 447230420481-06, Start date: 29 Jan 2016. **Aims** Promote general practice and the defence of professional freedom in the best interests of patients. **Structure** General Assembly (twice a year). Presidency and Secretariat provided by a national association member (4-year term). **Languages** English, French, German, Italian, Spanish. **Staff** provided by host organization. **Finance** Sources: members' dues. **Activities** Events/meetings; monitoring/evaluation. **Events** *Spring General Assembly* Brussels (Belgium) 2022, *Fall General Assembly* Ljubljana (Slovenia) 2022, *Spring General Assembly* Bucharest (Romania) 2021, *Fall General Assembly* Ljubljana (Slovenia) 2021, *Fall General Assembly* Ljubljana (Slovenia) 2020. **Publications** *UEMO – 40 Years of Experience looking forward into the Future* (2007); *Criteria for General Practitioner Trainers* (1993); *The Future of General Practice in Europe* (1992); *Cancer Training for General Practitioners*; *Declaration on Medical Secrecy and the Use of Modern Communication Technologies (EDP) in Medicine*. Reports on such topics as: quality assessment, continuing medical education, preventive medicine, contents and role of general medicine; access requirements to medical practice in social security systems within the European Union countries; conference proceedings; policy statement.

Members National organizations in 25 countries:
Austria, Belgium, Bulgaria, Czechia, Denmark, Finland, Germany, Hungary, Iceland, Ireland, Italy, Lithuania, Luxembourg, Malta, Netherlands, Norway, Portugal, Serbia, Slovakia, Slovenia, Spain, Sweden, Switzerland, Türkiye, UK.

IGO Relations Recognized by: *European Commission (EC, #06633)*. **NGO Relations** Member of (1): *European Forum for Primary Care (EFPC, #07326)*. Approaches European authorities through the intermediary of: *Standing Committee of European Doctors (#19955)*. [2022.12.09/XD0890/**D**]

- ♦ European Union of Geosciences (inactive)
- ♦ European Union Geriatric Medicine Society / see European Geriatric Medicine Society (#07392)
- ♦ European Union for Grain, Oilseed and Fodder Trades and Derivatives / see Committee of the Trade in Cereals, Oilseeds, Pulses, Olive Oil, Oils and Fats, Animal Feed and Agrosupply of the EU (#04289)
- ♦ European Union Group of Institutes of Navigation / see European Group of the Institutes of Navigation (#07424)
- ♦ European Union of Gymnastics / see European Gymnastics (#07442)
- ♦ European Union of Hatters' Fur Manufacturers (inactive)
- ♦ European Union of Health Food Stores (no recent information)
- ♦ European Union of Hide and Skin Merchants (no recent information)
- ♦ European Union for the Hop Trade (inactive)
- ♦ European Union of Importers, Exporters and Dealers in Dairy Products / see European Association of Dairy Trade (#06003)
- ♦ European Union of Independent Home-Builders / see Build Europe (#03350)
- ♦ European Union of Independent Hospitals / see Union européenne de l'hospitalisation privée (#20397)

♦ European Union of Independent Lubricant Companies / see Union Européenne de l'Industrie des Lubrifiants (#20398)

♦ European Union Institute for Security Studies (EUISS) 08994

Institut d'études de sécurité de l'Union européenne

Dir 100 av de Suffren, 75015 Paris, France. T. +33156891930. Fax +33156891931.
Brussels Office Justus Lipsius Bldg, Rue de la Loi 175, 00-FG-14, 1048 Brussels, Belgium.
URL: http://www.iss.europa.eu/

History Jan 2002. Established as an autonomous agency under the Common Foreign and Security Policy (CFSP) Council Joint Action 2001/554 of *European Union (EU, #08967)*. Now regulated by Council Decision 2014/75/CFSP. Now an integral part of the new structures that underpin further development of the CFSP/CSDP. Transformed from *Western European Union (WEU, inactive)* project with title *WEU Institute for Security Studies – Institut d'études de sécurité de l'UEO*, set up 13 Nov 1989, Paris (France) and commenced operations 1 Jul 1990. **Aims** Provide analyses and fora for discussion that can be of use and relevance to the formulation of EU policy; act as an interface between European experts and decision-makers at all levels. **Structure** Board, chaired by the High Representative of the Union for Foreign Affairs and Security Policy (HR); Political and Security Committee (PSC). **Languages** English. **Staff** 25-35 FTE. **Finance** Funded by EU member states according to a GNI-based formula. Budget (annual): about euro 4 million. **Activities** Research/documentation; politics/policy/regulatory; events/meetings. **Events** *EU-Singapore Dialogue Meeting* Singapore (Singapore) 2019, *India-European Union forum on effective multilateralism* Delhi (India) 2009, *Annual EU-Washington forum* Washington, DC (USA) 2009. **Publications** *EUISS Newsletter*; *Issue Alerts*; *Issue Briefs*; *Yearbook (YES)*. *Chaillot Papers* – series. Reports.

Members EU member states (27):
Austria, Belgium, Bulgaria, Croatia, Cyprus, Czechia, Denmark, Estonia, Finland, France, Germany, Greece, Hungary, Ireland, Italy, Latvia, Lithuania, Luxembourg, Malta, Netherlands, Poland, Portugal, Romania, Slovakia, Slovenia, Spain, Sweden.

NGO Relations Member of (3): *Council for Security Cooperation in the Asia Pacific (CSCAP, #04919)*; *EU Agencies Network (EUAN, #05564)*; *Euro-Mediterranean Study Commission (EuroMeSCo, #05727)* (Observer). [2021/XE1617/j/**E***]

♦ European Union of Insurance and Social Security Medicine (EUMASS) 08995

Union européenne de médecine d'assurance et de sécurité sociale (UEMASS) – Europäische Union der Sozialen Sicherung und Versicherungsmedizin

Secretariat Rue Guimard 15, 1040 Brussels, Belgium. T. +3216337085. E-mail: secretariateumass@gmail.com.
URL: https://www.eumass.eu/

History Sep 1974, Brussels (Belgium). Registration: Banque-Carrefour des Entreprises, No/ID: 0770.712.708, Start date: 5 Jul 2021, Belgium. **Aims** Promote cooperation and exchange of information between countries to advance progress of social security medicine in Europe. **Structure** General Assembly; Executive Board; Scientific Committee. **Languages** English, French. **Staff** Voluntary. **Finance** Sources: members' dues. **Events** *Biennal Congress* Strasbourg (France) 2023, *Biennial Congress* Basel (Switzerland) 2021, *Biennial Congress* Basel (Switzerland) 2020, *Biennial Congress* Maastricht (Netherlands) 2018, *Biennial Congress* Ljubljana (Slovenia) 2016. **Publications** Congress and symposium proceedings.

Members Full in 23 countries:
Austria, Belgium, Bosnia-Herzegovina, Croatia, Czechia, Estonia, Finland, France, Germany, Greece, Iceland, Italy, Netherlands, Norway, Poland, Portugal, Romania, Serbia, Slovakia, Slovenia, Sweden, Switzerland, UK.

NGO Relations Member of (2): *Federation of European and International Associations Established in Belgium (FAIB, #09508)*; *Standing Committee of European Doctors (#19955)*. [2022/XD5950/**D**]

♦ European Union Intellectual Property Office (EUIPO) 08996

Office de l'Union Européenne pour la Propriété Intellectuelle – Amt der Europäischen Union für Geistiges Eigentum – Oficina de Propiedad Intelectual de la Unión Europea – Ufficio dell'Unione Europea per la Proprietà Intellettuale – Bureau voor Intellectuele Eigendom van de Europese Unie

Exec Dir Avda de Europa 4, 03008 Alicante, Castellón, Spain. T. +34965139100. Fax +34965131344. E-mail: information@euipo.europa.eu – userassociations@euipo.europa.eu.
URL: http://euipo.europa.eu/

History 14 Mar 1994. Established on coming into effect of a regulation adopted by *Council of the European Union (#04895)*, 20 Dec 1993. Activities commenced 1 Sep 1994. Applications accepted from 1 Jan 1996; registration procedure commenced 1 Apr 1996. Located in Alicante (Spain). A decentralized agency of *European Union (EU, #08967)* within the framework of *Treaty on European Union (Maastricht Treaty, 1992)*. The European Observatory on Infringements of Intellectual Property Rights (formerly European Observatory on Counterfeiting and Piracy) was transferred to the Office according to the Regulation (EU) No 386/2012 of the European Parliament and of the Council of 19 April 2012, which came into force on 5 Jun 2012. Former names and other names: *Office for Harmonization in the Internal Market – Trade Marks and Designs (OHIM)* – former; *Office de l'harmonisation dans le marché intérieur – marques, dessins et modèles (OHMI)* – former; *Oficina de Armonización del Mercado Interior – Marcas, Dibujos y Modelos (OAMI)* – former; *Harmonisierungsamt für den Binnenmarkt – Marken, Muster und Modelle (HABM)* – former; *Ufficio per l'Armonizzazione nel Mercato Interno – Marchi, Disegni e Modelli (UAMI)* – former. **Aims** Register Community trademarks and designs, providing a uniform protection throughout the *European Union* through filing of a single application; develop a comprehensive European Trade Mark and Design Network; protect and enforce *intellectual property rights*; help combat the threat of IP infringements that jeopardize the EU position as a world leader in the areas of creativity and innovation and the health and safety of EU consumers. **Structure** Management Board; Budget Committee. Observer organizations in governance: *Benelux Organization for Intellectual Property (BOIP, #03203)*; *BUSINESSEUROPE (#03381)*; *European Brands Association (#06397)*; *ECTA (#05341)*; *European Patent Office (EPO, #08166)*; *International Trademark Association (INTA, #15706)*; *MARQUES (#16588)*; *World Intellectual Property Organization (WIPO, #21593)*. Additional observer seats rotating between members of Users' Group. Boards of Appeal. **Languages** English, French, German, Italian, Spanish. **Staff** 800.00 FTE, paid. **Finance** Fees paid by applicants. Budget (2010): euro 179 million. **Activities** Acts as official trade marks and designs registration office of the European Union. The Community trade mark (CTM) and registered Community design (RCD) serve as gateway to the European Single Market. A Community trade mark is valid for 10 years and is renewable; a Community design is valid for 5 years and is renewable up to 25 years at most. **Events** *ASEAN-EUIPO Heads Meeting (ARISE plus IPR)* Alicante (Spain) 2018, *ID5 Annual Meeting* Seoul (Korea Rep) 2018, *TM5 Annual Meeting* Seoul (Korea Rep) 2018, *Seminar on IP in the Innovation Ecosystem, Key Players and Success Factors* Singapore (Singapore) 2018, *International IP Enforcement Summit* Berlin (Germany) 2017. **Publications** *Official Journal of EUIPO* (12 a year) in English, French, German, Italian, Spanish; *Alicante News*; *Community Designs Bulletin* – online in the 20 EU languages; *Community Trade Marks Bulletin* – online. Annual Report. Information Services: Legal documentation service. Provides online electronic filing and communication as well as online business-to-business solution whereby clients can send their Community trade mark and Community design applications directly from their own back-office systems to EUIPO. **Information Services** *CTM-AGENT* – database; *CTM-DOWNLOAD* – database; *CTM-ONLINE* – database; *RCD-ONLINE* – database.

Members Governments of the 27 EU member countries:
Austria, Belgium, Bulgaria, Croatia, Cyprus, Czechia, Denmark, Estonia, Finland, France, Germany, Greece, Hungary, Ireland, Italy, Latvia, Lithuania, Luxembourg, Malta, Netherlands, Poland, Portugal, Romania, Slovakia, Slovenia, Spain, Sweden.

IGO Relations Maintains constant relations with the European Commission and the national IP offices of EU member states. Reports to: *European Court of Auditors (#06854)*. Partners with: *European Patent Office (EPO, #08166)*; *World Intellectual Property Organization (WIPO, #21593)*.
NGO Relations Member of (2): *EU Agencies Network (EUAN, #05564)*; *International Council of Design (ICoD, #13013)*.
Multilateral cooperation with other IP offices through *European Trade mark and Design Network*. Partners with user and sectorial organizations in the Users' Group include:
- *Association des Praticiens du Droit des Marques et des Modèles (APRAM)*;
- *Benelux Association for Trademark and Design Law (#03199)*;
- *Bureau of European Design Associations (BEDA, #03359)*;
- *BUSINESSEUROPE (#03381)*;
- *Committee of National Institutes of Patent Agents (CNIPA, #04274)*;
- *Conseil européen de l'industrie chimique (CEFIC, #04687)*;
- *ECTA (#05341)*;
- *EURATEX – The European Apparel and Textile Confederation (EURATEX, #05616)*;
- *European Brands Association (#06397)*;
- *European Federation of Agents of Industry in Industrial Property (#07042)*;
- *European Federation of Pharmaceutical Industries and Associations (EFPIA, #07191)*;
- *Fédération Internationale des Conseils en Propriété Intellectuelle (FICPI, #09624)*;
- ico-D;
- *International Association for the Protection of Intellectual Property (#12112)*;
- *International Chamber of Commerce (ICC, #12534)*;
- *International Trademark Association (INTA, #15706)*;
- *MARQUES (#16588)*;
- *Union of European Practitioners in Intellectual Property (UNION, #20392)*;
- *World Design Organization (WDO, #21358)*.

[2022/XE2565/**E***]

♦ European Union of Jewish Students (EUJS) 08997

Union Européenne des Etudiants Juifs (UEEJ)

Pres address not obtained.
URL: http://www.eujs.org/

History 1978, Grenoble (France). Founded as a Continental Union of *World Union of Jewish Students (WUJS, #21878)*. Former names and other names: *Europäische Union Jüdischer Studenten* – former. Registration: EU Transparency Register, No/ID: 683799510920-11. **Aims** Strengthen Jewish communities and European society through Jewish student activism and advocacy. **Structure** Congress (every 2 years); Executive; Praesidium; Secretariat. **Languages** English, French. **Staff** 5.50 FTE, paid; 5.00 FTE, voluntary. **Finance** Sources: donations; revenue from activities/projects. Annual budget: 500,000 USD. **Activities** Events/meetings; training/education. **Events** *Annual Congress* Jerusalem (Israel) 2013, *Annual Congress* Jerusalem (Israel) 2012, *Youth seminar* Basel (Switzerland) 1998, *Annual congress / Annual Meeting* Leicester (UK) 1998, *International seminar on racism and xenophobia* Greece 1997. **Publications** *Campus News* (12 a year); *EUJS Magazine* (6 a year).

Members Associations in 31 countries and territories:
Austria, Belarus, Belgium, Bulgaria, Croatia, Czechia, Denmark, Estonia, Finland, France, Germany, Greece, Hungary, Italy, Latvia, Lithuania, Luxembourg, Netherlands, North Macedonia, Norway, Poland, Romania, Russia, Serbia, Slovakia, Spain, Sweden, Switzerland, Türkiye, UK, Ukraine.

Consultative Status Consultative status granted from: *ECOSOC (#05331)* (Special); *Council of Europe (CE, #04881)* (Participatory Status). **NGO Relations** Member of: *UNITED for Intercultural Action – European Network Against Nationalism, Racism, Fascism and in Support of Migrants and Refugees (UNITED, #20511)*; *European Youth Forum (#09140)*. Associate member of: *European Council of Jewish Communities (ECJC, #06825)*; *European Students' Union (ESU, #08848)*. [2020.06.24/XD6014/**D**]

♦ European Union of Judges in Commercial Matters (EUJC) 08998

Union européenne des magistrats statuant en matière commerciale (UEMC) – Europäische Union der Richter in Handelssachen (EURH) – Europese Unie der Rechters in Handelszaken (EURH)

Pres UEMC, Palais de Justice, Quai Finkmatt, 67000 Strasbourg, France.
Hon Pres Gorskistrasse 16, 1230 Vienna, Austria. T. +431616030327.
Hon Pres 38 route de Bischwiller, 67800 Bischheim, France. T. +33388610601.
URL: http://www.eujc.eu/

History 9 Jun 1989, Strasbourg (France). Founded when by-laws were adopted. Registration: EU Transparency Register, No/ID: 47490029357-81. **Aims** Establish/strengthen links among members; provide them with information; represent them with the European institutions; ensure coordination of their activities. **Structure** General Meeting (annual); Board of Directors; Head Office in Strasbourg (France). **Languages** Dutch, English, French, German. **Staff** Voluntary. **Finance** Members' dues. **Activities** Events/meetings; research/documentation. **Events** *General Assembly* Saalbach (Austria) 2015, *General Assembly* Saalbach (Austria) 2014, *General Assembly* Saalbach (Austria) 2013, *General Assembly* Saalbach (Austria) 2012, *General Assembly* Saalbach (Austria) 2011. **Publications** *Best Practice*; *Lettre du juriste européen*.

Members National organizations in 5 countries:
Austria, Belgium, France, Germany, Switzerland.

Consultative Status Consultative status granted from: *Council of Europe (CE, #04881)* (Participatory Status). [2020.03.05/XD5313/**D**]

♦ European Union – Latin America and the Caribbean Foundation (EU-LAC Foundation) 08999

Fundación Unión Europea-América Latina y el Caribe (Fundación EU-LAC)

Exec Dir Grosse Bleichen 35, 20354 Hamburg, Germany. T. +4940806011450. E-mail: info@eulacfoundation.org – press@eulacfoundation.org.
Main Website: http://eulacfoundation.org/

History Hamburg (Germany). Created as a result and initiative of the VI Summit of Heads of State and Government, May 2010. Operations started Nov 2011. The depositary of the Agreement establishing EU-LAC International Foundation is the European Council and has been opened for signature 25 Oct 2016 to the date of its entry into force. **Aims** Strengthen and promote the strategic bi-regional EU-LAC relationship, enhancing its visibility and fostering active participation of the respective civil societies. **Structure** Board of Governors; President; Executive Director. **Languages** English, Spanish. **Staff** 10.00 FTE, paid. **Finance** Sources: contributions of member/participating states. **Activities** Awards/prizes/competitions; knowledge management/information dissemination; projects/programmes. Active in: Antigua-Barbuda, Argentina, Bahamas, Barbados, Belize, Bolivia, Brazil, Chile, Colombia, Costa Rica, Cuba, Dominica, Ecuador, El Salvador, Grenada, Guatemala, Guyana, Haiti, Honduras, Jamaica, Mexico, Nicaragua, Panama, Paraguay, Peru, St Kitts-Nevis, St Lucia, St Vincent-Grenadines, Suriname, Uruguay, Venezuela. **Events** *EU-CELAC Academic Summit* Brussels (Belgium) 2015.

Members Governments (61):
Antigua-Barbuda, Argentina, Austria, Bahamas, Barbados, Belgium, Belize, Bolivia, Brazil, Bulgaria, Chile, Colombia, Costa Rica, Croatia, Cuba, Cyprus, Czechia, Denmark, Dominica, Dominican Rep, Ecuador, El Salvador, Estonia, Finland, France, Germany, Greece, Grenada, Guatemala, Guyana, Haiti, Honduras, Hungary, Ireland, Italy, Jamaica, Latvia, Lithuania, Luxembourg, Malta, Mexico, Netherlands, Nicaragua, Panama, Paraguay, Peru, Poland, Portugal, Romania, Slovakia, Slovenia, Spain, St Kitts-Nevis, St Lucia, St Vincent-Grenadines, Suriname, Sweden, Trinidad-Tobago, UK, Uruguay, Venezuela.
Regional entities:
Comunidad de Estados Latinoamericanos y Caribeños (CELAC, #04432); *European Union (EU, #08967)*.

IGO Relations Partner of (3): *Development Bank of Latin America (CAF, #05055)*; *Italian-Latin American Institute (ILAI, #16071)*; *United Nations Economic Commission for Latin America and the Caribbean (ECLAC, #20556)* (Region of Lombardy). **NGO Relations** Strategic partnership with: *Fundación Global Democracia y Desarrollo (FUNGLODE)*; Institut des Amériques, Regione Lombardia. Partners with: *College of Europe (#04105)*; *Consejo Europeo de Investigaciones Sociales de América Latina (CEISAL, #04710)*; *GIGA – German Institute of Global and Area Studies*; *Instituto Cervantes (#11329)*; *University of the West Indies (UWI, #20705)*; national universities and institutes. [2022.02.16/XM4987/**F***]

♦ European Union-Latin American and Caribbean Summit (meeting series)
♦ European Union – Latin America Relations Observatory (#17635)

♦ European Union Liaison Committee of Historians 09000

Groupe de liaison des professeurs d'histoire contemporaine auprès de la Commission des Communautés européennes

Sec Archives nationales de Luxembourg, Plateau de Saint-Esprit, L-1475 Luxembourg, Luxembourg. T. +35224776665.
URL: http://eu-historians.org/

History 1982, Luxembourg. Former names and other names: *European Community Liaison Committee of Historians* – former; *Groupe de liaison des historiens auprès la Communauté européenne* – former; *Liaison Group of Modern History Lecturers of European Community Universities* – former; *Groupe de liaison des historiens auprès de l'Union européenne* – former. **Aims** Gather and convey information about work on European history after World War II; advise the European Union on research projects concerning contemporary European history; enable researchers to make better use of the archival sources; promote research meetings to get an update of work in progress and stimulate new research. **Languages** English, French, German. **Staff**

17.00 FTE, voluntary. **Finance** Supported by European research programmes. **Activities** Events/meetings; publishing activities. **Events** *Colloquium* Cluj-Napoca (Romania) 2013, *Colloquium* Aarhus (Denmark) 2010, *Colloquium* Rome (Italy) 2007, *Colloquium* Groningen (Netherlands) 2005, *Colloquium* Essen (Germany) 1999. **Publications** *Journal of European Integration History/Revue d'histoire de l'intégration européenne/Zeitschrift für Geschichte der Europäischen Integration.* Integration proceedings of conferences organized by Liaison Group.
Members Individuals in 11 countries:
Austria, Belgium, Denmark, France, Germany, Italy, Luxembourg, Netherlands, Romania, Spain, UK.
IGO Relations *European Commission (EC, #06633).* [2020/XE6143/v/E]

♦ European Union of Local Authority Staffs (inactive)
♦ European Union of Medical Advisers' Associations (inactive)

♦ European Union of Medical Specialists (UEMS) 09001

Union Européenne des Médecins Spécialistes (UEMS)

CEO Rue de l'Industrie 24, Domus Medica Europaea, 1040 Brussels, Belgium. T. +3224307350. Fax +3226403730. E-mail: secretariat@uems.eu – ceo@uems.eu.
URL: http://www.uems.eu/

History 20 Jul 1958, Brussels (Belgium). Former names and other names: *Unión Europea de Médicos Especialistas* – former; *Europäische Vereinigung der Fachärzte* – former; *União Européia dos Médicos Especialistas* – former; *Unione Europea dei Medici Specialisti* – former; *Europese Specialisten Vereniging* – former; *Europaeiske Forening af Speciallaeger* – former. Registration: Banque-Carrefour des Entreprises, No/ID: 0469.067.848, Start date: 6 Jan 2000, Belgium. **Aims** Study, promote and harmonize the highest level of training of medical specialists, medical practice and health care within European Union; study and promote free movement of specialist doctors within the EU; represent the medical specialist profession in Member States of the EU, to EU authorities and any other authority and/or organization dealing with questions directly or indirectly concerning the medical profession, and any action which might further achievement of the aforementioned objectives. **Structure** Council; Board; Executive. Specialist Sections (currently 43) and their European Boards; Multidisciplinary Joint Committees (15); Divisions. *European Accreditation Council for Continuing Medical Education (EACCME, #05823); European Council for Accreditation of Medical Specialist Qualifications (ECAMSQ).* **Languages** English, French. **Staff** 15.00 FTE, paid. **Finance** Sources: members' dues. Other sources: support from any other origin approved by the Board.
Activities Events/meetings. Specialist sections (43) and Multidisciplinary Joint Committees (15), of which the following are listed in this Yearbook:
- *European Board of Neurology (EBN, #06364);*
- *European Board of Oro-Maxillo-Facial Surgery (EBOMFS, #06367);*
- *European Board of Pathology (EBP, #06370);*
- *European Board and College of Obstetrics and Gynaecology (EBCOG, #06357);*
- *European Board of Paediatrics (EBP, #06368),* set up with CESP;
- *European Board of Paediatric Surgery (EBPS, #06369);*
- *European Board of Gastroenterology and Hepatology (EBGH, #06359);*
- *European Board of Ophthalmology (EBO, #06366);*
- *European Board of Physical and Rehabilitation Medicine (#06371);*
- *European Board of Plastic, Reconstructive and Aesthetic Surgery (EBOPRAS, #06372);*
- *European Board of Dermatology and Venereology (EBDV, #06358).*

These boards are responsible for harmonizing medical training in their respective specialty or specialities in Europe, accrediting training centres and their staff and awarding European diplomas to successful candidates. With a view to the creation of the European Single Market in medicine, proposes creation of a Central European office to evaluate supply and demand of doctors in European Community countries.
Events *NASCE (Network of Accredited Skills Centres in Europe) Meeting* Brussels (Belgium) 2022, *Joint Conference on CME-CPD in Europe* Seville (Spain) 2022, *Meeting* Brussels (Belgium) 2021, *Virtual Joint Conference on CME-CPD in Europe* Seville (Spain) 2021, *Joint Conference on CME-CPD in Europe* Seville (Spain) 2020. **Publications** *Structure and Development of CME in European Countries; UEMS Newsletter. UEMS Yearbook* (1958-2008).
Members National associations – Full; Associate; Observer. Full in 31 countries:
Austria, Belgium, Bulgaria, Croatia, Cyprus, Czechia, Denmark, Estonia, Finland, France, Germany, Greece, Hungary, Iceland, Ireland, Italy, Latvia, Lithuania, Luxembourg, Malta, Netherlands, Norway, Poland, Portugal, Romania, Slovakia, Slovenia, Spain, Sweden, Switzerland, UK.
Associate in 4 countries:
Armenia, Israel, Serbia, Türkiye.
Observer in 5 countries:
Georgia, Iraq, Lebanon, Morocco, Tunisia.
IGO Relations Recognized by: *European Commission (EC, #06633); European Parliament (EP, #08146); WHO (#20950).* Participates in EC Groups and Workforces. **NGO Relations** Member of (3): *European Public Health Association (EUPHA, #08298)* (Associated); *Federation of European and International Associations Established in Belgium (FAIB, #09508); Global Allergy and Asthma European Network (GA2LEN, #10179).* Partner of (1): *European Psychiatric Association (EPA, #08290).* Instrumental in setting up (4): *European Board of Anaesthesiology (EBA, #06354); European Board of Urology (EBU, #06374); European Federation of Surgical Specialties (EFSS, #07222); Multidisciplinary Joint Committee on Paediatric Urology (JCPU, #16883).* Represented on: *European Board for Accreditation in Cardiology (EBAC, #06353).* Recognizes: *VAS-European Independent Foundation in Angiology/Vascular Medicine (VAS, #20748).* Recognized by: *World Federation for Medical Education (WFME, #21454).* Consultative status with: *European Health Policy Forum (EHPF, no recent information);* EU Open Health Forum. [2022.10.21/XD0894/D]

♦ European Union – Mercosur (inactive)
♦ European Union Military Committee (inactive)
♦ European Union Military Staff Office (inactive)
♦ European Union Monitoring Commission (inactive)

♦ European Union of Mountaineering Associations (EUMA) 09002

Contact c/o DAV, Von-Kahr-Str 24, 80997 Munich, Germany. T. +49891400356. E-mail: info@european-mountaineers.eu.
Registered Address Avenue de la Couronne 313-20, 1050 Brussels, Belgium.
URL: https://www.european-mountaineers.eu/

History Registration: Banque-Carrefour des Entreprises, No/ID: 0696.898.973, Start date: 25 Oct 2018, Belgium; EU Transparency Register, No/ID: 101635029817-49, Start date: 25 Jan 2018. **Aims** Include mountaineering in European Union priorities as an important factor of quality of life and to be recognised as the dialogue partner for mountaineering by EU institutions. **Structure** Presidium.
Members Associations uniting nearly 3,000,000 mountaineers. Full in 23 countries:
Albania, Austria, Belgium, Bosnia-Herzegovina, Croatia, Cyprus, Czechia, France, Germany, Greece, Italy, Liechtenstein, Malta, Montenegro, Netherlands, Norway, Poland, Romania, Serbia, Slovakia, Slovenia, Spain, UK.
Associated in 2 countries:
Italy, Portugal.
NGO Relations Member of (1): *European Environmental Bureau (EEB, #06996).* Partner of (2): *European Ramblers' Association (ERA, #08328); Union internationale des associations d'alpinisme (UIAA, #20420).* Cooperates with (2): *Balkan Mountaineering Union (BMU, #03079); Club Arc Alpin (CAA, #04030).* [2021/AA1438/D]

♦ European Union of Music Competitions for Youth (EMCY) 09003

Union européenne des concours de musique pour la jeunesse – Unión Europea de Concursos de Música para Jóvenes – Europäische Union der Musikwettbewerbe für die Jugend

SG Schwere-Reiter-Str 2B, Haus 2, 80637 Munich, Germany. T. +4917657829475. E-mail: info@emcy.org.
URL: http://www.emcy.org/

History Former names and other names: *European Union of National Music Competitions for the Young* – former; *Union européenne des concours nationaux de musique pour la jeunesse* – former; *Unión Europea de los Concursos Nacionales de Música por la Juventud* – former; *Europäische Union der Nationalen Musikwettbewerbe für die Jugend* – former; *Unión Europea de los Concursos de Música por la Juventud* – former. Registration: Germany. **Aims** Develop, support and promote musical education of young talents in the pre-professional stage, as well as collaboration and exchange between music competitions for youth on a European level. **Structure** General Assembly (every 2 years); Board; Secretary-General. **Languages** English, French, German. **Staff** 1.00 FTE, paid; 1.00 FTE, voluntary. **Finance** Sources: members' dues; sponsorship. **Activities** Awards/prizes/competitions; events/meetings. **Events** *General Assembly* Luxembourg (Luxembourg) 2014, *Conference* Bratislava (Slovakia) 2013, *Board Meeting* Munich (Germany) 2013, *General Assembly* Ohrid (Macedonia) 2012, *Conference* Ried (Austria) 2012. **Publications** Newsletters; brochures.
Members Organizers of music competitions for young people in Europe. Members in 23 countries:
Austria, Bulgaria, Czechia, Denmark, Estonia, France, Germany, Italy, Lithuania, Luxembourg, Netherlands, North Macedonia, Norway, Poland, Portugal, Russia, Slovakia, Slovenia, Spain, Sweden, Switzerland, UK, Ukraine.
NGO Relations Member of (4): *European Alliance for Culture and the Arts (#05866); European Music Council (EMC, #07837); International Music Council (IMC, #14199); World Federation of International Music Competitions (WFIMC, #21445)* (Associate). Cooperates with (1): *European Broadcasting Union (EBU, #06404).* [2021.06.12/XD4006/D]

♦ European Union of Musicians (inactive)
♦ European Union of National Associations of Water Suppliers / see European Federation of National Associations of Water and Waste Water Services (#07170)
♦ European Union of National Associations of Water Suppliers and Waste Water Services / see European Federation of National Associations of Water and Waste Water Services (#07170)
♦ European Union of National Geological Surveys / see EuroGeoSurveys (#05686)

♦ European Union National Institutes for Culture (EUNIC) 09004

Dir Rue Ravenstein 18, 1000 Brussels, Belgium. T. +3226408158. E-mail: admin@eunicglobal.eu.
URL: https://www.eunicglobal.eu/

History 2006. Registration: Banque-Carrefour des Entreprises, No/ID: 0473.098.395, Start date: 7 Dec 1999; EU Transparency Register, No/ID: 302379535219-87, Start date: 24 Jun 2019. **Aims** Become the delivery, research and training partner of choice for cultural diplomacy and cultural relations at European and international level. **Structure** Biannual Meeting of Heads; Board of Directors; President; Vice-President. **Languages** English. **Staff** 7.00 FTE, paid. **Finance** Sources: members' dues. Supported by: *European Union (EU, #08967).* Annual budget: 500,000 EUR. **Activities** Networking/liaising; politics/policy/regulatory; projects/programmes; training/education.
Members Full (36) in 28 countries:
Austria, Belgium, Bulgaria, Croatia, Cyprus, Czechia, Denmark, Estonia, Finland, France, Germany, Greece, Hungary, Ireland, Italy, Latvia, Lithuania, Luxembourg, Malta, Netherlands, Poland, Portugal, Romania, Slovakia, Slovenia, Spain, Sweden, UK.
Included in the above, 3 organizations listed in this Yearbook:
British Council; Dutch Centre for International Cooperation (DutchCulture); Goethe-Institut. [2021/XJ1567/y/E]

♦ European Union of National Music Competitions for the Young / see European Union of Music Competitions for Youth (#09003)
♦ European Union of the Natural Gas Industry / see Eurogas (#05682)

♦ European Union Network for the Implementation and Enforcement of Environmental Law (IMPEL) 09005

Secretariat Chemin des deux maisons 73, box 3, 1200 Brussels, Belgium. E-mail: info@impel.eu.
Secretariat address not obtained.
URL: http://impel.eu/

History Dec 1993, Chester (UK), within *European Commission (EC, #06633),* as *European Community Network for the Implementation and Enforcement of Environmental law (ECONET).* Current name adopted Nov 1994. Since 2008, transformed into an international non-profit association, registered in accordance with Belgian law. **Aims** Create the necessary impetus in the European Union to make progress on ensuring a more effective application of environmental legislation. **Structure** General Assembly; Board; Secretariat. Expert Teams. **Events** *General Assembly* Paris (France) 2022, *General Assembly* Lisbon (Portugal) 2021, *General Assembly* Brussels (Belgium) 2020, *General Assembly* Helsinki (Finland) 2019, *EU Environmental Enforcement Networks Conference* Utrecht (Netherlands) 2016.
Members Environmental authorities (50) in 35 countries:
Albania, Austria, Belgium, Bulgaria, Croatia, Cyprus, Czechia, Denmark, Estonia, Finland, France, Germany, Greece, Hungary, Iceland, Ireland, Italy, Kosovo, Latvia, Lithuania, Luxembourg, Malta, Netherlands, North Macedonia, Norway, Poland, Portugal, Romania, Slovakia, Slovenia, Spain, Sweden, Switzerland, Türkiye, UK.
Observers include 1 organization listed in this Yearbook:
International Network for Environmental Compliance and Enforcement (INECE, #14261).
NGO Relations Member of: *International Network for Environmental Compliance and Enforcement (INECE, #14261).* [2016/XF6599/F]

♦ European Union of Nonsmokers 09006

Union européenne des non-fumeurs (UEN)

SG BP 12, L-8001 Strassen, Luxembourg. Fax +352311637.
Pres BP 142, 78001 Versailles CEDEX, France. T. +33130218694. Fax +33139511348.

History 1987, Strasbourg (France). **Aims** Defend non-smokers' rights. **Structure** Administrative Council of 25; Executive Committee of 8. **Languages** English, French. **Staff** Voluntary. **Finance** Members' dues. Private donations. **Events** *General Assembly* 2010, *General Assembly* 2009, *General Assembly* 2008, *General Assembly* Ljubljana (Slovenia) 2005, *Meeting / General Assembly* Netherlands 2004.
Members Associations in 17 countries:
Belgium, Denmark, France, Germany, Ireland, Israel, Lithuania, Luxembourg, Netherlands, Norway, Romania, Slovakia, Slovenia, Spain, Sweden, Switzerland, UK.
NGO Relations Full member of: *European Network for Smoking and Tobacco Prevention (ENSP, #08002).* Member of: *Framework Convention Alliance (FCA, #09981); International Commission on Occupational Health (ICOH, #12709); International Network of Women Against Tobacco (INWAT, #14343).* Also member of several international high-level working groups. [2016/XD4146/D]

♦ European Union Observatory for Nanomaterials (EUON) 09007

Contact c/o ECHA, PO Box 400, FI-0121 Helsinki, Finland.
URL: https://euon.echa.europa.eu/

Aims Provide information about existing nanomaterials on the EU market. **Structure** Hosted and maintained by *European Chemicals Agency (ECHA, #06523).* **Finance** Funded by *European Commission (EC, #06633).*
Activities Research/documentation. [2018/XM8654/E]

♦ European Union of Ophthalmic Surgeons (inactive)
♦ European Union of Orthodox Israelite Communities (inactive)
♦ European Union for Packaging and the Environment (inactive)
♦ European Union of Paediatric Surgical Associations / see European Paediatric Surgeons' Association (#08130)
♦ European Union of Painters and Decorators (no recent information)
♦ European Union of Pankration Athlima (inactive)
♦ European Union of Paper, Board and Packaging Wholesalers / see European Paper Merchants Association (#08138)

♦ European Union of Paratroopers 09008

Union européenne des parachutistes (UEP)

SG c/o Union Nationale des Parachutistes (UNP), 76 rue Marc Sangnier, 94700 Maisons-Alfort, France. T. +33140560667. Fax +33140560875. E-mail: gestion@union-nat-parachutistes.org.
URL: http://www.union-nat-parachutistes.org/

Events *Conference* Saint-Michel (France) 2015, *International congress / Conference* Madrid (Spain) 2002.
Members Membership countries not specified. [2018/XD9082/D]

♦ European Union of Philatelic Associations (inactive)
♦ European Union of Physics Research Organizations (inactive)
♦ European Union of Piano Makers Associations / see Union of European Piano Builders' Associations (#20391)

♦ European Union of the Potato Processing Industry / see EUPPA – European Potato Processors' Association (#05592)
♦ European Union of the Potato Trade / see European Potato Trade Association (#08257)
♦ European Union of Practising Veterinary Surgeons / see Union européenne des vétérinaires praticiens (#20405)
♦ European Union for the Prevention of Cruelty to Animals (inactive)

♦ European Union of Private Higher Education (EUPHE) 09009

Union Européenne de l'enseignement supérieure privé – Unión de Educación Superior Privada – Europäische Union der Privathochschulen

Pres Rue Belliard 20 1°, 1040 Brussels, Belgium. T. +330140650933.
Head of International Office address not obtained.
URL: https://www.euphe.eu/

History Jun 2018, Brussels (Belgium). Registration: Banque-Carrefour des Entreprises, No/ID: 0715.444.977, Start date: 4 Dec 2018, Belgium; EU Transparency Regisgter, No/ID: 686513034091-83, Start date: 25 Feb 2019. **Aims** Create and promote favourable conditions for the establishment and conduct of private higher education in Europe. **Structure** General Assembly; Board of Directors. **Languages** English. **Staff** 1.00 FTE, paid; 20.00 FTE, voluntary. **Finance** Sources: members' dues. Annual budget: 16,000 EUR (2021). **Activities** Advocacy/lobbying/activism; awareness raising; capacity building; events/meetings; guidance/assistance/consulting; knowledge management/information dissemination; monitoring/evaluation; networking/liaising. European Union. **Publications** *Die Alternative – Nichtstaatliche Hochschulen in Europa – The Alternative – Non-State Higher Education in Europe* (1st ed 2021) by Prof Klaus Hekking in English, German – Political, legal an economic conditions for non-state universities in the European Union..
Members Organizations in 9 countries:
Austria, Croatia, France, Germany, Ireland, Poland, Portugal, Slovenia, Spain. [2023.02.14/AA0949/**D**]

♦ European Union of Private Hospitals (#20397)
♦ European Union of Production and Wholesale Centres of Consumers' Cooperative Societies (inactive)

♦ European Union for Progressive Judaism (EUPJ) 09010

Main Office c/o Sternberg Ctr, 80 East End Road, London, N3 2SY, UK. E-mail: administrator@eupj.org.
URL: http://eupj.org/

History Set up as a constituent of *World Union for Progressive Judaism (WUPJ, #21883)*. Former names and other names: *World Union for Progressive Judaism – European Region* – alias; *European Region of the World Union for Progressive Judaism* – alias. Registration: Charity, No/ID: 253000, England and Wales; EU Transparency Register, No/ID: 570348727424-31. **Aims** Promote development of Progressive Judaism in Central, Western Europe and Israel; encourage and facilitate the formation of Progressive Jewish communities; stimulate and encourage the study of Judaism and a recognition of its place in modern life. **Structure** All constituents are represented on the Executive. **Activities** Active in any place where there are Jews interested in learning about progressive Judaism. Helps, however possible, in the training of rabbis and lay leaders for newly emerging congregations so that they are able to help in the Jewish education of their families. **Events** *Biennial Conference* Prague (Czechia) 2018, *Biennial Conference* Amsterdam (Netherlands) 2012, *Biennial Conference* Vienna (Austria) 2008, *Biennial conference / Conference* Barcelona (Spain) 2002, *Biennial conference / Conference* Zurich (Switzerland) 2000.
Members Congregations in 13 countries:
Austria, Belgium, Czechia, Denmark, France, Germany, Hungary, Italy, Luxembourg, Netherlands, Spain, Switzerland, UK. [2018/XE2667/**E**]

♦ European Union for the Protection of Animals (inactive)
♦ European Union of Public Accountants (inactive)

♦ European Union of Public Relations (EUPR) 09011

Union européenne de relations publiques – Unión Europea de Relaciones Públicas – Europäische Vereinigung für Public Relations – Unione Europea di Relazioni Pubbliche (UERP)

Pres Centro Commerciale Europa, PO Box 306, 39100 Bolzano, Italy. T. +39471200612. Fax +39471200612. E-mail: eupri@tin.it.
URL: http://www.eupri.com/

History 1976, Brussels (Belgium). Former names and other names: *European Union of Public Relations – International Service Organization (EUPR)* – former; *Union européenne de relations publiques – Organisation internationale de services* – former; *Unión Europea de Relaciones Públicas – Organización Internacional de Servicios* – former; *Europäische Vereinigung für Public Relations – Internationale Dienstleistungs-Organisation* – former; *Unione Europea di Relazioni Pubbliche – Organizzazione Internazionale di Servizi (UERP)* – former. Registration: No/ID: 000120, Start date: 25 Feb 1985, End date: 25 Feb 2026, Italy, Alto Adige; Ministero dello sviluppo economico, No/ID: 0001183124, Start date: 21 Apr 2006, End date: 21 Apr 2026, Italy, Rome. **Aims** Promote improvement of methodology and public relations techniques; coordinate and rationalize work in the field in the context of social and economic conditions of countries to which members belong; promote professional activity of members through exchanges, studies and research; ensure that members' activities comply with principles of correctness, loyalty and devotion as set out by EUPR Code. **Structure** Seat located in Bolzano-Bozen (Italy). **Languages** English, French, Italian, Spanish. **Staff** 10.00 FTE, paid. **Finance** Sources: members' dues. **Activities** Events/meetings; guidance/assistance/consulting; research/documentation. Active in all member countries. **Events** *Assembly* Riva del Garda (Italy) 2012, *Assembly* Italy 2011, *Assembly* Austria 2009, *International conference* Malta 2007, *NGOs conference* Malta 2004. **Publications** *Informeuropa Newsletter* (annual). White book on economic benefits from heritage restoration in Europe. **Members** Individual Subscribing members in Western Europe; Associate members in Eastern Europe and non-European countries. Membership countries not specified. **Consultative Status** Consultative status granted from: *ECOSOC (#05331)* (Ros C); *UNIDO (#20336)*. [2023/XD4134/v/**D**]

♦ European Union of Public Relations – International Service Organization / see European Union of Public Relations (#09011)
♦ European Union of Railway Modellers and Friends of the Railway (#20400)

♦ European Union of Rechtspfleger 09012

Union européenne des rechtspfleger – Europäische Union der Rechtspfleger (EUR)

Pres address not obtained. E-mail: eur-president@email.de.
Gen Sec Marxergasse 1a/1510, 1030 Vienna, Austria.
Main Website: https://eur-online.eu/

History 6 Oct 1967, Karlsruhe (Germany). Former names and other names: *Union européenne des greffiers de justice* – alias. Registration: EU Transparency Register, No/ID: 715434330912-85. **Aims** Participate in training, development and harmonization of *law* at European and international level; represent ideals and material interests of members; solve issues at national level with governments. **Structure** General Assembly; Congress; Officers: President, General Secretary, Treasurer. **Languages** English, French, German. **Finance** Sources: contributions. **Activities** Events/meetings; training/education. **Events** *Congress* Lisbon (Portugal) 2019, *General Assembly* Bucharest (Romania) 2018, *General Assembly* Tangiers (Morocco) 2017, *Congress* Malaga (Spain) 2016, *General Assembly / Annual General Assembly* Dijon (France) 2015. **Publications** *White Paper for a Greffier – Rechtspfleger for Europe* (2016); *Green Paper for a European Rechtspfleger* (2008); *Statuts et fonctions du greffier – Etude comparative – Rechtspfleger* (3rd ed 2001).
Members National societies in 13 countries:
Austria, Bulgaria, Czechia, Denmark, Estonia, France, Germany, Italy, Luxembourg, Poland, Portugal, Romania, Spain.
Associate members in 6 countries:
Japan, Korea Rep, Mali, Mauritania, Morocco, Tunisia.
Consultative Status Consultative status granted from: *Council of Europe (CE, #04881)* (Participatory Status). **IGO Relations** Observer status with (1): *Commission européenne pour l'efficacité de la justice (CEPEJ, #04213)*. [2022.05.12/XD4389/**D**]

♦ European Union Recreational Marine Industry Group (inactive)
♦ European Union of Research Institutes for Shoes (no recent information)
♦ European Union Research Organizations Heads of Research Councils (inactive)

♦ European Union for Responsible Incineration and Treatment of Special Waste (EURITS) 09013

Pres Dijle 17a, 2800 Mechelen, Belgium. E-mail: admin@eurits.org.
URL: http://www.eurits.org/

History 7 Dec 1993. Registration: EU Transparency Register, No/ID: 46904231219-48, Start date: 24 Feb 2009. **Aims** Conduct hazardous waste incineration and treatment in a safe, legal and responsible way. **Finance** Sources: members' dues.
Members Companies in 14 countries:
Austria, Belgium, Denmark, Finland, France, Germany, Hungary, Ireland, Italy, Poland, Spain, Sweden, Switzerland, UK.
IGO Relations Accredited by (2): *Basel Convention on the Control of Transboundary Movements of Hazardous Wastes and Their Disposal (UNCRTD, 1989)*; *Stockholm Convention on Persistent Organic Pollutants (POP treaty, 2001)*. [2023.02.14/XD6782/**D**]

♦ European Union Road Federation (ERF) 09014

Dir Gen Rue Belliard 20, 1040 Brussels, Belgium. T. +3226445877. Fax +3226475934.
Communications Dir address not obtained.
URL: http://www.erf.be/

History Jun 1998, Brussels (Belgium). Founded by national road associations from European Union Member States. Registration: No/ID: 0470.591.441, Start date: 17 Feb 2000, Belgium; EU Transparency Register, No/ID: 017343011782-42, Start date: 2 Sep 2013. **Aims** Coordinate views and concerns of Europe's road sector; act as a European platform for dialogue; condense the road sector's input on mobility issues; promote research leading to more sustainable forms of road transport. **Structure** Plenary Assembly; Executive Committee; Secretariat. Fora (2): *Mobility for Prosperity in Europe (MPE, #16839)*; *European Noise Barrier Federation (ENBF, #08052)*. **Languages** English, French, Spanish. **Staff** 4.00 FTE, paid. **Finance** Sources: members' dues. Other sources: proceeds from research; other proceeds. **Activities** Events/meetings; knowledge management/information dissemination; politics/policy/regulatory; research and development. **Events** *Lab Seminar* Brussels (Belgium) 2019, *European Road Infrastructure Congress* Leeds (UK) 2016, *Seminar on Engineering and Financing Safer and Sustainable Roads* Warsaw (Poland) 2011, *European Motorcyclists Forum* Brussels (Belgium) 2010, *International Motorcyclists Conference* Brussels (Belgium) 2010. **Publications** *Engineering Safer Roads* (6 a year); *Policy and Action* (6 a year); *Voice of The European Road* (6 a year) – electronic newsletter. *European Road Transport Statistics*; *Guidelines to Black Spot Management*; *Putting You in the Driving Seat for Safer Roads*; *Socio-economic Benefits of Roads*.
Members Industry Sector; Association; Research/Academia sector; Notified bodies; National Administration. Members in 23 countries and territories:
Austria, Belgium, Bosnia-Herzegovina, Bulgaria, Croatia, Czechia, Finland, France, Germany, Greece, Ireland, Italy, Luxembourg, Netherlands, Poland, Portugal, Qatar, Russia, Slovenia, Spain, Sweden, UK.
Confederation of Organizations in Road Transport Enforcement (CORTE, #04574); *European Asphalt Pavement Association (EAPA, #05920)*; *European Bitumen Association (EUROBITUME, #06348)*; *European Concrete Paving Association (EUPAVE, #06697)*; *European Noise Barrier Federation (ENBF, #08052)*.
NGO Relations Member of (6): *Confederation of Organizations in Road Transport Enforcement (CORTE, #04574)*; *Construction Products Europe AISBL (#04761)* (Associate); *European Road Transport Research Advisory Council (ERTRAC, #08396)*; *European Tourism Manifesto (#08921)*; *Industry4Europe (#11181)*; *Mobility for Prosperity in Europe (MPE, #16839)*. Partner of (1): *International Road Federation (IRF, #14758)*. [2020/XD7513/y/**D**]

♦ European Union Satellite Centre (SatCen) 09015

Centre satellitaire de l'Union européenne

Director Apdo de Correos 511, Torrejón de Ardoz, 28850 Madrid, Spain. T. +34916786000. Fax +34916786006. E-mail: info@satcen.europa.eu.
URL: https://www.satcen.europa.eu/

History 1 Jan 2002, Torrejón de Ardoz (Spain). Established by decision of 20 July 2001 of *Council of the European Union (#04895)*. Supersedes *Western European Union Satellite Centre (inactive)*. An agency set up under Common Foreign and Security Policy of *European Union (EU, #08967)*. **Aims** Support the decision-making and actions of the European Union in the context of the Common Foreign and Security Policy (CFSP) by providing analysis resulting from exploitation of relevant space assets and collateral data, including satellite imagery and aerial imagery, and related services. **Structure** Based at Torrejón (Spain), under political supervision of *Political and Security Committee (PSC)* and operational direction of the High Representative; Board; Executive Body; Divisions (4). **Languages** English, French. **Staff** 155.00 FTE, paid; 5.00 FTE, voluntary. Specialists from EU member countries, including maintenance, finance and security staff supporting operational functions. **Finance** Sources: contributions of member/participating states; revenue from activities/projects. Supported by: *European Union (EU, #08967)*. Annual budget: 35,000,000 EUR (2021). **Activities** Conflict resolution; humanitarian/emergency aid; knowledge management/information dissemination; monitoring/evaluation; projects/programmes; research and development; training/education. Geospatial analysis and services in space and security. **Events** *Conference* Madrid (Spain) 2022, *EU SST Seminar on Building the Future of SST* Madrid (Spain) 2021, *Big Data from Space Conference* Paris (France) 2021, *EU SST Seminar on Operations in Space Surveillance and Tracking* Madrid (Spain) 2020, *Conference on Image Information Mining* Bucharest (Romania) 2014. **Publications** Annual Report.
Members Governments of 27 countries:
Austria, Belgium, Bulgaria, Croatia, Cyprus, Czechia, Denmark, Estonia, Finland, France, Germany, Greece, Hungary, Ireland, Italy, Latvia, Lithuania, Luxembourg, Malta, Netherlands, Poland, Portugal, Romania, Slovakia, Slovenia, Spain, Sweden.
IGO Relations Partner of (2): *EuroGEOSS (#05685)*; *Group on Earth Observations (GEO, #10735)*. Cooperates with (1): *European Commission (EC, #06633)*. Also links with national and international institutions (not specified). **NGO Relations** Member of (1): *EU Agencies Network (EUAN, #05564)*. [2022.11.16/XE4478/**E***]

♦ European Union of School and University Health and Medicine (EUSUHM) 09016

Union européenne d'hygiène et de médecine scolaires et universitaires (UEHMSU)

Contact address not obtained. E-mail: info@eusuhm.org.
URL: http://www.eusuhm.org/

Events *Congress* Split (Croatia) 2022, *Biennial Congress* Split (Croatia) 2021, *Biennial Congress* Rotterdam (Netherlands) 2019, *Biennial Congress* Tallinn (Estonia) 2015, *Biennial Congress* London (UK) 2013. **Members** Membership countries not specified. [2022/XD2392/**D**]

♦ European Union of Science Journalists' Associations (EUSJA) 09017

Union européenne des associations de journalistes scientifiques – Europäische Union der Gesellschaften der Wissenschaftsjournalisten

Secretariat c/o Euroscience, 1 quai Lezay-Marnésia, 67000 Strasbourg CEDEX, France. T. +33388241150. Fax +33388247556. E-mail: office@euroscience.org – eusja@euroscience.org.
URL: http://www.eusja.org/

History 8 Mar 1971, Antwerp (Belgium). Founded replacing *Union internationale des journalistes scientifiques*. Former names and other names: *European Union of Associations of Science Journalists* – alias. **Aims** Facilitate gathering of information; promote discussion on topics related to journalism; open a forum for broader reporting on European science. **Structure** General Assembly; Board. Secretariat facilities from *European Association for the Advancement of Science and Technology (EUROSCIENCE, #05927)*. **Languages** English. **Staff** 1.00 FTE, paid. **Finance** Members' dues. **Activities** Networking/liaising; events/meetings. **Events** *European Conference for Science Journalists* Strasbourg (France) 2021, *European Conference of Science Journalists* Toulouse (France) 2018, *European Conference of Science Journalists* Copenhagen (Denmark) 2017, *European Science Journalists Conference* Copenhagen (Denmark) 2014, *General Assembly* Vienna (Austria) 2014. **Publications** *EUSJA Newsletter*.
Members Organizations of science journalists, grouping over 2500 science journalists, in 21 countries:
Austria, Belgium, Croatia, Czechia, Denmark, Estonia, Finland, Germany, Greece, Hungary, Ireland, Italy, Poland, Portugal, Romania, Russia, Slovenia, Spain, Sweden, Switzerland, UK. [2021/XD2776/**D**]

♦ European Union for the Scientific Study of Glass (no recent information)
♦ The European Union's Observatory on Older People / see International Association on Social Quality (#12168)

- ♦ The European Union's Observatory on Social Exclusion / see International Association on Social Quality (#12168)
- ♦ European Union of Social, Mutual and Cooperative Pharmacies / see Union européenne des Pharmacies sociales (#20401)
- ♦ European Union of the Social Pharmacies (#20401)
- ♦ European Union of Societies for Experimental Biology (inactive)
- ♦ European Union of Soldiers' Wives (no recent information)
- ♦ European Union Strategy for the Alpine Region / see EU Strategy for the Alpine Region (#09203)
- ♦ European Union Studies Association (internationally oriented national body)
- ♦ European Union Studies Association Asia Pacific / see EU Studies Association Asia Pacific (#09204)
- ♦ European Union Studies Association of Korea (internationally oriented national body)
- ♦ European Union Studies Center, New York (internationally oriented national body)

♦ European Union of Supported Employment (EUSE) 09018

Secretariat Karen Warson, Kongostraat 7, 9000 Ghent, Belgium. E-mail: info@euse.org.
URL: http://www.euse.org/

History 7 Jul 1993, Rotterdam (Netherlands). Registration: Banque-Carrefour des Entreprises, No/ID: 0775.758.587, Start date: 14 Oct 2021, Belgium; Netherlands; EU Transparency Register, No/ID: 724573314136-30. **Aims** Provide information and support to affiliates in the field of employment integration of people with a *disability*; promote supported employment in the regular *labour market* in Europe; cooperate with employers and co-workers to ensure that their needs are also addressed; collect and exchange information on national methodologies for creation of job opportunities, both for disabled people and for support workers and others concerned with their rights and lives; promote exchange of knowledge and experience and maintain contacts with associations, institutions and organizations at European Community level. **Structure** Council; Executive Committee. **Languages** English. **Staff** Voluntary. **Finance** Sources: meeting proceeds; members' dues; revenue from activities/projects. **Activities** Awareness raising; events/meetings; guidance/assistance/consulting; knowledge management/information dissemination; networking/liaising; projects/programmes; research and development; standards/guidelines. **Events** *Conference on Supported Employment* Oslo (Norway) 2022, *Transitions, for supported employment within Europe* Amsterdam (Netherlands) 2019, *Conference* Lisbon (Portugal) 2015, *Conference* Dublin (Ireland) 2013, *Conference* Copenhagen (Denmark) 2011.

Members National associations in 21 countries and territories:
Austria, Belgium, England, Finland, France, Germany, Gibraltar, Greece, Ireland, Italy, Malta, Netherlands, Northern Ireland, Norway, Poland, Portugal, Scotland, Slovenia, Spain, Sweden, Switzerland.

NGO Relations Member of (3): *European Association of Service Providers for Persons with Disabilities (EASPD, #06204)*; *European Disability Forum (EDF, #06929)*; *World Association for Supported Employment (WASE, #21195)*. [2022/XD3505/D]

♦ European Union of Swimming Pool and Spa Associations (EUSA) .. 09019

Sec c/o Bundesverband Schwimmbad, An Lyskirchen 14, 50676 Cologne, Germany. T. +492212716692. E-mail: info@eusaswim.eu.
Official Address Av des Arts 8, 1210 Brussels, Belgium.
URL: http://www.eusaswim.eu/

History 2006. Registration: Belgium. **Aims** Ensure with European Union offices a unit guaranteeing representation of the interests of professional groups in the field of swimming pools and spas and related activities. **Structure** Membership Meeting; Board of Directors; Working Committees (4). **Languages** English, French. **Staff** Voluntary. **Finance** Members' dues. **Events** *Meeting* Oxford (UK) 2013, *Meeting* London (UK) 2012, *Meeting* Bologna (Italy) 2011.

Members Active; Associate. Members in 12 countries:
Austria, France, Germany, Greece, Hungary, Italy, Portugal, Romania, Spain, Sweden, Switzerland, UK.

NGO Relations Partner of (2): *Euro Chlor (#05659)*; *European Association of Pump Manufacturers (EUROPUMP, #06182)*. In liaison with technical committees of: *Comité européen de normalisation (CEN, #04162)*. [2022/XJ4968/D]

- ♦ European Union for Systemics (#20403)
- ♦ European Union of Tourist Officers (inactive)
- ♦ European Union of Travelling Tradesmen (no recent information)
- ♦ European Union of Veterinary Hygienists / see Union européenne des vétérinaires hygiénistes (#20404)
- ♦ European Union of Veterinary Practitioners (#20405)
- ♦ European Union of Violin and Bow Makers / see European Association of Violin and Bow Makers (#06273)
- ♦ European Union Water Initiative (inactive)

♦ European Union of Water Management Associations (EUWMA) 09020

SG Dutch Water Authorities, Postbus 93218, 2509 AE The Hague, Netherlands. T. +31703519751. E-mail: info@dutchwaterauthorities.com.
URL: http://www.euwma.org/

History 1996. EU Transparency Register: 158678022663-08. **Aims** Increase cooperation in the field of water management between European water management associations so as to provide relevant information, views, position papers and policy documents to national governments, European and other relevant institutions. **Activities** Events/meetings; networking/liaising; knowledge management/information dissemination; research and development.

Members Full in 9 countries:
Belgium, France, Germany, Hungary, Italy, Netherlands, Portugal, Spain, UK. [2020.03.04/XJ7597/D]

- ♦ European Union of Weightball Lifting / see International Union of Kettlebell Lifting (#15786)

♦ European Union of Wholesale in Eggs, Egg-Products, Poultry and Game (EUWEP) 09021

Union européenne du commerce de gros des oeufs, produits d'oeufs, volaille et gibier – Europäische Union des Grosshandels mit Eiern, Eiprodukten, Geflügel und Wild – Unione Europea del Commercio all'Ingrosso delle Uova, dei Prodotti d'Uova, del Pollame e della Selvaggina – Europese Unie van de Groothandel in Eieren, Eierproducten en Gevogelte – Europaeiske Union for Engros-Handelen med Aeg, Aeggeprodukter Fjerkrae og Vildt

Secretariat Vendelier 57D, 3905 PC Veenendaal, Netherlands. T. +31306378844. E-mail: info@euwep.org.
SG address not obtained.
URL: https://www.euwep.org/

History 5 Nov 1959, Milan (Italy). Statutes adopted 5 Feb 1973, Brussels (Belgium). Reorganized and new rules adopted, 5-6 Jun 1997, Vienna (Austria), when became the umbrella organization for the 3 independently-operating member European trading organizations. New rules adopted 13 March 2019, following establishment of secretariat in the Netherlands. Registration: EU Transparency Register, No/ID: 36546161539-21. **Aims** Protect and defend rights, commercial functions and professional interests of member organizations by: strengthening cooperation among members; maintaining contacts with other professional organizations; studying common professional problems so as to reach common solutions; representing members' interests with the European Union. **Structure** General Assembly (annual); Board; Committees. **Languages** English. **Staff** 2.00 FTE, paid. **Finance** Sources: members' dues. **Activities** Events/meetings; projects/programmes. **Events** *General Assembly* Bucharest (Romania) 2012, *General Assembly* Krakow (Poland) 2011, *General Assembly* Verona (Italy) 2010, *General Assembly* Porto (Portugal) 2009, *General Assembly* Apeldoorn (Netherlands) 2008.

Members Independently-operating member European trading organizations (2), listed in this Yearbook:
European Egg Packers and Traders Association (EEPTA, #06969); *European Egg Processors Association (EEPA, #06970)*.

National associations of wholesalers of eggs, egg products, poultry and game and of related processing industries which are also members of one of the above trading organizations; individuals. Members in 17 EU countries (" indicates individuals only):
Austria, Belgium, Denmark, Finland, France, Germany, Greece (*), Hungary, Ireland (*), Italy, Netherlands, Poland, Portugal (*), Romania, Spain, Sweden, UK.

IGO Relations Accredited by (1): *European Commission (EC, #06633)*. **NGO Relations** Member of (1): *European Liaison Committee for Agricultural and Agri-Food Trades (#07687)*. [2021.06.18/XD0885/y/D]

- ♦ European Union of the Wholesale Potato Merchants / see European Potato Trade Association (#08257)
- ♦ European Union of the Wholesale Potato Trade / see European Potato Trade Association (#08257)
- ♦ European Union of Wholesalers Specializing in Stationery (inactive)
- ♦ European Union of Winter Cycling Tracks / see Union internationale des vélodromes (#20440)

♦ European Union of Women (EUW) 09022

Union européenne féminine (UEF) – Europäische Frauen-Union (EFU)

Contact BP 444, 86011 Poitiers CEDEX, France. E-mail: emorinchartier.euw@gmail.com.
URL: http://www.europeanunionofwomen.com/

History 1953, Salzburg (Austria). Registered in accordance with Austrian law. **Aims** Promote cooperation among women in political and civic organizations in Europe through the regular exchange of ideas on practical issues in political and social reform; preserve liberty and promote social and economic progress; strengthen and increase the influence of women in the political and civic life of their country and of Europe; provide support, training and information for women of emerging democracies in Central and Eastern Europe. **Structure** General Assembly (every 2 years); Executive Committee; Council (annual); Political Commission; Specialist Commissions (6); National Sections. **Languages** English, French, German. **Staff** Voluntary. **Finance** Members' dues. Other source: donations. Budget (annual): about pounds30,000. **Activities** Knowledge management/information dissemination; networking/liaising; training/education. **Events** *International meeting* Dijon (France) 2009, *Biennial General Assembly* Athens (Greece) 2001, *Biennial general assembly* Athens (Greece) 2000, *Multiculturality in Europe* Malta 2000, *Biennial general assembly* Stockholm (Sweden) 1999. **Publications** Commission reports.

Members National sections (composed of women members of parliament, members of local authorities and women in public life, drawn from Christian Democrat, Conservative and other like-minded political parties or similar civic bodies) in 22 countries:
Austria, Belgium, Cyprus, Denmark, Estonia, Finland, France, Germany, Greece, Hungary, Italy, Lithuania, Luxembourg, Malta, Norway, Poland, Portugal, Slovenia, Spain, Sweden, Switzerland, UK.

Consultative Status Consultative status granted from: *ECOSOC (#05331)* (Special); *Council of Europe (CE, #04881)* (Participatory Status). **IGO Relations** Accredited by: *United Nations Office at Vienna (UNOV, #20604)*. **NGO Relations** Member of: *Committee of NGOs on Human Rights, Geneva (#04275)*; *Conference of Non-Governmental Organizations in Consultative Relationship with the United Nations (CONGO, #04635)*; *Vienna NGO Committee on Drugs (VNGOC, #20773)*; *Vienna NGO Committee on the Status of Women (#20775)*. Instrumental in setting up: *Lola Solar Fund (no recent information)*. [2015.01.12/XD0902/D]

♦ European Union Women Inventors and Innovators Network (EUWIIN) 09023

Dir address not obtained. E-mail: contact@globalwiin.com.
URL: http://www.euwiininternational.eu/

History Founded in 2006, by Bola Olabisi. **Aims** Build opportunities for creative, inventive and innovative women across Europe. **Structure** Steering Committee of 6 members. **Activities** Knowledge management/information dissemination; guidance/assistance/consulting; networking/liaising; capacity building; research and development; training/education. **Events** *Women Inventors, Innovators & Entrepreneurs Exhibition, Conference & Awards* Bari (Italy) 2017, *Women Inventors, Innovators & Entrepreneurs Exhibition, Conference & Awards* London (UK) 2015. **Publications** e-Newsletter (6 a year). **Members** Categories Standard; Gold; Platinum; Diamond. Membership countries not specified. **NGO Relations** Cooperates with (1): *Global Women Inventor and Innovator Network (GWiIN)*. Collaborates with: *Association of Organisations of Mediterranean Businesswomen (#02840)*. [2017/XJ2007/F]

♦ European Union Youth Orchestra (EUYO) 09024

Orchestre des jeunes de l'Union européenne (OJCE) – Joven Orquesta de la Unión Europea – Jugendorchester der Europäischen Union – Orquestra da Juventude da União Européia – Orchestra Giovanile dell'Unione Europea – Jeugdorkest van de Europese Union – Europæiske Union Ungdomsorkester

CEO Corso della Giovecca 38, 44121 Ferrara FE, Italy. T. +442072357671. Fax +442072357370. E-mail: info@euyo.eu.
URL: http://www.euyo.eu/

History 8 Mar 1976. Founded as a result of an all-party resolution agreed by *European Parliament (EP, #08146)*, following the organization of *International Festival of Youth Orchestras*. Former names and other names: *European Community Youth Orchestra (ECYO)* – former; *Orchestre des jeunes de la Communauté européenne (OJCE)* – former; *Joven Orquesta de la Comunidad Europea* – former; *Jugendorchester der Europäischen Gemeinschaft* – former; *Orquestra Juvenil da Comunidade Européia* – former; *Orchestra Giovanile della Comunità Europea* – former; *Jeugdorkest van de Europese Gemeenschap* – former; *EF Ungdomsorkester* – former; *Orhistra Neoleas tis Evropaikis Kinotitas* – former; *Ceolfhoireann Aoság an Chomhphobail Eorapaigh* – former. Registration: EU Transparency Register, No/ID: 859389815176-35. **Aims** Demonstrate the cooperation and creativity of European youth and produce more enlightened Europeans equipped to play a part in the welfare and betterment of European and other communities, by establishing an orchestra of talented and dedicated young musicians from member countries of the European Union. **Structure** Organized under the auspices of *International Youth Foundation of Great Britain*, set up for that purpose. **Languages** English, French, German, Italian. **Staff** 6.00 FTE, paid. **Finance** Sources: European Union through the Creative Europe programme; EU Member State funding; private contributions. **Activities** Events/meetings; networking/liaising; projects/programmes.

Members Orchestra composed of about 140 young musicians between the ages of 16 and 26 from the 27 countries of the European Union:
Austria, Belgium, Bulgaria, Croatia, Cyprus, Czechia, Denmark, Estonia, Finland, France, Germany, Greece, Hungary, Ireland, Italy, Latvia, Lithuania, Luxembourg, Malta, Netherlands, Poland, Portugal, Romania, Slovakia, Slovenia, Spain, Sweden.

NGO Relations Member of (1): *European Alliance for Culture and the Arts (#05866)*. [2022.10.19/XF6658/F]

♦ European Unitarian-Universalists (EUU) 09025

Pres address not obtained. E-mail: secretary@europeanuu.org – contact@europeanuu.org.
URL: http://www.europeanuu.org/

History 1982. Former names and other names: *Unitarian Universalists in Europe* – alias. **Aims** Provide a means of mutual support for people interested in Unitarian Universalism and for Unitarian Universalists in Europe; provide assistance to existing fellowships in Europe and aid individuals who want to set up new fellowships; share information, programmes and experiences. **Structure** General Meeting (annual); Coordinating Council; Officers; Fellowships; at-large Group. **Languages** English. **Staff** 0.50 FTE, paid. **Finance** Sources: contributions. **Activities** Events/meetings. Active in: Belgium, Czechia, France, Germany, Netherlands, Switzerland. **Publications** *Unifier* (regular) – online internal newsletter. **Members** Individuals (200). Membership countries not specified. **Consultative Status** Consultative status granted from: *International Council of Unitarians and Universalists (ICUU, #13089)* (General). **NGO Relations** Member of (1): *International Council of Unitarians and Universalists (ICUU, #13089)* (Founding member). Affiliated with (1): *Unitarian Universalist Association (UUA, #20494)*. [2022.02.09/XF3303/F]

- ♦ European and United Kingdom Pool Federation / see European Blackball Association (#06349)
- ♦ European Universities Continuing Education Network / see European University Continuing Education Network (#09030)

♦ European University Alliance for Global Health (EUGLOH) 09026

SG address not obtained.
URL: https://www.eugloh.eu/

Aims Train future generations of European innovators, practitioners, experts and leaders serving all sectors of the society, ready to face interdisciplinary societal challenges related to Global Health. **Structure** Governing Board; Project Management Team; Executive Board; Student Board; Advisory Committee. **Activities** Events/meetings; research/documentation; training/education. **Events** *Annual Summit* Paris (France) 2022, *Annual Student Research Conference* Paris (France) 2021, *Annual Summit* Porto (Portugal) 2021.

Members Universities (5) in countries:
France, Germany, Hungary, Portugal, Sweden.
Consortium partners (4) in 4 countries:
Germany, Norway, Serbia, Spain. [2022/AA2710/**D**]

♦ European University Association (EUA) 09027

Association européenne de l'université

SG EUA Brussels Office, Avenue de l'Yser 24, 1040 Brussels, Belgium. T. +3222305544. Fax +3222305751. E-mail: info@eua.eu.
URL: https://eua.eu/

History 31 Mar 2001, Salamanca (Spain). Founded by merger of *Association of European Universities (CRE, inactive)* and *Confederation of European Union Rectors' Conferences (inactive)*. Registration: Banque-Carrefour des Entreprises, No/ID: 0477.216.541, Start date: 15 Feb 2022, Belgium; Swiss Civil Code, Switzerland; EU Transparency Register, No/ID: 81122172998-09, Start date: 12 Jan 2010. **Aims** As a centre of expertise in higher education and research, support universities by: promoting policies to enable universities and other higher education institutions to respond to growing expectations regarding their contribution to the future development of a knowledge society for Europe; advocating these policies to decision makers at different levels and ensuring that the voice of universities is heard; informing members of policy debates affecting their development; developing knowledge and expertise through projects that involve and benefit individual institutions while also underpinning policy development; strengthening governance, leadership and management of institutions; developing partnerships in higher education and research between Europe and the rest of the world so as to strengthen the position of European universities in a global context. **Structure** General Assembly (annual); Council; Board; Secretariat in Brussels (Belgium). Includes *EUA Council for Doctoral Education (EUA-CDE, #05563)*. **Languages** English, French. **Staff** 40.00 FTE, paid. **Finance** Sources: contributions; government support; revenue from activities/projects; subscriptions. **Activities** Events/meetings; networking/liaising; politics/policy/regulatory; training/education. **Events** *European Quality Assurance Forum* Aveiro (Portugal) 2023, *European Learning & Teaching Forum* Bilbao (Spain) 2023, *Annual Conference* Gdansk (Poland) 2023, *EUA-CDE Annual Meeting* Lappeenranta (Finland) 2023, *Deepening, Widening, Focusing – How to Navigate Transnational University Cooperation into the Future?* Brussels (Belgium) 2022. **Publications** Annual Report; newsletters; studies; reports; policy positions.
Members Full (Individual and Collective); Associate (Individual and Collective); Affiliate. Universities and institutions (about 850) in 47 countries:
Albania, Andorra, Armenia, Austria, Azerbaijan, Belarus, Belgium, Bosnia-Herzegovina, Bulgaria, Croatia, Cyprus, Czechia, Denmark, Estonia, Finland, France, Georgia, Germany, Greece, Holy See, Hungary, Iceland, Ireland, Italy, Kazakhstan, Latvia, Lithuania, Luxembourg, Malta, Moldova, Montenegro, Netherlands, North Macedonia, Norway, Poland, Portugal, Romania, Russia, Serbia, Slovakia, Slovenia, Spain, Sweden, Switzerland, Türkiye, UK, Ukraine.
Consultative Status Consultative status granted from: *UNESCO (#20322)* (Associate Status). **IGO Relations** Cooperates with (2): *Council of Europe (CE, #04881)*; *European Commission (EC, #06633)*. **NGO Relations** Observer status with (1): *European Energy Research Alliance (EERA, #06989)*. Member of (5): *EFMD – The Management Development Network (#05387)*; *European Association for Quality Assurance in Higher Education (ENQA, #06183)*; *European Quality Assurance Register for Higher Education (EQAR, #08311)*; *Federation of European and International Associations Established in Belgium (FAIB, #09508)*; *International Association of Universities (IAU, #12246)*. Cooperates with (1): *European University Continuing Education Network (EUCEN, #09030)*. Signatory to agreement of *Coalition for Advancing Research Assessment (CoARA, #04045)*. [2023/XD8329/**D**]

- ♦ European University, Belgrade (internationally oriented national body)
- ♦ European University Centre for Cultural Heritage, Ravello (internationally oriented national body)

♦ European University College Association (EucA) 09028

SG Rue de Trèves 49/51 – bte 3, 1040 Brussels, Belgium. T. +3222806340. Fax +3222806338. E-mail: info@euca.eu.
URL: http://www.euca.eu/

History 2008. Registration: Banque-Carrefour des Entreprises, No/ID: 0898.721.925, Start date: 23 Jun 2008, Belgium; EU Transparency Register, No/ID: 96348421122-86, Start date: 11 Feb 2009. **Aims** Create an international network among university colleges; promote cultural and academic exchanges between European students and encourage active citizenship among young people. **Structure** General Assembly; Board of Management; Scientific Committee. **Finance** Sources: donations; gifts, legacies; members' dues. **Activities** Events/meetings; training/education. **Publications** *EucA Newsletter*.
Members Students (about 30,000); Halls of residence (194). Members in 13 countries:
Belgium, Croatia, France, Germany, Hungary, Italy, Poland, Portugal, Romania, Slovenia, Spain, Switzerland, UK.
IGO Relations Registered in the European Transparency Register. **NGO Relations** Member of (1): *Lifelong Learning Platform – European Civil Society for Education (LLLP, #16466)*. Partner of (1): *International Association of Student Affairs and Services (IASAS, #12189)*. [2021/XM4176/**D**]

♦ European University Consortium for Pharmaceutical Research (ULLA) 09029

Committee Assistant c/o LACDR, Einsteinweg 55, 2333 CC Leiden, Netherlands. E-mail: info@ullapharmsci.org.
URL: https://ullapharmsci.org/

History 1992. The acronym "ULLA" derives from the founding universities: Uppsala (Sweden); London (UK); Leiden (Netherlands); Amsterdam (Netherlands). **Aims** Enhance collaboration within education and research in pharmaceutical sciences between the European universities. **Activities** Organizes summer schools. Offers grants for studies at other institutions. Serves as a platform for inter-institutional cooperation. **Events** *Symposium on proteins, peptides and peptidomimetics* Uppsala (Sweden) 2011. **Publications** *ULLA Pharmacy Series*.
Members Universities in 7 countries:
Belgium, Denmark, France, Italy, Netherlands, Sweden, UK.
NGO Relations *European Federation for Pharmaceutical Sciences (EUFEPS, #07192)*. [2022/XJ3997/**D**]

♦ European University Continuing Education Network (EUCEN) 09030

Réseau européen en formation continue universitaire

Exec Dir Balmes 132, 08008 Barcelona, Spain. T. +34935421825. Fax +34935422975. E-mail: office@eucen.eu.
URL: http://www.eucen.eu/

History Founded May 1991, Bristol (UK). Previously also referred to as *European Universities Continuing Education Network*. Registered in accordance with Belgian law, 1994. EU Transparency Register: 27779561950-28. **Aims** Contribute to economic and cultural life of Europe through promotion and advancement of lifelong learning within higher education institutions in Europe and elsewhere; foster universities' influence in development of lifelong learning knowledge and policies throughout Europe. **Structure** General Assembly (annual); Steering Committee; Secretariat. **Languages** English, French, Italian, Spanish. **Staff** 3.50 FTE, paid. **Finance** Members' dues. Other sources: projects; conferences and events; consulting. **Activities** Training/education; events/meetings; liaising/networking; research/documentation; projects/programmes; guidance/assistance/consulting. **Events** *Annual Conference* Utrecht (Netherlands) 2023, *Annual Conference* Budapest (Hungary) 2022, *Annual Conference* Budapest (Hungary) 2020, *Annual Conference* Aveiro (Portugal) 2019, *Autumn Seminar* Barcelona (Spain) 2018. **Publications** *eJournal of ULLL*. Policy statements; position papers; conference proceedings.
Members Full (140) in 30 countries:
Albania, Austria, Belgium, Bosnia-Herzegovina, Czechia, Estonia, Finland, France, Georgia, Germany, Greece, Hungary, Ireland, Italy, Liechtenstein, Lithuania, Malta, Netherlands, Norway, Poland, Portugal, Romania, Russia, Slovakia, Slovenia, Spain, Sweden, Switzerland, Türkiye, UK.
Associate members (8) in 8 countries:
Belgium, Canada, Denmark, Germany, Greece, Lebanon, Luxembourg, Switzerland.
Affiliate (24) in 16 countries and territories:
Belgium, Colombia, Estonia, Hungary, Netherlands, Norway, Palestine, Poland, Portugal, Slovakia, Spain, Sweden, Switzerland, Türkiye, UK, USA.
IGO Relations *European Commission (EC, #06633)*; *European Quality Assurance in Vocational Education and Training (EQAVET, #08312)*. **NGO Relations** *Eurasian Universities Union (EURAS, #05615)*; *European Access Network (EAN, #05819)*; *European Association for the Education of Adults (EAEA, #06018)*; *European Association of Institutions of Higher Education (EURASHE, #06086)*; *Global University Network for Innovation (GUNI, #10641)*; *Lifelong Learning Platform – European Civil Society for Education (LLLP, #16466)*; *European University Association (EUA, #09027)*; *International Council for Open and Distance Education (ICDE, #13056)*; *Red Universitaria de Educación Continua de Latinoamérica y Europa (RECLA, #18734)*; national associations. [2020.02.05/XF3124/**F**]

- ♦ European University of Creative and Audiovisual Writing / see Institut Européen d'Ecriture

♦ European University Foundation – Campus Europae (EUF-CE) 09031

SG Rue du Parc 31, L-5374 Munsbach, Luxembourg. T. +352261510. Fax +35226151032. E-mail: isabel.catarino@uni-foundation.eu – contact@uni-foundation.eu.
URL: http://www.campuseuropae.org/

History Conceptualized, 1998, in the framework of German presidency of *European Union (EU, #08967)*. Secretariat set up at Munsbach (Luxembourg), 2004. Registration: Start date: 2008, Luxembourg; EU Transparency Register, No/ID: 600840014582-48, Start date: 2014. **Aims** Organize high quality *student exchange* aimed at: providing students with the opportunity to go abroad for full academic years; providing incentives to learn the language of their host country; providing additional recognition for their mobility period through the CE-Degree; allowing students to combine studying and working abroad. **Structure** General Assembly; Student Council; Subject Committees; Secretariat, managed by Secretary-General. **Publications** *Campus Europae Newsletter* (12 a year). *Campus Europae – A Laboratory for Mobility* (2013).
Members Universities (21) in 16 countries:
Austria, Cyprus, Estonia, Finland, France, Germany, Greece, Italy, Latvia, Lithuania, Luxembourg, Poland, Portugal, Russia, Serbia, Spain.
IGO Relations *European Commission (EC, #06633)*. **NGO Relations** Member of (1): *Lifelong Learning Platform – European Civil Society for Education (LLLP, #16466)*. [2020/XJ5777/t/**F**]

♦ European University Hospital Alliance (EUHA) 09032

Manager Passeig de la Vall d'Hebron 119, 08035 Barcelona, Spain. T. +3467340043. E-mail: secretariat@euhalliance.eu.
Registered Address Warmoesberg 26, 1000 Brussels, Belgium.
URL: https://www.euhalliance.eu/

History Registration: Banque-Carrefour des Entreprises, No/ID: 0772.718.430, Start date: 20 Aug 2021, Belgium. **Aims** Build a network of sustainable healthcare ecosystems in Europe which achieve the best possible quality of care with the resources available. **Structure** Members' Assembly; Steering Committee; Secretariat.
Members University hospitals (9) in 9 countries:
Austria, Belgium, France, Germany, Italy, Netherlands, Spain, Sweden, UK.
NGO Relations Signatory to agreement of: *Coalition for Advancing Research Assessment (CoARA, #04045)*. [2022/AA3078/**D**]

♦ European University Information Systems Organization (EUNIS) ... 09033

Pres Trinity College Dublin, Univ of Dublin, Dublin, CO. DUBLIN, Ireland. E-mail: a.pacholak@uw.edu.pl – president.eunis@uw.edu.pl.
Registered Address Maison des Universités, 103 bd Saint Michel, 75005 Paris, France.
URL: http://www.eunis.org/

History Founded 1993. Registered in accordance with French law. EU Transparency Register: 268294422937-21. **Aims** Encourage exchanges, cooperation and debates between those responsible for information systems in higher education or research institutes/organizations within Europe; establish relationships with supervisory organizations in charge of information systems in higher education and in research institutes in each country as well as at European level. **Structure** General Assembly; Board of Directors; Task Forces (4). **Languages** English. **Staff** 3.00 FTE, paid. **Finance** Members' dues. Sponsorship. **Activities** Guidance/assistance/consulting; events/meetings; research/documentation. **Events** *Annual Congress* Athens (Greece) 2021, *Annual Congress* Helsinki (Finland) 2020, *Annual Congress* Trondheim (Norway) 2019, *Annual Congress* Paris (France) 2018, *Conference of European Rectors* Porto (Portugal) 2018. **Publications** *EUNIS Newsletter*, *European Journal of Higher Education IT*. Surveys; reports; workshop reports.
Members Regular; Corresponding; Honorary; Corporate; Individual. Regular in 30 countries:
Austria, Bulgaria, Croatia, Cyprus, Czechia, Denmark, Estonia, Finland, France, Germany, Greece, Hungary, Ireland, Italy, Kosovo, Latvia, Lithuania, Netherlands, North Macedonia, Norway, Poland, Portugal, Romania, Serbia, Slovakia, Slovenia, Spain, Sweden, Switzerland, UK.
Corresponding members in 1 country:
USA.
NGO Relations Cooperates with: *euroCRIS (#05672)*; *European University Association (EUA, #09027)*; *GÉANT Association (#10086)*; *Trans-European Research and Education Networking Association (TERENA, inactive)*; *Transforming Education Through Information Technologies (EDUCAUSE)*; national organizations. [2016.10.19/XD6593/**D**]

♦ European University Institute (EUI) 09034

Institut universitaire européen – Europäisches Hochschulinstitut – Istituto Universitario Europeo (IUE) – Europees Universitair Instituut

SG Via dei Roccettini 9, 50014 San Domenico di Fiesole, Italy. T. +39554685778.
Pres address not obtained. T. +39554685235. Fax +39554685312. E-mail: president@eui.eu.
URL: http://www.eui.eu/

History 19 Apr 1972. Established on signature of Convention by the 6 original member states of the then European Community. Officially opened in autumn 1976. Registration: EU Transparency Register, No/ID: 742228039171-04, Start date: 7 Aug 2020. **Aims** Foster advancement of learning in fields which are of particular interest for the development of Europe through doctoral and postdoctoral programmes, executive training and research. **Structure** High Council; Academic Council; Budget and Finance Committee; Research Council; Principal; Secretary-General. Academic Departments (4): Economics; History; Law; Political and Social Science. Includes: *Academy of European Law, Florence (see: #09034)*; *Historical Archives of the European Union (HAEU, #10927)*; Max Weber Programme for Postdoctoral Studies; *Robert Schuman Centre for Advanced Studies (RSCAS, see: #09034)*; The School of Transnational Governance. **Languages** English, French, Italian. **Staff** Administrative: 217; Professors: 91; Research: 136. **Finance** Financed by: contracting Member States; *European Commission (EC, #06633)*; external public and private research funding sources. **Activities** Research/documentation; knowledge management/information dissemination; training/education; events/meetings. **Events** *European Energy Policy and Law Conference* Brussels (Belgium) 2019, *The State of the Union Conference* Florence (Italy) 2019, *Joint Workshop on Asia and the Global Reach of European Union Law* Singapore (Singapore) 2019, *Conference on Secular Stagnation, Growth and Real Interest Rates* Florence (Italy) 2015, *Workshop on Public History and the Media* Florence (Italy) 2015. **Publications** *EUI Times* – electronic magazine. *EUI Working Papers* – series. Policy Papers; technical reports. **Information Services** *Cadmus* – Research Repository.
Members Contracting States (23):
Austria, Belgium, Bulgaria, Cyprus, Denmark, Estonia, Finland, France, Germany, Greece, Ireland, Italy, Latvia, Luxembourg, Malta, Netherlands, Poland, Portugal, Romania, Slovenia, Spain, Sweden, UK.
Associated States (2):
Norway, Switzerland. [2020/XF3293/j/**F***]

- ♦ European University of International Management and Business (internationally oriented national body)
- ♦ European University Network for International Humanitarian Aid Studies / see Network on Humanitarian Action (#17034)

♦ European University on Responsible Consumption and Production (EURECA-PRO) 09035

Contact address not obtained. E-mail: info@eurecapro.eu.
URL: https://www.eurecapro.eu/

History EURECA-PRO phase I (2020-2023) co-funded by the Erasmus+ Programme of *European Union (EU, #08967)*. **Aims** Act as the global educational core hub and interdisciplinary research and innovation leader in qualitative environmental and social framework development for responsible consumption and production of goods. **Finance** Also supported at national level. Supported by: *European Union (EU, #08967)* (Erasmus+ Programme). **Activities** Networking/liaising; research/documentation; training/education. **Events** *Conference* Chania (Greece) 2023, *Conference* León (Spain) 2022, *Conference* Leoben (Austria) 2021. **Publications** *EURECA-PRO Newsletter*.
Members Universities (8) in 7 countries:
Austria, Belgium, Germany, Greece, Poland, Romania, Spain. [2023/AA2667/F]

♦ European University Sports Association (EUSA) 09036

Office Tomšičeva ulica 4, 1000 Ljubljana, Slovenia. T. +38612560056. Fax +38612560057. E-mail: office@eusa.eu.
Registered Office C/O ASVZ, ETH Zentrum, 8092 Zurich ZH, Switzerland.
URL: http://www.eusa.eu/
History 1999, Vienna (Austria). Registration: Swiss Civil Code, Switzerland. **Aims** Maintain and develop regular communication between the national federations; coordinate competitions, conferences, mass-sport-events and other activities both at university and national level; represent university sport in general and the member federations in particular in relation to European organizations; disseminate throughout Europe the ideals of university sport in close collaboration with the International University Sports Federation (FISU) and other European organizations. **Structure** General Assembly; Executive Board; Commissions. **Languages** English. **Finance** Members' dues. Other sources: sports events (games, championships, patronage); educational events (conferences, conventions); donations; other. **Activities** Sporting activities; training/education; projects/programmes. **Events** *General Assembly* Budapest (Hungary) 2021, *Conference* Aveiro (Portugal) 2019, *General Assembly* Aveiro (Portugal) 2019, *General Assembly* Madrid (Spain) 2018, *Conference* Coimbra (Portugal) 2017. **Publications** *European University Sports Association Year Magazine*; *EUSA Newsletter*. *European University Sports Association: first 10 years 1999-2009*.
Members Federations in 45 countries:
Albania, Armenia, Austria, Azerbaijan, Belarus, Belgium, Bosnia-Herzegovina, Bulgaria, Croatia, Cyprus, Czechia, Denmark, Estonia, Finland, France, Georgia, Germany, Greece, Hungary, Iceland, Ireland, Israel, Italy, Latvia, Liechtenstein, Lithuania, Malta, Moldova, Montenegro, Netherlands, North Macedonia, Norway, Poland, Portugal, Romania, Russia, Serbia, Slovakia, Slovenia, Spain, Sweden, Switzerland, Türkiye, UK, Ukraine.
Consultative Status Consultative status granted from: *Council of Europe (CE, #04881)* (Participatory Status).
IGO Relations Member of (1): *Enlarged Partial Agreement on Sport (EPAS, #05487)* (Consultative Committee). Consultative Status with: *European Commission (EC, #06633)* – EU Expert Group on Human Resources Development in Sport (XG HR). **NGO Relations** Memorandum of Understanding with (1): *European Sports Press Union (AIPS Europe, #08822)*. [2022/XM2976/D]

- ♦ European University at St Petersburg (internationally oriented national body)
- ♦ European University of Volunteerism (see: #02978)

♦ European University for Well-Being (EUniWell) 09037

Communication Manager Albertus-Magnus-Platz, 50923 Cologne, Germany. T. +492214702345. E-mail: info@euniwell.eu.
URL: https://www.euniwell.eu/
History 2020. Founded in response to invitation of *Council of the European Union (#04895)* for member states to pursue a horizontal, cross-sectoral, knowledge-based approach to advance the 'Economy of Wellbeing', 24 Oct 2019. **Aims** Research, measure, understand, rebalance and help improve the well-being of individuals, civic communities and society as a whole on regional, national, European and global level and based on joint values – democratic, inclusive, diverse, research- and challenge-based, inter- and transdisciplinary, entrepreneurial, and co-creational. **Structure** EUniWell Board; Student Board; Rectors' Assembly; External Advisory Board; Steering and Management Team. **Languages** English, French, German, Hungarian, Italian, Spanish, Swedish, Ukrainian. **Finance** Sources: contributions of member/participating states; international organizations. Supported by: *European Commission (EC, #06633)*. **Activities** Events/meetings; healthcare; publishing activities; research and development; research/documentation; training/education.
Members Universities (10) in 8 countries:
France (Nantes), Germany (Cologne, Konstanz), Hungary (Semmelweis), Italy (Florence), Spain (Murcia, Santiago de Compostela), Sweden (Linnaeus), UK (Birmingham), Ukraine (Taras Shevchenko National University of Kyiv).
[2023.02.22/AA1172/E]

- ♦ European Unmanned Vehicle Systems Association / see Unmanned Vehicle Systems International (#20708)
- ♦ European Unoriented PET Film Manufacturers Association / see European Association for Unoriented Polyester Films (#06261)
- ♦ European Unsaturated PET Film Manufacturers Association / see European Association for Unoriented Polyester Films (#06261)

♦ European UP/VE Resin Association 09038

Contact c/o CEFIC, Avenue Van Nieuwenhuyse 4, 1160 Brussels, Belgium. T. +3226767262. Fax +3226767447. E-mail: coo@cefic.be.
URL: http://www.upresins.org/
History Set up as a sector group of *Conseil européen de l'industrie chimique (CEFIC, #04687)*. **Members** Companies (4). Membership countries not specified. **NGO Relations** Sectoral organization of: *European Composites Industry Association (EuCIA, #06692)*. [2015/XM4371/D]

- ♦ European Urban Charter (1992 treaty)
- ♦ European Urban Data Management Society / see Urban Data Management Society (#20730)
- ♦ European Urban Green Infrastructure Conference (meeting series)

♦ European Urban Knowledge Network (EUKN) 09039

Contact Schenkkade 50, 2595 AR The Hague, Netherlands. T. +31708002055. E-mail: info@eukn.eu.
URL: http://www.eukn.eu/
History Launched May 2005, having been developed as a pilot project under the auspices of the 2004 Dutch Presidency of the European Union, supported by the URBACT programme. Awarded legal status of 'European Grouping for Territorial Cooperation (EGTC)', 2013. **Aims** Generate a professional community that shares expert urban knowledge and policy practice; connect policy-makers, practitioners and researchers in pursuit of evidence-based sustainable urban development policy. **Structure** Assembly of EU Member States; Secretariat. **Languages** Dutch, English, French, German, Spanish. **Staff** 5.00 FTE, paid. **Finance** Members' contributions. **Activities** Research/documentation; events/meetings; knowledge management/information dissemination. **Events** *Annual Conference* Brussels (Belgium) 2019, *Annual Conference* Amsterdam (Netherlands) 2014, *Conference / Annual Conference* Oradea (Romania) 2013, *Conference on side effects of free mobility* Helsinki (Finland) 2009, *International conference* Rotterdam (Netherlands) 2008. **Publications** *The Inclusive City: approaches to combat urban poverty and social exclusion in Europe* (2014); *Municipal Action for Energy Efficiency* (2013); *Youth Unemployment and Geographic Mobility in the EU* (2013); *Multilevel Urban Governance* (2011). Research papers.
Members Organizations and National Focal Points in 7 countries:
Belgium, Cyprus, Czechia, France, Germany, Netherlands, Poland. [2017.10.18/XJ0318/F]

♦ European Urban Research Association (EURA) 09040

Secretariat c/o Europaeische Planungskulturen (EPK), August Schmidt Str 6, GB I Rm 420, 44221 Dortmund, Germany. T. +492317552485. Fax +492317554787. E-mail: secretariat@eura.org.
URL: http://www.eura.org/
History Sep 1997, Brussels (Belgium). Launched during an international conference held in Brussels; following discussions held at 'Shaping the Urban Future' in Bristol (UK), July 1994. **Aims** Provide a European forum for people from different disciplines and policy backgrounds to exchange information about and findings from research on towns and cities as the basis for closer cooperation; encourage interdisciplinary and cross-national approaches to research in and education for urban and regional studies as a professional and academic field; bridge the gaps between academic, professional and policy interests; inform public debate and improve the quality of urban policy. **Structure** Governing Board, comprising President, Vice President and 19 members. **Languages** English. **Finance** Members' dues (annual): between pounds16 (euro 24) – pounds165 (euro 240). **Activities** Organizes conferences and workshops; links European researchers with their counterparts in the rest of the world. Plans to launch journal *Urban Research and Practice* in 2008. **Events** *Conference* Milan (Italy) 2022, *Conference* Oslo (Norway) 2021, *Conference* Oslo (Norway) 2020, *EURA-UAA joint conference* Dublin (Ireland) 2019, *Conference* Tilburg (Netherlands) 2018. **Publications** *Urban Research and Practice Journal* (3 a year); *EURA Newsletter* (2 a year).
Members Institutional; East European Institutional; Individual; Research Student; Colleagues in Eastern Europe Institutional members in 12 countries:
Belgium, Denmark, France, Germany, Italy, Netherlands, Norway, Russia, Spain, Sweden, UK, USA.
Individuals in 23 countries. Membership countries not specified.
NGO Relations Cooperates with: *Association of European Schools of Planning (AESOP, #02542)*.
[2021/XD8789/D]

♦ European Urogynaecological Association (EUGA) 09041

Contact address not obtained. T. +39523338391. Fax +395231860018. E-mail: info@eugaoffice.org.
URL: http://www.eugaoffice.org/
History 2002, Prague. Also referred to as *European Uro-Gynaecology Association*. **Aims** Facilitate study and analysis of all aspects of *urinary tract* and *pelvic floor* dysfunction, promoting European-wide education and setting the standards in urogynaecology. **Languages** English. **Activities** Events/meetings. **Events** *Annual Congress* Ljubljana (Slovenia) 2021, *Interactive Meeting* Tel Aviv (Israel) 2020, *Annual Congress* Tel Aviv (Israel) 2019, *Annual Congress* Milan (Italy) 2018, *Annual Congress* Barcelona (Spain) 2017. **Members** Membership countries not specified. [2019.02.19/XD9220/D]

- ♦ European Uro-Gynaecology Association / see European Urogynaecological Association (#09041)
- ♦ European Usher Syndrome Study Group / see Usher Study Group

♦ European Utilities Telecom Council (EUTC) 09042

Gen Sec Avenue de la Toisor d'Or 22, B1, 1050 Brussels, Belgium. T. +3226452677. E-mail: info@eutc.org – communications@eutc.org.
URL: http://www.eutc.org/
History Set up by the US 'Utilities Telecom Council (UTC)'. Registration: Banque-Carrefour des Entreprises, No/ID: 0759.718.747, Start date: 11 Dec 2020, Belgium; EU Transparency Register, No/ID: 743143938227-72, Start date: 20 May 2020. **Structure** Board of Directors; Executive Team. **Activities** Events/meetings; research/documentation. **Events** *Annual Event* Lisbon (Portugal) 2022, *Annual Conference* Lisbon (Portugal) 2017, *Annual Conference* Dublin (Ireland) 2015, *Annual Conference* Monte Carlo (Monaco) 2014, *Annual Conference* Amsterdam (Netherlands) 2013. **Members** Charter; Associate. Membership countries not specified. **NGO Relations** Memorandum of Understanding with (1): *European Energy Information Sharing and Analysis Centre (EE-ISAC, #06987)*. Member of (1): *European Telecommunications Standards Institute (ETSI, #08897)*. [2022/XJ7950/E]

♦ European Vaccine Initiative (EVI) 09043

Project Manager UniversitätsKlinikum Heidelberg, Im Neuenheimer Feld 326 – 3 OG, 69120 Heidelberg, Germany. T. +496221565974.
URL: http://www.euvaccine.eu/
History Set up by the universities of Stockholm (Sweden) and Heidelberg (Germany). Since Mar 2011, an organization of the type *European Economic Interest Grouping (EEIG, #06960)*. **Aims** Create an environment conducive to accelerating the development and clinical assessment of vaccine candidates for diseases of poverty; promote affordability and accessibility of vaccines for diseases of poverty in low-income populations; align major stakeholders and act as a focal point to ensure the successful development of vaccines for diseases of poverty for low-income populations; communicate to stakeholders and public the importance of EVI's work and progress towards the deployment of affordable and efficacious vaccine candidates for diseases of poverty. **Structure** Board; Scientific Advisory Committee. **Finance** Funding from governmental agencies from Ireland, Germany, Netherlands, Sweden and Denmark, including from *Irish Aid*, *Swedish International Development Cooperation Agency (Sida)* and *DANIDA*. **Publications** *EVI Newsletter*.
Members Institutions (6) in 5 countries:
Germany, Ireland, Netherlands, Sweden, UK.
NGO Relations Member of: *Developing Countries Vaccine Manufacturers Network (DCVMN, #05052)*.
[2015/XJ8385/D]

- ♦ European Vaccines Manufacturers / see Vaccines Europe (#20741)
- ♦ European Values Study (unconfirmed)
- ♦ European Vascular Biology Association (inactive)

♦ European Vascular Biology Organization (EVBO) 09044

Pres c/o Faculty of Biochemistry, Biophysics and Medical Biotechnology, Jagiellonian University, 7 Gronostajowa Street, 30-387 Krakow, Poland. T. +48126646375.
Honorary Sec c/o Imperial College London, Imperial Centre for Translational and Experimental Medicine, Hammersmith Hospital, Du Cane Road, London, W12 0NN, UK. T. +4478720850245.
URL: http://www.evbo.org/
History 2006, by representatives of *European Vascular Biology Association (inactive)* and *European Vascular Genomics Network (EVGN, inactive)*. **Activities** *European Meeting on Vascular Biology and Medicine (EMVBM)*. **Events** *European Meeting on Vascular Biology and Medicine* Maastricht (Netherlands) 2019, *International Vascular Biology Meeting* Helsinki (Finland) 2018, *European Meeting on Vascular Biology and Medicine* Geneva (Switzerland) 2017, *International Vascular Biology Meeting* Boston, MA (USA) 2016, *European Meeting on Vascular Biology and Medicine* Pisa (Italy) 2015. **NGO Relations** *European Society for Microcirculation (ESM, #08651)*. [2016/XM8276/D]

♦ European Vascular Surgeons in Training (EVST) 09045

Sec c/o ESVS, 244 bd Albert 1er, 33800 Bordeaux, France. T. +33556490307. E-mail: info@esvs.org.
URL: https://esvs.org/european-vascular-surgeons-in-training/
History 2006. Founded by the merger of *European Association of Vascular Surgeons in Training (EAVST, inactive)* and the Junior Members Section of *European Society for Vascular Surgery (ESVS, #08772)*. **Activities** European Vascular Course (EVC). **Members** Individuals (approx 2,000). Membership countries not specified.
[2022/XM8282/D]

♦ European Vasculitis Society (EUVAS) 09046

Secretariat Box 57, Dept of Renal Medicine, Addenbrooke's Hosp, Cambridge, CB2 2QQ, UK. T. +441223217259. Fax +441223586506. E-mail: info@vasculitis.org.
Sec address not obtained.
URL: http://www.vasculitis.org/
History 15 May 2011, evolving from *European Vasculitis Study Group*. Constitution adopted 15 May 2011. **Aims** Unite vasculitis researchers and clinicians, promoting the study and treatment of vasculitis. **Structure** General Assembly. Presidential Council, comprising President, Vice-President, Secretary, Treasurer and member. **Languages** English. **Events** *International Vasculitis and ANCA Workshop / Meeting* Paris (France) 2013, *Asia Pacific Meeting* Tokyo (Japan) 2012.
Members Ordinary; Associate. Individuals in 23 countries:
Australia, Austria, Belgium, Canada, Czechia, Denmark, Finland, France, Germany, Greece, Ireland, Italy, Latvia, Mexico, Netherlands, Norway, Poland, Russia, Spain, Sweden, Switzerland, Türkiye, UK. [2020/XJ6745/D]

- ♦ European Vasculitis Study Group / see European Vasculitis Society (#09046)
- ♦ European VAT Club (unconfirmed)

♦ European Vegetable Protein Association (EUVEPRO) 09047

Association européenne des protéines végétales – Asociación Europea de Proteinas Vegetales – Europäische Vereinigung für Pflanzliches Protein – Associazione Europea Proteine Vegetali – Europese Plantaardig Eiwit Associatie – Europaeisk Forening for Vegetabilsk Protein
SG c/o Kellen, Av de Tervueren 188A, Postbox 4, 1150 Brussels, Belgium. T. +3227611650. Fax +3227611699. E-mail: euvepro@kellencompany.com.
URL: http://www.euvepro.eu/

History 16 Dec 1977, Brussels (Belgium). Former names and other names: *European Vegetable Protein Federation (EUVEPRO)* – former (1977); *Fédération européenne des protéines végétales* – former (1977); *Federación Europea de Proteinas Vegetales* – former (1977); *Federazione Europea Proteine Vegetali* – former (1977); *Europese Plantaardig Eiwit Federatie* – former (1977). Registration: EU Transparency Register, No/ID: 265472912378-24, Start date: 3 Dec 2013. **Aims** Promote awareness and acceptance of vegetable protein products on the part of *food* manufacturers and consumers; increase recognition, in European, national and international legislation, of vegetable protein products as foodstuffs and ingredients in their own right; stimulate research and commercial development of a wide range of vegetable protein products from different sources, such as soya, peas, beans, rapeseed, sunflower and cereals; monitor sustainable agriculture issues related to soy; represent on scientific, technical and institutional levels, all problems affecting the industry. **Structure** General Assembly (annual); Management Committee; Communication Group. **Languages** English, French. **Staff** 0.50 FTE, paid. **Finance** Sources: members' dues. **Activities** Awareness raising; events/meetings; knowledge management/information dissemination; networking/liaising; politics/policy/regulatory; projects/programmes; research and development; standards/guidelines. **Events** *Annual General Assembly* Brussels (Belgium) 2027, *Annual General Assembly* 2021, *Annual General Assembly* 2020, *Annual General Assembly* Brussels (Belgium) 2019, *Annual General Assembly* Lille (France) 2018. **Publications** Position papers.
Members Full in 5 countries:
Belgium, France, Germany, Netherlands, Switzerland.
Associate in 1 country:
France.
IGO Relations Recognized by: *European Commission (EC, #06633)*. Participates as observer in the activities of: *Codex Alimentarius Commission (CAC, #04081)*. **NGO Relations** Member of (2): *Primary Food Processors (PFP, #18496)*; *Round Table on Responsible Soy Association (RTRS, #18983)*. [2022.10.19/XD8953/D]

♦ European Vegetable Protein Federation / see European Vegetable Protein Association (#09047)

♦ European Vegetarian Union (EVU) 09048

Union européenne des végétariens

Pres Meidlinger Hauptstrasse 63/6, 1120 Vienna, Austria. E-mail: info@euroveg.eu.
Gen Sec Friedhofstr 12, 67693 Fischbach, Germany.
URL: http://www.euroveg.eu/

History Dec 1985. Founded as a regional council of *International Vegetarian Union (IVU, #15842)*. Became independent. Registration: Rhineland-Palatinate District court, No/ID: VR 30328, Start date: 15 Nov 2010, Germany, Rhineland-Palatinate; EU Transparency Register, No/ID: 109356110578-03, Start date: 5 Feb 2013. **Aims** Promote vegetarianism, vegetarian issues and benefits of a vegetarian lifestyle. **Structure** General Meeting (annual); Board; Secretariat. **Languages** English. **Staff** Voluntary. **Finance** Members' dues. Donations. **Activities** Knowledge management/information dissemination; awareness raising; advocacy/lobbying/activism; events/meetings. **Events** *Congress / Biennial Congress* Dresden (Germany) 2008, *Annual General Meeting* Vienna (Austria) 2007, *Annual General Meeting* Weidenthal (Germany) 2006, *Annual General Meeting* Riccione (Italy) 2005, *Annual General Meeting* Mons (Belgium) 2004. **Publications** Electronic newsletter.
Members Full – societies advocating vegetarian ideals and whose executive authority is vested in vegetarians; associate (no voting rights) – other societies, commissions and corporate bodies with relevant objectives. Members in 30 countries:
Austria, Belgium, Canada, Croatia, Czechia, Denmark, Finland, France, Germany, Iceland, India, Ireland, Italy, Kosovo, Lithuania, Moldova, Netherlands, Norway, Poland, Portugal, Romania, Russia, Serbia, Slovakia, Spain, Sweden, Switzerland, Türkiye, UK, USA. [2021/XD5870/D]

♦ European Vending Association / see European Vending and Coffee Service Association (#09049)

♦ European Vending and Coffee Service Association (EVA) 09049

Dir Gen Rue Van Eyck 44, 1000 Brussels, Belgium. T. +3225120075. Fax +3225022342. E-mail: ew@vending-europe.eu – vending@vending-europe.eu.
Facebook: https://www.facebook.com/EuropeanVendingCoffeeServiceAssociation

History 1976. Founded as *European Federation of Vending Associations (EFVA)* – *Fédération européenne des associations de la distribution automatique* – *Vereinigung der Europäischen Automatenverbände*. Formerly also known in French as *Association européenne de la distribution automatique*. Subsequently changed title to: *European Vending Association (EVA)*. Restructuration and new name, 1994. New statutes adopted 1995, 1998, 2000 and 2013. . Registration: Banque-Carrefour des Entreprises, No/ID: 0420.516.576, Start date: 17 Jun 1980, Belgium; EU Transparency Register, No/ID: 21371808279-69, Start date: 7 Mar 2012. **Aims** Represent the interests of the whole European coffee service and vending industry vis-à-vis European Union institutions and other relevant authorities or bodies. **Structure** General Assembly (annual); Executive Committee; Working Groups; Committees (13); Permanent Secretariat in Brussels (Belgium). **Languages** English, French. **Staff** 4.00 FTE, paid. **Finance** Members' dues. **Events** *Annual General Assembly and Conference* Düsseldorf (Germany) 2019, *Annual General Assembly and Conference* Seville (Spain) 2018, *Annual General Assembly and Conference* Rome (Italy) 2017, *Annual General Assembly and Conference* Cannes (France) 2016, *Annual General Assembly and Conference* Malaga (Spain) 2015. **Publications** *EVA Flash* (5 a year); *EU-Newsletter* (11 a year); *Information for Members*. Annual Report; position papers; press releases; leaflets; guides; brochures.
Members National Vending Associations in 13 countries:
Austria, Denmark, France, Germany, Hungary, Italy, Poland, Romania, Russia, Spain, Sweden, Switzerland, UK.
Direct members – internationally acting companies member of at least 1 EVA-affiliated national association (53) – in 14 countries:
Austria, Belgium, Denmark, France, Germany, Israel, Italy, Latvia, Netherlands, Russia, Spain, Sweden, Switzerland, UK.
Supportive members (28) in 14 countries and territories:
Belgium, France, Germany, Hungary, Ireland, Japan, Netherlands, Russia, Saudi Arabia, Spain, Switzerland, Taiwan, UK, USA.
Associate members (2):
European Drinking Water Cooler Association (EDWCA); National Automatic Merchandising Association (NAMA).
IGO Relations Cooperates with: *Council of the European Union (#04895)*; *European Economic and Social Committee (EESC, #06963)*. **NGO Relations** Member of: *EU Platform for Action on Diet, Physical Activity and Health (inactive)*; *Federation of European and International Associations Established in Belgium (FAIB, #09508)*. Cooperates with: *Comité européen de normalisation (CEN, #04162)*; *European Committee for Electrotechnical Standardization (CENELEC, #06647)*. [2022/XD3283/D]

♦ European Venous Forum (EVF) 09050

Exec Dir PO Box 172, Greenford, UB6 9ZN, UK. T. +442085757044. E-mail: admin@europeanvenousforum.org.
Registered Office 2nd Floor, 10-12 Bourlet Close, London, W1W 7BR, UK.
URL: http://www.europeanvenousforum.org/

History Jul 2000, Lyon (France). Founded under the auspices of *International Union of Angiology (IUA, #15754)* and *International Union of Phlebology (#15797)*. Registration: Companies House, No/ID: 04354339, Start date: 16 Jan 2002, England and Wales. **Aims** Develop scientific knowledge, research, clinical expertise, training and education of the highest quality; establish standards in the field of venous disease. **Structure** Annual General Meeting; Executive Committee; Board. **Languages** English. **Finance** Sources: members' dues. **Activities** Awards/prizes/competitions; events/meetings; financial and/or material support. **Events** *Hands-on Workshop* Porto (Portugal) 2023, *Hands-on Workshop* Porto (Portugal) 2022, *Annual Meeting* Venice (Italy) 2022, *Annual Meeting* 2021, *Hands-on Workshop* Porto (Portugal) 2021. **Publications** *EVF Journal*. Books; CD-Roms. **Members** Doctors (over 200) worldwide. Membership countries not specified. [2022.11.01/XD7248/v/D]

♦ European Ventilation Hygiene Association (EVHA) 09051

Main Office Belfry House, Bell Lane, Hertford, SG14 1BP, UK. T. +447495128811. E-mail: info@evha.eu.
URL: https://www.evha.eu/

History 1999. **Aims** Promote the ventilation hygiene industry within Europe; lobby for legislation and being recognized as the sign of competence and quality. **Activities** Advocacy/lobbying/activism; certification/accreditation; training/education. **Events** *Annual General Meeting* Malaga (Spain) 2022, *Annual General Meeting* Athens (Greece) 2021, *Annual General Meeting* Hertford (UK) 2020, *Annual General Meeting* Brussels (Belgium) 2019, *Annual General Meeting* London (UK) 2013. **Publications** *EVHA Newsletter*.
Members Full; Associate; Affiliate. Companies in 15 countries:
Belgium, Czechia, Finland, Germany, Greece, Ireland, Kuwait, Latvia, Malta, Netherlands, North Macedonia, Slovakia, Sweden, UK, United Arab Emirates. [2022.10.18/XD8202/D]

♦ European Ventilation Industry Association (EVIA) 09052

Secretariat c/o Grayling, Avenue des Arts 46, 1000 Brussels, Belgium. E-mail: secretariat@evia.eu.
URL: http://www.evia.eu/

History Jul 2010, Brussels (Belgium). Registration: No/ID: 0840.789.466, Start date: 3 Nov 2011, Belgium; EU Transparency Register, No/ID: 05513338917-92, Start date: 6 Jun 2012. **Aims** Promote highly energy efficient ventilation applications across Europe, with high consideration for health and comfort aspects; contribute to the energy efficiency targets set by the EU. **Structure** General Assembly; Steering Committee. Working Groups (5), coordinated by the Secretariat: WG Residential Ventilation Units (WG RVU); WG Non-Residential Ventilation Units (WG NRVU); WG Fans; WG Ventilation2030; WG Connectivity. Task Forces. **Activities** Events/meetings. **Events** *Annual General Meeting* Brussels (Belgium) 2021, *Annual General Meeting* Brussels (Belgium) 2020, *Annual General Meeting* Brussels (Belgium) 2019, *Annual General Meeting* Brussels (Belgium) 2018, *Annual General Meeting* Brussels (Belgium) 2017. **Members** EVIA has currently 48 members, both national associations and companies. **NGO Relations** Member of (2): *Alliance for Internet of Things Innovation (AIOTI, #00697)*; *Industry4Europe (#11181)*. [2022.08.08/XJ6877/t/D]

♦ European Venture Capital Association / see Invest Europe – The Voice of Private Capital (#15997)

♦ European Venture Philanthropy Association (EVPA) 09053

Main Office Rue Royale 94, 1000 Brussels, Belgium. T. +3225132131. E-mail: info@evpa.ngo.
URL: http://www.evpa.ngo

History 2004. Launched by 5 trustees. Registration: Banque-Carrefour des Entreprises, No/ID: 0810.969.290, Start date: 6 Apr 2009, Belgium; EU Transparency Register, No/ID: 651029816401-19, Start date: 9 Mar 2015. **Aims** Promote and shape the future of venture philanthropy and social investment in Europe and beyond. **Structure** Chairperson; CEO. **Languages** English, French. **Staff** 24.00 FTE, paid. **Finance** Sources: grants; meeting proceeds; members' dues; revenue from activities/projects; sponsorship. **Activities** Events/meetings; politics/policy/regulatory; research/documentation. **Events** *Annual Conference* Porto (Portugal) 2021, *Annual Conference* Brussels (Belgium) 2020, *Creating Shared Value – The Key Role of Corporate Social Investors* Singapore (Singapore) 2020, *Annual Conference* The Hague (Netherlands) 2019, *Annual Conference* Warsaw (Poland) 2018. **Publications** Surveys; toolkits; reports.
Members Organizations (300) in 35 countries:
Andorra, Austria, Belgium, Bosnia-Herzegovina, Canada, Czechia, Denmark, Estonia, Finland, France, Georgia, Germany, Greece, Hungary, India, Ireland, Italy, Kenya, Luxembourg, Malta, Netherlands, North Macedonia, Norway, Poland, Portugal, Russia, Serbia, Singapore, Slovakia, Spain, Sweden, Switzerland, Türkiye, UK, USA.
NGO Relations Member of (1): *Worldwide Initiatives for Grantmaker Support (WINGS, #21926)*. Endorsed by: *Invest Europe – The Voice of Private Capital (Invest Europe, #15997)*. Associate of: *Asian Venture Philanthropy Network (AVPN, #01778)*. [2022.11.15/XJ0642/y/D]

♦ European Vermiculite Association (no recent information)
♦ European Veterans Athletic Association / see European Masters Athletics (#07750)

♦ European Veterinary Dental College (EVDC) 09054

Sec Dyretannklinikken AS, Andebuveien 3, 3170 Sem, Norway.
Registered office address 82B High Street, Sawston, Cambridge, CB22 3HJ, UK.
URL: http://www.evdc.org/

History May 1998. **Aims** Advance the art and science of veterinary dentistry. **Structure** Board of Directors; Committees appointed for specific purposes. **Languages** English. **Staff** Voluntary. **Finance** Members' dues. Other fees. Annual budget: euro 35,000. **Activities** Training/education; knowledge management/information dissemination; publishing activities; projects/programmes; networking/liaising; events/meetings; standards/guidelines; certification/accreditation. **Events** *European Veterinary Dental Forum* Krakow (Poland) 2023, *European Veterinary Dental Forum* Krakow (Poland) 2022, *European Veterinary Dental Forum* Utrecht (Netherlands) 2019, *European Veterinary Dental Forum* Innsbruck (Austria) 2018, *European Veterinary Dental Forum* Malaga (Spain) 2017. **Publications** *Journal of Veterinary Dentistry* (4 a year).
Members Diplomates (60) in 17 countries and territories:
Austria, Belgium, Canada, Denmark, Finland, France, Germany, Hong Kong, Israel, Italy, Poland, Slovenia, South Africa, Spain, Switzerland, UK, USA.
NGO Relations Member of: *European Board of Veterinary Specialisation (EBVS, #06375)*. [2019.06.26/XD6548/v/D]

♦ European Veterinary Dental Society (EVDS) 09055

Sec Zultseweg 191, 8790 Waregem, Belgium.
URL: http://www.evds.org/

History Founded 1992. UK Registered Charity: 1128783. **Aims** Promote study, science and education in veterinary *dentistry*. **Structure** Board. **Languages** English. **Staff** Voluntary. **Events** *European Veterinary Dental Forum* Krakow (Poland) 2023, *European Veterinary Dental Forum* Krakow (Poland) 2022, *European Veterinary Dental Forum* Utrecht (Netherlands) 2019, *European Veterinary Dental Forum* Innsbruck (Austria) 2018, *European Veterinary Dental Forum* Malaga (Spain) 2017. **Publications** *EVDS Forum* (3-4 a year) – journal. Congress proceedings.
Members Individuals (over 200) in 26 countries:
Austria, Belgium, Brazil, Czechia, Denmark, Egypt, Estonia, Finland, France, Germany, Greece, Hungary, Italy, Netherlands, Norway, Poland, Portugal, Romania, Russia, Slovenia, South Africa, Spain, Sweden, Switzerland, UK, USA. [2019/XD6107/v/D]

♦ European Veterinary Emergency and Critical Care Society (EVECCS) 09056

Société européenne de soins intensifs et de médecine d'urgence – Sociedad Europea Veterinaria de Urgencias y Cuidados Intensivos – Europäische Notfall- und Intensivmedizin Vereinigung – Sociedade Europeia de Urgência e Cuidados Intensivos Veterinarios – Societatea Europeana de Urgente si Terapie Intensiva Veterinara

Sec address not obtained. E-mail: secretary@eveccs.org.
URL: http://www.eveccs.org/

History Apr 2002. Registration: Start date: 27 Mar 2002, Netherlands. **Aims** Promote study, development and practice of veterinary emergency medicine and critical patient care in Europe. **Structure** Executive Board; other Boards. **Events** *Annual Congress* Ghent (Belgium) 2022, *EVECC Online Congress* 2021, *EVECC Online Congress* 2020, *Annual Congress* Porto (Portugal) 2020, *Annual Congress* Tallinn (Estonia) 2019. **Publications** *Journal of Veterinary Emergency and Critical Care*. **Members** Individuals. Membership countries not specified. **NGO Relations** Sister organization: Veterinary Emergency and Critical Care Society (VECCS), USA. [2022.05.10/XM4600/D]

♦ European Veterinary Immunology Group (EVIG) 09057

Sec Uni Bern, Abt Experimentelle Klinische Forschung, Länggassstr 124, 3001 Bern, Switzerland. T. +41316312330. Fax +41316312538.
URL: http://www.evig.org.uk/

History 2001, under the auspices of *European Federation of Immunological Societies (EFIS, #07142)*. Transformed into a registered society, in accordance with German law, Sep 2009. **Aims** Be a platform for communication and exchange, enhancing European research in particular. **Structure** Steering Committee; Advisory Committee. **Events** *European Veterinary Immunology Workshop* Utrecht (Netherlands) 2018, *European Veterinary Immunology Workshop* Vienna (Austria) 2015, *European Veterinary Immunology Workshop* Edinburgh (UK) 2012, *European Veterinary Immunology Workshop* Berlin (Germany) 2009, *European Veterinary Immunology Workshop* Paris (France) 2006. [2014/XJ8822/D]

♦ European Veterinary Parasitology College (EVPC) 09058

Sec Veterinary Research Institute, Hellenic Agricultural Organization – Demeter, 570 01 Thessaloniki, Greece. E-mail: evpcsecretary@gmail.com.
URL: http://www.eurovetpar.org/

History Set up 2003, following an initiative taken at 18th Congress of *World Association for the Advancement of Veterinary Parasitology (WAAVP, #21114)*, Aug 2001, Stresa (Italy). Inaugural meeting: 27 Sep 2003, Maison-Alfort (France). Recognition awarded by *European Board of Veterinary Specialisation (EBVS, #06375)*, provisionally Jun 2003, and definitively 12 Apr 2013. Previously also referred to as *European College of Veterinary Parasitology (ECVPar)*. Registered in accordance with French law. **Aims** Advance veterinary parasitology; promote a high standard of training in the field; examine and certify European specialists in the field. **Structure** General Meeting of all Diplomates (annual); Board; Committees (3). **Languages** English. **Staff** None. **Finance** Members' dues. **Activities** Training/education; certification/accreditation; events/meetings. **Events** *Annual Meeting* Copenhagen (Denmark) 2019, *Annual Meeting* Brussels (Belgium) 2018, *Annual Meeting* Dublin (Ireland) 2014, *Annual Meeting* Munich (Germany) 2013, *International Symposium on Ectoparasites in Pets* Munich (Germany) 2013. **Publications** *EVPC Newsletter*, *Veterinary Parasitology* – official journal.
Members Founding Diplomates; Diplomates; Associate; Honorary. Active members (155) in 26 countries:
Australia, Austria, Belgium, Brazil, Canada, Croatia, Czechia, Denmark, Finland, France, Germany, Greece, Hungary, Ireland, Italy, Lithuania, Morocco, Netherlands, Portugal, South Africa, Spain, Sweden, Switzerland, Türkiye, UK, USA.
Also members in the West Indies. Membership countries not specified.
NGO Relations *European Scientific Counsel Companion Animal Parasites (ESCCAP, #08445)*.
[2018/XE4712/**E**]

♦ European Veterinary Radiological Association / see European Association of Veterinary Diagnostic Imaging (#06269)

♦ European Veterinary Society for Small Animal Reproduction (EVSSAR) 09059

Association vétérinaire européenne pour la reproduction des petits animaux
Contact Chée de Bruxelles 484, 7850 Enghien, Belgium.
URL: https://www.evssar.org/
History 1998. Registration: Banque-Carrefour des Entreprises, No/ID: 0465.471.524, Start date: 11 Mar 1999, Belgium. **Aims** Further scientific and clinical progress in veterinary and comparative companion animal reproduction, paediatrics and neonatology. **Structure** General Assembly (annual); Executive Committee. **Languages** English, French. **Finance** Sources: meeting proceeds; members' dues. **Activities** Awards/prizes/competitions; events/meetings; financial and/or material support; knowledge management/information dissemination; training/education. **Events** *European Symposium on Animal Reproduction* Nantes (France) 2023, *Congress* Milan (Italy) 2022, *Congress* Milan (Italy) 2021, *Meeting* Milan (Italy) 2020, *Meeting* Berlin (Germany) 2019. **Publications** *EVSSAR Newsletter* (2 a year).
Members Full in 34 countries:
Algeria, Argentina, Australia, Austria, Belgium, Brazil, Canada, Chile, Czechia, Denmark, Finland, France, Germany, Greece, Hungary, Ireland, Israel, Italy, Japan, Mexico, Netherlands, Nigeria, Norway, Poland, Portugal, Russia, Spain, Sweden, Switzerland, Thailand, Türkiye, UK, Ukraine, USA.
NGO Relations Member of (1): *Federation of European Companion Animal Veterinary Associations (FECAVA, #09497)*. Cooperates with (1): *European Society of Domestic Animal Reproduction (ESDAR, #08586)*. Instrumental in setting up (1): *European College of Animal Reproduction (ECAR, #06605)*. [2023/XD7176/**D**]

♦ European VHL (von Hippel-Lindau) Federation (VHL-Europa) 09060

Sec address not obtained. E-mail: secretary@vhl-europa.org.
Pres address not obtained. E-mail: president@vhl-europa.org.
URL: http://www.vhl-europa.org/
History Founded 22 Oct 2014. Registered in accordance with Dutch law. **Aims** Support existing organizations and help set up new ones; improve the situation of people affected with VHL; promote and sustain research. **Structure** General Assembly; Board; Medical and Scientific Advisory Board. **Activities** Events/meetings. **Publications** *VHL-Europa Newsletter*.
Members Full in 10 countries:
Belgium, Denmark, France, Germany, Greece, Hungary, Italy, Netherlands, Romania, Spain.
NGO Relations Member of: *EURORDIS – Rare Diseases Europe (#09175)*. [2017/XM7455/**D**]

♦ European Violence in Psychiatry Research Group (EViPRG) 09061

Chair address not obtained.
URL: http://eviprg.eu/
History 1997, London (UK). **Aims** Seek funds for, and carry out research on the topic of violence in psychiatry; promote the sharing of expertise and knowledge among researchers into violence in psychiatry. **Structure** Board. **Languages** English. **Staff** None. **Finance** Self-funding. **Activities** Events/meetings. **Events** *European Congress on Violence in Clinical Psychiatry* Rotterdam (Netherlands) 2022, *European Congress on Violence in Clinical Psychiatry* Oslo (Norway) 2019, *European Congress on Violence in Clinical Psychiatry* Dublin (Ireland) 2017, *European Congress on Violence in Clinical Psychiatry* Copenhagen (Denmark) 2015, *European congress on violence in clinical psychiatry* Ghent (Belgium) 2013. **Publications** *Violence in Mental Health Settings: Causes, Consequences and Management* (2006) by D Richter and R Whittington.
Members Individuals in 18 countries:
Czechia, Denmark, Finland, Germany, Greece, Iceland, Ireland, Italy, Netherlands, Norway, Portugal, Slovenia, Spain, Sweden, Switzerland, Türkiye, UK, USA.
NGO Relations Cooperates with (1): *European Network of Training in the Management of Aggression (ENTMA08)*. [2020/XM0661/v/**F**]

♦ European Virtual Institute for Integrated Risk Management (EU-VRi) 09062

Main Office Fangelsbachstr 14, 70178 Stuttgart, Germany. E-mail: jovanovic@eu-vri.eu – info@eu-vri.eu.
URL: http://www.eu-vri.eu/
History Nov 2006. Founded as a *European Economic Interest Grouping (EEIG, #06960)*. Former names and other names: *European Risk & Resilience Institute* – alias. Registration: Germany.
Members Companies in 19 countries:
Belgium, Czechia, Denmark, Finland, France, Germany, Greece, Hungary, Israel, Italy, Netherlands, Norway, Poland, Romania, Serbia, Slovenia, Spain, Sweden, Switzerland. [2020/XJ2927/j/**F**]

♦ European Virtual Institute on Knowledge-Based Multifunctional Materials (KMM-VIN) 09063

Registered Office Rue du Trône 98, 1000 Brussels, Belgium. T. +3222134160. Fax +3227915536. E-mail: office@kmm-vin.eu.
URL: http://www.kmm-vin.eu/
History Mar 2007, under the auspices of *European Commission (EC, #06633)*. Registration: AISBL/IVZW, Belgium. **Aims** Offer integrated basic and applied commercial research, educational and innovation activities in the field of knowledge-based structural and multifunctional materials. **Structure** General Assembly (annual). Governing Council of up to 12 members. Board of Directors, comprising CEO and 2 Directors. Working Groups (4): Materials for Transport; Materials for Energy; Biomaterials; Modelling. **Events** *Annual General Assembly* Brussels (Belgium) 2016, *Annual General Assembly* Brussels (Belgium) 2013. **Publications** *KMM-VIN Newsletter*.
Members Core; Associate. Core in 11 countries:
Austria, Bulgaria, Czechia, France, Germany, Italy, Poland, Serbia, Slovakia, Spain, UK.
Associate in 10 countries:
Austria, Czechia, Finland, Germany, Italy, Lithuania, Netherlands, Sweden, Switzerland, UK. [2020/XJ5621/j/**E**]

♦ European Virtual Institute for Speciation Analysis (EVISA) 09064

CEO Univ of Münster, Inst of Inorganic and Analytical Chemistry, Corrensstrasse 48, 48149 Münster, Germany. T. +4917618300268. E-mail: info@speciation.net.
URL: http://www.speciation.net/
History Registration: France. **Aims** Give industry and other customers access to a wide array of expertise concerning chemical speciation analysis by bringing together the most prominent European capabilities in the sector. **Structure** Executive Board; CEO; Advisory Board. **Languages** English, French, German. **Finance** Initial funding from *European Commission (EC, #06633)*. **Activities** Guidance/assistance/consulting; research/documentation; training/education. **Publications** *Speciation Newsletter* (12 a year). **Members** Institutions. Membership countries not specified. [2022.06.08/XJ9074/j/**D**]

♦ European Virtual Observatory (EURO-VO) 09065

Contact Observatoire de Strasbourg, 11 rue de l'Université, 67000 Strasbourg, France. T. +33368852487.
URL: http://www.euro-vo.org/
Activities Centres (3): Data Centre Alliance (DCA); Facility Centre (VOFC); Technology Centre (VOTC). **IGO Relations** Partner: *European Space Agency (ESA, #08798)*. **NGO Relations** Member of: *International Virtual Observatory Alliance (IVOA, #15858)*. [2007.08.01/XM1804/**F**]

♦ European Virtual Private Network Users Association (EVUA) 09066

Secretary address not obtained.
History 1993. Former names and other names: *Global Telecom User Group* – former; *Enterprise VPN User Organization* – former. **Aims** Enable multinational network users to influence and gain knowledge of the latest developments in the ICT world, and therefore to take better strategic and operational decisions; serve as an independent, neutral supplier and global ICT network user group for multinational companies, and the ICT industry platform for global users and suppliers. **Structure** Board, comprising Chairman, Deputy Chairman/Treasurer and 6 members. All Board members work for multinationals and are at the CIO/Global Telecom manager level. National specialist groups: France; Finland; USA. **Languages** English. **Staff** 6.00 FTE, paid. **Finance** Sources: meeting proceeds; members' dues; revenue from activities/projects. Annual budget: 500,000 GBP. **Activities** Events/meetings. Managed by end-users using their buying position to influence the supply side of the industry. Network includes independent industry partners, working links with regulatory organizations and links with other user groups. Special Interest Groups (6): Benchmarking and Service Management; Data; Legal and Contracts; Mobile Services/Cellular; Strategy; Remote Worker. Other activities: Annual Surveys; benchmarking; member consultancy. **Events** *Global IP and convergence* Amsterdam (Netherlands) 2007, *Mobility* Budapest (Hungary) 2007, *ICT strategies* Rome (Italy) 2007, *Conference / Conference and Members Meeting* Brussels (Belgium) 2006, *Conference / Conference and Members Meeting* Madrid (Spain) 2006. **Publications** *EVUA Newsletter* (4 a year). Member surveys; benchmarking report; news bulletins; newsflashes. **Information Services** *Intelligence Database on ICT services and service providers*. **Members** Companies (over 75) in Europe, North America and Asia-Pacific. Approximately 50% of member companies is ranked in the global 200 fortune company list. Membership countries not specified. **NGO Relations** Associate relations with other national user groups. [2016/XF4414/**F**]

♦ European Virus Archive goes Global (EVAg) 09067

Coordination and Management Office 27 bd Jean Moulin, 13385 Marseille CEDEX 5, France. T. +33491828622. E-mail: teamevag@european-virus-archive.com.
URL: http://www.european-virus-archive.com/
Aims Mobilize a global network with expertise in virology to collect, amplify, characterize, standardize, authenticate, distribute, track, viruses and derived products. **Finance** Funding from *European Union (EU, #08967)*. **Activities** Research and development.
Members Partner laboratories/institutes. Core partners in 10 countries:
France, Germany, Italy, Netherlands, Russia, Slovakia, Slovenia, South Africa, Switzerland, UK.
Included in the above, 1 institute listed in this Yearbook:
Pasteur Institute.
Associate partners in 11 countries:
Australia, China, Greece, Haiti, Japan, Jordan, Russia, Spain, Sweden, Türkiye, USA.
NGO Relations *European Society for translational Antiviral Research (ESAR, #08764)*. [2022/XM4937/**F**]

♦ European Virus Bioinformatics Center (EVBC) 09068

Managing Dir address not obtained.
URL: http://evbc.uni-jena.de/
Structure Board of Directors. **Activities** Events/meetings; research/documentation. **Events** *International Workshop on Virus Evolution and Molecular Epidemiology* Hong Kong (Hong Kong) 2019, *International Workshop on Virus Evolution and Molecular Epidemiology* Berlin (Germany) 2018. **Publications** *EVBC Newsletter*.
Members Full (151) from 78 research institutions in 26 countries:
Austria, Belgium, Brazil, Canada, China, Cyprus, Czechia, Denmark, Finland, France, Germany, Greece, Hungary, India, Ireland, Israel, Italy, Netherlands, Poland, Portugal, Russia, Slovenia, Spain, Switzerland, UK, USA. [2019/XM8370/**D**]

♦ European Vision Institute (EVI) 09069

Contact Rue du Trônee 98, 1050 Brussels, Belgium. T. +41792983142. Fax +41442520412. E-mail: info@europeanvisioninstitute.org.
URL: http://www.europeanvisioninstitute.org/
History An organization of the type *European Economic Interest Grouping (EEIG, #06960)*. Also referred to as *European Alliance for the Promotion of Vision Research and Ophthalmology (EU-EYE)*. **Aims** Serve as a European alliance for the promotion of vision research and *ophthalmology* for the benefit of the whole community. **Structure** Steering Committee. Head office in Brussels (Belgium). Liaison Offices in: Tübingen (Germany); London (UK); Paris (France); Coimbra (Portugal). **NGO Relations** Member of: *European Alliance for Vision Research and Ophthalmology (EU-EYE, #05890)*. [2014/XJ8373/j/**E**]

♦ European Vision Institute Clinical Research Network (EVICR.net) . . 09070

CEO AIBILI, Azinhaga de Santa Comba, 3000-548 Coimbra, Portugal. T. +351239480146. E-mail: evicrnet@aibili.pt.
URL: https://www.evicr.net/
History 2010. An organization of the type *European Economic Interest Grouping (EEIG, #06960)*. **Aims** Perform multinational clinical research in ophthalmology. **Structure** General Assembly; Steering Committee; Coordinating Centre/Management Board. Expert Committees. Industry Advisory Board. **Activities** Certification/accreditation; networking/liaising; research/documentation; training/education.
Members Clinical Research Sites (95) in countries:
Austria, Belgium, Denmark, France, Germany, Greece, Ireland, Israel, Italy, Netherlands, Portugal, Slovakia, Spain, Switzerland, UK.
NGO Relations Member of (1): *European Alliance for Vision Research and Ophthalmology (EU-EYE, #05890)*.
[2021/AA1479/**F**]

♦ European Vision Society (no recent information)

♦ European Visual Artists (EVA) 09071

SG Rue du Prince Royal 87, 1050 Brussels, Belgium. T. +3222909248. E-mail: info@evartists.org.
URL: https://www.evartists.org/
History 1997. Founded by 9 European collective management societies for visual arts. Former names and other names: *European Visual Artists Network (EVAN)* – former. Registration: Banque-Carrefour des Entreprises, No/ID: 0461.142.849, Start date: 6 Jun 1997, Belgium; European Transparency Register, No/ID: 121604011075-40, Start date: 3 May 2013. **Aims** Represent the interests of authors' collective management societies for the visual arts; facilitate access to works, create legal certainty and ensure that artists receive an equitable share of any profit generated by others with the exploitation of works; improve European authors' rights. **Structure** General Assembly (twice a year); Board of Administrators. **Activities** Knowledge management/information dissemination; networking/liaising. **Events** *Meeting* Helsinki (Finland) 2001, *Meeting* Copenhagen (Denmark) 1999.
Members European collecting societies (28). Full members in 16 countries:
Austria, Belgium, Czechia, Denmark, Finland, France, Germany, Hungary, Ireland, Italy, Netherlands, Norway, Portugal, Slovakia, Spain, Sweden.
Observers in 11 countries:
Czechia, Estonia, Greece, Iceland, Ireland, Latvia, Lithuania, Romania, Serbia, Slovakia, UK.
Consultative Status Consultative status granted from: *World Intellectual Property Organization (WIPO, #21593)* (Permanent Observer Status). **NGO Relations** Member of (2): *Culture First Coalition (inactive)*; *International Federation of Reproduction Rights Organizations (IFRRO, #13527)*. Associate member of: *Confédération internationale des sociétés d'auteurs et compositeurs (CISAC, #04563)*.
[2022.05.04/XF6110/**F**]

♦ European Visual Artists Network / see European Visual Artists (#09071)

♦ **European VitreoRetinal Society (EVRS)** **09072**
CEO 61 chemin du Mayne de Jouan, 33160 Bordeaux, France. T. +33632570535. E-mail: evrsc@evrs.org.
URL: http://www.evrs.eu/
History Registered in accordance with German law. **Aims** Promote vitreoretinal surgery and the therapy of vitreoretinal disease; represent the interests of *ophthalmologists* active in vitreoretinal disease in Europe. **Structure** General Assembly (every 2 years); Board of Directors. **Languages** English. **Finance** Members' dues. **Events** *Annual Congress* Verona (Italy) 2021, *Annual Congress* Verona (Italy) 2020, *Annual Congress* Lisbon (Portugal) 2019, *Annual Congress* Prague (Czechia) 2018, *Annual Congress* Florence (Italy) 2017.
Members Individuals in 49 countries:
Austria, Belgium, Bosnia-Herzegovina, Brazil, Bulgaria, China, Croatia, Cyprus, Czechia, Denmark, Egypt, Finland, France, Germany, Greece, Hungary, Iceland, India, Iran Islamic Rep, Ireland, Israel, Italy, Japan, Kuwait, Lebanon, Luxembourg, Mexico, Morocco, Netherlands, Norway, Poland, Portugal, Qatar, Romania, Russia, Saudi Arabia, Serbia, Slovakia, Slovenia, South Africa, Spain, Sweden, Switzerland, Tunisia, Türkiye, UK, Ukraine, Uruguay, USA. [2016.10.18/XD9364/**D**]

♦ **European VLBI Group for Geodesy and Astrometry (EVGA)** **09073**
Sec Norwegian Mapping Authority, Ny-Ålesund Geodetic Observatory, Postboks 13, 9173 Ny-Ålesund, Norway.
Chair Chalmers Univ of Technology, Dept of Earth and Space Sciences, Onsala Space Observatory, SE-439 92 Onsala, Sweden.
URL: http://www.evga.org/
History Set up as a subgroup of *International VLBI Service for Geodesy and Astrometry (IVS, #15860)*. Original charter approved 23 Apr 2005. **Aims** Foster the use of European VLBI resources for deriving high quality reference frames and other scientific results; form a link between the different European VLBI components from observations to data analysis; promote and represent European geodetic and astrometric VLBI within the broader international scientific communities; provide and archive information and scientific results of European geodetic and astrometric VLBI. **Structure** Chairman; Secretary. **Activities** Research; information dissemination; meeting activities. **Events** *Meeting / Working Meeting* Espoo (Finland) 2013, *Working Meeting* Bonn (Germany) 2011, *Working Meeting* Bordeaux (France) 2009, *Working Meeting* Vienna (Austria) 2007, *Working Meeting* Noto (Italy) 2005.
Members European IVS associated members in 7 countries:
Finland, France, Germany, Italy, Norway, Russia, Sweden. [2014/XJ7906/**D**]

♦ **European VLBI Network (EVN)** **09074**
Chairman Jodrell Bank Centre For Astrophysics, The Manchester University, Manchester, M13 9PL, UK.
URL: http://www.evlbi.org/
History 1980. Full title: *European VLBI Network – Consortium for Very Long Baseline Interferometry in Europe*. **Aims** Coordinate operation of radio *telescopes* for doing high resolution imaging of radio sources. **Structure** Consortium Board of Directors, including Chair and Vice-Chair. **Activities** Organizes joint observations of European radio telescopes. Develops VLBI technology and procedures, exchange of students and personnel. Organizes symposia. **Events** *Symposium and users meeting / Symposium* Manchester (UK) 2010, *Meeting* Torun (Poland) 2010, *Meeting* Bonn (Germany) 2009, *Meeting* Manchester (UK) 2009, *Meeting* Onsala (Sweden) 2009. **Publications** *EVN Newsletter* (3 a year). Biennial report.
Members Radio astronomy institutes (14) and individuals () in 13 countries:
China, Finland, France (*), Germany, Italy, Netherlands, Poland, Puerto Rico, South Africa, Spain, Sweden, UK, USA.
Included in the above, 1 institute listed in this Yearbook:
Joint Institute for VLBI in Europe (JIVE, #16135). [2011.08.16/XF4737/**F**]

♦ European VLBI Network – Consortium for Very Long Baseline Interferometry in Europe / see European VLBI Network (#09074)

♦ **European Vocational Training Association (EVTA)** **09075**
Association européenne pour la formation professionnelle (AEFP)
Dir-Gen Rue Victor Oudart 7, 1030 Brussels, Belgium. T. +3227722858. E-mail: info@evta.eu.
URL: http://www.evta.eu/
History 11 Sep 1996. Registration: Banque-Carrefour des Entreprises, No/ID: 0463.618.725, Start date: 27 Nov 2003, Belgium; EU Transparency Register, No/ID: 677979425796-48, Start date: 8 Feb 2017. **Structure** General Assembly; Governing Council; Management Committee. **Languages** English, French, Italian. **Staff** 5.00 FTE, paid. **Finance** Sources: members' dues; revenue from activities/projects. **Activities** Advocacy/lobbying/activism; awareness raising; capacity building; certification/accreditation; events/meetings; guidance/assistance/consulting; knowledge management/information dissemination; networking/liaising; projects/programmes; training/education. **Events** *Conference* Verona (Italy) 2014, *Conference* Brussels (Belgium) 2013, *Conference* Toulouse (France) 2013, *Conference on Sharing Knowledge to Build a Stronger European Economy Driven by Human Capital* Brussels (Belgium) 2012, *Conference* Budapest (Hungary) 2005. **Publications** Glossaries; reports; studies.
Members Full (13) in 8 countries:
Belgium, France, Greece, Hungary, Italy, Netherlands, Portugal, Slovakia.
NGO Relations Member of (2): *European Association for the Education of Adults (EAEA, #06018)*; *Lifelong Learning Platform – European Civil Society for Education (LLLP, #16466).* [2022.10.19/XD8336/**D**]

♦ **European Voice Teachers Association (EVTA)** **09076**
Pres 21 Longmeadow Gardens, Birdham, Chichester, PO20 7HP, UK. T. +441243512881. E-mail: president@evta-online.eu – secretary@evta-online.eu – info@evta-online.eu.
URL: http://www.evta-online.eu/
History Jan 1989, Amsterdam (Netherlands). Reconstituted Oct 2004, Hanover (Germany). Registration: Start date: Oct 2004, Germany. **Aims** Promote cultural, pedagogical and scientific aspects of *vocal pedagogy* in all styles of music. **Structure** Council of Representatives; Executive Committee. **Languages** English, German. **Staff** Voluntary. **Finance** Sources: government support; members' dues; revenue from activities/projects; sponsorship. Supported by: *European Commission (EC, #06633)*. **Activities** Awareness raising; networking/liaising; projects/programmes; training/education. **Events** *EUROVOX Congress* Edinburgh (UK) 2020, *EUROVOX Congress* The Hague (Netherlands) 2018, *Jewels of European Voice of Pedagogy Meeting* Celje (Slovenia) 2016, *EUROVOX Congress* Riga (Latvia) 2015, *Eurovox Congress* Munich (Germany) 2012. **Publications** *EVTA Newsletter*. *Handbook: Digital Technology in Teaching Voice*.
Members National organizations (23) in 23 countries:
Austria, Belgium, Croatia, Denmark, Finland, France, Germany, Hungary, Iceland, Ireland, Italy, Latvia, Netherlands, Norway, Poland, Portugal, Serbia, Slovenia, Spain, Sweden, Switzerland, Türkiye, UK.
NGO Relations Member of (2): *European Music Council (EMC, #07837)*; *International Congress of Voice Teachers (ICVT)*. Advisory Board Member of: *Pan European Voice Conference (PEVOC).* [2022/XD4962/**D**]

♦ **European Volcanological Association** **09077**
Association volcanologique européenne (LAVE)
Pres 7 rue de la Guadeloupe, 75018 Paris, France. T. +33142057257. E-mail: lave@club-internet.fr.
URL: http://www.lave-volcans.com/
History Founded 1986, Paris (France), as a French speaking European Association. **Aims** Bring together professionals and amateurs of vulcanology; provide them with a francophone publication; organize activities to inform the public at large, such as exhibitions, conferences, audiovisual events; promote scientific exchange in the field of Earth sciences and enhance research in the field of vulcanology. **Languages** French. **Staff** 15.00 FTE, voluntary. **Publications** *Revue LAVE* (6 a year) in French – journal. Thematic memories.
Members Individuals in 19 countries:
Austria, Belgium, Canada, Cyprus, Ecuador, France, Germany, Indonesia, Ireland, Italy, Luxembourg, Netherlands, New Zealand, Nicaragua, Poland, Spain, Switzerland, USA, Vanuatu. [2015.09.02/XD1708/v/**D**]

♦ **European Volleyball Confederation** **09078**
Confédération européenne de volleyball (CEV)
Admin Dir Route de Longwy 488, L-1940 Luxembourg, Luxembourg. T. +3522546461. Fax +35225464640. E-mail: director@cev.eu.
URL: http://www.cev.eu/
History 1973, as a confederation of European volleyball federations. **Aims** Encourage development and growth of the *sport* of volleyball in all its forms within the territories of its national federations. **Structure** General Assembly (annual); Board of Administration; Executive Committee; Commissions (8); Legal Chamber; Working Groups. Head Office, based in Luxembourg. **Languages** English. **Staff** 30.00 FTE, paid. **Finance** National federations' dues and contributions. Other sources: revenue of its organizations; regulation levies accruing from sporting events; product of any fine; aid of all kinds. **Activities** Events/meetings; awards/prizes/competitions. **Events** *General Assembly and Congress* Luxembourg (Luxembourg) 2016, *Annual Congress and General Assembly* Sofia (Bulgaria) 2015, *Annual Congress and General Assembly* Copenhagen (Denmark) 2013, *Annual Congress and General Assembly* Vienna (Austria) 2011, *Annual congress and general assembly* Luxembourg (Luxembourg) 2006. **Publications** e-Newsletter.
Members National federations in 56 countries and territories:
Albania, Andorra, Armenia, Austria, Azerbaijan, Belarus, Belgium, Bosnia-Herzegovina, Bulgaria, Croatia, Cyprus, Czechia, Denmark, England, Estonia, Faeroe Is, Finland, France, Georgia, Germany, Gibraltar, Greece, Greenland, Hungary, Iceland, Ireland, Israel, Italy, Kosovo, Latvia, Liechtenstein, Lithuania, Luxembourg, Malta, Moldova, Monaco, Montenegro, Netherlands, North Macedonia, Northern Ireland, Norway, Poland, Portugal, Romania, Russia, San Marino, Scotland, Serbia, Slovakia, Slovenia, Spain, Sweden, Switzerland, Türkiye, Ukraine, Wales.
Zonal associations (6):
Balkan Volleyball Association (BVA, #03090); *CEV Small Countries Association (SCA, #03841)*; *Eastern European Volleyball Zonal Association (EEVZA, #05239)*; *Middle European Volleyball Zonal Association (MEVZA, #16794)*; *Northern European Volleyball Zonal Association (NEVZA, #17591)*; *Western European Volleyball Zonal Association (WEVZA, #20915).*
NGO Relations A regional confederation of: *Fédération internationale de volleyball (FIVB, #09670)*. Member of: *Association of European Team Sports (ETS, #02546).* [2019.10.15/XE3783/**E**]

♦ European Volunteer Centre / see Centre for European Volunteering (#03743)
♦ European Wallcovering Association (inactive)

♦ **European Walled Towns (EWT)** **09079**
SG PO Box 492, Old Bakery Street, Valletta, VLT 1000, Malta. T. +35699021961. E-mail: walled.ewt@gmail.com.
URL: http://www.walledtowns.com/
History 1989, Tenby (UK). Former names and other names: *Walled Towns Friendship Circle (WTFC)* – former. **Aims** Work towards *sustainable* development of walled towns, walled cities and fortified *historic* towns. **Structure** General Meeting (annual); Executive Committee; Secretariat headed by Secretary-General. **Languages** English. **Staff** 3.00 FTE, voluntary. **Finance** Sources: members' dues. **Activities** Events/meetings; research/documentation. **Events** *Annual Symposium* Derry (UK) 2013, *Annual Symposium* Gmunden (Austria) 2012, *Annual Symposium* Lucca (Italy) 2011, *Annual Symposium* Fredericia (Denmark) 2010, *Annual Symposium* Osmangazi (Turkey) 2009.
Members Full; Associate. Towns in 23 countries:
Austria, Azerbaijan, Croatia, Cyprus, Czechia, Denmark, Estonia, France, Germany, Hungary, Ireland, Italy, Latvia, Malta, Netherlands, Norway, Portugal, Russia, Slovakia, Slovenia, Spain, Türkiye, UK.
Associate organizations in 7 countries:
Croatia, Ireland, Italy, Netherlands, Portugal, Spain, UK.
NGO Relations Member of (1): *European Heritage Alliance 3.3 (#07477).* [2020.08.25/XF6534/**F**]

♦ European War Veterans' Confederation (#04537)
♦ European Waste-to-Advanced Biofuels Association (unconfirmed)

♦ **European Water Association (EWA)** **09080**
Association Européenne de l'Eau – Europäische Vereinigung für Wasserwirtschaft
SG Theodor-Heuss-Allee 17, 53773 Hennef, Germany. T. +492242872189. Fax +492242872135. E-mail: info@ewa-online.eu.
URL: http://www.ewa-online.eu/
History Statutes originally formally adopted, 22 June 1981, Munich (Germany FR). Statutes modified: 25 May 1984, Munich; 15 Apr 1985, Rome (Italy); 16 May 1988, Voss (Norway); 12 May 1993, Munich; 25 May 1998, Croatia; 6 May 1999, Munich; 27 Apr 2005, Munich; 19 May 2006, Barcelona (Spain); 26 Apr 2007, Dubrovnik (Croatia); 7 May 2008, Munich; 1 May 2009, London (UK); 4 Jun 2010, Strasbourg (France); 1 Jul 2010, Vienna (Austria); 7 May 2012, Munich; 13 Jun 2013, Tuusula (Finland); 5 May 2014, Munich; 13 May 2015, Tirana (Albania); 31 May 2016, Munich; 11 May 2017, Lisbon (Portugal); 29 May 2018, Munich (Germany). Former names and other names: *European Water Pollution Control Association (EWPCA)* – former (1981 to 1999); *Association européenne de contrôle de la pollution des eaux* – former; *Association européenne pour la maîtrise de l'eau* – former. Registration: North Rhine Westphalia District court, No/ID: VR 4849, Start date: 28 Feb 1983, Germany, Bonn; EU Transparency Register, No/ID: 121848610166-52, Start date: 10 Dec 2012. **Aims** Promote through initiatives and activities the sustainable management of the total water cycle for Society's needs. **Structure** Council (meets at least annually); Management Committee; Standing Committees (2); Working Groups (WGs); Secretariat, headed by Secretary-General. **Languages** English. **Staff** 3.00 FTE, paid. **Finance** Sources: members' dues. **Activities** Awards/prizes/competitions; events/meetings; knowledge management/information dissemination. **Events** *Brussels Annual Conference* Brussels (Belgium) 2022, *EWA/DWA Innovation Workshop* Munich (Germany) 2022, *Integration of the Water Sector in the Circular Economy"* Munich (Germany) 2022, *Joint Specialty Conference* Sendai (Japan) 2022, *Joint Specialty Conference* Sendai (Japan) 2021. **Publications** *Water Manifesto* (annual); *EWA Newsletter*; *EWA Yearbook*. Position papers; symposia, seminar and workshop proceedings.
Members National professional associations in 21 countries:
Albania, Austria, Belgium, Bulgaria, Croatia, Czechia, Denmark, Estonia, Finland, France, Germany, Hungary, Luxembourg, Norway, Portugal, Romania, Serbia, Slovakia, Slovenia, Spain, Switzerland.
Corporate members in 22 countries:
Albania, Austria, Belgium, Bulgaria, Czechia, Denmark, Finland, France, Germany, Hungary, Italy, Luxembourg, Netherlands, North Macedonia, Norway, Romania, Serbia, Slovakia, Slovenia, Spain, Switzerland, UK.
Research members in 10 countries:
Austria, Belgium, Finland, Germany, Greece, Italy, Luxembourg, Norway, Poland, Spain.
NGO Relations In liaison with technical committees of: *Comité européen de normalisation (CEN, #04162)*. Close contact with: *Chartered Institution of Water and Environmental Management (CIWEM)*; *European Federation for Agricultural Recycling (EFAR)*; *European Federation of National Associations of Water and Waste Water Services (#07170)*; *European Water Resources Association (EWRA, #09085)*; *International Commission on Irrigation and Drainage (ICID, #12694)*; *International Water Association (IWA, #15865)*; Japan Sewage Works Association (JSWA); *Water Environment Federation (WEF).* [2022.05.10/XD7366/**D**]

♦ European Water Conditioning Association / see European Water and Wastewater Industry Association (#09087)

♦ **European Water Jetting Institute (EWJI)** **09081**
Main Office Av Rey Juan Carlos 92 – PF – Of 10, Argalia Bldg – Rabuso, MADRID, 28916 Leganés, Madrid, Spain. E-mail: info@ewji.org.
Brussels Office c/o Rabuso, Atrim Bldg – Regus BC, Rue des Colonies 11 – 1, 1000 Brussels, Belgium. T. +3225880190.
URL: http://www.ewji.org/
History 2013. Registration: EU Transparency Register, No/ID: 935442532665-34. **Aims** Promote the water jetting industry and its applications in Europe, towards the highest standards of safety, professional integrity and quality of service. **Structure** General Assembly; Board of Directors; Secretariat. **Languages** English. **Finance** Sources: members' dues. **Activities** Events/meetings; research/documentation; standards/guidelines; training/education. **Events** *Annual Convention* Paris (France) 2020, *Forum* Brussels (Belgium) 2019, *Annual Convention* Brussels (Belgium) 2018, *Annual Convention* Madrid (Spain) 2017, *Annual Convention* Cologne (Germany) 2016. **Publications** Guide.
Members Specialized national associations, contractors, suppliers and asset owners in 13 countries:
Austria, Belgium, France, Germany, Italy, Netherlands, Norway, Poland, Spain, Sweden, Switzerland, UK, USA. [2021.02.23/XM4714/**D**]

♦ European Waterpark Association (EWA) 09082

Managing Dir Josephsplatz 4, 90403 Nürburg, Germany. T. +499112406145. Fax +499112406146. E-mail: info@ewa.info.
URL: http://european-waterpark.org/

History 1994. **Aims** Ensure commercial promotion, safety, economical aspect and the professional and status interests of members. **Structure** General Assembly (annual); Board; Executive Committee; Committee of Supporting Members; Commissions; Working Groups. **Languages** English, German. **Staff** 3.00 FTE, paid. **Finance** Members' dues. **Activities** Advocacy/lobbying/activism; knowledge management/information dissemination; training/education, events/meetings. **Events** *Congress* Berlin (Germany) 2018, *Congress* Gelsenkirchen (Germany) 2014, *Congress* Kaprun (Austria) 2012, *Congress* Brühl (Germany) 2010, *Meeting* Vienna (Austria) 2009. **Publications** *Moderne Bäder Welten* (2à17). *Die Zukunft der Bäder* (2015); *Baden in Erlebniswelten* (2010).
Members Full; Associate; Supportive; Honorary. Water parks in 7 countries:
Austria, Czechia, Germany, Luxembourg, Slovenia, Sweden, Switzerland. [2020.03.03/XJ0564/**D**]

♦ European Water Partnership (EWP) 09083

Mailing Address PO Box 1113, 8900 CC Leeuwarden, Netherlands.
Contact Bvd Louis Schmidt 64, 1040 Brussels, Belgium.
URL: http://www.ewp.eu/

History 2006. **Aims** Promote sustainable water use in Europe and internationally through strategic planning and projects. **Structure** Board of Directors. **Events** *Meeting on Piloting Water Stewardship in Urban Zones* Brussels (Belgium) 2011, *Annual water and energy exchange summit* Cyprus 2010, *Annual water and energy exchange summit* Benalmadena (Spain) 2009, *STRIVER final conference* Brussels (Belgium) 2009, *European regional process meeting for the fifth world water forum* Saragossa (Spain) 2009.
Members Full in 7 countries:
Belgium, Germany, Italy, Netherlands, Poland, Spain, UK.
Included in the above, 9 organizations listed in this Yearbook:
European Committee of Environmental Technology Suppliers Associations (EUCETSA, #06648); European Desalination Society (EDS, #06908); European Landowners' Organization (ELO, #07639); European Partners for the Environment (EPE, #08154); European Small Hydropower Association (ESHA, #08495); Greenovate! Europe (#10726); IHE Delft Institute for Water Education (#11110); International Federation of Private Water Operators (AquaFed, #13517); Women Engage for a Common Future (WECF, #20992).
IGO Relations Partner of (1): *Global Alliances for Water and Climate (GAfWaC, #10230).* **NGO Relations** Instrumental in setting up (1): *European Water Stewardship (EWS).* [2022/XJ8219/y/**F**]

♦ European Water Platform / see Water Europe (#20828)
♦ European Water Pollution Control Association / see European Water Association (#09080)

♦ European Waterproofing Association (EWA) 09084

Main Office Boulevard du Souverain 68, Box 1, 1170 Brussels, Belgium. E-mail: info@ewa-europe.com.
URL: http://www.ewa-europe.com/

History Set up by extension of *International Association for Asphalt in Building Construction (inactive)*, set up 1948, Brussels. Restructured 2005. Previously registered in accordance with UK law. Former names and other names: *International Waterproofing Association (IAV)* – former (1968); *Association internationale de l'étanchéité (AIE)* – former (1968); *Internationaler Abdichtungsverband (IAV)* – former (1968); *Bitumen Waterproofing Association (BWA)* – former. Registration: Banque Carrefour des Entreprises, No/ID: 0597-802-387, Start date: 2015, Belgium; EU Transparency Register, No/ID: 064379325038-09, Start date: 12 Dec 2016. **Aims** Link information and research organizations, laboratories and individuals in order to coordinate studies on waterproofing-related matters and create an international centre of information, documentation and research; facilitate exchange of knowledge concerning waterproofing materials and their use; advise international and regional intergovernmental institutions and official professional associations in the field of construction and public works. **Structure** General Meeting (annual); Board of Directors; Advisory Committee; Executive Committee. Other Standing Committees (4): Technical; European Legislation; Publicity and Public Relations; Congress Organizing. Chief Executive is assisted by technical consultants. **Languages** English. **Staff** 4.00 FTE, paid. **Finance** Members' dues and admission fees. **Activities** Events/meetings. **Events** *International symposium on health effects of occupational exposure to emissions from asphalt/bitumen* Dresden (Germany) 2006, *Congress / Triennial Congress* Florence (Italy) 2000, *Congress / Triennial Congress* Copenhagen (Denmark) 1998, *International symposium on roofing technology* Gaithersburg, MD (USA) 1997, *Latin American roofing congress* Sao Paulo (Brazil) 1995.
Members Members in 14 countries:
Austria, Belgium, Denmark, Finland, France, Germany, Italy, Lithuania, Norway, Poland, Portugal, Spain, Sweden, Türkiye.
NGO Relations Member of (1): *Construction Products Europe AISBL (#04761).* In liaison with technical committees of: *Comité européen de normalisation (CEN, #04162).* [2020/XD2808/**D**]

♦ European Water Regulators (unconfirmed)

♦ European Water Resources Association (EWRA) 09085

Secretariat School of Rural/Surveying Engineering, Natl Technical Univ of Athens, Iroon Polytechniou 9, Zografou, 157 73 Athens, Greece. T. +302107722631. Fax +302107722632. E-mail: ewra@ewra.net.
URL: http://www.ewra.net/

History 19 Mar 1991. Founded as a regional committee within *International Association of Hydrological Sciences (IAHS, #11954).* Former names and other names: *European Committee for Water Resources Management (ECOWARM)* – former. **Aims** Promote research and the application of scientific knowledge on water resources to practical *engineering* activities; promote exchange of scientific knowledge in the field and serve as a forum for discussion between European scientists and professional engineers; contribute to dissemination in other regions of the world of the results of scientific and technical advances in the field by European specialists. **Structure** General Assembly (annual); Board of Management; Executive Committee. **Languages** English. **Finance** Sources: members' dues. **Activities** Events/meetings; knowledge management/information dissemination; training/education. **Events** *World Congress* Madrid (Spain) 2019, *World Congress* Athens (Greece) 2017, *World Congress* Istanbul (Turkey) 2015, *International Conference* Porto (Portugal) 2013, *International conference on sustainable groundwater management and control in the 21st century* Alexandria (Egypt) 2008. **Publications** *EWRAnews* (4 a year) – newsletter; *Environmental Processes* – journal; *European Water* – journal; *Water Resources Management* – journal; *Water Utility Journal.* Proceedings.
Members Individuals and organizations in 28 countries:
Austria, Belgium, Bulgaria, Cyprus, Czechia, Denmark, Finland, France, Germany, Greece (*), Hungary, Iceland, Iran Islamic Rep, Ireland, Israel, Italy, Netherlands, Norway, Portugal (*), Romania, Russia, Serbia, Slovakia, Spain, Sweden, Switzerland, Türkiye, UK.
IGO Relations *UNESCO (#20322).* Working relations with: *International Hydrological Programme (IHP, #13826).* **NGO Relations** Memorandum of Understanding with (1): *European Water Association (EWA, #09080).* European Regional Working Group of *International Commission on Irrigation and Drainage (ICID, #12694); Mediterranean Agronomic Institute of Bari (Bari MAI, #16641).* Working relations with: *International Water Resources Association (IWRA, #15871); World Water Council (WWC, #21908).* [2021/XD4982/**D**]

♦ European Water Stewardship (unconfirmed)

♦ European Water Treatment Association (EWTA) 09086

Chairman Willebroekkaai 37, 1000 Brussels, Belgium. T. +3222122623.
URL: http://www.ewta.eu/

Aims Provide a single point of contact for the European point of entry (POE) and point of use (POU) water treatment industry. **Structure** Board of Directors, comprising Chairman and 6 Directors. **NGO Relations** In liaison with technical committees of: *Comité européen de normalisation (CEN, #04162).* [2012/XJ4965/**D**]

♦ European Water and Wastewater Industry Association (Aqua Europa) 09087

Pres Registered Office, Multiburo Business Centre, Square de Meeûs 38-40, 1000 Brussels, Belgium. T. +3224016194. Fax +3224016888. E-mail: info@aqua-europa.eu.
URL: https://aqua-europa.eu/

History 1977. Relaunched May 2006. Former names and other names: *European Water Conditioning Association* – former; *Fédération européenne du traitement de l'eau (AQUA EUROPA)* – former; *Federación Europea de Tratamiento del Agua* – former; *Europäische Vereinigung für Wasseraufbereitung* – former; *Federazione Europea Trattamento Acqua* – former; *Europese Federatie voor Waterbehandeling* – former; *European Federation for Water Treatment* – former. Registration: EU Transparency Register, No/ID: 986379335268-59. **Aims** Represent the interests of the supply chain of the European water and wastewater industry at the EU level, covering all aspects of the development of water infrastructure within the EU and EFTA areas as well was internationally where appropriate. **Structure** General Assembly (annual); Council; Executive Committee; Technical and Representational Committees. **Languages** English, French, German. **Finance** Sources: members' dues. Annual budget: 100,000 EUR. **Activities** Knowledge management/information dissemination; standards/guidelines; training/education. **Events** *Meeting* Amsterdam (Netherlands) 1994, *Meeting* Barcelona (Spain) 1994, *Meeting* Helsinki (Finland) 1994, *Meeting* London (UK) 1994, *Plenary Meeting* Oslo (Norway) 1994. **Publications** *Aqua Europa Newsletter.* Position papers.
Members National trade associations (12) representing all aspects of the European water and wastewater industry. Members in 7 countries (" indicates Associate):
Austria, Germany, Italy, Netherlands, Spain, UK, USA (*).
IGO Relations Recognized by: *European Commission (EC, #06633).* **NGO Relations** Partner of: *Conseil européen de l'industrie chimique (CEFIC, #04687).* Associate member of: *Comité européen de normalisation (CEN, #04162).* [2020.09.17/XD0672/t/**D**]

♦ European Wax Federation (EWF) 09088

Main Office Bd du Souverain 165, 1160 Brussels, Belgium. T. +3225669131. E-mail: contact@wax.org.
URL: http://www.wax.org/

History 1978. Registration: EU Transparency Register, No/ID: 35124162688-86. **Aims** Bring together the European companies manufacturing or blending wax and having their own organisation for the marketing of these products in Europe; provide a forum for debating questions, problems, facts and topics arising during the manufacture, storage, transport use and disposal of waxes. **Structure** General Assembly; Board of Directors; Technical Committee; Task Force. **Activities** Monitoring/evaluation; advocacy/lobbying/activism; knowledge management/information dissemination; awards/prizes/competitions. **Events** *Annual General Assembly* Barcelona (Spain) 2009, *Annual General Assembly* Brussels (Belgium) 2008, *Annual General Assembly* Cascais (Portugal) 2007, *Annual General Assembly* Berlin (Germany) 2006, *Annual General Assembly* Krakow (Poland) 2005.
Members Wax producers and blenders (33) in 12 countries:
Belgium, Canada, France, Germany, Israel, Italy, Netherlands, Poland, Portugal, Spain, UK, USA. [2018/XE5990/**E**]

♦ European Weed Research Council / see European Weed Research Society (#09089)

♦ European Weed Research Society (EWRS) 09089

Société européenne de malherbologie – Europäische Gesellschaft für Herbologie – Società Europea di Malerbologia

Treasurer Postbus 28, 6865 ZG Doorwerth, Netherlands. T. +31263708389. Fax +31263706896. E-mail: ewrs@bureaupost.nl.
URL: http://www.ewrs.org/

History 4 Mar 1959, Stuttgart-Hohenheim (Germany). Changed to provide for individual membership, 1 Dec 1975, Paris (France). Former names and other names: *Research Group on Weed Control* – former (4 Mar 1959); *European Weed Research Council* – former (6 Apr 1960). Registration: No/ID: 40123440, Netherlands. **Aims** Promote and encourage weed research and technology in Europe for the benefit of the community as a whole. **Structure** General Assembly (annual); Board; Scientific Committee. Working Groups. **Languages** English. **Staff** 10.00 FTE, voluntary. **Finance** Members' dues. Sale of publications; possible profit from symposia. **Activities** Events/meetings; research/documentation; training/education. **Events** *Lighting the Future of Weed Science* Athens (Greece) 2022, *Lighting the Future of Weed Science* Athens (Greece) 2021, *International Symposium on Weeds and Invasive Plants* Prague (Czechia) 2020, *Symposium* Ljubljana (Slovenia) 2018, *International Symposium on Weeds and Invasive Plants* Chios (Greece) 2017. **Publications** *Weed Research* (6 a year); *EWRS Newsletter* (3 a year). List of members. Proceedings of symposia and conferences.
Members Ordinary (797) in 60 countries:
Albania, Algeria, Argentina, Australia, Austria, Belarus, Belgium, Benin, Bosnia-Herzegovina, Brazil, Bulgaria, Canada, Chile, China, Costa Rica, Croatia, Czechia, Denmark, Egypt, Estonia, Ethiopia, Finland, France, Gabon, Germany, Greece, Hungary, India, Indonesia, Ireland, Israel, Italy, Japan, Kazakhstan, Kenya, Korea Rep, Latvia, Lithuania, Mauritius, Mexico, Morocco, Netherlands, New Zealand, Norway, Paraguay, Poland, Portugal, Romania, Russia, Serbia, Slovakia, Slovenia, Spain, Sweden, Switzerland, Tunisia, Türkiye, UK, Ukraine, USA.
Affiliated Member Organizations (27) in 18 countries:
Australia, Belgium, Cameroon, Canada, France, Germany, Greece, Italy, Kenya, Latvia, Netherlands, New Zealand, Philippines, Romania, Russia, Spain, Türkiye, UK.
Sustaining (5) in 3 countries:
Germany, Italy, Switzerland.
Honorary (8) in 6 countries:
Belgium, France, Germany, Netherlands, UK. [2020/XD0904/v/**D**]

♦ European Weightlifting Federation (EWF) 09090

Fédération européenne haltérophile – Europäischer Gewichtheber Verband – Evropejskaja Federacija Tjazeloj Atletiki

Gen Sec Knez Mihailova 7, Belgrade, Serbia. T. +905323632115. E-mail: secretariat@ewf.sport.
Pres address not obtained.
URL: http://www.ewf.sport/

History Founded 20 Sep 1969, Warsaw (Poland). **Aims** Promote and popularize the *sport* of weightlifting in Europe; strengthen friendship and cooperation among national federations and lifters; promote all Europe Weightlifting Championships for any sex/age section; support and apply IWF technical rules in European *championships*, tournaments and meetings; resolve disputes that may arise between member countries during meetings or competitions; register European records. **Structure** Congress (annual, at European Senior Championship); Executive Committee; Commissions (2); Committees (4). **Languages** English, French, German, Russian, Spanish. **Staff** 3.00 FTE, voluntary. **Finance** Members' dues. **Activities** Sporting activities; events/meetings. **Events** *Annual Congress* Førde (Norway) 2016, *Technical Officials Seminar* Košice (Slovakia) 2015, *Scientific Seminar for Coaches* Rome (Italy) 2015, *Annual Congress* Tbilisi (Georgia) 2015, *Scientific Seminar for Coaches* Tel Aviv (Israel) 2014. **Publications** *EWF Scientific Magazine* (3 a year). Calendar.
Members Full national federations in 45 countries and territories:
Albania, Armenia, Austria, Azerbaijan, Belarus, Belgium, Bosnia-Herzegovina, Bulgaria, Croatia, Cyprus, Czechia, Denmark, Estonia, Finland, France, Georgia, Germany, Great Britain, Greece, Hungary, Iceland, Ireland, Israel, Italy, Kosovo, Latvia, Lithuania, Luxembourg, Malta, Moldova, Monaco, Netherlands, Norway, Poland, Romania, Russia, San Marino, Serbia, Slovakia, Slovenia, Spain, Sweden, Switzerland, Türkiye, Ukraine.
NGO Relations Member of: *International Council for Coaching Excellence (ICCE, #13008).* [2022/XD5406/**D**]

♦ European Welding Association (EWA) 09091

Gen Manager c/o Symop, 45 rue Louis Leblanc, 92400 Courbevoie, France. T. +33147176722.
URL: http://www.european-welding.org/

History Founded on merger of *European Committee of Associations of Manufacturers of Welding Products (CEFE, inactive)* and *European Committee of Manufacturers of Electric Welding Equipment (inactive).* Registration: EU Transparency Register, No/ID: 711840531940-21. **Aims** Promote common interests of members in the field of welding materials and of related technologies; stimulate exchange of information on welding *technology*, standardization and *market* developments; reduce existing *trade* barriers and prevent new barriers from developing. **Structure** General Assembly; Executive Committee; Management Team; Technical Committees; Statistics Committee; General Manager. **Languages** English. **Staff** 1.50 FTE, paid. **Finance** Members' dues. **Activities** Events/meetings. **Events** *General Assembly* Türkiye 2023, *Ordinary and Extraordinary General Assembly* Frankfurt-Main (Germany) 2022, *General Assembly* Courbevoie (France) 2021, *General Assembly* Bordeaux (France) 2019, *General Assembly* Helsinki (Finland) 2018. **Publications** Annual statistics of the industry.

Members Member organizations in 4 countries:
France, Germany, Italy, UK.
Member companies in 13 countries:
Austria, Finland, France, Germany, Greece, Italy, Netherlands, Poland, Slovenia, Spain, Sweden, Türkiye, UK.
IGO Relations As CEFE, recognized by: *European Commission (EC, #06633).* **NGO Relations** In liaison with the technical committees of: *International Organization for Standardization (ISO, #14473).* [2020/XD1776/D]

♦ European Welding Federation / see European Federation for Welding, Joining and Cutting (#07233)
♦ European Well Control Forum / see International Well Control Forum (#15877)

♦ European Wergeland Centre (EWC) 09092

Exec Dir Karl Johans gate 2, 0154 Oslo, Norway. T. +4721014500. E-mail: post@theewc.org.
URL: http://www.theewc.org/
History following recommendations at the Warsaw Summit 2005 to the Secretariat of *Council of Europe (CE, #04881).* Cooperation agreement between Council of Europe and Norwegian Government signed 16 Sep 2008, Strasbourg (France). Statutes adopted 12 Jun 2008, Oslo (Norway). Centre opened Feb 2009. Full title: *European Resource Centre on Education for Intercultural Understanding, Human Rights and Democratic Citizenship.* **Aims** Act as a *resource centre* on education for *intercultural understanding*, human *rights* and *democratic citizenship* for the member states of the Council of Europe. **Structure** Governing Board. **Languages** English. **Events** *International Conference on Interculturalism in Historical Education* Warsaw (Poland) 2015, *Crossing Borders Conference* Trondheim (Norway) 2013, *Global forum on reimagining democratic societies* Oslo (Norway) 2011, *Forum on the universality of human rights* Oslo (Norway) 2010. **Publications** *EWC Newsletter* (about 12 a year). **IGO Relations** Agreement with: *Council of Europe (CE, #04881).* [2022/XJ2288/E*]

♦ European Wheat Aneuploid Co-operative / see European Cereals Genetics Co-operative (#06509)

♦ European Whey Products Association (EWPA) 09093

Association européenne des produits de lactosérum – Europäischer Molkenprodukte Verband
SG Avenue d'Auderghem 22-28, 1040 Brussels, Belgium. T. +3225405040.
URL: http://ewpa.euromilk.org/
History Registration: Banque-Carrefour des Entreprises, No/ID: 0457.241.766, Start date: 10 Jan 1995, Belgium. **Structure** General Assembly. Executive Committee. From Jan 1996, integrates the previous *Association of Lactose Manufacturers (ALM, inactive)* as a Lactose Group. **Languages** English. **Events** *International Whey Conference* Brussels (Belgium) 2020, *International Whey Conference* Rotterdam (Netherlands) 2014, *International whey conference* Paris (France) 2008, *General Assembly* Copenhagen (Denmark) 2006, *International whey conference / Conference* Chicago, IL (USA) 2005.
Members Whey producing companies in 7 countries:
Denmark, Finland, France, Germany, Ireland, Netherlands, UK. [2020/XD5359/D]

♦ European Wholesale Meat Trade Association (inactive)

♦ European Wilderness Society 09094

Contact Dechant Franz Fuchs Str 5, 5580 Tamsweg, Austria. T. +43647427029. E-mail: info@wilderness-society.org.
URL: https://wilderness-society.org/
History 2014. Registration: Zentraler Vereinsregister, No/ID: ZVR 305471009, Austria. **Aims** Identify, designate, steward and promote Europe's last wilderness. **Structure** Advisory Board. **Languages** English, French, German, Hungarian, Italian, Slovakian, Ukrainian. **Staff** 13.00 FTE, paid. **Finance** Private funding; projects. **Activities** Events/meetings; monitoring/evaluation; networking/liaising; projects/programmes; research/documentation. **Publications** *Wilderness Newsletter* (weekly); *European Wilderness Journal* (4 a year). *Wilderness Network Book.* **Members** Individuals (over 100) in 18 countries. Membership countries not specified. **IGO Relations** *European Commission (EC, #06633); UNEP (#20299); World Tourism Organization (UNWTO, #21861).* **NGO Relations** Member of (1): *Global Rewilding Alliance (GRA, #10579). CEEweb for Biodiversity (#03626); Ecological Tourism in Europe (ÖTE); Friends of the Earth International (FoEI, #10002); International Union for Conservation of Nature and Natural Resources (IUCN, #15766); Wild Europe Foundation (#20955); World Wide Fund for Nature (WWF, #21922).* [2021/XM5049/D]

♦ European Wildlife Disease Association (EWDA) 09095

Sec IZW, Dept of Wildlife Diseases, Alfred-Kowalke-Strasse 17, 10315 Berlin, Germany. E-mail: ewda.secretary@gmail.com.
Chairperson address not obtained.
URL: http://www.ewda.org/
History 1990. **Aims** Provide a forum for exchange of information on wildlife diseases and their management. **Structure** Board; Advisory Board; Working Groups (3). **Languages** English. **Staff** 1.00 FTE, voluntary. **Finance** Members' dues. Conference proceeds. **Activities** Networking/liaising; research/documentation; training/education. **Events** *Managing Wildlife Diseases for Sustainable Ecosystems* Cuenca (Spain) 2021, *Conference* Larissa (Greece) 2018, *Conference* Berlin (Germany) 2016, *Conference* Edinburgh (UK) 2014, *Conference* Lyon (France) 2012. **Publications** *EWDA Bulletin (WEBZINE); Wildlife Related Emerging Diseases and Zoonose (WIREDZ)* – online magazine. **Members** Membership countries not specified. **NGO Relations** *Wildlife Disease Association (WDA, #20959).* [2021/XD6655/D]

♦ European Wind Energy Association / see WindEurope (#20965)

♦ European Window Film Association (EWFA) 09096

Manager Place Saint-Lambert 22, Bte 3, 1200 Brussels, Belgium. T. +3427611655. E-mail: info@ewfa.org.
URL: https://iwfa.com/ewfa/
History 26 Oct 2000. A chapter of *International Window Film Association (IWFA).* Registered in accordance with Belgian law. Registration: EU Transparency Register, No/ID: 86497137168-71, Start date: 16 Nov 2011. **Aims** Represent and further the interests of the window film industry. **Structure** Council. **Finance** Members' dues. **Activities** Annual General Meeting. **Events** *Meeting* Bucharest (Romania) 2013. **Members** Companies. Membership countries not specified. [2020/XD8255/D]

♦ European Wind Tower Association (unconfirmed)
♦ European Wireless Conference (meeting series)
♦ European Wireless Infrastructure Association (unconfirmed)
♦ European Wire Rope Information Service / see European Federation of Steel Wire Rope Industries (#07221)
♦ European Wishu Federation / see European Wushu Kungfu Federation (#09126)
♦ European Women Alliance (internationally oriented national body)

♦ European Women on Boards (EWOB) 09097

Registered Address Rue de la Presse 4, 1000 Brussels, Belgium. E-mail: communication@europeanwomenonboards.eu.
URL: https://europeanwomenonboards.eu/
History Jun 2013, Brussels (Belgium). Registration: Belgium. **Aims** Increase gender diversity in C-Suite and Board roles. **Structure** Board of Directors; Advisory Board; Executive Committee. **Languages** English. **Finance** Sources: members' dues; revenue from activities/projects; sponsorship. **Activities** Advocacy/lobbying/activism; events/meetings; knowledge management/information dissemination; networking/liaising; projects/programmes; research/documentation; training/education. **Events** *Meeting* Berlin (Germany) 2017, *Meeting* Brussels (Belgium) 2016, *Mentees Program Meeting* Brussels (Belgium) 2016. **Publications** *Gender Diversity Index.*
Members Associations in 7 countries:
Czechia, Finland, Germany, Italy, Netherlands, Poland, Türkiye.
IGO Relations *European Union (EU, #08967).* [2023.02.22/XM5664/F]

♦ European Women Lawyers' Association (EWLA) 09098

Association européenne des femmes juristes
SG Liersesteenweg 21, 2640 Mortsel, Belgium. T. +34918288800. E-mail: info@ewla.org.
URL: http://www.ewla.org/
History 19 Mar 2000, Berlin (Germany). Registration: Banque-Carrefour des Entreprises, No/ID: 0871.481.355, Start date: 15 Jan 2005, Belgium; EU Transparency Register, No/ID: 730379225729-59, Start date: 22 Feb 2017. **Aims** Improve understanding of European legislation in relation to equal opportunities, with particular reference to women, and the impact of these measures on women; bring together women lawyers across the European Union, the European Economic Area (EEA) and the European Free Trade Area (EFTA); undertake studies, research and conferences; strengthen links between EU women lawyers. **Structure** General Assembly (every 2 years); Board; Presidium. Working groups. **Languages** English, French. **Staff** Voluntary. **Finance** Sources: members' dues. **Activities** Events/meetings; networking/liaising; research/documentation. **Events** *Congress* Madrid (Spain) 2019, *The fourth Industrial Revolution and Ethics Congress* Madrid (Spain) 2019, *Congress* Luxembourg (Luxembourg) 2017, *Congress* Lille (France) 2015, *Women in business and social development* Rome (Italy) 2013. **Publications** Congress proceedings. **Members** National women lawyers associations; Individuals. Full; Associate; Observers; Students/Trainees. Membership countries from EU Members States. Associated national women lawyers associations from non-EU Member States in Europe. Membership countries not specified. **IGO Relations** Participant in Fundamental Rights Platform of: *European Union Agency for Fundamental Rights (FRA, #08969).* **NGO Relations** Member of (1): *European Movement International (EMI, #07825).* [2022.11.16/XD8792/D]

♦ European Women in Mathematics (EWM) 09099

Mailing Address Mathematics, PO Box 11100, FI-00076 Aalto, Finland. E-mail: membership@europeanwomeninmaths.org – contact@europeanwomeninmaths.org.
URL: http://www.europeanwomeninmaths.org/
History 2 Dec 1993. Founded following proposals, Aug 1986, Berkeley CA (USA), during International Congress of Mathematics. Registration: Finland. **Aims** Encourage women to take up and continue mathematical studies; support women who have or desire careers in mathematics research and related fields and provide a meeting place for them; foster international scientific communication among women in the mathematics field; promote equal opportunity and treatment of women and men in the mathematical community. **Structure** General Assembly (every 2 years); Standing Committee; Coordinators; Committee for Women in Mathematics; Scientific Committee. **Languages** English. **Staff** Voluntary. **Finance** Members' dues. **Activities** Events/meetings; training/education. **Events** *General Meeting* Espoo (Finland) 2022, *General Meeting* Graz (Austria) 2018, *Biennial Conference* Cortona (Italy) 2015, *Biennial Conference* Bonn (Germany) 2013, *Biennial Conference* Barcelona (Spain) 2011. **Publications** *EWM Newsletter* (annual).
Members Full; Honorary; Supporting. Organizations in 36 countries:
Argentina, Austria, Azerbaijan, Belarus, Belgium, Bulgaria, Czechia, Denmark, Estonia, Finland, France, Germany, Greece, India, Italy, Latvia, Lebanon, Lithuania, Malta, Moldova, Morocco, Netherlands, North Macedonia, Norway, Poland, Portugal, Romania, Russia, Serbia, Spain, Sweden, Switzerland, Türkiye, UK, Ukraine, USA.
NGO Relations Member of (1): *European Mathematical Society (EMS, #07755).* [2022/XD6357/D]

♦ European Women Payments Network (EWPN) 09100

Contact address not obtained. T. +31652894169. E-mail: info@ewpn.eu.
URL: http://ewpn.eu/
History Registration: No/ID: 71428445, Netherlands. **Aims** Provide a platform that inspires, empowers and mentors women in payments to help them realize their full individual potential and position themselves for greater personal success while continuing to learn and contribute to the payments and fintech industries. **Structure** Executive Board; Advisory Board. **Activities** Events/meetings; awards/prizes/competitions. **Events** *Annual Conference* Amsterdam (Netherlands) 2020, *Annual Conference* Amsterdam (Netherlands) 2019, *Annual Conference* Amsterdam (Netherlands) 2018, *Annual Conference* Amsterdam (Netherlands) 2017. **Publications** *EWPN Newsletter.* [2021/XM8013/F]

♦ European Women Rectors Association (EWORA) 09101

Registered Address Rond Point Schuman 11, 1040 Brussels, Belgium. E-mail: info@ewora.org.
President's Office Levent Loft Büyükdere Cad, No 201 A Blok K:5 D:88, Sisli, 34394 Istanbul/Istanbul, Türkiye. T. +905546568.
URL: https://www.ewora.org/
History 2015. Registration: Banque-Carrefour des Entreprises, No/ID: 0643.794.047, Start date: 2 Dec 2015, Belgium. **Aims** Promote the role of women in leadership positions in the academic sector; advocate gender equality in higher education and research at European and international scales. **Structure** General Assembly; Board of Directors; Executive Committee; Scientific Advisory Board. **Activities** Events/meetings. **Events** *Conference* Istanbul (Türkiye) 2023, *Conference* Zurich (Switzerland) 2021, *Conference* Malmö (Sweden) 2019, *Conference* Brussels (Belgium) 2017. **NGO Relations** Signatory to agreement of *Coalition for Advancing Research Assessment (CoARA, #04045).* [2023/AA3086/D]

♦ European Women's Centre for Studies in a Changing Society (inactive)

♦ European Women's Lobby (EWL) 09102

Lobby européen des femmes (LEF)
Secretariat Rue Hydraulique 18, 1210 Brussels, Belgium. T. +3222179020. Fax +3222198451. E-mail: ewl@womenlobby.org.
URL: http://www.womenlobby.org/
History 22 Sep 1990, Brussels (Belgium). Founded at 1st General Assembly, after a decision taken at 5th European Colloquium of Women's Associations, Nov 1987, London (UK). New statutes adopted Sep 2002; revised Oct 2004. New statutes adopted Jan 2007; Jun 2009. Former names and other names: *LOBBY* – alias. Registration: Banque Carrefour des Entreprises, No/ID: 0446.526.137, Start date: 22 Jan 1992, Belgium; EU Transparency Register, No/ID: 85686156700-13, Start date: 16 Sep 2011. **Aims** Support the active involvement of women from different parts of Europe in working to achieve equality between women and men; support national members through information/lobbying resources and training to actively engage with EU policy shaping and implementation of legislation at national level; through analysis, evaluation and monitoring provide regular input on all areas of EU policy development and implementation that have an impact on women's lives and on the promotion of equality between women and men; monitor and raise awareness about the development and implementation of gender mainstreaming in order to ensure the full integration of women's rights, interests and perspective in all areas of EU policy; take into account the needs and perspective of different groups of women, and the diverse experiences of women at all stages of their life cycle. **Structure** General Assembly (annual). Board of Administration of 40 members, comprising one representative from each national coordination and 10 representatives from European NGOs. Executive Committee, comprising President, 2 Vice-Presidents, Treasurer and 3 Board members. Secretariat, headed by General Secretary. Includes: European Observatory on Violence Against Women. **Languages** English, French. **Staff** 8.00 FTE, paid. **Finance** Sources: members' dues. Other sources: subvention from *European Commission (EC, #06633)*; independent funding sources. **Activities** Politics/policy/regulatory. **Events** *Annual General Assembly* Brussels (Belgium) 2019, *Annual General Assembly* Brussels (Belgium) 2018, *Annual General Assembly* Brussels (Belgium) 2017, *Annual General Assembly* Brussels (Belgium) 2016, *Annual General Assembly* Brussels (Belgium) 2015. **Publications** Annual Report; reports; books; thematic newsletters; position papers.
Members National and European women's NGOs in 32 countries:
Austria, Belgium, Bulgaria, Croatia, Cyprus, Czechia, Denmark, Estonia, Finland, France, Germany, Greece, Hungary, Iceland, Ireland, Italy, Latvia, Lithuania, Luxembourg, Malta, Netherlands, North Macedonia, Poland, Portugal, Romania, Serbia, Slovakia, Slovenia, Spain, Sweden, Türkiye, UK.
European-wide organizations (17):
BPW Europe – European Region of BPW International (#03309); European Centre of the International Council of Women (ECICW, #06485); European Confederation of Independent Trade Unions (CESI, #06705); European Council of WIZO Federations (ECWF, #06850); European Disability Forum (EDF, #06929); European Network of Migrant Women (ENoMW, #07947); European Trade Union Confederation (ETUC, #08927); European Young Women's Christian Association (The European YWCA, #09135); Fédération européenne des femmes actives en famille (FEFAF, #09568); International Alliance of Women (IAW, #11639); International Council of Jewish Women (ICJW, #13036); International Federation of Women in Legal Careers (IFWLC, #13579); Medical Women's International Association (MWIA, #16630); Soroptimist International of Europe (SI/E, #19689); University Women of Europe (UWE, #20707); Women's International League for Peace and Freedom (WILPF, #21024); World Association of Girl Guides and Girl Scouts (WAGGGS, #21142).

Supporting members in 3 countries:
Albania, Luxembourg, Malta.
European Blind Union (EBU, #06350).
Consultative Status Consultative status granted from: *ECOSOC (#05331)* (Special); *Council of Europe (CE, #04881)* (Participatory Status). **IGO Relations** Participant in Fundamental Rights Platform of: *European Union Agency for Fundamental Rights (FRA, #08969).* **NGO Relations** Member of (7): *Conference of Non-Governmental Organizations in Consultative Relationship with the United Nations (CONGO, #04635); EU Alliance for a democratic, social and sustainable European Semester (EU Semester Alliance, #05565); EU Civil Society Contact Group (CSCG, #05572); European NGO Platform Asylum and Migration (EPAM, #08051);* NGOs Liaison Group with the European Economic Social Committee; *SDG Watch Europe (#19162); Social Platform (#19344).* [2021/XF1647/y/F]

♦ European Women's Management Development International Network (EWMD) 09103

Head Office EWMD Intl eV, Geisbergweg 6c, 65205 Wiesbaden, Germany. E-mail: presid-ents.international@ewmd.org – service.international@ewmd.org.
URL: https://www.ewmd.org/

History 1984. Founded under the auspices of *EFMD – The Management Development Network (#05387).* Independent since 1994. Former names and other names: *EWMD International* – alias. Registration: Hesse District court, No/ID: VR 3602, Start date: 8 May 2001, Germany, Wiesbaden; EU Transparency Register, No/ID: 548761648694-59, Start date: 20 Jan 2023. **Aims** Achieve more visibility and participation of qualified women in leading positions in business, commerce and wider society, thus raising and enriching quality levels in management through more women and greater diversity. **Structure** General Assembly (annual, at Conference); International Board; Managing Board. **Languages** English. **Staff** 1.00 FTE, paid. Several voluntary. **Finance** Sources: members' dues. **Activities** Awards/prizes/competitions; events/meetings; training/education. **Events** *International Conference* Turin (Italy) 2023, *Annual Conference* Vienna (Austria) 2019, *Annual Conference* Berlin (Germany) 2014, *Annual Conference* Brescia (Italy) 2013, *Annual Conference* Vienna (Austria) 2012. **Publications** *EWMD International Newsletter* (3 a year). Country newsletters.
Members Members (nearly 1,000) in 18 countries and territories:
Austria, Belgium, France, Germany, Hong Kong, India, Italy, Luxembourg, Netherlands, Romania, Singapore, South Africa, Spain, Sweden, Switzerland, Türkiye, UK, USA.
NGO Relations Member of (4): *CEC European Managers (#03623); EFMD – The Management Development Network (#05387); GlobeWomen* (Global Summit of Women); *Women's International Network (WIN, #21027).* [2023.02.16/XF9917/v/F]

♦ European Women and Sport Network (EWS) 09104

Réseau européen femmes et sport
SG 4th Fl Burwood House, 14-16 Caxton St, London, SW1H 0QT, UK. T. +442079763928.
URL: http://www.ews-online.org/

History 1989, by *European Sports Conference (ESC, no recent information)* as a working group on Women and Sport. Transformed into a free-standing body with permanent status, 1993, after presentation of a final report, with Associate Member status on the ESC Executive Committee since 1994. **Aims** Represent, defend and promote the interests of women in sport at a European level; support and further develop the participation of girls and women in sport; help increase the number of women in decision-making bodies and in administration of sport at all levels; educate women for decision-making in sport through mentor programmes; promote involvement of female representatives in local, regional and national delegations at sport-political, scientific and sport-practical events, conferences, seminars and workshops, at national and international levels; strengthen cooperation and encourage the exchange of experience on women and sport issues among European countries; cultivate relations with international organizations and bodies on women and sport issues and, where appropriate, establish links of cooperation; motivate international and sport bodies to support and finance projects on women and sport; encourage and increase scientific research projects in various sports sciences for initiating, supporting and adopting women's perspectives. **Structure** Meeting (every 4 years). Steering Group, comprising Chair and 7 members. Network of EWS Contact Persons. **Languages** English. **Finance** Support through governmental and/or non-governmental sports organizations. Budget (annual): about euro 16,000. **Activities** Organizes European Women and Sport Conference (every 4 years), organized alternatively with the EWS Meeting. **Events** *Biennial Conference* Stockholm (Sweden) 2016, *Biennial Conference* London (UK) 2014, *Biennial Conference* Limassol (Cyprus) 2009, *Biennial Conference* Vienna (Austria) 2006, *Biennial Conference* Paris (France) 2004. **Publications** *EWS Newsletter.*
Members in 48 countries:
Albania, Andorra, Armenia, Austria, Azerbaijan, Belarus, Belgium, Bosnia-Herzegovina, Bulgaria, Croatia, Cyprus, Czechia, Denmark, Estonia, Finland, France, Georgia, Germany, Greece, Hungary, Iceland, Ireland, Israel, Italy, Latvia, Liechtenstein, Lithuania, Luxembourg, Malta, Moldova, Monaco, Netherlands, North Macedonia, Norway, Poland, Portugal, Romania, Russia, San Marino, Serbia, Slovakia, Slovenia, Spain, Sweden, Switzerland, Türkiye, UK, Ukraine.
NGO Relations Associate member of: ESC; *European Non-Governmental Sports Organization (ENGSO, #08054); European Women's Lobby (EWL, #09102).* [2014/XF6669/F]

♦ European Women's Synod (meeting series)
♦ European Wood-Based Panels Federation / see European Panel Federation (#08137)

♦ European Wood Preservative Manufacturers Group (EWPM) 09105

Sec Hollandseweg 7G, 6706 KN Wageningen, Netherlands. T. +447770888055. E-mail: info@ewpm.org.
URL: https://www.ewpm.org/

History Jul 1977. Statutes amended: 2019. Registration: EU Transparency Register, No/ID: 133623210570-20. **Aims** Promote with integrity the correct use of wood preservatives including production, transportation, utilization and disposal. **Structure** General Assembly (annual); Executive Committee; Working Groups (5); Secretariat. **Languages** English. **Staff** 1.00 FTE, paid; 5.00 FTE, voluntary. **Finance** Sources: members' dues. **Activities** Advocacy/lobbying/activism; knowledge management/information dissemination; politics/policy/regulatory; standards/guidelines. **Publications** *EWPM/WEI Treated Wood – A Sustainable Choice* (2019); *EWPM/WEI Timber Treatment Installations: Code of Practice for their Safe Design and Operations* (2011).
Members Voting members: producers (14) in 6 countries:
Belgium, France, Germany, Netherlands, UK, USA.
Non-voting members: associations in 4 countries:
Austria, Belgium, Germany, UK.
Permanent guest:
European Institute for Wood Preservation (WEI-IEO, #07575).
NGO Relations Observer status with (1): *Comité européen de normalisation (CEN, #04162)* (Technical Committees 112, 124, 175, 38, 351). [2022.02.08/XF2223/y/F]

♦ European Woodworking Machinery Importers' Committee (inactive)
♦ European Workers Committee Against German Remilitarization (inactive)

♦ European Work Hazards Network (EWHN) 09106

Main Office Piazza della Pace 5, Sala Baganza, 43044 Parma PR, Italy.
URL: http://www.ewhn.eu/

History 1986. Also referred to as *European Network for Better Work Environment.* Constitution adopted Oct 1996. 2012, registered in accordance with Italian law. **Aims** Serve as a platform for information, projects and exchange of experience in the field of *occupational* hazards. **Structure** International Committee. International Secretariat in Copenhagen (Denmark). **Activities** Acts as a 'network of networks' which collects and distributes information, exchanges practical experience and research, and promotes and improves safety and health at the workplace and in the environment. Strives to raise awareness of work hazards and to inspire humane solutions in the working environment. Fights for an increasing role for European-wide initiatives in cooperation with the trade unions and other organizations for a better working environment. Sub-networks (located in 6 countries and territories): Chemical Sector; Stress; Micro Electronics; Construction; Health in Small Companies; New Management Techniques; Occupational Exposure Limits; Working Time; Occupational Health Service. **Events** *Conference* Copenhagen (Denmark) 2018, *Empowerment of workers and experts to neutralize deregulation and lack of precautions in an European context* Rotterdam (Netherlands) 2016, *Conference* Bologna (Italy) 2013, *Conference* Leeds (UK) 2010, *Conference* Bologna (Italy) 2008. **Publications** *Workers Health International Newsletter.* Conference reports.

Members National networks in 12 countries and territories:
Austria, Denmark, England and Wales, Finland, France, Germany, Ireland, Italy, Netherlands, Norway, Scotland, Spain. [2018/XF4363/F]

♦ European Working Community for Food Inspection and Consumer Protection (EWFC) 09107

SG 4 rue des Tilleuls, 57070 Metz, France.
URL: http://www.ewfc.org/

History 23 Feb 1991. Legal seat: Saint-Julien-lès-Metz (France). Registration: Start date: 19 Sep 1991, France, Metz; EU Transparency Register, No/ID: 52069834210-92, Start date: 20 Sep 2010. **Aims** Gather the professional and state federations of food inspection of the individual member countries of Europe; intensify and accelerate the exchange of experiences and informations; harmonize inspection activities in Europe; guarantee the protection of the consumers. **Structure** General Assembly (every 2 years). Board, comprising President, General Secretary, Treasurer, Deputy General-Secretary, Deputy Treasurer, 9 Vice-Presidents and Assessor. **Languages** English. **Activities** Events/meetings; training/education; networking/liaising. **Events** *General Assembly* Newport (UK) 2015, *Congress* Amnéville (France) 2011, *Meeting / Congress* Vienna (Austria) 2009, *Congress* Newport (UK) 2006, *Congress* Brussels (Belgium) 2003. **Publications** *Food Matters. Guidelines for Good Control Practice; Guidelines for Official Sampling.*
Members Organizations in 10 countries:
Austria, Belgium, Cyprus, France, Germany, Ireland, Luxembourg, Netherlands, Sweden, UK. [2022/XJ1403/E]

♦ European Working Group on Acoustic Emission (EWGAE) 09108

Chair c/o Office of Technical Inspection UDT, Szczesliwicka 34, 02-353 Warsaw, Poland. T. +48225722100.
URL: http://ewgae.eu/

History Founded 1972, as *European Stress Wave Emission Working Group.* Current title adopted, Sep 1973, at second Institute of Physics' Conference on Acoustic Emission. **Aims** Promote the exchange of information on acoustic emission, with particular emphasis on scientific and technical development; promote the use of standardized terminology in acoustic emission documentation; provide information about acoustic emission instrumentation; provide information about acoustic emission to interest parties outside the Group, and liaise with other groups having common interests; develop common standards for acoustic emission practice. **Structure** Committee. **Languages** English. **Staff** None. **Activities** Knowledge management/information dissemination; research and development; standards/guidelines. **Events** *Conference* Potsdam (Germany) 2024, *Conference* Ljubljana (Slovenia) 2022, *Conference* Granada (Spain) 2020, *Conference* Senlis (France) 2018, *Conference* Prague (Czechia) 2016. **NGO Relations** Instrumental in setting up: *International Institute of Innovative Acoustic Emission (I3AE, #13891).* [2018/XJ5932/c/D]

♦ European Working Group on Clinical Cell Analysis / see European Society for Clinical Cell Analysis (#08544)

♦ European Working Group 'Courage to Take a Moral Stance' 09109

Europäische Arbeitsgemeinschaft 'Mut zur Ethik'
Contact address not obtained. T. +41794005157.
URL: http://www.mut-zur-ethik.ch/

Events *Conference* Feldkirch (Austria) 2010, *Conference* Feldkirch (Austria) 2009, *Conference* Feldkirch (Austria) 2008, *Peoples and cultures – respecting each other, helping one another, learning from each other* Feldkirch (Austria) 2007, *Conference* Feldkirch (Austria) 1996.
Members Organizations (21) in 9 countries:
Austria, Belgium, Czechia, France, Germany, Hungary, Switzerland, UK, USA.
Included in the above, 3 organizations listed in this Yearbook:
Cercle civique européen, Lausanne; Internationale Hippokratische Gesellschaft, Zurich; World Federation of Doctors who Respect Human Life (WFDWRHL, #21432). [2007/XN7184/y/E]

♦ European Working Group for Cystic Fibrosis / see European Cystic Fibrosis Society (#06879)

♦ European Working Group for Dendrochronology (EuroDendro) 09110

Groupe de travail européen pour la dendrochronologie
Address not obtained.

Aims Decide location and host for annual or biennial European meeting of *dendrochronologists.* **Structure** Informal, variable and voluntary group of specialists. **Finance** No separate budget. **Events** *EuroDendro Conference* Cambridge (UK) 2021, *EuroDendro Conference* Riga (Latvia) 2020, *EuroDendro Conference* Brno (Czechia) 2019, *EuroDendro Conference* Tartu (Estonia) 2017, *EuroDendro Conference* Antalya (Turkey) 2015. [2011/XE2968/E]

♦ European Working Group on Drug Oriented Research (EWODOR) 09111

Grupo Europeo de Trabajo sobre Investigación en Drogas
Contact c/o TG De Kiem, Vluchtenboerstraat 7a, 9890 Gavere, Belgium. T. +3293896666. Fax +3293848307. E-mail: eftc@dekiem.be.
Contact Univ of Stirling, Dept of Applied Social Science, Sociology/Social Policy and Criminology Section, Stirling, FK9 4LA, UK. T. +441786467737. Fax +441786466299.

History 1986. **Aims** Provide a forum within which researchers in the field of drug/alcohol *treatment, prevention* and policy share experience and expertise, compare procedures, methods and results and subject their work to peer examination. **Structure** Scientific and Organizing Committee. **Finance** Symposium fees. **Activities** Events/meetings; knowledge management/information dissemination; research/documentation. **Events** *International Symposium on Substance Abuse Treatment* Ghent (Belgium) 2018, *International Symposium on Substance Abuse Treatment* Thessaloniki (Greece) 2012, *International symposium on substance abuse treatment* Oslo (Norway) 2007, *International symposium on substance abuse treatment* Helsinki (Finland) 2006. **Members** Full researchers from EU member and Associated member countries in universities or other research institutions; Associate researchers from European third countries. Membership countries not specified. **NGO Relations** *European Federation of Therapeutic Communities (EFTC, #07225)* is a member. [2018/XE4263/E]

♦ European Working Group on Earth Science Conservation / see International Association for the Conservation of the Geological Heritage (#11810)

♦ European Working Group on Gaucher Disease (EWGGD) 09112

Secretariat Internal Med F5-169, Academic Medical Ctr, PO Box 22700, 1100 DE Amsterdam, Netherlands. T. +31205668315. Fax +31206917682.
Chairman Dept Gastroenterology/Hematology/Infectious Diseases, Univ Hosp Düsseldorf, Moorenstrasse 5, 40225 Düsseldorf, Germany. T. +492118119648.
URL: http://www.ewggd.com/

History 1993, as an affiliate of *European Study Group on Lysosomal Diseases (ESGLD, #08850).* Registered in accordance with Dutch law, 23 Feb 2012. **Aims** Promote research on Gaucher disease and ultimately improve lives of patients who suffer from the disease. **Structure** Board; Executive Committee. **Languages** English. **Staff** 0.10 FTE, paid. **Finance** Members' dues. Sponsoring of workshops by pharmaceutical parties. **Activities** Meeting activities; research/documentation. **Events** *Meeting* Genoa (Italy) 2018, *Meeting* Saragossa (Spain) 2016, *Meeting* Haifa (Israel) 2014, *Meeting* Paris (France) 2012, *Meeting* Cologne (Germany) 2010. **Publications** Working group papers. **Members** Juristic persons; alliances without legal personality. Membership countries not specified. **NGO Relations** Affiliated to: *International Gaucher Alliance (IGA, #13701).* [2017/XE3553/E]

♦ European Working Group for Glow Discharge Spectroscopy (EW-GDS) 09113

Chairman address not obtained.
URL: https://www.ew-gds.com/

History 1992, Paris (France). **Aims** Promote the development of GDS Technologies for both surface and bulk analysis of materials. **Structure** Steering Committee. **Activities** Awards/prizes/competitions; events/meetings; knowledge management/information dissemination; networking/liaising; research and development. **Events** *International Glow Discharge Spectroscopy Symposium* Liverpool (UK) 2024, *International Glow Discharge Spectroscopy Symposium* Oviedo (Spain) 2022, *International Glow Discharge Spectroscopy Symposium* Oviedo (Spain) 2021, *International Glow Discharge Spectroscopy Symposium* Oviedo (Spain) 2020, *International Glow Discharge Spectroscopy Symposium* Berlin (Germany) 2018. [2023/XM8369/D]

♦ European Working Group on Human Gene Transfer and Gene Therapy / see European Society of Gene and Cell Therapy (#08608)

♦ European Working Group on Labour Law (EWLL) 09114

Contact c/o Europa-Uni Viadrina, Große Scharrnstr 59, 15230 Frankfurt-Oder, Germany. T. +4933555342778. E-mail: info@c-illas.de.
URL: https://ewll.eu/

History 1998. **Activities** Events/meetings; research/documentation. **Events** *Seminar* Naples (Italy) 2022, *Seminar* Leicester (UK) 2021, *Seminar* Poznań (Poland) 2020, *Seminar* Ciudad Real (Spain) 2018, *Seminar* Frankfurt-Main (Germany) 2017.
Members Professors in 7 countries:
France, Germany, Italy, Netherlands, Poland, Spain, UK.
NGO Relations Member of (1): *Labour Law Research Network (LLRN, #16215).* [2021/AA2078/v/F]

♦ European Working Group on MDS (EWOG MDS) 09115

Study Centre Univ Hosp, Dept Pediatric and Adolescent Medicine, Pediatric Hematology and Oncology, 79106 Freiburg, Germany. T. +4976127045060. Fax +4976127045180. E-mail: ewog-mds@uniklinik-freiburg.de.
URL: http://www.ewog-mds.org/

History 1993. MDS stands for *Myelodysplastic Syndrome.* **Aims** Bring together clinicians and researchers with an interest in childhood MDS and juvenile myelomonocytic *leukemia* (JMML); initiate collaborative studies; disseminate information about childhood MDS; serve as a resource for those interested in childhood MDS. **Structure** Regional Coordinators; Committees (4); Scientific Board. **Activities** Research/documentation; knowledge management/information dissemination; events/meetings; publishing activities. **Events** *International Symposium on Pediatric MDS (Myelodysplatic Syndrome) and Bone Marrow Failure Syndromes* Frankfurt-Main (Germany) 2018, *International Symposium on Pediatric MDS (Myelodysplatic Syndrome) and Bone Marrow Failure Syndromes* Rome (Italy) 2017, *Business Meeting* Zurich (Switzerland) 2014, *International congress on pediatric MDS (myelodysplatic syndrome) and bone marrow failure syndromes* Rotterdam (Netherlands) 2009.
Members Full in 16 countries:
Austria, Belgium, Czechia, Denmark, Finland, Germany, Hungary, Ireland, Italy, Netherlands, Norway, Poland, Slovakia, Spain, Sweden, Switzerland. [2018.09.06/XJ1451/F]

♦ European Working Group in Pediatric Otorhinolaryngology / see European Society of Pediatric Otorhinolaryngology (#08692)
♦ European Working Group of Practitioners and Specialists in Free Practice / see EANA – European Working Group of Physicians in Private Practice (#05154)

♦ European Working Group on Psychosocial Aspects of Children with Chronic Renal Failure (EWOPA) 09116

Chairperson Dept of Paediatric Nephrology, Evelina Children's Hospital, London, SE1 7EH, UK.
URL: http://www.ewopa-renalchild.com/

History 1971, Paris (France). **Aims** Through annual conferences, exchange information, in order to provide the best available care and treatment, not only including medical treatment but especially psychosocial well-being. **Structure** Coordination Group of 4 members. **Staff** Voluntary. **Finance** Conference fees, sponsorship. No budget. **Events** *Annual Conference* Nijmegen (Netherlands) 2022, *Annual Conference* Nijmegen (Netherlands) 2020, *Annual Conference* Helsinki (Finland) 2019, *Annual Conference* Heidelberg (Germany) 2016, *Annual Conference* Porto (Portugal) 2014.
Members Full in 17 countries:
Armenia, Austria, Belgium, Czechia, Finland, France, Germany, Hungary, Ireland, Israel, Italy, Netherlands, Poland, Spain, Sweden, Switzerland, UK. [2016/XE2544/E]

♦ European Working Group for Psychosomatic Cancer Research (inactive)
♦ European Working Party for Landscape Husbandry (inactive)

♦ European Workplace Drug Testing Society (EWDTS) 09117

Pres Regione Gonzole 10/1, 14403 Orbassano TO, Italy. T. +391190224232.
Treas Nullanderstraat 103, 6461 GC Kerkrade, Netherlands.
URL: http://www.ewdts.org/

History Mar 1998, Huddinge (Sweden), at 1st European Symposium on Workplace Drug Testing. Previously registered in accordance with Luxembourg law. Currently registered in accordance with Spanish law. **Aims** Ensure Workplace Drug Testing in Europe is performed to a defined quality standard and in a legally secured way; provide an independent forum for all aspects of Workplace Drug Testing. **Structure** Board of Directors; Committees (6). **Languages** English. **Staff** None. **Finance** Conference income. **Events** *Symposium* Orbassano (Italy) 2021, *Symposium* London (UK) 2019, *Symposium* Turin (Italy) 2017, *IALM Intersocietal Symposium* Venice (Italy) 2016, *Symposium* Lisbon (Portugal) 2015. **NGO Relations** Endorses: *International Forum for Drug and Alcohol Testing (IFDAT).* [2016.10.20/XM3311/D]

♦ European Workshop of Advanced Plastic Surgery (EWAPS) 09118

Contact Praxis für Plastische Chirurgie, Wilhelmshoher Allee 137, 34121 Kassel, Germany. T. +4956150898. Fax +4956153202.
URL: http://www.ewaps.org/

History Set up 1986. Rules approved 2005, Stockholm (Sweden). **Aims** Acts as a forum to discuss clinical and scientific advancement in plastic surgery. **Structure** Board. **Events** *Annual Symposium* Bern (Switzerland) 2015, *Workshop* Switzerland 2015, *Workshop* Austria 2014, *Annual Symposium* Velden am Wörthersee (Austria) 2014, *Annual Symposium / Workshop* France 2013.
Members Individuals in 14 countries:
Austria, Czechia, France, Germany, Greece, Italy, Norway, Poland, Russia, Slovenia, Spain, Sweden, Switzerland, UK. [2015/XJ9631/c/D]

♦ European Workshop on Computational Geometry (meeting series)
♦ European Workshop on Econometrics and Health Economics (meeting series)
♦ European Workshop on Economic Theory (meeting series)
♦ European Workshop on Efficiency and Productivity Analysis (meeting series)

♦ European Workshop on Industrial Computer Systems (EWICS) 09119

EWICS TC7 Chair Univ Erlangen-Nuremberg, Software Engineering – Informatik 11, Martensstr 3, 91058 Erlangen, Germany. T. +4991318527870. Fax +4991318528746.
Association Chair address not obtained.
URL: http://www.ewics.org/

History 21 Jun 1974, Stuttgart (Germany FR). Full title: *European Workshop on Industrial Computer Systems – Technical Committee 7: Reliability, Safety, Security (EWICS TC7).* **Aims** Promote economical and efficient realization of programmable industrial computer systems through education, information exchange and elaboration of standards and guidelines. **Structure** Officers: Chairperson; 2 Vice-Chairpersons. Subgroups. **Languages** English. **Staff** None. **Finance** No financing or annual budget. **Activities** Standards/guidelines; training/education; knowledge management/information dissemination; events/meetings. **Events** *SAFECOMP : International Conference on Computer Safety, Reality and Security* Erlangen (Germany) 2020, *SAFECOMP : International Conference on Computer Safety, Reality and Security* Turku (Finland) 2019, *SAFECOMP : International Conference on Computer Safety, Reality and Security* Trondheim (Norway) 2016, *SAFECOMP : International Conference on Computer Safety, Reality and Security / SAFECOMP Conference* Delft (Netherlands) 2015, *SAFECOMP : International Conference on Computer Safety, Reality and Security / SAFECOMP Conference* Florence (Italy) 2014. **Publications** *Dependability of Critical Computer Systems* – 2 vols; *The Standardization and Regulatory Environment for the Application of Worldwide Standards relevant to the Use of Programmable Electronic Systems in Safety Related and Security Applications.* Conference and workshop proceedings; position papers; guidelines. [2020/XF1450/t/F]

♦ European Workshop on Industrial Computer Systems – Technical Committee 7: Reliability, Safety, Security / see European Workshop on Industrial Computer Systems (#09119)
♦ European Workshop on Lipid Mediators (meeting series)
♦ European Workshop on Magnetic Resonance in Medicine / see European Magnetic Resonance Forum Foundation (#07724)

♦ European Workshop on Particulate Systems (EWPS) 09120

Address not obtained.
URL: http://www.ewps.org/

History 1998, Berlin (Germany), as a *European Network of Leading Institutes of Pharmacy/Departments of Pharmaceutics and Biopharmaceutics* Full title: *European Workshop on Particulate Systems in Nanomedicine (EWPS).* **Activities** Events/meetings. **Events** *European Workshop on Particulate Systems* Copenhagen (Denmark) 2017, *European Workshop on Particulate Systems* Utrecht (Netherlands) 2014, *European Workshop on Particulate Systems* Paris (France) 2010, *European Workshop on Particulate Systems* Berlin (Germany) 2008, *European Workshop on Particulate Systems* Geneva (Switzerland) 2006.
Members Partners in 6 countries:
Denmark, France, Germany, Netherlands, Switzerland, UK. [2017/XM6267/c/E]

♦ European Workshop on Particulate Systems in Nanomedicine / see European Workshop on Particulate Systems (#09120)
♦ European Workshop for Rheumatology Research (meeting series)
♦ European Work Study Federation / see European Federation of Productivity Services (#07196)

♦ European Wound Management Association (EWMA) 09121

Head of Project Management Nordre Fasanvej 113, 2nd Floor, 2000 Frederiksberg, Denmark. T. +4570200305. Fax +4570200315. E-mail: jnk@ewma.org.
URL: http://www.ewma.org/

History 1991, Cardiff (UK). Former names and other names: *Société européenne des blessures* – former; *Sociedad Europea de Tratamiento de Heridas* – former. Registration: Charity Commission for England and Wales, No/ID: 1042404, England and Wales; EU Transparency Register, No/ID: 557849227343-14. **Aims** Promote advancement of education and research into native epidemiology, pathology, diagnosis, prevention and management of wounds of all aetiologies; serve as the umbrella organization for European national wound care associations. **Structure** General Assembly (annual); Council; Executive Board; Committees/Panels (7). **Languages** English. **Staff** 15.00 FTE, paid. **Finance** Sources: members' dues; sponsorship. Project funding from public and institutional sources. **Activities** Advocacy/lobbying/activism; events/meetings; publishing activities; training/education. Active in all member countries. **Events** *Conference* Milan (Italy) 2023, *Joint EWMA and Journées Cicatrisations Conference* Paris (France) 2022, *Joint EWMA and Journées Cicatrisations Conference* Paris (France) 2021, *Conference* London (UK) 2020, *Conference* Gothenburg (Sweden) 2019. **Publications** *EWMA Journal* (2 a year); *Press Newsletter.* Education materials; treatment guides; documents; abstracts; e-posters; webcasts. **Members** Open to all health care professionals engaged in wound care. 3,500 individual members. Membership countries not specified. **NGO Relations** Also links with national associations. [2020.08.04/XD4673/D]

♦ European Wrist Arthroscopy Society (EWAS) 09122

Groupe européen pour l'arthroscopie du poignet (GEAP) – Sociedad Europea de Artroscopia de Muñeca

SG C/ Calderón de la Barca 16, Entlo Izda, 39002 Santander, Cantabria, Spain.
URL: http://www.wristarthroscopy.eu/

History 19 Mar 2005, on the initiative of Prof Christophe Mathoulin. Registered in accordance with French law. **Aims** Represent all surgeons interested in the field of wrist surgery and wrist arthroscopy; improve the standard of wrist arthroscopy and wrist surgery; rationalize and unify the training and educational structure for the development of wrist arthroscopy. **Structure** General Assembly. Executive Committee, comprising President, 1st Vice-President, Past-President, Secretary-General, Vice Secretary-General, Treasurer and Chairmen of 4 committees (IT; Scientific; Future Development; Teaching). **Languages** English. **Staff** 27.00 FTE, voluntary. **Finance** Members' dues (annual): euro 20. **Activities** Organizes Annual Meeting during annual Fessh Congress. Offers (annually): 4-6 Ircad-EWAS courses (basic and advanced) in Strasbourg (France), Lukang (Taiwan) and Barretos (Brazil); 6 EWAS-endorsed courses in Barcelona (Spain), Stuttgart (Germany), Miami FL (USA), Hong Kong (Hong Kong), Lisbon (Portugal) and Rotterdam (Netherlands). **Publications** *Arthrosopic Management of Distal Radius Fractures* (2010) by Pinal Francisco et al. **Members** Individuals (300) worldwide. Membership countries not specified. **NGO Relations** Cooperates with: *Federation of the European Societies for Surgery of the Hand (FESSH, #09549).* [2012/XJ8062/D]

♦ European Writers' Congress / see European Writers' Council (#09123)

♦ European Writers' Council (EWC-FAAE) 09123

Fédération des association européennes d'écrivains (EWC-FAEE)

Pres Rue du Prince Royal 85-87, 1050 Brussels, Belgium. E-mail: ewc.secretariat@europeanwriterscouncil.eu.
URL: http://www.europeanwriterscouncil.eu/

History Feb 1977, West Berlin (Germany). Founded at Congress held under the auspices of *Council of Europe (CE, #04881).* Statutes adopted: 1985; 1998; 2001; 2003. Registered as a new organization, in accordance with Belgian law, when the original EWC was dissolved. Former names and other names: *European Writers' Congress* – former; *Association d'écrivains européens* – former. Registration: Banque-Carrefour des Entreprises, No/ID: 0886.193.681, Start date: 8 Jan 2007, Belgium; EU Transparency Register, No/ID: 56788289570-24, Start date: 15 Sep 2012. **Aims** Defend legal, economic, social and professional interests of writers and literary translators throughout Europe, at governmental and non-governmental institutions at European, national and international levels – concerning in particular authors' rights in the digital environment, cultural cooperation and improvement of authors' contractual rights. **Structure** Board; Secretariat, headed by Secretary-General. **Languages** English. **Staff** 0.80 FTE, paid. **Finance** Sources: donations; members' dues. **Activities** Advocacy/lobbying/activism; events/meetings; research/documentation. **Events** *Mare Nostrum Forum* Valletta (Malta) 2013, *Mare Nostrum* Turku (Finland) 2011, *Mare Nostrum Forum* Marseille (France) 2009, *Mare Nostrum Forum* Trieste (Italy) 2007, *Congress* Brussels (Belgium) 2006. **Publications** *The Value of Writers' Works.*
Members Writers' and/or translators' organizations and unions (45 at national level) representing about 160,000 writers and literary translators in 31 countries:
Austria, Belgium, Bulgaria, Croatia, Cyprus, Denmark, Estonia, Finland, France, Germany, Greece, Hungary, Iceland, Ireland, Italy, Latvia, Lithuania, Luxembourg, Malta, Netherlands, Norway, Poland, Portugal, Romania, Russia, Slovakia, Slovenia, Spain, Sweden, Switzerland, UK.
Associate members in 2 countries:
Finland, Portugal.
Consultative Status Consultative status granted from: *World Intellectual Property Organization (WIPO, #21593)* (Permanent Observer Status). **IGO Relations** Cooperates with (3): *Council of Europe (CE, #04881); European Commission (EC, #06633); European Parliament (EP, #08146).* [2022.10.19/XF1799/F]

♦ European Writing Centers Association (EWCA) 09124

Chair Inst of English Studies, Fac of Philology, Univ of Lodz, Pomorska 171/173, 90-236 Lódz, Poland.
URL: http://writingcenters.eu/

History Founded 1998. **Aims** Solicit engagement with institutions and individuals interested in the interactive and collaborative work of writing centers everywhere. **Structure** Board; Advisory Board. **Languages** English. **Activities** Events/meetings. **Events** *Conference* Graz (Austria) 2022, *Conference* Graz (Austria) 2020, *Conference* Lódz (Poland) 2016, *Conference* Frankfurt-Oder (Germany) 2014, *Conference* Blagoevgrad (Bulgaria) 2012.
Members Individuals in 38 countries:

Albania, Australia, Austria, Azerbaijan, Bangladesh, Belgium, Bulgaria, Canada, Cyprus, Czechia, Denmark, Egypt, France, Germany, Greece, Hungary, Israel, Japan, Korea Rep, Lebanon, Malaysia, Morocco, Netherlands, New Zealand, Nigeria, Norway, Oman, Poland, Qatar, Russia, Singapore, South Africa, Switzerland, Türkiye, UK, Ukraine, United Arab Emirates, USA.
NGO Relations Regional affiliate of: *International Writing Centers Association (IWCA).*
[2016.03.08/XM2230/**D**]

♦ European Writing Instrument Manufacturer's Association (EWIMA) 09125
Verband Europäischer Schreib- und Zeichengeräte-Hersteller
Gen Manager Fürther Strasse 17A, 90429 Nuremberg, Germany. T. +4911272290. Fax +49911272911. E-mail: info@ewima.eu.
URL: http://www.ewima.eu
History 1 Nov 1983, Seville (Spain). Former names and other names: *Federation of European Writing Instruments Associations (FEWIA)* – former (1983 to 1993); *Fédération européenne des associations d'instruments à écrire* – former; *Federazione Europea di Fabbricanti di Attrezzi per Scrittura* – former. Registration: EU Transparency Register, No/ID: 8203543301-90. **Aims** Represent leading manufacturers of writing instruments as well as suppliers of components. **Structure** General Assembly (hosted each year in a different member country); Board of Officers; Committees and Sub-committees. **Languages** English. **Staff** 6.00 FTE, paid. **Finance** Sources: subscriptions; patents. **Activities** Events/meetings; knowledge management/information dissemination. **Events** *Annual Meeting* Lugano (Switzerland) 2017, *Annual Meeting* Sirmione (Italy) 2013, *Annual Meeting* Amsterdam (Netherlands) 2012, *Annual Meeting* Hamburg (Germany) 2011, *Annual Meeting* Bordeaux (France) 2010.
Members Companies (50) in 10 countries:
Czechia, France, Germany, Italy, Netherlands, Spain, Sweden, Switzerland, Türkiye, UK.
NGO Relations In liaison with technical committee of: *Comité européen de normalisation (CEN, #04162).*
[2022.05.11/XD0429/**D**]

♦ European Wrought Aluminium Association (inactive)

♦ European Wushu Kungfu Federation (EWUF) 09126
Pres 32 Hilltop View, Yateley, GU46 6LZ, UK. T. +442081233888.
URL: http://www.ewuf.org/
History 1985, Bologna (Italy). Former names and other names: *European Wishu Federation (EWUF)* – former. Registration: Companies House, No/ID: 9609005, Start date: 27 May 2015, England and Wales. **Aims** Promote and develop Chinese *martial arts*. **Structure** Congress (annual); Executive Board; Executive Council. Commissions (9); Management Executive; Technical Committee. Elections every 4 years. **Languages** English. **Staff** Voluntary. **Finance** Members' dues. **Activities** Events/meetings. **Events** *Congress* Moscow (Russia) 2019, *Annual Congress* Moscow (Russia) 2016, *European Taijiquan and Internal Styles Championships* Stara Zagora (Bulgaria) 2016, *Biennial congress / Annual Congress* Netherlands 2000, *Biennial congress / Annual Congress* Athens (Greece) 1998.
Members Full in 34 countries:
Armenia, Austria, Azerbaijan, Belarus, Belgium, Bulgaria, Croatia, Estonia, France, Georgia, Germany, Greece, Hungary, Ireland, Israel, Italy, Latvia, Lithuania, Moldova, Netherlands, Norway, Poland, Portugal, Romania, Russia, Serbia, Slovakia, Slovenia, Spain, Sweden, Switzerland, Türkiye, UK, Ukraine.
Passive members in 3 countries:
Luxembourg, Monaco, Montenegro.
NGO Relations Member of: *International Wushu Federation (IWUF, #15918).* [2019/XD4448/**D**]

♦ **European XFEL** European X-Ray Free-Electron Laser Facility (#09127)

♦ European X-Ray Free-Electron Laser Facility (European XFEL) 09127
Sec Holzkoppel 4, 22869 Schenefeld, Germany. T. +494089981664. Fax +494098891905. E-mail: contact@xfel.eu.
URL: http://www.xfel.eu/
History Registered as a non-profit limited liability company under German law. Shareholders are designated by governments of international partners committing themselves in an intergovernmental convention supporting construction and operation of the European XFEL. Construction started early 2009; commissioning of accelerator finished early 2017; user operation of first branch started 3rd quarter 2017 and completed early 2019. Operation at nominal bunch train parameters expected 2020. **Aims** Construct and operate the European XFEL facility. **Structure** Council; Management Board; Advisory Committees (5). **Languages** English, German. **Staff** 400.00 FTE, paid. **Finance** Shareholders from participating governments. Annual budget for operation (2021): euro 137,000,000. **Events** *European Big Science Business Forum* Granada (Spain) 2022, *European Big Science Business Forum* Granada (Spain) 2021, *European Big Science Business Forum* Granada (Spain) 2020, *European Big Science Business Forum* Copenhagen (Denmark) 2018, *International Conference on Biology and Synchrotron Radiation* Hamburg (Germany) 2013.
Members Participating governments (12):
Denmark, France, Germany, Hungary, Italy, Poland, Russia, Slovakia, Spain, Sweden, Switzerland, UK.
NGO Relations Regional organization of: *EIROforum (#05401).* [2020.03.11/XJ4024/**F***]

♦ European X-ray Spectrometry Association (EXSA) 09128
Contact Konkoly-Thege M út 29-33, 26 ép fsz 11, Budapest 1121, Hungary. Fax +3613922299. E-mail: excom@exsa.hu – webmaster@exsa.hu.
URL: http://www.exsa.hu/
History 2004. **Aims** Promote innovation and cooperation of X-ray spectroscopists and analysts within Europe. **Structure** General Assembly; Supervisory Board; Executive Committee. **Languages** English. **Staff** Voluntary. **Finance** Members' dues. Sponsorship. **Activities** Events/meetings; networking/liaising; training/education. **Events** *European Conference on X-ray Spectrometry* Bruges (Belgium) 2021, *European Conference on X-ray Spectrometry* Bruges (Belgium) 2020, *European Conference on X-Ray Spectrometry* Ljubljana (Slovenia) 2018, *European Conference on X-Ray Spectrometry* Gothenburg (Sweden) 2016, *European Conference on X-Ray Spectrometry* Vienna (Austria) 2012. **Publications** *EXSA Newsletter.* **Members** Regular; Institutional. Members worldwide but mostly in Europe. Membership countries not specified. [2019.12.19/XM0684/**D**]

♦ European Yachting Association / see European Boating Association (#06376)

♦ European Yoga Alliance (EYA) 09129
Pres c/o Centro de Yoga Vasudeva, c/Transradio 11, 28100 Madrid, Spain. T. +916613059. E-mail: yogavasudeva@yahoo.es.
URL: http://www.europeanyogaalliance.org/
Members Organizations in 20 countries:
Bulgaria, Czechia, France, Germany, Iceland, Ireland, Italy, Netherlands, North Macedonia, Norway, Portugal, Romania, Russia, Slovenia, Spain, Sweden, Switzerland, Türkiye, UK, Ukraine.
Also included in the above, 1 organization listed in this Yearbook:
International Yoga Institute (no recent information).
NGO Relations Full member of: *International Yoga Federation (IYF, #15923).* Links with other alliances: *Africa Yoga Federation (AYF); Yoga Alliance of South America (no recent information).* [2007/XF7060/**F**]

♦ European Yoga Council (EYC) 09130
Pres Raja Yoga Inst of Holland, Aalduikerweg 1, 1452 XK Ilpendam, Netherlands. T. +31204361174. E-mail: rajayoga@xs4all.nl.
NGO Relations Member of: *International Yoga Federation (IYF, #15923).* [2009/XE4674/**E**]

♦ European Yoga Union 09131
Union européenne de yoga – Unione Europea di Yoga (UEY)
Secretariat En Gérardrie 29, 4000 Liège, Belgium. T. +3243686269. Fax +3243685136. E-mail: admin@yogaeurop.com.
URL: https://www.europeanyoga.org/euyws/
History 1971, France. **Aims** Share Yogic values and share these values with all who are interested in Yoga. **Structure** General Assembly. Executive Committee. Bureau, comprising General Secretary, Treasurer, External Relations Officer, President of the Education Commission and a member. **Activities** Organizes annual meeting in Zinal (Switzerland). Runs an Initial Training Programme. **Events** *Annual meeting* Zinal (Switzerland) 2006, *Annual meeting* Zinal (Switzerland) 2001, *Annual meeting* Zinal (Switzerland) 1999.

Members Ordinary in 12 countries:
Austria, Belgium, Finland, France, Germany, Italy, Netherlands, Romania, Slovakia, Spain, Switzerland, UK.
Corresponding members in 1 country:
Ireland.
Associated organization in 1 country:
Netherlands. [2019/XD5983/**D**]

♦ European Young Academies (unconfirmed)

♦ European Young Bar Association (EYBA) 09132
Pres address not obtained. T. +447831848192. E-mail: info@eyba.org.
URL: http://www.eyba.org/
History 23 May 1993, Prague (Czech Rep), formalizing for the first time informal relations already existing among city-based young lawyers groups. **Aims** Promote interests, welfare, working conditions and professional standards of young *lawyers*; provide them with education and training; facilitate exchange among young lawyers in Europe; coordinate agendas of young bar organizations in Europe and produce a calendar of events; influence policies of European institutions which affect young lawyers act as a source of information and publications comparing judicial systems and procedures in member countries; support young bar organizations in difficulty or requesting support for particular projects. **Structure** General Meeting (annual). Executive Committee, consisting of President, Vice-President, Honorary Secretary, Treasurer and 3 members. European Committee, comprising one delegate per member group. **Languages** English. **Finance** Members' dues. Sponsorship. **Activities** Events/meetings; networking/liaising; projects/programmes; capacity building. **Events** *Spring Conference* Glasgow (UK) 2021, *Annual General Meeting and Conference* Kiev (Ukraine) 2021, *Spring Conference* Glasgow (UK) 2020, *Annual General Meeting and Conference* Kiev (Ukraine) 2020, *Annual General Meeting and Conference* Rome (Italy) 2019. **Publications** *Eurolawyer* (4 a year) – journal; *EYBA Letter from the President* (4 a year). Information Services: Database of member groups; database of young lawyers in Europe.
Members City-based or national () associations in 20 countries:
Belgium (2), Czechia (2), Denmark (*), Estonia (*), France, Germany, Ireland (*), Italy (2), Latvia (*), Lithuania (*), Luxembourg, Netherlands (5), Norway (*), Russia, Serbia, Slovenia (*), Spain, Sweden (*), Switzerland, UK (6).
Consultative Status Consultative status granted from: *Council of Europe (CE, #04881)* (Participatory Status).
NGO Relations *Council of Bars and Law Societies of Europe (CCBE, #04871); The European Law Students' Association (ELSA, #07660); Inter-American Bar Association (IABA, #11401)* (Young Lawyers Section); *International Bar Association (IBA, #12320); Union des avocats européens (UAE, #20365); Union Internationale des Avocats (UIA, #20422).* [2017.03.08/XD5545/**D**]

♦ European Young Chemists' Network (see: #06524)
♦ European Young Christian Democrats (inactive)
♦ European Young Christian Workers / see JOC Europe (#16118)
♦ European Young Conservatives (no recent information)

♦ European Young Engineers (EYE) 09133
SG address not obtained. E-mail: eye@e-y-e.eu.
URL: http://www.e-y-e.eu/
History Founded 1994, Netherlands. Current statutes adopted, 6 Jul 2002. EU Transparency Register: 578001221797-91. **Aims** Improve mutual understanding between European engineers, education systems and nations; create a network to develop personal skills; foster mobility of young engineers in Europe; create a forum for exchange of experiences on personal and professional levels. **Structure** Council; Task Force; Working Groups; Secretariat. **Languages** English. **Staff** Voluntary. **Finance** Members' voluntary contributions; bi-annual conference financed by organizing national associations. **Activities** Events/meetings. **Events** *Conference* Zagreb (Croatia) 2021, *Conference* Ohrid (North Macedonia) 2020, *Conference* Eindhoven (Netherlands) 2019, *Conference* Madrid (Spain) 2019, *Conference* Hannover (Germany) 2016. **Publications** *EYE-contact* – magazine.
Members National associations (21) in 16 countries:
Belgium, Bosnia-Herzegovina, Bulgaria, Denmark, Finland, France, Germany, Hungary, Ireland, Italy, Luxembourg, Malta, Netherlands, Norway, Portugal, UK. [2016.10.19/XD7677/**D**]

♦ European Young Innovators Forum (EYIF) 09134
Headquarters Rue de la Science 14B, 1040 Brussels, Belgium.
Facebook: https://www.facebook.com/eyif.eu/
History Formally launched at *European Parliament (EP, #08146).* Registration: No/ID: 833-092-616, Belgium; EU Transparency Register, No/ID: 167339718832-92. **Aims** Be the voice for the community of innovators, mentors, influencers and experts who lead the movement in making Europe the ideal location for entrepreneurs from around the globe. **Structure** Board of Advisors. **Languages** English, French. **Activities** Networking/liaising; guidance/assistance/consulting; projects/programmes. **Events** *Grow Global* Brussels (Belgium) 2017, *Unconvention* Brussels (Belgium) 2015. **NGO Relations** *Junior Enterprises Europe (JE Europe, #16169).*
[2020/XM4161/**F**]

♦ European Young Women's Christian Association (The European YWCA) 09135
Co-Chairwoman c/o KFUM Sverige, Borgmastargatan 11, SE-116 29 Stockholm, Sweden. E-mail: info@europeanywca.org.
URL: http://europeanywca.org/
History 1979, Geneva (Switzerland). Initiated 1971, Accra (Ghana) at World YWCA Council Meeting, with the idea of en European Liaison Group to be coordinated by representatives of national associations. Responsibility of the Secretariat of the European YWCA assumed by: YWCA UK (1971); YWCA Greece (1975); YWCA Belgium (1983). Constitution amended: 1987. European YWCA Administrative Office moved to Geneva (Switzerland), 2004. Former names and other names: *European YWCA's Liaison Group (ELG)* – former; *YWCA's European Committee* – former; *Alliance européenne des unions chrétiennes féminines* – former. Registration: Start date: 2014, Sweden. **Aims** Develop the leadership and collective power of women and girls to achieve women's rights, gender equality, justice, peace, health, human dignity, freedom, a world free of discrimination, and a sustainable environment for all people; unite member associations in a European movement and provide opportunities for mutual learning and exchange; represent interests of member associations and act on their behalf in matters for which it has received authority; influence the policy of European institutions on issues relevant to women and girls; promote youth and equality policy to increase the participation of young women in society as well as in decision-making processes. **Structure** General Assembly (every 2 years); European Board. Seat in Stockholm (Sweden). **Languages** English. **Staff** 0.00 FTE, paid; 10.00 FTE, voluntary. Only voluntary work. **Finance** Sources: contributions; contributions of member/participating states; donations; fundraising; government support; members' dues. Annual budget: 10,000 EUR. **Activities** Events/meetings; knowledge management/information dissemination; networking/liaising; training/education. Active in all member countries. **Events** *General Assembly* Antwerp (Belgium) 2023, *Study Session* Budapest (Hungary) 2022, *Extraordinary General Assembly* 2021, *General Assembly* Bucharest (Romania) 2018, *Study Session* Budapest (Hungary) 2018. **Publications** *Newsletter* (4 a year).
Members Full Member Associations in 19 countries and territories:
Albania, Armenia, Belarus, Belgium, Denmark, Estonia, Finland, France, Germany, Great Britain, Greece, Ireland, Italy, Malta, Norway, Romania, Sweden, Switzerland, Ukraine.
Associate Member Associations in 6 countries and territories:
Georgia, Latvia, Lithuania, Netherlands, Poland, Scotland.
NGO Relations Member of (2): *European Women's Lobby (EWL, #09102); European Youth Forum (#09140).* Collaboration with: *Conference of European Churches (CEC, #04593); YMCA Europe (#21977);* World YWCA.
[2022.11.07/XD6453/**E**]

♦ European Youth for Action (EYFA) 09136
Fondation de la jeunesse européenne pour la protection des forêts
International Office New Yorck im Bethanien, Mariannenplatz 2A, 10997 Berlin, Germany. T. +493061740102 – +4930(4915210105373. E-mail: eyfa@eyfa.org.
URL: http://eyfa.org/

History 1986. **Aims** Challenge current ecologically and socially unsustainable systems by exploring sustainable ways of living and working, and by combating environmental destruction and social injustice using non-violent means; reduce air pollution and climate change; halt forest die-back; raise awareness towards environmental problems among young people; influence decision-makers. **Structure** General Assembly (during ECOTOPIA); International Coordination Team (ICT); Enlarged International Coordination Team; International Office; National Representatives; Action Groups; Affiliates. **Languages** English. **Staff** Voluntary. **Finance** *European Commission (EC, #06633)* (Directorate-General XI); *European Cultural Foundation (ECF, #06868)*; *European Youth Foundation (EYF, #09141)*; various European Ministries; town councils; foundations; agencies. Budget (annual): euro 133,000. **Activities** Awareness raising; events/meetings. **Events** *Winter meeting* Barcelona (Spain) 2002, *Ecotopia annual meeting* Ireland 2002, *Winter Meeting* Poland 2001, *ECOTOPIA Annual Meeting* Finland 2000, *ECOTOPIA Annual Meeting* Romania 1999. **Publications** *The Verge* (6 a year).
Members Youth and environmental organizations (more than 300) in 44 countries:
Albania, Australia, Austria, Belarus, Belgium, Bosnia-Herzegovina, Bulgaria, Canada, Croatia, Czechia, Denmark, Estonia, Finland, France, Georgia, Germany, Greece, Hungary, Ireland, Italy, Japan, Latvia, Lithuania, Luxembourg, Malta, Netherlands, Nigeria, North Macedonia, Norway, Philippines, Poland, Portugal, Romania, Russia, Serbia, Slovakia, Slovenia, Spain, Sweden, Switzerland, Türkiye, UK, Ukraine, USA.
Individuals in 4 countries:
Canada, South Africa, USA, Zambia.
NGO Relations Member of: *Climate Justice Now ! (CJN!, inactive)*; *International Network for Sustainable Energy (INFORSE, #14331)*; *Rising Tide International (#18953)*; *UNITED for Intercultural Action – European Network Against Nationalism, Racism, Fascism and in Support of Migrants and Refugees (UNITED, #20511)*.
[2015.09.09/XF2055/f/**F**]

♦ European Youth Alliance / see World Youth Alliance – Europe (#21952)
♦ European Youth Association (inactive)

♦ European Youth Card Association (EYCA) 09137

Association européenne des Cartes jeunes (AECJ)
Dir Centre Dansaert, Rue D'Alost 7-11, 1000 Brussels, Belgium. T. +3228806843. E-mail: mail@eyca.org.
URL: http://www.eyca.org/
History 1987. Former names and other names: *European Conference of Youth Cards* – former (1992); *Conférence européenne des Cartes jeunes* – former (1992). Registration: France; EU Transparency Register, No/ID: 401442732242-59. **Aims** Stimulate more young people to be socially, culturally, educationally and economically mobile. **Structure** General Assembly (annual, at Conference); Governing Board; Executive; Office. Members are required to sign the "Lisbon Protocol" and ratify the "Charter of Brussels". Regions (7): UK and Ireland; Nordic and Baltic States; Central and Eastern Europe; Mediterranean Countries; Iberian Peninsula; Benelux and France; German-speaking Countries. **Languages** English, French. **Finance** Sources: members' dues. Additional budget from the Partial Agreement on Youth Cards of *Council of Europe (CE, #04881)*. Annual budget: 500,000 EUR. **Activities** Advocacy/lobbying/activism; events/meetings. **Events** *General Assembly* 2021, *Annual Conference and General Assembly* Slovenia 2019, *Conference and General Assembly* Gdansk (Poland) 2016, *Seminar on Mobility Towards Inclusion* Samobor (Croatia) 2016, *Conference and General Assembly* Gothenburg (Sweden) 2015. **Publications** *EYCAtcher* – newsletter. Annual Report; discount guide; pocket folder.
Members Card-organizations in 49 countries:
Albania, Andorra, Armenia, Austria, Azerbaijan, Belarus, Belgium, Bosnia-Herzegovina, Bulgaria, Croatia, Cyprus, Czechia, Denmark, Estonia, Finland, France, Georgia, Germany, Greece, Hungary, Iceland, Ireland, Italy, Kosovo, Latvia, Liechtenstein, Lithuania, Luxembourg, Malta, Moldova, Monaco, Montenegro, Netherlands, North Macedonia, Norway, Poland, Portugal, Romania, Russia, San Marino, Serbia, Slovakia, Slovenia, Spain, Sweden, Switzerland, Türkiye, UK, Ukraine.
Consultative Status Consultative status granted from: *Council of Europe (CE, #04881)* (Participatory Status).
IGO Relations *European Commission (EC, #06633)*; *Partial Agreement on Youth Mobility Through the Youth Card (#18224)*. **NGO Relations** Cooperates with (2): *Eurodesk Network (#05675)*; *European Youth Information and Counselling Agency (ERYICA, #09142)*.
[2022/XF5016/**E**]

♦ European Youth Centres (EYCs) 09138

Centres européens de la jeunesse (CEJ)
Admin Assistant EYF Strasbourg 30 rue Pierre de Coubertin, 67000 Strasbourg, France. T. +33388412300. E-mail: youth@coe.int – reception.eycs@coe.int.
Budapest – Exec Dir Zivatar utca 1-3, Budapest 1024, Hungary. T. +3612124078. Fax +3612124076. E-mail: coe.budapest@coe.int.
URL: https://www.coe.int/en/web/youth/eyc-strasbourg/
History Established 1 Jun 1972, Strasbourg (France), on setting up of *European Youth Centre Strasbourg (EYCS)*, within the framework of *Council of Europe (CE, #04881)*. Strasbourg centre extended to present capacity, 1978, following decision of 1975. Since 1993, comprises part of the Youth Department, Directorate of Democratic Citizenship and Participation of the Council of Europe. *European Youth Centre Budapest (EYCB)* inaugurated 1995, Budapest, following enlargement of the Council of Europe to include countries of Central and Eastern Europe. Strasbourg Centre renovated with extended capacity in 2008. **Aims** Supplement *training* of youth *leaders* in a European context; provide nongovernmental youth organizations with a meeting place to further *international understanding* in respect of human rights and fundamental freedoms and for detailed study of European problems; seek to ensure participation by young people in solving problems which concern them; promote research into youth problems through exchange of ideas and experience. **Structure** *'Advisory Council on Youth'*, comprising 20 members of *European Youth Forum (#09140)*: 13 representatives of international nongovernmental youth organizations (INGYOs), 7 representatives of national youth committees, 5 representatives of national youth councils and 10 representatives of non-governmental youth organizations which are not member of EYF. *'Joint Council on Youth Questions'*, comprising governmental partners – *Council of Europe (CE, #04881)* – European Steering Committee for Youth (CDEJ / CDEJ) – and nongovernmental partners – represented by the Advisory Council on Youth. *'Programming Committee on Youth'*, comprising 8 members of CDEJ and 8 of the Advisory Council on Youth. **Languages** English, French. **Finance** Annual budget adopted by Council of Europe's Committee of Ministers. Annual budget: about euro 3,000,000. **Activities** Training/education; networking/liaising. **Events** *International seminar of young non-professional journalists on the education to citizenship* Strasbourg (France) 2000, *Joint seminar on gender equality and youth participation in minority communities* Budapest (Hungary) 1999, *International forum on European citizenship, international solidarity, social and culture practice and appeals* Strasbourg (France) 1999, *International seminar on children commercial sexual exploitation and prostitution* Budapest (Hungary) 1997, *Symposium on the cooperation with Eastern and Central European countries in youth field* Strasbourg (France) 1997.
Members Member States of the Council of Europe (47):
Albania, Andorra, Armenia, Austria, Azerbaijan, Belgium, Bosnia-Herzegovina, Bulgaria, Croatia, Cyprus, Czechia, Denmark, Estonia, Finland, France, Georgia, Germany, Greece, Hungary, Iceland, Ireland, Italy, Latvia, Liechtenstein, Lithuania, Luxembourg, Malta, Moldova, Monaco, Montenegro, Netherlands, North Macedonia, Norway, Poland, Portugal, Romania, Russia, San Marino, Serbia, Slovakia, Slovenia, Spain, Sweden, Switzerland, Türkiye, UK, Ukraine.
National youth committees and coordinating structures in 41 countries:
Albania, Armenia, Austria, Azerbaijan, Belarus, Belgium, Bulgaria, Croatia, Cyprus, Czechia, Denmark, Estonia, Finland, France, Georgia, Germany, Greece, Hungary, Iceland, Ireland, Latvia, Lithuania, Luxembourg, Malta, Moldova, Montenegro, Netherlands, North Macedonia, Norway, Poland, Portugal, Romania, Russia, Serbia, Slovakia, Slovenia, Spain, Sweden, Switzerland, UK, Ukraine.
Cooperating Organizations (56), including 53 organizations listed in this Yearbook:
- *CISV International (#03949)*;
- *Cooperation and Development Network Eastern Europe (CDN, #04794)*;
- *Coordinating Committee for International Voluntary Service (CCIVS, #04819)*;
- *Council for National and International Relations of Organizations of Youth and Popular Education (CNAJEP)*;
- *Democrat Youth Community of Europe (DEMYC, #05037)*;
- *Deutsches Nationalkomitee für Internationale Jugendarbeit (DNK, no recent information)*;
- *East Africa Work Campers Association (EAWA, no recent information)*;
- *Ecumenical Youth Council in Europe (EYCE, #05352)*;
- *European Bureau for Conscientious Objection (EBCO, #06411)*;
- *European Confederation of Youth Clubs (ECYC, #06727)*;
- *European Drama Encounters (EDERED)*;
- *European Educational Exchanges – Youth for Understanding (EEE-YFU, #06965)*;
- *European Medical Students' Association (EMSA, #07764)*;
- *European Non-Governmental Sports Organization (ENGSO, #08054)*;
- *European Peer Training Organization (EPTO)*;
- *European Students' Union (ESU, #08848)*;
- *European Trade Union Confederation (ETUC, #08927)*;
- *European Union of Jewish Students (EUJS, #08997)*;
- *European Young Women's Christian Association (The European YWCA, #09135)*;
- *European Youth Forum (#09140)*;
- *European Youth Information and Counselling Agency (ERYICA, #09142)*;
- *Federation of Young European Greens (FYEG, #09715)*;
- *Forum of European Muslim Youth and Student Organisations (FEMYSO, #09909)*;
- *Forum of European Roma Young People (FERYP, #09914)*;
- *Global Youth Action Network (GYAN)*;
- *Human Rights Education Youth Network (HREYN, #10982)*;
- *International Association for Political Science Students (IAPSS, #12095)*;
- *International Federation of Hard-of-Hearing Young People (IFHOHYP, #13436)*;
- *International Federation of Liberal Youth (IFLRY, #13469)*;
- *International Lesbian, Gay, Bisexual, Transgender, Queer and Intersex Youth and Student Organization (IGLYO, #14032)*;
- *International Movement ATD Fourth World (#14193)*;
- *International Union of Socialist Youth (IUSY, #15815)*;
- *International Young Catholic Students (IYCS, #15926)*;
- *International Young Nature Friends (IYNF, #15929)*;
- *Minorities of Europe (MOE, #16818)*;
- *Mouvement international de la jeunesse agricole et rurale catholique (MIJARC, #16865)*;
- *Network for Voluntary Development in Asia (NVDA, #17063)*;
- *People to People International (PTPI, #18300)*;
- *Rural Youth Europe (#19007)*;
- *Service Civil International (SCI, #19238)*;
- *South East European Youth Network (SEEYN, #19821)*;
- *Taking IT Global (TIG)*;
- *UNITED for Intercultural Action – European Network Against Nationalism, Racism, Fascism and in Support of Migrants and Refugees (UNITED, #20511)*;
- *World Association of Girl Guides and Girl Scouts (WAGGGS, #21142)*;
- *World Organization of the Scout Movement (WOSM, #21693)*;
- *YMCA Europe (#21977)*;
- *Young European Media Professionals (YEMP, #21986)*;
- *Young Europe – Youth Network Against Racism and Intolerance (YNRI)*;
- *Young Humanists International (#21993)*;
- *Young Women from Minorities (WFM, no recent information)*;
- *Youth Action for Peace (YAP, inactive)*;
- *Youth Express Network (Y-E-N, #22017)*;
- *Youth for Exchange and Understanding (YEU, #22016)*.

[2022/XE0947/y/**E***]

♦ European Youth Circus Organisation (EYCO) 09139

Contact 13 rue Marceau, 93100 Montreuil, France. T. +33141582230. E-mail: direction@ffec.asso.fr – coordinator@eyco.org.
URL: http://www.eyco.org/
History Formal statutes registered 9 Nov 2009, Paris (France). Activities started 2010. Statutes revised 2015.
Aims Stimulate, promote and support, on a national and European level, the process of recognizing and structuring youth circus. **Structure** Management Board. **Languages** English, French. **Staff** 1.00 FTE, paid.
Finance Members' dues. Key Action 3 (KA3) grant. **Activities** Events/meetings; research and development; training/education; networking/liaising; advocacy/lobbying/activism. **Events** *Meeting* Berlin (Germany) 2011, *Meeting* London (UK) 2009, *Meeting* Amsterdam (Netherlands) 2008, *Meeting* Tampere (Finland) 2007, *Meeting* Paris (France) 2006.
Members Full; Candidate; Associate. National umbrellas in 13 countries and territories:
Austria, Belgium (Flemish Region), Denmark, Estonia, Finland, France, Germany, Italy, Netherlands, Poland, Spain, Switzerland, UK.
[2016.10.31/XJ5262/**D**]

♦ European Youth Deaf Council / see European Union of Deaf Youth (#08986)

♦ European Youth Forum 09140

Forum Européen de la Jeunesse
SG Rue de l'Industrie 10, 1000 Brussels, Belgium. T. +3227937520. Fax +3228932580. E-mail: youthforum@youthforum.org.
URL: https://www.youthforum.org/
History Founded on merger of *Council of European National Youth Committees (CENYC, inactive)*, *European Coordination Bureau of International Youth Organizations (ECB, inactive)* and *Youth Forum of the European Union (YFEU, inactive)*. Set up following proposals for a *Common European Youth Platform*, drawn up at a consultation meeting, 18 Sep 1994, Luxembourg. Former names and other names: *Youth Forum Jeunesse (YFJ)* – alias; *Youth Forum of the European Union* – alias; *Forum jeunesse de l'Union européenne* – alias. Registration: Banque-Carrefour des Entreprises, No/ID: 0877.890.382, Start date: 14 Dec 2005, Belgium; EU Transparency Registger, No/ID: 43251547769-22, Start date: 18 Jan 2012. **Aims** Empower young people to participate actively in society to improve their own lives by representing and advocating their needs and interests and those of their organizations. **Structure** General Assembly (every 2 years); Council of Members; Board; Expert Groups; Secretariat. **Languages** English, French. **Staff** 25.50 FTE, paid. **Finance** Sources: contributions; grants; members' dues; sponsorship. **Activities** Advocacy/lobbying/activism; events/meetings.
Events *Lifelong Learning Week Meeting* Brussels (Belgium) 2019, *Lifelong Learning Week Meeting* Brussels (Belgium) 2018, *Lifelong Learning Week Meeting* Brussels (Belgium) 2017, *Lifelong Learning Week Meeting* Brussels (Belgium) 2016, *Council of Members Meeting* Madrid (Spain) 2015. **Publications** *YO!News* (weekly); *Yo Mag* (annual). Annual Report; thematic reports; research reports; policy papers; resolutions and positions.
Members Full members: national youth councils in 37 countries:
Armenia, Austria, Azerbaijan, Belarus, Belgium, Bulgaria, Croatia, Cyprus, Czechia, Denmark, Estonia, Finland, France, Georgia, Germany, Greece, Iceland, Ireland, Italy, Latvia, Lithuania, Luxembourg, Malta, Moldova, Netherlands, Norway, Poland, Portugal, Romania, Russia, Serbia, Slovakia, Slovenia, Spain, Sweden, Switzerland, UK.
International full members (41):
- *Alliance of European Voluntary Service Organizations (ALLIANCE, #00677)*;
- *Association des états généraux des étudiants de l'Europe (AEGEE-Europe, #02495)*;
- *Democrat Youth Community of Europe (DEMYC, #05037)*;
- *Ecumenical Youth Council in Europe (EYCE, #05352)*;
- *Erasmus Student Network (ESN, #05529)*;
- *European Bureau for Conscientious Objection (EBCO, #06411)*;
- *European Confederation of Youth Clubs (ECYC, #06727)*;
- *European Coordination, International Young Catholic Students – International Movement of Catholic Students (European Coordination IYCS-IMCS, inactive)*;
- *European Democrat Students (EDS, #06901)*;
- *European Educational Exchanges – Youth for Understanding (EEE-YFU, #06965)*;
- *European Federation for Intercultural Learning (EFIL, #07146)*;
- *European Liberal Youth (LYMEC, #07690)*;
- *European Students' Union (ESU, #08848)*;
- *European Trade Union Confederation (ETUC, #08927)*;
- *European Union of Jewish Students (EUJS, #08997)*;
- *European Young Women's Christian Association (The European YWCA, #09135)*;
- *Federation of Young European Greens (FYEG, #09715)*;
- *International Falcon Movement – Socialist Educational International (IFM-SEI, #13327)*;
- *International Federation of Catholic Parochial Youth Movements (#13379)*;
- *International Federation of Liberal Youth (IFLRY, #13469)*;
- *International Federation of Medical Students' Associations (IFMSA, #13478)*;
- *International Lesbian, Gay, Bisexual, Transgender, Queer and Intersex Youth and Student Organization (IGLYO, #14032)*;
- *International Movement ATD Fourth World (#14193)*;
- *International Union of Socialist Youth (IUSY, #15815)*;
- *International Young Nature Friends (IYNF, #15929)*;
- *Mouvement international de la jeunesse agricole et rurale catholique (MIJARC, #16865)*;
- *Organising Bureau of European School Student Unions (OBESSU, #17829)*;
- *Rural Youth Europe (#19007)*;
- *Service Civil International (SCI, #19238)*;
- *Tutmonda Esperantista Junulara Organizo (TEJO, #20268)*;
- *World Association of Girl Guides and Girl Scouts (WAGGGS, #21142)*;
- *World Organization of the Scout Movement (WOSM, #21693)*;

European Youth Foundation
09141

alphabetic sequence excludes
For the complete listing, see Yearbook Online at

– World Scout Bureau – European Regional Office (#21771);
– World Student Christian Federation (WSCF, #21833) (European Region of);
– YMCA Europe (#21977);
– Young European Federalists (#21984);
– Young European Socialists (YES, #21989);
– Youth and Environment Europe (YEE, #22012);
– Youth for Exchange and Understanding (YEU, #22016);
– Youth of European Nationalities (YEN, #22013);
– Youth of the European People's Party (YEPP, #22014).
Candidate member organizations in 2 countries:
Belgium, North Macedonia.
National youth council observer member in 2 countries:
Hungary, Ukraine.
International observer members (18):
Board of European Students of Technology (BEST, #03294); CISV International (#03949); Conseil européen des jeunes agriculteurs (CEJA, #04689); Don Bosco Youth-Net (DBYN, #05119); European Confederation of Independent Trade Unions (CESI, #06705); European Free Alliance Youth (EFAY, #07357); European Non-Governmental Sports Organization (ENGSO, #08054) (Youth Committee); European Youth Press (EYP, #09146); International Coordination of Young Christian Workers (ICYCW, #12960); International Debate Education Association (IDEA, #13142) (Netherlands); International Federation of Hard-of-Hearing Young People (IFHOHYP, #13436); International Federation of Training Centres for the Promotion of Progressive Education (#13572); Jeunes entrepreneurs de l'Union européenne (JEUNE, #16109); Jeunesses Musicales International (JMI, #16110); Pax Christi – International Catholic Peace Movement (#18266); Red Cross and Red Crescent Youth (see: #13526); The Duke of Edinburgh's International Award Foundation (#05145); Young Democrats for Europe (YDE, #21980).
Consultative Status Consultative status granted from: UNESCO (#20322) (Consultative Status); ECOSOC (#05331) (Special); Council of Europe (CE, #04881) (Participatory Status). **IGO Relations** Cooperates with (2): Council of Europe (CE, #04881) (Advisory Council on Youth); European Youth Centres (EYCs, #09138). Liaison Group of: European Economic and Social Committee (EESC, #06963); European Union Agency for Fundamental Rights (FRA, #08969). **NGO Relations** Member of (11): A Soul for Europe (ASF, #19697); Centre for European Policy Studies (CEPS, #03741); Civil Society Europe; Conference of Non-Governmental Organizations in Consultative Relationship with the United Nations (CONGO, #04635); European Movement International (EMI, #07825); European Policy Centre (EPC, #08240); Federation of European and International Associations Established in Belgium (FAIB, #09508); SDG Watch Europe (#19162); Social Platform (#19344); Spring Alliance (inactive); Wellbeing Economy Alliance (WEAll, #20856). Cooperates with (1): Foro Latinoamericano de Juventud (FLAJ, #09881). Supports (2): European Alliance for the Statute of the European Association (EASEA, #05886); UNITED for Intercultural Action – European Network Against Nationalism, Racism, Fascism and in Support of Migrants and Refugees (UNITED, #20511). Instrumental in setting up (1): International Youth Health Organization (YHO, #15933). Consultative status with: World Assembly of Youth (WAY, #21113).

[2023/XD5676/y/D]

♦ European Youth Foundation (EYF) 09141
Fonds européen pour la jeunesse (FEJ)
Head c/o Council of Europe, DG Democracy and Human Dignity-Dir. Democratic Participation, 30 rue Pierre de Coubertin, 67000 Strasbourg, France. T. +33388412019. Fax +33390214964. E-mail: eyf@coe.int.
URL: http://eyf.coe.int/
History May 1972, Strasbourg (France). Established under the auspices of Council of Europe (CE, #04881) by Committee of Ministers of the Council of Europe (#04273). **Aims** Support young people in getting closer to their objectives and their vision of a better future; make the voice of youth heard at a top decision making level; support European non-governmental youth organizations and networks; promote youth cooperation in Europe by providing support to youth activities aimed at the promotion of peace, understanding and cooperation. **Structure** Programming Committee on Youth (CPJ). **Languages** English, French. **Staff** 5.00 FTE, paid. **Finance** Sources: members' dues. Annual budget: 3,700,000 EUR. **Activities** Events/meetings; financial and/or material support; guidance/assistance/consulting. **Events** Meeting Strasbourg (France) 1997, Meeting Strasbourg (France) 1996, Meeting Strasbourg (France) 1995, Meeting Strasbourg (France) 1994, Meeting Strasbourg (France) 1994. **Publications** EYF Newsletter (12 a year). All Different – All Equal Cookbook. Annual Report; leaflet.
Members All member states of the Council of Europe (46):
Albania, Andorra, Armenia, Austria, Azerbaijan, Belgium, Bosnia-Herzegovina, Bulgaria, Croatia, Cyprus, Czechia, Denmark, Estonia, Finland, France, Georgia, Germany, Greece, Hungary, Iceland, Ireland, Italy, Latvia, Liechtenstein, Lithuania, Luxembourg, Malta, Moldova, Monaco, Montenegro, Netherlands, North Macedonia, Norway, Poland, Portugal, Romania, San Marino, Serbia, Slovakia, Slovenia, Spain, Sweden, Switzerland, Türkiye, UK, Ukraine.
Also signatory states to the European Cultural Convention (4):
Belarus, Holy See, Kazakhstan, Russia.

[2022.10.11/XF4371/f/F*]

♦ European Youth Human Rights Network (internationally oriented national body)

♦ European Youth Information and Counselling Agency (ERYICA) 09142
Agence européenne pour l'information et le conseil des jeunes – Agencia Europea de Información y Asesoramiento para los Jóvenes – Agenzia Europea per l'Informazione e la Consulenza dei Giovani
Dir Route de Thionville 87, L-2611 Luxembourg, Luxembourg. T. +35224873992. Fax +35226293215. E-mail: secretariat@eryica.org.
Pres address not obtained.
URL: http://www.eryica.org/
History 17 Apr 1986, Madrid (Spain). Former names and other names: European Youth Information and Counselling Association – former; Association européenne pour l'information et le conseil des jeunes – former. Registration: Luxembourg; EU Transparency Register, No/ID: 064473227395-04. **Aims** Promote European cooperation in the field of youth information and counselling and the implementation of the Principles of the European Youth Information Charter; develop services in this area which meet needs of young people; promote the development of a European dimension in these fields. **Structure** General Assembly (annual). Governing Board, consisting of President, 2 Vice-Presidents, Treasurer, 4 Members and (ex officio) Secretary-General. Secretariat in Luxembourg (Luxembourg). **Languages** English. **Activities** Knowledge management/information dissemination; networking/liaising; research/documentation; training/education. **Events** Annual General Assembly Luxembourg (Luxembourg) 2021, Annual General Assembly Edinburgh (UK) 2020, Annual General Assembly Tallinn (Estonia) 2019, Nordic-Baltic Working Group Meeting Helsinki (Finland) 2018, Annual General Assembly Helsinki (Finland) 2016. **Publications** ERYICA Newsletter (irregular).
Members Members (28) in 19 countries:
Austria, Belgium, Croatia, Cyprus, Estonia, Finland, France, Germany, Ireland, Italy, Luxembourg, Malta, Norway, Portugal, Slovakia, Slovenia, Spain, Switzerland, UK.
Affiliated Organizations (5) in 5 countries:
Andorra, Finland, Ireland, Liechtenstein, Lithuania.
Cooperating Organizations (4) in 4 countries:
Bosnia-Herzegovina, North Macedonia, Serbia, Slovenia.
Consultative Status Consultative status granted from: Council of Europe (CE, #04881) (Participatory Status).
IGO Relations Partnership agreement with Youth Directorate of: Council of Europe (CE, #04881); European Commission (EC, #06633).

[2021/XD1039/D]

♦ European Youth Information and Counselling Association / see European Youth Information and Counselling Agency (#09142)

♦ European Youth Network for Nuclear Disarmament (BANg) 09143
Contact Goethestr 16, 71272 Renningen, Germany.
URL: http://fb.com/banallnukes/
History 2005. Also known as Ban All Nukes generation. **Aims** Bring young people together and share ideas on peace and disarmament; inform people on the threat of nuclear weapons and the urgency of disarmament; promote non-violent action for a more peaceful world; support and strengthen existing campaigns against nuclear weapons. **Structure** A loose network with chapters in Europe, Asia, US and Latin America. Coordinators Council. **Languages** English. **Staff** None paid. **Finance** Funding fro education purposes from European and national governmental organizations. **Activities** Events/meetings; training/education. **NGO Relations** Member of: International Campaign to Abolish Nuclear Weapons (ICAN, #12426).

[2019/XM4346/F]

♦ European Youth Network on Sexual and Reproductive Rights (YouAct) 09144
Coordinator 60 Goswell Road, London, EC1M 7AD, UK. E-mail: info@youact.org – coordinator@youact.org.
URL: http://www.youact.org/
History Founded May 2004, Portugal, during 'Are you ready to act' youth conference. **Aims** Realize the sexual and reproductive health and rights of adolescents and youth through youth-led advocacy, awareness raising and training. **Structure** General Meeting. **Activities** Advocacy/lobbying/activism; awareness raising; training/education. **Publications** YouAct Newsletter.
Members Individuals younger than 30 in the 47 Council of Europe member states:
Albania, Andorra, Armenia, Austria, Azerbaijan, Belgium, Bosnia-Herzegovina, Bulgaria, Croatia, Cyprus, Czechia, Denmark, Estonia, Finland, France, Georgia, Germany, Greece, Hungary, Iceland, Ireland, Italy, Latvia, Liechtenstein, Lithuania, Luxembourg, Malta, Moldova, Monaco, Montenegro, Netherlands, North Macedonia, Norway, Poland, Portugal, Romania, Russia, San Marino, Serbia, Slovakia, Slovenia, Spain, Sweden, Switzerland, Türkiye, UK, Ukraine.
NGO Relations Every Woman Every Child (EWEC, #09215); PMNCH (#18410).

[2021/XM2865/v/F]

♦ European Youth Parliament (EYP) 09145
Parlement européen des jeunes – Europees Jongerenparlement
Exec Dir Sophienstr 28-29, 10178 Berlin, Germany. T. +493097005095. E-mail: info@eyp.org.
URL: http://www.eyp.org/
History Founded 1987, Fontainebleau (France), as a network of independent National Committees. Also known under the title Young Europe. **Aims** Support development of young people into politically aware and responsible citizens by involving them in European political thinking and promoting intercultural understanding. **Structure** Board of National Committees (BNC); Governing Body (GB); EYP Members. From 2004, Schwarzkopf Foundation Young Europe (SF, #19136) functions as international umbrella organization for the National Committees. **Languages** English. **Staff** 6.00 FTE, paid. **Finance** Sources: Council of Europe (CE, #04881); European Commission (EC, #06633); national governments; institutions; corporations. **Activities** Events/meetings; training/education. **Events** Session Ljubljana (Slovenia) 2021, Session Milan (Italy) 2021, Session Warsaw (Poland) 2021, Rethinking today, shaping tomorrow Milan (Italy) 2020, Session Warsaw (Poland) 2020. **Publications** Annual Report.
Members National Committees in 40 countries:
Albania, Armenia, Austria, Azerbaijan, Belarus, Belgium, Bosnia-Herzegovina, Croatia, Cyprus, Czechia, Denmark, Estonia, Finland, France, Georgia, Germany, Greece, Hungary, Iceland, Ireland, Italy, Kosovo, Latvia, Lithuania, Luxembourg, Netherlands, Norway, Poland, Portugal, Romania, Russia, Serbia, Slovakia, Slovenia, Spain, Sweden, Switzerland, Türkiye, UK, Ukraine.

[2020/XF1816/F]

♦ European Youth Press (EYP) 09146
Contact Alt-Moabit 89, 10559 Berlin, Germany. T. +30394052500 ext 35. E-mail: office@youthpress.org.
URL: http://www.youthpress.org/
History 2004. Former names and other names: European Youth Press – Network of young media makers – full title. Registration: Germany; EU Transparency Register, No/ID: 280112516951-40. **Aims** Inspire young people to become involved in the media and take an active part in civil society by fostering objective and independent media. **Structure** General Assembly; Executive Board; Advisory Board; Secretariat, located in Berlin (Germany). **Languages** English. **Staff** 1.00 FTE, paid; 8.00 FTE, voluntary. **Finance** Supported by: Council of Europe (CE, #04881); European Commission (EC, #06633); European Parliament (EP, #08146); Jugend in Aktion. **Activities** Events/meetings; training/education; networking/liaising; capacity building; knowledge management/information dissemination. **Publications** EYE Report (2016); Free our Media (2015) – comic book; EYE Report; Report on the youth event in Sibiu.
Members Organizations (27) in 23 countries:
Armenia, Austria, Belarus, Belgium, Bosnia-Herzegovina, Croatia, Czechia, Denmark, France, Germany, Hungary, Italy, Latvia, Malta, Montenegro, Netherlands, Poland, Portugal, Russia, Serbia, Slovakia, Sweden, Ukraine.
NGO Relations Observer status with (1): European Youth Forum (#09140).

[2020.02.20/XM2681/E]

♦ European Youth Press – Network of young media makers / see European Youth Press (#09146)
♦ **The European YWCA** European Young Women's Christian Association (#09135)
♦ European YWCA's Liaison Group / see European Young Women's Christian Association (#09135)

♦ European Zebrafish Society (EZS) 09147
Main Office Mendelstr 7, 48149 Münster, Germany. E-mail: office@ezsociety.org.
URL: https://www.ezsociety.org/
History Founded as the successor to EuFishBioMed Network. Registration: Baden-Württemmberg District court, No/ID: VR 103672, Start date: 19 Sep 2012, Germany, Mannheim. **Aims** Foster zebrafish research, providing a platform for researchers and a framework for grant funding for young researchers. **Structure** Steering Board; Board. **Activities** Awards/prizes/competitions; events/meetings. **Events** European Zebrafish Meeting Krakow (Poland) 2023, European Zebrafish Meeting 2020.

[2023/AA3192/D]

♦ European Zen Association / see International Zen Association (#15940)

♦ European Zeolites Producers Association (EUZEPA) 09148
Manager CEFIC, Rue Belliard 40, Box 15, 1040 Brussels, Belgium. T. +3224369475. E-mail: jwi@cefic.be – lva@cefic.be.
URL: http://www.zeolites.eu/
History Jan 2006, on merger of Zeolites Adsorbents Sector Group and Association of Detergent Zeolite Producers (Zeodet, inactive), as a sector group of Conseil européen de l'industrie chimique (CEFIC, #04687).
Members Companies (11). Membership countries not specified.

[2020/XJ5957/E]

♦ European Zero Emissions Technology & Innovation Platform / see Zero Emissions Platform (#22032)

♦ European Zoo Nutrition Centre (EZNC) 09149
Contact Deltahof 9, 2181 EN Hillegom, Netherlands. T. +31235846008.
URL: http://www.eznc.org/
History Jan 2002. **Aims** Stimulate zoo nutrition in Europe. **Languages** English. **Staff** 2.00 FTE, paid. **Finance** Income from sponsors, sales, activities. **Events** Practical zoo animal nutrition Leipzig (Germany) 2005, Conference Antwerp (Belgium) 2003, Conference Colden Common (UK) 2000, Conference Rotterdam (Netherlands) 1999. **Publications** Zoo Nutrition Tables and Guidelines. Annual report; leaflets. **Members** Individuals (400) in 30 countries. Membership countries not specified.

[2015/XJ3394/E]

♦ European Zoo Nutrition Research Group (inactive)
♦ Europe ARISE (internationally oriented national body)
♦ Europea Rum Associazione (no recent information)

♦ Europe and the Balkans International Network (EBIN) 09150
Dir c/o IECOB, 117 C so della Repubblica, 47121 Forlì FC, Italy. T. +3954336304. Fax +39543377088. E-mail: unibo.eurobalk@unibo.it.
URL: http://www.iecob.net/
History 1993, by 12 scholars from 4 countries (Italy, UK, Greece, Denmark) with financial support of the European Commission (EC, #06633), under the Human Capital and Mobility Programme (HCM, inactive). **Aims** Develop research and training in the fields of politics, economics, law, history, linguistics and culture; promote in Europe the knowledge about Central Eastern and Balkan Europe; looking towards a wider European integration process, foster international talk and interdisciplinarity as a method of work; encourage dialogue and communication even in the context of severe suffering because of disastrous conflicts. **Structure** Coordinator; members. **Finance** Supported by: European Commission (EC, #06633); Alma Mater University of Bologna; City Council of Forlì; Region Emilia-Romegna; Italian Ministry of Foreign Affairs. **Activities** Promotes and collaborates with numerous research activities. Also promotes: since 1995, annual 'Summer

School on Post-Communist Transition and European Integration Processes', held in Cervia (Italy) and Ravenna (Italy); Master programmes in Forlì (Italy) and Sarajevo (Bosnia-Herzegovina); conferences, meetings, training courses and seminars. Collects specialized books (books, reviews, photos) concerning East and Central Europe and the Balkans. Has consultative status with: Region Emilia-Romegna; Italian Ministry of Foreign Affairs; CEMIS. **Events** *Regional cooperation, peace-enforcement and the role of the treaties in the Balkans* Forlì (Italy) 2006, *Russia and the EU* Forlì (Italy) 2006, *Round table* Washington, DC (USA) 2006, *Consistency and quality control scheme* Bertinoro (Italy) / Forlì (Italy) 2005, *The influence of CIS revolutions on the crisis of Russia – possible outcomes and prospects* Forlì (Italy) 2005. **Publications** *Electronic Newsletter* (6 a year); *Journal of Southeastern Europe*. *Series of Balkan and East European Studies*. Occasional papers; guides; research; country manual.

Members Scholars (150) in 34 countries and territories:
Albania, Austria, Azerbaijan, Belarus, Bosnia-Herzegovina, Bulgaria, Canada, Croatia, Czechia, Denmark, Egypt, Finland, France, Germany, Greece, Hungary, Italy, Kosovo, Moldova, Montenegro, Netherlands, North Macedonia, Poland, Romania, Russia, Serbia, Slovakia, Slovenia, Sweden, Switzerland, Türkiye, UK, Ukraine, USA.
Collaborators in 42 countries:
Albania, Austria, Bangladesh, Belgium, Bosnia-Herzegovina, Bulgaria, Canada, Croatia, Cyprus, Czechia, Denmark, Egypt, Estonia, Finland, France, Germany, Greece, Hungary, India, Italy, Latvia, Lithuania, Malta, Moldova, Montenegro, Netherlands, North Macedonia, Pakistan, Poland, Romania, Russia, Serbia, Slovakia, Slovenia, Spain, Sri Lanka, Sweden, Switzerland, Türkiye, UK, Ukraine, USA.

IGO Relations Formal contacts with: *Central European Initiative (CEI, #03708)*; *European Union (EU, #08967)*; *International Bank for Reconstruction and Development (IBRD, #12317)*; *UNESCO (#20322)*. [2012/XF4323/y/**F**]

♦ Europe Without Barriers (internationally oriented national body)

♦ Europe-Central Asia Monitoring (EUCAM) 09151

Coordinator c/o CESS, Lutkenieuwstr 31a, 9712 AW Groningen, Netherlands. T. +31503132520. E-mail: info@eucentralasia.eu.
URL: http://www.eucentralasia.eu/

History 2008. Set up by *Fundación para las Relaciones Internacionales y el Dialogo Exterior (FRIDE, inactive)*, as a project. Currently implemented by: *Centre for European Security Studies (CESS)*. **Aims** Raise the profile of European-Central Asian relations. **Structure** Advisory Group; Associated Staff. **Languages** English. Some publications in Russian. **Staff** 1.50 FTE, paid. **Finance** Mostly funding from European governments and international foundations. Budget part of *Centre for European Security Studies (CESS)*. **Activities** Awareness raising; events/meetings; knowledge management/information dissemination; monitoring/evaluation; training/education. Europe and Central Asia. **Publications** *EUCAM Watch* – newsletter. *Policy Briefs*. Working papers and reports; factsheets. **NGO Relations** Partners include: *European Neighbourhood Council (ENC, #07855)*; *Norwegian Institute of International Affairs (NUPI)*. [2023.02.14/XM5991/**E**]

♦ **EUROPECHE** Association des organisations nationales d'entreprises de pêche de l'UE (#02841)
♦ Europe Citizen Band Federation / see European Citizen's Band Federation (#06556)
♦ Europe Citizen's Band Association / see European Citizen's Band Federation (#06556)
♦ Europe+ – Civil Society for the Renewal of European Democracy (inactive)
♦ Europe créativité / see International Association for the Arts, the Media and Creativity by and with Disabled People (#11713)
♦ Europe of Cultures Forum (internationally oriented national body)
♦ Europe Deaf Tech (unconfirmed)
♦ Europe Écologie – Les Verts (internationally oriented national body)

♦ L'Europe de l'enfance 09152

Secretariat c/o Office de la Naissance, Chaussée de Charleroi 95, 1060 Brussels, Belgium. T. +3225421200.
URL: http://www.childoneurope.org

History 2000. Established as a permanent intergovernmental group within *European Union (EU, #08967)*. *European Network of National Observatories on Childhood (ChildONEurope, #07951)* serves as technical/scientific instrument. **Aims** Introduce children's rights into mainstream EU policies. **Structure** Composed of government representatives in charge of childhood policies in the EU countries. **Activities** Meets twice a year on an informal basis, on invitation of the country holding the EU Presidency. **Events** *Meeting* Copenhagen (Denmark) 2012, *Meeting* Budapest (Hungary) 2011, *Meeting* Antwerp (Belgium) 2010, *Meeting* Brussels (Belgium) 2010, *Meeting* Madrid (Spain) 2010. [2012/XM2622/**F***]

♦ Européenne d'Ethnographie de l'Education / see Société internationale d'ethnographie (#19480)

♦ Europe de l'enseignement agronomique (Europea) 09153

SG Frauentorgasse 72-74, 3430 Tulln, Austria. T. +432272611570. E-mail: europea.austria@aon.at.
Registered Office Centre Technique Horticole, Chemin de Sibérie 4, 5030 Gembloux, Belgium.
URL: http://www.europea.org/

History 28 Sep 1993. Also referred to as *EUROPEA International*. Registered in accordance with Belgian law. **Aims** In member countries of the *European Community*: develop and improve education in agronomy; promote mutual recognition of qualifications; facilitate student and staff exchanges; encourage cooperation between agronomic education and the professional world; develop decentralized and continuing education, specialized networks, relations with countries outside the Community – particularly those of *Eastern Europe* and *developing countries*, the study of a *language* other than the mother tongue and *intercultural* exchanges. **Structure** General Assembly (twice a year). Administrative Council, comprising up to 3 representatives of member country and the Bureau, consisting of President, 2 Vice-Presidents, Secretary, Deputy-Secretary, Treasurer and Deputy-Treasurer. **Languages** English, French. **Finance** Members' dues (annual): maximum euro 1,000. **Activities** Organizes: International Forestry Competition for student; European competition of animal judgement by young people (annually, in Paris, France). Current Leonardo projects (2004-2007): Formations Agronomiques et Nouvelles Compétences our une Agriculture Multiculturelle (FANCAM) – Europea Belgium; Authentic Learning in Land-Based Education (ALIE) – Europea Netherlands. **Events** *General Assembly* Bergen (Norway) 2013, *General Assembly* Wageningen (Netherlands) 2013, *General assembly and meeting / General Assembly* Bristol (UK) 2005, *General assembly and meeting / General Assembly* Luxembourg (Luxembourg) 2005, *General assembly and meeting / General Assembly* 's Hertogenbosch (Netherlands) 2004. **Publications** Directory of horticultural and agricultural education establishments in EC countries and of member institutes.

Members Full – national and sub-national regional associations; Associate (); Honorary. Full and Associate members in 20 countries:
Belgium, Czechia, Denmark, Estonia, Finland, France, Germany, Greece, Ireland, Italy, Latvia, Luxembourg, Malta, Netherlands, Norway (*), Portugal, Slovakia, Spain, Sweden, UK.

NGO Relations Member of: *Didaxis (no recent information)*. Close links with: *International Association of Students in Agricultural and Related Sciences (IAAS, #12191)*. [2018/XE1748/**E**]

♦ Les Européens dans le monde (#08839)

♦ Européens Sans Frontières (ESF) 09154

Contact address not obtained. E-mail: contact@europeenssansfrontieres.eu.
URL: http://www.europeenssansfrontieres.eu/

History May 2011. Registered in accordance with French law. **Structure** Board. [2016/XM5292/**F**]

♦ Europees Agentschap voor Chemische Stoffen (#06523)
♦ Europees Agentschap voor de Maritieme Veiligheid (#07744)
♦ Europees Agentschap voor de Veiligheid van de Luchtvaart (#08978)
♦ Europees Agentschap voor Voedselveiligheid / see European Food Safety Authority (#07287)
♦ Europees Arbitragehof / see European Court of Arbitration (#06853)
♦ Europees arrestatiebevel (2001 treaty)
♦ Europees Bondgenootschap van Burgemeesters (inactive)
♦ Europees Bureau voor Fraudebestrijding (#05906)
♦ Europees Bureau voor Volksontwikkeling / see European Association for the Education of Adults (#06018)
♦ Europees Centrum van Bonden voor Gemeentepersoneel (inactive)
♦ Europees Centrum voor Conservatie, Restauratie en Renovatie / see European Centre for Restoration Techniques
♦ Europees Centrum van Gemeenschapsbedrijven / see SGI Europe (#19253)
♦ Europees Centrum voor de Kleinhandel (inactive)
♦ Europees Centrum van de Ondernemingen met Overheidsdeelneming / see SGI Europe (#19253)
♦ Europees Centrum voor de Ontwikkeling van de Beroepsopleiding (#06474)
♦ Europees Centrum voor Opleiding en Vervolmaking in Kunstambachten en Historische Restauratie (internationally oriented national body)
♦ Europees Centrum voor Restauratietechnieken (internationally oriented national body)
♦ Europees Centrum voor Vermiste en Misbruikte Kinderen / see European Centre for Missing and Sexually Exploited Children
♦ Europees Centrum voor Vermiste en Seksueel Uitgebuite Kinderen (internationally oriented national body)
♦ Europees Centrum voor Weervoorspellingen op Middellange Termijn (#06490)
♦ Europees Centrum voor Ziektepreventie en -bestrijding (#06476)
♦ Europees Chromosoom 11 Netwerk (#06547)
♦ Europees Chromosoom 11q Netwerk / see European Chromosome 11 Network (#06547)
♦ Europees Comité der Bedrijfsgroeperingen van Importeurs en Verdelers-Grossiers in Voedingswaren (inactive)
♦ Europees Comité van Constructeurs van Textiel-Machines (#06672)
♦ Europees Comité voor de Educatie van Intellectueel Vroegrijpe, Hoogbegaafde en Getalenteerde Kinderen en Adolescenten (#06664)
♦ Europees Comité van Fabrikanten van Ventilatie en Droogmateriaal (inactive)
♦ Europees Comité van Fabrikanten van Weeginstrumenten (#04151)
♦ Europees Comité voor de Handel in Zetmeelprodukten en Derivaten (inactive)
♦ Europees Comité voor het Katholiek Onderwijs (#04156)
♦ Europees Comité van de Nationale Bonden in de Sectoren Lederwerking, Fabricage van Reisartikelen en Aanverwante Industrieën (inactive)
♦ Europees Comité van de Nationale Verenigingen van Importateurs-Handelaren in Materieel voor Openbare Werken en Goederenbehandeling (no recent information)
♦ Europees Comité voor de opstelling van standaarden voor de binnenvaart (#04160)
♦ Europees Comité van de Regio's (#06665)
♦ Europees Comité van Verenigingen voor Algemeen Belang / see European Council for Non-Profit Organizations (#06834)
♦ Europees Consortium voor Communicatie-onderzoek / see European Communication Research and Education Association (#06675)
♦ Europees Coördinerend Comité van Röntgen- en Elektromedische Industrie / see European Coordination Committee of the Radiological, Electromedical Healthcare IT Industry (#06792)
♦ Europees Economisch en Sociaal Comité (#06963)
♦ Europeese Vereniging voor Neuro-Linguistische Psychotherapie (#06131)
♦ Europees Fonds voor Regionale Ontwikkeling (#08342)
♦ Europees Forum (internationally oriented national body)
♦ Europees Forum van christelijke Lesbische, Homo, Biseksuele en Transgender groepen (#07318)
♦ Europees Forum voor Open Systemen (no recent information)
♦ Europees Genootschap voor Milieu en Ontwikkeling (inactive)
♦ Europees Genootschap voor Munt- en Penningkunde (internationally oriented national body)
♦ Europees Genootschap van Vertebratenpaeontologen (#06266)
♦ Europees Instituut voor het Belang van het Kind (internationally oriented national body)
♦ Europees Instituut voor Bestuurskunde / see European Institute of Public Administration (#07569)
♦ Europees Instituut voor Bio-ethiek (internationally oriented national body)
♦ Europees Instituut, Gent (internationally oriented national body)
♦ Europees Instituut voor Onderwijs en Sociale Politiek / see European Institute of Education and Social Policy (#07551)
♦ Europees Instituut Onderzoek Arbeidsverhoudingen Bouw (#07549)
♦ Europees Jongerenparlement (#09145)
♦ Europees Keramisch Werkcentrum (internationally oriented national body)
♦ Europees Komitee voor de Automobielhandel en -Herstelling / see European Council for Motor Trades and Repairs (#06832)
♦ Europees Milieuagentschap (#06995)
♦ Europees Milieubureau / see European Environmental Bureau (#06996)
♦ Europees Netwerk van Culturele Centra (#07888)
♦ Europees Netwerk van Groene Senioren (#07915)
♦ Europees Netwerk Kindvriendelijke Steden / see European Network Child Friendly Cities (#07877)
♦ Europees Netwerk van Politievrouwen (#07970)
♦ Europees Netwerk voor de Rechten van de Oorspronkelijke Bewoners van Australie (internationally oriented national body)
♦ Europees Netwerk voor Sociale Actie (#08499)
♦ Europees Netwerk Van Oudere Vrijwilligers / see European Network of Older-Volunteer Organizations
♦ Europees Ontwikkelingsfonds (#06914)
♦ Europees Parlement (#08146)
♦ Europees Parlement – Fractie van de Partij van Europese Liberalen en Democraten / see Renew Europe (#18840)
♦ Europees Parlement, Liberale en Democratische Fractie / see Renew Europe (#18840)
♦ Europees Platform – internationaliseren in onderwijs (internationally oriented national body)
♦ Europees Platform voor het Nederlandse Onderwijs / see European Platform – internationalising education
♦ Europees Samenwerkingsverband van Nationale Organisaties van Onafhankelijke Scholen (#06833)
♦ Europees Secretariaat van Fabrikanten van Lichtmetalen Verpakkingen (inactive)
♦ Europees Secretariaat voor de Vrije Beroepen / see European Council of Liberal Professions (#06828)
♦ Europees Secretariat der Vrije, Zelfstandige en Sociale Beroepen / see European Council of Liberal Professions (#06828)
♦ Europees Sociaal Fonds (#08501)
♦ Europees Spiritijns Centrum voor Ontwikkeling en Samenwerking (#16188)
♦ Europees Technologie-Instituut / see European Institute of Innovation and Technology (#07562)
♦ Europees Tuinennetwerk (#07378)
♦ Europees Universitair Instituut (#09034)
♦ Europees Vakbondsinstituut (#08928)
♦ Europees Verbindingscomité van Expediteurs en Bemiddelaars bij het Vervoer in de Gemeenschappelijke Markt / see CLECAT (#03993)
♦ Europees Verbond van de Cellulose-, Houtslijp-, Papier- en Kartonindustrie (inactive)
♦ Europees Verbond van de Groothandel in Vlees (inactive)
♦ Europees Verbond van de Huisdiervoederindustrie (#09571)
♦ Europees Verbond Schoengroothandel (inactive)
♦ Europees Verbond voor Schriftpsychologie (#08616)
♦ Europees Verbond van met de Wijnbouw Verwante Bedrijfstakken (inactive)
♦ Europees Volkshuis (internationally oriented national body)
♦ Europees Waarnemingscentrum voor Drugs en Drugsverslaving (#07820)
♦ Europees Waarnemingscentrum van de Meertaligheid (internationally oriented national body)

♦ Europe External Programme with Africa (EEPA) 09155

SG Rue Stévin 115, 1000 Brussels, Belgium. T. +3222311659. E-mail: admin@eepa.be.
URL: http://www.eepa.be/

EuropeFides
09156

alphabetic sequence excludes
For the complete listing, see Yearbook Online at

History 1990. Former names and other names: *European Solidarity towards Equal Participation of People (Eurostep)* – former; *Solidarité européenne pour une participation égale des peuples* – former; *Solidarité européenne pour une participation égalitaire entre les peuples* – former. Registration: Belgium; EU Transparency Register, No/ID: 574620429651-88. **Aims** Influence development cooperation policies and practices of the *European Union* so they contribute to building a global community based on principles of sustainability, justice and equity. **Structure** Board of Directors. **Languages** English. **Staff** 7.00 FTE, paid. **Finance** Subventions. Annual budget: euro 300,000. **Activities** Research and development; projects/programmes; guidance/assistance/consulting; humanitarian/emergency aid. **Events** *Half-yearly general assembly* Brussels (Belgium) 2010, *Half-yearly general assembly* Gdansk (Poland) 2010, *Half-Yearly General Assembly* Brussels (Belgium) 2009, *Half-Yearly General Assembly* Madrid (Spain) 2009, *Half-Yearly General Assembly* Brussels (Belgium) 2008. **Publications** Briefing papers. **Members** Organizations in Africa, Europe and North America. Membership countries not specified. **Consultative Status** Consultative status granted from: *ECOSOC (#05331)* (Special). **IGO Relations** *Organisation of African, Caribbean and Pacific States (OACPS, #17796); African Union (AU, #00488); European Commission (EC, #06633); European Parliament (EP, #08146).* Contacts with: Embassies. **NGO Relations** Member of (1): *Social Watch (#19350).* [2018.07.10/XF2265/y/**F**]

♦ EuropeFides 09156

Contact 5 rue Denis Poisson, 75017 Paris, France. T. +33145534127. Fax +33145534129. E-mail: office@europefides.eu.
URL: http://www.europefides.eu/

History 2008, Paris (France). Former names and other names: *European Accounting, Audit, Tax and Legal Association for medium-sized companies (EuropeFides)* – full title. Registration: France. **Aims** Bring together certified tax advisors, accountants, auditors and lawyers throughout Europe and worldwide so as to provide an all-round service to clients. **Structure** General Meeting; Executive Board. **Languages** English. **Activities** Capacity building; events/meetings; guidance/assistance/consulting; networking/liaising; training/education. Active in all member countries. **Events** *Annual General Meeting* Paris (France) 2021, *Half-Yearly Meeting* London (UK) 2020, *Annual General Meeting* Malaga (Spain) 2020, *Virtual General Meeting* Paris (France) 2020, *Half-Yearly Meeting* Shanghai (China) 2019.
Members Individuals in 25 countries and territories:
Algeria, Austria, Belgium, Bulgaria, China, Cyprus, Czechia, France, Germany, Hong Kong, Italy, Japan, Latvia, Lebanon, Liechtenstein, Malta, Netherlands, Portugal, Serbia, Spain, Switzerland, Türkiye, UK, United Arab Emirates, USA.
[2021.06.08/XJ9448/**D**]

♦ Europe+ Foundation 09157

Fondation Europe+

Exec Dir 11 Allée de l'Arche, 92037 Paris CEDEX, France. T. +33146938866 – +33146938770. Fax +33146938770.

Aims Serve the *European Union* as a tool for reflection and for development of recommendations in support of operational implementation of *reforms* provided for in the Lisbon Agenda. **Structure** Executive Board, comprising 2 Co-Chairmen and 7 members. **Finance** 45% from public sources; 55% from private sector. **Activities** Think Tank provides deliverables in 5 areas: Towards a Sustainable Healthcare Model in Europe; Green Cities, Green Growth; For a New Territorial Attractiveness and Competitiveness Policy; Govern European Attractiveness Policies and Promote Europe as a Whole (in partnership with WAIPA); Maritime Energies – New challenges. Organizes *La Baule World Investment Conference* (annual). **Events** *Brainpower forum* La Baule (France) 2009, *Transatlantic green platform conference* La Baule (France) 2009, *WIC : annual world investment conference* La Baule (France) 2009, *Euro-Mediterranean investment conference* La Baule (France) 2008, *Transatlantic green platform conference* La Baule (France) 2008. [2009/XJ0115/f/**F**]

♦ Europe Foundation (EPF) 09158

Permanent Office 3 Kavsadze Str, 0179 Tbilisi, Georgia. T. +995322253942 – +995322253943. Fax +995322253942 ext 112. E-mail: info@epfound.ge.
URL: http://www.epfound.ge

History 2007. Former names and other names: *Eurasia Partnership Foundation (EPF)* – former (2007 to Dec 2015). Registration: Georgia. **Aims** Engage citizens in social, economic, and political developments in order to effect substantive and sustainable positive socio-economic change at local, regional and national level through both operational programs and grantmaking. **Structure** Board of Trustees; President. **Languages** English, Georgian. **Finance** Sources: donations; private foundations. Supported by: *DANIDA; Swedish International Development Cooperation Agency (Sida); United States Agency for International Development (USAID).* **Activities** Advocacy/lobbying/activism; capacity building; financial and/or material support; monitoring/evaluation; networking/liaising; projects/programmes. Active in: Georgia. **NGO Relations** Member of (2): *Eastern Partnership Civil Society Forum (EaP CSF, #05247); Philanthropy Europe Association (Philea, #18358).* [2020.05.04/XM5654/f/**F**]

♦ Europe HOpes (internationally oriented national body)
♦ Gli Europei nel Mondo (#08839)
♦ Europe Institute / see Institute of Europe, Moscow
♦ Europe Institute, Vienna (internationally oriented national body)
♦ Europeiska Byrån för Bedrägeribekämpning (#05906)
♦ Europeiska Byrån för Luftfartssäkerhet (#08978)
♦ Europeiska Centrumet för Kontroll av Narkotika och Narkotikamissbruk (#07820)
♦ Europeiska Ekonomiska och Sociala Kommittén (#06963)
♦ Europeiska Federationen för Grossister i Papper, Papp och Emballage / see European Paper Merchants Association (#08138)
♦ Europeiska Federationen för Offentligaställdas Förbund (#07202)
♦ Europeiska Gemenskapernas Förstainstansratt (inactive)
♦ Europeiska Gemenskapernas Statistik Kontor / see Statistical Office of the European Union (#19974)
♦ Europeiska Grafologförbundet (#08616)
♦ Europeiska institutet för kriminalpolitik verksamt i anslutning till Förenta Nationerna (#07550)
♦ Europeiska Investeringsbanken (#07599)
♦ Europeiska Kammarmusikpedagogiska Föreningen rf (#06516)
♦ Europeiska Kemikaliemyndigheten (#06523)
♦ Europeiska Kommissionen (#06633)
♦ Europeiska Kommittén för Offentliga Tjänster / see European Federation of Public Service Unions (#07202)
♦ Europeiska Kvinnopriset (#20993)
♦ Europeiska Liberala och Demokratiska Partiet / see Alliance of Liberals and Democrats for Europe Party (#00703)
♦ Europeiska Ombudsmannen (#08084)
♦ Europeiska Rådet av Nationella Friskoleförbund (#06833)
♦ Europeiska regionkommittén (#06665)
♦ Europeiska revisionsrätten (#06854)
♦ Europeiska Röntgen- och Elektromedicinska Industrins Samordningskommitté / see European Coordination Committee of the Radiological, Electromedical Healthcare IT Industry (#06792)
♦ Europeiska Samarbetsorganet för Katolsk Vuxenutbildning (#05966)
♦ Europeiska Samarbetsorganisationen för Nationella Språkinstitutioner / see European Federation of National Institutions for Language (#07172)
♦ Europeiska Smafoåretagarealliansen av Oberoende Små- och Medelstora Företag (#08494)
♦ Europeiska Socialdemokraternas Parlamentsgrupp / see Group of the Progressive Alliance of Socialists and Democrats in the European Parliament (#10786)
♦ Europeiska Socialdemokraters Parti (#18249)
♦ Europeiska Socialfonden (#08501)
♦ Europeiska Terminologiföreningen (#06252)
♦ Europeiska Tjänstemäns Fackförening / see European Public Service Union (#08303)
♦ Europeiska Unionen (#08967)
♦ Europeiska Unionens Domstol (#04938)
♦ Europeiska Unionens Kör / see European Union Choir (#08980)
♦ Europeiska unionens publikationsbyrå (#18562)
♦ Europeiska Unionens Råd (#04895)
♦ Europeiska Unionens stadga om de grundläggande rättigheterna (2000 treaty)
♦ Europeiska Unionens Statistikkontor (#19974)
♦ Europeiska Unionens Ungdoms Forum (inactive)
♦ Europeiska Utrikestjänsten (#07018)
♦ Europeiska Vörbundet av Industri Optik och Fin Mekanik (#07193)
♦ Europeiske Borgere Aksjon Service / see European Citizen Action Service (#06555)
♦ Europeiske Fagforeningsinstitut (#08928)
♦ Europeiske Marche Imod Arbejdsløsighed Usikkre Jobs og Udstødelse (#07735)
♦ Europeiske Miljøbyrået (#06995)
♦ Europeiske Sammenslutning av Papir- Kartong- og Emballasjegrossister / see European Paper Merchants Association (#08138)
♦ De Europeiske Sosialdemokraters Parti (#18249)
♦ Europeisk Havbunadarfelagid / see Federation of European Aquaculture Producers (#09491)
♦ Europeisk Overvåkingssenter for Narkotika og Narkotikamisbruk (#07820)
♦ Europeiskt Centrum för Förebyggande och Kontroll av Sjukdomar (#06476)
♦ Europeiskt Centrum för Utveckling av Yrkesutbildning (#06474)
♦ Europeiskt Nätverk för Experimentell Arkeologi och Forntida Teknik / see EXARC (#09219)
♦ Europeiskt Rättsligt Nätverk på Privaträttens Område (#07616)
♦ Europeiskt Tekniskt Institut / see European Institute of Innovation and Technology (#07562)
♦ Europe Israel Press Association (unconfirmed)

♦ Europe Jacques Delors 09159

Dir-Gen Rue du Duc 139, 1200 Brussels, Belgium. T. +32471933613. E-mail: info@europejacquesdelors.eu.
URL: https://www.europejacquesdelors.eu/

History 2020, Belgium. Former names and other names: *Europe Jacques Delors – Thinking Europe* – full title. Registration: Banque-Carrefour des Entreprises, No/ID: 0736.695.796, Start date: 23 Oct 2019, Belgium; EU Transparency Register, No/ID: 784839644387-27, Start date: 28 Oct 2021. **Aims** Contribute to the debate on European integration, focusing on sustainable development. **Structure** Executive Board; Team. **Staff** 6.00 FTE, paid; 1.00 FTE, voluntary. **Activities** Events/meetings; knowledge management/information dissemination; publishing activities; research/documentation. **Publications** *Europe Jacques Delors Newsletter.* **NGO Relations** Sister organizations: *Jacques Delors Centre; Institut Jacques Delors (IJD).* [2021.12.24/AA2173/j/**E**]

♦ Europe Jacques Delors – Thinking Europe / see Europe Jacques Delors (#09159)

♦ Europe Jazz Network (EJN) 09160

Contact 9 rue Gabrielle Josserand, 93500 Pantin, France. E-mail: office@europejazz.net.
URL: http://www.europejazz.net/

History 1987. Sometimes also referred to as *European Jazz Network.* **Aims** Maintain high standards of *artistic* direction; improve organizational efficiency of planning and therefore working conditions of *musicians*, agents and other workers in the sector by establishing close and more direct relations among them; create a code of conduct and *professional* behaviour among jazz promoters; commission and support the creation of original musical events. **Structure** General Assembly; Board of Directors; Secretary General. **Finance** Members' dues. Support from cultural organizations. **Activities** Organizes project tours. **Events** *Conference* Marseille (France) 2023, *Conference* Sofia (Bulgaria) 2022, *Conference* Tallinn (Estonia) 2021, *Conference* Sofia (Bulgaria) 2020, *Conference* Novara (Italy) 2019. **Publications** *PAN – Performing Arts Network* (4 a year). Information Services: Database containing information on events, tours, musicians, agents, promoters.
Members Member organisations in 14 countries:
Belgium, Denmark, France, Germany, Israel, Italy, Netherlands, Norway, Russia, Spain, Sweden, Switzerland, Türkiye, UK, USA.
User organisations in 4 countries:
Austria, France, Germany, Italy.
NGO Relations Member of: *Culture Action Europe (CAE, #04981); European Music Council (EMC, #07837); International Music Council (IMC, #14199).* [2019/XF2646/**F**]

♦ Europejska Agencja Bezpieczenstwa Lotniczego (#08978)
♦ Europejska Agencja Chemikaliów (#06523)
♦ Europejska Akademie ds Badania Aspektów Zyciowych, Integracji oraz Spoteczenstwa Cywilnego (#05799)
♦ Europejska Organizacja Armatorów Sródladowych (#08491)
♦ Europejska Partia Liberalnych Demokratów Partia / see Alliance of Liberals and Democrats for Europe Party (#00703)
♦ Europejska Siec Grup Pacjentów Chorych na Spzpiczaka (inactive)
♦ Europejska Siec Sadownicza w Sprawach Cywilnych i Handlowych (#07616)
♦ Europejskie Centrum Monitorowania Narkotyków i Narkomani (#07820)
♦ Europejskie Centrum Wspólpracy Mlodziezy (internationally oriented national body)
♦ Europejskiego Instytutu Technologii / see European Institute of Innovation and Technology (#07562)
♦ Europejski Komitet Ekonomiczno-Spoleczny (#06963)
♦ Europejski Komitet Regionów (#06665)
♦ Europejski Rzecznik Praw Obywatelskich (#08084)

♦ Europe Makes Ceramics (EMC) 09161

Coordinator 5-4 Keramische Prozesstechnik und Biowerkstoffe, Unter den Eichen 44-46, 12203 Berlin, Germany. T. +493081041540.
Events Manager address not obtained.
URL: https://euroceram.org/

History 2015. An initative of *European Ceramic Society (ECerS, #06507)*, under the umbrella of its R&D working group. **Activities** Events/meetings. **Events** *young Ceramists Additive Manufacturing Forum (yCAM)* 2020, *young Ceramists Additive Manufacturing Forum (yCAM)* Mons (Belgium) 2019, *young Ceramists Additive Manufacturing Forum (yCAM)* Padua (Italy) 2018, *young Ceramists Additive Manufacturing Forum (yCAM)* Berlin (Germany) 2017.
Members Laboratories (12) in 7 countries:
Belgium, France, Germany, Italy, Russia, Türkiye, UK. [2020/AA2080/**F**]

♦ Europe and Middle East Young Friends (EMEYF) 09162

Sec c/o QCEA, Square Ambiorix 50, 1000 Brussels, Belgium. T. +3222304935. Fax +3222306370. E-mail: emeyf@qcea.org.
URL: http://emeyf.org/

History 1984, as a regional organization based at *Quaker Council for European Affairs (QCEA, #18587)* and in the framework of *Religious Society of Friends (Quakers, #18834).* **Aims** Create a network of young friends – *Quakers* – aged between 18 and 35, across Europe and the Middle East, encouraging international friendship and exchange on *spiritual* matters. **Activities** Organizes: Spring Gathering; annual meeting. **Events** *Annual Meeting* Brussels (Belgium) 2017, *Annual Meeting* Bad Pyrmont (Germany) 2010.
Members Full in 18 countries:
Austria, Belgium, Czechia, Denmark, Finland, France, Germany, Hungary, Ireland, Israel, Italy, Lebanon, Netherlands, Norway, Portugal, Russia, Sweden, UK. [2016/XK1892/**E**]

♦ Europe Must Act (unconfirmed)
♦ Europenan Committee for Wire Drawing (#04166)

♦ Europe of Nations and Freedom Group (ENF) 09163

Europe des nations et des libertés (ENL)

Co-Pres European Parliament, Office ATR 00L034, Rue Wiertz 60, 1047 Brussels, Belgium. E-mail: enf-sg@ep.europa.eu.
Co-Pres address not obtained.
URL: https://www.enfgroup-ep.eu/

History Set up Jun 2015, as a political party within *European Parliament (EP, #08146)*. **Languages** English, French. **Finance** Funding through *European Parliament (EP, #08146)*.
Members Parliamentarians (38) of 8 countries:
Austria, Belgium, France, Germany, Italy, Netherlands, Poland, Romania.
NGO Relations *Movement for a Europe of Nations and Freedom (MENF, #16870)*. [2018/XM4322/**F**]

- ♦ Europe des nations et des libertés (#09163)
- ♦ EurOpen – European Federation of Associations of Open Systems Users (no recent information)
- ♦ **EUROPEN** European Organization for Packaging and the Environment (#08110)
- ♦ EUROPEN / see EUROPEN-PEN International (#09165)

♦ Europengineers 09164

Executive Secretariat c/o CAOS, WG Plein 475, 1054 SH Amsterdam, Netherlands. T. +31205893232. E-mail: europengineers@caos.nl.
URL: http://www.europengineers.com/

History 1964. From 1999 until 2005 a grouping of the type *European Economic Interest Grouping (EEIG, #06960)*, when EEIG was dissolved and an Association was created. Former names and other names: *Europengineers EEIG (EE)* – former. Registration: Netherlands. **Aims** Through member associations, provide a network of *engineering* services from the original concept of a project to completion of construction and subsequent operation and maintenance. **Structure** General Assembly; Board of Directors; Executive Secretariat. **Languages** English. **Staff** 1.00 FTE, paid. **Finance** Sources: members' dues. **Activities** Events/meetings; knowledge management/information dissemination. **Events** *Annual general assembly / General Assembly* Madrid (Spain) 2006, *Annual general assembly / General Assembly* Athens (Greece) 2005, *Annual general assembly / General Assembly* Bath (UK) 2004, *Annual general assembly / General Assembly* Paris (France) 2003, *Annual general assembly / General Assembly* Zurich (Switzerland) 2002.
Members Companies (10) in 10 countries:
Finland, France, Greece, Ireland, Italy, Netherlands, Portugal, Spain, Switzerland, UK. [2023.02.14/XF0988/**F**]

- ♦ Europengineers EEIG / see Europengineers (#09164)

♦ EUROPEN-PEN International 09165

Exec Dir Karolinerstr 93, 45141 Essen, Germany. T. +4920180050389.
URL: http://www.penworldwide.org/

History Founded 1997, Essen (Germany), as *Worldwide Practice Firms Network (EUROPEN)*. Set up as a European project, 1993. Current name adopted, 2013. **Aims** Support, coordinate and develop value-added services for the Practice Enterprise activities carried out in national member networks; promote and enhance the concept of learning by doing in a simulated *business* environment; promote the Practice Enterprise concept in new countries. **Structure** Members' Meeting (2 a year, in different member countries); Managing Committee; Central Offices; International Coordination Center, located in Germany. **Languages** Chinese, English, French, German, Spanish. **Staff** 4.00 FTE, paid. **Finance** Has been supported, among others, by: *European Commission (EC, #06633)*; *International Bank for Reconstruction and Development (IBRD, #12317)* (World Bank); national ministries worldwide. **Activities** Events/meetings; research and development; training/education; knowledge management/information dissemination. **Events** *Members Meeting* Antwerp (Belgium) 2019, *Members Meeting* Dornbirn (Austria) 2018, *Members Meeting* Plovdiv (Bulgaria) 2018, *Members Meeting* Seoul (Korea Rep) 2017, *European congress* Copenhagen (Denmark) 2004.
Members Practice enterprises in 28 countries:
Austria, Belgium, Brazil, Bulgaria, Canada, China, Costa Rica, Czechia, Denmark, Finland, France, Germany, Indonesia, Italy, Korea Rep, Kosovo, Lithuania, Luxembourg, Montenegro, Netherlands, Poland, Romania, Slovakia, Slovenia, Spain, Sweden, Switzerland, USA. [2019.02.11/XF7130/**F**]

- ♦ EUROPENS – Association for Democratic Development and Cooperation (inactive)

♦ EuropeOn 09166

Gen Sec Rond-Point Schuman 3, 1040 Brussels, Belgium. E-mail: info@europe-on.org.
URL: https://europe-on.org/

History 22 Oct 1953, Paris (France). Former names and other names: *International Association of Electrical Contractors* – former (22 Oct 1953); *Association internationale des entreprises d'équipement électrique (AIE)* – former (22 Oct 1953); *Asociación Internacional de Empresarios de Electricidad* – former (22 Oct 1953); *International Vereinigung der Unternehmungen für Elektrische Ausrüstung* – former (22 Oct 1953); *Associazione Internationale Installatori Impianti Elettrici* – former (22 Oct 1953); *Association européenne des entreprises d'équipement électrique* – alias; *European Association of Electrical Contractors* – former; *Association européenne des entreprises de l'installation électrique (AIE)* – former; *Asociación Europea de Impresarios de Instalaciones Eléctricas* – former; *Europäische Vereinigung der Unternehmungen für Elektrische Anlagen* – former; *Associazione Europea Installatori Impianti Elettrici* – former. Registration: European Transparency Register, No/ID: 9089874181-55, Start date: 10 Jul 2008. **Aims** Promote and represent the common interests of European electrical contractors whenever appropriate; develop a common basis of understanding; promote increased and improved technical standardization to ensure safety and economically sound, efficient solutions; monitor the legislative process of the EU of sector-related issues and give information on market trends; promote the image of the electrotechnical installation industry and their companies. **Structure** General Assembly; Board; Secretariat. **Languages** English, French, German. **Staff** 1.50 FTE, paid. **Finance** Sources: members' dues. **Activities** Standards/guidelines; monitoring/evaluation; events/meetings. **Events** *Conference* Edinburgh (UK) 2015, *Annual Conference / Conference* Portoroz (Slovenia) 2014, *Annual Conference / Conference* Copenhagen (Denmark) 2013, *Annual Conference / Conference* Helsinki (Finland) 2012, *Conference* Brussels (Belgium) 2011. **Publications** *AIE Newsletter* (6 a year); *AIE Directory* (every 2 years). *Embracing 60 Years of AIE* (2014); *AIE International Vocabulary* in English, French, German.
Members National associations in 17 countries and territories:
Austria, Belgium, Denmark, England, Finland, France (2), Germany, Italy, Luxembourg, Netherlands, Norway, Portugal, Scotland, Spain, Sweden, Switzerland.
Associate members in 2 countries:
Hungary, Slovenia.
Corresponding members in 3 countries:
Australia, South Africa, USA.
Regional corresponding organization (1):
Federation of Asian and Pacific Electrical Contractors Associations (FAPECA, #09443).
IGO Relations Recognized by: *European Commission (EC, #06633)*. **NGO Relations** Member of (1): *Forum for European Electrical Domestic Safety (FEEDS)*. Observer to: *International Electrotechnical Commission (IEC, #13255)*. Technical Liaison Partner with: *European Committee for Electrotechnical Standardization (CENELEC, #06647)*. Instrumental in setting up: *International Forum of Electrical Contractors (IFEC, no recent information)*. [2022/XD1277/**D**]

- ♦ Los Europeos en el Mundo (#08839)
- ♦ Europe plurilingue (internationally oriented national body)

♦ Europe Region World Physiotherapy (ER-WPT) 09167

SG Avenue des Arts 56, 1000 Brussels, Belgium. E-mail: info@erwcpt.eu.
URL: https://www.erwcpt.eu/

History Sep 1998. Founded through a merger of *World Confederation for Physical Therapy (WCPT, #21293)* Europe and *Standing Liaison Committee of Physiotherapists of the EU (SLCP, inactive)*. Registration: EU Transparency Register, No/ID: 24516996887-24, Start date: 5 Oct 2011. **Aims** Lead and promote physiotherapy in Europe and to oversee all matters related to physiotherapy. **Structure** General Meeting; Executive Committee. Working Groups. Includes: European Foundation for Physiotherapy and Physical Activity of the European Region of the World Confederation for Physical Therapy. **Languages** English, French. **Finance** Sources: members' dues. **Activities** Advocacy/lobbying/activism; events/meetings; training/education. **Events** *European Congress – Physiotherapy Education* Brussels (Belgium) 2020.
Members Organizations in countries:
Austria, Belgium, Bosnia-Herzegovina, Bulgaria, Croatia, Cyprus, Czechia, Denmark, Estonia, Finland, Germany, Greece, Hungary, Iceland, Ireland, Israel, Italy, Kosovo, Latvia, Lebanon, Liechtenstein, Lithuania, Luxembourg, Malta, Montenegro, Netherlands, Norway, Portugal, Romania, Slovakia, Slovenia, Spain, Sweden, Switzerland, Türkiye, UK, Ukraine. [2023/AA3136/**E**]

- ♦ **EUROPERF** European Perforators Association (#08187)
- ♦ Europe et scoutisme (internationally oriented national body)
- ♦ Europese 11q Groep / see European Chromosome 11 Network (#06547)
- ♦ Europese Academie voor Rechtstheorie (#05798)
- ♦ Europese Advocaten Unie (#20365)
- ♦ Europese Alliantie van Initiatieven voor Toegepaste Antroposofie / see Alliance ELIANT (#00672)
- ♦ Europese Associatie voor Geografie / see Association of European Geographical Societies (#02512)
- ♦ Europese Associatie van Onafhankelijke Staalproducenten (inactive)
- ♦ Europese Associatie voor Samenwerking (inactive)
- ♦ Europese Associatie van Turkse Academići (inactive)
- ♦ Europese Beweging / see European Movement International (#07825)
- ♦ Europese Binnenvaart Unie (#06318)
- ♦ Europese Boeren Vereniging / see European Coordination Via Campesina (#06795)
- ♦ Europese Bond van Bouw- en Houtarbeiders / see European Federation of Building and Woodworkers (#07065)
- ♦ Europese Bond van Bouw- en Houtarbeiders in de EEG / see European Federation of Building and Woodworkers (#07065)
- ♦ Europese Brandwondenvereniging (#06414)
- ♦ Europese Buxus- en Vormsnoeivereniging (#06389)
- ♦ Europese Christen-Demokratische Unie (inactive)
- ♦ Europese Commissie (#06633)
- ♦ Europese Confederatie van Brandstoffenhandelaars (#06703)
- ♦ Europese Confederatie van de Gelaryngectomeerden (#06709)
- ♦ Europese Confederatie van oud-leerlingen van jezuïetencolleges (#04536)
- ♦ Europese Confederatie van de Schoenindustrie (#04544)
- ♦ Europese Conferentie van Orde van Geneesheren / see European Council of Medical Orders (#06830)
- ♦ Europese Culturele Stichting (#06868)
- ♦ Europese Dienst voor Extern Optreden (#07018)
- ♦ Europese Documentatiecentra (#06937)
- ♦ Europese Economische Samenwerkingsverbanden (#06960)
- ♦ Europese Federatie van Artsenverenigingen voor het Therapeutisch Pluralisme (#06816)
- ♦ Europese Federatie van Attraktieparken (inactive)
- ♦ Europese Federatie van Beeldende Therapie (#07047)
- ♦ Europese Federatie voor de Bevordering van de Produktiviteit (#07196)
- ♦ Europese Federatie van de Borstel- en Penseelindustrie (#06406)
- ♦ Europese Federatie van Bouw- en Houtarbeiders (#07065)
- ♦ Europese Federatie van Christelijke Bouwvakarbeiders en Houtbewerkersbonden (inactive)
- ♦ Europese Federatie van Christelijke Mijnwerkersbonden (inactive)
- ♦ Europese Federatie voor Dierengezondheid en Sanitaire Veiligheid (#09581)
- ♦ Europese Federatie Energie – Chemie – Diverse Bedrijven (inactive)
- ♦ Europese Federatie van Erfelijke Ataxieën (#07138)
- ♦ Europese Federatie van Fabrikanten en Distributeurs van Persoonlijke Beschermingsmiddelen (#08418)
- ♦ Europese Federatie van Familieverenigingen van Psychisch Zieke Personen / see European Federation of Associations of Families of People with Mental Illness (#07051)
- ♦ Europese Federatie van foie-grasproducenten (#09569)
- ♦ Europese Federatie van Importeurs van Gedroogde Vruchten, Conserven, Specerijen en Honing / see European Federation of the Trade in Dried Fruit, Edible Nuts, Processed Fruit and Vegetables, Processed Fishery Products, Spices, Honey and Similar Foodstuffs (#07229)
- ♦ Europese Federatie van Katholieke Artsenverenigingen (no recent information)
- ♦ Europese Federatie voor Katholiek Volwassenenvorming (#05966)
- ♦ Europese Federatie van Koffiebranders-Verenigingen (inactive)
- ♦ Europese Federatie van Mengvoederfabrikanten (#09566)
- ♦ Europese Federatie van Mijnhoutverenigingen (inactive)
- ♦ Europese Federatie van Milieudienstbedrijven / see European Federation of Waste Management and Environmental Services (#07232)
- ♦ Europese Federatie van Nationale Taalinstellingen / see European Federation of National Institutions for Language (#07172)
- ♦ Europese Federatie voor het Onderwijs aan Kinderen van de Trekkende Beroepsbevolking (inactive)
- ♦ Europese Federatie van Optische en Fijnmechanische Industrie (#07193)
- ♦ Europese Federatie van Organisaties van Familieleden van Mensen met een Psychische Ziekte / see European Federation of Associations of Families of People with Mental Illness (#07051)
- ♦ Europese Federatie van het Overheidspersoneel (#07106)
- ♦ Europese Federatie voor Pensioenvoorziening / see PensionsEurope (#18291)
- ♦ Europese Federatie van Psychologen Associaties (#07199)
- ♦ Europese Federatie van de Right to Die Societies / see Right to Die Europe (#18941)
- ♦ Europese Federatie van Tankreinigingsorganisaties (#07224)
- ♦ Europese Federatie van Taxi's (inactive)
- ♦ Europese Federatie van Veilingmeesters-Taxateurs / see European Federation of Auctioneers (#07057)
- ♦ Europese Federatie van Verenigingen van Familieleden van de Psychisch Zieken (#07051)
- ♦ Europese Federatie van Verenigingen voor Industrieel en Technisch Erfgoed (#07053)
- ♦ Europese Federatie van Verenigingen van Leasing Ondernemingen (#07111)
- ♦ Europese Federatie van Verenigingen van Organisatiedeskundigen (#07159)
- ♦ Europese Federatie van Verkeer en Milieu (#07230)
- ♦ Europese Federatie voor Vermiste en Seksueel Uitgebuite Kinderen (#07166)
- ♦ Europese Federatie voor Waterbehandeling / see European Water and Wastewater Industry Association (#09087)
- ♦ Europese Filmunie (inactive)
- ♦ Europese Gemeenschap (inactive)
- ♦ Europese Gemeenschap voor Atoomenergie (inactive)
- ♦ Europese Gemeenschap voor Chirurgische Oncologie (#08753)
- ♦ Europese Gemeenschap der Koks / see Euro-Toques International (#09190)
- ♦ Europese Gemeenschap voor Kolen en Staal (inactive)
- ♦ Europese Gemeenschap van Organisaties van Reclamebemiddelaars (inactive)
- ♦ Europese Gemeenschappen (inactive)
- ♦ Europese Gemeenschap van Verenigingen voor de Groothandel in Bier van de Lid-Staten van de EEG (#02555)
- ♦ Europese Generieke Geneesmiddelen Associatie / see Medicines for Europe (#16633)
- ♦ Europese Genootschap voor Ingenieursopleiding (#19462)
- ♦ Europese Groep voor Arbeidster Pastoraal (#10740)
- ♦ Europese Groepering van de Verenigingen van Reformwinkels (no recent information)
- ♦ Europese Groep voor de Studie van Normativiteiten (#10741)
- ♦ Europese Hoger Onderwijs Samenleving / see EAIR, The European Higher Education Society (#05153)
- ♦ Europese Huisartsen Vereniging / see European Union of General Practitioners / Family Physicians (#08993)
- ♦ Europese Investeringsbank (#07599)
- ♦ Europese Jonge Christen Democraten (inactive)
- ♦ Europese Juristen Vereniging (#07661)
- ♦ Europese Justitiële Netwerk in Burgerlijke en Handelszaken (#07616)
- ♦ Europese Kansspelvereniging (no recent information)
- ♦ Europese Katholieke Foyer (internationally oriented national body)
- ♦ Europese Liberale en Democratische Partij / see Alliance of Liberals and Democrats for Europe Party (#00703)
- ♦ Europese Medische Vereniging (#07761)
- ♦ Europese Metaal-Unie (#07785)

Europese Middenstands Unie
09167

alphabetic sequence excludes
For the complete listing, see Yearbook Online at

- ♦ Europese Middenstands-Unie (no recent information)
- ♦ Europese Middenstandsvereniging (inactive)
- ♦ Europese Noodnummer Associatie (#06978)
- ♦ Europese Ombudsman (#08084)
- ♦ Europese Ontwikkelingspool / see Association transfrontalière du pôle européen de développement (#02958)
- ♦ Europese Optometrie Vereniging (#08675)
- ♦ Europese Organisatie voor Geografische Informatie (#08964)
- ♦ Europese Organisatie der Groenten en Fruitverwerkende Industrie / see European Association of Fruit and Vegetable Processors (#06049)
- ♦ Europese Organisatie van de Jam en Vruchtenconservenindustrie (inactive)
- ♦ Europese Organisatie van Militaire Verenigingen / see European Organisation of Military Associations and Trade Unions (#08099)
- ♦ Europese Organisatie voor Onderzoek en Kankerbehandeling (#08101)
- ♦ Europese Organisatie ter Bescherming van de Rechtspositie van Gedetineerden (internationally oriented national body)
- ♦ Europese Organisatie der Tomatenconserves-industrieën / see European Organisation of Tomato Industries (#08104)
- ♦ Europese Organisatie voor de Veiligheid van de Luchtvaart / see EUROCONTROL (#05667)
- ♦ Europese Organisatie van Verenigingen en Instellingen voor Huisvesting en Bijstand aan Jeugdige Werknemers (inactive)
- ♦ Europese Organisatie voor Wetenschappelijk Plantenonderzoek (#08211)
- ♦ Europese Organisatie der Zagerijen (#08114)
- ♦ Europese Oudervereniging / see European Parents' Association (#08142)
- ♦ Europese Persfoto Unie (inactive)
- ♦ Europese Plantaardig Eiwit Associatie (#09047)
- ♦ Europese Plantaardig Eiwit Federatie / see European Vegetable Protein Association (#09047)
- ♦ Europese Politie-Akademie / see European Union Agency for Law Enforcement Training (#08970)
- ♦ Europese Raad (#06801)
- ♦ Europese Raad voor Jonge Landbouwers (#04689)
- ♦ Europese Raad voor Ruw Leder (inactive)
- ♦ Europese Reizigersfederatie (#08162)
- ♦ Europese Rekenkamer (#06854)
- ♦ Europese Rum Vereniging (no recent information)
- ♦ Europese Schippersorganisatie (#08491)
- ♦ Europese Spaarbankenvereniging / see European Savings and Retail Banking Group (#08426)
- ♦ Europese Specialisten Vereniging / see European Union of Medical Specialists (#09001)
- ♦ Europese Stichting voor Management Development / see EFMD – The Management Development Network (#05387)
- ♦ Europese Stichting tot verbetering van de levens- en arbeidsomstandigheden (#07348)
- ♦ Europese Tafelvoetbal Associatie (inactive)
- ♦ Europese Unie (#08967)
- ♦ Europese Unie voor Alkohol, Brandewijn en Gedistilleerde Dranken (inactive)
- ♦ Europese Unie der Bedartikelennijverheid (inactive)
- ♦ Europese Unie van Christen Demokratische Werknemers (#08981)
- ♦ Europese Unie van de Groothandel in Eieren, Eierprodukten en Gevogelte (#09021)
- ♦ Europese Unie van de Handel in Vee en Vlees (#20394)
- ♦ Europese Unie van Industriën van Aardappelprodukten / see EUPPA – European Potato Processors' Association (#05592)
- ♦ Europese Unie van Melkkleinhandelsorganisaties (inactive)
- ♦ Europese Unie van Nationale Verenigingen van Waterleidingbedrijven / see European Federation of National Associations of Water and Waste Water Services (#07170)
- ♦ Europese Unie van de Onafhankelijken in Smeerstoffen / see Union Européenne de l'Industrie des Lubrifiants (#20398)
- ♦ Europese Unie der Rechters in Handelszaken (#08998)
- ♦ Europese Unie van de Sociale Apoteken (#20401)
- ♦ Europese Unie van Tandartsen (inactive)
- ♦ Europese Unie van Vetsmelters (inactive)
- ♦ Europese Unie van Werknemers in Film en Televisie (inactive)
- ♦ Europese Vennootschap van Ingenieurs en van Industriëlen (internationally oriented national body)
- ♦ Europese Vereniging van Accountants / see European Accounting Association (#05820)
- ♦ Europese Vereniging Band-, Vlecht en Elastiek Artikelen (inactive)
- ♦ Europese Vereniging voor Bank- en Financieel Recht (#02564)
- ♦ Europese Vereniging van Beroepsbrandweerofficieren (no recent information)
- ♦ Europese Vereniging van Binnenhavens / see European Federation of Inland Ports (#07144)
- ♦ Europese Vereniging voor Bloemen en Groenvoorziening (#02570)
- ♦ Europese Vereniging voor Bouwrecht (#08566)
- ♦ Europese Vereniging van Cafeinevrije Koffiefabrikanten (inactive)
- ♦ Europese Vereniging voor Chromatofonie (inactive)
- ♦ Europese Vereniging der Fotografische Industrie (inactive)
- ♦ Europese Vereniging voor Geestelijke Gezondheid en Doofheid (#08649)
- ♦ Europese Vereniging tegen Geluidshinder door Vliegtuigen (#20395)
- ♦ Europese Vereniging van Groenvoeder-Drogerijen (#06896)
- ♦ Europese Vereniging van Groothandelsondernemingen in Zuivelprodukten (#06003)
- ♦ Europese Vereniging voor Haveninformatica (inactive)
- ♦ Europese Vereniging van Hoorapparaten / see European Association of Hearing Aid Professionals (#06066)
- ♦ Europese Vereniging voor Humane Reproductie en Embryologie (#08625)
- ♦ Europese Vereniging van Ijzer- en Staalproducerende Industrieën / see European Steel Association (#08835)
- ♦ Europese Vereniging van Individuele Beleggers (inactive)
- ♦ Europese Vereniging van de Instellingen voor de Inrichting van het Platteland (#06198)
- ♦ Europese Vereniging voor Inwendige Ziekten en Chirurgie bij Vogels / see European College of Zoological Medicine (#06631)
- ♦ Europese Vereniging van Kalkzansteenproducenten (#06430)
- ♦ Europese Vereniging van het Kuurwezen (#08805)
- ♦ Europese Vereniging voor Lichaamsgerichte Psychotherapie / see European Association for Body Psychotherapy (#05958)
- ♦ Europese Vereniging voor Luchtvaartspsychologie (#05950)
- ♦ Europese Vereniging van Merkartikelfabrikanten / see European Brands Association (#06397)
- ♦ Europese Vereniging van het Onderwijzend Personeel (#02565)
- ♦ Europese Vereniging der Podologen (inactive)
- ♦ Europese Vereniging van Producenten van Eéncellige Eiwitten (inactive)
- ♦ Europese Vereniging van Producentenorganisaties in de Visserijsector (#06041)
- ♦ Europese Vereniging van Producten van Industriële Mortels (#07822)
- ♦ Europese Vereniging van Professionele Duikinstructeurs (#06663)
- ♦ Europese Vereniging voor de Promotie van Vouwkartonnage / see Association of European Cartonboard and Carton Manufacturers (#02502)
- ♦ Europese Vereniging voor Scheepvaartinformatica (inactive)
- ♦ Europese Vereniging van Sloopwerken (#06902)
- ♦ Europese Vereniging van Spoorwegpersoneel (#02558)
- ♦ Europese Vereniging van Stafartsen (#02577)
- ♦ Europese Vereniging voor Tandheelkundige Ergonomie / see European Society of Dental Ergonomics (#08577)
- ♦ Europese Vereniging ter Bestrijding van de Vervuiling door de Vezels (inactive)
- ♦ Europese Vereniging ter Bevordering van de Poëzie (inactive)
- ♦ Europese Vereniging voor Terminologie (#06252)
- ♦ Europese Vereniging van Territoriale Vertegenwoordigers van de Staat (no recent information)
- ♦ Europese Vereniging voor Thanatologie (inactive)
- ♦ Europese Vereniging voor Thuiszorg (inactive)
- ♦ Europese Vereniging van Thuiszorgorganisaties (inactive)
- ♦ Europese Vereniging voor de Transfers van Technologie en Opleiding (no recent information)
- ♦ Europese Vereniging van Transportinstituten (inactive)
- ♦ Europese Vereniging voor Vergelijkende Proeven (inactive)
- ♦ Europese Vereniging Via Campesina (#06795)
- ♦ Europese Vereniging van Visproducerende Organisaties / see European Association of Fish Producers Organizations (#06041)
- ♦ Europese Vereniging van Voorzieningen voor Personen met een Handicap (#06204)
- ♦ Europese Vereniging van het Vrije Denken (#06048)
- ♦ Europese Verening voor Onderlinge Borgstelling / see European Association of Guarantee Institutions (#06061)
- ♦ Europese Voedselautoriteit / see European Food Safety Authority (#07287)
- ♦ Europese Volkspartij (#08185)
- ♦ Europese Vrije Alliantie / see European Free Alliance (#07356)
- ♦ Europese Warenbeurs / see European Commodities Exchange (#06674)
- ♦ Europese Wetenschappelijke Vereniging voor Residentiële Hulpverlening en Pleegzorg voor Kinderen en Adolescenten (inactive)
- ♦ Europe's Manufacturers of Building, Automotive and Transport Glass / see Glass for Europe (#10157)
- ♦ Europe's MediaLab (#09818)
- ♦ Europe et Société (#02586)
- ♦ Europe Soya / see Donau Soja (#05116)
- ♦ EUROPETEL / see European Federation for Managers in Technologies of Information and Communication (#07163)
- ♦ **EUROPET** European Pediatrics Thematic Network (#08178)
- ♦ Europe – Third World Association / see eu can aid (#05570)
- ♦ Europe – Third World Centre (internationally oriented national body)
- ♦ EUROPETNET – European Pet Network (unconfirmed)
- ♦ Europe Triathlon / see European Triathlon Union (#08948)
- ♦ EUROPEUM – Institut pro evropskou politiku (internationally oriented national body)
- ♦ Europe United / see European Federalist Party (#07036)
- ♦ EuroPEX / see Association of European Energy Exchanges (#02509)
- ♦ **EUROPEX** Association of European Energy Exchanges (#02509)
- ♦ **EUROPGEN** European Generating Set Association (#07385)

♦ Europharm SMC 09168

Gen Dir 12 Allée de la Recherche, 1070 Brussels, Belgium. T. +3225295842. Fax +3225295872. E-mail: ave@europharmsmc.org – info@europharmsmc.org.
URL: http://www.europharmsmc.org/

History 26 Nov 2001, Paris (France). Registration: Belgium; EU Transparency Register, No/ID: 444624223007-47. **Aims** Promote values of small and medium sized *pharmaceutical* companies; assist and encourage relationships between companies; promote business opportunities; promote information exchange. **Structure** General Assembly. Board. Committee, comprising President, 4 Vice-Presidents, Treasurer and Secretary. **Languages** English. **Staff** 1.00 FTE, paid; 10.00 FTE, voluntary. **Finance** Members' dues. Budget (annual): euro 250,000. **Activities** Working Groups (4): Commercial and Business; Manufacturing and Purchasing; R and D; Regulatory. **Events** *Meeting* Budapest (Hungary) 2020, *Pharma Synergty International Conference* Berlin (Germany) 2019, *Business to Business Meeting* Warsaw (Poland) 2016, *Annual General Meeting* Rome (Italy) 2009, *Annual general meeting* Barcelona (Spain) 2007.
Members Companies in 13 countries:
Austria, Belgium, Bulgaria, Finland, France, Germany, Italy, Poland, Portugal, Spain, Sweden, Switzerland, UK.
[2022/XD9020/**D**]

- ♦ EUROPHOT – Arbeitsgemeinschaft Europäischer Berufsphotographen (inactive)
- ♦ **EUROPHRAS** European Society of Phraseology (#08705)
- ♦ Europhysical Letters Association / see Europhysics Letters Association (#09169)
- ♦ Europhysics Conference on Macromolecular Physics (meeting series)

♦ Europhysics Letters Association (EPL Association) 09169

Editorial Office 6 rue des Frères Lumière, 68200 Mulhouse, France. T. +33389329444. Fax +33389329449. E-mail: editorial.office@epletters.net.
Chair IBM Research Laboratory, 8803 Rüschlikon ZH, Switzerland. T. +4117248522. Fax +4117240084. E-mail: rsl@zurich.ibm.com.
URL: http://www.epletters.net/

History 1986, by *European Physical Society (EPS, #08207)* and several national societies. Also referred to as *Europhysical Letters Association*. **Aims** Contribute to, and promote advancement of *physics*. **Structure** Board of Directors. **Languages** English. **Activities** Research/documentation; knowledge management/information dissemination. **Events** *International Thin-Film Transistor Conference* Tokyo (Japan) 2013. **Publications** *Europhysics Letters* – journal.
[2018.09.05/XG7881/**E**]

- ♦ Europia / see FuelsEurope (#10014)
- ♦ Europianet e Rinj Federaliste (#21984)
- ♦ **Europiano** Union of European Piano Builders' Associations (#20391)
- ♦ EUROPIC – European Study Group on the Molecular Biology of Picornaviruses (meeting series)
- ♦ EUROPILE / see European Portable Battery Association (#08255)
- ♦ EUROPIL – Fédération européenne pour la promotion et l'insertion par le logement et son environnement (inactive)
- ♦ EUROPILOTE – European Organisation of Airline Pilots Associations (inactive)
- ♦ Europ'iske Unions Statistiske Kontor (#19974)

♦ Europlanet Society 09170

Admin Dir c/o ESF, 1 quai Lezay Marnésia, BP 90015, 67080 Strasbourg CEDEX, France. E-mail: contact@europlanet-society.org.
URL: http://www.europlanet-society.org/

History 2018, Berlin (Germany). Launched at European Planetary Science Congress (EPSC). Constitution approved 20 Sep 2018. Registration: EU Transparency Register, No/ID: 114999630727-04. **Aims** Promote advancement of European *planetary science* and related fields for the benefit of the community. **Structure** General Assembly; Executive Board; Executive Office. Hosted by: *European Science Foundation (ESF, #08441)*. **Activities** Events/meetings. **Events** *Europlanet Science Congress (EPSC)* 2025, *Europlanet Science Congress (EPSC)* Helsinki (Finland) 2024, *Europlanet Science Congress* San Antonio, TX (USA) 2023, *European Planetary Science Congress* Granada (Spain) 2022, *European Planetary Science Congress* Helsinki (Finland) 2021. **Publications** *Outreach Newsletter*. **Members** Corporate; Individual. Membership countries not specified.
[2022/XM7492/**E**]

- ♦ EUROPLANT – Comité européen des constructeurs de grands ensembles industriels (no recent information)

♦ Europlate 09171

Contact 20 Marden Grove, Taunton, TA1 2RT, UK. E-mail: enquiries@europlate.org.
URL: http://www.europlate.org/

History 1972, UK. Also referred to as *European Registration Plate Association*. **Aims** Group *automobile license plate collectors*. **Languages** English. **Events** *Biennial Meeting* Vaduz (Liechtenstein) 2016, *Biennial Meeting* Thierhaupten (Germany) 2014, *Biennial Meeting* Trezzo sull'Adda (Italy) 2012, *Biennial Meeting* Paris (France) 2010, *Biennial Meeting* Lyndhurst (UK) 2008. **Publications** *Europlate Newsletter* (4 a year). *Registration Plates of the World* (1994, 2004) – online.

Members Individuals (over 350) in 36 countries:
Andorra, Argentina, Armenia, Australia, Austria, Belgium, Canada, Chile, Czechia, Estonia, Finland, France, Germany, Hungary, India, Ireland, Italy, Japan, Korea Rep, Luxembourg, Mexico, Netherlands, New Zealand, Norway, Portugal, Russia, Slovenia, South Africa, Spain, St Kitts-Nevis, Sweden, Switzerland, UK, United Arab Emirates, Uruguay, USA.
[2020.03.04/XD2487/v/**D**]

♦ Europlatforms / see European Logistic Platforms Association (#07709)
♦ **Europlatforms** European Logistic Platforms Association (#07709)
♦ **Europol** European Police Office (#08239)
♦ Europol Working Group on the Harmonisation of Cybercrime Investigation Training / see European Cybercrime Training and Education Group (#06874)

♦ Euro Pony Club (EPC) 09172

Sec PO Box 9, Kecskemét 6044, Hungary. T. +36703666494. Fax +3676472701.
Pres ringduvevägen 3, SE-541 56 Skövde, Sweden. T. +46500434484.
URL: http://www.europonyclub.eu/

History 1989. **Aims** Foster a greater understanding of individual cultures, languages and peoples through the promotion of youth riding, pony club exchanges, *equestrian* sports and education. **Structure** General Assembly; Board. **Events** *General Assembly* Dillenburg (Germany) 2015, *General Assembly* Germany 2015.
Members Full in 12 countries:
Austria, Belgium, France, Germany, Hungary, Ireland, Italy, Netherlands, Poland, Sweden, Türkiye, UK.
NGO Relations Acknowledged by: *Fédération Équestre Internationale (FEI, #09484).* [2015/XJ9442/**F**]

♦ Europos Audito Rumai (#06854)
♦ Europos Aviacijos Saugos Agentura (#08978)
♦ Europos Bendriju Teisingumo Teismas / see Court of Justice of the European Union (#04938)
♦ Europos cheminiu Medziagu Agentura (#06523)
♦ Europos Ekonomikos ir Socialiniu Reikalu Komitetas (#06963)
♦ Europos Gyvenimo Tyrimo, Integracijos ir Pilietines Visuomenes Akademija (#05799)
♦ Europos Komisija (#06633)
♦ Europos Liaudies Partijos – Krikscioniu Demokratu (#10775)
♦ Europos liberalu democratu ir reformu partija / see Alliance of Liberals and Democrats for Europe Party (#00703)
♦ Europos Ombudsmenas (#08084)
♦ Europos Parlamentas (#08146)
♦ Europos Sajunga (#08967)
♦ Europos Sajungos leidiniu biuras (#18562)
♦ Europos Sajungos Taryba (#04895)
♦ Europos Sajungos Teisingumo Teismas (#04938)
♦ Europos Teisminiu Instituciju Nagrinejanciu Civilenes ir Komercines bylas, Tinklas (#07616)
♦ Europos Vadovu Taryba (#06801)
♦ Europpalaiset Kristilliset Ystävykset (inactive)
♦ EUROPREFAB – Europäische Organisation für den Fertigbau (inactive)
♦ EUROPRESSJUNIOR – Association européenne des éditeurs de publications pour la jeunesse (inactive)
♦ EUROPREV / see European Network for Prevention and Health Promotion in Family Medicine and General Practice (#07974)
♦ **EUROPREV** European Network for Prevention and Health Promotion in Family Medicine and General Practice (#07974)
♦ **EuroPris** European Organisation of Prison and Correctional Services (#08100)
♦ EUROPRO / see European PRO Committee (#08280)
♦ **EUROPRO** European PRO Committee (#08280)
♦ Europrofiles – European Association of Bead and Lath Producers (unconfirmed)
♦ Európska Agentúra pre Bezpecnost' Letectva (#08978)
♦ Európska Akadémia pre Vyskum Zivota, Integraciu a Obciansku Spolocnost (#05799)
♦ Europska Akademija za Istrazivanje Zivota, Integraciju i Civilno Drustvo (#05799)
♦ Európska Chemicka Agentúra (#06523)
♦ Európska Federacia pre Rozvoj Produktivity (#07196)
♦ Európska Justicvna siet v Civilnih in Gospodarskih Zadevah (#07616)
♦ Európska Komisia (#06633)
♦ Europska Komisija (#06633)
♦ Európska liberalna, demokraticka a reformna strana / see Alliance of Liberals and Democrats for Europe Party (#00703)
♦ Európska Rada (#06801)
♦ Europska siet komunitneho organizovani (#06681)
♦ Europska Soudni sit ve Vecech Obcanskych a Obchoichnich (#07616)
♦ Európska Unia (#08967)
♦ Europska Unija (#08967)
♦ Europska zaklada za filantropiju i drusveni razvoj (internationally oriented national body)
♦ Európske Monitorovacie Centrum pre Drogy a Drogovú Zavislost (#07820)
♦ Europske Observatorium Multilingvizmu (internationally oriented national body)
♦ Europski Gospodarski i Socijalni Odbor (#06963)
♦ Europski odbor regija (#06665)
♦ Europski Ombudsman (#08084)
♦ Europski Parlament (#08146)
♦ Europski Revizorski Sud (#06854)
♦ Europsko Vijece (#06801)
♦ Europsku Sluzbu za Vanjsko Djelovanje (#07018)
♦ Európsky Dvor Auditorov (#06854)
♦ Európsky Hospodarsky a Socialny Vybor (#06963)
♦ Európsky Ombudsman (#08084)
♦ Európsky Parlament (#08146)
♦ Európsky výbor regiónov (#06665)
♦ EURO-PSO / see European Federation of National Psoriasis Patients Associations (#07175)
♦ **EUROPSO** European Federation of National Psoriasis Patients Associations (#07175)
♦ EUROPTICA – European Federation of Applied Optics (inactive)

♦ Europt(r)ode 09173

Contact Dept Organic Chemistry, Complutense Univ of Madrid, Av Séneca 2, 28040 Madrid, Spain. T. +34913944220. E-mail: contact@europtrode.org.
URL: https://www.europtrode.org/

History 1991, Graz (Austria). Former names and other names: *Permanent Steering Committee of the Conference on Optical Chemical Sensors and Biosensors* – full title. **Aims** Stimulate and spread the interest of the scientific and technical community, as well as the general public, for research, development and applications of optical chemical sensors and biosensors. **Structure** Permanent Steering Committee, headed by Chairman. **Languages** English. **Activities** Events/meetings; guidance/assistance/consulting; knowledge management/information dissemination; networking/liaising; research and development; training/education. **Events** *EUROPTRODE : European Conference on Optical Chemical Sensors and Biosensors* Birmingham (UK) 2024, *EUROPTRODE : European Conference on Optical Chemical Sensors and Biosensors* Warsaw (Poland) 2021, *EUROPTRODE : European Conference on Optical Chemical Sensors and Biosensors* Naples (Italy) 2018, *EUROPTRODE : European Conference on Optical Chemical Sensors and Biosensors* Graz (Austria) 2016, *EUROPTRODE : European Conference on Optical Chemical Sensors and Biosensors* Athens (Greece) 2014.
[2020.11.17/XJ6455/c/**E**]

♦ Europulp 09174

Sec address not obtained. E-mail: europulpsec@outlook.com.
Pres Turkish Pulp Club, Reis Pazarlama Ve Ticaret AS, Mektep Sok No 10, 34330 Istanbul/Istanbul, Türkiye.
URL: http://www.europulp.eu/

History 21 Jan 1999, Brussels (Belgium). **Aims** Promote the common interests of member associations and their members. **Structure** Meeting of Delegates (twice a year); Executive Committee. **Languages** English. **Staff** 1.00 FTE, voluntary. **Finance** Sources: members' dues. **Activities** Events/meetings. **Events** *Seminar* 2020, *Seminar* Barcelona (Spain) 2020. **Publications** *Europulp Port Stocks* (12 a year).
Members Full in 10 countries:
Belgium, France, Germany, Italy, Netherlands, Portugal, Spain, Switzerland, Türkiye, UK. [2020.08.10/XD7207/**D**]

♦ **EUROPUMP** European Association of Pump Manufacturers (#06182)
♦ **EUROPUR** European Association of Flexible Polyurethane Foam Blocks Manufacturers (#06042)
♦ EuroQSAR – European Quantitative Structure-Activity Relationships (meeting series)
♦ EURORAD – European Association of Manufacturers of Radiators (inactive)
♦ **EURORAI** European Organization of Regional External Public Audit Finance Institutions (#08113)
♦ **EuroRAP** European Road Assessment Programme (#08392)
♦ EURORDIS / see EURORDIS – Rare Diseases Europe (#09175)

♦ EURORDIS – Rare Diseases Europe 09175

CEO c/o Plateforme Maladies Rares, 96 rue Didot, 75014 Paris, France. T. +33156535210. Fax +33156535215. E-mail: eurordis@eurordis.org.
Gen Sec In den Dellen 21, 51515 Kürten, Germany. T. +4922849869.
URL: http://www.eurordis.org/

History Mar 1997, Paris (France). Founding members: French patient organizations (4) dealing with muscular dystrophy, cystic fibrosis, AIDS and cancer. Former names and other names: *European Organization for Rare Disorders (EURORDIS)* – former; *Organisation européenne des maladies rares* – former; *European Organisation for Rare Diseases (EURORDIS)* – former; *Association européenne des maladies rares* – former. Registration: RNA, No/ID: W751129742, Start date: 1997, France; SIREN, No/ID: 413459066, France; EU Transparency Register, No/ID: 93272076510-87, Start date: 30 Aug 2011. **Aims** Improve the lives of all persons living with a rare disease. **Structure** General Assembly (annual); Board of Directors; European Headquarters located in Paris (France). **Languages** English, French, German, Italian, Portuguese, Russian, Spanish. **Staff** 47.00 FTE, paid. **Finance** Sources: members' dues. Other sources: grants from *European Commission (EC, #06633)* and private sources. **Activities** Advocacy/lobbying/activism; awareness raising; events/meetings; networking/liaising. **Events** *Annual General Assembly* Paris (France) 2023, *EURORDIS Membership Meeting* Stockholm (Sweden) 2023, *Annual General Assembly* Paris (France) 2022, *European Conference on Rare Diseases and Orphan Products* Paris (France) 2022, *European PF Patient Summit* Gentbrugge (Belgium) 2021. **Publications** Position papers; fact-sheets.
Members Rare disease organizations (1,012): Full; Associate. Organizations 74 countries and territories:
Albania, Algeria, Andorra, Argentina, Armenia, Australia, Austria, Belarus, Belgium, Benin, Bosnia-Herzegovina, Brazil, Bulgaria, Burkina Faso, Canada, China, Colombia, Croatia, Cyprus, Czechia, Denmark, Estonia, Finland, France, Georgia, Germany, Greece, Guatemala, Hong Kong, Hungary, Iceland, India, Iran Islamic Rep, Ireland, Israel, Italy, Japan, Kazakhstan, Kosovo, Latvia, Lebanon, Lithuania, Luxembourg, Malaysia, Malta, Mexico, Moldova, Montenegro, Morocco, Nepal, Netherlands, New Zealand, North Macedonia, Norway, Poland, Portugal, Romania, Russia, Serbia, Singapore, Slovakia, Slovenia, South Africa, Spain, Sweden, Switzerland, Taiwan, Türkiye, UK, Ukraine, Uruguay, USA, Venezuela, Zimbabwe.
Full members organizations include 48 organizations listed in this Yearbook:
– *Aniridia Europe (#00845)*;
– *Association Francophone des Glycogénoses (AFG)*;
– *Association Ollier Maffuci Europe*;
– *Childhood Cancer International Europe (CCI Europe, #03872)*;
– *CMTC-OVM*;
– *Cutis Laxa Internationale (CLI)*;
– *Cystic Fibrosis Europe (CF Europe, #04991)*;
– *DEBRA International (#05021)*;
– *Dravet Syndrome European Foundation (DSEF, #05130)*;
– *Esophageal ATresia Global Support Groups (EAT, #05540)*;
– *European Alliance of Neuromuscular Disorders Associations (EAMDA, #05876)*;
– *European Association of Patients Organizations of Sarcoidosis and other Granulomatous Disorders (EPOS, #06144)*;
– *European Chromosome 11 Network (#06547)*;
– *European Federation of Associations of Patients with Haemochromatosis (EFAPH, #07056)*;
– *European Federation of Hereditary Ataxias (Euro-ATAXIA, #07138)*;
– *European Federation of National HSP Associations (EURO-HSP, #07171)*;
– *European Federation of Williams Syndrome (FEWS, #07234)*;
– *European Haemophilia Consortium (EHC, #07444)*;
– *European Huntington Association (EHA, #07509)*;
– *European Network for Ichthyosis (ENI)*;
– *European Network for Research on Alternating Hemiplegia (ENRAH, #07987)*;
– *European Polio Union (EPU, #08246)*;
– *European Tuberous Sclerosis Complex Association (ETSC, #08955)*;
– *Federation of European Patient Groups Affected by Renal Genetic Diseases (FEDERG, #09526)*;
– *FSHD Europe (#10011)*;
– *HHT Europe*;
– *Hypophosphatasie Europe*;
– *International Federation for Spina Bifida and Hydrocephalus (IF SBH, #13552)*;
– *International Federation of National CdLS Support Organizations (CDLS World)*;
– *International Gaucher Alliance (IGA, #13701)*;
– *International Mito Patients (IMP, #14171)*;
– *International Niemann-Pick Disease Alliance (INPDA, #14371)*;
– *International Patient Organization for Primary Immunodeficiencies (IPOPI, #14533)*;
– *International Prader-Willi Syndrome Organisation (IPWSO, #14633)*;
– *LGD Alliance Europe (LGDA Europe, #16451)*;
– *Marfan Europe Network (M.E.N., #16573)*;
– *MPS Europe (#16877)*;
– *NBIA Alliance (#16961)*;
– *Osteogenesis Imperfecta Federation Europe (OIFE, #17907)*;
– *Pierre Robin Europe*;
– *Retina International (RI, #18926)*;
– *Rett Syndrome Europe (RSE, #18928)*;
– *Ring14 International (#18950)*;
– *SMA Europe (#19310)*;
– *Thalassaemia International Federation (#20139)*;
– *The Dysmelia Network (DysNet, #05149)*;
– *Thyroid Cancer Alliance (TCA, #20157)*;
– *World Duchenne Organization (WDO, #21366)*.
Associate include 51 organizations listed in this Yearbook:
– *22q11 Europe (#22043)*;
– *AHC Federation of Europe (AHCFE, #00585)*;
– *Alström Syndrome International (ASI, #00750)*;
– *Association Francophone contre la Polychondrite Chronique Atrophiante (AFPCA)*;
– *Children's Tumor Foundation Europe (CTF Europe, #03880)*;
– *Christianson Syndrome Europe (CS-Europe)*;
– *Chromosome 18 Registry and Research Society Europe (Chromosome 18 Europe, #03910)*;
– *Cystinosis Foundation*;
– *Empty Nose Syndrome International Association (ENSIA, #05448)*;
– *European Cavernoma Alliance*;
– *European Cleft Organisation (ECO, #06572)*;
– *European CMT Federation (ECMTF, #06586)*;
– *European Congenital Heart Disease Organisation (ECHDO, #06738)*;
– *European Federation Lesch-Nyhan Disease (LNDE)*;
– *European FH Patient Network (FH Europe, #07243)*;
– *European Idiopathic Pulmonary Fibrosis and Related Disorders Federation (EU-IPFF, #07515)*;
– *European Lung Foundation (ELF, #07718)*;
– *European MEN Alliance (EMENA, #07779)*;
– *European Myasthenia Gravis Association (EuMGA, #07844)*;
– *European Network for Rare and Congenital Anaemias (ENERCA, #07982)*;
– *European Patient Organisation for Dysimmune and Inflammatory Neuropathies (EPODIN, #08169)*;
– *European Sarcoidosis Foundation*;
– *European Sickle Cell Federation (ESCF, #08484)*;
– *European Society for Phenylketonuria and Allied Disorders (ESPKU, #08697)*;
– *European VHL (von Hippel-Lindau) Federation (VHL-Europa, #09060)*;

- *Fabry International Network (FIN, #09231)*;
- *Familial Mediterranean Fever and Autoinflammatory Diseased Global Association (FMF & AID Global Association)*;
- *Federation of European Scleroderma Associations (FESCA, #09540)*;
- *Fondation Internationale Tierno et Mariam (FITIMA)*;
- *Global DARE Foundation (#10315)*;
- *HAE International (HAEi, #10846)*;
- *International Brain Tumour Alliance (IBTA, #12393)*;
- *International FOXG1 Foundation*;
- *International Huntington Association (IHA, #13824)*;
- *International Painful Bladder Foundation (IPBF, #14499)*;
- *International Pemphigus and Pemphigoid Foundation*;
- *International Porphyria Patient Network (IPPN, #14621)*;
- *International WAGR Syndrome Association (IWSA)*;
- *International Waldenstrom's Macroglobulinemia Foundation (IWMF)*;
- *Liver Patients International (LPI, #16498)*;
- *LUPUS EUROPE (#16524)*;
- *Myeloma Patients Europe (MPE, #16924)*;
- *Naevus Global*;
- *NephcEurope (#16974)*;
- *Pulmonary Hypertension Association Europe (PHA Europe, #18575)*;
- *SIOP Europe (SIOPE, #19288)*;
- *Sjögren Europe (#19302)*;
- *Thyroid Federation International (TFI, #20158)*;
- *World Alliance of Pituitary Organizations (WAPO, #21087)*;
- *World Federation for Incontinence and Pelvic Problems (WFIPP, #21440)*;
- *XLPDR International Association.*

Consultative Status Consultative status granted from: *ECOSOC (#05331)* (Special). **NGO Relations** Member of (10): *EU Health Coalition*; *European Alliance for Personalised Medicine (EAPM, #05878)*; *European Alliance for Transformative Therapies (TRANSFORM, #05889)*; *European Cancer Organisation (ECO, #06432)* (Patient Advisory Committee); *European Patients' Academy on Therapeutic Innovation (EUPATI, #08170)*; *European Patients' Forum (EPF, #08172)*; *International Alliance of Patients' Organizations (IAPO, #11633)*; *Rare Cancers Europe (RCE, #18620)*; *Rare Diseases International (RDI, #18621)* (Founding); *Workgroup of European Cancer Patient Advocacy Networks (WECAN, #21054)*. Stakeholder in: *European Network for Health Technology Assessment (EUnetHTA, #07921)*. [2022.10.28/XD6342/y/**D**]

- ♦ **EuroRec Institute** European Institute for Health Records (#07560)
- ♦ EUROREG / see Centre for European Regional and Local Studies
- ♦ EUROREG – Centre for European Regional and Local Studies (internationally oriented national body)
- ♦ Euroregional Center for Democracy (internationally oriented national body)

♦ Euroregion Baltic (ERB) 09176

Contact Warmińsko-Mazurskie Marshal's Office, Emilii Plater 1, 10-562 Olsztyn, Poland.
Contact address not obtained.
URL: http://www.eurobalt.org/

History 22 Feb 1998. Founded following a conference 28 Feb – 1 Mar 1997. Registration: Poland. **Aims** Improve *living conditions* of those living along *border regions*; intensify economic and country development, environment protection, local actions, development of culture and cultural centres, development of transborder infrastructure, creation of advantageous conditions to cooperation in the fields of science, education, tourism, health protection and public assistance, study of neighbouring languages and development of a media network. **Structure** Council of up to 48 Councillors, comprising up to 8 representatives of each country. Executive Board of 21 members. Praesidium, comprising one representative of each country. Officers: President; Vice-President. Presidency and Secretariat rotate. **Activities** Working Groups (5): Spatial Planning; Tourism; Social Affairs; Transport; Ecology. Organizes seminars, sessions and exhibitions. **Events** *Annual Forum of Euroregion Baltic Stakeholders / Annual Forum* Gdansk (Poland) 2015, *Annual Forum of Euroregion Baltic Stakeholders / Annual Forum* Gdansk (Poland) 2014, *Annual Forum of Euroregion Baltic Stakeholders / Annual Forum* Kalmar (Sweden) 2013, *Annual Forum of Euroregion Baltic Stakeholders / Annual Forum* Nexo (Denmark) 2012, *Annual Forum of Euroregion Baltic Stakeholders / Annual Forum* Gdansk (Poland) 2011. **Publications** *Baltyk* – bulletin in Polish. Annual report.
Members Cities in 6 countries:
Denmark, Latvia, Lithuania, Poland, Russia, Sweden. [2022/XD7511/**D**]

- ♦ **EUROROC** European and International Federation of Natural Stone Industries (#07587)
- ♦ **EURORSA** Rescue Swimmers Association (#18850)
- ♦ Eurorühm (#05689)
- ♦ Euroryhmä (#05689)

♦ EUROSAC 09177

General Delegate 23/25 rue d'Aumale, 75009 Paris, France. T. +33147237558. Fax +33147236753. E-mail: info@eurosac.org.
URL: http://www.eurosac.org/

History 30 Jun 1952, Paris (France). Full title: *Fédération européenne des fabricants de sacs papier à grande contenance (EUROSAC) – European Federation of Multiwall Paper Sack Manufacturers – Europäische Vereinigung der Papiersackfabrikanten – Federazione Europea dei Fabbricanti di Sacchi Carta a Grande Contenuto – Federación Europea de Fabricantes de Sacos de Papel de Gran Contenido*. EU Transparency Register: 44757608446-73. **Aims** Safeguard and promote the *paper sack* industry and defend its professional and economic interests; maintain mutual respect among members; offer a forum for members to define common positions. **Structure** General Assembly (annual); Executive Board; Committees (4). **Languages** English, French, German. **Staff** 2.00 FTE, paid. **Finance** Members' dues. **Events** *Annual Congress* Bilbao (Spain) 2021, *Annual Congress* Vienna (Austria) 2020, *Annual Congress* Ljubljana (Slovenia) 2019, *Annual Congress* Valletta (Malta) 2018, *Annual Congress* Hamburg (Germany) 2017. **Members** Ordinary; Corresponding; Associate. Membership countries not specified. **NGO Relations** Member of: *International Confederation of Paper and Board Converters in Europe (CITPA, #12866)*. In liaison with technical committees of: *International Organization for Standardization (ISO, #14473)*. [2020/XD0737/**D**]

♦ Eurosafe 09178

SG Burton Safes, Brockholes Business Park, Rock Mill Road, Holmfirth, HD7 7BN, UK. T. +441484663388. Fax +441484666338.
URL: http://www.eurosafe-online.com/

History 24 May 1988, Paris (France). Sub-title: *European Committee of Safe Manufacturers Associations*. **Aims** Represent the interests of the European safe industry including products for *burglary* and *fire resistance*. **Structure** General Assembly; Presidential Committee. **Languages** English. **Finance** Members' dues. **Activities** Networking/liaising; certification/accreditation; standards/guidelines.
Members National associations (14) in 14 countries:
Austria, Belgium, Bulgaria, Finland, France, Germany, Ireland, Italy, Lithuania, Netherlands, Slovenia, Spain, Sweden, UK.
NGO Relations Cooperates with: *European Fire and Security Group (EFSG, #07259)*. [2018.09.10/XF3024/**F**]

- ♦ **EuroSafe** European Association for Injury Prevention and Safety Promotion (#06083)
- ♦ **EUROSAF** European Sailing Federation (#08421)
- ♦ **EUROSAI** European Organization of Supreme Audit Institutions (#08115)
- ♦ **EUROSAM** European Society for Applied Mathematics (#08521)
- ♦ EuroScan / see international HealthTechScan (#13784)
- ♦ EuroScan international network / see international HealthTechScan (#13784)
- ♦ EUROSCIA – European Organization of Scientific Anti-Aging Medicine (inactive)
- ♦ **EUROSCIENCE** Association européenne pour la promotion de la science et de la technologie (#05927)
- ♦ **EUROSCIENCE** European Association for the Advancement of Science and Technology (#05927)
- ♦ **EuroSDR** European Spatial Data Research (#08806)
- ♦ **EUROSEAS** European Association for South-East Asian Studies (#06217)
- ♦ EuroSECT – European Society of Extracorporeal Technology (inactive)

♦ Euroseeds 09179

SG Avenue des Arts 52, 7th floor, 1000 Brussels, Belgium. T. +3227432860. E-mail: secretariat@euroseeds.eu.
URL: http://www.euroseeds.eu/

History Nov 2000. Founded on merger of *Association of Common Market Potato Breeders (inactive)*, *Association des établissements multiplicateurs de semences fourragères des CE (AMUFOC, inactive)*, *Association of Plant Breeders of the European Economic Community (COMASSO, inactive)* and *Comité des semences du Marché commun (COSEMCO, inactive)*. Since Nov 2010, also includes *Eastern European Seed Network (EESNET, inactive)*. Former names and other names: *European Seed Association (ESA)* – former. Registration: Banque-Carrefour des Entreprises, No/ID: 0478.219.205, Start date: 5 Sep 2002, Belgium; EU Transparency Register, No/ID: 11362308587-10, Start date: 16 Apr 2012. **Aims** Represent the interests of those active in research, breeding, production and marketing of seeds of agricultural, horticultural and ornamental plant species. **Structure** General Assembly; Board; Committees (2); Sections (7); General Secretariat. **Languages** English. **Staff** 12.00 FTE, paid. **Finance** Sources: members' dues. **Activities** Events/meetings. **Events** *Congress* Copenhagen (Denmark) 2024, *Congress* St Julian's (Malta) 2023, *Congress* Berlin (Germany) 2022, *Congress* Prague (Czechia) 2021, *Congress* Brussels (Belgium) 2020.
Members Association membership; Individual; Associate. Association members in 28 countries:
Austria, Belgium, Bulgaria, Croatia, Czechia, Denmark, Estonia, Finland, France, Germany, Greece, Hungary, Ireland, Italy, Latvia, Netherlands, Poland, Portugal, Romania, Serbia, Slovakia, Slovenia, Spain, Sweden, Switzerland, Türkiye, UK, Ukraine.
Individual in 9 countries:
Denmark, France, Germany, Ireland, Netherlands, Romania, Spain, Switzerland, UK.
Associate in 13 countries:
Belgium, Denmark, France, Germany, Ireland, Italy, Morocco, Netherlands, Russia, Serbia, Switzerland, UK, USA.
NGO Relations Member of (5): *Agri-Food Chain Coalition (AFCC, #00577)*; *European Network of Agricultural Journalists (ENAJ, #07864)* (Associate); *European Oilseed Alliance (EOA, #08080)* (Associate); *European Policy Centre (EPC, #08240)*; *European Technology Platform 'Plants for the Future' (Plant ETP, #08890)*. [2022/XD6731/**D**]

- ♦ Eurosensors (meeting series)
- ♦ Euroshareholders (inactive)
- ♦ Euroshareholders / see BETTER FINANCE (#03219)
- ♦ **EUROSHNET** European Occupational Safety and Health Network (#08074)

♦ Euroshore International 09180

SG Esplanade 1 – Box 87, 1020 Brussels, Belgium. T. +3227579170. E-mail: info@euroshore.com.
URL: http://www.euroshore.com/

History 1998. Registration: Belgium; EU Transparency Register, No/ID: 35204533304-65. **Aims** Promote and further the interests of companies active in *ships waste* collection, management and valorization. **Structure** Board; Executive Committee. **Languages** English. **Staff** 1.00 FTE, paid. **Finance** Members' dues. Annual budget: about euro 100,000. **Activities** Advocacy/lobbying/activism; monitoring/evaluation; events/meetings; training/education; guidance/assistance/consulting.
Members Full in 17 countries and territories:
Belgium, Bulgaria, Croatia, Denmark, France, Germany, Ghana, Gibraltar, Greece, Malta, Netherlands, Nigeria, Portugal, Spain, Türkiye, UK, United Arab Emirates.
IGO Relations *European Commission (EC, #06633)*; *European Maritime Safety Agency (EMSA, #07744)*; *European Parliament (EP, #08146)*; *International Maritime Organization (IMO, #14102)*. [2020.03.17/XM7217/**D**]

- ♦ Eurosif / see European Sustainable Investment Forum (#08865)
- ♦ **EUROSIF** European Sustainable Investment Forum (#08865)
- ♦ **EUROSIL** European Association of Industrial Silica Producers (#06082)
- ♦ EuroSim / see Trans-Atlantic Consortium for European Union Studies and Simulations (#20202)
- ♦ EuroSimE – International Conference on Thermal, Mechanical and Multi-Physics Simulation and Experiments in Microelectronics and Microsystems (meeting series)
- ♦ **EUROSIM** Federation of European Simulation Societies (#09544)
- ♦ EurOSInet – European Interoperability Testing Association (inactive)
- ♦ **EUROSIS** European Multidisciplinary Society for Modelling and Simulation Technology (#07832)

♦ Eurosite 09181

Network Development Manager Postbus 90154, 5000 LG Tilburg, Netherlands. T. +31135944400.
URL: http://www.eurosite.org/

History Nov 1989, Rochefort-sur-Mer (France). Derives from *European Natural Sites Twinning Programme*, set up 1987, uniting public and private organizations managing Europe's natural heritage. Also known as *European Network of Site Management Organizations*. EU Transparency Register: 40754955270-22. **Aims** Provide opportunities for practitioners to network and exchange experience on practical *nature* management. **Structure** Council; Board; Secretariat. **Languages** Dutch, English, French. **Staff** 3.00 FTE, paid. **Finance** Members' dues. Other sources: grants; public bodies. **Activities** Events/meetings. **Events** *Annual Meeting* Barcelona (Spain) 2021, *Annual Meeting* Budapest (Hungary) 2018, *Conference on How People and the Economy Can Benefit from Nature* Brussels (Belgium) 2017, *Annual Meeting* Espoo (Finland) 2017, *Annual Meeting* Haarlem (Netherlands) 2014. **Publications** *Eurosite Review* (annual). Workshop proceedings; special reports; management planning toolkit. **Information Services** *European Facilitation Service (EFS)*.
Members Organizations (64), including public bodies, private organizations and NGOs which have land holdings and manage natural areas in Europe in 19 countries:
Belgium, Cyprus, Czechia, Finland, France, Germany, Greece, Hungary, Ireland, Italy, Lithuania, Luxembourg, Netherlands, Poland, Romania, Slovenia, Spain, Sweden, UK.
Included in the above, 2 organizations listed in this Yearbook:
A Rocha International (#18965); *ECNC – European Centre for Nature Conservation (#05289)*.
IGO Relations *European Commission (EC, #06633)*. **NGO Relations** Instrumental in setting up: *EECONET Action Fund (EAF, #05383)*. Member of: *European Habitats Forum (EHF, #07443)*. [2018.06.01/XF2304/**F**]

- ♦ **EuroSIVA** European Society of Intravenous Anaesthesia (#08635)
- ♦ **EUROSKIN** European Society of Skin Cancer Prevention (#08735)
- ♦ Euroskupina (#05689)
- ♦ **EUROSLA** European Second Language Association (#08456)
- ♦ EUROSLAG (internationally oriented national body)
- ♦ Euro Slate – Association of European Slate Producers (inactive)

♦ EUROSMART 09182

Contact Square de Meeûs 35, 1000 Brussels, Belgium. T. +3228803635. E-mail: info@eurosmart.com.
URL: http://www.eurosmart.com/

History 1995, as *European Smart Card Group*. Subsequently changed name to *European Smart Card Industry Association (EUROSMART)*. Tagline: The Voice of the Smart Security Industry. Registered in accordance with Belgian law. EU Transparency Register: 21856815315-64. **Aims** Expand the Smart Secure Devices market worldwide; promote Smart Security standards; improve quality *security* applications and services. **Structure** General Assembly (annual). Steering Committee, comprising Chairman, 2 Vice Chairmen, Treasurer, General Secretary and all Executive members. Working Groups. **Activities** Advocacy/lobbying/activism. **Events** *Annual General Assembly* Brussels (Belgium) 2013, *Meeting on Security and Privacy in the Digital World* Brussels (Belgium) 2012, *Meeting* Brussels (Belgium) 2005, *Annual e-Smart conference* Sophia Antipolis (France) 2005, *Annual e-Smart conference* Sophia Antipolis (France) 2004. **Publications** Position papers. **Members** Executive (12); Active (5); Partners (2); Associate (3); Individuals (3). Membership countries not specified. [2019/XD6151/**E**]

♦ EUROSOLAR – European Association for Renewable Energy 09183

Europäische Vereinigung für Erneuerbare Energien

Main Office Kaiser-Friedrich-Str 11, 53113 Bonn, Germany. T. +49228362373. Fax +49228361279. E-mail: info@eurosolar.org.
URL: http://www.eurosolar.org/

History Founded 1988, as *European Association for Solar Energy (EUROSOLAR) – Europäische Sonnenenergievereinigung*. Sometimes also referred to as *European Solar Energy Organization*. **Aims** Promote renewable energy as a substitution for nuclear and fossil energy. **Structure** Assembly of Delegates; General Executive Committee; National Sections, each with Executive Committee. **Languages** English, French, German, Italian, Spanish. **Finance** Members' dues. **Activities** Politics/policy/regulatory; standards/guidelines; events/meetings. **Events** *IRES : International Renewable Energy Storage Conference* Bonn (Germany) 2021, *IRES : International Renewable Energy Storage Conference* Düsseldorf (Germany) 2019, *IRES : International Renewable Energy Storage Conference* Düsseldorf (Germany) 2018, *IRES : International Renewable Energy Storage Conference* Düsseldorf (Germany) 2017, *IRES : International Renewable Energy Storage Conference* Düsseldorf (Germany) 2016. **Publications** *Solarzeitalter – Politik und Ökonomie Erneuerbarer Energien* (4 a year). Memoranda; books; conference proceedings.
Members Individuals and organizations. National sections in 13 countries:
Austria, Bulgaria, Czechia, Denmark, Georgia, Germany, Hungary, Italy, Luxembourg, Russia, Spain, Türkiye, Ukraine.
IGO Relations *United Nations Framework Convention on Climate Change – Secretariat (UNFCCC, #20564)*. Proposed and works for an *International Renewable Energy Agency (IRENA, #14715)*. **NGO Relations** *Global 100% RE (#10160)*; *International Network for Sustainable Energy (INFORSE, #14331)*; *International Solar Energy Society (ISES, #15564)*; *World Council for Renewable Energy (WCRE, #21340)*; *World Wind Energy Institute (WWEI, #21938)*. Member of: *World Wind Energy Association (WWEA, #21937)*. [2020/XD2634/D]

- ♦ EUROSOLAR / see EUROSOLAR – European Association for Renewable Energy (#09183)
- ♦ **Eurosophia** European Association of University Classics Teachers (#06260)
- ♦ **EUROSPACE** Association of European Space Industry (#02544)
- ♦ Euro Space Foundation / see Euro Space Society
- ♦ Euro Space Society (internationally oriented national body)
- ♦ EUROSPACEWARD – European Spaceward Association (unconfirmed)

♦ EuroSpill Association 09184

Contact Antrobus House, 18 College Street, Petersfield, GU31 4AD, UK. T. +443334441890. E-mail: info@eurospill.com.
URL: https://eurospill.com/

History 2004, Trondheim (Norway), at Interspill event. Trading name for Eurospill Ltd, a non-for-profit company registered in the UK. **Aims** Provide a web-based network across European countries to enable companies in each country to be connected with European industry. **Finance** Members' dues. **Events** *Interspill International Conference* Amsterdam (Netherlands) 2022, *Interspill International Conference* Amsterdam (Netherlands) 2021, *Interspill International Conference* London (UK) 2018, *Interspill International Conference* Amsterdam (Netherlands) 2015, *Interspill International Conference* Marseille (France) 2009.
Members Full in 9 countries:
Belgium, Croatia, France, Netherlands, Norway, Spain, Sweden, Türkiye, UK.
Included in the above, 1 organization listed in this Yearbook:
Sea Alarm Foundation (#19164). [2022/XJ0082/y/E]

- ♦ **EUROSPINE** EUROSPINE – Spine Society of Europe (#09185)

♦ EUROSPINE – Spine Society of Europe (EUROSPINE) 09185

Contact c/o Pfister Treuhand, Bankstr 4, 8610 Uster ZH, Switzerland. E-mail: info@eurospine.org.
URL: http://www.eurospine.org/

History 26 Jun 1998, Innsbruck (Austria). Founded on merger of *European Spinal Deformities Society (ESDS, inactive)* and *European Spine Society (inactive)*. Registration: Belgium. **Aims** Stimulate exchange of knowledge and ideas in the field of research, prevention and treatment of spine diseases and related problems; coordinate efforts undertaken in European countries for further development in this field. **Structure** General Assembly; Executive Committee; Councils (5); Committees (11). **Languages** English. **Finance** Members' dues. Meeting proceeds. **Activities** Events/meetings; awards/prizes/competitions; training/education. **Events** *Annual Meeting* Frankfurt-Main (Germany) 2023, *Annual Meeting* Milan (Italy) 2022, *Spring Specialty Meeting* Frankfurt-Main (Germany) 2021, *Annual Meeting* Vienna (Austria) 2021, *Annual Meeting* Uster (Switzerland) 2020. **Publications** *European Spine Journal* (12 a year); *My EUROSPINE News* (12 a year); *EUROSPINE Bulletin* (6 a year). Annual Report. **Members** Active; Corresponding; Senior; Honorary; Young; Associated; Institutional. Individuals in over 65 countries. Membership countries not specified. [2022/XD6776/D]

- ♦ Eurosport (internationally oriented national body)
- ♦ EuroSTAR Software Testing Conference (meeting series)
- ♦ Eurostat / see Statistical Office of the European Union (#19974)
- ♦ **Eurostat** Statistical Office of the European Union (#19974)

♦ Euro-Par Steering Committee 09186

Main Office c/o GWDG, Am Fassberg 11, 37077 Göttingen, Germany. E-mail: gwdg@gwdg.de.
Chair c/o ENS Rennes, Av Robert Schuman, 35170 Rennes, France.
URL: http://www.euro-par.org/

Aims Promote and advance all aspects of parallel and distributed *computing*. **Structure** Steering Committee, including Chair and Vice-Chair. Advisory Board. **Activities** Offers Achievement Award. **Events** *EURO-PAR : European Conference on Parallel Distributed Computing* Glasgow (UK) 2022, *EURO-PAR : European Conference on Parallel Distributed Computing* Lisbon (Portugal) 2021, *EURO-PAR : European Conference on Parallel Distributed Computing* Göttingen (Germany) 2020, *EURO-PAR : European Conference on Parallel Distributed Computing* Göttingen (Germany) 2019, *EURO-PAR : European Conference on Parallel Distributed Computing* Milan (Italy) 2018. **Publications** Conference proceedings.
Members Individuals in 8 countries:
France, Germany, Greece, Italy, Netherlands, Portugal, Spain, UK. [2021/XJ6412/c/E]

- ♦ Eurostep / see Europe External Programme with Africa (#09155)
- ♦ Eurosur – European Union – Mercosur (inactive)
- ♦ Euro Synergy Network (inactive)
- ♦ **Eurotalc** Scientific Association of European Talc Industry (#19146)
- ♦ EUROTALENT / see European Committee Promoting the Education of Gifted and Talented Young People (#06664)
- ♦ **EUROTALENT** European Committee Promoting the Education of Gifted and Talented Young People (#06664)
- ♦ **EUROTAS- Global Transpersonal Network** European Transpersonal Association (#08937)
- ♦ Euro TB – Surveillance de la tuberculose dans les pays de la région Europe de l'OMS / see European Tuberculosis Surveillance Network (#08954)
- ♦ EuroTB – Surveillance of Tuberculosis in Europe / see European Tuberculosis Surveillance Network (#08954)
- ♦ EuroTB – Tuberculosis Cases Notified in Europe / see European Tuberculosis Surveillance Network (#08954)
- ♦ **EURO-TC** European Treatment Centers for Drug Addiction (#08947)
- ♦ EuroTech Universities / see EuroTech Universities Alliance (#09187)

♦ EuroTech Universities Alliance 09187

Main Office Square de Meeûs 23, 1000 Brussels, Belgium. T. +3222740532.
URL: http://eurotech-universities.eu/

History Set up as an alliance of universities. Contract on 'Establishment of a Strategic Alliance between universities of excellence' signed 2011. Alliance office in Brussels (Belgium) set up 2012. Former names and other names: *EuroTech Universities* – alias. Registration: EU Transparency Register, No/ID: 992618013978-09, Start date: 15 Jul 2014. **Aims** Find technical solutions which address the major challenges of modern society; collaborate across research, education and innovation to support the EU goals of smart, sustainable and inclusive growth. **Structure** Alliance of 6 universities of science and technology. Main Office in Brussels (Belgium). **Languages** English. **Staff** 4.30 FTE, paid. **Finance** Sources: members' dues. **Activities** Events/meetings; research and development; training/education. **Publications** Position papers.
Members Universities in 6 countries:
Denmark, France, Germany, Israel, Netherlands, Switzerland. [2022.10.24/XJ5944/D]

- ♦ Eurotest (inactive)

♦ EuroTEST 09188

Coordination Secretariat Rigshosp – Univ of Copenhagen – CHIP, Section 2100 Finsencentret, Blegdamsvej 9, 2100 Copenhagen, Denmark. T. +4535455757. Fax +4535455758. E-mail: eurotest.rigshospitalet@regionh.dk.
Policy Officer EATG, Place Raymond Blyckaerts 13, 1050 Brussels, Belgium. T. +3226269641. Fax +3226443307.
URL: http://www.eurotest.org/

History 2007. Former names and other names: *HIV in Europe* – former (2007 to Jan 2019); *EuroTEST – Working together for an integrated testing and earlier care – Addressing Hepatitis, HIV, STIs and TB* – full title. **Aims** Ensure that people living with HIV, viral hepatitis, STIs or TB have access to testing and enter care earlier in the course of their infection than is currently the case; study the decrease in the proportion presenting late for care. **Structure** Steering Committee; Secretariat. **Activities** Events/meetings; projects/programmes. **Events** *HepHIV Conference* Lisbon (Portugal) 2021, *HepHIV Conference* Bucharest (Romania) 2019. [2020/AA0319/F]

- ♦ EuroTEST – Working together for an integrated testing and earlier care – Addressing Hepatitis, HIV, STIs and TB / see EuroTEST (#09188)
- ♦ **Eurotex** European Centre for Knowledge and Technology Transfer (#06489)
- ♦ **EUROTHERM** European Committee for the Advancement of Thermal Sciences and Heat Transfer (#06640)
- ♦ **EUROTHON** European Tropical Tuna Trade and Industry Committee (#08951)

♦ Eurotopia 09189

Contact Postfach 65, 2882 St Ursanne JU, Switzerland.
URL: http://www.andigross.ch/

History 1991, Rostock (Germany). An informal network. **Aims** Work for participative *citizenship rights* at European level, a European constitution and the emergence of a *transnational democracy*. **Structure** Informal network of national and/or local Eurotopia organizations and groups. **Languages** English, French, German, Italian. **Staff** 4.00 FTE, voluntary. **Events** *Biannual Assembly* Stockholm (Sweden) 2007, *Biannual Assembly* Amsterdam (Netherlands) 2006, *Biannual Assembly* St Ursanne (Switzerland) 2006, *Biannual Assembly* Strasbourg (France) 2006, *Biannual Assembly* Zurich (Switzerland) 2005. **Publications** *Transnational Democracy: Quarterly for a New European Polity*. *The Rostock-Process* (2003).
Members Active in 20 countries:
Austria, Belgium, Denmark, Estonia, Finland, France, Germany, Hungary, Iceland, Ireland, Italy, Latvia, Lithuania, Netherlands, Norway, Slovenia, Spain, Sweden, Switzerland, UK.
NGO Relations Member of: *Permanent Forum of European Civil Society (#18322)*. Instrumental in setting up: *Inter Citizens Conferences Network (no recent information)*; *Network Direct Democracy Initiatives in Europe (NDDIE, inactive)*. [2016/XF4534/F]

- ♦ EURO-TOQUES / see Euro-Toques International (#09190)

♦ Euro-Toques International (ETI) 09190

Office Rue du Luxembourg 19, 1000 Brussels, Belgium. E-mail: info@eurotoques-oesterreich.at.
URL: https://www.eurotoques-international.eu/home.html

History 18 Nov 1986, Brussels (Belgium), when statutes were adopted, as a consultative body to the European Community. Original title: *European Community of Cooks – Communauté Européenne des Cuisiniers (EURO-TOQUES) – Comunidad Europea de Cocineros – Europäische Gemeinschaft der Köche – Comunità Europea dei Cuochi – Comunidade Européia dos Cozinheiros – Europese Gemeenschap der Koks – Kokke i de Europaeiske Faellesskaber – Evropaiki Kinotita Magiron*. Also referred to by French initials *CEC* and as *Toques d'Or International*. Registered in accordance with Belgian law. EU Transparency Register: 489413337653-25. **Aims** Support traditional artisan producers; promote quality products; preserve *culinary* traditions at world level; ensure responsible handling of food by affiliated certified restaurants and cooks. **Structure** General Assembly; Bureau; National Offices. **Languages** French. **Staff** Full-time. **Finance** Members' dues. **Activities** Advocacy/lobbying/activism. **Events** *General Assembly* Luxembourg (Luxembourg) 2010, *General Assembly* Sofia (Bulgaria) 2009, *Extraordinary general assembly* Brussels (Belgium) 2008, *General Assembly* Hilvarenbeek (Netherlands) 2008, *General Assembly* Logroño (Spain) 2008. **Publications** *Toques d'Or Magazine* (annual) in English, French. Yearbook.
Members Founder, Honorary, Active and Ordinary. Professional cooks in 19 countries:
Belgium, Bulgaria, Cyprus, Denmark, Finland, France, Germany, Greece, Ireland, Italy, Luxembourg, Netherlands, Poland, Portugal, Romania, San Marino, Spain, Sweden, Switzerland.
IGO Relations *European Commission (EC, #06633)*. [2020/XD0418/v/E]

♦ EUROTOX 09191

SG address not obtained. E-mail: secretariat@eurotox.com.
URL: http://www.eurotox.com/

History 21 Jul 1989, Brighton (UK), when statutes were adopted, on merger of *European Society of Toxicology (EST, inactive)*, set up 20 Sep 1962, Zurich (Switzerland), as *'European Society for the Study of Drug Toxicity'* (individual membership), with *Federation of European Societies of Toxicology (FEST, inactive)*, formed 1984 by 14 national societies of EST, and with whom it had previously sponsored congresses held every 2 years. Full title of EUROTOX: *Association of European Toxicologists and Societies of Toxicology*. Registered in Basel (Switzerland) in accordance with Swiss law. **Aims** Encourage and extend research in the field of *toxicology*; ensure regular exchange of information on toxicity and its evaluation; undertake related scientific work; represent national societies of toxicology in Europe. **Structure** Business Council (meets annually), composed of delegates representing national societies (one or 2 depending on membership) and one delegate for each 200 individual members. Executive Committee of 7 to 11 members, including President, Vice-President (President-Elect), Past-President, Secretary-General and Treasurer. Sub-Committees (6): Education and Training; Scientific Affairs; External Affairs and Public Relations; Publications; Membership; Nominations. Liaison Officer for Central and Eastern European countries. Working Groups. **Languages** English. **Staff** Voluntary. **Finance** Members' dues. **Activities** Programmes to further education and advance toxicology as a science; publishes toxicological information; organizes advanced education initiatives; develops policy regarding training and registration of toxicologists, especially through Task Force on Registration; interacts with regulatory bodies; initiates and assists in translating and publishing general toxicology courses in conjunction with the Open University of the Netherlands; offers continuing education programme; assists attendance at meetings. Organizes: annual *'EUROTOX'* congress; *'Gerhard Zbinden Memorial Lecture'* (annual); training and discussion programme for toxicologists from Central and Eastern Europe. Bestows annual Merit Award and annual Young Scientist's Poster Award. Working Groups study specific aspects, for example Postgraduate Training in Toxicology and Toxicopathology. **Events** *Annual Congress* Ljubljana (Slovenia) 2023, *International Congress of Toxicology* Maastricht (Netherlands) 2022, *Annual Congress* 2021, *Annual Congress* Copenhagen (Denmark) 2020, *Meeting* Milan (Italy) 2019. **Publications** *Toxicology Letters* – official journal. *Toxicology: Principles and Applications* (1996). Proceedings of congress (as supplement to Archives).
Members Individuals (600) in 54 countries and territories:
Algeria, Argentina, Australia, Austria, Belarus, Belgium, Bosnia-Herzegovina, Brazil, Bulgaria, Canada, China, Colombia, Croatia, Czechia, Denmark, Egypt, Finland, France, Georgia, Germany, Greece, Hong Kong, Hungary, India, Iran Islamic Rep, Ireland, Israel, Italy, Japan, Kuwait, Lithuania, Mexico, Netherlands, New Zealand, North Macedonia, Norway, Poland, Portugal, Romania, Saudi Arabia, Serbia, Singapore, Slovakia, Slovenia, South Africa, Spain, Sweden, Switzerland, Taiwan, Türkiye, UK, Ukraine, USA, Venezuela.
National and regional societies in 31 countries:
Austria, Belgium, Bulgaria, Croatia, Czechia, Denmark, Estonia, Finland, France, Germany, Greece, Hungary, Ireland, Italy, Latvia, Netherlands, North Macedonia, Norway, Poland, Portugal, Romania, Russia, Serbia, Slovakia, Slovenia, Spain, Sweden, Switzerland, Türkiye, UK, Ukraine.
Included in the above, 1 organization listed in this Yearbook:
European Association of Poisons Centres and Clinical Toxicologists (EAPCCT, #06155).
NGO Relations Observer at: *European Federation for Pharmaceutical Sciences (EUFEPS, #07192)*. Full member of and close working relations with: *International Union of Toxicology (IUTOX, #15824)* (represented on Committee). *European Society for Toxicology In Vitro (ESTIV, #08763)*. [2020/XD0858/y/D]

- ♦ EUROTOX – European Committee for the Protection of the Population Against the Hazards of Chronic Toxicity (inactive)

EuroTra Association européenne
09191

- **EuroTra** Association européenne des formateurs du transport (#02571)
- **Euro Trade Institute** / see EHI Retail Institute
- **EUROTRANS** Comité européen des associations de constructeurs d'engrenages et d'éléments de transmission (#06643)
- **Eurotransplant Foundation** / see Eurotransplant International Foundation (#09192)

♦ Eurotransplant International Foundation — 09192
Dir PO Box 2304, 2301 CH Leiden, Netherlands. T. +31715795700. Fax +31715790057.
URL: http://www.eurotransplant.org/
History 12 May 1969, The Hague (Netherlands), as *Eurotransplant Foundation (ET) – Fondation européenne pour la transplantation*. **Aims** Serve as a focal point of cooperation among *dialysis* centres, *tissue typing* laboratories and *transplant* centres; minimize the risks of transplanted organs through tissue typing and matching; achieve a high utilization rate of available donor organs; assist in the arrangement of *organ transplants*. **Structure** Board. **Finance** Cost reimbursement by public and private health insurance companies. Other sources: donations; legacies; gifts; grants. **Activities** Events/meetings. **Events** *Winter Meeting* Alpbach (Austria) 2019, *Winter Meeting* Alpbach (Austria) 2016, *Extramural Tissue Typers Meeting* Maastricht (Netherlands) 2016, *Winter Meeting* Alpbach (Austria) 2015, *Meeting* Leiden (Netherlands) 2014. **Publications** *Eurotransplant Newsletter*. Annual Report. Data bank of almost 12,000 patients provides information for rapid matching with suitable donors.
Members Full in 8 countries:
Austria, Belgium, Croatia, Germany, Hungary, Luxembourg, Netherlands, Slovenia.
NGO Relations Collaborates with similar organizations in Europe (not specified). Instrumental in setting up: *Donor Action Foundation* (#05121). [2019.07.10/XF0910/f/F]

- **EuroTube Foundation** (internationally oriented national body)

♦ Eurotunnel — 09193
Contact Channel Tunnel Group, UK Terminal, Ashford Road, Folkestone, CT18 8XX, UK. T. +441303282222. Fax +441303850360. E-mail: communicationinternet@eurotunnel.com.
Contact Eurotunnel, 19 boulevard Malesherbes, 75008 Paris, France. T. +33155273959. Fax +33155273775.
URL: http://www.eurotunnel.com/
Structure General Meeting (annual). Board of 14 directors. Executive Committee. Divisions (5): Shuttle services; Railway services; Planning and development; Technical; Business services. Committees (4): Audit; Remuneration; Nomination; Safety/Security. Group Secretariat. **Staff** 3597.00 FTE, paid. **Activities** Operates the *Channel Tunnel* linking the UK with the rest of Europe. **Events** *Conférence sur le tunnel sous la manche* London (UK) 1988. **Publications** Annual Report. **NGO Relations** Associate member of: *International Union of Railways* (#15813). [2018/XM1060/e/F]

- **EUROTURBO** European Turbomachinery Society (#08958)
- **EURO UVS** / see Unmanned Vehicle Systems International (#20708)
- **EuroValve** (meeting series)

♦ Eurovent — 09194
SG Bd A Reyers 80, 1030 Brussels, Belgium. T. +32466900401. E-mail: secretariat@eurovent.eu.
URL: http://www.eurovent.eu/
History Jun 1996, Lyon (France). Founded by merger of *European Committee of Air Handling and Air Conditioning Equipment Manufacturers (EUROVENT, inactive)*, set up in 1958 as '*Comité européen des constructeurs de matériel aéraulique (CECMA)*' by a protocol of cooperation between Belgian, Dutch, French, German and Italian associations, and *European Committee of Manufacturers of Refrigeration Equipment (CECOMAF, inactive)*. In 1982 first discussions on a merger between EUROVENT and CECOMAF started; both associations moved the general secretariats offices to Brussels (Belgium) in 1988. Former names and other names: *Eurovent/Cecomaf European Committee of Air Handling and Refrigeration Equipment Manufacturers* – former; *Eurovent/Cecomaf Comité européen de constructeurs de matériel aéraulique et frigorifique* – former; *European Committee of Air Handling and Refrigeration Equipment Manufacturers (EUROVENT)* – former (2007). Registration: Banque-Carrefour des Entreprises, No/ID: 0464.434.317, Start date: 5 Nov 1998, Belgium; EU Transparency Register, No/ID: 89424237848-89, Start date: 26 Jan 2012. **Aims** Represent national associations, manufacturers and related organizations in the area of indoor climate (HVAC), process cooling and food cold chain technologies. **Structure** General Assembly (annual); Board; Commission. **Languages** English. **Staff** 4.00 FTE, paid. **Activities** Advocacy/lobbying/activism; certification/accreditation; events/meetings; networking/liaising; research/documentation. **Events** *Summit* Antalya (Türkiye) 2022, *General Assembly* Malaga (Spain) 2022, *General Assembly* Brussels (Belgium) 2021, *General Assembly* Brussels (Belgium) 2020, *Meeting* Vienna (Austria) 2019. **Publications** Guidebooks; technical manuals; position papers; recommendations; industry monographs.
Members Associations (16) in 13 countries:
Belgium, Denmark, Finland, France, Germany, Italy, Netherlands, Norway, Portugal, Spain, Sweden, Switzerland, Türkiye. [2022/XD6636/E]

- **Eurovent/Cecomaf** Comité européen de constructeurs de matériel aéraulique et frigorifique / see Eurovent (#09194)
- **Eurovent/Cecomaf** European Committee of Air Handling and Refrigeration Equipment Manufacturers / see Eurovent (#09194)
- **EUROVENT** – Comité européen des constructeurs de matériel aéraulique (inactive)
- **EURO-VO** European Virtual Observatory (#09065)
- **EuroVR** / see EuroXR (#09197)

♦ EUROWAXPACK – European Association of Manufacturers of Waxed Packaging Materials (EUROWAXPACK) — 09195
Mailing Address PO Box 85612, 2508 CH The Hague, Netherlands. T. +31703123929. Fax +31703636348. E-mail: mail@eurowaxpack.org.
URL: http://www.eurowaxpack.org/
History 1998, Cologne (Germany). Former names and other names: *European Federation of Manufacturers of Waxed Packaging Materials* – former. **Aims** Communicate the advantages and benefits of waxed *paper* as an environmentally sound, cost effective and contemporary packaging material. **Structure** Board. **Languages** English. **Staff** 2.00 FTE, paid. **Activities** Events/meetings. **Publications** *EuroWaxPack Newsletter* (2 a year).
Members Companies in 7 countries:
France, Germany, Ireland, Italy, Netherlands, Switzerland, UK.
NGO Relations Member of: *International Confederation of Paper and Board Converters in Europe (CITPA, #12866)*. [2017.11.22/XD7491/D]

- **EUROWAXPACK** EUROWAXPACK – European Association of Manufacturers of Waxed Packaging Materials (#09195)

♦ EuroWindoor — 09196
Contact Walter-Kolb-Str 1-7, 60594 Frankfurt-Main, Germany. T. +49699550540. Fax +496995505411.
Registered Office Schuman Business Center, 40 Rue Breydel, 1040 Brussels, Belgium.
URL: http://www.eurowindoor.eu/
History Founded 21 Jan 1999, Munich (Germany), by *European Federation of Building Joinery Manufacturers (FEMIB, inactive)*, *European Plastic Window Association (EPW, inactive)* and *Fédération des associations européennes des constructeurs de fenêtres et de façades (FAECF, #09456)*. FEMIB and EPW qubsequently merged into EuroWindoor, Mar 2015. Registered in accordance with Belgian law. EU Transparency Register: 29749561729-18. **Aims** Represent the interests of the European *window*, *door* and *facade* (curtain walling) sector. **Languages** English, German. **Publications** *EuroWindoor AISBL Newsletter* (2 a year). Position papers.
Members National associations in 13 countries:
Austria, Belgium, Czechia, Denmark, Finland, France, Germany, Italy, Netherlands, Norway, Portugal, Sweden, Switzerland.
IGO Relations *European Commission (EC, #06633)*. **NGO Relations** *Comité européen de normalisation (CEN, #04162)*; *Confédération européenne des industries du bois (CEI Bois, #04545)*; *European Aluminium (#05893)*; *European Federation of Associations of Locks and Builders Hardware Manufacturers (ARGE, #07054)*; *European Trade Association of PVC Window System Supplies (EPPA, #08924)*; *European Solar Shading Organization (ES-SO, #08794)*; *Glass for Europe (#10157)*; *International Organization for Standardization (ISO, #14473)*. [2021/XE4722/E]

- **EURO Working Group on Combinatorial Optimization** / see European Chapter on Combinatorial Optimization (#06517)
- **Euro-X** / see Eurogroup (#05689)

♦ EuroXR — 09197
Pres Via Previati n 1/E, 23900 Lecco LC, Italy. E-mail: info@euroxr-association.org.
Registered Office Rue du Trone 98, 1050 Brussels, Belgium.
URL: https://www.euroxr-association.org/
History Oct 2010. Founded as a continuation of the work in the FP6 Network of Excellence INTUITION (2004 – 2008). Former names and other names: *European Association for Virtual Reality and Augmented Reality (EuroVR)* – former; *European Association for Extended Reality* – full title. Registration: Belgium. **Aims** Establish connections with National Associations and Chapters in relevant fields in order to promote research excellence and stimulate development and deployment of XR technologies in existing, new and emerging fields. **Structure** General Assembly; Executive Board; Executive Committee. **Languages** English. **Activities** Events/meetings; knowledge management/information dissemination; publishing activities; research and development. **Events** *EuroXR International Conference* Stuttgart (Germany) 2022, *Conference* Valencia (Spain) 2020, *Conference* Tallinn (Estonia) 2019, *Conference* London (UK) 2018, *Conference* Paris (France) 2013. **Publications** *EuroXR Newsletter*. **Members** Corporate; Individual; Other. Membership countries not specified. [2021.02.17/XJ6857/D]

♦ EUROYARDS — 09198
Address not obtained.
URL: http://www.euroyards.com/
History 1992. A grouping of the type *European Economic Interest Grouping (EEIG, #06960)*. **Aims** Foster the interests of its partners, both by adopting common positions before international Bodies that promulgate the policies of the sector and by implementing them through ad-hoc working teams. **Structure** Executive Committee. **Events** *Meeting* Amsterdam (Netherlands) 2019, *Meeting* Amsterdam (Netherlands) 2019.
Members Shipbuilding companies in 6 countries:
Finland, France, Germany, Italy, Netherlands, Spain. [2019/AA0792/E]

- **EURRA** – European Rubber Reclaimers' Association (no recent information)
- **EurSafe** European Society for Agricultural and Food Ethics (#08514)
- **EURSAFETY HEALTH-NET** – Euregionales Netzwerk für Patientensicherheit und Infektionsschutz (internationally oriented national body)
- **EURSA** Staff Association of the WHO Regional Office for Europe (#19941)
- **EuRuKo** – European Ruby Conference (meeting series)

♦ EU-Russia Civil Society Forum (CSF) — 09199
Exec Dir Badstr 44, 13357 Berlin, Germany. T. +493046064540. E-mail: info@eu-russia-csf.org.
URL: http://eu-russia-csf.org/
History Officially launched 29 Mar 2011, Prague (Czech Rep). **Aims** Contribute to integration between Russia and the EU based on common values of pluralistic democracy, rule of law, human rights and social justice. **Events** *General Assembly* Bratislava (Slovakia) 2019, *General Assembly* Sofia (Bulgaria) 2018, *General Assembly* Helsinki (Finland) 2017, *General Assembly* Budapest (Hungary) 2015, *General Assembly* Tallinn (Estonia) 2014. **Publications** Policy papers. **Members** Member and supporter organizations (152). Membership countries not specified. **Consultative Status** Consultative status granted from: *Council of Europe (CE, #04881)* (Participatory Status). [2018.09.05/XM6169/F]

- **EURYDICE** – Information Network on Education in Europe (inactive)
- **EURYPAA** European Convention of Young People in Alcoholics Anonymous (#06780)
- **Eurzaijos Zalos Mazinimo Asociacijos** (#05609)
- **EUSA AP** EU Studies Association Asia Pacific (#09204)
- **EUSA** Asia Pacific / see EU Studies Association Asia Pacific (#09204)
- **EUSAAT** European Society for Alternatives to Animal Testing (#08517)
- **EUSA** European School of Administration (#08427)
- **EUSA** – European Union Studies Association (internationally oriented national body)
- **EUSA** European Union of Swimming Pool and Spa Associations (#09019)
- **EUSA** European University Sports Association (#09036)
- **EUSA** Europese Unie van de Sociale Apoteken (#20401)
- **EU-SAGE** – European Sustainable Agriculture through Genome Editing (unconfirmed)
- **EUSA** Korea – European Union Studies Association of Korea (internationally oriented national body)
- **EUSALP** EU Strategy for the Alpine Region (#09203)
- **EUsalt** European Salt Producers Association (#08425)
- **EUSAMA** – European Shock Absorbers Manufacturers Association (inactive)
- **EUSARF** – European Scientific Association for Residential and Foster Care of Children and Adolescents (inactive)
- **EUSAS** European Society for Automatic Alarm Systems (#08527)
- **EUSCEA** / see European Science Engagement Association (#08439)
- **EuSC** / see European Council for Modelling and Simulation (#06831)
- **EUSC** / see European Union Satellite Centre (#09015)
- **EUSC** – European Union Studies Center, New York (internationally oriented national body)
- **EUSEA** / see European Science Engagement Association (#08439)
- **EUSEA** European Science Engagement Association (#08439)
- **EUSEB** – European Union of Societies for Experimental Biology (inactive)
- **EUSEC** – European Conference of Engineering Societies of Western Europe and the United States of America (inactive)
- **EUSE** European Union of Supported Employment (#09018)
- **EU Semester Alliance** EU Alliance for a democratic, social and sustainable European Semester (#05565)
- **EuSEM** European Society for Emergency Medicine (#08590)
- **EuSEN** European Society for Emergency Nursing (#08591)
- **EUS** European Union for Systemics (#20403)
- **EUSFLAT** European Society for Fuzzy Logic and Technology (#08603)
- **EUSGA** – European Seals and Gaskets Association (unconfirmed)
- **EU SHD Coalition** / see Structural Heart Disease Coalition (#20013)
- **EUSIDIC** – European Association of Information Services (no recent information)
- **EUSIPA** European Structured Investment Products Association (#08845)
- **EUSJA** European Union of Science Journalists' Associations (#09017)
- **Euskal Herriko UNESCO Zentroa** / see Centro UNESCO del Pais Vasco
- **EUSMCP** / see Union européenne des Pharmacies sociales (#20401)
- **EUSOBI** European Society of Breast Imaging (#08535)
- **EUSOMA** European Society of Breast Cancer Specialists (#08534)
- **EuSoMII** European Society of Medical Imaging Informatics (#08647)
- **EU** – South Africa Free Trade Agreement (1999 treaty)
- **EUSPA** European Union Agency for the Space Programme (#08974)

♦ EU Specialty Food Ingredients — 09200
Main Office Avenue Tervueren 13a, Box 7, 1040 Brussels, Belgium. T. +3227365354. Fax +3227323427. E-mail: info@specialtyfoodingredients.eu.
URL: http://www.specialtyfoodingredients.eu/
History 21 Mar 1983. Present Charter adopted 22 Mar 1995. Present by-laws adopted Apr 2005. Former names and other names: *European Liaison Committee (ELC)* – former (21 Mar 1983 to 1993); *Federation of European Food Additives and Food Enzymes Industries (ELC)* – former (1993 to 2005); *Federation of European Food Additives, Food Enzymes and Food Cultures Industries (ELC)* – former (2005 to 2010); *Federation of European Specialty Food Ingredient Industries (ELC)* – former (2010 to 2017); *European Industrial Food Additives and Food Enzymes Liaison Committee* – former alias. Registration: EU Transparency Register, No/ID: 6160532422-38. **Aims** Represent mutual interests of the European food *additives* industry, principally in

scientific, technological and *regulatory* matters; make representations to the European Commission and other relevant authorities on all aspects of current and proposed legislation affecting food additives; encourage maintenance of the highest standards in manufacturing practice and product specification. **Structure** General Assembly (annual); Board; Secretariat. Committee (3): Food Improvement Agents; Communications; Nutrition. Sustainability Group. **Languages** English. **Finance** Members' dues. **Events** *Annual General Meeting* Genval (Belgium) 2015, *European nutrition and lifestyle conference* Brussels (Belgium) 2011, *General Assembly* Brussels (Belgium) 2006, *General Assembly* Brussels (Belgium) 2005.
Members Associations (18):
Association of Manufacturers and Formulators of Enzyme Products (AMFEP, #02793); Biopolymer International (#03256); Conseil européen de l'industrie chimique (CEFIC, #04687); Danish Agriculture and Food Council; *European Association of Polyol Producers (EPA, #06157); European Food and Feed Cultures Association (EFFCA, #07282); European Food Emulsifier Manufacturers' Association (EFEMA, #07281); European Lecithin Manufacturers Association (ELMA, #07675); European Technical Caramel Association (EUTECA, #08877)*; Federchimica-Assochimica Food Group /Italy/; Food Additives Industry Association (FAIA) /UK/; *INEC – Association of Producers of Carob Bean Gum (INEC, #11183); International Pectin Producers' Association (IPPA, #14539); International Sweeteners Association (ISA, #15639); Natural Food Colours Association (NATCOL, #16953)*; SYNPA – Les ingrédients alimentaires de spécialité; Verband der Chemischen Industrie (VCI); *World Association of Seaweed Processors (MARINALG International, #21185)*.
Companies. Membership countries not specified.
IGO Relations Recognized by: *European Commission (EC, #06633)*. Participates as observer in the activities of: *Codex Alimentarius Commission (CAC, #04081)*. **NGO Relations** Member of: *Industry4Europe (#11181)*. Works with: *International Chewing Gum Association (ICGA, #12545)*. [2022/XE0567/y/**E**]

- ♦ **EUSPEN** European Society for Precision Engineering and Nanotechnology (#08710)
- ♦ **EUSP** European Union of the Social Pharmacies (#20401)
- ♦ EUSP – European University at St Petersburg (internationally oriented national body)
- ♦ **EUSPM** European Society of Predictive Medicine (#08711)
- ♦ **EUSPR** European Society for Prevention Research (#08712)
- ♦ **Eu-SPRI** European Forum for Studies of Policies for Research and Innovation (#07335)
- ♦ **EuSpRIG** European Spreadsheet Risks Interest Group (#08824)
- ♦ **EUSSER** European Society for Shoulder and Elbow Rehabilitation (#08734)
- ♦ **EUSSET** European Society of Socially Embedded Technologies (#08737)
- ♦ EUSSG / see Usher Study Group
- ♦ **EuSSS** European Society for Separation Science (#08732)
- ♦ **EUSTAFOR** European State Forest Association (#08832)
- ♦ **EUSTAS** European Stevia Association (#08838)

♦ EU STEM Coalition 09201

Coordinator c/o PTvT, Postbus 76, 2501 CD The Hague, Netherlands. E-mail: info@stemcoalition.eu.
URL: https://www.stemcoalition.eu/

History 2015. Created by the national STEM platforms of Denmark, Belgium (Flanders), the Netherlands and Estonia. STEM stands for: *Science, Technology, Engineering, Mathematics*. **Aims** Shape STEM education policies and practices that foster economic growth, opportunity and well-being for all. **Structure** A network of national and regional (government-funded) organizations. **Finance** Supported by: *European Union (EU, #08967)*. **Activities** Events/meetings; financial and/or material support; politics/policy/regulatory; projects/programmes. European Union and associated countries.
Members National STEM platforms in 13 countries:
Belgium, Bulgaria, Denmark, Estonia, Finland, Germany, Netherlands, Norway, Spain, Switzerland, Türkiye, UK, Ukraine.
European partners (6):
Board of European Students of Technology (BEST, #03294); Conference of European Schools for Advanced Engineering Education and Research (CESAER, #04599); CSR Europe (#04977); European Network of Science Centres and Museums (ECSITE, #07998); Fédération Européenne d'Associations Nationales d'Ingénieurs (FEANI, #09558); Science on Stage Europe (SonSEu, #19142); ThinkYoung (#20144).
National/associate partners in 5 countries:
Denmark, France, Greece, Hungary, Spain. [2020.06.24/AA0719/y/**D**]

- ♦ **EUSTM** European Society for Translational Medicine (#08765)

♦ EUSTORY 09202

Managing Dir Körber Foundation, Kehrwieder 12, 20457 Hamburg, Germany. T. +4940808192161. Fax +4940808192302. E-mail: eustory@koerber-stiftung.de.
URL: http://www.eustory.eu/

History Founded Sep 2001, by organizations from 14 European countries. Launched as a project of the Körber Foundation, following an empirical survey called "Youth and History" in 27 European countries in 1994-1995 supported by the Foundation and the European Commission. **Aims** Support a European perspective on local, regional and national history, shunning exclusion and promoting understanding; view *European history* from the grass roots and recognize the vast *diversity* of experience; emphasize the view of history as a workshop for *intercultural* understanding; contribute to European efforts towards peace and tolerance. **Structure** Annual Meeting; Steering Committee; Board of Patrons (honorary). **Activities** Networking/liaising; events/meetings; awards/prizes/competitions. **Events** *Annual Meeting* Helsingør (Denmark) 2015, *Network Meeting / Annual Meeting* Berlin (Germany) 2014, *Network Meeting / Annual Meeting* Riga (Latvia) 2013, *Annual General Assembly / Annual Meeting* Hamburg (Germany) 2012, *Annual General Assembly / Annual Meeting* Hamburg (Germany) 2011.
Members National organizations in 22 countries and territories:
Belarus, Belgium, Bulgaria, Czechia, Denmark, Estonia, France, Germany, Ireland, Israel, Italy, Latvia, Norway, Poland, Portugal, Russia, Slovakia, Slovenia, Spain, Switzerland, Ukraine, Wales.
NGO Relations Member of: *A Soul for Europe (ASF, #19697)*. Cooperates with: *European Association of History Educators (EUROCLIO, #06069)*. [2017.10.25/XM3102/**F**]

♦ EU Strategy for the Alpine Region (EUSALP) 09203

Stratégie de l'Union européenne pour la région Alpine (SUERA) – Strategie der EU für den Alpenraum

Contact c/o ANCT, 20 ave de Ségur, TSA 10717, 75334 Paris CEDEX 07, France. E-mail: ag1leader.communication.staff@alpine-region.eu.
Administrative Office c/o ALP2GOV, Reg Lombardy, Piazza Città di Lombardia 1, 20124 Milan MI, Italy.
URL: http://www.alpine-region.eu/

History Former names and other names: *European Union Strategy for the Alpine Region* – alias. **Aims** Balance development and protection through innovative approaches strengthening the Alpine region. **Structure** General Assembly; Executive Board; Action Groups. **Events** *Meeting & Launch of Presidency* Lyon (France) 2020, *Annual Forum* Milan (Italy) 2019, *Annual Forum* Innsbruck (Austria) 2018, *Energy Conference* Vienna (Austria) 2018, *Annual Forum* Munich (Germany) 2017. **Publications** *EUSALP Newsletter*.
Members Countries (7) and regions (48):
Austria, France, Germany, Italy, Liechtenstein, Slovenia, Switzerland.
IGO Relations *Convention for the Protection of the Alps (Alpine convention, 1991); European Commission (EC, #06633)*. [2021/XM5600/**F***]

- ♦ EU Structural Heart Disease Coalition / see Structural Heart Disease Coalition (#20013)

♦ EU Studies Association Asia Pacific (EUSA AP) 09204

Contact c/o NCRE, Private Bag 4800, Univ of Canterbury, Christchurch 8042, New Zealand. T. +6433642348. Fax +6433642634. E-mail: eusaap@canterbury.ac.nz.
URL: https://jeanmonnet.nz/eusaap/

History Dec 1999. Former names and other names: *European Union Studies Association Asia Pacific* – alias; *EUSA Asia Pacific* – alias. **Aims** Promote and coordinate EU studies in related field; cultivate and develop mutual understanding and friendly cooperation in the region and with the EU and its member states. **Structure** Board. **Activities** Events/meetings; research/documentation; knowledge management/information dissemination. **Events** *Conference* Seoul (Korea Rep) 2022, *International Conference* Shanghai (China) 2019, *International Conference* Taipei (Taiwan) 2018, *International Conference* Tokyo (Japan) 2017, *International Conference* Hong Kong (Hong Kong) 2016. **Publications** *Asia Pacific Journal of EU Studies*.
Members Studies societies in 10 countries and territories:
Australia, China, Hong Kong, India, Japan, Korea Rep, Macau, New Zealand, Taiwan, Thailand. [2022/XM4205/**E**]

- ♦ **EUSUHM** European Union of School and University Health and Medicine (#09016)
- ♦ EUSV / see Weltunion der Vereine für Deutsche Schäferhunde (#20858)
- ♦ EUSynBioS / see European Synthetic Biology Society (#08869)
- ♦ **EUSynBioS** European Synthetic Biology Society (#08869)
- ♦ **EUTC** European Utilities Telecom Council (#09042)
- ♦ EUTDS – Europäische Union der Tapezierer, Dekorateure und Sattler (no recent information)
- ♦ **EUTECA** European Technical Caramel Association (#08877)
- ♦ **EuTeCer** European Technical Ceramics Federation (#08878)
- ♦ EUTEC – European Technology Chamber (unconfirmed)
- ♦ **EUTELSAT IGO** European Telecommunications Satellite Organization (#08896)
- ♦ Eutelsat intérimaire / see European Telecommunications Satellite Organization (#08896)
- ♦ EUTi – European Federation of Tinnitus Association (inactive)
- ♦ EUTO – European Union of Tourist Officers (inactive)
- ♦ EUTOR – Union européenne pour la technopédie, l'orthopédie et la réadaptation (inactive)
- ♦ EUTRAPLAST – Committee of Plastic Converters Associations of Western Europe (inactive)

♦ eu travel tech 09205

SG Avenue Marnix 17, 1000 Brussels, Belgium. T. +3226694253. E-mail: info@eutraveltech.eu.
URL: https://eutraveltech.eu/

History 2009. Former names and other names: *European Technology and Travel Services Association (ETTSA)* – former. Registration: EU Transparency Register, No/ID: 70614728635-77, Start date: 20 Apr 2012. **Aims** Represent and promote the interests of global distribution systems (GDSs) and travel distributors, towards the industry, policy-makers, opinion formers, consumer groups and all other relevant European stakeholders. **Structure** Board of Directors; Secretariat. **Languages** English. **NGO Relations** Member of (1): *European Tourism Manifesto (#08921)*. [2019.02.13/XJ7592/**D**]

- ♦ **EUTROC** European Network for Translational Research in Ovarian Cancer (#08025)
- ♦ EUTSA – European Table Soccer Association (no recent information)
- ♦ **EUTurbines** European Association of Gas and Steam Turbine Manufacturers (#06050)
- ♦ **EUU** European Unitarian-Universalists (#09025)
- ♦ EU Umweltbüro (internationally oriented national body)
- ♦ EU-UN Association / see European Union Association
- ♦ **EUVAS** European Vasculitis Society (#09046)
- ♦ EUVEPRO / see European Vegetable Protein Association (#09047)
- ♦ **EUVEPRO** European Vegetable Protein Association (#09047)
- ♦ **EU-VRi** European Virtual Institute for Integrated Risk Management (#09062)
- ♦ **EUWA** Association of European Wheel Manufacturers (#02552)

♦ EU Watch AISBL 09206

Exec Dir Av Louise 326, 1050 Brussels, Belgium. T. +32485869584. E-mail: office@euwatch.be.
URL: https://www.euwatch.be/

History 4 Sep 2020, Belgium. Registration: Banque-Carrefour des Entreprises, No/ID: 0759.570.376, Start date: 8 Dec 2020, Belgium; EU Transparency Register, No/ID: 377643141797-21, Start date: 15 Mar 2021. **Aims** Support the values and principles of the European Union; ensure that they are respected in everyday decision-making. **Structure** Board of Directors. **Languages** English, French, German, Spanish. **Staff** 2.00 FTE, paid. **Activities** Monitoring/evaluation; politics/policy/regulatory; projects/programmes; publishing activities; research and development. [2022.05.04/AA1482/**F**]

- ♦ **EUWEP** European Union of Wholesale in Eggs, Egg-Products, Poultry and Game (#09021)
- ♦ **EUW** European Union of Women (#09022)
- ♦ EUWI – European Union Water Initiative (inactive)
- ♦ **EUWIIN** European Union Women Inventors and Innovators Network (#09023)
- ♦ EUWL / see International Union of Kettlebell Lifting (#15786)
- ♦ **EUWMA** European Union of Water Management Associations (#09020)
- ♦ **EUxIN** European Union Cross Identity Network (#08983)
- ♦ EUYD / see European Union of Deaf Youth (#08986)
- ♦ **EUYO** European Union Youth Orchestra (#09024)
- ♦ EU – Zahnärztlicher Verbindungs-Ausschuss / see Council of European Dentists (#04886)
- ♦ **EUZEPA** European Zeolites Producers Association (#09148)
- ♦ EUZ – Europäische Union der Zahnärzte (inactive)
- ♦ EVAA / see Electric Drive Transportation Association
- ♦ EVAA – Esperantista Virina Asocio en Afriko (unconfirmed)
- ♦ EVAA / see European Masters Athletics (#07750)
- ♦ **EVAAP** Electric Vehicle Association of Asia Pacific (#05418)
- ♦ EVA – Electronic Imaging – the Visual Arts and Beyond (meeting series)
- ♦ EVA / see European Vending and Coffee Service Association (#09049)
- ♦ **EVA** European Vending and Coffee Service Association (#09049)
- ♦ EVA – European Vermiculite Association (no recent information)
- ♦ **EVA** European Visual Artists (#09071)
- ♦ **EVAg** European Virus Archive goes Global (#09067)
- ♦ EVALa – Entrenamiento en Vía Aérea Latinoamérica (unconfirmed)

♦ EvalHum 09207

Registered Address Manoir de Kerfloch, 56320 Priziac, France. E-mail: evalhum@evalhum.eu.
URL: http://www.evalhum.eu/

History Full title: *EvalHum – Research Evaluation, Innovation and Impact Analysis for the Social Sciences and Humanities*. Registered in accordance with French law. **Structure** Board. **Finance** Members' dues. **Activities** Events/meetings. **NGO Relations** Member of: *European Alliance for the Social Sciences and Humanities (EASSH, #05885)*. [2017/XM6599/**F**]

- ♦ EvalHum – Research Evaluation, Innovation and Impact Analysis for the Social Sciences and Humanities / see EvalHum (#09207)
- ♦ EVAlliance (internationally oriented national body)
- ♦ **EvalMENA** Middle East and North Africa Evaluators Network (#16778)

♦ EvalPartners 09208

Coordinator 3-247 Barr Str, Renfrew ON K7V 1J6, Canada. E-mail: ioce@earthlink.net.
URL: http://mymande.org/evalpartners/

History Launched 2012, by *International Organisation for Cooperation in Evaluation (IOCE, #14426)* and *UNICEF (#20332)*. **Aims** Enhance capacities of *Civil Society* Organizations (CSOs), particularly Voluntary Organizations for Professional Evaluation (VOPEs), to engage in a strategic and meaningful manner in national *evaluation* processes, contributing to improved country-led evaluation systems and policies that are equity-focused and gender equality responsive. **Structure** Board; Management Group; Executive Committee. **Languages** Arabic, English, French, Spanish. **Staff** 1.00 FTE, paid. **Finance** Majority of initial funding from Ministry of Foreign Affairs of Finland; *UN Women (#20724); UNICEF (#20332); United States Agency for International Development (USAID)*. **Activities** Capacity building; events/meetings. **Publications** *EvalPartners Newsletter. Evaluation and Civil Society: Stakeholders' perspectives on National Evaluation Capacity Development; Voluntary Organizations for Professional Evaluation (VOPEs): Learning from Africa, Americas, Asia, Australiasia, Europe and Middle East.* **IGO Relations** Cooperates with: *African Development Bank (ADB, #00283); Swiss Agency for Development and Cooperation (SDC); UN Women (#20724); UNDP (#20292); UNICEF (#20332); United Nations Evaluation Group (UNEG, #20560); United Nations Volunteers (UNV, #20650); United States Agency for International Development (USAID)*. **NGO Relations** Cooperates with: *Active Learning Network for Accountability and Performance in Humanitarian Action (ALNAP, #00101); Africa Gender and Development Evaluators Network (AGDEN, #00177); African Evaluation Association (AfrEA, #00304); Asia-Pacific Evaluation Association (APEA, #01894); Commonwealth of Independent States (CIS, #04341)* International Program Evaluation Network (IPEN); *Community of Evaluators in South Asia (COE, #04398); European Evaluation Society (EES, #07009); International Development Evaluation Association*

(IDEAS, #13158); *International Federation of Red Cross and Red Crescent Societies (#13526)*; *International Organisation for Cooperation in Evaluation (IOCE, #14426)*; *Middle East and North Africa Evaluators Network (EvalMENA, #16778)*; national organizations; *Red de Seguimiento, Evaluación y Sistematización de América Latine y el Caribe (ReLAC)*; *The Rockefeller Foundation (#18966)*; *United Nations Evaluation Group (UNEG, #20560)*. [2016.12.14/XJ8544/y/**E**]

♦ Evaluation and Accreditation of Quality in Language Services (Eaquals) 09209

Services Manager PO Box 95, Budapest 1301, Hungary. T. +3617855890. E-mail: info@eaquals.org.
Registered Office 29/30 Fitzroy Square, London, W1T 6LQ, UK.
URL: http://www.eaquals.org/

History Dec 1991, Trieste (Italy), as *European Association for Quality Language Services*. **Aims** Promote high quality in language *education*. **Structure** Board. **Languages** English, French, German, Italian, Spanish. **Staff** 5.00 FTE, paid. **Finance** Annual budget: euro 313,000. **Activities** Certification/accreditation; publishing activities. **Events** *International Conference* Venice (Italy) 2022, *International Conference* Belfast (UK) 2021, *International Conference* Belfast (UK) 2020, *International Conference* Madrid (Spain) 2019, *General Assembly and Annual Conference* Prague (Czechia) 2018. **Publications** *EAQUALS-ALTE European Language Portfolio* – also electronic; *EAQUALS Management Training Seminars*; *QualitTraining Guide* – in cooperation with ECML Graz. Self-help guides.
Members Founding; Accredited (142); Associate (31). Members in 34 countries:
Belgium, Bosnia-Herzegovina, Bulgaria, Croatia, Czechia, Egypt, France, Germany, Greece, Hungary, Ireland, Italy, Kazakhstan, Kosovo, Latvia, Libya, Luxembourg, Malta, Montenegro, North Macedonia, Poland, Portugal, Qatar, Romania, Russia, Saudi Arabia, Serbia, South Africa, Spain, Switzerland, Türkiye, UK, Ukraine, United Arab Emirates.
Consultative Status Consultative status granted from: *Council of Europe (CE, #04881)* (Participatory Status).
NGO Relations Member of: *Global Alliance of Education and Language Associations (GAELA)*.
[2019/XD4242/**D**]

- ♦ Evaluation International (internationally oriented national body)
- ♦ EVAM – Ending Violence Against Migrants (internationally oriented national body)
- ♦ EVAN / see European Visual Artists (#09071)
- ♦ The Evangelical Alliance Mission (internationally oriented national body)
- ♦ Evangelical Alliance Relief Fund / see Tearfund, UK
- ♦ The Evangelical Alliance Relief Fund / see TearFund, Schweiz

♦ Evangelical Association of the Caribbean (EAC) 09210

Association évangélique des Caraïbes (AEC) – Asociación Evangélica del Caribe
SG PO Box 4947, Tunapuna, Trinidad-Tobago.
URL: http://www.caribbeanevangelical.org/

History 1977, by *Caribbean Evangelical Theological Association (CETA, #03499)*, and initially headquartered in Jamaica – currently CETA is a member of EAC. Headquarters moved, 1 Jan 2012, to Trinidad-Tobago. **Aims** Unite Evangelical Christians in the Caribbean, giving them a regional identity, voice and platform to extend the Kingdom of God though Christ-centred proclamation of the Gospel to all peoples, discipling the nations, and the transformation of society. **Structure** General Assembly (meets every 2 years); Regional Board. **Languages** Dutch, English, French, Spanish. **Staff** 3.00 FTE, paid. **Finance** Members' dues. Other sources: gifts and offerings. **Activities** Religious activities. **Events** *Congress* Basseterre (St Kitts-Nevis) 2013, *Congress and General Assembly* Piarco (Trinidad-Tobago) 2013, *Congress / Congress and General Assembly* Georgetown (Guyana) 2011, *Congress / Congress and General Assembly* Kingston (Jamaica) 2009, *Congress and General Assembly* Port-of-Spain (Trinidad-Tobago) 2007. **Publications** *EAC News* (4 a year); *Caribbean Journal of Evangelical Theology* (annual).
Members Categories of full membership island or national associations of Evangelicals; denominations which have churches in at least 3 Caribbean territories; evangelical para-church organizations which operate in at least 3 territories. Associate membership. National Associations in 11 countries and territories:
Antigua-Barbuda, Barbados, Grenada, Guyana, Haiti, Jamaica, St Kitts-Nevis, St Lucia, St Vincent-Grenadines, Trinidad-Tobago, Virgin Is USA.
Included in the above Full members, 6 organizations listed in this Yearbook:
Caribbean-Atlantic Assembly of the Church of God (no recent information); *Caribbean Evangelical Theological Association (CETA, #03499)*; *Pentecostal Assemblies of the West Indies International (PAWI, #18292)*; *Salvation Army (#19041)* (Caribbean Territory); *Wycliffe Bible Translators International (WBT International)* (Caribbean branch); *Youth with a Mission (YWAM, #22020)*.
Individuals in 1 country:
Dominican Rep.
NGO Relations Member of: *World Evangelical Alliance (WEA, #21393)*. [2015.12.04/XD9754/y/**D**]

- ♦ Evangelical Association of Theological Education in Latin America (#02326)
- ♦ Evangelical Center for Pastoral Studies in Central America (internationally oriented national body)
- ♦ Evangelical Community for Apostolic Action / see CEVAA – Communauté d'églises en mission (#03840)
- ♦ Evangelical Episcopal Church / see Communion of Evangelical Episcopal Churches (#04385)
- ♦ Evangelical Fellowship of Asia / see Asia Evangelical Alliance (#01275)
- ♦ Evangelical Fellowship of the South Pacific / see South Pacific Evangelical Alliance (#19886)
- ♦ Evangelical Free Church Mission / see EFCA ReachGlobal
- ♦ Evangelical International Workers' Union (inactive)
- ♦ Evangelical Latin American Commission on Christian Education (inactive)
- ♦ Evangelical Lutheran Church in America (internationally oriented national body)
- ♦ Evangelical Lutheran Church of Southern Africa (internationally oriented national body)
- ♦ Evangelical Mission Association / see Global Connections
- ♦ Evangelical Sisterhood of Mary (religious order)
- ♦ Evangelische Arbeitsgemeinschaft für Erwachsenenbildung in Europa (inactive)
- ♦ Evangelische Broeder-Uniteit (#06777)
- ♦ Evangelische Brüder-Unität (#06777)
- ♦ Evangelische Marienschwesternschaft (religious order)
- ♦ Evangelische Partners in Hulp en Ontwikkeling / see Tear
- ♦ Evangelischer Entwicklungsdienst / see Brot für die Welt
- ♦ Evangelisches Missionswerk in Deutschland (internationally oriented national body)
- ♦ Evangelische Zentralstelle für Entwicklungshilfe / see Brot für die Welt
- ♦ Evangelistic International Ministries (internationally oriented national body)
- ♦ Evankelis-luterilainen lähetysyhdistys kylväjä (internationally oriented national body)
- ♦ Evatt Foundation (internationally oriented national body)
- ♦ **EVBB** Europäischer Verband Beruflicher Bildungsträger (#06085)
- ♦ **EVBC** European Virus Bioinformatics Center (#09068)
- ♦ **EVB** Europäischer Verband der Binnenhäfen (#07144)
- ♦ EVB – Europese Vereniging van Individuele Beleggers (inactive)
- ♦ **EVBFR** Europese Vereniging voor Bank- en Financieel Recht (#02564)
- ♦ **EVBK** Europäische Vereinigung Bildender Künstler aus Eifel und Ardennen (#07415)
- ♦ **EVBO** European Vascular Biology Organization (#09044)
- ♦ **EVBR** Europese Vereniging voor Bouwrecht (#08566)
- ♦ EVCA / see Invest Europe – The Voice of Private Capital (#15997)
- ♦ EVC – Europese Vereniging voor Chromatofonie (inactive)
- ♦ EVdB – Europäische Vereinigung der Binnenschiffer (internationally oriented national body)
- ♦ **EVDC** European Veterinary Dental College (#09054)
- ♦ **EVDS** European Veterinary Dental Society (#09055)
- ♦ **EVEA** Europäische Vereinigung für Eifel und Ardennen (#07414)
- ♦ **EVECCS** European Veterinary Emergency and Critical Care Society (#09056)
- ♦ EVEN – Eco-Village European Network / see Global Ecovillage Network – Europe (#10332)
- ♦ Evens Foundation (internationally oriented national body)
- ♦ Evens Stichting (internationally oriented national body)

♦ Eventing Organisers Association 09211

Chairman Postbus 334, 7500 AH Enschede, Netherlands. T. +31534350104. Fax +31534303265.

History 1996, as *Alliance of Organizers Concours Complet International (AOCCI)*. Present name adopted, 2003. **Staff** Voluntary. **Activities** Organizes meetings.
Members Full in 17 countries and territories:
Argentina, Australia, Austria, Belgium, Denmark, England, Finland, France, Germany, Ireland, Italy, Netherlands, New Zealand, Spain, Sweden, Switzerland, USA.
NGO Relations Member of: *International Equestrian Organisers' Alliance (IEOA, #13289)*. [2009/XF6354/**F**]

- ♦ Event Riders Association (no recent information)

♦ Events Industry Council (EIC) 09212

CEO 1120 20th Street NW, Ste 750, Washington DC 20036, USA. T. +12027129059. E-mail: info@eventscouncil.org.
URL: http://www.eventscouncil.org/

History 3 Feb 1949, USA. Formally incorporated, 1981. Took over *Green Meeting Industry Council (GMIC, inactive)*, 2016. Rebranded 2017. Former names and other names: *Convention Liaison Committee (CLC)* – former (1949 to 1974); *Convention Liaison Council (CLC)* – former (1974 to 1999); *Convention Industry Council (CIC)* – former (1999 to 2017). **Aims** Be the global voice of the business events industry on advocacy, research, professional recognition and standards. **Activities** Certification/accreditation; events/meetings; networking/liaising; research/documentation; standards/guidelines; training/education. **Events** *AIBTM : Americas incentive business travel and meetings workshop* Orlando, FL (USA) 2014, *AIBTM : Americas Incentive Business Travel and Meetings Workshop* Chicago, IL (USA) 2013, *AIBTM : Americas incentive business travel and meetings workshop* Baltimore, MD (USA) 2012, *AIBTM : Americas incentive business travel and meetings workshop* Baltimore, MD (USA) 2011, *AIBTM : Americas incentive business travel and meetings workshop* Baltimore, MD (USA) 2010.
Members Organizations (over 30) representing individuals, firms and properties involved in the events industry. Members include the following 22 organizations listed in this Yearbook:
- *AMC Institute*;
- *ASAE*;
- *Association of Collegiate Conference and Events Directors – International (ACCED-I)*;
- *Association of Destination Management Executives International (ADMEI)*;
- *Convention Sales Professionals International (CSPI)*;
- *Destinations International (#05046)*;
- *Federación de Entidades Organizadoras de Congresos y Afines de América Latina (COCAL, #09299)*;
- *Hospitality Sales and Marketing Association International (HSMAI, #10948)*;
- *IACC*;
- *International Association of Exhibitions and Events (IAEE)*;
- *International Association of Professional Congress Organisers (IAPCO, #12103)*;
- *International Association of Speakers Bureaus (IASB)*;
- *International Association of Venue Managers (IAVM)*;
- *International Congress and Convention Association (ICCA, #12892)*;
- *International Exhibition Logistics Association (IELA, #13322)*;
- *International Live Events Association (ILEA)*;
- *Meeting Professionals International (MPI, #16695)*;
- *Professional Convention Management Association (PCMA)*;
- *Religious Conference Management Association (RCMA, #18832)*;
- *Society for Incentive Travel Excellence (SITE, #19574)*;
- *Southern African Association for the Conference Industry (SAACI)*;
- *US Travel Association*.

[2021.06.29/XJ8049/ty/**E**]

- ♦ **EVER** European Association for Vision and Eye Research (#06274)

♦ EverGreen Agriculture Partnership 09213

Chair c/o ICRAF, UN Avenue, Gigiri PO Box 30677, Nairobi, 00100, Kenya.
URL: http://evergreenagriculture.net/

History Proposed 2012. **Aims** Use EverGreen Agriculture systems to increase food and nutritional security and resilience while enabling climate change adaptation and mitigation across Africa. **Structure** Steering Group. **Publications** *EverGreen World Newsletter*.
Members Organizations, including 4 listed in this Yearbook:
African Forest Forum (AFF, #00318); *World Agroforestry Centre (ICRAF, #21072)*; *World Resources Institute (WRI, #21753)*; *World Vision International (WVI, #21904)*.
NGO Relations Member of: *Global Alliance for Climate-Smart Agriculture (GACSA, #10189)*. Charter member of: *Global Landscapes Forum (GLF, #10451)*. [2016/XJ9380/y/**F**]

- ♦ **EVERI** European Association of Veterinarians in Education, Research and Industry (#06267)
- ♦ EveryChild (internationally oriented national body)
- ♦ Every Home Campaign / see Every Home for Christ International (#09214)

♦ Every Home for Christ International (EHCI) 09214

Pres PO Box 64000, Colorado Springs CO 80962, USA. T. +17192608888. Fax +17192607408. E-mail: info@ehc.org.
URL: http://www.ehc.org/

History Founded 1946, Canada. The first *Every Home Crusade* was launched in Japan and Italy in 1953. Also referred to as *EHC International* and *Every Home Campaign*. **Aims** Assist Every Home Campaign (EHC) offices and national Christians around the world to serve, mobilize and train the Church to actively pray for and participate in the systematic, personal presentation of the printed or repeatable message of the Gospel of Jesus Christ to every home in the whole world, adding new believers as functioning members of the Body of Christ. **Structure** Each EHC office has its own local board and is registered as a local corporation. **Finance** Sources: free-will offerings; grants by foundations. **Activities** Events/meetings. **Events** *Annual meeting* USA 2001, *Anniversary meeting* Colorado Springs, CO (USA) 1996, *Anniversary meeting* Guelph, ON (Canada) 1996, *World congress* Colorado Springs, CO (USA) 1994. **Publications** *Every Home Journal* (12 a year). **Members** EHC offices in over 150 countries and territories. Membership countries not specified. **NGO Relations** *Association of Evangelicals in Africa (AEA, #02587)*; *Fédération africaine des associations nationales de parents d'élèves et étudiants (FAPE, #09398)*; *Forum of Bible Agencies International (#09903)*; *Regional Network of Local Authorities for the Management of Human Settlements (CITYNET, #18799)*; *Stamps for Evangelism*; *Stockholm Environment Institute (SEI, #19993)*; *World Evangelical Alliance (WEA, #21393)*.
[2020.01.31/XF1383/v/**F**]

- ♦ Every Mother Counts (internationally oriented national body)
- ♦ Everyone's Child / see Godfrey's Children

♦ Every Woman Every Child (EWEC) 09215

Contact address not obtained. E-mail: everywoman.everychild@un.org.
URL: http://www.everywomaneverychild.org/

History Launched Sep 2010, by UN Secretary-General Ban Ki-moon, to implement *Global Strategy for Women's and Children's Health* (2010-2015). Updated *Global Strategy for Women's, Children's and Adolescents' Health* (2016-2030), launched Sep 2015. **Aims** Address major *health* challenges facing women, children and adolescents around the world. **Structure** High-Level Advisory Group. **Finance** Financing arm: *Global Financing Facility (GFF, #10360)*. **Activities** Acts on *Global Strategy for Women's, Children's and Adolescents' Health*.
Members Governments; philanthropic institutions; funders; UN and other multi-lateral organizations; civil society and non-governmental organizations; business community; health-care workers and professionals; academic and research institutions. Governments committing to the Strategy (85):
Afghanistan, Angola, Australia, Bangladesh, Benin, Bolivia, Burkina Faso, Burundi, Cambodia, Cameroon, Canada, Central African Rep, Chad, China, Colombia, Comoros, Congo Brazzaville, Congo DR, Côte d'Ivoire, Denmark, Djibouti, Dominican Rep, Egypt, Eritrea, Ethiopia, Finland, France, Gambia, Germany, Ghana, Guinea, Guinea-Bissau, Guyana, Haiti, India, Indonesia, Israel, Japan, Kenya, Korea Rep, Kyrgyzstan, Laos, Lesotho, Liberia, Madagascar, Malawi, Mali, Mauritania, Mexico, Mongolia, Morocco, Mozambique, Myanmar, Nepal, Netherlands, Niger, Nigeria, Norway, Oman, Pakistan, Papua New Guinea, Philippines, Rwanda, Sao Tomé-Principe, Senegal, Sierra Leone, Solomon Is, South Africa, South Sudan, Sri Lanka, Sudan, Sweden, Tajikistan, Tanzania UR, Thailand, Togo, Uganda, UK, Uruguay, USA, Uzbekistan, Vietnam, Yemen, Zambia, Zimbabwe.
Philanthropic institutions include 11 listed in this Yearbook:

Bill and Melinda Gates Foundation (BMGF); Children's Investment Fund Foundation (CIFF); European Foundation for the Care of Newborn Infants (EFCNI, #07344); Ford Foundation (#09858); Global Fund for Women (GFW, #10384); MacArthur Foundation; The Rockefeller Foundation (#18966); The William and Flora Hewlett Foundation; United Nations Foundation (UNF, #20563); Wellbeing Foundation Africa (ABFA); Women's Funding Network.

Research and academic institutions listed include 11 organizations listed in this Yearbook:
Aga Khan University (AKU, #00546); Barcelona Institute for Global Health (ISGlobal); Guttmacher Institute; ICDDR,B (#11051); Institute of Tropical Medicine Antwerp (IMT); International Center for Research on Women (ICRW); International Federation of Medical Students' Associations (IFMSA, #13478); International Partnership for Microbicides (IPM, inactive); International Union Against Tuberculosis and Lung Disease (The Union, #15752); RTI International.

Civil society and NGOs not listed above, include 53 organizations listed in this Yearbook:
- *Deutsche Stiftung Weltbevölkerung (DSW);*
- *Enfants du Monde (EdM);*
- *EngenderHealth;*
- *European Youth Network on Sexual and Reproductive Rights (YouAct, #09144);*
- *Every Mother Counts;*
- *FHI 360;*
- *Girls not Brides (#10154);*
- *Global Alliance for Improved Nutrition (GAIN, #10202);*
- *Global Alliance to Prevent Prematurity and Stillbirth (GAPPS);*
- *Global Health Council (GHC, #10402);*
- *Health Alliance International (HAI);*
- *IMA World Health (IMA);*
- *International Baby Food Action Network (IBFAN, #12305);*
- *International Budget Partnership (IBP, #12406);*
- *International Diabetes Federation (IDF, #13164);*
- *International Federation of Pharmaceutical Manufacturers and Associations (IFPMA, #13505);*
- *International Federation of Pharmaceutical Wholesalers (IFPW, #13506);*
- *International Planned Parenthood Federation (IPPF, #14589);*
- *IntraHealth International;*
- *Iodine Global Network (IGN, #16004);*
- *IPAS (#16010);*
- *Johns Hopkins Program for International Education in Gynecology and Obstetrics (JHPIEGO);*
- *Junior Chamber International (JCI, #16168);*
- *Let There Be Light International;*
- *Management Sciences for Health (MSH);*
- *mothers2mothers (m2m, #16859);*
- *MSI Reproductive Choices;*
- *Nutrition International (#17627);*
- *ONE (#17728);*
- *Organisation d'Afrique francophone pour le Renforcement des Systèmes de Santé et de la Vaccination (OAFRESS);*
- *PAI (#18025);*
- *PATH (#18260);*
- *Pathfinder International (#18261);*
- *Population Council (#18458);*
- *Population Reference Bureau (PRB);*
- *PSI (#18555);*
- *Reproductive Health Supplies Coalition (RHSC, #18847);*
- *Restless Development;*
- *Save the Children Federation (SCF);*
- *Smile Train (#19328);*
- *Swedish Organization for Global Health (SOGH);*
- *Taking IT Global (TIG);*
- *Tostan (#20176);*
- *WaterAid (#20822);*
- *Water.org;*
- *White Ribbon Alliance for Safe Motherhood (WRA, #20934);*
- *WomanCare Global (WCG);*
- *Women Deliver (#20989);*
- *World Association of Girl Guides and Girl Scouts (WAGGGS, #21142);*
- *World Vision International (WVI, #21904);*
- *World Young Women's Christian Association (World YWCA, #21947);*
- *Youth Coalition (YCSRR, #22011);*
- *Youth Peer Education Network (Y-PEER).*

UN, Multinateral Organizations and Partnerships, include 26 organizations listed in this Yearbook:
- *African Union (AU, #00488);*
- *Caribbean Community (CARICOM, #03476);*
- *Clean Cooking Alliance (#03987);*
- *Climate and Clean Air Coalition (CCAC, #04010);*
- *East African Community (EAC, #05181);*
- *European Parliamentary Forum for Sexual & Reproductive Rights (EPF, #08149);*
- *Food Fortification Initiative (FFI, #09844);*
- *Gavi – The Vaccine Alliance (Gavi, #10077);*
- *Global Fund to Fight AIDS, Tuberculosis and Malaria (Global Fund, #10383);*
- *Global Health Workforce Alliance (GHWA, inactive);*
- *Global Polio Eradication Initiative (GPEI, #10553);*
- *International Bank for Reconstruction and Development (IBRD, #12317)* (World Bank);
- *Inter-Parliamentary Union (IPU, #15961);*
- *Islamic Development Bank (IsDB, #16044);*
- *Office of the United Nations High Commissioner for Human Rights (OHCHR, #17697);*
- *Organisation of Islamic Cooperation (OIC, #17813);*
- *Organization of African First Ladies for Development (OAFLAD, #17852);*
- *Partners in Population and Development (PPD, #18247);*
- *PMNCH (#18410);*
- *Stop TB Partnership (#19999);*
- *The NCD Alliance (NCDA, #16963);*
- *UNDP (#20292);*
- *United Nations Global Compact (#20567);*
- *United Nations Population Fund (UNFPA, #20612);*
- *West African Health Organization (WAHO, #20881);*
- *WHO (#20950).*

NGO Relations *Development Media International (DMI).* [2016/XM5150/y/**E**]

♦ Everywoman Everywhere / see Every Woman Treaty (#09216)

♦ Every Woman Treaty 09216

Admin Dir 3301 Burke Ave North, Suite 330, Seattle WA 98103, USA. T. +16468180145.
URL: https://everywoman.org/

History 2015. Former names and other names: *Everywoman Everywhere* – former (2015 to 2018). Registration: 501(c)(3), No/ID: EIN 47-3272024, USA. **Aims** Advance the creation, adoption, and implementation of a global treaty to end violence against women and girls. **Structure** CoFounders – Board of Directors **Staff** 15.00 FTE, paid. **Activities** Advocacy/lobbying/activism.
Members Women's rights advocates; organizations. Members in 64 countries and territories:
Afghanistan, Aruba, Australia, Bangladesh, Bolivia, Brazil, Bulgaria, Cambodia, Cameroon, Canada, Congo DR, Costa Rica, Croatia, Dominican Rep, Ecuador, Egypt, El Salvador, Eswatini, Ethiopia, France, Haiti, Hong Kong, India, Iran Islamic Rep, Iraq, Israel, Italy, Jordan, Kyrgyzstan, Lebanon, Libya, Lithuania, Madagascar, Mexico, Mongolia, Morocco, Nepal, New Zealand, Nicaragua, Nigeria, Pakistan, Philippines, Poland, Russia, Saudi Arabia, Serbia, Sierra Leone, Singapore, Solomon Is, Somalia, South Africa, South Sudan, Spain, Sri Lanka, Sudan, Switzerland, Thailand, Trinidad-Tobago, Tunisia, Uganda, UK, USA, Uzbekistan, Zimbabwe. [2023.02.16/AA0019/**F**]

♦ **evfdiakonie** Europäischer Verband Freikirchlicher Diakoniewerke (#06013)
♦ **evfdiakonie** Europäischer Verband Freikirchlicher Diakoniewerke (#05759)
♦ **EVF** Europäische Vereinigung der Fleckviehzüchter (#08487)
♦ **EVF** European Venous Forum (#09050)
♦ **EVGA** European VLBI Group for Geodesy and Astrometry (#09073)
♦ **EVGE** Europäische Vereinigung der Gemeinschaften zur Zertifizierung von Entsorgungsfachbetrieben (#05763)
♦ **EVHA** European Ventilation Hygiene Association (#09051)
♦ EVHA – Europese Vereniging voor Haveninformatica (inactive)
♦ **EVH** Europäische Vereinigung des Holzbaus (#20164)
♦ **EVIA** European Ventilation Industry Association (#09052)
♦ **EVICR.net** European Vision Institute Clinical Research Network (#09070)
♦ Evidence Action (internationally oriented national body)
♦ Evidence Aid (unconfirmed)

♦ Evidence Informed Policy and Practice in Education in Europe (EIPPEE) 09217

Contact Social Science Research Unit, UCL Inst of Education, Univ College London, 18 Woburn Square, London, WC1H 0NR, UK. T. +442076126580. E-mail: s.graziosi@ucl.ac.uk.
URL: http://www.eippee.eu/

History Developed out of a collaborative projects funded by *European Commission (EC, #06633)* (2011-2013). Also referred to as *EIPPEE Network.* **Aims** Develop awareness and knowledge about *research* use; enable increased access to relevant educational research; encourage mediation between research and its use; enable the use of research; study the use of research in decision-making and identify the barriers and facilitators to this. **Activities** Events/meetings; guidance/assistance/consulting; training/education. **Events** *Advancing the use of research in education across Europe* Copenhagen (Denmark) 2016, *Conference / Annual Conference* Oslo (Norway) 2014, *Conference / Annual Conference* Frankfurt-Main (Germany) 2013, *Annual Conference* The Hague (Netherlands) 2012, *Conference* The Hague (Netherlands) 2012. [2016/XM4119/**E**]

♦ EVI – Eesti Välispoliitika Instituut (internationally oriented national body)
♦ EVI – Europäischer Verein Individueller Investoren (inactive)
♦ **EVI** European Vaccine Initiative (#09043)
♦ **EVI** European Vision Institute (#09069)
♦ **EVI** Europees Vakbondsinstituut (#08928)
♦ **EVIG** European Veterinary Immunology Group (#09057)
♦ **EViPRG** European Violence in Psychiatry Research Group (#09061)
♦ **EVISA** European Virtual Institute for Speciation Analysis (#09064)
♦ **EVKD** Europäische Vereinigung der Krankenhausdirektoren (#06073)
♦ EVK – Europäische Vereinigung der Kongressstädte (inactive)
♦ **EVK** Europese Vereniging van het Kuurwezen (#08805)
♦ EVL / see European Sign Federation (#08485)
♦ EVL – Europäischer Verband lifestyle (internationally oriented national body)
♦ EVL – Europäische Vereinigung von Liebhaberorchestern (inactive)
♦ EVME – Europäischer Verband mittelständischer Energieunternehmer (internationally oriented national body)
♦ EVM / see Vaccines Europe (#20741)
♦ **EVN** European VLBI Network (#09074)
♦ **EVODEMOS** Evolutionary Demography Society (#09218)

♦ Evolutionary Demography Society (EVODEMOS) 09218

Sec address not obtained.
Co-Pres address not obtained.
Co-Pres address not obtained.
URL: http://www.evodemos.org/

History Founded 2013. **Aims** Support research in evolutionary demography. **Structure** Board. **Activities** Events/meetings. **Events** *Annual Meeting* Paris (France) 2023, *Meeting* Røros (Norway) 2020, *Meeting* Coral Gables, FL (USA) 2019, *Meeting* Sainte Foy-lès-Lyon (France) 2018, *Meeting* Charlottesville, VA (USA) 2016. [2023/XM7377/c/**C**]

♦ E-VOTE-ID – International Conference for Electronic Voting (meeting series)
♦ **EVPA** European Venture Philanthropy Association (#09053)
♦ **EVPC** European Veterinary Parasitology College (#09058)
♦ **EVP** Europäische Volkspartei (#08185)
♦ **EVP** Europese Volkspartij (#08185)
♦ **EVP** Fractie van de Europese Volkspartij – Christen-democraten (#10775)
♦ **EVP** Fraktion der Europäischen Volkspartei – Christdemokraten (#10775)
♦ EVP-Fraktion/Europarat / see Group of the European People's Party (#10774)
♦ EVRA' / see European Association of Veterinary Diagnostic Imaging (#06269)
♦ Evraziiskoe patentnoe vedomstvo (#05612)
♦ Evrejskaja Organizacija Uznikov Fasistskih Konclagerej, Getto 'RUF' (internationally oriented national body)
♦ Evropaiki Diaskepsi Dromon tu Inu (inactive)
♦ Evropaïkí Diáskepsi ton Perifereión Oínou / see Assembly of European Wine Regions (#02317)
♦ Evropaiki Ekfrassi (internationally oriented national body)
♦ Evropaiki Enosi (#08967)
♦ Evropaiki Enosi Eklegmenon ton Orinon Periohon (#06021)
♦ Evropaiki Enosi Mikromosaion (no recent information)
♦ Evropaiki Epitropi (#06633)
♦ Evropaiki Epitropi Ton Organosseon Kinu Kalu / see European Council for Non-Profit Organizations (#06834)
♦ Evropaiki Iatriki Enosi (#07761)
♦ Evropaiki Kinotita (inactive)
♦ Evropaiki Kinotita Anfraka ke Haliva (inactive)
♦ Evropaiki Kinotita Atomikis Energias (inactive)
♦ Evropaiki Kinotita Magiron / see Euro-Toques International (#09190)
♦ Evropaiki Kinotites (inactive)
♦ Evropaiki Omospondia Dimopraton Teksnis / see European Federation of Auctioneers (#07057)
♦ Evropaiki Organosi Viomihanion Metapiisis Tomatas / see European Organisation of Tomato Industries (#08104)
♦ Evropaiki Trapeza Ependiseon (#07599)
♦ Evropaiko Grafio Perivallontos / see European Environmental Bureau (#06996)
♦ Evropaiko Kentro Epihiriseos me Simmetohi tu Dimosiu / see SGI Europe (#19253)
♦ Evropaiko Kentro tis Dimosias Epihiriseos / see SGI Europe (#19253)
♦ Evropaiko Kinoniko Tamio (#08501)
♦ Evropaiko Kinovulio (#08146)
♦ Evropaiko Kinovulio – Euroopan Liberaali-ja Demokraattipouleen Ryhmä / see Renew Europe (#18840)
♦ Evropaiko Laiko Komma (#08185)
♦ Evropaiko Simvulio (#06801)
♦ Evropaiko Simvulio Neon Agroton (#04689)
♦ Evropaikos Sindesmos Podologias (inactive)
♦ Evropako Forumo e Romango thaj e Phirutnengo (#08402)
♦ Evropejskaja Antirevmaticeskaja Liga / see European Alliance of Associations for Rheumatology (#05862)
♦ Evropejskaja Associacija po Demograficeskim Issledovanijam (#06158)
♦ Evropejskaja Associacija Ucrezdenij Svobodnogo Vremeni Detej i Molodezi (#06087)
♦ Evropejskaja Ekonomiceskaja Komissija OON (#20555)
♦ Evropejskaja Federacija Psihologii Sporta (#07218)
♦ Evropejskaja Federacija Tjazeloj Atletiki (#09090)
♦ Evropejskaja Organizacija Vyssih Kontrolnyh Organov (#08115)
♦ Evropejskaja Rabocaja Gruppa po Psihosomaticeskomu Issledovaniju Raka (inactive)
♦ Evropejskij Centr Mira i Razvitija (#06496)
♦ Evropejskij Institut po Preduprezdeniju Prestupnosti i Borbe s nej svjazannyj s Organizaciej Obedinennyh Nacij (#07550)

Evropejskij Konsorcium Politiceskih
09218

alphabetic sequence excludes
For the complete listing, see Yearbook Online at

- ♦ Evropejskij Konsorcium Politiceskih Issledovanij (#06762)
- ♦ Evropejskij Sovet Dorog Vina (inactive)
- ♦ Evropejskoe Obscestvo Kultury (#08576)
- ♦ Evropolitis Drasi Ipiresia / see European Citizen Action Service (#06555)
- ♦ Evropska Adameija za Raviskovanje Zivljenja, Integracije in Civilno Druzbo (#05799)
- ♦ Evropska Agencija za Kemikalije (#06523)
- ♦ Evropska Agencija za Varnost v Letalstvu (#08978)
- ♦ Evropska Agentura pro Bezpecnost Letectvi (#08978)
- ♦ Evropska Agentura pro Chemické Latky (#06523)
- ♦ Evropska Akademie pro Vyskum Zivota, Integraci a Obcanskou Spolecnost (#05799)
- ♦ Evropska Asociace Zarizeni pro Volny Cas Deti a Mladeze (#06087)
- ♦ Evropska Federacija za Versko Izobrazevanje Odraslih (#05966)
- ♦ Evropska Komise (#06633)
- ♦ Evropska Komisija (#06633)
- ♦ Evropska liberalne democraticka a reformni strana / see Alliance of Liberals and Democrats for Europe Party (#00703)
- ♦ Evropska Pravosodna Mreza v Civilnih in gospodarskih Zadevah (#07616)
- ♦ Evropska Rada (#06801)
- ♦ Evropska sit' Organizaci Sdruzujicich Pacienty s Mnohocetnym Myelomem (inactive)
- ♦ Evropská společnost pro právní dijiny (unconfirmed)
- ♦ Evropska Unie (#08967)
- ♦ Evropska Unija (#08967)
- ♦ Evropské Horské Fórum (#07824)
- ♦ Evropské Monitorovaci Centrum pro Drogy a Drogovou Zavislost (#07820)
- ♦ Evropske Sluzbe za Zunanje Delovanje (#07018)
- ♦ Evropské Sluzby pro Vnejsi Cinnost (#07018)
- ♦ Evropski Centar za Mir i Razvoj (#06496)
- ♦ Evropski Center za Etnicne in Regionalne Študije – Univerza v Mariboru (internationally oriented national body)
- ♦ Evropski Center za Spremljanje Drog in Zasvojensoti z Drogami (#07820)
- ♦ Evropski Ekonomsko-Socialni Odbor (#06963)
- ♦ Evropski odbor regij (#06665)
- ♦ Evropski Parlament (#08146)
- ♦ Evropski Svet (#06801)
- ♦ Evropski varuh Clovekovih Pravic (#08084)
- ♦ Evropsko-Africka Asociace pro Rozvoj (internationally oriented national body)
- ♦ Evropsko Racunsko Sodisce (#06854)
- ♦ Evropsko Udruzenje Uzgjaca Smedjeg Goveda (#06405)
- ♦ Evropsky Hospodarsky a Socialni Vybor (#06963)
- ♦ Evropsky Parlament (#08146)
- ♦ Evropsky Technologicky Institut / see European Institute of Innovation and Technology (#07562)
- ♦ Evropsky Ucetni Dvur (#06854)
- ♦ Evropsky ve Ejny Ochrance Prav (#08084)
- ♦ Evroskupina (#05689)
- ♦ Evróvisir Upplsinganetio (#05675)
- ♦ **EVRS** European VitreoRetinal Society (#09072)
- ♦ **EVSA** Entomologiese Vereniging van Suidelike Afrika (#05494)
- ♦ **EVS** Europäischer Verband der Standesbeamtinnen und Standesbeamten (#05760)
- ♦ EVS – European Values Study (unconfirmed)
- ♦ EVS – European Vision Society (no recent information)
- ♦ **EVS** Europees Verbond voor Schriftpsychologie (#08616)
- ♦ **EVSSAR** European Veterinary Society for Small Animal Reproduction (#09059)
- ♦ **EVST** European Vascular Surgeons in Training (#09045)
- ♦ **EVTA** European Vocational Training Association (#09075)
- ♦ **EVTA** European Voice Teachers Association (#09076)
- ♦ **EVT** Europäische Vereinigung für Tierproduktion (#07046)
- ♦ **EVT** Europese Vereniging voor Terminologie (#06252)
- ♦ **EVUA** European Virtual Private Network Users Association (#09066)
- ♦ EVUB – Europäische Vereinigung der Umweltwissenschaftlichen Berufe (no recent information)
- ♦ EVU – Electric Vehicle Union (unconfirmed)
- ♦ **EVU** Europäische Verein für Unfallforschung und Unfall Analyse (#05925)
- ♦ **EVU** European Vegetarian Union (#09048)
- ♦ **EVVC** European Association of Event Centers (#06032)
- ♦ **EVVD** Europese Vereniging van het Vrije Denken (#06048)
- ♦ **EVVE** European Association for the Consumption-based Billing of Energy Costs (#05989)
- ♦ **EVVOD** Europäischer Verband der Versorgungseinrichtungen des Öffentlichen Dienstes (#06180)
- ♦ EWAA – European Wrought Aluminium Association (inactive)
- ♦ EWABA – European Waste-to-Advanced Biofuels Association (unconfirmed)
- ♦ **EWAC** European Cereals Genetics Co-operative (#06509)
- ♦ EWA – Entwicklungswerkstatt Austria (internationally oriented national body)
- ♦ EWA – European Wallcovering Association (inactive)
- ♦ **EWA** European Water Association (#09080)
- ♦ **EWA** European Waterpark Association (#09082)
- ♦ **EWA** European Waterproofing Association (#09084)
- ♦ **EWA** European Welding Association (#09091)
- ♦ EWA – European Women Alliance (internationally oriented national body)
- ♦ EWALT – Eastern and Western Association for Liver Tumors (unconfirmed)
- ♦ **EWAPS** European Workshop of Advanced Plastic Surgery (#09118)
- ♦ **EWAS** European Wrist Arthroscopy Society (#09122)
- ♦ EWB – Educators Without Borders (internationally oriented national body)
- ♦ EWB – Elephants Without Borders (internationally oriented national body)
- ♦ EWB – Europe Without Barriers (internationally oriented national body)
- ♦ **EWB International** Engineers Without Borders International (#05481)
- ♦ EWCA – East-West Center Association (see: #05263)
- ♦ **EWCA** European Writing Centers Association (#09124)
- ♦ EWCC – East-West Cultural Center (internationally oriented national body)
- ♦ **EWC** East-West Center (#05263)
- ♦ **EWC** European Wergeland Centre (#09092)
- ♦ **EWC-FAAE** European Writers' Council (#09123)
- ♦ **EWC-FAEE** Fédération des association européennes d'écrivains (#09123)
- ♦ EWCF / see International Well Control Forum (#15877)
- ♦ **EWCI** Estonian World Council (#05550)
- ♦ EWD / see Widows Rights International
- ♦ **EWDA** European Wildlife Disease Association (#09095)
- ♦ EWDD / see European Monitoring Centre for Drugs and Drug Addiction (#07820)
- ♦ **EWDTS** European Workplace Drug Testing Society (#09117)
- ♦ EWEA / see WindEurope (#20965)
- ♦ **EWEC** Every Woman Every Child (#09215)
- ♦ EWEI – Eastwest European Institute (internationally oriented national body)
- ♦ EW – Election-Watch.EU (internationally oriented national body)
- ♦ EWEPA – European Workshop on Efficiency and Productivity Analysis (meeting series)
- ♦ EWET – European Workshop on Economic Theory (meeting series)
- ♦ EW – European Wireless Conference (meeting series)
- ♦ EWF / see Ondernemers Zonder Grenzen
- ♦ **EWFA** European Window Film Association (#09096)
- ♦ **EWFC** European Working Community for Food Inspection and Consumer Protection (#09107)
- ♦ EWF – Eurasian Women's Forum (meeting series)
- ♦ **EWF** European Federation for Welding, Joining and Cutting (#07233)
- ♦ **EWF** European Wax Federation (#09088)
- ♦ **EWF** European Weightlifting Federation (#09090)
- ♦ EWF International / see Engineers Without Borders International (#05481)
- ♦ EWF-USA / see Engineers for a Sustainable World
- ♦ **EWGAE** European Working Group on Acoustic Emission (#09108)
- ♦ EWGCCA / see European Society for Clinical Cell Analysis (#08544)
- ♦ EWGCF / see European Cystic Fibrosis Society (#06879)
- ♦ **EW-GDS** European Working Group for Glow Discharge Spectroscopy (#09113)
- ♦ EWG – Energy Watch Group (unconfirmed)
- ♦ **EWGGD** European Working Group on Gaucher Disease (#09112)
- ♦ EWGGT / see European Society of Gene and Cell Therapy (#08608)
- ♦ EWGLINET / see European Legionnaires' Disease Surveillance Network (#07681)
- ♦ EWGPO / see European Society of Pediatric Otorhinolaryngology (#08692)
- ♦ EWH – Engineering World Health (internationally oriented national body)
- ♦ **EWHN** European Work Hazards Network (#09106)
- ♦ EWIA – European Wireless Infrastructure Association (unconfirmed)
- ♦ **EWICS** European Workshop on Industrial Computer Systems (#09119)
- ♦ EWICS TC7 / see European Workshop on Industrial Computer Systems (#09119)
- ♦ **EWI** EastWest Institute (#05264)
- ♦ **EWI** Ecumenical Women's Initiative (#05351)
- ♦ EWI – Europäisches Währungsinstitut (inactive)
- ♦ **EWIMA** European Writing Instrument Manufacturer's Association (#09125)
- ♦ **EWIV** Europäische Wirtschaftliche Interessenvereinigung (#06960)
- ♦ **EWJI** European Water Jetting Institute (#09081)
- ♦ **EWLA** European Women Lawyers' Association (#09098)
- ♦ **EWL** European Women's Lobby (#09102)
- ♦ **EWLL** European Working Group on Labour Law (#09114)
- ♦ EWLM – European Workshop on Lipid Mediators (meeting series)
- ♦ **EWMA** European Wound Management Association (#09121)
- ♦ EWMCS / see World Master Chefs Society (#21639)
- ♦ **EWMD** European Women's Management Development International Network (#09103)
- ♦ EWMD International / see European Women's Management Development International Network (#09103)
- ♦ **EWM** European Women in Mathematics (#09099)
- ♦ EWMI – East-West Management Institute (internationally oriented national body)
- ♦ **EWNE** East-West-Network Europe (#05265)
- ♦ **EWOB** European Women on Boards (#09097)
- ♦ **EWODOR** European Working Group on Drug Oriented Research (#09111)
- ♦ **EWOG MDS** European Working Group on MDS (#09115)
- ♦ EWON – European Neonatal Workshop (meeting series)
- ♦ **EWOPA** European Working Group on Psychosocial Aspects of Children with Chronic Renal Failure (#09116)
- ♦ **EWORA** European Women Rectors Association (#09101)
- ♦ **EWPA** European Whey Products Association (#09093)
- ♦ EWPCA / see European Water Association (#09080)
- ♦ **EWP** End Water Poverty (#05464)
- ♦ **EWP** European Water Partnership (#09083)
- ♦ **EWPM** European Wood Preservative Manufacturers Group (#09105)
- ♦ **EWPN** European Women Payments Network (#09100)
- ♦ EWPS / see European Workshop on Particulate Systems (#09120)
- ♦ **EWPS** European Workshop on Particulate Systems (#09120)
- ♦ **EWRA** European Water Resources Association (#09085)
- ♦ EWRIS / see European Federation of Steel Wire Rope Industries (#07221)
- ♦ **EWRIS** European Federation of Steel Wire Rope Industries (#07221)
- ♦ Ewropew Ghall-Azzjoni Esterna (#07018)
- ♦ EWRR – European Workshop for Rheumatology Research (meeting series)
- ♦ **EWRS** European Weed Research Society (#09089)
- ♦ EWS – European Water Stewardship (unconfirmed)
- ♦ **EWS** European Women and Sport Network (#09104)
- ♦ EWSF / see European Federation of Productivity Services (#07196)
- ♦ EWSN – International Conference on Embedded Wireless Systems and Networks (meeting series)
- ♦ **EWTA** European Water Treatment Association (#09086)
- ♦ EWTA – European Wind Tower Association (unconfirmed)
- ♦ **EWTCA** East-West Transport Corridor Association (#05266)
- ♦ EWT – Endangered Wildlife Trust (internationally oriented national body)
- ♦ **EWT** European Walled Towns (#09079)
- ♦ EWUF / see European Wushu Kungfu Federation (#09126)
- ♦ **EWUF** European Wushu Kungfu Federation (#09126)
- ♦ **EWV** Europäische Wandervereinigung (#08328)
- ♦ EXA – International Conference on Exotic Aoms and Related Topics (meeting series)
- ♦ EXALT – EXALT – The Global Extractivisms and Alternatives Initiative (unconfirmed)
- ♦ EXALT – The Global Extractivisms and Alternatives Initiative (unconfirmed)
- ♦ Examen Internacional de Ginecólogia Pediatrica y de la Adolescencia (#13585)

♦ EXARC 09219

Contact Frambozenweg 161, 2321 KA Leiden, Netherlands. T. +4593101029. E-mail: info@exarc.net.
URL: https://exarc.net/

History 16 Mar 2003, Lejre (Denmark). Founded following a series of meetings since Feb 2001. Former names and other names: *European Exchange on Archaeological Research and Communication (EXARC)* – former; *Europeiskt Nätverk för Experimentell Arkeologi och Forntida Teknik* – former; *EXARC – International Association of Archaeological Open-Air Museums and Experimental Archaeology* – former. Registration: Handelsregister, No/ID: 17279629, Start date: 22 Dec 2009, Netherlands; Sweden. **Aims** Investigate, contextualize, present and interpret archaeological and experimental *archaeological heritage* with an emphasis focusing on, but not limited to, archaeological open-air *museums*. **Structure** Members' Meeting (annual); Board. **Languages** English. **Staff** 50.00 FTE, voluntary. **Finance** Sources: members' dues. **Activities** Events/meetings. **Events** *Experimental Archaeology Conference* Netherlands 2021, *Experimental Archaeology Conference* Trento (Italy) 2019, *Experimental Archaeology Conference* Leiden (Netherlands) 2017, *Experimental Archaeology Conference* Dublin (Ireland) 2015, *International Conference* Mistelbach (Austria) 2015. **Publications** *EXARC Journal* (4 a year).

Members Institutes (approx. 175) and individuals (approx. 225) in 44 countries and territories:
Åland, Australia, Austria, Azerbaijan, Belgium, Brazil, Bulgaria, Canada, Cyprus, Czechia, Denmark, Egypt, Finland, France, Germany, Greece, Hungary, India, Ireland, Israel, Italy, Kazakhstan, Latvia, Lithuania, Malta, Moldova, Namibia, Netherlands, Nicaragua, Norway, Poland, Portugal, Romania, Russia, Serbia, Slovakia, Slovenia, South Africa, Spain, Sweden, Switzerland, UK, Ukraine, USA.

NGO Relations Member of (1): *Network of European Museum Organizations (NEMO, #17024).* Affiliated with (1): *International Council of Museums (ICOM, #13051).* [2022.05.04/XF7043/F]

- ♦ EXARC – International Association of Archaeological Open-Air Museums and Experimental Archaeology / see EXARC (#09219)
- ♦ **EXAR** European Association for the Advancement of Archaeology by Experiment (#05926)

♦ **EXCA** European Expanded Clay Association (#07013)

♦ Excellence in Medical Education (EXCEMED) 09220

Headquarters 14 rue du Rhône, 1204 Geheva, Switzerland. E-mail: info@excemed.org.
Representative Office Viale della Piramide Cestia 1c, 00153 Rome RM, Italy. T. +396420413320. Fax +396420413677.
URL: https://www.excemed.org/

History 2002, by (US) BioSymposia, as *Serono Symposia International Foundation (SSIF)*. Current title adopted Apr 2014. **Aims** Dedicated to the continuing medical education of *healthcare* professionals. **Structure** Board of Directors; Medical Advisors; Scientific Committee. **Activities** Events/meetings; training/education. **Events** *Multiple Sclerosis Conference* Dubai (United Arab Emirates) 2014, *World congress on controversies in obstetrics, gynecology and infertility* Paris (France) 2008, *Symposium on psoriasis* Barcelona (Spain) 2007, *Meeting on art in the 21st century* Amsterdam (Netherlands) 2006, *International symposium on structure-function relationship of gonadotropins* Paris (France) 1989. **Publications** *SSIF Newsletter*. [2018/XM2295/f/**F**]

♦ Excellence in Pediatrics Institute (EIP) 09221

Switzerland Rue des Vignerons 1B, c/o H and B Law, 1110 Morges VD 1, Switzerland. T. +41225182409. E-mail: secretariat@ineip.org.
URL: http://www.ineip.org/

History Registration: EU Transparency Register, No/ID: 814880937536-71; Switzerland. **Aims** Improve child health and healthcare globally by empowering all providers who care for children with the latest practical skills, expert advice and peer-led guidance. **Structure** 2 Co-Chairs. **Activities** Events/meetings; advocacy/lobbying/activism; training/education. **Events** *Excellence in Pediatrics Conference* Amsterdam (Netherlands) 2021, *Excellence in Pediatrics Conference* 2020, *Excellence in Pediatrics Conference* Copenhagen (Denmark) 2019, *Excellence in Pediatrics Conference* Prague (Czechia) 2018, *Excellence in Pediatrics Conference* Vienna (Austria) 2017. [2021/XM7945/**D**]

♦ **EXCEMED** Excellence in Medical Education (#09220)
♦ Excess/Surplus Lines Claims Association / see International Association of Claim Professionals (#11777)
♦ Exchange and Cooperation Centre for Latin America (internationally oriented national body)
♦ Exchange Group for Appropriate Technology (internationally oriented national body)
♦ Exchange of Letters Constituting an Agreement Concerning German-French-Luxembourg Cooperation (1980 treaty)
♦ Exchange of Letters Constituting an Agreement Concerning the Movement of Refugees (1964 treaty)
♦ Exchange of Letters Constituting an Agreement Concerning the Right of Return of Refugee Workers (1964 treaty)
♦ Exchange of Letters Constituting an Agreement Concerning the Use of the Seaman's Book as a Travel Document (1964 treaty)
♦ Exchange of Letters Constituting an Agreement Concerning the Use of Seamen's Books as Travel Documents (1964 treaty)
♦ Exchange Network of Parliaments of Latin America and The Caribbean (#18696)
♦ Exchange of Notes Constituting an Agreement Amending the Wheat Agreement of 22 April 1942 (1946 treaty)
♦ Exchange of Notes Constituting an Agreement Concerning the Exchange of Cut Flowers on a Commercial Basis (1955 treaty)
♦ Exchange of Notes Constituting an Agreement Concerning the Liberalization of Trade in Fishing Products (1954 treaty)
♦ Exchange of Notes Constituting an Agreement Relating to Scientific Investigations of the Fur Seals in the North Pacific Ocean (1952 treaty)

♦ EXCiPACT 09222

Contact Rue Marie de Bourgogne 52, 1000 Brussels, Belgium. E-mail: info@excipact.org.
URL: https://www.excipact.org/

History Former names and other names: *International Pharmaceutical Excipients Certification* – full title. Registration: Belgium. **Aims** Manage an independent, high quality, third party certification scheme available to pharmaceutical excipient manufacturers and distributors worldwide. **Structure** General Assembly; Board; Operations & Admin Team. **Languages** English. **Activities** Certification/accreditation; standards/guidelines; training/education. **Events** *New GWP Standard* Brussels (Belgium) 2021. **Publications** *EXCiPACTNews Alert*. Standards; policy documents; articles; position papers; workshop proceedings; brochure.
Members Full (5):
Fédération européenne du commerce chimique (Fecc, #09563); *International Pharmaceutical Excipients Council Europe (IPEC Europe, #14565)*; *International Pharmaceutical Excipients Council of the Americas (IPEC-Americas)*; PQG (UK); SSPEA (China). [2022.06.15/XM6993/y/**C**]

♦ EXCON – International Conference on Excitonic and Photonic Processes in Condensed Matter and Nano Materials (meeting series)
♦ Executive Board of the Health Ministers' Council for the Gulf Cooperation Council States / see Gulf Health Council (#10830)
♦ Executive Committee for the EEC of the European Brushware Federation / see European Brushware Federation (#06406)
♦ Executive Committee of Non-Governmental Organizations Associated with the United Nations Department of Public Information / see Global NGO Executive Committee (#10507)
♦ Executive Committee for the Preparation of International Congresses of the Blind (inactive)
♦ Executive Council on Diplomacy (internationally oriented national body)
♦ Executive Council on Foreign Diplomacy / see Executive Council on Diplomacy
♦ Executive Council on Foreign Diplomats / see Executive Council on Diplomacy

♦ Executive MBA Council (EMBAC) 09223

Exec Dir One University Drive, ASBE, Orange CA 92866, USA. T. +17146287345. Fax +17146287345. E-mail: info@embac.org.
URL: http://embac.org/

History Founded 1981. Subtitle: *Global Voice of the Executive MBA Industry*. **Structure** Board of Trustees. **Activities** Awards/prizes/competitions; events/meetings; knowledge management/information dissemination; research/documentation; training/education. **Events** *Conference* Orlando, FL (USA) 2019, *Conference* Madrid (Spain) 2018. **Publications** Corporate; Academic. Membership countries not specified. [2019/XM7685/**C**]

♦ Executives Without Borders (internationally oriented national body)
♦ Executive Secretariat of the Council of Electrification of Central America (#19191)
♦ Executive Secretariat of the Middle East and North Africa Economic Summit (no recent information)
♦ Executive Secretary of the Committee for the Meetings of Nobel Laureates in Lindau / see Council for the Lindau Nobel Laureate Meetings (#04909)
♦ Executives' Meeting of East Asian and Pacific Central Banks (meeting series)
♦ ExecWB – Executives Without Borders (internationally oriented national body)
♦ Exhibit Designers and Producers Association / see Experiential Designers and Producers Association
♦ **EXIBA** European Extruded Polystyrene Insulation Board Association (#07019)

♦ Exit International 09224

Contact PO Box 37781, Darwin NT 0821, Australia. Fax +61289059249. E-mail: contact@exitinternational.net.
UK Contact BM Box 6681, London, WC1 N3AX, UK. Fax +442078500828.
URL: http://exitinternational.net/

History 1997, as *Voluntary Euthanasia Research Foundation (VERF)*. **Aims** Inform members and support them in their end of life decision-making. **Finance** Members' dues. **Activities** Events/meetings; advocacy/lobbying/activism; research and development. **Publications** *Deliverance* (4 a year) – newsletter. *Peaceful Pill eHandbook* – series. [2019/XM6678/**F**]

♦ Exotic Pathology Society 09225

Société de Pathologie Exotique (SPE)

SG c/o Inst Pasteur, 25 rue du Docteur Roux, 75724 Paris CEDEX 15, France. T. +33109671799. E-mail: secretaire@pathexo.fr.
URL: http://www.pathexo.fr/

History Founded 1908, by Alphonse Laveran (Nobel Prize 1907). Recognized in accordance with French law, decree of 10 Dec 1962. **Aims** Study exotic diseases of men and animals, hygienic and sanitary measures to prevent extension of epidemics, and epizootics of exotic origin. **Structure** General Assembly; Council; Bureau. **Languages** French. **Staff** 2.50 FTE, voluntary. **Finance** Members' dues. Annual budget: about euro 10,000. **Activities** Events/meetings; training/education. **Events** *French Language International Congress of Tropical Medicine / International Congress* Dakar (Senegal) 2013, *French language international congress of tropical medicine* Vientiane (Laos) 2010, *Réunion sur le fonds mondial de lutte contre le sida, le paludisme et la tuberculose* Libreville (Gabon) 2009, *Centenary meeting* Paris (France) 2008, *Congrès francophone d'épidémiologie en milieu tropical* Ouidah (Benin) 2007. **Publications** *Bulletin de la Société de Pathologie Exotique* (5 a year) in English, French; *Annuaire de la Société de pathologie exotique*.
Members Individuals in 30 countries:
Algeria, Argentina, Belgium, Benin, Brazil, Burkina Faso, Cambodia, Cameroon, Comoros, Congo Brazzaville, Congo DR, Côte d'Ivoire, France, Gabon, Germany, Guinea, Guyana, Italy, Laos, Madagascar, Mali, Niger, Portugal, Senegal, Spain, Switzerland, Togo, Tunisia, UK, Vietnam. [2018.09.05/XD4819/v/**F**]

♦ Expanded Research Program / see International Lead Zinc Research Organization (#14011)
♦ Expérience de vie internationale (#21930)
♦ Experiential Designers and Producers Association (internationally oriented national body)
♦ Experimental Aircraft Association (internationally oriented national body)
♦ Experimental Center for Latin American Studies / see Centro de Estudios Americanos y Caribeños
♦ Experimental Chaos and Complexity Conference (meeting series)
♦ Experiment in International Living / see Worldwide Network of the Experiment in International Living (#21930)
♦ Experimento de Convivencia Internacional (#21930)
♦ Experiment Vereinigung für das Praktische Zusammenleben der Völker (#21930)

♦ Experts for Specialised Construction and Concrete Systems (EFNARC) 09226

Sec c/o Versuchsstollen Hagerbach AG, Polistrasse 1, Flums Hochwiese, 8893 Flums SG, Switzerland. T. +41817341412. E-mail: secretary@efnarc.org.
URL: http://www.efnarc.org/

History Mar 1989. Founded by national trading associations representing producers and applicators of specialist construction products in Europe. Former names and other names: *European Federation of National Associations of Specialist Contractors and Material Suppliers to the Construction Industry* – former (Mar 1989); *Fédération européenne des associations nationales des entrepreneurs spécialisés et des fabricants de matériaux pour l'industrie de construction* – former (Mar 1989); *Europäische Bund der Nationalen Verbände von Spezialisten der Unternehmer und der Lieferanten von Materialen* – former (Mar 1989); *European Federation of Producers and Applicators of Specialist Products for Structures* – former; *Fédération européenne des producteurs et applicateurs de produits spéciaux pour structures* – former; *Europäischer Verband der Hersteller und Anwender von Spezialprodukten im Bauwesen* – former; *European Federation for Specialist Construction Chemicals and Concrete Systems* – former. **Aims** Promote the general interests and develop the industry in the field of specialised construction and concrete systems, in particular in regards of sprayed concrete solutions. **Structure** General Assembly; Executive Committee; Specialist Focus Groups. **Languages** English. **Finance** Sources: members' dues. **Activities** Advocacy/lobbying/activism; certification/accreditation; research and development; standards/guidelines; training/education. **Members** Companies. Membership countries not specified. [2022.02.15/XD3577/**D**]

♦ Export Advertising Association / see International Advertising Association (#11590)
♦ Export Development and Agricultural Diversification Unit / see Organisation of Eastern Caribbean States/Competitive Business Unit (#17805)
♦ **EXPRA** Extended Producer Responsibility Alliance (#09227)
♦ Express Association of the Middle East (no recent information)
♦ Expression européenne (internationally oriented national body)
♦ Express Mail Services / see Global Express Association (#10351)
♦ **EXSA** European X-ray Spectrometry Association (#09128)

♦ Extended Producer Responsibility Alliance (EXPRA) 09227

Managing Dir Avenue des Olympiades 2, 1140 Brussels, Belgium. T. +491712017055. E-mail: info@expra.eu.
URL: http://www.expra.eu/

History 2013. Registration: No/ID: 0524.725.854, Start date: 21 Mar 2013, Belgium; EU Transparency Register, No/ID: 382147211686-77, Start date: 5 Aug 2013. **Aims** Ensure recovery and *recycling* of packaging *waste* in the most economically efficient and ecologically sound manner. **Languages** Bulgarian, English, German. **Staff** 2.00 FTE, paid. **Finance** Sources: members' dues.
Members Packaging and packaging waste recovery and recycling systems (26) in 24 countries:
Belgium, Bosnia-Herzegovina, Bulgaria, Canada, Cyprus, Czechia, Estonia, Finland, Greece, Hungary, Iceland, Israel, Italy, Luxembourg, Malta, Netherlands, North Macedonia, Norway, Romania, Slovakia, Slovenia, Spain, Sweden, Türkiye.
NGO Relations Member of (1): *Circular Plastics Alliance (#03936). European Federation of Glass Recyclers (#07134)*. [2020.03.11/XM8512/**D**]

♦ External Finance for Africa Group / see Development Finance International Group

♦ Extinction Rebellion (XR) 09228

Address not obtained.
URL: https://rebellion.global/

History 2018. **Aims** As a decentralized, international and politically non-partisan movement using non-violent direct action and civil disobedience, persuade governments to act justly on the Climate and Ecological Emergency.
Members Groups in 80 countries:
Argentina, Australia, Austria, Belgium, Brazil, Bulgaria, Burkina Faso, Canada, Chile, China, Colombia, Congo DR, Costa Rica, Croatia, Czechia, Denmark, Ecuador, Estonia, Ethiopia, Finland, France, Gambia, Germany, Ghana, Greece, Hungary, Iceland, India, Indonesia, Ireland, Israel, Italy, Japan, Kenya, Korea Rep, Kosovo, Lebanon, Lithuania, Luxembourg, Malta, Mexico, Moldova, Nepal, Netherlands, New Zealand, Nigeria, Norway, Pakistan, Peru, Philippines, Poland, Portugal, Qatar, Romania, Russia, Rwanda, Senegal, Serbia, Sierra Leone, Slovakia, Solomon Is, South Africa, Spain, Sri Lanka, Sudan, Sweden, Switzerland, Taiwan, Tanzania UR, Thailand, Tunisia, Türkiye, Uganda, UK, Ukraine, Uruguay, USA, Venezuela, Zambia, Zimbabwe. [2022/AA2963/**F**]

♦ Extracorporeal Life Support Organization (internationally oriented national body)

♦ Extractive Industries Transparency Initiative (EITI) 09229

Initiative pour la Transparence dans les Industries Extractives – Iniciativa para la Transparencia de las Industrias Extractivas

Exec Dir Rådhusgata 26, 0151 Oslo, Norway. T. +4722200800. E-mail: secretariat@eiti.org.
URL: http://www.eiti.org/

History Jun 2003, London (UK). Introduced by UK Prime Minister Tony Blair in a statement intended for the World Summit on Sustainable Development, Johannesburg (South Africa), Sep 2002. Established after *Department for International Development (DFID, inactive)* convened a meeting of civil society, company and government representatives who agreed that a reporting standard should be developed. Registration: Norway. **Aims** Promote understanding of natural resource management, strengthen public and corporate governance and accountability, provide the data to inform policy-making and multi-stakeholder dialogue in the extractive sector. **Structure** Members' Meeting; Board (elected every 3 years in connection with the Global Conference); International Secretariat, located in Oslo (Norway). **Languages** English, French, Russian, Spanish. **Staff** 45.00 FTE, paid. **Finance** Support from organizations and governments. Annual budget: 7,000,000 USD. **Activities** Events/meetings. *Multi-Donor Trust Fund for the EITI*. **Events** *Board meeting* 2022, *Board meeting* 2021, *Meeting* Oslo (Norway) 2021, *Meeting* Addis Ababa (Ethiopia) 2019, *Meeting* Paris (France) 2019. **Publications** Online newsletter.

Members Implementing countries (55):
Afghanistan, Albania, Argentina, Armenia, Burkina Faso, Cameroon, Central African Rep, Chad, Colombia, Congo Brazzaville, Congo DR, Côte d'Ivoire, Ecuador, Ethiopia, Gabon, Germany, Ghana, Guinea, Guyana, Honduras, Indonesia, Iraq, Kazakhstan, Kyrgyzstan, Liberia, Madagascar, Malawi, Mali, Mauritania, Mexico, Mongolia, Mozambique, Myanmar, Netherlands, Niger, Nigeria, Norway, Papua New Guinea, Peru, Philippines, Sao Tomé-Principe, Senegal, Seychelles, Sierra Leone, Suriname, Tajikistan, Tanzania UR, Timor-Leste, Togo, Trinidad-Tobago, Uganda, UK, Ukraine, Yemen, Zambia.
Supporting countries (15):
Australia, Belgium, Canada, Denmark, Finland, France, Germany, Japan, Netherlands, Norway, Spain, Sweden, Switzerland, UK, USA. [2022.05.04/XM4529/t/**F**]

- ♦ Extradition Agreement (1911 treaty)
- ♦ Extradition Agreement (1952 treaty)
- ♦ Extradition Convention, 1907 (1907 treaty)
- ♦ Extradition Convention, 1923 (1923 treaty)
- ♦ extraterritorial obligations / see ETO Consortium (#05560)
- ♦ Extremaduran Centre for Studies and Cooperation with Ibero-America / see Fundación Academia Europea e Iberoamericana de Yuste

♦ Extreme Light Infrastructure ERIC (ELI ERIC) 09230

Dir-Gen Za Radnicí 835, 252 41 Dolní Břežany, Czechia. T. +420266051263. E-mail: info@eli-laser.eu.
URL: https://eli-laser.eu/

History 30 Apr 2021. Established by *ELI Delivery Consortium International Association (ELI-DC, inactive)*. Granted legal status of European Research Infrastructure Consortium (ERIC) by *European Commission (EC, #06633)*. **Aims** Provide access to world-class high power and ultra-fast lasers for science; enable cutting-edge research in physical, chemical, materials, and medical sciences, as well as breakthrough technological innovations. **Structure** General Assembly; Administration and Finance Committee; International Scientific and Technical Advisory Committee. Multi-site research infrastructure based on 3 specialized and complementary facilities in Czech Rep (ELI Beamlines), Hungary (ELI-ALPS) and Romania (ELI-NP).
Members Host (*) and founding members (4):
Czechia (*), Hungary, Italy, Lithuania.
Founding Observers (2):
Bulgaria, Germany.
NGO Relations Member of (1): *Association of European-level Research Infrastructure Facilities (ERF-AISBL, #02518)*. [2023/AA3027/j/**E***]

- ♦ Extreme Traveler International Congress (meeting series)
- ♦ **EYA** European Yoga Alliance (#09129)
- ♦ EYA – European Young Academies (unconfirmed)
- ♦ EYA / see World Youth Alliance – Europe (#21952)
- ♦ **EYBA** European Young Bar Association (#09132)
- ♦ **EYCA** European Youth Card Association (#09137)
- ♦ EYCD – European Young Christian Democrats (inactive)
- ♦ **EYCE** Ecumenical Youth Council in Europe (#05352)
- ♦ **EYC** European Yoga Council (#09130)
- ♦ EYC – European Young Conservatives (no recent information)
- ♦ EYCN – European Young Chemists' Network (see: #06524)
- ♦ **EYCO** European Youth Circus Organisation (#09139)
- ♦ **EYCs** European Youth Centres (#09138)
- ♦ EYCW / see JOC Europe (#16118)
- ♦ EYDC / see European Union of Deaf Youth (#08986)
- ♦ **EYE** European Young Engineers (#09133)
- ♦ Eye Movement Desensitization and Reprocessing International Association / see EMDR International Association
- ♦ Eyes and Ears of Europe (internationally oriented national body)
- ♦ Eyes and Ears of Europe – Association for the Design, Promotion and Marketing of Audiovisual Media / see Eyes and Ears of Europe
- ♦ Eyesight International (internationally oriented national body)
- ♦ Eyes of the World Foundation (internationally oriented national body)
- ♦ Eye and Tissue Bank International / see KeraLink International
- ♦ Eyewitness Palestine (internationally oriented national body)
- ♦ **EYFA** European Youth for Action (#09136)
- ♦ **EYF** European Youth Foundation (#09141)
- ♦ EYHR-Net – European Youth Human Rights Network (internationally oriented national body)
- ♦ **EYIF** European Young Innovators Forum (#09134)
- ♦ **EYP** European Youth Parliament (#09145)
- ♦ **EYP** European Youth Press (#09146)
- ♦ EZA Dritte Welt – Entwicklungszusammenarbeit mit der Dritten Welt (internationally oriented national body)
- ♦ **EZA** Europäisches Zentrum für Arbeitnehmerfragen (#06505)
- ♦ **EZB** Europäische Zentralbank (#06466)
- ♦ EZE / see Brot für die Welt
- ♦ EZFF – Europäisches Zentrum für Föderalismus-Forschung (internationally oriented national body)
- ♦ **EZMW** Europäisches Zentrum für Mittelfristige Wettervorhersage (#06490)
- ♦ **EZNC** European Zoo Nutrition Centre (#09149)
- ♦ EZNRG – European Zoo Nutrition Research Group (inactive)
- ♦ **EZPWD** Europäisches Zentrum für Parlamentarische Wissenschaft und Dokumentation (#06495)
- ♦ **EZS** European Zebrafish Society (#09147)
- ♦ F4E / see European Joint Undertaking for ITER and the Development of Fusion Energy (#07611)
- ♦ FA / see Friendship Ambassadors Foundation
- ♦ FAAB / see Asian Boxing Confederation (#01363)
- ♦ **FAAE** Forum of Armenian Associations of Europe (#09899)
- ♦ **FAA** Federation of African Archery (#09400)
- ♦ FAA – Fédération arabe d'aviron (inactive)
- ♦ FAAF – Fédération africaine d'action familiale (inactive)
- ♦ **FAAFI** Fédération des associations d'anciens fonctionnaires internationaux (#09457)
- ♦ **FAAPA** Fédération Atlantique des Agences de Presse Africaines (#09462)
- ♦ FAAT – Fédération africaine des arts traditionnels (inactive)
- ♦ FAAW – Federation of Arab Agricultural Workers (inactive)
- ♦ FAB / see International Cat Care
- ♦ **FABA** Federation of Asian Biotech Associations (#09429)
- ♦ **FABC** Federation of Asian Bishops' Conferences (#09430)
- ♦ FABCOS – Foundation for African Business and Consumer Services (internationally oriented national body)
- ♦ **FABEC** Functional Airspace Block Europe Central (#10016)
- ♦ **FAB** International Network on Feminist Approaches to Bioethics (#14270)
- ♦ FABIO / see Pan-Africa Bicycle Information Network
- ♦ **FABI** Union arabe des bibliothèques et de l'information (#00947)
- ♦ FabLearn (unconfirmed)
- ♦ Fabricators and Manufacturers Association International (internationally oriented national body)

♦ Fabry International Network (FIN) 09231

Coordinator address not obtained. E-mail: info@fabrynetwork.org.
URL: http://www.fabrynetwork.org/

History 2005. Registration: Handelsregister, No/ID: KVK 04080030, Netherlands. **Aims** Raise awareness and educate the public about Fabry *disease*, a life-threatening genetic *lysosomal*-storage disorder. **Structure** Board of Directors. **Languages** Danish, Dutch, English, Finnish, Greek, Lithuanian. **Staff** 1.00 FTE, paid. **Finance** Educational grants. **Events** *Meeting* Barcelona (Spain) 2019, *European Round Table on Fabry Disease* Paris (France) 2015.
Members Patient organizations in 51 countries and territories:
Argentina, Australia, Austria, Belgium, Brazil, Bulgaria, Canada, Chile, China, Colombia, Croatia, Czechia, Denmark, Ecuador, Egypt, Estonia, Finland, France, Germany, Greece, Hong Kong, Hungary, India, Indonesia, Iran Islamic Rep, Italy, Japan, Korea Rep, Luxembourg, Malaysia, Netherlands, New Zealand, Norway, Peru, Philippines, Poland, Portugal, Romania, Russia, Singapore, Slovakia, Slovenia, South Africa, Spain, Sweden, Switzerland, Taiwan, Türkiye, UK, Uruguay, USA.
IGO Relations Member of (1): *European Medicines Agency (EMA, #07767)*. **NGO Relations** Member of (3): *EURORDIS – Rare Diseases Europe (#09175)*; *Rare Diseases International (RDI, #18621)*; *World Patients Alliance (WPA)*. [2022/XM1567/**C**]

- ♦ FAC / see Fonds de solidarité prioritaire
- ♦ **FACCE-JPI** Joint Programming Initiative on Agriculture, Food Security and Climate Change (#16145)
- ♦ FACC – Federation of African Chambers of Commerce (no recent information)
- ♦ FACCI / see Federation of African Chambers of Commerce, Industry, Agriculture and Professions (#09401)
- ♦ FACDIM – Fondazione Adkins Chiti: Donne in Musica (internationally oriented national body)
- ♦ FACDIS – West Virginia Consortium for Faculty and Course Development in International Studies (internationally oriented national body)

♦ Face Equality International (FEI) 09232

Hon Treas Moulière, La Banquette, Guernsey, Castel, GY5 7EQ, UK. E-mail: info@faceequalityinternational.org.
URL: https://faceequalityinternational.org/

History Nov 2018. Registration: No/ID: CH597, UK, Guernsey. **Aims** Improve the life prospects of any person anywhere in the world who has a facial difference or disfigurement, an unusual-looking, scarred or asymmetrical face (or body) from any cause. **Structure** Forum; Board of Trustees; Council of Representatives. **Languages** English. **Staff** 1.00 FTE, paid. **Finance** Sources: donations; members' dues. **Activities** Events/meetings.
Members Organizations in 15 countries and territories:
Australia, Belgium, Canada, Channel Is, Czechia, Italy, Korea Rep, Netherlands, Nicaragua, South Africa, Switzerland, Taiwan, Türkiye, UK, USA.
Included in the above, 2 organizations listed in this Yearbook:
European Cleft Organisation (ECO, #06572); *Smile Train (#19328)*. [2021.02.24/XM8396/y/**C**]

- ♦ Face to Face International (internationally oriented national body)
- ♦ **FACE** Federation of Aluminium Consumers in Europe (#09415)
- ♦ **FACE** Federation of ASEAN Consulting Engineers (#09424)
- ♦ **FACE** Fédération des associations de chasse et conservation de la faune sauvage de l'UE (#09459)
- ♦ **FACE** Fresh Arts Coalition Europe (#09995)
- ♦ FACE – International Federation of Associations of Computer Users in Engineering, Architecture and Related Fields (no recent information)
- ♦ **FAC** Federation of Arab Contractors (#09419)
- ♦ FAC – Food Aid Committee (inactive)
- ♦ FAC – Food Aid Convention, 1986 (1986 treaty)
- ♦ FAC – Food Aid Convention, 1999 (1999 treaty)
- ♦ **FAC** Food Assistance Committee (#09840)
- ♦ **FAC** Forum Africain de la Concurrence (#00260)
- ♦ Fachstelle Ferntourismus / see Tourism Watch
- ♦ Fachverband Europäischer Sicherheits- und Schlüsselfachgeschäfte (#07708)

♦ Facilité africaine de l'eau (FAE) 09233

African Water Facility (AWF)

Officer-in-Charge ADB, BP 323 – 1002, Belvédère, Tunis, Tunisia. T. +21671102055. Fax +21671103744. E-mail: africanwaterfacility@afdb.org.
URL: http://www.africanwaterfacility.org/

History 25 May 2004, Kampala (Uganda), during Board of Governors meeting of *African Development Bank (ADB, #00283)*. Inaugural meeting 8 Jul 2005, Tunis (Tunisia). **Aims** Provide investment support for water management programmes and projects in Africa; accelerate development, approval and implementation of integrated water management plans; facilitate commitment of additional funds to the water sector in Africa. **Structure** Council comprising 5 representatives from *African Ministers' Council on Water (AMCOW, #00376)*, 5 representatives from partner/donor agencies, 1 representative from *New Partnership for Africa's Development (NEPAD, #17091)*, 1 representative from UN Water/Africa and 1 representative of *African Development Bank (ADB, #00283)*. **Staff** 18.00 FTE, paid. **IGO Relations** Located at: ADB. Supports setting up of: *Volta Basin Authority (VBA, #20808)*. Supports: *Lake Chad Basin Commission (LCBC, #16220)*; *World Hydrological Cycle Observing System (WHYCOS, #21573)*. **NGO Relations** *Waterpreneurs (#20833)*. [2012/XM1736/**F***]

- ♦ Facilité africaine de soutien juridique (#00361)

♦ Facility for Antiproton and Ion Research in Europe (FAIR) 09234

Contact Planckstr 1, 64291 Darmstadt, Germany. T. +496159713032. Fax +496159713916.
URL: http://www.fair-center.eu/

History 4 Oct 2010, Wiesbaden (Germany), when international agreement on the construction of the accelerator facility FAIR was signed by governments of Germany, Finland, France, India, Poland, Romania, Russia, Slovenia and Sweden. Part of international agreement is setting up of *FAIR GmbH*, also set up 2010. **Aims** Explore the nature of matter. **Structure** Council; Management Board; Scientific Council Administrative and Finance Committee; Machine Advisory Board; Board of Fair Collaborations; In-Kind Review Board; Program Advisory Committee; Expert Committee Experiments; Resource Review Board. **Languages** English, German. **Finance** Contributions of shareholders, with Germany bearing 3/4 of total costs of about euro 1,000,000,000. **Activities** Research and development; awareness raising; capacity building; financial and/or material support; guidance/assistance/consulting; knowledge management/information dissemination; events/meetings; publishing activities; research/documentation; training/education. Active in: Russia, india, China, Europe, Iran Islamic Rep.
Members Governments (10):
Finland, France, Germany, India, Poland, Romania, Russia, Slovenia, Sweden, UK.
IGO Relations *European Organization for Nuclear Research (CERN, #08108)*. [2017.04.20/XM5690/**F***]

- ♦ **FACIM** Fondation pour l'action culturelle internationale en montagne (#09813)
- ♦ Facing Facts! / see Facing Facts (#09235)

♦ Facing Facts 09235

Contact address not obtained. T. +3223443444. E-mail: melissa.sonnino@ceji.org.
URL: http://facingfacts.eu/

History Founded 2011, as a partnership between 4 NGOs. Currently a civil society initiative. Previously known as *Facing Facts!*. **Aims** Tackle the issue of *hate crime* and hate speech in Europe. **Structure** Coordinated by: *CEJI (#03628)*. **Languages** English, French, Greek, Hungarian, Italian, Polish, Spanish. **Finance** Funding from: *European Union (EU, #08967)*; foundations; corporate entities. **Activities** Training/education; advocacy/lobbying/activism; research/documentation; events/meetings. **Events** *Facing all the Facts Conference* Brussels (Belgium) 2018. **Publications** Country reports; reports. **NGO Relations** Partners include: *CEJI (#03628)*; *European Network on Independent Living (ENIL, #07929)*; *European Roma Information Office (ERIO)*. Associate partners include: *European Network against Racism (ENAR, #07862)*; *European Network on Religion and Belief (ENORB, #07985)*; *European Roma Rights Centre (ERRC, #08401)*; *European Union of Jewish Students (EUJS, #08997)*; *ILGA-Europe (#11118)*; *International Network Against Cyber Hate (INACH, #14229)*; *Social Platform (#19344)*. [2020.01.16/XM7788/**E**]

- ♦ Facing History and Ourselves (internationally oriented national body)
- ♦ **FACO** Federation of Asian Clinical Oncology (#09432)
- ♦ FACOGAZ / see Association of European Manufacturers of Gas Meters, Gas Pressure Regulators, Safety Devices and Stations (#02521)
- ♦ FACPB – Federación de Asociaciones de Comerciantes en Productos Basicos (no recent information)
- ♦ FACPM – Forum Africain contra la peine de mort (internationally oriented national body)
- ♦ **FACS** Federation of Asian Chemical Societies (#09431)

♦ FACSS – Federation of Analytical Chemistry and Spectroscopy Societies (internationally oriented national body)
♦ FACT – Foundation for the Accreditation of Cellular Therapy (internationally oriented national body)
♦ Factor 10 Club / see Factor 10 Institute (#09236)

♦ Factor 10 Institute 09236

Institut du facteur 10

Address not obtained.

URL: http://www.factor10.de/

History Oct 1994, Carnoules (France), as *Factor 10 Club – Club du facteur 10*. **Aims** Draw attention to the need for substantially reducing *global material flows* in a timely manner. **Activities** Current topics include: changes in cultural and economic priorities; increase in resource productivity through new technological approaches; ecological tax reforms; role of work in a sustainable economy. Annual meetings in Carnoules (France). *Carnoules Declarations*.

Members Individuals (16) in 10 countries:
Austria, Canada, France, Germany, India, Japan, Netherlands, Switzerland, UK, USA. [2009/XF3396/jv/**F**]

♦ Factors Chain International / see FCI (#09278)
♦ Faculdade Latinoamericana de Ciências Sociais (#16316)
♦ Facultad Latinoamericana de Ciencias Ambientales / see Latin American Forum of Environmental Sciences (#16336)
♦ Facultad Latinoamericana de Ciencias Sociales (#16316)
♦ Faculté Européenne Des Sciences Du Foncier / see European Academy of Land Use and Development (#05797)
♦ Faculté internationale d'ostéopathie (internationally oriented national body)
♦ Faculteit voor Vergelijkende Godsdienstwetenschappen (internationally oriented national body)
♦ Faculté latinoaméricaine de sciences sociales (#16316)
♦ Faculté des sciences religieuses comparatives (internationally oriented national body)
♦ Faculty for Comparative Study of Religions (internationally oriented national body)
♦ FADAS – Federation of Asian Dental Anesthesiology Societies (unconfirmed)
♦ FADEAO – Fédération des associations des écrivains de l'Afrique de l'ouest (inactive)
♦ FADE – Fight Against Desert Encroachment (internationally oriented national body)
♦ **FADES** Fonds Arabe pour le Développement Economique et Social (#00965)
♦ **FAD** Fonds africain de développement (#00285)
♦ **FAD** Forum Asia Democracy (#09900)
♦ **FADIB** Foundation for African Development through International Biotechnology (#09939)
♦ **FADI** Fondation Africaine pour le Droit International (#00325)
♦ FADI – Fonds africain de développement industriel (unconfirmed)
♦ **FAEA** Federation of ASEAN Economic Associations (#09425)
♦ FAECF / see Fédération des associations européennes des constructeurs de fenêtres et de façades (#09456)
♦ **FAECF** Fédération des associations européennes des constructeurs de fenêtres et de façades (#09456)
♦ **FAE** Facilité africaine de l'eau (#09233)
♦ **FAE** Federation of Arab Engineers (#09420)
♦ FAE / see Fédération panafricaine des employés (#09700)
♦ FAE – Forum alternatives européennes (internationally oriented national body)
♦ FAEIY – Fundación Academia Europea e Iberoamericana de Yuste (internationally oriented national body)
♦ **FAELA** Federación de Asociaciones Educativas de América Latina y el Caribe (#09289)
♦ Det Faelles Forskningscenter (#16147)
♦ **FAEO** Federation of African Engineering Organisations (#09402)
♦ FAEP / see European Magazine Media Association (#07723)
♦ FAEPLA / see Federación de Asociaciones Educativas de América Latina y el Caribe (#09289)
♦ FAES – Fédération d'astrologie de l'Europe du sud (no recent information)
♦ **FAES** Fondation africaine de l'eau et de la santé (#10891)
♦ FAET – Fédération arabe pour l'enseignement technique (no recent information)
♦ **FA** Families Anonymous (#09248)
♦ **FAFCE** Fédération des associations familiales catholiques en Europe (#09468)
♦ FAFCO – Asian Federation of Corporate Football (unconfirmed)
♦ FAfD / see African Development Fund (#00285)
♦ **FAFE** Fédération africaine des femmes entrepreneurs (#00313)
♦ FAFEM – Fédération des associations francophones d'étude de la ménopause (no recent information)
♦ **FAF** Family of the Americas Foundation (#09250)
♦ FAF – Free Africa Foundation (internationally oriented national body)
♦ FAF – Friendship Ambassadors Foundation (internationally oriented national body)
♦ FAFIA – Canadian Feminist Alliance for International Action (internationally oriented national body)
♦ **FAFICS** Federation of Associations of Former International Civil Servants (#09457)
♦ Fafo – Fafo Research Foundation (internationally oriented national body)
♦ Fafo Research Foundation (internationally oriented national body)
♦ FAFPAS – Fédération des associations de fabricants de produits alimentaires surgelés de la CEE (inactive)
♦ FAFRAD / see Fédération Euro-Africaine de Solidarité
♦ **FAFVAC** Fédération des associations francophones de vétérinaires pour animaux de compagnie (#09458)
♦ **FAGACE** Fonds africain de garantie et de coopération économique (#00326)
♦ **FAGAT** Forum of AsianPacific Graphic Arts Technology (#09901)
♦ Fagforening – Europaeiske Offentlig Tjeneste / see Union Syndicale Fédérale (#20485)
♦ Faglige Sammenslutning af Kornoplagringsvirksomheder i EØF / see Unistock Europe (#20492)
♦ **FAGOS** Federation of Arab Gynecology Obstetric Societies (#09421)
♦ FAGS – Federation of Astronomical and Geophysical Data Analysis Services (inactive)
♦ FAGU – Fondation africaine de gestion urbaine (internationally oriented national body)
♦ Fahamu (internationally oriented national body)
♦ fahamu – Networks for Social Justice / see Fahamu
♦ FAH – Fédération arabe d'haltérophilie (inactive)
♦ **FAIA** Fédération arabe des industries alimentaires (#00946)
♦ **FAIAO** Fédération des associations des industriels de l'Afrique de l'Ouest (#09714)
♦ **FAIAR** Federación de Asociaciones Iberoamericanas de Aire Acondicionado y Refrigeración (#09290)
♦ **FAIB** Fédération des associations européennes et internationales établies en Belgique (#09508)
♦ FAIB / see Federation of European and International Associations Established in Belgium (#09508)
♦ **FAIB** Federation of European and International Associations Established in Belgium (#09508)
♦ FAICA – Federación de Asociaciones de Ingenieros del Caribe (inactive)
♦ **FAIC** Forum of Adriatic and Ionian Cities (#09892)
♦ FAI' / see Europe Air Sports (#05776)
♦ FAI – Fédération abolitionniste internationale (inactive)
♦ **FAI** Fédération aéronautique internationale (#09397)
♦ **FAI** Fédération Anaforcal International (#09417)
♦ **FAI** Federazione ACLI Internazionali (#13336)
♦ FAI – FilmAid International (internationally oriented national body)
♦ FAI – Fondation Assistance Internationale (internationally oriented national body)
♦ FAI / see International Federation of ACLI (#13336)
♦ FAIMER – Foundation for the Advancement of International Medical Education and Research (internationally oriented national body)
♦ FAIMER Global / see Foundation for the Advancement of International Medical Education and Research

♦ **FAIM** Federation of Asian Institute of Management Alumni Associations (#09433)
♦ FAIP / see European Forum of Farm Animal Breeders (#07310)
♦ **FAIP** Fédération arabe des industries de la pêche (#00945)
♦ Faireachlann Eorpach an Ilteangachais (internationally oriented national body)
♦ **FAIR** Facility for Antiproton and Ion Research in Europe (#09234)
♦ **FAIR** Federation of Afro-Asian Insurers and Reinsurers (#09413)
♦ fair-fish international (internationally oriented national body)

♦ Fairfood International 09237

Exec Dir Mauritskade 63, 1092 AD Amsterdam, Netherlands. T. +31628352232. E-mail: info@fairfood.org.

URL: http://www.fairfood.org/

History 2002. **Aims** Accelerate the change towards a sustainable food system. **Structure** Executive Board; Advisory Board; Supervisory Board. **Languages** Dutch, English. **Activities** Advocacy/lobbying/activism; guidance/assistance/consulting; research and development. **Consultative Status** Consultative status granted from: *ECOSOC (#05331)* (Special). **NGO Relations** Member of (1): *OECD Watch (#17694)*. [2021.05.19/XJ6049/**F**]

♦ **FAIR** Forum of African Investigative Reporters (#09894)
♦ FAIR GmbH / see Facility for Antiproton and Ion Research in Europe (#09234)
♦ Fair Labor Association (internationally oriented national body)
♦ FAIRMED (internationally oriented national body)
♦ Fair River International Association for Development (internationally oriented national body)

♦ Fair Trade Advocacy Office (FTAO) 09238

Exec Dir Village Partenaire – bureau 1, Rue Fernand Bernier 15, 1060 Brussels, Belgium. T. +3225431923. Fax +3225434444. E-mail: enssle@fairtrade-advocacy.org – brussels@fairtrade-advocacy.org.

URL: http://www.fairtrade-advocacy.org/

History 2004. Founded as an informal advocacy cooperation mechanism, as a joint initiative of *Fairtrade International (FLO, #09240), European Fair Trade Association (EFTA, #07026), Network of European World Shops (NEWS, inactive)* and *World Fair Trade Organization (WFTO, #21396)* – Europe. Formalized Dec 2010, when it became a legally-independent foundation. Registration: Handelsregister, No/ID: KVK 51415666, Netherlands; EU Transparency Register, No/ID: 860901940087-20, Start date: 28 Oct 2020. **Aims** Speak out on behalf of the Fair Trade movement for Fair Trade and Trade Justice so as to improve the livelihoods of marginalized producers and workers in the South. **Structure** Board of Directors. **Activities** Advocacy/lobbying/activism. **Events** *Conference on Sustainability and Competition Policy : Bridging two Worlds to Enable a Fairer Economy* Brussels (Belgium) 2019. **Publications** *FTAO Newsletter*. Annual Report; position papers; ad hoc reports. **NGO Relations** Member of (2): *Cooperatives Europe (#04801); SDG Watch Europe (#19162)*. [2022.05.04/XJ8982/t/**E**]

♦ Fairtrade Africa (FTA) 09239

Exec Dir PO Box 3308, Nairobi, 00200, Kenya. T. +254202721930.

Street Addres 5th Avenue Suite, Room 8 – 9, 5th Avenue Ngong, Ngong Road, Nairobi, Kenya.

URL: http://www.fairtradeafrica.net/

History Mar 2004, Addis Ababa (Ethiopia), as *African Fairtrade Network (AFN)*. Moved to Nairobi (Kenya), 2010. **Aims** Increase awareness of fairtrade in Africa. **Structure** General Assembly (every 2 years). Board, comprising one representative from each regional network and one elected member to represent Fairtrade Africa on FLO Board. Management Team. Fairtrade Africa Regional Networks (4): Southern Africa Network (FTA-SAN); West Africa Network (FTA-WAN); Eastern Africa Network (FTA-EAN); North Africa Network (FTA-NAN). **Events** *Meeting* Moshi (Tanzania UR) 2006. **Members** Membership countries not specified. **IGO Relations** *Bioversity International (#03262)*. **NGO Relations** Regional member of: *Fairtrade International (FLO, #09240)*. [2012/XJ0834/t/**F**]

♦ Fairtrade International (FLO) 09240

CEO Bonner Talweg 177, 53129 Bonn, Germany. T. +49228949230. Fax +492282421713. E-mail: info@fairtrade.net.

URL: http://www.fairtrade.net/

History Apr 1997. Former names and other names: *Fairtrade Labelling Organizations International (FLO International)* – former. Registration: North Rhine-Westphalia District court, No/ID: VR 7795, Start date: 28 Jul 1998, Germany, Bonn. **Aims** Set international Fairtrade standards; support Fairtrade producer networks and national organizations; develop global Fairtrade strategy; promote trade justice. **Structure** General Assembly; Board. **Languages** English, French, German, Spanish. **Staff** 62.00 FTE, paid. **Finance** Members' dues. Other sources: institutional donors; funding partners. **Activities** Certification/accreditation; standards/guidelines. **Events** *Conférence sur le commerce équitable* Lyon (France) 2009. **Publications** *Monitoring and Impact Report*. Annual report; impact studies; position papers; information sheets in English, French, Spanish; brochures; leaflets.

Members Regional Producer Networks (3); national Fairtrade organizations (20) in 22 countries:
Australia, Austria, Belgium, Canada, Denmark, Finland, France, Germany, Ireland, Italy, Japan, Luxembourg, Netherlands, New Zealand, Norway, Portugal, South Africa, Spain, Sweden, Switzerland, UK, USA.
Included in the above, 1 organization listed in this Yearbook:
Max Havelaar Foundation.
Regional Networks (3):
Fairtrade Africa (FTA, #09239); Latin American and Caribbean Network of Small Fairtrade Producers (#16282); Network of Asia and Pacific Producers (NAPP, #16995).

Consultative Status Consultative status granted from: *ECOSOC (#05331)* (Special). **IGO Relations** *Bioversity International (#03262); European Commission (EC, #06633)*. **NGO Relations** Member of: *European Banana Action Network (EUROBAN, #06310)*; German Initiative for Sustainable Cocoa (GISCO); *Global Coffee Platform (GCP, #10298); ISEAL (#16026); Sustainable Apparel Coalition (SAC)*. Partner of: *Brot für die Welt; Comic Relief*; Ethical Tea Partnership (ETP); *Global Call for Climate Action (GCCA, inactive)*; Global Living Wage Coalition; Gold Standard. Instrumental in setting up: *Fair Trade Advocacy Office (FTAO, #09238)*. Cooperates with: *IFOAM – Organics International (IFOAM, #11105); Social Accountability International (SAI); Social Agriculture Network (SAN, #19333). SOLIDARIDAD Network (#19681)* was instrumental in initiation of the organization. [2021/XD6881/ty/**D**]

♦ Fair Trade International Symposium (meeting series)
♦ Fairtrade Labelling Organizations International / see Fairtrade International (#09240)
♦ Fairtrade NAPP / see Network of Asia and Pacific Producers (#16995)
♦ Fairtrade – Network of Asia and Pacific Producers / see Network of Asia and Pacific Producers (#16995)
♦ Fair Trade Organisatie / see Fair Trade Original
♦ Fair Trade Original (internationally oriented national body)
♦ Fair Trade Tourism (internationally oriented national body)

♦ Fair Trade Towns International (International FTTs) 09241

Address not obtained.

URL: http://www.fairtradetowns.org/

Structure Steering Committee. **Activities** Events/meetings. **Events** *International Conference* Cardiff (UK) 2019, *International Conference* Madrid (Spain) 2018.

Members Towns (over 2,000) in 35 countries and territories:
Australia, Austria, Belgium, Brazil, Cameroon, Canada, Chile, Costa Rica, Czechia, Denmark, Ecuador, Estonia, Finland, France, Germany, Ghana, Honduras, India, Ireland, Italy, Japan, Korea Rep, Lebanon, Luxembourg, Netherlands, New Zealand, Norway, Paraguay, Poland, Spain, Sweden, Switzerland, Taiwan, UK, USA. [2019/XM7695/**E**]

♦ Fair Trials 09242

Global CEO 5 Castle Road, London, NW1 8PR, UK. E-mail: office@fairtrials.net.

Europe Avenue Brugmann 12A, 1060 Brussels, Belgium.

Dir 1100 13th Street NW, Suite 800, Washington DC 20005, USA.

URL: http://www.fairtrials.org/

Fair Trials Abroad
09242

alphabetic sequence excludes
For the complete listing, see Yearbook Online at

History 1992. Former names and other names: *Fair Trials Abroad (FTA)* – former; *Fair Trials International* – legal name; *Fair Trials Europe* – legal name; *Fair Trials Americas* – legal name. Registration: Charity Commission, No/ID: 1134586, England and Wales; Companies House, No/ID: 7135273, England and Wales; Crossroads Bank for Enterprises, No/ID: 0552.688.677, Start date: 14 May 2014, Belgium; 501(c)(3), No/ID: DLN17053243307017, USA; EU Transparency Register, No/ID: 302540016347-29, Start date: 4 Mar 2015. **Aims** Campaign for fairness, equality and justice in criminal legal systems around the world. **Structure** Board of Trustees. **Activities** Advocacy/lobbying/activism; awareness raising; capacity building; guidance/assistance/consulting; knowledge management/information dissemination; projects/programmes; research and development; research/documentation; training/education. **NGO Relations** Member of (2): *European Implementation Network (EIN, #07521); Human Rights and Democracy Network (HRDN, #10980).* [2022.10.19/XJ2195/**F**]

- ♦ Fair Trials Abroad / see Fair Trials (#09242)
- ♦ Fair Trials Americas / see Fair Trials (#09242)
- ♦ Fair Trials Europe / see Fair Trials (#09242)
- ♦ Fair Trials International / see Fair Trials (#09242)
- ♦ Fairventures Worldwide (internationally oriented national body)

♦ Fair Wear Foundation (FWF) 09243

Contact PO Box 69253, 1060 CH Amsterdam, Netherlands. T. +31204084255. Fax +31204084254. E-mail: info@fairwear.org.
Street address Koningin Welhelminaplein 13, Amsterdam, Netherlands.
URL: http://fairwear.org/

History EU Transparency Register: 988743535279-05. **Aims** Improve *labour* conditions in the *garment* industry. **Structure** Board. **Languages** English. **Finance** Members' dues. Donor-funded projects. **Activities** Awareness raising; monitoring/evaluation; advocacy/lobbying/activism; capacity building; standards/guidelines. **Publications** Annual Report; performance checks; studies; guidance and tools.
Members Companies in 10 countries:
Austria, Belgium, France, Germany, Italy, Netherlands, Portugal, Sweden, Switzerland, UK.
IGO Relations *ILO (#11123).* **NGO Relations** *Bread for All; Clean Clothes Campaign (CCC, #03986): Committee for Asian Women (CAW, #04243).* [2019/XJ4710/f/**F**]

♦ FairWild Foundation 09244

Secretariat David Attenborough Bldg, Pembroke Str, Cambridge, CB2 3QZ, UK. T. +441223331929. E-mail: secretariat@fairwild.org.
Registered Office Stampfenbachstr 38, 8006 Zurich ZH, Switzerland.
URL: https://www.fairwild.org/

History 2001. Evolved from 2 separate initiatives working within the context of wild plants trade. Officially founded 2008. Registration: Start date: May 2008, Switzerland. **Aims** Enable transformation of resource management and business practices to be ecologically, socially and economically sustainable throughout the supply chain of wild-collected products. **Structure** Board of Trustees; Advisory Panel. **Activities** Advocacy/lobbying/activism; certification/accreditation; standards/guidelines. [2022/AA2807/f/**F**]

- ♦ Fair World Association (internationally oriented national body)
- ♦ **FAIS** Federation of African Immunological Societies (#09403)
- ♦ Faith and Ethics Network for the International Criminal Court (internationally oriented national body)
- ♦ Faithful Companions of Jesus (religious order)
- ♦ Faithful Servants of Jesus (religious order)

♦ FaithInvest 09245

Main Office c/o Stone King LLP, Boundary House, 91-93 Charterhouse St, London, EC1M 6HR, UK. E-mail: info@faithinvest.org.
URL: https://www.faithinvest.org/

History 2019. Founded by *Alliance of Religions and Conservation (ARC, inactive)* following its 'Faith in Finance' conference. Registration: Charity Commission, No/ID: 1187015, England and Wales; Companies House, No/ID: 11862410, England and Wales. **Aims** Support faiths to invest in line with their values to achieve a just and sustainable world. **Structure** Trustees. **Finance** Sources: grants. [2022/AA3097/**F**]

♦ Faith and Light International 09246

Association internationale Foi et lumière

Gen Sec 3 rue du Laos, 75015 Paris, France. T. +33153694430. E-mail: international@foietlumiere.org.
URL: https://www.foietlumiere.org

History 1971, Lourdes (France). Encouraged and confirmed by Paul VI in 1975 and by John-Paul II in 1981 and 1984. Charter and Constitution proposed by General Assembly, 26 Oct 1980, Lourdes (France), and adopted provisionally for a one-year period; amended and adopted by General Assembly, 1982, Wetherby (UK); further amendments adopted by General Assemblies: 1984, Rome (Italy); 1986, Santo Domingo (Dominican Rep); 1990, Edinburgh (UK); 1994, Warsaw (Poland); 1998, Québec (Canada); 2002, Rome; 2006, Madrid (Spain); 2008, Lourdes; 2013, Leeds (UK); 2018, Beirut (Lebanon). **Aims** Promote the belief on which it is founded, that each person with an intellectual disability is fully a person with all the rights of a human being: above all the right to be loved, recognized and respected for himself or herself and in the choices he/she makes; the right also to receive whatever help is necessary in order to grow at every level, spiritual and human. **Structure** General Assembly (every 5 years, at International Meeting); Board of Directors (meets twice a year); International Coordinating Team (meets at least once a year). Provinces, headed by Coordinators, (meeting annually). Local Communities, consisting of 15-40 persons with an intellectual disability, their families, friends and a chaplain. **Languages** English, French, Spanish. **Staff** 3.00 FTE, paid. **Finance** Sources: contributions; donations. **Activities** Events/meetings; religious activities. Active in all member countries. **Events** *General Assembly* Beirut (Lebanon) 2018, *General Assembly* Leeds (UK) 2013, *General Assembly* Lourdes (France) 2008, *General Assembly* Madrid (Spain) 2008, *Meeting* 1994. **Publications** *Up Sails! – Hisse et Ho ! – Izar Velas!* (4 a year) – Newsletter. Annual guidelines; leaflets; booklets.
Members in 89 countries and territories:
Albania, Argentina, Armenia, Australia, Austria, Belgium, Benin, Bosnia-Herzegovina, Brazil, Burkina Faso, Burundi, Cameroon, Canada, Central African Rep, Chile, Colombia, Congo DR, Côte d'Ivoire, Croatia, Cyprus, Czechia, Denmark, Dominican Rep, Ecuador, Egypt, Estonia, France, Georgia, Germany, Gibraltar, Greece, Honduras, Hong Kong, Hungary, India, Iran Islamic Rep, Ireland, Israel, Italy, Japan, Jordan, Kenya, Korea Rep, Kuwait, Lebanon, Lithuania, Luxembourg, Madagascar, Malaysia, Martinique, Mauritius, Mexico, Netherlands, New Caledonia, New Zealand, Nicaragua, Nigeria, Norway, Pakistan, Paraguay, Peru, Philippines, Poland, Portugal, Réunion, Romania, Russia, Rwanda, San Salvador, Serbia, Seychelles, Singapore, Slovakia, Slovenia, South Africa, South Sudan, Spain, Sudan, Sweden, Switzerland, Syrian AR, Taiwan, Togo, Uganda, UK, Ukraine, USA, Zambia, Zimbabwe. [2022.10.19/XF1416/**F**]

- ♦ Faith Movement for Gender Justice / see Side by Side (#19265)
- ♦ Faith and Order Movement (inactive)
- ♦ Faith in Water (internationally oriented national body)
- ♦ FAI – The World Air Sports Federation / see Fédération aéronautique internationale (#09397)
- ♦ **FAJ** Federation of African Journalists (#09404)
- ♦ **FAJ** Federation of Arab Journalists (#09422)
- ♦ **FAJU** Federation of African Journalist Union (#09405)
- ♦ FAKT – Consult for Management, Training and Technologies (internationally oriented national body)
- ♦ FAKT – Fördergesellschaft für Angepasste Techniken in der Dritten Welt (internationally oriented national body)
- ♦ Fakultät für Vergleichende Religionswissenschaften (internationally oriented national body)
- ♦ FALAE / see Forum for East Asia-Latin America Cooperation (#09907)
- ♦ FALAN / see Federation of Latin American and Caribbean Neurosciences (#09684)
- ♦ **FALAN** Federation of Latin American and Caribbean Neurosciences (#09684)
- ♦ FALAN-LARC / see Federation of Latin American and Caribbean Neurosciences (#09684)
- ♦ FALA / see Youth Alliance for Leadership and Development in Africa (#22004)
- ♦ FAL – Convention on Facilitation of International Maritime Traffic (1965 treaty)
- ♦ FAL / see Foro de Autoridades Locales por la Inclusión Social y la Democracia Participativa (#09876)
- ♦ **FAL** Foro de Autoridades Locales por la Inclusión Social y la Democracia Participativa (#09876)
- ♦ Falk Foundation (internationally oriented national body)

♦ Falun Dafa 09247

Exec Dir Falun Dafa Information Center, PO Box 577, New York NY 10956-9998, USA. T. +18454184870. E-mail: contact@faluninfo.net.
URL: http://www.falundafa.org

History by Li Hongzhi, as a movement of practitioners of 'Falun Gong' exercises. Became known as a public movement in China in 1992. Also referred to as *Falun Gong*. Practitioners deny claims that this is a religion, sect or cult. **Aims** Promote practice of 'Falun Gong', which incorporates principles of *Buddhism* and *Taoism* in conjunction with *physical exercises* and is considered to be a part of the Chinese tradition of spiritual and physical exercises referred to as *Xulian* or *Qigong*. **Events** *European Cultivation Experience Sharing Conference* Madrid (Spain) 2014. **Members** Individuals (100 million) in 40 countries. Membership countries not specified. [2016/XF6079/v/**F**]

- ♦ Falun Gong / see Falun Dafa (#09247)
- ♦ FAMA / see Federation of Asian Muaythai Associations (#09436)
- ♦ **FAMA** Federation of Asian Muaythai Associations (#09436)
- ♦ FAMAR – Fourth Association of Model Auto Racing (unconfirmed)
- ♦ FAMCLAM – Federación de Asociaciones Médicas Católicas Latinoamericanas (no recent information)
- ♦ **FAMD** Foundation for Asian Management Development (#09940)
- ♦ FAMEDEV – Inter-African Network for Women, Media, Gender and Development (inactive)
- ♦ FAME – Forum for African Medical Editors (unconfirmed)
- ♦ FAM – Fédération artisans du monde (internationally oriented national body)
- ♦ **FAM** Feminist Articulation Marcosur (#09730)
- ♦ FaMiDo – Familles du Monde (internationally oriented national body)
- ♦ **FAMI** Federation of Asian Motorcycle Industries (#09435)
- ♦ Famiglia Missionaria Donum Dei (religious order)
- ♦ Familia del Cenaculo Misionero (religious order)
- ♦ Familial Mediterranean Fever and Autoinflammatory Diseased Global Association (unconfirmed)
- ♦ Familie Leben Mission (religious order)

♦ Families Anonymous (FA) 09248

Contact 701 Lee St, Ste 670, Des Plaines IL 60016, USA. T. +18472945877. Fax +18472945837. E-mail: famanon@familiesanonymous.org.
URL: http://www.familiesanonymous.org/

History 1971. Incorporated in the State of California (USA), 1972. **Aims** Support groups for individuals concerned with a loved one or friend in trouble with *drugs*, *alcohol* or related *behavior problems*, whose behavior is affecting their lives. **Structure** Board of Directors, consisting of up to 24 members. World Service Office. Standing Committees (6): Public Information; World Service Office; Literature; Newsletter; Groups Coordinator; International Groups and Policy. **Finance** Sale of publications; donations. **Activities** Organizes meetings. Publishing activity. **Events** *Annual convention and business meeting* Huntsville, AL (USA) 2009, *Annual convention / Annual Convention and Business Meeting* Albany, NY (USA) 2008, *Annual Convention and Business Meeting* Cleveland, OH (USA) 2007, *Annual Convention* Naperville, IL (USA) 2007, *Annual convention and business meeting* Atlanta, GA (USA) 2006. **Publications** *The Twelve Step Rag* (6 a year). Pamphlets; bookmarks; posters; audio tape formats; books.
Members Groups in 16 countries and territories:
Australia, Canada, Greece, Honduras, Hong Kong, India, Italy, Kenya, Mexico, Panama, Portugal, Russia, Spain, Sweden, UK, Venezuela. [2013/XF3250/**F**]

♦ Families Empowered and Supporting Treatment of Eating Disorders (FEAST) 09249

Main Office PO Box 1281, Warrenton VA 20185, USA. T. +15402278518. E-mail: info@feast-ed.org.
URL: http://www.feast-ed.org/

History 2008, USA. **Structure** Parent Council; Professional Advisory Council. **Members** Families; clinicians; patients; organizations in 8 countries. Membership countries not specified. [2018/XM8158/**F**]

- ♦ Families in Global Transition (internationally oriented national body)
- ♦ Families of the Missing (internationally oriented national body)
- ♦ Familis OMF – Organisation mondiale pour les familles (no recent information)
- ♦ Familis WOF – World Organisation for Families (no recent information)
- ♦ Famille Cor Unum (religious order)
- ♦ Famille Monastique de Bethléem, de l'Assomption de la Vierge et de Saint Bruno (religious order)
- ♦ Familles du Monde (internationally oriented national body)
- ♦ Family Africa (internationally oriented national body)
- ♦ Family Alliance / see Family for Every Child (#09252)

♦ Family of the Americas Foundation (FAF) 09250

Fundación para la Familia de las Américas

Contact address not obtained. E-mail: familyplanning@yahoo.com.
URL: http://www.familyplanning.net/

History 1979, by Mercedes Arzú Wilson. **Aims** Educate women in regards to the workings of their natural cycles of fertility and infertility. **Activities** Provides services, teacher training and educational materials for the Ovulation Method of Natural Family Planning (NFP). **Events** *International Congress* Bratislava (Czechoslovakia) 1992, *International Congress* Kaunas (Lithuania) 1992, *International Congress* Luxembourg (Luxembourg) 1992, *International Congress* Moscow (Russia) 1992, *International Congress* Brighton (UK) 1990.
Members Mostly a US body. Active in 58 countries:
Argentina, Bahamas, Bangladesh, Belize, Benin, Bolivia, Botswana, Brazil, Burkina Faso, Burundi, Cameroon, Canada, Chad, Chile, China, Colombia, Congo Brazzaville, Congo DR, Costa Rica, Côte d'Ivoire, Cuba, Dominican Rep, Ecuador, Egypt, El Salvador, Gambia, Ghana, Guatemala, Honduras, India, Indonesia, Iran Islamic Rep, Jamaica, Kenya, Lesotho, Madagascar, Malawi, Mali, Mauritius, Mexico, Mozambique, Namibia, Nigeria, Panama, Paraguay, Peru, Rwanda, Sierra Leone, South Africa, Sudan, Tanzania UR, Togo, Uganda, Uruguay, USA, Venezuela, Zambia, Zimbabwe. [2010/XF2938/f/**F**]

- ♦ Family Bereavement Network / see Bereavement Network Europe (#03211)
- ♦ Family Business Network / see The Family Business Network International (#09251)
- ♦ The Family Business Network Asia (see: #09251)

♦ The Family Business Network International (FBN-I) 09251

CEO PO Box 915, 1001 Lausanne VD, Switzerland. T. +41216180192. E-mail: info@fbn-i.org.
Street Address Chemin de Bellerive 23, 1001 Lausanne VD, Switzerland.
URL: http://www.fbn-i.org/

History Founded 1989, as *Family Business Network (FBN)*. **Aims** Promote success and sustainability of families in business worldwide. **Structure** General Assembly; Board of Directors. Committees (2): Nomination; Next Generation. **Languages** English. **Staff** 6.00 FTE, paid. **Activities** Events/meetings. **Events** *Annual conference* Budapest (Hungary) 2022, *Annual conference* Budapest (Hungary) 2021, *Annual conference* Udaipur (India) 2019, *Annual conference* Venice (Italy) 2018, *Annual Conference* Las Palmas de Gran Canaria (Spain) 2017. **Publications** *FBN Newsletter* (4 a year).
Members Associations (29) in 25 countries:
Austria, Belgium, Brazil, Bulgaria, Chile, Colombia, Ecuador, Finland, France, Germany, Hungary, India, Ireland, Italy, Japan, Netherlands, Poland, Singapore, Slovenia, Spain, Sweden, Switzerland, Türkiye, UK, Ukraine.
Regional Chapters (3):
FBN Adria; FBN North America; *The Family Business Network Asia (FBN Asia, see: #09251).*
NGO Relations Instrumental in setting up: *The Family Business Network Asia (FBN Asia, see: #09251).* [2016.10.24/XU2335/y/**F**]

- ♦ Family Care Foundation (internationally oriented national body)
- ♦ Family Education Trust (internationally oriented national body)

♦ **Family for Every Child** **09252**
Contact 75 King William Street, London, EC4N 7BE, UK. T. +442077492490. E-mail: info@familyforeverychild.org.
New Zealand Address 17B Farnham Street, Parnell, Auckland 1052, New Zealand. T. +6498892490. E-mail: info@familyforeverychild.org.nz.
US Address 3000 S Randolph Street, Apt 613, Arlington VA 22206, USA. T. +19178223623.
URL: https://www.familyforeverychild.org/
History Former names and other names: *Family for Every Child New Zealand Trust* – legal name; *Family Alliance* – legal name. Registration: Charity Commission, No/ID: 1149212, England and Wales; Companies House, No/ID: 08177641, Start date: 13 Aug 2012, England; Charities Services, No/ID: CC54645, Start date: 24 May 2017, New Zealand; No/ID: 2670471, New Zealand; 501(c)(3), No/ID: EIN 46-5518730, USA. **Structure** Board of Trustees. Subsidiary: *EveryChild*.
Members Organizations (43) in 37 countries:
Bangladesh, Brazil, Cambodia, Chile, Colombia, Egypt, Ethiopia, Germany, Ghana, Greece, Guatemala, Guyana, India, Ireland, Italy, Jamaica, Jordan, Kenya, Korea Rep, Kyrgyzstan, Lebanon, Liberia, Mexico, Morocco, Nepal, New Zealand, Paraguay, Philippines, Russia, Rwanda, Senegal, South Africa, Sri Lanka, Türkiye, UK, USA, Zimbabwe. [2022/AA1322/**F**]

♦ Family for Every Child New Zealand Trust / see Family for Every Child (#09252)
♦ The Family / see The Family International (#09253)
♦ Family Federation for World Peace / see Family Federation for World Peace and Unification
♦ Family Federation for World Peace and Unification (internationally oriented national body)
♦ Family Health International / see FHI 360

♦ **The Family International (TFI)** **09253**
Address not obtained.
URL: http://www.thefamilyinternational.org/
History 1969, California (USA), by merger of two American groups: 'Revolutionaries for Jesus' and 'Teens for Christ'. Until Feb 1978, referred to as *Children of God – Enfants de Dieu*. Subsequently reformed as *Family of Love*. Previous full title: *Fellowship of Independent Christian Missionary Communities (The Family) – Association de communautés chrétiennes missionnaires indépendantes*. Other titles: *Heaven's Magic*; *World Services*. Comprehensive reorganization, known as the Reboot, 2010, following which it functions as an online community. **Aims** Share the message of God's love with people around the globe. **Structure** TFI Services. **Languages** English, Japanese, Portuguese, Spanish. **Publications** *Activated* (12 a year) – magazine; *Viewpoints* – articles. Educational and devotional materials. **Members** Individuals (1,700) in about 80 countries. Membership countries not specified. [2019.02.14/XR7047/s/**F**]

♦ Family Life Mission (religious order)
♦ Family of Love / see The Family International (#09253)
♦ Family of Love, 1540 (inactive)
♦ Family Members of the Missionary Company of the Sacred Heart (religious order)

♦ **Family Online Safety Institute (FOSI)** **09254**
CEO US Office, 1440 G St NW, Washington DC 20005, USA. E-mail: srawlins@fosi.org.
UK Office 69 Old Broad Street, 7th Floor Dashwood House, London, EC2M 1QS, UK.
URL: http://www.fosi.org/
History UK Registered Charity: 1095268. EU Transparency Register: 13644439020-84. **Aims** Identify and promote best practices, tools and methods in the field of online safety. **Structure** Board. Offices (4): Barcelona (Spain); Brighton (UK); Cologne (Germany); Washington DC (USA). Includes ICRA. **Activities** Events/meetings. **Events** *Round Table* London (UK) 2017, *Annual Conference* Washington, DC (USA) 2017, *Annual Conference* Washington, DC (USA) 2016, *Conference* Washington, DC (USA) 2009, *International online safety conference* Washington, DC (USA) 2007. **Members** Companies and organizations. Membership countries not specified. [2018/XM2593/j/**E**]

♦ Family Planet (internationally oriented national body)

♦ **Family Planning 2030 (FP2030)** **09255**
Exec Dir UN Foundation, 1750 Pennsylvania Avenue NW, Suite 300, Washington DC 20006, USA. T. +12028879040. E-mail: commitments@fp2030.org.
URL: https://fp2030.org/
History Successor to *Family Planning 2020 (FP2020, inactive)*. **Aims** Advance the rights of people everywhere to access reproductive health services safely and on their own terms. **Structure** Board; FP2030 Support Network with regional hubs. **Languages** English, French, Spanish. **Activities** Advocacy/lobbying/activism; awareness raising; events/meetings; guidance/assistance/consulting; healthcare; humanitarian/emergency aid; knowledge management/information dissemination. Active in all member countries.
Members Commitment makers: governments and civil society organizations. Governments (18):
Benin, Burkina Faso, Côte d'Ivoire, Ethiopia, Guinea, India, Kenya, Madagascar, Mali, Mauritania, Niger, Nigeria, Pakistan, Rwanda, Senegal, Tanzania UR, Togo, Uganda.
Non-government committments (over 40) include 14 organizations listed in this Yearbook:
Africa Health Budget Network (AHBN); *Asian-Pacific Resource and Research Centre for Women (ARROW, #01629)*; *Bill and Melinda Gates Foundation (BMGF)*; *Blue Ventures*; *DKT International*; *FHI 360*; *Global Advocacy for HIV Prevention (AVAC, #10172)*; *International Confederation of Midwives (ICM, #12863)*; *International Planned Parenthood Federation (IPPF, #14589)*; *IntraHealth International*; *Latin American and Caribbean Youth Network for Sexual and Reproductive Health and Rights (REDLAC, #16289)*; *MSI Reproductive Choices*; *United Nations Population Fund (UNFPA, #20612)*; *Women Deliver (#20989)*. [2022.10.12/AA2815/y/**F**]

♦ Family Rosary International (religious order)
♦ Family Watch – Instituto Internacional de Estudios sobre la Familia (internationally oriented national body)
♦ Family Watch International (internationally oriented national body)
♦ Family and Youth Concern / see Family Education Trust
♦ Famine Early Warning System Network (internationally oriented national body)

♦ **FAMI-QS** **09256**
SG Av des Arts 6, 1210 Brussels, Belgium. T. +3225503452. E-mail: fffs_info@fami-qs.org.
URL: http://www.fami-qs.org/
History May 2004. Former names and other names: *European Feed Additives and Premixtures Quality System European Association* – former; *FAMI-QS – The Quality and Safety System for Specialty Feed Ingredients and their Mixtures* – full title. Registration: Banque-Carrefour des Entreprises, Belgium. **Aims** Address safety, quality and regulatory compliance of specialty *feed ingredients* and their mixtures. **Structure** General Assembly (annual). **Languages** Chinese, Dutch, English, French, German, Portuguese, Spanish. **Staff** 3.00 FTE, paid. **Activities** Certification/accreditation; politics/policy/regulatory. **Events** *Workshop* Jakarta (Indonesia) 2018, *Workshop* Mumbai (India) 2018. **Publications** Annual Report; leaflet. **Members** Full; Associate. Membership countries not specified. **NGO Relations** Sister organization: *FEFANA – EU Association of Specialty Feed Ingredients and their Mixtures (#09720)*. Member of: *International Accreditation Forum (IAF, #11584)*. [2021.09.02/XM2144/**D**]

♦ FAMI-QS – The Quality and Safety System for Specialty Feed Ingredients and their Mixtures / see FAMI-QS (#09256)
♦ **FAMPO** Federation of African Medical Physics Organizations (#09406)
♦ **FAMSA** Federation of African Medical Students' Associations (#09407)
♦ FAMSI – Fondo Andaluz de Municipios para la Solidaridad Internacional (internationally oriented national body)
♦ FAMW – Federation of African Media Women (no recent information)
♦ **FANA** Federation of Arab News Agencies (#09423)
♦ **FANAF** Fédération des Sociétés d'Assurance de Droit National Africaines (#09408)
♦ **FANBPO** Fédération des Associations Nationales des Bécassiers du Paléarctique Occidental (#09460)
♦ **FANCA** Freshwater Action Network – Central America (#18638)
♦ **FANCAP** Fundación para la Alimentación y Nutrición de Centro América y Panama (#10019)
♦ **FANRPAN** Food, Agriculture and Natural Resources Policy Analysis Network (#09839)
♦ **FANSA** Freshwater Action Network South Asia (#09996)
♦ **FANS** Federation of Asian Nutrition Societies (#09437)
♦ **FANUS** Federation of African Nutrition Societies (#09409)
♦ FAOB / see Federation of Asian and Oceanian Biochemists and Molecular Biologists (#09438)
♦ **FAOBMB** Federation of Asian and Oceanian Biochemists and Molecular Biologists (#09438)
♦ FAO Bureau régional pour l'Europe / see FAO Regional Office for Europe and Central Asia (#09267)
♦ FAO Bureau régional pour l'Europe et l'asie centrale (#09267)

♦ **FAO/CIHEAM International Network for the Research and Development of Pasture and Forage Crops** **09257**
Coordinator RHEA – Research Ctr for a Sustainable Rural Development and Ecosystem Management, Rue Warichet 4 Box 202, 1435 Mont-Saint-Guibert, Belgium.
URL: http://www.iamz.ciheam.org/research/networks/pasture_and_forage_crops/
History 1978, with the name *European Cooperative Research Network on Pasture and Fodder Crops*, as part of *European System of Cooperative Research Networks in Agriculture (ESCORENA, #08871)* within *FAO (#09260)*, through its *European Commission on Agriculture (ECA)*, and with the support of *CIHEAM – International Centre for Advanced Mediterranean Agronomic Studies (CIHEAM, #03927)*. Subsequently changed title to *FAO/CIHEAM Interregional Cooperative Research Network on Pasture and Fodder Crops*. **Aims** Study and improve forage crop production on irrigated and rain-fed land, development and management of typically Mediterranean rangelands; study forage feeding value. **Structure** Coordinator. Subnetworks (2): Mountain Pastures; Mediterranean Forage Resources. **Activities** Events/meetings; training/education; knowledge management/information dissemination. **Publications** *Herba* (annual). REU Technical Series.
Members Institutions in 34 countries:
Albania, Algeria, Australia, Belgium, Bulgaria, Chile, Cyprus, Egypt, Estonia, Finland, France, Germany, Greece, Iceland, Iran Islamic Rep, Israel, Italy, Latvia, Lebanon, Lithuania, Morocco, Netherlands, Norway, Poland, Portugal, Romania, Serbia, Slovakia, Slovenia, Spain, Sweden, Switzerland, Tunisia, UK. [2014/XK0919/**E**]

♦ **FAO/CIHEAM Inter-Regional Cooperative Research Network on Nuts (NUCIS)** **09258**
Coordinator IRTA-Mas de Bover, Ctra Reus-El Morell, 43120 Tarragona, Spain. T. +34977328424. Fax +34977344055.
URL: http://www.iamz.ciheam.org/
History 1990, Turkey. 1990, Yalova (Turkey), during Expert Consultation on the Promotion of Nut Production in Europe and the Near East, as part of *European System of Cooperative Research Networks in Agriculture (ESCORENA, #08871)* within *FAO (#09260)*, through its *European Commission on Agriculture (ECA)* and *CIHEAM – International Centre for Advanced Mediterranean Agronomic Studies (CIHEAM, #03927)*. Also referred to as: *FAO/CIHEAM Research Network on Nuts*; *European Cooperative Research Network on Nuts*. **Aims** Establish close links between researchers working on the same subject; develop joint applied research on selected subjects, matters of common interest according to an accepted methodology, agreed division of tasks and timetable; promote exchange of *nut germplasm*; promote voluntary exchange of information and experimental data in selected subject matters. **Structure** Coordination Board, comprising FAO and CIHEAM officers, Network Coordinator and Sub-network Liaison Officers. Coordination Centre, headed by Coordinator and Secretary. Specialized Sub-Networks (8): Almond; Chestnut; Hazelnut; Pistachio; Stone Pine; Walnut and Pecan; Genetic Resources; Economics. **Languages** English. **Finance** Supported by FAO and CIHEAM. **Activities** Organizes specific meetings and workshops; promotes R and D activities; organizes courses; provides training grants for young researchers. **Events** *Coordination Board Meeting* Spain 2009, *Coordination Board Meeting* Spain 2001, *Coordination Board Meeting* Italy 1997, *Technical Consultation* Morocco 1996, *Technical consultation* Morocco 1996. **Publications** *NUCIS Newsletter*. Technical series. Proceedings; reports.
Members Institutions in 29 countries:
Albania, Algeria, Bosnia-Herzegovina, Bulgaria, Croatia, Cyprus, Egypt, France, Georgia, Greece, Hungary, Iran Islamic Rep, Israel, Italy, Libya, Moldova, Morocco, Netherlands, Portugal, Romania, Serbia, Slovakia, Slovenia, South Africa, Spain, Syrian AR, Tunisia, Türkiye, Ukraine. [2019/XK0918/**E**]

♦ FAO/CIHEAM Interregional Cooperative Research Network on Pasture and Fodder Crops / see FAO/CIHEAM International Network for the Research and Development of Pasture and Forage Crops (#09257)
♦ FAO/CIHEAM Network of Cooperative Research on Sheep and Goats / see Inter-regional FAO-CIHEAM Network for Research and Development in Sheep and Goats (#15970)
♦ FAO/CIHEAM Research Network on Nuts / see FAO/CIHEAM Inter-Regional Cooperative Research Network on Nuts (#09258)
♦ FAO Comisión para la Lucha contra la Langosta del Desierto en el Noroeste de Africa / see FAO Commission for Controlling the Desert Locust in the Western Region (#09259)
♦ FAO Comité CFFSA/CFE/CFCO sobre Cuestiones Forestales del Mediterraneo – Silva Mediterranea (#00542)
♦ FAO Commission on African Animal Trypanosomiasis (inactive)
♦ FAO Commission for Controlling the Desert Locust in North-West Africa / see FAO Commission for Controlling the Desert Locust in the Western Region (#09259)

♦ **FAO Commission for Controlling the Desert Locust in the Western Region** **09259**
FAO Commission de lutte contre le criquet pèlerin dans la région occidentale
Information Officer c/o FAO, Viale delle Terme di Caracalla, 00100 Rome RM, Italy. T. +39657051 – +39657054021. Fax +39657055152 – +39657055271.
URL: http://www.fao.org/ag/locusts/en/info/info/index.html
History Aug 1971, within the framework of *FAO (#09260)*, by Article XIX of *Agreement for the Establishment of a Commission for Controlling the Desert Locust in North-west Africa*, approved by the Council of FAO in 1970, and amended 1977. Original title: *FAO Commission for Controlling the Desert Locust in North-West Africa (CCDLNWA) – FAO Commission de lutte contre le criquet pèlerin en Afrique du Nord-Ouest (CLCPANO) – FAO Comisión para la Lucha contra la Langosta del Desierto en el Noroeste de Africa*. Replaced *FAO North-West African Desert Locust Research and Control Coordination Sub-Committee*, a subsidiary of *FAO Desert Locust Control Committee*. Statutes registered in *'UNTS 1/11354'*. **Aims** Promote national and international research and action on control of the desert locust in North-West Africa. **Structure** Executive Committee, consisting of one representative per member country, meets twice between Commission sessions. **Languages** Arabic, English, French. **Finance** Financed by Member States. Budget (annual): US$ 143,000. **Activities** Annual or Biennial Session. Provides emergency assistance; promotes and coordinates locust research, survey and control; builds up adequate control potential; monitors vegetation development and mapping in areas favourable for desert locust breeding. **Events** *Session* Nouakchott (Mauritania) 2014, *Session* Tunis (Tunisia) 2012, *Session* Agadir (Morocco) 2009, *Session* Bamako (Mali) 2007, *Session* Tripoli (Libyan AJ) 2005. **Publications** Monthly reports on locust situation within the region.
Members Member Nations and Associate Members of the FAO situated in the region and accepting the Agreement. Other States situated in the region that are members may be accepted. Representatives of 5 governments:
Algeria, Libya, Mauritania, Morocco, Tunisia.
Observers (1):
France.
IGO Relations Annual and Biennial Sessions attended by representatives of: *European and Mediterranean Plant Protection Organization (EPPO, #07773)*; *League of Arab States (LAS, #16420)*; Government of France. [2011/XE9584/**E***]

♦ FAO Commission on Fertilizers (inactive)
♦ FAO Commission de lutte contre le criquet pèlerin en Afrique du Nord-Ouest / see FAO Commission for Controlling the Desert Locust in the Western Region (#09259)
♦ FAO Commission de lutte contre le criquet pèlerin dans la région occidentale (#09259)
♦ FAO Commission on Plant Genetic Resources / see Commission on Genetic Resources for Food and Agriculture (#04215)
♦ FAO Commission on Plant Genetic Resources for Food and Agriculture / see Commission on Genetic Resources for Food and Agriculture (#04215)

♦ FAO Commission de la trypanosomiase animale africaine (inactive)
♦ FAO Desert Locust Control Committee / see Commission for Controlling the Desert Locust in South-West Asia (#04209)
♦ FAOE / see Federation of African Engineering Organisations (#09402)
♦ FAO/EUFMD / see European Commission for the Control of Foot-and-Mouth Disease (#06635)
♦ FAO European Forestry Commission / see European Forestry Commission (#07299)
♦ FAO – Federation Asian of Oriental (inactive)

♦ FAO – Food and Agriculture Organization of the United Nations . . . 09260

Organisation des Nations Unies pour l'alimentation et l'agriculture – Organización de las Naciones Unidas para la Agricultura y la Alimentación

Dir-Gen Viale delle Terme di Caracalla, 00153 Rome RM, Italy. T. +39657051. Fax +39657053152.
E-mail: fao-hq@fao.org.
URL: https://www.fao.org/

History 16 Oct 1945, Québec, QC (Canada). Constitution signed in 1945 by 44 countries. Absorbed *International Institute of Agriculture (IIAG, inactive)*, set up as an intergovernmental organization on 7 Jun 1905, and *International Emergency Food Council (inactive)*, set up 1946. As a Specialized Agency of the *United Nations (UN, #20515)* within *United Nations System (#20635)*, reports annually to *ECOSOC (#05331)*. **Aims** Contribute towards an expanding world economy and ensure humanity's freedom from *hunger* by: raising the level of *nutrition* and *living standards* of people in member countries; securing improvement in the efficiency of production and distribution of all food and agricultural products; bettering the living conditions of rural populations.

Structure Significant restructuring from 1994 onwards has decentralized operations and streamlined procedures.

I. /Governing Bodies/:
'Conference', meets in odd-numbered years, comprising all Members and Associate Members, and includes Chairperson and Secretary-General. *'Council'*, normally holding at least 5 session in a biennium, and containing 49 Member Nations. *Committee on World Food Security (CFS, see: #09260)*. *'Regional Conferences'*: Africa (ARC); Asia and the Pacific (APRC); Europe (ERC); Latin America and the Caribbean (LARC); Near East (NERC). *'Council Committees'* (3): Programme; Finance; Constitutional and Legal Matters. *'Technical Committees'* (4): Agriculture (COAG); Commodity Problems (CCP); Fisheries (COFI); Forestry (COFO).

II. /Statutory Bodies/ – by subject matter:
– *'Agriculture'*:
  – *European Commission on Agriculture (ECA)*, set up 1949 monitors *European System of Cooperative Research Networks in Agriculture (ESCORENA, #08871)*;
  – *Panel of Eminent Experts on Ethics in Food and Agriculture.*
– *'Animal Production and Health'*:
  – *Animal Production and Health Commission for Asia and the Pacific (APHCA, #00839)*;
  – *Commission on Livestock Development in Latin America and the Caribbean (LDAC, #04233)*;
  – *European Commission for the Control of Foot-and-Mouth Disease (EUFMD, #06635)*;
  – *Panel of PAAT Advisory Group Coordinators.*
– *'Commodities and Trade'*:
  – *Consultative Sub-Committee on Surplus Disposal*;
  – *Intergovernmental Group on Bananas and on Tropical Fruits (#11486)*;
  – *Intergovernmental Group on Citrus Fruit (#11487)*;
  – *Intergovernmental Group on Grains (#11488)*;
  – *Intergovernmental Group on Hard Fibres (IGG on Hard Fibres, #11489)*;
  – *Intergovernmental Group on Jute, Kenaf and Allied Fibres (IGG on Jute, Kenal and Allied Fibres, #11490)*;
  – *Intergovernmental Group on Meat and Dairy Products (#11491)*, including
    – *Intergovernmental Group on Oilseeds, Oils and Fats (#11492)*;
    – *Intergovernmental Group on Rice (#11493)*;
    – *Intergovernmental Group on Tea (#11494)*.
  – *'Fisheries'*:
    – *Advisory Committee on Fisheries Research*;
    – *Asia-Pacific Fishery Commission (APFIC, #01907)*;
    – *Central Asian and Caucasus Regional Fisheries and Aquaculture Commission (CACFish, #03679)*;
    – *'COFI Sub-Committee on Aquaculture'*;
    – *'COFI Sub-Committee on Fish Trade'*;
    – *Comisión de Pesca Continental y Acuicultura para América Latina y el Caribe (COPESCAALC, #04142)*;
    – *Committee for Inland Fisheries and Aquaculture of Africa (CIFAA, #04261)*;
    – *'Coordinating Working Party on Fishery Statistics'*;
    – *European Inland Fisheries and Aquaculture Advisory Commission (EIFAAC, #07540)*;
    – *Fishery Committee for the Eastern Central Atlantic (CECAF, #09784)*;
    – *General Fisheries Commission for the Mediterranean (GFCM, #10112)*;
    – *Indian Ocean Tuna Commission (IOTC, #11162)*;
    – *Regional Commission for Fisheries (RECOFI, #18763)*;
    – *South West Indian Ocean Fisheries Commission (SWIOFC, #19894)*;
    – *Western Central Atlantic Fishery Commission (WECAFC, #20911).*
  – *'Food Policy and Nutrition'*:
    – *Codex Alimentarius Commission (CAC, #04081)*;
    – *Codex Committee on Cereals, Pulses and Legumes*;
    – *Codex Committee on Cocoa Products and Chocolate*;
    – *Codex Committee on Contaminents in Food*;
    – *Codex Committee on Fats and Oils*;
    – *Codex Committee on Fish and Fishery Products*;
    – *Codex Committee on Food Additives*;
    – *Codex Committee on Food Hygiene*;
    – *Codex Committee on Food Import and Export Inspection and Certification Systems*;
    – *Codex Committee on Food Labelling*;
    – *Codex Committee on Fresh Fruits and Vegetables*;
    – *Codex Committee on General Principles*;
    – *Codex Committee on Meat Hygiene*;
    – *Codex Committee on Methods of Analysis and Sampling*;
    – *Codex Committee on Milk and Milk Products*;
    – *Codex Committee on Natural Mineral Waters*;
    – *Codex Committee on Nutrition and Food for Special Dietary Uses*;
    – *Codex Committee on Pesticide Residues*;
    – *Codex Committee on Processed Fruits and Vegetables*;
    – *Codex Committee on Residues of Veterinary Drugs in Foods*;
    – *Codex Committee on Spices and Culinary Herbs*;
    – *Codex Committee on Sugars*;
    – *Codex Committee on Vegetable Proteins*;
    – Executive Committee of the Codex Alimentarius Commission;
    – *FAO/WHO Coordinating Committee for Africa (CCAFRICA)*;
    – *FAO/WHO Coordinating Committee for Asia (CCASIA)*;
    – *FAO/WHO Coordinating Committee for Europe (CCEURO)*;
    – *FAO/WHO Coordinating Committee for Latin America and the Caribbean (CCLAC)*;
    – *FAO/WHO Coordinating Committee for North America and the South West Pacific (CCCNASWP)*;
    – *FAO/WHO Coordinating Committee for the Near East*;
    – *Joint FAO/WHO Expert Committee on Food Additives (JECFA, #16129).*
  – *'Forestry'*:
    – *Advisory Committee on Sustainable Forest-based Industries (ACSFI)*;
    – *African Forestry and Wildlife Commission (AFWC, #00319)*;
    – *AFWC/EFC/NEFC Committee on Mediterranean Forestry Questions – Silva Mediterranea (#00542)*;
    – *Asia-Pacific Forestry Commission (APFC, #01909)*;
    – *European Forestry Commission (EFC, #07299)*;
    – *International Poplar Commission (IPC, #14619)*;
    – *Latin American and Caribbean Forestry Commission (LACFC, #16278)*;
    – *Near East Forestry Commission (NEFC, #16965)*;
    – *North American Forestry Commission (NAFC, #17565).*
  – *'Genetic Resources for Food and Agriculture'*:
    – *Ad Hoc Intergovernmental Technical Working Group on Aquatic Genetic Resources for Food and Agriculture*;
    – *Ad Hoc Technical Working Group on Access and Benefit-sharing for Genetic Resources for Food and Agriculture*;
    – *Commission on Genetic Resources for Food and Agriculture (CGRFA, #04215)*;
    – *Governing Body of Intergovernmental Technical Working Group on Animal Genetic Resources for Food and Agriculture (ITWG-AnGR, see: #09260)*;
    – *Intergovernmental Technical Working Group on Plant Genetic Resources for Food and Agriculture*;
    – *Panel of Experts on Forest Gene Resources.*
  – *'Land and Water Development'*:
  – *Agricultural and Land and Water Use Commission for the Near East (ALAWUC, #00570).*
– *'Plant Production and Protection'*:
  – *Asia and Pacific Plant Protection Commission (APPPC, #01997)*;
  – *Commission for Controlling the Desert Locust in the Central Region (CRC, #04208)*;
  – *Commission for Controlling the Desert Locust in South-West Asia (SWAC, #04209)*;
  – *FAO Commission for Controlling the Desert Locust in the Western Region (#09259)*;
  – *Commission on Phytosanitary Measures (CPM)*;
  – *FAO Desert Locust Control Committee (DLCC, no recent information)*;
  – *International Plant Protection Convention, 1951 (IPPC, 1951)*;
  – *Joint FAO/WHO Meeting on Pesticide Management (JMPM)*;
  – *Joint FAO/WHO Meeting on Pesticide Residues (JMPR)*;
  – *Joint FAO/WHO Meeting on Pesticide Specifications (JMPS)*;
  – *Standards Committee*;
  – *Subsidiary Body on Dispute Settlement (SBDS).*
– *'Statistics'*:
  – *African Commission on Agricultural Statistics (AFCAS, #00254)*;
  – *Asia and Pacific Commission on Agricultural Statistics (APCAS, #01873)*;
  – *FAO/ECE/CES Study Group on Food and Agricultural Statistics in Europe*;
  – *FAO/OEA-CIE/IICA Working Group on Agricultural and Livestock Statistics for Latin America and the Caribbean.*

III. /Regional Offices/ (5):
– *FAO Regional Office for Africa (FAO/RAF, #09265)*;
– *FAO Regional Office for Asia and the Pacific (RAP, #09266)*;
– *FAO Regional Office for Europe and Central Asia (FAO/REU, #09267)*;
– *FAO Regional Office for Latin America and the Caribbean (FAO/RLC, #09268)*;
– *FAO Regional Office for the Near East and North Africa (#09269).*

IV. /Director-General/ heads Offices, Departments and Divisions. Departments (6): Agriculture and Consumer Protection; Economic and Social Development; Fisheries and Aquaculture; Forestry; Corporate Services; Human Resources and Finance; Technical Cooperation. Programmes/projects functioning in the above departments include:
FAO GLOBEFISH (#09261); *FAO Investment Centre (#09264).*

Languages Arabic, Chinese, English, French, Russian, Spanish. **Staff** As of 31 Dec 2015, employed 1,738 professional and 1,510 support staff, of whom about 57% work at headquarters in Rome (Italy). Matters affecting former staff are dealt through *Former FAO and Other United Nations Staff Association (FFOA)*. Personnel negotiations through: *Union of Local and Non Local General Service Staff FAO/WFP (#20455)*. The *Administrative Tribunal of the International Labour Organization (ILO Tribunal, #00118)* is competent to settle disputes. **Finance** Contributions from member nations for implementation of regular programmes of work are based on per capita income, and the scale of contribution is set out in each Conference report. Approved effective working budget for biennium 2016-2017 is US$ 2,600 million.

Activities Main areas (5): Putting information within reach and supporting the transition to sustainable agriculture; Strengthening political will and sharing policy expertise; Bolstering public-private collaboration to improve smallholder agriculture; Bringing knowledge to the field; Supporting countries prevent and mitigate risks. A wide-ranging number of themes and topics highlight FAO priorities to win the battle against hunger, malnutrition and rural poverty.

Agreements concluded under FAO auspices:
– *Convention on the Privileges and Immunities of the Specialized Agencies (1947)*;
– *Plant Protection Agreement for the Asia and Pacific Region (1956)*;
– *International Convention for the Conservation of Atlantic Tunas (1966)*;
– *Convention on the Conservation of the Living Resources of the Southeast Atlantic (1969)*;
– *Convention on Assistance in the Case of Nuclear Accident or Radiological Emergency (1986)*;
– *Convention on Early Notification of a Nuclear Accident (1986)*;
– *Regional Convention on Fisheries Cooperation among African States Bordering the Atlantic Ocean (1991)*;
– *Agreement to Promote Compliance with the International Conservation and Management Measures by Fishing Vessels on the High Seas (1993)*;
– *Rotterdam Convention on the Prior Informed Consent Procedure for Certain Hazardous Chemicals and Pesticides in International Trade (Rotterdam convention, 1998)*;
– *International Treaty on Plant Genetic Resources for Food and Agriculture (2001)*;
– *Agreement on Port State Measures to Prevent, Deter and Eliminate Illegal, Unreported and Unregulated Fishing (2009)*;
– *International Plant Protection Convention, 1951 (IPPC, 1951).*

Events *World Teak Conference* Accra (Ghana) 2022, *Future-Proof Green Cities Make Future-Proof Countries* Budapest (Hungary) 2022, *International Plant Health Conference* London (UK) 2022, *Port State Measures (PSMA) Regional Coordination for Asia Meeting* Seoul (Korea Rep) 2022, *Catalyzing Nature-based Solutions for Biodiversity, Climate Change and Sustainable Development through Ecosystem Restoration* Tokyo (Japan) 2022. **Publications** *Unasylva* (4 a year) – forestry; *GLOBEFISH Highlights* (4 a year); *World Animal Review* (4 a year); *Yearbook of Forest Products Statistics* (2 a year); *FAO Commodity Review* (annual); *State of Food and Agriculture* (annual); *State of Food Insecurity* (annual); *State of World Fisheries and Aquaculture* (every 2 years); *State of World Forests* (every 2 years); *Animal Health Yearbook*; *FAO Statistical Yearbook*; *Yearbook of Fishery Statistics Vol I: Catches and Landings*; *Yearbook of Fishery Statistics Vol II: Fishery Commodities*. *FAO Agricultural Planning Studies*; *FAO Food and Nutrition Series*; *FAO Statistics Series*; *FAO Soils Bulletin*; *FAO Plant Production and Protection Papers*; *FAO Irrigation and Drainage Papers*; *FAO Forestry Series*; *FAO Forestry Papers*; *FAO Fisheries Technical Papers*; *FAO Agricultural Series*; *FAO Fisheries Reports*; *FAO Fertilizer and Plant Nutrition Bulletins*; *FAO Environment and Energy Papers*; *FAO Economic and Social Development Papers*; *FAO Conservation Guides*; *FAO Animal Production and Health Papers*; *FAO Agricultural Services Bulletins*; *FAO Training Series*. *FAO Legislative Studies*. Non-periodical technical publications; educational and training manuals, guides and kits; Conference and Council reports. Publications are issued in Arabic, Chinese, English, French, Spanish, Russian, Portuguese. Information services: Serves as a clearing-house for data published and made available in every medium – print, film, radio and TV, video, CDs and DVDs. Central database generates regular production, trade and fertilizer yearbooks, commodity and country tables and bulletins of statistics, and is also used to answer ad hoc requests and to prepare regular reviews of the current situation and outlook. Databases and information systems: *Global Information and Early Warning System on Food and Agriculture (GIEWS, #10416)* – issues monthly reports on the world food situation; *International Information System for the Agricultural Sciences and Technology (AGRIS, #13848)*; *World Agricultural Information Centre (WAICENT, see: #09260)*, opened Dec 1992, combines information from about 40 databases into 2 databases accessible through FAO's website. Many other FAO projects also maintain databanks of information on specific areas of rural development, agriculture, forestry and fisheries. **Information Services** *Aquatic Sciences and Fisheries Information System (ASFIS)*; *International Fish Marketing Indicators Database (GLOBEFISH)*; *Support to Agricultural Information and Documentation Projects (SPIDA)*; *SPECIESDAB* – fish species; *Seed Information System*; *Remote Sensing Database (ARTEMIS)*; *Plant Nutrition Data Bank*; *Land Resource Data Bank*; *INFOFISH*; *Current Agricultural Research Information System (CARIS)*; *Geographic Information System (GIS)*; *Forest Resources Information System (FORIS)*; *Fisheries Statistical Database (FISHDAB)*; *Fisheries Project Information System (FIPIS)*; *FAOSTAT Database*; *FAOINFO Database*; *World Forestry Resources Inventory*.

Members Full members: independent nations. Associate members: territories or groups of territories not responsible for the conduct of their own international relations. Total membership, 194 countries:
Afghanistan, Albania, Algeria, Andorra, Angola, Antigua-Barbuda, Argentina, Armenia, Australia, Austria, Azerbaijan, Bahamas, Bahrain, Bangladesh, Barbados, Belarus, Belgium, Belize, Benin, Bhutan, Bolivia, Bosnia-Herzegovina, Botswana, Brazil, Brunei Darussalam, Bulgaria, Burkina Faso, Burundi, Cambodia, Cameroon, Canada, Cape Verde, Central African Rep, Chad, Chile, China, Colombia, Comoros, Congo Brazzaville, Congo DR, Cook Is, Costa Rica, Côte d'Ivoire, Croatia, Cuba, Cyprus, Czechia, Denmark, Djibouti, Dominica, Dominican Rep, Ecuador, Egypt, El Salvador, Equatorial Guinea, Eritrea, Estonia, Eswatini, Ethiopia, Fiji, Finland, France, Gabon, Gambia, Georgia, Germany, Ghana, Greece, Grenada, Guatemala, Guinea, Guinea-Bissau, Guyana, Haiti, Honduras, Hungary, Iceland, India, Indonesia, Iran Islamic Rep, Iraq, Ireland, Israel, Italy, Jamaica, Japan, Jordan, Kazakhstan, Kenya, Kiribati, Korea DPR, Korea Rep, Kuwait, Kyrgyzstan, Laos, Latvia, Lebanon, Lesotho, Liberia, Libya, Lithuania, Luxembourg, Madagascar, Malawi, Malaysia, Maldives, Mali, Malta, Marshall Is, Mauritania, Mauritius, Mexico, Micronesia FS, Moldova, Monaco, Mongolia, Montenegro, Morocco, Mozambique, Myanmar, Namibia, Nauru, Nepal, Netherlands, New Zealand, Nicaragua, Niger, Nigeria, Niue, North Macedonia, Norway, Oman, Pakistan, Palau, Panama, Papua New Guinea, Paraguay, Peru, Philippines, Poland, Portugal, Qatar, Romania, Russia, Rwanda, Samoa, San Marino, Sao Tomé-Principe, Saudi Arabia, Senegal, Serbia, Seychelles, Sierra Leone, Singapore, Slovakia, Slovenia, Solomon Is, Somalia, South Africa, South Sudan, Spain, Sri Lanka, St Kitts-Nevis, St Lucia, St Vincent-Grenadines, Sudan, Suriname, Sweden, Switzerland, Syrian AR, Tajikistan, Tanzania UR, Thailand, Timor-Leste, Togo, Tonga, Trinidad-Tobago, Tunisia, Türkiye, Turkmenistan, Tuvalu, Uganda, UK, Ukraine, United Arab Emirates, Uruguay, USA, Uzbekistan, Vanuatu, Venezuela, Vietnam, Yemen, Zambia, Zimbabwe.

Associate member, 2 countries and territories:
Faeroe Is, Tokelau.
Regional integration EU entity (1):
European Union (EU, #08967).
IGO Relations Cooperates closely with other UN agencies and bodies, particularly:
- *UNEP (#20299);*
- *UN-OCEANS (#20711);*
- *UNDP (#20292);*
- *UNESCO (#20322);*
- *United Nations Economic Commission for Latin America and the Caribbean (ECLAC, #20556);*
- *United Nations Group on the Information Society (UNGIS, #20570);*
- *United Nations Population Fund (UNFPA, #20612);*
- *United Nations University (UNU, #20642);*
- *WHO (#20950);*
- *World Food Programme (WFP, #21510);*
- *World Intellectual Property Organization (WIPO, #21593)* (Permanent observer status);
- *World Meteorological Organization (WMO, #21649);*
- *World Trade Organization (WTO, #21864)* (Observer Status).

Specialized Consultative Statuts to: *International Centre for Integrated Mountain Development (ICIMOD, #12500).* Instrumental in setting up: *Africa Solidarity Trust Fund (ASTF, #00522); Global Crop Diversity Trust (Crop Trust, #10313); FAO-ICARDA International Technical Cooperation Network on Cactus (CACTUSNET, #09262); Inter-American Citrus Network (IACNET, #11407).* Partner of: *Regional Seas Programme (#18814); United Nations Institute for Training and Research (UNITAR, #20576).*
Cooperation agreements approved by FAO Conference:
- *African Union (AU, #00488);*
- *Arab Organization for Agricultural Development (AOAD, #01018);*
- *Centre for Marketing Information and Advisory Services for Fishery Products in the Arab Region (INFOSAMAK, #03772);*
- *Council of Europe (CE, #04881);*
- *Desert Locust Control Organization for Eastern Africa (DLCO-EA, #05042);*
- *INFOPECHE (#11191);*
- *INFOPESCA (#11192);*
- *Intergovernmental Organization for Marketing Information and Technical Advisory Services for Fishery Products in the Asia and Pacific Region (INFOFISH, #11497);*
- *International Commission for the Conservation of Atlantic Tunas (ICCAT, #12675);*
- *International Organisation for the Development of Fisheries and Aquaculture in Europe (EUROFISH, #14427);*
- *Lake Victoria Fisheries Organization (LVFO, #16222);*
- *League of Arab States (LAS, #16420);*
- *Network of Aquaculture Centres in Asia-Pacific (NACA, #16991);*
- *OAS (#17629);*
- *OIE – World Organisation for Animal Health (#17703);*
- *Regional Centre on Agrarian Reform and Rural Development for the Near East (#18755).*

Relationship agreements concluded under the form of Memorandum of Understanding, exchange of letters or other appropriate documents:
- *Africa Rice Center (AfricaRice, #00518);*
- *African-Asian Rural Development Organization (AARDO, #00203);*
- *Organisation of African, Caribbean and Pacific States (OACPS, #17796);*
- *African Oil Palm Development Association (AFOPDA, no recent information);*
- *African Timber Organization (ATO, no recent information);*
- *Alliance of Cocoa Producing Countries (COPAL, no recent information);*
- Commission of the *Andean Community (#00817);*
- *Arab Centre for the Studies of Arid Zones and Dry Lands (ACSAD, #00918);*
- *Arab Industrial Development, Standardization and Mining Organization (AIDSMO, #00981);*
- *Arab Planning Institute (API, #01027);*
- *ASEAN (#01141);*
- *Asian Productivity Organization (APO, #01674);*
- *CABI (#03393);*
- *Caribbean Community (CARICOM, #03476);*
- *CIHEAM – International Centre for Advanced Mediterranean Agronomic Studies (CIHEAM, #03927);*
- *Comisión Permanente del Pacífico Sur (CPPS, #04141);*
- *Comité permanent inter-Etats de lutte contre la sécheresse dans le Sahel (CILSS, #04195);*
- *Common Market for Eastern and Southern Africa (COMESA, #04296);*
- *Commonwealth Secretariat (#04362);*
- *Communauté économique et monétaire d'Afrique centrale (CEMAC, #04374);*
- *Communauté économique des pays des Grands Lacs (CEPGL, #04375);*
- *Comunidade dos Países de Língua Portuguesa (CPLP, #04430);*
- *Council of Arab Economic Unity (CAEU, #04859);*
- *Economic Community of West African States (ECOWAS, #05312);*
- *Economic Cooperation Organization (ECO, #05313);*
- *European and Mediterranean Plant Protection Organization (EPPO, #07773);*
- *Gulf Cooperation Council (GCC, #10826);*
- *Inter-American Institute for Cooperation on Agriculture (IICA, #11434);*
- *Inter-American Tropical Tuna Commission (IATTC, #11454);*
- *Inter-State School of Rural Equipment Engineers (inactive);*
- *International Cocoa Organization (ICCO, #12627);*
- *International Coffee Organization (ICO, #12630);*
- *International Cotton Advisory Committee (ICAC, #12979);*
- *International Council for the Exploration of the Sea (ICES, #13021);*
- *International Grains Council (IGC, #13731);*
- *International Institute of Refrigeration (IIR, #13918);*
- *International Institute for the Unification of Private Law (UNIDROIT, #13934);*
- *International Jute Study Group (IJSG, no recent information);*
- *International Olive Council (IOC, #14405);*
- *International Organization for Migration (IOM, #14454);*
- *International Organisation of Vine and Wine (OIV, #14435);*
- *International Pacific Halibut Commission (IPHC);*
- *International Pepper Community (IPC, #14557);*
- *International Rubber Study Group (IRSG, #14772);*
- *International Sericultural Commission (ISC, #14837);*
- *International Sugar Organization (ISO, #15623);*
- *International Tea Promotion Association (ITPA, inactive);*
- *International Whaling Commission (IWC, #15879);*
- *Italian-Latin American Institute (ILAI, #16071);*
- *Joint Anti-Locust and Anti-Aviarian Organization (OCLALAV, inactive);*
- *Latin American Fisheries Development Organization (#16335);*
- *Latin American Integration Association (LAIA, #16343);*
- *Mano River Union (MRU, #16566);*
- *The Mediterranean Science Commission (CIESM, #16674);*
- *North American Plant Protection Organization (NAPPO, #17567);*
- *North-East Atlantic Fisheries Commission (NEAFC, #17581);*
- *OECD (#17693);*
- *Organisation of Eastern Caribbean States (OECS, #17804);*
- *Organisation internationale de la Francophonie (OIF, #17809);*
- *Organisation of Islamic Cooperation (OIC, #17813);*
- *Organisation pour la mise en valeur du fleuve Gambie (OMVG, #17814);*
- *Pacific Community (SPC, #17942);*
- *Pacific Islands Forum Fisheries Agency (FFA, #17969);*
- *Pacific Islands Forum Secretariat (#17970);*
- *Pacific Salmon Commission (PSC);*
- *Permanent Consultative Committee of the Maghreb (PCCM, inactive);*
- *Permanent Council of International Convention of Stresa for the Use of Appellations d'Origine and Denominations of Cheeses (no recent information);*
- *Organismo Internacional Regional de Sanidad Agropecuaria (OIRSA, #17830);*
- *Secretaría Permanente del Tratado General de Integración Económica Centroamericana (SIECA, #19195);*
- *Secretariat of the Convention on International Trade in Endangered Species of Wild Fauna and Flora (CITES Secretariat, #19199);*
- *Secretariat of the Pacific Regional Environment Programme (SPREP, #19205);*
- *Sistema Económico Latinoamericano (SELA, #19294);*
- *South Asia Cooperative Environment Programme (SACEP, #19714);*
- *Southeast Asian Fisheries Development Center (SEAFDEC, #19767);*
- *Southern African Development Community (SADC, #19843);*
- *Unión de Países Exportadores de Banano (UPEB, inactive);*
- *World Tourism Organization (UNWTO, #21861).*

Other major multilateral funding institutions with which the FAO cooperates include:
- *International Bank for Reconstruction and Development (IBRD, #12317),* the single most important source, whose funds are channelled through *International Development Association (IDA, #13155);*
- *International Fund for Agricultural Development (IFAD, #13692);*
- *United Nations Capital Development Fund (UNCDF, #20524).*

With ICSU, UNESCO, UNEP and WMO, cooperating in design and planning phase of: *Global Terrestrial Observing System (GTOS, #10626).* Participates in developing and implementing: *West and Central African Action Plan (WACAF, no recent information).*
In addition, a number of United Nations and other intergovernmental bodies indicate close links with FAO. These include:
- *Abdus Salam International Centre for Theoretical Physics (ICTP, #00005);*
- *African Centre for Gender (ACG);*
- *African Regional Centre of Technology (ARCT, #00432);*
- *African University for Cooperative Development (AUCD, #00494);*
- *AGRHYMET Regional Centre (#00565);*
- *Andean Parliament (#00820);*
- *Arab Federation of Fish Producers (AFFP, #00945);*
- *Arab Gulf Programme for United Nations Development Organizations (AGFUND, #00971);*
- *Asian-African Legal Consultative Organization (AALCO, #01303);*
- *Association of Agricultural Research Institutions in the Near East and North Africa (AARINENA, #02364);*
- *Bioversity International (#03262);*
- *Caribbean Agricultural Research and Development Institute (CARDI, #03436);*
- *Caribbean Fisheries Training and Development Institute (CFTDI, #03507);*
- *Caribbean Food and Nutrition Institute (CFNI, inactive);*
- *Centre for Alleviation of Poverty through Sustainable Agriculture (CAPSA-ESCAP, inactive);*
- *Centre de coopération internationale en recherche agronomique pour le développement (CIRAD, #03733);*
- *Center for Information on Migration in Latin America (#03643);*
- *Centre on Integrated Rural Development for Africa (CIRDAFRICA, no recent information);*
- *CGIAR System Organization (CGIAR, #03843),* especially *International Crops Research Institute for the Semi-Arid Tropics (ICRISAT, #13116);*
- *Comisión Sudamericana para la Lucha contra la Fiebre Aftosa (COSALFA, #04143);*
- *Convention on Long-range Transboundary Air Pollution (#04787);*
- *Eastern Caribbean Institute of Agriculture and Forestry (ECIAF, #05234);*
- *ECOWAS Bank for Investment and Development (EBID, #05334);*
- *Environmental Training Network for Latin America and the Caribbean (inactive);*
- *European Space Agency (ESA, #08798);*
- *Food and Fertilizer Technology Center for the Asian and Pacific Region (FFTC/ASPAC, #09842);*
- *Institute of Nutrition of Central America and Panama (INCAP, #11285);*
- *Inter-African Phytosanitary Council (AU-IAPSC, #11386);*
- *Inter-Agency Working Group on Desertification (IAWGD, inactive);*
- *Intergovernmental Oceanographic Commission (IOC, #11496);*
- *Inter-Organization Programme for the Sound Management of Chemicals (IOMC, #15956);*
- *Inter-Secretariat Committee on Scientific Programmes Relating to Oceanography (ICSPRO, inactive);*
- *Interstate Statistical Committee of the Commonwealth of Independent States (CIS-Stat, #15983);*
- *Interafrican Bureau for Animal Resources (AU-IBAR, #11382);*
- *International Center for Agricultural Research in the Dry Areas (ICARDA, #12466);*
- *International Centre for Genetic Engineering and Biotechnology (ICGEB, #12494);*
- *International Centre for Promotion of Enterprises (ICPE, #12509);*
- *International Centre for Scientific and Technical Information (ICSTI, #12514);*
- *International Civil Service Commission (ICSC, #12587);*
- *International Computing Centre (ICC, #12839);*
- *International Hydrographic Organization (IHO, #13825);*
- *International Institute for Adult Education Methods (IIAEM, no recent information);*
- *International Institute of Biological Control (IIBC, inactive);*
- *International Nuclear Information System (INIS, #14378);*
- *International Programme on Chemical Safety (IPCS, #14650);*
- *International Red Locust Control Organization for Central and Southern Africa (IRLCO-CSA, no recent information);*
- *International Trade Centre (ITC, #15703);*
- *International Tropical Timber Organization (ITTO, #15737);*
- *IOC Intergovernmental Panel on Harmful Blooms (IPHAB, #16002);*
- *IOC Sub-Commission for the Western Pacific (WESTPAC, see: #11496);*
- *Joint Inspection Unit of the United Nations (JIU, #16133);*
- *Lake Chad Basin Commission (LCBC, #16220);*
- *Marine Environmental Data Information Referral System (MEDI, no recent information);*
- *Mediterranean Action Plan (MAP, #16638);*
- *Mekong River Commission (MRC, #16703);*
- *Middle Eastern Regional Radioisotope Centre for the Arab Countries (MERRCAC, #16761);*
- *OPEC Fund for International Development (OFID, #17745);*
- *Pan American Foot-and-Mouth Disease Center (PAFMDC, #18106);*
- *Pan American Health Organization (PAHO, #18108);*
- *Programme on Man and the Biosphere (MAB, #18526);*
- *Regional Institute for Population Studies (RIPS, no recent information);*
- *Regional Organization for the Protection of the Marine Environment (ROPME, #18805);*
- *Southeast Asian Regional Center for Graduate Study and Research in Agriculture (SEARCA, #19781);*
- *SEAMEO Regional Tropical Medicine and Public Health Network (SEAMEO TROPMED, #19184);*
- *Secretariat of the Convention on Biological Diversity (SCBD, #19197);*
- *Southeast Asian Ministers of Education Organization (SEAMEO, #19774);*
- *Southeast Asian Regional Centre for Tropical Biology (SEAMEO BIOTROP, #19782);*
- *Statistical, Economic and Social Research and Training Centre for Islamic Countries (SESRIC, #19971);*
- *Statistical Institute for Asia and the Pacific (SIAP, #19972);*
- *Sub-Regional Fisheries Commission (SRFC, #20026);*
- *UNEP DTIE Chemicals Branch (inactive);*
- *UNESCO Regional Office for Education in the Arab States (UNEDBAS, #20320);*
- *UNHCR (#20327);*
- *Union internationale pour la protection des obtentions végétales (UPOV, #20436);*
- *United Nations Framework Convention on Climate Change – Secretariat (UNFCCC, #20564);*
- *United Nations International Drug Control Programme (UNDCP, inactive);*
- *United Nations International Emergency Network (UNIENET, no recent information);*
- *United Nations Joint Staff Pension Fund (UNJSPF, #20581);*
- *United Nations Non-Governmental Liaison Service (NGLS, #20591);*
- *United Nations Research Institute for Social Development (UNRISD, #20623);*
- *United Nations Volunteers (UNV, #20650);*
- *WHO Pan African Emergency Training Centre (PTC-Addis, no recent information);*
- *WHO Regional Office for Europe (#20945);*
- *WHO Tobacco Free Initiative (TFI, #20949).*

NGO Relations FAO has entered into formal relations with international non-governmental organizations that help to promote its purposes. As part of the policy concerning these relations, the Conference has adopted principles relating to eligibility, privileges and obligations for NGOs with several categories of relationship:
(1) *'Consultative Status:'*
- *Associated Country Women of the World (ACWW, #02338);*
- *Caritas Internationalis (CI, #03580);*
- *International Chamber of Commerce (ICC, #12534);*
- *International Co-operative Alliance (ICA, #12944);*
- *International Council of Women (ICW, #13093);*
- *International Federation of Red Cross and Red Crescent Societies (#13526);*
- *International Trade Union Confederation (ITUC, #15708);*
- *International Union of Food, Agricultural, Hotel, Restaurant, Catering, Tobacco and Allied Workers Associations (IUF, #15772);*
- Commission of the Churches on International Affairs of *World Council of Churches (WCC, #21320);*
- *World Family Organization (WFO, #21399);*
- *World Federation of Trade Unions (WFTU, #21493);*
- *World Federation of United Nations Associations (WFUNA, #21499);*
- *World Union of Catholic Women's Organisations (WUCWO, #21876);*
- *The World Veterans Federation (WVF, #21900).*

(2) *'Specialized Consultative Status:'*

FAO
09260

alphabetic sequence excludes
For the complete listing, see Yearbook Online at

- *Action Group on Erosion, Technology and Concentration (ETC Group, #00091)*;
- *AOAC INTERNATIONAL (#00863)*;
- *Asia-Pacific Broadcasting Union (ABU, #01863)*;
- *Canners International Permanent Committee (CIPC, inactive)*;
- *Collaborative International Pesticides Analytical Council (CIPAC, #04099)*;
- *Comité Européen de Droit Rural (CEDR, #04155)*;
- *Consumers International (CI, #04773)*;
- *CropLife International (#04966)*;
- *Education International (EI, #05371)*;
- *European Federation of Animal Science (EAAP, #07046)*;
- *Fédération internationale d'oléiculture (FIO, inactive)*;
- *FoodDrinkEurope (#09841)*;
- *Grain and Feed Trade Association (GAFTA, #10692)*;
- *Inter-Parliamentary Union (IPU, #15961)*;
- *International Association of Agricultural Economists (IAAE, #11695)*;
- *International Association of Horticultural Producers (#11940)*;
- *International Cargo Handling Coordination Association (ICHCA, inactive)*, currently replaced by *ICHCA International Limited (IIL, #11053)*;
- *International Commission of Agricultural and Biosystems Engineering (#12661)*;
- *International Commission on Irrigation and Drainage (ICID, #12694)*;
- *International Committee for Animal Recording (ICAR, #12746)*;
- *International Dairy Federation (IDF, #13128)*;
- *International Federation of Agricultural Journalists (IFAJ, #13346)*;
- *International Federation of Beekeepers' Associations (APIMONDIA, #13370)*;
- *International Federation for Home Economics (IFHE, #13447)*;
- *International Foundation for Science (IFS, #13677)*;
- *International Life Sciences Institute (ILSI, #14044)*;
- *International Organization for Standardization (ISO, #14473)*;
- *International Planned Parenthood Federation (IPPF, #14589)*;
- *International Seed Federation (ISF, #14828)*;
- *International Union for Conservation of Nature and Natural Resources (IUCN, #15766)*;
- *International Union of Food Science and Technology (IUFoST, #15773)*;
- *International Union of Forest Research Organizations (IUFRO, #15774)*;
- *International Union of Leather Technologists and Chemists Societies (IULTCS, #15788)*;
- *International Union of Nutritional Sciences (IUNS, #15796)*;
- *International Union of Pure and Applied Chemistry (IUPAC, #15809)*;
- *International Union of Soil Sciences (IUSS, #15817)*;
- *International Water Association (IWA, #15865)*;
- *The Marine Ingredients Organisation (IFFO, #16579)*;
- *Mouvement international de la jeunesse agricole et rurale catholique (MIJARC, #16865)*;
- *Organisation of African Trade Union Unity (OATUU, #17798)*;
- *Pan African Institute for Development (PAID, #18053)*;
- *Population Council (#18458)*;
- *Safeguard for Agricultural Varieties in Europe (SAVE Foundation, #19027)*;
- *Trade Unions International of Agricultural, Forestry and Plantation Workers (TUIAFPW, inactive)*;
- *Women's International League for Peace and Freedom (WILPF, #21024)*;
- *World Assembly of Youth (WAY, #21113)*;
- *World Association for Animal Production (WAAP, #21117)*;
- *World Council of Credit Unions (WOCCU, #21324)*;
- *World Federation of Parasitologists (WFP, #21471)*;
- *World Veterinary Association (WVA, #21901)*;
- *World Young Women's Christian Association (World YWCA, #21947)*;
- *World's Poultry Science Association (WPSA, #21825)*.

(3) *'Liaison Status:'*

- *African Rural and Agricultural Credit Association (AFRACA, #00446)*;
- *American Fisheries Society (AFS)*;
- *American Oil Chemists' Society (AOCS)*;
- *Arab Fertilizer Association (AFA, #00958)*;
- *Asia Pacific Rural and Agricultural Credit Association (APRACA, #02019)*;
- *Asian Cultural Forum on Development Foundation (ACFOD, no recent information)*;
- *Asian NGO Coalition for Agrarian Reform and Rural Development (ANGOC, #01566)*;
- *International Association for Water Law (#12263)*;
- *Asociación Latinoamericana de Instituciones Financieras para el Desarrollo (ALIDE, #02233)*;
- *Association of Interbalkan Women's Cooperation Societies, Thessaloniki (AIWCS, #02653)*;
- *Association internationale des mouvements familiaux de formation rurale (AIMFR, #02719)*;
- *Association des universités partiellement ou entièrement de langue française (AUPELF, inactive)*;
- *Caribbean Agricultural Association (CACRA, inactive)*;
- *Caribbean Food Crops Society (CFCS, #03509)*;
- *Centre de coopération pour les recherches scientifiques relatives au tabac (CORESTA, #03735)*;
- *CIRFS – European Man-made Fibres Association (#03944)*;
- *Comité européen des fabricants de sucre (CEFS, #04159)*;
- *COPA – european farmers (COPA, #04829)*;
- *Confédération internationale du crédit agricole (CICA, #04560)*;
- *Coordinating Committee for International Voluntary Service (CCIVS, #04819)*;
- *Dairy Society International (DSI, inactive)*;
- *Environment Liaison Centre International (ELCI, no recent information)*;
- *EUCARPIA (#05571)*;
- *European Association of Agricultural Economists (EAAE, #05932)*;
- *European Association for the Trade in Jute and Related Products (Eurojute, #06256)*;
- *Association of Catering Excellence (ACE)*;
- *European Food Law Association (EFLA, #07286)*;
- *European Liaison Committee for Pulp and Paper (EUCEPA, #07688)*;
- *European Tea Committee (ETC, inactive)*;
- *Federation of European Aquaculture Producers (FEAP, #09491)*;
- *Fédération européenne des industries de corderie ficellerie et de filets (EUROCORD, #09573)*;
- *Fertilizers Europe (#09738)*;
- *Food for the Hungry (fh, #09845)*;
- *Global Aquaculture Alliance (GAA, #10238)*;
- *Global Pulse Confederation (GPC, #10562)*;
- *Greenpeace International (#10727)*;
- *Health for Animals (#10870)*;
- *Heifer International*;
- *ICC – International Association for Cereal Science and Technology (#11048)*;
- *IFOAM – Organics International (IFOAM, #11105)*;
- *Industry Council for Development Services (ICDS, inactive)*;
- *Institute of Cultural Affairs International (ICAI, #11251)*;
- *Insurance Europe (#11362)*;
- *CIDSE (CIDSE, #03926)*;
- *International Alliance of Women (IAW, #11639)*;
- *International Association of Seed Crushers (IASC, inactive)*;
- *International Association of Students in Agricultural and Related Sciences (IAAS, #12191)*;
- *International Catholic Rural Association (ICRA, #12461)*;
- *International Cell Research Organization (ICRO, #12463)*;
- *International Christian Union of Business Executives (#12566)*;
- *International Collective in Support of Fishworkers (ICSF, #12639)*;
- *International Confederation of European Beet Growers (CIBE, #12860)*;
- *International Council for Adult Education (ICAE, #12983)*;
- *International Council of Forest and Paper Associations (ICFPA, #13023)*;
- *International Council for Game and Wildlife Conservation (#13024)*;
- *International Council of Hides, Skins and Leather Traders Associations (ICHSLTA, #13029)*;
- *International Council on Jewish Social and Welfare Services (INTERCO, #13035)*;
- *International Council on Social Welfare (ICSW, #13076)*;
- *International Economic Association (IEA, #13222)*;
- *International Egg Commission (IEC, #13245)*;
- *International Federation of Business and Professional Women (BPW International, #13376)*;
- *International Federation for Information and Documentation (FID, inactive)*;
- *International Federation of Women in Legal Careers (IFWLC, #13579)*;
- *International Fertilizer Association (IFA, #13589)*;
- *International Food Policy Research Institute (IFPRI, #13622)*;
- *International Fruit and Vegetable Juice Association (IFU, #13687)*;
- *International Geographical Union (IGU, #13713)*;
- *International Institute for Applied Systems Analysis (IIASA, #13861)*;
- *International Institute of Sugar Beet Research (IIRB, #13928)*;
- *International Jacques Maritain Institute (#13967)*;
- *International Law Association (ILA, #14003)*;
- *International Meat Secretariat (IMS, #14125)*;
- *International Movement for the Defence of and the Right to Pleasure (Slow Food, #14194)*;
- *International Organisation for Biological Control (IOBC, #14424)*;
- *International Peatland Society (IPS, #14538)*;
- *International Potash Institute (IPI, #14626)*;
- *International Silk Association (ISA, inactive)*;
- *International Society for Horticultural Science (ISHS, #15180)*;
- *International Society for Plant Pathology (ISPP, #15371)*;
- *International Tea Committee (ITC, #15664)*;
- *International Technical Tropical Timber Association (ITTTA, #15668)*;
- *International Textile Manufacturers Federation (ITMF, #15679)*;
- *International Union of Biological Sciences (IUBS, #15760)*;
- *International Union of Microbiological Societies (IUMS, #15794)*;
- *International Union of Notaries (#15795)*;
- *International Union of Socialist Youth (IUSY, #15815)*;
- *International Wool Textile Organisation (IWTO, #15904)*;
- *International Young Christian Workers (IYCW, #15927)*;
- *Internationale Raiffeisen Union e.V. (IRU, #13291)*;
- *Liaison Committee of Mediterranean Citrus Producing Countries (CLAM, inactive)*;
- *Life Institute (no recent information)*;
- *Near East and North Africa Regional Agricultural Credit Association (NENARACA, inactive)*;
- *Organization of the Cooperatives of America (OCA, inactive)*;
- *Pan African Federation of Agricultural Trade Unions (PAFATU, inactive)*;
- *Pesticide Action Network (PAN, #18336)*;
- *Practical Action (#18475)*;
- *Rotary International (RI, #18975)*;
- *Society for International Development (SID, #19581)*;
- *Soroptimist International (SI, #19686)*;
- *Sulphur Institute, The (TSI, #20034)*;
- *Tropical Growers' Association (TGA, #20250)*;
- *Union internationale pour la coopération au développement (UNICOS, inactive)*;
- *United Schools International (USI, #20660)*;
- *UNUM OMNES International Council of Catholic Men (ICCM, #20720)*;
- *World Animal Protection (#21092)*;
- *World Association of Girl Guides and Girl Scouts (WAGGGS, #21142)*;
- *World Blind Union (WBU, #21234)*;
- *World Federation of Democratic Youth (WFDY, #21427)*;
- *World Federation of Engineering Organizations (WFEO, #21433)*;
- *World Humanity Action Trust (WHAT, inactive)*;
- *World Organization of the Scout Movement (WOSM, #21693)*;
- *World Packaging Organisation (WPO, #21705)*;
- *World Phosphate Institute (#21728)*;
- *World Savings Banks Institute (WSBI, #21764)*;
- *World Sugar Research Organization (WSRO, #21837)*;
- *World University Service (WUS, #21892)*.

(4) *'Relationships agreements:'*

- *International Committee of the Red Cross (ICRC, #12799)*;
- *International Olympic Committee (IOC, #14408)*.

Supports: *Africare (#00516)*; *World Education (WE)*. Partner of: *WorldFish (#21507)*. National Committees facilitate liaison between the Organization and the governments and peoples of countries. They are national institutions, with constitutions and functions normally laid down in a governmental or ministerial instrument. [2023/XB0971/**B***]

♦ FAO Global Network of Market Information and Technical Advisory Services for Fishery Products / see FAO GLOBEFISH (#09261)

♦ FAO GLOBEFISH 09261

Secretariat Products/Trade/Marketing Branch (FIPM), FAO Fisheries and Aquaculture Policy and Economics Div, Viale delle Terme di Caracalla, 00153 Rome RM, Italy. T. +39657052692. Fax +39657053020. E-mail: globefish@fao.org.
URL: http://www.globefish.org/

History Set up 1984 by FAO World Fisheries Conference. FAO GLOBEFISH databank and Services project set up, 1985, within the framework of *FAO (#09260)*. Full title: *FAO Global Network of Market Information and Technical Advisory Services for Fishery Products (FAO GLOBEFISH)*. **Aims** Provide information on international fish trade and related issues worldwide. **Structure** Unit within FAO Fisheries and Aquaculture Department. **Staff** 70.00 FTE, paid. **Activities** Publishing activities. **Events** *Tuna trade conference* Kuala Lumpur (Malaysia) 2002, *International small pelagic conference* Agadir (Morocco) 2001, *World conference on the shrimp industry and trade* Chennai (India) 2001, *Salmon summit* Copenhagen (Denmark) 1999, *International fisheries conference / Meeting* Dublin (Ireland) 1999. **Publications** *Globefish European Fish Price Report* (12 a year); *Commodity Update*; *Globefish Highlights*; *GLOBEFISH Research Programme*. **Information Services** *GLOBEFISH Databank*. **IGO Relations** Part of *FISHINFONetwork (FIN)*, along with 7 independent organizations: *INFOPESCA (#11192)* (South and Central America); *Intergovernmental Organization for Marketing Information and Technical Advisory Services for Fishery Products in the Asia and Pacific Region (INFOFISH, #11497)* (Asia and the Pacific); *INFOPECHE (#11191)* (Africa); *INFOSA (#11203)* (Southern Africa); *Centre for Marketing Information and Advisory Services for Fishery Products in the Arab Region (INFOSAMAK, #03772)* (Arab speaking countries); *International Organisation for the Development of Fisheries and Aquaculture in Europe (EUROFISH, #14427)* (Eastern and Central Europe); *'INFOYU'* (China). Partner of: *European Commission (EC, #06633)* (DG MARE). [2015/XF4072/**F***]

♦ FAO-ICARDA International Technical Cooperation Network on Cactus (CACTUSNET) 09262

General Coordinator Dept of Agroindustry and Enology, Fac of Agronomic Science, Univ of Chile, Av Santa Rosa 11315, 882 08 08 Santiago, Santiago Metropolitan, Chile.
URL: http://www.cactusnetwork.org/

History 1993, Guadalajara (Mexico), within *FAO (#09260)*, as *FAO International Technical Cooperation Network on Cactus Pear (CACTUSNET FAO)*. **Aims** Collect and disseminate information on cactus production; facilitate collection and utilization of germplasm; promote ecological and social benefits of cactus pear; develop new food and carminic acid uses; work with national partners to improve technical capability. **Structure** General Coordination; Regional Coordinators; Research Theme Coordinators. **Languages** Arabic, English, French, Spanish. **Activities** Knowledge management/information dissemination; research/documentation; advocacy/lobbying/activism; events/meetings. Online group information exchange service. **Events** *International Congress on Cactus Pear and Cochineal* João Pessoa (Brazil) 2022, *International Congress on Cactus Pear and Cochineal* Hammamet (Tunisia) 2020, *International Congress on Cactus Pear and Cochineal* Coquimbo (Chile) 2017, *International Congress on Cactus Pear and Cochineal* Mendoza (Argentina) 2016, *International Congress* Agadir (Morocco) 2010. **Publications** *CactusNet Newsletter*. **Members** Full (237) in 41 countries. Membership countries not specified. **IGO Relations** *FAO (#09260)*; *International Center for Agricultural Research in the Dry Areas (ICARDA, #12466)*. [2018.09.05/XK2156/**E***]

♦ FAOI / see Federation of African Engineering Organisations (#09402)
♦ FAO International Technical Cooperation Network on Cactus Pear / see FAO-ICARDA International Technical Cooperation Network on Cactus (#09262)

♦ FAO Inter-Regional Cooperative Research Network on Rice in the Mediterranean Climate Areas (MedRice Network) 09263

Réseau coopératif interrégional de la FAO de recherche sur le riz en climat méditerranéen
Coordinator Dipto di Agronomia, Selvicoltura e Gestione del Territorio, Univ di Turin, Via Leonardo da Vinci 44, 10095 Grugliasco TO, Italy. T. +39116708780. Fax +39116708798.
URL: http://www.escorena.net/

History Sep 1990, Arles (France), as part of *European System of Cooperative Research Networks in Agriculture (ESCORENA, #08871)*, within *FAO (#09260)*, through its *European Commission on Agriculture (ECA)*. Previously abbreviated as *MedNetRice Network*. Also referred to as *European Cooperative Research Network on Rice*. **Aims** Promote scientific exchanges among rice scientists working in the Mediterranean area and in the other world regions with Mediterranean climate. **Structure** Working Groups (6): Biotechnology; Breeding and Varietal Improvement; Rice Agronomy; Rice Processing and Technology; Economics and Marketing; Information. **Languages** English. **Staff** 1.50 FTE, paid. **Finance** Supported by: FAO, *FAO Regional Office for Europe and Central Asia (FAO/REU, #09267)*, *FAO Regional Office for the Near East and North Africa (#09269)*, Research institutions belonging to this network. **Activities** Exchange of varieties for field trials; cooperative research: in genetic resources (diversity and quality); on red rice (biological understanding and agricultural practices); on water management (economy and ecology). **Events** *Meeting* Skadovsk (Ukraine) 2008, *International conference on sustainable rice production / Meeting* Krasnodar (Russia) 2006, *Conference on challenges and opportunities for sustainable rice-based production systems / Meeting* Turin (Italy) 2004, *Meeting* Turin (Italy) 2002, *Meeting* Krasnodar (Russia) 2001. **Publications** *Medoryzae* in English, French – newsletter.

Members Rice producing countries from the Mediterranean, Eastern Europe and the Pacific (23):
Albania, Australia, Azerbaijan, Bulgaria, Egypt, France, Greece, Hungary, Iran Islamic Rep, Italy, Kazakhstan, Morocco, Portugal, Romania, Russia, Spain, Syrian AR, Türkiye, UK, Ukraine, Uruguay, USA, Uzbekistan. [2009.06.01/XF5176/**F**]

♦ FAO Investment Centre 09264

Centre d'investissement de la FAO – Centro de Inversiones de la FAO

Main Office c/o FAO Investment Centre Div, Viale delle Terme di Caracalla, 00153 Rome RM, Italy. E-mail: investment-centre@fao.org.
URL: https://www.fao.org/support-to-investment/en/

History 1964. Established within the framework of *FAO (#09260)*. **Aims** Lead FAO's efforts to promote increased public and private investment in *agriculture* and development; assist *developing countries* in directing external, domestic and private funding in operations aimed to achieve sustainable food security worldwide and improve rural livelihoods. **Finance** Multilateral development institutions; bilateral development agencies; Arab development funds; private sector development agencies. **Activities** Undertakes over 600 field missions annually in support for some 140 investment projects in around 100 countries. Provides assistance to governments in identifying and formulating investment programme proposals through a process of continuous dialogue with multilateral financing institutions providing loans, grants and credits for agricultural and rural development. Costs of investment-related analyses, and of project planning, preparation and implementation supervision and evaluation, are shared between financing institutions and the Centre, at no expense to the recipient country. Has helped prepare close to a third of all World Bank financed projects in agriculture since 1964.

IGO Relations Cooperation agreements signed by FAO with:
- *African Development Bank (ADB, #00283)*;
- *Arab Authority for Agricultural Investment and Development (AAAID, #00902)*;
- *Arab Bank for Economic Development in Africa (#00904)*;
- *Arab Fund for Economic and Social Development (AFESD, #00965)*;
- *Asian Development Bank (ADB, #01422)*;
- *Banque de développement des Etats de l'Afrique centrale (BDEAC, #03168)*;
- *Banque ouest africaine de développement (BOAD, #03170)*;
- *Caribbean Development Bank (CDB, #03492)*;
- *Central American Bank for Economic Integration (CABEI, #03658)*;
- *Development Bank of Latin America (CAF, #05055)*;
- *East African Development Bank (EADB, #05183)*;
- *Eurasian Development Bank (EDB, #05605)*;
- *European Bank for Reconstruction and Development (EBRD, #06315)*;
- *Global Environment Facility (GEF, #10346)*;
- *Inter-American Development Bank (IDB, #11427)*;
- *International Bank for Reconstruction and Development (IBRD, #12317)*;
- *International Development Association (IDA, #13155)*;
- *International Fund for Agricultural Development (IFAD, #13692)*;
- *Islamic Development Bank (IsDB, #16044)*;
- *UNDP (#20292)*;
- *United Nations Capital Development Fund (UNCDF, #20524)*;
- *World Food Programme (WFP, #21510)*. [2020/XE0361/**E***]

♦ **FAONS** Federation of Asian Oceanian Neuroscience Societies (#09439)
♦ **FAOPMA** Federation of Asian and Oceania Pest Managers Associations (#09441)
♦ **FAOPS** Federation of Asian and Oceanian Physiological Societies (#09440)
♦ **FAOPS** Federation of Asia-Oceania Perinatal Societies (#09452)
♦ **FAO/RAF** FAO Regional Office for Africa (#09265)
♦ FAO/RAP / see FAO Regional Office for Asia and the Pacific (#09266)
♦ FAO Regional Animal Production and Health Commission for Asia and the Pacific / see Animal Production and Health Commission for Asia and the Pacific (#00839)

♦ FAO Regional Office for Africa (FAO/RAF) 09265

NGO Liaison Officer PO Box 1628, FAO Bldg, 2 Gamel Abdul Nasser Road, Accra, Ghana. T. +23321675000 ext 2204 – +233217010930. Fax +23321668427. E-mail: fao-ro-africa@fao.org.
URL: http://www.fao.org/world/regional/raf/index_en.htm

History within the framework of *FAO (#09260)*. **Languages** Arabic, English, French. **Staff** 63.00 FTE, paid. **Finance** Budget (annual): US$ 27,647,000. **Activities** Provides secretariat for the following FAO bodies: *African Commission on Agricultural Statistics (AFCAS, #00254)*; *African Forestry and Wildlife Commission (AFWC, #00319)*; *Committee for Inland Fisheries and Aquaculture of Africa (CIFAA, #04261)*; *Fishery Committee for the Eastern Central Atlantic (CECAF, #09784)*. **Events** *Biennial Regional Conference for Africa* Khartoum (Sudan) 2018, *IPPC Regional Workshop for Africa* Lomé (Togo) 2017, *Biennial Regional Conference for Africa* Abidjan (Côte d'Ivoire) 2016, *IPPC Regional Workshop for Africa* Addis Ababa (Ethiopia) 2016, *Biennial Regional Conference for Africa* Tunis (Tunisia) 2014. **Publications** *Liaison* (4 a year) in English, French – news brief; *Nature and Faune – Wildlife and Nature* (4 a year) in English, French – journal. Monographs; catalogues; directories; guides; sudies; reports.

Members FAO Member Nations in the Africa Region (50):
Algeria, Angola, Benin, Botswana, Burkina Faso, Burundi, Cameroon, Cape Verde, Central African Rep, Chad, Comoros, Congo Brazzaville, Congo DR, Côte d'Ivoire, Equatorial Guinea, Eritrea, Eswatini, Ethiopia, Gabon, Gambia, Ghana, Guinea, Guinea-Bissau, Kenya, Lesotho, Liberia, Libya, Madagascar, Malawi, Mali, Mauritania, Mauritius, Morocco, Mozambique, Namibia, Niger, Nigeria, Rwanda, Sao Tomé-Principe, Senegal, Seychelles, Sierra Leone, South Africa, Sudan, Tanzania UR, Togo, Tunisia, Uganda, Zambia, Zimbabwe.

IGO Relations *United Nations Economic Commission for Africa (ECA, #20554)*. [2021/XE9659/**E***]

♦ FAO Regional Office in Asia and the Far East / see FAO Regional Office for Asia and the Pacific (#09266)

♦ FAO Regional Office for Asia and the Pacific (RAP) 09266

Main Office c/o Food and Agriculture Organizations of the UN, Maliwan Mansion, Phra Athit Road, Bangkok, 10200, Thailand. T. +6626974000. Fax +6626974445. E-mail: fao-rap@fao.org.
URL: http://www.fao.org/asiapacific/en/

History Nov 1948, Bangkok (Thailand), as *FAO Regional Office in Asia and the Far East*. Agreement between *FAO (#09260)* and the Government of Thailand regarding the permanent site approved by 22nd Session of FAO Council, Oct-Nov 1955. Present name adopted 1979. Also referred to by acronyms *FAO/RAP* and *RAPA*. **Aims** Assist Asia-Pacific countries to achieve *food security* for present and future generations by providing policy advice and technical *expertise* in agriculture, economic and social development, fisheries, forestry and sustainable development; work with governments, civil society and the private sector to promote food security and durable improvements in *living standards* of the *poor* without damage to natural resources and to ensure that men and women have equal chances to benefit from agricultural and rural development. **Structure** Office headed by FAO Assistant Director-General/Regional Representative for Asia and the Pacific, assisted by Deputy Regional Representative. Support Groups (5); Regional Initiatives (5); Commissions (5): *Asia and Pacific Commission on Agricultural Statistics (APCAS, #01873)*; *Asia-Pacific Fishery Commission (APFIC, #01907)*; *Asia and Pacific Plant Protection Commission (APPPC, #01997)*; *Asia-Pacific Forestry Commission (APFC, #01909)*; *Animal Production and Health Commission for Asia and the Pacific (APHCA, #00839)*. **Languages** English, Thai. **Staff** 205.00 FTE, paid. **Finance** Regular programme financed by member countries; field programme mainly funded by extra-budgetary donors. **Activities** Focuses on reaching small farmers through: farm-based livelihood programmes, especially for rice; reducing damage to farming due to natural disasters; assisting countries in getting the best deal from world trade rules relating to agriculture, fisheries and forestry; using modern science and indigenous knowledge to increase environmentally-friendly agricultural production. Implements: *'FAO Special Programme for Food Security (SPFS)'* in the 14 low-income, food-deficit countries (LIFDICs) of the region; FAO South-South Cooperation Scheme to promote exchange of agricultural expertise among developing countries; funding raised by *'FAO TeleFood Campaign'* for micro-input schemes in 26 countries of the region. **Events** *Biennial Regional Conference* Thimphu (Bhutan) 2020, *International Workshop on Food Loss and Waste Prevention targeting Southeast and East Asian Region* Tokyo (Japan) 2019, *Emergency Regional Consultation on African Swine Fever Risk Reduction and Preparedness* Bangkok (Thailand) 2018, *Biennial Regional Conference* Nadi (Fiji) 2018, *IPPC Regional Workshop for Asia* Busan (Korea Rep) 2017. **Publications** *Asian Livestock* (12 a year); *Maliwan* (4 a year) – newsletter; *Tiger Paper* (4 a year); *Directory of Livestock and Veterinary Contact in Asia and the Pacific* (2 a year); *Farm Management Notes* (2 a year); *Statistical Rural Energy Bulletin* (2 a year); *Selected Indicators of Food and Agriculture Development in Asia-Pacific Region* (annual); *Statistical Profile on Livestock Population* (annual). *FAO/RAPA Monographs* – series; *FAO/RAPA Technical Publications* – series. *Training Manual for Environment Assessment in Forestry* (1996). Reports of regional meetings, consultations, workshops and symposia.

Members FAO member states in the region (46):
Afghanistan, Australia, Bangladesh, Bhutan, Brunei Darussalam, Cambodia, China, Cook Is, Fiji, France, India, Indonesia, Iran Islamic Rep, Japan, Kazakhstan, Kiribati, Korea DPR, Korea Rep, Laos, Malaysia, Maldives, Marshall Is, Micronesia FS, Mongolia, Myanmar, Nauru, Nepal, New Zealand, Niue, Pakistan, Palau, Papua New Guinea, Philippines, Russia, Samoa, Singapore, Solomon Is, Sri Lanka, Thailand, Timor-Leste, Tonga, Tuvalu, USA, Uzbekistan, Vanuatu, Vietnam.

Observers in 5 countries and territories:
Canada, Holy See, Netherlands, Tokelau, UK.

IGO Relations Collaborates with:
- *Agricultural and Food Marketing Association for Asia and the Pacific (AFMA, #00569)*;
- *ASEAN (#01141)*;
- *Asia-Pacific Association of Agricultural Research Institutions (APAARI, #01830)*;
- *Asian Development Bank (ADB, #01422)*;
- *Asian and Pacific Development Centre (APDC, #01608)*;
- *Association of Natural Rubber Producing Countries (ANRPC, #02822)*;
- *Centre for Alleviation of Poverty through Sustainable Agriculture (CAPSA-ESCAP, inactive)*;
- *Centre on Integrated Rural Development for Asia and the Pacific (CIRDAP, #03750)*;
- *European and Mediterranean Plant Protection Organization (EPPO, #07773)*;
- *Intergovernmental Organization for Marketing Information and Technical Advisory Services for Fishery Products in the Asia and Pacific Region (INFOFISH, #11497)*;
- *International Crops Research Institute for the Semi-Arid Tropics (ICRISAT, #13116)*;
- Regional Office of *International Development Research Centre (IDRC, #13162)*;
- *International Jute Organization (IJO, inactive)*;
- *International Rice Research Institute (IRRI, #14754)*;
- *Pacific Community (SPC, #17942)*;
- *Southeast Asian Regional Center for Graduate Study and Research in Agriculture (SEARCA, #19781)*;
- *Southeast Asian Fisheries Development Center (SEAFDEC, #19767)*;
- *Southeast Asian Regional Centre for Tropical Biology (SEAMEO BIOTROP, #19782)*;
- *Statistical Institute for Asia and the Pacific (SIAP, #19972)*;
- *United Nations Economic and Social Commission for Asia and the Pacific (ESCAP, #20557)*.

NGO Relations Member of: *Asia-Pacific Regional Space Agency Forum (APRSAF, #02010)*; *Regional Energy Resources Information Center (RERIC, #18780)*. Collaborates with: *Asia Bio and Organic Fertilizer Network (no recent information)*; *Asia-Pacific Association of Forestry Research Institutions (APAFRI, #01841)*; *Asian Association of Agricultural Colleges and Universities (AAACU, #01312)*; *Asian Institute of Technology (AIT, #01519)*; *Asian Media Information and Communication Centre (AMIC, #01536)*; *Asian Network on Forestry Education (ANFE, no recent information)*; *Asian Network on Problem Soils (no recent information)*; *Asian NGO Coalition for Agrarian Reform and Rural Development (ANGOC, #01566)*; *Association of Voluntary Agencies for Rural Development (AVARD)*; *International Maize and Wheat Improvement Center (#14077)*; *Network for the Development of Agricultural Cooperatives in Asia and the Pacific (NEDAC, #17004)*. [2019.11.22/XE0151/**E***]

♦ FAO Regional Office for Europe / see FAO Regional Office for Europe and Central Asia (#09267)

♦ FAO Regional Office for Europe and Central Asia (FAO/REU) 09267

FAO Bureau régional pour l'Europe et l'asie centrale – Oficina Regional para Europa y Asia Central

Senior Communications Officer Benczur Utca 34, Budapest 1068, Hungary. T. +3618141266. E-mail: fao-ro-europe@fao.org.
Regional Representative address not obtained.
URL: http://www.fao.org/europe/en/

History 1947, Rome (Italy), as *FAO Regional Office for Europe (FAO/REU) – FAO Bureau régional pour l'Europe – Oficina Regional para Europa*, within the framework of *FAO (#09260)*. Also referred to by acronym *FAO/REUR*. **Staff** 12.00 FTE, paid. **Finance** Annual budget: US$ 7 million. **Events** *Biennial Regional Conference for Europe* Lódz (Poland) 2022, *Regional Symposium on Sustainable Food Systems for Healthy Diets in Europe and Central Asia* Budapest (Hungary) 2017, *Biennial Regional Conference for Europe* Antalya (Turkey) 2016, *IPPC Regional Workshop for Eastern Europe and Central Asia* Minsk (Belarus) 2016, *Biennial Regional Conference for Europe* Bucharest (Romania) 2014.

Members Member Nations (53):
Albania, Andorra, Armenia, Austria, Azerbaijan, Belarus, Belgium, Bosnia-Herzegovina, Bulgaria, Croatia, Cyprus, Czechia, Denmark, Estonia, Finland, France, Georgia, Germany, Greece, Hungary, Iceland, Ireland, Israel, Italy, Kazakhstan, Kyrgyzstan, Latvia, Lithuania, Luxembourg, Malta, Moldova, Monaco, Montenegro, Netherlands, North Macedonia, Norway, Poland, Portugal, Romania, Russia, San Marino, Serbia, Slovakia, Slovenia, Spain, Sweden, Switzerland, Tajikistan, Türkiye, Turkmenistan, UK, Ukraine, Uzbekistan.

Regional entity:
European Union (EU, #08967). [2020/XE9681/y/**E***]

♦ FAO Regional Office for Latin America and the Caribbean (FAO/RLC) 09268

Bureau régional de la FAO pour l'Amérique Latine et les Caraïbes – Oficina Regional de la FAO para América Latina y el Caribe

Regional Representative Avenida Dag Hammarskjöld 3241, Vitacura, PO Box 10095, Santiago, Santiago Metropolitan, Chile. T. +5629232100. Fax +5629232101. E-mail: fao-rlc@fao.org.
URL: http://www.fao.org/americas/en/

History Established 1955, Santiago (Chile), within the framework of *FAO (#09260)*. **Aims** Assist countries in Latin America and the Caribbean to substantially increase *agricultural* and *food production*; make this production more accessible to poorer sectors of the population and able to compete in international markets; promote cooperation among *developing countries*; encourage their *self-reliance* through acknowledgement of their own resources, knowledge and skills; strengthen technical capacity of national institutions; stimulate capabilities and training of *human resources*; accelerate *development* through more efficient utilization of human, physical and financial resources available in the region. **Structure** Regional Technical Cooperation Networks: *Inter-American Citrus Network (IACNET, #11407)*; *Technical Cooperation Network on Food and Nutrition Surveillance System in Latin America and the Caribbean (SISVAN Network, no recent information)*; *Technical Cooperation Network on National Parks, Other Protected Areas and Wildlife in Latin America and the Caribbean (#20117)*, including *Subred de Areas Protegidas del Amazonas (SURAPA, no recent information)* and *Subred de Fauna del Cono Sur (no recent information)*; *Technical Cooperation Network on Agricultural Biotechnology in Latin America and the Caribbean (no recent information)*; *Technical Cooperation Network among Veterinary Research and Diagnostic Laboratories in Latin America and the Caribbean (REDLAB, see: #09268)*; *Technical Cooperation Network on Watershed Management in Latin America and the Caribbean (no recent information)*. **Languages** English, Portuguese, Spanish. **Staff** 37.00 FTE, paid. **Finance** Member countries' contributions through Regular Programme of FAO headquarters. **Activities** Guidance/assistance/consulting; knowledge management/information dissemination. **Events** *Biennial Regional Conference for Latin America and the Caribbean* Managua (Nicaragua) 2020, *IPPC Regional Workshop for Caribbean* Rome

FAO Regional Office
09268
alphabetic sequence excludes
For the complete listing, see Yearbook Online at

(Italy) 2020, *Biennial Regional Conference for Latin America and the Caribbean* Montego Bay (Jamaica) 2018, *IPPC Regional Workshop for Caribbean* Port-of-Spain (Trinidad-Tobago) 2018, *IPPC Regional Workshop for Caribbean* Bridgetown (Barbados) 2017.
Members Governments of 33 countries:
Antigua-Barbuda, Argentina, Bahamas, Barbados, Belize, Bolivia, Brazil, Chile, Colombia, Costa Rica, Cuba, Dominica, Dominican Rep, Ecuador, El Salvador, Grenada, Guatemala, Guyana, Haiti, Honduras, Jamaica, Mexico, Nicaragua, Panama, Paraguay, Peru, St Kitts-Nevis, St Lucia, St Vincent-Grenadines, Suriname, Trinidad-Tobago, Uruguay, Venezuela.
IGO Relations Cooperates with: *Caribbean Action Plan (CAR, #03432)*. Instrumental in setting up: *Caribbean Fisheries Training and Development Institute (CFTDI, #03507)*. [2014.12.02/XE9569/**E***]

♦ FAO Regional Office for the Near East / see FAO Regional Office for the Near East and North Africa (#09269)

♦ FAO Regional Office for the Near East and North Africa 09269

Regional Representative 11 A-Eslah Al-Zerai Street, Dokki, PO Box 2223, Cairo, Egypt. T. +2023316000 – +2023316001 – +2023316007. Fax +20237495981 – +20233373419. E-mail: fao-rne@fao.org.
URL: http://www.fao.org/neareast/en/

History 29 Nov 1947, Cairo (Egypt), as *FAO Regional Office for the Near East (FAO/RNE)*, within the framework of *FAO (#09260)*, at 3rd Session of the FAO Conference. Formal agreement with host government, 17 Aug 1952, approved by FAO in Nov 1952. Transferred temporarily to Rome (Italy) in Jun 1980; returned to original seat in Cairo in 1991. Previously also referred to by acronym as *FAO/RNEA*. **Aims** Assist Member States in raising the levels of nutrition and standards of living of their people, improving the food security, production and distribution of *food* and *agricultural* products, and achieving food self-sufficiency, through the implementation of sound and sustainable agricultural and rural development programmes; play an active role in promoting South-South cooperation between the countries of the region through workshops, seminars and conferences at regional and/or (sub)regional and/or national levels; serve as a secretariat for intergovernmental regional bodies; provide a forum for Member States to agree on, discuss and resolve shared problems. **Structure** Regional Conference (NERC) convenes usually at Ministers of Agriculture level, at least every 2 years, in years when FAO General Conference does not meet in full session. Observers from countries outside region are also invited to Conference. Headed by Assistant Director/Regional Representative. Work carried out through Regional Commissions for which RNE serves as secretariat: *Agricultural and Land and Water Use Commission for the Near East (ALAWUC, #00570)*, including *Commission for Controlling the Desert Locust in the Central Region (CRC, #04208)*; Desert Locust Commission; *Near East Forestry Commission (NEFC, #16965)*; *Regional Commission for Fisheries (RECOFI, #18763)*. **Languages** Arabic, English, French. **Staff** 18.00 FTE, paid. **Finance** Budget (biennium): US$ 11,553,000 million (for regional office). **Activities** Provides technical assistance and policy advice to Member Governments; organizes capacity building activities in all fields related to food security and to rural and of agricultural development, including forestry and fisheries; organizes technical meetings and expert consultations to review agricultural issues of importance to the region; works closely with UN system organizations to promote the attainment of the Millennium Development Goals (MDGs) in Member Countries of the region and to monitor progress achieved at country and regional levels; undertakes in-depth sector and sub-sector assessments to identify the main constraints hampering agricultural development in the Region and to propose alternative solutions to overcome these constraints; acts as executing agency for the implementation of rural and agricultural development projects in the Region funded either by national governments or by bi-lateral and/or multilateral funding agencies; acts as a specialized advisory body to Member Governments to advice on the feasibility of development projects and to assess their potential economic, social and environmental impacts; encourages technical and economic cooperation among countries of the Region and promote the use of regional and national institutions; supports the FAO Country Representatives in the Region by assisting them in policy level negotiations, advising them on regional policies affecting their host country, and by making available, regional technical officers or consultants for country assignments; cooperates with regional organizations and other development partners in supporting rural and agricultural development projects and programmes in the Region; organizes and conducts FAO Regional Conference for the Near East and the sessions of the FAO Regional Commissions for the Near East in close collaboration with the technical divisions in FAO Headquarters; assists Member Governments in establishing regional networks for exchanging information and expertise and for strengthening technical cooperation; produces technical publications providing up-to-date information on technology in agriculture, forestry and fisheries, for use by agricultural practitioners and by government and non-government organizations in the Region. **Events** *Biennial Regional Conference for the Near East (NERC)* Oman 2020, *Biennial Regional Conference for the Near East* Rome (Italy) 2018, *IPPC Regional Workshop for Near East and North Africa* Gammarth (Tunisia) 2017, *IPPC Regional Workshop for Near East and North Africa* Algiers (Algeria) 2016, *Biennial regional conference for the Near East* Rome (Italy) 2016. **Publications** Documents of regional interest in English, French, Arabic.
Members Governments of 20 countries:
Algeria, Bahrain, Egypt, Iran Islamic Rep, Iraq, Jordan, Kuwait, Lebanon, Libya, Mauritania, Morocco, Oman, Palestine, Qatar, Saudi Arabia, Sudan, Syrian AR, Tunisia, United Arab Emirates, Yemen.
IGO Relations Invites a large number of organizations as observers (not specified). Member of: *Association of Agricultural Research Institutions in the Near East and North Africa (AARINENA, #02364)*. **NGO Relations** Invites a large number of organizations as observers (not specified). [2018/XE0365/**E***]

♦ FAO/REU / see FAO Regional Office for Europe and Central Asia (#09267)
♦ **FAO/REU** FAO Regional Office for Europe and Central Asia (#09267)
♦ FAO/REUR / see FAO Regional Office for Europe and Central Asia (#09267)
♦ **FAO/RLC** FAO Regional Office for Latin America and the Caribbean (#09268)
♦ FAO/RNEA / see FAO Regional Office for the Near East and North Africa (#09269)
♦ FAO/RNE / see FAO Regional Office for the Near East and North Africa (#09269)
♦ FAO/UNDP Network of Aquaculture Centres in Asia / see Network of Aquaculture Centres in Asia-Pacific (#16991)
♦ FAO/WHO Codex Alimentarius Commission / see Codex Alimentarius Commission (#04081)
♦ FAO/WHO/FNAf – Joint FAO/WHO/OAU Regional Food and Nutrition Commission for Africa (inactive)

♦ FAO/WHO International Food Safety Authorities Network (INFOSAN) 09270

Secretariat Dept of Food Safety and Zoonoses – WHO, Avenue Appia 20, 1211 Geneva 27, Switzerland. E-mail: infosan@who.int.
Contact Food Safety and Quality Unit – FAO, Viale delle Terme di Caracalla, 00153 Rome RM, Italy. E-mail: infosan@fao.org.
URL: https://www.who.int/groups/international-food-safety-authorities-network-infosan

History 2004. Founded by *WHO (#20950)* and *FAO (#09260)*. **Aims** Facilitate the rapid exchange of information across borders and between members, during food safety events. **Structure** Managed by *WHO (#20950)* and *FAO (#09260)*. **Activities** Events/meetings; guidance/assistance/consulting; knowledge management/information dissemination. **Events** *Global Meeting* Abu Dhabi (United Arab Emirates) 2019. **Publications** *INFOSAN Quarterly Summary* (4 a year). **Members** National food safety authorities (186). [2020/AA0461/**F***]

♦ **FAPAA** Federation of Asia Pacific Aircargo Associations (#09453)
♦ **FAPA** Federation of Asian Pharmaceutical Associations (#09445)
♦ **FAPA** Federation of Asian Photographic Art (#09446)
♦ **FAP ALC-UE** Foro Académico Permanente ALC-UE (#09874)
♦ **FAPECA** Federation of Asian and Pacific Electrical Contractors Associations (#09443)
♦ **FAPED** Forum of African Parliamentarians for Education (#09895)
♦ **FAPE** Fédération africaine des associations nationales de parents d'élèves et étudiants (#09398)
♦ FAPIA / see International Classified Marketplace Association (#12592)
♦ FAPMS – Federation of Asia-Pacific Microbiology Societies (inactive)
♦ FAPOL – Federación Americana de Psicoanalisis de la Orientación Lacaniana (unconfirmed)
♦ **FAPP** Federación Arabe de Productores Pesqueros (#00945)
♦ **FAPP** Federation of ASEAN Poultry Producers (#09426)
♦ FAPPI – Federation of ASEAN Pulp and Paper Industries (unconfirmed)
♦ FAPRA – Federation of African Public Relations Associations (inactive)
♦ FAPRA / see Federation of Asia-Pacific Retailers Association (#09454)
♦ **FAPRA** Federation of Asia-Pacific Retailers Association (#09454)
♦ **FAPS** Federation of Asian Perfusion Societies (#09444)
♦ **FAPS** Federation of Asian Polymer Societies (#09447)
♦ **FAPTA** Federation of Asian Professional Textile Associations (#09448)
♦ FARA / see Federation of Asia-Pacific Retailers Association (#09454)
♦ **FARA** Forum for Agricultural Research in Africa (#09897)
♦ Far East Advanced School of Theology / see Asian Pacific Theological Seminary
♦ Far East Bridge Federation / see Asia Pacific Bridge Federation (#01862)
♦ Far East Broadcasting Associates / see Feba Radio (#09283)
♦ Far East Broadcasting Association / see Feba Radio (#09283)
♦ Far East Broadcasting Company (internationally oriented national body)
♦ Far Eastern Association / see Association for Asian Studies, Ann Arbor
♦ Far Eastern Commission (inactive)
♦ Far Eastern Gospel Crusade / see SEND International
♦ Far Eastern Institute / see Henry M Jackson School of International Studies
♦ Far-Eastern Prehistory Association / see Indo-Pacific Prehistory Association (#11171)
♦ Far East Fracture Group / see Far East Oceanic Fracture Society (#09271)
♦ Far East Model Car Association (unconfirmed)

♦ Far East Oceanic Fracture Society (FEOFS) 09271

Contact Mechanical Eng, Pohang Univ of Science, Pohang NORTH GYEONGSANG 790-784, Korea Rep.

History 23 Apr 1987, Shanghai (China), as *Far East Fracture Group (FEFG)*, as a regional organization of *International Congress on Fracture (ICF, #12894)*. Current name adopted 5 Jul 1994, Xi'an (China). **Aims** Foster research in the Far East and Oceanic nations/regions in the mechanics and phenomena of fracture, *fatigue*, and *strength* of *materials*; promote cooperation among scientists and engineers in these fields. **Structure** Council, consisting of national/regional delegations, each of which is appointed by each nation/region (a delegation consists of no more than 5 members); Founder-President, former Presidents and former Secretary-Generals are ex officio members of the Council. Executive Committee, comprising President, Vice-Presidents, Directors, Treasurer and Secretary-General; Founder-President, former Presidents and former Secretary-Generals are ex-officio members of the Executive Committee. **Languages** English. **Finance** Voluntary. **Activities** Holds conferences, symposia, seminars and workshops. *International Conference on Fracture and Strength of Solids*. **Events** *International Conference on Fracture and Strength of Solids* Yogyakarta (Indonesia) 2018, *International Conference on Fracture and Strength of Solids* Tokyo (Japan) 2016, *International Conference on Fracture and Strength of Solids* Jeju (Korea Rep) 2013, *Conference* Kuala Lumpur (Malaysia) 2010, *Conference* Urumqi (China) 2007. **Publications** Proceedings of conferences, symposia, seminars and workshops.
Members Organizations; Individuals. Members in 9 nations/regions:
Australia, China, Hong Kong, Indonesia, Japan, Korea Rep, Singapore, Taiwan, Thailand.
NGO Relations Cooperates with: *European Structural Integrity Society (ESIS, #08844)*. [2018/XE0820/**E**]

♦ Far East and South Pacific Federation of Branches of the World's Poultry Science Association / see Asian Pacific Federation of the World's Poultry Science Association Branches (#01615)
♦ Far East and South Pacific Games Federation for the Disabled (inactive)
♦ **FARECOGAZ** Association of European Manufacturers of Gas Meters, Gas Pressure Regulators, Safety Devices and Stations (#02521)
♦ **FARE** Forum des aéroports régionaux européens (#09912)
♦ **FARE Network** Football Against Racism in Europe (#09853)
♦ FAR – Fellowship for African Relief (internationally oriented national body)
♦ FAR – Fondation André Ryckmans (internationally oriented national body)
♦ FAR – Foundation for Agronomic Research (internationally oriented national body)
♦ FARIAD – Fair River International Association for Development (internationally oriented national body)
♦ FAR / see Latin American Reserve Fund (#16367)
♦ Farmacéuticos Mundi (internationally oriented national body)
♦ Farmaceutiske Industrie Internationale Sammenslutning i Landene inden for de Europaeiske Faellesskaber (inactive)
♦ FARM-Africa – Food and Agricultural Research Management (internationally oriented national body)
♦ FARMAMUNDI – Farmacéuticos Mundi (internationally oriented national body)
♦ Farm Animal Industrial Platform / see European Forum of Farm Animal Breeders (#07310)
♦ FARMAPU-INTER and CECOTRAP-RCOGL (internationally oriented national body)

♦ Farm Concern International (FCI) 09272

Contact KALRO Campus, Waiyaki Way, PO Box 15185-00100, Nairobi, 15185, Kenya. T. +2542626017. E-mail: info@farmconcern.org.
URL: https://www.farmconcern.org/

Aims Build and implement innovative market-led business models that catalyze smallholder commercialization and entrepreneurship for economic growth of households and enterprises for systematic graduation into investment platforms for sustainable communities in Africa and beyond. **Structure** Board. **IGO Relations** Partner of (12): *AVRDC – The World Vegetable Center (#03051)*; *Common Market for Eastern and Southern Africa (COMESA, #04296)*; *DANIDA*; *Deutsche Gesellschaft für Internationale Zusammenarbeit (GIZ)*; *European Commission (EC, #06633)*; *FAO (#09260)*; *ILO (#11123)*; *International Bank for Reconstruction and Development (IBRD, #12317)*; *International Development Research Centre (IDRC, #13162)*; *International Fund for Agricultural Development (IFAD, #13692)*; *UNDP (#20292)*; *United States Agency for International Development (USAID)*.
NGO Relations Partner of (21):
- *Access Agriculture (#00047)*;
- *Adventist Development and Relief Agency International (ADRA, #00131)*;
- *African Rural and Agricultural Credit Association (AFRACA, #00446)*;
- *African Wildlife Foundation (AWF, #00498)*;
- *Agricultural Market Development Trust (AGMARK, #00572)*;
- *Alliance for a Green Revolution in Africa (AGRA, #00685)*;
- *Association for Strengthening Agricultural Research in Eastern and Central Africa (ASARECA, #02933)*;
- *Bill and Melinda Gates Foundation (BMGF)*;
- *Consultative Group to Assist the Poor (CGAP, #04768)*;
- *Cultivating New Frontiers in Agriculture (CNFA)*;
- *Food and Agricultural Research Management (FARM-Africa)*;
- *Ford Foundation (#09858)*;
- *Gatsby Charitable Foundation*;
- *Grameen Foundation (GF, #10694)*;
- *Humanistisch Instituut voor Ontwikkelingssamenwerking (Hivos)*;
- *International Centre for Tropical Agriculture (#12527)*;
- *International Institute of Tropical Agriculture (IITA, #13933)*;
- *International Potato Center (#14627)*;
- *Strømme Foundation (SF)*;
- *The Rockefeller Foundation (#18966)*;
- *World Vision International (WVI, #21904)*.

[2018/AA1256/**F**]

♦ Farm Europe 09273

Head Office Rond-Point Schuman 9, Postbus 6, 1040 Brussels, Belgium. T. +3222345620.
URL: https://www.farm-europe.eu/

History Registration: EU Transparency Register, No/ID: 961826727268-04, Start date: 24 May 2017. **Aims** Stimulate thinking on rural economies. **Structure** Scientific Committee; Team; Working Groups; Advisory Committee. **Activities** Events/meetings; politics/policy/regulatory. **Events** *Global Food Forum* Brussels (Belgium) 2019. [2020/AA0074/**F**]

♦ FARM – Fondation pour l'agriculture et la ruralité dans le monde (internationally oriented national body)
♦ Farming First (unconfirmed)

articles and prepositions
http://www.brill.com/yioo

FCI
09277

♦ **Farm Radio International** **09274**
Radios Rurales Internationales
Exec Dir 1404 Scott St, Ottawa ON K1Y 2N2, Canada. T. +16137613650. Fax +16137980990. E-mail: info@farmradio.org.
URL: http://www.farmradio.org/
History 1 May 1979, Toronto, ON (Canada). Founded by George Atkins, a Canadian farm radio broadcaster, after a travel in Zambian countryside in 1975. Created to align better with the needs of small-scale farmers and share low-cost and no-cost ideas by radio. The first package of scripts and tapes was mailed to 34 broadcasters in 26 countries. Former names and other names: *Developing Countries Farm Radio Network (DCFRN)* – former; *Réseau de radio rurale des pays en développement (RRRPD)* – former; *Red de Radio Rural de los Paises en Desarrollo (RRRPD)* – former. Registration: No/ID: 11888 4808 RR0001, Start date: 1986, Canada. **Aims** Improve access of information for development in rural areas; enhance capacity of radio broadcasters. **Structure** Board of Directors (Canada); Advisory boards in several country offices. **Languages** English, French. **Staff** 20.00 FTE, paid. **Finance** Sources: contributions; contributions of member/participating states; donations; fundraising; government support; grants; international organizations. Supported by: *Alliance for a Green Revolution in Africa (AGRA, #00685)*; *Bill and Melinda Gates Foundation (BMGF)*; *Deutsche Gesellschaft für Internationale Zusammenarbeit (GIZ)*; *Enabel*; *FAO (#09260)*; Global Affairs Canada; *Helen Keller International (HKI, #10902)*; *International Development Research Centre (IDRC, #13162)*; *International Fund for Agricultural Development (IFAD, #13692)*; *Irish Aid*; *Luxembourg Agency for Development Cooperation (LUXDEV)*; *The Rockefeller Foundation (#18966)*; *United States Agency for International Development (USAID)*; *World Food Programme (WFP, #21510)*. Annual budget: 7,370,000 CAD (2021). **Activities** Capacity building; knowledge management/information dissemination; networking/liaising; projects/programmes; training/education. Farm Radio International runs radio projects that support a network of thousands of sub-Saharan broadcasters improve their interactive radio programs for rural listeners. Active in: Burkina Faso, Côte d'Ivoire, Ethiopia, Ghana, Kenya, Liberia, Malawi, Mali, Mozambique, Nigeria, Senegal, Sierra Leone, Tanzania UR, Togo, Uganda, Zambia. **Publications** *Barza Wire (Farm Radio Weekly)* (bi-weekly) in Amharic, English, French, Hausa, Swahili; *Tuning In* (3 a year). Annual Report; brochure; scripts; training resources. **Information Services** *Farm Radio FM*; *Farm Radio Resource Packs* in English, French.
Members Network partners (over 1000) in 41 countries:
Angola, Benin, Botswana, Burkina Faso, Burundi, Cameroon, Central African Rep, Chad, Comoros, Congo Brazzaville, Congo DR, Côte d'Ivoire, Eswatini, Ethiopia, Gambia, Ghana, Guinea, Guinea-Bissau, Kenya, Lesotho, Liberia, Madagascar, Malawi, Mali, Mauritania, Mauritius, Mozambique, Namibia, Niger, Nigeria, Rwanda, Senegal, Sierra Leone, South Africa, South Sudan, Sudan, Tanzania UR, Togo, Uganda, Zambia, Zimbabwe.
IGO Relations Accredited to the Conference of the Parties of: *Secretariat of the United Nations Convention to Combat Desertification (Secretariat of the UNCCD, #19208)*. Associated with Department of Global Communications of the United Nations. **NGO Relations** Member of (1): *Cooperation Canada*.
[2022.02.09/XF8607/**F**]

- ♦ Farms International (internationally oriented national body)
- ♦ Farnham Castle International Briefing and Conference Centre (internationally oriented national body)
- ♦ **FARO** Federation of Asian Organizations for Radiation Oncology (#09442)
- ♦ FAROF – Freehearts Africa Reach out Foundation (internationally oriented national body)
- ♦ **FARO** Forum of Arctic Research Operators (#09898)
- ♦ Fårsaarten Faeroese talo (internationally oriented national body)
- ♦ FARS / see World Skate Africa (#21787)
- ♦ FASAAD – Fédération africaine des secrétaires et assistants et attachés de direction (inactive)
- ♦ FASAA – Fonds spécial d'aide arabe à l'Afrique (inactive)
- ♦ **FASA** African Rowing Federation (#00445)
- ♦ **FASA** Federación de Asociaciones Sudamericanas de Anestesiologia (#09291)
- ♦ **FASA** Federation of ASEAN Shipowners Associations (#09427)
- ♦ FASAS – Federation of Asian Scientific Academies and Societies (inactive)
- ♦ **FASAVA** Federation of Asian Small Animal Veterinary Associations (#09449)
- ♦ **FASBMB** Federation of African Societies of Biochemistry and Molecular Biology (#09410)
- ♦ **FASC** Federation of African Societies of Chemistry (#09411)

♦ **Fascia Research Society (FRS)** **09275**
Exec Dir 16192 Coastal Hwy, Lewes DE 19958, USA. E-mail: info@fasciaresearchsociety.org.
URL: https://fasciaresearchsociety.org/
History Developed out of the International Fascia Research Congresses. **Aims** Facilitate, encourage and support dialogue and collaboration between clinicians, researchers and academicians so as to further understanding of the properties and functions of fascia. **Structure** Board. **Activities** Events/meetings; training/education. **Events** *International Fascia Research Congress* Montréal, QC (Canada) 2022, *International Fascia Research Congress* Montréal, QC (Canada) 2021, *Congress* Berlin (Germany) 2018, *Congress* Reston, VA (USA) 2015, *Basic science and implications for conventional and complementary health care* Vancouver, BC (Canada) 2012. **Publications** *Journal of Bodywork and Movement Therapies*. [2022.10.11/XM8377/j/**C**]

- ♦ FASE – Federation of Acoustical Societies of Europe (inactive)
- ♦ **FASE** Forensic Anthropology Society of Europe (#09860)
- ♦ **FAS** Femmes Africa solidarité (#09732)
- ♦ **FASGO** Fédération arabe des sociétés de gynécologie – obstétrique (#09421)
- ♦ FASID – Foundation for Advanced Studies on International Development (internationally oriented national body)
- ♦ FASI – Fédération des Associations de Solidarité Internationale (internationally oriented national body)
- ♦ **FASMI** Federation of Asian Societies for Molecular Imaging (#09450)
- ♦ **FASNUDA** Fonds d'affectation spéciale des Nations Unies pour le développement de l'Afrique (#20640)
- ♦ FASPA – Fédération africaine des syndicats du pétrole et affinage (no recent information)
- ♦ FASRC – Federation of Arab Scientific Research Councils (no recent information)
- ♦ Fastenopfer (internationally oriented national body)
- ♦ **FAST** Finance Alliance for Sustainable Trade (#09763)
- ♦ **FAST** Foundation for Aviation and Sustainable Tourism (#09942)

♦ **Fast-Track Cities** **09276**
Address not obtained.
URL: https://www.fast-trackcities.org/
History 1 Dec 2014. Founded by 4 core partners: *International Association of Providers of AIDS Care (IAPAC)*; *Joint United Nations Programme on HIV/AIDS (UNAIDS, #16149)*; *United Nations Human Settlements Programme (UN-Habitat, #20572)*; City of Paris (France).
Members Cities and municipalities (over 350) in 78 countries and territories:
Algeria, Argentina, Australia, Austria, Belarus, Belgium, Benin, Bosnia-Herzegovina, Brazil, Burkina Faso, Cameroon, Canada, Central African Rep, Chile, Congo Brazzaville, Congo DR, Côte d'Ivoire, Cuba, Czechia, Djibouti, Ecuador, France, Gabon, Georgia, Germany, Ghana, Greece, Haiti, Honduras, India, Indonesia, Ireland, Israel, Italy, Jamaica, Kazakhstan, Kenya, Kyrgyzstan, Lebanon, Lesotho, Malawi, Mali, Mexico, Monaco, Montenegro, Morocco, Mozambique, Namibia, Netherlands, Nigeria, North Macedonia, Panama, Paraguay, Peru, Philippines, Portugal, Réunion, Romania, Russia, Rwanda, Senegal, Serbia, Seychelles, Sierra Leone, South Africa, Spain, Switzerland, Taiwan, Tanzania UR, Thailand, Uganda, UK, Ukraine, Uruguay, USA, Uzbekistan, Vietnam, Zambia.
NGO Relations Member of (1): *Pandemic Action Network (PAN, #18173)*. [2021/AA2287/**F**]

- ♦ FAST-zero – International Symposium on Future Active Safety Technology toward zero-traffic-accident (meeting series)
- ♦ **FASU** Fédération africaine du sport universitaire (#09412)
- ♦ **FASU** Federation of African University Sports (#09412)
- ♦ **FASU** Forum africain pour la sécurité urbaine (#00323)
- ♦ FATAA – Federation of Arab Travel Agents' Associations (inactive)
- ♦ FATA – Fédération arabe de tir à l'arc (no recent information)
- ♦ FATA / see Federation of ASEAN Travel Associations (#09428)
- ♦ **FATA** Federation of ASEAN Travel Associations (#09428)
- ♦ Fatebenefratelli – Ordine Ospedaliero di San Giovanni di Dio (religious order)
- ♦ FAT – Federation of Arab Teachers (no recent information)
- ♦ **FATF** Financial Action Task Force (#09765)
- ♦ Fathers of Picpus – Society of the Sacred Hearts of Jesus and Mary (religious order)
- ♦ FATIGUE – International Fatigue Congress (meeting series)
- ♦ Fatima Weltapostolat (religious order)
- ♦ **FATIPEC** Federation of Associations of Technicians for Industry of Paints in European Countries (#09461)
- ♦ FATO / see Fédération Africaine des Professionnels de la Réadaptation (#09399)
- ♦ **FATO** Fédération Africaine des Professionnels de la Réadaptation (#09399)
- ♦ Fatty Pig Interational Conference – Fatty Pig Science and Utilization International Conference (meeting series)
- ♦ Fatty Pig Science and Utilization International Conference (meeting series)
- ♦ FAUA – Federation of ASEAN Urological Associations (inactive)

♦ **Fauna & Flora International (FFI)** **09277**
Governance & Risk Manager David Attenborough Bldg, Pembroke Street, Cambridge, CB2 3QZ, UK. T. +441223571000. Fax +441223461481. E-mail: info@fauna-flora.org – joanna.colley@fauna-flora.org.
URL: http://www.fauna-flora.org/
History 1903, London (UK). Former names and other names: *Society for the Preservation of the Wild Fauna of the Empire* – former (1903 to 1921); *Society for the Preservation of the Fauna of the Empire* – former (1921 to 1952); *Fauna Preservation Society* – former (1952 to 1980); *Fauna and Flora Preservation Society (FFPS)* – former (1980 to 2001). Registration: Companies House, No/ID: 2677068, Start date: Jan 1992, UK; The Charity Commission, No/ID: 1011102, Start date: May 1992, UK. **Aims** Conserve threatened species and ecosystems worldwide. **Structure** Board of Trustees/Directors. **Languages** English. **Staff** 479.00 FTE, paid. **Finance** Sources: donations; grants; members' dues. Other sources: statutory funding; grants from charitable trusts and foundations; corporate partnerships. **Activities** Capacity building; networking/liaising; projects/programmes. **Events** *Workshop on business opportunities and constraints for sustainable use of wetlands* Illmitz (Austria) 2006, *International mammalian conservation symposium* London (UK) 1997. **Publications** *Oryx – International Journal of Conservation* (4 a year); *Update* (3 a year) – newsletter; *Fauna and Flora Magazine* (annual). **Members** Standard; Sponsor; Supporter; Concessionary; Life. Members in about 125 countries and territories. Membership countries not specified. **Consultative Status** Consultative status granted from: *ECOSOC (#05331)* (Ros B); *UNEP (#20299)*. **IGO Relations** Accredited observer to: *UNEP (#20299)*. **NGO Relations** Member of (2): *Global Interagency Security Forum (GISF, #10430)*; *ResponsibleSteel (#18921)*. [2022.10.11/XB4322/v/**B**]

- ♦ Fauna and Flora Preservation Society / see Fauna & Flora International (#09277)
- ♦ Fauna Preservation Society / see Fauna & Flora International (#09277)
- ♦ FAVA/CA / see Florida Association for Volunteer Action in the Caribbean and the Americas
- ♦ FAVACA – Florida Association for Volunteer Action in the Caribbean and the Americas (internationally oriented national body)
- ♦ **FAVA** Federation of Asian Veterinary Associations (#09451)
- ♦ FAVE – Forum der Agraringenieur-Verbände Europas (inactive)
- ♦ **FAWA** Federation of Asia-Pacific Women's Associations (#09455)
- ♦ **FAWCO** Federation of American Women's Clubs Overseas (#09416)
- ♦ FAWE / see African Federation of Women Entrepreneurs (#00313)
- ♦ **FAWE** Forum for African Women Educationalists (#09896)
- ♦ FAWEU / see EUROMARFOR (#05711)
- ♦ FBA – Folke Bernadotte Academy (internationally oriented national body)
- ♦ FBA / see Forum of Bible Agencies International (#09903)
- ♦ FBC / see Catholic Biblical Federation (#03600)
- ♦ **FBC** Federação Biblica Católica (#03600)
- ♦ **FBC** Fédération biblique catholique (#03600)
- ♦ **FBC** Federazione Biblica Cattolica (#03600)
- ♦ **FBC** Free Burma Coalition (#09984)
- ♦ **FBE** Fédération bancaire de l'Union européenne (#06312)
- ♦ **FBE** Fédération des Barreaux d'Europe (#06320)
- ♦ **FBE** Flow Batteries Europe (#09800)
- ♦ FBFI – Food Basket Foundation International (internationally oriented national body)
- ♦ FB – Fribaptistsamfundet (inactive)
- ♦ FB – Fundación Bariloche (internationally oriented national body)
- ♦ FBHC – International Conference on Food Bioactives and Health (meeting series)
- ♦ FBN Asia – The Family Business Network Asia (see: #09251)
- ♦ FBN / see The Family Business Network International (#09251)
- ♦ **FBN-I** The Family Business Network International (#09251)
- ♦ FBT – Fundación del Bosque Tropical (internationally oriented national body)
- ♦ **FBU** Fraternité blanche universelle (#20684)
- ♦ **FCAA** Federación Caribeña de Asociaciones de Arquitectos (#09465)
- ♦ **FCAA** Fédération Caraïbéenne des Associations d'Architectes (#09465)
- ♦ **FCAA** Federation of Caribbean Associations of Architects (#09465)
- ♦ **FCAA** Fédération des consultants africains et arabes (#09475)
- ♦ FCA – Federation of Commodity Associations (no recent information)
- ♦ **FCA** Fellowship of Confessing Anglicans (#09725)
- ♦ **FCA** Fencing Confederation of Asia (#09735)
- ♦ FCA – Finn Church Aid (internationally oriented national body)
- ♦ **FCA** Framework Convention Alliance (#09981)
- ♦ **FCAM** Fondo Centroamericano de Mujeres (#03677)
- ♦ FCAT / see Federative International Programme for Anatomical Terminology (#09716)
- ♦ **FCBCO** Federation of Catholic Bishops' Conferences of Oceania (#09467)
- ♦ FCCAC – Fédération des chambres de commerce de l'Afrique centrale (inactive)
- ♦ FCCAO – Fédération des chambres de commerce de l'Afrique de l'Ouest (no recent information)
- ♦ FCCC – Federation of Commonwealth Chambers of Commerce (inactive)
- ♦ **FCC** Federation of Cocoa Commerce (#09473)
- ♦ **FCC** Fédération du Commerce des Cacaos (#09473)
- ♦ FCC – Foreign Correspondents' Club of South Asia (internationally oriented national body)
- ♦ **FCCI** Future Convention Cities Initiative (#10047)
- ♦ FCCI-OI / see Cap Business Océan Indien (#03419)
- ♦ FCDP / see Equitas – International Centre for Human Rights Education
- ♦ FCD – Solidarité socialiste – Fonds de coopération au développement (internationally oriented national body)
- ♦ **FCE** Foro Cívico Europeo (#06562)
- ♦ **FCE** Forum civique européen (#06562)
- ♦ **FCE** Forum civique européen (#06563)
- ♦ **FCEM** Femmes chefs d'entreprises mondiales (#09733)
- ♦ **FCES** French-Speaking Comparative Education Association (#02610)
- ♦ FCF – Family Care Foundation (internationally oriented national body)
- ♦ FC – Filiae Crucis Leodiensis (religious order)
- ♦ FC – Filii Caritatis (religious order)
- ♦ FC – Fratres a Caritate (religious order)
- ♦ FC – Fundación Carolina (internationally oriented national body)
- ♦ **FCH JU** Fuel Cells and Hydrogen Joint Undertaking (#10013)
- ♦ FCI / see France Expertise Internationale

♦ FCI **09278**

SG Keizersgracht 559, 1017 DR Amsterdam, Netherlands. T. +31206270306. Fax +31206257628. E-mail: fci@fci.nl.
URL: https://fci.nl/

History 22 Nov 1968, Stockholm (Sweden). Statutes adopted 28 Jun 1969, Scheveningen (Netherlands). Former names and other names: *Factors Chain International (FCI)* – former; *FCI – the Global Association for Open Account Trade Finance* – full title. **Aims** Facilitate and promote international factoring through a correspondent factoring platform. **Structure** Council (meets at least once a year); Executive Committee. Committees (7); Chapters (6); Subdivision: *EU Federation for the Factoring and Commercial Finance Industry (EUF, #05583).* **Languages** English. **Staff** 6.00 FTE, paid. **Finance** Sources: members' dues. Applicants' equity (normally US$ 2,000,000). **Activities** Networking/liaising; training/education. **Events** *Annual Meeting* Washington, DC (USA) 2022, *Annual Meeting* Amsterdam (Netherlands) 2021, *Annual Meeting* Washington, DC (USA) 2021, *Annual Meeting* 2020, *FCIreverse Forum* Madrid (Spain) 2019. **Publications** *FCI IN-SIGHT* (4 a year).

Members Companies and departments of banks or finance companies providing a factoring service and not members of or associated with an organization dealing with factoring within restricted groups. Members in 91 countries and territories:
Argentina, Armenia, Australia, Austria, Azerbaijan, Bahrain, Bangladesh, Belarus, Belgium, Bosnia-Herzegovina, Botswana, Brazil, Bulgaria, Cambodia, Cameroon, Canada, Chile, China, Colombia, Congo Brazzaville, Costa Rica, Côte d'Ivoire, Croatia, Curaçao, Cyprus, Czechia, Denmark, Dominican Rep, Ecuador, Egypt, Estonia, Finland, France, Georgia, Germany, Greece, Guatemala, Honduras, Hong Kong, Hungary, India, Indonesia, Israel, Italy, Japan, Kenya, Korea Rep, Lebanon, Lithuania, Malaysia, Malta, Mauritius, Mexico, Moldova, Mongolia, Morocco, Netherlands, New Zealand, Nicaragua, Nigeria, Norway, Oman, Panama, Peru, Poland, Portugal, Qatar, Romania, Russia, Senegal, Serbia, Singapore, Slovakia, Slovenia, South Africa, Spain, Sri Lanka, Sweden, Switzerland, Taiwan, Thailand, Tunisia, Türkiye, UK, Ukraine, United Arab Emirates, Uruguay, USA, Vietnam, Zambia, Zimbabwe.

NGO Relations Member of (1): *SME Finance Forum (#19323).* [2022.10.11/XC0922/**B**]

♦ FCIA Europe – Fibre Channel Industry Association Europe (inactive)
♦ FCIA – Fibre Channel Industry Association (internationally oriented national body)
♦ FCIA – Fine Chocolate Industry Association (unconfirmed)

♦ FCIB **09279**

Headquarters 8840 Columbia 100 Pkwy, Columbia MD 21045-2158, USA. T. +14104231840. Fax +14104231845. E-mail: fcib_info@fcibglobal.com – fcib_global@fcibglobal.com.
URL: http://www.fcibglobal.com/

History 1919, USA, as an association of business executives. Acronym derives from *Finance, Credit and International Business.* **Aims** Promote the sharing of international trade credit and finance knowledge. **Languages** English. **Activities** Events/meetings; training/education; research/documentation. **Events** *Annual International Credit and Risk Management Summit* Madrid (Spain) 2015, *Global Conference* Miami, FL (USA) 2015, *Global Conference* Baltimore, MD (USA) 2014, *Global Conference* Philadelphia, PA (USA) 2012, *Annual global conference* Miami, FL (USA) 2010. **Publications** *Business Credit* (10 a year). Electronic newsletters; European and globals strategic briefs; credit and collections surveys; reports. Information Services: Online Knowledge database. **Members** Individuals (1,090) in 55 countries. Membership countries not specified. **NGO Relations** *EuroCollectNet (ECN, #05664).* [2023/XM4545/**F**]

♦ **FCIC** Federation of Consultants from Islamic Countries (#09476)
♦ **FCI** Farm Concern International (#09272)
♦ **FCI** Fédération colombophile internationale (#09474)
♦ **FCI** Fédération cynologique internationale (#09477)
♦ FCI – Folklore Canada International (internationally oriented national body)
♦ FCI – Frigoclub International (see: #20213)
♦ FCI – the Global Association for Open Account Trade Finance / see FCI (#09278)
♦ FCIM / see World Federation of International Music Competitions (#21445)
♦ FC – International Conference on Frontier Computing (meeting series)
♦ **FCIV** Fondation Caritas in Veritate (#03582)
♦ FCJ – Faithful Companions of Jesus (religious order)
♦ FCL – Federación Campesina Latinoamericana (inactive)
♦ FCMC – Fondo Centroamericano del Mercado Común (inactive)
♦ **FCM** Fédération des experts comptables méditerranéens (#09584)
♦ **FCMM** Fundación Cumbre Mundial de la Mujer (#21038)
♦ **FCMS** Federation of Centers for Migration Studies G B Scalabrini (#09469)
♦ FCM – Société des Filles du Coeur de Marie (religious order)
♦ FCOC – Frente Continental de Organizaciones Comunales (no recent information)
♦ FCPAE – Federation of Chinese Professional Associations in Europe (internationally oriented national body)
♦ **FCPF** Forest Carbon Partnership Facility (#09862)
♦ FCSCJ – Filles de la Charité du Sacré-Coeur de Jésus (religious order)
♦ **FCS** Flow Chemistry Society (#09801)
♦ FCS – Foundation for a Civil Society (internationally oriented national body)
♦ **FCS** Friends of the Countryside (#10000)
♦ **FCSI** Foodservice Consultants Society International (#09850)
♦ FCSSC – Finance Center for South-South Cooperation (internationally oriented national body)
♦ FCTC – Framework Convention on Tobacco Control (2003 treaty)
♦ FCT – International Symposium on Fundamentals of Computation Theory (meeting series)
♦ **FDA** Fédération dentaire africaine (#09280)
♦ FDA – Foundation for the Development of Africa (internationally oriented national body)
♦ FDAP / see Asia Pacific Dental Federation/Asian Pacific Regional Organization of the Fédération Dentaire Internationale (#01882)
♦ **FDAP-ORAP** Fédération dentaire Asie-Pacifique/Organisation régionale Asie Pacifique de la Fédération dentaire internationale (#01882)
♦ FdCC – Congregatio Filiorum a Caritate (religious order)
♦ FdCC – Filles de la Charité Canossiennes (religious order)
♦ FDC – Figlie della Divina Carità (religious order)
♦ FDC – Freedom from Debt Coalition (internationally oriented national body)
♦ **FDFE** Foundation for a Drug-Free Europe (#09946)
♦ fD – freeDimensional (internationally oriented national body)
♦ **FDH** Frères des hommes (#03339)
♦ FDHM – Fonds pour les droits humains mondiaux (internationally oriented national body)

♦ FDI African Regional Organization (ARO) **09280**

Fédération dentaire africaine (FDA)

SG Dépt d'Odonto-stomatologie, Université de Dakar, BP 5005, Dakar, Senegal. T. +2218254753. E-mail: soukeye@gmail.com.

History 21 Nov 1991, Dakar (Senegal). Regional organization of *FDI – World Dental Federation (#09281).* **Events** *African odontological days* Tunis (Tunisia) 1994.

Members Full in 18 countries:
Benin, Burkina Faso, Cameroon, Chad, Congo Brazzaville, Congo DR, Côte d'Ivoire, Guinea, Libya, Madagascar, Mali, Mauritius, Namibia, Niger, Nigeria, Rwanda, Tunisia, Zambia.

NGO Relations *Groupement des associations dentaires francophones (GADEF, #10757).* [2010/XD3331/**E**]

♦ FDI / see FDI – World Dental Federation (#09281)
♦ FDI – Fédération dentaire internationale (#09281)
♦ **FDIF** Fédération démocratique internationale des femmes (#21022)
♦ **FDI** Fonds pour le développement industriel (#11173)
♦ **FDIME** Foundation for the Development of Internal Medicine in Europe (#09944)
♦ **FDIM** Federación Democratica Internacional de Mujeres (#21022)

♦ FDI – World Dental Federation **09281**

FDI – Fédération dentaire internationale

Exec Dir Chemin de Joinville 26, 1216 Geneva, Switzerland. T. +41225608150. E-mail: info@fdiworlddental.org.
Communications Dir address not obtained.
URL: https://www.fdiworlddental.org/

History 15 Aug 1900, Paris (France). Founded as a permanent bureau for organization of future international dental congresses. Reorganized 1962 to more effectively represent national dental associations. Former names and other names: *International Dental Federation* – former (15 Aug 1900 to 1991); *Fédération dentaire internationale (FDI)* – former (15 Aug 1900 to 1991). Registration: Start date: 17 Jul 1948, End date: 19 Sep 1952, Belgium; Start date: 19 Sep 1952, End date: 14 Jul 1959, Belgium; Start date: 14 Jul 1959, Belgium; Start date: 1 Jan 2002, France. **Aims** Be the worldwide, authoritative and independent voice of the dental profession; promote optimal oral and general health for all people; support member associations in enhancing the ability of their members to provide oral healthcare to the public; advance and promote the art, science and practice of dentistry. **Structure** General Assembly; Council. Council Committees (3): Executive; Finance; Remuneration. Standing Committees (5): Dental Practice; Education; Membership Liaison and Support; Public Health; Science. Sections (3): Defence Forces Dental Services; Chief Dental Officer/Dental Public Health; Women Dentists Worldwide. Regional Organizations (5): *Asia Pacific Dental Federation/Asian Pacific Regional Organization of the Fédération Dentaire Internationale (APDF-APRO, #01882); European Regional Organization of the Fédération dentaire internationale (ERO, #08345); FDI African Regional Organization (ARO, #09280); Latin American Odontological Federation (#16357); North American Organization of the FDI (NARO).* **Languages** English, French, German, Spanish. **Staff** 17.00 FTE, paid. **Finance** Annual budget: 4,000,000 CHF (2017). **Activities** Advocacy/lobbying/activism; awareness raising; events/meetings; training/education. **Events** *World Dental Congress* Sydney, NSW (Australia) 2023, *World Dental Congress* Mumbai (India) 2022, *World Dental Congress* Sydney, NSW (Australia) 2021, *Annual World Congress* Shanghai (China) 2020, *Annual World Congress* San Francisco, CA (USA) 2019. **Publications** *Congress News* (12 a year) – electronic newsletter; *FDI News* (12 a year) – electronic newsletter; *Letter from the President* (12 a year) – electronic newsletter; *International Dental Journal* (6 a year).

Members 189: Regular; Affiliate; Associate; Supporting. Regular (141) – national dental associations in 132 countries and territories:
Afghanistan, Albania, Andorra, Angola, Argentina, Armenia, Australia, Austria, Azerbaijan, Bahamas, Bangladesh, Barbados, Belarus, Belgium, Benin, Bolivia, Bosnia-Herzegovina, Botswana, Brazil, Bulgaria, Burkina Faso, Cambodia, Cameroon, Canada, Chile, China, Colombia, Congo DR, Costa Rica, Côte d'Ivoire, Croatia, Cuba, Cyprus, Czechia, Denmark, Ecuador, Egypt, Estonia, Ethiopia, Fiji, Finland, France, Gabon, Georgia, Germany, Ghana, Greece, Guam, Guatemala, Haiti, Honduras, Hong Kong, Hungary, Iceland, India, Indonesia, Iran Islamic Rep, Iraq, Ireland, Israel, Italy, Japan, Jordan, Kazakhstan, Kenya, Korea Rep, Kosovo, Kyrgyzstan, Laos, Latvia, Lebanon, Lithuania, Luxembourg, Macau, Malaysia, Mali, Malta, Mauritius, Mexico, Moldova, Mongolia, Morocco, Mozambique, Myanmar, Nepal, Netherlands, New Zealand, Niger, Nigeria, North Macedonia, Norway, Pakistan, Palestine, Panama, Paraguay, Philippines, Poland, Portugal, Puerto Rico, Romania, Russia, Rwanda, Saudi Arabia, Senegal, Serbia, Seychelles, Singapore, Slovakia, Slovenia, South Africa, Spain, Sri Lanka, Sudan, Sweden, Switzerland, Syrian AR, Taiwan, Tanzania UR, Thailand, Timor-Leste, Togo, Tunisia, Türkiye, Uganda, UK, Ukraine, United Arab Emirates, Uruguay, USA, Vanuatu, Vietnam, Zimbabwe.

Affiliate (18) – international dental associations:
Academy of Dentistry International (ADI); Alpha Omega International Dental Fraternity; Associaçao Dentaria Lusofona (ADL); *Commonwealth Dental Association (CDA, #04321); Groupement des associations dentaires francophones (GADEF, #10757); International Academy of Periodontology (#11569); International Association for Dental Research (IADR, #11838); International Association for Disability and Oral Health (iADH, #11848); International Association of Dental Students (IADS, #11839); International Association of Dento-Maxillo-Facial Radiology (IADMFR, #11841); International Association of Paediatric Dentistry (IAPD, #12064); International College of Dentists (ICD, #12644); International Congress of Oral Implantologists (ICOI, #12899); International Federation of Dental Anesthesiology Societies (IFDAS, #13403); International Federation of Dental Educators and Associations (IFDEA, #13404); International Society of Computerized Dentistry (ISCD);* Iranian-German Implant Association (IGIA); *Pierre Fauchard Academy (PFA, #18372).*

Associate (7) – national dental associations in 7 countries and territories:
Argentina, Bosnia-Herzegovina, Chile, Germany, Hungary, Paraguay, Taiwan.

Supporting (23) – not-for-profit organizations and national organizations with an international role. Supporting in 13 countries:
Brazil, Georgia, Germany, Greece, Guatemala, Ireland, Japan, Poland, Portugal, Switzerland, UK, United Arab Emirates, USA.

Included in the above, 8 organizations listed in this Yearbook:
Association of Dental Dealers in Europe (#02466); Association of International Dental Manufacturers (IDM, #02661); Balkan Stomatological Society (BaSS, #03088); Fédération de l'industrie dentaire en Europe (FIDE, #09595); Fédération Internationale No-Noma (#09645); International College of Cranio-Mandibular Orthopedics (ICCMO, #12643); Toothfriendly Foundation (#20173); Young Dentists Worldwide (YDW, #21981).

Consultative Status Consultative status granted from: *ECOSOC (#05331)* (Ros C); *WHO (#20950)* (Official Relations). **IGO Relations** Associated with Department of Global Communications of the United Nations. [2022/XA1788/y/**A**]

♦ FdIS – Filles de la Sagesse (religious order)
♦ FDM – Fratelli di Nostra Signora della Misericordia (religious order)
♦ FDM – Fundación Dieta Mediterranea (internationally oriented national body)
♦ **FDMIE** Fondation pour le Développement de la Médecine Interne en Europe (#09944)
♦ FDNSC – Figlie di Nostra Signora del Sacro Cuore (religious order)
♦ FDNSC – Filles de Notre-Dame du Sacré-Coeur (religious order)
♦ FDP – Parvum Opus Divinae Providentiae (religious order)
♦ FDSA – Flying Doctors' Society of Africa (internationally oriented national body)
♦ FdS – Figlie della Sapienza (religious order)
♦ **FDSN** International Federation of Digital Seismograph Networks (#13407)

♦ FDT Group **09282**

Managing Dir Industrieweg 5, 3001 Heverlee, Belgium. T. +3210222251. E-mail: info@fdtgroup.org.
URL: http://www.fdtgroup.org/

History 2003. Initially founded as an informal group. Formally set up Sep 2005, when registered in accordance with Belgian law. "FDT" derives from: Flachdach Technology. Registration: Start date: 2005, Belgium. **Aims** Establish FDT *Technology* as an international standard with broad acceptance in the automation *industry.* **Structure** General Assembly. Board of Directors, headed by Chairman. Executive Committee, comprising Managing Director, Secretary of the Board, Treasurer, Vice-President Associations and Standards, Vice-President Technology and 10 Vice-Presidents at Large. **Finance** Sources: members' dues. **Publications** *FDT Newsletter.* **Members** Companies (82). Membership countries not specified. [2022/XJ5625/**C**]

♦ FEAC – Federation of African Consultants (inactive)
♦ **FEACO** Fédération Européenne des Associations de Conseils en Organisation (#07159)
♦ **FEACU** Fédération européenne des associations, clubs et centres UNESCO (#07231)
♦ FEAD / see European Federation of Waste Management and Environmental Services (#07232)
♦ **FEAD** Fédération européenne des activités de la dépollution et de l'environnement (#07232)
♦ **FEAEP** Fédération européenne des associations d'étudiants en psychologie (#07200)
♦ **FEA** Fédération Européenne des Aérosols (#09557)
♦ FEA – Fédération internationale pour l'éducation artistique (inactive)
♦ **FEAFFA** Federation of East African Freight Forwarders Associations (#09478)
♦ FEA – Fonds pour l'entreprise en Afrique (inactive)
♦ **FEA** Forum des éducatrices africaines (#09896)
♦ **FEAGA** Federation of European Art Galleries Associations (#09492)
♦ FEAGE – Fédération européenne des associations pour la gestion de l'énergie (inactive)
♦ FEAJA – Federation of East African Journalists' Associations (inactive)
♦ FEAJD – Fédération euro-arménienne pour la justice et la démocratie (internationally oriented national body)
♦ **FEALAC** Forum for East Asia-Latin America Cooperation (#09907)
♦ **FEALC** Federación Espeleológica de América Latina y el Caribe (#19917)
♦ Fe y Alegria Movimiento Internacional de Educación Popular Integral y Promoción Social / see International Federation of Fe y Alegria (#13425)

- FEAMA – Fédération européenne des fabricants d'articles de ménage et professionnels en aluminium (inactive)
- FEAMC – Fédération européenne des associations de médecins catholiques (no recent information)
- **FEAM** Federation of European Academies of Medicine (#09490)
- **FEAM** Fédération européenne des académies de médecine (#09490)
- **FEANI** Fédération Européenne d'Associations Nationales d'Ingénieurs (#09558)
- **FEANTSA** Fédération européenne d'associations nationales travaillant avec les sans-abri (#07174)
- FEAPA / see European Society for Paediatric Anaesthesiology (#08677)
- FEAP / see Culture Action Europe (#04981)
- **FEAP** Federation of European Aquaculture Producers (#09491)
- **FEAP** Fédération européenne des associations de psychologues (#07199)
- **FEAPH** Fédération Européenne des Associations de Patients de l'Hémochromatose (#07056)
- FEAP / see IFLA Europe (#11103)
- **FEAS** Federation of Euro-Asian Stock Exchanges (#09486)
- **FEAS** Fédération européenne de l'actionnariat salarié (#07105)
- FEASO – Fédération Euro-Africaine de Solidarité (internationally oriented national body)
- FEAST / see Asian Pacific Theological Seminary
- **FEAST** Families Empowered and Supporting Treatment of Eating Disorders (#09249)
- FEASTM – Fédération européenne des associations en sciences et technologies marines (inactive)
- FEBA / see European Food Banks Federation (#07280)
- **FEBA** European Food Banks Federation (#07280)
- FEBA / see Feba Radio (#09283)

♦ Feba Radio 09283

Contact Skywaves House, Ivy Arch Road, Worthing, BN14 8BX, UK. T. +441903286400. E-mail: lifegivingmedia@feba.org.uk.
URL: http://www.feba.org.uk/

History Oct 1968, Seychelles. Founded 1968. Set up in UK, 1969. Started transmission, May 1970, as a Christian station. Station decommissioned 2003. Former names and other names: *Far East Broadcasting Association (FEBA)* – former; *Far East Broadcasting Associates (FEBA)* – former. Registration: Charity Commission, No/ID: 257343, England and Wales; Companies House, No/ID: 940492, England and Wales. **Aims** Promote effective and creative use of radio and other audio media, to inspire people to follow Jesus Christ. **Structure** Office in the UK; partners across Africa, Asia and the Middle East. **Staff** 8.00 FTE, paid. **Finance** Sources: private individuals; churches; grant making trusts. **Events** *Annual conference* Hoddesdon (UK) 1990. **NGO Relations** Member of (4): Evangelical Alliance; *Far East Broadcasting Company*; *Global Connections*; *Micah Global (#16741)*. [2022.10.20/XF0263/**F**]

- FEB / see Confederation of European Baseball (#04518)
- **FEBEA** Fédération européenne de finances et banques éthiques et alternatives (#07113)
- **FEB** Fellowship of European Broadcasters (#09726)
- **FEBIC** Federación Biblica Católica (#03600)
- **FEBIS** Federation of Business Information Services (#09464)
- **FEBMA** Federation of European Bearing Manufacturers Associations (#09493)
- FEBO – Fédération européenne du négoce de bois (inactive)
- **FEBS** Federation of European Biochemical Societies (#09494)
- FEBS – Financial Engineering and Banking Society (internationally oriented national body)
- FECAEXCA / see Federación de Camaras y Asociaciones de Exportadores de Centroamérica y el Caribe (#09293)
- **FECAEXCA** Federación de Camaras y Asociaciones de Exportadores de Centroamérica y el Caribe (#09293)
- FECA – Fédération des consultants africains (inactive)
- FECA – Fédération européenne des chasseurs à l'arc (no recent information)
- FECAF – Fédération européenne des collectionneurs et des amateurs de curiosités, antiquités et folklore (inactive)
- FECAICA / see Federación de Cámaras y Asociaciones Industriales de Centroamérica y República Dominicana (#09294)
- **FECAICA** Federación de Cámaras y Asociaciones Industriales de Centroamérica y República Dominicana (#09294)
- **FECALAC** Federación Centroamericana del Sector Lacteo (#09297)
- **FECAMCO** Federación de Camaras de Comercio del Istmo Centroamericano (#09470)
- FECAMU – Federación Centroamericana de Mujeres Universitarias (no recent information)
- FECARBOX / see American Boxing Confederation (#00776)
- **FECATRANS** Federación Centroamericana de Transportes (#09298)
- **FECAVA** Federation of European Companion Animal Veterinary Associations (#09497)
- **FECB** Fédération européenne la Citizen's Band (#06556)
- FECC / see Federation of European Carnival Cities (#09496)
- **FECC** Federation of European Carnival Cities (#09496)
- **FECC** Fédération européenne des cadres de la construction (#09561)
- **Fecc** Fédération européenne du commerce chimique (#09563)
- **FECCIA** European Federation of Managerial Staff in the Chemical and Allied Industries (#07160)
- FECCIWA / see Fellowship of Christian Councils and Churches in West Africa (#09724)
- **FECCIWA** Fellowship of Christian Councils and Churches in West Africa (#09724)
- **FECCLAHA** Fellowship of Christian Councils and Churches in the Great Lakes and Horn of Africa (#09723)
- FECCOM – Federación de Centroamérica y el Caribe de Obesidad y Metabolismo (unconfirmed)
- FECCOPIA (inactive)
- FECEC / see European Federation of Managers in the Banking Sector (#07161)
- **FECEC** Fédération européenne des cadres des établissements de crédit (#07161)
- **FECECT** Foundation European Congress on Extracorporeal Circulation Technology (#09951)
- FECEP – Fédération européenne des constructeurs d'équipement pétrolier (inactive)
- **FECER** Fédération européenne des cadres de l'énergie et de la recherche (#09562)
- FEC – Far Eastern Commission (inactive)
- FEC / see Federation of European manufacturers of Cookware and cutlery (#09511)
- **FEC** Federation of European manufacturers of Cookware and cutlery (#09511)
- **FEC** Fédération européenne de croquet (#09564)
- **FEC** Fédération de l'industrie européenne de la coutellerie, des couverts de table, de l'orfèvrerie et des articles culinaires (#09511)
- FEC – Fondation de l'entre-connaissance (internationally oriented national body)
- **FEC** Fondation européenne de la culture (#06868)
- **FEC** Foundation for Environmental Conservation (#09948)
- FEC – Fundación por la Europa de los Ciudadanos (internationally oriented national body)
- **FEC** Fundación Europea de la Cultura (#06868)
- **FECIF** Fédération européenne des conseils et intermédiaires financiers (#07122)
- **FECMA** Federation of European Credit Management Associations (#09498)
- FEC / see Network of European Foundations (#17019)
- FECO / see Federation of Cartoonists Organisations (#09466)
- **FECO** Federation of Cartoonists Organisations (#09466)
- **FECOF** Fédération européenne des communes forestières (#07157)
- FECOLAC – Fundación Educativa de la Confederación Latinoamericana de Cooperativas de Ahorro y Crédito (see: #16302)
- FECOM – Fonds européen de coopération monétaire (inactive)
- FECONSUR – South Continent Boxing Federation (unconfirmed)
- **FECRIS** Fédération européenne des centres de recherche et d'information sur le sectarisme (#07072)
- FECRO / see Federation of Business Information Services (#09464)
- FECS / see European Cancer Organisation (#06432)
- FECS / see European Chemical Society (#06524)
- **FECS** Fédération européenne des fabricants de céramiques sanitaires (#07073)
- FECTS / see European Matrix Biology (#07756)
- **FECTU** Fédération Européenne du Cheval de Trait pour la promotion de son Utilisation (#06944)
- FECVI – Fédération européenne des conseils en valorisation de l'innovation (no recent information)
- FEDAJT / see European Travel Press (#08944)
- FEDALC – Federación de Distribuidoras Alternativas de América Latina y el Caribe (no recent information)
- FEDALFARBIO – Andean Federation for Pharmacy and Biochemistry (inactive)
- **FEDARENE** European Federation of Agencies and Regions for Energy and the Environment (#07041)
- FEDAS – Fédération des associations européennes des fournisseurs de laboratoires scientifiques (no recent information)
- FEDAS / see Sporting Goods Industry Data Harmonization Organization (#19924)
- **FEDAVICAC** Federación de Avicultores de Centroamérica y el Caribe (#09292)
- **FEDCAR** Federation of European Dental Competent Authorities and Regulators (#09501)
- **FeDDAF-AO** Femmes, droit et développement en Afrique-Afrique de l'Ouest (#21005)
- FEDEAU – Fédération pour le développement de l'artisanat utilitaire (inactive)
- FEDECAME – Federación Cafetalera de América (inactive)
- **FEDECATUR** Federación de Camaras de Turismo de Centroamérica (#09295)
- **FEDECENTRO** Federación Latinoamericana de Comisiones de Boxeo Profesional (#09351)
- **FEDEC** Fédération européenne des écoles de cirque professionnelles (#09565)
- FEDECO – Federación de Comunidades Judias de Centroamérica y Panama (inactive)
- FEDECRAIL Europäische Föderation der Museums- und Touristikbahnen (#09284)

♦ FEDECRAIL – European Federation of Museum and Tourist Railways 09284

FEDECRAIL – Fédération européenne des chemins de fer touristiques et historiques – FEDECRAIL Europäische Föderation der Museums- und Touristikbahnen

Sec Merellaan 11, 4461 RH Goes, Netherlands. T. +31613596032. E-mail: contact@fedecrail.org.
Registered Office c/o Advocatenkantoor van der Perre, Ganzenstraat 57, 8000 Bruges, Belgium.
URL: http://www.fedecrail.org/

History 16 Apr 1994, Leuven (Belgium). Statutes: adopted 8 Sep 1994; amended 16 Apr 1999, Prague (Czech Rep) and 1 Oct 2005, Volos (Greece).. Registration: Belgium; EU Transparency Register, No/ID: 6128433730-45. **Aims** Encourage mutual cooperation between railway organizations and their members; study and resolve problems and developments relating to museum, tourist, preserved and other similar railways or tramways, railway museums and railway preservation groups; represent members on an international basis. **Structure** General Meeting (annual); Council; Working Group. **Languages** Dutch, English, French, German. **Staff** Voluntary. **Finance** Members' dues. **Activities** Events/meetings; monitoring/evaluation; knowledge management/information dissemination; advocacy/lobbying/activism. **Events** *International Conference* Bilbao (Spain) 2020, *International Heritage Railway Conference* Wernigerode (Germany) 2019, *International Heritage Railway Conference* Edinburgh (UK) 2018, *International Railway Heritage Conference* Antwerp (Belgium) 2017, *Annual General Meeting and Conference* Dornbirn (Austria) 2016. **Publications** *FEDECRAIL Update* (4 a year).
Members Associations, museums and railways in 28 countries:
Austria, Belgium, Bulgaria, Czechia, Denmark, Estonia, Finland, France, Germany, Greece, Hungary, Ireland, Italy, Latvia, Lithuania, Luxembourg, Netherlands, Norway, Poland, Portugal, Romania, Russia, Serbia, Spain, Sweden, Switzerland, UK, Ukraine.

IGO Relations Member of: Group of Representative Bodies (GRB) of *European Union Agency for Railways (#08973)*. **NGO Relations** Member of (2): *Europa Nostra (#05767)*; *European Heritage Alliance 3.3 (#07477)*. [2021/XD7548/**D**]

- FEDECRAIL – Fédération européenne des chemins de fer touristiques et historiques (#09284)
- FedEE / see The Federation of International Employers (#09644)
- **FedEE** The Federation of International Employers (#09644)
- **FEDEFAM** Federación Latinoamericana de Asociaciones de Familiares de Detenidos-Desaparecidos (#09344)
- **FEDEFARMA** Federación Centroamericana de Laboratorios Farmacéuticos (#03669)
- **FEDE** Federation for EDucation in Europe (#09479)
- **FEDE** Fédération européenne des écoles (#09479)
- **FEDELAT** Federación Latinoamericana de Asociaciones para el Estudio del Dolor (#09343)
- **FEDELATIN** Federación Latinoamericana de Boxeo (#16259)
- Fedeli Compagne di Gesù (religious order)
- Fedeli Serve di Gesù (religious order)
- **FEDEMAC** Federation of European Movers Associations (#09519)
- **FEDEM** Fédération européenne de l'encadrement de la métallurgie (#07162)
- FEDENATUR – Fédération européenne des espaces naturels et ruraux métropolitains et périurbains (inactive)
- FEDEORAMA – Federación de Organizaciones para el Futuro de Orinoquia y Amazonia (unconfirmed)
- **FEDEPRICAP** Federación de Entidades Privadas de Centroamérica, Panama y Republica Dominica (#09300)
- FEDEPSY – Fédération européenne de psychanalyse et Ecole psychanalytique de Strasbourg (internationally oriented national body)
- Federação das Associações Católicas na Europa (#09468)
- Federação de Associações Lusófonas de Ciências da Comunicação (unconfirmed)
- Federação dos Barreau da Europa (#06320)
- Federação Biblica Católica (#03600)
- Federação Biblica Católica Mundial / see Catholic Biblical Federation (#03600)
- Federação Camponesa Latinoamericana (inactive)
- Federação de Deficientes da Africa Austral (#19829)
- Federação das Distribuidoras Alternativas da América Latina (no recent information)
- Federação de Editores Europeus (#09536)
- Federação dos Engenheiros de Telecomunicações da Comunidade Européia (#09597)
- Federação Europeia das Associações para o Ensino das Linguas Maternas aos Estrangeiros (no recent information)
- Federação Europeia das Associações do Património Industrial e Técnico (#07053)
- Federação Europeia da Indústria Optica e da Mecânica da Precisão (#07193)
- Federação Européia de Leiloeiros / see European Federation of Auctioneers (#07057)
- Federação Européia dos Médicos Assalariados (#07209)
- Federação Européia de Profissionais de Ambiente (no recent information)
- Federação Europeia de Profissionais de Pedagogia (unconfirmed)
- Federação Européia de Zoólogia (inactive)
- Federação da Função Publica Européia (#06567)
- Federação Iberoamericana de Acústica (#11021)
- Federação Ibero-Americana das Associações Financeiras (no recent information)
- Federação Iberoamericana de Engenharia Mecânica (#09313)
- Federação Ibero-Americana de Jovens Empresarios (#09314)
- Federação IberoPanamericana de Periodontia (#09328)
- Federação da Industria do Azeite da Olive da CEE (#09596)
- Federação da Indústria de los Oleos Vegetais da CE / see FEDIOL – The EU Vegetable Oil and Proteinmeal Industry (#09718)
- Federação das Indústrias de Produtos Intermédios para a Panificação e Pastelaria no EEE / see Federation of European Manufacturers of Ingredients to the Bakery, Confectionery and Patisserie Industries (#09513)
- Federação Interamericana de Advogados (#11401)
- Federação Interamericana de Associações de Relações Públicas / see Inter-American Confederation of Public Relations (#11418)

- ♦ Federação Internacional dos Arquios de Televisão / see International Federation of Television Archives (#13568)
- ♦ Federação Internacional des Associações de Pessoas Idosas (#09609)
- ♦ Federação Internacional para a Cooperação entre Centros de Pesquisa em Sistemas e Serviços de Saúde (no recent information)
- ♦ Federação internacional de Cooperativas e Mutualidades de Seguros / Associação Regional para As Américas (#12949)
- ♦ Federação Internacional da Cruz Azul / see International Blue Cross (#12364)
- ♦ Federação Internacional de Educação Física / see International Federation of Physical and Sport Education (#13510)
- ♦ Federação Internacional de Educação Física e Sportiva (#13510)
- ♦ Federação Internacional de Médicos Veterinarios Lusófonos / see Federação Internacional dos Veterinarios Lusófonos (#09285)
- ♦ Federação Internacional dos Movimentos de Adultos Rurais Católicos (#13535)
- ♦ Federação Internacional de Organizações de Doadores Voluntarios de Sangre (#13374)
- ♦ Federação Internacional dos Professores de Francês (#09652)

♦ Federação Internacional dos Veterinarios Lusófonos (FIVEL) 09285

International Federation of Lusophone Veterinarians

Pres Sia Trecho 6, Lotes 130/140, Ed Ceara – 14o Andar, Brasilia DF, Brazil. E-mail: cfmv@cfmv.org.br.

History Also referred to as *Federação Internacional de Médicos Veterinarios Lusófonos.* [2008/XJ8011/D]

- ♦ Federação International de Padres Católicos Casados (inactive)
- ♦ Federação Latino-Americana de Analise Bioenergética (internationally oriented national body)
- ♦ Federação Latinoamericana de Associações de Consultores / see Federación Panamericana de Consultores (#09379)
- ♦ Federação Latino-americana das Associações dos Quimicos e Técnicos da Indústria do Couro (unconfirmed)
- ♦ Federação Latino-Americana de Associações de Sementes (#16330)
- ♦ Federação Latinoamericana e Caribenha de Comerço Eletrônico e Internet (#09341)

♦ Federação Latino Americana de Endocrinologia (FELAEN) 09286

Federación Latinoamericana de Endocrinologia

Contact Avenida Agamenon Magalhães 4775 – Sala 302, Empresarial Thomas Edios, Ilha do Leite, Recife PE, Brazil. T. +558121257473. Fax +558121257473. E-mail: felaen@felaen.org.

URL: http://www.felaen.org/

History Current statutes adopted 10 Oct 2013. **Structure** Assembly; Executive Committee. **Events** *Latin American Congress of Endocrinology (CONLAEN)* Recife (Brazil) 2021, *Congreso Latinoamericano de Endocrinología (CONLAEN)* Buenos Aires (Argentina) 2020, *Congreso Latinoamericano de Endocrinología* Cartagena de Indias (Colombia) 2018, *Fórum Latino Americano de Diabetes – FLAD* Sao Paulo (Brazil) 2013.

Members Affiliated societies in 18 countries:
Argentina, Bolivia, Brazil, Chile, Colombia, Costa Rica, Cuba, Dominica, El Salvador, Guatemala, Honduras, Mexico, Nicaragua, Panama, Peru, Puerto Rico, Uruguay, Venezuela.

NGO Relations *Federación de Centroamérica y el Caribe de Obesidad y Metabolismo (FECCOM); International Society of Endocrinology (ISE, #15086); Latin American Diabetes Association (#16311).* [2021/XJ9500/D]

- ♦ Federação Latinoamericana de Executivas de Empresas Turisticas / see Federación Internacional de Asociaciones de Ejecutivas de Empresas Turisticas (#09336)
- ♦ Federação Latino Americana de Jornalistas de Tecnologia (no recent information)
- ♦ Federação Latino Americana de Leasing (#09356)
- ♦ Federação Latino-Americana de Magistrados (#09357)
- ♦ Federação Latino-americana de Psicoterapia Analitica de Grupo (#09361)
- ♦ Federação Latino-Americana de Psicoterapias Cognitivas e Comportamentais (#09363)
- ♦ Federação Latino-Americana de Psiquiatria da Infância e Adolescência e Profissões Afins (#09364)
- ♦ Federação Latino Americana de Quiropraxia (#09367)
- ♦ Federação Latinoamericana das Sociedades de Neurocirurgia (#16325)
- ♦ Federação Latinoamericana de Sociedades de Sono (#09685)
- ♦ Federação Latinoamericana de Trabalhadores da Educação e a Cultura (#09375)
- ♦ Federação Latinoamericana des Trabalhadores no Indústria de Construção de Madeira (inactive)
- ♦ Federação Latinoamericana de Trabalhadores Texteis Vestuario, Calçado, Couro e Conexos (inactive)
- ♦ Federação Latinoamericana de Trabalhadores do Transporte (no recent information)
- ♦ Federação Mundial de Segurança (no recent information)
- ♦ Federação Pan-Americana de Farmacia (no recent information)
- ♦ Federação Panamericana pró Doação Voluntaria do Sangri (inactive)
- ♦ Federação Panamericana de Sindicatos das Artes, Meios da Comunicação e Espectaculo (#18099)
- ♦ Federação Psicanalitica da América Latina (#09386)
- ♦ Federação das Sociedades de Cancerologia da América do Sul (#09391)
- ♦ Federação Sul-Americanas da Ciência em Animais de Laboratório (#09704)

♦ Federacia Vcelarskych Organizacii (Apislavia) 09287

Federation of Beekeeping Organizations

Secretariat Slovensky Zvaz Vcelarov, Svrcia ul 14, 842 08 Bratislava, Slovakia. T. +421265421460 – +421265427944. Fax +421265420303. E-mail: cconst@apimondiafoundation.org – sekretariat@vcelari.sk.

URL: http://www.apislavia.org/

History Set up 1910, Sofia (Bulgaria), as *All Slavic Beekeeping Union.* Activities suspended at World War I. Revived 1990, with activities fully resumed, 1991, when new statutes and title of *Federation of Slavic and Danube Regional Beekeeping Organizations* were adopted. Present title adopted 1996, Moscow (Russia). **Aims** Contribute to improvement and control of *bee* products; coordinate activities in bee diseases control; coordinate advertising and sales of bee products; coordinate activities in the field of *apitherapy*; improve and develop selection and breeding activities; promote better direct contacts and exchange of experience between beekeepers. **Structure** Congress; General Assembly. **Languages** English, Russian. **Finance** Members' dues. **Activities** Projects/programmes; knowledge management/information dissemination; events/meetings. **Events** *Congress* Almaty (Kazakhstan) 2016, *Congress* Almaty (Kazakhstan) 2016, *General Assembly* Banska Bystrica (Slovakia) 2015, *Congress* Mugla (Turkey) 2014, *General Assembly* Romania 2013.

Members Beekeeping organizations in 17 countries:
Azerbaijan, Belarus, Bulgaria, Czechia, Greece, Kazakhstan, Kyrgyzstan, North Macedonia, Poland, Romania, Russia, Serbia, Slovakia, Slovenia, Tajikistan, Türkiye, Ukraine.

Included in the above, 1 organization listed in this Yearbook:
Fundatia Institutul International de Tehnologie si Economie Apicola (FIITEA). [2015.06.29/XM1304/D]

- ♦ Federacija Akusticeskih Obscestv Evropy (inactive)
- ♦ Federacija Evropejskih Himiceskih Obscestv / see European Chemical Society (#06524)
- ♦ Federacija Mira I Soglacija (#13501)
- ♦ Federación de Aeroclubes del Caribe (inactive)
- ♦ Federación Americana de Psicoanalisis de la Orientación Lacaniana (unconfirmed)
- ♦ Federación para la Amistad Mundial (inactive)
- ♦ Federación Andina de la Industria para la Protección de Cultivos (no recent information)
- ♦ Federación Arabe para la Enseñanza Técnica (no recent information)
- ♦ Federación Arabe de Productores Pesqueros (#00945)
- ♦ Federación Asiatica de Asociaciones Médicas Católicas (#01455)
- ♦ Federación Asiatica contra la Desaparición Involuntaria (#01453)

♦ Federación de Asociaciones de América Latina, el Caribe, España y Portugal de Entidades de Tecnologias de Información y Comunicación (ALETI) 09288

Sec address not obtained.

URL: http://www.aleti.org/

History Set up as *Asociación Latinoamericana de Entidades de Tecnologia de la Información (ALETI) – Latin American Information Technology Industry Association.* **Events** *Assembly / Meeting* Panama (Panama) 2015, *Assembly* Santiago (Chile) 2015, *Assembly* Guadalajara (Mexico) 2014, *Assembly* Lisbon (Portugal) 2014, *Meeting* Sao Paulo (Brazil) 2014.

Members in 14 countries:
Argentina, Brazil, Chile, Colombia, Costa Rica, Cuba, Dominican Rep, Ecuador, Mexico, Panama, Paraguay, Peru, Uruguay, Venezuela. [2015/XD8781/D]

- ♦ Federación de Asociaciones de Banqueros de Centroamérica y Panama (inactive)
- ♦ Federación de las Asociaciones de Caza y Conservación de la Fauna Silvestre de la UE (#09459)
- ♦ Federación de las Asociaciones de Cazadores de la UE / see Federation of Associations for Hunting and Conservation of the EU (#09459)
- ♦ Federación de Asociaciones de Comerciantes en Productos Basicos (no recent information)
- ♦ Federación Asociaciones Cristianas Trabajadores Internacionales / see International Federation of ACLI (#13336)
- ♦ Federación de Asociaciones de Crohn y Colitis Ulcerosa (#07095)

♦ Federación de Asociaciones Educativas de América Latina y el Caribe (FAELA) 09289

Federation of Educational Associations of Latin America and the Caribbean – Fédération des associations éducatives latinoaméricaines et des Caraïbes

Pres Chacabuco 90, 2o Piso, 1069AAB Buenos Aires, Argentina. T. +541143427788. Fax +541143428604. E-mail: ezequiel.martinich@uai.edu.ar.

URL: http://www.faepla.org/

History Set up end 1984. Registered 8 March 1985, Buenos Aires (Argentina), as *Federation of Associations of Private Educational Entities of Latin America.* Subsequently changed title to *Federación de Asociaciones Educativas Privadas de América Latina y el Caribe (FAEPLA) – Federation of Private Educational Associations of Latin America and the Caribbean – Fédération des associations éducatives privées latinoaméricaines et des Caraïbes*, 1987. Current title adopted Jan 2018. Registered in accordance with Argentine Law: C-9477. **Aims** Defend the right to education and cultural expression with equal opportunity and free choice of institution in accordance with convictions. **Structure** General Assembly (annual); Board of Directors. **Languages** Portuguese, Spanish. **Staff** 34.00 FTE, voluntary. **Finance** Members' dues. **Activities** Awards/prizes/competitions; networking/liaising; politics/policy/regulatory; research and development; standards/guidelines; training/education; events/meetings. Active in: Argentina, Bolivia, Brazil, Chile, Costa Rica, Ecuador, El Salvador, Honduras, Jamaica, Paraguay, Peru, Puerto Rico, Uruguay, Venezuela. **Events** *Latin American Conference of Education* Cochabamba (Bolivia) 2014, *Latin American Conference of Education* Buenos Aires (Argentina) 2009, *Latin American Conference of Education* Santa Cruz (Bolivia) 2007, *Latin American Conference of Education* Buenos Aires (Argentina) 2004, *Latin American Conference of Education* Buenos Aires (Argentina) 2002.

Members Private schools and universities in 12 countries:
Argentina, Bolivia, Brazil, Chile, Costa Rica, El Salvador, Honduras, Jamaica, Paraguay, Peru, Uruguay, Venezuela.

IGO Relations Special cooperation agreements with: *UNESCO Office, Montevideo – Regional Bureau for Sciences in Latin America and the Caribbean (#20314).* **NGO Relations** *Confederación Mundial de Educación (COMED, #04464); Consejo Latinoamericano de Ciencias Sociales (CLACSO, #04718).* [2018.03.09/XD2507/D]

- ♦ Federación de Asociaciones Educativas Privadas de América Latina y el Caribe / see Federación de Asociaciones Educativas de América Latina y el Caribe (#09289)
- ♦ Federación de Asociaciones Europeas et Internacionales Establecidas en Bélgica (#09508)
- ♦ Federación de Asociaciones de Familias Católicas en Europa (#09468)
- ♦ Federación de Asociaciones de Funcionarios Internacionales (#09603)

♦ Federación de Asociaciones Iberoamericanas de Aire Acondicionado y Refrigeración (FAIAR) 09290

Federation of Iberoamerican Airconditioning and Refrigeration Associations

Contact Colegio de Ingenieros Civiles de Mexico City, Camino Sta Teresa 187, Col Paredes Pedregal, CP 14010 Mexico City CDMX, Mexico.

URL: http://www.faiar.com.mx/

History Mar 2001, Madrid (Spain). **Activities** *Congreso Ibero-Americano de Aire Acondicionado y Refrigeración (CIAR).* **Events** *Congress* Madrid (Spain) 2015, *Congress* Cartagena de Indias (Colombia) 2013, *Congress* Mexico City (Mexico) 2011, *Congress* Guayaquil (Ecuador) 2009, *Ibero-American congress on air conditioning and refrigeration* Montevideo (Uruguay) 2005. [2014/XJ4294/D]

- ♦ Federación de Asociaciones de Impresores Serigraficos Europeos / see FESPA (#09739)
- ♦ Federación de Asociaciones de Ingenieros del Caribe (inactive)
- ♦ Federación de Asociaciones Internacionales Establecidas en Bélgica / see Federation of European and International Associations Established in Belgium (#09508)
- ♦ Federación de Asociaciones Médicas Católicas Latinoamericanas (no recent information)
- ♦ Federación de Asociaciones Nacionales de Agentes de Carga de América Latina y del Caribe (#16276)
- ♦ Federación de Asociaciones Nacionales de Agentes de Carga y Operadores Logísticos Internacionales de América Latina y el Caribe / see Latin American and Caribbean Federation of National Associations of Cargo (#16276)

♦ Federación de Asociaciones Sudamericanas de Anestesiologia (FASA) 09291

Federation of South American Societies of Anesthesiologists

Contact c/o SPAAR, Edif Eucaliptos Ingr 4, Dpto 413, San Felipe – Jesús Maria, 11, Lima, Peru. E-mail: spaarperu@gmail.com.

Facebook: https://www.facebook.com/FASAoficial/

History 1 Feb 1988, Paraguay. **Aims** Carry out activities relevant to scientific and professional concerns of members. **Structure** Executive Committee lies with the country hosting the next conference – Bolivia for 1998-2000. Officers: President; Secretary-General; Scientific Secretary. **Activities** Biennial conference rotates among members. **Events** *Biennial Congress / Biennial Conference* Lima (Peru) 2014, *Biennial Conference* Bogota (Colombia) 2010, *Biennial Conference* Montevideo (Uruguay) 2009, *Biennial congress / Biennial Conference* La Paz (Bolivia) 2006, *Biennial congress / Biennial Conference* San Miguel de Tucuman (Argentina) 2004.

Members National societies (10) in ten countries:
Argentina, Bolivia, Brazil, Chile, Colombia, Ecuador, Paraguay, Peru, Uruguay, Venezuela. [2017/XD2596/D]

- ♦ Federación de Asociaciones Veterinarias Asiaticas (#09451)
- ♦ Federación Astrológica de Europa del Sur (no recent information)
- ♦ Federación Astronautica Internacional / see International Astronautical Federation (#12286)
- ♦ Federación Automovilistica Internacional (#09613)

♦ Federación de Avicultores de Centroamérica y el Caribe (FEDAVICAC) 09292

Federation of Central American and Caribbean Poultry Sciences

Pres Apartado 827-10-00, San José, San José, San José, Costa Rica. E-mail: presidencia@ternerina.com.

URL: http://www.fedavicac.com/

Events *Congress* Havana (Cuba) 2014, *Healthy aviculture – a commitment for development* San Pedro Sula (Honduras) 2004, *Congress* Havana (Cuba) 2002.
Members in 9 countries:
Costa Rica, Cuba, Dominican Rep, El Salvador, Guatemala, Honduras, Nicaragua, Panama, Puerto Rico.
IGO Relations *Consejo Regional de Cooperación Agricola de Centroamérica, México y la República Dominicana (CORECA, no recent information).* [2017/XD9463/**D**]

♦ Federación de Banqueros Internacionales de la Florida (internationally oriented national body)
♦ Federación Biblica Católica (#03600)
♦ Federación Biblica Católica Mundial / see Catholic Biblical Federation (#03600)
♦ Federación Cafetalera de América (inactive)

♦ Federación de Camaras y Asociaciones de Exportadores de Centroamérica y el Caribe (FECAEXCA) 09293

Federation of Export Chambers of Central America and the Caribbean
Contact c/o AGEXPORT, 15 av 14-72, Zona 13, 01013 Guatemala, Guatemala. T. +50224223400. Fax +50224223434. E-mail: fecaexca.sederegional@agexport.org.gt.
History 1985, as *Central American Federation of Export Chambers – Federación de Camaras de Exportadores de Centroamérica*. Also referred to as: *Federation of Chambers of Central American Exporters*; *Gremial de Exportadores de Productos no Tradicionales*; *Federación de Camaras y Asociaciones de Exportadores de Centroamérica, Panama y el Caribe (FECAEXCA)*. **IGO Relations** Member of: *Comisión Centroamericana de Transporte Maritimo (COCATRAM, #04131)*. **NGO Relations** Special member of: *Federación de Entidades Privadas de Centroamérica, Panama y Republica Dominica (FEDEPRICAP, #09300)*. [2014/XD7054/**D**]

♦ Federación de Camaras y Asociaciones de Exportadores de Centroamérica, Panama y el Caribe / see Federación de Camaras y Asociaciones de Exportadores de Centroamérica y el Caribe (#09293)
♦ Federación de Camaras y Asociaciones Industriales Centroamericanas / see Federación de Cámaras y Asociaciones Industriales de Centroamérica y República Dominicana (#09294)

♦ Federación de Cámaras y Asociaciones Industriales de Centroamérica y República Dominicana (FECAICA) 09294

Contact Ruta 6, 10-01 9-21 Zona 4, Edificio Cámara de Industria de Guatemala, 01004 Guatemala, Guatemala. T. +50223809000. E-mail: info@fecaica.com.
URL: https://fecaica.com/
History 1959. Founded as an adherent member of *Latin American Industrialists Association (#16341)*. Former names and other names: *Federation of Industrial Chambers and Associations in Central America* – former; *Fédération de chambres de commerce et associations industrielles en Amérique centrale* – former; *Federación de Camaras y Asociaciones Industriales Centroamericanas (FECAICA)* – former. **Aims** Promote industrialization, economic integration, and the creation of a common market in Central America; promote the establishment of industries, increase in productivity and in product quality. **Structure** Executive Council (meets twice a year), consisting of 2 representatives per federation. Officers: President, Vice-President, Directors, Secretary-General, Treasurer. **Languages** Spanish. **Finance** Sources: members' dues. **Activities** Events/meetings; knowledge management/information dissemination.
Members National chambers of commerce and associations of industries in 5 countries:
Costa Rica, El Salvador, Guatemala, Honduras, Nicaragua.
NGO Relations *Federación de Entidades Privadas de Centroamérica, Panama y Republica Dominica (FEDEPRICAP, #09300).* [2022/XD4182/t/**D**]

♦ Federación de Camaras de Comercio del Commonwealth (inactive)
♦ Federación de Camaras de Comercio del Istmo Centroamericano (#09470)
♦ Federación de Camaras de Exportadores de Centroamérica / see Federación de Camaras y Asociaciones de Exportadores de Centroamérica y el Caribe (#09293)

♦ Federación de Camaras de Turismo de Centroamérica (FEDECATUR) 09295

Federation of Central American Tourist Boards
Contact Col Lomas del Guijarro Sur, Calle París, Ave Niza, Casa # 1223, 11101 Tegucigalpa, Francisco Morazán, Honduras. E-mail: direccionejecutiva@fedecatur.ca.
Facebook: https://www.facebook.com/fedecaturca/
Aims Further initiatives related with *tourism* development for the private and governmental bodies in the field, promoting projects that could be of regional interest to visitors, and contribute to the integration of Central America through tourism. **Structure** Meets every 4 months in a Central American country by rotation. **Activities** Events/meetings. **IGO Relations** Member of (1): *World Tourism Organization (UNWTO, #21861)*. **NGO Relations** Member of (1): *Sustainable Tourism Certification Network of the Americas (STCNA, #20069)*. Instrumental in setting up (1): *Central American Tourism Agency (CATA, #03674)*. [2020/XD6278/**D**]

♦ Federación de Camares y Asociaciones de Empresas de Seguridad Privada de los Paises del Mercosur / see Federación de Seguridad Privada de los Paises del Mercosur (#09389)
♦ Federación Campesina Latinoamericana (inactive)
♦ Federación Caribeña de Asociaciones de Arquitectos (#09465)
♦ Federación Caribeña del Comité de Revitalización Juvenil (inactive)
♦ Federación Católica Internacional de Educación Fisica y Deportes (#12456)
♦ Federación de Centroamérica y el Caribe de Obesidad y Metabolismo (unconfirmed)
♦ Federación Centroamericana de Arquitectos (inactive)
♦ Federación Centroamericana de bancos (inactive)
♦ Federación Centroamericana de Boxeo / see American Boxing Confederation (#00776)
♦ Federación Centroamericana y del Caribe de Boxeo / see American Boxing Confederation (#00776)

♦ Federación Centroamericana y del Caribe de Neumologia y Cirugia de Tórax (NEUMOFEDECA) 09296

Office address not obtained. T. +50588838043. E-mail: presidencia@neumofedeca.org – secretaria@neumofedeca.org.
Facebook: https://www.facebook.com/Federación-Centroamericana-y-del-Caribe-de-Neumología-y-Cirugia-de-Tórax/
Events *Congress* Antigua (Guatemala) 2013, *Congress* Tegucigalpa (Honduras) 2011, *Congress* San Salvador (El Salvador) 2010, *Congress* San José (Costa Rica) 2009, *Congress* Managua (Nicaragua) 2008. [2017/XM3804/**D**]

♦ Federación Centroamericana y del Caribe de Productores Lacteos / see Federación Centroamericana del Sector Lacteo (#09297)
♦ Federación Centroamericana de Laboratorios Farmacéuticos (#03669)
♦ Federación Centroamericana de Mujeres Universitarias (no recent information)

♦ Federación Centroamericana del Sector Lacteo (FECALAC) 09297

Central American Dairy Federation
Pres CNPL, 250 Este Antiguo Itan, CP 2992-1000, San José, San José, San José, Costa Rica. T. +5062535720. Fax +5062536573.
History 1996, San Salvador (El Salvador), following Primera Conferencia Centroamericana del Sector Lacteo. Also referred to as *Federación Centroamericana y del Caribe de Productores Lacteos*. **Events** *Meeting* Managua (Nicaragua) 2000, *Meeting* San Salvador (El Salvador) 1998. **Members** Membership countries not specified. **IGO Relations** *Central American Agricultural Council (#03657).* [2018/XD9468/**D**]

♦ Federación Centroamericana de Transportes (FECATRANS) 09298

Central American Transport Federation
Sec c/o CANATRAC, Apartado 652-1150, San José, San José, San José, Costa Rica. E-mail: info@canatrac.co.cr.
History 1970, date approximate. Registered in accordance with Guatemalan law, 1996. [2017/XD6545/**D**]

♦ Federación del los Colegios de Abogados de Europa (#06320)
♦ Federación de Colegios y Asociaciones de Profesionales de Ciencias Económicas de Centroamérica y Panama (no recent information)
♦ Federación de Comunidades Judias de Centroamérica y Panama (inactive)
♦ Federación Cristiana Internacional para le Prevención del Alcoholismo y Otras Toxicomanias (no recent information)
♦ Federación Democratica Internacional de Mujeres (#21022)
♦ Federación de Distribuidoras Alternativas de América Latina y el Caribe (no recent information)
♦ Federación de Editores Europeos (#09536)
♦ Federación de Empresarios Internacionales (#09644)
♦ Federación de Empresas Afroasiaticas de Seguros y Reaseguros (#09413)
♦ Federación Endodóntica Ibero-Americana (inactive)

♦ Federación de Entidades Organizadoras de Congresos y Afines de América Latina (COCAL) 09299

Federation of Latin American Congress Organizing Entities and Related Activities
Main Office Uruguay 1134, piso 9 of A, C1060ABD Buenos Aires, Argentina. E-mail: secretaria@cocal.org.
URL: http://www.cocal.org/
History 1985. Former names and other names: *Latin American Association of Congress Organizers* – former; *Federación Latinoamericana de Organizadores de Congresos y Afines* – former; *Latin American Confederation of Congress Organizers* – former; *Confederation of Latin American Congress Organizing Entities and Related Activities* – former (2003); *Confederación de Entidades Organizadoras de Congresos y Afines de América Latina* – former (2003); *Confederación Latinoamericana de Organizadores de Congresos y Afines* – former. **Aims** Support professional development of members; agree upon and protect professional and commercial ethical principals and norms; promote and market Latin American region as a venue of international events; maintain constant links with people and entities from the public and private sector; train new professionals and foster the creation of new associations. **Structure** General Assembly (annually); Steering Committee; Committees (4). **Languages** English, Portuguese, Spanish. **Staff** Voluntary. **Finance** Sources: in-kind support; meeting proceeds; members' dues. **Activities** Events/meetings. **Events** *Congress* Cuba 2023, *Annual Congress* Panama (Panama) 2019, *Annual Congress* Asunción (Paraguay) 2018, *Annual Congress* Punta del Este (Uruguay) 2017, *Annual Congress* Guadalajara (Mexico) 2016.
Members Full in 16 countries:
Argentina, Brazil, Chile, Colombia, Costa Rica, Cuba, Ecuador, Guatemala, Mexico, Panama, Paraguay, Peru, Puerto Rico, Spain, Uruguay, Venezuela.
NGO Relations Member of (2): *Events Industry Council (EIC, #09212)*; *Joint Meetings Industry Council (JMIC, #16140)*. [2022/XD1155/**D**]

♦ Federación de Entidades Privadas de Centroamérica y Panama / see Federación de Entidades Privadas de Centroamérica, Panama y Republica Dominica (#09300)

♦ Federación de Entidades Privadas de Centroamérica, Panama y Republica Dominica (FEDEPRICAP) 09300

Federation of Private Entities of Central America, Panama and Dominican Republic – Fédération des entreprises privées d'Amérique centrale, Panama et République Dominicaine
Exec Sec Ruta 6, 9-21 Zona 4, 01004 Guatemala, Guatemala. T. +50222010000.
History 31 Jan 1987, San Salvador (El Salvador), as *Federación de Entidades Privadas de Centroamérica y Panama – Federation of Private Entities of Central America and Panama*. **Aims** Promote strategies for economic growth and development in Central America; devise mechanisms that lead to more efficient transportation systems, greater development and integration of capital markets, and increased trade promotion at regional level, emphasizing private sector-led export growth. **Structure** General Assembly; Executive Committee; President; Executive Secretary. **Languages** English, Spanish. **Staff** 12.00 FTE, paid. **Finance** Members' dues. Specific programmes funded by other sources. **Activities** Research and development; events/meetings; knowledge management/information dissemination. **Events** *General Assembly* San José (Costa Rica) 2015, *General Assembly* Tegucigalpa (Honduras) 2014, *General Assembly* San Salvador (El Salvador) 2013, *Centroamerican congress on free enterprise* San Salvador (El Salvador) 1992. **Publications** *Integración en Marcha* (6 a year). *Centroamérica: Hacia un Nuevo Modelo de Integración*; *Centro América y el GATT*; *Declaración de San Salvador*; *Declaración de Tegucigalpa*; *Flujos de Carga del Comercio Exterior de Paises Centroamericanos: Analisis Preliminar y Recomendaciones*; *Guia de Algunas Instituciones: Elementos Relevantes de Cada Una* (3rd ed); *Mercados de Capitales*. Proceedings of seminars and fora.
Members Private business organizations in 7 countries:
Costa Rica, Dominican Rep, El Salvador, Guatemala, Honduras, Nicaragua, Panama.
Special members (2):
Federación Centroamericana de Empresarios Juveniles (FECAEJ, no recent information); *Federación de Camaras y Asociaciones de Exportadores de Centroamérica y el Caribe (FECAEXCA, #09293).* [2019.02.12/XD1566/y/**D**]

♦ Federación Espeleológica de América Latina y el Caribe (#19917)
♦ Federación Espiritista Internacional (#15586)
♦ Federación de Estudiantes de Medicina Centroamericanos (inactive)
♦ Federación de Estudiantes Universitarios de Centroamérica (#09471)
♦ Federación Europea para las Actividades de Desecho / see European Federation of Waste Management and Environmental Services (#07232)
♦ Federación Europea de Alojamientos Históricos / see Historic Hotels of Europe (#10930)
♦ Federación Europea para los Ancianos (#05597)
♦ Federación Europea de Asesores e Intermediarios Financieros (#07122)
♦ Federación Europea de las Asociaciones para la Enseñanza de las Lenguas Maternas a los Extranjeros (no recent information)
♦ Federación Europea de Asociaciones de Fabricantes de Cerrajeros (#07054)
♦ Federación Europea de Asociaciones de Intervenientes en Drogodependencias (inactive)
♦ Federación Europea de Asociaciones de Patrimonio Industrial y Técnico (#07053)
♦ Federación Europea de Asociaciones de Peatones (inactive)
♦ Federación Europea de las Asociaciones al Servicio de la Juventud (inactive)
♦ Federación Europea de Asociaciones de Torrefactores de Café (inactive)
♦ Federación Europea de centros docentes (#09479)
♦ Federación Europea del Commercio Mayorista y Exterior de Juguetes (inactive)
♦ Federación Europea de Compas (inactive)
♦ Federación Europea de Cuadros de las Entidades de Crédito (#07161)
♦ Federación Europea de Destinos Turisticos Nauticos (internationally oriented national body)
♦ Federación Europea Energia – Quimica – Industrias Diversas (inactive)
♦ Federación Europea para la Enseñanza de la Gemologia (#09502)
♦ Federación Europea de Envases de Vidrio (#09583)
♦ Federación Europea de Espacios Naturales y Rurales Metropolitanos y Periurbanos (inactive)
♦ Federación Europea para el Estudio del Trabajo / see European Federation of Productivity Services (#07196)
♦ Federación Europea de Fabricantes de Alimentos Compuestos para Animales (#09566)
♦ Federación Europea de Fabricantes de Cartón Ondulado (#07091)
♦ Federación Europea de Fabricantes de Ceramicas Sanitarias (#07073)
♦ Federación Europea de Fabricantes y Distribuidores de Equipos de Protección Individual (#08418)
♦ Federación Europea de Fabricantes de Sacos de Papel de Gran Contenido / see EUROSAC (#09177)
♦ Federación Europea de los Fabricantes de Tableros de Fibras (inactive)
♦ Federación Europea del Foie Gras (#09569)
♦ Federación Europea de Geólogos (#07133)
♦ Federación Europea de la Industria de los Alimentos para Animales de Compañia (#09571)
♦ Federación Europea de la Industria Optica y de la Mecanica de Precisión (#07193)
♦ Federación Europea de las Industrias de Cuchilleria, Cuberteria, Orfebreria y Menaje de Cocina (#09511)
♦ Federación Europea de Industrias del Juguete (inactive)

Federación Europea Ingenieria
09300

alphabetic sequence excludes
For the complete listing, see Yearbook Online at

- ♦ Federación Europea de Ingenieria del Paisaje (#05751)
- ♦ Federación Europea de la Manutención / see European Materials Handling Federation (#07752)
- ♦ Federación Europea de Médicos Asalariados (#07209)
- ♦ Federación Europea de Padres de Niños con Discapacidad Auditiva (#09577)
- ♦ Federación Europea del Personal de los Servicios Públicos (#07106)
- ♦ Federación Europea de Profesionales de la Pedagogia (unconfirmed)
- ♦ Federación Europea de los Profesores de Lenguas Clasicas de la Enseñanza Superior (#06260)
- ♦ Federación Europea para la Protección de las Aguas (inactive)
- ♦ Federación Europea de Proteinas Vegetales / see European Vegetable Protein Association (#09047)
- ♦ Federación Europea de Ramas de la Asociación Mundial de Avicultura Cientifica (#07063)
- ♦ Federación Europea de Sindicatos Cristianos de Trabajadores de la Construcción y la Madera (inactive)
- ♦ Federación Europea de Sindicatos de Trabajadores de las Minas, de la Quimica y de la Energia (inactive)
- ♦ Federación Europea de Sociedades de Bioquimica (#09494)
- ♦ Federación Europea de Sociedades de Traumatologia y Ortopedia Deportiva (inactive)
- ♦ Federación Europea de Subastadores / see European Federation of Auctioneers (#07057)
- ♦ Federación Europea de los Trabajadores de la Construcción y la Madera (#07065)
- ♦ Federación Europea de los Trabajadores del Transporte (#08941)
- ♦ Federación Europea de Tratamiento del Agua / see European Water and Wastewater Industry Association (#09087)
- ♦ Federación Europea de Zoologia (inactive)
- ♦ Federación Europea de Zootecnia (#07046)
- ♦ Federación de Fabricantes Europeos de Materiales de Fricción (#09512)

♦ Federación Farmacéutica Centroamericana y del Caribe (FFCC) . . . 09301

Central American and Caribbean Pharmaceutical Federation

Contact Colonia Lara No 636, Av José Marti, Apartado Postal 758, Tegucigalpa, Francisco Morazán, Honduras. T. +5042368943. Fax +5042366832. E-mail: cqfarmaceuticos@hotmail.com.

History 1985, San Salvador (El Salvador), granted legal status. **Events** *Congress* Managua (Nicaragua) 2012, *Congress* El Salvador 2009, *Congress* Panama (Panama) 2007, *Congress* Havana (Cuba) 2005, *Congress* Santo Domingo (Dominican Rep) 2003. **NGO Relations** Member of: *Pharmaceutical Forum of the Americas (#18351).* [2017/XD8013/**D**]

♦ Federación Farmacéutica Sudamericana (FEFAS) 09302

Sec c/o Colegio de Farmacéuticos de Salta, Av Entre Rios 853, 4400 Salta, Argentina. E-mail: secretaria@fefas.org.

Pres address not obtained. E-mail: presidencia@fefas.org.

URL: http://www.fefas.org/

History 9 Aug 1991, Santiago (Chile). **Aims** Promote the union of all pharmaceutical professionals of South America so as to keep the fundamental principles of the profession. **Structure** General Assembly; Executive Council. **Languages** Spanish. **Staff** 4.00 FTE, paid. **Finance** Voluntary membership fees. Congress earnings. Annual budget: US$ 10,000. **Activities** Events/meetings. **Events** *Congress* Ciudad del Este (Paraguay) 2019, *Congress* Medellin (Colombia) 2018, *Congress* Lima (Peru) 2017, *Congress* Rio de Janeiro (Brazil) 2015, *Congress* Quito (Ecuador) 2014. **Publications** *Farmacia Sudamericana* (2 a year) – magazine; *FEFAS Newsletter.*

Members Full in 10 countries:

Argentina, Bolivia, Brazil, Chile, Colombia, Ecuador, Paraguay, Peru, Uruguay, Venezuela.

NGO Relations Member of: *International Pharmaceutical Federation (#14566); Pharmaceutical Forum of the Americas (#18351).* [2016/XD4372/**D**]

- ♦ Federación de la Función Pública Europea (#06567)
- ♦ Federación de Fundaciones pro Salud Mundial (inactive)
- ♦ Federación Ganadera Internacional (inactive)
- ♦ Federación General de Clubs de Mujeres (internationally oriented national body)
- ♦ Federación General de Mujeres Arabes (no recent information)
- ♦ Federación Grafica Internacional (inactive)
- ♦ Federación Iberoamericana de Acústica (#11021)
- ♦ Federación Iberoamericana de Artistas Intérpretes y Ejecutantes / see Federación Iberolatinoamericana de Artistas Intérpretes y Ejecutantes (#09325)

♦ Federación Iberoamericana de Asociaciones de Derecho e Informatica (FIADI) 09303

Iberoamerican Federation of Informatic Law Associations

Vice-Pres address not obtained. E-mail: secretaria@fiadi.org.

URL: http://www.fiadi.org/

History 1984, Santo Domingo (Dominican Rep). Founded during I *Congreso Iberoamericano de Informatica Juridica*, to continue the work of *Regional Centre of Studies in Informatics (inactive).* **Aims** Promote study, research and consulting activities in the different fields of the information age and law. **Structure** Executive Council, comprising President, 6 Vice-Presidents and Secretary. **Languages** Spanish. **Finance** No budget. **Events** *Congreso Iberoamericano de Derecho e Informática* Havana (Cuba) 2021, *Congreso Iberoamericano de Derecho e Informática* Sao Paulo (Brazil) 2019, *Congreso Iberoamericano de Derecho e Informática* Panama (Panama) 2018, *Congreso Iberoamericano de Derecho e Informática* San Luis Potosi (Mexico) 2017, *Congreso Iberoamericano de Derecho e Informática* Salamanca (Spain) 2016. **Publications** *Revista Iberoamericana de Derecho e Informatica.* [2021/XD7753/**D**]

- ♦ Federación Iberoamericana de Asociaciones Financieras (no recent information)
- ♦ Federación Iberoamericana de Asociaciones de Historia Económica (no recent information)

♦ Federación Iberoamericana de Asociaciones de Personas Adultas Mayores (FIAPAM) 09304

Pres C/ Vargas 47, Esc Izda, 2a planta, 39010 Santander, Cantabria, Spain. E-mail: correo@fiapam.org.

Sec Gen ASCATE, Bo Los Angeles, CP 182-7050, Cartago, Cartago, Costa Rica. E-mail: direccion@ascate.org.

URL: http://fiapam.org/

Structure General Assembly; Council; Executive Committee. **Events** *Congress* Camboriú (Brazil) 2014.

Members Full in 22 countries:

Argentina, Bolivia, Brazil, Chile, Colombia, Costa Rica, Cuba, Dominican Rep, Ecuador, El Salvador, France, Guatemala, Honduras, Italy, Mexico, Nicaragua, Panama, Paraguay, Peru, Portugal, Spain, Uruguay. [2020/XJ9325/**D**]

♦ Federación Iberoamericana de Asociaciones de Psicologia (FIAP) . . 09305

Iberoamerican Federation of Psychology Associations

Pres c/o COP, Calle Conde Peñalver 45, 5o Izq, 28006 Madrid, Spain. Fax +34913095615. E-mail: contacto@fiapsi.org.

Sec AA 33842, Bogota, Bogota DC, Colombia.

URL: http://www.fiapsi.org/

History Jul 2002, Bogota (Colombia), during III Congreso Iberoamericano de Psicologia. **Events** *Congress* Córdoba (Argentina) 2018, *Congress* Antigua (Guatemala) 2016, *Congress* Lisbon (Portugal) 2014, *Congress* Sao Paulo (Brazil) 2012, *Congress* Oviedo (Spain) 2010. **Members** National societies. Membership countries not specified. [2018/XM8280/**D**]

♦ Federación Iberoamericana de Asociaciones Veterinarias de Animales de Compañia (FIAVAC) 09306

Iberoamerican Federation of Small Animal Veterinary Associations

Sec Paseo San Gervasio 46-48, E-7, 08022 Barcelona, Spain. T. +34932531522. Fax +34934183979.

URL: http://www.fiavac.org/

Structure Board, comprising President, Vice-President, Secretary and Treasurer. **Events** *Annual Congress* Lima (Peru) 2022, *Congress* Cartagena de Indias (Colombia) 2008, *Congress* Viña del Mar (Chile) 2007, *Congress* Vitória (Brazil) 2006, *Congress* Mexico City (Mexico) 2005. **Publications** *Clinica Practica* (4 a year) – journal.

Members National organizations (15) in 15 countries:

Argentina, Brazil, Chile, Colombia, Costa Rica, Dominican Rep, Ecuador, Guatemala, Mexico, Peru, Portugal, Spain, Uruguay, USA, Venezuela. [2013/XM0120/**D**]

♦ Federación Iberoamericana de Asociaciones de Victimas contra la Violencia Vial (FICVI) 09307

Contact Por la Via por la Vida, Carrera 11a No 90/16, Oficina 506, Bogota, Bogota DC, Colombia. T. +5716793302.

URL: http://contralaviolenciavial.org/

History Feb 2010, Medellin (Colombia). Registered in accordance with Colombian law. **Structure** General Assembly; Board of Directors.

Members Full in 14 countries:

Argentina, Brazil, Chile, Colombia, Costa Rica, Ecuador, Guatemala, Mexico, Panama, Paraguay, Portugal, Spain, Uruguay, Venezuela.

NGO Relations *New Car Assessment Programme for Latin America and the Caribbean (Latin NCAP, #17077); Observatorio Iberoamericano de Seguridad Vial (OISEVI, #17641).* [2016/XM5016/**D**]

- ♦ Federación Iberoamericana de Bolsas (#11022)

♦ Federación Iberoamericana de Capacitación y Desarrollo (FIACYD) 09308

Pres c/o APG, Av Ant Aug de Aguiar 106, 7o piso, 1050-019 Lisbon, Portugal. T. +351213522717. Fax +351213522713.

Exec Dir address not obtained.

History Founded 1986, Buenos Aires (Argentina), as *Ibero-Latin American Federation of Training and Development Organizations – Federación Ibero-Latino-Americana de Capacitación y Desarrollo (FILACYD).* **Events** *Congress* Lisbon (Portugal) 1998, *Congress* Jerez de la Frontera (Spain) 1992. **Members** Membership countries not specified. [2013/XD3445/**D**]

- ♦ Federación Iberoamericana del Consejo Mundial del Niño Dotado y Talentoso (#11023)
- ♦ Federación Iberoamericana de Defensa del Pueblo / see Federación Iberoamericana de Ombudsman (#09317)
- ♦ Federación Iberoamericana de Estimulación Prenatal y Temprana (no recent information)

♦ Federación Iberoamericana de Fondos de Inversión (FIAFIN) 09309

Sec c/o AMIB, Paseo de la Reforma 255, 1er piso, Col Cuauhtémoc, 06500 Mexico City CDMX, Mexico. E-mail: soniag@amib.com.mx.

URL: http://www.fiafin.org/

Structure Directive Board, including President and Secretary. Committees (4). **Events** *Meeting* Costa Rica 2008, *Meeting* Buenos Aires (Argentina) 2007.

Members Full in 14 countries:

Argentina, Bolivia, Brazil, Chile, Colombia, Costa Rica, Dominican Rep, Ecuador, El Salvador, Mexico, Peru, Portugal, Spain, Venezuela.

NGO Relations Member of: *International Investment Funds Association (IIFA, #13952).* [2017/XJ0519/**D**]

♦ Federación Iberoamericana de Franquicias (FIAF) 09310

Ibero-American Federation of Franchising

Exec Dir Av das Nações Unidas 10989, 9o e 11o andar, Conj 92 e 112 Vl Olímpia, Sao Paulo SP, 04578-000, Brazil. E-mail: comunicaciones@portalfiaf.org.

URL: http://www.portalfiaf.com/

History 1997. Registration: Spain. **Structure** General Assembly. **Finance** Members' dues.

Members National institutions in 12 countries:

Argentina, Brazil, Colombia, Costa Rica, Guatemala, Mexico, Paraguay, Peru, Portugal, Spain, Uruguay, Venezuela. [2022/XM7322/**D**]

♦ Federación Iberoamericana de Go (FIG) 09311

Iberoamerican Go Federation

Sec address not obtained. E-mail: secretario@fedibergo.org.

Pres address not obtained. E-mail: presidente@fedibergo.org.

URL: http://www.fedibergo.org/

History Jun 1997, Sapporo (Japan), by representatives of 8 national associations. **Activities** Organizes tournaments. [2013/XD8223/**D**]

♦ Federación Iberoamericana del Hormigón Premezclado (FIHP) 09312

Exec Dir Calle 103 No 15-80, Bogota, Bogota DC, Colombia. T. +5716180018. Fax +5716234205.

URL: http://www.hormigonfihp.org/

History 12 Oct 1976, Saragossa (Spain). Registration: Panama. **Aims** Foster use of ready mixed concrete; disseminate technical information between members. **Structure** Management Team. **Languages** Portuguese, Spanish. **Staff** 1.00 FTE, paid; 5.00 FTE, voluntary. **Finance** Members' dues. Other contributions. **Activities** Knowledge management/information dissemination; events/meetings. **Events** *Congreso Iberoamericano de Pavimentos de Concreto* Barranquilla (Colombia) 2020, *Iberoamerican Congress on Housing* Guatemala (Guatemala) 2015, *Meeting of Concrete* Managua (Nicaragua) 2015, *Meeting on Integral Management Concrete Industry* Monterrey (Mexico) 2015, *Half-yearly Meeting / Biannual Meeting* Puerto Vallarta (Mexico) 2015. **Publications** *Horminotici'at's* – online.

Members Full in 19 countries:

Argentina, Bolivia, Brazil, Colombia, Costa Rica, Cuba, Ecuador, El Salvador, Guatemala, Mexico, Nicaragua, Panama, Paraguay, Peru, Portugal, Puerto Rico, Spain, Uruguay, Venezuela.

Corresponding members in 2 countries:

Canada, USA.

NGO Relations Member of: *Global Cement and Concrete Association (GCCA, #10275).* [2021/XD1916/**D**]

♦ Federación Iberoamericana de Ingenieria Mecanica (FeIbIM) 09313

Iberoamerican Mechanical Engineering Federation – Federação Iberoamericana de Engenharia Mecânica (FeIbEM)

Pres Depto Ingenieria Mecanica, Univ Politécnica de Madrid, C/ José Gutiérrez Abascal 2, 28006 Madrid, Spain.

SG address not obtained.

URL: http://www.feibim.org/

History 1991. Registered in accordance with Spanish law, 1996. **Aims** Promote development of mechanical engineering and cooperation among institutions involved in the Iberoamerican region. **Structure** General Assembly; Executive Committee. **Languages** Portuguese, Spanish. **Finance** Members' dues. Donations. **Activities** Events/meetings; awards/prizes/competitions. **Events** *Iberoamerican Congress of Mechanical Engineering* Lisbon (Portugal) 2017, *Iberoamerican Congress of Mechanical Engineering* Guayaquil (Ecuador) 2015, *International Symposium on Multibody Systems and Mechanics* Santa Maria Huatulco (Mexico) 2014, *Iberoamerican Congress of Mechanical Engineering* La Plata (Argentina) 2013, *Iberoamerican Congress of Mechanical Engineering* Porto (Portugal) 2011. **Publications** *Revista Iberoamericana de Ingenieria Mecanica* (2 a year). [2018.06.18/XM3534/**D**]

♦ Federación Iberoamericana de Jóvenes Empresarios (FIJE) 09314

Iberoamerican Federation of Young Entrepreneurs – Federação Ibero-Americana de Jovens Empresarios

SG address not obtained. T. +556139642424. E-mail: secretariageneral@fije.org – organizacion@fije.org – contato@fije.org.

URL: http://fije.org/

History 1996, as *Confederación Iberoamericana de Jóvenes Empresarios (CIJE) – Iberoamerican Confederation of Young Entrepreneurs.* Re-founded under current title 2008. **Members** in 20 countries, not specified. **NGO Relations** Member of (1): *Espacio Iberoamericano de Juventud (EIJ, no recent information).* Cooperation agreement with: *Young Entrepreneurs for Europe (YES for Europe, #21982).* [2015/XM1388/**D**]

♦ Federación Iberoamericana de Mantenimiento (FIM) 09315

Ibero American Maintenance Federation

Exec Sec Del Carmen 776, Piso 4o, 1019 Buenos Aires, Argentina.
Pres c/o AEM, Plaza Dr Letamendi 37 4o 2o, 08007 Barcelona, Spain.
URL: http://www.fim-mantenimiento.org/

History 21 Aug 1990, Belo Horizonte (Brazil). Statutes approved 9 Nov 1993, Viña del Mar (Chile). **Activities** Organizes: *Congreso Iberoamericano de Mantenimiento*; World Congress. **Events** *Iberoamerican congress / Ibero American Congress* Barcelona (Spain) 2011, *World congress* Buenos Aires (Argentina) 2010, *World congress* Haikou City (China) 2008, *Iberoamerican congress / Ibero American Congress* Cajamarca (Peru) 2007, *World congress* Basel (Switzerland) 2006.
Members Associations in 8 countries:
Argentina, Bolivia, Brazil, Chile, Ecuador, Peru, Portugal, Spain.
NGO Relations Founding member of: *Global Forum on Maintenance and Asset Management (GFMAM, #10374)*. World Congress coordinated jointly with *European Federation of National Maintenance Societies (EFNMS, #07173)*. [2015/XM4073/**D**]

- ♦ Federación Iberoamericana de Medicina Estética (no recent information)
- ♦ Federación Iberoamericana de Mujeres de Empresa / see Federación Iberoamericana de Mujeres Empresarias (#09316)

♦ Federación Iberoamericana de Mujeres Empresarias (FIDE) 09316

Iberoamerican Federation of Business Women

Sec c/o ASEME, Calle de Zurbaran 8, 28010 Madrid, Spain. T. +34911547400. E-mail: info@fideweb.org.
Americas Tucuman 1506, 3o piso of 306, CP AAF 1050, Buenos Aires, Argentina. T. +541143723120. Fax +541143730197.
URL: https://fideweb.org/

History 1990. Former names and other names: *Federación Iberoamericana de Mujeres de Empresa* – alias. **Aims** Support and promote the full development of women entrepreneurs; promote equality at work; improve their socio-economic life; support relations between Latin American women. **Structure** Chairwoman; 3 Honorary Chairwomen; 1st and 2nd Vice-Presidents; Secretary-General. **Languages** English, Spanish. **Activities** Organizes annual Congreso Iberoamericano de Mujeres de Empresa (CIME). **Events** *Congreso Iberoamericano de Mujeres Empresarias* Las Palmas de Gran Canaria (Spain) 2021, *Congreso Iberoamericano de Mujeres Empresarias* Paraguay 2020, *Congreso Iberoamericano de Mujeres Empresarias* Santander (Spain) 2018, *Symposium* Andong (Korea Rep) 2016, *Congreso Iberoamericano de Mujeres Empresarias* Madrid (Spain) 2016.
Members Full in 9 countries:
Argentina, Brazil, Ecuador, Mexico, Paraguay, Peru, Portugal, Spain, Venezuela.
Regional organization:
Federación Internacional de Asociaciones de Ejecutivas de Empresas Turísticas (FIASEET, #09336). [2021/XD1234/y/**D**]

♦ Federación Iberoamericana de Ombudsman (FIO) 09317

Ibero-American Federation of Ombudsmen

Technical Sec Defensor del Pueblo – C/ Eduardo Dato no 31, 28071 Madrid, Spain. T. +34917164042. Fax +34913105202. E-mail: secretaria.tecnica@portalfio.org.
Chairman address not obtained.
URL: http://www.portalfio.org/

History 1996, Antigua (Guatemala). Former names and other names: *Federación Iberoamericana de Defensa del Pueblo* – former. **Languages** Portuguese, Spanish. **Activities** Awareness raising; capacity building; conflict resolution; events/meetings; networking/liaising; politics/policy/regulatory; projects/programmes; training/education. **Events** *Annual Congress* Mexico City (Mexico) 2014, *International Congress* Madrid (Spain) 2013, *Annual Conference* Madrid (Spain) 2009, *Annual Congress* Peru 1998. **Publications** Annual Report.
Members Ombudsman Offices in 22 countries and territories:
Andorra, Argentina, Bolivia, Brazil, Chile, Colombia, Costa Rica, Dominican Rep, Ecuador, El Salvador, Guatemala, Honduras, Mexico, Nicaragua, Panama, Paraguay, Peru, Portugal, Puerto Rico, Spain, Uruguay, Venezuela.
IGO Relations Cooperates with (6): *Corte Interamericana de Derechos Humanos (Corte IDH, #04851); European Commission for Democracy through Law (Venice Commission, #06636); European Union (EU, #08967); Inter-American Commission on Human Rights (IACHR, #11411); OAS (#17629); Office of the United Nations High Commissioner for Human Rights (OHCHR, #17697).* **NGO Relations** Cooperates with (7): *Alianza Global del Ombudsperson Local (AGOL, #00629); Asian Ombudsman Association (AOA, #01589); Caribbean Ombudsman Association (CAROA, #03533); Global Alliance of National Human Rights Institutions (GANHRI, #10214); International Ombudsman Institute (IOI, #14411); Latin American Institute for the Ombudsman (#16342); Red de Instituciones Nacionales para la Promoción y Protección de los Derechos Humanos del Continente Americano (RINDHCA).* [2021.02.17/XD5113/**D**]

- ♦ Federación Ibero Americana de Prensa Periódica (inactive)
- ♦ Federación Iberoamericana de Productores de Árides (unconfirmed)

♦ Federación Iberoamericana de Productores Cinematograficos y Audiovisuales (FIPCA) 09318

Ibero-American Federation of Cinematographic and Audiovisual Producers (FIPCA)

Exec Sec Calle Luis Buñuel, 2-3 Edificio EGEDA – Ciudad de la Imagen, Pozuelo de Alarcón, 28223 Madrid, Spain. T. +34691382922. E-mail: antonio.lopez@fipca.org.
Pres address not obtained.
URL: http://www.fipca.org

History 19 Mar 1997, Guadalajara (Mexico). Former names and other names: *Latin-American Federation of Cinematographic and Audiovisual Producers* – former. **Structure** Board. **Languages** Portuguese, Spanish. **Finance** Members' contributions; cooperation agreements. **Activities** Awards/prizes/competitions; capacity building; events/meetings.
Members Associations in 18 countries and territories:
Argentina, Bolivia, Brazil, Chile, Colombia, Cuba, Dominican Rep, Ecuador, Guatemala, Mexico, Panama, Paraguay, Peru, Portugal, Puerto Rico, Spain, Uruguay, Venezuela. [2023.02.14/XD7868/**D**]

♦ Federación Iberoamericana de Sindrome de Down (FIADOWN) 09319

Main Office C/ Machaquito no 58, L-10, 32803 Madrid, Spain. T. +34913160710. Fax +34913000430. E-mail: fiadown@fiadown.org.
URL: http://fiadown.org/

History 2010. Formal constitution adopted, 15 Aug 2011. Registration: No/ID: 599304, Start date: 10 Feb 2012, Spain. **Aims** Strengthen cooperation between federations and national associations of Iberoamerican countries; support promotion of organizations of Down's syndrome. **Structure** General Assembly; Managerial Committee. **Languages** Portuguese, Spanish. **Staff** 1.00 FTE, paid. **Finance** Subventions of private entities. Budget (2015): euro 56,000. **Events** *Congress* Cartagena de Indias (Colombia) 2019, *Congress* Salamanca (Spain) 2016, *Congress* Monterrey (Mexico) 2013, *Congress* Granada (Spain) 2010. **Publications** *Programa Iberoamericano de Salud para Personas con Sindroma de Down.*
Members Full in 13 countries:
Argentina, Brazil, Chile, Colombia, Costa Rica, El Salvador, Honduras, Paraguay, Peru, Portugal, Spain, Uruguay, Venezuela.
IGO Relations *Ibero-American General Secretariat (#11024).* [2022/XM4707/**D**]

♦ Federación Iberoamericana de Sociedades de Educación Matematica (FISEM) 09320

SG c/o THALES, Fac de Matematicas, Apartado 1160, 41080 Seville, Sevilla, Spain. E-mail: sg@fisem.org.
URL: http://www.fisem.org

Structure Executive Committee; Board of Governors. Officers: President; Vice-President; Secretary-General; Treasurer. **Events** *Iberoamerican Congress of Mathematics Education (CIBEM)* Sao Paulo (Brazil) 2022, *Iberoamerican Congress of Mathematics Education (CIBEM)* Madrid (Spain) 2017, *Iberoamerican Congress of Mathematics Education (CIBEM)* Montevideo (Uruguay) 2013, *Iberoamerican Congress of Mathematics Education (CIBEM)* Puerto Montt (Chile) 2009, *Iberoamerican Congress of Mathematics Education (CIBEM)* Porto (Portugal) 2005. **Publications** *UNION – Revista Iberoamericana de Educación Matematica.*
Members Federations in 14 countries:
Argentina, Bolivia, Brazil, Chile, Colombia, Dominican Rep, Ecuador, Mexico, Paraguay, Peru, Portugal, Spain, Uruguay, Venezuela. [2013/XJ6456/**D**]

♦ Federación Iberoamericana de Sociedades de Fisica (FEIASOFI) ... 09321

Iberoamerican Federation of Physics Societies

Admin Secretariat RSEF, UCM – Fisicas, Avda Complutense sn, 28040 Madrid, Spain. T. +34913944350. Fax +34913944162. E-mail: rsef@fis.ucm.es.
URL: http://www.feiasofi.net/

History 4 Nov 1996, Havana (Cuba), as *Unión Iberoamericana de Sociedades de Fisica (UISF)*. Present name adopted, 2005. **Events** *Meeting* Madrid (Spain) 2000. **Publications** *Revista de la Unión Iberoamericana de Sociedades de Fisica.* [2018/XJ4405/**D**]

♦ Federación Iberoamericana de Tenis de Mesa (FIBE) 09322

Ibero-American Table Tennis Federation

Pres Univ Pablo de Olavide, Carretera de Utrera Km 1, 41013 Seville, Sevilla, Spain. T. +34915477726. Fax +34915429205.
URL: http://fibetm.org/

History 5 May 1995, Tianjin (China). **Aims** Develop table tennis in the membership countries. **Structure** Congress, Directives, Permanent Commission, Secretary General and Committees. **Languages** Portuguese, Spanish. **Staff** Staff of every National Association; volunteers. **Finance** Members' dues. **Activities** Ordinary and Extraordinary Congresses; Iberoamerican Championships. **Events** *Annual Assembly* Budapest (Hungary) 2019.
Members Full in 14 countries:
Argentina, Brazil, Chile, Colombia, Cuba, Ecuador, Guatemala, Panama, Paraguay, Portugal, Puerto Rico, Spain, Uruguay, Venezuela.
NGO Relations Recognized by: *International Table Tennis Federation (ITTF, #15650).* [2019/XD6750/**D**]

♦ Federación Iberoamericana de Ultrasonografistas en Obstetricia y Ginecologia (FIAUOG) 09323

Pres address not obtained.

History Founded Apr 2007. **Events** *Congress* Valencia (Venezuela) 2008, *Congress* Lima (Peru) 2007. **NGO Relations** *Sociedad Iberoamericana de Diagnóstico y Tratamiento Prenatal (SIADTP, no recent information).* [2013/XM8201/**D**]

♦ Federación Iberoamericana Urbanistas (FIU) 09324

Secretariat Calle Avinyo 15, 08002 Barcelona, Spain. T. +34933043322. E-mail: secretaria@fiurb.org.
URL: http://www.fiurb.org/

History Oct 2010, Santa Cruz de Tenerife (Spain), during 14th 'Congreso Iberoamericano de Urbanismo'. **Structure** Board of Directors.
Members Organizations and individuals in 20 countries:
Argentina, Bolivia, Brazil, Chile, Colombia, Costa Rica, Cuba, Dominica, Ecuador, El Salvador, Guatemala, Mexico, Nicaragua, Panama, Peru, Portugal, Puerto Rico, Spain, Uruguay, Venezuela.
IGO Relations *United Nations Human Settlements Programme (UN-Habitat, #20572).* **NGO Relations** Partner of: *World Urban Campaign (WUC, #21893).* [2015/XM4194/**D**]

♦ Federación Iberolatinoamericana de Artistas Intérpretes y Ejecutantes (FILAIE) 09325

Fédération ibéro-latinoaméricaine des artistes interprètes et exécutants – Ibero-Latin-American Federation of Performers

Pres c/o AIE, C/ Torrelara no 8, 28016 Madrid, Spain. T. +34917819854. Fax +34917819550. E-mail: presidenciafilaie@filaie.com – mariajose.rubio@aie.es – comunicacion.presidencia@aie.es.
URL: https://www.filaie.org/

History Founded 1981. Also referred to as *Latin American Federation of Performers – Fédération latinoaméricaine des artistes interprètes et exécutants (FLAIE)* and previously also as *Federación Iberoamericana de Artistas Intérpretes y Ejecutantes*. Previously also known under the English acronyms *LAFP* and *ILAFP*. Restructured under current title 1992. **Aims** Defend the intellectual property rights of performers. **Structure** General Assembly; Board; Committees (4). **Languages** Spanish. **Staff** 12.00 FTE, paid. **Activities** Events/meetings. **Events** *Assembly* Panama (Panama) 2017, *Assembly* Madrid (Spain) 2013.
Members Full in 19 countries:
Argentina, Barbados, Bolivia, Brazil, Chile, Colombia, Costa Rica, Dominican Rep, Ecuador, El Salvador, Guatemala, Mexico, Panama, Paraguay, Peru, Portugal, Spain, Uruguay, Venezuela.
Consultative Status Consultative status granted from: *World Intellectual Property Organization (WIPO, #21593)* (Permanent Observer Status). [2017.10.23/XD4647/**D**]

- ♦ Federación Ibero-Latino-Americana de Capacitación y Desarrollo / see Federación Iberoamericana de Capacitación y Desarrollo (#09308)

♦ Federación Ibero-Latinoamericana de Cirugia Plastica (FILACP) ... 09326

Ibero-Latin American Federation of Plastic Surgery

Pres Av Centenario, Costa del Este, Torre Ancón, Local 13-C, Panama, Panamá, Panama PANAMÁ, Panama. E-mail: info@filacp.org.
URL: http://www.filacp.org/

History 1974, Caracas (Venezuela). Founded during the XIII Congress of *Latin American Society of Plastic Surgery (inactive)*. Previously a section of: *International Confederation for Plastic, Reconstructive and Aesthetic Surgery (IPRAS, inactive)*. **Aims** Promote cooperation on educational, research and ethics issues among Latin American societies of plastic surgery. **Structure** Board of Directors; Executive Committee; Consultative Council. **Languages** Portuguese, Spanish. **Staff** Voluntary. **Finance** Sources: members' dues. **Activities** Organizes: annual courses; medico-social programme to provide surgical assistance to the poor; regional congresses. Special chapters include: Ethics; Education; Teaching. **Events** *Congress* Punta Cana (Dominican Rep) 2021, *Central American and Caribbean Regional Congress* Guatemala (Guatemala) 2015, *Congress* Cancún (Mexico) 2014, *Congress* Medellin (Colombia) 2012, *Congress* Panama (Panama) 2010. **Publications** *Cirugia Plastica Ibero Latinoamericana* (6 a year) – journal.
Members National societies in 22 countries and territories:
Argentina, Bolivia, Brazil, Chile, Colombia, Costa Rica, Cuba, Dominican Rep, Ecuador, El Salvador, Guatemala, Honduras, Mexico, Nicaragua, Panama, Paraguay, Peru, Portugal, Puerto Rico, Spain, Uruguay, Venezuela.
Regional organization (1):
Society of Latin American Plastic Surgeons in USA and Canada (SLAPS, no recent information).
NGO Relations Instrumental in setting up: *Comité Ibero Latinoamericano de Prevención y Asistencia del Quemado (CILAPAQ, inactive).* [2021/XD6455/**D**]

♦ Federación Ibero Latinoamericana de Sociedades Médicas de Acupuntura (FILASMA) 09327

Ibero-Latin American Federation of Medical Societies of Acupuncture

SG Av del Cabildo c/ Cortés, chalet "Ursala", 20 000 Maldonado, Uruguay. E-mail: filasmaacupuntura@gmail.com.
URL: http://www.filasma.org/

History 1992, Gramado (Brazil). Present title adopted at 3rd Congress, San Pablo (Brazil), 22-25 Nov 2000. Former names and other names: *Federación Latino-americana de Sociedades Médicas de Acupuntura (FLASMA)* – former (1992 to 2000). **Aims** Join efforts to obtain recognition of acupuncture by academic, trade union and healthcare organizations of member countries. **Structure** Officers. **Languages** English, Portuguese, Spanish. **Staff** 9.00 FTE, voluntary. **Finance** Sources: contributions. **Activities** Events/meetings. **Events** *Congress* Uruguay 2022, *Congress* Santiago de Querétaro (Mexico) 2019, *World Medical Acupuncture Congress* Mexico City (Mexico) 2017.
Members Full in 13 countries:
Argentina, Brazil, Chile, Colombia, Ecuador, Mexico, Paraguay, Peru, Portugal, Puerto Rico, Spain, Uruguay, Venezuela. [2020.08.15/XM5681/**D**]

♦ Federación Ibero Panamericana de Periodoncia / see Federación Iberopanamericana de Periodoncia (#09328)

♦ Federación Iberopanamericana de Periodoncia (FIPP) 09328

IberoPanamerican Federation of Periodontics (IPFP) – Federação IberoPanamericana de Periodontia

SG address not obtained. E-mail: info@fippcongreso.com – pacoromeroperiodista@gmail.com – miguel.lopez@sepa.es.
Pres address not obtained.
URL: http://www.fippdentalearning.org/

History 1972. Dissolved 2002, to be refounded as the federation listed under current title. Former names and other names: *Asociación Panamericana de Periodontologia* – former (1972 to 2002); *Federación Ibero Panamericana de Periodoncia* – alias. **Events** *Congress* 2021, *Congress* Quito (Ecuador) 2020, *Congress* Santiago (Chile) 2015, *Congress* Venezuela 2011, *Congress* Argentina 2008. **Publications** *FIPP DENTALearning* – newsletter.
Members Full in 12 countries:
Argentina, Bolivia, Chile, Colombia, Dominica, Ecuador, Guatemala, Panama, Peru, Spain, Uruguay, Venezuela.
[2021/XJ8965/D]

♦ Federación de la Industria del Aceite de Olive de la CEE (#09596)
♦ Federación de la Industria Aceitera de la CE / see FEDIOL – The EU Vegetable Oil and Proteinmeal Industry (#09718)
♦ Federación de la Industria y Comercio de Agroquimicos del Cono Sur (no recent information)
♦ Federación de Industrias de Productos Intermedios para la Panaderia y Pasteleria en la EEE / see Federation of European Manufacturers of Ingredients to the Bakery, Confectionery and Patisserie Industries (#09513)
♦ Federación de Ingenieros de Telecomunicación de la Comunidad Europea (#09597)
♦ Federación de Instituciones Centroamericanas de Desarrollo (inactive)
♦ Federación de Institutos y Servicios de Neurociencias de las Américas (no recent information)
♦ Federación Interamericana de Abogados (#11401)
♦ Federación Interamericana de Administración de Personal / see Federación Interamericana de Asociaciones de Gestión Humana (#09329)

♦ Federación Interamericana de Asociaciones de Gestión Humana (FIDAGH) 09329

Sec/Treas Av Justo Arosemena y cl 31, Edif APEDE, 1er piso, Panama, Panamá, Panama PANAMá, Panama. E-mail: info@fidaghoficial.org.
URL: https://fidaghoficial.org/

History 1976. Statutes revised 1991, Quito (Ecuador). Former names and other names: *Inter-American Federation of Personnel Administration* – former (1976); *Fédération interaméricaine pour l'administration du personnel* – former (1976); *Federación Interamericana de Administración de Personal* – former (1976); *Federación Interamericana de Asociaciones Profesionales para la Gestion Humana (FIDAP)* – former; *Interamerican Federation of Human Resource Management* – former; *Inter-American Federation of Personnel Management (IFPM)* – alias; *Fundación Federación Interamericana de Asociaciones de Gestión Humana ((FIDAGH)* – legal name (2009). Registration: Start date: 26 Jan 2009, Panama. **Structure** Council, consisting of President, Vice President, Secretary/Treasurer, Communications Officer, Vice President – North, Vice President – South and Council Chairman. **Languages** English, Spanish. **Events** *Congress* Santiago (Chile) 2014, *Congress* Guatemala 2007, *Congress* Santo Domingo (Dominican Rep) 2003, *Congress* Mexico City (Mexico) 2002, *Congress* Lima (Peru) 2001.
Members Full in 12 countries:
Argentina, Brazil, Chile, Colombia, Dominican Rep, Ecuador, Mexico, Panama, Paraguay, Peru, Uruguay, Venezuela.
NGO Relations Instrumental in setting up and regional member of: *World Federation of People Management Associations (WFPMA, #21474)*. Founding member of: *Secretariado Iberoamericano de Dirección de Personal (inactive)*.
[2021/XD2241/D]

♦ Federación Interamericana de Asociaciones Profesionales para la Gestion Humana / see Federación Interamericana de Asociaciones de Gestión Humana (#09329)
♦ Federación Interamericana de Asociaciones de Relaciones Públicas / see Inter-American Confederation of Public Relations (#11418)
♦ Federación Interamericana de Asociaciones de Secretarias (#11430)
♦ Federación Interamericana de Automóvil-Clubs / see Federación Internacional del Automóvil Region IV (#09337)
♦ Federación Interamericana de Camaras de la Construcción (inactive)
♦ Federación Interamericana de Camaras de Informatica, Telecomunicaciones y Electrónica (no recent information)

♦ Federación Interamericana del Cemento (FICEM) 09330

Inter-American Cement Federation (FICEM)

Contact Calle 118 No 19-52, Oficina 204, Bogota 110011, Bogota DC, Colombia. T. +5716582978. E-mail: ficem@ficem.org.
URL: http://www.ficem.org/

History 1973. Current Bylaws adopted by 5th General Assembly, 20 Oct 1993, Caraballeda (Venezuela). Former names and other names: *Latin American Group of Cement and Concrete Institutions* – former; *Grupo Latinoamericano de Instituciones del Cemento y del Concreto* – former; *FICEM-APCAC* – former. **Aims** Promote sustainable development of the cement industry in the region. **Structure** General Assembly; Board of Directors; Consultative Council; Executive Direction; Planning Committee; Technical Council; Technical Committees. **Languages** English, Spanish. **Activities** Advocacy/lobbying/activism; knowledge management/information dissemination; publishing activities; research/documentation. **Events** *Congreso Iberoamericano de Pavimentos de Concreto* Barranquilla (Colombia) 2020, *General Assembly* Punta Cana (Dominican Rep) 2019, *Technical Congress* Punta Cana (Dominican Rep) 2019, *Foro de Cambio Climático y Coprocesamiento* Vienna (Austria) 2019, *General Assembly* Panama (Panama) 2018. **Publications** *Cemento & Concreto*.
Members Cement production companies. Membership countries not specified.
Institutes, Associations and Chambers of the Cement and Concrete Industry. Membership countries not specified.
NGO Relations Member of (1): *Global Cement and Concrete Association (GCCA, #10275)*.
[2021.02.17/XE1606/D]

♦ Federación Interamericana de Educación de Adultos (inactive)

♦ Federación Interamericana de Empresas de Seguros (FIDES) 09331

Inter-American Federation of Insurance Companies – Fédération interaméricaine des compagnies d'assurances

SG Av Hernando de Aguirre 848, Providencia, Santiago, Santiago Metropolitan, Chile.
Pres Edif Castilla, Loayza 250, La Paz, Bolivia.
URL: http://www.fideseguros.com/

History 14 May 1946, New York, NY (USA). Statutes adopted 1982. Former names and other names: *Hemispheric Insurance Conference* – former (16 May 1946); *Conférence hémisphérique des assurances* – former (16 May 1946); *Conferencia Hemisférica de Seguros* – former (16 May 1946). **Aims** Encourage the development of insurance and reinsurance by supporting, disseminating and promoting the great benefits that the sector brings to the economies and people of the twenty member countries it represents. **Structure** General Assembly (annual, including every 2 years at biennial Conference); Presidential Council (meets twice a year). General Secretariat, headed by Secretary-General. Permanent Committees. Regional Commissions (4): Northern (USA and Mexico); Central and Caribbean (Central America, Panama and Caribbean); Andean (Bolivia, Colombia, Ecuador, Peru, Venezuela); Southern (Argentina, Brazil, Chile, Paraguay, Uruguay). Work Groups. **Languages** English, Portuguese, Spanish. **Staff** 3.00 FTE, paid. **Finance** Sources: members' dues. Annual budget: 175,000 USD. **Activities** Develops statistics and legal regulations at regional level. **Events** *Hemispheric Insurance Conference* Rio de Janeiro (Brazil) 2023, *Biennial hemispheric insurance conference* Lima (Peru) 2001, *Biennial hemispheric insurance conference* Panama (Panama) 1999, *Hemispheric insurance conference* Mexico City (Mexico) 1997, *World insurance congress* Mexico City (Mexico) 1997. **Publications** *Noticiario FIDES com* (weekly) – electronic bulletin; *El Seguro Iberoamericano en Cifras* (annual). *Continental Insurance Directory*.
Members Active national representative organizations of private insurance enterprises (or liaison units where none exists), representing nearly 1,000 affiliated companies in 20 countries:
Argentina, Bolivia, Brazil, Chile, Colombia, Costa Rica, Dominican Rep, Ecuador, El Salvador, Guatemala, Honduras, Mexico, Nicaragua, Panama, Paraguay, Peru, Spain, Uruguay, USA, Venezuela.
Consultative Status Consultative status granted from: *UNCTAD (#20285)* (Special Category). **IGO Relations** *OAS (#17629)*. **NGO Relations** Member of (1): *Microinsurance Network (#16747)*.
[2023/XD0217/D]

♦ Federación Interamericana de Filatelia (FIAF) 09332

Inter American Philatelic Federation – Fédération interaméricaine de philatélie

Sec Los Cisnes 143, 27, Lima, Peru. E-mail: irvincicuta@yahoo.com.
Pres PO Box 49553, Sarasota FL 34230, USA.
URL: https://filatelia-interamericana.com/

History 1969, Mexico City (Mexico). **Aims** Promote philately in the Western hemisphere. **Structure** Board of Directors, consisting of President, Vice-President, Past-President, Secretary, Treasurer and 4 Directors. **Languages** English, Portuguese, Spanish. **Finance** Members' dues. **Activities** Working Committees (7): Aerophilately; Maximaphilia; Postal History; Prevention of Harmful Issues; Traditional; Thematics; Youth. Gives patronage or auspices to exhibitions held in the Western Hemisphere. FIAF Medal (an award given for outstanding services to philately). Established, 1988, the 'Alvaro Bonilla Lara' Literature Award (presented annually to the best work written about our philately). **Events** *Annual Meeting and Exhibition* Havana (Cuba) 2014, *Annual meeting / Annual Meeting and Exhibition* Buenos Aires (Argentina) 2001, *Annual meeting / Annual Meeting and Exhibition* Madrid (Spain) 2000, *Annual meeting / Annual Meeting and Exhibition* Buenos Aires (Argentina) 1999, *Annual meeting / Annual Meeting and Exhibition* Buenos Aires (Argentina) 1998. **Publications** *Emilio Obregon* – series.
Members Philatelists (200,000) in 20 countries:
Argentina, Bolivia, Brazil, Canada, Chile, Colombia, Costa Rica, Cuba, Dominican Rep, Ecuador, Honduras, Mexico, Panama, Paraguay, Peru, Portugal, Spain, Uruguay, USA, Venezuela.
Associate members in 2 countries:
Guatemala, Puerto Rico.
NGO Relations Associate member of: *Fédération internationale de philatélie (FIP, #09650)*.
[2022/XD1199/v/D]

♦ Federación Interamericana de la Industria de la Construcción (FIIC) 09333

Fédération interaméricaine de l'industrie de la construction – Inter-American Federation of the Construction Industry

Main Office Av Periférico Sur 4839, Tlalpan, 14010 Mexico City CDMX, Mexico. T. +5254247457 – +5254247458 – +5254247459. Fax +5256062786. E-mail: f.interamericana@fiic.lat.
URL: http://www.fiic.la/

History 6 Nov 1960, Mexico City (Mexico). Founded at 2nd Congress. By-laws amended 10-16 Sep 1962, Rio de Janeiro (Brazil). New statutes adopted, 9-11 Nov 1988, Santiago (Chile). **Aims** Promote development of the construction industry throughout the American continent; encourage cooperation among contractors and workers and advance their interests; further technical improvements and means of reducing costs; extend the use of private construction companies in public and private projects; contribute to solution of common problems. **Structure** Congress (every 2 years). Management Council (meets annually), consisting of 2 representatives from each member body. Executive Committee, consisting of President, 2 Vice-Presidents and Secretary-General. Secretariat General. Consultative Council of former Presidents of the Executive Council. **Languages** Spanish. **Finance** Members' dues. Percentage of Congress fees. **Activities** Approved and ratified the 'Conditions of Contract (International) for Works of Civil Engineering Construction', in collaboration with: *Associated General Contractors of America (AGC)*; *European Construction Industry Federation (#06766)*; *International Federation of Asian and Western Pacific Contractors' Associations (IFAWPCA, #13359)*; *International Road Federation (IRF Global, #14759)*. Arranges the compiling and exchange of background material, reports, data and technical studies. Organizes: Inter-American Congresses (every 2 years), Housing Congresses (every 4 years); Central American regional meetings (every year). **Events** *Biennial Inter-American Congress* Santiago (Chile) 2010, *Biennial congress / Biennial Inter-American Congress* Cartagena de Indias (Colombia) 2006, *Biennial congress / Biennial Inter-American Congress* San José (Costa Rica) 2004, *Biennial congress / Biennial Inter-American Congress* Mexico City (Mexico) 2003, *Biennial congress / Biennial Inter-American Congress* Panama (Panama) 2000. **Publications** *Boletin de la Federación Interamericana de la Industria de la Construcción* (12 a year).
Members National chambers of the construction industry (19) in 18 countries:
Argentina, Bolivia, Brazil (2), Chile, Colombia, Costa Rica, Dominican Rep, Ecuador, El Salvador, Guatemala, Honduras, Mexico, Nicaragua, Panama, Paraguay, Peru, Uruguay, Venezuela.
NGO Relations Member of: *Confederation of International Contractors Associations (CICA, #04558)*.
[2021/XD1132/t/D]

♦ Federación Interamericana de Instituciones de Crédito y Asesoria Municipal (inactive)
♦ Federación Interamericana de Mineros (inactive)
♦ Federación Interamericana de Sociedades de Autores y Compositores (inactive)
♦ Federación Interamericana de Touring y Automóvil Clubes / see Federación Internacional del Automóvil Region IV (#09337)
♦ Federación Interamericana de Trabajadores del Espectaculo (inactive)
♦ Federación Internacinal de Asociaciones Médicas de Terapia Neural (#13476)
♦ Federación Internacional de Abogadas (#13578)
♦ Federación Internacional – Acción de los Cristianos para la Abolición de la Tortura / see International Federation of ACATs – Action by Christians for the Abolition of Torture (#13334)
♦ Federación Internacional de Acción Familiar (inactive)
♦ Federación Internacional de las ACLI (#13336)
♦ Federación Internacional del Actividad Fisica Adaptada (#13338)
♦ Federación Internacional de Actores (#13337)

♦ Federación Internacional de Administradoras de Fondos de Pensiones (FIAP) 09334

International Federation of Pension Funds Administrators

Gen Sec Av Nueva Providencia 2155, Tower B /Floor 8 – Office 810, Providencia, Santiago, Santiago Metropolitan, Chile. T. +56223811723 ext 10. E-mail: fiap@fiap.cl.
URL: http://www.fiapinternacional.org/en/

History Montevideo (Uruguay). **Aims** Contribute to the improvement and strengthening of financially sustainable private pension systems; develop exchange of experiences between countries that have adopted pension systems based on privately managed individually-funded savings. **Structure** General Meeting (annual); Board of Directors; Executive Secretary. **Languages** English, Spanish. **Staff** 3.00 FTE, paid. **Finance** Subscriptions. **Activities** Events/meetings; research/documentation. **Events** *International Seminar* Madrid (Spain) 2021, *International Seminar* Santiago (Chile) 2019, *Annual Meeting* Poland 2009, *Annual assembly and seminar* Warsaw (Poland) 2009, *Annual assembly and seminar* Peru 2008. **Publications** *FIAP Informative Bulletin*; *Pension's Notes*; *Progress of the Pension Systems*. Annual Reports; statistics; studies; books.
Members Full: trade associations of pension fund managers in 12 countries:
Bolivia, Chile, Colombia, Costa Rica, Dominican Rep, El Salvador, Kazakhstan, Mexico, Peru, Spain, Ukraine, Uruguay.
Cooperation partners: companies providing services and products to the pension fund management industry in 5 countries:
Chile, Luxembourg, Spain, UK, USA.
IGO Relations *International Bank for Reconstruction and Development (IBRD, #12317)*; *International Monetary Fund (IMF, #14180)*; *OECD (#17693)*. **NGO Relations** Member of (1): *World Pension Alliance (WPA, #21719)*. Supports (1): *United Nations Environment Programme Finance Initiative (UNEP FI, #20559)*.
[2022/XJ3101/D]

♦ Federación Internacional de Aficionados de Rugby / see Rugby Europe (#18998)
♦ Federación Internacional de Agencias de Extractos de Periódicos (#09617)

♦ Federación Internacional de Ajedrez (#09627)
♦ Federación Internacional de Albergues de la Juventud / see Hostelling International (#10950)
♦ Federación Internacional Amateur de Sambo / see Fédération internationale de SAMBO (#09655)
♦ Federación Internacional de Antiguos Alumnos Iberoamericanos del INAP España (internationally oriented national body)
♦ Federación Internacional de Archivos Filmicos (#13427)
♦ Federación Internacional de Archivos de Imagenes en Movimiento / see International Federation of Film Archives (#13427)
♦ Federación Internacional de Archivos de Televisión / see International Federation of Television Archives (#13568)
♦ Federación Internacional de Arquitectos Paisajistas (#13467)
♦ Federación Internacional del Arte Fotografico (#13509)
♦ Federación Internacional de Asociaciones de Almacenistas de Aceros, Tubos y Metales (inactive)
♦ Federación Internacional de Asociaciones de Apicultura (#13370)

♦ Federación Internacional de Asociaciones de Ayuda Social, Ecológica y Cultural (FIADASEC) 09335

Fédération internationale d'associations d'aide social, écologique et culturelle – International Federation of Associations of Social, Ecological and Culture Aid – Federações de Ajuda Social, Ecológica e Cultural

Contact Calle Eduardo Vicioso 56, Ensanche Bella Vista, Santo Domingo, Dominican Rep. T. +18095355868 – +18092278067. Fax +18095350441. E-mail: irmgardradefeldt@gmail.com.
URL: http://www.fiadasec.org/

History 11 Dec 2003, Santo Domingo (Dominican Rep). Registered in accordance with the law of the Dominican Rep, 24 Feb 2004. **Aims** Help people increase their levels of *self-consciousness*. **Structure** General Assembly of member associations; General Assembly of National Executive Coordinators; International Presidency. **Languages** English, Portuguese, Spanish. **Staff** 11.00 FTE, paid; 1000.00 FTE, voluntary. **Activities** Training/education; events/meetings. **Publications** Magazine; books.
Members Full in 14 countries:
Argentina, Bolivia, Brazil, Colombia, Dominican Rep, Ecuador, El Salvador, Italy, Mexico, Peru, Puerto Rico, Spain, Uruguay, USA.
Consultative Status Consultative status granted from: *ECOSOC (#05331)* (Special).
[2015.07.05/XM3509/**D**]

♦ Federación Internacional de Asociaciones de Bibliotecarios y de Bibliotecas (#13470)
♦ Federación Internacional de Asociaciones Católicas de Ciegos (#13377)
♦ Federación Internacional de las Asociaciones de Directores del Trafico Aéreo (#13350)
♦ Federación Internacional de Asociaciones para la Educación de los Trabajadores (#13580)

♦ Federación Internacional de Asociaciones de Ejecutivas de Empresas Turisticas (FIASEET) 09336

Pres address not obtained. T. +51959295180. E-mail: presidencia@fiaseet.org – fiaseet@gmail.com.
Sec address not obtained. T. +56966742264. E-mail: secretaria@fiaseet.org.
URL: http://www.fiaseet.org/

History 1983, as *Federación Latinoamericana de las Feminas Ejecutivas de Empresas Turisticas (FLAFEET) – Federação Latinoamericana de Executivas de Empresas Turisticas*. Present name adopted 1999. **Aims** Make visible the important role women play as an engine of positive transformation of sustainable tourism. **Structure** General Assembly; Board of Directors. **Languages** English, Portuguese, Spanish. **Activities** Events/meetings. **Events** *International Congress* Ciudad del Este (Paraguay) 2019, *International congress* Barcelona (Spain) 2018, *International congress* Valencia (Spain) 2003, *International meeting of business and executive women of tourism / Meeting* Madrid (Spain) 1999.
Members in 7 countries:
Argentina, Brazil, Chile, Colombia, Paraguay, Peru, Spain.
NGO Relations Member of: *Federación Iberoamericana de Mujeres Empresarias (FIDE, #09316)*; Regional Action Group of the Americas for the Prevention of Sexual Exploitation of Girls, Children and Adolescents in Travel and Tourism (GARA).
[2020.03.10/XD2829/**D**]

♦ Federación Internacional de Asociaciones de Especialistas de la Seguridad e Higiene del Trabajo (no recent information)
♦ Federación Internacional de Asociaciones de Estudiantes de Medicina (#13478)
♦ Federación Internacional de Asociaciones de Ferreteros y Almacenistas de Hierros / see International Federation of Hardware and Housewares Associations (#13437)
♦ Federación Internacional de Asociaciones de Filatélicos (#13557)
♦ Federación Internacional de Asociaciones de Maestros (inactive)
♦ Federación Internacional de Asociaciones de la Margarina (inactive)
♦ Federación Internacional de Asociaciones Médicas Católicas (#13378)
♦ Federación Internacional de Asociaciones de Multimedia (#13483)
♦ Federación Internacional de Asociaciones Nacionales de Especialistas de Neumatico y Recauchutadores / see BIPAVER – European Retread Manufacturers Association (#03264)
♦ Federación Internacional de Asociaciones Nacionales de Estudiantes de Ingenieria (inactive)
♦ Federación Internacional de las Asociaciones de Personas de Edad / see Fédération internationale des associations de personnes âgées (#09609)
♦ Federación Internacional de Asociaciones de Personas Mayores (#09609)
♦ Federación Internacional de Asociaciones de Pilotos de Linea Aérea (#13349)
♦ Federación Internacional de Asociaciones de Productores Cinematograficos (#13429)
♦ Federación Internacional de las Asociaciones de Quimicos y Coloristas Textiles (#13365)
♦ Federación Internacional de Asociaciones Vexilológicas (#09611)
♦ Federación Internacional de Asociaciones de Viudos y Viudas (inactive)
♦ Federación Internacional Atletismo Aficionada / see World Athletics (#21209)
♦ Federación Internacional de Automatización (#13367)

♦ Federación Internacional del Automóvil Region IV 09337

Manager 5to piso, 1850 Avda del Libertador, C1425AAR Buenos Aires, Argentina. T. +541148024385. Fax +541148024385. E-mail: fiaregion4@fia.com.
URL: http://www.fiaregion4.com/

History 21 Sep 1941, Mexico City (Mexico). Founded under auspices of 2nd Inter-American Travel Congress and 4th Pan-American Highway Congress. Former names and other names: *Inter-American Federation of Automobile Clubs* – former; *Fédération interaméricaine des automobiles clubs* – former; *Federación Interamericana de Automóvil-Clubs (FIAC)* – former; *Federación Interamericana de Touring y Automóvil Clubes (FITAC)* – former; *Fédération interaméricaine de touring et des automobile-clubs* – former; *Inter-American Federation of Touring and Automobile Clubs* – former. **Aims** Ensure unity in automobile activities and protect the interests of *motorists* in member countries; facilitate automobile travel; provide uniform inter-American regulation of automobile sport; encourage organization of automobile *clubs* in countries where they do not exist; promote construction of highways and adequate road service; promote tourism, motoring and better road safety; promote interamerican reciprocal services. **Structure** General Assembly (annual); Executive Committee; Board of Directors. **Languages** English, Portuguese, Spanish. **Staff** 3.00 FTE, paid. **Finance** Quotas from member clubs. **Activities** Organizes meetings, workshops and seminars. Services to motorists include: provision of international documents (international driver's license, international motoring certificate, international presentation licence, safety identification stamps, international maps, etc); information about the mutual services between member clubs, road conditions, etc. **Events** *Inter-American Seminar* Lima (Peru) 2013, *Inter-American Seminar* Lima (Peru) 2012, *Inter-American Seminar* Lima (Peru) 2011, *Inter-American Seminar* Lima (Peru) 2010, *Inter-American Seminar* Lima (Peru) 2009. **Publications** Online newsletter. Apps.
Members Travel and automobile clubs in 19 countries:
Argentina (2), Bolivia, Brazil, Canada, Chile, Colombia, Costa Rica, Ecuador, El Salvador, Italy, Mexico, Nicaragua, Paraguay, Peru, Portugal, Spain, Uruguay, USA, Venezuela.
Consultative Status Consultative status granted from: *OAS (#17629)*. **NGO Relations** *Fédération Internationale de l'Automobile (FIA, #09613)*.
[2020/XD1078/**D**]

♦ Federación Internacional para los Barcos de Salvamento / see International Maritime Rescue Federation (#14104)
♦ Federación Internacional de Béisbol (inactive)
♦ Federación Internacional de Béisbol Amateur (inactive)
♦ Federación Internacional de Biologia Celular (#13382)
♦ Federación Internacional de Bobsleigh y Toboganing / see International Bobsleigh and Skeleton Federation (#12375)
♦ Federación Internacional de Camping, Caravaning y Autocaravaning (#09618)
♦ Federación Internacional de Camping y Caravanning / see Fédération Internationale de Camping, Caravanning et Autocaravaning (#09618)
♦ Federación Internacional de Carreteras (#14758)
♦ Federación Internacional de Centros CICOP / see Federation of International Centres for the Preservation of the Architectural Heritage (#09602)
♦ Federación Internacional de Centros para la Conservación del Patrimonio (#09602)
♦ Federación Internacional de Centros Sociales y Centros Vécinales (#13538)
♦ Federación Internacional de Centros Turisticos (inactive)
♦ Federación Internacional de Ciegos (inactive)
♦ Federación Internacional de Cine Super 8 (inactive)
♦ Federación Internacional de Coaliciones para la Diversidad Cultural (#13394)
♦ Federación Internacional de Colegios de Cirurgia (#13560)
♦ Federación Internacional del Comercio del Cacao (inactive)
♦ Federación Internacional de Compras (inactive)
♦ Federación Internacional de Compras y Dirección de Materiales / see International Federation of Purchasing and Supply Management (#13525)
♦ Federación Internacional de Comunidades Infantiles / see Fédération internationale des communautés éducatives (#09622)
♦ Federación Internacional de las Comunidades de Juventud Católica Parroquial / see International Federation of Catholic Parochial Youth Movements (#13379)
♦ Federación Internacional de Consejos de Artes y Agencias Culturales (#13358)
♦ Federación Internacional de Cooperativas y Mutuales de Seguros (#12948)
♦ Federación Internacional de Cooperativas y Mutuales de Seguros / Asociación Regional para Las Américas (#12949)
♦ Federación Internacional de Deportes para Ciegos (#12363)
♦ Federación Internacional de Deportes para Minusvalidos (inactive)
♦ Federación Internacional de Deportes para Personas con Deficiencias Mentales / see Virtus: World Intellectual Impairment Sport (#20793)
♦ Federación Internacional de Deportes para Personas con Discapacidad Intelectual / see Virtus: World Intellectual Impairment Sport (#20793)
♦ Federación Internacional del Deporte Universitario (#15830)
♦ Federación Internacional por los Derechos Humanos (#13452)
♦ Federación Internacional del Derecho a la Vida (#14755)
♦ Federación Internacional de Diabetes (#13164)
♦ Federación Internacional de Directores de Publicidad (inactive)
♦ Federación Internacional de Doctores Ingenieros y de Ingenieros Doctores-ès-Scientiae (inactive)
♦ Federación Internacional para la Economia Familiar / see International Federation for Home Economics (#13447)
♦ Federación Internacional de Educación Fìsica / see International Federation of Physical and Sport Education (#13510)
♦ Federación Internacional de Educación Física e Sportiva (#13510)
♦ Federación Internacional para Educación de Padres (#13499)
♦ Federación Internacional de Empleados, Técnicos y Profesionales (inactive)
♦ Federación Internacional de Empleados, Técnicos y Profesionales (#20340)
♦ Federación Internacional de Empresarios de Limpieza (#09628)
♦ Federación Internacional de Enfermeros Anestesistas (#13492)
♦ Federación Internacional de Epidemiologia Psiquiatrica (#13521)
♦ Federación Internacional de Esclerosis Múltiple (#16899)
♦ Federación Internacional de las Escuelas Unidas (#20660)
♦ Federación Internacional de Esqui / see Fédération Internationale de Ski (#09659)
♦ Federación Internacional de Estudiantes de Farmacia (#14568)

♦ Federación Internacional de Estudios sobre América Latina y el Caribe (FIEALC) 09338

International Federation for Latin American and Caribbean Studies – Fédération internationale d'études pour l'Amérique latine et les Caraïbes

Contact c/o CIALC, Piso 8, Torre II de Humanidades, Ciudad Universitaria, 04510 Mexico City CDMX, Mexico. E-mail: ruizg@unam.mx.
Pres address not obtained.
URL: http://www.cialc.unam.mx/fiealc/

History Nov 1978, Mexico City (Mexico). Founded on the initiative of 1st 'Simposio para la Coordinación y Difusión de los Estudios Latinoamericanos'. Statutes approved at 2nd Symposium, 6-7 Jun 1980, Caracas (Venezuela). *Centro de Investigaciones sobre América y el Caribe (CIALC, #03810)* and *Programa Universitario de Difusión de Estudios Latinoamericanos (PUDEL, no recent information)*, both created by the Universidad Nacional Autónoma de México (UNAM), coordinate activities of FIEALC and of *Sociedad Latinoamericana de Estudios sobre América Latina y el Caribe (SOLAR, #19406)*. Former names and other names: *Asociación Internacional de Estudios Latinoamericanos y del Caribe* – alias. **Aims** Promote exchange of knowledge and ideas regarding Latinamerican studies among scholars and research institutes; encourage interdisciplinary approaches with respect for the work of each participant; collaborate on creation of libraries and specialized information centers on Latinamerican studies. **Structure** Executive Committee; General Coordination; Consultative Assembly. **Languages** English, French, Portuguese, Spanish. **Finance** Supported by the Universidad Nacional Autónoma de México (UNAM). **Events** *Congress* Szeged (Hungary) 2019, *Congress* Belgrade (Serbia) 2017, *Congress* Busan (Korea Rep) 2015, *Congress* Antalya (Turkey) 2013, *International Conference on the Identities of Latin American Societies and Integral Globalization* Busan (Korea Rep) 2013.
Members Institutions (113) in 25 countries:
Belgium, Canada, China, Côte d'Ivoire, Denmark, France, Germany, Hungary, India, Israel, Italy, Japan, Korea Rep, Morocco, Netherlands, Poland, Portugal, Russia, Serbia, South Africa, Spain, Sweden, Switzerland, UK, USA.
Of the above-mentioned 113 affiliates, 71 organizations listed in this Yearbook:
– *Asociación Complutense de Investigaciones Socioeconómicas sobre América Latina (ACISAL, no recent information)*;
– *Asociación Coreana de Estudios Latinoamericanos, Seoul (LASAK)*;
– *Asociación de Investigación y Especialización sobre Temas Iberoamericanos (AIETI)*;
– *Asociación pro Potenciación de las Relaciones entre España e Iberoamérica (APREI, no recent information)*;
– *Association française des sciences sociales sur l'Amérique latine (AFSSAL, no recent information)*;
– *Association of Historians of Latin America and the Caribbean (#02632)*;
– *Busan University of Foreign Studies*;
– *Canada-Americas Policy Alternatives (CAPA, inactive)*;
– *Canadian Association for Latin American and Caribbean Studies (CALACS)*;
– *Center for Latin American and Caribbean Studies, Champaign*;
– *Center for Latin American Studies, Gainesville (CLAS)*;
– *Center for Latin American Studies, San Diego CA*;
– *Center for Latin American Studies, Stanford CA (CLAS, Stanford CA)*;
– *Center for Latin American Studies, Tempe AZ*;
– *Center of Latin American Affairs, Louisiana (no recent information)*;
– *Center of Latin American Studies, University of Kansas*;
– *Centre de recherches latino-américaines, Nanterre (no recent information)*;
– *Centre d'études et de recherches sur la coopération internationale (CERCI)*;
– *Centre for Cooperative and Labour Studies Abraham Alon (inactive)*;
– *Centre for International Information and Documentation, Barcelona (CIDOB Foundation)*;
– *Centre for Latin American Studies, Nagoya (no recent information)*;

Federación Internacional Estudios
09338

alphabetic sequence excludes
For the complete listing, see Yearbook Online at

- *Centro de Estudios Latinoamericanos, Lisboa (no recent information);*
- *Centro de Estudios Latinoamericanos, Tel Aviv (no recent information);*
- *Centro de Estudios Latinoamericanos, Tokyo (no recent information);*
- *Centro de Estudios Latinoamericanos, Uppsala (no recent information);*
- *Centro de Investigación y Promoción Iberoamérica-Europa (CIPIE, no recent information);*
- *Centro Español de Estudios de América Latina, Madrid (CEDEAL, no recent information);*
- *Centro Extremeño de Estudios y Cooperación con Iberoamérica (CEXECI);*
- *Centro Studi Terzo Mondo (CSTM);*
- *Collège international de philosophie, Paris (CIPh);*
- *Consejo Europeo de Investigaciones Sociales de América Latina (CEISAL, #04710);*
- *Dirección General de Cooperación con Iberoamérica* (Centro de Altos Estudios Hispanicos);
- *Escuela de Estudios Hispano-Americanos, Sevilla;*
- *Florida International University (FIU);*
- *Forum F I (no recent information);*
- *Fundación CIDEAL de Cooperación e Investigación;*
- *Groupe d'études latino-américaines de l'Institut de sociologie, Bruxelles (GELA-IS);*
- *History World Institute, Beijing (no recent information);*
- *Ibero-America Institute for Economic Research of the University of Göttingen (IAI);*
- *Ibero-Amerikanisches Institut Preussischer Kulturbesitz (IAI);*
- *Institut Català de Cooperació Iberoamericana (ICCI);*
- *Institut d'études ibériques et ibéroaméricaines, Talence (no recent information);*
- *Institute for Development and International Relations (IRMO);*
- *Institute for Latin American Research and for Development Cooperation (no recent information);*
- *Institute for the Study of Human Issues (ISHI, no recent information);*
- *Institute for the Study of the Americas (ISA);*
- *Institute for World Economics of the Hungarian Academy of Sciences (IWE);*
- *Institute of Iberoamerican Thought, Salamanca;*
- *Institute of Latin American Studies, Chapel Hill NC;*
- *Institute of Latin-American Studies, Glasgow (no recent information);*
- *Institute of Latin America of the Russian Academy of Sciences (ILA);*
- *Institut für Lateinamerika-Studies (ILAS);*
- *Institut Mirovoj Ekonomiki i Mezdunarodnyh Otnosenij Rossijskoj Akademii Nauk (IMEMO);*
- *Instituto de América Latina de la Universidad de Szeged (no recent information);*
- *Instituto de Estudios Latinoamericanos, Lisboa (IELA, no recent information);*
- *Instituto de Estudios Politicos para América Latina y Africa (IEPALA);*
- *Instituto Intercultural para la Autogestión y la Acción Comunal (INAUCO, #11335);*
- *Institut Pluridisciplinaire pour les Études sur les Amériques à Toulouse (IPEAT);*
- *Istituto per le Relazioni tra Italia ed i Paesi dell'Africa, America Latina e Medio Oriente (IPALMO, no recent information);*
- *Latin American Research Group (no recent information);*
- *Latin American Society of Japan (LASJ);*
- *Latin American Studies Association (LASA, #16388);*
- *Nordic Institute of Latin American Studies (NILAS);*
- *OAS (#17629)* (Department of Cultural Affairs);
- *Research Institute for Developing Economies, Warsaw (RIDE, no recent information);*
- *School of International Studies, Delhi* (Latin American Studies Division);
- *Society for Iberian and Latin American Thought, Washington (SILAT, no recent information);*
- *Teresa Lozano Long Institute of Latin American Studies, Austin (LLILAS);*
- *Unisa Centre for Latin American Studies (UCLAS).* [2020.07.01/XD4035/y/**D**]

- ♦ Federación Internacional Farmacéutica (#14566)
- ♦ Federación Internacional de Farmacéuticos Católicos (#13380)
- ♦ Federación Internacional de Fe y Alegria (#13425)
- ♦ Federación Internacional de Filatelia (#09650)
- ♦ Federación Internacional de los Funcionarios Superiores de Policia (no recent information)
- ♦ Federación Internacional de Fútbol Asociación (#13360)
- ♦ Federación Internacional de Fútbol de Salón (inactive)
- ♦ Federación Internacional de Gimnasia (#09636)
- ♦ Federación Internacional de Ginecologia y Obstetricia (#09638)
- ♦ Federación Internacional de Guardaparques (#14697)
- ♦ Federación Internacional de Halterofilia (#15876)
- ♦ Federación Internacional de los Hombres Católicos (#20720)
- ♦ Federación Internacional de Hospitales / see International Hospital Federation (#13812)
- ♦ El Federación Internacional de la Iglesias Evangelicas Libres (#13433)
- ♦ Federación Internacional de la Industria Fonografica (#13508)
- ♦ Federación Internacional de la Industria del Medicamento / see International Federation of Pharmaceutical Manufacturers and Associations (#13505)
- ♦ Federación Internacional de Ingenieria y Arquitectura Hospitalaria (#13439)
- ♦ Federación Internacional de Ingenieria Médica y Biológica (#13477)
- ♦ Federación Internacional de Ingenieros Municipales / see International Federation of Municipal Engineering (#13484)
- ♦ Federación Internacional de Ingenieros en Técnicas Automotrices (#13369)
- ♦ Federación Internacional de Instituciones para la Enseñanza del Español (inactive)
- ♦ Federación Internacional de Institutos para Estudios Avanzados (inactive)
- ♦ Federación Internacional de los Institutos de Investigaciones Socio-Religiosas (inactive)
- ♦ Federación Internacional de Judo (#13975)
- ♦ Federación Internacional de la Juventud (#15932)
- ♦ Federación Internacional de la Juventud Católica (inactive)
- ♦ Federación Internacional de las Juventudes Liberales (#13469)
- ♦ Federación Internacional de las Juventudes Liberales y Radicales / see International Federation of Liberal Youth (#13469)
- ♦ Federación Internacional de Lecheria (#13128)
- ♦ Federación Internacional de Ligas y Asociaciones Maritimas y Navales (#13474)
- ♦ Federación Internacional de las Ligas de los Derechos Humanos / see International Federation for Human Rights (#13452)
- ♦ Federación Internacional de Marketing (#14106)

♦ Federación Internacional de Maxibasquetbol (FIMBA) 09339

International Maxibasketball Federation

SG Larrea 527, Piso 4to, Dto H, C1030AAA Buenos Aires, Argentina. T. +541149612925. Fax +541196129254. E-mail: fimba@fimba.net.
URL: http://www.fimba.net/

History 21 Aug 1991, Buenos Aires (Argentina). **Aims** Promote, sponsor, foment, develop, organize, lead and control the maxibasketball category, attending to *basketball* Olympic rules and international *regulations*. **Structure** Board of Directors, including President, Vice-President and Secretary. Regions (3): America; Europe; Central Caribbean. **Languages** English, Spanish. **Staff** Secretariat: 3 FTE, paid; 2.5 FTE, voluntary. Worldwide: 1 FTE, paid; 2 FTE, voluntary. **Finance** Percentage of every championship. Annual budget: 50,000 USD. **Activities** Events/meetings; sporting activities. **Events** *Second age and maxisport* Buenos Aires (Argentina) 2006, *Congress* Buenos Aires (Argentina) 2005. **Publications** *Overtime* – magazine. Books.

Members Full in 48 countries:
Argentina, Austria, Belarus, Bosnia-Herzegovina, Brazil, Canada, Chile, Colombia, Costa Rica, Croatia, Cuba, Czechia, Dominican Rep, Ecuador, El Salvador, Estonia, Finland, France, Germany, Greece, Guatemala, Honduras, India, Ireland, Israel, Italy, Latvia, Lithuania, Moldova, Montenegro, New Zealand, Nicaragua, North Macedonia, Panama, Peru, Poland, Puerto Rico, Russia, Serbia, Slovakia, Slovenia, Spain, Sweden, Switzerland, Ukraine, Uruguay, USA, Venezuela.
Organizations applying for membership in 8 countries:
Bolivia, China, Japan, Jordan, Paraguay, Türkiye. [2021.09.02/XD8815/**C**]

- ♦ Federación Internacional Médica de Ozono (#14136)
- ♦ Federación Internacional de Medicina Fisica y Rehabilitación (inactive)
- ♦ Federación Internacional de Mineros (inactive)
- ♦ Federación Internacional de Motonautica (#20431)
- ♦ Federación Internacional de Movimientos de Adultos Rurales Católicos (#13535)
- ♦ Federación Internacional de los Movimientos de Agricultura Biológica / see IFOAM – Organics International (#11105)
- ♦ Federación Internacional de Mujeres Juristas (#13579)
- ♦ Federación Internacional de Mujeres de Negocios y Profesionales (#13376)
- ♦ Federación Internacional de Mujeres Universitarias / see Graduate Women International (#10688)
- ♦ Federación Internacional para la Música Coral (#13388)
- ♦ Federación Internacional de Músicos (#13486)
- ♦ Federación Internacional de Mutilados, de Invalidos de Trabajo y de Invalidos Civiles / see International Federation of Persons with Physical Disability (#13504)
- ♦ Federación Internacional de Obreros del Calzado, Cueros y Similares (inactive)
- ♦ Federación Internacional de Oleicultura (inactive)
- ♦ Federación Internacional de Organizaciones de Correspondencia e Intercambios Escolares (inactive)
- ♦ Federación Internacional de las Organizaciones de Donadores de Sangre (#13374)
- ♦ Federación Internacional de Organizaciones de Registros Sanitarios / see International Federation of Health Information Management Associations (#13441)
- ♦ Federación Internacional de Organizaciones de Turismo Social (inactive)
- ♦ Federación Internacional de Organizadores de Salones Naúticos (#13375)
- ♦ Federación Internacional de Orientación (#14485)
- ♦ Federación Internacional para la Orientación Familiar (#13423)
- ♦ Federación Internacional de Pádel (#14496)
- ♦ Federación Internacional de Patinaje sobre Ruedas / see World Skate (#21786)
- ♦ Federación Internacional de Patologia Cervical y Colposcopia (#13385)

♦ Federación Internacional de Pelota Vasca (FIPV) 09340

Fédération internationale de pelote basque – International Federation of Pelota Vasca

Contact Pabellón ARENA, Casa del deporte Plaza Aizagerria, 31006 Pamplona, Navarre, Spain. T. +948164080. Fax +948162525. E-mail: info@fipv.net.
Pres address not obtained.
URL: https://fipv.net/

History May 1929, Buenos Aires (Argentina). **Aims** Promote and spread knowledge of pelota vasca; organize its international rules and international *tournaments* and championships. **Structure** General Assembly (every 2 years at World Championship); Executive Committee. **Languages** English, French, Spanish. **Activities** Sporting activities. **Events** *General Assembly and World Championship* Tarbes (France) 2012, *Biennial general assembly / General Assembly and World Championship* Pau (France) 2010, *Biennial general assembly / General Assembly and World Championship* Rosario (Argentina) 2008, *Biennial general assembly / General Assembly and World Championship* Mexico 2006, *Biennial general assembly / General Assembly and World Championship* Pamplona (Spain) 2002. **Publications** *Manual de Cesta Punta* (1996) by Gonzalo Beaskoetxea; *La Pelota Vasca en Cuba – Su Evolución hasta 1930* (1990) by Antonio Méndez Muñiz; *Pelota Vasca en Cuba – 1930-1960* by Antonio Méndez Muñiz.

Members Affiliates in 30 countries:
Argentina, Belgium, Bolivia, Brazil, Canada, Chile, Colombia, Costa Rica, Cuba, Dominican Rep, Ecuador, France, Greece, Guatemala, India, Italy, Mexico, Morocco, Netherlands, Nicaragua, Panama, Paraguay, Peru, Philippines, Puerto Rico, South Africa, Spain, Uruguay, USA, Venezuela.

NGO Relations Member of (2): *Association of the IOC Recognized International Sports Federations (ARISF, #02767); Olympic Movement (#17719).* Recognized International Federation member of: *International Olympic Committee (IOC, #14408).* [2022/XD1974/**D**]

- ♦ Federación Internacional de PEN Clubs / see International PEN (#14552)
- ♦ Federación Internacional de Periodistas (#13462)
- ♦ Federación Internacional de Periodistas Libres (inactive)
- ♦ Federación Internacional del Personal de los Servicios Públicos (#13410)
- ♦ Federación Internacional de Personas con Discapacidad Fisica (#13504)
- ♦ Federación Internacional de Planificación de la Familia (#14589)
- ♦ Federación Internacional de Podologos y Podiatras / see International Federation of Podiatrists (#13514)
- ♦ Federación Internacional de Polo (#09675)
- ♦ Federación Internacional de la Prensa Periódica / see FIPP (#09776)
- ♦ Federación Internacional de la Prensa Técnica (inactive)
- ♦ Federación Internacional de Productores Agropecuarios (inactive)
- ♦ Federación Internacional de Productores de Fonogramas y Videogramas / see International Federation of the Phonographic Industry (#13508)
- ♦ Federación Internacional de los Productores de Jugos de Frutas / see International Fruit and Vegetable Juice Association (#13687)
- ♦ Federación Internacional de Profesiones Inmobiliarias (#09653)
- ♦ Federación Internacional de Profesores de Francés (#09652)
- ♦ Federación Internacional de Profesores de Lenguas Vivas (#13468)
- ♦ Federación Internacional de Psicoterapia (#13523)
- ♦ Federación Internacional de Psicoterapia Médica / see International Federation for Psychotherapy (#13523)
- ♦ Federación Internacional de Química Clínica (#13392)
- ♦ Federación Internacional de Reproducción Sonora (inactive)
- ♦ Federación Internacional de Resistentes (#13529)
- ♦ Federación Internacional de Sacerdotes Católicos Casados (inactive)
- ♦ Federación Internacional de Salvamento Acuatico – Región de las Américas (#14041)
- ♦ Federación Internacional para Salvamento Maritimo (#14104)
- ♦ Federación Internacional de SAMBO (#09655)
- ♦ Federacion Internacional para la Seguridad de los Usuarios de la Electricidad (#09658)
- ♦ Federación Internacional de Seguros Cooperativos / see International Cooperative and Mutual Insurance Federation (#12948)
- ♦ Federación Internacional de Servicios Telefónicos de Emergencia (#13567)
- ♦ Federación Internacional Sindical de la Enseñanza (#09662)
- ♦ Federación Internacional de Sindicatos Cristianos de Mineros (inactive)
- ♦ Federación Internacional de Sindicatos del Personal del Transporte (inactive)
- ♦ Federación Internacional de Sociedades Aerofilatélicas (#13342)
- ♦ Federación Internacional de Sociedades de la Cruz Roja y de la Media Luna Roja (#13526)
- ♦ Federación Internacional de las Sociedades de Fertilidad (#13426)
- ♦ Federación Internacional de Sociedades de Filosofia (#13507)
- ♦ Federación Internacional de Sociedades e Institutos del Renacimiento (#13549)
- ♦ Federación Internacional de Sociedades de Investigaciones Operacionales (#13493)
- ♦ Federación Internacional de Sociedades Magicas (#13473)
- ♦ Federación Internacional de Sociedades de Microscopia Electrónica (#13550)
- ♦ Federación Internacional de Sociedades de Oftalmologia (inactive)
- ♦ Federación Internacional de Sociedades Psicoanaliticas (#13522)
- ♦ Federación Internacional de Softbol (inactive)
- ♦ Federación Internacional de Taekwon-do Tradicional (#15712)
- ♦ Federación Internacional de Taquigrafia y Dactilografia / see Fédération internationale pour le traitement de l'information et de la communication (#09667)
- ♦ Federación Internacional de Tenis (#15676)
- ♦ Federación Internacional de Tenis de Mesa (#15650)
- ♦ Federación Internacional Textil y Vestido (inactive)
- ♦ Federación Internacional de Tiro Deportivo (#14852)
- ♦ Federación Internacional de Trabajadores de la Construcción y la Madera (inactive)
- ♦ Federación Internacional de Trabajadores de las Industrias Metalúrgicas (inactive)
- ♦ Federación Internacional de Trabajadores Petroleros y Quimicos (inactive)
- ♦ Federación Internacional de los Trabajadores de las Plantaciones, Agricolas y Similares (inactive)
- ♦ Federación Internacional de Trabajadores de la Quimica, Energia e Industrias Diversas (inactive)
- ♦ Federación Internacional de Trabajadores Sociales (#13544)

♦ Federación Internacional de Trabajadores del Textil, Vestuario y Cuero (inactive)
♦ Federación Internacional de los Trabajadores del Transporte (#15726)
♦ Federación Internacional de Transportes Aéreos Privados (inactive)
♦ Federación Internacional para el Tratamiento de la Información (#13458)
♦ Federación Internacional de Universidades Católicas (#13381)
♦ Federación Internacional de la Vejez (#13345)
♦ Federación Internacional de Vinos y Espirituosos / see FIVS (#09789)
♦ Federación Internacional de Vinos y Licores / see FIVS (#09789)
♦ Federación Internacional de Vivienda y Urbanismo (#13450)
♦ Federación Internacional de Vóleibol (#09670)
♦ Federación Internacional de Yoga (#15923)
♦ Federación International de Ingenieros Consultores (#13399)
♦ Federación Islamica Internacional de Organizaciones de Estudiantes (inactive)
♦ Federación de la Juventud Latinoamericana para Estudios sobre el Ambiente Humano (inactive)

♦ Federación de Latinoamérica y el Caribe para Internet y el Comercio Electrónico (ECOM-LAC) 09341

Latin American and Caribbean Federation for Internet and Electronic Commerce – Federação Latinoamericana e Caribenha de Comerço Eletrônico e Internet

Contact Rambla Rep de México 6125, 11500 Montevideo, Uruguay. T. +59826042222. Fax +59826042222.
URL: http://ecomlac.lat/

History Mar 1999, Rio de Janeiro (Brazil). **Aims** Promote development of ICTs in Latin America and Caribbean; support initiatives to reduce the digital divide in the region; represent the private sector in international forums. **Languages** English, Portuguese, Spanish. **Staff** 2.00 FTE, paid. **Finance** Sources: members' dues.
Members Associations in 6 countries:
Argentina, Brazil, Ecuador, Mexico, Peru, Uruguay.
NGO Relations Cooperation agreement with: *Asia and Pacific Internet Association (APIA, #01936).*
[2021.02.22/XD9409/**D**]

♦ Federación Latinoamericana de Administradores de la Salud (unconfirmed)
♦ Federación Latino Americana de Analisis Bioenergético (internationally oriented national body)

♦ Federación Latinoamericana de Apicultura (FILAPI) 09342

Pres c/o RNA-Chile, Anibal Pinto 450, Local 7, Galeria Alessandri, Concepción, Bio Bío, Chile. E-mail: filapifg@gmail.com – misaelcuevas@vtr.net.
URL: http://www.filapi.org/

History Founded 12 Jul 2008, Chile. **Aims** Strengthen the development of Latin American beekeeping and the integration of its trade and productive institutions. **Structure** Executive Council; Secretariat. **Activities** Events/meetings. **Events** *Un planeta saludable con abejas* Concepción (Chile) 2020, *Congreso* Montevideo (Uruguay) 2018, *Congress* Puerto Iguazú (Argentina) 2014. **Publications** *FILAPI Newsletter.*
Members Full in 8 countries:
Argentina, Brazil, Chile, Cuba, Mexico, Peru, Uruguay, Venezuela. [2020.01.15/XJ8970/**D**]

♦ Federación Latinoamericana de Artes Marciales Mixtas (unconfirmed)
♦ Federación Latinoamericana de Asociaciones de Consultores / see Federación Panamericana de Consultores (#09379)
♦ Federación Latinoamericana de Asociaciones de Empresas Biotecnológia (unconfirmed)

♦ Federación Latinoamericana de Asociaciones para el Estudio del Dolor (FEDELAT) 09343

Federation of Latin American Associations for the Study of Pain

Sec c/o INNSZ, Av Vasco de Quiroga 15, Col Belisario Dominguez, Sección XVI, Del Tlalpan, 14080 Mexico City CDMX, Mexico.
URL: http://www.fedelat.com/

History 12 Oct 1992, Cartagena de Indias (Colombia), within *International Association for the Study of Pain (IASP, #12206).* **Aims** Promote active collaboration among Latin-American IASP Chapters. **Structure** Committees (6): Education; Finance; Health Politics; International Relations; Publications; Scientific Information. **Languages** English, Portuguese, Spanish. **Staff** 5.00 FTE, paid. **Activities** Training/education; events/meetings. **Events** *Ibero-American Congress* Mexico City (Mexico) 2019, *Latin American Pain Congress* Mexico City (Mexico) 2019, *Ibero-American Congress* Lisbon (Portugal) 2018, *Latin American Pain Congress* Santa Cruz (Bolivia) 2017, *Latin American Pain Congress* San José (Costa Rica) 2016.
Members National organizations (20) in 20 countries:
Argentina, Bolivia, Brazil, Chile, Colombia, Costa Rica, Cuba, Dominican Rep, Ecuador, El Salvador, Guatemala, Honduras, Mexico, Nicaragua, Panama, Paraguay, Peru, Puerto Rico, Uruguay, Venezuela. [2017.07.12/XM0635/**D**]

♦ Federación Latinoamericana de Asociaciones de Facultades de Comunicación Social / see Federación Latinoamericana de Facultades de Comunicación Social (#09353)

♦ Federación Latinoamericana de Asociaciones de Familiares de Detenidos-Desaparecidos (FEDEFAM) 09344

Fédération latinoaméricaine des associations des familles des détenus disparus – Latin American Federation of Associations for Relatives of the Detained and Disappeared

Exec Sec address not obtained. E-mail: fedefam2018@gmail.com.
URL: http://www.desaparecidos.org/fedefam/

History 23 Jan 1981, San José (Costa Rica). Registered legally in Venezuela, 6 Dec 1982. **Aims** Fight against the forced disappearance in Latin America and the Caribbean through denunciation of this misdemeanour, the clarification of the truth about the facts, the judgement and sanction of those responsible for the crime, the promotion of national and international legal norms which prevent the impunity and the education in the field of the human rights so that such facts occur never again. **Structure** Congress (every 2 years). Board of Directors (meets annually), consisting of Executive Committee (5 members) and one delegate for each member country. Officers: President; Secretary of Finances; Executive Secretary; 3 untitled. Support Groups, primarily in Europe and North America. **Languages** English, French, Portuguese, Spanish. **Staff** 2.50 FTE, paid. **Finance** Sources: international aid agencies; churches; members; solidarity activities. Budget (annual): about US$ 100,000. **Activities** Advocacy/lobbying/activism; financial and/or material support. **Events** *Congress* La Paz (Bolivia) 2001, *Congress* Mar del Plata (Argentina) 1999, *Human rights and impunity* Santiago (Chile) 1999, *Congress* Mexico 1997, *Congress* Mexico City (Mexico) 1997. **Publications** *Hasta Encontrarlos* (6 a year); *Memoria de Congreso* (every 2 years). Country reports; campaign materials; special pamphlets.
Members Local committees and associations of relatives of disappeared persons in 14 countries:
Argentina, Bolivia, Brazil, Chile, Colombia, Ecuador, El Salvador, Guatemala, Honduras, Mexico, Nicaragua, Paraguay, Peru, Uruguay.
Support groups in 5 countries:
Belgium, Germany, Netherlands, UK, USA.
Consultative Status Consultative status granted from: *ECOSOC (#05331)* (Special). **NGO Relations** Member of: *International Coalition against Enforced Disappearances (ICAED, #12605); World Organisation Against Torture (OMCT, #21685).* Member the Steering Committee of: *Coalition of NGOs Concerned with Impunity for Violators of Human Rights (no recent information).* Special links with: *Fundación Latinoamericana por los Derechos Humanos y el Desarrollo Social (FUNDALATIN, #10036).* [2018/XD0354/**D**]

♦ Federacion Latinoamericana de Asociaciones de Medicina Perinatal (FLAMP) 09345

Latin American Federation of Perinatology

Contact Kennedy Norte, Calle José Alavedra y Av. Francisco de Orellana, Guayaquil, Ecuador. E-mail: flampcursos@gmail.com.
Facebook: https://www.facebook.com/flamp.medicinaperinatal.9/

History 1980. **Events** *Congress* Santo Domingo (Dominican Rep) 2022. **Publications** *Revista Latinoamericana de Perinatología.* [2022/AA1906/**D**]

♦ Federación Latinoamericana de Asociaciones Quimicas (#16320)
♦ Federación Latinoamericana de Asociaciones de Semillas (#16330)

♦ Federación Latinoamericana de Asociaciones de Técnicos y Fabricantes de Pinturas y Tintas (LATINPIN) 09346

Secretariat Av Dr Cardoso de Melo 1340, Sao Paulo SP, 04548-004, Brazil. T. +551140830500. E-mail: secretariado@latinpin.com.
URL: http://www.latinpin.com/

History 28 May 2014, Buenos Aires (Argentina). Conceived 2013, at meeting of Asociación Brasileña de Fabricantes de Tintas (ABRAFATI). **Aims** Promote development of the productive chain of the sector of *paints, varnishes, inks* and *coatings* in Latin America. **Structure** Executive.
Members Full in 7 countries:
Argentina, Bolivia, Brazil, Colombia, Ecuador, Mexico, Uruguay. [2023.02.17/XM7662/**D**]

♦ Federación Latinoamericana de Auditores Internos / see Fundación Latinoamericana de Auditores Internos (#10035)
♦ Federación Latinoamericana de Autismo (inactive)
♦ Federación Latinoamericana de Bancos (#16254)
♦ Federación Latino Americana de Bonsai / see Latin American and Caribbean Bonsai Federation (#16266)
♦ Federación Latinoamericana de Boxeo (#16259)

♦ Federación Latinoamericana de Carbono (FLC) 09347

Latin American Carbon Federation

Contact address not obtained.
URL: http://fedlatcarbono.org/

History 2013. **Structure** Board of Directors. **Activities** Events/meetings.
Members Full in 6 countries:
Argentina, Brazil, Chile, Colombia, Mexico, Uruguay. [2020/AA1167/**D**]

♦ Federación Latinoamericana y del Caribe de Asociaciones de Exportadores (inactive)
♦ Federación Latinoamericana y del Caribe de Colegios Jesuitas e Ignacianos / see Latin American Federation of Jesuit Schools (#16323)

♦ Federación Latinoamericana y del Caribe de Instituciones de Bioética (FELAIBE) 09348

Latin American and Caribbean Federation of Bioethics Institutions

Pres address not obtained. T. +5689839111. E-mail: gibioetica@vtr.net.
URL: http://www.bioeticachile.cl/felaibe/

History 1991, Caracas (Venezuela). Previously referred to as *Federación Latinoamericana de Instituciones de Bioética.* **Events** *Congress* San Juan (Puerto Rico) 2019, *Congress* Buenos Aires (Argentina) 2017, *Congress* San José (Costa Rica) 2015, *Congress* Guanajuato (Mexico) 2013, *Congress* Viña del Mar (Chile) 2011.
[2017/XD8176/**D**]

♦ Federación Latinoamericana y Caribeña de Bonsai (#16266)
♦ Federación Latinoamericana y del Caribe de Trabajadores de la Hoteleria, Gastronomia, Casino y Turismo (inactive)

♦ Federación Latinoamericana de Cirurgia (FELAC) 09349

Federation of Latin American Surgeons

Pres Elect Calz General Anaya 330, Col Carmen, 04100 Coyoacan CHIS, Mexico. T. +525556582263 – +525556586133. Fax +525556582193. E-mail: samuelshuchleib@yahoo.com.mx.
URL: http://www.felacred.org/

History 19 Jul 1973, Rio de Janeiro (Brazil). **Aims** Promote best practice of surgery among Latin American surgeons. **Structure** President; Executive Director; Secretary. **Languages** Spanish. **Finance** Members' dues. **Activities** Events/meetings; training/education. **Events** *Biennial Congress* Mexico 2011, *Biennial Congress* Sao Paulo (Brazil) 2009, *Biennial Congress* Santiago (Chile) 2007, *Biennial Congress* Cartagena de Indias (Colombia) 2005, *Regional meeting* Havana (Cuba) 2004. **Publications** *Boletin Informativo de la FELAC* (4 a year).
Members National associations in 18 countries:
Argentina, Bolivia, Brazil, Chile, Colombia, Costa Rica, Cuba, Dominica, Ecuador, El Salvador, Guatemala, Mexico, Nicaragua, Panama, Paraguay, Peru, Uruguay, Venezuela.
Regional organization:
European Association for Endoscopic Surgery and Other Interventional Techniques (EAES, #06026).
NGO Relations Member of: *International Federation of Societies of Endoscopic Surgeons (IFSES, #13546).*
[2016.12.14/XD9393/**D**]

♦ Federación Latinoamericana de Ciudades, Municipios y Asociaciones de Gobiernos Locales (FLACMA) 09350

Latin American Federation of Cities, Municipalities and Associations of Local Governments

Exec Sec Rio Tiber 91 – Int 402, Cuauhtémoc, 06500 Mexico City CDMX, Mexico. T. +525557299637. E-mail: flacma@fenamm.org.mx.
URL: http://www.flacma.com.br/

History Constituted 17 Nov 1981, Quito (Ecuador) by *Latin American Chapter of IULA (inactive).* **Aims** Promote municipal causes and local agendas of the cities, municipalities and associations of local governments of Latin America and the Caribbean before international organizations and associations that work in favor of local strengthening at a regional and global level. **Structure** General Assembly; Executive Bureau; Technical Committee. **Languages** English, Spanish. **Finance** Members' dues. Funding. **Activities** Events/meetings; knowledge management/information dissemination; awards/prizes/competitions; networking/liaising; guidance/assistance/consulting. **Events** *Congress* Mexico City (Mexico) 2020, *Congress* Santiago (Chile) 2019, *Hemispheric Summit of Mayors and Local Authorities* Punta del Este (Uruguay) 2018, *Hemispheric Summit of Mayors* Pachuca de Soto (Mexico) 2017, *Congress* Puerto Iguazú (Argentina) 2013.
Members Municipalist National Associations in 21 countries:
Argentina, Belize, Bolivia, Brazil, Chile, Colombia, Costa Rica, Dominican Rep, Ecuador, El Salvador, Guatemala, Haiti, Honduras, Mexico, Nicaragua, Panama, Paraguay, Peru, Puerto Rico, Uruguay, Venezuela.
IGO Relations Cooperates with: *Deutsche Gesellschaft für Internationale Zusammenarbeit (GIZ); European Commission (EC, #06633).* **NGO Relations** Partnership for the promotion of municipalism with: *Alianza Eurolatinoamericana de Cooperación entre Ciudades (AL-LAs, #00628); Red Mercociudades (MC, #18721); Union of Ibero-American Capital Cities (#20412).* Member of: *Global Taskforce of Local and Regional Governments (Global Taskforce, #10622).* [2019.08.01/XD8833/**D**]

♦ Federación Latinoamericana de Colegios de la Compañia de Jesús (#16323)
♦ Federación Latinoamericana de Colegios Jesuitas / see Latin American Federation of Jesuit Schools (#16323)

♦ Federación Latinoamericana de Comisiones de Boxeo Profesional (FEDECENTRO) 09351

Central American Boxing Federation

Contact address not obtained. T. +5052663061. Fax +5052663064. E-mail: rbagnariol@avasa.com.ni.
URL: http://wbanews.com/artman/publish/fedecentrorankings/index.shtml

History by *World Boxing Association (WBA, #21241).* [2010/XD7728/**D**]

♦ Federación Latinoamericana de Comunidades Terapéuticas (FLACT) 09352

Latin American Federation of Therapeutic Communities

Contact Federaciónna de Comunidades Terapeuticas, Calle 57 No 43-20, Medellin 8558, Antioquia, Colombia. T. +5742844304 – +5742844305. Fax +5742549902. E-mail: flact.oficial@gmail.com – fchiosso.flact@gmail.com.

Facebook: https://www.facebook.com/federacionlatinoamericanaCT/
History 1986, Campinas (Brazil). Founded as a regional group of *World Federation of Therapeutic Communities (WFTC, #21491)*. **Aims** Consolidate national association members, strengthen their training programs and create permanent links among them. **Structure** General Assembly (every 2 years, at Conference). Plenary Assembly (annual), comprising all Presidents of member federations. Board of 5 Directors: President, Vice-President, Secretary, Treasurer and Spokesman. **Finance** US$ 75 programme registration; support from the US State Department. Budget (annual): about US$ 360,000. **Activities** Training programs comprise courses in each country. Hosts *Latin American Conference of Therapeutic Communities (CLACT)* (every 2 years). **Events** *Conference* Lima (Peru) 2021, *Conference* Lima (Peru) 2015, *Conference* Santiago (Chile) 2013, *Conference* Medellin (Colombia) 2011, *Conference* Lima (Peru) 2009. **Publications** *FLACT Bulletin* (4 a year). Research material; program reports.
Members Associations of therapeutic communities in 23 countries and territories:
Argentina, Aruba, Bolivia, Brazil, Chile, Colombia, Costa Rica, Cuba, Curaçao, Dominican Rep, Ecuador, El Salvador, Guatemala, Honduras, Mexico, Neth Antilles, Nicaragua, Panama, Paraguay, Peru, Puerto Rico, Uruguay, Venezuela.
NGO Relations Links with national institutions and narcotic organizations active in the field. [2020/XD1037/**E**]

♦ Federación Latinoamericana de Consejos de Usuarios del Transporte Internacional (no recent information)
♦ Federación Latinoamericana de la Edificación, Madera y Materiales de la Construcción (#16318)
♦ Federación Latinoamericana de Editores de Musica (inactive)
♦ Federación Latinoamericana de Endocrinologia (#09286)
♦ Federación Latinoamericana de Enfermeria en Cuidado Intensivo (unconfirmed)
♦ Federación Latino-Americana de Exhibidores y Distribuidores de Cine Independiente (#16321)

♦ Federación Latinoamericana de Facultades de Comunicación Social (FELAFACS) 09353

Fédération latinoaméricaine d'associations de facultés de communication sociales – Latin American Federation of Communication Schools
Exec Sec UAO Div Comunicación Social, Valle del Lili, Carretera Via Jamundi, Cali, Valle del Cauca, Colombia. T. +5723188000ext11524.
Pres address not obtained.
URL: http://www.felafacs.org/
History 28 Oct 1981, Melgar (Colombia), as *Latin American Federation of Associations of Communication Schools – Federación Latinoamericana de Asociaciones de Facultades de Comunicación Social*, at constituent assembly. **Aims** Contribute to permanent improvement of the education of professional social communicators in the scientific, technological and ethical aspects, as well as in acquisition of a social conscience guided towards independent development and social progress, taking into account various national realities; contribute to creation and development of post-graduate studies and specialization courses for professional improvement of social communications. **Structure** General Assembly (every 3 years); Council of Directors. **Languages** English, Portuguese, Spanish. **Staff** 4.00 FTE, paid. **Finance** Sources: *Agencia Española de Cooperación Internacional para el Desarrollo (AECID)*; *Konrad Adenauer Foundation (KAF)*; Open Society Institute Foundation; other sources including UNESCO and *Convenio Andrés Bello de integración educativa, cientifica y cultural de América Latina y España (Convenio Andrés Bello, #04785)*; Santander Universidades. **Activities** Training/education; publishing activities; financial and/or material support. **Events** *Latin American Meeting of Social Communication Faculties* Lima (Peru) 2012, *Latin American Meeting of Social Communication Faculties* Montevideo (Uruguay) 2012, *Latin American meeting of social communication faculties* Havana (Cuba) 2009, *Latin American Meeting of Social Communication Faculties* Bogota (Colombia) 2006, *Conference of the Americas* Coral Gables, FL (USA) 2004. **Publications** *FELAFACS/OPCION* (3 a year); *Revista Dialogos de la Comunicación* (2 a year).
Members Faculties of communication (300) in 11 national associations of communications schools in 11 countries:
Argentina, Bolivia, Brazil, Chile, Dominican Rep, Mexico, Panama, Paraguay, Peru, Puerto Rico, Venezuela.
Individual schools of communication (60) in 10 countries:
Canada, Costa Rica, El Salvador, Guatemala, Haiti, Honduras, Nicaragua, Spain, Uruguay, USA.
Honorary members institutions and individuals, including 11 organizations listed in this Yearbook:
Asociación de Televisión Educativa Iberoamericana (ATEI, #02303); Asociación Internacional de Jóvenes Investigadores en Comunicación (AIJIC); Asociación Latinoamericana de Comunicación Grupal (no recent information); Asociación Latinoamericana de Educación y Comunicación Popular (ALER, #02207); Asociación Latinoamericana de Investigadores de la Comunicación (ALAIC, #02237); Association mondiale des radiodiffuseurs communautaires (AMARC, #02810); Centro Internacional de Estudios Superiores de Comunicación para América Latina (CIESPAL, #03806); International Federation of Journalists (IFJ, #13462); Konrad Adenauer Foundation (KAF); Organización Católica Latinoamericana y Caribeña de Comunicación (OCLACC, #17833); World Association for Christian Communication (WACC, #21126) (Latin America).
Consultative Status Consultative status granted from: *UNESCO (#20322)* (Consultative Status). **IGO Relations** *UNESCO Regional Bureau for Education in Latin America and the Caribbean (#20318)*. **NGO Relations** Member of: *Confederación Iberoamericana de Asociaciones Científicas y Académicas de la Comunicación (CONFIBERCOM, #04448); World Journalism Education Council (WJEC, #21602)*. Partner of: *United Nations Academic Impact (UNAI, #20516)*. [2017/XD2608/y/**D**]

♦ Federación Latinoamericana de las Feminas Ejecutivas de Empresas Turisticas / see Federación Internacional de Asociaciones de Ejecutivas de Empresas Turisticas (#09336)
♦ Federación Latinoamericana de Fibrosis Quistica (no recent information)
♦ Federación Latinoamericana de Hospitales (#16322)

♦ Federación Latinoamericana e Ibérica de Sociedades de Meteorologia (FLISMET) 09354

Pres c/o Sociedade Brasileira de Meteorologia, Rua México 41, Sala 1304, Rio de Janeiro RJ, 20 031-144, Brazil.
URL: http://www.flismet.org/
History 1986. **Events** *Congress* Havana (Cuba) 2017, *Congress* Spain 2007, *CLIMET : Latin American and Iberian meteorological congress* Havana (Cuba) 2003, *Congress* Argentina 1996.
Members National organizations in 6 countries:
Argentina, Brazil, Cuba, Mexico, Spain, Uruguay.
NGO Relations Member of: *International Forum of Meteorological Societies (IFMS, #13644)*. [2016/XD8875/**D**]

♦ Federación Latinoamericana de la Industria Farmacéutica (#16328)
♦ Federación Latinoamericana de la Industria para la Salud Animal (no recent information)
♦ Federación Latinoamericana de las Industrias de la Confección (inactive)
♦ Federación Latinoamericana de Instituciones de Bioética / see Federación Latinoamericana y del Caribe de Instituciones de Bioética (#09348)
♦ Federación Latinoamericana de Jóvenes Ambientalistas (inactive)

♦ Federación Latinoamericana de Ju-Jitsu (FLJJ) 09355

Contact Dojo Okinawa Goju Ryu, Av Francisco de Miranda, Centro Perú local B7-1, Chacao, Caracas 1060 DF, Venezuela.
History 12 Oct 2007. **Aims** Unify and integrate all those who practice martial arts in Central and South America. **Structure** Board, comprising President, Vice-President, General Secretary, Treasurer and one member.
Members Full in 5 countries:
Argentina, Chile, Costa Rica, Mexico, Venezuela. [2010/XM4041/**D**]

♦ Federación Latinoamericana de Leasing (FELALEASE) 09356

Latin American Leasing Federation – Federação Latino Americana de Leasing
Pres Rua Diogo Moreira, 132 8 andar – conj 806, CEP 05423-010, Sao Paulo SP, 05423-010, Brazil. T. +551130959100. Fax +551130959105. E-mail: felalease@felalease.org.
URL: http://www.felalease.com/
History Founded 1972, Sao Paulo (Brazil). **Aims** Study questions of direct or indirect concern to business operations of leasing companies; create and enhance relations among national associations. **Structure** Board of Directors, consisting of the presidents of member associations and including President, 1st and 2 Vice-Presidents and 2 Directors. Chairman. **Languages** Spanish. **Staff** 2.00 FTE, paid. 2 FTE. **Finance** Members' dues. **Events** *Annual congress* Cartagena de Indias (Colombia) 1995. **Publications** *FELALEASE* (occasional).
Members National organizations in 11 countries:
Argentina, Brazil, Chile, Colombia, Costa Rica, Dominican Rep, Ecuador, Guatemala, Mexico, Peru, Venezuela.
NGO Relations Member of: *World Leasing Council (inactive)*. [2017.06.01/XD4300/**D**]

♦ Federación Latinoamericana de Magistrados (FLAM) 09357

Federação Latino-Americana de Magistrados
SG Edificio Alzamora, Av Abancay con Nicolas de Piérola, piso 11, 150001, Lima, Peru. T. +51999414135.
Pres address not obtained.
URL: http://www.flammagistrados.com/
History 1977, Santiago (Chile), during 1st Congreso de Magistrados Latinoamericanos. Reactivated, 1999, following a period of reduced activity. **Structure** Officers: President; 1st and 2nd Vice-Presidents; Secretary General; Administrative Secretary; Past Presidents. **Events** *Ordinary General Assembly* Toluca (Mexico) 2017, *Ordinary General Assembly* Mérida (Mexico) 2015, *Annual Meeting* Mar del Plata (Argentina) 2010, *Annual Meeting* San Juan (Puerto Rico) 2001, *Annual Meeting* San José (Costa Rica) 2000.
Members National associations in 16 countries and territories:
Argentina, Brazil, Chile, Colombia, Costa Rica, Dominican Rep, El Salvador, Mexico, Nicaragua, Panama, Paraguay, Peru, Portugal, Puerto Rico, Spain, Uruguay. [2017/XM4038/**E**]

♦ Federación Latinoamericana de Marketing (no recent information)
♦ Federación Latinoamericana de Mastologia (#16324)
♦ Federación Latinoamericana de Medicina y Cirugia de la Pierna y Pié (no recent information)
♦ Federación Latinoamericana de Mujeres Universitarias (#16334)
♦ Federación Latinoamericanana y del Caribe de Periodistas Deportivos / see AIPS America (#00599)
♦ Federación Latinoamericana de Neurocirugia (#16325)
♦ Federación Latino-Americana de Nutrición Parenteral y Enteral / see Latin American Federation of Nutritional Therapy, Clinical Nutrition and Metabolism (#16326)
♦ Federación Latinoamericana de Organizadores de Congresos y Afines / see Federación de Entidades Organizadoras de Congresos y Afines de América Latina (#09299)
♦ Federación Latinoamericana de Parasitologia / see Latin American Federation of Parasitologists (#16327)
♦ Federación Latinoamericana de Parasitólogos (#16327)

♦ Federación Latinoamericana de Patologia del Tracto Genital Inferior y Colposcopia (FLPTGIC) 09358

Contact Hospital Infatil Universitario de San José, Cra 52 No 67 A – 71, Centro Médico – Consultorio 211, Bogota, Bogota DC, Colombia. T. +5716609475.
Pres Elect address not obtained.
URL: http://www.colpolatin.org/
History Oct 1992, Buenos Aires (Argentina), during 1st Congreso Latinoamericano de Patologia del Tracto Genital Inferior y Colposcopia, as an integral part of *International Federation for Cervical Pathology and Colposcopy (IFCPC, #13385)*. **Structure** Board, including President, Past-President, President-Elect, Secretary and Treasurer. **Events** *Congress* Cartagena de Indias (Colombia) 2010, *Congress* Quito (Ecuador) 2007, *Congress* Santiago (Chile) 2004, *Congress* Acapulco (Mexico) 2001, *Congress* Asunción (Paraguay) 1998.
Members Affiliates in 16 countries:
Argentina, Bolivia, Brazil, Chile, Colombia, Costa Rica, Cuba, Dominican Rep, Ecuador, El Salvador, Guatemala, Mexico, Paraguay, Peru, Uruguay, Venezuela. [2014/XM4037/**E**]

♦ Federación Latinoamericana de Periodistas (FELAP) 09359

Fédération latinoaméricaine des journalistes – Federation of Latin American Journalists
Pres UTPBA Alsina No 779, Capital Federal CP 1087, Buenos Aires, Argentina. T. +541143433436 – +541143431135 – +541143431145. Fax +541143433436 – +541143431135. E-mail: presidencia@felap.org.
SG address not obtained.
URL: http://felap.org/
History Founded 7 Jun 1976, Mexico City (Mexico). The Latin American Code of Journalist Ethics adopted at 2nd Congress, 1979, Caracas (Venezuela). **Aims** Defend the freedom of the press and of access to information; improve working conditions; contribute to friendship among the peoples of Latin America and the Caribbean; show solidarity with journalists who are persecuted. **Structure** Board of Directors; Executive Committee. **Languages** Spanish. **Staff** 9.00 FTE, voluntary. **Finance** Members' dues. **Events** *Congress* Buenos Aires (Argentina) 2007, *Congress* Patzcuaro (Mexico) 2003, *Congress* Havana (Cuba) 1999, *Congress* Buenos Aires (Argentina) 1995, *Congress* Canela (Brazil) 1991. **Publications** *Boletin-FELAP* (6 a year); *Cuadernos de FELAP* (periodical).
Members National organizations and unions (28), totalling 80,000 members, in 24 countries and territories:
Argentina, Bolivia, Brazil, Chile, Colombia, Costa Rica, Cuba, Dominican Rep, Ecuador, El Salvador, Grenada, Guatemala, Guyana, Haiti, Honduras, Mexico, Nicaragua, Panama, Peru, Puerto Rico, St Lucia, Suriname, Uruguay, Venezuela.
Consultative Status Consultative status granted from: *ECOSOC (#05331)* (Ros C). **IGO Relations** Accredited by: *United Nations Office at Vienna (UNOV, #20604)*. **NGO Relations** Cooperates with: *Asociación Latinoamericana de Investigadores de la Comunicación (ALAIC, #02237); Confederation of ASEAN Journalists (CAJ, #04509); Federación Latinoamericana de Facultades de Comunicación Social (FELAFACS, #09353); Instituto Internacional de Periodismo 'José Marti' (IPJM, #11340); International Federation of Journalists (IFJ, #13462); International Red Cross and Red Crescent Movement (#14707); Latin American Institute of Transnational Studies (LAITS, no recent information); Union internationale des journalistes africains (UIJA, #20428)*. [2023/XD6670/**D**]

♦ Federación Latinoamericana de Periodistas y Escritores de Turismo (inactive)
♦ Federación Latinoamericana de Periodistas Tecnológicos (no recent information)
♦ Federación Latinoamericana de Productores de Fonogramas y Videogramas (inactive)
♦ Federación Latinoamericana de Psicologia en Emergencias y Desastres (no recent information)

♦ Federación Latinoamericana de Psiconeuroinmunoendocrinologia (FLAPNIE) 09360

Hon Pres c/o Univ Católica del Uruguay, Av 8 de Octubre 2738, CP 11600 Montevideo, Uruguay. E-mail: margadub@gmail.com – mdubourd@ucu.edu.uy.
Hon Pres c/o Univ Favaloro, Av Entre Rios 495, Buenos Aires, Argentina. E-mail: jmoguile@favaloro.edu.ar.
URL: http://www.flapnie.org/
History 2008. **Aims** Facilitate academic and scientific exchange between members. **Structure** Council of Representatives. **Languages** English, Spanish. **Finance** Member contributions. **Activities** Events/meetings; training/education; knowledge management/information dissemination. **Events** *Congress* Mexico City (Mexico) 2016. **Publications** Books.
Members Full in 9 countries:
Argentina, Bolivia, Chile, Colombia, Ecuador, Mexico, Peru, Uruguay, Venezuela.
NGO Relations *Asociación Latinoamericana de Psicoterapias Integrativas (ALAPSI, #02260)*. [2016.07.12/XM4039/**D**]

♦ Federación Latinoamericana de psicoterapia (#16329)

♦ Federación Latinoamericana de Psicoterapia Analitica de Grupo (FLAPAG) 09361

Federação Latino-americana de Psicoterapia Analitica de Grupo
Sec c/o AAPPG, Lavalle 3584, C1190AAR, Buenos Aires, Argentina. T. +541148626818. E-mail: flapagsecretaria@gmail.com – info@flapag.org.

URL: http://www.flapag.org/
Structure Officers: President; Vice-President; Secretary; Vice-Secretary; Treasurer; Vice-Treasurer. **Languages** Portuguese, Spanish. **Staff** Part-time, voluntary. **Finance** Members' dues. **Events** *Congress* Montevideo (Uruguay) 2015, *Congress* Buenos Aires (Argentina) 2013, *Congress* Buenos Aires (Argentina) 2011.
Members in 7 countries:
Argentina, Brazil, Chile, Colombia, France, Mexico, Uruguay. [2015/XM1308/**D**]

♦ Federación Latino-Americana de Psicoterapia Psicoanalitica y Psicoanalisis (FLAPPSIP) 09362

Latin American Federation of Psychotherapy and Psychoanalysis Associations
SG address not obtained.
URL: http://www.flappsip.com/
History 24 May 1998. **Aims** Promote psychoanalysis, its theory, clinical aspects and all mutual relationship between them; conduct study of the relationship between clinical practice and social issues. **Structure** General Meeting of Delegates (annual). Board of Directors, comprising President, General Secretary, Treasurer, Scientific Secretary and member at-large. Fiscal Committee. **Languages** Portuguese, Spanish. **Staff** 5.00 FTE, paid. **Finance** Members' dues. Other sources: online courses; conference and meeting proceeds. **Activities** Courses; forums; research work; interinstitutional activities; workshops. **Events** *Congress* Montevideo (Uruguay) 2019, *Psychoanalysis, a changing world – theory, clinic and culture* Porto Alegre (Brazil) 2017, *Congress* Lima (Peru) 2015, *Congress* Santiago (Chile) 2013, *Congress* Buenos Aires (Argentina) 2011. **Publications** Congress and meeting papers. [2016/XD8281/**D**]

♦ Federación Latinoamericana de Psicoterapias Cognitivas y Conductuales (ALAPCCO) 09363

Federação Latino-Americana de Psicoterapias Cognitivas e Comportamentais (ALAPCCO)
Pres Fac of Philosophy, Sciences and Languages, USP, Av Bandeirantes 3900, Vila Monte Alegre, Ribeirão Preto SP, 14040-901, Brazil.
URL: https://www.alapcco.com/
History Proposed 1995 and set up 1999, Rio de Janeiro (Brazil). Statutes adopted Mar 1999. Former names and other names: *Asociación Latinoamericana de Psicoterapias Cognitivas y Conductuales* – former. **Structure** Steering Committee, comprising President, Vice-President, Past-President, Secretary, Treasurer and Member. **Events** *Congress* Santiago (Chile) 2015, *Congress* Rio de Janeiro (Brazil) 2012, *Congress* Bogota (Colombia) 2010, *Congress* Buenos Aires (Argentina) 2006.
Members Full in 4 countries:
Argentina, Brazil, Chile, Uruguay.
NGO Relations Recognized by: *International Association of Cognitive Behavioral Therapy (IACBT, #11781).* [2020/XJ6733/**D**]

♦ Federación Latinoamericana de Psiquiatria Biológica (no recent information)

♦ Federación Latinoamericana de Psiquiatria de la Infancia, Adolescencia, Familia y Profesiones Afines (FLAPIA) 09364

Federação Latino-Americana de Psiquiatria da Infância e Adolescência e Profissões Afins
Pres Av Córdoba 2302 6o K, C1120AAS, Capital Federal, Buenos Aires, Argentina. T. +541149524689. Fax +541149524501. E-mail: cmagestec@globo.com.
History 1995, Curitiba (Brazil). In English referred to as *Latin American Association of Child Psychiatry.* **Events** *Congress* Colonia del Sacramento (Uruguay) 2013, *Congress* Buenos Aires (Argentina) 2011, *Congress* Buenos Aires (Argentina) 2009, *Congress* Montevideo (Uruguay) 2007, *Congress* Punta del Este (Uruguay) 2007. [2016/XD7694/**D**]

♦ Federación Latinoamericana de Quemaduras (FELAQ) 09365

Pres Don Carlos 2939, Of 306, Las Condes, Santiago, Santiago Metropolitan, Chile. E-mail: jlpceo@gmail.com.
Sec address not obtained. E-mail: lyapt@vtr.net.
URL: http://www.felaq.org/
History 25 Oct 1995, Posadas (Argentina). Also referred to as *Federación Latinoamericana de Sociedades de Quemaduras (FELAQUE).* **Aims** Encourage and support the collection, interpretation and application of medical data, so as to promote dissemination, research and advances in the treatment of *burns.* **Structure** Executive Committee, including President, President-Elect, Secretary, Treasurer and Past-President. **Events** *Congress* Rio de Janeiro (Brazil) 2013, *Congress* Guadalajara (Mexico) 2011, *Congress* Peru 2007, *Congress* Fortaleza (Brazil) 2006, *Congress* Havana (Cuba) 2005.
Members Full in 6 countries:
Argentina, Brazil, Chile, Ecuador, Mexico, Nicaragua. [2013/XM0147/**D**]

♦ Federación Latinoamericana de Quimicos Textiles (FLAQT) 09366

Latin American Federation of Textile Chemists
SG Simbrón 5756, C1408BHJ, Buenos Aires, Argentina. T. +541146447520. Fax +541146447520 – +541146443996. E-mail: info@flaqt.net.
URL: http://www.flaqt.net/
History 12 Nov 1964. **Structure** President; 2 Vice-Presidents; Treasurer; Executive Secretary General; Secretary. **Languages** Portuguese, Spanish. **Finance** Members' dues. Other sources: congresses; donations. **Activities** Events/meetings. **Events** *Congreso Latinoamericano de Química Textil* Medellin (Colombia) 2018, *Congress* Medellin (Colombia) 2013, *Congress* Lima (Peru) 2010, *Congress* Santiago (Chile) 2008, *Congress* Buenos Aires (Argentina) 2006. **Publications** *Revista Digital.*
Members National associations in 10 countries:
Argentina, Brazil, Chile, Colombia, Ecuador, Peru, Spain, Uruguay, USA, Venezuela.
IGO Relations *United Nations (UN, #20515).* **NGO Relations** Universities. [2018/XD5731/**D**]

♦ Federación Latinoamericana de Quiropractica (FLAQ) 09367

Latin America Chiropractic Federation – Federação Latino Americana de Quiropraxia
Exec Dir 20 Blythwood Rod, Toronto ON M4N 1A1, Canada. E-mail: directora.ejecutiva@flaq.org.
Pres address not obtained.
URL: http://www.flaq.org/
History 23 Mar 1988, Mexico City (Mexico). 2006, re-established following dormant period. **Aims** Promote development of health through chiropractic in Latin America. **Structure** Board of Directors; Executive. **Languages** English, Portuguese, Spanish. **Staff** 1.00 FTE, paid. **Activities** Advocacy/lobbying/activism. **Events** *Congress* Puerto Vallarta (Mexico) 1995, *Congress* Cancún (Mexico) 1994. **Publications** *FLAQ Newsletter* (4 a year).
Members Full in 15 countries:
Argentina, Belize, Bolivia, Brazil, Chile, Colombia, Costa Rica, Ecuador, Guatemala, Honduras, Mexico, Panama, Peru, Puerto Rico, Venezuela. [2020.03.03/XD2720/**D**]

♦ Federación Latinoamericana de Semiótica (no recent information)
♦ Federación Latinoamericana de Servicios de Salud Adolescente (no recent information)

♦ Federación Latinoamericana de Simulación Clínica y Seguridad del Paciente (FLASIC) 09368

Federção Latino Americana de Simulação Clínica e Segurança do Paciente
Contact address not obtained. E-mail: info@flasic.org.
URL: https://www.flasic.org/
History Jun 2007, Bogota (Colombia). **Structure** Board of Directors. **Activities** Events/meetings. **Events** *Congress* Cancún (Mexico) 2023. **Publications** *Revista Latinoamericana de Simulación Clínica* (3 a year).
Members Organizations in 6 countries:
Brazil, Chile, Costa Rica, Mexico, Peru, Uruguay.
Chapter in 1 country:
Colombia.
NGO Relations Member of (1): *Global Network for Simulation in Healthcare (GNSH, #10499).* [2023/AA3163/**D**]

♦ Federación Latinoamericana de Sociedades de Cancerologia (#16319)
♦ Federación Latinoamericana de Sociedades de Ciencias Cosméticas (unconfirmed)
♦ Federación Latinoamericana de Sociedades Cientificas de Estudiantes de Medicina (no recent information)

♦ Federación Latinoamericana de Sociedades de Climaterio y Menopausia (FLASCYM) 09369

Pres address not obtained.
URL: http://www.flascym.org/
History 16 Apr 1993, Bahia Blanca (Argentina). Founded during an international meeting. Constitution approved 2 Dec 1993, Panama (Panama). **Structure** Officers: President; 1st and 2nd Vice-Presidents; Secretary-General; Treasurer; Deputy Treasurer. Scientific Committee. **Events** *Congress* Asunción (Paraguay) 2022, *Congress* San José (Costa Rica) 2019, *Congress* Lima (Peru) 2016, *Congress* La Paz (Bolivia) 2013, *Congress* Cancún (Mexico) 2010. [2021/XJ6477/**D**]

♦ Federación Latinoamericana de Sociedades de Esterilidad y Fertilidad (inactive)
♦ Federación Latinoamericana de las Sociedades para estudio del Sueño (#09685)

♦ Federación Latinoamericana de Sociedades de Fisica (FELASOFI) .. 09370

Latin American Federation of Physics Societies
Sec Soc Mexicana de Fisica, 2do piso, Dept de Fisica, Fac de Ciencias, Ciudad Univ, 04510 Coyoacan CHIS, Mexico. T. +526224946. Fax +526224848. E-mail: smf@ciencias.unam.mx.
URL: http://www.felasofi.net/
History 1984. Statutes being approved by 2nd Meeting of Latin American Physics Societies, 4-7 Jul 1984, Sao Paulo (Brazil), and ratified during the Latin American Meeting of Representatives, 29-31 Mar 1989, Cholula (Mexico). **Aims** Promote and coordinate the development of physics in the Latin American and Caribbean region, thus contributing to the general progress of the region. **Structure** Board of Directors, comprising a representative of each of the member organizations. General Secretariat, headed by Secretary General. Manages *Red Latinoamericana de Fisica (RELAFI, no recent information)*, together with *Centro Latino-Americano de Fisica (CLAF, #03815).* **Staff** 4.00 FTE, paid. **Finance** Members' dues. Other sources: grants; FELASOFI activities. **Activities** Scientific inter-exchange; Latin American Congress and other conferences and meetings; publishing activity.
Members Full members national associations or organizations. Adhering members individuals and institutions. National organizations (16) in 16 countries:
Argentina, Bolivia, Brazil, Chile, Colombia, Costa Rica, Cuba, Dominica, Ecuador, Guatemala, Honduras, Mexico, Nicaragua, Peru, Uruguay, Venezuela.
Regional organization (1):
Central American and Caribbean Physical Society (#03664). [2013.10.04/XD6463/**D**]

♦ Federación Latinoamericana de Sociedades de Foniatria, Logopedia y Audiologia (inactive)

♦ Federación Latinoamericana de Sociedades Magicas (FLASOMA) .. 09371

Latin American Federation of Magicians Societies
SG Angel Gallardo 620, 2o piso B, 1405 Buenos Aires, Argentina. T. +541149838075.
URL: http://www.flasoma.org/
History 17 Oct 1982. **Events** *Congress* Buenos Aires (Argentina) 2017, *Congress* Montevideo (Uruguay) 2015, *Congress* Santiago (Chile) 2013, *Congress* Guatemala (Guatemala) 2011, *Congress* Lima (Peru) 2009.
Members Societies in 13 countries and territories:
Argentina, Brazil, Chile, Colombia, Ecuador, Guatemala, Mexico, Peru, Puerto Rico, Spain, Uruguay, USA, Venezuela.
NGO Relations *International Federation of Magic Societies (#13473).* [2016/XM4042/**D**]

♦ Federación Latino-americana de Sociedades Médicas de Acupuntura / see Federación Ibero Latinoamericana de Sociedades Médicas de Acupuntura (#09327)
♦ Federación Latinoamericana de Sociedades de Obesidad (#16332)

♦ Federación Latinoamericana de Sociedades de Obstetricia y Ginecologia (FLASOG) 09372

Latin American Federation of Obstetric and Gynecological Societies
Secretariat Av Balboa with Ramón Jurado Street, Edf RBS 8th Floor 805, Panama, Panamá, Panama PANAMá, Panama. T. +5073943936. E-mail: contacto@flasog.org.
URL: http://www.flasog.org/
Structure General Assembly; Executive Committee. **Events** *Congress* Valencia (Venezuela) 2015, *Congress* Managua (Nicaragua) 2011, *Pan American sexually transmitted infections/AIDS congress* Punta del Este (Uruguay) 2003, *Sexually transmitted infections* Punta del Este (Uruguay) 2003, *Congress* Santa Cruz (Bolivia) 2002.
Members in 20 countries:
Argentina, Bolivia, Brazil, Chile, Colombia, Costa Rica, Cuba, Dominican Rep, Ecuador, El Salvador, Guatemala, Haiti, Honduras, Mexico, Nicaragua, Panama, Paraguay, Peru, Uruguay, Venezuela.
NGO Relations Member of: *Reproductive Health Supplies Coalition (RHSC, #18847).* Allied regional federation of: *Fédération Internationale de Gynécologie et d'Obstétrique (FIGO, #09638).* [2018.06.25/XD7221/**D**]

♦ Federación Latinoamericana de Sociedades de Quemaduras / see Federación Latinoamericana de Quemaduras (#09365)
♦ Federación Latinoamericana de Sociedades de Sexologia y Educación Sexual (#16331)
♦ Federación Latinoamericana de Sociedades de Ultrasonido (#16333)
♦ Federación Latinoamericana de Terapia Nutricional, Nutrición Clinica y Metabolismo (#16326)
♦ Federación Latinoamericana de Termalismo (no recent information)
♦ Federación Latinoamericana de Trabajadores Agricolas, Pecuarios y Afines (no recent information)

♦ Federación Latinoamericana de Trabajadores Bancarios, de Seguros y Servicios Afines (FELATRABS) 09373

Latin American Federation of Bank and Insurance Workers – Fédération latinoaméricaine des travailleurs des banques et des assurances
Pres Rua do Rosario 77, sala 1105, Fortaleza CE, 60055-090 CENTRO, Brazil. T. +558532532885 – +558532511231. Fax +558532532886. E-mail: feebnn@veloxmail.com.br – fed.bancarios_seguros@netgate.com.uy.
History presumably to take over activities of *Confederación Americana de Empleados Bancarios (CADEB, inactive).* **Aims** Discuss, make decisions on, and execute global labour policy in the banking and insurance sector and allied services in Latin America. **Structure** Board; Executive Committee. **Languages** Portuguese, Spanish. **Staff** 4.00 FTE, voluntary. **Finance** Self-financed. **Events** *Congress* Buenos Aires (Argentina) 2013, *Congress* Caracas (Venezuela) 2008. **Members** Membership countries not specified. **NGO Relations** Affiliated to: *World Organization of Workers (WOW, #21697).* [2015.01.19/XD0458/**D**]

♦ Federación Latinoamericana de Trabajadores Campesinos y de la Alimentación (inactive)
♦ Federación Latinoamericana de Trabajadores del Comercio y Similares / see Federación de Trabajadores Latinoamericanos del Comercio, Oficinas y Empresas Privadas de Servicios (#09394)
♦ Federación Latinoamericana de Trabajadores de la Comunicación Social / see Federación Latinoamericana de Trabajadores de la Cultura y de la Comunicación Social (#09374)

♦ Federación Latinoamericana de Trabajadores de la Cultura y de la Comunicación Social (FELATRACCS) 09374

Pres Jr Huancavelica 320, 1, Lima, Peru. T. +5114270687. Fax +5114278493.
URL: http://www.felatraccs.org/
History 31 Jan 1976, San José (Costa Rica), as *Latin American Federation of Press Workers – Fédération latinoaméricaine des travailleurs de la presse – Federación Latinoamericana de Trabajadores de la Prensa (FELATRAP)*, during 1st Latin American Congress of Press Workers. A regional organization of *World Organization of Workers (WOW, #21697).* 2004, name changed to *Federación Latinoamericana de Trabajadores de la Comunicación Social (FELATRACS).* **Aims** Promote the organization of workers in the press sector in all countries of Latin America, providing material and technical assistance as necessary, and organizing

necessary services at the Latin American level, cooperating in national-level provision of such services; promote unity at the national level among all organizations in the sector to render their activities more effective; study, promote, defend and represent the interests of press workers with government bodies in Latin America and world-wide, in line with workers' rights and interests; defend and promote the right for free and democratic organization of all press workers; monitor respect for freedom of information and expression. **Structure** Congress (every 4 years). Executive Committee, including President, 5 Regional Vice-Presidents and Secretary General. **Languages** French, Portuguese, Spanish. **Staff** 7.00 FTE, paid. **Finance** Members' dues. Contributions from CLAT. **Activities** Denounces violations of the liberty of information and free expression in Latin America and the Caribbean and defends the physical integrity and the human rights of journalists and press workers. Organizes meetings, seminars, training workshops, correspondence courses. Holds Congresses (every 4 years). **Events** *Congress* Lima (Peru) 2004. **Publications** *Boletin FELATRAP* (6 a year). Congress proceedings.
Members National organizations representing journalists and workers in social communication media in 18 countries and territories:
Argentina, Aruba, Bolivia, Chile, Colombia, Costa Rica, Dominican Rep, El Salvador, Guatemala, Haiti, Honduras, Neth Antilles, Nicaragua, Panama, Peru, Puerto Rico, Uruguay, Venezuela.
IGO Relations *FAO (#09260); ILO (#11123); OAS (#17629); UNESCO (#20322); United Nations Economic Commission for Latin America and the Caribbean (ECLAC, #20556).* **NGO Relations** Cooperates with: *Comisión Latinoamericana por los Derechos y Libertades de los Trabajadores y los Pueblos (CLADEHLT, no recent information).* [2020/XD8487/D]

♦ Federación Latinoamericana de Trabajadores de la Educación y la Cultura (FLATEC) 09375

Latin American Federation for Education and Cultural Workers – Federação Latinoamericana de Trabalhadores da Educação e a Cultura
Contact address not obtained.
URL: http://www.flatec.org/
History Aug 1979, Santo Domingo (Dominican Rep). Founded at Constitutive Congress, continuing the work of *Comisión Latinoamericana de Trabajadores de la Educación (CLATEC)*, set up in 1971. **Aims** Promote the cooperation on a Latin American level between education and cultural workers in all the countries and the territories of the continent; study the situation and the problems of education and cultural workers in Latin America; promote, defend and represent the interests of the education and cultural workers of member organizations. **Structure** Latin American Congress (every 4 years). Latin American Council; Executive Committee; Executive Bureau. *Instituto Pedagógico Latinoamericano y del Caribe (IPLAC).* Sub-regional Councils. **Languages** Spanish. **Finance** Sources: contributions; fundraising; grants; members' dues. **Activities** Organizes quadrennial congress; regional seminars. **Events** *Congress* Buenos Aires (Argentina) 2013, *Congress* Venezuela 1998, *Congress* Venezuela 1997, *Congress* Mar del Plata (Argentina) 1992, *Congress* San José (Costa Rica) 1987. **Publications** *Boletin FLATEC* (6 a year); *El Tintero* (4 a year).
Members Affiliate organizations in 19 countries and territories:
Argentina, Bolivia, Brazil, Chile, Colombia, Costa Rica, Curaçao, Dominican Rep, Ecuador, El Salvador, Haiti, Honduras, Nicaragua, Panama, Paraguay, Peru, Suriname, Uruguay, Venezuela. [2020/XD4610/D]

- ♦ Federación Latinoamericana de Trabajadores Graficos y del Papel (inactive)
- ♦ Federación Latinoamericana de Trabajadores de la Industria (inactive)

♦ Federación Latinoamericana de Trabajadores de la Industria y la Construcción (FLATIC) 09376

Latin American Federation of Industrial and Construction Workers
Pres Rua 24 de Maio 104 – 12 andar, Sao Paulo SP, CENTRO CEP 01041-000, Brazil. T. +551168239555. Fax +551168239555. E-mail: wilson@sintecsp.org.br.
History 29 Nov 2001, Venezuela, by merger of *Federación Latinoamericana de Trabajadores de la Industria (FLATI, inactive)* and *Latin American Federation of Workers of the Construction Industry, Wood and Building Materials (FLATICOM, inactive).* **Aims** Correct, when possible, functional difficulties of the trade union movement and contribute to its strengthening; coordinate, consolidate and train national and local leaders on issues specific to their industry in Latin America. **Structure** Officers: President; Secretary General; 1st and 2nd Secretaries; 3 Secretaries of Finance. Board of Auditors. **Languages** Portuguese. **Staff** 2.00 FTE, paid. **Finance** Members' dues. Budget (annual): Real 300,000. **Activities** Organizes seminars. **Publications** *New Season Magazine; New Season Newsletter.*
Members Confederations, federations and workers organizations in 26 countries and territories:
Argentina, Aruba, Bolivia, Brazil, Chile, Colombia, Costa Rica, Cuba, Curaçao, Dominica, Dominican Rep, Ecuador, El Salvador, Guatemala, Guyana, Haiti, Honduras, Mexico, Nicaragua, Panama, Paraguay, Peru, Puerto Rico, Suriname, Uruguay, Venezuela.
IGO Relations *ILO (#11123).* **NGO Relations** Affiliated to: *Building and Wood Workers' International (BWI, #03355).* [2009.09.24/XD8685/t/D]

- ♦ Federación Latinoamericana de Trabajadores de la Industria de la Construcción, la Madera y los Materiales de Construcción (inactive)

♦ Federación Latinoamericana de Trabajadores de las Industrias Metalúrgicas, Mecanicas y Mineras (FLATIM) 09377

Pres Av Belgrano 665, Buenos Aires, Argentina. T. +541143407418. Fax +541143407400.
History 1991, Caracas (Venezuela). [2012/XM2087/t/D]

- ♦ Federación Latinoamericana de Trabajadores de la Industria del Textil, Vestido, Calzado y Cuero (inactive)
- ♦ Federación Latinoamericana de Trabajadores de la Prensa / see Federación Latinoamericana de Trabajadores de la Cultura y de la Comunicación Social (#09374)
- ♦ Federación Latinoamericana de Trabajadores del Transporte (no recent information)
- ♦ Federación Latinoamericana de Turismo Social (inactive)
- ♦ Federación Luterana Mundial (#16532)
- ♦ Federación Mesoamericana de Asociaciones Conservacionistas No-Gubernamentales (inactive)
- ♦ Federación de Mineros de Europa (inactive)
- ♦ Federación Mundial de Agencias de Salud para la Promoción de la Contracepción Quirúrgica Voluntaria (inactive)
- ♦ Federación Mundial de Amigos de los Museos (#21435)
- ♦ Federación Mundial de Asociaciones de Administración de Personal / see World Federation of People Management Associations (#21474)
- ♦ Federación Mundial de Asociaciones, Centros y Clubs UNESCO (#21498)
- ♦ Federación Mundial de Asociaciones de Centros de Toxicologia Clinica y Centros de Control de Intoxicaciones (inactive)
- ♦ Federación Mundial de Asociaciones de Dirección de Personal / see World Federation of People Management Associations (#21474)
- ♦ Federación Mundial de Asociaciones pro Naciones Unidas (#21499)
- ♦ Federación mundial de las asociaciones de salud pública (#21476)
- ♦ Federación Mundial de Béisbol Amateur (inactive)
- ♦ Federación Mundial de los Centros Recreativos Judios / see JCC Global (#16093)
- ♦ Federación Mundial de Ciudades Unidas (inactive)
- ♦ Federación Mundial de Communidades Terapéuticas (#21491)
- ♦ Federación Mundial de las Comunidades de Vida Cristiana / see Christian Life Community (#03905)
- ♦ Federación Mundial de Dirigentes de Institutos de Belleza y Estética (no recent information)
- ♦ Federación Mundial de Educación Médica (#21454)
- ♦ Federación Mundial de Empleados / see World Organization of Workers (#21697)
- ♦ Federación Mundial de Ergoterapeutas (#21468)
- ♦ Federación Mundial para Estudios sobre el Futuro (#21535)
- ♦ Federación Mundial de Hemofilia (#21437)
- ♦ Federación Mundial de Instituciones Financieras de Desarrollo (#21428)
- ♦ Federación Mundial de Juventud Católica (inactive)
- ♦ Federación Mundial de la Juventud Democratica (#21427)
- ♦ Federación Mundial de Juventudes Femeninas Católicos (inactive)
- ♦ Federación Mundial de Medicina y Biologia Nucleares (#21467)
- ♦ Federación Mundial de Medicina Tradicional (no recent information)
- ♦ Federación Mundial de Médicos que respetan la Vida Humana (#21432)
- ♦ Federación Mundial de la Metalurgia (inactive)
- ♦ Federación Mundial de Musicoterapia (#21459)
- ♦ Federación Mundial de Organizaciones Femeninas Ucranias (#21496)
- ♦ Federación Mundial de Periodistas y Escritores de Turismo (#21494)
- ♦ Federación Mundial Protectora de Animales (inactive)
- ♦ Federación Mundial de Quiropractica (#21420)
- ♦ Federación Mundial de Salud Mental (#21455)
- ♦ Federación Mundial Sefardi (#21778)
- ♦ Federación Mundial de Seguridad (no recent information)
- ♦ Federación Mundial de Sociedades de Anestesiólogos (#21482)
- ♦ Federación Mundial de Sociedades de Medicina Intensiva / see World Federation of Intensive and Critical Care (#21444)
- ♦ Federación Mundial de Sociedades de Neurocirugia (#21466)
- ♦ Federación Mundial de Sociedades de Psiquiatrica Biológica (#21483)
- ♦ Federación Mundial de Trabajadores Agricolas (inactive)
- ♦ Federación Mundial de Trabajadores de la Agricultura y la Alimentación (inactive)
- ♦ Federación Mundial de Trabajadores de la Alimentación, del Tabaco y de los Hoteles-CMT (inactive)
- ♦ Federación Mundial de Trabajadores Cientificos (#21480)
- ♦ Federación Mundial de Trabajadores de la Construcción y la Madera (inactive)
- ♦ Federación Mundial de Trabajadores de la Industria (inactive)
- ♦ Federación Mundial de Trabajadores Non Manuales / see World Organization of Workers (#21697)
- ♦ Federación Mundial de Veteranos de Guerra / see The World Veterans Federation (#21900)
- ♦ Federación Mundial de Voleibol y de Beach Voleibol (inactive)
- ♦ Federación Mundial de Zonas Francas (#09693)
- ♦ Federación Mundo de Tecnologia del Entretenimiento y el Espectaculo (#21384)
- ♦ Federación de Municipalidades de Centroamérica y Panama (inactive)

♦ Federación de Municipios del Istmo Centroamericano (FEMICA) . . . 09378

Federation of Municipalities of the Central American Isthmus
Contact address not obtained. T. +50223683373 – +50223682645. Fax +50223373530. E-mail: info@femica.org.
History Sep 1991, Tegucigalpa (Honduras). Takes over activities of *Federación de Municipalidades de Centroamérica y Panama (FERMUCAP, inactive).* **Aims** Promote the interests of *municipalities* and secure the strengthening of the modern municipality, having managerial capacity and political power to further the *development* processes and the strategies to fight *poverty* on a local level. **Structure** Annual Assembly of Mayors. Management Board, consisting of one member from each member country. Presidency (rotating), elected annually by the Annual Assembly of Mayors. Executive Committee. Council of Analysis and Projects; Regional Coordination Project on Gender Equality; Assistance Executive Board; Internal Audit; Secretariat. **Languages** English, Spanish. **Staff** 7.00 FTE, paid. **Finance** Members' dues. Supported by *United States Agency for International Development (USAID).* **Activities** Organizes/assists in: seminars; workshops; congresses; other meetings; dialogues. Priority projects in the municipal field focus on political, administrative, service and financial issues. Set up and organizes *Red Centroamericana de Legisladores por el Fortalecimiento y la Descentralización Municipal (no recent information).* **Events** *Annual Congress* Guatemala (Guatemala) 1996, *Central America regional meeting of social and municipal sectors* Managua (Nicaragua) 1996, *Annual Congress* Panama 1995, *Annual Congress* Costa Rica 1994, *Annual Congress* Nicaragua 1993. **Publications** *FEMICA* (periodical). Pamphlets; folders. Meeting reports.
Members National associations of municipalities in 6 countries:
Costa Rica, El Salvador, Guatemala, Honduras, Nicaragua, Panama.
IGO Relations Formal contacts with: *Central American Institute of Public Administration (#03670); Inter-American Development Bank (IDB, #11427); International Bank for Reconstruction and Development (IBRD, #12317); OAS (#17629).* **NGO Relations** As *IULA Central America (IULA CENTAM)*, functions as Central American chapter of: *International Union of Local Authorities (IULA, inactive).* [2013/XD4638/D]

- ♦ Federación Odontológica de Centroamérica y Panama (#17691)
- ♦ Federación Odontológica Latinoamericana (#16357)
- ♦ Federación Organismos Cristianos de Servicio Internacional Voluntario / see Federazione Organismi Cristiani Servizio Internazionale Volontario
- ♦ Federación de Organizaciones para el Futuro de Orinoquia y Amazonia (unconfirmed)
- ♦ Federación de Organizaciones de Ingenieros de Centro América y Panama (#09483)
- ♦ Federación de Organizaciones Magisteriales de Centroamérica (inactive)
- ♦ Federación Panamericana de Asociaciones de Arquitectos (#18098)
- ♦ Federación Panamericana de Asociaciones de Facultades y Escuelas de Medicina (#18100)

♦ Federación Panamericana de Consultores (FEPAC) 09379

Pan-American Federation of Consultants
SG Avenida Rivera Navarrete No 762, piso 11, San Isidro, 27, Lima, Peru. T. +5114414182. E-mail: secretariageneral@fepac.org.
URL: http://www.fepac.org/
History 1971, as *Latin American Federation of Consulting Engineers – Fédération latinoaméricaine des consultants – Federación Latinoamericana de Asociaciones de Consultores (FELAC) – Federação Latinoamericana de Associações de Consultores (FELAC).* Current structure and name adopted, 1993. Registered in accordance with the law of Peru. **Aims** Group existing representative institutions of consulting *engineers* in American countries and contribute to their creation in American countries where none exists; promote technical scientific advancement of the profession and protect professional interests; ensure observance of standards and rules of professional conduct in conformity with Ethical Code; play a consultative role with governments of member associations' countries and promote advantages of using consulting services for public sector projects; act as source of information on matters of mutual interest. **Structure** General Assembly (annual). Executive Committee, comprising 5 standing committees, each chaired by a principal director: Planning; Policy; Programme and Membership; Budget and Finances; Nominating and Election. President, Vice-President. Administered by Secretary-General. **Languages** English, Spanish. **Staff** 8.00 FTE, paid. **Finance** Budget (annual): US$ 200,000. **Events** *Annual General Assembly* Santiago (Chile) 2008, *Annual General Assembly* Rio de Janeiro (Brazil) 2006, *Annual General Assembly* Mexico City (Mexico) 2004, *Annual General Assembly* Madrid (Spain) 2003, *Annual General Assembly* Santiago (Chile) 2002. **Publications** *Guia General para Selección y Contratación de Consultores.*
Members National associations in 13 countries:
Argentina, Bolivia, Brazil, Chile, Colombia, Ecuador, El Salvador, Honduras, Mexico, Paraguay, Peru, Spain, Venezuela. [2018/XD5388/D]

- ♦ Federación Panamericana pro Donación Voluntaria de Sangre (inactive)
- ♦ Federación Panamericana de Facultades y Escuelas de Ciencias Veterinarias (#18105)
- ♦ Federación Panamericana de Farmacia (no recent information)
- ♦ Federación Panamericana de Hockey (#18110)
- ♦ Federación Panamericana e Ibérica de Sociedades de Medicina Critica y Terapia Intensiva (#18111)
- ♦ Federación Panamericana de Ingenieria Económica y de Costos (no recent information)

♦ Federación Panamericana de Ingenieria Oceanica y Costera (FEPIOC) 09380

Contact address not obtained.
URL: http://www.ciccba.com.ar/xxxv-convencion-panamericana-de-ingenieria -upadi-panamma-2016/
Events *Congress* Panama (Panama) 2016. **Members** Membership countries not specified. **NGO Relations** Cooperates with: *Unión Panamericana de Asociaciones de Ingenieros (UPADI, #20469).* [2016/XD3936/D]

♦ Federación Panamericana de Karate 09381

Panamerican Karate Federation (PKF)

Pres address not obtained. T. +541147829135. Fax +541147805053. E-mail: karate@fibertel.com.ar – info@pkfkarate.com.
URL: https://www.pkfkarate.com/

History 1 Oct 1975, Long Beach, CA (USA). A continental union of *World Karate Federation (WKF, #21608)*, previously of *World Union of Karatedo Organizations (WUKO, inactive)*. Former names and other names: *Pan American Union of Karatedo Organizations (PUKO)* – former. **Structure** Officers. Regions: (4): North America; South America; Central America; Caribbean. Referee Council. Committees (3): Technical; Medical; Marketing. **Languages** English, Spanish. **Staff** Voluntary. **Finance** Sources: organization of special courses; sale of marketing items; sponsorship. **Activities** Sporting activities. **Events** *Congress* Curaçao 1991.
Members Regular members in 43 countries and territories:
Antigua-Barbuda, Argentina, Aruba, Bahamas, Barbados, Belize, Bermuda, Bolivia, Bonaire Is, Brazil, Canada, Cayman Is, Chile, Colombia, Costa Rica, Cuba, Curaçao, Dominican Rep, Ecuador, El Salvador, Grenada, Guadeloupe, Guatemala, Guiana Fr, Guyana, Haiti, Honduras, Jamaica, Martinique, Mexico, Nicaragua, Panama, Paraguay, Peru, Puerto Rico, St Kitts-Nevis, St Lucia, St Vincent-Grenadines, Suriname, Trinidad-Tobago, Uruguay, USA, Venezuela.
NGO Relations Member of (1): *Asociación de Confederaciones Deportivas Panamericanas (ACODEPA, #02119)*. [2017/XD7303/**D**]

♦ Federación Panamericana de Lecheria (FEPALE) 09382

Pan American Dairy Federation

SG Luis Alberto de Herrera 1052, Edif Torres del Puerto Torre B, Of 1507, 11-300 Montevideo, Uruguay. T. +59826282262. Fax +59826220968. E-mail: secgral@fepale.org – info@fepale.org.
URL: http://www.fepale.org/

History 28 Nov 1991, Montevideo (Uruguay), statutes having been adopted 25-26 Nov 1991, Montevideo. Recognized by the Ministry of Foreign Affairs of Uruguay, 29 Sep 1992. Replaces *Latin American Association of Food Processors (ALICA, inactive)*. **Aims** Promote relations, cooperation and integration of institutions, companies and individuals of the Pan American dairy sector; preserve and represent the general interests of the dairy industry in the region, especially in Latin America and the Caribbean; help increase per capita milk availability in the region; make information available to the sector on production, industry, trade and technology; promote effective mechanisms to avoid or correct distortions in trade competitiveness; favour training and transfer of know-how in all the links of the dairy agribusiness chain. **Structure** General Assembly; Council of Directors; General Secretary. Committees (3): Normalization and Control; Training, Research and Technology; Primary Production. **Languages** English, Portuguese, Spanish. **Staff** 6.00 FTE, paid. **Finance** Members' dues. **Activities** Coordinates and sponsors workshops, seminars, meetings and conventions, training activities, including Pan American Dairy Course. Advises members. Committees that deal with specialized matters. **Events** *Congress* Quito (Ecuador) 2021, *Congress* Quito (Ecuador) 2020, *Congress* Buenos Aires (Argentina) 2018, *Congress* Puerto Varas (Chile) 2016, *Congress* Querétaro (Mexico) 2014. **Publications** Information Services: Information system on dairy production, trade and technology. **Members** Full private and/or public entities of producers and/or processors; processing or trading companies; research institutions; academic and training centres; manufacturers and dealers of dairy equipment, materials and services; other related agencies. Adhering interested institutions or companies. Members in 13 countries. Membership countries not specified. **Consultative Status** Consultative status granted from: *ECOSOC (#05331)* (Ros C). **IGO Relations** Cooperates with: *FAO (#09260)*; *Inter-American Institute for Cooperation on Agriculture (IICA, #11434)*; *OIE – World Organisation for Animal Health (#17703)*; *Pan American Health Organization (PAHO, #18108)*. **NGO Relations** Regular cooperation with: *International Dairy Federation (IDF, #13128)*. [2013/XD3590/**D**]

♦ Federación Panamericana de Profesionales de Enfermeria (#18104)

♦ Federación Panamericana de Seguridad Privada (FEPASEP) 09383

Admin Sec CAESI, Montevideo 666, 3e Piso-307, 1019 Buenos Aires, Argentina. T. +541143742278. Fax +541143742278. E-mail: direjecutiva@fibertel.com.ar – presidenciacaesi@fibertel.com.ar.
Pres ANDEVIP, Carrera 56 No 79B – 61, Bogota, Bogota DC, Colombia.
URL: http://caesi.org.ar/fepasep-2

History 7 Jan 2002. Proposed 28 May 2001, Curitiba (Brazil). **Structure** Board of Directors. **Languages** English, Portuguese, Spanish. **Staff** 5.00 FTE, paid. **Events** *Côngress* Buenos Aires (Argentina) 2014, *Congress* Medellin (Colombia) 2013, *Congress* Curitiba (Brazil) 2012, *Congress* Panama (Panama) 2011, *International congress / Congress* Asunción (Paraguay) 2010.
Members Full in 20 countries:
Argentina, Bolivia, Brazil, Chile, Colombia, Costa Rica, Dominican Rep, Ecuador, El Salvador, Guatemala, Honduras, Mexico, Nicaragua, Panama, Paraguay, Peru, Spain, Uruguay, USA, Venezuela.
Adherent member in 2 countries:
Argentina, Brazil.
NGO Relations *Federación de Seguridad Privada de los Paises del Mercosur (FESESUR, #09389)*; *World Security Federation (WSF, no recent information)*. [2015.01.13/XM0820/**D**]

♦ Federación Panamericana de Sindicatos de Artes, Medios de Comunicación y Espectaculo (#18099)

♦ Federación Panamericana de Squash (FPS) 09384

Panamerican Squash Federation

Pres Colinas de Bello Monte, Av Tocuyo, Edif Res Técnicas, Caracas 1050 DF, Venezuela.
URL: https://www.panamsquash.com/

History 18 Nov 1989. Regional federation of: *World Squash Federation (WSF, #21826)*. Registration: Start date: 7 Sep 2018, Cayman Is. **Aims** Unite North American, Central American, South American and Caribbean nations into one group for the sake of the *sport* of squash; comply as a recognized body for Pan American and Olympic Game status. **Structure** General Meeting (annual); Executive Board. **Languages** English, Spanish. **Staff** Voluntary. **Finance** Members' dues. Donations. **Activities** Events/meetings; sporting activities. **Events** *Annual meeting* San Salvador (El Salvador) 2001, *Annual meeting* Winnipeg, MB (Canada) 1999, *Annual meeting* Mexico City (Mexico) 1998, *Annual meeting* Rio de Janeiro (Brazil) 1997, *Annual meeting* Medellin (Colombia) 1996.
Members Full in 27 countries and territories:
Argentina, Bahamas, Barbados, Bermuda, Brazil, Canada, Cayman Is, Chile, Colombia, Costa Rica, Dominican Rep, Ecuador, El Salvador, Guatemala, Guyana, Jamaica, Mexico, Panama, Paraguay, Peru, St Kitts-Nevis, St Lucia, St Vincent-Grenadines, Trinidad-Tobago, Uruguay, USA, Venezuela.
Affiliates (2):
Caribbean Area Squash Association (CASA, #03442); *South American Confederation of Squash (#19702)*.
NGO Relations Member of (1): *Asociación de Confederaciones Deportivas Panamericanas (ACODEPA, #02119)*. [2023/XD2373/y/**D**]

♦ Federación Pan Americana de Vela (#18128)
♦ Federación de Partidos Liberales y Centristas de Centro América y del Caribe (inactive)

♦ Federación de Partidos Verdes de las Américas (FPVA) 09385

Federation of Green Parties of the Americas – Fédération des partis verts des amériques

Treas c/o Partido Verde Ecologista de México, Loma Bonita No 18, Distrito Federal, 119500 Mexico City CDMX, Mexico.
URL: http://www.fpva.org/

History Founded 24 Mar 1997. **Aims** Unify and strengthen the efforts of green *ecological* political parties, green political movements and community groups committed to the protection of the environment and human rights, the prevention of war and conflict, the promotion of social justice and cooperation among green ecological political parties and green political movements that share the purposes and actions of the Federation; respect and support indigenous peoples; stimulate and give support to organizations which are in the process of establishing themselves as green or ecological political parties. **Structure** General Assembly (annual); Executive Committee; technical and thematic commissions (6); Ombudsman. **Events** *Annual Meeting* La Paz (Bolivia) 2013, *Annual Meeting* Antigua (Guatemala) 2012, *Annual Meeting* Natal (Brazil) 2011, *Annual Meeting* Bogota (Colombia) 2010, *Annual Meeting* Santiago (Chile) 2009.
Members Ecological parties in 11 countries:
Argentina, Bolivia, Brazil, Canada, Chile, Colombia, Dominican Rep, Mexico, Peru, USA, Venezuela.
Observers in 1 countries:
Guatemala. [2019.08.13/XD6649/**D**]

♦ Federación de Periodistas Deportivos de América / see AIPS America (#00599)
♦ Federación de Profesionales Caribeños de Cine y Video (no recent information)

♦ Federación Psicoanalitica de América Latina (FEPAL) 09386

Psychoanalytical Association of Latin America – Federação Psicanalitica da América Latina

Admin Sec Luis B Cavia 2640, apto 603 esq, Av Brasil 11300, Montevideo, Uruguay. Fax +59827075026. E-mail: fepal@adinet.com.uy.
SG address not obtained.
URL: http://www.fepal.org/

History 1960, as *Comité Coordinador de Organizaciones Psicoanaliticas de América Latina (COPAL) – Conselho Coordenador das Organizações Psicanaliticas da América Latina*. Present name adopted 1980. **Events** *Congress* Lima (Peru) 2018, *Congress* Cartagena de Indias (Colombia) 2016, *Congress* Buenos Aires (Argentina) 2014, *Congress* Sao Paulo (Brazil) 2012, *Congress* Bogota (Colombia) 2010.
Members Associations in 8 countries:
Argentina, Brazil, Chile, Colombia, Mexico, Peru, Uruguay, Venezuela. [2014/XD7137/**D**]

♦ Federación de Radioprotección de America Latina y el Caribe (FRALC) 09387

Latin American and Caribbean Federation of Radiation Protection Societies

Pres Domingo Cueto 241, Dpto 701, 14, Lima, Peru. E-mail: sprperu2016@gmail.com – spr_peru@yahoo.com.
SG address not obtained.
URL: http://proteccion-radiologica.blogspot.com/

History 26 Nov 1993, Zacatecas (Mexico). **Events** *Iberian and Latin American Congress on Radiological Protection Societies* Rio de Janeiro (Brazil) 2013, *Meeting* Guadalajara (Mexico) 1997, *Meeting* Vienna (Austria) 1996, *Meeting* Cusco (Peru) 1995.
Members National organizations (6) in 6 countries:
Argentina, Brazil, Cuba, Mexico, Peru, Uruguay.
NGO Relations Member of: *Grupo Iberoamericano de Sociedades Cientificas de Protección Radiológica (GRIAPRA, no recent information)*. [2016/XD8881/**D**]

♦ Federación Regional de Informatica de la Salud para América Latina y el Caribe / see International Medical Informatics Association for Latin America and the Caribbean (#14135)
♦ Federación para el Respeto del Hombre y de la Humanidad (inactive)

♦ Federación Sefaradi Latinoamericana (FeSeLa) 09388

Federation of Sephardi Organizations of Latin America

Pres address not obtained. E-mail: esefarad@esefarad.com.
URL: http://www.fesela.com/

History 1972, within the framework of *World Sephardi Federation (WSF, #21778)*. **Structure** President; Secretary; Treasurer. **Languages** Spanish.
Members National Committees in 11 countries:
Argentina, Brazil, Chile, Colombia, Guatemala, Panama, Paraguay, Peru, Uruguay, USA, Venezuela. [2017.03.09/XE4565/**E**]

♦ Federación de Seguridad Privada de los Paises del Mercosur (FESESUR) 09389

Contact Rua Bernardino Fanganielo 691, Casa Verde 02512-000, Sao Paulo SP, Brazil. T. +55118587360 – +55118587837.
URL: http://www.forodeseguridad.com/instit/latam/fesesur.htm

History Full title: *Federación de Camares y Asociaciones de Empresas de Seguridad Privada de los Paises del Mercosur*. **Structure** General Assembly.
Members Full in 5 countries:
Argentina, Bolivia, Brazil, Paraguay, Uruguay. [2019.07.15/XJ2015/**D**]

♦ Federación Simmental-Fleckvieh Mundial (#21785)
♦ Federación Sindical Europea de Servicios Públicos (#07202)
♦ Federación Sindical de Funcionarios Internacionales (inactive)
♦ Federación Sindical Mundial (#21493)
♦ Federación de Sindicatos de Trabajadores de las Universidades de Centroamérica, México y el Caribe (#09712)
♦ Federación de Sociedades de Cancerología del Mercosur, Chile y Bolivia / see Federación de Sociedados de Cancerología de Sudamerica (#09391)

♦ Federación de Sociedades de Cirurgia Pediatrica del Cono sur de América (CIPESUR) 09390

Federation of Pediatric Surgery Societies in the Southern Cone of America

Pres c/o MP, Av Ricaldoni 2452, esq Campbell, Montevideo, Uruguay.
Contact c/o ACA CIP, Sanchez de Bustamante 305, PB 1, 1173 Buenos Aires, Argentina.

History 1993. **Events** *Congress* Bariloche (Argentina) 2019, *Congress* Asunción (Paraguay) 2017, *Congress* Gramado (Brazil) 2015, *Congress* Santa Cruz (Bolivia) 2013, *Congress* Punta del Este (Uruguay) 2011. **Publications** *Revista de Cirurgia Infantil* (4 a year).
Members National organizations (5) in 5 countries:
Argentina, Brazil, Chile, Paraguay, Uruguay. [2013/XM0812/**D**]

♦ Federación de Sociedades Sudamericanas en Ciencias de Animales de Laboratorio (#09704)

♦ Federación de Sociedados de Cancerología de Sudamerica (FESCAS) 09391

Federação das Sociedades de Cancerologia da América do Sul

Contact address not obtained. E-mail: info@fescas.com.
URL: http://www.fescas.com/

History Former names and other names: *Federación de Sociedades de Cancerología del Mercosur, Chile y Bolivia* – former (1993 to 2010). **Structure** Executive Commission. **Events** *Meeting* Buenos Aires (Argentina) 2000.
Members Organizations in 7 countries:
Argentina, Bolivia, Brazil, Chile, Paraguay, Peru, Uruguay. [2021/AA2072/**D**]

♦ Federación Sudamericana de Actividad Física Adaptada (FESAFA) . 09392

Contact address not obtained. E-mail: fesafa.safapa@gmail.com.
URL: https://fesafa.net/

History 7 Nov 2020. Founded following International Symposium of Adapted Physical Activity (*Simposio Internacional de Actividad Física Adaptada).*A regional organization of *International Federation of Adapted Physical Activity (IFAPA, #13338)*. **Aims** Bring together professionals, researchers and students from South American countries to promote and disseminate scientific knowledge in Adapted Physical Activity, encouraging professional training, interventions and research for the benefit of people with disabilities. **Structure** General Assembly; Advisory Council; Executive. **Activities** Events/meetings. **Events** *Congreso Sudamericano en Actividad Física Adaptada (COSUAFA) / South American Congress on Adapted Physical Activity* Chillan (Chile) 2022. **Publications** *Boletín FeSAFA*.
Members Full in 13 countries and territories:
Argentina, Bolivia, Brazil, Chile, Colombia, Ecuador, Guiana Fr, Guyana, Paraguay, Peru, Suriname, Uruguay, Venezuela.
NGO Relations Member of (1): *International Federation of Adapted Physical Activity (IFAPA, #13338)*. [2022/AA2977/**D**]

♦ Federación Sudamericana de Powerlifting (FESUPO) 09393

South America Powerlifting Federation

SG Av De los Estudiantes 1576, San Antonio de Padua, ZIP 1718 Buenos Aires, Argentina. T. +542204823722. E-mail: jose@powerlifting.com.ar.
Pres Rua Paranapanema 111, ap 32 Saude, Sao Paulo SP, SP CEP 04144-100, Brazil. T. +551132595852. E-mail: powerbrazil@uol.com.br.

URL: http://www.powerlifting.com.ar/index%20fesupo.htm
History A regional federation of *International Powerlifting Federation (IPF, #14630)*. **Activities** Awards/prizes/competitions.
Members Organizations in 9 countries:
Argentina, Brazil, Colombia, Ecuador, Guyana, Paraguay, Peru, Uruguay, Venezuela. [2014/XJ4258/**D**]

♦ Federación Sudamericana de Practicos (no recent information)
♦ Federación Sudamericana de Sociedades de Cirugia de Cabeza y Cuello (inactive)
♦ Federación Técnica Iberoamericana de la Celulosa y el Papel (no recent information)
♦ Federación Teosófica Interamericana (#11453)
♦ Federación de los Trabajadores en la Industria de Platano de América Latina y del Caribe (inactive)
♦ Federación de Trabajadores Latinoamericana de la Industria de la Alimentación, Bebidas, Hoteles y Tabacos (inactive)

♦ Federación de Trabajadores Latinoamericanos del Comercio, Oficinas y Empresas Privadas de Servicios (FETRALCOS) 09394

Federation of Latin American Trade, Office and Private Service Sector Workers

Pres Toro a Cardones, Edificio Fristol Local 3, Altagracia, Caracas DF, Venezuela. E-mail: info@fetralcos.org.ar.
URL: http://www.fetralcos.org.ar/

History as *Federación Latinoamericana de Trabajadores del Comercio y Similares*. **Languages** Spanish. **Staff** 27.00 FTE, paid. **Finance** Members' dues. Voluntary contributions. **Activities** include support for the self-employed. **Events** *Congress* Brasilia (Brazil) 2004, *Congress* Lima (Peru) 1988. **Publications** *FETRALCOS Informa* (periodical). **Members** Membership countries not specified. **NGO Relations** Regional federation of: *World Organization of Workers (WOW, #21697)*. [2011/XD1167/t/**D**]

♦ Federación de Trabajadores de la Salud de Centroamérica y Panama (inactive)
♦ Federación Universal de las Asociaciones de Agencias de Viajes / see United Federation of Travel Agents' Associations (#20509)
♦ Federación Universal de Movimientos Estudiantiles Cristianos (#21833)
♦ Federación de Universidades Católicas de Europa (#07070)
♦ Federación de Universidades Privadas de América Central y Panama / see Asociación de Universidades Privadas de Centroamérica y Panama (#02306)
♦ Federación Universitaria Sionista Latinoamericano – Sur (inactive)
♦ Federación Universitaria Sionista Latinoamericano – Norte (no recent information)

♦ Federación de Usuarios de Interent de latinoamerica y Caribe (FUILAC) 09395

Contact Salta 2041, Mar del Plata, B7600DFQ Buenos Aires, Argentina. T. +542234912925. Fax +542234950758. E-mail: info@fuilac.org.
URL: http://www.fuilac.org/

Structure Bureau.
Members Full in 8 countries:
Argentina, Brazil, Chile, Colombia, Dominican Rep, El Salvador, Peru, Venezuela. [2018/XJ3693/**D**]

♦ Federación de Veterinarios Europeos de la Industria y la Investigación / see European Association of Veterinarians in Education, Research and Industry (#06267)
♦ Federacja Miedzynarodowa Prasy Technicznej i Zawodowej (inactive)
♦ Federacja Spolecznosci Terapeutycznych Europy Centralnej i Wschodniej (#09707)
♦ Federações de Ajuda Social, Ecológica e Cultural (#09335)
♦ Fédéralistes, Les (inactive)
♦ Federalists (inactive)
♦ Federalistskij Sojuz Evropejskih Nacionalnyh Mensinstv (#09396)
♦ Federalist Union of European Minorities and Regions / see Federal Union of European Nationalities (#09396)
♦ Federal Trust for Education and Research (internationally oriented national body)
♦ Federal Union of European Ethnic Groups / see Federal Union of European Nationalities (#09396)

♦ Federal Union of European Nationalities (FUEN) 09396

Union fédéraliste des communautés ethniques européennes – Föderalistische Union Europäischer Nationalitäten – Federalistskij Sojuz Evropejskih Nacionalnyh Mensinstv

Pres FUEN Secretariat, Schiffbrücke 41, 24939 Flensburg, Germany. T. +4946112855. Fax +49461180709. E-mail: info@fuen.org.
URL: http://www.fuen.org/

History 19 Nov 1949, Versailles (France). Most recent statutes adopted 11 Sep 2021, Trieste (Italy). Former names and other names: *Federalist Union of European Minorities and Regions* – former; *Union fédéraliste des communautés et régions européennes* – former; *Federal Union of European Ethnic Groups* – former (2016); *Föderalistische Union Europäischer Volksgruppen (FUEV)* – former (2016); *UFCE* – former (2016). Registration: EU Transparency Register, No/ID: 331310413543-50. **Aims** Preserve and promote the identity, language and culture of minorities as a contribution to linguistic and cultural diversity, for preservation of inalienable values and the intellectual heritage of Europe. **Structure** Assembly of Delegates (in conjunction with annual Congress); Presidium (Executive Board), includes a representative of *Youth of European Nationalities (YEN, #22013)*; Secretariat General in Flensburg (Germany), with further offices in Berlin (Germany) and Brussels (Belgium). **Languages** English, French, German, Russian. **Staff** 8.00 FTE, paid; 7.50 FTE, voluntary. **Finance** Sources: contributions; members' dues; revenue from activities/projects. Supported by: *European Commission (EC, #06633)*. **Activities** Advocacy/lobbying/activism; events/meetings; knowledge management/information dissemination; politics/policy/regulatory. Works for ratification of *European Charter for Regional or Minority Languages (ECRML, 1992)* and *Framework Convention for the Protection of National Minorities (1995)*. **Events** *Annual Congress* Trieste (Italy) 2021, *Assembly of Delegates* Flensburg (Germany) 2020, *Annual Congress* Bratislava (Slovakia) 2019, *Annual Congress* Leeuwarden (Netherlands) 2018, *Annual Congress* Cluj-Napoca (Romania) 2017. **Publications** *Fundamental Rights. FUEN An Outline History 1949-1999*. Press releases; proceedings of Congress of Nationalities; other conference, seminar, workshop and film festival proceedings; videos of conferences.
Members Full (105) in 35 countries:
Albania, Austria, Azerbaijan, Belgium, Bosnia-Herzegovina, Bulgaria, Croatia, Czechia, Denmark, Estonia, France, Georgia, Germany, Greece, Hungary, Italy, Kazakhstan, Kosovo, Kyrgyzstan, Latvia, Moldova, Netherlands, North Macedonia, Poland, Romania, Russia, Serbia, Slovakia, Slovenia, Spain, Sweden, Switzerland, Türkiye, Ukraine, Uzbekistan.
Consultative Status Consultative status granted from: *ECOSOC (#05331)* (Special); *Council of Europe (CE, #04881)* (Participatory Status). **IGO Relations** *Committee on the Elimination of Racial Discrimination (CERD, #04251)*; *European Committee of the Regions (CoR, #06665)*; *European Commission (EC, #06633)*; *European Parliament (EP, #08146)*; *European Union Agency for Fundamental Rights (FRA, #08969)*; *Office of the United Nations High Commissioner for Human Rights (OHCHR, #17697)*; *Organization for Security and Cooperation in Europe (OSCE, #17887)*; *UNESCO (#20322)*; *UNHCR (#20327)*; *United Nations Human Rights Council (HRC, #20571)*. **NGO Relations** Member of: *Conference of Non-Governmental Organizations in Consultative Relationship with the United Nations (CONGO, #04635)*; *European Civil Society Platform for Multilingualism (ECSPM, #06569)*. [2022.02.16/XD0924/**D**]

♦ Federasi Internasional Perhimpunan Donor Darah Sukarela (#13374)
♦ Federatia Balcanică a Asociatiilor Apicole (#03073)
♦ Federatie van de Bakkerij- en Banketbakkerijgrondstoffenindustrie in de EER / see Federation of European Manufacturers of Ingredients to the Bakery, Confectionery and Patisserie Industries (#09513)
♦ Federatie van de Bakkerijgrondstoffenindustrie in de EEG / see Federation of European Manufacturers of Ingredients to the Bakery, Confectionery and Patisserie Industries (#09513)
♦ Federatie van Baksteen en Dakpannen Fabrikanten / see Tiles and Bricks Europe (#20163)
♦ Federatie van Bedrijfsverpleegkundigen in de Europese Unie (#09697)
♦ Federatie van Brandweerverenigingen in de Europese Unie (#09555)
♦ Federatie van Europese Motorrijders (inactive)
♦ Federatie Europese Narren (#09810)
♦ Federatie van Europese Uitgevers (#09536)
♦ Federatie van Europese Zoölogen (inactive)
♦ Federatie van Ingenieurs der Telecommunicatie in de Europese Gemeenschap (#09597)
♦ Federatie van Jaarbeurzen, Vakbeurzen en Tentoonstellingen in de Benelux (inactive)
♦ Federatie voor Marokkaanse Democratische Organisaties / see Federatie voor Mondiale Democratische Organisaties
♦ Federatie voor Mondiale Democratische Organisaties (internationally oriented national body)
♦ Federatie van Nationale Organisaties van Groothandelaren, Importeurs en Exporteurs van Vis van de EEG / see Comité des organisations nationales des importateurs et exportateurs de poisson de l'UE (#04194)
♦ Federatie van Nationale Organisaties van Groothandelaren, Importeurs en Exporteurs van Vis van de Europese Unie / see Comité des organisations nationales des importateurs et exportateurs de poisson de l'UE (#04194)
♦ Federatie van de Olie-Industrie in de EG / see FEDIOL – The EU Vegetable Oil and Proteinmeal Industry (#09718)
♦ Federatie van de Olijfolie-Industrie in de EEG (#09596)
♦ Federatie van Papier-, Karton- en Verpakkings-Groothandelaren in Europa / see European Paper Merchants Association (#08138)
♦ Federatie van Verenigingen voor Verwarming en Luchtbehandeling in Europa / see Federation of European Heating, Ventilation and Air-Conditioning Associations (#09507)
♦ Fédération abolitionniste internationale (inactive)
♦ Fédération des académies nationales de médecine et des institutions similaires de l'Union européenne / see Federation of European Academies of Medicine (#09490)
♦ Fédération des académies scientifiques asiatiques (inactive)
♦ Federation of Acoustical Societies of Europe (inactive)
♦ Fédération des aéroclubs des Caraïbes (inactive)

♦ Fédération aéronautique internationale (FAI) 09397

Contact Maison du Sport International, Avenue de Rhodanie 54, 1007 Lausanne VD, Switzerland. T. +41213451070. Fax +41213451077. E-mail: info@fai.org.
URL: http://www.fai.org/

History 14 Oct 1905, Paris (France). Former names and other names: *FAI – The World Air Sports Federation* – alias. **Aims** Promote air sports and recreational flying. **Structure** General Conference (annual); Executive Board; Secretariat, headed by Secretary General; Air Sport Commissions (12); Technical Commissions (3). **Languages** English, French, Russian, Spanish. **Finance** Sources: members' dues; revenue from activities/projects; sponsorship. **Activities** Awards/prizes/competitions; events/meetings; standards/guidelines. **Events** *Annual General Conference* Lausanne (Switzerland) 2022, *Annual General Conference* Lausanne (Switzerland) 2021, *Annual General Conference* Lausanne (Switzerland) 2020, *Annual General Conference* Marrakech (Morocco) 2019, *Annual General Conference* Luxor (Egypt) 2018. **Members** Active: organizations representing all relevant disciplines practiced in their country; Associate: organizations representing only one discipline; Temporary: national organizations intending to become an Active or Associate Member; International Affiliate: international organizations sharing common goals with FAI. Active in 88 countries and territories. Membership countries not specified. **IGO Relations** Member of (1): *International Committee on Global Navigation Satellite Systems (ICG, #12775)*. Maintains liaison on matters of mutual interest with: *International Civil Aviation Organization (ICAO, #12581)*. Associated with Department of Global Communications of the United Nations. **NGO Relations** Member of (3): *Association of the IOC Recognized International Sports Federations (ARISF, #02767)*; *International World Games Association (IWGA, #15914)*; *Olympic Movement (#17719)*. Cooperates with (1): *International Testing Agency (ITA, #15678)*. Recognized International Federation of: *International Olympic Committee (IOC, #14408)*. [2021.10.28/XB1140/y/**B**]

♦ Fédération africaine d'action familiale (inactive)
♦ Fédération africaine des arts traditionnels (inactive)

♦ Fédération africaine des associations nationales de parents d'élèves et étudiants (FAPE) 09398

Pres Immeuble APEEC, Avenue Paul Doumer, BP 1113, Brazzaville, Congo Brazzaville. T. +2422814996 – +2425515613. Fax +242830643.
FAPE-Paris 37 rue Louis Rolland, 92120 Montrouge, France. T. +33146579766.
URL: https://actufape.jimdofree.com/

History Jan 1995. **Aims** Promote recognition of the central role of parents as first *educators* and of the need to include them as responsible partners of educational institutions; establish real partnership among educational institutions, political and administrative authorities and parents' associations. **Structure** General Assembly; Managing Board; Executive Bureau. **Languages** French. **Staff** 7.00 FTE, paid. **Finance** Members' dues. Specific activities and projects supported by: UNESCO; *Agence française de développement (AFD)*; *Every Home for Christ International (EHCI, #09214)*. **Activities** Projects/programmes; training/education. **Events** *Congrès / Congress* Côte d'Ivoire 2001, *Congrès / Congress* Ouagadougou (Burkina Faso) 1998. **Publications** *Nous les parents* (2 a year).
Members National parent organizations and non-governmental organizations in 14 countries:
Benin, Burkina Faso, Cameroon, Central African Rep, Chad, Congo Brazzaville, Congo DR, Côte d'Ivoire, Gabon, Guinea, Mali, Niger, Senegal, Togo.
International organizations (2):
Confédération internationale des parents (CIP, no recent information); *International Federation for Parent Education (IFPE, #13499)*.
Consultative Status Consultative status granted from: *ECOSOC (#05331)* (Ros C); *UNESCO (#20322)* (Associate Status). **IGO Relations** Accredited by (1): *Organisation internationale de la Francophonie (OIF, #17809)*. ACCT. **NGO Relations** Member of (1): *Global Campaign for Education (GCE, #10264)*. [2022/XD6239/**D**]

♦ Fédération africaine des employés / see Fédération panafricaine des employés (#09700)
♦ Fédération africaine pour l'étude de la douleur (no recent information)
♦ Fédération africaine des femmes entrepreneurs (#00313)
♦ Fédération africaine d'haltérophilie (#20854)
♦ Fédération Africaine de Médecine d'Urgence (#00307)
♦ Fédération africaine des organisations d'ingénieurs / see Federation of African Engineering Organisations (#09402)

♦ Fédération Africaine des Professionnels de la Réadaptation (FATO) 09399

African Federation of Rehabilitation Professionals

Contact 06 BP 9882, Ouagadougou 06, Burkina Faso. T. +22625387741. E-mail: fato@fatoafrique.org.
URL: http://www.fatoafrique.org/

History Feb 1992, Lomé (Togo). Founded as *Fédération africaine des techniciens orthoprothésistes (FATO) – African Federation of Orthopedic Technologists*. Present title adopted 2019, retaining original acronym. Registration: Start date: 1999, Burkina Faso. **Aims** Gather African associations of prosthetic and orthopaedic professionals in a body that promotes exchanges, mutual assistance and self-fulfillment; work for rehabilitation of all persons with disabilities in Africa; help promote research on new technologies appropriate to the African context; create a framework for meetings, training and experience sharing between African countries and with the rest of the world. **Structure** Federal Conference (every 2 years); Board; Federal Board; Regional Assembly (every 2 years); Regions (5); Bureau. **Languages** English, French. **Staff** 6.00 FTE, paid. **Finance** Members' dues. Other sources: annual subscriptions; subsidies; money-making activities; gifts from individuals or corporations. **Activities** Networking/liaising; training/education; awareness raising; research/documentation; events/meetings. **Events** *Equitable and universal access to rehabilitation services in Africa* Marrakech (Morocco) 2022, *Equitable and universal access to rehabilitation services in Africa* Marrakech (Morocco) 2020, *Congress* Kigali (Rwanda) 2018, *Congress* Lomé (Togo) 2016, *Congress* Yamoussoukro (Côte d'Ivoire) 2013. **Publications** *FATO Info*.

Members Active – national organizations; Benefactor – individuals or corporations; Honorary – individuals.
National organizations in 14 countries:
Benin, Burkina Faso, Burundi, Cameroon, Central African Rep, Chad, Congo DR, Côte d'Ivoire, Mali, Mauritania, Niger, Rwanda, Senegal, Togo.
Individuals in 3 countries:
Morocco, Sierra Leone, Zimbabwe.
IGO Relations Partner of: *African Rehabilitation Institute (ARI, #00437).* **NGO Relations** Member of: *RI Global (#18948).* Partner of: *Humanity and Inclusion (HI, #10975);* national organizations. [2022/XJ3946/t/**D**]

- ♦ Fédération africaine des secrétaires et assistants et attachés de direction (inactive)
- ♦ Fédération africaine des sociétés d'immunologie (#09403)
- ♦ Fédération africaine du sport universitaire (#09412)
- ♦ Fédération africaine des syndicats du pétrole et affinage (no recent information)
- ♦ Fédération africaine des techniciens orthoprothésistes / see Fédération Africaine des Professionnels de la Réadaptation (#09399)
- ♦ Fédération africaine de tennis de table (#00478)

♦ Federation of African Archery (FAA) 09400

SG El Estad El Bahary St, Sports Federations' Bldg – Office No 2, Nasr City, Cairo, Egypt. T. +201001087376.
URL: http://www.africanarchery.org/

History Also known and *World Archery Africa* – as the African section of *World Archery (#21105).* **Aims** Ensure development of the *sport* on the African Continent; provide the infrastructure and know-how for member nations to develop the sport. **Structure** Council. **Activities** Sporting events.
Members Federations in 28 countries:
Algeria, Benin, Cameroon, Central African Rep, Chad, Comoros, Côte d'Ivoire, Egypt, Ghana, Guinea, Kenya, Liberia, Libya, Malawi, Mali, Mauritius, Morocco, Namibia, Niger, Nigeria, Rwanda, Senegal, Somalia, South Africa, Sudan, Tunisia, Uganda, Zimbabwe. [2017/XM4690/**D**]

- ♦ Federation of African Chambers of Commerce (no recent information)
- ♦ Federation of African Chambers of Commerce and Industry / see Federation of African Chambers of Commerce, Industry, Agriculture and Professions (#09401)

♦ Federation of African Chambers of Commerce, Industry, Agriculture and Professions (ACCIP) 09401

Secretariat Federation of Egyptian Chambers of Commerce and Industry, 4 E1 Falky Square, Cairo, Egypt. T. +2023551164.

History Apr 2005, Alexandria (Egypt), by 42 African Chambers of Commerce. Previously also referred to as *Federation of African Chambers of Commerce and Industry (FACCI).* **Events** *Extra-ordinary Assembly* Addis Ababa (Ethiopia) 2009. [2009/XJ3936/t/**D**]

- ♦ Federation of African Consultants (inactive)

♦ Federation of African Engineering Organisations (FAEO) 09402

Fédération des organisations d'ingénieurs en Afrique (FEIA)

Secretariat Ste 205, NEC Bldg, Natl Engineering Ctr, Off Natl Mosque, Labour House Road, Central Business District, Abuja, Federal Capital Territory, Nigeria. T. +2348033345810.
LinkedIn: https://www.linkedin.com/company/federation-of-african-engineering-organisations

History 1972, Cairo (Egypt). Founded following recommendations, 1971, Nairobi (Kenya), of a meeting organized by *World Federation of Engineering Organizations (WFEO, #21433)* under *UNESCO (#20322)* sponsorship. Dormant until 1988, when revitalized by UNESCO. Accepted as an international member of WFEO, 1989, Prague (Czechoslovakia). Constitution adopted, 8 May 2012, Nairobi (Kenya). Former names and other names: *Federation of African Organizations of Engineers (FAOE)* – former (1972 to 2012); *Fédération africaine des organisations d'ingénieurs (FAOI)* – former (1972 to 2012). **Aims** Serve humanity Through the use of practiced technology; represent the engineering profession in Africa, on an international level. **Structure** General Assembly (at WFEO General Congress). Executive Committee. Secretariat. Federations (5): Central (CAFEO); Eastern (EAFEO); North (NAFEO); Southern (SAFEO); West (WAFEO). Standing Committees. **Languages** English, French. **Staff** 2.00 FTE, paid. **Finance** Mostly financed by the Nigerian Society of Engineers. **Activities** Courses, seminars and workshops on major engineering issues in Africa. **Events** *Conference* 2023, *General Assembly* Nairobi (Kenya) 2012, *General assembly / Meeting* Nairobi (Kenya) 2003, *Meeting* Nairobi (Kenya) 1995, *General Assembly* Havana (Cuba) 1993. **Publications** *FAOE Newsletter.* Journals.
Members Organizations of engineers in 22 countries:
Algeria, Cameroon, Congo DR, Côte d'Ivoire, Egypt, Ethiopia, Ghana, Guinea, Kenya, Libya, Mali, Morocco, Nigeria, Senegal, Sierra Leone, Somalia, Sudan, Tanzania UR, Tunisia, Uganda, Zambia, Zimbabwe.
IGO Relations *UNDP (#20292); UNIDO (#20336).* **NGO Relations** Member of (2): *World Council of Civil Engineers (WCCE, #21321); World Federation of Engineering Organizations (WFEO, #21433).* [2022/XD2227/**D**]

♦ Federation of African Immunological Societies (FAIS) 09403

Fédération africaine des sociétés d'immunologie

Pres Immunology Dept, Habib Bourguiba Hospital, 3029 Sfax, Tunisia. T. +21674451660 – +2167474451660. E-mail: fosier@kemri-wellcome.org – contact@faisafrica.com.

History Founded 1992, as a regional federation of *International Union of Immunological Societies (IUIS, #15781).* **Aims** Promote immunology research and training through: triennial Congress; scholarships to students and junior researchers so they can participate in the congress; support to organizations of specialized immunology courses; participation in the elaboration of guidelines for good laboratory practices and quality control in Africa. **Structure** Congress (triennially); Council; Executive of 5 officers. Committees (2): Clinical Immunology; Education and Publications. **Languages** English, French. **Staff** Voluntary. **Finance** Members' dues. Subvention from IUIS. Budget (annual): US$ 20,000. **Activities** Training/education. **Events** *Immunity and immunotherapeutics in Africa – tackling the burden of disease* Lilongwe (Malawi) 2021, *Immunity and immunotherapeutics in Africa – tackling the burden of disease* Lilongwe (Malawi) 2020, *Congress* Hammamet (Tunisia) 2017, *Towards full integration of immunology into Africa's healthcare systems* Nairobi (Kenya) 2014, *Congress* Durban (South Africa) 2012.
Members National societies in 11 countries:
Cameroon, Congo DR, Egypt, Ghana, Kenya, Nigeria, Senegal, South Africa, Sudan, Tunisia, Zimbabwe.
Included in the above, 1 organization listed in this Yearbook:
West African Immunology Society (WAIS, no recent information). [2016/XD2931/**D**]

♦ Federation of African Journalists (FAJ) 09404

Fédération des journalistes africains (FJA)

Contact Maison de la Presse, 5 Rue x Corniche, Médina, 12900 Dakar, Senegal. E-mail: mohgar@yahoo.com.
URL: http://www.africanjournalists.org/

History Nov 2007, Abuja (Nigeria). Founded during African Journalists Conference, by affiliate members of *International Federation of Journalists (IFJ, #13462).* **Events** *Congress* Harare (Zimbabwe) 2010, *Congress* Nairobi (Kenya) 2008.
Members Includes the following organizations:
Central African Union of Journalists; Eastern African Journalists Association; Northern African Network of Journalists; *Southern Africa Journalists Association (SAJA, no recent information); West African Journalists' Union (#20885).*
Consultative Status Consultative status granted from: *African Commission on Human and Peoples' Rights (ACHPR, #00255)* (Observer). **NGO Relations** Member of (1): *Ethical Journalism Network (EJN, #05554).* [2019/XM8248/**D**]

♦ Federation of African Journalist Union (FAJU) 09405

Contact 22 Talat Harb St, Information Dept Bldg, Cairo, Egypt. T. +20225795121 – +20225795123 – +20225795126. Fax +20225795165 – +20225795103. [2008/XJ0212/**D**]

- ♦ Federation of African Media Women (no recent information)

♦ Federation of African Medical Physics Organizations (FAMPO) 09406

Gen Sec Dept of Medical Physics – Natl Hosp, PMB 425, Garki, Abuja FCT 900001, Federal Capital Territory, Nigeria. T. +23592908846. Fax +23592908846.
Pres Hop des Specialites Ono, Fondation Hassan II Pour la Prevention et la Lutte Contre les Maladies du Systeme Nerveux, BP 6444, 10101 Rabat, Morocco. T. +212537775958. Fax +212537645564.
URL: http://www.federation-fampo.org/

NGO Relations Regional member of: *International Organization for Medical Physics (IOMP, #14453).* [2013/XJ6626/**D**]

♦ Federation of African Medical Students' Associations (FAMSA) 09407

Fédération des associations des étudiants africains en médecine

HQ Administrator C/O Office of the Provost, College of Medicine, University of Ibadan, Ibadan 200212, Oyo, Nigeria. T. +2347061016356. Fax +2348090897732. E-mail: famsaarchives@gmail.com – hq@famsanet.org.
URL: http://www.famsanet.org/

History Sep 1968, Accra (Ghana). Founded after having first been put forward 1964, Kampala (Uganda). Permanent headquarters established 1977, Ibadan (Nigeria). Registration: Ministry of Justice, the Gambia., No/ID: 2022/C19796, Start date: 21 Nov 2022, Gambia. **Aims** Enhance and broaden the general and special education of member medical students and thus to contribute to improvement of medical education in Africa; project the image of the African Medical Students both on the continental and international scene; establish contact with every Medical Students Association in African on professional matters; promote exchange of news of medical interest; generate initiative in population and health surveys as well as in bio-medical research in African medical students; encourage and assist member associations in fulfilling the essence of this education, to contribute towards the improvement of health conditions in Africa. **Structure** General Assembly; Executive Council; Standing Committees (5); Permanent Headquarters located in Ibadan (Nigeria). **Languages** Arabic, English, French. **Staff** Voluntary. **Finance** Sources: donations; grants; members' dues; sponsorship. **Activities** Advocacy/lobbying/activism; awareness raising; capacity building; events/meetings; healthcare; networking/liaising; projects/programmes; research and development; research/documentation; training/education. Active in all member countries. **Events** *Scientific Conference and General Assembly* Serekunda (Gambia) 2023, *East Africa Regional Convention* 2022, *Scientific Conference and General Assembly* Lusaka (Zambia) 2022, *West Africa Regional Convention* Oyo (Nigeria) 2022, *Scientific Conference and General Assembly* Cotonou (Benin) 2021. **Publications** *FAMSA Newsletter* (3 a year) in English; *Afromedica Journal* in English. Booklets; conference proceedings.
Members Full membership: over 240 registered Medical Students' Associations across the 5 regions of Africa in 48 countries:
Algeria, Angola, Benin, Botswana, Burkina Faso, Burundi, Cameroon, Central African Rep, Chad, Comoros, Congo Brazzaville, Congo DR, Egypt, Equatorial Guinea, Eritrea, Ethiopia, Gabon, Gambia, Ghana, Guinea, Guinea-Bissau, Kenya, Lesotho, Liberia, Libya, Madagascar, Malawi, Mali, Mauritania, Mauritius, Morocco, Mozambique, Namibia, Niger, Nigeria, Rwanda, Senegal, Seychelles, Sierra Leone, Somalia, South Africa, Sudan, Tanzania UR, Togo, Tunisia, Uganda, Zambia, Zimbabwe.
Associate membership: MSAs who are interested in FAMSA and its activities, but are unable to due to geographical location. Membership countries not specified.
Honorary membership: individuals who have contributed significantly to FAMSA. Membership countries not specified.
NGO Relations Member of (2): *The Right to Research Coalition (no recent information); World Federation of Public Health Associations (WFPHA, #21476).* African Regional Office of *International Federation of Medical Students' Associations (IFMSA, #13478).* [2023.02.26/XD3871/**D**]

♦ Federation of African National Insurance Companies 09408

Fédération des Sociétés d'Assurance de Droit National Africaines (FANAF)

Contact Rue Amadou Assane Ndoye angle Saint-Michel, BP 308, Dakar, Senegal. T. +221338896838. Fax +221338223756.
URL: http://www.fanaf.com/

History 17 Mar 1976, Yamoussoukro (Côte d'Ivoire). **Aims** Promote the development of the insurance industry; favour the exchanges between member societies and the establishment of an insurance common market; ensure continuing training in the field. **Structure** General Assembly (annual); Executive Committee; Permanent Secretariat, headed by Permanent Secretary General. **Languages** French. **Staff** Voluntary. **Finance** Members' dues. **Events** *Annual General Assembly* Abidjan (Côte d'Ivoire) 2016, *Annual general assembly / General Assembly* Dakar (Senegal) 2011, *Forum AFRisques* Abidjan (Côte d'Ivoire) 2010, *Annual General Assembly* Kinshasa (Congo DR) 2010, *Annual general assembly / General Assembly* Yamoussoukro (Côte d'Ivoire) 2009. **Publications** *L'Assureur africain* (4 a year); *Annuaire statistique.* Brochure.
Members Insurance and reinsurance companies in 29 countries:
Algeria, Bahrain, Benin, Burkina Faso, Burundi, Cameroon, Central African Rep, Chad, Congo Brazzaville, Congo DR, Côte d'Ivoire, Equatorial Guinea, Gabon, Ghana, Guinea, Kenya, Madagascar, Mali, Mauritania, Morocco, Niger, Nigeria, Rwanda, Senegal, Sierra Leone, South Africa, Tanzania UR, Togo, Tunisia.
Consultative Status Consultative status granted from: *UNCTAD (#20285)* (Special Category). **IGO Relations** Partner of: *Inter-African Conference on Insurance Markets (#11385); Institut international des assurances, Yaoundé (IIA, #11309).* Member of: *Commission régionale de contrôle des assurances dans les Etats africains (CRCA, see: #11385).* [2017.07.07/XD7407/**D**]

♦ Federation of African Nutrition Societies (FANUS) 09409

SG Dept of Nutrition and Dietetics, Univ of Nigeria, Onitsha Road, Nsukka, Enugu, Nigeria. E-mail: info@fanus.org.
Contact address not obtained.
URL: http://www.fanus.org/

Aims Promote advancement of nutrition science in Africa. **Structure** Council; President. **Languages** English. **Finance** Sources: donations; members' dues. **Activities** Events/meetings; networking/liaising; training/education; research and development; knowledge management/information dissemination. **Events** *Conference* Somerset West (South Africa) 2023, *Nutrition in action for sustainable development in Africa* Kigali (Rwanda) 2019, *Nutrition in Africa at a turning point* Arusha (Tanzania UR) 2015, *Accelerating nutrition action for africa's development* Abuja (Nigeria) 2011, *Conference* Ouarzazate (Morocco) 2007. **Members** Full in 12 countries. Membership countries not specified. **NGO Relations** Affiliated Member of: *International Union of Nutritional Sciences (IUNS, #15796).* [2022/XM3542/**D**]

- ♦ Federation of African Organizations of Engineers / see Federation of African Engineering Organisations (#09402)
- ♦ Federation of African Public Relations Associations (inactive)
- ♦ Federation of African Roller Sports / see World Skate Africa (#21787)

♦ Federation of African Societies of Biochemistry and Molecular Biology (FASBMB) 09410

Fédération des sociétés africaines de biochimie et de biologie moléculaire

Pres Cadi Ayyad Univ, Fac Sciences, Unit Biotechnology-Biochemistry, PBox 2390, Marrakech, Morocco. T. +212661232285. Fax +212524437412.
Gen Sec Dept of Biochemistry, Univ of Zimbabwe, BOX MP167, Mount Pleasant, Harare, HARARE, Zimbabwe. E-mail: bmbsz01@gmail.com.
URL: http://www.fasbmb.org.za/

History Founded Sep 1996, Nairobi (Kenya). **Aims** Promote biochemistry and molecular biology in Africa. **Structure** Council; Executive Committee. **Languages** English. **Finance** Funding from: *International Union of Biochemistry and Molecular Biology (IUBMB, #15759).* **Activities** Events/meetings; training/education. **Events** *Joint meeting* Potchefstroom (South Africa) 2018, *Symposium on Biochemistry* Harare (Zimbabwe) 2017, *Congress* South Africa 2012, *Congress* Marrakech (Morocco) 2009, *Health and wealth for Africa through biochemistry and molecular biology* Abuja (Nigeria) 2006.
Members National societies in 16 countries:
Cameroon, Côte d'Ivoire, Egypt, Gambia, Ghana, Kenya, Mauritius, Morocco, Nigeria, Senegal, South Africa, Sudan, Tunisia, Uganda, Zambia, Zimbabwe.
NGO Relations Member of: *International Union of Biochemistry and Molecular Biology (IUBMB, #15759).* [2017.03.08/XD6472/**D**]

♦ **Federation of African Societies of Chemistry (FASC)** **09411**

Sec Addis Ababa Univ, Fac of Science, PO Box 2305, Addis Ababa, Ethiopia. T. +251911244704. E-mail: info@faschem.org.

URL: http://www.faschem.org/

History 23 Feb 2006, Addis Ababa (Ethiopia), by *UNESCO – International Institute for Capacity Building in Africa (IICBA, #20308)* and 4 individual Founding Members. **Aims** Promote advancement of chemical sciences and the practice of chemistry that could be instrumental to the fulfillment of the development aspirations and objectives of the people in Africa. **Structure** Annual General Assembly. Executive Committee, comprising President, Vice-President, Secretary, Treasurer and 7 members. **Activities** Enhances member chemical societies' positions as the source of the highest quality chemical information; assists member chemical societies to promote the development of a community of highly-skilled practitioners of chemistry; supports member chemical societies in their efforts to foster their respective societies' belief and investment in chemistry. **Events** *Congress* Gaborone (Botswana) 2019, *Congress* Marrakech (Morocco) 2013, *Symposium on analytical chemistry for sustainable development* Marrakech (Morocco) 2013.

Members Chemical societies in 6 countries:
Egypt, Ethiopia, Kenya, Nigeria, South Africa, Tunisia.

Regional organizations (1):
West African Chemical Society (#20873).

NGO Relations Member of: *International Union of Pure and Applied Chemistry (IUPAC, #15809).*
[2010/XJ1147/y/**D**]

♦ **Federation of African University Sports (FASU)** **09412**

Fédération africaine du sport universitaire (FASU)

SG CC Block Tower, CCE, Makerere University, PO Box 1557, Kampala, Uganda. T. +256772403086. E-mail: info@africauniversitysports.com.

Pres address not obtained.

URL: http://www.africauniversitysports.com/

History 1974, Accra (Ghana). Registration: Uganda Registration Service Bureau, Uganda. **Aims** Promote sports excellence within the framework of university education in Africa for the sustainability of both body and mind. **Structure** General Assembly; Executive Committee; General Secretariat. **Languages** English, French. **Staff** 5.00 FTE, paid. **Finance** Sources: grants; members' dues. Other sources: assistance from *International University Sports Federation (FISU, #15830)* grant, on request; FASU games fees. **Activities** Events/meetings; sporting activities; training/education. **Events** *Elective General Assembly* Entebbe (Uganda) 2019, *Ordinary General Assembly* Kigali (Rwanda) 2017, *General Assembly* Addis Ababa (Ethiopia) 2015, *General Assembly* Windhoek (Namibia) 2012, *General Assembly* Kampala (Uganda) 2010.

Members in 40 countries:
Algeria, Angola, Benin, Botswana, Burkina Faso, Burundi, Cameroon, Cape Verde, Central African Rep, Comoros, Congo DR, Côte d'Ivoire, Egypt, Eswatini, Ethiopia, Gambia, Ghana, Guinea, Kenya, Lesotho, Libya, Madagascar, Malawi, Mauritius, Morocco, Mozambique, Namibia, Niger, Nigeria, Rwanda, Sao Tomé-Principe, Senegal, Sierra Leone, Somalia, South Africa, Sudan, Tanzania UR, Uganda, Zambia, Zimbabwe.

NGO Relations . [2022.02.21/XD3530/**D**]

♦ Federation of African Women Entrepreneurs / see African Federation of Women Entrepreneurs (#00313)
♦ Federation of African Women's Networks on Peace (no recent information)

♦ **Federation of Afro-Asian Insurers and Reinsurers (FAIR)** **09413**

Fédération d'assureurs et de réassureurs afro-asiatiques – Federación de Empresas Afroasiaticas de Seguros y Reaseguros

SG 129 El Tahrir Street, 4th Floor, Office No 1, Doqi, Giza, Egypt. T. +20223923630 – +20223951815. Fax +20223921848 – +20223961007. E-mail: info@fair1964.org.

URL: http://www.fair.org.eg/

History Founded 5 Sep 1964, Cairo (Egypt), at a meeting of representatives of Afro-Asian insurance markets in cooperation with the then *Afro-Asian Organization for Economic Cooperation (AFRASEC, inactive).* **Aims** Promote and foster insurance and reinsurance collaboration between Afro-Asian countries and with outside markets; act as spokesman for the insurance world in Africa and Asia; encourage the provision of insurance training facilities. **Structure** Biennial General Meeting; Executive Committee. **Languages** Arabic, English, French. **Staff** 5.00 FTE, paid. **Finance** Members' dues. **Activities** Events/meetings; knowledge management/ information dissemination. **Events** *Biennial General Meeting* Marrakech (Morocco) 2019, *Biennial General Meeting* Manama (Bahrain) 2017, *Biennial General Meeting* Cairo (Egypt) 2015, *Biennial General Meeting* Beijing (China) 2013, *General Meeting* Cairo (Egypt) 2011. **Publications** *FAIR Quarterly Review* (4 a year). Conference proceedings; reports.

Members African and Asian insurance companies and associations (251) in 50 countries:
Algeria, Bahrain, Bangladesh, Botswana, China, Cyprus, Egypt, Eritrea, Ethiopia, Ghana, Hong Kong, India, Indonesia, Iran Islamic Rep, Iraq, Jordan, Kazakhstan, Kenya, Korea DPR, Korea Rep, Kuwait, Lebanon, Libya, Madagascar, Malaysia, Maldives, Morocco, Nigeria, Oman, Pakistan, Philippines, Qatar, Rwanda, Saudi Arabia, Seychelles, South Africa, Sri Lanka, Sudan, Syrian AR, Tanzania UR, Thailand, Togo, Tunisia, Türkiye, United Arab Emirates, Uzbekistan, Vietnam, Yemen, Zambia, Zimbabwe.

Included in the above, 1 regional organization:
African Reinsurance Corporation (AFRICA RE, #00438).

Correspondent members (3) in 3 countries:
Germany, Malaysia, Switzerland.

Consultative Status Consultative status granted from: *ECOSOC (#05331)* (Ros C); *UNCTAD (#20285)* (Special Category). **IGO Relations** Accredited by: *United Nations Office at Vienna (UNOV, #20604).* Associated with Department of Global Communications of the United Nations. [2022/XD0927/**D**]

♦ Fédération afro-asiatique des producteurs de tabac (inactive)

♦ **Fédération des Agences Internationales pour le Développement (AIDE Fédération)** **09414**

Federation of International Agencies for Development

Pres 29 rue Traversière, 75012 Paris, France. T. +33140199151. Fax +33143443840. E-mail: international@aide-federation.org – aide@aide-federation.org.

Bureau Geneva Rue des Savoises MA 15, 1205 Geneva, Switzerland. E-mail: geneve@aide-federation.org.

URL: http://www.aide-federation.org/

History 1986. Former names and other names: *Agence internationale pour le développement (AIDE)* – former; *Agency for International Development* – former; *Aide – Solidarité* – former. Registration: Start date: 19 Mar 1998, France. **Aims** Give a permanent food and clothing assistance to needy families; assist persons with difficulties in finding a professional employment; participate in economic and social development projects in the Third World countries. **Activities** Events/meetings; financial and/or material support. **Events** *Colloque européen sur l'égalité des droits dans la diversité culturelle* Paris (France) 2008, *Colloquium on memory and human rights* Geneva (Switzerland) 2006, *How to surmount the obstacles to achieve the goals of the millennium for the development?* Geneva (Switzerland) 2006, *Forum on issues of diversity in Europe and European citizenship* Paris (France) 2006, *NGO forum* Paris (France) 2006. **Publications** *Oui à la vie* (4 a year).

Members National organizations (10) in 11 countries:
Belgium, Benin, Burkina Faso, Chad, France, India, Mali, Morocco, Senegal, Spain.

Consultative Status Consultative status granted from: *ECOSOC (#05331)* (General). **IGO Relations** Accredited by: *United Nations Office at Vienna (UNOV, #20604).* **NGO Relations** Member of: *European Social Action Network (ESAN, #08499); UNITED for Intercultural Action – European Network Against Nationalism, Racism, Fascism and in Support of Migrants and Refugees (UNITED, #20511).* [2020/XD0346/**D**]

♦ Fédération des agences de presse arabes (#09423)
♦ Federation of the Agrochemical Industry and Market of the Southern Cone (no recent information)
♦ Fédération de l'aide à l'enfance (internationally oriented national body)
♦ Fédération des aides aux toxicomanes en Europe / see European Treatment Centers for Drug Addiction (#08947)
♦ Federation of Allied Combatants in Europe (no recent information)

♦ **Federation of Aluminium Consumers in Europe (FACE)** **09415**

SG Rond Point Schuman 6 – box 5, 1040 Brussels, Belgium.

URL: https://face-aluminium.com/

History May 1999. Registration: Banque-Carrefour des Entreprises, No/ID: 0479.386.371, Start date: 19 May 1999, Belgium; EU Transparency Register, No/ID: 663240848326-52, Start date: 8 Dec 2022. **Aims** Advocate for a level playing field for the continent's downstream aluminium sector. [2023/AA3105/**D**]

♦ Federation Amateur of Muaythai of Asia / see Federation of Asian Muaythai Associations (#09436)
♦ Federation of American Sanatoria / see American College of Chest Physicians (#00778)
♦ Federation of American Women's Clubs in Europe / see Federation of American Women's Clubs Overseas (#09416)

♦ **Federation of American Women's Clubs Overseas (FAWCO)** **09416**

Pres 99 Wall Street, Suite 1931, New York NY 10005-4301, USA. E-mail: vp-communications@fawco.org – president@fawco.org.

URL: http://www.fawco.org/

History 1931. Founded by Caroline Curtis Brown. Dormant during World War II; reactivated in 1947. Former names and other names: *Federation of American Women's Clubs in Europe* – former. Registration: New York State Office of the Attorney General, No/ID: 21-63-96, Start date: 5 Sep 2006, USA; IRS Charities & Nonprofits, No/ID: 98-0058485, Start date: 20 Apr 1988, USA; New York State Division of Corporations, No/ID: 774661, Start date: 8 Jun 1982, USA. **Aims** Build strong support networks for members; improve lives of women and girls; advocate for rights of US citizens overseas; mobilize the skills of membership in support of global initiatives for education, the environment, health and human rights. **Structure** Board. **Languages** English. **Finance** Sources: donations; members' dues; sale of publications; sponsorship. **Activities** Events/meetings; networking/liaising; projects/programmes. Active in all member countries. **Events** *Biennial Conference* Bratislava (Slovakia) 2023, *Interim Meeting* Luxembourg (Luxembourg) 2022, *Biennial Conference* New York, NY (USA) 2021, *Interim Meeting* Luxembourg (Luxembourg) 2020, *Biennial Conference* Edinburgh (UK) 2019. **Publications** *Inspiring Women* (4 a year) – online magazine, profiles the lives of members of FAWCO Clubs throughout the world who have used their skills and talents to make an impact in the global community..

Members Clubs (over 60) and associations in 30 countries:
Antigua-Barbuda, Australia, Austria, Belgium, Colombia, Denmark, Finland, France, Germany, Greece, India, Ireland, Italy, Kenya, Korea Rep, Lebanon, Liechtenstein, Luxembourg, Moldova, Morocco, Netherlands, Nigeria, Norway, Philippines, Russia, Spain, Sweden, Switzerland, UK, USA.

Consultative Status Consultative status granted from: *ECOSOC (#05331)* (Special). **IGO Relations** Associated with Department of Global Communications of the United Nations. **NGO Relations** Member of (6): *Committee of NGOs on Human Rights, Geneva (#04275); Conference of Non-Governmental Organizations in Consultative Relationship with the United Nations (CONGO, #04635); NGO Committee on Migration, New York (#17112); NGO Committee on the Status of Women, Geneva (#17117); NGO Committee on the Status of Women, New York NY (see: #04635); Vienna NGO Committee on the Status of Women (#20775).* Member of: Working Group on Girls, New York. [2022.10.19/XE2588/**E**]

♦ Fédération d'Amérique centrale des associations non-gouvernementales de conservation (inactive)
♦ Fédération d'Amérique latine des établissements financiers (no recent information)
♦ Fédération pour l'amitié mondiale (inactive)

♦ **Fédération Anaforcal International (FAI)** **09417**

Registered Address Ctr Hospitalier Saint Joseph-Saint Luc, Unité d'Allergologie, 20 quai Claude Bernard, 69007 Lyon, France. E-mail: fai.wrld@gmail.com.

History Registration: France. **Aims** Promote, develop and coordinate the activities of initial and continuing medical training in allergology in the European and French-speaking area. **Structure** General Assembly; Board. **Activities** Events/meetings; research/documentation. **Events** *Congrès Francophone d'Allergologie* Paris (France) 2019.

Members Full in 22 countries:
Algeria, Belgium, Benin, Burkina Faso, Cameroon, Congo Brazzaville, Congo DR, Côte d'Ivoire, Djibouti, France, Gabon, Lebanon, Madagascar, Mali, Mauritania, Morocco, Niger, Romania, Rwanda, Senegal, Togo, Tunisia. [2020/AA0882/**C**]

♦ Federation of Analytical Chemistry and Spectroscopy Societies (internationally oriented national body)
♦ Fédération des Antilles (inactive)
♦ Federation of Arab Agricultural Engineers / see Arab Agricultural Engineers Union (#00895)
♦ Federation of Arab Agricultural Workers (inactive)
♦ Federation of Arab Biologists (inactive)

♦ **Federation of Arab Businessmen** **09418**

Pres Queen Rania Al-Absallah St – Jordan Univ, villa 11, Amman 11942, Jordan. T. +96265338035. Fax +96265337617. E-mail: info@fab-jo.org.

URL: http://www.fab-jo.org/

History 1997. Also referred to as *Arab Businessmen Confederation.* **Activities** annual Arab Businessmen Forum; sectorial meetings. **IGO Relations** Specialized agency of: *League of Arab States (LAS, #16420).* [2017/XD8819/**D**]

♦ **Federation of Arab Contractors (FAC)** **09419**

Union des entrepreneurs arabes (UEA)

Contact 34 Adly Street, Cairo, Egypt. T. +2023959500. Fax +2023959522. [2010/XD4264/**D**]

♦ Fédération arabe des armateurs / see Arab Federation of Shipping (#00953)
♦ Fédération arabe d'athlétisme amateur (inactive)
♦ Fédération arabe d'aviron (inactive)
♦ Fédération arabe des bibliothèques et centres d'information / see Arab Federation for Libraries and Information (#00947)
♦ Fédération arabe des clubs et associations des automobiles et touring (inactive)
♦ Federation of Arab Economists (no recent information)
♦ Fédération arabe de coopération agricole (inactive)
♦ Fédération arabe pour l'enseignement technique (no recent information)
♦ Fédération arabe des géomètres (#00955)
♦ Fédération arabe d'haltérophilie (inactive)
♦ Fédération arabe des industries alimentaires (#00946)
♦ Fédération arabe pour les industries d'ingénierie (#00943)
♦ Fédération arabe des industries de la pêche (#00945)
♦ Fédération arabe des industries textiles (inactive)

♦ **Federation of Arab Engineers (FAE)** **09420**

Fédération des ingénieurs arabes

Contact 30 Ramsis Street, PO Box 9, Cairo, 11522, Egypt. T. +20227735610. E-mail: arabengs@hotmail.com.

URL: http://arabfedeng.org/

History Apr 1963, Damascus (Syrian AR). Official inauguration 18 May 1963, Cairo (Egypt). Current statutes adopted 1984, Baghdad (Iraq). Former names and other names: *Arab Engineering Union* – former. **Aims** Aggregate potential of Arab engineers and their efforts towards promoting unity and political and economic independence of the Arab nation; improve the image of the engineering profession and increase its scientific standards; preserve Arab engineering heritage and contribute to its growth and advancement; support national associations and work towards their establishment where none exists; improve social and moral standards of Arab engineers and upgrade their scientific, practical and professional capabilities; coordinate and cooperate with other Arab professional unions; facilitate freedom of work and travel for Arab engineers in the Arab world; consolidate scientific thinking in planning and practice in Arab countries; strengthen relations with other international engineering organizations; evaluate Arab and foreign scientific engineering qualifications. **Structure** Supreme Council (one regular and one follow-up session annually); Executive Bureau; General Secretariat. **Languages** Arabic, English. **Staff** 6.00 FTE, paid; 1.00 FTE, voluntary. **Finance** Sources: donations; meeting proceeds; members' dues. **Events** *Arab Engineering Conference* Muscat (Oman) 2018, *International Conference on Climate Change – Palestine* Al-Bireh (Palestine) 2017, *Arab Engineering Conference* Manama (Bahrain) 2016, *Arab Engineering Conference* Jeddah (Saudi Arabia) 2012, *Arab Engineering Conference* Tripoli (Libyan AJ) 2009. **Publications** *Engineering Education Committee's Magazine* (2 a year); *The Federation of Arab Engineers' Magazine* (2 a year).

Members Engineering associations in 15 countries:
Algeria, Bahrain, Egypt, Iraq, Jordan, Kuwait, Lebanon, Libya, Morocco, Palestine, Sudan, Syrian AR, Tunisia, United Arab Emirates, Yemen.
IGO Relations Close cooperation with: *Arab Federation for Technical Education (AFTE, no recent information)*. **NGO Relations** International member of: *Engineering Association of Mediterranean Countries (EAMC, #05480)*; *World Federation of Engineering Organizations (WFEO, #21433)*. Co-founder of: *Arab Arbitration Chamber for Engineering and Construction Contracts (no recent information)*. Founder of: *Arab Architects Organization (#00898)*; *Arab Association of Engineering Consultants (#00899)*; *Engineering Data Centre*. [2020/XD2839/**D**]

- ♦ Fédération arabe des organismes au service des sourds / see Arab Federation of Organizations Working with the Deaf (#00949)
- ♦ Fédération arabe des producteurs des engrais chimiques / see Arab Fertilizer Association (#00958)
- ♦ Fédération arabe de psychiatrie (#00952)
- ♦ Fédération arabe régionale des associations pour le contrôle volontaire des naissances (inactive)
- ♦ Fédération arabe des sociétés de gynécologie – obstétrique (#09421)
- ♦ Fédération arabe des sociologues (inactive)
- ♦ Fédération arabe de sucre (inactive)
- ♦ Fédération arabe de tir à l'arc (no recent information)
- ♦ Fédération arabe des transporteurs maritime (#00953)
- ♦ Fédération arabe des travailleurs agricoles (inactive)
- ♦ Fédération arabe des travailleurs de l'alimentation (inactive)
- ♦ Fédération arabe des travailleurs du bois et des matériaux de construction (no recent information)
- ♦ Fédération arabe des travailleurs du commerce (inactive)
- ♦ Fédération arabe des travailleurs de l'imprimerie et de l'information (inactive)
- ♦ Fédération arabe des travailleurs des institutions métallurgiques, mécaniques et électriques (no recent information)
- ♦ Fédération arabe des travailleurs du naphte et de la chimie (inactive)
- ♦ Fédération arabe des travailleurs des services de la santé (inactive)
- ♦ Fédération arabe des travailleurs du textile (inactive)
- ♦ Fédération arabe des travailleurs du transport (no recent information)

♦ Federation of Arab Gynecology Obstetric Societies (FAGOS) 09421

Fédération arabe des sociétés de gynécologie – obstétrique (FASGO)

SG PO Box 942003, Amman 11194, Jordan. T. +962795521980. E-mail: ahmadd500@yahoo.com.
URL: http://fagos.org/

History 1992, on the initiative of the Jordanian Society of Obstetricians and Gynaecologists. Previously referred to in English as *Arab Association of Obstetrics and Gynaecology Societies*. **Structure** General Council; Managing Board. Scientific Groups (5): Fetomaternal; Fertility and Assisted Reproduction; Menopause; Gyn-Oncology; Gyn-Urology. **Activities** Events/meetings. **Events** *Meeting* Beirut (Lebanon) 2019, *Meeting* Beirut (Lebanon) 2018, *African and Eastern Mediterranean Regional Congress* Dubai (United Arab Emirates) 2018, *Congress* Khartoum (Sudan) 2016, *Congress* Jordan 2015.
Members in 15 countries:
Algeria, Egypt, Iraq, Jordan, Kuwait, Lebanon, Libya, Morocco, Oman, Palestine, Qatar, Saudi Arabia, Syrian AR, Tunisia, Yemen.
NGO Relations *Arab Maternal – Fetal Medicine Expert Group (AMFMEG, #01005)*. [2018/XD8332/**D**]

♦ Federation of Arab Journalists (FAJ) 09422

Fédération des journalistes arabes (FJA)

SG 22 Talat Harb St, Information Dept Bldg, Cairo, Egypt. T. +20225795121 – +20225795123 – +20225795126. Fax +20225795165 – +20225795103. E-mail: info-faj@faj.org.eg.

History 21 Feb 1964, Cairo (Egypt), under the name *Arab Union of Journalists – Union des journalistes arabes*. Previously also referred to as *General Federation of Arab Journalists (GFAJ) – Fédération générale des journalistes arabes (FGJA)*. **Aims** Serve the objectives of the Arab people in their unity; defend the causes of Arab journalists and develop their talents and abilities; defend the rights and freedoms of Arab journalists and human rights. **Structure** General Congress (every 4 years). Permanent Bureau (meets annually). General Secretariat, comprising President, 5 Vice-Presidents, Secretary-General and 8 members. Committees (9): Foreign Relations and International Affairs; Palestine; Press Freedoms; Professional; Culture and Media; Social Affairs; Democratic Development and Human Rights; Organizational and Membership Affairs; Finance Resources Development. **Languages** Arabic. **Staff** 10.00 FTE, paid. Officers voluntary. **Finance** Members' dues. Other sources: host country (Egypt); donations from other sources on permission of Standing Bureau, provided no conditions are attached. **Activities** Supports and coordinates the activities of member organizations; collaborates with international press organizations and with organizations engaged in the defence of human rights and fundamental freedoms; organizes or sponsors meetings, fora, exhibitions, training courses and exchange of delegations. Publishing activity. **Events** *Quadrennial general congress* Cairo (Egypt) 2004, *Quadrennial general congress* Amman (Jordan) 2000, *Quadrennial general congress* Cairo (Egypt) 1996, *Quadrennial General Congress* Baghdad (Iraq) 1983, *Quadrennial General Congress* Baghdad (Iraq) 1979. **Publications** *CFAG News Bulletin* (12 a year); *The Arab Journalist* (periodical) – magazine; *Four Years of the Activities of the Federation of Arab Journalists*; *The Charter of Federation of Arab Journalists*; *The Federation of Arab Journalists: A Documentary Study*. *Arab Press Heritage* – series; *The Professional* – series. *A Free and Responsible Arab Press*; *A Proposal for a Unified Arab Press Law*; *Fluctuating Oil Prices and Arab Economies*; *Informative Palestinian Challenges against the Israeli Aaggression*; *Speech under Siege: The Black Record of Israeli Aggression on the Palestinian Press*; *The Arab Common Market*; *The Arab Media and the Palestinian Intifada*; *The Freedom of the Press and Legislative Restrictions*; *The Future of the Arab Press under the IT Revolution*; *The Terminology War*.
Members Syndicates, associations, national unions of journalists in 19 countries and territories:
Algeria, Bahrain, Egypt, Iraq, Jordan, Kuwait, Lebanon, Libya, Mauritania, Morocco, Oman, Palestine, Saudi Arabia, Somalia, Sudan, Syrian AR, Tunisia, United Arab Emirates, Yemen.
IGO Relations Observer status: *League of Arab States (LAS, #16420)*; *UNESCO (#20322)*; *United Nations Human Rights Council (HRC, #20571)*. **NGO Relations** Cooperates with: *Afro-Asian Peoples' Solidarity Organization (AAPSO, #00537)*; *Amnesty International (AI, #00801)*; *Arab Organization for Human Rights (AOHR, #01020)*; *Committee to Protect Journalists (CPJ, #04280)*; *Confederation of ASEAN Journalists (CAJ, #04509)*; *Federation of Arab News Agencies (FANA, #09423)*; *General Union of Arab Writers (no recent information)*; *International Confederation of Arab Trade Unions (ICATU, #12845)*; *International Federation of Journalists (IFJ, #13462)*; *International Journalism Institute (IJI, inactive)*; *Reporters sans frontières (RSF, #18846)*; *Union internationale des journalistes africains (UIJA, #20428)*. [2012/XD4959/**D**]

- ♦ Federation of Arab Lawyers / see Arab Lawyers' Union (#01002)

♦ Federation of Arab News Agencies (FANA) 09423

Fédération des agences de presse arabes

Contact Sin El-Fiel, St-George Centre, 8th Floor, PO Box 14/5156, Mazra'a, Lebanon. T. +9611485020. Fax +9611482256.
URL: http://www.fananews.com/

History 28 Oct 1964, Cairo (Egypt), within the framework of *League of Arab States (LAS, #16420)*. Constitution adopted at 1st Conference, 24 Jul 1965, Amman (Jordan); amended at 2nd Conference, Apr 1974, Baghdad (Iraq). Commenced operations Jan 1975, Beirut (Lebanon), following 3rd Conference, 1974, Beirut, when Secretary-General was elected. **Aims** Promote the expansion of and cooperation between existing national news agencies in the region; contribute to the development of news exchanges and promote technical cooperation among news agencies; contribute to the training of news agency *journalists*. **Activities** Holds international and regional (Euro-Arab, Arab-Latin) seminars; training programmes; raises and distributes funds for newly established African and Arab news agencies. **Publications** *FANA Magazine* in Arabic, English. Directories.
Members Active; Affiliated; Observer. Arab news agencies (18) in 18 countries:
Algeria, Iraq, Jordan, Kuwait, Lebanon, Libya, Mauritania, Morocco, Palestine, Qatar, Saudi Arabia, Sudan, Syrian AR, Tunisia, United Arab Emirates, Yemen.
IGO Relations *United Nations University (UNU, #20642)*. [2017/XF8329/**F**]

- ♦ Federation of Arab Red Crescent and Red Cross Societies / see Arab Red Crescent and Red Cross Organization (#01033)
- ♦ Federation of Arab Red Crescent Societies / see Arab Red Crescent and Red Cross Organization (#01033)
- ♦ Federation of Arab Republics (inactive)
- ♦ Federation of Arab Scientific Research Councils (no recent information)
- ♦ Federation of Arab Societies of Anaesthesia and Intensive Care / see Pan Arab Federation of Societies of Anesthesia, Intensive Care and Pain Management (#18144)
- ♦ Federation of Arab Teachers (no recent information)
- ♦ Federation of Arab Travel Agents' Associations (inactive)
- ♦ Fédération artisans du monde (internationally oriented national body)
- ♦ Fédération de l'art photographique d'Asie (#09446)

♦ Federation of ASEAN Consulting Engineers (FACE) 09424

SG 63-2 and 65-2 Medan Setia 1, Damansara Heights, 50490 Kuala Lumpur, Malaysia. T. +60320950031. Fax +60320953499. E-mail: sec@acem.com.my.

History Founded 5 Jun 1989, Kuala Lumpur (Malaysia). **Aims** Promote formulation and implementation of policies, plans and projects for the participation and advancement of the domestic consulting engineering industry in ASEAN region. **Languages** English. **Staff** None. **Finance** Members' dues.
Members Full in 5 countries:
Indonesia, Philippines, Singapore, Thailand, Vietnam.
Consultative Status Consultative status granted from: *ASEAN (#01141)*. [2015/XD7828/**D**]

♦ Federation of ASEAN Economic Associations (FAEA) 09425

Pres c/o Indonesian Economists Association, Jalan Daksa IV No 9, Kebayoran Baru, Jakarta Selatan, Jakarta 12110, Indonesia.
URL: http://www.pem.org.my/faea2.html/

History Founded 27 Oct 1976, Prapat (Indonesia). **Events** *Annual Conference* Singapore (Singapore) 2019, *Annual Conference* Quezon City (Philippines) 2018, *Annual Conference* Penang (Malaysia) 2017, *Conference* Hanoi (Vietnam) 2015, *Annual Conference* Singapore (Singapore) 2013.
Members Economic associations in 8 countries:
Brunei Darussalam, Cambodia, Indonesia, Malaysia, Philippines, Singapore, Thailand, Vietnam.
IGO Relations Affiliated with: *ASEAN (#01141)*. **NGO Relations** Member of: *International Economic Association (IEA, #13222)*. [2014/XE0617/**E**]

♦ Federation of ASEAN Poultry Producers (FAPP) 09426

Sec FAPP Cooperating Office, 313 CP Tower 22nd Floor, Silom Road, Bangkok, 10500, Thailand. T. +6626382199 – +6626382881. Fax +6626382536.

History 9 Nov 2000. **Aims** Enhance sustainable growth of poultry production in ASEAN; exchange and disseminate knowledge and information; promote fair and free trade in poultry in international market; coordinate and collectively implement various activities, policies and strategies. **Structure** President; Secretary. **Languages** English. **Staff** Part-time, voluntary. **Finance** Members' contributions. **Events** *Annual Meeting* Kuala Lumpur (Malaysia) 2009, *Annual Meeting* Bangkok (Thailand) 2007, *Annual Meeting* Bangkok (Thailand) 2005, *Annual Meeting* Kuala Lumpur (Malaysia) 2005, *Annual Meeting* Hanoi (Vietnam) 2004.
Members Poultry producers of 5 countries:
Indonesia, Malaysia, Philippines, Thailand, Vietnam. [2009.10.02/XJ7181/**D**]

- ♦ Federation of ASEAN Pulp and Paper Industries (unconfirmed)

♦ Federation of ASEAN Shipowners Associations (FASA) 09427

Secretariat 59 Tras Street, Singapore 078998, Singapore. T. +6563052260. Fax +6562225527. E-mail: office@fasa.org.sg – ssa.admin@ssa.org.sg.
URL: http://www.fasa.org.sg/

History Nov 1975, Jakarta (Indonesia). **Aims** Promote, develop and support the common interest of shipowner members in South East Asia; foster, develop and maintain close cooperation; extend assistance to any member; improve *shipping* services; represent members in their collective dealing. **Structure** Rotating Chairmanship; Secretary-General. **Languages** English. **Staff** 1.00 FTE, voluntary. **Finance** Members' dues. **Events** *Annual General Meeting* Singapore (Singapore) 2005, *Annual General Meeting* Singapore (Singapore) 1998, *Conference* Manila (Philippines) 1989, *General Meeting* Manila (Philippines) 1986.
Members National shipowners' associations in 7 countries:
Indonesia, Malaysia, Myanmar, Philippines, Singapore, Thailand, Vietnam.
Consultative Status Consultative status granted from: *ASEAN (#01141)*. **NGO Relations** Affiliated with: *Asian Shipowners Association (ASA, #01697)*. [2020/XE8530/**E**]

- ♦ Federation of ASEAN Travel Agents / see Federation of ASEAN Travel Associations (#09428)

♦ Federation of ASEAN Travel Associations (FATA) 09428

Exec Dir Wisma MATTA, 6 Jalan Metro Pudu, Fraser Business Park, 55100 Kuala Lumpur, Malaysia. T. +60392221155. E-mail: hello@fata.travel.
Pres address not obtained.
URL: http://www.fata.travel/

History Original title *Federation of ASEAN Travel Agents (FATA)*. **Aims** Unite members in common purpose; attain highest standards of services and facilities for travellers and tourists; uphold dignity and ethics of the tour and travel business and strive towards professionalism; encourage, support and contribute to develop tourism into and within the ASEAN region; foster and maintain best relations among ASEAN countries and people with other related organizations and associations within and outside ASEAN. **Structure** Board of Directors; Executive Board. **Finance** Members' dues. **Events** *Convention* Chiang Mai (Thailand) 2018.
Members Tour operators and travel agents in 9 countries:
Brunei Darussalam, Cambodia, Indonesia, Laos, Malaysia, Myanmar, Philippines, Singapore, Thailand.
NGO Relations Member of: *World Travel Agents Associations Alliance (WTAAA, #21870)*. [2020/XE2762/**E**]

- ♦ Federation of ASEAN Urological Associations (inactive)
- ♦ Federation of Asian Amateur Boxing / see Asian Boxing Confederation (#01363)

♦ Federation of Asian Biotech Associations (FABA) 09429

Sec 401 Lakshmi Nivas, Greenlands Ameerpet, Hyderabad, Telangana 500 016 AP, Hyderabad TELANGANA 500 016 AP, India. T. +914023415667 – +914023415668. Fax +914023415669.
URL: http://www.biofaba.org/

History 27 Feb 2004, Hyderabad (India), during BioAsia 2004: The Global Bio Business Forum. **Aims** Promote and safeguard the overall interests of *biotechnology* as a science, profession, industry or trade; promote collaboration between academia and industries engaged in biotechnology among member countries; promote development of biotechnology and establish just and equitable principles and practices among member countries. **Structure** Platform for exploring business opportunities, technology transfer and tie ups among members and other countries worldwide. **Languages** English. **Staff** 8.00 FTE, paid. **Finance** Members' dues of individual chapters. Conference proceeds. **Activities** Grants awards to persons and institutions for outstanding contributions in the furtherance of the objectives of the Association; coordinates the conduct of training programmes on emerging areas of biotechnology; creates a database on expertise and technologies available for use by the biotech industry; acts as a facilitator between industry and governments to encourage investments in the field of biotechnology and also cross border trade in terms of export, outsourcing of services and other related activities; cooperates with other federations, associations, institutions, groups and bodies within Asian countries or in the world having similar aims and objectives; undertakes publicity through media and publication and participate and organizes international conferences, trade fairs or exhibitions in member countries by rotation; co-organizes BioAsia Forum; collects and obtains all information on matters affecting members, makes representations to the various authorities and appears before any authority in the interest of, protection and betterment of the constituent members for carrying on any activity relating to biotechnology and publishes and disseminates the same to members and others. **Events** *Global bio business forum* Hyderabad (India) 2008.
Members in 20 countries:
Bangladesh, China, India, Indonesia, Iran Islamic Rep, Israel, Japan, Kazakhstan, Korea Rep, Malaysia, Nepal, Pakistan, Philippines, Russia, Saudi Arabia, Singapore, Sri Lanka, Thailand, Türkiye, United Arab Emirates.
Associate organizations (2), one of which is listed in this Yearbook:
CANPREP (Canada); *European Federation of Biotechnology (EFB, #07062)*. [2011.06.01/XM0451/**D**]

Federation Asian Bishops
09430

alphabetic sequence excludes
For the complete listing, see Yearbook Online at

♦ Federation of Asian Bishops' Conferences (FABC) 09430
Fédération des conférences épiscopales de l'Asie

SG 4/F Holy Cross Centre, 72 Yiu Hing Road, Sai Wan Ho, Hong Kong, Central and Western, Hong Kong. T. +85239041211. Fax +85239041124. E-mail: fabccentral@yahoo.com.
URL: http://www.fabc.org/

History 28 Nov 1970, Manila (Philippines). Statutes adopted by participating member conferences, 25 Aug 1972; approved by His Holiness the Pope, 16 Nov 1972, ad experimentum for 2 years. Statutes amended 22-27 Apr 1974, Taipei (Taiwan), at 1st Plenary Assembly; approved, 21 Nov 1974 ad experimentum for 2 years by *Congregation for the Evangelization of Peoples (CEP, #04670)*, with approval repeated 6 Apr 1977. Statutes amended again by 5th Plenary Assembly, 17-27 Aug 1990, Bandung (Indonesia) and approved ad experimentum with recommendations for additional amendments by CEP. Additional amendments made at 6th Plenary Assembly, 10-19 Jan 1995, Manila (Philippines) and approved by Holy See. Further amendments made at 9th Plenary Assembly, 10-16 Aug 2009, Manila (Philippines), and at 10th Plenary Assembly, 10-16 Dec 2012, Ho Chi Minh City (Vietnam), and approved by Holy See. **Aims** Foster among members solidarity and co-responsibility for the welfare of Church and society in Asia; promote and defend whatever is for the greater good. **Structure** Plenary Assembly (every 4 years); Central Committee; Standing Committee; Central Secretariat; Offices established according to need. **Languages** English. **Staff** 1.50 FTE, paid; 4.50 FTE, voluntary. **Finance** Annual contributions of members conferences; grants; voluntary contributions. **Events** *Meeting* Bangkok (Thailand) 2017, *Pastoral Leadership Seminar for Bishops* Bangkok (Thailand) 2017, *Study Days on the Family* Bangkok (Thailand) 2017, *South Asia Regional Meeting on Women* Mumbai (India) 2017, *East Asian Regional Conference on Family* Taoyuan (Taiwan) 2017. **Publications** *FABC Newsletter* (3-4 a year); *FABC Papers* (3-4 a year). Books on relevant topics.
Members Bishops' Conferences in 19 countries and territories:
Bangladesh, Brunei Darussalam, Cambodia, India, Indonesia, Japan, Kazakhstan, Korea Rep, Laos, Malaysia, Myanmar, Pakistan, Philippines, Singapore, Sri Lanka, Taiwan, Thailand, Timor-Leste, Vietnam.
Associate members in 8 countries and territories:
Hong Kong, Kyrgyzstan, Macau, Mongolia, Nepal, Tajikistan, Turkmenistan, Uzbekistan. [2018.08.31/XD5358/**D**]

♦ Federation of Asian Chemical Societies (FACS) 09431
Fédération asienne de sociétés de chimie

SG Dept of Chemistry, Bangladesh Univ of Engineering and Technology, Ramna, Dhaka 1000, Bangladesh.
Pres address not obtained.
SG-Elect address not obtained.
URL: http://www.facs-as.org/

History 15 Aug 1979, Bangkok (Thailand). **Aims** Promote advancement and appreciation of chemistry and the interests of professional chemists in the Asia-Pacific. **Structure** General Assembly of Council (every 2 years); Executive Council. **Languages** English. **Staff** Part-time, voluntary. **Finance** Members' dues: US$ 120 – US$ 600 per year. **Activities** Projects/programmes; events/meetings; awards/prizes/competitions. **Events** *Asian Chemical Congress* Istanbul (Türkiye) 2023, *General Assembly* Istanbul (Türkiye) 2023, *Asian Chemical Congress* Istanbul (Turkey) 2021, *General Assembly* Istanbul (Turkey) 2021, *Asian Chemical Congress* Taipei (Taiwan) 2019. **Publications** *FACS Newsletter* (2 a year) – in collaboration with Dutch institute. *20th Century Chemistry in Asia – vol 1* (1992).
Members Chemical societies (28) in 27 countries and territories:
Australia, Bangladesh, Brunei Darussalam, Cambodia, China, Hong Kong, India, Indonesia, Israel, Japan, Jordan, Korea Rep, Kuwait, Malaysia, Mongolia, Nepal, New Zealand, Pakistan, Papua New Guinea, Philippines, Russia, Saudi Arabia, Singapore, Taiwan, Thailand, Türkiye, Vietnam.
Regional society:
NGO Relations Member of: *Asian Coordinating Group for Chemistry (ACGC, no recent information)*; *International Union of Pure and Applied Chemistry (IUPAC, #15809)*. Instrumental in setting up *Asian Network of Analytical Chemistry (ANAC, #01546)*; *Asian-Pacific Chemical Education Network (ACEN, #01604)*; *International Chemical Information Network (ChIN, #12542)*. Cooperates with: *European Chemical Society (EuChemS, #06524)*. The: *Union of Arab Chemists (UAC, no recent information)* is an associated organization. Instrumental in setting up: *Phytochemical Society of Asia (PSA, #18369)*. [2018/XD9555/**D**]

♦ Federation of Asian Clinical Oncology (FACO) 09432

Contact c/o JSCO, TKi Bldg 2F, 3-3-1 Kanda-Misakicho, Chiyoda-ku, Tokyo, 101-0061 Japan. E-mail: faco-office@jsco.or.jp.
URL: http://faco-org.blogspot.com/

History Feb 2012. **Aims** Improve the standard of cancer treatment through the cooperate studies on more effective therapeutic strategies based on drugs, surgery and/or radiotherapy that are already in use and also through the development of new drugs and other innovative approaches in Asian Pacific area. **Activities** Events/meetings. **Events** *International Conference* Yokohama (Japan) 2021, *International Conference* Seoul (Korea Rep) 2020, *International Conference* Shanghai (China) 2019, *International Conference* Yokohama (Japan) 2018, *International Conference* Seoul (Korea Rep) 2017.
Members Full in 3 countries:
China, Japan, Korea Rep. [2022.05.27/XM7366/**D**]

♦ Federation of Asian Dental Anesthesiology Societies (unconfirmed)
♦ Federation of Asian Electric Workers' Unions (inactive)

♦ Federation of Asian Institute of Management Alumni Associations (FAIM) 09433

Contact AIM Alumni Office, 123 Paseo de Roxas, Legazpi, 1229 Makati, Philippines.
URL: http://www.aimalumni.org/

History 11 Mar 1978, Kuala Lumpur (Malaysia), under the auspices of *Asian Institute of Management (AIM, #01518)*. **Aims** Foster social and fraternal association amongst AIM Alumni Associations; maintain close relationship with AIM and promote and advance AIM programs and related activities. **Structure** International Conference (annual). Executive Board, consisting of Chairman, Vice-Chairman, Secretary-General, Treasurer and Board of Trustees. **Events** *Annual international management conference / Annual International Conference* San Francisco, CA (USA) 1997, *Annual international management conference / Annual International Conference* Jakarta (Indonesia) 1996, *Annual international management conference* San Francisco, CA (USA) 1995, *Annual international management conference / Annual International Conference* Bangkok (Thailand) 1994, *Annual international management conference / Annual International Conference* Manila (Philippines) 1993. **Publications** *AIM Link* (4 a year).
Members Alumni associations in 12 countries and territories:
Bangladesh, Hong Kong, India, Indonesia, Korea Rep, Malaysia, Pakistan, Philippines, Singapore, Taiwan, Thailand, USA. [2018/XE0889/**E**]

♦ Federation of the Asian Master Tailors 09434

Contact Tung Hing Bldg – 9th Floor, Flat D, 129-135 Johnston Rd, Wanchai, Hong Kong, Central and Western, Hong Kong. T. +85225733371. E-mail: info@hktahk.com.
URL: http://www.hkedma.com.hk/

History 1 Nov 1936, Hong Kong. **Aims** Foster and promote the development of trade of tailoring industry; protect and enhance members' benefits; strengthen exchange and communication with regional and international companies and encourage mutual economic cooperation. **Languages** Chinese. **Staff** None paid. **Finance** Members' dues. Rental income. **Events** *Congress* Kuala Lumpur (Malaysia) 2020, *Congress* Daegu (Korea Rep) 2018, *Congress* Ubon Ratchathani (Thailand) 2016, *Congress* Kobe (Japan) 2014, *Congress* Singapore (Singapore) 2012. **Publications** None. **Members** Membership countries not specified. **IGO Relations** None. [2019/XD0110/**D**]

♦ Federation of Asian Motorcycle Industries (FAMI) 09435

Contact c/o AISI, Kirana 2 Tower Level 10-A, Boulevard Timur 88, Jakarta 14240, Indonesia. E-mail: info@fami-motorcycle.org.
URL: http://www.fami-motorcycle.org/

History 1999. Registration: Singapore. **Aims** Promote consultation with regard to the development of the motorcycle industry in Asia; act as an advisory capacity in all aspects of the motorcycle industry in Asia; promote closer relations and ties among member countries; collect, compile, study, update and supply date, information and documentation on the motorcycle industry and related subjects. **Structure** General Assembly. Management Committee. Committees (2): Research and Planning; Technical. Officers: President; 7 Vice-Presidents; Treasurer; Secretary General. **Events** *Intellectual property rights symposium* Pasay City (Philippines) 2011, *Annual General Meeting* Kuching (Malaysia) 2010, *Annual General Meeting* Manila (Philippines) 2009, *Annual General Meeting* Taichung (Taiwan) 2008, *Annual General Meeting* Taiwan 2008.
Members Associations in 7 countries and territories:
Indonesia, Japan, Malaysia, Philippines, Singapore, Taiwan, Thailand.
NGO Relations Member of: *International Motorcycle Manufacturers Association (IMMA, #14186)*. [2019/XJ4801/t/**D**]

♦ Federation of Asian Muaythai Associations (FAMA) 09436

Main Office 70 Anson Road, No 19-01, Hub Synergy Point, Singapore 079905, Singapore. E-mail: admin@famamuaythai.org.
URL: http://www.famamuaythai.org/

History Founded Nov 2005, Thailand. Former names and other names: *Federation Amateur of Muaythai of Asia (FAMA)* – former. **Aims** Promote the *sport* of muaythai in Asia. **Structure** General Assembly. Board, comprising President, 5 Vice-Presidents, Secretary General, Treasurer and 5 further members. [2020/XM2567/**D**]

♦ Federation of Asian Nutrition Societies (FANS) 09437

SG c/o JSNFS, Favor Field Ikebukuro 203, 3-60-5 Ikebukuro, Toshima-ku, Tokyo, 171-0014 Japan. T. +81369020072.

History 1971, Hyderabad (India), during 1st Asian Congress of Nutrition, when the idea of organizing the nutritional scientists of Asia into a federation was launched. Formally organized during 2nd Asian Congress, 17 Jan 1973, Manila (Philippines). **Aims** Foster international fellowship and cooperation among nutrition scientists in the Asian region; serve as a forum for exchange of information and experiences in nutrition research, training, and action programs; act as a liaison between member countries and IUNS as well as the appropriate United Nations agencies. **Structure** General Assembly (every 4 years). Executive Council, comprising President, Secretary General, Immediate Past President, 5 Honorary members and 4 ordinary members. **Languages** English. **Staff** Voluntary. **Finance** Secretariat expenses borne by host country. **Events** *Asian Congress of Nutrition (ACN)* Chengdu (China) 2023, *Asian Congress of Nutrition* Bali (Indonesia) 2019, *Asian Congress of Nutrition* Yokohama (Japan) 2015, *Asian Congress of Nutrition* Singapore (Singapore) 2011, *Asian Congress of Nutrition* Taipei (Taiwan) 2007. **Publications** *FANS Newsletter* (every 2 years).
Members National societies in 18 countries and territories:
Bangladesh, China, Hong Kong, India, Indonesia, Iran Islamic Rep, Japan, Korea Rep, Lebanon, Malaysia, Mongolia, Pakistan, Philippines, Singapore, Sri Lanka, Taiwan, Thailand, Vietnam.
NGO Relations Member of: *International Union of Nutritional Sciences (IUNS, #15796)*. [2019/XD0095/**D**]

♦ Federation of Asian and Oceanian Biochemists / see Federation of Asian and Oceanian Biochemists and Molecular Biologists (#09438)

♦ Federation of Asian and Oceanian Biochemists and Molecular Biologists (FAOBMB) 09438

SG Dept Biological Sciences and Biotechnology, Fac of Science and Technology, Univ Kebangsaan Malaysia, 43600 Bangi, Selangor, Malaysia. T. +60389213862. Fax +60389252698. E-mail: info@faobmb.com.
URL: http://www.faobmb.com/

History 13 Aug 1989, Seoul (Korea Rep). Founded when officially incorporated, having previously existed unincorporated as *Federation of Asian and Oceanian Biochemists (FAOB)*, founded 1 Aug 1972, and later as *Federation of Asian and Oceanian Biochemists and Molecular Biology*. Statutes most recently amended 4 Dec 2016, Manilla (Philippines). Registration: No/ID: A0026594K, Start date: 8 Dec 1992, Australia, State of Victoria. **Aims** Promote the science of biochemistry and molecular biology, including education, research and their applications worldwide, and in particular in the Asian and Oceanian region. **Structure** Council; Executive Committee; Education Committee; Fellowships Committee. **Languages** English. **Staff** 0.50 FTE, paid. **Finance** Sources: members' dues. Assistance from IUBMB. **Activities** Awards/prizes/competitions; events/meetings; financial and/or material support. **Events** *Congress* Melbourne, VIC (Australia) 2024, *FAOBMB Conference* Bangkok (Thailand) 2023, *FAOBMB Conference* Shenzhen (China) 2022, *Congress* Christchurch (New Zealand) 2021, *Symposium* Colombo (Sri Lanka) 2020.
Members Constituent (societies or groups in the field in Asia, Australia and the Pacific and Indian Oceans); Special (other interested organizations); Honorary. Organizations in 20 countries and territories:
Australia, Bangladesh, China, Hong Kong, India, Indonesia, Iran Islamic Rep, Japan, Korea Rep, Malaysia, Myanmar, Nepal, New Zealand, Pakistan, Philippines, Singapore, Sri Lanka, Taiwan, Thailand, Vietnam. [2022.05.11/XD5902/**D**]

♦ Federation of Asian and Oceanian Biochemists and Molecular Biology / see Federation of Asian and Oceanian Biochemists and Molecular Biologists (#09438)

♦ Federation of Asian Oceanian Neuroscience Societies (FAONS) 09439

Sec Korea Brain Research Inst, 61,Cheomdan-ro, Sinseo-dong, Dong-gu, Daegu, Korea Rep.
Pres address not obtained.
URL: http://www.faons.org/

Structure Council. Executive Committee, including President, President-Past, Secretary, Treasurer and Honorary President. **Events** *Symposium* Bali (Indonesia) 2022, *Symposium* Bali (Indonesia) 2022, *Symposium* Bali (Indonesia) 2021, *Congress* Daegu (Korea Rep) 2019, *Congress* Wuzhen (China) 2015.
Members Full in 15 countries and territories:
Australia, China, Hong Kong, India, Iran Islamic Rep, Israel, Japan, Korea Rep, Malaysia, Philippines, Singapore, Sri Lanka, Taiwan, Thailand, Vietnam.
NGO Relations Member of: *International Brain Research Organization (IBRO, #12392)*. [2022/XD5712/**D**]

♦ Federation of Asian and Oceanian Physiological Societies (FAOPS) . 09440

Sec Dept of Physiology, Fac of Medicine, Univ Teknologi Mara, Sg Buloh Campus, 47100 Sg Buloh, 47000 Shah Alam, Selangor, Malaysia.
URL: http://faops.asia/

History Nov 1990. Founded current constitution was adopted. **Aims** Encourage advancement of, facilitate exchange and dissemination of knowledge in, and foster and encourage research in the field of physiological sciences in Asia and Oceania. **Structure** General Assembly (at Congress); Council; Commissions; Secretariat. **Languages** English. **Staff** None. **Finance** Members' dues. **Events** *Congress* Daegu (Korea Rep) 2023, *Congress* Kyoto (Japan) 2019, *Congress* Bangkok (Thailand) 2015, *Congress* Taipei (Taiwan) 2011, *Congress* Seoul (Korea Rep) 2006. **Publications** *FAOPS Newsletter* (3 a year).
Members Regular; Associate; Supporting; Honorary. Regular (17) in 17 countries and territories:
Australia, China, India, Iran Islamic Rep, Israel, Japan, Korea Rep, Malaysia, Myanmar, Nepal, New Zealand, Pakistan, Philippines, Sri Lanka, Taiwan, Thailand, United Arab Emirates.
Associate in 2 countries:
Uzbekistan, Vietnam.
NGO Relations Member of: *International Union of Physiological Sciences (IUPS, #15800)*. [2022/XD5893/**D**]

♦ Federation of Asian and Oceania Pest Managers Associations (FAOPMA) 09441

Secretariat Unit 6, 12 Navigator Place, Hendra QLD 4011, Australia. E-mail: info@faopma.com.
URL: http://www.faopma.com/

History 1989. Originally referred to as *Federation of Asia-Oceania Pest Management*. **Aims** Unite national pest control organizations in Asia and Oceania. **Structure** Executive Committee comprising: President, President-Elect, Executive Director, Vice President, Treasurer, Secretary. **Languages** English. **Staff** Voluntary. **Finance** Members' dues (annual). **Events** *FAOPMA-Pest Summit* Kyoto (Japan) 2022, *FAOPMA-Pest Summit* 2021, *FAOPMA-Pest Summit* 2020, *FAOPMA-Pest Summit* Daejeon (Korea Rep) 2019, *FAOPMA-Pest Summit* Shenzhen (China) 2018.
Members National pest control organizations in 15 countries and territories:
Australia, China, Hong Kong, India, Israel, Japan, Korea Rep, New Zealand, Papua New Guinea, Philippines, Singapore, Taiwan, Thailand, UK, USA. [2020/XD4756/**D**]

♦ Federation of Asian Organizations for Radiation Oncology (FARO) .. 09442

Office c/o Radiation Oncology, Graduate School of Medicine, Gunma Univ, Showa Machi 3-39-22, Maebashi-shi, Maebashi GUNMA, 371-8511 Japan. T. +81272208380.
URL: http://faro.asia/

History Nov 2014, Yogyakarta (Indonesia). **Aims** Foster the role of radiation oncology to improve the basic level of radiotherapy for the benefit of the patients in the Asian region. **Structure** Council; Advisory Board. **Activities** Research/documentation; events/meetings; knowledge management/information dissemination; training/education. **Events** *Meeting* Philippines 2021, *Meeting* Shenzhen (China) 2019, *Meeting* Bali (Indonesia) 2018, *ESTRO meets Asia Conference* Singapore (Singapore) 2018, *Meeting* Bangalore (India) 2017.
Members Organizations in 12 countries:
Bangladesh, China, India, Indonesia, Japan, Korea Rep, Malaysia, Pakistan, Philippines, Singapore, Sri Lanka, Thailand.
[2022/XM6545/**D**]

♦ Federation Asian of Oriental (inactive)
♦ Federation of Asian Pacific Branches of the World's Poultry Science Association / see Asian Pacific Federation of the World's Poultry Science Association Branches (#01615)

♦ Federation of Asian and Pacific Electrical Contractors Associations (FAPECA) 09443

Fédération des associations d'installations électriques d'Asie et du Pacifique
SG 8/F Kwong Ah Bldg, 195-197 Johnson Road, Wan Chai, Wanchai, Hong Kong. T. +85225720843. Fax +85228382532. E-mail: adm@hkeca.org.
Pres Thai Electrical and Mechanical Contractors Association, 216/6 7/F LPN Tower, Nanglinjee Road, Chong Nonsee, Yannaw, Bangkok, 10120, Thailand. T. +6622854546-7. Fax +6622854288. E-mail: temca@temcathai.com.
URL: http://www.fapeca.org/

History 1986, Seoul (Korea Rep). **Structure** President, Vice-President, Secretary-General, 4 Directors and 1 Auditor. **Languages** English. **Staff** 8.00 FTE, voluntary. **Finance** Members' dues. **Events** *Joint Conference* Gwangju (Korea Rep) 2019, *Joint Conference* Manila (Philippines) 2018, *Joint Conference* Kuala Lumpur (Malaysia) 2017, *Joint Conference* Singapore (Singapore) 2016, *Joint Conference* Taipei (Taiwan) 2014.
Members Organizations in 12 countries and territories:
Australia, Hong Kong, Indonesia, Japan, Korea Rep, Malaysia, Mexico, New Zealand, Philippines, Taiwan, Thailand, USA.
Included in the above, 1 regional organization listed in this Yearbook:
ASEAN Federation of Electrical Engineering Contractors (AFEEC, #01174).
NGO Relations Member of: *EuropeOn (#09166).* Instrumental in setting up: *International Forum of Electrical Contractors (IFEC, no recent information).* Cooperates with: *ASEAN Federation of Electrical Engineering Contractors (AFEEC, #01174).* [2016/XJ1743/**D**]

♦ Federation of Asian and Pacific Fishery Associations (inactive)
♦ Federation of Asian-Pacific Retailers Association / see Federation of Asia-Pacific Retailers Association (#09454)

♦ Federation of Asian Perfusion Societies (FAPS) 09444

Contact c/o JaSECT, 4-1011-1 Uedayama, Tempaku-ku, Nagoya AICHI, 468-0001 Japan.
2020 Conference: https://www.facebook.com/Faps2020-101681424710561/

History Founded, 2007, during 7thAsian Conference on Extracorporeal Circulation. Inaugural meeting Sep 2011, Singapore. **Aims** Promote the science and practice of extracorporeal circulation technology; facilitate the exchange of ideas in the field of extracorporeal circulation through scientific meetings and personal contacts among cardiovascular specialists. **Events** *Meeting (FAPS 2020)* New Delhi (India) 2020, *Meeting (FAPS 2018)* Shanghai (China) 2018, *Meeting* Kobe (Japan) 2015, *Inaugural Meeting* Singapore (Singapore) 2011. [2012/XJ5327/**D**]

♦ Federation of Asian Pharmaceutical Associations (FAPA) 09445

Fédération des associations pharmaceutiques d'Asie
Gen Sec 3F Unit 309 Surabaya Bldg, Raya Garden Condo, West Service Rd, SLEX, Brgy Merville, 1700 Parañaque METRO MANILA, Philippines. T. +63284044739. E-mail: fapaasiahq@gmail.com.
URL: http://fapa.asia/

History 1964, Manila (Philippines). Constitution amended 16 Nov 1970. Statutes amended 23 Oct 2018. Registration: Securities and Exchange Commission, No/ID: CN200609304, Philippines. **Aims** Guide Asian pharmacists and pharmacy organizations to achieve professional excellence and contribute towards making medicines safe, effective, accessible and affordable, thus ensuring optimum health outcomes. **Structure** Council; Bureau; Sections. **Languages** English. **Staff** 2.00 FTE, paid. **Finance** Sources: contributions; donations; gifts, legacies; members' dues. **Activities** Humanitarian/emergency aid; knowledge management/information dissemination; projects/programmes; research/documentation. **Events** *Congress* Kuala Lumpur (Malaysia) 2022, *Biennial Congress* Kuala Lumpur (Malaysia) 2020, *Biennial Congress* Manila (Philippines) 2018, *Biennial Congress* Bangkok (Thailand) 2016, *Biennial Congress* Kota Kinabalu (Malaysia) 2014.
Members National associations in 24 countries and territories:
Afghanistan, Australia, Bangladesh, Cambodia, Hong Kong, India, Indonesia, Japan, Jordan, Korea Rep, Macau, Malaysia, Mongolia, Myanmar, Nepal, Pakistan, Papua New Guinea, Philippines, Singapore, Sri Lanka, Taiwan, Thailand, United Arab Emirates, Vietnam. [2022.05.27/XD0089/**D**]

♦ Federation of Asian Photographic Art (FAPA) 09446

Fédération de l'art photographique d'Asie
Contact c/o Photographic Society, PO Box 661, 10070 Penang, Malaysia.

History Nov 1966, Taipei (Taiwan). **Aims** Study photo art. **Languages** Chinese, English. **Staff** 1.50 FTE, voluntary. **Finance** Members' fees. Contributions. **Activities** Holds meetings, world photo exhibitions, theme lectures, seminars. **Events** *Congress* Penang (Malaysia) 2014, *Congress* China 2012, *Congress* Kota Kinabalu (Malaysia) 2008, *Congress* Kaohsiung (Taiwan) 2006, *Congress* Bandar Seri Begawan (Brunei Darussalam) 2004.
Members Central photographic associations in 12 countries and territories:
Brunei Darussalam, Hong Kong, India, Indonesia, Japan, Korea Rep, Malaysia, Philippines, Singapore, Taiwan, Thailand, Vietnam. [2012/XD9056/**D**]

♦ Federation of Asian Polymer Societies (FAPS) 09447

Pres c/o Polymer Society, Taipei, Taiwan. E-mail: polymer@itri.org.tw – pb221136@mail.nsysu.edu.tw.
URL: http://www.faps-asia.org/

History Dec 2007. **Aims** Encourage and facilitate cooperation among the Asian Polymer scientists. **Structure** Council. Officers: President; Vice-President; Secretary-General; Secretary-Treasurer; Secretary. Secretariat. **Events** *Polymer Congress* Vladivostok (Russia) 2021, *Polymer Congress* Taipei (Taiwan) 2019, *Polymer congress* Jeju (Korea Rep) 2017, *Polymer congress* Kuala Lumpur (Malaysia) 2015, *Polymer congress* Beijing (China) 2011.
Members Full in 14 countries and territories:
Bangladesh, China, India, Indonesia, Japan, Korea Rep, Malaysia, Nepal, Pakistan, Russia, Singapore, Taiwan, Thailand, Vietnam.
NGO Relations Member of (1): *International Union of Pure and Applied Chemistry (IUPAC, #15809).*
[2021/XJ1500/**D**]

♦ Federation of Asian Professional Textile Associations (FAPTA) 09448

Contact Korea Fiber Soc, 635-4 Yeoksam-dong, Kangnam-ku, Seoul, Korea Rep.

History 1991. **Aims** Promote cooperation between professional textile associations in Asia. **Structure** General Body Meeting (every 2 years). Executive Council, including President, General Secretary and Treasurer. **Events** *Biennial Conference* China 2013, *Biennial Conference* Shanghai (China) 2013, *Biennial Conference* Daegu (Korea Rep) 2011, *Biennial Conference* Ueda (Japan) 2009, *Biennial Conference* Taichung (Taiwan) 2007. **Publications** *Journal of FAPTA.*
Members Full in 8 countries and territories:
Australia, China, Hong Kong, India, Iran Islamic Rep, Japan, Korea Rep, Taiwan. [2012/XD8059/t/**D**]

♦ Federation of Asian Retailers Association / see Federation of Asia-Pacific Retailers Association (#09454)
♦ Federation of Asian Scientific Academies and Societies (inactive)

♦ Federation of Asian Small Animal Veterinary Associations (FASAVA) 09449

Hon Sec PO Box 234, Bundoora VIC 3083, Australia. T. +61394672255. Fax +61394677369.
URL: http://fasava.org/

History 2002, Granada (Spain). Proposed 2002, Grenada (Spain), at 27th Congress of *World Small Animal Veterinary Association (WSAVA, #21795).* Decision to create FASAVE made 2005, Taipei (Taiwan). Registered in accordance with Australian law, 31 Jul 2007. **Aims** Act as a common Asia Pacific forum for companion animal practice. **Structure** General Meeting. Executive Committee, comprising Chairman, Past Chairman, Honorary Secretary, Honorary Treasurer and Executive member. **Events** *Congress* Tokyo (Japan) 2019, *Congress* Singapore (Singapore) 2018, *Congress* Gold Coast, QLD (Australia) 2017, *Congress* Kuala Lumpur (Malaysia) 2016, *Congress* Taipei (Taiwan) 2015.
Members Founding members in 12 countries and territories:
Australia, China, Hong Kong, India, Korea Rep, Malaysia, New Zealand, Philippines, Singapore, Sri Lanka, Taiwan, Thailand.
Invited members in 4 countries:
Iran Islamic Rep, Japan, Nepal, Vietnam. [2019/XJ2789/**E**]

♦ Federation of Asian Societies for Molecular Imaging (FASMI) 09450

Pres address not obtained. E-mail: fasmiorg@gmail.com.
URL: https://www.f-asmi.org/

History Founded 1 Sep 2006, Hawaii (USA). Jointly suggested by the Presidents of the National Societies for Molecular Imaging of Japan, Korea Rep and Taiwan during the inaugural meeting of the Japanese Society for Molecular Imaging, 23-24 May 2006, Kyoto (Japan). **Aims** Promote molecular imaging in Asian countries and worldwide; facilitate communication between researchers and clinicians working in the field of molecular imaging and related disciplines; stimulate and mediate collaborations between molecular imaging researchers and clinicians in Asian countries and throughout the world; provide the network infrastructure for multi-disciplinary education and collaborate research in molecular imaging. **Events** *FASMI International Conference* Taipei (Taiwan) 2020, *World Molecular Imaging Congress* Philadelphia, PA (USA) 2017, *Annual Meeting* Kobe (Japan) 2016, *World Molecular Imaging Congress* New York, NY (USA) 2016, *World Molecular Imaging Congress* Honolulu, HI (USA) 2015.
Members in 3 countries and territories:
Japan, Korea Rep, Taiwan.
Candidate member:
India.
NGO Relations Cooperates with (1): *European Society for Molecular Imaging (ESMI, #08655).* Joint conference with *World Molecular Imaging Society (WMIS, #21656).* [2021/XM3614/**D**]

♦ Federation of Asian Veterinary Associations (FAVA) 09451

Fédération des associations vétérinaires asiatiques – Federación de Asociaciones Veterinarias Asiaticas
SG 69/26 Soi Pratumwan Resort, Phayatai Road, Bangkok, 10400, Thailand. Fax +6622528773. E-mail: secretariat@favamember.org.
URL: http://www.favamember.org/

History 22 Feb 1978, Manila (Philippines). Founded following a decision taken by representatives of 6 Asian national veterinarians' associations, 18 Feb 1976. **Aims** Enhance quality of life of the people in the region through responsible animal care and welfare by a unified professional association. **Structure** Council (meets annually), comprising President, Vice-President, Secretary-General, Treasurer, Auditor and representative from members. **Languages** English. **Staff** Voluntary. **Finance** Members' dues (annual). **Activities** Coordinates and facilitates technical assistance for member associations; establishes mutually beneficial relationship with local and international agro-veterinary industries; encourages veterinarians to provide and educate the public on quality veterinary services; facilitates improvement of veterinary education (undergraduate, postgraduate levels) relevant to the region. Executive Board meetings (annual). Regional veterinary congresses (every 2 years) hosted by a member association. **Events** *Congress* Kuching (Malaysia) 2023, *Congress* Fukuoka (Japan) 2022, *Congress* Kuching (Malaysia) 2021, *Congress* Kuching (Malaysia) 2020, *Biennial Congress* Bali (Indonesia) 2018. **Publications** *FAVA News* – online. Proceedings of regional congresses – online.
Members Professional veterinary associations in 19 countries and territories:
Australia, Bangladesh, Hong Kong, India, Indonesia, Japan, Korea Rep, Malaysia, Mongolia, Myanmar, Nepal, New Zealand, Pakistan, Philippines, Singapore, Sri Lanka, Taiwan, Thailand, Vietnam.
Included in the above, 1 organization listed in this Yearbook:
Asian Society of Conservation Medicine (ASCM, #01714); Association vétérinaire Euro-Arabe (AVEA, #02975).
NGO Relations Supports (since 2008) Universal Declaration of Animal Welfare of: *World Animal Protection (#21092).* [2022/XD8404/**D**]

♦ Federation of Asian and Western Pacific Contractors' Associations / see International Federation of Asian and Western Pacific Contractors' Associations (#13359)
♦ Federation of Asian Women's Associations / see Federation of Asia-Pacific Women's Associations (#09455)

♦ Federation of Asia-Oceania Perinatal Societies (FAOPS) 09452

President Kyorin Univ, 5 Chome-5-4-1, Shimorenjaku, Mitaka TOKYO, 181-8612 Japan.
SG address not obtained.
URL: https://plaza.umin.ac.jp/FAOPS/

History 1978. **Aims** Foster the science and art of perinatology; promote maternal, foetal and neonatal welfare; encourage cooperation with international bodies and maintain liaison with other organizations and professions involved in the field; provide expert advice to governmental and other bodies; promote research and training. **Structure** General Assembly (annual, at Congress); Council. **Languages** English. **Staff** Voluntary. **Finance** Sources: members' dues. **Events** *Congress* Tokyo (Japan) 2023, *FAOPS Congress* Kuala Lumpur (Malaysia) 2022, *FAOPS Congress* Jakarta (Indonesia) 2021, *FAOPS Congress* Tokyo (Japan) 2020, *Biennial Congress* Manila (Philippines) 2018.
Members National societies, with membership drawn from nursing, midwifery and basic science as well as paediatrics and obstetrics, in 13 countries:
Australia, India, Indonesia, Japan, Korea Rep, Malaysia, Nepal, New Zealand, Pakistan, Philippines, Singapore, Taiwan, Thailand.
NGO Relations Member of (1): *PMNCH (#18410).* [2022.10.26/XD2294/**D**]

♦ Federation of Asia-Oceania Pest Management / see Federation of Asian and Oceania Pest Managers Associations (#09441)

♦ Federation of Asia Pacific Aircargo Associations (FAPAA) 09453

Secretariat c/o AFIF, Ste 403, Level 3, The Office Tower, 152 Bunnerong Road, Eastgardens NSW 2036, Australia. T. +61293143055. Fax +61293143116. E-mail: afif@afif.asn.au.
Main: http://www.fapaa.org/

History Founded 10 Mar 1986, Singapore (Singapore). **Aims** Promote, protect and develop the air cargo industry in the region; foster closer relationships among air cargo associations and members; represent members and act as negotiating body in dialogues with governments, carriers and relevant bodies; set and regulate standards of practice to be maintained by members. **Languages** English. **Finance** Members' dues. **Events** *Annual executive council meeting* Dhaka (Bangladesh) 2011, *Annual executive council meeting* Singapore (Singapore) 2010, *Annual executive council meeting* Singapore (Singapore) 2009, *Annual executive council meeting* Tokyo (Japan) 2008, *Annual executive council meeting* Hong Kong (Hong Kong) 2007.
Members Aircargo associations in 16 countries:
Australia, Bangladesh, Brunei Darussalam, Hong Kong, India, Japan, Korea Rep, Macau, Malaysia, Nepal, New Zealand, Philippines, Singapore, Sri Lanka, Taiwan, Thailand.
NGO Relations Member of: *Latin American and Caribbean Federation of National Associations of Cargo (#16276).* [2014/XD2405/**D**]

♦ Federation of Asia-Pacific Microbiology Societies (inactive)

♦ Federation of Asia-Pacific Retailers Association (FAPRA) 09454

Chairperson A-11-11 and A-11-12, Level 11 Tower A, Menara UOA Bangsar, 5 Jalan Bangsar, Utama 1, 59000 Kuala Lumpur, Malaysia. E-mail: evelyn@mra.com.my.
Secretariat 46 Dongsi West Street, Dongcheng District, 100711 Beijing, China. E-mail: cgcc_intl@aliyun.com – wang.jingshi@cgcc.org.cn.
URL: http://www.fapra.net/

History 1989. Former names and other names: *Federation of Asian Retailers Association (FARA)* – former (1989); *Federation of Asian-Pacific Retailers Association (FAPRA)* – alias. **Aims** Further develop the retail industry in the region. **Activities** Events/meetings. **Events** *Biennial Convention* Bali (Indonesia) 2021, *Biennial Convention* Chongqing (China) 2019, *Biennial Convention* Kuala Lumpur (Malaysia) 2017, *Biennial Convention* Manila (Philippines) 2015, *Biennial Convention* Istanbul (Turkey) 2013.
Members Full in 21 countries and territories:
Australia, China, Fiji, Hong Kong, India, Indonesia, Japan, Korea Rep, Kyrgyzstan, Malaysia, Mongolia, Myanmar, New Zealand, Philippines, Singapore, Sri Lanka, Taiwan, Thailand, Türkiye, USA, Vietnam. [2021.02.18/XD3522/**D**]

♦ Federation of Asia-Pacific Women's Associations (FAWA) 09455

Fédération des associations féminines d'Asie et du Pacifique
Pres 962 Josefa Llanes Escoda St, Ermita, 1000 Manila, Philippines. T. +6325235024 – +6325233082.
URL: http://www.fawainternational.com/

History 19 Jun 1959, Manila (Philippines), as *Federation of Asian Women's Associations*. Current title adopted 1999. **Aims** Strive for effective understanding and cooperation among women and among people in general in the Asian region; enhance the role of Asian women in the economic, cultural and spiritual development of the region, and increase their participation in world affairs; gain access of Asian women to educational and cultural activities. **Structure** Board; Administrative Council. **Languages** English. **Staff** Voluntary. **Finance** Members' dues. **Events** *Biennial Convention* Manila (Philippines) 2018, *Biennial Convention* Singapore (Singapore) 2016, *Biennial Convention* Seoul (Korea Rep) 2014, *Biennial Conference* Guam 2012, *Biennial Conference* Taiwan 2009. **Publications** *FAWA News Bulletin* (4 a year); *The Asia Forum*.
Members Clubs and organizations that have been in existence for at least one year in 10 countries and territories:
Guam, Hong Kong, Indonesia, Japan, Korea Rep, Myanmar, Philippines, Singapore, Taiwan, Thailand.
IGO Relations *UNESCO (#20322)*. [2018/XD0928/**D**]

- ♦ Federation of Asia Simulation Societies (unconfirmed)
- ♦ Fédération asiatique d'analystes financiers / see Asian Securities and Investments Federation (#01695)
- ♦ Fédération asiatique des associations de bibliothécaires (inactive)
- ♦ Fédération asiatique des associations médicales catholiques (#01455)
- ♦ Fédération asiatique de l'emballage (#01648)
- ♦ Fédération asiatique haltérophile (#01781)
- ♦ Fédération asiatique de tennis de table (inactive)
- ♦ Fédération d'Asie des associations de publicité (#01452)
- ♦ Fédération asienne de sociétés de chimie (#09431)
- ♦ Federation of Association and Enterprises of Industrial Culinary Product Producers in Europe / see CULINARIA EUROPE (#04980)
- ♦ Fédération des association européennes d'écrivains (#09123)
- ♦ Fédération des associations d'anciens fonctionnaires internationaux (#09457)
- ♦ Fédération des associations arabes d'agents de voyages (inactive)
- ♦ Fédération des associations d'archivistes, bibliothécaires, documentalistes de la Caraïbe (inactive)
- ♦ Fédération des associations des banquiers d'Amérique centrale et du Panama (inactive)
- ♦ Fédération des associations des capitales et villes européennes du sport (#06440)
- ♦ Fédération des associations de chasse et conservation de la faune sauvage de l'UE (#09459)
- ♦ Fédération des associations de chasseurs de la CE / see Federation of Associations for Hunting and Conservation of the EU (#09459)
- ♦ Fédération des associations de chasseurs de l'UE / see Federation of Associations for Hunting and Conservation of the EU (#09459)
- ♦ Fédération des associations chrétiennes travailleurs internationaux / see International Federation of ACLI (#13336)
- ♦ Fédération des associations et clubs UNESCO d'Asie et du Pacifique (#01614)
- ♦ Federation for Associations Connected to the International Humana People to People Movement (see: #13817)
- ♦ Fédération des associations d'échanges, 1925 (inactive)
- ♦ Fédération des associations des écrivains de l'Afrique de l'ouest (inactive)
- ♦ Fédération des associations d'éditeurs de périodiques de la CE / see European Magazine Media Association (#07723)
- ♦ Fédération des associations éducatives latinoaméricaines et des Caraïbes (#09289)
- ♦ Fédération des associations éducatives privées latinoaméricaines et des Caraïbes / see Federación de Asociaciones Educativas de América Latina y el Caribe (#09289)
- ♦ Fédération des associations d'entrepreneurs asiatiques et du Pacifique occidental / see International Federation of Asian and Western Pacific Contractors' Associations (#13359)
- ♦ Fédération des associations des étudiants africains en médecine (#09407)
- ♦ Fédération des associations européennes de l'automatique / see European Gaming and Amusement Federation (#07374)
- ♦ Fédération des associations européennes du commerce de gros et extérieur (inactive)
- ♦ Fédération des associations européennes des constructeurs de fenêtres / see Fédération des associations européennes des constructeurs de fenêtres et de façades (#09456)

♦ Fédération des associations européennes des constructeurs de fenêtres et de façades (FAECF) 09456

Federation of European Window and Curtain Walling Manufacturer Associations – Föderation der Europäischen Fenster- und Fassadenherstellerverbände
Gen Sec Council for Aluminium in Building, Bqnk House, Bonds Mill, Stonehouse, Gloucester, GL10 3RF, UK. T. +441453828851.
URL: http://www.faecf.eu/

History 21 Nov 1968, The Hague (Netherlands), as *Federation of European Window Manufacturers' Associations – Fédération des associations européennes des constructeurs de fenêtres (FAECF) – Föderation der Europäischen Fensterherstellerverbände*. Previously referred to as *Federation of European Window and Curtain Wall Manufacturers' Associations*. **Aims** Promote and defend the European fenestration industry. **Structure** Management Council; General Secretariat. **Languages** English, French, German. **Staff** 2.00 FTE, paid. **Finance** Members' dues. **Activities** Knowledge management/information dissemination; standards/guidelines. **Events** *Biennial congress / Congress* Berlin (Germany) 2006, *Biennial congress / Congress* Greece 2003, *Congress* Turkey 2001, *Congress* Malta 2000, *Biennial Congress* Spain 2000.
Members Full in 6 countries:
Austria, France, Italy, Netherlands, Spain, UK.
Associate member listed in this Yearbook:
IGO Relations Recognized by: *European Commission (EC, #06633)*. **NGO Relations** In liaison with technical committees of: *Comité européen de normalisation (CEN, #04162)*; *International Organization for Standardization (ISO, #14473)*. Member of: *METALS FOR BUILDINGS (#16737)*. [2017.06.27/XD1010/**E**]

- ♦ Fédération des associations européennes des fournisseurs de laboratoires scientifiques (no recent information)
- ♦ Fédération des associations européennes de galeries d'art (#09492)
- ♦ Fédération des associations européennes et internationales établies en Belgique (#09508)
- ♦ Fédération des associations européennes de journalistes d'entreprises / see European Association for Internal Communication (#06091)
- ♦ Fédération des associations européennes de matériaux (#09515)
- ♦ Fédération des associations européennes de mousse de polyuréthane rigide (#09538)
- ♦ Fédération des associations européennes de la presse d'entreprise / see European Association for Internal Communication (#06091)
- ♦ Fédération des associations européennes de sérigraphes / see FESPA (#09739)
- ♦ Fédération des associations européennes du tissu conjonctif / see European Matrix Biology (#07756)
- ♦ Fédération des associations européennes de vétérinaires spécialisés en animaux de compagnie (#09497)
- ♦ Fédération des associations de fabricants de produits alimentaires surgelés de la CEE (inactive)
- ♦ Fédération des associations familiales catholiques en Europe (#09468)
- ♦ Fédération des associations féminines d'Asie et du Pacifique (#09455)
- ♦ Fédération des associations de fonctionnaires internationaux (#09603)

♦ Federation of Associations of Former International Civil Servants (FAFICS) 09457

Fédération des associations d'anciens fonctionnaires internationaux (FAAFI)
Contact c/o AAFI-AFICS Bureau E-2078, Palais des Nations, 1211 Geneva 10, Switzerland. E-mail: gvafafics@gmail.com – secretary@fafics.org.
URL: http://www.fafics.org/

History 26 Jul 1975, Geneva (Switzerland), to link individuals who have served in organizations of the United Nations system. Most recent statutes adopted 1 Jul 1983. Registered in accordance with Swiss Civil Code. **Aims** Provide a framework for promoting and defending the interests of former civil servants, most notably in pension and health insurance issues. **Structure** Council (meets annually); Working Groups (2). **Languages** English, French, Spanish. **Staff** 3.00 FTE, voluntary. **Finance** Members' dues. **Activities** Knowledge management/information dissemination. **Events** *Annual Session* Vienna (Austria) 2019, *Annual Session* Montréal, QC (Canada) 1992. **Publications** Internal documents; directory.
Members Associations in over 60 countries. Membership countries not specified. Included in the above, 9 organizations listed in this Yearbook:
Included in the above, 9 organizations listed in this Yearbook:
Association of Former International Civil Servants – Geneva (AAFI-AFICS Geneva, #02599); Association of Former International Civil Servants – New York (AFICS New York, #02600); Association of Former UNESCO Staff Members (AFUS Paris, #02601); Association of Former United Nations Personnel in and of India (AFUNPI, #02603); Association of Retired International Civil Servants, Austria (ARICSA); British Association of Former United Nations Civil Servants (BAFUNCS); Canadian Association of Former International Civil Servants (CAFICS); Former FAO and Other United Nations Staff Association (FFOA); Former Officials Association Turin (FOA Turin).
Consultative Status Consultative status granted from: *ECOSOC (#05331)* (Special). **IGO Relations** Recognized representative of all persons receiving a pension or other benefit from the: *United Nations Joint Staff Pension Fund (UNJSPF, #20581)* (now over 40,000), FAFICS has 4 non-voting representatives and 2 alternate representatives participating in meetings of the Board. Associated with Department of Global Communications of the United Nations. [2023/XF6569/y/**F**]

- ♦ Federation of Associations and Foundations Supporting Opera Houses and Festivals (inactive)
- ♦ Fédération des associations franco-africaines de développement, Paris / see Fédération Euro-Africaine de Solidarité
- ♦ Fédération des associations francophones d'étude de la ménopause (no recent information)

♦ Fédération des associations francophones de vétérinaires pour animaux de compagnie (FAFVAC) 09458

Administrator c/o AMVQ, 199 boul Sainte-Rose, Laval QC H7L 1L5, Canada. T. +14509631952. E-mail: amvq@amvq.qc.ca.
URL: http://www.fafvac.org/

History Officially set up 2006. **Aims** Harmonize the activities of various veterinary associations members; facilitate the dissemination of scientific information in French; promote projects concerning the welfare of companion animals; promote quality exercise in Francophone countries; establish and maintain a collaboration with international professional organizations. **Structure** Council, comprising President, 3 Vice-Presidents, Secretary General, Deputy Secretary, Treasurer General, Deputy Treasurer and Administrator. **Events** *Annual Congress* Montréal, QC (Canada) 2014, *Annual Congress* Liège (Belgium) 2011, *Annual Congress* Geneva (Switzerland) 2010, *Annual Congress* Lille (France) 2009, *Annual Congress* Saint-Hyacinthe, QC (Canada) 2008.
Members Associations in 7 countries:
Belgium, Canada, France, Haiti, Morocco, Switzerland, Tunisia. [2014/XJ4985/**C**]

♦ Federation of Associations for Hunting and Conservation of the EU . 09459

Fédération des associations de chasse et conservation de la faune sauvage de l'UE (FACE) – Zusammenschluss der Verbände für Jagd und Wildtiererhaltung in der EU – Federación de las Asociaciones de Caza y Conservación de la Fauna Silvestre de la UE – Federazione delle Associazioni venatori e per la Conservazione della Fauna Selvatica dell'UE
Gen Sec Rue Belliard 205, 1040 Brussels, Belgium. T. +3224161613. E-mail: info@face.eu – communication@face.eu.
URL: http://www.face.eu/

History 9 Mar 1977, Brussels (Belgium). Commenced activities, 11 Sep 1977. Former names and other names: *Federation of the Hunting Associations of the EEC* – former; *Federation of Field Sports Associations of the EC* – former; *Fédération des associations de chasseurs de la CE* – former; *Zusammenschluss der Jagdschutzverbände in der EG* – former; *Federazione delle Associazioni dei Cacciatori della CE* – former; *Federation of Field Sports Associations of the EU* – former; *Fédération des associations de chasseurs de l'UE* – former; *Zusammenschluss der Jagdschutzverbände in der EU* – former; *Federación de las Asociaciones de Cazadores de la UE* – former; *Federazione delle Associazioni dei Cacciatori della UE* – former. Registration: Banque-Carrefour des Entreprises, No/ID: 0418.672.289, Start date: 18 May 1978, Belgium. **Aims** Ensure that knowledge and experience of European hunters is integrated into the EU decision-making process. **Structure** General Assembly; Board. **Languages** English, French, German. **Staff** 11.50 FTE, paid. **Finance** Members' dues. Support from *European Commission (EC, #06633)* DG Environment and annual LIFE NGO Grant funding. **Activities** Advocacy/lobbying/activism; politics/policy/regulatory; events/meetings; training/education. **Events** *Annual Spring Members Meeting* Noordwijk (Netherlands) 2019, *European Hunters Conference* Noordwijk (Netherlands) 2019, *Autumn General Assembly* Brussels (Belgium) 2018, *Conference on Young Hunters* Brussels (Belgium) 2017, *General Assembly* Brussels (Belgium) 2014. **Publications** *European Charter on Hunting and Biodiversity*; *Hunting, an added value for Biodiversity*; *Manifesto 2009-2014*. Annual Report.
Members Open to national organizations in all countries of the Council of Europe. Currently organizations representing 7 million hunters in 36 countries:
Albania, Austria, Belgium, Bosnia-Herzegovina, Bulgaria, Croatia, Cyprus, Czechia, Denmark, Estonia, Finland, France, Germany, Greece, Hungary, Iceland, Ireland, Italy, Latvia, Lithuania, Luxembourg, Malta, Montenegro, Netherlands, Norway, Poland, Portugal, Romania, Serbia, Slovakia, Slovenia, Spain, Sweden, Switzerland, Türkiye, UK.
Associate members (6):
Conservation Force (#04729); ESFAM; *European Association of the Civil Commerce of Weapons (#05975)*; *European Bowhunting Association (EBA, #06385)*; Safari Club International Foundation; *Safari Club International (SCI)*.
IGO Relations Accredited by General Assembly of *UNESCO (#20322)* Convention on Intangible Cultural Heritage. Liaises with: *European Commission (EC, #06633)*. Serves as secretariat for the 'Fieldsports, Fishing and Conservation Intergroup' of: *European Parliament (EP, #08146)*. Observer status at: Technical Committee of *African-Eurasian Migratory /Water Bird/ Agreement (AEWA, 1995)*; *Standing Committee to the Bern Convention on the Conservation of European Wildlife and Natural Habitats (#19949)*. **NGO Relations** Member of (3): *International Union for Conservation of Nature and Natural Resources (IUCN, #15766)*; *Wetlands International (#20928)*; *World Forum on Shooting Activities (WFSA, #21523)*. Partner of (1): *Association of European Manufacturers of Sporting Firearms (ESFAM, #02523)*. In liaison with technical committees of: *International Organization for Standardization (ISO, #14473)*. [2021/XE3774/**E**]

♦ Fédération des associations des industriels de l'Afrique de l'Ouest (#09714)
♦ Fédération des associations d'ingénieurs de l'Asie du Sud-Est et du Pacifique (#09480)
♦ Fédération des associations d'installations électriques d'Asie et du Pacifique (#09443)
♦ Fédération des associations internationales établies en Belgique / see Federation of European and International Associations Established in Belgium (#09508)
♦ Fédération des associations internationales poétiques (inactive)
♦ Fédération des associations des journalistes de l'Afrique de l'Est (inactive)
♦ Fédération des associations nationales des agents et courtiers maritimes de navires (#09694)

♦ Fédération des Associations Nationales des Bécassiers du Paléarctique Occidental (FANBPO) 09460

Federazione delle Associazioni Nazionali dei Beccacciai del Paleartico Occidentale – Federation of European Woodcock Associations of Western Palearctic

Pres Via Fausto Vagnetti 12, 52031 Anghiari AR, Italy. T. +393298627229.
Sec Planafaye 118, 1752 Villars-sur-Glane FR, Switzerland. T. +41792137852.
URL: https://www.fanbpo.org/

History 10 Jun 2001. Former names and other names: *Club international des bécassiers du paléarctique occidental* – former. **Aims** Promote *conservation* of the *woodcock* in the Western Palearctic, whilst allowing a rational use of this species through sustainable and controlled *hunting*. **Structure** General Assembly. **Languages** English, French. **Staff** 6.00 FTE, voluntary. **Finance** Sources: members' dues. Annual budget: 1,250 EUR. **Activities** Monitoring/evaluation; research/documentation. **Events** *Meeting* Sopron (Hungary) 2015, *Meeting* Gruyères (Switzerland) 2014, *Meeting* La Forêt Fouesnant (France) 2008. **Publications** *FANBPO Bulletin* (2 a year). Annual report.
Members National organizations in 7 countries and territories:
France, Ireland, Italy, Portugal, Spain, Switzerland, Wales.
Correspondants in 6 countries:
Estonia, Greece, Hungary, Türkiye, UK, USA. [2022/XM0640/**D**]

♦ Fédération des Associations Nationales des Ingénieurs Electriciens de l'Europe (#04788)
♦ Fédération des associations nordiques d'annonceurs (inactive)
♦ Federation of Associations of Periodical Publishers in EC / see European Magazine Media Association (#07723)
♦ Fédération des associations pharmaceutiques d'Asie (#09445)
♦ Federation of Associations of Private Educational Entities of Latin America / see Federación de Asociaciones Educativas de América Latina y el Caribe (#09289)
♦ Fédération des associations des professionnels en produits de base (no recent information)
♦ Fédération des associations de sapeurs-pompiers dans l'Union européenne (#09555)
♦ Fédération des Associations de Solidarité Internationale (internationally oriented national body)

♦ Federation of Associations of Technicians for Industry of Paints in European Countries (FATIPEC) 09461

Secretariat 5 rue Etex, 75018 Paris, France. T. +33142634591. Fax +33142633150. E-mail: info@fatipec.com.
Gen Sec c/o PPG Polifarb Cieszyn SA, ul Chemikow 16, PO Box 188, 43-400 Cieszyn, Poland.
URL: http://www.fatipec.com/

History 7 Jan 1950, Geneva (Switzerland). Previously known in English as *Federation of Associations of Technicians in the Paint, Varnish, Enamel, and Printing-Ink Industries of Continental Europe*; in German as *Vereinigung der Europäischen Verbände der Techniker der Farb-, Email- und Druckfarben-Industrien des Europäischen Festlandes*; in French as *Fédération d'associations de techniciens des industries des peintures, vernis, émaux et encres d'imprimerie de l'Europe continentale*. Registered in accordance with French law. **Aims** Stimulate research and exchange of ideas and expertise and publish the results of scientific and technological works; support activities for development of international cooperation between coatings scientists and technicians worldwide; provide a platform for communication in the coatings world. **Structure** Board; Executive Committee; European Scientific Committee. **Languages** English. **Staff** 0.30 FTE, paid. **Finance** Members' dues. **Activities** Events/meetings. **Events** *European Technical Coatings Congress* Krakow (Poland) 2022, *European Technical Coatings Congress* Krakow (Poland) 2021, *European Technical Coatings Congress* Krakow (Poland) 2020, *European Technical Coatings Congress* Amsterdam (Netherlands) 2018, *European Technical Coatings Congress* Birmingham (UK) 2016. **Publications** Congress proceedings.
Members National associations (13), totalling over 3,000 individuals, in 12 countries:
Belgium, Czechia, France, Germany, Greece, Hungary, Iran Islamic Rep, Italy, Netherlands, Poland, Russia, Switzerland.
NGO Relations Member of: *Coatings Societies International (CSI, #04075)*. Cooperates with: *Oil and Colour Chemists' Association (OCCA, #17707)*. [2022/XD0929/t/**D**]

♦ Federation of Associations of Technicians in the Paint, Varnish, Enamel, and Printing-Ink Industries of Continental Europe / see Federation of Associations of Technicians for Industry of Paints in European Countries (#09461)
♦ Fédération d'associations de techniciens des industries des peintures, vernis, émaux et encres d'imprimerie de l'Europe continentale / see Federation of Associations of Technicians for Industry of Paints in European Countries (#09461)
♦ Fédération d'associations de techniciens des industries des peintures et vernis de la Scandinavie (#09702)
♦ Federation of Associations and Unions of the International Civil Service (inactive)
♦ Fédération des associations vétérinaires asiatiques (#09451)
♦ Fédération des associations zoroastriennes d'Amérique du Nord (internationally oriented national body)
♦ Fédération d'assureurs et de réassureurs afro-asiatiques (#09413)
♦ Fédération d'astrologie de l'Europe du sud (no recent information)
♦ Federation of Astronomical and Geophysical Data Analysis Services (inactive)

♦ Fédération Atlantique des Agences de Presse Africaines (FAAPA) 09462

Atlantic Federation of African Press Agencies

SG 122 Avenue Allal Ben Abdellah, BP 1049, 10000 Rabat, Morocco. E-mail: faapa@map.ma.
URL: http://www.faapa.info/

History 14 Oct 2014, Casablanca (Morocco). **Aims** Encourage the exchange of experiences, information and multimedia products; promote the exchange of ideas on the future of news agencies and the role they must play in the 21st century. **Structure** Executive Council. **IGO Relations** Partner of (2): *Union for the Mediterranean (UfM, #20457)*; *Union of OIC News AGencies (UNA, #20467)*. **NGO Relations** Partner of (2): *Alliance of Mediterranean News Agencies (AMAN, #00708)*; *Organization of Asian-Pacific News Agencies (OANA, #17855)*. [2022/AA3033/**D**]

♦ Fédération des auberges de jeunesse des Communautés européennes / see European Union Federation of Youth Hostel Associations (#08988)
♦ Fédération des auberges de jeunesse de l'Union européenne (#08988)
♦ Federation of Auctioneers of the EEC / see European Federation of Auctioneers (#07057)
♦ Fédération des Augustines Hospitalières de la Miséricorde de Jésus (religious order)
♦ Fédération autonautique internationale (inactive)
♦ Fédération des Autorités Compétentes et Régulateurs Dentaires Européens (#09501)
♦ Federation of Balkanite Turks Immigrants and Refugee Associations / see Balkan Türkleri Göçmenleri ve Mülteci Dernekleri Federasyonu (#03089)
♦ Federation of Balkan Turk Migrants and Refugee Associations (#03089)
♦ Federation of Balkan Turks and Associations for Emigrés / see Balkan Türkleri Göçmenleri ve Mülteci Dernekleri Federasyonu (#03089)
♦ Federation of Balkan Turks Migrants and Refugees Associations / see Balkan Türkleri Göçmenleri ve Mülteci Dernekleri Federasyonu (#03089)
♦ Fédération bancaire de la Communauté européenne / see European Banking Federation (#06312)
♦ Fédération bancaire latinoaméricaine (#16254)
♦ Fédération bancaire de l'Union européenne (#06312)
♦ Federation of Bankers' Associations of Central America and Panama (inactive)
♦ Fédération baptiste européenne (#06316)
♦ Fédération des baptistes d'Asie et Pacifique (#01857)
♦ Fédération des Barreaux d'Europe (#06320)
♦ Federation of Beekeeping Organizations (#09287)
♦ Fédération biblique catholique (#03600)
♦ Fédération des biologistes arabes (inactive)
♦ Fédération des bourses de la Communauté européenne / see Federation of European Securities Exchanges (#09542)
♦ Fédération des bourses européennes / see Federation of European Securities Exchanges (#09542)
♦ Federation of British Caribbean Civil Service Association / see Caribbean Public Services Association (#03545)

♦ Federation of British International Schools in Asia (FOBISIA) 09463

CEO 39/4 Todsamon Clubhouse Bldg, M Fl Soi Lasalle 39/1, Sukhumvit 105, Bangna, Bangkok, 10260, Thailand. T. +66027444070. E-mail: info@fobisia.org – ceo@fobisia.org.
URL: http://www.fobisia.org/

History 1988. Former names and other names: *Federation for British International Schools in South and East Asia (FOBISSEA)* – former (1988 to 2013). Registration: Ministry of Home Affairs' Registry of Societies, No/ID: T02SS0078K, Start date: 28 Aug 2008, Singapore. **Aims** Be the premier Federation in Asia supporting and promoting high-quality British-style international education. **Structure** Board of Directors; Head Office located in Bangkok (Thailand). **Languages** English. **Staff** 7.00 FTE, paid. **Finance** Sources: members' dues. **Activities** Events/meetings. **Events** *Annual Leadership Conference* Bangkok (Thailand) 2022, *Annual Leadership Conference* Bangkok (Thailand) 2021, *Annual Leadership Conference* Bangkok (Thailand) 2020, *Annual Leadership Conference* Macau (Macau) 2019, *Annual Leadership Conference* Bangkok (Thailand) 2018.
Members British international schools (81) in 18 countries and territories:
Brunei Darussalam, China, Hong Kong, India, Indonesia, Kazakhstan, Korea Rep, Laos, Malaysia, Mongolia, Myanmar, Nepal, Philippines, Singapore, Sri Lanka, Taiwan, Thailand, Vietnam.
NGO Relations Cooperates with (1): *Council of British International Schools (COBIS, #04872)*. [2021.06.25/XD9310/**D**]

♦ Federation for British International Schools in South and East Asia / see Federation of British International Schools in Asia (#09463)

♦ Federation of Business Information Services (FEBIS) 09464

Secretariat Winsbergring 10, 22525 Hamburg, Germany. T. +4940890692990. Fax +4940890692999. E-mail: secretariat@febis.org.
URL: http://www.febis.org/

History 1973. Former names and other names: *Federation of European Credit Reporting Organizations (FECRO)* – former; *Fédération européenne des agences de renseignements commerciaux et d'informations économiques* – former; *Föderation der Europäischen Wirtschaftsauskunfteien* – former; *Federation of European Business Information Suppliers* – alias. Registration: Germany; EU Transparency Register, No/ID: 825169522150-13, Start date: 8 Jun 2016. **Aims** Serve the common interests of members while monitoring new legislation like data protection laws and insolvency laws; oversee application of public sources and information. **Languages** English, German. **Finance** Sources: members' dues. **Events** *Spring Meeting* Amsterdam (Netherlands) 2022, *Spring Meeting* Riga (Latvia) 2019, *General Assembly* Split (Croatia) 2019, *Spring Meeting* Madrid (Spain) 2018, *General Assembly* Vilamoura (Portugal) 2015.
Members Business information, debt collection agencies, credit insurance and software providers in 60 countries and territories:
Austria, Bangladesh, Belgium, Bulgaria, Canada, China, Colombia, Côte d'Ivoire, Croatia, Cyprus, Czechia, Denmark, Ecuador, Estonia, Finland, France, Germany, Greece, Hong Kong, Hungary, India, Ireland, Italy, Japan, Jordan, Kazakhstan, Kenya, Korea Rep, Latvia, Lithuania, Luxembourg, Mali, Malta, Mauritius, Mexico, Moldova, Morocco, Netherlands, Norway, Peru, Poland, Portugal, Romania, Russia, Serbia, Singapore, Slovakia, Slovenia, South Africa, Spain, Sweden, Switzerland, Taiwan, Thailand, Türkiye, UK, Ukraine, United Arab Emirates, USA, Vietnam. [2022.06.07/XD2716/**D**]

♦ Fédération Caraïbéenne des Associations d'Architectes (#09465)
♦ Fédération caraïbéenne des associations de planification familiale (#03502)

♦ Federation of Caribbean Associations of Architects (FCAA) 09465

Fédération Caraïbéenne des Associations d'Architectes (FCAA) – Federación Caribeña de Asociaciones de Arquitectos (FCAA)

Secretariat Seroe Biento 47, Santa Cruz, Aruba.

History 14 Jan 2000, Santo Domingo (Dominican Rep). Section of *Pan American Federation of Architects' Associations (#18098)*. **Aims** Bring together Caribbean architects in order to reinforce the professional, artistic, intellectual and friendly relations between them. **Structure** Board, including President, 5 Vice-Presidents and Secretary. **Languages** English, French, Spanish. **Events** *Biennial* Cuba 2009, *Congress* Guiana Fr 2008, *Congress* Guyana 2008, *Biennial* Curaçao 2007, *The impact of tourism on architecture and vice versa* Oranjestad (Aruba) 2006. **Publications** *Revue Espacio Caribeno*.
Members Member associations in 19 countries and territories:
Antigua, Aruba, Bahamas, Barbados, Cuba, Curaçao, Dominica, Dominican Rep, Guadeloupe, Guyana, Jamaica, Martinique, Montserrat, Nevis Is, Puerto Rico, St Lucia, Suriname, Trinidad-Tobago, Virgin Is USA. [2010.09.13/XD8659/**D**]

♦ Federation of Caribbean Cinema and Video Professionals (no recent information)
♦ Federation of Caribbean Engineering Associations (inactive)
♦ Fédération carmélitaine apostolique (religious order)

♦ Federation of Cartoonists Organisations (FECO) 09466

Fédération des organisations de cartoonistes

Pres Gen Leidsestraat 177, 2182 DL Hillegom, Netherlands.
Vice Pres Reuchlinstrasse 17A, 70178 Stuttgart, Germany. T. +497115283371. Fax +497113651290.
URL: http://www.fecocartoon.com/

History 1984, as *Federation of European Cartoonists Organizations (FECO) – Fédération des organisations de cartoonistes européennes*. **Aims** Encourage goodwill among cartoonists; increase dissemination of information regarding the *art* of the cartoon worldwide. **Structure** Board. **Languages** English. **Staff** 8.00 FTE, paid. **Finance** Members' dues (annual): euro 200 per country. **Activities** Knowledge management/ information dissemination; events/meetings. **Events** *Meeting* St-Just-Le-Martel (France) 2010. **Publications** *FECOBulletin* (6 a year) – online; *FECONEWS* (2 a year) – magazine.
Members Groups (28) and Organization members (8) in 30 countries and territories:
Argentina, Australia, Azerbaijan, Belgium, Brazil, Bulgaria, China, Croatia, Cyprus, Czechia, Egypt, France, Germany, Greece, Indonesia, Iran Islamic Rep, Japan, Korea Rep, Mexico, Netherlands, North Macedonia, Norway, Portugal, Romania, Serbia, Spain, Taiwan, Türkiye, UK, USA.
Individuals: professional cartoonists, painters, graphic designers and illustrators (about 3000). Membership countries not specified. [2015/XD7072/**D**]

♦ Federation of Catholic Bishops' Conferences of Oceania (FCBCO) 09467

Sec SVD, Catholic Bishops Conf of Papua New Guinea and Solomon Is, PO Box 398, Waigani NCD 131 MBA, Papua New Guinea. T. +6753239577. Fax +6753232551.
Pres PO Box 1032, Boroko NCD 111 NCD, Papua New Guinea. T. +6753251192. Fax +6753256103.

History Founded 28 Jul 1992, when statutes approved "ad experimentum et ad quinquennium" by *Congregation for the Evangelization of Peoples (CEP, #04670)*. **Aims** Promote and defend the common good; contribute to the common good of the Universal Church; promote well-being of the family of nations by drawing on cultural riches of the peoples of Oceania; give visible expression to unity in diversity; collegial spirit and strengthen solidarity among members; provide an ecclesial structure whereby the members of the 4 member-conferences can collaborate to carry out joint pastoral action for the faithful of their nations. **Structure** Plenary Assembly (every 4 years); Executive Committee. **Languages** English, French. **Finance** Contributions from members. **Events** *Quadrennial Plenary Assembly* Wellington (New Zealand) 2014, *Quadrennial plenary assembly* Sydney, NSW (Australia) 2010, *Quadrennial plenary assembly* Suva (Fiji) 2006, *Quadrennial plenary assembly* Rome (Italy) 1998.

Members Individuals in 15 countries:
Australia, Cook Is, Fiji, Kiribati, Marshall Is, Micronesia FS, New Caledonia, New Zealand, Papua New Guinea, Polynesia Fr, Samoa, Solomon Is, Tonga, Tuvalu, Vanuatu.
Included in the above, 2 regional conferences listed in this Yearbook:
Catholic Bishops' Conference of Papua New Guinea and Solomon Islands; *Conferentia Episcopalis Pacifici (CEPAC, #04659)*. [2018.08.22/XD4849/vy/**D**]

♦ Federation of Catholic Family Associations in Europe 09468

Fédération des associations familiales catholiques en Europe (FAFCE) – Federación de Asociaciones de Familias Católicas en Europa – Föderation der Katholischen Familienverbände in Europa – Federazione delle Associazioni Familiari Cattoliche in Europa – Federação das Associações Católicas na Europa

Main Office Sq de Meeus 19, 1050 Brussels, Belgium. E-mail: info@fafce.org.
URL: http://www.fafce.org/

History 3 Feb 1991, Oberwesel (Germany). Founded following a proposal made 25 Mar 1990, Aachen (Germany). Statutes adopted 19 Mar 1994, Paris (France). Former names and other names: *Steering Group of the Catholic Family Organizations in Europe* – former (3 Feb 1991 to 14 Jun 1997); *Coordination des organisations familiales catholiques en Europe* – former (3 Feb 1991 to 14 Jun 1997); *Arbeitsgemeinschaft der Katholischen Familienorganisationen in Europa* – former (3 Feb 1991 to 14 Jun 1997). Registration: Start date: 3 Feb 1991, France. **Aims** Foster family needs across Europe; represent the interests of the family based on marriage of a man and a woman open to the birth of children. **Structure** General Assembly; Council of President. **Languages** English, French, German. **Staff** 1.50 FTE, paid. **Finance** Members' dues. Private donations. **Activities** Networking/liaising. **Events** *The Experience of Woment in Times of Pandemic* Brussels (Belgium) 2022, *General Assembly* Brussels (Belgium) 2018, *General Assembly* Brussels (Belgium) 2014, *General Assembly* Bucharest (Romania) 2014, *Conference / General Assembly* Strasbourg (France) 2013. **Publications** *Family and Europe, Seen from Brussels* – newsletter.
Members Full national/regional associations of Catholic families in 13 countries and territories:
Austria, Czechia, France, Germany, Hungary, Ireland, Italy, Lithuania, Poland, Portugal, Romania, Slovakia, Trentino-South Tyrol.
Associate family organizations in 4 countries:
Croatia, Malta, UK, Ukraine.
Consultative Status Consultative status granted from: *Council of Europe (CE, #04881)* (Participatory Status).
IGO Relations Member of: Fundamental Rights Platform of *European Union Agency for Fundamental Rights (FRA, #08969)*. **NGO Relations** Cooperates with: *COFACE Families Europe (#04084)*; *European Union of Former Pupils of Catholic Education (#08992)*; *KOLPING INTERNATIONAL (#16203)*. Member of: *Conference of INGOs of the Council of Europe (#04607)*; *European Sunday Alliance (#08856)*; *Forum of Catholic Inspired NGOs (#09905)*. [2020/XD6917/**D**]

♦ Federation of Catholic Universities / see International Federation of Catholic Universities (#13381)
♦ Fédération catholique mondiale pour la pastorale biblique / see Catholic Biblical Federation (#03600)

♦ Federation of Centers for Migration Studies G B Scalabrini (FCMS) . 09469

Contact c/o CMS, 307 East 60th St, 4th Fl, New York NY 10022, USA. T. +12123373080. E-mail: cms@cmsny.org.
URL: http://www.simn-global.org/

History 1964, New York NY (USA). Incorporated in the State of New York (USA). **Aims** Encourage and facilitate the study of *socio-demographic*, economic, political, legislative, historical and pastoral aspects of human migration, *refugee* movements and *ethnic* group relations everywhere; unite the objectives and works of member centers. **Structure** Federation of centres, each with its own director and schedule. Directors meet as required. **Languages** English, Italian, Portuguese, Spanish. **Staff** None. **Finance** Contributions from member centres. **Publications** *Migration World Magazine* – journal. Individual centres publish periodicals, books and occasional papers.
Members Centres in 9 countries:
Argentina, Australia, Brazil, France, Italy, Philippines, Switzerland, USA, Venezuela.
Centres listed in this Yearbook (5):
Center for Migration Studies, New York (CMS); *Centre d'information et d'études sur les migrations internationales (CIEMI)*; *Centro de Estudios Migratorios Latinoamericanos (CEMLA)*; *Centro de Estudos Migratorios, São Paulo (CEM, no recent information)*; *Centro Studi Emigrazione, Roma (CSER)*.
IGO Relations Consultative Status with: *ECOSOC (#05331)*. **NGO Relations** Supported by: *Congregation of the Missionaries of St Charles, Scalabrinians (CS)*. Collaborates with: *Scalabrini International Migration Institute (SIMI, #19062)*. [2018/XD5866/y/**E**]

♦ Federation of Central African Chambers of Commerce (inactive)
♦ Federation of Central American and Caribbean Poultry Sciences (#09292)

♦ Federation of Central American Chambers of Commerce 09470

Fédération des chambres de commerce de l'Amérique centrale – Federación de Camaras de Comercio del Istmo Centroamericano (FECAMCO)

Pres 9a Avenida Norte y 5ta Calle Poniente, No 333, San Salvador, El Salvador. T. +150322313054 – +150322313011.
URL: http://www.fecamco.com/

History 1961.
Members Chambers of commerce in 6 countries:
Costa Rica, El Salvador, Guatemala, Honduras, Nicaragua, Panama.
IGO Relations *Central American Common Market (CACM, #03666)*. Member of: *Comisión Centroamericana de Transporte Maritimo (COCATRAM, #04131)*. **NGO Relations** Memorandum of Understanding with: *World Chambers Federation (WCF, #21269)*. [2017/XD1516/**D**]

♦ Federation of Central American Development Foundations (inactive)
♦ Federation of Central American Tourist Boards (#09295)

♦ Federation of Central American University Students 09471

Fédération des étudiants universitaires d'Amérique centrale – Federación de Estudiantes Universitarios de Centroamérica (FEUCA)

Contact address not obtained. E-mail: feuca@csuca.org.
URL: https://www.facebook.com/FEUCA.CA/

Structure Presidency. **Languages** English, Spanish. **Staff** 12.00 FTE, paid. **Finance** Support from: *Confederación Universitaria Centroamericana (CSUCA, #04497)*. **Activities** Events/meetings. **Events** *Congress* Managua (Nicaragua) 2009, *General Assembly* Paris (France) 2008.
Members Full in 8 countries:
Belize, Costa Rica, Dominican Rep, El Salvador, Guatemala, Honduras, Nicaragua, Panama. [2019.02.13/XD5229/**D**]

♦ Fédération centroaméricaine (inactive)
♦ Fédération centroaméricaine d'architectes (inactive)
♦ Fédération centroaméricaine des laboratoires pharmaceutiques (#03669)
♦ Fédération centroaméricaine de médecine sportive (#04444)
♦ Federation of Chambers of Central American Exporters / see Federación de Camaras y Asociaciones de Exportadores de Centroamérica y el Caribe (#09293)
♦ Fédération de chambres de commerce africaines (no recent information)
♦ Fédération des chambres de commerce de l'Afrique centrale (inactive)
♦ Fédération des chambres de commerce de l'Afrique de l'Ouest (no recent information)
♦ Fédération des chambres de commerce de l'Amérique centrale (#09470)
♦ Fédération de chambres de commerce et associations industrielles en Amérique centrale / see Federación de Cámaras y Asociaciones Industriales de Centroamérica y República Dominicana (#09294)
♦ Fédération des chambres de commerce du Commonwealth (inactive)
♦ Fédération des chambres de commerce de l'industrie de l'Océan Indien / see Cap Business Océan Indien (#03419)
♦ Fédération des Chefs de Cuisine Nordique (#17233)
♦ Fédération des chefs de cuisine nordique (no recent information)
♦ Federation of Chinese Professional Associations in Europe (internationally oriented national body)
♦ Fédération chrétienne internationale pour la prophylaxie de l'alcoolisme et des autres toxicomanies (no recent information)
♦ Federation of Christian Organisms for International Voluntary Service / see Federazione Organismi Cristiani Servizio Internazionale Volontario
♦ Federation of Civil Aviation Companies (inactive)

♦ Federation of Clinical Immunology Societies (FOCIS) 09472

Exec Dir N83 W13410 Leon Rd, Menomonee Falls WI 53051, USA. T. +14143591670. Fax +14143591671. E-mail: info@focisnet.org.
URL: http://www.focisnet.org/

History 2001. Incorporated in 2003. **Aims** Improve human health through immunology; foster interdisciplinary approaches to both understand and treat immune-based diseases. **Structure** Executive Committee; Board of Directors; Steering Committee. Executive Director. **Staff** 4.00 FTE, paid. **Activities** Events/meetings; training/education; knowledge management/information dissemination. **Events** *Annual Meeting* San Francisco, CA (USA) 2024, *Annual Meeting* Boston, MA (USA) 2023, *Annual Meeting* San Francisco, CA (USA) 2022, *Annual Meeting* Menomonee Falls, WI (USA) 2021, *Annual Meeting* Menomonee Falls, WI (USA) 2020. **Publications** *FOCIS E-Newsletter* (4 a year); *Translational Immunology Update* (4 a year).
Members Affiliate societies in 21 countries:
Australia, Austria, Canada, Croatia, Egypt, France, Georgia, Germany, India, Israel, Italy, Japan, Lithuania, Mexico, Netherlands, Qatar, Spain, Sweden, UK, Ukraine, USA.
International affiliate organizations (57):
Australasian Society of Clinical Immunology and Allergy (ASCIA); *Center for International Blood and Marrow Transplant Research (CIBMTR, #03645)*; *CIS Society of Allergology and Clinical Immunology (#03948)*; *Pan American Group for Immunodeficiencies (PAGID)*; *World Allergy Organization – IAACI (WAO, #21077)*.
NGO Relations Affiliate member of: *International Union of Immunological Societies (IUIS, #15781)*. Associate of: *The Transplantation Society (TTS, #20224)*. [2017.03.08/XD8906/y/**D**]

♦ Federation of Cocoa Commerce (FCC) 09473

Fédération du Commerce des Cacaos (FCC)

SG 2nd Floor, 30 Watling Street, London, EC4M 9BR, UK. T. +442037736200. Fax +442074894845. E-mail: fcc@cocoafederation.com.
URL: http://www.cocoafederation.com/

History 2002. Founded on merger of Cocoa Association of London (CAL), set up 1929, with Association Française du Commerce des Cacaos (AFCC), set up May 1935. Registration: Companies House, No/ID: 074547, UK. **Aims** Provide a commercial framework for the cocoa market, so as to achieve contract harmonization and provide supporting services including arbitration and education programmes. **Structure** Board; Council; Committees. **Languages** English, French. **Staff** 4.00 FTE, paid. **Finance** Sources: members' dues. **Activities** Events/meetings; projects/programmes; training/education.
Members Full in 36 countries and territories:
Armenia, Belgium, Brazil, Cameroon, China, Côte d'Ivoire, Dominican Rep, Ecuador, Estonia, France, Germany, Ghana, Hong Kong, Indonesia, Italy, Japan, Kazakhstan, Luxembourg, Madagascar, Malaysia, Mauritius, Mexico, Netherlands, New Zealand, Nigeria, Peru, Philippines, Poland, Russia, Singapore, Spain, Switzerland, Togo, Türkiye, UK, USA.
NGO Relations Liaison organization: *European Cocoa Association (ECA, #06599)*; *World Cocoa Foundation (WCF)*. [2022.10.13/XM4374/**C**]

♦ Federation of Coffee Growers of America (inactive)
♦ Federation of Coffee Growers of Central America (inactive)
♦ Federation of Colleges and Associations of Economic Sciences Professionals in Central America and Panama (no recent information)
♦ Fédération des collèges et associations d'économistes d'Amérique centrale et du Panama (no recent information)

♦ Fédération colombophile internationale (FCI) 09474

International Pigeon Fanciers Federation

Gen Sec Hasseltsesteenweg 61E, 3720 Kortessem, Belgium. E-mail: secretariat@pigeonsfci.org.
Pres Bimbó út 29, Budapest 1022, Hungary.
URL: http://www.pigeonsfci.com/

History 9 Jan 1948, Brussels (Belgium). **Aims** Develop the sport of pigeon fancying in all its forms; study general problems facing pigeon fanciers; develop and reinforce friendship among pigeon fanciers of all countries. **Structure** General Assembly (twice a year); Committee. **Languages** French. **Finance** Sources: members' dues. **Activities** Events/meetings; sporting activities. **Events** *Half-yearly general assembly* Brussels (Belgium) 1992, *Half-yearly general assembly* Brussels (Belgium) 1992, *Half-yearly general assembly* Brussels (Belgium) 1991, *Half-yearly general assembly* Brussels (Belgium) 1991, *Half-yearly general assembly* Brussels (Belgium) 1990.
Members Pigeon fanciers (about 600,000) in 62 countries and territories:
Albania, Argentina, Australia, Austria, Bahrain, Belgium, Bosnia-Herzegovina, Brazil, Bulgaria, Canada, Chile, China, Colombia, Costa Rica, Croatia, Cuba, Czechia, Denmark, France, Germany, Greece, Hong Kong, Hungary, India, Ireland, Italy, Japan, Kosovo, Kuwait, Latvia, Lithuania, Luxembourg, Malta, Mexico, Morocco, Netherlands, Nicaragua, Norway, Peru, Philippines, Poland, Portugal, Qatar, Romania, Russia, Saudi Arabia, Serbia, Slovakia, Slovenia, South Africa, Spain, Sweden, Switzerland, Taiwan, Thailand, Trinidad-Tobago, Türkiye, UK, Ukraine, United Arab Emirates, Uruguay, USA. [2022/XD8811/**C**]

♦ Fédération des combattants alliés en Europe (no recent information)
♦ Fédération du Commerce des Cacaos (#09473)
♦ Federation of Commercial Audiovisual Libraries International (internationally oriented national body)
♦ Federation of Commodity Associations (no recent information)
♦ Federation of the Common Market Furniture Removing Enterprises / see Federation of European Movers Associations (#09519)
♦ Federation of Commonwealth Chambers of Commerce (inactive)
♦ Federation of Commonwealth Open and Distance Learning Associations (inactive)
♦ Fédération des communautés juives d'Amérique centrale et du Panama (inactive)
♦ Fédération communiste des Balkans (inactive)
♦ Fédération des compagnies d'aviation civile (inactive)
♦ Fédération des concours internationaux de musique / see World Federation of International Music Competitions (#21445)
♦ Federation of the Condiment Sauce Industries, Mustard and Fruit and Vegetables Prepared in Oil and Vinegar of the European Union (inactive)
♦ Fédération des conférences épiscopales de l'Asie (#09430)
♦ Fédération des conseils arabes de la recherche scientifique (no recent information)
♦ Fédération des consultants africains (inactive)

♦ Fédération des consultants africains et arabes (FCAA) 09475

Pres c/o FMCI, 5 Rue Idriss Al Akbar, Quartier Hassan, Rabat, Morocco. E-mail: contact@fmci.ma.

History 2009, with support of *Arab Bank for Economic Development in Africa (#00904)*. **Aims** Promote cooperation between Arabs and Africans consultants; facilitate the exchange of knowledge; assist members to develop skills; increase the participation of African and Arab consultants on global level; provide information; promote ethical and social standards. **Structure** General Assembly. Executive Committee. **Events** *General Assembly* Rabat (Morocco) 2014, *General Assembly* Casablanca (Morocco) 2010. [2014/XJ2284/**D**]

♦ Federation of Consultants from Islamic Countries (FCIC) 09476

Exec Dir Dr Bulent Tarcan sok no 10 K 4, Fulya Mahalesi, Gayrettepe, 34934 Istanbul/Istanbul, Türkiye. T. +902164570867. E-mail: info@thefcic.org.
URL: http://thefcic.org/

History 1986, Istanbul (Türkiye). Founded under the patronage of *Islamic Development Bank (IsDB, #16044)*. Affiliated institution of *Organisation of Islamic Cooperation (OIC, #17813)*. **Aims** Provide assistance in developing and improving the consulting profession in Islamic countries. **Structure** General Assembly; Executive Committee; President; Executive Director. **Languages** English. **Finance** Sources: members' dues. **Activities** Capacity building; events/meetings; guidance/assistance/consulting; training/education. **Events**

International Engineering Forum Istanbul (Turkey) 2021, *International Engineering Forum* Istanbul (Turkey) 2019, *The Role of Consulting Engineers as well as the Procurement Function in Realizing Sustainable Development Goals (SDGs)* Marrakesh-Safi (Morocco) 2019, *Why We Need Arbitration?* Marrakesh-Safi (Morocco) 2019, *Islamic Finance Tools, IsDB Procurement Procedures and Relations Between: IFIs, Public Institutes and Consultant* Tashkent (Uzbekistan) 2019. **Members** Consulting firms (about 110) from Islamic countries (IsDB members). Membership countries not specified. [2022/XE0864/E]

♦ Fédération cynologique internationale (FCI) 09477

Exec Dir Place Albert Ier 13, 6530 Thuin, Belgium. T. +3271591238. E-mail: info@fci.be.
Main Website: http://www.fci.be/

History Statutes adopted 22 May 1911. Reconstituted 10 Apr 1921. Statutes revised May 2007, Acapulco (Mexico). Latest statutes adopted Aug 2018, Brussels (Belgium). Former names and other names: *International Federation of National Canine Organizations* – alias; *International Canine Federation* – alias; *International Federation of Kennel Clubs* – alias. Registration: Banque-Carrefour des Entreprises, No/ID: 0408.298.734, Start date: 5 Mar 1968, Belgium. **Aims** Encourage and promote *breeding*, registration and use of *pedigree dogs* ensuring their functional health and physical features meet the standards set for each respective breed, enabling them to work and carry out different functions in accordance with the specific characteristics of their breed and the purposes for which they were created. **Structure** General Assembly (every 2 years); General Committee; Executive Committee; Mandatory Commissions (3); Standards and Scientific, and non-mandatory Commissions (24). **Languages** English, French, German, Spanish. **Staff** 13.00 FTE, paid. **Finance** Sources: members' dues. **Activities** Awards/prizes/competitions; events/meetings; knowledge management/information dissemination; monitoring/evaluation. **Events** *General Assembly* Madrid (Spain) 2022, *General Assembly* Prague (Czechia) 2021, *General Assembly* Shanghai (China) 2019, *Extraordinary General Assembly* Brussels (Belgium) 2018, *General Assembly* Budapest (Hungary) 2013. **Members** Full; associate; contract partners; national Kennel Clubs (99). Membership countries not specified. **NGO Relations** Member of (1): *Federation of European and International Associations Established in Belgium (FAIB, #09508)*.
[2023.02.15/XC1940/C]

- ♦ Fédération démocratique internationale des femmes (#21022)
- ♦ Fédération dentaire africaine (#09280)
- ♦ Fédération dentaire arabe (#00936)
- ♦ Fédération dentaire Asie Pacifique / see Asia Pacific Dental Federation/Asian Pacific Regional Organization of the Fédération Dentaire Internationale (#01882)
- ♦ Fédération dentaire Asie-Pacifique/Organisation régionale Asie Pacifique de la Fédération dentaire internationale (#01882)
- ♦ Fédération dentaire internationale / see FDI – World Dental Federation (#09281)
- ♦ Federation for the Development of Utilitarian Crafts (inactive)
- ♦ Fédération pour le développement de l'artisanat utilitaire (inactive)
- ♦ Federation of Digital Broadband Seismograph Networks / see International Federation of Digital Seismograph Networks (#13407)
- ♦ Federation of Digital Seismograph Networks / see International Federation of Digital Seismograph Networks (#13407)
- ♦ Federation of Drugfree Treatment Centres in Europe / see European Treatment Centers for Drug Addiction (#08947)
- ♦ Federation of Earth (see: #21313)

♦ Federation of East African Freight Forwarders Associations (FEAFFA) 09478

Secretariat PO Box 22694-00400, Tom Mboya, Nairobi, Kenya. T. +254202684802. E-mail: info@feaffa.com.
Street Address Crescent 9, on Crescent Road (Off Parklands Road), Westlands, Nairobi, Kenya.
URL: http://www.feaffa.com/

History 2006. Registered in accordance with the laws of Tanzania. **Aims** Promote a professional freight logistics industry for trade facilitation and regional economic growth. **Structure** Secretariat. **Activities** Training/education; knowledge management/information dissemination. **Publications** *Freight Logistics* (4 a year) – magazine.
Members Ordinary; Associate; Honorary. Members in 5 countries:
Burundi, Kenya, Rwanda, Tanzania UR, Uganda.
NGO Relations Partner of: *TradeMark East Africa (TMEA, #20183)*. [2014/XJ8875/D]

- ♦ Federation of East African Journalists' Associations (inactive)
- ♦ Federation of East European Family History Societies / see Foundation for East European Family History Societies
- ♦ Fédération des éditeurs européens (#09536)
- ♦ Federation of Educational Associations of Latin America and the Caribbean (#09289)

♦ Federation for EDucation in Europe (FEDE) 09479

Fédération européenne des écoles (FEDE) – Europäischer Schulverband – Federazione european delle scuole – Federación Europea de centros docentes

Secretariat Rue du Rhône 114, 1204 Geneva, Switzerland. E-mail: mailbox@fede.education.
URL: https://fede.education/

History 9 Apr 1963, Barcelona (Spain). Former names and other names: *European Federation of Private Schools* – alias; *European Federation of Schools* – former. Registration: Switzerland; EU Transparency Register, No/ID: 313869925841-90, Start date: 10 Feb 2017. **Aims** Participate in the creation of a real European teaching sector; defend the freedom of teaching; develop student and teacher mobility; create, recognize and validate qualifications at European level; create a European network of schools and universities making exchanges easier; improve teaching in countries outside the EU and EFTA. **Structure** General Assembly (annual); Committee, including Executive Council and Presidents of International Commissions (2). **Languages** English, French. **Staff** 7.00 FTE, paid. **Finance** Members' dues. Other sources: grants; donations; legacies; revenue from activities. **Activities** International Commissions (2): *'International Commission of Research and Development (CIRED)'*; *'International Commission of the Organization and Management of Examinations (CIOGE)'*. Organizes and sponsors: congresses; exhibitions. Devises examination programmes. Promotes and encourages the introduction of innovative pedagogical actions and actions for the cross-border mobility of students and teachers, as well as cooperation, experimentation and partnership ventures. Maintains a library. **Events** *General Assembly* Paris (France) 2020, *General Assembly* Malaga (Spain) 2019, *General Assembly* Athens (Greece) 2018, *General Assembly* Lisbon (Portugal) 2017, *General Assembly* Paris (France) 2016. **Publications** *FEDE Bulletin* (3 a year). Members' Directory; proceedings of commission meetings; general guide; booklets and leaflets.
Members Private education establishments and independent universities (over 300 members, representing 250,000 students and pupils) in 16 countries:
Algeria, Cyprus, France, Germany, Greece, Ireland, Italy, Morocco, Poland, Portugal, Romania, Russia, Senegal, Spain, Switzerland, Tunisia.
Consultative Status Consultative status granted from: *Council of Europe (CE, #04881)* (Participatory Status); *UNESCO (#20322)* (Consultative Status). **IGO Relations** Accredited by (1): *Organisation internationale de la Francophonie (OIF, #17809)*. **NGO Relations** Member of (3): *Conference of INGOs of the Council of Europe (#04607)*; *European Movement International (EMI, #07825)*; *World Union of Professions (WUP, #21882)*. Member of Executive Council of: *Conseil des associations d'Europe (CAE, no recent information)*. Also links with a number of other organizations active in the field (not specified). [2020/XD3822/D]

- ♦ **Federation EIL** Worldwide Network of the Experiment in International Living (#21930)
- ♦ Fédération des éleveurs de bétail (inactive)
- ♦ Fédération des employeurs européens / see The Federation of International Employers (#09644)
- ♦ Fédération des employeurs ONG (internationally oriented national body)

♦ Federation of Engineering Institutions of Asia and the Pacific (FEIAP) 09480

Fédération des associations d'ingénieurs de l'Asie du Sud-Est et du Pacifique

SG Inst of Engineers, Malaysia, Bangunan Ingenieur, Lots 60/62, Jalan 52/4, PO Box 223, 46720 Petaling Jaya, Selangor, Malaysia. T. +6037684010. Fax +6037577678. E-mail: aer@iem.org.my – beo@iem.org.my.
Pres address not obtained.
URL: http://www.feiap.org/

History 6 Jul 1978, Chiang Mai (Thailand). Regional network of *UNESCO Office, Jakarta – Regional Bureau for Sciences in Asia and the Pacific (#20313)*. Current constitution adopted June 2008, Hanoi (Vietnam). Former names and other names: *Federation of Engineering Institutions of South-East Asia and the Pacific (FEISEAP)* – former (1978 to 2008). **Aims** Study problems concerning education, training and qualifications of engineers; foster development of technicians in the field of engineering; encourage engineers to work towards social and economic development of the countries in the region; encourage formation and foster activities of national institutions of engineers in the region. **Structure** General Assembly (annual); Executive Committee; Standing Committees (4); Permanent Secretariat in Petaling Jaya (Malaysia). **Languages** English. **Staff** 3.00 FTE, paid. **Finance** Sources: contributions; members' dues; revenue from activities/projects. **Activities** Events/meetings; knowledge management/information dissemination. **Events** *General Assembly* Ipoh (Malaysia) 2018, *Meeting* Singapore (Singapore) 2018, *Convention* 2015, *World Engineers Summit on Climate Change* Singapore (Singapore) 2015, *General Assembly* Beijing (China) 2014. **Publications** Guides; guidelines.
Members National institutions of engineers in 23 countries and territories:
Australia, Bangladesh, Cambodia, China, Hong Kong, India, Indonesia, Iraq, Japan, Korea Rep, Malaysia, Myanmar, Nepal, Nigeria, Pakistan, Papua New Guinea, Peru, Philippines, Rwanda, Singapore, Taiwan, Thailand, Timor-Leste.
NGO Relations Member of (2): *Asian Pacific Regional Coordinating Committee (no recent information)*; *World Federation of Engineering Organizations (WFEO, #21433)*. Cooperates with (1): *Association for Engineering Education in Southeast Asia and the Pacific (AEESEAP, #02487)*. Instrumental in setting up (1): *Cooperative Program in Technological Research and Higher Education in Southeast Asia and the Pacific (no recent information)*. [2022.02.15/XD7064/D]

♦ Federation of Engineering Institutions of Islamic Countries (FEIIC) . 09481

Contact Kuala Lumpur Regional Office, Level 2 – Block 2A, Fac of Engineering, Univ Putra Malaysia, 43400 UPM Serdang, Selangor, Malaysia. T. +60389466451. Fax +60389468481. E-mail: feiicorg@feiic.org.
URL: http://www.feiic.org/

History May 1989. **Aims** Lead global technological innovation; promote cooperation for the benefit of the Muslim world. **Structure** General Assembly. Executive Committee, including President, 3 Vice-Presidents and Secretary-General. **Languages** Arabic, English. **Staff** 3.00 FTE, paid. **Finance** Members' dues. **Activities** Events/meetings. **Events** *General Assembly* Almaty (Kazakhstan) 2012, *General Assembly* Kazakhstan 2012, *WEC : world engineering congress* Kuching (Malaysia) 2010, *International mechanical engineering congress* Karachi (Pakistan) 2003. **Publications** *International Journal for Engineering and Technology (IJET)*.
Members in 20 countries:
Afghanistan, Azerbaijan, Bangladesh, Egypt, Indonesia, Iran Islamic Rep, Iraq, Jordan, Kazakhstan, Kyrgyzstan, Libya, Malaysia, Pakistan, Senegal, Sudan, Syrian AR, Tajikistan, Turkmenistan, Uganda, Uzbekistan.
IGO Relations *Inter-Islamic Network on Water Resources Development and Management (INWRDAM, #11513)*. [2014/XD9010/D]

♦ Federation of Engineering Institutions of South and Central Asia (FEISCA) 09482

Pres 4th Floor, No 340 R A de Mel Mawatha, Colombo, 03, Sri Lanka. T. +94112575923. Fax +94112573647.
SG IEP Bldg 97 B D-1, Liberty Round About, Gulberg-III, Lahore, Pakistan. T. +924235754043. Fax +94112699202. E-mail: sultan1256@hotmail.com – feisca.sect@gmail.com.
URL: http://feisca.net/

History Apr 1979, Delhi (India). Apr 1979, NEW Delhi (India). **Aims** Foster cooperation and exchange of information among national members; encourage effective engineering manpower development and utilization in the region; encourage formation and foster goal-oriented activities; study problems concerning education, training and continuing education and to recommend solutions; motivate engineers to work towards social and economic development of the countries in the region; promote regional cooperation in utilizing science and technology for development. **Structure** General Assembly; Executive Committee; Divisions; Committees; Task Forces; Secretariat. **Languages** English. **Finance** Members' dues. **Activities** Events/meetings. **Events** *General Assembly* Chandigarh (India) 2006, *International mechanical engineering congress* Karachi (Pakistan) 2003, *Regional meeting* Kathmandu (Nepal) 2003, *World congress on sustainable development* Kolkata (India) 2000.
Members National; Associate; Benefactor. National professional engineering organizations in 5 countries:
Bangladesh, India, Nepal, Pakistan, Sri Lanka.
IGO Relations *UNESCO (#20322)*. **NGO Relations** Member of: *World Federation of Engineering Organizations (WFEO, #21433)*. [2019.09.02/XD3866/D]

- ♦ Federation of Engineering Institutions of South-East Asia and the Pacific / see Federation of Engineering Institutions of Asia and the Pacific (#09480)

♦ Federation of Engineering Organizations of Central America and Panama 09483

Federación de Organizaciones de Ingenieros de Centro América y Panama (FOICAP)

Pres address not obtained. E-mail: presidenciafoicap@cfia.cr.
URL: http://www.foicap.org/

Events *Congress* San José (Costa Rica) 2014. **NGO Relations** Collaborates with: *Unión Panamericana de Asociaciones de Ingenieros (UPADI, #20469)*. [2014/XD8979/D]

- ♦ Federation of the English and French Speaking African Countries (inactive)
- ♦ Fédération des enseignants arabes (no recent information)
- ♦ Fédération des entrepreneurs de l'électromécanique de l'ANASE (#01174)
- ♦ Fédération des entreprises de déménagements du Marché commun / see Federation of European Movers Associations (#09519)
- ♦ Fédération des entreprises privées d'Amérique centrale, Panama et République Dominicaine (#09300)
- ♦ Fédération Equestre Européenne (#07005)

♦ Fédération Équestre Internationale (FEI) 09484

International Equestrian Federation

Pres HM King Hussein I Bldg, Chemin de la Joliette 8, 1006 Lausanne VD, Switzerland. T. +41213104747. Fax +41213104760. E-mail: info@fei.org.
CEO/SG address not obtained.
URL: http://www.fei.org/

History 21 May 1921, Paris (France). 1st Congress held 15 Nov 1921, Paris. **Aims** Serve as the international body governing equestrian sport recognized by the International Olympic Committee (IOC), including Dressage and Para Equestrian Dressage, Jumping, Event, Driving and Para Equestrian Driving, Endurance and Vaulting. Drive and develop equestrian sport globally in a modern, sustainable and structured manner with guaranteed integrity, athlete welfare, equal opportunity and a fair and ethical partnership with the horse. **Structure** General Assembly (annual); Sports Forum (annual); Board; Executive Board; Technical Committees; Standing Committees; Temporary Committees; Regional Groups (9). Continental associations (4): *African Confederation of Equestrian Sport (A.C.E.S., #00262)*; *Asian Equestrian Federation (AEF, #01441)*; *European Equestrian Federation (EEF, #07005)*; *Pan-American Equestrian Confederation (PAEC, #18097)*. **Languages** English, French. **Staff** 100.00 FTE, paid. **Finance** Sources: members' dues; sponsorship. **Activities** Advocacy/lobbying/activism; events/meetings; standards/guidelines. **Events** *Annual General Assembly* Antwerp (Belgium) 2021, *Annual General Assembly* Lausanne (Switzerland) 2020, *Annual General Assembly* Moscow (Russia) 2019, *Annual General Assembly* Manama (Bahrain) 2018, *Annual General Assembly* Montevideo (Uruguay) 2017. **Publications** *FEI FOCUS* (4 a year) in English. Annual Report; directory; rule books; media guides.
Members Affiliated national equestrian federations in 136 countries and territories:

Albania, Algeria, Andorra, Angola, Antigua-Barbuda, Argentina, Armenia, Australia, Austria, Azerbaijan, Bahamas, Bahrain, Barbados, Belarus, Belgium, Bermuda, Bolivia, Bosnia-Herzegovina, Botswana, Brazil, Brunei Darussalam, Bulgaria, Cambodia, Canada, Cayman Is, Chile, China, Colombia, Congo DR, Costa Rica, Croatia, Cuba, Cyprus, Czechia, Denmark, Dominican Rep, Ecuador, Egypt, El Salvador, Estonia, Eswatini, Ethiopia, Finland, France, Georgia, Germany, Greece, Guatemala, Haiti, Honduras, Hong Kong, Hungary, Iceland, India, Indonesia, Iran Islamic Rep, Iraq, Ireland, Israel, Italy, Jamaica, Japan, Jordan, Kazakhstan, Kenya, Korea DPR, Korea Rep, Kuwait, Kyrgyzstan, Latvia, Lebanon, Libya, Liechtenstein, Lithuania, Luxembourg, Madagascar, Malawi, Malaysia, Malta, Mauritius, Mexico, Moldova, Monaco, Mongolia, Morocco, Myanmar, Namibia, Netherlands, New Zealand, Nicaragua, North Macedonia, Norway, Oman, Pakistan, Palestine, Panama, Paraguay, Peru, Philippines, Poland, Portugal, Puerto Rico, Qatar, Romania, Russia, San Marino, Saudi Arabia, Senegal, Serbia, Singapore, Slovakia, Slovenia, South Africa, Spain, Sri Lanka, Sudan, Sweden, Switzerland, Syrian AR, Taiwan, Thailand, Trinidad-Tobago, Tunisia, Türkiye, Turkmenistan, UK, Ukraine, United Arab Emirates, Uruguay, USA, Uzbekistan, Venezuela, Virgin Is USA, Yemen, Zambia, Zimbabwe.
NGO Relations Member of (7): *Association of Paralympic Sports Organisations (APSO, #02850)*; *Association of Summer Olympic International Federations (ASOIF, #02943)*; *European Horse Network (EHN, #07499)*; *International Council for Coaching Excellence (ICCE, #13008)*; *International Paralympic Committee (IPC, #14512)*; *Olympic Movement (#17719)*; *Sports Rights Owners Coalition (SROC, #19929)*. Cooperates with (1): *International Testing Agency (ITA, #15678)*. Instrumental in setting up (1): *International Horse Sports Confederation (IHSC, #13811)*. Recognized by: *International Olympic Committee (IOC, #14408)*
[2022.10.13/XB1807/**B**]

♦ Federation of Esophageal Atresia and Tracheo-Esophageal Fistula Support Groups / see Esophageal ATresia Global Support Groups (#05540)
♦ Federation of Ethnic Communities' Councils of Australia (internationally oriented national body)
♦ Fédération des étudiants en médecine d'Amérique centrale (inactive)
♦ Fédération des étudiants universitaires d'Amérique centrale (#09471)

♦ Federation of Eurasian Soil Science Societies (FESSS) 09485

Gen Sec address not obtained. E-mail: evgeny.shein@gmail.com.
Pres address not obtained.
URL: http://fesss.org/
History 2012, by 4 societies of Turkey, Russia, Azerbaijan and Kazakhstan. **Aims** Provide exchange of knowledge and information among soil scientists. **Structure** Officers. **Activities** Events/meetings; knowledge management/information dissemination; training/education. **Events** *Eurasian Congress* Almaty (Kazakhstan) 2018, *Eurasian Congress* Sochi (Russia) 2015, *Eurasion Congress* Antalya (Turkey) 2014.
Members Full in 4 countries:
Azerbaijan, Kazakhstan, Russia, Türkiye. [2016/XM4356/**D**]

♦ Fédération Euro-Africaine de Solidarité (internationally oriented national body)
♦ Fédération euro-arménienne pour la justice et la démocratie (internationally oriented national body)

♦ Federation of Euro-Asian Stock Exchanges (FEAS) 09486

SG 5b Mher Mkrtchyan, 0010 Yerevan, Armenia. T. +37444737727. E-mail: secretariat@feas.org.
URL: http://www.feas.org/
History 16 May 1995, Istanbul (Turkey), with 12 Founding Members, at instigation of Istanbul Stock Exchange. Charter expanded at 1st Annual General Assembly, 2-3 Oct 1995, Istanbul; revised May 2005, Sep 2009. Headquarters moved from Istanbul to Yerevan (Armenia) 2017. **Aims** Contribute to cooperation, development, support and promotion of capital markets in the Euro-Asian region (Europe, Asia and the Mediterranean Basin). **Structure** General Assembly (annual); Board; Working Committee; Secretariat in Yerevan (Armenia). **Languages** English. **Finance** Members' dues. **Activities** Knowledge management/ information dissemination; awareness raising; research/documentation; standards/guidelines; certification/ accreditation; networking/liaising. **Events** *Annual General Assembly* Athens (Greece) 2020, *Annual General Assembly* Bucharest (Romania) 2019, *Annual General Assembly* Abu Dhabi (United Arab Emirates) 2018, *Annual General Assembly* Yerevan (Armenia) 2017, *Annual General Assembly* Sharm el Sheikh (Egypt) 2016. **Publications** *FEAS News*; *FEAS Yearbook*; *InfoFEAS*. Case studies. **Members** Full (20); Affiliate (5); Observer (5); Partner (5). Members in 20 countries. Membership countries not specified. [2021/XD4817/y/**D**]

♦ Fédération Euro-Méditerranéenne contre les Disparitions Forcées (FEMED) 09487

Euro-Mediterranean Federation against Enforced Disappearances
Pres 77 bis rue Robespierre, 93100 Montreuil, France. T. +33953368114. Fax +33143448782. E-mail: secretariat.femed@disparitions-euromed.org.
URL: http://www.disparitions-euromed.org/
History Feb 2000. As an informal gathering. Formalized May 2007, Beirut (Lebanon). Officially set up 27 May 2007. Registration: Start date: 31 Jan 2008, France. **Aims** Fight the practice of enforced disappearances as well as impunity; support victims' families in their claim for truth and justice. **Structure** Assembly; Board of Directors; Executive Office. **Languages** English, French. **Activities** Advocacy/lobbying/activism; awareness raising; capacity building; events/meetings; guidance/assistance/consulting. **Publications** *Duty of Truth* (2 a year).
Members Organizations (26) in 12 countries:
Algeria, Bosnia-Herzegovina, Cyprus, Iraq, Kosovo, Lebanon, Libya, Morocco, Serbia, Spain, Syrian AR, Türkiye.
NGO Relations Member of (1): *International Coalition against Enforced Disappearances (ICAED, #12605)*.
[2023.02.14/XM4211/**D**]

♦ Fédération euro-méditerranéenne des laboratoires d'analyses de biologie médicale (FEMLAB) 09488

Registered Office Maison du Pharmacien, 56 rue Ibn Charaf, Belvédère, 1082 Tunis, Tunisia.
History Statutes adopted, 7 Nov 2008, Paris (France). Registered in accordance with the law of Tunisia. **Structure** Consultative Council; Executive Board, comprising President, Vice-President, Secretary-General, Deputy Secretary-General, Treasurer and Deputy Treasurer. **Finance** Members' dues.
Members National organizations in 6 countries:
Algeria, France, Italy, Lebanon, Morocco, Tunisia. [2009/XM3264/**D**]

♦ Fédération euroméditerranéenne des municipalités oléicoles (inactive)

♦ Fédération Pro Europa Christiana (FPEC) 09489

Contact 9 rue de Hargarten, 57150 Creutzwald, France. T. +33387821019. E-mail: fpec@outlook.fr – fpec.creutzwald@gmail.com.
Contact Rue du Taciturne 49, 1000 Brussels, Belgium. T. +3222310944.
URL: http://federation-pro-europa-christiana.org/
History 2003. Registered in accordance with French law. EU Transparency Register: 65395896737-91. **Aims** Bring together national associations that promote *Christian values* throughout Europe. **Languages** English, French. **Staff** 30.00 FTE, paid. **Finance** Donations. **Activities** Religious activities. Active in: Austria, Belgium, Croatia, Estonia, France, Germany, Hungary, Ireland, Italy, Lithuania, Netherlands, Poland, Portugal, Scotland, Spain. **Publications** *Confiance* (2 a year) – bulletin.
Members Organizations in 7 countries:
Austria, France, Germany, Italy, Poland, Portugal, Spain.
IGO Relations None. [2017.06.01/XM5675/**D**]

♦ Fédération EUROPARC (#05768)

♦ Federation of European Academies of Medicine (FEAM) 09490

Fédération européenne des académies de médecine (FEAM)
Scientific Policy Officer Rue d'Egmont 13, 1000 Brussels, Belgium. T. +3227930250. E-mail: info@ feam.eu.
URL: http://www.feam.eu/
History 29 Oct 1993, Madrid (Spain). Founded following proposals 28 Sep 1991, Brussels (Belgium), and decision of 22 Jan 1993, London (UK). Current statutes adopted Dec 2013. Former names and other names: *Fédération des académies nationales de médecine et des institutions similaires de l'Union européenne* – full title. Registration: Banque-Carrefour des Entreprises, No/ID: 0455.764.396, Start date: 31 Aug 1995, Belgium; EU Transparency Register, No/ID: 879658235260-39, Start date: 28 Jun 2019. **Aims** Promote cooperation between national Academies of Medicine, Pharmacy and Veterinary Science, or national Academies via their medical division, in the WHO European region; provide them with a platform to formulate and express their common position on European matters concerning human and animal medicine, biomedical research, education, and health; extend to the European authorities the advisory role that they exercise in their own countries on those matters. **Structure** Council; Board; Secretariat. **Languages** English, French. **Staff** 7.00 FTE, paid. **Finance** Sources: donations; gifts, legacies; members' dues. **Activities** Events/meetings; healthcare; projects/programmes; research and development; training/education. **Events** *Symposium on Adult Vaccination and Vaccine Hesitancy* Brussels (Belgium) 2022, *Migration, Health, and Medicine Conference* Brussels (Belgium) 2019, *Workshop on Regenerative Medicine* Brussels (Belgium) 2019, *Workshop on Vaccination* Brussels (Belgium) 2018, *Assemblée générale* Brussels (Belgium) 2004.
Members Member academies (23) in 19 countries:
Austria, Belgium, Croatia, Czechia, France, Germany, Greece, Hungary, Ireland, Israel, Italy, Lithuania, Netherlands, Portugal, Romania, Serbia, Spain, Switzerland, UK.
Academic partners include:
Academia Europaea (#00011); *ALLEA – ALL European Academies (#00647)*; *European Academies' Science Advisory Council (EASAC, #05778)*; *European Council of Applied Sciences, Technologies and Engineering (Euro-CASE, #06804)*.
NGO Relations Member of (1): *InterAcademy Partnership (IAP, #11376)*. [2023.02.14/XD5005/**D**]

♦ Federation of European Aerosol Associations / see Fédération Européenne des Aérosols (#09557)

♦ Federation of European Aquaculture Producers (FEAP) 09491

Office Manager Avenue des Arts 56, 1000 Brussels, Belgium. T. +3243382995. E-mail: secretariat@ feap.info.
Gen Sec address not obtained.
URL: http://www.feap.info/
History Mar 1968, Geneva (Switzerland). Former names and other names: *European Salmonid Producers Federation* – former; *European Salmon Breeding Federation* – former; *Federation of the European Salmon and Trout Growers* – former; *Fédération européenne de la salmoniculture (FES)* – former; *Europäischer Verband der Salmonidenzüchter* – former; *Federazione Europea degli Allevatori di Salmonidi* – former; *Europaeiske Sammenslutning af Ørredproducenter* – former; *Fédération européenne des associations piscicoles* – former; *Fédération européenne des producteurs aquacoles* – former; *Federazione Europea Produttori Acquacoltura* – former; *Cónaidhm Thairgeoirí Uiseshaothraithe na hEorpa* – former; *Euroopan Vesiviljelijöiden Liitto* – former; *Forbundet av Europeiske Akvakultur Produsenter* – former; *Europeisk Havbunadarfelagid* – former; *Sammenslutningen af Europaeiske Akvakultur Producenter* – former. Registration: Start date: 21 Jun 1996, France; Banque-Carrefour des Entreprises, No/ID: 0871319425, Start date: 14 Feb 2003, Belgium. **Aims** Study questions relating to production and marketing of *trout, salmon, sea bass, sea bream, carp* and similar aquacultured species. **Structure** General Assembly. **Languages** English, French. **Staff** 2.50 FTE, paid. **Finance** Members' levy on fish production tonnage. **Activities** Events/meetings. **Events** *General Assembly* Rome (Italy) 2021, *General Assembly* Brussels (Belgium) 2020, *General Assembly* Aarhus (Denmark) 2019, *General Assembly* Paris (France) 2018, *General Assembly* Venice (Italy) 2017. **Publications** Annual Report.
Members National associations in 23 countries:
Belgium, Croatia, Cyprus, Czechia, Denmark, Finland, France, Germany, Greece, Hungary, Iceland, Ireland, Italy, Malta, Netherlands, Norway, Poland, Portugal, Spain, Sweden, Switzerland, Türkiye, UK.
Consultative Status Consultative status granted from: *FAO (#09260)* (Liaison Status); *ECOSOC (#05331)* (Ros C). **IGO Relations** Observer status with (3): *European Inland Fisheries and Aquaculture Advisory Commission (EIFAAC, #07540)*; *General Fisheries Commission for the Mediterranean (GFCM, #10112)*; *International Commission for the Conservation of Atlantic Tunas (ICCAT, #12675)*. **NGO Relations** Member of (3): Aquaculture Advisory Council (AAC); *European Aquaculture Technology and Innovation Platform (EATiP, #05910)*; *Market Advisory Council (MAC, #16584)*. [2023.02.14/XD0845/**D**]

♦ Federation of European Art Galleries Associations (FEAGA) 09492

Fédération des associations européennes de galeries d'art
Gen Sec Koninginnegracht 71, 2514 AG The Hague, Netherlands. E-mail: info@europeangalleries.org.
Chairwoman address not obtained.
URL: http://www.europeangalleries.org/
History 1974. Former names and other names: *International Association of Original Art Diffusers* – former (1974 to 1997); *Association internationale des diffuseurs d'oeuvres d'art originales (AIDOAO)* – former (1974 to 1997). **Aims** Defend the best interests of galleries and collectors, respect for artists and distribution of their works. **Structure** Board. **Languages** English, French. **Staff** Voluntary. **Finance** Sources: members' dues. **Activities** Events/meetings. **Events** *Annual Assembly* 2021, *Meeting* Vienna (Austria) 1990. **Publications** *FEAGA Newsletter*.
Members As of 2020, professional European art gallery organizations, representing over 2,000 galleries in 16 countries:
Austria, Belgium, Denmark, Finland, France, Germany, Greece, Hungary, Italy, Netherlands, Portugal, Russia, Slovakia, Sweden, Switzerland, UK. [2021.09.01/XD1157/**D**]

♦ Federation of European Associations of Paediatric Anaesthesia / see European Society for Paediatric Anaesthesiology (#08677)

♦ Federation of European Bearing Manufacturers Associations (FEBMA) 09493

SG Lyoner Strasse 18, 60528 Frankfurt-Main, Germany. T. +496966031624. Fax +496966031459.
History 1977. EU Transparency Register: 59210242996-35. **Aims** Represent the interests of the *industry* at national and international organizations, including governmental and quasi-governmental authorities and institutions. **Members** National associations. Membership countries not specified. **NGO Relations** Co-founded *World Bearing Association (WBA, #21227)*. [2018.06.01/XD3023/**D**]

♦ Federation of European Biochemical Societies (FEBS) 09494

Fédération des sociétés européennes de biochimie – Federación Europea de Sociedades de Bioquímica
SG Suite B1, St Andrew's House, 59 St Andrew's Street, Cambridge, CB2 3BZ, UK. E-mail: admin@ febs.org.
Chief Administrator address not obtained.
URL: http://www.febs.org/
History 1 Jan 1964, London (UK). Registration: Companies House, No/ID: 8239097, Start date: 3 Oct 2012, England and Wales. **Aims** Contribute to and promote advancement of research and education for the public benefit in the sciences of biochemistry, molecular biology and related disciplines. **Structure** Council; Executive Committee; Committees; Working groups; Secretariat at seat of Secretary-General (3-year term). **Languages** English. **Finance** Sources: sale of publications. **Activities** Awards/prizes/competitions; events/ meetings; financial and/or material support; knowledge management/information dissemination; publishing activities; training/education. **Events** *Annual Congress and Young Scientists Forum* Milan (Italy) 2024, *Annual Congress and Young Scientists Forum* Tours (France) 2023, *The Biochemistry Global Summit* Lisbon (Portugal) 2022, *Annual Congress and Young Scientists Forum* Ljubljana (Slovenia) 2021, *Annual Congress and Young Scientists Forum* Krakow (Poland) 2019. **Publications** *FEBS Open Bio* (12 a year); *Molecular Oncology* (12 a year); *FEBS Journal* (24 a year (twice monthly)); *FEBS Letters* (24 a year (twice monthly)).
Members National societies in 39 countries:
Armenia, Austria, Belarus, Belgium, Bosnia-Herzegovina, Bulgaria, Croatia, Cyprus, Czechia, Denmark, Estonia, Finland, France, Georgia, Germany, Greece, Hungary, Israel, Italy, Latvia, Lithuania, Moldova, Morocco, Netherlands, Norway, Poland, Portugal, Romania, Russia, Serbia, Slovakia, Slovenia, Spain, Sweden, Switzerland, Tunisia, Türkiye, UK, Ukraine.
NGO Relations Member of (1): *Biomedical Alliance in Europe (#03251)*. Coordinating Committees with: *Federation of Asian and Oceanian Biochemists and Molecular Biologists (FAOBMB, #09438)*; *International Union of Biochemistry and Molecular Biology (IUBMB, #15759)*; *Pan American Association for Biochemistry and Molecular Biology (PABMB, #18080)*. [2022/XD0936/**D**]

♦ Federation of European Biological Systematic Societies (BioSyst EU) 09495

Contact Swedish Museum of Natural History, PO Box 50007, SE-104 05 Stockholm, Sweden.

URL: http://www.biosyst.eu/
History 3 Oct 2006, Vienna (Austria). **Aims** Represent European scientists dealing with topics of systematic biology. **Activities** Events/meetings; research/documentation; training/education; networking/liaising. **Events** *Quadrennial Conference* Gothenburg (Sweden) 2017, *Quadrennial Conference / Congress* Vienna (Austria) 2013, *Quadrennial conference / Congress* Leiden (Netherlands) 2009.
Members Organizations in 5 countries:
Austria, France, Germany, Sweden, Switzerland, UK. [2016/XJ1549/**D**]

♦ Federation of European Business Information Suppliers / see Federation of Business Information Services (#09464)
♦ Federation of European Cancer Societies / see European Cancer Organisation (#06432)

♦ Federation of European Carnival Cities (FECC) 09496

Pres Stora Gatan 72, SE-193 30 Sigtuna, SE-193 30 Sigtuna, Sweden.
Gen Sec address not obtained.
URL: https://carnivalcities.net/
History 1980, Amsterdam (Netherlands), as *Foundation of European Carnival Cities (FECC) – Fondation des cités carnavalesques européennes – Fundación de las Ciudades Carnavalescas Europeas – Stiftung der Europäischen Karnevalsstädte – Fondazione delle Città Europee del Carnevale – Stichting van de Europese Carnavalssteden – Sammenslutningen af Europaeiske Karnevalsbyer – Udruzenje Evropskih Karnevalskih Grazdova – Idrima Karnavalion ton Evropaikon Poleon.* Articles adopted by General Assembly, held during 12th Convention, 20 May 1990, Ålborg (Denmark). Current Statutes revised by General Assembly, held during 13 Convention, 20 May 1993, Curaçao and in 2004, Bulgaria. Registered in accordance with the laws of the Grand Duchy of Luxembourg. **Aims** Collect knowledge and experiences of organizing mass-events; preserve the carnival heritage; stimulate youth participation in national carnival activities. **Structure** General Assembly (annual). International Board, consisting of President, 4 Vice Presidents (West-Europe; Mediterranean; North Europe, Baltic and Russia; Balkan), Secretary General and Treasurer/Member Administration. Board of Directors of 35 members. Senators (advisers – 5). Audit Committee of 3. **Languages** English, German. **Staff** 7.00 FTE, voluntary. **Finance** Members' dues. Sponsoring (about 10% of annual income). **Activities** Exchange of delegates and carnival groups. Exchange of ideas and experiences. Organizes an annual convention (with exhibition). **Events** *Annual Convention* Bol (Croatia) 2015, *Annual Convention* Limassol (Cyprus) 2014, *Annual Convention* Yambol (Bulgaria) 2013, *Annual Convention* Prilep (Macedonia) 2012, *Annual Convention* Vrnjacka Banja (Serbia) 2011. **Publications** *FECC Digital Newsletter* (6 a year) – online; *FECC Magazin* (2 a year).
Members Governments of 28 countries and territories:
Aruba, Belgium, Bosnia-Herzegovina, Bulgaria, Chile, Croatia, Curaçao, Cyprus, France, Germany, Greece, Hungary, Italy, Luxembourg, Malta, Montenegro, North Macedonia, Poland, Portugal, Romania, Russia, San Marino, Serbia, Slovakia, Slovenia, Spain, Sweden, Tunisia.
National sections in 6 countries and territories:
Denmark, Finland, Romania, St Lucia, Uruguay, USA.
Out of above mentioned body, listed in this Yearbook:
International Festivals Association (IFA, no recent information).
NGOs and individuals in 27 countries:
Albania, Argentina, Austria, Barbados, Belarus, Botswana, Brazil, Canada, Colombia, Costa Rica, Cuba, Czechia, Dominican Rep, El Salvador, Latvia, Liechtenstein, Lithuania, Namibia, Netherlands, Pakistan, Switzerland, Trinidad-Tobago, Turkiye, UK, Ukraine, Uzbekistan, Venezuela. [2022/XF1442/f/**F**]

♦ Federation of European Cartoonists Organizations / see Federation of Cartoonists Organisations (#09466)
♦ Federation of European Catholic Universities / see European Federation of Catholic Universities (#07070)
♦ Federation of European Chemical Societies / see European Chemical Society (#06524)
♦ Federation of European Coin Machine Associations / see European Gaming and Amusement Federation (#07374)
♦ Federation of European Coin-Operated Amusement Machine Associations / see European Gaming and Amusement Federation (#07374)

♦ Federation of European Companion Animal Veterinary Associations (FECAVA) 09497

Fédération des associations européennes de vétérinaires spécialisés en animaux de compagnie
Office Manager Rue Victor Oudart 7, 1030 Brussels, Belgium. T. +3225337020. E-mail: info@fecava.org.
URL: http://www.fecava.org/
History 12 May 1990, Biel (Switzerland). Founded following activity initiated at companion animal veterinarian practitioner meeting. Former names and other names: *European Harmonisation Committee* – former. Registration: Banque-Carrefour des Entreprises, Start date: 2011, Belgium; Start date: 1990, End date: 2011, France. **Aims** Promote professional development and representation of companion animal veterinarians in Europe; improve veterinary care of pets; highlight the human-animal bond and the "One Health" concept. **Structure** Board of Directors; Executive Board. **Languages** English. **Staff** 1.00 FTE, paid. **Finance** Sources: members' dues. Income from advertising. **Activities** Events/meetings; training/education. **Events** *FECAVA Eurocongress* Prague (Czechia) 2022, *FECAVA Eurocongress* 2021, *Congress* Warsaw (Poland) 2020, *Congress* St Petersburg (Russia) 2019, *Congress* Tallinn (Estonia) 2018. **Publications** *FECAVA Newsletter* (12 a year). Factsheets; posters.
Members Organizations in 40 countries:
Armenia, Austria, Belarus, Belgium, Bosnia-Herzegovina, Bulgaria, Croatia, Cyprus, Czechia, Denmark, Estonia, Finland, France, Georgia, Germany, Greece, Hungary, Ireland, Italy, Latvia, Lithuania, Luxembourg, Malta, Montenegro, Netherlands, North Macedonia, Norway, Poland, Portugal, Romania, Russia, Serbia, Slovakia, Slovenia, Spain, Sweden, Switzerland, Türkiye, UK, Ukraine.
Associate members – regional organizations (4):
European College of Veterinary Internal Medicine – Companion Animals (ECVIM – CA, #06624); European Society of Veterinary Oncology (ESVONC, #08782); European Veterinary Society for Small Animal Reproduction (EVSSAR, #09059); Veterinary European Transnational Network for Nursing Education and Training (VETNNET, #20762).
NGO Relations Member of (1): *Union européenne des vétérinaires praticiens (UEVP, #20405).* Partner of (1): *International Veterinary Students' Association (IVSA, #15851).* In liaison with technical committees of: *International Organization for Standardization (ISO, #14473).* [2022.05.11/XD2482/y/**D**]

♦ Federation of European Connective Tissue Societies / see European Matrix Biology (#07756)

♦ Federation of European Credit Management Associations (FECMA) . 09498

Fédération européenne des associations de crédit management
Pres Computerweg 22, 3542 DR Utrecht, Netherlands. E-mail: info@fecma.eu.
URL: http://www.fecma.eu/
History 1986. Statutes modified: 10 May 1994; 15 may 2009. Registration: Belgium. **Aims** Promote best practice in credit management by enabling members to share their knowledge and experience. **Structure** General Assembly (annual). Administrative Council of at least 3, including President, Vice-President, Treasurer and (if desired) Secretary. **Languages** English. **Finance** Members' dues. **Events** *Pan European Credit Management Congress* Krakow (Poland) 2021, *Pan European Credit Management Congress* Krakow (Poland) 2020, *Pan European Credit Management Congress* St Julian's (Malta) 2018, *Pan European Credit Management Congress* Brussels (Belgium) 2015, *Pan European Credit Management Congress* Budapest (Hungary) 2013. **Publications** *FECMA Newsletter. Pan European Magazine on Credit* (2012) – electronic; *Managing Cashflow Guide.*
Members National credit management associations (15) in 15 countries:
Austria, Belgium, Czechia, Denmark, Finland, France, Germany, Hungary, Ireland, Italy, Malta, Netherlands, Spain, Sweden, UK. [2020/XD3836/**D**]

♦ Federation of European Credit Reporting Organizations / see Federation of Business Information Services (#09464)
♦ Federation of the European Cutlery, Flatware, Holloware and Cookware Industries / see Federation of European manufacturers of Cookware and cutlery (#09511)
♦ Federation of the European Cutlery and Flatware Industries / see Federation of European manufacturers of Cookware and cutlery (#09511)

♦ Federation of European Data & Marketing (FEDMA) 09499

Main Office Av des Arts 43, 1040 Brussels, Belgium. T. +3227794268. Fax +3227789922. E-mail: info@fedma.org.
Communications Manager address not obtained.
URL: http://www.fedma.org/
History 1997. Created on merger of *European Direct Marketing Association (EDMA, inactive)* and *Federation of European Direct Marketing (FEDIM, inactive).* Former names and other names: *Federation of European Direct Marketing Association* – former; *Federation of European Direct Marketing (FEDMA)* – former; *Fédération du marketing direct européen* – former. Registration: Banque-Carrefour des Entreprises, No/ID: 0464.157.569, Start date: 18 May 1998, Belgium; EU Transparency Register, No/ID: 39300567160-02, Start date: 16 Nov 2011. **Aims** Promote and protect the European data driven marketing industry by creating greater acceptance and usage of data marketing by European consumers and business communities. **Structure** Board; Secretariat. **Languages** English, French, Italian. **Staff** 3.00 FTE, paid. **Finance** Sources: members' dues. **Activities** Advocacy/lobbying/activism; awards/prizes/competitions; awareness raising; events/meetings; knowledge management/information dissemination; monitoring/evaluation; networking/liaising; standards/guidelines; training/education. **Events** *Global Attitudes to Privacy Research* 2022, *Keep Calm and Foster Trust* Brussels (Belgium) 2019, *Annual European e-commerce conference* Brussels (Belgium) 2009, *Congress* Strasbourg (France) 1999. **Publications** *Europe Direct* (12 a year) – electronic newsletter; *FEDMA Membership News* (12 a year) – electronic newsletter; *Weekly Update* (52 year) – electronic newsletter. Guides; reports; Studies.
Members Direct Marketing Associations (DMAs) in 20 countries:
Austria, Belgium, Croatia, Czechia, Finland, France, Germany, Greece, Hungary, Italy, Latvia, Netherlands, Norway, Poland, Portugal, Romania, Sweden, Switzerland, Türkiye, UK.
Members include 1 organization listed in this Yearbook:
European Letterbox Marketing Association (ELMA, #07683).
Industry members. Membership countries not specified.
IGO Relations Member of: *London Action Plan (LAP, #16509).* **NGO Relations** Member of (2): *European Advertising Standards Alliance (EASA, #05829); European Interactive Digital Advertising Alliance (EDAA, #07582).* Cooperates with (1): *International Chamber of Commerce (ICC, #12534).* In liaison with technical committees of: *Comité européen de normalisation (CEN, #04162).* Close relationship with: *World Federation of Advertisers (WFA, #21407).* [2022.05.19/XD6263/y/**D**]

♦ Federation of European Defence Technology Associations (EDTA) . . 09500

SG Prinsessegracht 23, 2514 AP The Hague, Netherlands. T. +31717113973. E-mail: info@fedta.eu – press@fedta.eu.
URL: http://www.fedta.eu/
History Founded 28 Feb 1992, Madrid (Spain), on signature of a declaration by 6 founding members, as *European Federation of Defence Technology Associations (EDA).* Statutes adopted 24 Mar 1994, The Hague (Netherlands). Current acronym adopted 28 Apr 2005. **Aims** Enhance fellowship and cooperation, exchange of information, improve technological knowledge and promotion of public interest in defence related technology. **Structure** Board (meeting annually as general meeting); Headquarters at office of incumbent President. **Languages** English. **Staff** 1.00 FTE, voluntary. **Finance** None; members pay their own expenses. **Activities** Events/meetings; politics/policy/regulatory; knowledge management/information dissemination. **Events** *International symposium* Madrid (Spain) 1999, *Symposium on the EUCLID programme 1989-1994* The Hague (Netherlands) 1994. **Publications** Studies; comments.
Members Full member associations (7) in 6 countries:
Denmark, France, Germany, Netherlands, Spain, Switzerland.
Associated member associations (4) in 4 countries:
Belgium, Czechia, Finland, UK.
IGO Relations *EURODEFENSE Network (#05674).* **NGO Relations** *European Training and Simulation Association (ETSA, #08935).* [2022/XD4361/**D**]

♦ Federation of European Dental Competent Authorities and Regulators (FEDCAR) 09501

Fédération des Autorités Compétentes et Régulateurs Dentaires Européens
SG c/o Conseil nat'l de l'Ordre des chirurgiens-dentistes, 22 rue Emile Ménier, 75761 Paris CEDEX 16, France. E-mail: info@fedcar.eu.
Contact Av des Arts 8, 1210 Brussels, Belgium. T. +3225068844.
URL: http://fedcar.eu/
History 3 Apr 2004, following a series of informal meetings since 2000, as *Conference of Orders and Assimilated Bodies of Dental Practitioners in Europe (CODE) – Conférence des ordres et organismes assimilés des praticiens de l'art dentaire européens.* Registered in accordance with French law. **Aims** Increase patient safety across Europe; promote a high standard of dental care; contribute to the safe facilitation of dental professional mobility within the European Union. **Structure** Board; Secretariat. **Languages** English, French. **Events** *Autumn meeting* Madrid (Spain) 2010, *Spring meeting* Luxembourg (Luxembourg) 2009, *Autumn meeting* Paris (France) 2009, *Autumn meeting* Paris (France) 2008, *Biannual Meeting* London (UK) 2007.
Members National councils (22) in 21 countries:
Albania, Belgium, Bosnia-Herzegovina, Croatia, Denmark, Estonia, France, Hungary, Ireland, Italy, Luxembourg, Malta, Monaco, Norway, Portugal, Slovakia, Slovenia, Spain, Sweden, Switzerland, UK.
IGO Relations EU institutions. [2018/XM3301/**F**]

♦ Federation of the European Dental Industry (#09595)
♦ Federation of European Dental Laboratory Owners / see Fédération européenne et internationale des patrons prothésistes dentaires (#09575)
♦ Federation of the European Dermatological and Surgical Societies (no recent information)
♦ Federation of European Direct Marketing / see Federation of European Data & Marketing (#09499)
♦ Federation of European Direct Marketing (inactive)
♦ Federation of European Direct Marketing Association / see Federation of European Data & Marketing (#09499)
♦ Federation of European Direct Selling Associations / see European Direct Selling Association (#06928)
♦ Federation of European Domestic Appliance Manufacturers / see APPLiA – Home Appliance Europe (#00877)

♦ Federation for European Education in Gemmology 09502

Federación Europea para la Enseñanza de la Gemologia (FEEG)
Registered Office/Contact c/o Dutch Gemmological Institute, Mr Kesperstraat 10, 2871 GS Schoonhoven, Netherlands. T. +31182303250. Fax +31182303251. E-mail: vakschool@zadkine.nl – info@feeg.net.
URL: http://www.feeg-education.com
History 29 Aug 1996, following discussions initiated in 1990. **Aims** Establish a European standard of certification. **Events** *Symposium* Paris (France) 2022, *Symposium* Schoonhoven (Netherlands) 2020, *Symposium* Vicenza (Italy) 2019, *Symposium* Madrid (Spain) 2017, *Symposium* Idar-Oberstein (Germany) 2016.
Members Organizations (12) in 8 countries:
Austria, Belgium, France, Germany, Italy, Netherlands, Spain, UK. [2016/XD1978/**D**]

♦ Federation of European Employers / see The Federation of International Employers (#09644)

♦ Federation of European Equine Veterinary Associations (FEEVA) . . . 09503

Contact c/o FVE, Ave de Tervueren 12, 1040 Brussels, Belgium.
URL: http://www.fve.org/about_fve/organisations.php
History 29 Sep 1999, Paris (France), during the 6th World Equine Veterinary Congress. **Aims** Represent potential threats to equine health and welfare. **Structure** General Assembly. Board of Directors. **Languages** English. **Staff** Provided by: *Federation of Veterinarians of Europe (#09713).* **Finance** Members' dues. **Activities** Annual meeting. **Events** *Half-yearly general assembly* Brussels (Belgium) 2011, *Seminar on antimicrobials* Brussels (Belgium) 2011, *Half-yearly general assembly* Copenhagen (Denmark) 2011, *Conference on animal welfare in the Baltic region* Vilnius (Lithuania) 2011, *Half-yearly general assembly* Brussels (Belgium) 2010. **Publications** Policy documents; meetings presentations.

Members Veterinarians in 17 countries:
Austria, Belgium, Denmark, Finland, France, Germany, Hungary, Ireland, Italy, Latvia, Netherlands, Norway, Portugal, Spain, Sweden, Switzerland, UK.
NGO Relations Member of: *European Horse Network (EHN, #07499).* [2019/XD7782/**D**]

♦ Federation of European Ergonomics Societies (FEES) 09504

Fédération Européenne des Sociétés d'Ergonomie

Pres 76 bd Pierre Sémard, 31500 Toulouse, France. T. +33608754936. E-mail: president@ergonomics-fees.eu – info@ergonomics-fees.eu – treasurer@ergonomics-fees.eu.
SG Univ of Belgrade, Fac Mechanical Engineering, Belgrade, PAK 11000, Serbia.
URL: http://ergonomics-fees.eu/

History 7 May 2003, Munich (Germany). Former names and other names: *Vereinigung der europäischen ergonomischen Gesellschaften eV* – legal name. Registration: Eintragung beim Amtsgericht Dortmund im Vereinsregister, No/ID: 314/5702/7146, Germany; EU Transparency Register, No/ID: 501038437857-45, Start date: 15 Apr 2020. **Aims** Enhance recognition of ergonomics contributing to economic development, quality of life, health and safety at work, and social progress in European countries. **Structure** Council; Executive Committee; Working Groups. **Languages** English. **Staff** None. **Finance** Sources: members' dues. **Activities** Projects/programmes. Europe. **Events** *Conference on Workers Contribution to Safer Workplaces* Brussels (Belgium) 2017, *European conference on ergonomics* Bruges (Belgium) 2010, *Symposium on work ability* Tampere (Finland) 2010, *Workshop on human factors/ergonomics in the 7th Framework Research Program* Brussels (Belgium) 2007.
Members Federated societies in 22 countries:
Belgium, Croatia, Czechia, Finland, France, Germany, Greece, Hungary, Ireland, Italy, Latvia, Netherlands, Poland, Portugal, Romania, Russia, Serbia, Slovakia, Spain, Switzerland, UK, Ukraine.
NGO Relations Memorandum of Understanding with (1): *European Safety Federation (ESF, #08418).* [2021.02.18/XJ3157/**D**]

♦ Federation of European Explosives Manufacturers (FEEM) 09505

SG Rue Th de Cuyper 100, 1200 Brussels, Belgium.
URL: http://www.feem-europe.org/

History 1972. Founded as a sector group of *Conseil européen de l'industrie chimique (CEFIC, #04687).* An autonomous organization since 2019. **Aims** Advance the commercial explosive industry in the widest sense and with particular regard to safety, quality, security and legal matters. **Structure** General Assembly; Executive Committee; Working Groups (3). **Languages** English. **Staff** 0.50 FTE, paid. **Activities** Standards/guidelines. **Events** *General Assembly* Madrid (Spain) 2008, *General Assembly* Cologne (Germany) 2007, *General Assembly* Krakow (Poland) 2006, *General Assembly* Geneva (Switzerland) 2005, *General Assembly* Copenhagen (Denmark) 2004. **Publications** *Explosives Technical Bulletin.* Code of Good Practice; Guidance notes.
Members Manufacturers (19) in 31 countries and territories:
Austria, Belgium, Bulgaria, Cyprus, Czechia, Denmark, Estonia, Fed of Bosnia & Herzegovina, Finland, France, Germany, Greece, Hungary, Ireland, Italy, Latvia, Lithuania, Luxembourg, Malta, Netherlands, Norway, Poland, Portugal, Romania, Slovakia, Slovenia, Spain, Sweden, Switzerland, UK, Ukraine.
NGO Relations Member of (1): *SAFEX International (#19030)* (as Associate Member). [2023.02.14/XD1068/y/**E**]

- ♦ Federation of European Factoring Associations (no recent information)
- ♦ Federation of European Film Directors / see Federation of European Screen Directors (#09541)
- ♦ Federation of European Florists Groups / see International Florist Organisation (#13616)
- ♦ Federation of European Food Additives, Food Enzymes and Food Cultures Industries / see EU Specialty Food Ingredients (#09200)
- ♦ Federation of European Food Additives and Food Enzymes Industries / see EU Specialty Food Ingredients (#09200)
- ♦ Federation of European Genetical Societies (no recent information)

♦ Federation of European Golf Greenkeepers Associations (FEGGA) . . 09506

Exec Officer address not obtained.
URL: http://www.fegga.org/

History Apr 1996, Amsterdam (Netherlands). **Aims** Promote educational standards and professional recognition along with other issues facing greenkeepers concerning the European Union and EU legalisation. **Structure** Officers: Secretary; Chairman; Vice-Chairman. **Events** *Conference* Lisbon (Portugal) 2017, *Conference* Brussels (Belgium) 2008, *Conference* Munich (Germany) 2000.
Members Associations in 23 countries:
Austria, Belgium, Bulgaria, Czechia, Denmark, Estonia, Finland, Germany, Hungary, Iceland, Ireland, Italy, Netherlands, Norway, Portugal, Russia, Slovakia, Slovenia, South Africa, Sweden, Switzerland, UK, USA.
NGO Relations Supports: *GEO Foundation (#10132).* [2021/XD8256/**D**]

- ♦ Federation of the European Granite Industry (inactive)
- ♦ Federation of European Heating and Air-Conditioning Associations / see Federation of European Heating, Ventilation and Air-Conditioning Associations (#09507)
- ♦ Federation of European Heating and Ventilating Associations / see Federation of European Heating, Ventilation and Air-Conditioning Associations (#09507)

♦ Federation of European Heating, Ventilation and Air-Conditioning Associations (REHVA) 09507

Dir Rue Washington 40, 1050 Brussels, Belgium. T. +3225141171. E-mail: info@rehva.eu.
URL: http://www.rehva.eu/

History 27 Sep 1963. 2nd meeting, 1964, in London (UK). Statutes adopted, 1969, when first Board and secretariat was formed and operation formalized. Former names and other names: *Federation of European Heating and Ventilating Associations* – former (23 Sep 1963); *Federation of European Heating and Air-Conditioning Associations (REHVA)* – former; *Federatie van Verenigingen voor Verwarming en Luchtbehandeling in Europa* – former; *Representatives of European Heating and Ventilation Associations (REHVA)* – alias (1964). Registration: Banque-Carrefour des Entreprises, No/ID: 0886.234.065, Start date: 1 Oct 2006, Belgium; EU Transparency Register, No/ID: 898872714, Start date: 3 Jun 2020. **Aims** Develop and disseminate economical, energy efficient, safe and healthy technology for mechanical services of building; serve its members and the field of building engineering (heating, ventilation and air conditioning) by facilitating knowledge exchange, supporting the development of related EU policies and their national level of implementation. **Structure** General Assembly (annual); Board; Standing Committees (5); Permanent Secretariat. **Languages** English. **Staff** 5.00 FTE, paid. **Finance** Sources: members' dues. Supporters' fees. **Activities** Events/meetings; projects/programmes; research and development; standards/guidelines. **Events** *Brussels Summit* Brussels (Belgium) 2022, *Clima : World Congress on Heating, Ventilation, Refrigeration and Air-Conditioning* Rotterdam (Netherlands) 2022, *Brussels Summit* Brussels (Belgium) 2021, *CLIMAMED : Heating, Ventilation and Air-Conditioning Mediterranean Congress* Lisbon (Portugal) 2021, *Triennial International Conference on Cold Climate Heating Ventilation and Air-Conditioning* Tallinn (Estonia) 2021. **Publications** *REHVA European HVAC Journal* (6 a year); *REHVA Newsletter* (6 a year); *Supporter's Bulletin* (6 a year). eShop – European guidebooks. **Information Services** *HVAC Guidebook repository* – online publication library collection; *REHVA HVAC Dictionary* – online translation service.
Members National associations in 27 countries:
Belgium, Croatia, Czechia, Denmark, Estonia, Finland, France, Germany, Hungary, Italy, Latvia, Lithuania, Moldova, Netherlands, Norway, Poland, Portugal, Romania, Russia, Serbia, Slovakia, Slovenia, Spain, Sweden, Switzerland, Türkiye, UK.
NGO Relations Member of (3): *Climate Positive Europe Alliance (CPEA, #04021)* (Founding); *Federation of European and International Associations Established in Belgium (FAIB, #09508); Indoor Environmental Quality – Global Alliance (IEQ Global Alliance, #11168).* In liaison with technical committees of: *Comité européen de normalisation (CEN, #04162).* Associate partner of: *Covenant of Mayors for Climate and Energy (#04939).* [2021/XD3159/**D**]

- ♦ Federation for European Homeopathic Education (inactive)
- ♦ Federation of European Independent Financial Advisers (internationally oriented national body)
- ♦ Federation of European Industrial Cooperative Research Organizations (inactive)
- ♦ Federation of European Industrial Editors Associations / see European Association for Internal Communication (#06091)
- ♦ Federation of European Internal Communications Associations / see European Association for Internal Communication (#06091)
- ♦ Federation of European Internal Editors Associations / see European Association for Internal Communication (#06091)

♦ Federation of European and International Associations Established in Belgium (FAIB) 09508

Fédération des associations européennes et internationales établies en Belgique (FAIB) – Federación de Asociaciones Europeas et Internacionales Establecidas en Bélgica – Verband der in Belgien Niedergelassenen Europäischen und Internationalen Vereinigungen – Verbond van Europese en Internationale in België Gevestigde Verenigingen

SG Rue Washington 40, 1050 Brussels, Belgium. T. +3226411195 – +3226411193. Fax +3226411193. E-mail: faib@faib.org.
Pres address not obtained.
URL: http://www.faib.org/

History 16 Jun 1949, Brussels (Belgium). Founded on the initiative of Union of International Associations. Statutes revised: Jun 1977; 1994; 2004; 2014. Former names and other names: *Federation of International Associations Established in Belgium* – former (16 Jun 1949 to 2004); *Fédération des associations internationales établies en Belgique (FAIB)* – former (16 Jun 1949 to 2004); *Federación de Asociaciones Internacionales Establecidas en Bélgica* – former (16 Jun 1949 to 2004); *Verband der in Belgien Niedergelassenen Internationalen Vereinigungen* – former (16 Jun 1949 to 2004); *Verbond van Internationale in België Gevestigde Verenigingen* – former (16 Jun 1949 to 2004). Registration: Banque-Carrefour des Entreprises, No/ID: 0408.370.889, Start date: 16 Jun 1949, Belgium; EU Transparency Register, No/ID: 25961565102-76, Start date: 26 Jan 2011. **Aims** Study, promote and defend the collective and material interests of members; secure through collective action any measure which facilitates members' activities and furthers their establishment in Belgium; assist members in the organization of their activities. **Structure** General Assembly (annual); Board of Directors. **Languages** Dutch, English, French. **Staff** Paid and voluntary. **Finance** Sources: members' dues. **Activities** Events/meetings; knowledge management/information dissemination; networking/liaising. **Events** *Annual General Assembly* Brussels (Belgium) 2022, *Employees Working Abroad* Brussels (Belgium) 2022, *Who Needs an Auditor and For What?* Brussels (Belgium) 2022, *Annual General Assembly* Brussels (Belgium) 2021, *Visual Leadership – A Practical Approach for International Associations* Brussels (Belgium) 2021. **Publications** *FAIB News* (4 a year). **Information Services** *FAQs.*
Members Effective, Associate, Corresponding and Honorary Membership. Effective Members – international organizations having headquarters or registered offices in Belgium (319):
– *Access Agriculture (#00047);*
– *Accountancy Europe (#00061);*
– ADHD ASC & LD Belgium;
– *ADHD-Europe (#00113);*
– *Affordable Medicines Europe (#00150);*
– *Africa-Europe Diaspora Development Platform (ADEPT, #00170);*
– *Air Conditioning and Refrigeration European Association (AREA, #00601);*
– *Airport Regions Council (ARC, #00610);*
– *Airports Council International (ACI, #00611);*
– *Alliance for Beverage Cartons and the Environment (ACE, #00658);*
– Alliance for Pulmonary Hypertension (AFPH);
– *Alliance of Rail New Entrants (ALLRAIL, #00714);*
– AMCHAM;
– *amfori (#00797);*
– *Amicus Curiae;*
– *Architects Council of Europe (ACE, #01086);*
– *Association déontologique européenne de graphologues (ADEG, #02468);*
– *Association européenne pour la coordination de la représentation des consommateurs pour la normalisation (ANEC, #02561);*
– *Association for Teacher Education in Europe (ATEE, #02949);*
– *Association internationale de la boulangerie industrielle (AIBI, #02674);*
– *Association Internationale des Charités (AIC, #02675);*
– *Association of Dental Dealers in Europe (#02466)* (ADDE);
– *Association of European Public Postal Operators (PostEurop, #02534);*
– *Association of European Vehicle Logistics (ECG, #02551);*
– *Association of Issuing Bodies (AIB, #02768);*
– *Association of Mutual Insurers and Insurance Cooperatives in Europe (AMICE, #02816);*
– *Association of Plastics Manufacturers in Europe (Plastics Europe, #02862);*
– *Association of the European Rail Supply Industry (UNIFE, #02536);*
– *Bantani Education (#03171);*
– Belgisch-Deutsche Juristen-Vereinigung (BDJV);
– *Benelux Phlebology Society (BPS, #03204);*
– *Biomedical Alliance in Europe (#03251);*
– *BIPAR – European Federation of Insurance Intermediaries (#03263);*
– *Breast International Group (BIG, #03319);*
– *Bromine Science and Environmental Forum (BSEF, #03337);*
– *Bureau Européen des Unions de Consommateurs (BEUC, #03360);*
– *Bureau of European Design Associations (BEDA, #03359);*
– *Bureau of International Recycling (BIR, #03368);*
– *CEMBUREAU – The European Cement Association (CEMBUREAU, #03634);*
– *Centre culturel européen Jean Monnet, Bruxelles* (CCEJM);
– *Centre européen pour la recherche, le développement et l'enseignement de la nutrition et de la nutrithérapie (CERDEN);*
– *Cereals and Europe (C and E, #03829);*
– *Chantiers d'Afrique (CHAFI);*
– *Churches' Commission for Migrants in Europe (CCME, #03912);*
– *CIRFS – European Man-made Fibres Association (#03944);*
– Comité Universitaire de Solidarité (CUS);
– *Committee of the Trade in Cereals, Oilseeds, Pulses, Olive Oil, Oils and Fats, Animal Feed and Agrosupply of the EU (COCERAL, #04289);*
– *Community of European Railway and Infrastructure Companies (CER, #04396);*
– *Concept pour le Développement du Football Africain (CODEFA);*
– *Confédération des associations nationales de tanneurs et mégissiers de la Communauté européenne (COTANCE, #04515);*
– *Confederation of European Paper Industries (CEPI, #04529);*
– *Conseil européen de l'industrie chimique (CEFIC, #04687);*
– *Conseil européen de l'industrie des peintures, des encres d'imprimerie et des couleurs d'art (CEPE, #04688);*
– *Conseil international du sport militaire (CISM, #04695);*
– *Cosmetics Europe – The Personal Care Association (#04852);*
– *Council of Bars and Law Societies of Europe (CCBE, #04871);*
– *Council of Bureaux (CoB, #04873);*
– *Council of European Dentists (CED, #04886);*
– *Covered Bond and Mortgage Council (CBMC, #04940);*
– *CropLife Europe (#04965);*
– *CropLife International (#04966);*
– *ECTA (#05341);*
– *EDANA, the voice of nonwovens (EDANA, #05353);*
– *EFMD – The Management Development Network (#05387);*
– *EMEA Synthetic Turf Council (ESTC, #05436);*
– *ENCATC (#05452);*
– *eu can aid (ECA, #05570);*
– *EURHODIP (#05624);*
– *Eurochild (#05657);*
– *EuroCommerce (EC, #05665);*
– *EuroGeographics (#05684);*
– *Euroheat and Power (EHP, #05694);*
– *EUROJURIS International (#05696);*
– *European AIDS Treatment Group (EATG, #05850);*
– *European Alliance of Companies for Energy Efficiency in Buildings (EuroACE, #05865);*
– *European Association for Coal and Lignite (EURACOAL, #05978);*
– *European Association for e-Identity and Security (EEMA, #06077);*
– *European Association for Electromobility (AVERE, #06024);*

- *European Association for Potato Research (EAPR, #06160);*
- *European Association for Storage of Energy (EASE, #06223);*
- *European Association for Theoretical Computer Science (EATCS, #06253);*
- *European Association of Automotive Suppliers (CLEPA, #05948);*
- *European Association of Bioindustries (EuropaBio, #05956);*
- *European Association of Dairy Trade (#06003)* (EUCOLAIT);
- *European Association of Electrical and Electronic Waste Take Back Systems (WEEE Forum, #06022);*
- *European Association of Hearing Aid Professionals (AEA, #06066);*
- *European Association of Hospital Pharmacists (EAHP, #06074);*
- *European Association of Mining Industries, Metal Ores and Industrial Minerals (EUROMINES, #06122);*
- *European Association of Plaster and Plaster Product Manufacturers (EUROGYPSUM, #06152);*
- *European Association of Research Managers and Administrators (EARMA, #06195);*
- *European Association of the Machine tool Industries and related Manufacturing Technologies (CECIMO, #06113);*
- *European Automated Clearing House Association (EACHA, #06298);*
- *European Automotive Research Partners Association (EARPA, #06301);*
- *European AVM Alliance (EAA, #06305);*
- *European Banking Federation (EBF, #06312);*
- *European Brain Council (EBC, #06391);*
- *European Broadcasting Union (EBU, #06404);*
- *European Bureau for Conscientious Objection (EBCO, #06411);*
- *European Business Council for Africa (EBCAM, #06416);*
- *European Calcified Tissue Society (ECTS, #06429);*
- *European Cancer Organisation (ECO, #06432);*
- *European Cancer Patient Coalition (ECPC, #06433);*
- *European Carbon and Graphite Association (ECGA, #06447);*
- *European Centre for Electoral Support (ECES, #06478);*
- *European Ceramic Industry Association (CERAME-UNIE, #06506);*
- *European Coalition on Homeopathic and Anthroposophic Medicinal Products (ECHAMP, #06595);*
- *European Coil Coating Association (ECCA, #06601);*
- *European Confederation of Institutes of Internal Auditing (ECIIA, #06707);*
- *European Conference for Aero-Space Sciences (EUCASS, #06728);*
- *European Construction Industry Federation (#06766)* (FIEC);
- *European Consumer Debt Network (ECDN, #06772);*
- *European Coordination Committee of the Radiological, Electromedical Healthcare IT Industry (COCIR, #06792);*
- *European Council of Spatial Planners (ECTP-CEU, #06843);*
- *European Diisocyanate and Polyol Producers Association (ISOPA, #06926);*
- *European Direct Selling Association (SELDIA, #06928);*
- *European Dredging Association (EuDA, #06946);*
- *European Educational Exchanges – Youth for Understanding (EEE-YFU, #06965);*
- *European Electronic Component Manufacturers Association (EECA, #06974);*
- *European Engineering Industries Association (EUnited, #06991);*
- *European Environmental Bureau (EEB, #06996);*
- *European Esperanto Union (#07006)* (EEU);
- *European Expanded Clay Association (EXCA, #07013);*
- *European Federation and Forum for Osteopathy (EFFO, #07128);*
- *European Federation for Colposcopy and Pathology of the Lower Genital Tract (EFC, #07081);*
- *European Federation for Intercultural Learning (EFIL, #07146);*
- *European Federation of Art Therapy (EFAT, #07047);*
- *European Federation of Corrosion (EFC, #07090);*
- *European Federation of Equipment Leasing Company Associations (LEASEUROPE, #07111);*
- *European Federation of Financial Advisers and Financial Intermediaries (#07122)* (FECIF);
- *European Federation of Hard of Hearing People (EFHOH, #07136);*
- *European Federation of Lighter Manufacturers (EFML, #07153);*
- *European Federation of Local Energy Companies (CEDEC, #07156);*
- *European Federation of National Associations of Water and Waste Water Services (#07170)* (EUREAU);
- *European Federation of Pharmaceutical Industries and Associations (EFPIA, #07191);*
- *European Federation of Psychologists Associations (EFPA, #07199);*
- *European Film Agency Directors Association (EFAD, #07245);*
- *European FinTech Association (EFA);*
- *European Fishing Tackle Trade Association (EFTTA, #07267);*
- *European Flavour Association (EFFA, #07269);*
- *European Food Information Resource (EuroFIR, #07285);*
- *European Forum for Good Clinical Practice (EFGCP, #07313);*
- *European Foundation Centre (EFC, inactive);*
- *European Foundation for Alcohol Research (ERAB, #07342);*
- *European Franchise Federation (EFF, #07354);*
- *European Fresh Produce Association (FRESHFEL Europe, #07361);*
- *European Fund and Asset Management Association (EFAMA, #07365);*
- *European Garage Equipment Association (EGEA, #07377);*
- *European Group for Rooflights and Smoke-Ventilation (EUROLUX, #07434);*
- *European Group for the Certification of Constructional Steels (CONSCERT, #07418);*
- *European Heart Network (EHN, #07467);*
- *European Heat Pump Association (EHPA, #07469);*
- *European Historic Houses Association (EHH, #07491)* (EHHA);
- *European Horizons* (EuH);
- *European Industrial Gases Association (EIGA, #07525);*
- *European Industrial Research Management Association (EIRMA, #07531);*
- *European Institute for Advanced Studies in Management (EIASM, #07544);*
- *European Institute for Industrial Leadership (EIIL);*
- *European Institute of Diplomacy and International Relations (Vasco da Gama);*
- *European Insulation Manufacturers Association (EURIMA, #07577);*
- *European Internet Forum (EIF, #07591);*
- *European Investment Casters' Federation (EICF, #07600);*
- *EuropeanIssuers (#07605);*
- *European Junior Doctors Association (EJD, #07620);*
- *European Language Industry Association (ELIA, #07648);*
- *European Liaison Committee for Agricultural and Agri-Food Trades (#07687)* (CELCAA);
- *European Lift Association (ELA, #07695);*
- *European Litter Prevention Association (ELPA, #07703);*
- *European Logistic Platforms Association (Europlatforms, #07709);*
- *European Lung Cancer Working Party (ELCWP, #07717);*
- *European Microwave Association (EuMA, #07796);*
- *European Money Markets Institute (EMMI, #07819);*
- *European Movement International (EMI, #07825);*
- *European Network for Accreditation of Engineering Education (ENAEE, #07859);*
- *European Nuclear Society (ENS, #08059);*
- *European Organisation for Research and Treatment of Cancer (EORTC, #08101);*
- *European Organisation of Military Associations and Trade Unions (EUROMIL, #08099);*
- *European Petrochemical Association, The (EPCA, #08192);*
- *European Petroleum Refiners Association (#08194);*
- *European Plant Science Organization (EPSO, #08211);*
- *European Platform of Women Scientists (EPWS, #08235);*
- *European Powder Metallurgy Association (EPMA, #08260);*
- *European Public Affairs Consultancies' Association (EPACA, #08294);*
- *European Quality Assurance Register for Higher Education (EQAR, #08311);*
- *European Ready Mixed Concrete Organization (ERMCO, #08330);*
- *European Road Hauliers Association (UETR, #08393);*
- *European Roma Equality Network (EREN, #08400);*
- *European Safety Federation (ESF, #08418);*
- *European Savings and Retail Banking Group (ESBG, #08426);*
- *European SocieTy for Radiotherapy and Oncology (ESTRO, #08721);*
- *European Society of Anaesthesiology and Intensive Care (ESAIC, #08518);*
- *European Society of Intensive Care Medicine (ESICM, #08632);*
- *European Specialist Printing Manufacturers Associations (ESMA, #08809);*
- *European Students' Union (ESU, #08848);*
- *European Telecommunications Network Operators' Association (ETNO, #08895);*
- *European Textile Services Association (ETSA, #08904);*
- *European Tissue Symposium (ETS, #08917);*
- *European Tyre and Rubber Manufacturers' Association (ETRMA, #08963);*
- *European Union National Institutes for Culture (EUNIC, #09004);*
- *European Union of Insurance and Social Security Medicine (EUMASS, #08995);*
- *European Union of Medical Specialists (UEMS, #09001);*
- *European University Association (EUA, #09027);*
- *European Vending and Coffee Service Association (EVA, #09049);*
- *European Whey Products Association (EWPA, #09093);*
- *European Youth Forum (#09140);*
- *Fédération cynologique internationale (FCI, #09477);*
- *Fédération des ingénieurs des télécommunications de la Communauté européenne (FITCE, #09597);*
- *Fédération européenne de l'industrie des aliments pour animaux familiers (FEDIAF, #09571);*
- *Fédération Européenne des Aérosols (FEA, #09557);*
- *Fédération européenne des fabricants d'aliments composés pour animaux (FEFAC, #09566);*
- *Fédération européenne des industries de colles et adhésifs (FEICA, #09572);*
- *Fédération européenne du verre d'emballage (FEVE, #09583);*
- *Fédération Internationale de Camping, Caravanning et Autocaravaning (FICC, #09618);*
- *Fédération internationale des grossistes importateurs et exportateurs en fournitures automobiles (FIGIEFA, #09635);*
- *Federation of European Heating, Ventilation and Air-Conditioning Associations (REHVA, #09507);*
- *Federation of European Rigid Polyurethane Foam Associations (PU Europe, #09538);*
- *Federation of European Risk Management Associations (FERMA, #09539);*
- *Federation of Veterinarians of Europe (#09713)* (FVE);
- *FEDIOL – The EU Vegetable Oil and Proteinmeal Industry (#09718);*
- *FEFANA – EU Association of Specialty Feed Ingredients and their Mixtures (#09720);*
- *Fertilizers Europe (#09738);*
- *FIDI Global Alliance (#09753);*
- *Fondation des Régions Européennes pour la Recherche, l'Education et la Formation (FREREF, #09828);*
- *Fondation Europ'Atlas (EUROPATLAS);*
- *FoodDrinkEurope (#09841);*
- Forestière;
- *Forum of European National Highway Research Laboratories (FEHRL, #09910);*
- *GIGAEurope AISBL (#10151);*
- *Glass Alliance Europe (#10156);*
- *Groupement International de la Répartition Pharmaceutique (GIRP, #10762);*
- *GS1 (#10809);*
- H2i – Human Innovation Hub;
- *Health Care Without Harm Europe (HCWH Europe, #10877);*
- *Hydrogen Europe (#10998);*
- *IGI – The Global Wallcoverings Association (IGI, #11107);*
- *Inclusion Europe – European Association of Societies of Persons with Intellectual Disability and their Families (Inclusion Europe, #11144);*
- *Industrial Minerals Association – Europe (IMA Europe, #11179);*
- *Inter-Cultural Association (ICA, #11465);*
- *Intergraf (#11505);*
- *International Amateur Theatre Association (AITA/IATA, #11647);*
- *International Association for Soaps, Detergents and Maintenance Products (#12166)* (AISE);
- *International Association of Public Transport (#12118)* (UITP);
- *International Association of Sedimentologists (IAS, #12155);*
- *International Association of Young Lawyers (#12282)* (AIJA);
- *International Catholic Migration Commission – Europe (ICMC – Europe, #12460);*
- *International Co-operative Alliance (ICA, #12944);*
- *International Council for Laboratory Animal Science (ICLAS, #13039);*
- *International Dairy Federation (IDF, #13128);*
- *International Institute of Administrative Sciences (IIAS, #13859);*
- *International Institute of Sugar Beet Research (IIRB, #13928);*
- *International Life Saving Federation (ILS, #14040);*
- *International Light Association (ILA, #14045);*
- *International Motor Vehicle Inspection Committee (CITA, #14187);*
- *International Planned Parenthood Federation (IPPF, #14589)* (European Network);
- *International Trade Union Confederation (ITUC, #15708);*
- *International Wool Textile Organisation (IWTO, #15904);*
- *International Zinc Association (IZA, #15942)* (IZA Europe);
- *IREG Observatory on Academic Ranking and Excellence (IREG Observatory, #16017);*
- *Irish in Europe Association (IEAI);*
- *Joint Programming Initiative on Healthy and Productive Seas and Oceans (JPI Oceans, #16146);*
- *Joint Secretariat of Agricultural Trade Associations (#16148)* (SACAR);
- *Kids in Need of Defense Europe (KIND Europe);*
- *LightingEurope (#16472);*
- *Liquid Gas Europe (#16488);*
- *Medicines for Europe (#16633);*
- *MedTech Europe (#16692);*
- *Méliès International Festivals Federation (MIFF, #16706);*
- *NATRUE (#16950);*
- *Natural Mineral Waters Europe (NMWE, #16955);*
- *Nonviolent Peaceforce (NP, #17153);*
- *Open Forum Europe;*
- Orange Together;
- *Orgalim – Europe's Technology Industries (#17794);*
- *ParadigMS Private Foundation (ParadigMS, #18193);*
- *Partnership for Advanced Computing Europe (PRACE, #18229);*
- *Professionals in Humanitarian Assistance and Protection (PHAP, #18515);*
- *Quisper;*
- *RECHARGE (#18627);*
- *Refugee Hub Europe;*
- *Regroupement Européen pour la FOrmation et la Reconnaissance des MEDecines non-conventionnelles (REFORMED, #18824);*
- *RemitFund;*
- *Réseau Européen pour l'Insertion Sociale et Professionnelle de Personnes Défavorisées (REIN, #18874);*
- *Seafood Importers and Processors Alliance (SIPA, #19166);*
- *Search for Common Ground (SFCG);*
- *Seas at Risk (SAR, #19189);*
- *Seniors of the European Public Service (SEPS, #19229);*
- *Service Civil International (SCI, #19238);*
- *Society of Environmental Toxicology and Chemistry Europe (SETAC Europe, #19552);*
- *Solar Heat Europe (SHE, #19674);*
- *SolarPower Europe (#19676);*
- *Standing Committee of European Doctors (#19955)* (CPME);
- *Stroke Alliance for Europe (SAFE, #20012);*
- *Tantalum-Niobium International Study Center (T.I.C., #20095);*
- *Terre des hommes Foundation (Tdh Foundation, #20132);*
- *The Brewers of Europe (#03324);*
- *The European Travel Agents' and Tour Operators' Associations (ECTAA, #08942);*
- *The Guild of European Research-Intensive Universities (The Guild, #10820);*
- *TIC Council (#20160);*
- *Toy Industries of Europe (TIE, #20179);*
- *Trade Promotion Europe (TPE, #20184);*
- *UNESDA Soft Drinks Europe (UNESDA, #20323);*
- *Union européenne du commerce du bétail et de la viande (UECBV, #20394);*
- *Union for the Cultural and Professional Future in Europe (#20373)* (UCAPE);
- *Union of International Associations (UIA, #20414);*
- *Union of the Electricity Industry – Eurelectric (#20379);*
- *Université Européenne Jean Monnet* (UEJM);
- *Vaccine monitoring Collaboration for Europe (VAC4EU, #20740);*
- *Victim Support Europe (VSE, #20767);*
- *Volontariato Internazionale Donna Educazione Sviluppo (VIDES, #20806);*
- *Water Europe (WE, #20828);*
- *WCMC Europe;*
- *World Association of Public Employment Services (WAPES, #21179);*
- *World Bladder Cancer Patient Coalition (WBCPC, #21233);*
- *World Catholic Association for Communication (SIGNIS, #21264);*
- *World Employment Confederation (WEC, #21376);*
- *World Fair Trade Organization (WFTO, #21396)* (Europe);
- *World Federation of Intensive and Critical Care (WFICC, #21444);*

– *World Steel Association (worldsteel, #21829)*;
– *World Veterinary Association (WVA, #21901)*;
– *World Wide Fund for Nature (WWF, #21922)* (European Policy Programme).
NGO Relations Also links with national associations. [2023/XE0945/y/**E**]

♦ Federation of European and International Dental Technician Laboratory Owners (#09575)
♦ Federation of European and International Majorettes (inactive)

♦ Federation of European Laboratory Animal Science Associations (FELASA) 09509

Hon Sec PO Box 372, Eye, IP22 9BR, UK. E-mail: felasa@felasa.eu – info@felasa.eu.
URL: http://www.felasa.eu/

History 1978. Registration: Companies House, No/ID: 3808138, Start date: 15 Jul 1999, England and Wales. **Aims** Represent common interests of constituent associations in furtherance of all aspects of laboratory animal science in Europe and beyond. **Structure** Annual General Meeting; Board of Management; Executive Committee. **Languages** English. **Staff** 8.00 FTE, voluntary. **Finance** Sources: members' dues. **Activities** Certification/accreditation; training/education; events/meetings. **Events** *FELASA Congress* Marseille (France) 2022, *Triennial Symposium* Prague (Czechia) 2019, *Triennial Symposium* Brussels (Belgium) 2016, *Triennial Symposium* Barcelona (Spain) 2013, *Triennial Symposium* Helsinki (Finland) 2010. **Publications** Reports of working groups.

Members Associations in 26 countries:
Belgium, Croatia, Czechia, Denmark, Estonia, Finland, France, Germany, Greece, Hungary, Israel, Italy, Latvia, Lithuania, Netherlands, Norway, Poland, Portugal, Romania, Russia, Slovenia, Spain, Sweden, Switzerland, Türkiye, UK.
Included in the above, 2 organizations listed in this Yearbook:
Baltic Laboratory Animal Science Association (Balt-LASA); *Scandinavian Society for Laboratory Animal Science (Scand-LAS, #19112)*.
IGO Relations *European Commission (EC, #06633)*; *European Cooperation in Science and Technology (COST, #06784)*. **NGO Relations** Member of (1): *AAALAC International*. [2021/XD1535/y/**D**]

♦ Federation of European Liberal, Democrat and Reform Parties / see Alliance of Liberals and Democrats for Europe Party (#00703)

♦ Federation of European Literacy Associations (FELA) 09510

Chairperson address not obtained. E-mail: felaliteracyeurope@gmail.com.
URL: http://www.literacyeurope.org/

History 2008. Created by the International Literacy Association's *International Development in Europe Committee (IDEC, inactive)*, which merged with FELA, Jan 2018. Statutes formally adopted Jan 2018; amended Aug 2020. Registration: No/ID: 3083392-7, Start date: Jan 2019, Finland, Helsinki; Start date: 2008, End date: 2018, Belgium. **Aims** Contribute to improvements in literacy at all levels in member countries; promote and develop empirical and theoretical research in Europe on the learning and teaching of literacy; develop education policies and contribute to the implementation of European recommendations concerning literacy and its development; promote the exchange and cooperation between member organizations and other organizations worldwide; raise awareness of the importance of literacy. **Structure** General Assembly; Executive Committee; Delegates representing member organizations. **Languages** English. **Staff** None. **Finance** Sources: members' dues. **Activities** Advocacy/lobbying/activism; awards/prizes/competitions; awareness raising; events/meetings; networking/liaising; politics/policy/regulatory; publishing activities; research/documentation. **Events** *European Conference on Literacy* Chania (Greece) 2024, *European Conference on Literacy* Dublin (Ireland) 2022, *Conference* Dublin (Ireland) 2021, *European Conference on Literacy & Nordic Literacy Conference* Copenhagen (Denmark) 2019, *European Conference on Literacy* Madrid (Spain) 2017. **Publications** Articles.

Members Full; Associate. Members in 28 countries:
Austria, Belgium, Bulgaria, Croatia, Czechia, Denmark, Estonia, Finland, Germany, Greece, Hungary, Iceland, Ireland, Israel, Italy, Latvia, Lithuania, Netherlands, North Macedonia, Portugal, Romania, Russia, Slovakia, Slovenia, Spain, Sweden, Switzerland, UK.
NGO Relations European partner of: *International Literacy Association (ILA, #14057)*. [2023/XM7343/**D**]

♦ Federation of European manufacturers of Cookware and cutlery (FEC) 09511

Fédération de l'industrie européenne de la coutellerie, des couverts de table, de l'orfèvrerie et des articles culinaires (FEC) – Federación Europea de las Industrias de Cuchilleria, Cuberteria, Orfebreria y Menaje de Cocina – Föderation der Europäischen Schneidwaren-, Besteck-, Tafelgeräte- und Küchengeschirrindustrie – Federazione delle Industrie Europee di Coltelleria, Posateria, Vasellame e Pentolame

Coordinator 39-41 rue Louis Blanc, 92400 Courbevoie, France. E-mail: contact@fecassociation.eu.
URL: https://fecassociation.eu/

History 1952, Cernobbio (Italy). 1990, merged with *Association of the European Manufacturers of Vitreous Enamelled Hollow Ware (EUREMAIL, inactive)*. Currently covers stainless steel, sterling silver, silver plated metal, aluminium, copper and lacquered tin-plate articles of cutlery, flatware, holloware, cookware. Former names and other names: *Federation of the European Cutlery and Flatware Industries* – former; *Fédération de l'industrie européenne de la coutellerie et des couverts de table* – former; *Föderation der Europäischen Schneidwaren- und Besteckindustrie* – former; *Federation of the European Cutlery, Flatware, Holloware and Cookware Industries (FEC)* – former (1991); *Föderation der Europäischen Schneidwaren-, Besteck-, Tafelgeräte-, Küchengeschirr- und Haushaltgeräteindustrie* – alias. **Aims** Promote cooperation between members; give help and support on economic and technical improvements; work to the definition of technical standards; officially represent the common interests of members before international authorities and particularly to the European Commission. **Structure** Directors' Committee (meets 4 times a year); Senior and Advisor Experts; Coordinator. **Languages** English, French. **Staff** 1.00 FTE, paid. **Finance** Sources: members' dues. **Activities** Advocacy/lobbying/activism; networking/liaising; projects/programmes; research and development. **Events** *Business Meeting* Brussels (Belgium) 2013, *Biennial Congress* Porto (Portugal) 2004, *Biennial Congress* Berlin (Germany) 2002, *Biennial Congress* London (UK) 2000, *Biennial Congress* Amsterdam (Netherlands) 1998.

Members Full; Associate. Organizations of EC or EFTA countries. Members in 14 countries:
Belgium, Croatia, Denmark, Finland, France, Germany, Italy, Netherlands, Norway, Portugal, Spain, Sweden, Switzerland, UK.
IGO Relations Recognized by: *European Commission (EC, #06633)*. **NGO Relations** In liaison with technical committees and other European associations or committees. [2020.06.23/XD6810/t/**D**]

♦ Federation of European Manufacturers of Friction Materials (FEMFM) 09512

Fédération des fabricants européens de matériaux de friction – Federación de Fabricantes Europeos de Materiales de Fricción

Contact Robert-Perthel-Strasse 49, 50739 Cologne, Germany. T. +49221938808-0. Fax +49221938808-29. E-mail: office@femfm.com.
URL: http://www.femfm.com/

History 1972, Paris (France). **Aims** Promote safe operation of road *vehicles* by establishing standards for friction materials and control of application of these standards; ensure that existence of such standards provides conditions of free competition between manufacturers who have adopted and apply them; develop and establish a common technical and commercial nomenclature. **Languages** English.

Members Manufacturers in 10 countries:
Denmark, France, Germany, Hungary, Italy, Poland, Slovakia, Spain, Türkiye, UK.
Consultative Status Consultative status granted from: *ECOSOC (#05331)* (Ros A). [2023.02.14/XD5259/**D**]

♦ Federation of European Manufacturers of Ingredients to the Bakery, Confectionery and Patisserie Industries (FEDIMA) 09513

Main Office Rue de la Loi 38, Box 5, 1000 Brussels, Belgium. E-mail: secretariat@fedima.org.
URL: http://www.fedima.org/

History 21 May 1969, Milan (Italy). Established following food quality standards raised in the 1960s across Europe by then European Economic Community. Secretariat moved to Brussels (Belgium), 1985, to be closer to the European Institutions. Former names and other names: *Federation of the Raw Materials and Improvers Industry for the Bakery and Confectionery Trades in the EEC* – former (1969 to 1994); *Fédération des industries de matières premières et des améliorants pour la boulangerie et la pâtisserie dans la CEE* – former (1969 to 1994); *Verband der Bäckereigrundstoff- und Backmittelhersteller in der EWG* – former (1969 to 1994); *Federazione Comunitaria delle Industrie delle Materie Prime e di Miglioranti per la Panificazione e la Pasticceria* – former (1969 to 1994); *Federatie van de Bakkerijgrondstoffenindustrie in de EEG* – former (1969 to 1994); *Sammenslutningen af Fabrikanter af Bageri- og Konditoriartikler i EØF* – former (1969 to 1994); *Federation of the Intermediate Products Industries for the Bakery and Confectionery Trades in the EEA* – former (1994); *Fédération des industries des produits intermédiaires pour la boulangerie et la pâtisserie de l'EEE (FEDIMA)* – former (1994); *Federación de Industrias de Productos Intermedios para la Panaderia y Pasteleria en la EEE* – former (1994); *Verband der Bäckmittel- und Backgrundstoffhersteller im EWR* – former (1994); *Federação das Indústrias de Produtos Intermédios para la Panificação e Pastelaria no EEE* – former (1994); *Federazione delle Industrie delle Materie Prime e dei Semilavorati per la Panificazione e la Pasticceria dello SEE* – former (1994); *Federatie van de Bakkerij- en Banketbakkerijgrondstoffenindustrie in de EER* – former (1994); *Omospondia Viomihagion Proton Olon ke Endiameson Proionon Artopopas ke Zaharoplastikis tis EOP* – former (1994); *Federation of the European Union Manufacturers and Suppliers of Ingredients to the Bakery, Confectionery and Patisserie Industries (FEDIMA)* – former (2019). Registration: EU Transparency Register, No/ID: 904362515084-73, Start date: 1 Dec 2014. **Aims** Engage at EU level on policy issues relevant to the bakery and pastry ingredients industry, ensuring its members' needs are heard; secure access to a single European market for its members and facilitate their business activities within the European Union; exchange of information between national associations at a technical and legislative level; represent members within other trade associations; contribute to discussions and decisions on topics of common interests with other associations and industry players. **Structure** General Assembly; Board; Committees (5); Expert Groups. **Languages** English. **Staff** 1.50 FTE, paid. **Finance** Self-financed. **Activities** Advocacy/lobbying/activism; awareness raising; events/meetings; knowledge management/information dissemination; monitoring/evaluation; networking/liaising; politics/policy/regulatory; research/documentation; standards/guidelines. **Events** *Annual General Assembly* Antwerp (Belgium) 2022, *Annual General Assembly* Brussels (Belgium) 2021, *Annual General Assembly* Brussels (Belgium) 2020, *Annual General Assembly* Milan (Italy) 2019, *Symposium on Bread Promotion Activities in Europe* Brussels (Belgium) 2018. **Publications** Annual Report; position papers; guidelines.

Members National associations in 13 countries:
Austria, Belgium, France, Germany, Greece, Italy, Netherlands, Poland, Portugal, Romania, Spain, Türkiye, UK.
IGO Relations *European Commission (EC, #06633)*. **NGO Relations** Member of (1): *FoodDrinkEurope (#09841)* (as Affiliated member of). [2022.11.21/XD5584/t/**E**]

♦ Federation of European Maritime Associations of Surveyors and Consultants (FEMAS) 09514

Contact address not obtained. E-mail: sec@femas.info.
URL: http://www.femas.info/

History 1989, Amsterdam (Netherlands). Statutes adopted Sep 1993, Netherlands. **Aims** Serve as a forum for consultation concerning matters affecting maritime safety and operations; promote cooperation in the field. **Structure** General Assembly; Executive Council. **Languages** English. **Staff** 0.50 FTE, paid. **Finance** Sources: subscriptions.

Members Organizations in 6 countries:
Belgium, France, Germany, Greece, Netherlands, UK. [2022.02.15/XD3600/**D**]

♦ Federation of European Marketing Research Associations (inactive)

♦ Federation of European Materials Societies (FEMS) 09515

Fédération des associations européennes de matériaux

Exec Sec Malendriesstraat 70, 3370 Boutersem, Belgium. E-mail: secretary@fems.org.
URL: http://www.fems.org/

History Jan 1987. Current statutes adopted 7 May 1992. Statutes revised 21 Jul 1998. Registration: Banque-Carrefour des Entreprises, No/ID: 0447.452.189, Start date: 15 Oct 1992, Belgium. **Aims** Overcome the fragmentation of the materials science and engineering discipline in Europe in terms of countries; specialities and disciplines. **Structure** General Assembly (annual, usually at EuroMat conference); Executive Committee. **Languages** English, French, German. **Finance** Administrative expenses shared among members by common agreement. **Activities** Awards/prizes/competitions; events/meetings; networking/liaising. **Events** *EUROMAT : European Conference on Advanced Materials and Processes* Frankfurt-Main (Germany) 2023, *Biennial Junior EUROMAT Conference* Coimbra (Portugal) 2022, *EUROMAT : European Conference on Advanced Materials and Processes* Graz (Austria) 2021, *Biennial Junior EUROMAT Conference* Granada (Spain) 2020, *EUROMAT : European Conference on Advanced Materials and Processes* Stockholm (Sweden) 2019. **Publications** *Euromaterials* (4 a year) – incorporating FEMS News; *European Journal of Materials*.

Members Full independent European, national or multinational associations (22 – up to 3 per country) in 20 countries:
Austria, Belgium, Czechia (2), Denmark, Estonia, France, Germany (2), Greece, Hungary, Italy, Latvia, Lithuania, Netherlands, Norway, Poland, Portugal, Slovakia, Slovenia, Spain, Sweden, UK.
Associate members include the following international organizations (1):
European Structural Integrity Society (ESIS, #08844).
NGO Relations Founding member of: *European Materials Forum (EMF, #07751)*; *International Organization of Materials, Metals and Minerals Societies (IOMMMS, no recent information)*. Close liaison and sponsorship of conferences with: *ASM International (ASM)*; *European Materials Research Society (E-MRS, #07753)*; *Minerals, Metals and Materials Society (TMS)*. Endorses: *International Conference on Microwave Materials and their Applications (MMA)*. [2021/XD2064/**D**]

♦ Federation of European Microbiological Societies (FEMS) 09516

Fédération européenne des sociétés de microbiologie

Business Office c/o Delftechpark 37a, 2628 XJ Delft, Netherlands. T. +31153020050. E-mail: fems@fems-microbiology.org.
Registered Office Salisbury House, Station Road, Cambridge, CB1 2LA, UK.
URL: http://fems-microbiology.org/

History 1974. Registration: Charity, No/ID: 1072117, England and Wales; Companies House, No/ID: 3565643, Start date: 18 May 1998, England and Wales; EU Transparency Register, No/ID: 270557139261-47, Start date: 20 Aug 2020. **Aims** Work closely with Members and their dedicated volunteers to build and harness collective influence to advance microbiology. **Structure** Council (annual); Board of Directors; Committees (3). **Languages** English. **Staff** 7.70 FTE, paid. **Finance** Sources: sale of publications; donations and legacies; investments; charitable activities; other trading activities. **Activities** Awards/prizes/competitions; events/meetings; networking/liaising; publishing activities; financial and/or material support; research/documentation. **Events** *Congress of European Microbiologists* Hamburg (Germany) 2023, *World Microbe Forum* 2021, *Congress of European Microbiologists* Hamburg (Germany) 2021, *Conference on Microbiology* Belgrade (Serbia) 2020, *International Conference on Yeast Genetics and Molecular Biology* Gothenburg (Sweden) 2019. **Publications** *FEMS Newsletter* (12 a year); *Fems Microbiology Ecology* – journal; *FEMS Microbiology Letters* – journal; *FEMS Microbiology Reviews* – journal; *FEMS Yeast Research* – journal; *Pathogens and Disease* – journal. Bulletin; other publications.

Members Microbiology Societies (53) in 38 countries:
Armenia, Austria, Belarus, Belgium, Bosnia-Herzegovina, Bulgaria, Croatia, Czechia, Denmark, Estonia, Finland, France, Germany, Greece, Hungary, Iceland, Ireland, Israel, Italy, Latvia, Lithuania, Moldova, Netherlands, North Macedonia, Norway, Poland, Portugal, Romania, Russia, Serbia, Slovakia, Slovenia, Spain, Sweden, Switzerland, Türkiye, UK, Ukraine.
Included in the above, 2 international organizations listed in this Yearbook (3):
European Culture Collections' Organization (ECCO, #06872); *The International Biodeterioration and Biodegradation Society (IBBS, #12344)*.
NGO Relations Member of (1): *International Union of Microbiological Societies (IUMS, #15794)*. [2022/XD5828/y/**D**]

♦ Federation of European Mineral Engineering Programs (FEMP) 09517

Contact c/o Dept of Geoscience and Engineering, Secretariat room 3-14, Stevinweg 1, 2828 CN Delft, Netherlands. T. +31152785001. Fax +31152781189. E-mail: info@femp.org.
Pres address not obtained.
URL: http://www.femp.org/

Structure Industrial Advisory Board (meets annually). **Events** *Meeting* Netherlands 2007, *Meeting* Germany 2005. **NGO Relations** *European Association of Mining Industries, Metal Ores and Industrial Minerals (EUROMINES, #06122).* [2018.06.21/XD7862/**D**]

♦ Federation of European Motorcyclists (inactive)

♦ Federation of European Motorcyclists' Associations (FEMA) 09518

Gen Sec Square de Meeûs 18, 1050 Brussels, Belgium. T. +31613269211. E-mail: general-secretary@femamotorcycling.eu – info@femamotorcycling.eu.
URL: http://www.femamotorcycling.eu/

History 1 Jan 1998. Founded by merger of *European Motorcyclists Association (EMA, inactive)* and *Federation of European Motorcyclists (FEM, inactive).* Registration: Banque-Carrefour des Entreprises, Belgium; EU Transparency Register, No/ID: 43691777818-34. **Aims** Promote and preserve the interests of road riding motorcyclists by cultivating relationships with relevant authorities at European and UN level; assist in framing acceptable road transport legislation. **Structure** Executive Committee (meeting 3 times a year); Management Board; Working Groups; Secretariat in Brussels (Belgium). **Languages** English. **Staff** 2.00 FTE, paid. **Finance** Sources: members' dues. Supported by: *Federation of Harley-Davidson Clubs of Europe (FH-DCE, #09592)*; Motoclub Kayldall asbl; Stowarzyszenie H-DC Iron Rebels Poland; Trail Riders Fellowship; *Women's International Motorcycle Association (WIMA, #21026).* Annual budget: 144,000 EUR (2020). **Activities** Advocacy/lobbying/activism; awards/prizes/competitions; events/meetings; guidance/assistance/consulting; projects/programmes. **Events** *European Motorcyclists Forum* Brussels (Belgium) 2015, *European Motorcyclists Forum* Brussels (Belgium) 2014, *European Motorcyclists Forum* Cologne (Germany) 2012, *European Motorcyclists Forum* Brussels (Belgium) 2010, *International Motorcyclists Conference* Brussels (Belgium) 2010. **Publications** Press releases.
Members National organizations (20) in 15 countries:
Cyprus, Czechia, Denmark, Finland, France, Germany, Greece, Iceland, Ireland, Norway, Romania, Spain, Sweden, Switzerland, UK.
Consultative Status Consultative status granted from: *ECOSOC (#05331)* (Special). **IGO Relations** Advises: *European Commission (EC, #06633)*; *OECD (#17693).* **NGO Relations** Also links with national organizations. [2021.06.09/XD6331/**D**]

♦ Federation of European Movers Associations (FEDEMAC) 09519

Contact Rheinstrasse 2, 65760 Eschborn, Germany. T. +4961739669525. E-mail: headquarters@fedemac.eu.
Pres c/o BKV/CBD, Rue Stroobants 48A, 1140 Brussels, Belgium.
URL: http://www.fedemac.eu/

History 1959. Former names and other names: *Federation of the Common Market Furniture Removing Enterprises* – former; *Fédération des entreprises de déménagements du Marché commun* – former. **Aims** Represent the moving industry at European level. **Structure** General Assembly; Board. **Languages** English. **Events** *European Young Movers Conference* Bucharest (Romania) 2019, *European Young Movers Conference* Brussels (Belgium) 2018, *European Young Movers Conference* Riga (Latvia) 2017, *European Young Movers Conference* Madrid (Spain) 2016, *European Young Movers Conference* Sofia (Bulgaria) 2015. **Publications** *FEDEMAC Directory*; *FEDEMAC News Bulletin*; *FEDEMAC Newsflash*; *FEDEMAC Newsletter.*
Members Full: national associations in 10 countries:
Austria, Belgium, Bulgaria, Denmark, Germany, Italy, Luxembourg, Netherlands, Spain, Sweden.
Associate member in 1 country:
Switzerland.
Direct Affiliate Member Companies (19) in 10 countries:
Croatia, Finland, France, Greece, Malta, Poland, Romania, Slovakia, Slovenia, UK.
Commercial Partners (10) in 4 countries:
France, Germany, Netherlands, UK.
IGO Relations Memorandum of Understanding signed with: *World Customs Organization (WCO, #21350).* **NGO Relations** Member of: *Mobility for Prosperity in Europe (MPE, #16839).* [2019/XE6001/**E**]

♦ Federation of European National Collection Associations (FENCA) .. 09520

Pres FENCA Office, Friedrichstr 50-55, 10117 Berlin, Germany. T. +4930206073630. E-mail: office@fenca.eu.
SG c/o AIA, Delnicka 12, 170 00 Prague, Czechia. T. +420277003745. Fax +420266793511.
URL: https://fenca.eu/

History 15 Jan 1993. Statutes amended 16 Jun 1994, 11 May 1995, 19 Jun 1997, 18 Sep 1998 and 25 Sep 2010. Registered in accordance with Norwegian law. **Aims** Protect and take care of the interests of national member associations; promote development of European legislation within the debt collection industry. **Structure** Annual General Meeting; Board of Directors. **Events** *Annual General Meeting and Congress* Lisbon (Portugal) 2019, *Annual General Meeting and Congress* Berlin (Germany) 2016, *Annual General Meeting and Congress* Stockholm (Sweden) 2015, *Annual General Meeting and Congress / Annual General Meeting* Dubrovnik (Croatia) 2014, *Annual General Meeting and Congress* Taormina (Italy) 2013. **Publications** *FENCA Newsletter.*
Members National associations in 21 countries:
Austria, Belgium, Bulgaria, Croatia, Czechia, France, Germany, Greece, Italy, Netherlands, Norway, Poland, Portugal, Romania, Russia, Slovakia, Spain, Sweden, Switzerland, UK, Ukraine.
Affiliate members in 15 countries:
Bahrain, Egypt, France, Germany, Greece, Italy, Mexico, Netherlands, Norway, Portugal, Romania, Russia, Switzerland, UK, USA. [2015/XJ5504/**D**]

♦ Federation of European National Statistical Societies (FENStatS) ... 09521

SG 13 rue Érasme, L-1468 Luxembourg, Luxembourg.
Main Website: https://www.fenstats.eu/

History Current statutes adopted 17 Oct 2018, Bamberg (Germany). Registration: Registre de Commerce et Sociétés, Luxembourg. **Aims** Promote mutual communication, co-operation and statistical research in Europe; develop statistics to society and relations to European institutions; support diffusion of statistical education in Europe; secure more European funds dedicated for research and education in statistical sciences by requiring it at the European Community level; collaborate with other international statistical organisations. **Structure** General Assembly; Council; Executive Committee. **Languages** English. **Finance** Sources: donations; fees for services; members' dues.
Members European National Statistical Societies and Corporate members in 26 countries:
Austria, Belgium, Croatia, Cyprus, Czechia, Denmark, Finland, France, Germany, Greece, Hungary, Ireland, Italy, Latvia, Luxembourg, Netherlands, Norway, Poland, Portugal, Romania, Slovakia, Slovenia, Spain, Sweden, Switzerland, UK.
NGO Relations Cooperates with (2): *European Network for Business and Industrial Statistics (ENBIS, #07871)*; *International Statistical Institute (ISI, #15603).* [2022.03.10/AA0622/**D**]

♦ Federation of European Neuroscience Societies (FENS) 09522

Exec Dir c/o Fondation Universitaire, Rue d'Egmont 11, 1000 Brussels, Belgium. T. +3225450406. E-mail: office@fens.org.
URL: http://www.fens.org/

History 1 Jul 1998, Berlin (Germany). Founded at 1st Forum of European Neuroscience. Took over activities from *European Neuroscience Association (ENA, inactive),* 1 Jul 2000. Registration: No/ID: 0641.800.005, Belgium. **Aims** Advance research and education in neurosciences, within and outside of Europe; facilitate interaction and coordination between members. **Structure** Council; Executive Council; Advisory Board; Presidents of Member Societies; Committee Chairs. **Languages** English. **Staff** 10.00 FTE, paid. **Finance** Sources: meeting proceeds; members' dues; sale of publications. **Activities** Events/meetings; knowledge management/information dissemination; training/education. . **Events** *Forum of Neuroscience* Madrid (Spain) 2026, *Forum of Neuroscience* Vienna (Austria) 2024, *FENS Regional Meeting (FRM)* Albufeira (Portugal) 2023, *Brain Conference* Copenhagen (Denmark) 2023, *Forum of Neuroscience* Paris (France) 2022. **Publications** *European Journal of Neuroscience (EJN)* (bi-weekly); *FENS News Alerts.*
Members Full; Associate. Member Societies in 33 countries:
Armenia, Austria, Belgium, Croatia, Czechia, Denmark, Finland, France, Georgia, Germany, Greece, Hungary, Iceland, Ireland, Israel, Italy, Lithuania, Malta, Netherlands, Norway, Poland, Portugal, Romania, Russia, Serbia, Slovakia, Slovenia, Spain, Sweden, Switzerland, Türkiye, UK, Ukraine.
Regional organizations (10), listed in this Yearbook:
European Behavioural Pharmacology Society (EBPS, #06327); *European Brain and Behaviour Society (EBBS, #06390)*; *European College of Neuropsychopharmacology (ECNP, #06612)*; *European Confederation of Neuropathological Societies (Euro-CNS, #06715)*; *European Sleep Research Society (ESRS, #08493)*; *European Society for Neurochemistry (ESN, #08662)*; *Federation of European Physiological Societies (FEPS, #09530)*; *International Behavioural and Neural Genetics Society (IBANGS, #12332)*; *Molecular and Cellular Cognition Society (MCCS, #16847)* (Europe); *SRNT Europe (#19935).*
NGO Relations Member of (3): *European Animal Research Association (EARA, #05903)*; *European Brain Council (EBC, #06391)*; *International Brain Research Organization (IBRO, #12392).* Also links with national foundations. [2022.10.18/XD6699/y/**D**]

♦ Federation of European Numismatic Trade Associations (FENAP) .. 09523

Fédération européenne des associations de numismates professionnels – Föderation Europäischer Münzhändlerverbände
Sec Böckelmannweg 5, 58730 Fröndenberg, Germany. E-mail: info@fenap.com.
Pres Maximiliansplatz 10, 80333 Munich, Germany.
URL: http://www.fenap.org/

History 1991. Previously also referred to in English as *Federation of European Professional Numismatic Associations.*
Members Full; national organizations (10) in 10 countries:
Austria, Belgium, Denmark, France, Germany, Italy, Netherlands, Spain, Sweden, UK.
Associate member (1) in 1 country:
Switzerland.
NGO Relations Member of: *International Numismatic Council (INC, #14385).* [2015/XD7915/t/**D**]

♦ Federation of European Nurses in Diabetes / see Foundation of European Nurses in Diabetes (#09953)

♦ Federation of European Nutrition Societies (FENS) 09524

Fédération européenne des sociétés de nutrition
Main Office c/o Nutrition Soc Boyd Orr House, 10 Cambridge Court, 210 Shepherd's Bush Road, London, W6 7NT, UK. E-mail: office@fensnutrition.org.
URL: https://fensnutrition.org/

History 25 Apr 1979, Lutry (Switzerland). Statutes adopted 19 Jun 1979, Uppsala (Sweden). Statutes revised 2011, Madrid (Spain). **Aims** Advance research and education in the science of nutrition. **Structure** General Assembly; Board. **Languages** English. **Staff** Part-time, voluntary. **Finance** Sources: members' dues. **Activities** Events/meetings. **Events** *European Nutrition Conference* Belgrade (Serbia) 2023, *Quadrennial European Nutrition Conference* Dublin (Ireland) 2019, *Quadrennial European Nutrition Conference* Berlin (Germany) 2015, *Quadrennial European Nutrition Conference* Madrid (Spain) 2011, *Quadrennial European Nutrition Conference* Paris (France) 2007. **Publications** *FENS Newsletter* (irregular); *Society News* in *Annals of Nutrition and Metabolism* (irregular).
Members National societies in 28 countries:
Austria, Belgium, Bosnia-Herzegovina, Bulgaria, Croatia, Czechia, Denmark, Finland, France, Georgia, Germany, Greece, Hungary, Iceland, Ireland, Italy, Montenegro, Netherlands, North Macedonia, Norway, Poland, Portugal, Romania, Serbia, Spain, Sweden, Switzerland, UK. [2023.02.14/XD1592/**D**]

♦ Federation of European Ophthalmology (FEOph) 09525

Contact c/o DOG, Platenstr 1, 80336 Munich, Germany. E-mail: geschaeftsstelle@dog.org.
URL: http://www.feoph-sight.eu/

History 2007. Founded by representatives of national societies of France, Germany, Italy, Spain and UK. **Aims** Improve information exchange; increase the level of communication between European societies and individual ophthalmologists in Europe. **Structure** Board. **Languages** English. **Activities** Events/meetings; knowledge management/information dissemination. **Events** *Symposium* Paris (France) 2017, *International Conference on Ocular Pharmacology and Eye Care* Rome (Italy) 2017, *Symposium* Berlin (Germany) 2016, *Symposium* Rome (Italy) 2016, *Symposium* Rome (Italy) 2016. **Publications** *FEOph Sight Newsletter.*
Members National societies in 23 countries:
Austria, Belgium, Bosnia-Herzegovina, Bulgaria, Czechia, Denmark, Estonia, Finland, France, Germany, Greece, Ireland, Italy, Netherlands, Norway, Poland, Portugal, Russia, Spain, Sweden, Switzerland, UK, Ukraine. [2023.03.03/XJ8369/**F**]

♦ Federation of European Patient Groups Affected by Renal Genetic Diseases (FEDERG) 09526

Secretariat Rue de la Gare 90, 1495 Villers-la-Ville, Belgium. T. +33467275524. E-mail: info@federg.org.
URL: http://www.federg.org/

History May 2012, Paris (France). Registration: Banque-Carrefour des Entreprises, No/ID: 0553.753.994, Start date: 12 Jun 2014, Belgium; EU Transparency Register, No/ID: 396079525406-90, Start date: 12 Jan 2017. **Aims** Improve the health and quality of life of all those affected by rare and/or genetic kidney diseases. **Structure** General Assembly (annual); Board; Bureau; Scientific Council. **Activities** Advocacy/lobbying/activism; knowledge management/information dissemination; networking/liaising; research/documentation.
Members Full in 7 countries:
Belgium, France, Germany, Netherlands, Spain, Switzerland, UK.
NephcEurope (#16974).
NGO Relations Member of (3): *European Kidney Health Alliance (EKHA, #07626)* (Affiliate); *EURORDIS – Rare Diseases Europe (#09175)*; *Rare Diseases International (RDI, #18621).* Partner of (1): *Cystinosis Network Europe (CNE, #04993).* [2020/XM7427/y/**D**]

♦ Federation of European Pedestrian Associations (inactive)
♦ Federation of European Petroleum Equipment Manufacturers (inactive)

♦ Federation of European Pharmacological Societies (EPHAR) 09527

SG address not obtained.
URL: http://www.ephar.org/

History 1990, Amsterdam (Netherlands). Founded during *XIth International Congress of Pharmacology.* Former names and other names: *European Federation of Pharmacologists (EFP)* – former (1990 to 1994). **Aims** Advance research and education in the science of pharmacology; promote cooperation between national/regional pharmacological societies in Europe. **Structure** Council (meets every 2 years). Executive Committee, consisting of President, President Elect or Past President, Treasurer, 6 Councillors and Scientific Secretary. **Languages** English. **Staff** None. **Finance** Members' dues. **Activities** Organizes courses and training programmes; provides for exchange of scientific information; supports members' events. **Events** *Congress* Prague (Czechia) 2021, *Congress* Prague (Czechia) 2020, *Congress* Istanbul (Turkey) 2016, *Congress* Granada (Spain) 2012, *Congress* Manchester (UK) 2008.
Members National societies of pharmacology (26) recognized by IUPAHR:
Austria, Belgium, Bulgaria, Croatia, Czechia, Denmark, Finland, France, Germany, Greece, Hungary, Italy, Latvia, Malta, Netherlands, Norway, Poland, Portugal, Russia, Slovakia, Slovenia, Spain, Sweden, Switzerland, Türkiye, UK.
NGO Relations Observer at: *European Federation for Pharmaceutical Sciences (EUFEPS, #07192).* [2020/XD2293/**D**]

♦ Federation of European Philatelic Associations (FEPA) 09528

Pres Tabladila 2, 41013 Seville, Sevilla, Spain.
URL: http://fepanews.com/

History Founded 1989. **Aims** Represent and promote European philately within the aims and objectives of FIP, representing a European viewpoint to other philatelic organizations and stimulating interest particularly among young *collectors.* **Structure** Meeting (annual); Management Committee. **Languages** English. **Staff** Voluntary. **Activities** Events/meetings; awards/prizes/competitions. **Events** *Annual Meeting* Paris (France) 2012, *Annual Meeting* Opatija (Croatia) 2011, *Meeting* Antwerp (Belgium) 2010, *Meeting* Essen (Germany) 2009, *Meeting* Vienna (Austria) 2008. **Publications** *FEPA News Bulletin* (2 a year).

Federation European Phycological
09529

alphabetic sequence excludes
For the complete listing, see Yearbook Online at

Members National associations of 42 countries:
Albania, Armenia, Austria, Belarus, Belgium, Bulgaria, Croatia, Cyprus, Czechia, Denmark, Egypt, Estonia, Finland, France, Germany, Greece, Hungary, Iceland, Ireland, Israel, Italy, Latvia, Liechtenstein, Lithuania, Luxembourg, Montenegro, Netherlands, North Macedonia, Norway, Poland, Portugal, Romania, Russia, Serbia, Slovakia, Slovenia, Spain, Sweden, Switzerland, Türkiye, UK, Ukraine.
NGO Relations *Fédération internationale de philatélie (FIP, #09650).* [2014.01.20/XD2557/**D**]

♦ Federation of European Phycological Societies (FEPS) 09529

Sec c/o School of Natural Sciences, University of Galway, University Road, Galway, CO. GALWAY, H91 TK33, Ireland.
URL: http://www.feps-algae.org/

History 23 Jul 2007, Oviedo (Spain). Founded 4th European Phycological Congress, when Charter was signed. **Aims** Promote the study, conservation and application of algae; support educational activities and lobbying at the European level on matters involving algae, their present and projected roles. **Structure** General Meeting (annual); Council; Officers. **Finance** Members' dues. **Events** *European Phycological Congress / Congrès Phycologique Européen* Brest (France) 2023, *Congress* Zagreb (Croatia) 2019, *Congress* London (UK) 2015, *Congress* Rhodes Is (Greece) 2011, *Congress* Oviedo (Spain) 2007. **Publications** *Perspectives in Phycology* (4 a year) – electronic journal. Congress abstracts. **Members** Full; Associate; Individual. Membership countries not specified. [2022/XJ8713/**D**]

♦ Federation of European Physiological Societies (FEPS) 09530

SG Medical University Vienna, Center for Physiology and Pharmacology, Schwarzspanierstrasse 17, 1090 Vienna, Austria. T. +436888131180. Fax +43140160 ext 931101. E-mail: info@feps.org.
President Univ of Liverpool, Dept of Cellular and Molecular Physiology, University Dept 1st Floor, Liverpool, L8 7SS, UK. T. +441517945306. Fax +441517945321.
URL: http://www.feps.org/

History 2 Jul 1991, Prague (Czechia). Founded during the Regional meeting of *International Union of Physiological Sciences (IUPS, #15800).* Registration: Germany. **Aims** Strengthen physiology in Europe and beyond. **Structure** Council (meets annually); Executive Committee. **Languages** English. **Staff** None. **Finance** Sources: donations; gifts, legacies; members' dues; subsidies. **Activities** Awards/prizes/competitions; events/meetings; training/education. **Events** *Physiology in Focus Joint Meeting* Tallinn (Estonia) 2023, *Biennial Joint Meeting* Copenhagen (Denmark) 2022, *Biennial Joint Meeting* Berlin (Germany) 2020, *Joint Meeting* Bologna (Italy) 2019, *Biennial Joint Meeting* London (UK) 2018. **Publications** *Acta Physiologica* – journal; *FEPS Newsletter.* **Information Services** *FEPS-database* – information about research and educational activities of interest to European physiologists.
Members Societies in 35 countries:
Armenia, Austria, Belgium, Bulgaria, Croatia, Czechia, Denmark, Estonia, Finland, France, Germany, Greece, Hungary, Iceland, Israel, Italy, Latvia, Lithuania, Malta, Netherlands, North Macedonia, Norway, Poland, Portugal, Romania, Russia, Serbia, Slovakia, Slovenia, Spain, Sweden, Switzerland, Türkiye, UK, Ukraine.
International regional member:
Scandinavian Physiological Society (SPS, #19097).
NGO Relations Member of (2): *Federation of European Neuroscience Societies (FENS, #09522); International Union of Physiological Sciences (IUPS, #15800).* [2023.02.16/XF1755/y/**D**]

♦ Federation of European Play Industries (inactive)
♦ Federation of the European Precast Concrete Industry (#03363)

♦ Federation of European Private Port Companies and Terminals (FEPORT) 09531

SG Av des Arts 3, 5th floor, 1210 Brussels, Belgium. T. +3222188819 – +3227367552. Fax +3227323149. E-mail: secretariat@feport.eu.
Office Manager address not obtained.
URL: http://www.feport.eu/

History 13 Jan 1993. Former names and other names: *Federation of European Private Port Operators (FEPORT)* – former. Registration: Banque-Carrefour des Entreprises, No/ID: 0451.518.469, Start date: 29 Oct 1993, Belgium; EU Transparency Register, No/ID: 801302611511-33, Start date: 3 Jul 2013. **Aims** Inform and advise members on European port-related matters; discuss and formulate common points of view with regard to European policies; serve as interlocutor for EU institutions and other national and international organizations; share technical and operation know-how. **Structure** General Assembly; Board of Directors; Standing Committees; Working Groups and Ad-hoc Groups; Secretariat. **Languages** English. **Staff** 4.00 FTE, paid. **Finance** Sources: members' dues. **Activities** Events/meetings; knowledge management/ information dissemination; monitoring/evaluation. **Events** *Annual Stakeholder Conference* Brussels (Belgium) 2022, *Annual Stakeholder Conference* Brussels (Belgium) 2021, *Annual Stakeholder Conference* Brussels (Belgium) 2020, *Annual Stakeholder Conference* Brussels (Belgium) 2019, *Annual Stakeholder Conference* Brussels (Belgium) 2018. **Publications** *FEPORT Newsletter.* Position papers.
Members National and regional sector associations. Country members in 13 countries:
Belgium, Bulgaria, Denmark, Finland, France, Germany, Italy, Lithuania, Netherlands, Portugal, Romania, Spain, Türkiye.
Company members. Membership countries not specified.
IGO Relations Observer status with (1): *Baltic Marine Environment Protection Commission – Helsinki Commission (HELCOM, #03126).* **NGO Relations** Member of (1): *European Logistics Platform (ELP, #07711).* Participant in: *WATERBORNE (#20823).* [2022/XD3529/**D**]

♦ Federation of European Private Port Operators / see Federation of European Private Port Companies and Terminals (#09531)

♦ Federation of European Producers of Abrasives (FEPA) 09532

Headquarters Tour First – 11th Floor, 1-2 place des Saisons, 92400 Courbevoie, France. T. +33145812590. E-mail: fepa@fepa-abrasives.org.
URL: http://www.fepa-abrasives.org/

History 1955. Former names and other names: *European Federation of the Manufacturers of Abrasive Products* – former (1955); *Fédération européenne des fabricants de produits abrasifs (FEPA)* – former (1955); *Europäische Vereinigung der Schleifmittel-Hersteller* – former (1955). **Aims** Elaborate European standards in the abrasive products industry. **Structure** Assembly; Management Committee; Secretariat. Commissions. **Languages** English, French, German. **Staff** 1.00 FTE, paid. **Finance** Members' dues. **Events** *Congress* Madrid (Spain) 2012, *Congress* Stockholm (Sweden) 2011, *Congress* Brussels (Belgium) 2010, *Congress / Annual International Congress* Athens (Greece) 2009, *Meeting* Vienna (Austria) 2008. **Publications** *FEPA Newsletter.*
Members National Associations in 7 countries:
Austria, France, Germany, Italy, Spain, Sweden, UK.
Companies. Membership countries not specified.
IGO Relations Recognized by: *European Commission (EC, #06633).* **NGO Relations** Member of: *Industry4Europe (#11181).* [2020/XD2494/**D**]

♦ Federation of European Production and Industrial Management Societies (inactive)
♦ Federation of European Professional Numismatic Associations / see Federation of European Numismatic Trade Associations (#09523)

♦ Federation of European Professional Photographers (FEP) 09533

Main Office Willebroekkaai 37, 1000 Brussels, Belgium. E-mail: secretariat@europeanphotographers.eu.
URL: http://www.europeanphotographers.eu/

History Registered in accordance with Belgian law. **Events** *Identical in diversity* Valencia (Spain) 2008, *Annual General Assembly* Orvieto (Italy) 2006, *Annual General Assembly* Gmunden (Austria) 2005. **Publications** *FEP Newsletter.*
Members National associations (30) in 27 countries:
Armenia, Austria, Azerbaijan, Belarus, Belgium, Czechia, Denmark, Finland, France, Georgia, Germany, Hungary, Ireland, Italy, Latvia, Malta, Netherlands, Norway, Poland, Portugal, Russia, Serbia, Slovakia, Spain, Sweden, UK, Ukraine.
NGO Relations Member of: *SMEunited (#19327).* [2018.09.07/XD8507/t/**D**]

♦ Federation of European Professionals Working in the Field of Drug Abuse (inactive)

♦ Federation of European Protistological Societies (FEPS) 09534

Gen Sec Dept Environment and Primary Prevention, Ist Superiore di Sanità, V le Regina Elena 299, 00161 Rome RM, Italy. T. +39649902311. Fax +39649902295.
URL: http://feps-protists.eu/

History Set up 2006. **Aims** Promote research and education in the whole field of protistology; stimulate and expand collaborations between groups from different European countries; support young protistologists. **Structure** Council (meets at quadrennial congress). Secretary General. **Languages** English. **Staff** All voluntary. **Finance** No financial budget. **Activities** Events/meetings. **Events** *ECOP-ISOP joint meeting* Vienna (Austria) 2023, *Quadrennial European Congress of Protistology* Rome (Italy) 2019, *Quadrennial European Congress of Protistology* Seville (Spain) 2015, *Quadrennial European Congress of Protistology* Berlin (Germany) 2011, *Quadrennial European Congress of Protistology* St Petersburg (Russia) 2007. **Publications** *European Journal of Protistology.*
Members Full in 13 countries:
Belgium, Canada, Czechia, Denmark, France, Germany, Israel, Italy, Poland, Russia, Spain, UK, Ukraine. [2016.10.26/XJ8456/**D**]

♦ Federation of European Psychodrama Training Organizations (FEPTO) 09535

Fédération des organismes européens de formation au psychodrame

Sec Rua do Corgo, 698 R/C Esa Frt, 4450-104 Matosinhos, Portugal. T. +351933286684. E-mail: secretary@fepto.com.
Pres 13 Vironos Street, 152 31 Athens, Greece. T. +306945162993. E-mail: president@fepto.com.
Registered Office Rue de Rivage 20, 5100 Dave, Belgium.
URL: http://www.fepto.com/

History 17 Feb 1996, Leuven (Belgium), when constitution was adopted. Registered in accordance with Belgian law. Current Statutes adopted 1998. **Aims** Support wider recognition of psychodrama, based on the theory and methodology developed by J L Moreno, within Europe and the Mediterranean area. **Structure** General Assembly (annual); Council; Committees (4). **Finance** Members' dues. **Activities** Research/ documentation; training/education; events/meetings. **Events** *Annual Meeting* Ohrid (North Macedonia) 2022, *Conference* Matosinhos (Portugal) 2021, *Annual Meeting* Ohrid (North Macedonia) 2021, *Annual Meeting* Ohrid (North Macedonia) 2020, *Conference* Ohrid (North Macedonia) 2020. **Publications** *FEPTO News.*
Members Founding (individuals); Training organizations; Accrediting organizations. Training organizations in 26 countries:
Austria, Belgium, Bulgaria, Estonia, Finland, France, Germany, Greece, Hungary, Israel, Italy, Latvia, Lithuania, Netherlands, North Macedonia, Norway, Poland, Portugal, Romania, Russia, Serbia, Spain, Sweden, Switzerland, Türkiye, UK.
Accrediting organizations in 9 countries:
Bulgaria, Finland, Germany, Israel, Italy, Netherlands, Russia, Switzerland, UK.
NGO Relations Member of: *European Association for Psychotherapy (EAP, #06176).* [2018/XD5523/**D**]

♦ Federation of European Publishers (FEP) 09536

Fédération des éditeurs européens (FEE) – Federación de Editores Europeos – Europäischer Verleger-Verband – Federação de Editores Europeus – Federazione Editori Europei – Federatie van Europese Uitgevers – Sammenslutningen af Europaeiske Forlaeggere – Omospondia Evropaion Ekdoton

Dir Chée d'Ixelles 29/35, Box 4, 1050 Brussels, Belgium. T. +3227701110. Fax +3227712071. E-mail: info@fep-fee.eu.
Pres address not obtained.
URL: http://www.fep-fee.eu/

History 19 Jan 1967, Brussels (Belgium). Statutes changed 1990. Former names and other names: *Book Publishers Group of EEC* – former; *Groupe des éditeurs de livres de la CEE (GELC)* – former; *Grupo de Editores de Libros de la CEE* – former; *Gruppe der Buchverleger in der EWG* – former; *Grupo de Editores de Livros da CEE* – former; *Gruppo degli Editori di Libri delle CEE* – former; *Groep van Uitgevers van Boeken in de EEG* – former; *Forlaeggersammenslutningen i EØF* – former; *Grup Ekdoton Horon Medon tis EOK* – former. Registration: Banque-Carrefour des Entreprises, No/ID: 0448.301.831, Start date: 24 Sep 1992, Belgium; EU Transparency Register, No/ID: 398541467-53, Start date: 25 Jun 2008. **Aims** Provide representation for publishers' associations with *European Union* institutions to preserve and defend the interests of publishing; communicate information to publishers. **Structure** Board; Secretariat. **Languages** English, French. **Staff** 4.00 FTE, paid. **Finance** Sources: members' dues. **Events** *General Assembly* Brussels (Belgium) 2013, *General Assembly* Amsterdam (Netherlands) 2004, *General Assembly* Bergen (Norway) 2004, *Forum des éditeurs de l'Union Européenne* Brussels (Belgium) 1999, *Forum des éditeurs de l'Union Européenne* Frankfurt-Main (Germany) 1999.
Members National organizations in 28 countries:
Austria, Belgium, Bulgaria, Czechia, Denmark, Estonia, Finland, France, Germany, Greece, Hungary, Iceland, Ireland, Italy, Latvia, Lithuania, Luxembourg, Netherlands, Norway, Poland, Portugal, Romania, Serbia, Slovakia, Slovenia, Spain, Sweden, UK.
IGO Relations Recognized by: *European Commission (EC, #06633); European Parliament (EP, #08146).* **NGO Relations** Member of (6): *Creative Media Business Alliance (CMBA, #04947);* CreativityWorks!; *EDItEUR (#05361); European Internet Forum (EIF, #07591); International Federation of Reproduction Rights Organizations (IFRRO, #13527)* (Associate); *International Publishers Association (IPA, #14675)* (Associate). [2022/XE0504/**E**]

♦ Federation of European Rice Millers (FERM) 09537

Union des riziers européens

Main Office Ave de Tervueren 13 A, Bte 7, 1040 Brussels, Belgium. T. +3227365354. Fax +3227323427. E-mail: ferm@ferm-eu.org.
URL: http://www.ferm-eu.org/

History EU Transparency Register: 31958409365-30. **Aims** Promote and defend the interests of Europe's rice milling industry; provide support to European institutions in all aspects of policy and legislation that affects the supply, milling, processing, marketing and sale of rice in the European Union; ensure European rice mills can satisfy the demands of European consumers for rice of all origins. **Languages** English. **Finance** Members' dues. **Activities** Standards/guidelines; events/meetings. **Events** *Convention* Lisbon (Portugal) 2019, *Convention* Portofino (Italy) 2017, *Convention* Dubrovnik (Croatia) 2015, *Convention* Valencia (Spain) 2013, *Convention* Venice (Italy) 2009.
Members Companies (21) in 9 countries:
Belgium, France, Germany, Greece, Italy, Netherlands, Portugal, Spain, UK.
National rice milling associations (5) in 5 countries:
France, Germany, Italy, Portugal, Spain.
NGO Relations Member of: *Industry4Europe (#11181).* [2019/XD9394/**D**]

♦ Federation of European Rigid Polyurethane Foam Associations (PU Europe) 09538

Fédération des associations européennes de mousse de polyuréthane rigide – Vereinigung der Europäischen Polyurethan-Hartschaum-Verbände

SG Rue Belliard 65, 1040 Brussels, Belgium. T. +3227863554. E-mail: secretariat@pu-europe.eu.
URL: http://www.pu-europe.eu/

History 1978. Founded with the acronym *BING* which derived from the acronym of the four founding national associations. First Statutes adopted, 27 Dec 2004; most recent version, 27 Mar 2020. Registration: Banque Carrefour des Entreprises, No/ID: 0870.426.629, Start date: 28 Oct 2004, Belgium; EU Transparency Register, No/ID: 27993486325-38, Start date: 28 Jul 2011. **Aims** Establish permanent liaison among national member associations representing the polyurethane *insulation* industry; study all issues common to the rigid polyurethane foam industry at international level; represent the industry at all levels and in all matters within Europe; coordinate research on rigid polyurethane foam at European level. **Structure** General Assembly (annual); Managing Committee; Working Committees. **Languages** English. **Staff** 3.00 FTE, paid. **Finance** Sources: members' dues. **Activities** Events/meetings; research/documentation. **Events** *Annual General Assembly* Copenhagen (Denmark) 2022, *Annual General Assembly* 2020, *Annual General Assembly* Rome (Italy) 2019, *Annual General Assembly* Stockholm (Sweden) 2018, *Annual General Assembly* Edinburgh (UK) 2017.

Members Full: national trade associations of rigid polyurethane foam in 11 countries:
Belgium, Denmark, Finland, France, Germany, Italy, Netherlands, Poland, Spain, Sweden, UK.
Associate membership open to suppliers of raw materials, chemicals and other materials and machinery used in the manufacture of rigid polyurethane foam industry. Members in 11 countries:
Belgium, Finland, France, Germany, Hungary, Italy, Netherlands, Poland, Spain, Switzerland, UK.
NGO Relations Partner of (9): *Coalition for Energy Savings (#04056)*; *Construction 2050 Alliance (#04760)*; *Construction Products Europe AISBL (#04761)*; *Energy Efficiency Industrial Forum (EEIF, #05470)*; *European Association for External Thermal Insulation Composite Systems (EAE, #06035)*; European Coalition for Chemical Recycling; *Industry4Europe (#11181)*; *Modern Building Alliance (#16842)*; Renovate Europe. Cooperates with (5): Build Up; *Comité européen de normalisation (CEN, #04162)*; *Covenant of Mayors for Climate and Energy (#04939)*; *European Diisocyanate and Polyol Producers Association (ISOPA, #06926)*; *International Organization for Standardization (ISO, #14473)*. [2022.06.28/XD5860/**D**]

♦ Federation of European Risk Management Associations (FERMA) .. 09539

Fédération européenne de risk management

Exec Dir Av de Tervuren 273/B12, 1150 Brussels, Belgium. T. +3227619432. Fax +3227718720. E-mail: enquiries@ferma.eu.
Communication Officer address not obtained.
URL: http://www.ferma.eu/

History 1974, Brussels (Belgium). Founded as *European Association of Insurers of Industries (AEAI) – Association européenne des assurés de l'industrie*. Subsequently changed name to *European Risk Management Association*. Previously also referred to as *Association européenne des assurés de l'industrie (AEAI)*. Present name adopted 1995. Registration: Banque-Carrefour des Entreprises, No/ID: 0414.927.002, Start date: 28 Jun 1974, Belgium; EU Transparency Register, No/ID: 018778010447-60, Start date: 11 Jan 2013. **Aims** Lead and enhance effective practice of risk management, risk financing and insurance. **Structure** General Assembly (annual); Board of Directors; Executive Board; Working Groups. **Languages** English, French. **Staff** 4.00 FTE, paid. **Activities** Research/documentation; networking/liaising; awareness raising; knowledge management/information dissemination; events/meetings. **Events** *Biennial Risk Management Forum* Copenhagen (Denmark) 2022, *Biennial Risk Management Forum* Berlin (Germany) 2019, *Biennial Risk Management Forum* Monte Carlo (Monaco) 2017, *Conference on Board Governance and Emerging Risks in the C21* Brussels (Belgium) 2015, *Biennial Risk Management Forum* Venice (Italy) 2015. **Publications** *FERMA Newsletter* (6 a year); *FERMA Newswire*. Reports; guidelines.
Members Full; Adhering; Individual; Corporate; Honorary. National associations, representing over 4,800 individuals in a range of business sectors (manufacturing, financial services, charities, health organizations and local government organizations), in 20 countries:
Belgium, Bulgaria, Czechia, Denmark, Finland, France, Germany, Italy, Luxembourg, Malta, Netherlands, Norway, Portugal, Russia, Slovenia, Spain, Sweden, Switzerland, Türkiye, UK.
IGO Relations *European Commission (EC, #06633)*; *OECD (#17693)*. **NGO Relations** Member of: *Federation of European and International Associations Established in Belgium (FAIB, #09508)*. [2021/XD7360/**D**]

- ♦ Federation of European Rope and Twine Industries / see Fédération européenne des industries de corderie ficellerie et de filets (#09573)
- ♦ Federation of European Rope, Twine and Net Industries (#09573)
- ♦ Federation of the European Salmon and Trout Growers / see Federation of European Aquaculture Producers (#09491)

♦ Federation of European Scleroderma Associations (FESCA) 09540

Registered Address Rue du Pont à Rieu 13 i, 7500 Tournai, Belgium. E-mail: info@fesca-scleroderma.eu.
URL: http://www.fesca-scleroderma.eu/

History 2006. Registration: Banque-Carrefour des Entreprises, No/ID: 0889.943.920, Start date: 2 Feb 2007, Belgium. **Aims** Promote advancement of knowledge, research and information in the field within medical, governmental and social arenas; increase awareness of the disease among the general public; secure for those with scleroderma the best possible treatments, care and, ultimately, a cure. **Structure** Board. **Languages** English. **Events** *Systemic Sclerosis World Congress* 2022, *Systemic Sclerosis World Congress* Prague (Czechia) 2020, *Systemic Sclerosis World Congress* Bordeaux (France) 2018, *Systemic Sclerosis World Congress* Lisbon (Portugal) 2016, *Systemic Sclerosis World Congress* Rome (Italy) 2014.
Members Full in 19 countries:
Belgium, Croatia, Cyprus, Denmark, Finland, France, Germany, Hungary, Ireland, Italy, Netherlands, Norway, Poland, Portugal, Romania, Spain, Sweden, Switzerland, UK.
NGO Relations Member of (2): *European Patients' Forum (EPF, #08172)*; *EURORDIS – Rare Diseases Europe (#09175)*. [2020/XM1568/**D**]

- ♦ Federation of European Scouting / see Union Internationale des Guides et Scouts d'Europe – Fédération du Scoutisme Européen (#20426)

♦ Federation of European Screen Directors 09541

Fédération européenne des réalisateurs de l'audiovisuel (FERA) – Verband Europäischer Filmregisseure

CEO Rue du Prince Royal 85/87, 1050 Brussels, Belgium. T. +3225510894. E-mail: office@filmdirectors.eu.
URL: https://screendirectors.eu/

History 1980, Venice (Italy). Founded following a number of informal meetings. Statutes approved, Jan 1981, Barcelona (Spain); modified Sep 2013. Former names and other names: *Federation of European Film Directors* – former. Registration: Belgium; EU Transparency Register, No/ID: 29280842236-21. **Aims** Promote policies that maximize the creative, social and commercial potential of the *audiovisual* industry; enhance recognition of the cultural significance of audiovisual works and defend their integrity in 21st century Europe. **Structure** General Assembly (annual); Executive Committee; Honorary President; Ambassadors. **Languages** English, French. **Staff** Paid and voluntary. **Finance** Sources: members' dues. **Activities** Events/meetings; politics/policy/regulatory. **Events** *Annual General Assembly* 2020, *Annual General Assembly* Bucharest (Romania) 2019, *Annual General Assembly* Copenhagen (Denmark) 2012, *Annual General Assembly* Budapest (Hungary) 2009, *General assembly / Annual General Assembly* Dublin (Ireland) 2008. **Publications** *FERA Seasonal Newsletter*. *European Survey on the remuneration of audiovisual authors* in English; *FERA Directors Contracts' Guidelines* in English.
Members Organizations (48) in 33 countries:
Austria, Azerbaijan, Belgium, Bosnia-Herzegovina, Bulgaria, Croatia, Cyprus, Czechia, Denmark, Estonia, Finland, France, Germany, Greece, Hungary, Iceland, Ireland, Italy, Latvia, Lithuania, Luxembourg, Montenegro, Netherlands, North Macedonia, Norway, Poland, Portugal, Serbia, Slovenia, Spain, Sweden, Switzerland, UK.
Associate in 8 countries:
France, Hungary, Israel, Norway, Romania, Slovenia, Sweden, USA.
Consultative Status Consultative status granted from: *World Intellectual Property Organization (WIPO, #21593)* (Permanent Observer Status). **IGO Relations** Collaborates with: *European Commission (EC, #06633)*; *European Parliament (EP, #08146)*; *UNESCO (#20322)*. **NGO Relations** Member of (1): *Culture First Coalition (inactive)*. [2021.06.08/XD1865/**D**]

- ♦ Federation of European Screen Printers Associations / see FESPA (#09739)

♦ Federation of European Securities Exchanges (FESE) 09542

Main Office Av de Cortenbergh 116, 1000 Brussels, Belgium. T. +3225510180. Fax +3225124905.
URL: http://www.fese.eu/

History 1974. Initially founded as an informal discussion group for Chairmen of main EEC Stock Exchanges. Secretariat set up 1980. Former names and other names: *Committee of Stock Exchanges in the European Economic Community* – former; *Comité des bourses de la Communauté économique européenne* – former; *Federation of Stock Exchanges in the European Community* – former; *Fédération des bourses de la Communauté européenne* – former; *Federation of European Stock Exchanges* – former (1993 to 2001); *Fédération des bourses européennes* – former (1993 to 2001). Registration: European Transparency Register, No/ID: 71488206456-23. **Aims** Promote cooperation and links among *stock exchanges* of the *European Union*; represent member exchanges, in particular with European Union institutions. **Structure** General Assembly (annual). Committee, comprising chairmen of main stock exchanges and stock exchange associations in the European Community, has been referred to in the press as *Association européenne des présidents de bourse*. Officers: President; Vice-President; Secretary General; Deputy Secretary General. Working Committee. Sub-committees (4): Economics and Statistics; European Forum Task Force; Investment Service Directive (ISD) Task Force; Regulatory Matters. **Languages** Dutch, English, French, German, Italian, Spanish, Welsh. **Staff** 9.00 FTE, paid. **Finance** Members' contributions. **Events** *Convention* Brussels (Belgium) 2022, *Convention* Brussels (Belgium) 2021, *Convention* Brussels (Belgium) 2020, *Convention* Dublin (Ireland) 2019, *Convention* Vienna (Austria) 2018. **Publications** *European Stock Exchange Statistics* (10 a year). Annual statistical report; European directory (online and printed).
Members Full stock exchanges and exchange associations in 30 countries:
Austria, Belgium, Bulgaria, Cyprus, Czechia, Denmark, Estonia, Finland, France, Germany, Greece, Hungary, Iceland, Ireland, Latvia, Lithuania, Luxembourg, Malta, Netherlands, Norway, Poland, Portugal, Romania, Slovakia, Slovenia, Spain, Sweden, Switzerland, Türkiye, UK.
IGO Relations Recognized by: *European Commission (EC, #06633)*. **NGO Relations** Founding member of: *European Capital Markets Institute (ECMI, #06439)*. Member of: *European Parliamentary Financial Services Forum (EPFSF, #08148)*. Institutional member of: *Centre for European Policy Studies (CEPS, #03741)*. [2020/XE5165/**D**]

- ♦ Federation of European Self Employed Dental Technicians and Dental Laboratory Owners / see Fédération européenne et internationale des patrons prothésistes dentaires (#09575)

♦ Federation of European Self Storage Associations (FEDESSA) 09543

CEO BluePoint, Bd Auguste Reyers 80, 1030 Brussels, Belgium. T. +32472943324. E-mail: info@fedessa.org.
URL: http://www.fedessa.org/

History Mar 2004. Registration: Banque-Carrefour des Entreprises, No/ID: 0864.622.267, Start date: 8 Apr 2004, Belgium. **Aims** Provide a voice for the European self storage industry; promote and defend the industry in Europe; improve communication and cooperation between members; promote a common standard. **Structure** Council (meets twice a year). **Languages** English. **Staff** 2.00 FTE, paid. **Finance** Sources: members' dues. **Events** *Conference* Rotterdam (Netherlands) 2023, *Conference* Vilamoura (Portugal) 2022, *Conference* Birmingham (UK) 2021, *Annual Conference* Vilamoura (Portugal) 2020, *Annual Conference* London (UK) 2019. **Publications** *FOCUS Magazine* (4 a year); *FEDESSA e-News* (2 a year).
Members National associations in 14 countries:
Belgium, Czechia, Denmark, Finland, France, Germany, Ireland, Italy, Netherlands, Norway, Spain, Sweden, Switzerland, UK. [2021/XM0376/**D**]

♦ Federation of European Simulation Societies (EUROSIM) 09544

Sec address not obtained.
Pres address not obtained.
URL: http://www.eurosim.info/

History 5 Sep 1989, Edinburgh (UK). Founded at 3rd European Simulation Congress. **Aims** Provide a European forum to promote advancement of *modelling* and simulation in industry, research and development. **Structure** Board. **Languages** English. **Staff** 3.00 FTE, voluntary. **Finance** Sources: meeting proceeds. Annual budget: 2,000 EUR. **Activities** Events/meetings; knowledge management/information dissemination; research/documentation. **Events** *EUROSIM Congress* Amsterdam (Netherlands) 2023, *EUROSIM Congress* Amsterdam (Netherlands) 2022, *MESM : Middle East Symposium on Simulation and Modeling* Dubai (United Arab Emirates) 2019, *Triennial Congress* Logroño (Spain) 2019, *MESM : Middle East Symposium on Simulation and Modeling* Dubai (United Arab Emirates) 2017. **Publications** *Simulation Notes Europe (SNE)* – newsletter/journal.
Members Language-based member societies and federations; organized modelling and simulation groups. Full (14) representing 21 countries:
Austria, Belgium, Croatia, Czechia, Denmark, Finland, France, Germany, Hungary, Iceland, Italy, Latvia, Netherlands, Norway, Poland, Slovakia, Slovenia, Spain, Sweden, Switzerland, UK.
Included in the above, 3 regional societies:
Arbeitsgemeinschaft Simulation (ASIM, #01083); *Scandinavian Simulation Society (SIMS, #19100)*; *Société francophone de simulation (FRANCOSIM, no recent information)*.
Observer in 3 countries:
Kosovo, Romania, Russia.
NGO Relations *European Council for Modelling and Simulation (ECMS, #06831)*; International Group on Aviation and Multimodal Transport Research; *Society for Modeling Simulation International (SCSI, #19598)*. [2021/XD2149/y/**D**]

♦ Federation of European Social Employers (FESE) 09545

Dir Rue du Commerce 72, 1040 Brussels, Belgium.
URL: http://socialemployers.eu/

History Launched 20 Oct 2017, Brussels (Belgium), at *European Economic and Social Committee (EESC, #06963)*. **Aims** Provide social services' employers with an effective voice at European level; find common solutions to the sector's challenges with both representatives of workers and the European institutions; lead the European Union towards more social and inclusive policies. **Structure** Board. **Events** *Meeting on Socially Responsible Public Procurement for Social Services* Brussels (Belgium) 2019, *Meeting* Brussels (Belgium) 2018, *Seminar* Brussels (Belgium) 2018. **NGO Relations** *European Association of Service Providers for Persons with Disabilities (EASPD, #06204)*. [2018.09.21/XM6141/**D**]

♦ Federation of European Societies for Chemotherapy and for Infections (FESCI) 09546

Pres Dept of Preclinical and Clinical Pharmacology, Univ of Florence, Viale Pieraccini 6, 50139 Florence FI, Italy. T. +39554281 ext 310. Fax +39554271 ext 280. E-mail: d.saccomani@oic.it.

History 1994. Registration: UK. **Aims** Promote the education and science of chemotherapy. **Structure** Council (meets annually); Executive Committee. **Languages** English. **Staff** Voluntary. **Events** *Southeast European Conference* Thessaloniki (Greece) 2015, *Southeast European Conference* Bled (Slovenia) 2014, *Southeast European Conference* Istanbul (Turkey) 2013, *Southeast European Conference* Dubrovnik (Croatia) 2012, *Southeast European Conference* Belgrade (Serbia) 2011.
Members National organizations in 26 countries:
Austria, Belarus, Bulgaria, Croatia, Cyprus, Czechia, France, Georgia, Germany, Greece, Hungary, Israel, Italy, Lebanon, Morocco, Netherlands, Poland, Portugal, Russia, Slovakia, Slovenia, Spain, Switzerland, Türkiye, UK, Ukraine.
International organizations (4):
European Society for Paediatric Infectious Diseases (ESPID, #08682); *International Society of Non-Antibiotics (ISN, #15307)*; *Mediterranean Society of Chemotherapy and Infection (MedSocChemI, #16675)*; *Nordic Society for Clinical Microbiology and Infectious Diseases (NSCMID, #17413)*.
NGO Relations European branch of: *International Society of Antimicrobial Chemotherapy (ISAC, #14925)*. [2013/XD7384/y/**D**]

- ♦ Federation of European Societies for Microsurgery / see European Federation of Societies for Microsurgery (#07216)

♦ Federation of the European Societies of Neuropsychology (ESN) ... 09547

Sec Travessa Espera 8, 1o Esq A, 1200-176 Lisbon, Portugal.
URL: http://www.fesn.eu/

History Officially launched Sep 2008, Edinburgh (UK), following preparatory meetings held 2004, Modena (Italy) and 2006, Toulouse (France). Constitution adopted 11 Jan 2008. **Aims** Further the scientific and professional issues within the field of neuropsychology, including cognitive neuropsychology, clinical neuropsychology, behavioural neurology, neuroimaging and neuropsychological rehabilitation. **Structure** Council. Management Committee, comprising President, Vice-President, Treasurer, Secretary, Past President and 2 members. Ad hoc Task Forces. **Events** *Scientific Meeting* Thessaloniki (Greece) 2023, *Scientific Meeting* Milan (Italy) 2019, *Scientific Meeting* Maastricht (Netherlands) 2017, *Scientific Meeting* Tampere (Finland) 2015, *Scientific Meeting* Berlin (Germany) 2013.
Members Individuals who are members of European Societies of neuropsychology participating in the Federation. National Societies in 16 countries:
Austria, Belgium, Denmark, Finland, France, Germany, Ireland, Italy, Netherlands, Norway, Portugal, Spain, Sweden, Switzerland, Türkiye, UK.
NGO Relations Associate member of: *European Federation of Psychologists Associations (EFPA, #07199)*. [2013/XJ4170/**D**]

♦ Federation of European Societies of Plant Biology (FESPB) 09548

SG Università Campus Bio-Medico di Roma, Via Alvaro del Portillo 21, 00128 Rome RM, Italy. T. +3906225419114. E-mail: admin@fespb.org – info@fespb.org.
URL: http://www.fespb.org/

History 1978. Former names and other names: *Federation of European Societies of Plant Physiology (FESPP)* – former. **Aims** Strengthen science of plant physiology in Europe and beyond; establish cooperation among member societies and individuals. **Structure** General Assembly (every 2 years, at Scientific Meeting); Council; Executive Committees. **Languages** English. **Staff** 6.00 FTE, voluntary. **Finance** Sources: members' dues. **Activities** Events/meetings; knowledge management/information dissemination. **Events** *Plant Biology Europe Conference* Marseille (France) 2023, *Plant Biology Europe Conference* Turin (Italy) 2021, *Plant Biology Europe Conference* Turin (Italy) 2020, *Plant Biology Europe Conference* Copenhagen (Denmark) 2018, *Conference* Prague (Czech Rep) 2016.
Members National societies of plant physiology (21, one for the Scandinavian countries) grouping 3,000 individuals in 26 countries:
Austria, Belarus, Bulgaria, Croatia, Czechia, Denmark, Finland, France, Germany, Greece, Hungary, Ireland, Italy, Netherlands, Norway, Poland, Portugal, Romania, Russia, Serbia, Slovakia, Slovenia, Spain, Sweden, UK, Ukraine.
Regional affiliate representing Scandinavian members:
Societas Physiologiae Plantarum Scandinavica (SPPS, #19452).
NGO Relations Member of (1): *Global Plant Council (#10550).* [2022.11.06/XD7060/**D**]

- ♦ Federation of European Societies of Plant Physiology / see Federation of European Societies of Plant Biology (#09548)

♦ Federation of the European Societies for Surgery of the Hand (FESSH) 09549

Fédération des sociétés européennes de chirurgie de la main
SG FESSH c/o Ostschweizerische Revisionsgesellschaft AG, Spisergasse 9a, 9004 St Gallen, Switzerland. E-mail: secretarygeneral@fessh.com – office@fessh.com.
Manager address not obtained.
URL: https://www.fessh.com/

History 1990, Paris (France). Former names and other names: *Federation of European Societies for Surgery and Rehabilitation of the Hand* – former; *Fédération européenne des sociétés de chirurgie et de rééducation de la main* – former. **Aims** As representative of national hand surgery societies in Europe: improve the standard of hand surgery throughout Europe; develop surgical resources by advising European authorities of the requirements and appropriate quality of hand care; rationalize and unify the training and educational structure for qualification of European hand surgery specialists. **Structure** Delegates Assembly; Council; Committees. **Languages** English. **Activities** Awards/prizes/competitions; awareness raising; certification/accreditation; events/meetings; financial and/or material support; guidance/assistance/consulting; projects/programmes; research/documentation; training/education. **Events** *Congress* Basel (Switzerland) 2026, *Congress* Helsinki (Finland) 2025, *Congress* Rotterdam (Netherlands) 2024, *Congress* Rimini (Italy) 2023, *Congress* London (UK) 2022. **Publications** *Journal of Hand Surgery (European Volume).*
Members Full in 27 countries:
Austria, Belgium, Bulgaria, Czechia, Denmark, Estonia, Finland, France, Germany, Greece, Hungary, Ireland, Italy, Latvia, Netherlands, Norway, Poland, Portugal, Romania, Russia, Serbia, Spain, Sweden, Switzerland, Türkiye, UK, Ukraine.
Associate in 1 country:
Israel.
Corresponding in 5 countries:
Egypt, Korea Rep, Lithuania, Slovakia, South Africa.
NGO Relations Cooperates with (3): *European Federation of National Associations of Orthopaedics and Traumatology (EFORT, #07169); European Society of Plastic, Reconstructive and Aesthetic Surgery (ESPRAS, #08708); European Wrist Arthroscopy Society (EWAS, #09122).* [2022.05.10/XD2678/**D**]

- ♦ Federation of European Societies for Surgery and Rehabilitation of the Hand / see Federation of the European Societies for Surgery of the Hand (#09549)
- ♦ Federation of European Societies of Toxicology (inactive)

♦ Federation of European Societies on Trace Elements and Minerals (FESTEM) 09550

Pres Dept Laboratory Medicine, Hosp Gregorio Maranón, Calle del Dr Esquerdo 46, 28007 Madrid, Spain. E-mail: secre@seqc.es.
Gen Sec Univ de Pau et des Pays de l'Adour, IPREM – UMR 5254 Hélioparc, 2 av du président Angot, 64053 Pau, France.
URL: http://www.festem.eu/

History 21 Mar 1997, Rome (Italy). Founded under the initiative of *'Associazione Italiana per lo Studio degli Elementi in Traccia negli Organismi Viventi (AISETOV)'; 'Gesellschaft für Mineralstoffe und Spurenelemente (GMS)'* and *Société Francophone d'Etude et de Recherche sur les Eléments Toxiques et Essentiels (SFERETE, #19469).* **Aims** Encourage all kinds of activities in the field of trace elements and minerals, including development of research or educational projects, organization of scientific meetings, search for financial support through private or international organizations, etc. **Structure** Executive Committee. **Languages** English. **Staff** 12.00 FTE, voluntary. **Finance** Sources: contributions; meeting proceeds. **Activities** Events/meetings; networking/liaising. **Events** *International Symposium* Madrid (Spain) 2022, *International Symposium* Potsdam (Germany) 2019, *International Symposium* Catania (Italy) 2016, *International symposium / Symposium* Avignon (France) 2013, *International symposium / Symposium* St Petersburg (Russia) 2010. **Publications** *Journal of Trace Elements in Medicine and Biology.*
Members Societies in 6 countries:
France, Germany, Italy, Romania, Russia, Spain.
NGO Relations Formal contacts with: *Trace Element – Institute for UNESCO.* [2022.05.10/XD8272/**D**]

♦ Federation of European Societies for Tropical Medicine and International Health (FESTMIH) 09551

Contact Hygiene-Institut, Abt Tropenhygiene und Öffentliches Gesundheitswesen, Im Neuenheimer Feld 324, 69120 Heidelberg, Germany. T. +496221564904. Fax +496221565204. E-mail: secretariat.festmih@gmail.com.
URL: http://www.festmih.eu/

History 1995, Hamburg (Germany). Founded during the first European Conference on Tropical Medicine. **Aims** Promote cooperation between societies dedicated to tropical medicine and international health. **Structure** Assembly Council, elects Executive Board, comprising President, Vice-President, Secretary, Treasurer and 3 members. **Languages** English, French. **Staff** 1.50 FTE, voluntary. **Finance** Sources: contributions; donations; members' dues. **Activities** Events/meetings. **Events** *European Congress on Tropical Medicine and International Health (ECTMIH)* Utrecht (Netherlands) 2023, *European Congress on Tropical Medicine and International Health* Bergen (Norway) 2021, *European Congress on Tropical Medicine and International Health* Liverpool (UK) 2019, *European Congress on Tropical Medicine and International Health* Antwerp (Belgium) 2017, *European Congress on Tropical Medicine and International Health* Basel (Switzerland) 2015. **Publications** *TM and IH – Tropical Medicine and International Health* (12 a year) – official journal.
Members National societies in 16 countries:
Austria, Belgium, Croatia, Czechia, Finland, France, Germany, Ireland, Italy, Netherlands, Norway, Portugal, Spain, Sweden, Switzerland, UK.
Included in the above, 2 organizations listed in this Yearbook:
German Society of Tropical Medicine and International Health (DTG); Spanish Society of Tropical Medicine and International Health (SEMTSI). [2022/XD7187/y/**D**]

- ♦ Federation of European Specialty Food Ingredient Industries / see EU Specialty Food Ingredients (#09200)

♦ Federation of the European Sporting Goods Industry (FESI) 09552

Fédération européenne de l'industrie du sport
SG Avenue des Arts 43, 1040 Brussels, Belgium. T. +3227628648. Fax +3227718746. E-mail: info@fesi-sport.org.
URL: http://www.fesi-sport.org/

History 1964, Cologne (Germany FR). Head office moved to Brussels (Belgium), Oct 1994. Current by-laws adopted Oct 2014. Registered in accordance with Belgian law. **Aims** Defend the interests of sporting goods manufacturers, notably of sports textile, footwear and hardware. **Structure** General Assembly (annual); Board; Executive Committee. **Languages** English, French, Italian. **Staff** 4.00 FTE, paid. **Finance** Members' dues. **Activities** Politics/policy/regulatory; events/meetings; research and development. **Publications** Documentation on policy, legislation, reports and meetings.
Members Regular (National Sports Industry Federations -NSIFs, Industry Suppliers being members of a NSIF); Associated (Industry suppliers); Sustaining; Honorary. Members in 12 countries:
Austria, Croatia, Czechia, Denmark, France, Germany, Greece, Italy, Netherlands, Spain, Türkiye, UK.
NGO Relations Member of (1): *World Federation of the Sporting Goods Industry (WFSGI, #21487).* [2018/XD7292/t/**D**]

- ♦ Federation of European Sporting Goods Retail Associations / see Sporting Goods Industry Data Harmonization Organization (#19924)
- ♦ Federation of European Stock Exchanges / see Federation of European Securities Exchanges (#09542)

♦ Federation for European Storytelling (FEST) 09553

Seat Kasteelstraat 6, 3740 Bilzen, Belgium. E-mail: festeurope@gmail.com.
URL: http://fest-network.eu/

History Registered in accordance with Belgian law. EU Transparency Register: 196024034882-43. **Aims** Empower the world of storytelling in Europe. **Structure** Board of Governors; Executive Committee. **Activities** Advocacy/lobbying/activism; events/meetings. **Publications** *FEST Newsletter.*
Members Full in 23 countries:
Belgium, Bosnia-Herzegovina, Canada, Croatia, Cyprus, Denmark, Finland, France, Germany, Greece, Hungary, Ireland, Italy, Lithuania, Netherlands, Norway, Poland, Portugal, Slovenia, Sweden, Switzerland, Türkiye, UK. [2019/XM8384/**D**]

♦ Federation of European Tank Storage Associations (FETSA) 09554

Exec Dir Diamant Bldg, Bv Auguste Reyers 80, 1030 Brussels, Belgium. T. +3222389787. E-mail: mdw@fetsa.eu.
Pres address not obtained.
URL: http://www.fetsa.eu/

History Founded 1993, Brussels (Belgium). Registered in accordance with Belgian law. EU Transparency Register: 60758835312-16. **Aims** Represent the European independent tank storage industry towards the European Union and other international organizations; promote exchange of know-how and expertise. **Structure** Board; Executive Committee; DS Committee. **Languages** English. **Staff** 0.50 FTE, paid. **Finance** Members' dues. **Events** *Annual Conference* Rotterdam (Netherlands) 2021, *Annual Conference* Rotterdam (Netherlands) 2020, *Annual General Meeting* Tarragona (Spain) 2019, *Annual General Meeting* Antwerp (Belgium) 2016, *Annual General Meeting* Amsterdam (Netherlands) 2012.
Members National organizations (7) in 7 countries:
Belgium, France, Germany, Italy, Netherlands, Spain, UK.
Associate members in 4 countries:
Hungary, Poland, Sweden, Türkiye.
IGO Relations Consultative Status with: *Central Commission for the Navigation of the Rhine (CCNR, #03687); United Nations Economic Commission for Europe (UNECE, #20555).* [2018.09.10/XD6216/**D**]

- ♦ Federation of European Tile-Fixers' Associations (#05762)
- ♦ Federation of European Trade Associations of Scientific Laboratory Suppliers (no recent information)

♦ Federation of the European Union Fire Officer Associations (FEU) .. 09555

Fédération des associations de sapeurs-pompiers dans l'Union européenne – Federatie van Brandweerverenigingen in de Europese Unie
Sec 3 The Orchard, Castlebar, CO. MAYO, Ireland.
Registered Address 112 Bvd Gen George S Patton, L-2316 Luxembourg, Luxembourg.
URL: http://www.f-e-u.org/

History 6 Jun 1995, Tampere (Finland). Registration: Luxembourg; EU Transparency Register, No/ID: 014681328548-06, Start date: 9 Oct 2017. **Aims** Enhance fire safety and provide expertise to European bodies in matters concerning the development of fire brigades and fire safety in Europe. **Structure** General Council. **Languages** English. **Staff** 2.00 FTE, voluntary. **Finance** Sources: members' dues. **Activities** Events/meetings; projects/programmes. **Events** *Meeting* Porto (Portugal) 2019, *Meeting* Tartu (Estonia) 2018, *Meeting* Oslo (Norway) 2017, *Meeting* Barcelona (Spain) 2016, *Meeting* Budapest (Hungary) 2016.
Members Organizations in 20 countries:
Austria, Cyprus, Czechia, Denmark, Estonia, Finland, Germany, Greece, Hungary, Ireland, Italy, Luxembourg, Netherlands, Norway, Poland, Portugal, Slovenia, Spain, Sweden, UK.
Observers in 6 countries:
Belgium, Croatia, France, Latvia, Malta, Türkiye.
NGO Relations Member of (1): *Forum for European Electrical Domestic Safety (FEEDS).* [2022/XD7849/**D**]

- ♦ Federation of the European Union Manufacturers and Suppliers of Ingredients to the Bakery, Confectionery and Patisserie Industries / see Federation of European Manufacturers of Ingredients to the Bakery, Confectionery and Patisserie Industries (#09513)
- ♦ Federation of European Unions of Honorary Consuls (#09709)
- ♦ Federation of European Veterinarians in Industry and Research / see European Association of Veterinarians in Education, Research and Industry (#06267)
- ♦ Federation of European Wholesale and International Trade Associations (inactive)
- ♦ Federation of European Williams Syndrome / see European Federation of Williams Syndrome (#07234)
- ♦ Federation of European Window and Curtain Walling Manufacturer Associations (#09456)
- ♦ Federation of European Window and Curtain Wall Manufacturers' Associations / see Fédération des associations européennes des constructeurs de fenêtres et de façades (#09456)
- ♦ Federation of European Window Manufacturers' Associations / see Fédération des associations européennes des constructeurs de fenêtres et de façades (#09456)
- ♦ Federation of European Woodcock Associations of Western Palearctic (#09460)
- ♦ Federation of European Writing Instruments Associations / see European Writing Instrument Manufacturer's Association (#09125)
- ♦ Federation of European Youth Hostels in the EC / see European Union Federation of Youth Hostel Associations (#08988)

♦ Federation of European Zeolite Associations (FEZA) 09556

Sec Ruder Boskovic Inst, Bijenicka 54, HR-10000 Zagreb, Croatia. T. +38514560991. Fax +38514680098. E-mail: info@feza-online.eu.
Chairman Univ della Calabria, Via Pietro Bucci, 87036 Arcavacata CS, Italy. E-mail: ggiordaunical@yahoo.it.
URL: https://www.feza-online.eu/

History 12 Jul 1995, Szombathely (Hungary). Statutes adopted 1996. **Aims** Advance education in the study of zeolite molecular sieves, including technology and application thereof in the areas of chemistry, geology, chemical engineering and other branches of science or engineering; improve communication and collaboration between researchers in Europe. **Structure** Committee. **Activities** Events/meetings; awards/prizes/competitions; training/education; networking/liaising. **Events** *Conference* Portoroz (Slovenia) 2023, *Conference* 2021, *Conference* Sofia (Bulgaria) 2017, *Conference* Leipzig (Germany) 2014, *Conference* Valencia (Spain) 2011.
Members National organizations in 18 countries:
Bulgaria, Croatia, Czechia, France, Georgia, Germany, Hungary, Italy, Netherlands, Poland, Portugal, Romania, Russia, Serbia, Slovakia, Slovenia, Spain, UK. [2021/XJ4199/**D**]

- ♦ Fédération européene de l'industrie textile du coton et des fibres connexes (#07093)
- ♦ Fédération européenne des académies de médecine (#09490)
- ♦ Fédération européenne pour l'accroissement de la productivité (#07196)
- ♦ Fédération européenne des actionnaires salariés pour l'actionnariat salarié et la participation / see European Federation of Employee Share Ownership (#07105)
- ♦ Fédération européenne de l'actionnariat salarié (#07105)

- ♦ Fédération européenne des activités du déchet / see European Federation of Waste Management and Environmental Services (#07232)
- ♦ Fédération européenne des activités du déchet et de l'environnement / see European Federation of Waste Management and Environmental Services (#07232)
- ♦ Fédération européenne des activités de la dépollution et de l'environnement (#07232)

♦ Fédération Européenne des Aérosols (FEA) 09557

European Aerosol Federation – Europäischer Aerosolverband

SG Bd du Souverain 165, 1160 Brussels, Belgium. T. +3226796280. E-mail: info@aerosol.org.
URL: http://www.aerosol.org/

History 1959, Paris (France). Former names and other names: *Federation of European Aerosol Associations* – former; *Fédération européenne des associations aérosols* – former; *Föderation Europäischer Aerosol-Verbände* – former. Registration: Banque-Carrefour des Entreprises, No/ID: 0422.796.670, Start date: 26 May 1982, Belgium; EU Transparency Register, No/ID: 32814201372-84, Start date: 15 Mar 2009. **Aims** Coordinate and defend the interests of the aerosol *industry*. **Structure** Assembly of Delegates; Board of Directors; Committees; Working Groups; Task Forces; Secretariat. **Languages** English, French. **Staff** 2.00 FTE, paid. **Finance** Sources: members' dues. **Activities** Advocacy/lobbying/activism; events/meetings. **Events** *Biennial Congress* Lisbon (Portugal) 2022, *Aerosol Today Conference* Brussels (Belgium) 2020, *Annual Autumn Meeting* Geneva (Switzerland) 2019, *Biennial Congress* Düsseldorf (Germany) 2018, *Triennial Congress* Istanbul (Turkey) 2016. **Publications** *FEA Guidelines*; *FEA Standards*; *FEA Statistics Report*.

Members Full, including 350 companies active in the aerosol industry, in 19 countries:
Austria, Belgium, Czechia, Denmark, Finland, France, Germany, Greece, Hungary, Italy, Luxembourg, Netherlands, Poland, Portugal, Spain, Sweden, Switzerland, Türkiye, UK.
Corresponding members in 11 countries:
Argentina, Australia, Brazil, Chile, China, Mexico, New Zealand, Russia, Ukraine, USA, Venezuela.

IGO Relations Recognized by: *European Commission (EC, #06633)*. Participates in the work of: *United Nations Economic Commission for Europe (UNECE, #20555)*. **NGO Relations** Member of: *Downstream Users of Chemicals Co-ordination group (DUCC, #05127)*; *Federation of European and International Associations Established in Belgium (FAIB, #09508)*; *Industry4Europe (#11181)*. In liaison with technical committees of: *Comité européen de normalisation (CEN, #04162)*; *International Organization for Standardization (ISO, #14473)*. [2022.05.12/XD0934/**D**]

- ♦ Fédération européenne des agences régionales de l'énergie et de l'environnement / see European Federation of Agencies and Regions for Energy and the Environment (#07041)
- ♦ Fédération Européenne des Agences et des Régions pour l'Energie et l'Environnement (#07041)
- ♦ Fédération européenne des agences de renseignements commerciaux et d'informations économiques / see Federation of Business Information Services (#09464)
- ♦ Fédération européenne d'Aikido (inactive)
- ♦ Fédération Européenne des Aires de Jeu (inactive)
- ♦ Fédération européenne pour l'apprentissage interculturel (#07146)
- ♦ Fédération européenne de l'approvisionnement (inactive)
- ♦ Fédération européenne pour l'architecture du paysage / see IFLA Europe (#11103)
- ♦ Fédération européenne de l'art du mime (inactive)
- ♦ Fédération européenne pour l'art populaire et l'artisanat (#07279)
- ♦ Fédération européenne des associations aérosols / see Fédération Européenne des Aérosols (#09557)
- ♦ Fédération européenne des associations des allergies et insuffisant respiratoires (#07045)
- ♦ Fédération européenne des associations d'allergiques (inactive)
- ♦ Fédération européenne des associations de l'asthme et des allergies / see European Federation of Allergy and Airways Diseases Patients' Associations (#07045)
- ♦ Fédération européenne des associations de l'automatique / see European Gaming and Amusement Federation (#07374)
- ♦ Fédération européenne des associations de bois de mine (inactive)
- ♦ Fédération européenne d'associations et centres d'etudes irlandaises (#07048)
- ♦ Fédération européenne des associations, clubs et centres UNESCO (#07231)
- ♦ Fédération Européenne des Associations de Conseils en Organisation (#07159)
- ♦ Fédération européenne des associations contre la lèpre / see International Federation of Anti-Leprosy Associations (#13355)
- ♦ Fédération européenne des associations de crédit management (#09498)
- ♦ Fédération européenne des associations pour la défense des victimes de la prévention des dommages médicaux (no recent information)
- ♦ Fédération Européenne des Associations déleveurs de Pur Sang Anglais (#07226)
- ♦ Fédération européenne des associations de détaillants en articles de sport / see Sporting Goods Industry Data Harmonization Organization (#19924)
- ♦ Fédération européenne des associations de diététiciens (#07050)
- ♦ Fédération européenne des associations de la distribution automatique / see European Vending and Coffee Service Association (#09049)
- ♦ Fédération européenne des associations des économistes d'entreprise (no recent information)
- ♦ Fédération européenne des associations pour l'enseignement des langues maternelles aux étrangers (no recent information)
- ♦ Fédération européenne des associations des établissements de crédit-bail (#07111)
- ♦ Fédération européenne d'associations d'étudiants chrétiens (#07076)
- ♦ Fédération européenne des associations d'étudiants en psychologie (#07200)
- ♦ Fédération Européenne des Associations de Fabricants de Serrures et de Ferrures (#07054)
- ♦ Fédération européenne des associations de familles de malades psychiques (#07051)
- ♦ Fédération européenne des associations et fondations pour le rayonnement des opéras (inactive)
- ♦ Fédération européenne des associations pour la gestion de l'énergie (inactive)
- ♦ Fédération européenne des associations de guides touristiques (#07228)
- ♦ Fédération européenne d'associations et d'industries pharmaceutiques (#07191)
- ♦ Fédération Européenne des associations infirmières (#07180)
- ♦ Fédération européenne des associations d'ingénieurs (inactive)
- ♦ Fédération européenne des associations des instituts de crédit (#07121)
- ♦ Fédération européenne des associations d'instruments à écrire / see European Writing Instrument Manufacturer's Association (#09125)
- ♦ Fédération européenne des associations d'intervenants en toxicomanie (inactive)
- ♦ Fédération européenne des associations de journalistes du tourisme / see European Travel Press (#08944)
- ♦ Fédération européenne des associations de malades de Crohn et rectocolite hémorragique (#07095)
- ♦ Fédération européenne des associations de management industriel (inactive)
- ♦ Fédération européenne des associations maristes (inactive)
- ♦ Fédération européenne des associations de médecins catholiques (no recent information)
- ♦ Fédération européenne des associations nationales des entrepreneurs spécialisés et des fabricants de matériaux pour l'industrie de construction / see Experts for Specialised Construction and Concrete Systems (#09226)

♦ Fédération Européenne d'Associations Nationales d'Ingénieurs (FEANI) 09558

European Federation of National Engineering Associations – Föderation Europäischer Nationaler Ingenieurverbände

SG Central Secretariat c/o REGUS EU Commission, Schuman Square 6, 5th Floor, 1040 Brussels, Belgium. T. +3222347878. E-mail: secretariat.general@feani.org.
URL: http://www.feani.org/

History 7 Sep 1951, Paris (France). Founded following decision, 22-24 Jul 1949, Constance (Switzerland) of the International Congress of Engineers, and a study session, 11 Jun 1950, Freiburg-Breisgau (Switzerland). Current statutes approved 5 Oct 2012, Rome (Italy). Former names and other names: *International Federation of National Associations of Engineers* – former; *Fédération internationale d'associations nationales d'ingénieurs* – former. Registration: French Ministerial Decree, Start date: 9 Jan 1952, France; Start date: 1997, Belgium; EU Transparency Register, No/ID: 71635694112-37. **Aims** Facilitate mutual recognition of engineering qualifications in Europe and strengthen the position, role and responsibility of engineers in society; affirm the professional identity of engineers of Europe; strive for a single voice for the engineering profession in Europe, while acknowledging its diversity. **Structure** General Assembly (annual); Executive Board; European Monitoring Committee (EMC); Working Groups; Secretariat in Brussels (Belgium), headed by Secretary-General. Congresses open; meetings closed. **Languages** English, French, German. **Staff** 3.00 FTE, paid. **Finance** Sources: grants; members' dues. **Activities** Events/meetings; networking/liaising; training/education. **Events** *Annual Conference and General Assembly* Reykjavik (Iceland) 2019, *Annual Conference and General Assembly* Valletta (Malta) 2018, *Annual Conference and General Assembly* Vienna (Austria) 2017, *Annual Conference and General Assembly* Stockholm (Sweden) 2016, *Annual Conference and General Assembly* Lisbon (Portugal) 2015. **Publications** *FEANI INDEX*; *FEANI News*. Press releases.

Members National associations (over 80, totalling about 4 million individual engineers) in 32 countries:
Austria, Belgium, Bulgaria, Croatia, Cyprus, Czechia, Denmark, Estonia, France, Germany, Greece, Iceland, Ireland, Italy, Kazakhstan, Malta, Netherlands, North Macedonia, Norway, Poland, Portugal, Romania, Russia, Serbia, Slovakia, Slovenia, Spain, Sweden, Switzerland, Türkiye, UK, Ukraine.

Consultative Status Consultative status granted from: *ECOSOC (#05331)* (Ros C); *UNIDO (#20336)*. **IGO Relations** Recognized by: *European Commission (EC, #06633)*, 10 Mar 1994. Accredited by: *United Nations Office at Vienna (UNOV, #20604)*. Member of: *European Economic and Social Committee (EESC, #06963)* Liaison Group. **NGO Relations** Founding member of: *World Federation of Engineering Organizations (WFEO, #21433)*. Member of: *Consejo de las Asociaciones Profesionales de Ingenieros Civiles de Lengua Oficial Portuguesa y Castellana (CECPC-CICPC, #04702)*; *European Network for Accreditation of Engineering Education (ENAEE, #07859)*; *Knowledge4Innovation (K4I, #16198)*. Associate member of: *Société européenne pour la formation des ingénieurs (SEFI, #19462)*. Observer member of: *European Council of Liberal Professions (#06828)*. [2020.06.25/XD0741/**D**]

- ♦ Fédération européenne des associations nationales de services d'eau et assainissement (#07170)
- ♦ Fédération européenne d'associations nationales travaillant avec les sans-abri (#07174)

♦ Fédération européenne des associations de négociants en aciers, tubes et métaux (EUROMETAL) 09559

European Federation of Associations of Steel, Tube and Metal Merchants

Dir-Gen 202b rue de Hamm, L-1713 Luxembourg, Luxembourg. T. +35226259026. Fax +35226459205.
Officer address not obtained. E-mail: office@eurometal.net.
URL: http://www.eurometal.net/

History 11 May 1999, by merger of *European Federation of Steel Stockholders (inactive)* and *Fédération internationale des associations de négociants en aciers, tubes et métaux (FIANATM, inactive)*. **Structure** Presidency comprising President and 2 Vice-Presidents. Executive Committee; Management Committee. **Events** *Regional Meeting Nordics* Helsinki (Finland) 2019, *Regional Meeting Central Europe* Vienna (Austria) 2018, *Steelnet Forum* Bilbao (Spain) 2015, *General Assembly* Frankfurt-Main (Germany) 2015, *General Assembly* Frankfurt-Main (Germany) 2014. **Publications** *Eurometal Newsletter* (4 a year).

Members National associations in 20 countries:
Austria, Belgium, Czechia, Denmark, Finland, France, Germany, Greece, Italy, Luxembourg, Netherlands, Norway, Poland, Portugal, Romania, Spain, Sweden, Switzerland, UK, USA. [2015/XD7075/**D**]

- ♦ Fédération européenne des associations de numismates professionnels (#09523)
- ♦ Fédération européenne des associations de parents d'enfants décédés de mort subite (inactive)
- ♦ Fédération Européenne des Associations de Patients de l'Hémochromatose (#07056)
- ♦ Fédération européenne des associations de patients pour la médecine anthroposophique (#07189)
- ♦ Fédération Européenne des Associations de Patrimoine Industriel et Technique (#07053)
- ♦ Fédération européenne des associations piscicoles / see Federation of European Aquaculture Producers (#09491)
- ♦ Fédération européenne des associations de professeurs de déficients auditifs (inactive)
- ♦ Fédération européenne des associations de professeurs de langues et de civilisations classiques / see EUROCLASSICA (#05663)
- ♦ Fédération européenne des associations de psychologues (#07199)
- ♦ Fédération européenne des associations en sciences et technologies marines (inactive)
- ♦ Fédération européenne des associations au service de la jeunesse (inactive)
- ♦ Fédération européenne des associations de sociétés d'affacturage (no recent information)
- ♦ Fédération européenne des associations de spécialistes en orthodontie (#07185)
- ♦ Fédération européenne des associations de torréfacteurs du café (inactive)
- ♦ Fédération européenne des ataxies héréditaires (#07138)

♦ Fédération européenne des auto-écoles (EFA) 09560

European Driving Schools Association – Europäische Fahrlehrer Assoziation

Contact Rue de la Loi 223, 1000 Brussels, Belgium. E-mail: info@efa-eu.com.
URL: http://www.efa-eu.com/

History 1982, Germany FR. 1982, Bielefeld (Germany FR). Previously also referred to as *Association européenne des moniteurs d'auto-école*. Registered in accordance with German law. EU Transparency Register: 838015634532-59. **Aims** Improve road safety; harmonize driving tuition, driving teachers' training and driving tests. **Structure** Board. **Languages** English, French, German. **Activities** Projects/programmes; events/meetings. **Events** *Meeting* Rome (Italy) 2014, *Meeting* Leuven (Belgium) 2013, *Meeting* Sopron (Hungary) 2013, *Congress* Madrid (Spain) 2012, *Meeting* Vienna (Austria) 2012. **Publications** *EFA Newsletter*.

Members Driving school organizations in 21 countries:
Albania, Austria, Belgium, Czechia, Denmark, Estonia, Finland, France, Germany, Hungary, Iceland, Ireland, Italy, Luxembourg, Moldova, Netherlands, Norway, Portugal, Slovakia, Spain, UK.

NGO Relations Member of: *eSafetyAware (#05533)*. [2019/XD5800/**D**]

- ♦ Fédération européenne des banques alimentaires / see European Food Banks Federation (#07280)
- ♦ Fédération européenne de baseball / see Confederation of European Baseball (#04518)
- ♦ Fédération européenne de biotechnologie (#07062)
- ♦ Fédération européenne des bouffons (#09810)

♦ Fédération européenne des cadres de la construction (FECC) 09561

Contact Rue de Londres 15, 75009 Paris, France. T. +33155317676. Fax +33155317633. E-mail: cannavo.eu@gmail.com – patrizia.forcina@federmanager.it.

History 1993. Registration: RNA, No/ID: W751109634, Start date: 15 Jul 2010, France. **NGO Relations** Member of (2): *CEC European Managers (#03623)*; *Circular Plastics Alliance (#03936)*. [2015/XD4080/**D**]

♦ Fédération européenne des cadres de l'énergie et de la recherche (FECER) 09562

European Federation of Executives in the Sectors of Energy and Research

Main Office c/o CFE-CGC, 59 rue du Rocher, 75008 Paris, France.
URL: http://www.fecer.eu/

History Founded 1992, Paris (France), by 10 national organizations. Registered in accordance with French law. **Aims** As a grouping of professional staff, represent and defend common, moral and economic interests of production and development company executives in the energy sector and in related mining research companies in fossil and non-fossil fuel sectors in Europe. **Structure** General Assembly (every 3 years). Steering Committee (meets once a year), consisting of one representative and a substitute from each member organizations. Executive Committee, composed of Chairman, one or several Vice-Chairmen, Secretary-General and Treasurer. **Languages** English, French. **Finance** Budget: ECU 15,500.

Members National associations in 9 countries:
Belgium, Denmark, France, Germany, Italy, Luxembourg, Norway, Spain, UK.

NGO Relations Member of: *CEC European Managers (#03623)*. [2019/XD3008/**D**]

- ♦ Fédération européenne des cadres des établissements de crédit (#07161)
- ♦ Fédération européenne du café (#06600)

- Fédération européenne de canicross et de bikejöring (#06437)
- Fédération européenne de caravaning (#06443)
- Fédération européenne des centres de recherche et d'information sur le sectarisme (#07072)
- Fédération européenne des céphalées (#07451)
- Fédération Européenne des Chambres de Commerce Bilatérales (#07060)
- Fédération européenne des chasseurs à l'arc (no recent information)
- Fédération Européenne du Cheval de Trait pour la promotion de son Utilisation (#06944)
- Fédération européenne des choeurs de l'Union (#07075)
- Fédération européenne la Citizen's Band (#06556)
- Fédération européenne de climatothérapie (inactive)
- Fédération européenne des clubs du tissu conjonctif / see European Matrix Biology (#07756)
- Fédération européenne des collectionneurs et des amateurs de curiosités, antiquités et folklore (inactive)
- Fédération européenne des commerçants en électronique domestique et électroménager (#07103)

♦ Fédération européenne du commerce chimique (Fecc) 09563

European Association of Chemical Distributors – Europäischer Verband des Chemiehandels

Dir Gen Rue du Luxembourg 16B, 1000 Brussels, Belgium. T. +3226790260.
URL: http://www.fecc.org/

History 1954, Brussels (Belgium). New statutes adopted 25 Jan 2005. Former names and other names: *European Federation of Chemical Trade* – former. Registration: No/ID: 0465.031.460, Start date: 6 Sep 1998, Belgium; EU Transparency Register, No/ID: 0346440357-87, Start date: 3 Sep 2008. **Aims** Be the voice for, inform and serve European chemical distribution. **Structure** General Assembly; Board; Executive Committee; Consultative Assembly of National Association Members; Consultative Assembly of Company Members; Working Committees; Secretariat. **Languages** English, French, German, Italian, Spanish. **Staff** 6.00 FTE, paid. **Finance** Sources: members' dues. **Activities** Events/meetings; guidance/assistance/consulting; monitoring/evaluation. **Events** *Annual Congress and General Assembly* Sitges (Spain) 2022, *Annual Congress and General Assembly* Milan (Italy) 2021, *Annual Congress and General Assembly* Milan (Italy) 2020, *Annual Congress and General Assembly* Sitges (Spain) 2019, *Annual Congress and General Assembly* Nice (France) 2018. **Publications** *Fecc Newsletter*. Annual Report; guides.

Members National associations in 15 countries:
Austria, Belgium, Czechia, Denmark, Finland, France, Germany, Ireland, Italy, Netherlands, Portugal, Spain, Sweden, Switzerland, UK.

Companies (40) in 19 countries:
Austria, Belarus, Belgium, Czechia, Denmark, Finland, France, Germany, Greece, Ireland, Italy, Netherlands, Portugal, Russia, Spain, Sweden, Switzerland, Türkiye, UK.

Associate (9). Membership countries not specified.

IGO Relations Accredited by (1): *European Commission (EC, #06633)*. **NGO Relations** Member of (5): *Conseil européen de l'industrie chimique (CEFIC, #04687)*; *Downstream Users of Chemicals Co-ordination group (DUCC, #05127)*; *EXCiPACT (#09222)*; *Industry4Europe (#11181)*; *International Council of Chemical Associations (ICCA, #13003)*. Also links with USA 'National Association of Chemical Distributors' (NACD).
[2021.06.09/XD1418/**D**]

- Fédération européenne du commerce en fruits secs, conserves, épices et miel / see European Federation of the Trade in Dried Fruit, Edible Nuts, Processed Fruit and Vegetables, Processed Fishery Products, Spices, Honey and Similar Foodstuffs (#07229)
- Fédération européenne du commerce de gros et extérieur en jouets (inactive)
- Fédération européenne du commerce de l'horlogerie en gros (inactive)
- Fédération européenne des commissaires-priseurs / see European Federation of Auctioneers (#07057)
- Fédération européenne des communautés de Sant'Egidio (#07082)
- Fédération européenne des communes forestières (#07157)
- Fédération européenne des conseillers en commerce internationale (inactive)
- Fédération européenne des conseils et intermédiaires financiers (#07122)
- Fédération européenne des conseils en valorisation de l'innovation (no recent information)
- Fédération européenne de constructeurs d'équipement de grandes cuisines (#07068)
- Fédération européenne des constructeurs d'équipement pétrolier (inactive)
- Fédération européenne de la construction en bois / see Timber Construction Europe (#20164)
- Fédération Européenne pour le Contrôle Non Destructif (#07179)
- Fédération européenne de la corrosion (#07090)
- Fédération européenne des couples bi-nationaux/bi-culturelles (#06731)

♦ Fédération européenne de croquet (FEC) 09564

European Croquet Federation

SG Catharijnesingel 124, 3511 GX Utrecht, Netherlands. T. +31433509041.
URL: http://eurocroquet.eu/

History 1993, Paris (France). **Aims** Promote the playing of croquet within Europe. **Structure** Central Management Committee, comprising President, Secretary, Treasurer and 2 members. **Languages** English. **Finance** Members' dues. **Activities** Organizes annual European championships.

Members National croquet associations in 20 countries and territories:
Austria, Belgium, Czechia, England, Finland, France, Germany, Ireland, Isle of Man, Italy, Jersey, Latvia, Luxembourg, Norway, Russia, Scotland, Spain, Sweden, Switzerland, Wales.
[2019/XD6574/**D**]

- Fédération européenne des cyclistes (#06877)
- Fédération Européenne de Destinations Touristiques Nautiques (internationally oriented national body)
- Fédération européenne de la diaconie (#07099)
- Fédération Européenne des Directeurs de la Photographie Cinématographique / see International Federation of Cinematographers (#13390)
- Fédération européenne pour la disparition de la prostitution (no recent information)
- Fédération européenne pour le droit à la stérilisation volontaire (inactive)
- Fédération européenne des écoles (#09479)

♦ Fédération européenne des écoles de cirque professionnelles (FEDEC) 09565

European Federation of Professional Circus Schools

Secretariat Rue du Meiboom 18, Office 4.12, 1070 Brussels, Belgium. T. +3225267009. E-mail: info@fedec.eu.
URL: http://www.fedec.eu/

History 1998. Founded on the initiative of 3 higher education institutions for circus arts: *'Ecole Supérieure des Arts du Cirque'* (Belgium); *'Centre National des Arts du Cirque'* (France); *'Circus Space'* (UK). **Aims** Support development and evolution of pedagogy and creation in the field of circus arts education. **Structure** General Assembly; Managing Board. **Languages** English, French. **Staff** 3.00 FTE, paid. **Finance** Sources: members' dues; sponsorship. Other sources: framework partnership agreement with *European Commission (EC, #06633)*; private partnership. **Activities** Advocacy/lobbying/activism; events/meetings; knowledge management/information dissemination; training/education. **Events** *Conference* Montpellier (France) 2020, *Conference* Berlin (Germany) 2019, *Conference* Brussels (Belgium) 2018, *Conference* Madrid (Spain) 2017. **Publications** *Charter on Ethics and Deontology in Circus Arts Education and Training*; *Directory of Circus Arts Training Centres in Europe and Beyond*. Instruction manuals; reports; surveys; studies.

Members Categories – Full; Associate; Partners. Members (585) in 243 countries:
Argentina, Australia, Austria, Belgium, Canada, Chile, Czechia, Denmark, Finland, France, Germany, Hungary, Italy, Netherlands, Norway, Peru, Poland, Portugal, Russia, Spain, Sweden, Switzerland, UK, USA.

IGO Relations Cooperates with (1): *European Commission (EC, #06633)*. **NGO Relations** Member of (2): *Circostrada Network (#03933)*; *Lifelong Learning Platform – European Civil Society for Education (LLLP, #16466)*. Cooperates with (4): *CircusNext (#03943)*; *European Circus Association (ECA, #06552)*; *European League of Institutes of the Arts (ELIA, #07670)*; *European Youth Circus Organisation (EYCO, #09139)*.
[2021/XD4517/t/**D**]

- Fédération européenne d'éditeurs de périodiques / see European Magazine Media Association (#07723)
- Fédération européenne pour l'éducation catholique des adultes (#05966)
- Fédération européenne de l'éducation et de la culture (inactive)
- Fédération européenne pour l'éducation des enfants de la population itinérante professionnelle (inactive)
- Fédération européenne des éleveurs de la race brune (#06405)
- Fédération européenne des éleveurs de la race pie rouge (#08487)
- Fédération européenne de l'emballage souple (inactive)
- Fédération européenne des emballeurs et distributeurs de miel (#07140)
- Fédération Européenne des Emplois de la Famille (#07118)
- Fédération européenne des employeurs sociaux (#07214)
- Fédération européenne de l'encadrement de la métallurgie (#07162)
- Fédération européenne énergie – chimie – industries diverses (inactive)
- Fédération européenne des énergies renouvelables (#08355)
- Fédération européenne des énergies renouvelables (inactive)
- Fédération européenne pour enfants disparus et sexuellement exploités (#07166)
- Fédération européenne des enseignants en sciences infirmières (#07102)
- Fédération européenne de l'enseigne et de la signalétique (#08485)
- Fédération européenne des entreprises de travaux de voie (#07205)
- Fédération Européenne des Épargnants et Usagers des Services Financiers / see BETTER FINANCE (#03219)
- Fédération européenne d'épargne et de crédit pour le logement (#07064)
- Fédération européenne des équipement routiers de sécurité (inactive)
- Fédération européenne des espaces naturels et ruraux métropolitains et périurbains (inactive)
- Fédération européenne pour l'étude des corps gras (inactive)
- Fédération européenne pour l'étude du travail / see European Federation of Productivity Services (#07196)
- Fédération européenne des étudiants âgés aux universités (#07181)
- Fédération Européenne des Experts en CyberSécurité (#07096)
- Fédération européenne des fabricants d'adjuvants pour la nutrition animale / see FEFANA – EU Association of Specialty Feed Ingredients and their Mixtures (#09720)

♦ Fédération européenne des fabricants d'aliments composés pour animaux (FEFAC) 09566

European Feed Manufacturers' Federation – Federación Europea de Fabricantes de Alimentos Compuestos para Animales – Europäischer Verband der Mischfutterindustrie – Federazione Europea dei Fabbricanti di Mangimi Composti per Animali – Europese Federatie van Mengvoederfabrikanten – Europaeiske Forbund af Fodderfabrikanter

SG Rue de la Loi 223, Bte 3, 1040 Brussels, Belgium. T. +3222850050. Fax +3222305722. E-mail: fefac@fefac.eu.
Exec Sec address not obtained.
URL: http://www.fefac.eu/

History 6 Jul 1959, Brussels (Belgium). Latest statutes adopted 2011. Registration: Banque-Carrefour des Entreprises, No/ID: 0408.295.071, Start date: 18 Dec 1964, Belgium; EU Transparency Register, No/ID: 77105321408-83, Start date: 23 Mar 2009. **Aims** Carry out scientific, technical and institutional studies of interest to the animal feed industry and its international economic integration, in particular as regards the European Union. **Structure** General Assembly (annual); Praesidium; Administrative Council; Experts' Committees; Ad-hoc Working Groups; Task Forces; Issue Teams. **Languages** English. **Staff** 8.00 FTE, paid. **Finance** Members' dues. **Events** *Congress* Ystad (Sweden) 2023, *Congress* Antwerp (Belgium) 2020, *Global Feed and Food Congress* Bangkok (Thailand) 2019, *Congress* Córdoba (Spain) 2017, *High-Level Conference* Brussels (Belgium) 2016. **Publications** *Feed Facts* (4 a year); *Feed and Food* (annual); *Statistical Leaflet* (annual). *FEFAX*.

Members National associations in 23 countries:
Austria, Belgium, Bulgaria, Croatia, Cyprus, Czechia, Denmark, Finland, France, Germany, Hungary, Ireland, Italy, Lithuania, Netherlands, Poland, Portugal, Romania, Slovakia, Slovenia, Spain, Sweden, UK.

Observers in 2 countries:
Russia, Serbia.

Associate members (7) in 4 countries:
Belgium, Norway, Switzerland, Türkiye.

IGO Relations Recognized by: *European Commission (EC, #06633)*. Participates as observer in the activities of: *Codex Alimentarius Commission (CAC, #04081)*. **NGO Relations** Member of: *Agri-Food Chain Coalition (AFCC, #00577)*; Animal Task Force (ATF); EU Feed and Food Chain Platform on the use of green biotechnology; *European Aquaculture Technology and Innovation Platform (EATiP, #05910)*; European Platform for the Responsible Use of Medicines in Animals (EPRUMA); *Federation of European and International Associations Established in Belgium (FAIB, #09508)*; Food Safety Platform; *Industry4Europe (#11181)*; *International Feed Industry Federation (IFIF, #13581)*. Associate member of: *European Network of Agricultural Journalists (ENAJ, #07864)*. In liaison with technical committees of: *International Organization for Standardization (ISO, #14473)*. Coordinates: EU Feed Chain Task Force on the Catalogue of Feed Materials.
[2021/XD0726/t/**D**]

- Fédération européenne des fabricants d'articles de ménage et professionnels en aluminium (inactive)
- Fédération européenne des fabricants de briquets (#07153)
- Fédération Européenne des Fabricants de Carton Ondulé (#07091)
- Fédération européenne des fabricants de céramiques sanitaires (#07073)
- Fédération européenne des fabricants et distributeurs d'équipements de protection individuelle (#08418)
- Fédération européenne des fabricants d'enveloppes / see Fédération européenne des producteurs d'enveloppes (#09578)
- Fédération européenne des fabricants de flexpak (inactive)

♦ Fédération européenne des fabricants de palettes et emballages en bois (FEFPEB) 09567

European Federation of Wooden Pallet and Packaging Manufacturers

Sec PO Box 4076, 5004 JB Tilburg, Netherlands. T. +31135944802. Fax +31135944749. E-mail: fefpeb@wispa.nl.
URL: http://www.fefpeb.eu/

History Jun 1946. **Aims** Promote timber packaging, determination and defence of the interests of the European Wooden Pallet and Packaging Industry; stimulate information exchange between members in connection to various international items. **Structure** General Assembly; Policy and Technical Committee; Executive Committee; Ad-Hoc Working Groups. **Events** *Congress* Florence (Italy) 2022, *Congress* Hamburg (Germany) 2019, *Congress* Maastricht (Netherlands) 2017, *Congress* Brussels (Belgium) 2016, *Congress* Valencia (Spain) 2012.

Members Manufacturers in 13 countries:
Austria, Belgium, France, Germany, Italy, Lithuania, Netherlands, Portugal, Spain, Sweden, Switzerland, Türkiye, UK.

NGO Relations Member of: *Confédération européenne des industries du bois (CEI Bois, #04545)*. In liaison with technical committees of: *International Organization for Standardization (ISO, #14473)*.
[2018.06.01/XD0744/**D**]

- Fédération européenne des fabricants de panneaux de fibres (inactive)
- Fédération européenne des fabricants de panneaux de moyenne densité (inactive)
- Fédération européenne des fabricants de produits abrasifs / see Federation of European Producers of Abrasives (#09532)
- Fédération européenne des fabricants de produits réfractaires (#08339)
- Fédération européenne des fabricants de revêtements de sol stratifiés (#02533)
- Fédération européenne des fabricants de sacs papier à grande contenance / see EUROSAC (#09177)
- Fédération européenne des fabricants de tuiles et de briques / see Tiles and Bricks Europe (#20163)
- Fédération Européenne des Fabricants de Tuyaux en Grès / see FEUGRES – European Clay Pipe Association (#09741)

♦ Fédération européenne des femmes actives en famille (FEFAF) 09568

European Federation of Parents and Carers at home

General Sec Avenue Père Damien 76, 1150 Brussels, Belgium. T. +3227712334.
URL: http://www.fefaf.be/

History 18 Nov 1983, Brussels (Belgium). Former names and other names: *Fédération européenne des femmes actives au foyer (FEFAF)* – former. Registration: Banque Carrefour des Entreprises, No/ID: 0453.904.867, Start date: 24 Nov 1994, Belgium. **Aims** For those men/women who choose/have chosen or wish to choose to undertake the care of their children, their elderly or disabled relatives at home, work towards: recognition of the human, social and economic value of the voluntary caring and educational work carried out at home and the collection of date on this family-based work in the statistics; valuing those men/women; adapted social welfare rights; a Family Policy guaranteeing the rights of families and children. **Structure** General Assembly (annual); Managing Committee. **Languages** English, French. **Staff** Voluntary. **Finance** Sources: members' dues. **Events** *Annual General Assembly* Geneva (Switzerland) 2012, *Annual General Assembly* Warsaw (Poland) 2011, *Annual General Assembly* Bratislava (Slovakia) 2010, *Annual General Assembly* London (UK) 2009, *Annual General Assembly* Brussels (Belgium) 2008.
Members National associations Founder; Active; Corresponding. Members in 17 countries:
Austria, Belgium, Bulgaria, Cyprus, Denmark, France, Germany, Hungary, Ireland, Italy, Latvia, Poland, Romania, Slovenia, Spain, Sweden, UK.
Consultative Status Consultative status granted from: *ECOSOC (#05331)* (Special). **NGO Relations** Member of: *European Women's Lobby (EWL, #09102)*; *Social Platform (#19344)*; *Vienna NGO Committee on the Family (#20774)*. Supports: *European Alliance for the Statute of the European Association (EASEA, #05886)*; *European Citizens' Initiative Campaign (ECI Campaign, #06558)*. [2019/XD2218/**D**]

- ♦ Fédération européenne des femmes actives au foyer / see Fédération européenne des femmes actives en famille (#09568)
- ♦ Fédération européenne 'Pro Fide et Ecclesia' (inactive)
- ♦ Fédération européenne des filiales de l'Association mondiale d'aviculture (#07063)
- ♦ Fédération européenne de finances et banques éthiques et alternatives (#07113)

♦ Fédération européenne du foie gras (EURO FOIE GRAS) 09569

European Federation of Foie Gras – Federación Europea del Foie Gras – Europese Federatie van foie-grasproducenten

Contact Rue de l'Industrie 11, 1000 Brussels, Belgium. T. +3227200073. E-mail: contact@eurofoiegras.com.
URL: https://www.eurofoiegras.com/

History 2008, Strasbourg (France). Registration: EU Transparency Register, No/ID: 617506516010-41, Start date: 11 Feb 2015; No/ID: 0812.070.934, Start date: 4 Jun 2009, Belgium. **Aims** Promote foie gras. **Structure** Bureau; Advisory Cabinet.
Members Groups in 5 countries:
Belgium, Bulgaria, France, Hungary, Spain. [2020/AA0082/**D**]

- ♦ Fédération européenne de fondeurs à modèles perdus (#07600)
- ♦ Fédération européenne des fonds et sociétés d'investissement / see European Fund and Asset Management Association (#07365)
- ♦ Fédération européenne pour la formation et le développement (#08933)
- ♦ Fédération européenne du franchising (inactive)
- ♦ Fédération européenne de la ganterie de peau (no recent information)
- ♦ Fédération européenne pour le génie biologique (#05751)
- ♦ Fédération européenne de génie chimique (#07074)
- ♦ Fédération européenne des gentlemen amateurs et cavalières du trot (#05896)
- ♦ Fédération européenne des géologues (#07133)
- ♦ Fédération européenne des greffés du coeur / see European Heart and Lung Transplant Federation (#07466)
- ♦ Fédération européenne des greffés du coeur et des poumons (#07466)

♦ Fédération européenne des grossistes en appareils sanitaires et de chauffage (FEST) 09570

European Federation of the Sanitary and Heating Wholesale Trade

Dir Gen Excelsiorlaan 91, 1930 Zaventem, Belgium. E-mail: info@festassociation.eu.
Manager address not obtained.
URL: http://festassociation.eu/

History 1958. **Aims** Provide merchants of sanitary and heating articles with support and advice needed to run their businesses in a competitive environment. **Structure** General Assembly; Presidency. **Languages** English, French, German, Italian, Spanish. **Staff** 1.00 FTE, paid. **Events** *Congress* Lisbon (Portugal) 2022, *General Assembly* Milan (Italy) 2020, *Congress* Vienna (Austria) 2018, *Congress* Brussels (Belgium) 2016, *General Assembly* Milan (Italy) 2016. **Publications** *FEST Facts* (12 a year); *Fest Quarterly Magazine* (3 a year).
Members Full in 16 countries. Membership countries not specified. **IGO Relations** *European Commission (EC, #06633)*. **NGO Relations** National associations. [2022.02.15/XD3704/t/**D**]

- ♦ Fédération Européenne des Grossistes Indépendants en Matériel Electrique / see FEGIME (#09721)
- ♦ Fédération européenne des groupements d'outre-mer et d'expulsés de l'Est (inactive)
- ♦ Fédération européenne des groups RPE (#07110)
- ♦ Fédération européenne de gymnastique / see Fédération internationale de gymnastique (#09636)
- ♦ Fédération européenne haltérophile (#09090)
- ♦ Fédération européenne de handball (#07446)
- ♦ Fédération européenne d'hébergements historiques / see Historic Hotels of Europe (#10930)
- ♦ Fédération européenne des herbages (#07406)
- ♦ Fédération européenne de hockey (#07494)
- ♦ Fédération européenne des hôpitaux et des soins de santé (#07501)
- ♦ Fédération européenne de l'hôtellerie de plein air (#07066)
- ♦ Fédération européenne des importateurs de fruits secs, conserves, épices et miel / see European Federation of the Trade in Dried Fruit, Edible Nuts, Processed Fruit and Vegetables, Processed Fishery Products, Spices, Honey and Similar Foodstuffs (#07229)
- ♦ Fédération européenne des importateurs de machines et d'équipements de bureau (inactive)
- ♦ Fédération européenne des indépendants et des cadres (inactive)

♦ Fédération européenne de l'industrie des aliments pour animaux familiers (FEDIAF) 09571

European Petfood Industry Federation – Federación Europea de la Industria de los Alimentos para Animales de Compañía – Europäischer Verband der Hersteller von Heimtiernahrung – Federazione Europea dell'Industria di Alimenti per Animali Domestici – Europees Verbond van de Huisdiervoederindustrie – Europaeiske Forbund for Industrien for Foder til Selskabscyr

SG Av Louise 89, 1050 Brussels, Belgium. T. +3225360520. E-mail: fediaf@fediaf.org.
URL: http://www.fediaf.org/

History 29 Sep 1970. Registration: Banque-Carrefour des Entreprises, No/ID: 0416.200.175, Start date: 1 Jul 1976, Belgium; EU Transparency Register, No/ID: 053117613298-41, Start date: 19 Mar 2014. **Aims** Elaborate a policy for protection of the pet food industry within the European Community. **Languages** English, French, German. **Staff** 3.00 FTE, paid. **Finance** Sources: members' dues. **Events** *Annual General Meeting* Brussels (Belgium) 2020, *Annual General Meeting* Prague (Czechia) 2019, *Annual General Meeting* Rotterdam (Netherlands) 2018, *Annual General Meeting* Aix-en-Provence (France) 2015, *Annual General Meeting* Madrid (Spain) 2014. **Publications** Educational materials; guidelines.
Members National organizations in 18 countries:
Austria, Belgium, Czechia, Denmark, Finland, France, Germany, Hungary, Ireland, Italy, Netherlands, Norway, Poland, Romania, Spain, Sweden, Switzerland, UK.
IGO Relations *European Union (EU, #08967)*. **NGO Relations** Member of (2): *FoodDrinkEurope (#09841)*; *Global Alliance of Pet Food Associations (GAPFA, #10218)*. Cooperates with (1): *AnimalhealthEurope (#00837)*. Instrumental in setting up (1): *Pet Alliance Europe (PetPower)*. In liaison with technical committees of: *Comité européen de normalisation (CEN, #04162)*; *International Organization for Standardization (ISO, #14473)*. [2021/XD5301/t/**D**]

- ♦ Fédération européenne de l'industrie de la brosserie et pinceauterie (#06406)
- ♦ Fédération européenne de l'industrie du contreplaqué (inactive)
- ♦ Fédération européenne de l'industrie électro-céramique (inactive)
- ♦ Fédération européenne de l'industrie du jouet (inactive)
- ♦ Fédération européenne de l'industrie de l'optique et de la mécanique de précision (#07193)
- ♦ Fédération Européenne de l'Industrie du Parquet (#07188)
- ♦ Fédération européenne des industries de câbles d'acier / see European Federation of Steel Wire Rope Industries (#07221)

♦ Fédération européenne des industries de colles et adhésifs (FEICA) 09572

Association of the European Adhesive and Sealant Industry (FEICA)

SG Rue Belliard 40 box 10, 1040 Brussels, Belgium. T. +3228969600. E-mail: info@feica.eu.
URL: http://www.feica.eu/

History 14 Nov 1972, Rome (Italy). Founded to replace *Liaison Bureau for Manufacturers of Vegetable and Synthetic Glue in the EEC Countries (inactive)*, set up 1968. Former names and other names: *Association of European Adhesives Manufacturers* – former; *Verband Europäischer Klebstoffindustrien* – former; *European Association of the Adhesive and Sealant Industry* – former. Registration: Banque Carrefour des Entreprises, No/ID: 0884.334.548, Start date: 17 Oct 2006, Belgium; EU Transparency Register, No/ID: 51642763262-89, Start date: 22 Feb 2010. **Aims** Represent the adhesive and sealant industry at European level; work with all relevant stakeholders to create a mutually beneficial economic and legislative environment. **Languages** English. **Staff** 6.00 FTE, paid. **Finance** Sources: members' dues. **Activities** Knowledge management/information dissemination; networking/liaising; politics/policy/regulatory; standards/guidelines. **Events** *Paper and Board for Food Contact* Brussels (Belgium) 2022, *World Adhesive and Sealant Conference* Chicago, IL (USA) 2022, *Conference* Hamburg (Germany) 2022, *Conference* Warsaw (Poland) 2021, *Conference* Warsaw (Poland) 2020. **Publications** *FEICA Connect*.
Members National associations representing 700 company members in 17 countries:
Austria, Belgium, Denmark, France, Germany, Greece, Ireland, Italy, Luxembourg, Netherlands, Poland, Portugal, Slovenia, Spain, Sweden, Switzerland, UK.
Company Members (24); Affiliate Company Members (20). Membership countries not specified.
IGO Relations Accredited by (1): *European Commission (EC, #06633)*. **NGO Relations** Member of (6): *Conseil européen de l'industrie chimique (CEFIC, #04687)* (Affiliate); *Construction 2050 Alliance (#04760)*; *Construction Products Europe AISBL (#04761)* (Associate); *Downstream Users of Chemicals Co-ordination group (DUCC, #05127)*; *Federation of European and International Associations Established in Belgium (FAIB, #09508)*; *Industry4Europe (#11181)*. In liaison with technical committees of: *Comité européen de normalisation (CEN, #04162)*. Supporter of Declaration of on Paper Recovery, maintained by *European Paper Recycling Council (EPRC, #08139)*. [2022.05.11/XD2910/t/**D**]

- ♦ Fédération européenne des industries de corderie-ficellerie / see Fédération européenne des industries de corderie ficellerie et de filets (#09573)

♦ Fédération européenne des industries de corderie ficellerie et de filets (EUROCORD) 09573

Federation of European Rope, Twine and Net Industries

Contact Rue Archimède 17, 1000 Brussels, Belgium. T. +3223664096. Fax +3222316605. E-mail: eurocord@eurocord.com.
URL: http://eurocord.com/

History Founded 1975, as *Federation of Western European Rope and Twine Industries – Fédération des industries de corderie-ficellerie de l'Europe occidentale*. Subsequently became *Federation of European Rope and Twine Industries – Fédération européenne des industries de corderie-ficellerie*. Present name adopted 1995, on absorbing *European Association of Netting Manufacturers (EURONEM, inactive)*. EU Transparency Register: 474697531319-18. **Aims** Promote dialogue and exchange in fields of common interest between industries; defend EU members against unfair competition; study and solve common problems; gather and disseminate publicly available technical information between members. **Structure** General Assembly; Board; Technical Committee; TWGs (3); EU Liaison Committee. Product Committees (3): Rope; Agriculture; Netting Fishing and Aquaculture. Raschel Net. Shares common premises and secretariat with: *European Federation of Steel Wire Rope Industries (EWRIS, #07221)*. **Languages** English. **Staff** 1.00 FTE, paid. **Finance** Members' dues. **Activities** Events/meetings; knowledge management/information dissemination. **Events** *Annual Meeting* Brussels (Belgium) 2018, *Congress* Porto (Portugal) 2016, *Congress* Atlanta, GA (USA) 2015, *Congress* Bratislava (Slovakia) 2014, *Congress* Dublin (Ireland) 2013. **Publications** *EUROCORD Newsletter*.
Members Active; Associate; Corresponding, Affiliate. National associations and/or companies in 23 countries:
Argentina, Austria, Belgium, Brazil, China, Czechia, Denmark, Finland, France, Germany, Greece, Iceland, Italy, Japan, Netherlands, Norway, Poland, Portugal, Spain, Switzerland, Türkiye, UK, USA.
Consultative Status Consultative status granted from: *ECOSOC (#05331)* (Ros C); *UNCTAD (#20285)* (Special Category); *FAO (#09260)* (Liaison Status). **IGO Relations** Accredited by: *United Nations Office at Vienna (UNOV, #20604)*. Associated with Department of Global Communications of the United Nations. **NGO Relations** Member of (4): *AEGIS Europe*; *Circular Plastics Alliance (#03936)*; *EURATEX – The European Apparel and Textile Confederation (EURATEX, #05616)*; *Industry4Europe (#11181)*. [2020/XD0962/t/**D**]

- ♦ Fédération européenne des industries du jouet – jeux, jouets, puériculture (inactive)

♦ Fédération européenne des industries de porcelaine et de faïence de table et d'ornementation (FEPF) 09574

European Federation of the Industries of Earthenware and China Tableware and Ornamental Ware – Europäischer Verband der Industrien von Porzellan- Steingut- Geschirr- und Zierkeramik

Coordinator Rue Belliard 12, 1040 Brussels, Belgium. T. +3228083880. Fax +3225115174. E-mail: sec@cerameunie.eu.
URL: http://www.cerameunie.eu/

History 20 Oct 1958, Paris (France). **Aims** Promote the interests of the European earthenware and *porcelain* industry. **Structure** General Assembly (meets twice a year). President; Secretariat, headed by Secretary-General. Committees (3): Steering; Technical; Economic and Social. **Languages** English, French, German. **Finance** Members' dues. **Activities** Matters currently dealt with: standardization; WTO Eastern Europe, China, protection of marks and designs, health and safety standards; environmental issues. **Events** *European Ceramic Days* Brussels (Belgium) 2019, *Meeting* Brussels (Belgium) 2010, *Meeting* Burton on Trent (UK) 2008, *Meeting* Paris (France) 2007, *Meeting* Wroclaw (Poland) 2006. **Publications** *Courrier*.
Members National associations and firms. Members in 7 countries:
France, Germany, Italy, Luxembourg, Portugal, Russia, UK.
NGO Relations Member of: *European Ceramic Industry Association (CERAME-UNIE, #06506)*; *Industry4Europe (#11181)*. In liaison with technical committees of: *International Organization for Standardization (ISO, #14473)*. [2017/XD0754/t/**D**]

- ♦ Fédération européenne de l'industrie du sport (#09552)
- ♦ Fédération européenne des industries de serrures de sécurité (#07708)
- ♦ Fédération européenne des industries techniques de l'image et du son (inactive)
- ♦ Fédération européenne d'informatique médicale / see European Federation for Medical Informatics (#07164)
- ♦ Fédération européenne des institutions d'épargne et de crédit ou de crédit différé pour la construction / see European Federation of Building Societies (#07064)
- ♦ Fédération européenne des institutions linguistiques nationales / see European Federation of National Institutions for Language (#07172)
- ♦ Fédération européenne des instituts de dirigeants financiers (#07124)
- ♦ Fédération européenne pour l'interdiction des armes nucléaires (inactive)
- ♦ Fédération européenne and internationale des industries de la pierre naturelle (#07587)

♦ Fédération européenne et internationale des patrons prothésistes dentaires (FEPPD) 09575

Federation of European and International Dental Technician Laboratory Owners – Europäischer Verband Selbstständiger Zahntechniker Labor Einhaber

Main Office 2-4 Rond-point Schuman, Etage 6 / Boîte 6, 1040 Brussels, Belgium.
Facebook: https://www.facebook.com/feppd
History 17 May 1953. Former names and other names: *Fédération internationale de la prothèse dentaire* – former (17 May 1953 to 1974); *Fédération internationale des patrons prothésistes dentaires (FIPPD)* – former (1974 to 27 Jan 1983); *Federation of European Self Employed Dental Technicians and Dental Laboratory Owners* – former (27 Jan 1983); *Federation of European Dental Laboratory Owners* – former; *Fédération européenne des patrons prothésistes dentaires (FEPPD)* – former; *Europäischer Verband selbstständiger Zahntechniker* – former. Registration: Luxembourg. **Aims** Represent and promote professional interests of independent dental technicians at European and international levels; represent interests of member federations and their members to international authorities and organizations; develop and maintain relations between associations of dental technicians and dental surgeons in the spirit of collaboration and mutual understanding. **Structure** General Meeting (annual); Council; Expert and Working Groups. **Languages** English, French, German. **Staff** 1.00 FTE, paid. **Finance** Members' dues. **Events** *General Assembly* Kirchberg (Luxembourg) 2014, *General Assembly* Brussels (Belgium) 2013, *General Assembly* Nice (France) 2012, *General Assembly* Venice (Italy) 2011, *General Assembly* Brussels (Belgium) 2010. **Publications** *eU-News* – online.
Members National federations of 18 countries:
Austria, Belgium, Croatia, Czechia, Denmark, Finland, France, Greece, Hungary, Italy, Luxembourg, Malta, Netherlands, Norway, Slovakia, Slovenia, Sweden, Switzerland.
NGO Relations Member of: *SMEunited (#19327).* [2021/XD0970/**D**]

- Fédération européenne des jeunesses libérales et radicales (inactive)
- Fédération européenne des journalistes (#07152)
- Fédération européenne des juges administratifs (#02497)
- Fédération européenne du lobbying et public affairs / see Society of European Affairs Professionals (#19553)
- Fédération européenne des logiciels de loisirs (#11380)
- Fédération européenne de lutte contre les très haute tensions (no recent information)
- Fédération européenne des maîtres ramoneurs (#05761)
- Fédération européenne des managers commerciaux (internationally oriented national body)
- Fédération européenne des mandataires de l'industrie en propriété industrielle (#07042)
- Fédération Européenne de la Manutention (#07752)
- Fédération européenne du marché de l'art (no recent information)
- Fédération européenne du marketing direct (inactive)
- Fédération européenne de médecine interne (#07147)
- Fédération européenne de médecine physique et réadaptation / see European Society of Physical and Rehabilitation Medicine (#08706)
- Fédération européenne des médecins de collectivité / see European Federation of Salaried Doctors (#07209)
- Fédération européenne des médecins de collectivités (inactive)
- Fédération européenne des médecins salariés (#07209)
- Fédération européenne de la métallurgie des poudres / see European Powder Metallurgy Association (#08260)
- Fédération européenne des métallurgistes (inactive)

♦ Fédération Européenne pour les Métiers du Patrimoine Bâti (FEMP) 09576

European Federation for Architectural Heritage Skills
Sec AWAP – Ctr des métiers du patrimoine "La Paix Dieu", Rue Paix-Dieu 1b, 4540 Amay, Belgium. T. +3285410354.
URL: https://femp.jimdofree.com/
History 12 Jan 2012, Amay (Belgium). Set up to continue the work of *Associates of the European Foundation for Heritage Skills (inactive).* Registration: No/ID: 0501.946.492, Start date: 13 Dec 2012, Belgium. **Aims** Support and develop traditional know-how and skills involved in heritage crafts and professions. **Structure** General Assembly; Board of Directors. **Finance** Sources: members' dues.
Members Full in 10 countries:
Belgium, Croatia, France, Germany, Italy, Netherlands, Romania, Spain, Switzerland, UK.
European Maritime Heritage (EMH, #07741).
NGO Relations Member of (1): *European Heritage Alliance 3.3 (#07477).* [2018/AA0960/**D**]

- Fédération européenne du mobilier de bureau (#08109)
- Fédération européenne des motels (inactive)
- Fédération européenne motocycliste (inactive)
- Fédération européenne des moyennes et grandes entreprises de distribution (inactive)
- Fédération Européenne de Naturopathie Vitaliste (unconfirmed)
- Fédération européenne du négoce de l'ameublement (#07132)
- Fédération européenne du négoce de bois (inactive)
- Fédération européenne du nettoyage industriel / see European Cleaning and Facility Services Industry (#06571)
- Fédération européenne des organisations des détaillants en tabacs / see European Confederation of Tobacco Retailers (#06725)
- Fédération européenne des organisations de physique médicale (#07183)
- Fédération européenne de panneaux à base de bois (#08137)
- Fédération européenne des parasitologistes (#07186)
- Fédération européenne des parcs d'attractions (inactive)

♦ Fédération Européenne des Parents d'Enfants Déficients Auditifs (FEPEDA) 09577

European Federation of Parents of Hearing Impaired Children – Federación Europea de Padres de Niños con Discapacidad Auditiva – Europäischer Verband der Eltern Hörgeschädigter Kinder
Secretariat c/o FIAPAS, Pantoja 5 – local, 28002 Madrid, Spain. E-mail: contact@fepeda.eu.
URL: http://www.fepeda.eu/
History Founded 23 Jun 1990, Luxembourg, at founding meeting, following efforts of a team lead by Fin Colov. Statutes registered in Luxembourg, 5 Jul 1991. **Aims** Represent associations of parents and friends of deaf and hard-of-hearing children at a European level. **Structure** General Assembly (annual); Management Committee; Bureau. **Languages** English, French, German, Spanish. **Staff** 1.00 FTE, voluntary. **Finance** Members' dues. Other sources: national subventions; European Union subvention. **Activities** Events/meetings; training/education. Management of treaties and agreements: *European Charter of Parents' Rights*, adopted at Annual Assembly, 2004, Garphyttan (Sweden). **Events** *Annual General Assembly* Bucharest (Romania) 2018, *Annual General Assembly* Madrid (Spain) 2014, *Annual Family Meeting* Turku (Finland) 2011, *Annual Family Meeting* Carlingford (Ireland) 2007, *Annual general assembly* Garphyttan (Sweden) 2004.
Members Founding; Full; Associate; Observing. National associations in 27 countries:
Austria, Belarus, Belgium, Bulgaria, Czechia, Denmark, Estonia, Finland, France, Germany, Greece, Iceland, Ireland, Italy, Latvia, Lithuania, Luxembourg, Netherlands, Poland, Portugal, Romania, Russia, Slovakia, Spain, Sweden, Switzerland, UK.
NGO Relations Member of: *European Disability Forum (EDF, #06929).* [2018/XD2944/**D**]

- Fédération Européenne des Parfumeurs Détaillants (#07206)
- Fédération européenne de parodontologie (#07190)
- Fédération européenne des patrons prothésistes dentaires / see Fédération européenne et internationale des patrons prothésistes dentaires (#09575)
- Fédération européenne du personnel d'encadrement des productions, des industries, des commerces et des organismes agroalimentaires (inactive)
- Fédération européenne du personnel des services publics (#07106)
- Fédération européenne des personnes âgées (#05597)
- Fédération européenne des petits mutilés de guerre (inactive)
- Fédération Européenne de Photocatalyse (#08203)
- Fédération européenne des pilotes de ligne (inactive)
- Fédération européenne de planification stratégique (no recent information)
- Fédération européenne des plats frais refrigérés (#06535)
- Fédération européenne des PME du funéraire (no recent information)
- Fédération européenne des PME de haute technologie (no recent information)
- Fédération Européenne du Portage Salarial (unconfirmed)
- Fédération européenne des ports intérieurs (#07144)
- Fédération européenne des press clubs (#07194)
- Fédération européenne des press clubs et centres internationaux de presse / see European Federation of Press Clubs (#07194)
- Fédération européenne de la presse gratuite (inactive)
- Fédération européenne des producteurs et applicateurs de produits spéciaux pour structures / see Experts for Specialised Construction and Concrete Systems (#09226)
- Fédération européenne des producteurs aquacoles / see Federation of European Aquaculture Producers (#09491)
- Fédération européenne des producteurs autonomes et des consommateurs industriels d'énergie (inactive)

♦ Fédération européenne des producteurs d'enveloppes (FEPE) 09578

European Envelope Manufacturers Association – Europäische Vereinigung der Briefumschlagfabrikanten
Dir Av Louise 250, Bte 81, 1050 Brussels, Belgium. T. +3227794001. E-mail: info@fepe.org – secretariat@fepe.org.
URL: http://www.fepe.org/
History 1957. Current statutes adopted, 20 Sep 2007. Originally registered in accordance with Swiss civil code. Former names and other names: *Fédération européenne des fabricants d'enveloppes* – former. Registration: Banque-Carrefour des Entreprises, No/ID: 0889.632.530, Start date: 24 May 2007, Belgium; EU Transparency Register, No/ID: 221411241881-16, Start date: 18 Mar 2021. **Aims** Promote the interests of envelope manufacturers in Europe; coordinate industry-good activities; represent FEPE towards authorities, other associations and the general public. **Structure** General Meeting (annual); Board. **Languages** English. **Staff** 1.00 FTE, paid. **Finance** Sources: members' dues. **Events** *Annual Congress* Ljubljana (Slovenia) 2022, *Annual Congress* Brussels (Belgium) 2021, *Annual Congress* Porto (Portugal) 2019, *Annual Congress* Tallinn (Estonia) 2018, *Annual Congress* Marseille (France) 2017.
Members Envelope manufacturers; supply industry (affiliate members). Members in 31 countries:
Austria, Belgium, Bulgaria, Croatia, Czechia, Denmark, Finland, France, Germany, Greece, Ireland, Israel, Italy, Lithuania, Luxembourg, Netherlands, Norway, Poland, Portugal, Romania, Russia, Serbia, Slovakia, Slovenia, Spain, Sweden, Switzerland, UK, Ukraine, United Arab Emirates, USA.
NGO Relations Member of (1): *Industry4Europe (#11181).* Cooperates with: *Association of European Public Postal Operators (PostEurop, #02534); Comité européen de normalisation (CEN, #04162); Confederation of European Paper Industries (CEPI, #04529); European Commission (EC, #06633); Intergraf (#11505);* EU Ecolabelling Board; Global Envelope Alliance; *International Post Corporation (IPC, #14624); Universal Postal Union (UPU, #20682).* Signatory to Declaration on Paper Recovery, maintained by *European Paper Recycling Council (EPRC, #08139).* [2022/XD1593/**D**]

- Fédération européenne des producteurs de fibres-ciment (#07120)
- Fédération européenne des producteurs de films plastiques (inactive)
- Fédération européenne des producteurs de verre plat / see Glass for Europe (#10157)
- Fédération européenne des professionnels de l'environnement (no recent information)
- Fédération Européenne des Professionnels de la Pédagogie (unconfirmed)
- Fédération européenne des professionnels du tourisme chinois (unconfirmed)
- Fédération européenne des professions du spectacle (inactive)
- Fédération européenne pour la promotion de l'agriculture durable (#06743)
- Fédération européenne pour la promotion et l'insertion par le logement et son environnement (inactive)
- Fédération européenne pour la promotion des marchés publics – textiles et cuir (inactive)
- Fédération européenne de promotion des transports par voie navigable / see Inland Navigation Europe (#11216)
- Fédération européenne pour la promotion de vente / see Integrated Marketing Communications Council of Europe (#11369)
- Fédération européenne de la propriété immobilière (#08286)
- Fédération européenne pour la protection des eaux (inactive)
- Fédération européenne des protéines végétales / see European Vegetable Protein Association (#09047)
- Fédération européenne de psychanalyse (#08292)
- Fédération européenne de psychanalyse et Ecole psychanalytique de Strasbourg (internationally oriented national body)
- Fédération européenne de psychologie des sports et des activités corporelles (#07218)

♦ Fédération européenne de psychothérapie socio- et somato-analytique 09579

Dir c/o EEPSSA, 42 rue du Général de Gaulle, 67640 Lipsheim, France. T. +33388685654. Fax +33388685655.
URL: http://www.eepssa.org/
History 2000, Dresden (Germany). **Aims** Train psychotherapists. **Structure** General Assembly (every 2 years at Congress). **Languages** French. **Staff** 3.00 FTE, paid; 1.00 FTE, voluntary. **Finance** Members' dues. Budget (annual): euro 10,000. **Activities** Provides professional training in 12 schools; organizes *'Congrès International de Somatoanalyse'.* **Events** *Congrès international / Congress* Paris (France) 2014, *Congrès international* Budapest (Hungary) 2010, *Congrès international de psychothérapie socio- et somato-analytique* Paris (France) 2010, *Congress* Strasbourg (France) 2010, *Congrès international* Bucharest (Romania) 2009.
Members Founding; Associate. Schools (16) in 13 countries:
Belgium, Cameroon, Denmark, France, Germany, Hungary, India, Moldova, Morocco, Poland, Romania, Switzerland, Tunisia.
NGO Relations *Ecole européenne de psychothérapie socio- et somato-analytique, Strasbourg (EEPSSA); European Federation for Somato-Psychotherapy (EFSP, no recent information); International Association of Somatotherapy (IAS, no recent information).* [2019/XD8391/**D**]

- Fédération européenne de la publicité extérieure / see World Out of Home Organization (#21702)
- Fédération européenne de la publicité lumineuse / see European Sign Federation (#08485)
- Fédération européenne des radios libres (inactive)
- Fédération Européenne de la Randonnée Pédestre (#08328)
- Fédération européenne des réalisateurs de l'audiovisuel (#09541)
- Fédération Européenne de Recherche sur l'Éducation et l'Écologie de la Personne et de ses Applications Sociales (internationally oriented national body)
- Fédération européenne de recherche sur le SIDA (inactive)
- Fédération Européenne des Recycleurs de Verre (#07134)
- Fédération européenne des réseaux de coopération scientifique et technique de coordination (#07114)
- Fédération européenne de la restauration collective sous-traitée / see FoodServiceEurope (#09851)

♦ Fédération européenne des retraités et des personnes âgées (FERPA) 09580

European Federation of Retired and Elderly Persons
SG c/o CES, Boulevard Roi Albert II 5, 1210 Brussels, Belgium. T. +3222240576. Fax +3222240567.
Assistant to SG address not obtained. T. +3222240442.
URL: http://www.ferpa.online/
History 29 Apr 1993, Madrid (Spain). Founded 29-30 Apr 1993, Madrid (Spain), at founding congress, when constitution, Charter and programme were adopted. Derives from a *Comité de coordination des travailleurs retraités (CCTR)*, following decision adopted, Dec 1991, Amsterdam (Netherlands), by Executive Committee of *European Trade Union Confederation (ETUC, #08927)*, and new structure presented, Jun 1992, Geneva (Switzerland). **Aims** Represent retired and elderly people in dialogue with European institutions; protect retired

workers in harmony with ETUC, within the framework of social dialogue and at a political and institutional level. **Structure** Executive Committee (meets twice a year); Steering Committee; Women's Committee (meets annually). **Languages** English, French, German. **Staff** 1.00 FTE, paid. **Finance** Members' dues. **Events** *Quadrennial Congress* Venice (Italy) 2011, *Quadrennial Congress* Brussels (Belgium) 2007, *Quadrennial Congress* Rome (Italy) 2003, *Quadrennial Congress* Rome (Italy) 2003, *World NGO forum on ageing* Madrid (Spain) 2002. **Publications** Annual Report; congress reports; reports on pensions, health, dependent persons, etc.
Members National organizations of retired people (members of ETUC) in 23 countries:
Austria, Belgium, Cyprus, Denmark, Finland, France, Germany, Greece, Hungary, Ireland, Italy, Luxembourg, Malta, Netherlands, Norway, Poland, Portugal, Romania, Spain, Sweden, Switzerland, UK.
NGO Relations Member of: *Permanent Forum of European Civil Society (#18322).* [2017/XD3364/**E**]

- ♦ Fédération européenne de risk management (#09539)
- ♦ Fédération européenne de la salmoniculture / see Federation of European Aquaculture Producers (#09491)
- ♦ Fédération européenne de la santé animale (inactive)

♦ Fédération européenne pour la santé animale et la sécurité sanitaire (FESASS) 09581

European Federation for Animal Health and Sanitary Security – Europäische Vereinigung für Tiergesundheit und Gesundheitliche Sicherheit – Federazione Europea della Sanità Animale e della Sicurezza Sanitaria – Europese Federatie voor Dierengezondheid en Sanitaire Veiligheid
Pres Place du Nouveau Marché aux Grains 21, 1000 Brussels, Belgium. T. +3227594407. E-mail: fesass@fesass.eu.
Contact 37 rue de Lyon, 75000 Paris, France.
URL: http://www.fesass.eu/
History Founded Dec 2001. Previously also known under the acronym *EFAHSS*. **Aims** Improve animal health and welfare by: promoting effective measures of animal health management; developing and implementing coordinated, systemic control and eradication programmes for significant animal diseases; promoting uniform standards and equivalencies of guarantees for certification of animal health status. **Structure** General Assembly (annual). Executive Committee. **Languages** English, French. **Staff** 1.00 FTE, paid. **Finance** Members' dues. **Activities** Events/meetings. **Events** *General Assembly* Brussels (Belgium) 2020, *General Assembly* Brussels (Belgium) 2019.
Members Full in 10 countries:
Austria, Belgium, France, Germany, Ireland, Italy, Luxembourg, Netherlands, Portugal, Spain. [2020.03.06/XD8677/**D**]

- ♦ Fédération européenne des sciences sociales (no recent information)
- ♦ Fédération européenne de la sécurité routière (inactive)
- ♦ Fédération européenne des services en efficacité et intelligence énergétique (#07145)
- ♦ Fédération européenne des Services à la personne (#07212)
- ♦ Fédération Européenne des Sites Clunisiens (internationally oriented national body)
- ♦ Fédération européenne des sites fortifiés (#07127)
- ♦ Fédération européenne des sociétés d'acoustique (inactive)
- ♦ Fédération européenne des sociétés d'activité chrétienne (inactive)
- ♦ Fédération européenne des sociétés de chirurgie et de rééducation de la main / see Federation of the European Societies for Surgery of the Hand (#09549)
- ♦ Fédération européenne des sociétés de cytologie (#07097)
- ♦ Fédération Européenne des Sociétés d'Ergonomie (#09504)
- ♦ Fédération européenne des sociétés d'immunologie (#07142)
- ♦ Fédération européenne de sociétés pour la médecine et la biologie des ultra-sons (#07217)
- ♦ Fédération européenne des sociétés de microbiologie (#09516)
- ♦ Fédération européenne des sociétés de microchirurgie (#07216)
- ♦ Fédération européenne des sociétés nationales de chirurgie esthétiques (inactive)
- ♦ Fédération européenne des sociétés nationales d'entretien (#07173)
- ♦ Fédération européenne des sociétés de nutrition (#09524)
- ♦ Fédération européenne des sociétés de toxicologie (inactive)
- ♦ Fédération européenne du soudage, de l'assemblage et du coupage (#07233)
- ♦ Fédération européenne des spécialistes du minage (#07117)
- ♦ Fédération européenne des sports corporatifs (#07083)
- ♦ Fédération européenne des statisticiens de l'industrie pharmaceutique (#07220)
- ♦ Fédération européenne de surf (#08860)
- ♦ Fédération européenne des syndicats de la chimie et des industries diverses (inactive)
- ♦ Fédération européenne des syndicats chrétiens de mineurs (inactive)
- ♦ Fédération européenne des syndicats chrétiens d'ouvriers du bâtiment et du bois (inactive)

♦ Fédération européenne des syndicats d'entreprises d'isolation (FESI) 09582

European Federation of Associations of Insulation Contractors – Europäische Vereinigung der Verbände der Isolierunternehmungen – Federazione Europea delle Associazioni di Isolamento
SG TICA House, 34 Allington Way, Darlington, DL1 4QB, UK. T. +441325734140 – +441325466704.
URL: http://www.fesi.eu/
History 1970, Paris (France). **Aims** Represent firms concerned with thermal insulation, soundproofing, cold store and fire-proofing. **Languages** English, German. **Staff** 2.00 FTE, paid. **Events** *WIACO biennial congress / Biennial Congress* Paris (France) 2012, *World Congress* Dubrovnik (Croatia) 2006, *WIACO biennial congress / World Congress / Biennial Congress* Barcelona (Spain) 2004, *World Congress* Wiesbaden (Germany) 2002, *WIACO biennial congress / World Congress / Biennial Congress* Orlando, FL (USA) 2000. **Publications** *FESI Document* – series. *FESI Insulation Technical Lexicon* in Croatian, Dutch, English, French, German, Italian, Serbian, Spanish, Swedish.
Members National organizations in 17 countries:
Austria, Croatia, Denmark, Finland, France, Germany, Greece, Hungary, Italy, Lithuania, Netherlands, Norway, Poland, Spain, Sweden, Switzerland, UK.
IGO Relations Recognized by: *European Commission (EC, #06633).* **NGO Relations** In liaison with technical committees of: *International Organization for Standardization (ISO, #14473).* Instrumental in setting up: *European Industrial Insulation Foundation (EiiF, #07527); World Insulation and Acoustics Congress Organization (WIACO, #21591).* [2018.10.18/XD5743/**D**]

- ♦ Fédération européenne des syndicats de fabricants de jouets (inactive)
- ♦ Fédération européenne des syndicats de fabricants de menuiseries du bâtiment (inactive)
- ♦ Fédération européenne des syndicats de fabricants de panneaux de particules (inactive)
- ♦ Fédération européenne des syndicats de fabricants de parquets / see European Federation of the Parquet Industry (#07188)
- ♦ Fédération européenne des syndicats des mines, de la chimie et de l'energie (inactive)
- ♦ Fédération européenne des syndicats des secteurs de l'alimentation, de l'agriculture et du tourisme et des branches connexes / see European Federation of Food, Agriculture and Tourism Trade Unions (#07125)
- ♦ Fédération européenne de timeshare / see Resort Development Organisation (#18913)
- ♦ Fédération européenne du traitement de l'eau / see European Water and Wastewater Industry Association (#09087)
- ♦ Fédération européenne des transformateurs de tabac (#07227)
- ♦ Fédération européenne pour le transport et l'environnement (#07230)
- ♦ Fédération européenne des transports aériens privés (inactive)
- ♦ Fédération européenne des travailleurs de l'agriculture (inactive)
- ♦ Fédération européenne de travailleurs de l'alimentation et industries connexes – OE/CMT (inactive)
- ♦ Fédération européenne des travailleurs du bâtiment et du bois (#07065)
- ♦ Fédération européenne des travailleurs du bâtiment et du bois dans la CEE / see European Federation of Building and Woodworkers (#07065)
- ♦ Fédération Européenne des Travailleurs des Transports (#08941)
- ♦ Fédération européenne des unions professionelles de fleuristes / see International Florist Organisation (#13616)
- ♦ Fédération européenne des unions professionnelles d'experts en dommages après incendie et risques divers (#07158)
- ♦ Fédération européenne des usagers de la médecine naturelle (no recent information)
- ♦ Fédération européenne du velours (inactive)
- ♦ Fédération européenne pour la vente et le service à domicile / see European Direct Selling Association (#06928)

♦ Fédération européenne du verre d'emballage (FEVE) 09583

European Container Glass Federation – Federación Europea de Envases de Vidrio – Europäischer Behälterglasindustrie-Verband
SG Av Louise 89, Boîte 4, 1050 Brussels, Belgium. T. +3225360080. Fax +3225393752. E-mail: secretariat@feve.org.
URL: http://www.feve.org/
History 26 Sep 1977. Registration: Banque-Carrefour des Entreprises, No/ID: 0417.651.811, Start date: 22 Nov 1977, Belgium; EU Transparency Register, No/ID: 1550133398-72, Start date: 15 Sep 2008. **Aims** Represent at international level, from economic and technical points of view, the common interests of the container glass and mechanical glass *tableware* industry. **Structure** Annual General Meeting; Board of Directors; Permanent and Ad-hoc Committees; Working Groups of Experts. **Languages** English, French. **Staff** 5.00 FTE, paid. **Finance** Sources: members' dues. **Activities** Advocacy/lobbying/activism. **Publications** *The Gob* (annual); *FEVE News* (11 a year).
Members Companies in 22 countries:
Austria, Belgium, Bulgaria, Croatia, Czechia, Denmark, Estonia, France, Germany, Greece, Hungary, Italy, Netherlands, Poland, Portugal, Romania, Slovakia, Spain, Sweden, Switzerland, Türkiye, UK.
IGO Relations Recognized by: *European Commission (EC, #06633); European Parliament (EP, #08146).* **NGO Relations** Member of: *AEGIS Europe; European Food Sustainable Consumption and Production Round Table (European Food SCP Roundtable, #07289); European Network on Silica (NEPSI, #08001); Federation of European and International Associations Established in Belgium (FAIB, #09508); Glass Alliance Europe (#10156); Industry4Europe (#11181).* Partner of: *Wine in Moderation (WIM, #20967).* Regular contacts with: *International Technical Centre for Bottling and Packaging (#15667); BUSINESSEUROPE (#03381).* Contacts on packaging waste problems with various organizations, including: *Association of Plastics Manufacturers in Europe (Plastics Europe, #02862); FoodDrinkEurope (#09841); European Aluminium (#05893); European Brands Association (#06397).* [2021.03.12/XD1028/t/**D**]

- ♦ Fédération européenne des vétérans de guerre / see Confédération Européenne des Anciens Combattants (#04537)
- ♦ Fédération européenne des vétérinaires de l'industrie et de la recherche / see European Association of Veterinarians in Education, Research and Industry (#06267)
- ♦ Fédération Européenne des Victimes de la Route (#07207)
- ♦ Fédération européenne des villes de congrès (inactive)
- ♦ Fédération européenne des voyageurs (#08162)
- ♦ Fédération européenne de zoologie (inactive)
- ♦ Fédération européenne de zootechnie (#07046)
- ♦ Fédération Européen des Races Bovines de L'Arc Alpin (#05752)
- ♦ Fédération d'Europe des entraîneurs d'athlétisme (#06292)
- ♦ Fédération des experts-comptables européens / see Accountancy Europe (#00061)

♦ Fédération des experts comptables méditerranéens (FCM) 09584

Federation of Mediterranean Certified Accountants
SG c/o CNDCEC, Piazza de la Repubblica 59, 00185 Rome RM, Italy. T. +396699221120. Fax +39662209128. E-mail: secretariat@fcmweb.org.
URL: http://www.fcmweb.org/
History 28 Oct 1999, Rome (Italy). **Aims** Promote cooperation among professional accountancy bodies in the region, both in the private and in the public sectors; share knowledge and provide technical assistance to members to help them achieve and maintain high professional and quality assurance standards. **Structure** General Assembly (annually). Council, consisting of one representative from each member institute. Executive, comprising President, Deputy President and up to 8 Vice-Presidents. **Events** *Digital Conference* Rome (Italy) 2020, *Conference* Tirana (Albania) 2013, *Conference* Nicosia (Cyprus) 2012, *Conference* Rome (Italy) 2010, *Conference* Athens (Greece) 2007.
Members Institutes (21) in 16 countries:
Albania, Bulgaria, Cyprus, Egypt, France, Greece, Israel, Italy, Kosovo, Malta, Morocco, Romania, Serbia, Spain, Tunisia, Türkiye.
Associate members (2):
Association of Chartered Certified Accountants (ACCA); Fédération internationale des experts-comptables francophones (FIDEF, #09630).
NGO Relations Memorandum of Understanding with: *European Federation of Accountants and Auditors for SMEs (EFAA, #07037).* Affiliated to: *International Federation of Accountants (IFAC, #13335).* [2020/XD8343/**D**]

- ♦ Fédération des exportateurs d'Amérique latine et des Caraïbes (inactive)
- ♦ Federation of Export Chambers of Central America and the Caribbean (#09293)
- ♦ Fédération des fabricants européens de matériaux de friction (#09512)
- ♦ Federation of Fairs and Trade Shows of Benelux (inactive)
- ♦ Fédération des familles pour la paix mondiale / see Family Federation for World Peace and Unification

♦ Federation of Family History Societies (FFHS) 09585

Admin PO Box 62, Sheringham, NR26 9AR, UK. E-mail: admin@ffhs.org.uk.
URL: http://www.ffhs.org.uk/
History 1974, UK. Granted charitable status in 1982. UK Registered Charity: 1038721. **Aims** Coordinate and assist the work of societies or other bodies interested in family history, *genealogy* and *heraldry*; foster mutual cooperation and regional projects in these subjects. **Structure** Board of trustees. **Languages** English. **Finance** Members' dues. **Activities** Knowledge management/information dissemination; training/education; events/meetings. **Events** *Half-yearly meeting* Coventry (UK) 2004, *Half-yearly meeting* Loughborough (UK) 2004, *Half-yearly meeting* Colchester (UK) 2003, *Half-yearly meeting* Exeter (UK) 2003, *Half-yearly meeting* Warwick (UK) 2002. **Publications** *FFHS Ezine* (7 a year).
Members Family history societies (about 180) in 6 countries:
Australia, Canada, Ireland, New Zealand, UK, USA. [2018.06.01/XF4203/**F**]

- ♦ Fédération des femmes africaines spécialistes des médias (no recent information)
- ♦ Federation of Field Sports Associations of the EC / see Federation of Associations for Hunting and Conservation of the EU (#09459)
- ♦ Federation of Field Sports Associations of the EU / see Federation of Associations for Hunting and Conservation of the EU (#09459)
- ♦ Federation of Film and Audiovisual Composers of Europe (inactive)
- ♦ Fédération des foires et salons du Benelux (inactive)
- ♦ Fédération des Fonctionnaires Internationaux des Nations Unies (#20579)
- ♦ Fédération de la fonction publique européenne (#06567)
- ♦ Fédération des fondations du développement de l'Amérique centrale (inactive)
- ♦ Fédération des fondations pour la santé mondiale (inactive)
- ♦ Fédération forestière nordique (no recent information)
- ♦ Fédération et Forum Européens pour l'Ostéopathie (#07128)
- ♦ Fédération française de la photocatalyse / see European Photocatalysis Federation (#08203)
- ♦ Fédération du français universel (inactive)

♦ Fédération francophone des amis de l'orgue (FFAO) 09586

Francophone Federation of Friends of the Organ
Registered seat 13 rue de Balzac, 93600 Aulnay-sous-Bois, France. E-mail: ffao@ffao.com.
URL: http://www.ffao.com/

History 1 Dec 1983. Registered in accordance with French law: JO 1983/12/13. **Aims** Promote the use of the *pipe organ*. **Structure** Administration Council; Board of Directors. **Languages** French. **Staff** Voluntary. **Finance** Members' dues. **Events** *Assemblée Générale* Bondues (France) 2022, *Assemblée Générale* Paris (France) 2022, *Annual Conference* France 2014, *Annual Conference* Saint-Étienne (France) 2013, *Annual Conference* Saint-Étienne (France) 2013. **Publications** *Orgue francophone En Bref* (4 a year); *Revue Orgue francophone* (2 a year).
Members Full in 21 countries:
Australia, Austria, Belgium, Brazil, Canada, Denmark, France, Germany, Italy, Japan, Luxembourg, Netherlands, New Zealand, Norway, Poland, Romania, Spain, Sweden, Switzerland, UK, USA.
IGO Relations French Ministry of Culture. [2020.03.05/XD6957/**D**]

♦ Fédération francophone et germanophone des associations de coopération au développement (ACODEV) 09587

Main Office Quai du Commerce, 9, 1000 Brussels, Belgium. T. +3222198855. E-mail: info@acodev.be.
URL: http://www.acodev.be/

History 1 Oct 1997, Belgium. Founded by merger of *Fédération francophone des ONG d'envoi de coopérants ONG (CODEF, inactive)* and *Association des ONG francophones et germanophones pour la coopération avec le Tiers-monde (ADO, inactive)*. Registration: Banque-Carrefour des Entreprises, Belgium. **Aims** Represent and promote interests of member *nongovernmental organizations* with public authorities and funding organizations; offer services to the members to help them improve the quality of their work. **Structure** General Assembly; Administrative Council, comprising President and 15 members; Secretariat, headed by Secretary-General; Work Groups. **Languages** French. **Staff** 12.00 FTE, paid. **Finance** Sources: government support. Mainly funded by Belgian government. Annual budget: 800,000 EUR. **Activities** Events/meetings; knowledge management/information dissemination; networking/liaising. **Events** *Assemblée générale* Brussels (Belgium) 2022, *Assemblée générale* Brussels (Belgium) 2006. **Publications** *ACODEV actualités* – electronic newsletter.
Members National and international organizations; individual (1), based in Belgium, including 62 organizations listed in this Yearbook:
- *ACTEC – Association for Cultural, Technical and Educational Cooperation*;
- *ActionAid France – Peuples Solidaires*;
- *Action pour le développement – SOS Faim (SOS Faim)*;
- *Association des Rotary clubs belges pour la coopération au développement (ARCB-CD)*;
- *Autre Terre (#03044)*;
- *Avocats Sans Frontières (ASF, #03050)*;
- *Brothers to All Men (BAM, #03339)*;
- *Bureau international des Médecins sans frontières (MSF International, #03366)* (Belgian Section);
- *Centre tricontinental (CETRI)*;
- *Chain of Hope – Belgium*;
- *CNCD Opération 11 11 11*;
- *Collectif d'échanges pour la technologie appropriée (COTA)*;
- *Collectif Stratégies Alimentaires (CSA)*;
- *Comité d'aide aux calaminois du Tiers-Monde (CACTM)*;
- *Comité pour l'annulation de la dette du Tiers-monde (CADTM, #04148)*;
- *Commission justice et paix (CJP)*;
- *Conseil des communautés africaines en Europe/Belgique (CCAE/B)*;
- *Cooperation for the Development of the Craft Industry (Codéart)*;
- *Coopération par l'éducation et la culture (CEC)*;
- *Damien Foundation – Voluntary Organization for Leprosy and TB Control (AF)*;
- *Défi Belgique-Afrique (DBA)*;
- *Dienst voor Internationale Samenwerking aan Ontwikkelingsprojecten (DISOP)*;
- *Dynamo International – Street Workers Network*;
- *Echos communication*;
- *Enfance Tiers Monde*;
- *Entraide et fraternité*;
- *Fondation André Ryckmans (FAR)*;
- *Fondation universitaire pour la coopération internationale au développement (FUCID)*;
- *Fonds Ingrid Renard (FIR)*;
- *Friends of the Islands of Peace (Islands of Peace)*;
- *Humanity and Inclusion (HI, #10975)* (Belgian Section);
- *International Relief Service of Caritas Catholica, Belgium (CSI)*;
- *ITECO – Centre de formation pour le développement*;
- *Light for the World (#16474)*;
- *Louvain Coopération*;
- *Max Havelaar Foundation*;
- *Médecins du Monde – International (MDM, #16613)*;
- *Medical Aid for the Third World (G3W)*;
- *MEMISA*;
- *Oxfam Trading*;
- *Partenaire libéral pour le développement (PARTENAIRE)*;
- *Plan International (#18386)* (Belgian Section);
- *Quinoa*;
- *RCN Justice et Démocratie (RCN J&D)*;
- *Red Cross EU Office (#18643)* (Belgian Section);
- *Research Group for an Alternative Economic Strategy (GRESEA)*;
- *Sensorial Handicap Cooperation (SHC)*;
- *Service Civil International (SCI, #19238)* (Belgium);
- *Service d'information et formation Amérique Latine – Tiers Monde (SEDIF)*;
- *Solidarité étudiants du Monde (SETM)*;
- *Solidarité protestante*;
- *Solidarité socialiste – Fonds de coopération au développement (FCD)*;
- *SOS Layettes*;
- SOS Villages d'enfants – Belgium;
- *Soutien aux ONG à l'Est et au Sud (SONGES)*;
- *The World According to Women*;
- *UNICEF (#20332)* (Belgian Committee);
- *Vétérinaires Sans Frontières International (VSF International, #20760)* (Belgian Section);
- *VIA Don Bosco (#20766)*;
- *Viva Africa*;
- World Wildlife Fund Belgium;
- *WSM*.

NGO Relations Member of (1): *Fédération des employeurs ONG (FEONG)*. [2022.02.02/XE3874/y/**E**]

♦ Fédération francophone Internationale de Soins Palliatifs (FISP) . . . 09588

Contact address not obtained. E-mail: ffisp@ffisp.org.
URL: https://www.ffisp.org/

History 2013, Montréal, QC (Canada). Former names and other names: *Fédération Internationale de Soins Palliatifs (FISP)* – former (2017). **Aims** Develop information, training, promotion and research in palliative care in Francophone countries. **Structure** Committee. **Activities** Events/meetings. **Events** *Congress* Dakar (Senegal) 2021, *Congress* Paris (France) 2019, *Congrès International Francophone de Soins Palliatifs* Geneva (Switzerland) 2017, *Congrès International Francophone de Soins Palliatifs* Tunis (Tunisia) 2015, *Congrès International Francophone de Soins Palliatifs* Montréal, QC (Canada) 2013. **Members** Assocations (6). Membership countries not specified. [2020/XM6045/**C**]

- ♦ Fédération fraternelle universelle (inactive)
- ♦ Federation of French-Language Gynecologists and Obstetricians (inactive)

♦ Federation of Gay Games 09589

Co-Pres 584 Castro St, Suite 343, San Francisco CA 94114, USA. T. +18664591261. E-mail: contact@gaygames.net.
Co-Pres address not obtained.
URL: http://www.gaygames.org/

History Founded 1982, as *San Francisco Arts and Athletics*, as the international governing body for the Gay Games. Current title adopted 1989. **Aims** Promote equality through organizing the premier international LGBTQ and gay-friendly sports and cultural event known as the Gay Games. **Structure** Board of Directors; Committees; Task Forces. **Languages** English. **Staff** None. **Finance** Annual budget: about US$ 100,000. **Activities** Events/meetings; awards/prizes/competitions; sporting activities. **Events** *Annual Meeting* Paris (France) 2018, *Annual Meeting* Paris (France) 2017, *Annual Meeting* Sydney, NSW (Australia) 2016, *Annual Meeting* Cleveland, OH (USA) 2014, *Annual Meeting* Cleveland, OH (USA) 2013. **Publications** *Participate* – newsletter. News releases; stories; updates.
Members Organizations (56) in 20 countries and territories:
Argentina, Australia, Brazil, Bulgaria, Canada, China, England, Finland, France, Germany, Ireland, Israel, Mexico, Netherlands, Russia, Scotland, Slovenia, South Africa, Taiwan, USA.
Included in the above, 6 organizations listed in this Yearbook:
International Association of Gay and Lesbian Martial Artists (IAGLMA); *International Front Runners (IFR)*; *International Gay and Lesbian Aquatics (IGLA, #13702)*; *International Gay and Lesbian Football Association (IGLFA, #13703)*; *International Gay Bowling Organization*; *Wrestlers Without Borders*. [2020.03.03/XD6142/y/**D**]

♦ Federation of GCC Chambers (FGCCC) 09590

Contact PO Box 2198, Dammam 31451, Saudi Arabia. E-mail: info@fgccc.org – fgccc@fgccc.org.
URL: http://www.fgccc.org/

History 14 Oct 1979, Kuwait. Founded, and bylaws approved, during 2nd Conference of Arab Gulf Countries' Chambers. Launched in 1980. Former names and other names: *Union of Chambers of Commerce, Industry, and Agriculture of the Arab Gulf States* – former (1979 to 1990); *Federation of GCC Chambers of Commerce, Industry and Agriculture* – full title (1990); *Federation of the Gulf Cooperation Council Chambers* – alias. **Aims** Support and reinforce efforts aimed at integrating and coordinating the GCC states economies in *commerce*, *industry*, agriculture and services, in order to insure their growth and development, and to protect such economies, individually and collectively, from dangers from any source; identify and promote economic and productive capabilities of the GCC states, both within the area and abroad. **Structure** Council, consisting of chairmen of member chambers of commerce and industry and FGCCC Secretary General. General Secretariat, comprising 2 main sections: Economic and Legal Affairs; Administration and Financial. **Languages** Arabic. **Staff** 17.00 FTE, paid. **Finance** Members' dues. **Activities** Advocacy/lobbying/activism; knowledge management/information dissemination; standards/guidelines. **Events** *Mauritania's Livestock Investment Forum* Nouakchott (Mauritania) 2017, *Annual Conference* London (UK) 2002, *Joint INTERPRISE meeting* Dubai (United Arab Emirates) 1999, *Seminar on agriculture and economic development* Muscat (Oman) 1990, *Conference on Gulf chambers of commerce in 1992* Paris (France) 1990. **Publications** Studies; reports; brochures; resolutions and recommendations; working papers of regional conferences and seminars; proceedings of workshops.
Members Chambers of commerce and industry in 6 countries:
Bahrain, Kuwait, Oman, Qatar, Saudi Arabia, United Arab Emirates.
IGO Relations Cooperation agreements with: *Arab Organization for Agricultural Development (AOAD, #01018)*; *Council of Arab Economic Unity (CAEU, #04859)*; *Gulf Cooperation Council (GCC, #10826)*; *Gulf Organization for Industrial Consulting (GOIC, #10837)*; *Islamic Development Bank (IsDB, #16044)*. Memorandum of understanding with: *Council of Arab Ministers for Social and Economic Affairs (#04864)*. **NGO Relations** Through Global Chamber Platform, links with: *Association des chambres de commerce et d'industrie européennes (EUROCHAMBRES, #02423)*. [2021/XD8839/**D**]

- ♦ Federation of GCC Chambers of Commerce, Industry and Agriculture / see Federation of GCC Chambers (#09590)
- ♦ Fédération générale arabe d'assurance / see General Arab Insurance Federation (#10104)
- ♦ Fédération générale des clubs de femmes (internationally oriented national body)
- ♦ Fédération générale des femmes arabes (no recent information)
- ♦ Fédération générale des journalistes arabes / see Federation of Arab Journalists (#09422)

♦ Fédération des géomètres francophone (FGF) 09591

Main Office 40 avenue Hoche, 75008 Paris, France. T. +33153838800. E-mail: fgf@geometres-francophones.org.
URL: http://geometres-francophones.org/

History Constitutive Assembly held 24 Nov 2005, Rabat (Morocco), when statutes were approved. Statues modified 17 May 2011, Marrakech (Morocco) and 22 Oct 2013, Yaoundé (Cameroon). **Structure** General Assembly; Board. **Languages** French. **Activities** Training/education. **Events** *General Assembly* Québec, QC (Canada) 2014.
Members Full in 19 countries:
Algeria, Benin, Burkina Faso, Cameroon, Canada, Central African Rep, Chad, Congo Brazzaville, Congo DR, Côte d'Ivoire, Gabon, Guinea, Madagascar, Mali, Morocco, Niger, Senegal, Togo, Tunisia.
IGO Relations Accredited by (1): *Organisation internationale de la Francophonie (OIF, #17809)*. **NGO Relations** *International Federation of Surveyors (FIG, #13561)*; *Council of European Geodetic Surveyors (#04890)*; *Global Land Tool Network (GLTN, #10452)*; *Union Méditerranéenne des Géomètres (UMG, #20460)*. [2019/XJ9414/**C**]

- ♦ Federation of Global Governments (internationally oriented national body)
- ♦ Federation Global Initiative on Psychiatry / see Human Rights in Mental Health (#10988)
- ♦ Fédération des grandes tours du monde (#21436)
- ♦ Fédération graphique internationale (inactive)
- ♦ Federation of Green Parties of the Americas (#09385)
- ♦ Federation of the Gulf Cooperation Council Chambers / see Federation of GCC Chambers (#09590)
- ♦ Fédération des gynécologues et obstétriciens de langue française (inactive)
- ♦ Fédération haltérophile du Commonwealth (#04368)
- ♦ Fédération haltérophile internationale / see International Weightlifting Federation (#15876)

♦ Federation of Harley-Davidson Clubs of Europe (FH-DCE) 09592

Sec Vanhankyläntie 16, Pernajan Vanhakylä, FI-07740 Lovisa, Uusimaa, Finland. T. +358405597757. E-mail: info@fhdce.eu.
Treas address not obtained. E-mail: treasurer@fhdce.eu.
URL: http://www.fhdce.eu/

History 1991. Accepted as a *European Economic Interest Grouping (EEIG, #06960)*, 2002. Registration: Start date: 2019, Switzerland. **Aims** Solidify, consolidate and promote links and contacts between Harley-Davidson Clubs in Europe in accordance with the existing customs and traditions of the Harley-Davidson riders. **Languages** English. **Staff** None paid. **Activities** Networking/liaising.
Members Clubs (120), gathering some 38,000 individuals, in 26 countries:
Austria, Belgium, Bulgaria, Cyprus, Czechia, Denmark, Estonia, Finland, France, Germany, Greece, Iceland, Ireland, Italy, Lithuania, Luxembourg, Malta, Netherlands, Norway, Poland, Russia, Slovakia, Spain, Sweden, Switzerland, UK.
NGO Relations *Federation of European Motorcyclists' Associations (FEMA, #09518)*. [2022.10.19/XM6202/**E**]

- ♦ Federation of Health Societies in Latin America / see International Medical Informatics Association for Latin America and the Caribbean (#14135)
- ♦ Federation of Health Workers of Central America and Panama (inactive)
- ♦ Fédération de hockey d'Océanie (#17664)

♦ Federation of Horses in Education and Therapy International (HETI) 09593

Exec Dir/Sec 28 Willow Vale, Ballybrack, Dublin, CO. DUBLIN, A96 C2R4, Ireland. E-mail: office@hetifederation.org – education@hetifederation.org.
Pres address not obtained.
URL: http://www.hetifederation.org/

History 1980. Formally constituted 15 Aug 1991, Århus (Denmark). Former names and other names: *Federation of Riding for the Disabled International (FRDI)* – former (1980); *Fédération internationale d'équitation thérapeutique* – former (1980). Registration: Belgium. **Aims** Encourage worldwide links between countries and centers offering equine assisted activities (therapy and learning); assist in the development of new programmes; support scientific research efforts and distribution of education material. **Structure** International Council (meets every 3 years); Executive Committee. **Languages** English. **Staff** 0.50 FTE, paid. **Finance** Sources: donations; members' dues; sale of publications. **Events** *Triennial Therapeutic Riding Congress* Seoul

(Korea Rep) 2021, *Asia Forum* Seoul (Korea Rep) 2020, *Triennial Therapeutic Riding Congress* Dublin (Ireland) 2018, *Triennial Therapeutic Riding Congress* Taipei (Taiwan) 2015, *Triennial Therapeutic Riding Congress* Athens (Greece) 2012. **Publications** *HETI e-Newsletter* (6 a year); *Annual Membership Directory*; *Scientific Educational Journal of Therapeutic Riding*. Congress proceedings.
Members Full national organizations (53); Associate. Members in 45 countries and territories:
Argentina, Australia, Austria, Belgium, Brazil, Canada, China, Croatia, Czechia, Ecuador, Finland, France, Georgia, Germany, Greece, Honduras, Hong Kong, Hungary, Ireland, Israel, Italy, Japan, Korea Rep, Luxembourg, Mali, Mexico, Netherlands, New Zealand, Norway, Peru, Poland, Portugal, Russia, Saudi Arabia, Singapore, South Africa, Spain, Sweden, Switzerland, Taiwan, Thailand, Türkiye, UK, United Arab Emirates, USA.
NGO Relations Associate member of: *International Association of Human-Animal Interaction Organizations (IAHAIO, #11944).* [2022.06.15/XD3310/**C**]

- ♦ Fédération humaniste européenne (#07507)
- ♦ Federation of the Hunting Associations of the EEC / see Federation of Associations for Hunting and Conservation of the EU (#09459)
- ♦ Fédération hypothécaire auprès de la Communauté économique européenne / see Covered Bond and Mortgage Council (#04940)
- ♦ Fédération hypothécaire européenne / see Covered Bond and Mortgage Council (#04940)
- ♦ Federation of IAP2 / see International Association for Public Participation (#12117)
- ♦ Fédération ibéroaméricaine des bourses (#11022)
- ♦ Fédération ibéroaméricaine d'endodontie (inactive)
- ♦ Federation of Iberoamerican Airconditioning and Refrigeration Associations (#09290)
- ♦ Fédération ibéro-latinoaméricaine des artistes interprètes et exécutants (#09325)
- ♦ Fédération immobilière de l'Asie et du Pacifique (inactive)

♦ Federation of Immunological Societies of Asia-Oceania (FIMSA) . . . 09594

SG Inst of Immunology, Second Military Medical Univ, 800 Xiang Yin Road, 200433 Shanghai, China. Fax +862165382502.
URL: http://www.fimsa.org/

History Founded Feb 1992. Regional Federation of: *International Union of Immunological Societies (IUIS, #15781). European Federation of Immunological Societies (EFIS, #07142).* **Aims** Foster development of immunology in the region through close contact and interaction between immunological societies and communication and collaboration between immunologists; facilitate exchange of scientific information and personnel. **Structure** Governing Council, comprising President, Past-President, 2 Vice-Presidents, Secretary-General, Treasurer and 3 further councillors, plus representatives of observer countries. **Languages** English. **Staff** 2.00 FTE, paid. **Finance** Supported by grants from *International Council for Science (ICSU, inactive)* and IUIS. Donations or voluntary contributions from scientific bodies/institutions. **Activities** Events/meetings; training/education; networking/liaising. **Events** *Immunology for Humanity* Busan (Korea Rep) 2021, *Crosstalk between innate and adaptive immunity in health and disease* Bangkok (Thailand) 2018, *Frontiers in immune modulation* Singapore (Singapore) 2015, *Translation and disease* Delhi (India) 2012, *Congress* Taipei (Taiwan) 2008. **Publications** *FIMSA Newsletter*.
Members National organizations, members of IUIS, in 12 countries and territories:
Australia, China, Hong Kong, India, Iran Islamic Rep, Japan, Korea Rep, New Zealand, Papua New Guinea, Sri Lanka, Taiwan, Thailand.
Include in the above, 1 organization listed in this Yearbook:
Australasian Society for Immunology (ASI).
Observers in 4 countries (" indicates 2 observers, one for the Commonwealth of Independent States):
Bangladesh, Israel, Russia (*), Singapore. [2017/XD3076/y/**D**]

- ♦ Federation of Industrial Chambers and Associations in Central America / see Federación de Cámaras y Asociaciones Industriales de Centroamérica y República Dominicana (#09294)
- ♦ Federation Industrial Paints and Coats of Mercosul / see Industrial Federation Paints and Coats of Mercosul (#11175)

♦ Fédération de l'industrie dentaire en Europe (FIDE) 09595

Federation of the European Dental Industry – Vereinigung der Europäischen Dental-Industrie

Office Dir PO Box 400663, 50836 Cologne, Germany. T. +4922150068723. Fax +4922150068721. E-mail: info@fide-online.org.
Street address Aachener Strasse 1053-1055, 50858 Cologne, Germany.
URL: http://www.fide-online.org/

History 20 May 1957, Frankfurt-Main (Germany). Registration: EU Transparency Register, No/ID: 668712822914-86, Start date: 3 Aug 2016. **Aims** Represent common interests of European dental manufacturers associations, particularly before international bodies and promote their cooperation; liaise with institutions of the European Union; maintain relations with European associations of dealers, dentists and dental technicians. **Structure** General Assembly (every 2 years); Executive Committee. **Languages** English, French, German. **Staff** Part-time, voluntary. **Finance** Sources: members' dues. **Activities** Events/meetings; knowledge management/information dissemination; politics/policy/regulatory; standards/guidelines. **Events** *General Assembly* Cologne (Germany) 2023, *General Assembly* Cologne (Germany) 2021, *General Assembly* Cologne (Germany) 2019, *Dental Stakeholder Meeting* Brussels (Belgium) 2017, *General Assembly* Cologne (Germany) 2017. **Publications** *Survey on the European Dental Trade Market Trends* (annual) – in cooperation with ADDE.
Members National associations in 10 countries:
Austria, Belgium, Denmark, France, Germany, Italy, Netherlands, Spain, Switzerland, UK. [2022.10.19/XD0960/t/**D**]

- ♦ Fédération de l'industrie européenne de la construction (#06766)
- ♦ Fédération de l'industrie européenne de la coutellerie et des couverts de table / see Federation of European manufacturers of Cookware and cutlery (#09511)
- ♦ Fédération de l'industrie européenne de la coutellerie, des couverts de table, de l'orfèvrerie et des articles culinaires (#09511)
- ♦ Fédération de l'industrie granitière européenne (inactive)

♦ Fédération de l'industrie de l'huile d'olive de la CEE (FEDOLIVE) . . . 09596

Federation of the Olive Oil Industry of the EEC – Federación de la Industria del Aceite de Olive de la CEE – Verband der Olivenölindustrie der EWG – Federação da Industria do Azeite da Olive da CEE – Federazione dell'Industria dell'Olio d'Oliva della ECC – Federatie van de Olijfolie-Industrie in de EEG – Sammenslutninginden for Olivenolieindustrien i EØF – Sindesmos Viomihanias Eleoladu tis EOK

Main Office Piazza Campitelli 3, 00186 Rome RM, Italy. E-mail: info@fedolive.com.
URL: https://www.fedolive.com/

History 13 May 1969. **Aims** Create, maintain and develop among members a spirit and links of solidarity and defend the activity of members; examine in commun all the problems faced by the olive oil industry in the *European Union* member countries; determine and settle a common policy corresponding to the interests of the whole olive oil industry of EU member countries. **Structure** General Assembly (meets at least once a year). Executive Committee, consisting of President of the Federation, 2 representatives for each association, Executive Vice-President, assisted by the Directors and Secretaries of these associations. President, elected by the General Assembly. Vice-Presidents (5, one for each national delegation) and the Executive Vice-President nominated by General Assembly at the proposal of President. **Languages** French. **Finance** Members' dues.
Members National associations in 5 countries:
France, Greece, Italy, Portugal, Spain.
IGO Relations Recognized by: *European Commission (EC, #06633).* [2020/XE5620/t/**E**]

- ♦ Fédération de l'industrie de l'huilerie de la CE / see FEDIOL – The EU Vegetable Oil and Proteinmeal Industry (#09718)
- ♦ Fédération de l'industrie marbrière et de l'industrie granitière de la Communauté économique européenne / see European and International Federation of Natural Stone Industries (#07587)
- ♦ Fédération des industries de corderie-ficellerie de l'Europe occidentale / see Fédération européenne des industries de corderie ficellerie et de filets (#09573)
- ♦ Fédération des industries graphiques de l'Asie et du Pacifique (inactive)
- ♦ Fédération des industries de matières premières et des améliorants pour la boulangerie et la pâtisserie dans la CEE / see Federation of European Manufacturers of Ingredients to the Bakery, Confectionery and Patisserie Industries (#09513)
- ♦ Fédération des industries nordiques de fibres agglomérées (inactive)
- ♦ Fédération des industries des produits intermédiaires pour la boulangerie et la pâtisserie de l'EEE / see Federation of European Manufacturers of Ingredients to the Bakery, Confectionery and Patisserie Industries (#09513)
- ♦ Fédération des industries des sauces condimentaires, de la moutarde et des fruits et légumes préparés à l'huile et au vinaigre de l'Union européenne (inactive)
- ♦ Fédération de l'industrie textile africaine et malgache (inactive)
- ♦ Federation of Infectious Diseases Societies of Southern Africa (internationally oriented national body)
- ♦ Fédération d'ingénierie industrielle de l'Asie et du Pacifique (inactive)
- ♦ Fédération des ingénieurs arabes (#09420)

♦ Fédération des ingénieurs des télécommunications de la Communauté européenne (FITCE) 09597

Federation of Telecommunications Engineers in the European Community – Federación de Ingenieros de Telecomunicación de la Comunidad Europea – Föderation der Hochschule-Ingenieure des Fernmeldewesens der Europäischen Gemeinschaft – Federação dos Engenheiros de Telecomunicações da Comunidade Européia – Federazione degli Ingegneri delle Telecommunicazioni della Comunità Europea – Federatie van Ingenieurs der Telecommunicatie in de Europese Gemeenschap – Fíderationen af Telekommunikations Ingeniírer i det Europaeiske Faellesskab – Omospondia ton Tilepikinoniakon Mihanikon tis Evropaikis Kinotitas – Cónaidhm Inneatóirí Teileachumarsaide an Chomhphobail Eorphaigh

SG Bd Reyers 80, 1030 Brussels, Belgium. T. +32475714135. E-mail: info@fitce.org.
Treas St-Adriaanweg 15, 3190 Boortmeerbeek, Belgium. T. +32475840785. Fax +3215500050.
URL: http://www.fitce.org/

History 6 Oct 1961, Brussels (Belgium). Registration: Banque-Carrefour des Entreprises, No/ID: 0409.561.219, Start date: 4 Apr 1962, Belgium. **Aims** Act as a forum for ICT and media professionals to exchange views and gain insight in new developments and challenges related to technical, regulatory, societal and economic aspects of ICT and media technologies and services. **Structure** General Assembly (annual); Executive Committee; Bureau. **Languages** English, French. **Finance** Sources: members' dues. **Activities** Training/education; events/meetings; networking/liaising; research/documentation; knowledge management/information dissemination. **Events** *Future Telecommunications* Rome (Italy) 2022, *Annual Congress* Vienna (Austria) 2021, *Annual Congress* Krakow (Poland) 2020, *Annual Congress* Ghent (Belgium) 2019, *Annual Congress* Manchester (UK) 2018. **Publications** *FITCE Forum* (3 a year) – newsletter; *IEEE ComSoc Newsletter*. Congress proceedings.
Members National organizations in 11 countries:
Austria, Belgium, Czechia, Germany, Greece, Italy, Luxembourg, Poland, Romania, Spain, UK.
Individuals in 28 countries:
Austria, Belgium, Bulgaria, Croatia, Czechia, Denmark, Finland, France, Germany, Greece, Hungary, Ireland, Italy, Latvia, Lithuania, Luxembourg, Netherlands, Norway, Poland, Portugal, Romania, Slovakia, Slovenia, Spain, Sweden, Switzerland, Türkiye, UK.
IGO Relations Recognized by: *European Commission (EC, #06633).* **NGO Relations** Member of: *Federation of European and International Associations Established in Belgium (FAIB, #09508).* [2021/XE0959/**E**]

- ♦ Fédération d'initiatives chrétiennes pour l'Europe (inactive)
- ♦ Federation for Innovation in Democracy Europe (unconfirmed)

♦ Federation of Institutes of Food Science and Technology of ASEAN (FIFSTA) 09598

Contact address not obtained. E-mail: manager@fostat.org.

Aims Enhance development of food science technology as a profession; support development of the food industry in the ASEAN region. **Languages** English. **Events** *ASEAN food conference* Kuching (Malaysia) 2023, *Food Innovation Asia Conference* Bangkok (Thailand) 2021, *Food Innovation Asia Conference* Bangkok (Thailand) 2018, *Food Innovation Asia Conference* Bangkok (Thailand) 2017, *Food Innovation Asia Conference* Bangkok (Thailand) 2014.
Members Institutes of food science and technology in 9 countries:
Brunei Darussalam, Cambodia, Indonesia, Malaysia, Myanmar, Philippines, Singapore, Thailand, Vietnam.
IGO Relations *ASEAN (#01141).* **NGO Relations** Member of: *International Union of Food Science and Technology (IUFoST, #15773).* [2019.06.27/XD7669/**D**]

- ♦ Federation of Institutes and Services of Neurosciences of the Americas (no recent information)
- ♦ Federation of Institutions Concerned with the Study of the Adriatic Sea (inactive)

♦ Fédération des Institutions Internationales établies à Genève (FIIG) 09599

Federation of International Institutions based in Geneva

Pres Case 20, 1211 Geneva 20, Switzerland. T. +41227336717. Fax +41227347082. E-mail: info@fiig-geneva.org.
URL: https://www.fiig-geneva.org/

History Jun 1929, Geneva (Switzerland), as *Federation of Semi-Official and Private International Institutions established in Geneva – Fédération des institutions internationales semi-officielles et privées établies à Genève (FIIG) – Vereinigung von Halbamtlichen und Privaten in Genf Niedergelassenen Internationalen Organisationen*. Established in accordance with Swiss Law. **Aims** Facilitate establishment and activities of semi-official and private international organizations in Geneva, and promote and defend their interests. **Structure** General Assembly (annual) in Geneva (Switzerland); Committee. **Languages** French. **Staff** 1.00 FTE, voluntary. **Finance** Members' dues. **Events** *Annual General Assembly* Geneva (Switzerland) 2008, *World civil society conference* Montréal, QC (Canada) 1999, *Annual General Assembly* Geneva (Switzerland) 1994, *Annual General Assembly* Geneva (Switzerland) 1993, *Annual General Assembly* Geneva (Switzerland) 1992.
Members International organizations having headquarters or offices in Geneva (85):
- *Aga Khan Foundation (AKF, #00545);*
- Aga Khan Trust Fund for Culture;
- *Alliance internationale de tourisme (AIT, #00694);*
- *Amnesty International (AI, #00801);*
- *Association for the Prevention of Torture (APT, #02869);*
- *Building and Wood Workers' International (BWI, #03355);*
- *Centre for Humanitarian Dialogue (The HD Centre);*
- *Centre international réformé John Knox;*
- *Child Rights Connect (#03884);*
- *Consensus for Sustainable People, Organisations and Communities (CSPOC);*
- *Council for International Organizations of Medical Sciences (CIOMS, #04905);*
- *Council on Health Research for Development (COHRED, no recent information);*
- *Defence for Children International (DCI, #05025);*
- *Development Innovations and Networks (#05057);*
- Don du Livre;
- *European University Association (EUA, #09027);*
- *Fédération Internationale de l'Automobile (FIA, #09613);*
- *Fédération Internationale de Motocyclisme (FIM, #09643);*
- *Fondation pour l'économie et le développement durable des régions d'Europe (FEDRE, #09817);*
- Fondation RAFAD – *Recherches et applications de financements alternatifs au développement (Fondation RAFAD, #09827);*
- Fondation Webster;
- *Food for the Hungry (fh, #09845);*
- Foundation of the International School of Geneva;
- *Friedrich-Ebert-Stiftung (FES);*
- *Geneva International Peace Research Institute (GIPRI);*
- *Human Rights Information and Documentation Systems, International (HURIDOCS, #10985);*
- *Hunger Project (#10994);*
- *Indigenous Peoples' Center for Documentation, Research and Information (DOCIP);*
- *Institut d'action culturelle (IDAC);*
- *International Academy of Ceramics (IAC, #11540);*

- *International Association of Conference Interpreters (#11807)*;
- *International Baby Food Action Network (IBFAN, #12305)*;
- *International Baccalaureate (IB, #12306)*;
- *International Catholic Child Bureau (#12450)*;
- *International Catholic Migration Commission (ICMC, #12459)*;
- *International Commission of Jurists (ICJ, #12695)*;
- *International Council of Nurses (ICN, #13054)*;
- *International Council of Voluntary Agencies (ICVA, #13092)*;
- *International Electrotechnical Commission (IEC, #13255)*;
- *International Federation of Air Traffic Controllers' Associations (IFATCA, #13350)*;
- *International Federation of Pharmaceutical Manufacturers and Associations (IFPMA, #13505)*;
- *International Federation of Red Cross and Red Crescent Societies (#13526)*;
- *International Institute of Humanitarian Law (IIHL, #13885)*;
- *International Institute of Psychoanalysis and Psychotherapy Charles Baudouin (#13913)*;
- *International Organisation of Employers (IOE, #14428)*;
- *International Organization for Standardization (ISO, #14473)*;
- *International Peace Bureau (IPB, #14535)*;
- *International Pipe Line and Offshore Contractors Association (IPLOCA, #14586)*;
- *International Road Transport Union (IRU, #14761)*;
- *International Schools Association (ISA, #14789)*;
- *International Service for Human Rights (ISHR, #14841)*;
- *International Social Security Association (ISSA, #14885)*;
- *International Social Service (ISS, #14886)*;
- *International Standing Conference on Philanthropy (INTERPHIL, #15600)*;
- *International Trade Union Confederation (ITUC, #15708)* (replacing International Confederation of Free Trade Unions ICFTU and World Confederation of Labour WCL);
- *International Union of Food, Agricultural, Hotel, Restaurant, Catering, Tobacco and Allied Workers Associations (IUF, #15772)*;
- *International Youth and Student Movement for the United Nations (ISMUN, inactive)*;
- *Lucis Trust (LT, #16519)*;
- Medicines for Malaria Venture;
- *Migrants Rights International (MRI, #16799)*;
- *Norwegian Refugee Council (NRC)*;
- *ONG HOPE International*;
- *Pan African Institute for Development (PAID, #18053)*;
- *Pugwash Conferences on Science and World Affairs (#18574)*;
- *Quaker United Nations Office (QUNO, #18588)*;
- *Religions for Peace (RfP, #18831)*;
- Save the Children, Geneva;
- *UNI Global Union (#20338)*;
- *Union for International Cancer Control (UICC, #20415)*;
- *United Nations Watch (UN Watch)*;
- *Women's International League for Peace and Freedom (WILPF, #21024)*;
- *World Alliance of Young Men's Christian Associations (YMCA, #21090)*;
- *World Association for the School as an Instrument of Peace (#21184)*;
- *World Council of Churches (WCC, #21320)*;
- *World Economic Forum (WEF, #21367)*;
- *World Federation for Mental Health (WFMH, #21455)*;
- *World Federation of United Nations Associations (WFUNA, #21499)*;
- *World Heart Federation (WHF, #21562)*;
- *World Jewish Congress (WJC, #21599)*;
- *World ORT (WO, #21698)*;
- *World Scout Bureau (WSB, see: #21693)*;
- *World Student Christian Federation (WSCF, #21833)*;
- *World Vision International (WVI, #21904)*;
- *World Young Women's Christian Association (World YWCA, #21947)*;
- *Y's Men International (#19326)*. [2018.04.09/XE0956/y/**E**]

♦ Fédération des institutions internationales semi-officielles et privées établies à Genève / see Fédération des Institutions Internationales établies à Genève (#09599)
♦ Fédération des instituts d'études sur la mer Adriatique (inactive)
♦ Fédération interalliée des anciens combattants (inactive)
♦ Fédération interalliée des évadés de guerre et des passeurs (inactive)
♦ Fédération interaméricaine pour l'administration du personnel / see Federación Interamericana de Asociaciones de Gestión Humana (#09329)
♦ Fédération interaméricaine des associations de relations publiques / see Inter-American Confederation of Public Relations (#11418)
♦ Fédération interaméricaine des automobiles clubs / see Federación Internacional del Automóvil Region IV (#09337)
♦ Fédération interaméricaine des avocats (#11401)
♦ Fédération interaméricaine des compagnies d'assurances (#09331)
♦ Fédération interaméricaine des écoles catholiques de journalisme (inactive)
♦ Fédération interaméricaine d'éducation des adultes (inactive)
♦ Fédération interaméricaine des groupements de construction (inactive)
♦ Fédération interaméricaine de l'industrie de la construction (#09333)
♦ Fédération interaméricaine des institutions de crédit et d'assistance municipale (inactive)
♦ Fédération interaméricaine de journalistes et écrivains du tourisme (inactive)
♦ Fédération interaméricaine des organisations de journalistes (inactive)
♦ Fédération interaméricaine de philatélie (#09332)
♦ Fédération interaméricaine des secrétaires (#11430)
♦ Fédération interaméricaine des sociétés d'auteurs et de compositeurs (inactive)
♦ Fédération interaméricaine de touring et des automobile-clubs / see Federación Internacional del Automóvil Region IV (#09337)
♦ Fédération interaméricaine des travailleurs de la mine (inactive)
♦ Fédération interaméricaine des travailleurs du spectacle (inactive)

♦ Federation of Inter-Asian Philately (FIAP) 09600

Contact 3 Kian Teck Way, Singapore 628732, Singapore. T. +6567952075. Fax +6567953831. E-mail: fiapasia@yahoo.com.
URL: http://www.asiaphilately.com/

History 14 Sep 1974, Singapore (Singapore), when officially registered in Singapore. **Aims** Promote philatelic knowledge in the area, and assist the hobby's development throughout the region; promote international philatelic friendship worldwide. **Structure** Congress (previously every 2 years, currently every 4 years) elects Executive Committee (meeting twice a year), consisting of President, 2 Vice-Presidents, Secretary-General, Treasurer and 10 members. **Languages** English. **Finance** Members' dues. Donations. Budget (annual): about Singapore $ 5,000. **Activities** Promotes FIAP International Stamp Exhibitions within the region as well as full FIP World Stamp Exhibitions. The host nation of the Executive Committee meeting usually organizes a philatelic exhibition to coincide, where possible, with a national event. **Events** *Quadrennial Congress* Singapore (Singapore) 2019, *Quadrennial Congress* Seoul (Korea Rep) 2009, *Quadrennial Congress* Singapore (Singapore) 1995, *Biennial congress / Quadrennial Congress* Tokyo (Japan) 1991. **Publications** *FIAP Newsletter* (3 a year).
Members Philatelic federations in 31 countries and territories:
Australia, Azerbaijan, Bahrain, Bangladesh, Brunei Darussalam, China, Georgia, Hong Kong, India, Indonesia, Iran Islamic Rep, Iraq, Japan, Korea Rep, Kuwait, Macau, Malaysia, Mongolia, Nepal, New Zealand, Pakistan, Philippines, Qatar, Saudi Arabia, Singapore, South Africa, Sri Lanka, Taiwan, Thailand, United Arab Emirates, Vietnam.
NGO Relations *Fédération internationale de philatélie (FIP, #09650)*. [2012/XD1114/**D**]

♦ Federation of the Intermediate Products Industries for the Bakery and Confectionery Trades in the EEA / see Federation of European Manufacturers of Ingredients to the Bakery, Confectionery and Patisserie Industries (#09513)
♦ Federation of International Agencies for Development (#09414)
♦ Federation of International Associations Established in Belgium / see Federation of European and International Associations Established in Belgium (#09508)

♦ Federation of International Bandy (FIB) 09601

SG Box 91, SE-826 23 Söderhamn, Sweden. T. +462703232698. Fax +4627018014.
URL: http://www.worldbandy.com/

History 12 Feb 1955, Stockholm (Sweden). Founded by Finnish Bandy Federation, Norwegian Bandy Association, Russian Bandy Federation and Swedish Bandy Association. Current name adopted during Congress, 2001, Budapest (Hungary), according to request by IOC the same year, with acronym IBF being occupied. Former names and other names: *International Bandy Federation (IBF)* – former (1957 to 2001); *Internationella Bandyförbundet* – former (1957 to 2001). **Aims** Promote the *sport* of bandy; share and keep in practice the principles and articles of the Olympic Charter, including the policy with regard to anti-doping controls; promote overall development of bandy and rink-bandy sports within member countries and carry on propaganda for the importance and advantages of the sport; promote introduction and membership of new nations to FIB. **Structure** Meeting (annual, at Congress). Executive Committee, comprising President, 4 Vice-Presidents and Secretary General. Board, consisting of Executive Committee (excluding Secretary General) and 6 members. IOC Task Force Group. Committees (7): Election; Women's; Technical; Rules and Referee; Development; Disciplinary; Arbitration. Auditors. **Languages** English. **Staff** 0.50 FTE, paid. **Finance** Budget (annual): US$ 500,000. **Activities** Sporting activities. **Events** *Congress and annual meeting* Stockholm (Sweden) 2006, *Congress and annual meeting* Stockholm (Sweden) 2005, *Congress and annual meeting* Arkhangelsk (Russia) 2003, *Congress and annual meeting* Budapest (Hungary) 2001, *Congress and Annual Meeting* Norway 2000. **Publications** Activity reports.
Members Affiliated Clubs in 21 countries:
Australia, Belarus, Canada, Estonia, Finland, Hungary, India, Ireland, Italy, Kazakhstan, Kyrgyzstan, Latvia, Mongolia, Netherlands, Norway, Poland, Russia, Serbia, Sweden, Switzerland, USA.
NGO Relations Member of (2): *Association of the IOC Recognized International Sports Federations (ARISF, #02767)*; *Olympic Movement (#17719)*. Fully recognized by: *International Olympic Committee (IOC, #14408)*. [2021/XD1555/**D**]

♦ Federation of International Centres for the Preservation of the Architectural Heritage 09602

Federación Internacional de Centros para la Conservación del Patrimonio

Main Office Casa de los Capitanes, C/Obispo Rey Redondo 5, 38201 La Laguna, Santa Cruz de Tenerife, Spain. E-mail: federacioncicop@gmail.com.
URL: https://www.federacioncicop.org/

History 1992. Former names and other names: *International Federation Centres of CICOP* – alias; *Federación Internacional de Centros CICOP* – alias. **Events** *International Symposium Wooden Heritage Conservation* Chiloe Is (Chile) 2022, *Congress* Sao Paulo (Brazil) 2014, *Congress* Cascais (Portugal) 2012, *Biennial congress / Congress* Santiago (Chile) 2010, *Biennial congress / Congress* Seville (Spain) 2008. **NGO Relations** *Centro Internacional para la Conservación del Patrimonio (CICOP)*. [2023/XD8879/**D**]

♦ Federation of International Christian Workers Associations / see International Federation of ACLI (#13336)

♦ Federation of International Civil Servants' Associations (FICSA) ... 09603

Fédération des associations de fonctionnaires internationaux – Federación de Asociaciones de Funcionarios Internacionales – Bund der Personalverbände der Internationalen Beamten

Headquarters Palais des Nations, Office VB 03/04, 1211 Geneva 10, Switzerland. T. +41229173150. E-mail: ficsa@un.org – ficsagensec@un.org.
URL: http://www.ficsa.org/

History 26 Jan 1952, Paris (France). **Aims** Promote the interests of staff of the United Nations and its specialized agencies; seek fair treatment for all staff in matters of remuneration and benefits and conditions of security at all duty stations; enable member associations to coordinate their policies and activities in order to help attain the aims set forth in the Charter of the United Nations; promote development of an international *civil service* and protect the interests of international civil servants; represent staff at interagency level; strive to improve the image of the international civil service in the eyes of member states, the media and the public. **Structure** Council (annual) of delegates of member associations/unions. Executive Committee (meets at least once between Council sessions), consisting of President, General Secretary, Treasurer and 2 members for Compensation Issues, one member for Regional Field Issues and one Member without Portfolio, elected from candidates nominated by member associations/unions to represent the Federation and not their respective association/union. Permanent Secretariat in Geneva (Switzerland); Office in New York NY (USA). Standing Committees (7): General Service Questions; Professional Salaries and Allowances; Conditions of Service in the Field; Social Security/Occupational Health and Safety; Human Resources Management; Legal Questions; Staff/Management. Ad hoc committees and working groups. *International Civil Service (#12586)* comprises all civil servants whose allegiance is primarily inter-governmental rather than to a single government. **Languages** English, French. **Staff** 2.00 FTE, paid. **Finance** Sources: members' dues. **Activities** Defends interests of international civil servants before inter-agency bodies and legislative organs of the United Nations on common system issues; coordinates use of the appeal process against measures or decisions of doubtful legal validity; participates in cost-of-living surveys; organizes seminars, workshops and working groups; coordinates staff action and keeps staff representatives and the press aware of current issues; undertakes missions to duty stations where staff problems arise; provides support and material assistance on request and intervenes to safeguard staff interests. As part of the staff system, liaises with: *United Nations System Chief Executives Board for Coordination (CEB, #20636)*; *International Civil Service Commission (ICSC, #12587)* (and subsidiary organs); and, together with these bodies, with the United Nations General Assembly Fifth Committee. **Events** *Council Session* London (UK) 2020, *Annual Council Session* Vienna (Austria) 2019, *Annual Council Session* Bonn (Germany) 2018, *Annual Council Session* Kuala Lumpur (Malaysia) 2017, *Annual Council Session* Montréal, QC (Canada) 2016. **Publications** *FICSA Circular*; *FICSA Magazine*. News; press releases.
Members Staff associations of the United Nations and the specialized agencies (26):
- *Association of Professionals in FAO (AP in FAO, inactive)*;
- *IARC Staff Association (#11006)*;
- *IFAD Staff Association (#11099)*;
- *IMO Staff Association (#11135)*;
- *International Tribunal for the Law of the Sea (ITLOS, #15731)*;
- *IOM Global Staff Association Committee (GSAC, #16008)*;
- *PAHO/WHO Staff Association (#18024)*;
- SCBD Staff Association;
- *Staff Association of the International Atomic Energy Agency (#19938)*;
- *Staff Association of the WHO Regional Office for Africa (no recent information)*;
- *Staff Association of the WHO Regional Office for Europe (EURSA, #19941)*;
- *Staff Association of the World Intellectual Property Organization (WIPO Staff Association, #19942)*;
- *Staff Union of the International Training Centre of the ILO (ITCILO Staff Union)*;
- *UNAIDS Secretariat Staff Association (USSA, see: #16149)*;
- *UNESCO Staff Union (STU, #20321)*;
- *Union of Local and Non Local General Service Staff FAO/WFP (#20455)*;
- United Nations Logistics Base – LSU (Special Status);
- *Universal Postal Union (UPU, #20682)* (Staff);
- *UNRWA Area Staff Union (no recent information)* (West Bank, Lebanon);
- *UNRWA International Staff Association (ISA, no recent information)*;
- *UNWTO Staff Association, Madrid*;
- *WHO Eastern Mediterranean Region Staff Association, Cairo (EMRSA, no recent information)*;
- *WHO-HQ Staff Association, Geneva (WHO-HQ SA, #20938)*;
- *WHO Regional Office for the Western Pacific (WPRO, #20947)*;
- WHO/SEARO Staff Association;
- *WMO Staff Association (#20979)*.

Associate members (16):
Bioversity International (#03262) (Staff Association); *CERN Staff Association (#03834)*; *Commonwealth Secretariat (#04362)* (Staff Association); *Comprehensive Nuclear-Test-Ban Treaty Organization (CTBTO, #04420)* (Staff Council); *European Central Bank (ECB, #06466)*; European Central Bank Staff Association; *European Southern Observatory Staff Association (ESO Staff Association, #08797)*; *Global Fund to Fight AIDS, Tuberculosis and Malaria (Global Fund, #10383)*; *International Cocoa Organization (ICCO, #12627)* (Staff Association); *International Coffee Organization Staff Association (ICOSA, #12631)*; *International Olive Council (IOC, #14405)*; *International Organization for Migration (IOM, #14454)*; *ITER International Fusion Energy*

Organization (ITER Organization, #16072); Organisation for the Prohibition of Chemical Weapons (OPCW, #17823); Organization for Security and Cooperation in Europe (OSCE, #17887); World Trade Organization (WTO, #21864).
IGO Relations Accredited by (1): *United Nations Office at Vienna (UNOV, #20604).*
NGO Relations Consultative status offered to:
- *Asian Development Bank Staff Association and Staff Council (#01424);*
- *Association coopérative financière des fonctionnaires internationaux (AMFIE, #02455);*
- *Association internationale des traducteurs de conférence (AITC, #02748);*
- *European Molecular Biology Laboratory Staff Association (EMBL Staff Association, #07814);*
- *European Organisation for the Exploitation of Meteorological Satellites Staff Association Committee (EUMETSAT Staff Association Committee, #08097);*
- *Federation of Associations of Former International Civil Servants (FAFICS, #09457);*
- *Former FAO and Other United Nations Staff Association (FFOA);*
- *IDB Staff Association (#11092);*
- *IMF Staff Association (#11128);*
- *International Association of Conference Interpreters (#11807);*
- *OAS Staff Association (#17631);*
- Staff Association of the International Oil Pollution Compensation Fund;
- *Staff Council of the African Development Bank (#19943);*
- *Staff Union of the European Patent Office (SUEPO, #19944);*
- *United Nations Women's Guild – Geneva (UNWG – Geneva);*
- *World Bank Group Staff Association (#21219).*

Observer status offered to the federations of UN staff associations in Egypt, Paraguay, Uruguay, Argentina, Peru, Côte d'Ivoire, Philippines, Bangladesh, Cameroon, Pakistan, Lebanon, Mexico, Myanmar, India, Nigeria, Chile, Lesotho, Congo Brazzaville, Guinea, Benin and Sao Tomé-Principe. [2021.08.19/XC0946/y/**C**]

♦ Federation for International Cooperation of Health Services and Systems Research Centers (no recent information)
♦ Federation of International Cricketers Associations (internationally oriented national body)

♦ Federation of International Dance Festivals (FIDAF) 09604

Contact 3F – 5 – Seongjeong 8-gil, Seobuk-gu, Cheonan-si, Chungnam 331-934, Korea Rep. T. +82419007020 – +82419007021. Fax +82419000213. E-mail: cutylsh1@gmail.com – jinsil@cfac.or.kr.
URL: http://www.fidaf.net/

History Prior to inaugural meeting in Oct 2012, promoters' meeting held Sep 2011. **Aims** Establish a system of cooperation of dance festivals around the world; seek ways for mutual development; build a global network of dance festivals through exchanges among dance festivals around the world. **Structure** General Congress; Executive Committee; Secretariat. Regions (5): Asia; Africa; Europe; America; Oceania. **Languages** English. **Activities** Events/meetings; networking/liaising. **Events** *Congress* Cheonan (Korea Rep) 2021, *Congress* Seoul (Korea Rep) 2018, *Congress* Seoul (Korea Rep) 2016, *Congress* Seoul (Korea Rep) 2014.
Members Regular; Individual; Advisors. Members in 55 countries and territories:
Argentina, Armenia, Bangladesh, Benin, Bosnia-Herzegovina, Botswana, Brazil, Bulgaria, Colombia, Costa Rica, Egypt, Fiji, France, Georgia, Germany, Guam, India, Indonesia, Ireland, Israel, Italy, Japan, Jordan, Kenya, Korea Rep, Kosovo, Lithuania, Malaysia, Mexico, Micronesia FS, Montenegro, Nepal, Netherlands, North Macedonia, Northern Cyprus, Panama, Peru, Philippines, Poland, Portugal, Romania, Russia, Samoa, Senegal, Serbia, Singapore, Slovakia, Spain, Taiwan, Thailand, Tonga, Türkiye, Uganda, UK, Uruguay. [2020.04.03/XJ9650/**B**]

♦ Federation of International Danube Symposia on Diabetes Mellitus / see Federation of International Danube Symposia on Diabetes Mellitus – Central European Diabetes Association (#09605)

♦ Federation of International Danube Symposia on Diabetes Mellitus – Central European Diabetes Association (FID) 09605

Föderation der Internationalen Donau-Symposia über Diabetes Mellitus – Zentraleuropäische Diabetesgesellschaft
Gen Sec c/o Klin Abt f Endokrinologie und Stoffwechsel, Klinik für Innere Medizin III, Medizinische Univ Wien, Währinger Gürtel 18-20, 1090 Vienna, Austria.
URL: https://ceda-diabetes.eu/

History Prior to 1977, as *Federation of International Danube Symposia on Diabetes Mellitus – Föderation der Internationalen Donau-Symposia über Diabetes Mellitus.* Current title adopted, 2007. **Aims** Promote scientific interests and cooperation among active researchers, doctors and other professionals in the field of Diabetes Mellitus in Central and Eastern Europe. **Structure** Board. **Languages** English, German. **Staff** 1.00 FTE, paid. **Activities** Meeting activities; publishing activities; training/education. **Events** *Congress* Vienna (Austria) 2022, *Congress* Budapest (Hungary) 2021, *Congress* Belgrade (Serbia) 2020, *Symposium* Kiev (Ukraine) 2019, *Symposium* Krakow (Poland) 2018. [2018/XD8950/**E**]

♦ Fédération internationale des ACAT – Action des chrétiens pour l'abolition de la torture (#13334)
♦ Fédération internationale des accueils français / see Fédération Internationale des Accueils Français et francophones d'Expatriés (#09606)
♦ Fédération internationale des accueils français à l'étranger / see Fédération Internationale des Accueils Français et francophones d'Expatriés (#09606)
♦ Fédération internationale des accueils français et francophones à l'étranger / see Fédération Internationale des Accueils Français et francophones d'Expatriés (#09606)

♦ Fédération Internationale des Accueils Français et francophones d'Expatriés (FIAFE) 09606

SG 91 rue du faubourg Saint-Honoré, 75008 Paris, France. E-mail: secretaire@fiafe.org – communication@fiafe.org.
URL: http://www.fiafe.org/

History 24 Jan 1984, as *Fédération internationale des accueils français (FIAF).* Name changed, 1989, to *Fédération internationale des accueils français à l'étranger.* Name changed, 1992, to *Fédération internationale des accueils français et francophones à l'étranger (FIAFE).* Present name adopted 28 Mar 2017. Registered in accordance with French law. **Aims** Help French and French speaking expatriates settle well in their new city and country. **Structure** Board. **Languages** English. **Staff** 7.00 FTE, voluntary. **Finance** Members' dues. Other sources: subsidies; sponsorship. **Publications** Yearbook; leaflet. **Members** Associations (150) in 90 countries. Membership countries not specified. **NGO Relations** Member of: *Association francophone d'amitié et de liaison (AFAL, #02605).* [2019.06.18/XF2969/**F**]

♦ Fédération internationale des ACLI (#13336)
♦ Fédération internationale des acteurs (#13337)
♦ Fédération internationale de l'action catholique / see Forum international d'action catholique (#09919)
♦ Fédération internationale de l'action des chrétiens pour l'abolition de la torture / see International Federation of ACATs – Action by Christians for the Abolition of Torture (#13334)
♦ Fédération internationale d'action familiale (inactive)
♦ Fédération internationale de l'activité physique adaptée (#13338)
♦ Fédération internationale des administrateurs de biens conseils immobiliers / see Fédération internationale des professions immobilières (#09653)
♦ Fédération internationale des agences catholiques de presse (inactive)
♦ Fédération internationale des agences de voyages (inactive)
♦ Fédération internationale d'aikido (#11605)
♦ Fédération internationale amateur de sambo / see Fédération internationale de SAMBO (#09655)
♦ Fédération internationale d'ambulanciers (inactive)
♦ Fédération internationale des amies de la jeune fille (inactive)
♦ Fédération internationale des amis de la terre / see Friends of the Earth International (#10002)
♦ Fédération internationale des anciens combattants alliés (inactive)
♦ Fédération internationale des anciens prisonniers politiques du fascisme (inactive)
♦ Fédération internationale de l'approvisionnement (inactive)
♦ Fédération internationale de l'approvisionnement et de l'achat / see International Federation of Purchasing and Supply Management (#13525)
♦ Fédération Internationale de l'Arbre (internationally oriented national body)
♦ Fédération internationale des architectes d'intérieur (#13460)
♦ Fédération internationale des architectes paysagistes (#13467)
♦ Fédération internationale des archives du film (#13427)
♦ Fédération Internationale des Archives de Télévision (#13568)
♦ Fédération internationale des armateurs (inactive)
♦ Fédération internationale des armateurs pétroliers contre la pollution / see ITOPF Ltd (#16073)
♦ Fédération internationale de l'artisanat (inactive)
♦ Fédération Internationale de l'Art Photographique (#13509)
♦ Fédération internationale des arts, des lettres et des sciences (inactive)
♦ Fédération internationale des arts martiaux (#14108)
♦ Fédération internationale des assistants sociaux et des assistantes sociales / see International Federation of Social Workers (#13544)
♦ Fédération internationale d'associations d'aide social, écologique et culturelle (#09335)
♦ Fédération internationale des associations d'anatomistes (#13361)
♦ Fédération internationale des associations d'apiculture (#13370)
♦ Fédération internationale des associations d'auteurs de films /cinéma et télévision/ (inactive)
♦ Fédération internationale des associations de bibliothécaires / see International Federation of Library Associations and Institutions (#13470)
♦ Fédération internationale des associations de bibliothécaires et des bibliothèques (#13470)
♦ Fédération internationale des associations catholiques d'aveugles (#13377)
♦ Fédération internationale des associations de chefs de publicité d'annonceurs (inactive)
♦ Fédération Internationale des Associations de Chimistes du Textile et de la Couleur (#13365)
♦ Fédération internationale des associations contre la lèpre (#13355)
♦ Fédération internationale des associations de contrôleurs du trafic aérien (#13350)
♦ Fédération internationale des associations de défense, de recherche et d'enseignement de la phytothérapie (inactive)
♦ Fédération Internationale des Associations d'Étudiants en Médecine (#13478)
♦ Fédération internationale des associations de distributeurs de films (#13428)
♦ Fédération internationale des associations du dossier de santé / see International Federation of Health Information Management Associations (#13441)
♦ Fédération internationale des associations d'économistes d'entreprise (inactive)
♦ Fédération internationale des associations pour l'éducation des travailleurs (#13580)
♦ Fédération internationale des associations de l'électronique de sécurité du trafic aérien (#13351)
♦ Fédération internationale des associations endodontiques (#13411)
♦ Fédération internationale des associations d'entrepreneurs asiatiques et du Pacifique occidental (#13359)

♦ Fédération internationale des associations d'études classiques (FIEC) 09607

International Federation of the Societies of Classical Studies
SG Inst du monde antique et byzantin – Philologie classique, Univ de Fribourg, Rue Pierre-Aeby 16, 1700 Fribourg, Switzerland. T. +41263007832.
Pres Univ Autónoma de Madrid, Filología Clásica, C/ Francisco Tómas y Valiente, 1, 28049 Madrid, Spain.
URL: http://www.fiecnet.org/

History Sep 1948, Paris (France). Founded under the auspices of *UNESCO (#20322).* **Aims** Encourage research concerning the *ancient civilizations* of Greece and Rome, understood in the broadest sense; link the main associations in each country which aim at advancement of *Greek* or *Latin* studies. **Structure** General Assembly (at least twice in 5 years, including at Congress); Bureau. Membership closed. Meetings open. **Languages** English, French. **Staff** 10.00 FTE, voluntary. **Finance** Sources: members' dues. **Activities** Events/meetings; research/documentation. **Events** *International Congress* Wroclaw (Poland) 2025, *International Congress* Mexico City (Mexico) 2022, *International Congress* London (UK) 2019, *General Assembly* Bordeaux (France) 2014, *International Congress* Bordeaux (France) 2014.
Members National associations (75) in 52 countries:
Argentina, Australia, Austria, Belgium, Bolivia, Brazil, Bulgaria, Canada, Chile, China, Costa Rica, Côte d'Ivoire, Croatia, Czechia, Denmark, Egypt, Estonia, Finland, France, Germany, Greece, Hungary, Ireland, Israel, Italy, Japan, Korea Rep, Malawi, Mexico, Montenegro, Netherlands, New Zealand, Nigeria, North Macedonia, Norway, Peru, Poland, Portugal, Romania, Russia, Senegal, Serbia, Slovenia, South Africa, Spain, Sweden, Switzerland, Türkiye, UK, Uruguay, USA, Zimbabwe.
International organizations (16):
Association internationale de papyrologues (AIP, #02725); Association internationale d'études patristiques (AIEP, #02692); Association internationale pour l'étude de la mosaïque antique (AIEMA, #02689); Association pour l'antiquité tardive; Associazione Internazionale di Archeologia Classica (AIAC, #02988); Australasian Society for Classical Studies (ASCS); Centro Internazionale per lo Studio dei Papiri Ercolanesi "Marcello Gigante" (CISPE); Comité international permanent des études mycéniennes (CIPEM, #04181); International Association for Byzantine Studies (#11751); International Association for Greek and Latin Epigraphy (#11924); International Association for Neo-Latin Studies (IANLS, #12048); International Plato Society (#14603); International Union of Institutes of Archaeology, History and Art History in Rome (#15782); Pôle alpin de recherches sur les sociétés anciennes (PARSA, #18412); Société internationale de bibliographie classique (SIBC, #19474); Thesaurus Linguae Graecae.
NGO Relations Member of (2): *European Alliance for the Social Sciences and Humanities (EASSH, #05885); International Council for Philosophy and Human Sciences (CIPSH, #13061).* [2022.12.01/XA2030/y/**A**]

♦ Fédération internationale des associations d'eugénique (inactive)
♦ Fédération internationale des associations d'experts (inactive)
♦ Fédération internationale des associations de fabricants de produits d'entretien (inactive)
♦ Fédération internationale des associations de filatures de lin et d'étoupe (inactive)
♦ Fédération internationale des associations de hockey féminin (inactive)
♦ Fédération internationale des associations d'instituteurs (inactive)
♦ Fédération internationale des associations d'inventeurs (#13461)
♦ Fédération internationale des associations de libraires (inactive)
♦ Fédération internationale des associations de la margarine (inactive)
♦ Fédération internationale des associations de médecins de l'industrie pharmaceutique (#13363)
♦ Fédération internationale des associations médicales anthroposophiques (#13314)
♦ Fédération internationale des associations médicales catholiques (#13378)
♦ Fédération internationale des associations de multimedia (#13483)
♦ Fédération internationale des associations nationales d'athlètes olympiques / see World Olympians Association (#21682)
♦ Fédération internationale des associations nationales de droit de l'informatique (#13398)
♦ Fédération internationale d'associations nationales d'élèves ingénieurs (inactive)

♦ Fédération internationale des associations nationales d'exploitants de téléphériques, funiculaires et autres transports par câbles pour voyageurs (FIANET) 09608

International Federation of National Associations of Passenger Transport by Rope Railways – Internationaler Verband der nationalen Vereinigungen der Seilbahnen
Contact Domaines Skiables de France, Syndicat Nat des Téléphériques de France, Alpespace – Bât Annapurna, 24 rue St Exupéry, 73800 Francin, France.
History Prior to 1954. **Events** *Meeting* Kuusamo (Finland) 2006. **NGO Relations** *International Organization for Transportation by Rope (#14481).* [2016/XD9068/**D**]

♦ Fédération internationale d'associations nationales d'ingénieurs / see Fédération Européenne d'Associations Nationales d'Ingénieurs (#09558)
♦ Fédération internationale des associations nationales de normalisation (inactive)
♦ Fédération internationale des associations de négociants en aciers, tubes et métaux (inactive)
♦ Fédération internationale des associations de patrons de navires (#13539)

♦ **Fédération internationale des associations de personnes âgées (FIAPA)** 09609

International Federation of Associations of the Elderly – Federación Internacional de Asociaciones de Personas Mayores – Internationale Organisation für Senioren – Federazione Internazionale delle Associazioni di Persone Anziane – Federação Internacional des Associações de Pessoas Idosas

Assistant Coordinator 163 rue Charenton, 75012 Paris, France. T. +33986336326. E-mail: info@fiapa.net.
Pres address not obtained.
URL: http://www.fiapa.net/

History 26 Sep 1980, Paris (France). Founded by associations for the elderly in 4 European countries (Belgium, France, Italy, Spain). Former names and other names: *Federación Internacional de las Asociaciones de Personas de Edad* – former alias. **Aims** Promote the role and place of the elderly in social development; publicize the image and needs of the elderly, carrying their message to international organizations; fight against abuse of the elderly, including financial abuse. **Structure** General Meeting; Board of Directors; Scientific Council. **Languages** Arabic, Chinese, English, French, Italian, Russian, Spanish. **Activities** Research/documentation; events/meetings; advocacy/lobbying/activism. **Events** *International Congress* Nice (France) 2022, *Symposium* Paris (France) 2014, *Symposium* Paris (France) 2013, *Symposium* Brussels (Belgium) 2009, *Symposium* Santiago (Chile) 2007. **Publications** *Cahiers de la FIAPA* (2 a year); *FIAPA Contact*; *FIAPA Infos* in English, French, Spanish – magazine. Conference proceedings.
Members National, regional and district associations, grouping over 300 million people, in 47 countries:
Andorra, Argentina, Australia, Austria, Belgium, Benin, Bolivia, Brazil, Burkina Faso, Burundi, Cameroon, Canada, Chile, China, Colombia, Congo DR, Costa Rica, Côte d'Ivoire, Cuba, Dominican Rep, Ecuador, France, Germany, Hungary, Italy, Lithuania, Luxembourg, Mali, Malta, Mauritius, Mexico, Netherlands, Norway, Poland, Portugal, Romania, Russia, Rwanda, Senegal, Spain, Switzerland, Tunisia, UK, Ukraine, Uruguay, Venezuela, Vietnam.
Consultative Status Consultative status granted from: *ECOSOC (#05331)* (General); *UNESCO (#20322)* (Consultative Status); *Council of Europe (CE, #04881)* (Participatory Status). **IGO Relations** Member of: Liaison Committee of *European Commission (EC, #06633)*. Accredited by: *United Nations Office at Vienna (UNOV, #20604)*. Agreement with the UN Department for Policy Coordination and Sustainable Development for the preparations of the International Year of Older Persons. Associated with Department of Global Communications of the United Nations. **NGO Relations** Together with: *Eurolink Age (inactive)* and *European Platform of Seniors' Organizations (EPSO, no recent information)*, set up: *AGE Platform Europe (#00557)*. [2021/XD8096/**D**]

♦ Fédération internationale des associations de pilotes de ligne (#13349)
♦ Fédération internationale des associations pour la pratique des normes / see International Federation of Standards Users (#13558)
♦ Fédération internationale des associations de producteurs de films (#13429)
♦ Fédération internationale des associations de professeurs de sciences (#12997)
♦ Fédération internationale des associations de quincailliers et marchands de fer / see International Federation of Hardware and Housewares Associations (#13437)
♦ Fédération internationale des associations de spécialistes de la sécurité et de l'hygiène du travail (no recent information)
♦ Fédération internationale des associations de thanatologues (#13569)
♦ Fédération internationale des associations touristiques de cheminots (inactive)

♦ **Fédération internationale des associations de transitaires et assimilés (FIATA)** 09610

International Federation of Freight Forwarders Associations – Internationale Föderation der Spediteurorganisationen

Dir Gen Rue Kléberg 6, 1201 Geneva, Switzerland. E-mail: info@fiata.org.
URL: http://www.fiata.com/

History 31 May 1926, Vienna (Austria). Statutes revised: 8 Jun 1937, Paris (France); 22 Sep 1951, Badgastein (Austria); 9 Oct 1957, Amsterdam (Netherlands); 10 Oct 1961, Vienna; 26 Sep 1963, Lucerne (Switzerland); 21 Sep 1967, Opatija (Yugoslavia); 29 Sep 1977, Los Angeles CA (USA); 23 Oct 1988, Limassol (Cyprus); 23 Sep 1998, Sydney (Australia); 13 Oct 2001, Cancún (Mexico); 22 Oct 2007, Dubai (United Arab Emirates); 8 Oct 2016, Dublin (Ireland); 5 Oct 2019, Cape Town (South Africa). Former names and other names: *International Federation of Forwarding Organizations* – former (31 May 1926); *Fédération internationale des associations des transporteurs et assimilés (FIATA)* – former (31 May 1926). Registration: Switzerland; EU Transparency Register, No/ID: 439801633394-18. **Aims** Improve the quality of services of freight forwarders and promote and protect their interests world-wide. **Structure** General Meeting (annual); Presidency; Advisory Bodies (3); Institutes (3) with Working Groups. Airfreight Institute (includes 4 Working Groups); Multimodal Transport Institute (includes 3 Working Groups: Sea, Rail and Road Transport); Customs Affairs Institute; some Institutes have permanent contact groups with carriers' organizations: *International Air Transport Association (IATA, #11614)*, *International Road Transport Union (IRU, #14761)* and *International Union of Railways (#15813)*. **Languages** English. **Finance** Sources: members' dues. **Activities** Events/meetings; guidance/assistance/consulting; publishing activities; training/education. **Events** *World Congress* Panama (Panama) 2024, *World Congress* Brussels (Belgium) 2023, *World Congress* Busan (Korea Rep) 2022, *Multimodality in the Year of Rail* 2021, *World Congress* Brussels (Belgium) 2021. **Publications** *FIATA Review* (5 a year).
Members Ordinary – national associations (107) in 98 countries and territories:
Argentina, Australia, Austria, Bangladesh, Belarus, Belgium, Bosnia-Herzegovina, Brazil, Brunei Darussalam, Bulgaria, Cambodia, Cameroon, Canada, Chile, China, Colombia, Costa Rica, Croatia, Cyprus, Czechia, Denmark, Djibouti, Dominican Rep, Ecuador, Egypt, El Salvador, Estonia, Ethiopia, Finland, France, Georgia, Germany, Ghana, Greece, Guatemala, Honduras, Hong Kong, Hungary, India, Indonesia, Iran Islamic Rep, Ireland, Israel, Italy, Japan, Jordan, Kazakhstan, Kenya, Korea Rep, Kyrgyzstan, Latvia, Lebanon, Lithuania, Malaysia, Malta, Mauritius, Mexico, Moldova, Mongolia, Morocco, Myanmar, Netherlands, New Zealand, Nicaragua, Norway, Pakistan, Panama, Paraguay, Philippines, Poland, Portugal, Romania, Russia, Saudi Arabia, Serbia, Singapore, Slovakia, Slovenia, South Africa, Spain, Sri Lanka, Sweden, Switzerland, Syrian AR, Taiwan, Tanzania UR, Thailand, Türkiye, Uganda, UK, Ukraine, United Arab Emirates, Uruguay, USA, Uzbekistan, Vietnam, Zambia, Zimbabwe.
Associate – 5,291 individual affiliated firms (Categories A, B and C) – in 151 countries and territories:
Afghanistan, Albania, Algeria, Angola, Argentina, Armenia, Australia, Austria, Azerbaijan, Bahrain, Bangladesh, Belarus, Belgium, Benin, Bolivia, Bosnia-Herzegovina, Brazil, Brunei Darussalam, Bulgaria, Burundi, Cambodia, Cameroon, Canada, Chile, China, Colombia, Congo DR, Costa Rica, Côte d'Ivoire, Croatia, Cuba, Cyprus, Czechia, Denmark, Djibouti, Dominican Rep, Ecuador, Egypt, El Salvador, Estonia, Ethiopia, Fiji, Finland, France, Georgia, Germany, Ghana, Gibraltar, Greece, Guatemala, Guinea, Haiti, Honduras, Hong Kong, Hungary, Iceland, India, Indonesia, Iran Islamic Rep, Iraq, Ireland, Israel, Italy, Jamaica, Japan, Jordan, Kazakhstan, Kenya, Korea Rep, Kuwait, Kyrgyzstan, Laos, Latvia, Lebanon, Libya, Lithuania, Macau, Madagascar, Malaysia, Maldives, Malta, Mauritius, Mexico, Moldova, Mongolia, Montenegro, Morocco, Mozambique, Myanmar, Namibia, Nepal, Netherlands, New Zealand, Nicaragua, Niger, Nigeria, North Macedonia, Northern Mariana Is, Norway, Oman, Pakistan, Palestine, Panama, Papua New Guinea, Paraguay, Peru, Philippines, Poland, Portugal, Puerto Rico, Qatar, Romania, Russia, Saudi Arabia, Senegal, Serbia, Singapore, Slovakia, Slovenia, Somalia, South Africa, Spain, Sri Lanka, Sudan, Suriname, Sweden, Switzerland, Syrian AR, Taiwan, Tajikistan, Tanzania UR, Thailand, Togo, Trinidad-Tobago, Tunisia, Türkiye, Turkmenistan, Uganda, UK, Ukraine, United Arab Emirates, Uruguay, USA, Uzbekistan, Vanuatu, Venezuela, Vietnam, Virgin Is UK, Yemen, Zambia, Zimbabwe.
Consultative Status Consultative status granted from: *ECOSOC (#05331)* (Ros A); *UNCTAD (#20285)* (Special Category); *UNEP (#20299)*. **IGO Relations** Cooperates with: *United Nations Economic Commission for Europe (UNECE, #20555)* and its *'Working Party on Facilitation of International Trade Procedures'*. Accredited by: *United Nations Office at Vienna (UNOV, #20604)*. Memorandum of Understanding signed with: *World Customs Organization (WCO, #21350)*. Associated with Department of Global Communications of the United Nations. **NGO Relations** Member of: *Bureau international des containers et du transport intermodal (BIC, #03364)*. Consultative member of: *Comité maritime international (CMI, #04192)*. Cooperates with: *International Organization for Standardization (ISO, #14473)*. [2022/XC1916/**B**]

♦ Fédération internationale des associations des transporteurs et assimilés / see Fédération internationale des associations de transitaires et assimilés (#09610)
♦ Fédération internationale des associations de veufs et de veuves (inactive)

♦ **Fédération internationale des associations vexillologiques (FIAV)** .. 09611

International Federation of Vexillological Associations – Federación Internacional de Asociaciones Vexilológicas – Internationale Föderation Vexillologischer Gesellschaften

SG PO Box 836, Pinegowrie, 2123, South Africa. T. +27113133502. E-mail: sec.gen@fiav.org.
Pres Pazinska 50, HR-10110 Zagreb, Croatia. T. +385915639391. E-mail: pres@fiav.org.
URL: http://www.fiav.org/

History Founded 3 Sep 1967, Rüschlikon (Switzerland). Officially launched when statutes adopted, 7 Sep 1969, Boston MA (USA); statutes amended 29 Sep 1983. Statutes were replaced by current constitution, adopted 27 Sep 1989, and amended 12 Aug 1997, 29 Jul 1999, 23 Jul 2001, 7 Aug 2007, 14 Jul 2009 and 8 Aug 2017. **Aims** Unite those associations and institutions throughout the world whose object is the pursuit of vexillology, which is the creation and development of a body of knowledge about *flags* of all types, their forms and functions and of scientific theories and principles based on that knowledge. **Structure** General Assembly; Board. **Languages** German. **Staff** 3.00 FTE, voluntary. **Finance** None. **Activities** Events/meetings. **Events** *Biennial Congress* Ljubljana (Slovenia) 2022, *Biennial Congress* Ljubljana (Slovenia) 2021, *Biennial Congress* San Antonio, TX (USA) 2019, *Biennial Congress* London (UK) 2017, *Biennial Congress* Sydney, NSW (Australia) 2015. **Publications** *Info-FIAV* (2 a year). Congress proceedings.
Members National associations (51) in 45 countries:
Angola, Argentina, Australia, Belgium, Botswana, Bulgaria, Canada, Chile, China, Croatia, Czechia, Denmark, Eswatini, Finland, France, Georgia, Germany, Hungary, Iceland, India, Ireland, Italy, Japan, Lesotho, Madagascar, Malawi, Moldova, Mozambique, Namibia, Netherlands, New Zealand, North Macedonia, Norway, Poland, Russia, Slovenia, South Africa, Spain, Sweden, Switzerland, UK, Ukraine, USA, Zambia, Zimbabwe.
IGO Relations None. **NGO Relations** None. [2020.01.03/XD2038/**C**]

♦ **Fédération internationale des associés professionnels de l'avortement et de la contraception (FIAPAC)** 09612

International Federation of Professional Abortion and Contraception Associates – Internationale Vereinigung von Fachkräften und Verbänden zu Schwangerschaftsabbruch und Kontrazeption – Federazione Internazionale degli Operatori di Aborto e Contraccezione

Secretariat Orga-Med Congress Office, Opalfenweg 3, 1740 Ternat, Belgium. T. +3225820852. Fax +3225825515. E-mail: admin@fiapac.org.
Registered Address Maison des Associations de Paris 14, av rené boylesve, 75016 Paris, France.
URL: http://www.fiapac.org/

History 25 Jan 1997. **Aims** Provide a platform for all practical and ethical aspects of unwanted pregnancy and abortion. **Structure** General Assembly; Board; Executive Committee. **Languages** English, French, German. **Finance** Members' dues. **Activities** Events/meetings; knowledge management/information dissemination. **Events** *Conference* Riga (Latvia) 2022, *Conference* Berlin (Germany) 2020, *Conference* Nantes (France) 2018, *Conference* Lisbon (Portugal) 2016, *Task sharing in abortion care* Ljubljana (Slovenia) 2014. **Publications** *FIAPAC Newsletter* (3 a year). [2021/XD8495/t/**D**]

♦ Fédération internationale d'astronautique (#12286)
♦ Fédération internationale d'athlétisme amateur / see World Athletics (#21209)
♦ Fédération internationale des auberges de la jeunesse / see Hostelling International (#10950)
♦ Fédération internationale d'auteurs de films (inactive)

♦ **Fédération Internationale de l'Automobile (FIA)** 09613

International Automobile Federation – Federación Automovilistica Internacional

Pres 8 place de la Concorde, 75008 Paris, France. T. +33143124455. Fax +33143124466.
SG Mobility address not obtained.
SG Sport Chemin de Blandonnet 2, 1215 Geneva 15, Switzerland. T. +41225444500. Fax +41225444550.
URL: https://www.fia.com/

History 20 Jun 1904, Bad Homburg (Germany). New Statutes adopted in 1970 and again on 22 Mar 2001. Statutes modified: 5 Oct 2001; 2 Oct 2002; 16 Oct 2003; 1 Jul 2004; 14 Oct 2004; 31 Mar 2005; 20 Oct 2006; 26 Oct 2007; 7 Nov 2008; 23 Oct 2009; 5 Nov 2010; 9 Dec 2011. Former names and other names: *Association générale de l'automobile (AGA)* – former (1904 to 1906); *Association internationale des automobile-clubs reconnus (AIACR)* – former (1906 to 1946). Registration: EU Transparency Register, No/ID: 84839535366-67; No/ID: 78435412800018, France. **Aims** Uphold interest of members in all international matters concerning automobile mobility and *tourism* and *motor sport*; promote freedom of mobility through affordable, safe and clean motoring; defend the rights of consumers when travelling; promote development of motor sport; improve safety of the sport; enact, interpret and enforce common rules applicable to the organization and fair and equitable running of motor sport events; promote development of facilities and services of Member Clubs, Associations and Federations, and coordination of reciprocal services between Member Clubs for the benefit of their individual members when travelling abroad; exercise jurisdiction pursuant to disputes of a sporting nature and any disputes arising between Members, or in relation to any Members having contravened obligations laid down by the Statutes, the International Sporting Code and the Regulations; preserve and conserve all documents and artefacts concerning world motoring in order to retrace its history.
Structure General Assembly (annual), comprising delegates of Member Clubs, Associations and Federations. *World Council for Automobile Mobility and Tourism (see: #09613)*, comprising FIA President, Deputy President for Automobile Mobility and Tourism, 7 Vice-Presidents and 17 members. *World Motor Sport Council (see: #09613)*, comprising FIA President, Deputy President for Sport, 7 Vice-Presidents for Sport and 17 members. Senate, comprising President, FIA President, Deputy President for Automobile Mobility and Tourism, Deputy President for Sport, 4 members elected by World Council for Automobile Mobility and Tourism, 4 members elected by World Motor Sport Council and up to 4 members promoted by FIA President. FIA Academy, consisting of FIA President and 6 members elected by General Assembly. President presides over the Federation, with assistance from Deputy Presidents and Vice-Presidents. Automobile Mobility and Tourism Regions (4): Europe, Middle East and Africa; Asia and Pacific; North America; South America. International Tribunal and International Court of Appeal, including joint Congress. FIA International Historic Commission; Permanent or temporary commissions or sub-commissions. Committees (3): Audit; Judicial Appointment; Anti-Doping Disciplinary.
Sporting Commissions (22) assist World Motor Sport Council:
- Electric and New Energy Championships;
- Circuits;
- Cross-Country Rally;
- Drag Racing;
- Endurance;
- Formula One;
- Grand Touring Car;
- Hill-Climb;
- Historic Motor Sport;
- Homologation;
- International Karting;
- Land Speed Records;
- Manufacturers';
- Medical;
- Officials and Volunteers;
- Off-Road;
- Rally;
- Safety;
- Single-Seaters;
- Touring Car;
- Truck Racing;
- Women in Motor Sport;
- World Rally Championship.

General Judicial Secretariat; Secretariat located in Paris (France).
Languages English, French, Spanish. **Staff** Paid. **Finance** Members' dues (annual). Other sources: income and interest from personal estate or real estate owned by FIA; fees and taxes as decided by General Assembly; income arising directly or indirectly from sporting activities, including FIA Championships; income arising directly or indirectly from automobile mobility and tourism activities. **Activities** Participated in the drafting of the following conventions and agreements: *Customs Convention on the Temporary Importation of Commercial Road Vehicles (1956)*; *Agreement concerning the Adoption of Harmonized Technical United Nations Regulations for Wheeled Vehicles, Equipment and Parts which can be Fitted and/or be Used on Wheeled Vehicles and the Conditions for Reciprocal Recognition of Approvals Granted on the Basis of these United Nations Regulations (1958)*; *European Convention on the Punishment of Road Traffic Offences (1964)*; *Convention on Road Signs and Signals (1968)*; *Agreement on Minimum Requirements for the Issue and*

Validity of Driving Permits (APC, 1975); European Agreement on Main International Traffic Arteries (AGR, 1975). Participated and in the extension and amendment of the 1958 Agreement and the 1954, 1956 and 1968 Conventions. Participates in the drafting of minimum requirements for Professional Driving Instruction. Together with International Touring Alliance, set up *AIT/FIA Foundation – Mobility and Society (inactive)* (1993-2003). **Events** *Annual General Assembly* Bologna (Italy) 2022, *Annual General Assembly* Paris (France) 2021, *Annual General Assembly* Geneva (Switzerland) 2020, *Joint Sport and Mobility Conference* Paris (France) 2020, *Annual General Assembly* Paris (France) 2019. **Publications** *Bulletin officiel de la Fédération internationale de l'automobile* (4 a year); *FIA Legal Handbook* (annual); *FIA Yearbook*; *Karting Yearbook*; *Yearbook of Automobile Sport*. *Auto-Motive*. AIT and FIA Public Policy Statements; brochure on customs duties for permanent importation of vehicles.

Members Voting members (only one per country): National Automobile Clubs or National Automobile Associations (ACN) – activity must embrace entire national territory and cover road traffic, touring, defence of rightful interests of users and their safety on the one hand, and motor sport on the other. Clubs, Associations or Federations – activity embraces entire national territory and covers road traffic, touring or camping; Clubs, Associations or Federations (ASN) – activity embraces entire national territory and exclusively concerns motor sport. Sport Clubs (57); Mobility Clubs (97); Sport and Mobility Clubs (72). Voting members in 121 countries and territories:

Albania, Algeria, Andorra, Argentina, Australia, Austria, Azerbaijan, Bahrain, Bangladesh, Barbados, Belarus, Belgium, Bolivia, Bosnia-Herzegovina, Botswana, Brazil, Bulgaria, Canada, Chile, China, Colombia, Costa Rica, Côte d'Ivoire, Croatia, Cyprus, Czechia, Denmark, Dominican Rep, Ecuador, Egypt, El Salvador, Eritrea, Estonia, Ethiopia, Finland, France, Georgia, Germany, Greece, Guatemala, Hong Kong, Hungary, Iceland, India, Indonesia, Iran Islamic Rep, Iraq, Ireland, Israel, Italy, Jamaica, Japan, Jordan, Kazakhstan, Kenya, Korea Rep, Kuwait, Lebanon, Libya, Liechtenstein, Lithuania, Luxembourg, Macau, Macedonia, Madagascar, Malaysia, Malta, Mauritania, Mauritius, Mexico, Moldova, Monaco, Mongolia, Montenegro, Morocco, Mozambique, Netherlands, New Zealand, Nicaragua, Nigeria, North Macedonia, Norway, Oman, Pakistan, Palestine, Panama, Paraguay, Peru, Philippines, Poland, Portugal, Puerto Rico, Qatar, Romania, Russia, San Marino, Saudi Arabia, Senegal, Serbia, Singapore, Slovakia, Slovenia, South Africa, Spain, Sri Lanka, Sudan, Sweden, Switzerland, Syrian AR, Taiwan, Tanzania UR, Thailand, Trinidad-Tobago, Tunisia, Türkiye, Uganda, UK, Ukraine, United Arab Emirates, Uruguay, USA, Venezuela, Yemen.

Non-voting members: Associate – new Club, Association or Federation, accepted by General Assembly, which meets requirements defined in Statutes, initially without the right to vote for 2 years. Associate members in 35 countries and territories:

Algeria, Armenia, Austria, Belarus, Burundi, Cambodia, Congo Brazzaville, Cuba, Egypt, Finland, France, Georgia, Holy See, Italy, Jamaica, Lithuania, Madagascar, Malta, Moldova, Morocco, Namibia, Nepal, North Macedonia, Pakistan, Portugal, Russia, Rwanda, Sweden, Switzerland, Taiwan, Türkiye, UK, Ukraine, Zambia, Zimbabwe.

Included in Associate members, 4 organizations listed in this Yearbook:

Circuits International (#03934); European Road Assessment Programme (EuroRAP, #08392); Fédération internationale des véhicules anciens (FIVA, #09669); International Road Assessment Programme (iRAP, #14757).

Consultative Status Consultative status granted from: *ECOSOC (#05331)* (Special). **IGO Relations** Affiliate member of: *World Tourism Organization (UNWTO, #21861)*. Represented at European Union level by the AIT and FIA European Bureau in Brussels (Belgium). Cooperates with: *International Civil Aviation Organization (ICAO, #12581); UNEP (#20299); WHO (#20950).*

NGO Relations Member of (13): *Alliance for the Freedom of Car Repair in the EU (AFCAR, #00682); Association of the IOC Recognized International Sports Federations (ARISF, #02767); ERTICO ITS Europe (#05532); eSafetyAware (#05533); European New Car Assessment Programme (EURO NCAP, #08046); European Road Transport Research Advisory Council (ERTRAC, #08396); European Travel and Tourism Advisory Group (ETAG, #08946); Forum for Mobility and Society (FMS, #09924); Fédération des Institutions Internationales établies à Genève (FIIG, #09599); Global Road Safety Partnership (GRSP, #10581); International Road Federation (IRF, #14758); Mobility for Prosperity in Europe (MPE, #16839); Olympic Movement (#17719).* Cooperates with (1): *Alliance internationale de tourisme (AIT, #00694).*

Recognized by: *International Olympic Committee (IOC, #14408)*. In liaison with technical committees of: *International Organization for Standardization (ISO, #14473)*. Supports: *European Road Assessment Programme (EuroRAP, #08392)*. Regular working relations with:

- *European Broadcasting Union (EBU, #06404);*
- *Federación Internacional del Automóvil Region IV (#09337);*
- *Fédération Internationale de Motocyclisme (FIM, #09643);*
- *International Council on Monuments and Sites (ICOMOS, #13049);*
- *International Hotel and Restaurant Association (IH&RA, #13813);*
- *International Organization of Motor Vehicle Manufacturers (#14455);*
- *International Road Transport Union (IRU, #14761);*
- *World Road Association (PIARC, #21754).*

[2022/XB1386/y/**B**]

- ♦ Fédération internationale des autorités hippiques de courses au galop (#13449)
- ♦ Fédération internationale des aveugles (inactive)
- ♦ Fédération internationale Balint (#12307)
- ♦ Fédération internationale du balut (no recent information)
- ♦ Fédération internationale des banques de terminologie (inactive)

♦ Fédération internationale de basketball (FIBA) 09614

International Basketball Federation

SG Route Suisse 5, 1295 Mies VD, Switzerland. T. +41225450000. Fax +41225450099. E-mail: communications@fiba.basketball.
URL: http://www.fiba.basketball/

History 18 Jun 1932, Geneva (Switzerland). Since 1 Jun 2002, includes activities of the previous *International Committee for Mini-Basketball (inactive)* and its 5 Zone Commissions – *African Mini-Basketball Commission (inactive); Asian Mini-Basketball Commission (inactive); FIBA Mini-Basketball European Committee (inactive); Americas – Mini COPABA (inactive); Oceania Mini-Basketball Commission (inactive)* – integrated into FIBA. Current statutes and internal regulations adopted at 20th Congress, 2014, Seville (Spain). Former names and other names: *International Amateur Basketball Federation* – former (1932 to 1986); *Fédération internationale de basketball amateur* – former (1932 to 1986). **Aims** Develop and promote the game of basketball in order to bring people together and unite communities. **Structure** Congress (every 4 years with Mid-term Congress in-between); Central Board; Executive Committee; Commissions (8); Regional Offices (5): *FIBA Africa (#09744); FIBA Americas (#09745)*, comprising *International Basketball Federation – North American Zone (#12326), Comisión de la Zona Centroamericana y del Caribe de la Confederación Panamericana de Basquetbol (CONCENCABA, #04146)* and *Confederación Sudamericana de Básquetbol (CONSUBASQUET, #04482); FIBA-Asia (#09746); FIBA-Europe (#09747); FIBA Oceania (#09748)*. Recognized organizations (3): Basketball Arbitral Tribunal (BAT); *World Association of Basketball Coaches (WABC, #21119); International Wheelchair Basketball Federation (IWBF, #15882). The FIBA Foundation* functions as an education arm. **Languages** English, French, Spanish. **Staff** 190.00 FTE, paid. **Finance** Sources: members' dues; sale of publications. Other sources: registration fees; television and advertising rights. **Activities** Awards/prizes/competitions; sporting activities. **Events** *World Congress* Manila (Philippines) 2023, *Mid-Term Congress* Mies (Switzerland) 2021, *World Congress* Beijing (China) 2019, *Mid-Term Congress* Hong Kong (Hong Kong) 2017, *Extraordinary World Congress* Istanbul (Turkey) 2014. **Publications** Standards; guidelines; rules; reports. Information Services: *International Centre for the Documentation and Research of Basketball, Alcobendas (ICDRB).*

Members Affiliated National Federations (212), grouping about 400 million members in 212 countries and territories:

Afghanistan, Albania, Algeria, Andorra, Angola, Antigua-Barbuda, Argentina, Armenia, Aruba, Australia, Austria, Azerbaijan, Bahamas, Bahrain, Bangladesh, Barbados, Belarus, Belgium, Belize, Benin, Bermuda, Bhutan, Bolivia, Bosnia-Herzegovina, Botswana, Brazil, Brunei Darussalam, Bulgaria, Burkina Faso, Burundi, Cambodia, Cameroon, Canada, Cape Verde, Cayman Is, Central African Rep, Chad, Chile, China, Colombia, Comoros, Congo DR, Cook Is, Costa Rica, Côte d'Ivoire, Croatia, Cuba, Cyprus, Czechia, Denmark, Djibouti, Dominica, Dominican Rep, Ecuador, Egypt, El Salvador, Equatorial Guinea, Eritrea, Estonia, Eswatini, Ethiopia, Fiji, Finland, France, Gabon, Gambia, Georgia, Germany, Ghana, Gibraltar, Great Britain, Greece, Grenada, Guam, Guatemala, Guinea, Guinea-Bissau, Guyana, Haiti, Honduras, Hong Kong, Hungary, Iceland, India, Indonesia, Iran Islamic Rep, Iraq, Ireland, Israel, Italy, Jamaica, Japan, Jordan, Kazakhstan, Kenya, Kiribati, Korea DPR, Korea Rep, Kosovo, Kuwait, Kyrgyzstan, Laos, Latvia, Lebanon, Lesotho, Liberia, Libya, Lithuania, Luxembourg, Macau, Macedonia, Madagascar, Malawi, Malaysia, Maldives, Mali, Malta, Marshall Is, Mauritania, Mauritius, Mexico, Micronesia FS, Moldova, Monaco, Mongolia, Montenegro, Montserrat, Morocco, Mozambique, Myanmar, Namibia, Nauru, Nepal, Netherlands, New Caledonia, New Zealand, Nicaragua, Niger, Nigeria, Norfolk Is, North Macedonia, Northern Mariana Is, Norway, Oman, Pakistan, Palau, Palestine, Panama, Papua New Guinea, Paraguay, Philippines, Poland, Portugal, Puerto Rico, Qatar, Romania, Russia, Rwanda, Samoa, Samoa USA, San Marino, Sao Tomé-Principe, Saudi Arabia, Senegal, Serbia, Seychelles, Sierra Leone, Singapore, Slovakia, Slovenia, Solomon Is, Somalia, South Africa, South Sudan, Spain, Sri Lanka, St Kitts Is, St Lucia, St Vincent-Grenadines, Sudan, Suriname, Sweden, Switzerland, Syrian AR, Tahiti Is, Taiwan, Tajikistan, Tanzania UR, Thailand, Timor-Leste, Togo, Tonga, Trinidad-Tobago, Tunisia, Türkiye, Turkmenistan, Turks-Caicos, Tuvalu, Uganda, Ukraine, United Arab Emirates, Uruguay, USA, Uzbekistan, Vanuatu, Venezuela, Vietnam, Virgin Is UK, Virgin Is USA, Yemen, Zambia, Zimbabwe.

NGO Relations Member of (4): *Association of Summer Olympic International Federations (ASOIF, #02943); International Association of Sports Law (IASL, #12180); International Masters Games Association (IMGA, #14117); Olympic Movement (#17719).* Cooperates with (1): *International Testing Agency (ITA, #15678).* Supports (1): *Deaf International Basketball Federation (DIBF, #05017).* Recognized by: *International Olympic Committee (IOC, #14408).* Officially recognized organizations: *European Basketball Players' Union (UBE).* Maintains relations with: *Virtus: World Intellectual Impairment Sport (#20793).* [2023.02.16/XB1154/**B**]

- ♦ Fédération internationale de basketball amateur / see Fédération internationale de basketball (#09614)
- ♦ Fédération internationale de basketball en fauteuil roulant (#15882)
- ♦ Fédération internationale pour les bateaux de sauvetage / see International Maritime Rescue Federation (#14104)
- ♦ Fédération internationale du bâtiment et des travaux publics / see European Construction Industry Federation (#06766)

♦ Fédération internationale du béton (FIB) 09615

International Federation for Structural Concrete

SG fib c/o EPFL, Office GC A2 424, Chemin du Barrage, Station 18, 1015 Lausanne VD, Switzerland. T. +41216932747. Fax +41216936245. E-mail: fib@epfl.ch.
Communications & Events Specialist address not obtained.
URL: https://www.fib-international.org/

History 1998. Founded by merger of *Euro-International Committee for Concrete (CEB, inactive)* and *Fédération internationale de la précontrainte (FIP, inactive).* **Aims** Develop study of scientific and practical matters capable of advancing the technical, economic, aesthetic and environmental performance of concrete *construction.* **Structure** General Assembly; Technical Council; Praesidium; Commissions; Task Groups. **Languages** English. **Activities** Events/meetings; knowledge management/information dissemination; research and development; standards/guidelines. **Events** *Congress* Oslo (Norway) 2022, *Symposium on Concrete Structures* Lisbon (Portugal) 2021, *International PhD Symposium in Civil Engineering* Paris (France) 2021, *International Conference on Concrete Sustainability* Prague (Czechia) 2021, *International Conference on Concrete Sustainability* Prague (Czechia) 2020. **Publications** *fib Bulletin*; *Structural Concrete* – journal. *The fib Model Code for Concrete Structures* (2010).

Members Full in 45 countries:

Argentina, Australia, Austria, Belgium, Brazil, Canada, China, Cyprus, Czechia, Denmark, Finland, France, Germany, Greece, Hungary, India, Indonesia, Iran Islamic Rep, Israel, Italy, Japan, Korea Rep, Lebanon, Luxembourg, Netherlands, New Zealand, Norway, Poland, Portugal, Romania, Russia, Serbia, Slovakia, Slovenia, South Africa, Spain, Sweden, Switzerland, Thailand, Tunisia, Türkiye, UK, Ukraine, United Arab Emirates, USA.

NGO Relations Member of: *Liaison Committee of International Associations of Civil Engineering (#16453).* [2022/XC0104/**C**]

- ♦ Fédération internationale des bijoutiers, horlogers et orfèvres détaillants (inactive)
- ♦ Fédération internationale de billard (inactive)
- ♦ Fédération internationale de biologie cellulaire (#13382)
- ♦ Fédération internationale de bobsleigh et de tobogganing / see International Bobsleigh and Skeleton Federation (#12375)

♦ Fédération internationale de boules (FIB) 09616

International Bocce Federation

SG 1558 rue Claires Fontaines, 01150 Saint-Vulbas, France. T. +33474464939. Fax +33474464947. E-mail: contact@fiboules.org – fiboules@sfr.fr.
Pres address not obtained.
URL: http://www.fiboules.org/

History 14 Apr 1946, Ville-la-Grand (France). Former names and other names: *International Bocce Association* – alias. Registration: RNA, No/ID: W052002557, Start date: 13 Apr 1989, France. **Aims** Act as the international authority controlling the *sport* of 'Bocce'; encourage its development and promote friendly contact between players in all parts of the world. **Structure** Congress (every 2 years); Permanent Directing Committee (meeting twice a year); Discipline Council; Call Council. Commissions (4). Committees (5). Continental Delegates (8): Africa; North America; South America; Asia; China; Central Europe; Northern Europe; Oceania. Permanent Secretariat located in Gap (France). **Languages** French, Italian. **Staff** 1.00 FTE, paid. **Finance** Sources: members' dues. **Activities** Sporting activities. **Events** *Annual Congress* Santiago (Chile) 1987, *Annual Congress* Monte Carlo (Monaco) 1986. **Publications** *Bulletin de la FIB.*

Members National organizations, totalling 300,000 members, in 52 countries:

Algeria, Andorra, Argentina, Armenia, Australia, Belgium, Bolivia, Bosnia-Herzegovina, Brazil, Bulgaria, Burkina Faso, Cameroon, Chile, China, Congo Brazzaville, Côte d'Ivoire, Croatia, Denmark, Dominican Rep, Estonia, Finland, France, Germany, Guinea, Hungary, Italy, Japan, Luxembourg, Mauritania, Monaco, Montenegro, Morocco, Netherlands, Pakistan, Paraguay, Peru, Russia, San Marino, Senegal, Serbia, Singapore, Slovenia, Spain, Switzerland, Taiwan, Tonga, Tunisia, Türkiye, Uruguay, USA, Venezuela.

NGO Relations Accredited by (1): *International Olympic Committee (IOC, #14408).* Instrumental in setting up (1): *Confédération mondiale des sports de boules (CMSB, inactive).* [2022/XC1404/**D**]

- ♦ Fédération internationale des bourses de valeurs / see World Federation of Exchanges (#21434)

♦ Fédération internationale des bureaux d'extraits de presse (FIBEP) 09617

International Federation of Press Cutting Agencies – Federación Internacional de Agencias de Extractos de Periódicos – Internationaler Verband der Zeitungsausschnittbüros

Sec Gen c/o Observer, Lessinggasse 21, 1020 Vienna, Austria. T. +431213220.
URL: http://www.fibep.info/

History May 1953, Paris (France). Registered in accordance with French law. Also referred to in English as *International Federation of Press Clipping and Media Monitor Bureaux.* **Aims** Safeguard the interests of press cutting agencies. **Structure** General Assembly (annual). Executive Committee, comprising President, 3 Vice-Presidents, General Secretary and Treasurer. Commissions (3). **Languages** English, French, German. **Staff** 2.00 FTE, paid. **Finance** Entrance fee: euro 1130; annual dues: euro 1000. **Activities** Commissions (3): Fair-trade; Business Development; Marketing and Communications. **Events** *Congress* Dublin (Ireland) 2022, *Congress* 2021, *Congress* 2020, *Congress* Lima (Peru) 2019, *Congress* Copenhagen (Denmark) 2018.

Members Bureaux (80) in 43 countries and territories:

Argentina, Australia, Austria, Belgium, Bulgaria, Canada, Chile, China, Croatia, Czechia, Denmark, France, Germany, Greece, Hong Kong, Hungary, Iceland, India, Ireland, Israel, Italy, Japan, Kenya, Lithuania, Malaysia, Netherlands, New Zealand, Peru, Poland, Portugal, Romania, Russia, Slovakia, Slovenia, South Africa, Spain, Sweden, Switzerland, Taiwan, Türkiye, UK, United Arab Emirates, USA.

Consultative Status Consultative status granted from: *World Intellectual Property Organization (WIPO, #21593)* (Permanent Observer Status). [2019/XC1985/**C**]

- ♦ Fédération internationale des bureaux de justification de la diffusion (#13366)
- ♦ Fédération internationale des bureaux de voyages de la jeunesse (inactive)
- ♦ Fédération internationale des cadres de l'agriculture (inactive)
- ♦ Fédération internationale des cadres de la chimie et des industries annexes / see European Federation of Managerial Staff in the Chemical and Allied Industries (#07160)
- ♦ Fédération internationale des cadres des établissements de crédit et institutions financières (unconfirmed)
- ♦ Fédération internationale des cadres des mines et de l'energie (no recent information)
- ♦ Fédération internationale des cadres supérieurs de l'hôtellerie (no recent information)
- ♦ Fédération internationale des cadres des transports (#07730)
- ♦ Fédération internationale de caisses d'assurance volontaires / see International Federation of Health Plans (#13442)
- ♦ Fédération internationale des calvinistes (inactive)
- ♦ Fédération internationale de camping et de caravaning / see Fédération Internationale de Camping, Caravanning et Autocaravaning (#09618)

Fédération Internationale Camping
09618

alphabetic sequence excludes
For the complete listing, see Yearbook Online at

♦ Fédération Internationale de Camping, Caravanning et Autocaravaning (FICC) 09618

International Federation of Camping, Caravanning, and Motorcaravanning – Federación Internacional de Camping, Caravaning y Autocaravaning – Internationaler Camping, Caravaning- und Motorcaravaningverband – Federazione Internazionale Campeggio, Caravanning e Autocaravaning (FICC)

Pres Rue Belliard 20, bte 15, 1040 Brussels, Belgium. T. +3225138782. Fax +3225138783. E-mail: info@ficc.org.
URL: http://www.ficc.org/

History 1932, Sassenheim (Netherlands). Statutes adopted at 1st official meeting 4 May 1933, Hampton Court (UK), during 1st International Rally. Statutes modified: 1957; 1961; 1969; 1981; 1987; 1996; 2002; 2005; 2011. Former names and other names: *Fédération internationale de camping et de caravaning (FICC)* – former (1932); *International Federation of Camping and Caravanning* – former (1932); *Federación Internacional de Camping y Caravanning* – former (1932); *Internationaler Camping-und Caravaningverband* – former (1932); *Federazione Internazionale Campeggio Caravanning (FICC)* – former (1932). Registration: Banque-Carrefour des Entreprises, No/ID: 0434.924.838, Start date: 10 Oct 1988, Belgium. **Aims** Protect the interests of campers and caravanners at international level; promote this growing form of tourism. **Structure** General Assembly (annual, at International Rally); International Council; Executive Committee; Commissions (4); Permanent Secretariat. Meetings closed. **Languages** English, French, German. **Staff** 2.00 FTE, paid. Voluntary. **Finance** Sources: members' dues. **Activities** Awareness raising; events/meetings; guidance/assistance/consulting; research/documentation. **Events** *World Congress* Verrières-le-Buisson (France) 2022, *World Congress* Lisbon (Portugal) 2018, *International Rally* Korea Rep 2015, *International Rally* Novalja (Croatia) 2015, *International Rally* Pori (Finland) 2014. **Publications** *FICC Info*; *FICC Newsletter*.
Members Federations, clubs and associations in 39 countries and territories:
Australia, Austria, Belgium, Bulgaria, China, Croatia, Czechia, Estonia, Finland, France, Germany, Hungary, Iceland, Ireland, Israel, Italy, Japan, Korea Rep, Lithuania, Luxembourg, Malta, Netherlands, Norway, Poland, Portugal, Romania, Russia, San Marino, Serbia, Slovakia, Slovenia, Spain, Sweden, Switzerland, Taiwan, Türkiye, UK, Ukraine, United Arab Emirates.
IGO Relations Affiliated member of: *World Tourism Organization (UNWTO, #21861)*. **NGO Relations** Member of: *Federation of European and International Associations Established in Belgium (FAIB, #09508)*. Cooperates with: *International Organization for Standardization (ISO, #14473)*. [2020/XC1873/**C**]

- ♦ Fédération internationale de canoë (#12437)
- ♦ Fédération internationale catholique d'éducation physique et sportive (#12456)
- ♦ Fédération internationale catholique des organismes missionnaires de jeunes (inactive)
- ♦ Fédération internationale catholique et pédagogique (inactive)
- ♦ Fédération internationale des centres d'entraînement aux méthodes d'éducation active (#13572)

♦ Fédération internationale des centres l'étude et de documentation libertaires (FICEDL) 09619

Contact c/o CIRA, 24 ave de Beaumont, 1012 Lausanne VD, Switzerland. E-mail: info@cira.ch.
URL: https://ficedl.info/
NGO Relations *Centre international de recherches sur l'anarchisme (CIRA)* is a member. [2022/XF4664/**F**]

- ♦ Fédération internationale des centres de préparation au mariage (#13475)
- ♦ Fédération internationale des centres sociaux et communautaires (#13538)
- ♦ Fédération internationale de centres touristiques (inactive)
- ♦ Fédération internationale de la céramique (inactive)
- ♦ Fédération Internationale des Chambres Syndicales de Négociants en Timbres-Poste (#13557)
- ♦ Fédération internationale des charpentiers (inactive)
- ♦ Fédération internationale des chasseurs de son (inactive)
- ♦ Fédération internationale des chauffeurs-conducteurs, mécaniciens, électriciens et automobilistes (inactive)
- ♦ Fédération internationale des cheminots espérantistes (#13415)
- ♦ Fédération internationale des cheminots pour la sobriété (inactive)
- ♦ Fédération Internationale de Chimie Clinique (#13392)

♦ Fédération Internationale de Chiropratique du Sport (FICS) 09620

International Federation of Sports Chiropractic

Contact Av De Rhodanie 54, Maison du Sport Intl, 1007 Lausanne VD, Switzerland. T. +61417324384. E-mail: admin@ficsport.org.
URL: https://fics.sport/

History 1987, London (UK). Initiated in 1987 by Dr. Stephen Press. Former names and other names: *Fédération internationale de chiropratique sportive* – former. Registration: Swiss Civil Code, Start date: 1998, Switzerland. **Aims** Provide equitable access to sports chiropractic care, education, mentoring and research to all athletes and sports chiropractors regionally, nationally and internationally. **Structure** Executive Council (ExCo), representing 7 regions: Africa; Asia; Eastern Mediterranean; Europe; Latin America; North America; Pacific. Executive Management Team (EMT). Commissions (7): Education, Membership, Research, Marketing, Games, Student, Finance. Headquarters located in Lausanne (Switzerland). Administrative Management located in Canberra (Australia). **Languages** English, French. **Staff** Contracted service providers; several voluntary. **Finance** Sources: fees for services; meeting proceeds; members' dues; sponsorship. Annual budget: 250,000 CHF (2020). **Activities** Certification/accreditation; events/meetings; healthcare; networking/liaising; training/education. **Events** *Global Symposium* Paris (France) 2023, *Global Symposium* 2022, *Global Sports Chiropractic Symposium* 2021, *Symposium and General Assembly* Berlin (Germany) 2019, *Symposium and General Assembly* Washington, DC (USA) 2017. **Publications** *FICS International E-News* (4 a year); *Journal of Sports Chiropractic and Rehabilitation* (4 a year). *International Field Doctor's Guide*; *Sports Chiropractic Manual*; *The Role of Chiropractic in Sport*.
Members National Chiropractic Sports Councils in 31 countries and territories:
Australia, Bahrain, Belgium, Botswana, Canada, Denmark, England, France, Germany, Greece, Hong Kong, Ireland, Israel, Italy, Japan, Malaysia, Mexico, Namibia, Netherlands, New Zealand, Norway, Philippines, South Africa, Spain, Sweden, Switzerland, Taiwan, Türkiye, UK, USA, Vietnam.
NGO Relations Member of (2): *Olympic Movement (#17719)*; *World Federation of Chiropractic (WFC, #21420)*. Recognized by: *International Olympic Committee (IOC, #14408)*. [2022.11.30/XD2028/**B**]

- ♦ Fédération internationale de chiropratique sportive / see Fédération Internationale de Chiropratique du Sport (#09620)
- ♦ Fédération internationale des chronométreurs (#09717)
- ♦ Fédération internationale des ciné-clubs (#13430)
- ♦ Fédération internationale du cinéma non professionnel / see Union internationale du cinéma (#20423)
- ♦ Fédération internationale du cinéma super-8 (inactive)
- ♦ Fédération internationale du cinéma et de la télévision sportifs (#15588)
- ♦ Fédération internationale des cités-jardins et de l'urbanisme / see International Federation for Housing and Planning (#13450)
- ♦ Fédération internationale de citoyens européens opposés à l'entrée de la Turquie dans l'Union européenne (unconfirmed)
- ♦ Fédération internationale des clubs de camping-cars / see Fédération internationale des clubs de motorhomes (#09621)
- ♦ Fédération internationale des clubs motocyclistes / see Fédération Internationale de Motocyclisme (#09643)

♦ Fédération internationale des clubs de motorhomes (FICM) 09621

International Federation of Motorhome Clubs

Headquarters 8 rue de la Croix de Grès, 62000 Arras, France. E-mail: info@ficm-aisbl.eu.
Pres address not obtained.
URL: http://www.ficm-aisbl.eu/

History 1976. Current statutes modified 1995; 2005. Former names and other names: *Fédération internationale des clubs de camping-cars (FICCC)* – former. Registration: Start date: 2011, France; Banque-Carrefour des Entreprises, Belgium; EU Transparency Register, No/ID: 281777435616-61. **Aims** Facilitate contacts among motorhome drivers; respect nature and the environment, particularly camp sites, through judicious, limited and non-polluting parking; promote reputation of motorhome users through the good behaviour, politeness and tolerance of members. **Structure** General Assembly; Administrative Council. **Languages** Dutch, English, French, German, Italian, Portuguese, Spanish. **Staff** 44.00 FTE, voluntary. **Finance** Sources: members' dues. **Activities** Events/meetings; networking/liaising. **Events** *Annual meeting* Germany 2008, *Annual meeting* Switzerland 2007, *Annual meeting* Kampen (Netherlands) 2006, *Annual meeting* Portomaggiore (Italy) 2005, *Annual meeting* Tournai (Belgium) 2004.
Members National federations and clubs in 10 countries:
Belgium, France, Germany, Italy, Luxembourg, Netherlands, Portugal, Spain, Switzerland, UK. [2021.02.18/XD1814/**D**]

- ♦ Fédération internationale des clubs de publicité (inactive)
- ♦ Fédération internationale des coalitions pour la diversité culturelle (#13394)
- ♦ Fédération internationale des coiffeurs (inactive)
- ♦ Fédération internationale des collections de culture de microorganismes (inactive)
- ♦ Fédération internationale des collèges de chirurgie (#13560)
- ♦ Fédération internationale des coloniaux et anciens coloniaux (inactive)
- ♦ Fédération internationale des comités de coopération européenne (inactive)
- ♦ Fédération internationale des comités permanents d'expositions (inactive)
- ♦ Fédération internationale pour la commande automatique (#13367)
- ♦ Fédération internationale de commerce alternatif / see World Fair Trade Organization (#21396)
- ♦ Fédération internationale du commerce du cacao (inactive)
- ♦ Fédération internationale du commerce de la chaussure indépendant (inactive)
- ♦ Fédération internationale de commerce equitable / see World Fair Trade Organization (#21396)
- ♦ Fédération internationale du commerce de la fourrure / see International Fur Federation (#13696)
- ♦ Fédération internationale du commerce et de l'industrie (inactive)
- ♦ Fédération internationale du commerce et des industries du camping (inactive)
- ♦ Fédération internationale du commerce philatélique (inactive)
- ♦ Fédération internationale du commerce des semences (inactive)
- ♦ Fédération internationale des communautés de l'Arche / see L'Arche International (#01085)

♦ Fédération internationale des communautés éducatives (FICE-International) 09622

International Federation of Educative Communities – Internationale Gesellschaft für Erzieherische Hilfen (IGfH)

Contact 50a 1000 William Gladstone Street Center, Sofia, Bulgaria. T. +3599501710. E-mail: fice.inter@gmail.com.
Registered Office Hasengasse 60/14, Hasengasse 60/14, 1100 Vienna, Austria.
URL: https://www.ficeinter.net/

History 10 Jul 1948, Trogen (Switzerland), under the auspices of UNESCO, during Pestalozzi Village Study Sessions. Original title: *International Federation of Children's Communities – Fédération internationale des communautés d'enfants (FICE) – Federación Internacional de Comunidades Infantiles – Internationale Vereinigung der Erziehungsgemeinschaften*. Also referred to in German as *Internationale Gesellschaft für Heimerziehung*. Registered in accordance with Swiss law. **Aims** In accordance with the Universal Declaration of Human Rights, support endeavours to further global realization of the international rights of the child; focus on the disadvantaged child, on the child at risk and on how to improve its potentially detrimental living conditions and family surroundings; promote international exchange of knowledge and experience in the field of childcare; endeavour to improve extra-familial care; represent institutions in which children and adolescents live for shorter or longer periods; encourage the family as the original system; encourage reform and development in all types of child care; act as an international forum for exchange of experience among practitioners and academics in the field of care and education for children and young people both within and outside their families; coordinate with members in assisting children without families or whose families are only partially able to carry out social, educational or health care responsibilities; show special concern for children and youth who grow up in residential or community care, or in conditions which arrest their physical, emotional and social development. **Structure** General Assembly (every 3 years). Federal Council (meets twice a year), comprising representatives of national sections (2 per country). Executive Committee (meets 4 times a year), consisting of President, Secretary-General and Treasurer. Vice-Presidents (3) for: cooperation with Baltic countries and CIS states; professional questions, training and post-graduate training; questions concerning rights of the child. Honorary Presidents; Honorary members. Regional group: FICE-Europe. **Languages** English, French, German. **Staff** 1.00 FTE, paid. **Finance** Contributions of national sections; grants from foundations. **Activities** Events/meetings; networking/liaising; research/documentation. **Events** *World Congress* Tel Aviv (Israel) 2019, *Biennial Congress and General Assembly* Vienna (Austria) 2016, *Biennial Congress and General Assembly / Congress* Bern (Switzerland) 2013, *Biennial Congress and General Assembly* Israel 2012, *Biennial Congress and General Assembly / Congress* Stellenbosch (South Africa) 2010. **Publications** *FICE Bulletin* (2 a year) in English, French, German. *Recent Changes and New Trends in Extrafamilial Child Care: An International Perspective* (1994); *Training of Residential Child and Youth Care Staff* (1993); *Von den Kindergemeinschaften zur Ausserfamiliären Erziehung: Die Geschichte der FICE-International* (1992) by Irene Knöpfel-Nobs; *Glossary of Child, Social Care and Social Work Terms* (1991) in English, French, German; *Residential Child Care: An International Reader* (1991). Annual Report; congress proceedings.
Members National sections, comprising residential homes and other child care units, schools and workshops for disabled persons, education and training centres for professional staff and individual professionals and academics in the field. Members in 33 countries:
Austria, Belgium, Bosnia-Herzegovina, Bulgaria, Canada, Croatia, Czechia, Denmark, England, Estonia, Finland, France, Germany, Hungary, India, Israel, Italy, Luxembourg, Montenegro, Morocco, Netherlands, North Macedonia, Poland, Romania, Russia, Serbia, Slovakia, Slovenia, South Africa, Sweden, Switzerland, USA, Wales.
International corresponding members (3):
Eurydiom (no recent information); *International Association of Social Educators (#12167)*; *International Forum for Child Welfare (IFCW, #13633)*.
Consultative Status Consultative status granted from: *ECOSOC (#05331)* (Ros C); *UNICEF (#20332)*. **IGO Relations** Accredited by: *United Nations Office at Vienna (UNOV, #20604)*. Informal links with: *UNESCO (#20322)*. **NGO Relations** Member of: *International Conference of NGOs (#12883)*; *Conference of Non-Governmental Organizations in Consultative Relationship with the United Nations (CONGO, #04635)*; *European Network for Social Action (ENSACT, #08003)*; *Child Rights Connect (#03884)*; *NGO Committee on UNICEF (#17120)*. [2022/XD2517/y/**C**]

- ♦ Fédération internationale des communautés d'enfants / see Fédération internationale des communautés éducatives (#09622)
- ♦ Fédération internationale des communautés de jeunesse catholique paroissiales / see International Federation of Catholic Parochial Youth Movements (#13379)
- ♦ Fédération internationale des communautés utilisatrices de matériel agricole (inactive)
- ♦ Fédération internationale des compositeurs et musicologues progressistes (inactive)

♦ Fédération Internationale des Confréries Bachiques (FICB) 09623

International Federation of Wine Brotherhoods

Pres Chairman Musée du Vin, 5 square Charles Dickens – rue des Eaux, 75016 Paris, France. T. +33145256226. E-mail: info@winebrotherhoods.org.
URL: http://www.winebrotherhoods.org/

History 1964, Paris (France). Registered in accordance with French law. Adoption of *'International Charter of Wine Brotherhoods'* 2014. **Aims** Promote and network wine brotherhoods, regions and traditions; promote responsible wine consumption; educate the consumer in wine tasting and rating. **Structure** General Assembly; Administration Board; Executive Committee. **Languages** English, French. **Staff** 3.00 FTE, voluntary. **Finance** Sources: members' dues. **Activities** Events/meetings. **Events** *Congress* Portugal 2022, *Congress* Alba (Italy) / Grinzane Cavour (Italy) 2021, *Congress* Alba (Italy) / Grinzane Cavour (Italy) 2020, *General Assembly* Paris (France) 2020, *Congress* Skopje (Macedonia) 2018. **Publications** *FICB Newsletter* (2 a year).

Members Wine Brotherhoods and their chapters in 26 countries and territories:
Austria, Canada, Egypt, Estonia, Finland, France, Hong Kong, Hungary, Italy, Japan, Korea Rep, Macau, Madagascar, Moldova, Netherlands, North Macedonia, Portugal, Réunion, Romania, Serbia, Slovakia, Slovenia, Spain, Switzerland, UK, USA.
NGO Relations Partnership with: *Wine in Moderation (WIM, #20967)*. [2020.03.03/XU0147/**C**]

- ♦ Fédération Internationale des Conseils des Arts et des Agences Culturelles (#13358)
- ♦ Fédération internationale des conseils juridiques et fiscaux (inactive)
- ♦ Fédération internationale des conseils en propriété industrielle / see Fédération Internationale des Conseils en Propriété Intellectuelle (#09624)

♦ Fédération Internationale des Conseils en Propriété Intellectuelle (FICPI) 09624

International Federation of Intellectual Property Attorneys – Internationale Föderation von Patentanwälten

Secretariat Holbeinstrasse 36-38, 4003 Basel BS, Switzerland. E-mail: secretariat@ficpi.org.
SG c/o Sugrañes SLP, Calle Provenza 304, 08008 Barcelona, Spain. T. +34932151917. Fax +34932153723.
URL: http://www.ficpi.org/

History 1 Sep 1906, Milan (Italy). Statutes modified: 1927, Geneva (Switzerland); 1947, Scheveningen (Netherlands); 1957, Gjøvik (Norway); 1960, Rome (Italy); 1969, Ebeltoft (Denmark); 1973, Vienna (Austria); 1977, Buenos Aires (Argentina); 1980, Bergen (Norway); 1982, Berlin West (Germany FR); 1986, Funchal (Portugal); 1986, Melbourne (Australia); 1989, Venice (Italy); 1991, Johannesburg (South Africa); 1991, Harrogate (UK); 1992, Igls (Austria); 1993, Vejle (Denmark); 1994, Vienna (Austria); 1997, Hong Kong; 1998, Florence (Italy); 2000, Cape Town (South Africa); 2001, Seville (Spain); 2002, Prague (Czech Rep); 2003, Berlin (Germany); 2005, Seoul (Korea Rep); 2008, Sydney (Australia); 2010, Munich (Germany); 2011, Cape Town (South Africa); 2012, Melbourne (Australia); 2013, Cartagena de Indias (Colombia); 2014, Kyoto (Japan), Barcelona (Spain); 2016, Zurich (Switzerland); 2017, Hangzhou (China); 2018, Toronto ON (Canada); 2019, Turin (Italy); 2020 (Virtually); 2022, Cannes (France). Former names and other names: *International Federation of Patent Agents* – former; *Fédération internationale des conseils en propriété industrielle* – former; *International Federation of Industrial Property Attorneys* – former; *International Federation of Patent Attorneys* – alias. Registration: EU Transparency Register, No/ID: 34137929067-33. **Aims** Support members who are intellectual property attorneys established in private practice; bring value to intellectual property. **Structure** World Congress (triennial); Executive Committee; Bureau; Advisory Council. **Languages** English, French, German. **Staff** 1.50 FTE, paid. **Finance** Sources: meeting proceeds; members' dues. **Activities** Advocacy/lobbying/activism; projects/programmes; training/education. **Events** *Open Forum* London (UK) 2023, *World Congress* Cannes (France) 2022, *Virtual Open Forum* 2021, *Triennial World Congress* London (UK) 2021, *Virtual Open Forum* 2020. **Publications** *FICPI Newsletter* (irregular). Special publications.
Members National associations (14) in 14 countries:
Australia, Canada, Denmark, Finland, France, Germany, Italy, Japan, Norway, Portugal, South Africa, Sweden, Switzerland, UK.
National sections (23) in 23 countries:
Argentina, Austria, Belgium, Brazil, Chile, China, Czechia, Greece, Hungary, India, Ireland, Israel, Korea Rep, Malaysia, Mexico, Netherlands, New Zealand, Romania, Russia, Singapore, Spain, Türkiye, USA.
Regional section (1): FICPI Andean Section comprising 5 countries:
Bolivia, Colombia, Ecuador, Peru, Venezuela.
Individuals in 44 countries and territories:
Algeria, Bangladesh, Belarus, Bulgaria, Cameroon, China, Cyprus, Dominican Rep, Egypt, Estonia, Haiti, Hong Kong, Iceland, Indonesia, Iran Islamic Rep, Jersey, Jordan, Kazakhstan, Kenya, Latvia, Lebanon, Lithuania, Luxembourg, Macau, Morocco, Nigeria, North Macedonia, Oman, Pakistan, Panama, Paraguay, Philippines, Poland, Qatar, Serbia, Slovakia, Sri Lanka, Taiwan, Thailand, Tunisia, Ukraine, United Arab Emirates, Uruguay, Vietnam.
Consultative Status Consultative status granted from: *UNCTAD (#20285)* (Special Category); *World Intellectual Property Organization (WIPO, #21593)* (Permanent Observer). **IGO Relations** Observer to: *Union internationale pour la protection des obtentions végétales (UPOV, #20436)*. EU Members Commission cooperates with: *European Union Intellectual Property Office (EUIPO, #08996)*. **NGO Relations** Member of: *European Council of Liberal Professions (#06828)*. [2022.10.11/XB1972/**B**]

- ♦ Fédération internationale de coopération des centres de recherche sur les systèmes et services de santé (no recent information)
- ♦ Fédération internationale des coopératives d'assurances / see International Cooperative and Mutual Insurance Federation (#12948)
- ♦ Fédération Internationale des Coopératives et Mutuelles d'Assurance / Association Régionale pour les Amériques (#12949)
- ♦ Fédération internationale des coopératives et mutuelles d'assurances (#12948)
- ♦ Fédération internationale de la corderie (inactive)
- ♦ Fédération internationale des corps et associations consulaires / see World Federation of Consuls (#21422)
- ♦ Fédération internationale de course d'orientation (#14485)
- ♦ Fédération internationale de crémation (#13104)
- ♦ Fédération internationale de la Croix-Bleue / see International Blue Cross (#12364)
- ♦ Fédération internationale des cuisiniers (inactive)

♦ Fédération internationale culturelle féminine (FICF) 09625

Women's International Cultural Federation

Pres 51 rue Pergolèse, 75116 Paris, France. T. +33145016942. Fax +33145016942. E-mail: nvld@free.fr – contact@ficfart.org.
URL: http://www.ficfart.org/

History 1961, by Marguerite Perigot de la Tour, developing from *Club international féminin (CIF)* which she set up, Jun 1951, Paris (France). Constitutive Assembly 1962, Paris. Registered under French law. **Aims** Allow women *artists* of many countries the opportunity to share cultural ideals, information and opinions on modern society through international exhibitions of their works (paintings or sculptures). **Structure** General Meeting (annual, at Congress); Council; Committee. Administrative Secretariat in Paris (France) – International Secretary and Treasurer are always French nationals. International Bureau approves national groups. **Languages** English, French, German, Italian. **Staff** Voluntary. **Finance** Members' dues. **Activities** Organizes roundtables on topical matters; international artistic exhibitions. **Events** *Congress* Bucharest (Romania) 2009, *Congress* Istanbul (Turkey) 2009, *Congress* Ibbenbüren (Germany) 2008, *Congress* Istanbul (Turkey) 2007, *Congress* Paris (France) 2006. **Publications** *FICF Bulletin* (annual) in English, French, German.
Members National groups in 7 countries:
Belgium, Czechia, France, Germany, Greece, Italy, Poland.
Individuals in 16 countries:
Belgium, France, Germany, Greece, Iran Islamic Rep, Italy, Japan, Korea Rep, Norway, Peru, Poland, Romania, Spain, Sweden, UK, USA. [2015/XD3437/**D**]

- ♦ Fédération internationale de culture physique / see International Fitness and Bodybuilding Federation (#13610)
- ♦ Fédération internationale de curling, 1898 (inactive)
- ♦ Fédération internationale d'éducation physique / see International Federation of Physical and Sport Education (#13510)
- ♦ Fédération internationale des déménageurs internationaux / see FIDI Global Alliance (#09753)
- ♦ Fédération internationale pour le développement de l'enseignement ménager / see International Federation for Home Economics (#13447)
- ♦ Fédération internationale pour le développement de l'herboristerie médicinale, aromatique et des plantes similaires (inactive)
- ♦ Fédération internationale pour le développement participatif (inactive)
- ♦ Fédération internationale du diabète (#13164)

♦ Fédération Internationale de la Diaspora Afar (FIDA) 09626

Afar Diaspora International Federation

Project Manager Place de la Querelle 1 – Bte 13, 1000 Brussels, Belgium. T. +32467747525. E-mail: fida.afar@gmail.com.
URL: http://fida-afar.business.site/

History Set up 31 Mar 2013, as *Afar Diaspora Network (ADN)*. Registered under current title, in accordance with Belgian law, Feb 2015. **Aims** Promote and support the Afar people's physical, economic, social and cultural infrastructure, community development programmes and projects. **Structure** Board of Directors. **Languages** English, French. **Staff** 10.00 FTE, paid. **Finance** Members' dues. Other sources: donations; subsidies from the City of Brussels. Annual budget (2019): euro 6,200. **Activities** Advocacy/lobbying/activism; humanitarian/emergency aid; projects/programmes; events/meetings. **Events** *International Conference on Human Rights Situation in the Horn of Africa Area and in the AFAR Triangle Territories* Brussels (Belgium) 2018.
Members Full in 5 countries:
Belgium, Canada, France, Sweden, UK.
NGO Relations Cooperates with: City of Brussels. [2019.12.11/XM4669/**E**]

- ♦ Fédération internationale des dockers et marins / see International Transport Workers' Federation (#15726)
- ♦ Fédération internationale des docteurs-en-sciences (inactive)
- ♦ Fédération internationale des droguistes (inactive)
- ♦ Fédération internationale pour le droit européen (#13419)
- ♦ Fédération internationale des droits de l'homme / see International Federation for Human Rights (#13452)
- ♦ Fédération Internationale pour les Droits Humains (#13452)
- ♦ Fédération internationale du droit à la vie (#14755)
- ♦ Fédération internationale pour les échanges éducatifs d'enfants et d'adolescents (no recent information)

♦ Fédération internationale des échecs (FIDE) 09627

World Chess Federation – Federación Internacional de Ajedrez – Weltschachverband

Headquarters Ave de Rhodanie 54, 1007 Lausanne VD, Switzerland. T. +41216010039. E-mail: office@fide.com.
URL: http://www.fide.com/

History 20 Jul 1924, Paris (France). **Aims** Promote the art, sport and science of chess; establish close international cooperation between chess-players; regulate world *championships*; issue official code of rules; award international chess titles. **Structure** General Assembly (annual); Presidential Board; Executive Board; Commissions. **Languages** Arabic, English, French, German, Portuguese, Russian, Spanish. **Staff** 5.50 FTE, paid. **Finance** Sources: members' dues. Other sources: Percentage prize fund of FIDE events. **Activities** Sporting activities. **Events** *Annual Congress* Khanty-Mansiysk (Russia) 2021, *Annual Congress* Abu Dhabi (United Arab Emirates) 2020, *Annual Congress* Khanty-Mansiysk (Russia) 2020, *Annual Congress* Batumi (Georgia) 2018, *Annual Congress* Antalya (Turkey) 2017. **Publications** *Rating List* (6 a year); *Arbiter's Magazine* (2 a year); *Address List* (annual); *FIDE Trainer's Commission Yearbook* (annual); *FIDE Handbook* (every 2 years). Congress books.
Members National Organizations in 188 countries and territories:
Afghanistan, Albania, Algeria, Andorra, Angola, Argentina, Armenia, Aruba, Australia, Austria, Azerbaijan, Bahamas, Bahrain, Bangladesh, Barbados, Belarus, Belgium, Bermuda, Bhutan, Bolivia, Bosnia-Herzegovina, Botswana, Brazil, Brunei Darussalam, Bulgaria, Burkina Faso, Burundi, Cambodia, Cameroon, Canada, Cape Verde, Central African Rep, Chile, China, Colombia, Comoros, Congo Brazzaville, Costa Rica, Côte d'Ivoire, Croatia, Cuba, Cyprus, Czechia, Denmark, Djibouti, Dominican Rep, Ecuador, Egypt, El Salvador, England, Eritrea, Estonia, Eswatini, Ethiopia, Faeroe Is, Fiji, Finland, France, Gabon, Gambia, Georgia, Germany, Ghana, Greece, Guam, Guatemala, Guernsey, Guyana, Haiti, Honduras, Hong Kong, Hungary, Iceland, India, Indonesia, Iran Islamic Rep, Iraq, Ireland, Israel, Italy, Jamaica, Japan, Jersey, Jordan, Kazakhstan, Kenya, Korea Rep, Kosovo, Kuwait, Kyrgyzstan, Laos, Latvia, Lebanon, Lesotho, Liberia, Libya, Liechtenstein, Lithuania, Luxembourg, Macau, Madagascar, Malawi, Malaysia, Maldives, Mali, Malta, Mauritania, Mauritius, Mexico, Moldova, Monaco, Mongolia, Montenegro, Morocco, Mozambique, Myanmar, Namibia, Nauru, Nepal, Netherlands, New Zealand, Nicaragua, Nigeria, North Macedonia, Norway, Oman, Pakistan, Palau, Palestine, Panama, Papua New Guinea, Paraguay, Peru, Philippines, Poland, Portugal, Puerto Rico, Qatar, Romania, Russia, Rwanda, San Marino, Sao Tomé-Principe, Saudi Arabia, Scotland, Senegal, Serbia, Seychelles, Sierra Leone, Singapore, Slovakia, Slovenia, Solomon Is, Somalia, South Africa, South Sudan, Spain, Sri Lanka, Sudan, Suriname, Sweden, Switzerland, Syrian AR, Taiwan, Tajikistan, Tanzania UR, Thailand, Timor-Leste, Togo, Trinidad-Tobago, Tunisia, Türkiye, Turkmenistan, Uganda, Ukraine, United Arab Emirates, Uruguay, USA, Uzbekistan, Venezuela, Vietnam, Virgin Is UK, Virgin Is USA, Wales, Yemen, Zambia, Zimbabwe.
NGO Relations Member of (3): *Association of the IOC Recognized International Sports Federations (ARISF, #02767)*; *International University Sports Federation (FISU, #15830)*; *Olympic Movement (#17719)*. Instrumental in setting up (1): *International Mind Sports Association (IMSA, #14164)*. Recognized by: *International Olympic Committee (IOC, #14408)*. Collaborates with: *African Chess Union (#00245)*; *Arab Chess Federation (ACF, #00919)*; *Commonwealth Chess Association (CCA, #04317)*; *Confederation of Chess for the Americas (CCA, #04516)*; *European Chess Union (ECU, #06528)*; *International Braille Chess Association (IBCA, #12388)*; *International Chess Committee of the Deaf (ICCD, #12544)*; *International Computer Games Association (ICGA, #12836)*; *International Correspondence Chess Federation (ICCF, #12971)*; *International Physically Disabled Chess Association (IPCA, #14577)*; *Nordic Chess Federation (#17234)*. [2021/XB3482/**B**]

- ♦ Fédération internationale des échecs par correspondance (#12971)
- ♦ Fédération internationale de l'école et de la famille (inactive)
- ♦ Fédération internationale des écoles catholiques de journalisme (inactive)
- ♦ Fédération internationale des écoles de chiens guides d'aveugles / see International Guide Dog Federation (#13763)
- ♦ Fédération internationale des écoles de parents et d'éducateurs / see International Federation for Parent Education (#13499)
- ♦ Fédération internationale des écoles unies (#20660)
- ♦ Fédération internationale pour l'économie familiale / see International Federation for Home Economics (#13447)
- ♦ Fédération internationale des écrivains de langue française (no recent information)
- ♦ Fédération internationale des éditeurs de médailles / see International Art Medal Federation (#11675)
- ♦ Fédération internationale des éducateurs espérantistes progressistes (inactive)
- ♦ Fédération internationale pour l'éducation artistique (inactive)
- ♦ Fédération internationale d'éducation concernant les stupéfiants (inactive)
- ♦ Fédération internationale pour l'éducation des parents (#13499)
- ♦ Fédération internationale d'éducation physique et sportive (#13510)
- ♦ Fédération internationale des Eglises évangéliques libres (#13433)
- ♦ Fédération internationale des électriciens, électroniciens et spécialistes de l'automobile (inactive)
- ♦ Fédération internationale d'électroencéphalographie et de neurophysiologie clinique / see International Federation of Clinical Neurophysiology (#13393)
- ♦ Fédération internationale d'électronique médicale / see International Federation for Medical and Biological Engineering (#13477)
- ♦ Fédération internationale de l'élevage caprin (inactive)
- ♦ Fédération internationale d'éleveurs de poneys (inactive)
- ♦ Fédération internationale des employés de banque et de bourse (inactive)
- ♦ Fédération internationale des employés de commerce (inactive)
- ♦ Fédération internationale des employés municipaux / see Public Services International (#18572)
- ♦ Fédération internationale des employés des PTT (inactive)
- ♦ Fédération internationale des employés, techniciens et cadres (inactive)
- ♦ Fédération internationale de l'emulsion de bitume (#12356)
- ♦ Fédération internationale de l'encadrement des industries métallurgiques / see European Federation of Managers in the Steel Industry (#07162)
- ♦ Fédération internationale des Enfants de Marie Immaculée (religious order)
- ♦ Fédération internationale des enseignants de rythmique (#13418)
- ♦ Fédération internationale pour l'enseignement des arts du dessin (inactive)
- ♦ Fédération internationale pour l'enseignement du dessin et des arts appliqués à l'industrie (inactive)
- ♦ Fédération internationale pour l'enseignement ménager / see International Federation for Home Economics (#13447)
- ♦ Fédération internationale des entrepreneurs de la construction / see European Construction Industry Federation (#06766)
- ♦ Fédération internationale des entrepreneurs européens de bâtiment et de travaux publics / see European Construction Industry Federation (#06766)

Fédération internationale entreprises
09627
alphabetic sequence excludes
For the complete listing, see Yearbook Online at

♦ Fédération internationale des entreprises de couverture / see International Federation for the Roofing Trade (#13534)

♦ Fédération internationale des entreprises de nettoyage (FIDEN) . . . 09628

International Association of Building Service Contractors – Federación Internacional de Empresarios de Limpieza – Internationale Gemeinschaft des Gebäudereinigungs-Gewerbes – Federazione Internazionale delle Imprese di Pulizia

Contact Richard Wagnerstrasse 19, 80333 Munich, Germany. T. +498952304055. Fax +498952304050. E-mail: info@fiden.org.
URL: https://fiden.org/

History 1956. Former names and other names: *International Association of Cleaning Companies* – former; *Internationaler Verband der Reinigungsunternehmen* – former; *International Association of Building Contractors* – former. Registration: North Rhine-Westphalia District court, No/ID: VR 5393, Start date: 24 Nov 1986, Germany, Bonn. **Aims** Offer a platform for building *cleaning* companies to exchange experience and best practices; make business and personal contacts at European and international level. **Structure** General Assembly; Managing Committee; Steering Committee; Permanent Secretariat in Munich (Germany). **Languages** English, French, German, Italian, Spanish. **Staff** 2.00 FTE, paid. **Finance** Members' dues. **Activities** Events/meetings; guidance/assistance/consulting; networking/liaising. **Events** *International Congress* Dubrovnik (Croatia) 2022, *International Congress* Palma (Spain) 2021, *International Congress* Palma (Spain) 2020, *International Congress* Maastricht (Netherlands) 2019, *International Congress* Venice (Italy) 2018.
Members Full in 8 countries:
Austria, Germany, Greece, Hungary, Italy, Romania, Spain, Switzerland.
NGO Relations National associations. [2021/XD4138/**D**]

♦ Fédération internationale d'épidémiologie psychiatrique (#13521)
♦ Fédération internationale d'équitation thérapeutique / see Federation of Horses in Education and Therapy International (#09593)

♦ Fédération internationale d'escrime (FIE) 09629

International Fencing Federation

CEO Maison du Sport Int'l, Ave de Rhodanie 54, 1007 Lausanne VD, Switzerland. T. +41213203115. Fax +41213203116. E-mail: admin@fie.ch – info@fie.ch.
URL: http://fie.org/

History 29 Nov 1913, Paris (France). Founded following a fencing Congress in Ghent (Belgium). **Aims** Promote international development of fencing and strengthen ties of friendship between *amateur* fencers in all countries; ensure that contests are organized in accordance with official rules; investigate and decide all fencing questions involving international relations. **Structure** Congress; Executive Committee; Bureau; Permanent Commissions (7). **Languages** English, French, Spanish. **Staff** 12.00 FTE, paid. **Finance** Sources: members' dues; sponsorship. Other sources: licenses; TV fees. **Activities** Sporting activities. **Events** *Congress* Lausanne (Switzerland) 2019, *Congress* Paris (France) 2018, *Congress* Dubai (United Arab Emirates) 2017, *Congress* Rome (Italy) 2014, *Congress* Paris (France) 2013. **Publications** *Escrime XXI* (5 a year); *Lettre d'informations et urgentes de la FIE*. *Livre des statuts FIE*. Rules; Anti-Doping Code; handbooks for organization of Grand Prix competitions, World Championships, Zonal Championships; handbook for protocol.
Members National federations in 151 countries and territories:
Afghanistan, Albania, Algeria, Antigua-Barbuda, Argentina, Armenia, Aruba, Australia, Austria, Azerbaijan, Bahamas, Bahrain, Bangladesh, Barbados, Belarus, Belgium, Belize, Benin, Bermuda, Bolivia, Botswana, Brazil, Brunei Darussalam, Bulgaria, Burkina Faso, Cambodia, Cameroon, Canada, Chile, China, Colombia, Congo Brazzaville, Congo DR, Costa Rica, Côte d'Ivoire, Croatia, Cuba, Cyprus, Czechia, Denmark, Dominica, Dominican Rep, Ecuador, Egypt, El Salvador, Equatorial Guinea, Estonia, Finland, France, Gabon, Georgia, Germany, Ghana, Greece, Guam, Guatemala, Guinea, Guyana, Honduras, Hong Kong, Hungary, Iceland, India, Indonesia, Iran Islamic Rep, Iraq, Ireland, Israel, Italy, Jamaica, Japan, Jordan, Kazakhstan, Korea DPR, Korea Rep, Kuwait, Kyrgyzstan, Latvia, Lebanon, Libya, Lithuania, Luxembourg, Macau, Madagascar, Malaysia, Mali, Malta, Mauritania, Mauritius, Mexico, Moldova, Monaco, Mongolia, Montenegro, Morocco, Myanmar, Namibia, Nepal, Netherlands, New Zealand, Nicaragua, Niger, Nigeria, North Macedonia, Norway, Palestine, Panama, Paraguay, Peru, Philippines, Poland, Portugal, Puerto Rico, Qatar, Romania, Russia, Rwanda, Samoa, San Marino, Saudi Arabia, Senegal, Serbia, Sierra Leone, Singapore, Slovakia, Slovenia, Somalia, South Africa, Spain, Sri Lanka, Sweden, Switzerland, Syrian AR, Taiwan, Tajikistan, Thailand, Togo, Tunisia, Türkiye, Turkmenistan, Uganda, UK, Ukraine, United Arab Emirates, Uruguay, USA, Uzbekistan, Venezuela, Vietnam, Virgin Is USA, Yemen.
NGO Relations Member of (5): *Association of Summer Olympic International Federations (ASOIF, #02943)*; *International Committee for Fair Play (#12769)*; *International Council for Coaching Excellence (ICCE, #13008)*; *Olympic Movement (#17719)*; *World Anti-Doping Agency (WADA, #21096)*. Cooperates with (3): *International Committee of the Mediterranean Games (ICMG, #12783)*; *International Paralympic Committee (IPC, #14512)*; *International University Sports Federation (FISU, #15830)*. Recognized by: *International Olympic Committee (IOC, #14408)*. [2021/XB2051/**B**]

♦ Fédération internationale de l'esthétique-cosmétique (#13344)
♦ Fédération internationale d'études pour l'Amérique latine et les Caraïbes (#09338)
♦ Fédération internationale des étudiants 'Corda Fratres' (inactive)
♦ Fédération internationale des étudiants en droit (inactive)
♦ Fédération Internationale des Etudiants en Pharmacie (#14568)
♦ Fédération internationale des étudiants ès sciences politiques (inactive)
♦ Fédération internationale/européenne des cadres de la chimie et des industries annexes / see European Federation of Managerial Staff in the Chemical and Allied Industries (#07160)
♦ Fédération internationale européenne de la construction / see European Construction Industry Federation (#06766)
♦ Fédération internationale des experts en automobile (#13368)

♦ Fédération internationale des experts-comptables francophones (FIDEF) 09630

International Federation of French-Speaking Accountants

General Delegate 200-216 rue Raymond Losserand, 75014 Paris, France. T. +33144156295. E-mail: fidef@fidef.org.
URL: http://www.fidef.org/

History 15 Apr 1982. Founded following decision of a meeting Sep 1981. Registration: RNA, No/ID: W751060308, France. **Aims** Promote abilities, ethics and practice of accountants; develop cooperation between professional organizations of French-speaking accountants which are recognized by national authorities, in areas related to their profession and especially regarding the following: theoretical and continuing education, diploma, professional standards and quality control, deontology and ethics, juridical and accounting matters; exchange information on national regulation and practice; support the establishment and functioning of national professional organizations representing accountants and auditors in public practice; represent the profession of French-speaking accountants in international institutions. **Structure** General Assembly; Board of Management; Bureau. **Finance** Members' dues. **Activities** Events/meetings; standards/guidelines; training/education; networking/liaising. **Events** *Quelle profession au service des besoins de nos économies, une vision pour demain* Antananarivo (Madagascar) 2016, *Economie informelle, économie émergente, la profession comptable francophone s'engage* Saly (Senegal) 2014, *Annual General Assembly* Dijon (France) 2013, *Annual General Assembly* Paris (France) 2012, *Annual General Assembly* Tunis (Tunisia) 2005. **Publications** *FIDEF en bref* (periodical).
Members Active; Associate. Organizations in 23 countries:
Albania, Belgium, Benin, Bulgaria, Burkina Faso, Cameroon, Canada, Congo Brazzaville, Congo DR, Côte d'Ivoire, France, Guinea, Lebanon, Madagascar, Mali, Mauritania, Morocco, Niger, Romania, Senegal, Syrian AR, Togo, Tunisia.
Consultative Status Consultative status granted from: *Organisation internationale de la Francophonie (OIF, #17809)*; *UNCTAD (#20285)* (Special). **IGO Relations** Accredited by (1): *Organisation internationale de la Francophonie (OIF, #17809)*. **NGO Relations** Member of (3): *Association francophone d'amitié et de liaison (AFAL, #02605)*; *Fédération des experts comptables méditerranéens (FCM, #09584)* (Associate); *International Federation of Accountants (IFAC, #13335)* (Associate). [2018/XD1568/**D**]

♦ Fédération internationale pour l'extension et la culture de la langue française (inactive)

♦ Fédération internationale des fabricants des papiers gommés (FIPAGO) 09631

International Federation of Manufacturers of Gummed Paper – Internationaler Verband von Herstellern Gummierter Papiere

Delegate lordensstraat 70, 2012 HE Haarlem, Netherlands. T. +31653236970. E-mail: info@fipago.org.
URL: http://www.fipago.org/

History Founded 15 Mar 1957, The Hague (Netherlands). **Aims** Promote the interests of members by: carrying out research and studies; investigating commercial and economic policy questions, possibilities for quality improvement and unification of measures; compiling statistical data. **Structure** General Assembly (annual); Board of Directors; Technical and Marketing Committee. Meetings closed; annual congress open. **Languages** English. **Staff** 1.00 FTE, paid. **Finance** Members' dues. **Activities** Advocacy/lobbying/activism; standards/guidelines; research/documentation; knowledge management/information dissemination; events/meetings. **Events** *Annual Congress* St Gallen (Switzerland) 2014, *Annual Congress* Seville (Spain) 2012, *Annual Congress* Bologna (Italy) 2011, *Annual Congress* Dublin (Ireland) 2010, *Annual Congress* Sicily (Italy) 2009.
Members Manufacturers in 7 countries:
Argentina, Germany, India, Netherlands, Spain, Switzerland, USA. [2019.02.13/XC1926/**D**]

♦ Fédération internationale des fabricants et transformateurs d'adhésifs et thermocollants sur papiers et autres supports / see FINAT (#09773)

♦ Fédération internationale féline (FIFe) 09632

Gen Sec Na Vrsku 470/11, 671 67 Hrusovany nad Jevisovkou, Czechia. T. +420541227824. E-mail: general-secretary@fifeweb.org.
Pres address not obtained.
URL: http://www.fifeweb.org/

History 1949, France. Founded by Mme Ravel. Registration: Start date: 1998, Luxembourg. **Aims** Unite clubs and federations of clubs interested in *cats* of domestic origin, *pedigreed* or not; encourage breeding of cats, improvement of breeds and promotion of their welfare. Particular concerns: standardizing regulations governing shows, judges and international titles; defining and standardizing breeds; recognizing and harmonizing national pedigree registers, whilst endeavouring to institute a unique register of each type in each country; instituting and regulating an international register of prefixes or cattery names. **Structure** General Assembly (annual); Board; Commissions (5). **Languages** English, French, German. **Staff** 1.00 FTE, paid; 5.00 FTE, voluntary. **Finance** Sources: members' fees for holding shows; registering cattery names; judging examinations; etc. Annual budget: 200,000 EUR. **Activities** Certification/accreditation; events/meetings; monitoring/evaluation. **Events** *Annual General Assembly* Bratislava (Slovakia) 2019, *Annual General Assembly* Monte Gordo (Portugal) 2018, *Annual General Assembly* Bratislava (Slovakia) 2017, *Annual General Assembly* Lisbon (Portugal) 2016, *Annual General Assembly* Monte Gordo (Portugal) 2015. **Publications** *Colours and Patterns in EFG*; *FIFe 50 Year Jubilee Book*.
Members Full: national associations (42) in 40 countries:
Argentina, Austria (2 members), Belarus, Belgium, Brazil, Bulgaria, China, Colombia, Croatia, Czechia, Denmark, Estonia, Finland, France, Germany, Greece, Hungary, Iceland, Indonesia, Italy, Latvia, Liechtenstein, Lithuania, Luxembourg, Malaysia, Mexico, Moldova, Netherlands (2 members), Norway, Poland, Portugal, Romania, Russia, Slovakia, Slovenia, Spain, Sweden, Switzerland, UK, Ukraine.
IGO Relations Formal contacts with: *Council of Europe (CE, #04881)*. **NGO Relations** Founding member of: *World Cat Congress (WCC, #21262)*. In liaison with technical committees of: *International Organization for Standardization (ISO, #14473)*. [2023.02.14/XC0044/**C**]

♦ Fédération internationale des femmes des carrières juridiques – magistrats, avocats, avoués, notaires, professeurs de droit ou exerçant une autre carrière juridique (#13579)
♦ Fédération internationale des femmes de carrières libérales et commerciales (#13376)
♦ Fédération internationale des femmes diplômées des universités / see Graduate Women International (#10688)
♦ Fédération Internationale Des Femmes Juristes (#13578)
♦ Fédération internationale des femmes magistrats et avocats ou qui exercent une autre carrière juridique / see International Federation of Women in Legal Careers (#13579)
♦ Fédération internationale des femmes Mazdaznan (inactive)
♦ Fédération internationale des filateurs et fabricants de coton (inactive)
♦ Fédération internationale du film sur l'art (inactive)
♦ Fédération internationale de la filterie (inactive)
♦ Fédération internationale des fonctionnaires (inactive)
♦ Fédération internationale des fonctionnaires de police (inactive)
♦ Fédération internationale des fonctionnaires des services publiques / see International Federation of Employees in Public Services (#13410)
♦ Fédération internationale des fonctionnaires supérieurs de police (no recent information)
♦ Fédération Internationale de Football Association (#13360)
♦ Fédération Internationale de Football Corporatif (unconfirmed)

♦ Fédération internationale des footballeurs professionnels (FIFPRO) 09633

International Federation of Professional Footballers' Associations

Pres Scorpius 161, 2132 LR Hoofddorp, Netherlands. T. +31235546970. Fax +31235546971. E-mail: info@fifpro.org.
URL: http://www.fifpro.org/

History 1965, Paris (France). One of *International Trade Federations (ITF, inactive)* (World Secretariat for Trade Action) of *World Confederation of Labour (WCL, inactive)*. Registered in accordance with French law. WCL merged with *International Confederation of Free Trade Unions (ICFTU, inactive)* to form *International Trade Union Confederation (ITUC, #15708)*, Nov 2006. Registration: EU Transparency Register, No/ID: 730054141160-88, Start date: 1 Feb 2021. **Aims** Protect the rights of professional football players worldwide. **Structure** General Assembly (annual); Board; Global Player Council. **Languages** English, French, German, Italian, Spanish. **Finance** Members' dues. Other sources: contributions; donations; subsidies; income from events. **Events** *General Assembly* Sydney, NSW (Australia) 2019, *Annual Legal Conference* Amsterdam (Netherlands) 2015, *General Assembly* Tokyo (Japan) 2014, *Meeting* Brussels (Belgium) 2009, *General Assembly* Budapest (Hungary) 2009. **Publications** *Prestige* – magazine.
Members Associations in 62 countries and territories:
Argentina, Australia, Austria, Belgium, Bolivia, Botswana, Bulgaria, Cameroon, Chile, Colombia, Congo DR, Costa Rica, Croatia, Cyprus, Czechia, Ecuador, Egypt, England, Finland, France, Gabon, Ghana, Greece, Guatemala, Honduras, Hungary, India, Indonesia, Ireland, Israel, Italy, Japan, Kenya, Korea Rep, Malaysia, Malta, Mexico, Montenegro, Morocco, Netherlands, New Zealand, North Macedonia, Norway, Panama, Paraguay, Poland, Portugal, Qatar, Romania, Scotland, Serbia, Slovenia, South Africa, Spain, Sweden, Switzerland, Türkiye, Ukraine, Uruguay, USA, Venezuela, Zimbabwe.
IGO Relations Recognized by: *European Commission (EC, #06633)*. **NGO Relations** Accepted as representative by: *International Federation of Association Football (#13360)*. [2020/XD6919/t/**D**]

♦ Fédération internationale de football féminin (inactive)
♦ Fédération internationale de football de table (#15649)

♦ Fédération Internationale Francophone de Coelio-Chirurgie (FIFCC) 09634

Pres Clinique de la Source, Dans l'enceinte de la Clinique, Avenue Vinet 28, 1004 Lausanne VD, Switzerland. T. +41216483285. Fax +41216483287.

History 30 Sep 2005. Also referred to as *Fédération Internationale Francophone des sociétés Coelio-Chirurgie*. Current statutes adopted 26 Nov 2005, Tunis (Tunisia). Registered in accordance with French law. **Structure** Board of Directors. Executive Committee, including President, Vice-President, Secretary-General, Deputy Secretary-General and Treasurer. **Languages** English, French. **Events** *Congrès International de Coelio-Chirurgie* Lyon (France) 2011, *Congrès international de coelio-chirurgie* Lyon (France) 2010.
Members Individuals in 13 countries:
Algeria, Belgium, France, Iran Islamic Rep, Italy, Luxembourg, Mali, Morocco, Switzerland, Syrian AR, Tunisia, Türkiye, USA. [2013.06.29/XJ2366/v/**C**]

♦ Fédération internationale francophone de psychiatrie (internationally oriented national body)

- Fédération Internationale Francophone des sociétés Coelio-Chirurgie / see Fédération Internationale Francophone de Coelio-Chirurgie (#09634)
- Fédération internationale des gantiers (inactive)
- Fédération internationale de génétique (#13711)
- Fédération internationale du génie médical et biologique (#13477)
- Fédération internationale des géomètres (#13561)
- Fédération internationale de la gerbille (no recent information)
- Fédération internationale de golf sur pistes / see World Minigolf Sport Federation (#21653)

♦ Fédération internationale des grossistes importateurs et exportateurs en fournitures automobiles (FIGIEFA) 09635
International Federation of Automotive Aftermarket Distributors
CEO Bd de la Woluwe 42 (Bte 5), 1200 Brussels, Belgium. T. +3227619510. Fax +3227621255. E-mail: figiefa@figiefa.eu.
URL: http://www.figiefa.eu/
History 10 Mar 1956, Geneva (Switzerland). Founded as *International Federation of Wholesalers and Importers in Automobile Fittings – Fédération internationale des grossistes et importateurs en fournitures automobiles.* Registration: Banque-Carrefour des Entreprises, No/ID: 0472.205.007, Start date: 1 Oct 1999, Belgium; EU Transparency Register, No/ID: 69678928900-56, Start date: 5 Jun 2012. **Aims** Represent independent wholesalers and retailers of automotive replacement parts and their associated repair chains in Europe. **Structure** General Assembly (annual); Board of Directors. **Languages** English, French. **Staff** Paid. **Finance** Members' dues. **Activities** Monitoring/evaluation; awareness raising; research and development; networking/liaising; advocacy/lobbying/activism; standards/guidelines. **Events** *Annual Congress* Warsaw (Poland) 2011, *Annual congress* Istanbul (Turkey) 2009, *Annual congress* Brussels (Belgium) 2006, *Annual Congress* Lisbon (Portugal) 2004, *Annual Congress* Madrid (Spain) 2002.
Members National associations (20) in 19 countries:
Austria, Belgium, Czechia, Denmark, Finland, France, Germany, Ireland, Italy, Latvia, Netherlands, Norway, Poland, Portugal, Spain, Sweden, Switzerland, Türkiye, UK.
Associate members in 3 countries:
Australia, Canada, USA.
Consultative Status Consultative status granted from: *ECOSOC (#05331)* (Special). **NGO Relations** Member of: *Alliance for the Freedom of Car Repair in the EU (AFCAR, #00682); Federation of European and International Associations Established in Belgium (FAIB, #09508); SMEunited (#19327).* In liaison with technical committees of: *Comité européen de normalisation (CEN, #04162).*
[2021/XD2040/**D**]

- Fédération internationale des grossistes et importateurs en fournitures automobiles / see Fédération internationale des grossistes importateurs et exportateurs en fournitures automobiles (#09635)
- Fédération internationale des guides interprètes et touristiques (inactive)

♦ Fédération internationale de gymnastique (FIG) 09636
International Gymnastic Federation – Federación Internacional de Gimnasia – Internationaler Turnerbund
SG Av de la Gare 12A, 1003 Lausanne VD, Switzerland. T. +41213215510. Fax +41213215529. E-mail: info@fig-gymnastics.org.
URL: http://www.gymnastics.sport
History 23 Jul 1881, Liège (Belgium). Founded by the Belgian national association. *f* Has taken over activities of *International Federation of Sports Acrobatics (IFSA, inactive)* and *International Trampoline Federation (FIT, inactive).* Former names and other names: *Fédération européenne de gymnastique (FEG)* – former; *Bureau des fédérations européennes de gymnastique* – former. **Aims** Develop the practice of gymnastics; organize championships, participate at Olympic Games. **Structure** Congress; Council (meets annually); Executive Committee; Technical Committees (7); Commissions (12); Appeal Tribunal; Foundation Council. **Languages** English, French, German, Russian, Spanish. **Staff** 34.00 FTE, paid. **Activities** Sporting activities. **Events** *Congress* Antalya (Turkey) 2021, *Meeting* Swakopmund (Namibia) 2021, *Congress* Antalya (Turkey) 2020, *Meeting* Swakopmund (Namibia) 2020, *Meeting* St Petersburg (Russia) 2019. **Publications** *FIG Bulletin* (3 a year); *FIG Flash.*
Members Affiliated federations (154) in 154 countries and territories. Membership countries not specified.
Continental affiliated unions (5):
African Gymnastic Union (#00334); Asian Gymnastics Union (AGU, #01499); European Gymnastics (#07442); Oceania Gymnastics Union (OGU); *Union Panamericana de Gimnasia (UPAG, #20471).*
Associated federations in 2 territories:
Antigua, Macau.
IGO Relations *UNESCO (#20322).* **NGO Relations** Member of (5): *Association of Summer Olympic International Federations (ASOIF, #02943); International Committee for Fair Play (#12769); International Council of Sport Science and Physical Education (ICSSPE, #13077); International World Games Association (IWGA, #15914); Olympic Movement (#17719).* Recognized by: *International Olympic Committee (IOC, #14408).*
[2021.11.11/XB2094/y/**B**]

- Fédération internationale de gymnastique éducative / see International Federation of Physical and Sport Education (#13510)
- Fédération internationale de gymnastique Ling / see International Federation of Physical and Sport Education (#13510)

♦ Fédération internationale de gynécologie infantile et juvénile (FIGIJ) 09637
International Federation of Paediatric and Adolescent Gynaecology
Pres The Woodland Hospital, Rothwell Rd, Kettering, NN16 8XF, UK.
SG St Medica Hosp, Bul P Dapcevic 21, Belgrade, PAK 11000, Serbia.
URL: https://www.figij.org/
History Feb 1971, Lausanne (Switzerland). Founded on the occasion of 1st Symposium. Former names and other names: *International Federation of Infantile and Juvenile Gynecology* – former. Registration: France. **Aims** Improve reproductive health of young people worldwide by raising the bar for clinical care, research and education in the field of pediatric and adolescent gynecology. **Structure** General Assembly; Executive Committee. **Languages** English. **Finance** Sources: members' dues. **Activities** Events/meetings. **Events** *World Congress* Melbourne, VIC (Australia) 2019, *World Congress* Florence (Italy) 2016, *World Congress* Hong Kong (Hong Kong) 2013, *World congress* Montpellier (France) 2010, *European congress* St Petersburg (Russia) 2008. **Publications** *Pediatric and Adolescent Gynecology.*
Members National organizations in 34 countries:
Argentina, Australia, Austria, Belgium, Brazil, Canada, Chile, Cyprus, Czechia, Finland, France, Germany, Greece, Hong Kong, Hungary, Israel, Italy, Japan, Korea Rep, Lithuania, Malaysia, Mexico, Netherlands, Paraguay, Philippines, Poland, Russia, Serbia, Slovakia, Switzerland, UK, Uruguay, USA, Venezuela.
Individuals in 13 countries:
Bulgaria, China, Indonesia, Ireland, Kazakhstan, Latvia, Luxembourg, Mali, Mexico, Pakistan, Saudi Arabia, Spain, Ukraine.
NGO Relations Member and integral part of: *Fédération Internationale de Gynécologie et d'Obstétrique (FIGO, #09638).* Examinations of *International Fellowship of Paediatric and Adolescent Gynaecology (IFEPAG, #13585)* held at world congress.
[2022.06.14/XD6816/**C**]

♦ Fédération Internationale de Gynécologie et d'Obstétrique (FIGO) 09638
International Federation of Gynecology and Obstetrics – Federación Internacional de Ginecología y Obstetricia
Admin Dir Figo House, Waterloo Court – Suite 3, 10 Theed Street, London, SE1 8ST, UK. T. +442079281166. Fax +442079287099. E-mail: figo@figo.org.
URL: http://www.figo.org/
History 26 Jul 1954, Geneva (Switzerland). Founded when Constitution was adopted by General Assembly, following suggestions made at Congress, 1950, New York NY (USA). Former names and other names: *IFGO* – former. Registration: Swiss Civil Code, Switzerland; Charity Commission, No/ID: 1113263, England and Wales; Start date: 28 Nov 2001, USA, State of Illinois. **Aims** Promote the health and wellbeing of women worldwide and improve the practice of gynaecology and obstetrics; promote educational activities and strengthen communication links with and between member societies; further close relations with academic institutions, nongovernmental organizations, governments, intergovernmental organizations and the private sector. **Structure** General Assembly (meets every two years); Board of Trustees (elected for two-year terms); FIGO Council (meets at least once every year); FIGO Secretariat. **Languages** English, French, Spanish. **Staff** 35.00 FTE, paid. **Finance** Sources: contributions; fundraising; meeting proceeds; members' dues; sale of publications. **Activities** Awareness raising; capacity building; events/meetings; healthcare; knowledge management/information dissemination; networking/liaising; projects/programmes; publishing activities; research/documentation; standards/guidelines; training/education. Active in all member countries.
Events *FIGO World Congress of Gynecology and Obstetrics* Paris (France) 2023, *Latin American Regional Congress* Cartagena de Indias (Colombia) 2022, *World Congress of Gynecology and Obstetrics* 2021, *African and Eastern Mediterranean Regional Congress* Kigali (Rwanda) 2020, *World Congress of Gynecology and Obstetrics* Rio de Janeiro (Brazil) 2018. **Publications** *International Journal of Gynecology and Obstetrics* (12 a year); *Recommendations on Ethical Aspects of Human Reproduction* (every 3 years); *Report on Gynaecological Cancer* (every 3 years); *World Report on Women's Health* (every 3 years). *FIGO Gynaecological Endoscopy Series.* Slide atlas.
Members National societies in 135 countries and territories:
Afghanistan, Albania, Algeria, Argentina, Armenia, Australia, Azerbaijan, Bangladesh, Belarus, Belgium, Benin, Bolivia, Brazil, Bulgaria, Burkina Faso, Cambodia, Cameroon, Canada, Chile, China, Colombia, Congo DR, Costa Rica, Côte d'Ivoire, Croatia, Cuba, Cyprus, Czechia, Denmark, Dominican Rep, Ecuador, Egypt, El Salvador, Eritrea, Estonia, Ethiopia, Fiji, Finland, France, Gabon, Georgia, Germany, Ghana, Greece, Guatemala, Guinea, Haiti, Honduras, Hong Kong, Hungary, Iceland, India, Indonesia, Iran Islamic Rep, Iraq, Ireland, Israel, Italy, Jamaica, Japan, Jordan, Kenya, Korea Rep, Kosovo, Kuwait, Kyrgyzstan, Latvia, Lebanon, Liberia, Libya, Lithuania, Luxembourg, Macau, Malawi, Malaysia, Mali, Malta, Mexico, Moldova, Mongolia, Morocco, Mozambique, Myanmar, Nepal, Netherlands, New Zealand, Nicaragua, Niger, Nigeria, North Macedonia, Norway, Oman, Pakistan, Palestine, Panama, Papua New Guinea, Paraguay, Peru, Philippines, Poland, Portugal, Romania, Russia, Rwanda, Saudi Arabia, Senegal, Serbia, Sierra Leone, Singapore, Slovakia, Slovenia, South Africa, South Sudan, Spain, Sri Lanka, Sudan, Sweden, Switzerland, Syrian AR, Taiwan, Tanzania UR, Thailand, Tunisia, Türkiye, Uganda, UK, Ukraine, United Arab Emirates, Uruguay, USA, Uzbekistan, Venezuela, Vietnam, Zambia, Zimbabwe.
Consultative Status Consultative status granted from: *ECOSOC (#05331)* (Ros C); *WHO (#20950)* (Official Relations). **IGO Relations** Accredited by (1): *United Nations Office at Vienna (UNOV, #20604).* **NGO Relations** Member of (4): *Global Alliance for Maternal Mental Health (GAMMH, #10208); International Childbirth Initiative (ICI, #12547)* (Founding); *PMNCH (#18410); Reproductive Health Supplies Coalition (RHSC, #18847).* Instrumental in setting up (1): *World Association of Trainees in Obstetrics & Gynecology (WATOG, #21199).* Joint initiatives with: *International Society for the Study of Hypertension in Pregnancy (ISSHP, #15475).*
[2022.03.01/XB1927/**B**]

- Fédération internationale de l'habitation et de l'urbanisme / see International Federation for Housing and Planning (#13450)
- Fédération internationale pour l'habitation, l'urbanisme et l'aménagement des territoires (#13450)
- Fédération internationale haltérophile / see International Weightlifting Federation (#15876)
- Fédération internationale haltérophile et culturiste / see International Weightlifting Federation (#15876)
- Fédération internationale d'haltérophilie (#15876)
- Fédération Internationale de Handball (#13771)
- Fédération internationale de handball amateur (inactive)
- Fédération internationale de l'harmonica (inactive)
- Fédération internationale pour l'histoire publique (#13524)
- Fédération internationale pour l'histoire et les statistiques du football (#13432)
- Fédération internationale de hockey (#13802)
- Fédération internationale de hockey sur glace (#13831)
- Fédération internationale des hommes d'action catholique / see UNUM OMNES International Council of Catholic Men (#20720)
- Fédération internationale des hommes catholiques (#20720)
- Fédération internationale des hôpitaux / see International Hospital Federation (#13812)
- Fédération internationale des hôtesses de l'air / see International Federation of Air Hostesses and Flight Nurses (#13347)
- Fédération Internationale des Hôtesses et Convoyeuses de l'Air (#13347)
- Fédération internationale d'hygiène, de médecine préventive et sociale (inactive)
- Fédération internationale des imprimeurs sur tissus (inactive)
- Fédération internationale de l'industrie de l'habillement (#11659)
- Fédération internationale de l'industrie du médicament / see International Federation of Pharmaceutical Manufacturers and Associations (#13505)
- Fédération internationale de l'industrie phonographique (#13508)
- Fédération internationale des industries des aliments diététiques (#15576)
- Fédération internationale des industries et du commerce en gros des vins, spiritueux, eaux-de-vie et liqueurs / see FIVS (#09789)
- Fédération internationale des industries consommatrices d'énergie (inactive)
- Fédération internationale des industries consommatrices d'énergie, Europe (#13456)
- Fédération internationale des industries de glucose (inactive)
- Fédération internationale des industries graphiques – CMT (inactive)
- Fédération internationale des industries des produits diététiques incluant tous les aliments de l'enfance / see International Special Dietary Food Industries (#15576)
- Fédération internationale des industries textiles (#15679)
- Fédération internationale des industries textiles cotonnière et connexes / see International Textile Manufacturers Federation (#15679)
- Fédération internationale des infirmiers anesthésistes (#13492)
- Fédération internationale d'information et de documentation (inactive)
- Fédération internationale pour l'information sur le don d'organes et de tissus humains (inactive)
- Fédération internationale d'ingénierie municipal (#13484)
- Fédération internationale d'ingénierie hospitalière (#13439)
- Fédération internationale des ingénieurs-conseils (#13399)
- Fédération internationale des ingénieurs municipaux / see International Federation of Municipal Engineering (#13484)
- Fédération internationale des institutions d'enseignement de l'espagnol (inactive)

♦ Fédération internationale des instituts d'études médiévales (FIDEM) 09639
International Federation of Institutes for Medieval Studies
SG address not obtained. E-mail: secretary.general@fidemweb.org.
Pres Inst Supérieur de Philosophie, Collège Mercier, 14 Place Cardinal Mercier, 1348 Louvain-la-Neuve, Belgium. T. +3210474613 – +3210474614. E-mail: fidem@fidemweb.org.
URL: http://fidemweb.org/
History Founded 21 May 1987, Louvain-la-Neuve (Belgium). Headquarters moved to Porto (Portugal) 2009. **Aims** Promote collaboration between institutes and centres of medieval studies, national associations of medieval scholars and international societies; promote open exchange of information and coordination of study programmes and major research projects; be recognized as a reference organism and an organ for coordination of study and research on the Middle Ages. **Structure** General Assembly. Administrative Council (Board), comprising 2 Honorary Presidents, President, Vice-President, Secretary and 6 assessors. Committee. President; Secretary. **Languages** English, French, Italian. **Staff** 1.00 FTE, paid. **Finance** Members' dues. **Activities** Training/education; events/meetings. **Events** *European Congress of Medieval Studies* Basel (Switzerland) 2023, *European Congress* Basel (Switzerland) 2018, *Annual Meeting* Barcelona (Spain) 2017, *Annual Meeting* Cluj-Napoca (Romania) 2015, *European Congress* Porto (Portugal) 2013. **Publications** *Bulletin d'informations FIDEM. El Florilegio, Espacio de Encuentro de los Autores Antiguos y Medievales; International Directory of Medievalists – Répertoire international de médiévalistes; José Pablo Barragan Nieto, El de secretis mulierum at ribuido a Alberto Magno – Estudio, edición crítica y traducción; L'Antichità Classica nel Pensiero Medievale: A cura di A Palazzo; Mots Médiévaux Offerts à Ruedi Imbach; Rethinking and Recontextualizing Glosses: New Perspectives in the Study of Late Anglo-Saxon Glossography; Thèmes et études du Moyen Age.* Congress proceedings.

Fédération internationale instituts
09639

alphabetic sequence excludes
For the complete listing, see Yearbook Online at

Members Directors of institutions, centres and associations in 35 countries:
Argentina, Austria, Belgium, Brazil, Bulgaria, Canada, Chile, China, Cyprus, Czechia, Denmark, Finland, France, Germany, Greece, Holy See, Hungary, Iceland, Israel, Italy, Japan, Luxembourg, Netherlands, Norway, Peru, Poland, Portugal, Romania, Russia, Spain, Sweden, Switzerland, UK, USA, Venezuela.
[2023/XD3103/**D**]

♦ Fédération internationale des instituts de l'Europe du centre est (no recent information)
♦ Fédération internationale des instituts des hautes études (inactive)
♦ Fédération internationale des instituts de recherches socio-religieuses (inactive)
♦ Fédération internationale des instructeurs de sport de neige (#13542)
♦ Fédération internationale des intellectuels agricoles (inactive)

♦ **Fédération internationale d'inter-crosse (FIIC)** **09640**
Pres 317 6e Avenue, Lasalle QC H8P 2L5, Canada. T. +15145024556. E-mail: fiicofficial@gmail.com.
Facebook: https://www.facebook.com/FIICOfficial/
History Jun 1985, Paris (France). **Aims** Contribute, through the promotion of the sport of inter-crosse, to the education of a better citizen. **Structure** Board of Directors. **Languages** Czech, English, French, Italian, Swedish. **Staff** 4.00 FTE, voluntary. **Finance** Sources: members' dues. **Activities** Sporting activities.
Members in 23 countries. Membership countries not specified.
[2021.03.11/XD7919/**D**]

♦ **Fédération Internationale des Jardins Familiaux** **09641**
SG Rue de Bragance 20, L-1255 Luxembourg, Luxembourg. T. +352453231. Fax +352453412. E-mail: federation-internationale@jardins-familiaux.org.
URL: http://www.jardins-familiaux.org/
History 3 Oct 1926, Luxembourg. Reconstituted, 1949, following World War 2. Former names and other names: *International Office of Allotment Gardens Leagues* – former; *International Office of Allotment and Leisure Garden Societies* – former; *Office international des jardins familiaux* – former; *Internationales Büro der Kleingärtnerverbände* – former; *Internationales Büro der Kleingärtnerorganisationen* – former. Registration: No/ID: F 672, Luxembourg. **Aims** Support national *allotment* and leisure *garden* federations in Europe and Japan, sensitize national and international bodies to their concerns; stimulate both natural gardening, the protection of nature as well as environment and the integration and health purposes among their members. **Structure** General Assembly; Management Board; General Secretariat. **Languages** English, French, German. **Finance** Sources: donations; government support; grants; international organizations; members' dues. **Activities** Events/meetings; knowledge management/information dissemination; publishing activities; training/education. **Events** *International Congress* Vienna (Austria) 2016, *International Congress / Congress* Utrecht (Netherlands) 2014, *International congress / Congress* Copenhagen (Denmark) 2011, *International congress / Congress* Krakow (Poland) 2008, *International seminar* Vienna (Austria) 2006. **Publications** *Le trait d'union* (3 a year) in English, French, German. Newsletter.
Members Organizations of allotment gardens (one per country) in 13 countries:
Austria, Belgium, Denmark, Finland, France, Germany, Japan, Luxembourg, Netherlands, Norway, Sweden, Switzerland, UK.
Consultative Status Consultative status granted from: *Council of Europe (CE, #04881)* (Participatory Status).
[2022.05.10/XD2226/**D**]

♦ Fédération internationale du jazz (inactive)
♦ Fédération internationale du jeu de dames / see Fédération Mondiale du Jeu de Dames (#09690)
♦ Fédération Internationale des Jeunes (#15932)
♦ Fédération internationale pour les jeunes malentendants (#13436)
♦ Fédération internationale de la jeunesse catholique (inactive)
♦ Fédération internationale de la jeunesse pour l'étude et la conservation de l'environnement (inactive)
♦ Fédération internationale des jeunesses bons templiers (inactive)
♦ Fédération internationale des jeunesses libérales (#13469)
♦ Fédération internationale des jeunesses libérales et radicales / see International Federation of Liberal Youth (#13469)
♦ Fédération Internationale des jeunesses musicales / see Jeunesses Musicales International (#16110)
♦ Fédération internationale des jouets et de l'enfance (inactive)
♦ Fédération internationale des journalistes (#13462)
♦ Fédération internationale des journalistes agricoles (#13346)
♦ Fédération internationale des journalistes catholiques (inactive)
♦ Fédération internationale des journalistes et écrivains du tourisme (#21494)
♦ Fédération internationale des journalistes et écrivains des vins et spiritueux (#13577)
♦ Fédération internationale des journalistes de l'environnement (inactive)
♦ Fédération internationale des journalistes et informateurs de plein air (inactive)
♦ Fédération internationale des journalistes libres (inactive)
♦ Fédération internationale des journalistes des pays alliés et libres (inactive)
♦ Fédération internationale des journalistes professionnels de l'aéronautique et de l'astronautique (inactive)
♦ Fédération internationale de judo (#13975)
♦ Fédération internationale de korfbal / see International Korfball Federation (#13992)
♦ Fédération Internationale du Lait (#13128)
♦ Federation internationale de laiterie / see International Dairy Federation (#13128)
♦ Fédération internationale des langues et littératures modernes (#13480)
♦ Fédération internationale latine des juristes et avocats (inactive)
♦ Fédération internationale des libraires (inactive)
♦ Fédération internationale libre des déportés et internés de la résistance (inactive)
♦ Fédération internationale des ligues contre l'antisémitisme (inactive)
♦ Fédération internationale des ligues pour la défense des droits de l'homme et du citoyen / see International Federation for Human Rights (#13452)
♦ Fédération internationale des ligues des droits de l'homme / see International Federation for Human Rights (#13452)
♦ Fédération internationale des lithographes, imprimeurs-lithographes et professions similaires (inactive)
♦ Fédération Internationale de Luge (#14066)
♦ Fédération internationale de Luge de Course / see International Luge Federation (#14066)
♦ Fédération internationale de lutte amateur / see United World Wrestling (#20665)
♦ Fédération internationale des luttes associées / see United World Wrestling (#20665)
♦ Fédération internationale des luttes celtiques (#13383)
♦ Fédération internationale des maçons (inactive)
♦ Fédération internationale des Maisons de l'Europe (inactive)
♦ Fédération internationale des maîtres-tailleurs / see World Federation of Master Tailors (#21453)
♦ Fédération internationale des malentendants (#13435)
♦ Fédération internationale des marchands-tailleurs (inactive)
♦ Fédération internationale de marche (inactive)
♦ Fédération internationale du marketing (#14106)
♦ Fédération internationale de la médaille / see International Art Medal Federation (#11675)
♦ Fédération Internationale de la Médaille d'Art (#11675)

♦ **Fédération internationale de médecine manuelle (FIMM)** **09642**
International Federation of Manual/Musculoskeletal Medicine – Internationale Gesellschaft für Manuelle Medizin
SG FAAO, 1431 Thames Drive, Indianapolis IN 46143, USA. E-mail: atstill21@hotmail.com.
Pres Medisch Centrum ForceMed, Gagelboschplein 1, 5654 KN Eindhoven, Netherlands. E-mail: h.bultman@nvamg.nl.
URL: http://www.fimm-online.com/
History 25 Sep 1965, London (UK), at Congress of Manual Medicine. Statutes modified when registered according to Belgian law, 25 Feb 1968. Current statutes adopted 2002. Has been referred to in English as *International Federation of Manual Medicine*. **Aims** Promote scientific research and develop standards for quality management in the field; harmonize pre- and post-graduate education and support foundation of scientific associations and legal representation in the field in various countries; represent the interests of manual medicine in dealing at international level with official authorities and organizations. **Structure** General Assembly (annual); Executive Council. **Languages** English, French, German. **Staff** 3.50 FTE, voluntary. **Finance** Members' dues: Swiss Fr 200 plus Swiss Fr 5 per individual member. **Events** *General Assembly* Elche (Spain) 2019, *Conference* Seoul (Korea Rep) 2019, *General Assembly* Paris (France) 2018, *General Assembly* Paris (France) 2018, *General Assembly* Utrecht (Netherlands) 2017. **Publications** *Manuelle Medizin* in German.
Members Societies in 23 countries and territories:
Australia, Belgium, Bulgaria, Canada, Czechia, Denmark, Finland, France, Germany, Hong Kong, Hungary, Israel, Italy, Japan, Kazakhstan, Netherlands, Poland, Russia, Slovakia, Spain, Switzerland, Türkiye, USA.
NGO Relations *International Academy of Manual/Musculoskeletal Medicine (IAMMM, #11557)*.
[2020/XD1948/**C**]

♦ Fédération internationale de médecine physique et réadaptation (inactive)
♦ Fédération internationale de médecine sportive (#13554)
♦ Fédération internationale des métallurgistes (inactive)
♦ Fédération internationale du métier de couvreur (#13534)
♦ Fédération internationale des mineurs (inactive)
♦ Fédération internationale pour la mission intérieure et le service chrétien / see European Federation for Diaconia (#07099)
♦ Fédération internationale de motoculture (inactive)

♦ **Fédération Internationale de Motocyclisme (FIM)** **09643**
CEO Route de Suisse 11, 1295 Mies VD, Switzerland. T. +41229509500. Fax +41229509501. E-mail: info@fim.ch.
Pres address not obtained.
URL: http://www.fim-moto.com/
History 21 Dec 1904, Paris (France). Re-constituted 28 Nov 1912, London (UK). Former names and other names: *Fédération internationale des clubs motocyclistes (FICM)* – former (1904 to 1949); *Fédération international motocycliste* – former (1949 to 1997). Registration: EU Transparency Register, No/ID: 275954910173-88. **Aims** Control and develop sporting, touring and road safety aspects of *motorcycling*; render effective an international control of the *sport* by prescribing and enforcing a code of international rules for *competitions*; encourage international touring and maintain cordial relations between the motorcyclists of all countries; generally assure the unity of the motorcycle movement and safeguard the material and moral interests of its members throughout the world; represent the interests of motorcycle users within the European Community, as well as worldwide. **Structure** General Assembly of delegates (annual); Board of Directors; Executive Board. Commissions (13): Road Racing; Motocross; Trial; Enduro; Cross-Country Rallies; Track Racing; Technical; Women in Motorcycling; Leisure Motorcycling; Public Affairs; Environment; Medical; Judicial. **Languages** English, French. **Staff** 45.00 FTE, paid. **Finance** Sale of TV licenses, calendars. Annual budget: 20,000,000 CHF. **Activities** Awards/prizes/competitions; awareness raising; certification/accreditation; events/meetings; networking/liaising; projects/programmes; research and development; sporting activities; standards/guidelines. **Events** *Women in Motorsports Conference* Lahti (Finland) 2019, *General Assembly* Berlin (Germany) 2016, *Women and Sustainability Conference* Jerez de la Frontera (Spain) 2015, *Annual Congress* Monte Carlo (Monaco) 2013, *Asia General Assembly* Singapore (Singapore) 2012. **Publications** *FIM Yearbook*. Rule booklets; results and record lists; articles; press releases.
Members National motorcycle federations in 115 countries and territories:
Algeria, Andorra, Angola, Argentina, Australia, Austria, Bahrain, Belarus, Belgium, Bolivia, Bosnia-Herzegovina, Botswana, Brazil, Bulgaria, Cambodia, Canada, Chile, China, Colombia, Costa Rica, Côte d'Ivoire, Croatia, Cuba, Cyprus, Czechia, Denmark, Dominican Rep, Ecuador, Egypt, El Salvador, Estonia, Finland, France, Germany, Greece, Guam, Guatemala, Honduras, Hong Kong, Hungary, Iceland, India, Indonesia, Iran Islamic Rep, Iraq, Ireland, Israel, Italy, Japan, Jordan, Kazakhstan, Kenya, Korea Rep, Kuwait, Kyrgyzstan, Latvia, Lebanon, Libya, Liechtenstein, Lithuania, Luxembourg, Macau, Madagascar, Malaysia, Malta, Mauritania, Mexico, Moldova, Monaco, Mongolia, Montenegro, Morocco, Mozambique, Namibia, Nepal, Netherlands, New Zealand, Nicaragua, North Macedonia, Norway, Oman, Palestine, Paraguay, Peru, Philippines, Poland, Portugal, Puerto Rico, Qatar, Romania, Russia, San Marino, Saudi Arabia, Serbia, Singapore, Slovakia, Slovenia, South Africa, Spain, Sri Lanka, Sweden, Switzerland, Taiwan, Thailand, Tunisia, Türkiye, Uganda, UK, Ukraine, United Arab Emirates, Uruguay, USA, Venezuela, Zambia, Zimbabwe.
Continental unions (6):
FIM Africa (#09758); *FIM Asia (#09759)*; *FIM Europe (#09760)*; *FIM Latin America (FIM LA, #09762)*; FIM North America; *FIM Oceania*.
Associate members (4):
British Speedway Promoters Association (BSPA); *Circuits International (#03934)*, *International Road Racing Press Association (IRRPA, #14760)*; *Riders for Health II (#18940)*.
IGO Relations Affiliate member of: *World Tourism Organization (UNWTO, #21861)*. **NGO Relations** Member of (4): *Association of the IOC Recognized International Sports Federations (ARISF, #02767)*; *Fédération des Institutions Internationales établies à Genève (FIIG, #09599)*; *International Committee for Fair Play (#12769)*; *Olympic Movement (#17719)*. Recogized by: *International Olympic Committee (IOC, #14408)*. Liaison Organization of: *Comité européen de normalisation (CEN, #04162)*.
[2022.02.02/XC2270/y/**B**]

♦ Fédération internationale des mouvements d'adultes ruraux catholiques (#13535)
♦ Fédération internationale des mouvements d'agriculture biologique / see IFOAM – Organics International (#11105)
♦ Fédération Internationale des Mouvements Catholiques d'Action Paroissiale (#13379)
♦ Fédération internationale des mouvements d'école moderne (#13481)
♦ Fédération internationale des mouvements ouvriers chrétiens (inactive)

♦ **The Federation of International Employers (FedEE)** **09644**
Federación de Empresarios Internacionales
SG Adam House, 7-10 Adam Street, The Strand, London, WC2N 6AA, UK. E-mail: admin@fedee.com.
Contact Pindou 8, Chloe Court, Office 301, CY-8011 Paphos, Cyprus. T. +35726220427.
URL: https://www.fedee.com/
History Jun 1988, London (UK). Former names and other names: *European Union Employers' Network (EUEN)* – former (1988 to 25 May 1998); *European Employers' Network (EEN)* – former (1988 to 25 May 1998); *Réseau européen des employeurs (REE)* – former; *Federation of European Employers (FedEE)* – former (25 May 1998 to 2014); *Fédération des employeurs européens* – former (25 May 1998 to 2014). **Aims** Support and educate senior management of multinational enterprises to deal with a wide range of employment related issues. **Structure** Main Board; Secretariat. Chaired by The Ford Motor Company. **Languages** Chinese, English, French, German, Greek, Italian. **Staff** Variable. **Finance** Sources: fees for services; meeting proceeds; members' dues; revenue from activities/projects; sale of publications. **Activities** Advocacy/lobbying/activism; events/meetings; guidance/assistance/consulting; knowledge management/information dissemination; monitoring/evaluation; networking/liaising; training/education. **Publications** Ebooks; reports; guides. **Information Services** Newswire.
Members Corporate in 82 countries and territories:
Albania, Algeria, Andorra, Angola, Argentina, Australia, Austria, Belgium, Brazil, Bulgaria, Cambodia, Canada, Chile, China, Colombia, Croatia, Curaçao, Cyprus, Czechia, Denmark, Estonia, Finland, France, Germany, Ghana, Gibraltar, Greece, Hong Kong, Hungary, Iceland, India, Indonesia, Ireland, Isle of Man, Italy, Jamaica, Japan, Kenya, Korea Rep, Latvia, Liechtenstein, Lithuania, Luxembourg, Macau, Malawi, Malaysia, Malta, Mexico, Monaco, Mongolia, Montenegro, Morocco, Myanmar, Namibia, Nepal, Netherlands, New Zealand, Nigeria, Norway, Oman, Pakistan, Peru, Philippines, Poland, Portugal, Romania, Russia, Rwanda, Singapore, Slovakia, Slovenia, Spain, Sweden, Switzerland, Taiwan, Thailand, Türkiye, UK, Ukraine, USA, Vietnam, Zimbabwe.
[2022.10.31/XF3953/**F**]

♦ Fédération internationale des musiciens (#13486)
♦ Fédération internationale de la musique chorale (#13388)
♦ Fédération Internationale Musique espérance (#13487)
♦ Fédération internationale des mutilés, des invalides du travail et des invalides civils / see International Federation of Persons with Physical Disability (#13504)
♦ Fédération internationale de la mutualité (inactive)
♦ Fédération internationale de natation / see World Aquatics (#21100)
♦ Fédération internationale de natation amateur / see World Aquatics (#21100)
♦ Fédération internationale des naturopathes (inactive)
♦ Fédération internationale de navigabilité aérospatiale (#13352)
♦ Fédération internationale des négociants en photo et cinéma (inactive)

♦ Fédération internationale de neurophysiologie clinique (#13393)

♦ Fédération Internationale No-Noma 09645

International NoNoma Federation

Contact c/o Winds of Hope Foundation, Ch de Messidor 5, 1006 Lausanne VD, Switzerland. T. +41213207722. E-mail: info@nonoma.org.
URL: http://www.nonoma.org/

History Set up 20 Mar 2003, Geneva (Switzerland), by *Winds of Hope Foundation.* Current articles adopted Oct 2011, Ferney-Voltaire (France). Also referred to as *International Noma Federation* and Registered in accordance with Swiss Civil Code. **Aims** Strengthen the battle against the disease noma worldwide, by connecting all active organizations working against Noma. **Structure** General Assembly; Presidency. **Languages** English, French. **Activities** Advocacy/lobbying/activism; awareness raising; events/meetings; healthcare; research and development; training/education. **NGO Relations** Supporting member of: *FDI – World Dental Federation (#09281).* Partners: *Chaîne de l'Espoir, Mercy Ships (#16724).* [2020.02.20/XM6417/**C**]

♦ Fédération internationale de numismatique olympique (inactive)
♦ Fédération internationale pour l'observation du dimanche (inactive)
♦ Fédération internationale d'oléiculture (inactive)
♦ Fédération internationale des opérateurs de tours (#13571)
♦ Fédération internationale des organes artificiels (#13357)
♦ Fédération internationale des organisateurs de salons nautiques (#13375)
♦ Fédération internationale pour l'organisation de rencontres de handicapés (inactive)
♦ Fédération internationale des organisations d'anciens combattants / see The World Veterans Federation (#21900)
♦ Fédération internationale des organisations de correspondances et d'échanges scolaires (inactive)
♦ Fédération internationale des organisations défendant les droits de reproduction (#13527)
♦ Fédération internationale des organisations de donneurs de sang (#13374)
♦ Fédération internationale des organisations d'hôteliers, restaurateurs et cafetiers (inactive)
♦ Fédération internationale des organisations de sciences sociales (#13543)
♦ Fédération internationale des organisations de service de données / see International Federation of Data Organizations for the Social Sciences (#13402)
♦ Fédération internationale des organisations de services des données en sciences sociales (#13402)
♦ Fédération internationale des organisations syndicales du personnel des transports (inactive)
♦ Fédération internationale des organisations de tourisme social (inactive)
♦ Fédération internationale des organisations de travailleurs de la métallurgie (inactive)
♦ Fédération internationale des organisations de voyage de femmes (inactive)

♦ Federation internationale des organismes de formation à la Gestalt (FORGE) 09646

International Federation of Gestalt Training Organizations

Pres Sognsvannnsy 41, 0372 Oslo, Norway.
Contact Norsk Gestalt Inst, Pilestredet 75, 0354 Oslo, Norway. T. +4792037569.
Registered Office 183 rue Lecourbe, 75015 Paris, France.
URL: http://www.gestalt.lv/forge/

History Founded 1991, Paris (France). Statutes adopted 4 Oct 1993, Paris; modified 29 Jul 1993, London (UK) and 4 Jul 1997, Brussels (Belgium). Registered in accordance with French law. **Aims** Promote international collaboration and sharing of research in the field of training in Gestalt Therapy. **Structure** General Assembly (every 2 years); Board. **Languages** English. **Staff** Voluntary. **Finance** Members' dues. **Activities** Events/meetings. **Events** *Meeting* Krakow (Poland) 2013, *Meeting* Paris (France) 2012, *Meeting* Riga (Latvia) 2011, *Meeting* Berlin (Germany) 2010, *Meeting* Oslo (Norway) 2009.
Members Institutions (30) in 21 countries:
Belgium, Brazil, Canada, Denmark, France, Germany, Italy, Latvia, Malta, Mexico, North Macedonia, Norway, Poland, Romania, Russia, Serbia, Spain, Sweden, UK, Ukraine, USA.
Included in the above, 1 institution listed in this Yearbook:
Centre international de Gestalt (CIG, no recent information).
NGO Relations Member of: *European Association for Psychotherapy (EAP, #06176).* [2015.01.05/XD2504/y/**D**]

♦ Fédération internationale des organismes de psychologie médicale (inactive)
♦ Fédération internationale des ouvriers brasseurs (inactive)
♦ Fédération internationale des ouvriers de la chaussure et du cuir (inactive)
♦ Fédération internationale des ouvriers employés à la construction des routes (inactive)
♦ Fédération internationale des ouvriers de fabrique (inactive)
♦ Fédération internationale des ouvriers pelletiers (inactive)
♦ Fédération internationale des ouvriers tailleurs (inactive)
♦ Fédération internationale des ouvriers du transport (#15726)
♦ Fédération internationale des parcs de La Francophonie (inactive)
♦ Fédération internationale de pathologie cervicale et colposcopie (#13385)
♦ Fédération internationale de patinage à roulettes / see World Skate (#21786)
♦ Fédération internationale des patrons prothésistes dentaires / see Fédération européenne et internationale des patrons prothésistes dentaires (#09575)

♦ Fédération internationale des patrouilles de ski (FIPS) 09647

International Ski Patrol Federation (ISPF)

Sec address not obtained. E-mail: secretary@fips-skipatrol.org.
Pres address not obtained. E-mail: president@fips-skipatrol.org.
URL: http://www.fips-skipatrol.org/

History Set up 1979, Canada. **Aims** Promote prevention of skiing accidents and proper management of skiing accidents worldwide; encourage the gathering and exchange of ideas and information related to ski patrolling; help communications among ski patrol organizations. **Structure** Board of Directors. Officers: President; Secretary; Treasurer. **Languages** English, French. **Staff** 3.00 FTE, voluntary. **Finance** Members' dues. Annual budget: about Canadian $ 15,000. **Activities** Networking/liaising. **Events** *Biennial World Conference* Ponte di Legno (Italy) 2016, *Biennial World Conference* Kelowna, BC (Canada) 2014, *Biennial World Conference* Châtel (France) 2012, *Biennial World Conference* Åre (Sweden) 2009, *Biennial world conference* Åre (Sweden) 2009. **Publications** No regular publications.
Members National organizations in 17 countries:
Argentina, Australia, Canada, Chile, Finland, France, Italy, Japan, Korea Rep, New Zealand, Norway, Romania, Russia, Sweden, Switzerland, UK, USA.
NGO Relations No official formal contacts. [2016.10.18/XD7188/**D**]

♦ Fédération internationale des paveurs (inactive)
♦ Fédération internationale de la pêche sportive en eau douce (see: #04562)
♦ Fédération internationale de la pêche sportive en mer (see: #04562)
♦ Fédération internationale de pêche sportive mouche (see: #04562)
♦ Fédération internationale de pelote basque (#09340)
♦ Fédération internationale des PEN clubs / see International PEN (#14552)
♦ Fédération internationale du personnel d'encadrement des industries et commerces agricoles et alimentaires (inactive)
♦ Fédération internationale du personnel des services publics (#13410)
♦ Fédération internationale des personnes atteintes de spina-bifida et d'hydrocéphalie (#13552)
♦ Fédération internationale des personnes handicapées physiques (#13504)
♦ Fédération internationale de pétanque sur glace / see International Federation Icestocksport (#13455)

♦ Fédération internationale de pétanque et jeu provençal (FIPJP) 09648

International Federation of Pétanque and Provençal Game

Sec address not obtained. E-mail: fipjp@fipjp.com.
Pres address not obtained.
URL: https://www.fipjp.org/index.php/fr/

History 1958. **Aims** Promote petanque and the Provençal *game* in France and in the world. **Structure** Executive Committee of 12 members (half of membership being renewed every 2 years by the International Congress), including President (4 year term), Secretary General and Treasurer General. Commissions (5). **Languages** French. **Staff** Voluntary; administrative functions provided by the secretariat of *'La Fédération Française'.* **Finance** Sources: members' dues. Other sources: Subvention from the French Minister in charge of sports: euro 4,500. Annual budget: 20,000 EUR. **Activities** Advocacy/lobbying/activism; financial and/or material support; sporting activities; standards/guidelines. **Events** *Annual Meeting* Marseille (France) 2012, *Annual Meeting* Kemer (Turkey) 2011, *Annual meeting* Izmir (Turkey) 2010, *Annual meeting* Suphanburi (Thailand) 2009, *Annual Meeting* Dakar (Senegal) 2008.
Members Full national federations in 91 countries and territories:
Algeria, Andorra, Argentina, Armenia, Australia, Austria, Belarus, Belgium, Benin, Bermuda, Brunei Darussalam, Bulgaria, Burkina Faso, Cambodia, Cameroon, Canada, China, Comoros, Congo Brazzaville, Côte d'Ivoire, Croatia, Czechia, Denmark, Djibouti, Dominican Rep, Egypt, England, Estonia, Finland, France, Gabon, Georgia, Germany, Gibraltar, Guinea, Haiti, Hungary, India, Indonesia, Iran Islamic Rep, Ireland, Israel, Italy, Japan, Jersey, Laos, Latvia, Lebanon, Libya, Lithuania, Luxembourg, Madagascar, Malaysia, Mali, Mauritania, Mauritius, Mexico, Moldova, Monaco, Morocco, Netherlands, New Zealand, Niger, Norway, Pakistan, Philippines, Poland, Portugal, Qatar, Romania, Russia, San Marino, Scotland, Senegal, Serbia, Seychelles, Singapore, Slovakia, Slovenia, Spain, Sweden, Switzerland, Taiwan, Thailand, Tunisia, Türkiye, Ukraine, USA, Vanuatu, Vietnam, Wales.
NGO Relations Instrumental in setting up (1): *Confédération mondiale des sports de boules (CMSB, inactive).* [2022/XD1538/**C**]

♦ Fédération internationale des petites et moyennes entreprises commerciales (inactive)
♦ Fédération internationale des petites et moyennes entreprises industrielles (inactive)

♦ Fédération internationale des petits chanteurs (FIPC) 09649

International Federation of Pueri Cantores – Foederatio Internationalis Pueri Cantores (FIPC)

Sec Via Silvio Pellico 10, 28100 Novara NO, Italy. T. +393404099537.
URL: http://www.puericantores.org/

History 1949. Statutes approved by Pope Pius XII, 6 Apr 1951. Acknowledged, 1996, by the *Pontifical Council for the Laity (inactive)* as a private international association of the faithful, of pontifical right, with legal status. Former names and other names: *International Federation of Young Singers* – alias. **Aims** Develop *musical* education of boys and girls, particularly in the *liturgy*, so as to allow all young people to join together to sing the praises of God and so bring peace and goodwill to all mankind as promised at the first Christmas. **Structure** General Assembly (every 2 years); Council of Administration; Advisory Committees (2). **Languages** English, French, German, Italian, Spanish. **Staff** Voluntary. **Finance** Sources: grants; members' dues. **Activities** Events/meetings; networking/liaising; religious activities. **Events** *Congress* Vatican City (Vatican) 2023, *Rejoice and be glad!* Florence (Italy) 2022, *Rejoice and be glad!* Florence (Italy) 2021, *Congress* Florence (Italy) 2020, *Congress* Barcelona (Spain) 2018. **Publications** *FIPC Electronic Newsletter* (4 a year).
Members Children's choirs (boys, girls, mixed choirs with and without voices of men), specializing in liturgy and affiliated to National Federations in 23 countries:
Austria, Belgium, Brazil, Canada, Congo DR, France, Germany, Haiti, India, Ireland, Italy, Korea Rep, Latvia, Mexico, Netherlands, Poland, Portugal, Rwanda, Spain, Sri Lanka, Sweden, Switzerland, USA.
Correspondents in 17 countries:
Argentina, Benin, Burundi, Cameroon, Chile, Colombia, Denmark, Gabon, Hungary, Japan, Lebanon, Panama, Peru, Romania, Slovakia, Slovenia, Venezuela.
NGO Relations Member of (1): *International Federation for Choral Music (IFCM, #13388).* [2021.10.04/XD3740/**C**]

♦ Fédération internationale des petits frères des pauvres (#13471)
♦ Fédération internationale pharmaceutique (#14566)
♦ Fédération internationale des pharmaciens catholiques (#13380)

♦ Fédération internationale de philatélie (FIP) 09650

International Philatelic Federation – Federación Internacional de Filatelia – Internationaler Philatelisten-Verband

SG Hougang Central Post Office, PO Box 048, Singapore 915302, Singapore.
URL: http://www.f-i-p.ch/

History 18 Jun 1926, Paris (France). **Aims** Promote philately worldwide; represent philately at international level; support national federations; help combat forgery and other issues detrimental to philately. **Structure** Congress (every 2 years); Council; Executive Committee. **Languages** English, French, German, Spanish. **Staff** 1.50 FTE, paid. Voluntary. **Finance** Sources: grants; members' dues. **Activities** Commissions: Aerophilately with the Section Astro-Philately; Fight against Falsifications and Undesirable Issues; Maximaphily; Philatelic Literature; Postal History; Postal Stationery; Thematic Philately; Traditional Philately; Youth Philately; Revenues. Organizes philatelic competitions and exhibitions. **Events** *Congress* Jakarta (Indonesia) 2020, *Meeting* Stockholm (Sweden) 2019, *Congress* Bangkok (Thailand) 2018, *Meeting* Prague (Czechia) 2018, *Congress* Taipei (Taiwan) 2016. **Publications** *Flash* (4 a year). *FIP Competition Classes*; *FIP Guide for Judging Traditional/Postal History Exhibits*; *Origin and Evolution of the FIP.* Regulations and Guidelines – online.
Members National federations or societies in 85 countries and territories:
Albania, Argentina, Armenia, Australia, Austria, Bangladesh, Belarus, Belgium, Bolivia, Brazil, Bulgaria, Canada, Chile, China, Colombia, Congo Brazzaville, Costa Rica, Croatia, Cuba, Cyprus, Czechia, Denmark, Dominican Rep, Egypt, Estonia, Finland, France, Georgia, Germany, Greece, Honduras, Hong Kong, Hungary, Iceland, India, Indonesia, Ireland, Israel, Italy, Japan, Korea DPR, Korea Rep, Latvia, Libya, Liechtenstein, Lithuania, Luxembourg, Malaysia, Malta, Mexico, Mongolia, Montenegro, Nepal, Netherlands, New Zealand, Nigeria, Norway, Pakistan, Paraguay, Peru, Philippines, Poland, Portugal, Qatar, Romania, Russia, Saudi Arabia, Serbia, Singapore, Slovakia, Slovenia, South Africa, Spain, Sweden, Switzerland, Taiwan, Thailand, Türkiye, UK, Ukraine, United Arab Emirates, Uruguay, USA, Venezuela, Vietnam.
NGO Relations *International Federation of Aero-Philatelic Societies (#13342),* through Aerophilatelic Commission. [2019/XB2355/**B**]

♦ Fédération internationale de la philatélie maritime (inactive)
♦ Fédération internationale des phonothèques (inactive)
♦ Fédération Internationale de la Photographie de Nature (inactive)
♦ Fédération internationale de phytosociologie (inactive)
♦ Fédération internationale des piétons (#13502)
♦ Fédération internationale pour la planification familiale (#14589)
♦ Fédération internationale pour le planning familial / see International Planned Parenthood Federation (#14589)
♦ Fédération Internationale des Podiatres et Podologues / see International Federation of Podiatrists (#13514)
♦ Fédération internationale de podologie / see International Federation of Podiatrists (#13514)
♦ Fédération Internationale des Podologues (#13514)
♦ Fédération internationale des podologues et podiatres / see International Federation of Podiatrists (#13514)
♦ Fédération internationale des porcelainiers (inactive)
♦ Fédération internationale des potiers (inactive)
♦ Fédération internationale de powerlifting / see International Powerlifting Federation (#14630)
♦ Fédération internationale de praticiens de thérapeutiques naturelles (inactive)
♦ Fédération internationale de la précontrainte (inactive)
♦ Fédération internationale de la presse agricole (inactive)

♦ Fédération internationale de la presse cinématographique (FIPRESCI) 09651

International Federation of Film Critics

Gen Sec Schleissheimerstrasse 83, 80797 Munich, Germany. T. +4989182303. Fax +4989184766. E-mail: info@fipresci.org.
Sec address not obtained.
URL: http://www.fipresci.org/

Fédération internationale presse
09651

History 6 Jun 1930, Brussels (Belgium). Former names and other names: *International Federation of the Cinematographic Press* – former. **Aims** Develop at an international level the activities of national groups concerned with cinematographic press; organize and facilitate study sessions for *journalists* and critics; affirm freedom of criticism and cinematographic information; promote the cinema as a means of artistic expression, cultural formation and civic consciousness; discuss, define and affirm the rights and responsibilities specific to film criticism and journalism. **Structure** General Assembly (annual); Executive Bureau. **Languages** English, French. **Finance** Sources: members' dues. **Activities** Awards/prizes/competitions; events/meetings. **Events** *Annual General Assembly* Miskolc (Hungary) 2022, *Annual General Assembly* Miskolc (Hungary) 2021, *Annual General Assembly* Miskolc (Hungary) 2019, *Annual General Assembly* Bari (Italy) 2018, *Annual General Assembly* Bari (Italy) 2017. **Publications** *Newsletter and Documentation* (4 a year).
Members National associations (up to 2 per country); Individuals. National organizations in 62 countries and territories:
Argentina, Armenia, Australia, Austria, Bangladesh, Belgium, Bosnia-Herzegovina, Brazil, Bulgaria, Cameroon, Canada, Chile, Colombia, Croatia, Cuba, Czechia, Denmark, Egypt, Estonia, Finland, France, Germany, Greece, Hong Kong, Hungary, India, Israel, Italy, Japan, Kazakhstan, Korea Rep, Latvia, Malaysia, Mexico, Morocco, Netherlands, North Macedonia, Norway, Pakistan, Peru, Philippines, Poland, Portugal, Romania, Russia, Serbia, Singapore, Slovakia, Slovenia, Spain, Sri Lanka, Sweden, Switzerland, Tanzania UR, Thailand, Tunisia, Türkiye, UK, Uruguay, USA, Venezuela.
NGO Relations Bureau Member of: *International Council for Film, Television and Audiovisual Communication (IFTC, #13022)*. [2022.10.12/XC2025/**C**]

- ♦ Fédération internationale de la presse gastronomique, vinicole et touristique (inactive)
- ♦ Fédération internationale de la presse de langue française (inactive)
- ♦ Fédération internationale de la presse orientale (inactive)
- ♦ Fédération internationale de la presse périodique / see FIPP (#09776)
- ♦ Fédération internationale de la presse socialiste et démocratique (no recent information)
- ♦ Fédération internationale de la presse technique et professionnelle (inactive)
- ♦ Fédération internationale de prêtres catholiques mariés (inactive)
- ♦ Fédération internationale des producteurs agricoles (inactive)
- ♦ Fédération internationale des producteurs de films indépendants (no recent information)
- ♦ Fédération internationale des producteurs de jus de fruits / see International Fruit and Vegetable Juice Association (#13687)
- ♦ Fédération internationale des producteurs de phonogrammes et vidéogrammes / see International Federation of the Phonographic Industry (#13508)
- ♦ Fédération internationale des professeurs de l'enseignement secondaire officiel (inactive)

♦ Fédération internationale des professeurs de français (FIPF)   **09652**
International Federation of Teachers of French – Federación Internacional de Profesores de Francés – Federação Internacional dos Professores de Francês
Contact 9 rue Jean de Beauvais, 75005 Paris, France. T. +33156240355. E-mail: contact@fipf.org.
URL: http://fipf.org/

History 17 Jul 1969, Paris (France). Most recent statutes adopted 16 Jul 1992, Lausanne (Switzerland). **Aims** Bring together associations of teachers of French and individuals responsible for teaching French throughout the world; facilitate exchange of their experience and research in order to further the teaching both of French and of *French-speaking* culture; encourage and facilitate other forms of exchange, in particular discussion among different categories of French teachers. **Structure** General Assembly (from 1984, every 4 years), consisting of delegates of active member-associations. Administrative Council (meets at least annually), including President, 2 Vice-Presidents, founding Vice-President and immediate Past-President (one Vice-President must represent a country where French is taught as the mother tongue). Executive Bureau (meets at least annually), comprising President, 2 Vice-Presidents and Secretary-General. Interregional Commissions (8): Africa-Indian Ocean (APFA-OI); Arab World Commission (CMA); Asia and Pacific (CAP); North America (CAN); Western Europe (CEO); Eastern and Central Europe (CECO); Latin America and Caribbean (COPALC); French as Mother Tongue (CFLM), each of which organizes meetings and produces its own publications. Working groups. **Languages** French. **Staff** 3.50 FTE, paid. **Finance** Sources: gifts, legacies; grants; members' dues; sale of publications. **Activities** Encourages the creation of associations of teachers of French where none exists; organizes and supports international congresses, meetings, colloquia, study tours and seminars; annual study days at Sèvres (France). Instrumental in setting up: *Fonds mondial pour l'enseignement du français (FMEF, no recent information)*. **Events** *World Congress* Besançon (France) 2025, *Congrès Régional* Hammamet (Tunisia) 2022, *World Congress* Nabeul (Tunisia) 2021, *World Congress* Nabeul (Tunisia) 2020, *Congrès SEDIFRALE* Bogota (Colombia) 2018. **Publications** *Français dans le Monde* (6 a year); *Echanges* (4 a year); *Francophonies du Sud* (3 a year); *Recherches et Applications* (2 a year); *Dialogues et Cultures* (annual).
Members Active: associations of teachers of French in 131 countries and territories:
Afghanistan, Albania, Algeria, Angola, Argentina, Armenia, Australia, Austria, Azerbaijan, Bangladesh, Belarus, Belgium, Benin, Bolivia, Bosnia-Herzegovina, Botswana, Brazil, Bulgaria, Burkina Faso, Burundi, Cambodia, Cameroon, Canada, Central African Rep, Chad, Chile, China, Colombia, Congo Brazzaville, Congo DR, Costa Rica, Côte d'Ivoire, Croatia, Cuba, Cyprus, Czechia, Denmark, Djibouti, Dominican Rep, Ecuador, Egypt, El Salvador, Equatorial Guinea, Estonia, Ethiopia, Finland, France, Gabon, Georgia, Germany, Ghana, Greece, Guatemala, Guinea, Guinea-Bissau, Haiti, Honduras, Hong Kong, Hungary, Iceland, India, Indonesia, Iran Islamic Rep, Ireland, Israel, Italy, Japan, Kazakhstan, Kenya, Korea Rep, Kosovo, Latvia, Lebanon, Lithuania, Luxembourg, Madagascar, Malawi, Malaysia, Mali, Malta, Mauritania, Mauritius, Mexico, Moldova, Mongolia, Montenegro, Morocco, Mozambique, Netherlands, New Zealand, Niger, Nigeria, North Macedonia, Norway, Panama, Paraguay, Peru, Philippines, Poland, Portugal, Puerto Rico, Romania, Russia, Rwanda, Senegal, Serbia, Seychelles, Sierra Leone, Slovakia, Slovenia, South Africa, Spain, Sri Lanka, Sudan, Sweden, Switzerland, Taiwan, Tanzania UR, Thailand, Togo, Tunisia, Türkiye, Uganda, Ukraine, Uruguay, USA, Vanuatu, Venezuela, Vietnam, Zambia, Zimbabwe.
Consultative Status Consultative status granted from: *UNESCO (#20322)* (Consultative Status); *Council of Europe (CE, #04881)* (Participatory Status); *Organisation internationale de la Francophonie (OIF, #17809)*. **IGO Relations** Formal contacts with: *European Commission (EC, #06633)*. **NGO Relations** Member of (2): *Association francophone d'amitié et de liaison (AFAL, #02605)*; *Union des organisations internationales non-gouvernementales établies en France (UOIF, inactive)*. Affiliated to: *Association for French Studies in Southern Africa (AFSSA)*; *International Federation of Language Teacher Associations (#13468)*. Registered office with: *International Centre for Educational Research, Sèvres (CIEP)*. Through Interregional Commission for Africa, contacts and joint activities with: *Association des professeurs de français en Afrique (APFA, no recent information)*. [2021/XC2022/**B**]

- ♦ Fédération internationale des professeurs de langues vivantes (#13468)
- ♦ Fédération internationale des professionnels de l'assistance (inactive)

♦ Fédération internationale des professions immobilières (FIABCI)   **09653**
International Real Estate Federation – Federación Internacional de Profesiones Inmobiliarias – Internationaler Verband der Immobilienberufe
SG 3 rue de l'Arrivée, 75015 Paris, France. T. +33145382635. E-mail: info@fiabci.org.
Events Manager address not obtained.
URL: http://www.fiabci.org/

History 2 Jun 1951, Paris (France). Founded by national associations of Austria, Belgium, France, Germany FR and USA, following the setting up, 1948, Paris, of *International Federation of Real Estate Board Managers – Alliance internationale des administrateurs de biens immobiliers*. Recognized by French Ministerial Decree, 8 Oct 1951. Statutes last modified May 2013, Taichung (Taiwan). Former names and other names: *Confédération internationale des administrateurs de biens immobiliers* – former; *Alliance internationale des administrateurs de biens immobiliers* – former; *International Federation of Property Managers and Real Estate Consultants* – former; *Fédération internationale des administrateurs de biens conseils immobiliers* – former. **Aims** Provide access and opportunity for real estate professionals interested in gaining knowledge, sharing information and conducting international business with each other. **Structure** General Assembly (twice a year); Board of Directors; Executive Committee; General Secretariat based in Paris (France). Regional Structure: Asia-Pacific Region – 14 chapters; American Regions, with Americas Committee – 6 chapters; Africa and Near East Region – 5 chapters; Europe with European Committee and Regional European Committee – 22 chapters. Divisions (3): Administration; Professional; International Relations. **Languages** English, French, German, Japanese, Spanish. **Finance** Sources: contributions; meeting proceeds; members' dues. Other sources: global partners; education programmes. **Activities** Awards/prizes/competitions; events/meetings; knowledge management/information dissemination; networking/liaising; training/education. **Events** *World Real Estate Congress* Paris (France) 2022, *World Real Estate Congress* Manila (Philippines) 2020, *Global Business Summit* Ghent (Belgium) 2019, *Digital Era of Real Estate* Moscow (Russia) 2019, *Annual World Congress* Dubai (United Arab Emirates) 2018. **Publications** *E-newsletter* (12 a year).
Members Real estate professionals (individuals; companies; associations). Direct: Chapters; Multinational; Principal; Corporate; Public Sector; Honorary. Members of Chapters: Principal; Regular; Special; Corporate; Academic; Public Sector; Honorary. Companies and associations in 70 countries and territories. Membership countries not specified. Individuals in 46 countries and territories:
Andorra, Australia, Austria, Belgium, Brazil, Bulgaria, Canada, Colombia, Cyprus, Egypt, France, Georgia, Germany, Greece, Hungary, India, Indonesia, Iran Islamic Rep, Italy, Japan, Korea Rep, Luxembourg, Macau, Malaysia, Mexico, Monaco, Mongolia, Netherlands, New Zealand, Nigeria, Norway, Panama, Philippines, Portugal, Singapore, Slovenia, South Africa, Spain, Switzerland, Taiwan, Thailand, Türkiye, UK, Ukraine, USA, Vietnam.
Consultative Status Consultative status granted from: *ECOSOC (#05331)* (Special). **IGO Relations** Cooperates with (1): *United Nations Economic Commission for Europe (UNECE, #20555)*. Associated with Department of Global Communications of the United Nations. **NGO Relations** Member of (2): *International Ethics Standards Coalition (IES Coalition, #13307)*; *International Property Measurement Standards Coalition (IPMSC, #14656)*. [2021.03.04/XB2402/ty/**B**]

- ♦ Fédération internationale pour la protection des droits des minorités ethniques, religieuses, linguistiques et autres (inactive)
- ♦ Fédération internationale pour la protection des populations (inactive)
- ♦ Fédération internationale pour la protection des races indigènes contre l'alcoolisme (inactive)
- ♦ Fédération internationale protestante de l'enseignement (#11770)
- ♦ Fédération internationale de la prothèse dentaire / see Fédération européenne et internationale des patrons prothésistes dentaires (#09575)
- ♦ Fédération internationale de psychothérapie (#13523)
- ♦ Fédération internationale de psychothérapie médicale / see International Federation for Psychotherapy (#13523)
- ♦ Fédération internationale des quartiers anciens (inactive)
- ♦ Fédération internationale des quilleurs / see International Bowling Federation (#12384)
- ♦ Fédération internationale des radio-amateurs cheminots (#12122)
- ♦ Fédération internationale des radios et télévisions estudiantines (no recent information)
- ♦ Fédération internationale des radio-télégraphistes (inactive)
- ♦ Fédération internationale pour la recherche en histoire des femmes (#13528)
- ♦ Fédération internationale de recherches sur les systèmes (#13564)
- ♦ Fédération internationale de la recherche théâtrale (#13570)
- ♦ Fédération internationale des reconstructeurs de moteurs / see Fédération internationale des rectifieurs et reconstructeurs de moteurs (#09654)

♦ Fédération internationale des rectifieurs et reconstructeurs de moteurs (FIRM)   **09654**
International Association of Engine Rebuilders and Remanufacturers – Internationale Vereinigung der Motoreninstandsetzungsbetriebe
Pres Parc Av Jules Bordet 154, 1140 Brussels, Belgium. T. +491732519010. E-mail: president@firm-org.eu.
URL: http://www.firm-org.eu/

History May 1958, Brussels (Belgium). Previously also referred to in English and French as *International Federation of Engine Reconditioners – Fédération internationale des reconstructeurs de moteurs*. **Aims** Study and promote the interests of the profession in all fields, excluding political. **Structure** General Assembly (annual); Bureau; Executive Committee. **Languages** English. **Staff** Part-time. **Finance** Annual budget: about euro 16,000. **Activities** Knowledge management/information dissemination. **Events** *General Assembly / Assembly* Frankfurt-Main (Germany) 2014, *General Assembly / Assembly* Rimini (Italy) 2014, *General Assembly / Assembly* Paris (France) 2013, *General Assembly / Assembly* Frankfurt-Main (Germany) 2012, *General Assembly / Assembly* Istanbul (Turkey) 2012. **Publications** *FIRM Bulletin* (2 a year) in English, French; *ReMeTecNews*. Technical documentation.
Members National associations in 9 countries:
Austria, Belgium, Denmark, France, Germany, Netherlands, Sweden, Türkiye, UK.
IGO Relations Recognized by: *European Commission (EC, #06633)*. [2018.10.12/XD0057/**D**]

- ♦ Fédération internationale de recyclage (#14706)
- ♦ Fédération internationale des rédacteurs en chef (inactive)
- ♦ Fédération internationale des rédacteurs scientifiques (no recent information)
- ♦ Fédération Internationale des Relais Enfants Parents (unconfirmed)
- ♦ Fédération internationale des relieurs et professions similaires (inactive)
- ♦ Fédération internationale des résistants (#13529)
- ♦ Fédération internationale de roller-skating / see World Skate (#21786)
- ♦ Fédération internationale de roller sports / see World Skate (#21786)
- ♦ Fédération internationale des routiers, chauffeurs, magasiniers et aides d'Amérique (internationally oriented national body)
- ♦ Fédération internationale de rugby amateur / see Rugby Europe (#18998)
- ♦ Fédération internationale des salles municipales de sports et polyvalentes / see European Association of Event Centers (#06032)

♦ Fédération internationale de SAMBO (FIAS)   **09655**
International SAMBO Federation – Federación Internacional de SAMBO (FIAS)
Gen Dir Maison du Sport Internationale, Av de Rhodanie 54, 1007 Lausanne VD, Switzerland. T. +41216017014. Fax +41216017016. E-mail: swissoffice@sambo-fias.com.
Pres Gazetny pereulok 17/9 bld 2, Moscow MOSKVA, Russia, 125009. E-mail: info@sambo-fias.com.
URL: https://www.sambo.sport/en/

History 13 Jun 1984, Madrid (Spain). Founded at first General Assembly, when statutes were adopted. Constitutive Congress 16 May 1985, Bilbao (Spain). Former names and other names: *Fédération internationale amateur de sambo (FIAS)* – former; *International Amateur Sambo Federation* – former; *Federación Internacional Amateur de Sambo (FIAS)* – former. **Aims** Develop the *sport* of Sambo worldwide. **Structure** Congress (annual); Executive Committee; Commissions. **Languages** English, French, Russian, Spanish. **Staff** 15.00 FTE, paid. **Finance** Sources: donations; members' dues; revenue from activities/projects; sponsorship. license fees. **Activities** Events/meetings; sporting activities. **Publications** Statutes; bylaws; rules and regulations.
Members National organizations (one per country) in 94 countries and territories:
Afghanistan, Algeria, Angola, Argentina, Armenia, Australia, Austria, Azerbaijan, Bahrain, Bangladesh, Belarus, Belgium, Brazil, Cameroon, Canada, Chile, Colombia, Costa Rica, Croatia, Cyprus, Czechia, Dominican Rep, El Salvador, Estonia, Finland, France, Georgia, Germany, Greece, Guatemala, Hong Kong, Hungary, India, Indonesia, Iran Islamic Rep, Iraq, Ireland, Israel, Italy, Japan, Jordan, Kazakhstan, Korea Rep, Kyrgyzstan, Latvia, Lebanon, Lithuania, Macau, Malaysia, Mali, Mauritius, Mexico, Moldova, Mongolia, Montenegro, Morocco, Nepal, Netherlands, Nicaragua, Niger, North Macedonia, Pakistan, Palestine, Panama, Peru, Philippines, Poland, Portugal, Romania, Russia, Senegal, Serbia, Seychelles, Sierra Leone, Singapore, Slovakia, Slovenia, Spain, Sri Lanka, Switzerland, Syrian AR, Taiwan, Tajikistan, Thailand, Trinidad-Tobago, Tunisia, Türkiye, Turkmenistan, UK, Ukraine, USA, Uzbekistan, Venezuela, Vietnam, Yemen.
IGO Relations Accredited by (1): *United Nations Framework Convention on Climate Change (UNFCCC, 1992)*. Member of (1): *Enlarged Partial Agreement on Sport (EPAS, #05487)* (Consultative Committee). **NGO Relations** Accredited by (4): *Association internationale de la presse sportive (AIPS, #02729)*; *Olympic Council of Asia (OCA, #17718)*; *Peace and Sport*; *World Anti-Doping Agency (WADA, #21096)*. Member of (7): *Alliance of Independent recognised Members of Sport (AIMS, #00690)* (Associate); *Association of the IOC Recognized International Sports Federations (ARISF, #02767)*; *Conseil international du sport militaire (CISM, #04695)*; *International School Sport Federation (ISF, #14792)*; *International University Sports Federation (FISU, #15830)*; *International World Games Association (IWGA, #15914)*; *Olympic Movement (#17719)*. Cooperates with (1): *International Testing Agency (ITA, #15678)*. Recognized by *International Olympic Committee (IOC, #14408)*. [2021.06.18/XD6480/**C**]

- ♦ Fédération internationale pour la santé de la famille (#13424)
- ♦ Fédération internationale pour la santé publique (inactive)
- ♦ Fédération internationale de saut à la corde (inactive)
- ♦ Fédération internationale de sauvetage aquatique (inactive)
- ♦ Fédération internationale de sauvetage en mer (#14104)

♦ **Fédération Internationale de Savate (FISav)** **09656**

International Savate Federation

Contact 5 rue Alexandre Darracq, 94320 Thiais, France. E-mail: fisavate.office@gmail.com.
URL: http://www.savate.sport/

History Mar 1985. **Structure** Bureau; Comité Directeur (CDI). Commissions. **Languages** English, French. **Activities** Sporting activities. Active in all member countries. **NGO Relations** Member of (2): *Alliance of Independent recognised Members of Sport (AIMS, #00690)*; *Olympic Movement (#17719)*. Recognized by: *International Olympic Committee (IOC, #14408)*. [2022.06.23/XM4777/**C**]

♦ Fédération internationale de sclérose en plaques (#16899)

♦ **Fédération internationale de scrabble francophone (FISF)** **09657**

International Federation of French-Speaking Scrabble

Pres Chemin des Sources 5, 2114 Fleurier NE, Switzerland. E-mail: contact@fisf.net.
URL: http://www.fisf.net/

History 1978. New statutes adopted Nov 1997. Registration: Banque-Carrefour des Entreprises, No/ID: 0447.452.684, Start date: 7 May 1992, Belgium. **Aims** Develop rules of scrabble suitable for *competitions* in francophone countries. **Structure** General Assembly; Administrative Council; Steering Committee; Technical Commissions. **Languages** French. **Staff** 6.00 FTE, paid. **Finance** Members' dues. Annual budget: US$ 30,000. **Activities** Organizes world championships for francophone scrabble. Promotes exchanges between national federations. **Publications** *Officiel du Scrabble (ODS)*.

Members Individuals (about 20,000) from 27 national federations in 30 countries and territories:
Algeria, Angola, Belgium, Benin, Burkina Faso, Cameroon, Canada, Central African Rep, Chad, Congo Brazzaville, Congo DR, Côte d'Ivoire, France, Gabon, Guinea, Lebanon, Luxembourg, Madagascar, Mali, Mauritania, Mauritius, Morocco, New Caledonia, Niger, Romania, Senegal, Switzerland, Togo, Tunisia, UK. [2021/XE3941/**E**]

♦ **Fédération internationale pour la sécurité des usagers de l'électricité (FISUEL)** **09658**

International Federation for the Safety of Electricity Users – Federacion Internacional para la Seguridad de los Usuarios de la Electricidad

Secretariat 17 rue de l'Amiral Hamelin, 75783 Paris CEDEX 16, France. T. +33156795010. Fax +33156795015. E-mail: fisuel@fisuel.org.
URL: http://www.fisuel.org/

History 1 Feb 2002. Registration: Law 1901, Start date: 2002, France. **Aims** Promote the creation of standards, regulations, and installation inspection systems, if they do not already exist, based on the model of systems which are already established in other countries and have been thoroughly tested. Promote jointly all electrical safety at an international level, and encourage contact and sharing of experiences between countries with a common goal: increasing the level of safety in electrical installations; aiming at convergence between systems of reference. **Structure** Board of Directors, comprising President, Past President, Vice-President and Treasurer, 2 Vice-Presidents and 3 members. **Events** *Annual General Meeting* Tokyo (Japan) 2021, *Annual General Meeting* Tokyo (Japan) 2020, *Annual General Meeting* Paris (France) 2015, *International Forum on Electrical Safety* Seoul (Korea Rep) 2015, *Annual General Assembly* Madrid (Spain) 2011.

Members Full national and regional legal bodies in charge electrical safety levels. Member in 16 countries:
Argentina, Belgium, Benin, Côte d'Ivoire, France, Gabon, Ireland, Japan, Korea Rep, Lebanon, Luxembourg, Morocco, Portugal, Senegal, Spain, UK.

Associate bodies which give support to FISUEL. Members in 4 countries:
Cameroon, France, Portugal, Senegal.

Included in the above Associate Members, 2 organizations listed in this Yearbook:
European Copper Institute (ECI, #06796); *International Union for Electricity Applications (#15770)*.

NGO Relations Member of (1): *Forum for European Electrical Domestic Safety (FEEDS)*. [2022/XJ0886/y/**C**]

♦ Fédération internationale des semaines d'arts (inactive)
♦ Fédération internationale des services des espaces verts et de la récréation (inactive)
♦ Fédération internationale des services d'exposition / see International Federation of Exhibition and Event Services (#13420)
♦ Fédération internationale des services d'exposition et d'événement (#13420)
♦ Fédération internationale de services latino-américains et asiatiques de promotion de l'habitation populaire / see Servicio Latinoamericano, Africano y Asiatico de Vivienda Popular (#19246)
♦ Fédération internationale des services de secours par téléphone (#13567)

♦ **Fédération Internationale de Ski (FIS)** **09659**

International Ski Federation – Internationaler Ski Verband

Pres Marc Hodler House, Blochstrasse 2, 3653 Oberhofen-Thunersee BE, Switzerland. T. +41332446161. Fax +41332446171. E-mail: communications@fisski.com – mail@fisski.com.
SG address not obtained.
URL: http://www.fis-ski.com/

History 2 Feb 1924, Chamonix (France). Founded during the first Olympic Winter Games. Former names and other names: *Federación Internacional de Esquí* – former. **Aims** Promote the sport of skiing and snowboarding; direct the development of all ski and snowboarding activities world-wide. **Structure** Congress (every 2 years); Council; Committees (10); Special Committees (8); Technical Officials (11). **Languages** English, French, German, Russian. **Staff** 51.00 FTE, paid. Hundreds voluntary. **Finance** Annual budget: 30,000,000 CHF. **Activities** Sporting activities. **Events** *International Ski Congress* Reykjavik (Iceland) 2024, *International Ski Congress* Oberhofen-Thunersee (Switzerland) 2023, *International Ski Congress* Milan (Italy) 2022, *International Ski Congress* Oberhofen-Thunersee (Switzerland) 2021, *Biennial Congress* Pattaya (Thailand) 2020. **Publications** *FIS-Bulletin* in English, French, German; *FIS Directory*; *FIS World Statistics*.

Members National associations in 131 countries and territories:
Afghanistan, Albania, Algeria, Andorra, Argentina, Armenia, Australia, Austria, Azerbaijan, Bahamas, Barbados, Belarus, Belgium, Bermuda, Bolivia, Bosnia-Herzegovina, Brazil, Bulgaria, Cameroon, Canada, Cayman Is, Chile, China, Colombia, Costa Rica, Croatia, Cyprus, Czechia, Denmark, Dominica, Dominican Rep, Ecuador, Egypt, El Salvador, Eritrea, Estonia, Eswatini, Ethiopia, Fiji, Finland, France, Georgia, Germany, Ghana, Great Britain, Greece, Grenada, Guatemala, Guyana, Haiti, Honduras, Hong Kong, Hungary, Iceland, India, Iran Islamic Rep, Ireland, Israel, Italy, Jamaica, Japan, Jordan, Kazakhstan, Kenya, Korea DPR, Korea Rep, Kosovo, Kuwait, Kyrgyzstan, Latvia, Lebanon, Lesotho, Liechtenstein, Lithuania, Luxembourg, Madagascar, Malaysia, Malta, Mexico, Moldova, Monaco, Mongolia, Montenegro, Morocco, Nepal, Netherlands, New Zealand, Nigeria, North Macedonia, Norway, Pakistan, Palestine, Paraguay, Peru, Philippines, Poland, Portugal, Puerto Rico, Romania, Russia, Samoa USA, San Marino, Senegal, Serbia, Singapore, Slovakia, Slovenia, South Africa, Spain, Sri Lanka, Sudan, Sweden, Switzerland, Taiwan, Tajikistan, Thailand, Timor-Leste, Togo, Tonga, Trinidad-Tobago, Türkiye, Uganda, Ukraine, United Arab Emirates, Uruguay, USA, Uzbekistan, Venezuela, Virgin Is UK, Virgin Is USA, Zimbabwe.

NGO Relations Member of (3): *Association of the International Olympic Winter Sports Federations (AIOWF, #02757)*; *International Masters Games Association (IMGA, #14117)*; *Olympic Movement (#17719)*. Cooperates with (1): *International Testing Agency (ITA, #15678)*. Recognized by: *International Olympic Committee (IOC, #14408)*. [2019.09.25/XC2465/**B**]

♦ Fédération internationale de skibob (#14868)
♦ Fédération internationale des socialistes religieux (#14022)
♦ Fédération internationale des sociétés aérophilatéliques (#13342)
♦ Fédération internationale des sociétés d'amateurs d'exlibris (#13421)

♦ **Fédération internationale des sociétés artistiques et intellectuelles de cheminots (FISAIC)** **09660**

International Federation of Railwaymen's Art and Intellectual Societies – Internationaler Verband Kulturpflegender Eisenbahner

Gen Sec Münchener Str 49, 60329 Frankfurt-Main, Germany. Fax +4916090907684.
Pres 9 rue du Château-Landon, 75010 Paris, France. E-mail: assistante.fisaic@orange.fr.
URL: http://www.fisaic.org/

History 1952, Strasbourg (France). **Aims** Promote cultural activities between European railwaymen. **Structure** General Assembly (every 2 years). Officers: General President; Deputy Governor. Technical commissions (11). **Languages** English, French, German. **Staff** 5.00 FTE, voluntary. **Finance** Members' dues: about euro 2,000. **Activities** Organizes: congresses; festivals; competitions; Praesidium (every 2 years in alternating years to the General Assembly). Organizes an average of 3 to 4 events a year in the following categories: paintings and sculpture; photography; choirs; folklore; music; philately; radio amateurs; model railway; bridge; film-video. **Events** *General Assembly* Baden (Austria) 2012, *General Assembly* UK 2008, *General Assembly* Warsaw (Poland) 2006, *General Assembly* Zilina (Slovakia) 2004, *General Assembly* Obernai (France) 2002.

Members in 25 countries:
Austria, Belgium, Bulgaria, Croatia, Czechia, Denmark, Finland, France, Germany, Greece, Hungary, Italy, Luxembourg, Netherlands, North Macedonia, Norway, Poland, Romania, Serbia, Slovakia, Slovenia, Spain, Sweden, Switzerland, UK. [2022/XD1992/**D**]

♦ Fédération internationale des sociétés d'auteurs / see International Federation of Reproduction Rights Organizations (#13527)
♦ Fédération internationale des sociétés d'aviron / see World Rowing (#21756)
♦ Fédération internationale des sociétés des chimistes cosméticiens (#13545)
♦ Fédération internationale des sociétés de chirurgie de la main (#13551)
♦ Fédération internationale des sociétés Chopin (#13387)
♦ Fédération internationale des sociétés de la Croix-Bleue / see International Blue Cross (#12364)
♦ Fédération internationale des sociétés de la Croix-Rouge et du Croissant-Rouge (#13526)
♦ Fédération internationale des sociétés des droits de reproduction mécanique / see International Bureau of the Societies Administering the Rights of Mechanical Recording and Reproduction (#12416)
♦ Fédération internationale des sociétés de l'éducation ouvrière / see International Federation of Workers' Education Associations (#13580)
♦ Fédération internationale des sociétés de fertilité (#13426)
♦ Fédération internationale des sociétés d'histochimie et de cytochimie (#13548)
♦ Fédération internationale des sociétés d'ingénieurs des techniques de l'automobile (#13369)
♦ Fédération internationale des sociétés et instituts pour l'étude de la Renaissance (#13549)
♦ Fédération Internationale des Sociétés Magiques (#13473)
♦ Fédération internationale des sociétés de microscopie électronique (#13550)
♦ Fédération internationale des sociétés d'ophtalmologie (inactive)
♦ Fédération internationale des sociétés oto-rhino-laryngologiques (#13496)
♦ Fédération internationale des sociétés de pathologistes toxicologues (no recent information)
♦ Fédération internationale des sociétés de philosophie (#13507)
♦ Fédération internationale des sociétés professionnelles des gens de lettres / see Confédération internationale des sociétés d'auteurs et compositeurs (#04563)
♦ Fédération internationale des sociétés de publicité ferroviaire (inactive)
♦ Fédération internationale des sociétés de recherche opérationnelle (#13493)
♦ Fédération internationale des sociétés de rééducation de la main (#13547)
♦ Fédération internationale des sociétés de tempérance de la Croix-Bleue / see International Blue Cross (#12364)
♦ Fédération internationale des sociétés théâtrales d'amateurs (inactive)
♦ Fédération internationale de softball (inactive)
♦ Fédération internationale de la soie (inactive)
♦ Fédération Internationale de Soins Palliatifs / see Fédération francophone Internationale de Soins Palliatifs (#09588)
♦ Fédération internationale du sport automobile (inactive)
♦ Fédération internationale sportive de l'enseignement catholique (#15589)
♦ Fédération internationale du sport médical pour l'aide à la recherche cancérologique (inactive)
♦ Fédération internationale des sports acrobatiques (inactive)
♦ Fédération Internationale du Sport Scolaire (#14792)
♦ Fédération Internationale de Sports d'Obstacles (#21679)
♦ Fédération internationale de sports pour handicapés (inactive)
♦ Fédération internationale de sports pour personnes ayant une déficience intellectuelle / see Virtus: World Intellectual Impairment Sport (#20793)
♦ Fédération internationale des sports pour les personnes handicapées mentales / see Virtus: World Intellectual Impairment Sport (#20793)
♦ Fédération internationale des sports populaires (#13515)

♦ **Fédération internationale Sport pour tous (FISpT)** **09661**

International Sport for All Federation

Dir-Gen PO Box 33329, Manama 323, Bahrain. E-mail: fispt@outlook.com – fispteurope@gmail.com.
URL: https://www.fisptsportforall.org/

History 3 Apr 1982, Strasbourg (France). Statutes adopted 24 Feb 1983, Strasbourg (France). Moved to Bahrain, 2009. **Aims** Promote 'Sport for All' and establish contact among concerned organizations and people; be an action-oriented and consultative organization encouraging international exchanges in 'Sport for All' as a factor of *self-fulfilment* and a means of bringing people and nations together for mutual understanding. **Structure** General Assembly (every 4 years); Board of Directors; Presidency; nominated General Director and Sport Director. **Languages** Arabic, English, French, Italian, Spanish. **Staff** 10.00 FTE, voluntary. **Finance** Sources: contributions; grants; members' dues; revenue from activities/projects; sponsorship. **Events** *World congress on sport for all* Barcelona (Spain) 1998, *World congress on sport for all* Seoul (Korea Rep) 1996, *General Assembly* Blankenberge (Belgium) 1995, *World congress on sport for all* Uruguay 1994, *Seminar* Barcelona (Spain) 1992. **Members** Individual; National; Founding. Membership countries not specified. **NGO Relations** Recognized by: *International Olympic Committee (IOC, #14408)*. Instrumental in setting up: *African Confederation of Sports for All (inactive)*; *European Academy – Sport for All – on Tour (EAT, no recent information)*. [2022.11.14/XD0537/**B**]

♦ Fédération Internationale du Sport Universitaire (#15830)
♦ Fédération internationale de sténographie et de dactylographie / see Fédération internationale pour le traitement de l'information et de la communication (#09667)

♦ **Fédération internationale syndicale de l'enseignement (FISE)** **09662**

World Federation of Teachers' Unions – Federación Internacional Sindical de la Enseñanza – Internationale Vereinigung Lehrergewerkschaften – Mezdunarodnaja Federacija Profsojuzov Rabotnikov Prosvescenija

Gen Sec address not obtained.
Pres address not obtained. E-mail: topline_bangladesh@yahoo.com.
URL: http://wftufise.org/

History 7 Jul 1946, Paris (France). Founded by fusion of: *Internationale des travailleurs de l'enseignement (ITE, inactive)*, set up 1922 and with headquarters in Mexico City (Mexico) during World War II; *International Federation of Free Teachers' Unions (IFFTU, inactive)*, formed 1926; Confederation of American Educators, created 1929. Following split in the international trade union, 1947-1949, adhered to *World Federation of Trade Unions (WFTU, #21493)* in 1949 as a professional department; close relationship with WFTU developed, 1969, into a fully independent organization (TUI autonomy). Latest amendments to Constitution adopted by 12th Statutory Conference, 12 Jun 1981, Budapest (Hungary). Headquarters moved to Delhi (India) in 1997. **Aims** Build a democratic educational system in all countries; fight against illiteracy and for peace and disarmament; unite teachers' *trade unions* and promote teachers' trade union and *professional rights*; organize solidarity among teachers so as to achieve democratic schooling in each country, placing education at the service of peace and understanding among peoples. **Structure** Statutory Conference; Administrative Committee; Bureau; Secretariat. **Languages** Arabic, English, French, German, Russian, Spanish. **Staff** 12.00 FTE, paid. **Finance** Sources: members' dues. **Activities** Events/meetings; networking/liaising; research/documentation. **Events** *International Congress* Bhubaneswar (India) 2019, *International Congress* Mexico City (Mexico) 2018, *Statutory Conference* Delhi (India) 2015, *Statutory conference* Delhi (India) 2007, *Statutory Conference* Delhi (India) 2002. **Publications** *Teachers of the World* (4 a year) in English – journal; *FISE Information Letter* (8 a year) in Arabic, English, French, German, Portuguese, Russian, Spanish. Circular letters; brochures; reports.

Members Trade Unions (156), totalling over 26 million members, in 40 countries:
Argentina, Bangladesh, Bolivia, Brazil, Burkina Faso, Cape Verde, Chile, China, Colombia, Congo Brazzaville, Cuba, Ecuador, Ethiopia, France, Greece, India, Iraq, Jamaica, Kazakhstan, Korea DPR, Kuwait, Laos, Lebanon, Libya, Mexico, Morocco, Mozambique, Nepal, Nicaragua, Pakistan, Palestine, Peru, Philippines, Senegal, Sri Lanka, Syrian AR, Togo, United Arab Emirates, Vietnam, Yemen.

Also includes regional organizations (3), listed in this Yearbook:
Confederación de Educadores Americanos (CEA, #04446); *Federation of Arab Teachers (FAT, no recent information)*; *Federation of University Workers Unions of Central America, the Caribbean and Mexico (#09712)*.

Consultative Status Consultative status granted from: *ECOSOC (#05331)* (Ros C); *UNESCO (#20322)* (Consultative Status). **IGO Relations** Accredited by: *United Nations Office at Vienna (UNOV, #20604)*. **NGO Relations** Member of: *International Centre for Trade Union Rights (ICTUR, #12525)*; Trade Union Internationals (TUIs). [2023/XB3535/y/**B**]

- ♦ Fédération internationale des syndicats chrétiens des chemins de fer et des tramways (inactive)
- ♦ Fédération internationale des syndicats chrétiens d'employés / see World Organization of Workers (#21697)
- ♦ Fédération internationale des syndicats chrétiens d'employés (inactive)
- ♦ Fédération internationale des syndicats chrétiens d'employés techniciens et cadres / see World Organization of Workers (#21697)
- ♦ Fédération internationale des syndicats chrétiens d'employés, techniciens, cadres et voyageurs de commerce / see World Organization of Workers (#21697)
- ♦ Fédération internationale des syndicats chrétiens d'employés, techniciens ingénieurs et cadres / see World Organization of Workers (#21697)
- ♦ Fédération internationale des syndicats chrétiens de mineurs (inactive)
- ♦ Fédération internationale des syndicats chrétiens d'ouvriers agricoles (inactive)
- ♦ Fédération internationale des syndicats chrétiens d'ouvriers d'usine et de transports (inactive)
- ♦ Fédération internationale des syndicats chrétiens du personnel des services publiques / see International Federation of Employees in Public Services (#13410)
- ♦ Fédération internationale de syndicats chrétiens des postes, des télépostes, des télégraphes et des téléphones (inactive)
- ♦ Fédération internationale des syndicats ouvriers de l'industrie textile (inactive)
- ♦ Fédération internationale des syndicats des travailleurs de l'audio-visuel (inactive)
- ♦ Fédération internationale des syndicats des travailleurs de la chimie, de l'énergie, des mines et des industries diverses (inactive)
- ♦ Fédération internationale des systèmes de recherche agricole pour le développement (no recent information)
- ♦ Fédération internationale de Tai Chi Chuan Orient-Occident (inactive)
- ♦ Fédération internationale de Tchoukball (#15661)
- ♦ Fédération internationale des techniciens de la bonneterie (#13465)
- ♦ Fédération internationale de technologie et de navigabilité spatiale / see International Federation of Airworthiness (#13352)
- ♦ Fédération internationale de tennis (#15676)
- ♦ Fédération internationale de tennis de table (#15650)

♦ Fédération Internationale de Teqball (FITEQ) 09663

International Federation of Teqball

Registered Address 5-7 Expo Square, Budapest 1101, Hungary. E-mail: info@fiteq.org.
URL: https://www.fiteq.org/

History Mar 2017. Current statutes adopted Dec 2019. Registration: Company Registry Court of the Budapest-Capital Regional Court, No/ID: 01-02-0017651, Hungary. **Aims** Enable every person to participate in teqball or para teqball; allow all involved to reach their full potential, whatever level that might be; inspire the world through sporting success. **Structure** General Assembly; Executive Board. Committees. **Finance** Sources: members' dues. **Activities** Advocacy/lobbying/activism.
Members Federations in 97 countries and territories:
Afghanistan, Albania, Algeria, Antigua-Barbuda, Armenia, Austria, Bahamas, Bahrain, Benin, Bermuda, Bosnia-Herzegovina, Brunei Darussalam, Bulgaria, Burundi, Cambodia, Cameroon, Canada, Cape Verde, Chad, Cook Is, Côte d'Ivoire, Czechia, Djibouti, Eswatini, France, Gambia, Georgia, Ghana, Guam, Guatemala, Guinea, Guinea-Bissau, Guyana, Haiti, Hong Kong, Hungary, India, Indonesia, Iran Islamic Rep, Iraq, Italy, Jamaica, Japan, Jordan, Kazakhstan, Kenya, Korea Rep, Kosovo, Kuwait, Kyrgyzstan, Lebanon, Lesotho, Liberia, Luxembourg, Madagascar, Malawi, Malaysia, Mali, Mauritius, Moldova, Mongolia, Nepal, New Caledonia, Nigeria, Norway, Pakistan, Palestine, Papua New Guinea, Peru, Philippines, Poland, Portugal, Romania, Samoa USA, Senegal, Serbia, Seychelles, Sierra Leone, Slovakia, Somalia, South Africa, Sri Lanka, Switzerland, Syrian AR, Tajikistan, Thailand, Timor-Leste, Tunisia, Turkmenistan, Tuvalu, Ukraine, Uruguay, Vanuatu, Venezuela, Yemen, Zambia, Zimbabwe.
NGO Relations Member of (3): *Alliance of Independent recognised Members of Sport (AIMS, #00690)*; *Olympic Movement (#17719)*; *Organisation of Sports Federations of Oceania (OSFO, #17828)*. Cooperates with (1): *International Testing Agency (ITA, #15678)*. Recognized by: *International Olympic Committee (IOC, #14408)*. Officially recognized by: *Association of National Olympic Committees of Africa (ANOCA, #02820)*; *Olympic Council of Asia (OCA, #17718)*. [2022/AA1447/**C**]

- ♦ Fédération internationale Terre des hommes / see Terre des Hommes International Federation (#20133)
- ♦ Fédération internationale textile et habillement (inactive)

♦ Fédération internationale des thérapies et relations d'aide par la médiation (FITRAM) 09664

International Federation for Therapy and Assistance through Mediation

Contact 97a rue du Château, 67330 Ernolsheim-lès-Saverne, France. T. +33388703442.
History 13 Mar 2005, Strasbourg (France).
Members Full in 7 countries:
Belgium, France, Luxembourg, Poland, Romania, Slovakia, Spain.
Consultative Status Consultative status granted from: *Council of Europe (CE, #04881)* (Participatory Status). [2015.01.01/XM1393/**D**]

- ♦ Fédération internationale du thermalisme et du climatisme / see Fédération mondiale du thermalisme et du climatisme (#09692)
- ♦ Fédération internationale de tir à l'arc / see World Archery (#21105)

♦ Fédération Internationale de Tir aux Armes Sportives de Chasse (FITASC) 09665

International Federation for Sports Shooting

Pres 10 rue Mederic, 75017 Paris, France. T. +33142934053. Fax +33142935822. E-mail: fitasc@fitasc.com.
URL: http://www.fitasc.com/

History Founded 1921, as *Union internationale de chasse (UIC) – International Union of Hunting*. Present name adopted, 1938. **Aims** Unite national federations in non-olympic shooting disciplines. **Structure** Technical Commissions. **Events** *General Assembly* Madrid (Spain) 1997, *General Assembly* Porto (Portugal) 1996, *General Assembly* Malaga (Spain) 1995, *General Assembly* Toluca (Mexico) 1994, *General Assembly* Vilamoura (Portugal) 1993.
Members National federations (65) in 55 countries and territories:
Andorra, Argentina, Australia, Austria, Azerbaijan, Belarus, Belgium, Brazil, Canada, Chile, Colombia, Cyprus, Czechia, Denmark, Egypt, Estonia, Finland, France, Georgia, Germany, Greece, Hungary, Ireland, Italy, Kazakhstan, Kuwait, Latvia, Lithuania, Mexico, Monaco, Morocco, Netherlands, New Zealand, Norway, Poland, Portugal, Romania, Russia, San Marino, Singapore, Slovakia, Slovenia, South Africa, Spain, Sweden, Switzerland, Tahiti Is, Thailand, Tunisia, UK, Ukraine, United Arab Emirates, USA, Venezuela, Zimbabwe. [2015.01.06/XD5281/**C**]

- ♦ Fédération internationale de tir sportif (#14852)

♦ Fédération Internationale de Tourisme Équestre (FITE) 09666

International Federation of Equestrian Tourism

Secretary Parc Equestre Fédéral – La Colonie, 41600 Lamotte-Beuvron, France. E-mail: info@fite-net.org.
URL: https://fite-net.org/

History Founded 13 May 1975, Dublin (Ireland). Previously also known under the English acronym *IFET*. Current statutes adopted Sep 2016. Registered in accordance with French law. EU Transparency Register: 828428637647-22. **Aims** Bring together National Equestrian Tourism Organisations (NETOs) throughout the world, represent them, coordinate their action and contribute to development of all tourism activities linked to the use of horses. **Structure** General Assembly (annual); Board of Directors. **Languages** English, French. **Staff** Voluntary. **Finance** Sources: members' dues. **Activities** Certification/accreditation; events/meetings; sporting activities; training/education. **Events** *Congress* Liptovsky Mikulas (Slovakia) 2013, *Congress* Paris (France) 2011.
Members National associations in 21 countries:
Andorra, Austria, Belgium, Bulgaria, Canada, France, Germany, Hungary, Iceland, Ireland, Italy, Luxembourg, Netherlands, Portugal, Romania, Russia, Spain, Sweden, Switzerland, UK, USA.
NGO Relations Member of: *European Horse Network (EHN, #07499)*; *European Network of Outdoor Sports (ENOS, #07961)*. [2020/XD5452/**C**]

- ♦ Fédération internationale du tourisme social (inactive)
- ♦ Fédération internationale des traducteurs (#13574)
- ♦ Fédération internationale pour le traitement de l'information / see Fédération internationale pour le traitement de l'information et de la communication (#09667)
- ♦ Fédération internationale pour le traitement de l'information (#13458)

♦ Fédération internationale pour le traitement de l'information et de la communication (INTERSTENO) 09667

International Federation for Information and Communication Processing – Internationale Föderation für Informations und Kommunikationsverarbeitung

SG Kapellestraat 124, 8020 Oostkamp, Belgium. T. +32476265960. Fax +3250750154. E-mail: generalinquiries@intersteno.org.
URL: http://www.intersteno.org/

History 1954, Vevey (Switzerland). First Articles adopted 1 Aug 1955, Monaco; latest modifications adopted 15 Jul 2011, Paris (France). Former names and other names: *International Federation for Stenography and Typewriting* – former (1954); *Fédération internationale de sténographie et de dactylographie* – former (1954); *Federación Internacional de Taquigrafía y Dactilografía* – former (1954); *Internationale Föderation für Kurzschrift und Maschinenschreiben* – former (1954); *Federazione Internazionale di Stenografia e Dattilografia* – former (1954); *Fédération internationale pour le traitement de l'information* – former; *International Federation for Information Processing* – former; *Internationale Föderation für Informationsverarbeitung* – former. Registration: Germany, Bonn. **Aims** Associate professional stenographers, typists, reporters and word processing teachers of all countries; centralize, exchange and disseminate information of a *professional* character; establish personal contacts among members; advance joint studies concerning the profession; defend moral and material interests of national groups of professional stenographers and typists. **Structure** General Assembly (every 2 years during Congress); Council; Board. **Languages** English. **Staff** Voluntary. **Finance** Members' dues. Subscriptions; sale of publications; subsidies; donations; legacies; competition fees. **Activities** Training/education; events/meetings; knowledge management/information dissemination; publishing activities. **Events** *Intersteno Congress* Maastricht (Netherlands) 2022, *Intersteno Biennial Congress* Cagliari (Italy) 2019, *Intersteno Biennial Congress* Berlin (Germany) 2017, *Intersteno Biennial Congress / Biennial Congress* Budapest (Hungary) 2015, *Intersteno Congress* Ghent (Belgium) 2013. **Publications** *E-news*. **Members** National Groups; Individuals; Associated Companies. Membership countries not specified. [2022/XC2004/**F**]

- ♦ Fédération internationale de trampoline (inactive)
- ♦ Fédération internationale des transports aériens privés (inactive)
- ♦ Fédération internationale des transports commerciaux par automobiles (inactive)
- ♦ Fédération internationale des travailleurs du bâtiment (inactive)
- ♦ Fédération internationale des travailleurs du bâtiment et du bois (inactive)
- ♦ Fédération internationale des travailleurs de la chimie, de l'énergie et des industries diverses (inactive)
- ♦ Fédération internationale des travailleurs chrétiens réfugiés et émigrés (inactive)
- ♦ Fédération internationale des travailleurs de fonderies (inactive)
- ♦ Fédération internationale des travailleurs de l'habillement (inactive)
- ♦ Fédération internationale des travailleurs du pétrole et de la chimie (inactive)
- ♦ Fédération internationale des travailleurs des plantations (inactive)
- ♦ Fédération internationale des travailleurs des plantations, de l'agriculture et des secteurs connexes (inactive)
- ♦ Fédération internationale des travailleurs sociaux (#13544)
- ♦ Fédération internationale des travailleurs du tabac (inactive)
- ♦ Fédération internationale des travailleurs du textile, de l'habillement et du cuir (inactive)

♦ Fédération internationale Una Voce (FIUV) 09668

Foederatio Internationalis Una Voce – International Federation Una Voce

Contact address not obtained. E-mail: president@fiuv.org – secretary@fiuv.org – treasurer@fiuv.org.
URL: http://www.fiuv.org/

History 1965. **Aims** Ensure that the traditional Roman Mass as codified in the Missale Romanum edited by Pope John XXIII, and other ancient rites and usages of the Latin Church is maintained, both in practice and in law, as one of the forms of *liturgical* celebration which are recognized and honoured in the universal liturgical life of the Roman Catholic Church; obtain freedom of use for all the other Roman liturgical books enshrining previous liturgy and discipline of the Latin tradition; safeguard and promote the use of Latin, Gregorian *chant* and sacred polyphony in the liturgy of the *Roman Catholic Church*; encourage establishment of non-territorial parishes and/or chaplaincies in which only the liturgy as used in 1962 are employed. **Structure** General Assembly (biennial, in Rome, Italy); Council. **Languages** English. **Staff** Voluntary. **Finance** Members' dues. Charitable donations. **Activities** Events/meetings; guidance/assistance/consulting; religious activities. **Events** *General Assembly* 2021. **Publications** *Gregorius Magnus* (2 a year) – magazine. *Una Voce Studies on the Traditional Latin Mass* (2018); *The Case for Liturgical Restoration*. Position papers.
Members National associations in 39 countries and territories:
Argentina, Australia, Austria, Belarus, Brazil, Canada, Chile, China, Colombia, Costa Rica, Dominican Rep, England and Wales, Estonia, France, Germany, India, Ireland, Italy, Japan, Latvia, Malaysia, Malta, Mexico, Netherlands, New Zealand, Nigeria, Norway, Peru, Philippines, Poland, Puerto Rico, Russia, Scotland, Singapore, South Africa, Spain, Taiwan, Ukraine, USA. [2022/XD1203/**D**]

- ♦ Fédération internationale des unions intellectuelles (inactive)
- ♦ Fédération internationale et universelle des sociétés de crémation (inactive)
- ♦ Fédération internationale des universités catholiques (#13381)

♦ Fédération internationale des véhicules anciens (FIVA) 09669

International Federation of Historic Motor Vehicle Clubs

Gen Sec Villa Rey, Strada Val San Martino Superiore 27/B, 10131 Turin TO, Italy. T. +393917259962. E-mail: secretary@fiva.org.
Registered Office 8 place de la Concorde, 75008 Paris, France.
URL: http://www.fiva.org/

History 1 Mar 1966, Paris (France). Current statutes agreed 17 Nov 2018. Registration: France; EU Transparency Register, No/ID: 801754021924-61, Start date: 25 May 2016. **Aims** Protect and promote interest for vintage vehicles; support and encourage the study and classification of their history. **Structure** General Assembly; General Committee. Commissions. **Languages** English, French. **Finance** Annual budget: 200,000 CHF. **Activities** Awards/prizes/competitions; events/meetings. **Events** *General Assembly* Paris (France) 2016, *World Rally* Féchy (Switzerland) 2015, *World Rally* Luxembourg (Luxembourg) 2014, *World Rally* Cyprus 2013, *World Rally* Pesaro (Italy) 2012. **Publications** *FIVA Newsletter*.
Members National Clubs; Federations of Owners' Clubs. Members in 71 countries and territories:
Andorra, Argentina, Australia, Austria, Belgium, Bosnia-Herzegovina, Brazil, Bulgaria, Canada, Chile, China, Colombia, Croatia, Cyprus, Czechia, Denmark, Ecuador, Egypt, Finland, France, Germany, Gibraltar, Greece, Hungary, India, Iran Islamic Rep, Ireland, Israel, Italy, Japan, Jordan, Kuwait, Latvia, Lebanon, Libya, Liechtenstein, Lithuania, Luxembourg, Malaysia, Malta, Mexico, Moldova, Monaco, Morocco, Nepal, Netherlands, New Zealand, Norway, Paraguay, Peru, Poland, Portugal, Romania, Russia, San Marino, Serbia, Slovakia, Slovenia, South Africa, Spain, Sri Lanka, Sweden, Switzerland, Syrian AR, Thailand, Türkiye, UK, Ukraine, United Arab Emirates, Uruguay, USA.
Professional members: International companies; Museums and institutions; Media. Membership countries not specified.
Consultative Status Consultative status granted from: *UNESCO (#20322)* (Consultative Status). **NGO Relations** Associate member of: *Fédération Internationale de l'Automobile (FIA, #09613)*. [2020/XD2735/**D**]

- ♦ Fédération internationale des verriers (inactive)
- ♦ Fédération internationale de la vidéo (#15852)

♦ Fédération internationale du vieillissement (#13345)
♦ Fédération Internationale des Vins et Spiritueux / see FIVS (#09789)

♦ Fédération internationale de volleyball (FIVB) 09670

International Volleyball Federation – Federación Internacional de Vóleibol

Pres Château Les Tourelles, Chemin Edouard-Sandoz 2-4, 1006 Lausanne VD, Switzerland. T. +41213453535. Fax +41213453545. E-mail: administration@fivb.com – president.office.sec@fivb.com.

URL: https://www.fivb.com/

History 20 Apr 1947, Paris (France). Headquarters established in Lausanne (Switzerland) since 1984. Current Constitution adopted at Congress, 2000, Seville (Spain). Registration: Switzerland. **Aims** Encourage expansion, and organize and supervise the playing of volleyball and beach volleyball in all their forms in all parts of the world. **Structure** Congress (every 2 years); Board of Administration; Executive Committee; Commissions (11). **Languages** Arabic, English, French, Russian, Spanish. **Staff** 20.00 FTE, paid. **Finance** Sources: members' dues; sponsorship. Other sources: TV rights; marketing rights. **Activities** Events/meetings. **Events** *FIVB World Congress* Phuket (Thailand) 2021, *Biennial Congress* Phuket (Thailand) 2020, *Biennial Congress* Punta Cana (Dominican Rep) 2018, *Biennial Congress* Buenos Aires (Argentina) 2016, *Biennial Congress* Milan (Italy) 2014. **Publications** *FIVB X-Press* (12 a year) in English, French – information bulletin; *VolleyWorld* (6 a year) in Arabic, English, French, Spanish; *Coach Magazine* (4 a year) in English, French – technical magazine. *Rules of Volleyball*. Technical manuals.

Members Affiliate national federations ('F' indicates founder member) in 218 countries and territories:
Afghanistan, Albania, Algeria, Andorra, Angola, Anguilla, Antigua-Barbuda, Argentina, Armenia, Aruba, Australia, Austria, Azerbaijan, Bahamas, Bahrain, Bangladesh, Barbados, Belarus, Belgium (F), Belize, Benin, Bermuda, Bhutan, Bolivia, Bosnia-Herzegovina, Botswana, Brazil (F), Brunei Darussalam, Bulgaria, Burkina Faso, Burundi, Cambodia, Cameroon, Canada, Cape Verde, Cayman Is, Central African Rep, Chad, Chile, China, Colombia, Comoros, Congo Brazzaville, Congo DR, Cook Is, Costa Rica, Côte d'Ivoire, Croatia, Cuba, Cyprus, Czechia (F), Denmark, Djibouti, Dominica, Dominican Rep, Ecuador, Egypt (F), El Salvador, England, Equatorial Guinea, Eritrea, Estonia, Eswatini, Ethiopia, Faeroe Is, Fiji, Finland, France (F), Gabon, Gambia, Georgia, Germany, Ghana, Gibraltar, Greece, Greenland, Grenada, Guadeloupe, Guam, Guatemala, Guiana Fr, Guinea, Guinea-Bissau, Guyana, Haiti, Honduras, Hong Kong, Hungary (F), Iceland, India, Indonesia, Iran Islamic Rep, Iraq, Ireland, Israel, Italy (F), Jamaica, Japan, Jordan, Kazakhstan, Kenya, Kiribati, Korea DPR, Korea Rep, Kuwait, Kyrgyzstan, Laos, Latvia, Lebanon, Lesotho, Liberia, Libya, Liechtenstein, Lithuania, Luxembourg, Macau, Madagascar, Malawi, Malaysia, Maldives, Mali, Malta, Marshall Is, Martinique, Mauritania, Mauritius, Mexico, Micronesia FS, Moldova, Monaco, Mongolia, Montserrat, Morocco, Mozambique, Myanmar, Namibia, Nauru, Nepal, Netherlands, New Zealand, Nicaragua, Niger, Nigeria, Niue, North Macedonia, Northern Ireland, Northern Mariana Is, Norway, Oman, Pakistan, Palau, Palestine, Panama, Papua New Guinea, Paraguay, Peru, Philippines, Poland (F), Polynesia Fr, Portugal (F), Puerto Rico, Qatar, Romania (F), Russia, Rwanda, Samoa, Samoa USA, San Marino, Sao Tomé-Principe, Saudi Arabia, Scotland, Senegal, Serbia, Seychelles, Sierra Leone, Singapore, Slovakia, Slovenia, Solomon Is, Somalia, South Africa, Spain, Sri Lanka, St Kitts-Nevis, St Lucia, St Vincent-Grenadines, Sudan, Suriname, Sweden, Switzerland, Syrian AR, Taiwan, Tajikistan, Tanzania UR, Thailand, Togo, Tonga, Trinidad-Tobago, Tunisia, Türkiye, Turkmenistan, Tuvalu, Uganda, Ukraine, United Arab Emirates, Uruguay (F), USA (F), Uzbekistan, Vanuatu, Venezuela, Vietnam, Virgin Is UK, Virgin Is USA, Wales, Yemen, Zambia, Zimbabwe.

Regional confederations (5):
Asian Volleyball Confederation (AVC, #01779); Confederación Sudamericana de Voleibol (CSV, #04495); Confédération africaine de volley-ball (CAVB, #04503); European Volleyball Confederation (#09078); North-Central American and Caribbean Volleyball Confederation (#17576).

NGO Relations Member of (4): *Association of Summer Olympic International Federations (ASOIF, #02943); International Committee for Fair Play (#12769); International Masters Games Association (IMGA, #14117); Olympic Movement (#17719).* Recognized by: *International Olympic Committee (IOC, #14408).* [2021/XB2804/y/**B**]

♦ Fédération internationale de Vo Viêtnam (#13576)

♦ Federation International Football Skating (FIFS) 09671

Contact 700 Lavaca St, Ste 1401, Austin TX 78701, USA. E-mail: info.footballskating@gmail.com – info@footballskating.com – info@iptcertification.com.

URL: http://footballskating.com/

History Founded on merger of RollerSoccer and Futins. Both organizations became 2 independent federations, 2016, but merged again under listed title, Feb 2017. Former names and other names: *RollerSoccer International Federation (RSIF)* – former (Feb 2017). **Aims** Promote the practice of Football Skating. **Structure** Congress; Board. Regional federations: Football Skating Africa Conferederation (FSAC); Football Skating Europe Confederation (FSEC); Football Skating North America Federation; Football Skating Asia Federation; Football Skating South Asia Federation (FSSAF); Football Skating GCC Development. **Activities** Certification/accreditation; sporting activities.

Members Full in 38 countries:
Angola, Argentina, Benin, Brazil, Canada, China, Congo Brazzaville, Egypt, France, Guinea, India, Indonesia, Iran Islamic Rep, Italy, Kenya, Korea Rep, Kuwait, Malta, Nepal, Nigeria, Pakistan, Philippines, Russia, Rwanda, Saudi Arabia, Senegal, Sierra Leone, Slovenia, South Africa, Sri Lanka, Switzerland, Tanzania UR, Türkiye, Uganda, UK, United Arab Emirates, USA, Uzbekistan.

NGO Relations Member of (2): *General Association of Asia Pacific Sports Federations (GAAPSF, #10106); International Sport Network Organization (ISNO, #15592).* [2022/AA1088/**C**]

♦ Federation for International FootGolf (FIFG) 09672

Pres Place Saint-François 7, 1003 Lausanne VD, Switzerland. E-mail: board@fifg.org – info@fifg.org.

URL: http://www.fifg.org/

History 3 Jun 2012, Hungary. **Aims** Promote worldwide recognition of the sport of FootGolf. **Structure** Board of Directors. **Activities** Awards/prizes/competitions; events/meetings; sporting activities; standards/guidelines.

Members Organizations in 40 countries and territories:
Argentina, Australia, Belgium, Bolivia, Brazil, Canada, Chile, China, Czechia, England, France, Germany, Honduras, Hungary, Ireland, Italy, Japan, Korea Rep, Luxembourg, Malaysia, Mexico, Netherlands, New Zealand, Norway, Paraguay, Poland, Portugal, Russia, Scotland, Slovakia, Slovenia, South Africa, Spain, Sweden, Switzerland, Taiwan, Türkiye, Uruguay, USA, Wales.

NGO Relations Member of (1): *Alliance of Independent recognised Members of Sport (AIMS, #00690)* (Observer). [2023/AA1357/**C**]

♦ Federation of International Geo-Engineering Societies (FedIGS) . . . 09673

Pres address not obtained.

URL: https://www.geoengineeringfederation.org/

History 2007. Set up as an umbrella federation. **Aims** Facilitate cooperation within the geo-engineering profession; coordinate activities in areas of overlapping interest; raise public awareness and the profile of the geo-engineering profession. **Structure** Board. **Activities** Awareness raising; knowledge management/information dissemination; training/education.

Members Organizations (4):
International Association of Engineering Geology and the Environment (IAEG, #11872); International Geosynthetics Society (IGS, #13716); International Society for Rock Mechanics and Rock Engineering (ISRM, #15428); International Society for Soil Mechanics and Geotechnical Engineering (ISSMGE, #15452). [2019/AA0037/y/**B**]

♦ Federation of International Institutions based in Geneva (#09599)
♦ Federation of International Lacrosse / see World Lacrosse (#21616)
♦ Fédération international de lancer / see International Casting Sport Federation (#12447)
♦ Fédération international motocycliste / see Fédération Internationale de Motocyclisme (#09643)
♦ Federation of International Music Competitions / see World Federation of International Music Competitions (#21445)
♦ Federation of International Ninja Athletics (unconfirmed)
♦ Federation of International Nurse Education / see European Federation of Educators in Nursing Sciences (#07102)

♦ Federation of International Nurses in Endocrinology (FINE) 09674

Contact PO Box 23194, Tigard OR 97281, USA. E-mail: finenurses@gmail.com.

URL: https://finenurses.org/

Aims Promote excellence in clinical care by advancing the science and art of endocrine nursing throughout the world. **Activities** Events/meetings; networking/liaising; training/education.

Members Individuals in 22 countries:
Australia, Belgium, Canada, China, Denmark, Georgia, Germany, Ghana, India, Italy, Kenya, Netherlands, New Zealand, Nigeria, South Africa, Spain, Sweden, Thailand, Türkiye, UK, USA, Vietnam.

NGO Relations *International Society of Endocrinology (ISE, #15086); World Alliance of Pituitary Organizations (WAPO, #21087).* [2022/XM9011/v/**C**]

♦ Federation of International Poetry Associations (inactive)

♦ Federation of International Polo (FIP) 09675

Federación Internacional de Polo (FIP)

Admin Office Miraflores 1656, 11500 Montevideo, Uruguay. E-mail: office@fippolo.com.

URL: http://www.fippolo.com/

History 1983. Restructured 1989 by national organizations, when current by-laws adopted; by-laws modified 1991, UK; 1992, Chile; Sep 2014, Montevideo (Uruguay), at Special General Assembly. Former names and other names: *International Polo Federation (IPF)* – former. Registration: Start date: 25 Nov 1985, End date: 1989, Argentina, Buenos Aires; Start date: Mar 1989, Uruguay, Montevideo. **Aims** Promote polo as a sport throughout the world; channel the international games of polo as well as international activities; provide international rules of the game of polo (as established by the Asociacion Argentina de Polo, the Hurlingham Polo Association and the United States Polo Association); coordinate the criteria of its members; establish an international list of handicaps applicable to its tournaments; present educational regional courses for its members; promote improvement and visibility of the sport of polo internationally. **Structure** General Assembly (annual, in December); Council of Administration; Executive Committee; Committees. **Languages** English, Spanish. **Staff** 2.00 FTE, paid. **Finance** Sources: meeting proceeds; members' dues; sponsorship. **Activities** Events/meetings; sporting activities. **Events** *General Assembly* Buenos Aires (Argentina) 2019, *General Assembly* Buenos Aires (Argentina) 2018, *General Assembly* Buenos Aires (Argentina) 2017, *General Assembly* Buenos Aires (Argentina) 2016, *General Assembly* Buenos Aires (Argentina) 2015. **Publications** *FIP Newsletter* (4 a year). *FIP Guide to Commentating*; *FIP History*; *FIP The Olympic Years*.

Members National associations in 51 countries:
Argentina, Australia, Austria, Azerbaijan, Belgium, Brazil, Canada, Chile, China, Costa Rica, Ecuador, Egypt, England, France, Germany, Guatemala, Hungary, India, Iran Islamic Rep, Ireland, Italy, Japan, Kazakhstan, Kuwait, Malaysia, Mexico, Monaco, Mongolia, Morocco, Netherlands, New Zealand, Nigeria, Oman, Pakistan, Paraguay, Peru, Philippines, Portugal, Russia, Saudi Arabia, Singapore, Slovakia, South Africa, Spain, Sweden, Switzerland, Thailand, Ukraine, United Arab Emirates, Uruguay, USA.

NGO Relations Member of (3): *Association of the IOC Recognized International Sports Federations (ARISF, #02767); International Committee for Fair Play (#12769); Olympic Movement (#17719).* Recognized by: *International Olympic Committee (IOC, #14408).* [2023.02.17/XD3588/**C**]

♦ Federation of International Respiratory Societies (internationally oriented national body)

♦ Federation of International Retail Associations (FIRA) 09676

Chairman c/o NRF, 1101 New York Ave NW, Ste 1200, Washington DC 20005, USA. T. +12027837971. Fax +120277836520. E-mail: contact@nrf.com.

URL: https://nrf.com/about-usnrf-membership/fira-membership/

History Informal gatherings convened since 1990; formalized as *International Retail Forum (IRF)*, 1997. Renamed *Forum for International Retail Association Executives (FIRAE)*, 2003. Current title adopted 2018. **Aims** Promote networking, collaboration and information exchange among retail trade association executives around the world; enhance the success of global retail industry through the development of more informed and effective retail trade associations. **Structure** Officers. Secretariat, headed by staff of NRF. **Languages** English. **Staff** 1.00 FTE, paid. **Finance** Sources: members' dues. Other sources: Support from NRF. **Activities** Events/meetings; networking/liaising. **Events** *Annual Meeting* New York, NY (USA) 2020, *Annual Meeting* New York, NY (USA) 2019, *Half-Yearly Meeting* Dublin (Ireland) 2018, *Annual Meeting* New York, NY (USA) 2018, *Half-Yearly Meeting* Cernobbio (Italy) 2017. **Publications** *FIRA Chairman Update Newsletter* (2-4 a year).

Members National retail associations (39) in 22 countries and territories:
Australia, Austria, Belgium, Bolivia, Brazil, Canada, China, Denmark, Finland, France, Germany, India, Ireland, Italy, Japan, Mexico, Netherlands, Norway, Philippines, Sweden, United Arab Emirates, USA. [2019.07.10/XM3532/**C**]

♦ Federation of International Robosoccer Association (FIRA) 09677

Gen Sec address not obtained.

URL: http://www.firaworldcup.org/

History 5 Jun 1996, Daejeon (Korea Rep). 5 Jun 1996, Daejon (Korea Rep). **Aims** Promote the sport of *robot soccer* and associated research. **Structure** General Assembly. Executive Committee, including President, 3 Vice-Presidents, General Secretary and Treasurer. Advisory Committee. **Staff** 1.00 FTE, paid. **Activities** Organizes congresses and championships. **Events** *Robot World Congress* Changwon (Korea Rep) 2019, *Robot World Congress* Daejeon (Korea Rep) 2015, *Robot World Congress* Denver, CO (USA) 2014, *Robot World Congress* Kuala Lumpur (Malaysia) 2013, *Robot World Congress / Annual World Congress* Bristol (UK) 2012. **Publications** *FIRA Newsletter*. Congress proceedings. [2020/XD9050/**D**]

♦ Federation of International Societies for Pediatric Gastroenterology, Hepatology and Nutrition (FISPGHAN) 09678

Sec/Treas c/o Ctr for Clinical & Translational Science & Training, Univ of Cincinnati College of Medicine, 240 Albert Sabin Way, Location S, Ste 2 500, Cincinnati OH 45229, USA. T. +15138032612. Fax +15138031039. E-mail: info@fispghan.org.

URL: http://fispghan.org/

History to promote and organize the *World Congress of Paediatric Gastroenterology, Hepatology and Nutrition*. **Structure** Council, including President, Secretary-Treasurer and Executive Director. **Events** *Quadrennial World Congress of Pediatric Gastroenterology, Hepatology and Nutrition* Vienna (Austria) 2021, *Quadrennial World Congress of Pediatric Gastroenterology, Hepatology and Nutrition* Copenhagen (Denmark) 2020, *Quadrennial World Congress of Pediatric Gastroenterology, Hepatology and Nutrition* Montréal, QC (Canada) 2016, *Quadrennial World Congress of Pediatric Gastroenterology, Hepatology and Nutrition* Taipei (Taiwan) 2012, *Quadrennial world congress on pediatric gastroenterology, hepatology and nutrition* Foz do Iguaçu (Brazil) 2008.

Members Founding members (4):
Asian Pan-Pacific Society for Paediatric Gastroenterology, Hepatology, and Nutrition (APPSPGHAN, #01651); European Society for Paediatric Gastroenterology, Hepatology and Nutrition (ESPGHAN, #08680); Latinamerican Society for Pediatric Gastroenterology, Hepatology and Nutrition (LASPGHAN, #16382); North American Society for Paediatric Gastroenterology, Hepatology and Nutrition (NASPGHAN).

NGO Relations Member of: *International Pediatric Association (IPA, #14541).* [2020/XF7102/y/**D**]

♦ Federation of International Sports, Aerobics and Fitness International / see FISAF International (#09783)

♦ Federation of International Table-Tennis Manufacturers (FIT) 09679

Pres Quellenstrasse 33, 9500 Wil SG, Switzerland.

URL: http://www.tt-manufacturers.com/

History 1994, Birmingham (UK). **Aims** Defend and promote common interests of members in basic aspects of table tennis; represent them with other sports organizations, governments and other authorities; create conditions for international cooperation among them. **Structure** General Assembly (annual). Board comprising President, 2 Vice-Presidents and Treasurer. Working Groups. **Finance** Members' dues. **Events** *General Assembly* 1997.

Members Full members (38) in 12 countries and territories:
Belgium, China, France, Germany, Hong Kong, India, Japan, Korea Rep, Malaysia, Netherlands, Sweden, USA.

Associated members (4) in 3 countries:
Germany, Japan, USA.

NGO Relations Recognized by: *International Table Tennis Federation (ITTF, #15650).* [2018/XD4124/**D**]

♦ Federation of International Touch (FIT) 09680

Chair address not obtained. E-mail: secretary-general@internationaltouch.org.

URL: https://www.internationaltouch.org/

History 1985. Current version of constution adopted Nov 2021. **Aims** Promote, foster, improve, extend and govern the sport of Touch. **Structure** Annual General Meeting; Board; Committees. **Finance** Sources: members' dues.

Members National federations in 46 countries and territories:
Australia, Austria, Belgium, Bulgaria, Canada, Chile, China, Cook Is, Czechia, England, Estonia, Fiji, France, Germany, Guernsey, Hong Kong, India, Ireland, Italy, Japan, Jersey, Kiribati, Luxembourg, Malaysia, Netherlands, New Zealand, Niue, Papua New Guinea, Philippines, Portugal, Qatar, Samoa, Scotland, Singapore, Solomon Is, South Africa, Spain, Sri Lanka, Sweden, Switzerland, Taiwan, Thailand, Tokelau, Tonga, USA, Wales.
NGO Relations Oceania region is member of: *Organisation of Sports Federations of Oceania (OSFO, #17828).* [2022/AA2505/**C**]

- ♦ Federation of International Trade Associations (internationally oriented national body)
- ♦ Federation International Triathlon / see World Triathlon (#21872)
- ♦ Federation of International Women's Associations in London (internationally oriented national body)
- ♦ Fédération international de yoseikan budo et disciplines assimilées (inactive)
- ♦ Federation of International Youth Travel Organizations (inactive)
- ♦ Fédération Inter-Universitaire pour l'Université médicale virtuelle francophone / see Université Numérique Francophone des Sciences de la Santé et du Sport

♦ Federation of Islamic Medical Associations (FIMA) 09681

Pres FIMA Headquarters, 101 West 22nd St, Suite 106, Lombard IL 60148, USA. T. +16309320000. Fax +16309300005.
URL: http://www.fimaweb.net/

History Dec 1981, Orlando, FL (USA). Founded at forum sponsored by *Islamic Medical Association of North America (IMANA).* Registration: Start date: 18 Jan 1982, USA, Indiana; Start date: 30 Mar 1999, USA, Illinois. **Aims** Stimulate collaboration among member organizations in various countries in medical relief for needy communities, and during disasters; provide medical education, training and research; provide exchange of experiences and information, in the area of health; promote application of sound ethical standards in the practice of health care and medical research. **Structure** Council; Executive Committee; Executive Director. **Languages** English. **Staff** 1.00 FTE, paid; 2.00 FTE, voluntary. **Finance** Members' dues. Donations for specific relief projects. Annual budget: US$ 19,000. **Activities** Healthcare; humanitarian/emergency aid; training/education; projects/programmes; events/meetings; knowledge management/information dissemination. **Events** *Scientific Convention* Arusha (Tanzania UR) 2014, *Scientific Convention* Cape Town (South Africa) 2013, *Scientific Convention* Kuala Lumpur (Malaysia) 2012. **Publications** *FIMA Newsletter*, *FIMA Reliev E-Bulletin*; *FIMA Yearbook.* Books; reports; articles.
Members Full in 27 countries and territories:
Afghanistan, Algeria, Bangladesh, Bosnia-Herzegovina, Egypt, Germany, India, Indonesia, Iraq, Jordan, Lebanon, Malaysia, Mauritania, Morocco, Nigeria, Pakistan, Palestine, Saudi Arabia, South Africa, Sudan, Sweden, Türkiye, Uganda, UK, USA, Yemen, Zimbabwe.
Associate in 13 countries:
Australia, Azerbaijan, Cambodia, India, Kenya, Kosovo, Philippines, Singapore, Somalia, Sri Lanka, Tanzania UR, Thailand, Tunisia.
Consultative Status Consultative status granted from: *ECOSOC (#05331)* (Special). **IGO Relations** *WHO Regional Office for the Eastern Mediterranean (EMRO, #20944).* [2021/XD5595/**D**]

♦ Federation of Islamic Organisations in Europe (FIOE) 09682

Contact Rue de la Pacification 34, 1210 Brussels, Belgium. T. +3227423150. Fax +3227423155.
URL: http://fioe.org/

History Founded 1989. **Aims** Disseminate Islamic *culture* amongst the Muslims of Europe; assist in performing religious duties, preserving cultural identity and catering for social and religious needs; increase cooperation with Muslim organisations and promote cultural dialogue between Muslims and groups belonging to other faiths and ideologies. **Structure** General Secretariat. Departments (9): Relations; Da'wa and Introduction of Islam; Media; Education; Planning; Eastern Europe; Finance; Muslim Woman; Youth and Student. Central organizations: *European Institute for Human Science (IESH, see: #09682)*, comprising of European College for Islamic Studies, Arabic Language Institute, Institute for the Training of Imams and Institute for Learning the Holy Quran; *European Council for Fatwa and Research (ECFR, see: #09682)*; *Association of Muslim Schools in Europe (see: #09682).* Projects: Islamic schools; Al-Europiyya Periodical; Civilizational continuance. Set up: *European Association of Media Personnel (see: #09682)*; *Islamic-Catholic Liaison Committee (see: #09682).* **Publications** *Al-Europiya* – magazine.
Members in 19 countries:
Austria, Belgium, Bosnia-Herzegovina, Bulgaria, Czechia, Denmark, Finland, France, Germany, Hungary, Italy, Moldova, Netherlands, Poland, Romania, Sweden, Switzerland, UK, Ukraine.
IGO Relations Cooperation agreement with: *Islamic World Educational, Scientific and Cultural Organization (ICESCO, #16058).* **NGO Relations** Instrumental in setting up: *European League of Imams and Chaplains (inactive).* Member of: *European Network on Religion and Belief (ENORB, #07985).* [2017.06.01/XD7822/**D**]

- ♦ Federation of Jesuit and Ignatians Schools in Latin America and the Caribbean / see Latin American Federation of Jesuit Schools (#16323)
- ♦ Federation of Jesuit Schools in Latin America / see Latin American Federation of Jesuit Schools (#16323)
- ♦ Fédération des jeunes chambres économiques des pays utilisant le français dans leurs relations communes (inactive)
- ♦ Fédération des jeunes chefs d'entreprises européens (inactive)
- ♦ Fédération des jeunes écologistes européens / see Federation of Young European Greens (#09715)
- ♦ Fédération des jeunes entreprises d'Europe / see JA Europe (#16085)
- ♦ Fédération des jeunes verts européens (#09715)
- ♦ Fédération des jeux du Commonwealth (#04332)
- ♦ Federation of Jewish Child Survivors of the Holocaust / see World Federation of Jewish Child Survivors of the Holocaust and Descendants (#21448)
- ♦ Federation of Jewish Communities of Central America and Panama (inactive)
- ♦ Fédération des journalistes africains (#09404)
- ♦ Fédération des journalistes arabes (#09422)
- ♦ Federation of Junior Economic Chambers in Francophone Countries (inactive)
- ♦ Fédération des juristes africaines (#00500)

♦ Federation of Khoja Shia Ithna-Asheri Jamaats of Africa 09683

Head Office PO Box 3739-00506, Nairobi, Kenya. T. +254204348851 – +254204348852. Fax +254204348786. E-mail: secretariat@africafederation.org.
Branch PO Box 6710, Dar es Salaam, Tanzania UR. T. +255222150897. Fax +255222150964.
URL: http://www.africafederation.org/

History 1946. **Aims** Maintain brotherhood and unity, with primary emphasis on mobilizing youth towards education and community service and on progressively providing ladies with the opportunity to participate in communal affairs within the framework of the *Sharia.* **Structure** Trustees; Board. Officers: Chairman; Vice-Chairmen; Honorary Secretary; Assistant Secretary; Honorary Treasurer, Assistant Treasurer. Secretariat, headed by Executive Secretary. **Languages** English, Gujarati. **Staff** 8.00 FTE, paid. 8. **Events** *Triennial Conference* Arusha (Tanzania UR) 2007, *Triennial Conference* Nairobi (Kenya) 2004, *Triennial Conference* Dar es Salaam (Tanzania UR) 2001, *Triennial Conference* Arusha (Tanzania UR) 1998, *Triennial Conference* Dar es Salaam (Tanzania UR) 1998. **Publications** *Federation Samachar 9* (4 a year).
Members Communities (29) in 10 countries and territories:
Burundi, Congo DR, Kenya, Madagascar, Mauritius, Mozambique, Réunion, South Africa, Tanzania UR, Uganda.
NGO Relations Member of: *World Federation of Khoja Shia Ithna-Asheri Muslim Communities (World Federation of KSIMC, #21449).* [2014/XD6404/**D**]

- ♦ Fédération lainière internationale (#15904)
- ♦ Fédération LAMIE (internationally oriented national body)
- ♦ Federation of Latin America and the Caribbean Environmental Organizations (inactive)
- ♦ Federation of Latin American Associations for the Study of Pain (#09343)

♦ Federation of Latin American and Caribbean Neurosciences (FALAN) 09684

Pres IFIBYNE-UBA CONICET, Pab II Ciudad Univ, Buenos Aires, Argentina. T. +541145763368 – +541145763386.
URL: http://falan-ibrolarc.org/

History 2 Apr 2009, Montevideo (Uruguay), as *Federation of Neuroscience Societies in Latin America, the Caribbean and the Iberian Peninsula (FALAN).* Previously also referred to under the acronym *FALAN-LARC.* Current title adopted 2013. Registered in accordance with the laws of Chile. **Aims** Promote the study and research of neuroscience; promote linkage and exchange among affiliated entities and national, regional and international bodies related to the discipline. **Structure** General Assembly; Board of Directors; Scientific Committee. **Languages** English, Portuguese, Spanish. **Staff** 1.00 FTE, paid. **Finance** Support from: *International Brain Research Organization (IBRO, #12392)* – Latin American Committee; member societies. No fixed budget. **Activities** Events/meetings; standards/guidelines; networking/liaising; knowledge management/information dissemination. **Events** *Congress* Buenos Aires (Argentina) 2016, *Congress* Cancún (Mexico) 2012.
Members Full; Affiliate; Associate. Societies in 13 countries:
Argentina, Brazil, Chile, Colombia, Costa Rica, Cuba, Mexico, Peru, Portugal, Puerto Rico, Spain, Uruguay, Venezuela.
NGO Relations Member of: *International Brain Research Organization (IBRO, #12392).* [2016.12.14/XJ6704/**D**]

- ♦ Federation of Latin American Congress Organizing Entities and Related Activities (#09299)
- ♦ Federation of Latin American Journalists (#09359)

♦ Federation of Latin American Sleep Societies (FLASS) 09685

Federación Latinoamericana de las Sociedades para estudio del Sueño – Federação Latinoamericana de Sociedades de Sono

Contact address not obtained. E-mail: flassoficial@gmail.com – info@fedelass.com.
URL: https://fedelass.com/

History Founded as *Sociedad Latinoamericana del Sueño – Latin American Sleep Society.* As of 2016, assumed ceased to exist. **Structure** Officers: President; Vice-President; Secretary; Treasurer. **Staff** 1.00 FTE, paid. **Finance** Staff salary provided by AFIP, a foundation for the development of science, based in Sao Paulo. **Activities** Organizes congress (every 2 years). **Events** *Congress* Chile 2020, *Congress* Punta del Este (Uruguay) 2018, *Congress* Medellin (Colombia) 2016, *Congress* Mexico City (Mexico) 2014, *Congress* Bogota (Colombia) 2012. **Publications** *Hypnos* (3 a year) – electronic.
Members National societies in 10 countries:
Argentina, Brazil, Chile, Colombia, Cuba, Mexico, Paraguay, Peru, Uruguay, Venezuela. [2020/XD7084/**D**]

- ♦ Federation of Latin American Surgeons (#09349)
- ♦ Federation of Latin American Trade, Office and Private Service Sector Workers (#09394)
- ♦ Fédération latine des sociétés d'électroradiologie médicale (inactive)
- ♦ Fédération latinoaméricaine des artistes interprètes et exécutants / see Federación Iberolatinoamericana de Artistas Intérpretes y Ejecutantes (#09325)
- ♦ Fédération latinoaméricaine d'associations de facultés de communication sociales (#09353)
- ♦ Fédération latinoaméricaine des associations des familles des détenus disparus (#09344)
- ♦ Fédération latinoaméricaine et caraïbéenne de bonsaï (#16266)
- ♦ Fédération latinoaméricaine et des Caraïbes des associations nationales de charge (#16276)
- ♦ Fédération latinoaméricaine et de Caraïbes des travailleurs de l'hôtellerie, de la gastronomie, des casinos et du tourisme (inactive)
- ♦ Fédération latinoaméricaine des conseils des utilisateurs du transport international (no recent information)
- ♦ Fédération latinoaméricaine des consultants / see Federación Panamericana de Consultores (#09379)
- ♦ Fédération latino-américaine des exploitants et distributeurs de cinéma indépendant (#16321)
- ♦ Fédération latinoaméricaine des hôpitaux (#16322)
- ♦ Fédération latinoaméricaine de l'industrie pharmaceutique (#16328)
- ♦ Fédération latinoaméricaine des jeunes écologistes (inactive)
- ♦ Fédération latinoaméricaine de la jeunesse latinoaméricaine pour les études sur l'environnement humain (inactive)
- ♦ Fédération latinoaméricaine des journalistes (#09359)
- ♦ Fédération latinoaméricaine des parasitologues (#16327)
- ♦ Fédération latinoaméricaine de paysans (inactive)
- ♦ Fédération latinoaméricaine des sociétés de chimie (#16320)
- ♦ Fédération latino-américaine des syndicats des travailleurs de la construction et du bois (#16318)
- ♦ Fédération latinoaméricaine du thermalisme et climatisme (no recent information)
- ♦ Fédération latinoaméricaine de tourisme social (inactive)
- ♦ Fédération latinoaméricaine des travailleurs de l'agriculture et de la nutrition (inactive)
- ♦ Fédération latinoaméricaine des travailleurs des banques et des assurances (#09373)
- ♦ Fédération latinoaméricaine des travailleurs de l'industrie (inactive)
- ♦ Fédération latinoaméricaine des travailleurs de l'industrie de la construction, du bois et du matériel de bâtiment (inactive)
- ♦ Fédération latinoaméricaine des travailleurs des industries alimentaires, du tabac et de l'hôtellerie (inactive)
- ♦ Fédération latinoaméricaine des travailleurs des industries graphique et papetière (inactive)
- ♦ Fédération latinoaméricaine des travailleurs de la métallurgie et des mines (inactive)
- ♦ Fédération latinoaméricaine des travailleurs du pétrole (inactive)
- ♦ Fédération latinoaméricaine des travailleurs des plantations (inactive)
- ♦ Fédération latinoaméricaine des travailleurs de la presse / see Federación Latinoamericana de Trabajadores de la Cultura y de la Comunicación Social (#09374)
- ♦ Fédération latinoaméricaine des travailleurs du textile, de l'habillement, du cuir et de la chaussure (inactive)
- ♦ Fédération latinoaméricaine des travailleurs du transport (no recent information)
- ♦ Federation of Liberal and Centrist Parties of Central America and the Caribbean (inactive)
- ♦ Federation of Liberal and Democratic Parties in the European Community / see Alliance of Liberals and Democrats for Europe Party (#00703)
- ♦ Federation of Liberal, Democrat and Reform Parties of the European Community / see Alliance of Liberals and Democrats for Europe Party (#00703)
- ♦ Fédération luthérienne mondiale (#16532)

♦ Fédération Maghrébine de Gynécologie Obstétrique (FEMGO) 09686

Contact c/o Royale Marocaine de Gynécologie Obstétrique, Résidence du Centre, Angle Boulevard de la Résistance et Rue Liboune, 20000 Casablanca, Morocco. T. +21222304971. Fax +21222304983.

History 29 Nov 1997, Tunis (Tunisia). Former names and other names: *Fédération des Sociétés Nationales de Gynécologie-Obstétrique des pays du Maghreb Arabe* – former. **Structure** General Assembly. Executive Committee. **Events** *Congress* Blida (Algeria) 2019, *Congress* Gammarth (Tunisia) 2017, *Conference* Casablanca (Morocco) 2011.
Members Full in 4 countries:
Algeria, Mauritania, Morocco, Tunisia. [2019/XJ3658/**D**]

- ♦ Fédération maghrébine de médecine du sport (no recent information)
- ♦ Fédération des majorettes européennes et internationales (inactive)
- ♦ Federation of the Marble Industry and the Granite Industry of the European Economic Community / see European and International Federation of Natural Stone Industries (#07587)
- ♦ Fédération du marketing direct européen / see Federation of European Data & Marketing (#09499)
- ♦ Fédération de médecine nucléaire et de biologie de l'Asie et de l'Océanie (#01795)
- ♦ Fédération médicale arabe / see Arab Medical Union (#01007)
- ♦ Federation of Mediterranean Certified Accountants (#09584)
- ♦ Fédération méditerranéenne de gynécologie – obstétrique / see Federation of National Societies of Gynaecology and Obstetrics in the Mediterranean Countries (#09695)
- ♦ Fédération des mineurs d'Europe (inactive)

♦ **Federation of Mining and Metallurgical Workers' Unions of the Commonwealth of Independent States** 09687

Gen Sec 5/6 Bolshaya Dmitrovka St, Moscow MOSKVA, Russia, 101520. T. +74956926720 – +74956924925. Fax +74956925007. E-mail: kazprofmet@dan.kz.
URL: http://en.vkp.ru/

Members Trade unions in the CIS region (membership countries not specified). **NGO Relations** Member of: *General Confederation of Trade Unions (GCTU, #10108).* [2021/XM2459/D]

♦ **Fédération de missions évangéliques francophones (FMEF)** 09688

Coordinator 54 Rue Victor Schoelcher, 21800 Quetigny, France.
URL: http://ctamission.org/

History Founded 3 Mar 1968, by directors of evangelical missions in France and Switzerland. Registered in accordance with French law, 2 May 1988. **Aims** Act as spokesman for spiritual unity of the different francophone evangelical missions; promote the missionary interests of churches in francophone *Europe.* **Structure** General Assembly (annual); Executive Committee. **Languages** French. **Staff** 9.00 FTE, voluntary. **Finance** Members' dues. Budget: euro 34,000. **Activities** Organizes: annual 2-week "Cours d'entraînement missionnaire" for would-be missionaries; Mission(dot)net congress; member care for missionaries.
Members Full, including 14 organizations listed in this Yearbook:
Action biblique internationale (ABI); Association de soutien des missions des assemblées de France (ASMAF); Association internationale missionnaire (AIM); Groupes missionnaires (GM); Leprosy Mission International (TLMI, #16446); Mission chrétienne européenne, France (no recent information); Open Doors International (#17749); Operation Mobilisation (#17772) (Switzerland); *Service d'entraide et de liaison (SEL); Service missionnaire évangélique (SME); SIM International; Vision africa (VIA); WEC International (WEC, #20850)* (Switzerland); *World Evangelical Alliance (WEA, #21393).*
NGO Relations *Association d'églises de professants des pays francophones (AEPF, inactive); European Evangelical Mission Association (EEMA, #07011).* [2013.11.28/XD5853/y/D]

- ♦ Fédération mondial de dance de jazz (inactive)
- ♦ Fédération mondiale des agences de santé pour la promotion de la contraception chirurgicale volontaire (inactive)
- ♦ Fédération mondiale des amis des musées (#21435)
- ♦ Fédération mondiale des anciens combattants (#21900)
- ♦ Fédération mondiale des annonceurs (#21407)
- ♦ Fédération mondiale de l'art de guérir (inactive)
- ♦ Fédération mondiale des associations, centres et clubs UNESCO (#21498)
- ♦ Fédération mondiale des associations des centres de toxicologie clinique et des centres anti-poison (inactive)
- ♦ Fédération mondiale des associations de chirurgiens pédiatres (#21411)
- ♦ Fédération mondiale d'associations et de communautés diaconales (#21429)
- ♦ Fédération mondiale des associations de direction de personnel / see World Federation of People Management Associations (#21474)
- ♦ Fédération mondiale des associations pour le droit de mourir dans la dignité (#21477)
- ♦ Fédération mondiale des associations d'éducation (inactive)
- ♦ Fédération mondiale des associations pour les Nations Unies (#21499)
- ♦ Fédération mondiale des associations de santé publique (#21476)
- ♦ Fédération mondiale des associations de sociétés de commerce (no recent information)
- ♦ Fédération Mondiale Boules & Pétanque (#21721)
- ♦ Fédération mondiale des bourses de diamants (#21430)
- ♦ Fédération mondiale de bridge (#21246)
- ♦ Fédération mondiale du carillon (#21260)
- ♦ Fédération mondiale des centres communautaires juifs / see JCC Global (#16093)
- ♦ Fédération mondiale de chiropratique (#21420)
- ♦ Fédération mondiale des chirurgiens rhumatologues (inactive)

♦ **Fédération Mondiale du Cirque** 09689

Exec Dir 5 av des Ligures, 98000 Monte Carlo, Monaco. T. +37792052600. E-mail: admin@circusfederation.org.
URL: http://www.cirquemondial.org/

History 2008, Monaco. **Aims** Bring together the global circus community to preserve and promote circus arts and culture around the world. **Structure** Board of Directors, comprising President, Vice-President, Treasurer, Secretary and Directors-at-large. **Languages** English, French. **Finance** Sources: donations; fundraising; members' dues. Annual budget: 100,000 EUR.
Members National organizations in 7 countries:
Afghanistan, Australia, China, Japan, Monaco, South Africa, USA.
Regional organization, representing about 25 countries:
IGO Relations *UNESCO (#20322); Secretariat of the Convention on International Trade in Endangered Species of Wild Fauna and Flora (CITES Secretariat, #19199).* [2017.11.29/XJ0264/y/C]

- ♦ Fédération mondiale des cités unies (inactive)
- ♦ Fédération mondiale du Coeur / see World Heart Federation (#21562)
- ♦ Fédération mondiale des combattants, des résistants et des déportés juifs (no recent information)
- ♦ Fédération mondiale des communautés séphardites (inactive)
- ♦ Fédération mondiale des communautés thérapeutiques (#21491)
- ♦ Federation mondiale des communautés de vie chrétienne / see Christian Life Community (#03905)
- ♦ Fédération mondiale des concours internationaux de musique (#21445)
- ♦ Fédération mondiale des congrégations mariales / see Christian Life Community (#03905)
- ♦ Fédération mondiale des dirigeants des instituts de beauté et de l'esthétique (no recent information)
- ♦ Fédération mondiale des docteurs d'état et diplômés des universités de France (internationally oriented national body)
- ♦ Fédération mondiale des écoles arabo-islamiques internationales (inactive)
- ♦ Fédération mondiale de l'éducation médicale / see World Federation for Medical Education (#21454)
- ♦ Fédération mondiale pour l'éducation et les recherches en santé publique (inactive)
- ♦ Fédération mondiale des éleveurs de mérinos (#21456)
- ♦ Fédération mondiale des employés / see World Organization of Workers (#21697)
- ♦ Fédération mondiale pour l'enseignement médical (#21454)
- ♦ Fédération mondiale des entreprises de nettoyage (#21416)
- ♦ Fédération mondiale des ergothérapeutes (#21468)
- ♦ Fédération mondiale pour les études sur le futur (#21535)
- ♦ Fédération mondiale des fabricants de spécialités pharmaceutiques grand public / see Global Self-Care Federation (#10588)
- ♦ Fédération mondiale de femmes méthodistes / see World Federation of Methodist and Uniting Church Women (#21457)
- ♦ Fédération mondiale des grands concours internationaux de vins et spiritueux (#21452)
- ♦ Fédération mondiale de l'hémophilie (#21437)
- ♦ Fédération mondiale de l'industrie d'articles de sport (#21487)
- ♦ Fédération mondiale des infirmiers en neurochirurgie (#21465)
- ♦ Fédération mondiale des institutions financières de développement (#21428)
- ♦ Fédération mondiale des institutions juridiques internationales (inactive)
- ♦ Fédération mondiale des israélites britanniques (#03331)

♦ **Fédération Mondiale du Jeu de Dames (FMJD)** 09690

World Draughts Federation – Wereldddambond

Pres Cukrowa 49/2, 71-004 Szczecin, Poland. T. +48500048001. E-mail: webmaster@fmjd.org.
Gen Sec address not obtained.
URL: http://www.fmjd.org/

History 16 Sep 1947, Paris (France). Founded by representatives from Belgium, France, Netherlands and Switzerland. Former names and other names: *Fédération internationale du jeu de dames* – former (1957). **Aims** Promote development of international draughts on the 100 square board and all other types of draughts; obtain uniformity of rules for international competitions. **Structure** General Assembly (every 2 years); Managing Board; Executive Committee; Permanent Commissions (5). **Languages** English, French, Russian. **Staff** None. **Finance** Sources: grants; members' dues. Other sources: auspices fees. **Activities** Events/meetings. **Events** *Biennial General Assembly* Tallinn (Estonia) 2021, *Biennial General Assembly* Izmir (Turkey) 2019, *Biennial General Assembly* Tallinn (Estonia) 2017, *Biennial General Assembly* Aydin (Turkey) 2015, *Biennial General Assembly* Wageningen (Netherlands) 2013. **Publications** *Classement FMJD des joueurs internationaux* (4 a year); *Almanac* (annual). *Course in Draughts* by Tjalling Goedemoed in Chinese, Czech, English, French, Italian, Japanese, Mongolian, Portuguese, Spanish – free electronic books; *The Fascinating World of Draughts.*
Members Federations in 70 countries and territories:
Armenia, Aruba, Australia, Azerbaijan, Barbados, Belarus, Belgium, Benin, Brazil, Bulgaria, Burkina Faso, Cameroon, Canada, China, Congo Brazzaville, Congo DR, Costa Rica, Côte d'Ivoire, Curaçao, Cyprus, Czechia, Denmark, Dominican Rep, England, Estonia, France, Gambia, Georgia, Germany, Grenada, Guadeloupe, Guinea, Haiti, Hungary, India, Indonesia, Ireland, Israel, Italy, Japan, Kazakhstan, Kenya, Latvia, Lithuania, Mali, Mauritania, Moldova, Mongolia, Netherlands, New Zealand, Northern Ireland, Pakistan, Poland, Portugal, Russia, Scotland, Senegal, Slovenia, Somalia, South Africa, Suriname, Switzerland, Trinidad-Tobago, Türkiye, Turkmenistan, Uganda, Ukraine, USA, Uzbekistan, Wales.
Asian Draughts Confederation (ADC, #01432); European Draughts Confederation (EDC, #06945); Pan American Draughts and Checkers Confederation (PAMDCC, #18095).
NGO Relations Member of (3): *Alliance of Independent recognised Members of Sport (AIMS, #00690); International Mind Sports Association (IMSA, #14164)* (Founding); *Olympic Movement (#17719).* Recognized by: *International Olympic Committee (IOC, #14408).* Set up, as a legal entity of FMJD Section 64: *International Draughts Federation (IDF, #13199).* [2021.09.04/XD2161/C]

- ♦ Fédération mondiale de la jeunesse catholique (inactive)
- ♦ Fédération mondiale de la jeunesse démocratique (#21427)
- ♦ Fédération mondiale de la jeunesse hébraïque / see JCC Global (#16093)
- ♦ Fédération mondiale de la jeunesse orthodoxe / see World Fellowship of Orthodox Youth (#21504)
- ♦ Fédération mondiale des jeunesses féminines catholiques (inactive)
- ♦ Fédération mondiale des journalistes scientifiques (#21479)
- ♦ Fédération mondiale du judaïsme marocain (unconfirmed)
- ♦ Fédération mondiale des juifs originaires de Hongrie (#21439)
- ♦ Fédération mondiale de karaté (#21608)
- ♦ Fédération mondiale des maîtres-tailleurs (#21453)
- ♦ Fédération mondiale de médecine et de biologie nucléaires (#21467)
- ♦ Fédération mondiale de médecine et biologie des ultra-sons (#21497)
- ♦ Fédération mondiale des médecins pour le respect de la vie humaine (#21432)
- ♦ Fédération mondiale de la métallurgie (inactive)
- ♦ Fédération mondiale des missions islamiques (no recent information)
- ♦ Fédération mondiale de neurologie / see World Federation of Neurology (#21461)
- ♦ Fédération mondiale de neuroradiologie interventionnelle (#21446)
- ♦ Fédération mondiale des organisations de la construction et du bois (inactive)
- ♦ Fédération mondiale des organisations des femmes ukrainiennes (#21496)
- ♦ Fédération Mondiale des Organisations d'Ingénieurs (#21433)
- ♦ Fédération mondiale des parasitologues (#21471)
- ♦ Fédération mondiale des pilotes de ligne / see International Federation of Air Line Pilots' Associations (#13349)
- ♦ Fédération mondiale du poker (unconfirmed)
- ♦ Fédération mondiale de promotion des véhicles électriques (#21374)
- ♦ Fédération mondiale pour la protection des animaux (inactive)
- ♦ Fédération mondiale de psychothérapie (#21337)
- ♦ Fédération mondiale pour la santé mentale (#21455)
- ♦ Fédération mondiale de sécurité (no recent information)
- ♦ Fédération mondiale Simmental-Fleckvieh (#21785)
- ♦ Fédération mondiale des sociétés d'acupuncture (#21405)
- ♦ Fédération mondiale des sociétés d'anesthésiologistes (#21482)
- ♦ Fédération mondiale des sociétés de cuisiniers (#21124)
- ♦ Fédération mondiale des sociétés pour la culture de la rose (#21478)
- ♦ Fédération mondiale des sociétés de médecine chinoise (#21419)
- ♦ Fédération mondiale des sociétés de neurochirurgie (#21466)
- ♦ Fédération mondiale des sociétés de psychiatrie biologique (#21483)
- ♦ Fédération mondiale des sociétés de soins intensifs et de réanimation / see World Federation of Intensive and Critical Care (#21444)

♦ **Fédération mondiale de sophrologie caycédienne (FMSC)** 09691

Contact Edifici Areny 39, Bloc E, Planta Baixa 2, AD400 Arinsal, Andorra. T. +376838648. Fax +376838644. E-mail: sofrocay@sofrocay.com.
URL: http://www.sofrocay.com/

History as one of the 3 sections of *'Fondation Docteur Alfonso Caycédo (FAC)'.* **Events** *Congrès / World Congress* Paris (France) 1993. **Publications** *Sophrologie caycédienne en médecine et en prophylaxie sociale* – official journal. *Dictionnaire fondamental de la sophrologie* (1996) by Prof Alfonso Caycédo; *Sophrologie – Fondements et méthodologie* (2nd ed 1996) by Dr Patrick-André Chéné.
Members Schools and academies in 6 countries:
Belgium, France, Italy, Portugal, Spain, Switzerland. [2015/XE2243/E]

- ♦ Fédération mondiale des sourds / see World Federation of the Deaf (#21425)
- ♦ Fédération mondiale de squash (#21826)
- ♦ Fédération mondiale des syndicats de l'énergie, de la chimie et des industries diverses (inactive)

♦ **Fédération mondiale du thermalisme et du climatisme (FEMTEC)** .. 09692

World Federation of Hydrotherapy and Climatotherapy – Federazione Mondiale del Termalismo e del Climatismo – Weltverband für Balneologie und Klimatologie

Pres Centro di Ricerche in Bioclimatologia Medica, Univ degli Studi di Milan, Via Cicognara 7, 20129 Milan MI, Italy. T. +39250318458. Fax +39250318461. E-mail: simona.busato@libero.it.
Dir Intl Office Affairs address not obtained.
URL: http://www.femteconline.org/

History 1947, Prague (Czech Rep), as *International Federation of Thermalism and Climatism – Fédération internationale du thermalisme et du climatisme (FITEC) – Internationale Vereinigung für Balneologie und Klimatologie.* Also referred to as *International Federation on Hydrotherapy and Climatotherapy.* **Aims** Encourage closer international cooperation in theoretical and practical solution of scientific, medical, technical, economic, administrative, legal and tourist problems among public and private agencies concerned with thermalism and climatism. **Structure** Delegate Assembly (annual); Executive Committee; Technical Committees (10). **Languages** English, French, German, Italian, Russian, Spanish. **Staff** 5.00 FTE, paid; 10.00 FTE, voluntary. **Finance** Sources: members' dues. **Activities** Events/meetings; knowledge management/information dissemination; networking/liaising. **Events** *General Assembly and International Scientific Congress* Bologna (Italy) 2022, *General Assembly and International Scientific Congress* Chalkidiki (Greece) 2019, *General Assembly and International Scientific Congress* Batumi (Georgia) 2018, *General Assembly and International Scientific Congress* Ischia (Italy) 2017, *General Assembly and International Scientific Congress* Yerevan (Armenia) 2016. **Publications** *Thermae and Spa Medicine* – journal. Annual Report; congress proceedings.
Members National federations or central organizations in 27 countries:
Algeria, Andorra, Argentina, Armenia, Azerbaijan, Brazil, China, Cuba, Georgia, Hungary, Italy, Japan, Kazakhstan, Korea Rep, Latvia, Lithuania, Poland, Portugal, Romania, Russia, San Marino, Slovenia, Spain, Tunisia, Türkiye, Ukraine, Uzbekistan.
International organization (1):
Latin American Federation of Thermalism and Climatism (FLT, no recent information).
Consultative Status Consultative status granted from: *WHO (#20950)* (Official Relations). **NGO Relations** Member of: *Global Alliance Against Chronic Respiratory Diseases (GARD, #10182).* [2019/XC2032/y/C]

Fédération Mondiale Tir
09692

- Fédération Mondiale de Tir à l'Arc (#21105)
- Fédération mondiale de travailleurs agricoles (inactive)
- Fédération mondiale des travailleurs de l'agriculture et de l'alimentation (inactive)
- Fédération mondiale des travailleurs de l'industrie (inactive)
- Fédération mondiale de travailleurs des industries alimentaires, du tabac et hôtelière-CMT (inactive)
- Fédération mondiale des travailleurs non manuels / see World Organization of Workers (#21697)
- Fédération mondiale des travailleurs scientifiques (#21480)
- Fédération mondiale de twirling bâton (#21225)
- Fédération mondiale de vente directe (#21431)
- Fédération mondiale de volleyball et de beach volleyball (inactive)

♦ **Fédération Mondiale des Zones Franches (FEMOZA)** **09693**
World Federation of Free Zones – Federación Mundial de Zonas Francas
Secretariat Rue de Savoises 15, 1205 Geneva, Switzerland. E-mail: secretariat@femoza.org.
URL: http://www.femoza.org/
History Dec 1999. Registered under Swiss Civil Code. **Aims** Assist free and special economic zones around the world, especially in emergent countries. **Structure** Executive Committee; Secretariat, based in Geneva (Switzerland). **Languages** English, French, Spanish. **Staff** Voluntary. **Finance** Donors; sponsors; affiliates; professional services. **Activities** Networking/liaising; guidance/assistance/consulting; training/education; events/meetings. **Events** *General Assembly* Geneva (Switzerland) 2011, *General Assembly* Geneva (Switzerland) 2010, *International conference on free zones and science parks* Dubai (United Arab Emirates) 2003, *Latin American free zones conference* Colón (Panama) 2001, *WEPZA conference / Conference* London (UK) 2001. **Publications** *FEMOZA's World Free and Special Economic Zones Directory*; *The World of Free Zones*. Strategic plan; best practices; technical issues. **Members** Affiliate in 132 countries. Membership countries not specified. **Consultative Status** Consultative status granted from: *UNCTAD (#20285)* (General Category); *UNIDO (#20336)*.
[2019.09.27/XF6564/**F**]

- Fédération du Moyen-Orient contre le cancer (inactive)
- Federation of Municipalities of the Central American Isthmus (#09378)
- Federation of Municipalities of Central America and Panama (inactive)
- Federation of National Associations of Freight Forwarders and International Logistics Operators of Latin America and the Caribbean / see Latin American and Caribbean Federation of National Associations of Cargo (#16276)

♦ **Federation of National Associations of Shipbrokers and Agents** **09694**
(FONASBA)
Fédération des associations nationales des agents et courtiers maritimes de navires
Gen Manager 7th Floor, Walsingham House, 35 Seething Lane, London, EC3N 4AH, UK. T. +442076233113. E-mail: generalmanager@fonasba.com – admin@fonasba.com.
URL: http://www.fonasba.com/
History 23 Apr 1969, London (UK). **Aims** Act as consultant and authority for ship brokers and agents on all matters relating to the *shipping* profession, being sufficiently extensive and reputable to participate with national and/or international bodies, departments, authorities, associations or organizations on matters of concern; encourage fair and equitable practice of the professions of ship broker and agent. **Structure** Council; Executive Committee. Includes: *European Community Association of Ship Brokers and Agents (ECASBA, #06677)*. **Languages** English. **Staff** 1.50 FTE, paid. **Finance** Subscriptions from member associations on the basis of costs of Secretariat. **Events** *Annual Meeting* Antwerp (Belgium) 2021, *Annual Meeting* Genoa (Italy) 2020, *Annual Meeting* Miami, FL (USA) 2019, *Annual Meeting* Cancún (Mexico) 2018, *Annual Meeting* Dubai (United Arab Emirates) 2017.
Members Full: national associations in 48 countries:
Algeria, Angola, Argentina, Australia, Belgium, Brazil, Bulgaria, China, Costa Rica, Côte d'Ivoire, Croatia, Cyprus, Denmark, Egypt, Finland, France, Georgia, Germany, Greece, Hungary, Iran Islamic Rep, Ireland, Israel, Italy, Japan, Jordan, Kenya, Lebanon, Malta, Mexico, Morocco, Netherlands, Panama, Peru, Poland, Portugal, Russia, Slovenia, South Africa, Spain, Sweden, Syrian AR, Türkiye, UK, Ukraine, United Arab Emirates, Uruguay, USA.
Associate in 23 countries and territories:
Albania, Aruba, Bonaire Is, Cameroon, Cape Verde, Congo Brazzaville, Curaçao, Dominican Rep, Estonia, Georgia, India, Libya, Lithuania, Malaysia, Mauritania, Montenegro, Mozambique, Nigeria, North Macedonia, Romania, Tunisia, Venezuela, Yemen.
BIMCO (#03236); *Comité maritime international (CMI, #04192)*; *International Association of Dry Cargo Shipowners (INTERCARGO, #11853)*; *International Association of Independent Tanker Owners (INTERTANKO, #11959)*; *International Port Community Systems Association (IPCSA, #14623)*; International Transport Intermediaries Club; The Baltic Exchange.
Consultative Status Consultative status granted from: *International Maritime Organization (IMO, #14102)*; *UNCTAD (#20285)* (Special Category). **IGO Relations** Official relations (Special Category) with: *United Nations Commission on International Trade Law (UNCITRAL, #20531)*. Memorandum of Understanding signed with: *World Customs Organization (WCO, #21350)*. **NGO Relations** Cooperates with (2): *International Association of Ports and Harbors (IAPH, #12096)*; *International Chamber of Shipping (ICS, #12535)*. Associate Member of: *BIMCO (#03236)*; *International Association of Independent Tanker Owners (INTERTANKO, #11959)*; *International Port Community Systems Association (IPCSA, #14623)*. Working relations with: *Institute of Chartered Shipbrokers (#11247)*; *Comité maritime international (CMI, #04192)*; *International Ship Suppliers and Services Association (ISSA, #14850)*.
[2023.02.14/XD4092/**C**]

- Federation of National Associations of Women in Business in Eastern and Southern Africa / see COMESA Federation of National Associations of Women in Business (#04126)
- Fédération nationale des associations omnisports des jeunes Turcs de France / see COJEP International – Conseil pour la Justice, l'Egalité et la Paix (#04090)
- Federation of National European Menopause Societies (no recent information)
- Federation of National Organizations of EEC Fish Wholesalers, Importers and Exporters / see Comité des organisations nationales des importateurs et exportateurs de poisson de l'UE (#04194)
- Federation of National Organizations Fish Wholesalers, Importers and Exporters of the European Union / see Comité des organisations nationales des importateurs et exportateurs de poisson de l'UE (#04194)

♦ **Federation of National Societies of Gynaecology and Obstetrics in** **09695**
the Mediterranean Countries
Fédération des sociétés nationales de gynécologie-obstétrique des pays méditerranéens (FGOM)
Pres c/o STGO, 16 rue de Touraine, Mahrajène, 1082 Tunis, Tunisia.
Gen Sec ObyGyn Dept Brulo Inst, Via dell'Istria 65/1, 34100 Trieste TS, Italy.
History 28 Oct 1999, Marrakech (Morocco). Previously referred to as *Fédération méditerranéenne de gynécologie – obstétrique*. **Events** *Congress* Tunis (Tunisia) 2010, *Congress* Palermo (Italy) 2004, *Congress* Marrakech (Morocco) 2001, *Congrès* Marrakech (Morocco) 2001.
[2010/XD8333/**D**]

- Federation of Nature and National Parks of Europe / see EUROPARC Federation (#05768)
- Fédération naturiste internationale (#14219)

♦ **Federation of Neurogastroenterology and Motility (FNM)** **09696**
Contact c/o ESNM, Vienna Medical Academy, Alser Str 4, 1090 Vienna, Austria. T. +431405138331. Fax +4314078274. E-mail: info@esnm.eu.
History Set up by *European Society of Neurogastroenterology and Motility (ESNM, #08663)* and American Neurogastroenterology and Motility Society (ANMS). **Aims** Serve as common voice of all members; articulate perspectives of the scientific discipline to national and international agencies, foundations, philanthropic organizations and industry. **Activities** Events/meetings. **Events** *Meeting* Bangkok (Thailand) 2024, *Meeting* Bangkok (Thailand) 2022, *Meeting* Adelaide, SA (Australia) 2021, *Meeting* Adelaide, SA (Australia) 2020, *Meeting* Amsterdam (Netherlands) 2018.
Members Organizations (3):
American Neurogastroenterology and Motility Society (ANMS); *Asian Neurogastroenterology and Motility Association (ANMA, #01563)*; *European Society of Neurogastroenterology and Motility (ESNM, #08663)*.
Associate (2):
Australasian Neurogastroenterology and Motility Association (ANGMA); *Sociedad Latinoamericana de Neurogastroenterologia (SLNG, #19416)*.
[2020/XM6345/y/**C**]

- Federation of Neuroscience Societies in Latin America, the Caribbean and the Iberian Peninsula / see Federation of Latin American and Caribbean Neurosciences (#09684)
- Federation of Norden Associations / see Föreningarna Nordens Förbund (#09859)
- Federation of Nordic Amateur Symphony Orchestras (inactive)
- Federation of Nordic Anglers' Associations (inactive)
- Federation of Nordic Cereal Societies (no recent information)
- Federation of Nordic Fibreboard Industries (inactive)
- Federation of Nordic Police Unions / see Nordiska Polisförbundet (#17489)
- Federation of Nordic Travel Agents' Associations (inactive)
- Fédération Nordique du Béton (#17251)
- Fédération nordique des échecs (#17234)
- Fédération nordique des employées municipaux (#16204)
- Fédération nordique pour la formation médicale (no recent information)
- Fédération nordique des opérateurs de machines (#17279)
- Fédération nordique des ouvriers électriciens (no recent information)
- Fédération nordique de la presse commerciale et technique (inactive)
- Fédération nordique des propriétaires de forêts (inactive)
- Fédération nordique des travailleurs du bâtiment et du bois (#17283)
- Fédération nordique des travailleurs du transport (#17496)
- Fédération nordique de travailleurs d'usines (inactive)

♦ **Federation of Occupational Health Nurses within the European** **09697**
Union (FOHNEU)
Federatie van Bedrijfsverpleegkundigen in de Europese Unie
Pres address not obtained.
Sec address not obtained.
URL: http://www.fohneu.org/
History 1993. **Aims** Ensure that OHNs are competent and fully equipped to contribute to the health, safety and wellbeing of the EU's working populations; encourage OHNs to carry out research in areas of practice, education and management and to publish the results; establish links between occupational health and safety practitioners in the different countries so they can support each other, share ideas and best practices in order to provide cost effective, quality health care for all EU workers; engage in dialogue and support the main EU organizations responsible for health and safety as well as nursing authorities; ensure that the OHNs' role in workplace health care is recognized by governments, employers and worker representatives. **Structure** Includes Congress Committee. Executive Officers: President; Vice-President; Secretary; Treasurer. **Events** *New occupational health horizons* Rotterdam (Netherlands) 2016, *Meeting* Helsinki (Finland) 2015, *Meeting* Leuven (Belgium) 2015, *Meeting* Athens (Greece) 2014, *Meeting* Düsseldorf (Germany) 2014.
Members Occupational Health Nursing Associations within the European Union. Observer members outside the EU. Members in 16 countries (" indicates observer):
Austria, Belgium, Denmark, Finland, France, Germany, Greece, Ireland, Italy, Netherlands, Norway, Portugal, Spain, Sweden, Switzerland, UK.
IGO Relations Recognized by: *European Commission (EC, #06633)*; *WHO Regional Office for Europe (#20945)*.
[2014/XE2811/**E**]

- Federation of Oceania Rugby Unions / see Oceania Rugby (#17672)
- Fédération odontologique d'Amérique centrale et du Panama (#17691)
- Fédération odontologique de l'Amérique latine (#16357)
- Federation of Oils, Seeds and Fats Associations / see FOSFA International (#09935)
- Federation of the Olive Oil Industry of the EEC (#09596)
- Fédération des ONG allemandes de politique de développement et de l'aide humanitaire (internationally oriented national body)
- Federation of Ophthalmological Societies of Non-Aligned and SAARC Countries (inactive)
- Fédération des organisateurs de ventes publiques de la CEE / see European Federation of Auctioneers (#07057)
- Fédération des organisations de cartoonistes (#09466)
- Fédération des organisations de cartoonistes européennes / see Federation of Cartoonists Organisations (#09466)
- Fédération des organisations d'enseignants de l'Amérique centrale (inactive)
- Fédération des organisations européennes de recherches coopératives industrielles (inactive)
- Fédération des organisations d'ingénieurs en Afrique (#09402)
- Fédération des organisations nationales des grossistes, importateurs et exportateurs en poisson de la CEE / see Comité des organisations nationales des importateurs et exportateurs de poisson de l'UE (#04194)
- Fédération des organisations nationales des grossistes, importateurs et exportateurs en poisson de l'Union Européenne / see Comité des organisations nationales des importateurs et exportateurs de poisson de l'UE (#04194)
- Fédération des organisations non-gouvernementales de développement / see Verband Entwicklungspolitik und Humanitäre Hilfe e.V.

♦ **Fédération des Organisations Patronales de l'Afrique de l'Ouest** **09698**
(FOPAO)
Pres Abidjan Plateau, Avenue Lamblin, 01 BP 8666, Abidjan 01, Côte d'Ivoire. T. +22520305950. Fax +22520311009. E-mail: infos@fopao.org.
URL: http://www.fopao.net/
History 1996, Lomé (Togo). **Aims** Maintain a constant link and organize a framework of permanent and dynamic cooperation among members. **Structure** General Assembly; Executive Bureau. **Languages** English, French, Portuguese. **Staff** 3.00 FTE, paid; 9.00 FTE, voluntary. **Finance** Members' dues. Other sources: subventions; gifts; legacies. **Activities** Advocacy/lobbying/activism; training/education; guidance/assistance/consulting; knowledge management/information dissemination. **Events** *General Assembly* Abidjan (Côte d'Ivoire) 2014, *General Assembly* Lomé (Togo) 2013.
Members Organisations in 15 countries:
Benin, Burkina Faso, Cape Verde, Côte d'Ivoire, Gambia, Ghana, Guinea-Bissau, Liberia, Mali, Mauritania, Niger, Nigeria, Senegal, Sierra Leone, Togo.
[2018/XJ1657/**D**]

- Fédération des organisations scientifiques et techniques des pays socialistes (inactive)
- Fédération organismes chrétiens de service international volontaire / see Federazione Organismi Cristiani Servizio Internazionale Volontario
- Fédération des organismes européens de formation au psychodrame (#09535)

♦ **Federation of Orthopaedic Trainees in Europe (FORTE)** **09699**
Contact address not obtained. E-mail: info@forteortho.org.
URL: http://www.forteortho.org/
History 2005, Lisbon (Portugal). **Structure** Executive Board/Committee; Committees (9). **Activities** Training/education. **Publications** *FORTE Newsletter*.
[2018.10.04/XM6299/**D**]

- Fédération ouest-africaine des associations pour la promotion des personnes handicapées (no recent information)
- Fédération ouest-européenne nationale-socialiste (inactive)
- Federation of Outdoor Advertising / see World Out of Home Organization (#21702)
- Fédération ouvrière internationale des teinturiers-dégraisseurs (inactive)
- Fédération panafricaine des associations et clubs OUA (no recent information)
- Fédération panafricaine des associations d'oto-rhino-laryngologie (#18051)
- Fédération panafricaine des associations pour les personnes handicapées mentales (no recent information)
- Fédération panafricaine des cinéastes (no recent information)

♦ Fédération panafricaine des employés (FPE) 09700

Pan-African Federation of Clerical Workers (PAFCW)

SG BP 3058, Lomé, Togo. T. +2282221117. Fax +2282224441. E-mail: koffizoun1@yahoo.fr – zounkoffi@yahoo.fr.
URL: http://www.wownetwork.be/about-wow/organizational-structure/fpe/

History Founded 24 Oct 1997, as *African Federation of Clerical Workers (AFCW) – Fédération africaine des employés (FAE)*, as a regional federation of *World Organization of Workers (WOW, #21697)*. **Aims** Strength the position of members; exchange information and experiences through seminars. **Structure** Congress; Governing Board. **Languages** English, French. **Finance** Members' dues. Other sources: legacies; donations; grants. **Activities** Events/meetings; networking/liaising. **Events** *Congress* Medan (Indonesia) 2004, *Congress and seminar* 1997.
Members Affiliate national organizations (18) in 14 countries:
Burkina Faso, Cameroon, Chad, Congo DR, Gabon, Guinea, Madagascar, Mauritania, Morocco, Namibia, Niger, Sierra Leone, South Africa, Togo. [2015/XD6563/**D**]

- ♦ Fédération panafricaine des syndicats de l'agriculture (inactive)
- ♦ Fédération panafricaine des syndicats de l'éducation (no recent information)
- ♦ Fédération panafricaine des travailleurs de l'agriculture et de l'alimentation (inactive)
- ♦ Fédération panafricaine des travailleurs du bois et de la construction (no recent information)
- ♦ Fédération panafricaine des travailleurs de l'industrie (no recent information)
- ♦ Fédération panafricaine des travailleurs des industries alimentaires (no recent information)
- ♦ Fédération panafricaine des travailleurs du textile, habillement et cuir (no recent information)
- ♦ Fédération panafricaine des travailleurs du transport (inactive)
- ♦ Fédération panaméricaine des associations d'architectes (#18098)
- ♦ Fédération panaméricaine des associations des facultés de médecine (#18100)
- ♦ Fédération panaméricaine pour le don volontaire du sang (inactive)
- ♦ Fédération panaméricaine de hockey (#18110)
- ♦ Fédération panaméricaine de l'ingénierie économique et des coûts (no recent information)
- ♦ Fédération panaméricaine de médecine sportive (no recent information)
- ♦ Fédération panaméricaine de pharmacie (no recent information)
- ♦ Fédération panaméricaine des sociétés de géographie / see Pan American Institute of Geography and History (#18113)
- ♦ Fédération panaméricaine du travail (inactive)
- ♦ Fédération pan européenne des associations d'affaires réglementaires (inactive)
- ♦ Fédération Pan-Européenne des Sociétés de MTC (no recent information)
- ♦ Fédération Pan-Européenne des Spécialistes de Médecine Traditionelle Chinoise (#18175)
- ♦ Fédération pan-pacifique des relations publiques (inactive)
- ♦ Fédération des parcs naturels et nationaux d'Europe / see EUROPARC Federation (#05768)
- ♦ Fédération des partis libéraux et démocratiques de la Communauté européenne / see Alliance of Liberals and Democrats for Europe Party (#00703)
- ♦ Fédération des partis libéraux, démocratiques et réformateurs de la Communauté européenne / see Alliance of Liberals and Democrats for Europe Party (#00703)
- ♦ Fédération des partis libéraux, démocratiques et réformateurs européens / see Alliance of Liberals and Democrats for Europe Party (#00703)
- ♦ Fédération des partis verts des amériques (#09385)
- ♦ Federation for Peace and Conciliation / see International Federation for Peace and Conciliation (#13501)
- ♦ Federation of Pediatric Surgery Societies in the Southern Cone of America (#09390)
- ♦ Fédération des peuples d'ici et d'ailleurs (#18298)
- ♦ Federation of the Pharmaceutical Industry Associations in the EEC (inactive)
- ♦ Fédération des planteurs de café de l'Amérique (inactive)
- ♦ Fédération des planteurs de café d'Amérique centrale (inactive)
- ♦ Federation of Private Educational Associations of Latin America and the Caribbean / see Federación de Asociaciones Educativas de América Latina y el Caribe (#09289)
- ♦ Federation of Private Entities of Central America and Panama / see Federación de Entidades Privadas de Centroamérica, Panama y Republica Dominica (#09300)
- ♦ Federation of Private Entities of Central America, Panama and Dominican Republic (#09300)
- ♦ Federation of Private Universities of Central America / see Asociación de Universidades Privadas de Centroamérica y Panama (#02306)
- ♦ Federation of Private Universities of Central America and Panama / see Asociación de Universidades Privadas de Centroamérica y Panama (#02306)
- ♦ Fédération professionnelle arabe des travailleurs de la construction, du bois et des industries des matériaux de construction (inactive)
- ♦ Fédération professionnelle asiatique pour l'enseignement (no recent information)
- ♦ Fédération prohibitioniste internationale (inactive)
- ♦ Fédération de la publicité extérieure / see World Out of Home Organization (#21702)
- ♦ Federation of the Raw Materials and Improvers Industry for the Bakery and Confectionery Trades in the EEC / see Federation of European Manufacturers of Ingredients to the Bakery, Confectionery and Patisserie Industries (#09513)

♦ Federation of Regional Growth Actors in Europe (FEDRA) 09701

SG Square de Meeûs 18, 1050 Brussels, Belgium. T. +32477506612.
URL: http://www.fedra.eu/

History Registration: Banque-Carrefour des Entreprises, No/ID: 0648.590.401, Start date: 11 Feb 2016, Belgium. **Aims** Inform, educate and assist members and partners to engage in concrete European regional and interregional projects. **Structure** Advisory Board; Officers. Honorary Committee. **Languages** English. **Staff** 2-3. **Activities** Projects/programmes. **IGO Relations** *European Committee of the Regions (CoR, #06665); European Commission (EC, #06633); European Parliament (EP, #08146).* **NGO Relations** *European Business Summit (EBS, #06427).* [2018/XM5312/**D**]

- ♦ Fédération des républiques arabes (inactive)
- ♦ Fédération pour le respect de l'homme et de l'humanité (inactive)
- ♦ Federation for the Respect of Man and Humanity (inactive)
- ♦ Federation of Retired People of the PES / see European Senior Organization (#08465)
- ♦ Federation of Riding for the Disabled International / see Federation of Horses in Education and Therapy International (#09593)
- ♦ Fédération Routière Internationale (#14758)
- ♦ Fédération du Saumon Atlantique (internationally oriented national body)
- ♦ Fédération scandinave pour les animaux de laboratoires / see Scandinavian Society for Laboratory Animal Science (#19112)
- ♦ Fédération scandinave des importateurs du charbon (no recent information)
- ♦ Fédération scandinave de la jeunesse juive (no recent information)
- ♦ Fédération scandinave des télégraphes et des téléphones (inactive)

♦ Federation of Scandinavian Paint and Varnish Technologists 09702

Fédération d'associations de techniciens des industries des peintures et vernis de la Scandinavie – Vereinigung der Skandinavischen Farben und Lacktechniker – Skandinaviska Lackteknikers Förbund (SLF)

SG Becker Acroma KB, PO Box 2016, Märsta, SE-195 02 Stockholm, Sweden. T. +4638126260. E-mail: general.secretary@slfpaint.org.
Pres address not obtained. E-mail: slf.president@slfpaint.org.
URL: http://www.slfpaint.org/slf/hjem/

History 3 Jan 1953, Gothenburg (Sweden). **Aims** Promote cooperation between member associations and develop friendship among their members; arrange joint Scandinavian meetings; promote contact between Scandinavian and international associations. **Structure** Federation Meetings (every 3 years). Board (meets annually), composed of Chairmen of member associations, who hold the Presidency in rotation (3-year term). **Languages** Danish, English, Finnish, Norwegian, Swedish. **Staff** Part-time, voluntary. **Finance** Expenses shared according to national associations' membership. **Events** *Triennial Congress* Drammen (Norway) 2022, *Triennial Congress* Copenhagen (Denmark) 2018, *Triennial Congress* Gothenburg (Sweden) 2015, *Triennial Congress* Helsinki (Finland) 2012, *Triennial Congress* Sandefjord (Norway) 2009. **Publications** *Färg och Lack Scandinavia* (5 a year).
Members National associations, totalling over 1,800 individuals, in 4 countries:
Denmark, Finland, Norway, Sweden.
NGO Relations Member of: *Coatings Societies International (CSI, #04075).* [2011/XD0955/t/**D**]

♦ Fédération des Scénaristes d'Europe (FSE) 09703

Federation of Screenwriters in Europe

Management c/o UNI-Europa, Rue Joseph II 40, 1000 Brussels, Belgium. T. +442032873366. E-mail: office@federationscreenwriters.eu.
URL: https://federationscreenwriters.eu/

History Jun 2001, Athens (Greece), as *Federation of Scriptwriters in Europe.* Registered in accordance with Belgian law. **Aims** Advocate for freedom of expression, artistic creation and working conditions for screenwriters within the audiovisual field; protect national cultural identity and diversity of members. **Structure** General Assembly (annual); Executive Committee. **Languages** English, French. **Staff** 1.00 FTE, paid. **Finance** Members' dues. **Activities** Advocacy/lobbying/activism; events/meetings. **Events** *World Conference* Copenhagen (Denmark) 2021, *World Conference* Copenhagen (Denmark) 2020, *World Conference* Berlin (Germany) 2018, *World Conference* Warsaw (Poland) 2014, *World Conference* Barcelona (Spain) 2012. **Publications** *FSE Newsletter.* Information leaflets.
Members National and regional organizations (totalling about 7,000 writers) in 19 countries:
Austria, Belgium, Bulgaria, Denmark, Finland, France, Germany, Greece, Iceland, Ireland, Italy, Netherlands, Norway, Poland, Slovenia, Spain, Sweden, Switzerland, UK.
Consultative Status Consultative status granted from: *World Intellectual Property Organization (WIPO, #21593)* (Permanent Observer Status). [2020/XD9023/**D**]

- ♦ Federation of Scientific and Technical Organizations in Socialist Countries (inactive)
- ♦ Federation of Screenwriters in Europe (#09703)
- ♦ Federation of Scriptwriters in Europe / see Fédération des Scénaristes d'Europe (#09703)
- ♦ Federation of Secular Institutes in Latin America (#04451)
- ♦ Federation of Semi-Official and Private International Institutions established in Geneva / see Fédération des Institutions Internationales établies à Genève (#09599)
- ♦ Federation of Sephardi Organizations of Latin America (#09388)
- ♦ Fédération séphardite mondiale (#21778)
- ♦ Federation of Sewage and Industrial Wastes Associations / see Water Environment Federation
- ♦ Federation of Sewage Works Associations / see Water Environment Federation
- ♦ Federation of Slavic and Danube Regional Beekeeping Organizations / see Federacia Vcelarskych Organizacii (#09287)
- ♦ Fédération des sociétés africaines de biochimie et de biologie moléculaire (#09410)
- ♦ Fédération des Sociétés d'Assurance de Droit National Africaines (#09408)
- ♦ Fédération des sociétés chimiques européennes / see European Chemical Society (#06524)
- ♦ Fédération des sociétés de droits d'exécution (inactive)
- ♦ Fédération des sociétés de droits de représentation (inactive)
- ♦ Fédération des sociétés européennes de biochimie (#09494)
- ♦ Fédération des sociétés européennes de chirurgie de la main (#09549)
- ♦ Fédération des sociétés européennes oncologiques / see European Cancer Organisation (#06432)
- ♦ Fédération des sociétés latinoaméricaines de cancérologie (#16319)
- ♦ Fédération des Sociétés Nationales de Gynécologie-Obstétrique des pays du Maghreb Arabe / see Fédération Maghrébine de Gynécologie Obstétrique (#09686)
- ♦ Fédération des sociétés nationales de gynécologie-obstétrique des pays méditerranéens (#09695)
- ♦ Fédération des Sociétés Nationales des Ingénieurs Electriciens de l'Europe / see Convention of National Associations of Electrical Engineers of Europe (#04788)
- ♦ Fédération des sociétés théosophiques d'Europe / see Theosophical Society in Europe (#20142)
- ♦ Federation of Societies for Coatings Technology (internationally oriented national body)
- ♦ Federation of Societies for Rights of Performance (inactive)
- ♦ Federation of Societies for Rights of Representation (inactive)
- ♦ Federation of South American Societies of Anesthesiologists (#09291)

♦ Federation of South American Societies and Associations of Laboratory Animal Science Specialists 09704

Federación de Sociedades Sudamericanas en Ciencias de Animales de Laboratorio (FESSACAL) – Federação Sul-Americanas da Ciência em Animais de Laboratório

SG address not obtained.
Pres address not obtained.
URL: http://www.fessacal.com/

History 1999, Palma de Mallorca (Spain), during triennial symposium of *Federation of European Laboratory Animal Science Associations (FELASA, #09509).* Current statutes approved 13 Apr 2013. **Structure** General Assembly; Governing Board; Executive Committee. **Events** *International Congress* Buenos Aires (Argentina) 2014, *Ordinary Assembly* Punta del Este (Uruguay) 2013, *International Congress* Sao Paulo (Brazil) 2012, *Regional meeting / Congress* Montevideo (Uruguay) 2009, *Congress* Buenos Aires (Argentina) 2004.
Members Associations in 5 countries:
Argentina, Brazil, Chile, Uruguay, Venezuela. [2014/XM0872/**D**]

- ♦ Fédération de spécialistes en chirurgie plastique de l'ANASE (#01183)
- ♦ Fédération spéléologique de la Communauté Européenne / see Fédération Spéléologique Européenne (#09705)

♦ Fédération Spéléologique Européenne (FSE) 09705

European Speleological Federation

SG BP 3067, L-1030 Luxembourg, Luxembourg. E-mail: contact@eurospeleo.eu – communication@eurospeleo.eu.
URL: http://www.eurospeleo.eu/

History 8 Sep 1990. Founded under the auspices of *International Union of Speleology (#15818).* Former names and other names: *Speleological Federation of the European Community* – former; *Fédération spéléologique de la Communauté Européenne (FSCE)* – former; *Fédération spéléologique de l'Union Européenne (FSUE)* – former; *Speleological Federation of the European Union* – former. **Aims** Gather and represent cavers, speleological federations and *caving* clubs throughout Europe; support and promote European-wide actions and information exchange in the field of speleology and caving. **Structure** General Assembly (annual); Bureau. **Languages** English, French. **Staff** Voluntary. **Finance** Sources: members' dues. **Activities** Events/meetings. Active in all member countries. **Events** *EuroSpeleo Forum* Burgos (Spain) 2022, *General Assembly* Le Bourget-du-Lac (France) 2022, *General Assembly* 2021, *General Assembly* 2020, *EuroSpeleo Forum* Burgos (Spain) 2020. **Publications** *EuroSpeleo Newsletter.*
Members Full in 31 countries and territories:
Armenia, Austria, Belgium, Bulgaria, Croatia, Denmark, Finland, France, Georgia, Germany, Great Britain, Greece, Hungary, Ireland, Italy, Lithuania, Luxembourg, Moldova, Netherlands, Norway, Poland, Portugal, Romania, Serbia, Slovakia, Slovenia, Spain, Sweden, Switzerland, Türkiye, Ukraine.
NGO Relations Member of (1): *European Environmental Bureau (EEB, #06996).* [2023.02.27/XE2037/**D**]

- ♦ Fédération spéléologique de l'Union Européenne / see Fédération Spéléologique Européenne (#09705)
- ♦ Fédération spirite internationale (#15586)
- ♦ Federation for Sport at Altitude / see International Skyrunning Federation (#14873)
- ♦ Fédération sportive européenne des sapeurs pompiers (#07261)
- ♦ Fédération sportive pour la solidarité islamique (#16052)
- ♦ Federation of the Staff Associations of the United Nations and its Specialized Agencies in Delhi (internationally oriented national body)

- ♦ Federation of Staff Associations of United Nations and its Specialized Agencies in the Philippines (internationally oriented national body)

♦ Federation of Staff Associations of the United Nations and its Specialized Agencies in Santiago (FUNSA Santiago) 09706

Contact c/o ECLAC Staff Association, Casilla 179-D, Santiago, Santiago Metropolitan, Chile. T. +5622102215 – +5622102261. Fax +5622080252 – +5622081946. E-mail: consejo@cepal.org.
URL: http://www.eclac.org/

NGO Relations Observer status with: *Federation of International Civil Servants' Associations (FICSA, #09603).* [2011/XE4351/v/**E**]

- ♦ Federation of the Staff Associations of the United Nations and its Specialized Agencies and their Affiliated Bodies in Denmark (internationally oriented national body)
- ♦ Federation of State Insurance Organizations of SAARC Countries (inactive)
- ♦ Federation of Stock Exchanges in the European Community / see Federation of European Securities Exchanges (#09542)
- ♦ Fédération sympadent internationale / see Toothfriendly International
- ♦ Fédération syndicale européenne pour les secteurs de l'agriculture, de l'alimentation et de l'hôtellerie (#07125)
- ♦ Fédération syndicale européenne des services publics (#07202)
- ♦ Fédération syndicale européenne du textile, de l'habillement et du cuir (inactive)
- ♦ Fédération syndicale des fonctionnaires internationaux (inactive)
- ♦ Fédération syndicale internationale (inactive)
- ♦ Fédération syndicale mondiale (#21493)
- ♦ Fédération des syndicats chrétiens de l'Europe centrale (inactive)
- ♦ Fédération des syndicats des transports dans l'Union européenne / see European Transport Workers' Federation (#08941)
- ♦ Fédération des syndicats des travailleurs universitaires de l'Amérique centrale, du Mexique et des Caraïbes (#09712)
- ♦ Federation of Teachers Organizations of Central America (inactive)
- ♦ Federation of Telecommunications Engineers in the European Community (#09597)
- ♦ Fédération de tennis de table des Caraïbes (no recent information)
- ♦ Federation of Theosophical Societies in Europe / see Theosophical Society in Europe (#20142)
- ♦ Fédération théosophique mondiale des jeunes (inactive)

♦ Federation of Therapeutic Communities of Central and Eastern Europe (FTCCEE) 09707

Federacja Spolecznosci Terapeutycznych Europy Centralnej i Wschodniej

Pres 11 48 32 Debowa Street 5, 44-100 Gliwice, Poland. T. +48322702102. Fax +48322703758. E-mail: czpilu@mp.pl.

Aims Support the development of the programmes of therapeutic communities in rehabilitation of drug takers and those others who would benefit from the therapeutic community approach.
Members Full in 6 countries:
Bulgaria, Czechia, Hungary, Lithuania, Poland, Slovakia, Slovenia.
NGO Relations Member of: *World Federation of Therapeutic Communities (WFTC, #21491).* [2014/XJ5030/**D**]

♦ Federation of Timber and Related Industries Workers' Unions of the Commonwealth of Independent States 09708

Pres 42 Leninsky Prospekt, Moscow MOSKVA, Russia, 119119. T. +74959388202. Fax +74959388204. E-mail: fed@lesprofsng.ru.

Members Trade unions in the CIS region (membership countries not specified). **IGO Relations** *Commonwealth of Independent States (CIS, #04341).* **NGO Relations** Member of: *General Confederation of Trade Unions (GCTU, #10108).* [2014/XM2464/t/**D**]

- ♦ Federation of Transport Worker's Unions in the European Union / see European Transport Workers' Federation (#08941)
- ♦ Fédération des travailleurs de l'industrie bananière d'Amérique latine et des Caraïbes (inactive)

♦ Fédération de l'Union Européenne des Consuls Honoraires (FUECH) 09709

Federation of European Unions of Honorary Consuls

Contact Residence Lady, Av Winston Churchill 249/16, 1180 Brussels, Belgium. T. +32475587826. E-mail: office@fuech.cc – president@fuech.cc.
URL: http://www.fuech.cc/

History 17 Apr 2004, Grenoble (France). Former names and other names: *European Federation of Unions of Honorary Consuls* – alias. Registration: France; Austria; EU Transparency Register, No/ID: 2401666440-09. **Aims** Encourage ties among various consular associations; promote positive relations with the respective receiving states as well as with institutions of the European Union. **Structure** General Assembly; Managing Committee. **Languages** English, French, German. **Staff** 9.00 FTE, voluntary. **Finance** Sources: members' dues. **Events** *General Assembly* Vienna (Austria) 2017, *General Assembly* Valencia (Spain) 2016.
Members Federations in 17 countries and territories:
Albania, Austria, Belgium, France, Germany, Hungary, Italy, Lithuania, Málaga, Malta, Montenegro, Moravia-Silesia, Netherlands, Romania, San Marino, Slovenia, Valencia. [2021.06.10/XM6910/**E**]

- ♦ Federation for Universal French (inactive)
- ♦ Fédération universelle des associations d'agences de voyages / see United Federation of Travel Agents' Associations (#20509)
- ♦ Fédération Universelle des Associations Chrétiennes d'Etudiants (#21833)
- ♦ Fédération universelle des associations pédagogiques (inactive)
- ♦ Fédération universelle des étudiants chrétiens / see World Student Christian Federation (#21833)
- ♦ Fédération universelle d'étudiants contre l'alcoolisme (inactive)
- ♦ Fédération universelle des sociétés d'hôteliers (inactive)
- ♦ Fédération universitaire internationale pour les principes de la Société des Nations (inactive)
- ♦ Fédération des universités catholiques / see International Federation of Catholic Universities (#13381)
- ♦ Fédération des universités catholiques européennes (#07070)
- ♦ Fédération des Universités Catholiques d'Europe et du Liban / see European Federation of Catholic Universities (#07070)
- ♦ Fédération des universités du monde islamique (#09710)
- ♦ Fédération d'universités privés d'Amérique centrale et du Panama / see Asociación de Universidades Privadas de Centroamérica y Panama (#02306)

♦ Federation of the Universities of the Islamic World (FUIW) 09710

Fédération des universités du monde islamique (FUMI)

SG c/o ISESCO, Avenue des FAR – Hay Ryad, PO Box 2275, 10104 Rabat, Morocco. T. +21237566052 – +2123737566053. Fax +21237566012 – +21237566013. E-mail: fumi@isesco.org.ma.
URL: https://www.isesco.org.ma/fuiw.org/en/

History 30 Nov 1987, Rabat (Morocco). 30 Nov-1 Dec 1987, Rabat (Morocco), under the auspices of *Islamic World Educational, Scientific and Cultural Organization (ICESCO, #16058),* when statutes were adopted. Foundation followed recommendations of *OIC Ministerial Standing Committee on Scientific and Technological Cooperation (COMSTECH, #17702).* **Aims** Enhance level of scientific research in all fields, exchange findings and link them with the developmental and civilizational requirements of the Islamic Ummah; upgrade and develop higher education to address the needs of *Muslim* societies and benefit by the scientific and technological new developments in line with the Islamic Ummah's civilizational constants; further cooperation in such a way as to enhance the exchange of experiences, studies, programmes and visits in the fields of education, science, culture and technology; encourage the teaching of the language of the Holy Quran and the Islamic culture in member universities; step up the efforts of higher education institutions to address the current issues and entrench the values of understanding, coexistence and peace among the peoples of the Islamic Ummah and the world as a whole; upgrade member universities' knowledge and human capacities; care for the Islamic heritage by publicizing, translating and authenticating it, and focusing on the contribution of its scholars to human civilizational building. **Structure** General Conference (every 3 years); Executive Council; Secretary-General (Director-General of ISESCO, ex officio) heads General Secretariat at ISESCO headquarters. **Languages** Arabic, English, French. **Staff** Provided by ISESCO. **Finance** Members' dues. Other sources: annual subsidy and student scholarships from ISESCO; donations; grants; sales of publications. **Activities** Training/education; events/meetings; networking/liaising; knowledge management/ information dissemination. **Events** *General Conference* Kuwait 2007, *Session* Sharjah (United Arab Emirates) 2006, *Session* Kuwait (Kuwait) 2005, *General Conference* Sharjah (United Arab Emirates) 2004, *Session / General Conference* Sharjah (United Arab Emirates) 2004. **Publications** *Al-Ittihad/The Federation* (3 a year) in Arabic, English, French – newsletter; *Al-Jamia/The Federation* in Arabic, English, French – journal. *Directory of the Universities of the Islamic World* in Arabic, English, French; *Guide to Quality and Accreditation for the Universities of the Islamic World*; *Guide to Research Centres in the Member Universities.* Conference proceedings; strategy.
Members Universities and equivalents (214) in 39 countries and territories:
Azerbaijan, Bahrain, Bangladesh, Bosnia-Herzegovina, Brunei Darussalam, Burkina Faso, Chad, Comoros, Egypt, Guinea, Indonesia, Iran Islamic Rep, Iraq, Jordan, Kuwait, Kyrgyzstan, Lebanon, Libya, Malaysia, Mali, Mauritania, Morocco, Niger, Oman, Pakistan, Palestine, Qatar, Saudi Arabia, Senegal, Somalia, Sudan, Suriname, Syrian AR, Tajikistan, Tunisia, Türkiye, Uganda, United Arab Emirates, Yemen.
Member Universities in non-OIC member states in 10 countries:
India, Kenya, Netherlands, Northern Cyprus, Russia, Spain, Sri Lanka, Thailand, UK, USA.
Included in the above membership, 13 universities listed in this Yearbook:
Arabian Gulf University (AGU, #00976); Beirut Arab University (BAU); Graduate School of Islamic and Social Sciences (GSISS); International Islamic University Malaysia (IIUM, #13961); International University of Africa (IUA); International University of Kyrgyzstan (IUK); Islamic Civilization Institute, Moscow (no recent information); Islamic University in Niger (#16054); Islamic University in Uganda (IUIU, #16056); Islamic University – Medinah Munawwarah (no recent information); Islamic University of Rotterdam (IUR); Naif Arab University for Security Sciences (NAUSS, #16929); Universidad Islamica Internacional Averroes de Al-Andalus (no recent information).
NGO Relations Associate member of: *International Association of Universities (IAU, #12246).* Cooperation agreements with: *Association of African Universities (AAU, #02361); Association of Arab Universities (AARU, #02374); League of Arab Institutions for Higher Education (no recent information); League of Islamic Universities (#16425).* [2017.06.03/XD1634/y/**E**]

♦ Federation of University Women of Africa (FUWA) 09711

Pres PO Box 7178, Kampala, Uganda. T. +2567724540587 – +256772401855.
URL: http://www.graduatewomen.org/who-we-are/our-membership/regional-groups/africa- federation-of-university-women-of-africa-fuwa/

History as a regional grouping of *Graduate Women International (GWI, #10688).* **Events** *Conference* Lagos (Nigeria) 2009, *General Assembly* Kampala (Uganda) 2008. **Members** National organizations. Membership countries not specified. [2015/XD3418/**D**]

♦ Federation of University Workers Unions of Central America, the Caribbean and Mexico 09712

Fédération des syndicats des travailleurs universitaires de l'Amérique centrale, du Mexique et des Caraïbes – Federación de Sindicatos de Trabajadores de las Universidades de Centroamérica, México y el Caribe (FESITRAUCAMC)

Contact Asociación de Trabajadores Docentes, UNAN Leon, Planta Ed Central, Aptdo Postal 68, Contiguo a lg La Merced, León, Nicaragua. T. +505311-2421.

History Dec 1975, Costa Rica. **Events** *Congreso Latinoamericano de Sindicatos Universitarios* León (Nicaragua) 2012, *Congreso Latinoamericano de Sindicatos Universitarios* Lima (Peru) 2008. **NGO Relations** *Fédération internationale syndicale de l'enseignement (FISE, #09662).* [2013/XD1180/**D**]

- ♦ Fédération des Verts Africains (#00331)
- ♦ Fédération des vétérinaires de la Communauté européenne / see Federation of Veterinarians of Europe (#09713)
- ♦ Fédération des vétérinaires européens (#09713)

♦ Federation of Veterinarians of Europe 09713

Fédération des vétérinaires européens (FVE)

Exec Dir Rue Victor Oudart 7, 1030 Brussels, Belgium. T. +3225337020. E-mail: info@fve.org.
Office Manager address not obtained.
URL: http://www.fve.org/

History 8 Feb 1961. Restructured, 1974. New statutes adopted: May 1999; Jun 2005. Former names and other names: *Liaison Committee of Veterinarians of the EEC* – former (1961 to 1974); *Comité de liaison des vétérinaires de la CEE* – former (1961 to 1974); *Federation of Veterinarians of the European Community* – former (1974 to 1993); *Fédération des vétérinaires de la Communauté européenne* – former (1974 to 1993). Registration: Banque-Carrefour des Entreprises, No/ID: 0851.035.537, Start date: 1 Jul 2000; EU Transparency Register, No/ID: 3959733732-78, Start date: 5 Dec 2008. **Aims** Unite the European veterinary profession politically and professionally for the benefit of animal health, animal welfare and public health. **Structure** General Assembly (biannually, with autumn meeting always in Brussels, Belgium); Board of Officers; Sections (4); Working Groups. **Languages** Dutch, English, French, German. **Staff** 5.00 FTE, paid. **Finance** Sources: members' dues. **Activities** Advocacy/lobbying/activism; events/meetings. **Events** *General Assembly* London (UK) 2022, *General Assembly* Brussels (Belgium) 2021, *General Assembly* Brussels (Belgium) 2021, *General Assembly* Brussels (Belgium) 2020, *General Assembly* Brussels (Belgium) 2020. **Publications** *FVE Newsletter* (4 a year); *FVE News* (irregular).
Members Organizations (45) in 37 countries:
Albania, Austria, Belgium, Bosnia-Herzegovina, Bulgaria, Croatia, Cyprus, Czechia, Denmark, Estonia, Finland, France, Germany, Greece, Hungary, Iceland, Ireland, Italy, Latvia, Lithuania, Luxembourg, Malta, Montenegro, Netherlands, North Macedonia, Norway, Poland, Portugal, Romania, Serbia, Slovakia, Slovenia, Spain, Sweden, Switzerland, Türkiye, UK.
Observers in 4 countries:
Armenia, Russia, Türkiye, Ukraine.
Included in the above, 4 organizations listed in this Yearbook:
European Association of State Veterinary Officers (EASVO, #06221); European Association of Veterinarians in Education, Research and Industry (EVERI, #06267); Union européenne des vétérinaires hygiénistes (UEVH, #20404); Union européenne des vétérinaires praticiens (UEVP, #20405).
IGO Relations Recognized by: *European Commission (EC, #06633).* **NGO Relations** Special links with: *Federation of European Companion Animal Veterinary Associations (FECAVA, #09497).* Represented on: *Eurogroup for Animals (#05690); European Platform for the Responsible Use of Medicines in Animals (EPRUMA, #08231).* Attends the meetings of: *European Board of Veterinary Specialisation (EBVS, #06375).* Founding member of: *European Coordination Committee for Veterinary Training (ECCVT, #06793).* Member of: *Federation of European and International Associations Established in Belgium (FAIB, #09508).* Associate member of: *World Veterinary Association (WVA, #21901).* In liaison with technical committees of: *International Organization for Standardization (ISO, #14473).* Partner of: *International Veterinary Students' Association (IVSA, #15851).* Provides staff for: *European Association of Porcine Health Management (EAPHM, #06159); Federation of European Equine Veterinary Associations (FEEVA, #09503);* Veterinary Continuous Education in Europe (VetCEE). [2022.05.11/XE0516/y/**E**]

- ♦ Federation of Veterinarians of the European Community / see Federation of Veterinarians of Europe (#09713)
- ♦ Federation of West African Chambers of Commerce (no recent information)

♦ Federation of West African Manufacturers Associations (FEWAMA) 09714

Fédération des associations des industriels de l'Afrique de l'Ouest (FAIAO)

Admin Sec 77 Obafemi Awolowo Way, Ikeja, PO Box 3835, Lagos, Nigeria. T. +23414542700 – +23414542701. Fax +23414974240 – +23414974243.

History Founded 1988, Lagos (Nigeria). **Aims** Encourage formation of national manufacturers associations in West African countries. **Structure** General Assembly (annual); Executive Council. **Languages** English, French. **Staff** 1.00 FTE, paid. Secretariat staff seconded from Nigerian association member. **Finance** Members' dues. **Activities** Events/meetings; knowledge management/information dissemination; guidance/assistance/ consulting. **Events** *Annual general assembly / General Assembly* Lagos (Nigeria) 1996, *Annual general assembly / General Assembly* Lagos (Nigeria) 1994, *FEWAMA international seminar on penetrating community markets in ECOWAS sub-region* Lagos (Nigeria) 1993, *Annual general assembly / General Assembly* Niamey (Niger) 1992, *General Assembly* Lagos (Nigeria) / Cotonou (Benin) 1991. **Publications** *West African Industrial Directory* (1992). Information Services: Library on trade and industry in West Africa; information unit.
Members Manufacturers associations in 13 countries:
Benin, Burkina Faso, Côte d'Ivoire, Ghana, Guinea, Liberia, Mali, Mauritania, Niger, Nigeria, Senegal, Sierra Leone, Togo.
IGO Relations Observer status with: *Economic Community of West African States (ECOWAS, #05312)*.

[2019.09.24/XD2326/t/**D**]

♦ Federation of West African Pharmaceutical Students Associations (inactive)
♦ Federation of Western European Rope and Twine Industries / see Fédération européenne des industries de corderie ficellerie et de filets (#09573)
♦ Federation of West Thrace Turks in Europe (internationally oriented national body)
♦ Federation of Workers in the Banana Industry of Latin American and the Caribbean (inactive)
♦ Federation of World Health Foundations (inactive)
♦ Federation of World Peace and Love (internationally oriented national body)
♦ Federation of World Volunteer Firefighters Associations (no recent information)
♦ Federation of Young European Ecologists / see Federation of Young European Greens (#09715)
♦ Federation of Young European Employers (inactive)

♦ Federation of Young European Greens (FYEG) 09715
Fédération des jeunes verts européens (FJVE)
SG Rue Wiertz 31, 1050 Brussels, Belgium. T. +32495129601 – +3226260727. E-mail: office@fyeg.org.
URL: http://www.fyeg.org/
History 1988. Originally referred to as *Federation of Young European Ecologists – Fédération des jeunes écologistes européens (FJEE)*. Registered in accordance with Belgian law. EU Transparency Register: 756739622445-07. **Aims** Bring together young environmental and green *political* groups from all over Europe so as to encourage both mutual understanding and mutual action to promote a greener Europe; strive for *environmental* and social justice on a European level. **Structure** General Assembly (annual); Executive Committee. **Languages** English, French. **Staff** 3.50 FTE, paid. **Activities** Advocacy/lobbying/activism; events/ meetings; training/education. **Events** *General Assembly* Brussels (Belgium) 2021, *General Assembly* Brussels (Belgium) 2020, *General Assembly* Istanbul (Turkey) 2019, *General Assembly* Utrecht (Netherlands) 2018, *General Assembly* Madrid (Spain) 2017. **Publications** *E-newsletter* (12 a year); *Ecosprinter* (3 a year) – magazine.
Members Full: Youth groups of 'green' parties and green youth NGOs in 27 countries:
Albania, Belgium, Bulgaria, Cyprus, Czechia, Finland, France, Georgia, Germany, Greece, Hungary, Ireland, Italy, Luxembourg, Malta, Netherlands, North Macedonia, Norway, Poland, Portugal, Serbia, Spain, Sweden, Switzerland, Türkiye, UK, Ukraine.
Organization with Observer Status (1):
Cooperation and Development Network Eastern Europe (CDN, #04794).
IGO Relations Member of: *Anna Lindh Euro-Mediterranean Foundation for the Dialogue between Cultures (Anna Lindh Foundation, #00847)*. **NGO Relations** Official youth wing of: *European Green Party (EGP, #07409)*. Member of: *European Youth Forum (#09140)*.

[2019.10.02/XD2121/**E**]

♦ Federation of Zarathushti Associations of North America / see Federation of Zoroastrian Associations of North America
♦ Federation of Zoroastrian Associations of North America (internationally oriented national body)
♦ Federative Committee on Anatomical Terminology / see Federative International Programme for Anatomical Terminology (#09716)
♦ Federative International Committee on Anatomical Terminology / see Federative International Programme for Anatomical Terminology (#09716)

♦ Federative International Programme for Anatomical Terminology 09716
(FIPAT)
Communication Sec/Interim-Chair Radboud Univ Medical Centre, Dept Neurology, PO Box 9101, 6500 HB Nijmegen, Netherlands. T. +31654364692.
Informatics Sec Dalhousie Univ, Dept Medical Neuroscience, PO Box 15000, Halifax NS B3H 4R2, Canada.
URL: http://www.unifr.ch/ifaa/
History Founded 1989, Rio de Janeiro (Brazil), as *Federative Committee on Anatomical Terminology (FCAT)*, by *International Federation of Associations of Anatomists (IFAA, #13361)* on the occasion of the General Assembly of the XIIIth Congress of Anatomy, as successor to: *International Nomenclature Committee*, set up 1936, Milan (Italy), and dissolved 1939; and *International Anatomical Nomenclature Committee (IANC) – Comité de nomenclature anatomique internationale*, also set up by the Federation, 1950, Oxford (UK). Changed name at the XV International Congress of Anatomy, 1999, Rome (Italy), to *Federative International Committee on Anatomical Terminology (FICAT)*. Following a change in the IFAA Constitution on the occasion of the XVII IFAA Congress, 2009, Cape Town (South Africa), became a programme of IFAA, and adopted current title. Established under new name, 2010, after FICAT had been dissolved. **Aims** Provide high-level and simple to use biomedical anatomical terminology, relevant to the international anatomical community, health science in general, as well as to scientists, educators, writers, and general public; enhance communication within and between disciplines; enable continual revision and reorganization in order to meet new developments. **Structure** Working Groups (7); Subcommittees (2). **Languages** English. **Staff** Voluntary. **Finance** Grants from: *International Federation of Associations of Anatomists (IFAA, #13361)*; national anatomical societies. Support from Fribourg and Dalhousie Universities. **Activities** Knowledge management/information dissemination; events/meetings. **Events** *Meeting* Istanbul (Turkey) 2015, *Anatomy, from gross to molecular and digital* Beijing (China) 2014, *Meeting* Taormina (Italy) 2010, *Meeting* Cape Town (South Africa) 2009, *Meeting* Toronto, ON (Canada) 2006. **Publications** *Terminologia Embryologica – TE* (2013); *Terminologia Histologica – TH* (2008); *Terminologia Anatomica – TA* (1998). PDFs tables. **Information Services** *Terminologia Embryologica – 2nd edition* – 2017; *Terminologia Neuroanatomica* – 2017.
Members Individuals (48) in 22 countries:
Argentina, Australia, Brazil, Canada, China, Czechia, Germany, Grenada, India, Italy, Japan, Korea Rep, Netherlands, New Zealand, Portugal, Russia, South Africa, Spain, Sweden, Switzerland, UK, USA.

[2018.09.17/XE3833/v/**E**]

♦ Federazione ACLI Internazionali (#13336)
♦ Federazione delle Associazioni dei Cacciatori della CE / see Federation of Associations for Hunting and Conservation of the EU (#09459)
♦ Federazione delle Associazioni dei Cacciatori della UE / see Federation of Associations for Hunting and Conservation of the EU (#09459)
♦ Federazione Associazioni Cristiane Lavoratori Internazionali / see International Federation of ACLI (#13336)
♦ Federazione delle Associazioni Europee del Commercio all'Ingrosso ed Esterno (inactive)
♦ Federazione delle Associazioni dei Fabbricanti di Prodotti Alimentari Surgelati della CEE (inactive)
♦ Federazione delle Associazioni Familiari Cattoliche in Europa (#09468)
♦ Federazione delle Associazioni Nazionali dei Beccacciai del Paleartico Occidentale (#09460)
♦ Federazione delle Associazioni venatori e per la Conservazione della Fauna Selvatica dell'UE (#09459)
♦ Federazione Astrologica dell'Europa del Sud (no recent information)
♦ Federazione Biblica Cattolica (#03600)
♦ Federazione Cattolica Mondiale per l'Apostolato Biblico / see Catholic Biblical Federation (#03600)
♦ Federazione Comunitaria delle Industrie delle Materie Prime e di Miglioranti per la Panificazione e la Pasticceria / see Federation of European Manufacturers of Ingredients to the Bakery, Confectionery and Patisserie Industries (#09513)
♦ Federazione Editori Europei (#09536)
♦ Federazione Euromediterranea Municipalités Oléicoles (inactive)
♦ Federazione Europea degli Allevatori della Razza Bruna (#06405)
♦ Federazione Europea degli Allevatori di Salmonidi / see Federation of European Aquaculture Producers (#09491)
♦ Federazione Europea delle Aree Naturali e Rurali Metropolitane e Periurbane (inactive)
♦ Federazione Europea delle Associazioni de Consulenti in Materia Organizzativa (#07159)
♦ Federazione Europea delle Associazioni degli Economisti d'Impresa (no recent information)
♦ Federazione Europea delle Associazioni per l'Insegnamento delle Lingue (no recent information)
♦ Federazione Europea delle Associazioni di Isolamento (#09582)
♦ Federazione Europea delle Associazioni per il Legno da Miniera (inactive)
♦ Federazione Europea delle Associazioni per il Patrimonio Industriale e Tecnico (#07053)
♦ Federazione Europea delle Associazioni di Società di Factoring (no recent information)
♦ Federazione Europea delle Associazioni dei Torrefattori di Caffè (inactive)
♦ Federazione Europea della Citizen's Band (#06556)
♦ Federazione Europea di Climatoterapia (inactive)
♦ Federazione Europea del Commercio all Ingrosso ed Estero in Giocattoli (inactive)
♦ Federazione europea dei Consulenti e Intermediari Finanziari (#07122)
♦ Federazione Europea di Fabbricanti di Attrezzi per Scrittura / see European Writing Instrument Manufacturer's Association (#09125)
♦ Federazione Europea dei Fabbricanti di Cartone Ondulato (#07091)
♦ Federazione Europea dei Fabbricanti e Distributori di Dispositivi di Protezione Individuali (#08418)
♦ Federazione Europea dei Fabbricanti di Mangimi Composti per Animali (#09566)
♦ Federazione Europea dei Fabbricanti di Prodotti Refrattari (#08339)
♦ Federazione Europea dei Fabbricanti di Sacchi Carta a Grande Contenuto / see EUROSAC (#09177)
♦ Federazione Europea per la Gestione dei Rifiuti / see European Federation of Waste Management and Environmental Services (#07232)
♦ Federazione Europea degli Importatori di Frutta Secca, Conserve, Spezie e Miele / see European Federation of the Trade in Dried Fruit, Edible Nuts, Processed Fruit and Vegetables, Processed Fishery Products, Spices, Honey and Similar Foodstuffs (#07229)
♦ Federazione Europea dell'Industria di Alimenti per Animali Domestici (#09571)
♦ Federazione Europea dell'Industria dell'Ottica e della Meccanica di Precisione (#07193)
♦ Federazione Europea dell'Industria delle Spazzole e dei Pennelli (#06406)
♦ Federazione Europea per l'Ingegneria Naturalistica (#05751)
♦ Federazione Europea delle Istituzioni Linguistiche Nazionali / see European Federation of National Institutions for Language (#07172)
♦ Federazione Europea dei Lavoratori Edili e del Legno (#07065)
♦ Federazione Europea dei Lavoratori Edili e del Legno nella CEE / see European Federation of Building and Woodworkers (#07065)
♦ Federazione Europea Libere Associazioni (inactive)
♦ Federazione Europea dei Medici a Rapporto d'Impiego (#07209)
♦ Federazione european delle scuole (#09479)
♦ Federazione Europea dei Parchi Divertimento (inactive)
♦ Federazione Europea delle Persone Anziane (#05597)
♦ Federazione Europea Produttori Acquacoltura / see Federation of European Aquaculture Producers (#09491)
♦ Federazione Europea dei Professionisti dell'Ambiente (no recent information)
♦ Federazione Europea dei Professionisti della Pedagogia (unconfirmed)
♦ Federazione Europea Proteine Vegetali / see European Vegetable Protein Association (#09047)
♦ Federazione Europea della Pubblicità Esterna / see World Out of Home Organization (#21702)
♦ Federazione Europea della Razza Bruna (no recent information)
♦ Federazione Europea Delle Razze Bovine del Sistema Alpino (#05752)
♦ Federazione Europea della Sanità Animale e della Sicurezza Sanitaria (#09581)
♦ Federazione Europea dei Servizi di Produzione (#07196)
♦ Federazione Europea dei Trasformatori di Tabacco (#07227)
♦ Federazione Europea Trattamento Acqua / see European Water and Wastewater Industry Association (#09087)
♦ Federazione Europea di Venditori all'Aste / see European Federation of Auctioneers (#07057)
♦ Federazione Europea di Zoologia (inactive)
♦ Federazione della Funzione Pubblica Europea (#06567)
♦ Federazione dell'Industria Olearia della CE / see FEDIOL – The EU Vegetable Oil and Proteinmeal Industry (#09718)
♦ Federazione dell'Industria dell'Olio d'Oliva della ECC (#09596)
♦ Federazione delle Industrie Europee di Coltelleria, Posateria, Vasellame e Pentolame (#09511)
♦ Federazione delle Industrie delle Materie Prime e dei Semilavorati per la Panificazione e la Pasticceria dello SEE / see Federation of European Manufacturers of Ingredients to the Bakery, Confectionery and Patisserie Industries (#09513)
♦ Federazione degli Ingegneri delle Telecomunicazioni della Comunità Europea (#09597)
♦ Federazione Internazionale dell'Artigianato (inactive)
♦ Federazione Internazionale delle Associazioni Cattoliche Ciechi (#13377)
♦ Federazione Internazionale delle Associazioni di Chimica Tessile e Coloristica (#13365)
♦ Federazione Internazionale delle Associazioni dei Commercianti in Acciai, Tubi e Metalli (inactive)
♦ Federazione Internazionale delle Associazioni di Persone Anziane (#09609)
♦ Federazione Internazionale Campeggio Caravanning / see Fédération Internationale de Camping, Caravanning et Autocaravaning (#09618)
♦ Federazione Internazionale Campeggio, Caravanning e Autocaravaning (#09618)
♦ Federazione Internazionale delle Case d'Europa (inactive)
♦ Federazione Internazionale dei Centri di Aiuto per Telefono (#13567)
♦ Federazione Internazionale dei Centri ed Istituti di Bioetica di Ispirazione Personalista (unconfirmed)

♦ Federazione Internazionale Cronometristi (FIC) 09717
Fédération internationale des chronométreurs – International Timekeepers Federation
Main Office Via Della Moscova 39, 20121 Milan MI, Italy. E-mail: internationaltimekeepingfeder@gmail.com.
Facebook: https://www.facebook.com/people/Federazione-Internazionale-Cronometristi/100054501397636/
History 7 Dec 1957, Monte Carlo (Monaco), by adhering bodies of 7 countries, a *Centro Internazionale Permanente per il Perfezionamento del Cronometraggio Sportivo*, or *Centro Internazionale di Cronometraggio (CIO)*, having been set up 8 Jun 1949. Most recent statutes adopted 1994, Rome (Italy). Also referred to in English as *International Timekeeping Federation*. **Aims** Standardize *sports* time-keeping procedures to comply with principles of universality and equality in sport and ensure reliable and effective time-keeping; foster collaboration among national federations and safeguard their common interests. **Structure** Congress (General Assembly); Board of Director/Management Committee; Executive Committee; School of Timekeeping; Technical Commission; Permanent headquarters in Rome (Italy). **Languages** English, French. **Finance** Members' dues. **Activities** Training/education; standards/guidelines. **Publications** Textbooks; videos; CD-ROMs. **Members** Affiliated and officially recognized organizations (32) in 28 countries. Membership countries not specified. **NGO Relations** Recognized by: *International Olympic Committee (IOC, #14408)*.

[2021/XD5815/**D**]

♦ Federazione Internazionale dei Dirigenti dell' Agricoltura (inactive)
♦ Federazione Internazionale Farmacisti Cattolici (#13380)
♦ Federazione Internazionale delle Imprese di Pulizia (#09628)
♦ Federazione Internazionale di Ingegneria Ospedaliera (#13439)
♦ Federazione Internazionale dei Lavoratori Edili e del Legno (inactive)
♦ Federazione Internazionale degli Operatori di Aborto e Contraccezione (#09612)
♦ Federazione Internazionale delle Organizzazioni dei Donatori di Sangue (#13374)
♦ Federazione Internazionale Podologi e Podiatri / see International Federation of Podiatrists (#13514)
♦ Federazione Internazionale dei Preti Cattolici Sposati (inactive)

- ♦ Federazione Internazionale delle Scuole di Storia di Famiglia (no recent information)
- ♦ Federazione Internazionale dei Sindacati Metalmeccanici (inactive)
- ♦ Federazione Internazionale delle Società per la Pubblicità Ferroviaria (inactive)
- ♦ Federazione Internazionale della Stampa Gastronomica e Vinicola (inactive)
- ♦ Federazione Internazionale della Stampa Periodica / see FIPP (#09776)
- ♦ Federazione Internazionale della Stampa Tecnica (inactive)
- ♦ Federazione Internazionale di Stenografia e Dattilografia / see Fédération internationale pour le traitement de l'information et de la communication (#09667)
- ♦ Federazione Internazionale del Turismo Sociale (inactive)
- ♦ Federazione dei Medici Europei per il Pluralismo in Medicina (#06816)
- ♦ Federazione Mondiale delle Città Unite (inactive)
- ♦ Federazione Mondiale delle Comunità Terapeutiche (#21491)
- ♦ Federazione Mondiale delle Comunità di Vita Cristiana / see Christian Life Community (#03905)
- ♦ Federazione Mondiale della Gioventù Cattolica (inactive)
- ♦ Federazione Mondiale Studi sul Futuro (#21535)
- ♦ Federazione Mondiale del Termalismo e del Climatismo (#09692)
- ♦ Federazione degli Ordini Forensi di Europa (#06320)
- ♦ Federazione Organismi Cristiani Servizio Internazionale Volontario (internationally oriented national body)
- ♦ Federazione Sport Alta Quota / see International Skyrunning Federation (#14873)
- ♦ Federção Latino Americana de Simulação Clínica e Segurança do Paciente (#09368)
- ♦ **FEDER** Fonds européen de développement régional (#08342)
- ♦ **FEDERG** Federation of European Patient Groups Affected by Renal Genetic Diseases (#09526)
- ♦ FEDERLIBAS – Federazione Europea Libere Associazioni (inactive)
- ♦ FEDESA – Fédération européenne de la santé animale (inactive)
- ♦ FEDES – Fédération européenne de l'emballage souple (inactive)
- ♦ **FEDES** Fédération européenne des employeurs sociaux (#07214)
- ♦ **FEDESSA** Federation of European Self Storage Associations (#09543)
- ♦ FEDETON – European Federation of Nautical Tourism Destinations (internationally oriented national body)
- ♦ Fedevasi Kesehatan Keluarga Internasional (#13424)
- ♦ **FED** Fondo Europeo de Desarrollo (#06914)
- ♦ **FED** Fonds européen de développement (#06914)
- ♦ FED – Forum pour l'Europe démocratique (internationally oriented national body)
- ♦ FED – Foundation for Enterprise Development (internationally oriented national body)
- ♦ **FED** Fundo Europeu de Desenvolvimento (#06914)
- ♦ Fed Hitech – Fédération européenne des PME de haute technologie (no recent information)
- ♦ **FEDIAF** Fédération européenne de l'industrie des aliments pour animaux familiers (#09571)
- ♦ **FedIGS** Federation of International Geo-Engineering Societies (#09673)
- ♦ FEDIMA / see Federation of European Manufacturers of Ingredients to the Bakery, Confectionery and Patisserie Industries (#09513)
- ♦ **FEDIMA** Federation of European Manufacturers of Ingredients to the Bakery, Confectionery and Patisserie Industries (#09513)
- ♦ FEDIM – Federation of European Direct Marketing (inactive)
- ♦ FEDIOL – The EU Oil and Proteinmeal Industry / see FEDIOL – The EU Vegetable Oil and Proteinmeal Industry (#09718)

♦ FEDIOL – The EU Vegetable Oil and Proteinmeal Industry 09718

Dir Gen Av de Tervueren 168 – Bte 12, 1150 Brussels, Belgium. T. +3227715330. Fax +3227713817. E-mail: fediol@fediol.eu.
URL: http://www.fediol.eu/

History 28 Mar 1957. Former names and other names: *EC Seed Crushers' and Oil Processors' Federation* – former; *Fédération de l'industrie de l'huilerie de la CE* – former; *Federación de la Industria Aceitera de la CE* – former; *Vereinigung der Ölmühlenindustrie der EG* – former; *Federação da Indústria de los Oleos Vegetais da CE* – former; *Federazione dell'Industria Olearia della CE* – former; *Federatie van de Olie-Industrie in de EG* – former; *Brancheforeningen for Oliefabrikker i EF* – former; *Branchforeningen for Olje-och Fett-Industrin i EG* – former; *Öljynpuristamoiden ja -Puhdistamoiden Liito* – former; *FEDIOL – The EU Oil and Proteinmeal Industry* – former. Registration: Banque-Carrefour des Entreprises, No/ID: 0843.946.520, Start date: 24 Feb 2012, Belgium; EU Transparency Register, No/ID: 85076002321-31, Start date: 24 Sep 2009. **Aims** Create, maintain and develop solidarity among members; defend their activities; centralize and study together problems affecting the oil *processing industry* in *European Union* countries and formulate a common policy in its interests; represent the oil processing industries of EU countries to EU agencies and to other international bodies; if necessary, intervene with these agencies and maintain a permanent liaison with them to achieve these objectives; study all scientific, technical and industrial matters affecting the industry. **Structure** General Assembly (annual); Executive Board; Consultative Committee; Secretariat. Permanent Working Groups (7): Marketing; Technical; Renewable Resources; Nutrition; Food Safety; Contaminants; Feed Standard. Ad-hoc groups. **Staff** 9.00 FTE, paid. **Activities** Advocacy/lobbying/activism. **Events** *European Palm Oil Conference* Brussels (Belgium) 2014, *Meeting on Sustainable Palm Oil* Brussels (Belgium) 2014, *Conference* Amsterdam (Netherlands) 2012, *Meeting* Aarhus (Denmark) 1993.
Members National associations in 10 countries:
Belgium, Denmark, Finland, France, Germany, Italy, Netherlands, Poland, Spain, UK.
Associate members in 8 countries:
Austria, Czechia, Greece, Hungary, Poland, Portugal, Romania, Sweden.
IGO Relations Recognized by: *European Commission (EC, #06633)*. Participates as observer in the activities of: *Codex Alimentarius Commission (CAC, #04081)*. **NGO Relations** Member of (7): *European Bioeconomy Alliance (EUBA, #06334)*; *European Feed and Food Ingredients Safety Certification (EFISC-GTP, #07236)*; *European Feed Ingredients Platform (EFIP, #07237)*; *European Oilseed Alliance (EOA, #08080)* (Associate); *Primary Food Processors (PFP, #18496)*; *Round Table on Responsible Soy Association (RTRS, #18983)*; *Roundtable on Sustainable Palm Oil (RSPO, #18986)*. Partner of (1): *Livestock Environmental Assessment and Performance Partnership (LEAP, #16500)*. [2022/XE0961/t/**E**]

- ♦ FEDIP – Fédération européenne pour la disparition de la prostitution (no recent information)
- ♦ **FEDIYMA** European Federation of DIY Manufacturers (#07100)
- ♦ FEDMA / see Federation of European Data & Marketing (#09499)
- ♦ **FEDMA** Federation of European Data & Marketing (#09499)
- ♦ **FEDOLIVE** Fédération de l'industrie de l'huile d'olive de la CEE (#09596)
- ♦ FEDOM – Fédération européenne des associations pour la défense des victimes de la prévention des dommages médicaux (no recent information)
- ♦ FEDORA – Federation of Associations and Foundations Supporting Opera Houses and Festivals (inactive)
- ♦ **FEDRA** Federation of Regional Growth Actors in Europe (#09701)
- ♦ **FEDRE** Fondation pour l'économie et le développement durable des régions d'Europe (#09817)
- ♦ FEDSA / see European Direct Selling Association (#06928)
- ♦ FEDSS – Federation of the European Dermatological and Surgical Societies (no recent information)
- ♦ FEE / see Accountancy Europe (#00061)
- ♦ **FEECA** Fédération européenne pour l'éducation catholique des adultes (#05966)
- ♦ FEEC – Fédération européenne de l'éducation et de la culture (inactive)
- ♦ **FEECS** Fédération Européenne des Experts en CyberSécurité (#07096)
- ♦ Feedback EU (internationally oriented national body)
- ♦ Feed the Children (internationally oriented national body)
- ♦ **FEED** Foundation for European Economic Development (#09952)
- ♦ Feed – International Feed Conference (meeting series)
- ♦ **FEEDLATINA** Asociación de la Industrias de Alimentación Animal de América Latina y Caribe (#02158)
- ♦ **FEEDLATINA** Associação das Indústrias de Alimentação Animal da América Latina e Caribe (#02158)
- ♦ **FEEDM** Fédération européenne des emballeurs et distributeurs de miel (#07140)

♦ Feed the Minds 09719

Main Office The Foundry, 17-19 Oval Way, London, SE11 5RR, UK. E-mail: info@feedtheminds.org.
URL: http://www.feedtheminds.org/

History 1964. UK Registered Charity: 291333. **Aims** Improve through education, the material and *spiritual* lives of communities worldwide; support the provision of education to the global *church* and the poor and marginalized, of any faith and none. **Structure** Executive Committee; Trustees. **Languages** English. **Staff** 10.00 FTE, paid. **Finance** Members' dues. Other sources: individuals donations; grants. **Activities** Training/education. **Publications** *Connect* – newsletter. Annual Review. **Members** Individuals and several member bodies in the UK. Membership countries not specified. [2018/XF2751/y/**F**]

- ♦ Feed My Starving Children (internationally oriented national body)
- ♦ FEEDS – Forum for European Electrical Domestic Safety (unconfirmed)
- ♦ FEEE / see Foundation for Environmental Education (#09949)
- ♦ **FEE** Fédération des éditeurs européens (#09536)
- ♦ **FEEF** Fédération Européenne des Emplois de la Famille (#07118)
- ♦ FEEFHS – Foundation for East European Family History Societies (internationally oriented national body)
- ♦ **FEE** Foundation for Environmental Education (#09949)
- ♦ **FEEG** Federación Europea para la Enseñanza de la Gemologia (#09502)
- ♦ **FEEM** Federation of European Explosives Manufacturers (#09505)
- ♦ FEEM – Fondazione Eni Enrico Mattei (internationally oriented national body)
- ♦ FEEP – Foundation for European Environmental Policy (see: #11261)
- ♦ FEER – Fédération européenne des énergies renouvelables (inactive)
- ♦ **FEES** Federation of European Ergonomics Societies (#09504)
- ♦ **FEET** Fellowship of European Evangelical Theologians (#09727)
- ♦ **FE** European Federation of Catholic Married Priests (#07069)
- ♦ **FEEVA** Federation of European Equine Veterinary Associations (#09503)
- ♦ **FEFAC** Fédération européenne des fabricants d'aliments composés pour animaux (#09566)
- ♦ FEFAF / see Fédération européenne des femmes actives en famille (#09568)
- ♦ **FEFAF** Fédération européenne des femmes actives en famille (#09568)
- ♦ FEFA – Fondation pour l'Education des Femmes Africaines (internationally oriented national body)
- ♦ **FEFA** Forum européen des droits de l'homme et de la famille (#07315)

♦ FEFANA – EU Association of Specialty Feed Ingredients and their Mixtures 09720

Association Européenne des Ingrédient Spécifiques pour la nutrition animale et leur mélanges – Europäischer Verband für Wirkstoffe und Vormischung in der Tiernährung
SG Ave des Arts 56, 1000 Brussels, Belgium. E-mail: info@fefana.org.
URL: http://www.fefana.org/

History 22 Jan 1963. Dissolved, 30 Jan 2001. Re-established 13 Oct 2004. Current statutes adopted June 2010. Former names and other names: *European Federation for Additives in Animal Nutrition* – former; *European Federation of Manufacturers of Feed Additives* – former; *European Federation of Animal Feed Additive Manufacturers* – former; *Fédération européenne des fabricants d'adjuvants pour la nutrition animale (FEFANA)* – former; *Europäischer Verband für Wirkstoffe in der Tierernährung* – former; *FEFANA – European Feed Additive and Premixtures Association* – former. Registration: Banque-Carrefour des Entreprises, No/ID: 0870.060.405, Start date: 18 Nov 2004, Belgium; EU Transparency Register, No/ID: 20132976103-18, Start date: 28 Jun 2011. **Aims** Represent the interests of the specialty ingredients industry with products that enter the food chain via feed, whether produced in Europe or imported from third countries. **Structure** General Assembly (annual); Board; Strategic Groups (4). **Languages** Bulgarian, English, French, German, Italian, Spanish, Turkish. **Staff** 7.00 FTE, paid. **Finance** Sources: members' dues. **Activities** Knowledge management/information dissemination; politics/policy/regulatory. **Events** *High-Level Conference* Brussels (Belgium) 2016, *Meeting* Brussels (Belgium) 2016, *General Assembly* Brussels (Belgium) 1990.
Members Feed manufacturers, premixers and exporters in 16 countries:
Austria, Belgium, Denmark, Finland, France, Germany, Iceland, Ireland, Italy, Netherlands, Norway, Poland, Spain, Sweden, Switzerland, UK.
NGO Relations Member of (5): *Agri-Food Chain Coalition (AFCC, #00577)*; *European Food Sustainable Consumption and Production Round Table (European Food SCP Roundtable, #07289)*; *Federation of European and International Associations Established in Belgium (FAIB, #09508)*; *Industry4Europe (#11181)*; *International Feed Industry Federation (IFIF, #13581)*. In liaison with technical committees of: *Comité européen de normalisation (CEN, #04162)*. Associate member of: *European Network of Agricultural Journalists (ENAJ, #07864)*. Fellow organizations: *EU Specialty Food Ingredients (#09200)*; *European Association of Bioindustries (EuropaBio, #05956)*; *FAMI-QS (#09256)*; *Fédération européenne des fabricants d'aliments composés pour animaux (FEFAC, #09566)*; *Fédération européenne de l'industrie des aliments pour animaux familiers (FEDIAF, #09571)*; *General Confederation of Agricultural Cooperatives in the European Union (#10107)*. [2023/XD0736/**D**]

- ♦ FEFANA – European Feed Additive and Premixtures Association / see FEFANA – EU Association of Specialty Feed Ingredients and their Mixtures (#09720)
- ♦ FEFANA / see FEFANA – EU Association of Specialty Feed Ingredients and their Mixtures (#09720)
- ♦ **FEFAS** Federación Farmacéutica Sudamericana (#09302)
- ♦ **FEFB** Fédération européenne des fabricants de briquets (#07153)
- ♦ **FEFCO** Fédération Européenne des Fabricants de Carton Ondulé (#07091)
- ♦ **FEFD** Fédération européenne pour la formation et le développement (#08933)
- ♦ **FE** Fertility Europe (#09737)
- ♦ FEF – Fédération européenne du franchising (inactive)
- ♦ FEFG / see Far East Oceanic Fracture Society (#09271)
- ♦ **FEFPEB** Fédération européenne des fabricants de palettes et emballages en bois (#09567)
- ♦ FEFSI / see European Fund and Asset Management Association (#07365)
- ♦ FEGAP – Fédération européenne de la ganterie de peau (no recent information)
- ♦ **FEGAT** Fédération européenne des gentlemen amateurs et cavalières du trot (#05896)
- ♦ FEGC / see SEND International
- ♦ FEGC / see European Heart and Lung Transplant Federation (#07466)
- ♦ **FEGCP** Fédération européenne des greffés du coeur et des poumons (#07466)
- ♦ **FEG** Federación Europea de Geólogos (#07133)
- ♦ **FEG** Fédération européenne des associations de guides touristiques (#07228)
- ♦ **FEG** Fédération européenne des géologues (#07133)
- ♦ FEG / see Fédération internationale de gymnastique (#09636)
- ♦ FEG – Föderation Europäischer Gewässerschutz (inactive)
- ♦ **FEGGA** Federation of European Golf Greenkeepers Associations (#09506)

♦ FEGIME 09721

Managing Dir Gutenstttter Str 8e, 90449 Nürburg, Germany. T. +499116418990. Fax +499116418993. E-mail: info@fegime.com.
URL: http://www.fegime.com/

History Originated from an agreement between Spanish and French electrical wholesalers, signed 1989. When more groups joined FEGIME was founded 1993. Original full title: *Fédération Européenne des Grossistes Indépendants en Matériel Electrique (FEGIME) – European Federation of Independent Electrical Wholesalers*. Registered in accordance with German law. **Structure** Supervisory Board; Managing Director. **Publications** *FEGIME Voice* – newsletter.
Members Full in 20 countries:
Argentina, Cyprus, Denmark, Finland, France, Germany, Greece, Hungary, Ireland, Israel, Italy, Netherlands, Norway, Poland, Portugal, Romania, Russia, Spain, UK, Ukraine. [2019/XM8499/**D**]

- ♦ FEGOME – Fédération européenne des groupements d'outre-mer et d'expulsés de l'Est (inactive)
- ♦ FEGRO – European Federation for the Wholesale Watch Trade (inactive)

- ♦ FEGS – Federation of European Genetical Societies (no recent information)
- ♦ FEHE – Federation for European Homeopathic Education (inactive)
- ♦ **FEH** Fédération européenne de hockey (#07494)
- ♦ FEHH / see Historic Hotels of Europe (#10930)
- ♦ **FEHPA** Fédération européenne de l'hôtellerie de plein air (#07066)
- ♦ FEHRL / see Forum of European National Highway Research Laboratories (#09910)
- ♦ **FEHRL** Forum of European National Highway Research Laboratories (#09910)
- ♦ **FEIA** Fédération des organisations d'ingénieurs en Afrique (#09402)
- ♦ FEIA – Forum économique international des Amériques (internationally oriented national body)
- ♦ **FEIAP** Federation of Engineering Institutions of Asia and the Pacific (#09480)
- ♦ **FEIASOFI** Federación Iberoamericana de Sociedades de Fisica (#09321)
- ♦ **FeIbEM** Federação Iberoamericana de Engenharia Mecânica (#09313)
- ♦ **FeIbIM** Federación Iberoamericana de Ingenieria Mecanica (#09313)
- ♦ **FEIBP** Fédération européenne de l'industrie de la brosserie et pinceauterie (#06406)
- ♦ **FEICA** Association of the European Adhesive and Sealant Industry (#09572)
- ♦ **FEICA** Fédération européenne des industries de colles et adhésifs (#09572)
- ♦ FEIC – Fédération européenne de l'industrie du contreplaqué (inactive)
- ♦ FEICRO – Federation of European Industrial Cooperative Research Organizations (inactive)
- ♦ Feidearalacha Na Ehropa (#21984)
- ♦ FEIEA / see European Association for Internal Communication (#06091)
- ♦ **FEIEA** European Association for Internal Communication (#06091)
- ♦ **FEI** Face Equality International (#09232)
- ♦ FEIFA – Federation of European Independent Financial Advisers (internationally oriented national body)
- ♦ FEI – Federación Endodóntica Ibero-Americana (inactive)
- ♦ **FEI** Fédération Équestre Internationale (#09484)
- ♦ FEI – Financial Executives International (internationally oriented national body)
- ♦ FEIF / see International Federation of Icelandic Horse Associations (#13454)
- ♦ **FEIF** International Federation of Icelandic Horse Associations (#13454)
- ♦ **FEI** Fonds européen d'investissement (#07601)
- ♦ FEI – France Expertise Internationale (internationally oriented national body)
- ♦ **FEIIC** Federation of Engineering Institutions of Islamic Countries (#09481)
- ♦ FEILN / see European Federation of National Institutions for Language (#07172)
- ♦ FEIM – Fédération européenne des importateurs de machines et d'équipements de bureau (inactive)
- ♦ FEIN – Fondazione Europea Il Nibbio (internationally oriented national body)
- ♦ Feinstein International Center (internationally oriented national body)
- ♦ Feinstein International Famine Center / see Feinstein International Center
- ♦ **FEISCA** Federation of Engineering Institutions of South and Central Asia (#09482)
- ♦ FEISEAP / see Federation of Engineering Institutions of Asia and the Pacific (#09480)
- ♦ FEITIS – Fédération européenne des industries techniques de l'image et du son (inactive)
- ♦ **FEJA** Fédération européenne des juges administratifs (#02497)
- ♦ FEJC / see European Choral Association – Europa Cantat (#06541)
- ♦ FEJ – Fédération européenne des industries du jouet – jeux, jouets, puériculture (inactive)
- ♦ **FEJ** Fédération européenne des journalistes (#07152)
- ♦ **FEJ** Fonds européen pour la jeunesse (#09141)
- ♦ FEJLR – Fédération européenne des jeunesses libérales et radicales (inactive)
- ♦ **FEJS** Forum for European Journalism Students (#09908)
- ♦ FEJS International / see Forum for European Journalism Students (#09908)
- ♦ FELAA – Foro Latinoamericano de Estudiantes de Antropologia y Arqueologia (meeting series)
- ♦ **FELABAN** Federación Latinoamericana de Bancos (#16254)
- ♦ **FELAB** Latin American and Caribbean Bonsai Federation (#16266)
- ♦ FELACEX – Federación Latinoamericana y del Caribe de Asociaciones de Exportadores (inactive)
- ♦ FELAC – Federación Latinoamericana de Autismo (inactive)
- ♦ **FELAC** Federación Latinoamericana de Cirurgia (#09349)
- ♦ FELAC / see Federación Panamericana de Consultores (#09379)
- ♦ FELACUTI – Federación Latinoamericana de Consejos de Usuarios del Transporte Internacional (no recent information)
- ♦ FELAEB – Federación Latinoamericana de Asociaciones de Empresas Biotecnológia (unconfirmed)
- ♦ **FELAEN** Federação Latino Americana de Endocrinologia (#09286)
- ♦ **FELAFACS** Federación Latinoamericana de Facultades de Comunicación Social (#09353)
- ♦ **FELA** Federation of European Literacy Associations (#09510)
- ♦ Félag Norraenna Fagurfraedinga (#17411)
- ♦ FELAH / see Latin American Federation of Hospitals (#16322)
- ♦ **FELAIBE** Federación Latinoamericana y del Caribe de Instituciones de Bioética (#09348)
- ♦ FELAINCO – Federación Latinoamericana de las Industrias de la Confección (inactive)
- ♦ **FELALEASE** Federación Latinoamericana de Leasing (#09356)
- ♦ FELAM – Federación Latinoamericana de Marketing (no recent information)
- ♦ **FELANPE** Federación Latinoamericana de Terapia Nutricional, Nutrición Clinica y Metabolismo (#16326)
- ♦ FELANPE / see Latin American Federation of Nutritional Therapy, Clinical Nutrition and Metabolism (#16326)
- ♦ **FELAP** Federación Latinoamericana de Periodistas (#09359)
- ♦ **FELAQ** Federación Latinoamericana de Quemaduras (#09365)
- ♦ FELAQUE / see Federación Latinoamericana de Quemaduras (#09365)
- ♦ **FELASA** Federation of European Laboratory Animal Science Associations (#09509)
- ♦ FELASCC – Federación Latinoamericana de Sociedades de Ciencias Cosméticas (unconfirmed)
- ♦ **FELAS** Federación Latinoamericana de Asociaciones de Semillas (#16330)
- ♦ **FELASOFI** Federación Latinoamericana de Sociedades de Fisica (#09370)
- ♦ FELASSA – Federación Latinoamericana de Servicios de Salud Adolescente (no recent information)
- ♦ **FELATRABS** Federación Latinoamericana de Trabajadores Bancarios, de Seguros y Servicios Afines (#09373)
- ♦ **FELATRACCS** Federación Latinoamericana de Trabajadores de la Cultura y de la Comunicación Social (#09374)
- ♦ FELATRACS / see Federación Latinoamericana de Trabajadores de la Cultura y de la Comunicación Social (#09374)
- ♦ FELATRAP / see Federación Latinoamericana de Trabajadores de la Cultura y de la Comunicación Social (#09374)
- ♦ FELATURS – Federación Latinoamericana de Turismo Social (inactive)
- ♦ **FELCINE** Federación Latino-Americana de Exhibidores y Distribuidores de Cine Independiente (#16321)
- ♦ **FEL** Foundation for Endangered Languages (#09947)
- ♦ FELH / see Latin American Federation of Hospitals (#16322)
- ♦ FELICA – Federación de Partidos Liberales y Centristas de Centro América y del Caribe (inactive)
- ♦ Felician Sisters – Congregation of Sisters of St Felix of Cantalice (religious order)
- ♦ Feline Advisory Bureau / see International Cat Care
- ♦ Fellesrådet for Afrika (internationally oriented national body)
- ♦ Fellowship for African Relief (internationally oriented national body)

♦ Fellowship of Asian Methodist Bishops 09722

Contact c/o The Bishop's Office, Methodist Church in Singapore, 70 Barker Road, Methodist Centre, Singapore 309936, Singapore. T. +6564784784. Fax +6564784794.

History 1988, Manila (Philippines). **Aims** Provide a platform for consultation on matters of common interest to all Methodist churches in Asia. **Languages** English, Korean. **Staff** None. **Finance** No budget. **Events** *Meeting* Hong Kong (Hong Kong) 2011, *Meeting* Hong Kong (Hong Kong) 2011, *Meeting* Taipei (Taiwan) 2010, *Meeting* Delhi (India) 2009, *Meeting* Singapore (Singapore) 2008.

Members Full in 11 countries and territories:
Bangladesh, Hong Kong, India, Indonesia, Korea Rep, Malaysia, Myanmar, Philippines, Singapore, Sri Lanka, Taiwan.
NGO Relations Involved in setting up: *Asian Methodist Council (AMC, #01539).* [2011.07.06/XF3113/v/**F**]

♦ Fellowship of Christian Councils and Churches in the Great Lakes and Horn of Africa (FECCLAHA) 09723

General Secretariat PO Box 10033, Nairobi, 00100, Kenya. T. +254202730270 – +254202728289. Fax +254202721626. E-mail: info@fecclaha.org.
Street address 1st Floor – Old Administration Bldg, Nairobi Baptist Church, Off Ngong Road, Nairobi, Kenya.
URL: http://www.fecclaha.org/

History 3 Mar 1999, Nairobi (Kenya). **Aims** Promote peace and justice in the region. **Structure** General Assembly; Executive Committee; Secretariat. **Languages** English, French. **Publications** *FECCLAHA Newsletter.*
Members National councils in 10 countries:
Burundi, Congo DR, Eritrea, Ethiopia, Kenya, Rwanda, South Sudan, Sudan, Tanzania UR, Uganda.
IGO Relations Memorandum of Understanding with: *Regional Centre on Small Arms and Light Weapons in the Great Lakes Region, the Horn of Africa and Bordering States (RECSA, #18760).* **NGO Relations** Member of: *ACT Alliance (#00081); International Action Network on Small Arms (IANSA, #11585); Side by Side (#19265).* [2018.06.29/XD8392/**D**]

♦ Fellowship of Christian Councils and Churches in West Africa (FECCIWA) 09724

Association des conseils chrétiens et eglises en afrique de l'ouest (ACCEAO)
Main Office c/o AACC, 1235 Rue de la Paix, BP 2268, Lomé, Togo. E-mail: secretarygeneral@fecciwa.org.
URL: http://fecciwa.org/

History Feb 1994, as *Fellowship Meeting of Christian Councils in West Africa (FECCIWA).* Previously referred to as *Fellowship of Councils of Churches in West Africa.* **Aims** Promote fellowship and effective witness to the faith in the Lord and Saviour Jesus Christ among Christian Councils and Churches in the West African region; encourage the setting up of Christian Councils in countries where they do not exist; promote the Councils and Churches' involvement in holistic development in the sub-region. **Structure** General Assembly; Executive Committee; Secretariat. **Languages** English, French. **Staff** 3.50 FTE, paid; 0.50 FTE, voluntary. **Finance** Members' dues. Other sources: grants; donations. Annual budget: US$ 100,000. **Activities** Organizes meetings, workshops and seminars. Sets up projects. **Events** *General Assembly* Freetown (Sierra Leone) 2003, *Capacity building workshop* Abidjan (Côte d'Ivoire) 2002, *General Assembly* Bingerville (Côte d'Ivoire) 1999, *General Assembly* Banjul (Gambia) 1997, *General Assembly* Accra (Ghana) 1995.
Members Christian Councils and Churches in 13 countries:
Benin, Burkina Faso, Chad, Côte d'Ivoire, Gambia, Ghana, Guinea, Liberia, Niger, Nigeria, Senegal, Sierra Leone, Togo.
NGO Relations Member of: *Civil Society Platform for Peacebuilding and Statebuilding (CSPPS, #03970); Ecumenical Advocacy Alliance (EAA, inactive).* [2019/XF4887/**F**]

- ♦ Fellowship of Christian Councils in Southern Africa (unconfirmed)

♦ Fellowship of Confessing Anglicans (FCA) 09725

Secretariat Unit 42/43, Kingspark Business Centre, 152-178 Kingston Road, New Malden, KT3 3ST, UK. E-mail: operations@gafcon.org.
Registered Address 5 Fleet Place, London, EC4M 7RD, UK.
URL: http://fca.net/

History 29 Jun 2008, Jerusalem, by about 1,100 conservative orthodox Anglicans – many from developing countries – meeting at *Global Anglican Future Conference (Gafcon),* when "Jerusalem Declaration" was produced. Also referred to previously by initials *FOCA.* Registration: Charity Commision, No/ID: 1144227, England and Wales; Companies House, No/ID: 07759253, England and Wales. **Aims** As a group of *traditionalist* Anglicans: create a global network to combat modern trends and "false" *Gospels* in the *Church* such as ordination of gay clergy; rescue people from the forces of militant *secularism* and *pluralism* created by spiritual decline; emphasize an orthodox interpretation of the Bible. **Structure** Primates Council (meeting twice a year). **Events** *Global Anglican Future Conference* Jerusalem (Israel) 2018, *Global Anglican Future Conference* Nairobi (Kenya) 2013, *Global Anglican Future Conference* Jerusalem (Israel) 2008. **NGO Relations** *Anglican Communion (#00827).* [2020/XM7212/**E**]

- ♦ Fellowship of Councils of Churches in West Africa / see Fellowship of Christian Councils and Churches in West Africa (#09724)

♦ Fellowship of European Broadcasters (FEB) 09726

Address not obtained.
Twitter: https://twitter.com/febonline

History 1991. **Aims** Connect, serve and represent Christian organizations and individuals involved in communication throughout Europe; encourage cooperation and coordination between Christians in the European broadcasting and other communications media, both nationally and internationally. **Structure** Board of Management. **Languages** English. **Finance** Sources: members' dues. **Activities** Events/meetings; knowledge management/information dissemination; networking/liaising. **Events** *Conference* Dublin (Ireland) 2018, *Annual Conference* Soesterberg (Netherlands) 2016, *Using media to bring hope* Stansted (UK) 2015, *Conference* Stansted (UK) 2013, *The Christian voice in our society* Dresden (Germany) 2012. **Publications** *Email Snippets; FEB Update.*
Members Corporate members include the following organization listed in this Yearbook:
Trans World Radio (TWR). [2021.05.21/XF6820/y/**F**]

♦ Fellowship of European Evangelical Theologians (FEET) 09727

Association européenne de théologiens évangéliques (AETE) – Gemeinschaft Europäischer Evangelikaler Theologen (GEET)
Sec Fichtenweg 33, 57078 Siegen, Germany. T. +4927177007300.
Treas Karl-Broll-Strasse 7, 35619 Braunfels, Germany. T. +4964425218. Fax +4964195262712. E-mail: kasse@afet.de.
Chair 33 Avenue Jules Ferry, 13100 Aix-en-Provence, France. T. +33442271292.
URL: https://feet-europe.org/

History Sep 1977, Heverlee (Belgium). **Aims** Advance the *Christian* religion in Europe through promotion and encouragement of the study of Evangelical Christian Theology in a spirit of loyalty to the Bible with a view to serving the renewal of theological thinking, strengthening the work of the churches and promoting the task of theological research and education. **Structure** Executive Committee; Chairperson. **Languages** English, French, German. **Staff** 11.00 FTE, voluntary. **Finance** Members' dues. Other sources: donations; proceeds from conferences. **Activities** Research/documentation; knowledge management/information dissemination; events/meetings. **Events** *Conference* Prague (Czechia) 2022, *Conference* Prague (Czechia) 2020, *Christian identity and mission in a divided Europe* Prague (Czechia) 2018, *The reformation – its theology and its legacy* Lutherstadt Wittenberg (Germany) 2016, *Conference* Paris (France) 2014. **Publications** *European Journal of Theology.*
Members Full in 26 countries:
Austria, Belgium, Bulgaria, Croatia, Czechia, Denmark, Estonia, Finland, France, Germany, Greece, Hungary, Italy, Montenegro, Netherlands, Norway, Poland, Portugal, Romania, Serbia, Slovakia, Spain, Sweden, Switzerland, UK, Ukraine.
NGO Relations *European Council for Theological Education (ECTE, #06846); European Evangelical Alliance (EEA, #07010).* [2022/XD7220/**D**]

- ♦ Fellowship of European Oncology Nursing Societies / see European Oncology Nursing Society (#08086)
- ♦ Fellowship of Francophone Organizations and Churches on the Five Continents (#04387)
- ♦ Fellowship of Independent Christian Missionary Communities / see The Family International (#09253)
- ♦ Fellowship of Intentional Communities / see Foundation for Intentional Community
- ♦ Fellowship for Intentional Community / see Foundation for Intentional Community
- ♦ Fellowship International Mission (internationally oriented national body)

♦ Fellowship of the Least Coin (FLC) 09728

Communauté du moindre sou – Gemeinschaft der Kleinsten Münze

Exec Sec c/o CPBC HQ, Fajardo St, Jaro, 5000 Iloilo ILI, Philippines. T. +639182075477. E-mail: icflcph@gmail.com.

Hon Treas address not obtained.

URL: https://www.fellowshipoftheleastcoin.org/

History 1956. Founded by Mrs Shanti Solomon of India. Officially launched 1958 at the first Assembly of the Asian Church Women's Conference (ACWC) held in Hong Kong. International Committee for the FLC (ICFLC) was formed in 1979. Former names and other names: *International Committee for the Fellowship of the Least Coin (ICFLC)* – alias. **Aims** As an *ecumenical* movement: bring *Christian women* together in a fellowship of prayer, demonstrating solidarity with one another through common concern and love for humankind; reflect on issues of peace, reconciliation, justice and the empowerment of women. **Structure** International Committee comprises: President, a representative of *Asian Church Women's Conference (ACWC, #01377)*; one representative each from international ecumenical women's organizations, such as *International Committee for World Day of Prayer (#12811)* and WCC Program on Just Community of Women and Men; one woman representative from each region invited from the ecumenical women organizations or regional ecumenical organizations. **Languages** English. **Staff** 1.00 FTE, paid; 1.00 FTE, voluntary. **Finance** Through FLC Offerings. **Activities** Events/meetings; religious activities. **Events** *Meeting* Bahamas 2012, *Meeting* Dhour El Choueir (Lebanon) 2011, *Annual Meeting* Toronto, ON (Canada) 2008, *Annual Meeting* Tonga 2007, *Meeting* Malaysia 2006. **Publications** *Circle of Prayer* (every 2 years). *Shanti Means Peace. FLC In-Gathering Liturgy* (every year); *FLC Messages and Reports* (every year). Devotional and promotional material; messages; reports; brochure. **Members** Membership countries not specified. [2023.02.14/XE1793/**E**]

♦ Fellowship Meeting of Christian Councils in West Africa / see Fellowship of Christian Councils and Churches in West Africa (#09724)

♦ Fellowship of the Middle Eastern Evangelical Churches (FMEEC) .. 09729

Gen Sec PO Box 213, Ain Aar, Lebanon.

Events *International Conference* Cairo (Egypt) 2014, *International Conference* Beirut (Lebanon) 2012.

Members Full in 11 countries and territories:

Algeria, Cyprus, Egypt, Iran Islamic Rep, Jordan, Kuwait, Lebanon, Palestine, Sudan, Syrian AR, Tunisia.

[2011.06.01/XF4623/**F**]

♦ Fellowship of World Religions (inactive)
♦ FELM – Finnish Evangelical Lutheran Mission (internationally oriented national body)
♦ FELPA / see Society of European Affairs Professionals (#19553)
♦ FELS – Federación Latinoamericana de Semiótica (no recent information)
♦ FELSOCEM – Federación Latinoamericana de Sociedades Científicas de Estudiantes de Medicina (no recent information)
♦ FELTACA – Federación Latinoamericana de Trabajadores Campesinos y de la Alimentación (inactive)
♦ FELTRA – Federación Latinoamericana de Trabajadores Agrícolas, Pecuarios y Afines (no recent information)
♦ FEMAC – Federación Mesoamericana de Asociaciones Conservacionistas No-Gubernamentales (inactive)
♦ **FEMA** Federation of European Motorcyclists' Associations (#09518)
♦ Female Europeans of Medium and Small Enterprises (inactive)
♦ **FEMAS** Federation of European Maritime Associations of Surveyors and Consultants (#09514)
♦ FEMBA – Federación Mundial de Béisbol Amateur (inactive)
♦ **FEMB** Fédération européenne du mobilier de bureau (#08109)
♦ FEMCA – Far East Model Car Association (unconfirmed)
♦ FEMCA – Federación de Estudiantes de Medicina Centroamericanos (inactive)
♦ FemCities (unconfirmed)
♦ FEMCOM / see COMESA Federation of National Associations of Women in Business (#04126)
♦ Femconsult – Consultants on Gender and Development (internationally oriented national body)
♦ **FEMED** Fédération Euro-Méditerranéenne contre les Disparitions Forcées (#09487)
♦ FEM – Federation of European Motorcyclists (inactive)
♦ **FEM** Fédération Européenne de la Manutention (#07752)
♦ FEM – Fédération européenne des métallurgistes (inactive)
♦ FEM – Fédération européenne des motels (inactive)
♦ FEM – Female Europeans of Medium and Small Enterprises (inactive)
♦ FEM – Fennoscandian Exploration and Mining Conference (meeting series)
♦ **FEMFM** Federation of European Manufacturers of Friction Materials (#09512)
♦ **FEM** Fonds pour l'environnement mondial (#10346)
♦ FEMGED – Fédération européenne des moyennes et grandes entreprises de distribution (inactive)
♦ **FEMGO** Fédération Maghrébine de Gynécologie Obstétrique (#09686)
♦ FEMIBE – Fédération mondiale des dirigeants des instituts de beauté et de l'esthétique (no recent information)
♦ FEMIB – Fédération européenne des syndicats de fabricants de menuiseries du bâtiment (inactive)
♦ **FEMICA** Federación de Municipios del Istmo Centroamericano (#09378)
♦ **FEMIDE** Federación Mundial de Instituciones Financieras de Desarrollo (#21428)
♦ Femina Europa (internationally oriented national body)
♦ Féminin Pluriel (internationally oriented national body)
♦ Féminin pluriel international / see Féminin Pluriel

♦ Feminist Articulation Marcosur (FAM) 09730

Articulación Feminista Marcosur (AFM)

Exec Sec Cotidiano Mujer, San José 1436, CP 11200, Montevideo, Uruguay. T. +59829018782 – +59829020393. Fax +59829018782 – +59829020393. E-mail: cotidian@cotidianomujer.org.uy.

URL: http://www.mujeresdelsur-afm.org.uy/

History Founded Sep 2000, Montevideo (Uruguay). **Aims** Influence political discussion and systems that extend *citizenship* and deepen *democracy*; strengthen areas of joint communication among social movements; in particular reinforce these spheres with a feminist presence; serve as a thinktank for regional organizations based on national organizational processes, so as to harness the political incidence of women in the integration process and in defence of economic, social and cultural *rights*. **Structure** Coordination of 7 representatives. **Languages** English, Portuguese, Spanish. **Finance** Funds from: *Oxfam International (#17922)*. **Activities** Launched the campaign "Against fundamentalisms, people are fundamental". Work is reflected with *World Social Forum (WSF, #21797)* events. Organizes "Feminist Dialogues (FD)". Organizes seminars. **Publications** Books.

Members Organizations in 6 countries:

Argentina, Bolivia, Brazil, Paraguay, Peru, Uruguay.

Included in the above, 2 organizations listed in this Yearbook:

International Gender and Trade Network (IGTN, #13707); Red de Educación Popular entre Mujeres de América Latina y el Caribe (REPEM LAC, #18647).

NGO Relations *African Women's Development and Communication Network (FEMNET, #00503); Development Alternatives with Women for a New Era (DAWN, #05054); IO – Facilitating Space for Feminist Conversations (Io, #16005); Latin American and Caribbean Committee for the Defense of Women's Rights (#16268); Latin American and Caribbean Women's Health Network (LACWHN, #16288); Latin American and Caribbean Youth Network for Sexual and Reproductive Health and Rights (REDLAC, #16289).* [2013.07.30/XJ3409/y/**F**]

♦ Feminist International Radio Endeavour (internationally oriented national body)
♦ Feminist Network Against Domestic and Sexual Violence / see Latin American and Caribbean Feminist Network Against Domestic and Sexual Violence (#16277)
♦ **FEMIPI** Fédération européenne des mandataires de l'industrie en propriété industrielle (#07042)

♦ Femise Network 09731

Réseau femise

Gen Manager CMCI, 2 rue Henri Barbusse, 13241 Marseille CEDEX 01, France. T. +33491315195. Fax +33491315038. E-mail: contact@femise.org.

URL: http://www.femise.org/

History 1997. Full title: *Forum euroméditerranéen des instituts de sciences économiques*. Registered under French law. **Aims** Provide a platform that reinforces dialogue between stakeholders; conduct and communicate policy research on priority *EuroMed* issues. **Structure** Executive Committee; Board of Trustees; Specialized Committees (3). **Languages** Arabic, English, French. **Staff** 5.00 FTE, paid. **Finance** Supported by: *European Commission (EC, #06633)*. **Activities** Research/documentation; events/meetings; knowledge management/information dissemination; publishing activities. **Events** *Neighbours of neighbours – relations and cooperation of the EU-MED towards Africa* Valletta (Malta) 2018, *Conference* Casablanca (Morocco) 2017, *Two Decades after Barcelona : Rethinking the EU-Med Partnership* Athens (Greece) 2016, *Conference* Marrakech (Morocco) 2012, *The Arab awakening and the role of the EU-Med partnership* Marseille (France) 2011. **Publications** *Inside FEMISE* (3 a year) – newsletter. Annual Report; policy briefs; research reports; thematic reports; papers; articles; country profiles; edited volumes; conference papers.

Members Institutions (100) in 26 countries and territories:

Algeria, Austria, Belgium, Cyprus, Denmark, Egypt, Finland, France, Germany, Greece, Ireland, Israel, Italy, Jordan, Lebanon, Luxembourg, Malta, Morocco, Netherlands, Palestine, Portugal, Spain, Sweden, Tunisia, Türkiye, UK.

Included in the above, 16 organizations listed in this Yearbook:

Arab Centre for the Studies of Arid Zones and Dry Lands (ACSAD, #00918); Centre for Development Studies, Bath (CDS); Centre for Economic Research on Mediterranean Countries (CREM); Centre for Mediterranean and International Studies, Tunis (no recent information); Centre for Mediterranean Studies, Ankara (no recent information); European Network on Innovation and Co-Development (no recent information); European University Institute (EUI, #09034); French Leading Center for International Economic Studies, Paris (CEPII); Institut de recherche sur le Maghreb contemporain, Tunis (IRMC); Institute for European Studies, Malta; Institute for International Economic Studies (IIES); International Institute of Social Studies, The Hague (ISS); Istituto di Studi e Programmi per il Mediterraneo (ISPROM, no recent information); Kiel Institute for the World Economy (IfW); School of Oriental and African Studies (SOAS); Sussex European Institute (SEI).

NGO Relations Coordinated by: *Economic Research Forum (ERF, #05318); Université de la Méditerranée, Marseille.* [2018.06.01/XF5928/y/**F**]

♦ **FEMLAB** Fédération euro-méditerranéenne des laboratoires d'analyses de biologie médicale (#09488)
♦ femLINKpacific (internationally oriented national body)

♦ Femmes Africa solidarité (FAS) 09732

Exec Dir Rue du Vieux-Billard 8, PO Box 5037, 1211 Geneva 11, Switzerland. T. +41223288050. Fax +41223288052. E-mail: info@fasngo.org.

URL: http://www.fasngo.org/

History Jun 1996. Registration: Civil Code, Switzerland. **Aims** Foster, strengthen and promote the leading role of women in prevention, management and resolution of conflict on the African continent. **Structure** General Assembly (every 2 years); Executive Board; consisting Advisory Board; Secretariat in Geneva (Switzerland); Regional Office in Dakar (Senegal). **Languages** English, French. **Finance** Contributions from: governments of Netherlands, Switzerland and Finland; *Catholic Organization for Relief and Development (Cordaid); Ford Foundation (#09858); Joint United Nations Programme on HIV/AIDS (UNAIDS, #16149); OAU Peace Fund (inactive); Organisation internationale de la Francophonie (OIF, #17809); UNDP (#20292); UNHCR (#20327); Westminster Foundation for Democracy (WFD)*. **Activities** Advocacy/lobbying/activism; conflict resolution; capacity building. **Events** *International NGO forum on economic, social and cultural rights of women* Geneva (Switzerland) 2009, *Meeting on engendering the peace process in West Africa* Abuja (Nigeria) 2000, *Workshop on linking HIV/AIDS to women's peace advocacy* Addis Ababa (Ethiopia) 2000. **Publications** *FAS Advocacy News* (2 a year). *Les Meilleures pratiques des femmes en Afrique* – series; *Women's Best Practices in Africa* – series. *Implication des Femmes dans le conflit en région naturelle de la Casamance*. Brochures; reports.

Members Individuals; organizations. Members in 20 countries:

Algeria, Burundi, Cameroon, Central African Rep, Congo DR, Côte d'Ivoire, Ghana, Liberia, Mali, Mauritius, Mozambique, Nigeria, Rwanda, Senegal, Sierra Leone, Somalia, South Africa, Togo, Tunisia, Zambia.

Consultative Status Consultative status granted from: *African Commission on Human and Peoples' Rights (ACHPR, #00255)* (Observer); *ECOSOC (#05331)* (General); *UNESCO (#20322)* (Consultative Status). **IGO Relations** Observer to: *International Organization for Migration (IOM, #14454)*. Associated with Department of Global Communications of the United Nations. **NGO Relations** Member of: *Conference of Non-Governmental Organizations in Consultative Relationship with the United Nations (CONGO, #04635); Sudan Consortium (#20031); NGO Committee on the Status of Women, Geneva (#17117).* [2020/XF5923/**F**]

♦ Femmes chefs d'entreprises mondiales (FCEM) 09733

World Association of Women Entrepreneurs – Welt-Vereinigung von Unternehmerinnen

Pres Forum Francophone des Affaires, 3 Place de la Coupole, BP 98, 94223 Charenton CEDEX, France. T. +33609932818. E-mail: worldpresident@fcem.org.

URL: https://www.fcem.org/

History Founded 1945, France. Fully international since 1956. Statutes adopted 5 Jun 1965, Paris. Former names and other names: *European Association of Women Executives* – former (1952); *Association européenne des femmes chefs d'entreprise* – former (1952); *World Association of Women Business Owners* – former; *Association mondiale des femmes chefs d'entreprises* – former; *Asociación Mundial del Ejecutivas de Empresa* – former; *Asociación Mundial de Mujeres Empresarias* – former; *WAWE* – former. Registration: France. **Aims** Promote women's entrepreneurial initiative and reinforce national associations of women business owners. **Structure** World Congress (annual); Regional General Assemblies; Board (meets twice a year); FCEM Commissioners of Europe, Africa, Pacific Rim, Far East, and Americas; World Committee of national representatives (annual); Task Forces (9). **Languages** English, French, Spanish. **Staff** 9.00 FTE, paid. **Finance** Sources: members' dues. **Activities** Awards/prizes/competitions; events/meetings; guidance/assistance/consulting; networking/liaising; research/documentation. **Events** *Congress* Marrakech (Morocco) 2022, *Congress* Istanbul (Türkiye) 2021, *Annual World Congress* Lima (Peru) 2019, *Annual World Congress* Moscow (Russia) 2018, *Annual World Congress* Rome (Italy) 2017. **Publications** *FCEM News* (annual) in English, French, Spanish; *FCE News Digest* (periodical) in English, French, Spanish; *International Trade Directory* – annual directory of member firms. National bulletins and newsletters.

Members National associations (one per country), representing about 500,000 women entrepreneurs. Full in 36 countries and territories:

Algeria, Argentina, Armenia, Australia, Belgium, Benin, Brazil, Cameroon, Comoros, Congo Brazzaville, Congo DR, Côte d'Ivoire, Croatia, Czechia, Dominican Rep, Egypt, Equatorial Guinea, France, Gabon, Germany, Iceland, Italy, Korea Rep, Madagascar, Mauritius, Mexico, Morocco, Peru, Senegal, Seychelles, Sudan, Taiwan, Togo, Tunisia, Uruguay, USA.

Observer in 18 countries:

Australia, Bahrain, Congo DR, Greece, Jordan, Kuwait, Lebanon, Luxembourg, Monaco, Oman, Pakistan, Romania, Russia, Switzerland, Syrian AR, Türkiye, UK, Yemen.

Consultative Status Consultative status granted from: *ECOSOC (#05331)* (Roster); *Council of Europe (CE, #04881)* (Participatory Status); *World Intellectual Property Organization (WIPO, #21593)* (Observer Status). **NGO Relations** Member of: *Conference of Non-Governmental Organizations in Consultative Relationship with the United Nations (CONGO, #04635)*. Participant of: *United Nations Global Compact (#20567)*.

[2023/XC3476/**C**]

♦ Femmes démocrates-chrétiennes d'Amérique (#03900)
♦ Femmes en dialogues (internationally oriented national body)
♦ Femmes, droit et développement en Afrique-Afrique de l'Ouest (#21005)
♦ Femmes dans l'Emploi Informel: Globalisation et Organisation (#21003)

♦ Femmes de l'Eurégio Meuse-Rhin 09734

Frauen in der Euregio Maas-Rhein – Vrouwen in de Euregio Maas-Rijn

Address not obtained.

History 1975.

Members Women in 3 countries:

Belgium, Germany, Netherlands.

[2010/XE1729/**E**]

- ♦ Femmes d'Europe / see Association femmes d'Europe
- ♦ Femmes européennes des moyennes et petites entreprises (inactive)
- ♦ Femmes internationales murs brisés (internationally oriented national body)
- ♦ Femmes sous lois musulmanes (#21007)
- ♦ Femmes sous lois musulmanes – Réseau international de solidarité / see Women Living under Muslim Laws (#21007)
- ♦ Femmes pour un monde meilleur (internationally oriented national body)
- ♦ Femmes mondiales faisantes avances la liberté et l'égalité (unconfirmed)
- ♦ Femmes de Paix Autour de Monde (#18283)
- ♦ Femmes pour la paix, Suisse (internationally oriented national body)
- ♦ Femmes du PPE/UEDC / see EPP Women (#05516)
- ♦ Femmes dans la science, l'ingénierie et la technologie (#06276)
- ♦ Femmes et sport dans les pays méditerranéens (no recent information)
- ♦ Femmes pour l'union des pays libres (inactive)
- ♦ Femmes et villes international (internationally oriented national body)
- ♦ Femme et Terre (internationally oriented national body)
- ♦ **FEMNET** African Women's Development and Communication Network (#00503)
- ♦ FEMO – Fédération euroméditerranéenne des municipalités oléicoles (inactive)
- ♦ **FEMOZA** Fédération Mondiale des Zones Franches (#09693)
- ♦ **FEMP** Federation of European Mineral Engineering Programs (#09517)
- ♦ **FEMP** Fédération Européenne pour les Métiers du Patrimoine Bâti (#09576)
- ♦ FEMRA – Federation of European Marketing Research Associations (inactive)
- ♦ **FEMS** Federation of European Materials Societies (#09515)
- ♦ **FEMS** Federation of European Microbiological Societies (#09516)
- ♦ **FEMS** Fédération européenne des médecins salariés (#07209)
- ♦ FEMS – Federation of National European Menopause Societies (no recent information)
- ♦ FEMTAA – Federación Mundial de Trabajadores de la Agricultura y la Alimentación (inactive)
- ♦ FEMTAA – Fédération mondiale des travailleurs de l'agriculture et de l'alimentation (inactive)
- ♦ **FEMTEC** Fédération mondiale du thermalisme et du climatisme (#09692)
- ♦ Femtochemistry Conference (meeting series)
- ♦ FEMTO – Femtochemistry Conference (meeting series)
- ♦ FEMYSO / see Forum of European Muslim Youth and Student Organisations (#09909)
- ♦ **FEMYSO** Forum of European Muslim Youth and Student Organisations (#09909)
- ♦ **FENA** Fédération européenne du négoce de l'ameublement (#07132)
- ♦ **FENAP** Federation of European Numismatic Trade Associations (#09523)
- ♦ FENAVI – Fédération Européenne de Naturopathie Vitaliste (unconfirmed)
- ♦ **FENCA** Federation of European National Collection Associations (#09520)

♦ Fencing Confederation of Asia (FCA) 09735

Contact PSC Fencing Ctr, Philsports Complex, Meralco Avenue, 1600 Pasig City RIZ, Philippines. E-mail: asianfencing@gmail.com.
Pres 38 San Agustin St, Captol 8, Pasig City RIZ, Philippines. T. +6326715010. Fax +6326715015.
URL: http://www.asianfencing.com/

History Founded 1972, at the Congress of the Fédération international d'escrime (FIE), Munich (Germany) 1972, held during the Olympic Games. Original title: *Asian Fencing Confederation (AFC)*. **Aims** Promote and develop the sport of fencing in Asia; form and stimulate international opinion in favour of providing proper and better fencing facilities in Asia; coordinate fencing activities within Asia; cooperate with existing national/territorial fencing bodies within the region; offer financial, administrative, and technical support to existing national/territorial fencing bodies where necessary and possible; approve and enforce uniform policies and rules for encouragement and regulation of the sport of fencing in Asia and deal with any infringements thereof; reconcile or arbitrate in differences which may arise among national/territorial fencing bodies; foster the spirit of the Olympic Movement. **Structure** General Assembly (annual, at Congress). Executive Committee. Commissions (7): Technical; Referees; Propaganda; SEMI; Athlete; Women; Veteran. **Finance** Members' dues. **Activities** Sporting events. **Events** *Asian Juniors and Cadet Fencing Championships* Abu Dhabi (United Arab Emirates) 2015, *Asian Fencing Championships* Singapore (Singapore) 2015, *Asian Juniors and Cadet Fencing Championships* Bangkok (Thailand) 2013, *Asian Fencing Championships* Shanghai (China) 2013, *Asian Juniors and Cadet Fencing Championships* Bali (Indonesia) 2012.
Members Federations in 38 countries and territories:
Afghanistan, Bahrain, Bangladesh, Brunei Darussalam, Cambodia, China, Hong Kong, India, Indonesia, Iran Islamic Rep, Iraq, Japan, Jordan, Kazakhstan, Korea Rep, Kuwait, Kyrgyzstan, Lebanon, Macau, Malaysia, Mongolia, Myanmar, Nepal, Palestine, Philippines, Qatar, Saudi Arabia, Singapore, Sri Lanka, Syrian AR, Taiwan, Tajikistan, Thailand, Turkmenistan, United Arab Emirates, Uzbekistan, Vietnam, Yemen.
[2014/XD0676/**D**]

- ♦ **FEND** Foundation of European Nurses in Diabetes (#09953)
- ♦ **FEN** Föderation Europäischer Narren (#09810)
- ♦ FENI / see European Cleaning and Facility Services Industry (#06571)
- ♦ Fennoscandian Exploration and Mining Conference (meeting series)
- ♦ Fenno-Ugria (internationally oriented national body)
- ♦ **FENS** Federation of European Neuroscience Societies (#09522)
- ♦ **FENS** Federation of European Nutrition Societies (#09524)
- ♦ **FENStatS** Federation of European National Statistical Societies (#09521)
- ♦ FENTO – Fédération des organisations scientifiques et techniques des pays socialistes (inactive)
- ♦ **FENU** Fonds d'équipement des Nations unies (#20524)
- ♦ FENU – Fuerza de Emergencia de las Naciones Unidas (inactive)
- ♦ FEODT / see European Confederation of Tobacco Retailers (#06725)
- ♦ FEO / see Euro+Med PlantBase (#05732)
- ♦ **FEO** Foederatio Europea Orthodontica (#09811)
- ♦ **FEOFS** Far East Oceanic Fracture Society (#09271)
- ♦ FEONG – Fédération des employeurs ONG (internationally oriented national body)
- ♦ **FEOph** Federation of European Ophthalmology (#09525)
- ♦ FEPACE – Fédération européenne des producteurs autonomes et des consommateurs industriels d'énergie (inactive)
- ♦ **FEPAC** Federación Panamericana de Consultores (#09379)
- ♦ FEPACI – Fédération panafricaine des cinéastes (no recent information)
- ♦ FEPAFAR – Federación Panamericana de Farmacia (no recent information)
- ♦ FEPA – Federation of European Pedestrian Associations (inactive)
- ♦ **FEPA** Federation of European Philatelic Associations (#09528)
- ♦ FEPA / see Federation of European Producers of Abrasives (#09532)
- ♦ **FEPA** Federation of European Producers of Abrasives (#09532)
- ♦ **FEPAFEM** Federación Panamericana de Asociaciones de Facultades y Escuelas de Medicina (#18100)
- ♦ FEPA – Fonds für Entwicklung und Partnerschaft in Afrika (internationally oriented national body)
- ♦ **FEPALE** Federación Panamericana de Lecheria (#09382)
- ♦ **FEPAL** Federación Psicoanalitica de América Latina (#09386)
- ♦ FEPANDOSA – Federación Panamericana pro Donación Voluntaria de Sangre (inactive)
- ♦ FEPAPHAM – Fédération panafricaine des associations pour les personnes handicapées mentales (no recent information)
- ♦ FEPASA – Fédération panafricaine des syndicats de l'agriculture (inactive)
- ♦ FEPASE – Fédération panafricaine des syndicats de l'éducation (no recent information)
- ♦ **FEPASEP** Federación Panamericana de Seguridad Privada (#09383)
- ♦ FEPATAA – Fédération panafricaine des travailleurs de l'agriculture et de l'alimentation (inactive)
- ♦ **FEPAV** Federación Pan Americana de Vela (#18128)
- ♦ **FEPD** Fédération Européenne des Parfumeurs Détaillants (#07206)
- ♦ FEPEDA / see AIPS America (#00599)
- ♦ **FEPEDA** Fédération Européenne des Parents d'Enfants Déficients Auditifs (#09577)
- ♦ FEPEDICA – Fédération européenne du personnel d'encadrement des productions, des industries, des commerces et des organismes agroalimentaires (inactive)
- ♦ **FEPE** Fédération européenne des producteurs d'enveloppes (#09578)
- ♦ FEPE – Fédération européenne des professionnels de l'environnement (no recent information)
- ♦ FEPE – Fédération européenne pour la protection des eaux (inactive)
- ♦ FEPE International / see World Out of Home Organization (#21702)
- ♦ FEPEM – Federation of European Petroleum Equipment Manufacturers (inactive)
- ♦ FEP / see European Federation of the Parquet Industry (#07188)
- ♦ **FEP** European Federation of the Parquet Industry (#07188)
- ♦ FEPE / see World Out of Home Organization (#21702)
- ♦ **FEP** Federation of European Professional Photographers (#09533)
- ♦ **FEP** Federation of European Publishers (#09536)
- ♦ **FEP** Fédération européenne de psychanalyse (#08292)
- ♦ **FEPF** Fédération européenne des industries de porcelaine et de faïence de table et d'ornementation (#09574)
- ♦ **FEPF** Fédération européenne des producteurs de fibres-ciment (#07120)
- ♦ FEPIEC – Federación Panamericana de Ingenieria Económica y de Costos (no recent information)
- ♦ FEPI / see European Nursing Council (#08063)
- ♦ FEPI – Federation of European Play Industries (inactive)
- ♦ **FEPI** Fédération européenne des ports intérieurs (#07144)
- ♦ **FEPI** Fédération européenne de la propriété immobilière (#08286)
- ♦ **FEPIMCTI** Federación Panamericana e Ibérica de Sociedades de Medicina Critica y Terapia Intensiva (#18111)
- ♦ FEPIMS – Federation of European Production and Industrial Management Societies (inactive)
- ♦ **FEPIOC** Federación Panamericana de Ingenieria Oceanica y Costera (#09380)
- ♦ FEPORT / see Federation of European Private Port Companies and Terminals (#09531)
- ♦ **FEPORT** Federation of European Private Port Companies and Terminals (#09531)
- ♦ FEPPD / see Fédération européenne et internationale des patrons prothésistes dentaires (#09575)
- ♦ **FEPPD** Fédération européenne et internationale des patrons prothésistes dentaires (#09575)
- ♦ **FEPPEN** Federación Panamericana de Profesionales de Enfermeria (#18104)
- ♦ FEPP – Fédération Européenne des Professionnels de la Pédagogie (unconfirmed)
- ♦ **FEPSAC** Fédération européenne de psychologie des sports et des activités corporelles (#07218)
- ♦ **FEPS** Federation of European Phycological Societies (#09529)
- ♦ **FEPS** Federation of European Physiological Societies (#09530)
- ♦ **FEPS** Federation of European Protistological Societies (#09534)
- ♦ FEPS – Fédération Européenne du Portage Salarial (unconfirmed)
- ♦ **FEPS** Foundation for European Progressive Studies (#09954)
- ♦ **FEPTO** Federation of European Psychodrama Training Organizations (#09535)
- ♦ FEPV / see Integrated Marketing Communications Council of Europe (#11369)
- ♦ **FERA** Fédération européenne des réalisateurs de l'audiovisuel (#09541)
- ♦ **F.E.R.B.A.** Fédération Européen des Races Bovines de L'Arc Alpin (#05752)
- ♦ FERCO / see FoodServiceEurope (#09851)
- ♦ FERDI – Fondation pour les études et recherches sur le développement international (internationally oriented national body)
- ♦ FEREEPAS – Fédération Européenne de Recherche sur l'Éducation et l'Écologie de la Personne et de ses Applications Sociales (internationally oriented national body)
- ♦ FERES – Fédération internationale des instituts de recherches socio-religieuses (inactive)
- ♦ Fer Europ (inactive)
- ♦ FERFAP – Federation of African Women's Networks on Peace (no recent information)
- ♦ **FER** Fédération européenne des réseaux de coopération scientifique et technique de coordination (#07114)
- ♦ FER – Fonds européen pour les réfugiés (inactive)
- ♦ FERI / see Roosevelt Institute
- ♦ FERL – Fédération européenne des radios libres (inactive)
- ♦ **FERMA** Federation of European Risk Management Associations (#09539)
- ♦ **FERM** Federation of European Rice Millers (#09537)
- ♦ FERMUCAP – Federación de Municipalidades de Centroamérica y Panama (inactive)

♦ Fern 09736

Coordinator Rue d'Edimbourg 26, 1050 Brussels, Belgium. T. +3228944690. E-mail: info@fern.org.
URL: http://www.fern.org/

History 1995. Founded by Saskia Ozinga. Former names and other names: *FERN – Forests and the European Union Resource Network* – former (1995). Registration: Banque-Carrefour des Entreprises, Start date: 3 Jun 2002, Belgium, 0851.515.983; EU Transparency Register, No/ID: 40538475090-82, Start date: 25 Jan 2011. **Aims** Achieve greater environmental and social justice, focusing on forests and forest people's rights in the policies and practices of the European Union. **Structure** Board. Offices in: Brussels (Belgium); Moreton-in-Marsh (UK). **Languages** Catalan, Dutch, English, French, German, Russian, Spanish. **Staff** 18.00 FTE, paid. **Finance** Sources: government support; international organizations; private foundations. Supported by: *European Commission (EC, #06633)*. **Activities** Advocacy/lobbying/activism. **Publications** *EU Forest Watch* (10 a year). Briefing notes; reports; videos. **Members** Not a membership organization. **IGO Relations** Observer status with (1): *Ministerial Conference on the Protection of Forests in Europe (FOREST EUROPE, #16817)*. **NGO Relations** Member of (1): *European Environmental Bureau (EEB, #06996)*. Coordinates: *Forest Movement Europe (FME, #09864)*. On Steering Committee of: *Environmental Paper Network (EPN, #05507)*.
[2023.02.15/XF5594/**F**]

- ♦ Fernand Braudel Institute of World Economics (internationally oriented national body)
- ♦ FERN – Forests and the European Union Resource Network / see Fern (#09736)
- ♦ FEROPA – European Federation of Fibreboard Manufacturers (inactive)
- ♦ **FERPA** Fédération européenne des retraités et des personnes âgées (#09580)
- ♦ **FERP** Fédération Européenne de la Randonnée Pédestre (#08328)
- ♦ **FERPRESS** Union internationale de presse ferroviaire (#20434)
- ♦ FERS – Fédération européenne de recherche sur le SIDA (inactive)
- ♦ **FERSI** Forum of European Road Safety Research Institutes (#09913)
- ♦ FERT – FAO Commission on Fertilizers (inactive)

♦ Fertility Europe (FE) 09737

Office Manager Clos de la Ballade 11, 1140 Evere, Belgium. E-mail: office@fertilityeurope.eu.
URL: https://fertilityeurope.eu/

History Oct 2007. Initially founded as a sub-Group of *International Consumer Support for Infertility Community (iCSi, #12932)*. Later became an independent organization. Former names and other names: *European Infertility Alliance* – former. Registration: Banque-Carrefour des Entreprises, No/ID: 0812.730.732, Start date: 23 Jun 2009, Belgium; EU Transparency Register, No/ID: 013325324971-78, Start date: 8 Dec 2016. **Aims** Build a strong cross-border network among European patients and professionals so as to achieve the exchange of best practice; provide education in the field of protection of reproductive *health* and a pro-active approach to family planning; monitor, evaluate and improve the situation concerning the rights of those affected by difficulties in conceiving in various areas. **Structure** Executive Committee. Working Groups. Office Manager. **Languages** English. **Staff** 0.50 FTE, paid. **Finance** Diverse sources. **Activities** Advocacy/lobbying/activism; events/meetings; projects/programmes. **Publications** *Fertility Europe Magazine*. Leaflets; posters.
Members Full (11) in 10 countries:
Belgium, Czechia, Finland, Israel, Italy, Netherlands, Norway, Slovakia, Switzerland, UK.
Candidate (14) in 12 countries:
Austria, Bulgaria, Croatia, France, Greece, Hungary, Latvia, Poland, Portugal, Romania, Spain, Sweden.
NGO Relations Member of (2): *European Patients' Forum (EPF, #08172)*; *World Patients Alliance (WPA)*.
[2023/XM2538/**E**]

Fertilizers Europe
09738

alphabetic sequence excludes
For the complete listing, see Yearbook Online at

♦ Fertilizers Europe 09738

Dir General Ave des Nerviens 9-31, 1040 Brussels, Belgium. T. +3226753550. E-mail: administration@fertilizerseurope.com.
URL: http://www.fertilizerseurope.com/

History 1 Jan 1988. Founded by merger of *Common Market Committee of the Nitrogenous and Phosphatic Fertilizers Industry (inactive), European Nitrogen Producers' Association (APEA, inactive)* and *Nitrogen Study Centre (inactive)*. Former names and other names: *European Fertilizer Manufacturers Association (EFMA)* – former (1998 to 2010). Registration: EU Transparency Register, No/ID: 80788715017-29. **Aims** Represent the interests of European fertilizer producers within EU institutions and the wider community. **Structure** General Assembly (annual); Board; Standing Committees (3); Working Groups; Task Forces; Director General heads Secretariat in Brussels (Belgium), assisted by Issue Managers and other staff. **Languages** English. **Staff** 12.00 FTE, paid. **Finance** Sources: members' dues. **Activities** Advocacy/lobbying/activism; events/meetings; knowledge management/information dissemination. **Events** *Summit of the Organic and organo-mineral Fertilisers Industries in Europe (SOFIE)* Brussels (Belgium) 2023, *New fertilizer regulation: Where do we go?* Brussels (Belgium) 2019, *Workshop on Fertilizing Poduct Regulation Implementation Issues* Brussels (Belgium) 2019, *Safety Seminar* Lisbon (Portugal) 2019, *Plant Nutrition Forum* London (UK) 2019. **Publications** *Forecast of Food, Farming and Fertilizer Use in the European Union* (annual); *Annual Overview. Energy Strategy Fertilizers Europe*; *Fertilizers Europe Statistical Handbook*; *Growing Together*; *Infinite Product Stewardship*; *Mind The Gap*; *Modern Agriculture Feeds the World*; *Modern Fertilizer Production and Use*; *Towards Smart Agriculture (DAN)*. Information Services: Provides members with market information, including consumption forecasts, trade and production statistics and surveys of performance.

Members European enterprises, and national associations of enterprises, producing or distributing ammonia and/or chemically produced simple or complex nitrogen fertilizers. Corporate (17), national association (8). Members in 16 countries:
Austria, Belgium, Croatia, Czechia, France, Germany, Greece, Italy, Lithuania, Netherlands, Norway, Poland, Portugal, Romania, Spain, UK.

Consultative Status Consultative status granted from: *ECOSOC (#05331)* (Ros A). **NGO Relations** Member of (3): *European Sustainable Phosphorus Platform (ESPP, #08866)*; *Federation of European and International Associations Established in Belgium (FAIB, #09508)*; *Industry4Europe (#11181)*. Associate member of: *Critical Raw Materials Alliance (CRM Alliance, #04959)*; *European Network of Agricultural Journalists (ENAJ, #07864)*.
[2021.02.23/XD1719/**D**]

- ♦ FERTYP / see Forum of European Roma Young People (#09914)
- ♦ **FERVER** Fédération Européenne des Recycleurs de Verre (#07134)
- ♦ **FERV** Forum européen des Roms et des gens du voyage (#08402)
- ♦ **FERYP** Forum of European Roma Young People (#09914)
- ♦ **FESAC** Foundation for European Societies of Arms Collectors (#09955)
- ♦ **FESAFA** Federación Sudamericana de Actividad Física Adaptada (#09392)
- ♦ FESA – Finnish European Studies Association (internationally oriented national body)
- ♦ FESANDINA – Federación Andina de la Industria para la Protección de Cultivos (no recent information)
- ♦ **FESASS** Fédération européenne pour la santé animale et la sécurité sanitaire (#09581)
- ♦ **FESAT** Fondation européenne des services d'accueil téléphonique drogues et toxicomanies (#09819)
- ♦ **FESCA** Federation of European Scleroderma Associations (#09540)
- ♦ **FESCAS** Federación de Sociedados de Cancerología de Sudamerica (#09391)
- ♦ FESCBB – Fédération européenne des syndicats chrétiens d'ouvriers du bâtiment et du bois (inactive)
- ♦ FESCC / see European Federation of Clinical Chemistry and Laboratory Medicine (#07080)
- ♦ FESCID – Fédération européenne des syndicats de la chimie et des industries diverses (inactive)
- ♦ **FESCI** Federation of European Societies for Chemotherapy and for Infections (#09546)
- ♦ FESCO / see European Securities and Markets Authority (#08457)
- ♦ **FESE** Federation of European Securities Exchanges (#09542)
- ♦ **FESE** Federation of European Social Employers (#09545)
- ♦ **FeSeLa** Federación Sefaradi Latinoamericana (#09388)
- ♦ **FESESUR** Federación de Seguridad Privada de los Paises del Mercosur (#09389)
- ♦ FESET – Association européenne des centres de formation au travail socio-éducatif / see Formation d'éducateurs sociaux européens (#09873)
- ♦ **FESET** Formation d'éducateurs sociaux européens (#09873)
- ♦ FES / see Federation of European Aquaculture Producers (#09491)
- ♦ FESF / see European Academy of Land Use and Development (#05797)
- ♦ **FES** Fondo Europeo de Sviluppo (#06914)
- ♦ FES – Friedrich-Ebert-Stiftung (internationally oriented national body)
- ♦ **FESI** Federation of the European Sporting Goods Industry (#09552)
- ♦ **FESI** Fédération européenne des syndicats d'entreprises d'isolation (#09582)
- ♦ **FESI** Fundación para la Educación Superior Internacional (#13794)
- ♦ **FESITRAUCAMC** Federación de Sindicatos de Trabajadores de las Universidades de Centroamérica, México y el Caribe (#09712)
- ♦ FESM / see European Federation of Societies for Microsurgery (#07216)
- ♦ FESNCE – Fédération européenne des sociétés nationales de chirurgie esthétiques (inactive)

♦ FESPA 09739

CEO Holmbury, The Dorking Business Park, Station Road, Dorking, RH4 1HJ, UK. T. +441737240788. E-mail: info@fespa.com.
URL: http://www.fespa.com/

History 27 Feb 1962, Hamburg (Germany). Former names and other names: *Federation of European Screen Printers Associations* – full title; *Fédération des associations européennes de sérigraphes* – full title; *Federación de Asociaciones de Impresores Serigraficos Europeos* – full title; *Föderation der Europäischen Siebdruck-Verbände* – full title. Registration: Netherlands; Companies House, No/ID: 2449446, Start date: 5 Dec 1989, England. **Aims** Be the leading globally connecting imaging community reinvesting profits for the purpose of inspiring, educating and growing the industry. **Structure** General Assembly; Executive Board, composed of 10 members. **Languages** English, French, German, Lithuanian, Mandarin Chinese, Mandarin Chinese, Romanian, Spanish, Thai, Turkish. **Staff** 35.00 FTE, paid. **Finance** Sources: fees for services; members' dues. **Activities** Events/meetings; training/education. **Events** *Global Summit* Bangkok (Thailand) 2020, *Southern European Print Congress* Madrid (Spain) 2019, *Asia Conference* Bangkok (Thailand) 2017, *Global Summit* Amsterdam (Netherlands) 2015, *General Assembly* Madrid (Spain) 2015. **Publications** *FESPA World Magazine* (26 a year) in English.

Members National associations in 36 countries:
Australia, Austria, Belgium, Bulgaria, China, Croatia, Czechia, Denmark, Finland, France, Germany, Greece, Hungary, India, Italy, Japan, Korea Rep, Mexico, Nepal, Netherlands, Norway, Philippines, Poland, Portugal, Romania, Russia, Serbia, Slovakia, South Africa, Spain, Sweden, Switzerland, Thailand, Türkiye, UK, Ukraine.
Individuals in 3 countries and territories:
Canada, Hong Kong, USA.
Associate members in 6 countries:
Australia, China, India, Japan, Korea Rep, Thailand.
[2021/XD0940/y/**D**]

- ♦ **FESPB** Federation of European Societies of Plant Biology (#09548)
- ♦ FESPIC Federation – Far East and South Pacific Games Federation for the Disabled (inactive)
- ♦ FESPP / see Federation of European Societies of Plant Biology (#09548)
- ♦ FESR – Fédération européenne de la sécurité routière (inactive)
- ♦ **FESSACAL** Federación de Sociedades Sudamericanas en Ciencias de Animales de Laboratorio (#09704)
- ♦ FESS – Foundation for Environmental Security and Sustainability (internationally oriented national body)
- ♦ **FESSH** Federation of the European Societies for Surgery of the Hand (#09549)
- ♦ **FESSS** Federation of Eurasian Soil Science Societies (#09485)
- ♦ **FESTEM** Federation of European Societies on Trace Elements and Minerals (#09550)
- ♦ **FEST** Federation for European Storytelling (#09553)
- ♦ **FEST** Fédération européenne des grossistes en appareils sanitaires et de chauffage (#09570)
- ♦ FEST – Fédération européenne des sociétés de toxicologie (inactive)
- ♦ FEST – Forschungsstätte der Evangelischen Studiengemeinschaft (internationally oriented national body)
- ♦ **FESTMIH** Federation of European Societies for Tropical Medicine and International Health (#09551)
- ♦ FESU / see European Forum for Urban Security (#07340)
- ♦ FES / see Union Internationale des Guides et Scouts d'Europe – Fédération du Scoutisme Européen (#20426)
- ♦ **FESUPO** Federación Sudamericana de Powerlifting (#09393)
- ♦ FESV – Fédération européenne pour le droit à la stérilisation volontaire (inactive)
- ♦ FESYP – Fédération européenne des syndicats de fabricants de panneaux de particules (inactive)
- ♦ Fetal Medicine Foundation (internationally oriented national body)

♦ Fetal and Neonatal Physiological Society (FNPS) 09740

Pres Dept of Physiology/Development/Neuroscience, Univ of Cambridge, Downing Street, Cambridge, CB2 3DY, UK. E-mail: dag26@cam.ac.uk.
Scribe address not obtained.
URL: https://research.pdn.cam.ac.uk/fnps/

History Founded 1974, Oxford, during an informal meeting. Original title: *Conference on Fetal Breathing*. Between 1981 and 1983 referred to as *International Conference on Fetal Breathing and other Movements*. From 1984 until 1995 known as *Society for the Study of Fetal Physiology*. Since 1996 known under current title. **Structure** Board. **Activities** Awards/prizes/competitions; events/meetings; training/education. **Events** *Annual Meeting* Pescara (Italy) 2022, *Annual Meeting* 2021, *Annual Meeting* Erice (Italy) 2020, *Annual Meeting* Melbourne, VIC (Australia) 2019, *Annual Meeting* Maastricht (Netherlands) 2018. **Publications** Abstract books.
[2020.03.11/XM7811/c/**C**]

- ♦ FETAP – Fédération européenne des transports aériens privés (inactive)
- ♦ **FETBB** Fédération européenne des travailleurs du bâtiment et du bois (#07065)
- ♦ **FETBB** Federazione Europea dei Lavoratori Edili e del Legno (#07065)
- ♦ **FETCM** Federación Europea de los Trabajadores de la Construcción y la Madera (#07065)
- ♦ FETELAC – Foro de Educación Teológica Ecuménica de América Latina y el Caribe (unconfirmed)
- ♦ FETIBALC – Federación de los Trabajadores en la Industria de Platano de América Latina y del Caribe (inactive)
- ♦ FETLA – Federación de Trabajadores Latinoamericana de la Industria de la Alimentación, Bebidas, Hoteles y Tabacos (inactive)
- ♦ **FETRALCOS** Federación de Trabajadores Latinoamericanos del Comercio, Oficinas y Empresas Privadas de Servicios (#09394)
- ♦ FETRASCAP – Federación de Trabajadores de la Salud de Centroamérica y Panama (inactive)
- ♦ **FETRATAB** Fédération européenne des transformateurs de tabac (#07227)
- ♦ **FETSA** Federation of European Tank Storage Associations (#09554)
- ♦ FETS – Fondo Especial para la Transformación Social de Centroamérica (see: #03658)
- ♦ **FEUCA** Federación de Estudiantes Universitarios de Centroamérica (#09471)
- ♦ FEUCAL – Union of Federations of Latin American Catholic University Students (inactive)
- ♦ **FEU** Federation of the European Union Fire Officer Associations (#09555)

♦ FEUGRES – European Clay Pipe Association (FEUGRES e.V.) 09741

Contact Europaallee 63, 50226 Frechen, Germany. T. +492234507271. E-mail: info@feugres.eu.
URL: https://www.feugres.eu/

History 25 Apr 1957, Zurich (Switzerland). Former names and other names: *European Clay Pipe Association* – alias; *European Federation for the Vitrified Clay Pipe Industry* – former; *Fédération Européenne des Fabricants de Tuyaux en Grès (FEUGRES)* – former; *Europäische Vereinigung der Steinzeugröhrenindustrie* – former. Registration: North Rhine-Westphalia District court, No/ID: VR 20382, Start date: 4 Jun 2020, Germany, Köln. **Aims** Contribute to the solution of all scientific, technical and economic problems of joint concern to the European clay pipe industry. **Structure** General Assembly (annual); Board of Directors; Office. **Languages** English, French, German. **Finance** Sources: members' dues. **Events** *General Assembly* Brussels (Belgium) 2019, *Triennial international meeting of drainage experts* Budapest (Hungary) 2007, *Triennial international meeting of drainage experts* Sorrento (Italy) 2004, *Triennial international meeting of drainage experts* Barcelona (Spain) 2001, *Triennial international congress of drainage experts / Triennial International Meeting of Drainage Experts* Prague (Czech Rep) 1998.

Members Full in 3 countries:
Belgium, Germany, UK.

NGO Relations Member of (2): *European Ceramic Industry Association (CERAME-UNIE, #06506)* (as full member); *Industry4Europe (#11181)*.
[2020/XD0756/t/**D**]

- ♦ **FEUGRES e.V.** FEUGRES – European Clay Pipe Association (#09741)
- ♦ FEUGRES / see FEUGRES – European Clay Pipe Association (#09741)
- ♦ FEUPF / see International Florist Organisation (#13616)
- ♦ **FEVA** Fédération des Verts Africains (#00331)
- ♦ FEVC – Fédération européenne des villes de congrès (inactive)
- ♦ **FEVE** Fédération européenne du verre d'emballage (#09583)
- ♦ FEVEL – Fédération européenne du velours (inactive)
- ♦ FEVIR / see European Association of Veterinarians in Education, Research and Industry (#06267)
- ♦ FEVP / see International Forum for Volunteering in Development (#13659)
- ♦ **FEVR** Fédération Européenne des Victimes de la Route (#07207)
- ♦ FEVSD / see European Direct Selling Association (#06928)
- ♦ **FEWAMA** Federation of West African Manufacturers Associations (#09714)
- ♦ FEW – Formal Epistemology Workshop (meeting series)
- ♦ FEWIA / see European Writing Instrument Manufacturer's Association (#09125)
- ♦ FEWITA – Federation of European Wholesale and International Trade Associations (inactive)
- ♦ FEWS / see European Federation of Williams Syndrome (#07234)
- ♦ **FEWS** European Federation of Williams Syndrome (#07234)
- ♦ FEWS NET – Famine Early Warning System Network (internationally oriented national body)
- ♦ **FEZA** Federation of European Zeolite Associations (#09556)
- ♦ FEZANA – Federation of Zoroastrian Associations of North America (internationally oriented national body)
- ♦ **FEZ** Federación Europea de Zootecnia (#07046)
- ♦ FEZ – Fédération européenne de zoologie (inactive)
- ♦ **FEZ** Fédération européenne de zootechnie (#07046)
- ♦ FFACE – Federation of Film and Audiovisual Composers of Europe (inactive)
- ♦ **FFA** Foro Farmacéutico de las Américas (#18351)
- ♦ **FFA** Forum francophone des affaires (#09916)
- ♦ **FFA** Fur Free Alliance (#10043)
- ♦ **FFAO** Fédération francophone des amis de l'orgue (#09586)
- ♦ **FFA** Pacific Islands Forum Fisheries Agency (#17969)
- ♦ FFCAI – Frank Foundation Child Assistance International (internationally oriented national body)
- ♦ **FFCC** Federación Farmacéutica Centroamericana y del Caribe (#09301)
- ♦ FFE / see Freight Forward International (#09991)
- ♦ FFEM – Fonds français pour l'environnement mondial (internationally oriented national body)
- ♦ FFfF – Föreningen för Fredsforskning i Finland (internationally oriented national body)
- ♦ **FFF** Fossil Fuel Foundation of Africa (#09937)
- ♦ **FFF** Fridays For Future (#09997)
- ♦ **FFF** IHRA Foundation for the Future (#11113)
- ♦ FFF – International Symposium on Field- and Flow-Based Separations (meeting series)
- ♦ FF – Forschungsinstitut für Friedenspolitik, Weilheim (internationally oriented national body)
- ♦ FFHC / see Manos Unidas
- ♦ **FFHS** Federation of Family History Societies (#09585)
- ♦ **FFI** Fauna & Flora International (#09277)

♦ FFI – Fly Fishers International (unconfirmed)
♦ FFI / see Food Fortification Initiative (#09844)
♦ **FFI** Food Fortification Initiative (#09844)
♦ **FFI** Freight Forward International (#09991)
♦ FFI – Friendship Force International (internationally oriented national body)
♦ **FFII** Foundation for a Free Information Infrastructure (#09956)
♦ **FFINU** Fédération des Fonctionnaires Internationaux des Nations Unies (#20579)
♦ **FFLA** Fundación Futuro Latinoamericano (#10022)
♦ **FFL** Food for Life Global (#09847)
♦ FFMed – Fonds pour les Femmes en Méditerranée (internationally oriented national body)
♦ FFM / see International Mediterranean Women's Forum (#14143)
♦ **FFN** Fragility Fracture Network (#09980)
♦ FFOA – Former FAO and Other United Nations Staff Association (internationally oriented national body)
♦ FFOA Rome / see Former FAO and Other United Nations Staff Association
♦ **FFPE** Fédération de la fonction publique européenne (#06567)
♦ FFP – Food for the Poor (internationally oriented national body)
♦ **FFP** Foundations for Peace (#09974)
♦ FFP – Fund for Peace (internationally oriented national body)
♦ **FFPI** Free and Fair Post Initiative (#09986)
♦ FFPO – Fonds francophone de préparation olympique (see: #04634)
♦ FFPS / see Fauna & Flora International (#09277)
♦ FFRC – Finland Futures Research Centre (internationally oriented national body)
♦ FFSC – Institutum Fratrum Franciscalium a Santa Cruce (religious order)
♦ FFSI – Institutum Fratrum Filiorum Sancti Iosephi, vulgo Bayozefiti (religious order)
♦ FFSM – Fédération des fondations pour la santé mondiale (inactive)
♦ **FFTC/ASPAC** Food and Fertilizer Technology Center for the Asian and Pacific Region (#09842)
♦ FFW – International Conference on Fracture Fatigue and Wear (meeting series)
♦ FFWP / see Family Federation for World Peace and Unification
♦ FFWPU – Family Federation for World Peace and Unification (internationally oriented national body)
♦ FGAA / see General Arab Insurance Federation (#10104)
♦ FGB – Fondazione Giacomo Brodolini (internationally oriented national body)
♦ **FGBMFI** Full Gospel Business Men's Fellowship International (#10015)
♦ **FGCCC** Federation of GCC Chambers (#09590)
♦ FGED – Functional Genomics Data Society (inactive)
♦ FGEF – French Global Environment Facility (internationally oriented national body)
♦ **FGF** Fédération des géomètres francophone (#09591)
♦ FGI – Fédération graphique internationale (inactive)
♦ **FGIP** Human Rights in Mental Health (#10988)
♦ FGJA / see Federation of Arab Journalists (#09422)
♦ FGL – Fondazione Giovanni Lorenzini (internationally oriented national body)
♦ FGOLF – Fédération des gynécologues et obstétriciens de langue française (inactive)
♦ **FGOM** Fédération des sociétés nationales de gynécologie-obstétrique des pays méditerranéens (#09695)
♦ FGS – Fundação Gonçalo da Silveira (internationally oriented national body)
♦ **FH-DCE** Federation of Harley-Davidson Clubs of Europe (#09592)
♦ **FHE** Fédération humaniste européenne (#07507)
♦ **FH Europe** European FH Patient Network (#07243)
♦ FHF / see International Federation of Health Plans (#13442)
♦ **fh** Food for the Hungry (#09845)
♦ FHI / see FHI 360
♦ FHI 360 (internationally oriented national body)
♦ FHI / see Food for the Hungry (#09845)
♦ FHI – Future Hope International (internationally oriented national body)
♦ FHI / see International Weightlifting Federation (#15876)
♦ FHS – Fish Health Section of the Asian Fisheries Society (see: #01483)
♦ FHSSA / see Global Partners in Care
♦ **FIAA** Fédération internationale des associations d'anatomistes (#13361)
♦ **FIAA** Foundation for International Arbitration Advocacy (#09960)
♦ FIAAIINAPE – Federación Internacional de Antiguos Alumnos Iberoamericanos del INAP España (internationally oriented national body)
♦ FIABCI-CEE / see European Association of Real Estate Professions (#06186)
♦ FIABCI-CE / see European Association of Real Estate Professions (#06186)
♦ FIABCI Communauté européenne / see European Association of Real Estate Professions (#06186)
♦ **FIABCI** Fédération internationale des professions immobilières (#09653)
♦ **FIAB** Federación Iberoamericana de Bolsas (#11022)
♦ **FIAB** Forum international des autochtones sur la biodiversité (#13837)
♦ FIAB / see International Federation of Library Associations and Institutions (#13470)
♦ FIABV / see Ibero-American Federation of Exchanges (#11022)
♦ FIACA – Fédération internationale des anciens combattants alliés (inactive)
♦ **FIACAT** Fédération internationale des ACAT – Action des chrétiens pour l'abolition de la torture (#13334)
♦ FIAC / see Federación Internacional del Automóvil Region IV (#09337)
♦ FIAC – Fédération internationale des agences catholiques de presse (inactive)
♦ **FIAC** Forum international d'action catholique (#09919)
♦ **FIAC** Forum Internazionale di Azione Cattolica (#09919)
♦ **FIACYD** Federación Iberoamericana de Capacitación y Desarrollo (#09308)
♦ **FIADASEC** Federación Internacional de Asociaciones de Ayuda Social, Ecológica y Cultural (#09335)
♦ FIADELSO – Fundación Internacional de Apoyo al Desarrollo Local y Social (internationally oriented national body)
♦ **FIAD** Fédération internationale des associations de distributeurs de films (#13428)
♦ FIADHE – Federación Iberoamericana de Asociaciones de Historia Económica (no recent information)
♦ **FIADI** Federación Iberoamericana de Asociaciones de Derecho e Informatica (#09303)
♦ **FIADOWN** Federación Iberoamericana de Sindrome de Down (#09319)
♦ FIADREP – Fédération internationale des associations de défense, de recherche et d'enseignement de la phytothérapie (inactive)
♦ FIAE – Federación Iberoamericana de Estimulación Prenatal y Temprana (no recent information)
♦ **FIAET** Federación Internacional de Asociaciones para la Educación de los Trabajadores (#13580)
♦ **FIAET** Fédération internationale des associations pour l'éducation des travailleurs (#13580)
♦ **FIA** Federação Iberoamericana de Acústica (#11021)
♦ **FIA** Federación Interamericana de Abogados (#11401)
♦ **FIA** Fédération internationale des acteurs (#13337)
♦ **FIA** Fédération internationale d'aikido (#11605)
♦ FIA – Fédération Internationale de l'Arbre (internationally oriented national body)
♦ FIA – Fédération internationale de l'artisanat (inactive)
♦ **FIA** Fédération Internationale de l'Automobile (#09613)
♦ FIA – Fédération internationale des aveugles (inactive)
♦ FIAFE / see Fédération Internationale des Accueils Français et francophones d'Expatriés (#09606)
♦ **FIAFE** Fédération Internationale des Accueils Français et francophones d'Expatriés (#09606)
♦ **FIAF** Federación Iberoamericana de Franquicias (#09310)
♦ **FIAF** Federación Interamericana de Filatelia (#09332)
♦ FIAF / see Fédération Internationale des Accueils Français et francophones d'Expatriés (#09606)
♦ **FIAF** Fédération internationale des archives du film (#13427)
♦ **FIAFIN** Federación Iberoamericana de Fondos de Inversión (#09309)
♦ FIA – Food Industry Asia (unconfirmed)
♦ FIA – Forschungsstelle für Internationale Agrar- und Wirtschaftsentwicklung, Heidelberg (internationally oriented national body)

♦ FIA Foundation 09742

Headquarters 60 Trafalgar Square, London, WC2N 5DS, UK. T. +447879893222. E-mail: k.turner@fiafoundation.org.
URL: http://www.fiafoundation.org/

History 2001. Founded through a donation of *Fédération Internationale de l'Automobile (FIA, #09613)*. Former names and other names: *FIA Foundation for the Automobile and Society* – former. Registration: Charity Commission, No/ID: 1088670, England and Wales. **Aims** Support an international programme of activities promoting road safety, the environment and sustainable mobility, as well as funding motor sport safety research. **Structure** Board of Trustees headed by Chairman. **Finance** Donation from *Fédération Internationale de l'Automobile (FIA, #09613)*: US$ 300,000,000. **Events** *Annual General Assembly* Doha (Qatar) 2014.
Members Founding (152); other members (13). Members in 102 countries and territories:
Andorra, Argentina, Armenia, Australia, Austria, Bahrain, Belarus, Belgium, Bolivia, Bosnia-Herzegovina, Brazil, Bulgaria, Canada, Chile, China, Colombia, Costa Rica, Côte d'Ivoire, Croatia, Cyprus, Czechia, Denmark, Dominican Rep, Ecuador, Egypt, El Salvador, Estonia, Finland, France, Georgia, Germany, Greece, Hong Kong, Hungary, Iceland, India, Indonesia, Iran Islamic Rep, Ireland, Israel, Italy, Jamaica, Japan, Jordan, Kazakhstan, Kenya, Korea Rep, Kuwait, Latvia, Lebanon, Libya, Lithuania, Luxembourg, Macau, Malaysia, Mexico, Moldova, Monaco, Montenegro, Mozambique, Netherlands, New Zealand, Nicaragua, North Macedonia, Norway, Oman, Pakistan, Panama, Paraguay, Peru, Philippines, Poland, Portugal, Qatar, Romania, Russia, Saudi Arabia, Serbia, Singapore, Slovakia, Slovenia, South Africa, Spain, Sri Lanka, Sweden, Switzerland, Syrian AR, Taiwan, Tanzania UR, Thailand, Trinidad-Tobago, Tunisia, Türkiye, Uganda, UK, United Arab Emirates, Uruguay, USA, Venezuela, Yemen, Zambia, Zimbabwe.
Included in the above, 1 regional organization:
European Road Assessment Programme (EuroRAP, #08392).
Consultative Status Consultative status granted from: *ECOSOC (#05331)* (Ros A). **NGO Relations** Member of (2): *Climate and Clean Air Coalition (CCAC, #04010); Global Alliance for Surgical, Obstetric, Trauma and Anaesthesia Care (G4 Alliance, #10229).* Cooperates with (4): *Global Forum on Agricultural Research (GFAR, #10370); Global Fuel Economy Initiative (GFEI, #10381); Partnership for Clean Fuels and Vehicles (PCFV, #18231); Partnership on Sustainable, Low Carbon Transport Foundation (SLoCaT Foundation, #18244).* Supports (2): *Global New Car Assessment Programme (Global NCAP, #10506); New Car Assessment Programme for Latin America and the Caribbean (Latin NCAP, #17077).* [2022.02.08/XJ1766/fy/F]

♦ FIA Foundation for the Automobile and Society / see FIA Foundation (#09742)
♦ FIA – Futures Industry Association (internationally oriented national body)
♦ **FIAGC** Foro Iberoamericano de Agencias Gubernamentales de Protección al Consumidor (#09877)
♦ FIAGU / see African Foundation for Urban Management
♦ FIAI – Fédération internationale des associations d'instituteurs (inactive)
♦ FIAJF – Fédération internationale des amies de la jeune fille (inactive)
♦ FIAJ / see Hostelling International (#10950)
♦ **FIAMC** Fédération internationale des associations médicales catholiques (#13378)
♦ FIAM – Federación Internacional de Asociaciones de Maestros (inactive)
♦ **FIAM** Fédération internationale des associations de multimedia (#13483)
♦ FIANAO / see World Olympians Association (#21682)
♦ FIANATM – Fédération internationale des associations de négociants en aciers, tubes et métaux (inactive)
♦ FIANEI – Fédération internationale d'associations nationales d'élèves ingénieurs (inactive)
♦ **FIANET** Fédération internationale des associations nationales d'exploitants de téléphériques, funiculaires et autres transports par câbles pour voyageurs (#09608)
♦ FIAN / see FIAN International (#09743)
♦ FIAN-International / see FIAN International (#09743)

♦ FIAN International 09743

Information et réseau d'action pour le droit à se nourrir
Contact Willy-Brandt-Platz 5, 69115 Heidelberg, Germany. T. +4962216530030. Fax +4962216530033. E-mail: contact@fian.org.
Geneva Office Maison des Associations, 15 Rue des Savoises, 1205 Geneva, Switzerland. T. +41223280341. Fax +41223280342.
URL: http://www.fian.org/

History 1986. Founded as an international human rights organization. Statutes amended: May 1994, Vienna (Austria); Nov 2014, La Foresta (Belgium). Former names and other names: *Foodfirst Information and Action Network (FIAN)* – former; *FIAN-International (FIAN)* – former. **Aims** Promote the *human right* to adequate *food*, campaigning in both North and South against human rights violation in the field of *hunger* and *malnutrition*; focus on land rights. **Structure** International Council (every 3 years); International Executive Committee; Secretariat; Sections and Coordinations in: Austria; Belgium; Brazil; Burkina Faso; Colombia; Ecuador; Germany; Honduras; India; Indonesia; Mexico; Nepal; Norway; Paraguay; Sir Lanka; Sweden; Switzerland; Uganda; Zambia. **Languages** English, French, Spanish. **Staff** 18.00 FTE, paid. **Finance** Sources: donations; grants; members' dues. **Activities** Advocacy/lobbying/activism; guidance/assistance/consulting; research/documentation; training/education. **Events** *Vienna +20 Human Rights Experts Conference* Vienna (Austria) 2013, *International Council Meeting* Brasilia (Brazil) 2012, *International Council Meeting* Brussels (Belgium) 2010, *International Council Meeting* Vienna (Austria) 2008, *Biennial international conference* India 2001. **Publications** *Right to Food and Nutrition Watch* (annual); *Right to Food Journal* (annual). Booklets; policy papers; documentation; parallel reports to the UN; Fact Finding Mission Reports.
Members National Sections (19); Individuals. Members in 20 countries:
Austria, Belgium, Brazil, Burkina Faso, Colombia, Ecuador, Germany, Honduras, India, Indonesia, Mexico, Nepal, Norway, Paraguay, Portugal, Sri Lanka, Sweden, Switzerland, Uganda, Zambia.
Consultative Status Consultative status granted from: *African Commission on Human and Peoples' Rights (ACHPR, #00255)* (Observer); *ECOSOC (#05331)* (Ros A). **NGO Relations** Member of (6): *EU-LAT Network (#05585); Geneva Global Health Hub (G2H2, #10122); International Network for Economic, Social and Cultural Rights (ESCR-Net, #14255); International NGO/CSO Planning Committee for Food Sovereignty (IPC, #14365); Verband Entwicklungspolitik und Humanitäre Hilfe e.V. (VENRO); World Social Forum (WSF, #21797).* Cooperates with (2): *Alliance Against Hunger and Malnutrition (AAHM, no recent information); Transnational Institute (TNI, #20219).* Member of and provides secretariat for: *ETO Consortium (ETOs, #05560); Right to Food and Nutrition Watch Consortium (#18943).* [2022/XF1740/F]

♦ **FIAPAC** Fédération internationale des associés professionnels de l'avortement et de la contraception (#09612)
♦ **FIAPA** Fédération internationale de l'activité physique adaptée (#13338)
♦ FIAPA – Fédération internationale des associations de chefs de publicité d'annonceurs (inactive)
♦ **FIAPA** Fédération internationale des associations de personnes âgées (#09609)
♦ **FIAPAM** Federación Iberoamericana de Asociaciones de Personas Adultas Mayores (#09304)
♦ **FIAP** Federación Iberoamericana de Asociaciones de Psicologia (#09305)
♦ **FIAP** Federación Internacional de Administradoras de Fondos de Pensiones (#09334)
♦ **FIAP** Federation of Inter-Asian Philately (#09600)
♦ **FIAP** Fédération Internationale de l'Art Photographique (#13509)
♦ **FIAPF** Fédération internationale des associations de producteurs de films (#13429)
♦ FIAPP – Federación Ibero Americana de Prensa Periódica (inactive)
♦ FIAPP – Fédération internationale des anciens prisonniers politiques du fascisme (inactive)
♦ **FIAPS** Fédération internationale des associations de professeurs de sciences (#12997)
♦ FIARP / see Inter-American Confederation of Public Relations (#11418)
♦ **FIASEET** Federación Internacional de Asociaciones de Ejecutivas de Empresas Turisticas (#09336)
♦ **FIAS** Federación Interamericana de Asociaciones de Secretarias (#11430)
♦ **FIAS** Federación Internacional de SAMBO (#09655)
♦ FIAS / see Fédération internationale de SAMBO (#09655)
♦ **FIAS** Fédération internationale de SAMBO (#09655)
♦ FIAS – Force internationale d'assistance à la sécurité (inactive)
♦ FIATA / see Fédération internationale des associations de transitaires et assimilés (#09610)
♦ **FIATA** Fédération internationale des associations de transitaires et assimilés (#09610)

Fiatal Európai Föderalistak
09743

alphabetic sequence excludes
For the complete listing, see Yearbook Online at

- ♦ Fiatal Európai Föderalistak (#21984)
- ♦ FIATC – Fédération internationale des associations touristiques de cheminots (inactive)
- ♦ **FIAT** Fédération Internationale des Archives de Télévision (#13568)
- ♦ **FIAT** Fédération internationale des associations de thanatologues (#13569)
- ♦ **FIAU** International Federation Amateur Unifight (#13353)
- ♦ **FIAUOG** Federación Iberoamericana de Ultrasonografistas en Obstetricia y Ginecologia (#09323)
- ♦ **FIAVAC** Federación Iberoamericana de Asociaciones Veterinarias de Animales de Compañia (#09306)
- ♦ FIAV – Fédération internationale des agences de voyages (inactive)
- ♦ FIAV – Fédération internationale des associations de veufs et de veuves (inactive)
- ♦ **FIAV** Fédération internationale des associations vexillologiques (#09611)
- ♦ **FIBAA** Foundation for International Business Administration Accreditation (#09961)

♦ FIBA Africa 09744

Regional Dir Bd De Gaulle, face à la piscine d'Etat de Treichville, Abidjan BP 4482 01, Côte d'Ivoire. T. +22521598144. Fax +22521598145. E-mail: yacouba.yira@fiba.basketball – ali.boukari@fiba.basketball – info-africa@fiba.basketball.
URL: http://www.fiba.basketball/africa/

History 11 Jun 1961, Cairo (Egypt). Founded 11-14 Jun 1961, Cairo (Egypt), on the initiative of the first leaders of African National Basketball Federations, at a General Assembly organized by the Egyptian Basketball Federation under the aegis of *Fédération internationale de basketball (FIBA, #09614)*, and attended by 12 African National Federations. Original title: *Association of African Amateur Basketball Federations – Association des fédérations africaines de basketball (AFABA)*. 1 Jan 2015, became a FIBA Regional Office in the concept of "ONE FIBA", the world basketball family. **Aims** Promote *basketball* on the African continent; educate trainers, referees and managers. **Structure** General Assembly; Executive Committee; Bureau. Commissions (4): Technical; Competition; Development; Juridical. **Languages** English, French. **Staff** 22.00 FTE, paid. **Finance** Members' dues. Other sources: FIBA; proceeds from competitions. **Activities** Events/meetings; training/education; sporting activities. **Events** *Congress and General Assembly / General Assembly* Antananarivo (Madagascar) 2014, *General Assembly* Egypt 2012. **Publications** *Spotnews* (12 a year); *Women's AfroBasket News*.
Members National federations (members of FIBA) in 54 countries:
Algeria, Angola, Benin, Botswana, Burkina Faso, Burundi, Cameroon, Cape Verde, Central African Rep, Chad, Comoros, Congo Brazzaville, Congo DR, Côte d'Ivoire, Djibouti, Egypt, Equatorial Guinea, Eritrea, Eswatini, Ethiopia, Gabon, Gambia, Ghana, Guinea, Guinea-Bissau, Kenya, Lesotho, Liberia, Libya, Madagascar, Malawi, Mali, Mauritania, Mauritius, Morocco, Mozambique, Namibia, Niger, Nigeria, Rwanda, Sao Tomé-Principe, Senegal, Seychelles, Sierra Leone, Somalia, South Africa, South Sudan, Sudan, Tanzania UR, Togo, Tunisia, Uganda, Zambia, Zimbabwe. [2019.12.11/XD3641/E]

♦ FIBA Americas 09745

Pres 3480 Main Highway, Miami FL 33133, USA. E-mail: info-americas@fiba.basketball.
Exec Dir address not obtained.
URL: https://www.fiba.basketball/americas

History 1975. Founded within the framework of *Fédération internationale de basketball (FIBA, #09614)*. Former names and other names: *Pan American Basketball Confederation* – former; *Confederación Panamericana de Baloncesto (COPABA)* – former. **Structure** General Assembly; Board; Executive. Committees (6): Finance; Competitions; Development; Youth Basketball; Medical; Club and League Competitions. Sub-zones (3): *International Basketball Federation – North American Zone (#12326)*; *Comisión de la Zona Centroamericana y del Caribe de la Confederación Panamericana de Basquetbol (CONCENCABA, #04146)*; *Confederación Sudamericana de Básquetbol (CONSUBASQUET, #04482)*. **Languages** English, Portuguese, Spanish.
Members National federations in 42 countries and territories:
Antigua-Barbuda, Argentina, Aruba, Bahamas, Barbados, Belize, Bolivia, Brazil, Canada, Cayman Is, Chile, Colombia, Costa Rica, Cuba, Dominica, Dominican Rep, Ecuador, El Salvador, Grenada, Guatemala, Guyana, Haiti, Honduras, Jamaica, Mexico, Montserrat, Nicaragua, Panama, Paraguay, Puerto Rico, St Kitts-Nevis, St Lucia, St Maarten, St Vincent-Grenadines, Suriname, Trinidad-Tobago, Turks-Caicos, Uruguay, USA, Venezuela, Virgin Is UK, Virgin Is USA.
NGO Relations Member of (1): *Asociación de Confederaciones Deportivas Panamericanas (ACODEPA, #02119)*. [2022/XD0177/E]

♦ FIBA-Asia 09746

Exec Dir Bourj Hamoud, 52 Aboud Street, Harboyan Trade Center – 3rd Floor, Beirut, Lebanon. T. +9611267888. Fax +9611267888. E-mail: info-asia@fiba.com.
Communications Coordinator address not obtained.
URL: http://www.fibaasia.net/

History Jan 1960, Manila (Philippines), *FIBA-Asia Basketball Confederation*, as a continental confederation of *Fédération internationale de basketball (FIBA, #09614)*. Original title: *Asian Basketball Confederation (ABC)*. Constitution amended: 1963; Nov 1969, Bangkok (Thailand); Nov 1971, Tokyo (Japan); 1983, Hong Kong; Jan 1986, Kuala Lumpur (Malaysia); 2014, Istanbul (Turkey). **Aims** Promote, develop and regulate *basketball* in Asia according to FIBA standards; elevate its standard and foster closer friendly relations among members; produce world-class players, quality coaches and competent, fair and honest referees. **Structure** Congress; Central Board; Permanent Committees (11); Sub-zones (6). **Languages** English. **Staff** Voluntary. **Finance** Members' dues. Other sources: contributions; income from TV and sponsorship rights. **Activities** Standards/guidelines; networking/liaising; sporting events. **Events** *Meeting* Seoul (Korea Rep) 1997, *Congress* Seoul (Korea Rep) 1995, *Election od office bearers* Bangkok (Thailand) 1987, *Meeting* Seoul (Korea Rep) 1986.
Members National basketball federations or associations (one per country), which are members of FIBA, in 44 countries and territories:
Afghanistan, Bahrain, Bangladesh, Bhutan, Brunei Darussalam, Cambodia, China, Hong Kong, India, Indonesia, Iran Islamic Rep, Iraq, Japan, Jordan, Kazakhstan, Korea DPR, Korea Rep, Kuwait, Kyrgyzstan, Laos, Lebanon, Macau, Malaysia, Maldives, Mongolia, Myanmar, Nepal, Oman, Pakistan, Palestine, Philippines, Qatar, Saudi Arabia, Singapore, Sri Lanka, Syrian AR, Taiwan, Tajikistan, Thailand, Turkmenistan, United Arab Emirates, Uzbekistan, Vietnam, Yemen. [2016.10.20/XD3876/E]

- ♦ FIBA-Asia Basketball Confederation / see FIBA-Asia (#09746)

♦ FIBA-Europe 09747

Exec Dir Ismaningerstr 21, 81675 Munich, Germany. T. +49897806080. Fax +498978060859. E-mail: info@fibaeurope.com – info-europe@fiba.com.
URL: http://www.fibaeurope.com/

History Founded 1957, with the title *Standing Conference of Delegates of the National Basketball Federations of Europe – Conférence permanente des délégués des fédérations nationales de basketball de l'Europe*, as a permanent commission of *Fédération internationale de basketball (FIBA, #09614)*. Changed to *Standing Conference of National Basketball Federations of Europe – Conférence permanente des fédérations nationales de basketball de l'Europe*, 1991. Present name adopted 2002. **Aims** Promote, supervise and direct basketball in Europe. **Structure** General Assembly (annual); Board; Executive Committee; Permanent Commissions (8). **Languages** English. **Staff** 35.00 FTE, paid. **Activities** Events/meetings; sporting activities. **Events** *Annual General Assembly* Munich (Germany) 2014, *Annual General Assembly* Newport (UK) 2013, *Annual General Assembly* Ljubljana (Slovenia) 2012, *Meeting* Stockholm (Sweden) 2012, *Annual General Assembly* Sintra (Portugal) 2011.
Members National federations (members of FIBA) in 50 countries and territories:
Albania, Andorra, Armenia, Austria, Azerbaijan, Belarus, Belgium, Bosnia-Herzegovina, Bulgaria, Croatia, Cyprus, Czechia, Denmark, Estonia, Finland, France, Georgia, Germany, Gibraltar, Great Britain, Greece, Hungary, Iceland, Ireland, Israel, Italy, Kosovo, Latvia, Lithuania, Luxembourg, Malta, Moldova, Monaco, Montenegro, Netherlands, North Macedonia, Norway, Poland, Portugal, Romania, Russia, San Marino, Serbia, Slovakia, Slovenia, Spain, Sweden, Switzerland, Türkiye, Ukraine.
NGO Relations Member of: *Association of European Team Sports (ETS, #02546)*. [2019/XE0273/E]

- ♦ FIBA – Federación Internacional de Béisbol Amateur (inactive)
- ♦ **FIBA** Fédération internationale de basketball (#09614)
- ♦ FIBAFIN – Federación Iberoamericana de Asociaciones Financieras (no recent information)
- ♦ FIBA – Florida International Bankers' Association (internationally oriented national body)
- ♦ FIBA – Fondation internationale du Banc d'Arguin (internationally oriented national body)

♦ FIBA Oceania 09748

Regional Dir Ste 1801, Level 8, Tower 1, 56 Scarborough Street, Southport QLD 4215, Australia. T. +61756682570. E-mail: info-oceania@fiba.com.
URL: http://www.fibaoceania.com/

History 1968, as *Oceania Basketball Confederation (OBC)*, when recognized as a self-governing continental zone of *Fédération internationale de basketball (FIBA, #09614)*, following suggestion, 1967, of Al Ramsay. **Aims** Represent members' interests within FIBA; develop all aspects of basketball in the region and ensure that it is conducted according to FIBA rules and regulations; conduct qualification tournaments on behalf of FIBA for men's and women's world championships and for the Olympic Games; conduct regional and sub-regional competitions. **Structure** Congress (every 4 years, at a regional tournament). Executive (Management Committee), comprising President, Secretary-General and 5 members. Administrative Headquarters at Toormina (Australia). **Languages** English. **Staff** 3.00 FTE, paid. 6 national basketball development officers in 6 Pacific Island nations, paid (salaries subsidized by FIBA Oceania). **Finance** Members' dues. Other sources: grants from FIBA; Australian Department of Foreign Affairs; Oceania National Olympic Committee; National Olympic Confederations; sponsorships. **Activities** Organizes: FIBA Oceania Youth Tournament; All Star Tour; Oceania Championship; Coaches Study Tour; Coaching, Refereeing, Score Table, Statistics and Administration Courses. **Events** *Congress* Port Moresby (Papua New Guinea) 1991, *Meeting* Polynesia Fr 1989. **Publications** *Oceania Bulletin* (4 a year).
Members National federations (members of FIBA) in 21 countries and territories:
Australia, Cook Is, Fiji, Guam, Kiribati, Marshall Is, Micronesia FS, Nauru, New Caledonia, New Zealand, Norfolk Is, Northern Mariana Is, Palau, Papua New Guinea, Samoa, Samoa USA, Solomon Is, Tahiti Is, Tonga, Tuvalu, Vanuatu.
NGO Relations Member of: *Organisation of Sports Federations of Oceania (OSFO, #17828)*. [2017/XD0841/E]

- ♦ **FIBE** Federación Iberoamericana de Tenis de Mesa (#09322)
- ♦ **FIBEP** Fédération internationale des bureaux d'extraits de presse (#09617)
- ♦ Fiber Broadband Association (internationally oriented national body)

♦ Fiber Connect Council MENA 09749

Director General Creative City Media Free Zone, 4442, Fujairah, United Arab Emirates. E-mail: info@fiberconnectmena.org.
URL: https://fiberconnectmena.org/index.php/en/

History 2011. Founded by member companies (MOSECO, Draka, CISCO, Alcatel-Lucent, MEFC) as sister organization of: *Fibre-to-the-Home Council Europe (FTTH Council Europe, #09751)*. Former names and other names: *FTTH Council Middle East and North Africa* – former. Registration: Fujairah Culture and Media Authority, No/ID: 13260/2018, United Arab Emirates, Fujairah. **Aims** Accelerate Fiber to the Home (FTTH) adoption in Middle East and North Africa through information sharing and promotion in order to enhance the quality of life; contribute to a better environment and increased competitiveness. **Structure** Board; Committees. **Languages** Arabic, English. **Activities** Events/meetings; knowledge management/information dissemination. **Events** *Annual Conference* Cairo (Egypt) 2019, *Annual Conference* Beirut (Lebanon) 2018, *Annual Conference* Tunis (Tunisia) 2017, *Annual Conference* Kuwait (Kuwait) 2016, *Annual Conference* Muscat (Oman) 2015. **NGO Relations** . [2021.09.01/XJ2720/E]

- ♦ **FIB** Federation of International Bandy (#09601)
- ♦ **FIB** Fédération internationale du béton (#09615)
- ♦ **FIB** Fédération internationale de boules (#09616)
- ♦ **FIB** ICC Financial Investigation Bureau (#11046)
- ♦ FIBIP – Federazione Internazionale dei Centri ed Istituti di Bioetica di Ispirazione Personalista (unconfirmed)
- ♦ **FiBL** Forschungsinstitut für biologischen Landbau (#18857)
- ♦ FIBRAL – Fibral Material Alliance (unconfirmed)
- ♦ Fibral Material Alliance (unconfirmed)
- ♦ Fibre Channel Industry Association (internationally oriented national body)
- ♦ Fibre Channel Industry Association Europe (inactive)
- ♦ Fibre to the Home Council Americas / see Fiber Broadband Association

♦ Fibre-to-the-Home Council Asia-Pacific (FTTH Council Asia-Pacific) 09750

Address not obtained.
URL: http://www.ftthcouncilap.org/

History 2005, following sister organizations in US and Europe – *Fibre-to-the-Home Council Europe (FTTH Council Europe, #09751)*. **Aims** Educate the industry and the general public on the opportunities and benefits of FTTH solutions. **Structure** Board of Directors, comprising President, Vice-President, Secretary, Treasurer and 3 members. Working Committees (5). **Activities** Working Committees (5): Technologies and Architecture; Market Development; Membership; Planning Communications and Events; Regional and Government Relations. **Events** *Annual Conference* Delhi (India) 2017, *Annual Conference* Bangkok (Thailand) 2016, *Annual Conference* Jakarta (Indonesia) 2015, *Annual Conference* Penang (Malaysia) 2014, *General Meeting* Manila (Philippines) 2013. **NGO Relations** *Digital Council Africa*. [2016/XM2998/E]

♦ Fibre-to-the-Home Council Europe (FTTH Council Europe) 09751

Dir Gen Rue de la Presse 4, 1000 Brussels, Belgium. T. +32460974697. E-mail: info@ftthcouncil.eu.
URL: http://www.ftthcouncil.eu/

History 24 Mar 2004, Brussels (Belgium). Registration: No/ID: 0867.660.545, Start date: 6 Oct 2004, Belgium; EU Transparency Register, No/ID: 09838612482-61, Start date: 9 Oct 2009. **Aims** Accelerate availability of fibre-based, *broadband* access networks to consumers and businesses. **Structure** General Assembly; Board; Committees (5). **Languages** English. **Staff** 5.00 FTE, paid. **Finance** Members' dues. **Activities** Knowledge management/information dissemination; politics/policy/regulatory; events/meetings. **Events** *Annual Conference* Berlin (Germany) 2020, *Annual Conference* Amsterdam (Netherlands) 2019, *Annual Conference* Valencia (Spain) 2018, *Annual Conference* Marseille (France) 2017, *Annual Conference* Luxembourg (Luxembourg) 2016. **Publications** Handbook; guides.
Members Companies in 27 countries:
Austria, Belgium, Canada, China, Czechia, Denmark, Finland, France, Germany, Greece, India, Israel, Italy, Japan, Luxembourg, Netherlands, Norway, Poland, Portugal, Slovenia, Spain, Sweden, Switzerland, Taiwan, Türkiye, UK, USA.
IGO Relations *European Commission (EC, #06633)*. **NGO Relations** Sister organizations: Fibre Broadband Association and its LATAM chapter; *Fibre-to-the-Home Council Asia-Pacific (FTTH Council Asia-Pacific, #09750)*; *Digital Council Africa*; *Fiber Connect Council MENA (#09749)*. [2020/XJ3279/E]

- ♦ **FIBR** Fédération internationale de basketball en fauteuil roulant (#15882)
- ♦ FIBT – Fédération internationale des banques de terminologie (inactive)
- ♦ FIBT / see International Bobsleigh and Skeleton Federation (#12375)
- ♦ FIBV / see World Federation of Exchanges (#21434)
- ♦ FIC / see International Cardijn Association
- ♦ FICAB / see World Anti-Bullying Forum (#21094)
- ♦ FICAC – Fédération internationale des coloniaux et anciens coloniaux (inactive)
- ♦ FICAC / see World Federation of Consuls (#21422)
- ♦ **FICAC** World Federation of Consuls (#21422)
- ♦ FICA – Federation of International Cricketers Associations (internationally oriented national body)
- ♦ FICA – Flemish International Cooperation Agency (internationally oriented national body)
- ♦ **FICA** Forum for International Conciliation and Arbitration (#09920)
- ♦ FICAH / see Making Change
- ♦ FICA / see International Cooperative and Mutual Insurance Federation (#12948)
- ♦ FICASUR – Federación de la Industria y Comercio de Agroquimicos del Cono Sur (no recent information)
- ♦ FICAT / see Federative International Programme for Anatomical Terminology (#09716)
- ♦ **FICB** Fédération Internationale des Confréries Bachiques (#09623)
- ♦ FICCC / see Fédération internationale des clubs de motorhomes (#09621)
- ♦ FICC – Federación Interamericana de Camaras de la Construcción (inactive)
- ♦ FICC / see Fédération Internationale de Camping, Caravanning et Autocaravaning (#09618)
- ♦ **FICC** Fédération Internationale de Camping, Caravanning et Autocaravaning (#09618)
- ♦ **FICC** Fédération Internationale de Chimie Clinique (#13392)
- ♦ **FICC** Fédération internationale des ciné-clubs (#13430)
- ♦ **FICC** Federazione Internazionale Campeggio, Caravanning e Autocaravaning (#09618)

- ♦ FICCIA / see European Federation of Managerial Staff in the Chemical and Allied Industries (#07160)
- ♦ FICCIA/FECCIA / see European Federation of Managerial Staff in the Chemical and Allied Industries (#07160)
- ♦ FICC / see International Federation of Clinical Chemistry and Laboratory Medicine (#13392)
- ♦ FIC – Congregatio Fratrum Immaculatae Conceptionis Beatae Mariae Virginis (religious order)
- ♦ **FICDC** Fédération internationale des coalitions pour la diversité culturelle (#13394)
- ♦ FICEC – Fédération internationale des cadres des établissements de crédit et institutions financières (unconfirmed)
- ♦ **FICEDL** Fédération internationale des centres l'étude et de documentation libertaires (#09619)
- ♦ FICE – Fédération d'initiatives chrétiennes pour l'Europe (inactive)
- ♦ FICE / see Fédération internationale des communautés éducatives (#09622)
- ♦ **FICE-International** Fédération internationale des communautés éducatives (#09622)
- ♦ FICEM-APCAC / see Federación Interamericana del Cemento (#09330)
- ♦ **FICEMEA** Fédération internationale des centres d'entraînement aux méthodes d'éducation active (#13572)
- ♦ **FICEM** Federación Interamericana del Cemento (#09330)
- ♦ **FICEM** Inter-American Cement Federation (#09330)
- ♦ FICEPA – Federación Técnica Iberoamericana de la Celulosa y el Papel (no recent information)
- ♦ **FICEP** Fédération internationale catholique d'éducation physique et sportive (#12456)
- ♦ FIC EUROPE – Federation of the Condiment Sauce Industries, Mustard and Fruit and Vegetables Prepared in Oil and Vinegar of the European Union (inactive)
- ♦ **FIC** Fédération internationale de canoë (#12437)
- ♦ **FIC** Federazione Internazionale Cronometristi (#09717)
- ♦ FIC – Feinstein International Center (internationally oriented national body)
- ♦ **FICF** Fédération internationale culturelle féminine (#09625)
- ♦ FIC – Foundation for Intentional Community (internationally oriented national body)
- ♦ FIC – Freedom in Christ (internationally oriented national body)
- ♦ **FIC** Fundación InterAmericana del Corazón (#11432)
- ♦ **FICHL** Forum for International Criminal and Humanitarian Law (#09921)
- ♦ FICICA – Fédération internationale du personnel d'encadrement des industries et commerces agricoles et alimentaires (inactive)
- ♦ FICIC – Fédération internationale du commerce et des industries du camping (inactive)
- ♦ FIC / see InterAmerican Heart Foundation (#11432)
- ♦ FICJF – Fédération internationale des conseils juridiques et fiscaux (inactive)
- ♦ FIC – John E Fogarty International Center (internationally oriented national body)
- ♦ FICME – Fédération internationale des cadres des mines et de l'energie (no recent information)
- ♦ **FICM** Fédération internationale des clubs de motorhomes (#09621)
- ♦ FICM / see Fédération Internationale de Motocyclisme (#09643)
- ♦ FICO – Forum international de la course océanique (no recent information)
- ♦ FICOM-J – Fédération internationale catholique des organismes missionnaires de jeunes (inactive)
- ♦ **FICOMUNDYT** Federación Iberoamericana del Consejo Mundial del Niño Dotado y Talentoso (#11023)
- ♦ FICOSSER – Federation for International Cooperation of Health Services and Systems Research Centers (no recent information)
- ♦ FICP – Fédération internationale des clubs de publicité (inactive)
- ♦ **FICPI** Fédération Internationale des Conseils en Propriété Intellectuelle (#09624)
- ♦ FICP – Institutum Fratrum Instructionis Christianae de Ploërmel (religious order)
- ♦ **FICPM** Fédération internationale des centres de préparation au mariage (#13475)
- ♦ **FICSA** Federation of International Civil Servants' Associations (#09603)
- ♦ FICSAS – Federation of Institutions Concerned with the Study of the Adriatic Sea (inactive)
- ♦ FICS – Fédération internationale des chasseurs de son (inactive)
- ♦ **FICS** Fédération Internationale de Chiropratique du Sport (#09620)
- ♦ **FICT** Fédération internationale des cadres des transports (#07730)
- ♦ FICT – Fédération internationale de centres touristiques (inactive)
- ♦ **FICTS** Fédération internationale du cinéma et de la télévision sportifs (#15588)
- ♦ **FICTS** International Sporting Cinema and Television Federation (#15588)
- ♦ FICUMA – Fédération internationale des communautés utilisatrices de matériel agricole (inactive)
- ♦ **FICVI** Federación Iberoamericana de Asociaciones de Victimas contra la Violencia Vial (#09307)
- ♦ FIDA / see Development Training International
- ♦ **FIDACA** Fédération internationale des associations catholiques d'aveugles (#13377)
- ♦ FIDAC – Fédération interalliée des anciens combattants (inactive)
- ♦ **FIDAC** Fondos Internacionales de Indemnización de Daños Debidos a la Contaminación por Hidrocarburos (#14402)
- ♦ FIDAC / see The World Veterans Federation (#21900)
- ♦ **FIDA** Federación Internacional de Abogadas (#13578)
- ♦ **FIDA** Fédération internationale de la Diaspora Afar (#09626)
- ♦ **FIDA** Fédération Internationale Des Femmes Juristes (#13578)
- ♦ FIDAF – Federación Internacional de Acción Familiar (inactive)
- ♦ **FIDAF** Federation of International Dance Festivals (#09604)
- ♦ FIDAF – Fédération internationale d'action familiale (inactive)
- ♦ FIDAF / see International Federation of Hardware and Housewares Associations (#13437)
- ♦ **FIDA** Fondo Internacional de Desarrollo Agricola (#13692)
- ♦ **FIDA** Fonds international de développement agricole (#13692)
- ♦ FIDAGH / see Federación Interamericana de Asociaciones de Gestión Humana (#09329)
- ♦ **FIDAGH** Federación Interamericana de Asociaciones de Gestión Humana (#09329)
- ♦ Fida International (internationally oriented national body)
- ♦ **FIDA** International Federation of Women Lawyers (#13578)
- ♦ **FIDALMAR** Federación Internacional de Ligas y Asociaciones Maritimas y Navales (#13474)
- ♦ **FIDAMERICA** Network of IFAD Supported Projects in Latin America and the Caribbean (#17035)
- ♦ FIDAP / see Federación Interamericana de Asociaciones de Gestión Humana (#09329)
- ♦ FIDAQ / see International Federation of Hardware and Housewares Associations (#13437)
- ♦ FIDCA – Fédération internationale des cadres de l'agriculture (inactive)
- ♦ FIDEA – Federación Interamericana de Educación de Adultos (inactive)
- ♦ FIDEC – Fighting Infectious Diseases in Emerging Countries (internationally oriented national body)
- ♦ **FIDE** Federación Iberoamericana de Mujeres Empresarias (#09316)
- ♦ **FIDE** Fédération de l'industrie dentaire en Europe (#09595)
- ♦ FIDE – Federation for Innovation in Democracy Europe (unconfirmed)
- ♦ **FIDE** Fédération internationale pour le droit européen (#13419)
- ♦ **FIDE** Fédération internationale des échecs (#09627)
- ♦ **FIDEF** Fédération internationale des experts-comptables francophones (#09630)
- ♦ FIDEGEP – Fédération interalliée des évadés de guerre et des passeurs (inactive)
- ♦ **FIDEG** Fundación Internacional para el Desafio Económico y Global (#10029)
- ♦ FIDE / see Latin Evangelical Alliance (#16397)
- ♦ Fidèles Compagnes de Jésus (religious order)
- ♦ FIDELF – Fédération internationale des écrivains de langue française (no recent information)
- ♦ **FIDEM** Fédération internationale des instituts d'études médiévales (#09639)
- ♦ **FIDEM** Fédération Internationale de la Médaille d'Art (#11675)
- ♦ **FIDEN** Fédération internationale des entreprises de nettoyage (#09628)
- ♦ FIDEP – Fédération internationale pour le développement participatif (inactive)
- ♦ FIDEPS – Fonds international pour le développement de l'éducation physique et du sport (no recent information)
- ♦ Fiderationen af Telekommunikations Ingeniirer i det Europaeiske Faellesskab (#09597)
- ♦ **FIDESCO** Fondation internationale pour le développement au service des coopérants et de communautés de base (#09821)
- ♦ **FIDES** Federación Interamericana de Empresas de Seguros (#09331)
- ♦ FIDES – Fondation internationale pour le développement économique et social (internationally oriented national body)
- ♦ **FID** Federación Internacional de Diabetes (#13164)
- ♦ **FID** Federation of International Danube Symposia on Diabetes Mellitus – Central European Diabetes Association (#09605)
- ♦ **FID** Fédération internationale du diabète (#13164)
- ♦ FIDH-AE – Association Européenne pour la défense des Droits de l'Homme (no recent information)
- ♦ **fidh** Fédération Internationale pour les Droits Humains (#13452)
- ♦ FIDH / see International Federation for Human Rights (#13452)
- ♦ FIDIAM – Fondation internationale pour l'état de droit et l'indépendance des avocats et des magistrats (internationally oriented national body)
- ♦ **FIDIC** Fédération internationale des ingénieurs-conseils (#13399)

♦ FIDIC Group of African Member Associations (GAMA) 09752

Secretariat c/o ACEK-KENYA, PO Box 72643, City Square, Nairobi, Kenya. T. +254202249085.
URL: http://regions.fidic.ch/gama/

History 1994, as a regional grouping of *International Federation of Consulting Engineers (#13399)*. **Aims** Provide a forum for free exchange of information between FIDIC member associations in the African region; foster the *profession* of independent *consulting engineering* and of national associations of such engineers in the African continent. **Structure** Executive Committee. **Languages** English. **Staff** 3.00 FTE, paid. **Finance** Members' dues. Conferences. **Activities** Events/meetings; training/education; networking/liaising. **Events** *Annual Meeting* Maputo (Mozambique) 2014, *Annual meeting* Tunis (Tunisia) 2008, *Annual meeting* Gaborone (Botswana) 2007, *Annual meeting* Bagamoyo (Tanzania UR) 2006, *Annual meeting* Kampala (Uganda) 2005.
Members National associations of independent consulting engineers, members of FIDIC, in 16 African countries:
Botswana, Egypt, Ghana, Kenya, Malawi, Mali, Morocco, Mozambique, Nigeria, South Africa, Sudan, Tanzania UR, Tunisia, Uganda, Zambia, Zimbabwe. [2017.08.03/XE3117/**E**]

- ♦ FIDI / see FIDI Global Alliance (#09753)

♦ FIDI Global Alliance 09753

Gen Manager Fountain Plaza Bldg 501, 1st Floor, Belgicastraat 1, 1930 Zaventem, Belgium. T. +3224265160. E-mail: fidi@fidi.org.
URL: http://www.fidi.org/

History 16 Jul 1950, Estavayer-le-Lac (Switzerland). Former names and other names: *International Federation of International Furniture Removers* – former; *Fédération internationale des déménageurs internationaux (FIDI)* – former; *Internationale Föderation Internationaler Möbelspediteure* – former; *FIDI Global Alliance* – legal name (2007). Registration: Banque-Carrefour des Entreprises, No/ID: 0428.774.246, Start date: 16 Apr 1986, Belgium. **Aims** Represent the interests of companies specializing in international removals and *relocation*. **Structure** General Assembly (annual, at Conférence); Board of Directors; Delegates Meeting. **Languages** English. **Staff** 13.00 FTE, paid. **Finance** Sources: meeting proceeds; members' dues; revenue from activities/projects; sale of publications. **Activities** Certification/accreditation; events/meetings; research/documentation; training/education. **Events** *Annual Congress and General Assembly* Bangkok (Thailand) 2023, *Annual Congress and General Assembly* Cannes (France) 2022, *Annual Congress and General Assembly* Osaka (Japan) 2021, *Annual Congress and General Assembly* Osaka (Japan) 2020, *Essentials in International Moving Seminar* Seoul (Korea Rep) 2019. **Publications** *FIDI Focus Magazine*; *FIDI Newsletter*. Import and export customs guides.
Members Full national and regional moving associations (25); Affiliates moving company members of national associations. Affiliates (610) in 100 countries and territories:
Algeria, Argentina, Australia, Austria, Azerbaijan, Bahrain, Bangladesh, Belgium, Bolivia, Botswana, Brazil, Bulgaria, Canada, Chile, China, Colombia, Costa Rica, Côte d'Ivoire, Curaçao, Cyprus, Czechia, Denmark, Dominican Rep, Ecuador, Egypt, El Salvador, Estonia, Ethiopia, Finland, France, Germany, Ghana, Greece, Guatemala, Honduras, Hong Kong, Hungary, India, Indonesia, Ireland, Israel, Italy, Jamaica, Japan, Jordan, Kazakhstan, Kenya, Korea Rep, Kuwait, Lebanon, Luxembourg, Madagascar, Malawi, Malaysia, Mexico, Morocco, Mozambique, Namibia, Netherlands, New Zealand, Nigeria, Norway, Oman, Pakistan, Panama, Paraguay, Peru, Philippines, Poland, Portugal, Puerto Rico, Qatar, Romania, Russia, Saudi Arabia, Senegal, Serbia, Singapore, Slovakia, Slovenia, South Africa, Spain, St Maarten, Switzerland, Syrian AR, Taiwan, Thailand, Trinidad-Tobago, Tunisia, Türkiye, Uganda, UK, United Arab Emirates, Uruguay, USA, Venezuela, Vietnam, Virgin Is USA, Zambia, Zimbabwe.
Consultative Status Consultative status granted from: *ECOSOC (#05331)* (Ros A). **NGO Relations** Member of (1): *Federation of European and International Associations Established in Belgium (FAIB, #09508)*.
[2022.11.30/XB0947/**B**]

- ♦ FIDIIDS – Federación Internacional de Doctores Ingenieros y de Ingenieros Doctores-ès-Scientiae (inactive)
- ♦ FID – International Federation for Information and Documentation (inactive)
- ♦ **FIDM** Forum Internazionale delle Donne del Mediterraneo (#14143)
- ♦ **FID NANE** Organisation régionale pour les pays d'Afrique du Nord et du Proche-Orient (#17824)
- ♦ FIDO Alliance (unconfirmed)
- ♦ FIDR – Foundation for International Development / Relief (internationally oriented national body)
- ♦ FIDSSA – Federation of Infectious Diseases Societies of Southern Africa (internationally oriented national body)
- ♦ **FIEA** Fédération internationale des experts en automobile (#13368)
- ♦ **FIEALC** Federación Internacional de Estudios sobre América Latina y el Caribe (#09338)
- ♦ **FIEC** Fédération de l'industrie européenne de la construction (#06766)
- ♦ **FIEC** Fédération internationale des associations d'études classiques (#09607)
- ♦ FIED – Fédération internationale des étudiants en droit (inactive)
- ♦ FIEEA – Fédération internationale pour les échanges éducatifs d'enfants et d'adolescents (no recent information)
- ♦ **FIEEL** Fédération internationale des Eglises évangéliques libres (#13433)
- ♦ FIEESA – Fédération internationale des électriciens, électroniciens et spécialistes de l'automobile (inactive)
- ♦ **FIE** Fédération internationale d'escrime (#09629)
- ♦ FIEF – Fédération internationale de football féminin (inactive)
- ♦ FIEF – Forum international pour l'exploitation forestière (internationally oriented national body)
- ♦ FIEF / see International Federation for Home Economics (#13447)
- ♦ Field Science Office for South Asia / see UNESCO Asia-Pacific Regional Bureau for Communication and Information (#20300)
- ♦ Field Service Staff Union / see United Nations Field Staff Union (#20561)
- ♦ Fields of Life Trust (internationally oriented national body)
- ♦ Field Studies Council Overseas (internationally oriented national body)
- ♦ Fieles Siervas de Jesús (religious order)
- ♦ FIEL – Fundación de Investigaciones Económicas Latinoamericanas (internationally oriented national body)
- ♦ FIEM / see European Federation of Managers in the Steel Industry (#07162)
- ♦ FIEM / see International Federation for Home Economics (#13447)
- ♦ **FIEP** Federación Internacional de Epidemiologia Psiquiatrica (#13521)
- ♦ **FIEP** Fédération internationale pour l'éducation des parents (#13499)
- ♦ **FIEP** Fédération internationale d'épidémiologie psychiatrique (#13521)
- ♦ FIEP / see International Federation of Physical and Sport Education (#13510)
- ♦ **FIEPS** Fédération internationale d'éducation physique et sportive (#13510)
- ♦ **FIER** Fédération internationale des enseignants de rythmique (#13418)
- ♦ FIERI – Forum Internazionale ed Europeo di Ricerche sull' Immigrazione (internationally oriented national body)
- ♦ FIET – Fédération internationale des employés, techniciens et cadres (inactive)
- ♦ **FIFA** Fédération Internationale de Football Association (#13360)
- ♦ **FIFARMA** Federación Latinoamericana de la Industria Farmacéutica (#16328)
- ♦ FI – Farms International (internationally oriented national body)

- ♦ **FIFCC** Fédération Internationale Francophone de Coelio-Chirurgie (#09634)
- ♦ **FIFCJ** Fédération internationale des femmes des carrières juridiques – magistrats, avocats, avoués, notaires, professeurs de droit ou exerçant une autre carrière juridique (#13579)
- ♦ FIFCO – Fédération Internationale de Football Corporatif (unconfirmed)
- ♦ FIFDS – Football International Federation for Players with Down syndrome (unconfirmed)
- ♦ FIFDU / see Graduate Women International (#10688)
- ♦ FIFE – Fédération internationale des associations de fabricants de produits d'entretien (inactive)
- ♦ **FIFe** Fédération internationale féline (#09632)
- ♦ FIF – Fédération internationale de la filterie (inactive)
- ♦ FIfF – Forum Informatikerinnnen für Frieden und Gesellschaftliche Verantwortung (internationally oriented national body)
- ♦ **FIFG** Federation for International FootGolf (#09672)
- ♦ **FI** Fireball International (#09777)
- ♦ FIFMAS – Fonds international pour la fabrication de matériel d'animation sportive (see: #04634)
- ♦ **FIFM** Forum international des femmes de la méditerranée (#14143)
- ♦ FIFP – Fédération internationale francophone de psychiatrie (internationally oriented national body)
- ♦ **FIFPRO** Fédération internationale des footballeurs professionnels (#09633)
- ♦ FIFPSS – Forum international francophone de pédagogie des sciences de la santé (meeting series)
- ♦ **FI** Franciscans International (#09982)
- ♦ **FIFS** Federation International Football Skating (#09671)
- ♦ FIFSP – Federación Internacional de los Funcionarios Superiores de Policia (no recent information)
- ♦ FIFSP – Fédération internationale des fonctionnaires supérieurs de police (no recent information)
- ♦ **FIFSTA** Federation of Institutes of Food Science and Technology of ASEAN (#09598)
- ♦ Fifth Protocol to the General Agreement on Privileges and Immunities of the Council of Europe (1990 treaty)

♦ Fifty-One International (FOI) 09754

SG 16/5 Bd Paepsemlaan, 1070 Brussels, Belgium. T. +3224529770. E-mail: info@fifty-one-international.org.
URL: http://www.fifty-one-international.org/

History Founded by former members of: *Round Table International (RTI, #18982)*. Registration: Banque-Carrefour des Entreprises, Belgium. **Aims** Promote friendship, esteem and tolerance; encourage and develop mutual understanding. **Languages** Dutch, English, French, German. **Events** *Congres and General Assembly* Enghien (Belgium) 2021, *Congress and general assembly* Ghent (Belgium) 2010, *Congress* Namur (Belgium) 2005, *Congress* Thiméon (Belgium) 2004. [2022.02.16/XE4419/**E**]

- ♦ FIFUSA – Federación Internacional de Fútbol de Salón (inactive)
- ♦ **FIFyA** International Federation of Fe y Alegria (#13425)
- ♦ FIGE – Fédération de l'industrie granitière européenne (inactive)
- ♦ **FIG** Federación Iberoamericana de Go (#09311)
- ♦ **FIG** Federación Internacional de Guardaparques (#14697)
- ♦ **FIG** Fédération internationale des géomètres (#13561)
- ♦ **FIG** Fédération internationale de gymnastique (#09636)
- ♦ **FIG** Fonds international de garantie (#13761)
- ♦ Fight Against Desert Encroachment (internationally oriented national body)

♦ Fight the Fakes 09755

Secretariat c/o IFPMA, Chemin des Mines 9, PO Box 195, 1211 Geneva 20, Switzerland. E-mail: info@fightthefakes.org.
URL: http://fightthefakes.org/

Aims Raise awareness about the dangers of fake medicines. **Structure** Secretariat. **Activities** Awereness raising; advocacy/lobbying/activism.
Members Partners include:
Active Citizenship Network (ACN); Alliance for Safe Online Pharmacy – EU (ASOP EU, #00720); Global Pharma Health Fund (GPHF); Groupement International de la Répartition Pharmaceutique (GIRP, #10762); Institute of Research Against Counterfeit Medicines (IRACM); International Association for Medical Assistance to Travellers (IAMAT); International Council of Nurses (ICN, #13054); International Federation of Pharmaceutical Manufacturers and Associations (IFPMA, #13505); International Federation of Pharmaceutical Wholesalers (IFPW, #13506); International Pharmaceutical Federation (#14566); International Pharmaceutical Students' Federation (IPSF, #14568); Malaria Consortium; Medicines for Europe (#16633); Medicines for Malaria Venture (MMV, #16634); Pharmaceutical Security Institute (PSI, #18355); Roll Back Malaria Partnership (RBM, #18968); The NCD Alliance (NCDA, #16963); World Heart Federation (WHF, #21562); World Medical Association (WMA, #21646). [2016/XM5027/y/**F**]

- ♦ Fighting Infectious Diseases in Emerging Countries (internationally oriented national body)
- ♦ Fight for Peace (internationally oriented national body)
- ♦ **FIGIEFA** Fédération internationale des grossistes importateurs et exportateurs en fournitures automobiles (#09635)
- ♦ **FIGIJ** Fédération internationale de gynécologie infantile et juvénile (#09637)
- ♦ **FIG** International Federation of Surveyors (#13561)
- ♦ Figli della Beata Vergine Immacolata di Francia (religious order)
- ♦ Figli della Carità (religious order)
- ♦ Figli della Carità – Canossiani (religious order)
- ♦ Figlie del Buon Salvatore (religious order)
- ♦ Figlie della Carità Canossiane (religious order)
- ♦ Figlie della Carità del Sacro Cuore di Gesù (religious order)
- ♦ Figlie della Chiesa (religious order)
- ♦ Figlie della Croce (religious order)
- ♦ Figlie della Croce – Suore di Santa Andrea (religious order)
- ♦ Figlie della Divina Carità (religious order)
- ♦ Figlie della Divina Provvidenza di Créhen (religious order)
- ♦ Figlie di Gesù, Salamanca (religious order)
- ♦ Figlie di Maria (religious order)
- ♦ Figlie di Maria Ausiliatrice (religious order)
- ♦ Figlie di Maria e di Giuseppe (religious order)
- ♦ Figlie di Maria Immacolata (religious order)
- ♦ Figlie di Maria Santissima dell'Orto (religious order)
- ♦ Figlie della Natività di Maria (religious order)
- ♦ Figlie di Nostra Signora della Misericordia (religious order)
- ♦ Figlie di Nostra Signora al Monte Calvario (religious order)
- ♦ Figlie di Nostra Signora del Rifugio in Monte Calvario (religious order)
- ♦ Figlie di Nostra Signora del Sacro Cuore (religious order)
- ♦ Figlie della Provvidenza di Saint-Brieuc (religious order)
- ♦ Figlie dei Sacri Cuori – Suore Maestre di Santa Dorotea, Figlie dei Sacri Cuori (religious order)
- ♦ Figlie di San Giuseppe (religious order)
- ♦ Figlie di San Paolo – Pia Società delle Figlie di Santo Paolo (religious order)
- ♦ Figlie di Santa Anna (religious order)
- ♦ Figlie di Santa Maria della Divina Provvidenza (religious order)
- ♦ Figlie di Santa Maria della Presentazione (religious order)
- ♦ Figlie della Sapienza (religious order)
- ♦ Figli dell'Immacolata Concezione (religious order)
- ♦ Figli della Madre di Dio Addolorata (religious order)
- ♦ Figli di Maria Immacolata – Pavoniani (religious order)
- ♦ FIGL / see International Federation of Physical and Sport Education (#13510)
- ♦ Figli della Sacra Famiglia (religious order)
- ♦ Figli di Santa Maria Immacolata (religious order)
- ♦ **FIGO** Fédération Internationale de Gynécologie et d'Obstétrique (#09638)
- ♦ FIGT – Families in Global Transition (internationally oriented national body)
- ♦ FIHAC / see UNUM OMNES International Council of Catholic Men (#20720)
- ♦ **FIHCA** Fédération Internationale des Hôtesses et Convoyeuses de l'Air (#13347)
- ♦ **FIHC** Fédération internationale des hommes catholiques (#20720)
- ♦ FIHC / see International Weightlifting Federation (#15876)
- ♦ FIH – Fédération internationale de l'harmonica (inactive)
- ♦ **FIH** Fédération internationale de hockey (#13802)
- ♦ FIH / see International Hospital Federation (#13812)
- ♦ FIH / see International Weightlifting Federation (#15876)
- ♦ FIHMPS – Fédération internationale d'hygiène, de médecine préventive et sociale (inactive)
- ♦ **FIHP** Federación Iberoamericana del Hormigón Premezclado (#09312)
- ♦ **FIHP** Fédération internationale pour l'histoire publique (#13524)
- ♦ **FIHUAT** Fédération internationale pour l'habitation, l'urbanisme et l'aménagement des territoires (#13450)
- ♦ FIIA – Finnish Institute of International Affairs (internationally oriented national body)
- ♦ FIIAP / see Fundación Internacional y para Iberoamérica de Administración y Politicas Públicas (#10030)
- ♦ **FIIAPP** Fundación Internacional y para Iberoamérica de Administración y Politicas Públicas (#10030)
- ♦ **FIIB** Foro Internacional Indigena por la Biodiversidad (#13837)
- ♦ **FIIC** Federación Interamericana de la Industria de la Construcción (#09333)
- ♦ **FIIC** Fédération internationale d'inter-crosse (#09640)
- ♦ FIICYT – Fondo Iberoamericano de Integración Cientifica y Tecnológica (unconfirmed)
- ♦ FIIDOT – Fédération internationale pour l'information sur le don d'organes et de tissus humains (inactive)
- ♦ FIIEE – Federación Internacional de Instituciones para la Enseñanza del Español (inactive)
- ♦ **FIIEL** El Federación Internacional de las Iglesias Evangelicas Libres (#13433)
- ♦ FIIG / see Fédération des Institutions Internationales établies à Genève (#09599)
- ♦ **FIIG** Fédération des Institutions Internationales établies à Genève (#09599)
- ♦ FIIG – Fédération internationale des industries graphiques – CMT (inactive)
- ♦ **FIIH** Fédération internationale d'ingénierie hospitalière (#13439)
- ♦ **FIIM** Fédération internationale d'ingégnierie municipal (#13484)
- ♦ FIIM / see International Federation of Municipal Engineering (#13484)
- ♦ FIIM / see International Federation of Pharmaceutical Manufacturers and Associations (#13505)
- ♦ **FIIS** Forum international de l'innovation sociale (#13651)
- ♦ FIITEA – Fundatia Institutul International de Tehnologie si Economie Apicola (internationally oriented national body)
- ♦ FIIT – Fédération internationale des imprimeurs sur tissus (inactive)
- ♦ FIIT – Fundación Interamericana de Investigación Tropical (internationally oriented national body)
- ♦ **FIJA** Fédération internationale des journalistes agricoles (#13346)
- ♦ FIJC – Fédération internationale de la jeunesse catholique (inactive)
- ♦ **FIJC** Fundació Internacional Josep Carreras per a la Lluita contra la Leucèmia (#16153)
- ♦ **FIJC** Fundación Internacional José Carreras para la Lucha contra la Leucemia (#16153)
- ♦ **FIJE** Federación Iberoamericana de Jóvenes Empresarios (#09314)
- ♦ FIJE – Fédération internationale des journalistes de l'environnement (inactive)
- ♦ **FIJET** Fédération internationale des journalistes et écrivains du tourisme (#21494)
- ♦ **FIJEV** Fédération internationale des journalistes et écrivains des vins et spiritueux (#13577)
- ♦ FIJ – Fédération internationale du jazz (inactive)
- ♦ **FIJ** Fédération internationale des journalistes (#13462)
- ♦ **FIJ** Fédération internationale de judo (#13975)
- ♦ FIJL – Fédération internationale des journalistes libres (inactive)
- ♦ FIJM / see Jeunesses Musicales International (#16110)
- ♦ FIJPAA – Fédération internationale des journalistes professionnels de l'aéronautique et de l'astronautique (inactive)
- ♦ FIJUG / see International Fruit and Vegetable Juice Association (#13687)
- ♦ FIJU / see International Fruit and Vegetable Juice Association (#13687)
- ♦ **FIK** International Kendo Federation (#13982)
- ♦ **FILAC** Fondo para el Desarrollo de los Pueblos Indigenas de América Latina y el Caribe (#09832)
- ♦ **FILAC** Fund for the Development of the Indigenous Peoples of Latin America and the Caribbean (#09832)
- ♦ **FILACP** Federación Ibero-Latinoamericana de Cirugia Plastica (#09326)
- ♦ FILACYD / see Federación Iberoamericana de Capacitación y Desarrollo (#09308)
- ♦ **FILAIE** Federación Iberolatinoamericana de Artistas Intérpretes y Ejecutantes (#09325)
- ♦ **FILAPI** Federación Latinoamericana de Apicultura (#09342)
- ♦ FILASA – Federación Latinoamericana de la Industria para la Salud Animal (no recent information)
- ♦ **FILASMA** Federación Ibero Latinoamericana de Sociedades Médicas de Acupuntura (#09327)
- ♦ FILA / see United World Wrestling (#20665)
- ♦ **FILC** Fédération internationale des luttes celtiques (#13383)
- ♦ FILDIR – Fédération internationale libre des déportés et internés de la résistance (inactive)
- ♦ **FIL** Fédération Internationale du Lait (#13128)
- ♦ FIL – Fédération internationale des libraires (inactive)
- ♦ **FIL** Fédération Internationale de Luge (#14066)
- ♦ **FIL** Fundación Internacional para la Libertad (#10031)
- ♦ Filhas de Nossa Senhora do Sagrado Coração (religious order)
- ♦ Filhas de Sant'Ana (religious order)
- ♦ Filiación Cordimariana (religious order)
- ♦ Filiae Crucis Leodiensis (religious order)
- ♦ Filiae Mariae Auxiliatricis (religious order)
- ♦ Filiae Mariae Immaculatae (religious order)
- ♦ Filii Caritatis (religious order)
- ♦ Filii Immaculatae Conceptionis (religious order)
- ♦ Filii Matris Dei Dolorosae (religious order)
- ♦ Filii Sacrae Familiae Jesu, Mariae et Ioseph (religious order)
- ♦ **FIL** Internationaler Rodelverband (#14066)
- ♦ FIL / see International Luge Federation (#14066)
- ♦ **FIL** International Luge Federation (#14066)
- ♦ Filles de la Charité Canossiennes (religious order)
- ♦ Filles de la Charité du Sacré-Coeur de Jésus (religious order)
- ♦ Filles du Coeur Immaculé de Marie (inactive)
- ♦ Filles de la Croix (inactive)
- ♦ Filles de la Croix de Liège (religious order)
- ♦ Filles de la Croix – Soeurs de Saint-André de La Puye (religious order)
- ♦ Filles de la Divine Charité (religious order)
- ♦ Filles de la Divine Providence de Créhen (religious order)
- ♦ Filles de Jésus de Salamanque (religious order)
- ♦ Filles de Jésus Sauveur (religious order)
- ♦ Filles de Marie (religious order)
- ♦ Filles de Marie-Auxiliatrice (religious order)
- ♦ Filles de Marie-Immaculée (religious order)
- ♦ Filles de Marie et de Joseph (religious order)
- ♦ Filles de Notre-Dame d'Afrique (religious order)
- ♦ Filles de Notre-Dame de la Miséricorde de Savona (religious order)
- ♦ Filles de Notre-Dame du Sacré-Coeur (religious order)
- ♦ Filles de la Providence de Saint-Brieuc (religious order)

♦ Filles de la Providence de Sainte-Thérèse (religious order)
♦ Filles de la Sagesse (religious order)
♦ Filles de Saint-Camille (religious order)
♦ Filles de Sainte Anne (religious order)
♦ Filles de Sainte Marie de la Divine Providence (religious order)
♦ Filles de Sainte Marie du Jardin (religious order)
♦ Filles de Sainte-Marie de la Présentation (religious order)
♦ Filles de Sainte-Marie de la Providence de Saintes (religious order)
♦ Filles du Saint Esprit (religious order)
♦ Filles de Saint Paul – Pieuse Société des Filles de Saint Paul (religious order)
♦ Filles des Saints Coeurs – Enseignantes de Sainte Dorothée, Filles des Saints Coeurs (religious order)
♦ **FILLM** Fédération internationale des langues et littératures modernes (#13480)
♦ FilmAid International (internationally oriented national body)
♦ Filme für die Erde (internationally oriented national body)

♦ Filmkontakt Nord – Nordisk Panorama Foundation 09756

Managing Dir Vognmagergade 10, 1st floor, 1120 Copenhagen K, Denmark. T. +4533115152. Fax +4533112152. E-mail: post@nordiskpanorama.com.
URL: http://nordiskpanorama.com/

History 1991. **Aims** Act as an information and promotion centre for *Nordic documentaries* and short *films*; assist facilitate presentation of Nordic short Nordic independent film-makers in distribution. **Structure** Board. **Languages** English. **Staff** 4.00 FTE, paid. **Finance** Supported by: national subsidies from Denmark, Finland, Iceland, Norway; Sweden; *Nordic Council of Ministers (NCM, #17260)*; Nordic Film and TV Fund; City of Malmö (Sweden); Regional of Skåne and Film i Skåne. **Activities** Events/meetings; advocacy/lobbying/activism; knowledge management/information dissemination. **Events** *Annual Film Festival* Aarhus (Denmark) 2011, *Annual Film Festival* Bergen (Norway) 2010, *Annual Film Festival* Reykjavik (Iceland) 2009, *Annual Film Festival* Malmö (Sweden) 2008, *Annual Film Festival* Oulu (Finland) 2007. **Publications** *Nordisk Panorama Newsletter* (6 a year). Information Services: Database with information on Nordic documentaries and short films; video library.

Members Covers 5 countries:
Denmark, Finland, Iceland, Norway, Sweden. [2019.02.17/XF2532/F]

♦ Film Register Treaty Union / see Union for the International Registration of Audiovisual Works (#20444)
♦ Films for the Earth (internationally oriented national body)
♦ Films pour la Terre (internationally oriented national body)
♦ Film and Television Archives Advisory Committee / see Association of Moving Image Archivists
♦ Fils de la Charité (religious order)
♦ Fils de la Charité – Canossiens (religious order)
♦ Fils de l'Immaculée-Conception (religious order)
♦ Fils de Marie-Immaculée – Pavoniens (religious order)
♦ Fils de Marie Immaculée, Pères de Chavagnes (religious order)
♦ Fils de la Mère de Dieu Douloureuse (religious order)
♦ Fils de la Petite Oeuvre de la Divine Providence (religious order)
♦ Fils de Sainte Marie Immaculée (religious order)

♦ Filtration Society, The 09757

Sec 2 Bottoms Lane, Chester, CH4 7AP, UK.

History 1964, London (UK). Registration: Companies House, No/ID: 01780838, England and Wales. **Aims** Advance knowledge in the design and use of filtration and separation techniques in industry, commerce and every walk of life. **Structure** Council. Regional Chapters: *Nordic Filtration Society (NoFS, #17289)*; Japan Association. **Languages** English. **Finance** Members' dues. **Activities** Awards/prizes/competitions; events/meetings; financial and/or material support; knowledge management/information dissemination. **Events** *World Filtration Congress* San Diego, CA (USA) 2022, *World Filtration Congress* San Diego, CA (USA) 2021, *World Filtration Congress* San Diego, CA (USA) 2020, *World Filtration Congress* Taipei (Taiwan) 2016, *FILTECH EUROPE : International Conference for Filtration and Separation Technology* Wiesbaden (Germany) 2013. **Publications** *Filtration* (4 a year) – journal.

Members Individuals any individual, particularly those working for manufacturers, users, universities and research organizations; Chapters and Groups (). Members in 50 countries and territories:
Australia, Austria, Bangladesh, Belgium (*), Brazil, Canada, China, Cyprus, Czechia, Denmark, Finland, France, Germany, Ghana, Greece, Hong Kong, India, Indonesia, Iraq, Ireland, Israel, Italy, Japan (*), Korea DPR, Korea Rep, Malaysia, Mexico (*), Netherlands (*), New Zealand, Nigeria, Norway, Pakistan, Poland, Portugal, Romania, Russia, Saudi Arabia, Singapore, South Africa, Spain, Sri Lanka, Sweden, Switzerland, Taiwan, Thailand, Türkiye, UK (*), United Arab Emirates, USA, Zimbabwe. [2022/XF1786/F]

♦ FIL / see World Lacrosse (#21616)
♦ **FIMA** Federation of Islamic Medical Associations (#09681)

♦ FIM Africa 09758

Secretariat address not obtained. E-mail: fimafrica@fim-africa.com.
URL: http://www.fim-africa.com/

History 1998, with the title *African Motorcycle Union (AMU)*, as a continental union of *Fédération Internationale de Motocyclisme (FIM, #09643)*. **Aims** Promote and ensure the growth of all *motorcycling* (sport and leisure) throughout Africa. **Structure** General Assembly; Secretary General; Executive Director; Commissions; Working Groups. **Languages** English. **Staff** No full-time staff. **Finance** Funding from FIM; licence and permit fees. **Activities** Events/meetings. **Events** *General Assembly* Johannesburg (South Africa) 2015, *General Assembly / Congress* Johannesburg (South Africa) 2014, *General Assembly / Congress / General Assembly* Johannesburg (South Africa) 2013, *Seminar* Kampala (Uganda) 2012, *General Assembly* Kempton Park (South Africa) 2012.

Members Full in 15 countries:
Algeria, Angola, Botswana, Egypt, Kenya, Libya, Madagascar, Mauritania, Morocco, Namibia, South Africa, Tunisia, Uganda, Zambia, Zimbabwe. [2019.12.11/XD7067/E]

♦ **FIMARC** Fédération internationale des mouvements d'adultes ruraux catholiques (#13535)

♦ FIM Asia 09759

Pres c/o AAM, 225 Block 4 No 7, Persiaran Sukan, Laman Seri Business Park, section 13, 41000 Shah Alam, Selangor, Malaysia. T. +60355113429. Fax +60355112505. E-mail: wannzza18@gmail.com – corporate@aam.org.my.
URL: http://www.fim-asia.com/

History Continental union of *Fédération Internationale de Motocyclisme (FIM, #09643)*. Original title: *Asian Motorcycle Union (UAM)*. Current title adopted 30 Nov 2012.

Members Full in 26 countries and territories:
Bahrain, China, Guam, Hong Kong, India, Indonesia, Iran Islamic Rep, Japan, Jordan, Korea Rep, Kuwait, Kyrgyzstan, Lebanon, Macau, Malaysia, Mongolia, Nepal, Philippines, Qatar, Saudi Arabia, Singapore, Sri Lanka, Taiwan, Tajikistan, Thailand, United Arab Emirates. [2015/XD7074/E]

♦ **FIMBA** Federación Internacional de Maxibasquetbol (#09339)
♦ FIMB – Femmes internationales murs brisés (internationally oriented national body)
♦ **FIMCAP** Fédération Internationale des Mouvements Catholiques d'Action Paroissiale (#13379)
♦ **FIMC** Fédération internationale de la musique chorale (#13388)
♦ FIME – Federación Iberoamericana de Medicina Estética (no recent information)
♦ FIME – Fédération internationale des Maisons de l'Europe (inactive)
♦ **FIME** Fédération internationale Musique espérance (#13487)
♦ FIMELA / see MOKA International Foundation (#16846)
♦ **FIMEM** Fédération internationale des mouvements d'école moderne (#13481)

♦ FIM Europe 09760

Secretariat Viale delle Arti 181, 00054 Fiumicino, Italy. E-mail: office@fim-europe.com.
Registered Office 11 route Suisse, 1295 Mies VD, Switzerland.
URL: http://www.fim-europe.com/

History 5 Sep 1995, Munich (Germany). Founded by representatives of 7 national motorcycle federations (France, Italy, Switzerland, Greece, Slovakia, Portugal and Germany), in order to address European-specific motorcycling issues. Statutes approved 17 Feb 1996, Paris (France). Officially recognized as a Continental Union (CONU) of *Fédération Internationale de Motocyclisme (FIM, #09643)*, 1997, during the conference in Athens (Greece). New statutes and current title adopted 30 Nov 2012. Former names and other names: *Union européenne de motocyclisme (UEM)* – former (5 Sep 1995 to 30 Nov 2012); *European Motorcycle Union* – former (5 Sep 1995 to 30 Nov 2012). **Aims** Develop and promote all forms of motorcycling in Europe as well as cooperation and friendship between members; examine all questions related to development of motorcycling in Europe; organize European Championships and establish competitions; cooperate with FIM in all matters relating to the organization of international events and motorcycling in general; support creation and development of motorcycling activities in all European countries; promote motorcycling among young people, both as sport and motorcycling in general; encourage the use of motorcycles in European countries and to develop motorcycle tourism; represent the interests of motorcyclists before European authorities; promote in the media the sport of motorcycling and the use of motorcycles in all of Europe. **Structure** General Assembly; Management Council of 10 members; Executive Board of 5 members; Sporting Council, comprising 8 sporting commissions; Non-Sporting Council, comprising 4 non-sporting commissions. Panels (2): Judicial; Medical. **Languages** English, French. **Staff** 5.00 FTE, paid. **Activities** Events/meetings; sporting activities. Organizes European Motorcycle Championship and Cups for: Road Racing; Dragbike; Motocross and Snocross; Supermoto; Trial; Enduro and Bajas; Track Racing; Vintage; Motoball. **Events** *Congress* Zagreb (Croatia) 2019, *Congress* Nantes (France) 2018, *Congress* Rome (Italy) 2017, *Congress* Kavala (Greece) 2016, *Congress* Valletta (Malta) 2015. **Publications** *FIM Europe MAG.*

Members National federations in 47 countries:
Andorra, Austria, Azerbaijan, Belarus, Belgium, Bosnia-Herzegovina, Bulgaria, Croatia, Cyprus, Czechia, Denmark, Estonia, Finland, France, Germany, Great Britain, Greece, Hungary, Iceland, Ireland, Israel, Italy, Kazakhstan, Latvia, Liechtenstein, Lithuania, Luxembourg, Malta, Moldova, Monaco, Montenegro, Netherlands, North Macedonia, Norway, Poland, Portugal, Romania, Russia, San Marino, Serbia, Slovakia, Slovenia, Spain, Sweden, Switzerland, Türkiye, Ukraine. [2022/XD6716/E]

♦ **FIM** Federación Iberoamericana de Mantenimiento (#09315)
♦ FIM – Fédération internationale des mineurs (inactive)
♦ **FIM** Fédération Internationale de Motocyclisme (#09643)
♦ **FIM** Fédération internationale des musiciens (#13486)
♦ FIM – Fellowship International Mission (internationally oriented national body)
♦ FIM / see FIM-Forum for Democratic Global Governance (#09761)
♦ **FIM** FIM-Forum for Democratic Global Governance (#09761)

♦ FIM-Forum for Democratic Global Governance (FIM) 09761

Pres and CEO 4573 Sherbrooke St West, Ste 200, Westmount QC H3Z 1E9, Canada. T. +15144999468. Fax +15149871567.

History Founded 1998, as *Montreal International Forum (MIF) – Forum international de Montréal (FIM) – Foro Internacional de Montreal*. **Aims** Support and advance the goals of the *United Nations* System by improving the influence of international *civil society* in multilateral agencies; strengthen the influence of the voice of Southern civil society in debates and activities affecting global governance. **Structure** Southern-Based International Board of Directors; Secretariat. **Finance** Funding from governments, multilateral organizations, non-governmental organizations and foundations. **Activities** Events/meetings. **Events** *International conference on global democracy* Montréal, QC (Canada) 2005, *Global governance conference* Montréal, QC (Canada) 2002. **Publications** *Global Governance, Civil Society and Participatory Democracy: A View from Below* (2014) by Nigel Martin and Rajesh Tandon; *Democratizing Global Governance: Ten years of Case Studies and Reflections by Civil Society Activists* (2009). Case studies.

Members Individuals and organizations. FIM Network includes the following 28 organizations listed in this Yearbook:
- *Academic Council on the United Nations System (ACUNS, #00020)*;
- *Arab NGO Network for Development (ANND, #01016)*;
- *Australian Council for International Development (ACFID)*;
- *Bridge Initiative International (BI)*;
- *Canadian International Development Agency (CIDA, inactive)*;
- *Centre for Global Studies, Victoria (CFGS)*;
- *Centre for International Governance Innovation (CIGI)*;
- *CIVICUS: World Alliance for Citizen Participation (#03962)*;
- *Conference of Non-Governmental Organizations in Consultative Relationship with the United Nations (CONGO, #04635)*;
- *Cooperation Canada*;
- *Council of Non-Governmental Organizations for Development Support (#04911)*;
- *Ford Foundation (#09858)*;
- *Heinrich Böll Foundation*;
- *International Development Research Centre (IDRC, #13162)*;
- *International Fund for Agricultural Development (IFAD, #13692)*;
- *International Political Science Association (IPSA, #14615)*;
- *International Studies Association (ISA, #15615)*;
- *League of Arab States (LAS, #16420)*;
- *Organisation internationale de la Francophonie (OIF, #17809)*;
- *Organisation of Islamic Cooperation (OIC, #17813)*;
- *Oxfam GB*;
- *Oxfam Novib*;
- *Rockefeller Brothers Fund (RBF)*;
- *Society for Participatory Research in Asia (PRIA)*;
- *Swedish International Development Cooperation Agency (Sida)*;
- *UBUNTU – World Forum of Civil Society Networks (inactive)*;
- *UNDP (#20292)*;
- *United Nations Non-Governmental Liaison Service (NGLS, #20591)*. [2014.11.19/XG2498/y/F]

♦ FIM – Forum International de la Météo et du Climat (meeting series)
♦ **FIMFR** – Federación Internacional de Medicina Fisica y Rehabilitación (inactive)
♦ FIM – Frontier Internship in Mission (internationally oriented national body)
♦ **FIM Group** MOKA International Foundation (#16846)
♦ FIMH – International Conference on Functional Imaging and Modeling of the Heart (meeting series)
♦ **FIMI** Foro Internacional de Mujeres Indigenas (#13838)
♦ FIMIGCEE / see European and International Federation of Natural Stone Industries (#07587)
♦ **FIMITIC** International Federation of Persons with Physical Disability (#13504)
♦ **FIM LA** FIM Latin America (#09762)

♦ FIM Latin America (FIM LA) 09762

FIM Latín América

Main Office Jr Barlovento 149, Of 202, 15038, Lima, Peru. E-mail: direccion.general@fim-latinamerica.com.
URL: http://fim-latinamerica.com/

History 24 Jan 1975, Caracas (Venezuela). Continental union of *Fédération Internationale de Motocyclisme (FIM, #09643)*. Former names and other names: *Latin American Motorcycling Union* – former; *Unión Latinoamericana de Motociclismo (ULM)* – former. **Aims** Develop motorcycle sports, motorcycle leisure and road safety. **Structure** Board of Directors.Sporting Commissions (5); Non-Sporting Commissions (8). **Languages** Spanish. **Staff** 2.00 FTE, paid. **Activities** Events/meetings. **Events** *Congress* Bogota (Colombia) 2015, *Congress* Jerez de la Frontera (Spain) 2014, *Congress* Montevideo (Uruguay) 2013, *Congress* Monte Carlo (Monaco) 2012, *Congress* San José (Costa Rica) 2011.

Members Affiliate members in 20 countries:
Argentina, Bolivia, Brazil, Chile, Colombia, Costa Rica, Cuba, Dominican Rep, Ecuador, El Salvador, Guatemala, Honduras, Mexico, Nicaragua, Panama, Paraguay, Peru, Puerto Rico, Uruguay, Venezuela. [2020/XD9184/E]

♦ FIM Latín América (#09762)
♦ **FIMM** Fédération internationale de médecine manuelle (#09642)
♦ **FIMM** Fórum Internacional de las Mujeres del Mediterraneo (#14143)
♦ FIMM International Academy of Manual/Musculoskeletal Medicine / see International Academy of Manual/Musculoskeletal Medicine (#11557)
♦ FIM Oceania (internationally oriented national body)

- ♦ FIMOC – Fédération internationale des mouvements ouvriers chrétiens (inactive)
- ♦ FIMPR – Fédération internationale de médecine physique et réadaptation (inactive)
- ♦ FIMRC – Foundation for International Medical Relief of Children (unconfirmed)
- ♦ **FIMSA** Federation of Immunological Societies of Asia-Oceania (#09594)
- ♦ **FIMS** Fédération internationale de médecine sportive (#13554)
- ♦ FIMU / see Graduate Women International (#10688)
- ♦ FINA – Federation of International Ninja Athletics (unconfirmed)
- ♦ Final Act and Agreement for the Revision of the Telecommunications Agreement (1949 treaty)
- ♦ Final Act of the Intergovernmental Conference on the Adoption of a Travel Document for Refugees (1946 treaty)
- ♦ Final Act of the International Conference on Safety of Life at Sea (1948 treaty)
- ♦ Final Act of the Second International Peace Conference (1907 treaty)
- ♦ Final Acts of the World Administrative Radio Conference for Dealing with Frequency Allocations in Certain Parts of the Spectrum (1992 treaty)
- ♦ Final Act of the United Nations Conference on Customs Formalities for the Temporary Importation of Private Road Motor Vehicles and for Tourism (1954 treaty)
- ♦ Final Act of the United Nations Conference on International Commercial Arbitration (1958 treaty)
- ♦ Final Act of the United Nations Conference on the Law of the Sea (1958 treaty)
- ♦ Final Articles Revision Convention (1946 treaty)
- ♦ Final Declaration of the International Conference in Tangier (1956 treaty)
- ♦ Final Protocol of a Conference for the Unification of Allied Economic Action (1916 treaty)
- ♦ Final Protocol of the Naval Conference (1909 treaty)
- ♦ Final Protocol of the Preliminary Conference Respecting Wireless Telegraphy (1903 treaty)
- ♦ Final Protocol Relative to the Adoption of General Rules Respecting the Dimensions of Goods Trucks (1912 treaty)
- ♦ Final Protocol Relative to the Sealing of Trucks before Passing Customs (1907 treaty)
- ♦ Final Protocol for the Resumption of Friendly Relations (1901 treaty)
- ♦ Final Protocol for the Technical Unification of Railways (1907 treaty)

♦ Finance Alliance for Sustainable Trade (FAST) 09763

Contact 1255 Bd Robert Bourassa, Suite 801, Montréal QC H3B 3W3, Canada. T. +15146264848.
Facebook: https://www.facebook.com/FASTInt/

History Launched May 2007, following activities initiated in 2002. Secretariat operational as of 2008. **Aims** Facilitate efficiency and transparency in financial markets for sustainable SMEs in emerging economies by providing objective data while developing and promoting reporting and quality standards. **Structure** General Assembly (all full and associate members); Core Assembly (all full members); Board; Executive Committee. **Languages** English, French, Spanish. **Staff** 4.00 FTE, paid; 7.00 FTE, voluntary. **Finance** Sources: members' dues. Other sources: International cooperation funding. Annual budget: 684,309 USD. **Activities** Events/meetings; knowledge management/information dissemination; projects/programmes. **Events** *Round Table on Bridging Micro and Agricultural SME Finance* Beirut (Lebanon) 2014, *Annual General Meeting* Seattle, WA (USA) 2014. **Publications** *FAST Newsletter* (12 a year). Reports.
Members Financial institutions and sustainable producers (142) in 29 countries:
Belgium, Bolivia, Burundi, Canada, Colombia, Costa Rica, Côte d'Ivoire, Denmark, Dominican Rep, El Salvador, Ethiopia, Germany, Guatemala, Honduras, India, Kenya, Malawi, Mexico, Netherlands, Nicaragua, Peru, Philippines, Rwanda, Slovakia, Switzerland, Tanzania UR, Uganda, UK, USA.
Included in the above, 4 organizations listed in this Yearbook:
African Fine Coffees Association (AFCA, #00316); Catholic Organization for Relief and Development (Cordaid); International Institute for Sustainable Development (IISD, #13930); Société de coopération pour le développement international (SOCODEVI).
NGO Relations Member of: *Aspen Network of Development Entrepreneurs (ANDE, #02310).* Partner of: *Global Call for Climate Action (GCCA, inactive); Tropical Forest Alliance (TFA, #20249).* Supports: *Farming First.* [2018/XJ8237/ty/**C**]

- ♦ Finance Center for South-South Cooperation (internationally oriented national body)
- ♦ Finance, Credit and International Business / see FCIB (#09279)

♦ Finance Watch 09764

SG Rue Ducale 67 b3, 1000 Brussels, Belgium. T. +3228800430. Fax +3228886380. E-mail: office.manager@finance-watch.org – contact@finance-watch.org.
Head of Communications & Operations address not obtained.
URL: http://www.finance-watch.org/

History Founded following a call for action entitled "Call for a finance watch", Jul 2010, by a cross-party group of 22 Members of the European Parliament (MEPs) in response to the rising requests to meet with representatives of the financial industry and the increasingly technical financial legislation in the wake of the financial crisis that began in 2007. Beginning In Dec 2010, and over the course of 120 meetings with representatives of civil society and other organizations, a set of concrete proposals for the creation of Finance Watch was drawn up. Founding General Assembly took place 30 Jun 2011, Brussels (Belgium), when statutes were adopted and the Board was elected. Registration: Banque-Carrefour des Entreprises, No/ID: 0836.636.381, Start date: 30 May 2011, Belgium; EU Transparency Register, No/ID: 37943526882-24, Start date: 5 Oct 2011. **Aims** Act as a public interest counterweight to the financial lobby; strengthen the voice of society in the reform of financial regulation by conducting advocacy and representing public interest arguments to lawmakers and citizens. **Structure** General Assembly (annual); Board of Directors; Committee of Transparency and Independence. **Languages** English, French, German. **Staff** 17.00 FTE, paid. **Finance** Sources: donations; gifts, legacies; grants; members' dues. Supported by: *European Union (EU, #08967).* Annual budget: 2,800,000 EUR (2022). **Activities** Advocacy/lobbying/activism; events/meetings; guidance/assistance/consulting; knowledge management/information dissemination. **Events** *Climate crisis and the financial sector: Climate-related risks and the transformation to a sustainable economy* Brussels (Belgium) 2022, *Financing Local Green Enterprises in Developing and Emerging Countries* Brussels (Belgium) 2022, *Gender Perspective in Financial Inclusion* Brussels (Belgium) 2021, *How to reform the EU fiscal framework?* Brussels (Belgium) 2021, *Sustainable Corporate Governance: Setting the incentives and obligations for companies to transition towards sustainability* Brussels (Belgium) 2021. **Publications** Newsletter; consultation responses; technical briefings; position papers; reports.
Members National organizations in 21 countries:
Austria, Belgium, Bulgaria, Czechia, Denmark, France, Germany, Greece, Ireland, Italy, Luxembourg, Netherlands, Norway, Poland, Portugal, Romania, Slovakia, Spain, Sweden, Switzerland, UK.
International organizations (67), including 14 organizations listed in this Yearbook:
AGE Platform Europe (#00557); Bureau Européen des Unions de Consommateurs (BEUC, #03360); COFACE Families Europe (#04084); European Trade Union Confederation (ETUC, #08927); Fondation pour la Nature et l'Homme (FNH); Green Economy Coalition (GEC, #10717); Housing Europe – The European Federation for Public Cooperative and Social Housing (Housing Europe, #10956); New Economics Foundation (NEF, #17082); Nordic Financial Unions (#17292); Oxfam International (#17922); Secours catholique – Caritas France; Stichting Onderzoek Multinationale Ondernemingen (SOMO); Transparency International (TI, #20223) (EU Office); *UNI Global Union – Europa (UNI Europa, #20342).*
Individual experts in 21 countries:
Austria, Belgium, Bulgaria, Czechia, Denmark, France, Germany, Greece, Ireland, Italy, Luxembourg, Netherlands, Norway, Poland, Portugal, Romania, Slovakia, Spain, Sweden, Switzerland, UK.
NGO Relations Member of (9): 2°C Investing Initiative; Civil Society Convention; *European Financial Reporting Advisory Group (EFRAG, #07254); Global Alliance for Banking on Values (GABV, #10186); Green Economy Coalition (GEC, #10717);* Pacte Finance Climat; Promoting Economic Pluralism; Transforming Finance Network; *Wellbeing Economy Alliance (WEAll, #20856).* [2022.11.08/XJ8347/y/**F**]

♦ Financial Action Task Force (FATF) 09765

Groupe d'action financière (GAFI)

Exec Sec c/o OECD, 2 rue André Pascal, 75775 Paris CEDEX 16, France. T. +33145249090. Fax +33144306137. E-mail: contact@fatf-gafi.org.
URL: http://www.fatf-gafi.org/

History Jul 1989, Paris (France). Established at Economic Summit of the then *'Group of Seven'*, currently *Group of Eight (G-8, #10745).* Secretariat provided by *OECD (#17693).* Former names and other names: *Financial Action Task Force on Money Laundering* – former; *Groupe d'action financière sur le blanchiment de capitaux* – former. **Aims** Establish and refine global standards for combating *money laundering* and *terrorist* financing; foster and monitor countries' implementation of these standards; expand the geographic reach and implementation of FATF standards through a limited increase in membership and enhanced relationships with FSRBs and non-member countries; identify money laundering and terrorist financing threats; conduct outreach to relevant stakeholders. **Structure** Plenary; Steering Group; Working Groups; rotating Presidency and Vice-Presidency; Secretariat. Independent task force of experts from finance and justice ministries, financial regulators, financial intelligence units and law enforcement agencies. **Languages** English, French. **Staff** 36.00 FTE, paid. **Finance** Sources: contributions of member/participating states. **Activities** Standards/guidelines; monitoring/evaluation. Developed a series of Recommendations recognized as the international standard for combating money laundering and the financing of terrorism and proliferation of weapons of mass destruction. FATF Working Group and Plenary Meetings take place in February, Jun and October of each year. **Events** *Plenary Meeting* Paris (France) 2023, *Plenary Meeting* Paris (France) 2023, *Plenary Meeting* Paris (France) 2022, *Plenary Meeting* Paris (France) 2022. **Publications** Annual Report; FATF standards with interpretative notes and best practices papers; reports on money laundering and terrorist financing typologies; reports of mutual evaluations of member jurisdictions' anti-money laundering and terrorist financing systems; guidance papers.
Members Jurisdictions (37):
Argentina, Australia, Austria, Belgium, Brazil, Canada, China, Denmark, Finland, France, Germany, Greece, Hong Kong, Iceland, India, Ireland, Israel, Italy, Japan, Korea Rep, Luxembourg, Malaysia, Mexico, Netherlands, New Zealand, Norway, Portugal, Russia, Saudi Arabia, Singapore, South Africa, Spain, Sweden, Switzerland, Türkiye, UK, USA.
In addition to the above, 2 regional organizations:
European Commission (EC, #06633); Gulf Cooperation Council (GCC, #10826).
Observer country:
Indonesia.
Associate Members (9):
Asia/Pacific Group on Money Laundering (APG, #01921); Caribbean Financial Action Task Force (CFATF, #03505); Committee of Experts on the Evaluation of Anti-Money Laundering Measures and the Financing of Terrorism (MONEYVAL, #04257); Eastern and Southern African Anti-Money Laundering Group (ESAAMLG, #05252); Eurasian Group on Combating Money Laundering and Financing of Terrorism (EAG, #05608); Groupe d'Action contre le Blanchiment d'Argent en Afrique Centrale (GABAC); Grupo de Acción Financiera de Latinoamérica (GAFILAT, #10799); Intergovernmental Action Group against Money Laundering in West Africa (#11471); Middle East and North Africa Financial Action Task Force (MENAFATF, #16779).
IGO Relations Observers:
- *African Development Bank (ADB, #00283);*
- Anti-Money Laundering Liaison Committee of the Franc Zone (CLAB);
- *Asian Development Bank (ADB, #01422);*
- *Egmont Group of Financial Intelligence Units (#05396);*
- *Eurojust (#05698);*
- *European Bank for Reconstruction and Development (EBRD, #06315);*
- *European Central Bank (ECB, #06466);*
- *European Police Office (Europol, #08239);*
- *Inter-American Development Bank (IDB, #11427);*
- *International Bank for Reconstruction and Development (IBRD, #12317)* (World Bank);
- *International Criminal Police Organization – INTERPOL (ICPO-INTERPOL, #13110);*
- *International Monetary Fund (IMF, #14180);*
- *OAS (#17629);*
- *Inter-American Drug Abuse Control Commission (#11429)* and *Inter-American Committee Against Terrorism (#11412);*
- *OECD (#17693);*
- *Organization for Security and Cooperation in Europe (OSCE, #17887);*
- *United Nations Office on Drugs and Crime (UNODC, #20596)* and
- *Counter-Terrorism Committee (CTC, #04928);*
- *World Customs Organization (WCO, #21350).*

NGO Relations Observer status with (4): *Basel Committee on Banking Supervision (BCBS, #03183); Group of International Finance Centre Supervisors (GIFCS, #10782); International Association of Insurance Supervisors (IAIS, #11966); International Organization of Securities Commissions (IOSCO, #14470).* [2023/XF3051/y/**F***]

- ♦ Financial Action Task Force of Latin America (#10799)
- ♦ Financial Action Task Force on Money Laundering / see Financial Action Task Force (#09765)
- ♦ Financial Action Task Force of South America / see Grupo de Acción Financiera de Latinoamérica (#10799)
- ♦ Financial Cooperative Association of International Civil Servants (#02455)
- ♦ Financial Engineering and Banking Society (internationally oriented national body)
- ♦ Financial Executives International (internationally oriented national body)
- ♦ Financial Fund for the Development of the River Plate Basin (#09833)
- ♦ Financial Fund for the Plata Basin Development / see Fondo Financiero para el Desarrollo de la Cuenca del Plata (#09833)

♦ Financial Inclusion Equity Council (CIEF) 09766

Manager 10 Fawcett Str, Ste 204, Cambridge, MA 02138, UK. T. +16176257080. E-mail: info@accion.org.
URL: http://www.fiecouncil.com/

History Original title: *Council of Microfinance Equity Funds (CMEF).* **Aims** Represent private entities making active, long term, and sustainable equity investments in institutions focusing on under- or un-served clients, so as to achieve greater financial inclusion. **Structure** Advisory Board; Secretariat. **Activities** Events/meetings; knowledge management/information dissemination. **Events** *Meeting* Zeist (Netherlands) 2016, *Meeting* Washington, DC (USA) 2015, *Meeting* New York, NY (USA) 2014, *Meeting* Zurich (Switzerland) 2014, *Meeting* London (UK) 2013.
Members Organizations, including the following listed in this Yearbook (5):
ACCION International; FINCA International; Oikocredit International (Oikocredit, #17704); Opportunity International (#17776). [2016/XM1729/y/**F**]

- ♦ Financial Intermediation Research Society (internationally oriented national body)

♦ Financial Markets Association (FMA) 09767

Office Manager 8 rue du Mail, 75002 Paris, France. T. +33142975115. E-mail: secretariat@acifma.com.
URL: https://acifma.com/

History Jun 1955, France. Founded on the initiative of the Bank of England and the Banque de France. Former names and other names: *ACI International* – alias; *Association cambiste internationale (ACI)* – former (1955 to 1996); *ACI – Financial Markets Association* – alias. **Aims** Contribute to market development and market practice through education programmes and "The Model Code". **Structure** Management Board. Standing Committees. **Languages** English. **Staff** 4.00 FTE, paid. **Finance** Members' dues. Certification. **Activities** Arbitration services; certification; meeting activities. **Events** *World Congress* 2022, *World Congress* Moscow (Russia) 2022, *World Congress* Dubai (United Arab Emirates) 2021, *World Congress* Dubai (United Arab Emirates) 2020, *World Congress* Colombo (Sri Lanka) 2019. **Publications** *ACI Briefing* (5 a year).
Members National associations and individuals representing a total of 13,000 individuals. Affiliated national associations in 63 countries and territories:
Argentina, Australia, Austria, Bahrain, Belgium, Bulgaria, Canada, Channel Is, Croatia, Czechia, Denmark, Egypt, Finland, France, Germany, Ghana, Greece, Hong Kong, Hungary, Iceland, India, Indonesia, Ireland, Israel, Italy, Japan, Jordan, Kenya, Korea Rep, Kuwait, Lebanon, Luxembourg, Macau, Malaysia, Malta, Mauritius, Monaco, Netherlands, New Zealand, Nigeria, North Macedonia, Norway, Pakistan, Philippines, Poland, Portugal, Romania, Russia, Serbia, Singapore, Slovakia, Slovenia, South Africa, Sri Lanka, Sweden, Switzerland, Tanzania UR, Thailand, Tunisia, UK, United Arab Emirates, USA, Zambia.
NGO Relations Cooperates with (1): *Interarab Cambist Association (ICA, #11455).* [2021/XC1281/**F**]

♦ Financial Planning Standards Board (FPSB) 09768

Dir Marketing and Communications 707 17th St, Ste 2925, Denver CO 80202, USA. T. +17204071914. Fax +17209171921.

URL: http://www.fpsb.org/
History Founded 1990, as *International CFP Council*. Current name adopted Oct 2004. Incorporated in the State of Delaware (USA). **Aims** Advance the profession of personal financial planning; protect financial planning consumers; foster professionalism in financial planning through ongoing development and enforcement of relevant international competency and ethics standards; promote greater global recognition of CFP certification and its related marks as the international hallmarks of financial planning professionals. **Structure** Board of Directors; FPSB Council (Advisory Council). Committees (4): Audit; Compensation; Nominations; ISC Task Force. Subcommittees; Task Forces; Headquarters in Denver CO (USA). **Staff** 10.00 FTE, paid. **Activities** Training/education; certification/accreditation; standards/guidelines. **Events** *Meeting* Brussels (Belgium) 2019, *Meeting* Bangkok (Thailand) 2018, *Meeting* Kuala Lumpur (Malaysia) 2017, *Meeting* Cape Town (South Africa) 2016, *Meeting* Toronto, ON (Canada) 2016.
Members Affiliates organizations representing over 150,000 CFP professionals, in 24 countries and territories:
Australia, Austria, Brazil, Canada, China, Colombia, France, Germany, Hong Kong, India, Indonesia, Ireland, Japan, Korea Rep, Malaysia, Netherlands, New Zealand, Singapore, South Africa, Switzerland, Taiwan, Thailand, UK, USA.
Associates in 2 countries:
Israel, Türkiye. [2015.01.07/XD8394/**D**]

♦ Financial Sector Reform and Strengthening Initiative (FIRST Initiative) 09769

Contact World Bank, 1818 H Str NW, MSNI 9-904, Washington DC 20433, USA. T. +12024732765. Fax +12025227466. E-mail: first@worldbank.org.
URL: http://www.firstinitiative.org/
History 2002, by *Canadian International Development Agency (CIDA, inactive)*, *Department for International Development (DFID, inactive)*; *International Bank for Reconstruction and Development (IBRD, #12317)*, *International Monetary Fund (IMF, #14180)* and *Swedish International Development Cooperation Agency (Sida)*. **Aims** Support growth and poverty reduction in low- and middle-income countries through the promotion of robust and diverse financial sectors. **Structure** Council (meets annually), including Chairman and Vice-Chairman. Programme Management Unit (PMU). **Events** *Meeting / Consultative Group Meeting* Rabat (Morocco) 2015, *Meeting / Consultative Group Meeting* London (UK) 2011, *Meeting / Consultative Group Meeting* Nairobi (Kenya) 2008, *Meeting / Consultative Group Meeting* Bern (Switzerland) 2004. **Publications** Annual Report; brochure. **NGO Relations** Supports: *ASEAN Insurance Training and Research Institute (AITRI, #01202)*. Member of: *Making Finance Work for Africa (MFW4A, #16555)*. [2016/XM3253/**F**]

♦ Financial Services Institute of Australasia (internationally oriented national body)
♦ Financial Services Volunteer Corps (internationally oriented national body)

♦ Financial Stability Board (FSB) 09770

Contact c/o Bank for Intl Settlements, Centralbahnplatz 2, 4002 Basel BS, Switzerland. T. +41612808298. Fax +41612809100. E-mail: fsb@bis.org.
URL: http://www.fsb.org/
History Feb 1999. Established by G7 – currently *Group of Eight (G-8, #10745)* – Finance Ministers and Central Bank Governors, as *Financial Stability Forum (FSF)*. Re-established under current title, Apr 2009, by leaders of *Group of Twenty (G20, #10793)*, who endorsed the Charter formally establishing the Board. Registration: Start date: Jan 2013, Switzerland, Basel. **Aims** Coordinate at international level the work of national financial authorities and international standard setting bodies so as to develop and promote the implementation of effective regulatory, supervisory and other financial sector policies; address vulnerabilities affecting financial systems in the interest of global financial stability; promote members' implementation of international standards and agreed G20 and FSB commitments and policy recommendations. **Structure** Plenary (twice a year), comprising Chairperson and members: national authorities (60) plus *European Central Bank (ECB, #06466)* and *European Commission (EC, #06633)*; international financial institutions (4); international standard-setting, regulatory, supervisory and central bank bodies (6). **Languages** English. **Staff** 34.00 FTE, paid. Staff mostly seconded from member institutions, including IMF and World Bank. **Finance** Operational and administrative expenses carried by BIS. **Activities** Monitoring/evaluation. Assesses vulnerabilities affecting the global financial system and identifies and reviews regulatory, supervisory and related actions needed to address them and their outcomes; promotes coordination and information exchange among authorities responsible for financial stability; undertakes joint strategic reviews of the policy development work of the international standard setting bodies to ensure their work is timely, coordinated, focused on priorities and addressing gaps; sets guidelines for and support establishment of supervisory colleges; supports contingency planning for cross-border crisis management, particularly with respect to important firms; collaborates to conduct Early Warning Exercises. Ad-hoc engagement with industry and other stakeholders as necessary for policy development and implementation tracking. **Events** *ASEAN Conference on the Recommentations of the TCFD* Singapore (Singapore) 2018, *Regional Consultative Group for Middle East and North Africa Meeting* Abu Dhabi (United Arab Emirates) 2017, *International Financial Architecture Working Group Meeting* Seoul (Korea Rep) 2017, *Shadow Banking Experts Group Meeting* Tokyo (Japan) 2017, *International Financial Architecture Working Group Meeting* Seoul (Korea Rep) 2016. **Publications** Reports; statements; press releases.
Members National and financial authorities of 24 countries and territories:
Argentina, Australia, Brazil, Canada, China, France, Germany, Hong Kong, India, Indonesia, Italy, Japan, Korea Rep, Mexico, Netherlands, Russia, Saudi Arabia, Singapore, South Africa, Spain, Switzerland, Türkiye, UK, USA.
Regional authority (2):
European Central Bank (ECB, #06466); *European Commission (EC, #06633)*.
International financial institutions (4):
Bank for International Settlements (BIS, #03165); *International Bank for Reconstruction and Development (IBRD, #12317)* (World Bank); *International Monetary Fund (IMF, #14180)*; *OECD (#17693)*.
International standard-setting, regulatory, supervisory and central bank bodies (6):
Basel Committee on Banking Supervision (BCBS, #03183); *Committee on Payment and Settlement Systems (CPSS, inactive)*; *Committee on the Global Financial System (CGFS, #04258)*; *International Accounting Standards Board (IASB, #11583)*; *International Association of Insurance Supervisors (IAIS, #11966)*; *International Organization of Securities Commissions (IOSCO, #14470)*.
IGO Relations Cooperates with: *Financial Action Task Force (FATF, #09765)*. **NGO Relations** Cooperates with: *International Auditing and Assurance Standards Board (IAASB, #12296)*; *International Federation of Accountants (IFAC, #13335)*; *International Forum of Independent Audit Regulators (IFIAR, #13639)*. [2021/XF4879/y/**F***]

♦ Financial Stability Forum / see Financial Stability Board (#09770)

♦ Financial Stability Institute (FSI) 09771

Contact Bank for International Settlements, 4002 Basel BS, Switzerland. T. +41612809989. Fax +41612809100. E-mail: fsi@bis.org.
URL: http://www.bis.org/fsi/aboutfsi.htm
History 1999, by *Bank for International Settlements (BIS, #03165)* and *Basel Committee on Banking Supervision (BCBS, #03183)*. **Aims** Assist financial sector supervisors around the world in improving and strengthening their financial systems. **Activities** Organizes meetings, conferences and seminars. **Events** *Asia-Pacific High Level Meeting on Banking Supervision* Sydney, NSW (Australia) 2019, *Asia-Pacific High Level Meeting on Banking Supervision* Singapore (Singapore) 2018, *Regional Seminar on Problem Bank Identification, Supervision and Early Intervention* Singapore (Singapore) 2016, *Regional Seminar on Enterprise Risk Management for Solvency Purposes* Singapore (Singapore) 2014, *Regional Seminar on Resolution Frameworks and Crisis Management* Singapore (Singapore) 2013. **Publications** Occasional papers; Award papers. **Information Services** *FSI Connect* – online information and learning resource. **IGO Relations** Technical cooperating partner of: *Macroeconomic and Financial Management Institute of Eastern and Southern Africa (MEFMI, #16539)*. Partner of: *South East Asian Central Banks Research and Training Centre (SEACEN Centre, #19760)*. [2011/XM1515/j/**E***]

♦ Financial Transparency Coalition (FTC) 09772

Admin Dir c/o TSNE MissionWorks, 89 South St Suite 700, Boston MA 02111, USA. E-mail: info@financialtransparency.org.
URL: http://www.financialtransparency.org/
History 2009. Former names and other names: *Task Force on Financial Integrity and Economic Development* – former (2009). **Aims** Curtail illicit financial flows through promotion of a transparent, accountable and sustainable financial system. **Structure** Coordinating Committee of 9 partners: Centre for Budget and Governance Accountability; *Christian Aid*; *European Network on Debt and Development (EURODAD, #07891)*; *Global Financial Integrity (GFI, #10358)*; *Global Witness (GW)*; *Red Latinoamericana sobre Deuda, Desarrollo y Derechos (LATINDADD, #18711)*; *Tax Justice Network (TJN, #20100)*; *Tax Justice Network-Africa (TJN-A, #20101)*; *Transparency International (TI, #20223)*. **Finance** Major funding from: Finnish and Norwegian Ministries of Foreign Affairs; *The William and Flora Hewlett Foundation*; Omidyar Network; *Open Society Foundations (OSF, #17763)*. **Events** *Financial Transparency Conference* Bangkok (Thailand) 2020, *Financial Transparency Conference* Helsinki (Finland) 2017, *Financial Transparency Conference* Jakarta (Indonesia) 2015, *Conference* Lima (Peru) 2014, *Conference* Dar es Salaam (Tanzania UR) 2013.
Members Allied organizations (over 150) in 48 countries:
Afghanistan, Argentina, Azerbaijan, Bangladesh, Belgium, Bolivia, Brazil, Bulgaria, Cameroon, Congo DR, Ecuador, El Salvador, Ethiopia, Finland, France, Honduras, Hungary, Iceland, India, Indonesia, Kenya, Lebanon, Malaysia, Mexico, Montenegro, Morocco, Mozambique, Nepal, Netherlands, Nicaragua, Nigeria, North Macedonia, Norway, Pakistan, Philippines, Portugal, Senegal, Sierra Leone, South Africa, Spain, Sweden, Switzerland, Tanzania UR, Thailand, Tunisia, Uganda, UK, USA.
Included in the above, 38 organizations listed in this Yearbook:
- *ActionAid (#00087)*;
- *Africa Centre for Open Governance (AfriCOG)*;
- *Africa Development Interchange Network (ADIN)*;
- *African Citizens Development Foundation (ACDF)*;
- *African Monitor (AM)*;
- *African Network for Environment and Economic Justice (ANEEJ)*;
- *African Solutions to African Problems (ASAP)*;
- *ARTICLE 19 (#01121)*;
- *Association on Third World Affairs (ATWA, no recent information)*;
- *Catholic Agency for Overseas Development (CAFOD)*;
- *Consumer Unity and Trust Society (CUTS)*;
- *Edmund Rice International (ERI, #05362)*;
- *Foundation for the Development of Africa (FDA)*;
- *Global Health Council (GHC, #10402)*;
- *Global Network for Good Governance (GNGG, #10490)*;
- *Global South Initiative (GSI)*;
- *HELIO International (inactive)*;
- *Hope for the Nations (HFTN, #10944)*;
- *Institut arabe des chefs d'entreprises (IACE, #11236)*;
- *International Budget Partnership (IBP, #12406)*;
- *International NGO Forum on Indonesian Development (INFID, #14366)*;
- *International Trade Union Confederation (ITUC, #15708)*;
- *Jubilee South – Asian Peoples' Movement on Debt and Development (JSAPMDD, #16160)*;
- *Maryknoll Office for Global Concern (MOGC)*;
- *New Economics Foundation (NEF, #17082)*;
- *Open Knowledge International*;
- *Oxfam International (#17922)*;
- *Partnership for Transparency Fund (PTF, #18245)*;
- *Public Eye*;
- *Publish What You Fund*;
- *Social Accountability International (SAI)*;
- *South Asia Alliance for Poverty Eradication (SAAPE, #19712)*;
- *Suomalaiset Kehitysjärjestöt (Fingo)*;
- *Swedish NGO Centre for Development Cooperation (Forum Syd)*;
- *Transnational Institute (TNI, #20219)*;
- *UniversalGiving*;
- *World Business Academy (#21251)*;
- *World Policy Institute (WPI)*.

NGO Relations Supports: *European Network on Debt and Development (EURODAD, #07891)*. [2021/XJ7708/y/**F**]

♦ FINAT 09773

Managing Dir PO Box 85612, 2508 CH The Hague, Netherlands. T. +31703123910. Fax +31703636348. E-mail: info@finat.com.
Events & Publication Manager address not obtained.
URL: http://www.finat.com/
History 7 Nov 1958, Paris (France). Moved to The Hague (Netherlands), 1969. Former names and other names: *International Federation of Manufacturers and Converters of Pressure-Sensitive and Heatseals on Paper and Other Base Materials* – former; *Fédération internationale des fabricants et transformateurs d'adhésifs et thermocollants sur papiers et autres supports (FINAT)* – former; *Internationale Vereinigung der Hersteller und Verarbeiteiz von Selbstklebenden und Heissiegelfähigen und andere Stoffen* – former; *Association for the European Self-Adhesive Labelling and Adjacent Narrow Web Converting Industries* – full title. **Aims** Promote the interests of converters and suppliers of the *self-adhesive label* industry. **Structure** General Assembly (annual); Board; Executive Board; Committees; Sub-Committees. **Languages** English. **Staff** 3.00 FTE, paid. **Finance** Sources: members' dues; sponsorship. Other sources: advertising. **Activities** Advocacy/lobbying/activism; events/meetings; knowledge management/information dissemination; research/documentation; standards/guidelines; training/education. **Events** *European Label Forum* Vienna (Austria) 2023, *European Label Forum* Baveno (Italy) 2022, *European Label Forum* 2021, *European Label Forum* Rome (Italy) 2020, *European Label Forum* Copenhagen (Denmark) 2019. **Publications** *FINAT Radar* (2 a year); *FINAT Yearbook* (annual) in English; *FINAT E-newsletter* (24 a year). Technical Handbook; Educational Handbook. **Members** Ordinary (A – label manufacturers; B – manufacturers of self-adhesive and heat-seal materials, presses, inks, dies, application machinery, auxiliary equipment and materials); Extraordinary (C – manufacturers of papers, films, foils, adhesives, silicones, release liners, coating equipment, service providers; D – national associations of label manufacturers, institutes, information media; E – Honorary members). Enterprises (about 500) in 42 countries. Membership countries not specified. **NGO Relations** Member of (4): Celab-Europe; *European Platform for Chemicals Using Manufacturing Industries (CheMI, #08223)*; *International Confederation of Paper and Board Converters in Europe (CITPA, #12866)*; *Plastics Recyclers Europe (PRE, #18394)*. Supporter of Declaration of on Paper Recovery, maintained by *European Paper Recycling Council (EPRC, #08139)*. [2022.10.19/XD1951/**D**]

♦ FINA / see World Aquatics (#21100)
♦ FINCA / see FINCA International
♦ FINCA International (internationally oriented national body)
♦ FinCoNet – International Financial Consumer Protection Organisation (unconfirmed)
♦ FINDES – Fondation internationale pour le développement économique et social, Paris (internationally oriented national body)
♦ **FIND** Foundation for Innovative New Diagnostics (#09959)

♦ Findhorn Foundation 09774

Contact Communications Dept, The Park, Findhorn, Forres, IV36 3TZ, UK. T. +441309690311. Fax +441309691301. E-mail: enquiries@findhorn.org.
Cluny Hill St Leonards Road, Forres, IV36 3RD, UK. T. +441309678020. Fax +441309678021.
URL: http://www.findhorn.org/
History 17 Nov 1962, Findhorn (UK). Registered as a charitable Trust 1972. **Aims** As a *spiritual* community, holistic learning centre and ecovillage, help to unfold a new human consciousness and create a positive and sustainable future; explore the challenges and task of creating new ways of living that promote sustainability, peaceful relationships, cooperation with nature and a deep sense of inner wellbeing. **Structure** Board of Trustees (meets at least twice a year); Management Team. **Languages** English. **Staff** 90.00 FTE, paid. 50-70 voluntary. **Finance** Proceeds from workshops. Other sources: facilities rental; fundraising; donors; Global Network. Budget (annual): pounds1.6 million. **Activities** Training/education; assistance/advice/consulting; events/meetings. **Events** *Conference on nonviolent communication* Findhorn (UK) 2006, *International conference / Conference* Findhorn (UK) 2003, *International conference* Findhorn (UK) 2002, *International conference* Findhorn (UK) 2001, *International conference* Findhorn (UK) 2001. **Publications** Books; tapes.
Members Individuals resource people and stewards in 36 countries and territories:

Argentina, Armenia, Australia, Austria, Belgium, Bolivia, Brazil, Bulgaria, Canada, Chile, Colombia, Denmark, Finland, France, Germany, Greece, Hong Kong, India, Ireland, Israel, Italy, Japan, Luxembourg, Netherlands, New Zealand, Northern Ireland, Poland, Portugal, Russia, South Africa, Spain, Sweden, Switzerland, Türkiye, UK, USA.
IGO Relations Designated in an advisory capacity by the *United Nations (UN, #20515)*. CIFAL Findhorn is part of the Local Development Programme (LDP) of: *United Nations Institute for Training and Research (UNITAR, #20576)*. Annual Findhorn Foundation Ecovillage Training programme is part of the United Nations effort to promote basic principles of sustainable economic and social development and has the institutional endorsement of *United Nations Institute for Training and Research (UNITAR, #20576)*. Associated with Department of Global Communications of the United Nations. **NGO Relations** Founding member of: *NGO Forum on Environment (FOE, #17125)*. Member of: *EarthAction (EA, #05159)*; *Global Ecovillage Network (GEN, #10331)*. [2019/XF1780/fv/**F**]

- ♦ Find Your Feet (internationally oriented national body)
- ♦ Fine Chocolate Industry Association (unconfirmed)
- ♦ FINE / see European Federation of Educators in Nursing Sciences (#07102)
- ♦ **FINE** European Federation of Educators in Nursing Sciences (#07102)
- ♦ **FINE** Federation of International Nurses in Endocrinology (#09674)
- ♦ **FIN** Fabry International Network (#09231)
- ♦ **FIN** Fireflyers International Network (#09778)
- ♦ Fingo – Suomalaiset Kehitysjärjestöt (internationally oriented national body)
- ♦ FINICAM – Federación Interamericana de Instituciones de Crédito y Asesoria Municipal (inactive)
- ♦ Finland Futures Research Centre (internationally oriented national body)
- ♦ Finländsak Kommittén för Europeisk Säkerhet / see Finnish Committee for European Security
- ♦ Finlands Flyktinghjälp (internationally oriented national body)
- ♦ Finlands Fredsförbund (internationally oriented national body)
- ♦ Finländska utvecklingsföreningar rf (internationally oriented national body)
- ♦ Finlands Svenska Biblioteksförening (internationally oriented national body)

♦ FinMark Trust (FMT) 09775

CEO PO Box 61674, Sanofi House, Second Floor, 2 Bond Street, Grand Central Office Park, Midrand, 1632, South Africa. T. +27113159197. E-mail: info@finmark.org.za.
URL: http://www.finmark.org.za/

History Mar 2002. Founded with funding from *Department for International Development (DFID, inactive)*, originally for a five-year-term. **Aims** Make financial markets work for the poor, ensuring economic inclusivity and linking financial inclusion to the real economy. **Structure** Trustees (5), including Chair. **Staff** 40.00 FTE, paid. **Finance** Initial funding from: *Department for International Development (DFID, inactive)*. Current funding from: DFID/UKAID; *Bill and Melinda Gates Foundation (BMGF)*; MasterCard Foundation; *United Nations Capital Development Fund (UNCDF, #20524)*. **Activities** Capacity building; financial and/or material support; guidance/assistance/consulting; knowledge management/information dissemination; monitoring/evaluation; politics/policy/regulatory; projects/programmes. Active in: Botswana, Eswatini, Lesotho, Malawi, South Africa, Zimbabwe. **Events** *Segmenting loan performance in South Africa* Johannesburg (South Africa) 2015. **Information Services** *Knowledge Hub*. **NGO Relations** Spin-off organizations: *African Union for Housing Finance (AUHF, #00491)*; *Centre for Affordable Housing Finance in Africa (CAHF, #03723)*. Member of: *FSD Africa (#10010)*. Founding partner of: *Access to Insurance Initiative (A2ii, #00051)*. [2022.05.06/XJ4541/f/**F**]

- ♦ FinMUN – Finnish Model United Nations (internationally oriented national body)
- ♦ Finnchurchaid / see Finn Church Aid
- ♦ Finn Church Aid (internationally oriented national body)
- ♦ FINNFUND – Teollisen Yhteistyön Rahasto (internationally oriented national body)
- ♦ FINNIDA / see Department for International Development Cooperation
- ♦ Finnish Comittee for European Security / see Finnish Committee for European Security
- ♦ Finnish Committee for European Security (internationally oriented national body)
- ♦ Finnish Development NGOs (internationally oriented national body)
- ♦ Finnish European Studies Association (internationally oriented national body)
- ♦ Finnish Evangelical Lutheran Mission (internationally oriented national body)
- ♦ Finnish Export Institute / see Finnish Institute for International Trade
- ♦ Finnish Free Foreign Mission / see Fida International
- ♦ Finnish Fund for Industrial Cooperation (internationally oriented national body)
- ♦ Finnish Institute of International Affairs (internationally oriented national body)
- ♦ Finnish Institute for International Trade (internationally oriented national body)
- ♦ Finnish International Development Agency / see Department for International Development Cooperation
- ♦ Finnish International Studies Association (internationally oriented national body)
- ♦ Finnish League for Human Rights (internationally oriented national body)
- ♦ Finnish Lutheran Overseas Mission (internationally oriented national body)
- ♦ Finnish Model United Nations (internationally oriented national body)
- ♦ Finnish Peace Committee – Peace Fund (internationally oriented national body)
- ♦ Finnish Peace Research Association (internationally oriented national body)
- ♦ Finnish Refugee Council (internationally oriented national body)
- ♦ Finnish Society for Development Research (internationally oriented national body)
- ♦ Finnish Society for Development Studies / see Kehitystutkimuksen Seura
- ♦ Finnish Society for Futures Studies (internationally oriented national body)
- ♦ Finnish-Swedish Library Association (internationally oriented national body)
- ♦ Finnska Missionssällskapet (internationally oriented national body)
- ♦ FINO – Fédération internationale de numismatique olympique (inactive)
- ♦ **FINO** Fondation internationale Olympafrica (#09823)
- ♦ FiNo – Fonologi i Norden (meeting series)
- ♦ FINSIA – Financial Services Institute of Australasia (internationally oriented national body)
- ♦ FINTRA – Finnish Institute for International Trade (internationally oriented national body)
- ♦ **FINUL** Force intérimaire des Nations Unies au Liban (#20577)
- ♦ FIOCC – Fédération internationale des ouvriers de la chaussure et du cuir (inactive)
- ♦ FIOCES – Fédération internationale des organisations de correspondances et d'échanges scolaires (inactive)
- ♦ **FIODS** Fédération internationale des organisations de donneurs de sang (#13374)
- ♦ **FIOE** Federation of Islamic Organisations in Europe (#09682)
- ♦ FIO – Faculté internationale d'ostéopathie (internationally oriented national body)
- ♦ **FIO** Federación Iberoamericana de Ombudsman (#09317)
- ♦ FIO – Fédération internationale d'oléiculture (inactive)
- ♦ **FIOH** Future in Our Hands (#10050)
- ♦ FIOM – Fédération internationale des organisations de travailleurs de la métallurgie (inactive)
- ♦ FIOOT / see International Medical Ozone Federation (#14136)
- ♦ FIOPM – Fédération internationale des organismes de psychologie médicale (inactive)
- ♦ FIORH – Fédération internationale pour l'organisation de rencontres de handicapés (inactive)
- ♦ **FIORP** Fundación Internacional ORP (#10032)
- ♦ **FIOSS** Fédération internationale des organisations de sciences sociales (#13543)
- ♦ FIOST – Fédération internationale des organisations syndicales du personnel des transports (inactive)
- ♦ FIOW – First International Organization of Welcome (inactive)
- ♦ FIPAD – Fondation internationale pour un autre développement (inactive)
- ♦ FIPAD – Fundación Internacional para Alternativas de Desarrollo (inactive)
- ♦ FIPA – Federación Iberoamericana de Productores de Árides (unconfirmed)
- ♦ FIPA – Fédération internationale de la presse agricole (inactive)
- ♦ FIPA – Fédération internationale des producteurs agricoles (inactive)
- ♦ FIPA – Fédération internationale des professionnels de l'assistance (inactive)
- ♦ FIPA – Federation of International Poetry Associations (inactive)
- ♦ **FIPAGO** Fédération internationale des fabricants des papiers gommés (#09631)
- ♦ FIPA / see ParlAmericas (#18206)
- ♦ **FIPAT** Federative International Programme for Anatomical Terminology (#09716)
- ♦ **FIPCA** Federación Iberoamericana de Productores Cinematograficos y Audiovisuales (#09318)
- ♦ **FIPCA** Ibero-American Federation of Cinematographic and Audiovisual Producers (#09318)
- ♦ **FIPC** Fédération internationale des petits chanteurs (#09649)
- ♦ **FIPC** Fédération internationale des pharmaciens catholiques (#13380)
- ♦ **FIPC** Foederatio Internationalis Pueri Cantores (#09649)
- ♦ FIPC – Fonds international pour la promotion de la culture (inactive)
- ♦ FIPCM – Fédération internationale de prêtres catholiques mariés (inactive)
- ♦ **FIPD** Fondation de l'Institut Panafricain pour le Développement (#09820)
- ♦ **FIPE** Forum international pour la protection de l'enfance (#13633)
- ♦ FIPESO – Fédération internationale des professeurs de l'enseignement secondaire officiel (inactive)
- ♦ **FIP** Federación Internacional de Pádel (#14496)
- ♦ **FIP** Federación Internacional de Periodistas (#13462)
- ♦ **FIP** Federación Internacional de Polo (#09675)
- ♦ **FIP** Federación Internacional de Psicoterapia (#13523)
- ♦ **FIP** Fédération internationale pharmaceutique (#14566)
- ♦ **FIP** Fédération internationale de philatélie (#09650)
- ♦ FIP – Fédération internationale des phonothèques (inactive)
- ♦ FIP – Fédération internationale de phytosociologie (inactive)
- ♦ **FIP** Fédération internationale des piétons (#13502)
- ♦ **FIP** Fédération Internationale des Podologues (#13514)
- ♦ FIP – Fédération internationale de la précontrainte (inactive)
- ♦ **FIP** Fédération internationale de psychothérapie (#13523)
- ♦ **FIP** Federation of International Polo (#09675)
- ♦ **FIPF** Fédération internationale des professeurs de français (#09652)
- ♦ FIPFI – Fédération internationale des producteurs de films indépendants (no recent information)
- ♦ FIP / see Forus (#09934)
- ♦ **FIPFP** Fédération internationale des petits frères des pauvres (#13471)
- ♦ **FIP** Groupement pour les facilités de circulation internationale du personnel des chemins de fer (#02465)
- ♦ FIP / see International Federation of Podiatrists (#13514)
- ♦ **FIP** International Padel Federation (#14496)
- ♦ FIP / see International Powerlifting Federation (#14630)
- ♦ **FIPJP** Fédération internationale de pétanque et jeu provençal (#09648)
- ♦ FIPLF – Fédération internationale de la presse de langue française (inactive)
- ♦ **FIPLV** Fédération internationale des professeurs de langues vivantes (#13468)
- ♦ FIPMEC – Fédération internationale des petites et moyennes entreprises commerciales (inactive)
- ♦ FIPMI – Fédération internationale des petites et moyennes entreprises industrielles (inactive)
- ♦ FIPM / see International Federation for Psychotherapy (#13523)
- ♦ FIPOD – Fédération internationale pour l'observation du dimanche (inactive)
- ♦ FIPO – Fédération internationale de la presse orientale (inactive)
- ♦ FIPOI – Fondation des immeubles pour les organisations internationales (internationally oriented national body)
- ♦ **FIPOL** Fonds internationaux d'indemnisation pour les dommages dus à la pollution par les hydrocarbures (#14402)

♦ FIPP 09776

CEO 1st Floor, 48 Chancery Lane, London, WC2A 1JF, UK. T. +447921648138. E-mail: info@fipp.com.
Contact address not obtained.
URL: http://www.fipp.com/

History 26 Jul 1910, Brussels (Belgium). Reorganized 1925, Paris (France). Statutes adopted in 1927; revised: 1935; 1953; 1971; 2010. Former names and other names: *International Federation of the Periodical Press* – former; *Fédération internationale de la presse périodique (FIPP)* – former; *Federación Internacional de la Prensa Periódica* – former; *Internationaler Verband der Zeitschriftenpresse* – former; *Federazione Internazionale della Stampa Periodica* – former; *Internationale Federatie van de Periodieke Pers* – former; *Worldwide magazine media association* – former; *FIPP – the network for global media* – former; *FIPP – Connecting Global Media* – full title. Registration: Companies House, No/ID: 1006977, Start date: 5 Apr 1971, UK. **Aims** Empower media owner members to build market-leading international media businesses through intelligence, solutions and partnerships. **Structure** Management Board; President; CEO. **Languages** English. **Staff** 5.00 FTE, paid. Freelance contributors and consultants. **Finance** Sources: fees for services; meeting proceeds; members' dues; revenue from activities/projects; sale of publications; sponsorship. Annual budget: 1,000,000 GBP (2020). **Activities** Awards/prizes/competitions; events/meetings. **Events** *World Media Congress* Cascais (Portugal) 2022, *FIPP Direct-to-Consumer World* UK 2021, *Global Digital Innovators Summit* Berlin (Germany) 2020, *Global Digital Innovators Summit* Berlin (Germany) 2020, *World Media Congress* London (UK) 2020. **Publications** *FIPP World* (weekly) – newsletter; *Innovation in Media World* (annual). **Members** National associations of periodical publishers (35); Magazine publishing companies (160); Associate companies (40). Membership countries not specified. **Consultative Status** Consultative status granted from: *ECOSOC (#05331)* (Ros C); *UNESCO (#20322)* (Consultative Status); *World Intellectual Property Organization (WIPO, #21593)* (Permanent Observer Status). **IGO Relations** Accredited by (1): *United Nations Office at Vienna (UNOV, #20604)*. Represents magazine interests to: *Universal Postal Union (UPU, #20682)*. Invited to sessions of Intergovernmental Council of: *International Programme for the Development of Communication (IPDC, #14651)*. Associated with Department of Global Communications of the United Nations. **NGO Relations** Member of (3): *European Magazine Media Association (EMMA, #07723)*; *International Advertising Association (IAA, #11590)*; *International Federation of Reproduction Rights Organizations (IFRRO, #13527)*. In liaison with technical committees of: *International Organization for Standardization (ISO, #14473)*. [2023.02.20/XC2027/**C**]

- ♦ FIPP – Connecting Global Media / see FIPP (#09776)
- ♦ FIPPD / see Fédération européenne et internationale des patrons prothésistes dentaires (#09575)
- ♦ **FIPP** Federación Iberopanamericana de Periodoncia (#09328)
- ♦ FIPP – Fédération internationale pour la protection des populations (inactive)
- ♦ **FIPP** Fondation internationale pénale et pénitentiaire (#14553)
- ♦ FIPP / see International Federation of Podiatrists (#13514)
- ♦ FIPP – the network for global media / see FIPP (#09776)
- ♦ FIPREGA – Fédération internationale de la presse gastronomique, vinicole et touristique (inactive)
- ♦ **FIPRESCI** Fédération internationale de la presse cinématographique (#09651)
- ♦ FIPR / see World Skate (#21786)
- ♦ FIPS Casting (see: #04562)
- ♦ FIPSed – Fédération internationale de la pêche sportive en eau douce (see: #04562)
- ♦ **FIPS** Fédération internationale des patrouilles de ski (#09647)
- ♦ FIPS mer – Fédération internationale de la pêche sportive en mer (see: #04562)
- ♦ FIPS-M – International Sea Sportfishing Federation (see: #04562)
- ♦ FIPS Mouche – Fédération internationale de pêche sportive mouche (see: #04562)
- ♦ **FIPV** Federación Internacional de Pelota Vasca (#09340)
- ♦ FIQ / see International Bowling Federation (#12384)
- ♦ FIQ-WTBA Asian Zone / see Asian Bowling Federation (#01362)
- ♦ FIRA-AER / see Rugby Europe (#18998)
- ♦ FIRA – Association européenne de rugby / see Rugby Europe (#18998)
- ♦ **FIRAC** Fédération internationale des radio-amateurs cheminots (#12122)
- ♦ FIRAE / see Federation of International Retail Associations (#09676)
- ♦ **FIRA** Federation of International Retail Associations (#09676)
- ♦ **FIRA** Federation of International Robosoccer Association (#09677)
- ♦ FIRA / see Rugby Europe (#18998)

♦ FIR – association antifasciste / see International Federation of Resistance Movements (#13529)
♦ FIRE AID (internationally oriented national body)
♦ FIRE AID and International Development / see FIRE AID

♦ Fireball International (FI) 09777

Commodore Afflington Lookout Barn, Corfe Castle, BH20 5LR, UK. T. +441929439165.
Sec address not obtained.
URL: http://www.fireball-international.com/

History 1960, as an International Centreboard Boat Class Association of *World Sailing (#21760)*. Has also been referred to as *International Fireball Class Association*. **Aims** Promote and further the interests of International Fireball Class *yachting* throughout the world; maintain the design characteristics of the Fireball; coordinate and manage the affairs of the class; make recommendations to and agreements with ISAF concerning rules of the Class. **Structure** General Meeting (at World Championship Regatta). Council; Executive; Rules and Technical Committee; Secretariat. **Events** *Annual General Meeting* France 2009, *Annual General Meeting* Thailand 2008, *Annual General Meeting* St Moritz (Switzerland) 2007, *Annual General Meeting* Victoria, BC (Canada) 2006, *Annual General Meeting* Teignmouth (UK) 2005. **Publications** *International Fireball Magazine* (2 a year).
Members National associations in 22 countries and territories:
Australia, Belgium, Canada, Channel Is, Czechia, France, Germany, Hawaii, Ireland, Italy, Japan, Kenya, Namibia, Netherlands, Nigeria, South Africa, Sweden, Switzerland, Thailand, UK, USA, Zimbabwe. [2016/XE0799/**E**]

♦ FIREC – Fédération internationale des rédacteurs en chef (inactive)
♦ FIRE – Feminist International Radio Endeavour (internationally oriented national body)

♦ Fireflyers International Network (FIN) 09778

Hon Sec Malaysian Nature Soc, JKR 641, Jalan Kelantan, Bukit Persekutuan, 50480 Kuala Lumpur, Malaysia. E-mail: conservation2@mns.org.my.
URL: https://fireflyersinternational.net/

History 2007. **Aims** Serve as a leader and catalyst for the conservation of fireflies and their habitats. **Structure** Steering Committee. **Activities** Advocacy/lobbying/activism; events/meetings; research/documentation; training/education. **Events** *International Firefly Symposium* Tlaxcala (Mexico) 2025, *International Firefly Symposium* Avintes (Portugal) 2022, *International Firefly Symposium* 2020. **Members** Scientists (over 200) in over 20 countries. Membership countries not specified. [2022/AA2911/v/**F**]

♦ **FIRE** Fundación Internacional para la Restauración de Ecosistemas (#10033)
♦ Firelight Foundation (internationally oriented national body)

♦ Firemen without Borders 09779

Pompiers sans frontières (PoSF) – Bomberos Unidos sin Fronteras (BoSF)

Pres 12 rue Charloun Rieu, Groupe Scolaire Joseph d'Arbaud, 13090 Aix-en-Provence, France. T. +33442914722. Fax +33442914722. E-mail: contact@pompiers-sans-frontieres.org.
URL: http://www.pompiers-sans-frontieres.org/

History Jan 1991. In Spanish also known under the acronym *BUSF*. Registered in accordance with French law. Registered office in Aix-en-Provence (France). **Aims** Rehabilitate the system of civil security in emergent countries; develop research and training programmes on *disaster preparedness* in favour of the population, civil security and local institutions as a component of sustainable development; participate in *emergency* actions to help refugees and convey humanitarian *aid* in support of civil security structures which are victims of armed conflicts; provide intervention by specialized teams in countries where natural disasters occur. **Structure** Board of Directors. Director. Permanent Offices in: Haiti; Madagascar; Peru; Senegal. **Languages** English, French, Spanish. **Staff** 5.00 FTE, paid; 400.00 FTE, voluntary. **Finance** Public and private funds. Budget (annual): about euro 800,000. **Activities** Runs development programmes in Haiti, Madagascar, Morocco, Peru and Senegal. **Publications** *Pompiers Sans Frontières* (4 a year) – newsletter; *Pompiers sans frontières* (annual) – magazine.
Members Active; Associate; Honorary. Individuals in 10 countries:
Bolivia, Chile, France, Haiti, Indonesia, Madagascar, Mexico, Morocco, Peru, Senegal.
NGO Relations Member of: *Coordination SUD*. [2019/XG1548/**F**]

♦ Fire Safe Europe (FSEU) 09780

Managing Dir Rue Mercelis 57, 1050 Brussels, Belgium. T. +32487124467. E-mail: secretariat@firesafeeurope.eu.
URL: http://firesafeeurope.eu/

History 2011. **Aims** Improve fire safety in buildings for people and society. **Languages** English, French. **Activities** Awareness raising; advocacy/lobbying/activism; knowledge management/information dissemination; networking/liaising.
Members Organizations; companies. Organizations (3):
Concrete Europe (#04433); *European Association of Producers of Flame Retardant Olefinic Cable Compounds (FROCC, #06166)*; *European Autoclaved Aerated Concrete Association (EAACA, #06297)*.
Companies (7). Membership countries not specified. [2019.02.25/XM5822/y/**D**]

♦ **FIR** Fédération internationale de recyclage (#14706)
♦ **FIR** Fédération internationale des résistants (#13529)
♦ FIR – Fonds Ingrid Renard (internationally oriented national body)
♦ **FIRHF** Fédération internationale pour la recherche en histoire des femmes (#13528)
♦ Firilite – Federation of International Research Institutes on Law and Information Technology in Europe (inactive)
♦ Firilite – Firilite – Federation of International Research Institutes on Law and Information Technology in Europe (inactive)
♦ **FIRM** Fédération internationale des rectifieurs et reconstructeurs de moteurs (#09654)
♦ **FIRN** Frontiers in Immunology Research Network (#10006)
♦ FIRS – Financial Intermediation Research Society (internationally oriented national body)
♦ **FIRS** Forum of International Respiratory Societies (#09922)
♦ First African Bicycle Information Office / see Pan-Africa Bicycle Information Network

♦ First Aid Education European Network 09781

Contact address not obtained. E-mail: firstaid.refcentre@croix-rouge.fr.
URL: http://www.firstaidinaction.net/

History as *Red Cross and Red Crescent European Group for First Aid Education*. [2008/XG5949/**E**]

♦ First Church of Christ, Scientist 09782

Première Eglise du Christ, Scientiste

Contact 210 Massachussetts Ave, Boston MA 02115, USA. E-mail: info@churchofchristscientist.org.
URL: http://www.christianscience.com/

History 1879, Boston MA (USA), by Mary Baker Eddy and her followers. Reorganized under current name, 1892. Churches of Christ, Scientist worldwide are regarded as branches. Body corporate under General Laws of Commonwealth of Massachusetts (USA). **Aims** Commemorate the word and works of our Master Jesus, which should reinstate primitive Christianity, including healing of sickness and sin through reliance on the divine power of God's love. **Structure** Board of Directors; Board of Trustees; Local branch churches; Christian Science Publishing Society. **Languages** Publications in various languages. **Finance** Members' dues. Voluntary contributions. **Activities** Religious activities; events/meetings; publishing activities. **Events** *Annual Meeting* Boston, MA (USA) 2006, *International conference* Boston, MA (USA) 1998, *Annual meeting* Boston, MA (USA) 1995, *Annual meeting* Boston, MA (USA) 1994, *Meeting for young Christian scientists* Cardiff (UK) 1993. **Publications** *The Christian Science Sentinel* (weekly); *The Christian Science Journal* (12 a year); *Herald of Christian Science* (12 a year) in French, German, Portuguese, Spanish; *The Christian Science Monitor* (daily online and weekly in print); *Christian Science Quarterly Weekly Bible Lessons*. *Manual of The Mother Church* by Mary Baker Eddy; *Science and Health with Key to the Scriptures* by Mary Baker Eddy. Other writings by Mary Baker Eddy.
Members Congregations in 63 countries and territories:
Angola, Argentina, Australia, Austria, Barbados, Belgium, Benin, Bermuda, Brazil, Burundi, Cameroon, Canada, Chile, Colombia, Congo Brazzaville, Congo DR, Cuba, Denmark, Ecuador, Finland, France, Germany, Ghana, Greece, Grenada, Guatemala, Hong Kong, India, Indonesia, Ireland, Italy, Jamaica, Japan, Kenya, Korea Rep, Mexico, Netherlands, New Zealand, Nigeria, Peru, Philippines, Poland, Portugal, Puerto Rico, Russia, Rwanda, Singapore, South Africa, Spain, Sweden, Switzerland, Tanzania UR, Thailand, Togo, Trinidad-Tobago, Uganda, UK, Ukraine, Uruguay, USA, Venezuela, Zambia, Zimbabwe.
IGO Relations *European Commission (EC, #06633)*. [2019.10.07/XF0275/**F**]

♦ First Conference for the Exploitation and Conservation of Marine Resources in the South Pacific / see Comisión Permanente del Pacífico Sur (#04141)
♦ **FIRST** Forum of Incident Response and Security Teams (#09918)
♦ **FIRST Initiative** Financial Sector Reform and Strengthening Initiative (#09769)
♦ First International Newsreel and Television Association (inactive)
♦ First International Organization of Welcome (inactive)
♦ First Multilateral Monetary Clearing Agreement (1947 treaty)
♦ First Multipurpose Women Cooperative in Gassim (internationally oriented national body)
♦ FIRS / see World Skate (#21786)
♦ **FIRT** Fédération internationale pour la recherche théâtrale (#13570)
♦ FISAC – Federación Interamericana de Sociedades de Autores y Compositores (inactive)
♦ FISAC – Federation internationale de saut à la corde (inactive)
♦ **FISAE** International Federation of Ex-Libris Societies (#13421)
♦ FISA – Fédération internationale des semaines d'arts (inactive)
♦ **FISA** Fédération internationale des sociétés aérophilatéliques (#13342)
♦ FISA – Fédération internationale du sport automobile (inactive)
♦ FISAF / see FISAF International (#09783)
♦ FISA – Finnish International Studies Association (internationally oriented national body)

♦ FISAF International 09783

Exec Dir Ohradské nám 7a/1628, Stodůlky, 155 00 Prague, Czechia. E-mail: info@fisafinternational.com.
URL: https://www.fisafinternational.com/

History Former names and other names: *Federation of International Sports, Aerobics and Fitness International (FISAF)* – former. **Structure** Executive Committee. International Technical Committees (2): Sports Aerobics and Fitness; Hip Hop. Educational Comittee; Supervisory Board.
Members Full in 31 countries and territories:
Australia, Belgium, China, Côte d'Ivoire, Cyprus, Czechia, Denmark, Finland, France, Germany, India, Iran Islamic Rep, Italy, Korea Rep, Malaysia, Maldives, Mexico, Morocco, Netherlands, New Zealand, Poland, Portugal, Russia, Serbia, Singapore, South Africa, Spain, Switzerland, Taiwan, Trinidad-Tobago, UK.
NGO Relations Member of (2): *International Health and Fitness Association (IHFA)*; *International Sport Network Organization (ISNO, #15592)*. Partner of (1): *European Esports Observatory (EEO)*. [2020/AA1352/**C**]

♦ FISA – Fisheries Society of Africa (no recent information)
♦ **FISAIC** Fédération internationale des sociétés artistiques et intellectuelles de cheminots (#09660)
♦ FISA International Coaching Academy (internationally oriented national body)
♦ **FISav** Fédération Internationale de Savate (#09656)
♦ FISA / see World Rowing (#21756)
♦ **FISB** Fédération internationale de skibob (#14868)
♦ FISCETCV / see World Organization of Workers (#21697)
♦ FISCETC / see World Organization of Workers (#21697)
♦ **FISC** Fundación Internacional de Solidaridad Compañia de Maria (#10034)
♦ Fischerei-Übereinkommen (1964 treaty)
♦ FISC / see International Cooperative and Mutual Insurance Federation (#12948)
♦ FISCM – Fédération internationale des syndicats chrétiens de mineurs (inactive)
♦ **FISEC** Fédération internationale sportive de l'enseignement catholique (#15589)
♦ **FISE** Fédération internationale syndicale de l'enseignement (#09662)
♦ **FISEM** Federación Iberoamericana de Sociedades de Educación Matematica (#09320)
♦ FISE / see UNICEF (#20332)
♦ FIS – Fédération internationale du commerce des semences (inactive)
♦ FIS – Fédération internationale de sauvetage aquatique (inactive)
♦ **FIS** Fédération Internationale de Ski (#09659)
♦ **FISF** Fédération internationale de scrabble francophone (#09657)
♦ FIS – Fondation internationale scientifique (inactive)
♦ **FIS** Fondation islamique du salut (#09824)
♦ FISG – Forschungsinstitut für Spiritualität und Gesundheit (internationally oriented national body)
♦ FISGV – Federazione Internazionale della Stampa Gastronomica e Vinicola (inactive)
♦ Fisheries Society of Africa (no recent information)

♦ Fishery Committee for the Eastern Central Atlantic (CECAF) 09784

Comité des pêches pour l'Atlantique centre-Est (COPACE)

Sec FAO Regional Office, PO Box 1628, Accra, Ghana.
URL: http://www.fao.org/fishery/rfb/cecaf/

History 19 Sep 1967, Rome (Italy), by Article VI-2 of the Constitution of *FAO (#09260)*, following decision of FAO Council to replace *Regional Fisheries Commission for Western Africa (RFCWA)*, abolished by FAO Conference, 1967. First session Mar 1969. Rules of Procedure adopted 1969 and amended 1977. **Aims** Promote, coordinate and assist national and regional programmes of research and development, leading to rational utilization of the *marine fishery* resources of the CECAF area; assist member governments in establishing a scientific basis for regulation measures on conservation and improvement of marine fishery resources; encourage education and training through establishment or improvement of national and regional institutions and by promotion and organization of seminars, study tours and training centres; assist in collection, interchange, dissemination and analysis or study of statistical, biological and environmental data and other marine fishery information; assist member governments in formulating programmes to be implemented through sources of international aid to help achieve the above mentioned objectives; promote liaison and cooperation among competent institutions within the sea area served. **Structure** Committee elects Chairman and up to 3 Vice-Chairmen. Secretariat located at *FAO Regional Office for Africa (FAO/RAF, #09265)*. Currently under review for upgrading to Commission status. **Languages** English, French, Spanish. **Finance** FAO Regular Programme; extra budgetary funds for special studies and resource surveys. **Activities** Makes recommendations on: mesh size of trawls; limits to fishing efforts; integrated coastal management. **Events** *Session* Dakar (Senegal) 2016, *Session* Rabat (Morocco) 2012, *Session* Cotonou (Benin) 2008, *Session* Douala (Cameroon) 2006, *Session* Dakar (Senegal) 2004. **Publications** *CECAF Statistical Bulletin*. Session reports; data on fisheries resources and general fisheries information on request.
Members FAO member nations and associate members selected by FAO Director General. Governments of 32 countries:
Benin, Cameroon, Cape Verde, Congo Brazzaville, Congo DR, Côte d'Ivoire, Cuba, Equatorial Guinea, France, Gabon, Gambia, Ghana, Greece, Guinea, Guinea-Bissau, Italy, Japan, Korea Rep, Liberia, Mauritania, Morocco, Netherlands, Nigeria, Norway, Poland, Romania, Sao Tomé-Principe, Senegal, Sierra Leone, Spain, Togo, USA.
International organization (1):
European Union (EU, #08967).
Observers – governments of 4 countries:
Angola, Canada, Portugal, UK.
IGO Relations *Regional Fisheries Committee for the Gulf of Guinea (#18785)*; *Economic Community of West African States (ECOWAS, #05312)*; *Mano River Union (MRU, #16566)*; Ministerial Conference on Fisheries Cooperation among African States bordering the Atlantic Ocean; *African Union Scientific Technical Research Commission (AU STRC, #00493)*. [2010/XE9778/**E***]

♦ Fish Health Section of the Asian Fisheries Society (see: #01483)
♦ Fish Marketing Information, Promotion and Technical Advisory Services for Arab Countries / see Centre for Marketing Information and Advisory Services for Fishery Products in the Arab Region (#03772)
♦ **FISIER** Fédération internationale des sociétés et instituts pour l'étude de la Renaissance (#13549)
♦ **FISI** Fédération internationale des instructeurs de sport de neige (#13542)
♦ **FISITA** Fédération internationale des sociétés d'ingénieurs des techniques de l'automobile (#13369)
♦ FISMARC – Fédération internationale du sport médical pour l'aide à la recherche cancérologique (inactive)
♦ **FISM** Fédération Internationale des Sociétés Magiques (#13473)
♦ FISM – Federazione Internazionale dei Sindacati Metalmeccanici (inactive)

FISNA Forest Invasive
09784

alphabetic sequence excludes
For the complete listing, see Yearbook Online at

- ♦ **FISNA** Forest Invasive Species Network for Africa (#09863)
- ♦ **FISO** Fédération Internationale de Sports d'Obstacles (#21679)
- ♦ **FISO** Fundación Iberoamericana de Seguridad y Salud Ocupacional (#10027)
- ♦ FISP / see International Federation of Popular Sports (#13515)
- ♦ **FISP** Federación Internacional de Sociedades de Filosofia (#13507)
- ♦ FISP / see Fédération francophone Internationale de Soins Palliatifs (#09588)
- ♦ **FISP** Fédération francophone Internationale de Soins Palliatifs (#09588)
- ♦ **FISP** Fédération internationale des sociétés de philosophie (#13507)
- ♦ **FISPGHAN** Federation of International Societies for Pediatric Gastroenterology, Hepatology and Nutrition (#09678)
- ♦ **FISP** Internationale Vereinigung Philosophischer Gesellschaften (#13507)
- ♦ **FISP** International Federation of Philosophical Societies (#13507)
- ♦ **FISPMED** International Federation for Sustainable Development and Fight to Poverty in the Mediterranean-Black Sea (#13562)
- ♦ **FISpT** Fédération internationale Sport pour tous (#09661)
- ♦ fisrad – Fédération internationale des systèmes de recherche agricole pour le développement (no recent information)
- ♦ FISSF – Federazione Internazionale delle Scuole di Storia di Famiglia (no recent information)
- ♦ **FISS** Foundation for International Studies on Social Security (#09963)
- ♦ FISTAV – Fédération internationale des syndicats des travailleurs de l'audio-visuel (inactive)
- ♦ FISTED – Fondation islamique pour la science, la technologie et le développement (inactive)
- ♦ **FISU América** Organización Deportiva Universitaria Panamericana (#17835)
- ♦ **FISUEL** Fédération internationale pour la sécurité des usagers de l'électricité (#09658)
- ♦ **FISU** Federación Internacional del Deporte Universitario (#15830)
- ♦ **FISU** Fédération Internationale du Sport Universitaire (#15830)
- ♦ **FISU** International University Sports Federation (#15830)

♦ FISU Oceania 09785

Secretariat c/- Ste 1-12, Sports House, 150 Caxton Street, Milton QLD 4064, Australia. E-mail: office@fisuoceania.com.
URL: http://www.fisuoceania.com/

History 2008. A continental association of *International University Sports Federation (FISU, #15830)*. Former names and other names: *Oceania University Sports Association (OUSA)* – former. **Structure** Executive Committee.
Members Federations in 12 countries and territories:
Australia, Cook Is, Fiji, Guam, Marshall Is, Micronesia FS, New Caledonia, New Zealand, Northern Mariana Is, Papua New Guinea, Samoa, Samoa USA.
NGO Relations Member of (1): *Organisation of Sports Federations of Oceania (OSFO, #17828)*.
[2022/XM6867/**D**]

- ♦ FIT / see Robert Triffin International
- ♦ FITAC / see Federación Internacional del Automóvil Region IV (#09337)
- ♦ FITA – Federation of International Trade Associations (internationally oriented national body)
- ♦ FITAM – Fédération de l'industrie textile africaine et malgache (inactive)
- ♦ FITAP – Fédération internationale des transports aériens privés (inactive)
- ♦ **FITASC** Fédération Internationale de Tir aux Armes Sportives de Chasse (#09665)
- ♦ FITA / see World Archery (#21105)
- ♦ FITBB – Fédération internationale des travailleurs du bâtiment et du bois (inactive)
- ♦ **FITB** Fédération internationale de Tchoukball (#15661)
- ♦ **FITB** Fédération internationale des techniciens de la bonneterie (#13465)
- ♦ **FITB** International Tchoukball Federation (#15661)
- ♦ FITCA – Fédération internationale des transports commerciaux par automobiles (inactive)
- ♦ FITCCOROC – Fédération internationale de Tai Chi Chuan Orient-Occident (inactive)
- ♦ **FITCE** Fédération des ingénieurs des télécommunications de la Communauté européenne (#09597)
- ♦ **FITC** French Intensive Care Society (#19512)
- ♦ FITCM – Federación Internacional de Trabajadores de la Construcción y la Madera (inactive)
- ♦ FITCRE – Fédération internationale des travailleurs chrétiens réfugiés et émigrés (inactive)
- ♦ FITDH / see Terre des Hommes International Federation (#20133)
- ♦ FITEC / see Fédération mondiale du thermalisme et du climatisme (#09692)
- ♦ FITE – Federación Interamericana de Trabajadores del Espectaculo (inactive)
- ♦ **FITE** Fédération Internationale de Tourisme Équestre (#09666)
- ♦ FITEL – Federación Interamericana de Camaras de Informatica, Telecomunicaciones y Electrónica (no recent information)
- ♦ **FITEQ** Fédération Internationale de Teqball (#09663)
- ♦ **FIT** Federación Internacional de Tenis (#15676)
- ♦ **FIT** Fédération internationale de tennis (#15676)
- ♦ **FIT** Fédération internationale des traducteurs (#13574)
- ♦ FIT – Fédération internationale de trampoline (inactive)
- ♦ **FIT** Federation of International Table-Tennis Manufacturers (#09679)
- ♦ **FIT** Federation of International Touch (#09680)
- ♦ FIT – Fondazione Internazionale Trieste per il Progresso e la Libertà delle Scienze (internationally oriented national body)
- ♦ **FIT** Fondo Internacional Trans (#15720)
- ♦ FITH-CMT – Fédération internationale textile et habillement (inactive)
- ♦ FITIMA – Fondation Internationale Tierno et Mariam (unconfirmed)
- ♦ FITIM – Federación Internacional de Trabajadores de las Industrias Metalúrgicas (inactive)
- ♦ **FITO** Fondation internationale pour la trêve olympique (#14410)
- ♦ FITPASC – Fédération internationale des travailleurs des plantations, de l'agriculture et des secteurs connexes (inactive)
- ♦ FITPAS – Federación Internacional de los Trabajadores de las Plantaciones, Agricolas y Similares (inactive)
- ♦ FITPC – Fédération internationale des travailleurs du pétrole et de la chimie (inactive)
- ♦ FITPQ – Federación Internacional de Trabajadores Petroleros y Quimicos (inactive)
- ♦ **FITRAM** Fédération internationale des thérapies et relations d'aide par la médiation (#09664)
- ♦ FITS – Fédération internationale du tourisme social (inactive)
- ♦ FITS – Forum international tourisme solidaire et développement durable (internationally oriented national body)
- ♦ **FITT** Fédération internationale de tennis de table (#15650)
- ♦ FITT – Forum for International Trade Training (internationally oriented national body)
- ♦ FITTHC – Fédération internationale des travailleurs du textile, de l'habillement et du cuir (inactive)
- ♦ FITTVC – Federación Internacional de Trabajadores del Textil, Vestuario y Cuero (inactive)
- ♦ FITV-CMT – Federación Internacional Textil y Vestido (inactive)
- ♦ **FIUC** Federación Internacional de Universidades Católicas (#13381)
- ♦ **FIUC** Fédération internationale des universités catholiques (#13381)
- ♦ **FIU** Federación Iberoamericana Urbanistas (#09324)
- ♦ FIU – Florida International University (internationally oriented national body)
- ♦ **FIUP** Forum international des universités publiques (#13648)
- ♦ FIU-UMVF / see Université Numérique Francophone des Sciences de la Santé et du Sport
- ♦ **FIUV** Fédération internationale Una Voce (#09668)
- ♦ FIV / see Economic and Social Development Bank
- ♦ **FIVA** Fédération internationale des véhicules anciens (#09669)
- ♦ FIVAS / see Foreningen for Internasjonale Vannstudier
- ♦ FIVAS – Foreningen for Internasjonale Vannstudier (internationally oriented national body)
- ♦ **FIVB** Fédération internationale de volleyball (#09670)
- ♦ **FIVC** Fundación Interamericana Ciencia y Vida (#10028)

♦ Five Eyes (FVEY) 09786

Address not obtained.

History Origins traced to *Atlantic Charter (1941)*, issued Aug 1941. *British-US Communication Intelligence Agreement (BRUSA Agreement)*, signed May 1943 to facilitate cooperation. Treaty formalized as *United Kingdom United States Agreement (UKUSA agreement, 1947)*, Mar 1946.
Members Governments (5):
Australia, Canada, New Zealand, UK, USA.
[2016/XM5290/**F***]

♦ Five IP Offices (IP5) 09787

Contact address not obtained.
URL: https://www.fiveipoffices.org/

Aims Improve efficiency and address the growing backlogs in applications worldwide. **Activities** Events/meetings. **Events** *Meeting* Japan 2021, *Meeting* Incheon (Korea Rep) 2019.
Members Intellectual property offices (5):
China, Japan, Korea Rep, USA.
European Patent Office (EPO, #08166).
[2022/AA0254/y/**C**]

- ♦ **FIVEL** Federação Internacional dos Veterinarios Lusófonos (#09285)
- ♦ **Five plus Five Group** Cooperation Process in the Western Mediterranean (#04798)
- ♦ Five-Power Defence Agreement (1957 treaty)

♦ Five Power Defence Arrangements (FPDA) 09788

Address not obtained.

History 1971, on signature of series of agreements between New Zealand, Australia, UK, Singapore (Singapore) and Malaysia. Developed from *'Anglo-Malayan defence agreement'*, signed Aug 1957, since Nov 1959 *Five-Power Defence Agreement (FPDA, 1957)*. **Aims** Function as a multilateral *security* organization in *Southeast Asia*; build up trust among members and enhance security *cooperation*; consult in the event of any form of armed attack against Malaysia or Singapore (Singapore); provide assistance in the training and development of the *armed forces* of Singapore and Malaysia. **Activities** Forces of member countries undertake joint manoeuvres although, for economic reasons, Malaysia withdrew from the 1998 exercise programme.
Members Governments of 5 countries:
Australia, Malaysia, New Zealand, Singapore, UK.
[2009/XF6878/**F***]

- ♦ Five Talents International (internationally oriented national body)
- ♦ Five Years Meeting of Friends in America / see Friends United Meeting
- ♦ **FIV** Fédération internationale du vieillissement (#13345)
- ♦ **FIVH** Framtiden i Våre Hender (#10050)
- ♦ FIVOL – Fondazione Italiana per il Volontariato (internationally oriented national body)

♦ FIVS 09789

Deputy SG 1 cour du Havre, 75008 Paris, France.
URL: http://www.fivs.org/

History 1950, Paris (France). Before FIVS became known under its acronym only, its full title was: *International Federation of Wines and Spirits – Fédération Internationale des Vins et Spiritueux (FIVS) – Federación Internacional de Vinos y Licores*. Registered by French Ministerial Decree, 20 Jul 1951. Former names and other names: *International Union of Wine, Spirits, Brandy and Liqueur Industrialists and Wholesalers* – former; *Fédération internationale des industries et du commerce en gros des vins, spiritueux, eaux-de-vie et liqueurs* – former; *Federación Internacional de Vinos y Espirituosos* – former; *International Federation of Wines and Spirits* – former; *Fédération Internationale des Vins et Spiritueux (FIVS)* – former; *Federación Internacional de Vinos y Licores* – former. **Aims** Promote a successful global alcohol beverage industry, operating on the principles of economic, social and environmental sustainability in an environment free from *trade*-distorting factors; offer a forum for members to discuss and collaborate on areas of common interest. **Structure** General Assembly; Presidential Council; Working Groups (3); Committees (3); Secretariat. **Languages** English, French, Spanish. **Activities** Advocacy/lobbying/activism; events/meetings; knowledge management/information dissemination; networking/liaising; politics/policy/regulatory. **Events** *Meeting* Brussels (Belgium) 2022, *Virtual Sustainability Symposium* Brussels (Belgium) 2020, *Spring Conference* Geneva (Switzerland) 2019, *Global Trade Policy Conference* Brussels (Belgium) 2016, *General Assembly* Brussels (Belgium) 2015. **Members** Producers; distributors; importers; exporters; trade associations. Members (about 50) in over 20 countries. Membership countries not specified. **Consultative Status** Consultative status granted from: *World Intellectual Property Organization (WIPO, #21593)* (Permanent Observer Status). **IGO Relations** Observer status with: *Codex Alimentarius Commission (CAC, #04081)*; *International Organisation of Vine and Wine (OIV, #14435)*.
[2022/XC2792/**C**]

- ♦ **FIVU** Federación Internacional de Vivienda y Urbanismo (#13450)
- ♦ FIWAL – Federation of International Women's Associations in London (internationally oriented national body)

♦ FIWARE Foundation 09790

CEO Franklinstr 13A, 10587 Berlin, Germany.
URL: https://www.fiware.org/foundation/

History 2016. Founded by Atos, Engineering, Orange and Telefónica. Registration: Berlin District Court, No/ID: VR 35344, Start date: 28 Oct 2016, Germany, Charlottenburg. **Aims** Promote, augment, protect and validate the FIWARE technologies, as well as the activities of the FIWARE community. **Structure** General Assembly; Board of Directors; Board of officers; Technical Steering Committee; Team. Mission Support Committees. **Languages** English, French, German, Japanese, Spanish. **Staff** 30.00 FTE, paid; 10000.00 FTE, voluntary. **Activities** Advocacy/lobbying/activism; events/meetings; standards/guidelines. **Events** *FIWARE Global Summit* Malaga (Spain) 2020, *FIWARE Global Summit* Berlin (Germany) 2019. **Publications** *FIWARE for different domains* (2021). **Members** Full (over 400) in over 35 countries. Membership countries not specified.
[2021.05.19/AA0753/t/**F**]

- ♦ FIYBDA – Fédération international de yoseikan budo et disciplines assimilées (inactive)
- ♦ FIYE – Foundation for International Youth Exchange (internationally oriented national body)
- ♦ FIYTO – Federation of International Youth Travel Organizations (inactive)
- ♦ **FJA** Fédération des journalistes africains (#09404)
- ♦ **FJA** Fédération des journalistes arabes (#09422)
- ♦ FJCEE – Fédération des jeunes chefs d'entreprises européens (inactive)
- ♦ FJCEPF – Fédération des jeunes chambres économiques des pays utilisant le français dans leurs relations communes (inactive)
- ♦ FJCSH / see World Federation of Jewish Child Survivors of the Holocaust and Descendants (#21448)
- ♦ FJEE / see Federation of Young European Greens (#09715)
- ♦ FJJ – Fondation Jean-Jaurès (internationally oriented national body)
- ♦ **FJVE** Fédération des jeunes verts européens (#09715)
- ♦ FKN – Folkekirkens Nødhjaelp (internationally oriented national body)
- ♦ FK Norway / see Norwegian Agency for Exchange Cooperation
- ♦ FKRE – Forschungsstelle Kriege, Rustung und Entwicklung (internationally oriented national body)
- ♦ FLAAB – Federação Latino-Americana de Analise Bioenergética (internationally oriented national body)
- ♦ FLAAMM – Federación Latinoamericana de Artes Marciales Mixtas (unconfirmed)
- ♦ **FLACAM** Foro Latinoamericano de Ciencias Ambientales (#16336)
- ♦ FLACAM / see Latin American Forum of Environmental Sciences (#16336)
- ♦ **FLACMA** Federación Latinoamericana de Ciudades, Municipios y Asociaciones de Gobiernos Locales (#09350)
- ♦ **FLACSI** Federación Latinoamericana de Colegios de la Compañia de Jesús (#16323)
- ♦ **FLACSO** Facultad Latinoamericana de Ciencias Sociales (#16316)
- ♦ **FLACT** Federación Latinoamericana de Comunidades Terapéuticas (#09352)
- ♦ FLACTUR – Federación Latinoamericana y del Caribe de Trabajadores de la Hoteleria, Gastronomia, Casino y Turismo (inactive)
- ♦ FLADEM – Federación Latinoamericana de Editores de Musica (inactive)
- ♦ **FLADEM** Foro Latinoamericano de Educación Musical (#09879)

- ♦ FLAD – Fundação Luso-Americana para o Desenvolvimento (internationally oriented national body)
- ♦ FLA – Fair Labor Association (internationally oriented national body)
- ♦ FLAFEET / see Federación Internacional de Asociaciones de Ejecutivas de Empresas Turisticas (#09336)
- ♦ FLAFQ – Federación Latinoamericana de Fibrosis Quistica (no recent information)
- ♦ FLAGC / see Foro Iberoamericano de Agencias Gubernamentales de Protección al Consumidor (#09877)
- ♦ FLAIE / see Federación Iberolatinoamericana de Artistas Intérpretes y Ejecutantes (#09325)
- ♦ **FLAI** Fundación Latinoamericana de Auditores Internos (#10035)
- ♦ FLAJA – Federación Latinoamericana de Jóvenes Ambientalistas (inactive)
- ♦ **FLAJ** Foro Latinoamericano de Juventud (#09881)
- ♦ Flamands dans le monde – Travail coopératif de développement (internationally oriented national body)
- ♦ FLAMECIPP – Federación Latinoamericana de Medicina y Cirugia de la Pierna y Pié (no recent information)
- ♦ Flame International (internationally oriented national body)

♦ Flame Retardants Europe (FRE) 09791

Contact Rue de Luxembourg 22-24, 1000 Brussels, Belgium. T. +3227616691.

History 5 Sep 1990. Founded as a sector group of *Conseil européen de l'industrie chimique (CEFIC, #04687)*. Since May 2011, integrates *European Brominated Flame Retardant Industry Panel (EBFRIP, inactive)*. Former names and other names: *European Flame Retardants Association (EFRA)* – former. Registration: EU Transparency Register, No/ID: 961627032521-50. **Aims** Enhance *fire safety* and the understanding of flame retardant technologies. **Structure** Secretariat. **Languages** English. **Publications** *EFRA Newsletter* (irregular). Brochures; factsheets; reports.

Members European manufacturers and users of flame retardants (13) in 9 countries:
Belgium, China, Germany, Israel, Italy, Netherlands, Poland, UK, USA.

NGO Relations Member of: *Industry4Europe (#11181)*. [2020/XE1692/y/E]

- ♦ **FLAM** Federación Latinoamericana de Magistrados (#09357)
- ♦ **FLAM** Federación Latinoamericana de Mastología (#16324)
- ♦ **FLAMP** Federacion Latinoamericana de Asociaciones de Medicina Perinatal (#09345)
- ♦ **FLAMU** Federación Latinoamericana de Mujeres Universitarias (#16334)
- ♦ **FLANC** Federación Latinoamericana de Neurocirugia (#16325)
- ♦ **FLAPAG** Federación Latinoamericana de Psicoterapia Analitica de Grupo (#09361)
- ♦ FLAPB – Federación Latinoamericana de Psiquiatria Biológica (no recent information)
- ♦ FLAPED – Federación Latinoamericana de Psicologia en Emergencias y Desastres (no recent information)
- ♦ **FLAPE** Foro Latinoamericano de Politicas Educativas (#09882)
- ♦ **FLAP** Federación Latinoamericana de Parasitólogos (#16327)
- ♦ FLAPF – Federación Latinoamericana de Productores de Fonogramas y Videogramas (inactive)
- ♦ **FLAPIA** Federación Latinoamericana de Psiquiatria de la Infancia, Adolescencia, Familia y Profesiones Afines (#09364)
- ♦ **FLAPNIE** Federación Latinoamericana de Psiconeuroinmunoendocrinologia (#09360)
- ♦ **FLAPPSIP** Federación Latino-Americana de Psicoterapia Psicoanalitica y Psicoanalisis (#09362)
- ♦ **FLAPSI** Federación Latinoamericana de psicoterapia (#16329)
- ♦ **FLAQ** Federación Latinoamericana de Asociaciones Quimicas (#16320)
- ♦ **FLAQ** Federación Latinoamericana de Quiropractica (#09367)
- ♦ **FLAQT** Federación Latinoamericana de Quimicos Textiles (#09366)
- ♦ FLAQTIC – Federação Latino-americana das Associações dos Quimicos e Técnicos da Indústria do Couro (unconfirmed)
- ♦ **FLARE** Forests and Livelihoods: Assessment, Research, and Engagement (#09868)
- ♦ FLARE Network / see Forests and Livelihoods: Assessment, Research, and Engagement (#09868)
- ♦ **FLAR** Fondo Latinoamericano para Arroz de Riego (#10041)
- ♦ **FLAR** Fondo Latinoamericano de Reservas (#16367)
- ♦ **FLASCA** Federación Latinoamericana de Sociedades de Cancerologia (#16319)
- ♦ **FLASCYM** Federación Latinoamericana de Sociedades de Climaterio y Menopausia (#09369)
- ♦ FLASEF – Federación Latinoamericana de Sociedades de Esterilidad y Fertilidad (inactive)
- ♦ FLAS – Federación Latinoamericana de Administradores de la Salud (unconfirmed)
- ♦ FLASFLA – Federación Latinoamericana de Sociedades de Foniatria, Logopedia y Audiologia (inactive)
- ♦ **FLASIC** Federación Latinoamericana de Simulación Clínica y Seguridad del Paciente (#09368)
- ♦ FLASMA / see Federación Ibero Latinoamericana de Sociedades Médicas de Acupuntura (#09327)
- ♦ **FLASO** Federación Latinoamericana de Sociedades de Obesidad (#16332)
- ♦ **FLASOG** Federación Latinoamericana de Sociedades de Obstetricia y Ginecologia (#09372)
- ♦ **FLASOMA** Federación Latinoamericana de Sociedades Magicas (#09371)
- ♦ **FLASSES** Federación Latinoamericana de Sociedades de Sexologia y Educación Sexual (#16331)
- ♦ **FLASS** Federation of Latin American Sleep Societies (#09685)
- ♦ **FLASUD** Foro Latinoamericano para la Seguridad Urbana y la Democracia (#09883)
- ♦ **FLATEC** Federación Latinoamericana de Trabajadores de la Educación y la Cultura (#09375)
- ♦ FLATEVECU – Federación Latinoamericana de Trabajadores de la Industria del Textil, Vestido, Calzado y Cuero (inactive)
- ♦ FLATGRAPA – Federación Latinoamericana de Trabajadores Graficos y del Papel (inactive)
- ♦ **FLATIC** Federación Latinoamericana de Trabajadores de la Industria y la Construcción (#09376)
- ♦ FLATICOM – Federación Latinoamericana de Trabajadores de la Industria de la Construcción, la Madera y los Materiales de Construcción (inactive)
- ♦ FLATI – Federación Latinoamericana de Trabajadores de la Industria (inactive)
- ♦ **FLATIM** Federación Latinoamericana de Trabajadores de las Industrias Metalúrgicas, Mecanicas y Mineras (#09377)
- ♦ FLATPLAN – Latin American Plantation Workers' Federation (inactive)
- ♦ FLATREP – Comité Pro-Federación Latinoamericana de Trabajadores del Espectaculo Público (inactive)
- ♦ FLATT – Federación Latinoamericana de Trabajadores del Transporte (no recent information)
- ♦ **FLAUS** Federación Latinoamericana de Sociedades de Ultrasonido (#16333)
- ♦ Flavins – International Symposium on Flavins & Flavoproteins (meeting series)
- ♦ Flavobacterium Conference (meeting series)
- ♦ **FLC** Federación Latinoamericana de Carbono (#09347)
- ♦ **FLC** Fellowship of the Least Coin (#09728)
- ♦ **FLD** Front Line Defenders (#10008)
- ♦ **FLEAD** Fundación Latinoamericana para la Educación a Distancia (#10037)
- ♦ FLECI – Federación Latinoamericana de Enfermeria en Cuidado Intensivo (unconfirmed)

♦ Fleet Forum 09792

Exec Dir c/o Alber & Rolle, Chemin Frank-Thomas 34, 1208 Geneva, Switzerland. E-mail: info@fleetforum.org.
URL: http://fleetforum.org/

History 2003. Founded by *World Food Programme (WFP, #21510)*. Registration: Start date: 2011, Switzerland. **Aims** Provide leadership and support to *aid*, *development* and commercial *transport* sectors in low-to-middle income countries, in the areas of *road safety*, environmental impact, effectiveness and cost efficiency. **Structure** Board; Management Team. **Languages** English, French, Spanish, Swahili. **Staff** 4.00 FTE, paid. **Finance** Members' dues. Other sources: grants; proceeds from commercial activities. **Activities** Awards/prizes/competitions; events/meetings; training/education; standards/guidelines; advocacy/lobbying/activism; guidance/assistance/consulting; knowledge management/information dissemination; accreditation/certification. **Events** *Annual Conference* Copenhagen (Denmark) 2018, *Annual Conference* Brindisi (Italy) 2017, *Annual Conference* Dublin (Ireland) 2016, *Annual Conference* Rome (Italy) 2015, *Annual Conference* Budapest (Hungary) 2014. **Publications** Safety guide; toolkit; standards.

Members NGOs; international organizations; academic institutions; donors; corporate partners. Members include the following 9 organizations listed in this Yearbook:
Catholic Relief Services (CRS, #03608); *GOAL*; *International Rescue Committee (IRC, #14717)*; *MSI Reproductive Choices*; *Plan International (#18386)*; *UNHCR (#20327)*; *UNICEF (#20332)*; *World Food Programme (WFP, #21510)*; *World Vision International (WVI, #21904)*.

NGO Relations Member of: *Partnership for Clean Fuels and Vehicles (PCFV, #18231)*. Partner of: *North Star Alliance (#17605)*. [2019/XJ8597/F]

♦ Fleischner Society (FS) 09793

Main Office 1061 E. Main St, Ste 300, East Dundee IL 60118, USA. E-mail: info@fleischner.org.
URL: http://www.fleischner.org/

History 1969. Founded as an international group of prominent radiologists and other medical specialists interested in lung diseases. Named in honour of Dr Felix Fleischner. Former names and other names: *Fleischner Society for Thoracic Imaging and Diagnosis* – full title. **Aims** Foster the continuing development of *chest radiology* as an art and a science; to improve methods of teaching *radiological diagnosis* of chest *disease*; stimulate research in chest *radiology*. **Structure** Executive Committee; Nominating Committee; Academic Development Committee; Scientific Meeting Subcommittee; Ad hoc Committees. **Staff** 1.00 FTE, paid. **Activities** Training/education; awards/prizes/competitions; knowledge management/information dissemination; standards/guidelines. **Events** *Annual Meeting* Rome (Italy) 2021, *Joint Meeting* Paris (France) 2019, *Annual Conference* Beverly, MA (USA) 2017, *Annual Conference* New York, NY (USA) 2016, *Joint Meeting* Barcelona (Spain) 2015. **Publications** White papers; guidelines.

Members Physicians (78) interested in the radiological aspects of pulmonary disease and the basic disciplines of anatomy, physiology, pathology, and clinical medicine upon which radiological interpretation rests. Members in 13 countries:
Austria, Belgium, Canada, France, Germany, Greece, Italy, Japan, Korea Rep, Sweden, Switzerland, UK, USA.
[2021/XE1121/v/E]

- ♦ Fleischner Society for Thoracic Imaging and Diagnosis / see Fleischner Society (#09793)
- ♦ **FLEMACON** Federación Latinoamericana de la Edificación, Madera y Materiales de la Construcción (#16318)
- ♦ Flemings in the World – Development Cooperation (internationally oriented national body)
- ♦ Flemish Association for Development Cooperations and Technical Assistance (internationally oriented national body)
- ♦ Flemish Association for Training Programmes in Foreign Countries / see Vlaamse Vereniging voor Ontwikkelingssamenwerking en Technische Bijstand
- ♦ Flemish Federation of NGOs for Development Cooperation (internationally oriented national body)
- ♦ Flemish International Centre / see KIYO
- ♦ Flemish International Cooperation Agency (internationally oriented national body)
- ♦ **FLEP** Food Law Enforcement Practitioners (#09846)
- ♦ Fletcher School of Law and Diplomacy (internationally oriented national body)
- ♦ **F and L** European Freight and Logistics Leaders Forum (#07359)
- ♦ **FLEUROSELECT** International Association of Breeders and Distributors of Ornamental Plant Varieties (#11735)

♦ Flexible Packaging Europe (FPE) 09794

Exec Dir Mörsenbroicher Weg 200, 40470 Düsseldorf, Germany. T. +4921138732602. E-mail: enquiries@flexpack-europe.org.
URL: http://www.flexpack-europe.org/

History 29 Apr 1998, The Hague (Netherlands). Current statutes adopted, 20 Jun 2002. Became a division of *European Aluminium Foil Association (EAFA, #05894)*, 31 Dec 2005. Former names and other names: *EUROFLEX – European Forum for the Flexible Packaging Industry* – full title (20 Jun 2002); *EUROFLEX* – former (29 Apr 1998 to 20 Jun 2002). Registration: EU Transparency Register, No/ID: 616597915313-68, Start date: 18 Dec 2014. **Aims** Promote the flexible packaging industry; represent interests of the sector at the highest levels in Europe. **Languages** Dutch, English, French, German. **Finance** Members' dues. **Activities** Advocacy/lobbying/activism. **Events** *Annual Congress* Athens (Greece) 2005, *Annual Congress* Juan-les-Pins (France) 2004, *Annual Congress* Juan-les-Pins (France) 2004, *Annual Congress* Seville (Spain) 2003, *Annual Congress* Berlin (Germany) 2002. **Publications** *FlexAffairs Briefing* – newsletter. Report; congress proceedings.

Members Direct company; Associate; Affiliate; Academia. Members in 15 countries:
Austria, Czechia, Denmark, France, Germany, Greece, Italy, Netherlands, Poland, Russia, Spain, Sweden, Switzerland, Türkiye, UK.

International member (1):
International Packaging Institute (IPI).

NGO Relations Member of (3): *Circular Plastics Alliance (#03936)*; *European Food Sustainable Consumption and Production Round Table (European Food SCP Roundtable, #07289)*; *European Platform for Chemicals Using Manufacturing Industries (CheMI, #08223)*. Instrumental in setting up (1): *Fédération européenne de l'emballage souple (FEDES, inactive)*. [2022/XD8148/E]

- ♦ Flexographic Technical Association / see FTA Europe (#10012)
- ♦ **FLH** Federación Latinoamericana de Hospitales (#16322)
- ♦ **FLI** Fédération lainière internationale (#15904)

♦ Flight Safety Foundation (FSF) 09795

Fondation pour la sécurité aérienne

CEO-Pres 801 N Fairfax St, Ste 250, Alexandria VA 22314-1774, USA. T. +17037396700. Fax +17037396708.
URL: http://www.flightsafety.org/

History Founded 1945. Incorporated in the State of New York (USA). **Aims** Provide impartial, independent expert safety guidance and resources for the commercial and business *aviation* industry whose survival depends on safe operations. **Structure** Board of Governors, consisting up to 50 members of which a third retire each year; Executive Committee. **Finance** Members' dues. Other sources: seminars proceeds, sales of products; endowment. **Activities** Projects/programmes. **Events** *Annual Safety Forum* Brussels (Belgium) 2022, *Annual Business Aviation Safety Summit* Savannah, GA (USA) 2022, *International Air Safety Summit* Alexandria, VA (USA) 2021, *Annual Business Aviation Safety Summit* Savannah, GA (USA) 2021, *Annual Singapore Aviation Safety Seminar* Singapore (Singapore) 2021. **Publications** *AeroSafety World*. **Members** Industry leaders representing over 1,200 manufacturers, suppliers, insurance companies, regulators, corporate operators, airports, airlines and other companies, and individuals. Membership countries not specified. **NGO Relations** Cooperates with: *International Air Transport Association (IATA, #11614)*. *International Federation of Air Line Pilots' Associations (IFALPA, #13349)* is member. [2020/XF0967/f/F]

- ♦ flinovia – flow induced noise and vibration issues and aspects (unconfirmed)
- ♦ FLINS – International FLINS Conference on Robotics and Artificial Intelligence (meeting series)
- ♦ **FLISMET** Federación Latinoamericana e Ibérica de Sociedades de Meteorologia (#09354)
- ♦ **FLJJ** Federación Latinoamericana de Ju-Jitsu (#09355)
- ♦ FLM / see Fondazione Mediterraneo
- ♦ FLM – Family Life Mission (religious order)
- ♦ **FLM** Fédération luthérienne mondiale (#16532)
- ♦ **FLNJ** Front de libération des nains de jardin (#10671)

♦ Floating University (FU) 09796

Contact address not obtained. T. +33145684016. Fax +33145685812.
URL: http://www.ioc-cd.org/

History 1991, by *UNESCO (#20322)* and *European Science Foundation (ESF, #08441)*. Executed by *Intergovernmental Oceanographic Commission (IOC, #11496)*. Also known as *Training Through Research Programme (TTR)*. **Aims** Provide high-level training in *marine geosciences* by involving students and young scientists in advanced research projects; advance knowledge of *geological* and geosphere-biosphere coupling processes on the *sea* floor. **Structure** International Executive Committee. Scientific Committee. **Languages** English. **Staff** 1.50 FTE, paid. **Finance** Core support from IOC and participating countries. **Activities** Organizes: annual training cruises in the Atlantic Ocean, Black and Mediterranean Seas; international research conferences for presentation of cruise results; exchange by students and scientists between cooperating institutions. Related education and training activities promoted by setting up of: *'UNESCO Moscow*

(Russia) State University Research and Training Centre in Marine Geosciences'; 'UNESCO Chair in Marine Geosciences'. **Events** *Annual international research conference* Bremen (Germany) 2007, *Annual international research conference* Moscow (Russia) 2006, *Annual international research conference* Marrakech (Morocco) 2005, *Annual international research conference* Copenhagen (Denmark) 2004, *Annual international research conference* Bologna (Italy) 2003. **Publications** Cruise reports; Conference proceedings; Scientific papers.
Members Participation from 29 countries:
Algeria, Belgium, Brazil, Bulgaria, Chile, Denmark, France, Georgia, Germany, Greece, Ireland, Israel, Italy, Malta, Morocco, Mozambique, Netherlands, Norway, Pakistan, Poland, Portugal, Russia, Saudi Arabia, Senegal, Spain, Switzerland, Tunisia, Türkiye, UK, Ukraine, USA. [2010/XF3418/**F**]

♦ Flock Association of Europe (unconfirmed)
♦ **FLO** Fairtrade International (#09240)
♦ FLO International / see Fairtrade International (#09240)
♦ FLOODrisk – European Conference on Flood Risk Management (meeting series)
♦ Flora Europaea Organization / see Euro+Med PlantBase (#05732)
♦ Flora Europaea Residuary Body / see Euro+Med PlantBase (#05732)
♦ **Florence Network** Florence Network for Nursing and Midwifery (#09797)

♦ Florence Network for Nursing and Midwifery (Florence Network) .. 09797

Pres address not obtained. E-mail: scaa@zhaw.ch – florencenetworkpresident@gmail.com.
URL: https://theflorencenetwork.coventry.domains/

History 1995. **Aims** Develop and improve the quality of European higher education in nursing and midwifery by means of international cooperation in the field of education, scientific research and development. **Activities** Events/meeting; research/documentation. **Events** *Annual Meeting* Madrid (Spain) 2023, *Annual Meeting* 2021, *Annual meeting* Kuopio (Finland) 2020, *Annual meeting* Coventry (UK) / Northampton (UK) 2019, *Annual meeting* Brussels (Belgium) 2018.
Members Universities and schools of higher education in 19 countries and territories:
Belgium, Czechia, Denmark, England, Finland, Germany, Greece, Italy, Latvia, Netherlands, Norway, Portugal, Scotland, Slovakia, Slovenia, Spain, Sweden, Switzerland, Türkiye. [2021/XJ1344/**F**]

♦ Florence Nightingale International Foundation (FNIF) 09798

Fondation internationale Florence Nightingale – Fundación Internacional Florence Nightingale
Address not obtained.
URL: https://www.icn.ch/who-we-are/foundations

History 1934, London (UK). Not a public foundation, does not supply financial assistance. Registration: Charity Commission, No/ID: 1074773., England and Wales. **Aims** Support the advancement of nursing education, research and services for the public good. **Structure** Board of Directors of 6 members. **NGO Relations** Supports and complements work of: *International Council of Nurses (ICN, #13054).* [2018/XG8264/f/**E**]

♦ FloreSer – Asociación Centroamericana de Terapeutas Florales (no recent information)
♦ Floresta USA / see Plant With Purpose
♦ Florida Association of Voluntary Agencies for Caribbean Action / see Florida Association for Volunteer Action in the Caribbean and the Americas
♦ Florida Association for Volunteer Action in the Caribbean and the Americas (internationally oriented national body)
♦ Florida International Bankers' Association (internationally oriented national body)
♦ Florida International University (internationally oriented national body)
♦ **FLORINT** International Florist Organisation (#13616)

♦ FLORNET 09799

Registered Office c/o AOC de Groene Welle, Koggelaa 7, PO Box 552, 8000 AN Zwolle, Netherlands.
URL: http://flornet.eu/

History Set up May 2000, as *European network for professional education in floristry – FLORNET.* Since 17 Apr 2009, Melnik (Czech Rep), an organization of the type *European Economic Interest Grouping (EEIG, #06960).* Also known as *FLORNET European Economic Interest Grouping (FLORNET EEIG).* Registered in accordance with Dutch law. **Structure** General Assembly; Board of Directors. **Languages** English. **Events** *General Assembly* Paris (France) 2014, *General Assembly* Weihenstephan (Germany) 2013, *General Assembly* Langenlois (Austria) 2011. **Publications** *FLORNET Newsletter.*
Members Organizations in 14 countries:
Austria, Czechia, Estonia, Finland, France, Germany, Italy, Netherlands, Norway, Slovakia, Slovenia, Spain, Sweden, UK.
NGO Relations *International Florist Organisation (FLORINT, #13616).* [2017/XJ9823/**F**]

♦ FLORNET EEIG / see FLORNET (#09799)
♦ FLORNET European Economic Interest Grouping / see FLORNET (#09799)
♦ Flour Fortification Initiative / see Food Fortification Initiative (#09844)
♦ Flour Milling Associations Group of the EU Countries / see European Flour Millers' Association (#07272)

♦ Flow Batteries Europe (FBE) 09800

SG Avenue Adolphe Lacomblé 59, 1030 Brussels, Belgium. T. +3227432981.
Policy Officer address not obtained.
URL: https://www.flowbatterieseurope.eu/

History Registration: Banque-Carrefour des Entreprises, No/ID: 0782.985.582, Start date: 8 Mar 2022, Belgium; EU Transparency Register, No/ID: 633311345900-80, Start date: 22 Mar 2022. **Aims** Gather interested stakeholders to advance the research and development as well as the commercialization and deployment of flow batteries in Europe. **Structure** Executive Board; Secretariat. [2022/AA2555/**D**]

♦ Flow Chemistry Society (FCS) 09801

Contact Schulstrasse 14, 8451 Kleinandelfingen ZH, Switzerland. E-mail: info@flowchemistrysociety.com.
URL: https://flowchemistrysociety.com/

History 2010. **Aims** Stimulate development and advancement of flow chemistry for the benefit and progress of the chemistry community; provide a highlevel scientific forum for organic chemistry laboratories within the academic and industrial sector as well as in green chemistry and novel catalysis research. **Languages** English. **Activities** Awards/prizes/competitions; events/meetings; knowledge management/information dissemination; publishing activities; training/education. **Events** *Attila Pavláth Scientific Symposium* Budapest (Hungary) 2022, *FROST8 Frontiers in Organic Synthesis Technology Conference* Budapest (Hungary) 2021, *FCS India Annual Conference* Chandigarh (India) 2021, *Flow Chemistry Europe* Cambridge (UK) 2020, *FROST7 Frontiers in Organic Synthesis Technology Conference* Budapest (Hungary) 2019. **Publications** *Journal of Flow Chemistry* (4 a year). [2022.06.17/AA2095/**C**]

♦ flow induced noise and vibration issues and aspects (unconfirmed)
♦ Flow Regimes from International Experimental and Network Data (see: #13826)
♦ FLPT – Federación Latinoamericana de Periodistas Tecnológicos (no recent information)
♦ **FLPTGIC** Federación Latinoamericana de Patologia del Tracto Genital Inferior y Colposcopia (#09358)
♦ FLT – Federación Latinoamericana de Termalismo (no recent information)
♦ Flüchtlingsbetreuung der Evangelischen Kirche / see DIAKONIE – Evangelischer Flüchtlingsdienst
♦ Fluctuations of Glaciers Service / see World Glacier Monitoring Service (#21539)

♦ Fluid Power Net International (FPNI) 09802

Address not obtained.

History 1998. Founded as a joint initiative of: Fluidteknikk, Institutt for Termisk Energi og Vannkraft (Norwegian University of Science and Technology, Norway); Institute of Heavy Duty Machines (Krakow University of Technology, Poland); Department of Control and Engineering Design (Technical University of Denmark); Subsea Engineering Research Group, Department of Mechanical Engineering (Monash University, Australia). Most recent statutes adopted, Jun 2006, Sarasota FL (USA), during 4th PhD Symposium. Registered in the USA, 2012. 2016, ceased to exist following merger with *Network of Fluid Power Centres in Europe (FPCE, inactive)* to become *Global Fluid Power Society (GFPS, #10363).* **Aims** As a worldwide community for networking in the area of fluid power and fluid techniques; bring people together; provide information about fluid power developments and publications; strengthen the standing of fluid power and fluid techniques in industry; promote fluid power and fluid techniques as an autonomous scientific/technical discipline; promote the multi-disciplinary nature of modern fluid power systems. **Structure** Scientific Board; Secretariat. **Languages** English. **Activities** Events/meetings; networking/liaising; knowledge management/information dissemination. **Events** *Symposium / Biennial Fluid Poser PhD Symposium* Lappeenranta (Finland) 2014, *Biennial Fluid Poser PhD Symposium* Reggio Emilia (Italy) 2012, *Symposium* Reggio Emilia (Italy) 2012, *Symposium / Biennial Fluid Poser PhD Symposium* West Lafayette, IN (USA) 2010, *Symposium / Biennial Fluid Poser PhD Symposium* Krakow (Poland) 2008. **Publications** *International Journal of Fluid Power.* **Members** in 21 countries. Membership countries not specified. [2014.12.15/XF6949/**F**]

♦ **Flupa** Association francophone des professionnels de l'expérience utilisateur (#02618)
♦ Flux – Flux: The Society for Developmental Cognitive Neuroscience (internationally oriented national body)

♦ FLUXNET 09803

Contact address not obtained. E-mail: fluxdata-support@fluxdata.org.
URL: https://fluxnet.org/

History 1997. Project started with support from National Aeronautics and Space Administration (NASA) to provide ground support for *Earth Observing System (EOS)* and the Modis Resolution Imaging Spectroradiometer (MODIS) carried on the Terra and Aqua satellites. FLUXNET 2nd generation (2007-2011). FLUXNET revived for 3rd generation, 2014. **Aims** Facilitate communication and sharing of data and research ideas in the field of the eddy covariance flux measurements. **Structure** Community Council. **Staff** All voluntary. **Activities** Knowledge management/information dissemination; research/documentation. **NGO Relations** Cooperates with (2): *AsiaFlux (#01279); Integrated Carbon Observation System (ICOS, #11368).* Cooperates with various national organizations. [2022/AA2920/**F**]

♦ Flux: The Society for Developmental Cognitive Neuroscience (internationally oriented national body)
♦ Fly Fishers International (unconfirmed)
♦ Flying Doctors Service / see Amref Health Africa (#00806)
♦ Flying Doctors' Society of Africa (internationally oriented national body)
♦ Flyktninghjelpen / see Norwegian Refugee Council
♦ **FMAC** Fédération mondiale des anciens combattants (#21900)
♦ **FMACU** Federación Mundial de Asociaciones, Centros y Clubs UNESCO (#21498)
♦ **FMACU** Fédération mondiale des associations, centres et clubs UNESCO (#21498)
♦ **FMA** European Parliament Former Members Association (#08151)
♦ FMA – Fabricators and Manufacturers Association International (internationally oriented national body)
♦ **FMA** Fédération mondiale des annonceurs (#21407)
♦ FMAF – Fonds monétaire africain (unconfirmed)
♦ FMA – Filiae Mariae Auxiliatricis (religious order)
♦ **FMA** Financial Markets Association (#09767)
♦ **FMA** Fonds Monétaire Arabe (#01009)
♦ **FMA** Foro Mundial de las Alternativas (#21513)
♦ **FMA** Forum mondial des alternatives (#21513)
♦ **FMAM** Federación Mundial de Amigos de los Museos (#21435)
♦ **FMAM** Fédération mondiale des amis des musées (#21435)
♦ **FMANU** Fédération mondiale des associations pour les Nations Unies (#21499)
♦ FMATH-CMT – Federación Mundial de Trabajadores de la Alimentación, del Tabaco y de los Hoteles-CMT (inactive)
♦ FMATH-CMT – Fédération mondiale de travailleurs des industries alimentaires, du tabac et hôtelière-CMT (inactive)
♦ **FMBP** Fédération Mondiale Boules & Pétanque (#21721)
♦ FMCB – Fédération mondiale des organisations de la construction et du bois (inactive)
♦ **FMC** Fédération mondiale du carillon (#21260)
♦ FMC – Frères Missionnaires des Campagnes (religious order)
♦ **FMCIM** Fédération mondiale des concours internationaux de musique (#21445)
♦ FMCU – Federación Mundial de Ciudades Unidas (inactive)
♦ FMCU – Fédération mondiale des cités unies (inactive)
♦ FMCVX / see Christian Life Community (#03905)
♦ FMD – Fédération mondiale des docteurs d'état et diplômés des universités de France (internationally oriented national body)
♦ **FMD** Fondation Mattei Dogan (#09826)
♦ FMDJ – Fédération mondial de dance de jazz (inactive)
♦ FMDO / see Federatie voor Mondiale Democratische Organisaties
♦ FMDO – Federatie voor Mondiale Democratische Organisaties (internationally oriented national body)

♦ FMDV 09804

Exec Dir 35 Boulevard des Invalides, 75007 Paris, France. T. +33153857382. E-mail: contact@fmdv.net.
URL: http://www.fmdv.net/

History 7 Oct 2010, at the initiative of *World Association of the Major Metropolises (Metropolis, #21158), World Organization of United Cities and Local Governments (UCLG, #21695)* and 34 founding members. Full title: *Global Fund for Cities Development – Fonds mondial pour le développement des villes – Fondo Mundial par el Desarrollo de las Ciudades.* **Aims** Strengthen solidarity and financial capacity by and among *local authorities.* **Structure** General Assembly. Board of Directors, comprising President, 6 Vice-Presidencies, Treasurer and Executive Director. Project Selection Committee. Executive Office, in Paris (France). Regional Offices: Latin America (Mexico City, Mexico); Africa (Rabat, Morocco); Asia (Mashhad, Iran Islamic Rep). **Events** *EMDS : Meeting of Municipalities with Sustainable Development* Brasilia (Brazil) 2017.
Members Founding; Permanent; Organizations. Members in 22 countries and territories:
Belgium, Brazil, Canada, China, Congo Brazzaville, Côte d'Ivoire, Ethiopia, France, Iran Islamic Rep, Madagascar, Mali, Mauritania, Mexico, Morocco, Niger, Palestine, Philippines, Russia, Senegal, Spain, Türkiye, Venezuela.
Included in the above, 3 organizations listed in this Yearbook:
Association internationale des régions francophones (AIRF, #02739); World Association of the Major Metropolises (Metropolis, #21158); World Organization of United Cities and Local Governments (UCLG, #21695).
NGO Relations Member of: *Cities Climate Finance Leadership Alliance (CCFLA, #03952); Global Taskforce of Local and Regional Governments (Global Taskforce, #10622).* Associate partner of: *World Urban Campaign (WUC, #21893).* [2016/XJ6603/fy/**F**]

♦ **FMEEC** Fellowship of the Middle Eastern Evangelical Churches (#09729)
♦ FME – Federación de Mineros de Europa (inactive)
♦ FME – Fédération des mineurs d'Europe (inactive)
♦ **FMEF** Fédération de missions évangéliques francophones (#09688)
♦ **FME** Forest Movement Europe (#09864)
♦ **FME** Formal Methods Europe (#09872)
♦ FMEP – Foundation for Middle East Peace (internationally oriented national body)
♦ FMES – Fondation méditerranéenne d'études stratégiques (internationally oriented national body)
♦ FME / see World Organization of Workers (#21697)
♦ FMF & AID Global Association – Familial Mediterranean Fever and Autoinflammatory Diseased Global Association (unconfirmed)
♦ FMF – Fetal Medicine Foundation (internationally oriented national body)
♦ FMF – Frederick Mulder Foundation (internationally oriented national body)
♦ FMFSGP / see Global Self-Care Federation (#10588)
♦ **FMGCIVS** Fédération mondiale des grands concours internationaux de vins et spiritueux (#21452)
♦ FMI – Congregatio Filiorum Beatae Virginis Mariae Immaculatae (religious order)
♦ FMI – Filiae Mariae Immaculatae (religious order)
♦ **FMI** Fondo Monetario Internacional (#14180)
♦ **FMI** Fonds monétaire international (#14180)
♦ FMJC – Federación Mundial de Juventud Católica (inactive)
♦ FMJC – Fédération mondiale de la jeunesse catholique (inactive)

♦ **FMJD** Federación Mundial de la Juventud Democratica (#21427)
♦ **FMJD** Fédération Mondiale du Jeu de Dames (#09690)
♦ **FMJD** Fédération mondiale de la jeunesse démocratique (#21427)
♦ FMJFC – Fédération mondiale des jeunesses féminines catholiques (inactive)
♦ FMJM – Fédération mondiale du judaïsme marocain (unconfirmed)
♦ **FMK** Fédération mondiale de karaté (#21608)
♦ FMMA – Fratres Misericordiae Mariae Auxiliatricis (religious order)
♦ FMM/CMT – Federación Mundial de la Metalurgia (inactive)
♦ FMM/CMT – Fédération mondiale de la métallurgie (inactive)
♦ FMM – Franciscan Missionaries of Mary (religious order)
♦ FMM – Franciscan Missionaries of Mary in the World (religious order)
♦ FMM – Fratres de Misericordia (religious order)
♦ FMM – Fundación Monte Mediterraneo (internationally oriented national body)
♦ FMND – International Workshop in Financial Markets and Nonlinear Dynamics (meeting series)
♦ FMN / see World Federation of Neurology (#21461)
♦ **FMOI** Fédération Mondiale des Organisations d'Ingénieurs (#21433)
♦ FMO – Nederlandse Financierings-Maatschappij voor Ontwikkelingslanden (internationally oriented national body)
♦ FMPA – Fédération mondiale pour la protection des animaux (inactive)
♦ **FMPVE** Fédération mondiale de promotion des véhicules électriques (#21374)
♦ FMR – Association femmes méditerranée rencontres (inactive)
♦ **FMRPS** Fondation mondiale recherche et prévention SIDA (#21525)
♦ **FMSC** Fédération mondiale des sociétés de cuisiniers (#21124)
♦ **FMSC** Fédération mondiale de sophrologie caycédienne (#09691)
♦ FMSC – Feed My Starving Children (internationally oriented national body)
♦ **FMSCF** Fonds mondial de solidarité contre la faim (#09836)
♦ **FMSD** Forum Mondial Sciences et Démocratie (#21522)
♦ **FMS** Federacija Mira I Soglacija (#13501)
♦ **FMS** Forum for Mobility and Society (#09924)
♦ FMS – Foundation Max van der Stoel (internationally oriented national body)
♦ **FMSI** Marist International Solidarity Foundation Onlus (#09831)
♦ FMS – Institutum Fratrum Maristarum a Scholis (religious order)
♦ FMS / see International Federation for Peace and Conciliation (#13501)
♦ **FMSM** Fédération mondiale pour la santé mentale (#21455)
♦ FMS / see World Federation of the Deaf (#21425)
♦ FMTA-CMT – Federación Mundial de Trabajadores Agricolas (inactive)
♦ FMTA-CMT – Fédération mondiale de travailleurs agricoles (inactive)
♦ FMTCM – Federación Mundial de Trabajadores de la Construcción y la Madera (inactive)
♦ **FMT** FinMark Trust (#09775)
♦ FMTI – Federación Mundial de Trabajadores de la Industria (inactive)
♦ FMTI – Fédération mondiale des travailleurs de l'industrie (inactive)
♦ **FMTL** Fórum Mundial de Teologia e Libertação (#21524)
♦ FMTNM / see World Organization of Workers (#21697)
♦ **FMTS** Fédération mondiale des travailleurs scientifiques (#21480)
♦ FMVB – Federación Mundial de Voleibol y de Beach Voleibol (inactive)
♦ FMVB – Fédération mondiale de volleyball et de beach volleyball (inactive)
♦ FNB – Food not Bombs (internationally oriented national body)
♦ **FNCA** Forum for Nuclear Cooperation in Asia (#09926)
♦ FNCF – Forente Nordiske Castingforbund (unconfirmed)
♦ FNC Group – Freight Network Corporation Group (internationally oriented national body)
♦ **FNCL** Fundación del Nuevo Cine Latinoamericano (#09967)
♦ FN – Congregatio Sacrae Familiae a Nazareth (religious order)
♦ FND – Fraternité Notre Dame (religious order)
♦ FNDL – Fratres Nostrae Dominae Lurdensis (religious order)
♦ **FNDS** Functional Neurological Disorder Society (#10018)
♦ **FNF** Föreningarna Nordens Förbund (#09859)
♦ FNF – Frauennetzwerk für Frieden (internationally oriented national body)
♦ FNH – Fondation pour la Nature et l'Homme (internationally oriented national body)
♦ **FNI** Fédération naturiste internationale (#14219)
♦ **FNIF** Florence Nightingale International Foundation (#09798)
♦ FNI – Fridtjof Nansen Institute (internationally oriented national body)
♦ **FNM** Federation of Neurogastroenterology and Motility (#09696)
♦ FNPI / see Fundación Gabo
♦ FNPI – Fundación Gabriel García Márquez para el Nuevo Periodismo Iberoamericano / see Fundación Gabo
♦ FNPI – Gabriel García Márquez Foundation for New Ibero-American Journalism / see Fundación Gabo
♦ **FNPS** Fetal and Neonatal Physiological Society (#09740)
♦ **FNRBA** Forum of Nuclear Regulatory Bodies in Africa (#09927)
♦ **FNS** Friedrich Nietzsche Society (#09998)
♦ FN's Regionale Informationskontor (#20621)
♦ FNSt / see Friedrich Naumann Foundation for Freedom
♦ **FNSU** Forbundet Nordens Socialdemokratiske Ungdom (#09855)
♦ FNTDI / see Industrial Development Fund (#11173)
♦ **FNUDC** Fondo de las Naciones Unidas para el Desarrollo de la Capitalización (#20524)
♦ **FNUOD** Force des Nations Unies chargée d'observer le dégagement (#20553)
♦ **FNUOS** Fuerza de las Naciones Unidas para la Observación de la Separación (#20553)
♦ **FNUPI** Fonds des nations unies pour les partenariats internationaux (#20565)
♦ FNUR – Fonds des Nations Unies pour les réfugiés (inactive)
♦ **FNV** Förbundet Nordisk Vuxenupplysning (#09856)
♦ FOA – Friends of Animals (internationally oriented national body)
♦ FOA – Futures and Options Association (internationally oriented national body)
♦ FOAI – Fonds ouest africain d'investissement (see: #03170)
♦ FOAI – Friends of Africa International (internationally oriented national body)
♦ FOAL – Fundación ONCE para América Latina (internationally oriented national body)
♦ FOAPH – Fédération ouest-africaine des associations pour la promotion des personnes handicapées (no recent information)
♦ FOA-TURIN / see Former Officials Association Turin
♦ FOA Turin – Former Officials Association Turin (internationally oriented national body)
♦ FOB – European Federation for Freedom of Belief (internationally oriented national body)
♦ **FOBISIA** Federation of British International Schools in Asia (#09463)
♦ FOBISSEA / see Federation of British International Schools in Asia (#09463)
♦ FOCA / see Fellowship of Confessing Anglicans (#09725)
♦ FOCAC – Forum on China-Africa Cooperation (internationally oriented national body)
♦ **FOCA International** Open City International Foundation (#17748)
♦ **FOCALAE** Foro de Cooperación América Latina-Asia del Este (#09907)
♦ FOCAL International – Federation of Commercial Audiovisual Libraries International (internationally oriented national body)

♦ Focal Therapy Society (FTS) 09805

Contact 4100 Duff Place LL, Seaford NY 11783, USA. T. +15165201224. E-mail: info@focaltherapy.org – focal@focaltherapy.org.
URL: https://focaltherapy.org/

History Officially encorporated by joining with *Endourology Society (#05463)*, Oct 2019. **Aims** Advance and position minimally invasive treatments and image-targeted cancer treatment in a safe and effective gland-preserving manner to extend and maintain one's quality of life. **Structure** Board. **Events** *International Symposium on Focal Therapy and Imaging in Prostate and Kidney Cancer* Washington, DC (USA) 2020, *International Symposium on Focal Therapy and Imaging in Prostate and Kidney Cancer* Kyoto (Japan) 2019. [2021/AA0157/**C**]

♦ **FOCAP** Federación Odontológica de Centroamérica y Panama (#17691)
♦ FOCCISA – Fellowship of Christian Councils in Southern Africa (unconfirmed)
♦ **FOCIS** Federation of Clinical Immunology Societies (#09472)
♦ **FoCM** Foundations of Computational Mathematics (#09973)
♦ FOCODLA – Federation of Commonwealth Open and Distance Learning Associations (inactive)

♦ Focolare Movement 09806

Mouvement des Focolari – Movimento dei Focolari

Communication Manager Via Frascati 306, Rocca di Papa, 00040 Rome RM, Italy. E-mail: ufficio.comunicazione@focolare.org.
URL: http://www.focolare.org/

History 1943, Trento (Italy). Founded by Chiara Lubich, as a movement of spiritual and social renewal. Although part of the Catholic Church, the Movement involves other churches and religions, as well as with non-believers. Approved by the Holy See in 1964; declared a 'Private, Universal Association of Faithful of Pontifical Right' in 1990. Former names and other names: *Work of Mary (WM – Oeuvre de Marie)* – alias (1962); *Opera di Maria (OM)* – alias (1962). **Aims** Promote brotherhood and to achieve a more united world in which people respect and value diversity. **Structure** General Council; Co-Presidents (a lay woman and a male priest). **Languages** English, French, Italian, Portuguese, Spanish. Languages of the official website. **Activities** Events/meetings; knowledge management/information dissemination; projects/programmes; publishing activities; training/education. **Events** *United World Week Workshop* Brussels (Belgium) 2021, *United World Week Workshop* 2020. **Publications** *Big* (12 a year); *Teen's* (12 a year); *Word of Life* (12 a year); *Nuova Humanità* (6 a year); *Ekklesía. Pathways of Communion and Dialogue* (4 a year); *Città Nuova*. **Members** Individual members (about 110,000) and adherents/sympathizers (2,000,000). Membership countries not specified. **NGO Relations** Instrumental in setting up (6): *Action for a United World (AUW)*; *New Families Movement (#17085)*; *New Humanity (#17088)*; *Parish Movement (no recent information)*; *Teenagers for Unity (no recent information)*; *Youth for a United World (YUW, see: #09806)*. [2021.05.19/XF3806/F]

♦ Focolarini (religious order)
♦ **Focus** Focus on the Global South (#09807)

♦ Focus on the Global South (Focus) 09807

Main Office c/o CUSRI, Chulalongkorn University, Phyathai Road, Bangkok, 10330, Thailand. T. +6622187363 – +6622187364 – +6622187365. Fax +6622559976. E-mail: admin@focusweb.org.
URL: http://focusweb.org/

History Jan 1995. **Aims** Combine policy research, advocacy, activism and *grassroots* capacity building so as to generate critical analysis and encourage debate on national and international *policies* related to corporate-led globalization, neo-liberalism, militarization and climate justice. **Structure** Board of Directors. Offices in Bangkok (Thailand), Manila (Philippines) and Delhi (India). **Languages** English, Filipino, French, Hindi, Malayalam, Spanish, Thai. **Staff** 15.00 FTE, paid. **Activities** Programme areas (4): (1) De-globalization, Finance, Trade, Alternative Regionalism, Critical Discourse on Alternatives; (2) Reclaiming the Commons, Challenging Capitalist Agriculture, Peoples' Food Sovereignty, De-commodification and Agrarian Reform, Essential Goods and Services, Project on Sustainable Critics; (3) Peace and Democracy; (4) Climate Justice, International/Regional, China, Mekong Region and India. Organizes international courses and workshops. **Events** *Meeting on economic sovereignty in a globalising world* Thailand 1999, *Asia-Europe people's forum* London (UK) 1998, *International security conference* Manila (Philippines) 1998. **Publications** *Focus on the Global South News* (4 a year). Annual Report; books; dossiers; occasional papers; manual; guide; programmes produce papers and other publications. **Members** Not a membership organization. **Consultative Status** Consultative status granted from: *UNCTAD (#20285)* (General Category). **IGO Relations** Observer to: *United Nations Framework Convention on Climate Change – Secretariat (UNFCCC, #20564)*. **NGO Relations** Member of: *ASEAN Peoples Forum (APF)*; *Asia-Europe People's Forum (AEPF, #01274)*; *Climate Justice Now ! (CJN!, inactive)*; *ETO Consortium (ETOs, #05560)*; *Globalization Studies Network (GSN, #10440)*; *Just Net Coalition (JNC, #16173)*; *NGO Forum on ADB (#17123)*; *Our World is Not for Sale (OWINFS, #17917)*; *South Asia Peoples' Alliance (SAPA)*; *World Social Forum (WSF, #21797)*; national organizations. Instrumental in setting up: *Land Research Action Network (LRAN, #16228)*. [2013.07.19/XF4506/F]

♦ Focus Humanitarian Assistance 09808

Secretariat Ste 201, 789 Don Mills Road, Don Mills ON M3C 1T5, Canada. T. +14164220177. Fax +14164225032. E-mail: ficc@focushumanitarian.org.
Europe Office 205-209 Addiscombe Road, Croydon, CR0 6SP, UK. T. +442086546131. Fax +442086551649. E-mail: focuseurope@focushumanitarian.org.
URL: http://www.akdn.org/focus

History Registered in Canada, India, Pakistan, Portugal, UK and USA. UK Registered Charity: 1054174. **Aims** As an international group of agencies established by the Ismaili Muslim community: facilitate provision of emergency humanitarian assistance, principally in the developing world; enable communities to prepare for and, as far as possible, mitigate the impact of natural and man-made disasters; facilitate repatriation of displaced persons and resettlement of refugees.
Members Registered/liaison offices in 10 countries:
Afghanistan, Canada, France, India, Pakistan, Portugal, Russia, Tajikistan, UK, USA.
NGO Relations Affiliate of: *Aga Khan Development Network (AKDN, #00544)*. Programme partner of: *Aga Khan Foundation (AKF, #00545)*. [2018/XF4941/F]

♦ Focusing Resources on Effective School Health (FRESH) 09809

Contact Sect for Education and HIV and AIDS, Div of Education for Peace and Sustainable Development, UNESCO, 7 place de Fontenoy, 75352 Paris 07-SP, France. T. +33145681438. Fax +33145685636. E-mail: aids@unesco.org.
URL: http://www.unesco.org/education/fresh/

History Apr 2000, during Dakar (Senegal) World Education Forum, by *UNESCO (#20322)*, *UNICEF (#20332)*, *WHO (#20950)*, *International Bank for Reconstruction and Development (IBRD, #12317)* (World Bank) and *Education International (EI, #05371)*, replacing *Programme of Education for the Prevention of AIDS (inactive)*. **Aims** Serve as the common international framework to guide partners around the world on the basic principles for implementing school health programmes. **Structure** Advisory Board. Coordinating Committee, currently including: *UNESCO (#20322)*; *UNICEF (#20332)*; *United Nations Office on Drugs and Crime (UNODC, #20596)*; *Save the Children International (#19058)*; *Partnership for Child Development (PCD)*; *Education Development Center (EDC)*; American Institute for Research; *International Bank for Reconstruction and Development (IBRD, #12317)*. **Activities** Basic components (4): School health policies; Water, sanitation and the environment; Life skills education or skills-based health education; School health and nutrition services. [2015/XE4370/**E***]

♦ Focus on Microscopy (meeting series)
♦ Föderalistische Union Europäischer Nationalitäten (#09396)
♦ Föderalistische Union Europäischer Volksgruppen / see Federal Union of European Nationalities (#09396)
♦ Föderation der Drogenhilfen in Europa / see European Treatment Centers for Drug Addiction (#08947)
♦ Föderation der Europäischen Fenster- und Fassadenherstellerverbände (#09456)
♦ Föderation der Europäischen Fensterherstellerverbände / see Fédération des associations européennes des constructeurs de fenêtres et de façades (#09456)
♦ Föderation der Europäischen Kommunalwälder / see European Federation of Local Forest Communities (#07157)
♦ Föderation der Europäischen Parkett-Industrie (#07188)
♦ Föderation der Europäischen Parkett-Industrie-Verbände / see European Federation of the Parquet Industry (#07188)

Föderation Europäischen Schneidwaren
09809
alphabetic sequence excludes
For the complete listing, see Yearbook Online at

- ♦ Föderation der Europäischen Schneidwaren- und Besteckindustrie / see Federation of European manufacturers of Cookware and cutlery (#09511)
- ♦ Föderation der Europäischen Schneidwaren-, Besteck-, Tafelgeräte-, Küchengeschirr- und Haushaltgeräteindustrie / see Federation of European manufacturers of Cookware and cutlery (#09511)
- ♦ Föderation der Europäischen Schneidwaren-, Besteck-, Tafelgeräte- und Küchengeschirrindustrie (#09511)
- ♦ Föderation der Europäischen Siebdruck-Verbände / see FESPA (#09739)
- ♦ Föderation der Europäischen Wirtschaftsauskunfteien / see Federation of Business Information Services (#09464)
- ♦ Föderation Europäischer Aerosol-Verbände / see Fédération Européenne des Aérosols (#09557)
- ♦ Föderation Europäischer Chemischer Gesellschaften / see European Chemical Society (#06524)
- ♦ Föderation Europäischer Gewässerschutz (inactive)
- ♦ Föderation Europäischer Islandpferde Freunde / see International Federation of Icelandic Horse Associations (#13454)
- ♦ Föderation Europäischer Münzhändlerverbände (#09523)

♦ Föderation Europäischer Narren (FEN) 09810

Fédération européenne des bouffons – Federatie Europese Narren – European Federation of the Nars

Pres Quellenweg 3, 63639 Flörsbachtal, Germany.
URL: http://www.fenvlaanderen.be/

History 20 Jun 1970, Essen (Germany). **Aims** Promote the development and appreciation of *folklore, carnival,* majorettes, and gastronomic fraternities. **Events** *Annual General Meeting* Bad Gögging (Germany) 2015. **Members** Full in 3 countries:
Belgium, Germany, Netherlands. [2020/XD1293/**D**]

- ♦ Föderation Europäischer Nationaler Ingenieurverbände (#09558)
- ♦ Föderation Europäische Zoologen (inactive)
- ♦ Föderation EUROPARC (#05768)
- ♦ Föderation der Hochschule-Ingenieure des Fernmeldewesens der Europäischen Gemeinschaft (#09597)
- ♦ Föderation der Internationalen Donau-Symposia über Diabetes Mellitus / see Federation of International Danube Symposia on Diabetes Mellitus – Central European Diabetes Association (#09605)
- ♦ Föderation der Internationalen Donau-Symposia über Diabetes Mellitus – Zentraleuropäische Diabetesgesellschaft (#09605)
- ♦ Föderation der Katholischen Familienverbände in Europa (#09468)
- ♦ Föderation der Nationalen Elektrotechnischen Vereinigungen Europas (#04788)
- ♦ Föderation der Nationalen Elektrotechnischen Vereinigungen Westeuropas / see Convention of National Associations of Electrical Engineers of Europe (#04788)
- ♦ Föderation der Nationalkomitees im Internationalen Kulturellen Jugendaustausch / see International Cultural Youth Exchange (#13122)
- ♦ Föderation der Natur- und Nationalparke Europas / see EUROPARC Federation (#05768)
- ♦ Föderation der Westthrazien Türken in Europa (internationally oriented national body)

♦ Foederatio Europea Orthodontica (FEO) 09811

European Federation of Orthodontics

SG Avda Andalucia 67 1oA-B, 11007 Cadiz, Cádiz, Spain. T. +34956257952. Fax +34956263719.
Pres 95-97 Mavromichali Street, 114 72 Athens, Greece.
URL: http://www.feo-online.com/

History 24 May 1997, Brussels (Belgium). **Aims** Promote orthodontics and dento-facial orthopaedics in Europe by: improving understanding and cooperation between the constituent associations; harmonizing programs and training sessions; encouraging research. **Structure** General Assembly (annual). Executive Board, comprising President, Vice-President, Secretary-General, Adjunct Secretary-General, Treasurer, Webmaster and Administrator. **Languages** English. **Staff** None. **Finance** Members' dues. **Activities** Grants annual FEO Award to best scientific paper produced in English. Organizes: joint meeting (every 4-5 years); European day. **Events** *General Assembly* Athens (Greece) 2020, *General Assembly* Athens (Greece) 2014, *General Assembly* Dresden (Germany) 2011, *General Assembly* Thessaloniki (Greece) 2009, *General Assembly* Venice (Italy) 2008.
Members Individuals in 20 countries:
Albania, Belgium, Bulgaria, Croatia, Cyprus, France, Germany, Greece, Ireland, Italy, Luxembourg, North Macedonia, Portugal, Romania, Russia, Serbia, Slovenia, Spain, Türkiye, UK.
Corresponding member in 3 countries:
Egypt, Israel, Lebanon.
NGO Relations Affiliated with: *World Federation of Orthodontists (#21469).* [2013/XG8079/**D**]

- ♦ Foederatio Internationalis Pueri Cantores (#09649)
- ♦ Foederatio Internationalis Una Voce (#09668)
- ♦ Foederatio Mundialis Associationum Nationalium Internationalium Pediatricae Scientiae Chirurgicae (#21411)
- ♦ Foederatio Universitatum Catholicarum / see International Federation of Catholic Universities (#13381)
- ♦ **FoEE** Friends of the Earth Europe (#10001)
- ♦ **FoEI** Friends of the Earth International (#10002)
- ♦ FoEME / see EcoPeace Middle East (#05325)
- ♦ **FOE** NGO Forum on Environment (#17125)
- ♦ FOFCO – Oceanic Federation of Corporate Football (unconfirmed)
- ♦ Fogarty International Center of the National Institutes of Health / see John E Fogarty International Center
- ♦ **FOGGS** Foundation for Global Governance and Sustainability (#09958)
- ♦ FogQuest / see FogQuest: sustainable water solutions
- ♦ FogQuest: sustainable water solutions (internationally oriented national body)
- ♦ **FOHNEU** Federation of Occupational Health Nurses within the European Union (#09697)
- ♦ **FOIAnet** Freedom of Information Advocates Network (#09985)
- ♦ **FOICAP** Federación de Organizaciones de Ingenieros de Centro América y Panama (#09483)
- ♦ **FOI** Fifty-One International (#09754)
- ♦ FOI – Fraternité oecuménique internationale (internationally oriented national body)
- ♦ FOKUS – Forum for Kvinner og Utviklingsspørsmål (internationally oriented national body)
- ♦ **FOLA** Federación Odontológica Latinoamericana (#16357)
- ♦ **FOLATUR** Foro Latinoamericano de Turismo (#09884)
- ♦ Folke Bernadotte Academy (internationally oriented national body)
- ♦ Folke Bernadotte Academy – Swedish Agency for Peace, Security and Development / see Folke Bernadotte Academy
- ♦ Folkekirkens Nødhjaelp (internationally oriented national body)
- ♦ Folkliga Reseorganisationernas Internationella Federation (inactive)
- ♦ Folklore Canada International (internationally oriented national body)
- ♦ **FoLLI** Association of Logic, Language and Information (#02789)
- ♦ Folmer Wisti Fondation pour la compréhension internationale (internationally oriented national body)
- ♦ Folmer Wisti Fondon for International Forståelse (internationally oriented national body)
- ♦ Folmer Wisti Foundation for International Understanding (internationally oriented national body)
- ♦ Folmer Wisti Fundación para el Entendimiento Internacional (internationally oriented national body)
- ♦ Folmer Wisti Stiftung für Internationale Verständigung (internationally oriented national body)
- ♦ FOLU – Food and Land Use Coalition (unconfirmed)
- ♦ FOMA / see International Association of Operative Millers
- ♦ FOMCA – Federación de Organizaciones Magisteriales de Centroamérica (inactive)
- ♦ FOMETRO – Fonds médical tropical (internationally oriented national body)
- ♦ FOM – Families of the Missing (internationally oriented national body)
- ♦ FOM – Focus on Microscopy (meeting series)
- ♦ **FOMIN** Fondo Multilateral de Inversiones (#16887)
- ♦ FOMULAC – Fondation médicale de l'Université catholique de Louvain en Afrique centrale (internationally oriented national body)
- ♦ **FONASBA** Federation of National Associations of Shipbrokers and Agents (#09694)
- ♦ FONCABA – Formation de cadres africains (internationally oriented national body)
- ♦ Fondacija za mir i Resavanje Kriza (internationally oriented national body)

♦ FONDACIO 09812

Contact Maison de Fondacio en Belgique, Rue des Mimosas 64, 1030 Brussels, Belgium. T. +322413357. E-mail: belgium@fondacio.be.
URL: http://www.fondacio.be/

History Also referred to as *FONDACIO – Christians for the World – FONDACIO – Chrétiens pour le monde – FONDACIO – Cristianos para el mundo.* **Aims** As a mouvement based on a Christian community, build a more human world and share, with those wishing to, what gives meaning to the lives of members of the community. **Structure** Council. **Languages** English, French, Spanish. **Activities** Networking/liaising; training/education. **Members** Individuals (about 3,000). A further 10,000 individuals support the mission and spread it around the world. Membership countries not specified. **NGO Relations** Member of: *Crescendo Worldwide Network (#04950); Forum of Catholic Inspired NGOs (#09905).* [2022/XJ5001/f/**F**]

- ♦ FONDACIO – Chrétiens pour le monde – FONDACIO – Cristianos para el mundo / see FONDACIO (#09812)
- ♦ FONDACIO – Christians for the World / see FONDACIO (#09812)
- ♦ Fondación Italiana para el Voluntariado (internationally oriented national body)
- ♦ **FONDAD** Forum on Debt and Development (#09906)
- ♦ Fondafrica – African Rural Development Fund (see: #11233)
- ♦ Fondajo Afriko (see: #20676)
- ♦ Fondajo Azio (see: #20676)

♦ Fondation pour l'action culturelle internationale en montagne (FACIM) 09813

International Foundation for Cultural Cooperation in the Mountains – Fundación para la Acción Cultural Internacional en las Montañas – Stiftung für Internationales Kulturschaffen in Gebirge

Dir 59 rue du Commandant Perceval, 73000 Chambéry, France. T. +33479605900. Fax +33479605901. E-mail: info@fondation-facim.fr.
URL: http://www.fondation-facim.fr/

History 21 Jun 1970, Courchevel (France). **Aims** Value the cultural heritage in Savay. **Structure** Administrative Board elects Bureau of 4 for 1 year term. International Board. **Languages** English, French, German, Italian. **Staff** 11.00 FTE, paid. **Activities** Language laboratories; concerts; performances; meetings; colloquiums. **Events** *Meeting* Chambéry (France) 1991. **Publications** Reports. **Members** French Committees and associated Committees in 20 countries. [2010.06.30/XF4311/f/**F**]

- ♦ Fondation Adriano Olivetti (internationally oriented national body)
- ♦ Fondation Africaine pour le Droit International (#00325)
- ♦ Fondation africaine de l'eau et de la santé (#10891)
- ♦ Fondation africaine de gestion urbaine (internationally oriented national body)
- ♦ Fondation africaine pour le renouveau moral, l'apprentissage professionelle, universitaire international et le commerce électronique et la coordination des trades points aux Rwanda, République démocratique du Congo et Grands Lacs / see FARMAPU-INTER and CECOTRAP-RCOGL
- ♦ Fondation Afrique (see: #20676)
- ♦ Fondation Aga Khan (#00545)
- ♦ Fondation pour l'agriculture et la ruralité dans le monde (internationally oriented national body)
- ♦ Fondation AIH pour l'avenir / see IHRA Foundation for the Future (#11113)
- ♦ Fondation Alexander von Humboldt (internationally oriented national body)
- ♦ Fondation Alfried Krupp von Bohlen und Halbach (internationally oriented national body)
- ♦ Fondation Alliance française / see Fondation des Alliances Françaises (#09814)

♦ Fondation des Alliances Françaises (AF) 09814

SG 101 bd Raspail, 75006 Paris, France. T. +33153630803. Fax +33145486911. E-mail: info@fondation-alliancefr.org.
URL: https://www.fondation-alliancefr.org/

History 21 Jul 1883, Paris (France). Re-established by decree as a foundation uniting the individual Alliances, 23 Jul 2007. Former names and other names: *Alliance française* – former (21 Jul 1883 to 23 Jul 2007); *Fondation Alliance française (AF)* – former (23 Jul 2007). Registration: France. **Aims** Coordinate individual Alliances françaises worldwide, offering support and advice in pedagogic, administrative and management matters; promote teaching of the French language worldwide, its use and appreciation; develop knowledge of and taste for French-speaking cultures; encourage friendly relations between people from France and other countries. **Structure** Board; Secretariat General in Paris (France), headed by Secretary General. Maintains: *Ecole internationale de langue et de civilisation françaises (see: #09814).* Individual, autonomous Alliances françaises have their own Boards of Directors, are registered under local law and administered by volunteers in their host town or country; but they also constitute part of the international mouvement. **Languages** French. **Staff** 15.00 FTE, paid. **Finance** Sources: government support. Own resources; assistance from French government. **Activities** Events/meetings; guidance/assistance/consulting; networking/liaising; training/education. **Events** *Congrès Mondial* Paris (France) 2020, *Etats Généraux des Alliances Françaises d'Europe* Madrid (Spain) 2016, *International Colloquium* Paris (France) 2012, *International Colloquium* Paris (France) 2011, *Latin America and Caribbean Conference* Rio de Janeiro (Brazil) 2011. **Publications** *Le Fil d'Alliances.* Newsletter; conference and colloquium proceedings; activity report; brochures. **Members** Alliances Françaises (832) in 131 countries and territories. Membership countries not specified. **IGO Relations** Accredited by (1): *Organisation internationale de la Francophonie (OIF, #17809).* Cooperates with (1): *TV5Monde (TV5, #20269).* **NGO Relations** Cooperates with (1): *Radio France internationale (RFI).* [2022/XE3159/f/**F**]

- ♦ Fondation d'Amérique latine pour les droits de l'homme (#10036)
- ♦ Fondation André Ryckmans (internationally oriented national body)
- ♦ Fondation Antenna Technologies / see Antenna Technology
- ♦ Fondation Antonio Bana pour la recherche des migrations ornithologiques et la protection de l'environnement / see European Foundation Il Nibbio
- ♦ Fondation Apimondia / see Fundatia Institutul International de Tehnologie si Economie Apicola
- ♦ Fondation Arias pour la paix et le progrès humain (internationally oriented national body)
- ♦ Fondation pour les arts à Bruxelles (internationally oriented national body)
- ♦ Fondation l'art de vivre (internationally oriented national body)
- ♦ Fondation asiatique pour la prévention de la cécité (#01496)
- ♦ Fondation asiatique pour la prévention du crime (#01263)
- ♦ Fondation Asie (see: #20676)
- ♦ Fondation pour l'Asie (internationally oriented national body)
- ♦ Fondation Asie Pacifique du Canada (internationally oriented national body)
- ♦ Fondation Assistance Internationale (internationally oriented national body)
- ♦ Fondation assistance médicale internationale (internationally oriented national body)
- ♦ Fondation autrichienne pour la recherche dans le domaine du développement (internationally oriented national body)
- ♦ Fondation avocats pour avocats (internationally oriented national body)
- ♦ Fondation Bernard van Leer (internationally oriented national body)
- ♦ Fondation Bertelsmann (internationally oriented national body)
- ♦ Fondation Bertrand Russell pour la paix (#03213)
- ♦ Fondation pour le bien-être et l'éducation des peuples d'Asie (internationally oriented national body)
- ♦ Fondation Bill et Melinda Gates (internationally oriented national body)
- ♦ Fondation bouddhiste internationale (internationally oriented national body)

- Fondation Bruno Kreisky pour les services rendus aux droits humains (internationally oriented national body)
- Fondation canadienne des droits de la personne / see Equitas – International Centre for Human Rights Education
- Fondation Caritas in Veritate (#03582)
- Fondation catholique de bourses d'études pour africains / see Formation de cadres africains
- Fondation catholique de bourses d'études pour le Congo / see Formation de cadres africains
- Fondation du Centre Orient-Occident (see: #05263)
- Fondation 'Centres européens langues et civilisations / see Foundation for Language and Educational Centres (#09964)
- Fondation 'Centres langues et civilisations' (#09964)
- Fondation Charles Darwin pour les Iles Galapagos (#03852)

♦ Fondation Charles Léopold Mayer pour le progrès de l'homme (FPH) 09815

Charles Léopold Mayer Foundation for the Progress of Humankind – Fundación Charles Léopold Mayer para el Progreso del Hombre – Charles Léopold Mayer Stiftung für den Fortschritt des Menschen

Dir Gen FPH Secretariat, 38 rue Saint Sabin, 75011 Paris, France. T. +33143147575. Fax +33143147599. E-mail: contact.fph@fph.ch – direction@fph.ch.
Registered Office Route de Praz-Véguey 29, BP 907, 1022 Chavannes-près-Renens VD, Switzerland. T. +41213425010. E-mail: contact.fph@fph.ch.
URL: http://www.fph.ch/

History 1982. Founded as *Foundation for the Progress of Humanity – Fondation pour le progrès de l'homme – Fundación para el Progreso del Hombre – Stiftung für den Fortschritt des Menschen.* Also sometimes referred to as *International Foundation for Human Progress.* Present name adopted Feb 1996. Registration: Swiss Civil Code. **Aims** Contribute to long-term mutations of our societies by supporting the emergence of a world community capable of designing and conducting 3 major mutations: new social, political and institutions regulations from local to global (the governance revolution); a common ethical foundation (the Charter of Human Responsibilities); new development models. Seek a constant coming and going between diversity, expressed in its different dimensions, and unity, expressed through a constant attention to the management of relations and to territorial consistency. **Structure** Board; Management committee; Teams (2). **Languages** French. **Staff** 12.00 FTE, paid. **Finance** Budget (annual): Swiss Fr 11 million. **Activities** Awards/prizes/competitions; financial and/or material support; guidance/assistance/consulting; advocacy/ loybbying/activism. **Events** *Biennial China-Europe forum* Brussels (Belgium) 2007, *Asian forum for solidarity economy* Manila (Philippines) 2007, *Réunion sur les industries culturelles et la mondialisation* Paris (France) 2001, *Biennial China-Europe forum* China 1995. **Publications** *Editions Charles Léopold Mayer (ECLM).* **NGO Relations** *Alliance internationale des éditeurs indépendants; Alliance for Rebuilding Governance in Africa (ARGA, #00715); Alliance for a Responsible and United World (inactive); Institute for Research and Debate on Governance (IRG); West African Association for the Development of Artisanal Fisheries (WADAF, #20867); World Forum of Fisher Peoples (WFFP, #21517).* [2021/XF3029/f/F]

- Fondation Chrëschte mam Sahel (internationally oriented national body)
- Fondation Chrétiens pour le Sahel (internationally oriented national body)
- Fondation cinfo / see Centre for Information, Counseling and Training Professions Relating to International Cooperation and Humanitarian Aid
- **Fondation CIOMAL** Campagne Internationale de l'Ordre de Malte contre la lèpre (#03403)
- Fondation des cités carnavalesques européennes / see Federation of European Carnival Cities (#09496)
- Fondation des citoyens du monde (internationally oriented national body)
- Fondation Collège de l'Europe Hambourg (internationally oriented national body)
- Fondation du Commonwealth (#04330)
- Fondation pour la compréhension internationale / see Folmer Wisti Foundation for International Understanding
- Fondation de l'entre-connaissance (internationally oriented national body)
- Fondation pour la conservation de l'environnement (#09948)
- Fondation contre le commerce de femmes / see Coördinatiecentrum Mensenhandel
- Fondation contre le trafic de femmes / see Coördinatiecentrum Mensenhandel
- Fondation pour la coopération internationale / see Mandat International
- Fondation Cordell Hull pour l'éducation dans le monde (internationally oriented national body)
- Fondation Coudenhove-Kalergi / see European Society Coudenhove-Kalergi (#08573)
- Fondation Cousteau / see Cousteau Society
- Fondation culturelle des amériques (internationally oriented national body)
- Fondation Dag Hammarskjöld (#04995)
- Fondation Damien – Association de lutte contre la lèpre / see Damien Foundation – Voluntary Organization for Leprosy and TB Control
- Fondation Damien – Mouvement de lutte contre la lèpre (internationally oriented national body)
- Fondation pour la Décennie internationale de la promotion d'une culture de la paix et de la non-violence au profit des enfants du monde (internationally oriented national body)
- Fondation Denis de Rougemont pour l'Europe (internationally oriented national body)

♦ Fondation Déserts du Monde 09816

World Deserts Foundation

Main Office Parc des Grands Vents, 22 Route Oulet Fayet, Dely Brahim, 16000 Algiers, Algeria. T. +21321917036. Fax +21321373516. E-mail: fondationdesertsdumonde@hotmail.com.
Europe Office Rue de la Synagogue 34, 1204 Geneva, Switzerland. T. +41228002200. Fax +41228002201. E-mail: contact@fondationderougemont.org.
URL: http://www.desertsdumonde.com/

History Dec 2002, Algeria, on the initiative of Cherif Rahmani. **Aims** Fight desertification; involve local actors in creation of strategies, programs and projects; conserve desert ecosystems through inventory, classification and promotion of deserts; promote a durable development strategy; preserve the cultures and traditions of desert people around the world. **Structure** Sponsoring Committee. **Languages** Arabic, English, French. **Activities** Promotes awareness raising; provides information and training; organizes workshops and seminars nationally and internationally; organizes the Festival of Cultures and Civilizations of the Peoples of the Deserts of the World. **Publications** *Newsletter* in English, French. *A Traveler's Guide in the Deserts* in English, French; *Charter of Deserts* in Arabic, English, French. **Members** Individuals. Membership countries not specified. **IGO Relations** Accredited to: *ECOSOC (#05331)*; the Conference of the Parties of: *Secretariat of the United Nations Convention to Combat Desertification (Secretariat of the UNCCD, #19208).* [2012.06.01/XJ8274/f/F]

- Fondation pour un développement écologique (internationally oriented national body)
- Fondation pour le Développement de la Médecine Interne en Europe (#09944)
- Fondation pour le droit continental (internationally oriented national body)
- Fondation Earth Focus (internationally oriented national body)

♦ Fondation pour l'économie et le développement durable des régions d'Europe (FEDRE) 09817

Foundation for the Economy and Sustainable Development of the Regions of Europe

Exec Sec 17 rue François Dussaud, Les Acacias, 1227 Geneva, Switzerland. T. +41228071717. E-mail: info@fedre.org.
URL: http://www.fedre.org/

History 25 Apr 1996, Geneva (Switzerland), having been proposed by individual members of *Congress of Local and Regional Authorities of the Council of Europe (#04677),* when endorsed at CLRAE's First East/ West Economic Forum of the Regions of Europe, Jan 1996. **Aims** Offer urban and rural regions, towns, economic organizations and enterprises the opportunity to make themselves known and to establish direct relations favouring sustainable and regional development; support the economy and sustainable development of all regions of Western, Central and Eastern Europe and the countries of the Mediterranean; reinforce the regional dimension of political and economic activities in Europe; stimulate cooperation among European regions, particularly East/West; support endogenous development at local and regional level. **Structure** Governing Board, comprising Chairman and President, 3 Vice-Chairmen and Vice-Presidents and 2 other Members; Executive Secretary; Advisors in the fields of finance and banking, equipment and construction, trade, agriculture and environment. **Finance** Supported by: Council of Europe and its CLRAE; the Swiss Confederation; *Swiss Agency for Development and Cooperation (SDC)*; the Republic and Canton of Geneva (Switzerland); the City of Geneva; its partners (regions, towns, associations and enterprises). **Activities** Organizes Economic Fora at least once a year and other forum on specific themes at the request of regional actors; provides services for making contacts, finding partners, transfer of technology for development and markets; supports for the search of economic and financial information. **Events** *International forum* Geneva (Switzerland) 2007, *European forum on climate changes / Euroregions Forum* Geneva (Switzerland) 2006, *Summit economic forum* Tirana (Albania) 2006, *Forum of cities and regions of South-East Europe* Budva (Serbia-Montenegro) 2004, *Thematic forum on sustainable development* Geneva (Switzerland) 2004. **Publications** *Regions – European Partners/Partenaires de l'Europe* (12 a year) in English, French; *FEDRE Newsletter.* **Information Services** *Euroregions Web* – on Internet. **Consultative Status** Consultative status granted from: *Council of Europe (CE, #04881)* (Participatory Status); *ECOSOC (#05331)* (Special). **IGO Relations** Cooperates with: *European Bank for Reconstruction and Development (EBRD, #06315); European Commission (EC, #06633); United Nations Economic Commission for Europe (UNECE, #20555); United Nations Institute for Training and Research (UNITAR, #20576); World Meteorological Organization (WMO, #21649).* **NGO Relations** Cooperates with: *Assembly of European Regions (AER, #02316).* Member of: *Fédération des Institutions Internationales établies à Genève (FIIG, #09599).* Associate member of: *Network of Associations of Local Authorities of South-East Europe (NALAS, #16997).* [2019/XF3907/f/F]

- Fondation éducatif Helen Dwight Reid (internationally oriented national body)
- Fondation pour l'éducation à l'environnement (#09949)
- Fondation pour l'éducation à l'environnement en Europe / see Foundation for Environmental Education (#09949)
- Fondation pour l'Education des Femmes Africaines (internationally oriented national body)
- Fondation éducative de la Confédération latinoaméricaine des coopératives d'épargne et de crédit (see: #16302)
- Fondation Elie Wiesel pour l'humanité (internationally oriented national body)
- Fondation Énergies pour le Monde (internationally oriented national body)
- Fondation énergies pour le monde (internationally oriented national body)
- Fondation énergies pour le monde – Comité d'action pour le solaire / see Fondation énergies pour le monde
- Fondation pour enfants disparus et sexuellement exploités / see European Centre for Missing and Sexually Exploited Children
- Fondation ensemble (internationally oriented national body)
- Fondation espace Afrique (internationally oriented national body)
- Fondation éthique planétaire (internationally oriented national body)
- Fondation des études américaines (internationally oriented national body)
- Fondation d'études méditerranéennes (internationally oriented national body)
- Fondation pour les études et recherches sur le développement international (internationally oriented national body)
- Fondation euractiv / see Fondation Euractiv PoliTech (#09818)

♦ Fondation Euractiv PoliTech 09818

Europe's MediaLab

SG Intl Press Ctr, Blvd Charlemagne 1, Bte 1, 1041 Brussels, Belgium. T. +3222265819. E-mail: fondation@euractiv.com.
URL: https://europemedialab.eu/

History 2004. Former names and other names: *Fondation euractiv* – former (2004 to 2012). Registration: Banque-Carrefour des Entreprises, No/ID: 0862.453.031, Start date: 31 Dec 2003, Belgium; EU Transparency Register, No/ID: 485832526193-89, Start date: 3 Mar 2017. **Aims** Bring together individuals and organizations seeking to shape or influence *European Union policies.* **Structure** Management Board; Orientation Committee; Advisory Council. **Finance** Grants and payments. **Events** *Forum on Galileo's Role in the Transition towards Fully Autonomous Driving* Brussels (Belgium) 2018, *Forum sur l'avenir de l'Europe Sociale* Paris (France) 2018, *Table Ronde sur le Futur du Travail en Europe* Paris (France) 2018, *Annual EuroConference on Association Effectiveness through the Exchange of Best Practices* Brussels (Belgium) 2016, *Annual EuroConference on Association Effectiveness through the Exchange of Best Practices* Brussels (Belgium) 2015. [2021/XM7415/f/F]

- Fondation Eurasie (#05600)
- Fondation euroarabe de hautes études (internationally oriented national body)
- Fondation euro-méditerranéenne Anna Lindh pour le dialogue entre les cultures (#00847)
- Fondation euro-méditerranéenne de soutien aux défenseurs des droits de l'Homme (#05720)
- Fondation Europalia International (internationally oriented national body)
- Fondation Europ'Atlas (unconfirmed)
- Fondation Europe+ (#09157)
- Fondation européenne pour l'accréditation des écoles hôtelières (#07341)
- Fondation européenne pour l'amélioration des conditions de vie et de travail (#07348)
- Fondation européenne pour l'architecture du paysage / see IFLA Europe (#11103)
- Fondation européenne Charcot / see European Charcot Foundation (#06518)
- Fondation européenne de la culture (#06868)
- Fondation européenne pour le développement du management / see EFMD – The Management Development Network (#05387)
- Fondation européenne des droits de l'homme (inactive)
- Fondation européenne de l'énergie / see European Energy Forum (#06986)
- Fondation européenne d'études progressistes (#09954)
- Fondation européenne pour la formation (#08934)
- Fondation européenne pour la recherche dans l'accident vasculaire cérébral (internationally oriented national body)
- Fondation européenne de la science (#08441)
- Fondation européenne du Scoutisme (#08451)

♦ Fondation européenne des services d'accueil téléphonique drogues et toxicomanies (FESAT) 09819

European Foundation of Drug Helplines

Pres c/o VAD, Rue Vanderlinden 15, 1030 Brussels, Belgium.

History 1993. Registration: EU Transparency Register, No/ID: 044708725004-19, Start date: 9 Dec 2016. **Aims** Stimulate and develop cooperation between drug helplines in member states; enlarge the network by addition of drug helpline services from countries of central and eastern Europe and from all applicant countries. **Structure** Board; Working Groups (7); Permanent bureau in Brussels (Belgium). **Languages** English. **Staff** Voluntary. **Finance** Members' dues. Funding from: *European Commission (EC, #06633).* **Activities** Training/ education; knowledge management/information dissemination; projects/programmes; networking/liaising; standards/guidelines. **Events** *Conference* Lisbon (Portugal) 2007, *European conference of associated services* Barcelona (Spain) 2004, *Conference of associated services* Milan (Italy) 2003, *European conference of drug helplines* Berlin (Germany) 2001, *European conference of drug helplines* Lisbon (Portugal) 1992. **Publications** *FESAT Newsletter* (5 a year); *FESAT Monitoring Reports* (2 a year); *Lines Magazine. Drug Helplines and Legal Aspects; Equal Access for All Ethnic Minorities and Drug Helplines; Families and Drug Helplines.* Guidelines; conference and educational partnership reports.

Members European drug helpline services (about 30) in 17 countries:
Austria, Belgium, Cyprus, Czechia, Finland, France, Germany, Greece, Hungary, Ireland, Malta, Netherlands, Norway, Portugal, Romania, Sweden, UK.

IGO Relations Collaborates with: *European Monitoring Centre for Drugs and Drug Addiction (EMCDDA, #07820).* Member of: *European Commission (EC, #06633)* – Civil Society Forum on Drugs (DG Migration and Home Affairs). [2019/XF3917/f/F]

- Fondation européenne pour la transplantation / see Eurotransplant International Foundation (#09192)
- Fondation Europe et société / see Association Europe and Society (#02586)
- Fondation Evens (internationally oriented national body)
- Fondation des facultés universitaires Notre-Dame de la Paix pour la coopération internationale au développement / see Fondation universitaire pour la coopération internationale au développement
- Fondation Félix Houphouët-Boigny / see Fondation internationale Houphouët-Boigny pour la paix
- Fondation Félix Houphouët-Boigny pour la recherche de la paix / see Fondation internationale Houphouët-Boigny pour la paix
- Fondation des Femmes de l'Euro-Méditerranée (#05729)
- Fondation Ford (#09858)
- Fondation du forum universale (internationally oriented national body)
- Fondation de France (internationally oriented national body)
- Fondation François Visine / see European Merit Foundation
- Fondation Franz Weber (internationally oriented national body)
- Fondation Friedrich Ebert (internationally oriented national body)
- Fondation Friedrich Naumann / see Friedrich Naumann Foundation for Freedom
- Fondation Friedrich Naumann pour la liberté (internationally oriented national body)
- Fondation Fritz Thyssen (internationally oriented national body)
- Fondation Giovanni Agnelli (internationally oriented national body)
- Fondation GIPRI / see Geneva International Peace Research Institute
- Fondation Global Play (internationally oriented national body)
- Fondation GoodPlanet (internationally oriented national body)
- Fondation du Groupe de travail pour la recherche internationale sur les oiseaux d'eau et les zones humides (#09976)
- Fondation Hanns Seidel (internationally oriented national body)
- Fondation Henri la Fontaine (internationally oriented national body)
- Fondation de Hesse pour les recherches sur la paix et les conflits / see Peace Research Institute Frankfurt
- Fondation Hindemith (#10919)
- Fondation Hirondelle – Media for Peace and Human Dignity (internationally oriented national body)
- Fondation humanus – Humanus International (internationally oriented national body)
- Fondation IGF – Fondation Internationale pour la Gestion de la Faune (internationally oriented national body)
- Fondation IHRA pour l'avenir (#11113)
- Fondation des immeubles pour les organisations internationales (internationally oriented national body)
- Fondation pour l'Institut africain de gestion urbaine / see African Foundation for Urban Management

♦ Fondation de l'Institut Panafricain pour le Développement (FIPD) .. 09820

Contact Rue de Varembé 3, CP 116, 1211 Geneva 20, Switzerland. T. +41227336016 – +41227522937. E-mail: info@fondationipd.org.
URL: http://www.fondationipd.org/

History 6 Dec 2012, Geneva (Switzerland). Set up by *Pan African Institute for Development (PAID, #18053)* as a distinctive and autonomous foundation. Registration: Swiss Civil Code, Switzerland. **Aims** Contribute to consolidation, support and progressive sustainability of the financing of PAID and its activities. **Structure** Council; International Scientific and Educational Council; International Council of Sponsors. **Finance** Initial funding from *Pan African Institute for Development (PAID, #18053)*. **Activities** Advocacy/lobbying/activism; financial and/or material support; training/education. [2020.04.30/XM6822/f/**F**]

- Fondation inter-américaine (#11431)
- Fondation interaméricaine du barreau (see: #11401)
- Fondation international pour les arbres (internationally oriented national body)
- Fondation international Cardijn / see International Cardijn Association
- Fondation internationale pour un autre développement (inactive)
- Fondation internationale du Banc d'Arguin (internationally oriented national body)
- Fondation internationale carrefour (internationally oriented national body)
- Fondation internationale chrétienne pour la paix (inactive)
- Fondation internationale pour le développement économique et social (internationally oriented national body)
- Fondation internationale pour le développement économique et social, Paris (internationally oriented national body)

♦ Fondation internationale pour le développement au service des coopérants et de communautés de base (FIDESCO) 09821

Dir bd Auguste Blanqui, 75013 Paris, France. T. +33158107480. E-mail: contact@fidesco.fr.
URL: http://www.fidesco-international.org/

History 1981, France, by *Communauté de l'Emmanuel*, as a Catholic organization for international development. Also referred to as *Organisation Catholique de Solidarité Internationale*. Registered in accordance with French law. **Aims** Send volunteers at the request of the local *Catholic Church* to serve local populations without regard to religion, ethnicity or culture. **Structure** Council supervises national entities. Offices in: Australia; Austria; Belgium; France; Germany; Netherlands; Poland; Portugal; USA. **Languages** English, French. **Staff** Headquarters: 10 paid; other offices: 2 paid; several voluntary. **Finance** Private donors (about 70%); Government of France (about 30%) for training and medical insurance. **Activities** Religious activities; projects/programmes.
Members Volunteers (117) in 32 countries:
Angola, Benin, Brazil, Burkina Faso, Cambodia, Cameroon, Chile, Colombia, Congo DR, Côte d'Ivoire, Cuba, Guinea, Haiti, India, Indonesia, Israel, Kenya, Madagascar, Nigeria, Papua New Guinea, Peru, Philippines, Rwanda, Senegal, South Africa, Taiwan, Tanzania UR, Thailand, Timor-Leste, Togo, USA, Zambia.
NGO Relations Member of: *Forum of Catholic Inspired NGOs (#09905)*. Cooperates with: *Coordination SUD*; *Délégation catholique pour la coopération (DCC)*; *Guilde européenne du raid (GER)*. [2022/XF2991/f/**F**]

- Fondation internationale d'eidétique / see Eidetics Academy (#05400)
- Fondation internationale pour l'état de droit et l'indépendance des avocats et des magistrats (internationally oriented national body)
- Fondation internationale Florence Nightingale (#09798)
- Fondation Internationale pour la Gestion de la Faune (internationally oriented national body)

♦ Fondation internationale pour une histoire de la civilisation européenne 09822

International Foundation for a History of European Civilization
Address not obtained.

History 1994, Geneva (Switzerland). **Aims** Elaborate a European public opinion concerning the main issues of the European society so as to build up a united or coordinated Europe. **Structure** Council; Board of Honour; National Boards. **Languages** English, French, German, Italian, Portuguese, Spanish. **Finance** Public and private subsidies. Budget (annual): around euro 200,000. **Activities** Organizes: annual symposium; annual meetings of academics; "Club of European Cities". **Publications** *Note* (4 a year); *Cahier de la Fondation* (annual). Online guide.
Members Full in 8 countries:
Belgium, Germany, Italy, Netherlands, Portugal, Spain, Switzerland, UK. [2008/XF6485/f/**F**]

- Fondation internationale Houphouët-Boigny pour la paix (internationally oriented national body)
- Fondation internationale des immigrants (internationally oriented national body)
- Fondation internationale de l'innovation sociale / see International Forum for Social Innovation (#13651)
- Fondation internationale Ion Voicu (internationally oriented national body)
- Fondation internationale Ludmila Jivkova / see St Cyril and St Methodius International Foundation
- Fondation internationale Menarini (internationally oriented national body)
- Fondation internationale MOKA (#16846)
- Fondation internationale Moka El-Aboubakar / see MOKA International Foundation (#16846)

♦ Fondation internationale Olympafrica (FINO) 09823

Olympafrica International Foundation
Exec Dir BP 22519, Dakar, Senegal. E-mail: olympaf@orange.sn – olympaf@sentoo.sn.
URL: http://www.facebook.com/Olympafrica-F-Internationale-218294211683727/

History Jun 1993, Lausanne (Switzerland). **Aims** Use the impact of *sport* to motivate *young people* and provide the opportunity for their involvement in *development* activities; develop young people's talents through local sports programmes; improve *living conditions* in *rural* areas so as to encourage young people to remain or return there; protect young people from delinquency, drug addiction, sexually transmitted diseases, truancy, vagrancy, unemployment and under-employment; promote implementation of a network of centres in *African* countries to propagate Olympic ethics, peace, brotherhood and fair-play. **Finance** Sponsors include: *European Commission (EC, #06633)*; *International Olympic Committee (IOC, #14408)*; *International Bank for Reconstruction and Development (IBRD, #12317)*; *UNESCO (#20322)*. **NGO Relations** Recognized by: International Olympic Committee. [2016.07.05/XF3298/f/**F**]

- Fondation internationale pénale et pénitentiaire (#14553)
- Fondation internationale pour la population et le développement (#13674)
- Fondation internationale A S Pouchkine (internationally oriented national body)
- Fondation Internationale Prix Balzan (#12309)
- Fondation internationale pour la protection des défenseurs des droits humains / see Front Line Defenders (#10008)
- Fondation internationale pour les recherches sur l'art (internationally oriented national body)
- Fondation internationale Roncalli (internationally oriented national body)
- Fondation internationale pour la sauvegarde de la faune (#13667)
- Fondation internationale pour la sauvegarde du gibier / see International Foundation for the Conservation of Wildlife (#13667)
- Fondation internationale pour la sauvegarde des grues (#13102)
- Fondation internationale pour la science (#13677)
- Fondation internationale scientifique (inactive)
- Fondation internationale des stations scientifiques à haute altitude de Jungfraujoch et du Gornergrat (#13671)
- Fondation internationale des systèmes électoraux (#13669)
- Fondation Internationale Tierno et Mariam (unconfirmed)
- Fondation internationale pour la trêve olympique (#14410)
- Fondation internationale Triffin / see Robert Triffin International

♦ Fondation islamique du salut (FIS) 09824

Address not obtained.

History 1984, by Oussama bin Laden, initially to resist Soviet domination of Afghanistan. A precursor to *Al-Qa'ida (#00748)*. **Structure** Includes *Maison des compagnons* which deployed Muslim volunteers against the Soviet Army in Afghanistan. **Activities** Allegedly finances *Worldwide Intifada*.
Members Said to be active in 13 countries:
Albania, Iraq, Jordan, Lebanon, Malaysia, Morocco, Netherlands, Pakistan, Romania, Russia, Syrian AR, Türkiye, United Arab Emirates.
NGO Relations *Human Concern International (HCI)*. [2009/XF3700/f/**F**]

- Fondation islamique pour la science, la technologie et le développement (inactive)
- Fondation ISMU – Initiatives et études sur la multiethnicité (internationally oriented national body)
- Fondation italienne pour le volontariat (internationally oriented national body)
- Fondation Jean-Jaurès (internationally oriented national body)

♦ Fondation Jean Monnet pour l'Europe 09825

Jean Monnet Foundation for Europe
Dir Ferme de Dorigny, 1015 Lausanne VD, Switzerland. T. +41216922090. Fax +41216922095. E-mail: secr@fjme.unil.ch.
URL: http://www.jean-monnet.ch/

History Oct 1978, Lausanne (Switzerland). Founded by Jean Monnet (1888-1979) and Henri Rieben (1921-2006). **Aims** Contribute to the efforts dedicated to the construction of Europe by being inspired by the thought, method and action of Jean Monnet. **Structure** General Assembly; Executive Council; Scientific Committee. **Languages** English, French. **Staff** 8.00 FTE, paid. **Finance** Public subsidies; gifts from individuals and enterprises. **Activities** Events/meetings; financial and/or material support; networking/liaising; publishing activities; research/documentation; training/education. **Events** *Comment parler d'Europe?* Lausanne (Switzerland) 2022, *Annual General Assembly* Lausanne (Switzerland) 1993, *Annual General Assembly* Lausanne (Switzerland) 1990, *Annual general assembly* Lausanne (Switzerland) 1988. **Publications** *Cahiers rouges* – series, created in 1957, 219 issues to date; *Debates and Documents Collection* – created in 2014, 26 issues to date. Information Services: Media library; library; web portal for scanned archives; publications in open acces on website. Makes written archives related to the inception and development of the European Union available to researchers, including those of Jean Monnet, Robert Schuman, Robert Marjolin, Jacques Delors and other important protagonists. **Information Services** *European Documentation Centre*.
Members Full in 20 countries:
Austria, Belgium, China, France, Germany, Greece, Hungary, India, Ireland, Italy, Liechtenstein, Luxembourg, Netherlands, Norway, Poland, Portugal, Spain, Switzerland, UK, USA.
NGO Relations Cooperates with institutions of higher education and other foundations, associations and archives dealing with European affairs (not specified). [2023.02.16/XF1255/f/**F**]

- Fondation Jean Paul II pour le Sahel (#16121)
- Fondation de la jeunesse européenne pour la protection des forêts (#09136)
- Fondation KAF (internationally oriented national body)
- Fondation Karl Jaspers (#16180)
- Fondation Karl Kübel / see Karl Kübel Foundation for Child and Family
- Fondation Karl Kübel pour l'enfance et la famille (internationally oriented national body)
- Fondation Kim Phuc internationale (internationally oriented national body)
- Fondation Latsis internationale (internationally oriented national body)
- Fondation Léon Mba (internationally oriented national body)
- Fondation Léopold Sédar Senghor (internationally oriented national body)
- Fondation Liliane (internationally oriented national body)
- Fondation de logements coopératifs / see Global Communities
- Fondation des logiciels libre pour l'Afrique (#09989)
- Fondation de Louvain pour la coopération au développement / see Louvain Coopération
- Fondation luthérienne pour la recherche oecuménique (#16529)
- Fondation de la maison des sciences de l'homme (internationally oriented national body)
- Fondation des maisons familiales rurales dans le monde (internationally oriented national body)
- Fondation Marangopoulos pour les droits de l'homme (internationally oriented national body)
- Fondation Marcel Hicter / see Association Marcel Hicter
- Fondation Marcel Mérieux / see Mérieux Foundation
- Fondation Martin Ennals (#16590)

♦ Fondation Mattei Dogan (FMD) 09826

Pres Fondation Maison des sciences de l'homme, 54 bd Raspail, 75006 Paris, France. T. +33637728617. E-mail: president@fondationmatteidogan.org.
URL: http://www.fondationmatteidogan.org/

History 2001. Registration: Fondation reconnue d'utilité publique, France; USA. **Aims** Study the major issues of advanced or post-industrial societies from a comparative and interdisciplinary perspective by methods practised in the *social sciences*. **Structure** Executive Board; Board, comprising President, General Secretary and Treasurer. **Languages** English, French. **Staff** 2.00 FTE, voluntary. **Finance** Sources: donations; gifts, legacies; investments. **Activities** Awards/prizes/competitions. **Events** *Mattei Dogan – Pionnier de la Recherche Comparative Internationale en Sciences Sociales* Bucharest (Romania) 2021. **Publications** *Fondation philanthropiques en Europe et aus Etats-Unis* (2007); *The Legitimacy of Philanthropic Foundations* (2006). Online publications. **Members** Individuals. Membership countries not specified. **NGO Relations** Also links with national organizations. [2022.05.03/XM2916/f/F]

- ♦ Fondation pour la médecine et la recherche en Afrique / see Amref Health Africa (#00806)
- ♦ Fondation pour les Médias en Afrique de l'Ouest (#16617)
- ♦ Fondation médicale de l'Université catholique de Louvain en Afrique centrale (internationally oriented national body)
- ♦ Fondation Médicale de l'Université Catholique de Louvain au Congo / see Fondation médicale de l'Université catholique de Louvain en Afrique centrale
- ♦ Fondation Medicines Patent Pool / see Medicines Patent Pool (#16635)
- ♦ Fondation Mediterranea (internationally oriented national body)
- ♦ Fondation méditerranéenne d'études stratégiques (internationally oriented national body)
- ♦ Fondation pour la Mémoire de la Shoah (internationally oriented national body)
- ♦ Fondation Mentor / see Mentor International (#16716)
- ♦ Fondation Mentor Internationale (#16716)
- ♦ Fondation Mérieux (internationally oriented national body)
- ♦ Fondation du mérite européen (internationally oriented national body)
- ♦ Fondation MOA / see MOA International
- ♦ Fondation monde sans mines (internationally oriented national body)
- ♦ Fondation mondiale pour les guides et les éclaireuses (#21526)
- ♦ Fondation mondiale Pedro Arrupe / see Pedro Arrupe World Association (#18287)
- ♦ Fondation mondiale Pestalozzi / see Pestalozzi Children's Foundation
- ♦ Fondation mondiale recherche et prévention SIDA (#21525)
- ♦ Fondation mondiale de secours et d'amitié (#14713)
- ♦ Fondation mondiale pour le Waqf (#21906)
- ♦ Fondation des Nations Unies pour l'habitat et les établissements humains (inactive)
- ♦ Fondation pour la Nature et l'Homme (internationally oriented national body)
- ♦ Fondation Nestlé pour l'étude des problèmes de l'alimentation dans le monde (#16975)
- ♦ Fondation Nicolas Hulot pour la nature et l'homme / see Fondation pour la Nature et l'Homme
- ♦ Fondation Nobel (internationally oriented national body)
- ♦ Fondation nordique de la jeunesse (inactive)
- ♦ Fondation le Nouveau Monde (internationally oriented national body)
- ♦ Fondation Otto Benecke (internationally oriented national body)
- ♦ Fondation paix et développement (internationally oriented national body)
- ♦ Fondation pour la paix et la gestion des crises (internationally oriented national body)
- ♦ Fondation panaméricaine de développement (#18094)
- ♦ Fondation Partage Luxembourg (internationally oriented national body)
- ♦ Fondation pour la pathologie mondiale (#21714)
- ♦ Fondation pour la pathologie mondiale de la WASPaLM / see World Pathology Foundation (#21714)
- ♦ Fondation Patrimoine sans frontières / see Cultural Heritage without Borders
- ♦ Fondation Paul Ango Ela de géopolitique en Afrique centrale (internationally oriented national body)
- ♦ Fondation Paul Gérin-Lajoie (internationally oriented national body)
- ♦ Fondation de la Pensée Arabe (#01056)
- ♦ Fondation Peter Hesse – Solidarité dans le partenariat (internationally oriented national body)
- ♦ Fondation pour les peuples du Pacifique Sud / see Counterpart International
- ♦ Fondation polaire internationale (internationally oriented national body)
- ♦ Fondation pour une politique européenne de l'environnement (see: #11261)
- ♦ Fondation 'Populorum Progressio' (#09969)
- ♦ Fondation de la presse en Asie (inactive)
- ♦ Fondation pour le progrès de l'homme / see Fondation Charles Léopold Mayer pour le progrès de l'homme (#09815)
- ♦ **Fondation RAFAD** Fondation RAFAD – Recherches et applications de financements alternatifs au développement (#09827)

♦ Fondation RAFAD – Recherches et applications de financements alternatifs au développement (Fondation RAFAD) 09827

RAFAD Foundation

Contact Rue de Varembé 1, CP 117, 1211 Geneva 20, Switzerland. T. +41227335073. Fax +41227347083.

History Jul 1985, Geneva (Switzerland). Also known as *Research and Applications for Alternative Financing for Development – Investigación y Aplicación de Financiamientos Alternativos al Desarrollo*. **Aims** Improve *financing* alternatives for micro and small enterprises in developing countries through technical assistance. **Structure** Board of Directors, comprising President and 3 members. Secretariat. **Languages** English, French, Spanish. **Staff** 1.00 FTE, paid; 2.00 FTE, voluntary. **Finance** Annual budget: US$ 300,000. **Activities** Research and development of alternative finance instruments for financing micro and small entreprises in developing countries. Mandated for the evaluation of Guarantee Funds. **Events** *Meeting* Lima (Peru) 1997. **Publications** Annual Report.

Members Partners in 13 countries:
Benin, Burkina Faso, Burundi, Chile, Ecuador, El Salvador, Guatemala, Honduras, Mali, Nicaragua, Peru, Senegal, Togo.

NGO Relations Member of: *European Microfinance Platform (E-MFP, #07793)*; *International Guarantee Fund (IGF, #13761)*. [2018.01.29/XF2975/f/F]

- ♦ Fondation des recherches économiques latinoaméricaines (internationally oriented national body)
- ♦ Fondation pour la recherche stratégique (internationally oriented national body)

♦ Fondation des Régions Européennes pour la Recherche, l'Education et la Formation (FREREF) 09828

Project Manager Parc du Lyonnais, 392 rue des Mercières, Rillieux-la-Pape, 69140 Lyon, France. T. +33478556439. E-mail: freref@freref.eu.

URL: http://www.freref.eu/

History Statutes adopted 14 Mar 1991. Registered in accordance with Belgian law. **Aims** Promote European cooperation and exchange of practices between actors of lifelong learning. **Structure** General Assembly; Administrative Council; Scientific Council; Consultative Committees (2); Regional Representatives; Scientists. **Finance** Members' dues. Project funding from *European Commission (EC, #06633)*. **Activities** Training/ education; events/meetings; projects/programmes. **Events** *Regional specifics in education and traning, Research wanted?* Barcelona (Spain) 1995.

Members Regions (12) in 6 countries:
Belgium, France, Italy, Poland, Spain, Switzerland.
Institutions (5) in 2 countries:
France, Spain.

NGO Relations Member of: *Federation of European and International Associations Established in Belgium (FAIB, #09508)*. Associate member of: *Lifelong Learning Platform – European Civil Society for Education (LLLP, #16466)*. [2018.06.20/XF5391/f/F]

- ♦ Fondation René Seydoux pour le monde méditerranéen (internationally oriented national body)
- ♦ Fondation pour le renforcement des capacités en Afrique (#00233)
- ♦ Fondation Ricky Martin (internationally oriented national body)
- ♦ Fondation Robert Schuman (internationally oriented national body)
- ♦ Fondation Roger Riou – aide aux pays en voie de développement / see Association Roger Riou
- ♦ Fondation Roi Baudouin (internationally oriented national body)
- ♦ Fondation Rotary (#18974)
- ♦ Fondation des Rotary Clubs belges pour la coopération au développement / see Association des Rotary clubs belges pour la coopération au développement
- ♦ Fondation du rotary international de Belgique-Luxembourg pour l'aide au Tiers-monde / see Association des Rotary clubs belges pour la coopération au développement
- ♦ Fondation Royaumont pour le progrès des sciences de l'homme (internationally oriented national body)
- ♦ Fondation Rui (internationally oriented national body)
- ♦ Fondation rurale de l'Afrique de l'ouest (#20902)
- ♦ Fondation russe pour la paix (internationally oriented national body)
- ♦ Fondation SADAOC / see Foundation for Sustainable Food Security in Central West Africa (#09975)
- ♦ **Fondation SADAOC** Fondation pour la sécurité alimentaire durable en Afrique de l'Ouest centrale (#09975)
- ♦ Fondation de la santé et des droits de l'homme (inactive)
- ♦ Fondation Sasawaka pour la paix (internationally oriented national body)
- ♦ Fondation Sciences Citoyennes / see Sciences Citoyennes
- ♦ Fondation du scoutisme mondial (#21772)
- ♦ Fondation pour la sécurité aérienne (#09795)
- ♦ Fondation pour la sécurité alimentaire durable en Afrique de l'Ouest centrale (#09975)
- ♦ Fondation Segré (internationally oriented national body)
- ♦ Fondation Sentinelles / see Sentinelles
- ♦ Fondation Sommet mondial des femmes (#21038)
- ♦ Fondation St-Galloise d'études internationales / see ISC-Foundation
- ♦ Fondation suisse de déminage (internationally oriented national body)
- ♦ Fondation suisse pour la paix / see Swisspeace
- ♦ Fondation suisse pour la Paix – Institut pour la résolution de conflits / see Swisspeace
- ♦ Fondation Syngenta pour une Agriculture Durable (internationally oriented national body)

♦ Fondation Temimi pour la recherche scientifique et l'information (FTERSI) 09829

Founder and Gen Dir Immeuble Al-Imtiaz, Centre Urbain Nord, 1003 Tunis, Tunisia. T. +21671231444 – +21671751164. Fax +21671236677.

URL: http://temimi.refer.org/

History Apr 1995, Zaghouan (Tunisia), expanding and widening the activities of *Centre d'études et de recherches ottomanes, morisques, de documentation et d'information (CEROMDI, inactive)*, which had been set up in 1985. Official inauguration Mar 1997. **Aims** Create a centre for information on *Ottoman* and Moriscos Andalusian *history*, documentation, humanities and social sciences. **Structure** General Director; Secretary General. A consulting committee for each published review. **Languages** Arabic, English, French. **Staff** 9.00 FTE, paid. **Finance** Personal funds of Prof A Temimi. **Activities** Provides secretariat for: *Arab Committee for Ottoman Studies (ACOS, no recent information)*; *Arab Federation for Libraries and Information (AFLI, #00947)*; *International Committee for Moriscos Studies (#12788)*. **Events** *Congrès international de la recherche scientifique en sciences humaines et sociales* Zaghouan (Tunisia) 1999, *Symposium international d'études morisques* Zaghouan (Tunisia) 1999, *Congrès international de la recherche scientifique en sciences humaines et sociales* Zaghouan (Tunisia) 1998, *Congrès international sur les Chrétiens et Musulmans à l'époque de la Renaissance* Zaghouan (Tunisia) 1998, *International symposium for Ottoman studies / International Symposium* Zaghouan (Tunisia) 1998. **Publications** *La recherche scientifique en sciences humaines* (4 a year) in Arabic, French – bulletin; *Arab Historical Review for Ottoman Studies (AHROS)*; *La revue d'histoire maghrébine (RHM)*; *Revue arabe d'archives, de documentation et d'information (RAADI)*. *Archéologie Ottomane* – series; *Documentation, information et index* – series; *Etudes d'histoire Morisque* – series; *Histoire du Maroc et d'Afrique* – series; *Les provinces arabes à l'époque Ottomane* – series; *Monde arabe et Turquie à l'époque contemporaine* – series; *Recherche scientifique en sciences humaines* – series. Congress proceedings; monographs; studies. **NGO Relations** Member of: *International Union for Oriental and Asian Studies (IUOAS, inactive)*. [2011/XE2021/f/E]

- ♦ Fondation TerrEspoir (internationally oriented national body)
- ♦ Fondation Thomson Reuters (internationally oriented national body)
- ♦ Fondation du Tiers-monde (#20150)
- ♦ Fondation Toison d'Or / see Fondation Toison d'Or – Académie Européenne d'Histoire (#09830)

♦ Fondation Toison d'Or – Académie Européenne d'Histoire 09830

Pres Rue de la Procession 4, 1331 Rosières, Belgium. T. +3226535324. Fax +3226541908.

History 1969, Brussels (Belgium), as *Conseil de la Toison d'Or*. Changed to *Fondation Toison d'Or* in 1995, after merger with *Académie européenne d'histoire (inactive)*. Registered in accordance with Belgian law. **Aims** Upgrade the historic and cultural heritage of countries, regions, towns and cities associated with the Order of the Golden Fleece; emphasize their common civilization, interests and destiny. **Languages** French. **Finance** Members' dues. **Activities** Organizes exhibitions; runs the 'Espace Muséal Toison d'Or'. **Publications** *Toison d'Or – Présence de l'histoire* (irregular) – review. **NGO Relations** Instrumental in setting up: *Association européenne des villes de la toison d'or (#02584)*. [2011.07.31/XF1726/f/F]

- ♦ Fondation pour l'UNESCO – Education des enfants en détresse / see YOU Stiftung – Bildung für Kinder in Not
- ♦ Fondation universitaire pour la coopération internationale au développement (internationally oriented national body)
- ♦ Fondation Universitaire de la Mer Noire
- ♦ Fondation des universités néerlandaises pour la coopération internationale / see Netherlands Organization for International Cooperation in Higher Education
- ♦ Fondation Ushuaïa / see Fondation pour la Nature et l'Homme
- ♦ Fondation Vaticane "Centre International Famille de Nazareth" (#20750)
- ♦ Fondation Pro Victimis (internationally oriented national body)
- ♦ Fondation Village d'enfants Pestalozzi (internationally oriented national body)
- ♦ Fondation Volkswagen (internationally oriented national body)
- ♦ Fondation Voltaire (internationally oriented national body)
- ♦ Fondazione Adkins Chiti: Donne in Musica (internationally oriented national body)
- ♦ Fondazione Adriano Olivetti (internationally oriented national body)
- ♦ Fondazione AVSI (internationally oriented national body)
- ♦ Fondazione Barilla Center for Food and Nutrition (internationally oriented national body)
- ♦ Fondazione BCFN – Fondazione Barilla Center for Food and Nutrition (internationally oriented national body)
- ♦ Fondazione Canossiana Voica (internationally oriented national body)
- ♦ Fondazione Cariplo per le Iniziative e lo Studio della Multietnicità / see ISMU Foundation – Foundation for Initiatives and Studies on Multi-ethnicity
- ♦ Fondazione Centesimus Annus – Pro Pontifice (#03654)
- ♦ Fondazione Centro Euro-Mediterraneo sui Cambiamenti Climatici / see Centro Euro-Mediterraneo per i Cambiamenti Climatici
- ♦ Fondazione Centro Internazionale Radio Medico (internationally oriented national body)
- ♦ Fondazione delle Città Europee del Carnevale / see Federation of European Carnival Cities (#09496)
- ♦ Fondazione Comboniane nel Mondo (internationally oriented national body)
- ♦ Fondazione Eni Enrico Mattei (internationally oriented national body)
- ♦ Fondazione Europea Antonio Bana per la Ricerca Ornitologica sulle Migrazioni e per la Tutela dell'Ambiente / see European Foundation Il Nibbio
- ♦ Fondazione Europea per il Migliramento delle Condizioni di Vita e di Lavoro (#07348)
- ♦ Fondazione Europea Il Nibbio (internationally oriented national body)
- ♦ Fondazione Giacomo Brodolini (internationally oriented national body)
- ♦ Fondazione Giovanni Agnelli (internationally oriented national body)

- ♦ Fondazione Giovanni Lorenzini (internationally oriented national body)
- ♦ Fondazione Giuseppe Tovini / see Fondazione Tovini
- ♦ Fondazione Idis-Città della Scienza (internationally oriented national body)
- ♦ Fondazione IMC – Centro Marino Internazionale ONLUS / see International Marine Centre
- ♦ Fondazione Internazionale Menarini (internationally oriented national body)
- ♦ Fondazione Internazionale Premio Balzan (#12309)
- ♦ Fondazione Internazionale Trieste per il Progresso e la Libertà delle Scienze (internationally oriented national body)
- ♦ Fondazione ISMU – Iniziative e Studi sulla Multietnicità (internationally oriented national body)
- ♦ Fondazione Italiana per il Volontariato (internationally oriented national body)
- ♦ Fondazione Laboratorio Mediterraneo / see Fondazione Mediterraneo
- ♦ Fondazione Lelio e Lisli Basso – ISSOCO (internationally oriented national body)
- ♦ Fondazione Livorno Euro Mediterranea (internationally oriented national body)

♦ Fondazione Marista per la Solidarietà Internazionale Onlus 09831

Marist International Solidarity Foundation Onlus (FMSI)

Pres Piazzale Marcellino Champagnat 2, 00144 Rome RM, Italy. T. +396545171. Fax +39654517500. E-mail: fmsi@fms.it.
URL: http://fmsi.ngo/

History Oct 2007. Inspired by St. Marcellin Champagnat and established by the Congregation of the Marist Brothers of the Schools. **Aims** Promote education as an effective tool to protect and respect young people's rights and making them active agents of social transformation in their communities. **Structure** Board of Directors. **Languages** English, Italian, Spanish. **Staff** 5.00 FTE, paid. **Finance** Sources: contributions; donations; fundraising; government support; grants; international organizations; private foundations. **Activities** Advocacy/lobbying/activism; awareness raising; capacity building; financial and/or material support; humanitarian/emergency aid; monitoring/evaluation; networking/liaising; projects/programmes; religious activities; training/education. Active in all member countries. **Publications** Annual Report. **Members** Partners (130) in 56 countries. Membership countries not specified. **Consultative Status** Consultative status granted from: *ECOSOC (#05331)* (Special). **IGO Relations** *Inter-American Children's Institute (IACI, #11406).* **NGO Relations** Formal contacts with: *Solidaridad, Educación y Desarrollo (SED); VIVAT International (#20801).* Member of: Australian Marist Solidarity (AMS); *Federazione Organismi Cristiani Servizio Internazionale Volontario (Volontari nel Mondo – FOCSIV); Forum of Catholic Inspired NGOs (#09905);* Fundación Marista (FUNDAMAR); *International Catholic Centre of Geneva (ICCG, #12449); International Catholic Child Bureau (#12450).* Observer member of: *Movimiento Mundial por la Infancia de Latinoamérica y El Caribe (MMI-LAC, #16873).* [2020.04.29/XM8137/f/**F**]

- ♦ Fondazione Mediterranea (internationally oriented national body)
- ♦ Fondazione Mediterraneo (internationally oriented national body)
- ♦ Fondazione Mondiale Pestalozzi / see Pestalozzi Children's Foundation
- ♦ Fondazione Novae Terrae (internationally oriented national body)
- ♦ Fondazione per la Patologia (#21714)
- ♦ Fondazione per la Patologia della WASPaLM / see World Pathology Foundation (#21714)
- ♦ Fondazione Pia Autonoma Servizio dei Gesuiti per i Rifugiati / see Jesuit Refugee Service (#16106)
- ♦ Fondazione 'Populorum Progressio' (#09969)
- ♦ Fondazione Rui (internationally oriented national body)
- ♦ Fondazione SIPEC (internationally oriented national body)
- ♦ Fondazione svizzera per la Pace / see Swisspeace
- ♦ Fondazione svizzera per la Pace – Institute per la Risoluzione di Conflitti / see Swisspeace
- ♦ Fondazione Terra Madre (#20130)
- ♦ Fondazione Tovini (internationally oriented national body)
- ♦ Fondazione Vaticana "Centro Internazionale Famiglia di Nazareth (#20750)
- ♦ Fondazione Villaggio Pestalozzi per Bambini (internationally oriented national body)
- ♦ Fondem – Fondation Énergies pour le Monde (internationally oriented national body)
- ♦ Fonden för Mänskliga Rättigheter (internationally oriented national body)
- ♦ Fondi Internazionali di Indennizzo per i Danni Dovut All'Inquinamento Mediante Idrocarburi / see International Oil Pollution Compensation Funds (#14402)
- ♦ Fond des jeunes entrepreneurs des amériques (internationally oriented national body)
- ♦ Fond norvégien des droits de l'homme (internationally oriented national body)
- ♦ Fondo Africano de Desarrollo (#00285)
- ♦ Fondo Andaluz de Municipios para la Solidaridad Internacional (internationally oriented national body)
- ♦ Fondo Andino de Reservas / see Latin American Reserve Fund (#16367)
- ♦ Fondo para la Aplicación de Normas y el Fomento del Comercio (#19948)
- ♦ Fondo de Apoyo al Tercer Mundo (internationally oriented national body)
- ♦ Fondo Arabe para el Desarrollo Económico y Social (#00965)
- ♦ Fondo Asiatico de Desarrollo (#01425)
- ♦ Fondo de Asistencia Internacional de los Estudiantes y Académicos Noruegos (internationally oriented national body)
- ♦ Fondo Central para la Acción en Casos de Emergencias (#20525)
- ♦ Fondo Centroamericano de Inversion en la Pequeña Empresa (internationally oriented national body)
- ♦ Fondo Centroamericano del Mercado Común (inactive)
- ♦ Fondo Centroamericano de Mujeres (#03677)
- ♦ Fondo Cooperativo para el Carbono de los Bosques (#09862)
- ♦ Fondo Cristiano para Niños / see ChildFund International (#03869)
- ♦ Fondo para los Derechos Humanos Mundiales (internationally oriented national body)
- ♦ Fondo de Desarrollo (internationally oriented national body)

♦ Fondo para el Desarrollo de los Pueblos Indigenas de América Latina y el Caribe (FILAC) 09832

Fund for the Development of the Indigenous Peoples of Latin America and the Caribbean (FILAC) – Fonds pour le développement des peuples indigènes d'Amérique latine et des Caraïbes

Secretariat Av 20 de Octubre 2287, esq Rosendo Gutierrez, La Paz, Bolivia. T. +59122423233. E-mail: filac@filac.org.
URL: https://www.filac.org/

History 24 Jul 1992, Madrid (Spain). stalbished, at 2nd 'Ibero-American Summit of Chiefs of State and Government'. Former names and other names: *Fonds pour le développement des populations autochtones d'Amérique latine et des Caraïbes* – alias. **Aims** Assist the processes of *self development* of indigenous peoples, communities and organizations in Central America and the Caribbean. **Structure** General Assembly (annual); Governing Board; Technical Secretariat. **Events** *General Assembly* Madrid (Spain) 2017. **Publications** *Boletin Informativo del Fondo para el Desarrollo de los Pueblos Indigenas de América Latina y el Caribe. Serie Documentos.*

Members Governments of 22 countries:
Argentina, Belgium, Bolivia, Brazil, Chile, Colombia, Costa Rica, Cuba, Dominican Rep, Ecuador, El Salvador, Guatemala, Honduras, Mexico, Nicaragua, Panama, Paraguay, Peru, Portugal, Spain, Uruguay, Venezuela.

IGO Relations Observer status with (1): *United Nations (UN, #20515)* (General Assembly). **NGO Relations** Member of (1): *Red Iberoamericana de Organismos y Organizaciones contra la Discriminación (RIOOD, #18678).* [2021/XF3240/f/**F***]

- ♦ Fondo Especial de las Naciones Unidas (inactive)
- ♦ Fondo Especial de las Naciones Unidas, 1974 (no recent information)
- ♦ Fondo Especial para la Transformación Social de Centroamérica (see: #03658)
- ♦ Fondo Europeo di Cooperazione Monetaria (inactive)
- ♦ Fondo Europeo de Desarrollo (#06914)
- ♦ Fondo Europeo de Sviluppo (#06914)

♦ Fondo Financiero para el Desarrollo de la Cuenca del Plata (FONPLATA) 09833

Fonds fiduciaire pour la mise en valeur du bassin du Rio de la Plata – Financial Fund for the Development of the River Plate Basin – Fundo Financiero para o Desenvolvimento da Bacia do Prata

Headquarters Edificio La Vitalicia, Calle Cochabamba esq Saavedra, Piso 9, Casilla 2690, Santa Cruz, Bolivia. T. +59133159400. Fax +59133371713. E-mail: contacto@fonplata.org – fonplata@fonplata.org.
URL: http://www.fonplata.org/

History 12 Jun 1974, within the framework of *Comité Intergubernamental Coordinador de los Paises de la Cuenca del Plata (CIC, #04172),* at 6th *Meeting of Ministers of Foreign Affairs of the River Plate Basin Countries,* on signature of an agreement which entered into force 14 Oct 1976; operations commenced in 1977. Also referred to in English as *Financial Fund for the Plata Basin Development.* **Aims** Promote harmonious development and physical integration of the River Plate Basin and its areas of influence. **Structure** Board of Governors; Board of Executive Directors; Executive President. Project office in Asunción (Paraguay). **Languages** Portuguese, Spanish. **Staff** 51.00 FTE, paid. **Finance** Member country contributions. Current average annual lending capacity: US$ 250,000,000. **Activities** Projects/programmes; financial and/or material support.

Members Governments of 5 countries:
Argentina, Bolivia, Brazil, Paraguay, Uruguay. [2016.09.20/XF9800/f/**F***]

- ♦ Fondo Global Para Mujeres (#10384)
- ♦ Fondo Iberoamericano de Integración Cientifica y Tecnológica (unconfirmed)
- ♦ Fondo Ignacio Martin-Baró por la Salud Mental y los Derechos Humanos / see Martín-Baró Initiative for Wellbeing and Human Rights
- ♦ Fondo para la Industrialización de los Paises en Desarrollo / see Investeringsfonden for Udviklingslande
- ♦ Fondo Internacional de Desarrollo Agricola (#13692)
- ♦ Fondo Internacional para el Desarrollo de la Educación Fisica y el Deporte (no recent information)
- ♦ Fondo Internacional para la Promoción de la Cultura (inactive)
- ♦ Fondo Internacional Trans (#15720)
- ♦ Fondo de Inversiones de Venezuela / see Economic and Social Development Bank
- ♦ Fondo para Jóvenes Empresarios de las Américas (internationally oriented national body)
- ♦ Fondo Kuwaiti para el Desarrollo Económico Arabe (internationally oriented national body)
- ♦ Fondo Latinoamericano para Arroz de Riego (#10041)
- ♦ Fondo Latinoamericano de Reservas (#16367)
- ♦ Fondo Mondiale per la Natura (#21922)
- ♦ Fondo Mondiale di Solidarietà (#21818)
- ♦ Fondo Monetario Internacional (#14180)
- ♦ Fondo Multilateral de Inversiones (#16887)
- ♦ Fondo Mundial par el Desarrollo de las Ciudades / see FMDV (#09804)
- ♦ El fondo mundial de lucha contra el SIDA, la tuberculosis y la malaria (#10383)
- ♦ Fondo Mundial para la Naturaleza (#21922)
- ♦ Fondo Mundial de Solidaridad contra el Hambre (#09836)
- ♦ Fondo de las Naciones Unidas para Actividades en Materia de Población / see United Nations Population Fund (#20612)
- ♦ Fondo de las Naciones Unidas para la Ciencia y la Tecnologia para el Desarrollo (inactive)
- ♦ Fondo de las Naciones Unidas para la Colaboración Internacional (#20565)
- ♦ Fondo de la Naciones Unidas para la Democracia (#20551)
- ♦ Fondo de las Naciones Unidas para el Desarrollo de la Capitalización (#20524)
- ♦ Fondo de las Naciones Unidas para la Infancia (#20332)
- ♦ Fondo de las Naciones Unidas para los Refugiados (inactive)
- ♦ Fondon för Industriellt Samarbete med U-Länder / see Swedfund – International
- ♦ Fondon for International Forståelse / see Folmer Wisti Foundation for International Understanding
- ♦ Fondo Nórdico de Desarrollo (#17271)
- ♦ Fondo Noruego de los Derechos Humanos (internationally oriented national body)
- ♦ Fondo de la OPEP para el Desarrollo Internacional (#17745)
- ♦ Fondo Panamericano Leo S Rowe (#16445)
- ♦ Fondo del Patrimonio Mundial (#21568)
- ♦ Fondo para el Patrimonio Mundial Africano (#00505)
- ♦ Fondo de Población de las Naciones Unidas (#20612)
- ♦ Fondo para la Protección del Patrimonio Cultural y Natural Mundial de Valor Universal Excepcional / see World Heritage Fund (#21568)

♦ Fondo Regional de Tecnologia Agropecuaria (FONTAGRO) 09834

Regional Fund for Agricultural Technology – Fonds régional pour la technologie agricole

Exec Sec c/o IICA, 1889 F St NW, Ste 360, Washington DC 20006, USA. E-mail: fontagro@fontagro.org.
URL: http://www.fontagro.org/

History 1998. Established by 14 Latin American countries: Argentina; Bolivia; Chile; Colombia; Costa Rica; Ecuador; Honduras; Nicaragua; Panama; Paraguay; Peru; Dominican Rep; Uruguay; Venezuela. Spain joined in 2006. **Aims** Promote the agricultural sector's increase in competitiveness, while protecting natural resources and reducing poverty in the region, through the generation of agricultural technologies with international public goods characteristics, and by facilitating the exchange of scientific knowledge among research organizations within the region, as well as with other regions. **Structure** Board, comprising one representative from each member country. Technical and Administrative Secretariat, located at IDB Headquarters in Washington DC (USA). **Languages** English, Spanish. **Staff** 4.00 FTE, paid. **Finance** About US$ 100 million invested by member countries; counterpart project funding and other resources provided by sponsors and other research development organizations. **Activities** As a competitive grant programme, finances regional research projects. For each Call for Proposals, research priorities are defined in themes. Call for Proposals announced in FONTAGRO's website around February every year. **Publications** *Innovaciones de Impacto: Lecciones de la Agricultura Familiar en América Latina y el Caribe* (2013); *Plan de Mediano Plazo 2010-2015* (2011); *Guia para la Gestión de la Propiedad Intelectual en Consorcios Regionales de Investigación Agricola* (2010).

Members in 15 countries:
Argentina, Bolivia, Chile, Colombia, Costa Rica, Dominican Rep, Ecuador, Honduras, Nicaragua, Panama, Paraguay, Peru, Spain, Uruguay, Venezuela.

IGO Relations Sponsored by: *Inter-American Development Bank (IDB, #11427); Inter-American Institute for Cooperation on Agriculture (IICA, #11434).* [2022/XF6128/f/**F***]

- ♦ Fondo Rotatorio de las Naciones Unidas para la Exploración de los Recursos Naturales (inactive)
- ♦ **Fondo Rowe** Fondo Panamericano Leo S Rowe (#16445)
- ♦ **Fondo SAM** Fondo para el Sistema Arrecifal Mesoamericano (#09835)
- ♦ Fondos Internacionales de Indemnización de Daños Debidos a la Contaminación por Hidrocarburos (#14402)

♦ Fondo para el Sistema Arrecifal Mesoamericano (Fondo SAM) 09835

Mesoamerican Reef Fund (MAR Fund)

Contact 22 Avenia 0-59, Zona 15 Vista Hermosa II, CA 01015 Guatemala, Guatemala. T. +50223693188 – +50223691978. E-mail: info@marfund.org.
URL: http://www.marfund.org/

History Founded 2004. **Aims** Enable innovative, transnational solutions to critical Mesoamerican reef issues. **Structure** Board of Directors; Executive Management. Committees (5): Governance; Investment; Audit; Grants and Evaluation; Development. **Activities** Financial and/material support; guidance/assistance/consulting.

Members Full in 4 countries:
Belize, Guatemala, Honduras, Mexico.

NGO Relations Member of: *Red de Fondos Ambientales de Latinoamérica y el Caribe (RedLAC, #18656).* [2018/XM7582/f/**F**]

- Fondo Sociale Europeo (#08501)
- Fondo Social Europeo (#08501)
- Fondo de Solidaridad para las Luchas de Liberación Social en el Tercer Mundo (internationally oriented national body)
- Fondo di Solidarietà per le Lotte di Liberazione Sociale nel Terzo Mondo (internationally oriented national body)
- Fonds d'Abou Dhabi pour le développement (internationally oriented national body)
- Fonds d'affectation spéciale pour l'assistance à la lutte antimines / see United Nations Voluntary Trust Fund for Assistance in Mine Action (#20649)
- Fonds d'affectation spéciale des Nations Unies pour le développement de l'Afrique (#20640)
- Fonds d'affectation spéciale des Nations Unies pour l'élimination de la violence à l'égard des femmes (#20716)
- Fonds d'affectation spéciale pour la protection de la Mer méditerranéenne contre la pollution / see Mediterranean Trust Fund (#16686)
- Fonds africain d'appui au développement rural (see: #11233)
- Fonds africain de développement (#00285)
- Fonds africain de développement industriel (unconfirmed)
- Fonds africain de garantie et de coopération économique (#00326)
- Fonds d'aide et de coopération / see Fonds de solidarité prioritaire
- Fonds andin de réserve / see Latin American Reserve Fund (#16367)
- Fonds pour les animaux (internationally oriented national body)
- Fonds pour l'application des normes et le développement du commerce (#19948)
- Fonds arabe de développement (no recent information)
- Fonds Arabe pour le Développement Economique et Social (#00965)
- Fonds asiatique de développement (#01425)
- Fonds pour l'Assainissement et l'Hygiène (#19050)
- Fonds autorenouvelable des Nations Unies pour l'exploration des ressources naturelles (inactive)
- Fonds un pour cent pour le développement (#17733)
- Fonds Central pour les Interventions d'Urgence (#20525)
- Fonds centroaméricain du Marché commun (inactive)
- Fonds chrétien pour l'enfance / see ChildFund International (#03869)
- Fonds Clara Lachmanns pour promouvoir la compréhension inter-nordique (#03977)
- Fonds de cohésion (#04087)
- Fonds du Commonwealth pour la coopération technique (#04331)
- Fonds commun pour les produits de base (#04293)
- Fonds de consolidation de la paix des Nations Unies (#20607)
- Fonds de contributions volontaires des Nations Unies pour les handicapés (#20648)
- Fonds culturel nordique (#17264)
- Fonds culturel de l'OUA (no recent information)
- Fonds pour le développement et la collaboration en Afrique (internationally oriented national body)
- Fonds pour le développement industriel (#11173)
- Fonds pour le développement des peuples indigènes d'Amérique latine et des Caraïbes (#09832)
- Fonds pour le développement des populations autochtones d'Amérique latine et des Caraïbes / see Fondo para el Desarrollo de los Pueblos Indigenas de América Latina y el Caribe (#09832)
- Fonds de développement social du Conseil de l'Europe / see Council of Europe Development Bank (#04897)
- Fonds de développement des villes arabes (#01058)
- Fonds pour les droits humains mondiaux (internationally oriented national body)
- Fonds Dzivibai Baltijas Jura (internationally oriented national body)
- Fonds pour l'entreprise en Afrique (inactive)
- Fonds für Entwicklung und Partnerschaft in Afrika (internationally oriented national body)
- Fonds pour l'environnement mondial (#10346)
- Fonds d'équipement des Nations unies (#20524)
- Fonds européen de coopération / see Network of European Foundations (#17019)
- Fonds européen de coopération monétaire (inactive)
- Fonds Européen pour la Démocratie (#06983)
- Fonds européen de développement (#06914)
- Fonds européen de développement régional (#08342)
- Fonds européen d'investissement (#07601)
- Fonds européen pour la jeunesse (#09141)
- Fonds européen pour les réfugiés (inactive)
- Fonds Européen de Soutien à la Coproduction et la Diffusion des Oeuvres de Création Cinématographiques et Audiovisuelles (#08859)
- Fonds pour les Femmes en Méditerranée (internationally oriented national body)
- Fonds fiduciaire pour la mise en valeur du bassin du Rio de la Plata (#09833)
- Fonds français pour l'environnement mondial (internationally oriented national body)
- Fonds francophone de préparation olympique (see: #04634)
- Fonds de garantie et de coopération de l'OCAM / see African Fund for Guarantee and Economic Cooperation (#00326)
- Fonds de garantie des investissements privés en Afrique de l'Ouest (see: #03170)
- Fonds GARI – Fonds de garantie des investissements privés en Afrique de l'Ouest (see: #03170)
- Fonds pour l'industrialisation des pays en développement / see Investeringsfonden for Udviklingslande
- Fonds Ingrid Renard (internationally oriented national body)
- Fonds international pour le bien-être des animaux / see International Fund for Animal Welfare (#13693)
- Fonds international de coopération et développement (internationally oriented national body)
- Fonds international de développement agricole (#13692)
- Fonds international pour le développement de l'éducation physique et du sport (no recent information)
- Fonds international pour la fabrication de matériel d'animation sportive (see: #04634)
- Fonds international de garantie (#13761)
- Fonds international des Nations Unies pour le secours à l'enfance / see UNICEF (#20332)
- Fonds international pour la promotion de la culture (inactive)
- Fonds international de la recherche mondiale contre le cancer (internationally oriented national body)
- Fonds international Virginia Gildersleeve pour les femmes diplômées des universités / see Women First International Fund (#20996)
- Fonds internationaux d'indemnisation pour les dommages dus à la pollution par les hydrocarbures (#14402)
- Fonds koweïtien pour le développement économique arabe (internationally oriented national body)
- Fonds latinoaméricain de réserve (#16367)
- Fonds pour le livre en Europe centrale et orientale (#10040)
- Fonds médical tropical (internationally oriented national body)
- Fonds mémorial pour la culture juive / see Memorial Foundation for Jewish Culture
- Fonds voor Midden- en Oosteuropese Boekprojecten (#10040)
- Fonds mondial pour le développement des villes / see FMDV (#09804)
- Fonds Mondial pour les Femmes (#10384)
- Le Fonds mondial de lutte contre le sida, la tuberculose et le paludisme (#10383)
- Fonds mondial pour les monuments (#21657)
- Fonds mondial pour la nature (#21922)
- Fonds mondial de solidarité (#21818)

♦ Fonds mondial de solidarité contre la faim (FMSCF) 09836

World Community Fund Against Hunger – Fondo Mundial de Solidaridad contra el Hambre – Fundo Mundial de Solidariedade contra a Fome – Monda Funduso de Solidareco kontraŭ la Malsato – Weltfond der Solidarität gegen Hunger

Federal Sec/Pres 1 Ruelle Haute, 21120 Gémeaux, France. E-mail: info@globidar.org.
URL: http://www.globidar.org/

History 1982. Founded by *Peoples' Congress*. Registration: Start date: 1 Apr 1982, France, Bourgogne-Franche-Comté. **Aims** Favour regional and local *food self-sufficiency*. **Structure** Management Board, consisting of 12 members. **Languages** English, Esperanto. **Finance** Members' dues. Other sources: donations. Budget (annual): euro 20,000. **Activities** Projects/programmes. **Events** *General Assembly* Gémeaux (France) 2022, *General Assembly* Poitiers (France) 2016, *General Assembly for West Africa* Ouagadougou (Burkina Faso) 2013, *General Assembly* Joué-Lès-Tours (France) 2007, *General Assembly* Saint-Georges-les-Baillargeaux (France) 2001. **Publications** *Monda Solidareco* (4 a year) in Esperanto, French.
Members Individuals (1,050); Communities. Members in 29 countries and territories:
Albania, Algeria, Argentina, Belgium, Benin, Brazil, Burkina Faso, Cameroon, Central African Rep, Congo DR, Côte d'Ivoire, Cuba, Czechia, France, Germany, Haiti, Japan, Madagascar, Mauritania, Montserrat, Nigeria, Norway, Poland, Rwanda, Senegal, Spain, Sweden, Tanzania UR, Togo.
NGO Relations Supports: *Global Call for Action Against Poverty (GCAP, #10263)*. Also links with a large number of national bodies. [2022/XF1404/f/F]

- Fonds monétaire africain (unconfirmed)
- Fonds Monétaire Arabe (#01009)
- Fonds monétaire international (#14180)
- Fonds multilatéral d'investissement (#16887)
- Fonds national juif (#16113)
- Fonds des Nations Unies pour les activités en matière de population / see United Nations Population Fund (#20612)
- Fonds des Nations unies pour la démocratie (#20551)
- Fonds des Nations Unies pour le développement industriel / see Industrial Development Fund (#11173)
- Fonds des Nations Unies pour l'enfance (#20332)
- Fonds des nations unies pour les partenariats internationaux (#20565)
- Fonds des Nations Unies pour la population (#20612)
- Fonds des Nations Unies pour les réfugiés (inactive)
- Fonds des Nations Unies pour la science et la technique au service du développement (inactive)
- Fonds nordique de développement (#17271)
- Fonds nordique de projets d'exportations (#17490)
- Fonds voor Ontwikkelingssamenwerking – Socialistische Solidariteit (internationally oriented national body)
- Fonds OPEP pour le développement international (#17745)
- Fonds ouest africain d'investissement (see: #03170)
- Fonds panaméricain Léo S Rowe / see Leo S Rowe Pan American Fund (#16445)
- Fonds de partenariat pour le carbone forestier (#09862)
- Fonds du patrimoine mondial (#21568)
- Fonds pour le Patrimoine Mondial Africain (#00505)
- Fonds pour la protection du patrimoine mondial culturel et naturel de valeur universelle exceptionnelle / see World Heritage Fund (#21568)
- Fonds de rééetablissement du Conseil de l'Europe / see Council of Europe Development Bank (#04897)
- Fonds régional pour la technologie agricole (#09834)
- Fonds de réserve pour les opérations de maintien de paix (no recent information)

♦ Fonds Roberto Cimetta (FRC) 09837

Roberto Cimetta Fund (RCF)

Contact c/o ONDA, 13bis rue Henri Monnier, 75009 Paris, France. T. +33145263374.
URL: http://www.cimettafund.org/

History Founded 1999, by cultural professionals. Registered in accordance with Belgian law. EU Transparency Register: 808728714828-67. **Aims** Reduce the isolation of artists and operators by improving their mobility in the Euro-Arab zone; further individual movement of *artists* and professionals so they can find opportunities, partners and the means to realize personal or collective artistic projects; encourage meetings, networking and encounters between artists to further collaboration and build up artistic teams in the region; promote exchange of experience and the creation of artistic projects and projects of *cultural* cooperation; enable artists to take part in residencies and training programmes; establish partnerships with foundations and institutions providing international support to artistic mobility; take part in civil society platforms to integrate contemporary artistic and cultural projects in advocacy at the Euro-Mediterranean level; establish partnerships with operators in the region. **Structure** General Assembly (annual). Council, including President, Secretary and Treasurer. Board of Directors, comprising Chairman, Treasurer and 6 members. Secretary General. **Languages** Arabic, English, French, Turkish. **Staff** One. **Finance** Support from foundations and national, regional or local funding bodies. Current funding partners include: *Calouste Gulbenkian Foundation*; *Anna Lindh Euro-Mediterranean Foundation for the Dialogue between Cultures (Anna Lindh Foundation, #00847)*; French governmental agencies; Puglia Region (Italy); Marseille Provence (2013); Conseil Général des Bouches du Rhône, France. **Activities** Financial and/or material supports; events/meetings. **Publications** *Mad in Med* (2007). Impact assessment reports on the mobility programme (2012 and 2013). **NGO Relations** Member of: *Culture Action Europe (CAE, #04981)*. [2019/XF5667/f/F]

- Fonds Rowe / see Leo S Rowe Pan American Fund (#16445)
- Fonds rural pour le développement du Tiers-monde (internationally oriented national body)
- Fonds saoudien pour le développement (internationally oriented national body)
- Fonds social européen (#08501)

♦ Fonds de solidarité africain (FSA) 09838

African Solidarity Fund

Gen Dir BP 382, Niamey, Niger. T. +227722632 – +227722633 – +227722634. Fax +227733044. E-mail: fsa@fondsolidariteafricain.org.
URL: https://www.fondsolidariteafricain.org/

History 21 Dec 1976, following decision of Conference of Heads of State of French-Speaking Countries, Mar 1975, Bangui (Central African Rep). Became operational Sep 1979. **Aims** Contribute to economic development and poverty reduction within Member States by facilitating investment project financing in both public and private sectors, and microfinance activities. **Structure** General Meeting of Shareholders. Board of Directors, appoints the Managing Director. Registered office in Niamey (Niger). **Languages** French. **Staff** 30.00 FTE, paid. **Finance** Sources: appropriations made up of shareholders' contributions to the share capital; income generated by operations; investment income; grants; resources allocated to specific missions undertaken as part of fund management for third parties. Authorized capital fixed at about euro 228.7 million, including roughly euro 45.7 million representing the capital to be called up; remainder amounting to about euro 183 million is the callable capital. Callable capital is used as guarantee for commitments contracted by the Fund. **Activities** Finances selected investment projects. Methods of intervention: financial guarantee of bank loans and bond issues intended, on one hand for funding investment projects initiated in the territory of Member States by both public and private business, and on the other hand, for funding activities of microfinance institutions; interest rebate in favour of Member States through subsidies to make concessional funds mobilized by countries and their subdivisions; extension of loan tenor granted to SMEs/SMIs through a refinancing mechanism. Operations in all economic sectors: basic infrastructure; rural development; industry; agro-industry; telecommunications; energy; tourism and hotel industry; real estate; transport; education; health. Business activities are excluded from the Fund's scope of intervention. As at 31 Dec 2010, cumulative guarantees stood at about euro 355.2 million for 141 projects. These operations made it possible to mobilize funds in an amount of nearly euro 703 million. **Events** *Ordinary General Assembly* Abidjan (Côte d'Ivoire) 2012. **Publications** Annual Report.

Members Membership open to all African countries (regional members) as well as non-African countries and regional and international financial institutions (non-regional members). Member States (13):
Benin, Burkina Faso, Burundi, Central African Rep, Chad, Côte d'Ivoire, Gabon, Mali, Mauritius, Niger, Rwanda, Senegal, Togo.
IGO Relations Cooperation agreement with: *African Fund for Guarantee and Economic Cooperation (#00326)*; *Banque ouest africaine de développement (BOAD, #03170)*; *ECOWAS Bank for Investment and Development (EBID, #05334)*. **NGO Relations** Member of: *Association of African Development Finance Institutions (AADFI, #02353)*. [2020/XF8389/f/**F***]

- ♦ Fonds de solidarité et d'intervention pour le développement de la Communauté économique de l'Afrique de l'Ouest (inactive)
- ♦ Fonds de solidarité islamique (#16051)
- ♦ Fonds de solidarité pour les luttes de libération sociale dans le Tiers-monde (internationally oriented national body)
- ♦ Fonds de solidarité mondiale / see WSM
- ♦ Fonds de solidarité prioritaire (internationally oriented national body)
- ♦ Fonds de Soutien au Cinéma Européen / see European Support Fund for the Co-Production and Distribution of Creative Cinematographic and Audiovisual Works (#08859)
- ♦ Fonds de soutien "Eurimages" / see European Support Fund for the Co-Production and Distribution of Creative Cinematographic and Audiovisual Works (#08859)
- ♦ Fonds de soutien Tiers-monde (internationally oriented national body)
- ♦ Fonds spécial d'aide arabe à l'Afrique (inactive)
- ♦ Fonds spécial d'assistance d'urgence pour la lutte contre la sécheresse et la famine en Afrique (#19908)
- ♦ Fonds spécial des Nations unies (inactive)
- ♦ Fonds spécial des Nations Unies, 1974 (no recent information)
- ♦ Fonds spécial du Nigéria (internationally oriented national body)
- ♦ Fonds structurels de la Communauté européenne (inactive)
- ♦ Fonds voor Wereldsolidariteit / see WSM
- ♦ FONGAF – General Forum of the Arabic and African Nongovernmental Organizations (unconfirmed)
- ♦ FONOLA-SOL – Asociación Nórdica-Latinoamericana para la Educación Popular (no recent information)
- ♦ Fonologi i Norden (meeting series)
- ♦ **FONPLATA** Fondo Financiero para el Desarrollo de la Cuenca del Plata (#09833)
- ♦ **FONTAGRO** Fondo Regional de Tecnologia Agropecuaria (#09834)
- ♦ FONUR – Fondo de las Naciones Unidas para los Refugiados (inactive)
- ♦ Food and Agricultural Research Management (internationally oriented national body)
- ♦ Food and Agricultural Research Mission / see Food and Agricultural Research Management

♦ Food, Agriculture and Natural Resources Policy Analysis Network (FANRPAN) 09839

CEO 141 Cresswell Street, Weavind Park 0184, PB X2087, Silverton, Pretoria, 0127, South Africa. T. +27128042966. Fax +27128040600. E-mail: communications@fanrpan.org.
URL: http://www.fanrpan.org/

History 1997, Harare (Zimbabwe). Founded by Ministers of Agriculture from Eastern and Southern Africa. **Aims** Generate and promote independent research evidence to inform policy development and harmonization in the FANR (Food, Agriculture and Natural Resource) sector across the African continent. **Structure** General Meeting (annual); Board of Governors; Secretariat. **Languages** English. **Staff** 15.00 FTE, paid. **Activities** Advocacy/lobbying/activism; capacity building; politics/policy/regulatory; research/documentation. **Events** *Regional policy dialogue on biotechnology, agriculture and food security in Southern Africa* Johannesburg (South Africa) 2003.
Members Stakeholders from government, private sector, farming unions, research institutes and NGOs, grouped in country nodes in 17 countries:
Angola, Benin, Botswana, Congo DR, Eswatini, Kenya, Lesotho, Madagascar, Malawi, Mauritius, Mozambique, Namibia, South Africa, Tanzania UR, Uganda, Zambia, Zimbabwe. [2020.05.06/XG2771/**E**]

- ♦ Food and Agriculture Organization of the United Nations (#09260)
- ♦ Food Aid Charter / see Réseau de prévention des crises alimentaires (#18905)
- ♦ Food Aid Committee (inactive)
- ♦ Food Aid Convention, 1986 (1986 treaty)
- ♦ Food Aid Convention, 1995 (1994 treaty)
- ♦ Food Aid Convention, 1999 (1999 treaty)
- ♦ Food For All / see Making Change

♦ Food Assistance Committee (FAC) 09840

Contact c/o Intl Grains Council Secretariat, 1 Canada Square, Canary Wharf, London, E14 5AE, UK. T. +442075131122. Fax +442075130630. E-mail: fac@foodassistanceconvention.org.
URL: http://www.foodassistanceconvention.org/

History 1 Jan 2013. Set up as a replacement of *Food Aid Committee (FAC, inactive)*, which ended 2012. **Aims** Contribute to global food security; improve the ability of the international community to respond to emergency food situations and other food needs of developing countries. **Structure** Chair; Vice-Chair. Secretariat based at *International Grains Council (IGC, #13731)*. **Languages** English, French. **Finance** Sources: contributions of member/participating states. **Activities** Events/meetings. **Events** *Session* London (UK) 2021, *Session* London (UK) 2021, *Session* London (UK) 2020, *Session* London (UK) 2019, *Session* London (UK) 2019. **Publications** Annual Narrative Report.
Members Parties in 15 countries:
Australia, Austria, Canada, Denmark, Finland, France, Japan, Korea Rep, Luxembourg, Russia, Slovenia, Spain, Sweden, Switzerland, USA.
Regional member:
European Union (EU, #08967). [2021.11.02/XJ7930/**E***]

- ♦ Food Assistance Convention (2012 treaty)
- ♦ Food Basket Foundation International (internationally oriented national body)
- ♦ Food Basket International / see Food Basket Foundation International
- ♦ Food Crisis Prevention Network (#18905)

♦ FoodDrinkEurope 09841

Dir Gen Av des Nerviens 9-31, 1040 Brussels, Belgium. T. +3225141111. Fax +3225112905. E-mail: info@fooddrinkeurope.eu.
URL: http://www.fooddrinkeurope.eu/

History 3 Feb 1959, Brussels (Belgium). Founded within the framework of the then *'Union of Industries of the European Community'*, currently *BUSINESSEUROPE (#03381)*. Transformed into an independent confederation, 16 Dec 1981. Statutes adopted: 6 May 1982; 5 Oct 1989; Jan 1995; 21 Nov 2000. Former names and other names: *Committee of the Agriculture and Food Industries of the Union of Industries of the European Economic Community* – former (3 Feb 1959 to 16 Dec 1981); *Commission des industries agro-alimentaires de l'Union des industries de la Communauté économique européenne (CIAA – UNICE)* – former (3 Feb 1959 to 16 Dec 1981); *Confederation of the Food and Drink Industries of the EU* – former (16 Dec 1981 to Jan 1995); *Confédération des industries agro-alimentaires de l'UE* – former (16 Dec 1981 to Jan 1995); *CIAA – Confederation of the Food and Drink Industries of the EU* – former (Jan 1995 to 23 Jun 2011); *CIAA – Confédération des industries agro-alimentaires de l'UE* – former (Jan 1995 to 23 Jun 2011). Registration: Banque-Carrefour des Entreprises, No/ID: 0419.460.266, Start date: 1 Jun 1979, Belgium; EU Transparency Register, No/ID: 75818824519-45, Start date: 12 Nov 2010. **Aims** Facilitate development of an environment in which all European food and drink companies, whatever their size, can meet the needs of consumers and society while competing effectively for sustainable growth. **Structure** General Assembly; Board of Directors; Committees; Expert Groups; ad hoc Groups and Task Forces; Secretariat. **Languages** English, French. **Staff** 24.00 FTE, paid. **Finance** Sources: members' dues. **Activities** Events/meetings; politics/policy/regulatory; projects/programmes. **Events** *ENG Annual Global Food Safety Summit* Amsterdam (Netherlands) 2015, *Conference on Ensuring Sustainable Employment and Competitiveness in the EU Food and Drink Industry* Brussels (Belgium) 2013, *Biennial Congress* Brussels (Belgium) 2012, *Nanotechnology Stakeholder Dialogue Day* Brussels (Belgium) 2012, *Workshop on Impact of the Food Enzymes Legislation* Brussels (Belgium) 2012. **Publications** *Data and Trends*; *Electronic Press Pack*; *EU Food Law*; *Food and Drink Statistics*. Annual Report; memorandum; press releases; brochures; position papers.
Members Full: national federations representing the food and drink industries (24) in 24 countries:
Austria, Belgium, Croatia, Czechia, Denmark, Estonia, Finland, France, Germany, Greece, Hungary, Ireland, Italy, Latvia, Luxembourg, Netherlands, Poland, Portugal, Romania, Slovakia, Slovenia, Spain, Sweden, UK.
Observers: national federations in 2 countries:
Norway, Türkiye.
Liaison Committee members – companies (21) in 9 countries:
Belgium, France, Germany, Ireland, Luxembourg, Netherlands, Switzerland, Türkiye, UK.
European Sector Associations (28):
- *Association of the Chocolate, Biscuit and Confectionery Industries of the EU (CAOBISCO, #02427)*;
- *Comité européen des fabricants de sucre (CEFS, #04159)*;
- *Confédération des Fabricants de Levure de l'Union Européenne (COFALEC, #04551)*;
- *CULINARIA EUROPE (#04980)*;
- *EUPPA – European Potato Processors' Association (#05592)*;
- *EUROGLACES – European Ice Cream Association (Euroglaces, #05688)*;
- *European Association of Fruit and Vegetable Processors (PROFEL, #06049)*;
- *European Breakfast Cereal Association (CEEREAL, #06399)*;
- *European Coffee Federation (ECF, #06600)*;
- *European Dairy Association (EDA, #06883)*;
- *European Federation of Honey Packers and Distributors (#07140)*;
- *European Fruit Juice Association (AIJN, #07362)*;
- *European Herbal Infusions Association (EHIA, inactive)*;
- *European Margarine Association (IMACE, #07736)*;
- *European Plant-Based Foods Association (ENSA, #08210)*;
- *European Snacks Association (ESA, #08498)*;
- *European Spice Association (ESA, #08814)*;
- *European Tea Committee (ETC, inactive)*;
- *Fédération européenne de l'industrie des aliments pour animaux familiers (FEDIAF, #09571)*;
- *Federation of European Manufacturers of Ingredients to the Bakery, Confectionery and Patisserie Industries (FEDIMA, #09513)*;
- *Liaison Centre for the Meat Processing Industry in the EU (#16452)*;
- *Natural Mineral Waters Europe (NMWE, #16955)*;
- *Specialised Nutrition Europe (SNE, #19909)*;
- *spiritsEUROPE (#19921)*;
- *Starch Europe (#19966)*;
- *The Brewers of Europe (#03324)*;
- *UNESDA Soft Drinks Europe (UNESDA, #20323)*;
- *Union of Organizations of manufacturers of Pasta Products of the EU (#20468)*.

Consultative Status Consultative status granted from: *ECOSOC (#05331)* (Ros C); *FAO (#09260)* (Special Status). **IGO Relations** Liaises with: *European Union (EU, #08967)*. Recognized by: *European Commission (EC, #06633)*. Participates as observer in the activities of: *Codex Alimentarius Commission (CAC, #04081)*. Links with the following Community Institutions: *Council of the European Union (#04895)*; *European Economic and Social Committee (EESC, #06963)*; *European Parliament (EP, #08146)*. Contacts with: *Council of Europe (CE, #04881)*; *OECD (#17693)*; *UNEP (#20299)*; *UNIDO (#20336)*; *WHO (#20950)*; *World Trade Organization (WTO, #21864)*.
NGO Relations Member of (7): *Agri-Food Chain Coalition (AFCC, #00577)*; *Alliance for a Competitive European Industry (ACEI, #00670)*; *Circular Plastics Alliance (#03936)*; *EU Platform for Action on Diet, Physical Activity and Health (inactive)*; *EU Specialty Food Ingredients (#09200)*; *Federation of European and International Associations Established in Belgium (FAIB, #09508)*; *Industry4Europe (#11181)*. Cooperates with (1): *International Chewing Gum Association (ICGA, #12545)*.
Founding Member of: *European Food Sustainable Consumption and Production Round Table (European Food SCP Roundtable, #07289)*. Member of: *The Consumer Goods Forum (CGF, #04772)*. In liaison with technical committees of: *Comité européen de normalisation (CEN, #04162)*. Associate expert of: *Business and Industry Advisory Committee to the OECD (BIAC, #03385)*. Regular cooperation with: *Conseil européen de l'industrie chimique (CEFIC, #04687)*; *Fédération européenne du verre d'emballage (FEVE, #09583)*; *European Federation of Pharmaceutical Industries and Associations (EFPIA, #07191)*; *European Flavour Association (EFFA, #07269)*; *Natural Food Colours Association (NATCOL, #16953)*; *World Federation of Advertisers (WFA, #21407)*. Contacts with:
- *Association of Manufacturers and Formulators of Enzyme Products (AMFEP, #02793)*;
- *Bureau Européen des Unions de Consommateurs (BEUC, #03360)*;
- *Committee of the Trade in Cereals, Oilseeds, Pulses, Olive Oil, Oils and Fats, Animal Feed and Agrosupply of the EU (COCERAL, #04289)*;
- *Conseil européen de l'industrie des peintures, des encres d'imprimerie et des couleurs d'art (CEPE, #04688)*;
- *EuroCommerce (EC, #05665)*;
- *European Brands Association (#06397)*;
- *European Food Information Council (EUFIC, #07284)*;
- *European Liaison Committee for Agricultural and Agri-Food Trades (#07687)*;
- *European Plastics Converters (EuPC, #08216)*;
- *European Vending and Coffee Service Association (EVA, #09049)*;
- *Federation of the European Sporting Goods Industry (FESI, #09552)*;
- *General Confederation of Agricultural Cooperatives in the European Union (#10107)*;
- *International Organization for Standardization (ISO, #14473)*;
- *International Sweeteners Association (ISA, #15639)*. [2022.05.04/XE0970/y/**E**]

- ♦ Food Export Association of the Midwest USA (internationally oriented national body)

♦ Food and Fertilizer Technology Center for the Asian and Pacific Region (FFTC/ASPAC) 09842

Dir 5th Floor, 14 Wenchow Street, Taipei 10648, Taiwan. T. +886223626239. Fax +886223620478. E-mail: info@fftc.org.tw.
URL: https://www.fftc.org.tw/

History 24 Apr 1970, Taipei (Taiwan). Set up following signature of an agreement, Jun 1969, Kawana (Japan), by member states of the then *Asian and Pacific Council (ASPAC, inactive)*, which has been dormant since 1973. **Aims** Help farmers in the Asian and Pacific region by providing pertinent and timely information on the latest agricultural technologies and policies to help improve their yields, achieve higher incomes and enhance the sustainable agriculture and rural development in the region; contribute to the attainment of the UN's Sustainable Development Goals (SDGs). **Structure** Executive Board (meets annually); Working Group; Technical Advisory Committee (meets bienially); Administrative Section; Technical Section. **Languages** English. **Staff** 12.00 FTE, paid. **Finance** Sources: contributions of member/participating states. **Activities** Capacity building; knowledge management/information dissemination; networking/liaising; projects/programmes; training/education. **Events** *GCTF Workshop on the Challenges and Strategies for the Industrialization of Smart Agriculture* Taipei (Taiwan) 2022, *Joint Seminar on Intelligent Production of Livestock Industry and Aquaculture* Taipei (Taiwan) 2022, *Joint Symposium on the Establishment of an Intelligent Production System for Seeds and Seedlings* Taipei (Taiwan) 2022, *International Symposium on Climate Change and Food System* Tsukuba (Japan) 2022, *Joint Symposium on Climate Change and Food System* Tsukuba (Japan) 2022. **Publications** *FFTC Newsletter* (regular); *Quarterly Statistics of Commodity Prices in the Asian and Pacific region*. *FFTC Book Series*. Technical and Extension Bulletins; Seminar Papers. Information Services: Manages and maintains website on agricultural policies in Asia.
Members Governments of 6 countries and territories:
Japan, Korea Rep, Philippines, Taiwan, Thailand, Vietnam.
IGO Relations Supports (1): *Bioversity International (#03262)*. [2023.02.14/XE3954/**E***]

- ♦ Foodfirst Information and Action Network / see FIAN International (#09743)
- ♦ Food First – Institute for Food and Development Policy (internationally oriented national body)

♦ FOODforce 09843

Main Office c/o WUR, Droevendaalsesteeg 4, 6708 PB Wageningen, Netherlands. E-mail: info@foodforcenetwork.eu.
URL: http://www.foodforcenetwork.eu/

Aims As a network of leading *European research* provider organisations active in the areas of *food, nutrition* and *health*, provide a forum for discussion on delivery of *best practice* and societal impact; facilitate international aspects of knowledge exchange and innovation, both within and outside the European Union. **Activities** Spring meeting usually held in Brussels; Fall meeting hosted by a member. **Events** *Meeting* Dublin (Ireland) 2022.
Members Full in 16 countries:
Belgium, Denmark, France, Germany, Ireland, Italy, Netherlands, Norway, Poland, Portugal, Romania, Serbia, Slovakia, Spain, Sweden, UK.
Regional network:
European Association for Food Safety (SAFE Consortium, #06044). [2022/XM7898/**F**]

♦ Food Fortification Initiative (FFI) 09844

Dir 1518 Clifton Road NE, Atlanta GA 30322, USA. E-mail: info@ffinetwork.org.
URL: http://www.ffinetwork.org
History 2002, Atlanta, GA (USA). Former names and other names: *Flour Fortification Initiative (FFI)* – former (2002 to 2019). **Aims** Champion effective fortification of industrially milled flour and rice globally through multi-sector partnerships. **Staff** 11.00 FTE, paid. **Publications** Annual Report.
Members Partners include private and public/civic/educational bodies, including the following 12 organizations listed in this Yearbook:
Global Alliance for Improved Nutrition (GAIN, #10202); Helen Keller International (HKI, #10902); International Federation for Spina Bifida and Hydrocephalus (IF SBH, #13552); Iodine Global Network (IGN, #16004); Nutrition International (#17627); Pan American Health Organization (PAHO, #18108); UNICEF (#20332); United States Agency for International Development (USAID); WHO (#20950); WHO Regional Office for the Eastern Mediterranean (EMRO, #20944); World Food Programme (WFP, #21510); World Vision International (WVI, #21904).
NGO Relations Cooperates with (1): *Every Woman Every Child (EWEC, #09215).* [2023.02.16/XJ5829/y/**F**]

♦ Food for the Hungry (fh) 09845

Fundación contra el Hambre – Fundação Contra Fome
Headquarters 1224 E Washington St, Phoenix AZ 85034-1102, USA. T. +14809983100. Fax +14808895401. E-mail: hunger@fh.org.
URL: https://www.fh.org/
History Feb 1971, Glendale, CA (USA). Former names and other names: *Food for the Hungry International (FHI)* – former. Registration: Switzerland. **Aims** Respond to human suffering and graduate communities from extreme poverty. **Structure** Board of Directors (meets twice a year); Executive Committee. **Staff** 3100.00 FTE, paid. Staff of 30 nationalities, 98% working in their country of birth. **Finance** Private and public funding from a range of partners including the United Nations, governments, corporations and private foundations. **Activities** Financial and/or material support; awareness raising; capacity building; humanitarian/emergency aid. **Events** *Annual international management team meeting* Canada 2000, *Annual International Management Team Meeting* Philippines 1998, *Annual international management team meeting* Dominican Rep 1993, *Annual International Management Team Meeting* Japan 1992, *Annual International Management Team Meeting* Kenya 1990.
Members International and autonomous national offices in 24 countries:
Bangladesh, Bolivia, Burundi, Cambodia, Canada, Congo DR, Dominican Rep, Ethiopia, Guatemala, Haiti, India, Indonesia, Japan, Kenya, Korea Rep, Mozambique, Nicaragua, Peru, Philippines, Rwanda, South Sudan, Switzerland, Uganda, USA.
Members also in Middle Eastern countries. Membership countries not specified.
Consultative Status Consultative status granted from: *ECOSOC (#05331)* (Ros A); *FAO (#09260)* (Liaison Status). **IGO Relations** Observer to: *International Organization for Migration (IOM, #14454).* Associated with Department of Global Communications of the United Nations. **NGO Relations** Member of (10): *Alliance for Food Aid; British Overseas NGO's for Development (BOND)* (Full); *Consortium of Christian Relief and Development Association (CCRDA); CORE Group; Global Connections; Global Relief Alliance; InsideNGO (inactive); Joint Learning Initiative on Faith and Local Communities (JLI, #16139); Millennium Water Alliance (MWA); World Evangelical Alliance (WEA, #21393)* (Associate). Cambodian office is member of: *Cooperation Committee for Cambodia (CCC).* Partner of: *1,000 Days; United Against Hunger (UAH).* [2019/XF0136/f/**F**]

♦ Food for the Hungry, Canada / see Hope International Development Agency
♦ Food for the Hungry International / see Food for the Hungry (#09845)
♦ Food Industry Asia (unconfirmed)
♦ Food Industry Crusade Against Hunger / see Making Change
♦ Food and Land Use Coalition (unconfirmed)

♦ Food Law Enforcement Practitioners (FLEP) 09846

Contact Chartered Inst of Environmental Health, 15 Hatfields, London, SE1 8DJ, UK. T. +442078275835. Fax +442078276322.
URL: http://www.flep.org/
History Oct 1990, The Hague (Netherlands). **Aims** Develop mutual confidence and trust in the resolution of practical food control problems; promote adoption of good practices. **Structure** General Meeting (annual). Steering Group, including Chairman and Secretary. Secretariat. **Languages** English. **Staff** 9.00 FTE, voluntary. **Finance** Attendance fees. **Activities** Organizes: European forum (every 8 months); annual topic focused event. **Events** *Forum* Berlin (Germany) 2015, *Forum* Rome (Italy) 2014, *Forum* Utrecht (Netherlands) 2011, *Forum* Gozo Is (Malta) 2010, *Forum* Aarhus (Denmark) 2009. **Publications** Online reports.
Members Full in 24 countries:
Austria, Belgium, Czechia, Denmark, Finland, France, Germany, Greece, Hungary, Iceland, Ireland, Italy, Lithuania, Luxembourg, Malta, Netherlands, Norway, Portugal, Romania, Slovakia, Spain, Sweden, Switzerland, UK. [2013/XD7976/**F**]

♦ Food for Life / see Food for Life Global (#09847)

♦ Food for Life Global (FFL) 09847

Main Office 3911 Concord Pike, Ste 8030, SMB 1714, Wilmington DE 19803, USA. E-mail: contact@ffl.org.
URL: http://www.ffl.org/
History 1995, Potomac, MD (USA). Closed in 2015 and moved to Slovenia where it operated for two years. Former names and other names: *Food for Life* – former (1974). Registration: No/ID: 36-4887167, Start date: 6 Dec 2017, USA, Delaware. **Aims** Bring peace and prosperity to the world through the liberal distribution of pure plant-based meals prepared with loving intention; assit humanitarian efforts by coordinating and expanding the distribution of plant-based meals all over the world to the disadvantaged, malnourished and victims of disaster; promote the art and science of food yoga to nourish body, mind and soul. **Structure** Board of Directors; Executive Committee. **Languages** English, Hindi, Italian, Portuguese, Spanish. **Staff** 10.00 FTE, paid; 6.00 FTE, voluntary. Food for Life Global operates a virtual office, thus reducing our overhead costs, with staff working from home in 6 countries. **Finance** Annual budget: 1,000,000 USD (2021). **Activities** Advocacy/lobbying/activism; financial and/or material support; humanitarian/emergency aid; training/education. Active in all member countries.
Members Individuals in 81 countries and territories:
Argentina, Armenia, Australia, Austria, Bangladesh, Belarus, Belgium, Bolivia, Bosnia-Herzegovina, Botswana, Brazil, Bulgaria, Canada, Chile, Colombia, Costa Rica, Côte d'Ivoire, Croatia, Czechia, Denmark, Dominican Rep, Ecuador, El Salvador, Fiji, Finland, France, Georgia, Germany, Ghana, Guatemala, Guyana, Honduras, Hong Kong, Hungary, Indonesia, Ireland, Israel, Italy, Japan, Kazakhstan, Kenya, Kyrgyzstan, Latvia, Lithuania, Malaysia, Mauritius, Mexico, Moldova, Mozambique, Nepal, Netherlands, New Zealand, Nicaragua, Nigeria, North Macedonia, Norway, Paraguay, Peru, Philippines, Poland, Portugal, Romania, Russia, Serbia, Singapore, Slovakia, Slovenia, South Africa, Spain, Sri Lanka, Sweden, Taiwan, Tajikistan, Turkmenistan, Uganda, UK, Ukraine, Uruguay, USA, Uzbekistan, Zimbabwe.
NGO Relations Member of (1): *International Vegetarian Union (IVU, #15842).* Partner of (1): *Global Hunger Alliance (no recent information).* [2022.10.19/XE3682/**E**]

♦ Food not Bombs (internationally oriented national body)
♦ Food and Nutrition Foundation of Central America and Panama (#10019)

♦ Food Packaging Forum (FPF) 09848

Managing Dir Staffelstr 8, 8045 Zurich ZH, Switzerland. T. +41445155255. E-mail: info@fp-forum.org.
URL: https://www.foodpackagingforum.org/
History Registered in accordance with Swiss Civil Code. EU Transparency Register: 461883237039-87. **Aims** Enhance basic understanding of scientific principles and recent scientific findings that are relevant to the topic of food contact *chemicals* and their health impacts on humans and the *environment*. **Structure** Foundation Board. **Publications** *FPF Newsletter.* [2020/XM8750/f/**F**]

♦ Food Peace Campaign / see Oxfam Australia
♦ Food for the Poor (internationally oriented national body)
♦ Food Processing Machinery Europe (inactive)
♦ Food Quality and Health Association / see International Research Association for Organic Food Quality and Health (#14719)

♦ Food Security Cluster (FSC) 09849

Cluster sécurité alimentaire – Cluster de Seguridad Alimentaria
Global Coordinator c/o WFP HQ, Via Cesare Giulio Viola 68, 00148 Rome RM, Italy. T. +39665133518.
URL: http://foodsecuritycluster.org/
History Founded under the co-leadership of *FAO (#09260)* and *World Food Programme (WFP, #21510).* Formally endorsed by *Inter-Agency Standing Committee (IASC, #11393)*, 15 Dec 2010. **Aims** Coordinate the food security response during a *humanitarian* crisis, addressing issues of food availability, access and utilization. **Structure** Global Support Team; Technical Working Groups. **Finance** Funding from: *Department for International Development (DFID, inactive); ECHO (inactive); FAO (#09260); World Food Programme (WFP, #21510)*; Governments of Finland, Germany, Norway, Sweden, Switzerland. **Activities** Humanitarian/emergency aid; guidance/assistance/consulting; training/education; capacity building; advocacy/lobbying/activism; knowledge management/information dissemination. **IGO Relations** *FAO (#09260); World Food Programme (WFP, #21510).* **NGO Relations** Partners include: *International Federation of Red Cross and Red Crescent Societies (#13526)*; NGOs; UN agencies. [2014.12.30/XJ5123/**E**]

♦ Foodservice Consultants Society International (FCSI) 09850

Exec Dir 144 Parkedge Street, Rockwood ON N0B 2K0, Canada. T. +15198560783. Fax +15198560648. E-mail: info@fcsi.org.
URL: http://www.fcsi.org/
History May 1979, as a result of a merger of *'Food Facilities Consultants Society (FFCS)'*, set up 1955, with *International Society of Food Service Consultants (ISFSC, inactive)*, founded 1958. **Aims** Promote the profession of foodservice consulting on a global basis with emphasis on ethical business practice, professionalism, continuing education and independence from the supply chain; link professionals in the practice industry; encourage interest in foodservice design, engineering and management; broaden members' interests and encourage life-long learning, education, business relations, standards, efficiency and productivity. **Structure** Business meeting (annual). Operating Divisions (3): Americas; Europe/Africa/Middle East; Asia Pacific. Local Units/Chapters operating in: France, Germany-Austria, Netherlands, UK-Ireland, Switzerland, Italy, Canada, Pacific-Northwest (USA), New England (USA), California-Nevada (USA), Australia/New Zealand. **Languages** English. **Staff** 3.00 FTE, paid. **Finance** Members' dues. Other sources: event sponsorship; advertising sales. **Activities** Organizes: worldwide and divisional conferences; educational seminars; speakers bureau; intra-industry connections. Grants industry awards; promotes code of ethics; conducts Continuing Professional Growth program for consultant members. **Events** *Americas Division Conference* Montréal, QC (Canada) 2022, *Europe/Africa/Middle East Conference* Rotterdam (Netherlands) 2018, *Europe/Africa/Middle East Conference* Vienna (Austria) 2017, *Europe/Africa/Middle East Conference* Madrid (Spain) 2015, *Asia Pacific Annual Conference* Singapore (Singapore) 2012. **Publications** *The Consultant* (5 a year). Membership roster.
Members Consultant (Professional, Senior Associate, Associate, Emeritus and Student); Allied (Corporate and Individual Allied); Affiliate (Individual). Members (over 1,400) in 47 countries and territories:
Australia, Austria, Belgium, Canada, Chile, China, Czechia, Denmark, Dominican Rep, Egypt, El Salvador, Finland, France, Germany, Greece, Hong Kong, Hungary, Iceland, India, Indonesia, Ireland, Israel, Italy, Japan, Korea Rep, Lebanon, Liechtenstein, Malaysia, Mexico, Monaco, Netherlands, New Zealand, Peru, Philippines, Portugal, Qatar, Singapore, Slovenia, South Africa, Sweden, Switzerland, Thailand, Trinidad-Tobago, Türkiye, UK, United Arab Emirates, USA.
NGO Relations Links with a number of organizations, including the following listed in this Yearbook: *International Foodservice Manufacturers Association (IFMA); International Flight Services Association (IFSA).* [2012/XD0138/**F**]

♦ FoodServiceEurope 09851

SG Rue de Collège 27, 1050 Brussels, Belgium. T. +3228080644. E-mail: info@foodserviceeurope.org.
Main: http://www.foodserviceeurope.org/
History 1990, Brussels (Belgium). Former names and other names: *Fédération européenne de la restauration collective sous-traitée (FERCO)* – former (1990); *European Federation of Contract Catering Organizations* – former (1990). Registration: Belgium. **Aims** Provide constructive and intelligent solutions to the key socio-economic challenges that concern the industry. **Structure** General Assembly (twice a year); Board; Secretariat. **Languages** English, French. **Staff** 2.00 FTE, paid. **Finance** Members' dues. Annual budget: euro 200,000 – 250,000. **Activities** Advocacy/lobbying/activism; events/meetings. **Events** *Half-yearly general assembly* Brussels (Belgium) 2019, *Half-yearly general assembly* Madrid (Spain) 2018, *Half-yearly general assembly* Brussels (Belgium) 2017, *Half-yearly general assembly* Vienna (Austria) 2017, *Half-yearly general assembly* Helsinki (Finland) 2007. **Publications** *Guide to the Economically Most Advantageous Offer in the Contract Catering Sector* (2006). Annual statistics on the contract catering market.
Members National associations in 10 countries:
Austria, Belgium, France, Hungary, Italy, Netherlands, Portugal, Spain, Sweden, UK.
Associate 5 contract catering companies. Membership countries not specified.
NGO Relations Member of: Advisory Group on the Food Chain, Animal and Plant Health; *European Business Services Alliance (EBSA, #06426).* [2022/XD2866/**D**]

♦ Food Supplements Europe 09852

Contact Rue de l'Association 50, 1000 Brussels, Belgium. T. +3222091151. Fax +3222197342. E-mail: secretariat@foodsupplementseurope.org.
URL: http://www.foodsupplementseurope.org/
History 1998, as *European Responsible Nutrition Alliance (ERNA).* Serves as European voice of *International Alliance of Dietary Food Supplement Associations (IADSA, #11627).* Registered in accordance with Belgian law. EU Transparency Register: 638153011554-79. **Aims** Promote and encourage scientific research into supplementation from vitamins, minerals, herbs and other micronutrients. **Structure** General Assembly (annual). Officers: Chairman; Secretary-General; Treasurer. **Finance** Members' dues. **Events** *Joint conference* Berlin (Germany) 2005. **Members** Organizations; Companies. Membership countries not specified. [2015/XF5991/**F**]

♦ Food Systems for the Future (internationally oriented national body)
♦ Food Tank (internationally oriented national body)
♦ Food and Trees for Africa (internationally oriented national body)
♦ foodwatch (unconfirmed)

♦ Football Against Racism in Europe (FARE Network) 09853

Football contre le racisme en Europe – Fútbol contra el Racismo en Europa – Fussball gegen Rassismus in Europa – Calcio contro il Razzismo in Europa
Main Office Kanaalstaat 82-A, 1054 XL Amsterdam, Netherlands. E-mail: info@farenet.org.
URL: http://www.farenet.org/
History 1999, Vienna (Austria), at *European Commission (EC, #06633).* **Aims** Fight racism and discrimination in football across Europe. **Structure** Network of independent organizations, including: *European Gay and Lesbian Sport Federation (EGLSF, #07382).* **Languages** English. **Staff** 7.50 FTE, paid. **Finance** Support from: *King Baudouin Foundation (KBF)*; public funds, including from *European Commission (EC, #06633)* and *Council of Europe (CE, #04881); European Union Agency for Fundamental Rights (FRA, #08969).* Private sponsoring. **Activities** Advocacy/lobbying/activism; networking/liaising; sporting activities; training/education. **Events** *Respect Conference* Helsinki (Finland) 2012, *Seminar on Institutional Discrimination* Amsterdam (Netherlands) 2011, *Networking against racism and discrimination in European football – the role of fans, football clubs and ethnic minorities* Gelsenkirchen (Germany) 2004.

Members Partners (13) in 11 countries:
Austria, France, Germany, Hungary, Italy, Netherlands, Poland, Slovakia, Spain, Switzerland, UK.
Included in the above, 2 organizations listed in this Yearbook:
International League Against Racism and Antisemitism (#14014); Vienna Institute for International Dialogue and Cooperation (VIDC).
IGO Relations Participant in Fundamental Rights Platform of: *European Union Agency for Fundamental Rights (FRA, #08969).* Member of: *Enlarged Partial Agreement on Sport (EPAS, #05487).* **NGO Relations** Member of: *UNITED for Intercultural Action – European Network Against Nationalism, Racism, Fascism and in Support of Migrants and Refugees (UNITED, #20511).* [2020/XD8369/y/**D**]

♦ Football contre le racisme en Europe (#09853)
♦ Football International Federation for Players with Down syndrome (unconfirmed)

♦ Football Supporters Europe (FSE) 09854

Coordinator Postfach 30 62 18, 20328 Hamburg, Germany. T. +494037087741. Fax +494037087750. E-mail: info@fanseurope.org.
URL: http://www.footballsupporterseurope.org/
History 2008, as *Football Supporters International (FSI).* Present name adopted, 2009. Registered in accordance with German law. **Aims** Represent the interests and issues of football fans in Europe, especially at European level, but also at national and local levels where needed; encourage and exchange experience and (fan) culture amongst football fans in Europe; encourage responsible self-organization of football fans at national and local levels; disseminate information; use the positive potential of sport to promote tolerance, fan culture, gender equality, good governance, fairplay and grassroots football fans. **Structure** General Meeting (annual). Committee; Coordination (executive body). On-topic divisions; Working groups. **Languages** English, German. **Staff** 1.00 FTE, paid; 5.00 FTE, voluntary. **Activities** Projects, including "Fans' Embassies go East". Grassroots anti-discrimination campaigning. **Events** *Congress* Lisbon (Portugal) 2019, *Congress / Conference* Hamburg (Germany) 2009, *Congress / Conference* London (UK) 2008. **Publications** *FSE Newsletter* (every 6-8 weeks). Congress reports. Information Services: Database.
Members Full in 3 countries:
Austria, Belgium, Germany.
IGO Relations *Council of Europe (CE, #04881); European Commission (EC, #06633).* [2014/XJ8090/**F**]

♦ Football Supporters International / see Football Supporters Europe (#09854)
♦ **Footwork** International Podoconiosis Initiative (#14607)
♦ **FOPAO** Fédération des Organisations Patronales de l'Afrique de l'Ouest (#09698)
♦ FOPREL / see Foro de presidentes y presidentas de Poderes Legislativos de Centroamérica y el Caribe (#09887)
♦ **FOPREL** Foro de presidentes y presidentas de Poderes Legislativos de Centroamérica y el Caribe (#09887)
♦ **FORAGRO** Foro de las Américas para la Investigación y Desarrollo Tecnológico Agropecuario (#09875)
♦ An Foras Eirennach Gnóthal Eorpacha / see Leuven Institute for Ireland in Europe
♦ **ForATL** Forum of Asian Theological Librarians (#09902)
♦ FORATOM / see nucleareurope (#17616)
♦ Forbindelsescentret for det Europaeiske Økonomiske Faellesskabs Kog Forarbejdningsindustrier / see Liaison Centre for the Meat Processing Industry in the EU (#16452)
♦ Forbundet for Europas Zoologer (inactive)
♦ Forbundet av Europeiske Akvakultur Produsenter / see Federation of European Aquaculture Producers (#09491)
♦ Forbundet af Foreninger for i Udland Bosiddende EF Borgere / see Europeans throughout the World (#08839)
♦ Forbundet for Møllerisammenslutninger i det EU Lande / see European Flour Millers' Association (#07272)

♦ Forbundet Nordens Socialdemokratiske Ungdom (FNSU) 09855

Nordic Young Social Democrats
Address not obtained.
Events *Nordic and Baltic Young Social Democrats Meeting* Espoo (Finland) 2016.
Members Full in 9 countries:
Denmark, Estonia, Faeroe Is, Finland, Greenland, Iceland, Latvia, Norway, Sweden.
NGO Relations *Nordic Youth Council (NYC, #17474).* [2013.12.03/XD1831/**D**]

♦ Förbundet Nordisk Vuxenupplysning (FNV) 09856

Nordic Association for Adult Education
Gen Sec FNV Secretariat, Box 190, SE-101 23 Stockholm, Sweden. T. +46739413044.
Street address SV, Klarabergsviadukten 63, 2 tr, SE-101 23 Stockholm, Sweden.
URL: http://www.fnv.se/
History 1970, Stockholm (Sweden). **Aims** Represent and strengthen Nordic ideas and pedagogical models; develop and spread the Nordic model of folkbildning; promote popular adult education in general. **Structure** General Meeting; Board; Council. **Languages** Danish, English, Faroese, Icelandic, Norwegian, Swedish. **Staff** 1.00 FTE, paid. Project members. **Finance** Sources: grants; members' dues; revenue from activities/projects. **Activities** Events/meetings; projects/programmes. **Events** *Nordens östkust och Baltikums västkust* Cesu (Latvia) 1998, *Gränsregionalt samarbete* Copenhagen (Denmark) 1998, *Kustens döttrar och söner* Grebbestad (Sweden) 1998, *Norden, Europa och livslångt lärande* Reykjavik (Iceland) 1998, *Traditioner, livskvalitet och utkomstmöjligheter* Vilnius (Lithuania) 1998. **Publications** *FNV-informations* (periodical).
Members Organizations (8) working in the area of non formal adult education in 4 countries:
Denmark, Finland, Norway, Sweden.
NGO Relations Links with NGOs in Nordic and Baltic countries (not specified). [2021.06.22/XD1835/**D**]

♦ **FORCCE** Forum sur le commerce Canada-Europe (#03410)

♦ Force 11 (FORCE11) 09857

Registered Office 3026 Award Row, San Diego CA 92122, USA. E-mail: info@force11.org.
URL: http://www.force11.org/
History Grew out of of the FORCE Workshop, Aug 2011, Dagstuhl (Germany). Full title: *FORCE11 – The Future of Research Communications and e-Scholarship.* Registered in the State of California (USA). Current bylaws adopted Mar 2016. **Structure** Board of Directors. **Activities** Events/meetings. **Events** *Conference* San Diego, CA (USA) 2021, *Conference* San Diego, CA (USA) 2020, *Conference* Los Angeles, CA (USA) 2019, *Conference* Montréal, QC (Canada) 2018. [2019/XM7914/**C**]

♦ **FORCE11** Force 11 (#09857)
♦ FORCE11 – The Future of Research Communications and e-Scholarship / see Force 11 (#09857)
♦ Force aérienne de détection lointaine de l'OTAN (#16942)
♦ Force intérimaire des Nations Unies au Liban (#20577)
♦ Force internationale d'assistance à la sécurité (inactive)
♦ Force multinationale d'interposition (inactive)
♦ Force des Nations Unies chargée du maintien de la paix à Chypre (#20608)
♦ Force des Nations Unies chargée d'observer le dégagement (#20553)
♦ Force non-violente de paix / see Nonviolent Peaceforce (#17153)
♦ Force de paix interaméricaine (inactive)
♦ Forces alliées du Nord Europe / see Allied Joint Force Command Brunssum (#00734)
♦ Force d'urgence des Nations Unies (inactive)
♦ Fördergesellschaft für Angepasste Techniken in der Dritten Welt (internationally oriented national body)
♦ Förderverein Interkultur / see INTERKULTUR (#11516)

♦ Ford Foundation 09858

Fondation Ford
Pres 320 East 43rd St, New York NY 10017, USA. T. +12125735000. Fax +12123513677.
URL: http://www.fordfoundation.org/
History 1936, by Henry Ford and his son Edsel B Ford. Since 1950 moved to a national and international program. **Aims** Strengthen *democratic* values; reduce *poverty* and *injustice*; promote international cooperation; advance human achievement. **Structure** Board of Trustees of 15 members. Officers: President; Executive Vice-President, Secretary and General Counsel; Vice-President – Communications; Vice-President and Chief Investment Officer; Vice-Presidents (Democracy, Rights and Justice; Economic Opportunity and Assets; Education, Creativity and Free Expression); Treasurer and Chief Financial Officer; Deputy Vice-President – Program Management; Deputy Vice-President – Global Initiative on HIV-AIDS; Assistant Secretary and Associate General Counsel. Directors (11). Committees (11): Executive; Audit; Investment; Transactions; Membership; Proxy; Management and Governance; Transactions (subcommittee); plus 3 programme committees. Overseas field offices (10). **Languages** English. **Staff** 274.00 FTE, paid. **Finance** Endowment. As of 30 Sep 2009, total programme approvals: US$ 510,688,255. **Activities** Types of support: conferences and seminars; general purposes; matching funds; publications; research program-related investments; seed money; special projects; technical assistance; endowment funds; fellowships; individual grants. Programme areas (3): (1) *'Democracy, Rights and Justice'* with 3 sections – Democratic and Accountable Government; Human Rights; Social Justice Philanthropy. (2) *'Economic Opportunity and Assets'* with 3 sections – Economic Fairness; Metropolitan Opportunity; Sustainable Development. (3) *'Education, Creativity and Free Expression'* with 3 sections – Educational Opportunity and Scholarship; Freedom of Expression; Sexuality and Reproductive Health and Rights. Through 2007, spent over US$ 15,000 million on programs and grants in the US and other countries around the world. **Events** *Global Conference on Community Participatory Mapping of Indigenous People's Territories* Samosir Is (Indonesia) 2013, *MenEngage Africa symposium* Johannesburg (South Africa) 2009, *International meeting on the promotion of local music heritage in the age of globalization / General Assembly* Amman (Jordan) 2000, *International symposium in medical geography* Montréal, QC (Canada) 2000, *Regional symposium on common property and land tenure* Kampala (Uganda) 1996. **Publications** *The Ford Foundation Report* (2 a year). *Current Interests of the Ford Foundation* – booklet that includes grant application guidelines. Monographs; booklets and pamphlets; documentary films. **Members** Not a membership organization. **Consultative Status** Consultative status granted from: *ECOSOC (#05331)* (Special). **IGO Relations** Associated with Department of Global Communications of the United Nations. **NGO Relations** Supports a large number of organizations worldwide. [2021/XF0239/f/**F**]

♦ ForDIA – Concern for Development Initiatives in Africa (internationally oriented national body)
♦ Ford Institute for Human Security (internationally oriented national body)
♦ Fördraget om upprättandet av Europeiska Kol- och Stålgemenskapen (1951 treaty)
♦ Fördrag om upprättande av en Konstitution för Europa (2004 treaty)
♦ Foreign Correspondents' Club of South Asia (internationally oriented national body)
♦ Foreign Economic and Trade Arbitration Commission / see China International Economic and Trade Arbitration Commission
♦ Foreign Mission Board SBC / see International Mission Board
♦ Foreign Missions of Yarumal (religious order)
♦ Foreign Policy Association (internationally oriented national body)
♦ Foreign Policy Centre, London (internationally oriented national body)
♦ Foreign Policy Institute, Ankara (internationally oriented national body)
♦ Foreign Policy Research Institute (internationally oriented national body)
♦ Foreign Policy and United Nations Association of Austria (internationally oriented national body)
♦ Foreign Trade Arbitration Commission / see China International Economic and Trade Arbitration Commission
♦ Foreign Trade Association / see amfori (#00797)
♦ Foreign Trade Bank of Latin America (#03159)
♦ Foreininga for ei regulering og demokratisering av finansverda til beste for menneska (#02947)
♦ Forenede Nordiske Castingforbund (unconfirmed)
♦ Föreningarna Nordens Förbund (#09859)

♦ Föreningarna Nordens Förbund (FNF) 09859

Confederation of the Norden Associations – Föreningarna Nordens Förbund – Pohjola Norden Yhdistysten Liitto (NYL) – Samband Norraenu Felaganna
Sec Snaregade 10A, 1205 Copenhagen K, Denmark. T. +46762345414. E-mail: info@fnfnorden.org – thomas@fnfnorden.org.
URL: http://www.fnfnorden.org/
History History 16 Jul 1965, Reykjavik (Iceland), at 1st Congress, as a coordinating organ to interlink the various national Norden associations which had previously worked together informally. The latter were set up: 1919 in Denmark, Norway and Sweden; 1922 in Iceland; 1924 in Finland and the Faeroes; an associations was subsequently set up in Åland, 1970, and in Greenland, 1986. The Confederation was originally a *Consultative Group of Nordic Cooperatives – Nordiska Kooperativa Samrådsgruppen.* Joint platform adopted 1966; revised 1973 and 1997. Also previously referred to in English as: *League of Norden Associations; Union of Nordic Associations; Federation of Norden Associations.* **Aims** Develop and integrate *Nordic cooperation* within all sectors of society; expand cultural, social, political and economic contacts between Nordic peoples; initiate programmes of information on Nordic cooperation; increase knowledge of neighbouring countries within the region. **Structure** Praesidium; Working sessions of directors of National Norden Associations and Managing Director. **Languages** Danish, Finnish, Icelandic, Norwegian, Swedish. **Staff** 12.00 FTE, paid; 6.00 FTE, voluntary. **Finance** Members' dues. Official support for specific sectors (annually): about Danish Kr 15,000,000. **Activities** Networking/liaising. **Events** *General Assembly* Mikkeli (Finland) 2009, *Seminar for new employed at Nordic cooperation organs, institutions and firms* Gothenburg (Sweden) 1998, *Meeting* Finland 1996, *Meeting* Jyväskylä (Finland) 1987. **Publications** Brochures. **Information Services** *Nordic Information Offices* – set up following NMR decision, 1981, to provide information on official Nordic cooperation, coordinate Nordic activities in local regions and act as regional offices of Norden associations. As of 1998, there are 9 such offices: Denmark – at the Norden Association and in Sydslesvig; Finland – in Jyväskylä and Vasa; Iceland – in Akureyri; Norway – in Alta and Arendal; Sweden – in Umeå and Gothenburg.
Members National associations in 8 countries and territories:
Åland, Denmark, Faeroe Is, Finland, Greenland, Iceland, Norway, Sweden.
IGO Relations *Nordic Council of Ministers (NCM, #17260).* Holds joint meetings with Praesidium of: *Nordic Council (NC, #17256).* **NGO Relations** Instrumental in setting up: *Nordic Youth Orchestra (#17475).* Manages: *Nordic Network (#17348).* [2022/XD1244/**D**]

♦ Föreningen Acta Odontologica Scandinavica (#00083)
♦ Foreningen af Europaeiske Advokater (#20365)
♦ Foreningen af Europaeiske Staalproducenter / see European Steel Association (#08835)
♦ Foreningen Europa – Tredje Verden / see eu can aid (#05570)
♦ Foreningen af Fiskemel- og Fiskeolieproducenter i det Europaeiske Faelleskab / see European Fismeal and Fish Oil Producers (#07268)
♦ Föreningen för Folkbildning Norden-Latinamerika (no recent information)
♦ Föreningen för Fredsforskning i Finland (internationally oriented national body)
♦ Föreningen för Glassindustrin i EU / see EUROGLACES – European Ice Cream Association (#05688)
♦ Foreningen for Internasjonale Vann-og Skogstudier / see Foreningen for Internasjonale Vannstudier
♦ Foreningen for Internasjonale Vannstudier (internationally oriented national body)
♦ Föreningen för Internationella Studier (internationally oriented national body)
♦ Foreningen for en Levende Østersjíen (internationally oriented national body)
♦ Foreningen af Margarine-Industrier i EF-Landene / see European Margarine Association (#07736)
♦ Föreningen Norden (internationally oriented national body)
♦ Föreningen Nordiska Pappershistoriker (#02831)
♦ Föreningen Nordiska Teaterforskare (#02833)
♦ Foreningen for Nordisk Dialyse og Transplantation Personale (#02827)
♦ Foreningen for Organisationen af Fiskemelproducenter i de Europaeiske Økonomiske Faelleskaber / see European Fismeal and Fish Oil Producers (#07268)

♦ Föreningen for Orientaliska Studier (internationally oriented national body)
♦ Foreningen Scandiatransplant (#19066)
♦ Foreningen for Skandinaviske Sjomannshjem i Fremmende Havner (inactive)
♦ Föreningen för Spridandet av de Europeiska Språken / see Europe plurilingue
♦ Föreningen för Utveklingsforskning (internationally oriented national body)

♦ Forensic Anthropology Society of Europe (FASE) 09860

Pres Dipto Scienze Biomediche per la Salute, Univ degli Studi di Milano, Via Mangiagalli 37, 20133 Milan MI, Italy. E-mail: fase.fase@gmail.com.
URL: http://www.forensicanthropology.eu/

History 2003. Functions as a subsection of *International Academy of Legal Medicine (IALM, #11555)*. **Aims** Bring together anthropologists, forensic pathologists, odontologists, geneticists and other experts in the fields of forensic medicine and forensic science in the scientific and academic promotion and development of the discipline of forensic anthropology across Europe. **Structure** Board; Advisory Board. **Activities** Certification/accreditation; events/meetings; training/education. **Events** *Essentials on forensic anthropology* Bali (Indonesia) 2016, *Forensic anthropology* Coimbra (Portugal) 2016, *IALM Intersocietal Symposium* Venice (Italy) 2016, *Symposium* Heidelberg (Germany) 2013, *Workshop* Istanbul (Turkey) 2012. **Publications** *FASE Newsletter*. [2016/XM4785/**E**]

♦ Forente Nordiske Castingforbund (unconfirmed)

♦ Forest-Based Sector Technology Platform (FTP) 09861

Managing Dir European Forestry House, Rue du Luxembourg 66, 1000 Brussels, Belgium. T. +3222392303.
URL: http://www.forestplatform.org/

History 2004, by *Confederation of European Forest Owners (CEPF, #04525)*; *Confederation of European Paper Industries (CEPI, #04529)* and *Confédération européenne des industries du bois (CEI Bois, #04545)*. **Aims** Promote research and innovation in the forest-based sector; define and implement the sector's research and development roadmap for the future. **Structure** Board; Advisory Committee; National Support Groups; Managing Director. **Languages** English. **Staff** 3.00 FTE, paid. **Finance** Supported by: *Confederation of European Forest Owners (CEPF, #04525)*; *Confederation of European Paper Industries (CEPI, #04529)*; *Confédération européenne des industries du bois (CEI Bois, #04545)*; *European State Forest Association (EUSTAFOR, #08832)*; companies. **Activities** Research and development; knowledge management/information dissemination. **Events** *Joint Partnering Event for Horizon 2020* Munich (Germany) 2015, *Inspiring horizon, a new strategic research and innovation agenda for the forest- based sector* Barcelona (Spain) 2013, *Pacing innovation for the bioeconomy* Warsaw (Poland) 2011, *From research to business* Stockholm (Sweden) 2009, *Growing towards the future* Kranjska Gora (Slovenia) 2008. **Publications** *FTP Newsletter* (6 a year). Key documents.

Members National Support Groups in 23 countries:
Austria, Bulgaria, Czechia, Denmark, Estonia, Finland, France, Germany, Hungary, Italy, Latvia, Lithuania, Netherlands, Norway, Poland, Romania, Russia, Slovakia, Slovenia, Spain, Sweden, Switzerland, UK.
International organizational members (4):
Confédération européenne des industries du bois (CEI Bois, #04545); *Confederation of European Forest Owners (CEPF, #04525)*; *Confederation of European Paper Industries (CEPI, #04529)*; *European State Forest Association (EUSTAFOR, #08832)*.
NGO Relations Member of: *European Bioeconomy Alliance (EUBA, #06334)*. [2019/XM3099/**E**]

♦ Forest Carbon Partnership Facility (FCPF) 09862

Fonds de partenariat pour le carbone forestier – Fondo Cooperativo para el Carbono de los Bosques

Contact c/o Carbon Finance Unit, World Bank, 1818 H St NW, Washington DC 20433, USA. T. +12024731000. Fax +12025227432. E-mail: fcpfsecretariat@worldbank.org.
URL: http://www.forestcarbonpartnership.org/

History within *International Bank for Reconstruction and Development (IBRD, #12317)*. Announced, Dec 2007, Bali, during 13th Annual Conferences of the parties to *United Nations Framework Convention on Climate Change (UNFCCC, 1992)*. Became operational in Jun 2008. Charter setting up FCPF, revised 2 Mar 2010. **Aims** Assist *developing countries* in their efforts to reduce *emissions* from *deforestation* and forest degradation; foster conservation, *sustainable* management of forests and enhancement of forest carbon stock (REDD+) by providing value to standing forests. **Structure** Participants Assembly (annual). Participants Committee, consisting of 28 members elected by REDD Country Participants and financial contributors. Observers (6). IBRD is Trustee of Readiness Fund and Carbon Fund and provides Secretariat. **Finance** Readiness Fund: as of Nov 2011 – US$ 232 million pledged. Carbon Fund: as of Nov 2011 – US$ 215 million pledged. **Activities** Mechanisms (2): Readiness Mechanism – technical assistance and capacity building for REDD; Carbon Finance Mechanism – provides financing from the Carbon Fund, through which pilot incentive programs for REDD based on a system of compensated reductions are implemented. **Events** *Meeting* Paris (France) 2012.

Members REDD Country Participants from tropical and subtropical regions, which are members of IDA or IBRD, located between 35th parallel of latitude north and 35th parallel of latitude south; Donor Participants (governmental, private or public entities); Carbon Fund Participants (governmental, private or public entities).
REDD Country Participants (37):
Argentina, Bolivia, Cambodia, Cameroon, Central African Rep, Chile, Colombia, Congo Brazzaville, Congo DR, Costa Rica, El Salvador, Equatorial Guinea, Ethiopia, Gabon, Ghana, Guatemala, Guyana, Honduras, Indonesia, Kenya, Laos, Liberia, Madagascar, Mexico, Mozambique, Nepal, Nicaragua, Panama, Papua New Guinea, Paraguay, Peru, Suriname, Tanzania UR, Thailand, Uganda, Vanuatu, Vietnam.
Donor Fund and/or Carbon Fund Participants – Governments (11):
Australia, Denmark, Finland, Germany, Japan, Netherlands, Norway, Spain, Switzerland, UK, USA.
Donor Organizations (3):
Agence française de développement (AFD); *European Commission (EC, #06633)*; *The Nature Conservancy (TNC)*.
IGO Relations *International Development Association (IDA, #13155)*; *United Nations Collaborative Programme on Reducing Emissions from Deforestation and Forest Degradation in Developing Countries (UN-REDD Programme, #20528)*. [2011.11.14/XM3196/y/**F***]

♦ **FOREST EUROPE** Ministerial Conference on the Protection of Forests in Europe (#16817)

♦ Forest Invasive Species Network for Africa (FISNA) 09863

Réseau sur les espèces forestières envahissantes en Afrique

secretariat Forestry Research Institute of Malawi (FRIM), Kufa Road, PO Box 270, Zomba, Malawi.
URL: http://www.fao.org/forestry/fisna/en/

History Dec 2004, Zomba (Malawi), during a Task Force Meeting. **Aims** Coordinate the collation and dissemination of information relating to forest invasive species in sub-Saharan Africa for sustainable forest management and conservation of biodiversity. **Structure** Executive Committee.
Members Governments of 7 countries:
Ghana, Kenya, Malawi, South Africa, Tanzania UR, Uganda, Zambia. [2010/XJ1572/**E***]

♦ Forest Movement Europe (FME) 09864

Contact c/o FERN, Rue d'Edimbourg 26, 1050 Brussels, Belgium. T. +3228944690. E-mail: info@fern.org.
URL: http://www.fern.org/

History 1989. Founded at a meeting of European NGOs. In 1992, changed name to *European Rainforest Movement*. Current name adopted, 1994. Coordinated by *Fern (#09736)*. **Aims** Share information; develop joint strategies and a wider European perspective on forest issues; support *NGOs* and *indigenous* peoples in the South in their activities to *protect* forests. **Structure** An informal network of European NGOs working on forest-related issues, meeting annually. **Events** *Annual Meeting* Elbiku (Estonia) 2018, *Annual Meeting* Brasov (Romania) 2017, *Annual Meeting* Biggar (UK) 2016, *Annual Meeting* Brussels (Belgium) 2015, *Annual Meeting* Vienna (Austria) 2014.
Members NGOs (about 45) in 15 countries:
Austria, Belgium, Denmark, Finland, France, Germany, Ireland, Italy, Netherlands, Norway, Portugal, Spain, Sweden, Switzerland, UK.
NGO Relations Member of: *Abolition 2000 – Global Network to Eliminate Nuclear Weapons (Abolition 2000, #00006)*. [2018/XF1526/**F**]

♦ Forest Peoples Programme (FPP) 09865

Dir Registered Office, 1c Fosseway Business Ctr, Stratford Road, Moreton-in-Marsh, GL56 9NQ, UK. T. +441608652893. Fax +441608652878. E-mail: info@forestpeoples.org.
Contact Nieuwe Keizersgracht 45, 1018 VC Amsterdam, Netherlands.
URL: http://www.forestpeoples.org/

History 1990. Registration: Start date: 1997, Netherlands; Charity, No/ID: 1082158, Start date: 2000, England and Wales. **Aims** Create political space for forest peoples to secure their rights, control their lands and decide their own futures. **Structure** Board of Directors. **Staff** 45.00 FTE, paid. **Publications** *FPP E-Newsletter*.
Members Indigenous peoples' organizations, community groups and NGOs. Partners include 4 organizations listed in this Yearbook:
Asia Indigenous Peoples Pact (AIPP, #01282); *Indigenous Peoples' International Centre for Policy Research and Education (Tebtebba Foundation)*; *International Alliance of the Indigenous Tribal Peoples of the Tropical Forests (IAITPTF, #11629)*; *International Indigenous Forum on Biodiversity (IIFB, #13837)*.
Consultative Status Consultative status granted from: *African Commission on Human and Peoples' Rights (ACHPR, #00255)* (Observer); *UNEP (#20299)*; *UNESCO (#20322)* (Consultative Status). **IGO Relations** Accredited by (1): *Green Climate Fund (GCF, #10714)*. **NGO Relations** Member of (7): *European Network on Indigenous Peoples (ENIP, #07932)*; *GEF CSO Network (GCN, #10087)*; *HCV Network Ltd (HCV Network, #10865)*; *ICCA Consortium (#11041)*; *International Partnership for the Satoyama Initiative (IPSI, #14525)*; *International Union for Conservation of Nature and Natural Resources (IUCN, #15766)*; *World Heritage Watch (WHW)*. Partner of: *Tropical Forest Alliance (TFA, #20249)*; *Wetlands International (#20928)*. [2020/XJ8501/y/**F**]

♦ Forestry Mechanization (meeting series)

♦ Forestry Research Network for Sub-Saharan Africa (FORNESSA) . . 09866

Réseau de recherche forestière en Afrique subsaharienne

Coordinator CSIR-Forestry Research Inst of Ghana, PO Box UP 63 KNUST, Kumasi, Ghana. T. +233322060373 – +233322060123. Fax +233322060121.
Chairman Council for Scientific and Industrial Research, PO Box M32, Accra, Ghana. T. +2333027776514. Fax +233302777665.
URL: http://www.fornessa.org/

History 7 Jul 2000, Accra (Ghana). **Aims** Strengthen forestry research for greater impact on management and conservation of forest and tree resources for sustainable development in Sub-Saharan Africa. **Structure** Steering Committee. **Languages** English, French. **Staff** 3.00 FTE, paid. **Finance** Support from: *International Union of Forest Research Organizations (IUFRO, #15774)* Special Programme for Development of Capacities (SPDC). **Activities** Publishing activities; training/education; capacity building; knowledge management/information dissemination; events/meetings. **Events** *Regional Congress on Forests and Trees / Quinquennial Congress* Nairobi (Kenya) 2012. **Publications** Reports; book syntheses; factsheets. **Members** Individual; Honouring; Organizational. Institutions (109) in 36 countries. Membership countries not specified. **IGO Relations** Partners: *Bioversity International (#03262)*; *Centre de coopération internationale en recherche agronomique pour le développement (CIRAD, #03733)*; *European Commission (EC, #06633)*; *FAO (#09260)*. **NGO Relations** Partners: *African Academy of Sciences (AAS, #00193)*; *African Forest Forum (AFF, #00318)*; *Asia-Pacific Association of Forestry Research Institutions (APAFRI, #01841)*; *Center for International Forestry Research (CIFOR, #03646)*; *European Tropical Forest Research Network (ETFRN, #08950)*; *International Union of Forest Research Organizations (IUFRO, #15774)*; Northeast Asian Forest Forum (NEAFF); *World Agroforestry Centre (ICRAF, #21072)*. [2015.08.31/XM1894/**F**]

♦ Forestry and Timber Utilization Conference for Asia and the Pacific / see Asia-Pacific Forestry Commission (#01909)

♦ Forestry Workforce Network (FORWORKNET) 09867

Contact Sectoral Policies Dept, International Labour Office, Route des Morillons 4, 1211 Geneva 22, Switzerland. T. +41227996036. E-mail: sector@ilo.org.
URL: http://www.ilo.org/sector/lang – en/index.htm

History Sep 1993, jointly by the Industrial Activities Branch of *ILO (#11123)* and the *Joint FAO/ECE/ILO Committee on Forest Technology, Management and Training (inactive)*. Secretariat provided by ILO. Currently (2018) inactive/dormant. **Aims** Enable members to communicate directly with each other; open new opportunities for international exchange and collaboration; keep members abreast of new developments; serve as a "quick response" basis for international information. **Structure** Secretariat based at ILO, Geneva (Switzerland). **Finance** No membership fee. **Activities** Research/documentation; knowledge management/information dissemination; training/education. **Publications** *Forwork Update* in English, French, Spanish. *Membership Register – The Forestry Workforce Network*. Information Services: Specialized databases for references and statistics. **Members** Individuals and institutions (350) in 70 countries. Membership countries not specified. [2018.06.01/XF3138/d/**F**]

♦ **ForestSAT** Association for Forest Spatial Analysis Technologies (#02598)

♦ Forests and Livelihoods: Assessment, Research, and Engagement (FLARE) 09868

Secretariat School for Environment and Sustainability, Univ of Michigan, 440 Church Str, Ann Arbor MI 48109, USA. T. +17346474171. E-mail: flare.network@umich.edu.
URL: http://www.forestlivelihoods.org/

History Also referred to as *FLARE Network*. **Aims** Advance the state of knowledge regarding forest-based livelihoods. **Structure** Steering Committee; Secretariat. Working Groups. **Activities** Events/meetings; advocacy/lobbying/activism. **Events** *Annual Meeting* Ann Arbor, MI (USA) 2019, *Annual Meeting* Copenhagen (Denmark) 2018, *Annual Meeting* Stockholm (Sweden) 2017, *Annual Meeting* Edinburgh (UK) 2016, *Annual Meeting* Paris (France) 2015. [2019/XM7553/**F**]

♦ Forest Stewardship Council (FSC) 09869

Main Office Adenauerallee 134, 53113 Bonn, Germany. T. +49228367660. Fax +492283676630. E-mail: fsc@fsc.org – info@fsc.org.
URL: http://www.fsc.org/

History 1 Oct 1993, Toronto, ON (Canada). Set up at founding assembly. Also referred to as *FSC International*. Registration: EU Transparency Register, No/ID: 03556915643-37, Start date: 12 Apr 2011. **Aims** Promote responsible forest management worldwide, based on principles which ensure that all forests are managed in ways that are *environmentally* appropriate, socially beneficial and economically viable; provide a place where people with different interests can agree what responsible management means, translating that means into standards; facilitate market-based incentives for forest managers to adopts and implement those standards. **Structure** General Assembly; Board of Directors of 9 members; International Secretariat. Regional Offices (4): Africa; Asia Pacific; CIS countries; Latin America. **Languages** English, Spanish. **Finance** Members' dues. Other sources: accreditation program; commercial services; donation program. **Activities** Certification/accreditation; advocacy/lobbying/activism. **Events** *General Assembly* Kota Kinabalu (Malaysia) 2011, *General Assembly* Cape Town (South Africa) 2008, *General Assembly* Manaus (Brazil) 2005, *Annual Conference* Bonn (Germany) 2004, *General Assembly* Oaxaca (Mexico) 2002. **Publications** Annual Report; factsheets; case studies; technical guides.
Members Individuals in 79 countries and territories:
Argentina, Australia, Belgium, Bolivia, Bosnia-Herzegovina, Brazil, Bulgaria, Burkina Faso, Cameroon, Canada, Central African Rep, Chile, China, Colombia, Congo Brazzaville, Congo DR, Costa Rica, Côte d'Ivoire, Croatia, Ecuador, El Salvador, Estonia, Ethiopia, Fiji, Finland, France, Gabon, Germany, Ghana, Guatemala, Guyana, Honduras, Hungary, India, Indonesia, Italy, Japan, Kenya, Korea Rep, Latvia, Luxembourg, Malaysia, Montenegro, Morocco, Mozambique, Nepal, Netherlands, New Zealand, Nicaragua, Nigeria, Panama, Papua New Guinea, Peru, Poland, Portugal, Romania, Russia, Senegal, Serbia, Slovakia, South Africa, Spain, Sri Lanka, Sweden, Switzerland, Taiwan, Tanzania UR, Thailand, Togo, Tunisia, Uganda, UK, Ukraine, United Arab Emirates, Uruguay, USA, Venezuela, Vietnam, Zimbabwe.
Organizations in 59 countries:
Argentina, Australia, Austria, Belgium, Bolivia, Brazil, Bulgaria, Cameroon, Canada, Cayman Is, Chile, China, Colombia, Congo DR, Costa Rica, Côte d'Ivoire, Czechia, Denmark, Ecuador, Estonia, Fiji, Finland, France, Gabon, Germany, Guatemala, Honduras, Indonesia, Ireland, Israel, Italy, Japan, Latvia, Luxembourg, Malaysia, Mexico, Nepal, Netherlands, New Zealand, Nicaragua, Nigeria, Norway, Papua New Guinea, Peru, Poland, Romania, Russia, Singapore, South Africa, Spain, Sweden, Switzerland, Thailand, Uganda, UK, United Arab Emirates, Uruguay, USA, Vietnam.

Included in the above, 9 organizations listed in this Yearbook:
Fauna & Flora International (FFI, #09277); Greenpeace International (#10727) (Canada, China, Netherlands, New Zealand, UK, USA); *ICCO – Interchurch Organization for Development Cooperation; Rainforest Action Network (RAN, #18614); Rainforest Alliance; Soil Association; Verdens Skove; Wilderness Society; World Wide Fund for Nature (WWF, #21922).*
Consultative Status Consultative status granted from: *ECOSOC (#05331)* (Special); *UNEP (#20299).* **IGO Relations** Accredited by: *Ministerial Conference on the Protection of Forests in Europe (FOREST EUROPE, #16817); United Nations Framework Convention on Climate Change – Secretariat (UNFCCC, #20564).* Member of: *Congo Basin Forest Partnership (CBFP, #04662).* Observer status with: *Intergovernmental Negotiating Committee for a Legally Binding Agreement on Forests in Europe (INC-Forests, inactive).* **NGO Relations** Cooperates with (1): *European Sustainable Tropical Timber Coalition (STTC).* In liaison with technical committees of: *International Organization for Standardization (ISO, #14473).* Member of: *GEF CSO Network (GCN, #10087); Global Platform for Sustainable Natural Rubber (GPSNR, #10552); HCV Network Ltd (HCV Network, #10865); ISEAL (#16026); International Union for Conservation of Nature and Natural Resources (IUCN, #15766).* Charter member of: *Global Landscapes Forum (GLF, #10451).* Partner of: *Global Partnership on Forest and Landscape Restoration (GPFLR, #10535); Green Economy Coalition (GEC, #10717); Tropical Forest Alliance (TFA, #20249).* [2020/XF3541/y/**F**]

- Forests, Trees and People Programme in Asia / see RECOFTC – The Center for People and Forests (#18628)
- Forests of the World (internationally oriented national body)

♦ Forest Trends 09870
Main Office 1203 19th St NW, 4th Fl, Washington DC 20036, USA. T. +12022983000. Fax +12022983014. E-mail: info@forest-trends.org.
URL: http://www.forest-trends.org/
History 1998. **Aims** Maintain and restore forest *ecosystems* by promoting incentives that diversify *trade* in the forest sector. **Structure** Board of 19 members. **IGO Relations** Member of: *Congo Basin Forest Partnership (CBFP, #04662).* **NGO Relations** Member of: *GEF CSO Network (GCN, #10087); InsideNGO (inactive); International Union for Conservation of Nature and Natural Resources (IUCN, #15766).* Instrumental in setting up and partner of: *EcoAgriculture Partners (#05290); Rights and Resources Initiative (RRI, #18947).* Partner of: *Tropical Forest Alliance (TFA, #20249).* [2019/XF7132/**F**]

- The Forest Trust / see Earthworm Foundation (#05172)
- FOREX – Asia Pacific Foreign Exchange Congress (meeting series)
- Forex Club Interarab / see Interarab Cambist Association (#11455)
- **FORGE** Federation internationale des organismes de formation à la Gestalt (#09646)
- The Forgotten International (internationally oriented national body)
- FORIM – Forum des Organisations de Solidarité Internationale issues des Migrations (internationally oriented national body)
- Foring – Forum für Internationale Gesundheit (internationally oriented national body)
- foring – Forum for International Health (internationally oriented national body)
- Forlaeggersammenslutningen i EØF / see Federation of European Publishers (#09536)

♦ Formacare 09871
Contact c/o CEFIC, Rue Belliard 40, Box 15, 1040 Brussels, Belgium. T. +3224369451. E-mail: formacare@cefic.be.
URL: http://www.formacare.org/
History A sector group of *Conseil européen de l'industrie chimique (CEFIC, #04687).* **Aims** Provide a platform for open and constructive dialogue among *formaldehyde* manufacturers, downstream users and key regulators at both national and *European* levels. **Structure** General Assembly; Executive Committee; Secretary General. **Languages** English. [2019/XJ5958/**E**]

- Formal Epistemology Workshop (meeting series)
- Formal Ethics Conference (meeting series)
- Formal Ethics – Formal Ethics Conference (meeting series)

♦ Formal Methods Europe (FME) 09872
Contact Box 337, SE-751 05 Uppsala, Sweden. E-mail: info@fmeurope.org.
URL: http://www.fmeurope.org/
History 1984. Registration: Start date: 1998. **Aims** Stimulate use of formal methods of developing *computing systems* and *software* by European industry; promote international cooperation among researchers and users of formal methods so as to exchange ideas, identify common interests and make links between research and areas of application. **Structure** Board; Advisory Group; Working Groups. **Languages** English. **Activities** Events/meetings; networking/liaising. **Events** *International Symposium* Beijing (China) 2021, *International Symposium* Porto (Portugal) 2019, *International Symposium* Oxford (UK) 2018, *International Symposium* Limassol (Cyprus) 2016, *International Symposium* Oslo (Norway) 2015.
Members Full (about 350) in 43 countries and territories:
Algeria, Argentina, Australia, Austria, Belgium, Brazil, Canada, China, Czechia, Denmark, Estonia, Finland, France, Germany, Greece, Hong Kong, India, Iran Islamic Rep, Ireland, Israel, Italy, Japan, Korea Rep, Luxembourg, Macau, Netherlands, New Zealand, Norway, Pakistan, Poland, Portugal, Romania, Singapore, Slovakia, South Africa, Spain, Sweden, Switzerland, Türkiye, UK, Ukraine, Uruguay, USA.
NGO Relations Member of (1): *International Federation for Computational Logic (IFCoLog, #13397).* [2022.02.09/XF4331/**F**]

- Formation de cadres africains (internationally oriented national body)
- Formation pour la développement international (internationally oriented national body)

♦ Formation d'éducateurs sociaux européens (FESET) 09873
European Social Educator Training
Sec address not obtained.
Pres address not obtained.
URL: http://www.feset.org/
History 1989. Statutes adopted May 1991; amended Apr 1995, Oct 1998, Mar 2004, Apr 2016 and May 2018. Former names and other names: *European Association for Training Centres for Socio-Educational Care Work (EATCSECW)* – former; *Association européenne des centres de formation au travail socio-éducatif* – former; *FESET – Association européenne des centres de formation au travail socio-éducatif* – alias. **Aims** Promote education and training for socio-educational purposes; participate in programmes of different European bodies; ensure that the training centres be represented at the institutions of the European Union, the Council of Europe as well as other international organisations; encourage exchanges and understanding between training centres in EU Member States, Member States of the Council of Europe and in other European States; promote terms of mutual recognition of diplomas. **Structure** General Assembly; Board; Executive Committee. **Languages** English, French. **Staff** Voluntary. **Finance** Sources: members' dues. **Activities** Events/meetings; networking/liaising; research/documentation. **Events** *New horizons for social education* Turku (Finland) 2014, *Socio-pedagogical approaches in social professions* Osnabrück (Germany) 2010, *IFSW European seminar* Parma (Italy) 2007, *Biennial congress* Alicante (Spain) 2004, *Biennial congress* Stockholm (Sweden) 2001. **Publications** *European Journal of Social Education – Journal Européen d'Education Sociale* (2 a year) – journal. Magazine.
Members Ordinary; Associate institutions in 11 countries:
Austria, Belgium, Denmark, Finland, France, Germany, Hungary, Norway, Portugal, Spain, Switzerland.
Consultative Status Consultative status granted from: *Council of Europe (CE, #04881)* (Participatory Status). **NGO Relations** Member of: *European Network for Social Action (ENSACT, #08003).* Cooperates with: *European Association of Schools of Social Work (EASSW, #06200); European Centre for Community Education (ECCE, no recent information); International Federation of Social Workers (IFSW, #13544).* [2021/XD6709/**D**]

- FORMATS – International Conference on Formal Modeling and Analysis of Timed Systems (meeting series)
- FORMEC – Forestry Mechanization (meeting series)
- ForMENA – Council for MENA Affairs (unconfirmed)
- Former FAO and Other United Nations Staff Association (internationally oriented national body)
- Former Officials Association Turin (internationally oriented national body)
- Former Officials of the European Civil Service / see Seniors of the European Public Service (#19229)
- Formosa Gospel Crusades / see OC International (#17688)
- **FORNESSA** Forestry Research Network for Sub-Saharan Africa (#09866)
- Foro Abierto de Ciencias de America Latina y el Caribe (meeting series)

♦ Foro Académico Permanente ALC-UE (FAP ALC-UE) 09874
Academic Permanent Forum LAC-EU – Forum Académique Permanent ALC-UE
Contact Univ Miguel de Cervantes, Mac Iver 370, Santiago, Santiago Metropolitan, Chile. T. +5629273451.
Contact address not obtained. T. +33144398660.
URL: http://www.fap-alcue.org/
History Oct 2012, to ensure continuity of Academic Summits. **Structure** Bi-Regional Academic Council; Permanent Reflection Groups; Executive Secretariat. **Activities** Events/meetings. **Events** *EU-CELAC Academic Summit* Brussels (Belgium) 2015. [2016/XM4989/**F**]

- Foro de Alto Nivel sobre la Eficacia de la Ayuda (meeting series)
- Foro América Latina-Asia del Este / see Forum for East Asia-Latin America Cooperation (#09907)

♦ Foro de las Américas para la Investigación y Desarrollo Tecnológico Agropecuario (FORAGRO) 09875
Forum for the Americas on Agricultural Research and Technological Development
Exec Secretariat IICA, Apartado 55-2200, San Isidro de Coronado, San José, San José, San José, 11101, Costa Rica. T. +50622160180. E-mail: secretaria.foragro@iica.int.
URL: http://foragro.org/
Aims Promote dialogue, actively discuss needs and opportunities, generate analysis and proposals and foster partnerships to strengthen science, technology and innovation systems for sustainable development of agriculture in the Americas. **Structure** Assembly; Steering Committee; Executive Secretariat. **Languages** English, Spanish. **Events** *Meeting* Lima (Peru) 2012, *Meeting* Montevideo (Uruguay) 2008, *Meeting* Panama 2005, *Meeting* Panama (Panama) 2005, *Meeting* Brasilia (Brazil) 2002. **IGO Relations** Secretariat provided by: *Inter-American Institute for Cooperation on Agriculture (IICA, #11434).* [2020.03.10/XJ4033/**F**]

- Foro de Autoridades Locales por la Inclusión Social / see Foro de Autoridades Locales por la Inclusión Social y la Democracia Participativa (#09876)

♦ Foro de Autoridades Locales por la Inclusión Social y la Democracia Participativa (FAL) 09876
Forum of Local Authorities for Social Inclusion and Participatory Democracy – Forum des autorités locales pour l'inclusion sociale et la démocratie participative
Contact address not obtained. T. +34952608073. Fax +34952608010.
URL: http://www.redfal.org/
History 2001, within *World Social Forum (WSF, #21797),* as *Foro de Autoridades Locales por la Inclusión Social (FAL) – Forum of Local Authorities for Social Inclusion.* **Events** *Forum* Dakar (Senegal) 2011, *Forum* Belém (Brazil) 2009, *Forum* Caracas (Venezuela) 2006, *Forum* Barcelona (Spain) 2005, *Forum* Porto Alegre (Brazil) 2005. [2012/XM1358/**F**]

- Foro Cívico Europeo (#06562)
- Foro Civico Mundial (#21277)
- Foro de Cooperación América Latina-Asia del Este (#09907)
- Foro de Directores de los Servicios Meteorológicos e Hidrológicos del Africa del Oeste / see Conference of Directors of the West African National Meteorological and Hydrological Services (#04589)
- Foro de dirigentes de Asia y el Pacifico sobre of VIH/SIDA y el desarrollo (#01942)
- Foro de Educación Teológica Ecuménica de América Latina y el Caribe (unconfirmed)
- Foro Empresarial Mercosur Unión – Europea (internationally oriented national body)
- Foro europeo para Maestros de la Educación Religiosa (#07337)
- Foro Europeo de la Montaña (#07824)
- Foro Europeo de Rociadores Automaticos (#07262)
- Foro Farmacéutico de las Américas (#18351)
- Foro de Federaciones (internationally oriented national body)
- **FORO** Foro Iberoamericano de Organismos Reguladores Radiológicos y Nucleares (#09878)
- Foro Global de la Economia Social (#10603)
- Foro Global de Gobierno Corporativo (inactive)
- Foro Global de Investigación Agropecuaria (#10370)
- Foro Global para los Servicios de Asesoria Rural (#10378)

♦ Foro Iberoamericano de Agencias Gubernamentales de Protección al Consumidor (FIAGC) 09877
Presidency Dir Nac Defensa Consumidor, Av Julio A Roca 651, 4o Piso, Buenos Aires, Argentina. T. +541143494182. E-mail: dndc@produccion.gob.ar – internacional.dndc@produccion.gob.ar.
URL: http://www.fiagc.org/
History 2001, as *Foro Latinoamericano de Agencias Gubernamentales de Protección al Consumidor (FLAGC).* Current title adopted 2006. **Aims** Promote cooperation between government agencies of consumer protection in Ibero-America. **Structure** Presidency; Technical Secretariat. **Activities** Knowledge management/information dissemination; events/meetings. **Publications** *FIAGC Bulletin.*
Members Governmental institutions (one per country) of 22 countries:
Argentina, Bolivia, Brazil, Chile, Colombia, Costa Rica, Cuba, Dominican Rep, Ecuador, El Salvador, Guatemala, Honduras, Mexico, Nicaragua, Panama, Paraguay, Peru, Portugal, Puerto Rico, Spain, Uruguay, Venezuela.
Observer members include:
Consumers International (CI, #04773); International Bank for Reconstruction and Development (IBRD, #12317) (World Bank); *OAS (#17629); UNCTAD (#20285).*
IGO Relations Observer status with (1): *International Consumer Protection and Enforcement Network (ICPEN, #12930).* [2021/XM5892/**F***]

- Foro Iberoamericano y del Caribe de Mejores Practicas (#11019)
- Foro Iberoamericano de Dialogo Evangélico / see Latin Evangelical Alliance (#16397)

♦ Foro Iberoamericano de Organismos Reguladores Radiológicos y Nucleares (FORO) 09878
Iberoamerican Forum of Radiological and Nuclear Regulatory Organisations
Secretariat Av del Libertador 8250, Piso 1o Ofic 1334 A, C1429BNP Buenos Aires, Argentina. T. +541163231748. Fax +541147047079. E-mail: info@foroiberam.org.
URL: http://www.foroiberam.org/
History 9 Jul 1997. Established through Veracruz Agreement. Constitution adopted Jul 2010; amended Jun 2015, Lima (Peru). Functions within *Global Nuclear Safety and Security Network (GNSSN, #10509)* of *International Atomic Energy Agency (IAEA, #12294).* **Aims** Promote a high level of radiation and nuclear safety in all practices using radioactive materials in the region. **Structure** Board of Directors (Plenary); Technical Executive Committee; Secretary. **Languages** Spanish. **Finance** Sources: contributions of member/participating states. Through IAEA extra-budgetary programme. **Activities** Knowledge management/information dissemination. **Events** *Plenary Meeting* Buenos Aires (Argentina) 2020, *Plenary Meeting* Buenos Aires (Argentina) 2020, *Plenary Meeting* Santiago (Chile) 2019, *Plenary Meeting* Brasilia (Brazil) 2018, *Plenary Meeting* Buenos Aires (Argentina) 2017. **Publications** Standards/guidelines. **Information Services** *RED Network.*
Members Radiological and nuclear regulatory agencies from 10 countries:
Argentina, Brazil, Chile, Colombia, Cuba, Mexico, Paraguay, Peru, Spain, Uruguay.
NGO Relations Memorandum of Understanding with (1): *European Technical Safety Organisations Network (ETSON, #08880).* [2020.08.29/XJ7396/**F***]

♦ Foro Intergubernamental sobre Seguridad Quimica (inactive)
♦ Foro internacional de Acción Católica (#09919)
♦ Foro Internacional para el Bienestar de la Infancia (#13633)
♦ Foro Internacional de Constalaciones Sistémicas en Organizaciones (#13656)
♦ Foro Internacional del Enfoque Centrado en la Persona (meeting series)
♦ Foro Internacional Indigena por la Biodiversidad (#13837)
♦ Foro Internacional de Montreal / see FIM-Forum for Democratic Global Governance (#09761)
♦ Foro Internacional de Mujeres Indigenas (#13838)
♦ Foro Internacional de las Plataformas Nacionales de ONGs / see Forus (#09934)
♦ Foro Internacional para el Transporte Rural y el Desarrollo (#13650)
♦ Foro Interparlamentario de las Américas / see ParlAmericas (#18206)
♦ Foro de la Juventud de la Unión Europea (inactive)
♦ Foro Latinoamericano de Agencias Gubernamentales de Protección al Consumidor / see Foro Iberoamericano de Agencias Gubernamentales de Protección al Consumidor (#09877)
♦ Foro Latinoamericano de Ciencias Ambientales (#16336)

♦ Foro Latinoamericano de Educación Musical (FLADEM) 09879

Latin American Musical Education Forum

SG Monte Athos 116, Col Lomas de Chapultepec, 11000 Mexico City CDMX, Mexico.
Hon Pres address not obtained.
URL: http://fladem.ning.com/

History 1995, San José (Costa Rica). **Activities** Seminar; Annual Assembly. **Events** *Seminar* Córdoba (Argentina) 2009, *Seminar* Mérida (Mexico) 2008, *Seminar* Lima (Peru) 2007, *Seminar* Bogota (Colombia) 2006, *Seminar* San José (Costa Rica) 2005. **Members** Membership countries not specified.

[2009/XJ8025/**F**]

♦ Foro Latinoamericano de Entes Reguladores de Telecomunicaciones (REGULATEL) 09880

Contact c/o Subsecretaria de Telecomuniciones, Ministerio de Transporte y Telecomunicaciones, Amunategui 139 – 50o piso, Santiago, Santiago Metropolitan, Chile. T. +56225888000ext3753. E-mail: durbina@subtel.gob.cl.
URL: http://www.regulatel.org/

Aims Promote cooperation and coordination between regulatory organizations; promote improvement of telecommunications in Latin America. **Structure** Pleanary Assembly; Executive Committee; Executive Secretariat. **Activities** Politics/policy/regulatory; events/meetings.
Members Authorities of 23 countries and territories:
Argentina, Bolivia, Brazil, Chile, Colombia, Costa Rica, Cuba, Dominican Rep, Ecuador, El Salvador, Guatemala, Honduras, Italy, Mexico, Nicaragua, Panama, Paraguay, Peru, Portugal, Puerto Rico, Spain, Uruguay, Venezuela. [2017/XM5903/**F***]

♦ Foro Latinoamericano de Estudiantes de Antropologia y Arqueologia (meeting series)

♦ Foro Latinoamericano de Juventud (FLAJ) 09881

Forum latinoaméricain des jeunes – Latin American Youth Forum

Address not obtained.
Sec address not obtained.
Pres address not obtained.

History Dec 1993, Puebla (Mexico), by: Inter-American Scout Committee (ISC); International Falcon Movement Socialist Educational International (IFM-SEI); International Union of Socialist Youth (IUSY); World Federation of Democratic Youth (WFDY); COPPPAL Youth; National Youth Council of Chile; National Youth Council El Salvador; National Youth Council of Uruguay; National Youth Council of Peru. Also referred to in English as *Coordination Platform of Youth Organizations in Latin America.* **Aims** Be an area for the convergence of national, social international and political international platforms and NGOs specializing in youth; develop and strengthen youth association as a means to achieve the protagonist participation of *young people* in the development strategies of Latin American countries and the improvement of the quality of life for young people on the continent; be an interlocutor and agent of consultation and debate with youth organizations, NGOs, international cooperation agencies and bodies, governmental structures and supranational bodies; encourage and coordinate joint research, policies and work among member youth organizations; strengthen the technical management ability of members; foment the creation of public agencies dealing with youth. **Structure** General Assembly. Leadership Committee, comprising 8 full member organizations. Executive Secretariat. Emergency Resolutions Committee, composed of 2 full member organizations plus Executive Secretariat. **Activities** Organizes *Euro-Latin American Youth Forum (FEULAT)* with *European Youth Forum (#09140).* **Events** *European Union – Latin America and the Caribbean youth summit* Madrid (Spain) 2010, *FEULAT : Euro-Latin American youth forum* Mollina (Spain) 2009, *General Assembly* Panama (Panama) 2008, *FEULAT : Euro-Latin American youth forum* Mollina (Spain) 2006, *FEULAT : Euro-Latin American youth forum* Mollina (Spain) 2004.
Members Full; Observer. Youth organizations in 16 countries:
Argentina, Brazil, Chile, Colombia, Costa Rica, Cuba, Ecuador, El Salvador, Guatemala, Honduras, Mexico, Panama, Paraguay, Peru, Uruguay, Venezuela.
International and regional full members (7):
Christian Workers Youth of America; *Inter-American Scout Committee (ISC, #11445); International Falcon Movement – Socialist Educational International (IFM-SEI, #13327); International Union of Socialist Youth (IUSY, #15815); Organización Continental Latinoamericana y Caribeña de Estudiantes (OCLAE, #17834); World Association of Girl Guides and Girl Scouts (WAGGGS, #21142); World Federation of Democratic Youth (WFDY, #21427).*
Observer members (2):
Consejo Episcopal Latinoamericano (CELAM, #04709) (Youth Section); *Latin American and Caribbean Alliance of YMCAs (LACA, #16264).* [2013/XF3433/y/**F**]

♦ Foro Latinoamericano de Politicas Educativas (FLAPE) 09882

Coordinator Gen LPP, Tucuman 1650, 2do E, C1050AAF Buenos Aires, Argentina.
Exec Sec address not obtained.
Blog: https://forolatinoflape.blogspot.com/

History 23 Oct 2003, Mexico City (Mexico). [2009/XF7152/**F**]

♦ Foro Latinoamericano para la Seguridad Urbana y la Democracia (FLASUD) 09883

Latin American Forum for Urban Security and Democracy

Address not obtained.

History 2001, Mexico City (Mexico). **Aims** Contribute to the development and consolidation of a social and democratic state of rule of law in the global scenario. **Activities** Offers courses.
Members Full; Associate. Full in 4 countries:
Argentina, Brazil, Colombia, Mexico.
Associate in 5 countries:
Argentina, Brazil, Italy, Mexico, Spain.
NGO Relations Supports: *African Forum for Urban Security (AFUS, #00323).* [2010/XM3973/**F**]

♦ Foro Latinoamericano de Turismo (FOLATUR) 09884

Address not obtained.
URL: http://www.folatur.com/

Structure General Assembly.
Members Full in 11 countries:
Argentina, Bolivia, Brazil, Chile, Colombia, Ecuador, Mexico, Paraguay, Peru, Uruguay, Venezuela.
NGO Relations Member of: *World Travel Agents Associations Alliance (WTAAA, #21870).* [2017/XM6603/**F**]

♦ Foro de Ministros de Cultura y Responsables de Politicas Culturales de América Latina y el Caribe (no recent information)
♦ Foro de Ministros de Medio Ambiente de América Latina y el Caribe (#09923)
♦ Foro Mondial de Educación (#21371)
♦ Foro de Montañas para América Latina / see Latin American Network on Andean Mountains (#16350)
♦ Foro de Mujeres y Cuestiones de Desarrollo (internationally oriented national body)
♦ Foro Mundial de las Alternativas (#21513)
♦ Foro Mundial Bananero (#21215)
♦ Foro Mundial Comunidades Pesqueras (#21517)
♦ Foro Mundial sobre Derecho, Justicia y Desarrollo (#10373)
♦ Foro Mundial de los GLP / see World LPG Association (#21629)
♦ Foro Mundial de Productores de Café (meeting series)
♦ Foro Mundial de la Sociedad Civil (#21278)
♦ Foro Mundial de Teologia y Liberación (#21524)
♦ Foro de las Naciones Unidas sobre los Bosques (#20562)
♦ Foro de Organismos de Acreditación de América (#11396)

♦ Foro de los Países de América Latina y el Caribe sobre el Desarrollo Sostenible 09885

Forum of the Countries of Latin America and the Caribbean on Sustainable Development

Address not obtained.
URL: https://foroalc2030.cepal.org/

History May 2016. Established by resolution 700 (XXXVI), Mexico Resolution, by *United Nations Economic Commission for Latin America and the Caribbean (ECLAC, #20556)*, at its 36th session. **Aims** Function as the regional mechanism to follow up and review the implementation of the 2030 Agenda for Sustainable Development, including the Sustainable Development Goals and targets, and its means of implementation, including the Addis Ababa Action Agenda adopted at the Third International Conference on Financing for Development. **Events** *Meeting* 2021, *Meeting* Santiago (Chile) 2019, *Meeting* Santiago (Chile) 2018, *Meeting* Mexico City (Mexico) 2017. [2021/AA2094/c/**F**]

♦ Foro Parlamentario sobre Armas Pequeñas y Ligeras (#18218)
♦ Foro Permanente para las Cuestiones Indigenas (#20609)

♦ Foro Permanente de Tiempo Libre y Recreación 09886

Permanent Forum for Leisure and recreation

Secretariat Centro Recreandonos, José Llupes 4551, 11900 Montevideo, Uruguay. T. +59823063075. Fax +59823054397. E-mail: recreandonosr@hotmail.com.
URL: http://forotiempolibre.blogspot.com/

History 20 Oct 1995, Montevideo (Uruguay). **Events** *Congreso internacional sobre juego, recreacion y tiempo libre* Montevideo (Uruguay) 2005. [2018/XJ4415/**F**]

♦ Foro de Presidentes de Poderes Legislativos de Centroamérica / see Foro de presidentes y presidentas de Poderes Legislativos de Centroamérica y el Caribe (#09887)
♦ Foro de Presidentes de Poderes Legislativos de Centroamérica y Otros Organismos Conexos / see Foro de presidentes y presidentas de Poderes Legislativos de Centroamérica y el Caribe (#09887)

♦ Foro de presidentes y presidentas de Poderes Legislativos de Centroamérica y el Caribe (FOPREL) 09887

Exec Sec address not obtained. E-mail: info@foprel.org.ni – comunicacion@foprel.org.ni.
URL: https://foprel.digital/

History 26 Aug 1994, Managua (Nicaragua). Former names and other names: *Foro de Presidentes de Poderes Legislativos de Centroamérica y Otros Organismos Conexos* – former (Aug 1994 to May 2001); *Foro de Presidentes de Poderes Legislativos de Centroamérica (FOPREL)* – former (May 2001); *Forum of Presidents of Legislative Authorities of Central America* – former (May 2001). **Aims** Promote the legislative integration of Central American countries through the development of parliamentary institutions and the harmonization of laws; accelerate the creation of integration mechanisms. **Structure** Advisory Council; Parliamentary Committees; Permanent Secretariat. Permanent auxiliary body: *Instituto Internacional de Estudios Legislativos del FOPREL (IIEL-FOPREL, #11338).* **Finance** Sources: contributions of member/participating states. **Activities** Awards/prizes/competitions. **Events** *Forum* El Salvador 2001, *Forum* Honduras 1999, *Forum* San José (Costa Rica) 1999, *Forum* Managua (Nicaragua) 1998, *Forum* San José (Costa Rica) 1997. **Publications** *Plenario Centroamericano* (4 a year) in Spanish.
Members Member countries and territories (10):
Belize, Costa Rica, Dominican Rep, El Salvador, Guatemala, Honduras, Mexico, Nicaragua, Panama, Puerto Rico.
IGO Relations Memorandum of Understanding with (1): *OAS (#17629).* **NGO Relations** *Red de Información Legislativa para América Central y el Caribe (RILCA, no recent information).* [2022/XF5660/**F***]

♦ Foro para el Progreso y Desarrollo de América del Sur (PROSUR) .. 09888

Forum for the Progress and Development of South America (FPDSA) – Fórum para o Progresso e Desenvolvimento da América do Sul (PROSUL)

Address not obtained.

History Initiative proposed 14 Jan 2019, by presidents of Chile and Colombia, as an integration body to replace *Union of South American Nations (#20481).* Santiago Declaration signed 22 Mar 2019. **Aims** Renew and strengthen regional integration.
Members Governments (8):
Argentina, Brazil, Chile, Colombia, Ecuador, Guyana, Paraguay, Peru. [2020/XM8984/**F***]

♦ Foro Social Mundial de las Economias Transformadoras (meeting series)

♦ Foro Social Pan-Amazônico (FSPA) 09889

Pan-Amazonic Social Forum – Fórum Social Pan-Amazônico

Address not obtained.

Events *Forum* Santarem (Brazil) 2010, *Another Amazon is possible, diversity, sovereignty and peace* Manaus (Brazil) 2005, *Forum* Ciudad Guayana (Venezuela) / Guayana (Venezuela) 2004, *Forum* Belém (Brazil) 2003, *Forum* Belém (Brazil) 2002. **NGO Relations** Observer to: *World Social Forum (WSF, #21797).*

[2009/XJ4233/**F**]

♦ Foro Técnico IIRSA (inactive)
♦ Foro del Tercer Mundo (#20149)
♦ Foro Urbano Internacional (internationally oriented national body)
♦ forRefugees (unconfirmed)
♦ FoRS – Ceske Fórum pro Rozvojovou Spolupraci (internationally oriented national body)
♦ Forschungs- und Dokumentationszentrum für Kriegsverbrecherprozesse (internationally oriented national body)
♦ Forschungsgesellschaft für das Weltflüchtlingsproblem (#02942)
♦ Forschungsinstitut für biologischen Landbau (#18857)
♦ Forschungsinstitut für Europafragen der Wirtschaftsuniversität Vienna / see Europe Institute, Vienna
♦ Forschungsinstitut für Fragen des Donauraumes / see Institut für den Donauraum und Mitteleuropa
♦ Forschungsinstitut für Friedenspolitik, Weilheim (internationally oriented national body)
♦ Forschungsinstitut für Internationale Politik und Sicherheit / see Stiftung Wissenschaft und Politik
♦ Forschungsinstitut für Spiritualität und Gesundheit (internationally oriented national body)
♦ Forschungsinstitut für Verbands- und Genossenschafts-Management (internationally oriented national body)
♦ Forschungskooperation "Europäische Kulturen in der Wirtschaftskommunikation" / see Europäische Kulturen in der Wirtschaftskommunikation (#05754)
♦ Forschungsschwerpunkt Entwicklungssoziologie / see Transnationalisation and Development Research Centre, Bielefeld
♦ Forschungsstätte der Evangelischen Studiengemeinschaft (internationally oriented national body)
♦ Forschungsstelle für Internationale Agrarentwicklung, Heidelberg / see Forschungsstelle für Internationale Agrar- und Wirtschaftsentwicklung, Heidelberg
♦ Forschungsstelle für Internationale Agrar- und Wirtschaftsentwicklung, Heidelberg (internationally oriented national body)
♦ Forschungsstelle Kriege, Rustung und Entwicklung (internationally oriented national body)
♦ Forschungsstelle Osteuropa (internationally oriented national body)

- Forschungsstelle für Sicherheitspolitik und Konfliktanalyse / see Center for Security Studies
- Forschungs- und Studienzentrum für Agrar- und Forstwissenschaften der Tropen und Subtropen (internationally oriented national body)
- Forschungszentrum Kriege, Rustung und Entwicklung / see Forschungsstelle Kriege, Rustung und Entwicklung
- Forskningspolitiska Institutet, Lund (internationally oriented national body)
- Fort van de Democratie / Fortress of Democracy / see Stichting Vredeseducatie
- **FORTE** Federation of Orthopaedic Trainees in Europe (#09699)
- Fortress Study Group (internationally oriented national body)

♦ Forum 18 09890

Contact Postboks 6603, Rodeløkka, 0502 Oslo, Norway. E-mail: f18news@editor.forum18.org.
URL: https://www.forum18.org/

History Registration: Danish Tax Authority, No/ID: 34929998, Denmark. **Aims** Work for freedom of religion or belief for all on the basis of the Article 18 of the Universal Declaration of Human Rights. **Structure** Board. **Publications** *Forum 18 News Service.*
Members Full in 3 countries:
Denmark, Norway, Sweden. [2022.05.04/AA1911/F]

- Forum Académique Permanent ALC-UE (#09874)
- Forum sur l'Administration Fiscale Africaine (#00479)

♦ Forum of the Adriatic and Ionian Chambers of Commerce (AIC FORUM) 09891

Secretariat c/o Ancona Chamber of Commerce, Piazza XXIV Maggio 1, 60124 Ancona AN, Italy. T. +39715898249 – +39715898266. E-mail: segreteria.forum@an.camcom.it.
URL: http://www.forumaic.org/

History 2001. Founded as a non-profit and transnational association. **Aims** Strengthen the synergies and opportunities for *socio-economic development* of the Adriatic and Ionian area; establish and develop economic, environmental and cultural integration among the Chamber bodies of Adriatic and Ionian Sea area; provide contribution to European integration through the development of the entrepreneurial spirit and support to small and medium enterprises; foster debate on topics such as Sustainable Tourism, Circular Economy, Creative and Cultural Industries, and Energy Efficiency. **Structure** Board of Governors; Secretary-General. **Languages** Croatian, English, Italian. **Staff** 1.00 FTE, paid. **Finance** Sources: members' dues. **Activities** Awareness raising; events/meetings; networking/liaising. **Events** *Congress of Women's Entrepreneurship of the Adriatic and Ionian Area* Pescara (Italy) 2022, *Forum of the Adriatic and Ionian Chambers of Commerce, Cities and Universities* Budva (Montenegro) 2019, *Forum of the Adriatic and Ionian Chambers of Commerce, Cities and Universities* Split (Croatia) 2018, *Forum* Pescara (Italy) / Chieti (Italy) 2017, *Forum* Ancona (Italy) 2016. **Publications** *AIC FORUM Newsletter.*
Members Full (37) in 8 countries:
Albania, Bosnia-Herzegovina, Croatia, Greece, Italy, Montenegro, Serbia, Slovenia.
NGO Relations Member of (1): *Association des chambres de commerce et d'industrie européennes (EUROCHAMBRES, #02423).* [2023.02.20/XJ6164/F]

♦ Forum of Adriatic and Ionian Cities (FAIC) 09892

Forum delle Città dell'Adriatico e dello Ionio

SG c/o Ancona Municipality, Piazza XXIV Maggio 1, 60123 Ancona AN, Italy. T. +39712222401 – +39712222484 – +39712222487. Fax +39712222495. E-mail: faic@comune.ancona.it.
URL: http://www.faic.eu/

History 1999, Ancona (Italy), as *Forum of Adriatic and Ionian Cities and Towns.* **Aims** Strengthen and develop the economic, social, environmental and cultural heritage of Adriatic and Ionian cities; collaborate on European integration and enlargement. **Structure** Assembly of Members; Governing Board. **Languages** English, Italian. **Staff** 4.00 FTE, paid. **Finance** Municipality of Ancona and other member cities. **Activities** Events/meetings; training/education. **Events** *Plenary Session* Pescara (Italy) / Chieti (Italy) 2017, *Plenary Session* Kotor (Montenegro) 2015, *Plenary Session* Pescara (Italy) 2014, *Plenary Session* Brindisi (Italy) 2013.
Members Towns and cities in 8 countries:
Albania, Bosnia-Herzegovina, Croatia, Greece, Italy, Montenegro, Serbia, Slovenia.
IGO Relations *Adriatic and Ionian Initiative (AII, #00121); European Union (EU, #08967).* **NGO Relations** Partner of: *Conference of European Cross-border and Interregional Cities Network (CECICN, #04595).* Collaborates with: *Conference of Peripheral Maritime Regions of Europe (CPMR, #04638); Forum of the Adriatic and Ionian Chambers of Commerce (AIC FORUM, #09891); Virtual University of the Adriatic-Ionic Basin (UniAdrion, #20792).* [2018.09.05/XJ2079/F]

- Forum of Adriatic and Ionian Cities and Towns / see Forum of Adriatic and Ionian Cities (#09892)
- Forum des aéroports régionaux européens (#09912)
- Forum Africain de la Concurrence (#00260)
- Forum Africain contra la peine de mort (internationally oriented national body)
- Forum africain pour la réglementation des services publics (#00324)
- Forum africain pour la sécurité urbaine (#00323)

♦ Forum for African Archaeology and Cultural Heritage 09893

Address not obtained.

History 1992, Rome (Italy). **Aims** Promote the exchange of knowledge among scholars in the field of archaeology and *anthropology.* **Structure** President; Permanent Secretary; Executive Committee; Counsellor. **Activities** Organizes workshops. **Events** *Cultural heritage management and field-training in Africa* Rome (Italy) 1998. **Publications** *Forum for African Archaeology and Cultural Heritage Newsletter* (annual). *Dynamics of Populations, Movements and Responses to Climatic Change in Africa* (1997) by B E Barich and H C Gatto.
Members Individuals (92) in 24 countries:
Austria, Belgium, Cameroon, Canada, Chad, Egypt, Ethiopia, France, Gabon, Germany, Ghana, Italy, Kenya, Mali, Morocco, Niger, Norway, Poland, Senegal, South Africa, Sweden, Tunisia, USA, Zimbabwe. [2008/XF4308/v/F]

♦ Forum of African Investigative Reporters (FAIR) 09894

Main Office 4th Floor, Mentone Media Centre, 1 Park Road, Richmond, Johannesburg, 2092, South Africa. T. +27114828493. Fax +27114827208.
URL: https://fairreporters.wordpress.com/

Aims Promote the interests of African investigative journalists in the written, visual or broadcast media; foster solidarity, excellence and cooperation among African investigative journalists; provide a forum for the dissemination of information useful to African investigative journalists. **Structure** General Meeting (annual). Board (meets 4 times a year). Executive Committee, comprising Chairperson, Deputy Chairperson and Secretary-Treasurer. **Activities** Sub-Committees (6): Defence of Media Freedom and Access to Information; Education and Training; Ethics and Professional Standards; Fund Raising; Legal Issues; Membership and Membership Services. **NGO Relations** Member of: *Global Investigative Journalism Network (GIJN, #10433).* [2013/XM1821/F]

- Forum for African Medical Editors (unconfirmed)
- Fórum Africano das Administrações Tributárias (#00479)

♦ Forum of African Parliamentarians for Education (FAPED) 09895

Contact UNESCO Dakar Regional Bureau for Education, Route de Ngor, Enceinte Hotel Ngor Diarama, BP 3311, Dakar, Senegal. T. +221338649600.

History 17 Oct 2001, Paris (France). Constitutive Conference organized 2002, Dar es Salaam (Tanzania UR). **Aims** Promote Education for All (EFA). **Events** *Session* Port Louis (Mauritius) 2011, *Session / Forum* Dakar (Senegal) 2009, *Southern African regional meeting* Mangochi (Malawi) 2006, *Southern African regional meeting* Livingstone (Zambia) 2005, *Southern African regional meeting* Windhoek (Namibia) 2004. **IGO Relations** *UNESCO (#20322).* [2009/XF6591/F*]

♦ Forum for African Women Educationalists (FAWE) 09896

Forum des éducatrices africaines (FEA)

Exec Dir PO Box 21394-00505, Ngong Road, Nairobi, Kenya. T. +254714606629 – +25473638700. Fax +2543874150. E-mail: fawe@fawe.org.
Street Address c/o FAWE House, Chania Avenue, Off Wood Avenue, Kilimani, Nairobi, Kenya.
URL: http://www.fawe.org/

History 1992. Registration: Start date: 25 Jun 1993, Kenya. **Aims** Work at all levels to reinforce policies and practices that promote gender equity in access, retention and quality, within the context of achieving education for all – a human right and development necessity; encourage governments to pay attention to factors constraining the access, survival and achievement of girls in education; act as a think tank and pressure group to effect positive changes in female education in Africa; improve the quality of basic education to benefit more girls; provide a forum for continual debate on girls' education; highlight priorities and build consensus around such priorities; document and disseminate information on innovative strategies and encourage their replication; build essential links between educational research, policy, planning and implementation. **Structure** General Assembly (every 3 years). Executive Committee; Secretariat. National chapters (34). **Languages** English, French. **Staff** 10.00 FTE, paid.
Finance Supported by:
- *Africa Network Campaign on Education for All (ANCEFA, #00302);*
- *African Academy of Sciences (AAS, #00193);*
- *Aga Khan Foundation (AKF, #00545);*
- *Association for the Development of Education in Africa (ADEA, #02471)* Secretariat;
- *Canadian International Development Agency (CIDA, inactive);*
- *Carnegie Corporation of New York;*
- *DANIDA;*
- *David and Lucile Packard Foundation;*
- *Department for International Development (DFID, inactive);*
- *Deutsche Gesellschaft für Internationale Zusammenarbeit (GIZ);*
- *Ford Foundation (#09858);*
- *International Bank for Reconstruction and Development (IBRD, #12317);*
- *International Development Research Centre (IDRC, #13162);*
- *Islamic Development Bank (IsDB, #16044);*
- National Foreign Ministries (Netherlands, Finland, Ireland);
- National organizations;
- *Norwegian Agency for Development Cooperation (Norad);*
- *The Rockefeller Foundation (#18966);*
- *Swedish International Development Cooperation Agency (Sida);*
- *UNESCO (#20322);*
- *UNICEF (#20332);*
- *The United Methodist Church (UMC, #20514);*
- *United Nations Girls' Education Initiative (UNGEI, #20566);*
- *United Nations Population Fund (UNFPA, #20612);*
- *United States Agency for International Development (USAID);*
- *Women Thrive Alliance.*

Activities Advocacy/lobbying/activism; awards/prizes/competitions; knowledge management/information dissemination. **Events** *General Assembly* Lusaka (Zambia) 2017, *General Assembly* Nairobi (Kenya) 2014, *General Assembly* Nairobi (Kenya) 2011, *General Assembly* Nairobi (Kenya) 2008, *General assembly* Nairobi (Kenya) 2005. **Publications** *FAWE Newsletter* in English, French. *Girls Education Series.* Annual Reports; handbooks; books; surveys; press releases; behavioral change communication posters; information education communication materials; audiovisual material.
Members National chapters in 32 countries:
Benin, Burkina Faso, Burundi, Cameroon, Chad, Comoros, Congo DR, Eswatini, Ethiopia, Gabon, Gambia, Ghana, Guinea, Kenya, Liberia, Madagascar, Malawi, Mali, Mozambique, Namibia, Nigeria, Rwanda, Senegal, Seychelles, Sierra Leone, Somalia, Sudan, Tanzania UR, Togo, Uganda, Zambia, Zimbabwe.
Consultative Status Consultative status granted from: *UNESCO (#20322)* (Associate Status); *United Nations Population Fund (UNFPA, #20612).* **IGO Relations** Key partner of: *United Nations Girls' Education Initiative (UNGEI, #20566).* **NGO Relations** Member of: *Girls not Brides (#10154); Next Einstein Forum (NEF, #17098); NGO-UNESCO Liaison Committee (#17127).* Support from: *Charities Aid Foundation of America (CAF America).* Partnership with: *African Women's Development and Communication Network (FEMNET, #00503).* Collaborates with: *Higher Education for Development Cooperation (HEDCO); Institute of Development Studies, Brighton (IDS).* Memorandum of Understanding with: *Global e-Schools and Communities Initiative (GESCI); International Day of the African Child and Youth (IDAY, #13140).* [2021/XF2578/F]

- Forum Afrika (internationally oriented national body)
- Forum der Agraringenieur-Verbände Europas (inactive)

♦ Forum for Agricultural Research in Africa (FARA) 09897

Exec Dir 7 Flower Avenue, Mile 7, New Achimota, PMB CT173, Accra, Ghana. T. +233302744888. E-mail: info@faraafrica.org – babugri@faraafrica.org.
URL: http://faraafrica.org/

History Evolving out of *Special Programme for African Agricultural Research (SPAAR, inactive),* set up in 1985. Formally founded, Apr 2001, by *Association for Strengthening Agricultural Research in Eastern and Central Africa (ASARECA, #02933), West and Central African Council for Agricultural Research and Development (WECARD, #20907)* and *Southern African Centre for Cooperation in Agricultural Research and Training (SACCAR, inactive).* Formally launched at General Assembly, July 2002, Maputo (Mozambique). Serves as technical arm of *African Union (AU, #00488)* on matters concerning agriculture science, technology and innovation. **Aims** Create broad-based improvements in agricultural productivity, competitiveness and markets by supporting Africa's sub-regional organizations in strengthening capacity for agricultural innovation. **Structure** General Assembly (every 3 years); Board of Directors. Secretariat, headed by Executive Director. **Languages** English, French. **Staff** 25 recruited internationally; 9 recruited regionally; 32 recruited locally. **Finance** Funding from: *African Development Bank (ADB, #00283); Canadian International Development Agency (CIDA, inactive); CGIAR System Organization (CGIAR, #03843); Department for International Development (DFID, inactive); European Commission (EC, #06633); International Bank for Reconstruction and Development (IBRD, #12317)* (World Bank); *United States Agency for International Development (USAID);* governments of Denmark, France, Germany, Ireland, Netherlands and Norway. Annual budget: 2,200,000 USD. **Activities** Projects/programmes. **Events** *Science and Partnerships for Agriculture Conference* Accra (Ghana) 2022, *General Assembly* Ouagadougou (Burkina Faso) 2010, *African agricultural science week* Johannesburg (South Africa) 2007, *Conference on capacity strengthening, information exchange, learning and foresight for agricultural innovation* Johannesburg (South Africa) 2007, *General Assembly* Johannesburg (South Africa) 2007. **Publications** *FARA Bulletin* (12 a year); *FARA Quarterly Newsletter.* Annual Report; project documents; peer reviewed publications. **Members** Founding members and other North African Sub-Regional Organizations. Core; Ordinary; Investor; Honorary. Membership countries not specified. **IGO Relations** Technical arm of: *New Partnership for Africa's Development (NEPAD, #17091).* Partner of: *African Union (AU, #00488); Centre for Coordination of Agricultural Research and Development for Southern Africa (CCARDESA, #03736);* CGIAR centres; *Southern African Development Community (SADC, #19843)* – Directorate of Food, Agriculture and Natural Resources (FANR); *West African Science Service Center on Climate Change and Adapted Land Use (WASCAL, #20897).* Supports: *International Crops Research Institute for the Semi-Arid Tropics (ICRISAT, #13116).* **NGO Relations** Member of: *Global Forum on Agricultural Research (GFAR, #10370).* Cooperates with: *African Technology Policy Studies Network (ATPS, #00481); Association for Strengthening Agricultural Research in Eastern and Central Africa (ASARECA, #02933); International Centre for Tropical Agriculture (#12527); International Fertilizer Development Center (IFDC, #13590); West and Central African Council for Agricultural Research and Development (WECARD, #20907).* Partner in: *Platform for African – European Partnership on Agricultural Research for Development (PAEPARD, #18398).* Supports: *International Institute of Tropical Agriculture (IITA, #13933).* Works with: *Young Professionals for Agricultural Development (YPARD, #21996).* [2022.10.27/XF4296/F]

- Forum alternatives européennes (internationally oriented national body)
- Forum for the Americas on Agricultural Research and Technological Development (#09875)

♦ Forum of Arctic Research Operators (FARO) 09898

Secretariat c/o Bioscience Dept, Aarhus University, PO Box 358, 4000 Roskilde, Denmark. E-mail: faro-arctic@bios.au.dk.
URL: http://www.faro-arctic.org/

History Aug 1998. **Aims** Facilitate and optimize logistics and operational support for scientific research in the Arctic; encourage international collaboration in Arctic research. **Structure** Executive Committee. **Activities** Organizes annual meeting during Arctic Science Summit Week (ASSW). **Events** *Annual Arctic Science Summit* Arkhangelsk (Russia) 2019, *Annual Meeting* Arkhangelsk (Russia) 2019, *Annual Arctic Science Summit* Davos (Switzerland) 2018, *Annual Arctic Science Summit* Prague (Czechia) 2017, *ISAR : International Symposium on the Arctic Research* Prague (Czechia) 2017.
Members in 17 countries and territories:
Canada, China, Finland, France, Germany, Greenland, Iceland, Italy, Japan, Korea Rep, Netherlands, Norway, Poland, Russia, Sweden, UK, USA. [2014/XM2344/F]

♦ Forum of Armenian Associations of Europe (FAAE) 09899

Forum des associations arméniennes d'Europe – Forum Armenischer Vereinigungen in Europa
Pres Krajna 86, 821 04 Bratislava, Slovakia. E-mail: faae@faaeurope.eu.
URL: http://www.faaeurope.eu/

History 19 Jul 1998, Geneva (Switzerland), on the initiative of Toros Sagherian. Registered in accordance with Swiss law. **Aims** Increase cooperation among Armenian organizations throughout Europe. **Structure** General Assembly (annual); Executive Committee. **Languages** Armenian, English, Russian, Slovakian. **Events** *Annual Conference* Venice (Italy) 2003, *Annual Conference* Uppsala (Sweden) 2002, *Annual Conference* Bonn (Germany) 2001, *Annual Conference* Budapest (Hungary) 2000.
Members Organizations in 17 countries:
Belarus, Belgium, Bulgaria, Estonia, France, Germany, Hungary, Italy, Latvia, Lithuania, Moldova, Netherlands, Romania, Russia, Sweden, Switzerland, UK. [2018.09.12/XF6264/F]

♦ Forum Armenischer Vereinigungen in Europa (#09899)
♦ **FORUM-ASIA** Asian Forum for Human Rights and Development (#01491)

♦ Forum Asia Democracy (FAD) 09900

Forum Asie démocratie
Contact address not obtained. T. +33145983085. Fax +33145983261.

History Jul 2001. **Aims** Promote freedom, democracy and the rule of law in Asia. **NGO Relations** Instrumental in setting up: *World Forum for Democratization in Asia (WFDA, #21515).* [2008/XM1152/F]

♦ Forum of AsianPacific Graphic Arts Technology (FAGAT) 09901

Contact c/o JAGAT, 1-29-11 Wada, Suginami-ku, Tokyo, 166-8539 Japan. T. +81333843111. Fax +81333843481.
URL: http://www.jagat.or.jp/asia/

Aims Facilitate exchange of *printing* technology; promote progress in the printing industry in *Asian* countries through development of cooperative relationships, with a view to internationalization. **Events** *Forum* Sydney, NSW (Australia) 2011, *Forum* Beijing (China) 2007, *Forum* Sri Lanka 2006, *Forum* Kuala Lumpur (Malaysia) 2004, *Forum* Singapore (Singapore) 2002.
Members Full in 9 countries:
Australia, China, Japan, Korea Rep, Malaysia, Philippines, Singapore, Sri Lanka, Thailand. [2011/XJ4844/F]

♦ Forum of Asian Theological Librarians (ForATL) 09902

Convenor 119 Ilocos Sur St, Bago Bantay, Quezon City, Manila, Philippines.
Sec Jakarta Theological Seminary, Jl Proklamasi No 27, Jakarta 10320, Indonesia. T. +62213904237. Fax +62213906096. E-mail: hildakorpala@yahoo.com.
URL: http://www.foratl.org/

History Founded 25 May 1991, Chiang Mai (Thailand), during the Consultation of Asian Theological Librarians organized by *Programme for Theology and Cultures in Asia (PTCA, inactive).* **Aims** Facilitate development and exchange of resources for *theology* in the Asian context; encourage and support formation of national theological library associations or networks, national depositories of Christian literature and union listings, directory of Asian theological libraries, guidelines, indexes, bibliographies etc for publication; promote cooperation among, and training of, theological librarians; develop an Asia-wide network of theological libraries. **Structure** Executive Committee; Area Representatives; Task Forces. **Languages** English. **Staff** Voluntary. **Finance** Funds from ecumenical partner organizations. **Activities** Training/education; events/meetings. **Events** *Indonesia cantik – innovation and transformation in Asian theological libraries* Jakarta (Indonesia) 2018, *Speed of change – Asian theological librarians in rapid transition* Bangkok (Thailand) 2015, *Workshop / Consultation of Asian Theological Librarians* Manila (Philippines) 2012, *Workshop / Consultation of Asian Theological Librarians* Singapore (Singapore) 2009, *Workshop / Consultation of Asian Theological Librarians* Seremban (Malaysia) 2006. **Publications** *ForATL News* (2 a year). *Directory of Asian Theological Libraries (DATL) and Who's Who in DATL* (2nd ed 2002). Information Services: Internet Database of Asian Journals.
Members Individuals (50) in 17 countries and territories:
Australia, China, Hong Kong, India, Indonesia, Korea Rep, Malaysia, Myanmar, Nepal, New Zealand, Philippines, Singapore, Sri Lanka, Taiwan, Thailand, Tonga, Vanuatu. [2017.10.25/XF6247/v/F]

♦ Forum asiatique sur les droits humains et le développement (#01491)
♦ Forum asiatique pour la liturgie (#01530)
♦ Forum Asie démocratie (#09900)
♦ Forum des associations arméniennes d'Europe (#09899)
♦ Forum Atomique Européen / see nucleareurope (#17616)
♦ Forum for Automobile and Society / see Forum for Mobility and Society (#09924)
♦ Forum des autorités locales pour l'inclusion sociale et la démocratie participative (#09876)
♦ Forum of Bible Agencies / see Forum of Bible Agencies International (#09903)

♦ Forum of Bible Agencies International 09903

Contact Church St Station, PO Box 2457, New York NY 10008, USA. E-mail: info@forum-intl.net.
URL: http://www.ifoba.org/

History 1990, Horsleys Green (UK), as an informal network. Previously referred to as *Forum of Bible Agencies (FBA)* and *International Forum of Bible Agencies.* **Aims** Cooperate to maximize worldwide access and impact of God's word. **Structure** Associate. **Staff** 1.00 FTE, paid. **Events** *Annual Meeting* Albuquerque, NM (USA) 2019, *Annual Meeting* Washington, DC (USA) 2018, *Annual Meeting* Jerusalem (Israel) 2017.
Members Organizations and agencies (25), including the following 18 organizations listed in this Yearbook:
Audio Scripture Ministries; Ethnos360; Every Home for Christ International (EHCI, #09214); Global Recordings Network (GRN) (Australia); Institute for Bible Translation; Lutheran Bible Translators (LBT); OneHope; Open Doors International (#17749); Pioneer Bible Translators (PBT); Scripture Union International Council (#19161); SGM Lifewords; SIM International; Talking Bibles International; Trans World Radio (TWR); United Bible Societies (UBS, #20498); Word for the World, The (TWFTW International, #21048); World Mission; Wycliffe Bible Translators International (WBT International). [2016/XG3560/y/F]

♦ FORUMBrussels International (unconfirmed)
♦ Forum on Business and Social Responsibility in the Americas (internationally oriented national body)
♦ Forum des caisses d'épargne postales (see: #21764)
♦ Forum des Caraïbes (#09904)

♦ Forum of Caribbean States (CARIFORUM) 09904

Forum des Caraïbes
SG c/o CARICOM Secretariat, Turkeyen, Georgetown, Guyana. T. +5922220001. Fax +5922220172. E-mail: cariforum@caricom.org.
Contact c/o ACP Group, Avenue Georges Henri 451, 1200 Brussels, Belgium. T. +3227430600. Fax +3227355573.

History 19 Oct 1992. Established to group states of *Organisation of African, Caribbean and Pacific States (OACPS, #17796)* in the Caribbean region under the terms of the *Fourth ACP-EEC Convention (Lomé IV, 1989).* Former names and other names: *Caribbean Forum of ACP States* – alias; *Caribbean Forum* – alias. **Aims** Programme and coordinate the allocation and monitoring of available European Development Fund resources for the purpose of financial regional projects in the Caribbean region, which fall within the framework of the Lomé (Togo) IV Convention and the Cotonou (Benin) Agreement. **Structure** Council of Ministers (meets annually). Secretariat, comprising Secretary-General and Programming Unit. Programme Policy Boards or Executive Committees; Implementing Agencies. **Finance** Total value of regional programmes financed by EDF: about euro 300 million. **Activities** Politics/policy/regulatory. **Events** *Joint meeting* 2003, *Ministers meeting* 2003, *FIU supervisor's symposium* Antigua-Barbuda 2003, *Special meeting of ministers* Barbados 2003, *Regional conference on national umbrella organisation* Belize 2003. **Publications** *CARIFORUM – Cultural Review of the Caribbean* in English, French, Spanish.
Members Governments of 16 Caribbean states and territories:
Antigua-Barbuda, Bahamas, Barbados, Belize, Cuba, Dominica, Dominican Rep, Grenada, Guyana, Haiti, Jamaica, St Kitts-Nevis, St Lucia, St Vincent-Grenadines, Suriname, Trinidad-Tobago.
IGO Relations Develops programmes under *European Development Fund (EDF, #06914).* Relevant treaty: *ACP-EU Partnership Agreement (Cotonou agreement, 2000).* Special links with: *Caribbean Community (CARICOM, #03476).* Instrumental in setting up: *Caribbean Export Development Agency (Caribbean Export, #03501); Caribbean Regional Information and Translation Institute (CRITI, #03548).* [2008/XF4117/F*]

♦ Forum of Catholic Inspired NGOs 09905

Secretariat Piazza Can Calisto 16, 00153 Rome RM, Italy. E-mail: forum@foruminternational.org.
URL: https://foruminternational.org/

History Founded 2007. **Aims** Develop its role as a social observatory and offer a space for analysis, reflection and exchange of expertise so as to strengthen the Catholic voice in the public debate and in its advocacy before intergovernmental bodies specifically. **Structure** Forum; Secretariat.
Members Organizations (103):
– *ADF International (#00112);*
– *Africa-Europe Faith and Justice Network (AEFJN, #00171);*
– *Aid to the Church in Need (#00587);*
– *Apostolat Militaire International (AMI);*
– *Association Catholique Internationale de Services pour la Jeunesse Féminine (ACISJF/In Via, #02417);*
– *Association Internationale des Charités (AIC, #02675);*
– *Association Points-Coeur (#02863);*
– *Associazione Comunità Papa Giovanni;*
– *AVSI Foundation;*
– *Caritas Internationalis (CI, #03580);*
– *Caritas in Veritate Foundation (#03582);*
– *Catholic International Education Office (#03604);*
– *Catholic Relief Services (CRS, #03608);*
– *Catholic Youth Network for Environmental Sustainability in Africa (CYNESA, #03611);*
– *Center for Family and Human Rights (C-Fam);*
– *Christian Life Community (CLC, #03905);*
– *CIDSE (CIDSE, #03926);*
– *Comité Européen pour l'Enseignement Catholique (CEEC, #04156);*
– *Community of Sant'Egidio;*
– *Company of the Daughters of Charity of St Vincent de Paul (DC);*
– *Congregation of the Mission (Vincentians);*
– *Congregations of St Joseph (CSJs, #04673);*
– *Crescendo Worldwide Network (#04950);*
– Dominican Leadership Conference;
– *Dominicans for Justice and Peace (OP, #05113);*
– *Don Bosco International (DBI, #05117);*
– *Edmund Rice International (ERI, #05362);*
– *European Centre for Law and Justice (ECLJ);*
– *Federation of Catholic Family Associations in Europe (#09468);*
– *Femina Europa;*
– *FONDACIO (#09812);*
– *Fondation internationale pour le développement au service des coopérants et de communautés de base (FIDESCO, #09821);*
– *Fondazione Marista per la Solidarietà Internazionale Onlus (#09831);*
– *Fondazione Novae Terrae;*
– *Fracarita International (#09979);*
– Frente Nacional por la Familia;
– Fundación Inclueyndo México;
– *Fundación Promoción Social;*
– *HOSPITALITY EUROPE (#10947);*
– *Institut de la Bienheureuse Vierge Marie (Dames Anglaises);*
– *Instituto Politica Familiar Federación Internacional (IPF);*
– *International Catholic Child Bureau (#12450);*
– *International Catholic Committee of Nurses and Medico-social Assistants (#12451);*
– *International Catholic Cooperation Centre for UNESCO (CCIC, #12454);*
– *International Catholic Migration Commission (ICMC, #12459);*
– *International Catholic Rural Association (ICRA, #12461);*
– *International Center of Law, Life, Faith and Family (ICOLF);*
– *International Christian Union of Business Executives (#12566);*
– *International Commission of Catholic Prison Pastoral Care (ICCPPC, #12670);*
– *International Confederation of the Society of St Vincent-de-Paul (#12870);*
– *International Coordination of Young Christian Workers (ICYCW, #12960);*
– *International Federation of Catholic Medical Associations (#13378);*
– *International Federation of Catholic Parochial Youth Movements (#13379);*
– *International Federation of Catholic Universities (IFCU, #13381);*
– *International Federation of Fe y Alegria (FIFyA, #13425);*
– *International Federation of Rural Adult Catholic Movements (#13535);*
– *International Movement ATD Fourth World (#14193);*
– *International Movement of Apostolate of Children (IMAC, #14192);*
– *International Organization for the Right to Education and Freedom of Education (#14468);*
– *International Solidarity and Human Rights Institute (ISHRI);*
– *International Young Catholic Students (IYCS, #15926);*
– *Istituto Internazionale Maria Ausiliatrice delle Salesiane di Don Bosco (IIMA);*
– *Jesuit European Social Centre (JESC, #16103);*
– *Jesuit Refugee Service (JRS, #16106);*
– *Knights of Columbus (K of C);*
– *KOLPING INTERNATIONAL (#16203);*
– *Laudato Si' Movement (#16403);*
– *MaterCare International (MCI, #16597);*
– *Medical Mission Sisters;*
– *Mediterraneo Senza Handicap;*
– *Mercy International Association (MIA, #16723);*
– *Missionary Oblates of Mary Immaculate (OMI);*
– *Mouvement international d'apostolat des milieux sociaux indépendants (MIAMSI, #16864);*
– *Mouvement international de la jeunesse agricole et rurale catholique (MIJARC, #16865);*
– *New Humanity (#17088);*
– *New Women for Europe (NWFE);*
– *Order of St Augustine (Augustinians International);*
– *Organisation mondiale des anciens élèves de l'enseignement catholique (OMAEC, #17816);*
– *Partnership for Global Justice;*
– *Passionists International (PI, #18254);*
– *Pax Christi – International Catholic Peace Movement (#18266);*
– *Pax Romana, International Movement of Catholic Students (IMCS, #18268);*
– Priests for Life;
– *Religious of the Sacred Heart of Mary (RSHM);*
– Salesian Missions;
– *School Sisters of Notre Dame (SSND);*
– *Society for the Protection of Unborn Children (SPUC);*
– Society of Catholic Social Scientists;
– *Society of Mary (Marianists);*
– *Society of the Sacred Heart of Jesus (St Madeleine-Sophie Barat);*

Forum China Africa
09905

alphabetic sequence excludes
For the complete listing, see Yearbook Online at

– Soeurs de Notre-Dame de Namur (SNDN);
– SOS Chrétiens d'Orient;
– Teresian Association;
– UMEC-WUCT (#20280);
– Union Internationale des Guides et Scouts d'Europe – Fédération du Scoutisme Européen (UIGSE-FSE, #20426);
– UNUM OMNES International Council of Catholic Men (ICCM, #20720);
– Vie montante internationale (VMI, #20769);
– Volontariato Internazionale Donna Educazione Sviluppo (VIDES, #20806);
– World Catholic Association for Communication (SIGNIS, #21264);
– World Movement of Christian Workers (WMCW, #21660);
– World Union of Catholic Women's Organisations (WUCWO, #21876);
– World Youth Alliance (WYA, #21949). [2019/XM8823/y/F]

♦ Forum on China-Africa Cooperation (internationally oriented national body)
♦ Forum delle Città dell'Adriatico e dello Ionio (#09892)
♦ ForumCiv (internationally oriented national body)
♦ Forum Civil Peace Service (internationally oriented national body)
♦ Forum civique européen (#06562)
♦ Forum civique européen (#06563)
♦ Forum des collectivités territoriales européennes pour la sécurité urbaine / see European Forum for Urban Security (#07340)
♦ Forum sur le commerce Canada-Europe (#03410)
♦ Forum on Contemporary Europe, Stanford CA (internationally oriented national body)
♦ Forum sur la coopération sino-africaine (internationally oriented national body)
♦ Forum of the Countries of Latin America and the Caribbean on Sustainable Development (#09885)
♦ Forum de Crans Montana (#04944)

♦ Forum on Debt and Development (FONDAD) 09906
Dir Nieuwendammerdijk 421, 1023 BM Amsterdam, Netherlands. T. +31206371954. Fax +31206371954.
URL: http://www.fondad.org/
History 1987, The Hague (Netherlands). **Aims** Provide factual background information and practical strategies on North-South problems – primarily international financial issues – to policymakers and other interested groups in both industrial and developing countries; stimulate adoption of measures which improve the functioning of the international monetary system and the financing of development. **Structure** Advisory Board, consisting of Chairman and 9 members. **Staff** 2.00 FTE, paid. **Activities** Organizes high-level seminars and conferences. **Events** Conference Kuala Lumpur (Malaysia) 2007, Conference New York, NY (USA) 2006, Conference The Hague (Netherlands) 2006, Conference Amsterdam (Netherlands) 2005, Conference Pretoria (South Africa) 2005. **Publications** Global Imbalances and Developing Countries: Remedies for a Failing International Financial System (2007); Global Imbalances and the US Debt Problem: Should Developing Countries Support the US Dollar ? (2006); Africa in the World Economy: The National, Regional and International Challenges (2005); Protecting the Poor: Global Financial Institutions and the Vulnerability of Low-Income Countries (2005); Helping the Poor: The IMF and Low-Income Countries (2005); HIPC Debt Relief: Myths and Reality (2004); Diversity in Development: Reconsidering the Washington Consensus (2004); China's Role in Asia and the World Economy: Fostering Financial Stability and Growth (2004); Financial Stability and Growth in Emerging Economies: The Role of the Financial Sector (2003); The Crisis that Was Not Prevented: Lessons for Argentina, the IMF and Globalization (2003); A Regional Approach to Financial Crisis Prevention: Lessons from Europe and Initiatives in Asia, Latin America and Africa (2002); Reforming the International Financial System: Crisis Prevention and Response (2001); New Challenges of Crisis Prevention: Addressing Economic Imbalances in the North and Boom Bust Cycles in the South (2001); Management of Global Financial Markets (2000); Private Capital Flows to Africa: Perception and Reality (1999); Regional Integration and Multilateral Cooperation in the Global Economy (1998); Policy Challenges of Global Financial Integration (1998); Regional Integration Arrangements in Economic Development: Panacea or Pitfall ? (1997); Regionalism and the Global Economy: The Case of Central and Eastern Europe (1997); Regionalism and the Global Economy: The Case of Africa (1996); Resolving Africa's Multilateral Debt Problem: A Response to the IMF and the World Bank (1996); Can Currency Crises be Prevented or Better Managed ? Lessons from Mexico (1996); Regionalism and the Global Economy: The Case of Latin America and the Caribbean (1995); Multilateral Development Banks: An Assessment of their Financial Structures, Policies and Practices (1995); Multilateral Debt: An Emerging Crisis ? (1994); The Pursuit of Reform: Global Finance and the Developing Countries (1993); Fragile Finance: Rethinking the International Monetary System (1992); African Debt Revisited: Procrastination or Progress ? (1991). [2013/XF2449/F]

♦ Forum for Development Cooperation with Indigenous Peoples (internationally oriented national body)
♦ Forum for Development and Environment (internationally oriented national body)
♦ Forum sur le développement participatif (internationally oriented national body)
♦ Forum des Directeurs des Services Météorologiques et Hydrologiques de l'Afrique d'Ouest / see Conference of Directors of the West African National Meteorological and Hydrological Services (#04589)
♦ Forum of Directors of the West African National Meteorological and Hydrological Services / see Conference of Directors of the West African National Meteorological and Hydrological Services (#04589)
♦ Forum des dirigeants de la région Asie-Pacifique sur le VIH/sida et le développement (#01942)
♦ Forum delle Donne del Mediterraneo / see International Mediterranean Women's Forum (#14143)

♦ Forum for East Asia-Latin America Cooperation (FEALAC) 09907
Foro de Cooperación América Latina-Asia del Este (FOCALAE)
Secretariat 60 Sajikro 8gil, Jongno-gu, Seoul 03172, Korea Rep. T. +82220018539. Fax +82220018535. E-mail: cybersecretariat@fealac.org – fealac@mofa.go.kr.
URL: http://www.fealac.org/
History Sep 1999, Singapore (Singapore). Proposed Sept, 1998 by Singapore's Prime Minister during official visit to Chile in order to increase cooperation between East Asia and Latin America. Officially launched at first Senior Officials' Meeting. Former names and other names: East Asia-Latin America Forum (EALAF) – former; Foro América Latina-Asia del Este (FALAE) – former. **Aims** Promote better understanding, political dialogue and cooperation so as to achieve more effective and fruitful relations and closer cooperation between the two regions. **Structure** Foreign Ministers' Meetings (every 2 years); Troika Foreign Ministers' Meeting (annual); Senior Officials' Meeting (annual); Coordination Meeting; Working Groups (4). **Languages** English. **Activities** Events/meetings. **Events** Cyber Secretariat Workshop Seoul (Korea Rep) 2020, TROIKA Foreign Ministers Meeting New York, NY (USA) 2019, Business Innovation Forum Santo Domingo (Dominican Rep) 2019, Foreign Ministers Meeting Santo Domingo (Dominican Rep) 2019, Senior Officials Meeting Santo Domingo (Dominican Rep) 2019. **Publications** FEALAC Factsheet in English; FEALAC Guide in English.
Members Member States (36):
Argentina, Australia, Bolivia, Brazil, Brunei Darussalam, Cambodia, Chile, China, Colombia, Costa Rica, Cuba, Dominican Rep, Ecuador, El Salvador, Guatemala, Honduras, Indonesia, Japan, Korea Rep, Laos, Malaysia, Mexico, Mongolia, Myanmar, New Zealand, Nicaragua, Panama, Paraguay, Peru, Philippines, Singapore, Suriname, Thailand, Uruguay, Venezuela, Vietnam.
Including 2 organizations listed in the Yearbook:
United Nations Economic and Social Commission for Asia and the Pacific (ESCAP, #20557); United Nations Economic Commission for Latin America and the Caribbean (ECLAC, #20556). [2020.07.09/XF6279/F*]

♦ Forum économique international des Amériques (internationally oriented national body)
♦ Forum des éducatrices africaines (#09896)
♦ Forum EMPRESA – Forum on Business and Social Responsibility in the Americas (internationally oriented national body)
♦ Forum euroméditerranéen des instituts de sciences économiques / see Femise Network (#09731)
♦ Forum Europa der Kulturen (internationally oriented national body)
♦ Forum for European Electrical Domestic Safety (unconfirmed)
♦ **FORUM** European Forum of Heritage Associations (#07314)
♦ **Forum** European Forum of Official Gazettes (#07325)
♦ Forum of European Freshwater Research Organisations / see European Network of Freshwater Research Organisations (#07911)
♦ Forum of European Highway Research Laboratories / see Forum of European National Highway Research Laboratories (#09910)

♦ Forum for European Journalism Students (FEJS) 09908
Contact Hranilniska ulica 10, 1000 Ljubljana, Slovenia. E-mail: sec@fejsint.org – fejssec@gmail.com.
Main Website: http://www.fejs.info
History 1985. Founded by Danish and Dutch students. Former names and other names: Forum for European Journalism Students international (FEJS International) – alias. Registration: Belgium. **Aims** Create understanding between European journalism students. **Structure** General Assembly (annual); Supervisory Board; Secretariat (rotates every 2 years). **Events** Annual Congress Ljubljana (Slovenia) 2023, Annual Congress Utrecht (Netherlands) 2013, Annual Congress Antwerp (Belgium) 2012, Annual Meeting Matera (Italy) 2011, Annual Meeting Ljubljana (Slovenia) 2010. [2023.03.01/XF4899/F]

♦ Forum for European Journalism Students international / see Forum for European Journalism Students (#09908)
♦ Forum of European Muslim and Youth Organizations / see Forum of European Muslim Youth and Student Organisations (#09909)

♦ Forum of European Muslim Youth and Student Organisations (FEMYSO) 09909
Gen Sec Rue Archimède 50, 1000 Brussels, Belgium. T. +3222806921. Fax +3222806923. E-mail: info@femyso.org.
URL: http://www.femyso.org/
History 1 Sep 1996, Leicester (UK). Former names and other names: Forum of European Muslim and Youth Organizations (FEMYSO) – former. Registration: Belgium. **Aims** Serve as a platform for cooperation for Muslim youth organizations in Europe. **Structure** General Assembly (every 2 years); Executive Committee; Board of Trustees; Office. **Finance** Sources: members' dues. **Activities** Events/meetings; networking/liaising; training/education.
Members Organizations in 21 countries:
Albania, Austria, Belgium, Bosnia-Herzegovina, Czechia, Finland, France, Germany, Hungary, Ireland, Italy, Lithuania, Moldova, North Macedonia, Norway, Poland, Romania, Slovakia, Sweden, UK, Ukraine.
Consultative Status Consultative status granted from: Council of Europe (CE, #04881) (Participatory Status).
IGO Relations Member of: European Youth Centres (EYCs, #09138). **NGO Relations** Member of: European Network against Racism (ENAR, #07862); Islamic Conference Youth Forum for Dialogue and Cooperation (ICYF-DC, #16040); UNITED for Intercultural Action – European Network Against Nationalism, Racism, Fascism and in Support of Migrants and Refugees (UNITED, #20511). Associate member of: European Students' Union (ESU, #08848). [2020.05.07/XF6752/F]

♦ Forum of European National Highway Research Laboratories (FEHRL) 09910
Forum des laboratoires européens de recherche routière
SG Bd de la Woluwe 42, Bte 3-B, 1200 Brussels, Belgium. T. +3227758245. E-mail: info@fehrl.org.
Office Assistant address not obtained.
URL: http://www.fehrl.org/
History 1989. Former names and other names: Forum of European Highway Research Laboratories (FEHRL) – former (1989). Registration: Banque-Carrefour des Entreprises, No/ID: 0472.087.221, Start date: 15 Jun 2000, Belgium. **Aims** Provide scientific input to EU and national government policy on highway engineering and road transport matters; create and maintain an efficient and safe road network in Europe; increase innovation in European road construction and road-using industries; improve energy efficiency of highway engineering and operations; protect the environment and improve quality of life. **Structure** General Assembly (twice a year); Executive Committee; Secretariat, located in Brussels (Belgium). **Languages** English. **Staff** 5.00 FTE, paid. **Finance** Sources: members' dues; revenue from activities/projects. **Activities** Events/meetings; research/documentation. **Events** Infrastructure Research Meeting (FIRM) Brussels (Belgium) 2021, Infrastructure Research Meeting Brussels (Belgium) 2019, Infrastructure Research Meeting Brussels (Belgium) 2017, Workshop Brussels (Belgium) 2016, Infrastructure Research Meeting Brussels (Belgium) 2013. **Publications** FEHRL Newsletter (6 a year); FEHRL Infrastructure Research Magazine (FIRM). Annual Report; reports; papers.
Members Full: national laboratories in 30 countries:
Austria, Belgium, Bulgaria, Croatia, Czechia, Denmark, France, Germany, Greece, Hungary, Ireland, Israel, Italy, Latvia, Lithuania, Luxembourg, Netherlands, Norway, Poland, Portugal, Serbia, Slovakia, Slovenia, Spain, Sweden, Switzerland, Türkiye, UK, Ukraine, USA.
IGO Relations Cooperates with: specialized programme of OECD (#17693). **NGO Relations** Member of (5): European Construction Technology Platform (ECTP, #06768); European Green Vehicles Initiative Association (EGVIA, #07410); European Road Transport Research Advisory Council (ERTRAC, #08396); European Transport Research Alliance (ETRA, #08939); Federation of European and International Associations Established in Belgium (FAIB, #09508). [2022.05.04/XF3269/F]

♦ Forum for European Philosophy (internationally oriented national body)

♦ Forum for European e-Public Services (e-Forum) 09911
Hôte européen pour les services publics (HESPEL)
Pres address not obtained.
URL: http://www.eu-forum.org/
History Founded 2002, Brussels (Belgium). Registered in accordance with Belgian law. **Aims** Improve the use of information and communication technologies within the public services sector; support exchange of best practices in the same field. **Structure** General Meeting (annual). Board of Directors. Executive Committee, comprising President, Secretary, Treasurer and Executive Director. **Languages** English, French. **Staff** 1.00 FTE, paid; 10.00 FTE, voluntary. **Finance** Budget (annual): euro 250,000. **Events** Summit Beijing (China) 2012, Summit Yantai (China) 2012, Summit Beijing (China) 2011, Summit Beijing (China) 2010, Summit Paris (France) 2010.
Members Full in 37 countries (indicates founding members):
Algeria, Austria, Belgium (*), Bulgaria, Burkina Faso, Cape Verde, China, Cyprus, Czechia, Denmark (*), Estonia, Finland, France (*), Georgia, Germany (*), Greece, Hungary, Iceland, Ireland, Italy, Luxembourg (*), Malta, Netherlands, Norway, Poland, Portugal, Romania, Russia, Slovakia, Slovenia, Spain (*), Sweden, Switzerland, Tunisia, Türkiye, UK (*), USA.
IGO Relations Participant in Fundamental Rights Platform of: European Union Agency for Fundamental Rights (FRA, #08969). [2013.06.01/XF6655/F]

♦ Forum of European Regional Airports 09912
Forum des aéroports régionaux européens (FARE)
Contact address not obtained. T. +3226493533. Fax +3226492593.
History 2 Feb 2005, Stansted (UK), following a series of meetings in 2004. **Aims** Represent and promote the interests of European regional airports. **Structure** General Assembly. Executive Committee, comprising Chairman and 4 Vice-Chairmen.
Members Regional airports (33) in 8 countries:
Belgium, Denmark, France, Germany, Italy, Netherlands, Sweden, UK. [2009/XM0664/F]

♦ Forum of European Road Safety Research Institutes (FERSI) 09913
Forum européen des Instituts de Recherche sur la Sécurité Routière
Sec SWOV Inst for Road Safety Research, PO Box 93113, 2509 AC The Hague, Netherlands. T. +31703173352. Fax +31703201261. E-mail: fersi@swov.nl.
Registered Address Chaussée de Haecht 1405, 1130 Brussels, Belgium.
URL: http://www.fersi.org/
History Mar 1991, Copenhagen (Denmark). Registration: Banque-Carrefour des Entreprises, No/ID: 0844.756.172, Start date: 27 Mar 2012, Belgium. **Aims** Promote or coordinate high quality research on road safety issues; consult on implementation of research results; scientifically evaluate implementation outcomes. **Structure** General Assembly (twice a year); Executive Board; Thematic working groups. **Languages** English. **Staff** 0.20 FTE, paid. **Finance** Sources: members' dues. Annual budget: 61,000 EUR. **Activities** Awards/prizes/competitions; events/meetings; knowledge management/information dissemination; networking/liaising; research and development. **Events** Conference The Hague (Netherlands) 2022,

Conference The Hague (Netherlands) 2021, *General Assembly* Madrid (Spain) 2016, *Conference* Bergisch-Gladbach (Germany) 2014, *International Conference on Road Safety on Four Continents* Beijing (China) 2013. **Publications** *E-scooters in Europe: legal status, usage and safety; results of a survey in FERSI countries* (2020) by Kas Kamphuis and Ingrid van Schagen in English; *Safety through automation? Ensuring that automated and connected driving contribute to a safer transportation system* (2020) by Anna Anund and Anders Lindström et al in English; *Guidelines for assessing the prevalence of mobile phone use in traffic* (2019) by M Vollrath and M Schumacher et al in English; *Safety through automation? Ensuring that automated and connected driving contribute to a safer transportation system* (2018) in English; *Country survey: State of the art of MAIS 3+ assessment in the FERSI Member States and EU/EEA countries (2016)* (2016) in English; *Towards safer roads in Europe – Nine key challenges for road safety research for the next decade* (2014) in English; *Uniform approach to classification of injuries – Research and implementation measures* (2014) in English. **Members** National road safety research institutions (one per country) authorized by national government. Members in 22 countries:
Austria, Belgium, Croatia, Czechia, Denmark, Finland, France, Germany, Greece, Hungary, Ireland, Italy, Netherlands, Norway, Poland, Portugal, Russia, Serbia, Slovenia, Spain, Sweden, Switzerland.
IGO Relations Road and Transport Research Programme of: *OECD (#17693)*. **NGO Relations** Member of (1): *European Transport Research Alliance (ETRA, #08939)*. [2022/XF3103/F]

♦ Forum of European Roma and Travellers Young People / see Forum of European Roma Young People (#09914)

♦ Forum of European Roma Young People (FERYP) 09914

Pres 1 rue de l'Ancienne Ecole, 67100 Strasbourg, France. E-mail: info@feryp.org.
Facebook: https://www.facebook.com/feryp.org/

History 26 Feb 2003. Former names and other names: *Forum of European Roma and Travellers Young People (FERTYP)* – alias. **Aims** Prepare the new/future generation of young Roma to act for the improvement of the situation of the Roma communities in Europe. **Activities** Events/meetings; networking/liaising; projects/programmes; publishing activities; training/education. **Events** *Study Session* Strasbourg (France) 2014, *International seminar* Sofia (Bulgaria) 1999. **Members** Organizations and individuals. Membership countries not specified. **IGO Relations** Member INGYO of: *European Youth Centres (EYCs, #09138)*. [2021/XF4028/F]

♦ Forum of European Securities Commissions / see European Securities and Markets Authority (#08457)
♦ Forum of the European Societies of Clinical Chemistry and Laboratory Medicine / see European Federation of Clinical Chemistry and Laboratory Medicine (#07080)
♦ Forum Europe des cultures (internationally oriented national body)
♦ Forum pour l'Europe démocratique (internationally oriented national body)
♦ Forum Européen d'Alpbach (#07304)
♦ Forum européen pour les arts et le patrimoine / see Culture Action Europe (#04981)
♦ Forum européen des associations nationales de l'industrie de l'ascenseur / see European Lift Association (#07695)
♦ Forum européen des associations pour le patrimoine (#07314)
♦ Forum européen de l'assurance accidents du travail et maladies professionnelles (#07317)
♦ Forum Européen des Comités Nationaux des Laïcs (#07322)
♦ Forum européen pour la démocratie et la solidarité (#07307)
♦ Forum Européen des Directeurs du Patrimoine (#07478)
♦ Forum européen des droits de l'homme et de la famille (#07315)
♦ Forum Européen de l'Energie (#06986)
♦ Forum européen de l'enseignement de la culture religieuse à l'école (internationally oriented national body)
♦ Forum Européen des Femmes Musulmanes (#07321)
♦ Forum européen fréquence et temps (#07360)
♦ Forum européen des gestionnaires de santé (no recent information)
♦ Forum européen des groupes chrétiens LGBT (#07318)
♦ Forum Européen des Instituts de Recherche sur la Sécurité Routière (#09913)
♦ Forum Européen de la Jeunesse (#09140)
♦ Forum Européen pour la Liberté dans l'Education (#07311)
♦ Forum européen du logement (#07504)
♦ Forum européen de management / see World Economic Forum (#21367)
♦ Forum européen de la médecine complémentaire et alternative pour un service de santé intégré en Europe / see European Federation for Complementary and Alternative Medicine (#07084)
♦ Forum européen de la montagne (#07824)
♦ Forum européen des personnes handicapées (#06929)
♦ Forum européen de politique criminelle appliquée (internationally oriented national body)
♦ Forum européen des politiques architecturales (#07306)
♦ Forum européen des professeurs d'éducation religieuse (#07337)
♦ Forum Européen de la Psychomotricité (#07327)
♦ Forum européen des Roms et des gens du voyage (#08402)
♦ Forum européen de secours aux victimes / see Victim Support Europe (#20767)
♦ Forum européen pour la sécurité urbaine (#07340)
♦ Forum européen des systèmes ouverts (no recent information)
♦ FORUM européen du volontariat pour le développement / see International Forum for Volunteering in Development (#13659)
♦ Forum Europeo de Asociaciones Arqueológicas (#07314)
♦ Forum Europeo dell'Assicurazione Contro gli Infortuni sul Lavoro e le Malattie Professionali (#07317)
♦ Forum Europeo delle Associazioni Archeologiche (#07314)
♦ Forum Europeo dei Comitati Nazionali dei Laici (#07322)
♦ Forum Europeo per l'Insegnamento Scolastico della Religione (internationally oriented national body)
♦ Forum Europeo de Psicomotricidad (#07327)
♦ Forum Europeo para la Seguridad Urbana / see European Forum for Urban Security (#07340)
♦ FORUM Europeo de Voluntariado para el Desarrollo / see International Forum for Volunteering in Development (#13659)
♦ Forum des fédérations (internationally oriented national body)
♦ Forum of Federations (internationally oriented national body)
♦ Forum des femmes de la méditerranée / see International Mediterranean Women's Forum (#14143)
♦ Forum Fisheries Agency / see Pacific Islands Forum Fisheries Agency (#17969)
♦ Forum pour la formation en commerce international (internationally oriented national body)

♦ Forum for Former African Heads of State and Government (Africa Forum) 09915

Executive Secretariat PO Box 6541, Pretoria, South Africa. T. +27123548048. Fax +27123548161. E-mail: emilia.haworth@africaforum.org.
URL: http://www.africaforum.org/

History 11 Jan 2006, Maputo (Mozambique), as an informal network. Former names and other names: *AF* – former. **Aims** Harness the experience, moral authority and good offices of former African Heads of State and Government; advance African development, particularly by promoting sustainable peace and security, enhancing and sustaining democratic governance in Africa and promoting human rights. **Structure** General Assembly; Executive Secretariat; Committees. **Languages** English, French, Portuguese. **Staff** 15.00 FTE, paid. **Finance** Funding. Annual budget: about US$ 2,500,000. **Activities** Advocacy/lobbying/activism; monitoring/evaluation; events/meetings; guidance/assistance/consulting; networking/liaising. **Events** *General Assembly* Addis Ababa (Ethiopia) 2016, *General Assembly* Oyala (Equatorial Guinea) 2016, *General Assembly* Addis Ababa (Ethiopia) 2015, *General Assembly* Johannesburg (South Africa) 2006.
Members Individuals (40) from 19 countries:
Benin, Botswana, Burundi, Cape Verde, Ethiopia, Gambia, Ghana, Kenya, Liberia, Malawi, Mauritius, Mozambique, Namibia, Nigeria, Sao Tomé-Principe, South Africa, Tanzania UR, Togo, Zambia. [2019.12.11/XM5961/v/F]

♦ **Forum** Forum International du Volontariat pour le Développement (#13659)
♦ ForUM – Forum for Utvikling og Miljø (internationally oriented national body)

♦ Forum francophone des affaires (FFA) 09916

International Pres 3 place de la Coupole, BP 98, 94223 Charenton CEDEX, France. T. +33143962606. Fax +33143534180. E-mail: ffa.org@orange.fr – contact@ffa-int.org.
URL: http://www.ffa-int.org/

History Sep 1987, Québec, QC (Canada). Founded during 2nd *Conférence au sommet des chefs d'Etat et de gouvernement des pays ayant le français en partage (Sommet de la Francophonie, #04648)*. International Secretariat officially inaugurated 30 May 1990, Montréal QC (Canada). **Aims** Promote *industrial, technological* and *commercial* exchanges. **Languages** French. **Staff** 80.00 FTE, paid. **Activities** Networking/liaising; knowledge management/information dissemination; events/meetings. **Events** *Forum* Dakar (Senegal) 2014, *Forum* Kinshasa (Congo DR) 2012, *Forum* Montreux (Switzerland) 2010, *Forum* Québec, QC (Canada) 2008, *Forum* Québec, QC (Canada) 2008. **Publications** *Croissance Actualités*; *La Gazette*. **Members** National Committees in all francophone countries, and Spanish, Portuguese and Arab speaking countries (111 in total). Membership countries not specified. **Consultative Status** Consultative status granted from: *ECOSOC (#05331)* (Ros C); *UNIDO (#20336)*. **IGO Relations** Cooperation agreement with: *Agence intergouvernementale de la Francophonie (inactive)*. **NGO Relations** Member of: *Association francophone d'amitié et de liaison (AFAL, #02605)*. [2017.01.05/XF3258/F]

♦ Forum for the Future (internationally oriented national body)
♦ Forum de Genève (internationally oriented national body)
♦ Forum della Gioventù dell'Unione Europea (inactive)
♦ Forum and Haut Niveau sur l'Efficacité de l'Aide (meeting series)

♦ Forum of Heads of ASEAN Power Utilities/Authorities (HAPUA) 09917

Sec 3rd Floor Adityawarman Bldg, Jl Adittyawarman No 42, Kebayoran Baru, Jakarta 12160, Indonesia. T. +62818123286. Fax +6281872786252. E-mail: syaiful@pln.co.id – epalupi@pln.co.id.
URL: http://www.hapuasecretariat.org/

History 1981, by governments of Indonesia, Malaysia, Philippines, Singapore and thailand. Within the framework of *ASEAN (#01141)*. **Structure** Council; Secretariat; Country Coordinators; Project Coordinators for Working Groups. Working Group, set up, Apr 2000, to formulate an *'ASEAN Interconnection Master Plan'* for *ASEAN Power Grid (#01224)*. **Events** *Meeting* Melaka (Malaysia) 2015, *Meeting* Cambodia 2014, *Meeting* Hua Hin (Thailand) 2010, *Meeting* Vientiane (Laos) 2005, *Meeting* Siem Reap (Cambodia) 2004.
Members Governments (10):
Brunei Darussalam, Cambodia, Indonesia, Laos, Malaysia, Myanmar, Philippines, Singapore, Thailand, Vietnam.
IGO Relations *ASEAN Council on Petroleum (ASCOPE, #01164)*. [2015/XK2208/F*]

♦ Forum for Ibero-American Dialogue of Evangelicals / see Latin Evangelical Alliance (#16397)
♦ Forum des Iles du Pacifique (#17968)

♦ Forum of Incident Response and Security Teams (FIRST) 09918

Secretariat 2500 Regency Pkwy, Cary NC 27518, USA. E-mail: first-sec@first.org.
URL: http://www.first.org/

History 1990. Founded as a consortium of computer incident response and security teams. Most recent statutes adopted 9 Feb 1999. **Aims** Foster cooperation among *information technology* constituents in the effective prevention, detection and recovery from *computer security* incidents; provide members with technical information, tools, methods, assistance and guidance; coordinate proactive liaison activities and analytical support; encourage development of quality products and services; improve national and international information security. **Structure** Conference (annual). Steering Committee, comprising Chair, Vice-Chair and 8 members. Officers: President; Secretary; Chief Financial Officer. Task Forces; Secretariat. **Finance** Members' dues (annual): Corporate (Full) US$ 600; Personal (Liaison) US$ 240. **Activities** Events/meetings; guidance/assistance/support. ing; Symposia. **Events** *Annual Conference* Fukuoka (Japan) 2024, *Annual Conference* Montréal, QC (Canada) 2023, *Technical Colloquium* Amsterdam (Netherlands) 2022, *Annual Conference* Dublin (Ireland) 2022, *Technical Colloquium on Cold Incident Response* Oslo (Norway) 2021.
Members Teams in 27 countries and territories:
Australia, Brazil, Canada, Chile, China, Croatia, Denmark, France, Germany, Israel, Italy, Japan, Korea Rep, Mexico, Netherlands, New Zealand, Norway, Poland, Russia, Singapore, Slovenia, Spain, Sweden, Switzerland, Taiwan, UK, USA.
NGO Relations Input or influence on aspects of development or regulation of: *Internet (#15948)*. [2021/XF6903/F]

♦ Forum Informatikerinnen für Frieden und Gesellschaftliche Verantwortung (internationally oriented national body)
♦ Forum intergouvernemental sur la sécurité chimique (inactive)
♦ Fórum Internacional da Abordagem Centrada na Pessoa (meeting series)
♦ Fórum Internacional de las Mujeres del Mediterraneo (#14143)
♦ Forum Internacional para la Naturaleza y el Turismo (internationally oriented national body)
♦ Fórum Internacional das Plataformas Nacionais de ONGs / see Forus (#09934)
♦ FORUM Internacional de Voluntariado para el Desarrollo (#13659)

♦ Forum international d'action catholique (FIAC) 09919

International Forum of Catholic Action (IFCA) – Foro internacional de Acción Católica – Forum Internazionale di Azione Cattolica (FIAC)

Coordinator Via della Conciliazione 1, 00193 Rome RM, Italy. T. +396661321. Fax +3966868755. E-mail: info@catholicactionforum.org.
URL: http://www.catholicactionforum.org/

History 1991, Rome (Italy). Former names and other names: *Fédération internationale de l'action catholique* – former. **Structure** General Assembly. **Events** *Assembly* Rome (Italy) 2004, *General Assembly* Rome (Italy) 2004, *International congress on catholic action* Rome (Italy) / Loreto (Italy) 2004, *Assembly* Rome (Italy) 2000, *General Assembly* Rome (Italy) 2000.
Members in 12 countries:
Argentina, Colombia, Italy, Luxembourg, Malta, Mexico, Myanmar, Paraguay, Romania, Spain, Switzerland, Venezuela.
Observers in 4 countries:
Burundi, Peru, Poland, Slovenia.
NGO Relations Member of: *Crescendo Worldwide Network (#04950)*; *Laudato Si' Movement (#16403)*. [2020/XF5740/F]

♦ Forum International de l'Approche Centrée sur la Personne (meeting series)
♦ Forum international des autochtones sur la biodiversité (#13837)
♦ Forum international des avocats des voyages et du tourisme / see International Forum of Travel and Tourism Advocates (#13657)
♦ Forum for International Commercial Arbitration / see Forum for International Conciliation and Arbitration (#09920)

♦ Forum for International Conciliation and Arbitration (FICA) 09920

Chairman 9, Dora Carr Close, Headington, Oxford, OX3 9RF, UK. T. +44186575195 – +447990888990. E-mail: info@fica-disputeresolution.com.
URL: https://fica-disputeresolution.com/

History 1996. Former names and other names: *Forum for International Commercial Arbitration* – former. **Aims** Promote effective dispute resolution through traditional and non-traditional processes designed to provide efficient dispute resolution tailored to each situation. **Structure** Chairman; Management Committee; Directors. **Languages** English, French, German. **Staff** 8.00 FTE, voluntary. **Activities** Advocacy/lobbying/activism; networking/liaising; projects/programmes. **Members** Individuals. Membership countries not specified. **IGO Relations** Observer to: *United Nations Commission on International Trade Law (UNCITRAL, #20531)*. [2020.05.08/XM3370/F]

♦ Forum international de la course océanique (no recent information)

♦ **Forum for International Criminal and Humanitarian Law (FICHL)** . . . **09921**
Dir c/o CILRAP, Via S. Gallo135r, 50129 Florence FI, Italy.
Registered Address Av des Saisons 100-102, 1050 Brussels, Belgium.
URL: http://www.fichl.org/
History Set up as a department of *Centre for International Law Research and Policy (CILRAP, #03756)*. Registered in accordance with Belgian law. Registration: Crossroads Bank for Enterprises, No/ID: 0827.424.153, Start date: 1 Jul 2010, Belgium. **Aims** Identify, frame and host discourses on key issues in international criminal and humanitarian law, transitional justice and in law more widely. **Structure** Coordination Group; Advisory Board; Fellows. Director. **Activities** Events/meetings; training/education. **Publications** *FICHL Occasional Paper Series*; *FICHL Policy Brief Series*. [2022/XJ9754/**F**]

♦ Forum internationale de la communication (#12816)
♦ Forum für Internationale Gesundheit (internationally oriented national body)
♦ Forum international pour l'exploitation forestière (internationally oriented national body)
♦ Forum international des femmes de la méditerranée (#14143)
♦ FORUM / see International Forum for Volunteering in Development (#13659)
♦ **Forum** International Forum for Volunteering in Development (#13659)
♦ Forum international francophone de pédagogie des sciences de la santé (meeting series)
♦ Forum for International Health (internationally oriented national body)
♦ Forum international des industries maritimes (inactive)
♦ Forum international de l'innovation sociale (#13651)
♦ Forum International de la Météo et du Climat (meeting series)
♦ Forum international de Montréal / see FIM-Forum for Democratic Global Governance (#09761)
♦ Forum international des ONG pour le développement en Indonésie (#14366)
♦ Forum international des organisations défendant les droits de reproduction / see International Federation of Reproduction Rights Organizations (#13527)
♦ Forum international des organisations de droit de réprographie / see International Federation of Reproduction Rights Organizations (#13527)
♦ Forum international de la paix (inactive)
♦ Forum International des Plateformes National d'ONG / see Forus (#09934)
♦ Forum international pour la protection de l'enfance (#13633)

♦ **Forum of International Respiratory Societies (FIRS)** **09922**
Exec Dir Avee Ste-Luce 4, 1003 Lausanne VD, Switzerland.
URL: http://www.firsnet.org/
History 22 Jan 2002, Geneva (Switzerland) by *Asociación Latinoamericana del Tórax (ALAT, #02273)*, American Thoracic Society (ATS), American College of Chest Physicians (ACCP), *Asian Pacific Society of Respirology (APSR, #01643)*, *European Respiratory Society (ERS, #08383)* and *International Union Against Tuberculosis and Lung Disease (The Union, #15752)*. **Aims** Promote advocacy in matters of global respiratory health and the identification of new areas for global initiatives.
Members Organizations (7):
American College of Chest Physicians (ACCP); American Thoracic Society (ATS); *Asian Pacific Society of Respirology (APSR, #01643)*; *Asociación Latinoamericana del Tórax (ALAT, #02273)*; *European Respiratory Society (ERS, #08383)*; *International Union Against Tuberculosis and Lung Disease (The Union, #15752)*; *Pan-African Thoracic Society (PATS, #18070)*.
NGO Relations Participates in: *Global Alliance Against Chronic Respiratory Diseases (GARD, #10182)*. [2019/XJ2264/y/**F**]

♦ Forum for International Retail Association Executives / see Federation of International Retail Associations (#09676)
♦ Forum international des scouts juifs (#13643)
♦ Forum international tourisme solidaire et développement durable (internationally oriented national body)
♦ Forum for International Trade Training (internationally oriented national body)
♦ Forum international des transport (#15725)
♦ Forum international pour le transport rural et le développement (#13650)
♦ Forum international des universités publiques (#13648)
♦ Forum international des villes de Graz (internationally oriented national body)
♦ Forum International du Volontariat pour le Développement (#13659)
♦ Forum Internazionale dell'Approccio Centrato sulla Persona (meeting series)
♦ Forum Internazionale di Azione Cattolica (#09919)
♦ Forum Internazionale delle Donne del Mediterraneo (#14143)
♦ Forum Internazionale ed Europeo di Ricerche sull' Immigrazione (internationally oriented national body)
♦ Fórum Interparlamentar das Américas / see ParlAmericas (#18206)
♦ Forum interparlementaire des Amériques / see ParlAmericas (#18206)
♦ Forum de la jeunesse d'Asie et du Pacifique (#01647)
♦ Forum jeunesse de l'Union européenne / see European Youth Forum (#09140)
♦ Forum jeunesse de l'Union européenne (inactive)
♦ Forum des juges de l'Union européenne pour l'environnement (unconfirmed)
♦ Forum da Juventude da Comunidade Européia (inactive)
♦ Forum da Juventude da União Europeia (inactive)
♦ Forum for Kvinner og Utviklingsspørsmål (internationally oriented national body)
♦ Forum des laboratoires européens de recherche routière (#09910)
♦ Forum latinoaméricain des jeunes (#09881)
♦ **Forum LGBT** European Forum of Lesbian, Gay, Bisexual and Transgender Christian Groups (#07318)
♦ Forum Libéral Européen (#07689)
♦ Forum of Local Authorities for Social Inclusion / see Foro de Autoridades Locales por la Inclusión Social y la Democracia Participativa (#09876)
♦ Forum of Local Authorities for Social Inclusion and Participatory Democracy (#09876)
♦ Forum of the Local and Regional Authorities of Europe for Urban Security / see European Forum for Urban Security (#07340)
♦ Forum maghrébin pour l'environnement et le développement (unconfirmed)
♦ Forum of Ministers of Culture and Officials responsible for Cultural Policy in Latin America and the Caribbean (no recent information)

♦ **Forum of Ministers of the Environment of Latin America and the Caribbean** **09923**
Foro de Ministros de Medio Ambiente de América Latina y el Caribe
Contact ONU Medio Ambiente Avda Morse, Corregimiento de Ancón, Edificio 103, Clayton, Ciudad del Saber, Apartado Postal 0843-03590, Panama, Panamá, Panama PANAMá, Panama. T. +15073053100. Fax +15073053105. E-mail: enlace@pnuma.org.
URL: http://www.pnuma.org/
Events *Meeting* Los Cabos (Mexico) 2014, *Meeting* Santo Domingo (Dominican Rep) 2008, *Meeting* Panama 2003, *Meeting* Rio de Janeiro (Brazil) 2001, *Meeting* Bridgetown (Barbados) 2000. **IGO Relations** *Environmental Training Network for Latin America and the Caribbean (inactive)*; *UNEP (#20299)*. [2017.08.08/XF6261/c/**F***]

♦ **Forum for Mobility and Society (FMS)** **09924**
Secretariat Rue de la Science 41, 1040 Brussels, Belgium. T. +3222820817. E-mail: secretariat@debatingmobility.eu.
URL: http://www.debatingmobility.eu/
History 16 May 2000, Brussels (Belgium). Founded as *Forum for Automobile and Society*. Registration: EU Transparency Register, No/ID: 05046148043-73, Start date: 10 Feb 2012. **Aims** Serve as a forum for the exchange of information and views for all those interested in automotive issues. **Languages** English. **Staff** 0.50 FTE, paid. **Activities** Organizes debates and workshops. **Events** *Conference on Connected and Automated Driving* Brussels (Belgium) 2019.
Members Political: members of the European Parliament (40). Membership countries not specified. Corporate: companies and organizations (22), including 4 organizations listed in this Yearbook:
Corporate: companies and organizations (22), including 4 organizations listed in this Yearbook:
ERTICO ITS Europe (#05532); *European Association of Automotive Suppliers (CLEPA, #05948)*; *European Automobile Manufacturers' Association (ACEA, #06300)*; *Fédération Internationale de l'Automobile (FIA, #09613)*.
IGO Relations *European Parliament (EP, #08146)*. [2016/XF6371/y/**F**]

♦ Forum mondial des alternatives (#21513)
♦ Forum mondial de la banane (#21215)
♦ Forum mondial pour le conseil rural (#10378)
♦ Forum Mondial sur le Droit, la Justice et le Développement (#10373)
♦ Forum mondial de l'économie sociale (#10603)
♦ Forum mondial de l'éducation (#21371)
♦ Forum mondial des GPL / see World LPG Association (#21629)

♦ **Forum Mondial Heracles (HERACLES)** **09925**
Pres UFC – Dept de Français Langue Etrangère, 30 rue Mégevand, 25000 Besançon, France.
URL: https://forummondialheracles.wixsite.com/heracles/
History Set up21 Jul 2008, Québec QC (Canada), at the intiative of *Agence universitaire de La Francophonie (AUF, #00548)*. **Aims** Gather professional groups, university *language teaching* centres. **Events** *Forum* Montréal, QC (Canada) 2018. **Publications** *Bulletin HERACLES* (4 a year). **NGO Relations** *Fédération internationale des professeurs de français (FIPF, #09652)*. [2018/XM7906/**F**]

♦ Forum mondial sur la migration et le développement (#10376)
♦ Forum mondial de la participation citoyenne (#21277)
♦ Forum mondial des populations de pêcheurs (#21517)
♦ Forum mondial des producteurs de café (meeting series)
♦ Forum mondial de la recherche agricole (#10370)
♦ Forum Mondial Sciences et Démocratie (#21522)
♦ Forum mondial des sciences de la vie (unconfirmed)
♦ Forum mondial de la société civile (#21278)
♦ Forum Mondial de Théologie et Libération (#21524)
♦ Forum mondial sur la transparence et l'échange de renseignements à des fins fiscales (#10379)
♦ Fórum de las Mujeres del Mediterraneo / see International Mediterranean Women's Forum (#14143)
♦ Fórum Mundial de Educação (#21371)
♦ Fórum Mundial de Teologia e Libertação (#21524)
♦ Forum du musée européen (#07836)
♦ Forum des Nations Unies sur les forêts (#20562)
♦ Forum Neoleas tis Evropaikis Enosis (inactive)
♦ Forum for Nordisk Jernbanesamarbeide (#17395)
♦ Forum for Nordisk Jernbane Samarbejde (#17395)
♦ Forum för Nordiskt JärnvägsSamarbete (#17395)

♦ **Forum for Nuclear Cooperation in Asia (FNCA)** **09926**
Main Office IARD-NSRA, 5-18-7 Shimbashi, Minato-ku, Tokyo, 105-0004 Japan. T. +813547011983. Fax +81354701991. E-mail: fnca@fnca.mext.go.jp.
URL: http://www.fnca.mext.go.jp/
History Apr 1999, following an agreement during the 10th International Conference for Nuclear Cooperation in Asia. **Aims** Promote regional cooperation toward peaceful use of nuclear technology. **Structure** Ministerial Level Meeting; Senior Officials Meeting; Coordinators Meeting; Study Panels; Projects. **Activities** Events/meetings; projects/programmes. **Events** *Study Panel Meeting* Tokyo (Japan) 2021, *Coordinators Meeting* Tokyo (Japan) 2019, *Ministerial Meeting* Tokyo (Japan) 2018, *Study Panel Meeting* Tokyo (Japan) 2018, *Ministerial Meeting* Astana (Kazakhstan) 2017. **Publications** *Biofertilizer Newsletter*; *FNCA Newsletter*; *Radioactive Waste Management Newsletter*. *FNCA Brochure*.
Members Participating countries (12):
Australia, Bangladesh, China, Indonesia, Japan, Kazakhstan, Korea Rep, Malaysia, Mongolia, Philippines, Thailand, Vietnam.
NGO Relations Member of: *World Council of Isotopes (WCI, #21331)*. [2018/XF6631/**F***]

♦ **Forum of Nuclear Regulatory Bodies in Africa (FNRBA)** **09927**
Contact c/o IAEA – VIC, PO Box 100, 1400 Vienna, Austria. E-mail: fnrba.contact-point@iaea.org.
URL: http://gnssn.iaea.org/main/FNRBA/
History Established 26 Mar 2009. Comes under the umbrella of *Global Nuclear Safety and Security Network (GNSSN, #10509)* within *International Atomic Energy Agency (IAEA, #12294)*. **Aims** Be instrumental to the enhancement, strengthening and harmonization of *radiation* protection, nuclear *safety* and security regulatory infrastructure and framework among members. **Structure** Plenary Body; Steering Committee; Secretariat – based at *International Atomic Energy Agency (IAEA, #12294)*. Technical Groups. **Activities** Training/education; knowledge management/information dissemination; events/meetings. **Events** *Coordination Meeting* Vienna (Austria) 2017, *FNRBA Plenary Meeting* Vienna (Austria) 2016. **Publications** Surveys.
Members Active Member States (31):
Angola, Botswana, Burkina Faso, Cameroon, Chad, Congo DR, Côte d'Ivoire, Egypt, Ethiopia, Gabon, Ghana, Kenya, Madagascar, Malawi, Mali, Mauritania, Mauritius, Morocco, Namibia, Niger, Nigeria, Senegal, Seychelles, Sierra Leone, South Africa, Sudan, Tanzania UR, Tunisia, Uganda, Zambia, Zimbabwe.
IGO Relations *European Commission (EC, #06633)*; national governmental agencies. [2018/XM6492/**F***]

♦ Forum oecuménique de femmes chrétiennes d'Europe (#05347)
♦ Forum des Organisations de Solidarité Internationale issues des Migrations (internationally oriented national body)
♦ Forum de Paris sur la Paix (internationally oriented national body)
♦ Fórum dos Parlamentos dos Países de Língua Portuguesa (inactive)
♦ Forum parlementaire inter-européen sur la population et le développement / see European Parliamentary Forum for Sexual & Reproductive Rights (#08149)
♦ Forum pour le Partenariat avec l'Afrique (#00510)
♦ Forum permanent de la société civile européenne (#18322)
♦ Forum PET Europe (unconfirmed)
♦ Forum of Postal Savings Banks (see: #21764)
♦ Forum of Presidents of Legislative Authorities of Central America / see Foro de presidentes y presidentas de Poderes Legislativos de Centroamérica y el Caribe (#09887)
♦ Forum per i Problemi della Pace e della Guerra (internationally oriented national body)
♦ Forum for the Problems of Peace and War (internationally oriented national body)
♦ Forum for the Progress and Development of South America (#09888)
♦ Forum progressiste mondial des jeunes (#10558)
♦ Forum progressive mondial (#10557)
♦ Fórum para o Progresso e Desenvolvimento da América do Sul (#09888)
♦ Forum de psychiatrie de l'enfant et de l'adolescent de l'ANASE (meeting series)
♦ Forum régional d'analyse et de concertation (meeting series)
♦ Forum régional de l'ASEAN (#01228)

♦ **Forum Regional Security Committee (FRSC)** **09928**
Contact c/o Pacific Islands Forum Secretariat, Private Mail Bag, Suva, Fiji. T. +6793312600. Fax +6793220230. E-mail: info@forumsec.org.
History 1991, within the framework of *Pacific Islands Forum (#17968)*. **Aims** Consider a regional approach on *transnational crime* in the *South Pacific*. **Activities** Developed the 1992 Honiara Declaration of Law Enforcement Cooperation, which provides for a regional law enforcement network and sets out initial priorities in areas such as drugs, training and development of legislative frameworks. **Events** *Meeting* Nadi (Fiji) 2006, *Meeting* Auckland (New Zealand) 2005, *Meeting* Nadi (Fiji) 2004. [2020/XK0564/**F***]

♦ Forum Scoial Mondial des Economies Transformatrices (meeting series)

- ♦ Forum Secretariat / see Pacific Islands Forum Secretariat (#17970)
- ♦ Forum social africain (#00457)
- ♦ Forum social mondial (#21797)
- ♦ Fórum Social Mundial (#21797)
- ♦ Fórum Social Mundialé (#21797)
- ♦ Fórum Social Pan-Amazônico (#09889)
- ♦ Forum de la société civile de l'Afrique de l'ouest (#20864)
- ♦ Forum Syd – Swedish NGO Centre for Development Cooperation (internationally oriented national body)
- ♦ Forum synergies (internationally oriented national body)

♦ Forum for Telecom Operators of Small States (Teleforum) 09929

Address not obtained.
URL: https://teleforum.org/

History Sep 2000, London (UK). Established through a meeting held in London in September 2000 by CEOs of GO Malta, Siminn, Faroese Telecom, Gibtelecom, TELE-POST Greenland, Guyana T & T, Telecom Liechtenstein, POST Luxembourg and Monaco Telecom. **Aims** Allow participants to share experiences, address issues faced by small operators, undertake group initiatives of mutual benefit and lobby for common interests; encourage initiatives which include knowledge sharing, consultancies, training, pooling of resources and discussions on the legal, regulatory, technical and commercial environment of the telecommunications industry. **Structure** Annual Conference; Chairman. **Languages** English. **Finance** Sources: members' dues. **Activities** Events/meetings; politics/policy/regulatory. Organisation Committee Meetings; Lead Country Concept Events; Workshops on Specialized Telecoms Topics and Information Dissemination; Specialized Group on EU Regulatory Aspects. **Events** *Teleforum* St Julian's (Malta) 2022, *Teleforum* Greenland 2021, *Teleforum* Greenland 2020, *Teleforum* Mariehamn (Finland) 2019, *Teleforum* Luxembourg (Luxembourg) 2018.
Members Registered telecommunications operators who are national incumbents or former incumbents established in small states, territories or dependencies with a population which does not exceed 2 million inhabitants. Members in 16 countries and territories:
Åland, Andorra, Cape Verde, Cyprus, Faeroe Is, Gibraltar, Greenland, Guernsey, Iceland, Isle of Man, Jersey, Liechtenstein, Luxembourg, Malta, Monaco, Suriname. [2020.06.19/AA0429/F]

- ♦ Forum du Tiers-monde (#20149)

♦ Forum Train Europe (FTE) 09930

Acting Managing Dir Hilfikerstrasse 3, 3000 Bern 65, Switzerland. T. +41512850615. Fax +41512201242. E-mail: info@forumtraineurope.eu.
Events Manager address not obtained.
URL: http://www.forumtraineurope.eu/

History 1 Jan 1997. Founded on merger of *European Goods Trains Timetable Conference (CEM, inactive)*, set up 1 Jan 1924, and *European Passenger Train Timetable Conference (CEH, inactive)*, formed 1 Jan 1923, Bern (Switzerland). Registration: EU Transparency Register, No/ID: 955440948173-56, Start date: 22 Nov 2022. **Aims** Determine and optimize international passenger *rail* and *maritime* services and organize the international movement of trains scheduled for goods traffic, including routing of parcels in full wagons; coordinate timetables of the various administrations and the connections at frontier stations; reduce the length of frontier stops; maximize use of rolling stock. **Structure** Executive Board. **Languages** English, French, German, Russian. **Staff** 5.00 FTE, paid. **Finance** Sources: members' dues. Annual budget: 1,000,000 CHF. **Events** *Conference on maintenance and infrastructure renewal* London (UK) 1999. **Publications** *FTE Info.*
Members Full (95) in 32 countries:
Austria, Belarus, Belgium, Bosnia-Herzegovina, Bulgaria, Croatia, Czechia, Denmark, Finland, France, Germany, Greece, Hungary, Italy, Luxembourg, Montenegro, Netherlands, North Macedonia, Norway, Poland, Portugal, Romania, Russia, Serbia, Slovakia, Slovenia, Spain, Sweden, Switzerland, Türkiye, UK, Ukraine. [2022/XF4256/F]

- ♦ Forumul Montan European (#07824)
- ♦ Forum Umwelt und Entwicklung (internationally oriented national body)
- ♦ Forum UNESCO – Université et patrimoine (#09931)

♦ Forum UNESCO – University and Heritage (FUUH) 09931

Forum UNESCO – Université et patrimoine (FUUP)

Contact Camino de Vera s/n, 46022 Valencia, Spain. T. +34963877780. Fax +34963877789. E-mail: forum@fuuh.upv.es.
URL: http://www.universityandheritage.net/

History 1995, as a joint programme between the Culture Sector of *UNESCO (#20322)* and the Polytechnic University of Valencia (Spain). Previously also referred to as *International Network of Universities Forum UNESCO – University and Heritage.* **Aims** Mobilize universities with cultural or natural heritage disciplines or disciplines that are linked to it; share knowledge, know-how and competences; reinforce cooperation between universities, disciplines, heritage professionals; courage professors' and students' participation in heritage safeguarding projects; promote inter-cultural dialogue through heritage; set up synergies with existing networks. **Finance** Financed by: *Agencia Española de Cooperación Internacional para el Desarrollo (AECID)*; *World Heritage Centre (WHC, #21566)*; Polytechnical University of Valencia (UPV Spain). **Activities** Organizes: international seminars; workshops; summer/field youth workcamps; summer universities; conservation projects; thematic research teams; academic exchange programme. Manages: thesis database; membership database; network communication tools. **Events** *International seminar / Annual Seminar* Hanoi (Vietnam) 2009, *International symposium on sharing heritages* Valencia (Spain) 2008, *International seminar / Annual Seminar* Florence (Italy) 2006, *International seminar* Newcastle upon Tyne (UK) 2005, *International seminar* Buenos Aires (Argentina) 2004. **Publications** *FUUH Bulletin* (12 a year) – electronic.
Members Individuals (2,662) and universities (830) in 126 countries and territories. Membership countries not specified. International organizations (2):
International organizations (2):
Council of Europe (CE, #04881); *European Commission (EC, #06633).* [2014/XF6455/F]

- ♦ Forum Universale Foundation / see Fondation du forum universale

♦ Forum Urodynamicum 09932

Contact Urologische Klinik und Poliklinik der Ludwig-Maximilians-Universität München, Klinikum Grosshadern, Marchioninistrasse 15, 81377 Munich, Germany. T. +4989440076527. Fax +4989440078734. E-mail: info@forum-urodynamicum.de.
URL: http://www.forum-urodynamicum.de/

Aims Advance interdisciplinary research and postgraduate education in the fields of prevention, diagnosis, and treatment of lower *urinary* tract dysfunction, as well as in *female* urology. **Events** *Annual Meeting* Giesen (Germany) 2014, *Annual Meeting* Giesen (Germany) 2014, *Annual Meeting* Heidelberg (Germany) 2013, *Annual Meeting* Zurich (Switzerland) 2012, *Annual Meeting* Mönchengladbach (Germany) 2011.
Members Full in 3 countries:
Austria, Germany, Switzerland. [2018/XJ5259/F]

- ♦ Forum for Utvikling og Miljø (internationally oriented national body)
- ♦ Forum for Women and Development (internationally oriented national body)

♦ Forum of Worldwide Music Festivals (FWMF) 09933

Contact Dr Theo Tutsstraat 20, 2530 Boechout, Belgium. T. +3234556944. E-mail: info@fwmf.world.
URL: http://www.fwmf.world/

History 1991. Former names and other names: *European Forum of Worldwide Music Festivals (EFWMF)* – former. Registration: Banque-Carrefour des Entreprises, No/ID: 0461.869.359, Start date: 20 Nov 1997, Belgium. **Aims** Increase interest and knowledge of world, *ethnic* and *traditional* music. **Structure** General Meeting; Board; Permanent Office. **Languages** English. **Finance** Sources: members' dues. **Activities** Events/meetings; knowledge management/information dissemination; networking/liaising. **Events** *Annual WOMEX Conference* Copenhagen (Denmark) 2011, *Annual WOMEX conference* Copenhagen (Denmark) 2010, *Annual WOMEX conference* Copenhagen (Denmark) 2009, *Members meeting* Oslo (Norway) 2006, *Annual WOMEX conference / Annual Worldwide Music Expo – WOMEX* Seville (Spain) 2006.
Members Major European festivals (42) in 21 countries and territories:
Belgium, Brazil, Czechia, Denmark, Estonia, Finland, France, Germany, Hungary, Israel, Italy, Korea Rep, Morocco, Netherlands, North Macedonia, Norway, Palestine, Slovenia, Spain, Sweden, Switzerland. [2023.02.15/XF3373/F]

- ♦ forumZFD – Forum Ziviler Friedensdienst (internationally oriented national body)
- ♦ Forum Ziviler Friedensdienst (internationally oriented national body)
- ♦ FORU / see Oceania Rugby (#17672)

♦ Forus 09934

Dir 14 passage Dubail, 75010 Paris, France. T. +33144728012. E-mail: contact@forus-international.org.
URL: http://forus-international.org/

History Oct 2008, with cooperation programme initiated between French and Brazilian platforms as early as 2003. Original title: *International Forum of National NGO Platforms (IFP) – Forum International des Plateformes National d'ONG (FIP) – Foro Internacional de las Plataformas Nacionales de ONGs (FIP) – Fórum Internacional das Plataformas Nacionais de ONGs (FIP).* Current title adopted Oct 2018. Full title: *Forus – Connect Support Influence.* **Aims** Promote a fair and sustainable world where the most vulnerable populations have a voice, *human rights* are respected and inequalities and injustice are combatted. **Structure** General Assembly; Council; Secretariat. **Languages** English, French, Portuguese, Spanish. **Finance** Public and private resources. **Events** *General Assembly* Dakar (Senegal) 2011.
Members NGO Platforms (69) in 68 countries:
Angola, Argentina, Belgium, Benin, Bolivia, Botswana, Brazil, Burkina Faso, Burundi, Cambodia, Cameroon, Canada, Cape Verde, Central African Rep, Chad, Chile, China, Colombia, Congo Brazzaville, Congo DR, Cook Is, Côte d'Ivoire, Czechia, Denmark, Dominican Rep, Fiji, Finland, France, Gambia, Guatemala, Guinea, Honduras, Hungary, India, Indonesia, Ireland, Japan, Kiribati, Korea Rep, Latvia, Lithuania, Madagascar, Mali, Malta, Mauritius, Morocco, Mozambique, Nepal, New Zealand, Nigeria, Paraguay, Peru, Philippines, Portugal, Romania, Rwanda, Sao Tomé-Principe, Senegal, Seychelles, Slovenia, Spain, Taiwan, Togo, Uganda, UK, Uruguay, USA, Zambia.
Included in the above, 11 organizations listed in this Yearbook:
American Council for Voluntary International Action (InterAction); *British Overseas NGO's for Development (BOND)*; *Cooperation Canada*; *Coordination SUD*; *Council for International Development (CID)*; *Globalt Fokus*; *International NGO Forum on Indonesian Development (INFID, #14366)*; *Irish Association of Non-Governmental Development Organisations (Dóchas)*; *Japanese NGO Center for International Cooperation (JANIC)*; *Korea NGO Council for Overseas Development Cooperation (KCOC)*; *Taiwan Alliance in International Development (Taiwan AID).*
Regional organizations (7):
Asia Development Alliance (ADA, #01266); *Confédération européenne des ong d'urgence et de développement (CONCORD, #04547)*; *Mesa de Articulación de Asociaciones Nacionales y Redes de ONGs de América Latina y el Caribe (La Mesa de articulación, #16727)*; *Pacific Islands Association of Non-Governmental Organizations (PIANGO, #17961)*; *Réseau des Plateformes des ONG de l'Afrique Centrale (REPONGAC, #18903)*; *Réseau des Plate-formes nationales d'ONG d'Afrique de l'Ouest et du Centre (REPAOC, #18902)*; *Southern African Development Community (SADC, #19843).* [2020.01.03/XJ5904/y/F]

- ♦ Forus – Connect Support Influence / see Forus (#09934)
- ♦ FORUT – Solidaritetsaksjon for utvikling (internationally oriented national body)
- ♦ Forward Edge International (internationally oriented national body)
- ♦ FORWARD – Foundation for Women's Health Research and Development (internationally oriented national body)
- ♦ FORWARD International / see Foundation for Women's Health Research and Development
- ♦ **FORWORKNET** Forestry Workforce Network (#09867)
- ♦ **FOSCAO** Forum de la société civile de l'Afrique de l'ouest (#20864)
- ♦ FOS Collective / see Foundations of Success
- ♦ FOSDA – Foundation for Security and Development in Africa (internationally oriented national body)
- ♦ FOSDEM – Free and Open Source Software Developers' European Meeting (meeting series)

♦ FOSFA International 09935

Chief Exec 4-6 Throgmorton Ave, London, EC2N 2DL, UK. T. +442073742346. Fax +442073748574. E-mail: contact@fosfa.org.
URL: http://www.fosfa.org/

History 1971, London (UK). Predecessor organization dates back to 1863. Former names and other names: *Federation of Oils, Seeds and Fats Associations* – former. Registration: Companies House, No/ID: 00926329, England and Wales. **Aims** Act as a contract-issuing and arbitration body in respect of international trade in *oilseeds, oils* and fats and *groundnuts/peanuts*; represent producers, shippers, traders, brokers, refiners, crushers, end-users and all related service industries/providers. **Structure** Council; Committee Structure. **Languages** English. **Staff** 7.00 FTE, paid. **Finance** Sources: members' dues; sale of products. **Activities** Events/meetings; training/education. **Events** *Annual General Assembly* London (UK) 2010, *Annual General Assembly* Barcelona (Spain) 2009, *Annual General Assembly* London (UK) 2008, *Annual meeting* London (UK) 2006, *Annual meeting* Geneva (Switzerland) 2005. **Members** Companies (about 1,200), including multinationals, in 89 countries and territories. Membership countries not specified. **IGO Relations** Observer status with (1): *Codex Alimentarius Commission (CAC, #04081).* **NGO Relations** In liaison with technical committees of: *International Organization for Standardization (ISO, #14473).* [2023.02.15/XD1964/F]

- ♦ FOS – Fonds voor Ontwikkelingssamenwerking – Socialistische Solidariteit (internationally oriented national body)
- ♦ FOS – Föreningen for Orientaliska Studier (internationally oriented national body)
- ♦ FOS – Foundations of Success (internationally oriented national body)
- ♦ FOSIDEC – Fonds de solidarité et d'intervention pour le développement de la Communauté économique de l'Afrique de l'Ouest (inactive)
- ♦ **FOSI** Family Online Safety Institute (#09254)

♦ FOSSASIA 09936

Co-Founder 12 Eu Tong Sen Street No 8-169, Singapore 059819, Singapore. E-mail: fossasia@googlegroups.com.
URL: https://fossasia.org/

History 2009. Name derives from the acronym FOSS: *free and open-source software.* Registration: No/ID: 201702892N, Singapore. **Aims** Develop Open Source software applications and Open Hardware together with a global community from its base in Asia. **Activities** Events/meetings; projects/programmes. **Events** *Summit* Singapore (Singapore) 2021, *PostgreSQL Asia Pacific Conference* Singapore (Singapore) 2019, *Summit* Singapore (Singapore) 2019, *PostgreSQL Asia Pacific Conference* Singapore (Singapore) 2018, *Workshop* Singapore (Singapore) 2016. [2021/AA2084/D]

- ♦ **FOSSFA** Free Software and Open Source Foundation for Africa (#09989)

♦ Fossil Fuel Foundation of Africa (FFF) 09937

Co-Dir PO Box 1549, Houghton, Johannesburg, 2193, South Africa. T. +27112606815 – +2711(27824514743.
Manager address not obtained. T. +27114869447.
URL: http://www.fossilfuel.co.za/

History 1994. **Aims** Further education, science and technology in the coal, carbon and energy *industry* in Africa. [2014/XF6254/f/F]

♦ Fossil Fuels Forum 09938

Secretariat DG Energy, European Commission, 1049 Brussels, Belgium.
URL: http://ec.europa.eu/energy/oil/berlin_forum/berlin_forum_en.htm

History by *European Commission (EC, #06633)* – DG TREN. Also referred to as *Berlin Forum* and *Berlin Forum on Fossil Fuels.* First forum organized, 2005. **Aims** Provide a platform for structured dialogue between European Commission services and the stakeholder community from the *EU energy* sector, including corporations, industry associations, member state administrations and European civil society. **Structure** Plenary (annual). Working Parties. **Activities** Organizes annual forum, always in Berlin (Germany). [2010/XM1585/E*]

- ♦ Foster Europe (internationally oriented national body)
- ♦ Foster Europe – Foundation for strong European Regions / see Foster Europe
- ♦ Foster Parents Plan International / see Plan International (#18386)

♦ **FOSWAL** Foundation of SAARC Writers and Literature (#09972)
♦ Foucauld – Piccoli Fratelli di Gesù (religious order)
♦ Foundation for the Accreditation of Cellular Therapy (internationally oriented national body)
♦ Foundation for Advanced Studies on International Development (internationally oriented national body)
♦ Foundation for the Advancement of International Medical Education and Research (internationally oriented national body)
♦ Foundation for Advancement of International Science (internationally oriented national body)
♦ Foundation Africa (see: #20676)
♦ Foundation for African Business and Consumer Services (internationally oriented national body)

♦ Foundation for African Development through International Biotechnology (FADIB) 09939

Pres PO Box 1457, Enugu, Nigeria. T. +23442459360. Fax +23442453202 – +23442330611.
History Founded 11 Mar 1992, Awka (Nigeria). Constitution adopted 25 Sep 1992. Registered in accordance with Nigerian law; also registered in the States of Iowa and South Carolina (USA). **Aims** Develop utilization of the biotechnology revolution in Africa by: training Africans in gene cloning and related sciences and biotechnologies, with particular attention to candidates from sub-Saharan Africa; developing improvisation in equipment use and laboratory procedures in genetic engineering and related fields so as to ameliorate endemic infrastructural problems and shortage of funds, and transmit these developments to trainees; providing equipment and materials for qualified trainees to adapt newly-acquired techniques, so as to improve life quality in their home environments; research into applications of genetic engineering and related fields of relevance to development of Africa, including the environment, and disseminating results of this research. **Structure** General Meeting (annual). Council of Trustees (meets annually), consisting of members from the various regions of Africa and the international community. Executive Committee, comprising the Officers and Executive Member-at-large. **Languages** English. **Staff** 1.00 FTE, paid; 3.00 FTE, voluntary. **Finance** Grants from: *Commonwealth Secretariat (#04362)*; *International Centre for Genetic Engineering and Biotechnology (ICGEB, #12494)*; *International Union of Biochemistry and Molecular Biology (IUBMB, #15759)*; *UNESCO (#20322)*. **Activities** Training/education; events/meetings; research/documentation; knowledge management/information dissemination. **Events** *Workshop on biotechnology* Enugu (Nigeria) 2000, *International conference on biotechnology for development in Africa* Enugu (Nigeria) 1997, *Workshop on gene cloning* Enugu (Nigeria) 1996, *Biotechnology and the environment* 1995, *Genetic engineering* Awka (Nigeria) 1995. **Publications** *FADIB Newsletter* (4 a year). Workshop materials; papers.
Members Ordinary; Executive; Trustee. Members in 37 countries:
Algeria, Belgium, Benin, Botswana, Burkina Faso, Burundi, Cameroon, Canada, Congo Brazzaville, Congo DR, Côte d'Ivoire, Egypt, Ethiopia, France, Gabon, Gambia, Germany, Ghana, Guinea, India, Israel, Kenya, Madagascar, Malawi, Mali, Nigeria, Senegal, Sierra Leone, South Africa, Sudan, Sweden, Tanzania UR, Uganda, UK, USA, Zambia, Zimbabwe.
IGO Relations Close cooperation with ICGEB, which has a trustee on the Council. **NGO Relations** Member of: *International Union of Microbiological Societies (IUMS, #15794)*; *Consortium on Science, Technology and Innovation for the South (COSTIS, no recent information).* [2016/XF2880/f/F]

♦ Foundation for the African Urban Management Institute / see African Foundation for Urban Management
♦ Foundation Against Trafficking in Women / see Coördinatiecentrum Mensenhandel
♦ Foundation for Agronomic Research (internationally oriented national body)
♦ Foundation Amazon Fund (unconfirmed)
♦ Foundation for the Application and Teaching of Sciences (internationally oriented national body)
♦ Foundation for the Arts in Brussels (internationally oriented national body)
♦ Foundation Asia (see: #20676)

♦ Foundation for Asian Management Development (FAMD) 09940

Address not obtained.
History 1 Apr 1983, Tokyo (Japan), as a private, non-profit Japanese organization. **Aims** Promote management development and *manpower* improvement of small and medium-sized *enterprises* in Asian nations, particularly the member countries of *ASEAN*. **Structure** Board of Trustees, consisting of Chairman, 2 Vice Chairmen, Managing Director, 6 Executive Trustees, 6 Trustees and 2 Auditors. Board of Councillors, consisting of 16 members. **Finance** Contributions of member companies. **Activities** Extends grants for locally conducted programs focusing on management development for SME's in electronics, including: seminars, workshops and symposia; management personnel training programs; research and field study; publication and translation. **Events** *Conference on harnessing SME growth through japanese initiatives / Conference* Manila (Philippines) 1996, *Conference* Tokyo (Japan) 1993, *Conference on management development of small and medium enterprises in Asia / Conference* Tokyo (Japan) 1989, *Symposium on Asian small and medium sized enterprises management development* Japan 1988, *International workshop on women entrepreneurship* Singapore (Singapore) 1988. **Publications** *Asia Pacific Newsletter* (2 a year). **NGO Relations** *Asian Network for Industrial Technology Information and Extension (TECHNONET ASIA, no recent information)*; national organizations. [2010/XF1979/f/F]

♦ Foundation of Asia-Pacific Development Centre on Disability (APCD Foundation) 09941

Exec Dir APCD Bldg, 255 Rajvithi Rd, Rajthevi, Bangkok, 10400, Thailand. T. +6623547505. Fax +6623547507. E-mail: nongnuch@apcdfoundation.org – info@apcdproject.org.
URL: http://www.apcdfoundation.org/
History 1 Aug 2002, Bangkok (Thailand). Founded as a legacy of the Asia and Pacific Decade of Disabled Persons (1993-2002). Endorsed by UNESCAP as a regional cooperative base for its Biwako Millennium Framework for an inclusive society in the Asian and Pacific Decade of Disabled Persons (2003-2012). Under Royal Patronage of HRH Princess Maha Chakri Sirindhorn. **Aims** Promote a barrier-free, inclusive and rights-based society for all in Asia and the Pacific through empowerment of persons with disabilities and disabled people's organizations. **Activities** Training/education; knowledge management/information dissemination; networking/liaising. **Events** *ASEAN-Japan Senior Officials Meeting on International Cooperation and Disability* Tokyo (Japan) 2015, *Workshop for the capacity development of self-help organizations of persons with disabilities* Bangkok (Thailand) 2010, *International Conference on Tsunami Preparedness of Persons with Disabilities* Bangkok (Thailand) 2007. **Publications** Newsletters; training reports; booklets; caroons; DVDs. **Members** Government Focal Points – Ministries – in over 40 countries in Asia and the Pacific; Associate Organizations – DPOs and other NGOs (over 200). Membership countries not specified. **IGO Relations** Collaborates with: *ASEAN (#01141)* for the Institute on Disability and Public Policy in the ASEAN Region; *FAO (#09260)*; *Japan International Cooperation Agency (JICA)*; *United Nations Economic and Social Commission for Asia and the Pacific (ESCAP, #20557)*. **NGO Relations** Serves as secretariat for: *CBR Asia-Pacific Network (CBR AP Network, #03617)*. [2017/XE4657/f/F]

♦ Foundation for Aviation and Sustainable Tourism (FAST) 09942

Dir Gen 2nd Floor – Old Vayudoot Bldg, Air India Complex, Safdurjung Airport, Delhi 110 003, DELHI 110 003, India. T. +911124627100. Fax +911124610377. E-mail: infofastindia@gmail.com.
URL: http://www.fastindia.org.in/
History Founded Apr 1992, Delhi (India). Registered in accordance with Indian law. **Aims** Function as an institutional base for study of all aspects of civil aviation and tourism, including management; act as a think tank for promoting an objective, realistic and innovative approach to policies in civil aviation and tourism; disseminate knowledge and exchange information through appropriate channels; serve as a resource centre and databank for matters relating to civil aviation and tourism; identify, highlight and promote the interest of the traveller and other consumers connected with civil aviation and tourism; study and sketch the scope and pattern of sustainable growth in tourism that would be in harmony with the socio-cultural and ecological milieu; act as an anchor and catalyst in order to maximize the availability of technological and managerial resources in developing countries of the world in the field of civil aviation and tourism; act as a bridge for North-South cooperation in the field. **Structure** Advisory Council; Executive Committee; Board of Trustees. **Languages** English. **Staff** 5.00 FTE, paid; 20.00 FTE, voluntary. **Finance** Members' dues. Other sources: donations; income from consultancy/advisory services and seminar/conference sponsorship. **Activities** Events/meetings; guidance/assistance/consulting; research/documentation. **Events** *International conference* Delhi (India) 2004, *International conference* Delhi (India) 2000, *International conference* Delhi (India) 1998. **Publications** *FAST Bulletin* (3 a year). *Aviation and Tourism: Synergy to Success* (2003); *Airborne for Progress* (2001); *Flight into the Millennium – Aviation and Tourism* (1998); *New Horizons in Travel and Tourism – Asian Approach* (1996); *Emerging Trends in Aviation and Sustainable Tourism* (1994); *100 Years of Civil Aviation in India*.
Members Advisory Council in 13 countries:
Canada, Côte d'Ivoire, France, India, Japan, Malaysia, Mauritius, Nepal, Netherlands, Russia, Sri Lanka, UK, Zambia. [2015/XF3309/f/F]

♦ Foundation for Baltic and East European Studies (internationally oriented national body)
♦ Foundation BOS / see Vereniging Tropische Bossen

♦ Foundation Care4BrittleBones (Care4BrittleBones) 09943

Stichting Care4BrittleBones (Care4BrittleBones)
CEO Het Kerkehout 3a, 2245 XM Wassenaar, Netherlands. E-mail: info@care4brittlebones.org.
Main Website: http://www.care4brittlebones.org/
History Feb 2012, Netherlands. Registration: KvK, No/ID: 54665256, Netherlands; RSIN, No/ID: 851392854, Netherlands. **Aims** Enable a better quality of life for people with Osteogenesis Imperfecta. **Structure** Board; Advisory Boards; Core Team. **Languages** English, German. **Activities** Events/meetings; research/documentation. **Events** *International Conference on Quality of Life for Osteogenesis Imperfecta* 2019. **Publications** *Care4Bones Newsletter*; *Care4BrittleBones Newsletter*. [2021.05.19/AA0798/f/F]

♦ Foundation Center / see Candid
♦ Foundation for a Civil Society (internationally oriented national body)
♦ Foundation College of Europe Hamburg (internationally oriented national body)
♦ Foundation for Cooperative Housing / see Global Communities
♦ Foundation for Cultural Heritage without Border / see Cultural Heritage without Borders
♦ Foundation for a Culture of Peace (internationally oriented national body)
♦ Foundation of December 10 1986 / see LEGO Foundation
♦ Foundation for Democracy in Africa (internationally oriented national body)
♦ Foundation for the Development of Africa (internationally oriented national body)
♦ Foundation for Development Cooperation (internationally oriented national body)

♦ Foundation for the Development of Internal Medicine in Europe (FDIME) 09944

Fondation pour le Développement de la Médecine Interne en Europe (FDMIE) – Stiftung für die Förderung der Inneren Medizin in Europa (SFIME)
Contact c/o Fiduciaire Verifid SA, Rue du Rhône 100, 1204 Geneva, Switzerland. E-mail: contact@fdime.org.
URL: https://www.fdime.org/
History 17 Jan 2003, Geneva (Switzerland). Registration: Swiss Civil Code. **Aims** Raise funds to support and promote research projects on rare diseases and auto-immune diseases; provide grants and bursaries, and offer advanced training courses and seminars for Young Internists. **Structure** Council; Management Committee. **Staff** 12.00 FTE, voluntary. **Finance** Sources: donations. **Activities** Financial and/or material support; training/education. Europe. [2022.10.30/XM8986/f/F]

♦ Foundation for the Development of International Law in Asia (DILA) 09945

Contact address not obtained.
URL: http://www.dilafoundation.org/
History 21 Dec 1989, The Hague (Netherlands). Registered in accordance with Dutch law. **Aims** Promote the study and analysis of topics and issues in the field of international law, in particular from an Asian perspective; promote the study and dissemination of knowledge of international law in Asia; promote contacts and cooperation between people and institutions actively dealing with questions of international law relating to Asia. **Structure** Governing Board. **Languages** Dutch, English. **Events** *International Conference on Reshaping International Law in the Asian Century* Seoul (Korea Rep) 2020, *International Conference on Emerging Political and Economic Issues in North-East Asia* Incheon (Korea Rep) 2019, *International Conference on Critical International Legal Issues Affecting Asia* Seoul (Korea Rep) 2019, *International Conference on Encyclopedia of Public International Law in Asia* Seoul (Korea Rep) 2019, *Asia Pacific Ocean Law Institutions Alliance Conference* Busan (Korea Rep) 2015. **Publications** *Asian Yearbook of International Law*. [2014/XJ7774/f/F]

♦ Foundation for Development and Partnership in Africa (internationally oriented national body)
♦ Foundation DIAKONIA World Federation of Diaconal Associations and Diaconal Communities / see World Federation of Diaconal Associations and Diaconal Communities (#21429)
♦ Foundation Diakonia / see World Federation of Diaconal Associations and Diaconal Communities (#21429)
♦ Foundation Dorcas Aid International / see Dorcas (#05123)

♦ Foundation for a Drug-Free Europe (FDFE) 09946

Contact Operational Office, Rue Dumonceau 2, 1000 Brussels, Belgium. T. +32488232423. E-mail: contact@fdfe.eu.
Registered Office Reimersholmsgatan 9, SE-117 40 Stockholm, Sweden.
URL: http://fdfe.eu/
History Founded Mar 2004, on the initiative of *Church of Scientology International (CSI, #03922)*. Registered in accordance with Swedish law. **Aims** Prevent and stop debilitating drug use through educating youth and non-users concerning the harmful effects that drugs can inflict upon the body, mind and personality, and by finding and directing users to programmes that can help them achieve comfortable abstinence for life. **Structure** Advisory Board. **Languages** English. **Staff** 6.00 FTE, voluntary. **Finance** Donations from members and general public. **Activities** Events/meetings; advocacy/lobbying/activism; training/education. **Events** *Conference* Vienna (Austria) 2017. **Publications** Educational materials; articles; public service announcements; DVD.
Members Full in 23 countries:
Austria, Belgium, Bulgaria, Czechia, Denmark, Finland, France, Germany, Greece, Hungary, Ireland, Italy, Netherlands, Norway, Portugal, Russia, Slovakia, Slovenia, Spain, Sweden, Switzerland, UK, USA.
IGO Relations Member of: Civil Society Forum on Drugs. **NGO Relations** Member of: Drug Policy Futures; *Vienna NGO Committee on Drugs (VNGOC, #20773)*; *World Federation Against Drugs (WFAD, #21408)*. [2018.08.21/XM3587/f/F]

♦ Foundation for Dutch Forestry Development Cooperation / see Vereniging Tropische Bossen
♦ Foundation of Dutch Volunteers / see SNV Netherlands Development Organisation
♦ Foundation for East European Family History Societies (internationally oriented national body)
♦ Foundation for Ecological Development (internationally oriented national body)
♦ Foundation for the Economy and Sustainable Development of the Regions of Europe (#09817)

♦ Foundation for Endangered Languages (FEL) 09947

Chairman 129 High Street, Hungerford, RG17 0DL, UK. T. +441488208563.
URL: http://www.ogmios.org/
History Founded 1996, London (UK). UK Registered Charity. **Aims** Support, enable and assist the documentation, protection and promotion of endangered languages, with particular focus on revitalization activities. **Structure** Committee. **Languages** English. **Staff** 0.50 FTE, paid. **Finance** Members' dues. Other sources: sales of publications; donations; consultancy projects. Annual budget: about US$ 50,000. **Activities** Events/meetings; financial and/or material support. **Events** *Conference* Sydney, NSW (Australia) 2019, *Conference* Reykjavik (Iceland) 2018, *Conference* Alcanena (Portugal) 2017, *Conference* Hyderabad (India) 2016, *Conference* New Orleans, LA (USA) 2015. **Publications** *Ogmios Newsletter* (3 a year). Congress proceedings.
Members Full in 40 countries and territories:
Australia, Belgium, Brunei Darussalam, Canada, Congo Brazzaville, Cyprus, Denmark, Finland, France, Gambia, Germany, Hungary, India, Indonesia, Iran Islamic Rep, Ireland, Israel, Italy, Japan, Kenya, Latvia, Malaysia, Mongolia, Morocco, Nepal, Netherlands, New Zealand, Norway, Pakistan, Papua New Guinea, Poland, Russia, South Africa, Spain, Sweden, Taiwan, Tajikistan, Uganda, UK, USA. [2018.10.17/XJ0634/f/F]

♦ Foundation for Enterprise Development (internationally oriented national body)

♦ Foundation for Environmental Conservation (FEC) 09948
Fondation pour la conservation de l'environnement

Pres Rue de l'Avenir 1, 1110 Morges VD, Switzerland.
URL: https://foundationforec.org/

History 1975, Geneva (Switzerland). Founded by *International Union for Conservation of Nature and Natural Resources (IUCN, #15766)*, *World Wide Fund for Nature (WWF, #21922)* and Prof Nicholas Polunin (died 1997). Prof Polunin's leadership succeeded by his son Nicholas "Nick" V C Polunin. Instrumental in setting up: *World Council For The Biosphere (WCB, inactive)*. Registration: Switzerland. **Aims** Help promote environmental conservation. **Structure** Governing Board. Organizes: *International Conferences on Environmental Future (ICEF)*. **Finance** Sources: donations; sale of publications. **Activities** Awards/prizes/competitions; events/meetings. **Events** *International Conference on Environmental Future* Honolulu, HI (USA) 2018, *International Conference on Environmental Future* Newcastle upon Tyne (UK) 2011, *International Conference on Environmental Future* Zurich (Switzerland) 2003, *Symposium on the imperative of biosphere conservation* 1998, *International Conference on Environmental Future – ICEF* Budapest (Hungary) 1990. **Publications** *Environmental Conservation* (4 a year). *Cambridge Studies in Environmental Policy* – series; *Environmental Challenges: From Stockholm to Rio and Beyond* – series; *Environmental Monographs and Symposia* – series. *Aquatic Ecosystems* (2008); *World Who Is Who and Does What in Environment and Conservation* (1997); *Surviving With The Biosphere*. Conference proceedings, invited review papers also published in the journal Environmental Conservation. [2022.05.10/XF5358/f/F]

♦ Foundation for Environmental Education (FEE) 09949
Fondation pour l'éducation à l'environnement – Stiftung für Umwelterziehung – Stichting voor Milieueducatie

CEO Scandiagade 13, 2450 Copenhagen SV, Denmark. T. +4561248080. E-mail: info@fee.global.
URL: http://www.fee.global/

History Founded 1981. Original name: *Foundation for Environmental Education in Europe – Fondation pour l'éducation à l'environnement en Europe (FEEE) – Stiftung für Umwelterziehung in Europa – Stichting voor Milieueducatie in Europa*. Current Statutes adopted by General Assembly, 2014. **Aims** Promote *sustainable development* through environmental education both by carrying out programmes and by creating an awareness of the concept of environmental education across the world. **Structure** General Assembly (every 2 years); Board of Directors; Head Office located in Copenhagen (Denmark). **Languages** English. **Staff** 16.00 FTE, paid. **Finance** Members' dues. Programme participation financed through combination of national financing (sponsoring, support from government agencies or local authorities, funds) and sponsors. **Activities** Training/education; awareness raising. **Publications** *YRE Yearbook*. Annual Report.

Members Full; Associate. National organizations in 76 countries and territories:
Australia, Bahamas, Belgium, Bermuda, Brazil, Bulgaria, Canada, China, Colombia, Comoros, Croatia, Cyprus, Czechia, Denmark, Dominican Rep, England, Estonia, Finland, France, Germany, Ghana, Greece, Iceland, India, Iran Islamic Rep, Ireland, Israel, Italy, Japan, Jordan, Kazakhstan, Kenya, Korea Rep, Latvia, Lithuania, Madagascar, Malaysia, Malta, Mauritius, Mexico, Mongolia, Montenegro, Morocco, Netherlands, New Zealand, North Macedonia, Northern Ireland, Norway, Poland, Portugal, Puerto Rico, Qatar, Romania, Russia, Scotland, Serbia, Singapore, Slovakia, Slovenia, South Africa, Spain, St Maarten, Sweden, Switzerland, Tanzania UR, Thailand, Trinidad-Tobago, Tunisia, Türkiye, Uganda, Ukraine, United Arab Emirates, USA, Virgin Is USA, Wales.

Honorary and Affiliate in 15 countries and territories:
Belgium, Colombia, Denmark, Estonia, Finland, Germany, Latvia, Montenegro, Netherlands, Northern Ireland, Norway, Sweden, Trinidad-Tobago, United Arab Emirates, Virgin Is USA.

Members also in Indian Ocean States, not specified.

Consultative Status Consultative status granted from: *UNESCO (#20322)* (Consultative Status); *UNEP (#20299)*. **IGO Relations** Member of: *World Tourism Organization (UNWTO, #21861)*. Cooperates with: [2017.10.19/XF1380/f/F]

- ♦ Foundation for Environmental Education in Europe / see Foundation for Environmental Education (#09949)
- ♦ Foundation for Environmental Security and Sustainability (internationally oriented national body)
- ♦ Foundation for the Euro-Mediterranean Civil Forum / see Euro-Mediterranean Foundation of Support to Human Rights Defenders (#05720)
- ♦ Foundation Europalia International (internationally oriented national body)
- ♦ Foundation European Art Manifestation / see International Foundation Manifesta (#13673)
- ♦ Foundation of European Carnival Cities / see Federation of European Carnival Cities (#09496)

♦ Foundation on European Citizens' Rights, Involvement and Trust (ECIT Foundation) 09950

Dir Rue d'Arlon 53, 1040 Brussels, Belgium. E-mail: info@ecit-foundation.eu.
Registered Address Rue Washington 40, 1050 Brussels, Belgium. T. +32477206706. E-mail: ecit.omondi@gmail.com.
URL: http://www.ecit-foundation.eu/

History 3 Jun 2015. Registration: Banque-Carrefour des Entreprises, No/ID: 0631.739.521, Start date: 3 Jun 2016, Belgium; EU Transparency Register, No/ID: 494832735094-65, Start date: 11 Jun 2019. **Aims** Develop a holistic approach to European citizenship; become a multidisciplinary resource bringing together different aspects of this transnational citizenship; place Union citizenship in a broader framework, bringing about a more coherent citizenship within the European Union and introducing reforms for a full-scale European citizenship. **Structure** Board of Directors. **Languages** English, French. **Staff** 2.00 FTE, paid. **Finance** Donations; services; exchange programmes. **Activities** Training/education; events/meetings; publishing activities. **Events** *Annual Conference* Brussels (Belgium) 2022, *Annual Conference* Brussels (Belgium) 2021, *Annual Conference on European Citizenship* Brussels (Belgium) 2020, *Summer University* Brussels (Belgium) 2019, *Summer University* Brussels (Belgium) 2018. **Members** Not a membership organization. **NGO Relations** Member of: *European Association for Local Democracy (ALDA, #06110)*; *Federation of European and International Associations Established in Belgium (FAIB, #09508)*. Located at: *International Association Centre (MAI)*. [2021/XM4375/f/F]

♦ Foundation European Congress on Extracorporeal Circulation Technology (FECECT) 09951

Secretariat PO Box 84 115, 3009 CC Rotterdam, Netherlands. T. +31104527004 – +3110(31629229655. E-mail: office@fecect.org.
Street address c/o Moonen Conference Organizers, Pearl Buckplaats 37, 3069 BZ Rotterdam, Netherlands.
URL: http://www.fecect.org/

History following a series of congresses organized by national societies. Set up by Dutch Society, 1989, and confirmed 1992, Arles (France). **Aims** Create an international platform for exchange of knowledge in regard to extracorporeal circulation technology and related areas for *perfusionists*, clinical, and non-clinical researchers in cooperation with representatives of Eastern and Western European countries or representatives of areas within Europe, with the same language or cultural background. **Structure** Executive Board; Organizing Committee; Scientific Committee. **Events** *European Congress on Extracorporeal Circulation Technology* Riga (Latvia) 2021, *European Congress on Extracorporeal Circulation Technology* Salerno (Italy) 2019, *European Congress on Extracorporeal Circulation Technology* Marseille (France) 2017, *European Congress on Extracorporeal Circulation Technology* Krakow (Poland) 2015, *European Congress on Extracorporeal Circulation Technology* Toledo (Spain) 2013. [2013.10.04/XM2993/cf/E]

- ♦ Foundation for European Development Assistance / see Network for European Monitoring and Development Assistance

♦ Foundation for European Economic Development (FEED) 09952

Chair 23 Preston Drove, Brighton, BN1 6LA, UK.
Sec address not obtained.
URL: https://charity-feed.org/

History Nov 1990, by *European Association for Evolutionary Political Economy (EAEPE, #06033)*. Registration: Charity Commission, No/ID: 1001277, England and Wales. **Aims** Advance education throughout Europe in the field of political economy, with particular regard to evolutionary and institutional approaches to economic theory and policy. **Structure** Board of Trustees, including Chairperson, Secretary and Treasurer. **Languages** English. **Staff** Voluntary. **Finance** Donations; investments. Budget (annual): pounds7,000. **Activities** Education; research. **Publications** None. **Members** Not a membership organization. [2022/XK0985/f/F]

- ♦ Foundation for European Environmental Policy (see: #11261)
- ♦ Foundation for European Language and Educational Centres / see Foundation for Language and Educational Centres (#09964)
- ♦ Foundation for European Monitoring and Development Assistance / see Network for European Monitoring and Development Assistance

♦ Foundation of European Nurses in Diabetes (FEND) 09953

Pres 24 Holmesdale Avenue, London, SW14 7BQ, UK. T. +442088766122. E-mail: info@fend.org.
Registered office 37 Earls Drive, Newcastle upon Tyne, NE15 7AL, UK.
URL: https://www.fend.org/

History 1995. Former names and other names: *Federation of European Nurses in Diabetes* – former. Registration: Companies House, No/ID: 07114723, Start date: 31 Dec 2009, England; Charity Commission, No/ID: 1134995, England and Wales; EU Transparency Register, No/ID: 550318321992-41, Start date: 29 May 2016. **Aims** Develop and promote the professional role of the diabetes nurse in Europe; influence European *health care* policy relevant to diabetes care and research; promote acceptable standards and equity of care for people with diabetes throughout Europe. **Structure** Executive Committee. **Languages** English. **Staff** Voluntary. **Finance** Sources: members' dues; sponsorship. **Activities** Advocacy/lobbying/activism; events/meetings; healthcare; research/documentation; standards/guidelines; training/education. **Events** *Annual Conference* London (UK) 2021, *Annual Conference* 2020, *Annual Conference* Barcelona (Spain) 2019, *Annual Conference* Berlin (Germany) 2018, *Annual Conference* Lisbon (Portugal) 2017. **Publications** *International Diabetes Nursing*. *Diabetes – The Policy Puzzle: The State We Are In* (4th ed 2014); *Diabetes EU Policy Recommendations* (2006); *Diabetes – The Policy Puzzle: Towards Benchmarking in the EU 25* (2006); *Diabetes – The Policy Puzzle: Is Europe Making Progress?* (3rd ed). **Members** Individuals. Membership countries not specified. **NGO Relations** Member of (4): *European Alliance for Diabetes Research (EURADIA, #05868)*; *European Coalition for Diabetes (ECD, #06592)*; *European Diabetes Forum (EUDF, #06916)*; *European Foundation for the Study of Diabetes (EFSD, #07351)*. [2021.06.08/XD7538/f/D]

♦ Foundation for European Progressive Studies (FEPS) 09954
Fondation européenne d'études progressistes

Admin Officer Av des Arts 46, 1000 Brussels, Belgium. T. +3222346900. Fax +3222800383. E-mail: info@feps-europe.eu.
URL: http://www.feps-europe.eu/

History Dec 2007. Registration: Banque-Carrefour des Entreprises, No/ID: 0896.230.213, Start date: 6 Mar 2008, Belgium. **Aims** Develop innovative research, policy advice, training and debates to inspire and inform progressive politics and policies across Europe. **Structure** General Assembly; Bureau; Scientific Council. **Languages** English, French. **Staff** 22.00 FTE, paid. **Finance** Since Sep 2008, co-financed by *European Parliament (EP, #08146)*. **Activities** Events/meetings; research/documentation. **Events** *Call to Europe VI Conference* Brussels (Belgium) 2016, *Conference on the Future of the Digital Single Market* Brussels (Belgium) 2016, *Seminar* Brussels (Belgium) 2016, *Middle East – challenges for progressive politics in Israel* Brussels (Belgium) 2014, *Symposium* Brussels (Belgium) 2014. **Publications** *Progressive Post* (4 a year) – magazine. *Next Left Book*. Books; studies; reports; articles.

Members National political foundations and think tanks (43) in 23 countries:
Austria, Belgium, Bulgaria, Czechia, Denmark, Estonia, Finland, France, Germany, Greece, Hungary, Ireland, Italy, Latvia, Luxembourg, Malta, Netherlands, Poland, Portugal, Romania, Slovenia, Spain, Sweden, UK.

Included in the above, 6 organizations listed in this Yearbook:
Foundation Max van der Stoel (FMS); *Friedrich-Ebert-Stiftung (FES)*; *Jean-Jaurès Foundation (FJJ)*; *Olof Palme International Center, Stockholm*; *Samarbetsorganisationen för de Nordiska Socialdemokratiska Parterna och Fackföreningsrörelsen (SAMAK, #19045)*; *SOLIDAR (#19680)*.

Observers in 7 countries:
Albania, Australia, Canada, Chile, Croatia, Israel, Italy, Mexico, Netherlands, North Macedonia, Serbia, Switzerland, Türkiye, UK, USA.

Included in the above, 2 organizations listed in this Yearbook:
Central and Eastern European Network for Gender Issues (CEE Gender Network, #03695); *European Forum for Democracy and Solidarity (EFDS, #07307)*.

Ex-officio members (5):
Group of the Progressive Alliance of Socialists and Democrats in the European Parliament (S and D, #10786); *Party of European Socialists (PES, #18249)*; PES in Committee of Regions; PES Women; *Young European Socialists (YES, #21989)*.

Consultative Status Consultative status granted from: *ECOSOC (#05331)* (Special). **NGO Relations** Member of: *SOLIDAR (#19680)*. Closely linked with: *Group of the Progressive Alliance of Socialists and Democrats in the European Parliament (S and D, #10786)*; *Party of European Socialists (PES, #18249)*. Supports: *Change Partnership*. [2022.05.04/XJ0457/fy/F]

♦ Foundation for European Societies of Arms Collectors (FESAC) 09955

Chairman Unit One – Fist Floor, Clock Tower Block, Tigne' Point, Sliema, SLM 3190, Malta. T. +35621411600. E-mail: chairman@fesac.eu.
URL: https://fesac.eu/

History 1993, Maastricht (Netherlands). **Events** *Conference* Sliema (Malta) 2020. **NGO Relations** Member of (1): *World Forum on Shooting Activities (WFSA, #21523)*. Partner of (1): *Association of European Manufacturers of Sporting Firearms (ESFAM, #02523)*. [2018/XM2883/f/F]

- ♦ Foundation for European Studies – European Institute, Lodz (internationally oriented national body)
- ♦ Foundation Europe and Society / see Association Europe and Society (#02586)

♦ Foundation for a Free Information Infrastructure (FFII) 09956

Main Office Geschäftsstelle, Malmöer Str 6, 10439 Berlin, Germany. T. +493041722597. Fax +4930721509663769. E-mail: berlin@ffii.org.
Contact Avenue du Diamant 196, 1030 Brussels, Belgium. T. +32484566109. Fax +49721509663769.
URL: http://www.ffii.org/

History 1998. **Aims** Support the development of public information goods based on *copyright*, free *competition* and open standards. **Events** *PostgreSQL Asia Pacific Conference* Singapore (Singapore) 2019, *Summit* Singapore (Singapore) 2019, *PostgreSQL Asia Pacific Conference* Singapore (Singapore) 2018, *FOSSASIA Summit* Singapore (Singapore) 2017. **Consultative Status** Consultative status granted from: *World Intellectual Property Organization (WIPO, #21593)* (Permanent Observer Status). **NGO Relations** Member of: *ETO Consortium (ETOs, #05560)*. [2020/XM1269/f/F]

♦ Foundation for Gaia 09957

Contact 8 Redington House, Priory Green, London, N1 9QQ, UK. E-mail: contact@foundation-for-gaia.org.
URL: http://www.foundation-for-gaia.org/

History 1983. Registration: Charity Commission, No/ID: 327843, England and Wales. **Aims** Call for all humankind to act in partnership with nature in protecting the complex life-support system of the planet, to husband resources appropriately, to modify ecological relationships wisely, to establish satisfactory recycling mechanisms in harmony with natural ones, to develop clean energy sciences and to move towards a new ecological economic system that makes a clear distinction between wholesome and cancerous forms of growth. **Structure** Board of Trustees. **Languages** English. **Staff** Voluntary. **Activities** Advocacy/lobbying/activism; politics/policy/regulatory; research and development; knowledge management/information dissemination; networking/liaising; training/education; projects/programmes. **Publications** Articles. **Members** Not a membership organization. **Consultative Status** Consultative status granted from: *ECOSOC (#05331)* (Special). **NGO Relations** Founding member of: *NGO Forum on Environment (FOE, #17125)*. Member of: *NGO Alliance on Global Concerns and Values (NGO Alliance, #17102)*. Steering Committee member of: *IUCN WCPA*

Specialist Group on Cultural and Spiritual Values of Protected Areas (CSVPA, #16080). **Partners**: Associazione Italiana Wilderness; *Center for International Environmental Law (CIEL)* Human Rights and Climate Change Working Group; *Global Ecovillage Network (GEN, #10331); Global Ecovillage Network – Europe (GEN Europe, #10332); Planetary Association for Clean Energy (PACE, #18381).* [2016.06.01/XJ0983/f/F]

- ♦ Foundation for Global Community – Global Initiatives Team for the CSCE (internationally oriented national body)
- ♦ Foundation for the Global Compact (internationally oriented national body)
- ♦ Foundation Global Ethic / see Global Ethic Foundation

♦ Foundation for Global Governance and Sustainability (FOGGS) 09958

Exec Dir Rue Abbé Cuypers 3, 1040 Brussels, Belgium. E-mail: info@foggs.org.
URL: https://www.foggs.org/

History 2013, Brussels (Belgium). Statutes modified: 2018; 2020; 2021. Registration: Banque-Carrefour des Entreprises, No/ID: 0537.478.384, Start date: 14 Aug 2013, Belgium. **Aims** Develop and promote a Grand Narrative of hope, for a people-centred, planet-friendly, inclusive and sustainable globalisation in a digital world; help address major global challenges through a revamped global governance system and engaged, responsible and informed global citizens; nsure that the rapid and transformative technological and digital advances contribute to a more just and equitable world, with a better life for all people. **Structure** Executive Board; Advisory Board; Secretariat. **Languages** English. Occasional publications or events in other languages. **Activities** Events/meetings; knowledge management/information dissemination; politics/policy/regulatory. **Publications** *FOGGS Newsletter.* [2022.05.20/AA2249/f/F]

- ♦ Foundation for Global Sports Development (internationally oriented national body)
- ♦ Foundation Global Values Alliance (internationally oriented national body)
- ♦ Foundation for Grassroots Initiatives in Africa (internationally oriented national body)
- ♦ Foundation The Hague Joint Conferences on International Law (internationally oriented national body)
- ♦ Foundation for Health and Human Rights (inactive)
- ♦ Foundation for Hospices in Sub-Saharan Africa / see Global Partners in Care
- ♦ Foundation For Human Rights And Freedoms And Humanitarian Relief / see HH Humanitarian Relief Foundation
- ♦ Foundation ILCOP – International Liaison Committee for Peace Foundation (see: #14535)
- ♦ Foundation IMC – International Marine Centre ONLUS / see International Marine Centre

♦ Foundation for Innovative New Diagnostics (FIND) 09959

Main Office Campus Biotech, 9 Chemin des Mines, 1202 Geneva, Switzerland.
URL: https://www.finddx.org/

History 2003, at a meeting of *WHO (#20950)*, with initial funding from *Bill and Melinda Gates Foundation (BMGF)*. Registered in accordance with Swiss Civil Code. **Aims** Bring diagnostic solutions to the very societies where treatable *diseases* are rampant and where poverty and poor health are closely intertwined. **Structure** Board of Directors, headed by Chairman. Head office in Geneva (Switzerland). Offices in India and Uganda. **Finance** Funded by: *Bill and Melinda Gates Foundation (BMGF)*; governments of Netherlands and Germany; *Department for International Development (DFID, inactive); European Commission (EC, #06633); United States Agency for International Development (USAID); Irish Aid; Unitaid (#20493).* **NGO Relations** Member of: *Global Health Technologies Coalition (GHTC).* [2020/XJ5768/f/F]

- ♦ Foundation for Intentional Community (internationally oriented national body)
- ♦ Foundation of Interessengemeinschaft Zitrussäfte / see SGF International (#19252)
- ♦ Foundation of the Internatioanl Medical Radio Center (internationally oriented national body)

♦ Foundation for International Arbitration Advocacy (FIAA) 09960

Pres Rue du Pré-de-la-Bichette 1 – 11th floor, 1202 Geneva, Switzerland. T. +41223080000. Fax +41223080001. E-mail: info@fiaa.com.
URL: https://www.fiaa.com/

Aims Provide advocacy training specifically designed for international arbitration. **Structure** Board of Trustees; Executive Committee; Advisory Council. **Activities** Events/meetings; training/education. **Events** *FIAA International Arbitration Advocacy Workshop* Singapore (Singapore) 2013. [2021/AA2085/f/F]

♦ Foundation for International Business Administration Accreditation (FIBAA) 09961

Manager Berliner Freiheit 20-24, 53111 Bonn, Germany. T. +492282803560. E-mail: info@fibaa.org.
Zurich Office c/o economiesuisse I Verband der Schweizer Unternehmen, Hegibachstrasse 47, 8032 Zurich ZH, Switzerland.
URL: http://www.fibaa.org/

History Oct 1994. **Aims** Support maintenance and enhancement of quality standards in *teaching* and *learning* in *higher education*; promote accreditation of study programmes and higher education institutions as well as certification of continuing education courses and corporate learning units. **Structure** Managing Directors. **Languages** English, German. **Staff** 17.00 FTE, paid. **Activities** Certification/accreditation; guidance/assistance/consulting.

Members Organizations and individuals in 4 countries:
Austria, Germany, Netherlands, Switzerland.

NGO Relations Member of (5): *Asia-Pacific Quality Network (APQN, #02004); Central and Eastern European Network of Quality Assurance Agencies in Higher Education (CEENQA, #03696); EFMD – The Management Development Network (#05387); European Quality Assurance Register for Higher Education (EQAR, #08311); International Network of Quality Assurance Agencies in Higher Education (INQAAHE, #14312).* Also links with national organizations. [2016/XF7185/f/F]

- ♦ Foundation for International Community Assistance / see FINCA International

♦ Foundation of the International Congress on Hyperbaric Medicine (ICHM) 09962

Sec-Treas Hyperbaric Medicine, Level 1, Prince of Wales Hospital, Barker Street, Randwick NSW 2031, Australia.

History 1987, Sydney, NSW (Australia). Founded at 9th International Congress on Hyperbaric Medicine. **Aims** Promote and support the international congress on hyperbaric medicine. **Finance** Members' dues. **Events** *International Congress on Hyperbaric Medicine* Rio de Janeiro (Brazil) 2020, *Biennial Congress* Belgrade (Serbia) 2017, *Triennial Congress* Buenos Aires (Argentina) 2014, *Triennial Congress / International Congress on Hyperbaric Medicine* Cape Town (South Africa) 2011, *Triennial congress / International Congress on Hyperbaric Medicine* Beijing (China) 2008. **Publications** *Oxygen* – newsletter. Congress' proceedings. [2020/XF5926/f/F]

- ♦ Foundation for an International Court of the Environment / see International Court of the Environment Foundation (#13097)
- ♦ Foundation for the International Decade for a Culture of Peace and Non-Violence for the Children of the World (internationally oriented national body)
- ♦ Foundation for International Development Africa / see Development Training International
- ♦ Foundation for International Development / Relief (internationally oriented national body)
- ♦ Foundation for International Development Study and Research (internationally oriented national body)
- ♦ Foundation for International Medical Relief of Children (unconfirmed)
- ♦ Foundation for International Organizations Buildings (internationally oriented national body)
- ♦ Foundation of International Servant Leadership Exchange Association (internationally oriented national body)

♦ Foundation for International Studies on Social Security (FISS) 09963

SG c/o Herman Deleeck Ctr for Social Policy, Fac of Social Sciences, Univ of Antwerp, St-Jacobstr 2, 2000 Antwerp, Belgium. T. +3232755790. Fax +3232755374.
Chair Univ New South Wales, Fac of Arts and Social Sciences, Sydney NSW 2052, Australia.
URL: http://www.fiss-socialsecurity.org/

History May 1987. **Aims** Promote international multidisciplinary research on social security, including its relationships with other aspects of society such as the labour market, unemployment, poverty, income redistribution, savings, housing, family, health and well-being. **Structure** Board of Governors, comprising President, Secretary-General, Treasurer and 9 Governors. **Languages** English. **Staff** 3.00 FTE, voluntary. **Finance** Grants from universities and research institutes. Budget (annual): about euro 10,000. **Activities** Events/meetings; awards/prizes/competitions. **Events** *Annual International Research Seminar* Sigtuna (Sweden) 2016, *Annual International Research Seminar / Conference* Hong Kong (Hong Kong) 2015, *Annual International Research Seminar / Conference* Sigtuna (Sweden) 2014, *Annual International Research Seminar / Conference* Sigtuna (Sweden) 2013, *Annual International Research Seminar / Conference* Sigtuna (Sweden) 2012. **Publications** *International Studies on Social Security* – book series in 16 vols.

Members Individuals and institutions in 17 countries:
Argentina, Australia, Belgium, Denmark, Finland, France, Germany, Greece, Israel, Italy, Japan, Netherlands, Norway, Sweden, Switzerland, UK, USA. [2015.06.01/XF5619/f/F]

- ♦ Foundation for International Understanding, Denmark / see Folmer Wisti Foundation for International Understanding
- ♦ Foundation for International Voluntary Service (internationally oriented national body)
- ♦ Foundation for International Work Camps / see Foundation for International Voluntary Service
- ♦ Foundation for International Youth Exchange (internationally oriented national body)
- ♦ Foundation JIN / see JIN Climate and Sustainability
- ♦ Foundation Joint Implementation Network / see JIN Climate and Sustainability

♦ Foundation for Language and Educational Centres (EUROCENTRES) 09964

Fondation 'Centres langues et civilisations' – Stiftung für Sprach- und Bildungszentren

CEO Seestrasse 247, 8038 Zurich ZH, Switzerland. T. +41444855040 – +41444855215. Fax +41444816124. E-mail: info@eurocentres.com.
URL: http://www.eurocentres.com/

History Founded 1960, as a non-profitmaking foundation. Former title: *Foundation for European Language and Educational Centres (EUROCENTRES) – Fondation 'Centres européens langues et civilisations' – Stiftung für Europäische Sprach- und Bildungszentren.* **Aims** Enable persons of either sex from any country to study *foreign languages* and get acquainted with the characteristics of other peoples and their *cultures*, by providing full-time training with high quality *teaching*, equipment, resources and premises, at reasonable fees. **Languages** Chinese, English, French, German, Italian, Japanese, Russian, Spanish. **Activities** Intensive Courses; Compact Courses; Teacher Training and Development; Holiday Courses; Business Professional English. **Events** *Biennial council meeting* Rapperswil (Switzerland) 1989, *Biennial council meeting* Cologne (Germany FR) 1987. **Information Services** *my Eurocentres* – virtual learning environment.

Members Schools (about 40) in 18 countries (not specified). Associated Schools in 3 countries. Membership countries not specified.
Associated Schools in 3 countries. Membership countries not specified.

Consultative Status Consultative status granted from: *Council of Europe (CE, #04881)* (Participatory Status). [2013.09.02/XF4930/f/F]

♦ Foundation LEAD Network 09965

Contact Keizersgracht 59A, 1015 CE Amsterdam, Netherlands. E-mail: info@lead-eu.net.
URL: http://www.lead-eu.net/

History First meeting organized 2011. Full title: *LEAD Network – Leading Executives Advancing Diversity.* Registered in accordance with Dutch law, 2014: 853 084 518. **Aims** Attract, retain and advance *women* in the *retail* and consumer *goods* industry in *Europe* through education, leadership and business development. **Structure** Executive Committee; Steering Committee. Advisory Board. **Languages** English. **Staff** 3.00 FTE, paid. **Finance** Funded by partners. **Activities** Events/meetings. **Events** *Network Event* Madrid (Spain) 2019, *Conference* London (UK) 2018. **Members** Full in 26 countries. Membership countries not specified. [2020.02.06/XM7981/f/F]

♦ Foundation for Legal Knowledge Systems (JURIX) 09966

Address not obtained.
URL: http://www.jurix.nl/

History 1988. **Structure** Executive Committee; Steering Committee. **Activities** Events/meetings. **Events** *International Conference on Legal Knowledge Systems* Madrid (Spain) 2019, *International Conference on Legal Knowledge Systems* Groningen (Netherlands) 2018, *International Conference on Legal Knowledge Systems* Luxembourg (Luxembourg) 2017, *International Conference on Legal Knowledge Systems* Nice (France) 2016, *International Conference on Legal Knowledge Systems* Braga (Portugal) 2015. [2018/XW0313/f/F]

- ♦ Foundation for a Living Baltic Sea (internationally oriented national body)
- ♦ Foundation for Male Contraception / see Male Contraceptive Initiative
- ♦ Foundation Max van der Stoel (internationally oriented national body)
- ♦ Foundation for Mediterranean Studies (internationally oriented national body)
- ♦ Foundation for Middle East and Balkan Studies (internationally oriented national body)
- ♦ Foundation for Middle East Peace (internationally oriented national body)
- ♦ Foundation for Missing and Sexually Exploited Children / see European Centre for Missing and Sexually Exploited Children
- ♦ Foundation myclimate (internationally oriented national body)
- ♦ Foundation "Nansen-Centre" / see Nansen International Environmental and Remote Sensing Centre (#16935)
- ♦ Foundation for a New Ibero-American Journalism / see Fundación Gabo

♦ Foundation of New Latin American Cinema 09967

Fundación del Nuevo Cine Latinoamericano (FNCL)

Dir Gen Quinta Santa Barbara calle 212 esq 31, Rpto La Coronela, La Lisa, Havana, Cuba. T. +5372718967 – +5372718311. Fax +5372736364. E-mail: fcine@cubarte.cult.cu.
URL: http://www.cinelatinoamericano.org/

History 4 Dec 1985, under the auspices of *Comité de Cineastas de América Latina y el Caribe (CCAL, no recent information).* **Aims** Help strengthening the Latin American cinema, in particular the newly emerging cinematographies, by promoting its production, distribution, and exhibition; foster research, teaching, conservation, maintenance of film, archives and cultural dissemination of the Latin American cinematographic work; further a growing and effective solidarity within the Latin American cinematography in the framework of the preservation of the cultural heritage of Latin American peoples, as well as their dignity and social justice. **Structure** President; Executive Board, comprising 4 members. **Finance** Sources: contributions from governments, private bodies and international organizations; donations from artists and other individuals. **Activities** Guidance/assistance/consulting; training/education; advocacy/lobbying/activism. Acts as information center specialized in cinema and video, consisting of 19 databases. **Events** *Seminar* Havana (Cuba) 2001, *Conference of Latin American producers and distributors* Havana (Cuba) 1998, *Conference of Latin American producers and distributors* Havana (Cuba) 1996. **Publications** *Guiones Cinematograficos* – series. Monographs; directories; studies.

Members National representatives in 31 countries and territories:
Argentina, Belize, Bolivia, Brazil, Chile, Colombia, Costa Rica, Cuba, Dominican Rep, Ecuador, El Salvador, Germany, Guatemala, Guyana, Haiti, Honduras, Italy, Jamaica, Martinique, Mexico, Neth Antilles, Nicaragua, Panama, Paraguay, Peru, Puerto Rico, Spain, Uruguay, USA, Venezuela, Zimbabwe.

Affiliate organizations in 5 countries:
Bolivia, Mexico, Panama, Peru, Venezuela.

IGO Relations Links with various bodies, of which listed in this Yearbook: *Agencia Española de Cooperación Internacional para el Desarrollo (AECID); Conferencia de Autoridades Cinematograficas de Iberoamérica (CACI, no recent information); International Fund for the Promotion of Culture (IFPC, inactive); International Programme for the Development of Communication (IPDC, #14651); Swedish International Development Cooperation Agency (Sida); UNDP (#20292); UNESCO (#20322).*

NGO Relations Links with a large number of bodies active in the field, of which listed in this Yearbook:
- *International Cinema and Television School (#12572);*
- *Asociación Imagenes del Caribe (no recent information);*
- *Association des distributeurs alternatifs de l'Amérique latine et des Caraïbes (FEDALC, no recent information);*

- *CILECT Ibero América (CIBA, see: #11771);*
- *Confederación Universitaria Centroamericana (CSUCA, #04497);*
- *Coordinadora Latinoamericana de Archivos de Imagenes en Movimiento (CLAIM, no recent information);*
- *Dirección General de Cooperación con Iberoamérica;*
- *Federación Iberoamericana de Productores Cinematograficos y Audiovisuales (FIPCA, #09318);*
- *Federación Latinoamericana de Facultades de Comunicación Social (FELAFACS, #09353);*
- *Federación de Profesionales Caribeños de Cine y Video (no recent information);*
- *Institute for Latin America (inactive);*
- *International Federation of Film Archives (#13427);*
- *MacArthur Foundation;*
- *Memorial Foundation of Latin America;*
- *Pan African Federation of Film Makers (FEPACI, no recent information);*
- *Unión de Cinematecas de América Latina (UCAL, no recent information).* [2022/XF2111/f/**F**]

♦ Foundation for Peace (internationally oriented national body)
♦ Foundation for Peace Education / see Stichting Vredeseducatie
♦ Foundation for Peace Studies Aotearoa/New Zealand (internationally oriented national body)
♦ Foundation PEN Emergency Fund (internationally oriented national body)
♦ Foundation People for Peace and Defense of Human Rights / see Global Refugee Leaders Forum
♦ Foundation for the Peoples of the South Pacific / see Counterpart International

♦ Foundation of the Peoples of the South Pacific International (FSPI) 09968

Contact address not obtained. T. +6793312250. Fax +6793312298.
URL: http://www.fspi.org.fj/

History Mar 1989, Los Angeles CA (USA), as *Pacific Islands Development Association (PIDA)*, in the *'Los Angeles Accord'*. Present title adopted Dec 1989, following poll of member agencies. Formal agreement signed Nov 1990, Fiji. An *NGO Pacific Council for Development* had previously been set up provisionally, Sep 1984, in the *'Tonga Covenant'*. First registered in accordance with the law of Papua New Guinea, 1991; re-registered in accordance with the law of Vanuatu, 1999. Also referred to as *FSP International*. **Aims** Facilitate the process of self-help development for people of the Pacific, particularly the *poor* and the rural majorities. **Structure** General Meeting (annually). Board. Executive Committee, including Chairman, Deputy Chairman, Treasurer, Secretary and Executive Director. **Staff** 8.00 FTE, paid. **Finance** Mainly through project grants and contracts. Major donors include: New Zealand Government; *Department for International Development (DFID, inactive)*; *European Commission (EC, #06633)*. **Activities** Facilitates and promotes members' work in integrated rural development; designs and plans multi-country projects implemented through local member NGOs; manages regional projects. Major sectors include: Conservation; Forestry, Coastal/Marine; Small Enterprise Development; Community Health. **Events** *Meeting* Suva (Fiji) 1991. **Publications** Sector newsletters; Annual Report; project reports.
Members Independent and metropolitan () membership in 11 countries:
Australia (*), Fiji, Kiribati, Papua New Guinea, Samoa, Solomon Is, Tonga, Tuvalu, UK (*), USA (*), Vanuatu.
Included in the above, 4 organizations listed in this Yearbook:
Counterpart International (FSP); Just World Partners; Timor Aid.
IGO Relations Cooperates with: *Pacific Community (SPC, #17942); Secretariat of the Pacific Regional Environment Programme (SPREP, #19205).* Operational agreements with various regional IGOs. **NGO Relations** Member of: *EarthAction (EA, #05159); GEF CSO Network (GCN, #10087); Pacific Islands Association of Non-Governmental Organizations (PIANGO, #17961).* Part of: *Pacific Islands Regional Non-governmental Organizations (PRNGO, #17978).* Participates in: *Global Island Partnership (GLISPA, #10436); Global Partnership for Oceans (GPO, #10537).* [2013/XF2208/fy/**F**]

♦ Foundation 'Populorum Progressio' 09969

Fondation 'Populorum Progressio' – Fundación 'Populorum Progressio' – Stiftung 'Populorum Progressio' – Fundação 'Populorum Progressio' – Fondazione 'Populorum Progressio'
Office c/o Pontificio Consiglio Cor Unum, Palazzo San Pio X, Via della Conciliazione 5, 00120 Vatican City, Vatican. T. +39669889411. Fax +39669887301 – +39669887311. E-mail: corunum@corunum.va.
Admin Council Segretaria del Consejo de Administración, Carrera 7B bis No 124-78, Bogota, Bogota DC, Colombia. T. +5712134043. Fax +5716204297.
URL: http://www.corunum.va/

History 13 Feb 1992, Vatican City, by Pope John-Paul II. **Aims** Support projects aimed at integral human development of the poorest communities of rural peoples in *Latin America* and the *Caribbean* as a gesture of *pontifical* solidarity with marginalized indigenous and mixed-race populations, indios and campesinos, according to a just and appropriate application of the social teaching of the Church. **Structure** Council of Administration (meets annually), comprising 6 bishops from different Latin American countries. President; Vice-President. Secretariat. **Finance** Contributions; offerings; bequests. **Activities** Provides financial assistance to projects in Latin America and Caribbean countries; encourages episcopal conferences to collect funds for this purpose. **Events** *Annual Latin America meeting* 2001, *Annual Latin America meeting* 2000, *Annual Latin America meeting* 1999.
Members Full in 34 countries and territories:
Antigua-Barbuda, Argentina, Barbados, Belize, Bolivia, Brazil, Chile, Colombia, Costa Rica, Cuba, Dominica, Dominican Rep, Ecuador, El Salvador, Grenada, Guatemala, Guyana, Haiti, Honduras, Jamaica, Mexico, Neth Antilles, Nicaragua, Panama, Paraguay, Peru, Puerto Rico, St Kitts-Nevis, St Lucia, St Vincent-Grenadines, Suriname, Trinidad-Tobago, Uruguay, Venezuela. [2013.08.08/XF3571/f/**F**]

♦ Foundation PPDR / see Global Refugee Leaders Forum

♦ Foundation for the Preservation of the Mahayana Tradition (FPMT) . 09970

Pres/CEO 1632 SE 11th Ave, Portland OR 97214-4702, USA. T. +15038081588. Fax +15032320557. E-mail: info@fpmt.org.
Exec Assistant address not obtained.
URL: http://www.fpmt.org/

History 1971. Founded by Buddhist masters Lama Thubten Yeshe and Lama Thubten Zopa Rinpoche. **Aims** Transmit Mahayana *Buddhist* tradition and values worldwide through teaching, meditation and community service; provide education through which people's minds and hearts can be transformed into their highest potential for the benefit of others, inspired by an attitude of universal responsibility; create harmonious environments and help all beings develop their full potential of infinite wisdom and compassion. **Structure** Composed of over 150 Buddhist monasteries, city and country retreat centres, communities, publishing houses and health and healing centres. *International Mahayana Institute (IMI, #14074)* is the group of non-Tibetan monks and nuns practising and working within the FPMT. International Office: Portland OR (USA); Regional Offices (4); National Offices (6). **Languages** English. **Staff** 11.00 FTE, paid; 2.00 FTE, voluntary. **Finance** Sources: donations. **Activities** Projects/programmes. **Events** *International meeting* Melbourne, VIC (Australia) 1991.
Members International network of individuals (about 6,000), grouped in 150 FPMT Centers, in 30 countries and territories:
Australia, Austria, Brazil, Canada, China, Colombia, Denmark, France, Germany, Greece, Iceland, India, Indonesia, Italy, Japan, Latvia, Malaysia, Mexico, Mongolia, Nepal, Netherlands, New Zealand, Russia, Singapore, Spain, Sweden, Switzerland, Taiwan, UK, USA. [2022.02.16/XF2037/fv/**F**]

♦ Foundation for the Progress of Humanity / see Fondation Charles Léopold Mayer pour le progrès de l'homme (#09815)
♦ Foundation to Publish ERAE / see European Agricultural and Applied Economics Publications Foundation (#05845)
♦ Foundation for the Refugee Education Trust / see RET International (#18927)
♦ Foundation for Regional Development (internationally oriented national body)
♦ Foundation for Religious Tolerance / see International Foundation for Human Rights and Tolerance
♦ Foundation for Research on International Environment, National Development and Security (internationally oriented national body)
♦ Foundation for the Research of Turkestan, Azerbaijan, Crimea, Caucasus and Siberia / see Research Centre for Turkestan and Azerbaijan

♦ Foundation for Responsible Robotics (FRR) 09971

Contact Sleedoornstr 14, 2565 WN The Hague, Netherlands. E-mail: info@responsiblerobotics.org.
URL: http://responsiblerobotics.org/

History Set up, Twente (Netherlands). **Aims** Promote responsible design, development, implementation, and policy of robots embedded in society; influence the future development and application of robotics such that it embeds the standards, methods, principles, capabilities, and policy points, as they relate to the responsible design and deployment of robotic systems. **Structure** Co-Directors; Executive Advisory Board. Committees (3): Technical Expertise; Legal Expertise; Organizing. **Languages** English. **Staff** 5.00 FTE, voluntary. **Finance** Members' dues. **Activities** Guidance/assistance/consulting; networking/liaising; projects/programmes; publishing activities; research and development; research/documentation; training/education; events/meetings. **Publications** *FRR Newsletter*. Documents. [2020/XM5918/f/**F**]

♦ Foundation of SAARC Writers and Literature (FOSWAL) 09972

Pres 4/6 Siri Fort Institutional Area, Delhi 110 049, DELHI 110 049, India. T. +91116498070 – +91116494444. Fax +91116496542.
URL: http://www.foundationsaarcwriters.com/

History 1975, Delhi (India). Recognized body of *South Asian Association for Regional Cooperation (SAARC, #19721)*, since Jan 2002. Previously also known under the acronym *FSWL*. **Activities** Organizes conferences. Programmes: Youth Outreach; Writers-in-Residence. Setting up an *International Centre of Women's Literature*. **Events** *Conference* Aligarh (India) 2005, *Conference* Delhi (India) 2004, *Conference* Dhaka (Bangladesh) 2004, *Conference* Lahore (Pakistan) 2004, *Conference* Kaafu Atoll (Maldives) 2003. **Publications** *Beyond Borders* (3 a year) – journal. Anthologies; translations. [2017/XF6967/f/**F**]

♦ Foundations of Computational Mathematics (FoCM) 09973

Sec address not obtained.
Chair address not obtained.
URL: http://focm-society.org/

Aims Support and promote research at the interface of mathematics and computation. **Structure** Board of Directors; Executive Committee. **Activities** Events/meetings; awards/prizes/competitions. **Events** *Conference* Barcelona (Spain) 2017. **Publications** *FoCM Journal*. [2018.09.05/XM5463/c/**F**]

♦ Foundation for Security and Development in Africa (internationally oriented national body)
♦ Foundation for Self-Sufficiency in Central America / see EcoViva
♦ Foundation for a Smoke-Free World (unconfirmed)
♦ Foundation for the Social Promotion of Culture / see Fundación Promoción Social
♦ Foundation for Solidarity and Peace 'Serafin Aliaga' (internationally oriented national body)

♦ Foundations for Peace (FFP) 09974

Secretariat Community Foundation Northern Ireland, City Link Business Park, Albert Street, Belfast, BT12 4BU, UK.
Contact address not obtained.
URL: http://foundationsforpeace.com/

History Founded 14 Oct 2003, UK, by organizations based in areas of conflict. Formally launched, 2006, New York NY (USA). A legally registered Charity in Northern Ireland. **Aims** Serve as a platform for social justice, inclusion and peacebuilding; support foundations' work in their own communities. **Languages** English. **Staff** Voluntary. **Finance** Philanthropic donations. Annual budget: about US$ 80,000. **Activities** Events/meetings. **Events** *Meeting* Brussels (Belgium) 2004. **Publications** *Foundations for Peace Newsletter*. Conference reports.
Members Organizations in 9 countries and territories:
Bangladesh, Georgia, India, Indonesia, Nepal, Northern Ireland, Palestine, Serbia, Sri Lanka. [2020/XF7184/**F**]

♦ Foundation for Spreading the Knowledge to Unify Humanity (internationally oriented national body)
♦ Foundations of Success (internationally oriented national body)
♦ Foundation for Studies on Turkish-Arab Relations / see Ortadogu ve Balkan Incelemeleri Vakfi
♦ Foundation for the Support of International Medical Training (internationally oriented national body)
♦ Foundation for Support for the Latin American Blind / see Fundación ONCE para América Latina
♦ Foundation for Sustainable Development Intercultural Exchange (internationally oriented national body)
♦ Foundation for Sustainable Development in Latin America (#10021)
♦ Foundation for the Sustainable Development of the South American Chaco (internationally oriented national body)

♦ Foundation for Sustainable Food Security in Central West Africa (SADAOC Foundation) 09975

Fondation pour la sécurité alimentaire durable en Afrique de l'Ouest centrale (Fondation SADAOC)
Exec Sec 06 BP 9256, Ouagadougou 06, Burkina Faso. E-mail: bkouassi1@gmail.com.
URL: http://www.sadaoc.bf/

History 1 Jun 1992, as *Network on Sustainable Food Security in Central West Africa – Réseau de sécurité alimentaire durable en Afrique de l'Ouest centrale*, on the initiative of the Netherlands Ministry of Development Cooperation (DGIS) and Dutch universities. Previously also referred to in French as *Réseau de recherche SADAOC* and *Réseau SADAOC*. Added, 18 Jun 1996, a foundation, *Fondation SADAOC*, registered in Maastricht (Netherlands), to channel funds for its activities. **Aims** Develop a new structural approach to improving food security in West Africa by strengthening local research capacity and stimulating high quality research that supports policy design; develop methods for effective and structured consultation between researchers and policy makers; enhance regional cooperation and coordination for food security policies. **Structure** International Management Board; National Networks; Executive Secretariat hosted in Burkina Faso. **Finance** Funding from DGIS. Estimated annual budget: US$ 750,000. **Activities** Events/meetings; networking/liaising; research and development; projects/programmes; capacity building. **Events** *Round table on a regional food policy issue* 2003, *Round table* 2003, *Round Table* Abidjan (Côte d'Ivoire) 2002, *International conference on food security* Bamako (Mali) 2002, *Round table / International Conference on Food Security* Accra (Ghana) 2001. **Publications** *SADAOC Info* (2 a year) – bulletin. Research reports.
Members National networks (") and universities and other bodies in 6 countries:
Burkina Faso (*), Côte d'Ivoire (*), Ghana (*), Mali, Netherlands (*), Togo.
Included in the above, 1 organization listed in this Yearbook:
Centre for Development Studies, Cape Coast (CDS, no recent information). [2017.09.15/XF2717/f/**F**]

♦ Foundations of Utility and Risk Conference (meeting series)
♦ Foundation for Teaching Aids at Low Cost / see Health Books International
♦ Foundation for Theological Education in South East Asia (internationally oriented national body)
♦ Foundation for the Third Millennium (internationally oriented national body)
♦ Foundation for Tolerance International (internationally oriented national body)
♦ Foundation UNESCO – Education for Children in Need / see YOU Stiftung – Bildung für Kinder in Not
♦ Foundation United Cultures Organization / see United Cultures Foundation
♦ Foundation for Universal Responsibility of His Holiness The Dalai Lama (internationally oriented national body)
♦ Foundation Voice of Africa / see Stichting Stem van Afrika
♦ Foundation for the Welfare and Education of Asian People (internationally oriented national body)
♦ Foundation for Women's Health Research and Development (internationally oriented national body)

♦ Foundation Working Group International Waterbird and Wetland Research (WIWO) 09976

Fondation du Groupe de travail pour la recherche internationale sur les oiseaux d'eau et les zones humides – Stichting Werkgroep Internationaal Wad- en Watervogelonderzoek
Secretary PO Box 6521, 6503 GA Nijmegen, Netherlands.
Chair address not obtained.
URL: http://www.wiwo.org/

History Founded 1983. **Aims** Stimulate, initiate and execute scientific research into *waders* and other waterbirds and their haunts, for the benefit of *nature conservation* as well as the transfer of knowledge; promote transfer of knowledge of management of wetlands and wetland bird populations. **Structure** Board of 7 members. **Finance** Subsidies, including more recently from the following organizations or agreements listed in this Yearbook: *African-Eurasian Migratory /Water Bird/ Agreement (AEWA, 1995)*; *BirdLife International (#03266)*; *Wetlands International (#20928)*. **Activities** Research/documentation; networking/liaising. **Events** *Annual Meeting* Utrecht (Netherlands) 2010, *Annual meeting* Utrecht (Netherlands) 2008, *Annual Meeting* Utrecht (Netherlands) 2005. **Publications** *WIWO Reports* – series. [2015.11.26/XE3584/f/**F**]

- ♦ Foundation World Without Mines (internationally oriented national body)
- ♦ Foundation for Worldwide International Student Exchange (internationally oriented national body)
- ♦ **FourA** Asian Academic Accounting Association (#01292)

♦ Four Dragons 09977

Address not obtained.

History Also referred to as *Four Tigers*, *East Asian Tigers* and *Asia's Four Little Dragons*. **Aims** Unite the 4 small *Asian less developed* countries that have experienced unusually rapid *economic* growth between the early 1960s and 1990s.

Members Governments of 4 countries and territories:
Hong Kong, Korea Rep, Singapore, Taiwan. [2008/XF5628/**F***]

- ♦ Four Paws International (#20776)
- ♦ Four plus Five Group / see Cooperation Process in the Western Mediterranean (#04798)
- ♦ Foursquare Church / see International Church of the Foursquare Gospel
- ♦ Fourth ACP-EEC Convention (1989 treaty)
- ♦ Fourth Additional Protocol to the European Convention on Extradition (2012 treaty)
- ♦ Fourth Association of Model Auto Racing (unconfirmed)
- ♦ Fourth Freedom Forum (internationally oriented national body)
- ♦ Fourth International (inactive)
- ♦ Fourth Protocol to the General Agreement on Privileges and Immunities of the Council of Europe (1961 treaty)
- ♦ The Fourth World / see Fourth World General Council (#09978)

♦ Fourth World General Council 09978

Conseil général du quart monde

Contact c/o Fourth World, PO Box 2410, Swindon, SN5 4XN, UK. T. +441793772214.

History Aug 1980, in preparation for the first Assembly. Also referred to as *The Fourth World*. **Aims** Strengthen communications links working for down-scaling of military, industrial, commercial and governmental complexes so as to help avert the threat of global war and ecological disaster; combat giantism of social institutions and work for a human scale and a non-centralized, multi-cellular, power-dispersed world order. **Structure** Includes: League of Real Nations; The Academic Inn; The Middlebury Institute; The Kohr Schumacher Trust; Neighbourhood Democracy Network; Purton Fourth World University. Offices in: Australia; India; New Zealand; USA. **Finance** Members' dues: variable – individually self-determined; libraries and institutions – pounds25. **Events** *Annual assembly of the fourth world* UK 1994, *Assembly* UK 1994, *Annual Assembly of the Fourth World* Wales (UK) 1994, *Assembly / Annual Assembly of the Fourth World* Barcelona (Spain) 1993, *Assembly / Annual Assembly of the Fourth World* London (UK) 1991. **Publications** *Purton Today* (4 a year); *Academic Inn Papers*; *Fourth World Review* – temporarily suspended. *Fourth World Papers* – series. **Members** Representatives of small nations; groups working for autonomy and independence; minority groups; groups in the fields of peace action, ecology, economics, energy resources, women's liberation; alternative groups. Members in 59 countries and territories:
Australia, Austria, Bangladesh, Belgium, Botswana, Brazil, Canada, China, Colombia, Cuba, Czechia, Denmark, Egypt, Eswatini, Fiji, Finland, France, Germany, Ghana, Greece, Haiti, Hong Kong, Hungary, India, Indonesia, Ireland, Italy, Lesotho, Liechtenstein, Luxembourg, Malawi, Mauritius, Mexico, Morocco, Mozambique, Netherlands, New Zealand, Nicaragua, Nigeria, Norway, Pakistan, Papua New Guinea, Peru, Philippines, Poland, Romania, Saudi Arabia, Senegal, Singapore, Slovakia, Slovenia, South Africa, Spain, Sweden, Trinidad-Tobago, United Arab Emirates, USA, Zambia, Zimbabwe. [2011.06.01/XF4477/**F**]

- ♦ Four Tigers / see Four Dragons (#09977)
- ♦ FOV – Friends of Vellore (internationally oriented national body)
- ♦ **FOVU** Nordisk Folkeoplysnings- og Voksenundervisningssamarbejde (#17504)
- ♦ FOW – Friends of Ostomates Worldwide (internationally oriented national body)
- ♦ FOWPAL – Federation of World Peace and Love (internationally oriented national body)
- ♦ Foyer catholique européen (internationally oriented national body)
- ♦ Foyer Cattolico Europeo (internationally oriented national body)
- ♦ **FP2030** Family Planning 2030 (#09255)
- ♦ **FPAA** Federación Panamericana de Asociaciones de Arquitectos (#18098)
- ♦ FPAE – Fondation Paul Ango Ela de géopolitique en Afrique centrale (internationally oriented national body)
- ♦ FPA – Foreign Policy Association (internationally oriented national body)
- ♦ **FPA** Forum pour le Partenariat avec l'Afrique (#00510)
- ♦ **FP-AP** Association Européenne des Anciens Parlementaires (#06047)
- ♦ **FP-AP** European Association of Former Parliamentarians (#06047)
- ♦ FPC – Foreign Policy Centre, London (internationally oriented national body)
- ♦ FPC – Funding for Peace Coalition (internationally oriented national body)
- ♦ FPC / see International Federation for Peace and Conciliation (#13501)
- ♦ FPCP – Fratres Piae Congregationis a Praesentatione (religious order)
- ♦ FPDA / see AIPS America (#00599)
- ♦ FPDA – Five-Power Defence Agreement (1957 treaty)
- ♦ **FPDA** Five Power Defence Arrangements (#09788)
- ♦ **FPDSA** Forum for the Progress and Development of South America (#09888)
- ♦ **FPEC** Fédération Pro Europa Christiana (#09489)
- ♦ **FPE** Fédération panafricaine des employés (#09700)
- ♦ **FPE** Flexible Packaging Europe (#09794)
- ♦ **FPFECV** Federación Panamericana de Facultades y Escuelas de Ciencias Veterinarias (#18105)
- ♦ FP – Féminin Pluriel (internationally oriented national body)
- ♦ **FPF** Food Packaging Forum (#09848)
- ♦ FPG / see Féminin Pluriel
- ♦ FP Global / see Féminin Pluriel
- ♦ **FPH** Fondation Charles Léopold Mayer pour le progrès de l'homme (#09815)
- ♦ **FPH** Frente Parlamentario Contra el Hambre de América Latina y el Caribe (#09994)
- ♦ FPHV – Fundación Pro Humanae Vitae (internationally oriented national body)
- ♦ FPI – Fédération prohibitioniste internationale (inactive)
- ♦ FPI – Foreign Policy Institute, Ankara (internationally oriented national body)
- ♦ FPI – Forskningspolitiska Institutet, Lund (internationally oriented national body)
- ♦ FPI – Johns Hopkins Foreign Policy Institute, Washington DC (internationally oriented national body)
- ♦ FPL – International Conference on Field-Programmable Logic and Applications (meeting series)
- ♦ FPLP – Fórum dos Parlamentos dos Países de Língua Portuguesa (inactive)
- ♦ **FPMA** Fonds pour le Patrimoine Mondial Africain (#00505)
- ♦ **FPMA** Fundo para o Património Mundial Africano (#00505)
- ♦ FPME – Food Processing Machinery Europe (inactive)
- ♦ **FPMT** Foundation for the Preservation of the Mahayana Tradition (#09970)
- ♦ FPN / see Americans for Peace Now
- ♦ **FPNI** Fluid Power Net International (#09802)
- ♦ **FPNUL** Fuerza Provisional de las Naciones Unidas en el Libano (#20577)
- ♦ **FPP** Forest Peoples Programme (#09865)
- ♦ FPPG – Forum per i Problemi della Pace e della Guerra (internationally oriented national body)
- ♦ FPRA – Finnish Peace Research Association (internationally oriented national body)
- ♦ FPRI – Foreign Policy Research Institute (internationally oriented national body)
- ♦ **FPSAC** Permanent Program Committee of the Formal Power Series and Algebraic Combinatorics (#18329)
- ♦ **FPSB** Financial Planning Standards Board (#09768)
- ♦ FPSC / see Fundación Promoción Social
- ♦ FPS – European Conference on Fluid-Particle Separation (meeting series)
- ♦ **FPS** Federación Panamericana de Squash (#09384)
- ♦ FPS – International Symposium on Foundations and Practice of Security (meeting series)
- ♦ FPTBC – Fédération panafricaine des travailleurs du bois et de la construction (no recent information)
- ♦ FPT – Friends Peace Teams (internationally oriented national body)
- ♦ FPTI – Fédération panafricaine des travailleurs de l'industrie (no recent information)
- ♦ FPTT – Fédération panafricaine des travailleurs du transport (inactive)
- ♦ FPTTH – Fédération panafricaine des travailleurs du textile, habillement et cuir (no recent information)
- ♦ **FPVA** Federación de Partidos Verdes de las Américas (#09385)
- ♦ FPV – Fondation Pro Victimis (internationally oriented national body)
- ♦ **FQH** International Research Association for Organic Food Quality and Health (#14719)

♦ Fracarita International 09979

General Coordinator Boeveriestraat 14, 8000 Bruges, Belgium. T. +3250440690. E-mail: fracarita-international@fracarita.net.

URL: https://www.fracarita-international.org/

History Set up as the non-profit organization of *Brothers of Charity (FC)*. Registration: Banque-Carrefour des Entreprises, No/ID: 0811.110.832, Start date: 10 Apr 2009, Belgium. **Aims** Support the services of the congregation in Latin America, Africa, Asia and Europe. **Structure** General Assembly; Governing Board; Executive Committee; International Development Office. **Consultative Status** Consultative status granted from: *ECOSOC (#05331)* (Special). **NGO Relations** Member of (1): *Forum of Catholic Inspired NGOs (#09905)*. [2022/XM8826/**E**]

- ♦ FRAC – Forum régional d'analyse et de concertation (meeting series)
- ♦ Fractie van de Europese Volkspartij – Christen-democraten (#10775)
- ♦ Fractie van de Europese Volkspartij in het Comité van de Regio's (#10776)
- ♦ Fractie de Groenen in het Europees Parlement / see Group of the Greens – European Free Alliance (#10781)
- ♦ Fractie de Groenen – Vrije Europese Alliantie (#10781)
- ♦ Fractie van de Partij van de Europese Sociaaldemokraten / see Group of the Progressive Alliance of Socialists and Democrats in the European Parliament (#10786)
- ♦ **FRA** European Union Agency for Fundamental Rights (#08969)

♦ Fragility Fracture Network (FFN) 09980

Central Office c/o MCI Schweiz, Schaffhauserstr 550, 8052 Zurich ZH, Switzerland. T. +41448094286. Fax +41448094201. E-mail: ff-network@mci-group.com.

URL: http://fragilityfracturenetwork.org/

History Current articles revised Jul 2018. Former names and other names: *Fragility Fracture Network of the Bone and Joint Decade* – full title. Registration: Switzerland. **Aims** Disseminate globally the best multidisciplinary practice in preventing and managing fragility fractures; promote research aimed at better treatments of osteoporosis, sarcopenia and fracture; drive policy change that will raise fragility fracture higher up the healthcare agenda in all countries. **Structure** General Assembly (annual); Board; Executive Committee; Corporate Advisory Council. **Languages** English. **Staff** 1.00 FTE, paid. **Activities** Events/meetings. **Events** *Global Congress* Melbourne, VIC (Australia) 2022, *Annual Global Congress* 2021, *Annual Global Congress* Oxford (UK) 2019, *Annual Global Congress* Dublin (Ireland) 2018, *Annual Global Congress* Malmö (Sweden) 2017. **Publications** *FFN Newsletter* (3 a year).

Members Full in 46 countries and territories:
Albania, Argentina, Australia, Austria, Belgium, Brazil, Bulgaria, Canada, China, Colombia, Denmark, Estonia, Finland, France, Germany, Greece, Hong Kong, Iceland, India, Indonesia, Iran Islamic Rep, Iraq, Ireland, Italy, Japan, Korea Rep, Lebanon, Lithuania, Netherlands, New Zealand, Norway, Philippines, Poland, Russia, Saudi Arabia, Serbia, Slovenia, Spain, Sweden, Switzerland, Taiwan, Thailand, Türkiye, UK, United Arab Emirates, USA. [2021/XJ7580/**F**]

- ♦ Fragility Fracture Network of the Bone and Joint Decade / see Fragility Fracture Network (#09980)
- ♦ Fraktion der Allianz der Liberalen und Demokraten für Europa / see Renew Europe (#18840)
- ♦ Fraktion die Grünen im Europäischen Parlament / see Group of the Greens – European Free Alliance (#10781)
- ♦ Fraktion der Europäischen Volkspartei im Ausschuss der Regionen (#10776)
- ♦ Fraktion der Europäischen Volkspartei – Christdemokraten (#10775)
- ♦ Fraktion der Grünen – Freie Europäische Allianz (#10781)
- ♦ Fraktion der Progressiven Allianz der Sozialdemokraten im Europäischen Parlament (#10786)
- ♦ Fraktion der Socialdemokratischen Partei Europas / see Group of the Progressive Alliance of Socialists and Democrats in the European Parliament (#10786)
- ♦ **FRALC** Federación de Radioprotección de America Latina y el Caribe (#09387)
- ♦ Frame Relay Forum / see Broadband Forum (#03334)
- ♦ Framework Agreement on BIMSTEC Free Trade Area (2004 treaty)
- ♦ Framework Agreement for the Conservation of Living Marine Resources on the High Seas of the South Pacific (2000 treaty)
- ♦ Framework Agreement on Enhancing ASEAN Economic Cooperation (1992 treaty)
- ♦ Framework Agreement on Facilitation of Cross-border Paperless Trade in Asia and the Pacific (2016 treaty)

♦ Framework Convention Alliance (FCA) 09981

Exec Dir c/o HealthBridge, 1 Nicholas Street, Ste 1004, Ottawa ON K1N 7B7, Canada. T. +16132413927. E-mail: mackaseya@fctc.org.

Contact Rue de la Fontaine 2, Case Postale 3484, 1211 Geneva 3, Switzerland.

URL: https://fctc.org/

History 1999. Founded to support the development of the global tobacco control treaty: *Framework Convention on Tobacco Control (FCTC, 2003)*. Also referred to as *Framework Convention Alliance on Tobacco Control*. Registration: Swiss Civil Code, Switzerland. **Aims** Help develop and implement the Framework Convention on *Tobacco Control* (FCTC) as the basis for effective global tobacco control. **Structure** General Assembly (annual). Board of Directors, consisting of 3 members at-large elected independently of any regional considerations, and 6 members elected to represent WHO's 6 regional divisions: Africa, South-East Asia, Europe, Eastern Mediterranean, Americas and Western Pacific. **Languages** Arabic, Chinese, English, French, Russian, Spanish. **Activities** Promotes and supports tobacco control through development and implementation of the FCTC; strengthens and influences the FCTC process; mobilizes and strengthens the capacity of regional and local civil society; monitors implementation of the FCTC, its guidelines and protocols. **Events** *International Conference on Public Health Priorities in the 21st Century* Delhi (India) 2013.
Publications *Tobacco Watch*.

Members Regional and national organizations (nearly 400) in 93 countries and territories:
Algeria, Argentina, Armenia, Australia, Azerbaijan, Bahrain, Bangladesh, Barbados, Benin, Brazil, Bulgaria, Cambodia, Cameroon, Canada, Chad, Chile, China, Congo Brazzaville, Congo DR, Costa Rica, Czechia, Egypt, Finland, France, Georgia, Germany, Ghana, Greece, Honduras, Hong Kong, Hungary, India, Indonesia, Iran Islamic Rep, Ireland, Israel, Jamaica, Japan, Jordan, Kenya, Korea Rep, Kyrgyzstan, Lithuania, Malawi, Mali, Mauritius, Mexico, Mongolia, Morocco, Mozambique, Nepal, New Zealand, Niger, Nigeria, Norway, Pakistan, Palau, Panama, Papua New Guinea, Paraguay, Peru, Philippines, Portugal, Romania, Russia, Saudi Arabia, Senegal, Serbia, Slovakia, South Africa, Spain, Sri Lanka, St Lucia, Sudan, Sweden, Switzerland, Syrian AR, Taiwan, Tanzania UR, Thailand, Togo, Trinidad-Tobago, Türkiye, Uganda, UK, Ukraine, Uruguay, USA, Uzbekistan, Vietnam, Yemen, Zambia, Zimbabwe.

Included in the above, 13 organizations listed in this Yearbook:
African Centre for Empowerment and Gender Advocacy; *Africa Tobacco Control Regional Initiative (ATCRI, #00524)*; *Association of European Cancer Leagues (ECL, #02500)*; *Campaign for Tobacco-Free Kids*; *CorpWatch*; *European Heart Network (EHN, #07467)*; *European Medical Association on Smoking and Health (EMASH, #07762)*; *European Network for Smoking and Tobacco Prevention (ENSP, #08002)*; *European Respiratory Society (ERS, #08383)*; *European Union of Nonsmokers (#09006)*; *Observatoire du tabac en Afrique francophone (OTAF, #17638)*; *Pan-African Thoracic Society (PATS, #18070)*; *Smoke Free Partnership (SFP, #19329)*.

International organizations (22):
– *Adventist Development and Relief Agency International (ADRA, #00131)*;
– *Commonwealth Medical Association (CMA, #04351)*;
– *Consumers International (CI, #04773)* (Regional Office for Asia and Pacific);
– *FDI – World Dental Federation (#09281)*;
– *InterAmerican Heart Foundation (IAHF, #11432)*;
– *International Alliance of Women (IAW, #11639)*;
– *International Council of Women (ICW, #13093)*;
– *International Federation of Medical Students' Associations (IFMSA, #13478)*;
– *International Network of Women Against Tobacco (INWAT, #14343)*;
– *International Non Governmental Coalition Against Tobacco (INGCAT, no recent information)*;
– *International Pharmaceutical Federation (#14566)*;
– International Tobacco Control;
– *International Union Against Tuberculosis and Lung Disease (The Union, #15752)*;
– *International Union for Health Promotion and Education (IUHPE, #15778)*;
– *Medical Women's International Association (MWIA, #16630)*;
– *Southeast Asian Tobacco Control Alliance (SEATCA, #19785)*;
– *Union for International Cancer Control (UICC, #20415)*;
– *Women's Environment and Development Organization (WEDO, #21016)*;
– *World Assembly of Youth (WAY, #21113)*;
– *World Federation of Public Health Associations (WFPHA, #21476)*;
– *World Heart Federation (WHF, #21562)*;
– *World Vision International (WVI, #21904)*.

Consultative Status Consultative status granted from: *ECOSOC (#05331)* (Special); *WHO (#20950)* (Official Relations). **NGO Relations** Together with American Cancer Society, coordinates: *Global Smokefree Partnership (GSP, #10602)*. [2022/XF6318/y/**F**]

♦ Framework Convention Alliance on Tobacco Control / see Framework Convention Alliance (#09981)
♦ Framework Convention for the Protection of the Marine Environment of the Caspian Sea (2003 treaty)
♦ Framework Convention for the Protection of National Minorities (1995 treaty)
♦ Framework Convention on Tobacco Control (2003 treaty)
♦ Framework for Northeast Asian Subregional Programme of Environmental Cooperation / see North East Asian Centre for Environmental Data and Training (#17578)
♦ Framtiden i Våre Hender (#10050)
♦ Framtidsjorden (internationally oriented national body)
♦ France Amérique latine (internationally oriented national body)
♦ France Coopération Internationale / see France Expertise Internationale
♦ France Expertise Internationale (internationally oriented national body)
♦ France Libertés – Fondation Danielle Mitterrand (internationally oriented national body)
♦ Francescane Missionarie di Maria (religious order)
♦ Francescane Missionarie di Maria nel Mondo (religious order)
♦ France terre d'asile (internationally oriented national body)
♦ France Volontaires (internationally oriented national body)
♦ Franciscaines de l'Adoration Perpétuelle d'Olpe (religious order)
♦ Franciscaines de l'Immaculée-Conception (religious order)
♦ Franciscaines de la Miséricorde (religious order)
♦ Franciscaines Missionnaires de Marie (religious order)
♦ Franciscaines missionnaires de Marie à travers le monde (religious order)
♦ Franciscaines Missionnaires de Notre-Dame (religious order)
♦ Franciscaines Missionnaires du Sacré-Coeur (religious order)
♦ Franciscaines de Montpellier (religious order)
♦ Franciscaines de la Pénitence et de la Charité Chrétienne d'Heythuizen (religious order)
♦ Franciscaines Petites Soeurs de Jésus (religious order)
♦ Franciscaines de la Propagation de la Foi (religious order)
♦ Franciscaines de Sainte-Blandine de Metz (religious order)
♦ Franciscaines de Sainte-Marie des Anges (religious order)
♦ Franciscaines du Saint-Esprit (religious order)
♦ Franciscaines de Seillon (religious order)
♦ Franciscaines Servantes de Marie (religious order)
♦ Franciscains International – Familia Franciscana Internacional / see Franciscans International (#09982)
♦ Franciscanas Misioneras de Maria (religious order)
♦ Franciscanas Misioneras de Maria en el Mundo (religious order)
♦ Franciscanas Misioneras de Nuestra Señora (religious order)
♦ Franciscanas Missionarias de Nossa Senhora (religious order)
♦ Franciscan Brothers of the Holy Cross (religious order)
♦ Franciscan Brothers of the Third Order Regular, Mountbellew (religious order)
♦ Franciscan Clarist Congregation (religious order)
♦ Franciscan Friars of the Atonement (religious order)
♦ Franciscan International University / see Pontifical University Antonianum
♦ Franciscan Media (internationally oriented national body)
♦ Franciscan Missionaries of Mary (religious order)
♦ Franciscan Missionaries of Mary in the World (religious order)
♦ Franciscan Missionaries of our Lady (religious order)
♦ Franciscan Multiversity of Latin America (unconfirmed)

♦ Franciscans International (FI) 09982

Exec Dir Rue de Vermont 37-39, 1202 Geneva, Switzerland. T. +41227794010. E-mail: geneva@franciscansinternational.org – director@franciscansinternational.org.
Permanent Office 246 East 46th Street, Suite 1F, New York NY 10017-2937, USA. T. +19176751075. E-mail: newyork@franciscansinternational.org.
URL: http://www.franciscansinternational.org/

History 27 Jun 1985, New York, NY (USA). Founded as an inter-familial organization representing the Franciscans at the United Nations. Former names and other names: *Franciscains International – Familia Franciscana Internacional* – former; *Fransiscains International* – former. **Aims** Work for promotion, protection and respect of *human rights*, as well as social and environmental *justice* through advocacy, with specific reference to business and human rights, extreme poverty and human rights, sustainable development, and women and children (birth registration). **Structure** International Board of Directors, appointed by the Conference of the Franciscan Family. **Languages** English, French, German, Spanish. **Staff** 10.50 FTE, paid. **Finance** Franciscan community donations and funding agencies. **Activities** Advocacy/lobbying/activism. **Events** *Meeting* Rome (Italy) 1998, *Working group meeting* Rome (Italy) 1998, *Meeting* Rome (Italy) 1997, *Working group meeting* Rome (Italy) 1997, *Meeting* New York, NY (USA) 1996. **Publications** *FI Newsletter* (3-4 a year) in English, French, German, Italian, Portuguese, Spanish; *Franciscans International Annual Report* in English, French, German, Italian, Spanish. *A UN Special Rapporteur on human rights and climate change? Regional perspectives* (2021) in English, French, Spanish; *Human Rights, Sustainable Development and Climate Policies: Connecting the Dots* (2nd ed 2021) in English, French, Spanish; *New Migration Dynamics in Northern Central America, Mexico and the United States: Central American exodus caravans, COVID-19, and serious human rights violations* (2021) in English, Spanish; *30 years at the United Nations*, (2020) in English, French, German, Italian, Portuguese, Spanish; *Tearing Down the Walls: Challenging myths about migration from a human rights perspective* (2020) in English, German, Italian, Portuguese, Spanish; *Making Human Rights Work for People in Extreme Poverty: Handbook for implementing the UN Guiding Principles on Extreme Poverty and Human Rights* (2015) in English, French; *Franciscans in West Papua: The journey of Dutch OFM friars with the Papuans in the stuggle for their dignity* (2014) in English; *Development: sustainable for whom?* (2013) in English, French; *Modern Slavery in India* (2012) in English; *The Right to Water and Sanitation* (2011) in English; *World Poverty* (2007) in English, French, German. **Consultative Status** Consultative status granted from: *African Commission on Human and Peoples' Rights (ACHPR, #00255)* (Observer); *ECOSOC (#05331)* (General). **IGO Relations** Accredited by: *United Nations Commission on Sustainable Development (CSD, inactive)*; *United Nations Framework Convention on Climate Change – Secretariat (UNFCCC, #20564)*; Beijing Women's Conference. Associated with Department of Global Communications of the United Nations. **NGO Relations** Member of: *European Network for Central Africa (EurAc, #07874)*; *Laudato Si' Movement (#16403)*. [2022.02.09/XF3144/**F**]

♦ Franciscan Sisters (religious order)
♦ Franciscan Sisters, Daughters of the Sacred Hearts of Jesus and Mary (religious order)
♦ Franciscan Sisters of the Immaculate Heart of Mary's Congregation (religious order)
♦ Franciscan Sisters of Mary (religious order)
♦ Franciscan Sisters of Perpetual Adoration (religious order)
♦ Franciscan Sisters of the Poor (religious order)
♦ Franciscans of Saint Mary of the Angels (religious order)
♦ Franco Arab Chamber of Commerce (internationally oriented national body)
♦ Franco-Iberian Union for Coordinating the Production and Transmission of Electricity (inactive)
♦ François-Xavier Bagnoud Center for Health and Human Rights (internationally oriented national body)
♦ Francophone Asian-Pacific Regional Centre (internationally oriented national body)
♦ Francophone Association for Cardiovascular Prevention and Rehabilitation (#02617)
♦ Francophone Club of Retina Specialists (unconfirmed)
♦ Francophone Ergonomics Society (#19460)
♦ Francophone Federation of Friends of the Organ (#09586)
♦ Francophone Fund for Olympic Preparation (see: #04634)
♦ Francophone International Federation of Psychiatry (internationally oriented national body)
♦ Francophone International LGBTQI Network (unconfirmed)
♦ Francophone Network of Age-Friendly Cities (internationally oriented national body)
♦ Francophone Society of Psychosomatic Dermatology (#19467)

♦ Francophonie pongiste internationale 09983

SG c/o Fédération Française de Tennis de Table, 3 rue Dieudonnée Costes, 75013 Paris, France. T. +33153945000. E-mail: secretariat@fpi-internationale.fr.
URL: http://www.fpi-internationale.fr/historique/

Members Membership countries not specified. **NGO Relations** Member of: *International Table Tennis Federation (ITTF, #15650)*. [2019.07.01/XD2845/**F**]

♦ **FRANCOPOL** Réseau international francophone de formation policière (#18894)
♦ Franc Zone (#22037)
♦ Frank Bold Society (internationally oriented national body)
♦ Frank Foundation Child Assistance International (internationally oriented national body)
♦ Frank Internationale Kinderhilfe (internationally oriented national body)
♦ Franklin and Eleanor Roosevelt Institute / see Roosevelt Institute
♦ Franklin Knowledge Corps (internationally oriented national body)
♦ Fransiscains International / see Franciscans International (#09982)
♦ Franziskanerbrüder vom Heiligen Kreuz (religious order)
♦ Franziskaner Helfen / see Missionszentrale der Franziskaner
♦ Franziskanerinnen von der ewigen Anbetung in Olpe (religious order)
♦ Franziskanerinnen, Töchter der Heiligen Herzen Jesu und Mariä (religious order)
♦ Franziskanerinnen von der Unbefleckten Empfängnis (religious order)
♦ Franziskanerinnen vom Heiligen Martyrer Georg zu Thuine (religious order)
♦ Franz Weber Foundation (internationally oriented national body)
♦ **FRAO** Fondation rurale de l'Afrique de l'ouest (#20902)
♦ Fratellanza Bianca Universale (#20684)
♦ Fratelli della Beata Vergine Maria, Madre della Misericordia (religious order)
♦ Fratelli della Carità (religious order)
♦ Fratelli Celliti o Alessiani di Aquisgrana (religious order)
♦ Fratelli Cristiani (religious order)
♦ Fratelli dalla Croce – Canonici Regolari della Santa Croce (religious order)
♦ Fratelli Figli Giuseppini del Rwanda (religious order)
♦ Fratelli Francescani della Santa Croce (religious order)
♦ Fratelli di Huybergen – Fratelli dell'Immacolata Concezione della Beata Vergine Maria, Madre di Dio (religious order)
♦ Fratelli dell'Immacolata Concezione della Beata Vergine Maria, Madre di Dio (religious order)
♦ Fratelli dell'Istruzione Cristiana di Ploërmel (religious order)
♦ Fratelli dell'Istruzione Cristiana di San Gabriele (religious order)
♦ Fratelli Maristi delle Scuole (religious order)
♦ Fratelli della Misericordia (religious order)
♦ Fratelli della Misericordia di Maria Ausiliatrice (religious order)
♦ Fratelli Missionari di San Francesco d'Assisi (religious order)
♦ Fratelli di Nostra Signora di Lourdes (religious order)
♦ Fratelli di Nostra Signora della Misericordia (religious order)
♦ Fratelli dei Poveri di San Francesco Serafico (religious order)
♦ Fratelli della Presentazione (religious order)
♦ Fratelli della Sacra Famiglia di Belley (religious order)
♦ Fratelli del Sacro Cuore (religious order)
♦ Fratelli di San Francesco Saverio (religious order)
♦ Fratelli di San Giuseppe Benedetto Cottolengo (religious order)
♦ Fratelli di San Luigi Gonzaga (religious order)
♦ Fratelli di Santo Patrizio (religious order)
♦ Fratelli Saveriani – Fratelli di San Francesco Saverio (religious order)
♦ Fratelli delle Scuole Cristiane (religious order)
♦ Fratelli Servi di Maria Immacolata (religious order)
♦ Fratelli del Terz'Ordine Regolare di San Francesco d'Assisi di Mountbellew (religious order)
♦ Fratelli dell'Uomo (#03339)
♦ **FRATEL** Réseau francophone de la régulation des télécommunications (#18886)
♦ Frater – Fraternidad Cristiana Intercontinental de Personas con Discapacidad (religious order)
♦ Frater – Fraternité chrétienne intercontinentale de personnes avec handicap (religious order)
♦ Frater – Intercontinental Christian Fraternity of People with Disabilities (religious order)
♦ Fraternal Democrats (inactive)
♦ Fraternidad Blanca Universal (#20684)
♦ Fraternidad Cristiana Intercontinental de Personas con Discapacidad (religious order)
♦ Fraternidade Branca Universal (#20684)
♦ Fraternidad Mundial de las Asambleas de Dios (#21111)
♦ Fraternidad de Sindicalistas de Asia (inactive)
♦ Fraternità delle Piccole Sorelle di Gesù (religious order)
♦ Fraternitas Rosarii (religious order)
♦ Fraternitas Sacerdotalis Sancti Petri (religious order)
♦ Fraternitatea Albă Universală (#20684)
♦ Fraternité Africaine / see Solidagro
♦ Fraternité blanche universelle (#20684)
♦ Fraternité chrétienne intercontinentale de personnes avec handicap (religious order)
♦ Fraternité Europe Asie (internationally oriented national body)
♦ Fraternité évangélique latinoaméricaine (#04660)
♦ Fraternité internationale des magiciens (#12402)
♦ Fraternité internationale des prisons (#18503)
♦ Fraternité islamique (#16915)
♦ Fraternité des Missionnaires de Sainte-Thérèse de l'Enfant-Jésus (religious order)
♦ Fraternité mondiale Baden-Powell (#03055)
♦ Fraternité mondiale de la jeunesse orthodoxe (#21504)

- ♦ Fraternité mondiale des organisations de la jeunesse orthodoxe / see World Fellowship of Orthodox Youth (#21504)
- ♦ Fraternité Notre Dame (religious order)
- ♦ Fraternité oecuménique internationale (internationally oriented national body)
- ♦ Fraternité des Petits Frères de l'Evangile (religious order)
- ♦ Fraternité religieuse internationale (no recent information)
- ♦ Fraternité Sacerdotale (religious order)
- ♦ Fraternité sacerdotale internationale Saint-Pie X (#18494)
- ♦ Fraternité du Saint-Esprit (religious order)
- ♦ Fraternité des syndicalistes d'Asie (inactive)
- ♦ Fraternité théologique africaine (#00483)
- ♦ Fraternité de la Vierge des Pauvres (religious order)
- ♦ Fraternity of Operative Millers of America (FOMA) / see International Association of Operative Millers
- ♦ Fraters van Onze Lieve Vrouw, Moeder van Barmhartigheid (religious order)
- ♦ Frati Francescani dell'Atonement (religious order)
- ♦ Fratres a Caritate (religious order)
- ♦ Fratres Immaculatae Conceptionis Beatissimae Virginis Mariae Matris Dei (religious order)
- ♦ Fratres de Misericordia (religious order)
- ♦ Fratres Misericordiae Mariae Auxiliatricis (religious order)
- ♦ Fratres Nostrae Dominae Lurdensis (religious order)
- ♦ Fratres Piae Congregationis a Praesentatione (religious order)
- ♦ Fratres de Sacco (inactive)
- ♦ Fratres a Sacratissimo Corde Iesu (religious order)
- ♦ Fratres Tertii Ordinis Sancti Francisci Capulatorum a Beata Virgine Perdolente (religious order)
- ♦ Fratri Predicatori (religious order)
- ♦ Frauen in der Euregio Maas-Rhein (#09734)
- ♦ Frauen Europäische Mittel- und Kleinbetriebe (inactive)
- ♦ Frauen Europas / see Association femmes d'Europe
- ♦ Frauen für den Frieden, Schweiz (internationally oriented national body)
- ♦ Frauengilde der Vereinten Nationen in Wien (internationally oriented national body)
- ♦ Frauen in Naturwissenschaft, Ingenieurwesen und Technologie (#06276)
- ♦ Frauennetzwerk für Frieden (internationally oriented national body)
- ♦ Frauensolidarität – Entwicklungspolitische Initiativen für Frauen in der Dritten Welt (internationally oriented national body)
- ♦ FRB – Fondation Roi Baudouin (internationally oriented national body)
- ♦ FRC – Finnish Refugee Council (internationally oriented national body)
- ♦ **FRC** Fonds Roberto Cimetta (#09837)
- ♦ FRD – Fonds rural pour le développement du Tiers-monde (internationally oriented national body)
- ♦ FRD – Fund for Reconciliation and Development (internationally oriented national body)
- ♦ FRDI / see Federation of Horses in Education and Therapy International (#09593)
- ♦ Frederick Mulder Foundation (internationally oriented national body)
- ♦ Fred Hollows Foundation (internationally oriented national body)
- ♦ Fredsfonden (internationally oriented national body)
- ♦ Fredskämparna i Finland rf (internationally oriented national body)
- ♦ Fredskorpset / see Norwegian Agency for Exchange Cooperation
- ♦ Free and Accepted Colored Masons of America / see Modern Free and Accepted Masons of the World
- ♦ Free Ads Papers International Association / see International Classified Marketplace Association (#12592)
- ♦ Free Africa Foundation (internationally oriented national body)

♦ Free Burma Coalition (FBC) 09984

Address not obtained.
URL: http://www.freeburmacoalition.org/

History 1995, USA. 1995, Madison WN (USA). **Aims** Serve as an umbrella group of organizations working for freedom and democracy in Burma; build a grassroots movement inspired by and modeled after the anti-apartheid movement in South Africa; support Daw Aung San Suu Kyi and the National League for Democracy as the sole legitimate leader of Burma. **Structure** Coordinating office located in Washington DC (USA). Regional divisions. **Finance** Membership donations, private donors, private foundations. Annual budget: US$ 80,000. **Activities** Coordinates campaigns opposing the junta ruling Burma, including: suspension of UN General Assembly seat; consumer boycotts of companies investing or operating in Burma. Organizes annual strategy conference. **Events** *Conference* Washington, DC (USA) 1998. **Publications** *Free Burma Now* (4 a year) – newsletter; *FBC Digest* (52 a year) – electronic news digest; *FBC Kiosk* (100 a year) – electronic news bulletin.
Members Colleges, groups, organizations and universities (over 200) in 30 countries:
Australia, Bangladesh, Belgium, Benin, Brazil, Canada, Finland, France, Germany, India, Indonesia, Israel, Jamaica, Japan, Malaysia, Myanmar, Netherlands, New Zealand, Nicaragua, Norway, Philippines, Russia, Saudi Arabia, Slovenia, South Africa, Spain, Switzerland, Taiwan, Thailand, USA.
Included in the above, 2 organizations listed in this Yearbook:
Buddhist Peace Fellowship (BPF); International Council for Adult Education (ICAE, #12983).
NGO Relations Cooperates with a number of national organizations active in the field. [2008/XF4725/y/**E**]

- ♦ Free the Children / see WE Charity (#20849)
- ♦ freeDimensional (internationally oriented national body)
- ♦ Freedom in Christ (internationally oriented national body)
- ♦ Freedom from Debt Coalition (internationally oriented national body)
- ♦ Freedom Forum (internationally oriented national body)
- ♦ The Freedom Fund (internationally oriented national body)
- ♦ Freedom House (internationally oriented national body)

♦ Freedom of Information Advocates Network (FOIAnet) 09985

Coordinator Access Info Africa, Plot 436/431 Mawanda Road Suite A4, PO Box 35643, Kampala, Uganda. T. +256414533554. E-mail: info@africafoicentre.org.
Chairperson address not obtained.
URL: http://www.foiadvocates.net/

History 28 Sep 2002, Sofia (Bulgaria). Originally designated 28 September as International Right to Know Day, which was recognised by UN General Assembly in 2019 as International Day for Universal Access to Information. **Aims** Promote the right to access information held by public authorities or the right to information; facilitate debates about right to information issues and engage with other players in this area; support our members to promote and protect the right to information in their own countries. **Structure** Steering Committee, elected by civil society organizations. **Languages** English. **Activities** Awareness raising; events/meetings; knowledge management/information dissemination; networking/liaising. Active in all member countries. **Publications** *10-10-10 Statement*; *World Advocacy Update.*
Members Individuals; civil society organizations. Organisations (over 250) in 76 countries:
Albania, Argentina, Armenia, Australia, Austria, Azerbaijan, Bangladesh, Bosnia-Herzegovina, Brazil, Bulgaria, Cambodia, Canada, Chile, Colombia, Croatia, Cyprus, Czechia, Denmark, Dominican Rep, Ecuador, Egypt, Georgia, Germany, Ghana, Guatemala, Honduras, Hungary, India, Indonesia, Israel, Italy, Jamaica, Japan, Jordan, Kazakhstan, Kenya, Kosovo, Kyrgyzstan, Latvia, Lebanon, Lithuania, Mexico, Moldova, Mongolia, Montenegro, Morocco, Mozambique, Namibia, Nepal, Nicaragua, Nigeria, North Macedonia, Pakistan, Palestine, Panama, Paraguay, Peru, Philippines, Poland, Romania, Russia, Senegal, Serbia, Sierra Leone, Slovakia, South Africa, Spain, Sweden, Tajikistan, Türkiye, Uganda, UK, Ukraine, Uruguay, USA, Venezuela.
Included in the above, 20 organizations listed in the Yearbook:
Access Info Europe; Africa Freedom of Information Centre (AFIC, #00175); African Network of Constitutional Lawyers (ANCL, #00384); African Women's Development and Communication Network (FEMNET, #00503); ARTICLE 19 (#01121); Bank Information Center (BIC); Civil Rights Defenders; Commonwealth Human Rights Initiative (CHRI, #04340); Due Process of Law Foundation (DPLF, #05144); Global Witness (GW); International Renaissance Foundation (IRF); International Research and Exchanges Board (IREX); Media Institute of Southern Africa (MISA, #16619); NATO Watch (#16949); Open Knowledge International; Oxfam International (#17922); Publish What You Fund; The Access Initiative (TAI, #00050); The Carter Center; The Trust for the Americas (#20252). [2022.05.11/XM0731/y/**F**]

- ♦ Freedom Now (internationally oriented national body)

♦ Free and Fair Post Initiative (FFPI) 09986

Contact Rue du Luxembourg 22-24, 1000 Brussels, Belgium. T. +3222131300. Fax +3222131313.

History Oct 2000, Brussels (Belgium). Registration: EU Transparency Register, No/ID: 326647527646-54. **Aims** Promote liberalization of postal services and fair *competition* in the postal sector. [2020/XF6451/**F**]

- ♦ FREE – Future of Rural Energy in Europe (unconfirmed)
- ♦ Freehearts Africa Reach out Foundation (internationally oriented national body)
- ♦ Free International Federation of Deportees and Resistance Internees (inactive)
- ♦ Free International University of Moldova (internationally oriented national body)
- ♦ Freeman Spogli Institute for International Studies (internationally oriented national body)

♦ Free Methodist World Conference 09987

Sec-Treas c/o Wilmore FMC, 1200 Lexington Rd, Wilmore KY 40390, USA. E-mail: wcec.sec.treas@gmail.com.

History Founded Jun 1999, Anderson IN (USA). Replaced *Free Methodist World Fellowship (inactive).* **Aims** Coordinate worldwide activities of the Free Methodist Church denomination; promote fellowship and mutual understanding in the Free Methodist *Church* globally. **Structure** Council of Bishops; Executive Committee. Area Fellowships (7): Central/East Africa; Southern Africa; West Africa; Asia; Europe; Latin America; North America. **Finance** Dues from member General Conferences and Annual Conferences; donations from individuals and foundations. **Activities** Events/meetings. **Events** *Quadrennial World Conference / World Conference* Durban (South Africa) 2015, *Quadrennial World Conference / World Conference* Bujumbura (Burundi) 2011, *Quadrennial world conference / World Conference* Sao Paulo (Brazil) 2007, *Quadrennial World Conference / World Conference* Harare (Zimbabwe) 2003, *General Conference* Toronto, ON (Canada) 2002. **Publications** None.
Members Individuals in 71 countries and territories:
Antigua-Barbuda, Argentina, Australia, Bahamas, Belgium, Benin, Bolivia, Botswana, Brazil, Burundi, Cambodia, Cameroon, Canada, Chile, Colombia, Congo DR, Costa Rica, Dominican Rep, Ecuador, Egypt, El Salvador, Ethiopia, France, Gabon, Ghana, Greece, Guiana Fr, Haiti, Honduras, Hong Kong, Hungary, India, Iraq, Japan, Jordan, Kenya, Korea Rep, Liberia, Malawi, Malaysia, Mexico, Mozambique, Myanmar, Nepal, Netherlands, Nicaragua, Nigeria, Panama, Paraguay, Peru, Philippines, Portugal, Puerto Rico, Romania, Rwanda, South Africa, Spain, Sri Lanka, Sweden, Taiwan, Tanzania UR, Thailand, Togo, Uganda, UK, Ukraine, Uruguay, USA, Venezuela, Zambia, Zimbabwe. [2014.12.07/XF5557/v/**F**]

♦ Freemuse 09988

Contact Jagtvej 223, 3rd floor, 2100 Copenhagen, Denmark. T. +4553871027. E-mail: freemuse@freemuse.org.
URL: https://freemuse.org/

History 1998. Set up following 1st World Conference on Music and Censorship. Former names and other names: *FREEMUSE – Freedom of Musical Expression* – full title. Registration: Denmark. **Aims** Advocate and defend musicians' rights to freedom of musical creation, performance and publishing and citizens' access to musical expressions as protected in the Universal Declaration of Human Rights. **Structure** General Assembly; Executive Committee; Board of Advisors; Secretariat. **Activities** Advocacy/lobbying/activism; research/documentation. **Consultative Status** Consultative status granted from: *ECOSOC (#05331)* (Special). [2022/AA2939/**D**]

- ♦ FREEMUSE – Freedom of Musical Expression / see Freemuse (#09988)
- ♦ Free and Open Source Software Developers' European Meeting (meeting series)
- ♦ Freeplay Foundation / see Lifeline Energy
- ♦ Free the Slaves (internationally oriented national body)
- ♦ Free Software Foundation Europe (internationally oriented national body)

♦ Free Software and Open Source Foundation for Africa (FOSSFA) . . . 09989

Fondation des logiciels libre pour l'Afrique
Address not obtained.

History 21 Feb 2003, Geneva (Switzerland). Founded during the World Summit on the Information Society. **Aims** Promote sustainable, viable and *cost* effective software products for Africa through education and local capacity building. **Activities** Events/meetings. **Events** *IDLELO : African Conference on Free Software and Open Source and the Digital Commons / Conference* Abuja (Nigeria) 2012. [2014/XF6829/f/**F**]

- ♦ Free Trade Europa (unconfirmed)

♦ Free Vietnam Alliance (FVA) 09990

Alliance Vietnam liberté (AVL)
Address not obtained.
URL: http://www.lmvntd.org/

History 15 Jul 1990, Paris (France), during the Conference of Movements for Vietnam's Freedom and Democracy. Affiliated with the Viet Tan – Vietnam Reform Party. **Aims** Bring about a pluralistic democracy in Vietnam through non-violent means. **Structure** Council of 15 members, including Secretary-General. Offices (4): Paris (France); Garden Grove CA (USA); Cabramatta (Australia); Tokyo (Japan). **Activities** Organizes conferences and campaigns. **Publications** *Viet Nam Dan Chu* (12 a year) in Vietnamese – magazine; *Vietnam Democracy* (12 a year) in English; *Vietnam Infos* (6 a year) in French. *Roadmap to a Democratic and Developed Vietnam.*
Members Organizations in 15 countries:
Australia, Belgium, Canada, Czechia, Denmark, France, Germany, Japan, Netherlands, New Zealand, Norway, Switzerland, UK, USA, Vietnam.
Individuals in 4 countries and territories:
Korea Rep, Russia, Taiwan, Vietnam. [2013/XF5575/**F**]

- ♦ Free Wheelchair Mission (internationally oriented national body)
- ♦ Free World Foundation (internationally oriented national body)
- ♦ Free World Institute (internationally oriented national body)
- ♦ **FRE** Flame Retardants Europe (#09791)
- ♦ Freie Hochschule für Geisteswissenschaft (#19134)
- ♦ Freight Forward Europe / see Freight Forward International (#09991)

♦ Freight Forward International (FFI) 09991

Contact address not obtained. T. +441344862964. Fax +441344744352.

History 1994, as *Freight Forward Europe (FFE)* by 8 of Europe's leading freight forwarding companies. **Aims** Provide global *logistics service providers* with a knowledge-sharing platform to better serve customer needs; reinforce the direct business advantage of large global logistics service providers through a united approach towards legislators and regulators, suppliers and client groups in relation to *standards* development and questions of mutual interest in the industry; provide leadership and direction for the freight forwarding and logistics industry for the benefit of the whole profession; act as an interlocutor with European policy-makers and cooperate with other sectors of the transport, trade and industry so as to enhance the direct business interest of participating companies; focus on policies to enable freight forwarders to perform their services and activities efficiently and to diversify the range and scope of their services as integrated-service providers; provide advice and facilitate information exchange among members. **Structure** CEO Committee, including Chairman and Vice-Chairman. Working Committees (4): Air Freight; Customs; Overland; Security. Task Forces. **Activities** Issues include: freedom to choose the best available transportation means; ability to rely on competitive carriers operating in an efficient infrastructure; availability of communication means; ability to operate in markets in fair competition with other service providers. **Publications** Sustainable Mobility Fact Sheets; positions papers; press releases. **Members** Logistics and freight forwarding companies (7). Membership countries not specified. [2008/XF7037/**F**]

- ♦ Freight Network Corporation Group (internationally oriented national body)
- ♦ Freiwilligen Programm der Vereinten Nationen (#20650)
- ♦ French Academic Network on Asian Studies (internationally oriented national body)
- ♦ French-African Summit Conference (meeting series)
- ♦ French Agency for International Business Development (internationally oriented national body)

♦ French Assistance Agency / see Fonds de solidarité prioritaire
♦ French Association for American Studies (internationally oriented national body)
♦ French Association for the Development of International Exchange of Food and Agricultural Products and Technologie / see Association for the Development of International Exchanges in Agricultural and Agrifood Products and Techniques
♦ French Community (inactive)
♦ French Cultural Union / see Union culturelle et technique de langue française (#20374)
♦ French Culture International Academy (inactive)
♦ French Equatorial Africa (inactive)
♦ French Executive Service Overseas / see ECTI – Professionnels Seniors Bénévoles
♦ French Farmers and International Development (internationally oriented national body)
♦ French Global Environment Facility (internationally oriented national body)
♦ French Institute of Andean Studies – Institut français d'études andines (internationally oriented national body)
♦ French Institute of International Relations (internationally oriented national body)
♦ French Institute for International and Strategic Affairs (internationally oriented national body)
♦ French Institute for Middle East (internationally oriented national body)
♦ French Institute for Middle East Archaeology / see Institut français du Proche-Orient
♦ French Institute for Research in Africa (internationally oriented national body)
♦ French Institute for Studies and Terminology in Environmental Matters / see Académie d'environnement d'expression francophone, philosophique et scientifique
♦ French Intensive Care Society (#19512)
♦ French-Language Association for Orthopaedics (#02842)
♦ French-Language Association for Research on Diabetes and Metabolic Diseases / see Société Francophone du Diabète (#19468)
♦ French-Language Association of Scientific Psychology (no recent information)
♦ French-Language Cultural and Technical Union (#20374)
♦ French-Language Infant Pneumology and Phthisiology Group (inactive)

♦ French Language Network for International Clinical Epidemiology . 09992

Réseau d'épidémiologie clinique international francophone (RECIF)

Coordinator Univ Claude Bernard Lyon 1, 7 rue Guillaume Paradin, Bât B 3ème ét, 69372 Lyon CEDEX 08, France. T. +33478785764.
Pres Unité de Recherche Clinique, RECIF – DIM, Hospices Civils de Lyon, 162 avenue Lacassagne, 69424 Lyon CEDEX, France. T. +33472115707. Fax +33472115711.
URL: http://recif.univ-lyon1.fr/

History 1988, by *Mérieux Foundation*, Université Claude Bernard Lyon (France) 1 and Hospices Civils de Lyon. Also referred to as *Euro-Mediterranean CLEN* or *EuroMed CLEN*. Previously also referred to as *French-Speaking International Clinical Epidemiological Network – Réseau d'épidémiologie clinique international francophone.* Regional network of *INCLEN Trust International (#11142).* **Aims** Promote teaching and applied research in clinical epidemiology in France and in French-speaking countries, and on a broader scale, for French-speaking doctors in Africa, Eastern Europe and in countries along the Mediterranean Sea. **Structure** General Meeting (annually, with INCLEN). Board, headed by President. Scientific Committee; Teaching Committee. Clinical Epidemiology Units (4). **Languages** English, French. **Staff** 1.50 FTE, paid; 3.50 FTE, voluntary. **Finance** Grants from: Region and government; INCLEN; universities and public institutions. **Activities** Develops teaching and collaborative research programmes; organizes diplomas, intensive seminars; supports and assists physicians in their clinical research protocols. Organizes: annual General Meeting; biennial General Conference. **Publications** *RECIF Newsletter. Recherche Cliknique: penser, réaliser, publier* (2010); *La Recherche Clinique – de l'idée à la publication* (1995).
Members Full in 7 countries:
Algeria, Canada, Denmark, France, Morocco, Romania, Switzerland.
NGO Relations Support network for clinical research of *Conférence internationale des doyens des facultés de médecine d'expression française (CIDMEF, #04616).* [2012.07.25/XF4368/**F**]

♦ French-Language Society of Bronchoesophagology and Gastroscopy (inactive)
♦ French-Language Society of Infectious Pathology (internationally oriented national body)
♦ French-Language Society of Nutrition and Dietetics / see Société française de nutrition
♦ French-Language Society of Pneumology (#19510)
♦ French-Language Society for Psychotherapeutic Research (no recent information)
♦ French-Language Writers' Association (#02481)
♦ French-Language Writers Syndicate (internationally oriented national body)
♦ French Leading Center for International Economic Studies, Paris (internationally oriented national body)
♦ French-Pacific Banking Agreement (#04422)
♦ French Peace Movement (#16867)
♦ French Promotion and Investment Company for Economic Cooperation (internationally oriented national body)
♦ French Research Institute for Exploitation of the Sea / see Ifremer
♦ French Society of Nutrition (internationally oriented national body)

♦ French Society for Thoracic and Cardiovascular Surgery (FSTCVS) . 09993

Société française de chirurgie thoracique et cardiovasculaire (SFCTCV)

Main Office 56 bd Vincent Auriol, 75013 Paris, France. T. +33142164210. Fax +33153629120. E-mail: secretariat@sfctcv.org.
URL: http://www.sfctcv.org/

History 1947, Paris (France), as *Société de chirurgie thoracique et cardio-vasculaire de langue française.* Registered in accordance with French law. Present name adopted 2001. **Aims** Carry out study and research in the field of thoracic and cardiovascular surgery. **Structure** General Assembly (annual). Board of Directors (meets annually) consisting of Founding President, President, 1-2 Vice-Presidents, Secretary-General, Treasurer, plus possibly Assistant Secretary-General and Assistant Treasurer. Supervisory Council, comprising past Presidents and Secretaries-General over the previous 3 years. **Languages** English, French. **Finance** Sources: members' dues. Other sources: Subventions. **Activities** Organizes 2 annual meetings. **Events** *European congress for bronchology and interventional pulmology* Marseille (France) 2011, *Congrès* Lille (France) 2009, *Congress* Paris (France) 2008, *Congrès* Paris (France) 2008, *Congrès* Paris (France) 2005. **Publications** *Journal de chirurgie thoracique et cardio-vasculaire* (2 a year).
Members Cardiovascular and thoracic surgeons in 49 countries:
Algeria, Argentina, Belgium, Bolivia, Brazil, Burkina Faso, Canada, China, Colombia, Côte d'Ivoire, Dominican Rep, Egypt, France, Gabon, Germany, Greece, India, Iran Islamic Rep, Italy, Japan, Lebanon, Luxembourg, Madagascar, Mali, Mauritania, Monaco, Morocco, Netherlands, Paraguay, Portugal, Romania, Russia, Saudi Arabia, Senegal, Spain, Sweden, Switzerland, Syrian AR, Tunisia, Türkiye, UK, Ukraine, United Arab Emirates. [2019/XD2118/**C**]

♦ French-Speaking Andrology Society (#19456)
♦ French-Speaking Association of Personal Data Protection Authorities (#02606)
♦ French-Speaking Association for Progress in Food Processing (no recent information)
♦ French-Speaking Association of Solids Mass Spectrometry (no recent information)
♦ French Speaking Cardiological Congress (meeting series)
♦ French-speaking Classification Society (#19465)
♦ French-Speaking Comparative Education Association (#02610)
♦ French Speaking Epidemiologist's Association (#02490)
♦ French-Speaking International Clinical Epidemiological Network / see French Language Network for International Clinical Epidemiology (#09992)
♦ French Speaking Linux and Free Software Users' Association (#02620)
♦ French-Speaking Neuropsychological Society (#19505)
♦ French-speaking Primatological Society (#19472)
♦ French-Speaking Radio and Television International Council (#04694)
♦ French Speaking Society of Chronobiology (internationally oriented national body)
♦ French-Speaking Society of Neurosurgery (#19503)
♦ French West Africa (inactive)
♦ Frente Continental de Organizaciones Comunales (no recent information)

♦ Frente Parlamentario Contra el Hambre de América Latina y el Caribe (FPH) 09994

Technical Sec Av Dag Hammarrskjöld 3241, Vitacura, Santiago, Santiago Metropolitan, Chile. T. +56229232100. E-mail: contacto@parlamentarioscontraelhambre.org.
URL: http://parlamentarioscontraelhambre.org/

History 2009. **Structure** Executive Coordinating Commission.
Members National Parliamentary Fronts in 21 countries:
Argentina, Belize, Bolivia, Brazil, Chile, Colombia, Costa Rica, Dominican Rep, Ecuador, El Salvador, Grenada, Guatemala, Haiti, Honduras, Mexico, Nicaragua, Panama, Paraguay, Peru, St Vincent-Grenadines, Uruguay.
IGO Relations Partner of (3): *Agencia Española de Cooperación Internacional para el Desarrollo (AECID); FAO (#09260); Parlamento Latinoamericano (PARLATINO, #18203).* [2021/AA2283/**F**]

♦ FREPI – Fédération Internationale des Relais Enfants Parents (unconfirmed)
♦ **FREREF** Fondation des Régions Européennes pour la Recherche, l'Education et la Formation (#09828)
♦ Frères Auxiliaires du Clergé (religious order)
♦ Frères de la Bienheureuse Vierge Marie, Mère de Miséricorde (religious order)
♦ Frères Cellites (religious order)
♦ Frères de la Charité (religious order)
♦ Frères de Chéméré (religious order)
♦ Frères de la Doctrine Chrétienne (religious order)
♦ Frères des Ecoles Chrétiennes (religious order)
♦ Frères Fils de Saint Joseph du Rwanda (religious order)
♦ Frères Franciscains de la Sainte Croix (religious order)
♦ Frères de la Fraternité de la Vièrge des Pauvres (religious order)
♦ Frères des hommes (#03339)
♦ Frères des hommes – Europe / see Brothers to All Men (#03339)
♦ Frères de Huybergen – Frères de l'Immaculée Conception de la Bienheureuse Vierge Marie, Mère de Dieu (religious order)
♦ Frères de l'Immaculée Conception de la Bienheureuse Vierge Marie, Mère de Dieu (religious order)
♦ Frères de l'Instruction Chrétienne de Ploërmel (religious order)
♦ Frères de l'Instruction Chrétienne de Saint Gabriel (religious order)
♦ Frères Maristes des Ecoles (religious order)
♦ Frères de la Miséricorde de Sainte Marie-Auxiliatrice (religious order)
♦ Frères Missionnaires des Campagnes (religious order)
♦ Frères Missionnaires de la Charité (religious order)
♦ Frères Missionnaires de Saint François d'Assise (religious order)
♦ Frères de Notre-Dame de Lourdes (religious order)
♦ Frères de Notre-Dame de la Miséricorde (religious order)
♦ Frères de la Présentation (religious order)
♦ Frères du Sacré-Coeur (religious order)
♦ Frères de Saint François Xavier (religious order)
♦ Frères de Saint Joseph-Benoît Cottolengo (religious order)
♦ Frères de Saint Louis de Gonzague (religious order)
♦ Frères de Saint Patrick (religious order)
♦ Frères Xavériens de Bruges (religious order)
♦ Frères Xavériens – Frères de Saint François Xavier (religious order)
♦ fresh20 (internationally oriented national body)

♦ Fresh Arts Coalition Europe (FACE) 09995

Contact c/o ONDA, 13 bis rue Henri Monnier, 75009 Paris, France. E-mail: info@fresh-europe.org.
URL: http://www.fresh-europe.org/

Aims Support contemporary cross-disciplinary art forms; facilitate international collaboration. **Structure** Board. **Activities** Events/meetings; projects/programmes.
Members Full (51) in 22 countries:
Australia, Austria, Belgium, Canada, Czechia, Denmark, Estonia, Finland, France, Germany, Greece, Italy, Lithuania, Malta, Netherlands, Slovakia, South Africa, Spain, Sweden, Switzerland, UK, USA.
NGO Relations Member of: *European Alliance for Culture and the Arts (#05866).* [2016/XM4838/y/**D**]

♦ **FRESHFEL Europe** European Fresh Produce Association (#07361)
♦ **FRESH** Focusing Resources on Effective School Health (#09809)
♦ Freshwater Action Network – Central America (#18638)

♦ Freshwater Action Network South Asia (FANSA) 09996

Convenor c/o LUMANTI, Manbhawan Road, Kumaripati Ward 5, Lalitpur, Nepal.
Facebook: https://www.facebook.com/fansouthasia/

History 2007. Formally launched Jan 2008, Nepal. **Aims** Strengthen the engagement of CSOs in policy-making and development initiatives to achieve the international targets on water and sanitation; improve regional cooperation between CSOs of differing perspectives, priorities and skills and increase the number of NGOs to advocate and communicate clearly on water policy issues and the broader agenda. **NGO Relations** Affiliate member of: *Freshwater Action Network (FAN, inactive).* Member of: *The Butterfly Effect (BE, #03389).* Partner of: *Sanitation and Water for All (SWA, #19051).* [2021/XJ5184/**E**]

♦ Freudenberg Foundation (internationally oriented national body)
♦ Freudenberg Stiftung (internationally oriented national body)
♦ Freunde der Erziehungskunst Rudolf Steiners (internationally oriented national body)
♦ Freunde der Friedensinseln (internationally oriented national body)
♦ Freunde der Friedensinseln und der Aktion Brot für den Frieden / see Friends of the Islands of Peace
♦ Freunde der Kunstbuchbinderei, Die / see ARA International (#01080)
♦ Freunde des Westlichen Buddhistischen Orden / see Triratna Buddhist Community (#20243)
♦ FRF / see Broadband Forum (#03334)
♦ FRH – Fédération pour le respect de l'homme et de l'humanité (inactive)
♦ **FRH** Future for Religious Heritage (#10051)
♦ Friars of the Sack (inactive)
♦ Fribaptistsamfundet (inactive)
♦ Fribourg Union, 1885 (inactive)
♦ **FRIDA** Young Feminist Fund (#21990)
♦ FridaysForFuture / see Fridays For Future (#09997)

♦ Fridays For Future (FFF) 09997

Address not obtained.
URL: https://fridaysforfuture.org/

History Aug 2018. Started when 15-year-old Greta Thunberg began a school strike for climate. Former names and other names: *FridaysForFuture* – alias. **Aims** Protest against the lack of action on the climate crisis. **Activities** Advocacy/lobbying/activism; awareness raising. **NGO Relations** Partner of (1): *Stop Ecocide International (SEI, #19998).* [2022/AA1301/**F**]

♦ Fridtjof-Nansen-Akademie für Politische Bildung (internationally oriented national body)
♦ Fridtjof Nansen Institute (internationally oriented national body)
♦ Fridtjof Nansens Institutt (internationally oriented national body)
♦ Fridtjof Nansen Stiftelsen på Polhøgda / see Fridtjof Nansen Institute
♦ Friedensforschungsinstitut, Oslo (internationally oriented national body)
♦ Friedensinseln / see Friends of the Islands of Peace
♦ Friedensinseln – Freunde der Friedensinseln (internationally oriented national body)
♦ Friedensuniversität (internationally oriented national body)
♦ Friedrich Ebert Foundation (internationally oriented national body)

Friedrich Ebert Stiftung
09997

alphabetic sequence excludes
For the complete listing, see Yearbook Online at

- ♦ Friedrich-Ebert-Stiftung (internationally oriented national body)
- ♦ Friedrich Naumann Foundation / see Friedrich Naumann Foundation for Freedom
- ♦ Friedrich Naumann Foundation for Freedom (internationally oriented national body)
- ♦ Friedrich Naumann Foundation for Liberty and Freedom / see Friedrich Naumann Foundation for Freedom
- ♦ Friedrich-Naumann-Stiftung / see Friedrich Naumann Foundation for Freedom
- ♦ Friedrich-Naumann-Stiftung für die Freiheit (internationally oriented national body)

♦ Friedrich Nietzsche Society (FNS) 09998

Sec address not obtained.
Pres address not obtained.
URL: http://fns.org.uk/

History Current constitution adopted, 11 Sep 2009. **Aims** Promote and develop the study of the life, work and influence of Friedrich Nietzsche across different disciplines, and different traditions and communities of Nietzsche scholarship. **Structure** Annual General Meeting; Executive Committee. **Staff** Voluntary. **Finance** Members' dues. **Activities** Events/meetings. **Events** *Nietzsche and humanity – (anti-)humanism, posthumanism, transhumanism* Tilburg (Netherlands) 2019, *Nietzsche and the politics of difference* Newcastle upon Tyne (UK) 2018, *Conference* Bath (UK) 2017, *Conference* Halle (Saale) (Germany) 2016, *Conference* Hull (UK) 2015. **Members** Individuals. Membership countries not specified. **NGO Relations** Member of: *International Federation of Philosophical Societies (FISP, #13507).* [2019/XW0190/**E**]

- ♦ FRIEND/Alpine and Mediterranean Hydrology (see: #13826)
- ♦ FRIEND/AMHY – FRIEND/Alpine and Mediterranean Hydrology (see: #13826)
- ♦ Friendasia (internationally oriented national body)
- ♦ FriendensFrauen Weltweit (#18283)
- ♦ FRIEND – Flow Regimes from International Experimental and Network Data (see: #13826)
- ♦ FRIEND / Hindu Kush-Himalayan (see: #13826)
- ♦ FRIEND/Nile Basin (see: #13826)
- ♦ FRIEND/Northern European (see: #13826)
- ♦ Friends / see World Anti-Bullying Forum (#21094)
- ♦ Friends of Africa / see Friends of Africa International
- ♦ Friends of Africa International (internationally oriented national body)
- ♦ Friends of Animals (internationally oriented national body)
- ♦ Friends of Art Bookbinding, The / see ARA International (#01080)

♦ Friends Without A Border (FWAB) 09999

Exec Dir 1123 Broadway, Ste 1210, New York NY 10010, USA. T. +12126910909. Fax +12123378052. E-mail: fwab@fwab.org.
URL: http://www.fwab.org/

History 1996. Founded by Kenro Izu. **Aims** Provide high-quality *medical* care to *children* in a compassionate environment; provide continuing *education* to healthcare professionals throughout Southeast Asia so they will become the clinicians and educators of the future; improve the health, nutrition and hygiene of local communities through outreach programmes and home care; stimulate research to develop sound healthcare practices appropriate for local conditions. **Structure** Board of Directors. **Finance** Annual budget: 2,133,790 USD (2019). **Activities** Healthcare. Active in: Cambodia, Laos. [2021.05.18/XM4238/**F**]

- ♦ Friends of a Corner of India and the World (internationally oriented national body)

♦ Friends of the Countryside (FCS) 10000

Coordinator Rue de Trèves 67, 1040 Brussels, Belgium. T. +3222343000. Fax +3222343009. E-mail: coordination@elo.org.
CEO & SG address not obtained.
URL: http://friendsofthecountryside.org/

History Registration: EU Transparency Register, No/ID: 76014811270-77, Start date: 27 Feb 2009. **Aims** Promote the holistic economic, social and environmental management of the countryside; support private business and rural property throughout the European Union and its adherent members. **Structure** General Assembly; Board; Secretariat. **Activities** Events/meetings. **Events** *General Assembly* Córdoba (Spain) 2021, *General Assembly* Belgium 2020, *General Assembly* Angers (France) 2019, *Conference* Brussels (Belgium) 2010. **NGO Relations** Founding member of: *Rural Investment Support for Europe Foundation (RISE Foundation, #19002).* [2022/XM2326/**E**]

♦ Friends of the Earth Europe (FoEE) 10001

Coordination européenne des Amis de la Terre Europe (CEAT) – Amigos de la Tierra Europa

Main Office Mundo-b Building, Rue d'Edimbourg 26, 1050 Brussels, Belgium. T. +3228931000. Fax +3228931035. E-mail: info@foeeurope.org.
URL: http://www.foeeurope.org/

History 1985, Brussels (Belgium). Founded as a regional coordinating body of *Friends of the Earth International (FoEI, #10002).* Former names and other names: *Friends of the Earth European Coordination* – former; *Coordination européenne des Amis de la terre* – former. **Aims** Campaign for sustainable and just societies and for the protection of the environment. **Structure** General Meeting (annual); Executive Committee; local groups. *Young Friends of the Earth Europe (Young FoEE, #21992).* **Languages** English. **Staff** 34.00 FTE, paid. **Finance** Members' dues. Other sources: operational and project grants from *European Commission (EC, #06633)*; grants from private funders and governments. Annual budget (2017): about euro 4,647,912. **Activities** Meeting activities; awareness raising; advocacy/lobbying/activism. **Events** *Post-Growth Conference* Brussels (Belgium) 2018, *Forum on making the EU Budget Work for People and Planet* Brussels (Belgium) 2013, *Conference on sustainability and solidarity* Gothenburg (Sweden) 2001, *Conference on Euro-Mediterranean free trade zone* Brussels (Belgium) 2000, *International conference on sustainable agriculture in the next millennium* Brussels (Belgium) 2000. **Publications** *Friends of the Earth Europe Annual Review.* Reports; documents.

Members Groups (33) in 31 countries:
Austria, Belgium, Bosnia-Herzegovina, Bulgaria, Croatia, Cyprus, Czechia, Denmark, Estonia, Finland, France, Georgia, Germany, Hungary, Ireland, Latvia, Lithuania, Luxembourg, Malta, Netherlands, North Macedonia, Norway, Poland, Russia, Slovakia, Slovenia, Spain, Sweden, Switzerland, UK, Ukraine.

NGO Relations Member of: *Climate Action Network Europe (CAN Europe, #04001)*; *Coalition for Energy Savings (#04056)*; *European Coalition for Corporate Justice (ECCJ, #06591)*; *Environmental Coalition on Standards (ECOS, #05499)*; *The Green 10 (#10711)*; *Our World is Not for Sale (OWINFS, #17917)*; *SDG Watch Europe (#19162)*; *Spring Alliance (inactive)*; *TP Organics – European Technology Platform (TP Organics, #20180).* [2021/XF1293/**E**]

- ♦ Friends of the Earth European Coordination / see Friends of the Earth Europe (#10001)

♦ Friends of the Earth International (FoEI) 10002

Amis de la Terre International – Amigos de la Tierra Internacional

International Coordinator PO Box 19199, 1000 GD Amsterdam, Netherlands. T. +31206221369.
Street address Nieuwe Looiersstraat 31 III, 1017 VA Amsterdam, Netherlands.
URL: http://www.foei.org/

History 1971, by national FOE groups in France, Germany FR, Sweden, UK and USA. Registered in Amsterdam (Netherlands). In 1992 became a 'federation' of organizations. Previously also referred to in French as *Réseau international des amis de la terre.* Also referred to in French as *Fédération internationale des amis de la terre.* As of 2004, integrated activities of *For Mother Earth (inactive).* **Aims** Work towards a peaceful and sustainable world based on societies living in harmony with *nature* and towards a society of interdependent people living in dignity, wholeness and fulfillment in which equity and human and peoples' rights are realized. **Structure** General Meeting (every 2 years); Executive Committee; International Secretariat, based in Amsterdam (Netherlands). Since 1986, FoEI's 3-tier structure – local, national and international – has been strengthened with the creation of *Friends of the Earth Europe (FoEE, #10001)*, FoEI's first regional network linking European member groups. **Languages** English, French, Spanish. **Staff** 20.00 FTE, paid. **Finance** Members' dues. Other sources: donations; subsidies. Special funds: Membership Support Fund. Annual budget: about US$ 2,000,000. **Activities** Advocacy/lobbying/activism; knowledge management/information dissemination; networking/liaising; events/meetings. **Events** *Biennial General Assembly* Kandy (Sri Lanka) 2014, *Biennial General Meeting* Sri Lanka 2014, *Biennial General Meeting* El Salvador 2012, *Biennial General Meeting* Penang (Malaysia) 2010, *Planet Diversity : world congress on the future of food and agriculture* Bonn (Germany) 2008. **Publications** Annual Report; thematic publications.

Members Organizations (73), with a combined membership of about 2 million individuals, in 71 countries and territories:
Argentina, Australia, Austria, Bangladesh, Belgium, Bosnia-Herzegovina, Brazil, Bulgaria, Cameroon, Canada, Chile, Colombia, Costa Rica, Croatia, Curaçao, Cyprus, Czechia, Denmark, El Salvador, Estonia, Finland, France, Georgia, Germany, Ghana, Grenada, Guatemala, Haiti, Honduras, Hungary, Indonesia, Ireland, Japan, Korea Rep, Latvia, Liberia, Lithuania, Luxembourg, Malaysia, Mali, Malta, Mauritius, Mexico, Mozambique, Nepal, Netherlands, New Zealand, Nigeria, North Macedonia, Norway, Palestine, Papua New Guinea, Paraguay, Philippines, Poland, Russia, Sierra Leone, Slovakia, South Africa, Spain, Sri Lanka, Sweden, Switzerland, Tanzania UR, Timor-Leste, Togo, Tunisia, Uganda, UK, Uruguay, USA.
NOAH International represents Danish section.

Consultative Status Consultative status granted from: *ECOSOC (#05331)* (Ros B); *International Maritime Organization (IMO, #14102)*; *UNEP (#20299).* **IGO Relations** Observer status at: *Convention on the Prevention of Marine Pollution by Dumping of Wastes and other Matter (LDC, 1972)*; *Convention for the Protection of the Marine Environment and the Coastal Region of the Mediterranean (Barcelona Convention, 1976)*; *Convention on Wetlands of International Importance Especially as Waterfowl Habitat (Convention on Wetlands, 1971)*; *FAO (#09260)*; *International Tropical Timber Organization (ITTO, #15737)*; *OSPAR Commission for the Protection of the Marine Environment of the North-East Atlantic (OSPAR Commission, #17905).* Participates in the meetings of: *Intergovernmental Panel on Climate Change (IPCC, #11499)*; *International Atomic Energy Agency (IAEA, #12294)*; *Montreal Protocol on Substances that Deplete the Ozone Layer (1987).* Participates in the work of: *United Nations Economic Commission for Europe (UNECE, #20555).* Accredited by: *Green Climate Fund (GCF, #10714)*; *United Nations Framework Convention on Climate Change – Secretariat (UNFCCC, #20564)*; *International Whaling Commission (IWC, #15879)*; *United Nations Office at Vienna (UNOV, #20604).* Accredited to the Conference of the Parties of: *Secretariat of the United Nations Convention to Combat Desertification (Secretariat of the UNCCD, #19208).* Associated with Department of Global Communications of the United Nations. Through Italian section, observer to: *Committee of International Development Institutions on the Environment (CIDIE, no recent information).*

NGO Relations Founding member of: *Global Forest Coalition (GFC, #10368).* Member of:
- *Abolition 2000 – Global Network to Eliminate Nuclear Weapons (Abolition 2000, #00006)*;
- *Asia-Pacific People's Environment Network (APPEN, no recent information)*;
- *BankTrack (#03166)*;
- *Campaign for a More Democratic United Nations (CAMDUN, inactive)*;
- *Climate Action Network (CAN, #03999)*;
- *Climate Justice Now ! (CJN!, inactive)*;
- *EarthAction (EA, #05159)*;
- *Environment Liaison Centre International (ELCI, no recent information)*;
- *Greenskies (inactive)*;
- *International Network for Sustainable Energy (INFORSE, #14331)*;
- *International Pollutants Elimination Network (IPEN, #14616)*;
- *Mediterranean Information Office for Environment, Culture and Sustainable Development (MIO-ECSDE, #16657)*;
- *NGO Forum on ADB (#17123)*;
- *Our World is Not for Sale (OWINFS, #17917)*;
- *Seas at Risk (SAR, #19189)*;
- *Taiga Rescue Network (TRN, inactive)*;
- *World Social Forum (WSF, #21797).*

Friends of the Earth EWNI is member of: *Crisis Action (#04957).* Represented on the Organizing Committee of: *Hague Appeal for Peace (HAP, #10848). GRET* is member. Participates in: *Antarctic and Southern Ocean Coalition (ASOC, #00849).* Signatory to: *Alter Summit.* In liaison with technical committees of: *International Organization for Standardization (ISO, #14473).* Collaborates with: *Third World Network (TWN, #20151).* Through constituent bodies, links with: *European Environmental Bureau (EEB, #06996).* American section is member of: *Advocacy Network for Africa (ADNA).* Signatory to the 'Publish What You Pay' appeal of: *Publish What You Pay Coalition (PWYP, #18573).* Supports: *Global Call for Action Against Poverty (GCAP, #10263).* [2019.07.04/XF4299/y/**F**]

- ♦ Friends of the Earth Middle East / see EcoPeace Middle East (#05325)

♦ Friends of Europe 10003

Amis de l'Europe, les

Contact Square de Meeûs 5-6, 1000 Brussels, Belgium. T. +3228939819. Fax +3228939828. E-mail: info@friendsofeurope.org.
URL: http://www.friendsofeurope.org/

History Jan 1999, Brussels (Belgium). A prominent Brussels-based think-tank for EU policy analysis and debate that is independent of EU institutions and without national or political bias. Incorporated *Security and Defence Agenda (SDA, inactive).* Registration: Belgium. **Aims** Connect people, stimulate debate and trigger change to create a more inclusive, sustainable and forward-looking Europe. **Events** *EU-Western Balkans Summit* Brussels (Belgium) 2022, *Europe-China Forum* Brussels (Belgium) 2022, *Health Innovation Summit* Brussels (Belgium) 2022, *Peace, Security and Defence Summit* Brussels (Belgium) 2022, *Annual Summit on Europe's Climate and Energy* Brussels (Belgium) 2019. [2021/XN8010/y/**F**]

- ♦ FRIENDS – Foundation for Research on International Environment, National Development and Security (internationally oriented national body)
- ♦ Friends of the Global Fight Against AIDS, Tuberculosis and Malaria (internationally oriented national body)
- ♦ Friends of the Global Fund Europe (internationally oriented national body)
- ♦ Friendship Ambassadors / see Friendship Ambassadors Foundation
- ♦ Friendship Ambassadors Foundation (internationally oriented national body)
- ♦ Friendship Force International (internationally oriented national body)
- ♦ Friendship North-South (internationally oriented national body)
- ♦ Friends International Center against Bullying / see World Anti-Bullying Forum (#21094)
- ♦ Friends International Centre / see Quaker United Nations Office (#18588)
- ♦ Friends International Ministries (internationally oriented national body)
- ♦ Friends of the Islands of Peace (internationally oriented national body)
- ♦ Friends of the Islands of Peace and of the Bread of Peace Campaign / see Friends of the Islands of Peace
- ♦ Friends of Literature Association / see IFLAC – International Forum for the Literature and Culture of Peace (#11102)
- ♦ Friends of the Orphans / see Nuestros Pequeños Hermanos
- ♦ Friends of Ostomates Worldwide (internationally oriented national body)
- ♦ Friends Peace Center (internationally oriented national body)
- ♦ Friends of Peace Now / see Americans for Peace Now
- ♦ Friends Peace Teams (internationally oriented national body)
- ♦ Friends of Scouting in Europe / see European Scout Foundation (#08451)
- ♦ Friends of the Third World (internationally oriented national body)
- ♦ Friends of Thomas More Association / see Amici Thomae Mori (#00799)
- ♦ Friends United Meeting (internationally oriented national body)
- ♦ Friends of the United Nations (internationally oriented national body)
- ♦ Friends of Vellore (internationally oriented national body)
- ♦ Friends of Waldorf Education (internationally oriented national body)
- ♦ Friends of the Western Buddhist Order / see Triratna Buddhist Community (#20243)
- ♦ Friends of WFP – Friends of the World Food Programme (internationally oriented national body)
- ♦ Friends World College / see Global College, Long Island University
- ♦ Friends World Committee / see Friends World Committee for Consultation (#10004)

♦ Friends World Committee for Consultation (FWCC) 10004

Comité consultatif mondial des Amis (CCMA) – Comité Mundial de la Consulta de los Amigos (CMCA) – Beratendes Weltkomitee der Freunde (BWF)

SG FWCC World Office, 173 Euston Rd, London, NW1 2AX, UK. T. +442076631199. Fax +442076631189. E-mail: world@fwcc.world.

URL: http://fwcc.world/
History 8 Sep 1937, Swarthmore, PA (USA). Founded at *Quaker World Conference*. Basic principles and key functions parallel the mandate given to early Quakers by George Fox. Previously also referred to in English and French as *Friends World Committee – Comité mondial des Amis*, and in French and Spanish as *Comité consultatif mondial de la société des Amis – Comité Consultivo Mundial de la Sociedad de los Amigos*. Registration: Charity Commission, No/ID: 211647, England and Wales. **Aims** Answering God's call to universal love, bring Friends of varying traditions and cultural experiences together in worship, communications and consultation, to express common heritage and the *Quaker* message to the world. **Structure** Meeting of representatives (every 7-10 years); Central Executive Committee; Special Committees. Autonomous regional sections (4): Africa; Americas; Asia-West Pacific; Europe and Middle East. Committee carries out international administration, while each country has its own *Religious Society of Friends (Quakers, #18834)*. National and regional (sub-national) Religious Societies of Friends are autonomous in their own right. Meetings closed. **Languages** English. **Staff** 4.00 FTE, paid. **Finance** Contributions from: constituent Yearly Meetings; individuals; private bodies. **Activities** Events/meetings; networking/liaising; knowledge management/information dissemination. International group of Friends attends in an observer capacity at United Nations General Assembly. Quaker programmes and initiatives include: *American Friends Service Committee (AFSC)*; *Church and Peace (#03916)*; *Europe and Middle East Young Friends (EMEYF, #09162)*; *Evangelical Friends Church, International (EFCI, no recent information)*; *Friends Peace Center (CAP)*; *Friends United Meeting (FUM)*; *Quaker Council for European Affairs (QCEA, #18587)*; *Quaker Peace and Social Witness (QPSW, see: #10004)*; *Quaker United Nations Office (QUNO, #18588)*; *Right Sharing of World Resources (RSWR)*; *Wider Quaker Fellowship (WQF, see: #10004)*. **Events** *Triennial Meeting* Dublin (Ireland) 2007, *Triennial Meeting* Auckland (New Zealand) 2004, *Triennial meeting* New Hampshire (USA) 2000, *Triennial Meeting* USA 2000, *Triennial Meeting* Birmingham (UK) 1997. **Publications** *Friends World News* (2 a year).
Members Representatives appointed by the Yearly Meetings; other groups and offices of Friends. Groups and individuals in 77 countries:
Australia, Austria, Belgium, Belize, Bolivia, Botswana, Brazil, Burundi, Cambodia, Canada, China, Colombia, Congo DR, Costa Rica, Cuba, Czechia, Denmark, Egypt, El Salvador, Estonia, Eswatini, Ethiopia, Finland, France, Germany, Ghana, Greece, Guatemala, Honduras, Hong Kong, Hungary, India, Indonesia, Ireland, Israel, Italy, Jamaica, Japan, Kenya, Korea Rep, Lebanon, Lesotho, Lithuania, Madagascar, Malawi, Mexico, Namibia, Nepal, Netherlands, New Zealand, Nigeria, Norway, Palestine, Papua New Guinea, Peru, Philippines, Poland, Qatar, Russia, Rwanda, Sierra Leone, Singapore, Slovakia, South Africa, Spain, Sri Lanka, Sweden, Switzerland, Taiwan, Tanzania UR, Thailand, Uganda, UK, Ukraine, USA, Zambia, Zimbabwe.
Consultative Status Consultative status granted from: *ECOSOC (#05331)* (General); *UNCTAD (#20285)* (General Category); *World Intellectual Property Organization (WIPO, #21593)* (Permanent Observer Status); *UNEP (#20299)*; *UNICEF (#20332)*. **IGO Relations** Observer to: *International Organization for Migration (IOM, #14454)*. Accredited by: *United Nations Office at Vienna (UNOV, #20604)*. Accredited to the Conference of the Parties of: *Secretariat of the United Nations Convention to Combat Desertification (Secretariat of the UNCCD, #19208)*. Associated with Department of Global Communications of the United Nations. **NGO Relations** Member of: *Alliance of NGOs on Crime Prevention and Criminal Justice (#00709)*; *Child Rights Connect (#03884)*; *International Network for a Culture of Nonviolence and Peace (#14247)*; *NGO Committee for Disarmament, Geneva (#17105)*; *NGO Committee on Disarmament, Peace and Security, New York NY (#17106)*; *NGO Committee on UNICEF (#17120)*. Working relations with: *World Council of Churches (WCC, #21320)*. [2020/XC0983/**E**]

♦ Friends of the World Food Programme (internationally oriented national body)
♦ Friends World Institute / see Global College, Long Island University
♦ Friends World Program / see Global College, Long Island University
♦ FriEnt – Arbeitsgemeinschaft Frieden und Entwicklung (internationally oriented national body)
♦ FRI – Family Rosary International (religious order)
♦ FRI – Fundación REDBIO Internacional
♦ Frigoclub International (see: #20213)
♦ Frisian International Contact (internationally oriented national body)
♦ Fritz Thyssen Foundation (internationally oriented national body)
♦ Fritz Thyssen Stiftung (internationally oriented national body)
♦ Frivilligorganisationernas Fond för Mänskliga Rättigheter / see Swedish Foundation for Human Rights
♦ FRMT – Fundación Rigoberta Menchú Tum (internationally oriented national body)
♦ **FROCC** European Association of Producers of Flame Retardant Olefinic Cable Compounds (#06166)
♦ FroCos – International Symposium on Frontiers of Combining Systems (meeting series)
♦ Front anti-communiste international (inactive)

♦ Frontex, the European Border and Coast Guard Agency 10005

Main Office Plac Europejski 6, 00-844 Warsaw, Poland. T. +48222059500. Fax +48222059501. E-mail: frontex@frontex.europa.eu.
URL: http://frontex.europa.eu/
History Council Regulation (EC) 2007/2004 of 26 Oct 2004 led to establishment of the European Agency for the Management of Operational Cooperation at the External Borders of the Member States of the European Union (Frontex). This Regulation was repealed by Regulation (EU) 2016/1624 of 14 Sep 2016, establishing Frontex, the European Border and Coast Guard Agency. The latest amendment of the Frontex mandate occurred when Regulation (EU) 2019/1896 of 13 Nov 2019 on the European Border and Coast Guard (OJ L 295, 14.11.2019, p. 1) came into force. **Aims** Promote, coordinate and develop European border management in line with the EU fundamental rights charter and the concept of Integrated Border Management. **Structure** Executive Director; Deputy Executive Directors (3); Divisions (9); Cabinet; Offices; Task Forces; Headquarters in Warsaw (Poland). **Staff** 1989.00 FTE, paid. **Finance** Annual budget: 754,375,142 EUR (2022). **Activities** Events/meetings; guidance/assistance/consulting; knowledge management/information dissemination; monitoring/evaluation; research and development. **Events** *Regional Workshop for Border Officials of Western Balkans* Belgrade (Serbia) 2021. **Publications** *2021 in brief* (annual); *Risk Analysis for 2021* (annual).
Members Members of Consultative Forum (Jan 2020):
Amnesty International – European Institutions Office (#00802); *Churches' Commission for Migrants in Europe (CCME, #03912)*; *Council of Europe (CE, #04881)*; *European Union Agency for Asylum (EUAA, #08968)*; *European Union Agency for Fundamental Rights (FRA, #08969)*; *International Commission of Jurists (ICJ, #12695)*; *International Organization for Migration (IOM, #14454)*; *Jesuit Refugee Service Europe (JRS Europe, #16107)*; *Office of the United Nations High Commissioner for Human Rights (OHCHR, #17697)*; *OSCE – Office for Democratic Institutions and Human Rights (OSCE/ODIHR, #17902)*; *Red Cross EU Office (#18643)*; *Save the Children International (#19058)*; *UNHCR (#20327)*.
IGO Relations Accredited by (1): *United Nations Office on Drugs and Crime (UNODC, #20596)*. Signed working arrangements with: *Eurojust (#05698)*; *European Union Agency for the Operational Management of Large-Scale IT Systems in the Area of Freedom, Security and Justice (eu-LISA, #08972)*; *European Fisheries Control Agency (EFCA, #07266)*; *European Maritime Safety Agency (EMSA, #07744)*; *European Police Office (Europol, #08239)*; *European Union Agency for Fundamental Rights (FRA, #08969)*; *European Union Agency for Law Enforcement Training (CEPOL, #08970)*; *International Centre for Migration Policy Development (ICMPD, #12503)*; *International Criminal Police Organization – INTERPOL (ICPO-INTERPOL, #13110)*; *International Organization for Migration (IOM, #14454)*; *UNHCR (#20327)*; *United Nations Office on Drugs and Crime (UNODC, #20596)*; *European External Action Service (EEAS, #07018)*; *Organization for Security and Cooperation in Europe (OSCE, #17887)*; *Geneva Centre for Security Sector Governance (DCAF, #10121)*. **NGO Relations** Member of (1): *EU Agencies Network (EUAN, #05564)*. [2022.10.18/XM2692/**E***]

♦ Frontex / see Frontex, the European Border and Coast Guard Agency (#10005)
♦ Frontier Conservation (internationally oriented national body)
♦ Frontier Internship in Mission (internationally oriented national body)
♦ Frontiers (internationally oriented national body)

♦ Frontiers in Immunology Research Network (FIRN) 10006

Contact 64 Holden St, Worcester MA 01605-3109, USA. T. +15088523937. Fax +15085950089. E-mail: hkan@firnweb.com.
URL: http://www.firnweb.com/
Aims Facilitate exchange of information and collaboration among scientists in academic and non-academic organizations as well as business and government. **Structure** Trustees. **Languages** English. **Activities** Events/meetings. **Events** *International Conference* Rome (Italy) 2021, *International Conference* Rome (Italy) 2020, *International Conference* Vienna (Austria) 2019, *International Conference* Lugano (Switzerland) 2018, *International Conference* Heraklion (Greece) 2017. **Publications** *International Journal of Immunological Studies (IJIS)* (4 a year). [2018.09.10/XJ1120/**C**]

♦ Front de libération des nains de jardin (#10671)

♦ Frontline AIDS 10007

Registered Office Preece House, 1st and 2nd Fl, 91-101 Davigdor Rd, Hove, BN3 1RE, UK. T. +441273718900. E-mail: mail@frontlineaids.org.
URL: http://www.frontlineaids.org/
History Dec 1993, London (UK), by *The Rockefeller Foundation (#18966)* and the development assistance agencies of *European Union (EU, #08967)*, France, Sweden, UK and USA. Original title *International HIV/AIDS Alliance – Alliance internationale contre le VIH/SIDA*. UK Registered Charity: 1038860. **Aims** Prevent HIV infection; facilitate access to treatment, care and support; lessen the impact of AIDS. **Structure** International Secretariat in Brighton (UK); representative country office in USA; linking organizations and country offices (29) in 24 countries. **Languages** English, French, Russian, Spanish. **Staff** 367 FET, of which 120 at International Secretariat.
Finance Supported by government departments and organizations, including the following listed in the Yearbook:
- *Agencia Española de Cooperación Internacional para el Desarrollo (AECID)*;
- *Bill and Melinda Gates Foundation (BMGF)*;
- *Canadian International Development Agency (CIDA, inactive)*;
- *Comic Relief*;
- *DANIDA*;
- *Department for International Development (DFID, inactive)*;
- *European Commission (EC, #06633)*;
- *Ford Foundation (#09858)*;
- *Global Fund to Fight AIDS, Tuberculosis and Malaria (Global Fund, #10383)*;
- *The William and Flora Hewlett Foundation*;
- *Joint United Nations Programme on HIV/AIDS (UNAIDS, #16149)*;
- *Norwegian Agency for Development Cooperation (Norad)*;
- *Swedish International Development Cooperation Agency (Sida)*;
- *UNDP (#20292)*;
- *United Nations Population Fund (UNFPA, #20612)*;
- *United States Agency for International Development (USAID)*;
- *WHO (#20950)*.

Activities Networking/liaising. **Publications** *Frontline Insights* (12 a year) – newsletter. Annual Review; policy reports; good practice reports; toolkits; CD-ROMs; e-bulletins.
Members Alliance linking organizations and country partners in 34 countries:
Bolivia, Botswana, Burkina Faso, Burundi, Cambodia, China, Côte d'Ivoire, Ecuador, Egypt, Eswatini, Ethiopia, Haiti, India, Indonesia, Jordan, Kenya, Kyrgyzstan, Lebanon, Malawi, Mexico, Morocco, Mozambique, Myanmar, Namibia, Nigeria, Peru, Senegal, South Africa, Tanzania UR, Tunisia, Uganda, Ukraine, Vietnam, Zimbabwe.
Consultative Status Consultative status granted from: *ECOSOC (#05331)* (Special). **IGO Relations** *Global Fund to Fight AIDS, Tuberculosis and Malaria (Global Fund, #10383)*; *Joint United Nations Programme on HIV/AIDS (UNAIDS, #16149)*; *WHO (#20950)*. **NGO Relations** Full member of: *British Overseas NGO's for Development (BOND)*; *Consortium for Street Children (CSC)*. Member of: *Regional Inter-Agency Task Team on Children and AIDS in Eastern and Southern Africa (RIATT-ESA, #18791)*; *Girls not Brides (#10154)*; *Global Health Council (GHC, #10402)*; *Global Health Workforce Alliance (GHWA, inactive)*; *International Treatment Preparedness Coalition (ITPC, #15729)*; *NonProfit Organizations Knowledge Initiative (NPOKI)*; *PMNCH (#18410)*; *TB Europe Coalition (TBEC, #20104)*; *UK Consortium on AIDS and International Development*. Associate member of: *International Initiative for Impact Evaluation (3ie, #13851)*. Cooperates with: *Action for Global Health (AfGH, #00090)*; *Caribbean Regional Network of People Living with HIV/AIDS (CRN+, #03549)*; *FHI 360*; *ICASO (#11040)*. Instrumental in setting up: *Health Communication Partnership (HCP)*. Supports: *Red de Trabajadoras Sexuales de América Latina y el Caribe (REDTRASEX, #18731)*. [2019.11.12/XF3949/**F**]

♦ Frontline Chaplains International / see International Fellowship of Chaplains

♦ Front Line Defenders (FLD) 10008

Exec Dir Avoca Court, 1st floor, Temple Road, Blackrock, CO. DUBLIN, A94 R7W3, Ireland. T. +35312123750. Fax +35312121001. E-mail: info@frontlinedefenders.org.
Brussels Office Square Marie-Louise 72, 1000 Brussels, Belgium. T. +3222309383. Fax +3222300028. E-mail: euoffice@frontlinedefenders.org.
URL: https://www.frontlinedefenders.org/
History 22 Feb 2001, Dublin (Ireland). Former names and other names: *International Foundation for the Protection of Human Rights Defenders (Front Line Defenders)* – legal name; *Fondation internationale pour la protection des défenseurs des droits humains* – legal name; *Fundación Internacional para la Protección de los/las Defensores/as de los Derechos Humanos* – legal name. Registration: No/ID: 593190, Ireland; No/ID: 20204494, Ireland. **Aims** Defend those who champion the Universal Declaration of Human Rights. **Structure** Board of Directors; International Advisory Council. **Languages** Arabic, English, French, Russian, Spanish. **Staff** 33.00 FTE, paid. **Finance** Donors, including the following organizations listed in this Yearbook: *American Jewish World Service (AJWS)*; *Bread for the World Institute (BFW Institute)*; *European Instrument for Democracy and for Human Rights (EIDHR, #07576)*; *Humanistisch Instituut voor Ontwikkelingssamenwerking (Hivos)*; *Irish Aid*; *Oak Foundation*; *Overbrook Foundation*; *Sigrid Rausing Trust*; *Swedish International Development Cooperation Agency (Sida)*; *Taiwan Foundation for Democracy (TFD)*. **Activities** Financial and/or material support; training/education; capacity building; advocacy/lobbying/activism; networking/liaising; awards/prizes/competitions; guidance/assistance/consulting. **Events** *Biennial Conference* Dublin (Ireland) 2013, *Biennial Conference* Dublin (Ireland) 2003. **Consultative Status** Consultative status granted from: *ECOSOC (#05331)* (Special); *African Commission on Human and Peoples' Rights (ACHPR, #00255)* (Observer Status). **IGO Relations** Member of: *European Economic and Social Committee (EESC, #06963)* Liaison Group. Cooperates with: *Council of Europe (CE, #04881)*. **NGO Relations** Member of (3): *Human Rights and Democracy Network (HRDN, #10980)*; *Irish Association of Non-Governmental Development Organisations (Dóchas)* (Associate); *ProtectDefenders.eu (#18546)*. [2022/XG9033/t/**F**]

♦ Front Line Defenders / see Front Line Defenders (#10008)
♦ Frontline Homeopathy / Homeopathy Action Trust (internationally oriented national body)
♦ Front du Maghreb (unconfirmed)
♦ Front d'unité et d'action de l'Afrique du Nord (inactive)
♦ FRPM – European Meeting on Fire Retardant Polymeric Materials (meeting series)
♦ **FRR** Foundation for Responsible Robotics (#09971)
♦ **FRSC** Forum Regional Security Committee (#09928)
♦ **FRS** Fascia Research Society (#09275)
♦ FRS – Fondation pour la recherche stratégique (internationally oriented national body)
♦ FRUCOM / see European Federation of the Trade in Dried Fruit, Edible Nuts, Processed Fruit and Vegetables, Processed Fishery Products, Spices, Honey and Similar Foodstuffs (#07229)
♦ **FRUCOM** European Federation of the Trade in Dried Fruit, Edible Nuts, Processed Fruit and Vegetables, Processed Fishery Products, Spices, Honey and Similar Foodstuffs (#07229)

♦ Fruit and Vegetable Dispute Resolution Corporation (DRC) 10009

Corporation de règlement des différends dans les fruits et légumes – Corporación de Solución de Controversias sobre Frutas y Hortalizas

CEO Bldg 75 – Central Experimental Farm, 960 Carling Avenue, Ottawa ON K1A 0C6, Canada. T. +16132340982. Fax +16132348036. E-mail: info@fvdrc.com.
URL: http://fvdrc.com/
History Set up 1996. **Aims** Serve the produce trade; educate members as to best practices so as to avoid disputes in the first place. **Structure** Board of Directors. **Activities** Guidance/assistance/consulting; standards/guidelines.
Members Active in 13 countries and territories:
Brazil, Canada, Chile, China, Dominican Rep, Honduras, Hong Kong, Israel, Peru, South Africa, Spain, Uruguay, USA.
IGO Relations Observer to: *Codex Alimentarius Commission (CAC, #04081)*. [2019/XM7042/**D**]

Frysk Ynternasjonaal Kontakt
10009
alphabetic sequence excludes
For the complete listing, see Yearbook Online at

- ♦ Frysk Ynternasjonaal Kontakt (internationally oriented national body)
- ♦ FSAD – Fondation Syngenta pour une Agriculture Durable (internationally oriented national body)
- ♦ **FSA** Fonds de solidarité africain (#09838)
- ♦ FSA / see International Skyrunning Federation (#14873)
- ♦ **FSB** Financial Stability Board (#09770)
- ♦ FSC / see Sciences Citoyennes
- ♦ FSCEC – Fédération des syndicats chrétiens de l'Europe centrale (inactive)
- ♦ FSCE / see Fédération Spéléologique Européenne (#09705)
- ♦ FSC – Field Studies Council Overseas (internationally oriented national body)
- ♦ **FSC** Food Security Cluster (#09849)
- ♦ **FSC** Forest Stewardship Council (#09869)
- ♦ FSC – Institutum Fratrum Scholarum Christianarum (religious order)
- ♦ FSC International / see Forest Stewardship Council (#09869)
- ♦ FSCT – Federation of Societies for Coatings Technology (internationally oriented national body)

♦ FSD Africa 10010

Contact Riverside Green Stes, Palm Ste, Riverside Drive, Nairobi, Kenya. T. +254204024000. E-mail: info@fsdafrica.org.
URL: http://www.fsdafrica.org/

History Created 2012. FSD stands for: *Financial Sector Development.* **Aims** Reduce *poverty* across sub-Saharan Africa by building financial markets that are efficient, robust and inclusive. **Finance** Funded by *Department for International Development (DFID, inactive).* Other main stakeholders: *Consultative Group to Assist the Poor (CGAP, #04768)*; Mastercard Foundation; *International Finance Corporation (IFC, #13597)*; *Alliance for Financial Inclusion (AFI, #00679)*; *Making Finance Work for Africa (MFW4A, #16555)*; *United Nations Capital Development Fund (UNCDF, #20524)*; *Deutsche Gesellschaft für Internationale Zusammenarbeit (GIZ).* **Activities** Training/education; advocacy/lobbying/activism. **Events** *AFSIC : Africa Financial Services Investment Conference* London (UK) 2021, *AFSIC : Africa Financial Services Investment Conference* London (UK) 2020, *AFSIC : Africa Financial Services Investment Conference* London (UK) 2019, *AFSIC : Africa Financial Services Investment Conference* London (UK) 2018, *AFSIC : Africa Financial Services Investment Conference* London (UK) 2017.
Members Full in 8 countries:
Kenya, Mozambique, Nigeria, Rwanda, South Africa, Tanzania UR, Uganda, Zambia.
Included in the above, 1 organization listed in this Yearbook:
NGO Relations Supports: *Access to Insurance Initiative (A2ii, #00051)*; *Centre for Affordable Housing Finance in Africa (CAHF, #03723).* [2018/XM6543/**F**]

- ♦ FSD – Fondation suisse de déminage (internationally oriented national body)
- ♦ FSDR – Finnish Society for Development Research (internationally oriented national body)
- ♦ **FSE** Fédération des Scénaristes d'Europe (#09703)
- ♦ **FSE** Fédération Spéléologique Européenne (#09705)
- ♦ **FSE** Fonds social européen (#08501)
- ♦ **FSE** Football Supporters Europe (#09854)
- ♦ **FSESP** Fédération syndicale européenne des services publics (#07202)
- ♦ **FSEU** Fire Safe Europe (#09780)
- ♦ FSFE – Free Software Foundation Europe (internationally oriented national body)
- ♦ FSF Europe / see Free Software Foundation Europe
- ♦ FSF / see Financial Stability Board (#09770)
- ♦ **FSF** Flight Safety Foundation (#09795)
- ♦ FSF – Food Systems for the Future (internationally oriented national body)
- ♦ FSF – Institutum Fratrum a Sancta Familia de Bellicio (religious order)
- ♦ **FS** Fleischner Society (#09793)
- ♦ FSFS – Finnish Society for Futures Studies (internationally oriented national body)
- ♦ FSFW – Foundation for a Smoke-Free World (unconfirmed)
- ♦ FSGC – Congregatio Fratrum a Sancto Ioseph Benedicto Cottolengo (religious order)
- ♦ FSG – Institutum Fratrum Instructionis Christianae a Sancto Gabriele (religious order)

♦ FSHD Europe 10011

Head of Communication Van Heutszlaan 6, 3743 JN Baarn, Netherlands.
Facebook: https://www.facebook.com/FSHDEurope/

History 2010, Baarn (Netherlands). Registration: No/ID: 40000172, Netherlands. **Aims** Be the voice and ears of people with Facioscapulohumeral *Muscular Dystrophy* (FSHD) throughout Europe and beyond; raise awareness, understanding and knowledge of FSHD; foster a culture of collaboration among stakeholders; provide an FSHD knowledge platform sharing information and best practices relevant to FSHD. **Structure** General Assembly (annual); Executive Board; Scientific Advisors. **Languages** Dutch, English, French, German, Italian, Russian, Spanish. **Staff** 10.00 FTE, voluntary. **Finance** Sources: members' dues.
Members Organizations in 6 countries:
France, Germany, Italy, Netherlands, Spain, UK.
IGO Relations *European Medicines Agency (EMA, #07767).* **NGO Relations** Member of: *EURORDIS – Rare Diseases Europe (#09175)*; *TREAT-NMD Neuromuscular Network (TREAT-NMD, #20231).*
[2020.06.23/XM7456/**D**]

- ♦ **FSI** Fédération spirite internationale (#15586)
- ♦ FSI – Fédération syndicale internationale (inactive)
- ♦ **FSI** Financial Stability Institute (#09771)
- ♦ FSI / see Football Supporters Europe (#09854)
- ♦ FSIMT – Foundation for the Support of International Medical Training (internationally oriented national body)
- ♦ FSIO – Federation of State Insurance Organizations of SAARC Countries (inactive)
- ♦ FSI Stanford – Freeman Spogli Institute for International Studies (internationally oriented national body)
- ♦ FSK / see Center for Security Studies
- ♦ FSMET – Foro Social Mundial de las Economias Transformadoras (meeting series)
- ♦ FSMET – Forum Social Mondial des Economies Transformatrices (meeting series)
- ♦ **FSM** Federación Sindical Mundial (#21493)
- ♦ **FSM** Fédération séphardite mondiale (#21778)
- ♦ **FSM** Fédération syndicale mondiale (#21493)
- ♦ **FSMF** Fondation Sommet mondial des femmes (#21038)
- ♦ FSM – Filles de Sainte-Marie de la Présentation (religious order)
- ♦ FSM – Franciscan Sisters of Mary (religious order)
- ♦ FSMI – Congregatio Filiorum Sanctae Mariae Immaculatae (religious order)
- ♦ FSN – Fonds spécial du Nigéria (internationally oriented national body)
- ♦ FSP / see Counterpart International
- ♦ FSP / see Swisspeace
- ♦ **FSPA** Foro Social Pan-Amazônico (#09889)
- ♦ FSP – Congregatio Fratrum a Sancto Patricio (religious order)
- ♦ FSP – Counterpart International (internationally oriented national body)
- ♦ FSP – Fonds de solidarité prioritaire (internationally oriented national body)
- ♦ **FSPI** Foundation of the Peoples of the South Pacific International (#09968)
- ♦ FSP International / see Foundation of the Peoples of the South Pacific International (#09968)
- ♦ FSPM – Femmes et sport dans les pays méditerranéens (no recent information)
- ♦ FSSCA / see EcoViva
- ♦ FSSCyC – Federación Sudamericana de Sociedades de Cirugia de Cabeza y Cuello (inactive)
- ♦ FSSP – Fraternitas Sacerdotalis Sancti Petri (religious order)
- ♦ **FSSPX** Fraternité sacerdotale internationale Saint-Pie X (#18494)
- ♦ FSSU / see United Nations Field Staff Union (#20561)
- ♦ FST / see Institut de recherche pour la gestion des associations et des coopératives, Fribourg
- ♦ **FSTCVS** French Society for Thoracic and Cardiovascular Surgery (#09993)
- ♦ FST / see European Transport Workers' Federation (#08941)
- ♦ FSUE / see Fédération Spéléologique Européenne (#09705)
- ♦ FSVC – Financial Services Volunteer Corps (internationally oriented national body)
- ♦ FSWL / see Foundation of SAARC Writers and Literature (#09972)
- ♦ F/TAAC / see Association of Moving Image Archivists
- ♦ FTA / see amfori (#00797)

♦ FTA Europe 10012

SG Av Louise 130-A, 1050 Brussels, Belgium. T. +3222308646. Fax +3222311464. E-mail: secretary.general@fta-europe.eu.
URL: http://www.fta-europe.eu/

History Feb 2015. Set up by national organizations in Spain, France, Italy, UK – *European Flexographic Industry Association (EFIA)* – and *European Flexographic Technical Association Benelux (EFTA-Benelux).* FTA stands for *Flexographic Technical Association.* Registration: AISBL/IVZW, No/ID: 0598.740.715, Start date: 5 Feb 2015, Belgium. **Aims** Represent the common interests of the European flexographic (flexo) *printing* industry. **Structure** Board. Committees (3): Education; Technical; Marketing. **Languages** English. **Staff** 1.00 FTE, paid. **Finance** Members' dues. **Activities** Projects/programmes; events/meetings; awards/prizes/competitions; networking/liaising; advocacy/lobbying/activism. **Events** *Packaging Conference* Brussels (Belgium) 2019, *Meeting* Brussels (Belgium) 2018. **Publications** *FTA Europe Best Practice Toolbox*; *FTA Europe Newsletter.*
Members Full in 7 countries:
Denmark, France, Italy, Netherlands, Spain, Sweden, UK.
NGO Relations *Intergraf (#11505)*; *Industry4Europe (#11181).* [2020/XM5703/**D**]

- ♦ **FTA** Fairtrade Africa (#09239)
- ♦ FTA / see Fair Trials (#09242)
- ♦ **FTA** Fraternité théologique africaine (#00483)
- ♦ **FTAO** Fair Trade Advocacy Office (#09238)
- ♦ **FTCCEE** Federation of Therapeutic Communities of Central and Eastern Europe (#09707)
- ♦ **FTC** Financial Transparency Coalition (#09772)
- ♦ FTC / see WE Charity (#20849)
- ♦ FTDA – France terre d'asile (internationally oriented national body)
- ♦ **FTE** Forum Train Europe (#09930)
- ♦ **FTERSI** Fondation Temimi pour la recherche scientifique et l'information (#09829)
- ♦ FTESEA – Foundation for Theological Education in South East Asia (internationally oriented national body)
- ♦ FTFA – Food and Trees for Africa (internationally oriented national body)
- ♦ FTFMD – International Society of Functional Thin Film Materials and Devices (unconfirmed)
- ♦ **FTI** Federación Teosófica Interamericana (#11453)
- ♦ FTI – Foundation for Tolerance International (internationally oriented national body)
- ♦ FTIS – Fair Trade International Symposium (meeting series)
- ♦ **FTM** Forum du Tiers-monde (#20149)
- ♦ **FTP** Forest-Based Sector Technology Platform (#09861)
- ♦ FTPP / see RECOFTC – The Center for People and Forests (#18628)
- ♦ **FTS** Focal Therapy Society (#09805)
- ♦ FTTH Council Africa / see Digital Council Africa
- ♦ FTTH Council Americas / see Fiber Broadband Association
- ♦ **FTTH Council Asia-Pacific** Fibre-to-the-Home Council Asia-Pacific (#09750)
- ♦ **FTTH Council Europe** Fibre-to-the-Home Council Europe (#09751)
- ♦ FTTH Council Middle East and North Africa / see Fiber Connect Council MENA (#09749)
- ♦ FTTH North America / see Fiber Broadband Association
- ♦ FTTX Council Africa / see Digital Council Africa
- ♦ FUAAV / see United Federation of Travel Agents' Associations (#20509)
- ♦ **FUACE** Fédération Universelle des Associations Chrétiennes d'Etudiants (#21833)
- ♦ **FUCE** Fédération des universités catholiques européennes (#07070)
- ♦ FUCID – Fondation universitaire pour la coopération internationale au développement (internationally oriented national body)
- ♦ FU.CO.IN. – Fundación para las Comunidades Internacionales (internationally oriented national body)
- ♦ FUDER – Fundación para el Desarrollo Regional (internationally oriented national body)
- ♦ **FUECH** Fédération de l'Union Européenne des Consuls Honoraires (#09709)
- ♦ **FUEDI** Fédération européenne des unions professionnelles d'experts en dommages après incendie et risques divers (#07158)

♦ Fuel Cells and Hydrogen Joint Undertaking (FCH JU) 10013

Exec Dir WA TO 56, 1049 Brussels, Belgium. T. +3222218148. E-mail: fch-ju@fch.europa.eu – communications@fch.europa.eu.
URL: https://www.fch.europa.eu/

History 2008. A Public-Private Partnership between *European Commission (EC, #06633)* and the industry. Will be replaced by *Clean Hydrogen Partnership.* **Aims** Accelerate the market introduction of fuel cell and hydrogen energy technologies, realising their potential as an instrument in achieving a carbon-clean energy system. **Structure** Governing Board; Executive Director; Scientific Committee; States Representatives Group; Stakeholder Forum.
Members Public:
European Commission (EC, #06633).
Private: Fuel cell and hydrogen industries and research community represented by:
Hydrogen Europe (#10998); Hydrogen Europe Research.
NGO Relations Member of (1): *EU Agencies Network (EUAN, #05564).* [2021/AA1428/**E**]

♦ FuelsEurope 10014

Dir Bd du Souverain 165, 3rd floor, 1160 Brussels, Belgium. T. +3225669100. Fax +3225669111. E-mail: info@fuelseurope.eu.
URL: https://www.fuelseurope.eu/

History 14 Sep 1989, Brussels (Belgium). Statutes amended: 16 May 1991; Mar 1993; Oct 1995. Along with *Oil Companies' European Association for Environment, Health and Safety in Refining and Distribution (CONCAWE, #17708)*, became a division of *European Petroleum Refiners Association (#08194)*, 1 Jan 2013. Former names and other names: *European Petroleum Industry Association (Europia)* – former (1989 to Jun 2014); *Association de l'industrie pétrolière européenne* – former (1989 to Jun 2014). Registration: Belgium. **Aims** Inform and provide expert advice to the EU institutions and other stakeholders about European *petroleum* refining and distributioin and its products in order to: contribute in a constructive way to development of technically feasible and cost effective EU policies and legislation; promote understanding amongst EU institutions and citizens of the contribution of European petroleum refining and distribution to European economic, technological and social progress. **Structure** General Assembly (annual); Board of Directors; Issue Management Committee; issue groups and task forces; secretariat. **Languages** English. **Staff** 12.00 FTE, paid. **Activities** Advocacy/lobbying/activism. **Events** *Annual Conference* Brussels (Belgium) 2019, *Annual Conference* Brussels (Belgium) 2018. **Publications** Activity report (annual). **Members** Companies (41) accounting for almost 100% of EU petroleum refining capacity and more than 75% of EU motor fuel retail sales. Membership countries not specified. **NGO Relations** Cooperates with: *Conseil européen de l'industrie chimique (CEFIC, #04687)*; *International Organization for Standardization (ISO, #14473).* Member of: *Alliance for a Competitive European Industry (ACEI, #00670)*; *Centre for European Policy Studies (CEPS, #03741)*; *European Energy Forum (EEF, #06986)*; *Industry4Europe (#11181)*; *Oil Companies' European Association for Environment, Health and Safety in Refining and Distribution (CONCAWE, #17708).* [2019/XD2455/**D**]

- ♦ **FUEN** Federal Union of European Nationalities (#09396)
- ♦ Fuerza de Emergencia de las Naciones Unidas (inactive)
- ♦ Fuerza de las Naciones Unidas para el Mantenimiento de la Paz en Chipre (#20608)
- ♦ Fuerza de las Naciones Unidas para la Observación de la Separación (#20553)

♦ Fuerza Provisional de las Naciones Unidas en el Libano (#20577)
♦ FUEV / see Federal Union of European Nationalities (#09396)
♦ **FU** Floating University (#09796)
♦ **FuHD – AL** Fundación Henry Dunant América Latina (#10024)
♦ **FUILAC** Federación de Usuarios de Interent de latinoamerica y Caribe (#09395)
♦ **FUIW** Federation of the Universities of the Islamic World (#09710)
♦ Fulbright Alumni Association / see Fulbright Association
♦ Fulbright Association (internationally oriented national body)

♦ Full Gospel Business Men's Fellowship International (FGBMFI) 10015

Communauté internationale des hommes d'affaires du plein Evangile – Geschaftslente des Vollen Evangeliums International

Corporate Office One Park Plaza, Suite 600, Irvine CA 92614, USA. T. +19495294688. E-mail: info.fgbmfi@gmail.com – media@fgbmfi.org.
URL: http://www.fgbmfi.org/

History 1953, Costa Mesa CA (USA). **Aims** Testify to the power of the living God in our world today; reach all men for *Jesus Christ*; bring greater unity among all members in the Body of Christ. **Structure** Founder/ President; Executive Vice-President; Executive Committee; International Directors; Chapter Officers. **Finance** Members' dues. Other sources: grants; sale of publications. Budget (annual): US$ 4 million. **Activities** Organizes Annual World Convention and regional conventions. Local groups and chapters meet regularly each month for praise, worship and fellowship. European chapter: *Full Gospel Business Men's Fellowship International Europe (see: #10015)*. **Events** *World Convention* Central Valley CA (USA) 2015, *Annual World Convention* Houston, TX (USA) 2015, *World Convention* Houston, TX (USA) 2014, *World convention* Fort Lauderdale, FL (USA) 2009, *Glory invasion meeting* Singapore (Singapore) 2008. **Publications** *Vision* – inter-organization magazine; *Voice* – magazine. *The Happiest People on Earth*. Books; booklets; brochures.
Members Chapters and local groups (over 4,000), totalling 50,000 individual members. About 1 million men worldwide meet regularly each month. Permanently represented in 133 countries and territories:
Albania, Angola, Antigua-Barbuda, Argentina, Armenia, Aruba, Australia, Austria, Bahamas, Barbados, Belgium, Belize, Benin, Bermuda, Bolivia, Brazil, Bulgaria, Burkina Faso, Burundi, Cameroon, Canada, Cayman Is, Central African Rep, Chad, Chile, China, Colombia, Congo Brazzaville, Congo DR, Costa Rica, Côte d'Ivoire, Croatia, Cuba, Curaçao, Cyprus, Czechia, Denmark, Dominica, Dominican Rep, Ecuador, El Salvador, Equatorial Guinea, Estonia, Eswatini, Fiji, Finland, France, Gabon, Gambia, Germany, Ghana, Gibraltar, Greece, Grenada, Guadeloupe, Guatemala, Guinea, Guyana, Honduras, Hong Kong, Hungary, Iceland, India, Indonesia, Ireland, Israel, Italy, Jamaica, Japan, Jersey, Kenya, Latvia, Liechtenstein, Lithuania, Luxembourg, Malawi, Malaysia, Mali, Malta, Martinique, Mexico, Montserrat, Myanmar, Netherlands, New Zealand, Nicaragua, Nigeria, Norway, Pakistan, Panama, Papua New Guinea, Paraguay, Peru, Philippines, Poland, Portugal, Puerto Rico, Romania, Russia, Rwanda, Saudi Arabia, Senegal, Serbia, Sierra Leone, Singapore, Slovakia, Slovenia, South Africa, Spain, Sri Lanka, St Croix Is, St Kitts-Nevis, St Lucia, St Maarten, St Thomas Is, St Vincent-Grenadines, Suriname, Sweden, Switzerland, Taiwan, Tanzania UR, Thailand, Togo, Trinidad-Tobago, Uganda, UK, Ukraine, Uruguay, USA, Venezuela, Virgin Is UK, Zambia, Zimbabwe.
[2022/XF0216/**F**]

♦ Full Gospel Business Men's Fellowship International Europe (see: #10015)
♦ Fulton Society (unconfirmed)
♦ **FUMEC** Federación Universal de Movimientos Estudiantiles Cristianos (#21833)
♦ FUM – Friends United Meeting (internationally oriented national body)
♦ **FUMI** Fédération des universités du monde islamique (#09710)
♦ FUMN – Fondation Universitaire de la Mer Noire
♦ FUNAP – Federation of Staff Associations of United Nations and its Specialized Agencies in the Philippines (internationally oriented national body)
♦ FUNCEJI – Fundación Comunidad Esperanza y Justicia Internacional (unconfirmed)

♦ Functional Airspace Block Europe Central (FABEC) 10016

Communication Cell address not obtained.
URL: https://www.fabec.eu/

History Declaration of Intent signed Nov 2008. Operates on the basis of the *Treaty relating to the establishment of the Functional Airspace Block "Europe Central" between the Federal Republic of Germany, the Kingdom of Belgium, the French Republic, the Grand Duchy of Luxembourg, the Kingdom of the Netherlands and the Swiss Confederation (FABEC Treaty)*, signed Dec 2010. Operational since June 2013. **Aims** Achieve optimal performance in the areas relating to safety, environmental sustainability, capacity, cost-efficiency, flight efficiency and military mission effectiveness, by the design of airspace and the organization of air traffic management in the airspace concerned regardless of existing boundaries. **Structure** Council; ANSP Strategic Board; ANSP Consultation Board. Permanent bodies: FABEC States Bureau; ANSP FABEC Group. Standing Committees for Operations, Safety, Technology, Environment, HR and Training, Social Dialogue and Institutional questions. **Publications** *FABEC Bulletin*. *Climate Change and the role of air traffic control* (2022); *Interdependencies within ATM Performance in the Context of a Dynamic Environment* (2021); *Fragmentation in Air Traffic and its Impact on ATM Performance* (2019). *FABEC Performance Report*.
Members Partners in 6 countries:
Belgium, France, Germany, Luxembourg, Netherlands, Switzerland.
Regional partner:
EUROCONTROL Maastricht Upper Area Control Centre (MUAC, #05670). [2023.02.14/XM8721/**F***]

♦ Functional Genomics Data Society (inactive)

♦ Functional Metagenomics International 10017

Contact Dept of Biology, Univ of Waterloo, 200 Univ Ave W, Waterloo ON N2L 3G1, Canada.
History 2011. Previously also referred to as *International Society for Functional Metagenomics*. **Aims** Promote interaction between functional metagenomics researchers around the world; provide a forum for discussion of the latest experimental advances and technical development in metagenomics based gene discovery and analysis, with clinical, industrial, and environmental applications. **Events** *Conference* Trondheim (Norway) 2019, *Conference* Inderøy (Norway) 2016, *Conference* Trondheim (Norway) 2016, *Functional Metagenomics Conference* Pretoria (South Africa) 2013. [2016.06.23/XJ7519/**E**]

♦ Functional Neurological Disorder Society (FNDS) 10018

Exec Dir 555 E Wells St, Suite 1100, Milwaukee WI 53202-3823, USA. T. +14149189814. E-mail: info@fndsociety.org.
Events Manager address not obtained.
URL: https://www.fndsociety.org/

History Proposed Sep 2017, Edinburgh (UK). Inaugural meeting, Jun 2020, Boston MA (USA). **Structure** Board of Directors; Program Committee. **Activities** Events/meetings. **Events** *International Conference on Functional Neurological Disorders* Boston, MA (USA) 2022, *International Conference on Functional Neurological Disorders* Boston, MA (USA) 2020, *International Conference on Functional Neurological Disorders* Edinburgh (UK) 2017. **NGO Relations** *World Federation of Neurology (WFN, #21461).* [2020/XM8740/**C**]

♦ the Fund / see Episcopal Relief and Development
♦ Fundação Assistência Médica Internacional (internationally oriented national body)
♦ Fundação Calouste Gulbenkian (internationally oriented national body)
♦ Fundação Centro Internacional de Educação, Capacitação e Pesquisa Aplicada em Aguas (internationally oriented national body)
♦ Fundação Contra Fome (#09845)
♦ Fundação Gonçalo da Silveira (internationally oriented national body)
♦ Fundação InterAmericana do Coração (#11432)
♦ Fundação Luso-Americana / see Fundação Luso-Americana para o Desenvolvimento
♦ Fundação Luso-Americana para o Desenvolvimento (internationally oriented national body)
♦ Fundação MacArthur (internationally oriented national body)
♦ Fundação Memorial de América Latina (internationally oriented national body)
♦ Fundação Oriente, Lisboa (internationally oriented national body)
♦ Fundação 'Populorum Progressio' (#09969)
♦ Fundação Portugal-Africa (internationally oriented national body)
♦ Fundação Rotaria (#18974)
♦ Fundação Rural da Africa do Oeste (#20902)
♦ Fundação SOS Amazonia / see Associação SOS Amazonia
♦ Fundació CIDOB – Centre d'Informació i Documentació Internacionals a Barcelona (internationally oriented national body)
♦ Fundació Institut Barcelona d'Estudis Internacionals (internationally oriented national body)
♦ Fundació Internacional Josep Carreras per a la Lluita contra la Leucèmia (#16153)
♦ Fundació Internacional Olof Palme (internationally oriented national body)
♦ Fundación Abogados para Abogados (internationally oriented national body)
♦ Fundación Academia Europea e Iberoamericana de Yuste (internationally oriented national body)
♦ Fundación Acceso (internationally oriented national body)
♦ Fundación para la Acción Cultural Internacional en las Montañas (#09813)
♦ Fundación AGRECOL Andes (internationally oriented national body)
♦ Fundación Agreste (unconfirmed)
♦ **Fundación ALAS** América Latina en Acción Solidaria (#16396)
♦ Fundación Alboan (internationally oriented national body)
♦ Fundación Alexander Von Humboldt (internationally oriented national body)

♦ Fundación para la Alimentación y Nutrición de Centro América y Panama (FANCAP) 10019

Food and Nutrition Foundation of Central America and Panama

Exec Sec c/o INCAP, Calzada Roosevelt, 6-25 Zona 11, PO Box 1188, 01901 Guatemala, Guatemala. T. +50224713299. Fax +50224409672. E-mail: lromero@fancap.org – info@fancap.org.
URL: http://www.fancap.org/

Aims Promote activities for solving food and nutrition problems in the region. [2017/XD7127/f/**F***]

♦ Fundación para las Américas (#20252)

♦ Fundación América Solidaria 10020

Exec Dir General Bustamante 26, 5th Floor, Providencia, Santiago, Santiago Metropolitan, Chile. T. +56226352125. E-mail: comunicaciones@americasolidaria.org.
URL: http://www.americasolidaria.org/

History 1998, Chile. Executive office established 2002. Registration: Ministerio de Justicia, No/ID: 161038, Start date: 15 Jan 2014, Chile. **Aims** Work collaboratively with most excluded communities in Latin America to promote leadership of children and adolescence in the exercise and defense of their rights. **Structure** Board of Directors; Executive Office. **Languages** Spanish. **Staff** 50.00 FTE, paid; 100.00 FTE, voluntary. **Finance** Sources: donations; fundraising; government support; international organizations; private foundations. Annual budget: 4,000,000 USD (2022). **Activities** Advocacy/lobbying/activism; awards/prizes/ competitions; awareness raising; capacity building; events/meetings; financial and/or material support; guidance/assistance/consulting; knowledge management/information dissemination; monitoring/evaluation; networking/liaising; projects/programmes; training/education. Active in: Argentina, Brazil, Chile, Colombia, Haiti, Mexico, Peru, Uruguay, USA. **Publications** *Bajo el Cielo de América* (2017).
Members Country offices in 7 countries:
Argentina, Chile, Colombia, Haiti, Peru, Uruguay, USA.
Consultative Status Consultative status granted from: *ECOSOC (#05331)* (Special).
[2023.02.16/XM7185/f/**F**]

♦ Fundación para la Aplicación y Enseñanza de las Ciencias (internationally oriented national body)
♦ Fundación Arias para la Paz y el Progreso Humano (internationally oriented national body)
♦ Fundación Arte de Vivir (internationally oriented national body)
♦ Fundación Athena Intelligence (internationally oriented national body)
♦ Fundación de Ayuda a los Ciegos de Hispanoamérica / see Fundación ONCE para América Latina
♦ Fundación Bariloche (internationally oriented national body)
♦ Fundación Bernard van Leer (internationally oriented national body)
♦ Fundación Bertelsmann (internationally oriented national body)
♦ Fundación del Bosque Tropical (internationally oriented national body)
♦ Fundación Calouste Gulbenkian (internationally oriented national body)
♦ Fundación Carolina (internationally oriented national body)
♦ Fundación Católicas por el Derecho a Decidir en América Latina / see Católicas por el Derecho a Decidir (#03612)
♦ Fundación CELARG – Centro de Estudios Latinoamericanos Rómulo Gallegos (internationally oriented national body)
♦ Fundación Centro Extremeño de Estudios y Cooperación con Iberoamérica / see Fundación Academia Europea e Iberoamericana de Yuste
♦ Fundación Charles Darwin para las Islas Galapagos (#03852)
♦ Fundación Charles Léopold Mayer para el Progreso del Hombre (#09815)
♦ Fundación Chol-Chol (internationally oriented national body)
♦ Fundación CIDEAL de Cooperación e Investigación (internationally oriented national body)
♦ Fundación CIDOB – Centro de Estudios y Documentación Internacionales de Barcelona (internationally oriented national body)
♦ Fundación Círculo de Montevideo / see Circulo de Montevideo (#03938)
♦ Fundación de las Ciudades Carnavalescas Europeas / see Federation of European Carnival Cities (#09496)
♦ Fundación CODESPA (internationally oriented national body)
♦ Fundación de Comunicaciones Latinoamericanas David Livingston (internationally oriented national body)
♦ Fundación para las Comunidades Internacionales (internationally oriented national body)
♦ Fundación Comunidad Esperanza y Justicia Internacional (unconfirmed)
♦ Fundación para la Conservación de la Biodiversidad y su Habitat (internationally oriented national body)
♦ Fundación contra el Hambre (#09845)
♦ Fundación Cordell Hull para Educación Internacional (internationally oriented national body)
♦ Fundación Cultural de las Américas (internationally oriented national body)
♦ Fundación Cultura de Paz (internationally oriented national body)
♦ Fundación Cumbre Mundial de la Mujer (#21038)
♦ Fundación Dag Hammarskjöld (#04995)
♦ Fundación para el Debido Proceso (#05144)
♦ Fundación para el Desarrollo Regional (internationally oriented national body)

♦ Fundación para el Desarrollo Sostenible en América Latina (FUNDES) 10021

Foundation for Sustainable Development in Latin America

Exec Dir address not obtained. E-mail: internacional@fundes.org.
URL: http://www.fundes.org/

History 1984, Panama. **Aims** Promote the competitive development of micro, small and medium-sized enterprises (MSMEs) in Latin America. **Languages** English, Spanish.
Members in 10 countries:
Argentina, Bolivia, Chile, Colombia, Costa Rica, El Salvador, Guatemala, Mexico, Panama, Venezuela.
NGO Relations Member of: *Aspen Network of Development Entrepreneurs (ANDE, #02310)*; *International Center for Economic Growth (ICEG, inactive).* [2017/XD6757/f/**F**]

♦ Fundación Desarrollo Sostenido (internationally oriented national body)
♦ Fundación para el Desarrollo Sustentable del Chaco Sudamericano (internationally oriented national body)
♦ Fundación para el Desarrollo de Zonas Secas y Semiaridas de Mesoamérica (internationally oriented national body)
♦ Fundación Dieta Mediterranea (internationally oriented national body)
♦ Fundación Directorio Legislativo (internationally oriented national body)

♦ Fundación Earth Train (internationally oriented national body)
♦ Fundación Ecologia y Desarrollo (internationally oriented national body)
♦ Fundación Educación y Cooperación / see EDUCO
♦ Fundación para la Educación Superior Internacional (#13794)
♦ Fundación Educativa de la Confederación Latinoamericana de Cooperativas de Ahorro y Crédito (see: #16302)
♦ Fundación para el Entendimiento Internacional / see Folmer Wisti Foundation for International Understanding
♦ Fundación Escuela Latinoamericana de Redes (internationally oriented national body)
♦ Fundación Etica Mundial (internationally oriented national body)
♦ **Fundación EU-LAC** Fundación Unión Europea-América Latina y el Caribe (#08999)
♦ Fundación Euroamérica (internationally oriented national body)
♦ Fundación Euroarabe de Altos Estudios (internationally oriented national body)
♦ Fundación por la Europa de los Ciudadanos (internationally oriented national body)
♦ Fundación Europea de la Cultura (#06868)
♦ Fundación Europea de Derechos del Hombre (inactive)
♦ Fundación Europea para la Innovación y Desarrollo de la Tecnología (unconfirmed)
♦ Fundación Europea de Medicina Tradicional China (internationally oriented national body)
♦ Fundación Europea para la Mejora de las Condiciones de Vida y de Trabajo (#07348)
♦ Fundación Europea Sociedad y Educación (internationally oriented national body)
♦ Fundación para la Familia de las Américas (#09250)
♦ Fundación Federación Interamericana de Asociaciones de Gestión Humana (/ see Federación Interamericana de Asociaciones de Gestión Humana (#09329)
♦ Fundación Friedrich Ebert (internationally oriented national body)

♦ Fundación Futuro Latinoamericano (FFLA) 10022

Main Office Shyris N37-313 y El Telégrafo, Quito, Ecuador. E-mail: info@ffla.net.
URL: http://www.ffla.net/

History 1 Nov 1993, Quito (Ecuador). Registration: Ecuador. **Aims** Promote constructive dialogue; strengthen citizen, political and institutional capacities; integrate processes for *sustainable development* in Latin America. **Structure** International Board of Directors; Advisory Board. Executive Director; Directors; Technical Staff. **Languages** Spanish. **Staff** 29.00 FTE, paid. **Finance** Budget (annual): about US$ 2.1 million. **Activities** Capacity building; research and development; events/meetings. **Publications** Reports; guides. **Consultative Status** Consultative status granted from: *UNCTAD (#20285)* (Special Category). **IGO Relations** Accredited organization of: *Green Climate Fund (GCF, #10714).* **NGO Relations** Founding member of: *International Centre for Trade and Sustainable Development, Geneva (ICTSD, #12524).* Member of: *Climate and Development Knowledge Network (CDKN, #04012); International Union for Conservation of Nature and Natural Resources (IUCN, #15766).* Also links with a number of national organizations and universities in Latin America active in the field. [2020/XF3611/f/F]

♦ Fundación Gabo (internationally oriented national body)
♦ **Fundación GEISER** Grupo de Enlace, Investigación y Soporte de Enfermedades Raras de Latino America (#10804)
♦ Fundación Global Democracia y Desarrollo (internationally oriented national body)
♦ Fundación Global Nature (internationally oriented national body)
♦ Fundación Global Play (internationally oriented national body)

♦ Fundación Hastinapura 10023

Hastinapura Foundation

Main Office Riobamba 1020, C1116ABF, Buenos Aires, Argentina. T. +541148119342. Fax +541148119342. E-mail: infocentral@hastinapura.org.ar.
URL: http://www.hastinapura.org.ar/

History 1981. **Aims** Promote *non-violent education* and *spiritual universalism.* **Structure** Board of Directors. **Languages** Spanish. **Staff** 4.00 FTE, paid. **Finance** Voluntary contributions. **Activities** Training/education; networking/liaising. **Publications** *Hastinapura Diario para el Alma* (6 a year). Translations; spiritual wiritings.
Members Individuals in 4 countries:
Argentina, Bolivia, Colombia, Uruguay.
IGO Relations Associated with Department of Global Communications of the United Nations. [2017.06.01/XF4183/fv/F]

♦ Fundación Help for the Andes (internationally oriented national body)

♦ Fundación Henry Dunant América Latina (FuHD – AL) 10024

Pres/Dir California 1892, Providencia, Santiago, Santiago Metropolitan, Chile. T. +5622055179. Fax +5622090657. E-mail: contacto@funhd.org.
URL: http://www.fundacionhenrydunant.org/

History Founded 2006, Santiago (Chile), as a sister organization and local representative of *Collège universitaire Henry Dunant (CUHD, #04111).* **Aims** Construct answers and public policy formulations that fulfill social rights. **Structure** Board. *'Association Henry Dunant France-Amérique Latine'.* Implemented by *Instituto Internacional Henry Dunant (see: #10024).* **Languages** English, French, Spanish. **Activities** Training/education; certification/accreditation; guidance/assistance/consulting; politics/policy/regulatory; events/meetings. **Publications** *Derecho a la Alimentación, Politicas Públicas e Instituciones contra el Hambre*; *Derechos Humanos, Pedagogia de la Memoria y Politicas Culturales*; *El Paradigma de los Derechos Universales, 2 vols*; *Exigibilidad y Realización de Derechos Sociales Impacto en la Politica Pública*; *La Travesia del Salitre Chileno: De la pampa a la tierra Holandesa* by Aafke Steenhuis; *Migración y Derechos Jumanos*; *Politicas Públicas: Exigibilidad y realización de derechos*; *Seguridad Alimentaria: Derecho a la alimentación y politicas públicas contra el hambre en América Central.* **IGO Relations** Cooperates with: *FAO (#09260); ILO (#11123)* – sub-regional office for Cono Sur; *Institute of Nutrition of Central America and Panama (INCAP, #11285); International Organization for Migration (IOM, #14454); Organization of Ibero-American States for Education, Science and Culture (#17871); Pan American Health Organization (PAHO, #18108); Secretariat of the United Nations Convention to Combat Desertification (Secretariat of the UNCCD, #19208); UNDP (#20292)* – Chile; *UNESCO (#20322); UNHCR (#20327); UNICEF (#20332); United Nations Office for Disaster Risk Reduction (UNDRR, #20595); United Nations Population Fund (UNFPA, #20612); United Nations System (#20635)* – Chile. **NGO Relations** Cooperates with: *Amnesty International (AI, #00801); Ford Foundation (#09858); Heinrich Böll Foundation; Instituto Centroamericano de Estudios Fiscales (ICEFI, #11325); International Federation of Red Cross and Red Crescent Societies (#13526); World Organisation Against Torture (OMCT, #21685)* – Centro Regional de Derechos Humanos y Justicia de Género; national organizations. [2020/XM3894/f/F]

♦ Fundación Pro Humanae Vitae (internationally oriented national body)

♦ Fundación Iberoamérica Europa Centro de Investigación, Promoción y Cooperación Internacional (CIPIE) 10025

Contact C/General Arrando 14, Bajo derecha (local), 28010 Madrid, Spain. T. +34915322828. E-mail: fundacionfie@fundacionfie.org.
URL: https://www.fundacionfie.org/

History 17 Jun 1981, Madrid (Spain). Founded by Chilean and Spanish politicians and other personalities as a Technical Agency for Development and Interconnection between European and Ibero-American private and governmental organizations to manage aid and advise on the implementation of specific Programs and Projects. **Aims** Promote cultural, economic, political and social cooperation in Latin America, Europe and any country or region in the world; support the dissemination and implementation of the values of the democratic system as a form of human coexistence, political pluralism, rule of law, and respect for Human Rights. **Structure** Board of Trustees; Management Team; International Cooperation Network. **Languages** English, Spanish. **Staff** 25.00 FTE, paid. **Activities** Awareness raising; capacity building; events/meetings; projects/programmes; publishing activities; research/documentation; training/education. Active in: Argentina, Bolivia, Brazil, Chile, Colombia, Costa Rica, Cuba, Dominican Rep, Ecuador, El Salvador, Guatemala, Mexico, Nicaragua, Panama, Paraguay, Peru, Uruguay, Venezuela. **Publications** *Estudios Iberoamericanos* in Spanish. Analysis; Notebooks; Art Catalogs. **NGO Relations** Collaborates with universities, study and research centers in Spain and Latin America. [2020.11.21/XM7516/f/F]

♦ Fundación Iberoamericana para la Gestión de la Calidad (FUNDIBEQ) 10026

Iberoamerican Foundation for Quality Management

Main Office c/Fernando el Santo 27 4B, 28010 Madrid, Spain. T. +34915488882. Fax +34913106683. E-mail: sg@fundibeq.org – admon@fundibeq.org.
URL: http://www.fundibeq.org/

History Founded 18 Mar 1998. **Aims** Promote and develop quality management in the region using the Iberoamerican Excellence Model. **Structure** Board. **Languages** Portuguese, Spanish. **Staff** 5.00 FTE, paid. **Activities** Awards/prizes/competitions; events/meetings. **Events** *Convencion Iberoamericana de Excelencia en la Gestion* Madrid (Spain) 2012, *Virtual Educa : international conference on education, training and new technologies* São José dos Campos (Brazil) 2007. **Publications** *Aprender de los Mejores – Buenas Practicas.*
Members in 17 countries:
Argentina, Bolivia, Brazil, Chile, Colombia, Costa Rica, Cuba, Dominican Rep, Ecuador, El Salvador, Mexico, Paraguay, Peru, Portugal, Spain, Uruguay, Venezuela. [2014.06.01/XD7953/f/F]

♦ Fundación Iberoamericana de Seguridad y Salud Ocupacional (FISO) 10027

Exec Dir Billinghurst 1833, Piso 6, C1425DTJ, Buenos Aires, Argentina. T. +541148114146. E-mail: info@fiso-web.org.
URL: http://www.fiso-web.org/

History Founded 2000, by private initiative of 3 major occupational risk management entities: Chilean Safety Association – ACHS; Occupational Risk Management – COLMENA (Colombia); Insurer Prevention ART (Argentina). **Aims** Stimulate development of investigation activities, qualification and professional pursuit of the systems of *occupational health* and risks, so as to improve *labour conditions* of the workers of Latin America and the Iberian Peninsula. **Languages** Spanish. **Activities** Financial and/or material support; events/meetings; training/education. **Publications** *NotiFISO* (twice a month) – newsletter; *TecniFISO* (twice a month) – newsletter.
Members Full in 4 countries:
Argentina, Chile, Colombia, Peru.
Associate in 1 country:
Peru. [2014.12.16/XM8237/f/F]

♦ Fundación IEPALA / see Instituto de Estudios Politicos para América Latina y Africa
♦ Fundación Instituto Forestal Latinoamericano / see Latin American Forestry Institute
♦ Fundación Instituto Iberoamericano de Administración Pública / see Fundación Internacional y para Iberoamérica de Administración y Politicas Públicas (#10030)
♦ Fundación Instituto para las Negociaciones Agricolas Internacionales (internationally oriented national body)
♦ Fundación Interamericana (#11431)
♦ Fundación Interamericana de Abogados (see: #11401)

♦ Fundación Interamericana Ciencia y Vida (FIVC) 10028

Contact ULIA, Departamento de Sociologia, Universidad de Valencia, Campus de los Naranjos, 46022 Valencia, Spain. E-mail: departament.sociologia@uv.es.
URL: http://www.ulia.org/ficv/fundicv.htm

History 1998 – 07, Guadalajara (Mexico). Founded Jul 1998, Guadalajara (Mexico). **Activities** Project: Universidad Libre Internacional de las Américas (ULIA). **Events** *Congress* Santiago (Chile) 2007, *Congress* Valencia (Spain) 2006, *Congress* Cancún (Mexico) 2005, *Congress* Montevideo (Uruguay) 2004, *Congress* Querétaro (Mexico) 2003. [2013.11.25/XM2590/f/F]

♦ Fundación InterAmericana del Corazón (#11432)
♦ Fundación Interamericana para la Cultura y el Desarrollo (internationally oriented national body)
♦ Fundación Interamericana de Investigación Tropical (internationally oriented national body)
♦ Fundación Intermón / see INTERMON OXFAM
♦ Fundación Internacional para Alternativas de Desarrollo (inactive)
♦ Fundación Internacional de Apoyo al Desarrollo Local y Social (internationally oriented national body)
♦ Fundación Internacional para la Asistencia Comunitaria / see FINCA International

♦ Fundación Internacional para el Desafio Económico y Global (FIDEG) 10029

International Foundation for Global Economic Development

Contact Bolonia, de Price Smart, 2 cuadras al Lago, Managua, Nicaragua. T. +50522668869. Fax +50522668711.
URL: http://www.fideg.org/

History 1990, Managua (Nicaragua). **Aims** Act as a think-thank on economics, social issues, household surveys, poverty measurement, microfinance and genre. **Structure** Executive Director; Sub-Director; Research Director; Administrative Director. **Languages** English, Spanish. **Staff** 2.50 FTE, paid. **Finance** Funding through projects. Budget (2010): US$ 250,800. **Activities** Socioeconomic research; surveys; studies. **Publications** *Observador Economico* (12 a year) – magazine. Surveys; program evaluations. **IGO Relations** Participating institution of: *Latin American and Caribbean Research Network (#16284).* **NGO Relations** Member of: *International Center for Economic Growth (ICEG, inactive)*; Nicaraguan Statistics Network. [2021/XF2684/f/F]

♦ Fundación Internacional Florence Nightingale (#09798)

♦ Fundación Internacional y para Iberoamérica de Administración y Politicas Públicas (FIIAPP) 10030

International and Ibero-American Foundation for Administration and Public Affairs

Main Office c/ Beatriz de Bobadilla 18, 2a planta, 28040 Madrid, Spain. T. +34915914600. Fax +34915914590. E-mail: info@fiiapp.org – comunicacion@fiiapp.org.
URL: http://www.fiiapp.org/

History 1997. Former names and other names: *Inter-American Institute of Administrative Sciences* – alias; *Fundación Instituto Iberoamericano de Administración Pública (FIIAP)* – alias. Registration: Spain; EU Transparency Register, No/ID: 76875858222-63. **Events** *High-Level Meeting of the Structured and Comprehensive EU/CELAC Dialogue on Migration* Brussels (Belgium) 2013, *Meeting on Migration and Development* Brussels (Belgium) 2013, *Senior Official MME Meeting* Brussels (Belgium) 2013, *International Congress on Gender-Based Violence* Madrid (Spain) 2013, *Meeting* Brussels (Belgium) 2009. **NGO Relations** Member of: *European Network of Implementing Development Agencies (EUNIDA, #07926); Global Action on Disability Network (GLAD, #10165); Practitioners' Network for European Development Cooperation (#18476).* Cooperates with: *International Federation of Former Iberoamerican Students of the INAP (FIAAIINAPE).* [2018/XD8057/f/D]

♦ Fundación Internacional José Carreras para la Lucha contra la Leucemia (#16153)

♦ Fundación Internacional para la Libertad (FIL) 10031

Contact address not obtained. E-mail: info@fundacionfil.org.
URL: https://fundacionfil.org/

History Founded Oct 2002. **Aims** Defend and promote the principles of freedom, democracy and the rule of law. **Structure** Board of Directors. **Activities** Events/meetings. [2019/XM7515/f/F]

♦ Fundación Internacional de Macroglobulemia de Waldenström (internationally oriented national body)

♦ Fundación Internacional ORP (FIORP) 10032

Contact C/ Buen Gobernador, 28027 Madrid, Spain. E-mail: info@fiorp.org.
URL: https://fiorp.org/

History *ORP* derives from: *Occupational Risk Prevention.* Registration: Spain. **Aims** Improve the quality of working life; enhance business innovation. **Structure** Scientific Committee. **Activities** Events/meetings. **Events** *ORP Conference* Barcelona (Spain) 2021, *ORP Conference* Madrid (Spain) 2019. **Publications** *ORPjournal* (4 a year). [2022/AA0562/f/F]

♦ Fundación Internacional Planeta Libre (internationally oriented national body)

- Fundación Internacional para la Protección de los/las Defensores/as de los Derechos Humanos / see Front Line Defenders (#10008)
- Fundación Internacional Raoul Wallenberg (#14698)

♦ Fundación Internacional para la Restauración de Ecosistemas (FIRE) 10033

Main Office C/ Princesa 3 dpdo, 7a planta, apto 703, 28008 Madrid, Spain. T. +34669902888. E-mail: luis.cayuela@urjc.es – info@fundacionfire.org.
URL: http://www.fundacionfire.org/

History 2006. Registered in accordance with Spanish law since 2006. **Aims** Restore and conserve ecosystems, transferring academic knowledge to operational projects with the highest possible social return. **Structure** Board of Directors; Offices in Chile and Paraguay. **Languages** English, Spanish. **Staff** 5.00 FTE, paid. **Finance** Public and private support. **Activities** Projects/programmes; research/documentation; training/education. **Publications** Manuals; books.
Members Full in 15 countries:
Argentina, Canada, Chile, Colombia, Costa Rica, Ecuador, Guatemala, Haiti, Mexico, Nicaragua, Panama, Paraguay, Spain, Uruguay, USA.
NGO Relations *International Analog Forestry Network (IAFN, #11650); International Union for Conservation of Nature and Natural Resources (IUCN, #15766); Society for Ecological Restoration International (SERI).*
[2018/XM4603/f/F]

♦ Fundación Internacional de Solidaridad Compañia de Maria (FISC) . 10034

International Solidarity Foundation of the Company of Mary
Main Office C/ Islas Aleutianas 26, 28035 Madrid, Spain. T. +34913112491 ext 4013. E-mail: fisc-ongd@fisc-ongd.org.
URL: http://www.fisc-ongd.org/

History Founded 1995, by The Company of Mary. **Aims** Promote solidarity, cooperation and education for development, prioritizing human rights, gender equality and capacity building of individuals and groups collaborating to build a more fair, inclusive society; promote peace and freedom. **Structure** Board of Trustees; Director. **Languages** Spanish. **Staff** 6.00 FTE, paid; 200.00 FTE, voluntary. **Finance** Donations; project income. **Activities** Training/education; capacity building. Active in: Argentina, Colombia, Congo DR, Nicaragua, Peru, Philippines. **Publications** *FISC informa* (periodical). Magazines; newsletters.
[2019.09.26/XM8138/f/F]

- Fundación de Investigaciones Económicas Latinoamericanas (internationally oriented national body)
- Fundación Japón (internationally oriented national body)
- Fundación Juan March (internationally oriented national body)
- Fundación Kim Phuc Internacional (internationally oriented national body)
- Fundación Konrad Adenauer (internationally oriented national body)

♦ Fundación Latinoamericana de Auditores Internos (FLAI) 10035

Contact address not obtained. E-mail: auditoresinternoslatam@gmail.com.
URL: https://www.laflai.org/

History 8 Sep 1995, Cancún (Mexico) as *Federación Latinoamericana de Auditores Internos.* **Events** *Congress* Lima (Peru) 2009, *Congress* Punta Cana (Dominican Rep) 2008, *Congress* Mexico City (Mexico) 2004, *Congress* La Paz (Bolivia) 2003, *Congress* Managua (Nicaragua) 2002.
Members in 8 countries:
Argentina, Brazil, Colombia, Costa Rica, Dominican Rep, Mexico, Nicaragua, Uruguay. [2019/XJ4296/D]

♦ Fundación Latinoamericana por los Derechos Humanos y el Desarrollo Social (FUNDALATIN) 10036

Fondation d'Amérique latine pour les droits de l'homme – Latin American Foundation for Human Rights and Social Development
Pres Final Av Alameda, El Rosal, Caracas 1062 DF, Venezuela. T. +582129535976. E-mail: fundalatin@gmail.com.
URL: http://fundalatin.org.ve/

History Jun 1978, Caracas (Venezuela). Also referred to in English as *Latin American Foundation of Detained and Disappeared People.* **Aims** Promote human rights, sustainable development, justice and peace, solidarity of peoples and Latin American integration. **Structure** Annual Meeting; President. **Languages** English, Spanish. **Staff** 4.00 FTE, paid. **Activities** Knowledge management/information dissemination. **Publications** *The Eternal Debt*; *The Other World*; *Wake Up America.* **Consultative Status** Consultative status granted from: *ECOSOC (#05331)* (Special). **IGO Relations** *Inter-American Commission on Human Rights (IACHR, #11411); United Nations Human Rights Council (HRC, #20571).* [2018.09.05/XF0774/f/F]

♦ Fundación Latinoamericana para la Educación a Distancia (FLEAD) 10037

Latin American Foundation for Distance Education
Contact Av Pedro Molina 461, Planta Baja Of 8, 5500 Mendoza, Argentina. T. +542614299177. Fax +542614255044.
URL: http://www.flead.org/

History 2004. **Events** *Latin American virtual congress on distance education* 2004. [2015/XJ3308/f/F]

- Fundación Latinoamericana de Transporte Público y Urbano (unconfirmed)
- Fundación LatinoAméricaPosible / see LatinoAméricaPosible (#16402)
- Fundación MacArthur (internationally oriented national body)
- Fundación Mediterranea (internationally oriented national body)
- Fundación Migrantes y Refugiados sin Fronteras (unconfirmed)
- Fundación Monte Mediterraneo (internationally oriented national body)
- Fundación Mundial de Destrucción Estatutaria de Explosivos / see World EOD Foundation (#21387)
- Fundación Mundial de EOD (#21387)
- Fundación Mundial Pedro Arrupe / see Pedro Arrupe World Association (#18287)
- Fundación Mundial de la Salud para el Desarrollo y la Paz (internationally oriented national body)
- Fundación Mundial de la Salud para la Paz / see World Health Foundation for Development and Peace
- Fundación Mundubat (internationally oriented national body)
- Fundación de las Naciones Unidas para el Habitat y los Asentamientos Humanos (inactive)
- Fundación del Nuevo Cine Latinoamericano (#09967)
- Fundación para un Nuevo Periodismo Iberoamericano / see Fundación Gabo
- Fundación Oceana (internationally oriented national body)
- Fundación ONCE para América Latina (internationally oriented national body)
- Fundación Panamericana para el Desarrollo (#18094)
- Fundación Panamericana de la Salud y Educación / see PAHO Foundation (#18022)
- Fundación por la Paz (internationally oriented national body)
- Fundación Paz y Solidaridad 'Serafin Aliaga' (internationally oriented national body)
- Fundación 'Populorum Progressio' (#09969)
- Fundación para el Progreso del Hombre / see Fondation Charles Léopold Mayer pour le progrès de l'homme (#09815)
- Fundación Promoción Social (internationally oriented national body)
- Fundación Promoción Social de la Cultura / see Fundación Promoción Social
- Fundación REDBIO Internacional
- Fundación Red Deporte y Cooperación (internationally oriented national body)
- Fundación Red Deporte – Fundación Red Deporte y Cooperación (internationally oriented national body)
- Fundación Ricky Martin (internationally oriented national body)
- Fundación Rigoberta Menchú Tum (internationally oriented national body)
- Fundación Rio Abierto (internationally oriented national body)
- Fundación Rotaria (#18974)
- Fundación Rusa por la Paz (internationally oriented national body)
- Fundación Santillana (internationally oriented national body)
- Fundación Scito (internationally oriented national body)
- Fundación para el Tercer Mundo / see INTERMON OXFAM
- Fundación Unión Europea-América Latina y el Caribe (#08999)
- Fundación Universitaria Holandesa de Cooperación Internacional / see Netherlands Organization for International Cooperation in Higher Education
- Fundación Vaticana "Centro Internacional Familia de Nazaret" (#20750)
- Fundación Wassu-UAB (internationally oriented national body)
- Fundació per la Pau (internationally oriented national body)
- Fundació Pau i Solidaritat / see Fundació Pau i Solidaritat – CCOO de Catalunya
- Fundació Pau i Solidaritat – CCOO de Catalunya (internationally oriented national body)
- Fundació Scito (internationally oriented national body)
- Fundació Ulls del Món (internationally oriented national body)
- Fundacja Centrum Prasowe dla Krajów Europy Srodkowej i Wschodniej (#03694)
- Fundacja ClientEarth (#03996)
- Fundacja ECCC (internationally oriented national body)
- Fundacja Ecobaltic (internationally oriented national body)
- Fundacja Nadzieja Dla Baltyyku (internationally oriented national body)

♦ Fundacja TechSoup 10038

Vice-Pres ul Bracka 25, 5th Floor, PL-00-028, Warsaw, Poland. T. +48221022135.
URL: http://fundacja-techsoup.org/

History May 2009, Poland, as the European office of *TechSoup Global (#20122).* Registered in accordance with Polish law. **Aims** Support development of *civil society* in Poland, Europe and worldwide. **Structure** Board, including Chair and Vice-Chair. **Staff** 8.00 FTE, paid. [2018/XM3874/f/F]

♦ Fundacom 10039

Sec Paseo de la Castellana 193, 1 Planta – Of 112, 28046 Madrid, Spain. T. +34917021377. E-mail: info@fundacom.lat.
URL: https://fundacom.lat/

History Former names and other names: *Fundacom – Fundación para el impulso de la comunicación en español y portugués en el mundo* – full title; *Fundacom – Fundação para a promoção da comunicação no mundo que fala espanhol e português* – full title. Registration: Spain. **Structure** Council of Patrons; Management Team. **Activities** Awards/prizes/competitions; events/meetings; research/documentation; training/education. **Events** *Cumbre Iberoamericana de Comunicación Estratégica* Madrid (Spain) 2019.
Members Associations in 11 countries:
Argentina, Brazil, Chile, Colombia, Dominican Rep, Guatemala, Mexico, Panama, Portugal, Spain, Uruguay.
[2020/AA0543/C]

- Fundacom – Fundação para a promoção da comunicação no mundo que fala espanhol e português / see Fundacom (#10039)
- Fundacom – Fundación para el impulso de la comunicación en español y portugués en el mundo / see Fundacom (#10039)
- FUNDAEC – Fundación para la Aplicación y Enseñanza de las Ciencias (internationally oriented national body)
- **FUNDALATIN** Fundación Latinoamericana por los Derechos Humanos y el Desarrollo Social (#10036)
- Fundalivingston – Fundación de Comunicaciones Latinoamericanas David Livingston (internationally oriented national body)
- Fund for Animals (internationally oriented national body)
- Fundatia Institutul International de Tehnologie si Economie Apicola (internationally oriented national body)
- Fundation PROA / see Open Arms

♦ Fund for Central and East European Book Projects (CEEBP) 10040

Fonds pour le livre en Europe centrale et orientale – Fonds voor Midden- en Oosteuropese Boekprojecten
Dir Nieuwe Prinsengracht 89, 1018 VR Amsterdam, Netherlands. T. +31205207390. E-mail: ceebp@ceebp.org.
URL: http://www.ceebp.org/

History Dec 1992, Amsterdam (Netherlands). Founded under the auspices of *European Cultural Foundation (ECF, #06868)*, as a sister and successor organization of *Central and East European Publishing Project (CEEPP, inactive)*, Oxford (UK). **Aims** Enhance quality publishing in Central and Eastern Europe through support of the translation and dissemination of seminal books in the field of literature and the humanities; advance a viable quality book trade in the countries of Central and Eastern Europe and its integration in the international book world. **Structure** Board of Trustees; Executive Committee; Advisory Board; Director. **Languages** English. **Staff** 0.20 FTE, voluntary. **Finance** Sources: donations; international organizations; private foundations. Sources have included: Allianz Cultural Foundation; Dutch Foundation for Literature; Dutch Ministry of Education, Culture and Science; Dutch Ministry of Foreign Affairs; ECF; Hamburger Stiftung zur Förderung von Wissenschaft und Kultur. Annual budget: 40,000 EUR. **Activities** Financial and/or material support; projects/programmes; training/education. Active in: Albania, Belarus, Bosnia-Herzegovina, Bulgaria, Croatia, Czechia, Estonia, Hungary, Kosovo, Latvia, Lithuania, Montenegro, North Macedonia, Poland, Romania, Serbia, Slovakia, Slovenia, Ukraine. **Publications** *CEEBP Newsletter*; *Publishers' Portraits: Publishing in Central and Eastern Europe. CEEBP Profile and Books* – online. Information Services: Website links to the book trade and literary Central and Eastern Europe. **Members** Not a membership organization. **NGO Relations** Links with national organizations. [2021.09.30/XF3356/f/F]

- Fund for Development Cooperation – Socialist Solidarity (internationally oriented national body)
- Fund for the Development of the Indigenous Peoples of Latin America and the Caribbean (#09832)
- FUNDEA – Fundación Euroarabe de Altos Estudios (internationally oriented national body)
- Fund for Education in World Order / see Fund for Peace
- FUNDESEM – Fundación para el Desarrollo de Zonas Secas y Semiaridas de Mesoamérica (internationally oriented national body)
- **FUNDES** Fundación para el Desarrollo Sostenible en América Latina (#10021)
- FUNDESO – Fundación Desarrollo Sostenido (internationally oriented national body)
- Fund for Global Human Rights (internationally oriented national body)
- **FUNDIBEQ** Fundación Iberoamericana para la Gestión de la Calidad (#10026)
- Funding for Peace Coalition (internationally oriented national body)

♦ Fund for Latin American Irrigated Rice 10041

Fondo Latinoamericano para Arroz de Riego (FLAR)
Main Office KM 17 Recta Cali, Palmira AA 6713, Cali, Valle del Cauca, Colombia. T. +5724450052 – +5724450093. Fax +5724450094.
URL: http://www.flar.org/

History 16 Jan 1995. **Aims** Serve as a forum of information on market needs and opportunities of member countries; increase sustainable rice production. **Structure** Steering Committee; Technical Commission; Executive Director. **Finance** Members' dues. **Events** *International rice meeting* Havana (Cuba) 2002. **Publications** *Foro Arrocero Latinoamericano* – newsletter.
Members National organizations (13) in 13 countries:
Argentina, Bolivia, Brazil, Chile, Colombia, Costa Rica, Cuba, Guatemala, Nicaragua, Panama, Paraguay, Uruguay, Venezuela.
International organizations (3):
Centre de coopération internationale en recherche agronomique pour le développement (CIRAD, #03733); International Centre for Tropical Agriculture (#12527); International Rice Research Institute (IRRI, #14754).
[2018/XF5762/fy/F]

- Fund for Nonviolence (internationally oriented national body)
- Fundo Cristão para Crianças / see ChildFund International (#03869)
- Fundo Europeu de Desenvolvimento (#06914)
- Fundo Financiero para o Desenvolvimento da Bacia do Prata (#09833)

- Fundo para Jovens Empresarios das Américas (internationally oriented national body)
- Fundo Mundial para a Natureza (#21922)
- Fundo Mundial de Solidariedade contra a Fome (#09836)
- Fundo Panamericano Leo S Rowe / see Leo S Rowe Pan American Fund (#16445)
- Fundo para o Património Mundial Africano (#00505)
- Fundo Rowe / see Leo S Rowe Pan American Fund (#16445)
- Fundo Social Europeu (#08501)
- Fundo de Solidariedade para as Lutas de Libertação Social no Terceiro Mundo (internationally oriented national body)
- Fundo Sueco de Cooperación Industrial con los Paises en Via de Desarrollo / see Swedfund – International
- Fund for Peace (internationally oriented national body)
- Fund for Peace: Peaceful Settlement of Territorial Disputes / see OAS Peace Fund (#17630)
- Fund for the Protection of the World Cultural and Natural Heritage of Outstanding Universal Value / see World Heritage Fund (#21568)
- Fund for Reconciliation and Development (internationally oriented national body)
- Fund for Solidarity and Economic Development of the West African Economic Community (inactive)
- FUN – Friends of the United Nations (internationally oriented national body)
- Fünftes zusatzprotokoll zum Allgemeinen abkommen über die privilegien und immunitäten (1990 treaty)
- FUNGLODE – Fundación Global Democracia y Desarrollo (internationally oriented national body)
- FUNPZA / see Asociación Latinoamericana de Parques Zoológicos y Acuarios (#02252)
- FUNSA Delhi – Federation of the Staff Associations of the United Nations and its Specialized Agencies in Delhi (internationally oriented national body)
- FUNSA Denmark – Federation of the Staff Associations of the United Nations and its Specialized Agencies and their Affiliated Bodies in Denmark (internationally oriented national body)
- **FUNSA Santiago** Federation of Staff Associations of the United Nations and its Specialized Agencies in Santiago (#09706)
- FUNU – Force d'urgence des Nations Unies (inactive)
- FUPAC / see Asociación de Universidades Privadas de Centroamérica y Panama (#02306)
- **FUPAD** Fundación Panamericana para el Desarrollo (#18094)

♦ Fur Europe 10042

Main Office Ave des Arts 3-4-5, 1210 Brussels, Belgium. T. +3222091170. E-mail: info@fureurope.eu.
URL: http://www.fureurope.eu/

History 2014. Founded on merger of *European Fur Breeders Association (EFBA, inactive)* with European members of *International Fur Federation (IFF, #13696)*. **Activities** Knowledge management/information dissemination; advocacy/lobbying/activism.
Members Full in 27 countries:
Austria, Belgium, Bosnia-Herzegovina, Bulgaria, Czechia, Denmark, Estonia, Finland, France, Germany, Greece, Hungary, Iceland, Ireland, Italy, Latvia, Lithuania, Netherlands, Norway, Poland, Romania, Slovakia, Slovenia, Spain, Sweden, Switzerland, UK.
NGO Relations Affiliated with: *COPA – european farmers (COPA, #04829)*. Subscribert to: *ISEAL (#16026)*. [2021/XM5953/**D**]

- FUR – Foundations of Utility and Risk Conference (meeting series)

♦ Fur Free Alliance (FFA) 10043

Contact Panamalaan 110, 1019 AZ Amsterdam, Netherlands. E-mail: info@anima.dk.
URL: http://www.furfreealliance.com/

Aims Seek, by appropriate legal and non-violent means, to bring and end to the killing and exploitation of all animals for their fur by raising public awareness about the cruelty and negative environmental impacts associated with the global fur trade; focus on the deprivation and cruelty suffered by fur bearing animals both in wild *trapping* and industrial fur farming. **Structure** Secretariat in Nottingham (UK). **Finance** Sources: contributions; members' dues. Affiliate organizations responsible for financing their own initiatives, or in the case of joint campaigns, financial costs are shared proportionately, according the their means. **Activities** Awards/prizes/competitions; knowledge management/information dissemination.
Members Affiliated national and international organizations in 22 countries and territories:
Belgium, Canada, Croatia, Czechia, Denmark, Finland, France, Germany, Hong Kong, Ireland, Italy, Japan, Latvia, Netherlands, Norway, Russia, Spain, Sweden, Switzerland, UK, Ukraine, USA.
International organizations (5):
Fund for Animals; *Global Action Network (GAN)*; *Humane Society International (HSI, #10966)*; *International Fund for Animal Welfare (IFAW, #13693)*; *World Animal Protection (#21092)*.
NGO Relations Secretariat located at: Respect for Animals. [2022/XF6260/y/**F**]

- Al Furqan Islamic Heritage Foundation (internationally oriented national body)

♦ Pro Fuse International 10044

Pres c/o Eaton MEM, Reddings Lane, Tyseley, Birmingham, B11 3EZ, UK. E-mail: profuseinternational@googlemail.com.
URL: http://www.profuseinternational.com/

History Sep 1988. **Aims** Promote the use and value of products which use *fuses* as a protective device. **Events** *International conference on electrical fuses and their applications* Clermont-Ferrand (France) 2007. **Members** Manufacturers of either fuses or fuse-based equipment in 20 European countries. Membership countries not specified. [2010/XM2375/**F**]

- **Fusion for Energy** European Joint Undertaking for ITER and the Development of Fusion Energy (#07611)
- FUSLA Sur – Federación Universitaria Sionista Latinoamericano – Sur (inactive)
- FUSLA Norte – Federación Universitaria Sionista Latinoamericano – Norte (no recent information)
- Fussball gegen Rassismus in Europa (#09853)
- Fútbol contra el Racismo en Europa (#09853)

♦ FUTURALLIA Association 10045

Association FUTURALLIA
Contact Téléport 1, 7 ave du Tour de France, CS 50146, Futuroscope cedex, 86961 Chasseneuil du Poitou, France. T. +33549003572. Fax +33549003567.
URL: http://www.futurallia.com/

History 2000, following a series of business conventions. **Aims** Develop and foster exchanges within the small and medium-sized *enterprises* (SME) worldwide network; meet multi-sector business managers from all over the world; discover techniques in managing the evolution of national and international markets; complete their range of products and enlarge their distribution network; identify new poles of development to explore new markets. **Structure** Board. **Languages** English, French. **Staff** 5.00 FTE, paid. **Activities** Events/meetings; networking/liaising. **Events** *International Business Development Forum* Bucharest (Romania) 2015, *International Business Development Forum* Lyon (France) 2014, *International Business Development Forum* Lyon (France) 2014, *International Business Development Forum* Istanbul (Turkey) 2013, *International Business Development Forum* Lille (France) 2012. [2016.06.01/XJ4195/**F**]

♦ Future Africa Forum 10046

Founder 107 Lower Kabete Road, Nairobi, 00604, Kenya. E-mail: info@futureafricaforum.org.
URL: https://futureafricaforum.org/

Aims Increase the participation of young African's in building the future of Africa. **Activities** Advocacy/lobbying/activism; events/meetings. **NGO Relations** Member of (1): *Pandemic Action Network (PAN, #18173)*. [2023/AA2288/**F**]

- Future African Leaders Alliance / see Youth Alliance for Leadership and Development in Africa (#22004)
- Future Agricultures (unconfirmed)

♦ Future Convention Cities Initiative (FCCI) 10047

Chair Seoul Tourism Org, 110-460 8 – 9Fl 49, Daehak-ro, Jongno-gu, Seoul, Korea Rep.
History 2010. **Aims** Investigate leading new trends in business events.
Members Cities (7) in 7 countries:
Australia, Canada, Korea Rep, South Africa, UK, United Arab Emirates, USA. [2015/XM4229/**F**]

♦ Future Earth 10048

Interim Executive Director Sustainability, Energy and Environment Complex (SEEC), MacAllister Building, Suite N292 4001, Discovery Drive, Boulder CO 80303, USA. E-mail: contact@futureearth.org.
URL: http://www.futureearth.org/

History 2012, Rio de Janeiro (Brazil). Announced at UN Conference on Sustainable Development, building on earlier science collaboration in programmes of *International Geosphere-Biosphere Programme (IGBP, inactive)*, *International Human Dimensions Programme on Global Environmental Change (IHDP, inactive)*, *World Climate Research Programme (WCRP, #21279)* and *DIVERSITAS – International Programme of Biodiversity Science (inactive)*. Became fully operational, 2015. Former names and other names: *Future Earth – research for global sustainability* – full title. **Aims** Accelerate transformations to global sustainability through research and innovation. **Structure** Governing Council, composed of: *Belmont Forum (#03197)*; *International Science Council (ISC, #14796)*; *UNEP (#20299)*; *UNESCO (#20322)*; *United Nations University (UNU, #20642)*; *World Meteorological Organization (WMO, #21649)*. Advisory Committee; Global Hubs (5); Regional Centres (4); Secretariat. Runs: *Global Land Programme (GLP, #10450)*; *Global Mountain Biodiversity Assessment (GMBA, #10477)*. **Languages** English. **Finance** Funded by: private and public foundations; government agencies; universities; other groups. **Activities** Projects/programmes; research and development. **Events** *Programme on Ecosystem Change and Society Conference* Montréal, QC (Canada) 2024, *SRI2022 Asia Spotlight Meeting* Kyoto (Japan) 2022, *Programme on Ecosystem Change and Society Conference* Montréal, QC (Canada) 2022, *Sustainability Research and Innovation Congress* Pretoria (South Africa) 2022, *Sustainability Research and Innovation Congress* Brisbane, QLD (Australia) 2021. **Publications** *Anthropocene Magazine*.
Members Organizations within the Alliance (9):
Belmont Forum (#03197); *International Science Council (ISC, #14796)*; *Science and Technology in Society Forum (STS forum, #19145)*; *Sustainable Development Solutions Network (SDSN, #20054)*; *UNEP (#20299)*; *UNESCO (#20322)*; *United Nations University (UNU, #20642)*; *World Meteorological Organization (WMO, #21649)*.
Consultative Status Consultative status granted from: *UNEP (#20299)*. **IGO Relations** Partner of (1): *Group on Earth Observations (GEO, #10735)*. **NGO Relations** Member of (3): *Global Commons Alliance*; *International Centre for Earth Simulation (ICES Foundation)*; *Science Based Targets Network*. Instrumental in setting up (1): *Earth Commission (#05163)*. An initiative of: *Science and Technology Alliance for Global Sustainability (Alliance, #19143)*. [2020.10.22/XJ6881/y/**F**]

- Future Earth (internationally oriented national body)

♦ Future Earth Coasts 10049

International Project Office Leibniz Centre for Tropical Marine Research, Fahrenheitstrasse 6, 28359 Bremen, Germany. T. +49421238000. E-mail: info@futureearthcoasts.org.
URL: https://www.futureearthcoasts.org/

History Founded 1992, as *Land-Ocean Interactions in the Coastal Zone Project (LOICZ) – Interaction terre-océan dans les zones côtières*, a Core Project of *International Geosphere-Biosphere Programme (IGBP, inactive)* and a Core Science Project of *International Human Dimensions Programme on Global Environmental Change (IHDP, inactive)*. Phase I: 1992-2002. Phase II: 2005-2012. As of 2015, a core project of *Future Earth (#10048)* and present name adopted. **Aims** Support sustainability and adaptation to global change in the coastal zone by providing the knowledge needed to coastal communities. **Structure** Executive Committee; International Project Office; Regional Nodes. **Languages** Chinese, English, German. **Staff** 1.70 FTE, paid. **Activities** Research/documentation; events/meetings; networking/liaising. **Events** *Open Science Meeting* Gold Coast, QLD (Australia) 2021, *Open Science Meeting* Gold Coast, QLD (Australia) 2020, *Open science meeting* Yantai (China) 2011, *Storm surges congress* Hamburg (Germany) 2010, *Scientific workshop on Arctic coastal zones at risk* Tromsø (Norway) 2007. **Publications** *State of the Arctic Coast 2010 – Scientific Review and Outlook* – in cooperation with IASC, IPA and AMAP. *Reports and Studies Series*. *Coastal Fluxes in the Anthropocene* (2005); *Carbon and Nutrient Fluxes in Continental Margins*; *Our Coastal Futures – A Strategy for the Sustainable Development of the World's Coasts*. Gef-booklet. **Members** Not a membership organization. National contacts in 55 countries, not specified. [2021/XK0794/**E**]

- Future Earth – research for global sustainability / see Future Earth (#10048)
- Future for Elephants (internationally oriented national body)
- Future Forest (internationally oriented national body)
- Future Generations (internationally oriented national body)
- Future Group International, The (unconfirmed)
- Future Hope International (internationally oriented national body)
- Future Learning Lab (internationally oriented national body)

♦ Future in Our Hands (FIOH) 10050

Framtiden i Våre Hender (FIVH)
Address not obtained.
URL: http://www.fiohnetwork.org/

History 25 Apr 1974, Norway. Developed into an international network of FIOH groups, since when also referred to as *Future in Our Hands International Network*. as an international movement. UK network *Future in Our Hands Education and Development Fund* is a UK Registered Charity: 1047953. **Aims** Work to alleviate *poverty* in the *developing world* and to prevent degradation of the environment worldwide; advocate the need to complement these efforts with a less materialistic *lifestyle* for the affluent societies. **Structure** Local Groups; National Secretariat. **Languages** Norwegian. **Staff** 24.00 FTE, paid. **Finance** Members' dues. Other sources: support from Norwegian Ministry of the Environment; *Norwegian Agency for Development Cooperation (Norad)*; individual gifts. **Activities** Advocacy/lobbying/activism; financial and/or material support. **Publications** *Folkevett* – magazine.
Members Branches and contacts (over 24,000) in 13 countries:
Cameroon, Ghana, India, Kenya, Liberia, Norway, Pakistan, Philippines, Sierra Leone, Sweden, Tanzania UR, UK, Zimbabwe.
NGO Relations Member of (3): *EarthAction (EA, #05159)*; *European Responsible Investment Network (ERIN)*; *Taiga Rescue Network (TRN, inactive)*. Instrumental in setting up (1): *Development Fund*. [2018/XF5482/**F**]

- Future in Our Hands Education and Development Fund / see Future in Our Hands (#10050)
- Future in Our Hands International Network / see Future in Our Hands (#10050)

♦ Future for Religious Heritage (FRH) 10051

Exec Officer Rue de Trèves 67, 1040 Brussels, Belgium. T. +3224007703. E-mail: info@frh-europe.org.
URL: http://www.frh-europe.org/

History Set up following earlier meetings in 2009 and 2010. Former names and other names: *European Network for Historic Places of Worship* – alias. Registration: No/ID: 0839.745.430, Start date: 29 Sep 2011, Belgium. **Aims** Promote, encourage and support the safeguard, maintenance, conservation, restoration, accessibility and embellishment of places of worship, their contents and their history. **Structure** Annual General Meeting; Council; Office. **Languages** English. **Staff** 2.00 FTE, paid. **Activities** Awareness raising; networking/liaising; knowledge management/information dissemination; research and development; projects/programmes; guidance/assistance/consulting. **Events** *Meeting* Barcelona (Spain) 2021, *Meeting* Blankenburg (Germany) 2021, *Meeting* Bologna (Italy) 2021, *Meeting* Brussels (Belgium) 2021, *Biennial Conference* Paris (France) 2018. **Members** Not-for-profit sector; universities; charities; religious organizations; local and national governments; individuals. Membership countries not specified. Full (over 70); Associate (over 900). Membership countries not specified. **NGO Relations** Member of (1): *European Heritage Alliance 3.3 (#07477)*. [2020/XJ7437/**D**]

- Future of Rural Energy in Europe (unconfirmed)
- Futures Industry Association (internationally oriented national body)
- Futures and Options Association (internationally oriented national body)

♦ **Futuribles International** **10052**
SG 47 rue de Babylone, 75007 Paris, France. T. +33153633770. Fax +33142226554.
URL: https://www.futuribles.com/
History 1960, Paris (France). Founded by Bertrand de Jouvenel. Reorganized in 1970 when joined by *'Centre d'études prospectives'*, and in 1971 when joined by *'Centre de recherche sur l'évolution des entreprises'*. In 1975 took over the work of *'Société d'études et de documentations économiques, industrielles and sociales (SEDEIS)'*. Former names and other names: *International Committee of Futuribles* – former; *Comité international futuribles* – former; *International Association Futuribles (IAF)* – former; *Association internationale futuribles (AIF)* – alias. Registration: SIRET, No/ID: 78431494000056, Start date: 1967, France; EU Transparency Register, No/ID: 021720248767-58, Start date: 31 Jan 2023. **Aims** Detect what is purely conjunctural or anecdotal in nature and what seems significant and indicative of key and emerging 'weak signals' trends that represent the real roots of possible futures; explore what may happen and how possible futures may develop, taking into account factors of inertia, discontinuity or rupture; examine what policies and strategies can be adopted according to the vision of the desirable and feasible future. **Structure** General Assembly (annual); Management Board; Executive Board; Network of Experts; Foreign Correspondents; Associated Researchers. **Languages** English, French. **Staff** 10.00 FTE, paid. **Finance** Sources: fees for services; members' dues; sale of publications. **Activities** Events/meetings; publishing activities; research/documentation; training/education. **Events** *Séminaire sur la Prospective Territoriale* Paris (France) 2021, *Séminaire sur les méthodes et les outils de la prospective stratégique* Paris (France) 2021, *Table Ronde* Paris (France) 2020, *Table ronde sur la réforme des retraites* Paris (France) 2003, *Séminaire sur la prospective territoriale et le développement local* Paris (France) 2002. **Publications** *Revue Futuribles* (6 a year) in French; *Bibliographie prospective* (11 a year) in French. *Etude Futuribles*; *Vigie* in French. **Members** Ordinary; Active; Patron; Corporate; Association. Membership countries not specified. **NGO Relations** Institutional member of: *Society for International Development (SID, #19581)*. [2023/XC4412/**C**]

♦ FUTURUM – Economic Association for the International Advancement of Industrial and Cultural Interests (inactive)
♦ **FUUH** Forum UNESCO – University and Heritage (#09931)
♦ **FUUP** Forum UNESCO – Université et patrimoine (#09931)
♦ **FUWA** Federation of University Women of Africa (#09711)
♦ **FVA** Free Vietnam Alliance (#09990)
♦ **FVE** Fédération des vétérinaires européens (#09713)
♦ **FVEY** Five Eyes (#09786)
♦ FVG – Faculteit voor Vergelijkende Godsdienstwetenschappen (internationally oriented national body)
♦ **FWAB** Friends Without A Border (#09999)
♦ FWACC – Federation of West African Chambers of Commerce (no recent information)
♦ FWAPSA – Federation of West African Pharmaceutical Students Associations (inactive)
♦ FWBO / see Triratna Buddhist Community (#20243)
♦ **FWCC** Friends World Committee for Consultation (#10004)
♦ FWEAP – Foundation for the Welfare and Education of Asian People (internationally oriented national body)
♦ **FWF** Fair Wear Foundation (#09243)
♦ FWF – Free World Foundation (internationally oriented national body)
♦ FWHF – Federation of World Health Foundations (inactive)
♦ FWI – Family Watch International (internationally oriented national body)
♦ **FWMF** Forum of Worldwide Music Festivals (#09933)
♦ FWM – Free Wheelchair Mission (internationally oriented national body)
♦ FWP / see Global College, Long Island University
♦ FWVFA – Federation of World Volunteer Firefighters Associations (no recent information)
♦ FXB International – Association François-Xavier Bagnoud (internationally oriented national body)
♦ **FYEG** Federation of Young European Greens (#09715)
♦ FYF – Find Your Feet (internationally oriented national body)
♦ FYK – Frysk Ynternasjonaal Kontakt (internationally oriented national body)
♦ Fyysisen Valtameritieteen Pohjoismainen Kollegio (inactive)
♦ G-10 – Group of Ten (inactive)
♦ **G112** Generation 112 (#10113)
♦ **G11** Group of Eleven (#10753)
♦ G-15 / see Group of Fifteen (#10778)
♦ **G-15** Group of Fifteen (#10778)

♦ **G200 Association** **10053**
Pres Rue du Rhône 14, CP 5670, 1211 Geneva 11, Switzerland. T. +41225182888.
URL: http://www.g200youthforum.org/
History Former names and other names: *G8 and G20 Alumni Association* – former. **Aims** Represent independent views and opinions of the new generation of *young leaders*; reunite G200 Forum *alumni* for further *professional* development; create a platform for interaction between alumni, young leaders, experts, representatives of business and governments of G200 countries; facilitate easier cooperation on a day to day basis; continue integration of alumni into the common global community so as to help solve current world problems. **Structure** Scientific Commission; Parliamentarians' Commission; Commission on Education; Young Leaders Commission; Executive Committee; Strategic Committee. President. Includes *G200 Youth Forum*. **Activities** Events/meetings; awards/prizes/competitions. **Events** *Youth Forum* Dubai (United Arab Emirates) 2017, *Youth Forum* Garmisch-Partenkirchen (Germany) 2016, *Youth Forum* Garmisch-Partenkirchen (Germany) 2015.
Members Individuals in 9 countries:
Australia, Belgium, Canada, China, Latvia, Russia, Slovakia, South Africa, Taiwan. [2020/XJ9946/v/**E**]

♦ **G20 Global Smart Cities Alliance on Technology Governance** **10054**
Secretariat address not obtained. E-mail: info@globalsmartcitiesalliance.org.
URL: https://globalsmartcitiesalliance.org/
History Jun 2019. Founded in partnership with *Group of Twenty (G20, #10793)*. **Aims** Advance the responsible and ethical use of smarty city technologies. **Structure** Secretariat maintained by *World Economic Forum (WEF, #21367)*. **Activities** Standards/guidelines. **Events** *Launch Meeting* Yokohama (Japan) 2019. **NGO Relations** Institutional partners include: *Commonwealth Local Government Forum (CLGF, #04348)*; *Global Initiative for Inclusive Information and Communication Technologies (G3ict, #10425)*; *Local Governments for Sustainability (ICLEI, #16507)*; *World Economic Forum (WEF, #21367)*; *World e-Governments Organization of Cities and Local Governments (WeGO, #21542)*; *World ENABLED (WE)*; *World Organization of United Cities and Local Governments (UCLG, #21695)*. [2019/AA0153/**E**]

♦ **G20** Group of Twenty (#10793)

♦ **G20 Interfaith Forum Association (IF20)** **10055**
Contact address not obtained. E-mail: media@g20interfaith.org.
URL: https://www.g20interfaith.org/
History 2014, Australia. **Aims** Advocate for global solutions by collaborating with religious thought leaders and political representatives. **Structure** Advisory Council; Secretariat. **Events** *Forum* Abu Dhabi (United Arab Emirates) 2022, *Forum* Kyoto (Japan) 2019. **IGO Relations** Cooperates with (2): *Deutsche Gesellschaft für Internationale Zusammenarbeit (GIZ)*; *UNDP (#20292)*. Key partners: *King Abdullah Bin Abdulaziz International Centre for Interreligious and Intercultural Dialogue (KAICIID, #16193)*; *United Nations Alliance of Civilizations (UNAOC, #20520)*. **NGO Relations** Cooperates with (18): *A Common Word Among the Youth (ACWAY)*; *African Consortium for Law and Religion Studies (ACLARS, #00266)*; *Association internationale pour la défense de la liberté religieuse (AIDLR, #02681)*; *Christian Aid*; *Community of Sant'Egidio*; *Consorcio Latinoamericano de Libertad Religiosa (#04732)*; *European Academy of Religion (EuARe, #05812)*; *Globethics.net Foundation (#10669)*; *International Consortium for Law and Religion Studies (ICLARS, #12918)*; *International Partnership on Religion and Sustainable Development (PaRD, #14524)*; *International Religious Liberty Association (IRLA)*; *International Shinto Foundation (ISF)*; *Religions for Peace (RfP, #18831)*; *United Religions Initiative (URI, #20658)*; *World Communion of Reformed Churches (WCRC, #21289)*; *World Faiths Development Dialogue (WFDD)*; *World Jewish Congress (WJC, #21599)*; *Worldwide Support for Development (WSD)*. [2020/AA0113/c/**E**]

♦ **G-20Y Association** **10056**
Contact c/o Swiss Financial Company and Trust SA, Rue du Rhône 14, CP 5670, 1211 Geneva 11, Switzerland. T. +41225181631. E-mail: g20@g20ys.org.
URL: http://www.g20ys.org/
History Full title: *G-20Y Summit International Organizing Committee Association*. **Aims** Act as a platform for *business leaders* addressing current challenges to shape a better *future*. **Structure** Founder/President; Advisory Board; Program Committee; Executive Committee. **Activities** Events/meetings. **Events** *Summit* Évian (France) 2018, *Summit* Évian (France) 2017, *Summit* St Moritz (Switzerland) 2016, *Annual Summit* Évian (France) 2015, *Summit* Évian (France) 2015. [2017/XM6225/c/**F**]

♦ **G20 YEA** G20 young Entrepreneurs' Alliance (#10057)

♦ **G20 young Entrepreneurs' Alliance (G20 YEA)** **10057**
Address not obtained.
URL: http://www.g20yea.com/
History Charter adopted Nov 2010, Incheon (Korea Rep). **Aims** Champion the importance of young entrepreneurs to the G20 member nations. **Activities** Events/meetings. **Events** *Annual Summit* Fukuoka (Japan) 2019, *Annual Summit* Buenos Aires (Argentina) 2018, *Annual Summit* Berlin (Germany) 2017, *Commerce Global Conference* Berlin (Germany) 2017, *Annual Summit* Beijing (China) 2016.
Members Full in 19 countries:
Argentina, Australia, Brazil, Canada, China, France, Germany, India, Indonesia, Italy, Japan, Korea Rep, Mexico, Russia, Saudi Arabia, South Africa, Türkiye, UK, USA.
Included in the above, 1 organization listed in this Yearbook:
Young Entrepreneurs for Europe (YES for Europe, #21982).
IGO Relations *Group of Twenty (G20, #10793)*. [2019/XM7095/**E**]

♦ G-20Y Summit International Organizing Committee Association / see G-20Y Association (#10056)
♦ G-22 – Group of Twenty-Two (inactive)
♦ G-24 / see Intergovernmental Group of Twenty-Four on International Monetary Affairs (#11495)
♦ G-24 – Group of Twenty Four (no recent information)
♦ **G2H2** Geneva Global Health Hub (#10122)

♦ **G-3** **10059**
Address not obtained.
History as an informal title for the group of three nations whose central banks most affect the world monetary situation.
Members Governments of 3 countries:
Germany, Japan, USA. [2008/XF1478/**F***]

♦ **G-3 (G3)** **10058**
Contact ULB – Intl Office, Avenue F D Roosevelt 50, 1050 Brussels, Belgium.
Contact Univ de Montréal – Dir Affairs Intl, 3744 rue Jean-Brillant, bureau 581-32, Montréal QC H3T 1P1, Canada.
Contact Univ of Geneva – Intl Relations and Partnerships Office, Boulevard du Pont-d'Arve 40, 1211 Geneva 4, Switzerland.
URL: https://g3univ.org/
History 26 Sep 2012, Brussels (Belgium). Created as a grouping of 3 universities in Montréal QC (Canada), Brussels, (Belgium) and Geneva (Switzerland). Former names and other names: *Le G3 de la Francophonie* – full title. **Aims** Foster trilateral collaboration in *research* and *education*. **Structure** Rectors; Steering Committee; Administrative Contact. **Languages** English, French. **Finance** Financed through member institutions.
Members Partners in 3 countries:
Belgium, Canada, Switzerland. [2022.02.09/XM7915/**F**]

♦ **G31000** Global Institute for Risk Management Standards (#10428)
♦ Le G3 de la Francophonie / see G-3 (#10058)
♦ **G3** G-3 (#10058)
♦ **G-3** Group of Three (#10791)
♦ **G-3** Group of Three ABM (#10792)
♦ **G-3** Grupo de los Tres (#10791)
♦ **G-3** Grupo de los Tres ABM (#10792)
♦ **G3ict** Global Initiative for Inclusive Information and Communication Technologies (#10425)
♦ G3W – Geneeskunde voor de Derde Wereld (internationally oriented national body)
♦ **G4 Alliance** Global Alliance for Surgical, Obstetric, Trauma and Anaesthesia Care (#10229)
♦ **G4** Global Gambling Guidance Group (#10385)
♦ **G-4** Group of Four (#10780)
♦ **G5+** Gender5+ (#10093)
♦ **G-5** Group of Five (#10779)

♦ **G5 Sahel** **10060**
Permanent Secretary Ilot A 742 Bis, Route des Ambassades, BP 6002, Nouakchott, Mauritania. T. +22245257730. E-mail: contact@g5sahel.org.
URL: https://g5sahel.org/
History Established 16 Feb 2014, Nouakchott (Mauritania). Convention signed 19 Dec 2014. **Aims** Ensure *development* and *security* conditions in member countries; provide a strategic framework for intervention to improve *living conditions* of the population; combine development and security, supported by democracy and good governance in a framework of mutually beneficial regional and international cooperation; promote inclusive and sustainable regional development. **Structure** Conference of Heads of State; Council of Ministers; Permanent Secretariat; Committee of Defence and Security; National committees of Coordination of action. **Activities** Policy/politics/regulatory. **Events** *Summit* Ouagadougou (Burkina Faso) 2019, *Summit* Niamey (Niger) 2018.
Members Governments (5):
Burkina Faso, Chad, Mali, Mauritania, Niger. [2019/XM7619/**E***]

♦ G-6 – Six Markets Group (no recent information)
♦ **G-77** Group of 77 (#10732)
♦ **G-7** Group of Seven (#10788)
♦ G7 Information Centre / see G8 Information Centre
♦ G7 Research Endowment Fund of Trinity College / see G8 Information Centre
♦ G7 SIG – G7 Support Implementation Group (no recent information)
♦ G7 Support Implementation Group (no recent information)
♦ G8 and G20 Alumni Association / see G200 Association (#10053)
♦ **G-8** Group of Eight (#10745)
♦ G8 Information Centre (internationally oriented national body)
♦ **GA2LEN** Global Allergy and Asthma European Network (#10179)
♦ **GA4GH** Global Alliance for Genomics and Health (#10199)
♦ GAA / see Welthungerhilfe
♦ **GAA** Global Aquaculture Alliance (#10238)
♦ GAA INTERASMA Global Asthma Association / see INTERASMA (#11457)
♦ **GAAMAC** Global Action Against Mass Atrocity Crimes (#10164)
♦ GAAPP / see Global Allergy and Airways Patient Platform (#10178)
♦ **GAAPP** Global Allergy and Airways Patient Platform (#10178)
♦ **GAAPSF** General Association of Asia Pacific Sports Federations (#10106)
♦ **GAATES** Global Alliance on Accessible Technologies and Environments (#10180)
♦ **GAATO** Global Alliance of Assistive Technology Organizations (#10185)
♦ **GAATW** Global Alliance Against Traffic in Women (#10184)
♦ GABAC – Groupe d'Action contre le Blanchiment d'Argent en Afrique Centrale (unconfirmed)
♦ GABA – Global Agricultural Biotechnology Association (inactive)
♦ **GABAOA** Groupe anti-blanchiment d'Afrique orientale et australe (#05252)
♦ GABC – Global Advances in Business and Communication (meeting series)
♦ GABC / see Global Alliance for Buildings and Construction (#10187)

- ♦ Gabo Foundation (internationally oriented national body)
- ♦ Gabungan Badminton Asia / see Badminton Asia (#03056)
- ♦ **GABV** Global Alliance for Banking on Values (#10186)
- ♦ GACD / see Aya Worldwide
- ♦ **GACD** Global Alliance for Chronic Diseases (#10188)
- ♦ GACE – Global Alliance for Community Empowerment (internationally oriented national body)
- ♦ **GACF** Global Alliance of Community Forestry (#10190)
- ♦ **GAC** GCC Accreditation Center (#10082)
- ♦ **GACG** Global Anti-Counterfeiting Group (#10236)
- ♦ GAC – Gulf Aluminium Council (unconfirmed)

♦ GACI Global 10061

Contact PO Box 123, Argyle TX 76226, USA. E-mail: info@gaciglobal.org.
URL: https://gaciglobal.org/

History Jan 2019. Registration: 501(c)(3) non-profit, USA. **Aims** Connect families affected by Generalized Arterial Calcification of Infancy or Hypophosphatemic Rickets caused by ENPP1 or ABCC6 Deficiencies to each other and to the medical community; provide current educational resources and support ongoing research. **Structure** Board of Directors; Medical Advisory Board. **Languages** Chinese, English, French, German, Italian, Japanese, Russian, Spanish. **Activities** Advocacy/lobbying/activism; awareness raising; events/meetings; healthcare; knowledge management/information dissemination; networking/liaising; projects/programmes; research and development; training/education. [2022.06.15/AA2351/**C**]

- ♦ **GACSA** Global Alliance for Climate-Smart Agriculture (#10189)
- ♦ **GACS** Global Alliance of Continuous Plankton Recorder Surveys (#10191)
- ♦ GADAA – Global Alzheimer's and Dementia Action Alliance (inactive)
- ♦ Gaddafi International Charity and Development Foundation (internationally oriented national body)
- ♦ Gaddafi International Foundation for Charity Associations / see Gaddafi International Charity and Development Foundation
- ♦ **GADeF** Global Alliance for Development Foundation (#10192)
- ♦ **GADEF** Groupement des associations dentaires francophones (#10757)
- ♦ **GADR** Global Alliance for Disaster Reduction (#10193)
- ♦ **GADRI** Global Alliance of Disaster Research Institutes (#10194)
- ♦ GADYLP – Global Alert for Defence of Youth and the Less Privileged (internationally oriented national body)
- ♦ **GAEBA** Global Alliance of Eye Bank Associations (#10197)
- ♦ **GAeF** Gesellschaft für Aerosolforschung (#10140)
- ♦ GAELA – Global Alliance of Education and Language Associations (unconfirmed)
- ♦ **GAELF** Global Alliance to Eliminate Lymphatic Filariasis (#10195)
- ♦ GAFCON / see Fellowship of Confessing Anglicans (#09725)
- ♦ GAFFI / see Global Action For Fungal Infections (#10166)
- ♦ **GAFFI** Global Action For Fungal Infections (#10166)
- ♦ GAF – Global Assistance Foundation (internationally oriented national body)
- ♦ **GA-FGM** Global Alliance against Female Genital Mutilation (#10183)
- ♦ **GAFIC** Groupe d'action financière des Caraïbes (#03505)
- ♦ **GAFI** Groupe d'action financière (#09765)
- ♦ **GAFILAT** Grupo de Acción Financiera de Latinoamérica (#10799)
- ♦ **GAFIMOAN** Groupe d'action financière du moyen-orient et de l'afrique du nord – (#16779)
- ♦ GAFISUD / see Grupo de Acción Financiera de Latinoamérica (#10799)
- ♦ **GAFSP** Global Agriculture and Food Security Program (#10174)
- ♦ **GAFTA** Grain and Feed Trade Association (#10692)
- ♦ **GAFTA** Greater Arab Free-Trade Area (#10700)
- ♦ **GAfWaC** Global Alliances for Water and Climate (#10230)
- ♦ GA / see GA – Society for Medicinal Plant and Natural Product Research (#10075)
- ♦ GA – Gesellschaft für Arzneipflanzen- und Naturstoff-Forschung (#10075)
- ♦ GAG – Global Accrediting Group (see: #21330)
- ♦ GA – Global Alliance (internationally oriented national body)
- ♦ **GA** Global Alliance for Public Relations and Communication Management (#10223)
- ♦ GAGTA – Geometric and Asymptotic Group Theory with Applications (meeting series)
- ♦ **GAHP** Global Association Hubs Partnership (#10242)
- ♦ GAHSSR – Global Association for Humanities and Social Science Research (internationally oriented national body)
- ♦ GAI / see Moynihan Institute of Global Affairs
- ♦ Gaia Foundation (internationally oriented national body)
- ♦ Gaia Foundation to Spread Knowledge of the New Whole Earth Consciousness / see Gaia Foundation
- ♦ GAIA – Global AIDS Interfaith Alliance (internationally oriented national body)
- ♦ **GAIA** Global Alliance for Incinerator Alternatives (#10203)

♦ Gaia Mater 10062

Administrative Head Office BP 22, Mairie square Leon Blum, 78340 Les Clayes-sous-Bois, France. E-mail: contact@gaiamater.org.
URL: http://www.gaiamater.org/

History Founded 1979. Restructured 1998; in trans-national reconstruction since 31 Dec 2008. Full title: *Gaia Mater – Eco-humanist International Network.* **Aims** Share resources; promote progress of human society; protect societal and environmental balances; improve the knowledge and sharing of the historical, philosophical and scientific bases of eco-humanism – common heritage of humanity for more than 26 centuries. **Languages** English, French, Spanish. **Activities** Voluntary service; cooperation; information and educational campaigns. **Publications** Books; reports; films. [2013.07.30/XJ2557/**F**]

- ♦ Gaia Mater – Eco-humanist International Network / see Gaia Mater (#10062)
- ♦ Gaian Democracy Network (internationally oriented national body)
- ♦ Gaia Trust, Denmark (internationally oriented national body)
- ♦ GAIA Vaccine Foundation (internationally oriented national body)
- ♦ GAIA VF – GAIA Vaccine Foundation (internationally oriented national body)
- ♦ Gaia-X – European Association for Data and Cloud (unconfirmed)
- ♦ **GAID** Global Alliance for ICT and Development (#10200)
- ♦ **GAIF** General Arab Insurance Federation (#10104)
- ♦ GAI – Griffith Asia Institute (internationally oriented national body)
- ♦ **GAIL** Global Alliance of Impact Lawyers (#10201)
- ♦ **GAILL** Groupement des allergologistes et immunologistes de langues latines (#10754)
- ♦ **GAIMH** German Speaking Association for Infant Mental Health (#10139)
- ♦ GAIN – Global Aggregates Information Network (unconfirmed)
- ♦ **GAiN** Global Aid Network (#10176)
- ♦ **GAIN** Global Alliance for Improved Nutrition (#10202)
- ♦ GAI – NUS Global Asia Institute (internationally oriented national body)
- ♦ GAISF – Global Association of International Sport Federations (inactive)
- ♦ GAITF – Global Academy Institute of Technology Foundation (internationally oriented national body)
- ♦ **GAJE** Global Alliance for Justice Education (#10205)
- ♦ GaL-AA – Gays and Lesbians in Alcoholics Anonymous (internationally oriented national body)

♦ Galactosemia Network (GalNet) 10063

Chair address not obtained.
URL: https://www.galactosemianetwork.org/

History 2012. Founded with the support of: *European Galactosaemia Society (EGS, #07372)*; national societies. **Aims** Advance research, diagnosis, treatment and follow-up care of galactosemic patients. **Structure** Steering Committee. **Activities** Events/meetings; research/documentation; standards/guidelines. **Events** *Annual Meeting* 2022, *Annual Meeting* 2021, *Joint Meeting* Amsterdam (Netherlands) 2021, *Annual Meeting* 2020, *Joint Meeting* Amsterdam (Netherlands) 2019.

Members Full in 21 countries:
Australia, Austria, Belgium, Bulgaria, Croatia, Czechia, Estonia, France, Germany, Greece, Ireland, Israel, Italy, Lithuania, Netherlands, Poland, Portugal, Spain, Switzerland, UK, USA.
Also members in South America. Membership countries not specified.
NGO Relations Cooperates with (2): *European Galactosaemia Society (EGS, #07372)*; *Society for the Study of Inborn Errors of Metabolism (SSIEM, #19648).* [2022.06.21/AA2114/**F**]

- ♦ GALA – GALA: Generative Approaches to Language Acquisition conference (meeting series)
- ♦ GALA: Generative Approaches to Language Acquisition conference (meeting series)
- ♦ **GALA** Global Advertising Lawyers Alliance (#10171)
- ♦ **GALA** Globalization and Localization Association (#10439)
- ♦ GALA – Grupo de Acústicos Latinoamericanos (inactive)
- ♦ Galapagos Agreement – Framework Agreement for the Conservation of Living Marine Resources on the High Seas of the South Pacific (2000 treaty)
- ♦ Galcom International (internationally oriented national body)
- ♦ GALE – Global Alliance of Lesbian, Gay, Bisexual and Transgender Education (internationally oriented national body)
- ♦ GALF – Global Audit Leadership Forum (meeting series)
- ♦ **GALF** Groupement des anthropologistes de langue française (#10756)
- ♦ Galgos Ethique Europe (internationally oriented national body)
- ♦ GALHA – Gay and Lesbian Humanist Association / see LGBT Humanists

♦ Galileo Services (GS) 10064

Contact 10 Cours Louis Lumière, 94300 Vincennes, France.
URL: http://www.galileo-services.org/

Aims Foster an "end to end" vision of the Galileo system in order to fully respond to user and market needs. **IGO Relations** *Galileo Satellite Navigation Project.* **NGO Relations** Cooperates with: *Eurisy (#05625).* [2012/XJ6247/**E**]

- ♦ Galizan Institute for International Security and Peace Studies (internationally oriented national body)
- ♦ Gallifrey Foundation (unconfirmed)
- ♦ **GalNet** Galactosemia Network (#10063)

♦ Galpin Society for the Study of Musical Instruments 10065

Pres address not obtained. E-mail: admin@galpinsociety.org.
URL: http://www.galpinsociety.org/

History Oct 1946. Registration: Charity Commission, No/ID: 306012, England and Wales. **Aims** Publish original research into the history, construction, development and use of musical instruments; organize symposia, conferences; visit collections worldwide. **Structure** General Meeting (annual); Council; Officers. **Finance** Sources: members' dues. **Activities** Events/meetings; research/documentation. **Publications** *Galpin Society Newsletter* (3 a year); *Galpin Society Journal* (annual).

Members Institutions in 18 countries:
Australia, Austria, Belgium, Canada, Denmark, Finland, France, Germany, Italy, Japan, Netherlands, Norway, Portugal, Spain, Sweden, Switzerland, UK, USA.
Individuals in 25 countries:
Australia, Austria, Belgium, Brazil, Canada, Chile, Czechia, Denmark, Finland, France, Germany, Greece, Hungary, Ireland, Italy, Japan, Netherlands, New Zealand, Norway, Portugal, Spain, Sweden, Switzerland, UK, USA. [2023.02.20/XE3951/**E**]

♦ GALVmed 10066

CEO Doherty Bldg, Pentlands Science Park, Bush Loan, Edinburgh, EH26 0PZ, UK. T. +441314456264. E-mail: info@galvmed.org.
Communications Manager address not obtained.
URL: http://www.galvmed.org/

History 2004. Former names and other names: *Global Alliance for Livestock Veterinary Medicines (GALVmed)* – full title. Registration: Charities Commission, No/ID: SC039197, Scotland; Charity Commission, No/ID: 1115606, England and Wales. **Aims** Protect livestock and improve human lives by making livestock vaccines, diagnostics and medicines accessible and affordable to small-scale livestock producers in Africa and South Asia. **Structure** Board of Directors. **Staff** 31.00 FTE, paid. **Finance** Supported by: *Bill and Melinda Gates Foundation (BMGF)*; *Department for International Development (DFID, inactive).* **Activities** Monitoring/evaluation; politics/policy/regulatory; projects/programmes; research and development. Africa and South Asia.

Members Agricultural NGOs, health and development agencies and pharmaceutical companies (11), including the following 2 organizations listed in this Yearbook (" indicates founder member):
Food and Agricultural Research Management (FARM-Africa); *International Livestock Research Institute (ILRI, #14062).*
Observers (5):
Bill and Melinda Gates Foundation (BMGF); *Department for International Development (DFID, inactive)*; *FAO (#09260)*; *Interafrican Bureau for Animal Resources (AU-IBAR, #11382)*; *OIE – World Organisation for Animal Health (#17703).* [2022.05.11/XJ0943/y/**F**]

- ♦ **GAMA** FIDIC Group of African Member Associations (#09752)
- ♦ GAMA – General Aviation Manufacturers Association (internationally oriented national body)
- ♦ **GAMAG** Global Alliance on Media and Gender (#10209)
- ♦ **GAMA** Global Acetate Manufacturers Association (#10163)
- ♦ Gambia River Basin Development Organization (#17814)
- ♦ Game Cultures Society (unconfirmed)
- ♦ **GAME** Global Alliance for Medical Education (#10210)

♦ Game Philosophy Network 10067

Contact address not obtained.
URL: http://gamephilosophy.org/

History Started 2005. **Aims** Facilitate discussions dealing with philosophical issues raised by *computer* games. **Structure** Informal structure: Steering Group. **Activities** Events/meetings. **Events** *Philosophy of Computer Games Conference* St Petersburg (Russia) 2019, *Philosophy of Computer Games Conference* Copenhagen (Denmark) 2018, *Philosophy of Computer Games Conference* Krakow (Poland) 2017, *Philosophy of Computer Games Conference* Msida (Malta) 2016, *Philosophy of Computer Games Conference* Berlin (Germany) 2015.

Members Individuals in 28 countries and territories:
Australia, Austria, Belgium, Canada, China, Denmark, Estonia, Finland, Germany, Greece, Hong Kong, India, Ireland, Italy, Japan, Lebanon, Malta, Netherlands, New Zealand, Norway, Poland, Singapore, Spain, Sweden, Switzerland, Türkiye, UK, USA. [2018/XM7542/v/**F**]

- ♦ Game Rangers Association of Africa (internationally oriented national body)

♦ Game Theory Society (GTS) 10068

Vice-Pres Communications 451 McNeil Bldg, Univ of Pennsylvania, 3718 Locust Walk, Philadelphia PA 19104, USA. T. +12158986777.
URL: http://www.gametheorysociety.org/

History 1999. Current bylaws adopted 20 Jul 2006; amended 20 Feb 2012. **Aims** Promote the investigation, teaching and application of game theory. **Structure** Council; Steering Committee. **Activities** Awards/prizes/competitions; events/meetings. **Events** *World Congress* Budapest (Hungary) 2021, *World Congress* Maastricht (Netherlands) 2016, *World Congress* Istanbul (Turkey) 2012, *World Congress* Evanston, IL (USA) 2008, *Workshop on stochastic methods in game theory* Erice (Italy) 2005. **Publications** *GTS Newsletter.* [2020/XM5055/**C**]

- ♦ GAM / see European Flour Millers' Association (#07272)
- ♦ **GAMH** Global Action on Men's Health (#10167)
- ♦ **GAMIAN Europe** Global Alliance of Mental Illness Advocacy Networks – Europe (#10211)
- ♦ GAMIAN – Global Alliance of Mental Illness Advocacy Networks (internationally oriented national body)

♦ Gaming Regulators European Forum (GREF) 10069
Chair c/o Jersey Gambling Commission, 2nd Flr Salisbury House, 1-9 Union St, St Helier, JE3 2RF, UK. E-mail: info@jgc.je – info@gref.net.
URL: http://www.gref.net/
History Set up 8 Sep 1989, The Hague (Netherlands). **Aims** Provide a forum in which European gaming regulators can meet, exchange views and information and discuss policy on gaming matters. **Structure** Executive Board. **Languages** English. **Finance** Members' dues. **Activities** Events/meetings. **Events** *Meeting* Limassol (Cyprus) 2019, *Meeting* Prague (Czechia) 2018, *Meeting* London (UK) 2017, *Meeting* St Julian's (Malta) 2016, *Meeting* Vilnius (Lithuania) 2015.
[2014.06.09/XF5981/**F**]

♦ **GAMIP** Global Alliance for Ministries and Infrastructures for Peace (#10212)
♦ **GAMMA** Global Alliance of Marketing and Management Associations (#10207)
♦ **GAMMA** Global Association of Mixed Martial Arts (#10243)
♦ **GAMM** – Gesellschaft für Angewandte Mathematik und Mechanik (internationally oriented national body)
♦ **GAMMH** Global Alliance for Maternal Mental Health (#10208)
♦ Gandhi 2008 International / see Gandhi International
♦ Gandhi Centre for the Service of Life and Humanity (internationally oriented national body)
♦ Gandhi International (internationally oriented national body)
♦ Gandhi Worldwide Education Institute (internationally oriented national body)
♦ **GANES** Global Alliance for Leadership in Nursing Education and Science (#10206)
♦ **GAN** – Global Action Network (internationally oriented national body)
♦ **GAN** Global Adaptation Network (#10170)
♦ **GAN** Global Apprenticeship Network (#10237)
♦ **GAN** – Green Asia Network (internationally oriented national body)
♦ **GANHRI** Global Alliance of National Human Rights Institutions (#10214)
♦ Gannett Foundation / see Freedom Forum
♦ **GA-NOC** / see Association of National Olympic Committees (#02819)
♦ **GAO** – Global Academy of Osseointegration (unconfirmed)
♦ **GAPAEL** – Garapen eta Pakerako Elkartasuna (internationally oriented national body)
♦ **GAPA** Global Alcohol Policy Alliance (#10177)
♦ **GAPA** Global Asphalt Pavement Alliance (#10239)
♦ **GAPE** – Global Association for People and the Environment (internationally oriented national body)
♦ **GAPFA** Global Alliance of Pet Food Associations (#10218)
♦ **GAP** Global Action Plan International (#10168)
♦ **GAP** Great Ape Project (#10698)
♦ **GAP** Groupe anti-blanchiment de l'Asie/Pacifique (#01921)
♦ **GAP** International / see Global Action Plan International (#10168)
♦ **GAP** International (internationally oriented national body)
♦ **GAPPA** Global Alliance of Partners for Pain Advocacy (#10217)
♦ **GAPPS** – Global Alliance to Prevent Prematurity and Stillbirth (internationally oriented national body)
♦ **GAPPS** / see Global Alliance for the Project Professions (#10220)
♦ **GAPPS** Global Alliance for the Project Professions (#10220)
♦ **GAPRI** / see Griffith Asia Institute

♦ garagErasmus Foundation (garagErasmus) 10070
Office Via Nicola Antonio Porpora 146, 20131 Milan MI, Italy.
Brussels Office c/o Regione Toscana, Rond-Point Schuman 14, 1040 Brussels, Belgium. T. +32489177660. E-mail: info@garagerasmus.org.
URL: http://www.garagerasmus.org/
History Founded 4 Oct 2012. Registered in accordance with Italian law. **Aims** Bring together a community of internationally minded people, who have had a professional or *study* experience *abroad*. **Structure** Board of Directors; High Level Council; Ethics Committee. Offices in Milan (Italy) and Brussels (Belgium). **Activities** Networking/liaising; guidance/assistance/consulting.
Members Universities; companies; cities/local authorities; local associations. Members in 12 countries: Austria, Belgium, France, Hungary, Ireland, Italy, Malta, Netherlands, Portugal, Russia, Spain, UK.
Included in the above, 2 organizations listed in this Yearbook:
Central European University (CEU, #03717); *Network of Universities from the Capitals of Europe (UNICA, #17061)*.
NGO Relations Partners include: *Erasmus Mundus Students and Alumni Association (EMA, #05527)*; *Erasmus Student Network (ESN, #05529)*; *Euronews (#05741)*; *Organisation for Cooperation, Exchange And Networking among Students (OCEANS, #17802)*. Instrumental in setting up: *Erasmus+ Student and Alumni Alliance (ESAA, #05528)*.
[2018/XM6580/fy/**F**]

♦ **garagErasmus** garagErasmus Foundation (#10070)
♦ **GARA** – Global AirRail Alliance (unconfirmed)
♦ **Garapen Bidean** – Human Rights and Development (internationally oriented national body)
♦ Garapen eta Pakerako Elkartasuna (internationally oriented national body)
♦ **GARC** Global Alliance for Rabies Control (internationally oriented national body)
♦ **GARD** / see Acting for Life
♦ Garden Gnome Liberation Front / see Gnome Liberation Front (#10671)
♦ Garden Organic / see Henry Doubleday Research Association
♦ **GARD** Global Alliance Against Chronic Respiratory Diseases (#10182)
♦ **Gare Européenne et Solidarité** Réseaux ferroviaires Européens Développement social et Solidarité dans les Gares (#18910)
♦ **GARMCO** – Gulf Aluminium Rolling Mill Company (no recent information)
♦ **GARM** Global Alliance for Responsible Media (#10224)
♦ **GARN** Global Alliance for the Rights of Nature (#10225)
♦ **GARP** Global Association of Risk Professionals (#10244)
♦ **GARP** – Global Atmospheric Research Programme (inactive)
♦ **GARTEUR** Group for Aeronautical Research and Technology in Europe (#10733)
♦ **GASA** Geostatistical Association of Southern Africa (#10137)
♦ **GASCA** – Global Alliance for Smart Cities in Africa (unconfirmed)
♦ **GASCDO** Global Alliance of Sickle Cell Disease Organizations (#10227)
♦ Gas Centrifuge Study Association (inactive)

♦ Gas Distributors For Sustainability (GD4S) 10071
Contact Av de Cortenbergh 66, 1000 Brussels, Belgium. T. +3222803994. E-mail: contact@gd4s.eu.
URL: http://gd4s.eu/
Aims Provide expertise regarding mobility packages; contribute to the development of gas market design; raise the voice of gas-only DSOs in the European debate; unlock the potential of renewable gas and gas grids. **Structure** General Assembly; Executive Committee; Executive Board. **Activities** Knowledge management/information dissemination; advocacy/lobbying/activism. **Events** *The Truth about Sector Coupling Seminar* Brussels (Belgium) 2021.
Members Gas distributors in 5 countries:
France, Italy, Portugal, Romania, Spain.
[2019/XM7572/**D**]

♦ **GASERC** Gulf Arab States Educational Research Centre (#10822)
♦ **GASET** – Global Alliance of Social Enterprises in Travel & Tourism (unconfirmed)

♦ Gas Exporting Countries Forum (GECF) 10072
SG PO Box 23753, Tornado Tower, 47th and 48th Floors, West Bay, Doha, Qatar. T. +97444048400. Fax +97444048415. E-mail: gecforum@qp.com.qa.
URL: http://www.gecf.org/

History 2001. **Aims** Support the sovereign rights of Member Countries over their natural gas resources and their ability to independently plan and manage the sustainable, efficient and environmentally conscious development, use and conservation of natural gas resources for the benefit of their people. **Structure** Executive Board; Secretariat; Departments (5): Gas Market Analysis; Energy Economics and Forecasting; Data and Information Services; Administration and Finance. **Events** *Biennial Asian Energy Ministerial Round Table* Abu Dhabi (United Arab Emirates) 2019, *Heads of State Summit & International Gas Seminar* Malabo (Equatorial Guinea) 2019, *International Gas Seminar* Malabo (Equatorial Guinea) 2019, *Ministerial Meeting* Port-of-Spain (Trinidad-Tobago) 2018, *Symposium on Natural Gas* Port-of-Spain (Trinidad-Tobago) 2018.
Members Full in 12 countries:
Algeria, Bolivia, Egypt, Equatorial Guinea, Iran Islamic Rep, Libya, Nigeria, Qatar, Russia, Trinidad-Tobago, United Arab Emirates, Venezuela.
Observers in 7 countries:
Azerbaijan, Iraq, Kazakhstan, Netherlands, Norway, Oman, Peru.
IGO Relations Cooperates with: *International Energy Forum (IEF, #13272)*.
[2020/XM8159/**F***]

♦ Gas Grid Group (internationally oriented national body)
♦ **GAS** / see Group-Analytic Society International (#10734)
♦ **GASI** Global Awareness Society International (#10247)
♦ **GASi** Group-Analytic Society International (#10734)

♦ Gas Infrastructure Europe (GIE) 10073
SG Av de Cortenbergh 100, 2nd floor, 1000 Brussels, Belgium. T. +3222090500. Fax +3222090501. E-mail: gie@gie.eu.
URL: http://www.gie.eu/
History 2002. Current title adopted when became umbrella organization for GTE, *GSE – Gas Storage Europe* and *GLE – Gas LNG Europe*, 10 Mar 2005. Former names and other names: *Gas Transmission Europe (GTE)* – former (2002); *GSE – Gas Storage Europe* – former; *GLE – Gas LNG Europe* – former. Registration: Banque-Carrefour des Entreprises, No/ID: 0478.897.017, Start date: 5 Dec 2002, Belgium; EU Transparency Register, No/ID: 76130992074-15, Start date: 28 Jul 2009. **Aims** Represent the sole interest of the infrastructure industry in the natural gas business such as Transmission System Operators, Storage System Operators and LNG Terminal Operators towards European institutions and policymakers. **Structure** General Assembly; Board; Sub-Groups (5); Secretariat; Subdivisions (3) have their own Executive Committee and Plenary. **Languages** English. **Staff** 7.00 FTE, paid. **Finance** Members' dues. Annual budget: euro 1,400,000. **Activities** Events/meetings; knowledge management/information dissemination. **Events** *Annual Conference* Budapest (Hungary) 2022, *Annual Conference* Lucerne (Switzerland) 2021, *Annual Conference* Lucerne (Switzerland) 2020, *Annual Conference* Paris (France) 2019, *Annual Conference* Bucharest (Romania) 2018. **Publications** Position papers; brochures; press releases; maps. **Information Services** *Aggregated Gas Storage Inventory (AGSI)*; *Aggregated LNG Storage Inventory (ALSI)*; *GIE Knowledge Centre*, *GLE Investment Database*; *GSE Investment Database*; *REMIT*.
Members Companies (68) in 26 countries:
Austria, Belgium, Bulgaria, Croatia, Czechia, Denmark, Finland, France, Germany, Greece, Hungary, Ireland, Italy, Latvia, Luxembourg, Netherlands, Norway, Poland, Portugal, Romania, Slovakia, Slovenia, Spain, Sweden, Switzerland, UK.
Observers (2) in 2 countries:
Greece, Ireland.
NGO Relations Member of (4): *European Association for the Streamlining of Energy Exchange-gas (EASEE-gas, #06224)*; *European Energy Forum (EEF, #06986)*; *European Policy Centre (EPC, #08240)*; *GasNaturally (#10074)*.
[2022/XD8378/**D**]

♦ **GASME** Global Alliance of SMEs (#10228)

♦ GasNaturally 10074
Secretariat address not obtained. E-mail: info@gasnaturally.eu.
URL: https://gasnaturally.eu/
Aims Highlight how, by using gas, a clean future can be made real. **Structure** Steering Committee. **Activities** Events/meetings.
Members Organizations (8):
Eurogas (#05682); *European Gas Research Group (#07380)*; *Gas Infrastructure Europe (GIE, #10073)*; *International Association of Oil and Gas Producers (IOGP, #12053)*; *International Gas Union (IGU, #13700)*; *Liquid Gas Europe (#16488)*; *MARCOGAZ – Technical Association of the European Natural Gas Industry (#16572)*; *NGVA Europe (#17130)*.
[2021/AA2761/y/**D**]

♦ GA – Society for Medicinal Plant and Natural Product Research ... 10075
GA – Gesellschaft für Arzneipflanzen- und Naturstoff-Forschung
Sec Havelstr 5, 64295 Darmstadt, Germany. T. +4961513305154. Fax +4961513305471. E-mail: ga-secretary@ga-online.org.
URL: http://www.ga-online.org/
History 1970. Founded as an international society, deriving from the German national association, set up 8 Apr 1953, Camberg-Taunus (Germany FR). Former names and other names: *Society for Medicinal Plant Research* – former; *Société de recherche des plantes médicinales* – former; *Gesellschaft für Arzneipflanzenforschung (GA)* – former. **Aims** Serve as an international focal point for those interested in: medicine, chemistry, biochemistry and cell culture of plants and other related fields; analytical methods for plants and plant products; regulatory aspects of herbal remedies – phytomedicines. **Structure** Members' Meeting (annual); Board of Directors; Advisory Board; Executive Council; Permanent Committees (4). **Languages** English, German. **Staff** Voluntary. **Finance** Sources: gifts, legacies; members' dues. **Activities** Awards/prizes/competitions; events/meetings; financial and/or material support; healthcare. **Events** *Annual Congress* Thessaloniki (Greece) 2022, *Annual Congress* Bonn (Germany) 2021, *Annual Congress* San Francisco, CA (USA) 2020, *International Congress on Natural Products Research* San Francisco, CA (USA) 2020, *Annual Congress* Innsbruck (Austria) 2019. **Publications** *Planta Medica* (12 a year) – journal; *Society for Medicinal Plant Research Newsletter* (2 a year).
Members Regular; Supporting; Honorary individual scientists in 82 countries. Membership countries not specified.
[2021.07.05/XD5907/v/**C**]

♦ Gas Processors Association – Europe (GPA Europe) 10076
Contact Willow Cottage, Stroud Lane, Fleet, GU51 5ST, UK. T. +441252625542. Fax +441252786260. E-mail: admin@gpaeurope.com.
URL: http://www.gpaeurope.com/
History Founded 1983, as a parallel organization to (US) Gas Processors Association and part of the umbrella organization *Global Gas Processors Alliance (GPA Global, #10387)*. Incorporated as a Company Limited by Guarantee in England and Wales, 2012. **Aims** Serve as a forum for the exchange of information on gas processing matters among operators, consultants and suppliers; promote technical and operational excellence throughout the European Gas industry. **Structure** Board of Directors; Management Committee; Sub-committees. **Languages** English. **Staff** 1.00 FTE, paid. **Finance** Members' dues. Conferences. **Activities** Awards/prizes/competitions; events/meetings; knowledge management/information dissemination. **Events** *Annual Conference* Barcelona (Spain) 2018, *Spring Meeting* Rome (Italy) 2018, *Annual Conference* Budapest (Hungary) 2017, *Annual Conference* Istanbul (Turkey) 2016, *Spring Meeting* Paris (France) 2016. **Publications** *In Brief* (twice a year) – magazine summarizing previous conferences. Conference reports.
Members Companies (144) in 14 countries:
Austria, Belgium, Canada, Denmark, France, Germany, Italy, Netherlands, Norway, Poland, Russia, Switzerland, UK, USA.
Individuals (about 300) in 13 countries:
Austria, Belgium, Canada, Denmark, France, Germany, Indonesia, Italy, Netherlands, Norway, Switzerland, UK, USA.
[2020.03.03/XD8191/**D**]

♦ Gastech Conference (meeting series)
♦ Gastech – Gastech Conference (meeting series)
♦ Gas Technology Institute (internationally oriented national body)
♦ Gaston Z Ortigas Peace Institute (internationally oriented national body)
♦ Gas Transmission Europe / see Gas Infrastructure Europe (#10073)
♦ **GATB** / see TB Alliance (#20103)
♦ **GATE** Global Action for Trans Equality (#10169)

Gateway Antarctica
10076

alphabetic sequence excludes
For the complete listing, see Yearbook Online at

- ♦ Gateway Antarctica (internationally oriented national body)
- ♦ **GATH-INTERNATIONAL** Global Academy of Tropical Health and Culture (#10162)
- ♦ GATJ – Global Alliance for Tax Justice (unconfirmed)
- ♦ GATM – Humanitarian Association of Turkmens of the World, Ashgabat (no recent information)
- ♦ Gatsby Charitable Foundation (internationally oriented national body)
- ♦ GATS – General Agreement on Trade in Services (1994 treaty)
- ♦ GATT 1947 – General Agreement on Tariffs and Trade, 1947 (1947 treaty)
- ♦ GATT 1994 – General Agreement on Tariffs and Trade, 1994 (1994 treaty)
- ♦ GATT – General Agreement on Tariffs and Trade (inactive)
- ♦ GATT Protocol – Protocol Relating to Trade Negotiations among Developing Countries (1971 treaty)
- ♦ GATW – Green Across the World (internationally oriented national body)
- ♦ The GAVI Alliance / see Gavi – The Vaccine Alliance (#10077)
- ♦ Gavi – L'Alliance du Vaccin (#10077)
- ♦ **Gavi** Gavi – L'Alliance du Vaccin (#10077)
- ♦ GAVI / see Gavi – The Vaccine Alliance (#10077)
- ♦ **Gavi** Gavi – The Vaccine Alliance (#10077)

♦ Gavi – The Vaccine Alliance (Gavi) 10077

Gavi – L'Alliance du Vaccin (Gavi)

CEO Global Health Campus, Chemin du Pommier 40, 1218 Le Grand-Saconnex GE, Switzerland. T. +41229096500. Fax +41229096550. E-mail: info@gavi.org.

Secretariat Washington DC 2099 Pennsylvania Ave NW, Suite 200, Washington DC 20006, USA. T. +12024781050. Fax +12024781060. E-mail: info@gavi.org.

URL: http://www.gavi.org/

History Jan 2000, Davos (Switzerland). Founded, by *Bill and Melinda Gates Foundation (BMGF)*, *UNICEF (#20332)* and *WHO (#20950)*, when officially launched to continue and build on the work of the previous *Children's Vaccine Initiative (CVI, inactive)*. Former names and other names: *Global Alliance for Vaccines and Immunization (GAVI)* – former; *The GAVI Alliance* – legal name. Registration: Switzerland; 501(c)(3), No/ID: EIN 91-2004617, USA; EU Transparency Register, No/ID: 078294941111-90, Start date: 27 Jan 2021. **Aims** Save children's lives and protect people's health by increasing access to immunization in poor countries. **Structure** Board of 28 members, consisting of 4 institutional seats – *UNICEF (#20332)*, *WHO (#20950)*, *International Bank for Reconstruction and Development (IBRD, #12317)* (World Bank) and *Bill and Melinda Gates Foundation (BMGF)* -, Governments implementing countries (5), Governments donor countries (5), Independent individuals (9), and one representative of Vaccine industry developing countries, Vaccine industry industrialized countries, Civil society organizations, and Research and technical health institutes, and Gavi CEO. Secretariat. **Languages** English. **Staff** 150.00 FTE, paid. **Finance** Sources: donations; government support. Supported by: *Bill and Melinda Gates Foundation (BMGF)*; *European Commission (EC, #06633)*; *International Finance Facility for Immunisation (IFFIm, #13598)*. **Activities** Financial and/or material support. **Events** *Global Vaccine Summit / Donor Pledging Conference* London (UK) 2020, *Technical Workshop on Mortality Surveillance in Africa* Addis Ababa (Ethiopia) 2019, *Replenishment Launch Meeting* Yokohama (Japan) 2019, *Mid-Term Review Meeting* Abu Dhabi (United Arab Emirates) 2018, *Meeting on the future of Harmonization for Health in Africa (HHA)* Dakar (Senegal) 2017. **Publications** Annual Report.

Members CSO Constituency includes 28 organizations listed in this Yearbook:

- *Action for Global Health (AfGH, #00090)*;
- *African Health Economics and Policy Association (AfHEA, #00335)*;
- *Amref Health Africa (#00806)*;
- *Bureau international des Médecins sans frontières (MSF International, #03366)*;
- *Catholic Organization for Relief and Development (Cordaid)*;
- *Catholic Relief Services (CRS, #03608)*;
- *Centre for Economic Governance and AIDS in Africa (CEGAA)*;
- *Christian Connections for International Health (CCIH)*;
- *Coalition against Typhoid (CaT, #04049)*;
- *CORE Group*;
- *Global Health Technologies Coalition (GHTC)*;
- *GOAL*;
- *International Federation of Red Cross and Red Crescent Societies (#13526)*;
- *Medical Women's International Association (MWIA, #16630)*;
- *ONE (#17728)*;
- *Pan African Treatment Access Movement (PATAM, #18071)*;
- *Partners in Health (PIH)*;
- *PCI Global*;
- *Plan International (#18386)*;
- *Réseau des Plate-formes nationales d'ONG d'Afrique de l'Ouest et du Centre (REPAOC, #18902)*;
- *RESULTS*;
- *Save the Children UK (SC UK)*;
- *Sightsavers International (#19270)*;
- *Task Force for Global Health (TFGH, #20098)*;
- *Transparency International (TI, #20223)*;
- *United States Fund for UNICEF (UNICEF USA)*.

IGO Relations Adheres to: *Global Partnership for Effective Development Co-operation (GPEDC, #10532)*. **NGO Relations** Accredited by (4): *Coalition against Typhoid (CaT, #04049)*; *Global Coalition Against Child Pneumonia (#10290)*; *Global Health Workforce Alliance (GHWA, inactive)*; *PMNCH (#18410)*. Partner of (3): *Every Woman Every Child (EWEC, #09215)*; *Global Financing Facility (GFF, #10360)*; *UHC2030 (#20277)*. Signatory to: *International Aid Transparency Initiative (IATI, #11604)*. Partners: *International Federation of Pharmaceutical Manufacturers and Associations (IFPMA, #13505)*; public health and research institutions. Partner of and supports: *International Vaccine Access Center (IVAC)*. [2021/XF5953/**F**]

- ♦ GAWC / see Global Alliances for Water and Climate (#10230)
- ♦ **GaWC** Globalization and World Cities Research Network (#10441)
- ♦ GAWF – General Arab Women Federation (no recent information)
- ♦ **GAWH** Global Alliance for Women's Health (#10233)
- ♦ GAWP – Global Action to Prevent War (internationally oriented national body)
- ♦ Gay Christian Europe (unconfirmed)
- ♦ GAYEDI – Great Africa Youth Empowerment and Development Initiative (internationally oriented national body)
- ♦ Gay Humanist Group / see LGBT Humanists

♦ Gay and Lesbian International Sport Association (GLISA) 10078

Address not obtained.

History 27 Mar 2004. Registered in accordance with Canadian law. **Aims** Organize competitive sporting opportunities for the diverse gender and sexual community athletes; assist in the development of LGBT sport associations, teams and clubs; increase awareness and visibility of gays, lesbians, bi-sexuals, transgendered, queer, and intersex persons in sports worldwide. **Structure** Board. Committees (6): Communications; Finance; Governance and Planning; Host Relations; Membership Services; Sport Technical. **Activities** Sporting activities. **Events** *International delegate congress* Antwerp (Belgium) 2007. **NGO Relations** Member of (1): *ILGA World (International Lesbian, Gay, Bisexual, Trans and Intersex Association, #11120)*. [2015/XM0895/**D**]

♦ Gay and Lesbian Rowing Federation (GLRF) 10079

Exec Dir 22647 Ventura Blvd, Suite 1030, Los Angeles CA 91364, USA. T. +13237711903. E-mail: rowing@glrf.info.

URL: http://www.glrf.info/

History 2000. Former names and other names: *Lambda Rowing International (LRI)* – former (2000 to 2007). Registration: USA, State of California. **Aims** Provide a means to connect lgbtq+ outdoor and indoor rowers, coxes, coaches and race officials. **Structure** Web-based organization. Management Team (administrative body); Policy Board of Directors. **Languages** English. **Staff** 1.00 FTE, paid. **Finance** Sources: donations; members' dues; sale of products; sponsorship. Other sources: product placement. **Activities** Networking/liaising; sporting activities.

Members Individuals Shoreside (free); OnTheWater (paid). Members (1,731) in 44 countries:

Argentina, Australia, Austria, Belgium, Brazil, Canada, Croatia, Czechia, Denmark, France, Germany, Greece, Hungary, India, Indonesia, Iran Islamic Rep, Ireland, Israel, Italy, Kenya, Malaysia, Mexico, Netherlands, New Zealand, Nigeria, Norway, Pakistan, Paraguay, Poland, Portugal, Qatar, Russia, Serbia, Slovakia, Slovenia, South Africa, Spain, Sweden, Switzerland, Türkiye, UK, United Arab Emirates, USA, Zimbabwe. [2021.06.08/XJ3803/**D**]

- ♦ Gay Police European Network / see European LGBT Police Association (#07686)
- ♦ Gays and Lesbians in Alcoholics Anonymous (internationally oriented national body)
- ♦ Gazette International Networking Institute / see Post-Polio Health International
- ♦ GBAC / see Graduate Management Admission Council (#10687)
- ♦ **GBA** Global Banking Alliance for Women (#10248)
- ♦ **GBA** Global Battery Alliance (#10249)
- ♦ **GBA** Global Biofoundries Alliance (#10253)
- ♦ **GBA** Global Biofoundries Alliance (#10252)
- ♦ **GBATA** Global Business and Technology Association (#10261)
- ♦ GBC / see GBCHealth
- ♦ GBC-Education – Global Business Coalition for Education (unconfirmed)
- ♦ **GBC** Global Business Coalition (#10257)
- ♦ GBCHealth (internationally oriented national body)
- ♦ GBCS – General Board of Church and Society of the United Methodist Church (internationally oriented national body)
- ♦ **GBDN** ILO Global Business and Disability Network (#11122)
- ♦ **GBEP** Global Bioenergy Partnership (#10251)
- ♦ **GBF** Graduate Business Forum (#10686)
- ♦ GBF – Great Bear Foundation (internationally oriented national body)
- ♦ GBG Foundation – Global Benefits Group Foundation (internationally oriented national body)
- ♦ **GB** Girls' Brigade International (#10152)
- ♦ GBGM / see Global Ministries of The United Methodist Church
- ♦ **GB** Grameen Bank (#10693)
- ♦ GBIC / see Girls' Brigade International (#10152)
- ♦ **GBIF** Global Biodiversity Information Facility (#10250)
- ♦ GBI Foundation – Global Basic Income Foundation (internationally oriented national body)
- ♦ GBI – Global Bioethics Initiative (internationally oriented national body)
- ♦ **GBI** The Global Business Initiative on Human Rights (#10259)
- ♦ GBIM / see Encompass World Partners
- ♦ GBM – Generic and Biosimilar Medicines of Southern Africa (internationally oriented national body)
- ♦ GBN – Global Biosaline Network (internationally oriented national body)
- ♦ **GBPN** Global Buildings Performance Network (#10256)
- ♦ GBS/CIDP Foundation International – Guillain-Barré Syndrome – Chronic Inflammatory Demyelinating Polyneuropathy Foundation International (internationally oriented national body)
- ♦ **GBSN** Global Business School Network (#10260)
- ♦ GBTA Europe (internationally oriented national body)
- ♦ GBTA – Global Business Travel Association (internationally oriented national body)
- ♦ GBTF – Global Biotechnology Transfer Foundation (unconfirmed)

♦ GBV Prevention Network 10080

Contact PO Box 6770, Kampala, Uganda. T. +256414531186. Fax +256414531249. E-mail: info@preventgbvafrica.org.

URL: http://www.preventgbvafrica.org/

History Sep 2003. GBV stands for *Gender-Based Violence*. **Aims** Become a vibrant space in the Horn, East and Southern *Africa* for innovation, expertise, experience and exchange on *Gender*-Based *Violence prevention*. **Structure** Advisory Committee. **Finance** Supported by: *Land and Agriculture Policy Centre (LAPC, no recent information)*; *Norwegian Agency for Development Cooperation (Norad)*.

Members Organizational and individual (over 800). Members in 23 countries:

Afghanistan, Angola, Botswana, Burundi, Congo DR, Eritrea, Eswatini, Ethiopia, Kenya, Malawi, Mauritius, Namibia, Nigeria, Pakistan, Rwanda, Sierra Leone, Somalia, South Africa, Sudan, Tanzania UR, Uganda, Zambia, Zimbabwe. [2017.03.10/XJ7450/**F**]

- ♦ GC3 – Global Coalition against Cervical Cancer (unconfirmed)
- ♦ **GCAE** Golf Course Association Europe (#10677)
- ♦ GCA – Global Center on Adaptation (unconfirmed)
- ♦ **GCA** Global Citizenship Alliance (#10282)
- ♦ GCA – Global Communication Association (internationally oriented national body)
- ♦ GCA – Global Cyber Alliance (internationally oriented national body)
- ♦ **GCAP** Global Call for Action Against Poverty (#10263)
- ♦ **GCAQE** Global Cabin Air Quality Executive (#10262)
- ♦ GCAS – Gulf Centre for Aviation Studies (internationally oriented national body)
- ♦ GCBC – Global Chinese Breast Cancer Organizations Alliance (internationally oriented national body)
- ♦ GCBCOA / see Global Chinese Breast Cancer Organizations Alliance

♦ GCC+3 10081

Address not obtained.

History *Gulf Cooperation Council (GCC, #10826)* plus Egypt, Iraq and Jordan. **Events** *Summit* Jeddah (Saudi Arabia) 2022.

Members Governments of 4 entities:

Egypt, Iraq, Jordan.

Gulf Cooperation Council (GCC, #10826). [2022/AA2914/**E***]

- ♦ GCC AA / see Advertising Business Group (#00136)
- ♦ GCCAAO – GCC Accounting and Auditing Organization (inactive)
- ♦ GCC Accounting and Auditing Organization (inactive)

♦ GCC Accreditation Center (GAC) 10082

Contact PO Box 85245, Riyadh 11691, Saudi Arabia. T. +966112061111. Fax +966114566479. E-mail: info@gac.org.sa.

URL: https://gac.org.sa/

History Established by governments of *Gulf Cooperation Council (GCC, #10826)*. **Aims** Provide specified accreditation services to laboratories within the territories of all Member States in the fields of calibration, *measurement*, testing, inspection and *certification* – *conformity* assessment. **Structure** Board of Directors; Director General; Stakeholders Advisory Committee. **Activities** Certification/accreditation; training/education.

Members Governments (7):

Bahrain, Kuwait, Oman, Qatar, Saudi Arabia, United Arab Emirates, Yemen.

NGO Relations Member of (2): *Asia Pacific Accreditation Cooperation (APAC, #01816)*; *International Halal Accreditation Forum (IHAF, #13769)*. [2023.02.15/XM7029/**E***]

- ♦ GCC Advertisers Association / see Advertising Business Group (#00136)
- ♦ GCC Advertising Association / see Advertising Business Group (#00136)
- ♦ **GCCA** Global Cement and Concrete Association (#10275)
- ♦ **GCCA** Global Cleantech Cluster Association (#10284)
- ♦ GCCA – Global Climate Change Alliance (inactive)
- ♦ **GCCA** Global Cold Chain Alliance (#10299)
- ♦ **GCCA** Global Colon Cancer Association (#10300)
- ♦ GCCA / see International Digital Enterprise Alliance (#13175)
- ♦ GCC AIR – GCC Association of Immunology and Rheumatology (unconfirmed)
- ♦ GCC Association of Immunology and Rheumatology (unconfirmed)
- ♦ **GCC BDI** GCC Board Directors Institute (#10083)

♦ **GCC Board Directors Institute (GCC BDI)** **10083**
Contact Emirates Financial Towers, Office 2201 – South Tower, PO Box 507007, Dubai, United Arab Emirates. T. +97145547967. E-mail: getinvolved@gccbdi.org.
URL: http://www.gccbdi.org/
History 2007. **Aims** Strengthen corporate governance in the GCC region through capability building, advocacy and promotion of sound governance practices. **Structure** Board of Governors. **Languages** Arabic, English. **Publications** Research; surveys; reports. **Members** Board directors and senior executives (over 1,200). Membership countries not specified. **NGO Relations** Member of: *Global Network of Director Institutes (GNDI, #10486).* [2019.02.19/XM6579/j/**D**]

♦ GCCEI – Grand Council of the Crees – Eeyou Istchee (internationally oriented national body)
♦ GCC – Global Cooperation Council (internationally oriented national body)
♦ **GCC** Global Cosmetics Cluster (#10309)
♦ **GCC** Gulf Cooperation Council (#10826)
♦ GCCI – Global Climate Change Institute, Tsinghua University (internationally oriented national body)
♦ GCCM / see Laudato Si' Movement (#16403)
♦ **GCCN** Global Cancer Coalitions Network (#10270)
♦ **GCC Patent Office** Patent Office of Cooperation Council for the Arab States of the Gulf (#18259)
♦ GCCQ / see Grand Council of the Crees – Eeyou Istchee
♦ GCCS – Global Center on Cooperative Security (internationally oriented national body)
♦ GCCSI / see Global CCS Institute (#10274)

♦ **GCC Standardization Organization (GSO)** **10084**
Contact GSO Building, AlGadeer – Olaya Str, PO Box 85245, Riyadh 11691, Saudi Arabia. T. +966112746655. Fax +966112105391. E-mail: csc@gso.org.sa.
URL: http://www.gso.org.sa/
History 31 Dec 2001, Muscat (Oman). Established on implementation of a resolution of *Gulf Cooperation Council (GCC, #10826).* Operational since May 2004. **Aims** Help the Gulf Cooperation Council (GCC) achieve the objectives set forth in its charter and in the GCC Economic Agreement by unifying the various standardization activities and following up application and compliance of the same in cooperation and coordination with the standardization bodies in the Member States in an endeavour to develop the *production* and *service* sectors, foster the Intra-GCC *trade*, protect the *consumer*, environment and public health, and encourage the GCC *industries* and *agricultural* production that would enhance the GCC *economy*, maintain the achievements of the Member States and minimize the technical trade barriers as envisaged by the objectives of the Customs Union. **Structure** Board of Directors (meets twice a year), comprising Ministers responsible for standardization of each Member State. Technical Council. General Secretariat, presided by Secretary-General. **Finance** Members' contributions. Other sources: donations; fees for services. **Activities** Standards/guidelines; training/education; knowledge management/information dissemination; guidance/assistance/consulting. **Events** *GCC Laboratory Proficiency Conference* Muscat (Oman) 2019, *Gulf Building Code Conference* Dubai (United Arab Emirates) 2017.
Members Standardization bodies of 7 countries:
Bahrain, Kuwait, Oman, Qatar, Saudi Arabia, United Arab Emirates, Yemen.
IGO Relations Instrumental in setting up (1): *Gulfmet (#10835).* Observer to: *Codex Alimentarius Commission (CAC, #04081).* **NGO Relations** Memorandum of Understanding with: *Comité européen de normalisation (CEN, #04162).* [2021/XJ3949/**D***]

♦ GCC-STAT / see Statistical Center for the Cooperation Council for the Arab Countries of the Gulf (#19970)
♦ **GCC Stat** Statistical Center for the Cooperation Council for the Arab Countries of the Gulf (#19970)
♦ GCC – YMCA Global Community Center (internationally oriented national body)
♦ **GCDFund** Global Child Dental Fund (#10279)
♦ GCD – Global Credit Data (unconfirmed)
♦ GCDN – Global Cultural Districts Network (unconfirmed)
♦ GCEA – Graphic Communications Education Association (internationally oriented national body)
♦ GCECEE / see European Savings and Retail Banking Group (#08426)
♦ **GCEC** Groupe consultatif européen des consommateurs (#06771)
♦ GCEF – Global Competitiveness Empowerment Forum (internationally oriented national body)
♦ GCE – Gay Christian Europe (unconfirmed)
♦ **GCE** Generation Climate Europe (#10114)
♦ GCEG – Global Community Earth Government (internationally oriented national body)
♦ **GCE** Global Campaign for Education (#10264)
♦ **GCERF** Global Community Engagement and Resilience Fund (#10303)
♦ **GCES** Gulf Comparative Education Society (#10825)
♦ GCET – Global Conference on Environmental Taxation (meeting series)
♦ GCF – Global Citizen Forum (unconfirmed)
♦ GCF – Global Citizen Forum (unconfirmed)
♦ **GCF** Global Climate Forum (#10287)
♦ **GCF** Green Climate Fund (#10714)
♦ **GCFI** Gulf and Caribbean Fisheries Institute (#10823)
♦ GCGF – IFC Global Corporate Governance Forum (inactive)
♦ **GCGI** Global Corporate Governance Institute (#10307)
♦ GCGI – Globalisation for the Common Good Initiative (unconfirmed)
♦ GC / see Global Coalition for Occupation Safety and Health (#10294)
♦ **GCHA** Global Climate and Health Alliance (#10288)
♦ **GCHERA** Global Confederation of Higher Education Associations for Agriculture and Life Sciences (#10304)
♦ GCH – Global Congress On Hysteroscopy (meeting series)
♦ GCHope – Giving Children Hope (internationally oriented national body)
♦ **GCHRAGD** Geneva Centre for Human Rights Advancement and Global Dialogue (#10120)
♦ GCHR – Gulf Center for Human Rights (internationally oriented national body)
♦ GCIA – Global Culinary Innovators Association (internationally oriented national body)
♦ **GCIAMT** Grupo Cooperativo Iberoamericano de Medicina Transfusional (#10801)
♦ GCIAN – Global Cochlear Implant Access Network (unconfirmed)
♦ GCIC – Groupement cinématographique international de conciliation (inactive)
♦ GCI – Gender Concerns International (internationally oriented national body)
♦ GCI – Global Cancer Initiative (internationally oriented national body)
♦ GCI – Global Change Institute (internationally oriented national body)
♦ GCI – Global Civil Initiatives (internationally oriented national body)
♦ GCI – Green Cooling Initiative (internationally oriented national body)
♦ **GCI** Green Cross International (#10715)
♦ GCI – Gwich'in Council International (internationally oriented national body)
♦ GCILL – Global Center for Indigenous Leadership and Lifeways (internationally oriented national body)
♦ **GCIRC** Groupe consultatif international de recherche sur le colza (#10736)
♦ GCISC – Global Change Impact Studies Centre (internationally oriented national body)
♦ GCL / see Customs Laboratories European Network (#04986)
♦ GCMC – George C Marshall European Centre for Security Studies, Garmisch Partenkirchen (internationally oriented national body)
♦ **GCM** Global Coalition on Migration (#10293)
♦ GCM – Global Community Monitor (internationally oriented national body)
♦ **GCNF** Global Child Nutrition Foundation (#10280)
♦ **GCN** GEF CSO Network (#10087)
♦ GCN – Global Challenges Network (internationally oriented national body)
♦ GCNU – Grupo de Comunicaciones de las Naciones Unidas (inactive)
♦ GCOA – Global Coalition on Aging (unconfirmed)
♦ **GCO** Gemeenschappelijk Centrum voor Onderzoek (#16147)
♦ GCO – Global Combat Sports Organization (unconfirmed)
♦ GCOM – Global Conference on Myositis (meeting series)
♦ **GCoM** Global Covenant of Mayors for Climate and Energy (#10312)
♦ GCOS / see Global Climate Observing System (#10289)
♦ **GCOS** Global Climate Observing System (#10289)
♦ GCP21 – Global Cassava Partnership for the 21st Century (unconfirmed)
♦ GCPA – Good Clinical Practice Alliance (unconfirmed)
♦ **GCPEA** Global Coalition to Protect Education from Attack (#10295)

♦ **GCP Europe** **10085**
SG Rond-Point Schuman 2-4, 1040 Brussels, Belgium. T. +32486352901. E-mail: info@gcpeurope.eu.
URL: http://www.gcpeurope.eu/
History 1949, Belgium. Set up by *International Union of Roofing and Plumbing Contractors (UICP, inactive).* Former names and other names: *GCP Europe – The voice of efficient building engineering services* – full title. Registration: Banque Carrefour des Entreprises, No/ID: 0479.214.345, Start date: 28 Nov 2001, Belgium; EU Transparency Register, No/ID: 495521635656-72, Start date: 16 Aug 2019. **Aims** Be the voice of the building services engineering sector, mechanical contractors, plumbers and HVAC installers; represent their interests at European Union level; contribute to the achievement of EU's climate, energy and prosperity goals. **Languages** English. **Activities** Advocacy/lobbying/activism; training/education. **Events** *Installers Summit* Luxembourg (Luxembourg) 2022.
Members Associations (17) in 12 countries:
Austria, Belgium, Denmark, Finland, Germany, Ireland, Luxembourg, Netherlands, Norway, Spain, Sweden, UK.
NGO Relations Member of (1): *Construction 2050 Alliance (#04760).* [2022.11.11/XM6656/**D**]

♦ GCP Europe – The voice of efficient building engineering services / see GCP Europe (#10085)
♦ GCPF / see CropLife International (#04966)
♦ **GCP** Global Carbon Project (#10272)
♦ **GCP** Global Coffee Platform (#10298)
♦ GCQHR – Global Congress for Qualitative Health Research (meeting series)
♦ **GCR2P** Global Centre for the Responsibility to Protect (#10277)
♦ GCR – Global Citizen's Rights (unconfirmed)
♦ GCR – Greek Council for Refugees (internationally oriented national body)
♦ GCRIO – US Global Change Research Information Office (internationally oriented national body)
♦ **GCRMN** Global Coral Reef Monitoring Network (#10306)
♦ **GCRSR** Global Coalition for Regulatory Science Research (#10296)
♦ GCS / see Global Cooperation Society
♦ GCSCC – Global Cyber Security Capacity Centre (internationally oriented national body)
♦ GCSD – Global Citizens for Sustainable Development (internationally oriented national body)
♦ GCS – Game Cultures Society (unconfirmed)
♦ GCS – Global Civic Sharing (internationally oriented national body)
♦ GCS International – Global Cooperation Society (internationally oriented national body)
♦ GCSM – Global Conference on Sustainable Manufacturing (meeting series)
♦ GCSP – Geneva Centre for Security Policy (internationally oriented national body)
♦ GCSS – Global Council of Sport Science (unconfirmed)
♦ **GCSS** Gulf Centre for Strategic Studies (#10824)
♦ **GCTF** Global Counterterrorism Forum (#10311)
♦ **GCTH** Grupo de Cooperação Técnica Horizontal da América Latina e Caribe sobre o HIV/Aids (#10945)
♦ GCTTN – Global Coalition of Think Tank Networks for SSC (unconfirmed)
♦ **GCTU** General Confederation of Trade Unions (#10108)
♦ **GCWA** Global Coalition on Women and AIDS (#10297)
♦ **GCWDA** Global Clean Water Desalination Alliance (#10285)
♦ **GCYDCA** Guidance, Counselling and Youth Development Centre for Africa (#10816)
♦ **GD4S** Gas Distributors For Sustainability (#10071)
♦ **GDAC** Global Dengue and Aedes-transmitted Diseases Consortium (#10316)
♦ **GDACS** Global Disaster Alert and Coordination System (#10322)
♦ GDAE – Global Development and Environment Institute (internationally oriented national body)
♦ **GDA** Global Dryland Alliance (#10326)
♦ **GDA** Grupo de Diarios América (#10803)
♦ Gdansk convention – Convention on Fishing and Conservation of the Living Resources in the Baltic Sea and the Belts (1973 treaty)
♦ GDC – Global Deaf Connection (internationally oriented national body)
♦ GDC – Global Developmental Corps (internationally oriented national body)
♦ **GDC** Global Diaspora Confederation (#10320)
♦ **GDC** Global Doctors for Choice (#10324)
♦ **GDE** Groupe des démocrates européens (#06744)
♦ GDF – Global Dairy Farmers (unconfirmed)
♦ **GDF** Global Diplomatic Forum (#10321)
♦ GDF – Global Diversity Foundation (internationally oriented national body)
♦ GDG – Global Development Group (internationally oriented national body)
♦ **GD** Graph Drawing (#10696)
♦ GDH / see Geneva for Human Rights – Global Training (#10124)
♦ **GDH** Genève pour le droits de l'homme – Formation internationale (#10124)
♦ GDI / see Dialogue Institute
♦ GDI – Global Democracy Initiative (internationally oriented national body)
♦ GDI – Global Development Incubator (unconfirmed)
♦ GDI – Global Disinformation Index (unconfirmed)
♦ GDI/JES / see Dialogue Institute
♦ **GDIN** Global Disaster Information Network (#10323)
♦ GDL / see Childreach International
♦ GDL – Gesellschaft Deutschsprachiger Lymphologen (internationally oriented national body)
♦ GDL – Global Diplomacy Lab (internationally oriented national body)
♦ **GDLN** Global Development Learning Network (#10317)
♦ **GDN** Gender and Disaster Network (#10096)
♦ GDN – Global Design Network (unconfirmed)
♦ **GDN** Global Development Network (#10318)
♦ **GDN** Green Diplomacy Network (#10716)
♦ **GDP** Global Dairy Platform (#10314)
♦ GDRC – Global Development Research Centre (internationally oriented national body)
♦ GDRC – Global Disaster Resilience Centre (internationally oriented national body)
♦ GDS – Global Doll Society (unconfirmed)
♦ GE4 / see Global Education: Exchanges for Engineers and Entrepreneurs (#10335)
♦ **Ge4** Global Education: Exchanges for Engineers and Entrepreneurs (#10335)
♦ GEAC – Gender Equality Advisory Council (unconfirmed)
♦ **GEAE** Groupement Européen des Ardennes et de l'Eifel (#07414)
♦ GEA – Gesellschaft der Europäischen Akademien (internationally oriented national body)
♦ GEA – Global Environmental Action (internationally oriented national body)
♦ **GEA** Global Express Association (#10351)
♦ GEAMR – Groupement européen des associations des maisons de réforme (no recent information)
♦ **GEAN** Global EV Association Network (#10349)
♦ GÉANT / see GÉANT Association (#10086)

♦ **GÉANT Association** **10086**
CEO City House, 126-130 Hills Road, Cambridge, CB2 1PQ, UK. T. +441223371300. Fax +441223371371. E-mail: info@geant.org.
Amsterdam Office Hoekenrode 3, 6th floor, 1102 BR Amsterdam, Netherlands. T. +31205304488. Fax +31205304499.

URL: http://www.geant.org/
History 1 Nov 2000. 2nd phase (GN2) ended 2009. 3rd phase *GN3* – Apr 2009-Mar 2013. *GN3plus* – Apr 2013-Apr 2015. *Delivery of Advanced Network Technology to Europe (DANTE, inactive)* and *Trans-European Research and Education Networking Association (TERENA, inactive)* set up association, 10 Oct 2014. Current articles adopted Nov 2015. Former names and other names: *GÉANT* – former; *GN3* – former; *GN3plus* – former. Registration: Handelsrregister, No/ID: KVK 40535155, Netherlands. **Aims** Develop, deliver and promote advanced networks and associated *e-infrastructure* services. **Structure** General Assembly; Board of Directors; Advisory Council. Committees; Working Groups. Offices: Amsterdam (Netherlands); Cambridge (UK). **Languages** English. **Staff** 80.00 FTE, paid. **Finance** Members' dues. Funding from: *European Commission (EC, #06633)*; European National Research and Education Networks (NRENs). **Activities** Guidance/assistance/consulting; knowledge management/information dissemination; networking/liaising; events/meetings; training/education; awards/prizes/competitions. **Events** *Pan-European Research and Education Networking Conference* Cambridge (UK) 2022, *Pan-European Research and Education Networking Conference* Cambridge (UK) 2021, *Pan-European Research and Education Networking Conference* Brighton (UK) 2020, *European Research Networking Conference* Tallinn (Estonia) 2019, *Digital Infrastructures for Research Conference* Lisbon (Portugal) 2018.
Members National; Representative; Associate. National members in 37 countries:
Albania, Armenia, Austria, Azerbaijan, Belarus, Belgium, Bulgaria, Croatia, Cyprus, Czechia, Estonia, France, Georgia, Germany, Greece, Hungary, Ireland, Israel, Italy, Latvia, Lithuania, Luxembourg, Malta, Moldova, Montenegro, Netherlands, North Macedonia, Poland, Portugal, Romania, Serbia, Slovakia, Slovenia, Spain, Switzerland, Türkiye, UK.
Representative member (1):
NORDUnet (#17553).
Associates in 12 countries:
Belgium, Canada, Denmark, Finland, Germany, Iceland, Italy, Netherlands, Norway, Sweden, Switzerland, UK.
Included in the above, 3 organizations listed in this Yearbook:
European Molecular Biology Laboratory (EMBL, #07813); *European Organization for Nuclear Research (CERN, #08108)*; *European Space Agency (ESA, #08798)*.
IGO Relations Partner of: *Group on Earth Observations (GEO, #10735)*. Collaborates with: *e-Infrastructure Reflection Group (e-IRG, #11208)*. **NGO Relations** Member of (1): *ORCID (#17790)*. Cooperates with (1): *European University Information Systems Organization (EUNIS, #09033)*. Instrumental in setting up (1): *Network Performing Arts Production Workshops (NPAPWS)*. [2022/XJ4897/y/**F**]

- ♦ GEAP – Global Embassy of Activists for Peace (unconfirmed)
- ♦ **GEAP** Groupe européen pour l'administration publique (#07430)
- ♦ **GEAP** Groupe européen pour l'arthroscopie du poignet (#09122)
- ♦ **GEBC** Groupement européen des banques coopératives (#05990)
- ♦ **GEBCO** Joint IOC/IHO Guiding Committee for the General Bathymetric Chart of the Oceans (#16137)
- ♦ GEB / see Community of European Railway and Infrastructure Companies (#04396)
- ♦ GEBN – Global Energy Balance Network (unconfirmed)
- ♦ **GEBTA** Guild of European Business Travel Agents (#10819)
- ♦ GEC / see Global Environment Centre
- ♦ GECA / see European Organisation for Research and Treatment of Cancer (#08101)
- ♦ GECE / see European Savings and Retail Banking Group (#08426)
- ♦ **GECE** Groupement européen des caisses d'épargne et banques de détail (#08426)
- ♦ **GECF** Gas Exporting Countries Forum (#10072)
- ♦ GEC – Global Environment Centre (internationally oriented national body)
- ♦ GEC – Global Environment Centre (internationally oriented national body)
- ♦ **GEC** Green Economy Coalition (#10717)
- ♦ **GEC** Groupe européen des charophytologues (#10772)
- ♦ GEC – Groupement européen des fabricants de celluloses (inactive)
- ♦ GECITEX – Groupement européen de coordination des industries textiles diverses (inactive)
- ♦ GECOOPS – Groupement européen de coopération sidérurgique (no recent information)
- ♦ **GEDC** Global Engineering Deans Council (#10344)
- ♦ **GEDIP** Groupe européen de droit international privé (#07429)
- ♦ GEDIS – Groupement européen des entreprises de distribution intégrée (inactive)
- ♦ **GEDnet** Global Type III Environmental Product Declarations Network (#10636)
- ♦ GEDRT – Groupe européen d'échange d'expériences sur la direction de la recherche textile (unconfirmed)
- ♦ GEECT – Groupement européen des écoles de cinéma et de télévision (see: #11771)
- ♦ GEEF / see European Family Businesses (#07028)
- ♦ GEE – Galgos Ethique Europe (internationally oriented national body)
- ♦ GEE / see GEO Foundation (#10132)
- ♦ GEE – Global Joint Seminar on Geo-Environmental Engineering (meeting series)
- ♦ GEEPHM – Groupement européen pour l'emploi des personnes avec handicap mental (no recent information)
- ♦ GEERES – Groupe européen d'échanges et de recherches en éducation sociale (no recent information)
- ♦ **GEET** Gemeinschaft Europäischer Evangelikaler Theologen (#09727)

♦ GEF CSO Network (GCN) 10087

Secretariat Save the Earth Cambodia, 3rd Floor, PS Office 217, Ste 358, Phnom Penh 122338, Cambodia. T. +85512599817. E-mail: chair.gcn@gmail.com.
History May 1995. Founded following the *Global Environment Facility (GEF, #10346)* Council's decision to enhance relationships between GEF and Civil Society Organizations (CSO). Former names and other names: *GEF-NGO Network* – former; *NGO Network of the Global Environment Facility* – alias. **Aims** Safeguard the global environment through strengthening *civil society* partnership with GEF by enhancing informed participation, contributing to policy development and stimulating local action. **Structure** Coordination Committee; Management Team; Sub-Committees; Task Forces; Regional Focal Points; Indigenous People's Representatives; Secretariat. **Languages** English. **Staff** None paid. **Finance** Grant from GEF Secretariat under the NGO Voluntary Fund, of US$ 50,000. **Activities** Awareness raising; capacity building; events/meetings; knowledge management/information dissemination; networking/liaising; politics/policy/regulatory. **Publications** *GEF CSO Quarterly E-newsletter*.
Members Organizations (about 500). Membership countries not specified.
Included as members, 83 organizations listed in this Yearbook:
- *Africa Foundation for Sustainable Development (AFSD, #00174)*;
- *African Conservation Centre (ACC)*;
- *African Conservation Foundation (ACF)*;
- *African Youth Movement (AYM, #00506)*;
- *Alliance Sud, Swiss Alliance of Development Organisations Swissaid – Catholic Lenten Fund – Bread for All – Helvetas – Caritas – Interchurch Aid*;
- *Amigos do Protocolo de Kyoto (APK)*;
- *Arab NGO Network for Environment and Development (RAED, #01017)*;
- *Arab Office for Youth and Environment (AOYE)*;
- *Asia Indigenous Peoples Pact (AIPP, #01282)*;
- *Asian Institute for Development Communication (Aidcom, #01515)*;
- *Asociación Centroamericana para la Economia, la Salud y el Ambiente (ACEPESA)*;
- *Atlantic States Legal Foundation (ASLF)*;
- *Bioresources Development and Conservation Programme (BDCP)*;
- *BirdLife International (#03266)*;
- *Both ENDS (#03307)*;
- *Caribbean Conservation Association (CCA, #03481)*;
- *Caucasus Environmental NGO Network (CENN, #03613)*;
- *CESVI Fondazione*;
- *Charles Darwin Foundation for the Galapagos Islands (CDF, #03852)*;
- *Clean Air Asia (#03983)*;
- *Climate Action Network Europe (CAN Europe, #04001)*;
- *Climate Institute*;
- *Conservation International (CI)*;
- *Earth Day Network (EDN, #05164)*;
- *Energy and Resources Institute (TERI)*;
- *Environmental Foundation for Africa (EFA)*;
- *Environment Liaison Centre International (ELCI, no recent information)*;
- *Environnement et développement du Tiers-monde (enda, #05510)*;
- *Fondation internationale du Banc d'Arguin (FIBA)*;
- *Forest Peoples Programme (FPP, #09865)*;
- *Forest Stewardship Council (FSC, #09869)*;
- *Forest Trends (#09870)*;
- *Foundation of the Peoples of the South Pacific International (FSPI, #09968)*;
- *Free World Foundation (FWF)*;
- *Fundación Ecológica Universal (FEU, no recent information)*;
- *German NGO Forum on Environment and Development*;
- *Global Environmental Forum (GEF)*;
- *Global Environment Centre (GEC)*;
- *Global Greengrants Fund*;
- *Global Witness (GW)*;
- *Green Asia Network (GAN)*;
- *Gulf Research Centre*;
- *ICCA Consortium (#11041)*;
- *Institute for Development and International Relations (IRMO)*;
- *Institute for Sustainable Power (ISP)*;
- *Institute for Transportation and Development Policy (ITDP)*;
- *Instituto para el Desarrollo Sustentable en Mesoamérica, Mexico (IDESMAC)*;
- *International Centre for Environmental Social and Policy Studies (ICESPS)*;
- *International Congo Aid-Smile African Children (ICASAC)*;
- *International Council of Environmental Law (ICEL, #13018)*;
- *International Environmental Law Research Centre (IELRC)*;
- *International Fund for Animal Welfare (IFAW, #13693)*;
- *International HCH and Pesticides Association (IHPA, #13776)*;
- *International Institute for Sustainable Development (IISD, #13930)*;
- *International Network for Sustainable Energy (INFORSE, #14331)*;
- *International Pollutants Elimination Network (IPEN, #14616)*;
- *International Scientific Forum 'Danube – River of Cooperation' (ISF "DRC")*;
- *International Snow Leopard Trust (ISLT)*;
- *International Society of Doctors for the Environment (ISDE, #15065)*;
- *International Union for Conservation of Nature and Natural Resources (IUCN, #15766)*;
- *Local Governments for Sustainability (ICLEI, #16507)*;
- *MacArthur Foundation*;
- *Mediterranean Association to Save the Sea Turtles (MEDASSET, #16647)*;
- *Mercy Corps International (MCI)*;
- *New World Hope Organization (NWHO)*;
- *Organization for Industrial, Spiritual and Cultural Advancement International (OISCA International, #17872)*;
- *Pacific Gender Climate Coalition*;
- *Partnership for African Environmental Sustainability (PAES)*;
- *Peace Parks Foundation (#18281)*;
- *Public Interest Intellectual Property Advisors (PIIPA)*;
- *Rare*;
- *Regional Environmental Centre for the Caucasus (REC Caucasus, #18781)*;
- *Safeguard for Agricultural Varieties in Europe (SAVE Foundation, #19027)*;
- *SMEFUNDS (#19324)*;
- *Society for Conservation and Protection of Environment (SCOPE)*;
- *South Asian Forum for Environment (SAFE)*;
- *Swiss Foundation for Mine Action (FSD)*;
- *The Nature Conservancy (TNC)*;
- *Transparency International (TI, #20223)*;
- *United Nations Foundation (UNF, #20563)*;
- *Wildlife Conservation Society (WCS)*;
- *World Resources Institute (WRI, #21753)*;
- *World Wide Fund for Nature (WWF, #21922)*. [2022.10.25/XM4939/y/**F**]

- ♦ **GEFDU** Groupe européen des femmes diplômées des universités (#20707)
- ♦ GEFF – Groupe des entomologistes forestiers francophones (unconfirmed)
- ♦ **GEF** Global Economist Forum (#10329)
- ♦ GEF – Global Education Fund (internationally oriented national body)
- ♦ GEF – Global Environmental Forum (internationally oriented national body)
- ♦ **GEF** Global Environment Facility (#10346)
- ♦ **GEF** Global ESports Federation (#10348)
- ♦ **GEF** Green European Foundation (#10718)
- ♦ GEF-NGO Network / see GEF CSO Network (#10087)
- ♦ GE – Géomètres experts fonciers européens (inactive)
- ♦ GEIC / see Global Environmental Outreach Centre
- ♦ **GEIDCO** Global Energy Interconnection Development and Cooperation Organization (#10342)
- ♦ GEIE GECOTTI-PE – Groupement Européen pour la mise en oeuvre des Programmes de COoperation Transfrontalière, Transnationale, Interrégionale et d'autres Programmes Européens (internationally oriented national body)
- ♦ **GEIE** Groupement européen d'intérêt économique (#06960)
- ♦ GEIFON – Global Educational Initiative For Nigeria (internationally oriented national body)
- ♦ GEIP – Groupe européen indépendant de programme (inactive)

♦ GEIR 10088

Postal Address c/o SEC Newgate EU, Rue Defacqz 52, 1050 Brussels, Belgium. T. +3228954497. E-mail: info@geir-rerefining.eu.
Registered Address Av des Arts 46, 1000 Brussels, Belgium.
URL: http://www.geir-rerefining.org/
History 1969. Set up as a section of *Union Européenne de l'Industrie des Lubrifiants (UEIL, #20398)*. Former names and other names: *Groupement européen de l'industrie de la régénération des huiles usagées (GEIR)* – former; *European Re-refining Industry Section* – former; *Groupement Européen de l'Industrie de la Régénération (GEIR)* – full title; *European Re-refining Industry Section of UEIL* – alias. **Aims** Defend the interests of the re-refining industry; promote information exchange on technology trends, health, safety and environmental topics and on economic and legal aspects of the industry.
Members Full in 11 countries:
Bulgaria, Denmark, Finland, France, Germany, Greece, Italy, Portugal, Spain, Türkiye, UK. [2023.02.13/XM1590/t/**E**]

- ♦ GEIR / see GEIR (#10088)
- ♦ GEJ / see European Federation of Journalists (#07152)
- ♦ **GEKE** Gemeinschaft Evangelischer Kirchen in Europa (#04405)
- ♦ GELA – Grupo Ethnobotanico Latinoamericano (no recent information)
- ♦ GELA-IS – Groupe d'études latino-américaines de l'Institut de sociologie, Bruxelles (internationally oriented national body)
- ♦ Gelatine Manufacturers in Europe / see Gelatin Manufacturers Association of Europe (#10090)

♦ Gelatin Manufacturers Association of Asia Pacific (GMAP) 10089

Contact 15 Holt Road, Taren Point NSW 2229, Australia. E-mail: gmap@bigpond.com.
URL: http://www.gmap-gelatin.com/
History Sep 1996.
Members Manufacturers in 7 countries:
Australia, China, India, Japan, Korea Rep, New Zealand, Taiwan.
NGO Relations Cooperates with: *Gelatin Manufacturers Association of Europe (GME, #10090)*; *South American Gelatin Manufacturers Association (SAGMA, #19703)*. [2016/XD6512/**D**]

♦ Gelatin Manufacturers Association of Europe (GME) 10090

Secretariat Rue Belliard 40, 1040 Brussels, Belgium. T. +3224369459. E-mail: info@gelatine.org.
URL: http://www.gelatine.org/

History 1974, as a sector group of *Conseil européen de l'industrie chimique (CEFIC, #04687)*. Also referred to as *Gelatine Manufacturers in Europe – Association européenne de fabricants de gélatine*. Also referred to in French as: *Bureau international des gélatines*; *Bureau international technique des gélatines*. **Structure** General Assembly; Committees (4); Working Groups. **Events** *General Assembly* Madrid (Spain) 1998, *Symposium* Madrid (Spain) 1998.
Members Manufacturers (11) in 9 countries:
Belgium, France, Germany, Italy, Netherlands, Slovakia, Spain, Sweden, UK.
NGO Relations Cooperates with: *Gelatin Manufacturers Association of Asia Pacific (GMAP, #10089)*; *South American Gelatin Manufacturers Association (SAGMA, #19703)*. [2019.06.21/XE6060/**E**]

♦ GELC / see Federation of European Publishers (#09536)
♦ GEL / see European Society of Lymphology (#08643)
♦ GELF – Groupe d'Endoscopie de Langue Française (internationally oriented national body)
♦ GEM4 – Global Enterprise for Micro-Mechanics and Molecular Medicine (no recent information)
♦ GEM – African Gender and Media Initiative (internationally oriented national body)
♦ GEMDEV / see Groupement d'intérêt scientifique pour l'étude de la mondialisation et du développement
♦ GEMDEV – Groupement d'intérêt scientifique pour l'étude de la mondialisation et du développement (internationally oriented national body)
♦ Gemeenschappelijk Centrum voor Onderzoek (#16147)
♦ Gemeenschap van Verenigingen van Krantenuitgevers in de EEG / see European Newspaper Publishers' Association (#08048)
♦ Gemeinde-Netzwerk – Allianz in den Alpen / see Alliance in the Alps (#00656)
♦ Gemeinnütziger Verein zur Förderung von Micro LGBT Geschäftsinitiativen in Österreicht und Zentral- und Osteuropa / see East meets West (#05260)
♦ Gemeinsame Forschungsstelle (#16147)
♦ Gemeinsamer Güterwägenpark (inactive)
♦ Gemeinschaft Emmanuel (religious order)
♦ Gemeinschaft der Europäischen Bahnen / see Community of European Railway and Infrastructure Companies (#04396)
♦ Gemeinschaft der Europäischen Bahnen und Infrastrukturgesellschaften / see Community of European Railway and Infrastructure Companies (#04396)
♦ Gemeinschaft des Europäischen Garten- Landschafts- und Sportplatzbaues (#07642)

♦ Gemeinschaft der Europäischen Transsibirien Operateure (GETO) . . 10091

Group of European Trans-Siberian Operators and Forwarders
Secretariat c/o TransInvest Holding AG, Zwinglistr 25, 9000 St Gallen, Switzerland. T. +41712271540. Fax +4171271550.
URL: http://www.geto.ch/
History Sep 1978. Previously also referred to as *Union of European Trans-Siberian Operators and Forwarders*. **Aims** Promote international transport on Eurasian railway routes. **Structure** Assembly; Board; Secretariat. **Languages** English. **Staff** Voluntary. **Finance** Members' dues. Annual budget: about Swiss Fr 4,000.
Members Full in 4 countries:
Austria, France, Germany, Switzerland. [2018.09.06/XD7865/v/**D**]

♦ Gemeinschaft Europäischer Evangelikaler Theologen (#09727)
♦ Gemeinschaft Evangelischer Kirchen in Europa (#04405)
♦ Gemeinschaft der Kleinsten Münze (#09728)
♦ Gemeinschaftliches Sortenamt (#04404)
♦ Gemeinschaft der Seligpreisungen (religious order)
♦ Gemeinschaft Umweltfreundlichen Teppichboden (#02489)
♦ Gemeinschaft der Unabhängigen Staaten (#04341)
♦ Gemeinschaft Unserer Lieben Frau vom Wege (religious order)
♦ Gemeinschaft der Zeitungsverlegerverbände der EWG / see European Newspaper Publishers' Association (#08048)
♦ GEMELA – Grupo de Estudios sobre la Mujer en España y las Américas (pre-1800) (internationally oriented national body)
♦ Gemengde Commissie van het Wegvervoerakkoord tussen de Benelux et de Baltische Staten (no recent information)
♦ Gemensamma Forskningscentret (#16147)
♦ Gemensam Nordisk Arbetsmarknad (no recent information)
♦ Gemensamt Nordiskt Organ inom Provnings- och Kontrollområdet / see Joint Nordic Organization for Technical Testing (#16142)
♦ Gemenskapens Växtsortsmyndighet (#04404)
♦ **GEM Foundation** Global Earthquake Model Foundation (#10327)
♦ **GEM** Global Education Motivators (#10336)
♦ GEM – Global Empowerment Movement (internationally oriented national body)
♦ **GEM** Global Entrepreneurship Monitor (#10345)
♦ GEM – Global Episcopal Mission Network (internationally oriented national body)
♦ GEM – Greater Europe Mission (internationally oriented national body)
♦ GEMI – Global Environmental Management Initiative (internationally oriented national body)

♦ Gemini Observatory 10092

Exec Sec NSF Astronomical Sci, 2415 Eisenhower Avenue, Room W 9152, Alexandria VA 22314, USA. T. +17032924907. E-mail: epenteco@nsf.gov.
URL: http://www.gemini.edu/
History on signature of the *International Gemini Agreement*. Managed by (US) national association of universities and (US) National Science Foundation. **Aims** Work as an international partnership to utilize *new technology* in building *astronomical telescopes* to produce sharper views of the universe. **Structure** Board, comprising members from each of the parties to the Agreement. International Project Office, headed by Project Director. **Activities** Building twin 8.1-metre telescopes, one on Mauna Kea, Hawaii (USA), the other on Cerro Pachón (Chile), together providing complete unobstructed coverage of both the Northern and Southern skies. Telescope on Mauna Kea became operational 1999. **Events** *Science Meeting* Seoul (Korea Rep) 2021, *Conference on astrophysical ages and time scales* Hilo, HI (USA) 2001. **Publications** *GEMINI Newsletter*. **Information Services** *Gemini Science Archive* – database.
Members Parties to the agreement, 7 countries:
Argentina, Australia, Brazil, Canada, Chile, UK, USA. [2018/XF4767/**F**]

♦ GEMM – Groupement européen du mobilier métallique (no recent information)
♦ **GEMNET** Global Emergency Medical Net (#10339)
♦ GEMO – Groupe Européen d'Étude des Métastases Osseuses (internationally oriented national body)
♦ **GEMSA** Gender and Media Southern Africa Network (#10099)
♦ GEMS/Water (see: #20299)
♦ GEN / see Accademia Europea di Scienza della Nutrizione (#00045)

♦ Gender5+ (G5+) 10093

Main Office Avenue d'Auderghem 322, 1040 Brussels, Belgium. E-mail: genderfive5plus@gmail.com.
URL: https://www.genderfiveplus.com/
History Also referred to as *Gender five plus*. Registration: No/ID: 0835.267.988, Start date: 7 Apr 2011, Belgium; EU Transparency Register, No/ID: 08506057684-79, Start date: 11 Jan 2012. **Aims** Promote women's rights and gender democracy from a *feminist* view point, so as to contribute to feminist vision to the process of transformation of society and European integration. **Structure** Executive Board. **Languages** English. **Staff** None paid. **Finance** Members' dues. Project income. **Activities** Activism/lobbying/activism; research/documentation; events/meetings. **IGO Relations** European institutions. **NGO Relations** *European Women's Lobby (EWL, #09102)*. [2020/XM5759/v/**F**]

♦ Gender Action 10094

Pres 925 H St NW, Ste 410, Washington DC 20001-4978, USA. T. +12022347722. E-mail: info@genderaction.org.
URL: http://www.genderaction.org/
History 2002. **Aims** Promote *women's* rights and gender equality and ensure women and men equally participate in and benefit from International Financial Institution (IFI) investments in developing countries. **Structure** Board of Directors; Advisory Council. **Activities** Advocacy/lobbying/activism. [2016/XM5280/**E**]

♦ **GenderCC** GenderCC – Women for Climate Justice (#10095)

♦ GenderCC – Women for Climate Justice (GenderCC) 10095

International Secretariat Anklamerstr 38, 10115 Berlin, Germany. T. +493021980088. E-mail: secretariat@gendercc.net.
Main Website: http://www.gendercc.net/
History Set up 2007, following impetus of 9th session of Conference of Parties of *United Nations Framework Convention on Climate Change (UNFCCC, 1992)*, 2003, Milan (Italy). Statutes adopted 4 Apr 2008; amended 2 July 2008. Registration: Germany. **Aims** Integrate gender justice into *climate change policy* at local, national and international levels. **Structure** General Members' Assembly; Steering Group; Board of Directors; International Secretariat. **Languages** Dutch, English, French, German, Spanish. **Publications** *GenderCC Newsletter*. Handbook; case studies; toolkit. **Consultative Status** Consultative status granted from: *ECOSOC (#05331)* (Special); *UNEP (#20299)*; *United Nations Framework Convention on Climate Change – Secretariat (UNFCCC, #20564)*. **IGO Relations** Accredited by (1): *Green Climate Fund (GCF, #10714)*. **NGO Relations** Member of (2): *Global Gender and Climate Alliance (GGCA, no recent information)*; Klima Allianz Deutschland. [2022.10.12/XJ9082/y/**C**]

♦ Gender Concerns International (internationally oriented national body)

♦ Gender and Disaster Network (GDN) 10096

Contact School of the Built and Natural Environment, Northumbria Univ, Newcastle upon Tyne, NE1 8ST, UK. T. +441912273757 – +441912274722. E-mail: gdn@gdnonline.org.
URL: http://www.gdnonline.org/
History 1997. **Aims** Advocate for gender mainstreaming in disaster risk reduction using the World Wide Web. **Structure** Steering Group. **Finance** Supporters: Northumbria University (UK); *UNDP (#20292)*; *United Nations Office for Disaster Risk Reduction (UNDRR, #20595)*; *United States Agency for International Development (USAID)*; USDA; *Swiss Agency for Development and Cooperation (SDC)*; *UN Women (#20724)* – South Asia. **Activities** Awards/prizes/competitions; knowledge management/information dissemination; advocacy/lobbying/activism. **NGO Relations** Member of: *Global Gender and Climate Alliance (GGCA, no recent information)*. [2015/XJ9419/**F**]

♦ Gender Equality Advisory Council (unconfirmed)
♦ Gender five plus / see Gender5+ (#10093)

♦ Gendering Asia Network 10097

Address not obtained.
URL: https://genderingasia.net/
History 2005. **Aims** Strengthen research and teaching on gender and Asia in the Nordic countries by facilitating contacts both internally among Nordic scholars and students, and also externally between *academia* in the *Nordic* countries and our counterparts in Asia and elsewhere in the world. **Structure** Steering Group. Coordinated by *NIAS-Nordisk Institut for Asienstudier (NIAS, #17132)*. **Activities** Networking/liaising; research/documentation; events/meetings. **Publications** *Gendering Asia Book Series*. [2016/XM8488/**F**]

♦ **GenderInSITE** Gender in science, innovation, technology and engineering (#10100)

♦ Gender Links (GL) 10098

CEO 9 Derrick Avenue, Cyrildene, Johannesburg, 2198, South Africa. T. +27116222877. Fax +27116224732. E-mail: execassistant@genderlinks.org.za.
Exec Dir address not obtained.
URL: http://www.genderlinks.org.za/
History 2001. Full title: *Gender Links for equality and justice*. Registered in accordance with South African law. **Aims** Work towards a region in which women and men are able to participate equally in all aspects of public and private life in accordance with the provisions of the Southern African Development Community (SADC) Protocol on Gender and Development. **Structure** Board of Directors, comprising Chairperson, Deputy Chairperson and 8 members. **Staff** 55.00 FTE, paid. **Activities** Coordinates *Southern Africa Gender Protocol Alliance (#19830)*.
Members Full in 15 countries:
Angola, Botswana, Congo DR, Eswatini, Lesotho, Madagascar, Malawi, Mauritius, Mozambique, Namibia, Seychelles, South Africa, Tanzania UR, Zambia, Zimbabwe.
IGO Relations *Southern African Development Community (SADC, #19843)*. [2015/XJ7287/**D**]

♦ Gender Links for equality and justice / see Gender Links (#10098)

♦ Gender and Media Southern Africa Network (GEMSA) 10099

Chair Gender Links, 9 Derrick Avenue, Cnr Marcia Avenue, Cyrildene, Johannesburg, 2198, South Africa. T. +27116226597. Fax +27116228674.
Aims Promote the mainstreaming of gender in the Southern African media as integral to the advocacy for freedom of expression, a free and independent media and for the development of democratic societies in the region. **Structure** General Meeting (every 2 years). Executive Committee, including Chairman, Deputy Chairman, Secretary and Treasurer. **Finance** Subscriptions.
Members Individuals and organizations in 13 countries:
Angola, Botswana, Eswatini, Lesotho, Malawi, Mauritius, Mozambique, Namibia, Seychelles, South Africa, Tanzania UR, Zambia, Zimbabwe.
Included in the above, 2 organizations listed in this Yearbook:
Federation of African Media Women (FAMW, no recent information); *Media Institute of Southern Africa (MISA, #16619)*. [2009/XM1960/**F**]

♦ Gender in science, innovation, technology and engineering (GenderInSITE) 10100

Secretariat c/o OWSD Secretariat, ICTP Campus, Adriatico Guesthouse, 7th floor, 34151 Trieste TS, Italy. E-mail: info@genderinsite.net.
URL: http://genderinsite.net/
Aims Inspire transformative actions and more effective development by understanding the impacts of science, innovation, technology and engineering (SITE) on *women* and men and how women and men can contribute to SITE. **Structure** Steering Committee; 2 Co-Chairs; Secretariat. Regional offices in: Argentina; Kenya; South Africa. **Finance** Support from: *Swedish International Development Cooperation Agency (Sida)*. **IGO Relations** *Latin American Faculty of Social Sciences (#16316)*; *UNESCO (#20322)*. [2016.06.28/XM4149/**F**]

♦ Gender Summit 10101

Contact c/o Portia, 9 Bonhill Street, London, EC2A 4DJ, UK. T. +442073675348. E-mail: team@gender-summit.com.
URL: http://gender-summit.com/
History 2011, originally as part of the *genSET* project. Full title: *Gender Summit – Quality Research and Innovation through Equality*. **Aims** Create regional and global multi-stakeholder communities committed to enhancing scientific excellence by: removing gender bias from science knowledge making; advancing gender equality in science structures and practices; and applying understanding of gender issues to advance more sustainable and effective research and innovation. **Structure** Steering Committee. **Activities** Events/meetings. **Events** *Gender Summit* Munich (Germany) 2021, *Gender Summit – Latin America and the Caribbean* Brazil 2020, *Gender Summit Africa* Nairobi (Kenya) 2020, *Gender Summit Asia Pacific* Seoul (Korea Rep) 2020, *Gender Summit Europe* Amsterdam (Netherlands) 2019. [2017/XM6315/c/**F**]

♦ Gender Summit – Quality Research and Innovation through Equality / see Gender Summit (#10101)

♦ Gender and Water Alliance (GWA) 10102

Alliance Genre et Eau – Alianza de Género y Agua – Aliança de Gênero e Agua

Exec Dir Hogestraat 20, 6953 AT Dieren, Netherlands. T. +31313427230. E-mail: secretariat@gwalliance.org.

URL: http://www.genderandwater.org/

History Mar 2000, The Hague (Netherlands). Established during 2nd World Water Forum, organized by *World Water Council (WWC, #21908)*. **Aims** Promote women's and men's equitable access to, and management of, safe and adequate water for domestic supply, sanitation, food security and environmental sustainability. **Structure** Steering Committee; Secretariat. **Languages** Arabic, English, French, Portuguese, Spanish. **Finance** Independently funded. **Activities** Advocacy/lobbying/activism; knowledge management/information dissemination; training/education. **Publications** Various publications available on website. **Members** Individuals (45% men, 55% women) and organizations (over 2,000) in 130 countries. Membership countries not specified. **Consultative Status** Consultative status granted from: *UNEP (#20299)*. **IGO Relations** Partners: *UNDP (#20292)*; *United Nations Human Settlements Programme (UN-Habitat, #20572)*. Partner of: *UN-Water (#20723)*. Accredited organization of: *Green Climate Fund (GCF, #10714)*. **NGO Relations** Member of: *End Water Poverty (EWP, #05464)*; *Global Gender and Climate Alliance (GGCA, no recent information)*; *Network for Capacity Building in Integrated Water Resources Management (CAP-Net, #17000)*; *Sustainable Sanitation Alliance (SuSanA, #20066)*. Partners include: *Both ENDS (#03307)*; *Global Water Partnership (GWP, #10653)*; *International Water Management Institute (IWMI, #15867)*; *International Waters Learning Exchange and Resource Network (IW-LEARN, #15873)*; *IRC (#16016)*; *Latin American Water Education and Training Network (LA-WETNET, #16393)*; *Water, Engineering and Development Centre (WEDC)*. [2020.09.12/XM0973/**B**]

- ♦ Geneeskunde voor de Derde Wereld (internationally oriented national body)
- ♦ GEN-E / see Global Ecovillage Network – Europe (#10332)
- ♦ **GENE** Global Education Network Europe (#10337)
- ♦ General Act of Arbitration: Pacific Settlement of International Disputes (1928 treaty)
- ♦ General Act of Conciliation, Arbitration and Judicial Settlement (1929 treaty)
- ♦ General Act Relative to African Slave Trade, 1885 (1885 treaty)
- ♦ General Agreement on Economic Regulations for International Road Transport (1954 treaty)
- ♦ General Agreement on Privileges and Immunities of the Council of Europe (1949 treaty)
- ♦ General Agreement on Tariffs and Trade (inactive)
- ♦ General Agreement on Tariffs and Trade, 1947 (1947 treaty)
- ♦ General Agreement on Tariffs and Trade, 1994 (1994 treaty)
- ♦ General Agreement on Trade in Services (1994 treaty)

♦ General Anthroposophical Society 10103

Société anthroposophique universelle – Allgemeine Anthroposophische Gesellschaft

Contact Goetheanum, Rüttiweg 45, 4143 Dornach SO 1, Switzerland. T. +41617064242. Fax +41617064314. E-mail: sekretariat@goetheanum.org.

URL: http://www.goetheanum.org/

History 24 Dec 1923, Dornach, (Switzerland). Derived from *Anthroposophical Society (inactive)*, set up in 1913. Legal entity of *School of Spiritual Science (#19134)*. Current constitution amended 23 Mar 2002, 15 Mar 2008, 16 Apr 2011 and 12 Apr 2014. Registered in accordance with Swiss Civil Code. **Aims** Make a spiritually based contribution to the life of humanity in the world of today and tomorrow. **Structure** General Meeting; Executive Council; Board of Trustees. **Finance** Members' dues. Donations. **Activities** Training/education; events/meetings; knowledge management/information dissemination. **Events** *General Meeting* Germany 1994. **Publications** *Anthroposophy Worldwide* (12 a year) – newsletter; *Das Goetheanum* (52 a year). Financial report.

Members Societies in 51 countries:

Argentina, Australia, Austria, Belgium, Brazil, Bulgaria, Canada, Chile, Colombia, Croatia, Czechia, Denmark, Ecuador, Egypt, Estonia, Finland, France, Georgia, Germany, Hungary, Iceland, India, Ireland, Israel, Italy, Japan, Latvia, Lithuania, Mexico, Namibia, Netherlands, New Zealand, Norway, Peru, Philippines, Poland, Portugal, Romania, Russia, Serbia, Slovakia, Slovenia, South Africa, Spain, Sweden, Switzerland, Thailand, UK, Ukraine, Uruguay, USA. [2016.06.22/XF0986/v/**F**]

♦ General Arab Insurance Federation (GAIF) 10104

Union générale arabe d'assurance (UGAA)

SG 10 Iran St Dokki, Giza, 11511, Egypt. E-mail: gaif@gaif.org.

Branch 8 Kasr El Nil St, Cairo, 11511, Egypt.

URL: http://www.gaif.org/

History 2 Sep 1964, Cairo (Egypt). Founded by *Council of Arab Economic Unity (CAEU, #04859)*. Former names and other names: *Fédération générale arabe d'assurance (FGAA)* – alias. **Aims** Strengthen links between Arab insurance markets and reveal their Arab status by preparation and collection of data; promote coordination of legislation and systems in member States, and Arabization of the insurance language. **Structure** General Conference; Council (meets annually); Executive Committee; General Secretariat. **Languages** Arabic, English, French. **Staff** 14.00 FTE, paid. **Finance** Sources: fees for services; members' dues; subscriptions. **Activities** Events/meetings; training/education. **Events** *General Conference* Oran (Algeria) 2022, *General Conference* Oran (Algeria) 2021, *General Conference* Hammamet (Tunisia) 2018, *General Conference* Beirut (Lebanon) 2016, *Regional Insurance Brokers Congress* Cairo (Egypt) 2015. **Publications** *GAIF Magazine* (4 a year); *GAIF Directory* (every 2 years) in Arabic, English. Meeting reports and resolutions; seminar and course papers; books.

Members Arab insurance and re-insurance companies and organizations (331) in 20 countries and territories:

Algeria, Bahrain, Egypt, Iraq, Jordan, Kuwait, Lebanon, Libya, Mauritania, Morocco, Oman, Palestine, Qatar, Saudi Arabia, Somalia, Sudan, Syrian AR, Tunisia, United Arab Emirates, Yemen.

Consultative Status Consultative status granted from: *UNCTAD (#20285)* (Special Category). [2022.10.23/XD0987/**D**]

- ♦ General Arab Women Federation (no recent information)
- ♦ General Assembly of European Students / see Association des états généraux des étudiants de l'Europe (#02495)
- ♦ General Assembly of National Olympic Committees / see Association of National Olympic Committees (#02819)

♦ General Assembly of Unitarian and Free Christian Churches 10105

Assemblée générale des églises chrétiennes libres et unitaires – Cymanfa Gyffredinol Eglwysi Undodaidd a Christnogion Rhydd

Chief Officer Unitarian Headquarters, Essex Hall, 1-6 Essex Street, London, WC2R 3HY, UK. T. +442072402384. E-mail: info@unitarian.org.uk.

URL: http://www.unitarian.org.uk/

History Founded 1928, by amalgamation of the British and Foreign Unitarian Association, set up in 1825, and the National Conference of Unitarian, Liberal Christian, Free Christian, Presbyterian and other Non-Subscribing or Kindred Congregations, created in 1881. Registered UK Charity Commission: 250788. **Aims** Promote a free and inquiring *religion* through the worship of God and the celebration of life, the service of humanity and respect for all creation and the upholding of liberal Christian tradition. **Structure** Annual Meeting; Executive Committee; District Associations; Member Congregations. **Languages** English, Welsh. **Staff** 9.00 FTE, paid. **Finance** Annual budget (2017/2018): income – pounds1,290,236; expenditure – pounds778,324. **Activities** Training/education; events/meetings; networking/liaising; publishing activities. **Publications** *The Inquirer* – independent periodical. Annual Report; annual directory; books; leaflets; worship packs.

Members (a) Full: (i) congregations, fellowships, representative (district) associations; (ii) ministers and lay pastors of congregations or fellowships; all Honorary Officers. (b) Associate. (c) Honorary. Affiliated member bodies in 8 countries:

Australia, Belgium, Canada, India, New Zealand, Nigeria, South Africa, USA.

NGO Relations Among affiliated societies a European body: *European Unitarian-Universalists (EUU, #09025)*. [2019.02.13/XF3526/**F**]

♦ General Association of Asia Pacific Sports Federations (GAAPSF) .. 10106

Contact No 1 Bldg, Longtanhu Sports Industry Area, 19 Zuoanmennei Ave, Dongcheng District, Beijing, China. T. +8610670930198008. E-mail: saaphbeijing@yahoo.com – chelucky@gaapsf.net.

URL: https://gaapsf.net/

History 20 Nov 2014, Macau. Former names and other names: *SportAccord Asia-Pacific Headquarters (SAAPH)* – former (2014 to 2018). **Aims** Promote friendships and sport exchanges among countries and districts of the Asia-Pacific region. **Structure** General Assembly; Executive Committee.

Members International; Continental; National. International include 37 organizations listed in this Yearbook:

- *Bukido World Federation (BWF, #03356)*;
- *Federation International Football Skating (FIFS, #09671)*;
- *International Association of Combative Sports (IACS, #11789)*;
- *International Council of Sqay (ICS)*;
- *International Diabolo Association (IDA, #13166)*;
- *International Kempo Federation (IKF, #13981)*;
- *International Pacific Sports Federation (IPSF)*;
- *International Parkour Federation (IPF, #14516)*;
- *International Pole Dance Fitness Association (IPDFA, #14609)*;
- *International Taekwon-do Forum (ITF)*;
- *Pole Sports & Arts World Federation (POSA, #18414)*;
- *Takeonejetsu Martial Arts World Federation*;
- *World Aerial Sports & Arts Federation (WAS&AF, #21071)*;
- *World Association of Majorette-sport and Twirling (WAMT)*;
- *World Boxing League (WBL)*;
- *World Budo Martial Arts Federation*;
- *World Dodgeball Association (WDA, #21365)*;
- *World Esports Consortium (WESCO, #21391)*;
- *World Ethnosport Society (#21392)*;
- *World Freerunning Parkour Federation (WFPF)*;
- *World Futsal Association (#21532)*;
- *World Hatha Yog Federation (#21554)*;
- *World Heavy Events Association (WHEA)*;
- *World Inclusive Dance Association (WIDA)*;
- *World Kabaddi Federation (WKF, #21606)*;
- *World Kettlebell Sport Federation (WKSF)*;
- *World Kickboxing League (WKL)*;
- *World Ninja Federation (WNF)*;
- *World O-Sport Federation (WOF, #21700)*;
- *World Pacific Sports Federation (WPSF)*;
- *World Rope Skipping Federation (WRSF)*;
- *World Silambam Association (WSA)*;
- *World Slingshot Sports Federation (WSSF, #21794)*;
- *World Sport Council (WCS)*;
- *World Strongmen Federation (WSF, #21832)*;
- *World Wellness Weekend (WWW)*;
- *World Yoga Association*.

National organizations in 22 countries and territories:

Afghanistan, Brazil, Colombia, Gambia, Hong Kong, India, Iran Islamic Rep, Italy, Macau, Malaysia, Malta, Nigeria, Pakistan, Poland, Portugal, Russia, Sierra Leone, Singapore, Spain, Switzerland, Taiwan, United Arab Emirates.

Continental organizations include 16 listed in this Yearbook:

Asia and Pacific Jump Rope Federation (APJRF, #01938); *Asia Diabolo Association (ADA)*; *Asia Freerunning Parkour Union (AFPU)*; *Asian Bodybuilding and Physique Sports Federation (ABBF, #01361)*; *Asian Bukido Federation (ABF)*; *Asian Draughts Confederation (ADC, #01432)*; *Asian O-Sport Federation (AOSF)*; *Asian Pencak Silat Federation (APSIF, #01660)*; *Asian Pickleball Federation (APF, #01665)*; *Asian Traditional Sports and Games Association (ATSGA)*; *Asian Weightlifting Federation (AWF, #01781)*; *European Boxing League (EBL)*; *Judo Union of Asia (JUA, #16162)*; *Pan American Electronic Sports Confederation (PAMESCO, #18096)*; *Silambam Asia (#19276)*; *Sqay Organization of Asia (SOA, #19932)*.

NGO Relations Partner of (11): *Asian Weightlifting Federation (AWF, #01781)*; *International Association of Combative Sports (IACS, #11789)*; *International Judo Federation (IJF, #13975)* (and its academy); *International Mind Sports Association (IMSA, #14164)*; *International Sport Network Organization (ISNO, #15592)*; *International Sport Organization (ISO)*; *International Weightlifting Federation (IWF, #15876)*; *International Wushu Federation (IWUF, #15918)*; *Judo Union of Asia (JUA, #16162)*; *World Bodybuilding and Physique Sports Federation (WBPF, #21237)*; *World Hatha Yog Federation (#21554)*. [2023.02.28/XM7392/y/**C**]

- ♦ General Association of Retired Volunteers (internationally oriented national body)
- ♦ General Association of Retired Volunteers for Cooperation and Development / see Association générale des intervenants retraités
- ♦ General Aviation Manufacturers Association (internationally oriented national body)
- ♦ General Baptist Foreign Mission Society (internationally oriented national body)
- ♦ General Baptist International Missions / see General Baptist Foreign Mission Society
- ♦ General Board of Christian Social Concerns / see General Board of Church and Society of the United Methodist Church
- ♦ General Board of Church and Society of the United Methodist Church (internationally oriented national body)
- ♦ General Board of Global Ministries / see Global Ministries of The United Methodist Church
- ♦ General Committee of Agricultural Cooperation in the EU / see General Confederation of Agricultural Cooperatives in the European Union (#10107)
- ♦ General Committee of Agricultural Cooperation in the European Community / see General Confederation of Agricultural Cooperatives in the European Union (#10107)
- ♦ General Committee of the Student Press (inactive)

♦ General Confederation of Agricultural Cooperatives in the European Union 10107

Confédération générale des coopératives agricoles de l'Union européenne (COGECA) – Confederación General de las Cooperativas Agrarias de la Unión Europea – Allgemeiner Verband der Landwirtschaftlichen Genossenschaften der Europäischen Union – Confederazione Generale delle Cooperative Agricole dell'Unione Europea

SG Rue de Trèves, 61, 1040 Brussels, Belgium. T. +3222872711. Fax +3222872700. E-mail: mail@copa-cogeca.eu.

URL: http://www.copa-cogeca.eu/

History 24 Sep 1959, The Hague (Netherlands). Secretariat merged with that of COPA on 1 Dec 1962. Integrated activities of *European Confederation of Agriculture (CEA, inactive)* with *COPA – european farmers (COPA, #04829)*, Jul 2006. Former names and other names: *General Committee of Agricultural Cooperation in the European Community* – former (1959); *Comité général de la coopération agricole de la Communauté européenne* – former (1959); *Allgemeiner Ausschuss des Ländlichen Genossenschaftswesens der Europäischen Gemeinschaft* – former (1959); *Comitato Generale della Cooperazione Agricola della Comunità Europea* – former (1959); *Specialized Committee on Fertilizers and Pesticides of Agricultural Cooperatives in the EEC Countries* – former; *Comité spécialisé des coopératives agricoles des pays de la CEE pour les engrais et pesticides* – former; *General Committee of Agricultural Cooperation in the EU* – former; *Comité général de la coopération agricole de l'UE (COGECA)* – former; *Allgemeiner Ausschuss des Ländlichen Genossenschaftswesens der EU* – former; *Comitato Generale della Cooperazione Agricola dell' UE* – former; *COGECA – european agri-cooperatives* – alias. Registration: Banque-Carrefour des Entreprises, No/ID: 0840.367.022, Start date: 18 Oct 2011, Belgium; EU Transparency Register, No/ID: 09586631237-74, Start date: 25 Feb 2009. **Aims** Represent the general and specific interests of the agricultural cooperative movement in discussions with EU institutions and other communities and bodies; undertake legal, economic, financial, social or other studies of concern to agricultural and *fisheries* cooperatives, in particular those illustrating the particular nature of agricultural and fisheries cooperatives as compared with non-cooperative enterprises, to the EU authorities and public opinion, and thus contribute to development of cooperative *enterprises* in general; promote contacts and cooperation between agricultural and fisheries cooperatives in EU countries and support and coordinate activities of organizations working in different spheres of agricultural cooperation in EC by creating or affiliating specialist committees; ensure liaison with COPA and any other organizations working in the agricultural or other economic or social fields, either at EU or at European and world level. **Structure** Conference (every 2 years), comprising representatives delegated by member organizations, associated and partner organizations. Praesidium is the highest decision-making body and consists of up to 3 representatives of each full member. Presidency; Liaison / Joint instruments with COPA: Coordination Committee; Finance and

Management Committee; Secretariat; Joint Working Parties. **Languages** English, French, German, Italian, Polish, Romanian, Spanish. **Staff** Permanent staff of the joint COPA/COGECA Secretariat: about 50. **Finance** Sources: members' dues. **Activities** Advocacy/lobbying/activism; events/meetings; politics/policy/regulatory. **Events** *Congress of European Farmers* Sibenik (Croatia) 2022, *Congress of European Farmers* Linz (Austria) 2018, *Conference on Availability of Animal Health Solutions for the Future of Livestock in Europe* Brussels (Belgium) 2017, *Symposium on Collecting and Sharing Data on Bee Health* Brussels (Belgium) 2017, *Workshop on Farmers, Forest Owners and their Cooperatives* Brussels (Belgium) 2017. **Publications** Fact sheets; position papers; press releases; congress brochure.
Members Full – national organizations (35) representing about 40,000 farmers' cooperatives in 26 EU countries:
Austria, Belgium, Cyprus, Czechia, Denmark, Estonia, Finland, France, Germany, Greece, Hungary, Ireland, Italy, Latvia, Lithuania, Luxembourg, Malta, Netherlands, Poland, Portugal, Romania, Slovakia, Slovenia, Spain, Sweden, UK.
Affiliate national organizations (4) in 3 countries:
France, Netherlands, Spain.
IGO Relations Liaises with: *European Committee of the Regions (CoR, #06665)*; *European Economic and Social Committee (EESC, #06963)*. *European Parliament (EP, #08146)*. Observer status with: *Intergovernmental Negotiating Committee for a Legally Binding Agreement on Forests in Europe (INC-Forests, inactive)*; *Union internationale pour la protection des obtentions végétales (UPOV, #20436)*. **NGO Relations** Member of (8): *Agri-Food Chain Coalition (AFCC, #00577)*; *Alliance for Internet of Things Innovation (AIOTI, #00697)*; *Circular Plastics Alliance (#03936)*; *Cooperatives Europe (#04801)*; *European Bioeconomy Alliance (EUBA, #06334)*; *European Technology Platform 'Plants for the Future' (Plant ETP, #08890)*; *TP Organics – European Technology Platform (TP Organics, #20180)*; *Water Europe (WE, #20828)*. Founding Member of: *European Food Sustainable Consumption and Production Round Table (European Food SCP Roundtable, #07289)*. Associate member of: *European Network of Agricultural Journalists (ENAJ, #07864)*. Observer to: *Wine in Moderation (WIM, #20967)*. Working relations with: *Intercoop Europe (ICE, #11464)*. Maintains contact with different EU cooperative organizations: *OITS/ European Commission for Social Tourism (CETS, #17713)*; *European Community of Consumer Cooperatives (EURO COOP, #06678)*; *Union européenne des Pharmacies sociales (UEPS, #20401)*. [2022.02.02/XE0989/**E**]

♦ General Confederation of Trade Unions (GCTU) 10108

Confédération générale des syndicats (CGS) – Vseobscaja Konfederacija Profsojuzov (VKP)
Gen Sec Leninsky Prospekt 42, Moscow MOSKVA, Russia, 119119. T. +74959380112. Fax +74959382155. E-mail: mail@vkp.ru – inter@vkp.ru.
URL: http://www.vkp.ru/
History 16 Apr 1992, Moscow (Russia). Founded at first congress, when constitution was approved. An international trade union organization reformed from the General Confederation of Trade Unions of the USSR, following recommendations, Mar 1992, by trade union organizations of *Commonwealth of Independent States (CIS, #04341)*. Constitution amended: 22 Sep 1993, at 2nd Congress; 18 Sep 1997, at 3rd Congress; 26 Mar 2004, at 5th Extraordinary congress. **Aims** Consolidate members' action in defence of rights of the employed, of youth in training and of pensioners, in the areas of *labour relations* and of professional, socio-economic and spiritual interests; promote protection of rights and guarantees for trade union activity; develop international trade union solidarity; support affiliates' bargaining campaign policies and international activities. **Structure** Congress (at least every 5 years) always in Moscow (Russia); Council; Executive Committee; Commissions (6). **Languages** Russian. **Staff** 50.00 FTE, paid. **Finance** Members' dues. **Activities** Guidance/assistance/consulting. **Events** *International conference* Moscow (Russia) 1996, *Congress* Moscow (Russia) 1993, *International trade union conference on social aspects of military conversion* Moscow (Russia) 1993, *Congress* Moscow (Russia) 1992. **Publications** *Vestnik Profsojuzov* (12 a year) in Russian; *Profsojuzi* (12 a year) in Russian; *Inform-Contact* (4 a year) in English, French.
Members National trade union centers in 10 countries:
Armenia, Azerbaijan, Belarus, Georgia, Kazakhstan, Kyrgyzstan, Moldova, Russia, Tajikistan, Ukraine.
Industry-based regional and international trade unions (27):
- *Confederation of Unions of Workers in Commerce, Restaurants, Consumers' Cooperatives and Various Forms of Business (#04577)*;
- *Consultative Council of Cultural Workers' Unions (CCCWU, #04766)*;
- *Federation of Mining and Metallurgical Workers' Unions of the Commonwealth of Independent States (#09687)*;
- *Federation of Timber and Related Industries Workers' Unions of the Commonwealth of Independent States (#09708)*;
- *International Amalgamation of Unions of Automobile and Farm Machinery Workers (IAUAFMW, #11644)*;
- *International Association of Chemical and Allied Industries Workers' Trade Unions (#11763)*;
- *International Association of Civil Aviation Workers' Unions (#11775)*;
- *International Association of Fishing Industry Workers' Unions (#11893)*;
- *International Association of Textile and Light Industry Workers' Unions (#12224)*;
- *International Association of Trade Unions of Workers in Scientific Research and Production Cooperatives and Enterprises (#12234)*;
- *International Community of Defence Industry Workers' Unions (ICDIWU, #12823)*;
- *International Confederation of Construction and Building Materials Industry Workers' Unions (#12853)*;
- *International Confederation of Health Workers' Unions (#12861)*;
- *International Confederation of Joint Venture Workers' Unions (#12862)*;
- *International Confederation of Railway Workers' and Transport Builders' Unions (#12869)*;
- *International Confederation of Trade Unions of Workers in the Oil and Gas Industries, and Construction Workers in the Oil and Gas Complex (#12872)*;
- *International Confederation of Water Transport Workers' Unions (ICWTWU, #12873)*;
- *International Federation of State and Public Employees (no recent information)*;
- *International Organisation of Agro-Industrial Trade Unions (#14422)*;
- *International Organisation of Communications Workers' Unions (#14425)*;
- *International Organisation of Metalworkers' Unions (#14431)*;
- *International Organisation of Trade Unions of Educational and Scientific Workers (IOTU Education and Science, #14434)*;
- *International Trade Union Alliance of Public Utilities, Local Industry and Services Workers (#15707)*;
- *International Trade Union "Elektroprofsoyuz" (Electrounion, #15710)*;
- *Interstate Federation of Atomic Energy Workers' Unions (#15980)*;
- Russian Trade Union of Radio and Electronic Workers;
- *Trade Union International of Workers in Geology, Geodesy and Cartography (#20189)*.

Consultative Status Consultative status granted from: *ECOSOC (#05331)* (Special); *ILO (#11123)* (Regional Status). [2014.06.19/XD3215/t/**D**]

♦ General Conference of the New Church (inactive)

♦ General Conference of Seventh-Day Adventists (SDA) 10109

Conférence générale des adventistes du septième jour – Asociación General de Adventistas del Séptimo Dia – General Konferenz der Siebenten-Tags-Adventisten – Associação Geral dos Adventistas do Sétimo Dia – Sjundedags Adventisternas Generalkonferens
Pres and Headquarters 12501 Old Columbia Pike, Silver Spring MD 20904, USA. T. +13016806000. E-mail: media@contact.adventist.org.
Main Website: https://gc.adventist.org/
History Founded in North America, the denominational name and basic organization having been adopted between 1860 and 1863. First European Conference: 1880, Denmark. **Aims** Proclaim to all peoples the everlasting gospel in the context of the three angels' messages of Revelation 14 6-12. **Structure** General Conference Session (every 5 years); General Executive Committee; Standing Committees. **Languages** 525. **Staff** 321410.00 FTE, paid. **Finance** Sources: tithe and offerings. **Activities** Covers: educational institutions from primary to university level; health and medical institutions; media centres; publishing houses; youth organizations; welfare activities. International services: *Adventist Development and Relief Agency International (ADRA, #00131)*; *Adventist World Radio (see: #10109)*. **Events** *Quinquennial World Conference* St Louis, MO (USA) 2022, *Quinquennial World Conference* Indianapolis, IN (USA) 2020, *Quinquennial World Conference* San Antonio, TX (USA) 2015, *Southern Asia-Pacific convention* Bangkok (Thailand) 2013, *Quinquennial World Conference* Atlanta, GA (USA) 2010. **Publications** *Adventist Review* (weekly); *SDA Annual Statistical Report* (annual). Periodicals (551). Literature available in 368 of the working languages.
Members Organized churches (88,718) totalling 21,414,779 individual members in 198 countries and territories:
Afghanistan, Albania, Algeria, Andorra, Angola, Anguilla, Antigua-Barbuda, Argentina, Armenia, Australia, Austria, Azerbaijan, Bahamas, Bahrain, Bangladesh, Barbados, Belarus, Belgium, Belize, Benin, Bermuda, Bolivia, Bosnia-Herzegovina, Botswana, Brazil, Bulgaria, Burkina Faso, Burundi, Cambodia, Cameroon, Canada, Cayman Is, Central African Rep, Chad, Chile, China, Colombia, Congo Brazzaville, Congo DR, Cook Is, Costa Rica, Côte d'Ivoire, Croatia, Cuba, Cyprus, Denmark, Dominica, Dominican Rep, Ecuador, Egypt, El Salvador, Equatorial Guinea, Eritrea, Estonia, Eswatini, Ethiopia, Faeroe Is, Fiji, Finland, France, Gabon, Gambia, Georgia, Germany, Ghana, Gibraltar, Greece, Grenada, Guadeloupe, Guam, Guatemala, Guiana Fr, Guinea, Guinea-Bissau, Guyana, Haiti, Honduras, Hong Kong, Hungary, Iceland, India, Indonesia, Iraq, Ireland, Israel, Italy, Jamaica, Japan, Jordan, Kazakhstan, Kenya, Kiribati, Korea Rep, Kuwait, Kyrgyzstan, Laos, Latvia, Lebanon, Lesotho, Liberia, Lithuania, Luxembourg, Madagascar, Malawi, Malaysia, Mali, Malta, Marshall Is, Martinique, Mauritania, Mauritius, Mexico, Micronesia FS, Moldova, Mongolia, Montserrat, Morocco, Mozambique, Myanmar, Namibia, Nauru, Nepal, Netherlands, New Caledonia, New Zealand, Nicaragua, Niger, Nigeria, Niue, Norfolk Is, North Macedonia, Norway, Oman, Pakistan, Palau, Panama, Papua New Guinea, Paraguay, Peru, Philippines, Pitcairn, Poland, Polynesia Fr, Portugal, Puerto Rico, Qatar, Réunion, Romania, Russia, Rwanda, Samoa, Samoa USA, Sao Tomé-Principe, Senegal, Serbia, Seychelles, Sierra Leone, Singapore, Slovakia, Slovenia, Solomon Is, South Africa, Spain, Sri Lanka, St Kitts-Nevis, St Lucia, St Vincent-Grenadines, Sudan, Suriname, Sweden, Switzerland, Taiwan, Tajikistan, Tanzania UR, Thailand, Timor-Leste, Togo, Tonga, Trinidad-Tobago, Tunisia, Türkiye, Turkmenistan, Tuvalu, Uganda, UK, Ukraine, United Arab Emirates, Uruguay, USA, Uzbekistan, Vanuatu, Venezuela, Vietnam, Virgin Is UK, Virgin Is USA, Wallis-Futuna, Zambia, Zimbabwe.
Individuals where no organized church exists, in 28 countries and territories:
Afghanistan, Åland, Andorra, Bhutan, Brunei Darussalam, Comoros, Djibouti, Gibraltar, Greenland, Guernsey, Holy See, Iran Islamic Rep, Jersey, Korea DPR, Maldives, Mauritania, Monaco, Morocco, Nauru, Sahara West, San Marino, Somalia, St Barthélemy, St Pierre-Miquelon, Syrian AR, Tokelau, Wallis-Futuna, Yemen.
Consultative Status Consultative status granted from: *ECOSOC (#05331)* (Special). **IGO Relations** *WHO (#20950)*. Associated with Department of Global Communications of the United Nations. **NGO Relations** Instrumental in setting up: *Adventist International Institute of Advanced Studies (AIIAS)*; *Asian Aid Organization*; *International Family Ministries and Counseling Association (IFMCA, no recent information)*. [2020.03.31/XB0991/**B**]

♦ General Convention of Inter-American Conciliation (1929 treaty)

♦ General Council of the Assemblies of God 10110

Conseil général des assemblées de Dieu
USA Office 1445 North Boonville Ave, Springfield MO 65802, USA. T. +14178622781. E-mail: info@ag.org.
Pres Continental Theological Seminary Kasteelstraat 48, 1600 Sint-Pieters-Leeuw, Belgium. T. +3223348555. Fax +3223348559. E-mail: info@ctsem.edu.
General: http://www.ag.org/
History 12 Apr 1914, Hot Springs, AR (USA). Constitution amended: 10 Oct 1916, St Louis MO (USA); 25 Sep 1919, St Louis MO (USA); 23 Aug 1965, Greene County MO (USA). Registration: USA. **Aims** Proclaim the Word of God in accordance with apostolic teaching and practice; labour for the *evangelization* of the world through the united efforts of the various Assemblies of God. **Structure** Autonomous and independent Assemblies of God organizations or fellowships. *Assemblies of God World Ministry (AoG World Ministries, see: #10110)* of the US Assemblies of God. Also includes: *Global University (see: #10110)*. **Languages** English. **Staff** 2699.00 FTE, paid. **Finance** Voluntary offerings of church members. **Activities** Study sessions; work among drug addicts and other needy youth; correspondence courses on post-graduate, college, Christian development and evangelism levels. Operates 166 missions (Africa 52, Asia Pacific 36, Eurasia 9, Latin America and Caribbean 38). Organizes annual conferences. Set up: 1981, *International Media Ministries (IMM, see: #10110)*; *Life Publishers International*; 1981, Center for Ministry to Muslims; 1984, Healthcare Ministries; *Continental Theological Seminary (CTS)*. Instrumental in setting up: *Global Teen Challenge*; *Asia Pacific Theological Association (APTA, see: #10110)*. **Events** *Meeting* Orlando, FL (USA) 2015, *Meeting* Orlando, FL (USA) 2013, *Meeting* Phoenix, AZ (USA) 2011, *Meeting* Orlando, FL (USA) 2009, *World congress* Lisbon (Portugal) 2008. **Publications** *La Voix chrétienne* – Belgium; *Pentecostal Evangel* – USA; *Pentecôte* – France. *Aux sources de la vérité biblique* by Myer Pearlman.
Members Individual members and adherents (65,398,796). Bible Schools (1,101); Extension Programmes (874). Members in 246 countries and territories:
Albania, Algeria, Angola, Anguilla, Antigua-Barbuda, Argentina, Armenia, Aruba, Australia, Austria, Azerbaijan, Bahamas, Bahrain, Bangladesh, Barbados, Belarus, Belgium, Belize, Benin, Bhutan, Bolivia, Bonaire Is, Bosnia-Herzegovina, Botswana, Brazil, Bulgaria, Burkina Faso, Burundi, Cambodia, Cameroon, Canada, Canaries, Cape Verde, Caroline Is, Cayman Is, Central African Rep, Chad, Chile, Chuuk, Colombia, Congo DR, Cook Is, Costa Rica, Côte d'Ivoire, Croatia, Curaçao, Czechia, Denmark, Dominica, Dominican Rep, Ecuador, Egypt, El Salvador, Equatorial Guinea, Estonia, Eswatini, Ethiopia, Fiji, Finland, France, French Antilles, Gabon, Gambia, Georgia, Germany, Ghana, Greece, Greenland, Grenada, Guadeloupe, Guam, Guatemala, Guiana Fr, Guinea, Guinea-Bissau, Guyana, Haiti, Honduras, Hungary, Iceland, India, Indonesia, Ireland, Israel, Italy, Jamaica, Japan, Jordan, Kazakhstan, Kenya, Kiribati, Korea Rep, Kyrgyzstan, Latvia, Lebanon, Lesotho, Liberia, Liechtenstein, Lithuania, Luxembourg, Madagascar, Malawi, Malaysia, Maldives, Mali, Malta, Marshall Is, Martinique, Mauritius, Mexico, Micronesia FS, Moldova, Mongolia, Montenegro, Montserrat, Mozambique, Namibia, Nauru, Netherlands, New Caledonia, New Zealand, Nicaragua, Niger, Nigeria, North Macedonia, Northern Mariana Is, Norway, Palau, Panama, Papua New Guinea, Paraguay, Peru, Philippines, Pohnpei, Poland, Polynesia Fr, Portugal, Rodriguez Is, Romania, Russia, Rwanda, Samoa, Samoa USA, Sao Tomé-Principe, Senegal, Serbia, Seychelles, Sierra Leone, Singapore, Slovakia, Slovenia, Solomon Is, South Africa, South Sudan, Spain, Sri Lanka, St Kitts-Nevis, St Lucia, St Vincent-Grenadines, Suriname, Sweden, Switzerland, Syrian AR, Taiwan, Tajikistan, Tanzania UR, Thailand, Timor-Leste, Togo, Tonga, Trinidad-Tobago, Turkmenistan, Turks-Caicos, Tuvalu, Uganda, UK, Ukraine, Uruguay, USA, Uzbekistan, Vanuatu, Venezuela, Yemen, Zambia, Zimbabwe.
There are 60 countries and territories not listed above due to the sensitive nature.
NGO Relations Congo DR mission member of: *Oikocredit International (Oikocredit, #17704)*. [2021/XD4455/**F**]

♦ General Council of the International Brotherhood of Workers (inactive)

♦ General Council for Islamic Banks and Financial Institutions (CIBAFI) 10111

Contact Office 51 Bldg 657, Road 2811 Block 428, Jeera 3 Tower, PO Box 24456, Seef Area, Manama, Bahrain. T. +97317357300. Fax +97317357307. E-mail: cibafi@cibafi.org.
URL: http://www.cibafi.org/
History 16 May 2001, Bahrain, by a recommendation and support from *Organisation of Islamic Cooperation (OIC, #17813)*, as the official umbrella for all Islamic financial institutions. Original title: *Council of Islamic Banks and Financial Institutions*. **Aims** Support Islamic financial services industry. **Structure** General Assembly; Board of Directors; Executive Committee; Secretariat. **Languages** Arabic, English. **Staff** 15.00 FTE, paid. **Activities** Politics/policy/regulatory; advocacy/lobbying/activism; research and development; awareness raising; knowledge management/information dissemination. **Publications** *CIBAFI InFocus Newsletter*. Activity reports; surveys; briefings. **Members** Over 120 members in 32 jurisdictions. Membership countries not specified. **IGO Relations** Affiliated institution of: *Organisation of Islamic Cooperation (OIC, #17813)*. [2017.10.12/XM2761/**E**]

♦ General Court of the European Communities (inactive)
♦ General Da'ud / see East Africa Consortium International
♦ General Directorate for Cooperation with Africa, Asia and Eastern Europe (internationally oriented national body)
♦ General Directorate for Cooperation with Latin America / see Dirección General de Cooperación con Iberoamérica
♦ General Federation of Arab Journalists / see Federation of Arab Journalists (#09422)
♦ General Federation of Arab Veterinarians (inactive)
♦ General Federation of Women's Clubs (internationally oriented national body)

♦ General Fisheries Commission for the Mediterranean (GFCM) 10112

Commission générale des pêches pour la Méditerranée (CGPM) – Comisión General de Pesca del Mediterraneo (CGPM)
Exec Sec Palazzo Blumenstihl, Via Vittoria Colonna 1, 00166 Rome RM, Italy. T. +39657055730. Fax +39657055827.
URL: http://www.fao.org/gfcm/
History 20 Feb 1952, Rome (Italy). Established under the provisions of Article XIV of the *FAO (#09260)* Constitution, and the Agreement for its establishment came into force, approved at the fifth session of the FAO Conference, 1949. Amendments to the Agreement approved: 22 May 1963, Rome; 1 Jul 1976, Rome; 16 Oct 1997, Rome; 20 May 2014, Rome. In 2011, launched process aiming to modernize the legal and institutional

framework, including a fourth amendment to the Constitutive Agreement. Former names and other names: *General Fisheries Council for the Mediterranean* – former; *Conseil général des pêches pour la Méditerranée* – former; *Consejo General de Pesca del Mediterraneo* – former. **Aims** Ensure *conservation* and sustainable use, at biological, social, economic and environmental levels, of living *marine resources* as well as sustainable development of aquaculture in the Mediterranean and the *Black Sea*. **Structure** Commission' sessions (annual); Bureau; Committees (4); Working Group; Secretariat located in Rome (Italy). **Languages** Arabic, English, French, Spanish. **Staff** 20.00 FTE, paid. **Finance** Autonomous budget: US$ 2,200,000. **Activities** Politics/policy/regulatory; monitoring/evaluation; research and development; knowledge management/information dissemination; advocacy/lobbying/activism; standards/guidelines; guidance/assistance/consulting. **Events** *Meeting* Madrid (Spain) 2016, *Session* Marrakech (Morocco) 2015, *Session* Milan (Italy) 2015, *Statutory Session of the Scientific and Advisory Committee* Rome (Italy) 2015, *Statutory Session of the Commission* Rome (Italy) 2014. **Publications** *The State of Mediterranean and Black Sea Fisheries* (every 2 years). *GFCM Studies and Reviews* – series. *Fisheries and Aquaculture Proceedings*. Session reports; brochures; technical papers.

Members Contracting Parties (24):
Albania, Algeria, Bulgaria, Croatia, Cyprus, Egypt, France, Greece, Israel, Italy, Japan, Lebanon, Libya, Malta, Monaco, Montenegro, Morocco, Romania, Slovenia, Spain, Syrian AR, Tunisia, Türkiye.
European Union (EU, #08967).
Cooperating non-Contracting Parties (2):
Georgia, Ukraine.
NGO Relations Also links with national associations. [2018.10.03/XE0994/y/**E***]

- ♦ General Fisheries Council for the Mediterranean / see General Fisheries Commission for the Mediterranean (#10112)
- ♦ General Forum of the Arabic and African Nongovernmental Organizations (unconfirmed)
- ♦ General Grand Chapter, Order of the Eastern Star (internationally oriented national body)
- ♦ General Grand Chapter of Royal Arch Masons / see General Grand Chapter of Royal Arch Masons International
- ♦ General Grand Chapter of Royal Arch Masons International (internationally oriented national body)
- ♦ General Inter-American Convention for Trade Mark and Commercial Protection (1929 treaty)
- ♦ General Konferenz der Siebenten-Tags-Adventisten (#10109)
- ♦ General Postal Union / see Universal Postal Union (#20682)
- ♦ General Secretariat of Abstaining Socialists (inactive)
- ♦ General Secretariat of Arab Red Crescent and Red Cross Societies / see Arab Red Crescent and Red Cross Organization (#01033)
- ♦ Generals for Peace and Disarmament / see Strategies for Peace (#20008)
- ♦ General Treaty on Central American Economic Integration, 1960 (1960 treaty)
- ♦ General Treaty on Central American Economic Integration, 1968 (1968 treaty)
- ♦ General Treaty of Inter-American Arbitration (1929 treaty)
- ♦ General Treaty of Peace and Amity, 1907 (1907 treaty)
- ♦ General Treaty of Peace and Amity, 1923 (1923 treaty)
- ♦ General Treaty of Peace and Friendship, Arbitration and Commerce (1906 treaty)
- ♦ General Treaty for the Redemption of the Schelde Tolls (1863 treaty)
- ♦ General Treaty for Renunciation of War as an Instrument of National Policy (1928 treaty)
- ♦ General Union of Arab Artists (inactive)
- ♦ General Union of Arab Peasants and Agricultural Cooperatives (no recent information)
- ♦ General Union of Arab Publishers (no recent information)
- ♦ General Union of Arab Students (no recent information)
- ♦ General Union of Chambers of Commerce, Industry and Agriculture for Arab Countries / see Union of Arab Chambers (#20350)
- ♦ General Union of Students of West Africa (inactive)
- ♦ General Union of Workers of Black Africa (inactive)
- ♦ Generalversammlung der Nationalen Olympischen Komittees / see Association of National Olympic Committees (#02819)

♦ Generation 112 (G112) 10113

Génération 112

Contact address not obtained. E-mail: remi.praud@generation112.eu – contact@generation112.eu.
SG address not obtained.
URL: http://www.generation112.eu/

History Aug 2009. Registered in accordance with French law. **Aims** Make Euro-*democracy* more concrete; play a role in the creation of a *European* public sphere, including politics, media, civil society and public opinion. **Structure** General Assembly. Board of Executives of 8 members. Administrative Board. Officers: President; Vice-President; Secretary General. **Members** Membership countries not specified. **NGO Relations** Partner of: *European Association for the Defence of Human Rights (AEDH, no recent information)*. [2012/XJ4725/**E**]

- ♦ Génération 112 (#10113)

♦ Generation Climate Europe (GCE) 10114

Contact address not obtained.
URL: https://gceurope.org/

History A coalition of youth-led organizations and networks. EU Transparency Register: 021591837250-68. **Aims** Empower *young* Europeans to advocate for stronger action on *climate change* and *environmental* issues. **Languages** English. **Activities** Advocacy/lobbying/activism.

Members Organizations (8):
Association des états généraux des étudiants de l'Europe (AEGEE-Europe, #02495); CliMates; *Erasmus Student Network (ESN, #05529)*; *European Students' Union (ESU, #08848)*; *International Federation of Catholic Parochial Youth Movements (#13379)*; *International Young Nature Friends (IYNF, #15929)*; *Organising Bureau of European School Student Unions (OBESSU, #17829)*; *Youth and Environment Europe (YEE, #22012)*. [2021/XM8848/**E**]

♦ Generation IV International Forum (GIF) 10115

Contact c/o OECD Nuclear Energy Agency, 46 quai Alphonse Le Gallo, 92100 Boulogne-Billancourt, France. E-mail: secretariat@gen-4.org.
URL: http://www.gen-4.org/

History Chartered Jul 2001; Extension signed 2011. Framework Agreement signed 2005 and registered with *United Nations (UN, #20515)* Secretariat in accordance with Article 102 of the Chart of the United Nations under No 50254 Multilateral; Extension signed Feb 2015. **Aims** Lead the collaborative efforts of leading *nuclear* technology nations to develop next-generation nuclear energy systems to meet the world's future *energy* needs. **Structure** Policy Group; System Steering Committee; Experts Group; Methodology Working Groups; Project Management Boards; Policy Secretariat. *Nuclear Energy Agency (NEA, #17615)* functions as Technical Secretariat. **Languages** English. **Staff** Secretariat: 5-7 FTE. **Finance** Secretariat funded by members. **Activities** Research and development; standards/guidelines; training/education; events/meetings. **Events** *Symposium* Paris (France) 2018, *Joint IAEA-GIF Technical Meeting on the Safety of High Temperature Gas Cooled Reactors* Vienna (Austria) 2018, *Joint IAEA-GIF Technical Meeting/Workshop on the Safety of Liquid Metal Cooled Fast Reactors* Vienna (Austria) 2018, *Global Symposium on Lead and Lead Alloy Cooled Nuclear Energy Science and Technology* Seoul (Korea Rep) 2017, *Policy Group Meeting* Busan (Korea Rep) 2012. **Publications** Annual Report; R+D Outlook; Roadmaps.

Members Governments having signed Charter and Framework Agreement (11):
Australia, Canada, China, France, Japan, Korea Rep, Russia, South Africa, Switzerland, UK, USA.
International member organization:
European Atomic Energy Community (Euratom, inactive).
Governments having signed Charter but not the Framework Agreement:
Argentina, Brazil.
Permanent observers (2):
International Atomic Energy Agency (IAEA, #12294); *Nuclear Energy Agency (NEA, #17615)*.
IGO Relations Observer to: *International Framework for Nuclear Energy Cooperation (IFNEC, #13681)*. [2019.07.03/XM3758/y/**F***]

♦ Generations for Peace 10116

CEO HQ – Al-Hussein Youth and Sport City, PO Box 963772, Amman 11196, Jordan. T. +96265004600. Fax +96265682954. E-mail: info@gfp.ngo.
Registered US Office 1800 Massachusetts Ave NW, Suite 401, Washington DC 20036, USA.
URL: http://www.gfp.ngo/

History Set up 2007 by HRH Prince Feisal Al Hussein of Jordan and Sarah Kabbani. Registered in accordance with the laws of Jordan; also registered in the State of Maryland: EIN 46-1577158. **Aims** Promote youth leadership, community empowerment, active tolerance and *responsible citizenship*. **Structure** Board (meets at least 4 times a year). **Languages** Arabic, English. **Staff** 70.00 FTE, paid. **Finance** Governmental donor funding from: Jordan and USA. Also funding from: *European Union (EU, #08967)*; *Fédération internationale de basketball (FIBA, #09614)*; *International Olympic Committee (IOC, #14408)*; *Laureus Sport for Good Foundation*; *Olympic Council of Asia (OCA, #17718)*; *UN Women (#20724)*; *UNDP (#20292)*; *UNICEF (#20332)*; individual donors. Annual budget (2019): US$ 9,000,000. **Activities** Conflict resolution; capacity building; events/meetings. **Publications** *e-Newsletter*. Annual Report; research publications.

Members Volunteers (over 12,500) in 37 countries and territories:
Afghanistan, Algeria, Armenia, Azerbaijan, Bosnia-Herzegovina, Burundi, Egypt, Georgia, Ghana, Indonesia, Iraq, Jordan, Kosovo, Kyrgyzstan, Lebanon, Libya, Nepal, Nigeria, North Macedonia, Pakistan, Palestine, Russia, Rwanda, Serbia, Sierra Leone, Somalia, South Sudan, Sri Lanka, Sudan, Timor-Leste, Tunisia, Uganda, Ukraine, USA, Yemen, Zambia, Zimbabwe.
IGO Relations *UNDP (#20292)*; *UNESCO (#20322)*; *UNICEF (#20332)*; United Nations Peacebuilding Support Office (UNPBSO); *United Nations Population Fund (UNFPA, #20612)*. Associated with Department of Global Communications of the United Nations. **NGO Relations** Recognized organization of *International Olympic Committee (IOC, #14408)*. [2020/XJ9415/**F**]

♦ Generative Linguistics in the Old World (GLOW) 10117

Contact GLOW Bureau, Utrecht University, UiL-OTS, Trans 10, 3512 JK Utrecht, Netherlands. E-mail: glow.gw@uu.nl.
Chairperson address not obtained.
URL: https://glowlinguistics.org/

History 1977. **Aims** Further the study of generative grammar; increase communication and cooperation among generative *grammarians*, particularly in Europe. **Structure** General Assembly (annual). Board of up to 9 members, including Chairman, Secretary, Treasurer and Congress President. **Events** *Annual Colloquium* Oslo (Norway) 2019, *Asia Conference* Seoul (Korea Rep) 2019, *Annual Colloquium* Brussels (Belgium) 2014, *Annual Colloquium / Asia Conference* Potsdam (Germany) 2012, *Asia Conference* Tsu (Japan) 2012. **Publications** *GLOW Newsletter* (2 a year); *Linguistic Review* – journal. [2020/XM0602/**F**]

- ♦ Generic and Biosimilar Medicines of Southern Africa (internationally oriented national body)
- ♦ Genesis Initiative (internationally oriented national body)
- ♦ **GENET** European NGO Network on Genetic Engineering (#08050)

♦ Genetic Epidemiology of Parkinson's Disease (GEO-PD) 10118

Contact Djavad Mowafaghian Ctr for Brain Health, 2215 Wesbrook Mall 5th Floor, Vancouver BC V6T 1Z3, Canada. T. +16048220322. E-mail: info@geopd.net.
URL: http://www.geopd.net/

History 2003. **Aims** Perform large-scale *genetic* association studies; serve as a replication engine. **Structure** Steering Committee; Executive. Cores (3): Clinical; Genotype; Statistical. **Events** *Annual Meeting* Omsk (Russia) 2021, *Annual Meeting* Milan (Italy) 2020, *Annual Meeting* Cape Town (South Africa) 2019, *Annual Meeting* Paris (France) 2018, *Meeting* Cairns, QLD (Australia) 2017.

Members Full in 29 countries:
Australia, Austria, Belgium, Brazil, Canada, China, Denmark, Estonia, France, Germany, Greece, India, Ireland, Italy, Japan, Korea Rep, Norway, Peru, Poland, Russia, Singapore, South Africa, Spain, Sweden, Taiwan, Tunisia, Türkiye, UK, USA. [2021/XM4291/**C**]

- ♦ Genetic Resources Action International / see GRAIN (#10691)
- ♦ Genetic Resources Center (see: #14754)
- ♦ Genetics of Industrial Microorganisms – International Commission / see Global Society for Industrial Microbiology (#10606)
- ♦ Genetics Society of AustralAsia (internationally oriented national body)
- ♦ Genetics Society of Australia / see Genetics Society of AustralAsia
- ♦ Génétique des microorganismes industriels – Commission internationale / see Global Society for Industrial Microbiology (#10606)
- ♦ GEN-Europe / see Global Ecovillage Network – Europe (#10332)
- ♦ **GEN Europe** Global Ecovillage Network – Europe (#10332)
- ♦ Geneva Act Concerning the International Classification of Goods and Services for the Purposes of the Registration of Marks (1977 treaty)
- ♦ Geneva Act of the The Hague Agreement Concerning the International Registration of Industrial Designs (1999 treaty)
- ♦ Geneva Appeal Association (internationally oriented national body)
- ♦ Geneva Asia Society (internationally oriented national body)

♦ Geneva Association 10119

Association de Genève – Asociación de Ginebra – Genfer Vereinigung

SG Talstrasse 70, 8001 Zurich ZH, Switzerland. T. +41442004900. Fax +41442004999. E-mail: secretariat@genevaassociation.org.
URL: http://www.genevaassociation.org/

History 27 Feb 1973, Geneva (Switzerland). Founded at Constituent Assembly, under the initiative of a committee which met for the first time 22 Sep 1971, Paris (France). Commenced operations 1 Jun 1973. Former names and other names: *International Association for the Study of Insurance Economics (Geneva Association)* – former; *Association internationale pour l'étude de l'économie de l'assurance (Association de Genève)* – former; *Asociación Internacional para el Estudio de la Economia del Seguro (Asociación de Ginebra)* – former; *Internationale Vereinigung für das Studium der Versicherungswirtschaft (Genfer Vereinigung)* – former. **Aims** Detect early ideas and emerging debates on political, economic and societal issues concerning the industry, notably climate change, health and ageing and new technologies and data. **Structure** General Assembly (annual); Board; Scientific Committee; General Secretariat. **Languages** Chinese, English, French, German. **Staff** 10.00 FTE, paid. **Finance** Annual budget: 6,000,000 CHF. **Activities** Awards/prizes/competitions; events/meetings; knowledge management/information dissemination; research/documentation. **Events** *Annual General Assembly* Buenos Aires (Argentina) 2019, *Biennial Joint Conference* Milan (Italy) 2019, *CEO Insurance Summit* Singapore (Singapore) 2019, *Annual General Assembly* Paris (France) 2018, *CEO Insurance Summit* Singapore (Singapore) 2018. **Publications** *Geneva Papers on Risk and Insurance*. Research reports; conference summaries.

Members Individuals in 22 countries and territories:
Argentina, Australia, Austria, Belgium, Bermuda, Brazil, Canada, China, Colombia, Finland, France, Germany, Italy, Japan, Korea Rep, Netherlands, Poland, Portugal, Spain, Switzerland, UK, USA.
NGO Relations Member of: *Fédération des Institutions Internationales établies à Genève (FIIG, #09599)*; *World Benchmarking Alliance (WBA, #21228)*. Cooperates with: *Asia-Pacific Risk and Insurance Association (APRIA, #02016)*; *European Association of Law and Economics (EALE, #06104)*; *European Group of Risk and Insurance Economists (EGRIE, #07433)*. [2020.08.18/XD4357/v/**C**]

- ♦ Geneva Call (internationally oriented national body)
- ♦ Geneva Centre for the Democratic Control of Armed Forces / see Geneva Centre for Security Sector Governance (#10121)

♦ Geneva Centre for Human Rights Advancement and Global Dialogue (GCHRAGD) 10120

Centre de Genève pour la Promotion de l'homme et le Dialogue Global

Contact Rue de Vermont 37-39, CP 186, 1211 Geneva 20, Switzerland. T. +41227482780. E-mail: info@gchragd.org.
URL: http://www.gchragd.org/

History Registered in accordance with Swiss civil code, Sep 2013. **Aims** Contribute to safeguarding human rights and dignity in accordance with established international standards; encourage global dialogue on the values of justice, tolerance and rejection of extremist and bigotry; promote human rights awareness among the general Arab and Muslim public and inter-cultural understanding; provide advice on human rights and global dialogue issues. **Structure** Executive Board; Headquarters in Geneva (Switzerland). **Languages** Arabic, English, French, Russian, Spanish. **Staff** 5.00 FTE, paid. **Activities** Research/documentation; awareness raising; capacity building; training/education; networking/liaising. **Events** *From Interfaith, Inter-Civilizational Cooperation to Human Solidarity* Vienna (Austria) 2019. **Publications** Proceedings. **Consultative Status** Consultative status granted from: *ECOSOC (#05331)* (Special). **IGO Relations** Memorandum of Understanding with: *European Public Law Organization (EPLO, #08299)*. cooperates with: *UNESCO (#20322)*; *United Nations Institute for Training and Research (UNITAR, #20576)*. **NGO Relations** Memorandum of Understanding with: EU Business School; *European Centre for Peace and Development (ECPD, #06496)*; *Oxford Centre for Islamic Studies (OCIS)*; *Rencontre africaine pour la défense des droits de l'homme (RADDHO)*. Agreements with: *Emirates Centre for Strategic Studies and Research (ECSSR)*; Geneva Academy for Peace and Mediation; Geneva Academy for Peace and Mediation. [2019.12.13/XM7186/**E**]

♦ Geneva Centre for Security Policy (internationally oriented national body)

♦ Geneva Centre for Security Sector Governance (DCAF) 10121

Centre de Genève pour la gouvernance du secteur de la sécurité – Centro de Ginebra para la Gobernanza del Sector de la Seguridad

Dir PO Box 1360, 1211 Geneva 1, Switzerland. E-mail: info@dcaf.ch.
Street Address Maison de la Paix, Chemin Eugène-Rigot 2E, 1202 Geneva, Switzerland.
URL: http://www.dcaf.ch/

History 27 Oct 2000, Geneva (Switzerland). Former names and other names: *Geneva Centre for the Democratic Control of Armed Forces (DCAF)* – former (2000 to 2019); *Centre pour la gouvernance du secteur de la sécurité – Genève* – former (2000 to 2019); *Genfer Zentrum für die Gouvernanz des Sicherheitssektors* – former (2000 to 2019). Registration: Switzerland. **Aims** Make people and the states they live in more secure through better security sector governance; contribute to improved security within a framework of democratic governance, the rule of law and human rights; assist partner states and international actors in improving governance of security sectors through inclusive and participatory reforms, based on international norms and good practices and in response to specific local contexts and challenges. **Structure** Foundation Council, comprising 63 Member States plus the Canton of Geneva (Switzerland) plus 6 permanent observers. Departments (4): Policy and Research; Operations; International Security Sector Advisor Team (ISSAT); Resources. Overseas offices in Bamako, Banjul, Beirut, Brussels, Ljubljana, Ramallah, Skopje, Tegucigalpa, Tripoli, Tunis. **Languages** English, French. **Staff** 170.00 FTE, paid. **Finance** Annual budget (2018): Swiss Fr 29,000,000. **Activities** Capacity building; knowledge management/information dissemination; guidance/assistance/consulting; standards/guidelines; research/documentation; monitoring/evaluation; projects/programmes; training/education. **Events** *Biennial International Security Forum* Geneva (Switzerland) 2016, *Biennial International Security Forum* Geneva (Switzerland) 2013, *Biennial international security forum / International Security Forum / Biennial International Security Forum* Geneva (Switzerland) 2009, *Young faces workshop* Geneva (Switzerland) 2007, *Workshop on roles and responsibilities of national security councils* Prague (Czech Rep) 2007. **Publications** *DCAF Backgrounders* – series; *DCAF Horizon 2015 Working Paper Series*; *DCAF Policy Papers* – series; *DCAF Yearly Book* – series; *SSR Papers* – series. Books; handbooks; gender tools and resources; occasional papers; policy papers; conference proceedings. All publications can be found on website.

Members Governments of 63 countries plus Canton of Geneva (Switzerland):
Albania, Argentina, Armenia, Austria, Azerbaijan, Belarus, Belgium, Bosnia-Herzegovina, Bulgaria, Burkina Faso, Burundi, Canada, Côte d'Ivoire, Croatia, Cyprus, Czechia, Denmark, Estonia, Finland, France, Georgia, Germany, Ghana, Greece, Hungary, Indonesia, Ireland, Italy, Kyrgyzstan, Latvia, Lebanon, Liechtenstein, Lithuania, Luxembourg, Madagascar, Mali, Malta, Moldova, Mongolia, Montenegro, Netherlands, Niger, Nigeria, North Macedonia, Norway, Philippines, Poland, Portugal, Romania, Russia, Senegal, Serbia, Slovakia, Slovenia, South Africa, Spain, Sweden, Switzerland, Tunisia, Türkiye, UK, Ukraine, USA.

IGO Relations Cooperates with: *Frontex, the European Border and Coast Guard Agency (#10005)*; *Southeast Europe Police Chiefs Association (SEPCA, #19824)*. Supports: *Police Cooperation Convention for Southeast Europe Secretariat (PCC SEE Secretariat, #18415)*. **NGO Relations** Cooperates with: *International Code of Conduct Association (ICoCA, #12629)*; *International Relations and Security Network (ISN, inactive)*. [2021/XE4425/**E***]

♦ Geneva Convention for the Amelioration of the Condition of the Wounded and Sick in Armed Forces in the Field, 1949 (1949 treaty)
♦ Geneva Convention for the Amelioration of the Condition of the Wounded and Sick in Armies in the Field, 1929 (1929 treaty)
♦ Geneva Convention for the Amelioration of the Condition of Wounded, Sick and Shipwrecked Members of Armed Forces at Sea (1949 treaty)
♦ Geneva convention – Convention for the Amelioration of the Condition of the Wounded in Armies in the Field, 1864 (1864 treaty)
♦ Geneva Convention – Convention for the Protection of Producers of Phonograms Against Unauthorized Duplication of Their Phonograms (1971 treaty)
♦ Geneva convention – Geneva convention for protection of the wounded in armies in the field, 1906 (1906 treaty)
♦ Geneva convention for protection of the wounded in armies in the field, 1906 (1906 treaty)
♦ Geneva Convention Relative to the Protection of Civilian Persons in Time of War (1949 treaty)
♦ Geneva Convention Relative to the Treatment of Prisoners of War (1949 treaty)
♦ Geneva Convention on Torture (1949 treaty)
♦ Geneva Forum (internationally oriented national body)

♦ Geneva Global Health Hub (G2H2) 10122

Exec Sec Route de Ferney 150, CP 2100, 1211 Geneva 2, Switzerland. T. +41796450137. E-mail: info@g2h2.org.
URL: http://g2h2.org/

History Statutes adopted 21 May 2016; revised 20 May 2018. Registration: Swiss Civil Code, Switzerland. **Aims** Promote *democratic* global governance to achieve comprehensive and equitable health for all by building a steady and strong *civil society* voice. **Structure** Annual General Meeting; Steering Committee; Working Groups; Secretariat. **Languages** English. **Staff** 0.15 FTE, paid. **Finance** Sources: contributions; donations; gifts, legacies; members' dues; private foundations. **Activities** Events/meetings; knowledge management/information dissemination; networking/liaising.

Members Organizations; Individuals. Organizations include 27 listed in this Yearbook:
- *African Centre for Global Health and Social Transformation (ACHEST)*;
- *Brot für die Welt*;
- *Catholic Organization for Relief and Development (Cordaid)*;
- *Cochrane Collaboration (#04078)*;
- *DIANOVA International (#05068)*;
- *Enfants du Monde (EdM)*;
- *European Association for Counselling (EAC, #05993)*;
- *FIAN International (#09743)*;
- *German Institute for Medical Mission (DIFÄM)*;
- *Global Policy Forum (GPF)*;
- *Harm Reduction International (HRI, #10861)*;
- *Health Poverty Action (HPA)*;
- *International Association for Hospice and Palliative Care (IAHPC, #11941)*;
- *International Federation of Anti-Leprosy Associations (ILEP, #13355)*;
- *International Federation of Social Workers (IFSW, #13544)*;
- *International Federation on Ageing (IFA, #13345)*;
- *Medact*;
- *Medico International*;
- *Medicus Mundi International – Network Health for All (MMI, #16636)*;
- *Movendi International (#16871)*;
- *Pan Pacific and South East Asia Women's Association (PPSEAWA, #18186)*;
- *People's Health Movement (PHM, #18305)*;
- *Public Services International (PSI, #18572)*;
- *Society for International Development (SID, #19581)*;
- *Viva Salud*;
- *WEMOS*;
- *World Federation of Public Health Associations (WFPHA, #21476)*.

IGO Relations Cooperates with (1): *WHO (#20950)*. [2022.10.19/XM7256/y/**E**]

♦ Geneva Global Hub for Education in Emergencies 10123

Coordinator Rue de Varembé 7, 1202 Geneva, Switzerland.
Facebook: https://www.facebook.com/EiEGenevaHub/

History 25 Jan 2021, Geneva (Switzerland). **Aims** Be a catalyst to accelerate progress towards SDG 4 in crises and displacement contexts; help realize the commitments set out in the Global Compact on Refugees.

Members Partners (10):
Switzerland.
Education Cannot Wait (ECW, #05369); *Global Education Cluster (#10333)*; *Institut de hautes études internationales et du développement (IHEID)*; *Inter-agency Network for Education in Emergencies (INEE, #11387)*; *International Committee of the Red Cross (ICRC, #12799)*; *UNESCO (#20322)*; *UNHCR (#20327)*; *UNICEF (#20332)*; University of Geneva. [2021/AA2140/y/**E**]

♦ Geneva for Human Rights – Global Training (GHR) 10124

Genève pour le droits de l'homme – Formation internationale (GDH) – Ginebra para los Derechos Humanos – Formación Internacional

Pres Ecumenical Ctr, Rte de Ferney 150, 1211 Geneva, Switzerland. T. +41223202727. Fax +41223202440. E-mail: acz.hr@bluewin.ch – info@gdh-ghr.org.
URL: http://www.gdh-ghr.org/

History 2003. Former names and other names: *Genève pour le droits de l'homme – Formation internationale (GDH)* – former; *Ginebra para los Derechos Humanos – Formación Internacional* – former. Registration: Swiss Civil Code, Switzerland. **Aims** Through training, study and protection, aim to contribute to human rights implementation inside countries; bridge the gap between standards of the UN and the follow-up of their decisions and recommendations; empower all those involved in promotion and protection of human rights. **Structure** General Assembly (annual); Executive Council; Working Groups; Secretariat based in Geneva (Switzerland). **Languages** English, French, Spanish. **Staff** Voluntary. **Finance** Training activities financed by donations, grants, registration fees and user contributions. **Activities** Training/education; events/meetings; capacity building.

Members Individuals in 22 countries:
Armenia, Belgium, Bolivia, Colombia, Congo Brazzaville, France, Germany, Guyana, Haiti, India, Indonesia, Ireland, Italy, Malta, Netherlands, Russia, Senegal, Spain, Switzerland, Timor-Leste, UK, USA.

Consultative Status Consultative status granted from: *ECOSOC (#05331)* (Special). **IGO Relations** Main partners include: *Office of the United Nations High Commissioner for Human Rights (OHCHR, #17697)*; UN Permanent Missions. [2019.12.14/XM8190/**E**]

♦ Geneva Infant Feeding Association (internationally oriented national body)
♦ Geneva Initiative on Psychiatry / see Human Rights in Mental Health (#10988)
♦ Geneva Initiative on Psychiatry – International Foundation for the Abolition and Prevention of Political Psychiatry / see Human Rights in Mental Health (#10988)
♦ Geneva Interfaith Intercultural Alliance (internationally oriented national body)
♦ Geneva International Academic Network (internationally oriented national body)
♦ Geneva International Centre for Humanitarian Demining (internationally oriented national body)

♦ Geneva International Centre for Justice (GICJ) 10125

Main Office PO Box 598, Vernier, 1214 Geneva, Switzerland. T. +41795365866. E-mail: info@gicj.org.
URL: http://www.gicj.org/

History Geneva (Switzerland). Registered in accordance with Swiss Civil Code. **Aims** Improve lives by tackling violations and all forms of violence and degrading or inhumane treatment through the strengthening of respect for human rights and combating impunity. **Structure** Executive Committee; Advisory Board. **Languages** Arabic, English, French. **Activities** Awareness raising; events/meetings; training/education. **Publications** *GICJ Newsletter*. **IGO Relations** UN institutions. **NGO Relations** NGOs; universities; research centres. [2019/XM4189/**E**]

♦ Geneva International Model United Nations (internationally oriented national body)
♦ Geneva International Peace Research Institute (internationally oriented national body)
♦ Geneva Peacebuilding Platform (internationally oriented national body)
♦ Geneva Protocol (1922 treaty)
♦ Geneva Research Centre (inactive)
♦ Geneva School of Diplomacy and International Relations (internationally oriented national body)

♦ Geneva Science and Diplomacy Anticipator (GESDA) 10126

SG c/o Fondation Campus Biotech, Chemin des Mines 9, 1202 Geneva, Switzerland. T. +41582010261. E-mail: info@gesda.global.
URL: https://gesda.global/

History 2019, Geneva (Switzerland). **Aims** Leverage the Geneva international ecosystem to anticipate, accelerate and translate into concrete actions the use of emerging science-driven topics. **Structure** Board of Directors; Academic Forum; Diplomacy Forum; Impact Fund; Executive Team. **Finance** Sources: government support; private foundations. [2021.05.26/AA1299/**E**]

♦ Geneva Securities Convention – UNIDROIT Convention on Substantive Rules for Intermediated Securities (2009 treaty)
♦ Geneva Summit – Geneva Summit for Human Rights and Democracy (meeting series)
♦ Geneva Summit for Human Rights and Democracy (meeting series)
♦ Geneva Treaty – Geneva Treaty on the International Recording of Scientific Discoveries (1978 treaty)
♦ Geneva Treaty on the International Recording of Scientific Discoveries (1978 treaty)
♦ Genève Asie Association (internationally oriented national body)
♦ Genève pour le droits de l'homme – Formation internationale (#10124)
♦ Genève – Tiers-monde (internationally oriented national body)
♦ Genfer Internationales Friedensforschungsinstitut (internationally oriented national body)
♦ Genfer Internationales Zentrum für Humanitäre Minenräumung (internationally oriented national body)
♦ Genfer protokolle (1922 treaty)
♦ Genfer Vereinigung (#10119)
♦ Genfer Zentrum für die Gouvernanz des Sicherheitssektors / see Geneva Centre for Security Sector Governance (#10121)
♦ Genfer Zentrum für Sicherheitspolitik (internationally oriented national body)
♦ **GEN** Global Ecolabelling Network (#10328)
♦ **GEN** Global Ecotourism Network (#10330)
♦ **GEN** Global Ecovillage Network (#10331)
♦ GEN – Global Entrepreneurship Network (unconfirmed)
♦ Génie climatique international – International Union of the Associations of Heating, Ventilating and Air Conditioning Contractors (inactive)
♦ GEN International / see Global Ecovillage Network (#10331)
♦ GENIVI Alliance / see Connected Vehicle Systems Alliance (#04681)
♦ Genocide Alert (internationally oriented national body)
♦ Genocide Convention – Convention on the Prevention and Punishment of the Crime of Genocide (1948 treaty)
♦ Genocide Watch (internationally oriented national body)
♦ Genodermatoses & Rare Skin Disorders in Mediterranean / see Rare Skin Diseases Network (#18622)
♦ Genodermatoses & Rare Skin Disorders Network / see Rare Skin Diseases Network (#18622)
♦ **GenoMEL** Melanoma Genetics Consortium (#16705)
♦ GENRI – Global Environment and Natural Resources Institute (internationally oriented national body)

Gensuikyo
10126

alphabetic sequence excludes
For the complete listing, see Yearbook Online at

♦ Gensuikyo (internationally oriented national body)
♦ GEN TEFL / see Global Educators Network Inc. (#10338)
♦ Pro Gentilezza: Association for the Spreading of Good and Human Feeling (inactive)
♦ Pro Gentilezza: Union pour la courtoisie (inactive)

♦ Gentle Learning International (GTI) 10127

Address not obtained.
URL: https://gentleteaching.com/

Aims Develop, promote and strengthen the values of Gentle Teaching every day. **Structure** Board of Directors. **Events** *International Conference* Ghent (Belgium) 2019.
Members Full in 14 countries – European members grouped within Gentle Teaching Europe:
Belgium, Brazil, Canada, Denmark, Dominican Rep, Iceland, India, Japan, Mexico, Netherlands, Portugal, Rwanda, UK, USA. [2019/XM8361/F]

♦ Gentle Teaching International (GTI) 10128

Contact address not obtained.
URL: https://gentleteaching.com/

History 2013. Registration: Canada. **Activities** Events/meetings. **Events** *Gentle Teaching International Conference* Ann Arbor, MI (USA) 2021, *Conference* Ghent (Belgium) 2019, *Conference* Amsterdam (Netherlands) 2018, *Conference* Vancouver, BC (Canada) 2017, *Conference* Kansas City, MO (USA) 2015. [2020/AA0273/F]

♦ **GENUNG** Groupe d'experts des Nations Unies sur les noms géographiques (#20569)
♦ **GEO*8** European Alliance for Earth Sciences (#05869)

♦ GEO Biodiversity Observation Network (GEO BON) 10129

Exec Sec Stewart Biology Bldg S3/18, McGill Univ, 1205 Docteur Penfield, Montréal QC H3A 1B1, Canada. E-mail: info@geobon.org.
URL: https://geobon.org/

History Part of *Group on Earth Observations (GEO, #10735)*, representing biodiversity, one of GEO's Societal-Benefit-Areas. Former names and other names: *Group on Earth Observations Biodiversity Observation Network (GEO BON)* – full title. **Aims** Improve the acquisition, coordination and delivery of biodiversity observations and related services to users including decision makers and the scientific community. **Structure** 2 Co-Chairs; Secretariat; Management Committee; Implementation Committee; Advisory Board. **Events** *Open Science Conference and All Hands Meeting* 2020, *All Hands Meeting* Beijing (China) 2018, *Open Science Conference and All Hands Meeting* Leipzig (Germany) 2016. **Members** Individuals (over 400) in 45 countries. Membership countries not specified. **NGO Relations** Cooperates with (1): *Marine Biodiversity Observation Network (MBON)*. [2022/AA2446/v/E]

♦ GEO BON / see GEO Biodiversity Observation Network (#10129)
♦ **GEO BON** GEO Biodiversity Observation Network (#10129)
♦ GEOC – Global Environmental Outreach Centre (internationally oriented national body)
♦ Geochemical Society (internationally oriented national body)

♦ GEODE 10130

SG Avenue Marnix 28, 1000 Brussels, Belgium. T. +3222044460. Fax +3222044469. E-mail: info@geode-eu.org.
URL: http://www.geode-eu.org/

History 1991. Founded by French and Spanish companies. Registration: EU Transparency Register, No/ID: 00098856602-24, Start date: 7 Sep 2011. **Aims** Establish equal opportunity access to *European* energy infrastructures for all those involved in serving the customer needs on *energy*, so as to create a truly competitive European energy *market*. **Structure** Board; Secretariat. Working Groups. **Publications** *Euroletter*. **Members** Companies (over 1400) in 15 countries:
Austria, Bulgaria, Denmark, Finland, France, Germany, Hungary, Ireland, Italy, Norway, Serbia, Slovenia, Spain, Sweden, UK. [2019.06.05/XM7049/D]

♦ geoENVia Association 10131

Sec Centre for Hydrogeology, Univ of Neuchâtel, 11 rue Emile Argand, 2007 Neuchâtel, Switzerland. T. +41327182690. Fax +41327182603. E-mail: contact@geoenvia.org.
URL: http://geoenvia.org/

Aims Promote use of *geostatistical* methods in *environmental* applications. **Structure** Council; Committee. **Finance** Members' dues. **Activities** *geonENV Conference*. **Events** *GeoENV : Biennial European Conference on Geostatistics for Environmental Applications* Parma (Italy) 2021, *GeoENV : Biennial European Conference on Geostatistics for Environmental Applications* Parma (Italy) 2020, *GeoENV : Biennial European Conference on Geostatistics for Environmental Applications* Belfast (UK) 2018, *GeoENV : Biennial European Conference on Geostatistics for Environmental Applications* Lisbon (Portugal) 2016, *GeoENV : Biennial European Conference on Geostatistics for Environmental Applications* Paris (France) 2014. **Members** Membership countries not specified. [2016/XF7089/F]

♦ GEO Foundation 10132

CEO 2 Quality Street, North Berwick, EH39 4HW, UK. T. +441620895100.
URL: https://sustainable.golf/

History Founded by *European Foundation for Golf and Environment (inactive)*, as *Golf Environment Europe (GEE)*. Subsequently referred to as *Golf Environment Organisation (GEO)*. Previously part of: UNEP Global Forum for Sport and Environment. **Aims** Help golf to deliver and be recognized for a positive impact for people and nature. **Structure** Board of Directors; Advisory Group; Expert Groups. **Staff** 13.00 FTE, paid. **Finance** Contributions from golfing organizations and from patrons and technical supporters. Also supported by: *UNEP (#20299)*; *European Commission (EC, #06633)*; *European Golf Association (EGA, #07399)*; *European Institute of Golf Course Architects (EIGCA, #07558)*; *Federation of European Golf Greenkeepers Associations (FEGGA, #09506)*; *Professional Golfers' Associations of Europe, The (PGAs of Europe, #18513)*. **Activities** Events/meetings; knowledge management/information dissemination. **Events** *COHAB : international conference on health and biodiversity* Galway (Ireland) 2008. **NGO Relations** Member of: *ISEAL (#16026)*; *Natural Capital Coalition (NCC, #16952)*. [2019/XM3028/t/F]

♦ GEO / see GEO Foundation (#10132)
♦ **GEO** Global Equity Organization (#10347)
♦ **GEO** Glosa Education Organization (#10670)
♦ Geographical Information Service Producers in Europe (no recent information)

♦ Geographical Information Systems International Group (GISIG) 10133

Coordinator Via Piacenza 54, 16138 Genoa GE, Italy. T. +39108355588. Fax +39108357190. E-mail: gisig@gisig.it.
Secretariat address not obtained.
URL: http://www.gisig.eu/

History 1992, as a European sectoral association on Geographical Information Systems (GIS), in the framework of *Community Programme in Education and Training for Technology (COMETT, inactive)*. **Aims** Group at European level universities, research institutions, companies and other private and public bodies dealing with geographical information systems and their applications through implementation of thematic networks for the various sectoral Geographical Information applications. **Structure** Executive Committee of 20 members; Auditors' Committee 3 members. **Languages** English. **Staff** 8.00 FTE, paid. 2 grant-holders. **Finance** Members' dues. Project contribution from *European Commission (EC, #06633)*; revenues from mapping services. **Activities** Implements thematic networks such as Web, conferences, training courses; carries out placement and exchange programmes. Organizes: International Symposium CoastGIS; ECO-GEOWATER events, a series of 6 EuroEvents between 2002-2004; ECO-IMAGINE, a series of 8 conferences and training courses between 2004-2007. Currently involved in a number of running European projects or proposals under evaluation. **Events** *ECO-IMAGINE thematic conference* Genoa (Italy) 2006, *GIS PLANET : conference on geographic information* Estoril (Portugal) 2005, *Nature-GIS conference* Turin (Italy) 2005, *Nature-GIS conference* Budapest (Hungary) 2004, *European conference and forum for integrated coastal management and geo-information research* Seville (Spain) 2004. **Publications** *GISIG Bulletin*. Proceedings.

Members Organizations (86) in 26 countries:
Austria, Belgium, Bulgaria, Croatia, Cyprus, Czechia, Denmark, France, Germany, Greece, Hungary, Iceland, Italy, Latvia, Lithuania, Malta, Netherlands, Poland, Portugal, Romania, Russia, Slovakia, Spain, Sweden, Türkiye, UK.
Included in the above, 2 organizations listed in this Yearbook:
International Centre for Coastal and Ocean Policy Studies (ICCOPS) (mutual membership); *Joint Research Centre (JRC, #16147)*.
NGO Relations Observer to: *European Umbrella Organization for Geographical Information (EUROGI, #08964)*. Member of: *European Geographic Information Network (EGIN, #07387)*. [2016/XE2617/y/E]

♦ Geographical Society of London / see Royal Geographical Society – with the Institute of British Geographers
♦ Geography of Innovation Conference (meeting series)
♦ **GEO** Group on Earth Observations (#10735)
♦ GeoHab – Marine Geological and Biological Habitat Mapping (unconfirmed)
♦ GeoICT – International Association of Geoinformation and Communication Technologies (internationally oriented national body)
♦ Geoinformatics Center (internationally oriented national body)
♦ Geoinformatics Center of AIT / see Geoinformatics Center
♦ Geo-Information for Disaster Management (meeting series)
♦ GEOINNO – Geography of Innovation Conference (meeting series)

♦ Geological Remote Sensing Group (GRSG) 10134

Chairman c/o Geological Soc, Burlington House, Piccadilly, London, W1J 0BD, UK. E-mail: chairman@grsg.org.uk.
URL: http://www.grsg.org.uk/

History A special interest group of the Geological Society of London (GeolSoc) and the Remote Sensing and Photogrammetry Society (RSPSoc). **Structure** Committee. **Finance** Members' dues. Sponsorship for events. **Activities** Events/meetings; knowledge management/information dissemination; networking/liaising; awards/prizes/competitions. **Events** *Annual General Meeting and Annual Conference* London (UK) 2018. **Publications** *GRSG Newsletter* (4 a year). **Members** Full (over 200) worldwide. Membership countries not specified. [2020.03.11/XM7983/E]

♦ Geological Society of Africa (GSAf) 10135

Société Géologique de l'Afrique

SG Dept of Geology, Univ of Zimbabwe, MP 167 Mt Pleasant, Harare, HARARE, Zimbabwe. T. +2637729066. Fax +2634336418.
Pres Dept of Geology, Univ of Ibadan, Oduduwa Road, Ibadan, Oyo, Nigeria.
URL: http://gsafr.org/

History 1970, Ibadan (Nigeria). Constitution most recently amended Nov 1992, Accra (Ghana) and Jan 2013, Addis Ababa (Ethiopia). Former names and other names: *GSA* – former. **Aims** Promote understanding of earth sciences in Africa; provide a forum for discussion, dissemination of information and cooperation among scientists and associations engaged in African geology; promote development of African earth resources for the benefit of Africa; improve natural hazards assessment and disaster mitigation. **Structure** General meeting (every 2 years); Council; Secretariat. **Languages** English, French. **Staff** 1.00 FTE, paid. **Finance** Sources: members' dues. Other sources: subvention from IUGS; special funds for international meetings. Annual budget: 12,000 USD. **Activities** Events/meetings; networking/liaising; publishing activities; research and development; training/education. **Events** *CAG: Colloquium of African Geology* Windhoek (Namibia) 2023, *Colloquium of African Geology* Fez (Morocco) 2021, *Conference* Fez (Morocco) 2021, *Colloquium of African Geology* Aveiro (Portugal) 2018, *Conference* Aveiro (Portugal) 2018. **Publications** *Africa Geonews* – newsletter; *Journal of African Earth Sciences* – official journal. Conference proceedings.
Members Regular, geologists; Associated, professionals; Institutional; Students; Honorary. Each country in Africa and all national geological societies are considered as members. Members in 64 countries:
Algeria, Angola, Australia, Austria, Belgium, Benin, Botswana, Burkina Faso, Burundi, Cameroon, Canada, Central African Rep, Chad, Congo Brazzaville, Congo DR, Côte d'Ivoire, Croatia, Czechia, Denmark, Egypt, Eritrea, Ethiopia, Finland, France, Gabon, Gambia, Germany, Ghana, Guinea, India, Ireland, Israel, Italy, Japan, Kenya, Libya, Madagascar, Malawi, Mali, Mauritania, Morocco, Mozambique, Namibia, Netherlands, Niger, Nigeria, Norway, Portugal, Russia, Saudi Arabia, Senegal, Serbia, Somalia, South Africa, Spain, Sudan, Sweden, Tanzania UR, Tunisia, Uganda, UK, USA, Zambia, Zimbabwe.
IGO Relations *United Nations Economic Commission for Africa (ECA, #20554)*. **NGO Relations** Affiliated member of: *International Union of Geological Sciences (IUGS, #15777)*. Cooperates with: *Association of Geoscientists for International Development (AGID, #02623)*. Partner of: *Earth Science Matters Foundation (ESM, #05169)*. Takes part in: *IUGS Commission on Management and Application of Geoscience Information (CGI, #16081)* and *International Geoscience Programme (IGCP, #13715)*. Special links with: *Pan African Network for a Geological Information System (PANGIS, no recent information)*. [2022.05.14/XD3798/D]

♦ Geological Society of America (internationally oriented national body)
♦ Geological Society of Southeast Asia (meeting series)
♦ Geólogos del Mundo (#21537)
♦ Geology for Global Development (internationally oriented national body)
♦ Géomètres experts fonciers européens (inactive)
♦ Geometric and Asymptotic Group Theory with Applications (meeting series)
♦ Geometric Science of Information (meeting series)
♦ GeoMod – Modelling in Geosciences (meeting series)
♦ **GEO-PD** Genetic Epidemiology of Parkinson's Disease (#10118)
♦ GeoProc – International Conference on Coupled THMC Processes in Geosystems (meeting series)
♦ Georg Eckert Institute for International Textbook Research (internationally oriented national body)
♦ Georg-Eckert-Institut für Internationale Schulbuchforschung (internationally oriented national body)
♦ George C Marshall European Centre for Security Studies, Garmisch Partenkirchen (internationally oriented national body)
♦ George Santayana Society (internationally oriented national body)
♦ Georgetown International Relations Association Inc (internationally oriented national body)
♦ George Washington Center for the Study of Globalization (internationally oriented national body)
♦ George Wright Society (internationally oriented national body)
♦ Geoscience InfoRmation in AFrica (unconfirmed)

♦ Geoscience Information Consortium (GIC) 10136

Exec Sec Geološki zavod Slovenije, Dimičeva ulica 14, 1000 Ljubljana, Slovenia. T. +386012809700. Fax +386012809753.
URL: http://www.g-i-c.org/

Aims Promote information exchange among geological surveys organizations (GSOs) related to the use and management of geoscience information systems in support of the earth sciences internationally. **Structure** Executive Committee; Steering Committee. **Activities** Events/meetings. **Events** *Annual Conference* Prague (Czechia) 2022, *Annual Conference* 2021, *Annual Conference* 2020, *Annual Conference* Madrid (Spain) 2019, *Annual Conference* Vienna (Austria) 2017.
Members Full in 31 countries:
Australia, Austria, Canada, China, Croatia, Czechia, Denmark, Finland, France, Germany, Hungary, Ireland, Italy, Japan, Lithuania, Namibia, Netherlands, New Zealand, North Macedonia, Norway, Poland, Romania, Saudi Arabia, Slovakia, Slovenia, South Africa, Spain, Sweden, Switzerland, UK, USA. [2022/XM5896/C]

♦ GEOSEA – Geological Society of Southeast Asia (meeting series)
♦ Geo-SEE Institute – South-East European Research Institute on Geo Sciences (internationally oriented national body)
♦ Geospatial World Forum (meeting series)

♦ Geostatistical Association of Southern Africa (GASA) 10137

Sec PO Box 62285, Marshalltown, 2107, South Africa. E-mail: member@gasa.org.za – support@gasa.org.za.
URL: http://www.gasa.org.za/

Aims Promote professional interests of geostatisticians by: increasing awareness of geostatistics and application of *spatial statistics* in Southern Africa; facilitating communication among practitioners; representing the opinions of professional geostatisticians to the public and to industry. **Structure** Council, including Chairman, Vice-Chairman, Secretary and Treasurer. **Events** *WCSB4 – World Conference on Sampling and Blending* Cape Town (South Africa) 2009. **Members** Membership countries not specified. [2017/XJ0567/**D**]

- ♦ GEOSUR – Asociación Sudamericana de Estudios Geopolíticos e Internacionales, Montevideo (no recent information)
- ♦ GEP / see Nottingham Centre for Research on Globalisation and Economic Policy
- ♦ **GEPC** Groupement européen des producteurs de champignons (#10758)
- ♦ GEPLACEA – Grupo de Paises Latinoamericanos y del Caribe Exportadores de Azúcar (inactive)
- ♦ GEP – Nottingham Centre for Research on Globalisation and Economic Policy (internationally oriented national body)
- ♦ **GEPO** Groupe européen de pastorale ouvrière (#10740)
- ♦ GEPROVAS – Groupe Européen de Recherche sur les Prothèses Appliquées à la Chirurgie Vasculaire (internationally oriented national body)
- ♦ GEPVP / see Glass for Europe (#10157)
- ♦ Gerald Durrell Wildlife Preservation Trust / see Durrell Wildlife Conservation Trust
- ♦ GERB / see Société Francophone de Chronobiologie
- ♦ **GERDDES-Africa** Study and Research Group on Democracy, Economic and Social Development in Africa (#20021)
- ♦ **GERDDES-Afrique** Groupe d'étude et de recherche sur la démocratie et le développement économique et social en Afrique (#20021)
- ♦ Gerecht van de Europese Gemeenschappen (inactive)
- ♦ GERES / see GERES
- ♦ GERES (internationally oriented national body)
- ♦ **GERFEC** Groupement Européen pour la Recherche et la Formation des Enseignants Chrétiens, Croyants et de toutes Convictions (#10759)
- ♦ **GERG** Groupe européen de recherches gazières (#07380)
- ♦ GER – Guilde européenne du raid (internationally oriented national body)
- ♦ Gerhard Kuentscher Society / see Gerhard Küntscher Society (#10138)
- ♦ Gerhard Küntscher Kreis – Association for the Advancement of Fracture Treatment / see Gerhard Küntscher Society (#10138)

♦ Gerhard Küntscher Society 10138

Sec c/o Dept for Trauma – Hand and Emergency Surgery, University of Rostock, Schillingalle 35, 18055 Rostock, Germany.
Pres c/o Dept of Trauma Surgery, Maastricht University Medical Center, P Debeyelaan 25, PO Box 5800, 6202 AZ Maastricht, Netherlands.
URL: http://www.kuentschersociety.org/

History 7 Dec 1973, Hamburg (Germany FR). Also referred to as *Gerhard Kuentscher Society*. Full official title: *Gerhard Küntscher Kreis – Association for the Advancement of Fracture Treatment*. Registered in accordance with German law. **Aims** Foster research in the field of *fracture* treatment so as to improve current methods and develop new ones. **Structure** General Assembly; Executive Board; Board of Trustees. **Languages** English, German. **Staff** None. **Finance** Members' dues. **Activities** Awards/prizes/competitions; events/meetings; publishing activities; training/education. **Events** *Osteosynthese International Annual Meeting* Aschaffenburg (Germany) 2016, *Osteosynthese International Annual Meeting* Brussels (Belgium) 2015, *Osteosynthese International Annual Meeting* Krems (Austria) 2014, *Osteosynthese International Annual Meeting* Izmir (Turkey) 2012, *Osteosynthese International Annual Meeting* Thessaloniki (Greece) 2011. **Publications** *INJURY* – journal.
Members Individuals in 15 countries:
Austria, Belgium, China, France, Germany, Greece, Hungary, India, Lithuania, Netherlands, Poland, Switzerland, Türkiye, UK, USA. [2016.06.01/XJ6478/**E**]

- ♦ Gericht der Europäischen Gemeinschaften (inactive)
- ♦ Gerichtshof der Europäischen Gemeinschaften / see Court of Justice of the European Union (#04938)
- ♦ Gerichtshofs der Europäischen Union (#04938)
- ♦ German Academic Exchange Service (internationally oriented national body)
- ♦ German Agro Action / see Welthungerhilfe
- ♦ German Agro Action – Freedom from Hunger – Freedom for People / see Welthungerhilfe
- ♦ German Association for American Studies (internationally oriented national body)
- ♦ German Association for Asian Studies (internationally oriented national body)
- ♦ German Association for East European Studies (internationally oriented national body)
- ♦ German Association for Economic Cooperation / see DEG – Deutsche Investitions- und Entwicklungsgesellschaft
- ♦ German Association for Historical Peace and Conflict Research (internationally oriented national body)
- ♦ German Association for Peace and Conflict Research (internationally oriented national body)
- ♦ German Atlantic Association (internationally oriented national body)
- ♦ German Catholic Bishops' Organisation for Development Cooperation (internationally oriented national body)
- ♦ German Catholic Bishops' Organisation for Development Cooperation – Campaign against Hunger and Disease in the World / see German Catholic Bishops' Organisation for Development Cooperation
- ♦ German Centre for International Migration and Development / see Centre for International Migration and Development
- ♦ German Council for Foreign Affairs / see Deutsche Gesellschaft für Auswärtige Politik
- ♦ German Council on Foreign Relations (internationally oriented national body)
- ♦ German Development Assistance Association for Social Housing (internationally oriented national body)
- ♦ German Development Bank (internationally oriented national body)
- ♦ German Development Institute (internationally oriented national body)
- ♦ German Doctors (internationally oriented national body)
- ♦ German Doctors Association for Humanitarian Cooperation (internationally oriented national body)
- ♦ German Doctors for Developing Countries / see German Doctors
- ♦ German Federal Coordination Internationalism (internationally oriented national body)
- ♦ German Finance Company for Investments in Developing Countries / see DEG – Deutsche Investitions- und Entwicklungsgesellschaft
- ♦ German Foundation for International Legal Cooperation (internationally oriented national body)
- ♦ German Foundation for Peace Research (internationally oriented national body)
- ♦ German Foundation for World Population (internationally oriented national body)
- ♦ German Humanitarian Foundation (internationally oriented national body)
- ♦ German Institute of African Research / see Institute of African Affairs, Hamburg
- ♦ German Institute for Agrarian Technology, Nienburg / see DEULA-Nienburg
- ♦ German Institute for International and Security Affairs / see Stiftung Wissenschaft und Politik
- ♦ German Institute for Medical Mission (internationally oriented national body)
- ♦ German Institute of Middle East Studies (internationally oriented national body)
- ♦ German Institute for Oriental Studies, Beirut (internationally oriented national body)
- ♦ German Investment and Development Company / see DEG – Deutsche Investitions- und Entwicklungsgesellschaft
- ♦ German Marshall Fund of the United States (internationally oriented national body)
- ♦ German Medical Aid Organization – action medeor (internationally oriented national body)
- ♦ German Medical Welfare Organization / see Deutsches Medikamenten-Hilfswerk – action medeor
- ♦ German Middle East Association / see German Near and Middle East Association
- ♦ German Middle East Studies Association for Contemporary Research and Documentation (internationally oriented national body)
- ♦ German Missionary Fellowship (internationally oriented national body)
- ♦ German National Committee of the FAO – Freedom from Hunger Campaign / see Welthungerhilfe
- ♦ German Near and Middle East Association (internationally oriented national body)
- ♦ German NGO Forum on Environment and Development (internationally oriented national body)
- ♦ German Oriental Society / see Deutsche Morgenländische Gesellschaft
- ♦ German Orient Institute / see Deutsches Orient-Institut
- ♦ German Overseas Institute Foundation / see GIGA – German Institute of Global and Area Studies
- ♦ German Peace Council (internationally oriented national body)
- ♦ German Peace Society – United War Resisters (internationally oriented national body)
- ♦ German Platform for Peaceful Conflict Management (internationally oriented national body)
- ♦ German Society for Global and Tropical Surgery (internationally oriented national body)
- ♦ German Society of Tropical Medicine and International Health (internationally oriented national body)
- ♦ German Society of Tropical Paediatrics and International Child Health (internationally oriented national body)

♦ German Speaking Association for Infant Mental Health (GAIMH) . . . 10139

Gesellschaft für Seelische Gesundheit in der Frühen Kindheit

Main Office c/o IFEF, Hernalser Hauptstrasse 15/2/9, 1170 Vienna, Austria. T. +436601852592. E-mail: info@gaimh.org.
URL: http://www.gaimh.org/

Aims Promote infant mental health; stimulate prevention and early detection of maldevelopments. **Structure** Board. **Events** *Annual Meeting* Salzburg (Austria) 2023, *Annual Meeting* Potsdam (Germany) 2022, *Annual Meeting* Switzerland 2021, *Annual Meeting* Vienna (Austria) 2020, *Annual Meeting* Hamburg (Germany) 2019.
Members Full in 3 countries:
Austria, Germany, Switzerland.
NGO Relations Member of: *World Association for Infant Mental Health (WAIMH, #21146).* [2020/XM8406/**D**]

- ♦ German-Speaking Mycology Society (#05051)
- ♦ German-Speaking Society for Hand Surgery (#05048)
- ♦ GERM – Groupement d'études et de recherches sur la méditerranée (internationally oriented national body)
- ♦ **GERN** Groupe européen de recherche sur les normativités (#10741)
- ♦ Gernika Gogoratuz Association / see Gernika Gogoratuz – Peace Research Center
- ♦ Gernika Gogoratuz – Centro de Investicación por la Paz (internationally oriented national body)
- ♦ Gernika Gogoratuz Peace Research Association / see Gernika Gogoratuz – Peace Research Center
- ♦ Gernika Gogoratuz – Peace Research Center (internationally oriented national body)
- ♦ Gernika Gogoratuz – Peace Research Group / see Gernika Gogoratuz – Peace Research Center
- ♦ Gerolamini (religious order)
- ♦ GERSO / see International Group for Scientific Research on Stomato-Odontology (#13755)
- ♦ GERTN / see DVB Project (#05147)
- ♦ **GESAC** Groupement Européen des Sociétés d'Auteurs et Compositeurs (#07422)
- ♦ **GESA** Global Energy Storage Alliance (#10343)
- ♦ GESAMP / see Joint Group of Experts on the Scientific Aspects of Marine Environmental Protection (#16131)
- ♦ **GESAMP** Joint Group of Experts on the Scientific Aspects of Marine Environmental Protection (#16131)
- ♦ Gesamtverband der Mühlenbetriebe der EU-Länder / see European Flour Millers' Association (#07272)
- ♦ Geschäftsführendes Sekretariat des Kuratoriums für die Tagungen der Nobelpreisträger in Lindau / see Council for the Lindau Nobel Laureate Meetings (#04909)
- ♦ Geschaftslente des Vollen Evangeliums International (#10015)
- ♦ GESCI – Global e-Schools and Communities Initiative (unconfirmed)
- ♦ GESCO / see Groupe International d'Experts en Systèmes vitivinicoles pour la CoOpération (#10748)
- ♦ **GESDA** Geneva Science and Diplomacy Anticipator (#10126)

♦ Gesellschaft für Aerosolforschung (GAeF) 10140

Association pour la recherche des aérosols – Association for Aerosol Research

Treas c/o Karlsruhe Inst of Technology, FTU, Postfach 3640, 76021 Karlsruhe, Germany. T. +4972160824800. Fax +4972160824857.
URL: http://www.gaef.de/

History 1972. **Aims** Promote all scientific branches of aerosol research. **Structure** Board at Large; Executive Board. **Languages** English, German. **Staff** 1.50 FTE, paid. **Finance** Members' dues. Registration fees. Annual budget: about euro 30,000. **Events** *Annual European aerosol conference / European Aerosol Conference* Granada (Spain) 2012, *Annual European aerosol conference / European Aerosol Conference* Manchester (UK) 2011, *Annual European aerosol conference* Helsinki (Finland) 2010, *International conference on workplace aerosols* Karlsruhe (Germany) 2010, *Annual European aerosol conference / European Aerosol Conference* Karlsruhe (Germany) 2009.
Members Individuals in 39 countries and territories:
Australia, Austria, Belarus, Belgium, Bulgaria, Canada, China, Czechia, Denmark, Egypt, Estonia, Finland, France, Germany, Greece, Hungary, India, Ireland, Israel, Italy, Japan, Kenya, Korea Rep, Liechtenstein, Morocco, Netherlands, New Zealand, Norway, Poland, Portugal, Russia, Slovenia, Spain, Sweden, Switzerland, Taiwan, UK, Ukraine, USA.
NGO Relations Member of: *International Aerosol Research Assembly (IARA, #11593).* [2016.11.11/XD8062/v/**D**]

- ♦ Gesellschaft für Angewandte Mathematik und Mechanik (internationally oriented national body)

♦ Gesellschaft für Arthroskopie und Gelenkchirurgie (AGA) 10141

Society for Arthroscopy and Joint-Surgery

Secretariat Porzellangasse 8/23, 1090 Vienna, Austria. T. +4314076432. Fax +43125330339035. E-mail: info@aga-online.ch.
Pres c/o Walder Wyss Ltd, PO Box 1236, Seefeldstrasse 123, 8034 Zurich ZH, Switzerland.
URL: http://www.aga-online.ch/

History 1983, Zurich (Switzerland). Founded as *Deutschsprachige Gesellschaft für Arthroskopie*. Registration: Switzerland. **Aims** Help and encourage young arthroscopists; foster close contact and mutual exchange among physicians practising arthroscopy. **Structure** Board, including President, Vice-President, Secretary and Treasurer. **Languages** German. **Events** *Congress* Vienna (Austria) 2022, *Congress* Innsbruck (Austria) 2021, *Congress* Munich (Germany) 2020, *Congress* Mannheim (Germany) 2019, *Congress* Linz (Austria) 2018. **Publications** *Arthroskopie* (4 a year) – magazine. **Members** Physicians and companies (over 3,400). Membership countries not specified. [2022/XJ6411/**D**]

- ♦ Gesellschaft für Arzneipflanzenforschung / see GA – Society for Medicinal Plant and Natural Product Research (#10075)
- ♦ Gesellschaft für Bedrohte Völker International (#19654)
- ♦ Gesellschaft für Biospeologie / see International Society of Biospeleology (#14975)
- ♦ Gesellschaft für Chronobiologie (#15010)
- ♦ Gesellschaft Deutschsprachiger Lymphologen (internationally oriented national body)
- ♦ Gesellschaften von Exlibris-Freunden (#13421)
- ♦ Gesellschaft der Europäischen Akademien (internationally oriented national body)
- ♦ Gesellschaft Europäischer Kammermusik-Lehrer (#06516)
- ♦ Gesellschaft Europäischer Schlüsseldienste / see European Locksmith Federation (#07708)
- ♦ Gesellschaft Europäischer Verbandsleiter / see European Society of Association Executives (#08526)
- ♦ Gesellschaft zur Foerderung der Literatur aus Afrika, Asien und Lateinamerika (internationally oriented national body)
- ♦ Gesellschaft zur Förderung der Europäischen Soziologie (#05928)
- ♦ Gesellschaft für Gestalttheorie und ihre Anwendungen (internationally oriented national body)
- ♦ Gesellschaft für Histochemie (#19568)
- ♦ Gesellschaft für Interkulturelle Seelsorge und Beratung (#19577)
- ♦ Gesellschaft für Kulturellen und Wissenschaftlichen Ost-West Austausch (no recent information)
- ♦ Gesellschaft für Lagerstättenforschung / see Society for Geology Applied to Mineral Deposits (#19565)
- ♦ Gesellschaft Mariens (religious order)

Gesellschaft Medizin Forschung
10141
alphabetic sequence excludes
For the complete listing, see Yearbook Online at

♦ Gesellschaft für Medizin und Forschung in Afrika / see Amref Health Africa (#00806)
♦ Gesellschaft für Menschenrechte / see International Society for Human Rights (#15183)
♦ Gesellschaft für Nahost Konföderation (inactive)

♦ Gesellschaft für Neuropädiatrie (GNP) 10142

Contact Pressestelle Berlin, Chausseestr 128-129, 10115 Berlin, Germany. E-mail: info@neuropaediatrie.com.
Contact Geschaeftsstelle Kempten, c/o ZiNK, Haubensteigweg 19, 87439 Kempten, Germany. T. +4983196076177. Fax +4983196076197.
URL: http://www.neuropaediatrie.com/

Aims Further research into neuropediatrics. **Structure** Board. **Languages** German. **Finance** Members' dues. Grants. **Activities** Events/meetings. **Publications** *Neuropediatrics* – journal.
Members Full in 3 countries:
Austria, Belgium, Switzerland.
Members also in:
Australia, Brazil, Canada, USA.
Other European countries. Membership countries not specified. [2018.01.03/XJ6672/**D**]

♦ Gesellschaft für Nuclearmedizin – Europa (inactive)
♦ Gesellschaft für Ökologie (#05301)
♦ Gesellschaft für Orthopädisch-Traumatologische Sportmedizin (#19614)
♦ Gesellschaft für Österreichisch-Arabische Beziehungen (internationally oriented national body)
♦ Gesellschaft für Ostnordische Philologie (#19223)
♦ Gesellschaft für Pädagogik und Information (inactive)

♦ Gesellschaft für pädiatrische Pneumologie (GPP) 10143

Office Medizinische Hochschule Hannover, Ztrm Kinderheilkunde / Jugendmedizin, Klinik für Pädiatrische Pneumologie, Allergologie und Neonatologie, Carl-Neuberg-Str 1, 30625 Hannover, Germany. T. +495115323220. E-mail: gpp.hp@mh-hannover.de.
Sec address not obtained. T. +495115329137. Fax +495115329125.
URL: http://www.paediatrische-pneumologie.eu/

History 1978, Hannover (Germany FR). **Structure** Board. **Events** *Annual Meeting* Munich (Germany) 2019, *Annual Meeting* Vienna (Austria) 2018, *Annual Meeting* Essen (Germany) 2017, *Annual Meeting* Dresden (Germany) 2016, *Annual Meeting* Basel (Switzerland) 2015. **Publications** *Zeitschrift der GPP*.
[2014/XJ8967/**D**]

♦ Gesellschaft für Schweisstechnik International (GSI-SLV) 10144

International Society for Welding Technology – Société internationale de technique de soudage

Secretariat address not obtained. T. +492033781119. E-mail: sekretariat@gsi-slv.de.
Commercial Manager address not obtained. T. +492033781123.
URL: http://www.gsi-slv.de/

History 1999, Germany, by the Deutscher Verband für Schweissen und verwandte Verfahren. Registered as a non-profit LLC. **Activities** Training/education. **Members** Membership countries not specified.
[2019/XJ8061/**D**]

♦ Gesellschaft für Seelische Gesundheit in der Frühen Kindheit (#10139)
♦ Gesellschaft für das Studium des Neuen Testaments (#19610)

♦ Gesellschaft für Terminologie und Wissenstransfer (GTW) 10145

Association pour la terminologie et le transfert des connaissances – Association for Terminology and Knowledge Transfer

Main Office Copenhagen Business School, Dalgas Have 15, 2000 Frederiksberg, Denmark. E-mail: hanneerdman@gmail.com.
URL: https://sf.cbs.dk/gtw/

History 1986, Trier (Germany FR). Reorganized, 2005, when moved to Copenhagen (Denmark). Registered in accordance with Danish law. **Aims** Promote knowledge and technology transfer by developing and investigating appropriate methods on modern *information technologies* and special languages. **Structure** Board. **Languages** Danish, English, French, German. **Staff** 5.00 FTE, voluntary. **Finance** Subsidies. **Activities** Events/meetings. **Events** *International Conference on Terminology and Knowledge Engineering* Copenhagen (Denmark) 2016, *International Conference on Terminology and Knowledge Engineering* Berlin (Germany) 2014, *International Conference on Terminology and Knowledge Engineering* Madrid (Spain) 2012, *International conference on terminology and knowledge engineering* Dublin (Ireland) 2010, *International congress on terminology and knowledge engineering* Copenhagen (Denmark) 2008. **Publications** *Mitteilungen für Terminologie und Wissenstransfer – Newsletter for Terminology and Knowledge Transfer – Bulletin de la terminologie et du transfert des connaissances* in English, French, German – newsletter; *TermNet News*. Reports.
Members Individuals and institutions in 33 countries:
Australia, Austria, Belgium, Bulgaria, Canada, China, Denmark, France, Germany, Greece, India, Indonesia, Ireland, Israel, Italy, Japan, Kuwait, Luxembourg, Mexico, Netherlands, Norway, Poland, Portugal, Russia, Saudi Arabia, Singapore, South Africa, Spain, Sweden, Switzerland, Thailand, UK, USA.
NGO Relations In liaison with technical committees of: *International Organization for Standardization (ISO, #14473)*. [2016.06.20/XF5041/**F**]

♦ Gesellschaft für Thrombose- und Hämostaseforschung (GTH) 10146

Society for Thrombosis and haemostasis Research

Office Gertrudenstr 9, 50667 Cologne, Germany. T. +4922142334646. Fax +4922142334620. E-mail: mail@gth-online.org.
URL: http://www.gth-online.org

History 1982. **Aims** Promote and support scientific research in the fields of thrombosis, hemostasis, and vascular medicine and biology. **Structure** Board. **Activities** Events/meetings; research/documentation; training/education. **Events** *Annual Meeting* Lausanne (Switzerland) 2021, *Annual Meeting* Bremen (Germany) 2020, *Annual Meeting* Berlin (Germany) 2019, *Annual Meeting* Vienna (Austria) 2018, *Annual meeting* Munich (Germany) 1994.
Members Full in 3 countries:
Austria, Germany, Switzerland.
NGO Relations Member of: *European Thrombosis and Haemostasis Alliance (ETHA, #08911)*.
[2020/XM7023/**D**]

♦ Gesellschaft für Tropenökologie (internationally oriented national body)
♦ Gesellschaft für Tropenpädiatrie und Internationale Kindergesundheit (internationally oriented national body)
♦ Gesellschaft für Vergleichende Erziehungswissenschaft in Europa (#04410)
♦ Gesellschaft für Versuchstierkunde (#19585)
♦ Gesellschaft für Virologie (internationally oriented national body)
♦ Gesellschaft zur wissenschaftlichen Untersuchung von Parawissenschaften (internationally oriented national body)
♦ **GeSI** Global Enabling Sustainability Initiative (#10340)

♦ Gestalt Academy of Scandinavia 10147

Gestalt-Akademin i Skandinavien

Contact Birger Jarlsgatan 58, SE-114 29 Stockholm, Sweden. E-mail: info@gestaltakademin.se.
URL: http://www.gestaltakademin.se/

NGO Relations *European Association for Psychotherapy (EAP, #06176)*. [2019/XE1993/**E**]

♦ Gestalt-Akademin i Skandinavien (#10147)
♦ GESTE – Groupe d'échanges scientifiques et technologiques éducation-environnement (internationally oriented national body)
♦ Gestionnaires européen de réseaux de transport / see European Network of Transmission System Operators for Electricity (#08026)
♦ Gestion des transformations sociales (#16562)
♦ Gesuiti – Compagnia di Gesù (religious order)
♦ Gesunde-Städte-Projekt / see WHO European Healthy Cities Network (#20936)
♦ **GET 2020** WHO Alliance for the Global Elimination of Trachoma (#20935)
♦ GETF – Global Environment and Technology Foundation (internationally oriented national body)
♦ GE-TM – Genève – Tiers-monde (internationally oriented national body)
♦ **GETO** Gemeinschaft der Europäischen Transsibirien Operateure (#10091)
♦ Getreide- und Futtermittel-Handelsvereinigung (#10692)
♦ GEVL – Groupement international d'étude pour l'exploitation des voitures-lits en Europe (inactive)
♦ Gewerkschaftlicher Verkehrsausschuss in der Europäischen Gemeinschaft / see European Transport Workers' Federation (#08941)
♦ Gewerkschaftsbund – Europäischer Öffentlicher Dienst / see Union Syndicale Fédérale (#20485)
♦ GEXSI – Global Exchange for Social Investment (internationally oriented national body)
♦ GFA – Global Finance Association (internationally oriented national body)
♦ **GFA** Global FinTech Association (#10361)
♦ **GFA** Global Flooring Alliance (#10362)
♦ GFA – Gospel for Asia (internationally oriented national body)
♦ GFAJ / see Federation of Arab Journalists (#09422)
♦ GFAN – Global Fund Advocates Network
♦ GFANZ – Glasgow Financial Alliance for Net Zero (unconfirmed)
♦ **GFAR** Global Forum on Agricultural Research (#10370)
♦ GFAS – Global Federation of Animal Sanctuaries (internationally oriented national body)
♦ GFAV – General Federation of Arab Veterinarians (inactive)
♦ **GfbV International** Gesellschaft für Bedrohte Völker International (#19654)
♦ **GFCC** Global Federation of Competitiveness Councils (#10355)
♦ **GFCE** Global Forum on Cyber Expertise (#10371)
♦ **GFCF** Global Fund for Community Foundations (#10382)
♦ GFC – Global Fashion Conference (meeting series)
♦ **GFC** Global Forest Coalition (#10368)
♦ GFC – Global Fund for Children (internationally oriented national body)
♦ **GFCM** General Fisheries Commission for the Mediterranean (#10112)
♦ **GFCS** Global Framework for Climate Services (#10380)
♦ GFDD – Global Foundation for Democracy and Development (internationally oriented national body)
♦ **GFDRR** Global Facility for Disaster Reduction and Recovery (#10352)
♦ GFEC – Green Finance and Economic Cooperation (unconfirmed)
♦ **GFEI** Global Fuel Economy Initiative (#10381)
♦ **GFEM** Gulf Federation of Emergency Medicine (#10827)
♦ GFEMS – Global Fund to End Modern Slavery (internationally oriented national body)
♦ GFF – Global Familymed Foundation (internationally oriented national body)
♦ **GFF** Global Financing Facility (#10360)
♦ GFF in support of / see Global Financing Facility (#10360)
♦ GFGD – Geology for Global Development (internationally oriented national body)
♦ **GFG** Global Forest Generation (#10369)
♦ GFGHNP / see Groupe francophone d'hépato-gastroentérologie et nutrition pédiatriques (#10742)
♦ **GF** Grameen Foundation (#10694)
♦ **GFHGNP** Groupe francophone d'hépato-gastroentérologie et nutrition pédiatriques (#10742)
♦ **GFHS** Global Forum on Human Settlements (#10372)
♦ **GFIA** Global Federation of Insurance Associations (#10356)
♦ GFI Europe – Good Food Institute Europe (unconfirmed)
♦ **GFI** Global Financial Integrity (#10358)
♦ GFI – Good Food Institute (internationally oriented national body)
♦ GF – International Groundfish Forum (meeting series)
♦ GFLA – Global First Ladies Alliance (unconfirmed)
♦ **GFLJD** Global Forum on Law, Justice and Development (#10373)
♦ GFLP – Global Family for Love and Peace (internationally oriented national body)
♦ **GFMA** Global Financial Markets Association (#10359)
♦ **GFMAM** Global Forum on Maintenance and Asset Management (#10374)
♦ GFMC – Global Fire Monitoring Centre (internationally oriented national body)
♦ **GFMD** Global Forum for Media Development (#10375)
♦ **GFMD** Global Forum on Migration and Development (#10376)
♦ GFMSA – Global Family Medicine Scientific Alliance (internationally oriented national body)
♦ GFNDR – Global Forum of NGOs for Natural Disaster Reduction (internationally oriented national body)
♦ **GFN** Global Farmer Network (#10354)
♦ **GFN** Global FoodBanking Network (#10365)
♦ **GfÖ** Gesellschaft für Ökologie (#05301)
♦ GFPD – Global Foundation for Peroxisomal Disorders (internationally oriented national body)
♦ **GFPF** Global Fluorocarbon Producers Forum (#10364)
♦ GFP – Global Flood Partnership (unconfirmed)
♦ GFPP – Global Forest Policy Project (internationally oriented national body)
♦ **GFPS** Global Fluid Power Society (#10363)
♦ **GFRAS** Global Forum for Rural Advisory Services (#10378)
♦ GFRUP – Groupe francophone de réanimation et urgences pédiatriques (internationally oriented national body)
♦ GFSE – Global Forum on Sustainable Energy (internationally oriented national body)
♦ **GFS** Gemeinsame Forschungsstelle (#16147)
♦ **GFSI** Global Food Safety Initiative (#10366)
♦ **GFSM** Groupe Francophone de Spectrométrie Mössbauer (#10744)
♦ **GFS World Council** Girls Friendly Society World Council (#10153)
♦ GFTA – International Symposium on Geometric Function Theory and Applications (meeting series)
♦ **GFU** Gran Fraternidad Universal (#20677)
♦ GfV – Gesellschaft für Virologie (internationally oriented national body)
♦ GFWC – General Federation of Women's Clubs (internationally oriented national body)
♦ GFW – Global Fishing Watch (internationally oriented national body)
♦ GFW – Global Forest Watch (internationally oriented national body)
♦ **GFW** Global Fund for Women (#10384)
♦ **GGBN** Global Genome Biodiversity Network (#10388)
♦ **GGC** Gulf of Guinea Commission (#10829)
♦ GGEN – Global Green Environmental Network (unconfirmed)
♦ GGEP / see Group of the Greens – European Free Alliance (#10781)
♦ GGF / see Institute for Geopolitical Research and Development (#11265)
♦ GGF / see Open Grid Forum (#17754)
♦ **GGGI** Global Ghost Gear Initiative (#10390)
♦ **GGGI** Global Green Growth Institute (#10392)
♦ GGI Global Alliance (unconfirmed)
♦ **GGI** Global Governance Institute (#10391)
♦ **GGIS** Global Green Island Summit (#10393)
♦ GGJ – Grassroots Global Justice Alliance (internationally oriented national body)
♦ **GGKP** Green Growth Knowledge Platform (#10719)
♦ GGLF / see Gnome Liberation Front (#10671)
♦ **GGN** Global Geoparks Network (#10389)
♦ GGN – Global Greeter Network Foundation (unconfirmed)
♦ GGN – Grameen Global Network (see: #10693)
♦ GGOS – Global Geodetic Observing System (see: #11914)
♦ **GGSD** Gulf Group for the Study of Diabetes (#10828)
♦ GGU – Global Green University (internationally oriented national body)

- ♦ GHA – Global Health Action (internationally oriented national body)
- ♦ **GHA** Gulf Heart Association (#10831)
- ♦ GHAI – Global Health Advocacy Incubator (internationally oriented national body)
- ♦ Ghana-Guinea Union (inactive)
- ♦ Ghaqda Ewropea Tal-Ghalliema (#02565)
- ♦ GHARF – Global Health Awareness Research Foundation (internationally oriented national body)
- ♦ **GHARP** Greater Horn of Africa Rainwater Partnership (#10701)
- ♦ **GHC** Global Health Cluster (#10401)
- ♦ GHC – Global Health Corps (internationally oriented national body)
- ♦ **GHC** Global Health Council (#10402)
- ♦ GHC – Global Hygiene Council (unconfirmed)
- ♦ **GHC** Gulf Health Council (#10830)
- ♦ **GHE** Global Health Europe (#10404)
- ♦ **GHEN** Global Higher Education Network (#10409)
- ♦ GHET / see Global Health through Education, Training and Service (#10403)
- ♦ **GHETS** Global Health through Education, Training and Service (#10403)
- ♦ **GHF** Global Hapkido Federation (#10397)
- ♦ GHF – Global Health Foundation (internationally oriented national body)
- ♦ GHF – Global Heritage Fund (internationally oriented national body)
- ♦ GHF – Global Housing Foundation (internationally oriented national body)
- ♦ GHF – Global Hydranencephaly Foundation (unconfirmed)
- ♦ GHGI – Global Health Group International (unconfirmed)
- ♦ **GHG Protocol** Greenhouse Gas Protocol (#10721)
- ♦ GHG Protocol Initiative / see Greenhouse Gas Protocol (#10721)
- ♦ **GHHF** Greater Horn Horizon Forum (#10702)
- ♦ **GHHIN** Global Heat Health Information Network (#10408)
- ♦ GHI Association – Globale Harmonisierungs Initiative für Gesetze und Verordnungen im Bereich Lebensmittel / see Global Harmonization Initiative (#10398)
- ♦ GHI Association – Global Harmonization Initiative for food regulations and legislation / see Global Harmonization Initiative (#10398)
- ♦ **GHI** Global Harmonization Initiative (#10398)
- ♦ GHI-net – Global Healthcare Information Network (internationally oriented national body)
- ♦ GHN / see Global Hope Network International (#10411)
- ♦ GHN – Groupe hygiène naturelle (inactive)
- ♦ **GHNI** Global Hope Network International (#10411)
- ♦ **GHOU** Global Hands-On Universe (#10395)
- ♦ **GHP** Global Handwashing Partnership (#10396)
- ♦ GHP – Global Health Partners (internationally oriented national body)
- ♦ **GHP** Global Humanitarian Platform (#10413)
- ♦ GHRD – Global Human Rights Defence (internationally oriented national body)
- ♦ GHRF – Global Health Research Foundation (internationally oriented national body)
- ♦ GHR Foundation (internationally oriented national body)
- ♦ **GHR** Geneva for Human Rights – Global Training (#10124)
- ♦ **GHSA** Global Health Security Agenda (#10405)
- ♦ **GHSI** Global Health Security Initiative (#10406)
- ♦ GHSN – Global Health Security Network (internationally oriented national body)
- ♦ GHTC – Global Health Technologies Coalition (internationally oriented national body)
- ♦ GHV – Global Health Visions (internationally oriented national body)
- ♦ GHW – Global Health Watch (internationally oriented national body)
- ♦ **GHWP** Global Harmonization Working Party (#10399)
- ♦ Gi4DM – Geo-Information for Disaster Management (meeting series)
- ♦ **GIABA** Groupe Intergouvernemental d'Action contre le Blanchiment d'Argent en Afrique de l'Ouest (#11471)
- ♦ GiA – Global Interaction (internationally oriented national body)
- ♦ **GIAIS** Global Infrastructure Alliance for Internet Safety (#10417)
- ♦ Gianelline – Figlie di Maria Santissima dell'Orto (religious order)
- ♦ Gianellines – Filles de Sainte Marie du Jardin (religious order)
- ♦ GIAN – Geneva International Academic Network (internationally oriented national body)

♦ Giant Screen Cinema Association (GSCA) 10148

Exec Dir 624 Holly Springs Rd, Ste 243, Holly Springs NC 27540, USA. T. +19193461123. Fax +19195739100.
URL: http://www.giantscreencinema.com/

History 1977, as 'Space Theater Consortium (STC), the professional organization for 15 Perf/70mm theatres and associations. 1993, name changed to *International Space Theatre Consortium (ISTC)*. 1999, name changed to *Giant Screen Theater Association (GSTA)*. Jan 2006, present name adopted upon merger with *Large Format Cinema Association (LFCA)*. **Aims** Serve as global forum for development and presentation of entertaining giant screen *film* experiences for lifelong learning. **Languages** English. **Activities** Organizes: international conference with trade show; Film Expo; symposia. **Events** *Annual Conference* Toronto, ON (Canada) 2014, *Annual Conference* Ottawa, ON (Canada) 2013, *Annual Conference* Sacramento, CA (USA) 2012, *Annual Conference* Austin, TX (USA) 2011, *Annual Conference* Chattanooga, TN (USA) 2010. **Publications** *The Big Frame* (4 a year); *Framework* – newsletter; *Rewind and Review* – newsletter. *GSTA Directory*. **Members** Regular; Developing; Associate. Individuals and organizations in 39 countries and territories: Australia, Austria, Belgium, Canada, China, Colombia, Denmark, Finland, France, Germany, Greece, India, Indonesia, Ireland, Israel, Italy, Japan, Korea Rep, Kuwait, Malaysia, Malta, Mexico, Netherlands, New Zealand, Norway, Pakistan, Philippines, Poland, Saudi Arabia, Singapore, South Africa, Spain, Sweden, Switzerland, Taiwan, Thailand, Türkiye, UK, USA.
[2015/XD6468/**D**]

- ♦ Giant Screen Theater Association / see Giant Screen Cinema Association (#10148)
- ♦ GIART – Groupement international des artistes interprètes ou exécutants (inactive)
- ♦ **GIBET** Groupement interuniversitaire Benelux des économistes des transports (#15985)
- ♦ **GIB Foundation** Global Infrastructure Basel Foundation (#10418)
- ♦ **GIB** Gulf International Bank (#10832)
- ♦ **GIBPOA** Grupo Iberoamericano de Polinomios Ortogonales y Aplicaciones (#10806)
- ♦ **GICA** Global Infrastructure Connectivity Alliance (#10419)
- ♦ GICCA – Grupo Iberoamericano de Implantes Cocleares y Ciencias Afines (unconfirmed)
- ♦ GICDF – Gaddafi International Charity and Development Foundation (internationally oriented national body)
- ♦ GIC – Geoinformatics Center (internationally oriented national body)
- ♦ **GIC** Geoscience Information Consortium (#10136)
- ♦ GIC – Gilman International Conservation Foundation (internationally oriented national body)
- ♦ GIC – Global Interdependence Center (internationally oriented national body)
- ♦ **GIC** Global Investor Coalition on Climate Change (#10434)
- ♦ GIC – Guilde internationale des coopératrices (inactive)
- ♦ **GIC** Gulf Investment Corporation (#10834)
- ♦ GICHD – Geneva International Centre for Humanitarian Demining (internationally oriented national body)
- ♦ **GICJ** Geneva International Centre for Justice (#10125)
- ♦ **GICNT** Global Initiative to Combat Nuclear Terrorism (#10424)
- ♦ GICRD – Groupe international de coopération et de recherche en documentation: planification territoriale – habitat – information (inactive)
- ♦ GICSV – Grupo Interamericano de Coordinación en Sanidad Vegetal (no recent information)
- ♦ GID-EMAN / see Euro-Mediterranean Academic Network (#05716)

♦ Gideons International (GI) 10149

Association internationale des gédéons

Main Office PO Box 140800, Nashville TN 37214-0800, USA. T. +16155645000. Fax +16155646000. E-mail: tgi@gideons.org.
Street Address 50 Century Blvd, Nashville TN 37214-0800, USA.
URL: http://www.gideons.org/

History 1 Jul 1899, Janesville WI (USA). **Aims** Win people for the Lord Jesus Christ through personal witness and the distribution of Bibles and New Testaments. **Languages** Over 90. **Staff** Over 100 paid; 125,000 volunteers in USA; over 150,000 volunteers outside USA. **Finance** Gifts. Budget (annual): about US$ 99 million. **Activities** Places Bibles and New Testaments in hotels, motels, hospitals, clinics and penal institutions. Distributes New Testaments free of charge to students, military, nurses and prisoners. **Events** *Annual Convention* Kansas City, MO (USA) 2006, *Annual Convention* Anaheim, CA (USA) 2005, *Annual Convention* Dallas, TX (USA) 2004, *Annual Convention* Birmingham, AL (USA) 2003, *Annual Convention* Louisville, KY (USA) 2002. **Publications** *The Gideon* (6 a year). **Members** Christian business and professional men in 193 countries and territories. Membership countries not specified. [2019/XD5394/v/**F**]

- ♦ **GID** Groupe interacadémique pour le développement (#10746)
- ♦ GIDRM – Global Initiative on Disaster Risk Management (internationally oriented national body)
- ♦ **GIEC** Groupe d'experts intergouvernemental sur l'évolution du climat (#11499)
- ♦ GIEDA / see International Group for Study of Intervertebral Spine Approaches (#13757)
- ♦ **GIEDA INTER RACHIS** Groupe international d'étude des approches intervertébrales du rachis (#13757)
- ♦ GIE EUMETNET / see Network of European Meteorological Services (#17022)
- ♦ **GIE** Gas Infrastructure Europe (#10073)
- ♦ **GIE** Grupo Iberamericano de Editores (#10805)
- ♦ **GIERAF** Groupe Interafricain d'Etudes, de Recherches et d'Application sur la Fertilité (#10747)
- ♦ **GIESCO** Groupe International d'Experts en Systèmes vitivinicoles pour la CoOpération (#10748)
- ♦ GI-ESCR – Global Initiative for Economic, Social and Cultural Rights (internationally oriented national body)
- ♦ **GIEWS** Global Information and Early Warning System on Food and Agriculture (#10416)
- ♦ GIFA – Geneva Infant Feeding Association (internationally oriented national body)
- ♦ GIFAP / see CropLife International (#04966)
- ♦ GIFCA / see Gaddafi International Charity and Development Foundation
- ♦ **GIFCS** Group of International Finance Centre Supervisors (#10782)
- ♦ **GIFFOCH** Groupe International Francophone pour la Formation aux Classifications du Handicap (#10749)
- ♦ **GIF** Generation IV International Forum (#10115)
- ♦ GIF – Global Innovation Fund (internationally oriented national body)
- ♦ GIFT – Global Institute of Flexible Systems Management (internationally oriented national body)

♦ Gift of Life International (GOL) 10150

Exec Dir address not obtained. T. +18455462104.
URL: http://giftoflife01.designinterventionsites.com/

History Set up as an organization based on *Rotary International (RI, #18975)*. **Aims** Provide hope to children from developing countries with heart disease regardless of their gender, creed or national origin. **Structure** Board of Directors. **Activities** Active in: El Salvador, Jamaica, Uganda. [2015/XJ9749/**F**]

- ♦ **GIFTS of Health** Global Initiative for Traditional Systems of Health (#10426)
- ♦ Gifts in Kind International / see Good360

♦ GIGAEurope AISBL 10151

Managing Dir Rondpoint Schuman 2-4, 5th floor, 1040 Brussels, Belgium. T. +3224033691. E-mail: office@gigaeurope.eu.
URL: https://gigaeurope.eu/

History 2 Sep 1955, Brussels (Belgium). New statutes adopted Mar 1994; again Dec 2009. Took over functions of *EuroCableLabs (ECL, inactive)*, 1 Jan 2002. Integrated *CTAM Europe (#04978)*, Aug 2015. Rebranded under current title, Nov 2019, with launch Nov 2020. Former names and other names: *International Alliance for Distribution by Cable* – former (2 Sep 1955 to 2 Sep 1955); *Alliance internationale de la distribution par câble (AID)* – former (2 Sep 1955 to Mar 1994); *European Cable Communications Association (ECCA)* – former (Mar 1994 to Feb 2007); *Cable Europe* – former (Feb 2007 to Nov 2019). Registration: No/ID: 0442.182.814, Start date: 12 Dec 1990, Belgium; EU Transparency Register, No/ID: 42178977290-80, Start date: 29 Nov 2011. **Aims** Support a strong and harmonized European Digital Single Market, with a clear focus on enabling regulatory and market conditions that allow for sustainable investment and innovation in Gigabit infrastructure and the Internet of Things; highlight the importance of EU policies based on long-term objectives, with regulatory intervention strictly limited to situations where the market fails to provide efficient outcomes; reduce market fragmentation and establish a level playing field across the whole digital ecosystem. **Structure** General Assembly; Board; Bureau. **Languages** English. **Staff** 4.00 FTE, paid. **Finance** Sources: members' dues. **Events** *Connectivity for a Gigabit Europe* 2021, *Trust in the Digital Decade – Making sure technology serves EU citizens* 2021, *Connecting for Recovery Launch Event* 2020, *Annual Congress and General Assembly* Berlin (Germany) 2019, *Annual Congress and General Assembly* Dublin (Ireland) 2018. **Members** Associate from connectivity and content sectors; industries and organizations from wider digital economy. Membership countries not specified. **Consultative Status** Consultative status granted from: *World Intellectual Property Organization (WIPO, #21593)* (Permanent Observer Status). **IGO Relations** Observer status with (2): *Intergovernmental Committee of the International Convention of Rome for the Protection of Performers, Producers of Phonograms and Broadcasting Organizations (#11474)*; *Union for the International Registration of Audiovisual Works (#20444)*. **NGO Relations** Member of (3): *European Internet Forum (EIF, #07591)* (as Associate member); *European Telecommunications Standards Institute (ETSI, #08897)*; *Federation of European and International Associations Established in Belgium (FAIB, #09508)*. Partner of (1): *European Committee for Electrotechnical Standardization (CENELEC, #06647)*.
[2021.09.07/XD1151/**D**]

- ♦ GIGA – German Institute of Global and Area Studies (internationally oriented national body)
- ♦ GIGA Institut für Asienstudien / see GIGA Institut für Asien-Studien
- ♦ GIGA Institut für Asien-Studien (internationally oriented national body)
- ♦ GIGA Institute of Asian Affairs / see GIGA Institut für Asien-Studien
- ♦ GIGA Institute for Asian Studies (internationally oriented national body)
- ♦ GIGA Institute of Middle East Studies, Hamburg (internationally oriented national body)
- ♦ GIGA Institut für Nahost-Studien, Hamburg (internationally oriented national body)
- ♦ **GIGANet** Global Internet Governance Academic Network (#10432)
- ♦ GIGAPP – Asociación Grupo de Investigación en Gobierno, Administración y Políticas Públicas (internationally oriented national body)
- ♦ GIGAPP – Association – Research Group in Government, Administration and Public Policies (internationally oriented national body)
- ♦ **GI** Gideons International (#10149)
- ♦ GI – Global Initiatives for Sustainable Development and Humanitarian Action (internationally oriented national body)
- ♦ GI – Grassroots International (internationally oriented national body)
- ♦ **GI Hub** Global Infrastructure Hub (#10420)
- ♦ Giiagda Zghazagh Ghal (#21984)
- ♦ GiiA – Geneva Interfaith Intercultural Alliance (internationally oriented national body)
- ♦ **GIIAP** Grupo Internacional de Investigación Sobre Actinomicetos Patógenos (#10807)
- ♦ GIIC – Global Information Infrastructure Commission (internationally oriented national body)
- ♦ **GIICS** Group of International Insurance Centre Supervisors (#10783)
- ♦ **GII** Global Implementation Initiative (#10415)
- ♦ **GIIGNL** Groupe international des importateurs de gaz naturel liquefié (#10750)
- ♦ GII – Goodwill Industries International (internationally oriented national body)
- ♦ **GIIN** Global Impact Investing Network (#10414)

GIIP
10151

alphabetic sequence excludes
For the complete listing, see Yearbook Online at

- ♦ GIIP – Groupement international de l'industrie pharmaceutique des pays de la CEE (inactive)
- ♦ GIIS / see Global Initiatives for Sustainable Development and Humanitarian Action
- ♦ GIJN Global Investigative Journalism Network (#10433)
- ♦ GIJTR – Global Initiative for Justice, Truth and Reconciliation (unconfirmed)
- ♦ GILCD / see Leadership exCHANGE
- ♦ Gilead Foundation (internationally oriented national body)
- ♦ Gilman International Conservation Foundation (internationally oriented national body)
- ♦ GIM Global Society for Industrial Microbiology (#10606)
- ♦ GIM-IC / see Global Society for Industrial Microbiology (#10606)
- ♦ GIMIC – International Association for Gastrointestinal Motility in Children (inactive)
- ♦ GIM International Committee / see Global Society for Industrial Microbiology (#10606)
- ♦ GIMUN – Geneva International Model United Nations (internationally oriented national body)
- ♦ GIN / see Intuition Network
- ♦ GINA Global Initiative on Asthma (#10422)
- ♦ Ginebra para los Derechos Humanos – Formación Internacional (#10124)
- ♦ Ginekis tis Evropis / see Association femmes d'Europe
- ♦ GINETEX Groupement International de l'Etiquetage pour l'Entretien des Textiles (#10761)
- ♦ GIN – Global Information Network (internationally oriented national body)
- ♦ GIN Global Islands Network (#10437)
- ♦ GIN Global Issues Network (#10438)
- ♦ GIN Greening of Industry Network (#10723)
- ♦ GIN Guidelines International Network (#10817)
- ♦ GINI / see Post-Polio Health International
- ♦ GINI – Governance Institutes Network International (internationally oriented national body)
- ♦ GI Norden Nordic Network for Geographic Information (#17355)
- ♦ GINREIKA / see Asian Federation of Laryngectomees' Associations (#01463)
- ♦ GIN-SSOGIE Global Interfaith Network for People of All Sexes, Sexual Orientation, Gender Identity and Expression (#10431)
- ♦ Giovani Democratici Cristiani Europei (inactive)
- ♦ Giovani per un Mondo Unito (see: #09806)
- ♦ Giovani nel Mondo (internationally oriented national body)
- ♦ Giovanni Agnelli Foundation (internationally oriented national body)
- ♦ Giovanni Lorenzini Medical Foundation (internationally oriented national body)
- ♦ Gioventù per i Diritti Umani Internazionale (#22019)
- ♦ Gioventù Federalista Europea (#21984)
- ♦ GIPC – Global Initiative for Positive Change (internationally oriented national body)
- ♦ Gipfel der Grossregion (meeting series)
- ♦ GIP Green Industry Platform (#10722)
- ♦ GIP / see Human Rights in Mental Health (#10988)
- ♦ GIPIS – Graduate Institute of Political and International Studies (internationally oriented national body)
- ♦ GIPRI – Geneva International Peace Research Institute (internationally oriented national body)
- ♦ GIRAF – Geoscience InfoRmation in AFrica (unconfirmed)
- ♦ GIRA – Georgetown International Relations Association Inc (internationally oriented national body)
- ♦ GIREDD / see Groupe international du rêve-éveillé en psychanalyse (#10752)
- ♦ GIRED / see Groupe international du rêve-éveillé en psychanalyse (#10752)
- ♦ GIREP Groupe international de recherche sur l'enseignement de la physique (#14731)
- ♦ GIREP Groupe international du rêve-éveillé en psychanalyse (#10752)
- ♦ GIRI Groupe International de Recherche sur l'Infinitésimal (#10751)
- ♦ Giri Institute of Development Studies (internationally oriented national body)
- ♦ Girl Effect (internationally oriented national body)
- ♦ The Girl Generation (unconfirmed)
- ♦ Girls' Brigade / see Girls' Brigade International (#10152)

♦ Girls' Brigade International (GB) 10152

Registered Office Cliff College, Calver, S32 3XG, UK. E-mail: home@gbworldwide.org.
URL: http://www.gbworldwide.org/
History 1893. Founded as 'Girls' Brigade'. Reconstructed 1965, as Girls' Brigade International Council (GBIC), to include 'Girls' Guildry', formed 1900, and 'Girls' Life Brigade", set up 1902. Confirmed 10 Jun 1968. Registration: Charity Commission, No/ID: 279811, England and Wales; Companies House, No/ID: 1460734, England and Wales. **Aims** Acting as a Christian organization – both international and interdenominational – help girls to become followers of Lord Jesus Christ and, through self control, reverence and a sense of responsibility, find true enrichment of life; provide activities designed to help girls to attain physical, mental and spiritual maturity and encourage girls to express what they learn through practical service to home, community and Church. **Structure** International Council, (meets at least every 4 years), comprising International President, 5 International Vice-Presidents (Chairpersons of the 5 Fellowships – Africa, Asia, Caribbean/Americas, Europe, Pacific), International Treasurer and representatives from member countries' National Councils. **Languages** English. **Staff** 0.50 FTE, paid. **Finance** Sources: grants; members' dues. Annual budget: 100,000 GBP. **Activities** Networking/liaising; training/education. **Events** Quadrennial Conference Kingston (Jamaica) 2022, Quadrennial Conference Zambia 2018, Quadrennial Conference Perth, WA (Australia) 2014, Quadrennial Conference Kuching (Malaysia) 2010, Quadrennial Conference Coleraine (UK) 2006.
Members Full in 42 countries and territories:
Anguilla, Antigua-Barbuda, Australia, Bahamas, Botswana, Canada, Cayman Is, Cook Is, Dominica, England, Eswatini, Ghana, Haiti, Hong Kong, Ireland, Jamaica, Kenya, Malawi, Malaysia, New Zealand, Nigeria, Niue, Northern Ireland, Papua New Guinea, Philippines, Romania, Scotland, Sierra Leone, Singapore, Solomon Is, South Africa, St Kitts-Nevis, St Maarten, St Vincent-Grenadines, Tanzania UR, Thailand, Trinidad-Tobago, USA, Virgin Is UK, Wales, Zambia, Zimbabwe.
Associate members in 11 countries and territories:
Belize, Bermuda, Brunei Darussalam, Congo DR, Montserrat, Samoa USA, St Eustatius, Tonga, Tuvalu, Uganda, Vanuatu.
Consultative Status Consultative status granted from: ECOSOC (#05331) (Special). **NGO Relations** Member of (1): Commonwealth Youth Exchange Council (CYEC).
[2023.02.28/XF0998/F]

- ♦ Girls' Brigade International Council / see Girls' Brigade International (#10152)
- ♦ Girls' Brigade Worldwide / see Girls' Brigade International (#10152)

♦ Girls Friendly Society World Council (GFS World Council) 10153

World Pres 15 Bridge Road, Bramley View, Johannesburg, 2090, South Africa. E-mail: gfsworldpres2020@gmail.com.
URL: http://www.gfsworld.org/
History 1955. Founded by the Presidents and Executive Secretaries of Girls Friendly Societies in 8 countries.
Aims Provide ministries in a safe and accepting environment where Christ's love is evident and the Gospel is proclaimed. **Structure** World Council (meets every 3 years), comprising World President, World Vice President, Secretary, Treasurer and World Youth Officer. **Languages** English. **Staff** Voluntary. **Finance** Sources: donations; members' dues. Annual budget: 20,000 USD. **Activities** Awards/prizes/competitions; projects/programmes; religious activities. **Events** Triennial Meeting Johannesburg (South Africa) 2021, Triennial Meeting South Africa 2020, Triennial Meeting Perth, WA (Australia) 2017, Triennial Meeting Swansea (UK) 2014, Triennial meeting Ireland 2011. **Publications** World Newsletter (4 a year).
Members Full in 33 countries and territories:
Angola, Australia, Cameroon, Canada, Congo DR, Dominican Rep, England, Eswatini, Ghana, Guyana, Honduras, Ireland, Japan, Kenya, Korea Rep, Liberia, Malawi, Mozambique, New Zealand, Papua New Guinea, Philippines, Rwanda, Sierra Leone, Solomon Is, South Africa, South Sudan, Sri Lanka, Tanzania UR, Uganda, USA, Wales, Zambia, Zimbabwe.
NGO Relations Accredited by (1): Green Anglicans.
[2022.02.02/XJ0533/E]

- ♦ Girls Learn International (internationally oriented national body)

♦ Girls not Brides 10154

Exec Dir Seventh Floor, 65 Leadenhall Street, London, EC3A 2AD, UK. E-mail: info@girlsnotbrides.org.
URL: http://girlsnotbrides.org/

History 2010. Former names and other names: Girls Not Brides – The Global Partnership to End Child Marriage – full title. **Aims** Bring child marriage to global attention; build an understanding of the necessities to end child marriage; call for laws, policies and programmes to be put in place, making a difference to the life of millions of girls. **Finance** Donors include: Canadian Department of Foreign Affairs, Trade and Development; The Elders Foundation (#05413); Ford Foundation (#09858); The William and Flora Hewlett Foundation; MacArthur Foundation; Open Society Foundations (OSF, #17763); private foundations. **Events** Global Meeting Kuala Lumpur (Malaysia) 2018, Workshop Amsterdam (Netherlands) 2016, Global Meeting Casablanca (Morocco) 2015, Workhop Istanbul (Turkey) 2013, Sub-Saharan Africa Regional Meeting Johannesburg (South Africa) 2012.
Members Civil society organizations (over 400) from 65 countries:
Afghanistan, Australia, Bangladesh, Belgium, Bhutan, Brazil, Bulgaria, Burkina Faso, Burundi, Cambodia, Cameroon, Canada, Chad, Congo DR, Côte d'Ivoire, Dominican Rep, Egypt, Ethiopia, France, Gambia, Georgia, Germany, Ghana, Guatemala, India, Iraq, Italy, Kazakhstan, Kenya, Kyrgyzstan, Lesotho, Liberia, Malawi, Malaysia, Mali, Morocco, Mozambique, Nepal, Netherlands, Nicaragua, Niger, Nigeria, Norway, Pakistan, Palestine, Paraguay, Rwanda, Saudi Arabia, Senegal, Sierra Leone, Somalia, South Africa, South Sudan, Sri Lanka, Sudan, Switzerland, Tajikistan, Tanzania UR, Türkiye, Uganda, UK, USA, Yemen, Zambia, Zimbabwe.
NGOs listed in this Yearbook (64):
- Accountability International (#00059);
- ActionAid (#00087);
- Advocates for Youth, Washington DC;
- African Child Education Right Initiative (ACERI);
- African Child Policy Forum (ACPF, #00246);
- African Development Aid Association (ADAA);
- Alliances for Africa (AfA);
- Anti-Slavery International (#00860);
- Arigatou International;
- Aura Freedom International;
- CARE International (CI, #03429);
- ChildFund International (#03869);
- ChildHope UK;
- EngenderHealth;
- Equality Now (#05518);
- Equilibres and Populations (Equipop);
- EveryChild;
- FHI 360;
- Forum for African Women Educationalists (FAWE, #09896);
- Foundation for Women's Health Research and Development (FORWARD);
- Free the Slaves;
- Frontline AIDS (#10007);
- Global Rights;
- Human Rights and Democracy Link Africa (RIDE AFRICA);
- Human Rights Watch (HRW, #10990);
- Hunger Project (#10994);
- Inter-African Committee on Traditional Practices Affecting the Health of Women and Children (IAC, #11384);
- International Center for Research on Women (ICRW);
- International Child Development Initiatives (ICDI);
- International Children's Center (ICC);
- International Foundation for Population and Development (IFPD, #13674);
- International Planned Parenthood Federation (IPPF, #14589);
- International Women's Health Coalition (IWHC);
- Men's Resources International (MRI);
- Moremi Initiative for Women's Leadership in Africa (Moremi Initiative);
- No Peace Without Justice (NPWJ, #17155);
- Norwegian Church Aid;
- Organisation of African Youth (OAYouth, #17799);
- PAI (#18025);
- Pan African Organisation for Research and Protection of Violence on Women and Children (PAORP-VWC);
- Parliamentarians for Global Action (PGA, #18208);
- Pathfinder International (#18261);
- Plan International (#18386);
- Population Council (#18458);
- Promundo;
- READ Global;
- Right to Play International (#18945);
- Royal Commonwealth Society (RCS, #18990);
- Save the Children UK (SC UK);
- Seeds to Sew International;
- Sonke Gender Justice Network;
- SOS-Kinderdorf International (#19693);
- Strømme Foundation (SF);
- TERRE DES FEMMES (#20131);
- Terre des hommes Foundation (Tdh Foundation, #20132);
- The Elders Foundation (#05413);
- United States Fund for UNICEF (UNICEF USA);
- Vital Voices Global Partnership (VVGP);
- WeForest (#20852);
- White Ribbon Alliance for Safe Motherhood (WRA, #20934);
- Women and Law in Southern Africa Research Trust (WLSA, #21006);
- Women Deliver (#20989);
- World Vision International (WVI, #21904);
- World Young Women's Christian Association (World YWCA, #21947).
Consultative Status Consultative status granted from: United Nations Population Fund (UNFPA, #20612).
[2022/XJ5478/y/F]

- ♦ Girls Not Brides – The Global Partnership to End Child Marriage / see Girls not Brides (#10154)
- ♦ GIRN Global Investor Relations Network (#10435)
- ♦ Giro Agreement, 1979 (1979 treaty)
- ♦ Giro Agreement, 1984 (1984 treaty)
- ♦ GIRP / see Groupement International de la Répartition Pharmaceutique (#10762)
- ♦ GIRP Groupement International de la Répartition Pharmaceutique (#10762)
- ♦ GIRSO Groupement international pour la recherche scientifique en stomatologie et odontologie (#13755)
- ♦ GIS Asie – Groupement d'intérêt scientifique Études asiatiques (internationally oriented national body)
- ♦ GIScience – International Conference on Geographic Information Science (meeting series)
- ♦ GISEH – Conférence Francophone en Gestion et Ingénierie des Systèmes Hospitaliers (meeting series)
- ♦ GISF Global Interagency Security Forum (#10430)
- ♦ GIS-GEMDEV / see Groupement d'intérêt scientifique pour l'étude de la mondialisation et du développement
- ♦ GISGUF Groupement international des secrétaires généraux des universités francophones (#10763)
- ♦ GIS Gulf Intervention Society (#10833)
- ♦ GISIG Geographical Information Systems International Group (#10133)
- ♦ GISPE – Geographical Information Service Producers in Europe (no recent information)
- ♦ GISPRI – Global Industrial and Social Progress Research Institute (internationally oriented national body)
- ♦ GITE Groupe international de travail sur l'éducation (#15909)
- ♦ GITES Groupement des industries européennes du tabac (#10760)
- ♦ GIT – Global Institute of Theology (see: #21289)
- ♦ GI-TOC Global Initiative Against Transnational Organized Crime (#10421)
- ♦ Giuseppini d'Asti – Oblati di San Giuseppe (religious order)
- ♦ Giuseppini del Belgio (religious order)
- ♦ Giuseppini del Murialdo – Congregazione di San Giuseppe (religious order)
- ♦ Givat Haviva Jewish-Arab Center for Peace (internationally oriented national body)
- ♦ Give2Asia (internationally oriented national body)
- ♦ Give Peace a Chance Trust (internationally oriented national body)

- ♦ Giving Children Hope (internationally oriented national body)
- ♦ Giving Global / see UniversalGiving
- ♦ Giving Institute: Leading Consultants to Non-Profits (internationally oriented national body)

♦ GivingTuesday 10155

Contact address not obtained. E-mail: info@givingtuesday.org.
URL: http://www.givingtuesday.org/

History Founded 2012, New York NY (USA), by 92nd Street Y in partnership with *United Nations Foundation (UNF, #20563)*. **Aims** Celebrate and support giving and *philanthropy*. **Activities** Networking/liaising.
Members Organizations in 38 countries and territories:
Argentina, Armenia, Australia, Barbados, Brazil, Canada, Chile, Croatia, Czechia, Dominican Rep, Germany, Hungary, India, Israel, Italy, Kazakhstan, Kenya, Liberia, Mexico, New Zealand, Norway, Panama, Puerto Rico, Romania, Russia, Rwanda, Singapore, Slovakia, Slovenia, Spain, Sweden, Switzerland, Tanzania UR, Uganda, UK, Uruguay, USA, Venezuela.
NGO Relations *Bill and Melinda Gates Foundation (BMGF).* [2018/XM7152/**F**]

- ♦ GIWA – Global Interfaith WASH Alliance (unconfirmed)
- ♦ **GIWEH** Global Institute for Water, Environment and Health (#10429)
- ♦ GIZ – Deutsche Gesellschaft für Internationale Zusammenarbeit (internationally oriented national body)
- ♦ GJARN – Global Jewish Assistance and Relief Network (internationally oriented national body)
- ♦ **GJASD International** Green Jobs and Sustainable Development International Centre (#10724)
- ♦ **GJBSA** Global Jesuit Business Student Association (#10442)
- ♦ GJC – Global Justice Center (internationally oriented national body)
- ♦ GJEP – Global Justice Ecology Project (internationally oriented national body)
- ♦ **GKPF** Global Knowledge Partnership Foundation (#10443)
- ♦ GKP / see Global Knowledge Partnership Foundation (#10443)
- ♦ Glaciological Society / see International Glaciological Society (#13718)
- ♦ GLADAOF / see Pan-American Retina and Vitreous Society (#18126)
- ♦ GLADEL – Grupo Latino Americano de Estudio de Lupus (unconfirmed)
- ♦ **GLAD** Global Action on Disability Network (#10165)
- ♦ GLADIO Network / see Allied Coordination Committee (#00733)
- ♦ **GLAFRI** Global Aluminium Foil Roller Initiative (#10234)
- ♦ **GLA** Global Logistics Associates (#10460)
- ♦ GLA – Global Lyme Alliance (internationally oriented national body)
- ♦ **GLANCE** Global Alliance for Newborn Care (#10215)
- ♦ GLAN / see European Network for Central Africa (#07874)
- ♦ **GLAP/IIAS** Grupo Latinoamericano por la Administración Pública (#16337)
- ♦ **GLAP/IIAS** Grupo Latino-americano pela Administração Pública (#16337)
- ♦ Glasgow Financial Alliance for Net Zero (unconfirmed)
- ♦ Glasindustrins Nordiska Samarbetskommitté (inactive)

♦ Glass Alliance Europe 10156

Coodinator Av Louise 89, Bte 5, 1050 Brussels, Belgium. T. +3225384446. Fax +3225378469. E-mail: info@glassallianceeurope.eu.
URL: http://www.glassallianceeurope.eu/

History 25 Sep 1964, Paris (France). Statutes updated: 2012; 2021. Former names and other names: *Standing Committee of Glass Industries of the EEC* – former; *Comité permanent des industries du verre de la CEE (CPIV)* – former; *Ständiger Ausschuss der Glas-Industrien in der EWG* – former; *Comitato Permanente delle Industrie del Vetro della CEE* – former; *Permanent Comité van de Glasindustriën van de EEG* – former; *Standing Committee of European Glass Industries* – former; *Comité permanent des industries du verre européennes (CPIV)* – former; *Ständiger Ausschuss der Glas-Industrien in Europa* – former; *Comitato Permanente delle Industrie del Vetro Europea* – former; *Permanent Comité van de Glasindustriën in Europa* – former. Registration: Banque-Carrefour des Entreprises, No/ID: 0418.388.615, Start date: 22 Jun 1978, Belgium; EU Transparency Register, No/ID: 74505036439-88, Start date: 17 Aug 2011. **Aims** Unite European glass industries to highlight the importance of glass making across Europe; promote an economic and policy environment allowing European-based glass manufacturing industries to continue flourishing and providing Europe with an innovative, stylish and sustainable material that is present in every aspect of our daily lives. **Structure** General Assembly (annual, since 1991) always in Brussels (Belgium); Executive Committee; Committees and Working Groups (8). **Languages** English, French, German. **Staff** 1.00 FTE, paid. **Finance** Sources: members' dues. **Activities** Advocacy/lobbying/activism; networking/liaising; research/documentation. **Events** *Annual General Assembly* Brussels (Belgium) 2002, *Annual General Assembly* Brussels (Belgium) 2001, *Annual General Assembly* Brussels (Belgium) 2000, *Annual General Assembly* Brussels (Belgium) 1999, *Annual General Assembly* Brussels (Belgium) 1998. **Publications** *Glass Alliance Europe Newsletter* (11 a year).
Members Full national and sectoral federations in 12 countries:
Austria, Belgium, Czechia, France, Germany, Italy, Netherlands, Poland, Slovakia, Spain, Türkiye, UK.
Sectoral Associations (5), listed in this Yearbook:
European Domestic Glass (EDG, #06938); European Special Glass Association (ESGA, #08807); Fédération européenne du verre d'emballage (FEVE, #09583); GlassFibreEurope (#10158); Glass for Europe (#10157).
NGO Relations Member of (1): *Industry4Europe (#11181).* [2021.05.25/XE3282/y/**E**]

- ♦ Glass in Building / see Glass for Europe (#10157)
- ♦ Glass in Building (inactive)

♦ Glass for Europe 10157

SG Rue Belliard 199/33, 1040 Brussels, Belgium. T. +3225384377. Fax +3222800281. E-mail: info@glassforeurope.com.
URL: http://www.glassforeurope.com/

History 15 Nov 1978, Brussels (Belgium). Founded on a formal, legalized basis. An extension of the earlier association, *Glass in Building (inactive)*, which represented some members since 1962. Former names and other names: *European Federation of Flat Glass Manufacturers* – former (1978); *Fédération européenne des producteurs de verre plat (GEPVP)* – former (1978); *Europäischer Verband der Flachglas-Hersteller* – former; *Glass in Building* – former; *Europe's Manufacturers of Building, Automotive and Transport Glass* – former; *Groupement européen des producteurs de verre plat* – former; *Glass for Europe – Europe's Manufacturers of Building, Automotive and Solar-Energy Glass* – full title. Registration: Banque Carrefour des Entreprises, No/ID: 0418.828.479, Start date: 15 Nov 1978, Belgium; EU Transparency Register, No/ID: 15997912445-80, Start date: 5 Oct 2009. **Aims** Support and enable a dynamic, influential and valued flat glass industry in the European Union. **Structure** General Assembly; Board of Directors; Committees; Task Forces. **Languages** English, French. **Staff** 5.00 FTE, paid. **Finance** Sources: members' dues. **Activities** Advocacy/lobbying/activism; guidance/assistance/consulting; knowledge management/information dissemination; standards/guidelines.
Members Major groups (5) with plants in 17 countries:
Belgium, Bulgaria, Czechia, Finland, France, Germany, Hungary, Italy, Luxembourg, Netherlands, Poland, Portugal, Romania, Spain, Sweden, Türkiye, UK.
IGO Relations Recognized by: *European Commission (EC, #06633); European Parliament (EP, #08146).*
NGO Relations Member of (6): *Construction 2050 Alliance (#04760); Construction Products Europe AISBL (#04761); European Association of Automotive Suppliers (CLEPA, #05948)* (Associate); *European Network on Silica (NEPSI, #08001); Glass Alliance Europe (#10156); Industry4Europe (#11181).* In liaison with technical committees of: *Comité européen de normalisation (CEN, #04162); International Organization for Standardization (ISO, #14473).* [2022.05.11/XD9209/**D**]

- ♦ Glass for Europe – Europe's Manufacturers of Building, Automotive and Solar-Energy Glass / see Glass for Europe (#10157)

♦ GlassFibreEurope 10158

SG Av Louise 89, Box 5, 1050 Brussels, Belgium. T. +3225384446. E-mail: info@glassfibreeurope.eu.
URL: http://www.glassfibreeurope.eu/

History 10 Jan 1987, as *Association des producteurs de fibres de verre européens (APFE) – European Glass Fibres Producers Association.* Registered in accordance with Belgian law. Registration: Belgium. **Aims** Promote positive contribution of reinforcement glass fibres to society. **Structure** General Assembly (annual); Management Board. **Languages** English, French, German. **Staff** 0.50 FTE, paid.
Members Reinforcement filament glass fibres producers in 12 countries:
Belgium, Czechia, France, Germany, Italy, Netherlands, Norway, Portugal, Slovakia, Spain, Türkiye, UK.
NGO Relations Member of: *AEGIS Europe; Conseil européen de l'industrie chimique (CEFIC, #04687); European Composites Industry Association (EuCIA, #06692); European Network on Silica (NEPSI, #08001); Glass Alliance Europe (#10156); Industry4Europe (#11181).* [2020/XD1735/**D**]

- ♦ Glassfibre Reinforced Cement Association / see International Glassfibre Reinforced Concrete Association
- ♦ Glass Molders, Pottery, Plastics and Allied Workers International Union (internationally oriented national body)
- ♦ Glass Performance Days (meeting series)
- ♦ Glasswing International (internationally oriented national body)
- ♦ Glaucoma Association / see International Glaucoma Association (#13719)

♦ Glaucoma Research Society (GRS) 10159

Pres 1276 South Park Street, 2W Victoria, Room 2035, Halifax NS B3H 2Y9, Canada. E-mail: bal@dal.ca.
sec Seoul Natl Univ – College of Medicine, 103 Daehak-ro, Jongno-gu, Seoul 110-799, Korea Rep.
URL: http://www.glaucomasociety.org/

History 1980, as *Glaucoma Society of the International Congress of Ophthalmology*, following meetings starting in the 1950s. Current by-laws last updated Aug 2014. Registered in accordance with Swiss Civil Code. **Aims** Provide a forum to discuss and stimulate compelling or innovative research to prevent glaucoma-related disability worldwide. **Structure** General Assembly (every 2 years); Executive Committee. **Languages** English. **Staff** 9.00 FTE, voluntary. **Finance** Sources: gifts, legacies; grants; members' dues. **Activities** Events/meetings. **Events** *Meeting* Halifax, NS (Canada) 2021, *Meeting* Halifax, NS (Canada) 2020, *Meeting* Parma (Italy) 2018, *Meeting* Seoul (Korea Rep) 2016, *Meeting* Jackson Hole, WY (USA) 2014. **Publications** *Glaucoma Update* (every 4 years).
Members Membership by nomination and election. Active (86); Emeritus (35); Honorary (6). Active in 20 countries and territories:
Australia, Austria, Brazil, Canada, China, Finland, Germany, Greece, India, Ireland, Israel, Italy, Japan, Korea Rep, New Zealand, Singapore, Switzerland, Taiwan, UK, USA.
Emeritus in 10 countries:
Australia, Belgium, Canada, France, Germany, Japan, New Zealand, Sweden, UK, USA.
Honorary in 3 countries:
Canada, Sweden, USA.
NGO Relations Assists *International Council of Ophthalmology (ICO, #13057)* with organization of: *International Congress of Ophthalmology* (every 4 years). [2017/XD8896/v/**C**]

- ♦ Glaucoma Society of the International Congress of Ophthalmology / see Glaucoma Research Society (#10159)
- ♦ GLCC – Global Lung Cancer Coalition (unconfirmed)
- ♦ GLCF – Global Land Cover Facility (internationally oriented national body)
- ♦ GLC – Great Lakes Commission (internationally oriented national body)
- ♦ **GLEAC** Global Legal Education Associations Consortium (#10456)
- ♦ GLEC – Global Logistics Emissions Council (unconfirmed)
- ♦ GLED – Grupo Latinoamericano de Epidemiologia de la Diabetes (unconfirmed)
- ♦ GLE – Gas LNG Europe / see Gas Infrastructure Europe (#10073)
- ♦ **GLEIF** Global Legal Entity Identifier Foundation (#10458)
- ♦ **GLE International** Internationale Gesellschaft für Logotherapie und Existenzanalyse (#13241)
- ♦ Glenmary Home Missioners (religious order)
- ♦ **GLEON** Global Lake Ecological Observatory Network (#10449)
- ♦ **GLEPHA** Global Law Enforcement and Public Health Association (#10453)
- ♦ **GLF** Global Landscapes Forum (#10451)
- ♦ GLF – Global Leadership Forum (unconfirmed)
- ♦ **GLF** Global Leadership Foundation (#10454)
- ♦ GLF – Global Legal Forum (unconfirmed)
- ♦ GLF / see Global Lighting Association (#10459)
- ♦ **GLF** Gnome Liberation Front (#10671)
- ♦ **GL** Gender Links (#10098)
- ♦ GLHEMA / see Asociación Latinoamericana de Aféresis y Terapias celulares (#02178)
- ♦ **GLHN** Global Labour History Network (#10446)
- ♦ **GLIA** Great Lakes Initiative on AIDS (#10704)
- ♦ GLIDE – Global Institute for Disease Elimination (unconfirmed)
- ♦ GLI – Girls Learn International (internationally oriented national body)
- ♦ **GLI** Global Labour Institute (#10447)
- ♦ GLI – Global Liver Institute (internationally oriented national body)
- ♦ **GLISA** Gay and Lesbian International Sport Association (#10078)
- ♦ **GLISPA** Global Island Partnership (#10436)
- ♦ GLiSS – Great Lakes Institute for Strategic Studies (internationally oriented national body)
- ♦ GLJ-ILRF – Global Labor Justice-International Labor Rights Forum (internationally oriented national body)
- ♦ GLMF – Giovanni Lorenzini Medical Foundation (internationally oriented national body)
- ♦ **GLMMS** Groupement latin et méditerranéen de médecine du sport (#16401)
- ♦ Globaïa (internationally oriented national body)
- ♦ Globaïa – Planetary Awareness through Science and Art / see Globaïa

♦ Global 100% RE 10160

Coordinator c/o WWEA, Charles-de-Gaulle-Str 5, 53113 Bonn, Germany. T. +49228324269800. Fax +4922824269802. E-mail: info@global100re.org.
URL: http://www.go100re.net/

History Former names and other names: *Global 100% Renewable Energy Platform* – alias. **Aims** Advocate for 100% *renewable energy*. **Structure** Executive Committee. **Activities** Capacity building; awareness raising; training/education.
Members Organizations include the following 6 listed in this Yearbook:
Climate Action Network (CAN, #03999); International Solar Energy Society (ISES, #15564); Local Governments for Sustainability (ICLEI, #16507); Sierra Club International Program (#19266); World Future Council Foundation (WFC, #21533); World Wind Energy Association (WWEA, #21937).
NGO Relations Member of: *EKOenergy (#05412).* Supporters include: *African Renewable Energy Alliance (AREA, #00439); Associação Lusófona de Energias Renovaveis (ALER); Climate Alliance (#04005); European Forum for Renewable Energy Sources (EUFORES, #07329); European Renewable Energies Federation (EREF, #08355); EUROSOLAR – European Association for Renewable Energy (#09183); IFOAM – Organics International (IFOAM, #11105); International Geothermal Association (IGA, #13717); European Federation of Citizen Energy Cooperatives (REScoop.eu, #07077).* [2020/XM5635/y/**F**]

- ♦ Global 100% Renewable Energy Platform / see Global 100% RE (#10160)
- ♦ GLOBAL 2000 (internationally oriented national body)
- ♦ Global 2000 – 2010 International (internationally oriented national body)

♦ Global 500 Environmental Forum 10161

Pres c/o Laurel Springs School, PO Box 1440, Ojai CA 93023, USA. Fax +18056460186.
URL: https://global500forum.org/

History 1992, Rio de Janeiro (Brazil). Founded during *United Nations Conference on Environment and Development (UNCED).* Former names and other names: *Global 500 Forum* – former alias. **Events** *International conference* Kuala Lumpur (Malaysia) 1995, *Meeting* Nairobi (Kenya) 1993, *Workshop* Nairobi (Kenya) 1992.
Members Individuals and organizations awarded UNEP's Global 500 Award for Environmental Achievement. Membership countries not specified. [2020/XE3171/**E**]

- ♦ Global 500 Forum / see Global 500 Environmental Forum (#10161)

♦ **GlobalABC** Global Alliance for Buildings and Construction (#10187)
♦ Global Academy Institute of Technology Foundation (internationally oriented national body)
♦ Global Academy of Osseointegration (unconfirmed)

♦ Global Academy of Tropical Health and Culture (GATH-INTERNATIONAL) 10162

Pres 59 Ramsis Street, Cairo, 11522, Egypt. Fax +20225750723.

History 1970, as a permanent study group within *International College of Surgeons (ICS, #12650)*. Launched, 1-3 Mar 2004, at Cairo (Egypt) *WHO Regional Office for the Eastern Mediterranean (EMRO, #20944)*. **Aims** Combat disease, ignorance and poverty. **Structure** Advisory Board of 3. Honorary Chairmen: 6. Nuclei: GATH-Europe; GATH-Sudan; GATH-Egypt; GATH-Sweden; GATH-Yemen; GATH-Zambia. **Activities** Study Groups (34). **Events** *Congress* Cairo (Egypt) 2009. **Publications** *Textbook of Tropical Surgery* (2004). [2009/XM2991/**E**]

♦ Global Accrediting Group (see: #21330)

♦ Global Acetate Manufacturers Association (GAMA) 10163

Contact Av Jules Bordet 142, 1140 Brussels, Belgium. T. +3227611616. Fax +3227611699.
Headquarters 355 Lexington Ave, 15th Floor, New York NY 10017, USA.
URL: http://acetateweb.com/

History 27 Jan 2000, Brussels (Belgium). Incorporated in the State of Delaware (USA), 2008. Registered in accordance with Belgian law. EU Transparency Register: 63323472608-78. **Aims** Provide information and support to members' efforts in the development and enhancement of the use of cellulose acetate and of products made therefrom. **Structure** General Assembly (annual). Officers: President; Vice-President; Treasurer. **Languages** English. **Finance** Members' dues. **Activities** Knowledge management/information dissemination; politics/policy/regulatory; projects/programmes. **Publications** *Cellulose Acetates: Properties and Application*. **Members** Producers of cellulose acetate flake, tow and filament. Membership countries not specified. [2016.06.01/XE4120/**E**]

♦ Global Action Against Mass Atrocity Crimes (GAAMAC) 10164

Support Office c/o Centre Jean-Jacques Gautier, Route de Ferney 10, 1202 Geneva, Switzerland. T. +41225521142. E-mail: contact@gaamac.org.
URL: https://www.gaamac.org/

History Mar 2013, Dar es Salaam (Tanzania UR). Founded following Regional Fora on the Prevention of Genocide, Dec 2008, Buenos Aires (Argentina); 2009, Tanzania UR; 2010, Switzerland; 2012, Cambodia. Created by States, civil society organizations and academic institutions with the support of *United Nations (UN, #20515)*. **Aims** Engage and support States everywhere to protect their populations from atrocity crimes by addressing root causes within their societies and to promote prevention at the national level as an upstream and permanent endeavor that builds on close collaboration between state actors and civil society. **Structure** Steering Group; Chair; Support Office, located in Geneva (Switzerland); Working Groups. **Languages** English, French. **Activities** Events/meetings; knowledge management/information dissemination; networking/liaising. **Events** *Biennial Meeting* 2021, *Biennial Meeting* The Hague (Netherlands) 2020, *Biennial Meeting* Kampala (Uganda) 2018, *Biennial Meeting* Manila (Philippines) 2016, *Biennial Meeting* San José (Costa Rica) 2014. **Publications** Any state, non-government organization and academic institution involved in atrocity prevention is eligible to become a partner of GAAMAC. Prospective partners should demonstrate an interest in or commitment to atrocity prevention and endorse GAAMAC's founding document. Partnerships are free, although financial and in-kind support is welcome. For more information, please contact the GAAMAC Support Office.

Members States (7):
Argentina, Armenia, Costa Rica, Denmark, Netherlands, Switzerland, Tanzania UR.
Some States are Steering Group members; others are partners.
Civil Society and academia, including 5 organizations listed in this Yearbook:
Comunità di Sant'Egidio – ACAP; *European Centre for the Responsibility to Protect (ECR2P)*; *Global Centre for the Responsibility to Protect (GCR2P, #10277)*; *Instituto Interamericano de Derechos Humanos (IIDH, #11334)*; *International Coalition for the Responsibility to Protect (ICRtoP, #12620)*.
The listed organizations are Steering Group members only. Partners and informal alliances are listed under "relations" below.

NGO Relations Cooperates with (20): African Coordination of Human Rights for the Armed Forces (CADHA); *Center for Global Nonkilling (#03642)*; *European Centre for the Responsibility to Protect (ECR2P)*; *Impunity Watch (#11138)*; *Instituto Interamericano de Derechos Humanos (IIDH, #11334)*; *International Coalition of Sites of Conscience (ICSC, #12621)*; Justice Access Point; *Montreal Institute for Genocide and Human Rights Studies (MIGS)*; *Parliamentarians for Global Action (PGA, #18208)*; *Peace Direct*; Platform for Peace and Humanity; Platform for Social Justice; Rights for Peace; Rwanda Youth Clubs for Peace Organization; The Oxford Programme on International Peace and Security; The Post-Conflict Research Center; The Sentinel Project; The West African Transitional Justice Centre; The Youth Association for Development; Yazda. [2022.06.15/AA0971/**C**]

♦ Global Action on Aging (internationally oriented national body)

♦ Global Action on Disability Network (GLAD) 10165

Contact Route de Ferney 150, PO Box 2100, 1211 Geneva 2, Switzerland. E-mail: glad@ida-secretariat.org.
URL: https://gladnetwork.net/

History Dec 2015, London (UK). **Aims** Support bilateral and multilateral donors and organizations, the private sector, foundations and others contributing resources to work together, in collaboration with organizations of persons with disabilities and partner governments, to enhance inclusion of persons with disabilities in international development and humanitarian action. **Structure** General Assembly; Steering Committee; Secretariat. Co-Chaired by *International Disability Alliance (IDA, #13176)* and Norwegian Ministry of Foreign Affairs. **Finance** Funded by: Australian and German Governments. Supported by: *Deutsche Gesellschaft für Internationale Zusammenarbeit (GIZ)*. **Activities** Advocacy/lobbying/activism; financial and/or material support; knowledge management/information dissemination; networking/liaising. **Events** *Meeting* Ottawa, ON (Canada) 2019, *Meeting* Helsinki (Finland) 2018. **Publications** *GLAD Newsletter*.

Members Organizations and ministry departments (37) in 11 countries:
Australia, Canada, Finland, Germany, Ireland, Japan, Netherlands, Norway, Sweden, UK, USA.
Included in the above, 23 organizations listed in this Yearbook:
- *Abilis Foundation*;
- *Agencia Española de Cooperación Internacional para el Desarrollo (AECID)*;
- *Asian Development Bank (ADB, #01422)*;
- *business disability international (bdi)*;
- *Department for International Development (DFID, inactive)*;
- *Disability Rights Fund (DRF, #05096)*;
- *European Commission (EC, #06633)*;
- *Fundación Internacional y para Iberoamérica de Administración y Politicas Públicas (FIIAPP, #10030)*;
- *Fundación ONCE para América Latina (FOAL)*;
- *Global Partnership for Education (GPE, #10531)*;
- *ILO (#11123)*;
- *International Bank for Reconstruction and Development (IBRD, #12317)* (World Bank);
- *International Disability Alliance (IDA, #13176)*;
- *Irish Aid*;
- *Japan International Cooperation Agency (JICA)*;
- *Nippon Foundation*;
- *Norwegian Agency for Development Cooperation (Norad)*;
- *Swedish International Development Cooperation Agency (Sida)*;
- *Swiss Agency for Development and Cooperation (SDC)*;
- *UNDP (#20292)*;
- *UNESCO (#20322)*;
- *UNICEF (#20332)*;
- *UN Women (#20724)*.

Advisors (4):
International Disability and Development Consortium (IDDC, #13177); *Office of the United Nations High Commissioner for Human Rights (OHCHR, #17697)*; Rotating representative of an Organization of Persons with Disabilities (DPO); UN Special Rapporteur on the Rights of Persons with Disabilities.
IGO Relations *Convention on the Rights of Persons with Disabilities (CRPD, 2006)*. [2022.05.04/XM5862/y/**F**]

♦ Global Action Fund for Fungal Infections / see Global Action For Fungal Infections (#10166)

♦ Global Action For Fungal Infections (GAFFI) 10166

Chief Exec Rue Le Corbusier 12, 1208 Geneva, Switzerland. E-mail: info@gaffi.org.
Contact Bridge House, Ashley Road, Hale, Altrincham, WA14 2UT, UK.
URL: https://www.gaffi.org/

History 2013. Former names and other names: *Global Action Fund for Fungal Infections (GAFFI)* – former. Registration: Swiss Civil Code, No/ID: CHE-476.655.939, Switzerland; Charity Commission, No/ID: 1170853, England and Wales. **Aims** Enable health systems especially in middle- and low-middle income countries to effectively diagnose and treat fungal disease. **Structure** Board; Executive. **Languages** English, French, Spanish. **Activities** Research and development; training/education. **Publications** Annual Report: https://gaffi.org/annual-reports/ **NGO Relations** Partner of (3): *European Confederation of Medical Mycology (ECMM, #06712)*; *International Society for Human and Animal Mycology (ISHAM, #15181)*; *International Society for Infectious Diseases (ISID, #15199)*. Also links with national institutions. [2022.05.12/AA1035/t/**F**]

♦ Global Action on Men's Health (GAMH) 10167

Contact address not obtained. E-mail: office@gamh.org.
URL: http://www.gamh.org/

History 2013. Founded as a collaborative project; officially launched June 2014. Registration: Charity Commission, Start date: 2019, England and Wales. **Aims** Create a world where all men and boys have the opportunity to achieve the best possible health and wellbeing wherever they live and whatever their backgrounds. **Structure** Board of Trustees. **Finance** Sources: donations; grants; members' dues. **Activities** Advocacy/lobbying/activism; guidance/assistance/consulting. **Publications** *GAMH eBulletin* (12 a year).

Members Full; Associate; Individual. Members (over 50) in 20 countries:
Australia, Brazil, Canada, Chile, Costa Rica, Denmark, Germany, Haiti, Ireland, Liberia, Malawi, Malaysia, Mexico, Mozambique, Nepal, New Zealand, Rwanda, South Africa, UK, USA.
Included in the above, 2 organizations listed in this Yearbook:
European Men's Health Forum (EMHF, #07783); *Promundo*. [2022.02.08/XM7832/y/**F**]

♦ Global Action Network (internationally oriented national body)
♦ Global Action Plan for the Earth / see Global Action Plan International (#10168)
♦ Global Action Plan for Environment and Development in the 21st Century (inactive)

♦ Global Action Plan International (GAP) 10168

Network Coordinator c/o Global Action Plan UK, 9-13 Kean Street, London, WC2B 4AY, UK. T. +442074204444. E-mail: team@globalactionplan.com.
URL: http://www.globalactionplan.com/

History 1989. Founded by David Gershon and Bessie Schadee, as *Global Action Plan for the Earth*. Also known as *GAP International*. **Aims** As a global leader of sustainable behaviour change, *empower* individuals and groups to act increasingly *sustainably*. **Structure** Board of Directors; GAP Network of independent national/regional organizations. **Languages** English. **Staff** 6.00 FTE, paid. **Finance** Members' dues. Other sources: sponsorship; international public project funds. **Activities** Guidance/assistance/consulting; monitoring/evaluation; research and development; training/education; networking/liaising. **Events** *Annual Meeting* Monteveglio (Italy) 2016, *Annual Meeting* Hôi An (Vietnam) 2015, *International Workshop* Johor (Malaysia) 2014, *International Workshop* Johor Bahru (Malaysia) 2014, *Annual Meeting* Madrid (Spain) / Miraflores de la Sierra (Spain) 2014. **Publications** *Drawing for Life* in Albanian, Belarusian, English, Macedonian, Russian, Ukrainian; *ESD Dialogues* in English, Russian. *Learning for Change* in English – iBook and pdf. Course books; school textbooks; teacher manuals; teacher training materials; workbooks; fact sheets; online programmes.

Members One or more organizations in each of 22 countries and territories:
Belarus, Belgium, Finland, Germany, Hungary, Iceland, India, Ireland, Kenya, Kosovo, Malaysia, Netherlands, Poland, Spain, Sweden, Switzerland, Türkiye, Uganda, UK, Ukraine, USA, Vietnam. [2020/XF2297/**F**]

♦ Global Action to Prevent War (internationally oriented national body)
♦ Global Action to Prevent War, Genocide and Internal Armed Conflict / see Global Action to Prevent War

♦ Global Action for Trans Equality (GATE) 10169

Main Office 580 Fifth Ave, Ste 820, New York NY 10036, USA. T. +16463411699. E-mail: info@gate.ngo.
URL: https://gate.ngo/

History 2010. **Aims** Work internationally on *gender* identity, gender expression, and bodily issues by defending human rights, making available critical knowledge, and supporting political organizing worldwide. **Structure** Board of Directors. **Finance** Supported by: Arcus Foundation; *Humanistisch Instituut voor Ontwikkelingssamenwerking (Hivos)*; *Open Society Foundations (OSF, #17763)*. **Activities** Advocacy/lobbying/activism. **NGO Relations** Cooperates with (1): *ILGA World (International Lesbian, Gay, Bisexual, Trans and Intersex Association, #11120)*. [2022.10.19/XJ9367/**F**]

♦ Global Action on Widowhood (internationally oriented national body)

♦ Global Adaptation Network (GAN) 10170

Contact CCAU-UNEP, PO Box 30552, Nairobi, 00100, Kenya.
URL: https://www.unenvironment.org/gan/

History Developed through *UNEP (#20299)* facilitated consultative processes with key partners and potential target groups between 2008 and 2010. **Aims** Help build *climate* resilience of *vulnerable* communities, *ecosystems* and economies through the mobilization of knowledge for adaptation. **Structure** Builds on 4 regional networks: Latin America and the Caribbean – *Regional Gateway for Technology Transfer and Climate Change Action (REGATTA, #18786)*; Asia Pacific – *Asia Pacific Adaptation Network (APAN, #01818)*; West Asia – *West Asia Regional Network on Climate Change (WARN-CC)*; Africa – *Africa Adaptation Knowledge Network (AAKNet)*. **Activities** Improving availability and accessibility of knowledge; Building capacity; Linking regional and thematic adaptation networks. **Events** *Forum* Abu Dhabi (United Arab Emirates) 2018. **Publications** *GAN News*. **NGO Relations** Participates in: *Global Center on Adaptation (GCA)*. [2020/XJ7848/**F**]

♦ Global Advances in Business and Communication (meeting series)

♦ Global Advertising Lawyers Alliance (GALA) 10171

Exec Dir 488 Madison Ave, 10th fl, New York NY 10022, USA. T. +12127054895. Fax +13474382185.
Sec-Treas c/o 5 Chancery Lane, Clifford's Inn, London, EC4A 1BL, UK.
URL: http://www.gala-marketlaw.com/

History 1989, as *European Advertising Lawyers Association (EALA)*, as a grouping of the type *European Economic Interest Grouping (EEIG, #06960)*. **Aims** Enhance members' ability to provide international compliance advice to commercial communicators around the world. **Languages** English, French, German, Spanish. **Finance** Members' dues. **Activities** Guidance/assistance/consulting. **Publications** *GALA Gazette*.

Members Advertising and marketing lawyers in 68 countries and territories:
Argentina, Australia, Austria, Belgium, Bolivia, Brazil, Bulgaria, Canada, Chile, China, Colombia, Costa Rica, Croatia, Cyprus, Czechia, Denmark, Dominican Rep, Ecuador, Egypt, El Salvador, Finland, France, Germany, Greece, Guatemala, Honduras, Hong Kong, Hungary, India, Ireland, Israel, Italy, Japan, Kenya, Luxembourg, Malaysia, Malta, Mexico, Mozambique, Netherlands, New Zealand, Nicaragua, Nigeria, Norway, Panama, Paraguay, Peru, Poland, Portugal, Puerto Rico, Romania, Russia, Serbia, Singapore, Slovakia, South Africa, Spain, Sweden, Switzerland, Türkiye, Uganda, UK, Ukraine, United Arab Emirates, Uruguay, USA, Venezuela, Zimbabwe.
Also members in the Caribbean. Membership countries not specified. [2019/XD5739/v/**D**]

♦ Global Advocacy for HIV Prevention (AVAC) 10172

Exec Dir 423 West 127th St, 4th Floor, New York NY 10027, USA. T. +12127966423. Fax +12123653452. E-mail: avac@avac.org.
URL: http://www.avac.org/

History 1995. Former names and other names: *Aids Vaccine Advocacy Coalition (AVAC)* – former. **Aims** Through education, policy analysis, advocacy and a network of global collaborations, accelerate the ethical development and global delivery of *AIDS* vaccines, male circumcision, microbicides, PrEP and other emerging HIV prevention options as part of a comprehensive response to the pandemic. **Structure** Board. **Staff** 21.00 FTE, paid. **Finance** Sources: donations. **Activities** Advocacy/lobbying/activism; events/meetings. **Consultative Status** Consultative status granted from: *ECOSOC (#05331)* (Special). **IGO Relations** *Joint United Nations Programme on HIV/AIDS (UNAIDS, #16149)*; *WHO (#20950)*.

NGO Relations Member of: *Global Health Technologies Coalition (GHTC)*. Stakeholder in: *Global HIV Vaccine Enterprise (#10410)*. Partners include:
- *Center for Health and Gender Equity (CHANGE); CONRAD; European AIDS Treatment Group (EATG, #05850); European Distribution System Operators' Association for Smart Grids (EDSO, #06931); FHI 360; MPact Global Action for Gay Men's Health and Rights (MPact, #16875); Global Network of People Living with HIV/AIDS (GNP+, #10494); Health Global Access Project (Health GAP); International AIDS Society (IAS, #11601); International AIDS Vaccine Initiative (IAVI, #11602); International Community of Women Living with HIV/AIDS (ICW, #12826); International Partnership for Microbicides (IPM, inactive); International Rectal Microbicide Advocates (IRMA); International Treatment Preparedness Coalition (ITPC, #15729); London School of Hygiene and Tropical Medicine (LSHTM); PATH (#18260); SRHR Africa Trust (SAT, #19934).*

[2021/XJ7312/**F**]

♦ Globaladvocaten 10173

Main Office Theaterarkaden – Oper, Kapuzinerstr 11, 53111 Bonn, Germany. T. +492289087280. E-mail: office@globaladvocaten.com.
URL: https://www.globaladvocaten.com/

History 1990. Established as a grouping of the type *European Economic Interest Grouping (EEIG, #06960)*. Former names and other names: *Globaladvocaten – The Global Law Group* – full title; *Euroadvocaten* – former; *The European Law Group* – former. Registration: Netherlands. **Aims** Help clients find the best and most cost-effective lawyers across the world.
Members Law firms in 26 countries:
Austria, Belarus, Belgium, Brazil, Bulgaria, Czechia, Denmark, France, Germany, Hungary, Italy, Montenegro, Netherlands, Norway, Poland, Portugal, Romania, Russia, Serbia, Slovakia, Spain, Switzerland, Türkiye, UK, Ukraine, USA.

[2020.11.25/XF4031/**F**]

- ♦ Globaladvocaten – The Global Law Group / see Globaladvocaten (#10173)
- ♦ Global Affairs Institute, Syracuse University / see Moynihan Institute of Global Affairs
- ♦ The Global Ageing Network / see International Association of Homes and Services for the Ageing (#11938)
- ♦ Global Aggregates Information Network (unconfirmed)
- ♦ Global Agricultural Biotechnology Association (inactive)

♦ Global Agriculture and Food Security Program (GAFSP) 10174

Coordination Unit c/o World Bank, 1818 H Str NW, MSN 5-510, Washington DC 20433, USA. E-mail: gafsp-info@gafspfund.org.
URL: https://www.gafspfund.org/

History Apr 2010. Set up as a multilateral mechanism – Financial Intermediary Fund – to assist the implementation of pledges made by the G20, Sep 2009, Pittsburgh PA (USA). **Aims** Improve incomes and food and nutrition security in low-income countries by boosting agricultural productivity. **Structure** Steering Committee; Technical Advisory Committee. Coordination Unit ran by *International Bank for Reconstruction and Development (IBRD, #12317)* (World Bank). Private sector window managed by *International Finance Corporation (IFC, #13597)*. **Finance** Funding from: public and private sectors of Australia, Canada, Germany, Ireland, Japan, Korea Rep, Netherlands, Spain, UK and USA; *Bill and Melinda Gates Foundation (BMGF)*. **Activities** Financial and/or material support; monitoring/evaluation.
Members Recipient countries (30):
Bangladesh, Benin, Bhutan, Burkina Faso, Burundi, Cambodia, Ethiopia, Gambia, Haiti, Honduras, Kenya, Kyrgyzstan, Laos, Liberia, Malawi, Mali, Mongolia, Nepal, Nicaragua, Niger, Rwanda, Senegal, Sierra Leone, Tajikistan, Tanzania UR, Timor-Leste, Togo, Uganda, Yemen, Zambia.
IGO Relations *International Bank for Reconstruction and Development (IBRD, #12317)* (World Bank). **NGO Relations** *Asian Farmers' Association for Sustainable Rural Development (AFA, #01450); International Fertilizer Development Center (IFDC, #13590); West African Network of Farmers' Organizations and Agricultural Producers (#20891).* [2022/XM5122/**E***]

♦ Global Aid Foundation 10175

Contact address not obtained.
URL: http://www.globalaidfoundation.org/

History Founded 1993, Astoria NY (USA), as *World Relief Foundation*. **Aims** Provide *relief aid* and *development* assistance to areas of *disaster* worldwide; empower *marginalized* communities with service centres and *volunteers*; act as liaison among relief agencies to channel resources where needed; train volunteers; advocate for universal social justice and peace; promote culture and art as a means of building stronger bonds among the human race; find and channel resources towards children education in underdeveloped countries. **Structure** Board of Trustees; Board of Directors. **Languages** English, Spanish. **Staff** Voluntary. **Finance** Private donations. Budget (annual): US$ 25,000 for operational expenses; all other financial donations are used in programmes. **Activities** Humanitarian/emergency aid. **Publications** *Global Aid Network* (3 a year).
Members Individuals in 17 countries:
Argentina, Austria, Bolivia, Brazil, Chile, Colombia, Ecuador, India, Mexico, Pakistan, Peru, Russia, Spain, Sri Lanka, UK, USA, Venezuela. [2015.09.01/XF3833/fv/**F**]

♦ Global Aid Network (GAiN) 10176

Address not obtained.
URL: http://gainworldwide.org/

History A worldwide humanitarian relief and development network. Registered in: Australia; Austria; Canada; Germany; Netherlands; Philippines; Korea Rep; Spain; Switzerland; UK, USA. **Aims** Reveal hope and restore life through *relief* and development initiatives for people living in crisis and injustice. [2018/XM7146/**F**]

- ♦ Global Aid Network (GAiN USA) / see Unto
- ♦ Global AIDS Interfaith Alliance (internationally oriented national body)
- ♦ Global AirRail Alliance (unconfirmed)

♦ Global Alcohol Policy Alliance (GAPA) 10177

Sec Torggata 1, 0181 Oslo, Norway. T. +4741622135. Fax +4723214501. E-mail: gapa@globalgapa.org.
Chairperson SHORE & Whariki Research Centre, College of Health, Massey University, P.O. Box 6137, Wellesley St, Auckland 1010, New Zealand. T. +6493666136.
URL: http://www.globalgapa.org/

History 2000, Syracuse, NY (USA). **Aims** Reduce alcohol-related harm worldwide by promoting science-based policies independent of commercial interests. **Structure** Advisory Board of 16 members drawn from all continents. **Languages** English. **Staff** Staff contributed by national organization represented by the Board. **Events** *Global Alcohol Policy Conference (GAPC)* Cape Town (South Africa) 2023, *Conference* Cape Town (South Africa) 2021, *Global Alcohol Policy Conference (GAPC)* Dublin (Ireland) 2020, *Global Alcohol Policy Conference (GAPC)* Melbourne, VIC (Australia) 2017, *Global Alcohol Policy Conference (GAPC)* Edinburgh (UK) 2015. **Publications** *The Globe*. [2022/XF6828/**F**]

- ♦ Global Alert for Defence of Youth and the Less Privileged (internationally oriented national body)

♦ Global Allergy and Airways Patient Platform (GAAPP) 10178

Exec Dir Altgasse 8-10, 1130 Vienna, Austria. T. +491717616923. E-mail: info@gaapp.org.
URL: https://gaapp.org/

History Dec 2009, Buenos Aires (Argentina). Constitution adopted Sep 2010, Barcelona (Spain). Former names and other names: *Global Allergy and Asthma Patient Platform (GAAPP)* – former. Registration: Landespolizeidirektion Wien, Referat Vereins-, Versammlungs- und Medienrechtsangelegenheiten, No/ID: ZVR-ZAHL 777551689, Start date: 8 Sep 2101, Austria, Vienna. **Aims** Support patients with allergies and asthma throughout the world by protecting their rights and insisting on the duties of governments, health-care professional organizations, and the general public. **Structure** Board. **Languages** English. **Staff** 3.00 FTE, paid; 6.00 FTE, voluntary. **Finance** Annual budget: 1,000,000 EUR (2022). **Events** *Global Respiratory Summit* Barcelona (Spain) 2022, *Scientific Meeting* Prague (Czechia) 2022, *Global Food Allergy Summit* Washington (USA) 2022. **Publications** More than 20 peer-reviewed publications: https://gaapp.org/gaapp-organization-info/publications*and*guidelines/
Members Founding members in 18 countries:
Argentina, Australia, Austria, Brazil, Canada, China, Czechia, Finland, France, Greece, Ireland, Italy, Lithuania, Poland, Portugal, South Africa, Sweden, Switzerland.
Included in the above, 2 organizations listed in this Yearbook:
European Federation of Allergy and Airways Diseases Patients' Associations (EFA, #07045); UNASMA – Fundación Internacional de Asma y Alergias (#20282).
NGO Relations Member of (1): *World Patients Alliance (WPA).* [2023.02.15/XJ6387/y/**C**]

♦ Global Allergy and Asthma European Network (GA2LEN) 10179

Main Office c/o DGAKI, Robert-Koch-Platz 7, 10115 Berlin, Germany. T. +4915156131844. E-mail: office@ga2len.net.
URL: http://www.ga2len.net/

History 12 Feb 2004, Brussels (Belgium). Registration: Amtsgericht Berlin – Charlottenburg, No/ID: VR27 531B, Germany. **Aims** Enhance quality and relevance of research in allergy and asthma; address all aspects of the disease; decrease the burden of allergy and asthma throughout Europe. **Structure** Executive Committee, comprising Chairman, 2 Vice-Chairpersons, Secretary General and Deputy Secretary General. **Finance** Funded by *European Commission (EC, #06633)* framework programme for research FP6. **Activities** Integration; joint research; spreading excellence. **Events** *Urticaria Conference* Hiroshima (Japan) 2021, *Global Urticaria Forum (GUF)* Berlin (Germany) 2020, *Global Urticaria Forum* Berlin (Germany) 2016, *Annual Conference* Berlin (Germany) 2010, *Symposium on asthma in adults and children* Warsaw (Poland) 2009.
Members Collaboration centres in 27 countries:
Austria, Belgium, Croatia, Cyprus, Czechia, Denmark, France, Germany, Greece, Hungary, Ireland, Israel, Italy, Lithuania, Luxembourg, Netherlands, North Macedonia, Poland, Portugal, Russia, Singapore, Slovenia, Spain, Sweden, Switzerland, Türkiye, UK.
Pan-European collaborating centres (3):
European Academy of Dermatology and Venereology (EADV, #05788); European Accreditation Council for Continuing Medical Education (EACCME, #05823); European Centre for Allergy Research Foundation (ECARF); European Union of Medical Specialists (UEMS, #09001).
Partners: research institutes and organizations in 14 countries:
Austria, Denmark, Finland, France, Germany, Greece, Italy, Netherlands, Norway, Poland, Portugal, Spain, Sweden, UK.
Regional organizations (2):
European Academy of Allergy and Clinical Immunology (EAACI, #05779); European Federation of Allergy and Airways Diseases Patients' Associations (EFA, #07045).
NGO Relations Member of: *Global Alliance Against Chronic Respiratory Diseases (GARD, #10182).*

[2021/XF7138/y/**F**]

- ♦ Global Allergy and Asthma Patient Platform / see Global Allergy and Airways Patient Platform (#10178)
- ♦ Global Alliance (internationally oriented national body)

♦ Global Alliance on Accessible Technologies and Environments (GAATES) 10180

Program Director 6300 Powers Ferry Rd, Suite 600-300, Atlanta GA 30339, USA. T. +12064378740. E-mail: info@gaates.org.
URL: http://www.gaates.org/

History Founded 2007, by an international consortium dedicated to promoting accessibility of built and virtual environments worldwide. Registered in accordance with Canadian law. **Aims** Promote understanding and implementation of accessibility of *sustainable* built, social and virtual environments, including architectural, infrastructural design, transportation systems, habitat and electronic information and communication technologies so that everyone, including people with *disabilities* and older persons are able to fully participate and contribute to society; support and encourage worldwide ratification and implementation of the UN Convention on the Rights of Persons with Disabilities. **Structure** Board; Executive Committee; Operational Committees; Volunteer Country Representatives. **Languages** English. **Staff** 2.50 FTE, paid. **Finance** Financed through projects and grants. **Activities** Guidance/assistance/consulting; knowledge management/information dissemination; standards/guidelines; politics/policy/regulatory; events/meetings. Management of treaties and agreements: *Convention on the Rights of Persons with Disabilities (CRPD, 2006)*. **Events** *Annual General Meeting* Montréal, QC (Canada) 2014, *Annual General Meeting* New York, NY (USA) 2013, *Annual Meeting / Annual General Meeting* Riyadh (Saudi Arabia) 2012, *Annual General Meeting* New York, NY (USA) 2011, *Annual General Meeting* Benghazi (Libyan AJ) 2010. **Publications** *Global Accessibility News* (weekly). Guidelines; handbooks; lesson plans; toolkit. **Members** Technical experts, individuals, organizations of people with disabilities, companies involved in information and communication technologies, architects, experts in emergency planning and life safety, and interested supporters. Members in over 120 countries (not specified). **Consultative Status** Consultative status granted from: *ECOSOC (#05331)* (Special). **IGO Relations** Cooperates with: *International Bank for Reconstruction and Development (IBRD, #12317)* (World Bank); *International Telecommunication Union (ITU, #15673)*; UN DESA; *UNESCO (#20322); UNICEF (#20332); United Nations Economic and Social Commission for Asia and the Pacific (ESCAP, #20557)*; various UN departments and agencies. **NGO Relations** Cooperates with: *World Wide Web Consortium (W3C, #21935); Global Initiative for Inclusive Information and Communication Technologies (G3ict, #10425).* [2020/XM2424/**F**]

♦ Global Alliance for Africa 10181

Exec Dir 703 West Monroe, Chicago IL 60661, USA. T. +13123820607. Fax +13123828850. E-mail: director@globalallianceafrica.org.
URL: http://www.globalallianceafrica.org/

History 1996, USA, by Thomas Derdak. **Aims** Develop *health care* and *education* programmes throughout Africa. **Structure** Board of Trustees. **NGO Relations** Member of: *Advocacy Network for Africa (ADNA).*

[2016/XF6785/**F**]

- ♦ Global Alliance Against Child Sexual Abuse Online / see WePROTECT Global Alliance (#20860)

♦ Global Alliance Against Chronic Respiratory Diseases (GARD) 10182

Contact Dept for Management of Noncommunicable Diseases, Disability, Violence and Injury Prevention (NVI), WHO, Avenue Appia 20, 1211 Geneva 27, Switzerland. Fax +41227914151. E-mail: gard@who.int.
URL: http://gard-breathefreely.org/

History 28 Mar 2006, Beijing (China), as a voluntary alliance of national and international organizations. **Aims** Raise recognition of the importance of chronic respiratory diseases (CRDs) at global and country levels; advocate the integration of prevention and control of such diseases into policies across all government departments; promote partnering for the prevention and control of CRDs. **Structure** General Meeting (annual); Planning Group; Executive Committee; Working Groups (7). Secretariat and technical leadership provided by *WHO (#20950)*. **Languages** English, French. **Staff** 2.50 FTE, paid. **Activities** Research/documentation. **Events** *General Meeting* Beijing (China) 2019, *General Meeting* Helsinki (Finland) 2018, *General Meeting* St Petersburg (Russia) 2012, *General Meeting* Toronto, ON (Canada) 2010, *General Meeting* Rome (Italy) 2009. **Publications** *GARD Newsletter*. Books; CD-Rom; flyer; meeting reports.
Members Participants organizations in 23 countries:
Belgium, Bulgaria, Cameroon, Canada, Cuba, Czechia, Denmark, Finland, France, Georgia, Greece, Italy, Japan, Korea Rep, Kyrgyzstan, Norway, Poland, Portugal, Russia, Syrian AR, Tunisia, Türkiye, USA.
Included in the above, 20 listed in this Yearbook:
Allergic Rhinitis and its Impact on Asthma Initiative (ARIA, #00648); Asian Allergy and Asthma Foundation (AAAF); Asian Pacific Society of Respirology (APSR, #01643); Asia Pacific Association of Allergy, Asthma and Clinical Immunology (APAAACI, #01831); Asociación Latinoamericana del Tórax (ALAT, #02273); European Centre for Allergy Research Foundation (ECARF); European Federation of Allergy and Airways Diseases Patients' Associations (EFA, #07045); Fédération mondiale du thermalisme et du climatisme (FEMTEC, #09692); Forum of International Respiratory Societies (FIRS, #09922); Global Allergy and Asthma European Network (GA2LEN, #10179); Global Initiative for Chronic Obstructive Lung Disease (GOLD, #10423); Global Initiative on Asthma (GINA, #10422); INTERASMA (#11457); International COPD Coalition (ICC, #12961); International Primary Care Respiratory Group (IPCRG, #14640); International Rhinologic Society (IRS, #14753); International Union Against Tuberculosis and Lung Disease (The Union, #15752); Société de pneumologie de langue française (SPLF, #19510); World Allergy Organization – IAACI (WAO, #21077); World Organization of Family Doctors (WONCA, #21690). [2018/XM1637/y/**F**]

♦ Global Alliance against Female Genital Mutilation (GA-FGM) 10183

Alliance globale contre les MGF (AG-MGF)

France 249 Route de Choudans, 01630 Saint-Jean-de-Gonville, France. T. +33445288564 – +334648908181. E-mail: info@global-alliance-fgm.org.
Switzerland Route de Ferney 150, 1211 Geneva, Switzerland. T. +41229200584.

URL: http://www.global-alliance-fgm.org/
History 2010. Also referred to as *Global Alliance against FGM*. Registered in accordance with French law. **Aims** Accelerate the total elimination of traditional *violence* against women worldwide. **Structure** General Assembly; Executive Board; International Conference Committee. **Activities** Advocacy/lobbying/activism. **Consultative Status** Consultative status granted from: *ECOSOC (#05331)* (Special). **IGO Relations** *Deutsche Gesellschaft für Internationale Zusammenarbeit (GIZ); UNESCO (#20322)*. **NGO Relations** Affiliated with: *Inter-African Committee on Traditional Practices Affecting the Health of Women and Children (IAC, #11384)*; national organizations. [2017/XM6176/**C**]

♦ Global Alliance against FGM / see Global Alliance against Female Genital Mutilation (#10183)

♦ Global Alliance Against Traffic in Women (GAATW) 10184

International Coordinator 191/41 6th floor, Sivalai Condominium, Soi 33 Itsaraphap Rd, Bangkok-yai, Bangkok, 10600, Thailand. T. +6628641427. Fax +6628641637. E-mail: gaatw@gaatw.org.
URL: http://www.gaatw.org/
History Oct 1994, Chiang Mai (Thailand), at an International Workshop on Migration and Traffic in Women. Formally registered as *Alliance Against Traffic in Women Foundation*, Thailand. **Aims** Ensure that human rights of *migrant* women are respected and protected by authorities and agencies; promote living and working conditions in countries of origin to provide women with more alternatives in their home countries; develop and disseminate information to women about migration, working conditions and their rights. **Structure** International Board (meets annually); Working Groups; Secretariat, based in Bangkok (Thailand). **Languages** English, Filipino, Hindi, Spanish. **Staff** 10.00 FTE, paid. **Finance** Private foundations. **Activities** Projects/programmes; advocacy/lobbying/activism; knwoledge management/information dissemination; research/documentation; networking/liaising. **Events** *Annual General Assembly* 1998.
Members NGOs (over 80) in 36 countries and territories:
Argentina, Austria, Bangladesh, Belarus, Bolivia, Brazil, Bulgaria, Cambodia, Canada, Colombia, Czechia, Germany, Guatemala, Hong Kong, India, Indonesia, Kenya, Mexico, Moldova, Mongolia, Nepal, Netherlands, Nigeria, North Macedonia, Peru, Philippines, Poland, Portugal, Romania, Singapore, Spain, Switzerland, Thailand, Türkiye, Ukraine, USA.
Regional member:
La Strada International (LSI, #20002).
Consultative Status Consultative status granted from: *ECOSOC (#05331)* (Special). **NGO Relations** Member of: *Association for Women's Rights in Development (AWID, #02980); UNCAC Coalition (#20283); United for Foreign Domestic Workers' Rights (UFDWR, #20510); Women in Migration Network (WIMN, #21008)*. [2020/XF4069/**F**]

♦ Global Alliance of Assistive Technology Organizations (GAATO) ... 10185

Registered Address Av Louis Casaï 81, Cointrin, 1216 Geneva, Switzerland. E-mail: secretary@gaato.org.
URL: https://www.gaato.org/
History 2000. Founded by 4 organizations, including *Association for the Advancement of Assistive Technology in Europe (AAATE, #02346)*. Current statutes approved June 2020. Former names and other names: *International Alliance of Assistive Technology Organizations (IAATO)* – former (2000 to 2020). Registration: Swiss Civil Code, Switzerland. **Aims** Advance the field of assistive technology (AT) and rehabilitation engineering (RE) to benefit people with disabilities and functional limitations of all ages; foster equitable and reliable access to assistive technology and rehabilitation; foster collaboration among members and with supranational and international organizations and organizations having similar or complementary goals; support assistive technology professional organizations in low- and middle-income countries. **Structure** General Assembly; Board; Executive Board of Directors; Secretariat headed by Secretary-General. **Languages** English. **Finance** Sources: donations; grants; members' dues; sponsorship; subsidies. **Activities** Advocacy/lobbying/activism; awareness raising; research/documentation; training/education.
Members Organizations (12) in 8 countries and territories:
Argentina, Australia, Austria, India, Japan, Korea Rep, Taiwan, USA.
Included in the above, 4 organizations listed in this Yearbook:
Association for the Advancement of Assistive Technology in Europe (AAATE, #02346); Global Assistive Technology Information Network (EASTIN Association, #10240); International Society for Prosthetics and Orthotics (ISPO, #15390); Raising the Floor (#18617). [2023.02.15/AA2106/y/**C**]

♦ Global Alliance for Banking on Values (GABV) 10186

Exec Dir Mauritskade 63, 1092 AD Amsterdam, Netherlands. T. +31615254228. E-mail: mail@gabv.org.
Head of Communications address not obtained.
URL: http://www.gabv.org/
History 2009, Netherlands. Founded by 10 sustainable banks from around the world. Registration: Netherlands. **Aims** Change the banking system so it is more transparent, supports economic, social and environmental sustainability, and is composed of a diverse range of banking institutions serving the real economy. **Languages** English. **Finance** Sources: members' dues. **Activities** Events/meetings. **Events** *Annual Meeting* New York, NY (USA) 2023, *European Meeting* Barcelona (Spain) 2017, *Annual Conference* Kathmandu (Nepal) 2017, *European Meeting* Olten (Switzerland) 2016, *North American Meeting* Washington, DC (USA) 2016. **Members** Financial institutions and strategic partners. Membership countries not specified. **NGO Relations** Member of (1): *Wellbeing Economy Alliance (WEAll, #20856)*. Partners include: *Aga Khan Development Network (AKDN, #00544)* Agency for Microfinance; *Association of Universities Entrusted to the Society of Jesus in Latin-America (#02969); CARE International (CI, #03429); CEMS – The Global Alliance in Management Education (#03635); The Rockefeller Foundation (#18966); SME Finance Forum (#19323)*; national organizations. [2023/XJ4663/**F**]

♦ Global Alliance of Banks / see Global Banking Alliance for Women (#10248)

♦ Global Alliance for Buildings and Construction (GlobalABC) 10187

Alliance mondiale pour les bâtiments et la construction
Secretariat United Nations Environment Programme, 1 rue Miollis, Building VII, 75015 Paris, France. T. +33145683756. Fax +33144371474. E-mail: global.abc@un.org – unep-economy-globalabc@un.org.
URL: http://www.globalabc.org/
History 3 Dec 2015, Paris (France). Founded at United Nations Climate Conference (COP21). **Aims** Work towards a zero-emission, efficient and resilient buildings and construction sector. **Activities** Advocacy/lobbying/activism; guidance/assistance/consulting; knowledge management/information dissemination; monitoring/evaluation; networking/liaising; politics/policy/regulatory; research and development. **Events** *SBE19 Tokyo : Sustainable Built Environment Tokyo Conference* Tokyo (Japan) 2019, *Round Table* Singapore (Singapore) 2016.
Members 256 members in 37 countries. Membership countries not specified.
Included in the above, 21 organizations listed in this Yearbook:
- *Arab Society for Academic Freedom;*
- *Architects Council of Europe (ACE, #01086);*
- *Buildings Performance Institute Europe (BPIE, #03354);*
- *Energy and Resources Institute (TERI);*
- *European Construction Industry Federation (#06766);*
- *Institut de la Francophonie pour le développement durable (IFDD, #11305);*
- *International Energy Agency (IEA, #13270);*
- *International Initiative for a Sustainable Built Environment (iiSBE, #13854);*
- *International Partnership for Energy Efficiency Cooperation (IPEEC, #14520);*
- *International Passive House Association (iPHA, #14527);*
- *International Renewable Energy Agency (IRENA, #14715);*
- *International Urban Development Association (INTA, #15832);*
- *Local Governments for Sustainability (ICLEI, #16507);*
- *Nubian Vault Association (#17614);*
- *Royal Institution of Chartered Surveyors (RICS, #18991);*
- *Sustainable Energy for All (SEforALL, #20056);*
- *UNEP (#20299);*
- *United Nations Human Settlements Programme (UN-Habitat, #20572);*
- *World Business Council for Sustainable Development (WBCSD, #21254);*
- *World Green Building Council (WorldGBC, #21544);*
- *World Resources Institute (WRI, #21753).* [2022.10.19/XM5751/y/**E**]

♦ Global Alliance for Chronic Diseases (GACD) 10188

Main Office c/o Wellcome Trust, 215 Euston Road, London, NW1 2BE, UK. E-mail: admin@gacd.org.
URL: http://www.gacd.org/
History Founded 15 Jun 2009, Seattle WA (USA), following the Grand Challenges Partnership, first announced in 'Nature' in 2007, which was inspired by a study published in 'Nature' involving a Delphi panel recruited from 50 countries around the world. **Aims** Initiate, facilitate and support joint research activities on chronic, non-communicable diseases (NCDs) in low- and middle-income countries (LMICs) and in vulnerable and indigenous communities in high-income countries (HIC); contribute to development and sharing of the evidence base with which policymakers draft and implement strategies for improving the health of their constituencies. **Structure** Board; Management Committee; Joint Technical Steering Committee; International Secretariat multinational research teams. **Activities** Events/meetings; financial and/or material support; research and development. **Events** *Annual Scientific Meeting* London (UK) 2022, *Annual Scientific Meeting* London (UK) 2021, *Annual Scientific Meeting* London (UK) 2020, *Annual Scientific Meeting* Bangkok (Thailand) 2019, *Annual Scientific Meeting* Sao Paulo (Brazil) 2018.
Members Public health research funders. Charter members in 12 countries:
Argentina, Australia, Brazil, Canada, China, India, Japan, Mexico, South Africa, Thailand, UK, USA.
Included in the above, one regional organization:
European Commission (EC, #06633).
Observer:
WHO (#20950).
NGO Relations Secretariat hosted by: *UCL Institute for Global Health (IGH)*. [2020/XJ5460/**C**]

♦ Global Alliance for Clean Cookstoves / see Clean Cooking Alliance (#03987)

♦ Global Alliance for Climate-Smart Agriculture (GACSA) 10189

Facilitation Unit FAO, Viale delle Terme di Caracalla, 00153 Rome RM, Italy. E-mail: acsa-facilitation-unit@fao.org.
URL: http://www.fao.org/gacsa/en/
History 23 Sep 2014, New York, NY (USA). Launched at UN Climate Summit, by President of Niger and Prime Minister of Netherlands. **Aims** Improve people's *food security* and *nutrition* in the face of *climate change*. **Structure** Annual Forum; Strategic Committee; Action Groups; Facilitation Unit.
Members Governmental and Development Agencies (32):
Armenia, Burkina Faso, Canada, Chile, Costa Rica, Cyprus, Denmark, France, Grenada, India, Ireland, Italy, Japan, Malawi, Mauritius, Mexico, Namibia, Nepal, Netherlands, Niger, Nigeria, Norway, Pakistan, Philippines, Sierra Leone, South Africa, Spain, Switzerland, Tanzania UR, Türkiye, UK, USA.
Inter-Governmental Groups (21):
- *African Development Bank (ADB, #00283);*
- *African Union (AU, #00488)* (Commission);
- *Centre de coopération internationale en recherche agronomique pour le développement (CIRAD, #03733);*
- *Common Market for Eastern and Southern Africa (COMESA, #04296);*
- *Commonwealth Secretariat (#04362);*
- Danish Agriculture and Food Council;
- *FAO (#09260);*
- *Food, Agriculture and Natural Resources Policy Analysis Network (FANRPAN, #09839);*
- *Global Environment Facility (GEF, #10346);*
- *Global Federation of Insurance Associations (GFIA, #10356);*
- Homabay Green;
- *Inter-American Development Bank (IDB, #11427);*
- *International Bank for Reconstruction and Development (IBRD, #12317)* (World Bank);
- *International Fund for Agricultural Development (IFAD, #13692);*
- Kyrgyz Association of Forest and Land Users;
- National Agricultural Research Centre Islamabad;
- National Council for Climate Change Sustainable Development and Public Leadership;
- National Institute of Agricultural Extension Management;
- *New Partnership for Africa's Development (NEPAD, #17091);*
- *UNHCR (#20327);*
- *World Food Programme (WFP, #21510).*

Non-governmental Organizations, including 13 organizations listed in this Yearbook:
African Forum for Agricultural Advisory Services (AFAAS, #00320); Africa Partnership on Climate Change Coalition (APCCC, #00509); BRAC (#03310); Centro Euro-Mediterraneo per i Cambiamenti Climatici (CMCC); Deutsche Gesellschaft für Internationale Zusammenarbeit (GIZ); Environmental Defense Fund (EDF); European Agroforestry Federation (EURAF, #05848); HELVETAS Swiss Intercooperation; INMED Partnerships for Children; Pro-Natura International (#16951); SNV Netherlands Development Organisation (SNV); Tearfund, UK; Women's Earth Alliance (WEA).
Farmer Organizations, include 3 organizations listed in this Yearbook:
Asian Farmers'Association for Sustainable Rural Development (AFA, #01450); Food and Agricultural Research Management (FARM-Africa); World Farmers' Organisation (WFO, #21401).
Research and Academic Institutions include 31 organizations listed in this Yearbook:
- *Acumen;*
- *Bioversity International (#03262);*
- *Caucasus Environmental NGO Network (CENN, #03613);*
- *Center for International Forestry Research (CIFOR, #03646);*
- *CGIAR System Organization (CGIAR, #03843);*
- *Commonwealth Scientific and Industrial Research Organization (CSIRO);*
- *EcoAgriculture Partners (#05290);*
- *EIT Climate-KIC (#05403);*
- *Emmaus International (#05445);*
- *European Synchrotron Radiation Facility (ESRF, #08868);*
- *EverGreen Agriculture Partnership (#09213);*
- *Forum for Agricultural Research in Africa (FARA, #09897);*
- *Global Forum on Agricultural Research (GFAR, #10370);*
- *Inter-American Institute for Cooperation on Agriculture (IICA, #11434);*
- *International Center for Biosaline Agriculture (ICBA, #12468);*
- *International Centre for Tropical Agriculture (#12527);*
- *International Coffee Organization (ICO, #12630);*
- *International Food Policy Research Institute (IFPRI, #13622);*
- *International Maize and Wheat Improvement Center (#14077);*
- *International Rice Research Institute (IRRI, #14754);*
- *International Union for Conservation of Nature and Natural Resources (IUCN, #15766);*
- *Joint Programming Initiative on Agriculture, Food Security and Climate Change (FACCE-JPI, #16145);*
- *Pan African Vision for the Environment (PAVE);*
- *Rainforest Alliance;*
- *Regional Universities Forum for Capacity Building in Agriculture (RUFORUM, #18818);*
- *The Nature Conservancy (TNC);*
- *Tropenbos International (TBI);*
- *Tropical Agriculture Research and Higher Education Center (#20246);*
- *West and Central African Council for Agricultural Research and Development (WECARD, #20907);*
- *World Agroforestry Centre (ICRAF, #21072);*
- *World Resources Institute (WRI, #21753).*

Private Groups, include 11 organizations listed in this Yearbook:
Crops For the Future (CFF, #04968); Fertilizers Europe (#09738); Global Biotechnology Transfer Foundation (GBTF); GLOBALG.A.P (#10386); Global Open Data for Agriculture and Nutrition (GODAN, #10514); International Agri-Food Network (IAFN, #11599); International Fertilizer Association (IFA, #13589); International Fertilizer Development Center (IFDC, #13590); International Humana People to People Movement (HPP, #13817); RTI International; World Business Council for Sustainable Development (WBCSD, #21254).
Non-profit organizations include 2 organizations listed in this Yearbook:
CABI (#03393); Terre et Humanisme (T and H).
Civil Society Organizations include 2 organizations listed in this Yearbook:
International Association of World Peace Advocates (IAWPA, #12281); Mouvement international de la jeunesse agricole et rurale catholique (MIJARC, #16865).
Regional alliances include 1 organization listed in this Yearbook:
Southern Africa Climate Change Coalition (SACCC). [2021/XJ9377/y/**E**]

- Global Alliance for Community Development / see Aya Worldwide
- Global Alliance for Community Empowerment (internationally oriented national body)

Global Alliance of Community Forestry (GACF) — 10190
Coordinator PO Box 8219, Babu Chiring Marg, Shanti Nagar Gate, Kathmandu, Nepal. T. +97714622271. Fax +97714485262.
Facebook: https://www.facebook.com/gacf.info/
History Nov 2004, by *Asociación Coordinadora Indigena y Campesina de Agroforesteria Comunitaria (ACICAFOC, #02120)* and Federation of Community Forest Users of Nepal (FECOFUN). **Aims** Increase cooperation in forest issues between community organizations worldwide; promote capacity and knowledge exchange between member organizations. **Structure** General Assembly. Executive Board. Secretariat, headed by Coordinator. **Events** Annual Meeting Lombok (Indonesia) 2011, Annual Meeting Cameroon 2008, International conference on community forest management and enterprises Rio Branco (Brazil) 2007, Annual Meeting Nepal 2006, Annual Meeting Guatemala 2004. **Publications** GACF E-Bulletin.
Members National organizations in 11 countries:
Cameroon, Colombia, Congo DR, Costa Rica, Ecuador, Finland, Indonesia, Mexico, Nepal, Papua New Guinea, Peru.
IGO Relations Participates in: *United Nations Forum on Forests (UNFF, #20562)*. **NGO Relations** Partners include: *Asociación Coordinadora Indigena y Campesina de Agroforesteria Comunitaria (ACICAFOC, #02120); RECOFTC – The Center for People and Forests (RECOFTC, #18628); Rights and Resources Initiative (RRI, #18947)*.
[2015.01.04/XM3123/F]

Global Alliance of Continuous Plankton Recorder Surveys (GACS) — 10191
Chair c/o SAHFOS, The Laboratory, Citadel Hill, Plymouth, PL1 2PB, UK. T. +441752633288. Fax +441752600015. E-mail: gacs@sahfos.ac.uk.
URL: http://www.globalcpr.org/
History Set up Sep 2011, with the support of *Sir Alister Hardy Foundation for Ocean Science (SAHFOS, inactive)*. Also referred to as *Global Alliance of CPR Surveys*. **Aims** Understand changes in plankton biodiversity at *ocean* basin scales through a global alliance of CPR surveys. **NGO Relations** Cooperates with: *Scientific Committee on Oceanic Research (SCOR, #19149)*.
[2017.06.01/XJ9562/E]

- Global Alliance of CPR Surveys / see Global Alliance of Continuous Plankton Recorder Surveys (#10191)

Global Alliance for Development Foundation (GADeF) — 10192
Co-Chairman Phinklife Inst, Tony's Lodge Street, SunCity Hub, Sunyani, Ghana. T. +233243823177 – +233200592979. E-mail: infogadef@gmail.com — info@gadef.net.
URL: http://www.gadef.net/
History 2008. Registration: Start date: 2010, Ghana. **Aims** Unleash the potentials of youth and community through philanthropy and social entrepreneurship to create a better future for young people and well-being of communities. **Structure** Board of Directors; Secretariat headed by President with Department Leads. **NGO Relations** African Youth Philanthropy Network (AYPN); GrassRoots Hub; *Worldwide Initiatives for Grantmaker Support (WINGS, #21926)*.
[2022.01.28/XJ9340/f/F]

Global Alliance for Disaster Reduction (GADR) — 10193
Address not obtained.
History 2001, when located at *Global Institute for Energy and Environmental Systems (GIEES, inactive)*. **Events** IDRC : regional international disaster reduction conference Harbin (China) 2007, IDRC : international disaster reduction conference Davos (Switzerland) 2006, International conference on energy, environment and disasters Charlotte, NC (USA) 2005.
[2011/XM0569/F]

Global Alliance of Disaster Research Institutes (GADRI) — 10194
SG Disaster Prevention Research Inst, Kyoto Univ – Uji Campus, Gokasho, Uji-shi, Kyoto, 611-0011 Japan. T. +81774384621. E-mail: secretariat-gadri@dpri.kyoto-u.ac.jp.
URL: http://gadri.net/
History Mar 2015, Kyoto (Japan). Founded at 2nd Global Summit of Research Institutes for Disaster Risk Reduction: Development of a Research Road Map for the Next Decade. **Aims** Contribute to enhancing disaster risk reduction and disaster resilience. **Structure** General Assembly; Board of Directors; Secretariat. **Activities** Events/meetings; knowledge management/information dissemination; research/documentation. **Events** Global Summit of Research Institutes for Disaster Risk Reduction Uji (Japan) 2023, Global Summit of Research Institutes for Disaster Risk Reduction Uji (Japan) 2021, Global Summit of Research Institutes for Disaster Risk Reduction Uji (Japan) 2019, Global Summit of Research Institutes for Disaster Risk Reduction Uji (Japan) 2017, Global Summit of Research Institutes for Disaster Risk Reduction Uji (Japan) 2015. **Publications** GADRI Actions. GADRI Book Series; Global Summit Series Resolutions. Annual Report.
Members Institutes in 44 countries and territories:
Algeria, Argentina, Australia, Austria, Bangladesh, Brazil, Bulgaria, Canada, China, Colombia, Ecuador, Egypt, France, Germany, Ghana, Hong Kong, India, Indonesia, Iran Islamic Rep, Israel, Italy, Japan, Korea Rep, Laos, Malaysia, Mexico, Morocco, Nepal, New Zealand, Oman, Philippines, Slovenia, South Africa, Sri Lanka, Sudan, Sweden, Switzerland, Taiwan, Thailand, Türkiye, UK, USA, Vietnam, Zimbabwe.
Asian Disaster Reduction Center (ADRC, #01427); Evidence Aid; Global Disaster Resilience Centre (GDRC); Global Earthquake Model Foundation (GEM Foundation, #10327); Global Risk Forum (GRF Davos); International Centre for Water Hazard and Risk Management (ICHARM); International Consortium on Landslides (ICL, #12917); International Institute for Applied Systems Analysis (IIASA, #13861); International Research Institute of Disaster Science (IRIDeS); Joint Research Centre (JRC, #16147); Open Partial Agreement on the Prevention of, Protection against and Organization of Relief in Major Natural and Technological Disasters (EUR-OPA Major Hazards Agreement, #17762); Overseas Development Institute (ODI); Stockholm Environment Institute (SEI, #19993); United Nations University Institute for Environment and Human Security (UNU-EHS, #20645).
[2020/AA0137/y/C]

- Global Alliance for EcoMobility / see EcoMobility Alliance (#05308)
- Global Alliance of Education and Language Associations (unconfirmed)

Global Alliance to Eliminate Lymphatic Filariasis (GAELF) — 10195
Sec c/o Liverpool School of Tropical Medicine, Pembroke Place, Liverpool, L3 5QA, UK. T. +441517053145. E-mail: gaelf@lstmed.ac.uk.
URL: http://www.gaelf.org/
History May 2000, Santiago de Compostela (Spain). **Aims** Bring together a diverse group of public/private health partners to eliminate lymphatic filariasis by mobilizing political, financial and technical resources to ensure success. **Structure** Steering Group; Representative Contact Group; Secretariat provided by Liverpool School of Tropical Medicine. **Languages** English. **Staff** Voluntary. **Finance** Sources: donations. **Activities** Events/meetings; monitoring/evaluation; projects/programmes. **Events** Biennial meeting / Meeting Seoul (Korea Rep) 2010, Biennial Meeting Tanzania UR 2008, Biennial Meeting Fiji 2006, Biennial Meeting Cairo (Egypt) 2004, Biennial meeting / Meeting Delhi (India) 2002. **Members** Participating Ministries of Health of 73 countries. Membership countries not specified. **NGO Relations** Partners include: *Bill and Melinda Gates Foundation (BMGF); The Carter Center; Catholic Medical Mission Board (CMMB); Health and Development International (HDI); Helen Keller International (HKI, #10902); Humanity and Inclusion (HI, #10975); IMA World Health (IMA); International Foundation for Dermatology (IFD, #13668); International Podoconiosis Initiative (Footwork, #14607); International Skin-Care Nursing Group (ISNG, #14872); International Volunteers in Urology (IVU, no recent information); Izumi Foundation; LEPRA Health in Action (LEPRA); Liverpool School of Tropical Medicine (LSTM); Sightsavers International (#19270).*
[2020/XF6583/F*]

Global Alliance for Energy Productivity — 10196
Secretariat c/o ASE, 1850 M St NW, Ste 610, Washington DC 20036, USA. T. +12028570666.
URL: http://www.globalproductivity.org/
History Launched 13 May 2015, as an initiative of *Alliance to Save Energy (ASE)*. **Aims** Double global energy productivity. **Structure** Steering Committee; Secretariat. Technical Advisory Committee.
Members Organizations in 11 countries:
Australia, Austria, Brazil, Canada, China, Denmark, Germany, India, Mexico, UK, USA.
Included in the above, 5 organizations listed in this Yearbook:
Climate Group (#04013); European Alliance to Save Energy (EU ASE, #05882); International Institute for Energy Conservation (IIEC, #13875); Sustainable Energy for All (SEforALL, #20056); We Mean Business.
NGO Relations Secretariat provided by *Alliance to Save Energy (ASE)*.
[2016/XM5934/y/E]

Global Alliance of Eye Bank Associations (GAEBA) — 10197
Administration Lions Eye Donation Service, Ctr for Eye Research Australia, Level 1, 32 Gisborn Str, Melbourne VIC 3002, Australia. T. +61399298377. Fax +61399298711. E-mail: info@gaeba.org.
Contact address not obtained.
URL: http://www.gaeba.org/
History 2012, when Memorandum of Understanding was signed by representatives of founding members. **Aims** Provide peer and professional support, knowledge exchange, advocacy, vigilance, surveillance and research and continual education opportunities, in line with local, national and international recommended Standards of Practice. **Structure** General Meeting (annual); Committee. **Activities** Events/meetings; training/education. **Events** World Eye Bank Symposium 2022, World Eye Bank Symposium Barcelona (Spain) 2018, World Eye Bank Symposium San Diego, CA (USA) 2015.
Members Founding Members (6):
Asociación Pan Americana de Bancos de Ojos (APABO, #02285); Association of Eye Banks of Asia (AEBA, #02591); European Eye Bank Association (EEBA, #07020); Eye Bank Association of America; Eye Bank Association of Australia and New Zealand (EBAANZ); Eye Bank Association of India (EBAI).
NGO Relations Member of: *International Council of Ophthalmology (ICO, #13057).* [2017/XM5912/y/C]

- Global Alliance in Favour of the Living Wages North and South Initiative / see Jus Semper Global Alliance

Global Alliance for the Future of Food — 10198
Exec Dir address not obtained. E-mail: info@futureoffood.org.
URL: https://futureoffood.org/
History Founded 2012. **Aims** Forge new insights and strengthen evidence for global systems change; convene key food systems actors and facilitate meaningful dialogue; stimulate local and global action for transformational change to realize healthy, equitable, renewable, resilient, interconnected, and culturally diverse food and agriculture systems shaped by people, communities, and their institutions. **Structure** Steering Committee; Coordinating Secretariat. **Activities** Monitoring/evaluation; research/documentation.
Members Organizations (25), including 7 organizations listed in this Yearbook:
Barilla Center for Food and Nutrition Foundation (BCFN Foundation); Christensen Fund (TCF); David and Lucile Packard Foundation; Heinrich Böll Foundation; McKnight Foundation; New Field Foundation; Oak Foundation; The Rockefeller Foundation (#18966); W K Kellogg Foundation (WKKF).
[2018/XM7661/y/C]

Global Alliance for Genomics and Health (GA4GH) — 10199
Headquarters MaRS Ctr – West Tower, 661 Univ Avenue, Suite 510, Toronto ON M5G 0A3, Canada. T. +16472598914. E-mail: info@ga4gh.org.
URL: https://www.ga4gh.org/
History Conceived Jan 2013. Constitution adopted Sep 2014. **Aims** Accelerate progress in genomic research and human health by cultivating a common framework of standards and harmonized approaches for effective and responsible genomic and health-related data-sharing. **Structure** Plenary Meeting; Steering Committee; Executive Committee; Strategic Advisory Board. **Activities** Events/meetings; research and development; standards/guidelines. **Events** Plenary Meeting Toronto, ON (Canada) 2020, Plenary Meeting Boston, MA (USA) 2019, Plenary Meeting Basel (Switzerland) 2018, Plenary Meeting Orlando, FL (USA) 2017, Plenary Meeting Vancouver, BC (Canada) 2016. **Publications** Books.
Members Full in 44 countries and territories:
Argentina, Australia, Austria, Bangladesh, Belgium, Brazil, Bulgaria, Canada, China, Denmark, Finland, France, Germany, Ghana, Greece, Hong Kong, India, Ireland, Israel, Italy, Japan, Korea Rep, Luxembourg, Malaysia, Mexico, Netherlands, New Zealand, Norway, Poland, Portugal, Qatar, Singapore, Slovenia, South Africa, Spain, Sri Lanka, Sweden, Switzerland, Taiwan, Türkiye, UK, United Arab Emirates, USA, Venezuela.
Included in the above, 11 organizations listed in this Yearbook:
European Molecular Biology Laboratory (EMBL, #07813); European Organisation for Research and Treatment of Cancer (EORTC, #08101); European Society of Human Genetics (ESHG, #08624); Human Genome Organization (HUGO, #10968); International Agency for Research on Cancer (IARC, #11598); International Cancer Genome Consortium (ICGC, #12432); International Rare Diseases Research Consortium (IRDiRC, #14699); International Society for Biological and Environmental Repositories (ISBER, #14964); Joint Research Centre (JRC, #16147); Pan African Bioinformatics Network for H3Africa (H3ABioNet); Wellcome Trust.
[2020.03.11/XM8399/y/C]

Global Alliance for ICT and Development (GAID) — 10200
Contact address not obtained.
History 19 Jun 2006, Kuala Lumpur (Malaysia), at the initiative of Kofi Annan, Secretary-General of *United Nations (UN, #20515)*, resulting from the *United Nations ICT Task Force*, set up 2001 with a 4-year mandate. Functions under the auspices of *ECOSOC (#05331)*. Full title: *Global Alliance for Information and Communication Technologies and Development*. **Aims** Respond to the need and demand for an inclusive global forum and platform for cross-sectoral policy dialogue, conducted in an open, multi-stakeholder and transparent manner, on the use of ICT for enhancing the achievement of internationally agreed development goals, including the Millennium Development Goals, notably reduction of poverty. **Structure** Strategy Council of 60 members. Steering Committee, comprising Chairman and several Co-Chairmen representing major constituencies, plus the UN Under-Secretary-General for Economic and Social Affairs and the Executive Coordinator of the Secretariat ex officio. Group of High-level Advisers; Network of Champions; Regional Networks; Communities of Expertise (thematic groups). Secretariat. **Languages** English. **Staff** 4.00 FTE, paid. 1 consultant; 3 interns. **Finance** Funded by voluntary contributions. **Events** ICT 4 all forum – Tunis +5 Tunis (Tunisia) 2010, Joint meeting on mobile technology, convergence and social networking tools for development and poverty alleviation and on the innovative uses of ICT in delivering digital health Geneva (Switzerland) 2009, ICT 4 all forum – Tunis+4 Hammamet (Tunisia) 2009, Annual meeting Monterrey (Mexico) 2009, Global forum on ICT and innovation for education Monterrey (Mexico) 2009. **Publications** Books; working papers; white guide. **IGO Relations** Support from: *Commonwealth Telecommunications Organisation (CTO, #04365)*. **NGO Relations** Instrumental in setting up: *e-Agriculture (#00575); Global Initiative for Inclusive Information and Communication Technologies (G3ict, #10425)*.
[2014/XM1513/F]

Global Alliance of Impact Lawyers (GAIL) — 10201
Secretariat 10 Queen Street Place, London, EC4R 1BE, UK. E-mail: contact@gailnet.org.
URL: https://gailnet.org/
History Feb 2022. Founded on merger of *esela – The legal network for social impact (esela, inactive)*, Benefit Company Bar Association (BCBA) and *Red Latinoamericana de Abogados de Impacto (RLAI, inactive)*. Registration: Companies House, No/ID: 09491407, Start date: 16 Mar 2015, England and Wales. **Aims** Grow the next generation of 'impact lawyers' who will advocate for and champion a rapid and just transition towards a truly sustainable and inclusive economy. **Structure** Board; Regional Boards; Executive Team; Secretariat. Regions: Asia Pacific; Europe; Latin America; North America; UK. **Events** Annual Summit London (UK) 2023.
Members Individuals in 27 countries and territories:
Argentina, Australia, Belgium, Brazil, Chile, China, Colombia, Costa Rica, Dominican Rep, Ecuador, Germany, Gibraltar, India, Italy, Japan, Mexico, Netherlands, New Zealand, Pakistan, Peru, Singapore, Spain, Sweden, Switzerland, UK, Uruguay, USA. Corporate members. Membership countries not specified.
[2023/AA3240/C]

Global Alliance for Improved Nutrition (GAIN) — 10202
Exec Dir Rue de Vermont 37-39, 1211 Geneva, Switzerland. T. +41227491850. Fax +41227491851. E-mail: communications@gainhealth.org.
URL: http://www.gainhealth.org/
History May 2002, New York, NY (USA). Founded during UN General Assembly Special Session on Children. Registered in accordance with Swiss Civil Code, 13 Mar 2003. Special international status granted by the Swiss Government, 2010. **Aims** End malnutrition by mobilizing public-private partnerships and providing financial and technical support to increase access to nutritious foods necessary for people, communities and economies to be stronger and healthier. **Structure** Board; Partnership Council; Secretariat. **Languages** English. **Staff** 125.00 FTE, paid. **Finance** Funding, including from: *Bill and Melinda Gates Foundation (BMGF); Department for International Development (DFID, inactive); Dutch Government; Irish Aid; United States Agency for International Development (USAID)*. **Activities** Advocacy/lobbying/activism. **Events** Sustainable Evidence-Based Actions for Change Workshop Singapore (Singapore) 2014, Forum Vienna (Austria) 2011, Conference

Global Alliance Incinerator
10203

Dubai (United Arab Emirates) 2010, *Forum* Amsterdam (Netherlands) 2009, *Conference* Brussels (Belgium) 2008. **Publications** *GAIN Newsletter* (3 a year). Annual Report. **Consultative Status** Consultative status granted from: *ECOSOC (#05331)* (Special); *WHO (#20950)*. **IGO Relations** Participates as observer in the activities of: *Codex Alimentarius Commission (CAC, #04081)*. Cooperates with: *African Union (AU, #00488)*; *UNICEF (#20332)*; *UNIDO (#20336)*; *World Bank Institute (WBI, #21220)*; *World Food Programme (WFP, #21510)*. **NGO Relations** Member of (3): *Aspen Network of Development Entrepreneurs (ANDE, #02310)*; *Global Open Data for Agriculture and Nutrition (GODAN, #10514)*; *World Benchmarking Alliance (WBA, #21228)*. Partner of various organizations, including: *1,000 Days*; *Every Woman Every Child (EWEC, #09215)*; *Food and Land Use Coalition (FOLU)*; *Helen Keller International (HKI, #10902)*; *Iodine Global Network (IGN, #16004)*; *Nutrition International (#17627)*; *PATH (#18260)*. [2021/XJ4029/**F**]

♦ **Global Alliance for Incinerator Alternatives (GAIA)** **10203**
International Coordinator 1958 University Avenue, Berkeley CA 94704, USA. T. +15108839490. Fax +15108839493. E-mail: info@no-burn.org.
Asia Pacific Regional Coordinator Unit 330, Eagle Court Condominium, 26 Matalino Street, Barangay Central, Quezon City, Philippines. T. +6324364733. Fax +6324364733.
Latin America Office Pasaje Paredes 1385, Concepción, Bio Bio, Chile. T. +56996526550.
URL: https://www.no-burn.org/
History Founded Dec 2000, South Africa. Previously also known as *Global Anti-Incinerator Alliance*. **Aims** Promote clean production and creation of a closed-loop, materials-efficient economy where all products are reused, repaired or recycled. **Structure** International Steering Committee; Global Coordination Team. **Languages** English. **Staff** 17.00 FTE, paid. **Finance** Sources: grants. **Activities** Events/meetings. **Events** *Asia Pacific Regional Meeting* Bali (Indonesia) 2017, *Global Meeting* Paris (France) 2015, *Global Meeting* Spain 2007, *Global Meeting* Malaysia 2003, *Global Meeting* South Africa 2000. **Publications** Articles; fact sheets. **Members** Grassroots groups, NGOs and individuals (over 800) in over 90 countries (not specified). **Consultative Status** Consultative status granted from: *UNEP (#20299)*. **IGO Relations** Accredited by: *Green Climate Fund (GCF, #10714)*. **NGO Relations** Member of: *Climate Justice Now ! (CJN!, inactive)*; *Health Care Without Harm (HCWH, #10875)*; *International Pollutants Elimination Network (IPEN, #14616)*; *NGO Forum on ADB (#17123)*. [2021/XM2076/**C**]

♦ **Global Alliance of Independent Firms (Praxity)** **10204**
Administrative Office Ste 2 – Beechwood, 57 Church Street, Epsom, KT17 4PX, UK. T. +441372738190. Fax +441372738199.
Registered Office Bellevue 5, Box 1001, 9050 Ghent, Belgium.
URL: http://www.praxity.com/
History Registered in accordance with Belgian law. **Aims** Be the most advanced alliance of strong, like-minded, independent and committed accounting and allied services firms that independently deliver client service and quality solutions globally. **Structure** General Meeting (annual). Governing Council. Management Board. **Members** Firms (69). Membership countries not specified. [2017/XJ5617/**D**]

♦ Global Alliance for Information and Communication Technologies and Development / see Global Alliance for ICT and Development (#10200)

♦ **Global Alliance for Justice Education (GAJE)** **10205**
Exec Sec Vanderbilt Law School, 131 21st Ave S, Nashville TN 37203-1181, USA. T. +16153224901. Fax +16153226631.
URL: http://www.gaje.org/
History 1996. Constitution adopted Dec 2001, Durban (South Africa). **Aims** Promote justice through education. **Structure** General Meeting. Steering Committee, consisting of one man and one woman from each of the regions (Africa, Australasia, East Asia, Eastern Europe, South America, South and Central Asia, North America, Western Europe). Executive Committee of 5. Officers: President; Secretary; Treasurer. **Activities** Events/meetings. **Events** *Conference* Bandung (Indonesia) 2019, *Conference* Puebla (Mexico) / Tlaxcala (Mexico) 2017, *Conference* Eskisehir (Turkey) 2015, *Worldwide Conference / Conference* Delhi (India) 2013, *Worldwide Conference / Conference* Valencia (Spain) 2011. **Publications** *GAJE E-Newsletter*. [2019/XJ5106/**B**]

♦ **Global Alliance for Leadership in Nursing Education and Science** **10206**
(GANES)
Contact American Assn of Colleges of Nursing, 655 K Street NW, Suite 750, Washington DC 20031, USA. T. +12024636930 ext 237.
URL: http://www.ganes.info/
Aims Work in partnership with global and national organizations to raise awareness of the key role of nurse education in the improvement of global health and quality of care.
Members National associations in 4 countries:
Australia, Canada, New Zealand, USA. [2020/XJ1819/**C**]

♦ Global Alliance of Lesbian, Gay, Bisexual and Transgender Education (internationally oriented national body)
♦ Global Alliance for Livestock Veterinary Medicines / see GALVmed (#10066)
♦ Global Alliance of Local Ombudsman (#00629)
♦ Global Alliance of the Local Ombudsperson / see Alianza Global del Ombudsperson Local (#00629)

♦ **Global Alliance of Marketing and Management Associations** **10207**
(GAMMA)
Pres College of Human Ecology, Yonsei Univ, 50 Yonsei-Ro, Seodeamun-Gu, Seoul 120-749, Korea Rep. T. +82221238361. Fax +82221233109. E-mail: gammaksms@gmail.com.
Central Office Dept of Business Admin, Changwon Natl Univ, 20 Changwondeahad-ro, Uichang-gu, Changwon SOUTH GYEONGSANG 641-773, Korea Rep. T. +82552133346. Fax +82552639096. E-mail: stride@changwon.ac.kr.
URL: http://www.gamma20.org/
History 21 Jul 2012. Founded by *European Marketing Academy (EMAC, #07745)*, *International Textile and Apparel Association (ITAA)* and national organizations in Australia, New Zealand, Japan and Korea.
Aims Obtain global benefits for members; stimulate global cooperation among participating organizations. **Structure** Officers; Global Offices; Directors. **Languages** English. **Activities** Events/meetings. **Events** *Global Fashion Management Conference* Seoul (Korea Rep) 2021, *Global Marketing Conference* Seoul (Korea Rep) 2020, *Global Fashion Management Conference* Paris (France) 2019, *Global Fashion Management Conference* Vienna (Austria) 2017, *Global Marketing Conference* Hong Kong (Hong Kong) 2016. **Publications** *Journal of Global Scholars of Marketing Science* (4 a year); *Journal of Global Fashion Marketing* (4 a year); *Journal of Global Sport Management* (4 a year); *GAMMA/KSMS Newsletter* (2 a year).
Members National organizations in 4 countries:
Australia, Japan, Korea Rep, New Zealand.
Regional associations (2):
European Marketing Academy (EMAC, #07745); *International Textile and Apparel Association (ITAA)*.
Partner organizations in 2 countries:
Greece, Spain. [2021/XM5614/y/**C**]

♦ **Global Alliance for Maternal Mental Health (GAMMH)** **10208**
Address not obtained.
URL: https://globalalliancematernalmentalhealth.org/
Aims Foster the translation of research in perinatal and maternal mental health into better care and outcomes for women and their families wherever they live. **Activities** Knowledge management/information dissemination.
Members Organizations (17):
African Alliance for Maternal Mental Health (AAMMH); *Childhood and Early Parenting Principles (CEPPs, #03873)*; *Fédération Internationale de Gynécologie et d'Obstétrique (FIGO, #09638)*; *International Association for Women's Mental Health (IAWMH, #12272)*; *International Foundation for Mother and Child Health (IFMCH)*; *International Marcé Society for Perinatal Mental Health (Marcé Society, #14089)*; *International Society for Developmental Origins of Health and Disease (DOHaD, #15055)*; *International Society of Psychosomatic Obstetrics and Gynaecology (ISPOG, #15402)*; Perinatal Mental Health Project; *Postpartum Depression: Action Towards Causes and Treatment Consortium (PACT Consortium, #18470)* (Mellow Parenting International); Postpartum Support, International (PSI); PRIME; *White Ribbon Alliance for Safe Motherhood (WRA, #20934)*; *World Association for Infant Mental Health (WAIMH, #21146)*; World Maternal Mental Health Day; *World Psychiatric Association (WPA, #21741)*. [2022/XM8404/y/**C**]

♦ **Global Alliance on Media and Gender (GAMAG)** **10209**
Secretariat 308 Main Street, Toronto ON M4C 4X7, Canada. T. +14166911999 ext 226. E-mail: gamag2017@gmail.com.
URL: https://gamag.net/
History 2 Dec 2013, Bangkok (Thailand). Launched by *UNESCO (#20322)* and over 500 organizations at the 1st Gobal Forum on Gender and Media. **Aims** Achieve gender equality in and through the media and ICTs in all formats and locations and across different forms of ownership. **Structure** International Steering Committee; Executive Committee. Regional Chapters: Africa; Asia-Pacific; Europe; Latin America and the Caribbean. Thematic Committees. [2021/AA1478/**E**]

♦ **Global Alliance for Medical Education (GAME)** **10210**
Exec Dir 122 W 26th Street, Suite 1100, New York NY 10001, USA. E-mail: info@gamecme.org.
URL: http://www.gamecme.org/
History 1995. **Aims** Advance innovation in medical education worldwide. **Structure** Board of Directors. **Events** *Futurist Forum* Budapest (Hungary) 2019, *Annual Meeting* Jersey City, NJ (USA) 2018, *Annual Meeting* Coral Gables, FL (USA) 2014, *Annual Meeting* Barcelona (Spain) 2013, *Annual Meeting* Toronto, ON (Canada) 2012. **Publications** *GAME Newsletter*.
Members Individuals in 13 countries:
Argentina, Australia, Brazil, Canada, Colombia, Germany, Italy, Japan, Mexico, Pakistan, Spain, UK, USA. [2021/XM1209/**F**]

♦ Global Alliance of Mental Illness Advocacy Networks (internationally oriented national body)

♦ **Global Alliance of Mental Illness Advocacy Networks – Europe** **10211**
(GAMIAN Europe)
Exec Dir Rue du Trône 60, 1050 Brussels, Belgium. E-mail: info@gamian.eu – executive.director@gamian.eu.
URL: http://www.gamian.eu/
History Mar 1997, Venice (Italy). Founded by 12 advocacy groups or associations dedicated to helping and sustaining those who suffer from mental illness. Statutes approved and registered in accordance with Belgian law, 2002. Statutes revised 2009. Registration: Start date: 1998, Switzerland, Zug; EU Transparency Register, No/ID: 50813891737-43, Start date: 22 May 2009. **Aims** Promote information, education and understanding of mental illness; encourage appropriate scientific research in the field. **Structure** General Assembly; Board of Directors; Executive Committee; Executive Director. **Languages** English. **Staff** Voluntary. **Finance** Sources: donations; grants; members' dues. **Activities** Advocacy/lobbying/activism; awards/prizes/competitions; events/meetings; training/education. **Events** *Annual Convention* Bucharest (Romania) 2019, *Annual Convention* Budapest (Hungary) 2017, *Annual Convention* Vienna (Austria) 2016, *Annual Convention* Budapest (Hungary) 2014, *Annual Convention* Vilnius (Lithuania) 2013. **Publications** *GAMIAN Europe Newsletter* (4 a year). Books; articles; leaflets; videos; audio cassettes; films.
Members Organizations (53) in 26 countries:
Armenia, Belgium, Croatia, Cyprus, Czechia, Estonia, France, Greece, Hungary, Ireland, Israel, Italy, Lithuania, Malta, Netherlands, Norway, Poland, Portugal, Romania, Russia, Slovakia, Slovenia, Spain, Sweden, Türkiye, UK.
Associate (individual) members in 8 countries:
Finland, Hungary, Ireland, Netherlands, Slovenia, Spain, Türkiye, UK.
Associate (familiy associations) in 9 countries:
Argentina, Australia, Brazil, Canada, Croatia, Italy, South Africa, Uganda, Venezuela.
Associate (professional association):
IGO Relations Contact with several EU Directorates (not specified). **NGO Relations** Member of (3): *European Patients' Forum (EPF, #08172)*; *International Alliance of Patients' Organizations (IAPO, #11633)*; *International Society for Bipolar Disorders (ISBD, #14977)*. Affiliated with (1): *World Psychiatric Association (WPA, #21741)*. [2022/XF6990/**F**]

♦ **Global Alliance for Ministries and Infrastructures for Peace** **10212**
(GAMIP) ....
Canada Office 7058 116 St, Delta BC V4E 1Y1, Canada. E-mail: info@gamip.org.
Contact Chemin de la Caracole 68, Genthod, 1294 Geneva, Switzerland. E-mail: info@gamip.org.
URL: http://www.gamip.org/
Aims Promote the development of infrastructures for peace at various levels. **Structure** Board of Directors. **Activities** Events/meetings. **Events** *Global Peace Summit* Tunja (Colombia) 2022, *Global Summit for Ministries and Departments of Peace* Geneva (Switzerland) 2013, *Global Summit for Ministries and Departments of Peace* Cape Town (South Africa) 2011, *Global Summit for Ministries and Departments of Peace* Costa Rica 2009, *Global Summit for Ministries and Departments of Peace* Japan 2007. **Members** Individuals worldwide. Membership countries not specified. **NGO Relations** *Peace Through Unity (PTU)*. Member of: *Global Movement for the Culture of Peace (GMCOP)*. [2022/XJ8503/v/**C**]

♦ **Global Alliance for Musculoskeletal Health (G-MUSC)** **10213**
Exec Secretariat Bone and Joint Research Office, The Knowledge Spa, Royal Cornwall Hosp Treliske, Truro, TR1 3HD, UK. T. +441872256438. E-mail: office@bjdonline.org.
URL: http://www.boneandjointdecade.org/
History 13 Jan 2000, Geneva (Switzerland), at headquarters of *WHO (#20950)*, as *Bone and Joint Decade (BJD)*. Full title: *Global Alliance for Musculoskeletal Health of the Bone and Joint Decade*. **Aims** Improve quality of life for people with *musculoskeletal* disorders worldwide. **Structure** International Coordinating Council; Business Advisory Committee. **Activities** Awareness raising; knowledge management/information dissemination; advocacy/lobbying/activism; research/documentation; awards/prizes/competitions. **Events** *World congress on sports trauma* Hong Kong (Hong Kong) 2008, *Annual world network conference* Beijing (China) 2004, *Annual world network conference* Berlin (Germany) 2003, *Annual world network conference* Rio de Janeiro (Brazil) 2002, *Annual world network conference* New York, NY (USA) 2001.
Members in 90 countries and territories:
Algeria, Argentina, Australia, Austria, Bangladesh, Belgium, Bolivia, Bosnia-Herzegovina, Brazil, Bulgaria, Canada, Chile, China, Colombia, Congo DR, Costa Rica, Cuba, Cyprus, Czechia, Denmark, Dominican Rep, Ecuador, Egypt, El Salvador, Estonia, Finland, France, Georgia, Germany, Greece, Guatemala, Haiti, Holy See, Honduras, Hong Kong, Hungary, Iceland, India, Indonesia, Iran Islamic Rep, Ireland, Italy, Japan, Jordan, Kenya, Korea Rep, Kuwait, Latvia, Lebanon, Libya, Lithuania, Malaysia, Mexico, Morocco, Netherlands, New Zealand, Nicaragua, Nigeria, North Macedonia, Norway, Oman, Pakistan, Panama, Peru, Philippines, Poland, Portugal, Puerto Rico, Qatar, Romania, Russia, Saudi Arabia, Singapore, Slovakia, Slovenia, South Africa, Spain, Sweden, Switzerland, Syria, Taiwan, Tanzania UR, Thailand, Tunisia, Türkiye, UK, Ukraine, Uruguay, USA, Venezuela, Vietnam.
IGO Relations *WHO (#20950)*. **NGO Relations** Founding member of: *Global Rehabilitation Alliance (#10565)*. *International Society of Orthopaedic Surgery and Traumatology (#15335)* is member. [2018/XF6936/**F**]

♦ Global Alliance for Musculoskeletal Health of the Bone and Joint Decade / see Global Alliance for Musculoskeletal Health (#10213)

♦ **Global Alliance of National Human Rights Institutions (GANHRI)** ... **10214**
Operations Manager UNOG – Palais des Nations, Office A573, 1211 Geneva 10, Switzerland. T. +41229172716. E-mail: info@ganhri.org.
Geneva Representative address not obtained.
URL: https://ganhri.org/
History 13 Dec 1993, Tunis (Tunisia). Constitution adopted 30 Jul 2008; amended 30 Mar 2012. Current statutes adopted 2 Mar 2019. Former names and other names: *International Coordinating Committee of National Institutions for the Promotion and Protection of Human Rights (ICC)* – former (1993 to 2016); *Comité international de coordination des institutions nationales pour la promotion et la protection des droits de l'homme (CIC)* – former (1993 to 2016); *Comité Internacional de Coordinación de las Instituciones Nacionales para la Promoción y Protección de los Derechos Humanos (CIC)* – former (1993 to 2016); *International Coordinating Committee (ICC)* – former (1993 to 2016); *Comité international de coordination (CIC)* – former (1993 to 2016); *Comité Internacional de Coordinación (CIC)* – former (1993 to 2016). Registration: Civil Code, Switzerland. **Aims** Promote and strengthen NHRIs to be in compliance with the Paris Principles and provide leadership for the promotion and protection of human rights; provide a framework for NHRIs to work together and cooperate at international level. **Structure** General Assembly; Bureau; Head Office. Sub-Committee on Accreditation; Finance Committee. Working Groups: Business and Human Rights; Rights of Persons with Disabilities; 2030 Agenda for Sustainable Development; Ageing. Regional networks (4): *Network of African National Human Rights Institutions (NANHRI, #16984)*; Asia Pacific Forum of National Human Rights

Institutions (APF, #01911); European Network of National Human Rights Institutions (ENNHRI, #07949); Red de Instituciones Nacionales para la Promoción y Protección de los Derechos Humanos del Continente Americano (RINDHCA). **Activities** Advocacy/lobbying/activism; awareness raising; certification/accreditation; events/meetings; guidance/assistance/consulting; knowledge management/information dissemination; monitoring/evaluation; projects/programmes; research and development; training/education. **Events** *Annual Meeting* Geneva (Switzerland) 2023, *Annual Meeting* 2022, *Annual Meeting* 2021, *General Meeting Annual Session* Geneva (Switzerland) 2016, *International Conference of National Human Rights Institutions* Mérida (Mexico) 2015.

Members A-Status members: NHRIs who comply fully with Paris Principles; B – Observer Status: not fully in compliance with the Paris Principles or insufficient information.

A-Status members (91):

Albania, Argentina, Armenia, Australia, Austria, Benin, Bolivia, Bosnia-Herzegovina, Bulgaria, Burundi, Cameroon, Canada, Chile, Colombia, Congo DR, Costa Rica, Croatia, Cyprus, Denmark, Ecuador, Egypt, El Salvador, Estonia, Ethiopia, Finland, France, Gambia, Georgia, Germany, Ghana, Great Britain, Greece, Guatemala, Haiti, Honduras, India, Indonesia, Iraq, Ireland, Jordan, Kenya, Korea Rep, Latvia, Liberia, Lithuania, Luxembourg, Madagascar, Malawi, Malaysia, Mali, Mauritania, Mauritius, Mexico, Moldova, Mongolia, Morocco, Namibia, Nepal, Netherlands, New Zealand, Nicaragua, Niger, Nigeria, Northern Ireland, Norway, Palestine, Panama, Peru, Philippines, Poland, Portugal, Qatar, Russia, Rwanda, Samoa, Scotland, Serbia, Sierra Leone, Slovenia, South Africa, Spain, Sri Lanka, Tanzania UR, Thailand, Timor-Leste, Togo, Uganda, Ukraine, Uruguay, Zambia, Zimbabwe.

B-Status members (28):

Algeria, Azerbaijan, Bahrain, Bangladesh, Belgium, Bulgaria, Chad, Congo Brazzaville, Côte d'Ivoire, Hungary, Kazakhstan, Kyrgyzstan, Libya, Maldives, Montenegro, Myanmar, Nicaragua, North Macedonia, Oman, Panama, Senegal, Slovakia, Sri Lanka, Sweden, Tajikistan, Tunisia, Türkiye, Venezuela. [2023/XJ2741/E]

♦ Global Alliance for Newborn Care (GLANCE) 10215

Contact c/o EFCNI, Hofmannstraße 7A, 81379 Munich, Germany. T. +498989083260. Fax +4989890832610. E-mail: info@glance-network.org.

URL: https://www.glance-network.org/

History 2018. Founded by *European Foundation for the Care of Newborn Infants (EFCNI, #07344).* **Aims** Create, empower and support a global patient voice in each region of the world while taking into account the respective cultural, historical and socio-economic backgrounds and needs of families. **Structure** Led by *European Foundation for the Care of Newborn Infants (EFCNI, #07344).* Founding Committee; Chair Committee; Working Groups. **NGO Relations** Partner of (1): *International Council of Multiple Birth Organisations (ICOMBO, #13050).* [2022/AA3149/C]

♦ Global Alliance of NGOs for Road Safety 10216

Admin Dir address not obtained. E-mail: admin@roadsafetyngos.org.

URL: http://www.roadsafetyngos.org/

History 2011. Set up by NGO members of the *United Nations Road Safety Collaboration.* Registration: Swiss Civil Code, Switzerland. **Aims** Unite, empower, and strengthen NGOs to stimulate collaborative advocacy, action, and accountability for road safety and road victims. **Structure** Board of Directors. **Activities** Advocacy/lobbying/activism; capacity building; events/meetings; networking/liaising. **Events** *Global Meeting of Nongovernmental Organizations Advocating for Road Safety and Road Victims* Budapest (Hungary) 2022, *Global Meeting of Nongovernmental Organizations Advocating for Road Safety and Road Victims* Stockholm (Sweden) 2019, *Global Meeting of Nongovernmental Organizations Advocating for Road Safety and Road Victims* Kuala Lumpur (Malaysia) 2017, *Global Meeting of Nongovernmental Organizations Advocating for Road Safety and Road Victims* Marrakech (Morocco) 2015, *Global Meeting of Nongovernmental Organizations Advocating for Road Safety and Road Victims* Antalya (Turkey) 2013. **Publications** *Good Practice Guide on Meaningful NGO Participation in the Field of Road Safety* (2021); *Safer Cycling Advocate Best Practice Guide* (2019); *The Day Our World Crumbled: The Human Impact of Inaction on Road Safety* (2019); *Walking the Talk* (2017). **Members** NGOs, over 280, active in over 90 countries (not specified). [2022.03.02/XJ5999/F]

♦ Global Alliance of Partners for Pain Advocacy (GAPPA) 10217

Contact c/o IASP, 1510 H St NW, Suite 600, Washington DC 20005-1020, USA. T. +12028567400. Fax +12028567401. E-mail: gappa@iasp-pain.org.

URL: https://www.iasp-pain.org/advocacy/global-alliance-of-partners-for-pain-advocacy-gappa/

History Sep 2018. An advocacy group within *International Association for the Study of Pain (IASP, #12206).* **Aims** Work together to improve the lives of people affected by pain through effective and equitable integration of the lived pain experience into all aspects of pain research, management, education, and advocacy, across the world, for all people. **Structure** Task Force. **Activities** Advocacy/lobbying/activism; events/meetings. **Events** *UPLiFT Conference* 2021. [2022/AA2534/v/E]

♦ Global Alliance of Pet Food Associations (GAPFA) 10218

Secretariat Avenue de Tervuren 13A, Bte 7, 1040 Brussels, Belgium. E-mail: secretariat@gapfa.org.

URL: http://www.gapfa.org/

History 2014, Belgium. **Aims** Support the health and wellbeing of dogs and cats; promote the benefits of living with them, by providing a forum to address industry consensus on key issues of mutual interest. **Structure** General Assembly; Executive Committee. **Languages** English. **Finance** Sources: members' dues. **Activities** Standards/guidelines.

Members Full in 12 countries:

Argentina, Australia, Brazil, Canada, Japan, Korea Rep, Mexico, New Zealand, Russia, South Africa, Thailand, USA.

Fédération européenne de l'industrie des aliments pour animaux familiers (FEDIAF, #09571).

[2020.08.19/XM4938/C]

♦ Global Alliance Powerfuels (unconfirmed)

♦ Global Alliance for the Prevention of Obesity and Related Chronic Disease 10219

Address not obtained.

History Feb 2005. At the initiative of *World Obesity (#21678).* **Aims** Provide coordinated NGO actions to help implement the WHO Global Strategy on Diet, Physical Activity and Health and the Global Strategy for the Prevention and Control of Non-communicable Diseases; encourage wider stakeholders to cooperate in unified actions and responses; develop best-practice prevention models, focusing on the prevention of childhood obesity as an essential first step towards preventing chronic diseases. **Structure** Presidential Council, headed by Chair. **Languages** English. **Finance** Voluntary support from members. **Activities** Advocacy and advice to government and policy makers.

Members International organizations (5):

International Diabetes Federation (IDF, #13164); International Pediatric Association (IPA, #14541); International Union of Nutritional Sciences (IUNS, #15796); World Heart Federation (WHF, #21562); World Obesity (#21678).

IGO Relations *WHO (#20950).* [2010/XM2432/y/F]

♦ Global Alliance to Prevent Prematurity and Stillbirth (internationally oriented national body)

♦ Global Alliance for Project Performance Standards / see Global Alliance for the Project Professions (#10220)

♦ Global Alliance for the Project Professions (GAPPS) 10220

Sec address not obtained. E-mail: info@globalpmstandards.org.

URL: https://www.pmprofessions.org

History First Global Steering Committee meeting held Aug 2002, London (UK). Originally referred to as *Global Performance Based Standards for Project Management Personnel* and subsequently as *Global Alliance for Project Performance Standards (GAPPS).* **Aims** Develop globally applicable project *management competence*-based standards, frameworks and mappings; provide relevant information for use by businesses, academic institutions, professional associations and government standards and qualifications bodies globally. **Structure** Global Steering Committee, headed by Chair. **Finance** Sources: members' dues. **Events** *Thought Leadership Forum* 2020, *Thought Leadership Forum* 2020, *Thought Leadership Forum* Sydney, NSW (Australia) 2020, *Thought Leadership Forum* Cabo San Lucas (Mexico) 2019, *Thought Leadership Forum* Lancaster (UK) 2019.

Members Active: Standards and Qualifications Organizations; Project Management Professional Associations; Academic/Training Institutions; Industry. Included in the above, 2 organizations listed in this Yearbook:

Green Project Management (GPM); International Project Management Association (IPMA, #14655).

[2021/XJ6712/ty/C]

♦ Global Alliance to Promote Fruits and Vegetable Consumption "5 a day" (AIAM5) 10221

Alianza Global de Promoción al Consumo de Frutas y Hortalizas "5 al dia" (AIAM5)

Coordinator Mercamadrid, Avda Villa de Vallecas, esq Calle 52, Parcela J4, 28053 Madrid, Spain. T. +34902365125. Fax +34902365126. E-mail: comitecientifico@5aldia.com – info@5aldia.com.

URL: http://aiam5.com/

History 2011, Madrid (Spain). Founded at 8th International Fruit and Vegetable Congress. *International Fruit and Vegetable Alliance (IFAVA, inactive)* merged into AIAM5, Mar 2015. Subsequently adopted current title. Former names and other names: *International Alliance of Associations and Movements 5 a day (AIAM5)* – former; *Alianza Internacional de Asociaciones y Movimientos "5 al dia" (AIAM5)* – former. **Aims** Create a powerful international network to promote and support efforts to increase consumption of fruit and vegetables by providing members with up-to-date information, support resources, and other communication tools. **Structure** Presidency; Working Groups; Secretariat. Headquarters in country organizing International Congress. **Languages** English, Spanish. **Activities** Advocacy/lobbying/activism; awards/prizes/competitions; awareness raising; capacity building; events/meetings; guidance/assistance/consulting; knowledge management/information dissemination; monitoring/evaluation; networking/liaising; projects/programmes; publishing activities; research and development; standards/guidelines; training/education. **Events** *Congress* Madrid (Spain) 2021, *Congress* Madrid (Spain) 2020, *Congress* Tuxtla Gutiérrez (Mexico) 2018, *Congress* Warsaw (Poland) 2017, *Congress* Bogota (Colombia) 2016. **Publications** *Mirador Salud* (12 a year) in Spanish; *Global Fruit and Vegetables Newsletter* (12 a year) in English, French, Spanish; *AIAM5 Newsflash* (4 a year) in English, Spanish.

Members Full – national associations in 31 countries:

Argentina, Bolivia, Brazil, Canada, Chile, Colombia, Costa Rica, Cuba, Dominican Rep, Finland, France, Germany, Honduras, Hungary, Italy, Japan, Lithuania, Mexico, New Zealand, Nicaragua, Norway, Paraguay, Peru, Poland, Portugal, Spain, Sweden, Switzerland, Uruguay, USA, Venezuela.

Collaborative (8):

Assemblée des Régions Européennes Fruitières, Légumières et Horticoles (AREFLH, #02314); AVRDC – The World Vegetable Center (#03051); European Fresh Produce Association (FRESHFEL Europe, #07361); European Union of the Fruit and Vegetable Wholesale, Import and Export Trade (EUCOFEL, inactive); FENAOMFRA (Federación Nacional de Operadores de Mercados Frutihortícolas de la República Argentina); *Institute of Nutrition of Central America and Panama (INCAP, #11285); Produce Marketing Association (PMA); World Union of Wholesale Markets (WUWM, #21889).* [2021.03.22/XM7357/C]

♦ Global Alliance for Public Relations and Communication Management (GA) 10223

Chief Admin Officer Via Geiuseppe Buffi 13, 6900 Lugano TI, Switzerland. E-mail: info@globalalliancepr.org.

URL: http://www.globalalliancepr.org/

History Formally started operating Jul 2002, following a pre-formation period starting 1996. **Aims** Enhance the role and value of public relations and communication management to organizations, and to global society. **Structure** Annual General Meeting; Council; Executive Board. **Activities** Awards/prizes/competitions; events/meetings; research/documentation; training/education. **Events** *World Public Relations Forum* Auckland (New Zealand) 2020, *World Public Relations Forum* Oslo (Norway) 2018.

Members Full in 35 countries and territories:

Argentina, Australia, Bangladesh, Belgium, Brazil, Canada, Chile, China, Croatia, Ecuador, Estonia, Finland, Germany, India, Indonesia, Ireland, Italy, Kenya, Lithuania, Malaysia, Mexico, New Zealand, Nigeria, Norway, Peru, Philippines, Portugal, Puerto Rico, Singapore, South Africa, Spain, Sweden, Switzerland, UK, USA.

Also a member in the Middle East. Membership countries not specified. Included in the above, 3 organizations listed in this Yearbook:

Included in the above, 3 organizations listed in this Yearbook:

African Public Relations Association (APRA); ASEAN Public Relations Network (APRN, #01226); Middle East Public Relations Association (MEPRA). [2020/XM8038/C]

♦ Global Alliance for Public Relations and Communication Management 10222

Chief Administrative Officer Via Ruggi 3, 6963 Lugano TI, Switzerland. E-mail: cao@globalalliancepr.org.

URL: http://www.globalalliancepr.org/

History 25 Oct 2000, Chicago, IL (USA). Founded by 25 national and international bodies. **Aims** Unify the public relations and communication management profession. Serve as a forum to: share ideas and best practice; identify common interests and develop global standards; provide a better understanding of the unique aspects of each culture in which practitioners operate. **Structure** Board; Secretariat in Switzerland. **Languages** English. **Finance** Sources: members' dues; revenue from activities/projects. **Activities** Awareness raising; events/meetings; knowledge management/information dissemination; research/documentation; standards/guidelines. **Events** *Biennial World Public Relations Forum* Auckland (New Zealand) 2020, *Biennial World Public Relations Forum* Oslo (Norway) 2018, *ASEAN Public Relation Regional Conference* Bali (Indonesia) 2017, *Annual General Meeting* New York, NY (USA) 2017, *Biennial World Public Relations Forum* Toronto, ON (Canada) 2016. **Publications** Research reports.

Members National associations in 30 countries:

Argentina, Australia, Bangladesh, Brazil, Canada, Chile, Croatia, Estonia, Finland, Germany, India, Indonesia, Ireland, Italy, Kenya, Lithuania, Malaysia, Mexico, New Zealand, Nigeria, Norway, Peru, Portugal, Singapore, South Africa, Spain, Sweden, Switzerland, UK, USA.

Also members in ASEAN and Middle East countries. Membership countries not specified.

IGO Relations Associated with Department of Global Communications of the United Nations.

[2021/XM0266/y/F]

♦ Global Alliance for Rabies Control (internationally oriented national body)

♦ Global Alliance for Responsible Media (GARM) 10224

Contact address not obtained. E-mail: garm@wfanet.org.

URL: https://wfanet.org/leadership/garm/about-garm

History 2019, Cannes (France). Founded by *World Federation of Advertisers (WFA, #21407).* Since nov 2019, a flagship project of *World Economic Forum (WEF, #21367)* Platform for Shaping the Future of Media, Entertainment and Culture. **Aims** Act as the forum for the creation of solutions that will improve online safety for both consumers and advertisers. **Structure** Chartered by *World Federation of Advertisers (WFA, #21407)* and reports to WFA Executive Committee. Steer Team. Working Groups. **Activities** Advocacy/lobbying/activism; standards/guidelines; training/education.

Members Advertisers; agencies; media companies; platforms; industry organizations.

European Association of Communications Agencies (EACA, #05983). [2021/AA2039/y/E]

♦ Global Alliance for the Rights of Nature (GARN) 10225

Address not obtained.

URL: http://therightsofnature.org/

History Set up Sep 2010, Patate (Ecuador). **Aims** Encourage recognition and effective implementation of Rights of Nature through the creation of a world network of individuals and organizations that, through active cooperation, collective action and legal tools based on Rights of Nature as an idea whose time has come, can change the direction humanity is taking the planet. **Structure** General Assembly; Executive Committee; Advisory Council. Working Groups. *International Rights of Nature Tribunal* with Steering Committee and Secretariat. **Activities** Founder and Secretariat for *International Rights of Nature Tribunal.*

Members Founding members in 9 countries:

Australia, Bolivia, Canada, Ecuador, India, Peru, South Africa, UK, USA.

Founding and other organizational members include 18 organizations listed in this Yearbook:

African Biodiversity Network (ABN, #00222); African Conservation Foundation (ACF); Biodynamic Agricultural Association of Southern Africa (BDAASA); Earth Law Alliance (ELA); Earth Law Center, Earth Partners Foundation; Food and Trees for Africa (FTFA); Gaia Foundation; Global Exchange (GX); Global Society for Ecology and Sound Economy (ECO2TERRA International); International Funders for Indigenous Peoples (IFIP); International Public Policy Institute (IPPI); Pachamama Alliance; Religious Society of Friends (Quakers,

#18834); Share the World's Resources (STWR); Solidaridad Internacional (SI); Women's Earth and Climate Action Network, International (WECAN); World Conscious Pact (WCP).
NGO Relations Member of: *Yes to Life, No to Mining (YLNM, #21976).* [2017/XM5867/y/**C**]

♦ Global Alliance for the Rights of Older People 10226
Secretariat Coordinator address not obtained. E-mail: info@rightsofolderpeople.org.
Chair address not obtained.
URL: https://rightsofolderpeople.org/
History 2011. **Aims** Support and enhance civil society's engagement at national, regional and international levels on the need for a new international instrument on the rights of older persons. **Structure** Steering Group; Secretariat. **Staff** 1.00 FTE, paid. [2022.06.14/XJ7483/y/**C**]

♦ Global Alliance of Sickle Cell Disease Organizations (GASCDO) 10227
Registered Address 260 Adelaide Street E, Unit 127, Toronto ON M5A 1N1, Canada. E-mail: connect@globalscd.org – gascdochair@gmail.com.
URL: https://www.globalscd.org/
History 21 Oct 2019, Canada. Proposed Mar 2019, London (UK). **Activities** Events/meetings; training/education. **Events** *Global Conference of Sickle Cell Disease Organizations* Accra (Ghana) 2022. **NGO Relations** Member of (1): *Rare Diseases International (RDI, #18621).* [2022/AA2328/**C**]

♦ Global Alliance for Smart Cities in Africa (unconfirmed)

♦ Global Alliance of SMEs (GASME) 10228
US Office 52 Bridge St, Metuchen NJ 08840, USA. T. +19083508296. Fax +19083508261.
Assia Office 800 Dongfang Road, Suite 1801, Pudong, Shanghai, China. T. +862150815730 – +862150815731. E-mail: gasmechina@163.com.
URL: http://www.globalsmes.org/
History Founded 1999. Set up the US-China Exchange Association (USCEA). **Aims** Create a bilateral / multilateral exchange platform for small and medium enterprises worldwide; enable mutually beneficial collaborations among SMEs worldwide; promote healthy and sustainable development of SMEs worldwide. **Structure** Global Leadership Council. Regional offices: New Jersey (USA); Shanghai (China); Paris (France); Tokyo (Japan); Phnom Penh (Cambodia); Nairobi (Kenya); Buenos Aires (Argentina). **Activities** Events/meetings; knowledge management/information dissemination; networking/liaising. **Events** *Seminar* Seoul (Korea Rep) 2016, *Seminar* Seoul (Korea Rep) 2016, *Meeting* Vienna (Austria) 2012. **Consultative Status** Consultative status granted from: *UNIDO (#20336).* [2019/XJ6717/**C**]

♦ Global Alliance of Social Enterprises in Travel & Tourism (unconfirmed)

♦ Global Alliance for Surgical, Obstetric, Trauma and Anaesthesia Care (G4 Alliance) 10229
Main Office 633 North St Clair Street, 20th Floor, Chicago IL 60611, USA. E-mail: contact@theg4alliance.org.
URL: http://www.theg4alliance.org/
History Proposed Oct 2014. Launched May 2015, Geneva (Switzerland), during *WHO (#20950)* World Health Assembly. Registration: USA. **Aims** Work to increase awareness, foster political will, shape policy, and mobilize resources to make access to quality, safe, timely, and affordable emergency and essential surgical, obstetric, trauma and anaesthesia (SOTA) care a global health priority and a reality for all. **Structure** Executive Team; Board of Directors; Permanent Council. **Finance** Sources: members' dues.
Members Federations; colleges/professional societies; academia; NGOs. Membership countries not specified. Included in the above, 10 organizations listed in this Yearbook:
Cure International; EngenderHealth; FIA Foundation (#09742); International Federation of Surgical Colleges (IFSC, #13560); Johns Hopkins Program for International Education in Gynecology and Obstetrics (JHPIEGO); Operation Smile; ReSurge International; Smile Train (#19328); West African College of Surgeons (WACS, #20876); World Federation of Societies of Anaesthesiologists (WFSA, #21482). [2022.06.17/XJ9657/y/**C**]

♦ Global Alliances for Water and Climate (GAfWaC) 10230
Alliances Mondiales pour l'Eau et le Climat (AMEC)
Contact address not obtained.
URL: http://www.water-climate-alliances.org/
History Declaration signed Nov 2016, Marrakech (Morocco), by representatives of *United Nations Economic Commission for Europe (UNECE, #20555), International Network of Basin Organizations (INBO, #14235), CDP (#03621),* SUEZ Eau France, (French) SIAAP, *Local Governments for Sustainability (ICLEI, #16507), Global Clean Water Desalination Alliance* and *International Renewable Energy Agency (IRENA, #14715).* Previously also known under the acronym *GAWC.* **Aims** Mobilize stakeholders to secure a place for water in climate summits, negotiations and financial mechanisms and actions; stimulate exchange of lessons learnt and best practices of efficient existing actions; identify and support new actions. **Structure** Structured around 4 Alliances: *"Paris Act" Alliance on water and climate adaptation in the basins of rivers, lakes and aquifers; Business Alliance for Water and Climate (BAFWAC); Megacities Alliance for Water and Climate (MAWAC, #16697); Global Clean Water Desalination Alliance (GCWDA, #10285).* Secretariat provided by *International Network of Basin Organizations (INBO, #14235).* Also includes: *Global Alliance for Water and Climate's Incubation Platform (GAWCIP).* **Events** *Partners Meeting* Cancún (Mexico) 2017, *International Summit on Water and Climate* Rome (Italy) 2017. **IGO Relations** Partners governments, local authorities and public organizations including: *African Ministers' Council on Water (AMCOW, #00376); Agence française de développement (AFD); Central Asia Regional Economic Cooperation (CAREC, #03684); Economic Community of Central African States (ECCAS, #05311); Economic Community of West African States (ECOWAS, #05312); Euro-Mediterranean Information System on Know-how in the Water Sector (EMWIS, #05722); European Regional Centre for Ecohydrology of the Polish Academy of Sciences, Lodz (ERCE PAS, #08341); International Hydrological Programme (IHP, #13826); OECD (#17693); United Nations Economic Commission for Europe (UNECE, #20555); The World Bank Group (#21218).*
NGO Relations Partners include:
- *Action Against Hunger (#00086);*
- *Alliance for Water Stewardship (AWS, #00727);*
- *Eau vive;*
- *European Federation of National Associations of Water and Waste Water Services (#07170);*
- *European Water Partnership (EWP, #09083);*
- *Green Cross International (GCI, #10715).*
- *Interbalkan Environment Center (i-BEC, #11458);*
- *International Network of Water Training Centres (INWTC, #14341);*
- *International Secretariat for Water (ISW, #14822);*
- *International Union for Conservation of Nature and Natural Resources (IUCN, #15766);*
- *International Water Resources Association (IWRA, #15871);*
- *Local Governments for Sustainability (ICLEI, #16507);*
- *The Mediterranean Wetlands Initiative (MedWet, #16688);*
- *The Nature Conservancy (TNC);*
- *Population Reference Bureau (PRB);*
- *Programme Solidarité eau (pS-Eau, #18529);*
- *Rivers without Boundaries (RwB);*
- *Wetlands International (#20928);*
- *World Business Council for Sustainable Development (WBCSD, #21254);*
- *World Council of Civil Engineers (WCCE, #21321);*
- *World Water Council (WWC, #21908);*
- *World Wide Fund for Nature (WWF, #21922).* [2018/XM5937/**E***]

♦ Global Alliance for Tax Justice (unconfirmed)
♦ Global Alliance for TB Drug Development / see TB Alliance (#20103)

♦ Global Alliance of Technological Universities (GlobalTech Alliance) . 10231
Contact Arcisstr 21, Room 1129, 80333 Munich, Germany. T. +498928922569. E-mail: globaltech@tum.de.
URL: http://globaltechalliance.org/
History Founded 2009. **Aims** Address global societal issues to which science and technology could be their solution. **Structure** Board. **Events** *Robotics Workshop* Sydney, NSW (Australia) 2018.
Members Institutions in 6 countries:
Australia, China, Germany, India, Singapore, UK. [2012/XM8008/**C**]

♦ Global Alliance for Trade Facilitation (the Alliance) 10232
Contact c/o ICC, 33-43 avenue du Président Wilson, 75116 Paris, France.
URL: http://www.tradefacilitation.org/
History Founded as a collaboration of international organizations, governments and businesses. **Aims** Enhance trade facilitation implementation by bringing together the public and private sectors as equal partners to identify and deliver commercially meaningful reforms in developing and least developed countries. **Structure** Led by *Center for International Private Enterprise (CIPE), International Chamber of Commerce (ICC, #12534)* and *World Economic Forum (WEF, #21367),* in cooperation with *Deutsche Gesellschaft für Internationale Zusammenarbeit (GIZ).* Steering Group; Management Team. **Finance** Funded by governments of USA, Canada, UK, Australia, Germany and Denmark. [2019/XM8416/t/**F**]

♦ Global Alliance for Tuberculosis Drug Development / see TB Alliance (#20103)
♦ Global Alliance for Vaccines and Immunization / see Gavi – The Vaccine Alliance (#10077)
♦ Global Alliance for Wild Cats (unconfirmed)
♦ Global Alliance on Women's Brain Health (unconfirmed)

♦ Global Alliance for Women's Health (GAWH) 10233
Alianza Global para la Salud de la Mujer
Contact address not obtained. T. +12122860424. Fax +12122869561. E-mail: wolfson@gawh.org.
URL: http://www.gawh.org/
History 1994, USA, by Dr Elaine Wolfson. **Consultative Status** Consultative status granted from: *ECOSOC (#05331)* (Special). **IGO Relations** Associated with Department of Global Communications of the United Nations. **NGO Relations** Member of: *Alliance for Health Promotion (A4HP, #00687).* [2016/XE2616/**E**]

♦ Global Alliance for Workers and Communities / see Global Alliance

♦ Global Aluminium Foil Roller Initiative (GLAFRI) 10234
Contact Moersenbroicher Weg 200, 40470 Düsseldorf, Germany. T. +4921138732602.
URL: http://www.global-alufoil.org/
History 2015. Founded when supporters of the 'informal' initiative decided to turn the activity into a legal trade association. **Aims** Promote foil innovation and position foil in the sustainability debate based on scientific evaluations as part of the solution to reduce *food waste.* **Structure** General Assembly; Board. **Languages** English. **Staff** 0.20 FTE, paid. **Finance** Sources: members' dues. **Activities** Advocacy/lobbying/activism; awareness raising; events/meetings; knowledge management/information dissemination; research and development. **Events** *Global Aluminium Foil Roller Conference* Istanbul (Türkiye) 2022, *Global Aluminium Foil Roller Conference* Dubai (United Arab Emirates) 2019, *Global Aluminium Foil Roller Conference – GLAFCO* Dubai (United Arab Emirates) 2014. **Members** Companies (63) in 28 countries. Membership countries not specified. **IGO Relations** Member of: Save Food Initiative of FAO/UNEP/Messe Düsseldorf. **NGO Relations** Member of (1): *Aluminium Stewardship Initiative (ASI, #00758).* [2022/XJ9376/**C**]

♦ Global Alzheimer's and Dementia Action Alliance (inactive)
♦ Global Anglican Future Conference / see Fellowship of Confessing Anglicans (#09725)

♦ Global Anti-Aggression Campaign 10235
SG address not obtained.
URL: http://www.qawim.org/
History 28 Apr 2003, Makkah (Saudi Arabia), by signatories to an anti-aggression declaration. **Aims** As a nongovernmental, independent, peaceful, educational campaign of volunteers: call on all peoples, governments, supporters of truth and justice and friends of peace to cooperate in rejecting aggression and spreading values of truth and justice; unite efforts of members of the Ummah in alerting the Muslim community on its right to self-defence; repel aggression by all possible legitimate and effective means; cooperate in righteousness and piety, aid the oppressed and repel aggressors; alert the Ummah on the plans of its enemies, calling on the community to protect its identity; reawaken the Islamic spirit among Muslims to serve their faith and nation and to defend their rights; clarify the true image of Islam, explain the humanitarian and ethical aspects of its laws and expose the falsehood of campaigns of prejudice against it; work for cooperation and coordination among both governmental and nongovernmental organizations in service to Muslim causes throughout the Islamic World; work for active cooperation among peoples, organizations and international bodies opposed to oppression and domination of peoples and their resources. **Members** Participation open to all members of the Ummah. Membership countries not specified. [2010/XF7166/**F**]

♦ Global Anti-Counterfeiting Group (GACG) 10236
Address not obtained.
URL: http://www.gacg.org/
History 1998. Registered in accordance with French law. EU Transparency Register: 60838305695-30. **Aims** Suppress counterfeiting of brand name merchandise, and patent and copyright piracy, through information exchange and legislative action; exchange and share information, participate in appropriate joint activities and cooperate in the resolution of specific IP problems and challenges in their respective national or regional areas. **Structure** Board. **Languages** English. **Activities** Events/meetings. **Events** *Autumn Meeting* Alicante (Spain) 2014, *Annual Meeting* London (UK) 2014, *Spring Meeting* London (UK) 2014, *Annual Meeting* Beijing (China) 2013, *Spring Meeting / Annual Meeting* Beijing (China) 2013.
Members National anti-counterfeiting organisations in 19 countries and territories:
Belgium, Canada, China, Denmark, Finland, France, Germany, Hong Kong, India, Italy, Kenya, Nigeria, Norway, Russia, Spain, Sweden, UK, Ukraine, USA.
International organizations (3):
Coalition for Intellectual Property Rights (CIPR); International Anticounterfeiting Coalition (IACC, #11656); MARQUES (#16588).
Consultative Status Consultative status granted from: *World Intellectual Property Organization (WIPO, #21593)* (Permanent Observer Status). **IGO Relations** *International Criminal Police Organization – INTERPOL (ICPO-INTERPOL, #13110); World Customs Organization (WCO, #21350).* [2017/XF5832/y/**F**]

♦ Global Anti-Incinerator Alliance / see Global Alliance for Incinerator Alternatives (#10203)

♦ Global Apprenticeship Network (GAN) 10237
Exec Dir Avenue Louis-Casaï 71, Cointrin, 1216 Geneva, Switzerland. T. +41229290011. E-mail: info@gan-global.org.
URL: http://www.gan-global.org/
History 2014, Initiated by *International Organisation of Employers (IOE, #14428)* and *Business and Industry Advisory Committee to the OECD (BIAC, #03385),* with the support of *ILO (#11123)* and *OECD (#17693).* Registered in accordance with Swiss Civil Code. **Aims** As a business-driven alliance, encourage and link *business* initiatives on skills and *employment* opportunities for *youth* – notably through apprenticeships and work readiness programmes. **Structure** Management Board. **Languages** English, French. **Staff** 77.00 FTE, paid. **Activities** Projects/programmes; training/education; networking/liaising; events/meetings. **Publications** Annual Report; catalogue of best practices and action; toolkits; flyer.
Members Partner institutions (4):
Business and Industry Advisory Committee to the OECD (BIAC, #03385); ILO (#11123); International Organisation of Employers (IOE, #14428); OECD (#17693).
National Networks in 9 countries:
Argentina, Colombia, France, Indonesia, Malawi, Mexico, Spain, Tanzania UR, Türkiye.
IGO Relations *Group of Twenty (G20, #10793)* – B20; *ILO (#11123); OECD (#17693).* [2017.11.06/XM4705/y/**F**]

♦ Global Aquaculture Alliance (GAA) 10238
Main Office 85 New Hampshire Ave, Ste 200, Portsmouth NH 03801, USA.
URL: http://www.aquaculturealliance.org/
History 1997. **Aims** Further environmentally responsible aquaculture to meet world food needs; work to improve production and marketing efficiencies and promote effective and coordinated regulatory and trade policies; develop certification standards and encourage the use of responsible aquaculture practices. **Structure** Board of Directors of 19 members. Central office. **Languages** English. **Finance** Members' dues. **Activities** Develops Best Aquaculture Practices (BAP) standards for certification of aquaculture facilities.

Organizes: GOAL Conference – Global Outlook for Aquaculture Leadership (annual), taking place on a different continent, reviews the production, demand and issues/solutions of raising seafood for the next 1-3 years; Board of Directors meetings (2 a year) during International Boston Seafood Trade Show (March) and GOAL Conference. **Events** *Conference* Portsmouth, NH (USA) 2020. **Publications** *Global Aquaculture Advocate* (6 a year) – magazine; *GAA Update* – electronic newsletter. **Members** Individual (producers, processors, marketers, retailers); Corporate; Associate; Individual Business. Membership countries not specified. **Consultative Status** Consultative status granted from: *FAO (#09260)* (Liaison Status). **NGO Relations** Participant in: *Global Partnership for Oceans (GPO, #10537).* [2020/XF5868/**F**]

♦ Global Asphalt Pavement Alliance (GAPA) 10239

Chairman Rue du Commerce 77, 1040 Brussels, Belgium. T. +3225025888. Fax +3225022358.
URL: https://globalasphalt.org/

History 2008. Founded by Australian Asphalt Pavement Association, *European Asphalt Pavement Association (EAPA, #05920)*, Japanese Road Contractors Association, National Asphalt Pavement Association and South African Bitumen Association. **Aims** Provide benefits to member organizations. **Activities** Awareness raising; events/meetings; knowledge management/information dissemination; networking/liaising. **Events** *Meeting* South Africa 2019. **Publications** *GAPA Magazine.*
Members Organizations in 6 countries:
Australia, Japan, Mexico, New Zealand, South Africa, USA.
European Asphalt Pavement Association (EAPA, #05920). [2019/AA1293/y/**C**]

♦ Global Assistance Foundation (internationally oriented national body)

♦ Global Assistive Technology Information Network (EASTIN Association) 10240

Pres Via del Piave 5, 32100 Belluno BL, Italy. T. +39043725775. E-mail: eastinassociation@gmail.com.
URL: http://www.eastin.eu/

History 2006. EASTIN information system initially created 2005 with support of *European Union (EU, #08967)*, within the eTEN initiative. EASTIN Association created to maintain and further develop the EASTIN system and the EASTIN network. Former names and other names: *European Assistive Technology Information Network (EASTIN)* – former. Registration: Italy.
Members Founding Partners (4) in 4 countries:
Denmark, Germany, Italy, UK.
Other full partners in 3 countries:
Australia, Belgium, France.
Affiliates in 8 countries and territories:
Cyprus, Israel, Latvia, Lithuania, Netherlands, Slovakia, Taiwan, Thailand.
NGO Relations Member of (1): *Global Alliance of Assistive Technology Organizations (GAATO, #10185).* [2023.02.14/AA2107/**E**]

♦ The Global Association of Art and Design Education and Research (Cumulus Association) 10241

SG Aalto Univ, School of Arts/Design/Architecture, PO Box 31000, FI-00076 Aalto, Finland. E-mail: contact@cumulusassociation.org.
Coordinator address not obtained.
President address not obtained.
URL: http://www.cumulusassociation.org/

History 1990. Statutes approved 22 Mar 2001, Rotterdam (Netherlands), during inaugural meeting. Former names and other names: *European Association of Universities and Colleges of Art, Design and Media (CUMULUS)* – former (1990 to 2006); *International Association of Universities and Colleges of Art, Design and Media (CUMULUS)* – former (2006 to 2021); *Cumulus* – alias. Registration: Finland. **Aims** Be a forum for knowledge exchange and best practices and a committed advocate for the positive role of designers and artists in shaping a better world. **Structure** General Assembly (annual); Executive Board. **Languages** English. **Staff** 2.00 FTE, paid. **Finance** Sources: members' dues. **Activities** Events/meetings; knowledge management/information dissemination; networking/liaising. **Events** *Design for adaptation* Detroit, MI (USA) 2022, *Un/Touchable – New Meanings and Values* Moscow (Russia) / St Petersburg (Russia) 2022, *Design culture(s)* Rome (Italy) 2021, *Design culture(s)* Rome (Italy) 2020, *Conference* St Petersburg (Russia) / Moscow (Russia) 2020. **Publications** *CUMULUS Kit.* Working papers; think tanks; exhibition catalogues; leaflets.
Members Full (340) and associate (10) in 64 countries and territories:
Argentina, Australia, Austria, Belgium, Bosnia-Herzegovina, Brazil, Bulgaria, Canada, Chile, China, Colombia, Cyprus, Czechia, Denmark, Ecuador, Estonia, Finland, France, Germany, Greece, Hungary, Iceland, India, Indonesia, Ireland, Israel, Italy, Japan, Jordan, Korea Rep, Latvia, Lebanon, Lithuania, Malaysia, Mexico, Morocco, Netherlands, New Zealand, Norway, Oman, Pakistan, Peru, Philippines, Poland, Portugal, Qatar, Russia, Singapore, Slovakia, Slovenia, South Africa, Spain, Sri Lanka, Sweden, Switzerland, Taiwan, Thailand, Türkiye, Uganda, UK, Ukraine, United Arab Emirates, Uruguay, USA.
Consultative Status Consultative status granted from: *UNESCO (#20322)* (Consultative Status). **NGO Relations** Member of (1): *Skillman Network (#19306)* (Alliance). Cooperates with (3): *European League of Institutes of the Arts (ELIA, #07670)*; *International Council of Design (ICoD, #13013)*; *UNLEASH.* Also links with national associations. [2023.02.14/XD8427/**D**]

♦ Global Association for Contact Center & Customer Engagement Best Practices (unconfirmed)

♦ Global Association Hubs Partnership (GAHP) 10242

Contact Rue Léon Deladrière 4, 1300 Limal, Belgium. T. +32475644996. E-mail: ms@associationhubs.org.
URL: http://www.associationhubs.org/

History Oct 2015, by 4 organizations from Dubai, Washington DC (USA), Singapore and Brussels (Belgium). **Aims** Assist *international associations* grow and better serve their overseas members by using respective partner *cities* as regional conduits to extend their efforts worldwide. **Structure** Annual Strategic Planning Meetings. **Languages** English. **Staff** 1.00 FTE, paid. **Finance** Members' dues. Annual budget: US$ 100,000. **Activities** Awareness raising; capacity building; events/meetings; guidance/assistance/consulting; knowledge management/information dissemination; networking/liaising; projects/programmes; research/documentation; training/education. **Events** *EAS : European Association Summit* Brussels (Belgium) 2019, *EAS : European Association Summit* Brussels (Belgium) 2018, *Dubai Association Conference* Dubai (United Arab Emirates) 2017. **Publications** *GAHP Newsletter* (4 a year).
Members Full in 4 countries:
Belgium, Singapore, United Arab Emirates, USA.
IGO Relations None. **NGO Relations** *ASAE*; *International Congress and Convention Association (ICCA, #12892)*; *Professional Convention Management Association (PCMA).* [2019/XM4212/**F**]

♦ Global Association for Humanities and Social Science Research (internationally oriented national body)
♦ Global Association of International Sport Federations (inactive)

♦ Global Association of Mixed Martial Arts (GAMMA) 10243

Contact PO Box 7884, 1008 AB Amsterdam, Netherlands. T. +31648455549. E-mail: info@gamma-sport.org.
Contact Laan van Kronenburg 14, 1183 AS Amstelveen, Netherlands.
URL: https://gamma-sport.org/

Aims Advocate martial arts' traditions of excellence, discipline, and respect to all levels of its community while promoting athlete safety, fair play, and acceptance to all who wish to participate. **Structure** Executive; Executive Board; Vice President Board. **NGO Relations** Cooperates with (1): *International Testing Agency (ITA, #15678).* [2022/AA3050/**C**]

♦ Global Association for People and the Environment (internationally oriented national body)

♦ Global Association of Risk Professionals (GARP) 10244

Pres GARP US Office, 111 Town Square Place, Ste 1215 07310, Jersey City NJ 07310, USA. T. +12017197210. Fax +12012225022.
Head of Marketing address not obtained.
UK Office 2nd Fl, Bengal Wing, 9A Devonshire Square, London, EC2M 4YN, UK. T. +442073979630. Fax +442076269300.
URL: http://www.garp.org/

History Founded Jul 1996, New York NY (USA). **Aims** As a global membership association for risk *managers*, help create a culture of risk awareness within organizations, from entry level to board level. **Structure** Board of Trustees; Executive Committee; FRM Committee; Regional Chapters (52). **Languages** English. **Staff** 75.00 FTE, paid. **Activities** Awards/prizes/competitions; certification/accreditation; events/meetings; projects/programmes; training/education. **Events** *Annual Risk Management Convention* New York, NY (USA) 2021, *Annual Risk Management Convention* New York, NY (USA) 2020, *Annual Risk Management Convention* New York, NY (USA) 2019, *Annual Risk Management Convention* New York, NY (USA) 2018, *Global Risk Forum* Tokyo (Japan) 2018. **Members** Financial risk management practitioners and researchers; regional central and global banks; asset management firms; insurance companies; securities regulators and commodities; government bodies; hedge funds; universities; corporations; multinationals. Members (over 150,000) in 195 countries and territories. Membership countries not specified. [2017.10.03/XB0008/tv/**B**]

♦ Global Association of Women in Payments / see Women in Payments (#21011)

♦ Global Asthma Network 10245

Contact Dept of Paediatrics: Child and Youth Health, Fac of Medical and Health Sciences – Univ of Auckland, Private Bag 92019 – Auckland Mail Ctr, Auckland 1142, New Zealand. T. +649373759981933. Fax +6493737602. E-mail: info@globalasthmanetwork.org.
URL: http://www.globalasthmanetwork.org/

History 2012. A collaboration between individuals of International Study of Asthma and Allergies in Childhood (ISAAC) and *International Union Against Tuberculosis and Lung Disease (The Union, #15752).* **Aims** Improve asthma care globally, with a focus on low- and middle-income countries. **Structure** Steering Group. **Activities** Capacity building; healthcare; research/documentation. [2020/AA0590/v/**F**]

♦ Global Atmospheric Research Programme (inactive)
♦ Global Audit Leadership Forum (meeting series)
♦ Global Autism Project (internationally oriented national body)

♦ Globalaw 10246

Secretariat Boulevard du Souverain 280, 1160 Brussels, Belgium. T. +3223202479. E-mail: secretariat@globalaw.net.
URL: http://www.globalaw.net/

History 1994. Previously known in full as *Globalaw – The International Law Group (Globalaw).* **Aims** Provide an effective platform to seamlessly address and meet global client needs. **Structure** Board of Directors; Secretariat. **Activities** Events/meetings; guidance/assistance/consulting. **Events** *European Regional Meeting* Amsterdam (Netherlands) 2016, *Annual Members Meeting* Dubai (United Arab Emirates) 2016, *Americas Regional Meeting* Miami, FL (USA) 2016, *North America Regional Meeting* Montréal, QC (Canada) 2015, *Asia Pacific Regional Meeting* Tokyo (Japan) 2015. **Members** Law firms (over 100). Membership countries not specified. [2020.01.17/XM4476/**F**]

♦ Global Awareness Society International (GASI) 10247

Main Office 804 East Second St, Bloomsburg PA 17815, USA. E-mail: 2030gasi@gmail.com.
URL: http://www.globalawarenesssociety.org/

History 1991. Registration: USA, Pennsylvania. **Aims** Promote awareness of the diversity of cultures within our global community; enhance understanding of the political, economic, social, demographic, technological and environmental issues among members of the global community; increase sensitivity to issues related to rapid globalization. **Structure** Officers: President; Vice-President; Secretary; Executive Director; Treasurer. **Languages** English. **Staff** 5.00 FTE, paid. **Finance** Members' dues. **Events** *Annual Conference* Bloomsburg, PA (USA) 2021, *Annual Conference* Las Vegas, NV (USA) 2020, *Annual Conference* Marrakech (Morocco) 2019, *Annual Conference* Atlanta, GA (USA) 2018, *Annual Conference* Heredia (Costa Rica) 2017. **Publications** *Journal of Global Awareness* (annual); *Global News.* Conference proceedings.
Members Individuals in 29 countries:
Australia, Austria, Bahamas, Barbados, Belgium, Brazil, Canada, China, Cuba, Egypt, France, Germany, Ghana, Hungary, India, Italy, Japan, Korea Rep, Kuwait, Mexico, New Zealand, Philippines, Poland, Saudi Arabia, Singapore, South Africa, Sweden, UK, USA. [2020/XD7189/v/**D**]

♦ Globalaw – The International Law Group / see Globalaw (#10246)
♦ Global AYA Accord (unconfirmed)

♦ Global Banking Alliance for Women (GBA) 10248

CEO 68 3rd St, Brooklyn NY 11231, USA. E-mail: info@gbaforwomen.org.
URL: http://www.gbaforwomen.org/

History 20 Jun 2001. Also referred to as *Global Alliance of Banks.* **Aims** Share best practices in order to accelerate the global growth and development of women's *businesses* and women's wealth creation. **Events** *Global SME Finance Forum* Beijing (China) 2016, *Summit* Singapore (Singapore) 2009, *Summit* London (UK) 2008, *Summit* Kampala (Uganda) 2007, *Summit* Glasgow (UK) 2006.
Members Banks (15) in 11 countries:
Australia, Canada, Egypt, El Salvador, Ireland, Nigeria, South Africa, Tanzania UR, Uganda, UK, USA.
IGO Relations Secretariat hosted by: *International Finance Corporation (IFC, #13597).* **NGO Relations** Member of: *Social Performance Task Force (SPTF, #19343).* Partner of: *SME Finance Forum (#19323).* [2018/XF7156/**F**]

♦ Global Basic Income Foundation (internationally oriented national body)

♦ Global Battery Alliance (GBA) 10249

Dir Route de la Capite 91-93, 1223 Cologny GE, Switzerland. E-mail: globalbatteryalliance@weforum.org.
URL: https://www.weforum.org/global-battery-alliance/home

History 2017. **Aims** Help establish a sustainable battery value chain. **Structure** Supervisory Council; Executive Board; Secretariat. Working Gropus; Partner Group. Secretariat at *World Economic Forum (WEF, #21367).*
Members Members (about 70): Industry; Public and International Organizations; NGOs, Foundations and Associations; Knowledge Partners; Trial Members. Membership countries not specified. Organizations include 21 listed in this Yearbook:
- *African Development Bank (ADB, #00283)*;
- *Alliance for Responsible Mining (ARM, #00717)*;
- *ClimateWorks Foundation (#04024)*;
- *Cobalt Institute (CI, #04076)*;
- *Deutsche Gesellschaft für Internationale Zusammenarbeit (GIZ)*;
- *European Federation for Transport and Environment (T and E, #07230)*;
- *Good Shepherd International Foundation (GSIF, #10680)*;
- *International Energy Agency (IEA, #13270)*;
- *International Institute for Environment and Development (IIED, #13877)*;
- *International Lead Association (ILA, #14009)*;
- *Nickel Institute (#17133)*;
- *OECD (#17693)*;
- *Pact (#18016)*;
- *Pure Earth (#18578)*;
- *RESOLVE*;
- *Responsible Business Alliance (RBA)*;
- *The World Bank Group (#21218)*;
- *UNEP (#20299)*;
- *UNICEF (#20332)*;
- *United Nations Economic Commission for Africa (ECA, #20554)*;
- *World Business Council for Sustainable Development (WBCSD, #21254).* [2021/AA1982/y/**C**]

♦ Global Benefits Group Foundation (internationally oriented national body)

♦ Global Biodiversity Information Facility (GBIF) **10250**
Exec Sec Universitetsparken 15, 2100 Copenhagen, Denmark. T. +4535321470. Fax +4535321480. E-mail: communication@gbif.org – info@gbif.org.
URL: http://www.gbif.org/

History Endorsed by science ministers of *OECD (#17693)*, 1999. Established as an intergovernmental initiative, Mar 2001. **Aims** Provide anyone, anywhere, open access to data about all types of life on Earth. **Structure** Governing Board (meets annually); Secretariat in Copenhagen (Denmark). **Languages** English. **Staff** 28.00 FTE, paid. **Finance** Annual contributions from Voting Participants. Supplementary Fund can accept grants and gifts in support of programme goals. **Activities** Standards/guidelines; knowledge management/ information dissemination; networking/liaising. **Events** *Governing Board Meeting* Brussels (Belgium) 2022, *Governing Board Meeting* Copenhagen (Denmark) 2021, *Governing Board Meeting* Copenhagen (Denmark) 2020, *Governing Board Meeting* Leiden (Netherlands) 2019, *Governing Board Meeting* Kilkenny (Ireland) 2018. **Publications** Technical publications on tools, standards and protocols on biodiversity informatics, IPRs and other related issues.
Members Memorandum of Understanding is open for signature to any country, economy or organization. Country participants in 62 countries and territories:
Andorra, Argentina, Australia, Belgium, Benin, Brazil, Bulgaria, Cameroon, Canada, Central African Rep, Chile, Colombia, Congo DR, Costa Rica, Cuba, Denmark, Ecuador, Estonia, Finland, France, Germany, Ghana, Guinea, Iceland, India, Indonesia, Ireland, Japan, Kenya, Korea Rep, Liberia, Luxembourg, Madagascar, Malawi, Mali, Mauritania, Mexico, Netherlands, New Zealand, Nicaragua, Niger, Nigeria, Norway, Peru, Poland, Portugal, Slovakia, Slovenia, South Africa, South Sudan, Spain, Sweden, Switzerland, Taiwan, Tanzania UR, Togo, Uganda, UK, Uruguay, USA, Vietnam, Zimbabwe.
Associate participants (46 organizations/economies), including the following 32 listed in our Yearbook:
- *Albertine Rift Conservation Society (ARCOS, #00620)*;
- *ASEAN Centre for Biodiversity (ACB, #01149)*;
- *Biodiversity Information Standards (TDWG, #03243)*;
- *BioNET INTERNATIONAL – Global Network for Taxonomy (BI, #03253)*;
- *Bioversity International (#03262)*;
- *Botanic Gardens Conservation International (BGCI, #03306)*;
- *CABI (#03393)* (Bioscience);
- *Consortium for the Barcode of Life (CBOL, #04737)*;
- *Consortium of European Taxonomic Facilities (CETAF, #04744)*;
- *Encyclopedia of Life (EOL, #05453)*;
- *Endangered Wildlife Trust (EWT)*;
- *European Environment Agency (EEA, #06995)*;
- Integrated Taxonomic Information System (ITIS);
- *Inter-American Biodiversity Information Network (IABIN, #11402)*;
- *International Barcode of Life (iBOL, #12323)*;
- *International Centre for Integrated Mountain Development (ICIMOD, #12500)*;
- *International Centre of Insect Physiology and Ecology (ICIPE, #12499)*;
- *International Commission on Zoological Nomenclature (ICZN, #12737)*;
- *International Long-Term Ecological Research Network (ILTER, #14065)*;
- *Local Governments for Sustainability (ICLEI, #16507)*;
- *Natural Science Collections Alliance (NSC Alliance)*;
- *NatureServe*;
- *Nordic Genetic Resource Centre (NordGen, #17303)*;
- *Programa Iberoamericano de Ciencia y Tecnologia para el Desarrollo (CYTED, #18524)*;
- *Scientific Committee on Antarctic Research (SCAR, #19147)*;
- *Society for the Preservation of the Natural History Collections (SPNHC)*;
- *Species 2000 (#19914)*;
- *Species360 (#19915)*;
- *UN Environment Programme World Conservation Monitoring Centre (UNEP-WCMC, #20295)*;
- *Wildscreen*;
- *World Federation for Culture Collections (WFCC, #21424)*.

IGO Relations Accredited by: *UNEP (#20299)*. **NGO Relations** NGOs participate at various levels.
[2022/XF4928/y/**F***]

♦ Global Bioenergy Partnership (GBEP) **10251**
Exec Sec FAO – Climate and Environment Div, Viale delle Terme di Caracalla, 00153 Rome RM, Italy. T. +39657052834. E-mail: gbep-secretariat@fao.org.
URL: http://www.globalbioenergy.org/

History Proposed Jul 2005, Gleneagles (UK), at Summit of *Group of Eight (G-8, #10745)*. Launched 11 May 2006, New York NY (USA), during 14th session of *United Nations Commission on Sustainable Development (CSD, inactive)*, when Terms of Reference were signed. Registered as a CSD Partnership, 18 Jan 2007. New mandates received by subsequent G8 and *Group of Twenty (G20, #10793)*. **Aims** Provide a forum for dialogue on effective policy frameworks, identifying ways to facilitate investment and transfer for technology; enhance collaborative project development and implementation, so as to optimize the contribution of bioenergy to sustainable development, taking account of environmental, social and economic factors; provide a framework for Partners to organize, articulate and implement targeted international research, development, deployment, demonstration and commercial activities, related to production, delivery, conversion, use and trade (local, regional or international), of bioenergy. **Structure** Steering Committee; Technical Working Group; Working Group on Capacity Building for Sustainable Bioenergy; Task Force on Sustainability; Secretariat. **Languages** English. **Staff** 4-5 FTE, paid; occasional voluntary. **Finance** Partners contribute funds at their own discretion. Secretariat mainly supported by Italy; additional support from Brazil Germany, Netherlands, Sweden, UK, USA, *FAO (#09260)*. **Activities** Events/meetings; advocacy/lobbying/activism. **Events** *Bioenergy Week of the Global Bioenergy Partnership* Manila (Philippines) 2019, *Meeting* The Hague (Netherlands) 2010. **Publications** Reports.
Members Governments of 23 countries:
Argentina, Brazil, Canada, China, Colombia, Fiji, France, Germany, Ghana, Italy, Japan, Mauritania, Mexico, Netherlands, Paraguay, Russia, Spain, Sudan, Sweden, Switzerland, Tanzania UR, UK, USA.
Organizations (15):
African Energy Commission (AFREC, #00298); *Economic Community of West African States (ECOWAS, #05312)*; *European Biomass Industry Association (EUBIA, #06339)*; *European Commission (EC, #06633)*; *FAO (#09260)*; *Inter-American Development Bank (IDB, #11427)*; *International Energy Agency (IEA, #13270)*; *International Renewable Energy Agency (IRENA, #14715)*; *UNCTAD (#20285)*; UN/DESA; *UNDP (#20292)*; *UNEP (#20299)*; *UNIDO (#20336)*; *United Nations Foundation (UNF, #20563)*; *World Council for Renewable Energy (WCRE, #21340)*.
Observer governments (29):
Angola, Australia, Austria, Cambodia, Chile, Denmark, Egypt, El Salvador, Ethiopia, Gambia, India, Indonesia, Jamaica, Kenya, Laos, Madagascar, Malaysia, Morocco, Mozambique, Nigeria, Norway, Panama, Peru, Philippines, Rwanda, South Africa, Thailand, Tunisia, Vietnam, Zimbabwe.
Observer organizations (12):
African Development Bank (ADB, #00283); *Asian Development Bank (ADB, #01422)*; *European Environment Agency (EEA, #06995)*; *Global Environment Facility (GEF, #10346)*; *International Bank for Reconstruction and Development (IBRD, #12317)* (World Bank); *International Civil Aviation Organization (ICAO, #12581)*; *International Fund for Agricultural Development (IFAD, #13692)*; *OAS (#17629)*; *Union économique et monétaire Ouest africaine (UEMOA, #20377)*; *United Nations Economic Commission for Latin America and the Caribbean (ECLAC, #20556)*; *World Agroforestry Centre (ICRAF, #21072)*; *World Business Council for Sustainable Development (WBCSD, #21254)*.
IGO Relations Hosted at *FAO (#09260)*. Several IGOs are partners and observers, not specified. **NGO Relations** Contributes to: *Sustainable Energy for All (SEforALL, #20056)*. [2019.12.16/XJ8799/**E***]

♦ Global Bioethics Initiative (internationally oriented national body)

♦ Global Biofoundries Alliance (GBA) **10253**
Chair address not obtained.
URL: https://biofoundries.org/

History 9 May 2019, Kobe (Japan). Proposed June 2018, London (UK). **Aims** Develop, promote, and support non-commercial biofoundries worldwide. **Structure** Steering Committee. Working Groups. **Activities** Advocacy/lobbying/activism; events/meetings; networking/liaising. [2021/AA1674/**C**]

♦ Global Biofoundries Alliance (GBA) **10252**
Chair address not obtained.
URL: https://biofoundries.org/

History 9 May 2019, Kobe (Japan). **Aims** Develop, promote, and support nonc-commercial biofoundries worldwide; intensity collaboration and communicaiton among biofoundries; collectively develop responses to technological, operational, and other types of common challenges; enhance visibility, impact and sustainability of non-commercial biofoundries; explore globally relevant and societally impactful grand challenge collaborative projects. **Structure** Interim Steering Committee. **Events** *Global Biofoundry Meeting* Montréal, QC (Canada) 2020, *Global Biofoundry Meeting* Kobe (Japan) 2019, *Global Biofoundry Meeting* London (UK) 2018. **Members** Publicly funded biofoundries. Membership countries not specified. [2019/AA0156/**C**]

♦ Global Biomass Network Project **10254**
Dir c/o BBI Int'l, 308 2nd Ave North, Ste 304, Grand Forks ND 58203, USA.
URL: http://www.globalbiomassnetwork.com/

Aims Promote *sustainable energy*, resource conservation and biomass utilization worldwide. **Events** *RETECH : international renewable energy technology conference* Las Vegas, NV (USA) 2009. **Information Services** *World Biomass Directory* – online. [2012/XJ0231/**F**]

♦ Global Biosaline Network (internationally oriented national body)
♦ Global Biotechnology Transfer Foundation (unconfirmed)

♦ Global Brigades **10255**
Headquarters 220 2nd Ave S, Seattle WA 98104, USA. T. +12064894789. E-mail: admin@globalbrigades.org.
URL: http://www.globalbrigades.org/

History 2007. Builds on the *Global Medical Relief (GMR)*, which existed 2003-2005. A 501(c)(3) nonprofit organization. **Aims** Empower volunteers and under-resourced communities to resolve global *health* and economic disparities and inspire all involved to collaboratively work towards an equal world. **Finance** Voluntary contributions. **Activities** Projects/programmes; advocacy/lobbying/activism. Active in: Ghana, Honduras, Nicaragua, Panama. [2018.09.05/XM5449/**F**]

♦ Global BrightLight Foundation (internationally oriented national body)

♦ Global Buildings Performance Network (GBPN) **10256**
Exec Dir 51 rue Sainte Anne, 75002 Paris, France. T. +33176218100.
URL: http://www.gbpn.org/

History 2011, by *ClimateWorks Foundation (#04024)*. **Aims** Significantly reduce greenhouse gas emissions associated with building energy use. **Structure** Board of Directors; Executive Committee; Strategic Advisory Group. Offices in: Paris (France); Beijing (China); Delhi (India); Brussels (Belgium); Washington DC (USA). **Activities** Policy Assistance; Research; Financial Expertise; Technical Support; Best Practices. **NGO Relations** *Buildings Performance Institute Europe (BPIE, #03354)*. Partners include: *ClimateWorks Foundation (#04024)*; *European Climate Foundation (ECF, #06574)*. [2015/XJ4600/**F**]

♦ Global Business Coalition (GBC) **10257**
Secretariat 55 avenue Bosquet, 75007 Paris, France. T. +33184176356.
Facebook: https://www.facebook.com/people/Global-Business-Coalition/100076959618812/

History Former names and other names: *B20 Coalition* – former (2012). **Aims** Bring together leading independent *business* associations from G20 economies; advocate on behalf of small, medium and large companies. **Structure** Steering Committee; Executive Committee; Business Leaders Forum; Chair. **Events** *Plenary Meeting* Seoul (Korea Rep) 2020, *Plenary Meeting* Istanbul (Turkey) 2015, *B20 Plenary Conference* Washington, DC (USA) 2015, *Kick-off Meeting* Washington, DC (USA) 2015, *Plenary Meeting* Paris (France) 2014.
Members Organizations in 14 countries:
Argentina, Australia, Brazil, Canada, France, Germany, India, Italy, Korea Rep, South Africa, Spain, Türkiye, UK, USA.
Regional federation:
BUSINESSEUROPE (#03381). [2018/XJ9715/y/**E**]

♦ Global Business Coalition for Education (unconfirmed)
♦ Global Business Council on HIV and AIDS / see GBCHealth
♦ Global Business Council on HIV/AIDS, Tuberculosis and Malaria / see GBCHealth

♦ Global Business Education Network (BUSINET) **10258**
Gen Manager address not obtained. E-mail: businet@gmx.com.
Pres Katholieke Hogeschool, Leuven, Belgium.
URL: http://www.businet.org.uk/

History 1987, as *Network for the Development of European Programmes in Higher Education – Réseau pour le développement de programmes européens en enseignement supérieur – Netwerk voor de Ontwikkeling van Europese Programmas in Hoger Onderwijs*. Subsequently changed title to *Network for the Development of Business Education Programmes*, 2000. Registered in accordance with Belgian law. **Aims** Develop international programmes in Business; promote opportunities for institutes of higher education, their staff and their students. **Structure** General Meeting (annual); Board of Management; Special Interest Groups. **Languages** English. **Staff** Voluntary. **Finance** Members' dues. Other sources: European Union or other government funding for specific projects (occasional). Annual budget: about euro 65,000. **Activities** Networking/liaising; events/meetings. **Events** *Annual Conference and General Assembly* Budapest (Hungary) 2016, *Annual Conference* Malta 2015, *Annual Conference and General Assembly* Valletta (Malta) 2015, *Annual Conference* Zagreb (Croatia) 2014, *Annual Conference* Valletta (Malta) 2013. **Publications** Weekly news update.
Members Institutions (90) in 29 countries:
Austria, Belgium, Bosnia, Croatia, Cyprus, Czechia, Denmark, Finland, France, Germany, Hungary, India, Ireland, Italy, Korea Rep, Latvia, Lithuania, Malta, Mexico, Netherlands, Norway, Poland, Portugal, Slovenia, South Africa, Spain, Switzerland, Türkiye, UK. [2019/XF2478/**F**]

♦ The Global Business Initiative on Human Rights (GBI) **10259**
Dir 19c Commercial Road, Eastbourne, BN21 3XE, UK.
URL: https://gbihr.org/

History Founded 2009, building on *Business Leaders Initiative on Human Rights (BLIHR, inactive)*. Registration: Companies House, No/ID: 06852108, UK. **Aims** Advance corporate respect for human rights through peer learning and disseminating practice-based insights to strengthen business practice. **Structure** CEO; Chair; Team; Steering Group; International Advisors. **Activities** Events/meetings; knowledge management/ information dissemination; monitoring/evaluation; politics/policy/regulatory; projects/programmes; training/ education. **Members** Corporations (22) headquartered and working across Asia, Europe, Latin America, Middle East, North Africa and North America. Membership countries not specified. [2021.08.31/XJ7820/**F**]

♦ Global Business School Network (GBSN) **10260**
CEO 1010 Vermont Ave, NW Ste 201, Washington DC 20005, USA. T. +12026289040.
URL: http://www.gbsn.org/

History 2003. **Aims** Tackle the developing world's severe shortage of management talent by building local management education capacity with programs, networking and events. **Structure** Board of Directors; Advisory Board; Academic Advisory Board. **Staff** 5.00 FTE, paid. **Activities** Networking/liaising; knowledge management/information dissemination; capacity building; advocacy/lobbying/activism. **Events** *Annual Conference* Miami, FL (USA) 2020, *Annual Conference* Lisbon (Portugal) 2019, *Annual Conference* Washington, DC (USA) 2017, *Joint Conference* Accra (Ghana) 2016, *Annual Conference* Manila (Philippines) 2015.
Members Schools (72) in 32 countries:
Australia, Austria, Barbados, Brazil, Canada, Chile, China, Colombia, Denmark, Egypt, France, India, Italy, Kenya, Mexico, Morocco, Netherlands, Nigeria, Pakistan, Philippines, Portugal, Russia, Senegal, Singapore, South Africa, Spain, Sweden, Switzerland, Tunisia, Türkiye, UK, USA.
Included in the above, 1 institute listed in this Yearbook:
INSEAD (#11228).
NGO Relations Member of: *EFMD – The Management Development Network (#05387)*. [2021/XJ9617/**F**]

♦ Global Business and Technology Association (GBATA) 10261

Founder PO Box 20277, Huntington Station, New York NY 11746, USA. T. +16316621336. Fax +16314992974. E-mail: info@gbata.org.
URL: http://gbata.org/

History 1998. **Aims** Promote research pertaining to business and technology issues currently faced in the global marketplace; improve communication and information exchange concerning these issues among interested college and university faculty members; facilitate association of all persons directly or indirectly concerned with these issues. **Structure** Board of Directors of 33. Leadership: President; Vice President; Vice-President-Program; Assistant Vice-President. **Finance** Sources: members' dues; sponsorship. **Events** *Annual Conference* Paris (France) 2019, *Annual Conference* Bangkok (Thailand) 2018, *Annual Conference* Vienna (Austria) 2017, *Annual Conference* Dubai (United Arab Emirates) 2016, *Annual Conference* Lisbon (Portugal) / Peniche (Portugal) 2015. **Publications** *Journal of Global Business and Technology (JGBAT). Conference Readings Book.* **Members** Full (over 2,500) in over 40 countries. Membership countries not specified.

[2019/XJ6739/**B**]

♦ Global Business Travel Association (internationally oriented national body)
♦ Global Business Women's Network / see GlobeWomen

♦ Global Cabin Air Quality Executive (GCAQE) 10262

Co-Chairman First Floor 10 Queen Street Place, London, EC4R 1BE, UK. T. +447968213862. E-mail: gcaqe@gcaqe.org.
URL: http://gcaqe.org/

History Set up 2006. **Aims** Effect the changes in the *aviation* industry necessary to prevent crew members, passengers and ground workers exposed to turbine *emissions* from being exposed to oil and hydraulic fluid in the ventilation air supplied to the cabin and flight deck. **Structure** Executive Board. Working Groups.
Members Full in 17 countries:
Australia, Austria, Belgium, Canada, Denmark, France, Germany, Italy, Luxembourg, Netherlands, Norway, Poland, Spain, Sweden, Switzerland, UK, USA.
NGO Relations Liaison Organization of: *Comité européen de normalisation (CEN, #04162).*

[2021/XM4809/**C**]

♦ Global Call for Action Against Poverty (GCAP) 10263

Action mondiale contre la pauvreté – Llamado Mundial a la Acción Contra la Pobreza

Dir c/o CIVICUS, PO Box 933, Southdale, Johannesburg, 2135, South Africa. T. +27118335959. Fax +27118339779. E-mail: info@gcap.global.
URL: https://gcap.global/

History 27 Jan 2005, Porto Alegre (Brazil), during *World Social Forum (WSF, #21797)*, following discussions, Sep 2003, Maputo (Mozambique), of a group of prominent civil society activists hosted by Graca Machel. GCAP Global Foundation is independent and is registered in accordance with Dutch law. **Aims** Support people in their struggles for justice; bring people and organizations together to challenge the institutions and processes that perpetuate poverty and inequalities across the world, to defend and promote human rights, gender justice, social justice and security needed for the dignity and peace of everyone. **Structure** Global Assembly; Global Council; Global Secretariat; Regional Councils; Global Foundation; *GCAP Global Foundation.* Constituency Groups. **Languages** Arabic, English, French, Portuguese, Spanish. **Staff** 7.00 FTE, paid. **Activities** Advocacy/lobbying/activism. **Events** *Conference on Building a Global Citizens Movement* Johannesburg (South Africa) 2013. **Publications** *GCAP Newsletter.*
Members Trade unions, community groups, faith groups, women and youth organizations, NGOs and other campaigners in over 100 countries (not specified). National coalitions in 110 countries and territories:
National coalitions in 110 countries and territories:
Afghanistan, Albania, Algeria, Angola, Argentina, Armenia, Australia, Austria, Azerbaijan, Bahrain, Bangladesh, Barbados, Belgium, Benin, Bolivia, Bosnia-Herzegovina, Botswana, Brazil, Bulgaria, Burkina Faso, Cameroon, Canada, Chile, China, Colombia, Congo Brazzaville, Congo DR, Costa Rica, Côte d'Ivoire, Czechia, Denmark, Dominican Rep, Ecuador, Egypt, El Salvador, Estonia, Ethiopia, Fiji, Finland, France, Gambia, Georgia, Germany, Ghana, Greece, Honduras, Hungary, Indonesia, Ireland, Italy, Japan, Jordan, Kenya, Korea Rep, Lebanon, Liberia, Luxembourg, Malawi, Mali, Malta, Mauritania, Mexico, Mongolia, Morocco, Mozambique, Namibia, Nepal, Netherlands, New Zealand, Nicaragua, Niger, Nigeria, Northern Ireland, Pakistan, Palestine, Panama, Paraguay, Peru, Philippines, Portugal, Romania, Russia, Rwanda, Scotland, Senegal, Serbia, Seychelles, Sierra Leone, Singapore, Slovakia, Slovenia, Somalia, South Africa, Spain, Sri Lanka, Sudan, Suriname, Switzerland, Tanzania UR, Togo, Tunisia, Uganda, UK, United Arab Emirates, Uruguay, USA, Vietnam, Yemen, Zambia, Zimbabwe.
IGO Relations Supporting organizations include: *Agence française de développement (AFD); UNDP International Policy Centre for Inclusive Growth (IPC-IG, #20289); UNICEF (#20332).*
NGO Relations Hosts: *Action for Sustainable Development (Action4SD).* Member of: *SDG Watch Europe (#19162).* Supporting organizations include:
- *Acción Internacional por la Salud – Latinoamérica and Caribe (AIS-LAC, #00056);*
- *ActionAid (#00087);*
- *ADD International;*
- *Africa Network Campaign on Education for All (ANCEFA, #00302);*
- *African Civil Society Network on Water and Sanitation (ANEW, #00250);*
- *African Dignity Foundation;*
- *African Forum and Network on Debt and Development (AFRODAD, #00321);*
- *African Monitor (AM);*
- *African Women's Development and Communication Network (FEMNET, #00503);*
- *Agency Coordinating Body for Afghan Relief (ACBAR);*
- *ALBOAN;*
- *Alianza Social Continental (ASC, #00635);*
- *All Africa Conference of Churches (AACC, #00640);*
- *Alliance Sud, Swiss Alliance of Development Organisations Swissaid – Catholic Lenten Fund – Bread for All – Helvetas – Caritas – Interchurch Aid;*
- *Alliance2015 (#00650);*
- *American Council for Voluntary International Action (InterAction);*
- *Amnesty International (AI, #00801);*
- *Ananda Marga Universal Relief Team (AMURT, #00811);*
- *Arab NGO Network for Development (ANND, #01016);*
- *Asia Pacific Network on Food Sovereignty (APNFS, #01965);*
- *Asia Pacific Women's Watch (APWW, #02077);*
- *Asian Forum for Human Rights and Development (FORUM-ASIA, #01491);*
- *Asian Forum for Human Rights and Development (FORUM-ASIA, #01491);*
- *Asociación Latinoamericana de Organizaciones de Promoción (ALOP, inactive);*
- *Association for the Taxation of Financial Transactions for the Aid of Citizens (#02947);*
- *Association for Women's Rights in Development (AWID, #02980);*
- *BRAC (#03310);*
- *British Council;*
- *British Overseas NGO's for Development (BOND);*
- *Cooperation Canada;*
- *CARE International (CI, #03429);*
- *Caritas Europa (#03579);*
- *Caritas Internationalis (CI, #03580);*
- *Catholic Agency for Overseas Development (CAFOD);*
- *Comité Catholique contre la Faim et pour le Développement-Terre Solidaire (CCFD-Terre Solidaire);*
- *Catholic Lenten Fund;*
- *Catholic Organization for Relief and Development (Cordaid);*
- *Center for Global Education and Experience (CGEE);*
- *Centre de recherche et d'information pour le développement, Paris (CRID);*
- *Center for Women's Global Leadership (CWGL);*
- *Centre for World Solidarity (CWS);*
- *Centro de Estudios Ecuménicos, México (CEE);*
- *Challenges Worldwide;*
- *ChildFund Alliance (#03868);*
- *Children in Crossfire;*
- *Christian Aid;*
- *CIMADE;*
- *CIVICUS: World Alliance for Citizen Participation (#03962);*
- *Comic Relief;*
- *Comité pour l'annulation de la dette du Tiers-monde (CADTM, #04148);*
- *Comité français pour la solidarité internationale (CFSI);*
- *Conference of Non-Governmental Organizations in Consultative Relationship with the United Nations (CONGO, #04635);*
- *Cooperazione Internazionale (COOPI);*
- *Coordination SUD;*
- *Craftsmen of the World Federation (FAM);*
- *Danish Refugee Council (DRC);*
- *Diakonia;*
- *Eau vive;*
- *Emmaus International (#05445);*
- *Engineers Without Borders International (EWB International, #05481);*
- *Entraide et fraternité;*
- *Europe External Programme with Africa (EEPA, #09155);*
- *European Network on Debt and Development (EURODAD, #07891);*
- *Federazione Organismi Cristiani Servizio Internazionale Volontario (Volontari nel Mondo – FOCSIV);*
- *Focus on the Global South (Focus, #09807);*
- *Freedom from Debt Coalition (FDC);*
- *Freshwater Action Network (FAN, inactive);*
- *Friends of the Earth International (FoEI, #10002);*
- *Global Campaign for Education (GCE, #10264);*
- *Global March Against Child Labour (#10463);*
- *Global Marshall Plan Initiative (#10466);*
- *Global Movement for Children (GMFC, inactive);*
- *Global Youth Action Network (GYAN);*
- *Habitat International Coalition (HIC, #10845);*
- *Human Rights Watch (HRW, #10990);*
- *Humanity and Inclusion (HI, #10975);*
- *ICASO (#11040);*
- *International Association for Democracy in Africa (#11836);*
- *International Co-operative Alliance (ICA, #12944);*
- *International Disability and Development Consortium (IDDC, #13177);*
- *International Falcon Movement – Socialist Educational International (IFM-SEI, #13327);*
- *International Movement ATD Fourth World (#14193);*
- *International Trade Union Confederation (ITUC, #15708);*
- *International Union for Conservation of Nature and Natural Resources (IUCN, #15766);*
- *IPS – Inter Press Service International Association (#16013);*
- *Italian Association Amici di Raoul Follereau (AIFO);*
- *Japan International Volunteer Centre (JVC);*
- *Jubilee Research (#16158);*
- *Jubilee South (#16159);*
- *Latin American and Caribbean Committee for the Defense of Women's Rights (#16268);*
- *MADRE;*
- *Manos Unidas;*
- *Never Again International;*
- *Norwegian Church Aid;*
- *Norwegian People's Aid (NPA);*
- *Oikos – Cooperação e Desenvolvimento (Oikos);*
- *ONE (#17728);*
- *One World Center;*
- *OneWorld Africa (see: #17738);*
- *OneWorld South Asia (OWSA, see: #17738);*
- *Oxfam International (#17922);*
- *Oxfam Novib;*
- *Pax Romana, International Movement of Catholic Students (IMCS, #18268);*
- *People's Health Movement (PHM, #18305);*
- *People's Movement for Human Rights Learning (PDHRE, #18307);*
- *Pesticide Action Network (PAN, #18336);*
- *Plan International (#18386);*
- *Public Services International (PSI, #18572);*
- *Red de Educación Popular entre Mujeres de América Latina y el Caribe (REPEM LAC, #18647);*
- *Religions for Peace (RfP, #18831);*
- *RESULTS;*
- *Save the Children International (#19058);*
- *Secours catholique – Caritas France;*
- *Shack-Slum Dwellers International (SDI, #19255);*
- *Broederlijk Delen;*
- *Social Watch (#19350);*
- *SOLIDAR (#19680);*
- *South Asian Network for Social and Agricultural Development (SANSAD);*
- *Swissaid;*
- *Tax Justice Network (TJN, #20100);*
- *Terre des Hommes International Federation (TDHIF, #20133);*
- *Third World Network (TWN, #20151);*
- *Transparency International (TI, #20223);*
- *Trocaire – Catholic Agency for World Development;*
- *UN Millennium Campaign (#20709);*
- *United Purpose (UP);*
- *Verband Entwicklungspolitik und Humanitäre Hilfe e.V. (VENRO);*
- *Voluntary Service Overseas (VSO);*
- *WIDE+ (#20951);*
- *Women and Law in Southern Africa Research Trust (WLSA, #21006);*
- *Women's Environment and Development Organization (WEDO, #21016);*
- *Women's Global Network for Reproductive Rights (WGNRR, #21019);*
- *Women's International League for Peace and Freedom (WILPF, #21024);*
- *WACI Health;*
- *World Federation of Diaconal Associations and Diaconal Communities (DIAKONIA, #21429);*
- *World Federation of United Nations Associations (WFUNA, #21499);*
- *World Organization of the Scout Movement (WOSM, #21693);*
- *World Vision International (WVI, #21904);*
- *World Wide Fund for Nature (WWF, #21922).*

Cooperates with: *Action Against Hunger (#00086); Global Call for Climate Action (GCCA, inactive).*

[2020/XJ4337/**F**]

♦ Global Campaign for Education (GCE) 10264

Campagne mondiale pour l'éducation (CME) – Campaña Mundial por la Educación

CEO no. 37 Bath Avenue, Rosebank, Johannesburg, 2196, South Africa. T. +27114474111. E-mail: info@campaignforeducation.org.
URL: http://www.campaignforeducation.org/

History 1999. **Aims** Promote education as a basic human right; mobilize public pressure to provide free, compulsory public basic education for all people; in particular for children, women and all disadvantaged, deprived sections of society. **Languages** Arabic, English, French, Portuguese, Spanish. **Staff** 10.00 FTE, paid. **Activities** Events/meetings. **Events** *World Assembly* 2021, *World Assembly* Kathmandu (Nepal) 2018, *World Assembly* Johannesburg (South Africa) 2015, *World Assembly* Paris (France) 2011, *World assembly* Sao Paulo (Brazil) 2008. **Publications** Annual School Report; annual Big Book and Big Film.
Members National organizations (over 120) in 84 countries:
Afghanistan, Albania, Algeria, Angola, Argentina, Armenia, Australia, Bangladesh, Benin, Bolivia, Brazil, Burkina Faso, Burundi, Cambodia, Cameroon, Canada, Chile, Colombia, Congo DR, Costa Rica, Denmark, Ecuador, Egypt, El Salvador, Ethiopia, France, Gabon, Gambia, Germany, Ghana, Guatemala, Guinea-Bissau, Haiti, India, Indonesia, Iraq, Ireland, Israel, Italy, Japan, Jordan, Kenya, Lebanon, Lesotho, Liberia, Malawi, Mali, Mauritius, Mexico, Mongolia, Morocco, Mozambique, Nepal, Netherlands, Nicaragua, Niger, Nigeria, Norway, Pakistan, Palestine, Papua New Guinea, Peru, Philippines, Portugal, Romania, Senegal, Sierra Leone, Solomon Is, Somalia, Spain, Sri Lanka, Sudan, Sweden, Switzerland, Tanzania UR, Timor-Leste, Togo, UK, USA, Vanuatu, Vietnam, Yemen, Zambia, Zimbabwe.
International and regional organizations (30), include the following 26 listed in this Yearbook:
- *ActionAid (#00087);*
- *Africa Network Campaign on Education for All (ANCEFA, #00302);*
- *Arab Network for Civic Education (ANHRE, #01011);*
- *Asia South Pacific Association for Basic and Adult Education (ASPBAE, #02098);*
- *CamFed International;*
- *Campaña Latinoamericana por el Derecho a la Educación (CLADE, #03407);*
- *ChildFund International (#03869);*

- *Comic Relief*;
- *Consejo de Educación de Adultos de América Latina (CEAAL, #04707)*;
- *Education International (EI, #05371)*;
- *Fédération africaine des associations nationales de parents d'élèves et étudiants (FAPE, #09398)*;
- *Inclusion International (#11145)*;
- *International Book Information Service (IBIS)*;
- *International Day of the African Child and Youth (IDAY, #13140)*;
- *International Federation of Fe y Alegria (FIFyA, #13425)*;
- *Light for the World (#16474)*;
- *Oxfam International (#17922)*;
- *PAMOJA Africa Reflect Network (PAMOJA)*;
- *Plan International (#18386)*;
- *Public Services International (PSI, #18572)*;
- *Red de Educación Popular entre Mujeres de América Latina y el Caribe (REPEM LAC, #18647)*;
- *RESULTS* (Educational Fund);
- *Save the Children International (#19058)*;
- *Sightsavers International (#19270)*;
- *Voluntary Service Overseas (VSO)*;
- *World Association of Girl Guides and Girl Scouts (WAGGGS, #21142)*.

Consultative Status Consultative status granted from: *ECOSOC (#05331)* (Special); *UNESCO (#20322)* (Consultative Status). **IGO Relations** Member of (2): *Global Partnership for Education (GPE, #10531)*; *International Task Force on Teachers for Education 2030 (#15657)*. **NGO Relations** Member of (2): *Global Coalition on Women and AIDS (GCWA, #10297)*; *Inter-agency Network for Education in Emergencies (INEE, #11387)*. Partner of (1): *International Day of the African Child and Youth (IDAY, #13140)*. Cooperates with (1): *ALBOAN*. Supports (1): *Global Call for Action Against Poverty (GCAP, #10263)*. [2022.02.18/XF6650/y/**F**]

♦ Global Campaign for Equal Nationality Rights 10265

Manager Women's Refugee Commission, 15 West 37th St, New York NY 10018, USA. T. +12125513115. Fax +12125513180.
URL: http://equalnationalityrights.org/

History Jun 2014. **Aims** Eliminate gender discrimination in nationality laws. **Structure** Steering Committee; coalition of regional, national and international NGOs. **Activities** Advocacy/lobbying/activism.
Members NGOs, academics, civil society partners, UN agencies and government allies in 9 countries:
Bahamas, Bahrain, Canada, Dominican Rep, Lebanon, Madagascar, Malaysia, Nepal, South Africa.
Included in the above, the following 8 organizations listed in this Yearbook:
Center for Justice and International Law (CEJIL, #03647); *Equality Now (#05518)*; *Equal Rights Trust (#05520)*; *Institute on Statelessness and Inclusion (ISI, #11295)*; *International Refugee Rights Initiative (IRRI, #14708)*; *UNHCR (#20327)*; *UN Women (#20724)*; *Women's Refugee Commission (WRC)*.
NGO Relations Member of: *Americas Network on Nationality and Statelessness (Red ANA)*. [2019.12.11/XM4204/y/**F**]

♦ Global Campaign for Good Urban Governance / see World Urban Campaign (#21893)

♦ Global Campaign for Peace Education 10266

Contact address not obtained. T. +12025561075. E-mail: news@peace-ed-campaign.org.
URL: https://www.peace-ed-campaign.org/

History May 1999, The Hague (Netherlands). Launched at conference organized by *Hague Appeal for Peace (HAP, #10848)*. **Aims** Promote peace education among schools, families and communities to transform the culture of violence into a culture of peace. **Structure** Global Advisory Committee; Campaign Coordinator. **Activities** Awareness raising; research and development; training/education. Active in all member countries.
Members Full in 13 countries:
Argentina, Canada, India, Japan, Nepal, Netherlands, Nicaragua, Pakistan, Switzerland, Thailand, Uganda, UK, USA. [2023,02.20/XK1939/**E**]

♦ Global Campaign for Ratification of the Convention on Rights of Migrants / see Global Campaign for Ratification of the Convention on the Rights of Migrant Workers (#10267)

♦ Global Campaign for Ratification of the Convention on the Rights of Migrant Workers 10267

Campagne mondiale en faveur de la ratification de la Convention sur les droits des travailleurs migrants – Campaña mundial por la ratificación de la Convención sobre los derechos de los trabajadores migratorios

Coordinator UN Office of the High Commissioner for Human Rights, Palais Wilson, 1211 Geneva 10, Switzerland. T. +41229179301. Fax +41229179008. E-mail: cmw@ohchr.org.

History Set up as a platform of international and non-governmental organizations. Former names and other names: *Global Campaign for Ratification of the Convention on Rights of Migrants* – former; *Campagne mondiale en faveur de la ratification de la Convention sur les droits des migrants* – former. **Aims** Promote ratification by national governments of the International Convention on the Protection of the Rights of All Migrant Workers and Members of their Families, adopted 18 Dec 1990 and entered into force 1 Jul 2003. **Structure** Steering Committee with representatives of NGOs and IGOs. **Languages** English, French. **Activities** Events/meetings. **Publications** Guides.
Members Steering Committee representatives:
Amnesty International (AI, #00801); *Global Migration Policy Associates (GMPA, #10473)*; *Human Rights Watch (HRW, #10990)*; *ILO (#11123)*; *International Advocacy and Resource Centre on the Human Rights of Migrant Workers (December 18)*; *International Catholic Migration Commission (ICMC, #12459)*; *International Federation for Human Rights (#13452)*; *International Organization for Migration (IOM, #14454)*; *International Trade Union Confederation (ITUC, #15708)*; *Migrant Forum in Asia (MFA, #16798)*; *Migrants Rights International (MRI, #16799)*; *Office of the United Nations High Commissioner for Human Rights (OHCHR, #17697)*; *Public Services International (PSI, #18572)*; *UNESCO (#20322)*; *World Council of Churches (WCC, #21320)*. [2022/XE3845/y/**E**]

♦ Global Camp Coordination and Camp Management Cluster (CCCM Cluster) 10268

Coordinator address not obtained. E-mail: globalsupport@cccmcluster.org.
URL: http://www.globalcccmcluster.org/

History Set up as a cluster within *Inter-Agency Standing Committee (IASC, #11393)*. **Aims** Coordinate humanitarian actors with regards to all services provided to displaced populations within any communal settings; work with the affected population to ensure representation, on-site governance and access to information about services provided. **Structure** Co-led by *International Organization for Migration (IOM, #14454)* and *UNHCR (#20327)*. Team; Global Strategic Advisory Group. **Activities** Capacity building; training/education; guidance/assistance/consulting. **IGO Relations** Partners: *International Organization for Migration (IOM, #14454)*; *UNHCR (#20327)*. **NGO Relations** Partners: *Agency for Technical Cooperation and Development (ACTED)*; *Danish Refugee Council (DRC)*; *The Lutheran World Federation (LWF, #16532)*; *Norwegian Refugee Council (NRC)*; *Shelter Centre*. Cooperates with: *IMPACT Initiatives*. [2018/XM7207/**E**]

♦ Global Campus of Human Rights 10269

SG Monastery of San Nicolò, Riviera San Nicolò 26, Lido, 30126 Venice VE, Italy. T. +39412720911. Fax +39412720914. E-mail: ema.secretariat@gchumanrights.org.
URL: https://gchumanrights.org/

History 15 Sep 2002, Venice (Italy). Registered in accordance with Italian law. Former names and other names: *Centre interuniversitaire européen pour les droits de l'homme et la démocratisation* – former; *European Inter-University Centre for Human Rights and Democratisation (EIUC)* – former. Registration: Italy. **Aims** Develop innovative master programmes, research activities and training seminars for all those working in the field of human rights; manage the Global Campus of Master's Programmes and Diplomas in Human Rights and Democratisation fostering communication and cooperation with its regional programmes supported by the European Union; develop the Human Rights Village together with the City of Venice. **Structure** General Assembly (annual); Board of Administrators; Advisory Board. **Languages** English, French, Italian. **Staff** 166.00 FTE, paid. **Finance** Supported by: *European Commission (EC, #06633)*; Region of Veneto; Municipality of Venice. Income from activities and contributions. **Activities** Training/education – including *Global Campus of Regional Masters*; events/meetings; research/documentation; advocacy/lobbying/activism. **Publications** *European Yearbook on Human Rights. Cambridge EIUC Series. EIUC Studies for the European Parliament.* Theses.
Members Participating universities (41) in 27 EU member states:
Austria, Belgium, Bulgaria, Cyprus, Czechia, Denmark, Estonia, Finland, France, Germany, Greece, Hungary, Ireland, Italy, Latvia, Lithuania, Luxembourg, Malta, Netherlands, Poland, Portugal, Romania, Slovakia, Slovenia, Spain, Sweden, UK.
IGO Relations Memorandum of Cooperation with: *UNESCO (#20322)*. Memorandum of Understanding with: *UNHCR (#20327)*. Participant in Fundamental Rights Platform of: *European Union Agency for Fundamental Rights (FRA, #08969)*. Agreement with: *Council of Europe (CE, #04881)*. **NGO Relations** Member of: *DataCite (#05011)*. Organizations member of Advisory Board: *Human Rights Watch (HRW, #10990)*; *International Commission of Jurists (ICJ, #12695)*; *International Committee of the Red Cross (ICRC, #12799)*; *International Rehabilitation Council for Torture Victims (IRCT, #14712)*; *No Peace Without Justice (NPWJ, #17155)*; *Terre des hommes Foundation (Tdh Foundation, #20132)*. [2018/XM0702/**E**]

♦ Global Cancer Care (internationally oriented national body)

♦ Global Cancer Coalitions Network (GCCN) 10270

Contact address not obtained. E-mail: info@globalccn.org.
URL: https://www.globalccn.org/

History May 2020. Created in response to concerns about the impact of COVID-19 on organizations. An informal, non-legal entity. **Aims** Share experiences and best practice.
Members Organizations (9):
ABC Global Alliance (#00004); *Global Colon Cancer Association (GCCA, #10300)*; *Global Lung Cancer Coalition (GLCC)*; *International Brain Tumour Alliance (IBTA, #12393)*; *International Kidney Cancer Coalition (IKCC, #13983)*; *Lymphoma Coalition (LC, #16535)*; *World Bladder Cancer Patient Coalition (WBCPC, #21233)*; *World Ovarian Cancer Coalition (#21703)*; *World Pancreatic Cancer Coalition (WPCC, #21708)*. [2020/AA2295/y/**F**]

♦ Global Cancer Initiative (internationally oriented national body)

♦ Global Canopy 10271

Head Office The Forest Hub, 3 Frewin Chambers, Frewin Court, Oxford, OX1 3HZ, UK. T. +441865724333. E-mail: info@globalcanopy.org – press@globalcanopy.org.
Main Website: http://www.globalcanopy.org/

History 2001. Former names and other names: *Global Canopy Programme (GPC)* – former. Registration: Charity Commission, No/ID: 1089110, England and Wales. **Aims** Target the market forces destroying nature; look at the production, trade and financing of key commodities responsible for agricultural expansion into tropical forests; work with companies, investors and governments to drive better decisions for nature, forests and people. **Structure** Board of Trustees. **Languages** English, Indonesian, Portuguese, Spanish. **Staff** 50.00 FTE, paid. **Finance** Sources: governmental and inter-governmental trusts; foundations; private individuals. **Activities** Advocacy/lobbying/activism; awareness raising; events/meetings; guidance/assistance/consulting; monitoring/evaluation; projects/programmes; research/documentation; training/education. Active in countries with large surviving tropical forests, particularly Latin America, Indonesia and parts of Africa. **Events** *Forest 500 Report Launch Seminar* Oxford (UK) 2023, *UNDP Nature for Life Hub* 2022, *CBD COP15: Using ENCORE to Assess Nature Exposure – a Deep-Dive Use Case* Montréal, QC (Canada) 2022, *COP27 – Amazon on the Verge of a New Future* Sharm el Sheikh (Egypt) 2022. **Publications** *Global Canopy newsletter. Forest 500 report* (2023) in English; *Little Book Series* in Bati (Indonesia), English, French, Mandarin Chinese, Spanish – The Little Book of Investing in Nature. Annual Report; insights; news releases. **IGO Relations** Accredited by (1): *Green Climate Fund (GCF, #10714)*. **NGO Relations** Member of (2): *Climate Knowledge Brokers (CKB, #04016)*; *Natural Capital Coalition (NCC, #16952)*. Partner of (2): *Global Call for Climate Action (GCCA, inactive)*; *Tropical Forest Alliance (TFA, #20249)*. [2023.02.21/XJ8899/**F**]

♦ Global Canopy Programme / see Global Canopy (#10271)
♦ Global Carbon Capture and Storage Institute / see Global CCS Institute (#10274)

♦ Global Carbon Project (GCP) 10272

Contact Center for Global Environmental Research, National Inst for Environmental Studies, Onogawa 16-2, Tsukuba IBARAKI, 305-8506 Japan. T. +81298502672. Fax +81298502960.
URL: http://www.globalcarbonproject.org/

History 2001 within *Earth System Science Partnership (ESSP, inactive)*. Jointly sponsored by *DIVERSITAS – International Programme of Biodiversity Science (inactive)*; *International Geosphere-Biosphere Programme (IGBP, inactive)*, *International Human Dimensions Programme on Global Environmental Change (IHDP, inactive)* and *World Climate Research Programme (WCRP, #21279)*. **Aims** Develop a complete picture of the global carbon cycle, including both its biophysical and human dimensions together with the interactions and feedbacks between them. **Languages** English. **Staff** 9.50 FTE, paid. **Events** *International symposium on realizing low carbon cities* Nagoya (Japan) 2009, *Towards low carbon cities international workshop* Nagoya (Japan) 2009, *Meeting* Banff, AB (Canada) 2003, *International ocean carbon coordination workshop* Paris (France) 2003. **IGO Relations** *Intergovernmental Panel on Climate Change (IPCC, #11499)*; *UNESCO (#20322)*. **NGO Relations** *International Council for Science (ICSU, inactive)*; *International Centre for Earth Simulation (ICES Foundation)*. [2019.10.31/XK2283/**E**]

♦ Global Career Services Summit (meeting series)

♦ Global Cashew Council 10273

Contact Carrer de la Fruita Seca, 4 Polígon Tecnoparc, 43204 Reus, Tarragona, Spain. T. +34977331416. E-mail: info@cashews.org.
URL: https://www.cashews.org/

History 21 May 2011, Budapest (Hungary). Agreement signed by main cashew producers, industry, *FAO (#09260)*, *United Nations Economic Commission for Europe (UNECE, #20555)* and *International Nut and Dried Fruit Council Foundation (INC, #14387)*. **Aims** Promote usage and consumption of cashews; initiate nutritional and health studies; promote food safety; develop quality standards; increase awareness of the health and nutritional benefits of cashews.
Members Signatories in 7 countries, and include 4 organizations:
Australia, Brazil, India, Netherlands, Singapore, USA, Vietnam.
African Cashew Alliance (ACA, #00234); *FAO (#09260)*; *International Nut and Dried Fruit Council Foundation (INC, #14387)*; *United Nations Economic Commission for Europe (UNECE, #20555)*. [2022/AA2746/y/**C**]

♦ Global Cassava Partnership for the 21st Century (unconfirmed)
♦ Global Catholic Climate Movement / see Laudato Si' Movement (#16403)
♦ Global Caucus on Community-Based Forest Management (unconfirmed)

♦ Global CCS Institute 10274

Contact PO Box 23335, Docklands, Melbourne VIC 8012, Australia. T. +61382607300. E-mail: info@globalccsinstitute.com.
Street address Level 16, 360 Elizabeth Street, Melbourne VIC 3000, Australia.
URL: http://www.globalccsinstitute.com/

History Founded Apr 2009, Canberra (Australia). Officially founded, 1 Jul 2009. Also referred to as *Global Carbon Capture and Storage Institute (GCCSI)* of *The Institute*. **Aims** Accelerate deployment of *carbon* capture and storage (CCS) as an imperative technology in tackling *climate change* and providing *energy* security. **Structure** Board of Directors. Offices: Melbourne VIC (Australia); Tokyo (Japan); Beijing (China); Brussels (Belgium); London (UK); Washington DC (USA). **Finance** Member funded. **Activities** Advocacy/lobbying/activism; capacity building; knowledge management/information dissemination; research and development. **Events** *CCS Symposium* Seoul (Korea Rep) 2013, *CCS symposium* Algiers (Algeria) 2010, *Asia Pacific clean coal forum* Tianjin (China) 2010, *CCS symposium* Beijing (China) 2009. **Publications** *Global Status of CSS* (annual) – report. Other reports; thought-leadership publications. **Members** Governments and governmental authorities of several countries and territories. Membership countries not specified. **IGO Relations** Cooperates with several international bodies. Accredited organization of: *Green Climate Fund (GCF, #10714)*. **NGO Relations** Member of: *Climate Technology Centre and Network (CTCN, #04023)*. Participant of: *United Nations Global Compact (#20567)*. [2020/XJ0111/j/**C**]

♦ Global Cement and Concrete Association (GCCA) 10275

Chief Exec Paddington Central, 6th Floor, 2 Kingdom Street, London, W2 6JP, UK. T. +442035804268. E-mail: info@gccassociation.org.
URL: https://gccassociation.org/

History Jan 2018. **Aims** Drive responsible industry leadership in the manufacture and use of cement and concrete; improve the global social and environmental impact of the sector's activities and products; foster innovation and collaboration with industry associations and inspiring architects, engineers and innovators across the globe and along the length of the built-environment value chain. **Structure** Board of Directors; Executive Team. **Activities** Events/meetings; research and development. **Events** *Annual Conference* Singapore (Singapore) 2019.
Members Full; Affiliate. Full – Membership countries not specified. Affiliate in 12 countries:
Affiliate in 12 countries:
Australia, Brazil, Canada, Germany, India, Ireland, Japan, Mexico, Russia, Spain, UK, USA.
Included in the above, 4 organizations listed in this Yearbook:
CEMBUREAU – The European Cement Association (CEMBUREAU, #03634); *Concrete Europe (#04433)*; *Federación Iberoamericana del Hormigón Premezclado (FIHP, #09312)*; *Federación Interamericana del Cemento (FICEM, #09330).*
NGO Relations *Arab Union for Cement and Building Materials (AUCBM, #01065).* [2020/XM8767/y/**C**]

- ♦ Global Center / see Center for Women's Global Leadership
- ♦ Global Center on Adaptation (unconfirmed)
- ♦ Global Center on Cooperative Security (internationally oriented national body)
- ♦ Global Center for Indigenous Leadership and Lifeways (internationally oriented national body)
- ♦ Global Centre for ICT in Parliament / see Global Centre for Information and Communication Technologies in Parliament (#10276)

♦ Global Centre for Information and Communication Technologies in Parliament 10276

Contact c/o IPU, 5 chemin du Pommier, CP 330, 1218 Le Grand-Saconnex GE, Switzerland.
Facebook: https://www.facebook.com/ictparliament/

History Nov 2005, Tunis (Tunisia), on the initiative of the Department of Economic and Social Affairs (UNDESA) of *United Nations (UN, #20515)* and *Inter-Parliamentary Union (IPU, #15961)*, during the World Summit on the Information Society (WSIS). Also referred to as *Global Centre for ICT in Parliament.* **Aims** Strengthen the role of parliaments in the promotion of the Information Society, through fostering ICT-related legislation; promote the use of ICT as a means to modernize parliamentary processes, increase transparency, accountability and participation, and improve inter-parliamentary cooperation. **Structure** Board, consisting of Speakers/ Presidents of Parliaments, and including 2 Co-Chairs, with IPU President and Under-Secretary-General for Economic and Social Affairs of the United Nations as ex officio members. Advisory Committee. **Events** *World e-parliament conference* Midrand (South Africa) 2010, *Annual meeting* Budapest (Hungary) 2009, *World e-parliament conference* Washington, DC (USA) 2009, *World e-parliament conference* Brussels (Belgium) 2008, *Parliamentary forum on shaping the information society* Hyderabad (India) 2008. [2014/XM8154/**E**]

♦ Global Centre for the Responsibility to Protect (GCR2P) 10277

Exec Dir Bunche Inst CUNY, 365 Fifth Ave, Ste 5203, New York NY 10016-4309, USA. T. +12128171989. E-mail: info@globalr2p.org.
URL: http://globalr2p.org/

History Feb 2008. Founded by supportive governments, leading figures from the human rights community, as well as by *International Crisis Group (Crisis Group, #13111)*, *Human Rights Watch (HRW, #10990)*, *Oxfam International (#17922)*, *Refugees International (RI)* and *World Federalist Movement – Movement for a Just World Order through a Strengthened United Nations (WFM, #21404) – Institute of Global Policy.* **Aims** Transform the principle of the Responsibility to Protect into a practical guide for action in the face of mass atrocities. **Structure** International Advisory Board; Patrons; Offices in New York NY (USA) and Geneva (Switzerland). Hosts *International Coalition for the Responsibility to Protect (ICRtoP, #12620).* **Languages** English, French. **Staff** 10.00 FTE, paid. **Finance** Sources: government support; private foundations. **Activities** Advocacy/lobbying/ activism; capacity building; events/meetings; guidance/assistance/consulting; networking/liaising; research/ documentation. **Events** *Meeting of the Global Network of R2P Focal Points* Brussels (Belgium) 2019, *Meeting of the Global Network of R2P Focal Points* Helsinki (Finland) 2018, *Meeting of the Global Network of R2P Focal Points* Doha (Qatar) 2017, *Meeting of the Global Network of R2P Focal Points* Seoul (Korea Rep) 2016, *Meeting of the Global Network of R2P Focal Points* Madrid (Spain) 2015. **Publications** *Atrocity Alert* (irregular); *R2P Monitor* (irregular). Commentary; media releases; occasional papers; open letters; policy briefs; statements; video. **NGO Relations** Member of (3): *Global Action Against Mass Atrocity Crimes (GAAMAC, #10164)*; *International Coalition for the Responsibility to Protect (ICRtoP, #12620)*; *NGO Working Group on the Security Council (#17128).* Also member of various other coalitions. [2020.05.06/XJ0898/**E**]

- ♦ Global Challenges Foundation (internationally oriented national body)
- ♦ Global Challenges Network (internationally oriented national body)
- ♦ Global Change Impact Studies Centre (internationally oriented national body)
- ♦ Global Change Institute (internationally oriented national body)
- ♦ Global Change System for Analysis, Research and Training / see Global Change System for Analysis, Research and Training (#10278)

♦ Global Change System for Analysis, Research and Training (START) 10278

Exec Dir 1440 G ST NW, Washington DC 20005, USA. T. +12024622213. E-mail: start@start.org.
URL: http://www.start.org/

History Proposed 1990 by *International Geosphere-Biosphere Programme (IGBP, inactive).* Launched 1992, under the aegis of *International Council for Science (ICSU, inactive)* and its 4 global change science programmes, as the capacity building arm of the global change programme work in Africa and Asia-Pacific. Previously known as *Global Change System for Analysis, Research and Training (START).* Now known only under acronym. Registered in accordance with USA law. **Aims** Increase opportunities for research, education and training that strengthen scientific capacities in developing countries to understand, communicate and motivate action on critical global *environmental* change challenges. **Structure** Board of Directors; International Secretariat. **Staff** 9.00 FTE, paid. **Activities** Capacity building; research and development; training/education. **Events** *International young scientists conference* Beijing (China) 2006, *South Asia regional conference on transitions towards sustainable development* Delhi (India) 2003, *International young scientists conference on global change* Trieste (Italy) 2003, *Meeting* Trieste (Italy) 2003, *Meeting* Hanoi (Vietnam) 2002. **Consultative Status** Consultative status granted from: *UNEP (#20299).* [2018.09.19/XK1089/**E**]

♦ Global Child Dental Fund (GCDFund) 10279

Chairman 26-29 Drury Lane, London, WC2B 5RL, UK. E-mail: info@gcdfund.org.
URL: http://www.gcdfund.org/

History 2008, building on achievements of *Global Child Dental Health Taskforce (GCDHT).* Registered Charity in England and Wales: 1125850. **Aims** Ensure that the most *disadvantaged* children, from the most deprived communities around the world, have access to dental care and do not suffer from obvious dental decay in their lifetime. **Structure** Trustees. **Activities** Healthcare; training/education; networking/liaising. **Publications** *GCDFund E-newsletter.* **NGO Relations** *Alliance for a Cavity-Free Future (ACFF, #00661).* [2018.10.05/XM6467/f/**F**]

♦ Global Child Nutrition Foundation (GCNF) 10280

Mailing Address P.O. Box 99435, Seattle WA 98139-0435, USA. T. +12064850405. E-mail: info@gcnf.org.
URL: http://www.gcnf.org/

History 2006, USA. Founded as the international arm of the US School Nutrition Association (SNA). Became wholly independent in 2013. Registration: 501(c)(3) organization, No/ID: EIN: 20-5094658, Start date: 2007, USA. **Aims** Expand opportunities for the world's children to receive adequate nutrition for learning and achieving their potential. **Structure** Board of Directors. **Languages** Arabic, English, French, Mandarin Chinese, Portuguese, Russian, Spanish. **Staff** 4.00 FTE, paid; 3.00 FTE, voluntary. A global team of 5 FTE consultants is also employed. **Finance** Sources: contributions; contributions of member/participating states; donations; fees for services; fundraising; gifts, legacies; grants; in-kind support; international organizations; members' dues; private foundations; revenue from activities/projects; sponsorship. Sources vary from year to year. Supported by: *Bill and Melinda Gates Foundation (BMGF)*; General Mills Foundation; US Department of Agriculture's Foreign Agricultural Service's McGovern-Dole Food for Education and Child Nutrition Program; West Star. Annual budget: 550,000 USD (2021). **Activities** Events/meetings; training/education. **Events** *Annual Forum* Montréal, QC (Canada) 2017. **Publications** *School Meal Programs Around the World* (2021). Global Survey Report. **IGO Relations** Member of (1): *School Meals Coalition.* Cooperates with (6): *Bioversity International (#03262)*; *Economic Community of West African States (ECOWAS, #05312)*; *FAO (#09260)*; *International Bank for Reconstruction and Development (IBRD, #12317)* (World Bank); *UNESCO (#20322)*; *World Food Programme (WFP, #21510).* Cooperates and/or partners with a wide variety of organizations globally. **NGO Relations** Member of (1): *Alliance to End Hunger.* Cooperates with (8): *Catholic Relief Services (CRS, #03608)*; *International Dairy Federation (IDF, #13128)*; *International Food Policy Research Institute (IFPRI, #13622)*; *JAM International (Joint Aid Management)*; *Nascent Solutions*; *Partnership for Child Development (PCD)*; *Save the Children International (#19058)*; *UN Nutrition (#20710).* Collaborates with a wide variety of organizations. [2022.04.21/XJ2837/f/**F**]

- ♦ Global Chinese Breast Cancer Organizations Alliance (internationally oriented national body)
- ♦ Global Choices (unconfirmed)

♦ Global Citizen 10281

CEO Ste 207, 594 Broadway, New York NY 10012, USA. E-mail: contact@globalcitizen.org – media@globalcitizen.org.
URL: http://www.globalcitizen.org/

History 2008. Platform founded 2012. **Aims** Act as a social platform for a global generation eager to solve the world's biggest challenges. **Structure** Board of Directors. **NGO Relations** *1,000 Days*; *Toilet Board Coalition (TBC, #20171).* [2017/XM5389/**F**]

- ♦ Global Citizen Forum (unconfirmed)
- ♦ Global Citizen Forum (unconfirmed)

♦ Global Citizenship Alliance (GCA) 10282

Pres/CEO Valkenauerstr 22, 5026 Salzburg, Austria. E-mail: info@globalcitizenshipalliance.org.
Contact Alice Seeger, PO Box 573, West Linn OR 97068, USA.
URL: http://globalcitizenshipalliance.org/

History 2015. **Aims** Promote education for engaged knowledge and responsible action in an interdependent world. **Structure** Board of Directors. **Activities** Events/meetings. **Events** *Seminar* Salzburg (Austria) 2018. [2022.02.02/XM7895/**C**]

♦ Global Citizenship Education Fund 10283

Spain Plaça Comercial 2, Entresuele 2a, 08003 Barcelona, Spain. T. +34931256980. E-mail: secretariat@globalcitizenshipeducation.fund.
Bogota Carrera 13 A no 87-11, Cundinamarca, Bogota, Bogota DC, Colombia. T. +5719161581.
URL: https://globalcitizenshipeducation.fund/

Aims Conceive, promote and monitor a sustainable programme of practice-oriented human rights education. **Structure** Board of Trustees; Executive President; Working Groups. **Activities** Advocacy/lobbying/activism. **IGO Relations** *Union for the Mediterranean (UfM, #20457).* **NGO Relations** Memorandum of Understanding with: *Asociación de las Camaras de Comercio e Industria del Mediterraneo (ASCAME, #02112).* [2021/XM8731/f/**F**]

- ♦ Global Citizen's Rights (unconfirmed)
- ♦ Global Citizens for Sustainable Development (internationally oriented national body)
- ♦ Global Civic Sharing (internationally oriented national body)
- ♦ Global Civil Initiatives (internationally oriented national body)
- ♦ Global Civil Society Forum (unconfirmed)

♦ Global Cleantech Cluster Association (GCCA) 10284

Chair Kirchgasse 42, 8001 Zurich ZH, Switzerland.
URL: http://www.globalcleantech.org/

History Launched 15 Nov 2010, Lahti (Finland). North American headquarters launched 30 Nov 2010, San Diego CA (USA). Registered in accordance with Swiss Civil Code. **Aims** Drive *sustainable* regional *economic* development, on a global scale. **Structure** Board. **Activities** Awards/prizes/competitions. **Events** *Asia-Pacific Cleantech Cluster Gateway Meeting* Singapore (Singapore) 2013.
Members Global Clusters (over 50) in 25 countries and territories:
Australia, Austria, Belgium, Bulgaria, Canada, China, Denmark, Finland, France, Germany, India, Ireland, Israel, Italy, Korea Rep, Mexico, Netherlands, New Zealand, Singapore, Sweden, Switzerland, Taiwan, UK, United Arab Emirates, USA. [2020/XJ9608/**C**]

♦ Global Clean Water Desalination Alliance (GCWDA) 10285

Chair address not obtained.

History 5 Dec 2015, Paris (France). Launched at 21st Conference of the Parties (COP21) of the United Nations Climate Change Conference. Registration: Swiss Civil Code, Start date: Feb 2018, Switzerland. **Aims** Take actions and promote dialogue on clean desalination and significantly reduce CO2 emissions in the desalination industry today and in the future. **Structure** Board; Executive Secretariat. Part of *Global Alliances for Water and Climate (GAfWaC, #10230).* **Finance** Sources: donations; members' dues. **Publications** *GCWDA Newsletter.*
Members Organizations in and governmental departments of 38 countries:
Australia, Belgium, Chile, China, Comoros, Côte d'Ivoire, Cyprus, Fiji, France, Germany, Greece, India, Indonesia, Israel, Italy, Japan, Jordan, Kenya, Korea Rep, Maldives, Morocco, Netherlands, Pakistan, Palau, Qatar, Saudi Arabia, Singapore, South Africa, Spain, St Kitts-Nevis, Sweden, Switzerland, Togo, Uganda, UK, United Arab Emirates, USA, Vietnam.
Included in the above, 7 organizations listed in this Yearbook:
African Development Bank (ADB, #00283); *IHE Delft Institute for Water Education (#11110)*; *International Desalination Association (IDA, #13152)*; *International Renewable Energy Agency (IRENA, #14715)*; *Middle East Solar Industry Association (MESIA)*; *TerraWatt Initiative (TWI)*; *UNEP (#20299).*
IGO Relations Partner of (2): *OECD (#17693)*; *UNESCO (#20322).* **NGO Relations** Partner of (1): *International Office for Water (IOW, #14399).* [2020.02.24/XM8608/**C**]

♦ Global Clearinghouse for Development Finance 10286

Exec Dir – Founder 182 Stissing Rd, Stanfordville NY 12581, USA. E-mail: barbara@globaldf.org.
URL: http://www.globalclearinghouse.org/

History 2002, Monterrey (Mexico), at United Nations Conference on Financing for Development. **Aims** Implement the Monterrey Consensus objective of mobilizing the private sector for development; advance the capacity of developing country governments and aid effectiveness of development agencies. **Finance** Supported by: *Ford Foundation (#09858)*; Governments of Norway and Switzerland; Samuels Associates; private sector experts. Sponsors include: *Swiss Agency for Development and Cooperation (SDC)*; *United Nations (UN, #20515)* Department of Economic and Social Affairs. **Activities** Provides Financing for Development Tools – e-communication technologies to enable more effective collaboration and catalytic exchange between governments, the private sector and development agencies, including: Development Finance Portal; INFRADEV; Government Investor Network. Capacity-building programmes. [2011.01.11/XJ1620/**E**]

- ♦ Global Climate Change Alliance (inactive)
- ♦ Global Climate Change Institute, Tsinghua University (internationally oriented national body)

♦ Global Climate Forum (GCF) 10287

Main office Neue Promenade 6, 10178 Berlin, Germany. T. +493020607380. Fax +4930206073833. E-mail: info@globalclimateforum.org.
URL: http://www.globalclimateforum.org/

History Sep 2001, Potsdam (Germany), as *European Climate Forum (ECF).* Present name adopted, Jan 2012. **Aims** Initiate and perform high-class research on *climate change* in close interaction with stakeholders; provide a communication platform for governments, local authorities, business and social movements. **Structure** General Assembly; Board of Directors. **Languages** English. **Staff** None. **Finance** Members' dues. Other sources: EC research projects; national funding agencies. **Activities** Research/documentation;

knowledge management/information dissemination; events/meetings. **Events** *Meeting* Incheon (Korea Rep) 2015, *Conference on Integrated Risk Governance in the Mediterranean Region* Barcelona (Spain) 2011, *Conference / European Conference* Venice (Italy) 2009, *Conference / European Conference* Alcala de Henares (Spain) 2008, *Conference / European Conference* Berlin (Germany) 2007. **Publications** Articles; working papers; reports.
Members Scientific Founding (7); Institutional (5); Government (1); NGOs (5); Scientific Institutions (13); Individual (35). Scientific Founding members include 5 organizations listed in this Yearbook:
Fondazione Eni Enrico Mattei (FEEM); International Research Centre on Environment and Development (CIRED); Nansen Environmental and Remote Sensing Center (NERSC); Potsdam Institute for Climate Impact Research (PIK); Tyndall Centre for Climate Change Research.
NGOs, include 2 organizations listed in this Yearbook:
European Business Council for a Sustainable Energy Future (e5, #06417); World Wide Fund for Nature (WWF, #21922).
Scientific institutions include 3 organizations listed in this Yearbook:
Centro Euro-Mediterraneo per i Cambiamenti Climatici (CMCC); Commonwealth Scientific and Industrial Research Organization (CSIRO); Wuppertal Institute for Climate, Environment and Energy.
NGO Relations Advisory member in: *European Business Council for a Sustainable Energy Future (e5, #06417).* Member of: Germanwatch. [2018.01.31/XF6668/y/**F**]

♦ Global Climate and Health Alliance (GCHA) 10288

Exec Dir address not obtained. E-mail: info@climateandhealthalliance.org.
URL: http://climateandhealthalliance.org/
History 2011, Durban (South Africa). Registration: Internal Revenue Service, No/ID: 46-1323531, Start date: 12 Mar 2014, USA. **Aims** Tackle *climate change*; protect and promote public health. **Structure** Board of Directors; Secretariat. **Languages** English, Spanish. **Staff** 5.00 FTE, paid. **Activities** Advocacy/lobbying/activism; awareness raising; capacity building; events/meetings; networking/liaising; politics/policy/regulatory; research/documentation.
Members Members include 12 organizations listed in this Yearbook:
European Environment and Health Youth Coalition (EEHYC, #07001); European Respiratory Society (ERS, #08383); FHI 360; Health and Environment Alliance (HEAL, #10879); Health Care Without Harm (HCWH, #10875); International Federation of Medical Students' Associations (IFMSA, #13478); International Network on Children's Health, Environment and Safety (INCHES, #14240); International Youth Alliance for Family Planning (IYAFP, #15931); Medact; Southern Africa Climate Change Coalition (SACCC); The NCD Alliance (NCDA, #16963); World Obesity (#21678).
IGO Relations Observer status with (2): *United Nations Framework Convention on Climate Change (UNFCCC, 1992); WHO (#20950)* (Civil Society Working Group on Climate and Health). [2022.02.14/XM9002/y/**C**]

♦ Global Climate Observing System (GCOS) 10289

Système mondial d'observation du climat (SMOC) – Sistema Mundial de Observación del Clima (SMOC)
Dir c/o WMO, Av de la Paix 7 bis, PO Box 2300, 1211 Geneva 2, Switzerland. T. +41227308067. Fax +41227308181. E-mail: gcos@wmo.int.
URL: https://gcos.wmo.int/
History 15 Apr 1992, Geneva (Switzerland). Established as a joint programme of *Intergovernmental Oceanographic Commission (IOC, #11496), International Council for Science (ICSU, inactive), UNEP (#20299)* and *World Meteorological Organization (WMO, #21649)*, following a Memorandum of Understanding signed Feb 1992. Revised Sep 1998. Former names and other names: *WMO-IOC-UNEP-ISC Global Climate Observing System (GCOS)* – full title. **Aims** Work with partners to ensure sustained provision of reliable physical, chemical and biological observations for the whole climate system. **Structure** Steering Committee; Secretariat located at Geneva (WMO) in Switzerland. **Languages** English. **Staff** 7.00 FTE, paid. **Finance** Sources: contributions of member/participating states; government support; international organizations; sponsorship. **Activities** Set up the 'GCOS Cooperation Mechanism (GCM)' through which renovation, installation and training projects are realized for improving climate observing systems in developing countries. Facilitates implementation of an operational system of atmospheric, oceanic and terrestrial observations for climate. Includes: *'GCOS Surface Network (GSN)'; 'GCOS Reference Surface Network (GRSN)'; 'GCOS Upper-Air Network (GUAN)'; 'GCOS Reference Upper-Air Network (GRUAN)'* and other networks in the oceanic and terrestrial domains. Defined a set of Essential Climate Variables (ECVs) for the atmospheric, oceanic and terrestrial domains for the purpose of UNFCCC and IPCC. All ECVs are technically and economically feasible for systematic observation. Regional activities: GCOS Regional Workshop Programme; Pacific Islands GCOS (PI-GCOS); Technical Support Projects (US GCOS); Climate for Development in Africa Programme; Report on the Progress on the Implementation of the Global Observing System for Climate in support of the UNFCCC COP 22; update of the Implementation Plan for the Global Observing System for Climate in Support of the UNFCCC (A2016, GCOS-200). **Events** *Climate Obervation Conference* 2021, *GCOS Conference on Global Climate Observation* Amsterdam (Netherlands) 2016, *Session* Geneva (Switzerland) 2014, *Session* Offenbach (Germany) 2013, *Session* Geneva (Switzerland) 2012. **Publications** Annual Report; implementation plan; brochures; reports; press releases; posters. **Members** Not a membership organization. **IGO Relations** Built on: *Global Ocean Observing System (GOOS, #10511).* Recognized as the Societal Benefit Area (SBA) Climate of: *Group on Earth Observations (GEO, #10735)* System of Systems (GEOSS). Works closely with: *Global Runoff Data Centre (GRDC, #10584).* **NGO Relations** Cooperates with (1): *Committee on Earth Observation Satellites (CEOS, #04249).* Instrumental in setting up (1): *Global Terrestrial Network for Permafrost (GTN-P, #10625).* [2021.03.17/XF1615/v/**F***]

♦ Global Coalition against Cervical Cancer (unconfirmed)

♦ Global Coalition Against Child Pneumonia 10290

Contact c/o IVAC, Johns Hopkins Bloomberg School of Public Health, 615 N Wolfe St, Baltimore MD 21205, USA. T. +14432872365.
URL: http://worldpneumoniaday.org/
History Apr 2009. **Aims** Raise awareness about the toll of pneumonia, the world's leading killer of children; advocate for global action to protect against, effectively treat and help prevent this deadly disease. **Activities** Organizes World Pneumonia Day (12 Nov). **Publications** *Coalition Newsletter.*
Members NGOs; community-based organizations; academic institutions; government agencies; foundations (over 125). Members include the following organizations listed in this Yearbook (22):
- *Clean Cooking Alliance (#03987);*
- *Earth Institute at Columbia University;*
- *Episcopal Relief and Development;*
- *Fighting Infectious Diseases in Emerging Countries (FIDEC);*
- *Gavi – The Vaccine Alliance (Gavi, #10077);*
- *Global Healthcare Information Network (GHI-net);*
- *Global Health Council (GHC, #10402);*
- *International Pediatric Association (IPA, #14541);*
- *International Rescue Committee (IRC, #14717);*
- *International Union Against Tuberculosis and Lung Disease (The Union, #15752);*
- *International Vaccine Access Center (IVAC);*
- *International Vaccine Institute (IVI, #15839);*
- *Medical Teams International (MTI);*
- *ONE (#17728);*
- *Pan-African Thoracic Society (PATS, #18070);*
- *PATH (#18260);*
- *Project HOPE;*
- *PSI (#18555);*
- *Save the Children Federation (SCF);*
- *Southern African Society for Paediatric Infectious Diseases (SASPID);*
- *Task Force for Global Health (TFGH, #20098);*
- *UNICEF (#20332).* [2019/XJ3028/y/**F**]

♦ Global Coalition against Daesh (Global Coalition) 10291

Address not obtained.
URL: http://theglobalcoalition.org/
History Established Sep 2014. Also referred to as *Global Coalition To Defeat ISIS.* **Aims** Degrade and ultimately defeat Daesh. **Activities** Advocacy/lobbying/activism. **Publications** *Counter Daesh Insight Bulletin.*
Members Governments (72):
Afghanistan, Albania, Australia, Austria, Bahrain, Belgium, Bosnia-Herzegovina, Bulgaria, Cameroon, Canada, Chad, Croatia, Cyprus, Czechia, Denmark, Djibouti, Egypt, Estonia, Ethiopia, Finland, France, Georgia, Germany, Greece, Guinea, Hungary, Iceland, Iraq, Ireland, Italy, Japan, Jordan, Korea Rep, Kosovo, Kuwait, Latvia, Lebanon, Libya, Lithuania, Luxembourg, Malaysia, Moldova, Montenegro, Morocco, Netherlands, New Zealand, Niger, Nigeria, North Macedonia, Norway, Oman, Panama, Philippines, Poland, Portugal, Qatar, Romania, Saudi Arabia, Serbia, Singapore, Slovakia, Slovenia, Somalia, Spain, Sweden, Taiwan, Tunisia, Türkiye, UK, Ukraine, United Arab Emirates, USA.
Regional institutions (5):
Community of Sahel-Saharan States (CEN-SAD, #04406); European Union (EU, #08967); International Criminal Police Organization – INTERPOL (ICPO-INTERPOL, #13110); League of Arab States (LAS, #16420); NATO (#16945). [2018/XM6944/**C***]

♦ Global Coalition on Aging (unconfirmed)
♦ Global Coalition for Change (internationally oriented national body)
♦ Global Coalition to Counter ISIL (unconfirmed)
♦ Global Coalition To Defeat ISIS / see Global Coalition against Daesh (#10291)

♦ Global Coalition to End Child Poverty 10292

Contact address not obtained. E-mail: coalitionchildpoverty@gmail.com.
URL: http://www.endchildhoodpoverty.org/
Aims Raise awareness about children living in poverty across the world and support global and national action to alleviate it. **Structure** No formal structure. **Activities** Advocacy/lobbying/activism. **Publications** *Newsletter.*
Members Organizations include 14 organizations listed in this Yearbook:
African Child Policy Forum (ACPF, #00246); Arigatou International; BRAC (#03310); ChildFund Alliance (#03868); Eurochild (#05657); Institute of Development Studies, Brighton (IDS); International Movement ATD Fourth World (#14193); OECD (#17693); Overseas Development Institute (ODI); Partnership for Economic Policy (PEP, #18233); Plan International (#18386); Save the Children Federation (SCF); SOS-Kinderdorf International (#19693); UNICEF (#20332). [2020/XM5572/y/**F**]

♦ **Global Coalition** Global Coalition against Daesh (#10291)

♦ Global Coalition on Migration (GCM) 10293

Contact CP 147, 1211 Geneva 20, Switzerland. T. +41225349313. Fax +41225349313.
URL: http://gcmigration.org/
History 3 Dec 2011, Geneva (Switzerland). **Structure** Secretariat hosted by *Migrants Rights International (MRI, #16799).* **Finance** Sources: international organizations. Supported by: *MacArthur Foundation.*
Members Organizations (14):
Espacio Sin Fronteras (ESF); *Global Migration Policy Associates (GMPA, #10473); International Catholic Migration Commission (ICMC, #12459); International Network on Migration and Development (INMD, #14296); International Trade Union Confederation (ITUC, #15708); La Via Campesina (#20765); Migrant Forum in Asia (MFA, #16798); Migrants Rights International (MRI, #16799);* National Alliance of Latin American and Caribbean Communities (NALACC); National Network for Immigrant and Refugee Rights (NNIRR); *Pan-African Network in Defense of Migrants' Rights (PANiDMR); Platform for International Cooperation on Undocumented Migrants (PICUM, #18401);* Transnational Migrant Platform; *Women in Migration Network (WIMN, #21008).*
NGO Relations Partner of: *Building and Wood Workers' International (BWI, #03355).* [2014/XJ8932/y/**C**]

♦ Global Coalition for Occupation Safety and Health 10294

Officer address not obtained. E-mail: labadmin-osh@ilo.org.
URL: http://www.ilo.org/
History As *Joint ILO/WHO Committee on Occupational Health*, within the framework of *ILO (#11123)* and *WHO (#20950).* Former names and other names: *Global OSH Coalition (GC)* – alias; *Global Coalition for Safety & Health at Work* – former; *Joint ILO/WHO Committee on Occupational Health* – former. **Aims** Stimulate collaboration between health and labour sectors to develop common solutions for workers' health and safety and to work across SDG3 and SDG8. **Structure** Led by *ILO (#11123), WHO (#20950)*, Finland, Singapore, *European Commission (EC, #06633), European Agency for Safety and Health at Work (EU-OSHA, #05843)* and *International Commission on Occupational Health (ICOH, #12709).* Steering Committee; Secretariat, based at ILO; Task Groups. **Events** *Meeting* Geneva (Switzerland) 2003.
Members Governments of 2 countries:
Finland, Singapore.
IGO Relations *European Commission (EC, #06633); ILO (#11123); WHO (#20950).* **NGO Relations** *International Commission on Occupational Health (ICOH, #12709).* [2019.04.24/XE2708/**E***]

♦ Global Coalition to Protect Education from Attack (GCPEA) 10295

Dir 350 Fifth Avenue, 34th Floor, New York NY 10118-3299, USA. T. +12123779413 – +12123779446. E-mail: gcpea@protectingeducation.org.
URL: http://protectingeducation.org/
History 2010, by organizations from the fields of education in emergencies and conflict-affected fragile states, higher education, protection, international human rights, and international humanitarian law. A project of the Tides Center. **Aims** Advocate for the protection of students, teachers, schools, and universities from attack. **Structure** Steering Committee. **Staff** 6.00 FTE, paid. **Finance** Funding, including from Protect Education in Insecurity and Conflict (PEIC), *UNICEF (#20332)*, and Columbia University's Program on Forced Migration and Health.
Members Organizations including 8 listed in this Yearbook:
Human Rights Watch (HRW, #10990); Institute of International Education (IIE); Inter-agency Network for Education in Emergencies (INEE, #11387); Norwegian Refugee Council (NRC); Save the Children Federation (SCF); Scholars at Risk (SAR); Studentenes og Akademikernes Internasjonale Hjelpefond (SAIH); UNHCR (#20327).
IGO Relations *UNESCO (#20322).* **NGO Relations** *Geneva Call; Inter-agency Network for Education in Emergencies (INEE, #11387).* [2016/XM4747/y/**E**]

♦ Global Coalition for Regulatory Science Research (GCRSR) 10296

Co-Chair Natl Ctr for Toxicological Research, FDA, 3900 NCTR Rd, Jefferson AR 72079, USA. T. +18705437000.
History Set up Sep 2013, USA, at 3rd Global Summit on Regulatory Science. **Structure** Executive Committee. **Events** *Annual Global Summit on Regulatory Science* Stresa (Italy) / Ispra (Italy) 2019, *Annual Global Summit on Regulatory Science* Beijing (China) 2018, *Annual Global Summit on Regulatory Science* Brasilia (Brazil) 2017, *Annual Global Summit on Regulatory Science* Bethesda, MD (USA) 2016, *Annual Global Summit on Regulatory Science* Parma (Italy) 2015.
Members Government departments of 7 countries:
Australia, Brazil, Canada, Japan, New Zealand, Singapore, USA.
Regional entity:
European Food Safety Authority (EFSA, #07287). [2019/XM4079/**E***]

♦ Global Coalition for Safety & Health at Work / see Global Coalition for Occupation Safety and Health (#10294)
♦ Global Coalition of Think Tank Networks for SSC (unconfirmed)

♦ Global Coalition on Women and AIDS (GCWA) 10297

Contact Avenue Appia 20, 1211 Geneva 27, Switzerland. T. +41227913370. Fax +41227914188.
URL: https://gcwa.unaids.org/
History 2 Feb 2004, London (UK). Set up as an initiative of *Joint United Nations Programme on HIV/AIDS (UNAIDS, #16149).* **Aims** Mobilize leadership and political will to influence laws, policies, programmes, and funding; promote action that gives girls and women the power to prevent *HIV* infection, and live fulfilling and productive lives when living with HIV. **Structure** Steering Committee, headed by 2 Co-chairs, one from civil society and one from UN. Secretariat, headed by Director. **Languages** English. **Staff** 2.50 FTE, paid. **Finance** Sources: *Joint United Nations Programme on HIV/AIDS (UNAIDS, #16149)*; donor funds. **Activities** Advocacy for the rights and needs of women and girls in the context of HIV. Participates in and convenes dialogue at international policy setting fora. **Publications** Reports; policy briefings.

Members Full from civil society, academic world, government and UN system (248), including 22 organizations listed in this Yearbook.
Caribbean Vulnerable Communities Coalition (CVC, #03565); Huairou Commission (#10960); International Center for Research on Women (ICRW); International Community of Women Living with HIV/AIDS (ICW, #12826); International Women's Health Coalition (IWHC); Joint United Nations Programme on HIV/AIDS (UNAIDS, #16149); Movimiento Latinoamericano y del Caribe de Mujeres Positivas Regional Argentina (MLCM+, no recent information); Voluntary Service Overseas (VSO); WHO (#20950). [2021/XF7137/y/F]

♦ Global Cochlear Implant Access Network (unconfirmed)

♦ Global Coffee Platform (GCP) 10298

Exec Dir Charles de Gaulle Str 5, 53113 Bonn, Germany. T. +49228850500. Fax +492282285020. E-mail: info@globalcoffeeplatform.org.
Secretariat Utrecht Nieuwekade 9, 3511 RV Utrecht, Netherlands. T. +31302305624. E-mail: info@globalcoffeeplatform.org.
URL: http://www.globalcoffeeplatform.org/

History Publicly launched Apr 2016, as a merger of *4C Association (inactive)* and the *Sustainable Coffee Program.* **Aims** Unite the whole coffee sector to tackle issues, multiply impact and improve farmer profitability; unite both public and private sector actors to create a sustainability vision for the sector. **Structure** Membership Assembly; Board; Secretariats – Bonn (Germany); Utrecht (Netherlands). Office: Piracicaba (Brazil).
Members Individual; Associate; Trade and Industry; Producers; Civil Society. Members in 46 countries and territories:
Australia, Austria, Belgium, Brazil, Burundi, China, Colombia, Costa Rica, Côte d'Ivoire, El Salvador, Ethiopia, Finland, France, Germany, Guatemala, Honduras, Hong Kong, India, Indonesia, Italy, Japan, Kenya, Laos, Madagascar, Malawi, Malaysia, Mexico, Netherlands, New Zealand, Nicaragua, Nigeria, Norway, Papua New Guinea, Peru, Rwanda, Singapore, South Africa, Spain, Sweden, Switzerland, Tanzania UR, Uganda, UK, USA, Vietnam, Zambia.
Included in the above, 7 organizations listed in this Yearbook:
African Fine Coffees Association (AFCA, #00316); European Coffee Federation (ECF, #06600); Fairtrade International (FLO, #09240); Rainforest Alliance; SNV Netherlands Development Organisation (SNV); SOLIDARIDAD Network (#19681); TechnoServe (#20120).
NGO Relations Member of: *ISEAL (#16026).* [2020/XM4919/y/F]

♦ Global Cold Chain Alliance (GCCA) 10299

Exec Vice-Pres 241 18th St S, Ste 620, Alexandria VA 22314, USA. T. +17033734300. Fax +17033734301. E-mail: email@gcca.org.
URL: http://www.gcca.org/

History 2007. Founded by *International Association of Refrigerated Warehouses (IARW, #12125)* and *World Food Logistics Organization (WFLO).* **Aims** Unite partners to advance excellence and innovation in the perishable *food industry.* **Events** *European Cold Chain Conference* Rotterdam (Netherlands) 2021, *European Cold Chain Conference* Rotterdam (Netherlands) 2020, *Latin America Cold Chain Congress* Mexico City (Mexico) 2013. **IGO Relations** Strategic partner: *International Institute of Refrigeration (IIR, #13918).* **NGO Relations** Core Partners: *International Association of Refrigerated Warehouses (IARW, #12125); World Food Logistics Organization (WFLO); International Institute of Ammonia Refrigeration (IIAR); International Refrigerated Transportation Association (IRTA); Controlled Environment Building Association (CEBA, #04783).* Affiliate Partners: national and multinational associations. Supporting Partners: companies and corporations. Strategic Partners, national and international associations and organizations including: *European Cold Storage and Logistics Association (ECSLA, #06603); Institute of International Container Lessors (IICL, #11273); International Dairy Foods Association (IDFA); Transfrigoroute International (TI, #20213); AIB International; Council of Supply Chain Management Professionals (CSCMP); International Packaged Ice Association (IPIA); International Cold Chain Technology (ICCT).* [2021/XJ8103/F]

♦ Global College, Long Island University (internationally oriented national body)

♦ Global Colon Cancer Association (GCCA) 10300

Exec Dir 333 City Ave, Ste PL-14, Bala Cynwyd PA 19004, USA.
URL: https://www.globalcca.org/

History 2011. Founded by heads of *Digestive Cancers Europe (DiCE, #05070)* and US Colon Cancer Alliance. Registration: 501(c)(3) not-for-profit, No/ID: 46-0657002, USA. **Aims** Create a global community in which people worldwide can unite and fight this disease with a unified voice. **Structure** Board of Directors. Executive Director. **Languages** English. **Staff** All voluntary. **Activities** Events/meetings. **Events** *Global Colorectal Cancer Congress* 2023, *Global Colorectal Cancer Congress* 2021, *Global Colorectal Cancer Congress* Orlando, FL (USA) 2020.
Members Full in 33 countries:
Australia, Belgium, Brazil, Canada, Cyprus, Czechia, El Salvador, Finland, France, Greece, India, Ireland, Israel, Latvia, Lebanon, Netherlands, New Zealand, Nigeria, North Macedonia, Peru, Poland, Portugal, Romania, Russia, Serbia, Slovakia, Slovenia, Spain, Türkiye, UK, United Arab Emirates, USA, Venezuela.
Included in the above, 1 organization listed in this Yearbook:
Digestive Cancers Europe (DiCE, #05070).
NGO Relations Member of (3): *Global Cancer Coalitions Network (GCCN, #10270); International Alliance of Patients' Organizations (IAPO, #11633); World Patients Alliance (WPA).* [2023/XJ5995/y/C]

♦ Global Combat Sports Organization (unconfirmed)

♦ Global Commission on Adaptation 10301

Contact c/o GCA, Wilhelmanakade 149C, 3072 AP Rotterdam, Netherlands. T. +12023214355.
Contact c/o WCI, 10 G St NE, Ste 800, Washington DC 20002, USA. T. +12027297736.
URL: http://gca.org/

History Launched 16 Oct 2018, The Hague (Netherlands). **Aims** Enhance the political visibility of adapting to *climate change.* **Structure** Leadership: Ban Ki-moon, former Secretary-General of *United Nations (UN, #20515)*; Bill Gates of *Bill and Melinda Gates Foundation (BMGF)* and Kristalina Georgieva, CEO of *International Bank for Reconstruction and Development (IBRD, #12317).* Commissioners (28). **Activities** Politics/policy/regulatory.
Members Countries, each with one commissioner (17):
Argentina, Bangladesh, Canada, China, Costa Rica, Denmark, Ethiopia, Germany, Grenada, India, Indonesia, Marshall Is, Mexico, Netherlands, Senegal, South Africa, UK.
Commissioners representing or having represented the following organizations (12):
African Development Bank (ADB, #00283); Alliance for a Green Revolution in Africa (AGRA, #00685); Bill and Melinda Gates Foundation (BMGF); BRAC (#03310); International Bank for Reconstruction and Development (IBRD, #12317); International Federation of Red Cross and Red Crescent Societies (#13526); Office of the United Nations High Commissioner for Human Rights (OHCHR, #17697); Shack-Slum Dwellers International (SDI, #19255); UNEP (#20299); United Nations Framework Convention on Climate Change (UNFCCC, 1992); United Nations (UN, #20515); World Resources Institute (WRI, #21753).
NGO Relations Managing partners: *Global Center on Adaptation (GCA); World Resources Institute (WRI, #21753).* [2018/XM7168/y/C]

♦ Global Commission on Drug Policy 10302

Exec Sec PO Box 1672, 1211 Geneva 1, Switzerland. T. +41229084375.
Communications Officer address not obtained.
URL: http://www.globalcommissionondrugs.org/

History Jan 2011. **Aims** Advocate for drug policies based on scientific evidence, human rights, public health and safety for all segments of the population. **Structure** Commissioners, including Chair and Honorary Chair; Secretariat, based in Geneva (Switzerland). **Finance** Sources: international organizations. Supported by: *Oak Foundation; Open Society Foundations (OSF, #17763)*; Swiss Federal Department of Foreign Affairs; Virgin Unite. **Publications** Reports; position papers.
Members Commissioners from 22 countries:
Brazil, Canada, Chile, Colombia, Czechia, Egypt, France, Greece, India, Mauritius, Mexico, New Zealand, Nigeria, Peru, Poland, Portugal, South Africa, Spain, Switzerland, Timor-Leste, UK, USA. [2019.06.06/XJ6069/v/C]

♦ Global Commons Alliance (unconfirmed)
♦ Global Commons Institute, London (internationally oriented national body)
♦ Global Communication Association (internationally oriented national body)
♦ Global Communities (internationally oriented national body)
♦ Global Community, The / see Global Community Earth Government
♦ Global Community Earth Government (internationally oriented national body)

♦ Global Community Engagement and Resilience Fund (GCERF) 10303

Exec Dir address not obtained. T. +41223060810. E-mail: info@gcerf.org.
Head of External Affairs address not obtained.
URL: http://www.gcerf.org/

History Signed Headquarters agreement with host country Switzerland, 26 May 2014. Registration: Swiss Civil Code, Start date: 9 Sep 2014, Switzerland; Registre du Commerce de Genève, No/ID: CHE-256.533.002, Switzerland. **Aims** Provide grants to community-level initiatives that address local drivers of violent extremism; strengthen resilience of communities to violent extremist agendas. **Structure** Board; Secretariat. **Languages** English. **Staff** 40.00 FTE, paid. **Finance** Voluntary contributions. As of Nov 2022, pledged/contributed: US$ 158,000,000. **Activities** Advocacy/lobbying/activism; events/meetings. Active in: Albania, Bangladesh, Bosnia-Herzegovina, Burkina Faso, Kenya, Kosovo, Mali, Mauritania, Niger, Nigeria, North Macedonia, Philippines, Somalia, Sri Lanka, Tunisia. **Events** *Meeting* Geneva (Switzerland) 2022, *Meeting* Tirana (Albania) 2022, *Meeting* Geneva (Switzerland) 2021, *Meeting* Paris (France) 2021, *Meeting* 2020. **Publications** Articles; essays; book chapters. **NGO Relations** Also links with national associations. [2023.02.22/XM4130/F]

♦ Global Community Monitor (internationally oriented national body)
♦ Global Compact / see United Nations Global Compact (#20567)
♦ Global Compact on Education (unconfirmed)
♦ Global Compact for Migration – Global Compact for Safe, Orderly and Regular Migration (2018 treaty)
♦ Global Compact for Safe, Orderly and Regular Migration (2018 treaty)
♦ Global Competitiveness Empowerment Forum (internationally oriented national body)
♦ Global Computer Network for Environment, Peace, Human Rights and Development / see GreenNet (#10725)
♦ Global Concern (internationally oriented national body)

♦ Global Confederation of Higher Education Associations for Agriculture and Life Sciences (GCHERA) 10304

SG address not obtained.
URL: http://www.gchera.com/

History Sep 1998, Kiev (Ukraine). Founded by presidents of 3 universities in USA, Ukraine and Germany. Former names and other names: *Global Consortium of Agricultural Universities* – former (Sep 1998 to 1999); *Global Consortium of Higher Education and Research for Agriculture* – former (1999 to 2011). **Aims** Encourage mutual understanding and cooperation among higher education associations and their constituent member universities; provide leadership in education, research, innovation and outreach in agricultural and life sciences; be a catalyst for sharing and adoption of best practices across membership. **Structure** General Assembly; Steering (Executive) Committee. **Languages** English. **Staff** 1.00 FTE, paid. **Activities** Awards/prizes/competitions; events/meetings; networking/liaising. **Events** *Global Conference* Bucharest (Romania) 2019, *Global Conference* Nanjing (China) 2017, *Global Conference* Beirut (Lebanon) 2015, *Conference on Agricultural Higher Education in the 21st century* Saragossa (Spain) 2015, *Conference on Food Security and Climate Change* Chihuahua, CHIH (Mexico) 2014.
Members National and regional university associations (over 900), including 7 organizations listed in this Yearbook:
African Network for Agriculture, Agroforestry and Natural Resources Education (ANAFE, #00380); Asian Association of Agricultural Colleges and Universities (AAACU, #01312); Asia-Pacific Association of Agricultural Research Institutions (APAARI, #01830); Association for European Life Science Universities (ICA, #02519); Central Asia and South Caucasus Consortium of Agricultural universities for Development (CASCADE, #03685); EARTH University (#05170); Regional Universities Forum for Capacity Building in Agriculture (RUFORUM, #18818).
NGO Relations Member of (2): *Global Forum for Rural Advisory Services (GFRAS, #10378); Young Professionals for Agricultural Development (YPARD, #21996).* Member of: Steering Committee of the *Global Forum on Agricultural Research (GFAR, #10370)*; Tropical Agriculture Platform, Global Task Force. [2021/XC0109/y/C]

♦ Global Confederation for Interprofessional Education and Collaborative Practice 10305

Interprofessional.Global
Contact Petrus Driessenstraat 3, tav Jeannette Bult, 9714 CA Groningen, Netherlands.
URL: http://interprofessional.global/

History Set up as *World Interprofessional Education and Collaborative Practice Co-ordinating Committee (WCC)*, the coordinating committee for the *All Together Better Health (ATBH)* conferences. Present name adopted, 2018. **Aims** Establish and maintain communication between networks of interprofessional *education* (IPE) and collaborative practice. **Structure** World Coordinating Committee. Administrative base chaired by CAIPE. **Events** *All Together Better Health Conference* Doha (Qatar) 2020, *All Together Better Health Conference* Auckland (New Zealand) 2018, *All Together Better Health Conference* Oxford (UK) 2016, *All Together Better Health Conference* Pittsburgh, PA (USA) 2014, *All Together Better Health Conference* Kobe (Japan) 2012.
Members Networks (8) in 5 countries:
Australia, Canada, Japan, UK, USA.
Regional networks (3):
Australasian Interprofessional Practice and Education Network (AIPPEN); European Interprofessional Education Network (EIPEN, #07595); Nordic Interprofessional Network (NIPNET, #17326). [2022/XM4114/ct/E]

♦ Global Confederation for Interprofessional Practice and Education / see Global Confederation for Interprofessional Education and Collaborative Practice (#10305)
♦ Global Conference on Environmental Taxation (meeting series)
♦ Global Conference on Myositis (meeting series)
♦ Global Conference on Sustainable Manufacturing (meeting series)
♦ Global Congress On Hysteroscopy (meeting series)
♦ Global Congress on Medicine and Health in Sport (meeting series)
♦ Global Congress on Molecular Pathology (meeting series)
♦ Global Congress for Qualitative Health Research (meeting series)
♦ Global Connections (internationally oriented national body)
♦ Global Connections Foundation (internationally oriented national body)
♦ Global Consortium of Agricultural Universities / see Global Confederation of Higher Education Associations for Agriculture and Life Sciences (#10304)
♦ Global Consortium of Higher Education and Research for Agriculture / see Global Confederation of Higher Education Associations for Agriculture and Life Sciences (#10304)
♦ Global Contract Foundation (internationally oriented national body)
♦ Global Convention on the Recognition of Qualifications concerning Higher Education (2019 treaty)
♦ Global Cool Foundation (internationally oriented national body)
♦ Global Cooperation for a Brighter Society, International / see Global Cooperation Society
♦ Global Cooperation Council (internationally oriented national body)
♦ Global Cooperation Society (internationally oriented national body)

♦ Global Coral Reef Monitoring Network (GCRMN) 10306

Coordinator Global Marine and Polar Progr, IUCN, Rue Mauverney 28, 1196 Gland VD, Switzerland.
URL: http://www.icriforum.org/gcrmn/

History Founded 1995, within the framework of *International Coral Reef Initiative (ICRI, #12965)*, following initiatives since 1991 by the 3 co-sponsors: *Intergovernmental Oceanographic Commission (IOC, #11496); International Union for Conservation of Nature and Natural Resources (IUCN, #15766); UNEP (#20299)*, with preparatory work by *UNEP-IOC-IUCN-WMO Global Task Team on the Implications of Climate Change on Coral*

Reefs (inactive). Currently hosted by IUCN Global Marine and Polar Programme. **Aims** Strengthen the existing capacity to assess coral reefs by providing a consistent monitoring program; identify processes and trends in coral reefs and discriminate between natural and anthropogenic and climatic changes; assess and report on the current status and future trends of coral reefs and how they are used and valued as resources; link existing organizations and individuals to effectively monitor ecological, social, cultural and economic aspects of coral reefs through collaborative regional networks; disseminate results locally, regionally and globally to advise policy, and to assist agencies to implement sustainable use and conservation of coral reefs and their resources. **Structure** Management Group comprises *Intergovernmental Oceanographic Commission (IOC, #11496), International Union for Conservation of Nature and Natural Resources (IUCN, #15766), International Bank for Reconstruction and Development (IBRD, #12317)* (World Bank), *UNEP (#20299), Secretariat of the Convention on Biological Diversity (SCBD, #19197), WorldFish (#21507)* and Great Barrier Reef Marine Park Authority, together with *International Coral Reef Initiative (ICRI, #12965)* Secretariat and Chairman of the Scientific and Technical Advisory Committee (GCRMN-STAC). Management Group cooperates with independent voluntary networks/nodes in East Asia, wider Caribbean region, Indian Ocean and Pacific region. Overall coordination currently managed by IUCN Global Marine and Polar Programme. **Languages** English, French, Indonesian, Spanish, Thai. **Staff** 1.00 FTE, paid. Voluntary node coordinators. **Finance** No funding. **Activities** Networking/liaising; monitoring/evaluation; knowledge management/information dissemination; training/education. Special monitoring projects (2): pilot programme to give a "snapshot" of reef status undertaken simultaneously in research institutes worldwide; tourist monitoring programme coordinated through tourist operators and Reef Check. **Events** *Meeting* Cebu City (Philippines) 2001. **Publications** Status reports; manuals; reports; brochures.

Members Governments, non-governmental organizations and international organizations. Members in 37 countries (" indicates Founding Members):

Australia (*), Barbados, Belize, Brazil, Colombia, Costa Rica, Cuba, Dominican Rep, Egypt, Fiji, France (*), Grenada, Honduras, India, Indonesia, Jamaica (*), Japan (*), Kenya, Korea Rep, Madagascar, Malaysia, Maldives, Mexico, Monaco, Netherlands, Palau, Panama, Philippines (*), Samoa, Seychelles, South Africa, Sweden (*), Tanzania UR, Thailand, UK (*), USA (*), Vietnam.

Organizations listed in this Yearbook (13):

Central Caribbean Marine Institute (CCMI); Conservation International (CI); Interamerican Association for Environmental Defense (#11398); International Coral Reef Society (#12966); Project AWARE Foundation; Reef-World Foundation; SeaWeb; Society for the Conservation of Reef Fish Aggregations (SCRFA, #19535); The Coral Reef Alliance (CORAL); The Nature Conservancy (TNC); Wildlife Conservation Society (WCS); World Resources Institute (WRI, #21753); World Wide Fund for Nature (WWF, #21922).

IGO Relations Cooperates with: *Global Ocean Observing System (GOOS, #10511); Global Terrestrial Observing System (GTOS, #10626); Regional Seas Programme (#18814); South Asia Cooperative Environment Programme (SACEP, #19714).* **NGO Relations** MSP's node: *International Ocean Institute – Pacific Islands (IOI-PI, see: #14394).* [2016.10.19/XF4038/**F**]

♦ Global Corporate Governance Institute (GCGI) 10307

Pres/CEO address not obtained. E-mail: csr.iarraiano@iscal.ipl.pt.
URL: http://www.gcg-csr.org/

History 2014, London (UK). **Aims** Rethink and integrate value issues into management practice, education and development. **Structure** Board of Directors; Executive Committee. **Activities** Events/meetings. **Events** *International Conference on Corporate Social Responsibility, Sustainability, Ethics and Governance* Baton Rouge, LA (USA) 2022, *International Conference on Corporate Social Responsibility, Sustainability, Ethics and Governance* Lisbon (Portugal) 2021, *International Conference on Corporate Social Responsibility, Sustainability, Ethics and Governance* Abu Dhabi (United Arab Emirates) 2019, *International Conference on Organization and Management* Abu Dhabi (United Arab Emirates) 2019, *International Conference on Corporate Social Responsibility, Sustainability, Ethics and Governance* Santander (Spain) 2018. [2020/XM8755/c/**C**]

♦ Global Corporate Real Estate Network (CORENET Global) 10308

CEO 133 Peachtree St NE, Ste 3000, Atlanta GA 30303, USA. T. +14045893210. Fax +14045893201. E-mail: media@corenetglobal.org.
URL: http://www.corenetglobal.org/

History 2001. Founded by merger of *International Development Research Council (IDRC, inactive)* and *Nacore International (inactive)*. **Activities** Events/meetings. **Events** *CoreNet Global Summit* Singapore (Singapore) 2023, *CoreNet Global Summit* Amsterdam (Netherlands) 2022, *CoreNet Global Summit – North America* Chicago, IL (USA) 2022, *Asia Pacific Summit* Singapore (Singapore) 2021, *Global Virtual Experience Session* Singapore (Singapore) 2020. **NGO Relations** Member of: *International Property Measurement Standards Coalition (IPMSC, #14656).* [2022/XF6301/**F**]

♦ Global Cosmetics Cluster (GCC) 10309

Contact 1 Place de la Cathédrale, 28000 Chartres, France. T. +33237183318. E-mail: hello@cosmetics-clusters.com.
URL: http://cosmeticsclusters.com/

History 2016, Paris (France). Former names and other names: *Cosmetics Clusters – International Network (CCIN)* – former (2016 to 2021). Registration: Préfecture d'Eure et Loir, No/ID: W281009777, Start date: 9 Apr 2021, France. **Aims** Develop the perfume-cosmetics industry worldwide. **Languages** English, French, Spanish. **Staff** 0.00 FTE, paid. **Events** *Cosmetics Cluster Rendez-vous on Cosmetic 360* Paris (France) 2021. **Members** Cosmetics associations in 16 countries and territories:

Belgium, Canada, China, Colombia, France, Italy, Japan, Korea Rep, Morocco, Portugal, Romania, Spain, Taiwan, Thailand, UK, USA. [2021.09.02/XM7292/**F**]

♦ Global Council for Anthropological Linguistics (GLOCAL) 10310

Communications Officer SOAS Univ of London, 10 Thornhaugh Street, Russell Square, London, WC1H 0XG, UK. E-mail: cala@soas.ac.uk.
URL: https://glocal.soas.ac.uk/

History 2016, Australia. Formed 2015; officially launched with first Central Committee, 2016. Innaugural annual conference held Jan 2019, Paññāsāstra University of Cambodia, Siem Reap. Former names and other names: *Conference on Asian Linguistic Anthropology (CALA)* – former. Registration: No/ID: 42937047321, Start date: 2016, Australia. **Aims** Elicit new understandings of Linguistic Anthropology by centering research and rhetoric on Asian contexts and a network of related fields; contribute to advanced efforts of other global societies and organizations in Linguistic Anthropology; strengthen conceptions of, and interest in, the Linguistic Anthropology of Asia, and connect scholars working in and on Asian regions with those in other regions. **Structure** Directorship; Communications; Administration; Scientific Committee. **Languages** English. **Staff** 4.00 FTE, paid; 10.00 FTE, voluntary. **Activities** Advocacy/lobbying/activism; awards/prizes/competitions; awareness raising; capacity building; events/meetings; financial and/or material support; guidance/assistance/consulting; knowledge management/information dissemination; networking/liaising; publishing activities; research/documentation; training/education. **Events** *Conference* Quezon City (Philippines) 2021, *Conference* Bintulu (Malaysia) 2020, *Conference* Siem Reap (Cambodia) 2019. **Publications** *Journal of Asian Linguistic Anthropology (The JALA).* Conference proceedings. **Members** Membership countries not specified. **NGO Relations** Constitutes *Global Network in Linguistic Anthropology*, together with *Conference on Mediterranean and European Linguistic Anthropology (COMELA, #04628), South and Central American Assembly on Linguistic Anthropology (SCAALA, #19752), Conference on Oceanian Linguistic Anthropology (COOLA, #04636), Middle Eastern Association of Linguistic Anthropology (MEALA, #16760)* and *African Assembly of Linguistic Anthropology (AFALA, #00204).* [2021.06.13/XM8713/c/**F**]

♦ Global Council of Sport Science (unconfirmed)

♦ Global Counterterrorism Forum (GCTF) 10311

Contact address not obtained. E-mail: adminunit@thegctf.org.
URL: https://www.thegctf.org/

History as a voluntary and not legally binding commitment. Launched, 22 Sep 2011, New York NY (USA). **Aims** Identify critical civilian counter-terrorism needs; mobilize the necessary expertise and resources to address these issues and build global political will; provide a venue for national CT officials and practitioners to meet. **Structure** Coordinating Committee, consisting of all members and co-chaired by 2 members from different regions. Working Groups. Administrative Unit. **Activities** Events/meetings. **Events** *Coordinating Committee Meeting* Tokyo (Japan) 2018, *Ministerial Meeting* New York, NY (USA) 2013, *Ministerial Meeting* Abu Dhabi (United Arab Emirates) 2012, *Ministerial Meeting* Istanbul (Turkey) 2012, *Ministerial Meeting* New York, NY (USA) 2011.

Members Governments (29):

Algeria, Australia, Canada, China, Colombia, Denmark, Egypt, France, Germany, India, Indonesia, Italy, Japan, Jordan, Morocco, Netherlands, New Zealand, Nigeria, Pakistan, Qatar, Russia, Saudi Arabia, South Africa, Spain, Switzerland, Türkiye, UK, United Arab Emirates, USA.

Regional community:

European Union (EU, #08967). [2022/XJ4621/**F***]

♦ Global Covenant of Mayors for Climate and Energy (GCoM) 10312

Global Secretariat Blvd Charlemagne 1, 1000 Brussels, Belgium. E-mail: info@globalcovenantofmayors.org.
URL: http://globalcovenantofmayors.org/

History Jun 2016. Founded on merger of *EU Covenant of Mayors*, set up 2008, and *Compact of Mayors*, launched Sep 2014. **Aims** Serve cities and local governments by mobilizing and supporting ambitious, measurable, planned climate and energy action in their communities by working with city/regional networks, national governments and other partners. **Structure** Mayoral Board including Co-Chairs; Strategic Advisory Committee; Regional and National Covenants of Mayors; Technical Working Groups. **Finance** Supported by: *Bloomberg Philanthropies; C40 (#03391); Climate Alliance (#04005); Council of European Municipalities and Regions (CEMR, #04891); Energy Cities (#05467); EUROCITIES (#05662); European Commission (EC, #06633); European Committee of the Regions (CoR, #06665); European Federation of Agencies and Regions for Energy and the Environment (FEDARENE, #07041); Local Governments for Sustainability (ICLEI, #16507); United Nations Human Settlements Programme (UN-Habitat, #20572); World Organization of United Cities and Local Governments (UCLG, #21695).* **Members** Over 11,500 cities and local governments in 142 countries,. Membership countries not specified. [2022.02.09/XM5346/**F**]

♦ Global Credit Data (unconfirmed)

♦ Global Crop Diversity Trust (Crop Trust) 10313

Exec Dir Platz er Vereinten Nationen 7, 53113 Bonn, Germany. T. +4922885427122. E-mail: info@croptrust.org.
URL: http://www.croptrust.org/

History Oct 2003. Founded by *FAO (#09260)* and *Bioversity International (#03262)* on behalf of *CGIAR System Organization (CGIAR, #03843).* Operates within the framework of *International Treaty on Plant Genetic Resources for Food and Agriculture (2001).* Headquarters Agreement signed with German Government, Dec 2012, with headquarters transferred to Bonn (Germany), 2013. **Aims** Ensure conservation and availability of crop diversity for food security worldwide. **Structure** Executive Board; Donors' Council. **Languages** English. **Finance** Sources: donations. Donors: country governments; civil society (foundations); private sector; farmers' organizations; individuals. **Activities** Events/meetings; knowledge management/information dissemination. **Events** *Simposio de recursos geneticos para América latina y el caribe* Montevideo (Uruguay) 2005.

Members Governments of 28 countries:

Australia, Cambodia, Cameroon, Cape Verde, Colombia, Ecuador, Egypt, Ethiopia, Germany, Ghana, India, Jordan, Kenya, Mali, Mauritius, Morocco, Pakistan, Peru, Romania, Samoa, Serbia, Slovakia, Sweden, Switzerland, Syrian AR, Togo, Tonga, Uganda.

IGO Relations Supports (4): *Africa Rice Center (AfricaRice, #00518); AVRDC – The World Vegetable Center (#03051); International Center for Agricultural Research in the Dry Areas (ICARDA, #12466); International Crops Research Institute for the Semi-Arid Tropics (ICRISAT, #13116).* **NGO Relations** Member of (1): *Global Open Data for Agriculture and Nutrition (GODAN, #10514).* Supports (2): *Coconut Genetic Resources Network (COGENT, #04080); International Institute of Tropical Agriculture (IITA, #13933).* [2022/XJ4086/**F***]

♦ Global Crop Protection Federation / see CropLife International (#04966)
♦ Global Culinary Innovators Association (internationally oriented national body)
♦ Global Cultural Districts Network (unconfirmed)
♦ Global Cyber Alliance (internationally oriented national body)
♦ Global Cyber Security Capacity Centre (internationally oriented national body)
♦ Global Dairy Farmers (unconfirmed)

♦ Global Dairy Platform (GDP) 10314

Exec Dir 10255 West Higgins Rd, Ste 820, Rosemont IL 60018-5616, USA. T. +18476273388. Fax +18476273380. E-mail: info@globaldairyplatform.com.
URL: http://www.globaldairyplatform.com/

History 2006, Rosemont, IL (USA). Registration: 501(c)(6) organization, No/ID: EIN: 90-0768957, Start date: 2012, USA. **Aims** Connect CEOs, executives, and researchers to collaborate on issues affecting the demand for dairy. **Structure** Board of Directors; Communications and Scientific Advisory Board; Operational Committee. **Languages** English. **Staff** 4.00 FTE, paid. **Finance** Sources: members' dues. **Events** *Reporting session* Parma (Italy) 2011. **Publications** *GDP Newsletter* (4 a year). Annual Review; Annual Meeting Document; Membership brochure.

Members Representation in 19 countries:

Australia, Belgium, Brazil, Canada, Denmark, Germany, Ireland, Israel, Japan, Kenya, Korea Rep, Netherlands, New Zealand, Norway, South Africa, Sweden, Switzerland, UK, USA.

Consultative Status Consultative status granted from: *ECOSOC (#05331)* (Special); *UNEP (#20299).* **NGO Relations** Member of: *International Agri-Food Network (IAFN, #11599).* [2022/XJ2834/**C**]

♦ Global DARE Foundation 10315

Contact PO Box 865, Windham ME 04062, USA. E-mail: info@globaldarefoundation.org.
URL: https://www.defeatadultrefsumeverywhere.org/

History DARE stands for: Defeat Adult Refsum Everywhere. Registration: No/ID: EIN 84-3343395, USA. **Aims** Promote world-wide awareness and better quality of life for all who are diagnosed with Adult Refsum Disease. **Structure** Board of Directors; Medical and Scientific Advisory Board. **NGO Relations** Member of (2): *EURORDIS – Rare Diseases Europe (#09175)* (Associate); *Global Genes* (RARE Foundation Alliance). [2021/AA2346/**C**]

♦ Global Deaf Connection (internationally oriented national body)
♦ Global Democracy Initiative (internationally oriented national body)

♦ Global Dengue and Aedes-transmitted Diseases Consortium (GDAC) 10316

Chair Duke-NUS Medical School, 8 College Road, Singapore 169857, Singapore.
Dir Intl Vaccine Inst, SNU Research Park, 1 Gwanak-ro, Gwanak-gu, Seoul 08826, Korea Rep. E-mail: gdacinfo@ivi.int.
URL: http://www.preventdengue.org/

History 31 Aug 2016, Mexico City (Mexico), under a Consortium Agreement, signed by *International Vaccine Institute (IVI, #15839), International Vaccine Access Center (IVAC), Partnership for Dengue Control (PDC, #18232)* and *Sabin Vaccine Institute (Sabin).* **Aims** Promote development and implementation of innovative and synergistic approaches for prevention and control of dengue and other Aedes-transmitted diseases. **Structure** Consortium Management Committee; Technical Advisory Group; Secretariat. **Languages** English. **Finance** Foundations; industry. **Activities** Advocacy/lobbying/activism; capacity building; healthcare; networking/liaising; research and development; research/documentation.

Members Organizations (4):

Duke-NUS MEdical School (Duke-NUS); *International Vaccine Access Center (IVAC); International Vaccine Institute (IVI, #15839); Partnership for Dengue Control (PDC, #18232).*

IGO Relations *WHO (#20950).* [2019.02.18/XM5062/y/**C**]

♦ Global Design Network (unconfirmed)
♦ Global Developmental Corps (internationally oriented national body)
♦ Global Development and Environment Institute (internationally oriented national body)
♦ Global Development Group (internationally oriented national body)
♦ Global Development Incubator (unconfirmed)

♦ Global Development Learning Network (GDLN) 10317

Secretariat World Bank Inst, MSN J2-200, 1818 H St NW, Washington DC 20433, USA. T. +12024588196. Fax +12025222005. E-mail: gdln.global@gmail.com – hb_chang@kdischool.ac.kr – info@gdln.net.
URL: http://www.gdln.org/

History 21 Jun 2000, as an initiative of *World Bank Institute (WBI, #21220)*. Previously also referred to as *Global Distance Learning Network*. **Aims** As a partnership of public, private and non-governmental organizations, serve the developing world; work together to take advantage of the most modern technologies, build local capacity; share learning and knowledge; develop a global community dedicated to fighting poverty. **Structure** Small Secretariat at World Bank Institute. Regional Secretariat (4): *Association of African Distance Learning Centres (AADLC, #02354)*; Asia and Pacific; Europe and Central Asia; Latin America and the Caribbean. **Activities** Links locally-owned and operated distance learning centres with content from multiple suppliers. **Events** *Virtual Educa : international conference on education, training and new technologies* São José dos Campos (Brazil) 2007.
Members Affiliates (some 120 learning centres) in 78 countries:
Afghanistan, Albania, Angola, Argentina, Armenia, Australia, Bangladesh, Benin, Bolivia, Bosnia-Herzegovina, Brazil, Bulgaria, Burkina Faso, Chile, China, Colombia, Costa Rica, Côte d'Ivoire, Croatia, Dominican Rep, Ecuador, Egypt, El Salvador, Ethiopia, France, Ghana, Greece, Guatemala, Honduras, Hungary, India, Indonesia, Italy, Jamaica, Japan, Jordan, Kazakhstan, Kenya, Korea Rep, Kosovo, Kuwait, Lithuania, Madagascar, Mauritania, Mexico, Moldova, Mongolia, Morocco, Mozambique, Nepal, Netherlands, Nicaragua, North Macedonia, Palestine, Papua New Guinea, Paraguay, Peru, Philippines, Portugal, Romania, Russia, Saudi Arabia, Senegal, Serbia, Singapore, Slovenia, South Africa, Spain, Sri Lanka, Tanzania UR, Thailand, Timor-Leste, Türkiye, Ukraine, Uruguay, USA, Venezuela, Vietnam.
Included in the above, 7 organizations listed in this Yearbook:
Asian Institute of Management (AIM, #01518); *IHE Delft Institute for Water Education (#11110)*; *Inter-American Institute for Cooperation on Agriculture (IICA, #11434)*; *International Development Law Organization (IDLO, #13161)*; *International Institute of Management LINK (IIM LINK)*; *Islamic Development Bank (IsDB, #16044)*; *Middle East Technical University (METU)*. [2016/XF6129/y/F]

♦ Global Development Links / see Childreach International

♦ Global Development Network (GDN) 10318

Main Office 2nd Floor West Wing, ISID Complex, 4 Vasant Kunj Inst Area, Delhi 110070, DELHI 110070, India. T. +911143239494 – +911126139494. Fax +911126136893. E-mail: communications@gdn.int.
URL: http://www.gdn.int/

History Dec 1999, as a public international organization, upon an agreement signed by representatives of (6) countries: Colombia; Egypt; India; Italy; Senegal; Sri Lanka. **Aims** Support researchers in developing and *transition countries* in generating and sharing applied *social science* research so as to advance social and economic development. **Structure** Board of 18 members. President. Headquarters in Delhi (India). Regional offices in Cairo (Egypt) and Washington DC (USA). **Finance** Support from: *Australian Aid (inactive)*; *Bill and Melinda Gates Foundation (BMGF)*; *Department for International Development (DFID, inactive)*; *Development Bank of Latin America (CAF, #05055)*; *Inter-American Development Bank (IDB, #11427)*; *International Bank for Reconstruction and Development (IBRD, #12317)*; *International Development Research Centre (IDRC, #13162)*; *Open Society Foundations (OSF, #17763)*; governments of Australia, France, Japan, Luxembourg, Netherlands. **Activities** Research/deocumentation; capacity building; awards/prizes/competitions; events/meetings. **Events** *Annual Conference* Lima (Peru) 2016, *Annual Conference* Accra (Ghana) 2014, *Annual Conference* Budapest (Hungary) 2012, *Annual Conference* Bogota (Colombia) 2011, *Annual conference* Prague (Czech Rep) 2010. **Publications** *Research Monitor*. Working Paper Series. Annual Report; books; policy briefs.
Information Services *GDNet Knowledge Services*.
Members Full in 4 countries:
Colombia, India, Spain, Sri Lanka.
IGO Relations Partners: *European Commission (EC, #06633)*; *OECD (#17693)*; *UNDP (#20292)*; *World Bank Institute (WBI, #21220)*.
NGO Relations Regional Network Partners:
– *African Economic Research Consortium (AERC, #00292)*; *Bureau for Research and Economic Analysis of Development (BREAD, #03373)*; *Central and Eastern European Regional Network (CERGE-EI)*; *East Asian Development Network (EADN, #05202)*; *Economic Research Forum (ERF, #05318)*; Economics Education and Research Consortium (EERC), Moscow (Russia); *European Development Research Network (EUDN, #06915)*; GDN-Japan; *Latin American and Caribbean Economics Association (LACEA, #16274)*; *Oceania Development Network (ODN, #17660)*; *South Asian Network of Economic Institutes*.
Hosts: *International Initiative for Impact Evaluation (3ie, #13851)*. Partners include:
– *Andes University (ULA)*; *Baltic-Nordic Minority Youth Network (no recent information)*; *Deutsches Institut für Entwicklungspolitik (DIE)*; *Institute of Development Studies, Brighton (IDS)*; *International Economic Association (IEA, #13222)*; *International Political Science Association (IPSA, #14615)*; *Japan International Cooperation Agency Ogata Sadako Research Institute for Peace and Development*; *Partnership for African Social and Governance Research (PASGR, #18230)*; *UNU World Institute for Development Economics Research (UNU-WIDER, #20722)*; *Wiener Institut für Internationale Wirtschaftsvergleiche (WIIW)*. [2017/XF5960/F]

♦ Global Development Research Centre (internationally oriented national body)

♦ Global Diagnostic Imaging, Healthcare IT, and Radiation Therapy Trade Association (DITTA) 10319

Main Office c/o COCIR, BluePoint Brussels, Bd A Reyers 80, 1030 Brussels, Belgium. E-mail: press@globalditta.org.
URL: http://globalditta.org/

History Officially incorporated 2012, as a non-profit association, registered in accordance with US law. **Aims** Act as one global voice for diagnostic imaging, radiation therapy, healthcare IT, electromedical and radiopharmaceutical manufacturers to better communicate, coordinate and collaborate on matters of common interest between participating associations and member companies so as to more effectively work with policymakers, organizations, professional associations and stakeholders at global level. **Structure** Chair; Vice-Chairs; Secretariat.
Members Organizations in 8 countries:
Brazil, Canada, China, Japan, Korea Rep, Russia, Thailand, USA.
Regional member:
European Coordination Committee of the Radiological, Electromedical Healthcare IT Industry (COCIR, #06792).
Consultative Status Consultative status granted from: *WHO (#20950)* (Official). [2020/XM5091/t/C]

♦ Global Dialogue (internationally oriented national body)
♦ Global Dialogue – for human rights and social change / see Global Dialogue
♦ Global Dialogue Institute / see Dialogue Institute

♦ Global Diaspora Confederation (GDC) 10320

Contact address not obtained. E-mail: virtual.reception@theglobaldiaspora.org.
URL: https://www.theglobaldiaspora.org/

History Jul 2020. Concept initiated Apr 2020, following the first Global Virtual Diaspora Exchange organized by *International Organization for Migration (IOM, #14454)*. Founded after it convened over 230 diaspora organizations from over 100 countries to publish a joint statement in solidarity with victims affected by xenophobia and discriminations. Registration: Handelsregister, No/ID: KVK 84850736, Netherlands. **Aims** Unify, support, develop and promote diaspora organizations across the world. **Structure** General Assembly; Council; Board of Trustees; Secretariat; Fellows. Departments (5): Administration; Marketing; Project; Human Resources; Healthcare. **Activities** Advocacy/lobbying/activism; awards/prizes/competitions; awareness raising; capacity building; certification/accreditation; events/meetings; guidance/assistance/consulting; humanitarian/emergency aid; knowledge management/information dissemination; networking/liaising; projects/programmes; research and development; research/documentation; standards/guidelines. **Members** Full and Associate – for diaspora organizations; non-member affiliates – for individuals and non-diaspora organziations. Membership countries not specified. [2022.10.13/AA2586/F]

♦ Global Digital Foundation (unconfirmed)
♦ Global Diplomacy Lab (internationally oriented national body)

♦ Global Diplomatic Forum (GDF) 10321

CEO 9th Floor, 6 Mitre Passage, Peninsula Square, London, SE10 0ER, UK. T. +442088533293. E-mail: enquiries@gdforum.org.
URL: http://www.gdforum.org/

Aims Facilitate the global exchange of ideas and knowledge; build bridges for understanding and cooperation. **Structure** Leadership Board; Advisory Board. **Activities** Advocacy/lobbying/activism; events/meetings; networking/liaising; training/education. **Events** *Young Diplomats Forum* London (UK) 2022, *Young Diplomats Forum* Brussels (Belgium) 2019, *Young Diplomats Forum* London (UK) 2019, *Young Diplomats Forum* Kuala Lumpur (Malaysia) 2018, *Young Diplomats Forum* London (UK) 2018. [2020.03.11/XM7975/F]

♦ Global Disaster Alert and Coordination System (GDACS) 10322

Secretariat address not obtained. E-mail: coordination@gdacs.org – secretariat@gdacs.org.
URL: http://portal.gdacs.org/

History A cooperation framework under the *United Nations (UN, #20515)* umbrella. **Aims** Provide alerts and impact estimations after major disasters through a multi-hazard disaster impact assessment service. **Structure** Advisory Group; Activation and Coordination Support Unit (ACSU) within *United Nations Office for the Coordination of Humanitarian Affairs (OCHA, #20593)* Geneva (Switzerland). serves as Secretariat. **Finance** Support from: *ECHO (inactive)*. **Activities** Guidance/assistance/consulting; standards/guidelines; knowledge management/information dissemination.
Members Founding partners (3):
Joint Research Centre (JRC, #16147); *United Nations Institute for Training and Research (UNITAR, #20576)* (UNOSAT); *United Nations Office for the Coordination of Humanitarian Affairs (OCHA, #20593)*.
NGO Relations Partners include: *Pacific Disaster Center (PDC)*. [2015/XJ9504/F*]

♦ Global Disaster Information Network (GDIN) 10323

Exec Dir Ste 201, 26128 Talamore Dr, South Riding VA 20152, USA. T. +12026475070. Fax +12026474628.
URL: http://www.gdin.org/

History 1998, following discussions between representatives of the UN, the EC and the UK. A voluntary association of nations, organizations and individuals. Registered in accordance with USA law. **Aims** Reduce impact of natural and technological disasters through better application of *information technology* to disaster management. **Structure** Executive Committee, comprising Chair and 6 members. Committees (11): Funding; GIS/Remote Sensing; Industry; Infectious Diseases; Information Facilitator; NGOs; Policy; Standards; Telecommunications; Peace Wing Pilot Project; Conference. Working Groups. Secretariat in South Riding VA (USA). **Activities** Main project: Standing Committee on Native American Disaster Information Needs. **Events** *IDRC : regional international disaster reduction conference* Harbin (China) 2007, *IDRC : international disaster reduction conference* Davos (Switzerland) 2006, *Conference* Washington, DC (USA) 2004, *International conference* Washington, DC (USA) 2003, *International conference* Rome (Italy) 2002. **NGO Relations** Partners: *Disaster Preparedness and Emergency Response Association, International (DERA International)*; *International Association of Emergency Managers (IAEM)*; national institutes and organizations. [2008/XF6539/F]

♦ Global Disaster Resilience Centre (internationally oriented national body)
♦ Global Disinformation Index (unconfirmed)
♦ Global Distance Learning Network / see Global Development Learning Network (#10317)
♦ Global Diversity Foundation (internationally oriented national body)

♦ Global Doctors for Choice (GDC) 10324

Exec Dir 1430 Broadway, Ste 1416, New York NY 10018, USA. E-mail: info@globaldoctorsforchoice.org.
URL: http://globaldoctorsforchoice.org/

History 2007. **Aims** Promote and defend women's *reproductive rights*; expand access to reproductive health services. **Structure** Board of Managers; Action Centers; Coordinating Team. **Languages** English, Spanish. **Finance** Foundations; individual donors. **Activities** Advocacy/lobbying/activism; events/meetings; training/education. Active in: Brazil, Colombia, Ghana, Mexico, South Africa.
Members Physicians (about 125) in 25 countries. Membership countries not specified. Partner organizations in 6 countries:
Partner organizations in 6 countries:
Brazil, Colombia, Ghana, Ireland, Mexico, South Africa. [2022/XJ7895/C]

♦ Global Doll Society (unconfirmed)

♦ Global Dressage Foundation 10325

Contact Koestraat 9, 5095 BD Hooge Mierde, Netherlands.
URL: https://www.globaldressageforum.com/global-dressage-foundation

History 7 Jul 2012. Registration: KVK, No/ID: 55934404, Netherlands. **Aims** Organize an annual meeting, the Global Dressage Forum. **Structure** Board. [2020/AA1188/cf/F]

♦ Global Dryland Alliance (GDA) 10326

Alliance Mondiale des Terres Arides

Exec Dir Onaiza, Zone 66, St 826 Villa 50, PO Box 22043, Doha, Qatar. T. +97440377200. Fax +97440377202. E-mail: info@globaldrylandalliance.com.
URL: http://www.globaldrylandalliance.org/

History Initial documents for establishment drafted 2011. Founding conference, 15 Oct 2017, Doha (Qatar), when foundation treaty was signed. An initiative of Sheikh Tamim bin Hamad Al Thani, Emir of State of Qatar. Former names and other names: *Making Drylands Food Secure* – alias. **Aims** Make dryland countries food secure and contribute to stability and peace in the world; work with local, regional, and international partners to identify, disseminate, and implement solutions for agricultural, water, and energy challenges of dryland countries. **Structure** Executive Council; Secretariat. **Languages** Arabic, English, French. **Activities** Events/meetings; knowledge management/information dissemination; research/documentation. **Events** *Founding Conference* Doha (Qatar) 2017.
Members Founding governments (11):
Benin, Burkina Faso, Guinea, Guinea-Bissau, Iraq, Mali, Morocco, Qatar, Senegal, Tanzania UR, Tunisia.
IGO Relations *African Development Bank (ADB, #00283)*; *Asian Development Bank (ADB, #01422)*; *Comité permanent inter-Etats de lutte contre la sécheresse dans le Sahel (CILSS, #04195)*; *FAO (#09260)*; *International Bank for Reconstruction and Development (IBRD, #12317)* (World Bank); *Islamic Development Bank (IsDB, #16044)*; *World Food Programme (WFP, #21510)*. **NGO Relations** *International Center for Biosaline Agriculture (ICBA, #12468)*. [2020.09.09/XM6164/D*]

♦ Global Dry Toilet Association of Finland (internationally oriented national body)
♦ Global Dry Toilet Club / see Global Dry Toilet Association of Finland

♦ Global Earthquake Model Foundation (GEM Foundation) 10327

SG Via Ferrata 1, 27100 Pavia PV, Italy. E-mail: info@globalquakemodel.org.
URL: http://www.globalquakemodel.org/

History 2009, Pavia (Italy). **Aims** Provide organizations and people with tools and resources for transparent assessment of earthquake risk anywhere in the world. **Structure** Governing Board; Scientific Board, Executive Committee; Secretariat, headed by Secretary-General. **Consultative Status** Consultative status granted from: *ECOSOC (#05331)* (Special). **IGO Relations** Participates in: *Group on Earth Observations (GEO, #10735)*. **NGO Relations** Member of (1): *Global Alliance of Disaster Research Institutes (GADRI, #10194)*. [2013/XJ7139/f/F]

♦ Global Ecolabelling Network (GEN) 10328

Secretariat PO Box 1807, Canberra ACT 2601, Australia. T. +61251102202. E-mail: gensecretariat@gmail.com – secretariat@globalecolabelling.net.
URL: http://www.globalecolabelling.net/

History 1994. Former names and other names: *International Eco-Labelling Committee* – former. **Aims** Improve, promote and develop ecolabelling of products and services around the world. **Structure** Board; Chair; Secretariat. **Languages** English. **Finance** Sources: members' dues. **Activities** Awareness raising; events/meetings; knowledge management/information dissemination; networking/liaising; standards/guidelines. **Events** *Annual General Meeting* 2020, *Annual General Meeting* Beijing (China) 2019, *Annual General Meeting* Berlin (Germany) 2018, *Annual General Meeting* Stockholm (Sweden) 2017, *Annual General Meeting* Kiev (Ukraine) 2016. **Publications** *GEN Magazine*; *GEN News*. Annual Report.
Members Type 1 ecolabelling organizations (27) representing over 50 countries. Members in 22 countries and territories:
Australia, Brazil, Canada, China, Germany, Hong Kong, India, Indonesia, Israel, Japan, Kazakhstan, Korea Rep, Malaysia, New Zealand, Philippines, Russia, Singapore, Sweden, Taiwan, Thailand, Ukraine, USA.
Included in the above, 2 organizations listed in this Yearbook:
European Commission (EC, #06633); *Nordic Swan Ecolabel (#17441)* (representing the 5).
Associate members in 8 countries:

Colombia, Indonesia, Netherlands, South Africa, Sri Lanka, Türkiye, USA, Vietnam.
Affiliate members include the following 2 organizations listed in this Yearbook:
International Green Purchasing Network (IGPN, #13736); ISEAL (#16026).
NGO Relations In liaison with technical committees of: *International Green Purchasing Network (IGPN, #13736); International Organization for Standardization (ISO, #14473); ISEAL (#16026).* [2022/XF4420/F]

♦ Global Economist Forum (GEF) 10329

Pres 62/1 Purana Paltan, Dhaka 1000, Bangladesh. T. +88029558318 – +88029558319. Fax +88029564091. E-mail: info@globaleconomistforum.org – president@globaleconomistforum.org.
Vice-Pres address not obtained.
URL: http://www.globaleconomistforum.org/

History 1904, London (UK). **Aims** Formulate global economic policy, alignment of wealth and facilities for all the citizens of every member states. **Structure** Executive Committee; Advisory Committee. **Languages** English. **Staff** 34.00 FTE, paid; 2200.00 FTE, voluntary. **Finance** Sources: donations. Supported by: *Asian Development Bank (ADB, #01422); International Bank for Reconstruction and Development (IBRD, #12317)* (World Bank); *International Monetary Fund (IMF, #14180); Islamic Development Bank (IsDB, #16044).* **Activities** Events/meetings; training/education. **Events** *World Economic and Sports Conference* Corfu (Greece) 2017, *World Economic and Sports Conference* Baroda (India) 2016. **Publications** *GEF Newsletter* (12 a year). Annual Report; Annual Research Book; Yearbook. **Members** Full in 104 countries. Membership countries not specified. **Consultative Status** Consultative status granted from: *ECOSOC (#05331)* (General).
[2022.05.09/XJ9771/F]

♦ Global Ecotourism Network (GEN) 10330

Sec address not obtained. E-mail: info@globalecotourismnetwork.org.
URL: http://www.globalecotourismnetwork.org/

History 2015. Set up by entire former advisory committee for *The International Ecotourism Society (TIES, #13225).* **Aims** Bring the world's regional and national ecotourism associations, networks and destinations, together with indigenous and rural peoples, global operators, professionals and academics, to grow the industry, provide advocacy, encourage through leadership and innovation, and add greater authenticity to ecotourism. **Structure** Executive Board. **Languages** English. **Activities** Advocacy/lobbying/activism; guidance/assistance/consulting; knowledge management/information dissemination; networking/liaising.
Members Ecotourism networks in 96 countries and territories:
Albania, Argentina, Armenia, Australia, Bangladesh, Belgium, Belize, Bhutan, Bolivia, Botswana, Brazil, Bulgaria, Cambodia, Cameroon, Canada, Chile, China, Colombia, Costa Rica, Côte d'Ivoire, Croatia, Cyprus, Denmark, Ecuador, Egypt, Ethiopia, Finland, France, Gambia, Georgia, Germany, Ghana, Greece, Guyana, Honduras, Hungary, India, Indonesia, Iran Islamic Rep, Ireland, Israel, Jamaica, Japan, Jordan, Kenya, Korea Rep, Kosovo, Laos, Lebanon, Madagascar, Malawi, Mexico, Mongolia, Montenegro, Morocco, Mozambique, Myanmar, Namibia, Nepal, Netherlands, New Zealand, Nigeria, Norway, Pakistan, Panama, Papua New Guinea, Peru, Philippines, Poland, Portugal, Puerto Rico, Romania, Russia, Rwanda, Serbia, Singapore, Slovakia, Slovenia, South Africa, Spain, Sri Lanka, Sweden, Switzerland, Taiwan, Tanzania UR, Thailand, Tunisia, Türkiye, Uganda, UK, Ukraine, United Arab Emirates, USA, Venezuela, Vietnam, Zimbabwe.
Regional networks (6):
African Ecotourism Network (AFEN); *Asian Ecotourism Network (AEN, #01433);* European Ecotourism Network (EEN); Latin American and Caribbean Ecotourism Network (LACEN); Middle East Ecotourism Network (MEEN); North America Ecotourism Network (NAEN). [2022.03.09/XM7024/F]

♦ Global Eco-Village Network / see Global Ecovillage Network (#10331)

♦ Global Ecovillage Network (GEN) 10331

Office Manager address not obtained. T. +441309692194. E-mail: welcome@ecovillage.org.
URL: http://ecovillage.org/

History Jun 1994, Denmark. Founded following initiatives of *Gaia Trust, Denmark.* Regional secretariats instituted during International Conference on Eco-Villages and Sustainable Communities, 1995, Findhorn (UK); inaugurated at UN Habitat Conference, Jun 1996, Istanbul (Turkey). Previously also written as *Global Eco-Village Network.* Also referred to as *GEN International.* Took over activities from *Earth Village Network (EVN, inactive).* Registration: Charity Commission, No/ID: SC043796, Start date: 19 Feb 2013, Scotland. **Aims** Serve as an umbrella organization for ecovillages, transition town initiatives, intentional communities and *ecologically*-minded individuals worldwide. **Structure** Network Steward Circle; Board of Directors. Regional networks: GEN-Africa; *Global Ecovillage Network – Europe (GEN Europe, #10332); Consejo de Asentamientos Sustentables de América Latina (CASA LATINA); GEN North America (GENNA); Global Ecovillage Network Oceania and Asia (GENOA);* NextGEN (Youth arm of the Global Ecovillage Network). Also includes: *Baltic Ecovillage Network (BEN, #03114).* **Languages** English, French, German, Italian, Polish, Portuguese, Russian, Spanish. **Staff** 10.00 FTE, paid; 1.00 FTE, voluntary. **Finance** Sources: donations; grants; sale of products. **Activities** Advocacy/lobbying/activism; events/meetings; guidance/assistance/consulting; networking/liaising; training/education. **Events** *Patterns and Practices of Regenerative Education* 2022, *Conference* Somogyvámos (Hungary) 2012, *Representatives meeting* Denmark 1998, *International congress* Alessano (Italy) 1996. **Publications** *Ecovillage Living* (periodical). **Information Services** *Global Ecovillage Information Service* – on WorldWideWeb (600 pages).
Members Ecovillages and related initiatives and individuals in 88 countries and territories:
Algeria, Argentina, Armenia, Australia, Austria, Bahamas, Bangladesh, Belarus, Belgium, Belize, Bolivia, Brazil, Bulgaria, Burkina Faso, Canada, Chile, China, Colombia, Costa Rica, Croatia, Cuba, Cyprus, Czechia, Denmark, Dominica, Dominican Rep, Ecuador, Egypt, El Salvador, Fiji, Finland, France, Germany, Ghana, Greece, Guatemala, Guinea, Honduras, Hungary, Iceland, India, Indonesia, Ireland, Israel, Italy, Jamaica, Japan, Kenya, Korea Rep, Laos, Lesotho, Luxembourg, Malaysia, Maldives, Mali, Mexico, Netherlands, New Zealand, Nicaragua, Norway, Pakistan, Palestine, Panama, Peru, Philippines, Poland, Portugal, Puerto Rico, Romania, Russia, Senegal, Serbia, Slovakia, Slovenia, South Africa, Spain, Sri Lanka, Sweden, Switzerland, Taiwan, Thailand, Türkiye, UK, Ukraine, Uruguay, USA, Venezuela, Vietnam.
Included in the above, 1 organization listed in this Yearbook:
Findhorn Foundation (#09774).
Ecovillage Networks in 47 countries and territories:
Argentina, Australia, Bangladesh, Belgium, Belize, Bolivia, Brazil, Canada, Chile, Colombia, Czechia, Denmark, Ecuador, Egypt, Finland, France, Germany, Greece, Guinea, Hungary, India, Indonesia, Israel, Italy, Japan, Korea Rep, Mexico, New Zealand, Norway, Pakistan, Palestine, Peru, Poland, Portugal, Puerto Rico, Russia, Senegal, South Africa, Spain, Sri Lanka, Sweden, Switzerland, Türkiye, UK, Uruguay, USA, Venezuela.
Consultative Status Consultative status granted from: *ECOSOC (#05331)* (Special); *UNEP (#20299).* **IGO Relations** Cooperates with (2): *Global Action Plan for Environment and Development in the 21st Century (Agenda 21, inactive); United Nations Institute for Training and Research (UNITAR, #20576).* **NGO Relations** Member of (4): *Conference of Non-Governmental Organizations in Consultative Relationship with the United Nations (CONGO, #04635); European Network for Community-Led Initiatives on Climate Change and Sustainability (ECOLISE, #07882); NGO Forum on Environment (FOE, #17125); Wellbeing Economy Alliance (WEAll, #20856).* Cooperates with (2): *Eco Earth Alliance (no recent information); Economy for the Common Good (ECG, #05323).* [2022.03.04/XF3890/F]

♦ Global Ecovillage Network – Europe (GEN Europe) 10332

Contact Ökodorf Sieben Linden, Sieben Linden 1, 38486 Beetzendorf, Germany. E-mail: info@gen-europe.org.
URL: http://www.gen-europe.org/

History Founded 1995, Findhorn (UK), as *EVEN – Eco-Village European Network,* during International Conference on Eco-Villages and Sustainable Communities; inaugurated at UN Habitat Conference, Jun 1996, Istanbul (Turkey). An autonomous regional network within the framework of *Global Ecovillage Network (GEN, #10331).* Also previously referred to as *GEN-Europe (GEN-E).* Registered in accordance with German law. **Aims** Assert the primacy of community, active citizenship and solidarity at the heart of all models for *sustainability*, giving equal weight to four core dimensions of sustainability – the economic, the ecological, the social and culture – as being mutually reinforcing, each essential to sustainable community development that truly meets the needs of people and the planet. **Structure** General Assembly. **Staff** 1.00 FTE, paid. **Finance** Members' dues. Other sources: conference fees; GAIA Trust; foundations; EU funding programmes. Budget (annual): about euro 500,000. **Activities** Networking/liaising; events/meetings; training/education; knowledge management/information dissemination; advocacy/lobbying/activism. **Events** *Summit* Findhorn (UK) 2015, *General Assembly* Germany 2015, *GEN-Europe Conference* Belzig (Germany) 2014, *General Assembly* Switzerland 2013, *General Assembly* Hungary 2012.
Members Ecovillages and ecovillage initiatives, and national/regional networks of ecovillages, in 28 countries:
Armenia, Austria, Belgium, Denmark, Estonia, Finland, France, Germany, Hungary, Iceland, Ireland, Israel, Italy, Latvia, Moldova, Netherlands, Norway, Portugal, Romania, Russia, Slovakia, Slovenia, Spain, Sweden, Switzerland, Türkiye, UK, Ukraine.
Also in the Baltic Sea Region. Membership countries not specified.
IGO Relations Cooperates with: *United Nations Institute for Training and Research (UNITAR, #20576).* **NGO Relations** Member of: *Eco Earth Alliance (no recent information); European Network for Community-Led Initiatives on Climate Change and Sustainability (ECOLISE, #07882).* [2014.12.08/XK1370/E]

♦ Global Educational Initiative For Nigeria (internationally oriented national body)
♦ Global Education Centre (internationally oriented national body)

♦ Global Education Cluster 10333

Coordinator address not obtained. E-mail: mgiordano@unicef.org – educationclusterunit@gmail.com.
Coordinator address not obtained.
URL: http://educationcluster.net/

History Set up as an open formal forum for coordination and collaboration on education in emergencies. **Aims** Ensure predictable, well coordinated and equitable provision of education for populations affected by humanitarian crises. **Structure** Education Cluster Unit; Working Group; country level Education Clusters. **Activities** Advocacy/lobbying/activism.
Members Global Partners; Associates. Global partners include 15 organizations listed in this Yearbook:
Catholic Relief Services (CRS, #03608); Finn Church Aid (FCA); Global Partnership for Education (GPE, #10531); Inter-agency Network for Education in Emergencies (INEE, #11387); International Institute for Educational Planning (IIEP, #13874); International Rescue Committee (IRC, #14717); Norwegian Refugee Council (NRC); Plan International (#18386); Save the Children International (#19058); UNESCO (#20322); UNHCR (#20327); UNICEF (#20332); Universal Human Rights Network; World Vision International (WVI, #21904); World Wide Education Project (WWEP).
NGO Relations Member of: *Inter-agency Network for Education in Emergencies (INEE, #11387).*
[2016/XM5009/y/F]

♦ Global Education Conference 10334

Address not obtained.
URL: http://www.globaleducationconference.org/

History Set up as a collaborative, world-wide community initiative. **Aims** Increase opportunities for building education-related connections around the globe while supporting cultural awareness, recognition of diversity, and educational access for all. **Structure** Global Advisory Board; Leadership Team. **Activities** Events/meetings. **NGO Relations** *Center for International Virtual Schooling (IVECA); Global Education Network Europe (GENE, #10337); Global Online Academy (GOA); Global STEM Education Center; International Research and Exchanges Board (IREX); Know My World (KMW); Taking IT Global (TIG).* [2017/XM6775/c/F]

♦ Global Education and Development (internationally oriented national body)
♦ Global Education for European Engineers and Entrepreneurs / see Global Education: Exchanges for Engineers and Entrepreneurs (#10335)

♦ Global Education: Exchanges for Engineers and Entrepreneurs (Ge4) 10335

President at IMT Mines Albi, Campus Jarlard, 81000 Albi Cedex 09, France. T. +33563493002. E-mail: info@ge4.org.
URL: http://www.ge4.org/

History 1996. Former names and other names: *Global Education for European Engineers and Entrepreneurs (GE4)* – former. Registration: SIREN, No/ID: 884 763 178, France. **Aims** Contribute to a mutual understanding between diverse cultures; stimulate education and personal development of young academics in an open and friendly environment. **Structure** International Advisory Board; Executive Board. **Languages** English, French, German, Spanish. **Staff** Voluntary. **Activities** Events/meetings; networking/liaising; training/education. **Events** *America-Europe global engineering meeting* Tampere (Finland) 2004. **Publications** *Best of Ge4* – newsletter. [2022.11.23/XJ4504/F]

♦ Global Education Fund (internationally oriented national body)

♦ Global Education Motivators (GEM) 10336

Pres c/o Chestnut Hill College, 9601 Germantown Ave, Philadelphia PA 19118-2695, USA. T. +12152481150. Fax +12152487056. E-mail: gem@chc.edu.
URL: http://www.gem-ngo.org/

History 1981, USA. Founded by Wayne Jacoby. Registration: USA. **Aims** Meet the complex needs of bringing the world into the classroom. **Structure** Board. **Activities** Awards/prizes/competitions; training/education; meeting activities. **Consultative Status** Consultative status granted from: *ECOSOC (#05331)* (Special). **IGO Relations** Associated with Department of Global Communications of the United Nations. **NGO Relations** Member of: *United Nations Academic Impact (UNAI, #20516).* [2020/XG5825/F]

♦ Global Education Network Europe (GENE) 10337

Registered Address Piet Heinkade 181H, 1019 HC Amsterdam, Netherlands. E-mail: ditta.dolejsiova@gene.eu.
URL: http://www.gene.eu/

History 2001. Registered in accordance with Dutch law: 34291232. **Aims** Support national structures in their work of improving quality and increasing provision of Global Education in Europe. **Structure** Board; Secretariat. **Languages** English. **Staff** 5-10 paid. **Finance** Members' dues. Funding from: *European Commission (EC, #06633).* **Activities** Networking/liaising; politics/policy/regulatory; guidance/assistance/consulting; events/meetings; publishing activities; awards/prizes/competitions; research/documentation. **Events** *Round Table* Brussels (Belgium) 2018, *Round Table* Oslo (Norway) 2018. **Publications** *The State of Global Education in Europe* (2018). National reports; policy briefings; brochures.
Members Ministries, agencies and other national bodies in the field of education. Members in 26 countries:
Austria, Belgium, Cyprus, Czechia, Denmark, Estonia, Finland, France, Germany, Greece, Ireland, Italy, Latvia, Lithuania, Luxembourg, Malta, Norway, Poland, Portugal, Romania, Slovakia, Slovenia, Spain, Sweden, Switzerland, UK.
Included in the above, 9 organizations listed in this Yearbook:
Agencia Española de Cooperación Internacional para el Desarrollo (AECID); Austrian Development Agency (ADA); Czech Development Agency (CzDA); Department for International Development (DFID, inactive); Deutsche Gesellschaft für Internationale Zusammenarbeit (GIZ); Enabel; Irish Aid; Nationale Commissie voor Internationale Samenwerking en Duurzame Ontwikkeling (NCDO); Norwegian Agency for Development Cooperation (Norad).
IGO Relations *Council of Europe (CE, #04881); OECD (#17693); UNESCO (#20322).*
[2018.10.11/XJ6029/y/F]

♦ Global Educators Network Inc. 10338

Pres 23/12 Prap Traichak Road, Muang, Phitsanulok, 65000, Thailand. T. +66801210087. E-mail: info@gentefl.org – gentefl15@gmail.com.
Exec Treas Apt 2, Brown House, Philippine Nazarene College, Pico Road, 2601 La Trinidad BEN, Philippines. T. +6309499088159.
URL: http://www.gentefl.org/

History 15 Dec 2014, Thailand. Former names and other names: *Global Educators Network Association of Teachers of English as a Foreign Language (GEN TEFL)* – former (2014 to 2021). Registration: Security and Exchange Commission, No/ID: 2022010037910-25, Start date: 10 Jan 2022, Philippines, CAR. **Aims** Create an innovating, connecting and mentoring atmosphere between educators. **Structure** Executive Board; Board of Advisors; Board of Directors; Editorial Board; Committees. **Languages** Chinese, English, Filipino, Indonesian, Irish Gaelic, Japanese, Polish, Russian, Thai, Vietnamese. **Staff** 30.00 FTE, voluntary. **Finance** Sources: in-kind support; members' dues; revenue from activities/projects. Annual budget: 10,000 THB (2020). **Activities** Awareness raising; events/meetings; guidance/assistance/consulting; knowledge management/information dissemination; networking/liaising; publishing activities; research/documentation; training/education. Active in: China, Indonesia, Jamaica, Malaysia, New Zealand, Philippines, Poland, Thailand, USA, Vietnam. **Events** *GEN TEFL International Conference* Danang (Vietnam) 2023, *GEN TEFL International Conference* Bangkok (Thailand) 2022, *International Education Conference* Bangkok (Thailand) 2022, *GEN TEFL International Conference* Bangkok (Thailand) 2021, *International Conference* Ho Chi Minh City (Vietnam) 2021. **Publications** *GEN TEFL Journal* in English; *Reflection – Official Bulletin* in English. *Book Of Abstracts* in English.

Members Full (25); Associate (371); Junior (15). Members in 32 countries and territories:
Algeria, Australia, Cambodia, Canada, China, India, Indonesia, Iran Islamic Rep, Iraq, Ireland, Israel, Jamaica, Japan, Jordan, Korea Rep, Laos, Malaysia, Mexico, Myanmar, Nepal, New Zealand, Philippines, Poland, Puerto Rico, Russia, South Africa, Sri Lanka, Thailand, UK, United Arab Emirates, USA, Vietnam.
IGO Relations Cooperates with (1): Department of Education Philippines. **NGO Relations** Affiliated with (1): *International Association of Teachers of English as a Foreign Language (IATEFL, #12222)*. Memorandum of Understanding with: Junior Chamber International, Bauang Fruit Basket Chapter (JCI BFB, Philippines).
[2022.01.13/XM5074/F]

♦ Global Educators Network Association of Teachers of English as a Foreign Language / see Global Educators Network Inc. (#10338)
♦ Global Elders / see The Elders Foundation (#05413)
♦ Global Embassy of Activists for Peace (unconfirmed)

♦ Global Emergency Medical Net (GEMNET) 10339

Pres Centre Médico Chirurgical, Rue Moxouris 21, 78150 Le Chesnay, France.
URL: http://www.gemnet.ch/
History Jan 2001, as *Urgences sans frontières*. Registered in accordance with French law. **Aims** Create an International Emergency Medical Team to give a rapid response in case of natural disaster in less than 24 hours. [2011/XJ4973/F]

♦ Global Empowerment Movement (internationally oriented national body)

♦ Global Enabling Sustainability Initiative (GeSI) 10340

Dir c/o Scotland House, Rond Point Schuman 6, 1040 Brussels, Belgium. T. +3222828442. Fax +3222828414. E-mail: info@gesi.org.
URL: http://www.gesi.org/
History 2001. Founded by a number of major ICT companies. Former names and other names: *Global e-Sustainability Initiative* – former. **Aims** Be a leading source of impartial information, resources and best practices for achieving integrated social and environmental sustainability through ICT. **Structure** Board; Management. Working Groups. **Languages** English. **Activities** Knowledge management/information dissemination. **Members** Service providers and vendors. Membership countries not specified. **IGO Relations** Partners include: *International Telecommunication Union (ITU, #15673)*; *UNEP (#20299)*; *United Nations Framework Convention on Climate Change (UNFCCC, 1992)*. **NGO Relations** Partner of: *Responsible Business Alliance (RBA)*; *World Business Council for Sustainable Development (WBCSD, #21254)*; *World Green Building Council (WorldGBC, #21544)*; *World Resources Forum Association (WRFA, #21752)*; *World Resources Institute (WRI, #21753)*. Member of: *Climate Technology Centre and Network (CTCN, #04023)*.
[2020.05.06/XJ4507/E]

♦ Global Energy Balance Network (unconfirmed)

♦ Global Energy Initiative 10341

Dir 866 UN Plaza, Ste 471, New York NY 10017, USA. T. +12125748138. Fax +16464762495. E-mail: info@globalenergyinitiative.org.
URL: http://globalenergyinitiative.org/
History Registered in the State of New York (USA). **Aims** Promote sustainable energy for all, fighting energy poverty, protecting the *environment*, and mitigating the effects of *climate change*. **Activities** Events/meetings; knowledge management/information dissemination; advocacy/lobbying/activism. **Consultative Status** Consultative status granted from: *ECOSOC (#05331)* (Special). [2017/XM6188/F]

♦ Global Energy Interconnection Development and Cooperation Organization (GEIDCO) 10342

Contact No 8 Xuanwumennei Str, Xicheng District, 100031 Beijing, China. T. +861063415760. Fax +861066598554. E-mail: info@geidco.org.
European Representative Office Markgrafenstr 34, 10117 Berlin, Germany.
URL: http://www.geidco.org/html/qqnycoen/index.html
History 2016, China. Registered in accordance with Chinese laws. **Aims** Promote the establishment of a GEI system; meet the global demand for electricity in a clean and green way; implement the United Nations "Sustainable Energy for All" and climate change initiatives; serve the sustainable development of humanity. **Structure** General Meeting; Council; Advisory Board. General Office. Committees (3): Economy and Law Professional; Clean Energy Professional; Strong and Smart Grid Professional. Bureaus (3): Development; Economic Information; General Affairs. Offices (7): Japan; Russia; Australia; Africa; Europe; South America; North America. **Languages** Chinese, English. **Staff** 70.00 FTE, paid; 100.00 FTE, voluntary. **Finance** Sources: donations; members' dues; revenue from activities/projects. Annual budget: about Chines Yuan 21,000,000. **Activities** Research and development. Active in: Australia, Brazil, China, France, Germany, Japan, Korea DPR, Russia, South Africa, UK, USA. **Events** *Global Energy Interconnection Asia Conference* Beijing (China) 2020, *Global Grid Forum* Vancouver, BC (Canada) 2019, *International Conference* Beijing (China) 2018, *African Seminar* Addis Ababa (Ethiopia) 2017, *High-Level Forum* Beijing (China) 2017.
Members Individuals; organzations; universities; research institutes; utilities; manufacturers; companies; financial institutions; firms. Members in 15 countries:
Australia, Brazil, China, Ethiopia, Germany, Italy, Japan, Korea Rep, Mongolia, Pakistan, Portugal, Russia, Tanzania UR, UK, USA.
Organizations include:
Eastern Africa Power Pool (EAPP, #05226).
Consultative Status Consultative status granted from: *UNEP (#20299)*. **IGO Relations** *African Union (AU, #00488)*; *ECOSOC (#05331)*; *European Union (EU, #08967)*; *International Energy Agency (IEA, #13270)*; *International Renewable Energy Agency (IRENA, #14715)*; *United Nations Economic and Social Commission for Asia and the Pacific (ESCAP, #20557)*. **NGO Relations** *Climate Parliament (#04019)*; *Global Infrastructure Connectivity Alliance (GICA, #10419)*; *International Electrotechnical Commission (IEC, #13255)*; *World Business Council for Sustainable Development (WBCSD, #21254)*. [2020/XM5287/C]

♦ Global Energy Storage Alliance (GESA) 10343

Contact c/o Stratgen, David Brower Ctr, 2150 Allston Way, Ste 210, Berkeley CA 94704, USA.
URL: http://www.globalesa.org/
History 2014, by *Alliance for Rural Electrification (ARE, #00719)* and national energy storage associations in the USA, Germany, China and India. **Aims** Advance education, collaboration, knowledge and proven frameworks about the benefits of energy storage and how it can be used to achieve a more efficient, cleaner, reliable, affordable and secure electric power system globally. **Structure** Board of Directors; Board of Advisors.
Members Full in 4 countries:
China, Germany, India, USA.
Regional member:
Alliance for Rural Electrification (ARE, #00719). [2015/XM4326/y/C]

♦ Global Engineering Deans Council (GEDC) 10344

Exec Sec GMU Volgenau School, 4400 University Dr, MS 4A3, Fairfax VA 22030, USA. E-mail: a.pappas@ifees.net.
URL: http://www.gedcouncil.org/
History 9 May 2008, Paris (France). Founded following meetings of a group of over 20 leaders of engineering education institutions and corporate partners, 9 Oct 2006, Rio de Janeiro (Brazil), and 30 Sep 2007, Istanbul (Turkey). Encouraged by the *International Federation of Engineering Education Societies (IFEES, #13412)*; modelled after the *American Society for Engineering Education (ASEE, #00790)* Engineering Deans Council (EDC). **Aims** Enhance the capabilities of engineering deans to transform schools in support of societies in a global economy; serve as a global network of engineering deans, and leverage on the collective strengths, for advancement of engineering education and research. **Structure** Leadership Team; Executive Committee. **Languages** Arabic, English, French, German, Greek, Portuguese, Russian, Spanish. **Staff** 2.00 FTE, paid. 3 consultants. **Activities** Events/meetings. **Events** *World Engineering Education Forum* Monterrey (Mexico) 2023, *EPOKA IFEES GEDC Regional Conference* Tirana (Albania) 2023, *GEDC Industry Forum* Cape Town (South Africa) 2022, *World Engineering Education Forum* Cape Town (South Africa) 2022, *World Engineering Education Forum* Madrid (Spain) 2021. **Publications** *Rising to the Top Volume III: Indian Women Engineering Leaders Share their Journeys to Professional Success* (2021) in English; *Rising to the Top Volume IV: African Women Engineering Leaders Share their Journeys to Professional Success* (2021) in English. *GlobalEngineer* (2022) in English.
Members Membership comprises persons-in-charge of: an engineering college, school or faculty in a university or institution of higher learning; an education institution of higher learning that is primarily focused on engineering education and research; engineering deans councils in respective countries and/or regions; or industry leaders that identify with the mission and vision of GEDC. Individuals consisting of: 179 Regular Members; 21 Former Deans; 9 Corporate Partners; 2 Ambassador Members; 1 Organizational Member. Members in 42 countries:
Argentina, Australia, Austria, Bosnia-Herzegovina, Brazil, Canada, Chile, China, Colombia, Ecuador, Ethiopia, France, Ghana, India, Iraq, Israel, Italy, Jamaica, Kenya, Korea Rep, Lebanon, Malawi, Malaysia, Mexico, Morocco, Nigeria, Pakistan, Panama, Paraguay, Peru, Qatar, Russia, Singapore, South Africa, Spain, Sudan, Türkiye, Uganda, UK, United Arab Emirates, USA, Zimbabwe. [2023.02.13/XJ1446/E]

♦ Global Enterprise for Micro-Mechanics and Molecular Medicine (no recent information)

♦ Global Entrepreneurship Monitor (GEM) 10345

Sec London Business School, Regents Park, London, NW1 4SA, UK. T. +447966908171. E-mail: info@gemconsortium.org.
URL: http://www.gemconsortium.org/
History 1999. Founded as a joint project between Babson College (USA) and London Business School (UK). **Aims** Increase understanding about the influence of entrepreneurship on economic growth, and identify factors that encourage or hinder it. **Structure** Board; National Teams. **Languages** English. **Staff** 8.00 FTE, paid. **Finance** Sources: members' dues; sponsorship. **Activities** Knowledge management/information dissemination; politics/policy/regulatory. **Events** *Annual Meeting* Miami, FL (USA) 2020. **Publications** Reports; academic papers.
Members Participating countries and territories (71):
Angola, Argentina, Armenia, Australia, Austria, Belarus, Belgium, Bosnia-Herzegovina, Brazil, Bulgaria, Canada, Chile, China, Colombia, Costa Rica, Croatia, Cyprus, Dominican Rep, Ecuador, Egypt, El Salvador, Estonia, Germany, Greece, Guatemala, India, Indonesia, Iran Islamic Rep, Ireland, Israel, Italy, Japan, Jordan, Kazakhstan, Korea Rep, Latvia, Lebanon, Luxembourg, Madagascar, Mexico, Morocco, Mozambique, Netherlands, North Macedonia, Norway, Oman, Pakistan, Panama, Paraguay, Peru, Poland, Portugal, Puerto Rico, Qatar, Russia, Saudi Arabia, Slovakia, Slovenia, South Africa, Spain, Sudan, Sweden, Switzerland, Taiwan, Thailand, Türkiye, UK, United Arab Emirates, Uruguay, USA, Vietnam.
IGO Relations *European Commission (EC, #06633)*; *International Bank for Reconstruction and Development (IBRD, #12317)* (World Bank); *International Development Research Centre (IDRC, #13162)*; *OECD (#17693)*. **NGO Relations** *World Economic Forum (WEF, #21367)*. [2020.05.06/XJ3212/E]

♦ Global Entrepreneurship Network (unconfirmed)
♦ Global Environmental Action (internationally oriented national body)
♦ Global Environmental Forum (internationally oriented national body)
♦ Global Environmental Information Exchange Network (inactive)
♦ Global Environmental Management Initiative (internationally oriented national body)
♦ Global Environmental Outreach Centre (internationally oriented national body)
♦ Global Environment Centre (internationally oriented national body)
♦ Global Environment Centre (internationally oriented national body)
♦ Global Environment Centre Foundation / see Global Environment Centre

♦ Global Environment Facility (GEF) 10346

Fonds pour l'environnement mondial (FEM)
CEO/Chairperson 1818 H St NW, MSN G6-602, Washington DC 20433, USA. T. +12024730508. Fax +12025223240 – +12023245. E-mail: secretariat@thegef.org.
URL: http://www.thegef.org/
History 1991, by Resolution 91-5 of the Executive Directors of the World Bank, as a 3-year pilot programme. Restructured and replenished, 16 Mar 1994, following agreement among GEF participants and requests from *Global Action Plan for Environment and Development in the 21st Century (Agenda 21, inactive)*, *United Nations Framework Convention on Climate Change (UNFCCC, 1992)* and *Convention on Biological Diversity (Biodiversity convention, 1992)*. Original implementing agencies: *International Bank for Reconstruction and Development (IBRD, #12317)*; *UNDP (#20292)* – through *Energy and Environment Group (see: #20292)*; *UNEP (#20299)*; *WMO Resource Mobilization Office (RMO, see: #21649)*. In 1999, other agencies were invited to execute GEF projects. **Aims** Forge international cooperation and finance activities to address 6 critical threats to the global environment: loss of biodiversity; climate change; degradation of international waters; ozone depletion; land degradation; persistent organic pollutants.
Structure Assembly (every 3-4 years) composed of all member countries or Participants. Council, comprising 32 members (14 from developed countries, 16 from developing countries and 2 from economies in transition). Secretariat, headed by CEO-Chairperson. Independent Evaluation Office (GEF IEO); Scientific and Technical Advisory Panel (STAP). Agencies are operational arm of GEF:
- *Asian Development Bank (ADB, #01422)*;
- *African Development Bank (ADB, #00283)*;
- *European Bank for Reconstruction and Development (EBRD, #06315)*;
- *FAO (#09260)*;
- *International Fund for Agricultural Development (IFAD, #13692)*;
- *Inter-American Development Bank (IDB, #11427)*;
- *UNDP (#20292)*;
- *UNEP (#20299)*;
- *UNIDO (#20336)*;
- *The World Bank Group (#21218)*;
- *Conservation International (CI)*;
- *Development Bank of Latin America (CAF, #05055)*;
- *Development Bank of Southern Africa (DBSA)*;
- Foreign Economic Cooperation Office – Ministry of Environmental Protection of China (FECO);
- Brazilian Biodiversity Fund (FUNBIO);
- *International Union for Conservation of Nature and Natural Resources (IUCN, #15766)*;
- *Banque ouest africaine de développement (BOAD, #03170)*;
- World Wildlife Fund-US.

Focal Points: political; operational. Conflict Resolution Commissioner.
Languages English. **Staff** 78.00 FTE, paid. **Finance** Contributions from 39 donor countries. Pledged contributions for 2014-2018 period: US$ 4,430,000,000. Additional cofinancing arrangements for projects and activities. Also seeks to procure funds from private sector and other sources. *Global Environment Trust Fund (GET)*, set up under the original Programme, has been replaced by *Global Environment Facility Trust Fund (GEF Trust Fund)*, to which a number of governments have made contributions, and to which *International Bank for Reconstruction and Development (IBRD, #12317)* acts as Trustee. **Activities** Financial and/or material support; projects/programmes; networking/liaising. Serves as "financial mechanism" to 5 conventions: *Convention on Biological Diversity (Biodiversity convention, 1992)*; *United Nations Framework Convention on Climate Change (UNFCCC, 1992)*; *Stockholm Convention on Persistent Organic Pollutants (POP treaty, 2001)*; *United Nations Convention to Combat Desertification (UNCCD, 1994)*; *Minamata Convention on Mercury (2013)*. **Events** *Integrated tools for managing the water, energy, and land nexus in large river basins* 2020, *Steering Committee Meeting* Laxenburg (Austria) 2019, *Towards the Establishment of an International Nitrogen Management System (INMS) Project General Assembly* Nairobi (Kenya) 2019, *Assembly* Danang (Vietnam) 2018, *Meeting* Washington, DC (USA) 2018. **Publications** *GEF Quarterly Operational Report (QOR)* (4 a year); *The Global Environment Facility (GEF)* (4 a year) – bulletin. *GEF Project Documents*; *GEF Working Papers*.
Members Open to all member states of the United Nations or one of its specialized agencies. States may become GEF participants by depositing a Notification of Participation with GEF Secretariat. As of May 2017, 183 participating states:
Afghanistan, Albania, Algeria, Angola, Antigua-Barbuda, Argentina, Armenia, Australia, Austria, Azerbaijan, Bahamas, Bangladesh, Barbados, Belarus, Belgium, Belize, Benin, Bhutan, Bolivia, Bosnia-Herzegovina, Botswana, Brazil, Bulgaria, Burkina Faso, Burundi, Cambodia, Cameroon, Canada, Cape Verde, Central African Rep, Chad, Chile, China, Colombia, Comoros, Congo Brazzaville, Congo DR, Cook Is, Costa Rica, Côte d'Ivoire, Croatia, Cuba, Czechia, Denmark, Djibouti, Dominica, Dominican Rep, Ecuador, Egypt, El Salvador, Equatorial Guinea, Eritrea, Estonia, Eswatini, Ethiopia, Fiji, Finland, France, Gabon, Gambia, Georgia, Germany, Ghana, Greece, Grenada, Guatemala, Guinea, Guinea-Bissau, Guyana, Haiti, Honduras, Hungary, India, Indonesia, Iran Islamic Rep, Iraq, Ireland, Israel, Italy, Jamaica, Japan, Jordan, Kazakhstan, Kenya, Kiribati, Korea DPR, Korea Rep, Kosovo, Kuwait, Kyrgyzstan, Laos, Latvia, Lebanon, Lesotho, Liberia, Libya, Lithuania, Luxembourg, Madagascar, Malawi, Malaysia, Maldives, Mali, Malta, Marshall Is, Mauritania, Mauritius, Mexico, Micronesia FS, Moldova, Mongolia, Montenegro, Morocco, Mozambique, Myanmar, Namibia, Nauru, Nepal, Netherlands, New Zealand, Nicaragua, Niger, Nigeria, Niue, North

Macedonia, Norway, Pakistan, Palau, Panama, Papua New Guinea, Paraguay, Peru, Philippines, Poland, Portugal, Romania, Russia, Rwanda, Samoa, Sao Tomé-Principe, Senegal, Serbia, Seychelles, Sierra Leone, Slovakia, Slovenia, Solomon Is, Somalia, South Africa, South Sudan, Spain, Sri Lanka, St Kitts-Nevis, St Lucia, St Vincent-Grenadines, Sudan, Suriname, Sweden, Switzerland, Syrian AR, Tajikistan, Tanzania UR, Thailand, Timor-Leste, Togo, Tonga, Trinidad-Tobago, Tunisia, Türkiye, Turkmenistan, Tuvalu, Uganda, UK, Ukraine, Uruguay, USA, Uzbekistan, Vanuatu, Venezuela, Vietnam, Yemen, Zambia, Zimbabwe.
IGO Relations Financial mechanism for: Convention on Biological Diversity; *Montreal Protocol on Substances that Deplete the Ozone Layer (1987)*; *Stockholm Convention on Persistent Organic Pollutants (POP treaty, 2001)*; UN Framework Convention on Climate Change; *United Nations Convention to Combat Desertification (UNCCD, 1994)*; *Vienna Convention for the Protection of the Ozone Layer (Ozone treaty, 1985)*. Associated with the following regional conventions: *Convention on the Conservation and Management of Highly Migratory Fish Stocks in the Western and Central Pacific Ocean (Pacific tuna convention, 2000)*; *Convention on Cooperation for the Protection and Sustainable Use of the Danube River (1994)*; *Framework Convention for the Protection of the Marine Environment of the Caspian Sea (Tehran Convention, 2003)*. **NGO Relations** Through *GEF CSO Network (GCN, #10087)*, cooperates with over 500 organizations. [2020/XF2335/f/**F***]

♦ Global Environment Information Centre / see Global Environmental Outreach Centre
♦ Global Environment and Natural Resources Institute (internationally oriented national body)
♦ Global Environment and Technology Foundation (internationally oriented national body)
♦ Globale Parlamentariergruppe für Habitat (#10525)
♦ Global Episcopal Mission Network (internationally oriented national body)

♦ Global Equity Organization (GEO) 10347

Exec Dir 1442 E Lincoln Ave, Ste 487, Orange CA 92865, USA. T. +17146302908. Fax +17144214900. E-mail: geoinfo@globalequity.org.
Events Managing Dir 10436 Ligthner Bridge Drive, Tampa FL 33636, USA.
URL: http://www.globalequity.org/
History 1999. **Aims** Advance knowledge and understanding of equity compensation worldwide through a global community of well-informed professionals. **Structure** Board of Directors; Provider Council; Advisory Council; Local Chapters. **Activities** Knowledge management/information dissemination; events/meetings; networking/liaising. **Events** *Annual Conference* Rome (Italy) 2017, *Annual Conference* Boston, MA (USA) 2016, *Annual Conference* London (UK) 2015, *Annual Conference* Miami, FL (USA) 2014, *International Conference* Munich (Germany) 2013. [2016/XM4826/**D**]

♦ Global ESports Federation (GEF) 10348

Contact 3 Stadium Drive, No 01-02, Singapore 397630, Singapore. E-mail: media@globalesports.org.
URL: https://globalesports.org/
History 2000. **Aims** Establish the credibility, legitimacy and prestige for esports. **Structure** Board. **Activities** Sporting activities.
Members Federations in countries and territories:
Argentina, Azerbaijan, Bahamas, Belarus, Belgium, Bosnia-Herzegovina, Brazil, Brunei Darussalam, Canada, Chile, China, Cuba, Czechia, Djibouti, Dominican Rep, Georgia, India, Indonesia, Iran Islamic Rep, Ireland, Italy, Jamaica, Japan, Kazakhstan, Lebanon, Malta, Mauritania, Moldova, Mongolia, Montenegro, Nepal, Nigeria, Pakistan, Paraguay, Peru, Philippines, Poland, Portugal, Saudi Arabia, Serbia, Singapore, South Africa, Sri Lanka, Suriname, Taiwan, Trinidad-Tobago, Tunisia, Türkiye, Turkmenistan, UK, Ukraine, Uruguay, USA, Venezuela.
IGO Relations Partner of (1): *International Telecommunication Union (ITU, #15673)*. **NGO Relations** Partner of (3): *Commonwealth Games Federation (CGF, #04332)*; *Olympic Council of Asia (OCA, #17718)*; *South American Sports Organization (SASO, #19708)*. [2021/AA1029/**C**]

♦ Global Ethic Foundation (internationally oriented national body)
♦ Global Ethic Foundation for Inter-Cultural and Inter-Religious Research, Education and Encounter / see Global Ethic Foundation

♦ Global EV Association Network (GEAN) 10349

Contact 215 Smart Bldg, 213-3, Cheomdan-ro, Jeju 63309, Korea Rep. T. +82647021580.
URL: http://www.globalev.org/
History EV stands for *Electric Vehicle*. **Aims** Expedite the adoption of EVs around the world as a key *climate change* effort. **Structure** Board of Directors. **Finance** Members' dues. **Events** *General Meeting* Jeju (Korea Rep) 2021, *General Meeting* Jeju (Korea Rep) 2020, *Conference* Jeju (Korea Rep) 2019, *Conference* Jeju (Korea Rep) 2018, *Conference* Jeju (Korea Rep) 2017.
Members Full in 20 countries and territories:
Azerbaijan, Belgium, Canada, China, Denmark, Dominican Rep, France, Hong Kong, Indonesia, Japan, Korea Rep, Malaysia, Mongolia, Myanmar, Netherlands, Norway, Philippines, Switzerland, Thailand, USA. [2019/XM8300/**F**]

♦ Globale Verantwortung – Arbeitsgemeinschaft für Entwicklung und Humanitäre Hilfe (internationally oriented national body)

♦ Global EverGreening Alliance 10350

Main Office 12/24 Lakeside Drive, East, Burwood VIC 3151, Australia.
URL: https://www.evergreening.org/
History 2012. **Aims** Cooperate with other organizations to restore degraded land and forests in order to capture carbon dioxide. **Structure** Board of Directors; Council of Fellows.
Members Member organizations include the following bodies listed in this Yearbook:
- *Botanic Gardens Conservation International (BGCI, #03306)*;
- *CARE International (CI, #03429)*;
- *Catholic Relief Services (CRS, #03608)*;
- *Concern Worldwide*;
- *Conservation International (CI)*;
- *Educational Concerns for Hunger Organization (ECHO)*;
- *European Agroforestry Federation (EURAF, #05848)*;
- *Fairventures Worldwide*;
- *Global Forest Generation (GFG, #10369)*;
- *Groundswell International (#10731)*;
- *International Tree Foundation (ITF)*;
- *Justdiggit*;
- *Oxfam International (#17922)*;
- *Plant-for-the-Planet Foundation (#18390)*;
- *Plant With Purpose*;
- *reNature Foundation*;
- *Self Help Africa (SHA, #19220)*;
- *SNV Netherlands Development Organisation (SNV)*;
- *SOS SAHEL (#19695)*;
- *The Nature Conservancy (TNC)*;
- *Trees for the Future (TFTF)*;
- *WeForest (#20852)*;
- *World Agroforestry Centre (ICRAF, #21072)*;
- *World Resources Institute (WRI, #21753)*;
- *World Vision International (WVI, #21904)*.

NGO Relations Member of (1): *Australian Council for International Development (ACFID)*. [2022/AA2905/y/**C**]

♦ Global Exchange (internationally oriented national body)
♦ Global Exchange for Social Investment (internationally oriented national body)

♦ Global Express Association (GEA) 10351

Dir Gen Rue du Mont-Blanc 26, 1201 Geneva, Switzerland. T. +41227165920. Fax +41227165921. E-mail: info@global-express.org.
URL: https://global-express.org/
History 1983. Former names and other names: *International Courier Conference* – former; *Express Mail Services* – former; *International Express Carriers Conference (IECC)* – former (1988). Registration: Switzerland. **Aims** Represent the interests of the international express *delivery* industry before international organizations. **Structure** Executive Committee. **Languages** English. **Finance** Members' dues. **Activities** Knowledge management/information dissemination; advocacy/lobbying/activism; publishing activities. **Events** *World express conference* New York, NY (USA) 1990. **Publications** *Express Delivery and Trade Facilitation: Impacts on the Global Economy* (2015); *The Impact of the Express Delivery Industry on the Global Economy* (2009).
Members Express carriers in 2 countries:
Germany, USA.
Affiliated regional associations (4):
Conference of Asia Pacific Express Carriers (CAPEC); *Conferencia Latino Americana de Compañias Express (CLADEC, #04654)*; *European Express Association (EEA, #07017)*; Express Association of America (EEA).
Consultative Status Consultative status granted from: *ECOSOC (#05331)* (Roster); *UNCTAD (#20285)* (General Category); *World Customs Organization (WCO, #21350)*. **IGO Relations** Registered with: *World Trade Organization (WTO, #21864)*. Invited to meetings of: *International Civil Aviation Organization (ICAO, #12581)*. Member of Consultative Committee of: *Universal Postal Union (UPU, #20682)*. Involved in the work of: *United Nations Committee of Experts on the Transport of Dangerous Goods and on the Globally Harmonized System of Classification and Labelling of Chemicals (Committee of Experts on TDG and GHS, #20543)*. [2022/XF1406/y/**F**]

♦ Global Facility for Disaster Reduction and Recovery (GFDRR) 10352

Head World Bank, 1818 H Str NW, Washington DC 20433, USA. T. +12024736253. Fax +12025223227. E-mail: gfdrr@worldbank.org.
URL: http://www.gfdrr.org/
History Sep 2006. Charter adopted by Consultative Group 23 Feb 2007. **Aims** Help high-risk, low-capacity developing countries better understand and reduce their vulnerabilities to natural hazards and adapt to *climate change* in the spirit of the Hyogo Framework for Action (HFA). **Structure** Managed by *International Bank for Reconstruction and Development (IBRD, #12317)* (World Bank). Consultative Group; Secretariat. Offices (4): Washington DC (USA); Brussels (Belgium); Tokyo (Japan); Geneva (Switzerland). **Staff** 31.00 FTE, paid. **Finance** Funded by 25 donor partners. **Events** *InterFLOOD Asia Conference* Singapore (Singapore) 2019, *InterMET Asia : Conference for Meteorology, Hydrology and Climate Services* Singapore (Singapore) 2019, *Workshop on Big Data Implications for Weather Data and Flood Management* Singapore (Singapore) 2019, *Workshop on Working Together Regionally* Singapore (Singapore) 2019, *InterMET Asia : Conference for Meteorology, Hydrology and Climate Services* Singapore (Singapore) 2018.
Members Governments (19):
Australia, Austria, Denmark, Djibouti, Germany, India, Japan, Korea Rep, Luxembourg, Mexico, Nigeria, Norway, Saudi Arabia, Spain, Sweden, Switzerland, Togo, UK, USA.
Regional entities (4):
European Union (EU, #08967); *Organisation of African, Caribbean and Pacific States (OACPS, #17796)*; *The World Bank Group (#21218)*; *United Nations Office for Disaster Risk Reduction (UNDRR, #20595)*.
Observer governments (24):
Bangladesh, Brazil, Canada, Chile, China, Colombia, Egypt, Finland, France, Haiti, Indonesia, Ireland, Italy, Malawi, Malaysia, Morocco, Netherlands, New Zealand, Philippines, Senegal, Solomon Is, South Africa, Türkiye, Vietnam.
Observer organizations (3):
International Federation of Red Cross and Red Crescent Societies (#13526); *Islamic Development Bank (IsDB, #16044)*; *UNDP (#20292)*.
NGO Relations *Global Resilience Partnership (GRP, #10577)*; *Understanding Risk Network (UR Network, #20287)*. [2020/XJ9477/**F***]

♦ Global Facility Management Association (Global FM) 10353

Contact Suite 4-01, 838 Collins Str, Docklands, Melbourne VIC 3008, Australia. T. +61386416666. E-mail: globalfmassociation@gmail.com – globalworldfmday@gmail.com.
URL: http://www.globalfm.org/
Aims Promote the strategic value and progress of the facilities management profession by leveraging member associations' strengths, knowledge and experience. **Structure** Board of Directors; Executive Committee. **Activities** Awards/prizes/competitions; events/meetings. **Events** *Global FM Summit* Amsterdam (Netherlands) 2019.
Members Organizations in 8 countries:
Australia, Brazil, Hungary, New Zealand, South Africa, UK, United Arab Emirates, USA.
Included in the above, 2 organizations listed in this Yearbook:
International Facility Management Association (IFMA, #13325); *Middle East Facility Management Association (MEFMA, #16763)*. [2018/XM7522/y/**C**]

♦ Global Family for Love and Peace (internationally oriented national body)
♦ Global Familymed Foundation (internationally oriented national body)
♦ Global Family Medicine Scientific Alliance (internationally oriented national body)

♦ Global Farmer Network (GFN) 10354

CEO 309 Court Avenue, Ste 214, Des Moines IA 50309, USA. T. +15152740800. Fax +12402018451. E-mail: info@globalfarmernetwork.org.
URL: http://globalfarmernetwork.org/
History 2000. **Aims** Insert the voice of farmers into the global dialogue regarding *food* and nutritional security. **Structure** Leadership. **Publications** *GFN Newsletter*. Annual Report. **Members** Individuals. Membership countries not specified. **Consultative Status** Consultative status granted from: *UNEP (#20299)*. **NGO Relations** Member of: *International Agri-Food Network (IAFN, #11599)*. [2017/XM6336/v/**F**]

♦ Global Fashion Conference (meeting series)
♦ Global Federation of Animal Sanctuaries (internationally oriented national body)

♦ Global Federation of Competitiveness Councils (GFCC) 10355

Exec Dir 900 17th Str NW, Ste 700, Washington DC 20006, USA. T. +12026824292.
URL: http://www.thegfcc.org/
Aims Share best practices among councils; create a network of global leaders committed to their national *prosperity* and the prosperity of the world. **Structure** Board. **Staff** 5.00 FTE, paid. **Events** *Global Innovation Summit* Washington, DC (USA) 2021, *Global Innovation Summit* Washington, DC (USA) 2020, *Global Innovation Summit* Buenos Aires (Argentina) 2018, *Global Innovation Summit* Kuala Lumpur (Malaysia) 2017, *Global Innovation Summit Annual Meeting* Banff, AB (Canada) 2014.
Members Federations in 18 countries:
Armenia, Brazil, Canada, Chile, Colombia, Egypt, India, Ireland, Japan, Mongolia, New Zealand, Panama, Qatar, Russia, Saudi Arabia, UK, United Arab Emirates, USA.
NGO Relations Supporting member of: *Inter-American Competitiveness Network (#11416)*. [2015/XJ9109/**C**]

♦ Global Federation of Insurance Associations (GFIA) 10356

Secretariat Insurance Europe, Rue du Champ de Mars 23, 1050 Brussels, Belgium. T. +3228943083. E-mail: secretariat@gfiainsurance.org.
URL: http://www.gfiainsurance.org/
History 9 Oct 2012. Founded after having previously existed as an informal network since 2008. **Aims** Represent national and regional insurance associations that serve the general interests of life, health and general insurance and reinsurance companies; advocate to national governments, international regulators and others on their behalf. **Structure** Executives: President; Vice-President; Secretary General; Treasurer; Membership Executive; Regional Representative; Working Group Chairs. **Publications** Annual Report; position papers. **Members** National and regional associations (40) and 1 Observer association representing 67 countries. Membership countries not specified. [2023.02.15/XJ7925/**C**]

♦ Global Fellowship of Christian Youth (Global Fellowship) 10357

General Manager Felden Lodge, Felden Lane, Hemel Hempstead, HP3 0BL, UK. E-mail: enquiries@globalfellowship.net – admin@globalfellowship.net.
URL: http://www.globalfellowship.net/
History 1963. Founded as *World Conference of The Boys' Brigade*, recognizing the autonomy and independence of members which had previously reported to The Boys' Brigade (UK). Previously also referred to as: *World Conference – a Family of Christian Youth Organizations*. Registration: Charity Commission, No/ID: 1188733, Start date: 24 Mar 2020, England and Wales. **Aims** Act as a network of Christian youth organizations. **Structure** Council of Representative Members (meets every 3 years); Executive Committee. National Member organizations are autonomous entities. Acts as international coordinating body for youth organizations: *Boys' Brigade, The (BB, #03308)* in over 50 countries; Frivilligt Drenge og Pige Forbund –

FDF/FPF (Denmark); Suomen Poikien ja Tyttojen Keskus – PTK (Finland); Neenah-Menasha Boys' and Girls' Brigade (USA); United Boys' and Girls' Brigade of America (USA); Junior Ministry (India). **Languages** English. **Staff** 1.00 FTE, paid. **Finance** Grants and donations from organizations and individuals. **Activities** Events/meetings; guidance/assistance/consulting; training/education. **Events** *Triennial Council and Conference* Lusaka (Zambia) 2019, *Triennial Council and Conference* London (UK) 2016, *Triennial Council and Conference* Singapore (Singapore) 2016, *Meeting* UK 2007, *Meeting* Partaharju (Finland) 2004. **Publications** *GF Update* (2 a year) – magazine.
Members Organizations, totalling about 500,000 members, in 58 countries and territories:
Antigua-Barbuda, Australia, Bahamas, Bangladesh, Barbados, Belize, Benin, Bermuda, Brazil, Brunei Darussalam, Cameroon, Canada, Congo DR, Cook Is, Côte d'Ivoire, Denmark, Dominica, Eswatini, Finland, Gambia, Ghana, Grenada, Guyana, Haiti, India, Indonesia, Ireland, Jamaica, Kenya, Lesotho, Malawi, Malaysia, Montserrat, Neth Antilles, New Zealand, Nigeria, Niue, Papua New Guinea, Rwanda, Samoa, Sierra Leone, Singapore, Solomon Is, South Africa, St Kitts-Nevis, St Lucia, St Vincent-Grenadines, Tanzania UR, Thailand, Tonga, Trinidad-Tobago, Tuvalu, Uganda, UK, USA, Vanuatu, Zambia, Zimbabwe.
NGO Relations *European Fellowship of Christian Youth (EF, #07238)* is a sub-grouping of some members. Member of: *Think Global – Development Education Association (DEA).* [2022/XF0702/**F**]

♦ The Global Fellowship of Confessing Anglicans / see Fellowship of Confessing Anglicans (#09725)
♦ **Global Fellowship** Global Fellowship of Christian Youth (#10357)
♦ Global Finance Association (internationally oriented national body)

♦ Global Financial Integrity (GFI) 10358

Managing Dir 1100 17th St NW, Ste 505, Washington DC 20036, USA. T. +12022930740. Fax +12022931720. E-mail: gfi@gfintegrity.org.
URL: http://www.gfintegrity.org/

History Sep 2006. **Aims** Promote national and multilateral policies, safeguards, and agreements aimed at curtailing the cross-border flow of illegal money. **Structure** Board of Directors. **Finance** Funded by: *African Development Bank (ADB, #00283); Financial Transparency Coalition (FTC, #09772); Ford Foundation (#09858);* Governments of Denmark and Spain; *Inter-American Development Bank (IDB, #11427);* Norwegian Research Council; various individual donors. **Consultative Status** Consultative status granted from: *ECOSOC (#05331)* (Special). **NGO Relations** On Coordinating Committee of: *Financial Transparency Coalition (FTC, #09772).* Member of: *International Corporate Accountability Roundtable (ICAR, #12968).* [2013/XJ7712/**F**]

♦ Global Financial Markets Association (GFMA) 10359

Main Office 1099 New York Av NW, 6th Fl, Washington DC 20005, USA.
URL: http://www.gfma.org/

Aims Develop strategies for global policy issues in the financial markets; promote coordinated advocacy efforts. **Events** *Green Finance Conference* Singapore (Singapore) 2018, *Green Finance Conference* Singapore (Singapore) 2017, *London Renminbi Conference* London (UK) 2016, *London Renminbi Markets Conference* London (UK) 2014. **Publications** News briefs.
Members Associations (3):
Asia Securities Industry and Financial Markets Association (ASIFMA, #02094); Association for Financial Markets in Europe (AFME, #02596); Securities Industry and Financial Markets Association (SIFMA). [2021/XJ2826/y/**C**]

♦ Global Financing Facility (GFF) 10360

Address not obtained.
URL: http://www.globalfinancingfacility.org/

History Launched Jul 2015, Addis Ababa (Ethiopia). Full title: *Global Financing Facility for Reproductive, Maternal, Newborn, Child and Adolescent Health (GFF) in support of Every Woman Every Child (EWEC, #09215),* of which it acts as financing arm. **Aims** Scale up the resources available for *reproductive,* maternal, *newborn, child* and adolescent health (RMNCAH); align partners round prioritized investments that generate results, while ensuring that countries are on a trajectory towards universal *health* coverage and *sustainable* health financing. **Structure** GFF Investors Group for the Global Strategy (Investors Group); GFF Trust Fund Committee. **Finance** Supported by: *The World Bank Group (#21218).* **Activities** Financial and/or material support. **Events** *Beating the Drum Conference* Oslo (Norway) 2018. **Publications** *GFF Newsletter.*
Members Partners include:
Gavi – The Vaccine Alliance (Gavi, #10077); Global Fund to Fight AIDS, Tuberculosis and Malaria (Global Fund, #10383).
IGO Relations Cooperates with: *H6 (#10844).* **NGO Relations** Member of: *UHC2030 (#20277).* [2017/XM6252/**F**]

♦ Global Financing Facility for Reproductive, Maternal, Newborn, Child and Adolescent Health / see Global Financing Facility (#10360)

♦ Global FinTech Association (GFA) 10361

Co-Founder Europaallee 39, 8004 Zurich ZH, Switzerland. E-mail: info@leonteq.com.
LinkedIn: https://www.linkedin.com/company/global-fintech-association/about/

History Articles of incorporation accepted 15 Jan 2016. Registered in accordance with Swiss Code. **Aims** Represent members' interest in the field of *financial* technologies. **Structure** General Assembly (annual); Board; Advisory Board; Administrative Office. **Languages** English. **Staff** None paid. **Finance** Sources: members' dues. **Activities** Events/meetings; knowledge management/information dissemination; networking/liaising. **Members** Companies. Membership countries not specified. [2017.07.21/XM5720/**C**]

♦ Global Fire Monitoring Centre (internationally oriented national body)
♦ Global First Ladies Alliance (unconfirmed)
♦ Global Fishing Watch (internationally oriented national body)
♦ Global Flood Partnership (unconfirmed)

♦ Global Flooring Alliance (GFA) 10362

Sec Campanula 20, 3317 HC Dordrecht, Netherlands. T. +31786187732. Fax +31785147833. E-mail: secretary@globalflooringalliance.com – info@globalflooringalliance.com.
URL: http://www.globalflooringalliance.com/

History 1989, as *European Parquet Alliance (Euparal).* Present name adopted, 2009. **Aims** Promote the use of *wooden flooring;* increase exchange of information in the field. **Languages** English. **Activities** Events/meetings. **Events** *Meeting* Toronto, ON (Canada) 2001.
Members Companies (14) in 14 countries:
Austria, Canada, Denmark, Finland, France, Iceland, Ireland, Italy, Netherlands, Portugal, Spain, Sweden, Switzerland, UK.
NGO Relations Member of: *European Federation of Parquet Importers (EFPI, #07187).* [2018/XD5159/**D**]

♦ Global Flow Measurement Workshop (meeting series)

♦ Global Fluid Power Society (GFPS) 10363

Chairman address not obtained.
URL: https://www.gfpsweb.org/

History 2016. Founded as a merger of *Network of Fluid Power Centres in Europe (FPCE, inactive)* and *Fluid Power Net International (FPNI, #09802).* Registration: Corporation, USA. **Aims** Bring people of the fluid power community together; provide information about fluid power developments and publications; strengthen the standing of fluid power and fluid techniques in industry and academia; promote fluid power and fluid techniques as scientific/technical discipline; promote collaborative projects and provide information about expertise in the field; promote the exchange of students and researchers among fluid power institutions. **Structure** General Assembly (annual); Board of Directors; Advisory Board. **Finance** Sources: members' dues. **Activities** Awards/prizes/competitions; events/meetings; knowledge management/information dissemination. **Publications** *International Journal of Fluid Power.*
Members Academic institutions in 16 countries:
Austria, Brazil, Canada, China, Denmark, Finland, France, Germany, Italy, Japan, Poland, Russia, Spain, Sweden, UK, USA.
Organizations and industries in 4 countries:
Germany, Italy, Switzerland, USA. [2022.06.14/AA0018/**C**]

♦ Global Fluorocarbon Producers Forum (GFPF) 10364

Contact c/o CEFIC, Av E Van Nieuwenhuyse 4, 1160 Brussels, Belgium.
URL: http://gfpf-forum.org/

History A Sector group of *Conseil européen de l'industrie chimique (CEFIC, #04687).* **Aims** Advocate for sensible reductions in the use of high global-warming fluorocarbons, especially in emissive applications; preserve choice for consumers and manufacturers; enable a practical timeline for adoption of replacement technology. [2017/XM6818/**F**]

♦ **Global FM** Global Facility Management Association (#10353)
♦ Global Focus (internationally oriented national body)
♦ Global Focus – Danish CSOs for Development Cooperation / see Globalt Fokus

♦ Global FoodBanking Network (GFN) 10365

Main Office 70 E. Lake St, Ste 1200, Chicago IL 60601, USA. T. +13127824560. Fax +13127824580. E-mail: info@foodbanking.org.
URL: http://www.foodbanking.org/

History 2006, by food bank networks in Argentina, Brazil, Canada, Mexico and USA. Registration: No/ID: 20-4268851, USA. **Aims** Create and strengthen food banks and national food bank networks, so as to alleviate *hunger.* **Structure** Board of Directors, comprising Chairman, Vice-Chairman and 17 members. **Activities** Set up: *Food Bank Leadership Institute.* **Publications** *Food* – magazine.
Members National Food Bank Networks in 8 countries:
Argentina, Australia, Canada, Guatemala, Mexico, South Africa, UK, USA.
Independent Certified Food Banks (3) in 2 countries:
Colombia, Japan.
NGO Relations Member of: *Organization of African Instituted Churches (OAIC, #17853).* Collaborates with: *European Food Banks Federation (FEBA, #07280).* [2020/XJ2798/**F**]

♦ Global Food Safety Initiative (GFSI) 10366

International Headquarters c/o Consumer Goods Forum, 47-53 rue Raspail, 92300 Levallois-Perret, France. T. +33182009595. Fax +33182009596. E-mail: gfsinfo@theconsumergoodsforum.com.
URL: http://www.mygfsi.com/

History Founded May 2000, by collaborative action of CEOs of the world's food retailers, working through their independent network *CIES – The Food Business Forum,* now the *The Consumer Goods Forum (CGF, #04772).* Registration: No/ID: W751029783, France. **Aims** Enhance food safety; ensure *consumer* protection; strengthen consumer confidence; set requirements for food safety management standards; improve cost efficiency throughout the food supply chain. **Structure** Board; Advisory Council; Technical Working Groups; Local Groups; Stakeholder Group. **Languages** English. **Staff** 5.50 FTE, paid. **Finance** Members' dues from *The Consumer Goods Forum (CGF, #04772)* (mother association). Other sources: events; sponsorship. **Activities** Standards/guidelines; meeting activities. Active in Europe and the following countries: Canada, China, India, Japan, Mexico, USA. **Events** *GFSI : Global Food Safety Initiative Conference* Barcelona (Spain) 2022, *GFSI : Global Food Safety Initiative Conference* Paris (France) 2021, *Global Food Safety Conference* Seattle, WA (USA) 2020, *Global Food Safety Conference* Paris (France) 2019, *Global Food Safety Conference* Tokyo (Japan) 2018. **Publications** *GFSI Newsletter.* [2021/XF6639/**F**]

♦ Global Footprint Network 10367

CEO 1528 Webster St, Oakland CA 94612, USA. T. +15108398879. E-mail: media@footprintnetwork.or.
Europe Av Louis-Casaï 18, 1209 Geneva, Switzerland. T. +41227477643.
URL: http://www.footprintnetwork.org/

History Operates through 2 separate legal entities: US based organization functioning as headquarters, and Swiss Foundation. **Aims** Provide *ecological* footprint accounting tools to drive informed policy decision in a resource-constrained world; work with local and national governments, investors and opinion leaders to ensure all people live well, within the means of one planet. **Structure** Board of Directors; Advisory Council. **Languages** English, French, German, Italian, Spanish. **Events** *Biennial Twin world congress* Nagoya (Japan) / Davos (Switzerland) 2009. **Publications** *Global Footprint Newsletter; Living Planet Report; Mediterranean Footprint Report; State of the States Report.* Annual Report. **Consultative Status** Consultative status granted from: *UNEP (#20299).* **NGO Relations** Member of: *Biodiversity Indicators Partnership (BIP, #03242); Mediterranean Information Office for Environment, Culture and Sustainable Development (MIO-ECSDE, #16657).* Sponsoring partner of: *Green Economy Coalition (GEC, #10717).* Partner of: *Global Call for Climate Action (GCCA, inactive); Local Governments for Sustainability (ICLEI, #16507).* [2020/XJ3320/**F**]

♦ Global Forest Coalition (GFC) 10368

Coalition mondiale des forêts (CMF) – Coalición Mundial por los Bosques
Main Office c/o Social Impact Factory, Vredenburg 40, 3511 BD Utrecht, Netherlands. E-mail: gfc@globalforestcoalition.org.
Exec Dir CC 13241, 1749 Asunción, Paraguay. T. +595981407375.
Chair Censat Ajua Viva, Cra 27a, Bogota 2410, Bogota DC, Colombia.
URL: http://www.globalforestcoalition.org/

History 2000. Founded by 19 NGOs, including *Friends of the Earth International (FoEI, #10002), International Alliance of the Indigenous Tribal Peoples of the Tropical Forests (IAITPTF, #11629)* and *World Rainforest Movement (WRM, #21745).* Registration: Start date: 2005, Netherlands. **Aims** Support and coordinate joint NGO/IPO campaigns focusing on raising awareness of the need for socially just and effective forest *policy,* challenging the underlying causes of forest loss and *rights* of *indigenous* and other forest peoples; facilitate informed participation of NGOs and indigenous peoples' organizations in the global policy debate relating to forests; promote and monitor the implementation of commitments made; defend the rights of indigenous and other forest peoples, with a special emphasis on women. **Structure** Board; Advisory Council; Regional Focal Points (5); Offices based in Amsterdam (Netherlands) and Asunción (Paraguay). **Languages** English, French, Russian, Spanish. **Staff** 4.00 FTE, paid. **Finance** Contributions from governments and private donors. Annual budget: about euro 480,000. **Activities** Advocacy/lobbying/activism; events/meetings; capacity building; networking/liaising. Management of treaties and agreements: *Convention on Biological Diversity (Biodiversity convention, 1992); United Nations Framework Convention on Climate Change (UNFCCC, 1992).* **Publications** *Forest Cover* (3 a year). Reports; toolkits; videos; briefing papers; photo essays.
Members Organizations (62) in 65 countries:
Argentina, Armenia, Australia, Bangladesh, Benin, Bolivia, Brazil, Bulgaria, Cameroon, Chile, China, Colombia, Congo Brazzaville, Congo DR, Costa Rica, Denmark, Dominican Rep, Ecuador, El Salvador, Ethiopia, France, Georgia, Germany, Ghana, India, Indonesia, Iran Islamic Rep, Ireland, Japan, Kazakhstan, Kenya, Korea Rep, Kyrgyzstan, Liberia, Malaysia, Morocco, Mozambique, Myanmar, Nepal, Netherlands, New Zealand, Nigeria, North Macedonia, Panama, Papua New Guinea, Paraguay, Philippines, Portugal, Russia, Samoa, Serbia, Solomon Is, South Africa, Sri Lanka, Sweden, Tajikistan, Tanzania UR, Thailand, Togo, Tunisia, Uganda, UK, Ukraine, USA, Vietnam.
Consultative Status Consultative status granted from: *ECOSOC (#05331)* (Special); *UNEP (#20299).* **IGO Relations** Accredited by: *Green Climate Fund (GCF, #10714).* **NGO Relations** Member of: *CBD Alliance (#03615); Climate Justice Now ! (CJN!, inactive); ICCA Consortium (#11041);* Women's Major Group for Sustainable Development. [2022/XJ3135/y/**F**]

♦ Global Forest Generation (GFG) 10369

CEO 5350 US Route 2, North Hero, VT 05474, USA. E-mail: info@globalforestgen.org.
URL: https://www.globalforestgeneration.org/

History 2018. Founded by: Constantino Aucca; Leslie Danoff; George Fenwick; Rita Fenwick. Registration: 501(c)3, No/ID: EIN 83-1150620, USA. **Aims** Protect and restore threatened, native forest ecosystems by empowering grassroots conservation leaders and their communities. **Structure** Board. **Activities** Advocacy/lobbying/activism; projects/programmes. **NGO Relations** Member of (1): *Global EverGreening Alliance (#10350).* [2022/AA2906/**F**]

♦ Global Forest Policy Project (internationally oriented national body)
♦ Global Forest Watch (internationally oriented national body)
♦ Global Forum (meeting series)

♦ Global Forum on Agricultural Research (GFAR) 10370

Forum mondial de la recherche agricole – Foro Global de Investigación Agropecuaria

Exec Sec c/o FAO, Viale delle Terme di Caracalla, 00153 Rome RM, Italy. T. +39657053413. Fax +39657053898. E-mail: gfar-secretariat@fao.org.

URL: http://www.gfar.net/

History Founded 31 Oct 1996. **Aims** Make agri-food research and innovation systems more effective, responsive and equitable, towards achieving Sustainable Development Goals. **Structure** Operates through GFAR Steering Committee, composed of 13 members, and National Agricultural Research Systems (NARS) Steering Committee, composed of chairpersons of the NARS regional fora on agricultural research (Asia and the Pacific, Central Asia and the Caucasus, Latin America and the Caribbean, Sub-Saharan Africa and West Asia and North Africa). GFAR support group under leadership of *International Fund for Agricultural Development (IFAD, #13692)*. Steering committees and support group meet 2 times a year. **Finance** Donors as of 1 Jan 2016: *European Commission (EC, #06633)*; *FAO (#09260)*; *International Fund for Agricultural Development (IFAD, #13692)*. **Events** *Global Science Conference on Climate Smart Agriculture* Montpellier (France) 2015, *Global Conference* Punta del Este (Uruguay) 2012, *Global conference on agricultural research for development* Montpellier (France) 2010, *Biennial science forum* Wageningen (Netherlands) 2009, *Triennial Conference* Delhi (India) 2006. **Information Services** *GFAR Document Repository* – online service.

Members National agricultural research systems (NARS). Membership countries not specified. Regional coordinators include 12 organizations listed in this Yearbook:

Asia-Pacific Association of Agricultural Research Institutions (APAARI, #01830); *Association for Strengthening Agricultural Research in Eastern and Central Africa (ASARECA, #02933)*; *Association of Agricultural Research Institutions in the Near East and North Africa (AARINENA, #02364)*; *Caribbean Agricultural Science and Technology Networking System (PROCICARIBE, no recent information)*; *European Forum on Agricultural Research for Development (EFARD, #07302)*; *Forum for Agricultural Research in Africa (FARA, #09897)*; *Inter-American Institute for Cooperation on Agriculture (IICA, #11434)*; *Programa Cooperative de Investigación, Desarrollo e Innovación Agrícola para los Trópicos Suramericanos (PROCITROPICOS, #18521)*; *Programa Cooperativo de Investigación y Transferencia de Tecnologia Agropecuaria para la Subregión Andina (PROCIANDINO, no recent information)*; *Programa Cooperativo para el Desarrollo Tecnológico Agroalimentario y Agroindustrial del Cono Sur (PROCISUR, #18522)*; *Sistema de Ciencia y Tecnologia Agroindustrial (SICTA, no recent information)*; *West and Central African Council for Agricultural Research and Development (WECARD, #20907)*.

IGO Relations Cooperates with: *AVRDC – The World Vegetable Center (#03051)*; *CABI (#03393)*; *Centre de coopération internationale en recherche agronomique pour le développement (CIRAD, #03733)*; national governmental organizations.

NGO Relations Hosts secretariat of: *Young Professionals for Agricultural Development (YPARD, #21996)*. Instrumental in setting up: *e-Agriculture (#00575)*; *Global Facilitation Unit for Underutilized Species (GFU, inactive)*; *Inter-regional Network on Cotton in Asia and North Africa (INCANA, #15972)*. Cooperates with:

- *African Model Forest Network (AMFN, #00377)*;
- *Arab Network for Women Farmers*;
- *Asian Farmers'Association for Sustainable Rural Development (AFA, #01450)*;
- *Asian NGO Coalition for Agrarian Reform and Rural Development (ANGOC, #01566)*;
- *Association for AgriCulture and Ecology (Agrecol)*;
- *Association for European Life Science Universities (ICA, #02519)*;
- *Association of International Research and Development Centers for Agriculture (AIRCA, #02760)*;
- *Caribbean Farmers Network (CaFAN, #03503)*;
- Comité para la Soberania Alimentaria América Latina y el Caribe (VTR);
- *Confederación de Organizaciones de Productores Familiares del MERCOSUR (COPROFAM)*;
- *Crawford Fund for International Agricultural Research*;
- *FIA Foundation (#09742)*;
- *Foro de las Américas para la Investigación y Desarrollo Tecnológico Agropecuario (FORAGRO, #09875)*;
- *Global Confederation of Higher Education Associations for Agriculture and Life Sciences (GCHERA, #10304)*;
- *Japan International Research Centre for Agricultural Sciences (JIRCAS)*;
- national organizations;
- *Pacific Island Farmers Organisation Network (PIFON, #17957)*;
- *PROLINNOVA (#18537)*;
- *Réseau maghrebin d'associations de développement local en milieu rural (REMADEL, #18898)*;
- *Royal Tropical Institute (KIT)*;
- *Tropical Agriculture Association (TAA)*;
- *West African Women's Association (WAWA, #20900)*;
- *World Farmers' Organisation (WFO, #21401)*;
- *World Neighbors (WN)* – Africa;
- World Rural Forum (WRF);
- World Rural Forum (WRF). [2016.06.01/XF5829/y/F]

♦ Global Forum on Cyber Expertise (GFCE) 10371

Dir Wilhelmina van Pruisenweg 104, 7th Floor, 2595 AN The Hague, Netherlands. T. +310702045030. E-mail: contact@thegfce.org.

URL: http://www.thegfce.org/

History Apr 2015, The Hague (Netherlands). Launched by the Dutch Government during the 2015 Global Conference on Cyber Space. **Aims** Strengthen cyber capacity and expertise globally through international collaboration and cooperation. **Structure** Advisory Board; Co-Chairs; Secretariat. **Languages** English, French, Spanish. **Finance** Sources: contributions of member/participating states; government support; grants; in-kind support; private foundations. **Activities** Advocacy/lobbying/activism; events/meetings; projects/programmes; research/documentation. **Events** *Annual Meeting* The Hague (Netherlands) 2019, *Annual Meeting* Singapore (Singapore) 2018, *Working Group Meeting* The Hague (Netherlands) 2018. **Publications** *Global Cyber Expertise Magazine* (2 a year) – online.

Members Countries; IGOs; NGOs; private companies. States (51):

Argentina, Australia, Austria, Bangladesh, Belgium, Canada, Chile, Côte d'Ivoire, Czechia, Dominica, Estonia, Finland, France, Gabon, Gambia, Germany, Guatemala, Hungary, India, Israel, Japan, Kenya, Korea Rep, Latvia, Mauritius, Mexico, Morocco, Netherlands, New Zealand, Nigeria, Norway, Peru, Philippines, Romania, Rwanda, Senegal, Serbia, Sierra Leone, Singapore, Spain, Suriname, Sweden, Switzerland, Tanzania UR, Thailand, Tunisia, Türkiye, UK, Ukraine, USA, Vietnam.

IGOs and NGOs (13):

African Union (AU, #00488); *Commonwealth Telecommunications Organisation (CTO, #04365)*; *Council of Europe (CE, #04881)*; *Economic Community of West African States (ECOWAS, #05312)*; *European Police Office (Europol, #08239)*; *European Union (EU, #08967)*; *International Association of Prosecutors (IAP, #12111)*; *International Bank for Reconstruction and Development (IBRD, #12317)* (World Bank); *International Chamber of Commerce (ICC, #12534)*; *International Criminal Police Organization – INTERPOL (ICPO-INTERPOL, #13110)*; *International Telecommunication Union (ITU, #15673)*; *OAS (#17629)*; *Organization for Security and Cooperation in Europe (OSCE, #17887)*.

IGO Relations *United Nations Office on Drugs and Crime (UNODC, #20596)*. **NGO Relations** Partners include: *Diplo Foundation*; *European Cybercrime Training and Education Group (ECTEG, #06874)*; *EastWest Institute (EWI, #05264)*; *Forum of Incident Response and Security Teams (FIRST, #09918)*; *Global Cyber Security Capacity Centre (GCSCC)*; *Norwegian Institute of International Affairs (NUPI)*. [2022.06.15/XM7841/y/F]

♦ Global Forum on Fighting Corruption and Safeguarding Integrity (meeting series)

♦ Global Forum on Human Settlements (GFHS) 10372

Contact 10 Waterside Plaza, Apt 20-E, New York NY 10010, USA. T. +19172561364.

Contact address not obtained.

URL: http://www.gfhsforum.org/

History Registered in the State of New York (USA). **Aims** Build sustainable human settlements; promote the UN Habitat agenda. **Structure** General Assembly; Board of Directors; Consultative Committee; Secretariat. **Activities** Awards/prizes/competitions; events/meetings; training/education. **Consultative Status** Consultative status granted from: *ECOSOC (#05331)* (Special). **IGO Relations** Associated with Department of Global Communications of the United Nations. **NGO Relations** Member of: *United Nations Global Compact (#20567)*. Associate partner of: *World Urban Campaign (WUC, #21893)*. [2017/XM4193/F]

♦ Global Forum on Law, Justice and Development (GFLJD) 10373

Forum Mondial sur le Droit, la Justice et le Développement – Foro Mundial sobre Derecho, Justicia y Desarrollo

Secretariat World Bank, Mail stop MC6-607, 1818 H St NW, Washington DC 20433, USA. T. +12024730304. E-mail: globalforumljd@worldbank.org.

URL: http://www.globalforumljd.org/

History Initiated 2010, by *International Bank for Reconstruction and Development (IBRD, #12317)* – World Bank, Legal Vice-Presidency. Officially launched Nov 2011. **Aims** Facilitate identification, discussion, production and/or sharing of innovative and customized legal and institutional tools to address global, regional or national development challenges. **Structure** Partners General Assembly; Steering Committee; Thematic Working Groups; Communities of Practice; Secretariat; Permanent Forum; ICT Knowledge Platform – Collaboration for Development (C4D). **Languages** English. **Staff** 3.50 FTE, paid. **Finance** Combination of voluntary financial and in-kind contributions (staff, premises, IT, etc) from partners. **Activities** Knowledge management/information dissemination; events/meetings. **Events** *Law, Climate Change and Environment Week Meeting* Washington, DC (USA) 2017, *Law, Climate Change and Environment Week Meeting* Washington, DC (USA) 2016.

Members Partners (180), including 68 listed in this Yearbook ('*' Founding Partners who signed before January 15, 2012 are members of the Interim Steering Committee):

- *Advocates for International Development (A4ID)*;
- *African Development Bank (ADB, #00283)* (*);
- *African Law Foundation (AFRILAW)*;
- *African Union (AU, #00488)* (Commission);
- *Arab Center for the Development of the Rule of Law and Integrity (ACRLI, #00912)* (*);
- *Asian Development Bank (ADB, #01422)*;
- *Auschwitz Institute for the Prevention of Genocide and Mass Atrocities*;
- *Basel Institute on Governance*;
- *Budapest Centre for the International Prevention of Genocide and Mass Atrocities*;
- *Catholic Organization for Relief and Development (Cordaid)*;
- *Centre for International Sustainable Development Law (CISDL)*;
- *Comisión Interamericana de Mujeres (CIM, #04137)*;
- *Council of Bars and Law Societies of Europe (CCBE, #04871)*;
- *Council of Europe (CE, #04881)*;
- *Department for International Development (DFID, inactive)*;
- *European Bank for Reconstruction and Development (EBRD, #06315)* (*);
- *European Club for Countertrade and Offset (ECCO, #06580)*;
- *European Law Institute (ELI, #07658)*;
- *European Network of Councils for the Judiciary (ENCJ, #07886)*;
- *European Public Law Organization (EPLO, #08299)*;
- *Fondation pour le droit continental*;
- *Global Legal Studies Network (GLSN)*;
- *Hague Institute for Innovation of Law (HIIL)*;
- *Institute on Disability and Public Policy (IDPP, #11255)*;
- *Institut international de droit d'expression et d'inspiration françaises (IDEF, #11310)*;
- *Inter-American Development Bank (IDB, #11427)*;
- *Inter-American Investment Corporation (IIC, #11438)*;
- *International Association for Water Law (#12263)* (*);
- *International Association of Penal Law (IAPL, #12074)* (*);
- *International Association of Prosecutors (IAP, #12111)*;
- *International Bank for Reconstruction and Development (IBRD, #12317)* (World Bank);
- *International Centre for Missing and Exploited Children (ICMEC, #12505)*;
- *International Civil and Commercial Law Centre Foundation (ICCLC)*;
- *International Criminal Court (ICC, #13108)*;
- *International Development Law Organization (IDLO, #13161)* (*);
- *International Development Research Centre (IDRC, #13162)*;
- *International Finance Corporation (IFC, #13597)*;
- *International Institute for the Unification of Private Law (UNIDROIT, #13934)* (*);
- *International Juvenile Justice Observatory (IJJO)*;
- *International Law Institute – African Centre for Legal Excellence (ILI – ACLE, #14005)*;
- *International Legal Foundation (ILF, #14026)* (*);
- *International Penal and Penitentiary Foundation (IPPF, #14553)* (*);
- *International Society of Criminology (ISC, #15038)* (*);
- *International Society of Social Defence and Humane Criminal Policy (ISSD, #15447)*;
- *International Union of Judicial Officers (#15785)*;
- *International Union of Notaries (#15795)*;
- *Islamic Development Bank (IsDB, #16044)*;
- *Istituto di Studi Giuridici Internazionali (ISGI)*;
- *Leuven Centre for Global Governance Studies*;
- *Multilateral Investment Guarantee Agency (MIGA, #16888)*;
- *Observatoire International du Bonheur (OIB)* (*);
- *OECD (#17693)*;
- *OPEC Fund for International Development (OFID, #17745)*;
- *PartnersGlobal*;
- *Penal Reform International (PRI, #18290)*;
- *Public Interest Intellectual Property Advisors (PIIPA)*;
- *South-East European Research Centre (SEERC)*;
- *The Hague Conference on Private International Law (HCCH, #10850)*;
- *UNEP (#20299)*;
- *Union Internationale des Avocats (UIA, #20422)*;
- *United Nations Commission on International Trade Law (UNCITRAL, #20531)*;
- *United Nations Human Settlements Programme (UN-Habitat, #20572)*;
- *United Nations Interregional Crime and Justice Research Institute (UNICRI, #20580)* (*);
- *United Nations Office on Drugs and Crime (UNODC, #20596)*;
- *United Nations (UN, #20515)* (Secretariat *);
- *United Nations University Institute for Environment and Human Security (UNU-EHS, #20645)*;
- *Women Enabled International (WEI, #20991)*;
- *World Resources Institute (WRI, #21753)*.

IGO Relations Links with UN agencies, international organizations, international financial institutions (see 'Members' for a partial list). [2018/XM5040/y/F]

♦ Global Forum on Leadership, Learning and Strategic Change (meeting series)

♦ Global Forum on Maintenance and Asset Management (GFMAM) .. 10374

Address not obtained.

URL: http://www.gfmam.org/

History by *European Federation of National Maintenance Societies (EFNMS, #07173)*, *Society for Maintenance and Reliability Professionals (SMRP)*, *Gulf Society for Maintenance Professionals (GSMP, #10840)*, *Federación Iberoamericana de Mantenimiento (FIM, #09315)* and national societies in Australia, Brazil, Canada, UK and South Africa. Registered in accordance with Swiss law. **Aims** Develop and promote knowledge, standards and education for the maintenance and asset management professions.

Members Organizations (9) in 6 countries:

Australia, Brazil, Canada, South Africa, UK, USA.

Included in the above, 5 organizations listed in this Yearbook:

European Federation of National Maintenance Societies (EFNMS, #07173); *Federación Iberoamericana de Mantenimiento (FIM, #09315)*; *Gulf Society for Maintenance Professionals (GSMP, #10840)*; *Society for Maintenance and Reliability Professionals (SMRP)*; *Southern African Asset Management Association (SAAMA)*. [2018/XM4075/y/F]

♦ Global Forum for Media Development (GFMD) 10375

Programmes and Policy Manager Rond Point Schuman 6, Box 5, 1040 Brussels, Belgium. T. +3222346306. E-mail: communications@gfmd.info.

Exec Dir address not obtained. E-mail: director@gfmd.info.

URL: http://gfmd.info/

History Oct 2005, at 1st conference, Amman (Jordan). Set up as membership organization, at 2nd conference, Dec 2008, Athens (Greece). **Aims** Support journalism and media; seek to foster viable and independent journalism, greater transparency and more pluralistic media environments. **Structure** Steering Committee; Secretariat based in Brussels (Belgium). **Languages** Arabic, English, French, Russian, Spanish. **Staff** 3.00 FTE, paid. **Finance** Members' dues. Contributions from donors, including: Deutsche Welle Akademie; Government of Flanders; *National Endowment for Democracy (NED)*; Norwegian Foreign Ministry; Open Society

Institute; *Swedish International Development Cooperation Agency (Sida)*; *UNDP (#20292)*; *UNESCO (#20322)*. **Activities** Knowledge management/information dissemination; guidance/assistance/consulting; projects/programmes; advocacy/lobbying/activism; events/meetings. **Events** *World Forum* Jakarta (Indonesia) 2016, *World Forum* Grahamstown (South Africa) 2012, *World forum* Brasilia (Brazil) 2011, *Asia regional forum* Jakarta (Indonesia) 2010, *World forum* Athens (Greece) 2008. **Publications** *Insider* (4 a year) – newsletter. Online resource centre.

Members Full; Associate. Members (190) include the following 13 organizations listed in this Yearbook:
Association of Caribbean Media Workers (ACM, #02408); *Balkan Investigative Reporting Network (BIRN, #03075)*; *BBC Media Action*; *Center for International Media Assistance (CIMA)*; *Fundación Gabo*; *International Center for Journalists (ICFJ)*; *International Federation of Journalists (IFJ, #13462)*; *International Foundation for Protection of Freedom of Speech – Adil Soz*; *International Media Support (IMS, #14128)*; *International Research and Exchanges Board (IREX)*; *Media Foundation for West Africa (MFWA, #16617)*; *Panos Network (#18183)*; *South East European Network for Professionalisation of the Media (SEENPM, #19817)*.

Consultative Status Consultative status granted from: *ECOSOC (#05331)* (Special). **IGO Relations** Cooperates with: *African Union (AU, #00488)*; *Council of Europe (CE, #04881)*; *European Commission (EC, #06633)*; *International Bank for Reconstruction and Development (IBRD, #12317)* (World Bank); *Internet Governance Forum (IGF, #15950)*; *OAS (#17629)*; *OECD (#17693)*; *Organization for Security and Cooperation in Europe (OSCE, #17887)*; *UNDP (#20292)*; *UNESCO (#20322)*. [2019/XM0625/cy/**F**]

♦ Global Forum on Migration and Development (GFMD) 10376

Forum mondial sur la migration et le développement

Contact Route des Morillons 15, Le Grand Saconnex, 1218 Geneva, Switzerland. T. +41227884946. Fax +41227884948. E-mail: gfmd@iom.int.
URL: http://gfmd.org/

History 2007. Set up as an informal, non-binding, voluntary and government-led process, at the initiative of *United Nations (UN, #20515)* Member States, to address migration and development interconnections in practical and action-oriented ways. **Aims** Foster practice and policy-oriented dialogue; build trust and partnerships among states; promote sharing of knowledge and good practices; reach out to the broader international community in identifying joint, coherent and cooperative responses to current and future challenges in the field of migration and development. **Structure** No formal structure. Chair-in-Office, assisted by: Chair's Taskforce, comprised of national and, if required by the annual Chair, some international experts; GFMD Support Unit (SU), based in Geneva (Switzerland); Country Focal Points; Troika, comprising current, past, and future Chairs; Steering Group (SG), comprising 37 governments; Friends of the Forum (FOF), comprised of all GFMD States Members. Except for Support Unit, supporting framework changes with the annual rotation of the Chairmanship. **Languages** English, French, Spanish. **Finance** Voluntary financial and in-kind contributions from governments. **Activities** Organizes Summit Meeting (annual), preceded by Civil Society Days (CSD), usually held in 2 days; results of the CSD are submitted as inputs to the Government Meeting; both meetings take place in the host country. During the period of the Chairmanship, varied preparatory activities take place, depending on the Chair's work priorities. Chair's Taskforce provides support for substantive preparations for the meeting; Support Unit provides administrative, financial and logistical assistance and administers the GFMD Platform for Partnerships; Country Focal Points enables liaison with participating governments and facilitates dialogue and greater coordination between different government offices and between government and other stakeholders at national level; Troika provides political and strategic guidance; Steering Group provides political and conceptual support to the process and the Chair; Friends of the Forum (FOF) advises on the agenda, structure and format of each Forum meeting. **Events** *Summit* Geneva (Switzerland) 2021, *Summit* Quito (Ecuador) 2020, *Summit* Marrakech (Morocco) 2018, *Summit* Berlin (Germany) 2017, *Summit* Dhaka (Bangladesh) 2016. **Publications** Report of Proceedings (annual).

Members Member States (193):
Afghanistan, Albania, Algeria, Andorra, Angola, Antigua-Barbuda, Argentina, Armenia, Australia, Austria, Azerbaijan, Bahamas, Bahrain, Bangladesh, Barbados, Belarus, Belgium, Belize, Benin, Bhutan, Bolivia, Bosnia-Herzegovina, Botswana, Brazil, Brunei Darussalam, Bulgaria, Burkina Faso, Burundi, Cambodia, Cameroon, Canada, Cape Verde, Central African Rep, Chad, Chile, China, Colombia, Comoros, Congo Brazzaville, Congo DR, Costa Rica, Côte d'Ivoire, Croatia, Cuba, Cyprus, Czechia, Denmark, Djibouti, Dominica, Dominican Rep, Ecuador, Egypt, El Salvador, Equatorial Guinea, Eritrea, Estonia, Eswatini, Ethiopia, Fiji, Finland, France, Gabon, Gambia, Georgia, Germany, Ghana, Greece, Grenada, Guatemala, Guinea, Guinea-Bissau, Guyana, Haiti, Holy See, Honduras, Hungary, Iceland, India, Indonesia, Iran Islamic Rep, Iraq, Ireland, Israel, Italy, Jamaica, Japan, Jordan, Kazakhstan, Kenya, Kiribati, Korea DPR, Korea Rep, Kuwait, Kyrgyzstan, Laos, Latvia, Lebanon, Lesotho, Liberia, Libya, Liechtenstein, Lithuania, Luxembourg, Madagascar, Malawi, Malaysia, Maldives, Mali, Malta, Marshall Is, Mauritania, Mauritius, Mexico, Micronesia FS, Moldova, Monaco, Mongolia, Montenegro, Morocco, Mozambique, Myanmar, Namibia, Nauru, Nepal, Netherlands, New Zealand, Nicaragua, Niger, Nigeria, North Macedonia, Norway, Oman, Pakistan, Palau, Panama, Papua New Guinea, Paraguay, Peru, Philippines, Poland, Portugal, Qatar, Romania, Russia, Rwanda, Samoa, San Marino, Sao Tomé-Principe, Saudi Arabia, Senegal, Serbia, Seychelles, Sierra Leone, Singapore, Slovakia, Slovenia, Solomon Is, Somalia, South Africa, South Sudan, Spain, Sri Lanka, St Kitts-Nevis, St Lucia, St Vincent-Grenadines, Sudan, Suriname, Sweden, Switzerland, Syrian AR, Tajikistan, Tanzania UR, Thailand, Togo, Tonga, Trinidad-Tobago, Tunisia, Türkiye, Turkmenistan, Tuvalu, Uganda, UK, Ukraine, United Arab Emirates, Uruguay, USA, Uzbekistan, Vanuatu, Venezuela, Vietnam, Yemen, Zambia, Zimbabwe.

IGO Relations Strong links with: *United Nations (UN, #20515)* through the Special Representative of the Secretary General on International Migration and Development, and the inter-agency Global Migration Group (GMG). **NGO Relations** Civil Society Coordinating office established upon invitation of the Swiss Chair, under the auspices of: *International Catholic Migration Commission (ICMC, #12459)*. While the primary purpose of the Forum is to facilitate a constructive dialogue among governments, the process has affirmed the crucial role of the civil society and other non-governmental actors (including the private sector) in enhancing coherence in policy making and institution building at the national, regional and international levels. [2022.02.08/XJ5844/**F***]

♦ Global Forum on Modern Direct Democracy (meeting series)
♦ Global Forum on MSM & HIV / see MPact Global Action for Gay Men's Health and Rights (#16875)
♦ Global Forum of NGOs for Natural Disaster Reduction (internationally oriented national body)

♦ Global Forum on Oceans, Coasts and Islands (GOF) 10377

Secretariat c/o Gerard J Mangone Center for Marine Policy, Univ of Delaware, Newark DE 19716, USA. T. +13028318086. Fax +13028313668.
URL: http://globaloceanforum.com/

History Sep 2002, Johannesburg (South Africa), during World Summit on Sustainable Development. Developed from WSSD Informal Coordinating Group on Oceans, Coasts and Islands. Also referred to as *Global Ocean Forum*. **Aims** Improve global, regional and national policies related to oceans, coasts and islands. **Structure** Steering Committee of 53 members. **Events** *Global Oceans Conference* Paris (France) 2010, *Global ocean policy day* Manado (Indonesia) 2009, *Global Oceans Conference* Hanoi (Vietnam) 2008, *Global Oceans Conference* Paris (France) 2006, *Global Oceans Conference* Paris (France) 2003. **Publications** *Global Forum on Oceans, Coasts, and Islands Newsletter* (6 a year). **Members** Membership countries not specified. **IGO Relations** Organizations involved: *Global Programme of Action for the Protection of the Marine Environment from Land-Based Activities (GPA, see: #20299)*; *Intergovernmental Oceanographic Commission (IOC, #11496)*. **NGO Relations** Participates in: *Global Partnership for Oceans (GPO, #10537)*. Secretariat housed at: *International Coastal and Ocean Organization (ICO, #12625)*. [2015/XF7032/**F**]

♦ Global Forum for Rural Advisory Services (GFRAS) 10378

Forum mondial pour le conseil rural – Foro Global para los Servicios de Asesoria Rural

Communications Manager c/o Agridea Eschikon 28, 8315 Lindau ZH, Switzerland. T. +41523549764. Fax +41523549797. E-mail: info@g-fras.org.
URL: http://www.g-fras.org/

History 2010, Lausanne (Switzerland). Charter approved 26 Mar 2010; came into effect 1 Jun 2011. **Aims** Provide advocacy and leadership on pluralistic, demand-driven rural advisory services within the global development agenda. **Structure** General Assembly; Board; operational activities under command of Executive Secretary. **Languages** Danish, Dutch, English, French, German, Portuguese, Spanish. **Staff** 3.00 FTE, paid. **Finance** Sources: contributions; donations. Supported by: *Bill and Melinda Gates Foundation (BMGF)*; *European Commission (EC, #06633)*; *International Fund for Agricultural Development (IFAD, #13692)*; *Swiss Agency for Development and Cooperation (SDC)*; *United States Agency for International Development (USAID)*. **Activities** Events/meetings; knowledge management/information dissemination; networking/liaising. **Events** *Meeting* 2021, *Annual Meeting* Buenos Aires (Argentina) 2014, *Annual Meeting* Berlin (Germany) 2013, *Annual Meeting* Manila (Philippines) 2012, *Annual Meeting* Nairobi (Kenya) 2011. **Members** Organizations and institutions. Membership countries not specified. **NGO Relations** Staff provided by: *International Food Policy Research Institute (IFPRI, #13622)*; Swiss Association for the Development of Agriculture and Rural Areas (Agridea). [2022.02.09/XJ7916/**F**]

♦ Global Forum on Sustainable Energy (internationally oriented national body)

♦ Global Forum on Transparency and Exchange of Information for Tax Purposes 10379

Forum mondial sur la transparence et l'échange de renseignements à des fins fiscales

Contact CTPA/GF Tax Cooperation, 2 rue André Pascal, 75775 Paris CEDEX 16, France. E-mail: gftaxcooperation@oecd.org.
URL: http://www.oecd.org/tax/transparency/

History 17 Sep 2009, by Council decision of *OECD (#17693)*, developing out of an earlier programme running since 2000. Original mandate expired 31 Dec 2012. Mandate renewed and revised 15 Nov 2012; renewed and revised again 27 Nov 2015 and will remain valid until 31 Dec 2020. **Aims** Implement internationally agreed standards of transparency and exchange of information in the tax area. **Structure** Steering Group: Peer Review Group; Automatic Exchange of Information Group Secretariat, based in OECD Centre for Tax Policy and Administration. **Languages** English, French. **Staff** 38.00 FTE, paid. **Finance** Members' dues. Budget (2018): euro 4,432,975. **Activities** Standards/guidelines; politics/policy/regulatory; monitoring/evaluation; guidance/assistance/consulting; knowledge management/information dissemination. **Events** *Meeting* Paris (France) 2019, *Meeting* Paris (France) 2018, *Meeting* Punta del Este (Uruguay) 2018, *Meeting* Yaoundé (Cameroon) 2017, *Meeting* Tbilisi (Georgia) 2016. **Publications** *Automatic Exchange of Information Implementation Report*. Annual Reports; Peer Review Reports; Handbook.

Members Governments of 152 countries and territories:
Albania, Andorra, Anguilla, Antigua-Barbuda, Argentina, Armenia, Aruba, Australia, Austria, Azerbaijan, Bahamas, Bahrain, Barbados, Belgium, Belize, Benin, Bermuda, Bosnia-Herzegovina, Botswana, Brazil, Brunei Darussalam, Bulgaria, Burkina Faso, Cambodia, Cameroon, Canada, Cape Verde, Cayman Is, Chad, Chile, China, Colombia, Cook Is, Costa Rica, Côte d'Ivoire, Croatia, Curaçao, Cyprus, Czechia, Denmark, Djibouti, Dominica, Dominican Rep, Ecuador, Egypt, El Salvador, Estonia, Eswatini, Faeroe Is, Finland, France, Gabon, Georgia, Germany, Ghana, Gibraltar, Greece, Greenland, Grenada, Guatemala, Guernsey, Guyana, Haiti, Hong Kong, Hungary, Iceland, India, Indonesia, Ireland, Isle of Man, Israel, Italy, Jamaica, Japan, Jersey, Kazakhstan, Kenya, Korea Rep, Kuwait, Latvia, Lebanon, Lesotho, Liberia, Liechtenstein, Lithuania, Luxembourg, Macau, Madagascar, Malaysia, Maldives, Malta, Marshall Is, Mauritania, Mauritius, Mexico, Monaco, Mongolia, Montenegro, Montserrat, Morocco, Nauru, Netherlands, New Zealand, Niger, Nigeria, Niue, North Macedonia, Norway, Pakistan, Panama, Papua New Guinea, Paraguay, Peru, Philippines, Poland, Portugal, Qatar, Romania, Russia, Rwanda, Samoa, San Marino, Saudi Arabia, Senegal, Serbia, Seychelles, Singapore, Slovakia, Slovenia, South Africa, Spain, St Kitts-Nevis, St Lucia, St Maarten, St Vincent-Grenadines, Sweden, Switzerland, Tanzania UR, Thailand, Togo, Trinidad-Tobago, Tunisia, Türkiye, Turks-Caicos, Uganda, UK, Ukraine, United Arab Emirates, Uruguay, USA, Vanuatu, Virgin Is UK.

Regional entity:
European Union (EU, #08967).

Observers (17):
African Development Bank (ADB, #00283); *African Tax Administration Forum (ATAF, #00479)*; *Asian Development Bank (ADB, #01422)*; *Caribbean Community (CARICOM, #03476)*; *Centre de rencontres et d'études des dirigeants des administrations fiscales (CREDAF, #03779)*; *Commonwealth Secretariat (#04362)*; *Council of Europe Development Bank (CEB, #04897)*; *European Bank for Reconstruction and Development (EBRD, #06315)*; *European Investment Bank (EIB, #07599)*; *Financial Action Task Force (FATF, #09765)*; *Inter-American Centre for Tax Administrations (#11405)*; *Inter-American Development Bank (IDB, #11427)*; *International Finance Corporation (IFC, #13597)*; *International Monetary Fund (IMF, #14180)*; *The World Bank Group (#21218)*; *United Nations (UN, #20515)*; *World Customs Organization (WCO, #21350)*. [2018.09.25/XM4852/**F***]

♦ Global Foundation for Democracy and Development (internationally oriented national body)
♦ Global Foundation for Peroxisomal Disorders (internationally oriented national body)
♦ Global Foundation for the Sustainability of Billion Minds (internationally oriented national body)

♦ Global Framework for Climate Services (GFCS) 10380

Secretariat c/o WMO, Av de la Paix 7bis, PO Box 2300, 1211 Geneva 2, Switzerland. T. +41227308579. Fax +41227308037.
URL: http://gfcs.wmo.int/

History Proposed 2009, Geneva (Switzerland), at 3rd World Climate Conference by Heads of States and Government Ministers. Office set up 2011, within *World Meteorological Organization (WMO, #21649)*. **Aims** Enable better management of the risks of climate variability and change and adaptation to *climate change*, through development and incorporation of science-based climate information and prediction into planning, policy and practice on global, regional and national scales. **Structure** Climate Coordination Panel (CCP); Partners Advisory Committee; Secretariat, accountable to WMO Secretary-General; sub-structures established as needed by CCP. **Languages** English, French. **Staff** 6.00 FTE, paid. **Finance** Members' contributions to Trust Fund or through bilateral and multi-lateral investments for projects. Sponsors: governments of Canada, UK, Ireland, Finland, France, Iran Islamic Rep, Australia, Korea Rep, Switzerland, Bangladesh, Qatar, Hong Kong, Norway, India, South Africa, Mexico, China and Germany. **Activities** Knowledge management/information dissemination; events/meetings; monitoring/evaluation; research/documentation; capacity building. **Events** *GCOS Conference on Global Climate Observation* Amsterdam (Netherlands) 2016, *Regional Consultation on GFCS in the Indian Ocean* Ebene (Mauritius) 2016, *Central Asia Observation Workshop* Bishkek (Kyrgyzstan) 2015, *Regional Consultation on Climate Services at the National Level for South East Europe* Antalya (Turkey) 2014, *Session* Geneva (Switzerland) 2014. **Publications** *GFCS Newsletter*. *Step-by-step Guidelines for Establishing a National Framework for Climate Services*. *GFCS Priority Needs* – brochure.

Members WMO members; inter- and non-governmental, regional, national and local stakeholders. Main partners:
- *European Centre for Medium-Range Weather Forecasts (ECMWF, #06490)*;
- *European Commission (EC, #06633)*;
- *European Organisation for the Exploitation of Meteorological Satellites (EUMETSAT, #08096)*;
- *FAO (#09260)*;
- *Global Water Partnership (GWP, #10653)*;
- *Group on Earth Observations (GEO, #10735)*;
- *HELVETAS Swiss Intercooperation*;
- *International Bank for Reconstruction and Development (IBRD, #12317)* (World Bank);
- *International Federation of Red Cross and Red Crescent Societies (#13526)*;
- *International Renewable Energy Agency (IRENA, #14715)*;
- *International Union of Geodesy and Geophysics (IUGG, #15776)*;
- *Norwegian Refugee Council (NRC)*;
- *Stockholm Environment Institute (SEI, #19993)*;
- *UNDP (#20292)*;
- *UNEP (#20299)*;
- *UNESCO (#20322)*;
- *United Nations Institute for Training and Research (UNITAR, #20576)*;
- *United Nations Office for Disaster Risk Reduction (UNDRR, #20595)*;
- *United Nations Office for Project Services (UNOPS, #20602)*;
- *WHO (#20950)*;
- *World Food Programme (WFP, #21510)*.

Other partners:
Centre for International Climate and Environmental Research, Oslo (CICERO); *Centro Interamericano de Capacitación en Administración Pública (CICAP, inactive)*; *CGIAR System Organization (CGIAR, #03843)* (Climate Change Agriculture and Food Security CCAFS); *Chr Michelsen Institute – Development Studies and Human Rights (CMI)*. [2019.09.02/XM4304/**E***]

♦ Global Free Software Organization (unconfirmed)

♦ Global Fuel Economy Initiative (GFEI) 10381

Exec Sec c/of FiA Foundation, 60 Trafalgar Square, London, WC2N 5DS, UK.
URL: http://www.fiafoundation.org/our-work/global-fuel-economy-initiative/

History Set up as a partnership of *FIA Foundation (#09742)*, *International Energy Agency (IEA, #13270)*, *Working Group on Sustainable Development (SDWG, #21061)*, *OECD (#17693)* – International Transport Forum (ITF), *International Council on Clean Transportation (ICCT, #13007)* and Institute for Transportation Studies – UC Davis. **Aims** Assist governments and transport stakeholders promote greater fuel economy. **Activities** Knowledge management/knowledge management; capacity building; awareness raising. **IGO Relations** *European Commission (EC, #06633)*; *Global Environment Facility (GEF, #10346)*. [2019.06.25/XJ9662/**E**]

- ♦ Global Fund Advocates Network
- ♦ Global Fund for Children (internationally oriented national body)
- ♦ Global Fund for Cities Development / see FMDV (#09804)

♦ Global Fund for Community Foundations (GFCF) 10382

Exec Dir PostNet Ste 135, Private Bag X2600 Houghton, Johannesburg, 2041, South Africa. T. +27114474396. E-mail: info@globalfundcf.org.
Street Address Fourth floor, 158 Jan Smuts Avenue, Rosebank, Johannesburg, 2196, South Africa.
UK Registered Office Community House, Citylink Business Park, Albert Street, Belfast, BT12 4HQ, UK.
URL: http://www.globalfundcommunityfoundations.org/

History Started Jan 2006, as a 3-year pilot project, initiated by *International Bank for Reconstruction and Development (IBRD, #12317)* (World Bank), *Ford Foundation (#09858)*, *Charles Stewart Mott Foundation* and *Worldwide Initiatives for Grantmaker Support (WINGS, #21926)*. Became an independent entity, 2009, when became a UK Registered Charity: XT18816. Set up head office in Johannesburg (South Africa), 2010, where it is registered as a Section 21 company. **Aims** Promote and support institutions of community philanthropy around the world. **Structure** Board, comprising Chair, Secretary, Treasurer and 3 members. **Staff** 4.00 FTE, paid. **Finance** Funding from: *Aga Khan Foundation (AKF, #00545)*; *Charles Stewart Mott Foundation*; *W K Kellogg Foundation (WKKF)*; *International Development Research Centre (IDRC, #13162)*; *King Baudouin Foundation (KBF)*; *TrustAfrica (#20251)*; *Rockefeller Brothers Fund (RBF)*; *Ford Foundation (#09858)*. **NGO Relations** *Network of European Foundations (NEF, #17019)*; *Worldwide Initiatives for Grantmaker Support (WINGS, #21926)*. [2018/XJ5657/f/**F**]

- ♦ Global Fund to End Modern Slavery (internationally oriented national body)
- ♦ Global Fund to End Slavery (unconfirmed)

♦ Global Fund to Fight AIDS, Tuberculosis and Malaria (Global Fund) . 10383

Le Fonds mondial de lutte contre le sida, la tuberculose et le paludisme – El fondo mundial de lucha contra el SIDA, la tuberculosis y la malaria

Exec Dir Global Health Campus, Chemin du Pommier 40, 1218 Le Grand-Saconnex GE, Switzerland. T. +41587911700. Fax +41445806820.
URL: http://www.theglobalfund.org/

History Jun 2001, Genoa (Italy). Founded by *Permanent Mechanism for Consultation and Political Coordination (Rio Group, inactive)*, following a proposal by Kofi Annan, Secretary-General of *United Nations (UN, #20515)*. Secretariat set up, Jan 2002. **Aims** Mobilize and invest nearly US$4 billion a year to support programmes run by local experts in countries and communities most in need to accelerate the end of AIDS, tuberculosis and malaria as epidemics. **Structure** Board; Technical Review Panel; Country Coordinating Mechanisms; Principal Recipients; Local Fund Agents; Partnership Forum; Inspector General; Technical Evaluation Reference Group; Secretariat. **Languages** Arabic, Chinese, English, French, Russian, Spanish. **Staff** 600.00 FTE, paid. *Administrative Tribunal of the International Labour Organization (ILO Tribunal, #00118)* is competent to settle disputes. **Finance** Contributions from donor countries, corporations, foundations and individuals, including: *Group of Eight (G-8, #10745)*; *(RED)*. **Activities** Financial and/or material support; networking/liaising. **Events** *Technical Workshop on Mortality Surveillance in Africa* Addis Ababa (Ethiopia) 2019, *Replenishment Conference* Lyon (France) 2019, *Meeting on the future of Harmonization for Health in Africa (HHA)* Dakar (Senegal) 2017, *Replenishment Conference* Montréal, QC (Canada) 2016, *Meeting* Tokyo (Japan) 2015. **Publications** Annual Report; regular progress reports; regional reviews; resource needs reports. **Members** Not a membership organization. **IGO Relations** Observer status with (1): *United Nations (UN, #20515)* (General Assembly). Cooperates with: *International Bank for Reconstruction and Development (IBRD, #12317)*, (World Bank); *Joint United Nations Programme on HIV/AIDS (UNAIDS, #16149)*; *Unitaid (#20493)*; *WHO (#20950)*. Supports: *SEAMEO TROPMED Regional Centre for Microbiology, Parasitology and Entomology (#19185)*; *UNICEF (#20332)*. Adheres to: *Global Partnership for Effective Development Co-operation (GPEDC, #10532)*. **NGO Relations** Member of: *Alliance for Malaria Prevention (AMP, #00706)*; *Federation of International Civil Servants' Associations (FICSA, #09603)*; *Inter-Agency Task Team on Children affected by AIDS (IATT, #11394)*; *International Partnership on Religion and Sustainable Development (PaRD, #14524)*; *Joint Learning Initiative on Faith and Local Communities (JLI, #16139)*; *Reproductive Health Supplies Coalition (RHSC, #18847)*; *Roll Back Malaria Partnership (RBM, #18968)*; *Stop TB Partnership (#19999)*. Partner of: *Global Financing Facility (GFF, #10360)*. Supports: *CARE International (CI, #03429)*; *Caribbean Regional Network of People Living with HIV/AIDS (CRN+, #03549)*; *Middle East and North Africa Harm Reduction Network (MENAHRA, #16780)*; *Robert Carr civil society Networks Fund (RCNF, #18956)*. Cooperates with: *International Aid Transparency Initiative (IATI, #11604)*; *UHC2030 (#20277)*. [2020/XF6560/I/**F***]

- ♦ **Global Fund** Global Fund to Fight AIDS, Tuberculosis and Malaria (#10383)
- ♦ Global Fund for Widows (internationally oriented national body)

♦ Global Fund for Women (GFW) 10384

Fonds Mondial pour les Femmes – Fondo Global Para Mujeres

Pres/CEO 800 Market Street, 7th Floor, San Francisco CA 94102, USA. T. +14152484800. Fax +14152484801.
URL: http://www.globalfundforwomen.org/

History Founded 1987, Palo Alto CA (USA), by Anne Firth Murray (Founding President), Frances Kissling, and Laura Lederer. Merged with *International Museum of Women (IMOW)*, Mar 2014. Registered in the State of California (USA). **Aims** Advance the movement for women's *human rights* by directing resources to, and raising the voices of, women worldwide. **Structure** Board of Directors; Executive Committee; Standing Committees (6); Standing Sub-Committees (2). **Languages** Arabic, English, French, Portuguese, Russian, Spanish. **Staff** 40.00 FTE, paid. **Finance** Grants from individuals, foundations, corporations and governments, including: Alice and Olivia; *Bill and Melinda Gates Foundation (BMGF)*; Dutch Government; Johnson and Johnson; JP Morgan Chase; *Levi Strauss Foundation (LSF)*; MAC AIDS Fund; Nike Foundation; *Oak Foundation*; PepsiCo; Symantec; Working Assets/CREDO. **Activities** Financial and/or material support; advocacy/lobbying/activism; capacity building; events/meetings. **Publications** Reports; Impact Reports; ENews. **Members** Not a membership organization. **Consultative Status** Consultative status granted from: *United Nations Population Fund (UNFPA, #20612)*. **IGO Relations** Associated with Department of Global Communications of the United Nations. **NGO Relations** Member of: *Association for Women's Rights in Development (AWID, #02980)*; *CIVICUS: World Alliance for Citizen Participation (#03962)*; *Global Philanthropy Project (GPP, #10546)*; *Prospera – International Network of Women's Funds (INWF, #18545)*; *Women's Funding Network*. Supports: *Caribbean Association for Feminist Research and Action (CAFRA, #03445)*; *Every Woman Every Child (EWEC, #09215)*; *International Federation of Women Lawyers (FIDA, #13578)*; *Feminist International Radio Endeavour (FIRE)*. [2018/XF2963/I/**F**]

- ♦ Global Future (unconfirmed)

♦ Global Gambling Guidance Group (G4) 10385

G4 Secretariat Pieter Calandlaan 317-319, NL-1068 NH, Amsterdam, Netherlands. T. +31204124403. E-mail: info@gx4.com.
URL: http://www.gx4.com/

History Founded 2004. **Aims** Minimize the impact of problem gambling by promoting a worldwide accreditation programme. **Structure** Board. **Languages** English. **Staff** 2.00 FTE, paid. **Finance** Financed by accredited and certified companies/organizations. **Activities** Accreditation/certification. **Publications** *G4 Newsletter* (10 a year). **Members** Organizations and companies. Membership countries not specified. [2022/XM0495/**D**]

♦ GLOBALG.A.P 10386

CEO c/o FoodPLUS GmbH, Spichernstrasse 55, 50672 Cologne, Germany. T. +492215799325. Fax +492215799389. E-mail: info@globalgap.org.
URL: http://www.globalgap.org/

History 1997. Founded by Euro-Retailer Produce Working Group (EUREP). GAP stands for *Good Agricultural Practice*. Former names and other names: *Global Partnership for Safe and Sustainable Agriculture (EUREPGAP)* – former (2007). **Aims** Promote global *harmonization*; set standards and procedures for the development of good *agricultural* practice, certification and benchmarking. **Structure** Board; Secretariat. Technical Committees (5): Crops; Aquaculture; Livestock; GRASP; Systems and Rules. Focus Groups. Certification Body Committee; Integrity Surveillance Committee (ISC). National Technical Working Groups. **Activities** Awards/prizes/competitions; certification/accreditation; events/meetings. **Events** *Conference* London (UK) 2010, *Conference* Cologne (Germany) 2008, *Conference* Bangkok (Thailand) 2007. **Publications** *Good Agricultural Practice – News*. Project reports.
Members Retail and Food Service Members in 18 countries:
Austria, Belgium, Finland, Germany, Hungary, Ireland, Italy, Japan, Latvia, Netherlands, Norway, Slovenia, South Africa, Spain, Sweden, Switzerland, UK, USA.
Producer/Supplier Members in 38 countries:
Argentina, Austria, Belgium, Brazil, Chile, China, Colombia, Denmark, Egypt, Estonia, Ethiopia, France, Germany, Hungary, India, Ireland, Israel, Italy, Kenya, Luxembourg, Mexico, Morocco, Myanmar, Netherlands, New Zealand, Norway, Peru, Romania, Spain, Sri Lanka, Sweden, Switzerland, Thailand, UK, United Arab Emirates, Uruguay, USA, Vietnam.
Associate in 42 countries:
Afghanistan, Argentina, Australia, Austria, Belgium, Brazil, Bulgaria, China, Colombia, Costa Rica, Czechia, Denmark, Dominican Rep, Ecuador, France, Germany, Greece, Guatemala, India, Ireland, Israel, Italy, Japan, Kenya, Korea Rep, Mexico, Myanmar, New Zealand, Nicaragua, Norway, Pakistan, South Africa, Spain, Suriname, Sweden, Türkiye, UK, United Arab Emirates, Uruguay, USA, Vietnam, Zimbabwe.
Included in the above, 6 organizations listed in this Yearbook:
CropLife Europe (#04965); *CropLife International (#04966)*; *CropLife Latin America (#04967)*; *Natural Resources Institute (NRI)*; *The Sustainability Consortium (TSC, #20049)*; *West African Power Pool (WAPP, #20894)*.
IGO Relations Cooperates with: *Deutsche Gesellschaft für Internationale Zusammenarbeit (GIZ)*. **NGO Relations** Member of: *Global Alliance for Climate-Smart Agriculture (GACSA, #10189)*; *International Accreditation Forum (IAF, #11584)*. [2021/XF6761/**F**]

♦ Global Gas Processors Alliance (GPA Global) 10387

Contact 60 60 American Plaza, Ste 700, Tulsa OK 74135, USA. T. +19184933872. Fax +19184933875.
URL: http://ggpa.gpaglobal.org/

History as an umbrella of regional gas processors associations. **Structure** Chapters (7): US GPA Midstream Association; Gas Processing Association Canada; *Gas Processors Association – Europe (GPA Europe, #10076)*; GPA Gulf Cooperation Council Chapter; Asia Pacific GPA (currently being developed); Venezuelan Gas Processors Association. [2016/XJ2262/**F**]

- ♦ Global Genes (internationally oriented national body)
- ♦ Global Genes – Allies in Rare Disease / see Global Genes

♦ Global Genome Biodiversity Network (GGBN) 10388

Secretariat Natl Museum of Natural History, Smithsonian Institution, PO Box 37012, SI Building, Room 153, MRC 010, Washington DC 20013-7012, USA. E-mail: ggbn@si.edu.
URL: http://ggbn.org/

Aims Foster collaborations among repositories of molecular biodiversity so as to ensure quality standards, improve best practices, secure interoperability, and harmonize exchange of material in accordance with national and international legislation and conventions; provide genome-quality samples from across the Tree of Life for research, training and development, thereby contributing to the conservation of global genetic diversity for generations to come. **Structure** International Steering Committee. Task Forces (3): Data Standards and Access; Policies and Practices; Marketing and Outreach. Secretariat. **Events** *International Conference on Biodiversity Biobanking* Vienna (Austria) 2018, *International Conference on Biodiversity Biobanking* Berlin (Germany) 2016, *International Conference on Biodiversity Biobanking* London (UK) 2014, *General Meeting* Berlin (Germany) 2013, *General Meeting* Copenhagen (Denmark) 2012.
Members Biorepositories, networks of biorepositories and research organizations. Members in 13 countries:
Australia, Austria, Brazil, China, Colombia, Croatia, Czechia, Denmark, Germany, Hungary, South Africa, UK, USA.
Included in the above, 2 organizations listed in this Yearbook:
Commonwealth Scientific and Industrial Research Organization (CSIRO); *Ocean Genome Legacy (OGL)*. [2017/XJ8728/y/**F**]

- ♦ Global Geodetic Observing System (see: #11914)

♦ Global Geoparks Network (GGN) 10389

Main Office 26 Baiwanzhuang Road, 100037 Beijing, China. E-mail: cgn.office@foxmail.com – ggn2004@gmail.com.
URL: http://www.globalgeopark.org/

History 1998, by *UNESCO (#20322)*. Originally referred to as *International Network of Geoparks*. Also referred to as *World Geoparks Network*. Present name adopted 2004. **Aims** Conserve and enhance the value of areas of geological significance in Earth history, including landscapes and geological formations, which are key witnesses to the evolution of our planet and determinants for our future; promote sustainable development through geo-tourism and education. **Structure** General Assembly; Executive Board; Advisory Committee; Committees; Task Forces; Working Groups; Operational Secretariat. Regional networks: *Asia Pacific Geoparks Network (APGN, #01916)*; *European Geoparks Network (EGN, #07389)*. **Languages** English. **Staff** 14.00 FTE, voluntary. **Activities** Awards/prizes/competitions; awareness raising; capacity building; certification/accreditation; events/meetings; guidance/assistance/consulting; knowledge management/information dissemination; monitoring/evaluation; networking/liaising; research and development; standards/guidelines. **Events** *International Conference on Geoparks* Jeju (Korea Rep) 2021, *International Conference on Geoparks* Jeju (Korea Rep) 2020, *International Conference on Geoparks* Shimabara (Japan) 2012, *International conference on geoparks* Langkawi (Malaysia) 2010, *Annual European geoparks conference* Idanha-a-Nova (Portugal) 2009. **Publications** *GGN Newsletter*.
Members Geoparks (120); Individuals (20). Members in 33 countries:
Austria, Brazil, Canada, China, Croatia, Cyprus, Czechia, Denmark, Finland, France, Germany, Greece, Hungary, Iceland, Indonesia, Ireland, Italy, Japan, Korea Rep, Malaysia, Morocco, Netherlands, Norway, Poland, Portugal, Romania, Slovakia, Slovenia, Spain, Türkiye, UK, Uruguay, Vietnam.
IGO Relations *International Geoscience Programme (IGCP, #13715)*; UNESCO – International Geosciences and Geoparks Programme (IGGP); *World Heritage Centre (WHC, #21566)*. **NGO Relations** *International Union for Conservation of Nature and Natural Resources (IUCN, #15766)*; *International Union of Geological Sciences (IUGS, #15777)*. [2021/XJ5706/**F**]

♦ Global Ghost Gear Initiative (GGGI) 10390

Secretariat c/o World Animal Protection, 222 Grays Inn Road, 5th Floor, London, WC1X 8HB, UK. E-mail: gggi@worldanimalprotection.org.
URL: http://www.ghostgear.org/

History Launched Sep 2015. **Aims** Improve the health of *marine ecosystems*; protect marine animals; safeguard human health and livelihoods. **Structure** Steering Group; Advisory Group; Secretariat. **Languages** English. **Finance** Annual budget (2017): US$ 780,000. **NGO Relations** *World Animal Protection (#21092)*. [2018.03.07/XM5177/**F**]

- ♦ GlobalGiving Foundation (internationally oriented national body)
- ♦ Global Ltd / see Global Maritime Education and Training Association (#10464)
- ♦ Global Governance Foundation / see Institute for Geopolitical Research and Development (#11265)

♦ Global Governance Institute (GGI) 10391

Office Hive 5 – Cours Saint Michel 30b, 1040 Brussels, Belgium. T. +3225390039. E-mail: info@globalgovernance.eu.
URL: http://www.globalgovernance.eu/

History Registration: Banque-Carrefour des Entreprises, No/ID: 0831.178.152, Start date: 18 Nov 2010, Belgium. **Aims** Promote comprehensive research, cutting-edge analysis and innovative advice on core policy issues, informed by a truly global perspective. [2021/XJ8398/j/**D**]

♦ Global Grassroots (internationally oriented national body)
♦ Global Green Environmental Network (unconfirmed)
♦ Global Greengrants Fund (internationally oriented national body)
♦ Global Green Growth Forum (unconfirmed)

♦ Global Green Growth Institute (GGGI) 10392

Dir-Gen Seoul Headquarters, 19-F Jeongdong Bldg, 21-15 Jeongdong-gil, Jung-gu, Seoul 100-784, Korea Rep. T. +82220969991. Fax +82220969990. E-mail: info@gggi.org.
URL: http://www.gggi.org/

History 16 Jun 2010. Launched as a non-profit foundation, on the initiative of Korea Rep President Lee Myung-bak, during East Asia Climate Forum. Signing Ceremony for the Agreement on the Establishment as an IGO held Jun 2012. Registration: Foundation, End date: Jun 2012, Korea Rep. **Aims** Pioneer and diffuse a new model of economic growth, known as 'green growth', that simultaneously targets key aspects of economic performance, such as poverty reduction, job creation and social inclusion, and those of environmental sustainability, such as mitigation of climate change and biodiversity loss and security of access to clean energy and water. **Structure** Assembly; Council; Executive Management. **Finance** An initial contribution of US$ 10 million per year for 3 years provided by government of Korean Rep. **Events** *Global Green Growth Week Conference* Seoul (Korea Rep) 2022, *Contributing to a Better World by Promoting and Advancing Green Growth* Seoul (Korea Rep) 2021, *Global Green Growth Week Conference* Seoul (Korea Rep) 2021, *Strengthening Partnership on Climate Action, Forest Restoration and Peace* Seoul (Korea Rep) 2021, *International New Energy Summit* Ulaanbaatar (Mongolia) 2021.
Members Governments (39):
Australia, Burkina Faso, Cambodia, China, Colombia, Costa Rica, Denmark, Ethiopia, Fiji, Guyana, Hungary, India, Indonesia, Jordan, Kiribati, Korea Rep, Laos, Mexico, Mongolia, Morocco, Mozambique, Myanmar, Nepal, Norway, Papua New Guinea, Paraguay, Peru, Philippines, Qatar, Rwanda, Senegal, Sri Lanka, Thailand, Tonga, Uganda, UK, United Arab Emirates, Vanuatu, Vietnam.
IGO Relations Accredited by (1): *Green Climate Fund (GCF, #10714)*. Observer status with (1): *United Nations (UN, #20515)* (General Assembly). Memorandum of Understanding with (4): *Asian Development Bank (ADB, #01422)*; *Deutsche Gesellschaft für Internationale Zusammenarbeit (GIZ)*; *Global Green Growth Forum (3GF)*; *United Nations Economic and Social Commission for Asia and the Pacific (ESCAP, #20557)*. Agreement with: *International Renewable Energy Agency (IRENA, #14715)*. **NGO Relations** Memorandum of Understanding with (1): *World Economic Forum (WEF, #21367)*. Member of (4): *Environmental Peacebuilding Association (EnPAx, #05509)*; *Green Industry Platform (GIP, #10722)*; *LEDS Global Partnership (LEDS GP, #16435)*; *World Water Council (WWC, #21908)*. Partner of (1): *Tropical Forest Alliance (TFA, #20249)*. Instrumental in setting up (2): *Green Growth Knowledge Platform (GGKP, #10719)*; *Inclusive Green Growth Partnership (IGGP, #11146)*. [2019/XM3877/j/**C***]

♦ Global Green Island Summit (GGIS) 10393

Secretariat address not obtained. T. +18085870051. E-mail: ggisforum@gmail.com.
URL: http://www.ggis-forum.org/sub/catalog.php?CatNo=12

History 27 Aug 2018, Jeju (Korea Rep). **Aims** Set up a cooperation network for all global islands; share sustainable models and best practices to enhance resilience against global environmental issues; promote leadership of global island governments; strengthen mutual cooperation that prioritizes clean energy, sustainable development and recovery. **Structure** Secretariat. **Activities** Events/meetings. **Events** *Global Green Island Summit Forum* Jeju (Korea Rep) 2018.
Members Islands (3) in 3 countries:
Japan (Okinawa), Korea Rep (Jeju), USA (Hawaii). [2020/AA0023/**F**]

♦ Global Greens 10394

Treas 31 Rue Wiertz, 1050 Brussels, Belgium. E-mail: secretary@globalgreens.org.
URL: http://www.globalgreens.org/

History Apr 2001, Canberra, ACT (Australia). Founded at the First Global Greens Congress, when Global Greens Charter was adopted and the collaboration mechanisms were set up. Registration: Banque-Carrefour des Entreprises, No/ID: 0552.785.578, Start date: 19 May 2014, Belgium. **Aims** Work cooperatively to implement the Global Greens Charter, which sets out core values of ecological wisdom, social justice, participatory democracy, nonviolence, sustainability and respect for diversity. **Structure** *Global Greens Coordination (GGC)* makes decisions on behalf of Global Greens in between Congresses, and consists of 3 members and 3 alternates of each of the 4 federations: *African Greens Federation (AGF, #00331)*; *Asia-Pacific Greens Federation (APGF, #01919)*; *European Green Party (EGP, #07409)*; *Federación de Partidos Verdes de las Américas (FPVA, #09385)*. **Languages** Chinese, English, French, Spanish. **Staff** 1.00 FTE, paid. **Finance** Donations. **Events** *Congress* Seoul (Korea Rep) 2023, *Congress* Liverpool (UK) 2017, *Congress* Dakar (Senegal) 2012, *Congress* Sao Paulo (Brazil) 2008, *Global conference / Congress* Canberra, ACT (Australia) 2001. **Publications** *Global Greens News and Newsletter*.
Members Green parties and political movements. Full (79) in 73 countries and territories:
Albania, Algeria, Andorra, Argentina, Australia, Austria, Belgium, Bolivia, Brazil, Bulgaria, Burkina Faso, Canada, Chad, Chile, Colombia, Congo Brazzaville, Congo DR, Côte d'Ivoire, Cyprus, Czechia, Dominican Rep, Egypt, Estonia, Finland, France, Georgia, Germany, Greece, Hungary, India, Ireland, Italy, Japan, Kenya, Korea Rep, Latvia, Lebanon, Luxembourg, Madagascar, Mali, Malta, Mauritius, Mexico, Moldova, Mongolia, Morocco, Mozambique, Nepal, Netherlands, New Zealand, Niger, North Macedonia, Norway, Pakistan, Peru, Poland, Portugal, Romania, Rwanda, Senegal, Slovenia, Spain, Sweden, Switzerland, Taiwan, Togo, Tunisia, Uganda, UK, Ukraine, USA, Venezuela, Zimbabwe.
Associate (15) in 12 countries and territories:
Azerbaijan, Bangladesh, Belarus, Burundi, Denmark, Fiji, Guatemala, India, Indonesia, Iraq, Palestine, Russia.
Candidate (2) in 2 countries:
Croatia, Türkiye.
Partners (2):
Global Young Greens (GYG, #10663); Taiwan Friends of the Global Greens.
IGO Relations Accredited by: *Green Climate Fund (GCF, #10714)*; *United Nations Framework Convention on Climate Change – Secretariat (UNFCCC, #20564)*. **NGO Relations** Affiliated Green foundations and institutes, not specified. [2022/XM0706/**F**]

♦ Global Green University (internationally oriented national body)
♦ Global Greeter Network Foundation (unconfirmed)
♦ Global Grid Forum / see Open Grid Forum (#17754)
♦ Global Groundwater Centre / see International Groundwater Resources Assessment Centre (#13739)
♦ Global Hand – Humanitarian Aid Network for Distribution (internationally oriented national body)

♦ Global Hands-On Universe (GHOU) 10395

Contact Largo dos Topazios 48 – 3 Frt, 2785-817 São Domingos de Rana, Portugal. E-mail: info@handsonuniverse.org.
URL: http://handsonuniverse.org/

History Hands-On Universe (HOU) project began 1990s, USA. GHOU founded when other countries became involved. **Aims** Train teachers on the use of modern tools and resources for science education and engage students in international scientific projects. **Activities** Events/meetings. **Events** *Annual Conference* Saint-Michel-L'Observatoire (France) 2019, *Annual Conference* Vienna (Austria) 2018. [2019/XM7993/**F**]

♦ Global Handwashing Partnership (GHP) 10396

Secretariat c/o FHI 360, 1825 Connecticut Ave NW, Washington DC 20009-5721, USA. T. +12028848000. Fax +12028848430.
URL: http://www.globalhandwashing.org/

History Founded 2001, as *Global Public-Private Partnership for Handwashing with Soap (PPPHW)*. Current title adopted Jan 2017. Grew out of two large-scale handwashing programmes whose success demonstrated the untapped synergies of public-private sector collaboration and the role of consumer research and consumer-centred marketing in driving handwashing behaviour change. Original members included multilateral organizations, academic institutions, non-governmental organizations, private sector companies and *United States Agency for International Development (USAID)*. **Aims** Promote handwashing with soap and the recognition of hygiene as a pillar of international development and public health. **Structure** Steering Committee; Resource Contributors; Secretariat. **Languages** English. **Staff** 2.00 FTE, paid; 1.00 FTE, voluntary. **Finance** Partner contributions. **Publications** *SOAPBOX* – newsletter. *Global Handwashing Day Planner's Guide*; *Handwashing 101 Distance Learning Course*; *Handwashing Advocacy Toolkit*. Research Summaries; Handwashing Factsheets.
Members Organizations, corporations and government agencies (15) including 8 organizations listed in this Yearbook:
FHI 360; *Global Soap Project*; *IRC (#16016)*; *London School of Hygiene and Tropical Medicine (LSHTM)*; *UNICEF (#20332)*; *United States Agency for International Development (USAID)*; *Water and Sanitation Programme (WSP, #20837)*; *Water Supply and Sanitation Collaborative Council (WSSCC, inactive)*.
NGO Relations Cooperates with: Clean, Fed and Nurtured Community of Practice; *Sanitation and Water for All (SWA, #19051)*. [2018/XM3916/j/**C**]

♦ Global Hapkido Federation (GHF) 10397

Pres address not obtained.
URL: http://www.globalhapkido.org/

History 1997, as *World Hapkido Games Federation (WHGF)*. Current title adopted, 2002. **Aims** Promote and instruct its members in the philosophy and techniques in traditional hapkido as it has been handed down from Masters to students. **Activities** World Hapkido Games. **Events** *Seminar* Seoul (Korea Rep) 1997.
Members Members in 13 countries:
Austria, Belgium, Brazil, Canada, France, Germany, Israel, Korea Rep, Netherlands, Russia, Spain, Switzerland, USA.
NGO Relations *International Hapkido Federation (IHF)*. [2013/XD7057/**D**]

♦ Global Harmonization Initiative (GHI) 10398

Contact Dept of Food Science and Technology, Univ für Bodenkultur, Muthgasse 18, 1190 Vienna, Austria. E-mail: info@globalharmonization.net.
URL: http://www.globalharmonization.net/

History 7 Nov 2007, Vienna (Austria). Constitution amended 18 Dec 2019. Former names and other names: *GHI Association – Global Harmonization Initiative for food regulations and legislation* – full title; *GHI Association – Globale Harmonisierungs Initiative für Gesetze und Verordnungen im Bereich Lebensmittel* – full title. Registration: No/ID: ZVR: 453446383, Austria. **Aims** Achieve consensus on the science of food regulations and legislation to ensure the global availability of safe and wholesome food products for all consumers. **Structure** Supervisory Board; Board; Working Groups; Ambassadors. **Languages** English. Important documents in up to 40 languages. **Staff** Voluntary. **Finance** Sources: donations; sale of publications. No budget. **Activities** Awareness raising; certification/accreditation; events/meetings; projects/programmes; standards/guidelines. Active worldwide. **Events** *Congress* St Petersburg (Russia) 2021, *Congress* Leiden (Netherlands) 2019. **Publications** *GHI Matters* (5 a year). *Nutrition and health aspects of traditional and ethnic foods*. *Food Safety Short Stories; A Collection of Real-Life Experiences* (1st ed 2022); *Food Safety Management; a practical guide for the food industry* (2nd ed 2022); *Ensuring Global Food Safety – Exploring Global Harmonization* (2nd ed); *Regulating Safety of Traditional and Ethnic Foods*.
Members Full (over 1,200) in 90 countries and territories:
Afghanistan, Albania, Argentina, Armenia, Australia, Austria, Bangladesh, Belgium, Bosnia-Herzegovina, Brazil, Bulgaria, Burkina Faso, Cambodia, Cameroon, Canada, Chile, China, Costa Rica, Côte d'Ivoire, Croatia, Cyprus, Czechia, Denmark, Egypt, England, Estonia, Ethiopia, Finland, France, Georgia, Germany, Ghana, Greece, Hong Kong, Hungary, India, Indonesia, Iran Islamic Rep, Ireland, Israel, Italy, Japan, Jordan, Kazakhstan, Kenya, Korea Rep, Latvia, Lebanon, Lithuania, Luxembourg, Malaysia, Malta, Mexico, Montenegro, Netherlands, New Zealand, Nigeria, North Macedonia, Northern Ireland, Norway, Pakistan, Peru, Poland, Portugal, Qatar, Romania, Russia, Saudi Arabia, Serbia, Singapore, Slovakia, Slovenia, South Africa, Spain, Sri Lanka, Sweden, Switzerland, Syrian AR, Taiwan, Tanzania UR, Thailand, Türkiye, Uganda, UK, Ukraine, Uruguay, USA, Venezuela, Vietnam, Zimbabwe. [2022.05.09/XM7897/**F**]

♦ Global Harmonization Working Party (GHWP) 10399

Secretariat Room 4, Unit 601,, Core Building 1, Hong Kong Science Park,, Pak Shek Kok, New Territories, Shatin, Hong Kong. E-mail: secretariat@ghwp.info.
URL: http://www.ghwp.info/

History 1996. Former names and other names: *Asian Harmonization Working Party (AHWP)* – former. **Aims** Strategically accelerate medical device regulatory convergence through promotion of an efficient and effective regulatory model for medical devices. **Structure** Chair and 2 Vice-Chairs; Secretariat Team; Administration Service; Technical Committee; Working Groups (9). **Languages** English. **Activities** Events/meetings; training/education. **Events** *Annual Meeting* 2021, *Annual Meeting* Muscat (Oman) 2019, *Annual Meeting* Kuala Lumpur (Malaysia) 2018, *Annual Meeting* Delhi (India) 2017, *Annual Meeting* Cebu City (Philippines) 2016. **Publications** *AHWP Newsletter*.
Members Experts from Medical Device Regulatory Authorities and the medical device industry. Members in 32 countries and territories:
Bahrain, Brunei Darussalam, Cambodia, Chile, China, Hong Kong, India, Indonesia, Jordan, Kazakhstan, Kenya, Korea Rep, Kuwait, Kyrgyzstan, Laos, Malaysia, Mongolia, Myanmar, Oman, Pakistan, Philippines, Saudi Arabia, Singapore, South Africa, Taiwan, Tanzania UR, Thailand, United Arab Emirates, USA, Vietnam, Yemen, Zimbabwe.
IGO Relations *International Medical Device Regulators Forum (IMDRF, #14132)*; *WHO (#20950)*. **NGO Relations** *International Organization for Standardization (ISO, #14473)*. [2022.05.04/XM3139/**F**]

♦ Global Health Action (internationally oriented national body)
♦ Global Health Advocacy Incubator (internationally oriented national body)

♦ Global Health Advocates 10400

Action Santé Mondiale
Contact 19 rue Portefoin, 75003 Paris, France. E-mail: info@ghadvocates.org.
Brussels Office Mundo J, Rue de l'Industrie 10, 1000 Brussels, Belgium.
URL: http://www.ghadvocates.org/

History 10 Sep 2001. Former names and other names: *Massive Effort Campaign (MEC)* – former (2001 to 2005); *Avocats pour la Santé dans le Monde* – former. Registration: Start date: 11 Mar 2008, France; EU Transparency Register, No/ID: 07720398190-53, Start date: 28 Feb 2012. **Aims** Advocate for policy change at the highest political level; mobilize resources to tackle major health threats and build sustainable health systems, focusing especially on AIDS, tuberculosis, malnutrition and other diseases of *poverty*. **Structure** Board of Directors. **Finance** Grants; pro bono support; project work with partners. **Activities** Advocacy/lobbying/activism; networking/liaising; meeting activities.
Members in 2 countries:
Belgium, France.
IGO Relations Cooperates with: *WHO (#20950)*. **NGO Relations** Cooperates with: *ACTION (#00085)*; *Christian Connections for International Health (CCIH)*; *International Union Against Tuberculosis and Lung Disease (The Union, #15752)*; *Malaria Foundation International (MFI, #16558)*; *World Vision International (WVI, #21904)*. Member of: *Alliance for Malaria Prevention (AMP, #00706)*; European Advocacy Coalition on Global Health Research and Development; *European Alliance for Responsible R and D and Affordable Medicines (#05879)*; *Coordination SUD*; *SDG Watch Europe (#19162)*. [2021/XF6716/**F**]

♦ Global Health Awareness Research Foundation (internationally oriented national body)
♦ Global Healthcare Information Network (internationally oriented national body)

♦ Global Health Cluster (GHC) 10401

Contact WHO, Avenue Appia 20, 1211 Geneva 27, Switzerland. E-mail: healthcluster@who.int.
URL: http://www.who.int/hac/global_health_cluster/en/

History 2005. Set under the leadership of *WHO (#20950)*. **Aims** Build consensus on *humanitarian* health *priorities* and related best practices; strengthen system-wide capacities to ensure an effective and predictable response. **Structure** Meeting (twice a year). Working Group. Policy and Strategy Team. **Publications** *GHC Newsletter*.
Members Partners. Cluster lead:
WHO (#20950).
UN Partners (5):
FAO (#09260); *UNHCR (#20327)*; *UNICEF (#20332)*; *United Nations Population Fund (UNFPA, #20612)*; *World Food Programme (WFP, #21510)*.
Non-UN Partners (29):
– *Africa Humanitarian Action (AHA)*;
– *American Refugee Committee (ARC)*;
– *CARE International (CI, #03429)*;
– *Catholic Relief Services (CRS, #03608)*;
– Centers for Disease Control and Prevention;
– Columbia University;

- *Concern Worldwide*;
- *Department for International Development (DFID, inactive)*;
- Harvard Humanitarian Initiative;
- *Humanity and Inclusion (HI, #10975)*;
- *International Centre for Migration, Health and Development (ICMHD, #12502)*;
- *International Council of Nurses (ICN, #13054)*;
- *International Council of Voluntary Agencies (ICVA, #13092)*;
- *International Federation of Red Cross and Red Crescent Societies (#13526)*;
- *International Medical Corps (IMC)*;
- *International Organization for Migration (IOM, #14454)*;
- *International Rescue Committee (IRC, #14717)*;
- Johns Hopkins University Center for Refugee and Disaster Response;
- *Médecins du Monde – International (MDM, #16613)*;
- *MSI Reproductive Choices*;
- Public Health Agency of Canada;
- *Save the Children Federation (SCF)*;
- *Save the Children UK (SC UK)*;
- *United States Agency for International Development (USAID)*;
- US Bureau of Population, Refugees and Migration;
- *World Association for Disaster and Emergency Medicine (WADEM, #21133)*;
- *World Vision International (WVI, #21904)*.

Observers (4):
American Council for Voluntary International Action (InterAction); *Bureau international des Médecins sans frontières (MSF International, #03366)*; *International Committee of the Red Cross (ICRC, #12799)*; *The Sphere Project (#19918)*. [2012/XJ5845/y/**E**]

♦ Global Health Corps (internationally oriented national body)

♦ Global Health Council (GHC) 10402

Mailing address c/o Global Impact, 1199 N Fairfax St, Ste 300, Alexandria VA 22314, USA. E-mail: communications@globalhealth.org.
Main Office 1875 K St NW, 4th Floor, Washington DC 20006, USA.
URL: http://www.globalhealth.org/

History Oct 1971, USA, as *National Council for International Health (NCIH)*. Operations suspended Jun 2012 and relaunched Jan 2013. **Aims** Promote better health around the world by assisting all who work for improvement and equity in global health to secure the information and resources they need to work effectively. **Structure** Board of Directors, including Chair, Vice-Chair, Secretary and Treasurer. **Events** *Annual Conference* Washington, DC (USA) 2012, *Annual conference* Washington, DC (USA) 2004, *Annual conference* Washington, DC (USA) 2003, *Annual conference* Washington, DC (USA) 2002, *Annual Conference* Washington, DC (USA) 2001. **Publications** *Global Health Magazine*.
Members Organizations, including 49 organizations listed in this Yearbook:
- *Adventist Development and Relief Agency International (ADRA, #00131)*;
- *Aeras Global TB Vaccine Foundation*;
- *African Methodist Episcopal Church Service and Development Agency (AME-SADA)*;
- *Alliance for the Prudent Use of Antibiotics (APUA)*;
- *American International Health Alliance (AIHA)*;
- *American Jewish World Service (AJWS)*;
- *American Leprosy Missions (ALM International)*;
- *American Society of Tropical Medicine and Hygiene (ASTMH)*;
- *Amref Health Africa (#00806)*;
- *Arogya World*;
- *Bread for the World Institute (BFW Institute)*;
- *CARE International (CI, #03429)*;
- *Catholic Medical Mission Board (CMMB)*;
- *Center for Global Development (CGD)*;
- *Center for Strategic and International Studies, Washington DC (CSIS)*;
- *Child Family Health International (CFHI)*;
- *Christian Connections for International Health (CCIH)*;
- *CORE Group*;
- *Curatio International Foundation (CIF)*;
- *Development Finance International Group (DFI)*;
- *DKT International*;
- *Earth Institute at Columbia University*;
- *Education Development Center (EDC)*;
- *EngenderHealth*;
- *Episcopal Relief and Development*;
- *Fair River International Association for Development (FARIAD)*;
- *FHI 360*;
- *Foundation for the Advancement of International Medical Education and Research (FAIMER)*;
- *Frontline AIDS (#10007)*;
- *General Board of Church and Society of the United Methodist Church (GBCS)*;
- *Global Alert for Defence of Youth and the Less Privileged (GADYLP)*;
- *Global Alliance to Prevent Prematurity and Stillbirth (GAPPS)*;
- *Global Communities*;
- *Global Health Action (GHA)*;
- *Global Impact*;
- *Global Partners in Care*;
- *Guttmacher Institute*;
- *Hesperian Health Guides*;
- *Humanity and Inclusion (HI, #10975)*;
- *IMA World Health (IMA)*;
- *Institute for Reproductive Health (IRH)*;
- *International Agency for the Prevention of Blindness (IAPB, #11597)*;
- *International AIDS Vaccine Initiative (IAVI, #11602)*;
- *International Association for the Study of Pain (IASP, #12206)*;
- *International Center for Research on Women (ICRW)*;
- *International Council on Women's Health Issues (ICOWHI, #13094)*;
- *International Food Information Council (IFIC)*;
- *RESULTS* (Educational Fund REF);
- *TB Alliance (#20103)*.

Consultative Status Consultative status granted from: *ECOSOC (#05331)* (Ros A); *WHO (#20950)* (Official Relations). **IGO Relations** Accredited by: *United Nations Office at Vienna (UNOV, #20604)*. Associated with Department of Global Communications of the United Nations. **NGO Relations** Works on greater involvement of people living with HIV/AIDS together with: *Global Network of People Living with HIV/AIDS (GNP+, #10494)*; *International Community of Women Living with HIV/AIDS (ICW, #12826)*. Allied partner of: *Financial Transparency Coalition (FTC, #09772)*. Partner of: *Every Woman Every Child (EWEC, #09215)*; *Stop TB Partnership (#19999)*. Member of: *American Council for Voluntary International Action (InterAction)*; *Global Coalition Against Child Pneumonia (#10290)*; *Global Health Workforce Alliance (GHWA, inactive)*; *Global Partnership for Sustainable Development Data (Data4SDGS, #10542)*; *PMNCH (#18410)*; *United Nations Global Compact (#20567)*. [2020/XG0269/y/**C**]

♦ Global Health through Education Training / see Global Health through Education, Training and Service (#10403)

♦ Global Health through Education, Training and Service (GHETS) . . . 10403

Office Administrator 8 North Main St, Ste 401, Attleboro MA 02703, USA. T. +15082265091. Fax +15084488346. E-mail: info@ghets.org.
URL: http://www.ghets.org/

History 2002, as *Global Health through Education Training (GHET)*. Current title adopted, 2003. **Aims** Improve health in developing countries through innovations in education and service. **Structure** Board, comprising President, Vice-President, Secretary, Treasurer and 8 members. **Activities** Programming priorities: Health Workforce Development; Women's Health; Worker and Community Health. [2010/XM0227/**E**]

♦ Global Health Europe (GHE) 10404

Secretariat address not obtained. E-mail: info@globalhealtheurope.org.
URL: http://globalhealtheurope.org/

History Jan 2008. Jointly set up and hosted by Graduate Institute of International and Development Studies, Global Health Programme, Geneva (Switzerland) and Department of International Health, Maastricht University (Netherlands). Former names and other names: *European Council on Global Health (PDF)* – former; *Global Health Europe – A Platform for European Engagement in Global Health* – full title. **Aims** Improve global health governance through a more coordinated, coherent, consistent and committed European engagement. **Structure** Steering Committee; Secretariat. **Activities** Knowledge management/information dissemination; capacity building; monitoring/evaluation; advocacy/lobbying/activism; events/meetings. **Publications** Position Statements; research papers; issue briefs; opinion pieces. [2022/XJ8767/**E**]

♦ Global Health Europe – A Platform for European Engagement in Global Health / see Global Health Europe (#10404)
♦ Global Health Foundation (internationally oriented national body)
♦ Global Health Group International (unconfirmed)
♦ Global Health Partners (internationally oriented national body)
♦ Global Health Promise (internationally oriented national body)
♦ Global Health Research Foundation (internationally oriented national body)

♦ Global Health Security Agenda (GHSA) 10405

Secretariat address not obtained. E-mail: ghsa.secretariat@gmail.com – thai.ghsacounit@gmail.com.
URL: http://www.ghsagenda.org/

History Feb 2014. Endorsed by *Group of Seven (G-7, #10788)*, Jun 2014. Mandate extended for another 5 years, by 2017 Kampala Declaration. **Aims** Advance a world safe and secure from infectious disease threats; bring together nations from all over the world to make new, concrete commitments; elevate global health security as a national leaders-level priority. **Structure** Ministerial-level meeting; Steering Group; Secretariat. **Activities** Capacity building; monitoring/evaluation. **Events** *Global Health Security Agenda Ministerial Meeting* Bangkok (Thailand) 2020, *Ministerial Meeting* Dakar (Senegal) 2019, *Ministerial Meeting* Nusa Dua (Indonesia) 2018, *Ministerial Meeting* Kampala (Uganda) 2017, *Ministerial Meeting* Rotterdam (Netherlands) 2016.
Members Member governments (65):
Afghanistan, Argentina, Australia, Azerbaijan, Bangladesh, Burkina Faso, Cameroon, Canada, Chile, China, Colombia, Congo Brazzaville, Congo DR, Côte d'Ivoire, Denmark, Ethiopia, Finland, France, Georgia, Germany, Ghana, Guinea, Guinea-Bissau, Haiti, India, Indonesia, Israel, Italy, Japan, Jordan, Kenya, Korea Rep, Laos, Liberia, Malaysia, Mali, Mexico, Mongolia, Netherlands, Nigeria, Norway, Pakistan, Peru, Philippines, Portugal, Saudi Arabia, Senegal, Sierra Leone, Singapore, South Africa, Spain, Sweden, Switzerland, Tanzania UR, Thailand, Togo, Türkiye, Uganda, UK, Ukraine, United Arab Emirates, USA, Vietnam, Yemen, Zimbabwe.
IGO Relations Advisory partners include: *Economic Community of West African States (ECOWAS, #05312)*; *European Union (EU, #08967)*; *FAO (#09260)*; *International Criminal Police Organization – INTERPOL (ICPO-INTERPOL, #13110)*; *United Nations Office for Disaster Risk Reduction (UNDRR, #20595)*; *WHO (#20950)*. [2021/XM7585/**F***]

♦ Global Health Security Initiative (GHSI) 10406

Secretariat Health Canada – Media Relations Unit, Public Affairs Branch, Brooke Claxton Bldg, 70 Colombine Driveway, Tunney's Pasture, Ottawa ON K1A 0K9, Canada. E-mail: ghsi.secretariat@phac-aspc.gc.ca.
URL: http://www.ghsi.ca/

History 7 Nov 2001, Ottawa (Canada), following the terrorist attacks, New York NY (USA), Sep 11 2001. **Aims** Strengthen public health response to the threat of international biological, chemical and radio-nuclear terrorism. **Events** *Ministerial Meeting* Tokyo (Japan) 2014, *Ministerial meeting* Brussels (Belgium) 2008, *Ministerial Meeting* USA 2007, *Ministerial meeting* Washington, DC (USA) 2007, *Ministerial meeting* Tokyo (Japan) 2006.
Members Governments of 8 countries:
Canada, France, Germany, Italy, Japan, Mexico, UK, USA.
Regional organizations (2):
European Commission (EC, #06633); *WHO (#20950)*.
IGO Relations Technical advisor: *WHO (#20950)*. [2022/XM3124/**F***]

♦ Global Health Security Network (internationally oriented national body)
♦ Global Health Service Corps / see Seed Global Health
♦ Global Health Technologies Coalition (internationally oriented national body)
♦ Global Health Visions (internationally oriented national body)
♦ Global Health Watch (internationally oriented national body)

♦ Global Heart Hub 10407

Contact Croi House, Moyola Lane, Newcastle, Galway, CO. GALWAY, H91 FF68, Ireland. T. +35391542404. E-mail: info@globalhearthub.org.
URL: https://globalhearthub.org/

History Former names and other names: *Global Heart Hub – The Alliance of Heart Patient Organisations* – former. **Aims** Provide a voice for those affected by cardiovascular disease.
Members Affiliates in 32 countries:
Australia, Austria, Belgium, Brazil, Canada, Chile, Colombia, Costa Rica, Czechia, Egypt, France, Germany, Greece, Hungary, Ireland, Israel, Italy, Japan, Latvia, Lebanon, Lithuania, Malaysia, Mexico, Netherlands, Poland, Portugal, Romania, Slovenia, Spain, Sweden, UK, USA.
NGO Relations Member of (4): *European Alliance for Cardiovascular Health (EACH, #05863)*; *European Patients' Forum (EPF, #08172)*; *World Heart Federation (WHF, #21562)*; *World Patients Alliance (WPA)*. [2022/AA1658/**C**]

♦ Global Heart Hub – The Alliance of Heart Patient Organisations / see Global Heart Hub (#10407)
♦ Global HearthWorks Foundation (internationally oriented national body)

♦ Global Heat Health Information Network (GHHIN) 10408

Contact address not obtained. E-mail: info@ghhin.org.
URL: https://www.ghhin.org/

History Jun 2016. Founded by experts and spearheaded by *WHO (#20950)* and *World Meteorological Organization (WMO, #21649)* Joint Office of Climate and Health, and US National Oceanic and Atmospheric Administration (NOAA). **Aims** Create a common space to promote evidence-driven interventions, shared-learning, co-production of information, synthesis of priorities, and capacity building that can empower multi-disciplinary actors to take more effective and informed life-saving preparedness and planning measures. **Structure** Steering Committee; Coordination Team. **Activities** Events/meetings; knowledge management/information dissemination; research/documentation. **Events** *Global Heat Health Forum* Copenhagen (Denmark) 2021, *Global Heat Health Forum* Copenhagen (Denmark) 2020, *Global Heat Health Forum* Hong Kong (Hong Kong) 2018. [2020/AA0932/**F**]

♦ Global Heritage Fund (internationally oriented national body)

♦ Global Higher Education Network (GHEN) 10409

Coordinator UMS NaHERI, Block C, Level 2, 10 Persiaran Bukit Jambul, 11900 Bayan Lepas, Penang, Malaysia. T. +6046535762. Fax +6046535771. E-mail: ghenetwork@usm.my.
URL: http://www.ghenetwork.usm.my/

History 2001, Penang (Malaysia). **Aims** Act as an international network of academics, policymakers, researchers and leaders of different fields; sustain research on higher education focusing on higher education futures and alternative perspectives. **Structure** Steering Committee; Secretariat. **Languages** English. **Staff** 2.00 FTE, paid. **Finance** Funded by University Sains Malaysia and Higher Education Ministry of Malaysia. **Activities** Events/meetings; research and development; networking/liaising. **Events** *Global Higher Education Forum* Penang (Malaysia) 2021, *Global Higher Education Forum* Putrajaya (Malaysia) 2018, *Global Higher Education Forum* Malaysia 2015, *Annual General Meeting* Sepang Utara (Malaysia) 2013, *Global Higher Education Forum* Sepang Utara (Malaysia) 2013.
Members Founding members in 7 countries:
Australia, Canada, Germany, India, Ireland, Malaysia, USA. [2022/XJ7036/**F**]

♦ **Global HIV Vaccine Enterprise** **10410**
Secretariat c/o IAS, Av de France 23, 1202 Geneva, Switzerland. T. +41227100870. E-mail: enterprise@iasociety.org.
URL: http://www.vaccineenterprise.org/
History 2003. **Aims** Accelerate development of preventive HIV vaccines through mutual coordination, collaboration, knowledge sharing and recruitment of new resources and funders to the field. **Structure** Board. **Events** *HIV Research for Prevention Conference (HIVR4P//Virtual)* Geneva (Switzerland) 2021, *HIVR4P : HIV Research for Prevention International Conference* Madrid (Spain) 2018, *HIVR4P : HIV Research for Prevention International Conference* Chicago, IL (USA) 2016, *HIVR4P : HIV Research for Prevention International Conference* Cape Town (South Africa) 2014, *AIDS Vaccine Conference* Barcelona (Spain) 2013. **Publications** *Global HIV Vaccine Enterprise Newsletter*. [2021.06.16/XJ9052/y/**C**]

♦ Global Hope Mobilization (internationally oriented national body)
♦ Global Hope Network / see Global Hope Network International (#10411)

♦ **Global Hope Network International (GHNI)** **10411**
Switzerland Office Chemin des Crêts-Pregny 27, Grand Saconnex, 1218 Geneva, Switzerland. T. +41227470083. E-mail: info.ch@ghni.org.
USA Office 934 N Magnolia Ave, Suite 310, Orlando FL 32803, USA. T. +14072073256. E-mail: info@ghni.org.
URL: http://www.globalhopenetwork.org/
History Also referred to as *Global Hope Network (GHN)*. **Aims** Provide relief and holistic, self-sustainable community development to the poorest, hidden people in Africa, the Middle East and Asia. **Structure** Resource Development Offices in Switzerland, UK and USA; Regional Field Leaders. **Languages** Arabic, English, French, German. Indian. **Staff** Over 150 paid and voluntary. **Finance** Public support. **Activities** Projects/programmes; humanitarian/emergency aid; research and development; capacity building. Active in: Afghanistan, Bangladesh, Burkina Faso, China, Egypt, Ethiopia, Greece, India, Indonesia, Iraq, Israel, Jordan, Kenya, Lebanon, Myanmar, Nepal, Niger, Nigeria, Sri Lanka, Tajikistan, Türkiye. **Events** *Geneva forum on social change* Geneva (Switzerland) 2009. **Consultative Status** Consultative status granted from: *ECOSOC (#05331)* (Special). [2019.09.27/XQ3048/**F**]

♦ Global Horizons (internationally oriented national body)
♦ **GlobalHort** Global Horticulture Initiative (#10412)

♦ **Global Horticulture Initiative (GlobalHort)** **10412**
Initiative mondiale pour l'horticulture
Exec Dir c/o Ctr for Development Research (ZEF), Univ of Bonn, Walter-Flex-Str 3, 53113 Bonn, Germany. T. +49228734476.
URL: http://www.globalhort.org/
History 2006, Montpellier (France), by 74 participants, representing 55 organizations, under the auspices of *AVRDC – The World Vegetable Center (#03051)*, *Centre de coopération internationale en recherche agronomique pour le développement (CIRAD, #03733)* and *International Society for Horticultural Science (ISHS, #15180)*. **Aims** Encourage and advocate for use of horticulture for development by fostering actions that endeavor a better employment of horticultural crop production, marketing and consumption to create wealth and improve human health and wellbeing in the world's poorest countries. **Structure** Organized as a Consortium; Board of Directors. **Languages** English, French. **Staff** 2.00 FTE, paid. **Activities** Advocacy/lobbying/activism; networking/liaising; capacity building; training/education; events/meetings. **Events** *All Africa Horticulture Congress* Nelspruit (South Africa) 2012, *All Africa horticulture congress* Nairobi (Kenya) 2009. **IGO Relations** Partners include: *AVRDC – The World Vegetable Center (#03051)*; *Bioversity International (#03262)*; *FAO (#09260)*. **NGO Relations** Partners include: *African Seed Trade Association (AFSTA, #00454)*; *International Society for Horticultural Science (ISHS, #15180)*; national organizations. Links with several NGOs including: *Crops For the Future (CFF, #04968)*; Prolinnova. [2014.07.08/XM2984/**E**]

♦ Global Housing Foundation (internationally oriented national body)

♦ **Global Humanitarian Platform (GHP)** **10413**
Contact c/o ICVA, 26-28 avenue Giuseppe Motta, 1202 Geneva, Switzerland. T. +41229509600. Fax +41229509609. E-mail: secretariat@icvanetwork.org.
URL: http://www.globalhumanitarianplatform.org/
History Jul 2006. **Structure** Steering Committee, comprising UN – represented by *United Nations Office for the Coordination of Humanitarian Affairs (OCHA, #20593)* – NGOs – represented by *International Council of Voluntary Agencies (ICVA, #13092)*, *American Council for Voluntary International Action (InterAction)*, *Steering Committee for Humanitarian Response (SCHR, #19978)* and *Voluntary Organisations in Cooperation in Emergencies (VOICE, #20809)* – and Red Cross/Red Crescent family, represented by *International Committee of the Red Cross (ICRC, #12799)*. **Activities** Events/meetings. **Events** *Meeting* Geneva (Switzerland) 2010, *Meeting* Geneva (Switzerland) 2008, *Meeting* Geneva (Switzerland) 2007. [2016.02.15/XM0042/**E**]

♦ Global Human Rights Defence (internationally oriented national body)
♦ Global Hydranencephaly Foundation (unconfirmed)
♦ Global Hygiene Council (unconfirmed)
♦ Global Impact (internationally oriented national body)
♦ Global Impact (internationally oriented national body)

♦ **Global Impact Investing Network (GIIN)** **10414**
Managing Dir One Battery Park Plaza, Suite 202, New York NY 10004, USA. T. +16468377430. E-mail: info@thegiin.org.
URL: https://thegiin.org/
History 2009. Currently a sponsored project of Rockefeller Philanthropy Advisors. Registration: 501(c)(3) non-profit, USA; EU Transparency Register, No/ID: 517822943889-09, Start date: 1 Sep 2021. **Aims** Increase the scale and effectiveness of impact investing. **Structure** Board of Directors. **Finance** Founding Supporters (3): JP Morgan; *The Rockefeller Foundation (#18966)*; *United States Agency for International Development (USAID)*. Additional supporters include: *Bill and Melinda Gates Foundation (BMGF)*; *W K Kellogg Foundation (WKKF)*. **Events** *GIIN Investor Forum* The Hague (Netherlands) 2022, *Forum* Amsterdam (Netherlands) 2019. **Publications** *GIIN News*. **NGO Relations** *IDP Foundation*; *World Benchmarking Alliance (WBA, #21228)*. [2021/XJ6219/**F**]

♦ **Global Implementation Initiative (GII)** **10415**
Address not obtained.
URL: https://globalimplementation.org/
History Incorporated Apr 2012. **Aims** Promote and establish coherent and collaborative approaches to implementation practice, science, and policy. **Structure** Board. **Finance** Members' dues. **Activities** Events/meetings. **Events** *Conference* Glasgow (UK) 2019. [2019/XM7552/**F**]

♦ Global Industrial and Social Progress Research Institute (internationally oriented national body)
♦ Global Information and Early Warning System / see Global Information and Early Warning System on Food and Agriculture (#10416)

♦ **Global Information and Early Warning System on Food and Agriculture (GIEWS)** **10416**
Système mondiale d'information et d'alerte rapide sur l'alimentation et l'agriculture (SMIAR) – Sistema Mundial de Información y Alerta sobre la Alimentación y la Agricultura (SMIA)
Contact FAO, Markets and Trade Division, Viale delle Terme di Caracalla, 00153 Rome RM, Italy. T. +390657054299. E-mail: giews1@fao.org.
URL: http://www.fao.org/giews/
History Apr 1975. Established within the framework of *FAO (#09260)*. Former names and other names: *Global Information and Early Warning System* – alias. **Aims** Monitor food supply and demand and other key indicators for assessing the overall food security situation in all countries of the world. **Languages** Arabic, Chinese, English, French, Russian, Spanish. **Activities** Capacity building; knowledge management/information dissemination; monitoring/evaluation; research/documentation; training/education. **Publications** *Food Price Monitoring and Analysis (FPMA)* (10 a year) in English – selected abstracts in Arabic, Chinese, French, Russian, Spanish; *Country Briefs* (4 a year) in English; *Crop Prospects and Food Situation* (4 a year) in English, French, Spanish; *Food Outlook* (2 a year) in English – summaries in Arabic, Chinese, French, Russian, Spanish. Special Reports/Alerts/Updates (ad-hoc) in Arabic, English, French, Russian, Spanish.
Members Governments participating in Global Information and Early Warning System on Food and Agriculture (117):
Algeria, Angola, Argentina, Australia, Austria, Bahamas, Bahrain, Bangladesh, Belgium, Benin, Bolivia (Plurinational State of), Brazil, Burkina Faso, Cameroon, Canada, Cape Verde, Chad, Chile, China, Colombia, Congo DR, Costa Rica, Côte d'Ivoire, Croatia, Cuba, Cyprus, Czechia, Denmark, Ecuador, Egypt, El Salvador, Estonia, Eswatini, Ethiopia, Fiji, Finland, France, Gabon, Germany, Ghana, Greece, Guatemala, Guinea, Guinea-Bissau, Guyana, Haiti, Honduras, Hungary, India, Indonesia, Iran Islamic Rep, Iraq, Ireland, Israel, Italy, Japan, Jordan, Kenya, Korea Rep, Lebanon, Liberia, Lithuania, Luxembourg, Madagascar, Malawi, Malaysia, Mali, Malta, Mauritius, Mexico, Moldova, Mongolia, Morocco, Myanmar, Nepal, Netherlands, New Zealand, Nicaragua, Niger, Nigeria, Norway, Pakistan, Panama, Paraguay, Peru, Philippines, Portugal, Qatar, Romania, Russia, Samoa, Saudi Arabia, Senegal, Sierra Leone, Singapore, Somalia, Spain, Sri Lanka, Sudan, Sweden, Switzerland, Syrian AR, Tanzania UR, Thailand, Togo, Trinidad-Tobago, Tunisia, Türkiye, UK, United Arab Emirates, Uruguay, USA, Venezuela (Bolivarian Republic of), Vietnam, Yemen, Zambia, Zimbabwe.
International participants, 3 organizations listed in this Yearbook:
European Union (EU, #08967); *Latin American Integration Association (LAIA, #16343)*; *Secretaria Permanente del Tratado General de Integración Económica Centroamericana (SIECA, #19195)*.
NGO Relations Cooperates with:
- *Action pour le développement – SOS Faim (SOS Faim)*;
- *ActionAid France – Peuples Solidaires*;
- *Afrique verte*;
- *American Friends Service Committee (AFSC)*;
- *Association européenne pour le développement et la santé (AEDES, #02562)*;
- *Australian Council for International Development (ACFID)*;
- *Baha'i International Community (#03062)*;
- *Brothers to All Men (BAM, #03339)*;
- *Bureau international des Médecins sans frontières (MSF International, #03366)*;
- *Cooperation Canada*;
- *CARE International (CI, #03429)*, including CARE Canada and Australia;
- *Caritas Internationalis (CI, #03580)*, including *'Caritas Neerlandica'*;
- *Catholic Agency for Overseas Development (CAFOD)*;
- *Comité Catholique contre la Faim et pour le Développement-Terre Solidaire (CCFD-Terre Solidaire)*;
- *Catholic Relief Services (CRS, #03608)*;
- *Centre de recherche et d'information pour le développement, Paris (CRID)*;
- *Centro Internazionale Crocevia (CIC)*;
- *Christian Aid*;
- *Church World Service (CWS)*;
- *CIMADE*;
- *Comité français pour la solidarité internationale (CFSI)*;
- *Development Innovations and Networks (#05057)*;
- *France Volontaires*;
- *German Catholic Bishops' Organisation for Development Cooperation (MISEREOR)*;
- *Groupe de recherche et de réalisations pour le développement rural dans le Tiers-monde (GRDR)*;
- *Institut de recherches et d'applications des méthodes de développement (IRAM)*;
- *International Committee of the Red Cross (ICRC, #12799)*;
- *The Lutheran World Federation (LWF, #16532)*;
- *Oxfam GB*;
- *Panos Network (#18183)*;
- *Save the Children UK (SC UK)*;
- *Solidarités agricoles et alimentaires (SOLAGRAL)*;
- *Steering Committee for Humanitarian Response (SCHR, #19978)*;
- *Terre des Hommes International Federation (TDHIF, #20133)*;
- *Trocaire – Catholic Agency for World Development*;
- *World Council of Churches (WCC, #21320)*;
- *World Vision International (WVI, #21904)*. [2021.09.06/XF9809/y/**F***]

♦ Global Information Infrastructure Commission (internationally oriented national body)
♦ Global Information Network (internationally oriented national body)
♦ Global Information Network for Small and Medium Enterprises (no recent information)

♦ **Global Infrastructure Alliance for Internet Safety (GIAIS)** **10417**
Contact address not obtained. E-mail: mgentles@microsoft.com.
History 24 Feb 2004, San Francisco CA (USA). **Aims** Provide technology and communications support to the worldwide service provider industry; facilitate collaboration in the field. **Structure** Working groups co-chaired by members and Microsoft.
Members Internet providers (67) in 24 countries:
Australia, Canada, Czechia, Denmark, Finland, France, Germany, India, Ireland, Israel, Italy, Japan, Korea DPR, Morocco, Netherlands, New Zealand, Norway, Poland, Russia, South Africa, Spain, Sweden, UK, USA. [2008/XF7148/**F**]

♦ **Global Infrastructure Basel Foundation (GIB Foundation)** **10418**
Contact Elisabethenstr 22, 4051 Basel BS, Switzerland. T. +41612051080. E-mail: info@gib-foundation.org.
URL: http://www.gib-foundation.org/
History 2008. Former names and other names: *Global Infrastructure Basel – The Sustainable Infrastructure Financing Summit* – full title. Registration: Swiss Civil Code, Switzerland. **Aims** Support development and financing of sustainable and resilient infrastructure and nature-based solutions. **Structure** Board. **Languages** English, German. **Staff** 5.00 FTE, paid. **Finance** Sources: government support; private foundations. Supported by: *European Commission (EC, #06633)*; *Ford Foundation (#09858)*; Swiss Government departments; *The Rockefeller Foundation (#18966)*. Annual budget: 1,500,000 USD. **Activities** Capacity building; events/meetings; politics/policy/regulatory; projects/programmes; standards/guidelines. **Events** *Annual Sustainable Infrastructure Summit* Basel (Switzerland) 2015, *Annual Sustainable Infrastructure Summit* Basel (Switzerland) 2014, *Annual Sustainable Infrastructure Summit*. Basel (Switzerland) 2013, *Annual Sustainable Infrastructure Summit* Basel (Switzerland) 2012, *Annual Sustainable Infrastructure Summit* Basel (Switzerland) 2011. **Publications** Reports. **Members** Not a membership organization. **IGO Relations** Cooperates with (3): *International Bank for Reconstruction and Development (IBRD, #12317)* (World Bank); *UNIDO (#20336)*; *United Nations Office for Disaster Risk Reduction (UNDRR, #20595)*. **NGO Relations** Member of (2): *Cities Climate Finance Leadership Alliance (CCFLA, #03952)*; *ISEAL (#16026)*. Partner of (2): *Long-term Infrastructure Investors Association (LTIIA, #16512)*; *Partnership on Sustainable, Low Carbon Transport Foundation (SLoCaT Foundation, #18244)*. Also links with national organizations. [2020.10.13/XJ9726/f/**F**]

♦ Global Infrastructure Basel – The Sustainable Infrastructure Financing Summit / see Global Infrastructure Basel Foundation (#10418)

♦ **Global Infrastructure Connectivity Alliance (GICA)** **10419**
Secretariat c/o The World Bank, 10 Marina Boulevard, Marina Bay Financial Center, Tower 2 No 12, Singapore 018983, Singapore. T. +6565013667. E-mail: gicasecretariat@worldbank.org.
URL: http://www.gica.global/
History Launched 2016, by *Group of Twenty (G20, #10793)*. **Aims** Support connectivity through cooperation and knowledge exchange. **Structure** Hosted by *The World Bank Group (#21218)* – Infrastructure Finance, PPS and Guarantees (IPG) Group.
Members include 10 organizations listed in this Yearbook:
Asian Development Bank (ADB, #01422); *Asian Infrastructure Investment Bank (AIIB, #01512)*; *Commonwealth Secretariat (#04362)*; *Eurasian Development Bank (EDB, #05605)*; *Global Energy Interconnection Development and Cooperation Organization (GEIDCO, #10342)*; *Global Infrastructure Hub (GI Hub, #10420)*; *Long-term Infrastructure Investors Association (LTIIA, #16512)*; *OECD (#17693)*; *The World Bank Group (#21218)*; *UNCTAD (#20285)*. [2020.02.11/XM8452/y/**E**]

♦ **Global Infrastructure Hub (GI Hub)** **10420**
CEO Level 23, 68 Pitt St, Sydney NSW 2000, Australia. T. +61283155300. E-mail: contact@gihub.org.
URL: http://www.gihub.org/
History 2014. Founded on the initiative of *Group of Twenty (G20, #10793)*. Registration: Australia. **Aims** Through cooperation with public and private sectors globally, increase the flow and quality of infrastructure projects around the world. liveable cities. **Structure** Board of Directors; Audit and Risk Committee. **Finance** Funding on a voluntary basis from G20 members and non-member countries. **Activities** Knowledge management/information dissemination; projects/programmes. **NGO Relations** Member of: *Global Infrastructure Connectivity Alliance (GICA, #10419)*. [2021/XM8453/**E**]

Global Inheritance
10420
alphabetic sequence excludes
For the complete listing, see Yearbook Online at

♦ Global Inheritance (internationally oriented national body)

♦ Global Initiative Against Transnational Organized Crime (GI-TOC) . . 10421

Co-Dir Avenue de France 23, 1202 Geneva, Switzerland. E-mail: secretariat@globalinitiative.net.
URL: https://globalinitiative.net/

History 2013. Born from a series of high-level discussions between law-enforcement officials from both developed and developing countries in New York NY (USA), 2011–2012. Former names and other names: *Global Initiative – Verein gegen transnationale organisiert Kriminalität* – former. Registration: Swiss Civil Code, No/ID: CHE-296 622. 305, Switzerland; No/ID: 102 464 2959, Austria; South Africa. **Aims** Provide a platform to promote greater debate and innovative approaches, which serve as the building blocks to an inclusive global strategy against organized crime. **Structure** Advisory Board; globally dispersed Secretariat; Headquarters in Geneva (Switzerland). **Staff** 90.00 FTE, paid. **Activities** Advocacy/lobbying/activism; awareness raising; events/meetings; networking/liaising. Initiatives include: *International Association for the Study of Organized Crime (IASOC).* **Members** Independent global and regional experts (over 500). Membership countries not specified. [2022.02.09/AA2228/v/**F**]

♦ Global Initiative on Asthma (GINA) 10422

Initiative mondiale pour l'asthme

Main Office PO Box 558, Fontana WI 53125, USA.
URL: http://www.ginasthma.com/

History 1992, by *WHO (#20950)* and (US) National Heart, Lung and Blood Institute. **Aims** Develop and implement an optimal strategy for asthma management and *prevention.* **Activities** Organizes *World Asthma Day (WAD).* **Events** *Triennial world asthma meeting* Bangkok (Thailand) 2004, *Triennial world asthma meeting* Chicago, IL (USA) 2001, *Triennial world asthma meeting* Barcelona (Spain) 1998. **NGO Relations** Member of: *Global Alliance Against Chronic Respiratory Diseases (GARD, #10182).* [2019/XF4251/**F**]

♦ Global Initiative for Chronic Obstructive Lung Disease (GOLD) 10423

Contact PO Box 558, Fontana WI 53125, USA.
Chair Institut Clinic del Tòrax, Hospital Clinic, Universitat de Barcelona, Vilarroel 170, CP 08036 Barcelona, Spain.
URL: https://goldcopd.org/

History 1997, by *WHO (#20950)* and 2 US health institutes. **Aims** Raise awareness of Chronic Obstructive Pulmonary Disease (COPD); improve prevention and treatment of COPD. **Structure** Executive Committee, including representatives from: *Asian Pacific Society of Respirology (APSR, #01643),* WHO and *World Organization of Family Doctors (WONCA, #21690).* Science Committee; Dissemination Committee; Workshop Panel. **Events** *International Conference* Philadelphia, PA (USA) 2019. **NGO Relations** Member of: *Global Alliance Against Chronic Respiratory Diseases (GARD, #10182). International COPD Coalition (ICC, #12961)* comprises patients organizations of GOLD. [2019/XM1888/**F**]

♦ Global Initiative to Combat Nuclear Terrorism (GICNT) 10424

Contact State Dept, 2201 C St NW, Washington DC 20520, USA. E-mail: globalinitiative@state.gov.
Main Website: https://www.gicnt.org/

History 16 Jul 2006, St Petersburg (Russia). Presidents George W Bush and Vladimir Putin jointly announced the organization of the Global Initiative to Combat Nuclear Terrorism (GICNT). First Plenary Meeting took place 30-31 Oct 2006, Rabat (Morocco). **Aims** Strengthen global capacity to prevent, detect and respond to nuclear terrorism by conducting multilateral activities that strengthen the plans, policies, procedures and interoperability of partner nations. **Structure** USA and Russia serve as Co-Chairs; Morocco leads the Implementation and Assessment Group (IAG) under the guidance of the Co-Chairs. **Activities** Multilateral activities and exercises. **Events** *Workshop* Seoul (Korea Rep) 2019, *Meeting* Helsinki (Finland) 2018, *Plenary Meeting* Tokyo (Japan) 2017, *Nuclear Security Summit* Washington, DC (USA) 2016, *Plenary Meeting* Helsinki (Finland) 2015.

Members Governments that have endorsed nuclear security principles (89):
Afghanistan, Albania, Algeria, Argentina, Armenia, Australia, Austria, Azerbaijan, Bahrain, Belarus, Belgium, Bosnia-Herzegovina, Bulgaria, Cambodia, Canada, Cape Verde, Chile, China, Côte d'Ivoire, Croatia, Cyprus, Czechia, Denmark, Estonia, Finland, France, Georgia, Germany, Greece, Hungary, Iceland, India, Iraq, Ireland, Israel, Italy, Japan, Jordan, Kazakhstan, Korea Rep, Kyrgyzstan, Latvia, Libya, Lithuania, Luxembourg, Madagascar, Malaysia, Malta, Mauritius, Mexico, Moldova, Montenegro, Morocco, Nepal, Netherlands, New Zealand, Nigeria, North Macedonia, Norway, Pakistan, Palau, Panama, Paraguay, Philippines, Poland, Portugal, Romania, Russia, Saudi Arabia, Serbia, Seychelles, Singapore, Slovakia, Slovenia, Spain, Sri Lanka, Sweden, Switzerland, Tajikistan, Thailand, Türkiye, Turkmenistan, UK, Ukraine, United Arab Emirates, USA, Uzbekistan, Vietnam, Zambia.

Official Observers (6):
European Union (EU, #08967); International Atomic Energy Agency (IAEA, #12294); International Criminal Police Organization – INTERPOL (ICPO-INTERPOL, #13110); United Nations Interregional Crime and Justice Research Institute (UNICRI, #20580); United Nations Office of Counter-Terrorism (UNOCT); *United Nations Office on Drugs and Crime (UNODC, #20596).* [2022.10.12/XJ2725/y/**E***]

♦ Global Initiative for Consensus in Pediatrics (unconfirmed)
♦ Global Initiative on Disaster Risk Management (internationally oriented national body)
♦ Global Initiative for Economic, Social and Cultural Rights (internationally oriented national body)
♦ Global Initiative to End All Corporal Punishment of Children / see End Corporal Punishment (#05457)
♦ Global Initiative for Inclusive ICTs / see Global Initiative for Inclusive Information and Communication Technologies (#10425)

♦ Global Initiative for Inclusive Information and Communication Technologies (G3ict) 10425

Pres/Exec Dir 6300 Powers Ferry Rd, Ste 600-300, Atlanta GA 30339, USA. T. +16785348518. Fax +14042520628. E-mail: info@g3ict.org.
URL: http://g3ict.org/

History Dec 2006, by *Global Alliance for ICT and Development (GAID, #10200)* and Secretariat of *Convention on the Rights of Persons with Disabilities (CRPD, 2006)* at UN DESA. Also referred to as *Global Initiative for Inclusive ICTs.* Subtitle: *Promoting the Rights of Persons with Disabilities in the Digital Age.* **Aims** Facilitate and support implementation of the dispositions of the Convention on the *Rights* of Persons with *Disabilities* on the accessibility of Information Communication Technologies (ICTs) and assistive technologies. **Structure** Board of Trustees; Steering Committee; Advisory Council. Division: *International Association of Accessibility Professionals (IAAP, #11680).* **Activities** Politics/policy/regulatory; advocacy/lobbying/activism; events/meetings; training/education; certification/accreditation. **Events** *M-enabling Summit* Washington, DC (USA) 2021, *M-enabling Summit* Washington, DC (USA) 2019.

Members Participating institutions (13):
Convention on the Rights of Persons with Disabilities (CRPD, 2006) (through UN Enable – UN Secretariat); *ILO (#11123); International Bank for Reconstruction and Development (IBRD, #12317)* (World Bank); *International Telecommunication Union (ITU, #15673);* ITU – Dynamic Coalition on Accessibility and Disability; *Office of the United Nations High Commissioner for Human Rights (OHCHR, #17697);* UN DESA; *UNESCO (#20322); United Nations Economic and Social Commission for Asia and the Pacific (ESCAP, #20557); United Nations Global Compact (#20567); United Nations Institute for Training and Research (UNITAR, #20576); WHO (#20950); World Intellectual Property Organization (WIPO, #21593).*

Consultative Status Consultative status granted from: *ECOSOC (#05331)* (Special). [2019/XJ9364/y/**E**]

♦ Global Initiative for Justice, Truth and Reconciliation (unconfirmed)
♦ Global Initiative for Positive Change (internationally oriented national body)
♦ Global Initiative on Psychiatry / see Human Rights in Mental Health (#10988)
♦ Global Initiative on Psychiatry – an international foundation for the promotion of humane, ethical and effective mental health care throughout the world / see Human Rights in Mental Health (#10988)
♦ Global Initiatives for Sustainable Development and Humanitarian Action (internationally oriented national body)

♦ Global Initiative for Traditional Systems of Health (GIFTS of Health) 10426

Chairman Green College, University of Oxford, Oxford, OX2 6HG, UK.
URL: http://www.giftsofhealth.org/

History Mar 1994, Ottawa (Canada). [2016/XF5931/**F**]

♦ Global Initiative – Verein gegen transnationale organisiert Kriminalität / see Global Initiative Against Transnational Organized Crime (#10421)
♦ Global Innovation Fund (internationally oriented national body)

♦ The Global Institute 10427

Pres PO Box 424, Portland ME 04112-0424, USA. T. +12076719131. E-mail: info@theglobalinstitute.org.
URL: https://theglobalinstitute.org/

History 2010, USA. Registration: USA, Maine. **Aims** As a social change organization, specializing in global leadership development, sustainable capacity building and strategic facilitation of social development initiatives, build movements and organizations that engage sustainable practices. **Structure** Head Office in USA; Independent operational hubs in Denmark, Germany and India. **Languages** Danish, English, Hindi, Spanish. **Staff** 6.50 FTE, paid; 22.00 FTE, voluntary. **Finance** Sources: donations; fees for services; grants. **Activities** Capacity building; events/meetings; knowledge management/information dissemination; monitoring/evaluation; networking/liaising; research/documentation; training/education. Active in: Denmark, Germany, India, USA. **NGO Relations** Member of (1): *Association for World Education (AWE, #02983).* [2021.03.18/AA1517/**F**]

♦ Global Institute for Disease Elimination (unconfirmed)
♦ Global Institute of Flexible Systems Management (internationally oriented national body)
♦ Global Institute for Leadership and Civic Development / see Leadership exCHANGE

♦ Global Institute for Risk Management Standards (G31000) 10428

Contact Rue des Colonies 11, 1000 Brussels, Belgium. E-mail: info@g31000.org.
Contact G31000 North America Inc, 340 Madison Avenue, 19th Floor, New York NY 10173-1921, USA. T. +12122209225.
URL: http://www.g31000.org/

History 2009. Registration: France. **Aims** Raise awareness for the ISO 31000 Risk Management Standard and associated documents. **Languages** English, French, Italian, Portuguese, Spanish. **Staff** 5-10. **Finance** Sources: members' dues. **Activities** Certification/accreditation; events/meetings; training/education. **Events** *Conference* Dubai (United Arab Emirates) 2017, *Conference* Cape Town (South Africa) 2015, *Conference* New York, NY (USA) 2014, *Conference* Toronto, ON (Canada) 2013, *Conference* Paris (France) 2012. **Members** Full in 122 countries. Membership countries not specified. **IGO Relations** None. [2018/XJ8851/j/**C**]

♦ Global Institute of Sustainability (internationally oriented national body)
♦ Global Institute of Theology (see: #21289)

♦ Global Institute for Water, Environment and Health (GIWEH) 10429

Exec Dir Rue du Chantepoulet 10, 1201 Geneva, Switzerland. T. +41227337511. Fax +41227348324. E-mail: info@giweh.ch.
URL: http://www.giweh.ch/

History Mar 2007. Registered in accordance with Swiss Civil Code. **Aims** Provide societies, individuals and institutions with educational, research, technical and scientific support to realize effective and sustainable use and management of water. **Structure** Steering Board; Scientific Committee. **Languages** English, French. **Staff** 7.00 FTE, paid. **Finance** Sources: donations. Other sources: Project-based; trainings; education; consultation. Annual budget: 350,000 CHF. **Activities** Awards/prizes/competitions; capacity building; certification/accreditation; conflict resolution; events/meetings; knowledge management/information dissemination; monitoring/evaluation; networking/liaising; research and development; training/education. **Events** *Conference on Water, Environment and Climate Change* Alexandria (Egypt) 2019, *International Conference on Water Resources and Environmental Management* Antalya (Turkey) 2014, *International Conference on Water Resources and Environmental management* Geneva (Switzerland) 2013, *International Conference on Water Resources and Environmental Management* Marrakech (Morocco) 2011. **Consultative Status** Consultative status granted from: *ECOSOC (#05331)* (Special). **IGO Relations** Collaborations and partnerships with: *OECD (#17693)* Water Governance Initiative. **NGO Relations** Collaborations and partnerships with: *Evian Group (inactive); Global Water Partnership (GWP, #10653); International Institute for Management Development (IMD); International Water Resources Association (IWRA, #15871); IHE Delft Institute for Water Education (#11110).* Member of: Asia Water Council; Swiss Water Partnership (SWP); *World Water Council (WWC, #21908).* [2018/XJ7939/j/**C**]

♦ Global Integrity (internationally oriented national body)
♦ Global Interaction (internationally oriented national body)

♦ Global Interagency Security Forum (GISF) 10430

Exec Dir Mines Advisory Group, Suite 3a, South Central, 11 Peter Street, Manchester, M2 5QR, UK. E-mail: gisf-admin@gisf.ngo – gisf-info@gisf.ngo.
Street Address CAFOD Head Office, Romero House, 55 Westminster Bridge Road, London, SE1 7JB, UK.
URL: https://gisf.ngo/

History 2006. Former names and other names: *European Interagency Security Forum (EISF)* – former (2006 to Apr 2020). **Aims** Have a positive impact on humanitarian security risk management (SRM) to keep aid workers safe and achieve sustainable access to populations in need. **Structure** Steering Group; Secretariat. **Languages** English, French, Spanish. **Finance** Supported by: *United States Agency for International Development (USAID).* Annual budget: 450,000 EUR. **Activities** Events/meetings; knowledge management/information dissemination; networking/liaising; research/documentation.

Members Organizations (145) in 18 countries:
Austria, Belgium, Czechia, Denmark, Finland, France, Germany, Ireland, Italy, Malta, Netherlands, Norway, Poland, Spain, Sweden, Switzerland, UK, USA.

- *ACT Alliance (#00081);*
- *Action Against Hunger (#00086);*
- *ActionAid (#00087);*
- *Agency for Technical Cooperation and Development (ACTED);*
- *Bureau international des Médecins sans frontières (MSF International, #03366);*
- *CARE International (CI, #03429);*
- *Caritas Internationalis (CI, #03580);*
- *Catholic Agency for Overseas Development (CAFOD);*
- *Catholic Organization for Relief and Development (Cordaid);*
- *Catholic Relief Services (CRS, #03608);*
- *Center for Civilians in Conflict (CIVIC);*
- *CESVI Fondazione;*
- *ChildFund International (#03869);*
- *Christian Aid;*
- *Christian Blind Mission (CBM);*
- *Concern Worldwide;*
- *Crisis Management Initiative (CMI);*
- *Danish Refugee Council (DRC);*
- *Deutsche Gesellschaft für Internationale Zusammenarbeit (GIZ);*
- *Diakonie Katastrophenhilfe;*
- *Education Development Center (EDC);*
- *EDUCO;*
- *Fauna & Flora International (FFI, #09277);*
- *Finn Church Aid (FCA);*
- *Food for the Hungry (fh, #09845);*
- *Global Communities;*
- *GOAL;*
- *GRET;*
- *Habitat for Humanity International (HFHI);*
- *HelpAge International (#10904);*
- *Help – Hilfe zur Selbsthilfe;*
- *HELVETAS Swiss Intercooperation;*
- *HIAS;*
- *Humanistisch Instituut voor Ontwikkelingssamenwerking (Hivos);*
- *Humanity and Inclusion (HI, #10975);*
- *iMMAP;*
- *INTERMON OXFAM;*

– *International Dryland Development Commission (IDDC, #13208)*;
– *International Medical Corps (IMC)*;
– *International Orthodox Christian Charities (IOCC)*;
– *International Rescue Corps (IRC)*;
– *INTERSOS*;
– *Islamic Relief Worldwide (IRWW, #16048)*;
– *Jesuit Refugee Service (JRS, #16106)*;
– *Johanniter-Unfall-Hilfe (JUH, #16120)*;
– *Kvinna till Kvinna Foundation*;
– *Legal Action Worldwide (LAW, #16438)*;
– *Malteser International*;
– *MEDAIR*;
– *Médecins du Monde – International (MDM, #16613)*;
– *Medical Teams International (MTI)*;
– *Medica Mondiale*;
– *Mennonite Economic Development Associates (MEDA)*;
– *Middle East Dietary Association (MEDA, no recent information)*;
– *Mines Advisory Group (MAG)*;
– *Mission East*;
– *Movement for Peace, Disarmament and Freedom (MPDL)*;
– *Norwegian Church Aid*;
– *Norwegian Refugee Council (NRC)*;
– *Oxfam GB*;
– *Oxfam International (#17922)*;
– *Oxfam Novib*;
– *PAX*;
– *People in Need (PIN)*;
– *Plan International (#18386)*;
– *Polish Humanitarian Action (PAH)*;
– *Première Urgence Internationale*;
– *Project HOPE*;
– *PSI (#18555)*;
– *Relief International*;
– *Saferworld*;
– *Salvation Army (#19041)*;
– *Save the Children International (#19058)*;
– *Secours catholique – Caritas France*;
– *ShelterBox*;
– *Sightsavers International (#19270)*;
– *Solidarités International*;
– *Swiss Interchurch Aid (EPER)*;
– *Tearfund, UK*;
– *The Lutheran World Federation (LWF, #16532)*;
– *Trocaire – Catholic Agency for World Development*;
– *Voluntary Service Overseas (VSO)*;
– *War Child International (#20817)*;
– *WaterAid (#20822)*;
– *Welthungerhilfe*;
– *Winrock International*;
– *Women for Women International (WFWI)*;
– *World Vision International (WVI, #21904)*;
– *ZOA*.

Associate members in 10 countries:
Australia, France, Germany, Israel, Netherlands, Portugal, Spain, Switzerland, UK, USA.
– *Access Now (#00052)*;
– *Amnesty International (AI, #00801)*;
– *Bill and Melinda Gates Foundation (BMGF)*;
– *British Council*;
– *Centre for Information, Counseling and Training Professions Relating to International Cooperation and Humanitarian Aid (CINFO)*;
– *Comic Relief*;
– *Conciliation Resources (CR)*;
– *Democracy Reporting International (DRI, #05034)*;
– *Deutsche Gesellschaft für Internationale Zusammenarbeit (GIZ)*;
– *European Commission (EC, #06633)*;
– *Fred Hollows Foundation*;
– *Geneva Call*;
– *Greenpeace International (#10727)*;
– *Human Rights Watch (HRW, #10990)*;
– *International Alert (#11615)*;
– *International Centre for Migration Policy Development (ICMPD, #12503)*;
– *International Committee of the Red Cross (ICRC, #12799)*;
– *International Federation of Red Cross and Red Crescent Societies (#13526)*;
– *International Planned Parenthood Federation (IPPF, #14589)*;
– *Israel Forum for International Humanitarian Aid (IsraAID)*;
– *Lumos Foundation*;
– *Mastercard Foundation*;
– *Medica Mondiale*;
– *Open Society Foundations (OSF, #17763)*;
– *Reprieve*;
– *Swiss Agency for Development and Cooperation (SDC)*;
– *Transparency International (TI, #20223)*;
– *United States Agency for International Development (USAID)*. [2023.02.15/AA2668/y/**F**]

♦ Global Interdependence Center (internationally oriented national body)

♦ Global Interfaith Network for People of All Sexes, Sexual Orientation, Gender Identity and Expression (GIN-SSOGIE) 10431

Exec Dir Corner Rabie Rd – Fourth Ave North, Fountainebleau, Randburg, 2032, South Africa. T. +27104461990. E-mail: info@gin-ssogie.org.
URL: http://www.gin-ssogie.org/

History Feb 2014. **Aims** Ensure that the views, values and rights of people of all sexes, sexual orientations, gender identities and expressions are recognized, respected, and valued. **Structure** Global Ambassadors; Governance Board. **Events** *Conference* Bangkok (Thailand) 2016. **NGO Relations** Member of (1): *European Forum of Lesbian, Gay, Bisexual and Transgender Christian Groups (Forum LGBT, #07318)*. [2020/XM5364/**F**]

♦ Global Interfaith WASH Alliance (unconfirmed)

♦ Global Internet Governance Academic Network (GIGANet) 10432

Chair Goldsmiths Univ of London, Dept of Media and Communications, 8 Lewisham Way, London, SE14 6NW, UK.
Sec Intl Relations Research Center (IRRC/NUPRI), Rua do Anfiteatro 181, Colméia-Favo 7, Cidade Univ, Sao Paulo SP, 05508-060, Brazil.
URL: https://www.giga-net.org/

History 2006, Athens (Greece), at 1st UN Internet Governance Forum. **Aims** Support establishment of a global network of scholars specializing in Internet governance issues; promote development of Internet governance as a recognized interdisciplinary field of study; advance theoretical and applied research on Internet governance; facilitate informed dialogue on policy issues and related matters between scholars and Internet governance stakeholders. **Staff** None. **Finance** No budget. **Activities** Events/meetings. **Events** *Symposium* Guadalajara (Mexico) 2016, *Symposium* João Pessoa (Brazil) 2015, *Symposium* Istanbul (Turkey) 2014, *Symposium* Bali (Indonesia) 2013, *Symposium* Baku (Azerbaijan) 2012. **Members** Individual researchers. Membership countries not specified. [2018.06.01/XJ8247/**F**]

♦ Global Intuition Network / see Intuition Network

♦ Global Investigative Journalism Network (GIJN) 10433

Réseau international de journalisme d'investigation – Red Global de Periodismo de Investigación

Exec Dir PO Box 7375, Silver Spring MD 20907, USA. E-mail: hello@gijn.org.
URL: https://gijn.org/

History 4 May 2003, Copenhagen (Denmark). Founded at 2nd Global Investigative Journalism Conference. **Aims** Support, promote and spread best practices in investigative and related data journalism; serve as a global hub, professional association and training centre for investigative journalists worldwide. **Structure** Board of Directors; Secretariat. **Languages** Arabic, Bengali, Chinese, English, French, German, Hindi, Indonesian, Portuguese, Russian, Spanish, Turkish, Urdu. **Staff** 32.00 FTE, paid. **Activities** Events/meetings; guidance/assistance/consulting; networking/liaising; training/education. Active in all member countries. **Events** *Global Investigative Journalism Conference (GIJC)* Gothenburg (Sweden) 2023, *Global Investigative Journalism Conference (GIJC22)* Sydney, NSW (Australia) 2022, *Forum on Media Practitioners* Tokyo (Japan) 2022, *Global Investigative Journalism Conference* 2021, *Asian Conference* Kuala Lumpur (Malaysia) 2020. **Publications** *GIJN Bulletin*. Conference programs; reports; articles.

Members Organizations (244) in 90 countries and territories. Membership countries not specified.
Included in the above, 8 organizations listed in this Yearbook:
African Network of Centres for Investigative Reporting (ANCIR); *European Journalism Centre (EJC, #07612)*; *Forum of African Investigative Reporters (FAIR, #09894)*; *International Consortium of Investigative Journalists (ICIJ)*; *International Media Support (IMS, #14128)*; *Southeast European Network for Computer-Assisted Reporting (SEENCAR, no recent information)*; *Southeast European Network for Investigative Reporting (SEENIR)*; *World Press Institute (WPI)*. [2023.02.14/XM1820/y/**F**]

♦ Global Investor Coalition on Climate Change (GIC) 10434

Contact address not obtained.
Contact address not obtained.
URL: https://globalinvestorcoalition.org/

History 2012. Launched by *Asia Investor Group op Climate Change (AIGCC, #01285)*, *CERES*, *Investor Group on Climate Change (IGCC)* and *Institutional Investors Group on Climate Change (IIGCC, #11317)*. **Aims** Increase investor education and engagement on climate change and climate-related policies. **Activities** Projects/programmes. [2020/AA1118/y/**E**]

♦ Global Investor Relations Network (GIRN) 10435

Contact Natl Investor Relations Inst, 225 Reinekers Lane, Ste 560, Alexandria VA 22314, USA.
URL: http://www.globalirnet.org/

History 4 Sep 2008, London (UK), on dissolving of *International Investor Relations Federation (IIRF, inactive)*. **Aims** Support the further development and practice of global investor relations requirements; raise credibility of investor relations; achieve best practices in global IR profession. **Structure** Steering Committee of 4. Chairman.

Members National IR societies in 23 countries:
Australia, Austria, Belgium, Brazil, Bulgaria, Canada, Denmark, Egypt, Finland, Germany, India, Japan, Malaysia, Norway, Poland, Portugal, Singapore, Spain, Switzerland, Türkiye, UK, Ukraine, USA. [2014/XJ2272/y/**C**]

♦ Globalisation for the Common Good Initiative (unconfirmed)

♦ Globalisation and Economic Policy Centre / see Nottingham Centre for Research on Globalisation and Economic Policy

♦ Global Island Partnership (GLISPA) 10436

Coordinator c/o IUCN, 1630 Connecticut Avenue NW, 3rd Floor, Washington DC 20009, USA. T. +12023412876. E-mail: info@glispa.org.
URL: http://glispa.org/

History 2005. Founded as a voluntary partnership of national and local governments, agencies and organizations. **Aims** Promote action for island *conservation* and *sustainable livelihoods*. **Structure** Board; Council; Steering Committee. Working Groups. Coordination Team.

Members Members in 16 countries and territories:
Aruba, Bahamas, France, Grenada, Guam, Hawaii, Italy, Marshall Is, Micronesia FS, New Caledonia, Niue, Palau, Polynesia Fr, Seychelles, USA, Virgin Is UK.
Atlantic Council; *Caribbean Biodiversity Fund (CBF)*; *Conservation International (CI)*; *Convention on Biological Diversity (Biodiversity convention, 1992)*; *Global Environment Facility (GEF, #10346)*; *International Union for Conservation of Nature and Natural Resources (IUCN, #15766)*; *Island Conservation (CI)*; *Okeanos Foundation for the Sea*; *Rare*; *Secretariat of the Pacific Regional Environment Programme (SPREP, #19205)*; *The Nature Conservancy (TNC)*; *Wildlife Conservation Society (WCS)*.

Friends in 9 countries and territories:
Bahamas, Cocos-Keeling Is, Germany, Micronesia FS, Palau, Seychelles, St Lucia, Tanzania UR, USA.
Commission de l'Océan Indien (COI, #04236); *Global Ocean Trust (GOT)*; *International Small Islands Studies Association (ISISA, #14876)*; *Local Governments for Sustainability (ICLEI, #16507)*; *Mountain Partnership (MP, #16862)*; *Pacific Islands Development Forum (PIDF, #17967)*; *UN Environment Programme World Conservation Monitoring Centre (UNEP-WCMC, #20295)*; *United Nations Office of the High Representative for the Least Developed Countries, Landlocked Developing Countries and Small Island Developing States (UN-OHRLLS, #20599)*; *World Federation for Coral Reef Conservation (WFCRC)*; *World Meteorological Organization (WMO, #21649)*.

IGO Relations Recognized as Best Practice Partnership by *United Nations Commission on Sustainable Development (CSD, inactive)*. **NGO Relations** Instrumental in setting up (1): *Coalition of Fragile Ecosystems (COFE)*. [2022/XJ5936/y/**F**]

♦ Global Islands Network (GIN) 10437

Exec Dir Struan House, Knockintorran, HS6 5ED, UK.
URL: http://www.globalislands.net/

History Jun 2002. A charitable company limited by guarantee. Scottish Registered Charity: SCO-33395. **Aims** Conduct and promote culturally appropriate, ecologically sound, economically sustainable and socially equitable development on islands worldwide. **Structure** Board of Directors.

Members National and international organizations. Membership countries not specified. Included in the above, 19 organizations listed in this Yearbook:
Included in the above, 19 organizations listed in this Yearbook:
American Society of International Law (ASIL); *Caribbean Alliance for Sustainable Tourism (CAST, #03439)*; *Caribbean Solar Energy Society (CSES, #03557)*; *Centre for Asia-Pacific Island Studies (CAPIS)*; *Centre for Tourism in Islands and Coastal Areas (CENTICA)*; *Durrell Wildlife Conservation Trust*; *Global Development Research Centre (GDRC)*; *Indo-Pacific Conservation Alliance (IPCA)*; *International Centre for Island Technology (ICIT)*; *International Research Foundation for Development (IRFD, #14724)*; *International Small Islands Studies Association (ISISA, #14876)*; *Islands and Small States Institute, Malta (ISSI, #16062)*; *Mediterranean Association to Save the Sea Turtles (MEDASSET, #16647)*; *Network of the Insular Chambers of Commerce and Industry of the European Union (INSULEUR, #17040)*; *Pacific-Asia Biodiversity Transect Network (PABITRA, #17929)*; *Pacific Islands Development Program (PIDP, see: #05263)*; *Pacific Islands Political Studies Association (PIPSA, #17976)*; *Pacific Tourism Organization (SPTO, #18008)*; *Secretariat of the Pacific Regional Environment Programme (SPREP, #19205)*.

NGO Relations Participates in: *Global Island Partnership (GLISPA, #10436)*. [2013.06.01/XM1876/y/**F**]

♦ Global Issues Network (GIN) 10438

Exec Dir address not obtained.
URL: http://globalissuesnetwork.org/

History Proposed 2003. Launched 2006. **Aims** Empower young people to *collaborate* locally, regionally, and globally in order to create project based sustainable solutions for shared global issues; recognize and nurture *youth empowerment*. **Structure** Board of Trustees; Administrative Team. **Activities** Events/meetings; projects/programmes. **Events** *Middle School GIN Conference* Bali (Indonesia) 2018, *High School GIN Conference* Shanghai (China) 2018, *Middle School GIN Conference* Hong Kong (China) 2017, *High School GIN Conference* Bali (Indonesia) 2016, *Middle School GIN Conference* Hangzhou (China) 2016. **NGO Relations** Partners include: *Association for the Advancement of International Education (AAIE)*; *Association of American Schools of Central America, Colombia, Caribbean and Mexico (Tri-Association, #02367)*; *American*

International Schools in the Americas (AMISA); Association of International Schools in Africa (AISA, #02761); East Asia Regional Council of Overseas Schools (EARCOS, #05214); Educational Collaborative for International Schools (ECIS, #05365). [2017/XM5779/F]

♦ **Globalization and Localization Association (GALA)** **10439**
Exec Dir 4701 SW Admiral Way, Suite 138, Seattle WA 98116, USA. T. +12064944686. E-mail: info@gala-global.org.
URL: http://www.gala-global.org/
History 15 Apr 2002. Registration: USA. **Aims** Support the global language services and technologies industry; promote use of multilingual content and communication to connect with audiences in their own languages and cultures via translation, localization and interpreting. **Structure** Board of Directors; Committees; SIGs. **Languages** English. **Staff** 5.00 FTE, paid. **Finance** Sources: members' dues; revenue from activities/projects; sponsorship. Annual budget: 900,000 USD (2022). **Activities** Awards/prizes/competitions; events/meetings; networking/liaising. **Events** *Annual Language of Business Conference* Dublin (Ireland) 2023, *Annual Language of Business Conference* San Diego, CA (USA) 2022, *Annual Language of Business Conference* Munich (Germany) 2019, *Annual Language of Business Conference* Boston, MA (USA) 2018, *Annual Language of Business Conference* Amsterdam (Netherlands) 2017. **Publications** *GALA Global Update* (12 a year) – newsletter.
Members Companies (430) in 52 countries and territories:
Argentina, Australia, Austria, Belgium, Brazil, Bulgaria, Canada, Chile, China, Czechia, Denmark, Egypt, Estonia, Finland, France, Germany, Greece, Guatemala, Hong Kong, Hungary, India, Ireland, Israel, Italy, Japan, Korea Rep, Latvia, Lithuania, Malaysia, Mexico, Netherlands, New Zealand, Norway, Philippines, Poland, Portugal, Romania, Russia, Saudi Arabia, Singapore, Slovakia, South Africa, Spain, Sweden, Taiwan, Thailand, Türkiye, UK, Ukraine, United Arab Emirates, USA, Vietnam.
[2022.11.08/XD9428/D]

♦ Globalization of Pharmaceutics Education Network (unconfirmed)
♦ Globalization Research Centre, Honolulu HI (internationally oriented national body)
♦ Globalization Research Centre, Taipei (internationally oriented national body)
♦ Globalization Research Network (internationally oriented national body)

♦ **Globalization Studies Network (GSN)** **10440**
Manager c/o ISS, Kortenaerkade 12, 2518 AX The Hague, Netherlands.
URL: http://gsnetwork.igloogroups.org/
History Jan 2003, Washington DC (USA). Inaugural conference Aug 2004, Warwick (UK). Dormant as of 2012. **Aims** Promote research and teaching collaborations involving world religions, cultures and disciplines. **Structure** General Meeting (annual). Steering Committee. **Events** *Conference* Waterloo, ON (Canada) 2008, *Conference* Kuala Lumpur (Malaysia) 2006, *Conference* Dakar (Senegal) 2005, *Conference* Warwick (UK) 2004, *Conference* Washington, DC (USA) 2003.
Members Research centres, programmes, university units, think tanks (110) in 45 countries:
Argentina, Australia, Bangladesh, Belgium, Brazil, Canada, Chile, China, Dominican Rep, Egypt, Ethiopia, Fiji, Finland, Germany, Ghana, Greece, India, Iran Islamic Rep, Ireland, Jamaica, Japan, Kenya, Lebanon, Malaysia, Mexico, Netherlands, Norway, Pakistan, Peru, Philippines, Poland, Portugal, Russia, Senegal, South Africa, Sri Lanka, Sweden, Taiwan, Tanzania UR, Thailand, Türkiye, Uganda, UK, USA, Venezuela.
Included in the above, 56 organizations listed in this Yearbook:
- *Africa Institute of South Africa (AISA);*
- *Asian Centre, University of the Philippines;*
- *Bandaranaike Centre for International Studies (BCIS);*
- *Carnegie Council for Ethics in International Affairs (CCEIA);*
- *Center for Global Accountabilities, Blacksburg VA;*
- *Center for Global Political Economy, Burnaby (CGPE);*
- *Center for Global Studies, Fairfax VA (CGS);*
- *Center for the Study of Global Change;*
- *Centre for Globalization Studies, Teheran;*
- *Centre for Global Political Economy, Brighton (CGPE);*
- *Centre for Global Research (inactive);*
- *Centre for Global Studies, Victoria (CFGS);*
- *Centre for International Governance Innovation (CIGI);*
- *Centre for Research on Globalization and Democratic Governance (GLODEM);*
- *Centre for the History of Globalization, Moscow (CHG);*
- *Centre for the Study of Global Ethics;*
- *Centre for the Study of Globalization, Aberdeen (CSG);*
- *Centre for the Study of Globalization and Regionalization (CSGR);*
- *Centre for the Study of Globalization, Athens (CSG);*
- *Centro de Estudios Globales y Regionales, Buenos Aires (CEGRE);*
- *Consejo Latinoamericano de Ciencias Sociales (CLACSO, #04718);*
- *Council for the Development of Social Science Research in Africa (CODESRIA, #04879);*
- *Dr Kiran C Patel Center for Global Solutions;*
- *Economic Research Forum (ERF, #05318);*
- *Focus on the Global South (Focus, #09807);*
- *George Washington Center for the Study of Globalization (CWCSG);*
- *Globalization Research Centre, Honolulu HI (GRC);*
- *Globalization Research Centre, Taipei;*
- *Globalization Research Network (GRN);*
- *GLOBUS – Institute for Globalization and Sustainable Development;*
- *Institute for Globalization Studies and Social Movements, Moscow (IGSO);*
- *Institute for Global Learning, Seaside CA;*
- *Institute for Global Studies (IGS);*
- *Institute for International Integration Studies (IIIS);*
- *Institute for International Trade (IIT);*
- *Institute for World Society Studies (IW);*
- *Institute of Commonwealth Studies, London (ICWS);*
- *Institute of Global Studies, Nankai University;*
- *Institute of International Studies, Wroclaw;*
- *Institute of Malaysian and International Studies (IKMAS);*
- *Institute on Globalization and the Human Condition;*
- *Institut Mirovoj Ekonomiki i Mezdunarodnyh Otnosenij Rossijskoj Akademii Nauk (IMEMO);*
- *Latin American Faculty of Social Sciences (#16316);*
- *Laurier Centre for Global Relations, Governance and Policy (CGRGP);*
- *Liu Institute for Global Issues (LIGI);*
- *Moynihan Institute of Global Affairs;*
- *Nottingham Centre for Research on Globalisation and Economic Policy (GEP);*
- *Organization for Social Science Research in Eastern and Southern Africa (OSSREA, #17888);*
- *Princeton School of Public and International Affairs;*
- *Research Network on International Governance, Globalization and the Transformations of the State (REGIMEN);*
- *School of Global Studies, Tempe AZ;*
- *School of International Studies, Delhi;*
- *Third World Network (TWN, #20151);*
- *Tropical Science Research Institute (IICT);*
- *UCLA Globalization Research Centre of Africa (GRCA);*
- *Yale Center for the Study of Globalization (YCSG).*

Associates organizations (15) in 6 countries:
Canada, Dominican Rep, Finland, Switzerland, UK, USA.
Included in the above 12 organizations listed in this Yearbook:
Center for Global Development (CGD); Center for Strategic and International Studies, Washington DC (CSIS); Charles Stewart Mott Foundation; Fundación Global Democracia y Desarrollo (FUNGLODE); Globalization and World Cities Research Network (GaWC, #10441); Global Studies Association (GSA); ILO (#11123); Network Institute for Global Democratization (NIGD); One World Trust (OWT); UNCTAD (#20285); United Nations Foundation (UNF, #20563); United Nations Research Institute for Social Development (UNRISD, #20623).
Supporters individuals (4) in 2 countries:
UK, USA. [2008/XM0398/dy/F]

♦ **Globalization and World Cities Research Network (GaWC)** **10441**
Dir Dept of Geography, Loughborough Univ, Loughborough, LE11 3TU, UK. T. +441509222794. Fax +441509223930.
URL: http://www.lboro.ac.uk/gawc/
History Loughborough (UK), as a spin-off from 'Global Observatory' website. Original title: *Globalization and World Cities Study Group and Network.* **Aims** Generate and support research on cities in globalization; provide a global platform for this research. **Structure** Decentralized collaborations through Loughborough University. **Languages** English. **Staff** No permanent staff. **Finance** Funded through project work. **Activities** Research projects; postgraduate projects; annual Lecture in Loughborough (UK). **Publications** *GaWC Research Bulletin.* Research reports.
Members Research collaborators in 20 countries:
Australia, Belgium, Brazil, China, France, Germany, Ireland, Israel, Italy, Mexico, Netherlands, Norway, Poland, Singapore, South Africa, Spain, Sweden, Switzerland, UK, USA.
NGO Relations Associate member of: *Globalization Studies Network (GSN, #10440).*
[2009.06.01/XM2186/F]

♦ Globalization and World Cities Study Group and Network / see Globalization and World Cities Research Network (#10441)

♦ **Global Jesuit Business Student Association (GJBSA)** **10442**
Exec Dir Univ of Detroit Mercy, 4001 W McNichols, Detroit MI 48221, USA. T. +13139931219. Fax +13139931052. E-mail: ulfertgw@udmercy.edu – director@iajbs.org.
URL: http://www.gjbsa.org/
Aims Recognize the academic achievements and community involvement of students attending Jesuit business schools. **Structure** Board.
Members Full in 26 countries and territories:
Argentina, Belgium, Bolivia, Brazil, Cameroon, Canada, Chile, Ecuador, El Salvador, France, India, Italy, Japan, Korea Rep, Lebanon, Mexico, Nicaragua, Peru, Philippines, Portugal, Spain, Taiwan, Thailand, Uruguay, USA, Venezuela.
NGO Relations *International Association of Jesuit Business Schools (IAJBS, #11974).*
[2016.06.01/XJ5214/E]

♦ Global Jewish Assistance and Relief Network (internationally oriented national body)
♦ Global Joint Seminar on Geo-Environmental Engineering (meeting series)
♦ Global Justice (internationally oriented national body)
♦ Global Justice Center (internationally oriented national body)
♦ Global Justice Ecology Project (internationally oriented national body)
♦ Global Justice Now (internationally oriented national body)
♦ Global Knowledge Initiative (internationally oriented national body)
♦ Global Knowledge Partnership / see Global Knowledge Partnership Foundation (#10443)

♦ **Global Knowledge Partnership Foundation (GKPF)** **10443**
Secretariat Dendermondsesteenweg 143, 9070 Destelbergen, Belgium.
URL: http://gkpfoundation.org/
History Founded 1997, Toronto (Canada), by *International Bank for Reconstruction and Development (IBRD, #12317),* as *Global Knowledge Partnership (GKP).* Registered as a foundation in accordance with Dutch law: KvK NL853261519B01. **Aims** Enhance the appropriate global and local uses of Information and Communications Technologies for Development (ICT4D); mobilize resources for member projects; mentor greater stakeholder engagement at all phases of projects. **Structure** Board of Trustees; Management Team; Advisory Committee. **Languages** Dutch, English, French, German, Spanish. **Activities** Awards/prizes/competitions; financial and/or material support; events/meetings; training/education. **Events** *Africa meeting* Addis Ababa (Ethiopia) 2008, *Annual meeting* Buenos Aires (Argentina) 2008, *Latin America and Caribbean regional meeting* Buenos Aires (Argentina) 2008, *Global knowledge conference* Kuala Lumpur (Malaysia) 2007, *Members wrap-up meeting* Kuala Lumpur (Malaysia) 2007. **IGO Relations** Partners: *African Development Bank (ADB, #00283); Commonwealth of Learning (COL, #04346); Commonwealth Secretariat (#04362);* Companies; *Deutsche Stiftung für Internationale Entwicklung (DSE, inactive); FAO (#09260);* Governments; *ILO (#11123); International Bank for Reconstruction and Development (IBRD, #12317)* (World Bank); *International Development Research Centre (IDRC, #13162); International Fund for Agricultural Development (IFAD, #13692); International Telecommunication Union (ITU, #15673); Islamic World Educational, Scientific and Cultural Organization (ICESCO, #16058); Swedish International Development Cooperation Agency (Sida); WHO (#20950).* **NGO Relations** Partners: *Association for Progressive Communications (APC, #02873); Bellanet Alliance of Social Entrepreneurs (BASE, #03196); British Council; Carnegie Corporation of New York; Globethics.net Foundation (#10669); International Institute for Sustainable Development (IISD, #13930); OneWorld International Foundation (OWIF, #17738); Panos Network (#18183).* Member of: *World Network for Linguistic Diversity (Maaya, #21671).* Instrumental in setting up: *e-Agriculture (#00575).*
[2015.10.01/XF4128/f/F]

♦ Global LAB – Global Learning Across Borders (internationally oriented national body)

♦ **Global Laboratory Network for Cholera and Other Diarrhoeal Infections (CHOLDInet)** **10444**
Contact Natl Inst of Cholera and Enteric Diseases, Indian Council of Medical Research, P-33 – CIT Road, Scheme-XM, Beliaghata, Kolkata, West Bengal 700 010, Kolkata WEST BENGAL 700 010, India. T. +913323633373 – +913323701176. Fax +913323632398 – +913323705066.
URL: http://www.niced.org.in/choldinet/default.htm
History Mar 2009, as an initiative of *WHO (#20950).* **Aims** Strengthen laboratory capacity for monitoring and rapid detection of cholera and other causes of diarrhoeal diseases to advance the application of control measures. **IGO Relations** *ICDDR,B (#11051).* [2011/XJ3757/E]

♦ Global Labor Justice-International Labor Rights Forum (internationally oriented national body)

♦ **Global Labor Organization (GLO)** **10445**
Pres Leimkugelstr 6, 45141 Essen, Germany. E-mail: office@glabor.org.
URL: https://glabor.org/
History Mar 2017. Registration: No/ID: HRB 23430, Start date: 12 Jan 2018, Germany. **Aims** Function as an international network and virtual platform for researchers, policy makers, practitioners and the general public interested in scientific research and its policy and societal implications on global labor markets, demographic challenges and human resources. **Structure** Management Board; Advisory Board. Research and Policy Cluster Leads; Country Leads.
Members Fellows and Affiliates (over 1500 individuals); Supporting institutions (35) in over 120 countries. Membership countries not specified.
Institutions include 5 listed in this Yearbook:
Center for Migration Studies, New York (CMS); Eurasia Business and Economics Society (EBES, #05599); International Economic Association (IEA, #13222); International Network of Business and Management Journal Editors (INBAM, #14237); International Security and Development Center (ISDC). [2020/AA0927/F]

♦ **Global Labour History Network (GLHN)** **10446**
Contact address not obtained. E-mail: info@socialhistoryportal.org.
URL: https://socialhistoryportal.org/glhn/
History 16 Jun 2015, Barcelona (Spain). **Aims** Promote research, the collection of data, the sharing and mobilization of knowledge, and preservation of archives and other historical materials. **Structure** Steering Committee. **Activities** Events/meetings; research/documentation. **Events** *Conference* Saint Louis (Senegal) 2022, *Conference* Stockholm (Sweden) 2020, *Conference* Delhi (India) 2017. [2022/AA2452/F]

♦ **Global Labour Institute (GLI)** **10447**
Contact Ave du Cardinal Mermillod 18, 1227 Carouge GE, Switzerland. T. +41223446363. Fax +41223446363. E-mail: gli@bluewin.ch.
URL: http://www.global-labour.org/
History Founded 1997, Geneva (Switzerland). Registered in accordance with Swiss Civil Code. **Aims** Support the efforts of the labour movement to deal with the globalization of world *economy* and its *social* and political consequences; strengthen links and networks between *trade unions* and other civil society organizations with similar or converging interests, particularly in the defence of human and democratic rights and social justice in all its aspects. **Structure** Board (meets at least annually). **Languages** English, French, German, Spanish. **Staff** 1.00 FTE, paid; 1.00 FTE, voluntary. **Finance** Sources: consultancy and author's fees; subsidies from public and private authorities or institutions; donations; sales of publications. **Activities** Training/education; research/documentation. **Members** Not a membership organization. **NGO Relations** Part of: GLI Network.
[2014.06.24/XE1762/j/E]

♦ Global Labour University (GLU) **10448**

Co-Exec Dir ICDD – University of Kassel, Dept of Social Sciences – (Fachbereich 5), Kleine Rosenstrasse 3, 34117 Kassel, Germany. T. +4956128610870. E-mail: info@global-labour-university.org – online@global-labour-university.org.
URL: https://global-labour-university.org

History Former names and other names: *Global Labour University – Freunde und Förderer* – legal name. Registration: Berlin District court, No/ID: VR 27701, Start date: 27 May 2008, Germany, Berlin. **Aims** Offer high-quality education programmes for trade unionists and other activists focusing on labour policies responding to the challenges of globalisation; engage in research and publication on how this globalisation impacts the world of work. **Structure** Council; Steering Committee. Operates as a network of trade unions, universities and the ILO. **Languages** English, German. **Activities** Events/meetings; research/documentation; training/education. **Events** *Global Labour University Conference* Berlin (Germany) 2019, *Global Labour University Conference* Sao Paulo (Brazil) 2018, *Conference* Berlin (Germany) 2014.
Members Full: international and national trade union organizations, universities, research institutes and other organizations. Associate institutional. Associated fellows. Full in 5 countries:
Brazil, Germany, India, South Africa, USA.
Building and Wood Workers' International (BWI, #03355); *Education International (EI, #05371)*; *European Trade Union Institute (ETUI, #08928)*; *Friedrich-Ebert-Stiftung (FES)*; *Global Union Federations (GUF, #10638)*; *ILO (#11123)* (Bureau for Workers' Activities (ACTRAV)); *IndustriALL Global Union (IndustriALL, #11177)*; *International Trade Union Confederation (ITUC, #15708)*; *International Transport Workers' Federation (ITF, #15726)*; *Public Services International (PSI, #18572)*; *Trade Union Advisory Committee to the OECD (TUAC, #20186)*; *UNI Global Union (#20338)*.
Associate Institutional in 2 countries:
Philippines, UK. [2023.02.21/AA0733/y/**F**]

♦ Global Labour University – Freunde und Förderer / see Global Labour University (#10448)

♦ Global Lake Ecological Observatory Network (GLEON) **10449**

Contact UW Ctr Limnology, 680 North Park St, Madison WI 53706, USA.
URL: http://www.gleon.org/

History Tagline: Networked Lake Science. **Aims** Conduct innovative science by sharing and interpreting high-resolution sensor data to understand, predict and communicate the role and response of lakes in a changing global environment. **Events** *Meeting* Chuncheon (Korea Rep) 2015, *Meeting* Lammi (Finland) 2007.
[2019/XM3746/**F**]

♦ Global Land Cover Facility (internationally oriented national body)

♦ Global Land Programme (GLP) **10450**

Contact Uni Bern Ctr for Development and Environment, Mittelstr 43, 3012 Bern, Switzerland. T. +41316318822. E-mail: admin@glp.earth.
URL: https://glp.earth/

History A global research project of *Future Earth (#10048)*. Former names and other names: *Global Land Project* – former. **Structure** Scientific Steering Committee; International Programme Office; Nodal Office Coordinators. **Activities** Events/meetings. **Events** *Open Science Meeting* Bern (Switzerland) 2019. **Publications** *E-News* (12 a year). **Members** Individuals. Membership countries not specified.
[2021/AA2192/v/**E**]

♦ Global Land Project / see Global Land Programme (#10450)

♦ Global Landscapes Forum (GLF) **10451**

Contact c/o CIFOR, Jalan CIFOR, Situ Gede, Bogor Barat, Bogor 16115, Indonesia. E-mail: info@globallandscapesforum.org.
URL: https://www.globallandscapesforum.org/

History 2013. Launched at COP19, Warsaw (Poland). Co-founded by *Center for International Forestry Research (CIFOR, #03646)*, *UNEP (#20299)* and *International Bank for Reconstruction and Development (IBRD, #12317)* (World Bank). **Aims** Create sustainable landscapes that are productive, prosperous, equitable and resilient and considers five cohesive themes of food and livelihood initiatives, landscape restoration, rights, finance and measuring progress. **Structure** Led by *Center for International Forestry Research (CIFOR, #03646)*. **Events** *GLF Climate Conference* Sharm el Sheikh (Egypt) 2022, *GLF Climate Conference* Glasgow (UK) 2021.
Members Charter members (28):
- *Center for International Forestry Research (CIFOR, #03646)*;
- *Centre de coopération internationale en recherche agronomique pour le développement (CIRAD, #03733)*;
- Climate Focus;
- *Conservation International (CI)*;
- *Deutsche Gesellschaft für Internationale Zusammenarbeit (GIZ)*;
- *EcoAgriculture Partners (#05290)*;
- *European Forest Institute (EFI, #07297)*;
- *EverGreen Agriculture Partnership (#09213)*;
- *Forest Stewardship Council (FSC, #09869)*;
- *Global Environment Facility (GEF, #10346)*;
- *IFOAM – Organics International (IFOAM, #11105)*;
- Indigenous Peoples Major Group for Sustainable Development (IPMG);
- *International Centre for Integrated Mountain Development (ICIMOD, #12500)*;
- *International Centre for Tropical Agriculture (#12527)*;
- *International Network for Bamboo and Rattan (INBAR, #14234)*;
- *International Union of Forest Research Organizations (IUFRO, #15774)*;
- *Rainforest Alliance*;
- *Rare*;
- *Rights and Resources Initiative (RRI, #18947)*;
- *Sustainable Agriculture Network (SAN, #20052)*;
- *The World Bank Group (#21218)*;
- *UNEP (#20299)*;
- Wageningen Centre for Development Innovation;
- *World Agroforestry Centre (ICRAF, #21072)*;
- *World Farmers' Organisation (WFO, #21401)*;
- *World Resources Institute (WRI, #21753)*;
- WWF Germany;
- Youth in Landscapes Initiative (YIL). [2021/XM9014/y/**F**]

♦ Global Land Tool Network (GLTN) **10452**

Contact ULLGB – UN-Habitat, PO Box 30030-00100, Nairobi, Kenya. T. +2542076238585.
URL: http://www.gltn.net/

History 2006, by *United Nations Human Settlements Programme (UN-Habitat, #20572)*, in cooperation with *Swedish International Development Cooperation Agency (Sida)*, Norwegian Ministry of Foreign Affairs and *International Bank for Reconstruction and Development (IBRD, #12317)*. **Aims** Contribute to *poverty* alleviation and the Millennium Development Goals through land reform, improved land management and security of tenure. **Structure** International Advisory Board of 7 members. Steering Committee. Secretariat, hosted by *United Nations Human Settlements Programme (UN-Habitat, #20572)*. **Events** *Partners Meeting* Nairobi (Kenya) 2011. **Publications** *GLTN Newsletter*.
Members Partners (69): Bilateral organizations; International professional bodies; International training/research institutions; Multilateral organizations; Rural/urban international civil societies. Individuals. Included in the above, 48 organizations listed in this Yearbook:
- *ActionAid (#00087)*;
- *African Institute for Strategic Research Governance and Development (AISRGD)*;
- *Alliance for a Green Revolution in Africa (AGRA, #00685)*;
- *Arab Federation of Surveyors (#00955)*;
- *Asian Coalition for Housing Rights (ACHR, #01381)*;
- *Asian NGO Coalition for Agrarian Reform and Rural Development (ANGOC, #01566)*;
- *Association of African Planning Schools (AAPS, #02359)*;
- *Bill and Melinda Gates Foundation (BMGF)*;
- *Cities Alliance (#03950)*;
- *Commonwealth Association of Surveying and Land Economy (CASLE, #04313)*;
- *Deutsche Gesellschaft für Internationale Zusammenarbeit (GIZ)*;
- *FAO (#09260)*;
- *Fédération des géomètres francophone (FGF, #09591)*;
- *GRET*;
- *Habitat for Humanity International (HFHI)*;
- *Habitat International Coalition (HIC, #10845)*;
- *Huairou Commission (#10960)*;
- *Institute for Housing and Urban Development Studies (IHS)*;
- *Institute for International Urban Development (I2UD)*;
- *International Alliance on Land Tenure and Administration (IALTA)*;
- *International Federation of Surveyors (FIG, #13561)*;
- *International Federation of Women Lawyers (FIDA, #13578)*;
- *International Fund for Agricultural Development (IFAD, #13692)*;
- *International Institute for Environment and Development (IIED, #13877)*;
- *International Institute of Rural Reconstruction (IIRR, #13921)*;
- *International Islamic University Malaysia (IIUM, #13961)*;
- *International Land Coalition (ILC, #13999)*;
- *International Research Group on Law and Urban Space (IRGLUS, #14729)*;
- *International Union for Land Value Taxation and Free Trade (The IU, #15787)*;
- *International Union of Notaries (#15795)*;
- *Landesa – Rural Development Institute (Landesa)*;
- *Les Afriques dans le monde (LAM)*;
- *Network-Association of European Researchers in Urbanisation in the South (N-AERUS, #16996)*;
- *Norwegian Refugee Council (NRC)*;
- *Open Source Geospatial Foundation (OSGeo, #17764)*;
- *Oxfam International (#17922)*;
- *Regional Centre for Mapping of Resources for Development (RCMRD, #18757)*;
- *Royal Institution of Chartered Surveyors (RICS, #18991)*;
- *Shack-Slum Dwellers International (SDI, #19255)*;
- *Swedish International Development Cooperation Agency (Sida)*;
- *Swiss Agency for Development and Cooperation (SDC)*;
- *The World Bank Group (#21218)*;
- *UNEP (#20299)*;
- *United Nations Economic and Social Commission for Asia and the Pacific (ESCAP, #20557)*;
- *United Nations Economic Commission for Africa (ECA, #20554)*;
- *United Nations Human Settlements Programme (UN-Habitat, #20572)*;
- *UN Women (#20724)*;
- *World Vision International (WVI, #21904)*. [2015/XJ4939/y/**E**]

♦ Global Law Enforcement and Public Health Association (GLEPHA) . . **10453**

Pres address not obtained.
URL: http://gleapha.wildapricot.org/

History Registered in accordance with Australian law. **Aims** Promote research, understanding and practice at the intersection of law enforcement and public health. **Structure** Annual General Meeting; Board; Special Interest Groups (SIGs). **Finance** Sources: members' dues. **Activities** Events/meetings; knowledge management/information dissemination. **Publications** *GLEPHA E-Newsletter*.
Members Founding in 3 countries:
Australia, Canada, USA.
NGO Relations *European Public Health Association (EUPHA, #08298)*. [2018/XM6421/**C**]

♦ Global Lawyers and Physicians (internationally oriented national body)
♦ Global Leadership Forum (unconfirmed)

♦ Global Leadership Foundation (GLF) **10454**

CEO 20 Little Britain, London, EC1A 7DH, UK. T. +442034571320. E-mail: secretariat@g-l-f.org.
Chair address not obtained.
Registered Address Andreas B Notter, Gerechtigkeitsgasse 50/52, 3011 Bern, Switzerland.
URL: http://www.g-l-f.org/

History Mar 2004. Founded by former prime ministers and presidents on the initiative of FW de Klerk. Registration: Swiss Civil Code, Switzerland. **Aims** Promote good governance (democratic institutions, open markets, human rights and the rule of law); contribute to prevention and resolution of conflict through resolution. **Structure** General Assembly (annual); Board of Directors; International Council; Strategy and Development Committee; Secretariat based in London (UK). **Languages** English, French, Spanish. **Staff** 4.00 FTE, paid. **Finance** Sources: private foundations. Other sources: corporations; private individuals. **Activities** Guidance/assistance/consulting.
Members Former Heads of State or Government; other leaders (all retired from active politics). Individuals in 34 countries:
Algeria, Australia, Austria, Botswana, Canada, Côte d'Ivoire, Denmark, Egypt, France, Ghana, Guatemala, India, Indonesia, Ireland, Jamaica, Latvia, Lebanon, Liberia, Mauritius, Mexico, New Zealand, Peru, Rwanda, Senegal, South Africa, Spain, Sweden, Switzerland, Tanzania UR, Thailand, Türkiye, UK, Uruguay, USA. [2023.02.13/XJ3056/f/**F**]

♦ Global Learning Across Borders (internationally oriented national body)

♦ Global Learning Initiative on Children and Ethnic Diversity (Una) . . **10455**

Administrator Ctr for Effective Education, School of Education, Queen's Univ Belfast, 69-71 University Street, Belfast, BT7 1HL, UK. T. +442890975952.
URL: http://www.unaglobal.org/

Aims Reduce racial and ethnic divisions and conflicts; build socially inclusive and respectful communities through the promotion of effective early childhood programmes. **Structure** Steering Group, consisting of Co-Chairs of each of the 6 Learning Groups and 2 Co-Directors. **Finance** Support from: *Bernard van Leer Foundation (BvLF)*; *Atlantic Philanthropies*; Queen's University Belfast (UK). **Activities** Dissemination; Research; Community Development; Evaluation. Learning Groups (6): Programme Development; Peacebuilding; Qualitative Methods; Quantitative Methods; Children's Rights; Social Change. **Events** *Biennial Conference on Building Peaceable Communities / Biennial Conference* Amsterdam (Netherlands) 2011.
Members Founding Partners (3):
Bernard van Leer Foundation (BvLF); *Bund Internationaler Detektive (BID)*; Queen's University Belfast.
Global Partners in 7 countries:
Australia, Belgium, Colombia, Indonesia, South Africa, UK, USA.
Included in the above, 1 organization listed in this Yearbook:
Diversity, Early Childhood Education and Training (DECET, #05106). [2012/XJ5290/y/**F**]

♦ Global Learning and Observations to Benefit the Environment (internationally oriented national body)

♦ Global Legal Education Associations Consortium (GLEAC) **10456**

Contact Univ Autònoma de Barcelona, Fac Dred, Carrer de la Vall Moronta s/n, 08193 Cerdanyola del Vallès, Barcelona, Spain. E-mail: info@elfa-edu.org.

History Apr 2018, Barcelona (Spain). Created by *European Law Faculties Association (ELFA, #07656)*, *Asociación de Facultades, Escuelas e Institutos de Derecho de América Latina (AFEIDAL, #02129)*, Southeastern Association of Law Schools (SEALS), China Association of Legal Education, Council of Australian Law Deans and *European Law Institute (ELI, #07658)*. Currently not an organization, but an agreement between founding institutions. **Aims** Act as a forum where members can discuss and debate current issues on legal education in a globalized world; prepare new drafts on international programmes and prepare joint academic curricular for global jurists; develop international joint seminars focusing on legal continuous education for practitioners. **Structure** Informal structure. **Languages** English. **Staff** 1.00 FTE, paid. **Activities** Events/meetings; training/education. [2022.10.13/XM7228/**E**]

♦ Global Legal Empowerment Network **10457**

Dir c/o Namati, 1616 P Street NW, Suite 101, Washington DC 20036, USA. T. +12027215600. Fax +12025300128.
URL: http://www.namati.org/network/

History 2010, by the Justice for the Poor Program of *International Bank for Reconstruction and Development (IBRD, #12317)* and Open Society Justice Initiative. Hosted by: *Namati (#16931)*. **Aims** Foster dialogue, tools sharing and, ultimately, a movement for legal empowerment worldwide. **Members** Organizations (over 1,400); Individuals (over 5,000). Membership countries not specified. **IGO Relations** Partners include: *Australian Aid (inactive); Department for International Development (DFID, inactive); Deutsche Gesellschaft für Internationale Zusammenarbeit (GIZ); International Development Law Organization (IDLO, #13161); UNICEF (#20332); United Nations Office on Drugs and Crime (UNODC, #20596); United States Agency for International Development (USAID).*
NGO Relations Partners include:
- *Alliances for Africa (AfA);*
- *Asia-Pacific Centre for Complex Real Property Rights (APCCRPR);*
- *Avocats Sans Frontières (ASF, #03050);*
- *BarefootLawyers International;*
- *BRAC (#03310);*
- *Children's Rights International (CRI, #03879);*
- *Commonwealth Human Rights Initiative (CHRI, #04340);*
- *Earth Security Initiative (ESI);*
- *Global Network for Public Interest Law (PILnet);*
- *Global Rights;*
- *Global Witness (GW);*
- *Habitat for Humanity International (HFHI);*
- *HelpAge International (#10904);*
- *Human Rights Education Associates (HREA);*
- *International Bridges to Justice;*
- *International Center for Transitional Justice (ICTJ);*
- *International Network to Promote the Rule of Law (INPROL, #14310);*
- *Landesa – Rural Development Institute (Landesa);*
- *Namati (#16931);*
- *Oxfam Novib;*
- *Oxfam GB;*
- *Rencontre africaine pour la défense des droits de l'homme (RADDHO);*
- *Women and Law in Southern Africa Research Trust (WLSA, #21006);*
- *The World Justice Project (WJP, #21605);*
- *World Resources Institute (WRI, #21753).* [2019/XJ5588/F]

♦ Global Legal Entity Identifier Foundation (GLEIF) 10458

Chairman St Alban-Vorstadt 5, PO Box, 4002 Basel BS, Switzerland. T. +41799193218.
CEO address not obtained.
URL: http://www.gleif.org/

History Jun 2014. Founded by *Financial Stability Board (FSB, #09770)*, on request of *Group of Twenty (G20, #10793)*. Statutes adopted 26 june 2014. Registration: Switzerland. **Aims** Develop and maintain the global Legal Entity Identifier (LEI) system; publish the LEI register, based on ISO 20275 ELF (Entity Legal Form) standard. **Structure** Board of Directors; Committees (5); LEI Regulatory Oversight Committee. **Languages** English. **Staff** 35.00 FTE, paid; 18.00 FTE, voluntary. **Finance** Annual budget (2019): US$ 9,500,000. **Activities** Awareness raising; certification/accreditation; knowledge management/information dissemination; publishing activities; standards/guidelines. **Events** *Legal Entity Identifier Regulatory Oversight Committee Plenary Meeting* Seoul (Korea Rep) 2019, *Seoul Meet the Market Seminar* Seoul (Korea Rep) 2019. **Members** Not a membership organization. **NGO Relations** *XBRL International (#21967).* [2019.12.30/XM6824/f/F]

♦ Global Legal Forum (unconfirmed)
♦ Global Legal Studies Network (internationally oriented national body)
♦ Global Legislators Organisation for a Balanced Environment – European Union / see GLOBE – European Union (#10667)
♦ Global Legislators Organization for a Balanced Environment International / see GLOBE International (#10668)

♦ Global Lighting Association 10459

SG PO Box 306, Carole Park, Ipswich QLD 4300, Australia. E-mail: info@globallightingassociation.org.
URL: http://www.globallightingassociation.org/

History Founded 2007, as *Global Lighting Forum (GLF)*. **Aims** Share information, within the limits of national and EU competition law, on political, scientific, business, social and environmental issues of relevance to the lighting industry; develop, implement and publish the position of the global lighting industry to relevant stakeholders in the international sphere. **Structure** Board (meets at least annually); Committees (3); Secretariat. **Languages** English. **Staff** 2.00 FTE, paid. **Finance** Members' dues. **Events** *Board Meeting* Tokyo (Japan) 2015, *Board Meeting* Seoul (Korea Rep) 2014, *Board Meeting* Delhi (India) 2013, *Annual Meeting / Board Meeting* Taipei (Taiwan) 2012, *Annual Meeting / Board Meeting* Sydney, NSW (Australia) 2011. **Publications** Customs classifications; position statements. papers; online publications.
Members Peak national and regional lighting associations representing over 5,000 lighting manufacturers, in 8 countries and territories:
Australia, Brazil, China, India, Japan, New Zealand, Taiwan, USA.
Regional organizations (2):
LightingEurope (#16472); Middle East Lighting Association (MELA, #16770). [2018.09.06/XJ5088/y/F]

♦ Global Lighting Forum / see Global Lighting Association (#10459)
♦ Global Links (internationally oriented national body)
♦ Global Links South / see Center for the Global South
♦ Global Liver Institute (internationally oriented national body)

♦ Global Logistics Associates (GLA) 10460

Head Office Augustapolder 72, Unit 1-3, 2992 SR Barendrecht, Netherlands. T. +31104229370. Fax +31104229854. E-mail: info@glanetwork.com.
URL: http://www.globallogisticsassociates.com/

History 1990. **Structure** General meeting (annual). **Activities** Operates *GlobeTrans International (GTI)* as a non-vessel-operating common carrier business unit. **Events** *Meeting* Goa (India) 2010, *Meeting* Antwerp (Belgium) 2009. **Members** Independent freight forwarders and customs brokers. Membership countries not specified. [2020/XJ8036/F]

♦ Global Logistics Emissions Council (unconfirmed)

♦ Global LPG Partnership (GLPGP) 10461

Headquarters 654 Madison Ave, Ste 1401, New York NY 10065, USA. T. +12128138360. E-mail: info@glpgp.org.
URL: http://glpgp.org/

History Set up 2012, as a United Nations-backed Public-Private Partnership, under the *Sustainable Energy for All (SEforALL, #20056)* initiative. Registered as a 501(c)3 charitable organization in the US. **Aims** Aggregate and deploy needed global resources to help developing countries transition large populations rapidly and sustainably to liquefied petroleum gas (LGP) for cooking. **Languages** English. **Finance** Institutional and individual donors. **Activities** Guidance/assistance/consulting; financial and/or material support.
Members Governments; NGOs; UN system; social impact investors; international LPG companies. Governments (5):
Cameroon, Ghana, Kenya, Tanzania UR, Uganda.
Other public sector organizations (8):
African Development Bank (ADB, #00283); ECOWAS Centre for Renewable Energy and Energy Efficiency (ECREEE, #05335); European Union (EU, #08967) (Infrastructure Trust Fund); *Investeringsfonden for Udviklingslande (IFU); Kreditanstalt für Wiederaufbau (KfW); SNV Netherlands Development Organisation (SNV); The World Bank Group (#21218); UNDP (#20292); UNIDO (#20336).*
NGOs/social impact organizations include 7 organizations listed in this Yearbook:
Clean Cooking Alliance (#03987); Climate and Clean Air Coalition (CCAC, #04010); Entrepreneurs du Monde; New Venture Fund (NVF); OPEC Fund for International Development (OFID, #17745); Sustainable Energy for All (SEforALL, #20056); United Nations Foundation (UNF, #20563).
Academic/research institutions include 3 organizations listed in this Yearbook:
Centre for International Climate and Environmental Research, Oslo (CICERO); Clean Air Asia (#03983); London School of Hygiene and Tropical Medicine (LSHTM).
IGO Relations *United Nations Framework Convention on Climate Change (UNFCCC, 1992).* **NGO Relations** Member of: *Oil and Gas Industry Energy Access Platform (EAP, #17710).* [2018.09.07/XM6557/y/F]

♦ Global Lung Cancer Coalition (unconfirmed)
♦ Global Lyme Alliance (internationally oriented national body)

♦ Globally Responsible Leadership Initiative (GRLI) 10462

Exec Dir Rue Gachard 88 – Box 5, 1050 Brussels, Belgium. E-mail: info@grli.org.
URL: http://www.grli.org/

History 2004. Founded by Board of Directors of *EFMD – The Management Development Network (#05387)*, in partnership with *United Nations Global Compact (#20567)*. Registration: Banque-Carrefour des Entreprises, No/ID: 0808.174.702, Start date: 4 Dec 2008, Belgium. **Aims** Develop a next generation of responsible leaders. **Structure** Council; Guardian Group; Board of Trustees; Executive Committee. **Events** *General Assembly* Oulu (Finland) 2014.
Members Institutional partners (68) in 22 countries:
Australia, Belgium, Brazil, Canada, China, Denmark, Finland, France, Germany, India, Netherlands, Norway, Pakistan, Paraguay, Peru, Philippines, Russia, South Africa, Spain, Sweden, UK, USA.
Included in the above, 5 organizations listed in this Yearbook:
AACSB International – Association to Advance Collegiate Schools of Business; Asian Institute of Management (AIM, #01518); China-Europe International Business School (CEIBS, #03888); EFMD – The Management Development Network (#05387); INSEAD (#11228); United Nations Global Compact (#20567).
NGO Relations Member of (1): *Wellbeing Economy Alliance (WEAll, #20856).* Co-convenor of: *Principles for Responsible Management Education (PRME, #18500).* [2022/XJ2426/fy/E]

♦ Global Mamas (internationally oriented national body)
♦ Global Management Accounting Research Symposium (meeting series)
♦ Global Mapping International (internationally oriented national body)

♦ Global March Against Child Labour 10463

Honorary Pres L-6, Kalkaji, Delhi 110019, DELHI 110019, India. T. +911149211111 – +911149211112. E-mail: joy.lawn@lshtm.ac.uk – march@lshtm.ac.uk.
URL: http://www.globalmarch.org/

History 20 Nov 1997. Not an organization but a movement instigated by *Child Rights International Network (CRIN, #03885)*. EU Transparency Register: 959137934771-01. **Aims** Mobilize worldwide efforts in order to protect and promote the *rights* of all children. **Languages** English, French, Spanish. **Activities** Events/meetings; advocacy/lobbying/activism. **Events** *Children's world congress on child labour and education* Delhi (India) 2005, *Children's world congress on child labour and education* Florence (Italy) 2004. **Publications** *Child Labour News Service.* **Members** in 140 countries. Membership countries not specified. **NGO Relations** Supports: *Global Call for Action Against Poverty (GCAP, #10263).* Board member of: *International Cocoa Initiative (ICI, #12626).* [2019/XF5914/F]

♦ Global March for Elephants and Rhinos (internationally oriented national body)
♦ Global March for Jesus (internationally oriented national body)
♦ Global Marina Institute (internationally oriented national body)

♦ Global Maritime Education and Training Association (GlobalMET) . . 10464

Dir 1070 10F Tower B1, Spaze iTech Park, Sohna Road, Sector 49, Gurugram, Haryana 122002, Gurugram HARYANA 122002, India. T. +911141761002. Fax +911126894188. E-mail: secretariat@globalmet.org – globalmet.secretariat@gmail.com.
Chair address not obtained.
URL: http://globalmet.org/

History Founded Sep 1996, Hong Kong, as *Association of Maritime Education and Training Institutions in Asia Pacific (AMETIAP)*. Current title adopted Oct 2006. Previously registered in accordance with Australian law, Dec 2002, as *AMETIAP (Global) Ltd.* Registered again, Feb 2007, as *GlobalMET Ltd.* **Aims** Promote, develop and support interests of members concerning development and quality of maritime education and training institutions; formulate a common stand on issues of interest to the Association related to maritime education, training, research and development; represent membership in its dealings with regional and international organizations. **Structure** General Meeting (annual); Board of Directors. **Languages** English. **Staff** 1.50 FTE, paid. **Finance** Members' dues. **Activities** Networking/liaising; events/meetings; training/education; guidance/assistance/consulting. **Events** *Annual Conference / Annual General Meeting* Manila (Philippines) 2015, *Annual General Meeting* Manila (Philippines) 2014, *Annual General Meeting* Manila (Philippines) 2013, *Annual General Meeting* Manila (Philippines) 2012, *Maritime Logistics International Forum* Singapore (Singapore) 2011. **Publications** *GlobalMET Newsletter.* Brochures.
Members Full; Associate; Honorary. Full in 37 countries:
Australia, Bangladesh, Belgium, Bulgaria, Canada, Chile, China, Cyprus, Georgia, Greece, India, Ireland, Japan, Kiribati, Malaysia, Maldives, Monaco, Montenegro, Myanmar, Netherlands, New Zealand, Norway, Pakistan, Panama, Papua New Guinea, Philippines, Russia, Singapore, South Africa, Sri Lanka, Sweden, Trinidad-Tobago, Türkiye, UK, United Arab Emirates, USA, Vietnam.
Associate in 5 countries:
Australia, Norway, Philippines, Singapore, UK.
Individuals in 9 countries:
Australia, Canada, India, New Zealand, Peru, Philippines, Singapore, South Africa, UK.
Honorary in 6 countries:
Australia, Japan, Philippines, Sweden, UK, USA.
IGO Relations Consultative status with: *International Maritime Organization (IMO, #14102).* [2022/XD8157/D]

♦ Global Maritime Forum 10465

Managing Dir Amaliegade 33B – 2nd Floor, 1256 Copenhagen K, Denmark. T. +4538401800. E-mail: ms@globalmaritimeforum.org – info@globalmaritimeforum.org.
URL: https://www.globalmaritimeforum.org/

History Registered in accordance with Danish law. **Aims** Shape the future of global seaborne trade to increase sustainable long-term economic development and human wellbeing. **Structure** Board of Directors; Advisory Council. **Activities** Events/meetings; knowledge management/information dissemination. **Publications** *Global Maritime Issues Monitor.* Annual Report. **NGO Relations** Member of: *High Level Panel for a Sustainable Ocean Economy (Panel, #10917)* – Advisory Council. [2022/XM8936/f/F]

♦ Global Marshall Plan Initiative 10466

Coordination Office Rosenstr 2, 20095 Hamburg, Germany. T. +494082290420. Fax +494082290421. E-mail: info@globalmarshallplan.org.
URL: http://www.globalmarshallplan.org/

History Founded 16 May 2003, Frankfurt-Main (Germany). **Aims** Support establishment of an effective, all encompassing plan for global *eco-social development.* **Finance** Two thirds through donations; one third through publication of books. *Global Marshall Plan Foundation* is financial base of the Initiative. **Events** *World commons forum* Salzburg (Austria) 2009. **Publications** Books.
Members Organizations and individuals in 28 countries and territories:
Argentina, Austria, Bangladesh, Belgium, Croatia, Denmark, Estonia, Finland, France, Germany, Greece, India, Jordan, Luxembourg, Mexico, Mozambique, Nepal, Netherlands, New Zealand, Nigeria, Russia, Slovenia, South Africa, Sweden, Taiwan, Türkiye, Ukraine, USA.
NGO Relations Member of (2): *Conference of Non-Governmental Organizations in Consultative Relationship with the United Nations (CONGO, #04635);* Klima-Allianz. Cooperates with (1): *Economy for the Common Good (ECG, #05323).* Supports: *Global Call for Action Against Poverty (GCAP, #10263).* Supported by a large number of national and international organizations, including: *Club of Budapest (#04032); Club of Rome (COR, #04038); Global Contract Foundation; United World Philharmonic Foundation; United World Philharmonic Youth Orchestra.* [2015.06.01/XJ3168/E]

♦ Global Mayors' Forum (GMF) 10467

Contact 16/F Intl Mayors Communication Ctr Bldg, Shennan Blvd, Shenzhen, 518053 Guangdong, China. T. +8675586100516. Fax +8675586100235. E-mail: secretary@globalmayorsforum.org – info@hk-imcc.com.
URL: http://www.globalmayorsforum.org/

History Initiated 2005, by *International Mayors Communication Centre (IMCC)*, of which it is a sub-brand. **Aims** Facilitate economic and cultural exchange and cooperation; search for sustainable development solutions; disseminate low carbon urban management ideas and technologies; facilitate the establishment of sister cities worldwide; set up a network for communication and cooperation between cities worldwide; promote urban development and world peace. **Structure** Council; Permanent Secretariat provided by IMCC. **Languages** Chinese, English. **Staff** 33.00 FTE, paid. **Activities** Research and development; advocacy/lobbying/activism; events/meetings. **Publications** *Dialogue to Global Mayors.* **Members** Cities (4800). Membership countries not specified. **Consultative Status** Consultative status granted from: *ECOSOC (#05331)* (Special). **IGO Relations** *UNDP (#20292)*; *UNEP (#20299)*; *United Nations Human Settlements Programme (UN-Habitat, #20572).* **NGO Relations** *EUROCITIES (#05662)*; *International Downtown Association (IDA)*; *Regional Network of Local Authorities for the Management of Human Settlements (CITYNET, #18799)*; *World Organization of United Cities and Local Governments (UCLG, #21695)*; *World Urban Campaign (WUC, #21893).* [2019.12.13/XM7239/**F**]

♦ Global Mechanism (GM) 10468

Managing Dir c/o UN Campus, Platz der Vereinten Nationen 1, 53113 Bonn, Germany. T. +492288152800 – +492288152856. E-mail: secretariat@unccd.int.
URL: https://www.unccd.int/about-us/global-mechanism

History 1998, as a subsidiary organ of *Secretariat of the United Nations Convention to Combat Desertification (Secretariat of the UNCCD, #19208)*, housed at *International Fund for Agricultural Development (IFAD, #13692).* **Aims** Support *developing countries* to increase *investment* in *sustainable land management*, so as to help reverse, control and prevent land degradation, whilst promoting economic and social development. **Activities** Regional Programmes (5): Asia and Pacific; East and Southern Africa; North Africa; Latin America and the Caribbean; West and Central Africa. Strategic Programmes (7): Economics and Financing Instruments; Market Access and Trade; Climate Change Finance; Innovative Finance and Private Sector; Civil Society; Policy and Investment Analysis; Forest Finance. **NGO Relations** *Réseau Sahel Désertification (ReSaD, #18906).* [2021/XJ5882/**E***]

♦ Global Media AIDS Initiative (GMAI) 10469

Contact address not obtained. T. +27117149111. Fax +27117149744.

History Jan 2004, on the initiative of former UN Secretary General Kofi Annan, in coordination with the Kaiser Family Foundation and UNAIDS. **Aims** Leverage the power of media to help prevent the spread of *HIV* and reduce the stigma facing those already living with the disease. [2012/XM3558/**F**]

♦ GlobalMedic (internationally oriented national body)
♦ Global Medical and Beauty Exchange Association (unconfirmed)

♦ Global Medical Technology Alliance (GMTA) 10470

Secretariat address not obtained. E-mail: info@globalmedicaltechnologyalliance.org.
URL: http://www.globalmedicaltechnologyalliance.org/

Aims Provide safe, effective and innovative medical technology that saves and enhances lives, benefiting people and society. **Languages** English. **Activities** Events/meetings. **Publications** Position papers.
Members National or regional medical technology associations. Full; Associate; Affiliate. Full in 16 countries:
Australia, Brazil, Canada, China, Denmark, Germany, Ireland, Japan, Korea Rep, Mexico, New Zealand, Russia, South Africa, Thailand, Türkiye, USA.
Regional full members (2):
Asia Pacific Medical Technology Association (APACMed, #01953); *Middle East Medical Devices and Diagnostics Trade Association (Mecomed, #16772).*
Associate in 1 country:
Colombia.
Affiliate in 1 country:
USA.
IGO Relations *WHO (#20950).* [2018/XJ7282/y/**C**]

♦ Global Medicare Foundation (unconfirmed)
♦ Global Medic Force (internationally oriented national body)
♦ Global Meeting of Generations (meeting series)
♦ GlobalMET Ltd / see Global Maritime Education and Training Association (#10464)
♦ **GlobalMET** Global Maritime Education and Training Association (#10464)

♦ Global Methane Initiative (GMI) 10471

Dir c/o EPA, 1201 Constitution Ave NW, Room 4353RR, Washington DC 20004, USA. T. +12023439683. Fax +12023432202. E-mail: asg@globalmethane.org.
URL: https://www.globalmethane.org/

History 2004. Launched as an international public-private initiative. **Aims** Target methane abatement, recovery, and use by focusing on biogas (which includes agriculture, municipal solid waste, and wastewater), coal mines, and oil and gas systems. **Structure** Steering Committee; Administrative Support Group. Subcommittees (3): Biogas; Coal Mines; Oil and Gas. Project Network. **Events** *Global Methane Forum* Geneva (Switzerland) 2020, *Global Methane Forum* Toronto, ON (Canada) 2018, *Global Methane Forum* Washington, DC (USA) 2016.
Members Partner countries (42):
Albania, Argentina, Australia, Brazil, Bulgaria, Canada, Chile, China, Colombia, Dominican Rep, Ecuador, Ethiopia, Finland, Georgia, Germany, Ghana, India, Indonesia, Italy, Japan, Jordan, Kazakhstan, Korea Rep, Mexico, Mongolia, Nicaragua, Nigeria, Norway, Pakistan, Peru, Philippines, Poland, Russia, Saudi Arabia, Serbia, Sri Lanka, Thailand, Türkiye, UK, Ukraine, USA, Vietnam.
Regional entity:
European Commission (EC, #06633).
Project Network Members (767) include the following organizations listed in this Yearbook:
Asian Development Bank (ADB, #01422); *Clean Air Asia (#03983)*; *Earth Charter International (ECI, #05161)*; *European Bank for Reconstruction and Development (EBRD, #06315)*; *GERES*; *Global Relief Foundation, Ghana (GREFA)*; *Instituto Internacional de Recursos Renovables (IRRI México)*; *International Bank for Reconstruction and Development (IBRD, #12317)* (World Bank); *International Solid Waste Association (ISWA, #15567)*; *NGVA Europe (#17130)*; *NGV Global (#17131)*; *Pan African Vision for the Environment (PAVE)*; *SNV Netherlands Development Organisation (SNV)*; *Water Environment Federation (WEF)*; *Winrock International*; *World Alliance for Decentralized Energy (WADE, #21081)*; *World Wide Fund for Nature (WWF, #21922).*
IGO Relations *United Nations Economic Commission for Europe (UNECE, #20555).* **NGO Relations** *Climate and Clean Air Coalition (CCAC, #04010).* [2021/XM5893/**E**]

♦ Global Microbial Identified Network (GMI Network) 10472

Administrative Coordinator Technical Univ of Denmark, Kemitorvet, Bldg 204, room 118, 2800 Kongens Lyngby, Denmark.
URL: https://www.globalmicrobialidentifier.org/

History Sep 2011, Brussels (Belgium). **Aims** Build a global system of DNA genome databases for microbial and infectious disease identification and diagnostics. **Structure** Steering Committee; Secretariat. **Activities** Events/meetings; knowledge management/information dissemination; research/documentation. **Events** *Meeting on Global Microbial Identifier* Vancouver, BC (Canada) 2021, *Meeting on Global Microbial Identifier* Vancouver, BC (Canada) 2020, *Meeting on Global Microbial Identifier* Singapore (Singapore) 2019, *Meeting on Global Microbial Identifier* Geneva (Switzerland) 2018, *Meeting on Global Microbial Identifier* Cabo San Lucas (Mexico) 2017. [2020/AA0181/**F**]

♦ Global Migration Group (inactive)

♦ Global Migration Policy Associates (GMPA) 10473

Pres Av de la Paix 11, 1201 Geneva, Switzerland. T. +41227338927.
URL: http://www.globalmigrationpolicy.org/

History Oct 2010. **Aims** Serve as an international research, policy development, advisory services and advocacy group; address international migration from a global, multidisciplinary and rights-based perspective. **Structure** Policy Board of Experts; Coordinating Team; Advisory Council; Secretariat. **Languages** English, French, Spanish. **Staff** 4.00 FTE, paid. **Finance** Members' dues. Other sources: contributions; projects. Budget (annual): about US$ 30,000. **Activities** Research/documentation; policy/politics/regulatory; capacity building; guidance/assistance/consulting; awareness raising; events/meetings. **Publications** Research reports; papers; articles; book chapters; conference presentations.
Members Global Migration Policy Associates in 19 countries:
Argentina, Australia, Austria, Dominican Rep, India, Ireland, Lebanon, Mauritania, Moldova, Morocco, Norway, Philippines, Russia, Senegal, South Africa, Sri Lanka, UK, Uruguay, USA.
Consultative Status Consultative status granted from: *ECOSOC (#05331)* (Special). **NGO Relations** Member of: *Global Coalition on Migration (GCM, #10293)*; Steering Committee for *Global Campaign for Ratification of the Convention on the Rights of Migrant Workers (#10267)*; *Women in Migration Network (WIMN, #21008).* Cooperates with many international and national NGOs/CSOs working in the field of migration. [2020/XJ5917/**F**]

♦ Global Military Advisory Council On Climate Change (GMACCC) ... 10474

Secretariat c/o EDRC, PO Box 121, 3090 Overijse, Belgium. T. +3226880243. E-mail: gmaccc@edrc.net.
URL: http://gmaccc.org/

History 2009. Founded at the initiative of *Institute for Environmental Security (IES).* **Aims** Highlight the potential security implications of a changing climate and advocating action, including by the military, to minimize the risks. **Structure** Bureau. **Events** *Conference on the Climate-Security Nexus* Brussels (Belgium) 2019, *The Climate-Security Nexus: Implications for the Military* Brussels (Belgium) 2019, *Conference* Madrid (Spain) 2019, *Enhancing Climate Diplomacy in a Changing Political Environment* Brussels (Belgium) 2017.
Members Individuals in 14 countries:
Australia, Bangladesh, Canada, France, Germany, Guyana, India, Ireland, Nepal, Netherlands, Pakistan, Türkiye, UK, USA.
Institutions (8) in 3 countries:
Bangladesh, Netherlands, USA.
Environment and Development Resource Centre (EDRC); *European Climate Foundation (ECF, #06574)*; *Institute for Environmental Security (IES)*; *Institute for Governance and Sustainable Development (IGSD).* [2021/AA1235/y/**E**]

♦ Global Millennium International NGO (internationally oriented national body)

♦ Global Mining Guidelines Group (GMG) 10475

CEO 26 Bridge Street, Ormstown QC 10S 1K0, Canada. T. +14508299000. E-mail: info@gmggroup.org.
URL: https://gmggroup.org/

History May 2012. Evolved from efforts by the Surface Mining Association for Research and Technology (SMART) members. Originally a committee under the CIM Surface Mining Society. Became an independent legal entity, Nov 2021. Former names and other names: *Global Mining Standards and Guidelines Group* – former. **Aims** Facilitate and drive the application, utilization and development of global mining standards and guidelines; enable a global community and knowledge hub to support standards and guidelines as positive tools for the global mining industry. **Structure** Executive Council; Governance Committee; Working Group Coordination Committee; Leadership Advisory Board; Regional Representatives. **Activities** Publishing activities; standards/guidelines. **Members** Corporate members (over 100) in 53 countries. Membership countries not specified. **NGO Relations** Supports (1): *Electric Mine Conference.* [2022/AA2462/**C**]

♦ Global Mining Standards and Guidelines Group / see Global Mining Guidelines Group (#10475)
♦ Global Ministries of The United Methodist Church (internationally oriented national body)

♦ Global mobile Suppliers Association (GSA) 10476

Secretariat PO Box 6092, Sheffield, S6 9HF, UK. T. +447976037327. E-mail: info@gsacom.com.
URL: https://gsacom.com/

History 2 Oct 1998. Founding during General Assembly, when Articles entered into force. Articles revised: 25 Sep 2002; June 2017. Registration: Swiss Civil Code, Switzerland. **Aims** Be the industry voice of the global mobile ecosystem by representing companies engaged in the supply of infrastructure, semiconductors, test equipment, devices, applications and mobile support services. **Structure** General Assembly; Executive Board; Operations Team; Working and Advisory Groups; Secretariat. **Languages** English. **Finance** Sources: members' dues; revenue from activities/projects; sponsorship; subscriptions. **Activities** Events/meetings; knowledge management/information dissemination; research/documentation. **Publications** Reports. **Information Services** *Industry Database*; *On-line Engagement Platform.*
Members Companies; Associates. Members in 18 countries and territories:
Brazil, Canada, China, Finland, France, Germany, Hong Kong, India, Italy, Malaysia, Russia, Spain, Sweden, Taiwan, UK, United Arab Emirates, USA, Vietnam.
IGO Relations Affiliated with (4): *Asia-Pacific Telecommunity (APT, #02064)*; CAICT; *Comisión Interamericana de Telecomunicaciones (CITEL, #04138)*; *Regional Commonwealth in the Field of Communications (RCC, #18767).* [2023.02.14/XJ8306/**C**]

♦ Global Mobility Alliance (unconfirmed)
♦ Global Mountain Action (internationally oriented national body)

♦ Global Mountain Biodiversity Assessment (GMBA) 10477

Exec Officer Inst of Plant Sciences, Univ of Bern, Altenbergrain 21, 3013 Bern, Switzerland. T. +41316314937. Fax +41316314942. E-mail: gmba@ips.unibe.ch.
URL: http://www.gmba.unibe.ch/

History Inaugurated as a cross-cutting network of *DIVERSITAS – International Programme of Biodiversity Science (inactive)* in fulfillment of *Global Action Plan for Environment and Development in the 21st Century (Agenda 21, inactive)*; initiated by the Swiss Academy of Sciences. Activities officially taken up by convening the First International Conference on Mountain Biodiversity, Rigi Kaltbad (Switzerland), Sep 2000. Currently a project of *Future Earth (#10048).* **Aims** Explore and explain the great biological richness of the mountains of the world and their responses to global change; provide input to policy makers and stakeholders for the *conservation* and *sustainable* use of biodiversity in mountain regions; synthesize hidden and fragmented results of research on mountain biodiversity; shape a global corporate identity for a scattered research community; increase visibility of mountain biodiversity issues; advocate studies on the human influence on natural and cultural landscapes in the mountains; encourage sustainable development of rural upland areas. **Structure** Scientific Steering Committee; International Project Office. **Staff** 2.00 FTE, paid. **Finance** Funded by Swiss National Science Foundation. **Activities** Events/meetings; research/documentation. **Events** *Conference on Mountains of Our Future Earth* Perth (Scotland) 2015. **Publications** *Data Mining for Global Trends in Mountain Biodiversity* (2010); *Mountain Biodiversity and Global Change* (2010); *Land Use Change and Mountain Biodiversity* (2006); *Global Mountain Biodiversity Assessment* (2005) by E M Spehn and Ch Körner; *Mountain Biodiversity: a global assessment* (2002) by Ch Körner; *Mountain Biodiversity Matters* (2001) by Ch Körner et al.
Members International organization (1):
International Centre for Integrated Mountain Development (ICIMOD, #12500).
NGO Relations Member of: *International Centre for Earth Simulation (ICES Foundation)*; *Mountain Partnership (MP, #16862).* [2018/XJ0700/y/**E**]

♦ Global Movement for the Culture of Peace (unconfirmed)
♦ Global Movement for a Culture of Peace and Non-Violence (see: #20322)

♦ Global Movement for Digital Freedom (Access) 10478

Exec Dir PO Box 20429, Greeley Square Station, 4 East 27th St, New York NY 10001-9998, USA. T. +18884140100. E-mail: info@accessnow.org.
URL: http://www.accessnow.org/

History following the Iranian elections of 2009. **Aims** Provide critical real-time technical support to human *rights* activists and pro-democracy dissidents in closed and semi-closed countries around the world. **Structure** Board of Directors; International Advisory Board; Technical Advisory Board. **Activities** Campaigns. [2016/XJ2204/F]

♦ Global Movement for Equality and Justice in the Muslim Family / see Musawah (#16905)
♦ Global Musa Genomics Consortium (inactive)
♦ Global Natural Health Alliance (internationally oriented national body)

♦ Global Nature Fund (GNF) 10479

Pres Fritz-Reichle-Ring 4, 78315 Radolfzell, Germany. T. +49773299950. Fax +497732999588. E-mail: info@globalnature.org.
URL: http://www.globalnature.org/

History 1998. Former names and other names: *International Foundation for Environment and Nature* – alias; *Internationale Stiftung für Umwelt und Natur* – alias. Registration: Germany; EU Transparency Register, No/ID: 350623540375-32, Start date: 30 Nov 2020. **Aims** Promote preservation and protection of the natural basis of life worldwide; support sustainable development in developing countries; promote international collaboration among organizations that carry out projects benefiting water bodies, wildlife and people. **Structure** Board of Directors; Founders Committee; Advisory Board. **Languages** English, German, Spanish. **Staff** 12.50 FTE, paid. **Finance** Sources: donations. Private funds; state and EU programmes; cooperation with business sector. Annual budget: 2,500,000 EUR. **Activities** Projects/programmes; events/meetings. **Events** *International Living Lakes Conference* Valencia (Spain) 2019, *International Living Lakes Conference* Nanchang (China) 2014, *Workshop* Brussels (Belgium) 2011, *International Living Lakes Conference* Johannesburg (South Africa) 2002. **Publications** *GNF Newsletter* (4 a year) in English, German. Annual Report in English, German. Thematic publications.

Members Full in 54 countries:
Argentina, Australia, Austria, Benin, Bolivia, Botswana, Brazil, Burundi, Cambodia, Cameroon, Canada, China, Colombia, Congo DR, Denmark, Estonia, Georgia, Germany, Greece, Guatemala, Hungary, India, Indonesia, Israel, Italy, Japan, Jordan, Kazakhstan, Kenya, Kyrgyzstan, Lithuania, Malawi, Mexico, Mongolia, Mozambique, Pakistan, Palestine, Paraguay, Peru, Philippines, Poland, Russia, Rwanda, South Africa, Spain, Sri Lanka, Switzerland, Tanzania UR, Türkiye, Uganda, UK, Uruguay, USA, Zambia.

IGO Relations Contacts with: *Secretariat of the Convention of Wetlands (#19200); UNEP (#20299).* **NGO Relations** Member of (5): *European Network for Sustainable Tourism Development (ECOTRANS, #08018); Freshwater Action Network (FAN, inactive); International Union for Conservation of Nature and Natural Resources (IUCN, #15766); Natural Capital Coalition (NCC, #16952); World Heritage Watch (WHW).* Also member of national organizations. [2018.09.12/XF6977/f/F]

♦ **Global NCAP** Global New Car Assessment Programme (#10506)
♦ GLOBALNET – Global Network of Women in Politics (internationally oriented national body)

♦ Global Net Neutrality Coalition 10480

Address not obtained.
URL: http://www.thisisnetneutrality.org/

History 25 Nov 2014. **Aims** Promote net neutrality, such that the *Internet* is be maintained as an open platform, on which network providers treat all content, applications and services equally, without discrimination.
Members Groups (over 35) in 19 countries (not specified), including 9 organizations listed in this Yearbook:
Access Now (#00052); ARTICLE 19 (#01121); Digital Defenders Partnership (DDP); Electronic Frontier Foundation (EFF); European Digital Rights (EDRi, #06924); Greenpeace International (#10727); Index on Censorship (Index); International PEN (#14552); Witness. [2014/XJ8985/y/C]

♦ Global Network for Advanced Management (unconfirmed)
♦ Global Network for Africa's Prosperity (internationally oriented national body)
♦ Global Network Against Weapons and Nuclear Power in Space (internationally oriented national body)

♦ Global Network for B2B Integration in High Tech Industries (EDIFICE) 10481

Secretariat Tiensestraat 12, 3320 Hoegaarden, Belgium. T. +3216437415.
URL: http://www.edifice.org/

History 1986, as *Electronic Data Interchange Forum for Companies with Interests in Computing and Electronics.* Subsequently changed title to: *Standardized Electronic Commerce Forum for Companies with Interests in Computing, Electronics and Telecommunication.* Registered in accordance with Belgian law, number 0506893789. EU Transparency Register: 556685530186-15. **Aims** Drive and enable global standardized B2B adoption through best practice, information sharing and influencing *standards* development. **Structure** Plenary Group; Task Groups; Permanent Secretariat. **Languages** English. **Finance** Members' dues. **Activities** Events/meetings. **Events** *Conference on B2B Challenges and Level of B2B Integration across Asia-Pacific* Singapore (Singapore) 2013. **Publications** Company Identification Numbers (CIN). Guidelines. **Members** Companies and organizations worldwide. Membership countries not specified. **IGO Relations** In liaison with technical committees of: *United Nations Centre for Trade Facilitation and Electronic Business (UN/ CEFACT, #20527).* **NGO Relations** In liaison with technical committees of: *Comité européen de normalisation (CEN, #04162); European Committee for Electrotechnical Standardization (CENELEC, #06647); International Electrotechnical Commission (IEC, #13255); International Organization for Standardization (ISO, #14473); Odette International (#17689).* [2018/XE1735/t/E]

♦ Global Network for Banking Innovation in Microfinance (GNBI) 10482

Red Global para la Innovación Bancaria en Microfinanzas

Contact c/o WWB, 122 East 42nd St, 42nd Floor, New York NY 10168, USA. T. +12127688513. Fax +1212768-8519.
URL: http://www.swwb.org/

History 7 Apr 2001, by *Women's World Banking (WWB, #21037).*
Members Financial institutions (21) in 16 countries:
Bangladesh, Bolivia, Chile, Dominican Rep, Germany, India, Indonesia, Kenya, Mexico, Netherlands, Paraguay, Peru, Sri Lanka, Switzerland, Thailand, USA. [2008.06.01/XF6409/F]

♦ Global Network of Basins Working on Climate Change Adaptation . . 10483

Address not obtained.

History 2013. Founded by *United Nations Economic Commission for Europe (UNECE, #20555),* in cooperation with *International Network of Basin Organizations (INBO, #14235),* following the 6th World Water Forum, Marseille (France). Former names and other names: *Global Network of River Basins on Climate Change Adaptation* – former. **Aims** Promote cooperation on adaptation in transboundary basins; compare different methodologies and approaches for adapting to climate change; promote a shared vision between participating basins. **Events** *Meeting* Geneva (Switzerland) 2019, *Meeting* Geneva (Switzerland) 2014, *Meeting* Geneva (Switzerland) 2013. **Members** Transboundary basins (16). [2020/XM7766/F]

♦ Global Network for Biosystematics of Arthropods, Nematodes and Microorganisms / see BioNET INTERNATIONAL – Global Network for Taxonomy (#03253)

♦ Global Network for Cacao Genetic Resources (CacaoNet) 10484

Coordinator c/o Bioversity International, Via dei Tre Denari 472/a, 00054 Maccarese RM, Italy.
URL: http://www.cacaonet.org/

History 2005. Officially launched Oct 2006, San José (Costa Rica). Former names and other names: *Global Network on Cacao Genetic Resources Conservation and Use* – alias. **Aims** Optimize the conservation and use of cacao genetic resources, as the foundation of a sustainable cocoa economy. **Structure** Secretariat hosted by: *Bioversity International (#03262).* **Finance** Funded by: US Department of Agriculture; Mars; *World Cocoa Foundation (WCF);* Cocoa Research Association. **IGO Relations** Partners include: *Alliance of Cocoa Producing Countries (COPAL, no recent information); Bioversity International (#03262); CABI (#03393); Centre de coopération internationale en recherche agronomique pour le développement (CIRAD, #03733); Common Fund for Commodities (CFC, #04293); Global Crop Diversity Trust (Crop Trust, #10313); International Cocoa Organization (ICCO, #12627); International Treaty on Plant Genetic Resources for Food and Agriculture (2001); Tropical Agriculture Research and Higher Education Center (#20246).* **NGO Relations** Partners include: *International Institute of Tropical Agriculture (IITA, #13933); World Agroforestry Centre (ICRAF, #21072); World Cocoa Foundation (WCF).* [2021/XM4842/F]

♦ Global Network on Cacao Genetic Resources Conservation and Use / see Global Network for Cacao Genetic Resources (#10484)

♦ Global Network of Civil Society Organizations for Disaster Reduction (GNDR) 10485

Red Global de Organizaciones de la Sociedad Civil para la Reducción de Desastres – Réseau mondial des Organisations de la Société civile pour la réduction des catastrophes

Team Administrator 8 Waldegrave Road, Teddington, London, TW11 8HT, UK. E-mail: info@gndr.org.
URL: http://www.gndr.org/

History Jun 2007, Geneva (Switzerland). Launched following World Conference, Jan 2005, Kobe (Japan), and supported by *United Nations Office for Disaster Risk Reduction (UNDRR, #20595).* Former names and other names: *Global Network for Disaster Reduction* – alias. Registration: Charity Commission, No/ID: 1141471, England and Wales; Companies House, No/ID: 07374358, Start date: 13 Sep 2010, England; EU Transparency Register, No/ID: 122058834948-39, Start date: 5 Jun 2019. **Aims** Constitute a voluntary network of civil society organizations, associations and individuals who are committed to working together, and engaging with partners and other stakeholders, to increase community resilience and reduce disaster risk around the world. **Structure** Global Board; Trustees; Secretariat, located in London (UK). **Languages** English, French, Spanish. **Staff** 18.00 FTE, paid. **Finance** Strategic partners; donor governments. **Activities** Advocacy/lobbying/activism; awareness raising; monitoring/evaluation; capacity building; networking/ liaisingknowledge management/information dissemination; politics/policy/regulatory. **Events** *Digital Global Summit* London (UK) 2020, *Meeting on Local Risk Profiling and Monitoring to Strengthen Resilience* Sendai (Japan) 2015, *Asian grassroots women's academy on resilience* Cebu City (Philippines) 2008. **Publications** *DRR Good Practice and Lessons Learnt* (2007, 2008). **Members** Individuals (1,600) from 850 civil society organizations in 140 countries. Membership countries not specified. **Consultative Status** Consultative status granted from: *ECOSOC (#05331)* (Special). **NGO Relations** Member of: *Transparency, Accountability and Participation Network (TAP Network, #20222).* [2022/XM3760/F]

♦ Global Network on Dental Education (unconfirmed)

♦ Global Network of Director Institutes (GNDI) 10486

Secretariat address not obtained. T. +27846064444.
URL: http://www.gndi.org/

Aims Develop and promote leading practices and programs that enhance the capability of directors to drive sustainable performance for the benefit of shareholders, the economy and society.
Members Full in 19 countries:
Argentina, Australia, Brazil, Canada, Germany, Hong Kong, Israel, Malaysia, Mauritius, New Zealand, Pakistan, Philippines, Russia, Singapore, South Africa, Switzerland, Thailand, UK, USA.
Regional entities (2):
European Confederation of Directors' Associations (ecoDa, #06702); GCC Board Directors Institute (GCC BDI, #10083). [2019/XM6578/F]

♦ Global Network for Disaster Reduction / see Global Network of Civil Society Organizations for Disaster Reduction (#10485)

♦ Global Network of Domestic Election Monitors (GNDEM) 10487

Réseau mondial d'observateurs nationaux des élections – Red Global de Monitores Electorales Nacionales

Contact address not obtained. E-mail: gndem09@gmail.com.
URL: http://www.gndem.org/

History 1986. **Aims** Safeguard electoral integrity; help create governmental and political accountability; contribute to mitigating potentials for politically motivated violence; promote the right of citizens to participate in public affairs.
Members Organizations (over 175) in 71 countries and territories:
Afghanistan, Albania, Angola, Argentina, Armenia, Azerbaijan, Bahrain, Bangladesh, Bolivia, Bosnia-Herzegovina, Burkina Faso, Burundi, Cambodia, Cameroon, Chad, Colombia, Congo DR, Côte d'Ivoire, Croatia, Ecuador, Egypt, Georgia, Ghana, Guatemala, Guinea, Haiti, Indonesia, Jordan, Kazakhstan, Kenya, Kyrgyzstan, Lebanon, Liberia, Madagascar, Malawi, Malaysia, Maldives, Mali, Mauritania, Moldova, Montenegro, Morocco, Mozambique, Nepal, Niger, Nigeria, North Macedonia, Pakistan, Palestine, Paraguay, Peru, Philippines, Romania, Russia, Senegal, Serbia, Sierra Leone, Slovakia, South Africa, South Sudan, Sudan, Taiwan, Thailand, Timor-Leste, Togo, Tunisia, Uganda, Ukraine, Venezuela, Yemen, Zambia.
Included in the above, 7 organizations listed in this Yearbook:
Centre for Africa Democratic Affairs (CADA); Instituto Centroamericano de Estudios Politicos (INCEP); International Society for Fair Elections and Democracy (ISFED); Latin American Faculty of Social Sciences (#16316); Rencontre africaine pour la défense des droits de l'homme (RADDHO); Southern African Catholic Bishops' Conference (SACBC, #19838); Southern African Centre for the Constructive Resolution of Disputes (SACCORD).
Regional Networks (9):
Acuerdo de Lima; Arab Network for Democratic Elections (ANDE); Asian Network for Free Elections (ANFREL, #01550); East and Horn of Africa Election Observers Network; Election Network Society in the Arab Region (ENAR); European Network of Election Monitoring Organizations (ENEMO, #07900); European Platform for Democratic Elections (EPDE, #08224); Southern Africa Development Community Election Support Network (SADC-ESN, #19827); West Africa Election Observers Network (WAEON, #20865). [2018/XJ7565/y/F]

♦ Global Network for Economics of Learning, Innovation and Competence Building Systems (GLOBELICS) 10488

Secretariat Centro Internacional de Política Económica, UNA Campus B Nuñez, Lagunilla, Heredia, Heredia, Heredia, 02393-30000, Costa Rica. T. +50625624300. E-mail: secretariat@globelics.org.
URL: http://globelics.org/

History 2001. Founded by economists and experts on innovation systems inspired by the work by Christopher Freeman and Richard Nelson. **Aims** Strengthen research capabilities worldwide in the field of innovation and competence building systems and, especially, promote capability building in this field in the less developed countries. **Structure** Scientific Board. Regional Chapters: *African Network for Economics of Learning, Innovation and Competence Building Systems (AFRICALICS, #00385); Asian Network for Learning, Innovation and Competence Building Systems (ASIALICS, #01551); European Network for the Economics of Learning, Innovation, and Competence Building Systems (EUROLICS, #07897); Latin American Network for Economics of Learning, Innovation and Competence Building Systems (LALICS, #16352); Mediterranean Network for the Knowledge Economy and Innovation (MEDAlics).* **Languages** English. **Finance** Supported by: *Swedish International Development Cooperation Agency (Sida).* **Activities** Capacity building; events/meetings; research/documentation; training/education. C. **Events** *GLOBELICS International Conference* Heredia (Costa Rica) 2021, *GLOBELICS International Conference* Accra (Ghana) 2018, *GLOBELICS International Conference* Athens (Greece) 2017, *GLOBELICS International Conference* Bandung (Indonesia) 2016, *GLOBELICS International Conference* Havana (Cuba) 2015. **Publications** *Globelics Thematic Reviews. Globelics Working Paper Series.* Reports. **Members** Scholars (over 1500) working on learning, innovation and competence building systems. Membership countries not specified. [2021/XM2524/F]

♦ Global Network of Export-Import Banks and Development Finance Institutions (G-NEXID) 10489

Contact Rue de Chantepoulet 10, 1201 Geneva, Switzerland. E-mail: contact@gnexid.com.
URL: https://gnexid.com/

History 13 Mar 2006. Registration: Swiss Civil Code, No/ID: 080.881.046, Switzerland, Geneva. **Aims** Facilitate cooperation among export-import banks and development finance institutions in support of South-South trade, investment and project finance. **Structure** General Assembly; Steering Committee; Presidency; Treasury; Secretariat. **Languages** English. **Activities** Capacity building; events/meetings; knowledge management/information dissemination; networking/liaising; research/documentation. **Events** *Green Sukuk and Resource Mobilisation for Sustainable Infrastructure in Sub-Saharan Africa* 2021, *Improving Access to Trade Finance for SMEs through Transactional Connectivity* 2021, *The COVID-19 Crisis and its Aftermath* 2021, *Impact Investment in the COVID-19 Era and its Aftermath* 2020, *The African Continental Free Trade Area and South-South Trade* 2020. **Publications** *G-NEXID: 10 Years of Promoting South-South Trade, Investment and Cooperation* (2016). Yearbook.

Members National institutions in 8 countries:
China, Ghana, India, Indonesia, Nigeria, Saudi Arabia, Thailand, Zambia.
Regional institutions (5):
African Export-Import Bank (Afreximbank, #00305); Banque de développement des Etats de l'Afrique centrale (BDEAC, #03168); ECOWAS Bank for Investment and Development (EBID, #05334); Islamic Corporation for the Insurance of Investment and Export Credit (ICIEC, #16041); Trade and Development Bank (TDB, #20181). [2021.06.09/XM6282/**F**]

♦ Global Network for Good Governance (GNGG) 10490

Global SG PO Box 607, Limbé, Cameroon. T. +23777536682. Fax +23733333175. E-mail: contact@gngg.us.
Street address Petit Papa Bldg, 2nd floor, off Saker Road, New Town, Limbé, Cameroon.
URL: http://www.gngg.us/

History Nov 1999, Rome (Italy). Launched 1 Jun 2002. Former names and other names: *Global Network for Good Governance and Development* – alias. Registration: Cameroon. **Aims** Promote and sustain the practice of good governance principles (GGP) as a prelude to sustainable development. **Structure** General Assembly; International Advisory Board; Management Committee. **Languages** English, French. **Staff** 3.00 FTE, paid; 7.00 FTE, voluntary. **Finance** Donors, including: *Catholic Relief Services (CRS, #03608); Deutsche Gesellschaft für Internationale Zusammenarbeit (GIZ); Organisation internationale de la Francophonie (OIF, #17809); Partnership for Transparency Fund (PTF, #18245); UNDP (#20292).* Annual budget: 35,000 USD. **Activities** Training/education; projects/programmes; awareness raising. **Publications** *GNGG News Glance* (12 a year); *Success Story Magazine; The Bell; The Good Governance Observer* – newsletter; *The Parrot.*
Members Individuals and institutions in 23 countries:
Bosnia-Herzegovina, Bulgaria, Cameroon, Ecuador, Eswatini, Ghana, Italy, Kenya, Malawi, Malta, Mauritius, Mozambique, Netherlands, Nigeria, Oman, Pakistan, Panama, Romania, South Africa, Tanzania UR, Togo, USA, Zimbabwe.
Consultative Status Consultative status granted from: *African Commission on Human and Peoples' Rights (ACHPR, #00255)* (Observer). **IGO Relations** *International Development Law Organization (IDLO, #13161).* Consultative status with: *African Union (AU, #00488); Organisation internationale de la Francophonie (OIF, #17809).* **NGO Relations** Member of: *African Coalition for Corporate Accountability (ACCA, #00252); African Federation for the Gifted and Talented (AFGT, #00308); Tax Justice Network (TJN, #20100); UNCAC Coalition (#20283).* Allied partner of: *Financial Transparency Coalition (FTC, #09772).* [2019.02.11/XM2543/**F**]

- ♦ Global Network for Good Governance and Development / see Global Network for Good Governance (#10490)
- ♦ Global Network Initiative (internationally oriented national body)
- ♦ Global Network of Internet and Society Research Centers / see Network of Internet and Society Research Centers (#17045)

♦ Global Network of Isotopes in Precipitation (GNIP) 10491

Contact Isotope Hydrology Section – IAEA, Wagramerstrasse 5, PO Box 100, 1400 Vienna, Austria. T. +431260021735 – +43126000. Fax +43126007. E-mail: gnip@iaea.org.
URL: https://www.iaea.org/services/networks/gnip

History Founded 1961, as a joint programme of *International Atomic Energy Agency (IAEA, #12294)* and *World Meteorological Organization (WMO, #21649).* Became operational within Isotope Hydrology Section of IAEA in Dec 1998, when a Memorandum of Understanding was signed between IAEA and WMO. Combined with the *'Isotope Hydrology Information System (ISOHIS)'* since early 2001. Integrated into the WISER ('Water Isotope System for Data Analysis, Visualization and Electronic Retrieval') web platform, 2004. **Aims** Collect basic meteorological data and isotope contents of precipitation (oxygen-18, deuterium and tritium) on a global scale to obtain basic data on the temporal and spatial variations of environmental isotopes in precipitation; provide basic isotope data for the use of environmental isotopes in hydrological investigations within the scope of water resources inventory, planning and development; provide input data to verify and further improve atmospheric circulation models as well as studies on climate change or ecology. **Structure** Scientific Steering Committee (meets as needed, usually in Vienna, (Austria)). **Languages** English. **Staff** 1.00 FTE, paid. **Finance** Members' dues. **Activities** Research/documentation; monitoring/evaluation. **Events** *International conference on isotopes in environmental studies* Monte Carlo (Monaco) 2004, *International symposium on quality assurance for analytical methods in isotope hydrology* Vienna (Austria) 2004, *International symposium* Vienna (Austria) 2003. **Information Services** *Water Isotope System for Data Analysis, Visualization and Electronic Retrieval (WISER).*
Members Participating National Networks, research institutes and laboratories in 87 countries:
Argentina, Australia, Austria, Bahrain, Bangladesh, Benin, Bolivia, Brazil, Burkina Faso, Cameroon, Canada, Central African Rep, Chad, Chile, China, Colombia, Congo DR, Costa Rica, Croatia, Cuba, Czechia, Denmark, Ecuador, Ethiopia, Finland, France, Gabon, Georgia, Germany, Ghana, Greece, Greenland, Honduras, Hungary, Iceland, India, Iraq, Ireland, Italy, Japan, Kazakhstan, Korea Rep, Latvia, Luxembourg, Madagascar, Malaysia, Mali, Mauritius, Mexico, Moldova, Monaco, Morocco, Mozambique, Netherlands, New Zealand, Nicaragua, Niger, Norway, Pakistan, Panama, Peru, Philippines, Poland, Portugal, Romania, Russia, Saudi Arabia, Senegal, Slovakia, Slovenia, South Africa, Spain, Sri Lanka, Sweden, Switzerland, Tanzania UR, Thailand, Togo, Tunisia, Türkiye, Uganda, UK, Ukraine, Uruguay, USA, Vietnam, Zambia.
IGO Relations *Global Terrestrial Network – Hydrology (GTN-H, #10624).* [2017.03.09/XF2549/**F**]

♦ Global Network of Japanese Language Education (GN) 10492

Contact address not obtained.

History Former names and other names: *Japanese Language Education Global Network* – alias. **Aims** Enable information exchange about Japanese language education around the world, so as to promote international cooperation, practical activities for learning and teaching Japanese and international development of academic research. **Events** *International Conference on Japanese Language Education* Venice (Italy) 2018, *ICJLE : International Conference of Japanese Language Education* Bali (Indonesia) 2016.
Members National associations in 9 countries and territories:
Australia, Canada, China, Hong Kong, Indonesia, Korea Rep, New Zealand, Taiwan, USA.
Regional association:
Association of Japanese Language Teachers in Europe (AJE, #02769). [2017/XM5487/**F**]

♦ Global Network on Local Governance (GNLG) 10493

Contact ISS, 8 Nelson Mandela Road, Delhi 110 070, DELHI 110 070, India. T. +911126121902 – +911126121909.
URL: http://www.gnlg.org/

History by *World Movement for Democracy (#21661).* **Aims** Develop an understanding of local governance and disseminate information; provide an interface for institutions working on issues of local governance to network and share information; provide an informal forum that seeks to harness ideas and solicit consensus of priority issues on local governance; promote a culture of good governance at the local level. **Publications** *GNLG Newsletter.*
Members Local governments in 6 countries:
Australia, China, Japan, Mexico, South Africa, UK. [2007/XM2433/**F**]

- ♦ Global Network of Mission Structures (unconfirmed)
- ♦ Global Network of Modding Extremists (unconfirmed)

♦ Global Network of People Living with HIV/AIDS (GNP+) 10494

Red Mundial de Personas con VIH y SIDA

Co-Exec Dir Eerste Helmersstraat 17 B3, 1054 CX Amsterdam, Netherlands. T. +31204234114. Fax +31204234224. E-mail: infognp@gnpplus.net.
URL: https://gnpplus.net/

History 1986. Founded as *International Steering Committee for People with HIV/AIDS* of the *International Conferences of People with HIV/AIDS.* Registration: No/ID: KVK 41214768, Netherlands, Amsterdam. **Aims** Improve the quality of life of people living with HIV. **Structure** Board. Regional networks: *Asia-Pacific Network of People Living with HIV/AIDS (APN+, #01973); Caribbean Regional Network of People Living with HIV/AIDS (CRN+, #03549); European Network of People Living with HIV/AIDS (ENP+, inactive); Latin American Network of People Living with HIV/AIDS (RED LA+, #16355); Network of African People Living with HIV and AIDS (NAP+, #16986);* GNP North America (GNPNA). **Languages** English. **Staff** 10.00 FTE, paid. **Activities** Advocacy/lobbying/activism; knowledge management/information dissemination; networking/liaising. **Events** *International AIDS conference* Melbourne, VIC (Australia) 2014, *International AIDS conference* Washington, DC (USA) 2012, *International AIDS conference* Vienna (Austria) 2010, *International AIDS conference* Mexico City (Mexico) 2008, *International AIDS Conference* Toronto, ON (Canada) 2006. **Publications** *CCM Handbook; Positive Development.* Manuals; guidelines; policy framework; good practice guide.
Members Active members in 94 countries and territories:
Argentina, Australia, Austria, Bahamas, Barbados, Belgium, Bermuda, Botswana, Brazil, Bulgaria, Burkina Faso, Burundi, Cambodia, Cameroon, Canada, Chile, China, Colombia, Comoros, Congo DR, Costa Rica, Côte d'Ivoire, Dominican Rep, El Salvador, Estonia, Eswatini, Fiji, Finland, France, Gambia, Germany, Ghana, Greece, Hong Kong, Hungary, India, Indonesia, Ireland, Israel, Italy, Jamaica, Japan, Kenya, Latvia, Lesotho, Liechtenstein, Luxembourg, Malawi, Malaysia, Mexico, Morocco, Mozambique, Namibia, Netherlands, New Zealand, Nicaragua, Niger, Nigeria, Norway, Pakistan, Panama, Papua New Guinea, Paraguay, Peru, Philippines, Poland, Portugal, Romania, Russia, Rwanda, Samoa, San Marino, Senegal, Sierra Leone, Singapore, South Africa, Spain, Sri Lanka, Suriname, Sweden, Switzerland, Taiwan, Thailand, Tonga, Trinidad-Tobago, Türkiye, Uganda, UK, Uruguay, USA, Venezuela, Vietnam, Zambia, Zimbabwe.
Consultative Status Consultative status granted from: *ECOSOC (#05331)* (Special); *WHO (#20950)* (Official Relations). **IGO Relations** Policy adviser to: *WHO (#20950)* and other UN organizations. **NGO Relations** Member of: *International Treatment Preparedness Coalition (ITPC, #15729).* Participates in: *HIV Young Leaders Fund (HYLF, no recent information).* Works on greater involvement of people living with HIV/AIDS together with: *Global Health Council (GHC, #10402); ICASO (#11040); International Community of Women Living with HIV/AIDS (ICW, #12826); International Network of People who Use Drugs (INPUD, #14301).* [2022/XF2817/**F**]

♦ Global Network for Perinatal and Reproductive Health (GNPRH) ... 10495

Coordinator OHSU Ctr for Women's Health, Oregon Health and Science Univ, Dept Obstetrics and Gynecology, 3181 SW Sam Jackson Park Rd, L-458, Portland OR 97239, USA. T. +15034942101. Fax +15034945296.
Coordinator Khon Kaen Univ, Dept Obstetrics and Gynecology, Khon Kaen, 40002, Thailand. T. +6643202470. Fax +6643202476.
URL: http://www.ohsu.edu/gnprh/index.htm

Aims Conduct clinical research in the area of reproductive health, identify and introduce the most cost-effective interventions and the best evidence-based clinical practices; develop capacity building and transference of skills; advance global knowledge on those diseased which affect the reproductive health of *women* and *children.* **Structure** Technical Advisory Committee. **Finance** Sources include: *The Rockefeller Foundation (#18966); INCLEN Trust International (#11142); United States Agency for International Development (USAID).* **NGO Relations** Member of: *PMNCH (#18410).* [2009/XM3792/**F**]

- ♦ Global Network for Public Interest Law (internationally oriented national body)

♦ Global Network of Religions for Children (GNRC) 10496

SG c/o Arigatou Intl – Nairobi, Crawford Business Park, State House Road, PO Box 43536, Nairobi, 00100, Kenya. T. +254202573920 – +254202573921. E-mail: info@gnrc.net.
URL: http://www.gnrc.net/

History May 2000. Inaugurated by *Arigatou International.* **Aims** Create a better environment for children through engaging in prayer, mutual enlightenment, dialogue and cooperation among people of different faiths, including children, on the local, national, regional and global levels. **Structure** Coordinators (7): Central Asia and Caucasus; Africa; South Asia; Europe; Latin America and Caribbean; Arab States; Israel. **Languages** Arabic, English, French, Spanish. **Activities** Events/meetings. **Events** *Global Forum* Dar es Salaam (Tanzania UR) 2012, *Global Forum* Hiroshima (Japan) 2008, *Global Forum* Geneva (Switzerland) 2004, *Global Forum* Tokyo (Japan) 2000.
Members in 82 countries. Membership countries not specified. Included in the above, one organization listed in this Yearbook:
Included in the above, one organization listed in this Yearbook:
Pan European Federation of TCM Societies (PEFOTS, no recent information). [2018/XM3686/**C**]

♦ Global Network for Resource Efficient and Cleaner Production (RECPnet) 10497

Secretariat Industrial Resource Efficiency Unit, Environment Branch, UNIDO, PO Box 300, 2400 Vienna, Austria. E-mail: recpnet@unido.org.
URL: http://www.recpnet.org/

History Formalized by its Charter and operational Nov 2010, with 41 founding members then adopting the *Nairobi RECPnet Declaration,* 2011. **Aims** Contribute to the effective and efficient development, application, adaptation, scaling up and mainstreaming of RECP concepts, methods, policies, practices and technologies in developing and transition economies. **Structure** Members' Assembly; Regional Chapters; Executive Committee; Secretariat. **Finance** Through donors, including Governments of Switzerland, Austria, Norway and Slovenia, and *European Commission (EC, #06633).* **Activities** Awareness raising; capacity building; knowledge management/information dissemination; advocacy/lobbying/activism; events/meetings. **Events** *Global Conference* Helsinki (Finland) 2017.
Members Organizations in 62 countries:
Albania, Argentina, Armenia, Australia, Austria, Bolivia, Brazil, Bulgaria, Cambodia, Cape Verde, China, Colombia, Costa Rica, Croatia, Cuba, Czechia, Dominican Rep, Egypt, El Salvador, Finland, Georgia, Germany, Ghana, Guatemala, Honduras, India, Indonesia, Israel, Jordan, Kenya, Korea Rep, Laos, Lebanon, Lithuania, Mexico, Moldova, Montenegro, Morocco, Mozambique, Namibia, Nicaragua, North Macedonia, Pakistan, Paraguay, Peru, Philippines, Romania, Russia, Rwanda, Senegal, Serbia, South Africa, Sri Lanka, Switzerland, Tanzania UR, Tunisia, Türkiye, Uganda, Ukraine, Uzbekistan, Vietnam, Zimbabwe.
Included in the above, 5 organizations listed in this Yearbook:
African Roundtable for Sustainable Consumption and Production (ARSCP, #00444); Asia Pacific Roundtable on Sustainable Consumption and Production (APRSCP, #02017); Asia Society for Social Improvement and Sustainable Transformation (ASSIST, #02097); Tunis International Centre for Environmental Technologies (CITET); Weitz Center for Development Studies. [2019/XM5067/y/**F**]

- ♦ Global Network for the Right to Food and Nutrition / see Right to Food and Nutrition Watch Consortium (#18943)
- ♦ Global Network of River Basins on Climate Change Adaptation / see Global Network of Basins Working on Climate Change Adaptation (#10483)

♦ Global Network of Sex Work Projects (NSWP) 10498

Secretariat The Matrix, 62 Newhaven Road, Edinburgh, EH6 5QB, UK. T. +441315532555. E-mail: secretariat@nswp.org.
URL: http://www.nswp.org/

History 1992, Amsterdam (Netherlands), during the International AIDS Conference, as an informal alliance with the title *Network of Sex Work Projects (NSWP).* Secretariat set up 1992, South Africa. Secretariat collapsed, 2004, when NSWP became an informal alliance again. Registered as a UK not-for-profit private company, 2008. Previously also referred to as *International Network of Sex Work Projects.* **Aims** Conduct a mix of pro-active and re-active policy advocacy to support human rights and evidence based approaches to female, male and transgendered sex workers and strengthening sex worker communities. **Structure** Board of Directors. **Languages** Chinese, English, French, Russian, Spanish. **Staff** 6.00 FTE, paid. **Finance** Donations. **Activities** Advocacy/lobbying/activism. **Events** *International AIDS conference* Melbourne, VIC (Australia) 2014. **Members** Full in over 40 countries. Membership countries not specified. **Consultative Status** Consultative status granted from: *ECOSOC (#05331)* (Special). **NGO Relations** Participates in: *HIV Young Leaders Fund (HYLF, no recent information).* Cooperates with: *ICASO (#11040).* [2018/XN9674/**F**]

♦ Global Network for Simulation in Healthcare (GNSH) 10499

Sec address not obtained. E-mail: executive@gnsh.org.
URL: https://www.gnsh.org/

History Aug 2010. Former names and other names: *Global Simulation Network for Simulation in Healthcare* – former. Registration: Section 501(c)(3), USA, Tennessee; Companies House, No/ID: 09921432, Start date: 17 Dec 2015, End date: 2 Nov 2021, England and Wales. **Aims** Enhance patient safety and quality of healthcare by promoting the appropriate use of simulation through collaboration, advocacy and support. **Structure** Board of Directors. **Activities** Events/meetings. **Events** *Summit* 2022, *Summit* Lisbon (Portugal) 2022, *Summit* 2021, *Summit* 2020, *Summit* Vienna (Austria) 2019.
Members Founding members in 3 countries:
Australia, UK, USA.

International Nursing Association for Clinical Simulation and Learning (INACSL); Society in Europe for Simulation Applied to Medicine (SESAM, #19555).
Non-Commercial and Commercial members. Membership countries not specified. In addition to founding members, also includes:
Federación Latinoamericana de Simulación Clínica y Seguridad del Paciente (FLASIC, #09368); International Pediatric Simulation Society (IPSS, #14546). [2022/AA3162/y/**D**]

♦ Global Network for SMART Organization Design 10500

Contact address not obtained.
Contact address not obtained.
URL: https://www.smartorganizationdesign.com/
History Started as a joint initiative of the STS Roundtable (North America) and the Ulbo de Sitter (USI) Institute (Netherlands and Belgium). **Aims** Promote and support international growth of local/regional networks committed to advancing SmarT theories and practices; facilitate communication and shared learning among diverse and dispersed researchers and practitioners. **Structure** Coordination Group. **Activities** Events/meetings. **Events** *Meeting* Austin, TX (USA) 2022, *Meeting* Trondheim (Norway) 2021, *Meeting* Trondheim (Norway) 2020, *Meeting* Los Angeles, CA (USA) 2019, *Meeting* Netherlands 2018.
Members Full in 4 countries:
Belgium, Netherlands, Norway, USA. [2022/AA2801/**F**]

♦ Global Network for Social Threefolding (GlobeNet3) 10501

Réseau mondial pour la triarticulation sociale – Red Global para la Trimembración Social – Globalt Nettverk for Sosial Tregrening
Secretariat 3201 Corinthian Executive Regency, Ortigas Avenue, Ortigas Center, Pasig City, 1605 Manila, Philippines.
URL: http://www.globenet3.org/
History Also referred to as *GN3*. **Aims** Promote harmonization and mobilization of economy, policy and culture towards comprehensive *sustainable development*. **Structure** Geographic Nodes (17); Functional Nodes (3): Global Secretariat; Funding; Research.
Members Geographic Nodes (17) in 11 countries:
Denmark, France, Germany, Israel, Japan, Netherlands, Norway, Philippines, South Africa, Sweden, USA.
[2010.01.28/XJ3213/**F**]

♦ Global Network for Sustainable Housing (GNSH) 10502

Contact c/o UN-Habitat, PO Box 30030, Nairobi, 00100, Kenya. T. +254207623120.
URL: https://unhabitat.org/network/global-network-for-sustainable-housing
History 2011. Initially set up through *United Nations Human Settlements Programme (UN-Habitat, #20572).* Now a partnership of international organizations. **Aims** Promote projects that demonstrate the capacity to enhance sustainable urban development and economic growth, increase employment opportunities, improve quality of life and contribute to poverty alleviation. **IGO Relations** Partners include: *International Network for Bamboo and Rattan (INBAR, #14234).* **NGO Relations** Partners include: *International Centre for Earth Construction (#12485); Habitat for Humanity International (HFHI); International Federation of Red Cross and Red Crescent Societies (#13526); Network for an Economical and Ecological Habitat (EcoSouth Network, #17007).* [2015/XM4199/**E**]

♦ Global Network of Women Peacebuilders (GNWP) 10503

CEO 777 UN Plaza, Ste 11-E, New York NY 10017, USA. T. +16466633230. E-mail: gnwp@gnwp.org – communications.gnwp@gmail.com.
URL: http://www.gnwp.org/
History Set up as a programme partner of *International Civil Society Action Network (ICAN, #12588)*, as a coalition working on UN Security Council Resolutions 1325 and 1820 on women and peace and security including supporting resolutions 1888, 889 and 1960 at local, national, regional and international levels. Registration: 501(c)(3) charity, USA. **Aims** Bridge the gap between policy discussions and implementation and action on the ground on women, peace and security issues. **Structure** Board of Directors; International Advisory Council. **Activities** Advocacy/lobbying/activism; events/meetings. **Publications** Briefs; reports.
Members Organizations (over 100) in Africa, Asia and Pacific, Europe and Latin America. Membership countries not specified. Included in the above, 7 organizations listed in this Yearbook:
Arab Renaissance for Democracy and Development (ARDD); femLINKpacific; Global Partnership for the Prevention of Armed Conflict (GPPAC, #10538); PeaceWomen Across the Globe (#18283); Permanent Peace Movement (no recent information); Red de Seguridad y Defensa de América Latina (RESDAL, #18730).
NGO Relations Member of (2): *International Peace Bureau (IPB, #14535); NGO Working Group for Women, Peace and Security (NGOWG, #17129).* [2022/XJ4565/y/**F**]

♦ Global Network of Women in Politics (internationally oriented national body)
♦ Global Network for Women's and Children's health Research (internationally oriented national body)

♦ Global Network of Women's Shelters (GNWS) 10504

Main Office address not obtained. E-mail: info@gnws.org.
URL: http://gnws.org/
History 2009. **Aims** Unite the women's shelter movement globally to end violence against women and their children. **Structure** Board, including representatives of *African Network of Women Shelters (ANWS, #00398), Asian Network of Women's Shelters (ANWS, #01562), Women Against Violence Europe (WAVE, #20986)* and *Red Interamericana de Refugios (RIRE).* Committees (3): Communications and Awareness; Policy; Membership and Governance. Set up: GNWS Foundation, 2014. **Activities** Advocacy/lobbying/activism; events/meetings; networking/liaising. **Events** *World Conference on Women's Shelters* Kaohsiung (Taiwan) 2019, *World Conference on Women's Shelters* The Hague (Netherlands) 2015, *World Conference on Women's Shelters / World Conference of Women's Shelters* Washington, DC (USA) 2012, *World Conference on Women's Shelters* Edmonton, AB (Canada) 2008. **Information Services** *Lila.help* in Chinese, English, French, Hindi, Japanese, Russian, Spanish – Lila.help is the lead international directory of vetted direct support services for victims of gender-based violence.. [2022.11.22/XJ9804/**F**]

♦ Global Neuro 10505

Managing Dir Clavadelerstr 8, 7270 Davos GR, Switzerland. T. +41814142533. E-mail: info@globalneuro.org.
URL: http://www.globalneuro.org/
History Founded 2013, as an initiative of *AO Foundation (#00866).* Developed into an independent organization. **Aims** Educate clinicians to improve patient outcomes in neurosurgery. **Structure** Board. **Activities** Awareness raising; knowledge management/information dissemination; training/education. **Events** *Symposium* Shenzhen (China) 2018. **Publications** *Global Neuro Newsletter.* [2019/XM8000/**C**]

♦ Global New Car Assessment Programme (Global NCAP) 10506

Administrator 60 Trafalgar Square, London, WC2N 5DS, UK. T. +442076374121. Fax +442076365330.
URL: http://www.globalncap.org/
History Memorandum and Articles of Association incorporated 2 Feb 2011. UK Registered Charity: 1141798. **Aims** Support the development of new consumer crash test programmes in emerging markets where vehicle growth is strong but indepenet consumer information on crashworthiness is frequently not readily available; promote public safety and public health, protection and preservation of human life; conserve, protect and improve the physical and natural environment. **Structure** Board of Trustees. **Finance** Funding support from: Bloomberg Philanthropies; *FIA Foundation (#09742); International Consumer Research and Testing (ICRT, #12931);* Road Safety Fund. **Consultative Status** Consultative status granted from: *ECOSOC (#05331)* (Special). **NGO Relations** *European New Car Assessment Programme (EURO NCAP, #08046); New Car Assessment Programme for Latin America and the Caribbean (Latin NCAP, #17077); New Car Assessment Program for Southeast Asian Countries (ASEAN NCAP, #17078).* Member of: *Partnership for Clean Fuels and Vehicles (PCFV, #18231).* [2018/XM5013/**F**]

♦ Global NGO Executive Committee (GNEC) 10507

Mailing Address PO Box 91, Mamaroneck NY 10543, USA. E-mail: info@gnec.ngo.
URL: https://gnec.ngo/
History 1962. Former names and other names: *Executive Committee of Non-Governmental Organizations Associated with the United Nations Department of Public Information (NGO/DPI Executive Committee)* – former (2020); *Comité exécutif des organisations non gouvernementales associées au Département de l'information des Nations Unies* – former (2020). Registration: USA, New York. **Aims** Act in an advisory and liaison capacity to channel information and represent the interests of NGOs in association with DPI; increase public understanding of the work and achievements of the United Nations and its bodies. **Structure** An elected body representing NGOs associated with the Department of Global Communications of the United Nations (DPI). Chair; 2 Vice-Chairpersons; Secretary; Treasurer; 18 Members; 4 Ex-Officio members. **Languages** English. **Finance** Contributions from member NGOs. **Activities** Guidance/assistance/consulting; networking/liaising; knowledge management/information dissemination; awareness raising; events/meetings. **Events** *Annual Conference* Gyeongju (Korea Rep) 2016, *Annual Conference* New York, NY (USA) 2014, *Annual conference* Bonn (Germany) 2011, *Annual conference* Melbourne, VIC (Australia) 2010, *Annual conference* Mexico City (Mexico) 2009. **Publications** *NGO/DPI Reporter* (4 a year). **Members** Membership open to organizations (over 1,500) granted association status with DPI. Membership not specified. **IGO Relations** *United Nations (UN, #20515).* [2022/XE4757/y/**E**]

♦ Global NPO Coalition on FATF 10508

Secretariat c/o HSC, Riviervismarkt 4, 2513 AM The Hague, Netherlands. E-mail: npos@fatfplatform.org.
URL: https://fatfplatform.org/
History Founded by Charity & Security Network (CSN), *European Center for Not-for-Profit Law (ECNL, #06463), Philanthropy Europe Association (Philea, #18358)* and *Human Security Collective (HSC).* **Aims** Mitigate the unintended consequences of countering the financing of terrorism (CFT) policies on civil society so that legitimate charitable activity is not disrupted. **Structure** Core Group; Technical Advisory Group.
Members Non-profit organizations in 14 countries and including 7 organizations listed in this Yearbook:
Belgium, Indonesia, Jordan, Kenya, Kosovo, Mexico, Netherlands, Nigeria, Pakistan, Switzerland, Tunisia, Uganda, UK, USA.
Community World Service Asia (#04407); European Center for Not-for-Profit Law (ECNL, #06463); Human Security Collective (HSC); International Center for Not-for-Profit Law (ICNL, #12471); Islamic Relief Worldwide (IRWW, #16048); Norwegian Refugee Council (NRC); Philanthropy Europe Association (Philea, #18358).
[2023/AA3242/y/**E**]

♦ Global Nuclear Energy Partnership / see International Framework for Nuclear Energy Cooperation (#13681)

♦ Global Nuclear Safety and Security Network (GNSSN) 10509

Contact c/o IAEA – VIC, PO Box 100, 1400 Vienna, Austria. T. +43126000. Fax +43126007. E-mail: gnssn.contact-point@iaea.org.
URL: http://gnssn.iaea.org/
History Launching formally announced, 2006, Moscow (Russia). Functions within *International Atomic Energy Agency (IAEA, #12294)*, as a human network, functioning as a key support element of the *Global Nuclear Safety and Security Framework (GNSSF).* **Aims** Share information and knowledge; facilitate multilateral cooperation and coordination; build capacity. **Structure** Steering Committee; Governance Board, comprising Executive, Advisory Group, Coordinators, Moderators and Assistants. Secretariat.
Activities coordinated among networks, subdivided into: Global networks; Regional networks; National platforms; Thematic networks; Capacity building and Networking. Global Networks (6):
– *International Regulatory Network (RegNet); Global Safety Assessment Network; Emergency and Preparedness Network; Nuclear Security Information Portal; Technical and Scientific Organization Forum; Global Nuclear Safety and Security Communication Network (GNSS COM).*
Regional Networks (8):
– *Arab Network of Nuclear Regulators (ANNuR, #01013);*
– *Asian Nuclear Safety Network (ANSN, #01572);*
– *European Nuclear Safety Regulators Group (ENSREG, #08058);*
– *Forum of Nuclear Regulatory Bodies in Africa (FNRBA, #09927);*
– *European Technical Safety Organisations Network (ETSON, #08880);*
– *Foro Iberoamericano de Organismos Reguladores Radiológicos y Nucleares (FORO, #09878);*
– *Ibero-American Platform for Operators in the Area of Nuclear Safety (IAEA PIANOS);*
– *European and Central Asian Safety Network (EuCAS, #06465).*
Thematic Networks (16):
– CANada Deuterium Uranium Reactor Regulators' Forum (CANDU); Control of Sources Network; Global Transport Networks; Water-Water Energetic Reactor Regulators' Forum (WWER); *Mediterranean Region Transport Network (MEDNET);* SMR Regulators' Forum; *International Low Level Waste Disposal Network (DISPONET);* Network of Environmental Management and Remediation (ENVIRONET); *International Decommissioning Network (IDN); International Predisposal Network (IPN); IAEA International Network of Laboratories for Nuclear Waste Characterization (LABONET);* Laboratory of RadioAnalyses and Environment (LRAE); Management System Network of Excellence (MSN); *International Network on Spent Fuel Management (SFM Network);* Underground Research Facilities Network for Geological Disposal (URF Network); Integrated Review Service for Radioactive Waste and Spent Fuel Management, Decommissioning and Remediation (ARTEMIS).
Events *Plenary Meeting* Vienna (Austria) 2019, *Meeting* Vienna (Austria) 2018, *Meeting* Vienna (Austria) 2018, *Plenary Meeting* Vienna (Austria) 2018, *Meeting* Vienna (Austria) 2017. **IGO Relations** Partners include: *Arab Atomic Energy Agency (AAEA, #00901); European Commission (EC, #06633);* national institutions.
[2018/XM6490/**F***]

♦ Global Nurses United (unconfirmed)
♦ Globalnye akcii chelovechestva protiv 'svobodnoy' torgovli i VTO (#18304)
♦ Global Observatory on Donation and Transplantation (internationally oriented national body)

♦ Global Observatory on Peer-to-Peer, Community Self-Consumption and Transactive Energy Models (GO-P2P) 10510

Operating Agent Univ College London, Central House, 14 Upper Woburn Place, London, WC1H 0NN, UK. E-mail: d.shipworth@userstcp.org – vikki@userstcp.org.
URL: https://userstcp.org/task/peer-to-peer-energy-trading/
History 2 Sep 2019, London (UK). Expected to run until 3 Mar 2023. **Aims** Understand the policy, regulatory, social and technological conditions necessary to support the wider deployment of peer-to-peer, community self-consumption and transactive energy models. **Activities** Events/meetings.
Members Individuals in 8 countries:
Australia, Belgium, Ireland, Italy, Netherlands, Switzerland, UK, USA. [2021.10.05/AA1572/v/**F**]

♦ Global Ocean (internationally oriented national body)
♦ Global Ocean Forum / see Global Forum on Oceans, Coasts and Islands (#10377)

♦ Global Ocean Observing System (GOOS) 10511

Système mondial d'observation de l'océan – Sistema Mundial de Observación de los Océanos
Head c/o IOC, 7 place de Fontenoy, 75352 Paris 007-SP, France. T. +33145683992. E-mail: goos@unesco.org.
URL: http://www.ioc-goos.org/
History Feb 1992, Paris (France), at first intergovernmental meeting. Memorandum of Understanding signed, 1993, by *Intergovernmental Oceanographic Commission (IOC, #11496), International Council for Science (ICSU, inactive), World Meteorological Organization (WMO, #21649)* and *UNEP (#20299).* As of 2005, oceanographic component of *Global Earth Observing System of Systems (GEOSS).* **Aims** Collect comprehensive information on properties and variability of the Earth's ocean system as basis for monitoring and forecasting its state under changing conditions; assist in detection of climate change and assessing its impact; provide a basis for development of national and international policies for resource management and coastal development and management, for assessing and preserving the health of the ocean and for promoting related capacity building in ocean science and its application; using already existing scientific research networks, gather, store and exploit data with a view to arriving at practical decisions concerning climate and ocean resources including fish and other living matter. **Structure** Steering Committee. Essential ocean Variables Panels: Ocean Observations Panel for Climate (OOPC); Biogeochemistry Panel; Biology and Ecology Panel. Implemented by: Regional Alliances *Joint WMO-IOC Technical Commission for Oceanography and*

Marine Meteorology (JCOMM, #16151); *International Oceanographic Data and Information Exchange (IODE, #14396)*; Programme Office (GPO); Regional Ocean Observation Systems (ROOS) and Regional Coastal Ocean Observation Systems (RCOOS). GRAs (12): *European Global Ocean Observing System (EuroGOOS, #07396)*; *Mediterranean Oceanography Network for the Global Ocean Observing System (MONGOOS, #16668)*; *'Black Sea GOOS'*; *'IO-GOOS (Indian Ocean GOOS)'*; *'NEAR-GOOS (North-East Asian Region GOOS)'*; *Pacific Islands GOOS (PI-GOOS, #17971)*; *'IOCARIBE-GOOS (Caribbean Region GOOS)'*; *Global Ocean Observing System for Africa (GOOS Africa, #10512)*; *'USA GOOS'*; *'Southeast Asian GOOS (SEA-GOOS)'*; *'OCEATLAN'*; *GOOS Regional Alliance for the South East Pacific (GRASP, #10682)*; *'IMOS Australian Integrated Marine Observing System'*. **Languages** English, French, Russian, Spanish. **Staff** 12.00 FTE, paid. **Finance** Sources for international coordination: UNESCO via IOC (60%); earmarked government contributions to IOC Trust Fund (40%). Paris (France) Secretariat provided by IOC; Regional GOOS Programme Office in Perth provided by Australian regional and federal government grants; Regional GOOS Programme office in Rio de Janeiro (Brazil) supported by IOC and Brazilian navy. Budget (annual), (excluding project implementation costs, including meetings and design panel implementation costs and salaries of coordination staff): US$ 2.7 million. **Activities** *'Main focus'*: modules (Coastal; Open Ocean) identifying user communities and requirements; designing end-to-end outputs to satisfy these requirements. *'Main methods'*: data and information management; ocean observation in situ and from space; snowcasting and forecasting; activities, including workshops. Includes: operational oceanographic observations and analyses; supporting research; timely distribution of data and products; data assimilation into numerical models leading to predictions; capacity building in participating member states to develop analysis and application capability, especially developing countries. Phased approach: (i) planning, including design and technical definition; (ii) operational demonstration (pilot projects); (iii) incorporation of suitable existing and new observing activities; (iv) gradual operational implementation of the permanent or ongoing GOOS; (v) continued assessment and improvement. *'Current projects'*: El Nino Southern Oscillation Observing and Forecasting System; development of national and regional programmes; Argo – seeding the ocean with 3,000 profiling floats for data collection; PIRATA – monitoring ocean's role in climate control; Global Ocean Data Assimilation Experiment – assimilating real time meteorological and ocean data into forecasting models; GOOS Regional Alliances Network Development (GRAND), supporting regional activities of GOOS. Organizes: I-GOOS Meeting (every 2 years); GOOS Forum (every 2 years). Regional Alliances organize regional conferences, seminars and workshops. **Events** *I-GOOS Meeting* Paris (France) 2011, *I-GOOS Meeting* Paris (France) 2007, *Session* Seoul (Korea Rep) 2007, *Forum of the GOOS regional alliances* Cape Town (South Africa) 2006, *Pan-African LMEs forum* Cape Town (South Africa) 2006. **Publications** Reports.
Members Member States (100):
Albania, Angola, Argentina, Australia, Barbados, Belgium, Benin, Bosnia-Herzegovina, Brazil, Bulgaria, Cameroon, Canada, Chile, China, Colombia, Comoros, Congo Brazzaville, Costa Rica, Côte d'Ivoire, Croatia, Cuba, Cyprus, Denmark, Ecuador, Egypt, Fiji, Finland, France, Gabon, Gambia, Georgia, Germany, Ghana, Greece, Guinea, Iceland, India, Indonesia, Iran Islamic Rep, Ireland, Israel, Italy, Japan, Kenya, Kiribati, Korea Rep, Madagascar, Malaysia, Malta, Marshall Is, Mauritania, Mauritius, Mexico, Micronesia FS, Morocco, Mozambique, Namibia, Nauru, Netherlands, New Zealand, Nigeria, Niue, Norway, Oman, Pakistan, Palau, Papua New Guinea, Peru, Philippines, Poland, Portugal, Romania, Russia, Samoa, Senegal, Serbia, Seychelles, Sierra Leone, Singapore, Slovenia, Solomon Is, South Africa, Spain, Sri Lanka, Sweden, Tanzania UR, Thailand, Togo, Tonga, Trinidad-Tobago, Tunisia, Türkiye, Tuvalu, UK, Ukraine, Uruguay, USA, Vanuatu, Venezuela, Vietnam.
IGO Relations *World Hydrological Cycle Observing System (WHYCOS, #21573)* is expected to be the freshwater equivalent system. Works closely with: *Global Climate Observing System (GCOS, #10289)*; *Global Terrestrial Observing System (GTOS, #10626)*. Involved in development and implementation of: *Regional Seas Programme (#18814)*. Participates in: *Group on Earth Observations (GEO, #10735)*. **NGO Relations** Member of (1): *Partnership for Observation of the Global Oceans (POGO, #18239)*. Participates in: *Ocean Observations Panel for Climate (OOPC, #17683)*. [2018/XF2537/**F***]

♦ Global Ocean Observing System for Africa (GOOS Africa) 10512

Project Office Dir Section Ocean Observations and Services, IOC/UNESCO, 1 rue Miollis, 75732 Paris CEDEX 15, France. T. +33145684040. Fax +33145485813.
Chairman Marine Fisheries Research Division, PO Box BT-62, Tema, Ghana. T. +22322208048. Fax +22322203066.
URL: http://www.ioc-goos.org/
History within *Global Ocean Observing System (GOOS, #10511)* of *Intergovernmental Oceanographic Commission (IOC, #11496)*. **NGO Relations** Member of (1): *World Association of Marine Stations (WAMS, #21161)* (as Founding member of). Cooperates with (1): *Mediterranean Oceanography Network for the Global Ocean Observing System (MONGOOS, #16668)*. [2014/XJ4234/**E**]

♦ Global Oceans (internationally oriented national body)
♦ Global Ocean Trust (unconfirmed)

♦ Global Off-Grid Lighting Association (GOGLA) 10513

Exec Dir Arthur van Schendelstraat 500, 3511 MH Utrecht, Netherlands. T. +31304100914. E-mail: info@gogla.org.
URL: http://www.gogla.org/
History 2012, as a public-private initiative of *International Bank for Reconstruction and Development (IBRD, #12317)* / *International Finance Corporation (IFC, #13597)* Lighting Africa and companies. **Aims** Help members build sustainable markets, delivering quality, affordable products and services to as many households, businesses and communities as possible across the developing world. **Structure** Board; Secretariat. **Languages** English. **Events** *International Off-Grid Lighting Conference* Dubai (United Arab Emirates) 2015. **Publications** *GOGLA Newsletter*. Guides; reports; briefing notes.
Members Organizations and companies. Included in the above, 3 organizations listed in this Yearbook:
International Finance Corporation (IFC, #13597); *Shell Foundation*; *SolarAid*. [2019.02.12/XJ9324/y/**E**]

♦ Global Oncology (internationally oriented national body)
♦ Global One (internationally oriented national body)
♦ Global One 2015 / see Global One
♦ Global Online Academy (internationally oriented national body)

♦ Global Open Data for Agriculture and Nutrition (GODAN) 10514

Communications Manager 21111 Lakeshore, Ste-Anne-de-Bellevue, Montréal QC H9X 3V9, Canada. T. +15143988675. E-mail: enquiries@godan.info.
URL: http://www.godan.info/
History Announced at Open Government Partnership Conference, Oct 2013. Governments of US and UK partnered to form the initiative. **Aims** Support global efforts to make agricultural and nutritionally relevant data available, accessible, and usable for unrestricted use worldwide. **Structure** Donor Steering Committee; Secretariat. **Languages** English, French. **Finance** Sources: government support; international organizations. Supported by: *CABI (#03393)*; *Centre universitaire de la Romania (inactive)*; *CGIAR System Organization (CGIAR, #03843)*; *Department for International Development (DFID, inactive)*; *FAO (#09260)*; Government of Netherlands; Open Data Institute; US Government. **Activities** Advocacy/lobbying/activism; awareness raising; capacity building; events/meetings; guidance/assistance/consulting; knowledge management/information dissemination; monitoring/evaluation; projects/programmes; research/documentation; standards/guidelines; training/education. **Events** *Summit* New York, NY (USA) 2016. **Publications** Papers; reports; standards; brochures.
Members Governments; donors; international and not-for-profit organizations; businesses. Partners (over 1,200) include:
- *African Centre for Technology Studies (ACTS, #00243)*;
- *African Development Bank (ADB, #00283)*;
- *African Fertilizer and Agribusiness Partnership (AFAP, #00314)*;
- *Alliance for a Green Revolution in Africa (AGRA, #00685)*;
- *Asia-Pacific Association of Agricultural Research Institutions (APAARI, #01830)*;
- *AVRDC – The World Vegetable Center (#03051)*;
- *Bill and Melinda Gates Foundation (BMGF)*;
- *CABI (#03393)*;
- *CGIAR System Organization (CGIAR, #03843)*;
- *FAO (#09260)*;
- *Global Alliance for Improved Nutrition (GAIN, #10202)*;
- *Global Crop Diversity Trust (Crop Trust, #10313)*;
- *Global Forum on Agricultural Research (GFAR, #10370)*;
- *Global Plant Council (#10550)*;
- *Initiative for Global Development (IGD)*;
- *Institute of Development Studies, Brighton (IDS)*;
- *Inter-American Institute for Cooperation on Agriculture (IICA, #11434)*;
- *International Bank for Reconstruction and Development (IBRD, #12317)*;
- *International Food Policy Research Institute (IFPRI, #13622)*;
- *International Livestock Research Institute (ILRI, #14062)*;
- *International Network for Bamboo and Rattan (INBAR, #14234)*;
- *International Society of Automation (ISA)*;
- *International Treaty on Plant Genetic Resources for Food and Agriculture (2001)*;
- *ONE (#17728)*;
- *Oxfam GB*;
- *PanAfrican Farmers' Organization (PAFO, #18049)*;
- *Practical Action (#18475)*;
- *RTI International*;
- *United Nations Global Compact (#20567)*;
- *United States Agency for International Development (USAID)*;
- *Web alliance for Regreening in Africa (W4RA)*;
- *World Agricultural Forum (WAF)*.

IGO Relations Partner of (1): *Group on Earth Observations (GEO, #10735)*. **NGO Relations** Member of (1): *Global Partnership for Sustainable Development Data (Data4SDGS, #10542)*. [2021.05.18/XM4437/y/**F**]

♦ Global Optimization Workshop (meeting series)

♦ Global Organic Textile Standard International Working Group (GOTS) 10515

Managing Director Global Standard, Rotebühlstr 102, 70178 Stuttgart, Germany. E-mail: mail@global-standard.org.
URL: http://www.global-standard.org/
History 2008. Registration: No/ID: HRB 726970, Germany, Stuttgart; EU Transparency Register, No/ID: 127596116563-01, Start date: 14 Mar 2015. **Aims** Develop, implement, verify, protect and promote the Global Organic Textile Standard. **Structure** Advisory Council; Standards Committee; Certifiers Council. **Activities** Standards/guidelines; certification/accreditation; events/meetings. **Events** *Regional Seminar* Dhaka (Bangladesh) 2019, *Regional Seminar* Izmir (Turkey) 2019, *Conference* Mumbai (India) 2015. **Publications** *GOTS News*.
Members Organizations (4):
International Natural Textile Association (#14217); Japan Organic Cotton Association (JOCA); *Organic Trade Association (OTA, #17795)*; *Soil Association*.
NGO Relations Subscriber to: *ISEAL (#16026)*. [2020/XM4127/y/**E**]

♦ Global Organisation for Bioinformatics Learning, Education and Training (GOBLET) 10516

Contact CMBI 260 Radboud Univ, Nijmegen Medical Ctr, Geert Grooteplein 26-28, 6525 GA Nijmegen, Netherlands. E-mail: info@mygoblet.org.
URL: https://www.mygoblet.org/
History Founded 2012, by *European Molecular Biology Network (EMBnet, #07815)*, *International Society for Computational Biology (ISCB, #15026)*, *Asia Pacific Bioinformatics Network (APBioNet, #01858)*, *African Society for Bioinformatics and Computational Biology (ASBCB, #00459)*, *Sociedad Iberoamericana de Bioinformatica (SoIBio, #19361)*, *International Society for Biocuration (ISB, #14959)*, NBIC, SeqAhead, *EMBL's European Bioinformatics Institute (EMBL-EBI, #05433)* and BTN. Former names and other names: *GOBLET Stichting* – legal name. Registration: Netherlands. **Aims** Cultivate the global bioinformatics trainer community; set standards; provide high-quality resources to support learning, education and training. **Structure** General Meeting (annual); Full Board; Executive Board. Committees (5): Fundraising; Learning, Education and Training; Outreach and PR; Standards; Technical. **Finance** Sources: members' dues. **Activities** Certification/accreditation; training/education. **Publications** Guides. [2019/XM8728/y/**C**]

♦ Global Organization for EPA and DHA Omega-3 (GOED) 10517

Exec Dir 222 South Main St, Ste 500, Salt Lake City UT 84101, USA. E-mail: info@goedomega3.com.
URL: http://www.goedomega3.com/
History 2006. Former names and other names: *GO3ETA Inc* – legal name. Registration: 501(c)(6), USA. **Aims** Support members who are committed to responsibly developing, sustaining and expanding markets for EPA and DHA Omega-3s, while promoting health benefits, supporting public education and safety, establishing ethical business and product quality standards, and advancing government, healthcare and industry relations. **Structure** Board of Directors; Sub-Committees (4). **Languages** English, Spanish. **Events** *GOED Exchange* 2024, *GOED Exchange* Fort Lauderdale, FL (USA) 2022, *GOED Exchange* Barcelona (Spain) 2020, *GOED Exchange* Seattle, WA (USA) 2018, *GOED Exchange* Santa Cruz de Tenerife (Spain) 2016. **IGO Relations** Observer to: *Codex Alimentarius Commission (CAC, #04081)*. [2021/XJ5381/**D**]

♦ Global Organization for Lysosomal Diseases (inactive)
♦ Global Organization for Maternal and Child Health (internationally oriented national body)

♦ Global Organization of Parliamentarians Against Corruption (GOPAC) 10518

Organisation mondiale des parlementaires contre la corruption – Organización Mundial de Parlamentarias contra la Corrupción
Exec Dir 1 Station A, Toronto ON M5W 1A2, Canada. E-mail: secretariat@gopacnetwork.org – info@gopacnetwork.org – ed@gopacnetwork.org.
Head Office The White Palace, Doha, Qatar. T. +97444774328.
URL: http://www.gopacnetwork.org/
History Oct 2002, Ottawa, ON (Canada). Founded as a result of a Global Conference. Registration: Start date: Sep 2003, Canada. **Aims** Fight corruption; promote integrity through the enhancement of the effectiveness of parliaments and legislatures; provide a voice for global parliamentarians fighting corruption; make parliaments more effective institutions of democratic oversight. **Structure** Annual General Meeting; Global Conference (every 2 years); Board of Directors; Executive Committee; Secretariat; Regional Chapters (5): *African Parliamentarians Network Against Corruption (APNAC, see: #10518)*; *Arab Region Parliamentarians Against Corruption (ARPAC, see: #10518)*; *GOPAC América Latina y el Caribe (see: #10518)*; *GOPAC Oceania (see: #10518)*; *South East Asia Parliamentarians Against Corruption (SEAPAC, see: #10518)*; National Chapters (64). **Languages** Arabic, English, French, Spanish. **Staff** 3.00 FTE, paid. **Finance** Principle in-kind contribution by the State of Qatar **Activities** Guidance/assistance/consulting; knowledge management/information dissemination; training/education. **Events** *Global Conference* Doha (Qatar) 2019, *Annual General Meeting* Bali (Indonesia) 2017, *Global Conference* Yogyakarta (Indonesia) 2015, *Global Conference* Manila (Philippines) 2013, *Global Conference* Mexico City (Mexico) 2011. **Publications** *GOPAC Newsletter* (12 a year). *Parliament's Role in Implementing the Sustainable Development Goals: A Parliamentary Handbook* (1st 2017) by GOPAC and Islamic Development Bank; *GOPAC Anti-Money Laundering Action Guide for Parliamentarians*; *Handbook on Parliamentary Ethics and Conduct: A guide for parliamentarians*; *Improving Democratic Accountability Globally: A handbook for legislators on congressional oversight in presidential systems*. Position papers.
Members Current or former legislators or legislators who have been denied their right to take office in 148 countries and territories:
Afghanistan, Albania, Algeria, Angola, Antigua-Barbuda, Argentina, Armenia, Aruba, Australia, Austria, Azerbaijan, Bahrain, Bangladesh, Barbados, Belgium, Belize, Benin, Bolivia, Bosnia-Herzegovina, Botswana, Brazil, Bulgaria, Burkina Faso, Burundi, Cambodia, Cameroon, Canada, Chad, Chile, China, Colombia, Congo Brazzaville, Congo DR, Cook Is, Costa Rica, Côte d'Ivoire, Croatia, Denmark, Djibouti, Dominica, Dominican Rep, Ecuador, Egypt, El Salvador, Fiji, France, Gabon, Gambia, Georgia, Germany, Ghana, Greece, Grenada, Guatemala, Guinea, Guyana, Haiti, Honduras, Hungary, India, Indonesia, Iran Islamic Rep, Iraq, Ireland, Italy, Jamaica, Japan, Jordan, Kazakhstan, Kenya, Kiribati, Korea Rep, Kuwait, Kyrgyzstan, Lebanon, Lesotho, Liberia, Libya, Lithuania, Luxembourg, Madagascar, Malawi, Malaysia, Maldives, Mali, Mauritania, Mauritius, Mexico, Micronesia FS, Moldova, Mongolia, Montenegro, Morocco, Mozambique, Myanmar, Namibia, Nauru, Nepal, Netherlands, New Zealand, Nicaragua, Niger, Nigeria, North Macedonia, Norway, Oman, Pakistan, Palestine, Panama, Papua New Guinea, Paraguay, Peru, Philippines, Poland, Romania, Russia, Rwanda, Saudi Arabia, Senegal, Serbia, Sierra Leone, Slovenia, South Africa, South Sudan, Spain, Sri Lanka, St Lucia, Sweden, Switzerland, Tajikistan, Tanzania UR, Thailand, Timor-Leste, Tonga, Trinidad-Tobago, Tunisia, Türkiye, Uganda, UK, Ukraine, United Arab Emirates, Uruguay, USA, Venezuela, Vietnam, Yemen, Zambia, Zimbabwe.

Consultative Status Consultative status granted from: *Council of Europe (CE, #04881)* (Participatory Status); *ECOSOC (#05331)* (Special); *UNEP (#20299)*. **IGO Relations** Observer status with (1): *Egmont Group of Financial Intelligence Units (#05396)*. **NGO Relations** Observer status with (1): *Inter-Parliamentary Union (IPU, #15961)*. Member of (1): *Transparency, Accountability and Participation Network (TAP Network, #20222)*.
[2022.10.16/XD8971/**C**]

♦ Global Organization for PHA (GO!PHA) 10519

Contact Oudebrugsteeg 9, 1012 JN Amsterdam, Netherlands. E-mail: gopha@gopha.org.
URL: https://www.gopha.org/

History 2019. Registration: Stichting, No/ID: KVK 75070790 860130071, Netherlands; EU Transparency Register, No/ID: 946264840278-51, Start date: 11 Nov 2020. **Aims** Accelerate the development of the PHA (Polyhydroxyalkanoate polymer)-platform industry. **Activities** Advocacy/lobbying/activism; knowledge management/information dissemination; research/documentation; training/education. **Events** *PHA-platform World Congress* Cologne (Germany) 2021. **Publications** *GO!PHA Newsletter* – electronic. White papers; position papers. [2020.12.09/AA1207/**F**]

♦ Global Oscillation Network Group (GONG) 10520

Program Manager NSO, 950 N Cherry Ave, Tucson AZ 85719-4933, USA. T. +15203188138.
URL: http://gong.nso.edu/

History 5 Oct 1997, when commenced operations. **Aims** Conduct detailed study of *solar* internal structure and dynamics, in particular differences in the sun's internal rotation speeds, using *helioseismology*. **Finance** (US) National Science Foundation. Budget (annual): about US$ 2 million. **Activities** Obtains nearly continuous observations of the Sun's "five-minute" oscillations, or pulsations through a 6-station network of extremely sensitive and stable solar velocity imagers located around the Earth. Facilitates the coordinated scientific investigation of these measurements through a major, distributed data reduction and analysis system. Organizes annual scientific meetings. **Events** *Biennial meeting / Annual Meeting* Sheffield (UK) 2006, *Biennial Meeting* New Haven, CT (USA) 2004, *Biennial Meeting* Big Bear Lake, CA (USA) 2002, *Annual Meeting* Big Bear Lake, CA (USA) 2000, *Biennial Meeting* Santa Cruz de Tenerife (Spain) 2000.
Members Individual members (150) in 31 countries and territories:
Algeria, Australia, Belgium, Canada, Chile, China, Czechia, Denmark, France, Germany, India, Iran Islamic Rep, Israel, Italy, Japan, Korea Rep, Mexico, Morocco, Netherlands, Norway, Poland, Portugal, Russia, South Africa, Spain, Sweden, Switzerland, Taiwan, UK, USA, Uzbekistan.
Partners (solar observatories) (6) in 5 countries:
Australia, Chile, India, Spain, USA (2). [2010/XF4415/**F**]

♦ Global OSH Coalition / see Global Coalition for Occupation Safety and Health (#10294)

♦ Global Outbreak Alert and Response Network (GOARN) 10521

Réseau mondial d'alerte et d'action en cas d'épidémie
Contact c/o WHO, Avenue Appia 20, 1211 Geneva 27, Switzerland. E-mail: goarn@who.int.
URL: http://www.who.int/csr/outbreaknetwork/en/

History Founded Apr 2000, Geneva (Switzerland), within *WHO (#20950)*. **Aims** Contribute towards global *health* security by: combating the international spread of outbreaks; ensuring that appropriate technical assistance reaches affected states rapidly; contributing to long-term epidemic preparedness and capacity building. **Structure** Steering Committee. **NGO Relations** Cooperates with: *African Field Epidemiology Network (AFENET, #00315)*. [2013.07.18/XJ3758/**E**]

♦ Global Outreach (internationally oriented national body)
♦ Global Outreach Doctors (internationally oriented national body)

♦ Global Paediatric Surgery Network (GPSN) 10522

Founder address not obtained.
URL: http://globalpaediatricsurgery.org/

History Registered in accordance with US law. **Aims** Serve as a clearinghouse for volunteer work performed by pediatric surgerions around the world. **Structure** Board of Directors. **NGO Relations** Endorsed by: *European Paediatric Surgeons' Association (EUPSA, #08130)*; *International Pediatric Endosurgery Group (IPEG, #14542)*; *Pacific Association of Pediatric Surgeons (PAPS, #17933)*; *Pan African Pediatric Surgical Association (PAPSA, #18059)*; *World Federation of Associations of Pediatric Surgeons (WOFAPS, #21411)*; national associations. [2015/XJ9660/**F**]

♦ Global Panel on Agriculture and Food Systems for Nutrition (GLOPAN) 10523

Secretariat c/o LIDC, 20 Bloomsbury Square, London, WC1A 2NS, UK. T. +442076127957. E-mail: secretariat@glopan.org.
URL: http://glopan.org/

History Formally set up Aug 2013, London (UK), by *Bill and Melinda Gates Foundation (BMGF)* and *Department for International Development (DFID, inactive)*. **Aims** Help governments in low and middle-income countries develop evidence-based policies that make high-quality diets safe, affordable and accessible. **Structure** Panel; Secretariat. **Activities** Events/meetings. **Members** Individuals. Membership countries not specified. **IGO Relations** Together with *African Development Bank (ADB, #00283)* and *African Union (AU, #00488)* Commission, instrumental in setting up *African Leaders for Nutrition (ALN)*. **NGO Relations** Hosted by: *London International Development Centre (LIDC)*. [2019.12.30/XM6562/v/**F**]

♦ Global Panel Foundation 10524

Chair Vězeňská 5, Old Town, 110 00 Prague 1, Czechia. E-mail: office@praguesociety.org.
Global Panel Australia Australia Square Level 39, 264-278 George Street, Sydney NSW 2000, Australia.
URL: http://globalpanel.org/

History 1989, Netherlands. **Aims** Support governments, institutions and the private sector, so as to facilitate solutions in conflict areas around the world. **Structure** General Meeting; Board of Directors; Supervisory Board; Board of Advisors. **Languages** English, German. **Staff** 25.00 FTE, paid. **Finance** Funding from private sector; sponsorship; donations; subscriptions. **Activities** Networking/liaising; conflict resolution; awards/prizes/competitions; events/meetings. **Publications** *Global Panel Newsletter*.
Members Statesmen, business leaders, scientists, ministers, secretaries of state, CEO's, lobbyists, scientists and entrepreneurs. Members in 28 countries:
Australia, Austria, Belgium, Canada, Czechia, Denmark, Egypt, Estonia, Finland, Germany, India, Israel, Japan, Korea Rep, Latvia, Lithuania, Morocco, Netherlands, New Zealand, Norway, Pakistan, Romania, Slovakia, Spain, Sweden, Switzerland, UK, USA.
NGO Relations Partner organization: *Prague Society for International Cooperation*. [2021/XM3202/fv/**F**]

♦ Global Parents for Eczema Research (internationally oriented national body)
♦ Global Parks (internationally oriented national body)

♦ Global Parliamentarians on Habitat (GPH) 10525

Groupe Mondial de Parlementaires pour l'Habitat – Grupo Mundial de Parlamentarios para el Habitat – Globale Parlamentariergruppe für Habitat
Sec address not obtained. E-mail: apolvcam@gmail.com.
URL: http://www.gph-habitat.de/

History 1987, Yokohama (Japan), during the International Year of Shelter for the Homeless. First Rules of Procedure adopted 1992, Vancouver BC (Canada). Current Rules approved by General Assembly, 30 Jan 1998, Cancún (Mexico). **Aims** Promote the implementation of the Habitat Agenda – a global plan of action setting out strategies for adequate, sustainable development in the area of shelter and human settlements. **Structure** General Assembly (every 2-3 years). Board of Directors, consisting of President, 4 regional Vice Presidents and Presidents of Advisory Council and of Former Parliamentarians Group. Regional Councils (4): Africa; America; Asia; Europe. Regional Boards of Directors. **Languages** English. **Staff** At least 5. **Finance** Conference costs financed by hosts of events; Individual members financed by respective parliaments; Office of President and Secretary-General currently financed by German Bundestag. **Activities** Meeting activities. **Events** *Global Forum on Parliamentarians on Habitat* Naples (Italy) 2012, *Global Forum* Zadar (Croatia) 2011, *Global Forum* Rio de Janeiro (Brazil) 2010, *Global parliamentarians meeting for Europe* The Hague (Netherlands) 2006, *Global forum on parliamentarians on habitat / Global Forum* Rabat (Morocco) 2005. **Publications** No regular publications. Studies. **Members** Individual; Former; Groups. Membership countries not specified. **IGO Relations** Close collaboration with: *United Nations Human Settlements Programme (UN-Habitat, #20572)*. **NGO Relations** Parnter of: *World Urban Campaign (WUC, #21893)*. [2014/XF4480/**F**]

♦ Global Parliamentarians Network to End Infectious Diseases (UNITE) 10526

Exec Dir Avda Franscisco Salgado Zenha 4, 1950-443 Lisbon, Portugal. E-mail: unitenetwork@unitenetwork.org.
URL: https://www.unitenetwork.org/

History 2017. Founded by Dr Ricardo Baptista Leite, under the auspices of *Joint United Nations Programme on HIV/AIDS (UNAIDS, #16149)*. Former names and other names: *UNITE Global Parliamentarians Network to end HIV/AIDS, Viral Hepatitis and other Infectious Diseases* – full title. **Aims** Achieve political impact towards ending infectious diseases as a global health threat. **Structure** Global Board; Secretariat; Regional Chapters (10). **Finance** Sources: donations. Funding from philanthropic sources, not from industry sources. **Activities** Advocacy/lobbying/activism; events/meetings. Active in all member countries. **Events** *Global Summit* 2021, *Global Summit* 2020.
Members Parliamentarians (over 150) in 56 countries and territories:
Argentina, Australia, Austria, Belgium, Bolivia, Botswana, Brazil, Canada, Chile, Côte d'Ivoire, Cuba, Cyprus, Estonia, Finland, France, Georgia, Germany, Greece, Honduras, India, Indonesia, Ireland, Italy, Kenya, Lithuania, Macau, Malaysia, Maldives, Malta, Mexico, Moldova, Morocco, Mozambique, Myanmar, Nauru, Nepal, Netherlands, Nigeria, Norway, Pakistan, Philippines, Portugal, Romania, Sao Tomé-Principe, Slovenia, South Africa, Spain, Switzerland, Tanzania UR, Tunisia, UK, Ukraine, USA, Yemen, Zambia, Zimbabwe.
NGO Relations Member of (1): *Pandemic Action Network (PAN, #18173)*. [2022.01.18/AA2285/v/**F**]

♦ Global Parliamentary Alliance Against Atrocity Crimes (unconfirmed)

♦ Global Parliament of Mayors (GPM) 10527

Exec Dir PO Box 12 600, 2500 DJ The Hague, Netherlands. E-mail: gpm@denhaag.nl.
Street Address Spui 70, The Hague, Netherlands.
URL: https://globalparliamentofmayors.org/

History Inaugural convening, Sep 2016, The Hague (Netherlands). **Aims** Build on the experience, expertise and leadership of mayors in tackling local challenges resulting from global problems. **Structure** General Meeting; Executive Committee; Advisory Committee; Secretariat. **Languages** English. **Staff** 1.00 FTE, paid. **Activities** Events/meetings. **Events** *Conference* Durban (South Africa) 2019. **Publications** Declarations.
Members Mayors in 23 countries and territories:
Afghanistan, Argentina, Belgium, Gambia, Germany, Italy, Jordan, Kosovo, Liberia, Mozambique, Nepal, Netherlands, Norway, Pakistan, Palestine, Portugal, Senegal, Sierra Leone, South Africa, Switzerland, Uganda, UK, USA.
IGO Relations *International Organization for Migration (IOM, #14454)*; *UNICEF (#20332)*; *United Nations Human Settlements Programme (UN-Habitat, #20572)*. **NGO Relations** Member of: *Global Taskforce of Local and Regional Governments (Global Taskforce, #10622)*. [2020.01.16/XM8604/v/**F**]

♦ Global Partners in Care (internationally oriented national body)

♦ Global Partnership Against the Spread of Weapons and Materials of Mass Destruction 10528

Address not obtained.

History Launched 27 Jun 2002, Canada, at *Group of Eight (G-8, #10745)* Summit, as a 10-year initiative. Expanded 2011 (2013-2018). **Aims** Fund and coordinate projects and activities in the areas of chemical, biological, nuclear and radiological security. **Structure** Chaired by Chair of *Group of Seven (G-7, #10788)*. **Activities** Financial and/or material support. **Events** *Nuclear Security Summit* Washington, DC (USA) 2016.
Members Governments of 27 countries:
Australia, Belgium, Brazil, Canada, China, Czechia, Denmark, Finland, France, Germany, Hungary, India, Ireland, Italy, Japan, Korea Rep, Mexico, Netherlands, New Zealand, Norway, Poland, Russia, South Africa, Sweden, Switzerland, UK, USA.
[2016/XM4966/**F***]

♦ Global Partnership on Artificial Intelligence (unconfirmed)

♦ Global Partnership on Children with Disabilities (GPcwd) 10529

Contact Anthony Lake, UNICEF House, Three United Nations Plaza, New York NY 10017, USA. T. +12123267000 – +12128246000. Fax +12128887465 – +12128887454.
URL: http://www.gpcwd.org/

History Mar 2011. **Aims** Advance the rights of children with disabilities at global, regional and country levels. **Structure** Currently led by *UNICEF (#20332)*. **Activities** Task Forces (4): Nutrition; Education; Humanitarian Action; Assistive Technology. **Events** *Forum* New York, NY (USA) 2013, *Forum* New York, NY (USA) 2012.
Members Organizations (over 240), including 61 listed in this Yearbook:
- *Able Child Africa*;
- *ADD International*;
- *Africa Disability Alliance (ADA)*;
- *Arab Organization of Disabled People (AODP, #01019)*;
- *Association for Aid and Relief – Japan (AAR)*;
- *Atlas Alliance*;
- *Australian Aid (inactive)*;
- *Best Buddies International (BBI)*;
- *Catholic Agency for Overseas Development (CAFOD)*;
- *Christian Blind Mission (CBM)*;
- *Commonwealth Secretariat (#04362)*;
- *Council for Exceptional Children (CEC)*;
- *Disability Rights International (DRI)*;
- *Disabled Peoples' International (DPI, #05097)*;
- *End Corporal Punishment (#05457)*;
- *Equip KIDS International (EKI)*;
- *European Christian Organisations in Relief and Development (EU-CORD, #06545)*;
- *European Union Agency for Fundamental Rights (FRA, #08969)*;
- *EveryChild*;
- *Global Alliance on Accessible Technologies and Environments (GAATES, #10180)*;
- *Global Partnership for Disability and Development (GPDD, #10530)*;
- *Global Partnership for Education (GPE, #10531)*;
- *Humanity and Inclusion (HI, #10975)*;
- *ILO (#11123)*;
- *Inclusion International (#11145)*;
- *Inter-agency Network for Education in Emergencies (INEE, #11387)*;
- *International Association for Special Education (IASE, #12174)*;
- *International Bank for Reconstruction and Development (IBRD, #12317)*;
- *International Centre for the Advancement of Community-Based Rehabilitation (ICACBR)*;
- *International Council for Education of People with Visual Impairment (ICEVI, #13015)*;
- *International Disability Alliance (IDA, #13176)*;
- *International Disability and Development Consortium (IDDC, #13177)*;
- *International Federation for Spina Bifida and Hydrocephalus (IF SBH, #13552)*;
- *International Federation of Anti-Leprosy Associations (ILEP, #13355)*;
- *International Research and Development Actions (IRDAC)*;
- *Italian Association Amici di Raoul Follereau (AIFO)*;
- *Leonard Cheshire Disability (#16443)*;
- *Leprosy Mission International (TLMI, #16446)*;
- *Light for the World (#16474)*;
- *Office of the United Nations High Commissioner for Human Rights (OHCHR, #17697)*;
- *Pan American Health Organization (PAHO, #18108)*;
- *Perkins International*;
- *Plan International (#18386)*;
- *Platform Handicap en Ontwikkelingssamenwerking (PHOS)*;
- *RI Global (#18948)*;
- *Save the Children Federation (SCF)*;
- *Sightsavers International (#19270)*;
- *Special Olympics International (SOI, #19910)*;
- *Stichting Liliane Fonds (SLF)*;
- *Swedish International Development Cooperation Agency (Sida)*;
- *UNDP (#20292)*;
- *UNESCO (#20322)*;
- *UNHCR (#20327)*;
- *UNICEF (#20332)*;

- *United Nations Economic Commission for Latin America and the Caribbean (ECLAC, #20556)*;
- *United Nations Mine Action Service (UNMAS, #20585)*;
- *United Nations Population Fund (UNFPA, #20612)*;
- *United States Agency for International Development (USAID)*;
- *WHO (#20950)*;
- *World Vision International (WVI, #21904)*;
- *World Wide Hearing (WWHearing, #21923)*. [2013/XJ7693/y/**E**]

♦ Global Partnership on Cities and Biodiversity / see Global Partnership on Local and Subnational Action for Biodiversity (#10536)

♦ Global Partnership for Disability and Development (GPDD) 10530

Secretariat c/o The World Bank, MS G8-803, 1818 H St NW, Washington DC 20433, USA.
URL: http://bbi.syr.edu/gpdd/index.html

History 2008, following activities initiated in 2002. **Aims** Promote the inclusion of the disabled in poverty alleviation and development projects. **Structure** Board of Directors of 12 voting members. Secretariat, headed by Executive Director.
Members Academia; disability and mainstream development NGOs; disabled people organizations; government organizations; financial institutions; foundations; unions; inter-governmental organizations. Included in the above 10 organizations listed in this Yearbook:
CBR Africa Network (CAN, #03616); *Community-Based Rehabilitation Network – South Asia (CBR Network South Asia, #04391)*; *European Association of Service Providers for Persons with Disabilities (EASPD, #06204)*; *Humanity and Inclusion (HI, #10975)*; *Leonard Cheshire Disability (#16443)*; *Light for the World (#16474)*; *MyRight – Empower People with Disabilities*; *Sightsavers International (#19270)*; *VSA*; *World Institute on Disability (WID)*.
IGO Relations Secretariat hosted by *International Bank for Reconstruction and Development (IBRD, #12317)*.
NGO Relations Participates in: *Global Partnership on Children with Disabilities (GPcwd, #10529)*.
[2008/XM8219/y/**F**]

♦ Global Partnership for Education (GPE) 10531

Partenariat mondial pour l'éducation

Acting CEO c/o World Bank, MSN J2-200, 1818 H St NW, Washington DC 20433, USA. T. +12024580825. Fax +12025223923. E-mail: information@globalpartnership.org.
Brussels Office Ave Marnix 17, 2nd floor, 1000 Brussels, Belgium.
URL: http://www.globalpartnership.org/

History 2002. Founded following consensus reached at Monterrey (Mexico). Former names and other names: *Education for All Fast Track Initiative (EFA FTI)* – former (2002 to 2011). **Aims** Mobilize partnerships and investments that transform education systems in developing countries, leaving no one behind. **Structure** Board of Directors; Secretariat. **Finance** Sources: government support. **Activities** Events/meetings; knowledge management/information dissemination; networking/liaising; training/education. **Events** *Global Education and Skills Forum* Dubai (United Arab Emirates) 2016.
Members Developing Countries; Donors and Agencies; Civil Society. Developing countries (43):
Developing countries (43):
Albania, Benin, Bhutan, Burkina Faso, Cambodia, Cameroon, Central African Rep, Djibouti, Ethiopia, Gambia, Georgia, Ghana, Guinea, Guinea-Bissau, Guyana, Haiti, Honduras, Kenya, Kyrgyzstan, Laos, Lesotho, Liberia, Madagascar, Malawi, Mali, Mauritania, Moldova, Mongolia, Mozambique, Nepal, Nicaragua, Niger, Papua New Guinea, Rwanda, Sao Tomé-Principe, Senegal, Sierra Leone, Tajikistan, Timor-Leste, Togo, Vietnam, Yemen, Zambia.
Donor governments (20):
Australia, Belgium, Canada, Denmark, France, Germany, Ireland, Italy, Japan, Luxembourg, Netherlands, Norway, Portugal, Romania, Russia, Spain, Sweden, Switzerland, UK, USA.
Donor agency:
European Commission (EC, #06633).
Multilateral agencies / partners (7):
African Development Bank (ADB, #00283); *Asian Development Bank (ADB, #01422)*; European Commission; *Inter-American Development Bank (IDB, #11427)*; *UNDP (#20292)*; *UNESCO (#20322)*; *UNICEF (#20332)*.
Civil Society Organization:
Global Campaign for Education (GCE, #10264).
IGO Relations *International Institute for Educational Planning (IIEP, #13874)*. Adheres to: *Global Partnership for Effective Development Co-operation (GPEDC, #10532)*. **NGO Relations** Member of (2): *Early Childhood Development Action Network (ECDAN, #05155)*; *Global Action on Disability Network (GLAD, #10165)*. Partner of (1): *Dubai Cares*. Supports (1): *Campaña Latinoamericana por el Derecho a la Educación (CLADE, #03407)*. Participates in: *Global Education Cluster (#10333)*; *Global Partnership on Children with Disabilities (GPcwd, #10529)*; *Inter-agency Network for Education in Emergencies (INEE, #11387)*. [2022/XJ1076/y/**F***]

♦ Global Partnership for Effective Development Co-operation (GPEDC) 10532

Partnerships and Coordination Specialist UNDP, One United Nations Plaza, New York NY 10017, USA. T. +12129065000. Fax +12129065364. E-mail: info@effectivecooperation.org.
Policy Analyst c/o OECD, 2 rue André Pascal, 75775 Paris CEDEX 16, France. T. +33145241979. Fax +33144306147.
URL: http://effectivecooperation.org/

History 1 Dec 2011, Busan (Korea Rep). Created at 4th *High Level Forum on Aid Effectiveness (HLF)*. Former names and other names: *Busan Partnership for Effective Development Co-operation* – former. **Aims** Drive development effectiveness, to maximize the effectiveness of all forms of co-operation for development for the shared benefits of people, planet, prosperity and peace. **Structure** Steering Committee of 25; 4 Co-Chairs. **Events** *High-Level Meeting* Geneva (Switzerland) 2022, *Busan Global Partnership Forum* Busan (Korea Rep) 2021, *Senior-Level Meeting* New York, NY (USA) 2019, *Busan Global Partnership Forum* Seoul (Korea Rep) 2019, *Meeting* Seoul (Korea Rep) 2019. **Publications** *Global Partnership Newsletter*.
Members Endorsed by 160 governments:
Afghanistan, Albania, Algeria, Angola, Armenia, Australia, Austria, Azerbaijan, Bangladesh, Belarus, Belgium, Benin, Bhutan, Bolivia, Bosnia-Herzegovina, Botswana, Brazil, Bulgaria, Burkina Faso, Burundi, Cambodia, Cameroon, Canada, Cape Verde, Central African Rep, Chad, China, Colombia, Comoros, Congo Brazzaville, Congo DR, Cook Is, Costa Rica, Côte d'Ivoire, Croatia, Cyprus, Czechia, Denmark, Djibouti, Dominican Rep, Ecuador, Egypt, El Salvador, Eritrea, Estonia, Ethiopia, Fiji, Finland, France, Gabon, Gambia, Georgia, Germany, Ghana, Greece, Guatemala, Guinea, Guinea-Bissau, Haiti, Holy See, Honduras, Hungary, Iceland, India, Indonesia, Iran Islamic Rep, Iraq, Ireland, Israel, Italy, Jamaica, Japan, Jordan, Kazakhstan, Kenya, Kiribati, Korea Rep, Kosovo, Kuwait, Kyrgyzstan, Laos, Latvia, Lebanon, Lesotho, Liberia, Lithuania, Luxembourg, Madagascar, Malawi, Malaysia, Maldives, Mali, Malta, Marshall Is, Mauritania, Mexico, Micronesia FS, Moldova, Mongolia, Morocco, Mozambique, Myanmar, Namibia, Nepal, Netherlands, New Zealand, Nicaragua, Niger, Nigeria, Norway, Pakistan, Palestine, Panama, Papua New Guinea, Paraguay, Peru, Philippines, Poland, Portugal, Romania, Russia, Rwanda, Samoa, Sao Tomé-Principe, Saudi Arabia, Senegal, Serbia, Sierra Leone, Singapore, Slovakia, Slovenia, Solomon Is, Somalia, South Africa, South Sudan, Spain, Sri Lanka, Sudan, Sweden, Switzerland, Tajikistan, Tanzania UR, Thailand, Timor-Leste, Togo, Tonga, Tunisia, Türkiye, Tuvalu, Uganda, UK, Ukraine, United Arab Emirates, Uruguay, USA, Vanuatu, Vietnam, Yemen, Zambia, Zimbabwe.
Regional entity:
European Union (EU, #08967).
Organizations adhering to the Partnership (56):
- *Abu Dhabi Fund for Development (Abu Dhabi Fund)*;
- *African Development Bank (ADB, #00283)*;
- *African Union (AU, #00488)* (Commission);
- *Arab Bank for Economic Development in Africa (#00904)*;
- *Arab Fund for Economic and Social Development (AFESD, #00965)*;
- *ASEAN (#01141)*;
- *Asian Development Bank (ADB, #01422)*;
- *Asia-Pacific Economic Cooperation (APEC, #01887)*;
- *BetterAid (inactive)*;
- *Bill and Melinda Gates Foundation (BMGF)*;
- *Black Sea Trade and Development Bank (BSTDB, #03278)*;
- *Business and Industry Advisory Committee to the OECD (BIAC, #03385)*;
- *Caribbean Community (CARICOM, #03476)*;
- *Caribbean Development Bank (CDB, #03492)*;
- *Central American Bank for Economic Integration (CABEI, #03658)*;
- *Common Market for Eastern and Southern Africa (COMESA, #04296)*;
- *Commonwealth Secretariat (#04362)*;
- *Consultative Group to Assist the Poor (CGAP, #04768)*;
- *Development Gateway (#05056)*;
- *European Bank for Reconstruction and Development (EBRD, #06315)*;
- *European Investment Bank (EIB, #07599)*;
- *Gavi – The Vaccine Alliance (Gavi, #10077)*;
- *Global Environment Facility (GEF, #10346)*;
- *Global Fund to Fight AIDS, Tuberculosis and Malaria (Global Fund, #10383)*;
- *Global Partnership for Education (GPE, #10531)*;
- *Inter-American Development Bank (IDB, #11427)*;
- *Intergovernmental Authority on Development (IGAD, #11472)*;
- *International Bank for Reconstruction and Development (IBRD, #12317)*;
- International Business Leaders Forum;
- *International Committee of the Red Cross (ICRC, #12799)*;
- *International Disability Alliance (IDA, #13176)*;
- *International Federation of Red Cross and Red Crescent Societies (#13526)*;
- *International Fund for Agricultural Development (IFAD, #13692)*;
- *International Monetary Fund (IMF, #14180)*;
- *International Vaccine Institute (IVI, #15839)*;
- *Inter-Parliamentary Union (IPU, #15961)*;
- *Islamic Development Bank (IsDB, #16044)*;
- *Kuwait Fund for Arab Economic Development (KFAED)*;
- *Learning Network on Capacity Development (LenCD)*;
- *New Partnership for Africa's Development (NEPAD, #17091)*;
- *OECD (#17693)*;
- *OPEC Fund for International Development (OFID, #17745)*;
- *Organisation internationale de la Francophonie (OIF, #17809)*;
- *Organisation of African, Caribbean and Pacific States (OACPS, #17796)*;
- *Organisation of Eastern Caribbean States (OECS, #17804)*;
- *Organization of Ibero-American States for Education, Science and Culture (#17871)*;
- *Pacific Islands Forum Secretariat (#17970)*;
- Pine Global Limited;
- *Saudi Fund for Development (SFD)*;
- *The African Capacity Building Foundation (ACBF, #00233)*;
- *United Nations Global Compact (#20567)*;
- *United Nations Office for Disaster Risk Reduction (UNDRR, #20595)*;
- *United Nations Sustainable Development Group (UNSDG, #20634)*;
- *United Regions Organisation/FOGAR (#20657)*;
- *World Business Council for Sustainable Development (WBCSD, #21254)*;
- *World Organization of United Cities and Local Governments (UCLG, #21695)*. [2023.02.23/XJ4994/**E***]

♦ Global Partnership for Emerging Leaders (internationally oriented national body)

♦ Global Partnership to End Violence Against Children (End Violence Against Children) 10533

Main Office 633 Third Ave, 25th Floor, New York NY 10017, USA. E-mail: secretariat@end-violence.org – info@end-violence.org.
URL: http://www.end-violence.org/

History Jul 2016. **Structure** Board; Executive Committee; Steering Committee of *End Violence Fund*. Secretariat. **Staff** 4.00 FTE, paid. **Events** *End Violence Solutions Summit* Stockholm (Sweden) 2018.
Members Governments; UN agencies; international organizations; civil society; faith groups; private sector; philanthropic foundations; individuals. Members include 60 organizations listed in this Yearbook:
- *African Child in Need (ACIN)*;
- *African Child Policy Forum (ACPF, #00246)*;
- *ChildFund Alliance (#03868)*;
- *ChildFund International (#03869)*;
- *Child Helpline International (CHI, #03870)*;
- *ChildPact (#03874)*;
- *Children Unite*;
- *Child Rights Coalition Asia (CRC Asia, #03883)*;
- *Child Rights International Network (CRIN, #03885)*;
- *Commonwealth Youth Peace Ambassadors Network (CYPAN)*;
- *Consortium for Street Children (CSC)*;
- *Defence for Children International (DCI, #05025)*;
- *Department for International Development (DFID, inactive)*;
- *Disability Rights International (DRI)*;
- *EDUCO*;
- *End Child Prostitution, Child Pornography and Trafficking of Children for Sexual Purposes (ECPAT, #05456)*;
- *End Corporal Punishment (#05457)*;
- *Enfants du Globe*;
- *European Foundation for Missing and Sexually Exploited Children (Missing Children Europe, #07166)*;
- *Firelight Foundation*;
- *Global Partnerships Forum (GPF, #10540)*;
- *Global Peace Development Organization (GPDO)*;
- *Global Social Service Workforce Alliance (#10604)*;
- *Global Support for Kids Initiative (GSK Initiative)*;
- *Human Rights Now (HRN)*;
- *Inclusion International (#11145)*;
- *International Bureau for Children's Rights (IBCR, #12412)*;
- *International Centre for Missing and Exploited Children (ICMEC, #12505)*;
- *International Federation of Red Cross and Red Crescent Societies (#13526)*;
- *International Justice Mission (IJM)*;
- *International Social Service (ISS, #14886)*;
- *It's a Penalty*;
- *Keeping Children Safe*;
- *Maestral International*;
- *Movendi International (#16871)*;
- *No Means No Worldwide (NMNW)*;
- *Oak Foundation*;
- *Observatory on Values and Education in Humanity (OveHum InterNational)*;
- *Penal Reform International (PRI, #18290)*;
- *Plan Børnefonden*;
- *Promundo*;
- *REPSSI (#18848)*;
- *Retrak*;
- *Saffron Social Development Global Foundation (Saffron SDGF)*;
- *Save the Children UK (SC UK)*;
- *Sexual Violence Research Initiative (SVRI, #19251)*;
- *SOS-Kinderdorf International (#19693)*;
- *South Asia Initiative to End Violence Against Children (SAIEVAC, #19719)*;
- *Terre des Hommes International Federation (TDHIF, #20133)*;
- *Together for Girls*;
- *UNHCR (#20327)*;
- *UNICEF (#20332)*;
- *United Nations Office on Drugs and Crime (UNODC, #20596)*;
- *Viva Network (#20800)*;
- *Watchlist on Children and Armed Conflict (Watchlist)*;
- *WHO (#20950)*;
- *Women's World Summit Foundation (WWSF, #21038)*;
- *World Council of Churches (WCC, #21320)*;
- *World Vision International (WVI, #21904)*;
- *ygap*. [2021/XM5573/y/**F**]

♦ Global Partnership for Financial Inclusion (GPFI) 10534

Contact c/o SME Finance Forum, 2121 Pennsylvania Ave NW, Washington DC 20433, USA.
URL: http://www.gpfi.org/

History Founded as the main implementing mechanism of the endorsed action plan by leaders of *Group of Twenty (G20, #10793)*. Officially launched 10 Dec 2010, Seoul (Korea Rep). **Aims** Help countries put into practice the Principles for Innovative Financial Inclusion; strengthen data for measuring financial inclusion develop methodologies for countries wishing to set targets. **Structure** Jointly chaired by the present, former and next leaders of *Group of Twenty (G20, #10793)*. Sub-Groups (3): G20 principles and Standard Setting Bodies (SSBs); SME Finance; Data and Measurement. **Activities** Work spearheaded by: *Alliance for Financial Inclusion (AFI, #00679)*; *Consultative Group to Assist the Poor (CGAP, #04768)*; *International Finance Corporation (IFC, #13597)*; *International Bank for Reconstruction and Development (IBRD, #12317)*. **Events** *Plenary Meeting* 2020, *Global SME Finance Forum* Amsterdam (Netherlands) 2019, *G20 High-Level Symposium on Aging and Financial Inclusion* Tokyo (Japan) 2019, *Plenary Meeting* Tokyo (Japan) 2019, *Global SME Finance Forum* Madrid (Spain) 2018. **NGO Relations** Partner of (1): *Responsible Finance Forum (RFF)*. [2020/XJ5271/**F***]

♦ Global Partnership on Forest and Landscape Restoration (GPFLR) . 10535

Coordinator c/o IUCN, 70 Mayfield Avenue, Toronto ON M6S 1K6, Canada. T. +14167633437. E-mail: gpflr@iucn.org.
Facilitator Wageningen UR Ctr for Development Innovation, PO Box 88, 6700 AB Wageningen, Netherlands. T. +31317481397.
URL: http://www.forestlandscaperestoration.org/

History Initiated 2003 by *International Union for Conservation of Nature and Natural Resources (IUCN, #15766)*, *World Wide Fund for Nature (WWF, #21922)* and Forestry Commission of Great Britain. Spearheaded by *International Union for Conservation of Nature and Natural Resources (IUCN, #15766)*. **Aims** Catalyze dynamic, voluntary action through sharing diverse experiences on restoration efforts which deliver tangible benefits to both local communities and nature through a landscape approach, while also fulfilling international commitments on forests. **Structure** Steering Committee; e-Secretariat (voluntary virtual). **Activities** Research/documentation; events/meetings. **Events** *Mediterranean Forest Week* Agadir (Morocco) 2017.
Members Governments; organizations; academic/research institutes; communities; individuals. Organizations (21):
- *Bioversity International (#03262)*;
- *Center for International Forestry Research (CIFOR, #03646)*;
- *Commonland Foundation*;
- *FAO (#09260)*;
- *Forest Stewardship Council (FSC, #09869)*;
- *International Bank for Reconstruction and Development (IBRD, #12317)* (World Bank);
- *International Model Forest Network (IMFN, #14175)*;
- *International Tropical Timber Organization (ITTO, #15737)*;
- *International Union for Conservation of Nature and Natural Resources (IUCN, #15766)*;
- *International Union of Forest Research Organizations (IUFRO, #15774)*;
- *Program on Forests (PROFOR, #18525)*;
- *Secretariat of the Convention on Biological Diversity (SCBD, #19197)*;
- *Secretariat of the United Nations Convention to Combat Desertification (Secretariat of the UNCCD, #19208)*;
- *Society for Ecological Restoration International (SERI)*;
- *Tropenbos International (TBI)*;
- *UN Environment Programme World Conservation Monitoring Centre (UNEP-WCMC, #20295)*;
- *UNEP (#20299)*;
- *United Nations Forum on Forests (UNFF, #20562)*;
- Wageningen University and Research;
- *World Agroforestry Centre (ICRAF, #21072)*;
- *World Resources Institute (WRI, #21753)*.

Governments (6):
Germany, Netherlands, Rwanda, Switzerland, UK, USA. [2023/XM5817/y/**F**]

♦ Global Partnership for Local Action (internationally oriented national body)

♦ Global Partnership on Local and Subnational Action for Biodiversity 10536

Address not obtained.
URL: http://www.cbd.cbd.int/subnational/partners-and-initiatives/

History Proposed during Meeting on Cities and Biodiversity, Mar 2007, Curitiba (Brazil). Formally launched, 7 Oct 2008, Barcelona (Spain), under the title *Global Partnership on Cities and Biodiversity*. **Aims** Provide a voice for local and subnational governments in the discussion on implementing the Convention on Biological Biodiversity through the contribution of these levels of government. **Structure** Advisory Committee of Cities; Advisory Committee of Subnational Governments; *Urban Biodiversity and Design (URBIO, #20729)*. Facilitated by *Secretariat of the Convention on Biological Diversity (SCBD, #19197)*. **Languages** English. **Staff** Part-time staff provided by *Secretariat of the Convention on Biological Diversity (SCBD, #19197)* and *Local Governments for Sustainability (ICLEI, #16507)*. **Finance** No specific budget. **Activities** Events/meetings.
Members Participants, include UN organizations, NGOs, a scientific network and an Advisory Committee on Cities and Biodiversity. Organizations listed in this Yearbook (11):
International Union for Conservation of Nature and Natural Resources (IUCN, #15766); *Local Governments for Sustainability (ICLEI, #16507)* (and its Local Action for Biodiversity Initiative); *Secretariat of the Convention on Biological Diversity (SCBD, #19197)*; *UNEP (#20299)*; *UNESCO (#20322)*; *United Nations Human Settlements Programme (UN-Habitat, #20572)*; *United Nations University Institute for the Advanced Study of Sustainability (UNU-IAS, #20643)*; *Urban Biodiversity and Design (URBIO, #20729)*; *WHO (#20950)*.
Cities (7) in 7 countries:
Brazil, Canada, France, Germany, Japan, Mexico, South Africa.
IGO Relations *Convention on Biological Diversity (Biodiversity convention, 1992)*. [2014.07.09/XJ4717/y/**E**]

♦ Global Partnership for Oceans (GPO) 10537

Contact address not obtained. E-mail: enb@iisd.org.

History Launched Feb 2012, Singapore (Singapore). 'Declaration for Healthy and Productive Oceans to Help Reduce Poverty' adopted, Jun 2012, at Rio+20 Conference. Until Jan 2015, Secretariat hosted by *International Bank for Reconstruction and Development (IBRD, #12317)*. **Aims** Tackle widely documented problems of *overfishing*, *pollution*, and habitat loss. **Structure** Interim Working Group of 30 representatives drawn from partner organizations.
Members Participants support Declaration: Governments and Government Agencies; Private Sector; Civil Society Organizations; Foundation; Regional and Multilateral Organizations; Research; UN Conventions.
Governments and government agencies from 23 countries:
Antigua-Barbuda, Australia, Belize, Cook Is, Denmark, Fiji, Finland, Germany, Grenada, Iceland, Jamaica, Kiribati, Korea Rep, Marshall Is, Mauritius, Monaco, New Zealand, Norway, Palau, Samoa, Seychelles, Sweden, USA.
Included in the above, 3 organizations listed in this Yearbook:
Deutsche Gesellschaft für Internationale Zusammenarbeit (GIZ); *Nordic Council of Ministers (NCM, #17260)*; *United States Agency for International Development (USAID)*.
Private Sector includes 1 organization listed in this Yearbook:
Global Aquaculture Alliance (GAA, #10238).
Civil Society Organizations include 27 organizations listed in this Yearbook:
- *Aquaculture Stewardship Council (ASC, #00885)*;
- *Blue Ventures*;
- *Conservation International (CI)*;
- *Counterpart International (FSP)*;
- *Environmental Defense Fund (EDF)*;
- *Fauna & Flora International (FFI, #09277)*;
- *Foundation of the Peoples of the South Pacific International (FSPI, #09968)*;
- *Global Aquaculture Alliance (GAA, #10238)*;
- *Global Development Research Centre (GDRC)*;
- *Global Forum on Oceans, Coasts and Islands (GOF, #10377)*;
- *Global Oceans (GO)*;
- *International Coalition of Fisheries Associations (ICFA, #12614)*;
- *International Seafood Sustainability Foundation (ISSF)*;
- *International Union for Conservation of Nature and Natural Resources (IUCN, #15766)*;
- *MarViva Foundation (#16591)*;
- *Oceana*;
- *Ocean Recovery Alliance (ORA, #17686)*;
- *PYXERA Global*;
- *SeaWeb*;
- *Stakeholder Forum for a Sustainable Future (SF)*;
- *Sustainable Fisheries Partnership (#20058)*;
- *The Nature Conservancy (TNC)*;
- *Volunteers for Economic Growth Alliance (VEGA)*;
- *Wildlife Conservation Society (WCS)*;
- *WorldFish (#21507)*;
- *World Ocean Council (WOC, #21680)*;
- *World Wide Fund for Nature (WWF, #21922)*.

Foundations include 2 organizations listed in this Yearbook:
MacArthur Foundation; *The Ocean Foundation (TOF)*.
Regional and Multilateral Organizations (9):
Global Environment Facility (GEF, #10346); *Inter-American Development Bank (IDB, #11427)*; *Organisation of African, Caribbean and Pacific States (OACPS, #17796)*; *Pacific Community (SPC, #17942)*; *Pacific Islands Forum Fisheries Agency (FFA, #17969)*; *Pacific Islands Forum Secretariat (#17970)*; *Secretariat of the Pacific Regional Environment Programme (SPREP, #19205)*; *The World Bank Group (#21218)*; Western Indian Ocean Coastal Challenge.
Research institutes include 3 organizations listed in this Yearbook:
Global Change Institute (GCI); *Institute for Marine and Antarctic Studies (IMAS)*; *University of the South Pacific (USP, #20703)*.
UN and Conventions (5):
Convention on Wetlands of International Importance Especially as Waterfowl Habitat (Convention on Wetlands, 1971); *FAO (#09260)*; *Intergovernmental Oceanographic Commission (IOC, #11496)*; *UNDP (#20292)*; *UNEP (#20299)*. [2015/XJ6767/y/**B**]

♦ Global Partnership on Output-Based Aid / see Global Partnership for Results-Based Approaches (#10539)

♦ Global Partnership for the Prevention of Armed Conflict (GPPAC) . . 10538

Partenariat mondial pour la prévention des conflits armés

Exec Dir Laan van Meerdervoort 70, 2517 AN The Hague, Netherlands. T. +31703110970. Fax +31703600194. E-mail: info@gppac.net.
URL: http://www.gppac.net/

History 2003. Founded by *Global Partnership for the Prevention of Armed Conflict Foundation (GPPAC Foundation)*. Former names and other names: *European Centre for Conflict Prevention (ECCP)* – former (2003); *European Conference on Conflict Prevention* – alias; *European Platform for Conflict Prevention* – alias. Registration: No/ID: 41217404, Netherlands. **Aims** Build a new international consensus and enable joint action, through a multi-stakeholder partnership including civil society, governments, regional organizations and the UN, to prevent violent conflict and promote peacebuilding, based on regional and global action agendas. **Structure** International Steering Group (ISG); *Global Partnership for the Prevention of Armed Conflict Foundation (GPPAC Foundation)*; Board; Global Secretariat; Regional Secretariats; Regional Steering Groups (RSGs); Programme Steering Committee; Working Groups; ISG Liaisons; Regions (15). **Languages** Arabic, English, French, Russian, Spanish. **Staff** 15.00 FTE, paid; 4.00 FTE, voluntary. **Finance** Sources: donations. Supported by: *Catholic Organization for Relief and Development (Cordaid)*; City of The Hague (Netherlands); Dutch Ministries of Foreign and of Economic Affairs; Federal Government of Belgium; *Netherlands Institute of International Relations – Clingendael*; Norwegian Ministry of Foreign Affairs; *Rockefeller Brothers Fund (RBF)*; Swedish Ministry of Foreign Affairs. **Events** *Conference on EU Civil Society Dialogue Network* Amsterdam (Netherlands) 2011, *DW Global Media forum* Bonn (Germany) 2008, *Global conference on civil society forging partnerships to prevent violent conflict and build peace* New York, NY (USA) 2005. **Publications** *GPPAC Newsletter*. Annual Report; articles.
Members Regional Secretariats (16):
African Centre for the Constructive Resolution of Disputes (ACCORD); *Coordinadora Regional de Investigaciones Económicas y Sociales (CRIES, #04812)*; *femLINKpacific*; *Foundation for Tolerance International (FTI)*; *Global Partnership for the Prevention of Armed Conflict Foundation (GPPAC Foundation)*; *Initiatives for International Dialogue*; *International Centre on Conflict and Negotiation (ICCN)*; *Nansen Center for Peace and Dialogue (NCPD, #16934)*; *Nonviolence International (NI, #17152)*; *NPI Africa*; *Peace Boat*; *Permanent Peace Movement (PPM)*; *Regional Centre for Strategic Studies, Colombo (RCSS)*; *Servicios y Asesoria para la Paz (SERAPAZ)*; *Southeast Asian Conflict Studies Network (SEACSN, #19762)*; *West Africa Network for Peacebuilding (WANEP, #20878)*.
Active members (about 200). Membership countries not specified.
NGO Relations Member of (5): *Asia Democracy Network (ADN, #01265)*; *Global Network of Women Peacebuilders (GNWP, #10503)*; *International Campaign to Abolish Nuclear Weapons (ICAN, #12426)*; *NGO Working Group for Women, Peace and Security (NGOWG, #17129)*; *NGO Working Group on the Security Council (#17128)*. Cooperates with (1): *Alliance for Peacebuilding*. Supports (1): *Civil Society Platform for Peacebuilding and Statebuilding (CSPPS, #03970)*. [2020/XJ3541/y/**F**]

♦ Global Partnership for the Prevention of Armed Conflict Foundation (internationally oriented national body)

♦ Global Partnership for Results-Based Approaches (GPRBA) 10539

Chair The World Bank, 1818 H St NW, Washington DC 20433, USA. T. +12024731000. E-mail: rbfinfo@gprba.org.
URL: http://www.gprba.org/

History 2003. Former names and other names: *Global Partnership on Output-Based Aid (GPOBA)* – former (2003 to 2019). **Aims** Fund, design, demonstrate, and document results-based financing (RBF) approaches to improve delivery of basic infrastructure and social services to the poor in developing countries. **Structure** Program Council, consisting of representatives from each of the partners, including World Bank representative serving as Chair. **Staff** 17.00 FTE, paid. **Activities** Financial and/or material support; projects/programmes. Active in: Armenia, Bangladesh, Bolivia, Brazil, Burkina Faso, Cameroon, Colombia, Ethiopia, Ghana, Honduras, India, Indonesia, Kenya, Lesotho, Liberia, Mali, Mongolia, Morocco, Mozambique, Myanmar, Nepal, Nigeria, Palestine, Philippines, Senegal, Solomon Is, Sri Lanka, Tanzania UR, Uganda, Uzbekistan, Vietnam, Yemen, Zambia. **Publications** Annual Report.
Members Partners (6):
Australian Aid (inactive); *Department for International Development (DFID, inactive)*; Dutch Directorate-General for International Cooperation (DGIS); *International Bank for Reconstruction and Development (IBRD, #12317)* (World Bank); *International Finance Corporation (IFC, #13597)*; *Swedish International Development Cooperation Agency (Sida)*.
NGO Relations Member of (1): *Global Water Operators' Partnerships Alliance (GWOPA, #10652)*. [2021.10.05/XJ6910/y/**E***]

♦ Global Partnership for Safe and Sustainable Agriculture / see GLOBALG.A.P (#10386)

♦ Global Partnerships Forum (GPF) 10540

Pres 55 Bank Street, White Plains NY 10606, USA. E-mail: info@partnerships.org.
URL: http://www.partnerships.org/

History 2010, New York, NY (USA). **Aims** Address economic and social challenges within a global forum through innovative partnerships; work with global *leaders* to create greater opportunity through collaboration. **Structure** Board of Directors; Ambassadors; International Advisory Board; Advisors. **Languages** English, French. **Staff** 4.00 FTE, paid. **Finance** Annual budget: 375,000 USD. **Activities** Capacity building; knowledge management/information dissemination; projects/programmes. **Events** *Symposium on One Ocean, achieving Sustainability Through Sanctuaries* New York, NY (USA) 2015, *Conference* London (UK) 2012. **Publications** *GPF Newsletter* (annual). **NGO Relations** Member of (1): *Global Partnership to End Violence Against Children (End Violence Against Children, #10533)*. Also links with national associations. [2023.03.01/XJ5018/**F**]

♦ **Global Partnership for Social Accountability (GPSA)** **10541**
Contact address not obtained. E-mail: gpsa@worldbank.org.
URL: http://www.worldbank.org/gpsa/
History Dec 2012. **Aims** Improve development results by supporting capacity building for enhanced beneficiary feedback and participation. **Structure** Steering Committee, chaired by *International Bank for Reconstruction and Development (IBRD, #12317)* and comprising a representation of CSOs, donors and governments. **Finance** GPSA Multi-donor Trust Fund of currently US$ 23 million. Donors: *International Bank for Reconstruction and Development (IBRD, #12317); Ford Foundation (#09858); Open Society Foundations (OSF, #17763)*. **Publications** *GPSA Newsletter*. **IGO Relations** Global partners include: *Banque ouest africaine de développement (BOAD, #03170); Latin American Centre for Development Administration (#16294); European Commission (EC, #06633); UNICEF (#20332)*.
NGO Relations Global partners include:
- *Africa Freedom of Information Centre (AFIC, #00175);*
- *Aga Khan Foundation (AKF, #00545);*
- *American Council for Voluntary International Action (InterAction);*
- *CARE International (CI, #03429);*
- *Catholic Organization for Relief and Development (Cordaid);*
- *CIVICUS: World Alliance for Citizen Participation (#03962);*
- *Consumer Unity and Trust Society (CUTS);*
- *Ford Foundation (#09858);*
- *Fundación CIDEAL de Cooperación e Investigación;*
- *German Marshall Fund of the United States (GMF);*
- *HELVETAS Swiss Intercooperation;*
- *Humanistisch Instituut voor Ontwikkelingssamenwerking (Hivos);*
- *Innovations, environnement, développement Afrique (IED);*
- *Inter-American Dialogue (IAD);*
- *Inter-American Foundation (IAF, #11431);*
- *INTERMON OXFAM;*
- *International Day of the African Child and Youth (IDAY, #13140);*
- *International Federation of Red Cross and Red Crescent Societies (#13526);*
- *Keystone Accountability (#16186);*
- *Open Society Foundations (OSF, #17763);*
- *Overseas Development Institute (ODI);*
- *Oxfam GB;*
- *Partnership for Transparency Fund (PTF, #18245);*
- *Society for Participatory Research in Asia (PRIA);*
- *TrustAfrica (#20251);*
- *Voluntary Service Overseas (VSO);*
- *World Federation of Engineering Organizations (WFEO, #21433);*
- *World Learning;*
- *World Vision International (WVI, #21904).*

[2013/XJ7663/**E***]

♦ Global Partnership to Stop TB / see Stop TB Partnership (#19999)

♦ **Global Partnership for Sustainable Development Data (Data4SDGS)** **10542**
Exec Dir address not obtained. E-mail: info@data4sdgs.org.
URL: http://www.data4sdgs.org/
History Launched Sep 2015. **Aims** Help stakeholders across countries and sectors fully harness the data revolution for sustainable development, using this new knowledge to improve lives and protect the planet. **Activities** Research and development; networking/liaising.
Members Data Champions Governments; NGOs; business. Governments of 10 countries:
Canada, Colombia, France, Italy, Kenya, Mexico, Nigeria, Senegal, UK, USA.
Organizations include 39 organizations listed in this Yearbook:
- *African Union (AU, #00488)* (Commission);
- *Africa's Voices Foundation;*
- *CARE International (CI, #03429);*
- *Children's Investment Fund Foundation (CIFF);*
- *CIVICUS: World Alliance for Citizen Participation (#03962);*
- *Ford Foundation (#09858);*
- *Gavi – The Vaccine Alliance (Gavi, #10077);*
- *Global Health Council (GHC, #10402);*
- *Global Integrity;*
- *Global Open Data for Agriculture and Nutrition (GODAN, #10514);*
- *Group on Earth Observations (GEO, #10735);*
- *ILO (#11123);*
- *International Association for Official Statistics (IAOS, #12052);*
- *International Institute for Sustainable Development (IISD, #13930);*
- *International Monetary Fund (IMF, #14180);*
- *International Statistical Institute (ISI, #15603);*
- *Internews;*
- *OECD (#17693);*
- *ONE (#17728);*
- *Plan International (#18386);*
- *Publish What You Fund;*
- *Restless Development;*
- *Southern Voice on Post-MDG International Development Goals (Southern Voice, #19880);*
- *Sustainable Development Solutions Network (SDSN, #20054);*
- *The William and Flora Hewlett Foundation;*
- *The World Bank Group (#21218);*
- *Transparency, Accountability and Participation Network (TAP Network, #20222);*
- *Transparency International (TI, #20223);*
- *UNDP (#20292);*
- *UNESCO Institute for Statistics (UIS, #20306);*
- *UNIDO (#20336);*
- *United Nations Economic and Social Commission for Asia and the Pacific (ESCAP, #20557);*
- *United Nations Economic Commission for Africa (ECA, #20554);*
- *United Nations Office for Project Services (UNOPS, #20602);*
- *UN Women (#20724);*
- *World Agroforestry Centre (ICRAF, #21072);*
- *World Council on City Data (WCCD);*
- *World Resources Institute (WRI, #21753);*
- *World Wide Web Foundation (#21936).*

NGO Relations *CartONG (#03591).* [2019.02.12/XM4975/y/**F**]

♦ **Global Partnership for Zero Leprosy** **10543**
Secretariat Task Force for Global Health, 330 West Ponce de Leon Ave, Decatur GA 30030, USA. E-mail: info@zeroleprosy.org.
URL: https://zeroleprosy.org/
History 2018. **Aims** Facilitate alignment of the leprosy community; accelerate effective collaborative action toward the goal of zero leprosy. **Structure** Leadership Team. Secretariat located at: *Task Force for Global Health (TFGH, #20098)*.
Members Partnership organizations, including 9 organizations listed in this Yearbook:
Acción Sanitaria y Desarrollo Social (ANESVAD); Damien Foundation – Voluntary Organization for Leprosy and TB Control (AF); FAIRMED; International Association for Integration, Dignity and Economic Advancement (IDEA, #11967); International Federation of Anti-Leprosy Associations (ILEP, #13355); Leprosy Mission International (TLMI, #16446); Novartis Foundation; Sasakawa Memorial Health Foundation; *Task Force for Global Health (TFGH, #20098).*
Observer:
WHO (#20950).
NGO Relations Member of (1): *Neglected Tropical Diseased NGO Network (NNN, #16969).*
[2020/AA1034/y/**F**]

♦ GlobalPartnersUnited (internationally oriented national body)
♦ Global Peace Campaign (internationally oriented national body)
♦ Global Peace Containers / see Peace Containers
♦ Global Peace Development Organization (internationally oriented national body)
♦ Global Peace and Development Service Alliance (unconfirmed)
♦ Global Peace Foundation (internationally oriented national body)

♦ **Global Peace Foundation (GPF)** **10544**
Main Office 9320 Annapolis Rd, Ste 100, Lanham MD 20706, USA. T. +12026434733. Fax +12404471709. E-mail: info@globalpeace.org.
Contact 6912 220th Str SW, Suite 200, Mountlake Terrace WA 98043, USA. T. +14255827901.
URL: http://www.globalpeace.org/
History Set up 2009. Registration: No/ID: 26-4599860, USA. **Aims** Promote an innovative, values-based approach to peacebuilding, guided by the vision of One Family under God. **Structure** Global Leadership Council. **Activities** Advocacy/lobbying/activism; events/meetings;. Active in: Brazil, Cambodia, India, Indonesia, Ireland, Japan, Kenya, Korea Rep, Malaysia, Mongolia, Nepal, Nigeria, Paraguay, Philippines, Tanzania UR, Uganda, Uruguay, USA. **Events** *International Forum on One Korea* Seoul (Korea Rep) 2021, *International Forum on One Korea* Seoul (Korea Rep) 2020, *International Forum on One Korea* Seoul (Korea Rep) 2020, *International Forum on One Korea* Seoul (Korea Rep) 2020, *Smart Technology for Sustainable Development and Procurement Conference* Suwon (Korea Rep) 2019. [2020/XM5413/f/**F**]

♦ Global Peace Service Network / see Global Peace Services USA
♦ Global Peace Services USA (internationally oriented national body)
♦ Global Peatlands Initiative (unconfirmed)

♦ **Global Pediatric Endocrinology and Diabetes (GPED)** **10545**
Contact Ste 334, 3381 Cambie Street, Vancouver BC V5Z 4R3, Canada. E-mail: info@globalpedendo.org.
URL: http://www.globalpedendo.org/
History 2010. Incorporated in Canada. Registered with charitable status, 2017. **Aims** Improve the care of children living in low and middle-income countries (LMICs) presenting with endocrine disorders or diabetes, through public advocacy, training and education of local *health* professionals, clinical collaborations and development of translational clinical research. **Structure** Executive Committee; Working Groups. **Languages** English. **Staff** Voluntary. **Finance** No membership fee. **Activities** Advocacy/lobbying/activism; healthcare; training/education. **Publications** *GPED Newsletter* (4 a year).
Members Organizations. National associations in 4 countries:
Canada, India, Japan, USA.
Regional associations (7):
African Society for Paediatric and Adolescent Endocrinology (ASPAE, #00465); Arab Society for Paediatric Endocrinology and Diabetes (ASPED, #01048); Asia Pacific Paediatric Endocrine Society (APPES, #01988); Australasian Paediatric Endocrine Group (APEG); European Society for Paediatric Endocrinology (ESPE, #08678); International Society for Pediatric and Adolescent Diabetes (ISPAD, #15344); Latin American Society for Pediatric Endocrinology (#16381).
NGO Relations *Caring and Living As Neighbours (CLAN).* [2018.09.06/XM5409/y/**C**]

♦ Global Pediatric MDS Initiative (unconfirmed)
♦ Global Peering Forum (internationally oriented national body)
♦ Global Penguin Society (internationally oriented national body)
♦ Global Pension Alliance / see World Pension Alliance (#21719)
♦ Global Performance Based Standards for Project Management Personnel / see Global Alliance for the Project Professions (#10220)
♦ Global Perspectives in Education / see American Forum for Global Education
♦ Global Pharma Health Fund (internationally oriented national body)
♦ Global Philanthropy Forum (internationally oriented national body)
♦ Global Philanthropy Partnership (internationally oriented national body)

♦ **Global Philanthropy Project (GPP)** **10546**
Contact c/o Community Initiatives, 1000 Broadway, Suite 480, Oakland CA 94607, USA. E-mail: info@globalphilanthropyproject.org.
URL: https://globalphilanthropyproject.org/
History Founded 2009. **Aims** Expand global philanthropic support to advance the human rights of lesbian, gay, bisexual, transgender, and intersex – *LGBTI* – people in the Global South and East. **Structure** Executive Committee. **Activities** Research/documentation; events/meetings.
Members Organizations (20), including 13 organizations listed in this Yearbook:
Baring Foundation; Ford Foundation (#09858); Fund for Global Human Rights (FDHM); Global Fund for Women (GFW, #10384); Humanistisch Instituut voor Ontwikkelingssamenwerking (Hivos); International Trans Fund (ITF, #15720); Mama Cash (#16560); Oak Foundation; Open Society Foundations (OSF, #17763); Sigrid Rausing Trust; The Other Foundation (#17913); UHAI EASHRI – East African Sexual Health and Rights Initiative (UHAI); Urgent Action Fund for Women's Human Rights (UAF).
NGO Relations Member of: *Ariadne – European Funders for Social Change and Human Rights (Ariadne, #01103); Worldwide Initiatives for Grantmaker Support (WINGS, #21926).* [2020.03.11/XM8810/y/**F**]

♦ **Global Phosphorus Research Initiative (GPRI)** **10547**
Co-Founder CSPR, Dept of Thematic Studies – Water and Environmental Studies, Linköping Univ, SE-581 83 Linköping, Sweden.
URL: http://phosphorusfutures.net/global-research/
History Co-founded 2008 by Australian and Swedish researchers. **Aims** Research how phosphorus security can ensure global food security. **Activities** Research and development; research/documentation.
Members Research institutes (6) in 5 countries:
Australia, Canada, France, Netherlands, Sweden. [2019/XM6906/**F**]

♦ Global Plan of Action for the Conservation, Management and Utilization of Marine Mammals (inactive)

♦ **Global Planners Network (GPN)** **10548**
Contact c/o APA, 205 N Michigan Ave, Suite 1200, Chicago IL 60601, USA. E-mail: global@planning.org.
URL: http://www.globalplannersnetwork.org/
History as an umbrella organization. **Events** *Connecting people and ideas* Sydney, NSW (Australia) 2014, *Congress* Montréal, QC (Canada) 2010, *Conference* ZhenJiang (China) 2008, *Congress* ZhenJiang (China) 2008, *Congress* Vancouver, BC (Canada) 2006.
Members Signatory: recognized professional planning associations of nations that have signed up to the Vancouver Declaration of 2006 in 6 countries:
Austria, Canada, Ireland, New Zealand, UK, USA.
Included in the above, 2 regional associations:
Commonwealth Association of Planners (CAP, #04307); European Council of Spatial Planners (ECTP-CEU, #06843).
Supporter members:
International Federation for Housing and Planning (IFHP, #13450); International Society of City and Regional Planners (ISOCARP, #15012). [2019/XM3561/y/**E**]

♦ **Global Planning Education Association Network (GPEAN)** **10549**
Contact address not obtained. E-mail: gpeannetwork@gmail.com.
URL: https://www.gpean-planning.org/
History Jul 2001. **Aims** Improve quality and visibility of planning and planning education worldwide. **Events** *World Planning Schools Congress* Bali (Indonesia) 2022, *World Planning Schools Congress* Lisbon (Portugal) 2021, *World planning schools congress* Rio de Janeiro (Brazil) 2016, *World planning schools congress* Perth, WA (Australia) 2011.
Members National organizations (6) in 6 countries:
Australia, Brazil, Canada, France, Indonesia, USA.
International organizations (5):
Asian Planning Schools Association (APSA, #01667); Asociación Latinoamericana de Escuelas de Urbanismo y Planeación (ALEUP, #02212); Association of African Planning Schools (AAPS, #02359); Association of European Schools of Planning (AESOP, #02542); Association pour la promotion de l'enseignement et de la recherche en aménagement et urbanisme (APERAU, #02875). [2021/XF7073/y/**F**]

♦ **Global Plant Council** **10550**
Communications Officer address not obtained. E-mail: info@globalplantcouncil.org.
URL: http://globalplantcouncil.org/
History 16 Jul 2009, Honolulu, HI (USA). Registration: Switzerland. **Aims** Increase awareness of the central role of *plant science* in resolving issues such as world hunger, energy, climate change, health and well-being, sustainability and environmental protection; define and engage in coordinated strategies to address these issues. **Structure** Executive Committee. Executive Director. **Events** *Annual Meeting* Saskatoon, SK (Canada) 2017, *Annual Meeting* Jeju (Korea Rep) 2012, *Annual Meeting* Qingdao (China) 2011, *Annual Meeting* Montréal, QC (Canada) 2010.
Members Organizations (19), including the following 5 listed in this Yearbook:
African Crop Science Society (ACSS, #00280); European Plant Science Organization (EPSO, #08211); Federation of European Societies of Plant Biology (FESPB, #09548); International Crop Science Society (ICSS, #13115); Societas Physiologiae Plantarum Scandinavica (SPPS, #19452).
NGO Relations Member of: *Global Open Data for Agriculture and Nutrition (GODAN, #10514)*. Cooperates with: *Global Forum on Agricultural Research (GFAR, #10370).* [2020/XJ0919/y/**B**]

♦ **GlobalPlatform** **10551**
Administrative Office 544 Hillside Rd, Redwood City CA 94062, USA. E-mail: secretariat@globalplatform.org.
URL: http://www.globalplatform.org/
Aims Identify, develop and publish specifications which facilitate the secure and interoperable deployment and management of multiple embedded applications on secure chip technology. **Structure** Board of Directors, including Chairman, Vice-Chairman and Secretary/Treasurer. Executive Team, comprising Executive Director, Technical Director and Operations Secretariat. Committees (3): Card; Device; Systems. Advisory Council. Task Forces (3): Mobile; Government; IP Connectivity. **Members** Full; Participating; Observer; Public Entity; Consultant. **NGO Relations** In liaison with technical committees of: *Comité européen de normalisation (CEN, #04162)*. Partner of: *oneM2M (#17732).* [2013/XJ4969/**F**]

♦ Global Platform for Higher Education in Emergencies (unconfirmed)

♦ **Global Platform for Sustainable Natural Rubber (GPSNR)** **10552**
Secretariat 2 Science Park Drive, 01-03 Ascent, Singapore 118222, Singapore. T. +6592970636. E-mail: info@gpsnr.org.
URL: https://www.gpsnr.org/
History Launched Oct 2018. Development initiated by CEOs of *World Business Council for Sustainable Development (WBCSD, #21254)*. **Aims** Lead improvements in the socioeconomic and environmental performance of the natural rubber value chain. **Structure** General Assembly; Executive Committee; Working Groups; Secretariat.
Members Companies; organizations. Membership countries not specified. Organizations, include 9 listed in this Yearbook:
Organizations, include 9 listed in this Yearbook:
BirdLife International (#03266); Conservation International (CI); Forest Stewardship Council (FSC, #09869); HCV Network Ltd (HCV Network, #10865); Mighty Earth; Rainforest Alliance; SNV Netherlands Development Organisation (SNV); World Resources Institute (WRI, #21753); World Wide Fund for Nature (WWF, #21922).
Affiliate members include 3 organizations listed in this Yearbook:
Center for International Forestry Research (CIFOR, #03646); Centre de coopération internationale en recherche agronomique pour le développement (CIRAD, #03733); European Tyre and Rubber Manufacturers' Association (ETRMA, #08963).
NGO Relations *International Rubber Study Group (IRSG, #14772); ISEAL (#16026).* [2020/XM8891/y/**F**]

♦ Global Play Foundation (internationally oriented national body)
♦ Global Policy Forum (internationally oriented national body)
♦ Global Policy Forum Europe / see GPF Europe (#10684)

♦ **Global Polio Eradication Initiative (GPEI)** **10553**
Contact WHO, Avenue Appia 20, 1211 Geneva 27, Switzerland. E-mail: polionews@who.int.
URL: http://www.polioeradication.org/
History 1988, by *WHO (#20950)*. **IGO Relations** Partner: *UNICEF (#20332)*. **NGO Relations** Partner: *Every Woman Every Child (EWEC, #09215); Rotary International (RI, #18975).* [2018.06.01/XF6600/**F**]

♦ Global Political Trends Center (internationally oriented national body)
♦ Global Potential (internationally oriented national body)

♦ **Global Power and Propulsion Society (GPPS)** **10554**
Main Office Landis Gyr-Str 1, 6300 Zug, Switzerland. T. +41446325072. E-mail: info@gpps.global.
URL: http://www.gpps.global/
Aims Provide an environment for professionals to meet and exchange results and ideas, with a specific focus on power generation and propulsion systems. **Structure** Executive Committee; Advisory Committee. **Activities** Awards/prizes/competitions; events/meetings. **Events** *International Forum for Aviation and Energy Systems* Zurich (Switzerland) 2021, *Conference* Chania (Greece) 2020, *International Forum for Aviation and Energy Systems* Zurich (Switzerland) 2020, *Conference* Beijing (China) 2019, *International Forum for Aviation and Energy Systems* Zurich (Switzerland) 2019. **Publications** *GPPS Journal*; *GPPS Newsletter*. [2021/XM7904/**C**]

♦ Global Precipitation Climatology Centre (internationally oriented national body)
♦ Global Press Institute (internationally oriented national body)

♦ **Global Privacy Assembly (GPA)** **10555**
Secretariat Info Commissioner's Office, Wycliffe House, Walter Lane, Wilmslow, SK9 5AF, UK. E-mail: secretariat@globalprivacyassembly.org.
URL: https://globalprivacyassembly.org/
History 1979. **Aims** Provide leadership at international level in data protection and privacy. **Structure** Executive Committee; Secretariat. **Activities** Events/meetings. **Events** *Conference* Tirana (Albania) 2019, *Conference* Brussels (Belgium) 2018, *Conference* Amsterdam (Netherlands) 2015, *Conference* Warsaw (Poland) 2013, *Conference* Punta del Este (Uruguay) 2012. **Publications** *Conference Newsletter*.
Members Public authorities (122). Accredited members in 74 countries and territories:
Albania, Andorra, Argentina, Armenia, Australia, Belgium, Benin, Bosnia-Herzegovina, Bulgaria, Burkina Faso, Canada, Cape Verde, Colombia, Costa Rica, Côte d'Ivoire, Croatia, Cyprus, Czechia, Denmark, Estonia, Finland, France, Georgia, Germany, Ghana, Gibraltar, Greece, Guernsey, Hong Kong, Hungary, Iceland, Ireland, Isle of Man, Israel, Italy, Japan, Jersey, Korea Rep, Kosovo, Latvia, Liechtenstein, Lithuania, Luxembourg, Mali, Malta, Mauritius, Mexico, Moldova, Monaco, Montenegro, Morocco, Netherlands, New Zealand, North Macedonia, Norway, Peru, Philippines, Poland, Portugal, Romania, Senegal, Serbia, Slovakia, Slovenia, South Africa, Spain, Sweden, Switzerland, Tunisia, Türkiye, UK, Ukraine, Uruguay, USA.
Regional accredited members (3):
Council of Europe (CE, #04881); European Union (EU, #08967); International Criminal Police Organization – INTERPOL (ICPO-INTERPOL, #13110).
NGO Relations Instrumental in setting up (1): *International Working Group on Data Protection in Telecommunications (IWGDPT, #15908). Association francophone des autorités de protection des données personnelles (AFAPDP, #02606).* [2021/XM1745/c/**F**]

♦ **Global Private Capital Association (GPCA)** **10556**
CEO 589 8th Ave, Floor 18, New York NY 10018, USA.
Asia Office 1 Nanson Road, Level 3, Singapore 238909, Singapore.
URL: https://www.globalprivatecapital.org/
History 2004. Former names and other names: *Emerging Markets Private Equity Association (EMPEA)* – former (2004 to 2021). **Aims** Catalyze private equity and venture capital investment in emerging markets. **Structure** Board of Directors, comprising Chairman, Vice-Chairman and 16 members. Advisory Council. Regional Councils (2): Africa; Asia. Legal and Regulatory Council. **Events** *Members Meeting* Singapore (Singapore) 2019. **Publications** *Newswatch*. Annual Report. **Members** Premier; Full; Associate. Firms (300) worldwide. **IGO Relations** *African Development Bank (ADB, #00283); Agencia Española de Cooperación Internacional para el Desarrollo (AECID); Asian Development Bank (ADB, #01422); Commonwealth Secretariat (#04362); DEG – Deutsche Investitions- und Entwicklungsgesellschaft; European Bank for Reconstruction and Development (EBRD, #06315); International Finance Corporation (IFC, #13597); Overseas Private Investment Corporation (OPIC)*. **NGO Relations** *Development Bank of Southern Africa (DBSA); Japan Bank for International Cooperation (JBIC); Association for Private Capital Investment in Latin America (LAVCA, #02871); Nederlandse Financierings-Maatschappij voor Ontwikkelingslanden (FMO); SME Finance Forum (#19323).* [2020/XJ5081/**C**]

♦ Global Programme of Action for the Protection of the Marine Environment from Land-Based Activities (see: #20299)
♦ Global Programme Against Money Laundering / see United Nations Global Programme Against Money Laundering, Proceeds of Crime and the Financing of Terrorism (#20568)

♦ **Global Progressive Forum (GPF)** **10557**
Forum progressive mondial
SG European Parliament, Rue Wiertz 60, 1047 Brussels, Belgium. E-mail: info@globalprogressiveforum.org.
URL: http://www.globalprogressiveforum.org/
History 29 Nov 2003, Brussels (Belgium). Founded on the initiative of *Group of the Progressive Alliance of Socialists and Democrats in the European Parliament (S and D, #10786), Party of European Socialists (PES, #18249)* and *Foundation for European Progressive Studies (FEPS, #09954)*, with the cooperation of *Socialist International (SI, #19340)*. **Aims** Create a global, progressive community for a fairer, more inclusive globalization. **NGO Relations** Partner of (1): *Progressive Alliance for Freedom, Justice and Solidarity (Progressive Alliance, #18530)*. Cooperates with (1): *Global Progressive Youth Forum (GPYF, #10558).* [2019/XM2534/**F**]

♦ **Global Progressive Youth Forum (GPYF)** **10558**
Forum progressiste mondial des jeunes
Contact MJS France, 10 rue de Solférino, 75007 Paris, France.
History by *Young European Socialists (YES, #21989)* and *International Union of Socialist Youth (IUSY, #15815)*. **NGO Relations** Member of: *Decent Work Alliance (inactive)*. Close cooperation with: *Global Progressive Forum (GPF, #10557).* [2007/XM2535/**F**]

♦ Global Project Against Hate and Extremism (internationally oriented national body)

♦ **Global Project Logistics Network (GPLN)** **10559**
Coordinator address not obtained. E-mail: coordinator@gpln.net.
URL: http://www.gpln.net/
History 2004. **Aims** Act as the professional projects logistics network of independent companies specializing in international projects movements by air, sea and land as well as specialized lifts and the special handling of oversized, out-of-gauge and heavy lift cargo. **Events** *Annual General Meeting* Rotterdam (Netherlands) 2022, *Annual General Meeting* Dubai (United Arab Emirates) 2017, *European Conference on Inland Terminals* Liège (Belgium) 2013. **Publications** *Global Project Logistics NEWSletter* (6 a year).
Members Full in 95 countries and territories:
Afghanistan, Angola, Argentina, Australia, Austria, Bahrain, Bangladesh, Belgium, Benin, Brazil, Bulgaria, Cameroon, Canada, Chile, China, Colombia, Congo DR, Costa Rica, Croatia, Czechia, Denmark, Dominican Rep, Egypt, Eritrea, Estonia, Finland, France, Germany, Ghana, Guatemala, Honduras, Hong Kong, Hungary, India, Indonesia, Iran Islamic Rep, Iraq, Ireland, Israel, Italy, Japan, Jordan, Kazakhstan, Kenya, Korea Rep, Kuwait, Lebanon, Libya, Lithuania, Madagascar, Malaysia, Maldives, Malta, Mexico, Morocco, Mozambique, Myanmar, Netherlands, New Zealand, Nigeria, Norway, Pakistan, Panama, Philippines, Poland, Portugal, Qatar, Réunion, Romania, Russia, Saudi Arabia, Singapore, Slovakia, Slovenia, South Africa, South Sudan, Spain, Sri Lanka, Sudan, Sweden, Switzerland, Syrian AR, Taiwan, Tanzania UR, Thailand, Tunisia, Türkiye, Uganda, UK, Ukraine, United Arab Emirates, Uruguay, USA, Venezuela, Vietnam. [2021/XM5263/**F**]

♦ **Global Protection Cluster (GPC)** **10560**
Coordinnator c/o UNHCR HQ, Case Postale 2500, DEPOT, 1211 Geneva 2, Switzerland. E-mail: gpc@unhcr.org.
URL: http://www.globalprotectioncluster.org/
History 2011. **Aims** Improve predictability, leadership, effectiveness and accountability of response to ensure that protection is central to humanitarian action. **Structure** Steering Committee; Support Cell; Coordination Team; *UNHCR (#20327)* acts as head. Includes *Child Protection Working Group (CPWG)*. **Languages** Arabic, English, French, Russian, Spanish. **Staff** 8.00 FTE, paid. **Activities** Events/meetings. **Publications** *Forced Migration Review*. **Members** Not a membership organization. **IGO Relations** Organizations involved include: *UNDP (#20292); UNHCR (#20327); UNICEF (#20332); United Nations Mine Action Service (UNMAS, #20585); United Nations Population Fund (UNFPA, #20612); World Food Programme (WFP, #21510).* [2020/XJ7692/**E**]

♦ Global Psychology and Language Research Association (internationally oriented national body)
♦ Global Public Policy Institute (internationally oriented national body)

♦ **Global Public Policy Network (GPPN)** **10561**
Contact address not obtained. E-mail: gppn.conference@sciencespo.fr.
URL: https://www.gppnetwork.org/
History 2005. Founded as a partnership between 3 educational institutes in UK, USA and France. **Aims** Address the most pressing public policy challenges of the 21st century. **Activities** Events/meetings; training/education. **Events** *Conference* Tokyo (Japan) 2021, *Conference* London (UK) 2020, *Conference* Singapore (Singapore) 2019, *Conference* Singapore (Singapore) 2019, *Conference* New York, NY (USA) 2018.
Members Universities in public policy (7) in 7 countries:
Brazil, France, Germany, Japan, Singapore, UK, USA. [2021/AA1632/**F**]

♦ Global Public-Private Partnership for Handwashing with Soap / see Global Handwashing Partnership (#10396)

♦ **Global Pulse Confederation (GPC)** **10562**
Main Office Silver Tower, DMCC Office no 1 – Lower Level, PO Box 340503, Dubai, United Arab Emirates. T. +97143633612. E-mail: office@globalpulses.com.
Exec Dir address not obtained.
URL: http://globalpulses.com/
History 25 Jun 1963, Paris (France). Former names and other names: *International Pulse Trade and Industry Confederation (IPTIC)* – former; *Confédération internationale du commerce et des industries des légumes secs (CICILS)* – former; *Confederación Internacional del Comercio e Industrias de Legumbres Secas* – former. Registration: United Arab Emirates, Dubai; France. **Aims** Serve as *documentation* centre for the industry; act as a single voice to represent its interests, particularly in relation to international institutions, and protect mutual interests; promote pulse consumption for both human and animal *nutrition*; take measures necessary to make international trade in the field easier; harmonize world *standards*. **Structure** General Assembly (every 2 years); Executive; Standing Committee. **Languages** English, French, German, Italian, Spanish. **Staff** 5.00 FTE, paid. **Finance** Sources: members' dues. **Activities** Advocacy/lobbying/activism; events/meetings; knowledge management/information dissemination; networking/liaising. **Events** *Annual Convention* Sydney, NSW (Australia) 2023, *Americas Pulses Congress* Cancún (Mexico) 2022, *Americas Pulses Congress* Cancún (Mexico) 2022, *Annual Convention* Dubai (United Arab Emirates) 2022, *Annual Convention* 2021.
Members Full National Associations; Associate Companies. Members in 40 countries and territories:
Algeria, Argentina, Australia, Belgium, Brazil, Bulgaria, Canada, Chile, China, Costa Rica, Denmark, Egypt, France, Germany, Greece, India, Italy, Japan, Jordan, Kenya, Lebanon, Libya, Mexico, Myanmar, Niger, Pakistan, Singapore, South Africa, Spain, Sri Lanka, Sudan, Sweden, Switzerland, Tanzania UR, Tunisia, Türkiye, UK, United Arab Emirates, USA, Venezuela.
Consultative Status Consultative status granted from: *ECOSOC (#05331)* (Ros C); *FAO (#09260)* (Liaison Status). **IGO Relations** Standing Committees liaise with: *OECD (#17693)*. Recognized by: *European Commission (EC, #06633)*. Observer to: *Codex Alimentarius Commission (CAC, #04081)*. **NGO Relations** Member of: *International Agri-Food Network (IAFN, #11599)*. In liaison with technical committees of: *International Organization for Standardization (ISO, #14473).* [2022/XC2389/**C**]

♦ Global Quality Assurance Conference (meeting series)

♦ **Global RCE Network Education for Sustainable Development** **10563**
Contact c/o UNU-IAS, 5-53-70 Jingumae, Shibuya-ku, Tokyo, 150-8925 Japan. T. +81354671212. Fax +81334992828. E-mail: rceservicecentre@unu.edu.
URL: http://www.rcenetwork.org/

History ESD project launched 2003, by *United Nations University Institute for the Advanced Study of Sustainability (UNU-IAS, #20643)*, in response to the UN resolution on the Decade of Education for Sustainable Development (UNDESD). ESD project functions through 2 initiatives of which the global multi-stakeholder global network of Regional Centres of Expertise on ESD (RCEs) is one. **Aims** Translate global objectives into the context of the local communities in which they operate. **Activities** Networking/liaising; research and development; training/education. **Events** *Europe RCE Meeting* Heraklion (Greece) 2019, *Africa RCE Meeting* Luyengo (Eswatini) 2019, *Global RCE Conference* Cebu City (Philippines) 2018, *Americas RCE Meeting* Posadas (Argentina) 2018, *Asia-Pacific Meeting* Sydney, NSW (Australia) 2018. **Publications** *RCE Bulletin* (12 a year). **NGO Relations** *UbuntuNet Alliance for Research and Education Networking (#20275)*.
[2019.05.30/XM8011/**F**]

♦ Global Real Estate Institute (unconfirmed)

♦ **Global Reconciliation** **10564**
Exec Dir Monash Univ, Dept of Medicine, Alfred Hospital, Commercial Road, Prahran VIC 3181, Australia.
URL: http://www.globalreconciliation.org/

History Founded as *Global Reconciliation Network*. **Aims** Engage individuals from different cultural, national, philosophical and religious traditions on issues, topics and projects of common interest and concern around the theme of reconciliation to work together. **Structure** Management Board; Executive Committee. **Languages** English. **Staff** 5 FTE, paid and voluntary. **Finance** Donations; philanthropic grants; competitive research grants. **Activities** Awareness raising. **Events** *Conference* Colombo (Sri Lanka) 2013, *Conference* Amman (Jordan) 2009, *Conference* Amman (Jordan) 2008, *Conference* Sarajevo (Bosnia-Herzegovina) 2005, *Conference* India 2004. [2018.10.27/XM2013/**F**]

♦ Global Reconciliation Network / see Global Reconciliation (#10564)
♦ Global Recordings Network (internationally oriented national body)
♦ Global Refuge (internationally oriented national body)
♦ Global Refugee Leaders Forum (internationally oriented national body)
♦ Global Regions Forum / see United Regions Organisation/FOGAR (#20657)
♦ Global Register of Migratory Species (internationally oriented national body)

♦ **Global Rehabilitation Alliance** **10565**
Contact c/o Dept of Rehabilitation Medicine, Hannover Medical School, Carl-Neuberg-Str 1, 30625 Hannover, Germany.
URL: http://www.global-rehabilitation-alliance.org/

History Founded 22 May 2018, Geneva (Switzerland) by 14 organizations. **Aims** Advocate for the *health* systems strengthening to provide rehabilitation, as an integral component of Universal Health Coverage. **Structure** Board. **Languages** English. **Activities** Advocacy/lobbying/activism; awareness raising.
Members Founding members (14):
American Speech-Language-Hearing Association (ASH); *Dementia Alliance International (DAI, #05028)*; *Global Alliance for Musculoskeletal Health (G-MUSC, #10213)*; *Humanity and Inclusion (HI, #10975)*; *ICRC MoveAbility Foundation (MoveAbility, #11087)*; *International Committee of the Red Cross (ICRC, #12799)*; *International Council of Nurses (ICN, #13054)*; *International Society for Prosthetics and Orthotics (ISPO, #15390)*; *International Society of Physical and Rehabilitation Medicine (ISPRM, #15366)*; *International Spinal Cord Society (ISCoS, #15581)*; *World Confederation for Physical Therapy (WCPT, #21293)*; *World Federation for NeuroRehabilitation (WFNR, #21464)*; *World Federation of Chiropractic (WFC, #21420)*; *World Federation of Occupational Therapists (WFOT, #21468)*.
IGO Relations *WHO (#20950)*. [2019.03.12/XM7372/y/**C**]

♦ Global Relief Alliance (internationally oriented national body)
♦ Global Relief Foundation, Ghana (internationally oriented national body)

♦ **Global Renewable Fuels Alliance (GRFA)** **10566**
Contact address not obtained. T. +14168476497.
URL: http://www.globalrfa.org/

History 25 Feb 2009, San Antonio TX (USA). **Aims** Promote expanded use of renewable fuels throughout the world through advocacy of sound public policy and responsible research. **Structure** Board. **Languages** English.
Members National fuel associations (3) in 3 countries:
Brazil, Canada, USA.
Regional association:
ePURE (#05517). [2017/XJ2860/y/**C**]

♦ Global Reporting Centre (internationally oriented national body)

♦ **Global Reporting Initiative (GRI)** **10567**
Chief Exec PO Box 10039, 1001 EA Amsterdam, Netherlands. T. +31205310000. Fax +3120205310031. E-mail: info@globalreporting.org – communications@globalreporting.org.
Street address Barbara Strozzilaan 336, 1083 HN Amsterdam, Netherlands.
URL: http://www.globalreporting.org/

History 1997. Founded by *CERES* and *Tellus Institute*. Formally inaugurated as a *UNEP (#20299)* collaborating organization, 2002. Registration: EU Transparency Register, No/ID: 01437575131-45, Start date: 28 Jan 2011; Stichting, Start date: 2002, Netherlands. **Aims** As an independent international organization, help businesses, governments and other organizations understand and communicate their sustainability impacts, enabled through GRI Standards. **Structure** Board of Directors; Global Sustainability Standards Board; Stakeholder Council; Regional Hubs (6); Secretariat. **Languages** English. **Staff** 90.00 FTE, paid. **Finance** Sources: donations; government support; members' dues; revenue from activities/projects. **Activities** Capacity building; events/meetings; guidance/assistance/consulting; knowledge management/information dissemination; publishing activities; standards/guidelines; training/education. **Events** *Global Conference* Amsterdam (Netherlands) 2020, *GRI Standards Launch Meeting* Abu Dhabi (United Arab Emirates) 2017, *Global Conference* Amsterdam (Netherlands) 2016, *Regional Conference on Aligning Corporate Sustainability with Sustainable Development Goals* Bangkok (Thailand) 2015, *Global Conference* Amsterdam (Netherlands) 2013. **Publications** *GRI Sustainability Reporting Standards (GRI Standards)*. **Information Services** *Sustainability Disclosure Database*.
Members Organizational members of the GRI GOLD Community include the following 2 organizations listed in this Yearbook:
CERES; *European Investment Bank (EIB, #07599)*.
Consultative Status Consultative status granted from: *ECOSOC (#05331)* (Special); *UNCTAD (#20285)* (Special). **IGO Relations** Cooperates with (1): *UNCTAD (#20285)*. Collaborating Centre of: *UNEP (#20299)*. Global strategic partnerships with: *OECD (#17693)*. **NGO Relations** Memorandum of Understanding with (4): *CDP (#03621)*; *Earth Charter International (ECI, #05161)*; *International Integrated Reporting Council (IIRC, inactive)*; *World Business Council for Sustainable Development (WBCSD, #21254)*. Member of (3): *Green Economy Coalition (GEC, #10717)*; *Natural Capital Coalition (NCC, #16952)*; *World Benchmarking Alliance (WBA, #21228)*. Global strategic partnership with: *United Nations Global Compact (#20567)*. Subscriber to: *ISEAL (#16026)*. [2021.05.20/XF1351/y/**F**]

♦ **Global Research on Acute Conditions Team (GREAT)** **10568**
Registered Office Via Antonio Serra 54, 00191 Rome RM, Italy. Fax +39699367613. E-mail: info@greatnetwork.org.
URL: http://www.greatnetwork.org/

History Registration: No/ID: 97603950581, Italy. **Aims** Build a new way in doing research through the concept of translational *medicine*. **Structure** General Assembly; Executive Committee; Scientific Committee; General Secretariat. **Languages** English, French, German, Italian. **Staff** 3.00 FTE, paid. **Events** *International Meeting* Florence (Italy) 2022, *International Meeting* Rome (Italy) 2021, *International Meeting* 2020, *International Meeting* Edinburgh (UK) 2019, *International Meeting* Venice (Italy) 2018.
Members Full in 40 countries:
Argentina, Australia, Austria, Belarus, Belgium, Brazil, China, Czechia, Denmark, Egypt, Finland, France, Germany, India, Ireland, Italy, Japan, Kenya, Korea Rep, Lebanon, Lithuania, Luxembourg, Netherlands, New Zealand, Norway, Poland, Portugal, Romania, Russia, Serbia, Singapore, South Africa, Spain, Sweden, Switzerland, Tunisia, Türkiye, UK, USA, Uzbekistan.
[2021/XM4313/**D**]

♦ **Global Research and Advocacy Group (GRAG)** **10569**
Contact PO Box 45030, FANN 12522 Dakar, Senegal. E-mail: info@globalresearchandadvocacygroup.org.
URL: http://www.globalresearchandadvocacygroup.org/

Aims Promote and protect minorities' rights to safeguard their *health* and make informed decisions regarding their *sexual* behavior, reproduction, and family formation. **Structure** Board of Directors; International Consultative Committee. **NGO Relations** Partners include: *Council on International Educational Exchange (CIEE, #04901)*; *Counterpart International (FSP)*; *FHI 360*; *MPact Global Action for Gay Men's Health and Rights (MPact, #16875)*; *Global Health Council (GHC, #10402)*; *Hope for African Children Initiative (no recent information)*; *International Rectal Microbicide Advocates (IRMA)*; *IntraHealth International*; *Joint United Nations Programme on HIV/AIDS (UNAIDS, #16149)*; *Population Council (#18458)*; *Save the Children International (#19058)*; *UNDP (#20292)*; *WHO (#20950)*; *Woodrow Wilson International Center for Scholars (WWICS)*.
[2015/XJ9372/**D**]

♦ **Global Research Alliance on Agricultural Greenhouse Gases (GRA)** . **10570**
Contact address not obtained. E-mail: secretariat@globalresearchalliance.org.
URL: https://globalresearchalliance.org/

History Launched Dec 2009, by a Charter. **Aims** Provide a framework for cooperation and investment in research activities that support the agricultural sector in meeting the growing demand for food while reducing greenhouse gas emissions intensity. **Structure** Council; Secretariat. **Languages** English, Spanish. **Activities** Awards/prizes/competitions; capacity building; knowledge management/information dissemination; research and development. **Events** *Annual Council Meeting* Santiago (Chile) 2022, *Annual Council Meeting* Canberra, ACT (Australia) 2021, *Annual Council Meeting* Bali (Indonesia) 2019, *Annual Council Meeting* Berlin (Germany) 2018.
Members Members in 66 countries:
Argentina, Australia, Bangladesh, Belgium, Benin, Bolivia, Brazil, Cameroon, Canada, Chile, China, Colombia, Congo DR, Costa Rica, Côte d'Ivoire, Cuba, Denmark, Dominican Rep, Ecuador, Egypt, Eswatini, Ethiopia, Finland, France, Germany, Ghana, Honduras, Indonesia, Ireland, Italy, Japan, Kenya, Korea Rep, Lithuania, Malawi, Malaysia, Mexico, Mongolia, Namibia, Netherlands, New Zealand, Nicaragua, Nigeria, Norway, Panama, Paraguay, Peru, Philippines, Poland, Samoa, Senegal, South Africa, Spain, Sri Lanka, Sweden, Switzerland, Thailand, Tunisia, Türkiye, Uganda, UK, Uruguay, USA, Vietnam, Zambia, Zimbabwe. [2022.10.28/XM8372/**C***]

♦ **Global Research Alliance for Sustainable Finance and Investment (The Alliance)** **10571**
Contact address not obtained. E-mail: info@sustainablefinancealliance.org.
URL: https://www.sustainablefinancealliance.org/

History Founded 2017. **Aims** Promote multi-disciplinary rigorous and impactful academic research on sustainable finance and investment. **Structure** Organizing Committee. **Activities** Events/meetings. **Events** *Conference* New Haven, CT (USA) 2023, *Conference* Zurich (Switzerland) 2022, *Conference* Beijing (China) 2021, *Conference* New York, NY (USA) 2020, *Conference* Oxford (UK) 2019.
Members Universities (25) in 11 countries:
Australia, Canada, China, France, Germany, Netherlands, New Zealand, Sweden, Switzerland, UK, USA.
[2020.03.16/XM7813/**C**]

♦ **Global Research Business Network (GRBN)** **10572**
Exec Dir address not obtained. E-mail: info@grbn.org.
URL: http://www.grbn.org/

History 2011, by *Americas Research Industry Alliance (ARIA)*, *Asia Pacific Research Committee (APRC, #02011)* and *European Federation of Associations of Market Research Organizations (EFAMRO, #07055)*. **Aims** Promote and advance the business of research by developing and supporting strong autonomous national research associations.
Members Organizations (3):
Americas Research Industry Alliance (ARIA); *Asia Pacific Research Committee (APRC, #02011)*; *European Federation of Associations of Market Research Organizations (EFAMRO, #07055)*. [2015/XJ9576/y/**F**]

♦ **Global Research Collaboration for Infectious Disease Preparedness (GLOPID-R)** **10573**
Contact address not obtained. E-mail: contact@glopid-r.org.
URL: https://www.glopid-r.org/

History Founded 2013. **Aims** Bring together research funding organizations on a global scale to facilitate an effective and rapid research of a significant outbreak of a new or re-emerging infectious disease with epidemic and pandemic potential. **Structure** Assembly; Board of Chairs; Secretariat. **Events** *World Forum on Research and Innovation for New Coronavirus* Geneva (Switzerland) 2020. **Publications** *GLOPID-R Newsletter*.
Members Full (28) in 20 countries:
Argentina, Australia, Brazil, Canada, Egypt, France, Germany, India, Italy, Japan, Kenya, Korea Rep, Mexico, Netherlands, Norway, South Africa, Spain, Thailand, UK, USA.
Included in the above, 10 organizations listed in this Yearbook:
African Academy of Sciences (AAS, #00193); *Bill and Melinda Gates Foundation (BMGF)*; *Department for International Development (DFID, inactive)*; *European Commission (EC, #06633)* (DG Research and Innovation); *International Development Research Centre (IDRC, #13162)*; *Wellcome Trust*.
Observers (2):
Coalition for Epidemic Preparedness Innovations (CEPI, #04057); *WHO (#20950)*. [2020/XM8859/y/**C**]

♦ Global Research Consortium on Economic Structural Transformation (unconfirmed)

♦ **Global Research Council (GRC)** **10574**
Exec Sec address not obtained. T. +441793418031. E-mail: grc@fapesp.br.
URL: https://www.globalresearchcouncil.org/

Aims Represent research funding agencies from around the world, dedicated to promote sharing of data and best practices for high-quality collaboration among funding agencies worldwide. **Structure** Annual Meeting; Governing Board; Regional Meetings. **Activities** Capacity building; events/meetings; knowledge management/information dissemination; research/documentation. **Events** *Annual Meeting* Panama (Panama) 2022, *Europe Regional Meeting* 2021, *Annual Meeting* Durban (South Africa) 2021, *Asia-Pacific Regional Meeting* Iran Islamic Rep 2021, *Middle East and North Africa Regional Meeting* Saudi Arabia 2020. **Publications** Action plans; discussion papers; statements; surveys. **Members** Engineering funding agencies. Membership countries not specified. **IGO Relations** *OECD (#17693)*; *United Nations (UN, #20515)*. **NGO Relations** Cooperates with (1): *TWAS (#20270)*. [2022/XJ7062/**F**]

♦ **Global Research Forum on Sustainable Production and Consumption (GRF)** **10575**
Contact address not obtained. E-mail: grfsustainable@gmail.com.
URL: https://grf-spc.weebly.com/

Aims Strengthen the community of researchers and practitioners engaged in research on the worldwide transition to sustainable production and consumption systems. **Structure** Executive Committee. **Activities** Events/meetings. **Events** *Transforming production and consumption – bridging sustainability research with policy and practice* Hong Kong (Hong Kong) 2019.
Members Individuals in 24 countries:
Brazil, Canada, Chile, China, Denmark, Eswatini, Germany, India, Japan, Latvia, Lithuania, Malaysia, Mexico, Netherlands, Norway, Philippines, Singapore, South Africa, Sweden, Switzerland, Türkiye, UK, Ukraine, USA.
NGO Relations *Sustainable Consumption Research and Action Initiative (SCORAI, #20053)*.
[2019/XM7550/v/**F**]

♦ **Global Research Management Network (GRMN)** **10576**
Contact Research Management / ACU, Woburn House, 20-24 Tavistock Square, London, WC1H 9HF, UK. T. +442073872655.
History Apr 2001. **Aims** Promote communication and sharing of best practices amongst members. **Structure** Managed by *Association of Commonwealth Universities, The (ACU, #02440)* in partnership with *Society of Research Administrators International (SRA)*. **Finance** Members' dues (annual): pounds55. **Publications** *Research Global* (3 a year) – magazine. E-mail briefings; reports. **Members** Full (about 400) in over 40 countries. Membership countries not specified. [2011/XJ0182/**E**]

♦ **Global Resilience Partnership (GRP)** **10577**
CEO Stockholm Resilience Cnt, Stockholm Univ, Kräftriket 2B, SE-114 19 Stockholm, Sweden. E-mail: info@globalresiliencepartnership.org.
URL: http://www.globalresiliencepartnership.org/
History Set up as a public-private partnership. **Aims** Work towards a resilient, sustainable and prosperous *future* for *vulnerable* people and places. **Structure** Advisory Council; Secretariat. Hosted by: *Stockholm Resilience Centre (#19995)*. **Finance** Sources: government support.
NGO Relations Partner of: *UN Climate Resilience Initiative (A2R, #20284)*.
Partners include 15 organizations listed in this Yearbook:
- *Alliance for Water Stewardship (AWS, #00727)*;
- *CARE International (CI, #03429)*;
- *Comité permanent inter-Etats de lutte contre la sécheresse dans le Sahel (CILSS, #04195)*;
- *Department for International Development (DFID, inactive)*;
- *Global Environment Facility (GEF, #10346)*;
- *Global Facility for Disaster Reduction and Recovery (GFDRR, #10352)*;
- *Intergovernmental Authority on Development (IGAD, #11472)*;
- *International Institute for Environment and Development (IIED, #13877)*;
- *Small Enterprise Education and Promotion Network (SEEP)*;
- *Swedish International Development Cooperation Agency (Sida)*;
- *Stockholm Resilience Centre (#19995)*;
- *UNDP (#20292)*;
- *United States Agency for International Development (USAID)*;
- *We Effect*;
- *Wetlands International (#20928)*.

Hosts: *Resilience Measurement Evidence and Learning Community of Practice (RMEL CoP, #18912)* [2021/XM7167/y/**F**]

♦ Global Resilient Cities Network (unconfirmed)
♦ Global Resource Action Center for the Environment (internationally oriented national body)
♦ Global Resource Bank (internationally oriented national body)
♦ Global Resource Foundation / see Global Resource Bank

♦ **Global Resource Information Database (GRID)** **10578**
Base de données mondiale d'information sur les ressources – Base de Datos de Recursos Mundiale
Dir GRID-Geneva, Science Div, UN Environment, Chemin des Anemones 11, Châtelaine, 1219 Geneva, Switzerland. T. +41229178237.
URL: https://www.unenvironment.org/about-un-environment/why-does-un-environment-mat ter/global-resource-information-database-grid/
History 1985, with centres in Geneva (Switzerland) and Nairobi (Kenya), as a function-specific element within the framework of *UNEP (#20299)*, incorporated into a Programme Activity Centre by decision 16/25 of 16th Session of Governing Council. Originally one of 6 main components of the now United Nations system-wide *Earthwatch (inactive)*; currently related to Earthwatch through UNEP's Programme, managed by UNEP Division of Early Warning and Assessment (DEWA). Also referred to as *UNEP/GRID*. **Aims** Underpin UNEP's assessment activities and its efforts to support global and regional *environmental* decision-making by improving access to high-quality data about the state of the world's environment. **Structure** A global network of governmental, non-governmental and academic centres of excellence in remotely sensed data gathering which also have geo-spatial capability to manage this data. Formerly coordinated through a Programme Activity Centre based at UNEP Headquarters; since 1995, centres tend to operate independently. Offices located in: Arendal (Norway); Brazil; Budapest (Hungary); Christchurch (New Zealand); Geneva (Switzerland); Moscow (Russia); Nairobi (Kenya); Sioux Falls SD (USA); Tbilisi (Georgia); Tsukuba (Japan); Warsaw (Poland). **Languages** English, French. **Finance** Sources: governments; international agencies. **Activities** Knowledge management/information dissemination; capacity building; training/education. **Events** *AfricaGIS conference* Abidjan (Côte d'Ivoire) 1995, *Workshop on indicators of sustainable development for decision making* Ghent (Belgium) 1995, *ENRIN Asia Pacific regional meeting* Kathmandu (Nepal) 1995. **Publications** A GEO related publications; foresight briefs. Information Services: Geospatial servers; statistics and indicators; spatial data infrastructure; cloud technology; multiple interactive platforms.
Members Affiliated centres in 11 countries:
Brazil, Georgia, Hungary, Japan, Kenya, New Zealand, Norway, Poland, Russia, Switzerland, USA.
IGO Relations As well as UNEP and its regional offices, cooperates in programmes with:
(1) within UNEP – Post-Conflict and Disaster Branch; Regional Office for Europe; Regional Office for Africa; Regional Office for West Asia; Regional Office for Asia and Pacific; *Convention on International Trade in Endangered Species of Wild Fauna and Flora (CITES, 1973)*; *Basel Convention on the Control of Transboundary Movements of Hazardous Wastes and Their Disposal (UNCRTD, 1989)*; *Global Environment Facility (GEF, #10346)* / Biosafety; Joint UNEP/OCHA Unit; UN Environment Chemicals; Minamata Convention; Barcelona Convention; Convention on Biological Diversity (CBD); Ramsar Convention. (2) Other UN Agencies – *FAO (#09260)*; *International Bank for Reconstruction and Development (IBRD, #12317)*; International Strategy for Disaster Risk Reduction (UNISDR); UNDP's Bureau of Crisis Prevention and Recovery (BCPR); *United Nations Office for the Coordination of Humanitarian Affairs (OCHA, #20593)*; *UNESCO (#20322)*; *United Nations Economic Commission for Europe (UNECE, #20555)*; *United Nations Human Settlements Programme (UN-Habitat, #20572)*; *United Nations Institute for Training and Research (UNITAR, #20576)*; *United Nations Office for Project Services (UNOPS, #20602)*; *WHO (#20950)*.
(3) Other agencies: *CGIAR System Organization (CGIAR, #03843)*.
Cooperates with: *Conservation of Arctic Flora and Fauna (CAFF, #04728)*.
NGO Relations Instrumental in setting up: *Cities Environment Report on the Internet (CEROI, no recent information)*. *International Science Initiative in the Russian Arctic (ISIRA)*. Partner of: *Many Strong Voices (MSV, #16568)*; *ProAct (#18506)*. [2019.12.12/XF2721/**F***]

♦ Global Resource Services (internationally oriented national body)
♦ Global Response Medicine (internationally oriented national body)
♦ GLOBAL RESPONSIBILITY – Austrian Platform for Development and Humanitarian Aid (internationally oriented national body)
♦ Global Resuscitation Alliance (unconfirmed)
♦ Global Reverse Phase Protein Array Workshop (meeting series)

♦ **Global Rewilding Alliance (GRA)** **10579**
Co-Dir WILD, 717 Poplar Ave, Boulder CO 80304, USA. E-mail: info@rewildingglobal.org.
Co-Dir address not obtained.
URL: https://rewildingglobal.org/
History 2020. Founded by *WILD Foundation (WILD, #20956)*. **Aims** Mobilize the power of people working together to rewild the Earth and stabilize the climate.
Members Full (over 125). Membership countries not specified. Included in the above, 12 organizations listed in this Yearbook:
African Conservation Foundation (ACF); *African Parks (AP, #00411)*; *Cheetah Conservation Fund (CCF)*; *Endangered Wildlife Trust (EWT)*; *European Wilderness Society (#09094)*; *Global Center for Indigenous Leadership and Lifeways (GCILL)*; *Peace Parks Foundation (#18281)*; *Rewilding Europe (#18933)*; *Save the Elephants (STE)*; *The European Nature Trust (TENT)*; *Wilderness Foundation Africa*; *Wild Europe Foundation (#20955)*.
NGO Relations Partner of (1): *WILD Foundation (WILD, #20956)*. [2022/AA2214/**C**]

♦ Global Rhetoric Society (unconfirmed)

♦ **Global Rice Science Partnership (GRiSP)** **10580**
Programme Dir c/o IRRI, APO Box 7777, Manila, Philippines. T. +632580560 ext 2707.
History Set up as research programme of *CGIAR System Organization (CGIAR, #03843)*, 2010. Led by *International Rice Research Institute (IRRI, #14754)*, *African Association for a Unified System of Business Laws (UNIDA, #00218)* and *International Centre for Tropical Agriculture (#12527)*, in collaboration with *Centre de coopération internationale en recherche agronomique pour le développement (CIRAD, #03733)*, *Institut de recherche pour le développement (IRD)*, *Japan International Research Centre for Agricultural Sciences (JIRCAS)* and 900 research and development partners worldwide. **Aims** Reduce poverty and hunger; improve human health and nutrition; reduce the environmental footprint; enhance the ecosystem resilience of rice production systems through high-quality international research research, partnership and leadership. **Finance** Budget (2015): US$ 112.6 million. **Activities** Research. **Events** *Africa Forum* Cotonou (Benin) 2015, *Africa Forum* Cotonou (Benin) 2014. [2015/XJ9834/**E**]

♦ Global Rights (internationally oriented national body)
♦ Global Rights Alert (internationally oriented national body)
♦ Global Risk Forum (internationally oriented national body)
♦ Global Rivers Environmental Education Network (internationally oriented national body)

♦ **Global Road Safety Partnership (GRSP)** **10581**
CEO c/o IFRC, PO Box 303, 1211 Geneva 19, Switzerland. T. +41227304222. Fax +41227330395. E-mail: grsp@ifrc.org.
URL: http://www.grsproadsafety.org/
History Feb 1999, by *The World Bank Group (#21218)*, *Department for International Development (DFID, inactive)* and *International Federation of Red Cross and Red Crescent Societies (#13526)*. **Aims** Reduce road-crash death and injury in low- and middle-income countries. **Structure** Steering Committee; Elected Executive Committee; Chief Executive; Secretariat. Implementation carried out by in-country teams. **Languages** English, French. **Staff** 37.50 FTE, paid. **Finance** Members' dues. Direct project funding. Budget (annual): US$ 7.47 million. **Activities** Networking/liaising; capacity building; training/education; advocacy/lobbying/activism. **Events** *International Conference on Road Safety on Four Continents* Abu Dhabi (United Arab Emirates) 2010, *Annual Asia road safety seminar* Singapore (Singapore) 2009, *ASEAN seminar* Hanoi (Vietnam) 2002, *ASEAN seminar* Tokyo (Japan) 2001. **Publications** *GRSP e-News* (regular). Annual Report; case studies; reports; fact sheets; road safety manuals.
Members Corporations; Foundations; Multi-Lateral Members. Included in the above, 11 organizations listed in this Yearbook:
Asian Development Bank (ADB, #01422); *Department for International Development (DFID, inactive)*; *Fédération Internationale de l'Automobile (FIA, #09613)* (Foundation for the Automobile and Society); *Inter-American Development Bank (IDB, #11427)*; *International Bank for Reconstruction and Development (IBRD, #12317)* (World Bank); *International Federation of Red Cross and Red Crescent Societies (#13526)*; *International SOS Foundation (ISOS Foundation, #15570)*; *United Nations Economic Commission for Europe (UNECE, #20555)*; *WHO (#20950)*; *World Business Council for Sustainable Development (WBCSD, #21254)* (Cement Sustainability Initiative (CSI)); *World Rescue Organisation (WRO, #21751)*.
IGO Relations Chair of Pillar 4: Safer Road Users of *United Nations (UN, #20515)* Road Safety Collaboration (UNRSC). **NGO Relations** Hosted by: *International Federation of Red Cross and Red Crescent Societies (#13526)*. Liaison Member of: 39001 Committee producing the Road Traffic Safety Standards of *International Organization for Standardization (ISO, #14473)*. Member of: International Consultative Committee for the Organization of the First Global Ministerial Conference on Road Safety; *La Prévention Routière Internationale (PRI, #18493)*. [2016.02.16/XF2191/y/**F**]

♦ **Global Robot Cluster (GRC)** **10582**
Secretariat 32 Seongseogongdan-ro 11-gil, Dalseo-gu, Daegu 42714, Korea Rep. T. +82533823130. Fax +82535853130. E-mail: jwshin@repa.or.kr.
URL: http://www.higrc.org/
History 15 Nov 2017. Founded on adoption of Daegu Declaration, by 5 clusters in 4 countries. Inauguration ceremony held, Nov 2018; Secretariat established, Sep 2019, Daegu (Korea Rep). **Aims** Support the development and business of robotics technology. **Structure** General Meeting; Board of Directors; Executive; Secretariat. **Activities** Events/meetings; research and development. **Events** *Daegu Global Robot Business Forum* Daegu (Korea Rep) 2022, *Collaborative Robot Impact on the New Society* Daegu (Korea Rep) 2021, *Daegu Global Robot Business Forum* Daegu (Korea Rep) 2021, *Global Robot Cluster Seminar* Daegu (Korea Rep) 2021, *The Evolution of Human Robot Interaction*. Daegu (Korea Rep) 2021.
Members Full in 17 countries:
Finland, France, Israel, Kazakhstan, Korea Rep, Kyrgyzstan, Malaysia, New Zealand, Pakistan, Philippines, Romania, Russia, Singapore, Spain, Türkiye, USA, Uzbekistan. [2022.01.14/AA1937/**C**]

♦ Global Round Table (unconfirmed)

♦ **Global Roundtable for Sustainable Beef (GRSB)** **10583**
Office Administrator 13570 Meadowgrass Drive, Suite 201, Colorado Springs CO 80921, USA. T. +17193552935. E-mail: information@grsbeef.org.
URL: https://grsbeef.org/
Aims Advance, support, and communicate continuous improvement in sustainability of the global beef value chain. **Structure** General Assembly; Board of Directors; Executive Committee; Technical Working Groups. **Events** *Global Conference* Colorado Springs, CO (USA) 2021, *Global Conference* Asunción (Paraguay) 2020, *Global Conference* Kilkenny (Ireland) 2018, *Global Conference* Banff, AB (Canada) 2016.
Members Producers and producer associations; commerce and processing sector; retail companies; civil society; national or regional roundtables; allied industry initiatives. Membership countries not specified. Included in the above, 5 organizations listed in this Yearbook:
Earth Innovation Institute (#05165); *Rainforest Alliance*; *SOLIDARIDAD Network (#19681)*; *Textile Exchange (#20135)*; *World Wide Fund for Nature (WWF, #21922)*.
NGO Relations Subscriber to: *ISEAL (#16026)*. [2021.06.03/XM8966/y/**F**]

♦ Global Routes (internationally oriented national body)

♦ **Global Runoff Data Centre (GRDC)** **10584**
Centre mondial de données sur l'écoulement – Centro Mundial de Datos de Escorrentia – Weltdatenzentrum Abfluss
Head Fed Inst of Hydrology, Am Mainzer Tor 1, 56068 Koblenz, Germany. T. +4926113065224. Fax +4926113065722. E-mail: grdc@bafg.de.
URL: http://grdc.bafg.de/
History 1988, Koblenz (Germany FR), within the Federal Institute of Hydrology. Also referred to as *WMO Global Runoff Data Centre*. Operated under the auspices of *World Meteorological Organization (WMO, #21649)*. Mandate reinforced by WMO Resolution 21 (CG-XII, 1995) and 25 (Cg-XIII, 1999). **Aims** Facilitate and optimize global information exchange on *surface water hydrology*, thus supporting international research in the fields of water resources, hydrology, *climatology* and global change, by collecting and disseminating a comprehensive and sound *river* discharge *database*. **Structure** International Steering Committee (every 2 years); Secretariat. **Staff** 4.00 FTE, paid. **Finance** Supported by Germany. **Activities** Knowledge management/information dissemination. **Events** *Global Workshop on Long-Term Observatories of Mountain Social-Ecological Systems* Reno, NV (USA) 2014. **Publications** *GRDC Report Series*. Database catalogues; annual status reports; data products. **Information Services** *GRDB* – comprises about 9,500 stations featuring 410,000 station years river discharge data from 160 countries – includes ARDB – Arctic Runoff Data Base.
Members Steering Committee members (12):
Federal Institute of Hydrology (BfG); *Flow Regimes from International Experimental and Network Data (FRIEND, see: #13826)*; *Global Precipitation Climatology Centre (GPCC)*; *International Association of Hydrological Sciences (IAHS, #11954)*; *International Data Centre on Hydrology of Lakes and Reservoirs (HYDROLARE, #13137)*; *International Groundwater Resources Assessment Centre (IGRAC, #13739)*; *UNEP (#20299)* (DEWA); *UNESCO (#20322)* (Water); UN GEMS/Water GEMStat Global Water Quality Database; WMO Climate and Water Department: Basic Systems in Hydrology; WMO Hydrology Commission; *World Meteorological Organization (WMO, #21649)*.
Observers (4):

Global Climate Observing System (GCOS, #10289); International Hydrological Programme (IHP, #13826) (HWRP German Secretariat); *World Climate Research Programme (WCRP, #21279); World Water Assessment Programme (WWAP, #21907).*
IGO Relations Counterpart: *GEMS/Water (see: #20299).* Cooperates with: *International Centre for Water Resources and Global Change (ICWRGC, #12528).* Network member of: *Global Terrestrial Network – Hydrology (GTN-H, #10624).* [2018.06.07/XK1065/**E***]

♦ Global Rust Initiative / see Borlaug Global Rust Initiative (#03305)

♦ Global Salmon Initiative (GSI) 10585

CEO address not obtained. T. +16045068414. E-mail: info@globalsalmoninitiative.org.
URL: http://globalsalmoninitiative.org/
History Launched 14 Aug 2013, following signing of Memorandum of Understanding, signed Apr 2012. **Aims** Provide a responsibly produced source of healthy food to feed the growing population, and work to reduce the *environmental* impacts of salmon farming. **Structure** Co-Chairs (2). **Activities** Standards/guidelines. **Publications** *Sustainability Report* (annual).
Members Companies from salmon farming industry with activities in 8 countries:
Australia, Canada, Chile, Faeroe Is, Ireland, New Zealand, Norway, UK.
Associate Members (8) from the pharmaceutical and feed industries. Member countries not specified.
IGO Relations Partners with: *FAO (#09260).* **NGO Relations** Member of: *High Level Panel for a Sustainable Ocean Economy (Panel, #10917)* – Advisory Network. [2020.01.15/XM4395/**F**]

♦ Global Sanitet Club of Finland / see Global Dry Toilet Association of Finland

♦ Global Satellite Operators' Association (GSOA) 10586

Main Office Avenue Marnix 17, 1000 Brussels, Belgium. E-mail: info@gsoasatellite.com.
URL: https://gsoasatellite.com/
History Mar 2002. Expanded to cover EMEA region, 2015; rebranded as global entity, 2021. Former names and other names: *European Satellite Operators Association (ESOA)* – former (2002); *Association européenne des opérateurs de satellites* – former (2002); *EMEA Satellite Operators Association (ESOA)* – former (2015). Registration: EU Transparency Register, No/ID: 530938126582-09; Belgium. **Aims** Lead a coordinated and impactful response to global challenges and opportunities for the commercial satellite communications sector by raising awareness of the reach, resilience, variety and capability of satellite services. **Structure** General Assembly (annual); Board of Directors; Permanent Secretary General; Working Group Coordinators. **Languages** English, French, German. **Staff** 2.00 FTE, paid. **Finance** Subscription fees. **Activities** Awareness raising. **Events** *Conference on the Future of Digital Content and Services* Brussels (Belgium) 2015, *ESTEL : International Conference on Telecommunication via Satellite* Rome (Italy) 2012.
Members Full members (11); Supporting (14). Members in 8 countries:
France, Italy, Luxembourg, Netherlands, Norway, Spain, Sweden, UK. [2020/XD8844/**D**]

♦ Global Scholars (internationally oriented national body)
♦ Global School for Advanced Studies (internationally oriented national body)
♦ Global e-Schools and Communities Initiative (unconfirmed)
♦ Global Scientific Information and Computing Center (internationally oriented national body)
♦ Global Seafood Ratings Alliance (unconfirmed)

♦ Global Security Industry Alliance (GSIA) 10587

CEO 360 Business Solutions Ltd, 510 Wayson Comm BLDG, 28 Connaught RD West, Hong Kong, Central and Western, Hong Kong.
Admin Office Bldg 18 Shangsha Technology Innovation Park, Bin He Road, Shenzhen, Futian District, 518048 Guangdong, China.
URL: http://www.gsialliance.net/
History Foundation laid 2001. Formally structured 2005. Revised charter, structure and new headquarters, 2009. **Aims** United the global security community around the principles of fairness, honesty, innovation, sharing, open communication and "win-win" strategic cooperation. **Structure** Advisory Boards (4); Vice-President's Council; Corporate Board. **Activities** Events/meetings; guidance/assistance/consulting; knowledge management/information dissemination.
Members Full; Strategic. Members in 17 countries and territories:
Australia, Bangladesh, Brazil, Canada, China, Hong Kong, India, Israel, Korea Rep, Malaysia, Philippines, Russia, Singapore, Thailand, United Arab Emirates, USA, Vietnam.
Included in the above, 3 organizations listed in this Yearbook:
Asian Anti-Counterfeit Association (AAA, #01308); Asociación Latinoamericana de Seguridad (ALAS); International Society of Crime Prevention Practitioners (ISCPP). [2016/XM4112/ty/**C**]

♦ Global Security Institute (internationally oriented national body)
♦ Global Security Research Institute / see Keio University Global Research Institute

♦ Global Self-Care Federation (GSCF) 10588

Dir Gen Avenue Alfred Cortot 7D, 1260 Nyon VD, Switzerland. T. +41223625384. E-mail: admin@wsmi.org.
URL: https://www.selfcarefederation.org/
History 1970. Founded by representatives of American, Canadian and European proprietary medicine associations. Former names and other names: *World Federation of Proprietary Medicine Manufacturers (WFPMM)* – former (1970 to 1997); *Fédération mondiale des fabricants de spécialités pharmaceutiques grand public (FMFSGP)* – former (1970 to 1997); *World Self-Medication Industry (WSMI)* – former (1997); *Industrie mondiale de l'automédication responsable* – former (1997). **Aims** Support development of industry associations around the world to aid in the understanding and development of responsible self-care and self-medication. **Structure** General Assembly; Board of Directors; Executive Committee; Directorate. **Languages** English. **Staff** 6.00 FTE, paid. **Finance** Sources: members' dues. Annual budget: 670,000 CHF. **Activities** Awareness raising; events/meetings; knowledge management/information dissemination; research/documentation; standards/guidelines. **Events** *World Congress* Cape Town (South Africa) 2022, *World Congress* Cape Town (South Africa) 2021, *World Congress* Cape Town (South Africa) 2020, *Asia Pacific Regional Conference* Beijing (China) 2019, *General Assembly* Sydney, NSW (Australia) 2017. **Publications** Booklets.
Members National and regional associations and manufacturers of non-prescription medicines in 21 countries and territories:
Argentina, Australia, Brazil, Canada, China, Colombia, India, Indonesia, Israel, Japan, Kenya, Korea Rep, Malaysia, Mexico, New Zealand, Philippines, South Africa, Switzerland, Taiwan, Thailand, USA.
Asia-Pacific Self-Medication Industry (APSMI, #02024); Asociación Latinoamericana de Autocuidado Responsable (ILAR, #02184); Association of the European Self-Care Industry (#02543); Middle-East, North Africa and Pakistan Self-Care Industry (MENAP-SCI, #16783).
Consultative Status Consultative status granted from: *ECOSOC (#05331)* (Roster); *WHO (#20950)* (Official Relations); *World Intellectual Property Organization (WIPO, #21593)* (Permanent Observer Status). **IGO Relations** Participates as observer in the activities of: *Codex Alimentarius Commission (CAC, #04081); WHO (#20950); World Intellectual Property Organization (WIPO, #21593).* **NGO Relations** Member of (1): *International Council on Harmonisation of Technical Requirements for Registration of Pharmaceuticals for Human Use (ICH, #13027).* Cooperates with (1): *International Federation of Pharmaceutical Manufacturers and Associations (IFPMA, #13505).* Associate Expert group of *Business and Industry Advisory Committee to the OECD (BIAC, #03385).* [2023/XD3997/y/**B**]

♦ Global Semiconductor Alliance (GSA) 10589

CEO 12400 Coit Road, Suite 650, Dallas TX 75251, USA. T. +19728667579. E-mail: contact@gsaglobal.org.
URL: https://www.gsaglobal.org/
History Former names and other names: *GSA – Where Leaders Meet* – alias. **Aims** Establish a profitable and sustainable semiconductor ecosystem. **Structure** Board of Directors; Advisory Group; Executive Management. Councils. **Activities** Awards/prizes/competitions; events/meetings. **Events** *European Executive Forum* Munich (Germany) 2022, *International Semiconductor Forum* Munich (Germany) 2011, *International Semiconductor Executive Forum* London (UK) 2010. [2021/AA2160/**C**]

♦ Global Sepsis Alliance (GSA) 10590

Manager c/o Charité Univ Hospital, Hindenburgdamm 27, 12203 Berlin, Germany.
Registered Address 12 Park Lane, Tilehurst, RG31 5DL, UK.
URL: http://www.globalsepsisalliance.com/
History by *International Society for the Performing Arts Foundation (ISPA, #15350), World Federation of Pediatric Intensive and Critical Care Societies (WFPICCS, #21473), International Sepsis Forum (ISF, #14836),* Sepsis Alliance and *World Federation of Critical Care Nurses (WFCCN, #21423).* Registration: Charity Commission, No/ID: 1142803, England and Wales; Companies House, No/ID: 7476120, England and Wales. **Aims** Elevate public, philanthropic and governmental awareness, understanding and support of sepsis; accelerate collaboration among researchers, clinicians, associated working groups and those dedicated to supporting them. **Structure** Council, comprising Chair, Executive Director, Managing Director and 11 members. **Events** *Middle East Awareness Day Meeting* Dubai (United Arab Emirates) 2017, *Middle East Awareness Day Meeting* Dubai (United Arab Emirates) 2016.
Members Founding members (5):
International Sepsis Forum (ISF, #14836); Sepsis Alliance; *World Federation of Critical Care Nurses (WFCCN, #21423); World Federation of Intensive and Critical Care (WFICC, #21444); World Federation of Pediatric Intensive and Critical Care Societies (WFPICCS, #21473).*
Organizations (25) in 16 countries:
Australia, Belize, Canada, Chile, China, Germany, Greece, India, Italy, Netherlands, New Zealand, Serbia, Spain, UK, United Arab Emirates, USA.
Included in the above, 7 organizations listed in this Yearbook:
Centre for International Child Health (CICH); European Society of Paediatric and Neonatal Intensive Care (ESPNIC, #08683); International Pan-Arab Critical Care Medicine Society (IPACCMS, #14503); Latin American Sepsis Institute (ILAS); Maventy Health International (MHI); Society of Critical Care Medicine (SCCM). [2021/XJ4699/y/**C**]

♦ Global Services Network (GSN) 10591

Contact Coalition of Service Industries, 1707 L St NW, Ste 1000, Washington DC 20036, USA. T. +12022897460.
URL: http://www.servicescoalition.org
History Apr 1998. An Internet based organization. **Aims** Support liberalization of international services trade through multilateral negotiations under the auspices of the World Trade Organisation (WTO). **Finance** Contributions.
Members Individuals in 41 countries and territories:
Argentina, Australia, Barbados, Belgium, Brazil, Canada, Chile, China, Colombia, Costa Rica, Denmark, Eswatini, Finland, France, Germany, Hong Kong, Hungary, India, Ireland, Italy, Jamaica, Japan, Korea Rep, Netherlands, Peru, Philippines, Portugal, South Africa, Spain, Sweden, Switzerland, Syrian AR, Taiwan, Thailand, Trinidad-Tobago, Tunisia, Türkiye, UK, Uruguay, USA, Vietnam.
NGO Relations *Services World Forum (SWF, no recent information).* [2016/XF6707/**F**]

♦ Global Shapers Community 10592

Contact c/o WEF, Route de la Capite 91-93, 1223 Cologny GE, Switzerland. E-mail: globalshapers@weforum.org.
URL: http://www.globalshapers.org/
History Founded 2011, by founder of *World Economic Forum (WEF, #21367).* Registered in accordance with Swiss Civil Code. **Aims** Empower young people to play an active role in shaping local, regional and global agendas. **Structure** Board of Directors. **Finance** Contributions from *World Economic Forum (WEF, #21367).* **Events** *Annual Summit* Geneva (Switzerland) 2019, *Asia Pacific Conference* Bangkok (Thailand) 2018. [2020/XM8074/**E**]

♦ Global Shea Alliance (GSA) 10593

Headquarters Jubilee House, 4th Lane, Kuku Hill, Osu, Accra, Ghana. T. +233302773393. E-mail: info@globalshea.com.
URL: http://www.globalshea.com/
History 2011. EU Transparency Register: 999592922120-36. **Aims** Design, develop, and deliver strategies that drive a *competitive* and *sustainable* shea *industry* worldwide, improving the *livelihoods* of rural African women and their communities. **Structure** General Assembly; Executive Committee. **Finance** Members' dues. **Activities** Events/meetings; training/education. **Publications** *Global Shea Alliance Newsletter.* [2014/XJ8849/**D**]

♦ Global Shelter Cluster (GSC) 10594

Coordinator c/o UNHCR, Rue Montbrillant 94, 1202 Geneva, Switzerland. E-mail: urquia@unhcr.org.
Coordinator c/o IFRC, Chemin des Crêts 17, 1209 Geneva, Switzerland.
URL: http://www.sheltercluster.org/
History Set up as an *Inter-Agency Standing Committee (IASC, #11393)* coordination mechanism. Through Memorandum of Understanding with *United Nations Office for the Coordination of Humanitarian Affairs (OCHA, #20593),* signed 2006, *International Federation of Red Cross and Red Crescent Societies (#13526)* assumed responsibility to complement leadership of *UNHCR (#20327).* **Aims** Enable better coordination among shelter actors, including local and national governments, so people who need shelter assistance get help faster and receive the right kind of support. **Structure** Lead Agencies (GCLAs): *International Federation of Red Cross and Red Crescent Societies (#13526)* – convenes in natural disaster situations; *UNHCR (#20327)* – leads in conflict situations. Strategic Advisory Group; Global Support Team; Donor Consultation Group; Working Groups; Communities of Practice; Country-level Shelter Clusters. **Languages** Arabic, English, French, Russian, Spanish, Ukrainian. **Staff** 13.50 FTE, paid. **Finance** Funding from various donors, including lead agencies and partner agencies. Annual budget: euro 2,500,000. **Activities** Guidance/assistance/consulting; humanitarian/emergency aid; events/meetings. **Events** *Annual Meeting* Geneva (Switzerland) 2019, *Annual Meeting* Le Grand-Saconnex (Switzerland) 2018, *Annual Meeting* Pregny-Chambésy (Switzerland) 2017. **Publications** Reports.
Members Partners include 35 organizations listed in this Yearbook:
- *Agency for Technical Cooperation and Development (ACTED);*
- *American Council for Voluntary International Action (InterAction);*
- *CARE International (CI, #03429);*
- *CartONG (#03591);*
- *Catholic Relief Services (CRS, #03608);*
- *Christian Aid;*
- *Danish Refugee Council (DRC);*
- *Department for International Development (DFID, inactive);*
- *Emergency Architects;*
- *European Union (EU, #08967)* (Humanitarian Aid and Civil Protection);
- *Global Communities;*
- *Habitat for Humanity International (HFHI);*
- *IMPACT Initiatives;*
- *International Centre for Earth Construction (#12485);*
- *International Organization for Migration (IOM, #14454);*
- *International Rescue Committee (IRC, #14717);*
- *MEDAIR;*
- *Norwegian Refugee Council (NRC);*
- *Oxfam International (#17922);*
- *People in Need (PIN);*
- *ProAct (#18506);*
- *Relief International;*
- *Royal Institution of Chartered Surveyors (RICS, #18991);*
- *Save the Children International (#19058);*
- *ShelterBox;*
- *Shelter Centre;*
- *Swiss Agency for Development and Cooperation (SDC);*
- *Swiss Resource Centre and Consultancies for Development (SKAT);*
- *TECHO (#20121);*
- *UNICEF (#20332);*
- *United Nations Human Settlements Programme (UN-Habitat, #20572);*
- *United Nations Office for the Coordination of Humanitarian Affairs (OCHA, #20593);*

– *United Nations Relief and Works Agency for Palestine Refugees in the Near East (UNRWA, #20622)*;
– *United States Agency for International Development (USAID)*;
– *World Vision International (WVI, #21904)*.

IGO Relations *International Organization for Migration (IOM, #14454)*; *United Nations Human Settlements Programme (UN-Habitat, #20572)*. **NGO Relations** *International Council of Voluntary Agencies (ICVA, #13092)*; *International Red Cross and Red Crescent Movement (#14707)*; *Steering Committee for Humanitarian Response (SCHR, #19978)*. [2019.03.11/XM7202/y/**E**]

♦ Global Shippers' Alliance (GSA) 10595

Contact Boulevard Auguste Reyers 80, 1030 Brussels, Belgium. T. +3227068186. E-mail: info@globalshippersalliance.org.
URL: http://globalshippersalliance.org/

Aims Intervene in the field of international *transport* and *trade* in a joint and coordinated way to promote the evolution of regulation, markets, and practices, which will enhance and better facilitate the flow of goods between the continents. **Activities** Advocacy/lobbying/activism.
Members Organizations (3):
American Association of Exporters and Importers (AAEI); *Asian Shippers' Council (ASC, #01698)*; *European Shippers' Council (ESC, #08477)*. [2017/XM6363/y/**C**]

♦ Global Shippers' Forum (GSF) 10596

Dir Unit A, Farriers Courtyard, Spelmonden Road Goudhurst, Cranbrook, TN17 1HE, UK. T. +441892552384. E-mail: secretariat@globalshippersforum.com.
URL: https://globalshippersforum.com/

History 1994. Former names and other names: *Tripartite Shippers' Group (TSG)* – former. Registration: Companies House, No/ID: 07667177, Start date: 13 Jun 2011, England and Wales. **Aims** Represent shippers and national and regional shippers associations to provide a single global voice for shippers in shaping international *transport* policy. **Structure** General Meeting (annual); Board of Directors; Secretariat. **Activities** Events/meetings; advocacy/lobbying/activism. **Events** *Global Liner Shipping Asia Conference* Singapore (Singapore) 2019, *Annual Meeting* Melbourne, VIC (Australia) 2018.
Members National organizations in 10 countries:
Argentina, Australia, Canada, Korea Rep, New Zealand, South Africa, Sri Lanka, Switzerland, UK, USA.
Regional members (2):
European Shippers' Council (ESC, #08477); *Union of African Shippers' Councils (UASC, #20348)*. [2021/XJ0933/y/**F**]

♦ Global Shrimp Forum Foundation 10597

Main Office Daalseplein 101, 3511 SX Utrecht, Netherlands.
URL: https://www.shrimp-forum.com/

History Founded by *Aquaculture Stewardship Council (ASC, #00885)* and partners. Registration: Handelsregister, No/ID: KVK 85718114, Netherlands. **Structure** Board. **Events** *Global Shrimp Forum* Utrecht (Netherlands) 2023, *Global Shrimp Forum* Utrecht (Netherlands) 2022. [2022/AA3295/t/**F**]

♦ Global Sickle Cell Disease Network (GSCDN) 10598

Dir Hosp for Sick Children, 525 University Avenue, Ste 777, Toronto ON M5G 2L3, Canada. T. +14168136194.
URL: http://www.globalsicklecelldisease.org/

Aims Collaborate to reduce the burden of sickle cell disease globally. **Structure** International Advisory Council; Working Groups. **Activities** Events/meetings. **Events** *Global Congress on Sickle Cell Disease and Bonne-Marrow Transplantation* Bhubaneswar (India) 2017, *Global Congress on Sickle Cell Disease and Bonne-Marrow Transplantation* Rio de Janeiro (Brazil) 2014, *Global Congress on Sickle Cell Disease and Bonne-Marrow Transplantation* Accra (Ghana) 2010. **Publications** Books. **NGO Relations** *SickKids International (SKI)*. [2016/XM5349/**F**]

♦ Global Sight Initiative 10599

Address not obtained.
URL: http://globalsightinitiative.org/

Aims Scale up sustainable eye care services worldwide.
Members Mentor institutions (8) in 5 countries:
Egypt, India, Nepal, Spain, Tanzania UR.
NGO Relations Collaborates with: *International Agency for the Prevention of Blindness (IAPB, #11597)*; *International Eye Foundation (IEF, #13324)*; *Seva Foundation (SF)*. [2013/XJ7295/**F**]

♦ Global Silicones Council (GSC) 10600

Exec Dir c/o ACC, 700 Second St NE, Washington DC 20002, USA.
URL: https://globalsilicones.org/

Aims Promote the safe use and stewardship of silicones globally. **Activities** Advocacy/lobbying/activism; monitoring/evaluation.
Members Regional Silicone Industry Associations (3):
CES – Silicones Europe (#03838); Silicone Industry Association of Japan (SIAJ); Silicones, Environmental, Health, and Safety Center (SEHSC). [2022/XM8926/y/**C**]

♦ Global Simulation Network for Simulation in Healthcare / see Global Network for Simulation in Healthcare (#10499)
♦ Global Sisters of Moral Fibre (internationally oriented national body)
♦ GlobalSkin / see International Alliance of Dermatology Patient Organizations (#11626)

♦ Global Smart Grid Federation (GSGF) 10601

Sec-Treas SmartGridIreland, Unit 16 – Innovation Ctr, NI Science Park, Queen's Road, Belfast, BT3 9DT, UK. T. +442890737950.
URL: http://www.globalsmartgridfederation.org/

History Apr 2010, Washington DC (USA). **Aims** Create smarter, cleaner electrical systems around the world. **Structure** Board of Directors. **Languages** English. **Events** *Smart Community Japan Meeting* Tokyo (Japan) 2015, *European Utility Week Conference* Vienna (Austria) 2015.
Members Organizations (12) in 12 countries and territories:
Australia, Belgium, Canada, France, India, Ireland, Japan, Korea Rep, Mexico, Norway, Taiwan, USA.
IGO Relations Collaborates with: *International Smart Grid Action Network (ISGAN, #14877)*. [2017.06.01/XJ2648/**E**]

♦ Global Smile Foundation (internationally oriented national body)

♦ Global Smokefree Partnership (GSP) 10602

Contact c/o Framework Convention Alliance, Rue de la Fontaine 2, Case Postale 3484, 1211 Geneva 3, Switzerland. E-mail: fca@fctc.org.
URL: http://www.globalsmokefreepartnership.org/

Aims Promote effective smokefree air policies worldwide. **Activities** Helps practitioners and advocates of smokefree policies to: access the evidence for smokefree policies; request assistance from a network of experts; take action in support of smokefree policies. **Publications** Newsletter. **NGO Relations** Member of: *New World Hope Organization (NWHO)*. Coordinated by American Cancer Society and *Framework Convention Alliance (FCA, #09981)*. Partners: *Union for International Cancer Control (UICC, #20415)*; *International Union Against Tuberculosis and Lung Disease (The Union, #15752)*; *Southeast Asian Tobacco Control Alliance (SEATCA, #19785)*; *World Heart Federation (WHF, #21562)*; *Vital Strategies*; national organizations. [2010/XJ1086/**F**]

♦ Global Soap Project (internationally oriented national body)

♦ Global Social Economy Forum (GSEF) 10603

Forum mondial de l'économie sociale – Foro Global de la Economia Social
SG Rm 319 Bldg 9, Seoul Innovation Park, Eunpyeong-gu, Seoul, Korea Rep. T. +8223524208. E-mail: gsef@gsef-net.org.
URL: http://gsef-net.org/

History Nov 2013, Seoul (Korea Rep), when Seoul Declaration was adopted. **Aims** Serve as a hub for sharing visions and experiences across international borders and cooperation based on multilateral (public-private-people) partnerships for a better world. **Structure** General Assembly; Steering Committee; Secretariat. **Languages** English, French, Spanish. **Staff** 5.00 FTE, paid. **Finance** Members' dues. City contributions. **Activities** Networking/liaising; events/meetings; advocacy/lobbying/activism; capacity building; research and development. **Events** *Meeting* Mexico City (Mexico) 2021, *Meeting* Mexico City (Mexico) 2020, *Meeting* Bilbao (Spain) 2018, *Asia Policy Dialogue* Seoul (Korea Rep) 2018, *CITIES Knowledge Transfer Projects Workshop* Seoul (Korea Rep) 2018. **Publications** *GSEF Newsletter*. Case studies.
Members Cities (16); Social Economy Networks (41). Members in 30 countries and territories:
Bangladesh, Cambodia, Canada, Cape Verde, China, Congo DR, Côte d'Ivoire, Ecuador, France, Haiti, India, Indonesia, Japan, Kenya, Korea Rep, Mali, Mexico, Morocco, Nepal, Pakistan, Palestine, Peru, Philippines, Senegal, Spain, Switzerland, Taiwan, Tunisia, Uganda, UK.
Organizations include the following 2 listed in this Yearbook:
Asian Venture Philanthropy Network (AVPN, #01778); *United Nations Research Institute for Social Development (UNRISD, #20623)*.
IGO Relations *ILO (#11123)* Academy on Social and Solidarity Economy; *United Nations Research Institute for Social Development (UNRISD, #20623)*. **NGO Relations** Active member of: *SSE International Forum (#19937)*. [2019.02.12/XM4379/y/**F**]

♦ Global Social Service Workforce Alliance 10604

Dir address not obtained. E-mail: contact@socialserviceworkforce.org.
URL: http://www.socialserviceworkforce.org/

History 6 Jun 2013, South Africa. Conceptualized Nov 2010, South Africa, at a conference organized by US Government's *'President's Emergency Plan for AIDS Relief (PEPFAR)'*. **Aims** Work toward a world in which a well-planned, developed and supported social service workforce engages people, structures and organizations to strengthen and build individual, child, family and community well-being and resilience. **Structure** Steering Committee. **Staff** 3.00 FTE, paid. **Finance** Supported by: *UNICEF (#20332)*; *United States Agency for International Development (USAID)*. **Activities** Advocacy/lobbying/activism; capacity building; events/meetings; knowledge management/information dissemination; networking/liaising. **Publications** Reports; toolkits. **Members** Individuals (2,800) in 143 countries from NGOs, government, UN agencies, donors, academic institutions, professional associations and other stakeholder groups. Membership countries not specified. **NGO Relations** Member of (1): *Global Partnership to End Violence Against Children (End Violence Against Children, #10533)*. [2022.02.03/XJ6893/**C**]

♦ Global Social Work Network (internationally oriented national body)

♦ Global Society of Cardiology (GSoC) 10605

Main Office address not obtained. E-mail: info@globalsocietyofcardiology.org.
URL: https://globalsocietyofcardiology.org/

Aims Act as the voice of all doctors who are working in fields of cardiovascular disease. **Events** *Metaverse Congress* 2023. [2023/AA3178/**C**]

♦ Global Society for Ecology and Sound Economy (internationally oriented national body)

♦ Global Society for Industrial Microbiology (GIM) 10606

Chair Jaio Tong Univ, 800 Dongchuan Rd, Minhang Dist, Shanghai, China.
URL: http://www.tau.ac.il/~coheng/other/gim.html

History 1970, Prague (Czechia). Founded at 1st International Symposium on 'Genetics of Industrial Microorganisms'. Previously came within the framework of *International Union of Microbiological Societies (IUMS, #15794)*. Originally affiliated with *International Commission for Microbial Genetics (ICMG, inactive)*. Former names and other names: *Globe Society for Industrial Microbiology* – alias; *International Committee for Genetics of Industrial Microorganisms (GIM International Committee)* – alias; *Genetics of Industrial Microorganisms – International Commission (GIM-IC)* – former; *Génétique des microorganismes industriels – Commission internationale* – former. **Aims** Initiate and enhance contacts and exchange of experience between genetics and industrial *microbiology*; further development of genetics and *molecular biology* of industrially used organisms, especially *microbes* and *cell cultures*. **Languages** English. **Activities** Events/meetings; training/education. **Events** *Triennial Symposium* Pisa (Italy) 2019, *Triennial Symposium* Cancún (Mexico) 2013, *Quadrennial symposium / Quadrennial GIM Symposium* Melbourne, VIC (Australia) 2010, *GIM quadrennial symposium / Quadrennial GIM Symposium* Prague (Czech Rep) 2006, *Quadrennial symposium / Quadrennial GIM Symposium* Seoul (Korea Rep) 2002. **Publications** Symposium proceedings.
Members Individuals in 14 countries:
Canada, China, Croatia, Czechia, Germany, Israel, Italy, Japan, Netherlands, New Zealand, Russia, Singapore, UK, USA.
Associate members in 6 countries:
Croatia, France, Italy, Switzerland, UK, USA. [2020/XE0850/v/**E**]

♦ Global Soil Biodiversity Initiative (GSBI) 10607

Scientific Chair School of Global Environmental Sustainability, Mail-Stop 1036, 108 Johnson Hall, Colorado State Univ, Fort Collins CO 80523, USA. T. +19704924215. E-mail: info@globalsoilbiodiversity.org.
URL: http://www.globalsoilbiodiversity.org/

History Launched Sep 2011. **Aims** Promote the translation of expert knowledge on soil biodiversity into environmental policy and sustainable land management for the protection and enhancement of ecosystem services. **Structure** Secretariat. **Events** *Global Soil Biodiversity Conference* Dublin (Ireland) 2023, *Global Soil Biodiversity Conference* Nanjing (China) 2017, *Global Soil Biodiversity Conference* Dijon (France) 2014.
Members Full (over 450) in 70 countries:
Algeria, Argentina, Australia, Austria, Bangladesh, Belgium, Bosnia-Herzegovina, Brazil, Bulgaria, Burundi, Canada, China, Colombia, Costa Rica, Croatia, Cyprus, Czechia, Denmark, Ecuador, Eritrea, Estonia, Ethiopia, Fiji, Finland, France, Germany, Ghana, Greece, Guadeloupe, Hungary, India, Indonesia, Iran Islamic Rep, Ireland, Israel, Italy, Jamaica, Japan, Kenya, Latvia, Mauritius, Mexico, Nepal, Netherlands, New Zealand, Nicaragua, Nigeria, North Macedonia, Norway, Pakistan, Peru, Portugal, Russia, Senegal, Serbia, Slovakia, Slovenia, South Africa, Spain, Sri Lanka, Suriname, Sweden, Switzerland, Thailand, Tunisia, Türkiye, UK, Uruguay, USA, Vietnam.
IGO Relations Partner of: *Global Soil Partnership (GSP, #10608)*. Collaborating institutions include: *Bioversity International (#03262)*; *Joint Research Centre (JRC, #16147)*. [2016/XJ7327/**F**]

♦ Global Soil Partnership (GSP) 10608

Partenariat mondial sur les sols – Alianza Mundial por el Suelo
Information/Communication Specialist c/o FAO, Viale delle Terme di Caracalla, 00153 Rome RM, Italy. T. +39657053843. E-mail: gsp-secretariat@fao.org – world-soil-day@fao.org.
URL: http://www.fao.org/global-soil-partnership/en/

History Full title: *Global Soil Partnership for Food Security and Climate Change Mitigation and Adaptation*. Following preparatory and participatory work by *FAO (#09260)*, a meeting was convened, Sep 2011, Rome (Italy), where members endorsed proposal to set up partnership. Technical Working Group of 76 voluntary members worldwide set up to prepare a draft of Terms of Reference. Initiative endorsed by FAO Committee on Agriculture (COAG), May 2012. **Aims** Improve governance of the limited soil resources of the planet in order to guarantee healthy and productive soils for a food secure world, as well as support other essential ecosystem services. **Structure** Plenary Assembly (annual); Intergovernmental Technical Panel on Soils (ITPS); Secretariat, hosted by *FAO (#09260)*; Regional and Sub-regional Soil Partnership; Regional Steering Committees; Regional Working Groups; Pillar Chairs and Pillars Working Group (composed by Regional Focal Points); GSP Partners and National Focal Points; Technical Networks. **Languages** Arabic, Chinese, English, French, Russian, Spanish. **Staff** 2.00 FTE, paid. **Finance** Projects approved by "Healthy Soils Facility". **Activities** Knowledge management/information dissemination; events/meetings; networking/liaising; capacity building; standards/guidelines. **Events** *Plenary Assembly* Rome (Italy) 2022, *Plenary Assembly* Rome (Italy) 2021, *Plenary Assembly* Rome (Italy) 2020, *Plenary Assembly* Rome (Italy) 2019, *Plenary Assembly* Rome (Italy) 2018. **Publications** Reports; guidelines; handbooks; booklets; technical documents; state-of-the-art publications; policy briefs; global assessments; outcome documents; concept notes.
Members FAO member countries are partners by default. Others partners are voluntary: governmental organizations; universities; institutions; academia; research centers; soil science societies; UN agencies; NGOs; private companies; farmer associations; donors; etc. Partner countries not specified. Included in the above, 20 organizations listed in this Yearbook:

African Conservation Tillage Network (ACT, #00265); Africa Soil Science Society (ASSS, #00520); Eurasian Center for Food Security; EuroGeoSurveys (#05686); European Commission (EC, #06633); European Society for Soil Conservation (ESSC, #08739); Global Soil Biodiversity Initiative (GSBI, #10607); International Center for Agricultural Research in the Dry Areas (ICARDA, #12466); International Center for Biosaline Agriculture (ICBA, #12468); International Centre for Tropical Agriculture (#12527); International Institute of Tropical Agriculture (IITA, #13933); International Soil Tillage Research Organization (ISTRO, #15562); International Union of Soil Sciences (IUSS, #15817); ISRIC – World Soil Information (#16068); Latin American Society of Soil Science (#16385); Mediterranean Agronomic Institute of Bari (Bari MAI, #16641); New World Hope Organization (NWHO); The James Hutton Institute; UNISFÉRA (#20491); West and Central African Council for Agricultural Research and Development (WECARD, #20907).

IGO Relations Joint FAO/IAEA Programme of Nuclear Techniques in Food and Agriculture; *Intergovernmental Panel on Climate Change (IPCC, #11499); Intergovernmental Science-Policy Platform on Biodiversity and Ecosystem Services (IPBES, #11500);* Science Policy Interface; *Secretariat of the United Nations Convention to Combat Desertification (Secretariat of the UNCCD, #19208); UNEP (#20299); World Meteorological Organization (WMO, #21649).* **NGO Relations** Links with numerous NGOs and civil society organizations. [2022/XJ7326/y/**E***]

♦ Global Soil Partnership for Food Security and Climate Change Mitigation and Adaptation / see Global Soil Partnership (#10608)

♦ Global Solar Council (GSC) 10609

Conseil mondial solaire

Contact address not obtained. T. +862133683167 ext 809. E-mail: qwang@apvia.org.
URL: http://www.globalsolarcouncil.org/

History Dec 2015, Paris (France), at COP21 Climate Change Conference. **Aims** Bring the value of solar energy to a wider audience; make solar a leader in the *energy* market. **Structure** General Meeting (annual); Board of Directors. **Events** *Global Green Energy Associations Meeting* Shanghai (China) 2019, *Global Solar Associations Meeting* Shanghai (China) 2018.

Members Full in 18 countries and territories:
Australia, Brazil, China, France, Germany, Greece, India, Israel, Italy, Korea Rep, Mexico, South Africa, Spain, Switzerland, Taiwan, Türkiye, UK, USA.

Included in the above, 6 organizations listed in this Yearbook:
Asian Photovoltaic Industry Association (APVIA, #01663); International Solar Energy Society (ISES, #15564); Middle East Solar Industry Association (MESIA); New Energy Industry Association for Asia and the Pacific (NEIAAP); PV CYCLE Association; SolarPower Europe (#19676).

NGO Relations Memorandum of Understanding with: *TerraWatt Initiative (TWI).* [2019/XM4317/y/**B**]

♦ Global SOL Network 10610

Chairperson 34 Woodland Road, Northampton MA 03862, USA.
Vice Chairperson address not obtained.
URL: https://globalsolcommunities.org

History 1997. Originally set up within (US) Society for Organizational Learning (SOL). Registration: Start date: 2020, Sweden, Stockholm. **Aims** Share Organizational Learning via the use of systems thinking tools and techniques globally. **Structure** Board Representatives from each of the Global Communities. **Languages** Afrikaans, English, French, Japanese, Portuguese, Singapore Sign Language, Spanish, Swedish. **Staff** 8.00 FTE, voluntary. **Events** *General Assembly* Stockholm (Sweden) 2012. **Publications** *Reflections – The SoL e-Journal.*

Members in 30 countries:
Argentina, Australia, Austria, Brazil, Chile, Colombia, Croatia, Denmark, Egypt, Finland, France, Germany, Hungary, India, Israel, Japan, Malaysia, Mexico, Netherlands, Norway, Peru, Portugal, Singapore, South Africa, Spain, Sweden, Switzerland, UK, USA, Venezuela. [2022.10.18/XF3134/**F**]

♦ Global Solutions Initiative Foundation 10611

Managing Dir Friedrichstr 194-199, 10117 Berlin, Germany.
SG address not obtained.
Events Management Askanischer Platz 3, 10963 Berlin, Germany. E-mail: contact@global-solutions.international.
URL: http://www.global-solutions-initiative.org

History Founded during the 2017 German G20 Presidency. **Aims** Propose policy responses to major global problems addressed by the G20, the G7 and other global governance fora. **Structure** Includes: Global Solutions Initiative Foundation gemeinnützige GmbH. **Languages** English, German. **Staff** An interdisciplinary team. **Activities** Events/meetings; guidance/assistance/consulting; projects/programmes; publishing activities; training/education. **Events** *Annual Global Solutions Summit* Berlin (Germany) 2021, *Annual Global Solutions Summit* Berlin (Germany) 2020, *Annual Global Solutions Summit* Berlin (Germany) 2019, *Annual Global Solutions Summit* Berlin (Germany) 2018, *Annual Global Solutions Summit* Berlin (Germany) 2017. **Publications** *G20 Insights; Global Solutions Journal. Global Solutions Papers.* **IGO Relations** *Asian Development Bank Institute (ADB Institute, #01423); Deutsche Gesellschaft für Internationale Zusammenarbeit (GIZ); Economic Research Institute for ASEAN and East Asia (ERIA, #05319); OECD (#17693).*

NGO Relations Partners include:
- *Argentine Council for International Relations (CARI);*
- *Bertelsmann Foundation;*
- *Bruegel;*
- *Centre for International Governance Innovation (CIGI);*
- *Centre for Strategic and International Studies, Jakarta (CSIS);*
- *Council for Global Problem-Solving (CGP, #04898);*
- *Friedrich-Ebert-Stiftung (FES);*
- *Institut français des relations internationales (IFRI);*
- *Institute for New Economic Thinking (INET);*
- *Italian Institute for International Political Studies (ISPI);*
- *Kiel Institute for the World Economy (IfW);*
- *Konrad Adenauer Foundation (KAF);*
- *Real Instituto Elcano de Estudios Internacionales y Estratégicos;*
- *Robert Bosch Foundation;*
- *Stiftung Mercator;*
- *Volkswagen Foundation;*
- *World Health Summit Foundation (WHS Foundation, #21560).* [2020.05.07/XM8584/f/**F**]

♦ Global Sourcing Association (internationally oriented national body)
♦ Global Sourcing Council (unconfirmed)
♦ Global South Initiative (internationally oriented national body)
♦ Global Spatial Data Infrastructure Association (inactive)

♦ Global Speakers Federation (GSF) 10612

Office address not obtained. T. +14164413650.
Pres address not obtained. T. +441344427977.
URL: http://www.globalspeakers.net/

History Jul 1997. Launched Jan 1998. Original title: *International Federation of Professional Speakers (IFFPS).* Current title adopted, 18 Jul 2009. Also referred to as *GSPGlobal.* **Aims** Advance the professional speaking community worldwide. **Structure** Executive Council, headed by Chair. **Languages** English. **Staff** 2.00 FTE, paid. **Finance** Sources: members' dues. **Activities** Events/meetings. **Events** *Global Speakers Summit* Vancouver, BC (Canada) 2013, *Global summit for professional speakers* 2011, *Global Speakers Summit* Noordwijk (Netherlands) 2011, *Global summit for professional speakers* Cape Town (South Africa) 2009, *Global summit for professional speakers* Dubai (United Arab Emirates) 2007. **Publications** *Professional Speaker Magazine* (10 a year); *Global Speakers Network News Brief* (twice a month).

Members Organizations (11) in 11 countries:
Australia, Canada, France, Germany, Malaysia, Netherlands, New Zealand, Singapore, South Africa, UK, USA. [2020/XM1693/**C**]

♦ Global Sports Alliance (GSA) 10613

Chairman GSA World Ctr, 4-8-207 Nampeidai-cho, Shibuya-ku, Tokyo, 150-0036 Japan. T. +81334613082.

History Nov 1999. Also referred to as *NPO Global Sports Alliance.* **Aims** Contribute to the creation of a sustainable society; develop environmentally aware sports cultures. **Structure** General Assembly (annual). Council. **Activities** Set up 'Ecoflag Movement'. **Events** *General Meeting* Tokyo (Japan) 2019.

Members Teams (14) in 11 countries:
Brazil, China, Japan, Kenya, Monaco, Nepal, Nigeria, Norway, Pakistan, Spain, USA.

IGO Relations Partner: *UNEP (#20299).* **NGO Relations** Partners: *1% for the Planet; Association européenne de cyclosport (AEC); Fédération internationale de volleyball (FIVB, #09670);* Sports and Environment Commission of *International Olympic Committee (IOC, #14408); International Table Soccer Federation (ITSF, #15649);* national organizations. [2014/XM2645/**F**]

♦ Global STEM Education Center (internationally oriented national body)
♦ Global Strategies (internationally oriented national body)
♦ Global Strategies for HIV Prevention / see Global Strategies
♦ Global Stroke Alliance (unconfirmed)
♦ Global Student Embassy (internationally oriented national body)

♦ Global Student Forum (GSF) 10614

Exec Dir Boulevard Bischoffsheim 15, 1000 Brussels, Belgium. T. +3222240611. E-mail: steering.committee@globalstudentforum.org.
URL: https://www.globalstudentforum.org/

History Founded by *All-Africa Students Union (AASU, #00644), Commonwealth Students' Association (CSA, #04363), European Students' Union (ESU, #08848), Organising Bureau of European School Student Unions (OBESSU, #17829)* and *Organización Continental Latinoamericana y Caribeña de Estudiantes (OCLAE, #17834).* **Aims** Build networks and facilitate active solidarity through digital campaigns and on the ground action. **Structure** Steering Committee; Secretariat. **Activities** Advocacy/lobbying/activism; capacity building; events/meetings; networking/liaising; training/education.

Members Membership covers 183 unions in 114 countries, as members of 5 regional organizations:
Algeria, Angola, Argentina, Armenia, Austria, Bangladesh, Belarus, Belgium, Benin, Bolivia, Bosnia-Herzegovina, Botswana, Brazil, Bulgaria, Burkina Faso, Burundi, Cape Verde, Central African Rep, Chad, Chile, Colombia, Comoros, Congo Brazzaville, Congo DR, Côte d'Ivoire, Croatia, Cyprus, Czechia, Denmark, Djibouti, Dominican Rep, Ecuador, Egypt, Equatorial Guinea, Eritrea, Estonia, Eswatini, Ethiopia, Fiji, Finland, France, Gabon, Gambia, Georgia, Germany, Ghana, Guatemala, Guinea, Guinea-Bissau, Hungary, Iceland, Ireland, Israel, Italy, Jamaica, Kenya, Kosovo, Latvia, Lesotho, Liberia, Libya, Lithuania, Luxembourg, Madagascar, Malawi, Malaysia, Mali, Malta, Mauritania, Mauritius, Mexico, Moldova, Montenegro, Morocco, Mozambique, Namibia, Netherlands, Nicaragua, Niger, Nigeria, North Macedonia, Norway, Panama, Peru, Poland, Portugal, Romania, Rwanda, Sao Tomé-Principe, Senegal, Serbia, Seychelles, Sierra Leone, Slovakia, Slovenia, Somalia, South Africa, South Sudan, Spain, St Lucia, Sudan, Sweden, Switzerland, Tanzania UR, Togo, Tunisia, Türkiye, Uganda, UK, Ukraine, Uruguay, Venezuela, Zambia, Zimbabwe.

All-Africa Students Union (AASU, #00644); Commonwealth Students' Association (CSA, #04363); European Students' Union (ESU, #08848); Organising Bureau of European School Student Unions (OBESSU, #17829); Organización Continental Latinoamericana y Caribeña de Estudiantes (OCLAE, #17834).

NGO Relations Partner of (3): *100 Million (#22042); Education International (EI, #05371); Open Society Foundations (OSF, #17763).* [2021/AA1587/y/**F**]

♦ Global Studies Association (internationally oriented national body)
♦ Global Studies Center (internationally oriented national body)
♦ Global Summit of National Bioethics Committees (meeting series)

♦ Global Superior Energy Performance Partnership (GSEP) 10615

Address not obtained.

History 20 Jul 2010, Washington, DC (USA). Founded at first *Clean Energy Ministerial (CEM, #03988).* Formally adopted as a task group under *Centro Latinoamericano de Educación y Cultura (CLADEC, no recent information).* **Aims** Reduce global energy use; encourage industrial facilities and commercial buildings to pursue continuous improvements in energy efficiency; promote public-private partnerships for cooperation on specific technologies or in individual energy-intensive sectors. **Activities** Working Groups (6): Certification; Cool Roofs and Pavement; Power; Steel; Cement; Combined Heat and Power. **Events** *Meeting* Tokyo (Japan) 2012.

Members Participating Governments (12):
Canada, Denmark, Finland, France, India, Japan, Korea Rep, Mexico, Russia, South Africa, Sweden, USA.

Regional Entity:
European Union (EU, #08967). [2012/XJ2650/**E***]

♦ Global Support for Kids Initiative (internationally oriented national body)
♦ Global Surgery Germany / see Deutsche Gesellschaft für Globale- und Tropenchirurgie
♦ Global Survival Network / see Wildlife Alliance (#20957)
♦ Global Survivors Fund (unconfirmed)

♦ Global Sustainability Coalition for Open Science Services (SCOSS) . 10616

Executive Group Chair address not obtained.
URL: https://scoss.org/

History 2017. **Aims** Help identify non-commercial services essential to Open Science; make qualified recommendations on which of these services should be considered for funding support. **Structure** Board; Executive Group; Advisory Group.

Members Organizations (10) in 6 countries:
Australia, Canada, France, Mexico, Qatar, USA.

Association of African Universities (AAU, #02361); Association of European Research Libraries (#02540); Electronic Information for Libraries (EIFL, #05425); SPARC Europe (#19902). [2023/AA1797/y/**C**]

♦ Global e-Sustainability Initiative / see Global Enabling Sustainability Initiative (#10340)

♦ Global Sustainable Electricity Partnership 10617

Secretariat World Trade Centre Montreal, 393 Saint-Jacques Street, Ste 258, Montréal QC H2Y 1N9, Canada. T. +15143928876. Fax +15143928900.
URL: http://www.globalelectricity.org/

History Founded 1992, following UN Conference on Environment and Development. Original title: *Network of Expertise for the Global Environment (e7).* Changed title to *Network of Expertise for the Global Environment (e8),* Jun 2006. Current title adopted, Jun 2011. **Aims** Promote sustainable energy development worldwide through implementation of electricity projects and capacity-building activities in developing and emerging countries. **Structure** Board of Directors; Rotating Chairmanship; Committees (3); General Secretariat, based in Montréal QC (Canada). **Languages** English, French, Spanish. **Activities** Events/meetings. Active in: Argentina, Benin, Bhutan, Burkina Faso, Ecuador, Indonesia, Maldives, Nepal, Niger, Philippines, Tuvalu, Uruguay. **Events** *Annual Summit* Osaka (Japan) 2019, *Annual Summit* Beijing (China) 2016, *Joint Workshop on the role of Public Private Partnerships in Promoting Energy Storage and Energy Access Initiative / Annual Summit* Rio de Janeiro (Brazil) 2015, *Annual Summit* Moscow (Russia) 2014, *Annual Summit* Washington, DC (USA) 2013. **Publications** Newsletter. Annual Report.

Members Electricity companies (12) in 10 countries:
Brazil, Canada, China, France, Germany, Italy, Japan, Russia, Spain, USA.

IGO Relations Cooperates with: *United Nations Economic Commission for Europe (UNECE, #20555)* International PPP Center of Excellence for the High-Level Dialogue Program on PPPs. **NGO Relations** Cooperates with: *Global BrightLight Foundation; World Business Council for Sustainable Development (WBCSD, #21254); World Energy Council (WEC, #21381)* in the Global Electricity Initiative (GEI). [2018/XF5644/**F**]

♦ Global Sustainable Seafood Initiative (GSSI) 10618

Exec Dir Donkere Spaarne 26 Rood, 2011 JG Haarlem, Netherlands. T. +31630680691 – +31653192492. E-mail: secretariat@ourgssi.org.
URL: https://www.ourgssi.org/

History Registration: Stichting, Netherlands. **Aims** Ensure confidence in the supply and promotion of certified seafood as well as to promote improvement in the seafood certification schemes. **Structure** Steering Board; Secretariat. **Activities** Knowledge management/information dissemination; networking/liaising. **Events** *Meeting* Amsterdam (Netherlands) 2019. **Publications** *GSSI Newsletter.*

Members Funding Partners (80). Membership countries not specified.

Affiliated partners include:
Centro Desarrollo y Pesca Sustenable (CeDePesca, #03796); Deutsche Gesellschaft für Internationale Zusammenarbeit (GIZ); FAO (#09260); The Sustainable Trade Initiative (IDH, #20070); World Wide Fund for Nature (WWF, #21922). [2021.05.19/AA0789/y/**F**]

♦ Global Sustainable Technology and Innovation Conference (meeting series)

♦ Global Sustainable Tourism Council (GSTC) 10619

CEO PO Box 96503 #51887, Washington DC 20090-6503, USA. E-mail: info@gstcouncil.org – members@gstcouncil.org.
Main Website: https://www.gstcouncil.org/

History Aug 2010. Founded following merger of *'Partnership for Global Sustainable Tourism'* and *'Sustainable Tourism Stewardship Council (STSC)'*. By-laws adopted 24 Sep 2010; amended 3 Nov 2011. Dec 2014, took over activities of *'Tour Operator Initiative (TOI)'*. Registration: USA. **Aims** Establish and manage global sustainable tourism standards with the aim of increasing sustainable tourism knowledge and practices among public and private stakeholders. **Structure** Board of Directors; Executive Committee; Election Committee; Assurance Panel; Working Groups (6). **Staff** 7.00 FTE, paid. **Activities** Certification/accreditation; knowledge management/information dissemination; standards/guidelines. **Events** *Asia-Pacific Sustainable Tourism Conference* Gunsan (Korea Rep) 2022, *Global Sustainable Tourism Conference* Seville (Spain) 2022, *Global Sustainable Tourism Conference* Angra do Heroismo (Portugal) 2019, *Asia-Pacific Sustainable Tourism Conference* Chiang Mai (Thailand) 2019, *Global Sustainable Tourism Conference* Maun (Botswana) 2018. **Publications** Annual Report.
Members Tourism stakeholders in 102 countries and territories:
Albania, Argentina, Australia, Austria, Bahamas, Bangladesh, Belgium, Belize, Bhutan, Bosnia-Herzegovina, Botswana, Brazil, Bulgaria, Cambodia, Canada, Cape Verde, Cayman Is, Chile, China, Colombia, Costa Rica, Croatia, Cyprus, Denmark, Dominican Rep, Ecuador, Egypt, England, Estonia, Ethiopia, Fiji, Finland, France, Georgia, Germany, Greece, Greenland, Guam, Guatemala, Guyana, Hong Kong, Hungary, Iceland, India, Indonesia, Ireland, Israel, Italy, Jamaica, Japan, Jordan, Kenya, Korea Rep, Laos, Latvia, Macau, Malaysia, Maldives, Malta, Mauritius, Mexico, Micronesia FS, Mongolia, Montenegro, Myanmar, Namibia, Nepal, Netherlands, New Zealand, Niue, North Macedonia, Norway, Palau, Panama, Papua New Guinea, Peru, Philippines, Poland, Portugal, Romania, Russia, Serbia, Seychelles, Singapore, Slovakia, Slovenia, Solomon Is, South Africa, Spain, Sri Lanka, St Kitts-Nevis, Sweden, Switzerland, Taiwan, Thailand, Timor-Leste, Türkiye, UK, Ukraine, United Arab Emirates, USA, Vanuatu.
Included in the above, 10 organisations listed in this Yearbook:
Asian Ecotourism Network (AEN, #01433); European Network for Sustainable Tourism Development (ECOTRANS, #08018); Fair Trade Tourism; Hostelling International (#10950); Pacific Asia Travel Association (PATA, #17932); Rainforest Alliance; Verdens Skove; World Centre of Excellence for Destinations (CED); World Tourism Organization (UNWTO, #21861); World Wide Fund for Nature (WWF, #21922).
NGO Relations Member of (2): *High Level Panel for a Sustainable Ocean Economy (Panel, #10917)* (Advisory Network); *Sustainable Tourism Certification Alliance Africa (STCAA, #20068).* Partner of (1): *Adventure Travel Trade Association (ATTA, #00135).* Subscriber to: *DATEX II.* [2020.05.08/XJ5301/y/**B**]

♦ Global System for the Conservation and Sustainable Utilization of Plant Genetic Resources for Food and Sustainable Agriculture (inactive)

♦ Global Tamil Forum (GTF) 10620

Contact PO Box 2048, Croydon, CR90 9LE, UK. E-mail: info@globaltamilforum.org.
URL: http://www.globaltamilforum.org/

History 24 Feb 2010, UK. **Aims** Establish an international, grassroots and youth based, Tamil democratic political organization that would generate constructive change through Collective Global Tamils. **Structure** General Meeting (annual). **Events** *International Conference on Human Rights* Sydney, NSW (Australia) 2011, *Tamil Diaspora Conference* Sydney, NSW (Australia) 2011.
Members Founding organizations in 8 countries:
Australia, Canada, Malaysia, Netherlands, Norway, Sweden, UK, USA. [2017/XJ5095/**E**]

♦ Global Tape Forum (GTF) 10621

Address not obtained.
URL: http://www.globaltapeforum.com/

History 2014. **Aims** Represent the world *self adhesive* tape industry. **Activities** Standards/guidelines; knowledge management/information dissemination; events/meetings. **Events** *Global Summit* Osaka (Japan) 2021, *Global Summit* Osaka (Japan) 2020, *Global Summit* Munich (Germany) 2018, *Global Summit* Beijing (China) 2016.
Members Organizations in 4 countries and territories:
China, Japan, Taiwan, USA.
Regional organization:
European Adhesive Tape Association (AFERA, #05826). [2021/XM6765/y/**F**]

♦ **Global Taskforce** Global Taskforce of Local and Regional Governments (#10622)

♦ Global Taskforce of Local and Regional Governments (Global Taskforce) 10622

Address not obtained.
URL: https://www.global-taskforce.org/

History Founded 2013. **Aims** Bring the perspectives of local and regional governments to the SDGs, climate change agenda and New Urban Agenda in particular. **Activities** Events/meetings.
Members Organizations (23):
- *Alianza Eurolatinoamericana de Cooperación entre Ciudades (AL-LAs, #00628);*
- *Arab Towns Organization (ATO, #01059);*
- *Association Internationale des Maires et responsables des capitales et métropoles partiellement ou entièrement Francophones (AIMF, #02715);*
- *C40 (#03391);*
- Cités Unies France;
- *Commonwealth Local Government Forum (CLGF, #04348);*
- *Council of European Municipalities and Regions (CEMR, #04891);*
- *European Aluminium Holloware Manufacturer's Association (EAHMA, inactive);*
- *Federación Latinoamericana de Ciudades, Municipios y Asociaciones de Gobiernos Locales (FLACMA, #09350);*
- *FMDV (#09804);*
- *Global Parliament of Mayors (GPM, #10527);*
- *Local Governments for Sustainability (ICLEI, #16507);*
- *PLATFORMA (#18397);*
- *Red Mercociudades (MC, #18721);*
- UCLG Eurasia;
- UCLG-NORAM;
- *Union of Ibero-American Capital Cities (#20412);*
- *United Cities and Local Governments Asia Pacific (UCLG ASPAC, #20501);*
- *United Cities and Local Governments of Africa (UCLG Africa, #20500);*
- *United Regions Organisation/FOGAR (#20657);*
- *World Association of the Major Metropolises (Metropolis, #21158);*
- *World Organization of United Cities and Local Governments (UCLG, #21695).* [2019/XM8603/y/**F**]

♦ **GlobalTech Alliance** Global Alliance of Technological Universities (#10231)
♦ Global Technology Network (see: #21629)
♦ Global Teen Challenge (internationally oriented national body)
♦ Globalteer (internationally oriented national body)
♦ Global Telecom User Group / see European Virtual Private Network Users Association (#09066)

♦ Global Telecom Women's Network (GTWN) 10623

Global Secretariat c/o Ariadne Capital, 28 Queen Str, London, EC4 R1BB, UK. E-mail: info@gtwn.org.
SG Tavistock House South, Tavistock Square, London, WC1H 9LE, UK. T. +441713880671. Fax +441713800623.
Registered Office Cologne Chamber of Commerce Untersachsenhausen 10-26, 50667 Cologne, Germany.
URL: http://www.gtwn.org/

History Mar 1991, Hannover (Germany). Registered in accordance with German law. **Aims** Provide a forum for executive women active in telecommunications to get together and "network"; provide a role model to younger women managers active in telecommunications; contribute to the evolving global information society in a positive manner. **Structure** International Board. **Finance** Sources: members' dues. **Activities** Awards/prizes/competitions; events/meetings; research/documentation; training/education. **Publications** *GTWN Newsletter.* [2016/XJ8375/**C**]

♦ Global Terrestrial Network – Hydrology (GTN-H) 10624

Coordinator Intl Center for Water Resources and GLobal Change, Federal Inst of Hydrology, Am Mainzer Tor 1, 56068 Koblenz, Germany.
URL: http://www.gtn-h.info/

History Set up 2001, as a joint effort of *World Meteorological Organization (WMO, #21649)* / Climate and Water Department, *Global Climate Observing System (GCOS, #10289)* and *Global Terrestrial Observing System (GTOS, #10626).* Also referred to as *GTN Hydrology.* **Aims** Support scientific advance and operational applications with regard to climate variability and change as well as water resources assessment and management. **Languages** English, German. **Finance** Support from: *Global Climate Observing System (GCOS, #10289); World Meteorological Organization (WMO, #21649);* German Government; Federal Institute of Hydrology. **Activities** Knowledge management/information dissemination; research/documentation; research and development. **Events** *Session* Koblenz (Germany) 2017.
Members Network members (12):
CNES/LEGOS Hydroweb; *FAO (#09260)* (Aquastat); *GEMS/Water (see: #20299); Global Network of Isotopes in Precipitation (GNIP, #10491);* Global Network of Isotopes in Rivers; *Global Precipitation Climatology Centre (GPCC); Global Runoff Data Centre (GRDC, #10584); International Data Centre on Hydrology of Lakes and Reservoirs (HYDROLARE, #13137); International Groundwater Resources Assessment Centre (IGRAC, #13739); International Soil Moisture Network (ISMN);* National Snow and Ice Data Centre (NSIDC); *World Glacier Monitoring Service (WGMS, #21539).*
IGO Relations Represents observational arm of *Group on Earth Observations (GEO, #10735)* / Integrated Global Water Cycle Observations Theme. [2018.09.06/XM6002/**F***]

♦ Global Terrestrial Network for Permafrost (GTN-P) 10625

Exec Dir Alfred Wegener Inst, Helmholtz Ctr for Polar and Marine Research, Am Handelshafen 12, 27570 Bremerhaven, Germany. E-mail: gtnp-secretariat@awi.de.
URL: https://gtnp.arcticportal.org/

History Developed 1999, by *Asia and Oceania Thyroid Association (AOTA, #01810), Global Climate Observing System (GCOS, #10289)* and *Global Terrestrial Observing System (GTOS, #10626).* **Aims** Obtain a comprehensive view of the spatial structure, trends, and variability of changes in the active layer thickness and permafrost temperature. **Structure** Steering Committee; Secretariat. **NGO Relations** *International Centre for Earth Simulation (ICES Foundation).* [2018/XM8994/**F**]

♦ Global Terrestrial Observing System (GTOS) 10626

Système global d'observation terrestre – Sistema Global de Observación Terrestre

Contact address not obtained. T. +39657054026. Fax +39657053369.
URL: https://www.fao.org/geospatial/projects/detail/en/c/1035185/

History Jan 1996. Memorandum of Understanding signed, 1997, by 5 co-sponsors: *FAO (#09260); International Council for Science (ICSU, inactive); UNESCO (#20322); UNEP (#20299); World Meteorological Organization (WMO, #21649).* **Aims** Provide policy makers, resource managers and researchers with access to the data needed to detect, quantify, locate, understand and warn of environmental changes (especially reductions) in the capacity of terrestrial ecosystems to support sustainable development, focusing on: changes in land quality; availability of freshwater resources; loss of biodiversity; *climate change;* impacts of pollution and toxicity. **Structure** Steering Committee (GTSC). Secretariat located at FAO in Rome (Italy). Working Groups; Technical Panels. **Languages** Arabic, Chinese, English, French, Spanish. **Activities** Networking/liaising; knowledge management/information dissemination. **Events** *Planning meeting* Rabat (Morocco) 1995. **Publications** Report (3 a year). Books; conference proceedings; biennial report. **Information Services** *Terrestrial Ecosystem Monitoring Sites (TEMS)* – database, registering and documenting existing long-term monitoring activities useful to the scientific and policy community. **IGO Relations** Complements: *Global Ocean Observing System (GOOS, #10511).* Involved in development and implementation of: *Regional Seas Programme (#18814).* Participates in: *Group on Earth Observations (GEO, #10735).* **NGO Relations** Takes part in: *International Long-Term Ecological Research Network (ILTER, #14065); Mountain Research Initiative (MRI, #16863).* Instrumental in setting up: *Global Terrestrial Network for Permafrost (GTN-P, #10625).* [2015/XF3429/**F***]

♦ Global TestNet 10627

Secretariat Plymouth Marine Laboratory, Prospect Place, Plymouth, PL1 3DH, UK. T. +441752633100. E-mail: twf@pml.ac.uk.
URL: http://www.globaltestnet.org/

History 21 Oct 2013. Established through Memorandum of Understanding signed by representatives of ballast water treatment system testing organizations. Not-for-profit member's association, accepted as a non-government organisation (NGO) with the UN's *International Maritime Organization (IMO, #14102).* Registration: Companies House, No/ID: 12548727, Start date: 7 Apr 2020, England and Wales. **Aims** Promote comparable and accurate test results on the performance evaluation of technologies and methodologies to control the risk of bio-invasion and *harmful species* introductions by *shipping,* through an open exchange of information, transparency in methodologies and advancing the science of testing. **Structure** Board of Directors; Steering Committee; Secretariat. **Languages** English. **Staff** None paid. **Finance** Annual budget: 15,000 GBP (2022). **Activities** Events/meetings; knowledge management/information dissemination. **Events** *Annual Forum* London (UK) 2020, *Annual Forum* London (UK) 2019, *Annual Forum* London (UK) 2018, *Annual Forum* London (UK) 2017, *Annual Forum* Montréal, QC (Canada) 2016.
Members Full in 10 countries:
China, Denmark, Germany, Japan, Korea Rep, Netherlands, Norway, Singapore, UK, USA. [2022.10.19/XM8380/**F**]

♦ Globalt Fokus (internationally oriented national body)
♦ Globalt Fokus – Folkelige organisationers udviklingssamarbejde / see Globalt Fokus
♦ Global Ties US (internationally oriented national body)

♦ Global Tiger Forum (GTF) 10628

Secretariat T-5 – Third Floor, Anupam Plaza Bldg, Sri Aurobindo Marg, Kalu Sarai, Delhi 110016, DELHI 110016, India. T. +911143586287. Fax +911140687453. E-mail: globaltigerforum@gmail.com.
URL: http://www.globaltigerforum.com/

History Mar 1994, Delhi, when resolution was passed. **Aims** Highlight the rationale for tiger preservation and provide leadership and common approach throughout the world so as to safeguard the survival of the tiger, its prey and its habitat. **Structure** General Assembly; Executive Committee. **Events** *Conservation Assured/Tiger Standards (CA/TS) Global Consultation Meeting* Bangkok (Thailand) 2015.
Members Tiger range countries; Non tiger range countries; International NGOs and Intergovernmental organizations; Honorary individual members; National NGOs. All Tiger Range Countries (7):
Bangladesh, Bhutan, Cambodia, India, Myanmar, Nepal, Vietnam.
Non Tiger Range country (1):
UK.
International organizations (3):
International Fund for Animal Welfare (IFAW, #13693); TRAFFIC International (#20196); World Wide Fund for Nature (WWF, #21922).
National organizations in 2 countries:
India, Nepal.
Associate member in 1 country:
USA.
NGO Relations *Global Tiger Initiative (GTI, #10629).* [2015/XJ9702/**F***]

♦ Global Tiger Initiative (GTI) 10629

Secretariat c/o World Bank, 1818 H St NW, Washington DC 20433, USA. T. +12024580466.
URL: http://globaltigerinitiative.org/

History 2008, by *International Bank for Reconstruction and Development (IBRD, #12317)* (World Bank), *Global Environment Facility (GEF, #10346), Smithsonian Institution, Save the Tiger Fund (STF)* and *International Tiger Coalition (ITC).* **Aims** Work together toward a common agenda to save wild tigers from extinction. **Structure** Secretariat, based at *International Bank for Reconstruction and Development (IBRD, #12317).*
Members Tiger range countries (13):
Bangladesh, Bhutan, Cambodia, China, India, Indonesia, Laos, Malaysia, Myanmar, Nepal, Russia, Thailand, Vietnam.

Institutions include 17 organizations listed in this Yearbook:
ASEAN Wildlife Enforcement Network (ASEAN-WEN, #01246); Environmental Investigation Agency (EIA); Global Environment Facility (GEF, #10346); Global Tiger Forum (GTF, #10628); International Bank for Reconstruction and Development (IBRD, #12317); International Criminal Police Organization – INTERPOL (ICPO-INTERPOL, #13110); International Fund for Animal Welfare (IFAW, #13693); Kreditanstalt für Wiederaufbau (KfW); Save the Tiger Fund (STF); Secretariat of the Convention on International Trade in Endangered Species of Wild Fauna and Flora (CITES Secretariat, #19199); Smithsonian Institution; UNDP (#20292); United Nations Office on Drugs and Crime (UNODC, #20596); United States Agency for International Development (USAID); Wildlife Conservation Society (WCS); World Customs Organization (WCO, #21350); World Wide Fund for Nature (WWF, #21922). [2015/XJ9699/y/**E**]

♦ Global Timber Tracking Network (GTTN) 10630

Contact c/o Bioversity Intl, PO Box 236, UPM Post Office, 43400 Serdang, Selangor, Malaysia. T. +60389423891. Fax +60389487655. E-mail: gttn@cgiar.org.
URL: http://www.globaltimbertrackingnetwork.org/

History Apr 2012, under the auspices of *Bioversity International (#03262)*. **Aims** Facilitate and promote the integrated use of technologies in timber tracking to reduce illegal logging and associated trade. **Structure** Steering Committee. Working Groups. Overall coordination through *Bioversity International (#03262)*. **Finance** Supported by: Federal Republic of Germany. **Activities** Networking/liaising; knowledge management/information dissemination; standards/guidelines. **Publications** *GTTN Newsletter*. **IGO Relations** Main partners: *Bioversity International (#03262); CGIAR System Organization (CGIAR, #03843).* [2016/XM4766/**F**]

♦ Globalt Nettverk for Sosial Tregrening (#10501)
♦ Global Tracheostomy Collaborative (unconfirmed)

♦ Global Trade Analysis Project (GTAP) 10631

Main Office Purdue – Ag-Econ, 403 W State St, West Lafayette IN 47907-2056, USA. T. +17654944199. Fax +17654961224. E-mail: contactgtap@purdue.edu.
URL: http://www.gtap.agecon.purdue.edu/

History 1992. **Aims** Improve the quality of quantitative analysis of global economic issues within an economy-wide framework. **Structure** Global network of researchers and policy makers (GTAP Consortium). **Languages** English. **Staff** 14.50 FTE, paid. **Finance** Members' dues (Consortium). Other sources: database sales; projects. **Activities** Offers data, models and resources for multi-region, applied general equilibrium analysis of global economic issues; undertakes research projects. Organizes: Annual Conference; annual professional short courses. **Events** *Annual Conference on Global Economic Analysis (GTAP)* Tokyo (Japan) 2020, *Annual Conference* Warsaw (Poland) 2019, *Annual Conference* Cartagena de Indias (Colombia) 2018, *Annual Conference* West Lafayette, IN (USA) 2017, *Annual Conference* Washington, DC (USA) 2016. **Publications** *Dynamic Modeling and Applications in Global Economic Analysis* by Elena Ianchovichina and Terrie L Walmsley; *Global Trade Analysis: Modelling and Applications* by Thomas W Hertel. **Members** Researchers (over 10,000) in over 160 countries. Membership countries not specified. **NGO Relations** Instrumental in setting up: *South Asian Network on Economic Modeling (SANEM, #19736).* [2021/XJ0125/tv/**F**]

♦ Global Trade and Innovation Policy Alliance (unconfirmed)
♦ Global Trade Professionals Alliance (internationally oriented national body)

♦ Global Traders Conference (GTC) 10632

Address not obtained.
Exec Pres address not obtained.

Consultative Status Consultative status granted from: *UNCTAD (#20285)* (General Category). [2012/XF6515/t/**F**]

♦ Global Trading Web Association / see Open Network for Commerce Exchange (#17758)

♦ Global Traditional Wing Chun Kung Fu Association (GTWCKFA) 10633

Contact Level 1, 2C Staley Street, Brunswick VIC 3056, Australia. T. +61396633588. E-mail: academy@cheungsmartialarts.com.
URL: http://www.cheungsmartialarts.com/

History 1978, Melbourne, VIC (Australia). Former names and other names: *World Wing Chun Kung Fu Association (WWCKFA)* – former. **Aims** Foster, develop and promote traditional Wing Chun Kung Fu *martial arts* worldwide. **Structure** Executive Committee; Administrative Committee. **Activities** Sporting activities; training/education.
Members Full in 17 countries and territories:
Australia, Bermuda, Canada, Croatia, Cyprus, Denmark, France, Greece, Italy, Namibia, Netherlands, New Zealand, North Macedonia (former Yugoslav Rep of), Poland, Serbia, UK, USA.
Branches (48) in 12 countries:
Australia, Bermuda, Canada, Cyprus, England, Greece, Guatemala, Italy, Namibia, Netherlands, North Macedonia, USA. [2022.02.15/XD6012/**D**]

♦ Global Training and Development Institute (internationally oriented national body)

♦ Global Transparency Initiative (GTI) 10634

Secretariat c/o BIC Central Office, 1023 15th St NW, 10th Floor, Washington DC 20005, USA. T. +12027377752. E-mail: info@bankinformationcenter.org.
URL: http://www.ifitransparency.org/

Aims Promote openness in the International Financial Institutions (IFIs); strengthen IFIs' accountability to the public interest and expand political space to debate development models. **Structure** Executive Committee. **Finance** Funded by: *Ford Foundation (#09858); Oxfam Novib.*
Members Organizations (10) in 8 countries:
Argentina, India, Mexico, Philippines, Poland, South Africa, UK, USA.
Included in the above, 4 organizations listed in this Yearbook:
ARTICLE 19 (#01121); Bank Information Center (BIC); Bretton Woods Project; CEE Bankwatch Network (#03624). [2011/XJ0559/y/**F**]

♦ Global Travel and Tourism Partnership (GTTP) 10635

Exec Dir Solar House, 282 Chase Road, London, N14 6NZ, UK. E-mail: execdirector@gttp.org.
URL: https://www.gttp.org/

History 1996, New York, NY (USA). Registration: Companies House, No/ID: 12712685, Start date: 2 Jul 2020, England and Wales. **Aims** Inspire and enable young people to build successful careers in travel and tourism. **Structure** Advisory Board.
Members Full in 16 countries and territories:
Brazil, Canada, China, France, Hong Kong, Hungary, India, Ireland, Jamaica, Kenya, New Zealand, Philippines, Russia, South Africa, Tanzania UR, UK.
Affiliate in 1 country:
USA.
NGO Relations Partner of (4): *International Youth Foundation (IYF); World Tourism Forum Lucerne; World Tourism Network (WTN, #21860); World Travel and Tourism Council (WTTC, #21871).* [2021.12.02/AA2231/**F**]

♦ Global Type III Environmental Product Declarations Network (GEDnet) 10636

Secretariat Sankt Paulsgatan 6, SE-118 80 Stockholm, Sweden. T. +46850636254. Fax +46850636259.

History Founded 1999. **Aims** Encourage information exchange between type III environmental product declarations system developers; discuss key issues in development of systems and harmonization of product specific requirements. **Languages** English. **Finance** Members' dues. **Activities** Events/meetings. **Events** *Meeting* Panama (Panama) 2014, *Meeting* Gaborone (Botswana) 2013, *Meeting* Bangkok (Thailand) 2012, *Meeting* Oslo (Norway) 2011. **Publications** *GEDnet Newsletter* – electronic. *International Guide to Environmental Product Declarations* – online.
Members Full in 10 countries:
China, Denmark, Germany, Japan, Korea Rep, Netherlands, Norway, Sweden, Taiwan, USA.
Associate in 2 countries:
Germany, Sweden. [2014.11.10/XJ4348/**F**]

♦ Global U7 Consortium / see Global U8 Consortium (#10637)

♦ Global U8 Consortium 10637

SG Inha Univ, 100 Inha-ro, Nam-gu, Incheon 402-751, Korea Rep. T. +82328607230. Fax +82328607232. E-mail: orir@inha.ac.kr.
URL: https://gu8.inha.ac.kr/

History Incheon (Korea Rep), as *Global U7 Consortium*. **Aims** Promote cross-cultural education through *student* exchange and the adoption of common curricula. **Structure** Steering Committee.
Members Universities (7) in 5 countries:
Australia, France, Israel, Korea Rep, USA. [2013/XJ3386/**E**]

♦ Global Union for Boeing Workers (unconfirmed)

♦ Global Union Federations (GUF) 10638

Coordinator Intl Trade Union House, Bd du Roi Albert II 5, 1210 Brussels, Belgium. T. +3222240211. Fax +3222015815.
URL: http://www.global-unions.org/

History 19 Sep 1913, Zurich (Switzerland), following International Trade Union Conference, 16-18 Sep 1913, to group individual industry and/or occupation International Trade Secretariats (ITS) which trade unions had started to organize internationally in the late 19th century. First links had been made 1885, London (UK); the first ITS (that for tobacco) was formed in 1889, and a first joint conference took place 1901, Copenhagen (Denmark), on the initiative of Scandinavian, British and German trade unions; by 1911 there were 28 ITS (21 based in Germany). *International Trade Secretariats Coordinating Committee – Comité de coordination des Secretariats professionnels internationaux*, set up Mar 1949, Bournemouth (UK), was replaced, Jun 1952 by *International Trade Secretariats Liaison Office (inactive)*, which soon ceased to function. In Dec 1949, *International Confederation of Free Trade Unions (ICFTU, inactive)* was formed of democratic national trade union central organizations. Original title: *International Trade Secretariats (ITS) – Secrétariats professionnels internationaux (SPI) – Secretariados Profesionales Internacionales – Internationale Berufssekretariate*. Current title adopted in 2002. The GUF (currently 11), while constitutionally independent, are formally associated and work closely with *International Trade Union Confederation (ITUC, #15708)* and *Trade Union Advisory Committee to the OECD (TUAC, #20186)*. All GUFs, ITUC and TUAC constitute *Council of Global Unions (CGU)*, created Jan 2007. **Aims** Represent the international trade union movement. **Languages** English, French, Spanish. **Staff** None. **Activities** GUF met together annually for a General Conference until 2007, when the Conference was replaced by *Council of Global Unions (CGU)* meetings. Each GUF has a programme of meetings and activities for unions in its own sector. **Events** *Annual coordination meeting* Singapore (Singapore) 2019, *Annual coordination meeting* Singapore (Singapore) 2018, *Annual coordination meeting* Singapore (Singapore) 2017, *Joint Global Unions – TUSSOs/Partners Strategy Workshop on the Asian Development Bank Engagement* Singapore (Singapore) 2013, *Annual coordination meeting* Singapore (Singapore) 2010. **Publications** *Getting the World to WORK: Global Union Strategies for Recovery; Making a World of Difference.*
Members GUFs (11):
Building and Wood Workers' International (BWI, #03355); Education International (EI, #05371); IndustriALL Global Union (IndustriALL, #11177); International Arts and Entertainment Alliance (IAEA, #11676); International Federation of Journalists (IFJ, #13462); International Trade Union Confederation (ITUC, #15708); International Transport Workers' Federation (ITF, #15726); International Union of Food, Agricultural, Hotel, Restaurant, Catering, Tobacco and Allied Workers Associations (IUF, #15772); Public Services International (PSI, #18572); Trade Union Advisory Committee to the OECD (TUAC, #20186); UNI Global Union (#20338).
NGO Relations Instrumental in setting up (1): *Global Unions Committee on Workers' Capital (CWC, #10639).* [2019/XF5824/y/**F**]

♦ Global Unions Committee on Workers' Capital (CWC) 10639

Comité sur le capital des travailleurs du groupement Global Unions – Comité sobre el Capital de los Trabajadores

Program Manager 789 West Pender Street, Suite 440, Vancouver BC V6C 1H2, Canada. T. +16046952038.
URL: https://www.workerscapital.org/

History 1999. A joint initiative of *International Trade Union Confederation (ITUC, #15708), Global Union Federations (GUF, #10638)* and *Trade Union Advisory Committee to the OECD (TUAC, #20186)*. **Aims** Promote information sharing and joint action on workers' capital. **Structure** Leadership Team; Secretariat. **Activities** Events/meetings. **Events** *Conference* Paris (France) 2019. **Members** Participants (over 700) in 25 countries. Membership countries not specified. [2022.10.19/AA0913/**E**]

♦ Global Universities in Distance Education (internationally oriented national body)
♦ Global University (see: #10110)

♦ Global University Leaders Forum (GULF) 10640

Contact c/o WEF, Route de la Capite 91-93, 1223 Cologny GE, Switzerland. T. +41228691212. Fax +41227862744. E-mail: gulf@weforum.org.
URL: http://www.weforum.org/communities/global-university-leaders-forum/

History 2006. Founded at the initiative of *World Economic Forum (WEF, #21367)*. **Aims** Act as a community to address educational, scientific and research agendas; act as an advisory body providing intellectual stewardship to the WEF. **Structure** Chair; Vice-Chairs. **Languages** English. **Staff** 1.00 FTE, paid. **Finance** Supported by: *World Economic Forum (WEF, #21367)*. **Activities** Guidance/assistance/consulting; networking/liaising. **Publications** None.
Members Heads of global universities (29) in 10 countries:
Canada, China, Italy, Japan, Korea Rep, Singapore, South Africa, Switzerland, UK, USA. [2022/XJ5853/**F**]

♦ Global University Network for Innovation (GUNI) 10641

Réseau mondial pour l'innovation dans l'enseignement supérieur (RMIES)

Dir Avda Tibidabo 39, 08035 Barcelona, Spain. T. +34935817099. E-mail: info@guninetwork.org.
URL: http://www.guninetwork.org/

History 1999. Founded by *UNESCO (#20322), United Nations University (UNU, #20642)* and Universitat Politècnica de Catalunya – BarcelonaTech (UPC). **Aims** Foster the role of higher education in society by supporting the renewal of its visions and policies around the world in terms of public service, relevance, social responsibility and innovation. **Structure** Executive Committee; Regional Networks (5) include: *Réseau européen de recherche et d'innovation dans l'enseignement supérieur (RERIES, #18877)*. **Languages** Catalan, English, Spanish. **Staff** 2.00 FTE, paid. **Activities** Events/meetings; networking/liaising; publishing activities. **Events** *World Conference on Higher Education* Barcelona (Spain) 2022, *International Conference on Sustainable Development Goals and Higher Education* Barcelona (Spain) 2020, *International Conference on Quality Assurance in Higher Education in Africa* Abuja (Nigeria) 2019, *Group of Experts on SDGs and Higher Education Meeting* Barcelona (Spain) 2018, *International Conference on Humanities and Higher Education* Barcelona (Spain) 2018. **Publications** *Higher Education Newsletter* (12 a year) – electronic; *Higher Education in the World* (annual). *GUNI Series on the Social Commitment of Universities.*
Members Higher Education UNESCO Chairs, higher education institutions, research centres and networks related to innovation and social commitment in higher education. Members (250) in 81 countries and territories. Membership countries not specified.
Included in the above, 15 organizations listed in this Yearbook:
African and Malagasy Council for Higher Education (#00364); Arab Open University (AOU); Association of Amazonian Universities (UNAMAZ, #02366); Association of Southeast Asian Institutions of Higher Learning (ASAIHL, #02920); Association of Universities of Latin America and the Caribbean (#02970); Centro Interuniversitario de Desarrollo (CINDA, #03809); Consortium for North American Higher Education Collaboration (CONAHEC, #04756); European Federation of Catholic Universities (#07070); International Centre for Higher Education Management (ICHEM); International Network of Quality Assurance Agencies in Higher Education (INQAAHE, #14312); Latin American Council of Business Schools (#16308); Latin American Faculty of Social Sciences (#16316); Network of Macrouniversities of Latin America and the Caribbean (#17047); UNESCO (#20322); United Nations University (UNU, #20642).
IGO Relations *UNESCO (#20322); United Nations University (UNU, #20642).* [2023.02.14/XF6314/y/**F**]

♦ Global Urban Competititeness Project (GUCP) 10642

Sec Room 722/723, Floor 7, No 28 Shuguangxili, Chaoyang, 100028 Beijing, China. E-mail: info@gucp-us.org.
Pres Dept of Economics – Bucknell Univ, Lewisburg PA 17837, USA.
URL: http://www.gucp-us.org/

Structure Council. **Activities** Events/meetings. **Events** *Global Urban Competitiveness Project International Conference* Incheon (Korea Rep) 2019. [2020/AA0252/v/**F**]

♦ Global Urban Development (GUD) 10643

Chairman/CEO PO Box 1510, Rehoboth Beach DE 19971, USA. T. +12025545891. E-mail: info@globalurban.org.
URL: https://www.globalurban.net/

History 2001. Former names and other names: *Prague Institute for Global Urban Development* – former (2001 to Oct 2005). Registration: USA, State of Delaware. **Aims** Increase research, teaching, discussion, publication and action on the major issues related to urban development worldwide. **Structure** Board of Directors. Executive Committee, comprising Chairman, President, 3 Vice-Chairs, Secretary-Treasurer and 7 further members. Advisory Board. Offices in: Barcelona (Spain); Beijing (China); Belo Horizonte (Brazil); Curitiba (Brazil); Hong Kong; Istanbul (Turkey); London (UK); Prague (Czech Rep); San Francisco CA (USA); Singapore (Singapore); Sydney (Australia); Toronto ON (Canada); Washington DC (USA). **Languages** English. **Staff** 2.00 FTE, paid. 17 senior fellows; 11 fellows. **Finance** Public support (contributions and grants); program service revenue. **Activities** Metropolitan Economic Strategy and Sustainable Economic Development. **Publications** *Global Urban Development Magazine*.

Members Full in 52 countries and territories:
Albania, Argentina, Australia, Austria, Bangladesh, Belgium, Brazil, Canada, Chile, China, Colombia, Czechia, Djibouti, Finland, France, Germany, Ghana, Greece, Guatemala, Hungary, India, Indonesia, Iran Islamic Rep, Israel, Italy, Kenya, Korea Rep, Mexico, Mongolia, Morocco, Netherlands, New Zealand, Nigeria, Pakistan, Palestine, Peru, Philippines, Poland, Portugal, Russia, Senegal, Singapore, Slovakia, South Africa, Spain, Sweden, Tanzania UR, UK, United Arab Emirates, USA, Vietnam, Zimbabwe.

NGO Relations Member of: *Association for Women's Rights in Development (AWID, #02980)*; *International Housing Coalition (IHC Global)*. Partner of: *Partnership on Sustainable, Low Carbon Transport Foundation (SLoCaT Foundation, #18244)*; *World Urban Campaign (WUC, #21893)*. [2022/XM2824/**E**]

♦ Global Utmaning (internationally oriented national body)

♦ Global UTM Association (GUTMA) 10644

Address not obtained.
URL: http://gutma.org/

History UTM stands for *Unmanned Aircraft Systems Traffic Management*. Current statutes adopted Jun 2017. Registered in accordance with Swiss Civil Code. **Aims** Foster the safe, secure and efficient integration of drones in national *airspace* systems. **Structure** General Assembly; Board of Directors. **Languages** English. **Activities** Events/meetings. **Events** *Annual Conference* Portland, OR (USA) 2019, *Annual Conference* Madrid (Spain) 2018, *Annual Conference* Montréal, QC (Canada) 2017. **Members** Full; Associate. Membership countries not specified. [2017/XM6249/**C**]

♦ Global Vaccine Data Network (GVDN) 10645

Project Manager Global CoordinatingCtr, C:- UniServices Univ Auckland, Waipapa Taumata Rau, Private Bag 92019, Auckland 1142, New Zealand. E-mail: gvdn@auckland.ac.nz.
URL: https://www.globalvaccinedatanetwork.org/

Aims Conduct globally coordinated epidemiological studies on the safety and effectiveness of vaccines, including COVID-19 vaccines. **Structure** Global Coordinating Centre; Scientific Advisory Committee. **Publications** *Safety by Numbers*.

Members Partner institutions in 17 countries and territories:
Argentina, Australia, Canada, China, Denmark, Ethiopia, Finland, France, Ghana, Hong Kong, India, Netherlands, New Zealand, South Africa, Taiwan, UK, USA.
INCLEN Trust International (#11142); *Vaccine monitoring Collaboration for Europe (VAC4EU, #20740)*. [2022/AA3235/y/**F**]

♦ Global Variome Limited / see Human Variome Project (#10992)
♦ Global Vascular Access Network (unconfirmed)
♦ Global Village Energy Partnership / see Energy 4 Impact (#05465)

♦ Global Virtual University (GVU) 10646

Contact Development Studies, School of Management, Agder Univ College, Gimlemoen, Serviceboks 422, 4604 Kristiansand, Norway. T. +4738141763. Fax +4738141028.

History 17 Jun 2003, Arendal (Norway). Branch of *United Nations University (UNU, #20642)*. An online network university. **Structure** Administrative centre in Arendal (Norway); headquarters in Tokyo (Japan). **Activities** Organizes on-line e-learning courses and programme with a focus on environment and development. **Publications** *The E-Learner* – newsletter.

Members Partners institutions (11) in 10 countries:
Australia, Costa Rica, Ethiopia, Ghana, Indonesia, Japan, Norway, Sweden, Tanzania UR, UK.

IGO Relations Partners: *UNEP (#20299)*. [2010/XF7110/**F**]

♦ Global Virus Network (GVN) 10647

Program Dir 725 West Lombard St, Room S413, Baltimore MD 21201, USA. T. +14107061966.
URL: http://gvn.org/

Aims Strengthen *medical research* and response to current viral causes of human *disease* and prepare against new viral *pandemic* threats. **Structure** Board of Directors. **Staff** 6.00 FTE, paid. **Activities** Advocacy/lobbying/activism; research/documentation; training/education. *Reinhard Kurth Scholarship Fund*. **Events** *Meeting* Barcelona (Spain) 2019, *Meeting* Veyrier-du-Lac (France) 2018, *Meeting* Melbourne, VIC (Australia) 2017, *Meeting* Sapporo (Japan) 2016, *Meeting* Beijing (China) 2015. **Publications** *GVN News*; *Virion Newsletter*.

Members Centers of Excellence in 16 countries:
Argentina, Australia, China, Germany, India, Ireland, Israel, Italy, Japan, Netherlands, Russia, South Africa, Spain, Sweden, UK, USA. [2019/XJ7872/**C**]

♦ Global Vision / see Global Vision Corporation (#10648)

♦ Global Vision Corporation 10648

Dir 29 Quai du Mont Blanc, 1201 Geneva, Switzerland. T. +41227328685.

History 1992. Former names and other names: *Global Vision* – former. **Aims** Promote the development of a *sustainable civilization* based on renewable resources and common sense. **Structure** Board of Directors. **Activities** Produces the *'Global Vision Project'*: international educational media campaign to "sell" the concept of sustainability as a global goal. Instrumental in setting up: *International Institute of Astro-Archaeology (no recent information)*. **IGO Relations** Partner of (8): *FAO (#09260)*; *UNDP (#20292)*; *UNEP (#20299)*; *UNESCO (#20322)*; *UNICEF (#20332)*; *United Nations Human Settlements Programme (UN-Habitat, #20572)*; *United Nations Population Fund (UNFPA, #20612)*; *WHO (#20950)*. Accredited to: *United Nations Commission on Sustainable Development (CSD, inactive)*. **NGO Relations** Partner of (10): *Earth Day Network (EDN, #05164)*; *Essence Economics Institute (no recent information)*; *European Broadcasting Union (EBU, #06404)*; *Global Access Television Service (WETV Initiative, no recent information)*; *International Union for Conservation of Nature and Natural Resources (IUCN, #15766)*; *Mega-Cities Project (#16698)*; *Princeton Institute for International and Regional Studies (PIIRS)*; *TVE International*; *World Game Institute (WGI, inactive)*; *World Wide Fund for Nature (WWF, #21922)*. [2016/XF4126/**F**]

♦ Global Vision International Charitable Trust (internationally oriented national body)
♦ Global Voice of the Executive MBA Industry / see Executive MBA Council (#09223)
♦ Global Voices (internationally oriented national body)
♦ Global Volcanism Network (internationally oriented national body)

♦ Global Volcano Model Network (GVM) 10649

Contact School of Earth Sciences, Univ of Bristol, Wills Memorial Bldg, Queens Road, Bristol, BS8 1RJ, UK. T. +441179545419. Fax +441179253385.
Contact BGS – Murchison House, West Mains Road, Edinburgh, EH9 3LA, UK. T. +441316500417. Fax +441316682683. E-mail: sclou@bgs.ac.uk.
URL: http://globalvolcanomodel.org/

Aims Create a sustainable, accessible information platform on volcanic hazard and risk. **Structure** Management Board; Scientific Steering Committee. **Activities** Research/documentation; knowledge management/information dissemination; standards/guidelines. **Publications** *GVM Newsletter*. **NGO Relations** *Asociación Latinoamericana de Volcanologia (ALVO)*; *European Plate Observing System (EPOS, #08220)*; *International Association of Volcanology and Chemistry of the Earth's Interior (IAVCEI, #12259)*; *International Centre for Earth Simulation (ICES Foundation)*; *International Centre for Numerical Methods in Engineering (CIMNE)*; *International Volcanic Health Hazard Network (IVHHN, see: #12259)*; *World Organization of Volcano Observatories (WOVO, #21696)*. [2019/XM7745/**F**]

♦ Global Voluntary Development Association (internationally oriented national body)
♦ Global Volunteer Network / see Bamboo Foundation
♦ Global Volunteers (internationally oriented national body)
♦ Global VSAT Forum / see GVF (#10842)

♦ Global Warming International Center (GWIC) 10650

Contact address not obtained. T. +16309101551. Fax +16309101561. E-mail: sinyan@gmail.com.
Street Address 22W381 75th Street, Naperville IL 60565-9245, USA.
URL: http://www.GlobalWarming.net/

History 1986. **Aims** Disseminate information on global warming science and policy. **Languages** Chinese, English, French, German. **Staff** 72.00 FTE, paid. **Finance** Members' dues. **Activities** Organizes conferences and workshops. Major projects: Global Treeline Project (GTP) – existence and magnitude of sub-arctic warming; Greenhouse Gas Reduction Benchmark (GHGRB); Himalayan Reforestation Project (HRP) – model biologically-engineered reforestation project for developing countries which require biomass commodities from severely steep hills; Extreme Event Index (EEI) – tracking economic impact of climate change. **Events** *Annual Global Warming International Conference* Beijing (China) 2009, *Annual conference / Annual Global Warming International Conference* Cambridge (UK) 2008, *Annual conference / Annual Global Warming International Conference* Miami, FL (USA) 2007, *Annual conference / Annual Global Warming International Conference* Miami, FL (USA) 2006, *Annual conference / Annual Global Warming International Conference* New York, NY (USA) 2005. **Publications** *World Resource Review* (4 a year) – journal. *Extreme Event Index (EEI)*. [2011.06.01/XE3651/**E**]

♦ Global WASH Cluster (GWC) 10651

Coordinator c/o UNICEF Geneva, Avenue de la Paix 5-7, 1211 Geneva, Switzerland. T. +41229095329. Fax +41229095902. E-mail: fbouvet@unicef.org – globalwashcluster@gmail.com.
URL: http://washcluster.net/

History Created 2006, as a cluster within *Inter-Agency Standing Committee (IASC, #11393)*, building on the success of an existing *Water, Sanitation and Hygiene (WASH)* working group. **Aims** Improve coordination in emergencies. **Structure** Led by *UNICEF (#20332)*. Strategic Advisory Group; Cluster Advocacy and Support Team; Field Support Team; Technical Working Groups. **Activities** Training/education.

Members Full; Associate; Standing Observer; Adhoc/special invitees. Members include the following 65 organizations listed in this Yearbook:

- *Action Against Hunger (#00086)*;
- *Active Learning Network for Accountability and Performance in Humanitarian Action (ALNAP, #00101)*;
- *Adventist Development and Relief Agency International (ADRA, #00131)*;
- *Agency for Technical Cooperation and Development (ACTED)*;
- *American Council for Voluntary International Action (InterAction)*;
- *Antenna Technology*;
- *Australian Aid (inactive)*;
- *Bremen Overseas Research and Development Association (BORDA)*;
- *Bureau international des Médecins sans frontières (MSF International, #03366)*;
- *CARE International (CI, #03429)*;
- *Catholic Agency for Overseas Development (CAFOD)*;
- *Catholic Relief Services (CRS, #03608)*;
- *Centre for Affordable Water and Sanitation Technology (CAWST)*;
- *Clean the World*;
- *Concern Worldwide*;
- *Department for International Development (DFID, inactive)*;
- *Deutsche Gesellschaft für Internationale Zusammenarbeit (GIZ)*;
- *Engineers Without Borders International (EWB International, #05481)*;
- *European Commission (EC, #06633)*;
- *Global Communities*;
- *GlobalMedic*;
- *GOAL*;
- *iMMAP*;
- *IMPACT Initiatives*;
- *International Federation of Red Cross and Red Crescent Societies (#13526)*;
- *International Medical Corps (IMC)*;
- *International Organization for Migration (IOM, #14454)*;
- *International Rescue Committee (IRC, #14717)*;
- *Islamic Relief Worldwide (IRWW, #16048)*;
- *London School of Hygiene and Tropical Medicine (LSHTM)*;
- *MEDAIR*;
- *MENTOR Initiative*;
- *Mercy Corps International (MCI)*;
- *Muslim Aid*;
- *Norwegian Church Aid*;
- *Norwegian Refugee Council (NRC)*;
- *Oxfam International (#17922)*;
- *Pan American Health Organization (PAHO, #18108)*;
- *Peace Corps*;
- *Plan International (#18386)*;
- *Polish Humanitarian Action (PAH)*;
- *Première Urgence Internationale*;
- *PSI (#18555)*;
- *Relief International*;
- *Save the Children International (#19058)*;
- *Shelter Centre*;
- *Solidarités International*;
- *Swedish International Development Cooperation Agency (Sida)*;
- *Swiss Agency for Development and Cooperation (SDC)*;
- *Tearfund, UK*;
- *Terre des hommes Foundation (Tdh Foundation, #20132)*;
- *UNDP (#20292)*;
- *UNEP (#20299)*;
- *UNHCR (#20327)*;
- *UNICEF (#20332)*;
- *United Nations Human Settlements Programme (UN-Habitat, #20572)*;
- *United Nations Office for the Coordination of Humanitarian Affairs (OCHA, #20593)*;
- *United Nations Organization Stabilization Mission in the Democratic Republic of Congo (MONUSCO, #20605)*;
- *United Nations Relief and Works Agency for Palestine Refugees in the Near East (UNRWA, #20622)*;
- *United States Agency for International Development (USAID)*;
- *Water, Engineering and Development Centre (WEDC)*;
- *Welthungerhilfe*;
- *WHO (#20950)*;
- *World Food Programme (WFP, #21510)*;
- *World Vision International (WVI, #21904)*. [2018/XM7211/y/**E**]

♦ Global Water (internationally oriented national body)
♦ Global Water Challenge (internationally oriented national body)

♦ Global Water Operators' Partnerships Alliance (GWOPA) 10652

Main Office UN-Habitat- Urban Services, Platz der Vereinten Nationen 1, UN Campus Bonn, 53113 Bonn, Germany. E-mail: info@gwopa.org.
URL: http://gwopa.org/

History Jan 2009, Nairobi (Kenya). Founded in response to the need for creating a mechanism for the collaboration of water utilities as highlighted in the "Hashimoto Action Plan" announced by the United Nations Secretary General's Advisory Board on Water and Sanitation (UNSGAB) during the 4th World Water Forum in Mexico. One of the recommendations of the Hashimoto Action Plan was the establishment of a global mechanism to promote Water Operators Partnerships (WOPs). Comes within *United Nations Human Settlements Programme (UN-Habitat, #20572)*. **Aims** Bring together a diversity of actors – networks, associations, financial institutions, and research and expert organizations – that stand to enrich WOPs with their knowledge and resources; build on the relative strengths of partners in order to make WOPs work. **Structure** General Assembly (every 2 years), in conjunction with Congress; Steering Committee (SC), comprising water operators, operator associations, WOP platforms from regions worldwide, private sector water operators, non-governmental and civil society organizations, labour union representatives, and substantive and financial partners. **Languages** English, French, Spanish. **Finance** Supported by the Government of Germany; other sources of funding for specific areas of the workplan. **Activities** Capacity building; events/meetings. Active in: Argentina, Australia, Bangladesh, Colombia, Honduras, Indonesia, Jamaica, Kenya, Mexico, Nigeria, Pakistan, South Africa, Spain. **Events** *Global Water Operators Partnerships (WOPs) Congress* Bonn (Germany) 2023, *General Assembly* Barcelona (Spain) 2015, *Global Water Operators Partnerships (WOPs) Congress* Barcelona (Spain) 2015, *Global Water Operators Partnerships (WOPs) Congress* Barcelona (Spain) 2013, *Advancing Water Operator Partnerships in Asia and the Pacific Seminar* Singapore (Singapore) 2012.
Members Public utilities/associations/regulators/WOP platforms; NGOs/CSOs; private operators and associations; labour unions; financial/substantial partners. Members and partners include 23 organizations listed in this Yearbook:
– *African Water Association (AfWA, #00497)*;
– *Agence française de développement (AFD)*;
– *Agencia Española de Cooperación Internacional para el Desarrollo (AECID)*;
– *Arab Countries Water Utilities Association (ACWUA, #00934)*;
– *Asian Development Bank (ADB, #01422)*;
– *Caribbean Water and Sewerage Association (CAWASA, #03567)*;
– *Caribbean Water and Wastewater Association (CWWA, #03568)*;
– *Deutsche Gesellschaft für Internationale Zusammenarbeit (GIZ)*;
– *Global Partnership for Results-Based Approaches (GPRBA, #10539)*;
– *Institut français de recherche en Afrique (IFRA)*;
– *Inter-American Association of Sanitary and Environmental Engineering (#11400)*;
– *Inter-American Development Bank (IDB, #11427)*;
– *International Federation of Private Water Operators (AquaFed, #13517)*;
– *International Water Association (IWA, #15865)*;
– *Network for Capacity Building in Integrated Water Resources Management (CAP-Net, #17000)*;
– *Pacific Water Association (PWA)*;
– *South East Asian Water Utilities Network (SEAWUN, #19787)*;
– *Stockholm International Water Institute (SIWI)*;
– *Transnational Institute (TNI, #20219)*;
– *United Nations University (UNU, #20642)*;
– *United States Agency for International Development (USAID)*;
– *Water and Sanitation Programme (WSP, #20837)*;
– *WHO (#20950)* (Water Safety Plan).

[2020.05.06/XJ6905/y/**E**]

◆ **Global Water Partnership (GWP)** 10653
Exec Sec PO Box 24177, SE-104 51 Stockholm, Sweden. T. +46812138609. E-mail: helena.gunnmo-lind@gwp.org.
Street address Linnégatan 87D, SE-115 23 Stockholm, Sweden.
General: http://www.gwp.org/
History Aug 1996, Stockholm (Sweden). **Aims** Advance governance and management of water resources for sustainable and equitable development; foster implementation of integrated water resources management (IWRM) – the coordinated development and management of water, land and related resources by maximizing economic and social welfare without compromising sustainability of ecosystems and the environment. **Structure** Network Meeting (annual); Steering Committee; GWP Technical Committee (TEC); Regional Water Partnerships (RWPs); Country Water Partnerships; Global Secretariat in Stockholm (Sweden). **Languages** English. **Staff** 35.00 FTE, paid. **Finance** Sources: contributions. Contributions from development agencies. Annual budget: 15,886,000 EUR (2021). **Activities** Advocacy/lobbying/activism; awareness raising; events/meetings; knowledge management/information dissemination; networking/liaising; publishing activities; training/education. Active in all member countries. **Events** *European River Symposium* Vienna (Austria) 2021, *European River Symposium* Vienna (Austria) 2016, *Consulting Partners Annual Meeting / Consulting Partners' Annual Meeting* Stockholm (Sweden) 2013, *Consulting Partners' Annual Meeting* Stockholm (Sweden) 2012, *Consulting Partners' Annual Meeting* Stockholm (Sweden) 2011. **Publications** *NewsFlow* (12 a year); *GWP in Action* – Annual Report. **Information Services** Integrated Water Resources Management.
Members Open to all organizations involved in the field, including government institutions in developing and developed countries, UN agencies, multilateral development banks, professional associations, research institutes, NGOs and the private sector. Partners (over 3,000) in over 180 countries and territories. Membership countries not specified.
Included in the above, 3 organizations listed in this Yearbook:
Coalition Clean Baltic (CCB, #04053); *Fundación Agreste*; *Institut International d'Ingénierie de l'Eau et de l'Environnement (2iE, #11313)*.
IGO Relations Observer status with (2): *Baltic Marine Environment Protection Commission – Helsinki Commission (HELCOM, #03126)* (Central and Eastern Europe); *UN DESA*. Member of (2): *International Commission for the Protection of the Danube River (ICPDR, #12720)*; *NDC Partnership (#16964)* (as Associate member of). Partner of (1): *Global Framework for Climate Services (GFCS, #10380)*. Cooperates with (3): *Niger Basin Authority (NBA, #17134)* (West Africa Water Partnership); *UN-Water (#20723)*; *Water and Sanitation Programme (WSP, #20837)*. **NGO Relations** Memorandum of Understanding with (1): *Nile Basin Discourse (NBD, #17139)*. Member of (2): *Network of Asian River Basin Organizations (NARBO, #16993)*; *WaterNet (#20832)*. Partner of (2): *Africa-EU Innovation Alliance for Water and Climate (AfriAlliance, #00169)*; *European Centre for River Restoration (ECRR, #06499)*. Cooperates with (6): *Global Institute for Water, Environment and Health (GIWEH, #10429)*; *International Association of Hydrogeologists (IAH, #11953)*; *Network for Capacity Building in Integrated Water Resources Management (CAP-Net, #17000)*; *Rainwater Partnership (no recent information)*; *Sanitation and Water for All (SWA, #19051)*; *Society for Conservation and Protection of Environment (SCOPE)*.

[2022.05.04/XF4132/**F**]

◆ **Global Water Research Coalition (GWRC)** 10654
Managing Dir PO Box 1008, Stirling SA 5152, Australia. E-mail: globalwaterresearch@gmail.com.
URL: http://www.globalwaterresearchcoalition.net/
History 2002. **Aims** Maintain a strong partnership between world leading water research organizations to generate, exchange and communicate knowledge through research collaborations to support safe and sustainable *water supply* and sanitation for the protection of public health and the aquatic environment. **Structure** Board of Directors. **Activities** Events/meetings; research/documentation.
Members Full in 9 countries:
Australia, Canada, France, Germany, Netherlands, Singapore, South Africa, UK, USA.
NGO Relations Affiliated to: *International Water Association (IWA, #15865)*.

[2021/XJ9642/**C**]

◆ **Global Water Solidarity (GWS)** 10655
Contact Chemin des Anémones 11-13, Chatelaine, 1219 Geneva, Switzerland. T. +41229178768.
History 2012, Marseille (France). Officially launched during the 6th World Water Forum, by *UNDP (#20292)* through its Geneva Representation Office. Former names and other names: *Global Water Solidarity – International Platform for the Promotion of Decentralized Solidarity Mechanisms* – alias. **Aims** Contribute to the achievement of MDG target 7-C and the human right to water and *sanitation*; promote, scale up and support decentralized action for water cooperation, through articulation of partners and interventions, exchange of knowledge and expertise and innovative financing mechanisms; develop, replicate and scale up decentralized solidarity mechanisms (DSMs); support existing DSMs at national and regional levels. **Languages** English, French, Spanish. **Finance** Funding from: French Ministry of Foreign Affairs (MAEF); *UNDP (#20292)*. **Activities** Awareness raising; financial and/or material support; knowledge management/information dissemination; networking/liaising; events/meetings.

Members Local, regional and national authorities, international and multilateral organizations, water operators, NGOs and private sector organizations. Founding Members (20); Partners and Members (over 100).
Included in Founding Members, 12 organizations listed in this Yearbook:
Action Against Hunger (#00086); *Both ENDS (#03307)*; *International Office for Water (IOW, #14399)*; *International Secretariat for Water (ISW, #14822)*; *Observatoire du Sahara et du Sahel (OSS, #17636)*; *Programme Solidarité eau (pS-Eau, #18529)*; *Projektgroep voor Technische Ontwikkelingssamenwerking (PROTOS)*; *Swiss Agency for Development and Cooperation (SDC)*; *UNDP (#20292)*; *United Nations Capital Development Fund (UNCDF, #20524)*; *Water and Sanitation for Africa (WSA, #20836)*; *World Organization of United Cities and Local Governments (UCLG, #21695)*.

[2015.06.01/XJ7126/y/**E**]

◆ Global Water Solidarity – International Platform for the Promotion of Decentralized Solidarity Mechanisms / see Global Water Solidarity (#10655)
◆ Global Wellness Institute (internationally oriented national body)
◆ GlobalWIIN / see Global Women Inventor and Innovator Network

◆ **Global Wind Energy Council (GWEC)** 10656
Communications Dir Rue de Commerce 31, 1000 Brussels, Belgium. E-mail: info@gwec.net.
Communications Officer address not obtained.
URL: http://www.gwec.net/
History 9 Mar 2005, Brussels (Belgium). Registration: Banque-Carrefour des Entreprises, No/ID: 0878.020.640, Start date: 20 Dec 2005, Belgium; EU Transparency Register, No/ID: 0614379494-67, Start date: 10 Oct 2008. **Aims** Ensure that wind power establishes itself as the answer to today's energy challenges, providing substantial environmental and economic benefits; create a better policy environment for wind power at international political level. **Languages** English, Mandarin Chinese. **Staff** 12.00 FTE, paid. **Finance** Sources: meeting proceeds; members' dues. **Activities** Events/meetings; politics/policy/regulatory; projects/programmes; research/documentation. **Events** *Global Offshore Wind Summit* Akita (Japan) 2022, *Global Offshore Wind Summit* Kitakyushu (Japan) 2021, *International New Energy Summit* Ulaanbaatar (Mongolia) 2021, *Asian Clean Energy Summit* Singapore (Singapore) 2019, *International New Energy Summit* Ulaanbaatar (Mongolia) 2019. **Publications** *Quarterly Market Outlook Update* (4 a year); *Global Wind Energy Outlook* (2 a year). *Global Offshore Wind Report*; *Global Wind Report*. Country Reports; Topical Reports.
Members Corporate; Association. Membership countries not specified. Included in the above, 3 organizations listed in this Yearbook:
Global Wind Organisation (GWO, #10657); *IMCA International Marine Contractors Association (IMCA, #11127)*; *WindEurope (#20965)*.
Consultative Status Consultative status granted from: *ECOSOC (#05331)* (Special); *UNEP (#20299)*. **NGO Relations** Instrumental in setting up (1): *Alliance for Rural Electrification (ARE, #00719)*.

[2022/XM0405/**E**]

◆ **Global Wind Organisation (GWO)** 10657
CEO Vesterbrogade 1c, 1620 Copenhagen, Denmark. E-mail: info@globalwindsafety.org.
URL: https://www.globalwindsafety.org
History Current Articles adopted Feb 2019. Registration: Denmark. **Aims** Strive for an injury free work environment in the wind turbine industry. **Structure** General Assembly; Executive Committee; Secretariat. **Finance** Sources: members' dues. **Activities** Awards/prizes/competitions; standards/guidelines. **Members** Turbine manufacturers and owners. Membership countries not specified. **NGO Relations** Member of (1): *Global Wind Energy Council (GWEC, #10656)*.

[2022/AA2298/**C**]

◆ GLOBAL WIP / see Global Network of Women in Politics
◆ Global Witness (internationally oriented national body)
◆ Global Woman / see Global Women P.E.A.C.E. Foundation
◆ Global Woman Peace Foundation / see Global Women P.E.A.C.E. Foundation
◆ Global Women Inventor and Innovator Network (internationally oriented national body)
◆ Global Women Inventors & Innovators Network / see Global Women Inventor and Innovator Network
◆ Global Women Leadership Program / see African Women Leaders in Agriculture and the Environment
◆ the global women network / see Féminin Pluriel
◆ Global Women P.E.A.C.E. Foundation (internationally oriented national body)

◆ **Global Women in PR (GWPR)** 10658
Founder Erskine House, 59 Davies Str, London, W1K 5JT, UK. T. +447710260743.
Founder address not obtained. T. +447860492914.
URL: http://www.globalwpr.com/
History Launched Oct 2015, Milan (Italy), at summit of *International Communications Consultancy Organisation (ICCO, #12815)*. **Aims** Act as an international forum for networking groups of senior Public Relations (PR) women to meet, share contacts, experiences and ideas for their mutual benefit; highlight the *gender imbalance and pay gap* that exists in the PR industry worldwide, alongside finding ways of increasing the representation of women in the boardroom and ensuring equal pay. **Structure** Committee of Senior PR Heads. **Languages** English. **Staff** 1.00 FTE, paid. All others voluntary. **Finance** Sponsorships. **Activities** Networking; liaising; research/documentation; events/meetings.
Members Groups in 4 countries:
Australia, Canada, UK, United Arab Emirates.
Emerging Groups in Europe and USA.
IGO Relations None. **NGO Relations** None.

[2016.06.01/XM4216/**E**]

◆ Global Women's Leadership and Gender Program / see African Women Leaders in Agriculture and the Environment

◆ **Global Women's Network for the Energy Transition (GWNET)** 10659
Exec Dir Auhofstr 12/2/4, 1130 Vienna, Austria. E-mail: info@globalwomennet.org.
URL: https://www.globalwomennet.org/
History 2017. Registration: Austria. **Aims** Address the current gender imbalances in the energy sector; promote gender-sensitive action around the energy transition in all parts of the world. **Structure** General Assembly; Governing Board; International Secretariat; Advisory Council. **Languages** English, French, German, Spanish. **Staff** 5.00 FTE, paid. **Publications** *GWNET Newsletter* (4 a year) in English. **Members** Individual and Corporate members (3,000) from over 140 countries. Membership countries not specified. **IGO Relations** Cooperates with (7): *Deutsche Gesellschaft für Internationale Zusammenarbeit (GIZ)*; *International Finance Corporation (IFC, #13597)*; *International Renewable Energy Agency (IRENA, #14715)*; *Organization for Security and Cooperation in Europe (OSCE, #17887)*; *Regional Center for Renewable Energy and Energy Efficiency (RCREEE, #18754)*; *The World Bank Group (#21218)*; *UNIDO (#20336)*. **NGO Relations** Member of (1): *IRENA Coalition for Action (#16018)*. Partner of (9): *Clean Cooking Alliance (#03987)*; *European Federation of Agencies and Regions for Energy and the Environment (FEDARENE, #07041)*; *Global Wind Energy Council (GWEC, #10656)*; *International Hydropower Association (IHA, #13828)*; *International Network on Gender and Sustainable Energy (ENERGIA, #14272)*; *International Solar Energy Society (ISES, #15564)*; *REN21 (#18836)*; *SolarPower Europe (#19676)*; *Sustainable Energy for All (SEforALL, #20056)*.

[2022.10.12/AA2826/**F**]

◆ Global Women Social Enterprise (unconfirmed)

◆ **Global Women's Strike (GWS)** 10660
Head Office c/o Crossroads Women's Centre, 25 Wolsey Mews, London, NW5 2DX, UK. T. +442074822496. Fax +442072677297. E-mail: gws@globalwomenstrike.net.
URL: http://www.globalwomenstrike.net
History 1972. Founded by Selma James. **Aims** Campaign internationally, in its capacity as a network of black and white *women*, for wages for house work for all women – to be paid by governments from military budgets and the profits of business and industry. **Structure** Autonomous groups/organizations within the Campaign include: *International Black Women for Wages for Housework* (no recent information); *International Prostitutes Collective (IPC)*; *International Wages Due Lesbians*; *Women With Visible and Invisible Disabilities (WinVisible)*. **Finance** Sources: fundraising; literature sales. **Activities** Events/meetings. **Events** *International conference* London (UK) 1992, *Wages for housework and counting women's work* Philadelphia, PA (USA) 1992.
Members Groups (7) in 4 countries:
Canada, Trinidad-Tobago, UK (2), USA (3).
NGO Relations Coordinates: *International Women Count Network (IWCN, #15894)*.

[2021/XF1847/**F**]

♦ **Global Wordnet Association (GWA)** **10661**
Co-Pres Princeton Computer Sci Dept, 35 Olden St, Princeton NJ 08540-5233, USA.
Co-Pres VU Amsterdam, De Boelelaan 1105, Room 11A-26, 1081 HV Amsterdam, Netherlands.
Registered Office Herensingel 168, 1382 VV Weesp, Netherlands.
URL: http://www.globalwordnet.org/
History Founded following Princeton Wordnet and EuroWordNet projects. Former names and other names: *WordNet Association* – alias. Registration: Netherlands. **Aims** Provide a platform for discussing, sharing and connecting wordnets for all languages in the world. **Structure** Board, comprising 2 Co-Presidents, Secretary-Treasurer and 8 members. **Events** *International Conference* San Sebastian (Spain) 2023, *International Conference* Pretoria (South Africa) 2021, *International Conference* Wroclaw (Poland) 2019, *International Conference* Singapore (Singapore) 2018, *International Conference* Bucharest (Romania) 2016. [2022/XM3865/**E**]

♦ Global Workers Justice Alliance / see Justice in Motion
♦ GlobalWorks Foundation (internationally oriented national body)

♦ **Global Young Academy (GYA)** **10662**
Managing Dir c/o Leopoldina, Emil Abderhalden Strasse 37, 06108 Halle (Saale), Germany. T. +4934547239170. E-mail: info@globalyoungacademy.net.
URL: http://www.globalyoungacademy.net/
History Feb 2010. Set up with support of *IAP – The Global Network of Science Academies (inactive)*. **Aims** Empower and mobilize young *scientists* to address issues of particular importance to early career scientists. **Structure** General Meeting (annual); Executive Committee; Senior Advisory Board; Working Groups. **Languages** English. **Staff** 9.00 FTE, paid. **Finance** Sources: government support; revenue from activities/projects. Annual budget: 815,000 EUR (2020). **Activities** Events/meetings; networking/liaising. **Events** *Annual General Meeting* Kigali (Rwanda) 2023, *International Conference of Young Scientists* Kigali (Rwanda) 2023, *General Meeting* Fukuoka (Japan) 2022, *International Conference of Young Scientists* Fukuoka (Japan) 2022, *International Conference of Young Scientists* Halle (Saale) (Germany) 2021. **Publications** *GYA Newsletter* (12 a year); *GYA Connections* (annual) – magazine; *Quarterly Bulletin*. Reports; statements; scientific publications.
Members Members (200) and alumni (366) in 101 countries and territories:
Albania, Argentina, Australia, Austria, Bahrain, Bangladesh, Belgium, Benin, Bosnia-Herzegovina, Brazil, Cambodia, Cameroon, Canada, Chile, China, Colombia, Côte d'Ivoire, Croatia, Cyprus, Denmark, Ecuador, Egypt, Estonia, Ethiopia, Finland, France, Germany, Ghana, Greece, Guatemala, Hong Kong, Hungary, Iceland, India, Indonesia, Iran Islamic Rep, Iraq, Ireland, Israel, Italy, Japan, Jordan, Kazakhstan, Kenya, Korea Rep, Kuwait, Lebanon, Lesotho, Lithuania, Madagascar, Malaysia, Malta, Mauritius, Mexico, Mongolia, Montenegro, Morocco, Namibia, Nepal, Netherlands, New Zealand, Nicaragua, Niger, Nigeria, Norway, Oman, Pakistan, Panama, Philippines, Poland, Portugal, Qatar, Romania, Russia, Rwanda, Saudi Arabia, Senegal, Serbia, Singapore, Slovenia, South Africa, Spain, Sri Lanka, Sudan, Sweden, Switzerland, Taiwan, Tanzania UR, Thailand, Tunisia, Türkiye, Uganda, UK, Ukraine, United Arab Emirates, Uruguay, USA, Uzbekistan, Venezuela, Vietnam, Zimbabwe.
NGO Relations Memorandum of Understanding with (1): *ALLEA – ALL European Academies (#00647)*. Member of (2): *European Young Academies (EYA)*; *InterAcademy Partnership (IAP, #11376)*. Cooperates with (1): *TWAS (#20270)*. Affiliated with (1): *International Science Council (ISC, #14796)*. Also links with national associations. [2023.02.20/XJ7957/v/**F**]

♦ **Global Young Greens (GYG)** **10663**
Main Office 34 Rue Du Taciturne, 1000 Brussels, Belgium. E-mail: secretary@globalyounggreens.org.
URL: http://www.globalyounggreens.org/
History Jan 2007, Nairobi (Kenya). **Aims** Empower young people within the framework of participatory *democracy*; create a space for young people to be active without being dominated by older generations; address inequalities between organizations and individuals; forge strong links between sectors and organizations; further the Green principles on planet Earth. **Structure** Network of youth activists (35 years of age and under). Congress (meets every 5 years); Steering Committee; Thematic Working Groups; Committees; Ad hoc Working Groups. **Staff** 8.00 FTE, voluntary. **Activities** Politics/policy/regulatory; networking/liaising. **Events** *Congress* Incheon (Korea Rep) 2023, *Conference* 2022, *Congress* Seoul (Korea Rep) 2021, *Congress* Liverpool (UK) 2017, *Congress* Dakar (Senegal) 2012. [2020/XM0721/**F**]

♦ Global Young Leaders Academy (unconfirmed)
♦ Global Youth Action Network (internationally oriented national body)

♦ **Global Youth Biodiversity Network (GYBN)** **10664**
Contact address not obtained. E-mail: melina.sakiyama@gmail.com – christian.schwarzer@gmail.com – gybninfo@gmail.com.
URL: http://www.gybn.org/
History Proposed 2008. Establishment process started 2010. Founding meeting Aug 2012, Berlin (Germany). Statutes adopted 1 Oct 2012; revised 25 Oct 2015. **Aims** Represent the voice of global youth in the negotiations under the United Nations Convention on Biological Diversity (CBD); raise awareness among young people of the values of biodiversity; connect individuals and youth organizations so as to build a global coalition to halt the loss of biodiversity. **Structure** Steering Committee; Alumni Board; Task Forces; Working Groups; Focal Points. Includes: *Latin America and the Caribbean (GYBN LAC)*. **Activities** Advocacy/lobbying/activism; events/meetings.
Members Organizations (115). National organizations in 31 countries:
Bahrain, Bangladesh, Benin, Bolivia, Cameroon, Canada, Colombia, Congo Brazzaville, Costa Rica, Ethiopia, France, Germany, Ghana, Greece, India, Indonesia, Italy, Kenya, Korea Rep, Mexico, Nepal, Nigeria, Portugal, Rwanda, Senegal, Spain, Sri Lanka, Sweden, Uganda, UK, USA.
International organization:
International Forestry Students' Association (IFSA, #13628).
IGO Relations *Convention on Biological Diversity (Biodiversity convention, 1992)*. [2017/XM5804/y/**F**]

♦ Global Youth Coalition Against Cancer (unconfirmed)
♦ Global Youth Innovation Network (internationally oriented national body)

♦ **Global Youth Mobilization** **10665**
Contact address not obtained. E-mail: info@globalyouthmobilization.org.
URL: https://globalyouthmobilization.org/
History 19 Apr 2021. Founded by *World Organization of the Scout Movement (WOSM, #21693)*, *World Alliance of Young Men's Christian Associations (YMCA, #21090)*, *World Young Women's Christian Association (World YWCA, #21947)*, *World Association of Girl Guides and Girl Scouts (WAGGGS, #21142)*, *International Federation of Red Cross and Red Crescent Societies (#13526)* and *The Duke of Edinburgh's International Award Foundation (#05145)*. **Aims** Act as a movement of young people taking action to improve their lives now and in a post-COVID-19 world. **Structure** Board; Management Team. **Activities** Advocacy/lobbying/activism; events/meetings; financial and/or material support. **Events** *Global Youth Summit* 2021. **IGO Relations** Partner of (1): *WHO (#20950)*. **NGO Relations** Partner of (1): *United Nations Foundation (UNF, #20563)*. [2021/AA1655/**F**]

♦ **Global Zero (GZ)** **10666**
Development Dir address not obtained. E-mail: globalzero@globalzero.org.
Exec Dir address not obtained.
URL: http://www.globalzero.org/
History Launched Dec 2008, Paris (France). Registered in accordance with US law, Jun 2012. Independent since Nov 2012. **Aims** Eliminate all *nuclear weapons*. **Activities** Advocacy/lobbying/activism. **Members** Individuals. Membership countries not specified. **Consultative Status** Consultative status granted from: *ECOSOC (#05331)* (Special). [2018/XJ5605/**F**]

♦ Globe Aware (internationally oriented national body)
♦ **GLOBE EU** GLOBE – European Union (#10667)

♦ **GLOBE – European Union (GLOBE EU)** **10667**
SG Rue des Deux Églises 14-16, 1000 Brussels, Belgium.
URL: https://www.globe-eu.org/
History The "EU chapter" of *GLOBE International (#10668)*. Works within the *European Parliament (EP, #08146)*. Former names and other names: *Global Legislators Organisation for a Balanced Environment – European Union* – legal name; *GLOBE European Union – The Network for Environmental Legislators* – alias. Registration: Banque-Carrefour des Entreprises, No/ID: 0445.031.842, Start date: 22 Aug 1991, Belgium. **Aims** Serve as a platform for discussing European Commission policy proposals and for coordinating political action among like-minded legislators in the European Parliament and at member state level; facilitate structured discussions between Members of the European Parliament, Commission officials, specialists, and a diversity of stakeholders. **Structure** Board of Directors; Advisory Council. **Activities** Events/meetings; networking/liaising. Networking with business and industry delegates through the GLOBE EU Bee Group. **Events** *Regenerative Agriculture: Dud or Silver Bullet?* Brussels (Belgium) 2022, *Think2030 conference* Brussels (Belgium) 2018.
Members Individuals in 15 countries:
Belgium, Denmark, Finland, France, Germany, Greece, Latvia, Lithuania, Malta, Netherlands, Poland, Portugal, Romania, Slovakia, Sweden.
NGO Relations Member of (1): *Brussels Dialogue on Climate Diplomacy (BDCD, #03341)*. Partner of (4): *Ellen MacArthur Foundation*; *International Union for Conservation of Nature and Natural Resources (IUCN, #15766)* (European Regional Office); *World Business Council for Sustainable Development (WBCSD, #21254)*; *World Green Building Council (WorldGBC, #21544)*. [2023/AA2420/**E**]

♦ GLOBE European Union – The Network for Environmental Legislators / see GLOBE – European Union (#10667)
♦ GLOBE – Global Learning and Observations to Benefit the Environment (internationally oriented national body)
♦ Globe International (internationally oriented national body)

♦ **GLOBE International** **10668**
Contact Ave des Volontaires 235/2, 1150 Brussels, Belgium. E-mail: secretariat@globelegislators.org.
Globe Europe 34 Boulevard de Waterloo, 1000 Brussels, Belgium.
URL: http://globelegislators.org/
History 31 Mar 1989, Brussels (Belgium). Former names and other names: *Global Legislators Organization for a Balanced Environment International (GLOBE International)* – former; *GLOBE International – The Global Legislators Organisation (GLOBE International)* – full title. Registration: Banque Carrefour des Entreprises, No/ID: 0445.593.551, Start date: 3 Sep 1991, Belgium. **Aims** Support national parliamentarians to develop and agree common legislative responses to major challenges posed by sustainable development. **Structure** International Board; International Secretariat located in Brussels (Belgium); National Directors. Includes: *GLOBE – European Union (GLOBE EU, #10667)*. **Languages** English, Filipino, French, German, Hindi, Italian, Portuguese, Spanish. **Staff** 10.00 FTE, paid. **Finance** Grants from: governmental sources of Brazil, Germany, Mexico and UK; *ClimateWorks Foundation (#04024)*; *Department for International Development (DFID, inactive)*; *Global Challenges Foundation*; *Global Environment Facility (GEF, #10346)*; *Norwegian Agency for Development Cooperation (Norad)*; *UNEP (#20299)*; Zennström Philanthropies. **Activities** Capacity building; knowledge management/information dissemination; financial and/or material support; events/meetings. **Events** *GLOBE COP26 Legislators Summit* Glasgow (UK) 2021, *GLOBE COP21 Legislators Summit* Paris (France) 2015, *GLOBE COP20 Legislators Summit* Lima (Peru) 2014, *World summit of legislators* Rio de Janeiro (Brazil) 2012, *Meeting* Nairobi (Kenya) 2009. **Publications** Newsletter; policy briefs; legislator toolkits. **Members** Individual legislators and others in over 100 countries. Membership countries not specified. **Consultative Status** Consultative status granted from: *ECOSOC (#05331)* (Special). **IGO Relations** Participates in the work of: *United Nations Economic Commission for Europe (UNECE, #20555)*. Accredited by: *United Nations Framework Convention on Climate Change – Secretariat (UNFCCC, #20564)*. Regular relations with: *Interparliamentary Assembly of Member Nations of the Commonwealth of Independent States (IPA CIS, #15958)*. **NGO Relations** Member of (1): *EarthAction (EA, #05159)*. [2021/XF0146/v/**F**]

♦ GLOBE International – The Global Legislators Organisation / see GLOBE International (#10668)
♦ GLOBE International / see GLOBE International (#10668)
♦ **GLOBELICS** Global Network for Economics of Learning, Innovation and Competence Building Systems (#10488)
♦ Globelink (internationally oriented national body)
♦ **GlobeNet3** Global Network for Social Threefolding (#10501)
♦ Globe Society for Industrial Microbiology / see Global Society for Industrial Microbiology (#10606)

♦ **Globethics.net Foundation** **10669**
Exec Dir Route de Ferney 150, 1211 Geneva 2, Switzerland.
URL: http://www.globethics.net/
History 2005. Registration: Civil Code, Start date: 2009, Switzerland; EU Transparency Register, No/ID: 070732339554-63, Start date: 11 Sep 2020. **Aims** Embed ethics in higher education. **Structure** Board; International Secretariat in Geneva (Switzerland), headed by Executive Director; Regional Offices (5). **Languages** Chinese, English, French, German, Indonesian, Portuguese, Spanish. **Staff** 12.00 FTE, paid. **Finance** Support from: *Catholic Lenten Fund*; Linsi Foundation; *Swiss Agency for Development and Cooperation (SDC)*. **Activities** Knowledge management/information dissemination; research/documentation. **Events** *Global Ethics Forum* Geneva (Switzerland) 2016, *Global Ethics Forum* Geneva (Switzerland) 2015, *Global Ethics Forum* Bangalore (India) 2014, *Global Ethics Forum* Geneva (Switzerland) 2013, *Global Ethics Forum / Annual Global Ethics Forum* Geneva (Switzerland) 2012. **Members** Institutions and individuals interested in various fields of applied ethics in 170 countries. Membership countries not specified. **Consultative Status** Consultative status granted from: *ECOSOC (#05331)* (Special). **NGO Relations** Member of (3): *Ethical Journalism Network (EJN, #05554)*; *International Federation of Library Associations and Institutions (IFLA, #13470)*; *International Partnership on Religion and Sustainable Development (PaRD, #14524)*. Cooperates with (1): *G20 Interfaith Forum Association (IF20, #10055)*. Partner of: *Alliance for Responsible and Sustainable Societies (#00718)*; *Association of Certified Anti-Money Laundering Specialists (ACAMS)*; *Business Ethics Network of Africa (BEN-Africa, #03380)*; *ECLOF International (#05287)*; *European Business Ethics Network (EBEN, #06418)*; *Europeana Foundation (#05839)*; *Fondation Charles Léopold Mayer pour le progrès de l'homme (FPH, #09815)*; *Global Knowledge Partnership Foundation (GKPF, #10443)*; *International Society of Business, Economics and Ethics (ISBEE, #14988)*; *Latin American Business Ethics Network (#16262)*; *World Association for Christian Communication (WACC, #21126)*; *World Council of Churches (WCC, #21320)*; *World Student Christian Federation (WSCF, #21833)*; national organizations. [2020.03.10/XJ1117/f/**F**]

♦ Globetree Foundation (internationally oriented national body)
♦ GlobeWomen (internationally oriented national body)
♦ GlobeWomen Research and Education Institute / see GlobeWomen
♦ GLOBSEC (internationally oriented national body)
♦ GLOBUS – Institute for Globalization and Sustainable Development (internationally oriented national body)
♦ Globus et Locus (internationally oriented national body)
♦ **GLOCAL** Global Council for Anthropological Linguistics (#10310)
♦ GLOCOM – Center for Global Communications (internationally oriented national body)
♦ GLODEM – Centre for Research on Globalization and Democratic Governance (internationally oriented national body)
♦ GloFin / see Global Finance Association
♦ **GLO** Global Labor Organization (#10445)
♦ GLOHOMO – Global Hope Mobilization (internationally oriented national body)
♦ **GLOPAN** Global Panel on Agriculture and Food Systems for Nutrition (#10523)
♦ **GloPent** European Research Network on Global Pentecostalism (#08373)
♦ **GLOPID-R** Global Research Collaboration for Infectious Disease Preparedness (#10573)

♦ **Glosa Education Organization (GEO)** **10670**
Address not obtained.
URL: http://www.glosa.org/

History Mar 1981, having developed from attempts to promote the use of the artificial language InterGlossa. Includes the previous *Glosa International Language Network (inactive)*. Registered in accordance with UK law. **Aims** Improve, simplify and economize international communications; develop use of Glosa, a phonetic *language* derived from InterGlossa, as a common auxiliary language for the European Union, for scientists and for computers worldwide; provide teaching materials and eventually establish study centres; help to link students and teachers of Glosa with schools in different countries where Glosa is taught. **Staff** 4.00 FTE, voluntary. **Finance** Subscription to publication; sales of publications; donations. **Activities** Limited by lack of funds, but organizes: penfriend service for Glosa speakers; meetings (monthly) in Richmond (UK) and other events (mainly in Africa); speakers' visits to schools. Study groups meet in various countries. **Publications** *Plu Glosa Nota* (4 a year). Dictionaries; teaching books; teaching cassettes; leaflets. Annual Report.
Members Individuals in 15 countries:
Australia, Belgium, Canada, China, France, Germany, India, Italy, Luxembourg, New Zealand, Spain, Tanzania UR, Uganda, UK, USA. [2011/XF4155/v/**F**]

- ♦ GLOSS – IOC Group of Experts on the Global Sea-Level Observing System (see: #11496)
- ♦ GLOTEC – Global Technology Network (see: #21629)
- ♦ GloVANet – Global Vascular Access Network (unconfirmed)
- ♦ **GLOW** Generative Linguistics in the Old World (#10117)
- ♦ GLoW – Global Action on Widowhood (internationally oriented national body)
- ♦ **GLP** Global Land Programme (#10450)
- ♦ **GLPGP** Global LPG Partnership (#10461)
- ♦ **GLRF** Gay and Lesbian Rowing Federation (#10079)
- ♦ **GLS** Gypsy Lore Society (#10843)
- ♦ GLS – International Conference on Gas-Liquid and Gas-Liquid-Solid Reactor Engineering (meeting series)
- ♦ GLSN – Global Legal Studies Network (internationally oriented national body)
- ♦ **GLTN** Global Land Tool Network (#10452)
- ♦ **GLU** Global Labour University (#10448)
- ♦ GLULAM – European Glued Laminated Timber Industries Association (no recent information)
- ♦ **GMACCC** Global Military Advisory Council On Climate Change (#10474)
- ♦ **GMAC** Graduate Management Admission Council (#10687)
- ♦ GMAEA – Global Medical and Beauty Exchange Association (unconfirmed)
- ♦ GMA – Global Mobility Alliance (unconfirmed)
- ♦ GMA – Global Mountain Action (internationally oriented national body)
- ♦ **GMAI** Global Media AIDS Initiative (#10469)
- ♦ **GMAP** Gelatin Manufacturers Association of Asia Pacific (#10089)
- ♦ GMARS – Global Management Accounting Research Symposium (meeting series)
- ♦ **GMBA** Global Mountain Biodiversity Assessment (#10477)
- ♦ GMC – Grupo Mercado Común del MERCOSUR (see: #19868)
- ♦ GMCOP – Global Movement for the Culture of Peace (unconfirmed)
- ♦ **GMCV** Grupo Mundial del Comercio del Vino (#21939)
- ♦ **GMDAC** IOM Global Migration Data Analysis Centre (#16007)
- ♦ **GME** Gelatin Manufacturers Association of Europe (#10090)
- ♦ GMEL – Groupement des mathématiciens d'expression latine (inactive)
- ♦ GMfC – GreenMicrofinance Center (internationally oriented national body)
- ♦ GMFER – Global March for Elephants and Rhinos (internationally oriented national body)
- ♦ GMF – German Marshall Fund of the United States (internationally oriented national body)
- ♦ **GMF** Global Mayors' Forum (#10467)
- ♦ GMF – Global Medicare Foundation (unconfirmed)
- ♦ **GMF** Group of European Municipalities with Nuclear Facilities (#10773)
- ♦ GMFJ – Global March for Jesus (internationally oriented national body)
- ♦ GMGC – Global Musa Genomics Consortium (inactive)
- ♦ GMG – Global Meeting of Generations (meeting series)
- ♦ GMG – Global Migration Group (inactive)
- ♦ **GMG** Global Mining Guidelines Group (#10475)
- ♦ **GM** Global Mechanism (#10468)
- ♦ GM – Groupes missionnaires (internationally oriented national body)
- ♦ GMI – Global Mapping International (internationally oriented national body)
- ♦ GMI – Global Marina Institute (internationally oriented national body)
- ♦ **GMI** Global Methane Initiative (#10471)
- ♦ **GMI** Gold Mercury International (#10676)
- ♦ **GMI Network** Global Microbial Identified Network (#10472)
- ♦ GMJO – Gustav Mahler Jugendorchester (internationally oriented national body)
- ♦ **GMPA** Global Migration Policy Associates (#10473)
- ♦ GMP – International Conference on Geometric Modeling and Processing (meeting series)
- ♦ GMSO – Standardization and Metrology Organization for Gulf Cooperation Council Countries (no recent information)
- ♦ **GMTA** Global Medical Technology Alliance (#10470)
- ♦ GMU – Giovani per un Mondo Unito (see: #09806)
- ♦ GM-UMC – Global Ministries of The United Methodist Church (internationally oriented national body)
- ♦ **G-MUSC** Global Alliance for Musculoskeletal Health (#10213)
- ♦ GN3 / see GÉANT Association (#10086)
- ♦ GN3 / see Global Network for Social Threefolding (#10501)
- ♦ GN3plus / see GÉANT Association (#10086)
- ♦ **GNAFCC** WHO Global Network for Age-friendly Cities and Communities (#20937)
- ♦ GNA – Gulf News Agency (inactive)
- ♦ GNAM – Global Network for Advanced Management (unconfirmed)
- ♦ GNAP – Global Network for Africa's Prosperity (internationally oriented national body)
- ♦ **GNBI** Global Network for Banking Innovation in Microfinance (#10482)
- ♦ **GNDEM** Global Network of Domestic Election Monitors (#10487)
- ♦ **GNDI** Global Network of Director Institutes (#10486)
- ♦ **GNDR** Global Network of Civil Society Organizations for Disaster Reduction (#10485)
- ♦ **GNEC** Global NGO Executive Committee (#10507)
- ♦ GNE – Groupement du nursing européen (inactive)
- ♦ GNEP / see International Framework for Nuclear Energy Cooperation (#13681)
- ♦ **G-NEXID** Global Network of Export-Import Banks and Development Finance Institutions (#10489)
- ♦ **GNF** Global Nature Fund (#10479)
- ♦ **GNGG** Global Network for Good Governance (#10490)
- ♦ **GN** Global Network of Japanese Language Education (#10492)
- ♦ GNHA – Global Natural Health Alliance (internationally oriented national body)
- ♦ GNI – Global Network Initiative (internationally oriented national body)
- ♦ Gniomhaireacht Solathair Euratom (#05617)
- ♦ **GNIP** Global Network of Isotopes in Precipitation (#10491)
- ♦ **GNLG** Global Network on Local Governance (#10493)
- ♦ GNMS – Global Network of Mission Structures (unconfirmed)
- ♦ GNOME Foundation (internationally oriented national body)
- ♦ GNOME – Global Network of Modding Extremists (unconfirmed)

♦ Gnome Liberation Front (GLF) 10671

Front de libération des nains de jardin (FLNJ)
Address not obtained.
French section: http://www.flnjfrance.com/
History Also referred to in English as *Garden Gnome Liberation Front (GGLF)*. **Aims** Promote the rights of garden gnomes; protect them from unstable *gardeners*. **Activities** *European Gnome Sanctuary*, Barga (Italy), is a place of refuge for all freedom loving gnomes. **Events** *Congress* Chemnitz (Germany) 2002. **NGO Relations** (US) 'Free the Gnomes'; (Belgian) 'Movement for the Liberation of Garden Gnomes (MTLNJ)'. [2008/XF6571/**F**]

- ♦ Le Gnomon / see Institut international d'histoire du notariat (#11312)
- ♦ **GNP** Gesellschaft für Neuropädiatrie (#10142)
- ♦ **GNP+** Global Network of People Living with HIV/AIDS (#10494)
- ♦ GNP Latin America / see Latin American Network of People Living with HIV/AIDS (#16355)
- ♦ **GNPRH** Global Network for Perinatal and Reproductive Health (#10495)
- ♦ **GNRC** Global Network of Religions for Children (#10496)
- ♦ **GNS** Gulf Neurosurgical Society (#10836)
- ♦ **GNSH** Global Network for Simulation in Healthcare (#10499)
- ♦ **GNSH** Global Network for Sustainable Housing (#10502)
- ♦ GNSH – Grey Nuns of the Sacred Heart (religious order)
- ♦ **GNSSN** Global Nuclear Safety and Security Network (#10509)
- ♦ GNUD / see United Nations Sustainable Development Group (#20634)
- ♦ GNU – Global Nurses United (unconfirmed)
- ♦ **GNWP** Global Network of Women Peacebuilders (#10503)
- ♦ **GNWS** Global Network of Women's Shelters (#10504)

♦ GO15 10672

SG 2502 Creekside Drive, Lansdale PA 19446, USA. T. +12674202082. E-mail: secretariat@go15.org.
URL: http://www.go15.org/
History 2004, as *Very Large Power Grid Operators Association (VLPGO)*. Full title: *GO15 – Reliable and Sustainable Power Grid*. Became a formal organization, 2009. **Aims** Reach international consensus on strategic issues; develop a common vision with respect to the technologies and best practices required to address those issues; facilitate implementation of the vision through informational exchanges, joint projects and cooperation with other international organizations in the industry. **Structure** Governing Board. Steering Board, comprising President and 2 Vice-Presidents (Past-President and Future President). Secretariat, headed by Secretary General. President. **Events** *Annual Meeting* New York, NY (USA) 2013, *Annual Meeting* Paris (France) 2012. **Publications** *GO15 Newsletter*.
Members Full in 14 countries:
Australia, Belgium, Brazil, China, France, India, Italy, Japan, Korea Rep, Russia, South Africa, Spain, UK, USA. [2014/XJ7581/**F**]

- ♦ GO15 – Reliable and Sustainable Power Grid / see GO15 (#10672)
- ♦ GO3ETA Inc / see Global Organization for EPA and DHA Omega-3 (#10517)
- ♦ GÖAB – Gesellschaft für Österreichisch-Arabische Beziehungen (internationally oriented national body)
- ♦ **GOAC** Greek Orthodox Archdiocesan Council of America (#10708)
- ♦ GOA – Global Online Academy (internationally oriented national body)
- ♦ GOAL (internationally oriented national body)
- ♦ GOAL / see Alianza Global del Ombudsperson Local (#00629)
- ♦ GOAL International / see GOAL
- ♦ GOAL USA / see GOAL
- ♦ **GOARN** Global Outbreak Alert and Response Network (#10521)
- ♦ Gobierno Mundial de Ciudadano/a/s Mundiales (#21543)
- ♦ **GOBLET** Global Organisation for Bioinformatics Learning, Education and Training (#10516)
- ♦ GOBLET Stichting / see Global Organisation for Bioinformatics Learning, Education and Training (#10516)
- ♦ **GODAN** Global Open Data for Agriculture and Nutrition (#10514)
- ♦ Godfrey's Children (internationally oriented national body)
- ♦ GODT – Global Observatory on Donation and Transplantation (internationally oriented national body)
- ♦ Godwin Osung International Foundation / see Cohesive Communities Development Initiative
- ♦ **GOED** Global Organization for EPA and DHA Omega-3 (#10517)
- ♦ GOER – Grupo de Operaciones Especiales en Rescate (internationally oriented national body)
- ♦ Goethe-Institut (internationally oriented national body)
- ♦ GOETO – Grand Order of European Travel Organizers (inactive)
- ♦ **GOF** Global Forum on Oceans, Coasts and Islands (#10377)
- ♦ **GOGLA** Global Off-Grid Lighting Association (#10513)
- ♦ GO – Global Oceans (internationally oriented national body)
- ♦ GO – Global Oncology (internationally oriented national body)
- ♦ Go Green Initiative (internationally oriented national body)
- ♦ **GO!** Growing Opportunities International (#10797)
- ♦ GOIAVE – Groupement océanien des instituts à vocation environnementale (inactive)
- ♦ **GOIC** Gulf Organization for Industrial Consulting (#10837)

♦ Going-Electric 10673

Pres Rue Royale 15, 1000 Brussels, Belgium. T. +32472991801. Fax +3223074704.
History May 2008. Founding Assembly, 29 Apr 2009, Brussels (Belgium). Former names and other names: *European Association for Battery Electric Vehicles* – former (May 2008 to Jun 2010); *Going-Electric – The Association for Electric Vehicles and Their Users in Europe* – full title. Registration: Start date: 24 Jun 2009, Belgium. **Aims** Ensure European policies and directives leading to the research subsidies and incentives to producers, consumers and cities that will enable Europe to become a leader in terms of production of EVs and their parts as well as of EV commercialization. **Structure** Board of Directors, comprising President, Vice-President and Secretary. [2013/XJ7683/**D**]

- ♦ Going-Electric – The Association for Electric Vehicles and Their Users in Europe / see Going-Electric (#10673)
- ♦ Goi Peace Foundation (internationally oriented national body)
- ♦ Golda Meir Mount Carmel International Training Centre (internationally oriented national body)

♦ Golden Flower T'ai Chi Association International 10674

Contact 612 North Trade St, Winston-Salem NC 27101, USA. T. +13367271131.
URL: http://www.goldenflower.org/
Members Schools in 4 countries:
Belgium, Netherlands, Russia, USA. [2010/XN7267/**D**]

♦ Golden Key International Honour Society 10675

Headquarters 1040 Crown Pointe Parkway, Ste 900, Atlanta GA 30338-4724, USA. T. +16786892200. Fax +16786892298. E-mail: memberservices@goldenkey.org.
URL: http://www.goldenkey.org/
History 1977, USA. An academic honour society. **Aims** Recognize and encourage scholastic achievement and excellence among college and university students from all academic disciplines. **Activities** International and regional conferences. Awards over US$ 400,000 annually through scholarship and award programmes. **Events** *Asia-Pacific conference* Sydney, NSW (Australia) 2010, *Asia Pacific conference* Canberra, ACT (Australia) 2009, *Conference* New Orleans, LA (USA) 2008, *International conference* Atlanta, GA (USA) 2007, *Asia Pacific regional conference* Surfers Paradise, QLD (Australia) 2007.
Members Chapters (350) in 7 countries:
Australia, Canada, Malaysia, New Zealand, South Africa, United Arab Emirates, USA. [2011/XM2839/**F**]

- ♦ Golden Palm International (internationally oriented national body)
- ♦ **GOLD** Global Initiative for Chronic Obstructive Lung Disease (#10423)
- ♦ GOLD – Global Organization for Lysosomal Diseases (inactive)
- ♦ Goldin Institute for International Partnership and Peace (internationally oriented national body)

♦ Gold Mercury International (GMI) 10676

Contact 13 Chesterfield Street, Mayfair, London, W1J 5JN, UK. T. +441212881210. E-mail: chon.kemp@goldmercury.org.
URL: http://www.goldmercury.org/

History 1961, Rome (Italy). Founded by Eduardo De Santis. Headquarters relocated from Rome to London (UK). **Aims** Work with corporations, governments, organizations and leaders to navigate global complexity and advance better governance, peace, sustainability and cooperation. **Structure** International Advisory Board; Awards Nomination Committee. **Languages** English. **Staff** 15.00 FTE, paid. Several voluntary. **Finance** Sources: fees for services; meeting proceeds; sale of publications; sponsorship. **Activities** Awards/prizes/competitions; events/meetings; guidance/assistance/consulting; monitoring/evaluation; politics/policy/regulatory; research/documentation; training/education. **Events** *Conference* London (UK) 2013, *Conference* Portugal 2011, *Conference* Colombia 2009, *Conference* London (UK) 2007, *Conference* Venice (Italy) 2007. **Publications** *Anticipatory Governance Series*; *Policy Report Series*. Strategic foresight and business model innovation publications. **Information Services** *GLOGO – Global Governance Monitoring System*.
[2021.05.18/XF6985/**F**]

♦ Golf Course Association Europe (GCAE) 10677

Main Office Zuiderweg 68a, 1456 NH Wijdewormer, Netherlands. T. +31203306103. E-mail: office@gcae.eu.
URL: http://www.gcae.eu/

History 2006, as *European Golf Course Owners Association (EGCOA)*. Present name adopted, 2018. **Aims** Professionalize the golf business on a European level; expand the game of golf and create a positive attitude towards the game; protect the industry's interests on a European level. **Structure** Board of Directors; Advisory Board. **Staff** 2.00 FTE, paid. **Events** *Conference* Cascais (Portugal) 2020, *Conference* Berlin (Germany) 2019, *Conference* Vienna (Austria) 2018, *Conference* Amsterdam (Netherlands) 2016, *Conference* Amsterdam (Netherlands) 2015.
Members National associations in 12 countries:
Austria, Czechia, Denmark, Finland, France, Germany, Italy, Netherlands, Portugal, Slovenia, Sweden, Switzerland.
NGO Relations Supports: *GEO Foundation (#10132)*. [2018/XM3040/**D**]

- ♦ Golf Environment Europe / see GEO Foundation (#10132)
- ♦ Golf Environment Organisation / see GEO Foundation (#10132)
- ♦ **GOL** Gift of Life International (#10150)
- ♦ Go-MCH – Global Organization for Maternal and Child Health (internationally oriented national body)
- ♦ Gondra Treaty – Treaty to Avoid or Prevent Conflicts between the American States (1923 treaty)
- ♦ Gondwana Research Group / see International Association for Gondwana Research (#11923)
- ♦ **GONG** Global Oscillation Network Group (#10520)
- ♦ Gonin Society / see Jules Gonin Club (#16165)
- ♦ Good360 (internationally oriented national body)

♦ GoodBirth Network 10678

Contact address not obtained. E-mail: stan@goodbirth.net.
URL: http://goodbirth.net/

History 1 Jan 2016, San Francisco, CA (USA). Registration: Section 501(c)(3), USA. **Aims** Share and promote good *birth* practices and birth home models in low-resource communities. **Structure** Global network of mid-wifery centres and researchers. **Activities** Knowledge management/information dissemination; standards/guidelines; training/education. **NGO Relations** Member of (1): *PMNCH (#18410)*. [2022.10.25/XM7013/**F**]

- ♦ Good Clinical Practice Alliance (unconfirmed)

♦ GoodElectronics 10679

Contact KNSM-laan 17, 1019 KA Amsterdam, Netherlands. T. +31206391291. E-mail: info@goodelectronics.org.
URL: https://goodelectronics.org/

Aims Contribute to improving corporate and public *policies* and practices with regard to protecting and respecting *human rights* and the *environment* in the global *electronics* supply chain, with a specific focus on big brand companies. **Structure** Steering Committee; International Network Coordinator. **Finance** Supported by: *European Union (EU, #08967)*.
Members Organizations, including 20 listed in this Yearbook:
African Resources Watch (AFREWATCH); *Asia Monitor Resource Centre (AMRC)*; *Basel Action Network (BAN, #03182)*; *Bread for All*; *Catholic Agency for Overseas Development (CAFOD)*; *Environmental Coalition on Standards (ECOS, #05499)*; *European Coalition for Corporate Justice (ECCJ, #06591)*; *European Environmental Bureau (EEB, #06996)*; *Global Labor Justice-International Labor Rights Forum (GLJ-ILRF)*; *Greenpeace International (#10727)*; *IndustriALL Global Union (IndustriALL, #11177)*; *Interfaith Center on Corporate Responsibility (ICCR)*; *International Campaign for Responsible Technology (I-CRT)*; *International Trade Union Confederation (ITUC, #15708)*; *People and Planet*; *Solidarity Center*; *Stichting Onderzoek Multinationale Ondernemingen (SOMO)*; *Worker Rights Consortium (WRC)*; *Workers Hub For Change (WH4C, #21052)*; *World Economy, Ecology and Development (WEED)*. [2023/XM7605/y/**F**]

- ♦ Good Energies Foundation (unconfirmed)
- ♦ Good Fish Foundation (internationally oriented national body)
- ♦ Good Food Institute (internationally oriented national body)
- ♦ Good Food Institute Europe (unconfirmed)
- ♦ Good Helpers (internationally oriented national body)
- ♦ The Good Lobby / see eLabEurope
- ♦ Good Neighbors International (internationally oriented national body)
- ♦ Good News Missionary Society (religious order)
- ♦ Good People International (internationally oriented national body)
- ♦ Good People World Family / see Good People International
- ♦ GoodPlanet Foundation (internationally oriented national body)

♦ Good Shepherd International Foundation (GSIF) 10680

Contact Via Raffaello Sardiello 20, 00165 Rome RM, Italy. T. +3906661791. E-mail: info@gsif.it.
URL: https://www.gsif.it/

History 2007, Italy. Founded by *Sisters of Our Lady of Charity of the Good Shepherd*, as a Mission Development Office. Became incorporated as a foundation, 2008. **Aims** Support the programs of the Good Shepherd sisters for vulnerable children, girls and women, promoting the rights of people living in poverty, affected by human trafficking, migration, gender-based violence and other forms of discrimination. **Structure** Assembly of Founders; Board of Directors; Congregational Leadership Team. **NGO Relations** Partner of (1): *Global Battery Alliance (GBA, #10249)*. [2020/AA1983/t/**F**]

- ♦ Good Shepherd Sisters of Quebec – Servants of the Immaculate Heart of Mary (religious order)

♦ GoodWeave International 10681

Main Office 1111 14th St NW, Ste 820, Washington DC 20005, USA. E-mail: info@goodweave.org.
URL: http://www.goodweave.net/

History 5 Sep 1994, on the initiative of *South Asian Coalition on Child Servitude (SACCS, #19725)*. Original title: *Rugmark Foundation (RMF)*; also referred to as *RugMark International (RMI)*. **Aims** End exploitative *child labour* in the *carpet* industry of South Asia; as an international, independent, legal, professional and non-commercial *certification* and monitoring system, provide an internationally credible monitoring and certification mechanism for carpets made without child labour; encourage adult employment with reasonable wages and facilities; through consumer education, promote trade prospects of firms and establishments genuine in their commitment to abide by GoodWeave criteria. **Structure** Offices in: Afghanistan; India; Nepal; UK; USA. **Languages** English. **Staff** 26.00 FTE, paid. **Finance** All country offices have individual budgets. **Activities** Develops the GoodWeave trademark. Inspects weaving factories; companies meeting strict no-child-labour standards are issued with unique, traceable certification labels for their rugs. Provides rehabilitation and education for former child weavers. Direct action to prevent child labour includes awareness work in producing and consumer communities and marketing campaigns. Works with *ISEAL (#16026)* to develop standards in the wider framework of environmental and social responsibility.
Members Individuals in 40 countries and territories:
Argentina, Australia, Austria, Bangladesh, Barbados, Belgium, Bhutan, Brazil, Canada, Côte d'Ivoire, Denmark, Finland, France, Germany, Greece, Hong Kong, India, Ireland, Italy, Japan, Malaysia, Mauritius, Mexico, Morocco, Nepal, Netherlands, New Zealand, Nigeria, Norway, Singapore, South Africa, Spain, Sudan, Sweden, Switzerland, Taiwan, Thailand, Trinidad-Tobago, USA, Zimbabwe.
Organizations in 3 countries:
Burkina Faso, Mauritania, Togo.
IGO Relations *UNICEF (#20332)*. **NGO Relations** Supported by: *Anti-Slavery International (#00860)*; *Asia Pacific Workers Solidarity Link (APWSL, #02078)*; *Asian American Free Labor Institute (AAFLI, no recent information)*; *Brot für die Welt*; *Christian Aid*; *German Catholic Bishops' Organisation for Development Cooperation (MISEREOR)*; *International Trade Union Confederation (ITUC, #15708)*; *Rädda Barnen – Save the Children Sweden*. Member of: *International Corporate Accountability Roundtable (ICAR, #12968)*.
[2018/XG3469/**E**]

- ♦ Goodwill Industries International (internationally oriented national body)
- ♦ **GOOS Africa** Global Ocean Observing System for Africa (#10512)
- ♦ **GOOS** Global Ocean Observing System (#10511)

♦ GOOS Regional Alliance for the South East Pacific (GRASP) 10682

Chief Officer GOOS Project Office, IOC Secretariat – UNESCO, 1 rue Miollis, 75732 Paris CEDEX 15, France. T. +33145683992.
URL: http://www.ioc-goos.org/

History May 2003, within *Intergovernmental Oceanographic Commission (IOC, #11496)* as part of *Global Ocean Observing System (GOOS, #10511)*. **Events** *Meeting* Lima (Peru) 2007. [2013/XE4614/**E**]

- ♦ **GO-P2P** Global Observatory on Peer-to-Peer, Community Self-Consumption and Transactive Energy Models (#10510)
- ♦ GOPAC América Latina y el Caribe (see: #10518)
- ♦ **GOPAC** Global Organization of Parliamentarians Against Corruption (#10518)
- ♦ GOPAC Oceania (see: #10518)
- ♦ GOPA / see European Political Strategy Centre (#08248)
- ♦ GOP – Green Our Planet (internationally oriented national body)
- ♦ **GO!PHA** Global Organization for PHA (#10519)
- ♦ Gorbachev Foundation – International Foundation of Socio-Economic and Political Studies (internationally oriented national body)
- ♦ Gorta – Self Help Africa / see Self Help Africa (#19220)
- ♦ Gospel for Asia (internationally oriented national body)
- ♦ Gospel Communications International (internationally oriented national body)
- ♦ Gospel Films / see Gospel Communications International
- ♦ Gospel Literature Worldwide (internationally oriented national body)
- ♦ Gospel Missionary Union / see Avant Ministries
- ♦ Gospel Outreach / see OC International (#17688)
- ♦ Gospel Recordings International / see Global Recordings Network
- ♦ GOSS – Gulf Obesity Surgery Society (unconfirmed)
- ♦ Gossner Mission (internationally oriented national body)
- ♦ GOT – Global Ocean Trust (unconfirmed)
- ♦ Gothenburg University, Department of Peace and Conflict Research / see Department of Peace and Development Research, Gothenburg University
- ♦ **GOTS** Gesellschaft für Orthopädisch-Traumatologische Sportmedizin (#19614)
- ♦ **GOTS** Global Organic Textile Standard International Working Group (#10515)

♦ Gottfried-Wilhelm-Leibniz-Gesellschaft (GWLG) 10683

Société internationale Gottfried-Wilhelm-Leibniz – International Gottfried-Wilhelm-Leibniz Society
Dir GWLB-NLB, Waterloostrasse 8, 30169 Hannover, Germany. T. +495111267331. Fax +495111267202. E-mail: info@leibnizgesellschaft.de.
Exec Officer address not obtained. E-mail: info@leibnizgesellschaft.de.
URL: http://www.gottfried-wilhelm-leibniz-gesellschaft.de/

History 1966, Hannover (Germany FR). **Aims** Advance the knowledge of the work and activity of Leibniz, of the manner in which Leibniz cultivates the relationship between the disciplines of sciences and inform wider circles on the conceptions of Leibniz. **Structure** General Assembly; Board; Scientific Committee. **Languages** German. **Activities** Events/meetings. **Events** *Congress* Hannover (Germany) 2011, *Congress* Hannover (Germany) 2006, *Congress* Berlin (Germany) 2001, *Leibniz and Europe* Hannover (Germany) 1994, *Congress* Hannover (Germany FR) 1988. **Publications** *Studia Leibnitiana* (2 a year); *Supplementa*. *Sonderhefte*.
Members Individuals and organizations (400) in 31 countries and territories:
Argentina, Australia, Austria, Belgium, Canada, Croatia, Cuba, Czechia, Denmark, Finland, France, Germany, Hungary, India, Ireland, Israel, Italy, Japan, Korea Rep, Mexico, Netherlands, Poland, Portugal, Romania, Serbia, Spain, Switzerland, Taiwan, UK, Ukraine, USA.
NGO Relations Member of: *International Federation of Philosophical Societies (FISP, #13507)*. Links with a number of national organizations interested in the field. [2018/XE0404/**E**]

- ♦ Gouvernement mondial des citoyen/ne/s du monde (#21543)
- ♦ Gov2u (unconfirmed)
- ♦ Governance Institutes Network International (internationally oriented national body)
- ♦ Governance International (internationally oriented national body)
- ♦ Governance Resource Centre / see Governance and Social Development Resource Centre
- ♦ Governance Risk Compliance Security International (unconfirmed)
- ♦ Governance and Social Development Resource Centre (internationally oriented national body)
- ♦ GOW – Global Optimization Workshop (meeting series)
- ♦ GP4HEiE – Global Platform for Higher Education in Emergencies (unconfirmed)
- ♦ GP 4 LA – Global Partnership for Local Action (internationally oriented national body)
- ♦ GPAAAC – Global Parliamentary Alliance Against Atrocity Crimes (unconfirmed)
- ♦ GPAC Trust – Give Peace a Chance Trust (internationally oriented national body)
- ♦ **GPA Europe** Gas Processors Association – Europe (#10076)
- ♦ **GPAFI** Groupement de prévoyance et d'assurance des fonctionnaires internationaux (#10764)
- ♦ **GPA Global** Global Gas Processors Alliance (#10387)
- ♦ **GPA** Global Privacy Assembly (#10555)
- ♦ GPA – Global Programme of Action for the Protection of the Marine Environment from Land-Based Activities (see: #20299)
- ♦ GPAHE – Global Project Against Hate and Extremism (internationally oriented national body)
- ♦ GPAI – Global Partnership on Artificial Intelligence (unconfirmed)
- ♦ GPC / see Peace Containers
- ♦ **GPCA** Global Private Capital Association (#10556)
- ♦ **GPCA** Gulf Petrochemicals and Chemicals Association (#10839)
- ♦ GPCC – Global Precipitation Climatology Centre (internationally oriented national body)
- ♦ GPCE / see Pharmaceutical Group of the European Union (#18352)
- ♦ GPC / see Global Canopy (#10271)
- ♦ GPC – Global Peace Campaign (internationally oriented national body)
- ♦ **GPC** Global Protection Cluster (#10560)
- ♦ **GPC** Global Pulse Confederation (#10562)
- ♦ **GPcwd** Global Partnership on Children with Disabilities (#10529)
- ♦ **GPDD** Global Partnership for Disability and Development (#10530)
- ♦ GPD – Glass Performance Days (meeting series)
- ♦ GPDO – Global Peace Development Organization (internationally oriented national body)
- ♦ GPDSA – Global Peace and Development Service Alliance (unconfirmed)
- ♦ GPD / see Strategies for Peace (#20008)
- ♦ GPE / see American Forum for Global Education
- ♦ **GPEAN** Global Planning Education Association Network (#10549)
- ♦ **GPEDC** Global Partnership for Effective Development Co-operation (#10532)
- ♦ **GPED** Global Pediatric Endocrinology and Diabetes (#10545)
- ♦ **GPE** Global Partnership for Education (#10531)
- ♦ **GPEI** Global Polio Eradication Initiative (#10553)
- ♦ GPEL – Global Partnership for Emerging Leaders (internationally oriented national body)

♦ GPEN – Globalization of Pharmaceutics Education Network (unconfirmed)
♦ GPER – Global Parents for Eczema Research (internationally oriented national body)

♦ GPF Europe 10684

Dir Königstr 37a, 53115 Bonn, Germany. T. +492289650510. Fax +492289638206. E-mail: europe@globalpolicy.org.
URL: https://www.globalpolicy.org

History 24 Sep 2004, Bonn (Germany). Founded as a legally and financially independent sister organization of *Global Policy Forum (GPF)*. Former names and other names: *Global Policy Forum Europe* – full title. Registration: Germany; EU Transparency Register, No/ID: 539713836884-33. **Aims** Monitor the work of the *United Nations* and scrutinize global policy making; promote *accountability* and citizen participation in decisions on peace and security, social justice and international law; analyse deep and persistent structures of power and rapidly-emerging issues and crises. **Activities** Advocacy/lobbying/activism; events/meetings; knowledge management/information dissemination; monitoring/evaluation; research/documentation. **NGO Relations** Member of (1): *Social Watch (#19350)*. [2021.05.27/XJ4592/**E**]

♦ **GPF** Global Partnerships Forum (#10540)
♦ **GPF** Global Peace Foundation (#10544)
♦ GPF – Global Peering Forum (internationally oriented national body)
♦ GPF – Global Policy Forum (internationally oriented national body)
♦ **GPF** Global Progressive Forum (#10557)
♦ **GPFI** Global Partnership for Financial Inclusion (#10534)
♦ **GPFLR** Global Partnership on Forest and Landscape Restoration (#10535)
♦ GP – Global Potential (internationally oriented national body)
♦ **GP** Groupe Polyphénols (#10767)
♦ GPHF – Global Pharma Health Fund (internationally oriented national body)
♦ **GPH** Global Parliamentarians on Habitat (#10525)
♦ **GPIC** Gulf Petrochemical Industries Company (#10838)
♦ **GPIE** Groupement des pharmaciens de l'industrie en europe (#07530)
♦ GPI – Global Press Institute (internationally oriented national body)
♦ GPI – Good People International (internationally oriented national body)
♦ **GPLN** Global Project Logistics Network (#10559)
♦ GPLRA – Global Psychology and Language Research Association (internationally oriented national body)
♦ **GPM** Global Parliament of Mayors (#10527)
♦ GPM – Green Project Management (unconfirmed)
♦ **GPML** United Nations Global Programme Against Money Laundering, Proceeds of Crime and the Financing of Terrorism (#20568)
♦ **GPN** Global Planners Network (#10548)
♦ GPOBA / see Global Partnership for Results-Based Approaches (#10539)
♦ **GPO** Global Partnership for Oceans (#10537)
♦ GPoT – Global Political Trends Center (internationally oriented national body)
♦ GPPAC Foundation – Global Partnership for the Prevention of Armed Conflict Foundation (internationally oriented national body)
♦ **GPPAC** Global Partnership for the Prevention of Armed Conflict (#10538)
♦ GPP – Geneva Peacebuilding Platform (internationally oriented national body)
♦ **GPP** Gesellschaft für pädiatrische Pneumologie (#10143)
♦ GPP – Global Philanthropy Partnership (internationally oriented national body)
♦ **GPP** Global Philanthropy Project (#10546)
♦ GPP / see Groupe de Recherche Petites Paysanneries (#10769)
♦ GPPi – Global Public Policy Institute (internationally oriented national body)
♦ **GPPN** Global Public Policy Network (#10561)
♦ **GPPS** Global Power and Propulsion Society (#10554)
♦ **GPRBA** Global Partnership for Results-Based Approaches (#10539)
♦ **GPRI** Global Phosphorus Research Initiative (#10547)
♦ GPRMC / see European Composites Industry Association (#06692)
♦ **GPSA** Global Partnership for Social Accountability (#10541)
♦ GPS – Global Penguin Society (internationally oriented national body)
♦ **GPSN** Global Paediatric Surgery Network (#10522)
♦ **GPSNR** Global Platform for Sustainable Natural Rubber (#10552)
♦ GPS-USA – Global Peace Services USA (internationally oriented national body)
♦ **GPUE** Groupement pharmaceutique de l'Union européenne (#18352)
♦ GPU – GlobalPartnersUnited (internationally oriented national body)
♦ **GPYF** Global Progressive Youth Forum (#10558)
♦ GQAC – Global Quality Assurance Conference (meeting series)
♦ GRAA – Game Rangers Association of Africa (internationally oriented national body)
♦ Le Graal / see The Grail – International Movement of Christian Women (#10689)
♦ Grace Brethren International Missions / see Encompass World Partners

♦ Grace Communion International 10685

Mailing address 3120 Whitehall Park Drive, Charlotte NC 28273, USA. T. +19804953975. E-mail: info@gci.org.
UK Office PO Box 7703, Market Harborough, LE16 7ZG, UK. E-mail: info@gracecom.church.
URL: http://www.gci.org/

History Founded 1934, when Herbert Armstrong began a radio ministry in the State of Oregon (USA) called 'Radio Church of God'. In 1947, incorporated the church in the State of California. In 1968, name changed to *Worldwide Church of God (WCG)*. Offices moved to Pasadena CA (USA) in 1947 and to Glendora CA (USA) in 2006. During 1990s, evaluated some of the foundational and non-traditional doctrines. At that time moved to the center of the historic, orthodox Christian faith; no longer teaches doctrine that Great Britain and the United States of America descended from two of the lost tribes of Israel; currently teaches the Trinity, that God is one divine Being in three eternal, co-essential, yet distinct persons. Other doctrines have also been evaluated and modified in light of Scripture. As a result of rejecting or modifying many of the teachings of Herbert W Armstrong, the denomination experienced the loss of well over half its membership, most of whom became part of over 200 splinter groups (not listed). Current title adopted, 2009, with some nations continuing to use the old name. **Aims** Proclaim the *gospel* of Jesus *Christ* worldwide; help members grow spiritually. **Structure** Based in the USA, with offices in Canada, UK, Europe, South Africa, Australia, Philippines, Caribbean and Latin America. **Languages** English, French, German, Italian, Portuguese, Spanish, Tagalog. **Staff** USA Headquarters: 30; 306 pastors in USA; about 360 internationally. **Finance** Budget (annual) – US Headquarters: about US$ 11 million. **Activities** Services consist of a sermon preceded by congregational singing, special music, church life presentations, prayer and local announcements. Sponsored *'Ambassador University'* in East Texas (closed operation in 1997). Also previously had media presence with *'World Tomorrow'* television programme (went off the air in 1994). Organizes international conferences. Sponsors various regional conferences, seminars, spiritual-enrichment programs and camps, retreats for the pastors and members of the church. **Events** *International Conference* Orlando, FL (USA) 2013, *Feast of the tabernacles* Bournemouth (UK) 2000, *Feast of the tabernacles* Eastbourne (UK) 1999, *Feast of the tabernacles* Eastbourne (UK) 1998, *Feast of the tabernacles* Rye (UK) 1997. **Publications** *Christian Odyssey* – US; *Face to Face* – South Africa; *GCI Today* – Australia; *La Vie Chrétienne* – France; *LifeLine* – Netherlands; *Nachfolge* – Germany; *Northern Light* – Canada; *Odisea Cristiana* – Latin America. **Members** Active in nearly 100 countries and territories, with about 42,000 members, in over 900 congregations. Membership countries not specified. **NGO Relations** Internationally, belongs to various evangelical organizations. Affiliated with: Grace Communion Seminary. Also member of a number of national evangelical organizations in the USA. [2022/XF1371/**F**]

♦ GRACE – Global Resource Action Center for the Environment (internationally oriented national body)
♦ **GRACE** Groupe francophone de Réhabilitation Améliorée après Chirurgie (#10743)
♦ GRACEH – Graduate Conference in European History (meeting series)
♦ Grâce international, la / see Dialogue Afrique-Europe
♦ Graduate Business Admission Council / see Graduate Management Admission Council (#10687)

♦ Graduate Business Forum (GBF) 10686

Address not obtained.
URL: http://graduatebusinessforum.com/

History 1983. Registration: 501(c)(3) nonprofit corporation, USA. **Aims** Be a catalyst organization for positive change in management education, business and society; inspire graduate leaders to adopt a global citizen mindset and internalize a holistic view of leadership and growth beyond profit also including people, planet and peace. **Structure** Board of Directors; Executive Team. **Activities** Events/meetings. **Events** *Conference* Paris (France) 2019. [2020/AA0893/**F**]

♦ Graduate Conference in European History (meeting series)
♦ Graduate Institute of International and Development Studies (internationally oriented national body)
♦ Graduate Institute of Political and International Studies (internationally oriented national body)

♦ Graduate Management Admission Council (GMAC) 10687

Mailing Address PO Box 2969, Reston VA 20195, USA. T. +17036689600. Fax +17036689601. E-mail: customercare@gmac.com.
Europe Office PO Box 70184, London, WC1A 9HZ, UK. E-mail: emea@gmac.com.
URL: http://www.gmac.com/

History 1970. Exam created 1953. Former names and other names: *Graduate Business Admission Council (GBAC)* – former (1970 to 1976). **Structure** Board of Directors, comprising Chair, Vice-Chair and 12 members. **Activities** Owns and administers *'Graduate Management Admission Test (GMAT)'* exam. **Events** *Annual Conference* Baltimore, MD (USA) 2022, *Leadership Conference* Baltimore, MD (USA) 2022, *Asia Pacific Conference* Bangkok (Thailand) 2016.
Members Schools in 27 countries and territories:
Australia, Belgium, Brazil, Canada, China, Costa Rica, Denmark, Egypt, France, Germany, Hong Kong, India, Ireland, Israel, Italy, Korea Rep, Netherlands, Russia, Singapore, South Africa, Spain, Sweden, Switzerland, Taiwan, Thailand, UK, USA.
Included in the above, 5 institutions listed in this Yearbook:
China-Europe International Business School (CEIBS, #03888); Escuela Superior de Administración y Dirección de Empresas (ESADE); ESMT Berlin; INSEAD (#11228); IPADE Business School.
NGO Relations Member of: *EFMD – The Management Development Network (#05387).* [2020/XJ7292/y/**C**]

♦ Graduate School of Asian and African Area Studies (internationally oriented national body)
♦ Graduate School of European and International Studies / see Graduate Institute of Political and International Studies
♦ Graduate School of International Relations (internationally oriented national body)
♦ Graduate School of International Studies, Denver / see Josef Korbel School of International Studies
♦ Graduate School of International Studies, Seoul (internationally oriented national body)
♦ Graduate School of International Trade and Business Administration, Laredo TX (internationally oriented national body)
♦ Graduate School of Islamic and Social Sciences (internationally oriented national body)
♦ Graduate School of Public and International Affairs, Pittsburgh (internationally oriented national body)

♦ Graduate Women International (GWI) 10688

Contact Chemin du Grand-Montfleury 48, 1290 Versoix GE, Switzerland. T. +41227312380.
URL: http://www.graduatewomen.org/

History Founded 11 Jul 1919, London (UK), as *International Federation of University Women (IFUW) – Fédération internationale des femmes diplômées des universités (FIFDU) – Federación Internacional de Mujeres Universitarias (FIMU)*. Current name adopted 2015. Moved to Geneva (Switzerland), 1972. Latest revision of Constitution: 2015, Manchester (UK). **Aims** Promote *lifelong education* for women and *girls*; promote international cooperation, friendship, peace and respect for human *rights* for all, whatever their gender, age, race, nationality, religion, political opinion, sexual orientation or other status; advocate for advancement of the status of women and girls; encourage and enable them to apply their knowledge and skills in leadership and decision-making in all forms of public and private life. **Structure** General Assembly (every 3 years). Standing Committees (5): Fellowships; Education; Membership; Resolutions; Finance. Special Committees (2): Project Development; Hegg-Hoffet Fund. Representative to the UN and Specialized Agencies: New York NY (USA) (ECOSOC); Geneva (Switzerland) (ECOSOC and ILO); Vienna (Austria) (ECOSOC); Paris (France) (UNESCO). Regional groupings (5): *Federation of University Women of Africa (FUWA, #09711); University Women of Asia (UWA, #20706); University Women of Europe (UWE, #20707); Latin American Federation of University Women (#16334); Pacific Graduate Women's Network (PGWNet).* **Languages** English. **Staff** 2.00 FTE, paid. **Finance** Capitation fees of individual members through national federations and associations; donations from members and others; legacies; grants from third parties for special projects. **Activities** Advocacy/lobbying/activism; events/meetings; financial and/or material support; projects/programmes; research/documentation; training/education. **Events** *Triennial Conference* Tokyo (Japan) 2022, *Triennial Conference* Geneva (Switzerland) 2019, *Triennial Conference* Cape Town (South Africa) 2016, *Asian Regional Workshop on Capacity Building* Singapore (Singapore) 2014, *Seminar on Increasing Access to Education for Girls and Women in Asia* Singapore (Singapore) 2014. **Publications** *GWI Update*; *IFUW Update*. Annual Report; policy updates; policy papers; internal newsletters.
Members National federations and associations in 54 countries and territories:
Argentina, Australia, Austria, Bangladesh, Bolivia, Bulgaria, Burkina Faso, Cameroon, Canada, Congo DR, Cyprus, Egypt, El Salvador, England, Fiji, France, Ghana, Haiti, Hong Kong, Iceland, India, Ireland, Israel, Japan, Kenya, Korea Rep, Lebanon, Lithuania, Mexico, Nepal, Netherlands, New Zealand, Nigeria, Northern Ireland, Norway, Pakistan, Panama, Paraguay, Russia, Rwanda, Scotland, Senegal, Sierra Leone, Singapore, Slovenia, Somalia, South Africa, Spain, Switzerland, Türkiye, Uganda, USA, Zambia, Zimbabwe.
Consultative Status Consultative status granted from: *ECOSOC (#05331)* (Special); *UNESCO (#20322)* (Consultative Status); *ILO (#11123)* (Special List); *UNICEF (#20332).* **NGO Relations** Member of: *Committee of NGOs on Human Rights, Geneva (#04275); Conference of Non-Governmental Organizations in Consultative Relationship with the United Nations (CONGO, #04635); International Conference of NGOs (#12883); NGO Committee on the Status of Women, Geneva (#17117); NGO Committee on Sustainable Development, Vienna (#17119); NGO Committee on UNICEF (#17120); Vienna NGO Committee on Drugs (VNGOC, #20773); Vienna NGO Committee on the Status of Women (#20775).* Instrumental in setting up *Women First International Fund (#20996).* [2020.02.07/XB2037/**B**]

♦ GRAEL / see Group of the Greens – European Free Alliance (#10781)
♦ **GRAG** Global Research and Advocacy Group (#10569)
♦ **GRA** Global Research Alliance on Agricultural Greenhouse Gases (#10570)
♦ GRA – Global Resuscitation Alliance (unconfirmed)
♦ **GRA** Global Rewilding Alliance (#10579)
♦ GRA – Global Rights Alert (internationally oriented national body)
♦ The Grail / see The Grail – International Movement of Christian Women (#10689)

♦ The Grail – International Movement of Christian Women 10689

Contact Nieuwegracht 51, 3512 LE Utrecht, Netherlands. E-mail: iltsecr@thegrail.org.
URL: http://www.thegrail.org/

History 1921, Nijmegen (Netherlands). Latest international structures adopted 2011, Kleinmond (South Africa), at International General Assembly. Former names and other names: *International Grail Movement* – former; *Mouvement international du Graal* – former; *The Grail* – former; *Le Graal* – former; *International Movement of Christian Women – The Grail* – former; *International Women's Grail Movement* – former. **Aims** As a spiritual, cultural and social international movement of women grounded in Christian faith, promote global solidarity, environmental sustainability, spiritual search and social, economic and racial justice. **Structure** International General Assembly; International Council; International Leadership Team; International Secretariat; Global Networks including: *Women of the Americas (see: #10689).* **Languages** English, Portuguese, Spanish. **Staff** 1.50 FTE, paid. **Finance** Sources: contributions; donations. *Grail International Solidarity Fund (ISF)* supports only Grail programmes and projects. **Activities** Events/meetings; training/education. **Events** *International Grail Finance Meeting* Fatima (Portugal) 2020, *International Council Meeting* USA 2020, *International Council Meeting* Lembeni (Tanzania UR) 2019, *General Assembly* Fatima (Portugal) 2017, *International Council Meeting* Sydney, NSW (Australia) 2015. **Publications** *Grail International Newsletter* (12 a year); *crossroads* (2 a year) – Bulletin. *Women of Vision* (2017). *Grail Entering the 21st Century* – Booklet. National publications.

Grail Movement
10690

alphabetic sequence excludes
For the complete listing, see Yearbook Online at

Members Grail circles or groups and individuals in 28 countries:
Angola, Australia, Belgium, Belize, Brazil, Canada, Cape Verde, Ecuador, France, Germany, India, Indonesia, Ireland, Italy, Kenya, Mexico, Mozambique, Netherlands, Papua New Guinea, Paraguay, Philippines, Portugal, South Africa, Sweden, Tanzania UR, Uganda, USA, Zimbabwe.
Consultative Status Consultative status granted from: *ECOSOC (#05331)* (Special). **NGO Relations** Member of (1): *Conference of Non-Governmental Organizations in Consultative Relationship with the United Nations (CONGO, #04635).* Instrumental in setting up (1): *Transnational Network for Young European Women (LIEN, see: #10689).* [2021.05.21/XF4372/v/**F**]

♦ Grail Movement 10690

Mouvement international du Graal

Contact 786 Jones Rd, Vestal NY 13850, USA. T. +18004279217. E-mail: info@grailmessage.com.
URL: http://www.grailnet.org/

Aims Spread the *'Message of the Grail'*, being the *spiritual* teachings of Oscar Ernest *Bernehardt*, also known as Abd-Ru-Shin, Son of Man promised by Jesus, on the knowledge of creation, its laws and man's place in it, giving the teachings of *Christ* in a language comprehensible to modern man; publish and disseminate Bernehardt's foretellings. **Publications** *Dans la lumière de la verité* by O E Bernehardt – in several languages. **Members** Individuals (about 15,000) in 62 countries:
Algeria, Angola, Argentina, Australia, Austria, Belgium, Bolivia, Brazil, Bulgaria, Burundi, Cameroon, Canada, Chile, China, Congo Brazzaville, Congo DR, Côte d'Ivoire, Czechoslovakia (unspecified), Denmark, Finland, France, Germany, Greece, Guatemala, Hong Kong, Hungary, India, Ireland, Italy, Japan, Jordan, Kenya, Liechtenstein, Luxembourg, Malawi, Malaysia, Mali, Mexico, Netherlands, New Zealand, Nigeria, Norway, Paraguay, Peru, Philippines, Poland, Portugal, Romania, Senegal, Serbia, South Africa, Spain, Sweden, Switzerland, Togo, Tunisia, Türkiye, UK, Uruguay, USA, Venezuela, Vietnam.
Members also in the former USSR; countries not specified. [2010/XF2260/v/**F**]

♦ GRAIN 10691

Main Office Casanova 118, escalera derecha 1° B, 08036 Barcelona, Spain. E-mail: grain@grain.org.
URL: http://www.grain.org/

History 1990. Founded developing from the former *'Seeds Campaign'* of *International Coalition for Development Action (ICDA, inactive).* Currently an independent organization. Original full title: *Genetic Resources Action International (GRAIN) – Action internationale pour les ressources génétiques – Acción Internacional en pro de los Recursos Genéticos.* Currently only uses acronym as title. Registration: Spain. **Aims** Support small *farmers* and social movements in their struggles for community-controlled and *biodiversity*-based food systems. **Structure** Board. **Languages** English, French, Spanish. **Staff** 14.00 FTE, paid. **Finance** Sources: grants from NGOs, governments and occasionally IGOs. Contributors include: *Bread for All*; *Brot für die Welt*; *Comité Catholique contre la Faim et pour le Développement-Terre Solidaire (CCFD-Terre Solidaire)*; *Catholic Lenten Fund*; *German Catholic Bishops' Organisation for Development Cooperation (MISEREOR)*; *New Field Foundation*; *Oxfam Novib*; *Swissaid.* Sporadic funding from: *European Union (EU, #08967).* **Activities** Networking/liaising; research/documentation; knowledge management/information dissemination; monitoring/evaluation; advocacy/lobbying/activism. **Events** *European NGO network meeting on genetic resources and biotechnology* Barcelona (Spain) 1991, *European NGO Network Meeting on Genetic Resources and Biotechnology* Copenhagen (Denmark) 1988. **Publications** *Biodiversidad: Sustente y Culturas* (4 a year); *Supermarket Watch Asia* (4 a year) – electronic bulletin. Book; reports. **Members** Not a membership organization. **IGO Relations** Links with various UN bodies, especially *FAO (#09260).* [2021/XF2334/**F**]

♦ Grain and Feed Trade Association (GAFTA) 10692

Getreide- und Futtermittel-Handelsvereinigung

Dir Gen 9 Lincoln's Inn Fields, London, WC2A 3BP, UK. T. +442078149666. Fax +442078148383. E-mail: post@gafta.com.
URL: https://www.gafta.com/

History 1878. Founded as London (UK) Corn Trade Association. Present name adopted, 1971, upon merger of Cattle Food Trade Association (CFTA) and London Corn Trade Association (LCTA). Incorporated *International General Produce Association (IGPA, inactive)*, 2009. Registration: No/ID: 1006456, England and Wales. **Aims** Promote international trade in agricultural commodities, spices and general produce; protect members' interests worldwide. **Structure** Annual General Meeting; Council. Offices in: Beijing (China); Singapore (Singapore); Geneva (Switzerland); Kiev (Ukraine); London (UK). **Languages** English. **Staff** 25.00 FTE, paid. **Finance** Sources: members' dues. **Activities** Advocacy/lobbying/activism; networking/liaising; politics/policy/regulatory; standards/guidelines. **Publications** *GAFTAWorld.* **Members** Member companies (over 1,900): trading companies and brokers involved in trading grain, animal feedingstuffs, pulses and rice at all stages of the supply chain from production to final consumption; Individual members, superintendents, arbitrators; Associate members: analysts, fumigators and professional firms that provide services to the trade. Members in 100 countries and territories. Membership countries not specified. **Consultative Status** Consultative status granted from: *ECOSOC (#05331)* (Ros C); *FAO (#09260)* (Special Status); *UNCTAD (#20285)* (Special Category); *UNEP (#20299).* **IGO Relations** Observer status with (1): *Codex Alimentarius Commission (CAC, #04081).* **NGO Relations** Member of (3): *Committee of the Trade in Cereals, Oilseeds, Pulses, Olive Oil, Oils and Fats, Animal Feed and Agrosupply of the EU (COCERAL, #04289)*; *International Agri-Food Network (IAFN, #11599)*; *International Grain Trade Coalition (IGTC, #13732).* [2021.06.15/XD3848/t/**D**]

♦ Grain and Feed Trade Committee of the EC / see Committee of the Trade in Cereals, Oilseeds, Pulses, Olive Oil, Oils and Fats, Animal Feed and Agrosupply of the EU (#04289)
♦ Grains Trade Convention (1994 treaty)
♦ GRAIPE / see European Rural and Isolated Practitioners Association (#08415)
♦ GRALAC – Centre for the Study of the Great Lakes Region of Africa (internationally oriented national body)
♦ GRAM / see Vision GRAM-International

♦ Grameen Bank (GB) 10693

Main Office Grameen Bank Bhaban, Mirpur 2, Dhaka 1216, Bangladesh. T. +88029031138. Fax +88029033559. E-mail: mdsecretariat@grameen.com.
URL: http://www.grameen.com/

History 2 Oct 1983, Bangladesh. Founded when officially founded as an independent bank, having originated, 1976, as an action research project of Chittagong University. Founder: Prof Muhammad Yunus. Received the Nobel Peace Price in 2006. **Aims** Eradicate *poverty* in Bangladesh by: using *credit* as a cost-effective weapon against poverty and as a catalyst in improving socio-economic conditions of the poor; extend banking facilities to poor women as well as men; eliminate exploitation of the poor by money lenders so as to create opportunity for self employment for unutilized and underutilized *manpower* resources; bring disadvantaged people into an organizational system that they can understand and operate and can find socio-political and economic strength through mutual support; reverse the vicious circle of low income to an expanding system of low income – credit – *investment* – more income – more credit – more investment – more income. **Structure** Includes: *Grameen Trust (GT, #10695)*; *Grameen Global Network (GGN, see: #10693).* **Finance** Paid-up share capital: Government of Bangladesh 25%; Bank borrowers 75%. Total disbursement of loan funds as of Jul 2000: US$ 3,000 million. Repayment rate 98%. **Activities** Financial and/or material support; training/education; networking/liaising. **Publications** Via Grameen Trust. **Members** Not a membership organization. [2019/XF3094/**F**]

♦ Grameen Foundation (GF) 10694

Pres/CEO 1400 K St NW, Ste 550, Washington DC 20005, USA. T. +12026283560. Fax +12026282341.
URL: http://www.grameenfoundation.org/

History 1997, inspired by the work of Nobel Prize winner Prof Muhammad Yunus. Registered in accordance with US law. **Aims** Enable the *poor*, especially women, to create a world without *hunger* and *poverty.* **Structure** Board of Directors. Subsidiaries (2): Grameen Foundation India; TaroWorks. Merged with *Freedom from Hunger (inactive)*, 2016. **Activities** Advocacy/lobbying/activism. **Publications** *GF eNewsletter.* **NGO Relations** Member of: *Alliance for Affordable Internet (A4AI, #00651)*; *Better Than Cash Alliance (#03220)*; *InsideNGO (inactive)*; *Partnership for Responsible Financial Inclusion (PRFI, #18241).* [2017.07.05/XM5383/f/**F**]

♦ Grameen Global Network (see: #10693)

♦ Grameen Trust (GT) 10695

Main Office Telecom Bhaban Level 3, 53/1 Box Nagar, Zoo Road, Mirpur-1, Dhaka 1216, Bangladesh. E-mail: info@grameentrust.org.
URL: http://www.grameentrust.org/

History 1989. Founded as sister organization to *Grameen Bank (GB, #10693).* **Aims** Support and promote programmes to reduce *poverty* within Grameen Bank projects; provide seed and scaling-up *funding* to replication projects working with the poorest, especially *women*, in different countries; provide training and technical assistance to global organizations; build a global network of people working for alleviation of poverty; bring about socio-economic changes in the lives of the poor. **Structure** Board of Trustees. **Staff** 46.00 FTE, paid. **Activities** Through Grameen Bank Replication Programme, provides financial, technical, training and information support to organizations implementing microcredit programmes for the poor, following the 'Grameen Bank Approach'. Forms local networks in a number of countries and coordinates *Grameen Global Network (GGN, see: #10693)* as a forum for exchange of experience, learning and information among partners, friends and supporters of Grameen so as to enable effective planning, coordination and monitoring of progress. In collaboration with these networks and with Grameen Bank, organizes: Grameen Dialogue Programmes for policymakers and NGOs; special training programmes; management workshops. **Publications** *Grameen Dialogue* (4 a year) – newsletter; *Grameen Poverty Research* (4 a year) – newsletter. *Grameen Manual* – series. *Grameen Trust: An Update* (1999) by H I Latifee; *Banker to the Poor* (1998) by Muhammad Yunus in Dutch, English, French, German, Gujarati, Italian, Japanese, Portuguese, Spanish, Turkish; *Grameen Bank: Tools and Techniques – Microfinance Technologies* (1998) by H I Latifee; *Poor but Strong: Women in the People's Economy of Bangladesh* (1997) by Ulrike Müller-Glodde; *Participation as Process – Process as Growth: What we can learn from Grameen Bank Bangladesh* (1993) by Andreas Fuglesang and Dale Chandler in Chinese, English; *Grameen Bank: Experiences and Reflections* by Muhammad Yunus in Chinese, Spanish, Vietnamese – translation and commentary of Ismail Hakki Bursevi. Training materials; manuals; booklets.
Members Projects (105) funded in 34 countries and territories:
Afghanistan, Bangladesh, Bolivia, Bosnia-Herzegovina, Cameroon, Central African Rep, China, Ecuador, Egypt, El Salvador, Ethiopia, India, Indonesia, Kenya, Korea Rep, Kosovo, Kyrgyzstan, Lesotho, Malaysia, Mauritania, Mexico, Myanmar, Nepal, Nigeria, Pakistan, Philippines, Samoa, Senegal, Tanzania UR, Togo, Uganda, Vietnam, Zambia, Zimbabwe.
Grameen Foundations in 3 countries:
Argentina, Australia, USA.
IGO Relations *Australian Aid (inactive)*; *Commonwealth Secretariat (#04362)*; *Deutsche Gesellschaft für Technische Zusammenarbeit (GTZ, inactive)*; *UNHCR (#20327)*; *United Nations Capital Development Fund (UNCDF, #20524)*; *United Nations Office for Project Services (UNOPS, #20602)*; *United States Agency for International Development (USAID)*; *The World Bank Group (#21218).* **NGO Relations** *Citi Foundation*; *MacArthur Foundation*; *Oikocredit International (Oikocredit, #17704)*; *The Rockefeller Foundation (#18966).* [2021/XF6126/**F**]

♦ Gran Consejo de los Crees (internationally oriented national body)
♦ Grand conseil des Cris (internationally oriented national body)
♦ Grand conseil des Cris du Québec / see Grand Council of the Crees – Eeyou Istchee
♦ Grand Council of the Crees – Eeyou Istchee (internationally oriented national body)
♦ Grand Council of the Crees of Québec / see Grand Council of the Crees – Eeyou Istchee
♦ Grande fraternité universelle (#20677)
♦ Grande fraternité universelle, Fondation Dr Serge Raynaud de la Ferrière / see Universal Great Brotherhood (#20677)
♦ Grande Loge Internationale du Druidisme (religious order)
♦ Grand International Brotherhood of Locomotive Engineers / see Brotherhood of Locomotive Engineers, International
♦ Grandmont (religious order)
♦ Grandmothers for Peace International (internationally oriented national body)
♦ Grand Orange Lodge / see Orange Order (#17782)
♦ Grand Order of European Travel Organizers (inactive)
♦ Grand-Ordre des organisateurs européens de voyages (inactive)
♦ Grand quartier général des puissances alliées en Europe (#20039)
♦ Grand Rite Malgache (see: #16593)
♦ Grands Carmes – Carmes de l'Ancienne Observance (religious order)
♦ Gran Fratellanza Universale (#20677)
♦ Gran Fratellanza Universale, Fundación Dr Serge Raynaud de la Ferrière / see Universal Great Brotherhood (#20677)
♦ Gran Fraternidad Universal (#20677)
♦ Gran Fraternidad Universal Fundación / see Universal Great Brotherhood (#20677)
♦ Gran Fraternidad Universal, Fundación Dr Serge Raynaud de la Ferrière / see Universal Great Brotherhood (#20677)
♦ Gränskommittén Østfold-Bohuslän / see SvinesundKommittén
♦ Gränskommittén Østfold-Bohuslän-Dalsland / see SvinesundKommittén
♦ Grantmakers Without Borders (internationally oriented national body)
♦ GRAO – Groupe régional de l'Afrique de l'Ouest (inactive)

♦ Graph Drawing (GD) 10696

Contact Dept Computer Science, Univ of Arizona, Tucson AZ 85721, USA. T. +15206265320. Fax +15206214246.
URL: http://graphdrawing.org/

History 1992, Marino (Italy). **Aims** Promote research on *network visualization* and its applications. **Structure** Steering Committee; Advisory Board. **Languages** English. **Staff** Voluntary. **Finance** No financial support. **Activities** Events/meetings. **Events** *International Symposium on Graph Drawing and Network Visualization* Tokyo (Japan) 2022, *International Symposium on Graph Drawing and Network Visualization* Tübingen (Germany) 2021, *International Symposium on Graph Drawing and Network Visualization* Vancouver, BC (Canada) 2020, *International Symposium on Graph Drawing* Prague (Czechia) 2019, *International Symposium on Graph Drawing* Barcelona (Spain) 2018. **Publications** Proceedings.
Members Individuals in 8 countries:
Australia, Canada, France, Germany, Greece, Italy, Japan, USA. [2022.05.05/XJ7003/**E**]

♦ Graphic Communications Association / see International Digital Enterprise Alliance (#13175)
♦ Graphic Communications Computer Association / see International Digital Enterprise Alliance (#13175)
♦ Graphic Communications Education Association (internationally oriented national body)
♦ **GRAPPA** Group for Research and Assessment of Psoriasis and Psoriatic Arthritis (#10787)
♦ **GRASP** GOOS Regional Alliance for the South East Pacific (#10682)
♦ **GRASP** Great Apes Survival Project (#10699)
♦ GrassRootsAfrica – Foundation for Grassroots Initiatives in Africa (internationally oriented national body)
♦ Grassroots Global Justice Alliance (internationally oriented national body)
♦ Grassroots International (internationally oriented national body)
♦ Grassroots Organizations Operating Together in Sisterhood (internationally oriented national body)

♦ Gravitational Wave International Committee (GWIC) 10697

Exec Sec address not obtained. E-mail: gwic-exsec@gravity.psu.edu.
URL: https://gwic.ligo.org/

History 1997. Functions as Working Group 11 of *International Union of Pure and Applied Physics (IUPAP, #15810).* **Aims** Facilitate international collaboration and cooperation in the construction, operation and use of the major gravitational wave detection facilities worldwide. **Structure** Chairperson; Executive Secretary. **Activities** Awards/prizes/competitions; events/meetings; research/documentation. **Events** *International LISA Symposium* Glasgow (UK) 2022, *Edoardo Amaldi Conference on Gravitational Waves* Melbourne, VIC (Australia) 2021, *International LISA Symposium* 2020, *Edoardo Amaldi Conference on Gravitational Waves* Valencia (Spain) 2019, *LISA : Biennial International Laser Interferometer Space Antenna Symposium* Zurich (Switzerland) 2016. [2022/XJ6645/**E**]

♦ Gray Panthers / see Gray Panthers Project Fund

- ♦ Gray Panthers Project Fund (internationally oriented national body)
- ♦ GRB – Global Resource Bank (internationally oriented national body)
- ♦ **GRBN** Global Research Business Network (#10572)
- ♦ GRCA / see International Glassfibre Reinforced Concrete Association
- ♦ GRCA International – International Glassfibre Reinforced Concrete Association (internationally oriented national body)
- ♦ GRCA – UCLA Globalization Research Centre of Africa (internationally oriented national body)
- ♦ GRC – Genetic Resources Center (see: #14754)
- ♦ GRC – Globalization Research Centre, Honolulu HI (internationally oriented national body)
- ♦ GRC – Global Reporting Centre (internationally oriented national body)
- ♦ **GRC** Global Research Council (#10574)
- ♦ GRC – Global Rhetoric Society (unconfirmed)
- ♦ **GRC** Global Robot Cluster (#10582)
- ♦ **GRC** Green Ark Committee (#10712)
- ♦ GRCN – Global Resilient Cities Network (unconfirmed)
- ♦ GRCSI – Governance Risk Compliance Security International (unconfirmed)
- ♦ **GRDC** Global Runoff Data Centre (#10584)
- ♦ GRDR – Groupe de recherche et de réalisations pour le développement rural dans le Tiers-monde (internationally oriented national body)
- ♦ Gréasan Eorpach na Oibrithe Deonacha Aosta / see European Network of Older-Volunteer Organizations
- ♦ Great Africa Youth Empowerment and Development Initiative (internationally oriented national body)

♦ Great Ape Project (GAP) 10698

Communications Manager Praça Isaac Oliver, 342 V Campestre, Sao Paulo SP, 04330-130, Brazil. T. +551155649595. Fax +551155649596. E-mail: projetogap@projetogap.org.br – imprensa@projetogap.org.br.
URL: http://www.greatapeproject.org/

History 1994. Former names and other names: *Great Ape Project International* – former. **Aims** Seek legal, moral and political protection for the nonhuman great apes (*chimpanzees, gorillas, orangutans* and bonobos); defend the rights of the great primates to life, freedom and non-torture; promote the World Declaration on Great Primates. **Languages** English, Portuguese, Spanish. **Finance** Sources: contributions; grants. **Publications** *Los Grandes Simios y sus derechos básicos – Great Apes and their basic rights* (2019/2020) by Pedro Pozas Terrados; *The Great Ape Project Census: Recognition for the Uncounted* (2002); *The Great Ape Project: Equality Beyond Humanity* (1993).
Members National groups/representatives in 13 countries:
Argentina, Austria, Brazil, Chile, Costa Rica, Côte d'Ivoire, France, Germany, Israel, Mexico, Portugal, Spain, UK.
[2022.02.11/XF4680/**F**]

- ♦ Great Ape Project International / see Great Ape Project (#10698)

♦ Great Apes Survival Project (GRASP) 10699

Projet pour la survie des grands singes

Contact c/o UN Environment, PO Box 30552, Nairobi, 00100, Kenya. T. +254207626712. E-mail: info@un-grasp.org.
URL: http://www.un-grasp.org/

History Set up by *UNEP (#20299)* and *UNESCO (#20322)*. **Aims** Lift the threat of immediate *extinction* facing most populations of great apes; work as a coherent partnership to conserve in their natural habitats wherever they exist wild populations of every kind of great ape; make sure that where apes and people interact, their interactions are mutually positive and sustainable; exemplify and relieve the threats faced by other kinds of animals, birds and plants sharing the forests where apes survive and illustrate what can be achieved through a partnership between all stakeholders in a fragile ecosystem. **Structure** Council, comprising a representative of each full member. Executive Committee, consisting of UNEP and UNESCO representatives, 4 range states representatives, 2 NGO partners, 2 donor governments and one Multilateral Environmental Agreement Secretariat. Scientific Commission; Technical Support Team; Patrons. Secretariat provided by UNEP and UNESCO. **Languages** English, French. **Staff** 4.00 FTE, paid; 1.00 FTE, voluntary. 2 consultants; 2 UNESCO staff contributing 10% of their time. **Finance** Supported by: UNEP; UNESCO; governments; foundations; private sector. **Activities** High-level national and intergovernmental dialogue to generate political will and influence policy for great ape conservation globally; Planning and monitoring at the national, regional and international levels to half bring the decline of great ape populations to a halt; Development and promotion of best practices, cooperation and technical support between stakeholders; Media, information and public awareness to mitigate the threats facing the great apes; New and additional funding for great ape conservation. **Events** *Meeting* Paris (France) 2019, *Intergovernmental meeting on great apes* Kinshasa (Congo DR) 2005, *Meeting* Kinshasa (Congo DR) 2005, *Workshop* Brazzaville (Congo Brazzaville) 2003, *Conference* Paris (France) 2003. **Publications** *The World Atlas of Great Apes and Their Conservation* (2005); *GRASP Strategy* (2002); *The Great Apes – The Road Ahead* (2002). Folder; newsletters; posters; leaflets; stickers.
Members Great ape range state partners in 23 countries:
Angola, Burundi, Cameroon, Central African Rep, Congo Brazzaville, Congo DR, Côte d'Ivoire, Equatorial Guinea, Gabon, Ghana, Guinea, Guinea-Bissau, Indonesia, Liberia, Malaysia, Mali, Nigeria, Rwanda, Senegal, Sierra Leone, Sudan, Tanzania UR, Uganda.
Non-great ape range states partners that directly or indirectly support or participate in programmes in 6 countries:
Belgium, Denmark, Germany, Ireland, Norway, UK.
Governmental partner (1):
European Union (EU, #08967).
IGO Relations Coordinated by UNEP and UNESCO. Partnership with environmental conventions: *Convention on Biological Diversity (Biodiversity convention, 1992)*; *Secretariat of the Convention on the Conservation of Migratory Species of Wild Animals (UNEP/CMS, #19198)*; *Secretariat of the Convention on International Trade in Endangered Species of Wild Fauna and Flora (CITES Secretariat, #19199)*; *World Heritage Centre (WHC, #21566)*. Member of: *Congo Basin Forest Partnership (CBFP, #04662)*.
NGO Relations Scientific Commission comprises members of *International Union for Conservation of Nature and Natural Resources (IUCN, #15766)* – Species Survival Commission (SSC). Partnership with NGOs in the field of great ape conservation, including the following listed in this Yearbook:
- *African Wildlife Foundation (AWF, #00498);*
- *Ape Alliance (#00871);*
- *Born Free Foundation;*
- *Conservation International (CI);*
- *Dian Fossey Gorilla Fund International;*
- *Fauna & Flora International (FFI, #09277);*
- *Great Apes World Heritage Species Project;*
- *Institute of Tropical Forest Conservation (IFTC);*
- *International Fund for Animal Welfare (IFAW, #13693);*
- *International Gorilla Conservation Programme (IGCP);*
- *Jane Goodall Institute (JGI, #16089);*
- *Orangutan Foundation International (OFI, #17784);*
- *Pan African Sanctuary Alliance (PASA, #18064);*
- *TUSK;*
- *Wild Chimpanzee Foundation (WCF);*
- *Wild for Life Campaign (Wild for Life, #20958);*
- *Wildlife Conservation Society (WCS);*
- *World Animal Protection (#21092);*
- *World Wide Fund for Nature (WWF, #21922).*

Other supporting partners include: *Living Earth Foundation.* [2020/XE4454/**E**]

- ♦ Great Apes World Heritage Species Project (internationally oriented national body)
- ♦ Great Bear Foundation (internationally oriented national body)

♦ Greater Arab Free-Trade Area (GAFTA) 10700

Contact League of Arab States, Midan Attahrir, Tahrir Square, PO Box 11642, Cairo, Egypt. T. +202750511. Fax +202740331.

History Feb 1998, as *Pan Arab Free Trade Area (PAFTA)*, on signature of a treaty by 18 members of *League of Arab States (LAS, #16420)*, following several years of negotiation commencing with signature, 1980, of the Charter for *Action économique arabe commune (AEAC, no recent information)* to ensure Arab economic integration. Came into existence under listed title, 1 Jan 2005, following *Agadir Agreement (2004)* establishing a free trade area between Jordan, Tunisia, Morocco and Egypt, projected to include all LEA members by 2015. **Aims** Eliminate trade barriers among members by gradually lowering regional *custom duties*. **Languages** Arabic, English. **IGO Relations** Together with *European Union (EU, #08967)*, expected to form part of the proposed *Euro-Mediterranean Free-Trade Area (EMEFTA)* within *Union for the Mediterranean (UfM, #20457)*.
[2019.12.10/XF5884/t/**F***]

- ♦ Greater Europe Mission (internationally oriented national body)

♦ Greater Horn of Africa Rainwater Partnership (GHARP) 10701

Information and Communication Officer Hurlingham, Rose Ave Off Argwings Kodhek Road, PO Box 10742-00100, Nairobi, Kenya. T. +254202710657. Fax +254202710657.

History Mar 2001. **Aims** Promote rainwater harvesting and management technologies. **Structure** Council.
Members National organizations (4) in 4 countries:
Ethiopia, Kenya, Tanzania UR, Uganda.
NGO Relations Partner of: *Rainwater Partnership (no recent information).* [2011.07.07/XM0976/**F**]

♦ Greater Horn Horizon Forum (GHHF) 10702

Contact 3 boulevard Cheik Osman, 2632, Djibouti, Djibouti. T. +253358449. E-mail: info@greater-horn-horizon-forum.org.
URL: http://www.greater-horn-horizon-forum.org/ghhf/

History Officially launched Nov 2007, Djibouti. **Aims** Foster dialogue on the future of the Horn of *Africa* in order to facilitate the formulation and implementation of *policies* conductive to mutual understanding, regional integration and peace in the region. **Structure** General Assembly. Executive Committee, comprising Chair, Vice-Chair, Treasurer, Reporter and 9 members. Executive Secretariat. **Events** *Conference on Migration and Institution Building in the Horn of Africa* Djibouti (Djibouti) 2014, *Biennial General Assembly* Djibouti (Djibouti) 2011, *Dialogue between youth, media, NGOs and intellectuals in the Horn of Africa* Djibouti (Djibouti) 2010, *Biennial General Assembly* Djibouti (Djibouti) 2009, *Conference on identity, citizenship and regional integration in the Horn of Africa* Djibouti (Djibouti) 2009. **Publications** *GHHF Newsletter*.
Members Full in 7 countries:
Djibouti, Eritrea, Ethiopia, Kenya, Somalia, Sudan, Uganda. [2019/XJ2060/**F**]

♦ Greater Tumen Initiative (GTI) 10703

Dir 1-1-142 Tayuan Diplomatic Compound, 1 Xindong Road, 100600 Beijing, China. T. +861065326871. Fax +861065326465. E-mail: gti.secretariat@undp.org.
URL: http://www.tumenprogramme.org/

History 1995, when member governments signed agreements to establish *Tumen River Area Development Programme*. Transition to an independent organization: 2010-2015. **Aims** Strengthen economic and technical *cooperation*; attain greater growth and *sustainable* development in North East *Asia*, especially the Greater Tumen Region. **Structure** Consultative Commission; Secretariat. **Events** *Workshop* Busan (Korea Rep) 2019, *Workshop* Jeju (Korea Rep) 2018.
Members Governments (4):
China, Korea Rep, Mongolia, Russia.
IGO Relations Supported by: *UNDP (#20292).* [2019/XM8294/**F***]

- ♦ **GREAT** Global Research on Acute Conditions Team (#10568)
- ♦ Great Lakes Advocacy Network / see European Network for Central Africa (#07874)
- ♦ Great Lakes Commission (internationally oriented national body)

♦ Great Lakes Initiative on AIDS (GLIA) 10704

Contact address not obtained. T. +250587344 – +2505872345. Fax +250587343. E-mail: info@greatlakesinitiative.org.
URL: http://www.greatlakesinitiative.org/

History 1998, and formally set up, 2004, following signing the GLIA Convention. Convention ratified, 2005. **Aims** Contribute to the reduction of *HIV* infections; mitigate the socio-economic impact of the epidemic in the Great Lakes Region by developing regional collaboration and implementing interventions that can add value to the efforts of each individual country. **Structure** Council of Ministers. Executive Committee of CEOS of National AIDS Coordinative Commissions (NACCs). Executive Secretariat, headed by Executive Secretary. **Languages** English, French. **Staff** 11.00 FTE, paid. **Finance** Members' dues. Project support from: *International Development Association (IDA, #13155)* and *International Bank for Reconstruction and Development (IBRD, #12317)*. Budget (annual): US$ 5 million. **Activities** GLIA Support Project. **Publications** Reports; brochures; strategic plan.
Members Governments of 6 countries:
Burundi, Congo DR, Kenya, Rwanda, Tanzania UR, Uganda. [2010/XJ0141/**E***]

- ♦ Great Lakes Institute for Strategic Studies (internationally oriented national body)

♦ Great Lakes Parliamentary Forum on Peace (Amani Forum) 10705

Contact address not obtained. T. +254202730802. Fax +254202730805.

History 1998, by parliamentarians in the Great Lakes region of Africa. **Aims** Eliminate armed conflict in the Great Lakes region; promote peace and democratic governance. **Structure** General Assembly (annual). Executive Committee, including Chairman, Secretary-General and Treasurer. Secretariat in Nairobi (Kenya). Chapters (6): Burundi; Congo DR; Kenya; Rwanda; Tanzania UR; Uganda; Zambia.
Members Parliamentarians (about 650) in 6 countries:
Burundi, Congo DR, Kenya, Rwanda, Tanzania UR, Uganda, Zambia.
Organizations (1):
Medicus Mundi International – Network Health for All (MMI, #16636). [2012/XM2310/y/**F**]

♦ Great Limpopo Transfrontier Park 10706

Coordinator Gonarezhou National Park, Dept of National Parks and Wildlife Management, Harare, HARARE, Zimbabwe. T. +2634790574 – +2634705344. Fax +2634726089.
URL: http://www.greatlimpopo.org/

History Nov 2000, on signature of an agreement by governments of Mozambique, South Africa and Zimbabwe. Memorandum of Understanding signed Dec 2002. **Aims** As a cross-border wildlife conservation park, promote biodiversity and eco-tourism. **Activities** Park, covering 35,000 sq km, comprises national parks in the 3 participating countries and includes 116 species of reptiles, 147 of mammals, 505 of birds and 2,000 of plants.
Members Participating countries (3):
Mozambique, South Africa, Zimbabwe. [2013/XF7199/**F***]

- ♦ "Great Silk Way" International Youth Union (internationally oriented national body)

♦ Great Transition Initiative (GTI) 10707

Coordinator Tellus Inst, 2 Garden St, Cambridge MA 02138-3631, USA. T. +16172665400. E-mail: contact@greattransition.org.
URL: http://www.greattransition.org/

History Founded Jun 2003, following the activities of *Global Scenario Group (GSG, inactive)*. Relaunched by *Tellus Institute*, 2014. **Aims** Develop and promote futures scenarios for *peaceful* and *sustainable* coexistence. **Structure** Core Team; Editorial Committee. **Languages** English. **Staff** Staff and office support provided by *Tellus Institute*. **Finance** Supported by *Tellus Institute*. Annual budget: about US$ 300,000. **Activities** Advocacy/lobbying/activism; networking/liaising; projects/programmes. **Publications** *MacroScope*. *Journey to Earthland: The Great Transition to Planetary Civilization* (2016) by Paul Raskin. **Members** Scholars and researchers (about 1,000). Membership countries not specified. [2019.02.13/XM4535/**F**]

- ♦ GReCEST – Global Research Consortium on Economic Structural Transformation (unconfirmed)

GRECO Groupe états
10707

alphabetic sequence excludes
For the complete listing, see Yearbook Online at

♦ **GRECO** Groupe d'états contre la corruption (#10789)
♦ Greek Centre of European Studies and Research (internationally oriented national body)
♦ Greek Committee for International Democratic Solidarity (internationally oriented national body)
♦ Greek Committee for International Detente and Peace (internationally oriented national body)
♦ Greek Council for Refugees (internationally oriented national body)

♦ Greek Orthodox Archdiocesan Council of America (GOAC) 10708

Conseil de l'Archevêché orthodoxe grec d'Amérique – Consejo del Arzobispado Ortodoxo Griego de América

Main office 8 East 79th St, New York NY 10075, USA. T. +12125703500. Fax +12125703569. E-mail: archdiocese@goarch.org.
URL: http://www.goarch.org/

History as *Greek Orthodox Archdiocesan Council of North and South America – Conseil de l'Archevêché orthodoxe grec d'Amérique du Nord et du Sud – Consejo del Arzobispado Ortodoxo Griego de América del Norte y del Sur.* **Aims** Promote the United Nations principles of: maintaining peace and security in the world; working together with the nations of the world to promote better welfare, education, health conditions and the protection of the environment; encouraging respect for the individual human rights and freedoms, including religious freedom; enhancing the status of women and of condemning racism and racial discrimination in the world. **Finance** Members' dues. **Activities** Organizes conferences, seminars and workshops. Supports programmes in developing countries. Organizes a biennal congress. **Events** *Biennial Congress* Nashville, TN (USA) 2006, *Biennial Congress* New Orleans, LA (USA) 1992, *Biennial Congress* Boston, MA (USA) 1988. **Publications** *Orthodox Observer* (1 or 2 a month); *OCMC Magazine.* Newsletters.
Members Organizations in 38 countries and territories:
Albania, Argentina, Bahamas, Bolivia, Brazil, Cameroon, Canada, Chad, Chile, Colombia, Costa Rica, Cuba, Cyprus, Ghana, Greece, Guatemala, Haiti, Hong Kong, India, Indonesia, Kenya, Korea Rep, Mexico, Nigeria, Panama, Paraguay, Peru, Philippines, Poland, Puerto Rico, Romania, Slovakia, Tanzania UR, Türkiye, Uganda, Uruguay, USA, Venezuela.
Consultative Status Consultative status granted from: *ECOSOC (#05331)* (General); *UNICEF (#20332).* **IGO Relations** Accredited by: *United Nations Office at Vienna (UNOV, #20604).* Associated with Department of Global Communications of the United Nations. **NGO Relations** Member of: *Conference of Non-Governmental Organizations in Consultative Relationship with the United Nations (CONGO, #04635); Mining Working Group at the UN (MWG, #16813); NGO Committee on Freedom of Religion or Belief, New York NY (#17109); NGO Committee on UNICEF (#17120).* [2010/XF1420/F]

♦ Greek Orthodox Archdiocesan Council of North and South America / see Greek Orthodox Archdiocesan Council of America (#10708)

♦ Greek Orthodox Patriarchate of Alexandria and All Africa 10709

Patriarcat grec-orthodoxe d'Alexandrie et de toute l'Afrique

Contact PO Box 2006, Alexandria, Egypt. T. +2034868595. Fax +2034875684. E-mail: patriarxeio.alexandreias@gmail.com.
URL: http://www.patriarchateofalexandria.com/

History According to the tradition the Church of Alexandria was founded by St Mark the apostle and evangelist. By the 4th century it had already extended across Egypt and Libya and had almost one hundred dioceses. The Church fathers Athanasios and Cyril fought for the preservation of Orthodox faith at the Councils of Nicea, 325, and Ephesus, 431. After the Council of Chalcedon, 451, there was a division, and part of the Church joined the Monophysites. Thus two patriarchates arose – the Egyptian, which is known as Coptic, and the Byzantine, which, since the capture of Constantinople by the Turks in 1453, has called itself Greek Orthodox. After the Turkish conquest of Egypt in 1517 the Greek Orthodox patriarchs were forced temporarily to seek refuge in Constantinople. During the Reformation in the West, the Alexandrian patriarchate was administered by the Cretan patriarchs Sylvester, Meletios I Pegas, Cyril Lukaris, Gerasimos I (1567-1630). The last of them, Metrophanes Kritopoulos, was elected patriarch in 1630. The present Pope and Patriarch of Alexandria and All Africa is His Beatitude THEDOROS II. **Structure** The Church is governed by the Patriarch in conjunction with the Synod. **Activities** Offers philanthropic help all over Africa. **Publications** *Analekta* in Greek – with articles in English, French, Arabic; *Eklesiatikos Pharos; Pantainos.* **Information Services** *Patricarchate's Library* – founded 10th century and containing 41,000 volumes, 542 manuscripts and 2,241 rare editions. **Members** Metropolitanates (28), Bishoprics (5), grouping 5,000,000 members, Metropolitans (28), Diocesan Bishops (5), Titular Metropolitans (5), Auxiliary Bishops (2), retired Bishops (5), and priests (1,000). Membership in Africa. Membership countries not specified. **NGO Relations** Member of: *Council of African Instituted Churches (no recent information); Holy and Great Council (#10937); Middle East Council of Churches (MECC, #16756); World Council of Churches (WCC, #21320).* [2018.07.09/XF5128/F]

♦ Greek Orthodox Patriarchate of Antioch and All the East 10710

Patriarcat grec-orthodoxe d'Antioche et de tout l'Orient

Patriarchate PO Box 9, Damascus, Syrian AR. T. +963115424400 – +963115424401 – +963115424403. Fax +963115424404. E-mail: secretary@antiochpatriarchate.org.
URL: http://antiochpatriarchate.org/

History reputedly 37 AD, Antioch (Syria), by St Peter the Apostle. Once spread throughout Asia and, by the 6th century, included 150 metropolitans and bishops. From 518, forced to move from Antioch to various locations, settling in Mardin (Turkey) during the 13th century. In 1933, transferred to Homs (Syria), and in 1957, to Damascus (Syrian AR). The Syrian Orthodox Church of Antioch dates back to the time of the Apostles and is the second established church in Christendom after Jerusalem (Israel) and the earliest of the Apostolic Churches, with Christians first being referred to as Christians in Antioch. Became more localised following: division of the Church; granting of independence to the Churches of Cyprus and Iberia; Islamic advance in the 7th century; formation of the Uniate Church in the 18th century; emigration in the 20th century. Also referred to in English as: *Syrian Orthodox Patriarchate of Antioch and All the East; Universal Syrian Orthodox Church.* **Aims** In accordance with the Nicene Creed, conform to the teachings of the 3 Ecumenical Councils of Nicea (AD 325), Constantinople (AD 381) and Ephesus (AD 431), while rejecting the Council of Chalcedon (AD 451). **Structure** Holy Synod (the highest ecclesiastical authority of Antioch) is the assembly of all the bishops with the Patriarch as President. Priesthood comprises 3 ranks: *'Episcopate'* – Patriarch, archbishop, bishop; *'Vicarate'* – chor-episcopos, pastor; *'Deaconate'* – archdeacon (one per diocese), evangelical deacon, subdeacon, lector or qoruya, singer or mzamrono. Each archdiocese is headed by an archbishop, who is under the jurisdiction of the Patriarch and accountable to the Holy Synod. The local Holy Synod in India is presided over by the Catholicos of the East, Malankara (India). Regional Churches: *Church in the Middle East; Church in India; Church in the Americas; Church in Europe,* including *Archdiocese of Central Europe and Benelux Countries* and *Archdiocese of Sweden and Scandinavia.* **Activities** Maintains responsibility for the people under the jurisdiction of the Patriarchate in the midst of a multi-religious society. Agenda includes authentic witness to the Christian faith, pastoral care of youth and reorganization of the establishment in order to express more clearly its apostolicity and its unity. Particular emphasis is laid on the coherence of the family, which is the centre of the Church and the source of spiritual development. Maintains theological seminaries in Damascus (Syrian AR) and Udayagiri. Particular characteristics of the Syrian Orthodox Church are: a Semitic form of Christianity with a culture similar to that experienced by Christ himself; a liturgy in the Syriac language, again similar to that used by Christ and the Apostles; one of the most ancient liturgies, handed from one generation to the next; a multi-ethnic congregation united as one in the body of Christ. **Publications** *Al-Kalima* in Arabic; *An-Nachra* in Arabic; *An-Nour* in Arabic; *Orthodoxia* in Spanish; *The World* in English.
Members The jurisdiction of the Patriarchate, comprising 22 dioceses, 750,000 members, 28 bishops, 496 parishes and 408 priests, covers all of Syria, Lebanon, Iraq and Iran, the Arabian peninsula, certain areas of Turkey and the whole Orient. It also extends to the Arab-speaking Orthodox who live in North and South America, Australia and New Zealand. Churches in 19 countries:
Argentina, Australia, Austria, Belgium, Brazil, Canada, France, Germany, India, Iraq, Israel, Lebanon, Netherlands, New Zealand, Sweden, Switzerland, Syrian AR, Türkiye, USA.
NGO Relations Member of: *Holy and Great Council (#10937); Middle East Council of Churches (MECC, #16756); Oikocredit International (Oikocredit, #17704); World Council of Churches (WCC, #21320).* [2016/XF5146/F]

♦ The Green 10 10711

Coordinator address not obtained. T. +48530141181. E-mail: secretariat@green10.org.
URL: https://green10.org/

History An informal grouping of initially 8 of the largest environmental NGOs in Europe. Former names and other names: *Green 8* – former; *Green 9* – former. **Aims** Work with *EU* law-making institutions, the European Commission, the European Parliament and the Council of Ministers to ensure that the *environment* is placed at the heart of policy-making. **Finance** Sources: members' dues. Other sources: core funding from European Commission (except for Greenpeace); some member organizations receive funding on a case-by-case basis for specific projects from governments and foundations and donations from industry. **Activities** Advocacy/lobbying/activism.
Members International organizations (10):
BirdLife International (#03266); CEE Bankwatch Network (#03624); Climate Action Network Europe (CAN Europe, #04001); European Environmental Bureau (EEB, #06996); European Federation for Transport and Environment (T and E, #07230); Friends of the Earth Europe (FoEE, #10001); Greenpeace International (#10727) (Europe); *Health and Environment Alliance (HEAL, #10879); Internationals amis de la nature (IAN, #14780); World Wide Fund for Nature (WWF, #21922)* (European Policy Office).
IGO Relations *European Commission (EC, #06633); European Parliament (EP, #08146); Council of the European Union (#04895).* **NGO Relations** Member of (2): *Civil Society Europe; EU Civil Society Contact Group (CSCG, #05572).* [2023/XF6672/y/F]

♦ Green 8 / see The Green 10 (#10711)
♦ Green 9 / see The Green 10 (#10711)
♦ Green Across the World (internationally oriented national body)
♦ Green Africa Directory (internationally oriented national body)
♦ Green Africa Foundation (internationally oriented national body)
♦ Green Alternative European Link / see Group of the Greens – European Free Alliance (#10781)

♦ Green Ark Committee (GRC) 10712

SG 38, Avenue Cliniques, PO Box 785, Gombe, Kinshasa, Congo DR. T. +243813819062. E-mail: greenarknetwork@gmail.com.
URL: http://www.green-ark.org/

History 21 Feb 2011, Kinshasa (Congo DR). Set up as a movement to address issues concerning biodiversity resources. Former names and other names: *Arche Verte* – former. Registration: No/ID: JUST/SG/20/2376/2014, Congo DR, Kinshasa. **Aims** Promote an environmentally sound society eager to uphold natural balances and prudent use of ecosystems' resources; preserve ecosystems in a bid to improve socio-economic conditions among the most vulnerable people, upholding equitable access to available resources for livelihoods and boosting up sustainable development across eco-friendly communities. **Structure** General Assembly; Board of Directors; General Secretariat. **Languages** English, French. **Staff** 12.00 FTE, paid; 3.00 FTE, voluntary. **Finance** Annual budget: 600,000 USD. **Activities** Advocacy/lobbying/activism; capacity building; events/meetings; guidance/assistance/consulting; humanitarian/emergency aid. Active in: Cameroon, Central African Rep, Congo DR. **Events** *International Conference* Kinshasa (Congo DR) 2016, *Meeting on Climate Change in Africa* Kinshasa (Congo DR) 2015. **Publications** *How to search and secure funds for your project? Guide for project leaders and NGOs from the South – Comment rechercher et mobiliser un Financement pour votre Projet? Guide pour les porteurs du projet et ONGs du Sud* (European University Editions (EUE) 2021); *Gender, Sex Equality and developpement: Which model for African Society? – Genre, Egalité des Sexes et developpement : Quel modèle pour la société africaine?* (European University Edition (EUE) 2020); *Sanitation and Development: Ensuring Sustainability in DRC* (2012); *Making an Ebola Free World, it is doable!. Green Ark Action Plan 2022-2026; Recommandations de la Campagne d'action pour la décennie de la biodiversité (2011-2020).* Conference and workshop reports. **NGO Relations** Partner of (7): *350.org; Advocates for International Development (A4ID); Climate Action Network (CAN, #03999); End Water Poverty (EWP, #05464); Gender and Water Alliance (GWA, #10102); Programme Solidarité eau (pS-Eau, #18529); World Federation Against Drugs (WFAD, #21408).* [2021.03.24/XJ5809/F]

♦ Green Asia Network (internationally oriented national body)
♦ Green Balkans Movement / see BALKANI Wildlife Society (#03076)

♦ Green Belt Movement 10713

Exec Dir – Headquarters Adams Arcade – Kilimani Lane off Elgeyo Marakwet Rd, PO Box 67545-00200, Nairobi, Kenya. T. +254203873057 – +254203860158. E-mail: gbm@greenbeltmovement.org.
Chair – Europe Office Development House, 56-64 Leonard Street, London, EC2A 4LT, UK. T. +442075490395. Fax +442075490396. E-mail: gbmi@greenbeltmovement.org.
URL: http://www.greenbeltmovement.org/

History 1977, Nairobi (Kenya). Founded, by National Council of Women of Kenya. European branch is UK Registered Charity: 1112639. **Aims** Avert *desertification* process throughout Kenya through *planting* of trees; promote *environment conservation* and sustainable development; promote indigenous *trees* and shrubs; promote planting of multipurpose trees with special reference to nutritional requirements of man and his livestock; encourage soil conservation and land reclamation through tree planting; develop methods for rational land use; create self-employment opportunities, especially for handicapped persons; create income-generating activity for rural women; develop a sustainable methodology for rural development. **Structure** General Meeting; Officers; Executive Committee. **Languages** English, Greek. **Staff** 35.00 FTE, paid. **Finance** Sources: donations; grants; members' dues. **Activities** Training/education; projects/programmes. *'Green Belt Safaris',* launched to act as the local funding source. *'The Naked Earth'* (film); *'Women at Work'* (film). **Publications** *Challenge for Africa* by Wangari Maathai; *Replenishing the Earth* by Wangari Maathai; *The Green Belt Movement – Sharing the Approach and the Experience* by Wangari Maathai; *Unbowed – memoir* by Wangari Maathai. Booklets.
Members Green belt movements set up or being set up in 22 countries:
Australia, Austria, Belgium, Brazil, Canada, Denmark, Ethiopia, Finland, Germany, Haiti, Ireland, Kenya, Netherlands, Norway, Sweden, Switzerland, Tanzania UR, Türkiye, Uganda, UK, USA, Zambia.
Consultative Status Consultative status granted from: *UNEP (#20299).* **IGO Relations** *United Nations Conference on Environment and Development (UNCED).* Invited to Governing Council sessions of: *International Fund for Agricultural Development (IFAD, #13692).* **NGO Relations** Member of (1): *Environment Liaison Centre International (ELCI, no recent information).* Partner of (1): *Southern and Eastern Africa Rainwater Network (SearNet, #19876).* [2020/XF2088/F]

♦ Green Without Borders (internationally oriented national body)

♦ Green Climate Fund (GCF) 10714

Exec Dir G-Tower, 175 Art Center-daero, Yeonsu-gu, Incheon 22004, Korea Rep. T. +82324586059. Fax +82324586094. E-mail: info@gcfund.org.
URL: https://www.greenclimate.fund/

History Established 2010 by 194 countries party to the *United Nations Framework Convention on Climate Change (UNFCCC, 1992).* An operating entity of the Convention's financial mechanism in accordance with Article 11 of the Convention. **Aims** Advance the goal of keeping the temperature increase on earth below 2 degrees Celsius. **Structure** Board; Secretariat; Trustee. Current observers (3): *Jubilee South – Asian Peoples' Movement on Debt and Development (JSAPMDD, #16160); Heinrich Böll Foundation; Climate Markets and Investment Association (CMIA, #04018).* **Languages** UN languages. **Staff** 224.00 FTE, paid. **Finance** Advanced economies have formally agreed to jointly mobilize US$ 100,000,000,000 per year by 2020, from a variety of sources, to address the pressing mitigation and adaptation needs of developing countries. **Activities** Financial and/or material support; events/meetings. **Events** *Conference of Private Investment for Climate* Incheon (Korea Rep) 2021, *International Conference on Climate Finance and Industry* Incheon (Korea Rep) 2021, *Meeting on Implementing the New Green Climate Fund Urban Strategy in Africa* Incheon (Korea Rep) 2021, *Meeting* Incheon (Korea Rep) 2021, *Meeting* Incheon (Korea Rep) 2021.
IGO Relations Accredited international entities:
– *Adaptation Fund (AF, #00109);*
– *African Development Bank (ADB, #00283);*
– *African Union (AU, #00488);*
– *Agence française de développement (AFD);*
– *Asian Development Bank (ADB, #01422);*
– *Banque ouest africaine de développement (BOAD, #03170);*
– *Commonwealth Secretariat (#04362);*

- *Deutsche Gesellschaft für Internationale Zusammenarbeit (GIZ)*;
- *Development Bank of Latin America (CAF, #05055)*;
- *ECOWAS Bank for Investment and Development (EBID, #05334)*;
- *European Bank for Reconstruction and Development (EBRD, #06315)*;
- *European Investment Bank (EIB, #07599)*;
- *FAO (#09260)*;
- *Global Green Growth Institute (GGGI, #10392)*;
- *Inter-American Development Bank (IDB, #11427)*;
- *International Bank for Reconstruction and Development (IBRD, #12317)*;
- *International Civil Aviation Organization (ICAO, #12581)*;
- *International Development Association (IDA, #13155)*;
- *International Finance Corporation (IFC, #13597)*;
- *International Fund for Agricultural Development (IFAD, #13692)*;
- *International Organization for Migration (IOM, #14454)*;
- *International Renewable Energy Agency (IRENA, #14715)*;
- *Multilateral Fund for the Implementation of the Montreal Protocol (#16885)*;
- *Nordic Development Fund (NDF, #17271)*;
- *OECD (#17693)*;
- *South Centre (#19753)*;
- *UNEP (#20299)*;
- *UN Women (#20724)*;
- *UNDP (#20292)*;
- *UNICEF (#20332)*;
- *UNIDO (#20336)*;
- *WHO (#20950)*;
- *World Food Programme (WFP, #21510)*;
- *World Meteorological Organization (WMO, #21649)*.

NGO Relations Accredited civil society organizations include:
- *ActionAid (#00087)*;
- *African Climate Finance Hub (ACFH)*;
- *African Women's Development Fund (AWDF, #00504)*;
- *American Jewish World Service (AJWS)*;
- *Asia Foundation*;
- *Asia Indigenous Peoples Pact (AIPP, #01282)*;
- *Asia Pacific Forum on Women, Law and Development (APWLD, #01912)*;
- *Asia Pacific Network on Food Sovereignty (APNFS, #01965)*;
- *Asian Institute of Technology (AIT, #01519)*;
- *BirdLife International (#03266)*;
- *Both ENDS (#03307)*;
- *BRAC (#03310)*;
- *Caribbean Natural Resources Institute (CANARI, #03525)*;
- *Catholic Agency for Overseas Development (CAFOD)*;
- *Caucasus Environmental NGO Network (CENN, #03613)*;
- *CEE Bankwatch Network (#03624)*;
- *Center for Clean Air Policy (CCAP)*;
- *Centre for European Policy Studies (CEPS, #03741)*;
- *Center for Global Development (CGD)*;
- *Center for International Environmental Law (CIEL)*;
- *Christian Aid*;
- *Civil Society Coalition on Climate Change (CSCCC, #03967)*;
- *Climate Action Network (CAN, #03999)*;
- *Climate Action Network South Asia (CANSA, #04003)*;
- *Climate Alliance (#04005)*;
- *Climate Analytics*;
- *Climate Policy Initiative (CPI, #04020)*;
- *CERES*;
- *Conservation International (CI)*;
- *Coordinadora de las Organizaciones Indígenas de la Cuenca Amazónica (COICA, #04811)*;
- *Deutsches Institut für Entwicklungspolitik (DIE)*;
- *E3G – Third Generation Environmentalism*;
- *Energy and Resources Institute (TERI)*;
- *Environmental Defense Fund (EDF)*;
- *Federation for Associations Connected to the International Humana People to People Movement (see: #13817)*;
- *Forest Peoples Programme (FPP, #09865)*;
- *Foundation myclimate*;
- *Freedom from Debt Coalition (FDC)*;
- *Friends of the Earth International (FoEI, #10002)*;
- *Fundación Futuro Latinoamericano (FFLA, #10022)*;
- *Future Forest*;
- *Gender and Water Alliance (GWA, #10102)*;
- *GenderCC – Women for Climate Justice (GenderCC, #10095)*;
- *Global Alliance for Incinerator Alternatives (GAIA, #10203)*;
- *Global Canopy (#10271)*;
- *Global CCS Institute (#10274)*;
- *Global Environment Centre (GEC)*;
- *Global Forest Coalition (GFC, #10368)*;
- *Global Greens (#10394)*;
- *Green Asia Network (GAN)*;
- *Greenpeace International (#10727)*;
- *Heinrich Böll Foundation*;
- *HELVETAS Swiss Intercooperation*;
- *Humanistisch Instituut voor Ontwikkelingssamenwerking (Hivos)*;
- *IBON International (#11037)*;
- *Indigenous Peoples' International Centre for Policy Research and Education (Tebtebba Foundation)*;
- *Institute for Global Environmental Strategies (IGES, #11266)*;
- *Interamerican Association for Environmental Defense (#11398)*;
- *International Association for the Advancement of Innovative Approaches to Global Challenges (IAAI, #11687)*;
- *International Centre for Environment Audit and Sustainable Development (iCED, #12489)*;
- *International Centre for Trade and Sustainable Development, Geneva (ICTSD, #12524)*;
- *International Child Welfare Organization (ICWO)*;
- *International Council on Clean Transportation (ICCT, #13007)*;
- *International Geothermal Association (IGA, #13717)*;
- *International Hydropower Association (IHA, #13828)*;
- *International Institute for Environment and Development (IIED, #13877)*;
- *International Rivers*;
- *International Solar Energy Society (ISES, #15564)*;
- *International Solid Waste Association (ISWA, #15567)*;
- *International Trade Union Confederation (ITUC, #15708)*;
- *International Union for Conservation of Nature and Natural Resources (IUCN, #15766)*;
- *International Work Group for Indigenous Affairs (IWGIA, #15907)*;
- *Jubilee South – Asian Peoples' Movement on Debt and Development (JSAPMDD, #16160)*;
- *LDC Watch (#16412)*;
- *Local Governments for Sustainability (ICLEI, #16507)*;
- *Mercy Corps International (MCI)*;
- *The Nature Conservancy (TNC)*;
- *SNV Netherlands Development Organisation (SNV)*;
- *Oil Change International*;
- *Overseas Development Institute (ODI)*;
- *Oxfam GB*;
- *Panafrican Climate Justice Alliance (PACJA, #18046)*;
- *Pesticide Action Network (PAN, #18336)*;
- *Practical Action (#18475)*;
- *Project Gaia (#18533)*;
- *Renewable Energy and Energy Efficiency Partnership (REEEP, #18837)*;
- *REN21 (#18836)*;
- *Réseau des Femmes Africaines pour la Gestion Communautaire des forêts (REFACOF)*;
- *South Asian Forum for Environment (SAFE)*;
- *Stockholm Environment Institute (SEI, #19993)*;
- *Stockholm International Water Institute (SIWI)*;
- *Third World Network (TWN, #20151)*;
- *Transparency International (TI, #20223)*;
- *WaterAid (#20822)*;
- *Wildlife Conservation Society (WCS)*;
- *Women in Informal Employment: Globalizing and Organizing (WIEGO, #21003)*;
- *Women Organizing for Change in Agriculture and Natural Resource Management (WOCAN)*;
- *Women's Environment and Development Organization (WEDO, #21016)*;
- *World Bioenergy Association (WBA, #21231)*;
- *World Farmers' Organisation (WFO, #21401)*;
- *World Future Council Foundation (WFC, #21533)*;
- *World Leadership Alliance – Club de Madrid (WLA-CdM, #21619)*;
- *World Resources Institute (WRI, #21753)*;
- *World Vision International (WVI, #21904)*;
- *World Wide Fund for Nature (WWF, #21922)*.

[2020/XJ2175/f/F*]

♦ Green Cooling Initiative (internationally oriented national body)
♦ Green Coordination of Green Parties / see European Green Party (#07409)

♦ Green Cross International (GCI) 10715
Croix verte internationale
Dir Rue du Pré-de-la-Bichette 1, 6th Floor – Nations Center, 1202 Geneva, Switzerland. T. +41227891662. Fax +41227891695. E-mail: hq@gcint.org.
URL: http://www.gcint.org/
History 18 Apr 1993. Founded by Mikhail Gorbachev (1931-2022), former leader of the USSR, after delegates at the Earth Summit, Jun 1992, Rio de Janeiro (Brazil), requested him to create and launch an organization that would apply the emergency response model of the Red Cross to ecological issues. **Aims** Respond to the combined challenges of security, poverty and environmental degradation to ensure a sustainable and secure future. **Structure** General Assembly (every 2 years); Board of Directors; Honorary Board; Secretariat in Geneva (Switzerland). **Languages** English. **Staff** 5.00 FTE, paid. **Finance** Funded by contributions from national organizations and donations from companies, other institutions, individuals and governments. **Activities** Advocacy/lobbying/activism; knowledge management/information dissemination. **Events** GMO Forum Seoul (Korea Rep) 2016, *Water for life forum* Foz do Iguaçu (Brazil) 2005, *International conference on environment, security and sustainable development* The Hague (Netherlands) 2004, *From conflict to cooperation in international water resources management conference* Delft (Netherlands) 2002, *Earth dialogues / Quadrennial Meeting* Lyon (France) 2002.
Members National organizations in 27 countries and territories:
Argentina, Australia, Belarus, Bolivia, Brazil, Burkina Faso, Canada, Côte d'Ivoire, Czechia, Denmark, Eswatini, France, Ghana, Hungary, Italy, Japan, Korea Rep, Netherlands, Poland, Russia, Spain, Sri Lanka, Sweden, Switzerland, Taiwan, Ukraine, USA.
Consultative Status Consultative status granted from: *ECOSOC (#05331)* (General); *UNESCO (#20322)* (Foundations). **IGO Relations** Member of: *United Nations Framework Convention on Climate Change – Secretariat (UNFCCC, #20564)*. Partner of: *Global Alliances for Water and Climate (GAfWaC, #10230)*; *Secretariat of the United Nations Convention to Combat Desertification (Secretariat of the UNCCD, #19208)*; *UNEP (#20299)*; *UNEP/ United Nations Office for the Coordination of Humanitarian Affairs (OCHA, #20593) Environmental Emergencies Section*; *United Nations Human Settlements Programme (UN-Habitat, #20572)*. **NGO Relations** Member of: *Coalition Eau*; *EarthAction (EA, #05159)*; *End Water Poverty (EWP, #05464)*; *Freshwater Action Network (FAN, inactive)*; *Water and Climate Coalition (WCC, no recent information)*; *World Water Council (WWC, #21908)*. Partner of: *1% for the Planet*.

[2021/XF5170/F]

♦ Green Diplomacy Network (GDN) 10716
Contact address not obtained. T. +420224182052. E-mail: press@mzv.cz.
URL: http://ec.europa.eu/external_relations/environment/gdn/index_en.htm
History 2003, as an informal network launched by *Council of Europe (CE, #04881)*. Also referred to as *EU Green Diplomacy Network*. **Aims** Increase the coherence, consistency and effectiveness of European action in the field of *environment*. **Structure** Coordination of Network resides in rotating Presidency of *European Commission (EC, #06633)*. **Activities** Orchestrates campaigns and courses. **Events** Meeting Prague (Czech Rep) 2009, Meeting Kranj (Slovenia) 2008, Meeting Paris (France) 2008, Meeting Germany 2007, Meeting Portugal 2007. **Publications** *EU Environment Policy Brief*.

[2010/XM2981/E]

♦ Green Earth Foundation (internationally oriented national body)

♦ Green Economy Coalition (GEC) 10717
Contact 80-86 Gray's Inn Road, London, WC1X 8NH, UK. T. +442034637399. Fax +442035149055.
URL: http://www.greeneconomycoalition.org/
History 2009. **Aims** Research, promote and deliver an inclusive transition to a sustainable green economy which will tackle inequality, protect natural resources and ecosystems and provide a sustainable future. **Structure** Steering Group; Secretariat. **Languages** English, French. **Staff** 7.00 FTE, paid. **Activities** Research and development; politics/policy/regulatory; Events/meetings; advocacy/lobbying/activism; networking/liaising. **Publications** Research papers.
Members NGOs; research institutes; UN organizations; business and trade unions. Members include the following 19 organizations listed in this Yearbook:
Caribbean Natural Resources Institute (CANARI, #03525); *Consumers International (CI, #04773)*; *Ecologic Institut (#05303)*; *Forest Stewardship Council (FSC, #09869)*; *Fundación Ecologia y Desarrollo (ECODES)*; *Global Footprint Network (#10367)*; *Global Reporting Initiative (GRI, #10567)*; *ILO (#11123)*; *Institute for Development, Environment and Peace (Vitae Civilis)*; *International Institute for Environment and Development (IIED, #13877)*; *International Institute for Sustainable Development (IISD, #13930)*; *International Trade Union Confederation (ITUC, #15708)*; *International Union for Conservation of Nature and Natural Resources (IUCN, #15766)*; *SEED (#19213)*; *STEPS Centre*; *The Natural Step (TNS, #16958)*; *UNEP (#20299)*; *World Business Council for Sustainable Development (WBCSD, #21254)*; *World Wide Fund for Nature (WWF, #21922)*.
IGO Relations Founding members: *ILO (#11123)*; *International Union for Conservation of Nature and Natural Resources (IUCN, #15766)*; *UNEP (#20299)*. Official partner: UN Partnership for Action on the Green Economy (UN-PAGE). **NGO Relations** Member of (2): *Natural Capital Coalition (NCC, #16952)*; *Wellbeing Economy Alliance (WEAll, #20856)*.

[2019.02.13/XJ2930/y/F]

♦ Green European Foundation (GEF) 10718
Acting Dir Mundo Madou, Av des Arts 7-8, 1210 Brussels, Belgium. T. +3223290050. E-mail: info@gef.eu.
Registered Office Rue du Fossé 3, L-1536 Luxembourg, Luxembourg.
URL: http://gef.eu/
History 2008. Established as the European-level political foundation associated with *European Green Party (EGP, #07409)* and *Group of the Greens – European Free Alliance (Greens/EFA, #10781)* in *European Parliament (EP, #08146)*. **Aims** Contribute to a lively European sphere of debate; foster greater involvement of citizens in European *politics*; create a common Green vision for Europe. **Structure** General Assembly; Board of Directors. **Languages** English. **Staff** 16.00 FTE, paid. **Finance** Supported by: *European Parliament (EP, #08146)*. **Activities** Awareness raising; capacity building; events/meetings; knowledge management/information dissemination; networking/liaising; training/education. **Publications** *GEF Newsletter*, *Green European Journal*. Educational materials.
Members Full in 17 countries:
Austria, Belgium, Croatia, Finland, France, Germany, Greece, Hungary, Ireland, Italy, Luxembourg, Netherlands, Poland, Spain, Sweden, Türkiye, UK.
Organization members (3):
European Green Party (EGP, #07409); *Federation of Young European Greens (FYEG, #09715)*; *Group of the Greens – European Free Alliance (Greens/EFA, #10781)*.

[2023.02.15/XM5774/f/F]

♦ Green Finance and Economic Cooperation (unconfirmed)
♦ GREEN – Global Rivers Environmental Education Network (internationally oriented national body)
♦ Green Group in the European Parliament / see Group of the Greens – European Free Alliance (#10781)

♦ **Green Growth Knowledge Platform (GGKP)** **10719**
Head Intl Environment House, Chemin des Anemones 11-13, 1219 Geneva, Switzerland.
URL: http://www.greengrowthknowledge.org/
History Set up Jan 2012, by *Global Green Growth Institute (GGGI, #10392)*, *OECD (#17693)*, *UNEP (#20299)* and *The World Bank Group (#21218)*. **Aims** Identify major knowledge gaps in green growth theory, policy and practice and address these gaps by promoting collaboration and coordinated research; use knowledge management and communication tools to provide practitioners, policymakers and other experts with opportunities to access, share and utilize green growth policy analysis, guidance, lessons learned, information and data. **Structure** Steering Committee, comprising founding organizations. Advisory Committee. Secretariat jointly hosted by *Global Green Growth Institute (GGGI, #10392)* and *UNEP (#20299)*. **Languages** English. **Staff** 4.00 FTE, paid. **Finance** Donor contributions. **Activities** Research/documentation; knowledge management/information dissemination; training/education. **Events** *Conference* Seoul (Korea Rep) 2019, *Inclusive solutions for the green transition – competitiveness, jobs/skills and social dimensions* Paris (France) 2018, *Transforming development through inclusive green growth* Jeju (Korea Rep) 2016, *Conference* Venice (Italy) 2015, *Conference / Annual Conference* Paris (France) 2013. **Publications** *Knowledge Update* (12 a year) – newsletter. Working paper series – online. Annual Report.
Members Knowledge partners (over 40) include 32 organizations listed in this Yearbook:
- *African Centre for Technology Studies (ACTS, #00243)*;
- *African Development Bank Group (ADB Group, #00284)*;
- *Arab Forum for Environment and Development (AFED, #00960)*;
- *Climate and Development Knowledge Network (CDKN, #04012)*;
- *Deutsche Gesellschaft für Internationale Zusammenarbeit (GIZ)*;
- *Deutsches Institut für Entwicklungspolitik (DIE)*;
- *Energy and Resources Institute (TERI)*;
- *Global Green Growth Institute (GGGI, #10392)*;
- *ILO (#11123)*;
- *Institut International d'Ingénierie de l'Eau et de l'Environnement (2iE, #11313)*;
- *International Center for Climate Governance (ICCG)*;
- *International Centre for Trade and Sustainable Development, Geneva (ICTSD, #12524)*;
- *International Institute for Sustainable Development (IISD, #13930)*;
- *International Monetary Fund (IMF, #14180)*;
- *International Trade Centre (ITC, #15703)*;
- *LEDS Global Partnership (LEDS GP, #16435)*;
- *Local Governments for Sustainability (ICLEI, #16507)*;
- *Mercator Research Institute on Global Commons and Climate Change (MCC)*;
- *Nordic Development Fund (NDF, #17271)*;
- *OAS (#17629)*;
- *OECD (#17693)*;
- *Renewable Energy and Energy Efficiency Partnership (REEEP, #18837)*;
- *The World Bank Group (#21218)*;
- UN – Department of Economic and Social Affairs;
- *UNDP (#20292)*;
- *UNEP (#20299)*;
- *UNIDO (#20336)*;
- *United Nations Economic and Social Commission for Asia and the Pacific (ESCAP, #20557)*;
- *United Nations Economic Commission for Africa (ECA, #20554)*;
- *United Nations Economic Commission for Europe (UNECE, #20555)*;
- *United Nations Institute for Training and Research (UNITAR, #20576)*;
- *World Wide Fund for Nature (WWF, #21922)*.

NGO Relations Member of: *LEDS Global Partnership (LEDS GP, #16435)*. [2016.02.08/XM4415/y/**F**]

♦ Greenheart International (internationally oriented national body)

♦ **Green Hotels Association** **10720**
Pres/Founder PO Box 420212, Houston TX 77242-0212, USA. T. +17137898889. Fax +17137899786. E-mail: green@greenhotels.com.
URL: http://www.greenhotels.com/
History 1993. **Aims** Encourage, promote and support ecological consciousness in the *hospitality* industry; help hotels save water, save energy and reduce solid waste; help protect *travel* destinations. **Languages** English. **Staff** 3.00 FTE, paid. **Publications** *Greening Newsletter* (6 a year). *Membership Conservation Guidelines and Ideas*.
Members Hotel members in 16 countries and territories:
Aruba, Brazil, Canada, Cayman Is, Colombia, Greece, India, Indonesia, Italy, Jamaica, Mexico, Namibia, Papua New Guinea, Philippines, Puerto Rico, USA. [2020.06.23/XD6752/**D**]

♦ **Greenhouse Gas Protocol (GHG Protocol)** **10721**
Dir WRI, 10 G St NE, Ste 800, Washington DC 20002, USA. T. +12027297777. Fax +12027297686.
Contact WBCSD, 4 chemin de Conches, 1231 Geneva, Switzerland. T. +41228393187. Fax +41228393131. E-mail: info@wbcsd.org.
URL: http://www.ghgprotocol.org/
History Founded 1998, by *World Business Council for Sustainable Development (WBCSD, #21254)* and *World Resources Institute (WRI, #21753)*. Original title: *Greenhouse Gas Protocol Initiative (GHG Protocol Initiative)*. **Aims** Build credible, effective and robust GHG accounting and reporting platforms that serve as a foundation to address climate change. **Structure** Multi-stakeholder partnership of businesses, NGOs, governments, academics and others convened by WBCSD and WRI. **Languages** Chinese, English, French, Japanese, Korean, Portuguese, Spanish. **Staff** 15.00 FTE, paid. **Finance** Grants. **Activities** Publishing activities; standards/guidelines; training/education, capacity building; guidance/assistance/consulting. **Publications** Standards and guidance documents. **IGO Relations** Collaborating organizations include: *European Bank for Reconstruction and Development (EBRD, #06315)*; *European Commission (EC, #06633)*; *International Bank for Reconstruction and Development (IBRD, #12317)*; *International Energy Agency (IEA, #13270)*; *International Finance Corporation (IFC, #13597)*; *OECD (#17693)*; *UNEP (#20299)*; *United Nations Framework Convention on Climate Change – Secretariat (UNFCCC, #20564)*; *United States Agency for International Development (USAID)*. **NGO Relations** Collaborating organizations include: *Confederation of European Paper Industries (CEPI, #04529)*; *Conservation International (CI)*; *Energy and Resources Institute (TERI)*; *Environmental Defense Fund (EDF)*; *International Aluminium Institute (IAI, #11643)*; *International Emissions Trading Association (IETA, #13262)*; *Pew Center on Global Climate Change*; *Union of Concerned Scientists (UCS)*; *World Steel Association (worldsteel, #21829)*; *World Wide Fund for Nature (WWF, #21922)*. [2017.10.25/XF6215/**F**]

♦ Greenhouse Gas Protocol Initiative / see Greenhouse Gas Protocol (#10721)

♦ **Green Industry Platform (GIP)** **10722**
Address not obtained.
URL: http://www.greenindustryplatform.org/
History Convened by *UNIDO (#20336)* and *UNEP (#20299)*. **Aims** Act as a forum to catalyze, mobilize and mainstream action on green industry around the world. **Structure** Advisory Board. Executive Board. Technical Expert Committee.
Members Businesses; Governments; organizations Business in 35 countries:
Austria, Bangladesh, Belgium, Brazil, Cambodia, Cameroon, China, Costa Rica, Denmark, Egypt, Ethiopia, France, India, Israel, Italy, Kenya, Laos, Lebanon, Malaysia, Mexico, Poland, Portugal, Russia, Serbia, Slovenia, South Africa, Spain, Sri Lanka, St Lucia, Sweden, Türkiye, Uganda, UK, USA, Zimbabwe.
Governments/government agencies of 28 countries:
Belarus, Bhutan, Burkina Faso, Colombia, Costa Rica, Côte d'Ivoire, Denmark, France, Guinea, Jamaica, Jordan, Kenya, Laos, Maldives, Mexico, Moldova, Myanmar, Netherlands, Nigeria, Philippines, Poland, Sierra Leone, South Africa, Sweden, Switzerland, Tuvalu, Ukraine, Vietnam.
Organizations in 27 countries:
Austria, Belgium, Cambodia, China, Colombia, Denmark, Egypt, France, Germany, Ghana, India, Israel, Korea Rep, Laos, Lebanon, Myanmar, Nigeria, Panama, Peru, Russia, Senegal, Spain, Trinidad-Tobago, UK, Uruguay, USA, Zimbabwe.
Included in the above, 12 organizations listed in this Yearbook:
Energy and Resources Institute (TERI); *European Commission (EC, #06633)* (Environment Directorate General); *Global Environment Facility (GEF, #10346)*; *Global Green Growth Institute (GGGI, #10392)*; *International Centre for Materials Technology Promotion (ICM, see: #20336)*; *International Chamber of Commerce (ICC, #12534)*; *Latin American Quality Institute (LAQI, #16364)*; *Plan Bleu pour l'environnement et le développement en Méditerranée (Plan Bleu, #18379)*; *Rainforest Alliance*; *UNIDO International Solar Energy Centre for Technology Promotion and Transfer (ISEC, #20334)*; *Weitz Center for Development Studies*; *Wuppertal Institute for Climate, Environment and Energy*. [2014/XJ8353/ty/**F**]

♦ **Greening of Industry Network (GIN)** **10723**
Coordinator CSTM Governance and Technology for Sustainability, Univ of Twente, PO Box 217, 7500 AE Enschede, Netherlands. T. +31534894234. E-mail: info-gin@utwente.nl.
URL: http://www.greeningofindustry.org/
History 1991. **Aims** Develop knowledge and transform practice to accelerate progress toward a sustainable society. **Structure** International Planning Board; Steering Committee; Coordinators (9). **Languages** English. **Activities** Events/meetings. **Events** *An Equitable, inclusive, and Environmentally Sound Circular Economy* 2020, *Pursuit of Sustainability in the Post-Covid Era* 2020, *Sustainability Science Post COVID-19 – Social Distancing Life, Approaching Natural Life* 2020, *Towards Circular Regions* Netherlands 2020, *International Conference* Mexico City (Mexico) 2019. **Publications** *GIN Newsletter*. *GIN book series*. **Members** in over 50 countries worldwide. Membership countries not specified. [2021.05.18/XF4646/t/**F**]

♦ **Green Jobs and Sustainable Development International Centre (GJASD International)** **10724**
Headquarters c/o l'Etude d'avocats, CPB Partners, Chemin des Carrés 37, Chancy, 1284 Geneva, Switzerland. T. +41763438687. E-mail: info@gjasd.org.
URL: http://www.gjasd.org/
History 10 Nov 2014, Geneva (Switzerland). Registration: Federal Commercial Register, No/ID: CHE-288.795.026, Start date: 25 Oct 2019, Switzerland, Geneva. **Aims** Enhance general awareness of the consequences of *climate change* and the importance of shifting toward a green and sustainable economy; promote greening enterprises and green sectors as the areas of significant opportunities for investment, growth and jobs; advance the mechanisms for measuring green growth and green labour market performance; assist countries in harnessing their green tourism potential. **Structure** General Assembly; Executive Committee. Headquarters located in Geneva (Switzerland). **Languages** English, French, German, Russian, Ukrainian. **Activities** Capacity building; guidance/assistance/consulting; knowledge management/information dissemination; networking/liaising; projects/programmes; research and development. Active in: Azerbaijan, Bangladesh, Georgia, Kyrgyzstan, Madagascar, Moldova, Philippines, Russia, Tajikistan, Ukraine. **NGO Relations** Member of (1): *World Alliance for Efficient Solutions*. [2022.06.17/XM7299/**C**]

♦ Green Lines Institute for Sustainable Development (unconfirmed)
♦ GREEN LINES – Instituto para o Desenvolvimento Sustentável (unconfirmed)
♦ GreenMicrofinance Center (internationally oriented national body)

♦ **GreenNet** **10725**
Contact The Green House, 244-254 Cambridge Heath Rd, London, E2 9DA, UK. T. +443303554011. E-mail: info@gn.apc.org.
URL: http://www.gn.apc.org/
History 1986, London (UK). Full title: *Global Computer Network for Environment, Peace, Human Rights and Development*. **Aims** As a computer-based *communications* system, helps environment, peace, human rights and development movements worldwide to communicate more effectively. **Structure** Run by an independent non-profit making organization. **Finance** Sources: users' fees; grants and gifts. **Activities** Knowledge management/information dissemination. **Publications** *GreenNet News*. Electronic mail service; past electronic conferencing system (over 250 subject areas).
Members Membership covers 44 countries (" indicates individual members only):
Angola, Bangladesh (*), Belgium, Bosnia-Herzegovina, Burundi, Cameroon, Croatia, Czechia, Denmark (*), Egypt (*), Eritrea, Ethiopia, France, Germany, Ghana, Hungary, India, Indonesia (*), Ireland, Israel (*), Jordan, Kenya, Madagascar, Morocco, Netherlands, Nigeria (*), Palestine, Philippines, Romania, Senegal, Serbia, Slovakia, Slovenia, South Africa, Spain, Sri Lanka, Sweden, Switzerland (*), Tanzania UR, Tunisia, Uganda, UK (*), Zambia, Zimbabwe.
NGO Relations Together with *Institute for Global Communications (IGC, inactive)*, instrumental in setting up: *Association for Progressive Communications (APC, #02873)*; GreenNet Educational Trust. [2019/XF1123/**F**]

♦ Green Our Planet (internationally oriented national body)

♦ **Greenovate! Europe** **10726**
Managing Dir Renewable Energy House, Rue d'Arlon 63-65, 1040 Brussels, Belgium. T. +3224001006. Fax +3224001009. E-mail: info@greenovate-europe.eu.
URL: http://www.greenovate-europe.eu/
History An organization of the type *European Economic Interest Grouping (EEIG, #06960)*. **Aims** Develop *sustainable business* by providing *innovation* support services at EU level to policy-makers, research laboratories, technology developers, companies willing to acquire or spin-out new technologies, and investors. **Structure** General Assembly; Board; Executive Board. **Languages** English, French, German. **Staff** 5.00 FTE, paid. **Events** *Conference on Opening Doors to Efficient Buildings* Brussels (Belgium) 2022, *Workshop on the Role of Multinational Companies and Supply Chains in Innovation* Brussels (Belgium) 2012. **Members** Full (25) in 14 countries. Membership countries not specified. **NGO Relations** Member of: *A.SPIRE (#02311)*; *European Water Partnership (EWP, #09083)*; *European Water Partnership (EWP, #09083)*; *WindEurope (#20965)*. [2021/XJ8757/**E**]

♦ **Greenpeace International** **10727**
Main Office Ottho Heldringstraat 5, 1066 AZ Amsterdam, Netherlands. T. +31207182000. Fax +31207182002. E-mail: info.int@greenpeace.org.
URL: https://www.greenpeace.org/international/
History 1971, Vancouver BC (Canada). Registered in accordance with Dutch law as *Stichting Greenpeace Council*, 1979. **Aims** Change attitudes and behaviour, protect and conserve the *environment* and promote peace. **Structure** General Meeting (annual); Board of Directors; National/Regional Offices; International Executive Director. **Languages** English. **Staff** About 135, plus 100 ships' crew. **Finance** Entirely funded by donations of individuals and private foundation grants. **Activities** Advocacy/lobbying/activism; awareness raising. **Events** *EMDS : Meeting of Municipalities with Sustainable Development* Brasilia (Brazil) 2017, *Green Asia Forum* Busan (Korea Rep) 2013, *Conference* Dalfsen (Netherlands) 2010, *Conference* Dalfsen (Netherlands) 2010, *Meeting* Dalfsen (Netherlands) 2010. **Consultative Status** Consultative status granted from: *ECOSOC (#05331)* (General); *FAO (#09260)* (Liaison Status); *International Maritime Organization (IMO, #14102)*; *UNEP (#20299)*; *Council of Europe (CE, #04881)* (Participatory Status). **IGO Relations** Observer to: *Western and Central Pacific Fisheries Commission (WCPFC, #20912)*; *Codex Alimentarius Commission (CAC, #04081)*; *Global Environment Facility (GEF, #10346)*; *Inter-American Tropical Tuna Commission (IATTC, #11454)*; International Whaling Commission; *OSPAR Commission for the Protection of the Marine Environment of the North-East Atlantic (OSPAR Commission, #17905)*; *United Nations Framework Convention on Climate Change (UNFCCC, 1992)*. Accredited by: *Green Climate Fund (GCF, #10714)*; *United Nations Framework Convention on Climate Change – Secretariat (UNFCCC, #20564)*; *International Whaling Commission (IWC, #15879)*; *United Nations Office at Vienna (UNOV, #20604)*. Associated with Department of Global Communications of the United Nations. Involved in: *Consultative Meeting of Contracting Parties to the London Convention/Meeting of Contracting Parties to the London Protocol (#04769)*; *Convention for the Protection of the Marine Environment and the Coastal Region of the Mediterranean (Barcelona Convention, 1976)*; *Intergovernmental Panel on Climate Change (IPCC, #11499)*; *Secretariat of the Basel Convention (SBC, #19196)*; *Secretariat of the Convention on Biological Diversity (SCBD, #19197)*; *Secretariat of the Convention on International Trade in Endangered Species of Wild Fauna and Flora (CITES Secretariat, #19199)*; *Stockholm Convention on Persistent Organic Pollutants (POP treaty, 2001)* Secretariat; *UNEP (#20299)* Mercury Assessment Group. **NGO Relations** Member of: *CHS Alliance (#03911)*; *EarthAction (EA, #05159)*; *Environment Liaison Centre International (ELCI, no recent information)*; *Global Call for Climate Action (GCCA, inactive)*; *The Green 10 (#10711)*; *High Seas Alliance (HSA, #10918)*; *InterEcoClub (IEC, no recent information)*; *International Network for Sustainable Energy (INFORSE, #14331)*; *Oilwatch (#17711)*; *Species Survival Network (SSN, #19916)*. European Unit is signatory to Founding Statement of: *Alliance for Lobbying Transparency and Ethics Regulation (ALTER-EU, #00705)*. Supports: *International Foundation for the Survival and Development of Humanity (no recent information)*; *International Pollutants Elimination Network (IPEN, #14616)*; *Taiga Rescue Network (TRN, inactive)*. [2021/XF4392/**F**]

♦ Green Project Management (unconfirmed)

- Green Schools Alliance (internationally oriented national body)
- **Greens/EFA** Group of the Greens – European Free Alliance (#10781)
- Greens / see Group of the Greens – European Free Alliance (#10781)

Green Spider Network (GSN) — 10728
Pres Ministry of Environment and Sustainable Development, Water Dept, 12 Libertatii Blvd, Sector 5, Bucharest, Romania. T. +40213162184. Fax +40213160282.
URL: http://ec.europa.eu/environment/networks/greenspider/
History 1995. **Aims** Promote relations between *EU* administration and national institutions; provide a platform for exchange of information and experience in the field of *environmental* communication. **Structure** Core group of 5-6 members. President. **Finance** Supported by *European Commission (EC, #06633)* (DG Environment). **Events** *Annual Meeting* Berlin (Germany) 2012, *Annual Meeting* Copenhagen (Denmark) 2011, *Annual meeting* Brussels (Belgium) 2010, *Annual meeting* Brussels (Belgium) 2009, *Annual meeting* Annecy (France) 2008.
Members Full in 28 countries:
Austria, Belgium, Bulgaria, Cyprus, Czechia, Denmark, Estonia, Finland, France, Germany, Greece, Hungary, Iceland, Ireland, Italy, Latvia, Lithuania, Malta, Netherlands, Norway, Poland, Portugal, Romania, Slovakia, Spain, Sweden, Türkiye, UK.
European institutions (3):
European Commission (EC, #06633) (DG Environment); *European Environment Agency (EEA, #06995)*; *European Environmental Communication Networks (EECN, #06997)*.
Permanent Observer:
UNEP (#20299). [2015/XM2924/y/**E**]

- Green Sports Alliance (internationally oriented national body)

Greenwich Mean Time — 10729
Head Office Royal Observatory Greenwich, National Maritime Museum, Park Row, Greenwich, London, SE10 9NF, UK. Fax +442083126632.
URL: https://greenwichmeantime.com/
History 1884, Washington DC (USA), on signature of an agreement by representatives of 26 countries at *International Meridian Conference*. Based on original calculations by Nevil Maskelyne, first published 1767. Based in the Royal Observatory Greenwich (UK) and managed as part of the National Maritime Museum. **Aims** Provide a basis for computation of precise longitude and time zones worldwide; operate a public *astronomy* service and public museum and archive; provide educational programmes. [2018/XF4306/**F**]

- Green World City Organisation (unconfirmed)
- **GREFA** – Global Relief Foundation, Ghana (internationally oriented national body)
- **GREF** Gaming Regulators European Forum (#10069)
- **GREF** – Groupement des retraités éducateurs sans frontières (internationally oriented national body)
- **GREF** Groupe des radiologistes enseignants d'expression française (#10768)
- **GRELL** Groupe de coordination pour l'épidémiologie et l'enregistrement du cancer dans les pays de langue latine (#10737)
- Gremial de Exportadores de Productos no Tradicionales / see Federación de Camaras y Asociaciones de Exportadores de Centroamérica y el Caribe (#09293)
- **GREMPA** Groupe de recherches méditerranéennes pour l'amandier – pistachier (#10770)
- **GREPA** Groupe de recherche européen sur la paroi abdominale (#07480)
- GRESAL / see Groupe de recherches en sciences sociales sur l'Amérique Latine
- GRESAL – Groupe de recherches en sciences sociales sur l'Amérique Latine (internationally oriented national body)
- **GRESEA** – Groupe de recherche pour une stratégie économique alternative (internationally oriented national body)
- **GRET** (internationally oriented national body)
- Grete Lundbeck European Brain Research Foundation (internationally oriented national body)
- **GRET** – Professionals for Fair Development / see GRET
- **GRET** – Professionnels du développement solidaire / see GRET
- Greycells – Association of Former International Civil Servants for Development (internationally oriented national body)

Grey Literature Network Service (GreyNet International) — 10730
Contact Javastraat 194-HS, 1095 CP Amsterdam, Netherlands. T. +31203312420. E-mail: info@greynet.org.
URL: http://www.greynet.org/
History 1992, Amsterdam (Netherlands). Founded during 1st International Conference on Grey Literature. Discontinued in 2000 and relaunched 2003. **Aims** Facilitate dialogue, research and communication between individuals and organizations in the field of grey literature; further seek, identify and distribute information on and about grey literature in networked environments, as well as curriculum development and instruction. **Structure** Committees (4): Research and Development; Publishing and Communication; Open Access; Education and Training. **Languages** English. **Staff** 1.00 FTE, paid. **Finance** Sources: fees for services; meeting proceeds; members' dues; sale of publications; sponsorship. **Activities** Events/meetings; publishing activities; research/documentation; training/education. **Events** *International Conference on Grey Literature* Bethesda, MD (USA) 2022, *International Conference on Grey Literature* Amsterdam (Netherlands) 2021, *International Conference on Grey Literature* Pisa (Italy) 2020, *International Conference on Grey Literature* Hannover (Germany) 2019, *International Conference on Grey Literature* New Orleans, LA (USA) 2018. **Publications** *The Grey Journal (TGJ): An International Journal on Grey Literature* (3 a year). *The GreyForum*. International Directory; Guides; Conference Memoranda. **Information Services** *DANS Data Archive*; *GreyGuide Portal and Repository*; *OpenGrey Repository*; *TIB Visual Series*.
Members Organizational (10) in 8 countries:
Austria, Czechia, Germany, Italy, Korea Rep, Netherlands, Slovakia, USA.
Partnerships:
France, USA.
International Council for Scientific and Technical Information (ICSTI, #13070).
WorldWide Science Alliance. [2022.05.04/XM2037/**F**]

- **GreyNet International** Grey Literature Network Service (#10730)
- Grey Nuns of the Sacred Heart (religious order)
- Grey Nuns – Sisters of Charity of Montreal (religious order)
- Grey Nuns – Sisters of Charity of Ottawa (religious order)
- Grey Nuns – Sisters of Charity of Quebec (religious order)
- Grey Nuns – Sisters of Charity of St Hyacinthe (religious order)
- Grey Sisters of the Immaculate Conception (religious order)
- **GRFA** Global Renewable Fuels Alliance (#10566)
- **GRF** Davos – Global Risk Forum (internationally oriented national body)
- **GRF** Global Research Forum on Sustainable Production and Consumption (#10575)
- **GRG** Committee / see International Society on General Relativity and Gravitation (#15138)
- **GRG** Society / see International Society on General Relativity and Gravitation (#15138)
- **GRIAPRA** – Grupo Iberoamericano de Sociedades Cientificas de Protección Radiológica (no recent information)
- **GRI** / see Borlaug Global Rust Initiative (#03305)
- **GRID**-Arendal (internationally oriented national body)
- **GRID** Global Resource Information Database (#10578)
- Griffith Asia Institute (internationally oriented national body)
- Griffith Asia Pacific Council / see Griffith Asia Institute
- Griffith Asia Pacific Research Institute / see Griffith Asia Institute
- Griggs University and International Academy (internationally oriented national body)
- **GRI** – Global Real Estate Institute (unconfirmed)
- **GRI** – Global Refuge (internationally oriented national body)
- **GRI** Global Reporting Initiative (#10567)

- **GRINSO** – Group for International Solidarity (internationally oriented national body)
- **GRIP** / see Groupe de recherche et d'information sur la paix et la sécurité
- **GRIP** – Groupe de recherche et d'information sur la paix et la sécurité (internationally oriented national body)
- **GRiSP** Global Rice Science Partnership (#10580)
- **GRLI** Globally Responsible Leadership Initiative (#10462)
- **GRM** – Global Response Medicine (internationally oriented national body)
- **GRM** – Grand Rite Malgache (see: #16593)
- **GRMN** Global Research Management Network (#10576)
- **GRN** – Globalization Research Network (internationally oriented national body)
- **GRN** – Global Recordings Network (internationally oriented national body)
- Groep van Apotekers van de Europese Gemeenschap / see Pharmaceutical Group of the European Union (#18352)
- Groepering van Apotekers van de Europese Unie (#18352)
- Groepering van Associaties van de Maisverwerkende Industrieën van de EEG-Landen / see Euromaisiers (#05709)
- Groepering van de Keramiektegel-Producenten van de Gemeenschappelijke Markt / see European Ceramic Tile Manufacturers' Federation (#06508)
- Groep van Uitgevers van Boeken in de EEG / see Federation of European Publishers (#09536)
- Gromadianska Initsiatyva (internationally oriented national body)
- **GROMS** – Global Register of Migratory Species (internationally oriented national body)
- Grönlannin Pohjola-Instituutti (internationally oriented national body)
- **GROOTS** – Grassroots Organizations Operating Together in Sisterhood (internationally oriented national body)
- Gross-Loge des Druidentums (religious order)
- Grotius Centre – Grotius Centre for International Legal Studies (internationally oriented national body)
- Grotius Centre for International Legal Studies (internationally oriented national body)

Groundswell International — 10731
Dir 1215 Kearney St NE, Washington DC 20017, USA. T. +12028329352. E-mail: csacco@groundswellinternational.org.
URL: http://www.groundswellinternational.org/
History Aug 2009, Rutland MA (USA). Registered in the State of Washington DC (USA). **Aims** Strengthen power and potential of family *farmers* in Africa, Americans and Asia to cultivate, grown and spread environmentally sound farming practices that work with nature, not against it. **Structure** International Council; Board of Directors. **Activities** Networking/liaising; training/education; advocacy/lobbying/activism; capacity building. Active in: Burkina Faso, Ecuador, Ghana, Guatemala, Haiti, Honduras, Mali, Nepal, USA. **Events** *Global Conference* Stony Point, NY (USA) 2015. [2015.10.09/XJ5894/**F**]

- Group of 11 / see Cartagena Group (#03589)
- Group of 15 / see Group of Fifteen (#10778)
- Group of 24 / see Intergovernmental Group of Twenty-Four on International Monetary Affairs (#11495)
- Group of 30 / see Group of Thirty (#10790)
- Group of 5 / see Group of Five (#10779)
- Group of 5 / see Group of Seven (#10788)

Group of 77 (G-77) — 10732
Groupe des 77 – Grupo de los 77
Secretariat United Nations Headquarters, Secretariat Bldg, Room S-0518, New York NY 10017, USA. T. +12129634777. Fax +12129633515. E-mail: secretariat@g77.org.
URL: http://www.g77.org/
History 15 Jun 1964, by 77 developing countries signatory to the '*Joint Declaration of the Seventy-Seven Countries*' issued at the end of the first session of *UNCTAD (#20285)*, Geneva (Switzerland). Permanent institutional structure developed gradually, commencing with the first Ministerial Meeting of the Group of 77, 10-25 Oct 1967, Algiers (Algeria), which adopted the Charter of Algiers, followed by the creation of Chapters of the Group of 77 with Liaison offices in Geneva (UNCTAD), Nairobi (Kenya) (UNEP), Paris (France) (UNESCO), Rome (Italy) (FAO/IFAD), Vienna (Austria) (UNIDO) and the Group of 24 in Washington DC (USA) (IMF and World Bank). Although membership of G-77 has increased to 134 countries, the original name is retained because of its historic significance. **Aims** As the largest intergovernmental organization of *developing states* in the United Nations, provide the means for the countries of the South to articulate and promote their collective economic interests and enhance their joint negotiating capacity on all major international *economic* issues in the *United Nations* system; promote South-South *cooperation* for development. **Structure** The work of G-77 in each Chapter is coordinated by a Chair who acts as its spokesperson. The Chairmanship rotates on a regional basis and is held for one year in all the Chapters. The Chairmanship is the highest political body. The supreme decision-making body is the South Summit, convened every 5 years. Meeting of the Ministers for Foreign Affairs, convened annually at the beginning of the regular session of the General Assembly of the United Nations in New York NY (USA) and periodically in preparation for UNCTAD sessions. Special Ministerial Meetings are also called as needed. Plenary body is *Intergovernmental Follow-up and Coordination Committee of the Group of 77 on Economic Cooperation among Developing Countries (IFCC, see: #10732)*. Secretariat led by Executive Secretary. **Languages** Arabic, English, French, Spanish. **Finance** Contributions by Member States.
Activities Besides formulating joint positions on resolutions and decisions within the framework of the United Nations, produces joint declarations and action programmes on development issues, including:
– Joint Declaration the Group of 77 Geneva, 15 Jun 1964;
– Algiers Charter, 10-25 Oct 1967;
– *Agreement on a Global System of Trade Preferences among Developing Countries (GSTP, 1988)*, 11-13 Apr 1988;
– 30th Anniversary Ministerial Declaration, 24 Jun 1994;
– Ministerial Statement on '*An Agenda for Development*', 1994;
– Declaration of the South Summit and the Havana Programme of Action, 10-14 Apr 2000;
– Sao Paulo Declaration/40th Anniversary Ministerial Declaration, 11-12 Jun 2004;
– Doha Declaration and Doha Plan of Action of the 2nd G-77 South Summit, 12-16 Jun 2005;
– 50th Anniversary Summit Declaration 14-15 Jun 2014.
Group also: makes statements at various Main Committees of the General Assembly, ECOSOC and other subsidiary bodies; sponsors and negotiates resolutions and decisions at major conferences and other meetings held under the aegis of the UN dealing with international economic cooperation and development; sponsors projects on South-South cooperation through funding from the Perez-Guerrero Trust Fund and convenes high-level meetings on thematic/sectoral issues.
Events *High-level United Nations conference on South-South cooperation* Nairobi (Kenya) 2009, *Meeting of Ministers of Science and Technology* Rio de Janeiro (Brazil) 2006, *South summit* Doha (Qatar) 2005, *Meeting of Ministers of Science and Technology* Hong Kong (Hong Kong) 2005, *High-level conference on South-South cooperation* Marrakech (Morocco) 2003. **Publications** *The Group of 77 at the United Nations* – third series, in 6 vols. *Directory of Institutions for Science, Technology, and Innovation in the South*.
Members Governments of 134 countries:
Afghanistan, Algeria, Angola, Antigua-Barbuda, Argentina, Bahamas, Bahrain, Bangladesh, Barbados, Belize, Benin, Bhutan, Bolivia, Bosnia-Herzegovina, Botswana, Brazil, Brunei Darussalam, Burkina Faso, Burundi, Cambodia, Cameroon, Cape Verde, Central African Rep, Chad, Chile, China, Colombia, Comoros, Congo Brazzaville, Congo DR, Costa Rica, Côte d'Ivoire, Cuba, Djibouti, Dominica, Dominican Rep, Ecuador, Egypt, El Salvador, Equatorial Guinea, Eritrea, Eswatini, Ethiopia, Fiji, Gabon, Gambia, Ghana, Grenada, Guatemala, Guinea, Guinea-Bissau, Guyana, Haiti, Honduras, India, Indonesia, Iran Islamic Rep, Iraq, Jamaica, Jordan, Kenya, Kiribati, Korea Rep, Kuwait, Laos, Lebanon, Lesotho, Liberia, Libya, Madagascar, Malawi, Malaysia, Maldives, Mali, Marshall Is, Mauritania, Mauritius, Micronesia FS, Mongolia, Morocco, Mozambique, Myanmar, Namibia, Nauru, Nepal, Nicaragua, Niger, Nigeria, Oman, Pakistan, Palestine, Panama, Papua New Guinea, Paraguay, Peru, Philippines, Qatar, Rwanda, Samoa, Sao Tomé-Principe, Saudi Arabia, Senegal, Seychelles, Sierra Leone, Singapore, Solomon Is, Somalia, South Africa, South Sudan, Sri Lanka, St Kitts-Nevis, St Lucia, St Vincent-Grenadines, Sudan, Suriname, Syrian AR, Tajikistan, Tanzania UR, Thailand, Timor-Leste, Togo, Tonga, Trinidad-Tobago, Tunisia, Turkmenistan, Uganda, United Arab Emirates, Uruguay, Vanuatu, Venezuela, Vietnam, Yemen, Zambia, Zimbabwe.
IGO Relations United Nations bodies:
– *Comprehensive Nuclear-Test-Ban Treaty Organization (CTBTO, #04420)*;
– *FAO (#09260)*;

- *ILO (#11123)*;
- *International Atomic Energy Agency (IAEA, #12294)*;
- *International Civil Aviation Organization (ICAO, #12581)*;
- *International Civil Service Commission (ICSC, #12587)*;
- *International Fund for Agricultural Development (IFAD, #13692)*;
- *International Maritime Organization (IMO, #14102)*;
- *International Monetary Fund (IMF, #14180)*;
- *International Organization for Migration (IOM, #14454)*;
- *International Telecommunication Union (ITU, #15673)*;
- *International Trade Centre (ITC, #15703)*;
- *Joint Inspection Unit of the United Nations (JIU, #16133)*;
- *Joint United Nations Programme on HIV/AIDS (UNAIDS, #16149)*;
- *Office of the United Nations High Commissioner for Human Rights (OHCHR, #17697)*;
- *Organisation for the Prohibition of Chemical Weapons (OPCW, #17823)*;
- *Pan Caribbean Partnership against HIV and AIDS (PANCAP, #18171)*;
- *UNEP (#20299)*;
- *UN Women (#20724)*;
- *UNCTAD (#20285)*;
- *UNDP (#20292)*;
- *UNESCO (#20322)*;
- *UNHCR (#20327)*;
- *UNICEF (#20332)*;
- *UNIDO (#20336)*;
- *United Nations (UN, #20515)*;
- *United Nations Economic Commission for Africa (ECA, #20554)*;
- *United Nations Economic Commission for Africa (ECA, #20554)*;
- *United Nations Economic Commission for Europe (UNECE, #20555)*;
- *United Nations Economic Commission for Latin America and the Caribbean (ECLAC, #20556)*;
- *United Nations Economic and Social Commission for Asia and the Pacific (ESCAP, #20557)*;
- *United Nations Economic and Social Commission for Western Asia (ESCWA, #20558)*;
- *United Nations Framework Convention on Climate Change – Secretariat (UNFCCC, #20564)*;
- *United Nations Human Settlements Programme (UN-Habitat, #20572)*;
- *United Nations Institute for Disarmament Research (UNIDIR, #20575)*;
- *United Nations Institute for Training and Research (UNITAR, #20576)*;
- *United Nations Office for Disaster Risk Reduction (UNDRR, #20595)*;
- *United Nations Interregional Crime and Justice Research Institute (UNICRI, #20580)*;
- *United Nations Office on Drugs and Crime (UNODC, #20596)*;
- *United Nations Office for Project Services (UNOPS, #20602)*;
- *United Nations Population Fund (UNFPA, #20612)*;
- *United Nations Relief and Works Agency for Palestine Refugees in the Near East (UNRWA, #20622)*;
- *United Nations Research Institute for Social Development (UNRISD, #20623)*;
- *United Nations System Staff College (UNSSC, #20637)*;
- *United Nations University (UNU, #20642)*;
- *Universal Postal Union (UPU, #20682)*;
- *WHO (#20950)*;
- *World Food Programme (WFP, #21510)*;
- *World Intellectual Property Organization (WIPO, #21593)*;
- *World Meteorological Organization (WMO, #21649)*;
- *World Tourism Organization (UNWTO, #21861)*;
- *World Trade Organization (WTO, #21864)*.

Sub-Regional, Regional, Inter-Regional organizations and economic groupings, including: *Non-Aligned Movement (NAM, #17146)*; *South Centre (#19753)*. [2018.09.04/XF0728/**F***]

- ♦ Group of 8 / see Group of Eight (#10745)
- ♦ Group of 9 / see Group of Nine (#10785)
- ♦ Group of Acousticians of Latin America (inactive)
- ♦ Group of Advisers on the Ethical Implications of Biotechnology / see European Group on Ethics in Science and New Technologies (#07420)

♦ Group for Aeronautical Research and Technology in Europe (GARTEUR) 10733

Groupe pour la recherche et la technologie aéronautique en Europe – Gruppe für Luftfahrt-Forschung und Technologie in Europa

Sec Box 5008, SE-165 10 Hasselby, Sweden. T. +4687595564. E-mail: secretariat@garteur.org.
URL: http://www.garteur.org/

History 1973, by representatives of government departments responsible for aeronautical research in France, Germany FR and UK. Netherlands joined in 1977, Sweden in 1991, Spain in 1996 and Italy in 2000. Memorandum of Understanding (MoU) among governments of member countries came into effect on 6 Apr 1981, with Addenda 1, 2 and 3 coming into effect on 28 Nov 1991, 18 Oct 1996 and 200 respectively, together with *'GARTEUR Charter'* under which the Group operates. MoU amended in 1986 by Appendix A (Rules for the Protection and Use of Intellectual Property in GARTEUR Cooperation) and in 1988 by Appendix B (GARTEUR Security Regulations). Permanent Instructions, amended from time to time to accommodate practical needs, comprise detailed operational guidelines and procedures. **Aims** Strengthen collaboration among European countries with major research capabilities and government funded programmes; stimulate advances in the aeronautical sciences and pursue topics of application-oriented research in order to maintain and strengthen the competitiveness of the European *aerospace industry* by concentrating existing resources in an efficient manner and seeking to avoid duplication of work; perform joint research work in fields suitable for collaboration and within research groups specifically established for this purpose; identify technology gaps and facility needs and recommend effective ways for the member countries to jointly overcome such shortcomings; exchange scientific and technical information among member countries. **Structure** I. *'Council'*, composed of representatives of each member country who constitute the national delegations. Executive Committee, consisting of one member of each national delegation. Secretary. No permanent Secretariat and headquarters. Chairmanship and Secretariat rotate every 2 years among members. Meetings of Council and Executive Committee are closed. II. *'Groups of Responsables'* (4), consisting of representatives from national research establishments, industry and academia. III. *'Action Groups'* – technical expert bodies for programme formulation of the research programme and execution of research work. **Languages** English. **Finance** Resources are made available by governments of member countries or by participating organizations on the basis of balanced contributions. **Activities** 'Groups of Responsables' (4) carry out research: Aerodynamics; Flight Mechanics, Systems and Integration; Helicopters; Structures and Materials. **Publications** Annual Report; technical publications. Available on website.

Members Member countries (7):
France, Germany, Italy, Netherlands, Spain, Sweden, UK. [2011.09.03/XE4050/**E***]

- ♦ Group of African, Caribbean and Pacific States / see Organisation of African, Caribbean and Pacific States (#17796)
- ♦ Group of Allied Mega-Biodiverse Nations / see Alliance Against Biopiracy (#00653)
- ♦ Group-Analytic Society / see Group-Analytic Society International (#10734)

♦ Group-Analytic Society International (GASi) 10734

Main Office 1 Daleham Gardens, London, NW3 5BY, UK. T. +442074356611. Fax +442074439576. E-mail: office@groupanalyticsociety.co.uk.
URL: https://groupanalyticsociety.co.uk/

History 1952, London (UK). Former names and other names: *Group-Analytic Society (GAS)* – former (1952 to 2011). Registration: Charity Commission, No/ID: 1174815, England and Wales. **Aims** Study and promote the development of clinical and applied aspects of *group analysis*. **Structure** Management Committee. **Finance** Subscriptions. **Activities** Organizes: scientific meetings (always in London), Annual Autumn Workshop, Annual Summer Workshop, Annual SH Foulkes Lecture; Spring Weekend Meeting – Study Day; international symposium and workshop (every 3 years). Sub-Committees. **Events** *International Symposium* Belgrade (Serbia) 2023, *Symposium* Barcelona (Spain) 2020, *International Symposium* Berlin (Germany) 2017, *International Symposium* Lisbon (Portugal) 2014, *Triennial European Symposium in Group Analysis* London (UK) 2011. **Publications** *Group Analysis* (4 a year) – journal; *Bulletin* (regular); *Contexts* – international newsletter; *International Directory of Members*. List of members' publications worldwide. Information Services: Library.

Members Full; Associate; Student. Individuals (800) in 31 countries:
Australia, Austria, Brazil, China, Croatia, Czechia, Denmark, Finland, Germany, Greece, Hungary, Iceland, Ireland, Italy, Japan, Lithuania, Malaysia, Mexico, New Zealand, Norway, Poland, Portugal, Russia, Serbia, Slovenia, South Africa, Spain, Sweden, Switzerland, UK, USA. [2021/XF4148/v/**F**]

- ♦ Group on the Balkan Agreement on Cooperation on Tourism (inactive)
- ♦ Group for Cancer Epidemiology and Registration in Latin Language Countries (#10737)
- ♦ Group DVB – Digital Video Broadcasting / see DVB Project (#05147)
- ♦ Groupe des 11 / see Cartagena Group (#03589)
- ♦ Groupe des 15 / see Group of Fifteen (#10778)
- ♦ Groupe des 30 / see Group of Thirty (#10790)
- ♦ Groupe des 5 / see Group of Five (#10779)
- ♦ Groupe des 77 (#10732)
- ♦ Groupe des 8 / see Group of Eight (#10745)
- ♦ Groupe des 9 / see Group of Nine (#10785)
- ♦ Groupe ABC (inactive)
- ♦ Groupe de l'Accord sur la coopération des pays balkaniques en matière de tourisme (inactive)
- ♦ Groupe d'Action contre le Blanchiment d'Argent en Afrique Centrale (unconfirmed)
- ♦ Groupe d'action financière (#09765)
- ♦ Groupe d'action financière sur le blanchiment de capitaux / see Financial Action Task Force (#09765)
- ♦ Groupe d'action financière des Caraïbes (#03505)
- ♦ Groupe d'action financière du moyen-orient et de l'afrique du nord – (#16779)
- ♦ Groupe d'actions contre la Marginalisation. / see Vision GRAM-International
- ♦ Groupe d'action du tourisme européen (#08946)
- ♦ Groupe d'aide aux réalisations pour le développement / see Acting for Life
- ♦ Groupe d'aide aux réfugiés et personnes déplacées / see Acting for Life
- ♦ Groupe de l'alliance progressiste des socialistes and démocrates au Parlement européen (#10786)
- ♦ Groupe des ambassadeurs latinoaméricains auprès des Communautés européennes (inactive)
- ♦ Groupe anti-blanchiment d'Afrique orientale et australe (#05252)
- ♦ Groupe anti-blanchiment de l'Asie/Pacifique (#01921)
- ♦ Groupe arabe des institutions supérieures de contrôle des finances publiques (#01021)

♦ Group on Earth Observations (GEO) 10735

Dir Avenue de la Paix 7 bis, Case Postale 2300, 1211 Geneva, Switzerland. T. +41227308505. Fax +41227308520. E-mail: secretariat@geosec.org.
URL: http://www.earthobservations.org/

History 16 Feb 2005, Brussels (Belgium). Founded during Third Earth Observation Summit, to develop the 10-year implementation plan for a *Global Earth Observation System of Systems (GEOSS)*. New Strategic Plan runs 2016-2025. **Aims** Build a Global Earth Observation System of Systems (GEOSS) over the next 10 years, which will work with and build upon existing national, regional and international systems to provide comprehensive, coordinated Earth observations from thousands of instruments worldwide, transforming the data they collect into vital information for society. **Structure** Plenary (at least annually); Executive Committee; Programme Board; Secretariat. Committees (4); Working Group. Regional initiatives (4): *AfriGEOSS*; *AmeriGEOSS (#00796)*; *Asia-Oceania GEOSS (AOGEOSS, #01800)*; *EuroGEOSS (#05685)*. **Languages** English. **Staff** 9 permanent; 3 short-term; 5 seconded experts. **Finance** Voluntary contributions. **Activities** Capacity building; events/meetings; knowledge management/information dissemination; projects/programmes. Priority engagement areas: UN 2030 Agenda for Sustainable Development; *Paris Agreement (2015)*; Sendai Framework for Disaster Risk Reduction. Work divided along 8 societal benefit areas: Biodiversity and Ecosystem Sustainability – through *GEO Biodiversity Observation Network (GEO BON, #10129)*; Disaster Resilience; Energy and Mineral Resource Management; Food Security and Sustainable Agriculture; Public Health Surveillance; Infrastructure and Transport Management; Sustainable Urban Development; Water Resources Management. **Events** *Asia-Oceania GEO Symposium* Japan 2021, *Symposium* Geneva (Switzerland) 2019, *AmeriGEOSS Week* Lima (Peru) 2019, *Meeting* Kyoto (Japan) 2018, *Meeting* Kyoto (Japan) 2018. **Publications** *GEO News* (6 a year) – electronic newsletter.

Members Governments of 104 countries:
Algeria, Argentina, Armenia, Australia, Austria, Bahamas, Bahrain, Bangladesh, Belgium, Belize, Brazil, Bulgaria, Burkina Faso, Cambodia, Cameroon, Canada, Central African Rep, Chile, China, Colombia, Congo Brazzaville, Costa Rica, Côte d'Ivoire, Croatia, Cyprus, Czechia, Denmark, Ecuador, Egypt, Estonia, Ethiopia, Finland, France, Gabon, Georgia, Germany, Ghana, Greece, Guinea, Guinea-Bissau, Honduras, Hungary, Iceland, India, Indonesia, Iran Islamic Rep, Ireland, Israel, Italy, Japan, Kazakhstan, Kenya, Korea Rep, Latvia, Luxembourg, Madagascar, Malaysia, Mali, Malta, Mauritius, Mexico, Moldova, Mongolia, Morocco, Nepal, Netherlands, New Zealand, Niger, Nigeria, Norway, Oman, Pakistan, Panama, Paraguay, Peru, Philippines, Poland, Portugal, Romania, Russia, Senegal, Serbia, Seychelles, Slovakia, Slovenia, Somalia, South Africa, Spain, Sudan, Sweden, Switzerland, Tajikistan, Thailand, Tunisia, Türkiye, Uganda, UK, Ukraine, United Arab Emirates, Uruguay, USA, Uzbekistan, Vietnam, Zimbabwe.

Regional organization (1):
European Commission (EC, #06633).

IGO Relations Participating organizations:
- *African Centre of Meteorological Applications for Development (ACMAD, #00242)*;
- *African Regional Centre for Space Science and Technology Education – English (ARCSSTE-E, #00431)*;
- *African Regional Institute for Geospatial Information Science and Technology (AFRIGIST, #00433)*;
- *AGRHYMET Regional Centre (#00565)*;
- *Bioversity International (#03262)*;
- *Caribbean Meteorological Organization (CMO, #03524)*;
- *Commission des forêts d'Afrique centrale (COMIFAC, #04214)*;
- *Central American Integration System (#03671)*;
- *Centre for Environment and Development for the Arab Region and Europe (CEDARE, #03738)*;
- *Commission on the Protection of the Black Sea Against Pollution (Black Sea Commission, #04237)*;
- *Convention on Biological Diversity (Biodiversity convention, 1992)*;
- *Coordination Group for Meteorological Satellites (CGMS, #04827)*;
- *European Centre for Medium-Range Weather Forecasts (ECMWF, #06490)*;
- *European Environment Agency (EEA, #06995)*;
- *European Organisation for the Exploitation of Meteorological Satellites (EUMETSAT, #08096)*;
- *European Space Agency (ESA, #08798)*;
- *European Union Satellite Centre (SatCen, #09015)*;
- *FAO (#09260)*;
- *Global Biodiversity Information Facility (GBIF, #10250)*;
- *Global Climate Observing System (GCOS, #10289)*;
- *Global Ocean Observing System (GOOS, #10511)*;
- *Global Terrestrial Observing System (GTOS, #10626)*;
- *Intergovernmental Oceanographic Commission (IOC, #11496)*;
- *International Centre for Integrated Mountain Development (ICIMOD, #12500)*;
- *International Hydrographic Organization (IHO, #13825)*;
- *Observatoire du Sahara et du Sahel (OSS, #17636)*;
- *Pacific Community (SPC, #17942)*;
- *Regional Centre for Mapping of Resources for Development (RCMRD, #18757)*;
- *Regional Remote Sensing Centre for North African States (#18807)*;
- *UNEP (#20299)*;
- *UNESCO (#20322)*;
- *UNICEF (#20332)*;
- *United Nations Convention to Combat Desertification (UNCCD, 1994)*;
- *United Nations Economic Commission for Africa (ECA, #20554)*;
- *United Nations Economic Commission for Latin America and the Caribbean (ECLAC, #20556)*;
- *United Nations Economic and Social Commission for Asia and the Pacific (ESCAP, #20557)*;
- *United Nations Framework Convention on Climate Change – Secretariat (UNFCCC, #20564)*;
- *United Nations Institute for Training and Research (UNITAR, #20576)*;
- *United Nations Office for Disaster Risk Reduction (UNDRR, #20595)*;
- *United Nations Office for Outer Space Affairs (UNOOSA, #20601)*;
- *Water Center for the Humid Tropics of Latin America and the Caribbean (#20824)*;
- *WHO (#20950)*;
- *The World Bank Group (#21218)*;
- *World Meteorological Organization (WMO, #21649)*.

Partner of: *United Nations Committee of Experts on Global Geospatial Information Management (UN-GGIM, #20540)*.

NGO Relations Participating organizations:
- *African Association of Remote Sensing of the Environment (AARSE, #00216);*
- *African Climate Change Research Centre (ACCREC);*
- *Afriterra Foundation;*
- *Arab States Research and Education Network (ASREN, #01051);*
- *Asian Disaster Preparedness Center (ADPC, #01426);*
- *Belmont Forum (#03197);*
- *Committee on Data for Science and Technology (CODATA, #04247);*
- *Committee on Earth Observation Satellites (CEOS, #04249);*
- *Committee on Space Research (COSPAR, #04287);*
- *Conservation International (CI);*
- *Creative Commons International (CCI);*
- *Earthmind;*
- *EIS-AFRICA (#05402);*
- *EUREC (#05619);*
- *Eurisy (#05625);*
- *EuroGeographics (#05684);*
- *EuroGeoSurveys (#05686);*
- *European Association of Remote Sensing Companies (EARSC, #06190);*
- *European Association of Remote Sensing Laboratories (EARSeL, #06191);*
- *European Plate Observing System (EPOS, #08220);*
- *European Severe Storms Laboratory (ESSL, #08471);*
- *Future Earth (#10048);*
- *Global Earthquake Model Foundation (GEM Foundation, #10327);*
- *Global Flood Partnership (GFP);*
- *Global Open Data for Agriculture and Nutrition (GODAN, #10514);*
- *GÉANT Association (#10086);*
- *IHE Delft Institute for Water Education (#11110);*
- *Institute of Electrical and Electronics Engineers (IEEE, #11259);*
- *Integrated Carbon Observation System (ICOS, #11368);*
- *Interbalkan Environment Center (i-BEC, #11458);*
- *International Association of Geodesy (IAG, #11914);*
- *International Astronautical Federation (IAF, #12286);*
- *International Cartographic Association (ICA, #12446);*
- *International Centre on Research El Niño (CIIFEN);*
- *International Council for Science (ICSU, inactive);*
- *International Council on Systems Engineering (INCOSE, #13083);*
- *International Federation of Digital Seismograph Networks (FDSN, #13407);*
- *International Institute for Applied Systems Analysis (IIASA, #13861);*
- *International Institute of Space Law (IISL, #13926);*
- *International Institute for Sustainable Development (IISD, #13930);*
- *International Long-Term Ecological Research Network (ILTER, #14065);*
- *International Ozone Commission (IO3C, #14495);*
- *International Society for Digital Earth (ISDE, #15061);*
- *International Society for Photogrammetry and Remote Sensing (ISPRS, #15362);*
- *International Union of Geodesy and Geophysics (IUGG, #15776);*
- *International Union of Geological Sciences (IUGS, #15777);*
- *International Water Management Institute (IWMI, #15867);*
- *ISC World Data System (ISC-WDS, #16024);*
- *UN-GGO: Geospatial Societies (UN-GGIM GS, #20324);*
- *Marine Technology Society (MTS);*
- *Mountain Research Initiative (MRI, #16863);*
- *Network of European Meteorological Services (EUMETNET, #17022);*
- *Open Geospatial Consortium (OGC, #17752);*
- *Partnership for Observation of the Global Oceans (POGO, #18239);*
- *Research Data Alliance (RDA, #18853);*
- *Secure World Foundation (SWF);*
- *Sustaining Arctic Observing Networks (SAON, #20071);*
- *United Nations University Institute for Environment and Human Security (UNU-EHS, #20645);*
- *World Climate Research Programme (WCRP, #21279);*
- *World Federation of Public Health Associations (WFPHA, #21476);*
- *World Ocean Council (WOC, #21680);*
- *World Resources Institute (WRI, #21753).*

Participates in: *International Working Group on Satellite-Based Emergency Mapping (IWG-SEM, #15911).* Observers include: *Global Change System for Analysis, Research and Training (START, #10278); Joint IOC/IHO Guiding Committee for the General Bathymetric Chart of the Oceans (GEBCO, #16137).* Member of: *Asia-Pacific Regional Space Agency Forum (APRSAF, #02010); Global Partnership for Sustainable Development Data (Data4SDGS, #10542).* In cooperation with technical committees of: *Comité européen de normalisation (CEN, #04162).* [2018/XM0470/**F***]

- ♦ Group on Earth Observations Biodiversity Observation Network / see GEO Biodiversity Observation Network (#10129)
- ♦ Groupe des associations économiques privées de la CEE axées sur l'Amérique latine (inactive)
- ♦ Groupe d'Australie (#03036)
- ♦ **Groupe BAD** Groupe de la Banque africaine de développement (#00284)
- ♦ Groupe de la Banque africaine de développement (#00284)
- ♦ Groupe de la Banque mondiale / see The World Bank Group (#21218)
- ♦ Groupe Banque mondiale (#21218)
- ♦ Groupe de Bellagio / see International Working Group on Education (#15909)
- ♦ Groupe Bilderberg / see Bilderberg Meetings (#03234)
- ♦ Groupe de Brazzaville – Union africaine et malgache (inactive)
- ♦ Groupe de Carthagène (#03589)
- ♦ Groupe de Casablanca – Etats africains de la Charte de Casablanca (inactive)
- ♦ Groupe des cinq (#10779)
- ♦ Groupe CITCS Afrique – Groupe communication internationale en technologie, cultures et services en Afrique (internationally oriented national body)
- ♦ Groupe Coimbra (#04089)
- ♦ Groupe communication internationale en technologie, cultures et services en Afrique (internationally oriented national body)
- ♦ Groupe des communications des Nations Unies (inactive)
- ♦ Groupe commun nordique pour les problèmes des pépinières forestières (inactive)
- ♦ Groupe consultatif actuariel européen / see Actuarial Association of Europe (#00105)
- ♦ Groupe consultatif sur les affaires économiques et monétaires internationales / see Group of Thirty (#10790)
- ♦ Groupe consultatif d'assistance aux plus pauvres (#04768)
- ♦ Groupe consultatif des associations d'actuaires des pays des Communautés européennes / see Actuarial Association of Europe (#00105)
- ♦ Groupe consultatif européen des consommateurs (#06771)
- ♦ Groupe Consultatif Européen sur l'Information Financière (#07254)
- ♦ Groupe consultatif international pour la paix et le désarmement (inactive)

♦ Groupe consultatif international de recherche sur le colza (GCIRC) . 10736

International Consultative Research Group on Rapeseed

Contact 11 rue de Monceau, CS 60003, 75378 Paris CEDEX 08, France. T. +33142820878.
URL: http://www.gcirc.org/

History 3 Nov 1977, Paris (France). Statutes adopted 4 Jun 1982; modified Mar 2007. Registered in accordance with French law. **Aims** Develop scientific and technical research, studies and experiments concerning improvement of rapeseed and its processed products from *agronomic*, technological and food points of view; ensure close links among researchers on this subject. **Structure** General Assembly (every 2 years); Board of Directors. **Languages** English. **Staff** 0.50 FTE, paid. **Finance** Members' dues. Other sources: income from property; subsidies; sponsorship of Technical Committees. Annual budget: about euro 12,195. **Activities** Research/documentation; events/meetings. **Events** *General Assembly* Berlin (Germany) 2019, *Quadrennial Congress* Berlin (Germany) 2019, *General Assembly* Alnarp (Sweden) 2017, *Technical Meeting* Alnarp (Sweden) 2017, *Quadrennial Congress* Saskatoon, SK (Canada) 2015. **Publications** *Bulletin GCIRC* – online. Congress proceedings.

Members Individuals; Active Members subject to sponsorship of other members and approval of the Board.
Members in 18 countries:
Australia, Belgium, Canada, China, Czechia, Denmark, Finland, France, Germany, India, Iran Islamic Rep, Poland, Slovakia, Spain, Sweden, Switzerland, UK, USA.
Organizations in 5 countries:
Canada, France, Germany, Sweden, UK.
NGO Relations National organizations. [2016.10.25/XD7884/**D**]

- ♦ Groupe consultatif international de la recherche et du sauvetage (#14816)
- ♦ Groupe consultatif mixte des politiques (no recent information)
- ♦ Groupe consultatif pour la recherche agricole internationale / see CGIAR System Organization (#03843)
- ♦ Groupe de coopération en matière de lutte contre l'abus et le trafic illicite des stupéfiants (#04796)
- ♦ Groupe de coopération nordique de recherche forestière (inactive)
- ♦ Groupe de coordination de l'énergie (inactive)

♦ Groupe de coordination pour l'épidémiologie et l'enregistrement du cancer dans les pays de langue latine (GRELL) 10737

Group for Cancer Epidemiology and Registration in Latin Language Countries

Secretariat c/o Registre des cancers du Tarn, BP 37, 81000 Albi, France. T. +33531156503 – +33563475951. E-mail: grell.latine@onco-occitanie.fr.
URL: https://www.grell-network.org/

History 1975. Previously referred to as *Groupe pour l'épidémiologie et l'enregistrement du cancer dans les pays de langue latine (RLL).* Also referred to as *Groupe des registres de langue latine.* **Aims** Promote *epidemiologic* cancer studies, especially those based on cancer registry data. **Structure** Board, comprising President, Secretary and Treasurer. **Languages** French, Italian, Portuguese, Spanish. **Staff** Voluntary. **Finance** No budget. **Activities** Organizes: Annual Scientific Meeting; other meetings; training courses. **Events** *Annual Meeting* Pamplona (Spain) 2020, *Annual Meeting* Lisbon (Portugal) 2019, *Annual Meeting* Trento (Italy) 2018, *Annual Meeting* Brussels (Belgium) 2017, *Annual Meeting* Geneva (Switzerland) 2014.
Members Individuals (20) in 9 countries:
Argentina, Belgium, Cuba, France, Italy, Portugal, Spain, Switzerland, Uruguay. [2020/XF5399/v/**E**]

- ♦ Groupe de coordination européenne des institutions nationales pour la promotion et la protection des droits de l'homme / see European Network of National Human Rights Institutions (#07949)
- ♦ Groupe de coordination inter-maghrébin pour les relations avec la CEE (meeting series)
- ♦ Groupe du démocrates-chrétiens / see Group of the European People's Party – Christian Democrats (#10775)
- ♦ Groupe des démocrates européens (#06744)
- ♦ Groupe développement / see Acting for Life
- ♦ Groupe de développement pour l'Amérique latine de la Communauté atlantique (inactive)
- ♦ Groupe des Dix (inactive)
- ♦ Groupe d'échanges scientifiques et technologiques éducation-environnement (internationally oriented national body)
- ♦ Groupe des éditeurs de livres de la CEE / see Federation of European Publishers (#09536)
- ♦ Groupe ELDR / see Renew Europe (#18840)
- ♦ Groupe pour l'élevage et la conservation de la faune malgache / see Madagascar Fauna and Flora Group (#16540)
- ♦ Groupe d'Endoscopie de Langue Française (internationally oriented national body)
- ♦ Groupe Energies renouvelables / see GERES
- ♦ Groupe énergies renouvelables et environnement / see GERES
- ♦ Groupe énergies renouvelables, environnement and solidarités / see GERES
- ♦ Groupe des entomologistes forestiers francophones (unconfirmed)
- ♦ Groupe pour l'épidémiologie et l'enregistrement du cancer dans les pays de langue latine / see Groupe de coordination pour l'épidémiologie et l'enregistrement du cancer dans les pays de langue latine (#10737)
- ♦ Groupe d'états contre la corruption (#10789)
- ♦ Groupe d'etude de l'infection osseuse articulaire / see European Bone and Joint Infection Society (#06380)
- ♦ Groupe d'étude international de jute (no recent information)
- ♦ Groupe d'étude international du nickel (#14370)
- ♦ Groupe d'étude international du plomb et du zinc (#14012)
- ♦ Groupe d'étude et de recherche sur la démocratie et le développement économique et social en Afrique (#20021)
- ♦ Groupe d'Etude des Rythmes Biologiques / see Société Francophone de Chronobiologie
- ♦ Groupe d'études interdisciplinaires Afrique-Europe (#00172)
- ♦ Groupe d'études interdisciplinaires Afrique-Europe en sciences humaines et sociales / see Africa-Europe Group for Interdisciplinary Studies (#00172)
- ♦ Groupe d'études international pour l'enseignement des mathématiques (inactive)
- ♦ Groupe d'études latino-américaines de l'Institut de sociologie, Bruxelles (internationally oriented national body)
- ♦ Groupe d'études sur la responsabilité chrétienne pour la collaboration européenne (inactive)
- ♦ Groupe d'études pour l'union douanière européenne (inactive)
- ♦ Groupe d'Etude des Systèmes de Conduite de la vigne / see Groupe International d'Experts en Systèmes vitivinicoles pour la CoOpération (#10748)
- ♦ Groupe d'étude des tanneurs et mégissiers de la CEE / see Confédération des associations nationales de tanneurs et mégissiers de la Communauté européenne (#04515)
- ♦ Groupe européen d'administration publique / see European Group for Public Administration (#07430)
- ♦ Groupe européen pour l'administration publique (#07430)
- ♦ Groupe européen pour l'arthroscopie du poignet (#09122)
- ♦ Groupe européen d'athérosclérose / see European Atherosclerosis Society (#06289)
- ♦ Groupe européen pour la certification de l'acier de construction (#07418)
- ♦ Groupe européen des charophytologues (#10772)
- ♦ Groupe européen de chimiothérapie anticancéreuse / see European Organisation for Research and Treatment of Cancer (#08101)
- ♦ Groupe européen de défense du monde animal (inactive)
- ♦ Groupe Européen d'Étude des Métastases Osseuses (internationally oriented national body)
- ♦ Groupe européen de droit international privé (#07429)
- ♦ Groupe européen de droit public (#07431)
- ♦ Groupe européen d'échange d'expériences sur la direction de la recherche textile (unconfirmed)
- ♦ Groupe européen d'échanges et de recherches en éducation sociale (no recent information)
- ♦ Groupe européen d'économistes en matière de risque et d'assurance (#07433)
- ♦ Groupe européen d'électrostimulation (inactive)
- ♦ Groupe européen d'éthique des sciences et des nouvelles technologies (#07420)
- ♦ Groupe européen d'éthique des sciences et des nouvelles technologies auprès de la Commission européenne / see European Group on Ethics in Science and New Technologies (#07420)
- ♦ Groupe européen pour l'étude des lysosomes (#08850)
- ♦ Groupe européen d'étude sur la prolifération cellulaire / see European Cell Proliferation Society (#06459)
- ♦ Groupe européen d'études de l'épiphyse / see European Biological Rhythms Society (#06337)
- ♦ Groupe européen pour les études organisationnelles (#07428)
- ♦ Groupe européen d'études sur la rupture / see European Structural Integrity Society (#08844)

♦ Groupe européen d'expertise en épidémiologie pratique (Epicentre) 10738

European Group of Expertise in Field Epidemiology

Postal Address 8 rue St Sabin, 75011 Paris, France. E-mail: epimail@epicentre.msf.org.
URL: http://www.epicentre.msf.org/

History 1987, Médecins sans frontières, France. Registered in accordance with French law. **Aims** Ascertain the imbalance growing between *care* offered and *health care* needed in *Third World* countries. **Structure** Team of 25 epidemiologists carry out research from offices in Paris (France), Geneva (Switzerland), Brussels (Belgium) and Uganda. **Activities** Creates and puts into place operational research projects and studies for diseases and topics which constitute public health priorities in developing countries, including: malaria; trypanosomiasis; meningitis; infectious tropical diseases; epidemiology of disasters; nutrition; vaccinology; therapeutic tests; investigation cases; epidemiologic monitoring. Conducts surveys, at the request of MSF, WHO and other NGOs, in developing countries, often in emergency situations, covering: evaluation of sanitary priorities in cases of displaced populations; epidemic investigations; putting in place and evaluation of epidemiological surveillance systems; evaluation of health programmes and care. Organizes theoretical and practical training sessions in public health and epidemiology open to health workers and European students of all levels, principally: rapid sanitary evaluation in emergency situations; survey methods in epidemiology; investigation of epidemics; epidemiological surveillance systems; training the trainer. Offers competences at the disposal of requesting organizations through expert ground missions in epidemiology in developing countries; develops software intended for medical and sanitary fields; organizes annual Scientific Day, in conjunction with international congress. **Events** *Annual scientific meeting* Paris (France) 2005. **Publications** Scientific publications covering results of studies. **Information Services** *Epitryps* – trypanosomiasis programme monitoring; *Epiview* – epidemiological surveillance; *FUCHIA* – HIV/AIDS programme monitoring.
Members Individuals in 3 countries:
Belgium, Switzerland, Uganda.
IGO Relations A *WHO (#20950)* Collaborating Centre for Research in Epidemiology and Response to Emerging Diseases since 1996. [2019/XK1844/v/**E**]

♦ Groupe européen des femmes diplômées des universités (#20707)
♦ Groupe Européen Francophone d'Études des Métastases Osseuses / see Groupe Européen d'Étude des Métastases Osseuses
♦ Groupe européen sur les immunodéficiences (#08630)
♦ Groupe européen indépendant de programme (inactive)

♦ Groupe européen de l'industrie papetière pour les affaires sociales (PEGS) 10739

Address not obtained.
History as a club of social experts; not a formal organization, having no statutes and no official task. [2016.01.21/XF2660/t/**F**]

♦ Groupe Européen des Instituts de Navigation (#07424)
♦ Groupe européen des journalistes / see European Federation of Journalists (#07152)
♦ Groupe européen des journaux pour la science et la technologie (inactive)
♦ Groupe européen de nutritionnistes / see Accademia Europea di Scienza della Nutrizione (#00045)

♦ Groupe européen de pastorale ouvrière (GEPO) 10740

European Group for Worker Pastoral – Grupo Europeo de Pastoral Obrera – Europäische Gruppe für Arbeiter Pastoral – Gruppo Europeo di Pastorale del Lavoro – Europese Groep voor Arbeidster Pastoraal

Coordinator Chée de Marche 60 A, 5330 Assesse, Belgium. T. +3283656073.
History Founded Oct 1972, Rome (Italy). Sometimes also referred to as *European Group for Pastoral Work*. **Aims** Reinforce *solidarity*; support participation in the *labour* movement in the fight against exclusion and poverty. **Structure** Executive; Coordination Team. **Languages** English, French, German, Portuguese. **Staff** 5.00 FTE, voluntary. **Finance** Members' dues. Other sources: receives funding from *Development Cooperation with the Third World (EZA Dritte Welt)*; subsidies. **Activities** Events/meetings. **Events** *Conference* Ludwigshafen (Germany) 2015, *Conference* Remich (Luxembourg) 2014, *Changer pour espérer – le sort des migrants et des autres travailleurs* Manchester (UK) 2013, *Conference* Barcelos (Portugal) 2011, *Conference* Mainz (Germany) 2009.
Members Representatives of the worker pastoral of 12 countries:
Belgium, Czechia, France, Germany, Italy, Luxembourg, Malta, Portugal, Romania, Spain, Switzerland, UK.
NGO Relations Member of: *European Centre for Workers' Questions (#06505)*. [2015.06.12/XD3416/**E**]

♦ Groupe européen de politique écologique (inactive)
♦ Groupe européen de psychologie mathématique (#07754)
♦ Groupe européen sur la radiodiffusion télévisuelle numérique / see DVB Project (#05147)

♦ Groupe européen de recherche sur les normativités (GERN) 10741

European Group of Research into Norms – Grupo Europeo de Investigación sobre Normatividades – Europäische Arbeitsgruppe Erforschung Normativer Systeme – Grupo Europeo de Investigação sobre as Normatividades – Gruppo Europeo di Ricerche sulle Normatività – Europese Groep voor de Studie van Normativiteiten

SG Immeuble Edison, 43 boulevard Vauban, 78280 Guyancourt, France. T. +33134521735. Fax +33134521732.
Dir address not obtained. T. +33134521730.
URL: http://www.gern-cnrs.com/
History 1985. **Aims** Bring together scientific centres and researchers from different disciplines (mainly sociology, history, political sciences, criminology) working on norms and *deviance* and *insecurity*. **Structure** Steering Committee. **Languages** English, French. **Staff** 2.00 FTE, paid. **Finance** Financed by CNRS and French Ministry of Justice. Funding from members and individual researchers. **Activities** Events/meetings; training/education. **Events** *Conference on working as a policeman / Colloquium* Caen (France) 2007, *Colloque international sur le crime et l'insécurité* Paris (France) 2005, *Journées d'étude sur les violences en temps de guerre* Brussels (Belgium) 2004, *Colloque sur la crise des normativités* Paris (France) 1993. **Publications** Newsletter; books; reports. **Members** Centres and researchers in the fields of sociology, history, law and political science. Membership countries not specified. [2018.06.19/XE1646/**E**]

♦ Groupe Européen de Recherche sur les Prothèses Appliquées à la Chirurgie Vasculaire (internationally oriented national body)
♦ Groupe européen de recherches sur la fibrose cystique / see European Cystic Fibrosis Society (#06879)
♦ Groupe européen de recherches gazières (#07380)
♦ Groupe européen de recherches sur les hautes pressions (#07486)
♦ Groupe européen pour les recherches psychosomatiques sur le cancer (inactive)
♦ Groupe européen de recherches spatiales (inactive)
♦ Groupe européen de statistiques de l'emballage (inactive)
♦ Groupe européen des systèmes atomiques (#07416)
♦ Groupe européen de travail d'aménagement paysagiste (inactive)
♦ Groupe européen sur le travail à domicile (#07497)
♦ Groupe d'experts intergouvernemental sur l'évolution du climat (#11499)
♦ Groupe d'experts des Nations Unies sur les noms géographiques (#20569)
♦ Groupe d'experts OMM/CESAP des cyclones tropicaux (#20976)
♦ Groupe féminin de liaison (inactive)
♦ **Groupe FIM** Fondation internationale MOKA (#16846)
♦ Groupe francophone de gastroentérologie hépatologie et nutrition pédiatrique / see Groupe francophone d'hépato-gastroentérologie et nutrition pédiatriques (#10742)

♦ Groupe francophone d'hépato-gastroentérologie et nutrition pédiatriques (GFHGNP) 10742

Main Office 330 Av de Grande Bretagne, 70034 Toulouse Cedex 9, France.
URL: http://www.gfhgnp.org/
History 1987. Former names and other names: *Groupe francophone de gastroentérologie hépatologie et nutrition pédiatrique (GFHGNP)* – former (1987). **Aims** Promote research in paediatric gastroenterology. **Structure** Council of 14, including President, 2 Vice-Presidents, Secretary-General and Treasurer. Working Groups. **Languages** French. **Staff** 7.00 FTE, voluntary. **Finance** Members' dues. Sponsoring from industry; grants. **Events** *Congrès* Bordeaux (France) 2022, *Congrès* Carcassonne (France) 2021, *Congrès* Bordeaux (France) 2020, *Congrès* Paris (France) 2019, *Congrès* Dijon (France) 2018.
Members Full in 16 countries:
Algeria, Belgium, Canada, Croatia, France, Gabon, Italy, Lebanon, Luxembourg, Morocco, Romania, Spain, Switzerland, Syrian AR, Tunisia, Vietnam. [2021/XM2022/**D**]

♦ Groupe francophone de réanimation et urgences pédiatriques (internationally oriented national body)

♦ Groupe francophone de Réhabilitation Améliorée après Chirurgie (GRACE) 10743

Address not obtained.
URL: http://www.grace-asso.fr/
History 2014. **Aims** Promote development and dissemination of improved rehabilitation after surgery. **Structure** Board of Directors; Bureau. [2018/XM6682/**F**]

♦ Groupe Francophone de Spectrométrie Mössbauer (GFSM) 10744

Sec Inst de Physique et de Chimie des Matériaux de Strasbourg, 23 rue du Loess, BP 43, 67034 Strasbourg CEDEX 2, France.
Pres Univ cath de Louvain, Inst of Condensed Matter and Nanosciences (IMCN/MOST), Place Louis Pasteur 1, 1348 Louvain-la-Neuve, Belgium.
URL: http://www.gfsm.fr/
History 1979, as 'Groupe Français de spectroscopie Mössbauer'. Current title adopted Dec 2004, when statutes were modified, when French-speaking laboratories were admitted to join. Registered in accordance with French law. **Aims** Promote, study and carry out scientific and cultural projects relating to individuals and research training or research and development using the Mössbauer spectroscopy as a technique of investigation. **Structure** Board. **Languages** French. **Staff** Voluntary. **Finance** Members' dues. **Activities** Events/meetings. Active in: Francophone areas in Europe and the Maghreb region. **Events** *Sondes nucléaires et instrumentation* Jülich (Germany) 2015, *Spectroscopie Mössbauer et énergie* Montpellier (France) 2014, *Nanomatériaux, matériaux pour l'énergie et l'environnement* Nancy (France) 2013, *Réunion* Rouen (France) 2012, *Réunion* Strasbourg (France) 2011. **IGO Relations** *Agence universitaire de La Francophonie (AUF, #00548)*. **NGO Relations** None. [2019/XM4390/**D**]

♦ Groupe FRIEND pour la région Alpes et Méditerrané (see: #13826)
♦ Groupe FRIEND pour la région du Nil (see: #13826)
♦ Groupe pour la gauche unitaire européenne (#10794)
♦ Groupe des huit (#10745)
♦ Groupe hygiène naturelle (inactive)

♦ Group of Eight (G-8) 10745

Groupe des huit

No fixed address address not obtained.
URL: http://www.g8.gc.ca/
History Derives from informal meetings of finance ministers arranged by Valéry Giscard d'Estaing of France and Helmut Schmidt of Germany in the early 1970s. When they became heads of government – respectively President of France and Chancellor of the Federal Republic of Germany – they decided to invite the heads of government of other "most industrialized countries" – Italy, Japan, United Kingdom and USA – to join the meetings, the first such being Nov 1975, Rambouillet (France). Canada was included at meetings from Jun 1976, from which time the Groups was referred to as *Group of Seven (G-7, #10788)*. The President of the then Commission of the European Communities (currently European Commission) was invited as an observer for the first time in 1978. Russia was included from 1997, since when the Group met under current title – or *Group of 8 – Groupe des 8* – when dealing with non-financial matters. Russia became full member during the Summit meeting in 2002. When finance ministers of Canada, Italy and Russia are not present, the Group is referred to as *Group of Five (G-5, #10779)*. Meetings together with the Netherlands, Belgium, Sweden and Switzerland comprise *Group of Ten (G-10, inactive)*. A wider and more representative *Group of Twenty-Two (G-22, inactive)* has been proposed by the USA and some other members.
The titles are not official, simply an informal description, originally for occasional meetings of ministers of finance of the most industrialized countries as described above and subsequently also of the summits of the heads of state and government of these countries. The latter meetings were also referred to as: *Seven-Power Summit – Sommet des sept*; *Summit of the Seven Most Industrialized Countries – Sommet des sept pays les plus industrialisés*. Summits including Russia are also referred to as: *Summit of the Most Industrialized Countries – Sommet des pays les plus industrialisés*; *Summit of the Eight Most Industrialized Countries – Sommet des huit pays les plus industrialisés*; *The Eight – Les huit*. Sometimes formal economic preparations for the summit are made at ministerial sessions of *OECD (#17693)*.
The *Plaza Agreement*, 22 Sep 1985, covers plans to achieve more balanced growth and bring exchange rates into line with underlying fundamentals. The *Louvre Accord*, Feb 1987, covers maintenance of currency stability.
Aims Exchange information and options and establish a rapport with each other; set the international agenda for the year ahead; focus *economic policy* and force decisions. As indicated in the Plaza Agreement: while recognizing progress in promoting convergence of favourable economic performance among participating countries, seek to achieve increased and more balanced growth and bring key *exchange rates* more into line with underlying fundamentals. As indicated in the Louvre Accord: coordinate activities of finance ministers so that *currency stability* may be maintained. **Events** *G-7 Annual Summit Meeting* Schloss Elmau (Germany) 2022, *G-7 Annual Summit Meeting* Cornwall (UK) 2021, *G-7 Annual Summit Meeting* Maryland (USA) 2020, *G-7 Annual Summit Meeting* Biarritz (France) 2019, *G-7 Annual Summit Meeting* La Malbaie, QC (Canada) 2018.
Members The 8 most industrialized countries:
Canada, France, Germany, Italy, Japan, Russia, UK, USA.
Observer:
European Commission (EC, #06633).
IGO Relations Supports (1): *Global Fund to Fight AIDS, Tuberculosis and Malaria (Global Fund, #10383)*. Instrumental in setting up (13): *Africa Partnership Forum (APF, #00510)*; *Assistance for Economic Restructuring in the Countries of Central and Eastern Europe (no recent information)*; *Financial Action Task Force (FATF, #09765)*; *Financial Stability Board (FSB, #09770)*; *G7 Support Implementation Group (G7 SIG, no recent information)*; *Global Information Network for Small and Medium Enterprises (no recent information)*; *Group of Twenty Four (G-24, no recent information)*; *Group of Twenty (G20, #10793)*; *Infrastructure Consortium for Africa (ICA, #11206)*; *International Advanced Robotics Programme (IARP, #11589)*; *International Commission on Missing Persons (ICMP, #12706)*; *International Partnership for Energy Efficiency Cooperation (IPEEC, #14520)*; *Versailles Project on Advanced Materials and Standards (VAMAS, #20757)*. **NGO Relations** Works with: *G8 Information Centre*. [2009/XF2036/**F***]

♦ Groupe Initiatives (internationally oriented national body)
♦ Groupe de l'instructeur du monde / see World Teacher Trust (#21848)

♦ Groupe interacadémique pour le développement (GID) 10746

Gen Sec 23 quai de Conti, 75006 Paris, France. E-mail: contact@g-i-d.org.
Pres address not obtained.
URL: http://www.g-i-d.org/
History 2007. Set up by 11 academic institutions in Africa and southern Europe. **Aims** Promote joint *European* and *African development*. **Structure** *Euro-Mediterranean Academic Network (EMAN, #05716)*; *GID-ESAN – Euro-Sub-Saharan Area*. **Activities** Research/documentation; training/education; knowledge management/ information dissemination. **Publications** *GID Letter*.
Members Academies in 5 countries:
Egypt, France, Italy, Morocco, Senegal.
IGO Relations *The Mediterranean Science Commission (CIESM, #16674)*. [2022/XM6703/**F**]

♦ Groupe Interafricain d'Etudes, de Recherches et d'Application sur la Fertilité (GIERAF) 10747

Admin Secretariat address not obtained. T. +23733428144 – +23777708374. E-mail: gieraf2011@live.fr.
URL: http://www.gieraf.org/

History Registered in accordance with the laws of Togo. **Structure** General Assembly; Executive Board; Board of Directors. **Events** *Congress* Brazzaville (Congo Brazzaville) 2015, *Congress* Dakar (Senegal) 2013, *Congress* Cotonou (Benin) 2011, *Congress* Douala (Cameroon) 2010, *Congress* Lomé (Togo) 2009.
Members Full in 9 countries:
Benin, Burkina Faso, Cameroon, Congo Brazzaville, Côte d'Ivoire, Madagascar, Mali, Senegal, Togo. [2015/XJ9282/**D**]

- ♦ Groupe intercontinental des grands magasins (#11461)
- ♦ Groupe Intergouvernemental d'Action contre le Blanchiment d'Argent en Afrique de l'Ouest (#11471)
- ♦ Groupe Intergouvernemental sur les Agrumes (#11487)
- ♦ Groupe intergouvernemental sur la banane et les fruits tropicaux (#11486)
- ♦ Groupe intergouvernemental sur les céréales (#11488)
- ♦ Groupe intergouvernemental COI chargé d'étudier les efflorescences algales nuisibles (#16002)
- ♦ Groupe intergouvernemental COI-FAO chargé d'étudier les efflorescences algales nuisibles / see IOC Intergovernmental Panel on Harmful Blooms (#16002)
- ♦ Sous-Groupe intergouvernemental sur des cuirs et peaux (#11502)
- ♦ Groupe intergouvernemental d'experts des normes internationales de comptabilité et de publication (#11503)
- ♦ Groupe intergouvernemental sur les fibres dures (#11489)
- ♦ Groupe intergouvernemental sur les graines oléagineuses et les matières grasses (#11492)
- ♦ Groupe intergouvernemental sur le jute, le kenaf et les fibres apparentees (#11490)
- ♦ Groupe intergouvernemental sur le riz (#11493)
- ♦ Groupe intergouvernemental sur le thé (#11494)
- ♦ Groupe intergouvernemental sur la viande et les produits laitiers (#11491)
- ♦ Groupe intergouvernemental des vingt-quatre pour les questions monétaires internationales (#11495)
- ♦ Groupe international de coopération et de recherche en documentation: planification territoriale – habitat – information (inactive)
- ♦ Groupe international d'étude des approches des disques intervertébraux / see International Group for Study of Intervertebral Spine Approaches (#13757)
- ♦ Groupe international d'étude des approches intervertébrales du rachis (#13757)
- ♦ Groupe international d'étude de la circulation cérébrale (inactive)
- ♦ Groupe international d'étude du dépistage et de la prévention du cancer (inactive)
- ♦ Groupe international d'étude du diabète de l'enfant et de l'adolescent / see International Society for Pediatric and Adolescent Diabetes (#15344)
- ♦ Groupe international d'étude des hormones stéroïdes (no recent information)
- ♦ Groupe international d'étude sur la laine (inactive)
- ♦ Groupe international d'études du caoutchouc (#14772)

♦ Groupe International d'Experts en Systèmes vitivinicoles pour la CoOpération (GiESCO) 10748

Group of international Experts of vitivinicultural Systems for CoOperation
Registered Office Montpellier SupAgro, 2 place Viala, 34060 Montpellier, France. E-mail: giesco_pav@yahoo.fr.
URL: http://www.giesco.org/

History Nov 1979, as *Groupe d'Etude des Systèmes de Conduite de la vigne (GESCO)*, a French organization. Became European, 1989. Turned international 1999. Current statutes adopted 17 Mar 2014. Registered in accordance with French law. **Aims** Promote science and technology linked to viticulture; communicate about new models of sustainable viticulture including meta-ethics; stimulate international cooperation on viticulture and links with oenology and socio-economy. **Structure** General Assembly; Board of Directors. **Languages** English, French. Also local languages at meetings. **Staff** 4.00 FTE, paid. **Finance** Members' dues. **Activities** Events/meetings. **Publications** Proceedings. **Members** Individuals (about 400) in about 40 countries. Membership countries not specified. **IGO Relations** *International Organisation of Vine and Wine (OIV, #14435).* [2017.12.11/XJ8988/**D**]

♦ Groupe International Francophone pour la Formation aux Classifications du Handicap (GIFFOCH) 10749

Main Office c/o IFPEK, Pôle Formation Continue – Conseil/Expertise, 12 rue Jean-Louis Bertrand, 35000 Rennes, France. T. +33299590182.
URL: http://giffoch.org/

History 6 Feb 2004. Also referred to as *Réseau francophone de formation et de recherche sur la classification internationale du fonctionnement, du handicap et de la santé (CIF).*
Members in 4 countries:
Belgium, Canada, France, Switzerland. [2019.07.29/XM2308/**F**]

♦ Groupe international des importateurs de gaz naturel liquefié (GIIGNL) 10750

International Group of Liquefied Natural Gas Importers
Gen Delegate 8 rue de l'Hôtel de Ville, 92200 Neuilly-sur-Seine, France. T. +33156655160. E-mail: central-office@giignl.org.
URL: http://www.giignl.org/

History 1971, Paris (France). **Aims** Promote development of activities related to liquefied natural gas (LNG), such as purchasing, importing, processing, transportation, handling, regasification and various uses; provide an overview of the state-of-the art technology in the LNG industry and its general economic state; enhance facility operations; diversify contractual techniques; develop positions to be taken in international agencies. **Structure** General Assembly (annual). **Languages** English, French, Japanese. **Staff** 3.50 FTE, paid. **Events** *General Assembly* Neuilly-sur-Seine (France) 2021, *General Assembly* Neuilly-sur-Seine (France) 2020, *General Assembly* Singapore (Singapore) 2019, *General Assembly* Fukuoka (Japan) 2018, *General Assembly* Brussels (Belgium) 2017. **Publications** *LNG Custody Transfer Handbook* (2nd ed 2001) – 3rd ed 2010. *The LNG Industry in 2012* – online.
Members in 21 countries and territories:
Argentina, Austria, Belgium, Canada, Chile, China, France, Germany, Greece, India, Italy, Japan, Korea Rep, Netherlands, Norway, Portugal, Spain, Taiwan, Türkiye, UK, USA. [2018/XD2689/**D**]

- ♦ Groupe international 'Laïcat et communauté chrétienne' (inactive)
- ♦ Groupe international de planification stratégique en microgravité (#14157)
- ♦ Groupe international de recherche sur l'enseignement de la physique (#14731)

♦ Groupe International de Recherche sur l'Infinitésimal (GIRI) 10751

International Research Group on Very Low Dose and High Dilution Effects
Sec Oxford Homeopathy, 30 Rosamund Road, Wolvercote, Oxford, OX2 8NU, UK. E-mail: info@oxford-homeopathy.org.uk.
Pres address not obtained.
URL: http://giri-society.org/

History Founded 1986, Monaco. **Aims** Encourage scientific work on low dose and high dilution effects including *homeopathy*. **Structure** General Assembly (annual). Board of 15 members. Executive Committee, comprising President, 2 Vice-Presidents, Secretary, Treasurer and Editor. Scientific Committee of 3. **Languages** English. **Staff** 14.00 FTE, paid. **Finance** Sources: members' dues; sponsorship. **Events** *Meeting* London (UK) 2019, *Symposium* Verona (Italy) 2015, *Meeting / Symposium* Russia 2014, *Symposium* Germany 2013, *Symposium* Switzerland 2013. **Publications** *International Journal of High Dilution Research.*
Members Individuals in 24 countries:
Argentina, Australia, Austria, Belgium, Brazil, Canada, Costa Rica, Côte d'Ivoire, France, Germany, Greece, India, Israel, Italy, Mexico, Monaco, Netherlands, Poland, Portugal, Romania, Russia, Switzerland, UK, USA. [2019/XJ1267/v/**C**]

- ♦ Groupe international de recherche sur la préservation du bois / see International Research Group on Wood Protection (#14733)
- ♦ Groupe international de recherche sur la protection du bois (#14733)
- ♦ Groupe international de recherche sur les protéines carcinoembryoniques / see International Society for Oncology and BioMarkers (#15323)
- ♦ Groupe international de recherche scientifique en stomatologie / see International Group for Scientific Research on Stomato-Odontology (#13755)
- ♦ Groupe international de recherches sur les ordures ménagères (inactive)
- ♦ Groupe international du rêve-éveillé de Desoille / see Groupe international du rêve-éveillé en psychanalyse (#10752)
- ♦ Groupe international du rêve-éveillé dirigé de Desoille / see Groupe international du rêve-éveillé en psychanalyse (#10752)

♦ Groupe international du rêve-éveillé en psychanalyse (GIREP) 10752

Main Office 80 rue de Vaugirard, 75006 Paris, France.
URL: http://www.girep.com/

History 1968, as *Groupe international du rêve-éveillé dirigé de Desoille (GIREDD)*, following 1960 creation of the 'Groupe de recherche sur le rêve-éveillé dirigé' within *Société de recherches psychothérapiques de langue française (no recent information).* 1982, name changed to *Groupe international du rêve-éveillé de Desoille (GIRED).* Present name adopted by General Assembly, 5 Apr 1987, Paris (France). Registered in accordance with French law. **Aims** Continue the research in *psychotherapy* of Robert *Desoille*; establish a means of expressing the *unconscious* in an analytical perspective. **Structure** General Assembly (every year). Administrative Council, consisting of 12 to 15 members. Bureau, composed of President, Vice President, Secretary General, Assistant Secretary General and Treasurer. **Activities** Training of practitioners. Meetings, seminars, symposia. **Events** *Colloquium* Paris (France) 1986, *International conference on psychotherapeutic studies* Paris (France) 1986. **Publications** *Etudes psychothérapiques* (4 a year).
Members Individuals Full (mainly) French nationals; other nationals (not more than 25% of all full members); Associate; Honorary. Affiliated Groups. Members in 9 countries:
Argentina, Belgium, Brazil, France, Germany, Italy, Switzerland, Uruguay, USA.
Affiliated groups in 3 countries:
Argentina, Brazil, Italy. [2015/XE3942/**E**]

- ♦ Groupe international de travail sur l'éducation (#15909)
- ♦ Groupe international de travail pour les équipements de sport et de loisirs / see Internationale Vereinigung Sport- und Freizeiteinrichtungen (#13319)
- ♦ Groupe juridique international des droits de l'homme / see Global Rights
- ♦ Group of Eleven / see Cartagena Group (#03589)

♦ Group of Eleven (G11) 10753

Address not obtained.

History *Lower-Middle Income Countries Initiative* conceived, Aug 2005, New York NY (USA). G11 officially launched at 1st Summit, Sep 2006, New York NY. **Aims** Prepare common platforms for soliciting additional support through increased aid and investment, facilitated trade and debt relief. **Structure** Meeting of Heads of State. **Events** *Meeting* Jordan 2009, *Meeting* Jordan 2007.
Members Governments (11):
Croatia, Ecuador, El Salvador, Georgia, Honduras, Indonesia, Jordan, Morocco, Pakistan, Paraguay, Sri Lanka. [2010/XJ1238/**F***]

- ♦ Groupe de liaison des entreprises européennes de spiritueux (#08817)
- ♦ Groupe de liaison des historiens auprès la Communauté européenne / see European Union Liaison Committee of Historians (#09000)
- ♦ Groupe de liaison des historiens auprès de l'Union européenne / see European Union Liaison Committee of Historians (#09000)
- ♦ Groupe de liaison international sur le tabac et la santé (internationally oriented national body)
- ♦ Groupe de liaison des professeurs d'histoire contemporaine auprès de la Commission des Communautés européennes (#09000)
- ♦ Groupe libéral, démocrate et réformateur / see Alliance of Liberals and Democrats for Europe (#00702)

♦ Groupement des allergologistes et immunologistes de langues latines (GAILL) 10754

Latin Languages Speaking Allergists and Immunologists
SG c/o CAIC, Rua Sampaio e Pina 16-4, 1070-249 Lisbon, Portugal. T. +351213874201.
Pres address not obtained.

History 21 Jul 1971, Paris (France). **Aims** Bring together scientists, professionals, practitioners, researchers, involved in immunology and allergy; collect, analyse, appreciate and promote methods, techniques, concepts, discoveries, and generally speaking any information relevant to allergy and immunology, including influences, connections and correlations on diseases, physiology and social medicine. **Languages** English, French, German, Italian, Portuguese, Spanish. **Staff** 2.00 FTE, voluntary. **Finance** Sources: contributions; grants; members' dues. Annual budget: 70,000 EUR. **Activities** Representation at the main international congresses. Post-graduate seminars in allergology and clinical immunology (annual). **Events** *Annual Meeting* Sintra (Portugal) 2014, *Annual Meeting* Sintra (Portugal) 2013, *Annual meeting* Como (Italy) 2011, *Annual meeting* Sintra (Portugal) 2010, *Annual Meeting* Lugano (Switzerland) 2009. **Publications** *Allergie et immunologie*; *European Annals of Allergology and Clinical Immunology.*
Members Founding; Active; Honorary. Individuals in 58 countries and territories:
Albania, Algeria, Argentina, Australia, Austria, Belgium, Benin, Bolivia, Brazil, Cameroon, Canada, Chile, Colombia, Côte d'Ivoire, Cuba, Czechia, Denmark, Ecuador, Egypt, Finland, France, Gabon, Germany, Greece, Guatemala, Hong Kong, Hungary, Israel, Italy, Laos, Luxembourg, Madagascar, Mauritius, Mexico, Mozambique, New Zealand, Peru, Philippines, Poland, Portugal, Romania, Saudi Arabia, Senegal, Serbia, Seychelles, South Africa, Spain, Switzerland, Thailand, Togo, Tunisia, Türkiye, UK, Uruguay, USA, Vanuatu, Venezuela, Vietnam. [2014/XD4696/v/**C**]

♦ Groupement AMPERE 10755

Gen Sec ETH Zürich – Lab Phys Chem, Vladimir-Prelog-Weg 2, 8093 Zurich ZH, Switzerland. T. +41446324259. Fax +41446331448. E-mail: contact@ampere-society.org.
URL: http://www.ampere-society.org/

History 1951, France. Former names and other names: *Atomes et Molécules Par Études Radio-Électriques* – full title. Registration: Swiss Civil Code, Start date: 1956, Switzerland. **Aims** Contribute to the progress of Radio Spectroscopy, Magnetic Resonance and Related Phenomena; maintain and expand services for the whole community engaged in Magnetic Resonance and Related Phenomena in Europe and worldwide; accommodate new developments in new areas which are progressively opened by the scientific evolution. **Activities** Events/meetings; training/education. **Events** *International Conference on Nuclear Hyperpolarization (HYP21)* Lyon (France) 2021, *International Conference on Nuclear Hyperpolarization (HYP20)* Lyon (France) 2020, *International Conference on Nuclear Hyperpolarization (HYP18)* Southampton (UK) 2018, *Annual European Magnetic Resonance Conference* Hersonissos (Greece) 2013, *Congress* Dublin (Ireland) 2012. **Publications** *AMPERE Bulletin.* [2022.02.09/XM2146/**F**]

♦ Groupement des anthropologistes de langue française (GALF) 10756

Group of French-Speaking Anthropologists
Pres VUB, Fac WE – Unit DBIO, Bureau 7F416, Pleinlaan 2, 1050 Brussels, Belgium. T. +3226293408. Fax +3226293407.

History 1972, as *Association anthropologique internationale de langue française*; present title adopted 1981, following re-constitution 19 Jun 1980, Paris (France). Previously also referred to as *Association des anthropologistes de langue française.* **Aims** Promote physical anthropology in French-speaking countries; facilitate exchanges between French-speaking anthropologists. **Structure** Group meets at least every 2 years; members elect Committee comprising President, 2 Vice-Presidents (one acting as Treasurer) Secretary. Acts as a club of professionals united by their language. **Languages** French. **Staff** None. **Finance** None. **Events** *Colloque* Bordeaux (France) 2022, *Colloque* Toulouse (France) 2016, *Colloque* Marseille (France) 2013, *Colloquium* Dakar (Senegal) 2011, *Colloquium* Bordeaux (France) 2009. **Publications** Colloquium papers.
Members Individuals in 14 countries:
Belgium, Canada, Czechia, France, Israel, Italy, Madagascar, Monaco, Morocco, Portugal, Romania, Spain, Switzerland, USA.
NGO Relations A number of national and the following international bodies: *International Association of Human Biologists (IAHB, #11945).* [2013/XD6037/v/**D**]

♦ **Groupement des associations dentaires francophones (GADEF) . . . 10757**
Contact 54 rue Ampère, 75017 Paris, France. T. +33156792065. Fax +33156792021. E-mail: gadef@gadef.fr.
History Founded Jun 1971. Registered in accordance with French law. **Aims** Contribute to progress in the science of dentistry and to worldwide promotion of the dental profession; defend the use of the French language and encourage its development for improved mutual international professional understanding; participate in safeguarding and improving public health. **Structure** General Assembly (annual); Administrative Council (meets annually); Bureau. **Languages** French. **Staff** 1.00 FTE, voluntary. **Finance** Members' dues. Subventions. **Activities** Training/education; events/meetings. **Events** *Triennial scientific and cultural days* Lomé (Togo) 2006, *Triennial scientific and cultural days* Cotonou (Benin) 2004, *Triennial scientific and cultural days* Yaoundé (Cameroon) 2002, *Triennial scientific and cultural days* Bamako (Mali) 1998, *Triennial scientific and cultural days* Sofia (Bulgaria) 1995.
Members Full dental associations and secretariats (30) in 29 countries and territories:
Andorra, Belgium, Benin, Bulgaria, Burkina Faso, Cameroon, Canada, Congo Brazzaville, Congo DR, Côte d'Ivoire, Djibouti, France, Gabon, Guinea, Haiti, Israel, Luxembourg, Madagascar, Mali, Mauritania, Mauritius, Morocco, Niger, Romania, Rwanda, Senegal, Switzerland, Togo, Tunisia.
NGO Relations Member of: *Association francophone d'amitié et de liaison (AFAL, #02605)*; *FDI – World Dental Federation (#09281)*. [2020/XD4513/**F**]

- ♦ Groupement des associations des maïsiers des pays de la CEE / see Euromaisiers (#05709)
- ♦ Groupement des associations meunières des pays de la UE / see European Flour Millers' Association (#07272)
- ♦ Groupement des banques coopératives de la CE / see European Association of Co-operative Banks (#05990)
- ♦ Groupement des caisses d'épargne de la Communauté économique européenne / see European Savings and Retail Banking Group (#08426)
- ♦ Groupement cinématographique international de conciliation (inactive)
- ♦ Groupement des coopératives d'épargne et de crédit de la CEE / see European Association of Co-operative Banks (#05990)
- ♦ Groupement pour les droits des minorités (#16820)
- ♦ Groupement d'éditeurs des Caraïbes (#03546)
- ♦ Groupement des éducateurs retraités sans frontières / see Groupement des retraités éducateurs sans frontières
- ♦ Groupement pour l'étude des lymphatiques / see European Society of Lymphology (#08643)
- ♦ Groupement d'études et de recherches sur la méditerranée (internationally oriented national body)
- ♦ Groupement d'études et de recherches – Notre Europe / see Institut Jacques Delors
- ♦ Groupement Européen des Ardennes et de l'Eifel (#07414)
- ♦ Groupement européen des artistes des Ardennes et de l'Eifel (#07415)
- ♦ Groupement européen des associations des maisons de réforme (no recent information)
- ♦ Groupement européen pour l'assurance des architectes (no recent information)
- ♦ Groupement européen des banques coopératives (#05990)
- ♦ Groupement européen des caisses d'épargne / see European Savings and Retail Banking Group (#08426)
- ♦ Groupement européen des caisses d'épargne et banques de détail (#08426)
- ♦ Groupement européen de coopération sidérurgique (no recent information)
- ♦ Groupement européen de coordination des industries textiles diverses (inactive)
- ♦ Groupement européen des écoles de cinéma et de télévision (see: #11771)
- ♦ Groupement européen pour l'emploi des personnes avec handicap mental (no recent information)
- ♦ Groupement européen des entreprises de distribution intégrée (inactive)
- ♦ Groupement européen d'étude et de recherche pour la formation des enseignants chrétiens / see Groupement Européen pour la Recherche et la Formation des Enseignants Chrétiens, Croyants et de toutes Convictions (#10759)
- ♦ Groupement européen de fabricants d'appareils d'éclairement zénithal et exutoires de fumées (#07434)
- ♦ Groupement européen des fabricants de celluloses (inactive)
- ♦ Groupement européen des fédérations et syndicats nationaux d'installateurs frigoristes dans tous les systèmes et applications (#00601)
- ♦ Groupement européen des importateurs et distributeurs des vins et spiritueux (#07235)
- ♦ Groupement Européen de l'Industrie de la Régénération / see GEIR (#10088)
- ♦ Groupement européen de l'industrie de la régénération des huiles usagées / see GEIR (#10088)
- ♦ Groupement européen d'intérêt économique (#06960)
- ♦ Groupement européen de lymphologie / see European Society of Lymphology (#08643)
- ♦ Groupement européen des médecins en pratique libre (#05154)
- ♦ Groupement Européen pour la mise en oeuvre des Programmes de COoperation Transfrontalière, Transnationale, Interrégionale et d'autres Programmes Européens (internationally oriented national body)
- ♦ Groupement européen du mobilier métallique (no recent information)
- ♦ Groupement européen des plastiques renforcés – Matériaux Composites / see European Composites Industry Association (#06692)

♦ **Groupement européen des producteurs de champignons (GEPC) . . 10758**
European Mushroom Growers' Group
Gen Sec 44 rue d'Alésia, 75014 Paris, France. T. +33153914444. Fax +33143209487. E-mail: contact@anicc.com.
URL: http://www.infochampi.eu/
History Created 1980, initially as an unofficial group. EU Transparency Register: 901422415532-12. **Aims** Defend the interests of the European fresh and processed cultivated mushroom sector. **Structure** General Meeting.
Members Delegations in 10 countries:
Belgium, Denmark, France, Germany, Hungary, Ireland, Italy, Netherlands, Poland, Spain.
NGO Relations *COPA – european farmers (COPA, #04829)*; *General Confederation of Agricultural Cooperatives in the European Union (#10107)*. [2017/XM6907/**D**]

- ♦ Groupement européen des producteurs de verre plat / see Glass for Europe (#10157)
- ♦ Groupement européen des produits oléochimiques et associés (#08081)
- ♦ Groupement européen de la publicité télévisée / see egta – association of television and radio sales houses (#05397)

♦ **Groupement Européen pour la Recherche et la Formation des Enseignants Chrétiens, Croyants et de toutes Convictions (GERFEC) 10759**
European Group for Research and Training of Teachers Holding Christian and Other Beliefs and Convictions
Pres 16 cour de Bretagne, 67100 Strasbourg, France. T. +33388140884. E-mail: rmgerfec@orange.fr.
URL: http://www.gerfec.eu/
History 1979. Previously referred to as *Groupement européen de recherches en formation pour l'enseignement catholique* and subsequently *European Research and Study Group for the Training of Christian Educators – Groupement européen d'étude et de recherche pour la formation des enseignants chrétiens*. **Aims** Encourage intercultural openness in Europe through the means of education. **Structure** Council representing 14 countries. **Consultative Status** Consultative status granted from: *Council of Europe (CE, #04881)* (Participatory Status). **NGO Relations** Instrumental in setting up *European Association of Research and Educational Exchanges (no recent information)*. [2016/XG4296/**D**]

- ♦ Groupement européen de recherche scientifique en stomato-odontologie / see International Group for Scientific Research on Stomato-Odontology (#13755)
- ♦ Groupement européen de recherches en formation pour l'enseignement catholique / see Groupement Européen pour la Recherche et la Formation des Enseignants Chrétiens, Croyants et de toutes Convictions (#10759)
- ♦ Groupement européen des retraités des caisses d'épargne, banques et institutions similaires / see Group of European Retired Staff and Pensioners from Savings Banks, Banks and Related Institutions (#10777)
- ♦ Groupement européen des retraités et des pensionnés des caisses d'epargne, banques et institutions similaires (#10777)
- ♦ Groupement Européen des Sociétés d'Auteurs et Compositeurs (#07422)
- ♦ Groupement pour les facilités de circulation internationale du personnel des chemins de fer (#02465)
- ♦ Groupement des fédérations des scieries européennes / see European Organization of the Sawmill Industry (#08114)
- ♦ Groupement francophone d'histoire de l'ophtalmologie / see Société francophone d'histoire de l'ophtalmologie
- ♦ Groupement des importateurs des vins et spiritueux de la CEE / see European Federation of Wine and Spirit Importers and Distributors (#07235)
- ♦ Groupement industriel européen d'études spatiales / see Association of European Space Industry (#02544)

♦ **Groupement des industries européennes du tabac (GITES) 10760**
Grouping of European Tobacco Industries
Pres Rue de Hollerich 31, PO Box 2202, L-1022 Luxembourg, Luxembourg. T. +3524939391. Fax +352493939409.
History 1990, when became registered in accordance with French law. Currently registered in accordance with Luxembourg law. EU Transparency Register: 16135192686-50. **Aims** Contribute to an efficient functioning of the European Union by paying particular attention to establishing trading conditions based on clear and fair rules and to working towards the interests of small and medium-sized firms active in tobacco industries; elaborate and diffuse common positions for its members concerning community politics regarding finished products of tobacco, primary tobacco products and other primary products for the manufacture of finished products of tobacco, as well as any other subject on which the tobacco industry legitimately could give an opinion. **Languages** English, French, German. **Finance** Members' dues.
Members Full in 4 countries:
France, Greece, Luxembourg, Spain. [2016.06.20/XD7294/t/**D**]

- ♦ Groupement de l'institution prévention de la sécurité sociale pour l'Europe / see EUROGIP
- ♦ Groupement d'intérêt scientifique 'Economie mondiale, Tiers-monde, Développement / see Groupement d'intérêt scientifique pour l'étude de la mondialisation et du développement
- ♦ Groupement d'intérêt scientifique pour l'étude de la mondialisation et du développement (internationally oriented national body)
- ♦ Groupement d'intérêt scientifique Études asiatiques (internationally oriented national body)
- ♦ Groupement international des artistes interprètes ou exécutants (inactive)
- ♦ Groupement international d'associations de langue et de culture françaises / see Union culturelle et technique de langue française (#20374)
- ♦ Groupement international des associations nationales de fabricants de pesticides / see CropLife International (#04966)
- ♦ Groupement international des associations nationales de fabricants de produits agrochimiques / see CropLife International (#04966)
- ♦ Groupement international des comités de l'étiquetage pour l'entretien des textiles / see Groupement International de l'Etiquetage pour l'Entretien des Textiles (#10761)
- ♦ Groupement international pour la coordination de la psychiatrie et des méthodes psychologiques (inactive)
- ♦ Groupement international d'éditeurs scientifiques, techniques et médicaux / see International Association of Scientific, Technical and Medical Publishers (#12154)

♦ **Groupement International de l'Etiquetage pour l'Entretien des Textiles (GINETEX) 10761**
International Association for Textile Care Labelling – Internationale Vereinigung für die Pflegekennzeichnung von Textilien
Dir-Gen 37 rue de Neuilly, 92110 Clichy, France. T. +33147563171. E-mail: ginetex@ginetex.net.
URL: http://www.ginetex.net/
History 4 Feb 1956, Paris (France). Former names and other names: *International Group of National Textile Care Labelling Committees* – former; *Groupement international des comités de l'étiquetage pour l'entretien des textiles* – former; *International Symposium for Textile Care Labelling* – former; *Symposium international pour l'étiquetage d'entretien des textiles* – former; *Internationalen Symposiums für Textilpflegekennzeichnung* – former; *International Group for Textile Care Labelling* – former. **Aims** Establish a correct International Care Labelling System by means of symbols registered as trademarks; assist consumers of textile products by promoting use of these symbols for labelling textiles according to the care they should be given in laundering, bleaching, ironing, tumble drying and dry-cleaning. **Structure** General Assembly; Governing Body; Technical Committee; Legal Committee; Liaison Committee. **Languages** English, French. **Staff** 6.00 FTE, paid. **Finance** Sources: members' dues. **Activities** Awareness raising; standards/guidelines. Eco-caring;sustainability.
Members National care labelling organizations, autonomous with respect to their members, in 23 countries:
Austria, Belgium, Brazil, Czechia, Denmark, Finland, France, Germany, Greece, Italy, Japan, Lithuania, Netherlands, Norway, Portugal, Slovakia, Slovenia, Spain, Sweden, Switzerland, Tunisia, Türkiye, UK.
IGO Relations Trademarks registered with: *World Intellectual Property Organization (WIPO, #21593)*. **NGO Relations** Agreement with: *Comité européen de normalisation (CEN, #04162)*. In liaison with technical committees of: *International Organization for Standardization (ISO, #14473)*. Cooperates with: *EURATEX – The European Apparel and Textile Confederation (EURATEX, #05616)*; *International Apparel Federation (IAF, #11659)*; *International Committee of Textile Care (#12809)*. [2020.08.26/XD2091/**F**]

- ♦ Groupement international d'étude pour l'exploitation des voitures-lits en Europe (inactive)
- ♦ Groupement international d'études sur les examens systématiques en médecine préventive et en médecine (inactive)
- ♦ Groupement international des fabricants de papiers peints / see IGI – The Global Wallcoverings Association (#11107)
- ♦ Groupement international des fabricants de revêtements muraux / see IGI – The Global Wallcoverings Association (#11107)
- ♦ Groupement international des fédérations cynologiques / see Union canine internationale (#20370)
- ♦ Groupement international de l'industrie pharmaceutique des pays de la CEE (inactive)
- ♦ Groupement international pour la recherche scientifique en stomatologie et odontologie (#13755)
- ♦ Groupement international de recherches sur l'emboutissage (#13143)

♦ **Groupement International de la Répartition Pharmaceutique (GIRP) 10762**
European Healthcare Distribution Association
Secretariat Rue de la Loi 26, 10th Floor, Box 14, 1040 Brussels, Belgium. T. +3227779977. Fax +3227703601. E-mail: girp@girp.eu.
URL: http://girp.eu/
History 4 Apr 1960. Statutes adopted 7 Jun 1998, Gothenburg (Sweden). Current bye laws adopted, 29 Nov 2000, Brussels (Belgium). Former names and other names: *International Group for Pharmaceutical Distribution in the Countries of the European Community* – former (1960 to 1990); *Groupement international de la répartition pharmaceutique des pays de la Communauté européenne* – former (1960 to 1990); *International Group for Pharmaceutical Distribution in the Countries of the European Community and other Countries in Europe* – former (1990 to 1992); *Groupement international de la répartition pharmaceutique des pays de la Communauté européenne et d'autres pays d'Europe* – former (1990 to 1992); *International Group for Pharmaceutical Distribution in Europe* – former; *Groupement international de la répartition pharmaceutique européenne (GIRP)* – former; *European Association of Pharmaceutical Wholesalers* – former; *International Group for Pharmaceutical Distribution in Europe* – former; *European Association of Pharmaceutical Full-line Wholesalers* – former (2015). Registration: Banque Carrefour des Entreprises, No/ID: 0464.770.352, Start date: 14 Jul 1998, Belgium; EU Transparency Register, No/ID: 0757172464-29, Start date: 3 Oct 2008. **Aims** Carry out common examination and study of questions relating to professional wholesale and

handling of *pharmaceuticals*. **Structure** General Assembly (twice a year); Board; Managing Board. **Languages** English. **Finance** Sources: members' dues. **Activities** Events/meetings; knowledge management/information dissemination; research/documentation. **Events** *Annual Meeting and Conference* Bucharest (Romania) 2023, *Supply Chain Conference* Madrid (Spain) 2023, *Annual Meeting and Conference* Berlin (Germany) 2022, *Autumn Meeting* Brussels (Belgium) 2022, *Supply Chain Conference* Dublin (Ireland) 2022.
Members Full National organizations; Full member companies; Associate; Liaison; Supporting. Full national organizations in 32 countries:
Austria, Belgium, Bulgaria, China, Croatia, Czechia, Denmark, Estonia, Finland, France, Germany, Greece, Hungary, Ireland, Italy, Latvia, Lithuania, Luxembourg, Malta, Norway, Poland, Portugal, Romania, Russia, Serbia, Slovakia, Slovenia, Spain, Sweden, Switzerland, Türkiye, UK.
IGO Relations Recognized by: *European Commission (EC, #06633)*. **NGO Relations** Member of (5): *Alliance for Safe Online Pharmacy – EU (ASOP EU, #00720); EU Health Coalition; European Alliance for Personalised Medicine (EAPM, #05878); Federation of European and International Associations Established in Belgium (FAIB, #09508); International Federation of Pharmaceutical Wholesalers (IFPW, #13506)*. Partner of (1): *Fight the Fakes (#09755)*. [2021/XE2088/**E**]

- ♦ Groupement international de la répartition pharmaceutique européenne / see Groupement International de la Répartition Pharmaceutique (#10762)
- ♦ Groupement international de la répartition pharmaceutique des pays de la Communauté européenne / see Groupement International de la Répartition Pharmaceutique (#10762)
- ♦ Groupement international de la répartition pharmaceutique des pays de la Communauté européenne et d'autres pays d'Europe / see Groupement International de la Répartition Pharmaceutique (#10762)

♦ Groupement international des secrétaires généraux des universités francophones (GISGUF) 10763

Contact Univ de Liège, 7 Place du XX Aout, 4000 Liège, Belgium. T. +3243665302. E-mail: administrateur@uliege.be.
Registered Office Maison des Universités, 103 bd St-Michel, 75006 Paris, France.
URL: http://www.gisguf.org/

History 1977, Toulouse (France). Registered in accordance with French law. **Aims** Pool together the competences of the Secretaries-General (or equivalent) of member universities and the activities of continued professional training adapted to the evolution of higher education and research; define a policy of exchange and communication between the Secretaries-General (or equivalent) of French-speaking universities worldwide. **Structure** General Assembly (every 2 years); Administrative Council; Bureau. **Languages** French. **Finance** Members' dues. Subsidies from represented countries and national or international organizations and associations. **Activities** Events/meetings. **Events** *Colloque biennal / Biennial Conference* Bordeaux (France) 2014, *Colloque biennal / Biennial Conference* Beirut (Lebanon) 2012, *Colloque biennal / Biennial Conference* Yaoundé (Cameroon) 2010, *Colloque biennal / Biennial Conference* Geneva (Switzerland) 2007, *Colloque biennal / Biennial Conference* Marrakech (Morocco) 2005. **Publications** Colloquia proceedings.
Members Secretaries-General (261) of French-speaking universities in 29 countries:
Algeria, Belgium, Benin, Brazil, Bulgaria, Burkina Faso, Cameroon, Canada, Congo DR, Côte d'Ivoire, Egypt, France, Guinea, Hungary, Lebanon, Mauritania, Mauritius, Moldova, Montenegro, Morocco, Niger, Romania, Senegal, Serbia, Switzerland, Togo, Tunisia, Türkiye, Vietnam.
NGO Relations Associate member of: *Agence universitaire de La Francophonie (AUF, #00548)*. [2020.03.06/XF3322/v/**F**]

- ♦ Groupement international des sociétés de sport-toto et du lotto (inactive)
- ♦ Groupement international de travail pour les affaires indigènes / see International Work Group for Indigenous Affairs (#15907)
- ♦ Groupement international de travail pour les peuples autochtones (#15907)
- ♦ Groupement interuniversitaire Benelux des économistes des transports (#15985)
- ♦ Groupement latin de médecine du sport / see Latin and Mediterranean Group of Sport Medicine (#16401)
- ♦ Groupement latin et méditerranéen de médecine du sport (#16401)
- ♦ Groupement des mathématiciens d'expression latine (inactive)
- ♦ Groupement de microbiologie de l'Europe du Nord-Ouest (inactive)
- ♦ Groupement mondial des ex-boxeurs (inactive)
- ♦ Groupement du nursing européen (inactive)
- ♦ Groupement océanien des instituts à vocation environnementale (inactive)
- ♦ Groupement pharmaceutique de la Communauté européenne / see Pharmaceutical Group of the European Union (#18352)
- ♦ Groupement pharmaceutique de l'Union européenne (#18352)
- ♦ Groupement des pharmaciens de l'industrie en europe (#07530)

♦ Groupement de prévoyance et d'assurance des fonctionnaires internationaux (GPAFI) 10764

Provident and Insurance Group of International Officials
Main Office Palais des Nations, Office B-214, 1211 Geneva 10, Switzerland. E-mail: gpafi@un.org.
URL: http://www.gpafi.com/

History Founded 1958, by *United Nations Staff Association, Coordinating Council – Geneva (no recent information)*. **Aims** Provide for international civil servants, active or retired and family members, complementary health insurance, accident insurance, loss of salary insurance in case of long-term sick leave and assistance coverage. **Finance** Members' dues (annual). [2020/XF0508/**E**]

- ♦ Groupement des producteurs de carreaux céramiques du Marché commun / see European Ceramic Tile Manufacturers' Federation (#06508)
- ♦ Groupement des producteurs de la CEE de céramiques techniques pour applications électroniques, électriques, mécaniques et autres / see European Technical Ceramics Federation (#08878)
- ♦ Groupement des producteurs européens de céramiques techniques pour applications électroniques, électriques, mécaniques et autres / see European Technical Ceramics Federation (#08878)
- ♦ Groupement des producteurs d'isolateurs et de pièces isolantes minérales à usage électro-technique de la CEE / see European Technical Ceramics Federation (#08878)
- ♦ Groupement des retraités éducateurs sans frontières (internationally oriented national body)
- ♦ Groupement des retraités et des pensionnés des caisses d'épargne européennes / see Group of European Retired Staff and Pensioners from Savings Banks, Banks and Related Institutions (#10777)
- ♦ Groupement de travailleurs syndicalistes d'Amérique latine (inactive)
- ♦ Groupement des unions nationales des agences et organisateurs de voyages de la CEE / see The European Travel Agents' and Tour Operators' Associations (#08942)
- ♦ Groupement des unions nationales des agences et organisateurs de voyages de l'UE / see The European Travel Agents' and Tour Operators' Associations (#08942)
- ♦ Groupement des unions nationales des agences de voyages de la CEE / see The European Travel Agents' and Tour Operators' Associations (#08942)
- ♦ Groupement des utilisateurs de matériaux réfractaires (inactive)
- ♦ Groupe mixte d'experts chargé d'étudier les aspects scientifiques de la pollution des mers / see Joint Group of Experts on the Scientific Aspects of Marine Environmental Protection (#16131)
- ♦ Groupe mixte d'experts chargé d'étudier les aspects scientifiques de la protection de l'environnement marin (#16131)
- ♦ Groupe mixte d'experts OMI/FAO/UNESCO-COI/OMM/OMS/AIEA/ONU/PNUE chargé d'étudier les aspects scientifiques de la protection de l'environnement marin / see Joint Group of Experts on the Scientific Aspects of Marine Environmental Protection (#16131)
- ♦ Groupe Mondial sur la Migration (inactive)
- ♦ Groupe Mondial de Parlementaires pour l'Habitat (#10525)
- ♦ Groupe de Monrovia – Organisation des Etats africains et malgaches (inactive)
- ♦ Le Groupe de Montréal (#16853)
- ♦ Groupe des Nations Unies pour le développement / see United Nations Sustainable Development Group (#20634)
- ♦ Groupe des Neuf (#10785)
- ♦ Groupe nordique pour les questions des bâtiments publiques (#17252)
- ♦ Groupe Nouvelle Europe (inactive)
- ♦ Groupe d'observateurs militaires des Nations Unies dans l'Inde et le Pakistan (#20584)

♦ Groupe oecuménique des Dombes 10765

Ecumenical Group of Dombes
Secretariat 21 rue Jean Bouchet, 86000 Poitiers, France. T. +33615527013. E-mail: secretairegdd@gmail.com.
Archives Abbaye St Joseph de Pradines, 42630 Pradines, France.
URL: http://www.groupedesdombes.org/

History 1937, by Abbot Paul Couturier and Pastor Richard Baümlin. **Aims** Promote the unity of *Churches* through prayer and theological reflection. **Structure** Co-Presidents (2); Coopted Members. **Languages** French. **Staff** Voluntary. **Finance** Self-financed. **Activities** Events/meetings. **Events** *Annual session* Pradines (France) 2001, *Annual session* Pradines (France) 2000, *Annual session* Pradines (France) 1999, *Annual session* Pradines (France) 1998, *Annual Session* Villars-les-Dombes (France) 1997. **Publications** *Communion et conversion des Eglises* (2014) in French; *Le Notre Père, un itinéraire de conversion pour les Eglises* (2010) in French; *Un seul Maître – L'autorité doctrinale dans l'Eglise* (2005) – in French, Italian, (2010) in English; *Marie dans le dessein de Dieu et la communion des saints* (1998) – in French, Italian, (1999) in German, (2002) in English, (2004) in Polish, (2005) in Brasilian, Korean; *Pour la conversion des Eglises* (1991) – in French, Italian, Spanish, (1993) in English, (1994) in German; *Pour la communion des Eglises – L'apport du Groupe des Dombes 1937-1987* (1988).
Members Ministers and lay people, men and women, Protestants (Lutheran and Reformed) and Catholics. Members in 4 countries:
Belgium, France, Italy, Switzerland. [2017.11.19/XF2058/**F**]

- ♦ Groupe oecuménique de femmes consacrées (#05348)
- ♦ Groupe des ONG pour la Convention relative aux droits de l'enfant / see Child Rights Connect (#03884)
- ♦ Groupe des onze / see Cartagena Group (#03589)
- ♦ Groupe des organismes de bassin européens pour l'application de la directive-cadre sur l'eau (#10771)
- ♦ Groupe parlementaire démocrate-chrétien /du Conseil de l'Europe/ / see Group of the European People's Party (#10774)
- ♦ Groupe parlementaire du Parti des socialistes européens / see Group of the Progressive Alliance of Socialists and Democrats in the European Parliament (#10786)
- ♦ Groupe parlementaire du PSE / see Group of the Progressive Alliance of Socialists and Democrats in the European Parliament (#10786)
- ♦ Groupe du Parti populaire européen / see Group of the European People's Party – Christian Democrats (#10775)
- ♦ Groupe du Parti populaire européen au Comité des régions (#10776)
- ♦ Groupe du Parti Populaire Européen – Démocrates-chrétiens (#10775)
- ♦ Groupe parti populaire Européen / Démocrates chrétiens à l'Assemblée parlementaire du Conseil de l'Europe (#10774)
- ♦ Groupe des pays d'Amérique latine et des Caraïbes (#10784)
- ♦ Groupe des pays latinoaméricains et des Antilles exportateurs de sucre (inactive)
- ♦ Groupe des pays de l'Undugu (meeting series)
- ♦ Groupe Petites Paysanneries / see Groupe de Recherche Petites Paysanneries (#10769)

♦ Groupe pluri-professionnelle européen de reflexion et de formation en santé (Euro Cos humanisme et santé) 10766

Contact Hôpitaux Univ de Strasbourg, 1 place de l'Hôpital, 67091 Strasbourg CEDEX, France. T. +33388115006. Fax +33388115068. E-mail: eurocos@chru-strasbourg.fr.
URL: http://eurocos.u-strasbg.fr/

History Jun 1992, Strasbourg (France), as *European Post-Graduate Training Institute in Health Care (Euro Cos and Santé)* – Groupe pluri disciplinaire et pluri professionnel européen de reflexion et de formation en santé, on signature of an agreement between *European Association of Hospital and Health Services Social Workers (EAHHSSW, inactive)* and 3 Strasbourg-based universities and hospitals. Statutes adopted by Constitutive General Assembly, 14 May 1994, Strasbourg. Present name adopted 2002. **Aims** Promote a global approach by tackling health problems at a European level through inter-professional pooling of competences, complementarities and differences of founding institutions; facilitate exchanges, discussions and understanding among different European health professionals on specific topics and specialties. **Structure** General Assembly (annual). Board of Management, consisting of 4 representatives of founding institutions and 3 qualified individuals. Executive Bureau, comprising President, Secretary and Treasurer. **Languages** French. **Finance** Members' dues. Includes subvention from *European Commission (EC, #06633)*. **Activities** Provides multi-disciplinary training; organizes seminars and discussions. Topics: AIDS; drug addiction; alcoholism; alternatives to hospitalization. **Events** *International Days* Strasbourg (France) 2014, *International days* Strasbourg (France) 2008, *International days* Strasbourg (France) 2007, *Rencontre francophone de santé publique* Prague (Czech Rep) 2006, *International days* Strasbourg (France) 2005. **Publications** Proceedings.
Members Qualified individuals, mostly in France but in a total of 8 countries:
Belgium, Canada, Czechia, France, Italy, Portugal, Spain, Switzerland.
IGO Relations *WHO (#20950); Council of Europe (CE, #04881)* (Health Division); *European Parliament (EP, #08146)* (Commission on Health and Environment). [2011.06.01/XE1781/t/**E**]

- ♦ Groupe de pneumologie et phtisiologie infantile de langue française (inactive)
- ♦ Groupe Polyphenols / see Groupe Polyphénols (#10767)

♦ Groupe Polyphénols (GP) 10767

Contact Univ Bordeaux Segalen, Lab de Pharmacognosie, BP 80, 146 Rue Léo Saignat, 33076 Bordeaux, France. T. +33557574715. Fax +33557574716.
URL: http://www.groupepolyphenols.com/

History 1972, France. Also referred to as *Groupe Polyphenols*. Current statutes adopted 1996. Registered in accordance with French law. **Aims** Promote the study of polyphenols in all fields involving these substances, both fundamental and applied; encourage research; facilitate information exchange between researchers. **Structure** General Assembly; Board. **Languages** English, French. **Finance** Members' dues. **Activities** Events/meetings; awards/prizes/competitions. **Events** *International Conference on Polyphenols* Turku (Finland) 2021, *International Conference on Polyphenols* Turku (Finland) 2020, *International Conference on Polyphenols* Madison, WI (USA) 2018, *International Conference on Polyphenols* Vienna (Austria) 2016, *International Conference on Polyphenols* Nagoya (Japan) 2014. **Publications** *Recent Advances in Polyphenol Research (RAPR)* – book series. *Polyphenols Communications* – conference proceedings. [2020/XJ6648/**F**]

- ♦ **Groupe Pompidou** Groupe de coopération en matière de lutte contre l'abus et le trafic illicite des stupéfiants (#04796)
- ♦ Groupe de projet pour la coopération technique du développement (internationally oriented national body)
- ♦ Groupe des quinze (#10778)

♦ Groupe des radiologistes enseignants d'expression française (GREF) 10768

Pres Radiologie A CHU J Minjoz, Bd Fleming, 25030 Besançon CEDEX, France. Fax +33381668495. E-mail: secretariat@cerf-radiologie.fr.
URL: http://www.sfrnet.org/sfr/societe/relations-internationales/index.phtml

History Jan 1989, Abidjan (Côte d'Ivoire). Network of *Conférence internationale des doyens des facultés de médecine d'expression française (CIDMEF, #04616)*. Registered in accordance with French law. Statutes amended Oct 2011. **Aims** Promote *education* in radiology and medical imaging. **Structure** General Assembly (annual). Bureau, comprising President, 3 Vice-Presidents, Secretary-General, Vice Secretary-General, Treasurer and 4 members. **Finance** Support from: the French Government; *Agence française de développement (AFD); Agence universitaire de La Francophonie (AUF, #00548)*; national organizations.

Groupe recherche crime
10768

alphabetic sequence excludes
For the complete listing, see Yearbook Online at

Members Active; Associate; Partners; Past Active; Honorary. Members in 40 countries:
Afghanistan, Algeria, Belgium, Benin, Bulgaria, Burkina Faso, Burundi, Cambodia, Cameroon, Canada, Central African Rep, Chad, Congo Brazzaville, Congo DR, Côte d'Ivoire, Czechia, France, Gabon, Guinea, Haiti, Hungary, Laos, Lebanon, Madagascar, Mali, Mauritius, Moldova, Morocco, Niger, Poland, Romania, Rwanda, Senegal, Slovakia, Switzerland, Syrian AR, Togo, Tunisia, Vietnam. [2022/XE4622/E]

- ♦ Groupe de recherche sur le crime transnational / see Joint Research Centre on Transnational Crime
- ♦ Groupe de recherche et d'échanges technologiques / see GRET
- ♦ Groupe de recherche et d'étude de la paroi abdominale / see European Hernia Society (#07480)
- ♦ Groupe de recherche européen sur la paroi abdominale (#07480)
- ♦ Groupe de recherche et d'information sur la paix / see Groupe de recherche et d'information sur la paix et la sécurité
- ♦ Groupe de recherche et d'information sur la paix et la sécurité (internationally oriented national body)

♦ Groupe de Recherche Petites Paysanneries (GRPP) 10769

Treas 4 rue des Fleurs, 63530 Enval, France.
Contact c/o Ladyss, Bât T-1er étage, 200 avenue de la République, 72001 Nanterre CEDEX, France. T. +33140977806. Fax +33140977155. E-mail: petites.paysanneries@gmail.com.
URL: http://paysanneries.hypotheses.org/

History Also works under the name *Groupe Petites Paysanneries (GPP)*. Current statutes published 30 Nov 2013. Registered in accordance with French law. **Aims** (Re)discover the little known/unknown peasant farms in their various configurations. **Structure** Board of Directors; Bureau; Scientific Committee. **Events** *Journées Petites Paysanneries* Marseille (France) 2017. [2017/XM6111/F]

- ♦ Groupe de recherche et de réalisations pour le développement rural dans le Tiers-monde (internationally oriented national body)
- ♦ Groupe de recherches et d'études économiques et sociales sur l'Amérique Latine / see Groupe de recherches en sciences sociales sur l'Amérique Latine

♦ Groupe de recherches méditerranéennes pour l'amandier – pistachier (GREMPA) 10770

Group of Mediterranean Research on Almond and Pistachios
Contact c/o Mediterranean Agronomic Institute of Saragossa, IAMZ/CIHEAM, Avda Montañana 1005, 50059 Saragossa, Spain. T. +34976716000. Fax +34976716001. E-mail: iamz@iamz.ciheam.org.
URL: http://www.iamz.ciheam.org/

History 19 Feb 1974, Saragossa (Spain). 19-20 Feb 1974, Saragossa (Spain), by *CIHEAM – International Centre for Advanced Mediterranean Agronomic Studies (CIHEAM, #03927)*, as a research group of *Mediterranean Agronomic Institute of Zaragoza (MAIZ, #16644)*, in collaboration with Agrimed group of the European Community. Original title: *Mediterranean Cooperative Research and Study Group on the Almond Tree*. Current title adopted 1987, when joined by research group on pistachio. Previously also referred to as *Mediterranean Group for Almond and Pistachio*. **Aims** Make a shared analysis of problems affecting almond and pistachio crops in the Mediterranean area; conduct a common search for results; enable exchange of results by harmonizing methodology and applied techniques. **Structure** Informal network meeting every 3-4 years. **Languages** English, French. **Staff** None. **Finance** Source: *European Commission (EC, #06633)*; *CIHEAM – International Centre for Advanced Mediterranean Agronomic Studies (CIHEAM, #03927)*; national and local funds. **Activities** Coordinated programs concern: (1) variety comparison tests; (2) singling out parents with outstanding characteristics; (3) exchange of genetic material: varieties and selections; (4) standardization of observation methods (blooming, ripening, shell hardness, etc), drafting the pomological schedule; (5) cooperation in the research on rootstocks; (6) constitution and preservation of botanical collections of the under-genus Amygdalus. **Events** *Meeting* Athens (Greece) 2007, *Meeting* Saronis (Greece) 2007, *Meeting* Mirandela (Portugal) 2003, *Meeting* Saragossa (Spain) 2001, *Meeting* Sanliurfa (Turkey) 1999. **Publications** Meeting reports.
Members Individuals in 19 countries:
Bulgaria, Croatia, Egypt, France, Greece, Hungary, India, Israel, Italy, Libya, Morocco, Portugal, Romania, Spain, Syrian AR, Tunisia, Türkiye, Ukraine, USA.
IGO Relations Currently under the auspices of: Mediterranean Agronomic Institute of Zaragoza; *OECD (#17693)*. **NGO Relations** *FAO/CIHEAM Inter-Regional Cooperative Research Network on Nuts (NUCIS, #09258)*. [2011.06.01/XE5970/v/E]

- ♦ Groupe de recherches en sciences sociales sur l'Amérique Latine (internationally oriented national body)
- ♦ Groupe de recherche pour une stratégie économique alternative (internationally oriented national body)
- ♦ Groupe pour la recherche et la technologie aéronautique en Europe (#10733)
- ♦ Groupe régional de l'Afrique de l'Ouest (inactive)
- ♦ Groupe régional européen / see European Music Council (#07837)
- ♦ Groupe des registres de langue latine / see Groupe de coordination pour l'épidémiologie et l'enregistrement du cancer dans les pays de langue latine (#10737)
- ♦ Groupe de Rio (inactive)
- ♦ Groupe de Royaumont (inactive)
- ♦ Groupe de Schengen (inactive)
- ♦ Groupe Scientifique Européen Tuber aestivum/uncinatum (meeting series)
- ♦ Groupe des sept pour la coopération économique avec l'Afrique / see European Business Council for Africa (#06416)
- ♦ Groupe des sept por la coopération du secteur privé européen avec l'Afrique / see European Business Council for Africa (#06416)
- ♦ Groupe des sept pour la coopération du secteur privé européen avec l'Afrique, les Caraïbes et le Pacifique / see European Business Council for Africa (#06416)
- ♦ Groupe des sept / see European Business Council for Africa (#06416)
- ♦ Groupes missionnaires (internationally oriented national body)
- ♦ Groupe socialiste de l'Assemblée parlementaire du Conseil de l'Europe / see Socialists, Democrats and Greens Group (#19342)
- ♦ Groupe socialiste au Conseil de l'Europe / see Socialists, Democrats and Greens Group (#19342)
- ♦ Groupe socialiste au Parlement européen / see Group of the Progressive Alliance of Socialists and Democrats in the European Parliament (#10786)
- ♦ Groupe socialiste du Parlement européen / see Group of the Progressive Alliance of Socialists and Democrats in the European Parliament (#10786)
- ♦ Groupe Socialistes, démocrates et verts (#19342)
- ♦ Groupe pour la solidarité internationale (internationally oriented national body)
- ♦ Groupe de soutien aux capacités africaines de maintien de la paix (no recent information)
- ♦ Groupe de spécialistes de l'acoustique d'Amérique latine (inactive)
- ♦ Groupe sudaméricain pour l'athérosclérose (inactive)
- ♦ Groupe de travail autochtone international sur le VIH et le SIDA (unconfirmed)
- ♦ Groupe de Travail "Bruxelles 1952 / see International Automotive Lighting and Light Signalling Expert Group (#12301)
- ♦ Groupe de travail sur les critères et les indicateurs de la conservation et de l'aménagement durable des forêts des régions tempérées et boréales (#21058)
- ♦ Groupe de Travail Désertification (internationally oriented national body)
- ♦ Groupe de travail sur l'emploi et les moyens de subsistance durables (inactive)
- ♦ Groupe de travail européen pour la dendrochronologie (#09110)
- ♦ Groupe de travail inter-agences sur la désertification (inactive)
- ♦ Groupe de travail international sur les femmes et le sport (#15912)
- ♦ Groupe de travail international des ONG sur les questions légales et institutionnelles (#14369)
- ♦ Groupe de travail international sur la surveillance de la résistance aux anti-tuberculeux / see Tuberculosis Surveillance Research Unit (#20256)
- ♦ Groupe de travail mixte COI/OMM/CPPS pour l'étude du phénomène El Niño / see Programa para el Estudio Regional del Fenómeno El Niño en el Pacifico Sudeste (#18523)
- ♦ Groupe de travail mondial sur les rapaces (#21945)
- ♦ Groupe de travail de la paix et la sécurité européenne (internationally oriented national body)
- ♦ Groupe de travail permanent des jeunes médecins européens / see European Junior Doctors Association (#07620)
- ♦ Groupe de travail permanent des jeunes médecins hospitaliers européens / see European Junior Doctors Association (#07620)
- ♦ Groupe de travail sur la promotion touristique de la région danubienne / see Danube Tourist Commission (#05005)
- ♦ Groupe de travail sur la publicité, les études de marché et d'opinion (inactive)
- ♦ Groupe des trente (#10790)
- ♦ Groupe de Trevi (inactive)
- ♦ Groupe des trois (#10791)
- ♦ Groupe des trois ABM (#10792)
- ♦ Groupe URD – Groupe urgence, réhabilitation et développement (internationally oriented national body)
- ♦ Groupe urgence, réhabilitation et développement (internationally oriented national body)

♦ Group of European Basin Organizations for the Implementation of the Water Framework Directive (EURO-INBO) 10771

Groupe des organismes de bassin européens pour l'application de la directive-cadre sur l'eau – Grupo de Organismos de Cuenca Europeos para la Implementación de la Directiva Marco sobre el Agua
Contact c/o RIOB, 21 rue de Madrid, 75008 Paris, France. T. +33144908860. Fax +33140080145. E-mail: secretariat@riob.org.

History Sep 2003, Valencia (Spain). Regional network of *International Network of Basin Organizations (INBO, #14235)*. **Aims** Enrich implementation of water policies in Europe, including the Common Implementation Strategy (CIS), through practical experience for supporting candidate countries and disseminating principles and tools of European water. **Structure** Annual Plenary Assembly. **Activities** Politics/policy/regulatory; networking/liaising; knowledge management/information dissemination; training/education; monitoring/evaluation. **Events** *Europe-INBO Conference* Paris (France) 2020, *Europe-INBO Conference* Lahti (Finland) 2019, *Europe-INBO Conference* Seville (Spain) 2018, *Europe-INBO Conference* Dublin (Ireland) 2017, *Europe-INBO Conference* Lourdes (France) 2016. **Publications** *Europe INBO* – electronic newsletter. **IGO Relations** *European Commission (EC, #06633)*. [2018/XJ3456/E]

♦ Group of European Charophytologists 10772

Groupe européen des charophytologues (GEC)
Contact Hydrobiological Inst Naum Ohridski 50, 6000 Ohrid, North Macedonia. E-mail: trajsa@hio.edu.mk.

History 1987. **Aims** Coordinate and exchange research dealing with recent and fossil charophytes. **Structure** Informal. **Events** *Meeting* Palermo (Italy) 2018, *Meeting / Annual Meeting* Ohrid (Macedonia) 2009, *Meeting / Annual Meeting* Belgrade (Serbia) 2007, *Meeting / Annual Meeting* Barcelona (Spain) 2006, *Meeting / Annual Meeting* Iffeldorf (Germany) 2003.
Members Full organizations in 18 countries:
Austria, Belgium, Croatia, Czechia, France, Germany, Netherlands, Norway, Poland, Romania, Russia, Serbia (Serbia and Montenegro), Slovakia, Spain, Sweden, Switzerland, UK, Ukraine.
NGO Relations Links with *International Research Group on Charophytes (IRGC, #14727)*. [2018/XF3475/F]

- ♦ Group of European Customs Laboratories / see Customs Laboratories European Network (#04986)

♦ Group of European Municipalities with Nuclear Facilities (GMF) ... 10773

Pres Gran Via 62, 10o derecha, 28013 Madrid, Spain. E-mail: gmf@gmfeurope.org.
URL: https://www.gmfeurope.org/

History 1993. **Aims** Defend and ensure that European nuclear municipalities take part in the discussion forums and the decisionmaking carried out in the European Union; promote information exchange between European nuclear municipalities. **Structure** Praesidium, comprising President and 3 Vice-Presidents. **Finance** Sources: members' dues. **Events** *General Assembly* Madrid (Spain) 2020, *Annual General Assembly* Vienna (Austria) 2018, *Annual General Assembly* Madrid (Spain) 2017, *Nuclear energy as a real option for future and stakeholder engagement* Paks (Hungary) 2015, *Annual General Assembly* Gundremmingen (Germany) 2014.
Members Municipalities in 13 countries:
Belgium, Bulgaria, Czechia, France, Hungary, Lithuania, Netherlands, Romania, Slovakia, Slovenia, Spain, Sweden, UK. [2021/XF6671/F]

- ♦ Group of European Nutritionists / see Accademia Europea di Scienza della Nutrizione (#00045)
- ♦ Group of the European People's Party / see Group of the European People's Party – Christian Democrats (#10775)

♦ Group of the European People's Party 10774

Groupe parti populaire Européen / Démocrates chrétiens à l'Assemblée parlementaire du Conseil de l'Europe
SG c/o Council of Europe, Bureau PAL 5139, 67075 Strasbourg CEDEX, France. T. +33388412676. Fax +33388412769.
URL: http://www.epp-cd.eu/

History Founded as a functional organization of *European Union of Christian Democrats (EUCD, inactive)*, within the framework of *Parliamentary Assembly of the Council of Europe (PACE, #18211)*. Currently parliamentary group of *European People's Party (EPP, #08185)*. Original title: *Christian Democrat Group /in the Parliamentary Assembly of the Council of Europe/ – Groupe parlementaire démocrate-chrétien /du Conseil de l'Europe/ – Grupo Parlamentario Demócrata Cristiano /del Consejo de Europa/ – EVP-Fraktion/Europarat*. Full English title: *Group of the European People's Party in the Parliamentary Assembly of the Council of Europe*. **Aims** As a *political* group, represent *Christian Democratic* and EPP views in the Parliamentary Assembly of the Council of Europe. **Structure** Bureau, comprising President and 14 Vice-Presidents. **Languages** English, French. **Staff** 1.50 FTE, paid. **Finance** Annual subvention from Assembly budget relative to number of members.
Members Parliamentarians (184) from 43 countries:
Albania, Armenia, Austria, Azerbaijan, Belgium, Bosnia-Herzegovina, Bulgaria, Croatia, Cyprus, Czechia, Denmark, Estonia, Finland, France, Georgia, Germany, Greece, Hungary, Ireland, Italy, Latvia, Liechtenstein, Lithuania, Luxembourg, Malta, Moldova, Monaco, Netherlands, North Macedonia, Norway, Poland, Portugal, Romania, San Marino, Serbia, Slovakia, Slovenia, Spain, Sweden, Switzerland, Türkiye, UK, Ukraine. [2016/XE0465/v/F]

♦ Group of the European People's Party – Christian Democrats (EPP) . 10775

Groupe du Parti Populaire Européen – Démocrates-chrétiens (PPE) – Grupo del Partido Popular Europeo – Demócrata-Cristianos (PPE) – Fraktion der Europäischen Volkspartei – Christdemokraten (EVP) – Grupo do Partido Popular Europeu – Democratas-Cristãos (PPE) – Gruppo del Partito Popolare Europeo – Democratici Cristiano (PPE) – Fractie van de Europese Volkspartij – Christen-democraten (EVP) – Det Europaeiske Folkepartis Gruppe – Kristelige Demokrater (EPP) – Euroopan Kansanpuolueen Rhymä – Kristillisdemokraatit (EPP) – Poslanecky Klub Evropské Lidové Strany – Krest'anskych Demokrat (ELS) – Poslanecky Klub Evrópske l'Udovej Strany – Krest'anskych Demokratov (ELS) – Klub Zastupnika Europske Pucke Stranke – Krscanski Demokrati (EPP) – Poslanska Skupina Evrovske Ljudske Stranke – Krscanskih Demokratov (ELS) – Európai Néppart – Kereszténydemokratak – Képviselócsoport (EPP) – Grupa Europejskiej Partii Ludowej – Chrzexcijanscy Demokraci (EPL) – Euroopa Rahvapartei – Kristlike Demokraatide Fraktsioon (ERP) – Eiropas Tautas Partijas – Kristigie Demokrati (ETP) – Europos Liaudies Partijos – Krikscioniu Demokratu (ELP) – Grupp tal-Partit Popolari Ewropew – Dokristjani (PPE) – Grupul Partidului Popular European – Crestin Democrat (PPE) – Grúpa Phairti an Phobail Eorpaigh – Na Daonlathaithe Criostai (PPE)
Chairman Rue Wiertz 60, 1047 Brussels, Belgium. T. +3222845890. Fax +3222849890.
URL: http://www.eppgroup.eu/

History Founded 23 Jun 1953, as the Christian-Democratic Group, as a political fraction in the *'Common Assembly of the European Coal and Steel Community'*. On 19 Mar 1958, the Common Assembly became *European Parliament (EP, #08146)*. In 1979, when the EP introduced direct, universal elections, became *Group of the European People's Party (Christian-Democratic Group) – Groupe du Parti populaire européen (Groupe du démocrates-chrétiens)*. Subsequent name changes, 1999-2009: *European People's Party (Christian Democrats); European Democrats*. Current title re-adopted, Jun 2009. **Aims** Bring together centre and centre-right pro-European political forces from the member states of the European Union; advance the goal of a more competitive and democratic Europe, closer to its citizens, and a social market economy. **Structure** Group Assembly; Bureau; Presidency; Working Groups. **Languages** Bulgarian, Croatian, Czech, Danish, Dutch, English, Estonian, Finnish, French, German, Hungarian, Irish Gaelic, Italian, Latvian, Lithuanian, Maltese, Polish, Portuguese, Romanian, Slovakian, Slovene, Spanish, Swedish. **Staff** 285.00 FTE, paid. **Finance** General budget of *European Parliament (EP, #08146)*. **Activities** Politics/policy/regulatory; meeting activities; training/education; networking/liaising. **Events** *Meeting* Amsterdam (Netherlands) 2013, *Meeting on Enforcement of Social Rules in Road Transport* Brussels (Belgium) 2012, *Meeting* Gödöllő (Hungary) 2011, *Seminar* Budapest (Hungary) 2010, *Seminar* Brussels (Belgium) 1994. **Publications** Annual Activity Report; policy papers; positions papers.

Members MEPs (217), elected by direct universal suffrage for a 5-year period, belonging to parties in 27 countries:

Austria, Belgium, Bulgaria, Croatia, Cyprus, Czechia, Denmark, Estonia, Finland, France, Germany, Greece, Hungary, Ireland, Italy, Latvia, Lithuania, Luxembourg, Malta, Netherlands, Poland, Portugal, Romania, Slovakia, Slovenia, Spain, Sweden.

IGO Relations Cooperates with: *European Committee of the Regions (CoR, #06665); Council of Europe (CE, #04881)*; Parliaments of the 27 member states of the European Union. **NGO Relations** Cooperates with: *African Foundation (no recent information); Centrist Democrat International (CDI, #03792); Christian Democratic Organization of America (#03899); Robert Schuman Foundation for Cooperation among Christian Democrats in Europe (RSF, #18957); European People's Party (EPP, #08185); European Union of Christian Democratic Workers (EUCDW, #08981); Youth of the European People's Party (YEPP, #22014)*. [2016.12.22/XF2703/v/**F**]

♦ Group of the European People's Party in the Committee of the Regions (EPP-CoR) 10776

Groupe du Parti populaire européen au Comité des régions – Grupo del Partido Popular Europeo en el Comite de las Regiones – Fraktion der Europäischen Volkspartei im Ausschuss der Regionen – Grupo do Partido Popular Europeu no Comité das Regiões – Fractie van de Europese Volkspartij in het Comité van de Regio's

Secretariat Rue Belliard 101, Office 7110, 1040 Brussels, Belgium. T. +3222822221 – +3222822250. Fax +3222822329. E-mail: epp@cor.europa.eu.
URL: https://www.eppcor.eu/

History 8 Mar 1994. Founded within the framework of *European Committee of the Regions (CoR, #06665)*. **Aims** Promote the ideals of the *Christian democratic* movements as broadly as possible, as well as a greater and systematic involvement of cities and regions in EU policy making. **Structure** Plenary Assembly of about 129 full and 128 alternate members. Bureau; Presidency; Coordinators; Secretariat, headed by Secretary-General. **Languages** English, French, German. **Staff** 11.00 FTE, paid. **Finance** Financed from the budget of COR. **Activities** Guidance/assistance/consulting. **Publications** *The REPPorter* – newsletter. *Your Guide*. Dedicated and thematic publications.

Members of the EPP Group in the CoR in 27 countries of the European Union:

Austria, Belgium, Bulgaria, Croatia, Cyprus, Czechia, Denmark, Estonia, Finland, France, Germany, Greece, Hungary, Ireland, Italy, Latvia, Lithuania, Luxembourg, Malta, Netherlands, Poland, Portugal, Romania, Slovakia, Slovenia, Spain, Sweden.

IGO Relations *Conference of the Regional and Local Authorities for the Eastern Partnership (CORLEAP, #04645)*. [2016/XE2123/**E**]

- ♦ Group of the European People's Party in the Parliamentary Assembly of the Council of Europe / see Group of the European People's Party (#10774)

♦ Group of European Retired Staff and Pensioners from Savings Banks, Banks and Related Institutions 10777

Groupement européen des retraités et des pensionnés des caisses d'epargne, banques et institutions similaires – Agrupación Europea de Jubilados y Pensionistas de Cajas de Ahorros, Bancos e Instituciones Afines – Europäische Gruppierung der Ruheständler und Rentner der Sparkassen, Banken und Ähnlichen Institutionen – Gruppo Europeo dei Pensionati delle Casse di Risparmio, Banche ed Enti Affini

Exec Pres C/Santiago 4, 03001 Alicante, Castellón, Spain. T. +34965211187. Fax +34965905826. E-mail: info@euroencuentros.org.
URL: http://www.euroencuentros.org/

History Founded as *Group of European Saving Banks Retired Staff and Pensioners – Groupement des retraités et des pensionnés des caisses d'épargne européennes – Agrupación de Jubilados y Pensionistas de las Cajas de Ahorros Europeas – Gruppe von Jubilierten und Pensionären von den Europäischen Sparkassen – Gruppo dei Pensionati delle Casse di Risparmio Europee – Vereniging der Gepensioneerden van Europese Spaarbanken*. Named changed to *Group of European Saving Banks, Banks and Related Institutions Retired Staff – Groupement européen des retraités des caisses d'épargne, banques et institutions similaires – Agrupación Europea de Jubilados de las Cajas de Ahorro, Bancos e Instituciones Afines – Vereinigung von Pensionären der Sparkassen, Banken und Ähnlichen Einrichtungen – Gruppo Europeo dei Pensionati delle Casse di Risparmio, Banche ed Enti Affini*, 31 Oct 2000, Lisbon (Portugal). Registered in accordance with Spanish law. **Aims** Defend criteria determining the social character of savings banks and the intentions in creating them, particularly promoting activities leading to respect for those who have reached retirement age in the service of such institutions. **Structure** Assembly (annual); Board of Directors; Executive Committee. **Languages** English, French, German, Italian, Portuguese, Spanish. **Staff** 1.00 FTE, paid. **Finance** Members' dues. **Activities** Events/meetings. **Events** *Meeting* Vienna (Austria) 2019, *Meeting* Chianciano Terme (Italy) 2016, *Meeting* La Coruña (Spain) 2015, *Meeting* Fuengirola (Spain) 2014, *Meeting* Tossa de Mar (Spain) 2013. **Publications** *EUROMEETINGS* (annual) in English, French, German, Italian, Portuguese, Spanish – magazine.

Members National, regional and local organizations in 8 countries:

Belgium, France, Germany, Italy, Portugal, Spain, Sweden, UK.

NGO Relations Member of: *AGE Platform Europe (#00557)*. [2015.09.01/XE1897/**E**]

- ♦ Group of European Saving Banks, Banks and Related Institutions Retired Staff / see Group of European Retired Staff and Pensioners from Savings Banks, Banks and Related Institutions (#10777)
- ♦ Group of European Saving Banks Retired Staff and Pensioners / see Group of European Retired Staff and Pensioners from Savings Banks, Banks and Related Institutions (#10777)
- ♦ Group of European Trans-Siberian Operators and Forwarders (#10091)
- ♦ Groupe des verts – Alliance libre européenne (#10781)
- ♦ Groupe des verts au Parlement européen / see Group of the Greens – European Free Alliance (#10781)
- ♦ Groupe des vingt (#10793)
- ♦ Groupe des vingt quatre (no recent information)
- ♦ **Groupe des vingt-quatre** Groupe intergouvernemental des vingt-quatre pour les questions monétaires internationales (#11495)
- ♦ Groupe de Visegrad (#20794)
- ♦ Groupe de Weimar (#20855)
- ♦ Group of Experts on Tax Treaties between Developed and Developing Countries / see United Nations Committee of Experts on International Cooperation in Tax Matters (#20541)

♦ Group of Fifteen (G-15) 10778

Groupe des quinze

Contact address not obtained. T. +41227916701 – +41227916298. Fax +41227916169. E-mail: info@group-of-fifteen.ch.
URL: http://www.g15.org/

History Sep 1989, as *Summit Level Group of Developing Countries*, following conclusion of 9th *Conference of Heads of State or Government of Non-Aligned Countries*, Belgrade (Serbia-Montenegro). Full title: *Group of Fifteen – Summit Level Group of Developing Countries (G-15)* Also referred to as *Group of 15 – Groupe des 15*. **Aims** Stimulate greater and mutually beneficial *cooperation* among *developing countries*, especially in the areas of investment, trade and technology; act as a catalyst for greater South-South cooperation, lending greater cohesion and credibility to developing countries in their efforts to pursue a more positive and productive North-South dialogue; facilitate national efforts for *development* and economic progress; serve as a forum for regular consultations among developing countries so as to coordinate policies and action of South countries at global level; assist in the formulation and implementation of programmes of cooperation. **Structure** Summit (rotating among the 3 developing regions of the South). Ministers of Foreign affairs meet annually in New York NY (USA) with other Ministerial Meetings held as necessary. Personal Representatives of Heads of State and Government meet regularly in Geneva (Switzerland). Steering Committee (TROIKA), comprising Foreign Ministers from the preceding, present and future Summit host countries, is responsible for overseeing and coordinating work of G-15. Troika Foreign Ministers are assisted by Troika Personal Representatives of Heads of State and Government (PRs) in Geneva. Each member country is represented by a PR in regular meetings of the Group. Technical Support Facility. **Languages** Arabic, English, French, Spanish. **Staff** 3.00 FTE, paid. **Finance** Annual contribution by members. **Activities** Participation in G-15 projects is open to all developing countries, not just G-15 members. **Events** *Annual Summit Meeting* Teheran (Iran Islamic Rep) 2010, *Annual Summit Meeting* Havana (Cuba) 2006, *Summit* Algiers (Algeria) 2005, *Summit / Annual Summit Meeting* Caracas (Venezuela) 2004, *Summit / Annual Summit Meeting* Jakarta (Indonesia) 2001. **Publications** *Group of Fifteen Booklet*.

Members Developing countries (17):

Algeria, Argentina, Brazil, Chile, Egypt, India, Indonesia, Iran Islamic Rep, Jamaica, Kenya, Malaysia, Mexico, Nigeria, Senegal, Sri Lanka, Venezuela, Zimbabwe. [2020/XF1525/**F***]

- ♦ Group of Fifteen – Summit Level Group of Developing Countries / see Group of Fifteen (#10778)
- ♦ Group of Fifty (internationally oriented national body)

♦ Group of Five (G-5) 10779

Groupe des cinq

Address not obtained.

History as follow-up to the *Plaza Agreement*, 22 Sep 1985. Not an organization – title is informal description referring to occasional meetings of Ministers of Finance of the 5 most industrialized countries. Also referred to as *Group of 5 – Groupe des 5*. When joined by Finance Ministers of Italy and Canada, referred to as *Group of Seven (G-7, #10788)*, which ultimately replaced G-5, 1986-1987. Joined further by Finance Ministers of the Netherlands, Belgium, Sweden and Switzerland this became *Group of Ten (G-10, inactive)*. A wider and more representative *Group of Twenty-Two (G-22, inactive)* has been proposed by the USA and some other members. **Aims** As indicated in the Plaza Agreement: while recognizing progress in promoting convergence of favourable *economic* performance among participating countries, seek to achieve increased and more balanced growth, and to bring key exchange rates more into line with underlying fundamentals.

Members Ministers of Finance of the 5 leading industrial countries:

France, Germany, Japan, UK, USA.

IGO Relations *International Monetary Fund (IMF, #14180)*. [2011/XF2680/c/**F***]

- ♦ Group of Five (#10800)

♦ Group of Four (G-4) 10780

Grupo de los Cuatro

Address not obtained.

History May 1992, on signing of the *Nueva Ocotepeque Agreement*, ratifying the objective of establishing a free trade area. This was established Jul 1993, having been operative *'de facto'* from Apr 1993. Members have also signed bilateral agreements. **Aims** As an informal collaboration between the countries of the Northern Triangle of *Central America*, work towards a *customs union* and further *economic* union. **Activities** *'Declaration of San Salvador'*, Aug 1993, and *'Declaration of Santo Tomas'*, Sep 1993, Guatemala (Guatemala), agreed to accelerate the integration process and adopted common policies in trade liberalization, facilities for migration movements, infrastructure and communications, aspects of common social interest, foreign relations. Currently negotiating on establishment of a regional capital market, regional stock exchange and regional institution to coordinate external assistance.

Members Governments of 4 countries:

El Salvador, Guatemala, Honduras, Nicaragua.

IGO Relations *Central American Common Market (CACM, #03666)*. [2010/XF3703/**F***]

- ♦ Group of French-Speaking Anthropologists (#10756)
- ♦ Group of Friends United against Human Trafficking (unconfirmed)

♦ Group of the Greens – European Free Alliance (Greens/EFA) 10781

Groupe des verts – Alliance libre européenne – Grupo de los Verdes – Alianza Libre Europea – Fraktion der Grünen – Freie Europäische Allianz – Grupo dos Verdes – Aliança Livre Europeia – Gruppo Verde – Alleanza Libera Europea – Fractie de Groenen – Vrije Europese Alliantie – Gruppen de Gröna – Europeiska Fria Alliansen – Gruppen de Gronne – Europaeiske Fri Alliance – Vihreät – Euroopan Vapaa Allianssi – Ryhmä

SG c/o Parlement européen, Central Secretariat, Office PHS02C27 – Paul Henri Spaak Bldg, Rue Wiertz 60, 1047 Brussels, Belgium. T. +3222842117. Fax +3222307837. E-mail: contactgreens@europarl.europa.eu.
URL: https://www.greens-efa.eu/

History 1984, as a subgroup of *Rainbow Group (inactive)*, under the title *Green Alternative European Link (GRAEL) – Alliance verte alternative européenne*. Name changed to *Green Group in the European Parliament (Greens) – Groupe des verts au Parlement européen (GVPE) – Grupo de los Verdes en el Parlamento Europeo – Fraktion die Grünen im Europäischen Parlament – Grupo dos Verdes no Parlamento Europeu – Gruppo i Verdi al Parlamento Europeo – Fractie de Groenen in the Europees Parlement – Gruppen de Gröna i Europaparlamentet – Gruppen de Grønne i Europa-Parlamentet – Euroopan Parlamentin Vihreä Ryhmä – I Prasini sto Evropaiko Kinovulio*. Also referred to under the English acronym *GGEP*. Part of: *European Free Alliance (EFA, #07356)*. **Aims** Defend green politics in Europe and in the world. **Structure** Comprises members of *European Parliament (EP, #08146)* representing 'green' parties in their own countries. Plenary Assembly (annual). Bureau; 2 Co-Presidents; Secretariat, headed by General Secretary. Working Groups. **Finance** Financed by European Parliament's funds. **Events** *Conference on climate migrations* Brussels (Belgium) 2008, *Conference on olympic games in China* Brussels (Belgium) 2008, *Conference on the European neighbourhood policy* Brussels (Belgium) 2008, *Conference on tourism and climate change* Brussels (Belgium) 2008, *Conference on basic income* Brussels (Belgium) 2007. **Publications** Charters; reports; dossiers; books; leaflets.

Members Members of the European Parliament (50) representing ecological parties in 16 countries:

Austria, Belgium, Croatia, Denmark, Estonia, Finland, France, Germany, Hungary, Italy, Latvia, Lithuania, Luxembourg, Netherlands, Slovenia, Spain, Sweden.

NGO Relations Member of: *European Energy Forum (EEF, #06986); European Network Against the Arms Trade (ENAAT, #07861)*. Coordinates: *European Agricultural Convention (EAC, no recent information)*. Instrumental in setting up: *European Network Against Trafficking in Women for Sexual Exploitation (ENATW, #07863)*, and many bodies in other fields. Links with a large number of organizations active in the field, including: *European Green Party (EGP, #07409); Green European Foundation (GEF, #10718)*. [2016/XE6091/**F**]

- ♦ Group of Independent Representatives / see European Conservatives Group (#06744)
- ♦ Grouping of European Tobacco Industries (#10760)
- ♦ Group of international Experts of vitivinicultural Systems for CoOperation (#10748)

♦ Group of International Finance Centre Supervisors (GIFCS) 10782

Chairman c/o Financial Supervision Commission, PO Box 58, Finch Hill House, Douglas, IM99 1DT, UK. T. +441624689300.
URL: http://www.gifcs.org/

History Founded Oct 1980, Basel (Switzerland), at the instigation of the *Basel Committee on Banking Supervision (BCBS, #03183)*. Original title: *Offshore Group of Banking Supervisors (OGBS)*. **Aims** Enable members to identify and discuss issues of mutual interest, establish an identity of purpose and share knowledge and experiences; participate with relevant international organizations in setting up and promoting implementation of international standards for the supervision of financial services and for combating money laundering/terrorist financing; encourage members to apply high standards of supervision based on internationally accepted principles; promote a general raising of standards among member jurisdictions through a peer group approach and mutual independent evaluation; agree on and promote a positive, constructive and coordinated response to the approaches made by other supervisory authorities for assistance; promote the adoption of the Group's Statement of Best Practice for trust and company service providers; promote the adoption of the principles of the Group's paper on hedge fund regulation. **Structure** Plenary Meeting (annual); Technical Meeting (annual). **Languages** English. **Staff** Administration by staff of Isle of Man Financial Supervision Commission. **Finance** Members' dues. **Activities** Networking/liaising; standards/guidelines; events/meetings. **Events** *Annual Meeting* London (UK) 2015, *Annual Meeting* Macau (Macau) 2015, *Annual Meeting* Tianjin (China) 2014, *Annual Meeting* Panama (Panama) 2013, *Annual Meeting* Istanbul (Turkey) 2012.
Members Full Members; Observers. Supervisory authorities in 19 countries and territories:
Aruba, Bahamas, Barbados, Bermuda, Cayman Is, Cook Is, Curaçao, Gibraltar, Guernsey, Isle of Man, Jersey, Macau, Mauritius, Panama, Samoa, St Maarten, Vanuatu, Virgin Is UK.
IGO Relations Observer status with: *Asia/Pacific Group on Money Laundering (APG, #01921)*; *Caribbean Financial Action Task Force (CFATF, #03505)*; *Committee of Experts on the Evaluation of Anti-Money Laundering Measures and the Financing of Terrorism (MONEYVAL, #04257)*; *Egmont Group of Financial Intelligence Units (#05396)*; *Financial Action Task Force (FATF, #09765)*. **NGO Relations** Member of: Consultative Group of *Basel Committee on Banking Supervision (BCBS, #03183)*. [2016/XD9548/v/**E**]

♦ Group of International Insurance Centre Supervisors (GIICS) 10783

Chair c/o GFSC, PO Box 128, Glategny Court, Glategny Esplanade, St Peter Port, GY1 3HQ, UK. Fax +441481726952.
URL: http://www.giics.org/

History Mar 1993, under written Constitution, as *Offshore Group of Insurance Supervisors (OGIS)*. Present name adopted, 2012. **Aims** Provide a forum for discussion between members, represent their interests at international forums and support them in implementing sound supervisory practices and meeting international regulatory standards. **Structure** General Meeting (annual); Executive Committee. **Finance** Members' dues. Receives funding from *International Association of Insurance Supervisors (IAIS, #11966)* when organizing particular seminars and workshops. **Activities** Events/meetings; training/education. **Events** *Annual General Meeting* Fort Lauderdale, FL (USA) 2007, *Annual Working Meeting* Guernsey (UK) 2007, *Annual Meeting* USA 2007, *Annual general meeting / Annual Meeting* Beijing (China) 2006, *Annual Working Meeting* St Lucia 2006. **Publications** Standards and guidance papers online.
Members in 18 countries and territories (also in Labuan, not listed below):
Anguilla, Aruba, Bahamas, Barbados, Belize, Bermuda, Cayman Is, Cook Is, Curaçao, Gibraltar, Guernsey, Isle of Man, Jersey, Macau, Samoa, Turks-Caicos, Vanuatu, Virgin Is UK. [2017.07.07/XF6315/**F**]

- ♦ Group for International Solidarity (internationally oriented national body)
- ♦ GROUPISOL / see European Technical Ceramics Federation (#08878)
- ♦ Group of Latin American Ambassadors to the European Communities (inactive)

♦ Group of Latin American and Caribbean States 10784

Groupe des pays d'Amérique latine et des Caraïbes (GRULAC) – Grupo de Paises de América Latina y el Caribe

Contact address not obtained. Fax +41227312069.

Events *Annual Assembly* Havana (Cuba) 2013, *Meeting* San José (Costa Rica) 2007, *Meeting* Lima (Peru) 2001. **IGO Relations** *UNICEF (#20332)*. [2012/XE4762/**E***]

- ♦ Group of Latin American and Caribbean Sugar Exporting Countries (inactive)
- ♦ Group for Latin American Studies of the Institute of Sociology, Free University of Brussels (internationally oriented national body)
- ♦ Group of Mathematicians of Romance Languages (inactive)
- ♦ Group of Mediterranean Research on Almond and Pistachios (#10770)
- ♦ Group of National Travel Agents' Associations within the EEC / see The European Travel Agents' and Tour Operators' Associations (#08942)
- ♦ Group of National Travel Agents' and Tour Operators' Associations within the EEC / see The European Travel Agents' and Tour Operators' Associations (#08942)
- ♦ Group of National Travel Agents' and Tour Operators' Associations within the EU / see The European Travel Agents' and Tour Operators' Associations (#08942)

♦ Group of Nine 10785

Groupe des Neuf

Address not obtained.

History as an informal group of countries meeting infrequently to discuss matters of mutual interest. Also referred to as *Group of 9 – Groupe des 9*.
Members Governments of 9 countries:
Austria, Belgium, Bulgaria, Denmark, Finland, Hungary, Romania, Serbia, Sweden. [2010/XF5101/**F***]

- ♦ Group for Pastoral Work for Circus and Showmen of All Confessions / see International Group of Priests for Circus and Showmen of All Confessions (#13752)
- ♦ Group of Policy Advisers / see European Political Strategy Centre (#08248)

♦ Group of the Progressive Alliance of Socialists and Democrats in the European Parliament (S and D) 10786

Groupe de l'alliance progressiste des socialistes and démocrates au Parlement européen – Grupo de la Alianza Progresista de Socialistas and Demócratas en el Parlamento Europeo – Fraktion der Progressiven Allianz der Sozialdemokrated im Europäischen Parlament – Gruppo dell'Alleanza Progressista di Socialisti and Democratici al Parlamento Europeo – Grupa Postepowego Sojuszu Socjalistów and Demokratów w Parlamencie Europejskim

SG European Parliament (ATR 05K022), Rue Wiertz, 1047 Brussels, Belgium. T. +32228411560.
Pres European Parliament (ATR 05K018), Rue Wiertz, 1047 Brussels, Belgium.
URL: http://www.socialistsanddemocrats.eu/

History 1954, as *Groupe socialiste du Parlement européen – Gruppo Socialista Parlamento Europeo – Sozialistische Fraktion Europäisches Parlament – Socialistische Fractie Europees Parlement*, to bring together Socialist members of *European Parliament (EP, #08146)*. Subsequently changed title to *Parliamentary Group of the Party of European Socialists – Groupe parlementaire du Parti des socialistes européens – Grupo Parlamentario del Partido de los Socialistas Europeos – Fraktion der Sozialdemokratischen Partei Europas – Grupo Parlamentare do Partido Socialista Europeu – Gruppo Parlamentare del Partido del Socialismo Europeo – Fractie van de Partij van de Europese Sociaaldemokraten – Europeiska Socialdemokraternas Parlamentsgrupp – Europaeiske Socialdemokraters Gruppe – Euroopan Sosialidemokraattisen Puolueen Parlamenttirhmä – Kinovulevtiki Omada tu Evropaiku Sisialistiku Kommatos*, 1995. Changed title to: *Socialist Group in the European Parliament – Groupe socialiste au Parlement européen – Grupo Socialista en el Parlamento Europeo – Sozialdemokratische Fraktion im Europäischen Parlament – Grupo Socialista no Parlamento Europeu – Gruppo Socialista al Parlamento Europeo – Sociaal-Democratische Fractie in the Europees Parlement – Socialdemokratiska Gruppen i Europaparlamentet – De Europaeiske Socialdemokraters Gruppe Euroopan Parlamentin Sosialidemokraattinen Ryhmä – Skupina Socialnich Demokratu v Evropském Parlamentu – Socialisticka Skupina v Európskom Parlamente – Az Európai Parlament Szocialista Képviselőcsoportja – Grupa Socjalistyczna w Parlamencie Europejskim – Skupina Socialdemokratov v Evropskem Parlamentu – Euroopa Parlamendi Sotsiaaldemokraatide Fraktsioon – Socialdemokratu Grupa Eiropas Parlamenta – Socialistu Frakcija Europos Parlamente*, 2004. Previously also referred to as *Groupe parlementaire du PSE*. **Aims** Work around key issues, such as: fair and inclusive society based on social justice and solidarity; a fair way out of the economic crisis based on investment in education, research, job creation and an ambitious EU industrial policy; greening the economy; create jobs and prosperity; defend human rights and civil liberties; put people first; promote equality. **Structure** Parliamentarians. Bureau; Coordinators (23); Secretariat. **Activities** Events/meetings; networking/liaising; politics/policy/regulatory. **Events** *An Alternative Energy Summit* Brussels (Belgium) 2011, *Conference on best practices for cohesion* Brussels (Belgium) 2008, *Meeting* Espoo (Finland) 1996, *North-South conference* Brussels (Belgium) 1991, *International conference* Amsterdam (Netherlands) 1988. **Publications** Brochures; leaflets.
Members Parliamentarians (195), members of the European Parliament, in 27 countries:
Austria, Belgium, Bulgaria, Croatia, Cyprus, Czechia, Denmark, Estonia, Finland, France, Germany, Greece, Hungary, Ireland, Italy, Latvia, Lithuania, Luxembourg, Malta, Netherlands, Poland, Portugal, Romania, Slovakia, Slovenia, Spain, Sweden.
IGO Relations Contact with European institutions, governments and parliamentary groups in the EU, wider Europe and world, including the following bodies listed in this Yearbook: *European Committee of the Regions (CoR, #06665)*; *Court of Justice of the European Union (CJEU, #04938)*; *European Central Bank (ECB, #06466)*; *European Commission (EC, #06633)*; *European Court of Auditors (#06854)*; *European Foundation for the Improvement of Living and Working Conditions (Eurofound, #07348)*; *European Investment Bank (EIB, #07599)*; *European Medicines Agency (EMA, #07767)*; *European Ombudsman (#08084)*; *European Police Office (Europol, #08239)*; *ILO (#11123)*; *Statistical Office of the European Union (Eurostat, #19974)*.
NGO Relations Contact with organizations that promote employment, sustainable economic development, peace, consumer protection, civil and human rights, fair trade and development, including the following bodies listed in this Yearbook:
- *European Anti-Poverty Network (EAPN, #05908)*;
- *European Forum for Democracy and Solidarity (EFDS, #07307)*;
- *European Movement International (EMI, #07825)*;
- *European Trade Union Confederation (ETUC, #08927)*;
- *Friedrich-Ebert-Stiftung (FES)*;
- *Inter-Parliamentary Union (IPU, #15961)*;
- *International Falcon Movement – Socialist Educational International (IFM-SEI, #13327)*;
- *Jean-Jaurès Foundation (FJJ)*;
- *Observatoire social européen (OSE)*;
- *Olof Palme International Center, Stockholm*;
- *Party of European Socialists (PES, #18249)*;
- *Social Platform (#19344)*;
- *SOLIDAR (#19680)*.

Instrumental in setting up: *Global Progressive Forum (GPF, #10557)*. [2018.02.02/XF2702/v/**F**]

- ♦ Group of Refractory Material Users (inactive)

♦ Group for Research and Assessment of Psoriasis and Psoriatic Arthritis (GRAPPA) 10787

Contact 3213 W Wheeler St, Ste 35, Seattle WA 98199, USA.
URL: http://www.grappanetwork.org/

History Founded 2003, inspired by Assessment in Ankylosing Spondylitis Working Group (ASAS). A US nonprofit of the type 501(c)3. **Aims** Facilitate sharing of information related to psoriasis and psoriatic arthritis; network among different medical disciplines that see psoriasis and psoriatic arthritis patients; enhance research, diagnosis and treatment of psoriasis and psoriatic arthritis. **Structure** Executive Committee; Steering Committee. Committees. **Activities** Awards/prizes/competitions; guidance/assistance/consulting; training/education; events/meetings. **Events** *Annual Meeting* Paris (France) 2019, *Annual Meeting* Toronto, ON (Canada) 2018. **Publications** *GRAPPA Newsletter*. [2019/XM8025/**F**]

- ♦ Group for Research and Information on Peace and Security (internationally oriented national body)
- ♦ Group for Research and Study of the Abdominal Wall / see European Hernia Society (#07480)
- ♦ Group of Retired IAEA, UNIDO and UN Staff in Austria / see Association of Retired International Civil Servants, Austria
- ♦ Group for Rural And Isolated Practitioners in Europe / see European Rural and Isolated Practitioners Association (#08415)
- ♦ Group of Schengen (inactive)

♦ Group of Seven (G-7) 10788

No fixed address address not obtained.

History 1975, when 7 major industrial countries began to hold annual economic summits. At the level of finance ministers and central bank governors, replaced *Group of Five (G-5, #10779)* as main policy coordination group during 1986-1987, particularly following the Louvre Accord of Feb 1987, agreed by G-5 plus Canada, and subsequently endorsed by G-7. Since 1987, G-7 finance ministers and central bank governors meet at least biannually. Managing Director of *International Monetary Fund (IMF, #14180)* usually participates, by invitation. When Russia joins, Group becomes *Group of Eight (G-8, #10745)*. Also referred to as *Group of 5*. **Aims** Monitor developments in the world *economy*; assess economic policies. **Events** *Ministerial Meeting on Gender Equality between Women and Men* Paris (France) 2019, *Health Experts Meeting* Tokyo (Japan) 2016.
Members Ministers of Finance of the 7 leading industrial countries:
Canada, France, Germany, Italy, Japan, UK, USA. [2011/XJ4647/c/**F***]

- ♦ Group of Seven for Economic Cooperation with Africa / see European Business Council for Africa (#06416)
- ♦ Group of Seven / see European Business Council for Africa (#06416)
- ♦ Group of Seven for European Private Sector Cooperation with Africa / see European Business Council for Africa (#06416)
- ♦ Group of Seven for European Private Sector Cooperation with Africa, Caribbean and Pacific / see European Business Council for Africa (#06416)
- ♦ Group of Shanghai / see Shanghai Cooperation Organization (#19256)
- ♦ Group of Six / see European Committee for Electrotechnical Standardization (#06647)

♦ Group of States Against Corruption 10789

Groupe d'états contre la corruption (GRECO)

Exec Sec Directorate General Human Rights and Rule of Law (DGI), Council of Europe, 67075 Strasbourg CEDEX, France. E-mail: webmaster.greco@coe.int.
URL: http://www.coe.int/greco/

History Established as an Enlarged Partial Agreement of *Council of Europe (CE, #04881)*, by Resolution (98) 7 of *Committee of Ministers of the Council of Europe (#04273)*, 5 May 1998. Formally set up, 1 May 1999 by Resolution (99) 5. Legal standards involved: *Civil Law Convention on Corruption (1999)* (ETS 174); *Criminal Law Convention on Corruption (1999)* (ETS 173) and *Additional Protocol to the Criminal Law Convention on Corruption (2003)* (ETS 191); Resolution of the Committee of Ministers of the Council of Europe on the Twenty Guiding Principles for the Fight against Corruption (Resolution (97) 24); Recommendation of the Committee of Ministers of the Council of Europe on Codes of Conduct for Public Officials (No R (2000) 10); Recommendation of the Committee of Ministers of the Council of Europe on Common Rules against Corruption in the Funding of Political Parties and Electoral Campaigns (Rec (2003) 4). **Aims** Improve policies, legislation and institutional set-ups for preventing and combating corruption in the GRECO member states. **Structure** Plenary; Bureau; Statutory Committee; Secretariat. **Languages** English, French. **Activities** Events/meetings; monitoring/evaluation; training/education. **Events** *Conference* Strasbourg (France) 2009. **Publications** *General Activity Report* (annual). Evaluation reports; compliance reports.
Members Enlarged Agreement open to Council of Europe member States and under certain conditions to non-member States. Parties to the Criminal or Civil Law Conventions on Corruption are automatically members. Governments of 48 countries:
Albania, Andorra, Armenia, Austria, Azerbaijan, Belgium, Bosnia-Herzegovina, Bulgaria, Croatia, Cyprus, Czechia, Denmark, Estonia, Finland, France, Georgia, Germany, Greece, Hungary, Iceland, Ireland, Italy, Kazakhstan, Latvia, Liechtenstein, Lithuania, Luxembourg, Malta, Moldova, Monaco, Montenegro, Netherlands, North Macedonia, Norway, Poland, Portugal, Romania, San Marino, Serbia, Slovakia, Slovenia, Spain, Sweden, Switzerland, Türkiye, UK, Ukraine, USA.
IGO Relations Organizations with observer status: *European Union (EU, #08967)*; *International Anti-Corruption Academy (IACA, #11654)*; *International Institute for Democracy and Electoral Assistance (International IDEA, #13872)*; *OAS (#17629)*; *OECD (#17693)*; *OSCE – Office for Democratic Institutions and Human Rights (OSCE/ODIHR, #17902)*; *United Nations Office on Drugs and Crime (UNODC, #20596)*. Contacts with: *Eurojust (#05698)*; *European Anti-Fraud Office (#05906)*; *European Commission (EC, #06633)*; *European Ombudsman*

(#08084). **NGO Relations** Contacts with: *Global Organization of Parliamentarians Against Corruption (GOPAC, #10518)*; *International Chamber of Commerce (ICC, #12534)*; *International Foundation for Electoral Systems (IFES, #13669)*; *Transparency International (TI, #20223)*. [2022.10.11/XE4422/**E***]

- ♦ Group for the Study of Biological Rhythms / see Société Francophone de Chronobiologie
- ♦ Group for the Study of the Human Companion Animal Bond / see Society for Companion Animal Studies
- ♦ Group of Temperate Southern Hemisphere Countries on the Environment (no recent information)
- ♦ Group of Ten (inactive)

♦ Group of Thirty 10790

Groupe des trente

Exec Dir 1701 K St NW, Ste 950, Washington DC 20006, USA. T. +12023312472. E-mail: info@group30.org.

URL: http://www.group30.org/

History 1978. Also known as *Consultative Group on International Economic and Monetary Affairs – Groupe consultatif sur les affaires économiques et monétaires internationales* and as *Group of 30 – Groupe des 30*. **Aims** Deepen understanding of international *economic* and *financial* issues; explore the international repercussions of decisions taken in the public and private sectors and examine the choices available to market practitioners and to policymakers; provide a forum within which to review trends within the international *banking* community. **Languages** English. **Staff** 3.50 FTE, paid. **Finance** Supported by contributions from private sources: foundations; banks; non-bank corporations; central banks; individuals. **Activities** Events/meetings. **Events** *International Banking Seminar* New York, NY (USA) 2016, *Plenary Session* New York, NY (USA) 2016, *Plenary Session* Singapore (Singapore) 2016, *International Banking Seminar* Lima (Peru) 2015, *Plenary Session* New York, NY (USA) 2015. **Publications** Annual Report; study group reports; occasional paper series.

Members Individuals in 18 countries:
Argentina, Brazil, China, Denmark, France, Germany, India, Israel, Italy, Japan, Kuwait, Mexico, Poland, Singapore, Spain, Switzerland, UK, USA. [2016.06.21/XF5228/v/**F**]

♦ Group of Three (G-3) 10791

Groupe des trois – Grupo de los Tres (G-3)

Address not obtained.

History Sep 1990. Treaty – *Free Trade Agreement of the Group of Three* – signed 13 Jun 1994, Cartagena de Indias (Colombia), entered into force 1 Jan 1995. **Aims** Establish a programme of *trade liberalization* over 10 years; establish a free trade area; become an important element of political and economic support to foster development in *Central America* and the *Caribbean*. **Activities** The Agreement provides for: granting of asymmetric trade conditions to Colombia and Venezuela; special treatment for most agricultural products and the automobile sector; special arrangements for Venezuela to dismantle textile tariffs. **Events** *Summit of heads of state and government of CARICOM and G3 and the vice-president of Suriname* Port-of-Spain (Trinidad-Tobago) 1993.

Members Governments of 3 countries:
Colombia, Mexico, Venezuela.

IGO Relations *Caribbean Community (CARICOM, #03476)*. [2009/XF3578/**F***]

♦ Group of Three ABM (G-3) 10792

Groupe des trois ABM – Grupo de los Tres ABM (G-3)

Address not obtained.

History Sep 1987. Title is informal description of occasional meetings of Ministers of Finance of the 3 American countries with the greatest national debt. **Aims** Bring together Ministers of *Finance* for informal discussions.

Members Ministers of Finance of 3 countries:
Argentina, Brazil, Mexico. [2010/XF1969/c/**F***]

♦ Group of Twenty (G20) 10793

Groupe des vingt

No fixed address address not obtained.

URL: http://www.g20.org/

History Established as a response both to the financial crises of the late 1990s and to a growing recognition that key emerging-market countries were not adequately included in the core of global economic discussion and governance, by *Group of Eight (G-8, #10745)*. Inaugural meeting took place 15-16 Dec 1999, Berlin (Germany), hosted by German and Canadian Finance Ministers. Superseded *Group of Twenty-Two (G-22, inactive)*. **Aims** Promote open and constructive discussion between industrial and emerging-market countries on key issues related to global *economic stability*; support growth and development across the globe by contributing to strengthening of the international *financial* architecture and providing opportunities for dialogue on national policies, international cooperation and international financial institutions. **Structure** No permanent Secretariat; activities and agenda led by the rotating Presidency. A troika, for continuity, is composed of the current, future and past Presidency nations. Informal *Forum of Finance Ministers and Central Bank Governors*, which meet at least annually; this meeting is preceded by deputies' meetings and extensive technical work. To ensure global economic fora and institutions work together, the Managing Director of the International Monetary Fund and the President of the World Bank, plus the chairs of the International Monetary and Financial Committee and Development Committee of the IMF and World Bank, also participate in G-20 meetings on an ex-officio basis. Chairmanship rotates between members and is selected from a different regional grouping of countries each year. **Staff** No permanent staff. **Activities** Organizes: meetings; workshops; study groups; working groups. *Global Partnership for Financial Inclusion (GPFI, #10534)* functions as main implementing organization for the G20 Financial Inclusion Action Plan. **Events** *Annual Summit of Heads of State and Government* Bali (Indonesia) 2022, *Sherpa Meeting* Florence (Italy) 2021, *Annual Summit of Heads of State and Government* Rome (Italy) 2021, *Health Ministers' Meeting* Rome (Italy) 2021, *Joint Finance and Health Ministers' Meeting* Rome (Italy) 2021.

Members Finance Ministers and Central Bank Governors of 19 countries:
Argentina, Australia, Brazil, Canada, China, France, Germany, India, Indonesia, Italy, Japan, Korea Rep, Mexico, Russia, Saudi Arabia, South Africa, Türkiye, UK, USA.

Also a member:
European Union (EU, #08967) (represented by the rotating Council presidency and the European Central Bank (ECB)).

IGO Relations Organizations whose Executive Directors or Chairpersons attend talks: *International Bank for Reconstruction and Development (IBRD, #12317)* (World Bank); *International Monetary and Financial Committee (IMFC, #14179)*; *International Monetary Fund (IMF, #14180)* and its Development Committee. Instrumental in setting up: *Financial Stability Board (FSB, #09770)*. **NGO Relations** *International Organization of Securities Commissions (IOSCO, #14470)* participates in working groups. [2021/XF5906/y/**F***]

- ♦ Group of Twenty Four (no recent information)
- ♦ **Group of Twenty-Four** Intergovernmental Group of Twenty-Four on International Monetary Affairs (#11495)
- ♦ Group of Twenty-Two (inactive)

♦ Group of the Unified European Left (UEL) 10794

Groupe pour la gauche unitaire européenne (GUE) – Gruppa Obedinennyh Evropejskih Levyh Sil (OEL)

SG Conseil de l'Europe, Bureau 5158/60, 67075 Strasbourg CEDEX, France. T. +33388413684. Fax +33388413766.

URL: http://www.gue-uel.org/

History within the framework of *Parliamentary Assembly of the Council of Europe (PACE, #18211)*. **Aims** Represent the broad spectrum of left views in the Parliamentary Assembly of the Council of Europe. **Structure** President, 3 Vice-Presidents and members; Secretariat. **Languages** English, French, German, Italian, Russian. **Staff** 0.80 FTE, paid. **Finance** Allocation to political groups from *Council of Europe (CE, #04881)* (Committee on the budget and the intergovernmental work programme). **Activities** Politics/policy/regulatory.

Members Parliamentarians (35) from 16 countries and territories:
Cyprus, Czechia, Denmark, Germany, Greece, Greenland, Iceland, Ireland, Moldova, Netherlands, Norway, Portugal, Russia, San Marino, Spain, Türkiye. [2017.03.13/XF1472/v/**F**]

♦ Grow Africa Partnership 10795

Exec Dir NEPAD Agency Headquarters, 230 15th Road, Randjespark, Midrand, Johannesburg, 1682, South Africa. T. +27112563534. E-mail: info@growafrica.com.

URL: http://www.growafrica.com/

History Partnership founded 2011, by *African Union (AU, #00488)*, *New Partnership for Africa's Development (NEPAD, #17091)* and *World Economic Forum (WEF, #21367)*. **Aims** Enable countries to realize the potential of the *agriculture* sector for economic growth and job creation, particularly among farmers, women and youth. **Structure** Steering Committee; Leadership Council, co-convened by *African Union (AU, #00488)* Commission and *World Economic Forum (WEF, #21367)*. Secretariat. **Finance** Supported by grants from: *United States Agency for International Development (USAID)*; *Swiss Agency for Development and Cooperation (SDC)*. **Activities** Networking/liaising; knowledge management/information dissemination; guidance/assistance/consulting. **Events** *Leadership for Agriculture Forum* Abidjan (Côte d'Ivoire) 2017.

Members Companies (over 200). Governments (12):
Benin, Burkina Faso, Côte d'Ivoire, Ethiopia, Ghana, Kenya, Malawi, Mozambique, Nigeria, Rwanda, Senegal, Tanzania UR.

IGO Relations Partners include: *African Union (AU, #00488)*; *New Partnership for Africa's Development (NEPAD, #17091)* – Planning and Coordinating Agency; *United States Agency for International Development (USAID)*; *World Food Programme (WFP, #21510)*. **NGO Relations** Partners include: *Alliance for a Green Revolution in Africa (AGRA, #00685)*; *Landesa – Rural Development Institute (Landesa)*; *World Economic Forum (WEF, #21367)*. [2017/XM6566/**F**]

- ♦ Grow Up Free from Poverty Coalition (internationally oriented national body)

♦ Growing Media Europe 10796

SG c/o COPA-COGECA, Rue de Trèves 61, 1040 Brussels, Belgium. T. +32483449917. E-mail: info@growing-media.eu.

URL: http://www.growing-media.eu/

History 1 Oct 2016. Set up when *European Peat and Growing Media Association (EPAGMA, inactive)* separated into 2 organizations, the other being *Energy Peat Europe (EPE, no recent information)*. Registration: Banque-Carrefour des Entreprises, No/ID: 0666.595.876, Start date: 23 Nov 2016, Belgium; EU Transparency Register, No/ID: 01873234294-62, Start date: 5 Oct 2010. **Aims** Promote optimum legislation for the manufacturing as well as the free and fair trade of growing media within Europe. **Structure** Secretariat. **NGO Relations** *International Peatland Society (IPS, #14538)*. [2022/XM5468/**D**]

♦ Growing Opportunities International (GO!) 10797

Exec Dir 291 Harcourt Str, Winnipeg MB R3J 3H4, Canada. T. +12048372778. E-mail: contact-gointernational@gmail.com.

URL: http://growingopportunitiesinternational.org/

History 2010. **Aims** Partner with motivated individuals in East Africa who have sustainable project ideas to positively impact their community. **Structure** Board. **NGO Relations** Member of: *Posner Center for International Development (Posner Center)*. [2015/XM4165/**F**]

♦ Growth Hormone Research Society (GRS) 10798

Office Dept of Endocrinology and Internal Medicine, Entrance G G94 level 4, Aarhus Univ Hosp, Palle Juul Jensens Bd 99, 8200 Aarhus, Denmark. E-mail: grs@clin.au.dk.

URL: http://www.ghresearchsociety.org/

History 5 Oct 1992, Madrid (Spain). Registration: Denmark. **Aims** Promote scientific exchange and research in the field of growth hormone and related substances. **Structure** General Assembly; Council; Executive Committee. **Finance** Sources: members' dues. **Events** *Joint Congress* Foz do Iguaçu (Brazil) 2020, *Joint Congress* Seattle, WA (USA) 2018, *Joint Congress* Tel Aviv (Israel) 2016, *Meeting* Manchester (UK) 2014, *Joint Congress / Meeting* Singapore (Singapore) 2014. **Publications** *Pituitary*. **Members** Active; associate; supporting. Individuals (about 400) in 30 countries. Membership countries not specified. **NGO Relations** Joint meetings with: *International Society for IGF Research (IGF Society, #15191)*. [2021.09.01/XD7848/**D**]

- ♦ **Growth Plus** Association internationale Europe's 500 (#02695)
- ♦ Growth Triangle / see Indonesia-Malaysia-Thailand Growth Triangle (#11167)
- ♦ Growth Triangle of Singapore, Malaysia's Jamore State and Indonesia's Riau Province / see Indonesia-Malaysia-Thailand Growth Triangle (#11167)
- ♦ **GRP** Global Resilience Partnership (#10577)
- ♦ **GRPP** Groupe de Recherche Petites Paysanneries (#10769)
- ♦ **GRSB** Global Roundtable for Sustainable Beef (#10583)
- ♦ **GRSG** Geological Remote Sensing Group (#10134)
- ♦ **GRS** Glaucoma Research Society (#10159)
- ♦ GRS – Global Resource Services (internationally oriented national body)
- ♦ **GRS** Growth Hormone Research Society (#10798)
- ♦ **GRSP** Global Road Safety Partnership (#10581)
- ♦ GRT – Global Round Table (unconfirmed)
- ♦ GRT – Gruppo per le Relazioni Transculturali (internationally oriented national body)
- ♦ **GRULAC** Groupe des pays d'Amérique latine et des Caraïbes (#10784)
- ♦ GRULA – Grupo de Embajadores de América Latina ante las Comunidades Europeas (inactive)
- ♦ An Grúpa Euro (#05689)
- ♦ Grupa Europejskiej Partii Ludowej – Chrzexcijanscy Demokraci (#10775)
- ♦ Grúpa Phairti an Phobail Eorpaigh – Na Daonlathaithe Criostai (#10775)
- ♦ Grupa Porozumienia Liberalów i Demokratów na rzecz Europy / see Renew Europe (#18840)
- ♦ Grupa Postepowego Sojuszu Socjalistów and Demokratów w Parlamencie Europejskim (#10786)
- ♦ Grupa Socjalistyczna w Parlamencie Europejskim / see Group of the Progressive Alliance of Socialists and Democrats in the European Parliament (#10786)
- ♦ Grup Ekdoton Horon Medon tis EOK / see Federation of European Publishers (#09536)
- ♦ Grup Llati i Mediterrani de Medicina de l'Esport (#16401)
- ♦ Grupo de los 77 (#10732)
- ♦ Grupo de Açao Financeira da América Latina (#10799)
- ♦ Grupo de Ação Financeira da América do Sul / see Grupo de Acción Financiera de Latinoamérica (#10799)
- ♦ Grupo de Acción Financiera del Caribe (#03505)

♦ Grupo de Acción Financiera de Latinoamérica (GAFILAT) 10799

Financial Action Task Force of Latin America – Grupo de Açao Financeira da América Latina

Sec Florida 939 – 10o A, C1005AAS Buenos Aires, Argentina. T. +541152529292. E-mail: contacto@gafilat.org.

URL: http://www.gafilat.org/

History 8 Dec 2000, Cartagena de Indias (Colombia), by *Financial Action Task Force (FATF, #09765)*, as *Financial Action Task Force of South America – Grupo de Acción Financiera de Sudamérica (GAFISUD) – Grupo de Ação Financeira da América do Sul*. Present name adopted during Plenary, 7-11 Jul 2014. **Aims** Develop and implement a comprehensive global strategy to combat *money laundering* and *terrorist* financing. **Structure** Plenary of Representatives; Council of Authorities; Executive Secretariat. **Languages** Spanish. **Staff** 9.00 FTE, paid. **Finance** Member States' contributions. Observers' contributions. **Activities** Monitoring/evaluation; networking/liaising; training/education. **Events** *Plenary Meeting* Buenos Aires (Argentina) 2009, *Plenary Meeting* Montevideo (Uruguay) 2009, *Plenary Meeting* Buenos Aires (Argentina) 2008, *Joint typologies meeting* Monte Carlo (Monaco) 2008, *Plenary Meeting* Santa María Huatulco (Mexico) 2008.

Members Governments of 17 countries:
Argentina, Bolivia, Brazil, Chile, Colombia, Costa Rica, Cuba, Dominican Rep, Ecuador, Guatemala, Honduras, Mexico, Nicaragua, Panama, Paraguay, Peru, Uruguay.

Observer governments (6):
Canada, France, Germany, Portugal, Spain, USA.

Observer organizations (14):

Grupo Acción Financiera
10799

alphabetic sequence excludes
For the complete listing, see Yearbook Online at

Alliance for Financial Inclusion (AFI, #00679); Asia/Pacific Group on Money Laundering (APG, #01921); Caribbean Financial Action Task Force (CFATF, #03505); Central American Bank for Economic Integration (CABEI, #03658); Counter-Terrorism Committee (CTC, #04928); European Commission (EC, #06633); Financial Action Task Force (FATF, #09765); Inter-American Committee Against Terrorism (#11412); Inter-American Development Bank (IDB, #11427); Inter-American Drug Abuse Control Commission (#11429) (of Organization of American States OAS); *International Bank for Reconstruction and Development (IBRD, #12317)* (World Bank); *International Criminal Police Organization – INTERPOL (ICPO-INTERPOL, #13110); International Monetary Fund (IMF, #14180); United Nations (UN, #20515).* [2019.12.11/XF6694/**F***]

♦ Grupo de Acción Financiera de Sudamérica / see Grupo de Acción Financiera de Latinoamérica (#10799)
♦ Grupo de Acústicos Latinoamericanos (inactive)
♦ Grupo da Aliança dos Democratas e Liberais pela Europa / see Renew Europe (#18840)
♦ Grupo de la Alianza Progresista de Socialistas and Demócratas en el Parlamento Europeo (#10786)
♦ Grupo de Australia (#03036)
♦ Grupo del Banco Mundial (#21218)
♦ Grupo de Cartagena (#03589)

♦ Grupo de los Cinco 10800

Group of Five

Address not obtained.

History by 5 Portuguese ex-colonies. **Aims** Promote *cooperation* among former colonies of Portugal in Africa. **Members** Representatives of 5 countries:
Angola, Cape Verde, Guinea-Bissau, Mozambique, Sao Tomé-Principe. [2010/XF2045/**F***]

♦ Grupo de los Cincuenta (internationally oriented national body)
♦ Grupo dos Cinqüenta (internationally oriented national body)
♦ **Grupo CLAHT** Grupo Cooperativo Latinoamericano de Hemostasia y Trombosis (#10802)
♦ Grupo Compostela de Universidades (#04419)
♦ Grupo de Comunicaciones de las Naciones Unidas (inactive)
♦ Grupo Consultativo de Ayuda a la Población Mas Pobre (#04768)
♦ Grupo Consultivo sobre Investigación Agricola Internacional / see CGIAR System Organization (#03843)
♦ Grupo de Cooperação Técnica Horizontal da América Latina e Caribe sobre o HIV/Aids (#10945)
♦ Grupo de Cooperación Técnica América Latina y Caribe en VIH/SIDA (#10945)

♦ Grupo Cooperativo Iberoamericano de Medicina Transfusional (GCIAMT) 10801

Pres c/o Edif Colegios Prof, Segundo Nivel, 0 calle 15-46, zona 15, Col El Maestro, Guatemala, Guatemala. E-mail: jjhuamans@gmail.com – boletingciamt@gmail.com.
URL: http://gciamt.org/

Structure Assembly; Board of Directors. **Events** *Congress* Belo Horizonte (Brazil) 2015, *Congress* Antigua (Guatemala) 2013.
Members Full in 9 countries:
Argentina, Bolivia, Colombia, Guatemala, Mexico, Panama, Peru, USA, Venezuela.
Included in the above, 1 organization listed in this Yearbook:
Asociación Latinoamericana de Aféresis y Terapias celulares (ALAyTeC, #02178).
IGO Relations *Pan American Health Organization (PAHO, #18108).* [2017/XJ8864/**D**]

♦ Grupo Cooperativo Latinoamericano de Hemostasia y Trombosis (Grupo CLAHT) 10802

Latin American Cooperative Group on Haemostasis and Thrombosis

SG address not obtained.
URL: http://www.grupoclaht.com.ar/

History Feb 1973, Havana (Cuba), under the auspices of the Inter-American Division of *International Society of Hematology (ISH, #15159).* **Aims** Increase research in haemostasis and thrombosis in Latin America. **Structure** Officers: President; 2 Vice-Presidents; Treasurer; Secretary; Scientific Secretary. Advisory Committee. **Languages** Portuguese, Spanish. **Staff** 4.50 FTE, voluntary. **Finance** Members' dues. **Activities** Organizes congresses, symposia and protocols of investigation and treatment in haemostasis and thrombosis in Latin America. **Events** *Congress* Sao Paulo (Brazil) 2015, *Congress* Cancún (Mexico) 2013, *Annual Symposium* Lima (Peru) 2010, *Biennial congress / Congress* Buenos Aires (Argentina) 2008, *Annual Symposium* Asunción (Paraguay) 2006.
Members in 15 countries:
Argentina, Bolivia, Brazil, Chile, Colombia, Costa Rica, Cuba, Dominican Rep, Ecuador, Mexico, Panama, Paraguay, Peru, Uruguay, Venezuela.
NGO Relations Formal contacts with: *Danubian League Against Thrombosis and Haemorrhagic Disorders (#05007); International Society on Thrombosis and Haemostasis (ISTH, #15511); European and Mediterranean League Against Thrombotic Diseases (EMLTD, #07771);* national organizations. [2014/XD8443/**D**]

♦ Grupo de los Cuatro (#10780)

♦ Grupo de Diarios América (GDA) 10803

Network of Latin American Newspapers

Main Office 777 Brickell Ave, Ste 500, Miami FL 33131, USA. T. +13055770094. Fax +13055770096. E-mail: consultas@gda.com.
URL: http://www.gda.com/

History 1991. Founded by 11 prominent Latin American newspapers. **Aims** Exchange of information, news, journalistic work and newspapers. among member newspapers. **Structure** Executive Board, comprising President, Vice-President and 9 members. **Events** *Seminar on analyzing journalism and governability* Miami, FL (USA) 2004.
Members Newspapers in 11 countries:
Argentina, Brazil, Chile, Colombia, Costa Rica, Ecuador, Mexico, Peru, Puerto Rico, Uruguay, Venezuela. [2020/XF2894/**F**]

♦ Grupo de los Diez (inactive)
♦ Grupo de Editores de Libros de la CEE / see Federation of European Publishers (#09536)
♦ Grupo de Editores de Livros da CEE / see Federation of European Publishers (#09536)
♦ Grupo de Embajadores de América Latina ante las Comunidades Europeas (inactive)

♦ Grupo de Enlace, Investigación y Soporte de Enfermedades Raras de Latino America (Fundación GEISER) 10804

Sec Nicolas Avellaneda 595, Mendoza, Argentina. T. +542614251523. E-mail: contacto@fundaciongeiser.org.
URL: http://fundaciongeiser.org/

History 2002. **Aims** Study the effect of rare diseases on the individual's quality of life. **Structure** Governing Body, including President, Vice-President, Secretary and Treasurer. **Events** *Latin American and Caribbean symposium* Buenos Aires (Argentina) 2010.
Members Full in 22 countries:
Argentina, Bolivia, Brazil, Chile, Colombia, Costa Rica, Cuba, Dominican Rep, Ecuador, El Salvador, Guatemala, Guyana, Haiti, Honduras, Jamaica, Mexico, Nicaragua, Panama, Peru, Suriname, Uruguay, Venezuela. [2011/XJ1294/t/**F**]

♦ Grupo de Estudio Internacional de Etnomatematica (#15618)
♦ Grupo de Estudios sobre la Mujer en España y las Américas (pre-1800) (internationally oriented national body)
♦ Grupo Ethnobotanico Latinoamericano (no recent information)
♦ Grupo Europeo de Cooperação Económica e Desenvolvimento (internationally oriented national body)
♦ Grupo Europeo de Institutos de Navegación (#07424)
♦ Grupo Europeo de Investigação sobre as Normatividades (#10741)
♦ Grupo Europeo de Investigación sobre Normatividades (#10741)
♦ Grupo Europeo de Pastoral Obrera (#10740)
♦ Grupo Europeo de Trabajo sobre Investigación en Drogas (#09111)
♦ Grupo Europeo de Tratamientos sobre SIDA / see European AIDS Treatment Group (#05850)
♦ Grupo Europeu das Caixas Económicas / see European Savings and Retail Banking Group (#08426)
♦ Grupo Europeu sobre o Trabalho no Domicilio (#07497)
♦ Grupo de Expertos de las Naciones Unidas en Nombres Geograficos (#20569)

♦ Grupo Iberamericano de Editores (GIE) 10805

Inter-American Publishers Group

Contact Rua Cristiano Viana 91, Pinheiros, Sao Paulo SP, 05411-000, Brazil. T. +551130691300. Fax +551130691303. E-mail: jie@gieditores.org – presidente.gie@gmail.com.
URL: http://gieditores.org/

History 1981. **Aims** Promote and assist free circulation of ideas and books; promote relations within the Latin American book industry. **Structure** Officers: President; 4 Vice Presidents; Secretary; Treasurer. **Finance** Members' dues. **Activities** Organizes: 4 annual meetings coinciding with Latin American book fairs; SILAR Program (Salon Interamericano del Libro Anual Rotativo); Congreso Iberoamericano de Editores (every 2 years). **Events** *Congreso Iberoamericano de Editores* Santa Cruz (Bolivia) 2016, *Congreso Iberoamericano de Editores* San Salvador (El Salvador) 2014, *Congreso Iberoamericano de Editores* Guadalajara (Mexico) 2012, *Congreso Iberoamericano de Editores* Madrid (Spain) 2006, *SILAR* Bogota (Colombia) 2004.
Members Associated chambers (26) in 22 countries:
Argentina, Bolivia, Brazil, Canada, Chile, Colombia, Costa Rica, Dominican Rep, Ecuador, El Salvador, Guatemala, Mexico, Nicaragua, Panama, Paraguay, Peru, Portugal, Puerto Rico, Spain, Uruguay, USA, Venezuela.
Adhering chambers (3) in 3 countries:
Cuba, El Salvador, Honduras.
IGO Relations Agreement with: *Regional Centre for the Promotion of Books in Latin America and the Caribbean (#18758); UNESCO (#20322)* (Publishing Department). **NGO Relations** Cooperates with (2): *International Association of Scientific, Technical and Medical Publishers (STM, #12154); International Federation of Reproduction Rights Organizations (IFRRO, #13527).* Affiliated with (1): *International Publishers Association (IPA, #14675).* [2020/XF1570/**F**]

♦ Grupo Iberoamericano de Implantes Cocleares y Ciencias Afines (unconfirmed)

♦ Grupo Iberoamericano de Polinomios Ortogonales y Aplicaciones (GIBPOA) 10806

Iberoamerican Group of Orthogonal Polynomials and Applications

Address not obtained.

History Founded Jun 2011, Bogota (Colombia), at first EIBPOA Workshop. Also known as *Grupo IBPOA.* **Aims** Promote the study and research of orthogonal polynomials in Latin America; establish collaboration networks between researchers. **Activities** Events/meetings; research/documentation. **Events** *Workshop* Madrid (Spain) 2018.
Members Full in 7 countries:
Argentina, Brazil, Colombia, Mexico, Portugal, Spain, Venezuela. [2018/XM7689/c/**E**]

♦ Grupo Iberoamericano de Sociedades Cientificas de Protección Radiológica (no recent information)
♦ Grupo IBPOA / see Grupo Iberoamericano de Polinomios Ortogonales y Aplicaciones (#10806)
♦ Grupo Industrial Europeo de Estudio Espacial / see Association of European Space Industry (#02544)
♦ Grupo Interamericano de Coordinación en Sanidad Vegetal (no recent information)
♦ Grupo InterGovernamental de Acção contra o Branqueamento de Dinheiro em Africa Ocidental (#11471)
♦ Grupo Intergubernamenal sobre Fibras Duras (#11489)
♦ Grupo Intergubernamental sobre Arroz (#11493)
♦ Grupo Intergubernamental sobre la Carne y los Productos Lacteos (#11491)
♦ Grupo Intergubernamental sobre Cereales (#11488)
♦ Grupo Intergubernamental de la FAO sobre Frutos Citricos (#11487)
♦ Grupo Intergubernamental sobre Semillas Oleaginosas, Aceites y Grasas (#11492)
♦ Grupo Intergubernamental sobre el Té (#11494)
♦ Grupo Intergubernamental de Trabajo de Expertos en Normas Internacionales de Contabilidad y Presentación de Informes (#11503)
♦ Grupo Internacional de Estudio del Depistaje y de la Prevención del Cancer (inactive)
♦ Grupo Internacional de Estudio sobre el Plomo y el Zinc (#14012)

♦ Grupo Internacional de Investigación Sobre Actinomicetos Patógenos (GIIAP) 10807

International Group for Research on Pathogenic Actinomycetes

Pres Univ Claude Bernard Lyon 1, 8 av Rockefeller, 69373 Lyon CEDEX, France.
Office Fac de Farmacia y Bioanalisis, Univ de los Andes, AP 164, Mérida 5101 ME, Venezuela. T. +582742403110-11.
URL: http://www.giiap.com/

History 1992, Mexico, following activities initiated in 1990. **Aims** Promote collaboration among researchers interested in pathogenic actinomycetes. **Structure** Executive President. Consultative Board, comprising former Presidents. **Languages** English, French, Spanish. **Staff** Voluntary. **Finance** No budget. **Activities** Organizes student exchanges, courses, conferences and seminars. Makes 'Cabeza Maya' award for extraordinary achievements in the field. **Events** *Conference* Toluca (Mexico) 2013, *International conference on the biology of nocardiae / Conference* Monterrey (Mexico) 2007, *International conference on the biology of nocardiae / Conference* Lyon (France) 2005, *International conference on the biology of nocardiae* Mérida (Venezuela) 2003, *International conference on the biology of nocardiae / Conference* Davis, CA (USA) 2000. **Publications** *Actinomicetoma; Manual de Diagnostico de Actinomicetos Patogenos.*
Members Individuals in 11 countries:
Brazil, France, Germany, Mexico, Portugal, Puerto Rico, Spain, Switzerland, UK, USA, Venezuela.
NGO Relations Close collaboration with: *Andes University (ULA); Latin American Council for Biomedical Research (CLABE, no recent information);* university departments. [2014.06.01/XD7589/v/**F**]

♦ Grupo Internacional del Trabajo sobre Asuntos Indigenos (#15907)
♦ Grupo Internacional de Trabajo para Instalaciones Deportivas y Recreativas / see Internationale Vereinigung Sport- und Freizeiteinrichtungen (#13319)
♦ Grupo de Investigación por la Paz – Gernika Gogoratuz / see Gernika Gogoratuz – Peace Research Center
♦ Grupo de Investigación para la Paz en la Universidad de Constanza (internationally oriented national body)
♦ Grupo Juridico Internacional de Derechos Humanos / see Global Rights
♦ Grupo Latinoamericano por la Administración Pública (#16337)
♦ Grupo Latinoamericano de Angeografia Ocular, Laser y Cirurgia Vitreo-retiniana / see Pan-American Retina and Vitreous Society (#18126)
♦ Grupo Latinoamericano de Epidemiologia de la Diabetes (unconfirmed)
♦ Grupo Latino Americano de Estudio de Lupus (unconfirmed)
♦ Grupo Latinoamericano de Hemaféresis / see Asociación Latinoamericana de Aféresis y Terapias celulares (#02178)
♦ Grupo Latinoamericano de Instituciones del Cemento y del Concreto / see Federación Interamericana del Cemento (#09330)
♦ Grupo Latino-americano pela Administração Pública (#16337)
♦ Grupo Latino y Mediterraneo de Medicina del Deporte (#16401)
♦ Grupo de Matematicos de Expresión Latina (inactive)
♦ Grupo Mercado Comum do MERCOSUL (see: #19868)
♦ Grupo Mercado Común del MERCOSUR (see: #19868)
♦ Grupo Mixto de Expertos sobre los Aspectos Cientificos de la Contaminación de las Aguas del Mar / see Joint Group of Experts on the Scientific Aspects of Marine Environmental Protection (#16131)
♦ Grupo Mixto de Expertos sobre los Aspectos Cientificos de la Protección del Medio Marino (#16131)

- ♦ Grupo Mixto de Expertos OMI/FAO/UNESCO-COI/OMM/OMS/OIEA/Naciones Unidas/PNUMA sobre los Aspectos Cientificos de la Protección del Medio Marino / see Joint Group of Experts on the Scientific Aspects of Marine Environmental Protection (#16131)
- ♦ Grupo Mixto de Trabajo COI-OMM-CPPS sobre las Investigaciones relativas a El Niño / see Programa para el Estudio Regional del Fenómeno El Niño en el Pacifico Sudeste (#18523)
- ♦ Grupo Mundial del Comercio del Vino (#21939)
- ♦ Grupo Mundial de Parlamentarios para el Habitat (#10525)
- ♦ Grupo Mundial de Trabajo sobre las Rapaces (#21945)
- ♦ Grupo de ONGs para la Convención sobre los Derechos del Niño / see Child Rights Connect (#03884)
- ♦ Grupo de Operaciones Especiales en Rescate (internationally oriented national body)
- ♦ Grupo de Operadores de Redes da América Latina e Caribe (unconfirmed)
- ♦ Grupo de Organismos de Cuenca Europeos para la Implementación de la Directiva Marco sobre el Agua (#10771)
- ♦ Grupo de Paises de América Latina y el Caribe (#10784)
- ♦ Grupo de Paises Latinoamericanos e do Caribe Exportadores de Açucar (inactive)
- ♦ Grupo de Paises Latinoamericanos y del Caribe Exportadores de Azúcar (inactive)
- ♦ Grupo Pan-Americano de Estudo em Imunodeficiências Primarias (internationally oriented national body)
- ♦ Grupo Panamericano de Inmunodeficiencias (internationally oriented national body)
- ♦ Grupo Parlamentare do Partido Socialista Europeu / see Group of the Progressive Alliance of Socialists and Democrats in the European Parliament (#10786)
- ♦ Grupo Parlamentario Demócrata Cristiano /del Consejo de Europa/ / see Group of the European People's Party (#10774)
- ♦ Grupo Parlamentario del Partido de los Socialistas Europeos / see Group of the Progressive Alliance of Socialists and Democrats in the European Parliament (#10786)
- ♦ Grupo del Partido Popular Europeo en el Comite de las Regiones (#10776)
- ♦ Grupo del Partido Popular Europeo – Demócrata-Cristianos (#10775)
- ♦ Grupo do Partido Popular Europeu – Democratas-Cristãos (#10775)
- ♦ Grupo do Partido Popular Europeu no Comité das Regiões (#10776)
- ♦ **Grupo La Rabida** Grupo de Universidades Iberoamericanas La Rabida (#10808)
- ♦ Grupo de Rio (inactive)
- ♦ Grupos Africa da Suécia (internationally oriented national body)
- ♦ Grupo de San José (no recent information)
- ♦ Grupo Socialista no Parlamento Europeu / see Group of the Progressive Alliance of Socialists and Democrats in the European Parliament (#10786)
- ♦ Grupo Socialista en el Parlamento Europeo / see Group of the Progressive Alliance of Socialists and Democrats in the European Parliament (#10786)
- ♦ Grupo Sudamericano de la Aterosclerosis (inactive)
- ♦ Grupo de Trabajo sobre Criterios e Indicadores para la Conservación y el Manejo Sustentable de los Bosques Templados y Boreales (#21058)
- ♦ Grupo de Trabajo Indigena Internacional frente al VIH y SIDA (unconfirmed)
- ♦ Grupo de Trabajo Internacionales sobre la Mujer y el Deporte (#15912)
- ♦ Grupo de Trabajo para los Pueblos Indigenas / see Netherlands Centre for Indigenous Peoples
- ♦ Grupo de Trabalho Amazônico (internationally oriented national body)
- ♦ Grupo de los Tres (#10791)
- ♦ Grupo de los Tres ABM (#10792)
- ♦ Grupo Trevi (inactive)

♦ Grupo de Universidades Iberoamericanas La Rabida (Grupo La Rabida) 10808

Contact Paraje La Rabida s/n, La Rabida, 21819 Palos de la Frontera, Spain. T. +34959350452. E-mail: secretaria.general@grupolarabida.org.
URL: http://grupolarabida.org/

History 1995. Current statutes adopted May 2010. **Aims** Contribute to training of *university* professors, scientists and professionals at *postgraduate* and *doctorate* level. **Structure** General Assembly; Executive Committee. **Activities** Training/education.
Members Universities in 16 countries:
Argentina, Bolivia, Brazil, Chile, Colombia, Costa Rica, Cuba, Dominican Rep, Ecuador, El Salvador, Mexico, Nicaragua, Panama, Peru, Puerto Rico, Spain. [2017/XM6264/**D**]

- ♦ Grupo dos Verdes – Aliança Livre Europeia (#10781)
- ♦ Grupo de los Verdes – Alianza Libre Europea (#10781)
- ♦ Grupo dos Verdes no Parlamento Europeu / see Group of the Greens – European Free Alliance (#10781)
- ♦ Grupo de los Verdes en el Parlamento Europeo / see Group of the Greens – European Free Alliance (#10781)
- ♦ Gruppa Obedinennyh Evropejskih Levyh Sil (#10794)
- ♦ Gruppe der Buchverleger in der EWG / see Federation of European Publishers (#09536)
- ♦ Gruppe der Europäischen Gasforschung (#07380)
- ♦ Gruppe von Jubilierten und Pensionären von den Europäischen Sparkassen / see Group of European Retired Staff and Pensioners from Savings Banks, Banks and Related Institutions (#10777)
- ♦ Gruppe für Luftfahrt-Forschung und Technologie in Europa (#10733)
- ♦ Gruppen Alliancen af Liberale og Demokrater for Europa / see Renew Europe (#18840)
- ♦ Gruppen Alliansen Liberaler och Demokrater för Europa / see Renew Europe (#18840)
- ♦ Gruppen de Gröna i Europaparlamentet / see Group of the Greens – European Free Alliance (#10781)
- ♦ Gruppen de Gröna – Europeiska Fria Alliansen (#10781)
- ♦ Gruppen de Gronne – Europaeiske Fri Alliance (#10781)
- ♦ Gruppen de Grønne i Europa-Parlamentet / see Group of the Greens – European Free Alliance (#10781)
- ♦ Gruppo Abele (internationally oriented national body)
- ♦ Gruppo dell'Alleanza dei Democratici e dei Liberali per l'Europa / see Renew Europe (#18840)
- ♦ Gruppo dell'Alleanza Progressista di Socialisti and Democratici al Parlamento Europeo (#10786)
- ♦ Gruppo delle Associazioni del Mugnai dei Paesi della UE / see European Flour Millers' Association (#07272)
- ♦ Gruppo degli Editori di Libri delle CEE / see Federation of European Publishers (#09536)
- ♦ Gruppo Europeo delle Casse di Risparmio / see European Savings and Retail Banking Group (#08426)
- ♦ Gruppo Europeo di Pastorale del Lavoro (#10740)
- ♦ Gruppo Europeo dei Pensionati delle Casse di Risparmio, Banche ed Enti Affini (#10777)
- ♦ Gruppo Europeo di Ricerche sulle Normatività (#10741)
- ♦ Gruppo Farmaceutico della Comunità Europea / see Pharmaceutical Group of the European Union (#18352)
- ♦ Gruppo Farmaceutico dell'Unione Europea (#18352)
- ♦ Gruppo Internazionale dell'Industria Farmaceutica dei Paesi della CEE (inactive)
- ♦ Gruppo Latino e Mediterraneo di Medicina Sportiva (#16401)
- ♦ Gruppo di Lavoro Europeo per la Ricerca Psicosomatica sul Cancro (inactive)
- ♦ Gruppo di Nutrizionisti Europea / see Accademia Europea di Scienza della Nutrizione (#00045)
- ♦ Gruppo Parlamentare del Partido del Socialismo Europeo / see Group of the Progressive Alliance of Socialists and Democrats in the European Parliament (#10786)
- ♦ Gruppo del Partito Popolare Europeo – Democratici Cristiano (#10775)
- ♦ Gruppo dei Pensionati delle Casse di Risparmio Europee / see Group of European Retired Staff and Pensioners from Savings Banks, Banks and Related Institutions (#10777)
- ♦ Gruppo per le Relazioni Transculturali (internationally oriented national body)
- ♦ Gruppo di Ricerca sulla Criminalità Transnazionale / see Joint Research Centre on Transnational Crime
- ♦ Gruppo Socialista Parlamento Europeo / see Group of the Progressive Alliance of Socialists and Democrats in the European Parliament (#10786)
- ♦ Gruppo Socialista al Parlamento Europeo / see Group of the Progressive Alliance of Socialists and Democrats in the European Parliament (#10786)
- ♦ Gruppo Stambecco Europa (#00744)
- ♦ Gruppo di Studio Internazionale di Etnomatematica (#15618)
- ♦ Gruppo Verde – Alleanza Libera Europea (#10781)
- ♦ Gruppo i Verdi al Parlamento Europeo / see Group of the Greens – European Free Alliance (#10781)
- ♦ Gruppo di Volontariato Civile (internationally oriented national body)
- ♦ Grupp ta'l- Alleanza tal-Liberali u d-Demokratici ghall-Ewropa / see Renew Europe (#18840)
- ♦ Grupp tal-Euro (#05689)
- ♦ Grupp tal-Partit Popolari Ewropew – Dokristjani (#10775)
- ♦ Grupul Latin Mediteranean de Medicina Sportiva (#16401)
- ♦ Grupul Partidului Popular European – Crestin Democrat (#10775)

♦ GS1 10809

Contact Av Louise 326, 1050 Brussels, Belgium. T. +3227887800. E-mail: helpdesk@gs1.org.
URL: http://www.gs1.org/

History 1977, Brussels (Belgium). Founded on the initiative of manufacturers and retailers from 12 European countries. From 1978, open to organizations from other continents. Former names and other names: *European Article Numbering Association (EAN)* – former (1977 to 1978); *Association européenne de numérotation des articles* – former (1977 to 1978); *International Article Numbering Association* – former (1978 to 1992); *Association internationale de numérotation des articles* – former (1978 to 1992); *EAN International* – former (1992 to 2005). Registration: No/ID: 0419.640.608, Start date: 30 Jul 1979, Belgium; EU Transparency Register, No/ID: 073756422825-22, Start date: 27 Jul 2016. **Aims** Establish a global *multi-industry* system to identify, capture and share information of products, services and locations based on internationally accepted and business-led GS1 standards; facilitate collaboration among trading partners, organizations and technology providers in order to solve *business* challenges that leverage standards and to ensure visibility along the entire supply chain. **Structure** General Assembly; Management Board; Global Office in Brussels (Belgium). **Languages** English. **Staff** 74.00 FTE, paid. **Finance** Sources: members' dues. **Activities** Standards/guidelines. **Events** *Healthcare Online Summit* Brussels (Belgium) 2021, *Healthcare Online Summit* Brussels (Belgium) 2021, *Annual General Assembly* Lisbon (Portugal) 2021, *weCONNECT Workshop on Helping Businesses Sell Efficiently and Effectively on e-Commerce* Singapore (Singapore) 2021, *weCONNECT Workshop on Helping Businesses Sell Efficiently and Effectively on e-Commerce* Singapore (Singapore) 2021. **Publications** Annual Report; brochures.
Members National organizations in 116 countries and territories:
Albania, Algeria, Argentina, Armenia, Australia, Austria, Azerbaijan, Bahrain, Belarus, Belgium, Bolivia, Bosnia-Herzegovina, Brazil, Bulgaria, Cambodia, Cameroon, Canada, Chile, China, Colombia, Costa Rica, Côte d'Ivoire, Croatia, Cuba, Cyprus, Czechia, Denmark, Dominican Rep, Ecuador, Egypt, El Salvador, Estonia, Finland, France, Georgia, Germany, Ghana, Greece, Guatemala, Honduras, Hong Kong, Hungary, Iceland, India, Indonesia, Iran Islamic Rep, Ireland, Israel, Italy, Japan, Jordan, Kazakhstan, Kenya, Korea DPR, Korea Rep, Kuwait, Kyrgyzstan, Latvia, Lebanon, Libya, Lithuania, Luxembourg, Macau, Malaysia, Malta, Mauritius, Mexico, Moldova, Mongolia, Montenegro, Morocco, Myanmar, Namibia, Netherlands, New Zealand, Nicaragua, Nigeria, Norway, Oman, Pakistan, Panama, Paraguay, Peru, Philippines, Poland, Portugal, Qatar, Romania, Russia, Saudi Arabia, Senegal, Serbia, Singapore, Slovakia, Slovenia, South Africa, Spain, Sri Lanka, Sweden, Switzerland, Syrian AR, Taiwan, Tajikistan, Tanzania UR, Thailand, Tunisia, Türkiye, Turkmenistan, UK, Ukraine, United Arab Emirates, Uruguay, USA, Uzbekistan, Venezuela, Vietnam.

Consultative Status Consultative status granted from: *ECOSOC (#05331)* (Special). **IGO Relations** Cooperates with (6): *International Telecommunication Union (ITU, #15673); Steering Committee on Trade Capacity and Standards (CTCS, #19979); United Nations Centre for Trade Facilitation and Electronic Business (UN/CEFACT, #20527); United Nations Economic Commission for Europe (UNECE, #20555)* (through its 'Working Party on Facilitation of International Trade Procedures'); *Universal Postal Union (UPU, #20682); World Customs Organization (WCO, #21350).* **NGO Relations** Observer status with (1): *Alliance for Safe Online Pharmacy – EU (ASOP EU, #00720).* Member of (1): *Alliance for Internet of Things Innovation (AIOTI, #00697).* Cooperates with (9): *Business and Industry Advisory Committee to the OECD (BIAC, #03385); Comité européen de normalisation (CEN, #04162); European Internet Forum (EIF, #07591); European Telecommunications Standards Institute (ETSI, #08897); Federation of European and International Associations Established in Belgium (FAIB, #09508); GS1 in Europe (#10810); GSM Association (GSMA, #10813);* Health Level 7 (HL7); *International Organization for Standardization (ISO, #14473).* [2022.06.17/XC8492/y/**C**]

♦ GS1 in Europe 10810

Coordinator Rue Royale 76, mailbox 1, 1000 Brussels, Belgium. T. +33678267501.
URL: http://www.gs1.eu/

Structure Regional Executive Committee; Working Groups.
Members Organizations (47) in 47 countries:
Albania, Armenia, Austria, Azerbaijan, Belarus, Belgium, Bosnia-Herzegovina, Bulgaria, Croatia, Cyprus, Czechia, Denmark, Estonia, Finland, France, Georgia, Germany, Greece, Hungary, Iceland, Ireland, Israel, Italy, Kazakhstan, Kyrgyzstan, Latvia, Lithuania, Moldova, Montenegro, Netherlands, North Macedonia, Norway, Poland, Portugal, Romania, Russia, Serbia, Slovakia, Slovenia, Spain, Sweden, Switzerland, Türkiye, Turkmenistan, UK, Ukraine, Uzbekistan.
NGO Relations Liaison Organization of: *Comité européen de normalisation (CEN, #04162).*
[2016/XM4810/**D**]

- ♦ GSA / see Geological Society of Africa (#10135)
- ♦ **GSAC** IOM Global Staff Association Committee (#16008)
- ♦ GSA / see European Union Agency for the Space Programme (#08974)
- ♦ **GSAf** Geological Society of Africa (#10135)
- ♦ GSA – Genetics Society of AustralAsia (internationally oriented national body)
- ♦ GSA – Geological Society of America (internationally oriented national body)
- ♦ **GSA** Global mobile Suppliers Association (#10476)
- ♦ **GSA** Global Semiconductor Alliance (#10589)
- ♦ **GSA** Global Sepsis Alliance (#10590)
- ♦ **GSA** Global Shea Alliance (#10593)
- ♦ **GSA** Global Shippers' Alliance (#10595)
- ♦ GSA – Global Sourcing Association (internationally oriented national body)
- ♦ **GSA** Global Sports Alliance (#10613)
- ♦ GSA – Global Studies Association (internationally oriented national body)
- ♦ GSA – Green Schools Alliance (internationally oriented national body)
- ♦ GSA – Green Sports Alliance (internationally oriented national body)
- ♦ GSAS – Global School for Advanced Studies (internationally oriented national body)
- ♦ **GSA** UNICEF Global Staff Association (#20330)
- ♦ GSA – Where Leaders Meet / see Global Semiconductor Alliance (#10589)
- ♦ **GSBI** Global Soil Biodiversity Initiative (#10607)
- ♦ **GSCA** Giant Screen Cinema Association (#10148)
- ♦ **GSCDN** Global Sickle Cell Disease Network (#10598)
- ♦ **GSCF** Global Self-Care Federation (#10588)
- ♦ **GSC** Global Shelter Cluster (#10594)
- ♦ **GSC** Global Silicones Council (#10600)
- ♦ **GSC** Global Solar Council (#10609)
- ♦ GSC – Global Sourcing Council (unconfirmed)
- ♦ GSC – Global Studies Center (internationally oriented national body)
- ♦ GSD – Foundation for Global Sports Development (internationally oriented national body)
- ♦ GSD – Geneva School of Diplomacy and International Relations (internationally oriented national body)
- ♦ GSDI Association – Global Spatial Data Infrastructure Association (inactive)
- ♦ GSDRC – Governance and Social Development Resource Centre (internationally oriented national body)
- ♦ GSE-AIESG / see Alpine Ibex European Specialist Group (#00744)
- ♦ **GSE-AIESG** Alpine Ibex European Specialist Group (#00744)
- ♦ G-SEC / see Keio University Global Research Institute

- ♦ GSE-European Alpine Ibex Specialist Group / see Alpine Ibex European Specialist Group (#00744)
- ♦ **GSEF** Global Social Economy Forum (#10603)
- ♦ GSE – Gas Storage Europe / see Gas Infrastructure Europe (#10073)
- ♦ GSE – Global Student Embassy (internationally oriented national body)
- ♦ **GSE** Gruppo Stambecco Europa (#00744)
- ♦ **GSE** Guide Share Europe (#10818)
- ♦ GSEIS / see Graduate Institute of Political and International Studies
- ♦ **GSEP** Global Superior Energy Performance Partnership (#10615)
- ♦ GSETAU – Groupe Scientifique Européen Tuber aestivum/uncinatum (meeting series)
- ♦ **GSF** Global Shippers' Forum (#10596)
- ♦ GSF – Global Smile Foundation (internationally oriented national body)
- ♦ **GSF** Global Speakers Federation (#10612)
- ♦ **GSF** Global Student Forum (#10614)
- ♦ GSF – Global Survivors Fund (unconfirmed)
- ♦ **GS** Galileo Services (#10064)
- ♦ **GSGF** Global Smart Grid Federation (#10601)
- ♦ GSH – Güteschutzgemeinschaft Hartschaum (internationally oriented national body)
- ♦ **GSIA** Global Security Industry Alliance (#10587)
- ♦ GSIC – Global Scientific Information and Computing Center (internationally oriented national body)
- ♦ GSIC – Grey Sisters of the Immaculate Conception (religious order)
- ♦ **GSIF** Good Shepherd International Foundation (#10680)
- ♦ GSI – Geometric Science of Information (meeting series)
- ♦ **GSI** Global Salmon Initiative (#10585)
- ♦ GSI – Global Security Institute (internationally oriented national body)
- ♦ GSI – Global South Initiative (internationally oriented national body)
- ♦ GSIS / see Josef Korbel School of International Studies
- ♦ GSIS – Graduate School of International Studies, Seoul (internationally oriented national body)
- ♦ GSIS – Institute for a Global Sustainable Information Society (The) (internationally oriented national body)
- ♦ **GSI-SLV** Gesellschaft für Schweisstechnik International (#10144)
- ♦ GSISS – Graduate School of Islamic and Social Sciences (internationally oriented national body)
- ♦ GSK Initiative – Global Support for Kids Initiative (internationally oriented national body)

♦ GSMA Europe 10811

Vice-Pres Europe Park View, 4th Floor, Ch d'Etterbeek 180, 1040 Brussels, Belgium. T. +3227920550. E-mail: gsmaeurope@gsma.com.
Head Office GSM Association, The Walbrook Bldg, Walbrook 25, London, EC4N 8AF, UK. T. +442073560600.
URL: http://www.gsma.com/gsmaeurope/

History as a Regional Interest Group of *GSM Association (GSMA, #10813)*. **Aims** Represent the interests of mobile operators, including hand set and device makers, software companies, equipment providers and internet companies, as well as organizations in adjacent industry sectors. **Activities** Networking/liaising; politics/policy/regulatory; events/meetings. **Publications** Position papers. **NGO Relations** Member of: *European Policy Centre (EPC, #08240).* [2017/XJ2101/**E**]

- ♦ **GSMA** GSM Association (#10813)

♦ GSM Arab World 10812

Chairman address not obtained. E-mail: gsmaw@gsm.org.
URL: http://www.gsmworld.com/gsmaw/index.shtml

History As a Regional Interest Group of *GSM Association (GSMA, #10813)*. **Aims** Represent mobile operators in the Arab region.
Members Mobile operators in 20 countries and territories:
Albania, Bahrain, Egypt, Iraq, Jordan, Kuwait, Lebanon, Libya, Mauritania, Morocco, Oman, Palestine, Qatar, Saudi Arabia, Somalia, Sudan, Syrian AR, Tunisia, United Arab Emirates, Yemen. [2010/XJ2104/**E**]

♦ GSM Association (GSMA) 10813

Dir-Gen Walbrook Building, 25 Wallbrook, London, EC4N 8AF, UK. T. +442073560600. Fax +4420773560601. E-mail: info@gsma.com.
URL: http://www.gsma.com/

History 1987. Former names and other names: *GSM Memorandum of Understanding Association (GSM MoU Association)* – former. **Aims** Represent the interests of the worldwide mobile *communications industry.* **Structure** Board; Executive Management Committee. Regional Interest Groups (3): *GSM Arab World (#10812); GSMA Europe (#10811); GSM Association Latin American Operators (#10814).* Head Office in London (UK). Also offices in: Atlanta GA (USA); Hong Kong; Shanghai (China); Brussels (Belgium); Santiago (Chile); Barcelona (Spain); Nairobi (Kenya); Delhi (India). **Activities** Awards/prizes/competitions; events/meetings. **Events** *MWC Conference* Barcelona (Spain) 2021, *4YFN Meeting* Barcelona (Spain) 2020, *MWC Conference* Barcelona (Spain) 2020, *4YFN Meeting* Shanghai (China) 2020, *MWC Conference* Shanghai (China) 2020.
Members Categories: Full – mobile operators (about 800); Associate – mobile carries, suppliers, clearing houses and open connectivity solution providers; Rapporteur – non-GSM licensed operators moving to LTE/HSPA or those wishing to roam on GSM. Full members in 224 countries and territories:
Afghanistan, Albania, Algeria, Andorra, Angola, Anguilla, Antigua-Barbuda, Argentina, Armenia, Aruba, Australia, Austria, Azerbaijan, Bahamas, Bahrain, Bangladesh, Barbados, Belarus, Belgium, Belize, Benin, Bermuda, Bhutan, Bolivia, Bosnia-Herzegovina, Botswana, Brazil, Brunei Darussalam, Bulgaria, Burkina Faso, Burundi, Cambodia, Cameroon, Canada, Cape Verde, Cayman Is, Central African Rep, Chad, Chile, China, Colombia, Comoros, Congo Brazzaville, Congo DR, Cook Is, Costa Rica, Côte d'Ivoire, Croatia, Cuba, Cyprus, Czechia, Denmark, Djibouti, Dominica, Dominican Rep, Ecuador, Egypt, El Salvador, Equatorial Guinea, Eritrea, Estonia, Eswatini, Ethiopia, Faeroe Is, Falklands/Malvinas, Fiji, Finland, France, Gabon, Gambia, Georgia, Germany, Ghana, Gibraltar, Greece, Greenland, Grenada, Guadeloupe, Guam, Guatemala, Guernsey, Guiana Fr, Guinea, Guinea-Bissau, Guyana, Haiti, Honduras, Hong Kong, Hungary, Iceland, India, Indonesia, Iran Islamic Rep, Iraq, Ireland, Isle of Man, Israel, Italy, Jamaica, Japan, Jersey, Jordan, Kazakhstan, Kenya, Kiribati, Korea DPR, Korea Rep, Kuwait, Kyrgyzstan, Laos, Latvia, Lebanon, Lesotho, Liberia, Libya, Liechtenstein, Lithuania, Luxembourg, Macau, Madagascar, Malawi, Malaysia, Maldives, Mali, Malta, Mauritania, Mauritius, Mayotte, Mexico, Micronesia FS, Moldova, Monaco, Mongolia, Montenegro, Montserrat, Morocco, Mozambique, Myanmar, Namibia, Nauru, Nepal, Netherlands, New Caledonia, New Zealand, Nicaragua, Niger, Nigeria, Niue, Norfolk Is, North Macedonia, Northern Mariana Is, Norway, Oman, Pakistan, Palau, Palestine, Panama, Papua New Guinea, Paraguay, Peru, Philippines, Poland, Polynesia Fr, Portugal, Puerto Rico, Qatar, Réunion, Romania, Russia, Rwanda, Samoa, Samoa USA, San Marino, Sao Tomé-Principe, Saudi Arabia, Senegal, Serbia, Seychelles, Sierra Leone, Singapore, Slovakia, Slovenia, Solomon Is, Somalia, South Africa, Spain, Sri Lanka, St Kitts-Nevis, St Lucia, St Pierre-Miquelon, St Vincent-Grenadines, Sudan, Suriname, Sweden, Switzerland, Syrian AR, Taiwan, Tajikistan, Tanzania UR, Thailand, Timor-Leste, Togo, Tonga, Trinidad-Tobago, Tunisia, Türkiye, Turkmenistan, Turks-Caicos, Uganda, UK, Ukraine, United Arab Emirates, Uruguay, USA, Uzbekistan, Vanuatu, Venezuela, Vietnam, Virgin Is UK, Virgin Is USA, Yemen, Zambia, Zimbabwe.
NGO Relations Member of: *European Financial Coalition against Commercial Sexual Exploitation of Children Online (EFC, #07249); Near Field Communication Forum (NFC Forum, #16968); PMNCH (#18410).* Associate expert of: *Business and Industry Advisory Committee to the OECD (BIAC, #03385).* Partner of: *Centro de Estudios Avanzados en Banda Ancha para el Desarrollo (CEABAD, #03797); Mastercard Foundation.* [2021/XE2891/**B**]

♦ GSM Association Latin American Operators 10814

Chairman c/o ITC, Torre de las Telecomunicaciones, Guatemala 1075 – Nivel 21, 11800 Montevideo, Uruguay.
URL: http://www.gsmlaa.org/

History As a Regional Interest Group of *GSM Association (GSMA, #10813).* **Structure** Plenary Meeting; Working Groups. **Events** *Plenary Meeting* Montevideo (Uruguay) 2014, *Plenary Meeting* Quito (Ecuador) 2014, *Plenary Meeting* Bogota (Colombia) 2013, *Plenary Meeting* Lima (Peru) 2013, *Plenary Meeting* Cancún (Mexico) 2010. **Publications** Position papers; studies.
Members Mobile operators in 28 countries and territories:
Argentina, Aruba, Belize, Bolivia, Brazil, Chile, Colombia, Costa Rica, Cuba, Dominican Rep, Ecuador, El Salvador, Falklands/Malvinas, Guatemala, Guyana, Haiti, Honduras, Mexico, Neth Antilles, Nicaragua, Panama, Paraguay, Peru, Suriname, Turks-Caicos, Uruguay, Venezuela, Virgin Is UK.
Members also in the French West Indies. [2010/XJ0851/**E**]

- ♦ GSM Memorandum of Understanding Association / see GSM Association (#10813)
- ♦ GSM MoU Association / see GSM Association (#10813)
- ♦ **GSMP** Gulf Society for Maintenance Professionals (#10840)
- ♦ **GSN** Globalization Studies Network (#10440)
- ♦ **GSN** Global Services Network (#10591)
- ♦ **GSN** Green Spider Network (#10728)
- ♦ GSN / see Wildlife Alliance (#20957)
- ♦ **GSOA** Global Satellite Operators' Association (#10586)
- ♦ **GSoC** Global Society of Cardiology (#10605)
- ♦ **GSO** GCC Standardization Organization (#10084)
- ♦ GSPGlobal / see Global Speakers Federation (#10612)
- ♦ **GSP** Global Smokefree Partnership (#10602)
- ♦ **GSP** Global Soil Partnership (#10608)
- ♦ GSPIA – Graduate School of Public and International Affairs, Pittsburgh (internationally oriented national body)
- ♦ **GSPR** Gulf Society of Pediatric Respirology (#10841)
- ♦ GSRA – Global Seafood Ratings Alliance (unconfirmed)
- ♦ GSSCRM – Gulf Society for Stem Cell Research and Regenerative Medicine (unconfirmed)
- ♦ GSS – George Santayana Society (internationally oriented national body)
- ♦ **GSSI** Global Sustainable Seafood Initiative (#10618)
- ♦ GSSWA / see Global Social Service Workforce Alliance (#10604)
- ♦ GSTA / see Giant Screen Cinema Association (#10148)
- ♦ **GSTC** Global Sustainable Tourism Council (#10619)
- ♦ G-STIC – Global Sustainable Technology and Innovation Conference (meeting series)
- ♦ GSTP – Agreement on a Global System of Trade Preferences among Developing Countries (1988 treaty)
- ♦ GSW International Youth Union – "Great Silk Way" International Youth Union (internationally oriented national body)
- ♦ GSWN – Global Social Work Network (internationally oriented national body)
- ♦ GTA – Grupo de Trabalho Amazônico (internationally oriented national body)
- ♦ **GTAP** Global Trade Analysis Project (#10631)
- ♦ GTA – Society for Gestalt Theory and its Applications (internationally oriented national body)
- ♦ GTB" / see International Automotive Lighting and Light Signalling Expert Group (#12301)
- ♦ **GTB** International Automotive Lighting and Light Signalling Expert Group (#12301)
- ♦ GTC – Global Tracheostomy Collaborative (unconfirmed)
- ♦ **GTC** Global Traders Conference (#10632)
- ♦ GTC – Grains Trade Convention (1994 treaty)
- ♦ GT-CS – International Society for Group Theory in Cognitive Science (no recent information)
- ♦ GTD – Groupe de Travail Désertification (internationally oriented national body)
- ♦ GTDI – Global Training and Development Institute (internationally oriented national body)
- ♦ GTE / see Gas Infrastructure Europe (#10073)
- ♦ **GTF** Global Tamil Forum (#10620)
- ♦ **GTF** Global Tape Forum (#10621)
- ♦ **GTF** Global Tiger Forum (#10628)
- ♦ **GT** Grameen Trust (#10695)
- ♦ **GTH** Gesellschaft für Thrombose- und Hämostaseforschung (#10146)
- ♦ GTI – Gas Technology Institute (internationally oriented national body)
- ♦ **GTI** Gentle Learning International (#10127)
- ♦ **GTI** Gentle Teaching International (#10128)
- ♦ **GTI** Global Tiger Initiative (#10629)
- ♦ **GTI** Global Transparency Initiative (#10634)
- ♦ **GTI** Greater Tumen Initiative (#10703)
- ♦ **GTI** Great Transition Initiative (#10707)
- ♦ **GTI** Groupe de travail international sur les femmes et le sport (#15912)
- ♦ GTIPA – Global Trade and Innovation Policy Alliance (unconfirmed)
- ♦ **GTN-H** Global Terrestrial Network – Hydrology (#10624)
- ♦ GTN Hydrology / see Global Terrestrial Network – Hydrology (#10624)
- ♦ **GTN-P** Global Terrestrial Network for Permafrost (#10625)
- ♦ GTÖ – Gesellschaft für Tropenökologie (internationally oriented national body)
- ♦ **GTOS** Global Terrestrial Observing System (#10626)
- ♦ GTPA – Global Trade Professionals Alliance (internationally oriented national body)
- ♦ GTP – Gesellschaft für Tropenpädiatrie und Internationale Kindergesundheit (internationally oriented national body)
- ♦ **GTS** Game Theory Society (#10068)
- ♦ **GTTN** Global Timber Tracking Network (#10630)
- ♦ **GTTP** Global Travel and Tourism Partnership (#10635)
- ♦ GTWA / see Open Network for Commerce Exchange (#17758)
- ♦ **GTWCKFA** Global Traditional Wing Chun Kung Fu Association (#10633)
- ♦ **GTW** Gesellschaft für Terminologie und Wissenstransfer (#10145)
- ♦ **GTWN** Global Telecom Women's Network (#10623)
- ♦ GUAAPC – General Union of Arab Peasants and Agricultural Cooperatives (no recent information)
- ♦ Guadalupe Missioners (religious order)
- ♦ Gualandi Mission for the Deaf (religious order)
- ♦ GUAM Group / see Organization for Democracy and Economic Development (#17861)
- ♦ **GUAM** Organization for Democracy and Economic Development (#17861)
- ♦ Guaranty and Cooperation Fund of AMCO / see African Fund for Guarantee and Economic Cooperation (#00326)
- ♦ GUAS – General Union of Arab Students (no recent information)
- ♦ Guatemala Protocol – Protocol to the General Treaty of Central American Economic Integration, 1993 (1993 treaty)
- ♦ Guayule Rubber Society / see Association for the Advancement of Industrial Crops
- ♦ GUCCIAAC / see Union of Arab Chambers (#20350)
- ♦ **GUCP** Global Urban Competititeness Project (#10642)
- ♦ **GUD** Global Urban Development (#10643)
- ♦ Guds kirke Jesus Kristus Ministerial International (religious order)
- ♦ Guds Kyrka Jesu Kristi Ministeriell Internationell (religious order)
- ♦ **GUE** Groupe pour la gauche unitaire européenne (#10794)
- ♦ GUE/NGL / see The Left in the European Parliament (#16436)

♦ Guerrand-Hermès Foundation for Peace 10815

CEO 199 Preston Road, Brighton, BN1 6AW, UK. T. +441273555022. Fax +441273555625. E-mail: info@ghfp.org.
Paris Office 26 boulevard Malesherbes, 3eme étage, 75008 Paris, France. T. +33153632520. Fax +33153632524. E-mail: sx@ghfp.org.
URL: http://www.ghfp.org/

History 1996. UK Registered Charity: 1134575. **Aims** Promote and support peace and a sustainable human *future*; identify and investigate key questions of human concern; develop an understanding of the dynamics of relevant topical issues. **Structure** Trustees. **Activities** Conducts research; initiates, supports and facilitates projects and processes; creates meeting and spaces for dialogue. **Publications** Annual Report. Position papers; books; conference proceedings. **Consultative Status** Consultative status granted from: *ECOSOC (#05331)* (Special). **NGO Relations** Member of: *European Peacebuilding Liaison Office (EPLO, #08176).* [2018/XJ4792/**t**/**F**]

- ♦ GUF / see Research Centre on Development and International Relations
- ♦ **GUF** Global Union Federations (#10638)
- ♦ Guidance Committee for Road Safety in the Nordic Countries (inactive)

♦ **Guidance, Counselling and Youth Development Centre for Africa (GCYDCA)** **10816**

Exec Dir PO Box 30058, Lilongwe, Malawi. T. +2651713181 – +2651713182. E-mail: info@gcydca.org.
URL: http://gcydca.org/

History 1994, by African Ministers of Education. **Aims** Develop and institutionalize guidance, counselling and youth development services as non-academic support with the needs of *girls* as a special focus. **Structure** Board of Directors; Technical Working Committee; Coordinating Offices; Executive Director. **Languages** English, Portuguese. **Finance** Members' dues. Grants. **Publications** *Journal for Guidance and Counselling.*
Members Governments (50):
Angola, Benin, Botswana, Burkina Faso, Burundi, Cameroon, Cape Verde, Central African Rep, Chad, Comoros, Congo Brazzaville, Côte d'Ivoire, Djibouti, Egypt, Equatorial Guinea, Eritrea, Eswatini, Ethiopia, Gabon, Gambia, Ghana, Guinea-Bissau, Kenya, Lesotho, Liberia, Libya, Madagascar, Malawi, Mali, Mauritania, Mauritius, Morocco, Mozambique, Namibia, Niger, Nigeria, Rwanda, Sao Tomé-Principe, Senegal, Seychelles, Sierra Leone, Somalia, South Africa, Sudan, Tanzania UR, Togo, Uganda, Zambia, Zimbabwe.
IGO Relations *Regional Center for Educational Planning (RCEP, #18752).* **NGO Relations** National Board for Certified Counsellors International (NBCC-I). [2016.07.01/XJ9386/**D***]

♦ GUIDE Association – Global Universities in Distance Education (internationally oriented national body)
♦ Guidelines International Ministries (internationally oriented national body)

♦ **Guidelines International Network (GIN)** **10817**

CEO address not obtained. E-mail: office@g-i-n.net – comms@g-i-n.net.
Registered Office J and H Mitchell WS, 51 Atholl Road, Pitlochry, PH16 5BU, UK.
URL: http://www.g-i-n.net/

History 2002. Registration: Companies House, No/ID: SC243691, Scotland; OSCR, No/ID: SC034047, Scotland. **Aims** Improve the quality of *health care* by promoting systematic development of *clinical* practice guidelines and their application into practice. **Structure** Board of Trustees; Executive Committee; Subcommittees (5); Working Groups (13); Regional Communities (7). **Languages** English. **Staff** 3.50 FTE, paid. **Finance** Sources: members' dues. **Activities** Events/meetings; healthcare; knowledge management/information dissemination; networking/liaising; standards/guidelines. **Events** *Conference* Glasgow (UK) 2023, *Conference* Toronto, ON (Canada) 2022, *Conference* Adelaide, SA (Australia) 2019, *Conference* Philadelphia, PA (USA) 2016, *Conference* Amsterdam (Netherlands) 2015. **Information Services** *GIN International Guideline Library & Registry* – online, open access.
Members Organizations (109) and individuals (118) in 51 countries:
Albania, Armenia, Australia, Austria, Belgium, Brazil, Cameroon, Canada, China, Colombia, Croatia, Cyprus, Czechia, Denmark, Ecuador, Egypt, El Salvador, Estonia, Ethiopia, Finland, France, Germany, Greece, India, Indonesia, Ireland, Italy, Japan, Kenya, Korea Rep, Luxembourg, Malaysia, Netherlands, New Zealand, Norway, Peru, Philippines, Poland, Portugal, Qatar, Romania, Saudi Arabia, Singapore, South Africa, Spain, Sweden, Switzerland, Tunisia, UK, Ukraine, USA.
Included in the above, 1 organization listed in this Yearbook:
World Confederation for Physical Therapy (WCPT, #21293) (European Region).
NGO Relations Partner of (2): *Cochrane Collaboration (#04078); International Network of Agencies for Health Technology Assessment (INAHTA, #14230).* [2023.02.14/XJ0102/y/**F**]

♦ **Guide Share Europe (GSE)** **10818**

Contact Gewerbestrasse 10, 6330 Cham ZG, Switzerland. T. +41417487020. Fax +41417487035. E-mail: gsehq@gse.org.
Main Website: https://www.gse.org/

History 1 Jan 1995. Founded by merger of *Guidance for Users of Integrated Data Processing Equipment (GUIDE, inactive)* and *SHARE Europe (SEAS, inactive).* **Aims** Encourage members to exchange experience and information related to *ICT*; influence ICT product and service providers; influence European standards in Information and Communication Technology. **Structure** General Assembly. **Languages** English. **Staff** 3.00 FTE, paid. **Finance** Sources: members' dues. **Activities** Events/meetings. **Events** *Nordic Region Technical Conference* Aarhus (Denmark) 2019, *Nordic Region Technical Conference* Oslo (Norway) 2017, *Management summit* Lisbon (Portugal) 2016, *Guide Executive Club Meeting* Madrid (Spain) 2016, *Nordic Region Technical Conference* Copenhagen (Denmark) 2014.
Members Organizations in 22 countries:
Austria, Belgium, Denmark, Finland, France, Germany, Greece, Hungary, Iceland, Ireland, Israel, Italy, Luxembourg, Netherlands, Norway, Portugal, Slovenia, Spain, Sweden, Switzerland, UK, USA. [2023.02.14/XF3358/**F**]

♦ Guilde européenne du raid (internationally oriented national body)
♦ Guilde internationale des coopératrices (inactive)
♦ Guilde internationale de maîtres-opticiens / see International Opticians Association (#14415)
♦ Guilde internationale des opticiens / see International Opticians Association (#14415)

♦ **Guild of European Business Travel Agents (GEBTA)** **10819**

SG Rue Dautzenberg 60, 1050 Brussels, Belgium. T. +3226442187. Fax +3226442421.

History Founded Jan 1990, London (UK). Registered in accordance with Belgian law. EU Transparency Register: 843162615419-55. **Aims** Speak and act in unity for the benefit of business travellers and the agents who serve them. **Structure** Board of Directors; Secretariat, located in Brussels (Belgium). **Events** *Annual Conference* Brussels (Belgium) 2012, *Annual meeting* Brussels (Belgium) 2007, *Annual Conference* Bruges (Belgium) 2005, *Annual Conference* London (UK) 2003, *Annual Conference* Lisbon (Portugal) 2002.
Members National Guilds, with over 300 institutional members, in 3 countries:
Italy, Spain, UK. [2018/XF5017/**F**]

♦ **The Guild of European Research-Intensive Universities (The Guild)** . **10820**

Main Office Rue du Trône 98, 3rd floor, 1050 Brussels, Belgium. E-mail: office@the-guild.eu.
URL: http://www.the-guild.eu/

History 2016, Brussels (Belgium). Founded by universities from Italy, Sweden, Netherlands, Poland, Germany and UK. Formally launched 21 Nov 2016. Registration: Banque-Carrefour des Enterprises, No/ID: 0660.794.583, Start date: 9 Aug 2016, Belgium. **Aims** Enhance the voice of academic institutions, their researchers and their students. **Structure** General Assembly; Board of Directors. **Activities** Advocacy/lobbying/activism; events/meetings; research/documentation; training/education. **Events** *ARUA – The Guild Virtual Conference on Strengthening the African Knowledge Society* 2021, *ARUA – The Guild Virtual Conference on Strengthening the African Knowledge Society* 2021, *National Strategies and the Role of Universities in Integrating International Students to the Local Labour Market* 2021, *Reimagining research-led higher education – how to build standards that help, not hinder?* 2021, *Transnational Collaboration and Lifelong Learning: Looking back – looking forward* 2021.
Members Universities (21) in 16 countries:
Austria, Belgium, Denmark, Estonia, France, Germany, Italy, Netherlands, Norway, Poland, Romania, Slovenia, Spain, Sweden, Switzerland, UK.
NGO Relations Member of (1): *Federation of European and International Associations Established in Belgium (FAIB, #09508).* [2021.12.01/XM4913/**F**]

♦ **The Guild** The Guild of European Research-Intensive Universities (#10820)
♦ Guild of Rôtisseurs / see Chaîne des Rôtisseurs – Association Mondiale de la Gastronomie (#03845)
♦ Guillain-Barré Syndrome – Chronic Inflammatory Demyelinating Polyneuropathy Foundation International (internationally oriented national body)
♦ Guillain-Barré Syndrome Foundation International / see Guillain-Barré Syndrome – Chronic Inflammatory Demyelinating Polyneuropathy Foundation International
♦ Guillain-Barré Syndrome Support Group / see Guillain-Barré Syndrome – Chronic Inflammatory Demyelinating Polyneuropathy Foundation International
♦ Guillain-Barré Syndrome Support Group International / see Guillain-Barré Syndrome – Chronic Inflammatory Demyelinating Polyneuropathy Foundation International

♦ **Gulf Air** **10821**

Corporate Communication PO Box 138, Manama, Bahrain. T. +97317338765.
URL: http://www.gulfair.com/

History 24 Mar 1950, Bahrain, as *Gulf Aviation Company*, by a group of local businessmen. With the coming of political independence to the region, the four owner States of United Arab Emirates, Bahrain, Oman and Qatar decided to establish a jointly-owned national carrier. Private shareholdings in Gulf Air were gradually acquired and the treaty establishing new joint ownership of the Gulf Air was declared by the four rulers on 1 Jan 1974. **Aims** Increase the economic cooperation between the member States and expand their resources, as well as unite their efforts and capabilities with the aim of supporting a prosperous air *transport* utility between their countries and the rest of the world. **Structure** General Assembly (annual). Board of Directors, consisting of 4 directors from each member State who are appointed for a renewable term of 3 years, the office of Chairman rotating in alphabetical order of the member States for each period of one year. **Staff** 5000.00 FTE, paid.
Members Governments of 4 countries and territories:
Abu Dhabi, Bahrain, Oman, Qatar. [2015/XM1051/e/**F***]

♦ Gulf Aluminium Council (unconfirmed)
♦ Gulf Aluminium Rolling Mill Company (no recent information)

♦ **Gulf Arab States Educational Research Centre (GASERC)** **10822**

Dir PO Box 12580, 71656 Shameya, Kuwait. T. +965483428 – +9654846898 – +9654830317. Fax +9654830571.
URL: http://www.gaserc.edu.kw/

History 1978, Riyadh (Saudi Arabia), by 2nd Conference of Gulf Ministers of Education, as a specialized institution of *Arab Bureau of Education for the Gulf States (ABEGS, #00910).* Became fully operational beginning of 1979. **Aims** Contribute to developing the educational movement in member states, ensure the efficiency, updating and integrating of that movement and make it an effective factor in developing *human resources* and in social and economic *development* of member states in particular and of the Arab world in general. **Structure** Board of Administration (meets twice a year), consisting of a representative educational specialist nominated by each member state (who alone has voting rights), Director of Education Department of ABEGS and the Director of GASERC. Technical Committee, comprising Director of GASERC, Counsellor and various expert staff. Divisions (2): *'Educational Planning'*, including Educational Planning and Economics Unit, Information and Documentation Unit; *'Curricula'*, including Curricula Unit, Preparation and Training Unit, Evaluation and Measurement Unit, Arabic Language Unit. Further Units (2): Adult and Continuing Education; Financial and Administration. **Finance** Contributions of member states. **Activities** Carries out studies and research on the situation of educational activity in member states; follows up new educational trends worldwide and adapts them to the Arab environment in the Region; performs and evaluates experiments in the educational system, generalizing those which prove to be useful; undertakes educational assessment of current techniques and methods. **Publications** *Al Hassad – Educational Bulletin* (6 a year) in Arabic. **Information Services** *ERIC Database* – on CD-ROM; *GASERC Bibliographic Database*; *Pro Quest Database* – on CD-ROM.
Members Governments of 7 countries:
Bahrain, Kuwait, Oman, Qatar, Saudi Arabia, United Arab Emirates, Yemen.
IGO Relations *Arab League Educational, Cultural and Scientific Organization (ALECSO, #01003); International Bureau of Education (IBE, #12413); Islamic World Educational, Scientific and Cultural Organization (ICESCO, #16058); UNESCO (#20322); UNESCO Regional Office for Education in the Arab States (UNEDBAS, #20320); UNESCO Office, Cairo – Regional Bureau for Sciences in the Arab States (ROSTAS, #20312).* [2016/XE1008/**E***]

♦ Gulf Association for Metrology / see Gulfmet (#10835)
♦ Gulf Aviation Company / see Gulf Air (#10821)

♦ **Gulf and Caribbean Fisheries Institute (GCFI)** **10823**

Institut de pêche du Golfe et des Caraïbes

Exec Dir c/o Florida Fish and Wildlife Conservation Commission, Marine Research Institute, 2796 Overseas Highway, Ste 119, Marathon FL 33050, USA.
Exec Sec c/o Florida Sea Grant, 8600 Picos Road – Suite 101, Fort Pierce FL 34946-3045, USA.
URL: http://www.gcfi.org/

History 1948, Miami FL (USA). **Aims** Support fisheries development and management activities throughout the Caribbean, Gulf of Mexico and adjacent regions; provide for acquisition and exchange of information on scientific findings, management techniques, fishing technology, *aquaculture* and other topics affecting the well being and the use of fishery resources of the region. **Structure** Board of Directors. Officers: Chairman; Vice Chairman; Treasurer; Executive Director; Executive Secretary. **Languages** English, Spanish. **Staff** 1.00 FTE, paid. **Activities** Annual meetings; workshops; extension programs; research activities; advisory services. **Events** *Annual Conference* Punta Cana (Dominican Rep) 2019, *Annual conference* San Andrés (Colombia) 2018, *Annual conference* Mérida (Mexico) 2017, *Annual Conference* San Juan (Puerto Rico) 2010, *Annual Conference* Cumana (Venezuela) 2009. **Publications** Conference proceedings; scientific reports; other documents. Information Services: Library.
Members Individual (Member, Honorary); Group; Sustaining; Library. Members in 67 countries and territories:
Argentina, Australia, Bahamas, Barbados, Belgium, Belize, Bermuda, Brazil, Canada, Chile, China, Colombia, Costa Rica, Côte d'Ivoire, Cuba, Denmark, Dominica, Dominican Rep, Ecuador, Egypt, El Salvador, Equatorial Guinea, Finland, France, Germany, Greece, Grenada, Guinea, Guyana, Haiti, Honduras, Hong Kong, Indonesia, Ireland, Israel, Italy, Jamaica, Japan, Kenya, Malaysia, Mexico, Monaco, Netherlands, New Zealand, Nicaragua, Norway, Panama, Philippines, Portugal, Puerto Rico, Saudi Arabia, Solomon Is, South Africa, Spain, Sri Lanka, St Kitts-Nevis, St Lucia, St Vincent-Grenadines, Suriname, Sweden, Switzerland, Trinidad-Tobago, UK, Uruguay, USA, Venezuela. [2015/XD1005/j/**E**]

♦ Gulf Center for Human Rights (internationally oriented national body)
♦ Gulf Centre for Aviation Studies (internationally oriented national body)

♦ **Gulf Centre for Strategic Studies (GCSS)** **10824**

Chairman GCSS Head Office, Davina House, 137-149 Goswell Road, Room No 106, London, EC1V 7ET, UK. T. +442074907101. Fax +442074907102. E-mail: gcss@btconnect.com.
URL: http://www.gcss-eg.org/

History 1985. UK Registered Company. **Aims** Conduct research on and analyse various issues concerning the Gulf region at the international level; document historical events and highlight significant developments at regional and international levels; disseminate awareness of Gulf regional issues at the international level; enhance bilateral cooperation with other international research and studies centres that have similar aims and interests. **Structure** Regional offices (3): Manama (Bahrain); Cairo (Egypt); United Arab Emirates. **Languages** Arabic, English. **Finance** Subscriptions; research commissions; book sales. **Activities** Research and development; publishing activities; knowledge management/information. **Events** *Euro-Arab information and media conference* Manama (Bahrain) 1998. **Publications** *Bahrain Brief* (12 a year) – newsletter; *Gulf Affairs Magazine* in Arabic; *Saudi Trends.* Books (over 300); monographs; studies; monographs; lectures.
Members Not a membership organization. **IGO Relations** Formal contacts with: *Gulf Cooperation Council (GCC, #10826); League of Arab States (LAS, #16420); UNDP (#20292).* **NGO Relations** Involved in: *Amnesty International (AI, #00801); Arab Lawyers' Union (ALU, #01002); Arab Organization for Human Rights (AOHR, #01020); Federation of Arab Journalists (FAJ, #09422); Human Rights Watch (HRW, #10990); Transparency International (TI, #20223).* [2018.06.01/XE2982/s/**E**]

♦ **Gulf Comparative Education Society (GCES)** **10825**

Secretariat Sheikh Saud bin Saqr Al Qasimi Foundation for Policy Research, PO Box 12050, Ra's al Khaymah, United Arab Emirates. E-mail: brian@alqasimifoundation.rak.ae.
URL: http://gces.ae/

History 2008. **Aims** Develop collaborative and individual research and activities that explore educational issues that impact the region. **Structure** Board; Secretariat. **Languages** Arabic, English. **Staff** 2.00 FTE, paid. **Finance** Members' dues. **Activities** Events/meetings. **Events** *Symposium* Ra's al Khaymah (United Arab Emirates) 2018, *Symposium* Kuwait (Kuwait) 2016, *Symposium* Dubai (United Arab Emirates) 2015, *Symposium* Dubai (United Arab Emirates) 2014, *Symposium / Annual Symposium* Muscat (Oman) 2013. **Publications** Proceedings. **NGO Relations** Member of: *World Council of Comparative Education Societies (WCCES, #21322).* [2018.02.04/XJ6305/**D**]

♦ Gulf Cooperation Council (GCC) **10826**
Conseil de coopération du Golfe (CCG)
SG PO Box 7153, Riyadh 11462, Saudi Arabia. T. +96614827777ext1238. Fax +96614829089.
URL: http://www.gcc-sg.org/
History 25 May 1981, Abu Dhabi (United Arab Emirates), on signature of Charter. Also referred to as *Cooperation Council for the Arab States of the Gulf (CCASG) – Conseil de coopération des Etats arabes du Golfe* and as *Arab Gulf Cooperation Council (AGCC) – Conseil de coopération du Golfe arabe.* Summit meeting 1981, Riyadh (Saudi Arabia), agreed to make the region an economic common market. Economic charter adopted, Nov 1981, whereby, from 1 Dec 1981, member states would open their frontiers to goods produced within the region. First stage of 'Unified Economic Agreement' commenced implementation 1 Mar 1983, following decision, Nov 1982, Bahrain, at 3rd session of Supreme Council. This agreement has since been replaced by the 'Economic Agreement', signed 31 Dec 2001. Supreme Council decision to launch *Gulf Common Market*, 1 Jan 2008. Statutes registered in *'UNTS 1/21244'.* **Aims** Effect coordination, integration and interconnection between member states in all fields in order to achieve unity among them; deepen and strengthen relations, links and areas of cooperation now prevailing among their peoples in various fields; formulate similar regulations in various fields, including economic and financial affairs, commerce, customs and communications, education and culture, social and health affairs, information and tourism and legislation and administrative affairs; stimulate scientific and technological progress in the fields of industry, mining, agriculture, water and animal resources; establish scientific research and joint ventures and encourage cooperation by the private sector for the good of their people. **Structure** Supreme Council, composed of heads of Member States, with rotating presidency (meets annually). Commissions (2): Consultative; Dispute Settlement. Ministerial Council, comprising Foreign Ministers or other ministers deputizing for them. Secretariat General, comprising Secretary-General,10 Assistant Secretaries-General and Directors-General of the functional divisions. Main organizations: *'Supreme Council'*, formed of heads of member states, is highest authority, meeting in 2 ordinary and consultative sessions a year. Presidency rotates, based on alphabetical order of names of member states. Attached to Supreme Council: (1) Commission for the Settlement of Disputes, Supreme Council establishing composition on ad-hoc basis in accordance with nature of the dispute; (2) Consultative Commission of 30 members (5 from each GCC member state); (3) Ministerial Council (meets every 3 months), formed of the Foreign Ministers of member states or other delegated ministers; (4) Secretariat General, comprising Secretary-General, Assistant Secretaries-General and staff as required, consists of the following sectors: Political Affairs; Military Affairs; Economic Affairs; Human and Environment Affairs; Legal Affairs; Finance and Administration Affairs; Information Centre; Information Department; Technical Telecommunication Bureau in Bahrain; GCC Delegation in Brussels (Belgium). *Patent Office of Cooperation Council for the Arab States of the Gulf (GCC Patent Office, #18259).* National Authority for the Control of Toxic Chemicals, established in each member state. **Languages** Arabic, English. **Staff** Paid. **Finance** Annual budget of the Secretariat shared by member states. **Activities** Politics/policy/regulatory activities. **Events** *EU-GCC Business Forum* Brussels (Belgium) 2022, *Electronic Warfare Conference* Abu Dhabi (United Arab Emirates) 2018, *Petroleum Media Forum* Abu Dhabi (United Arab Emirates) 2017, *Joint Ministerial Session* Manama (Bahrain) 2017, *Joint Ministerial Session* Brussels (Belgium) 2016. **Publications** *Al-Maseera* (12 a year) in Arabic; *Attaawun* (4 a year) in Arabic; *Legal Bulletin* (4 a year) in Arabic; *GCC Economic Bulletin* (annual) in Arabic; *Statistical Bulletin* (annual); *Directory of Media and Journalism Institutions of the GCC States.* Books; pamphlets.
Members Governments of 6 countries:
Bahrain, Kuwait, Oman, Qatar, Saudi Arabia, United Arab Emirates.
IGO Relations Permanent Observer to: *ECOSOC (#05331).* Observer to: *International Fund for Agricultural Development (IFAD, #13692); Regional Commission for Fisheries (RECOFI, #18763); Southeast European Law Enforcement Center (SELEC, #19815); World Trade Organization (WTO, #21864).* Accredited as observer to Governing Council of: *UNEP (#20299).* Participates in the activities of: *UNCTAD (#20285).* Relationship agreement with: *FAO (#09260); UNIDO (#20336).* Special links with: *ASEAN (#01141); UNICEF (#20332).* Accord to promote cooperation in energy-related training, exchange of data and expertise and information activities signed with: *Organization of Arab Petroleum Exporting Countries (OAPEC, #17854).* Member of: *CGIAR System Organization (CGIAR, #03843); Financial Action Task Force (FATF, #09765); Middle East and North Africa Financial Action Task Force (MENAFATF, #16779).* Working relations with: *International Mobile Satellite Organization (IMSO, #14174); International Telecommunication Union (ITU, #15673),* especially its Radiocommunication Sector; *Organisation of Islamic Cooperation (OIC, #17813).* Supports: *International Center for Agricultural Research in the Dry Areas (ICARDA, #12466).* Instrumental in setting up: *Gulf Aluminium Rolling Mill Company (GARMCO, no recent information); Gulf International Bank (GIB, #10832); Gulf Investment Corporation (GIC, #10834); Gulf Organization for Industrial Consulting (GOIC, #10837); Standardization and Metrology Organization for Gulf Cooperation Council Countries (GMSO, no recent information); GCC Standardization Organization (GSO, #10084).* **NGO Relations** Instrumental in setting up: *Advertising Business Group (ABG, #00136); Gulf Heart Association (GHA, #10831); Organisation des producteurs de ciment (no recent information); Water Science and Technology Association (WSTA, #20838).* [2016.01.28/XD9187/**D***]

♦ Gulf Federation of Emergency Medicine (GFEM) **10827**
Headquarters Al Mamzer Area, Al Wedha Road 46, Dubai, United Arab Emirates. T. +97142556655. E-mail: gfem2020@gmail.com – gfem.gcc@gmail.com.
Gen Sec address not obtained.
URL: https://www.gfem2020.com/
History 2017. **Aims** Achieve cooperation and integration in the areas of health emergency medicine with all its branches among GCC countries. **Structure** Board of Directors. **Languages** Arabic, English.
Members Full in 6 countries:
Bahrain, Kuwait, Oman, Qatar, Saudi Arabia, United Arab Emirates.
IGO Relations *Gulf Cooperation Council (GCC, #10826).* **NGO Relations** Member of: *International Federation for Emergency Medicine (IFEM, #13409).* [2020/XM9009/**D**]

♦ **GULF** Global University Leaders Forum (#10640)

♦ Gulf Group for the Study of Diabetes (GGSD) **10828**
Main Office c/o MCI Middle East, Level 9 World Trade Centre, Sheikh Zayed Road, Dubai, United Arab Emirates. E-mail: ggsd@mci-group.com.
URL: http://ggsd-diabetes.com/
History Founded 20 Jan 2000. **Aims** Improve and prolong the lives of people with diabetes. **Structure** Board. **Activities** Events/meetings; training/education. **Events** *Novel and innovative approaches to diabetes in 2020* Muscat (Oman) 2020, *Conference* Kuwait (Kuwait) 2018, *Conference* Manama (Bahrain) 2016, *Excellence in Diabetes Conference* Doha (Qatar) 2014, *Conference* Jeddah (Saudi Arabia) 2010. [2020/XJ9607/**D**]

♦ Gulf of Guinea Commission (GGC) **10829**
Comissão do Golfo da Guiné
Exec Sec Condominio Rosa Linda, Futungo de Belas, Entrada 1B, Luanda, Angola. E-mail: cgg@cggrps.org.
History 2001, Luanda (Angola). Established by the Treaty signed 3 Jul 2001, in Libreville (Gabon), by Angola, Congo, Gabon, Nigeria and Sao Tome and Principe. Joined by Cameroun and the Democratic Republic of Congo in 2008. Open to other states in the Gulf of Guinea region for purposes of transforming the sub region into a Zone of Peace and Security. **Aims** Serve as a permanent institutional framework of consultation among Member States for *cooperation* and *development*, as well as for the prevention, management and resolution of *conflicts* that may arise from the delimitation of borders and economic and commercial exploitation of natural resources within territorial boundaries of Member States, particularly in the overlapping Exclusive Economic Zones. **Structure** Assembly of Heads of States and Government; Council of Ministers; Secretariat; Ad-hoc Arbitration Mechanism. Executive Secretary; 2 Deputy Executive Secretaries; 2 Directors (Admin, Finance). **Languages** English, French, Portuguese, Spanish. **Finance** Sources: contributions of member/participating states. **Activities** Objectives: strengthen ties of cooperation and solidarity among member States; harmonize policies of Member States regarding matters of common interest, particularly concerning exploitation of natural resources; protect, preserve and improve the natural environment of the Gulf of Guinea and cooperate in the event of natural disaster; formulate a concerted immigration policy; develop a wide communication network.
Members Governments of 9 countries:
Angola, Cameroon, Congo Brazzaville, Congo DR, Equatorial Guinea, Gabon, Ghana, Nigeria, Sao Tomé-Principe.
IGO Relations Committed to principles and objectives of the Charters of: Treaty establishing the *African Economic Community (AEC, #00290); African Union (AU, #00488); United Nations (UN, #20515); United Nations Convention on the Law of the Sea (UNCLOS, 1982).* [2021.10.27/XJ2279/**F***]

♦ Gulf Health Council (GHC) **10830**
Gen Manager Diplomatic Quarters, Next to Chinese Embassy, PO Box 7431, Riyadh 11462, Saudi Arabia. T. +96614885262. Fax +96614885266. E-mail: info@ghc.sa.
URL: http://www.ghc.sa/
History Feb 1976, Riyadh (Saudi Arabia). Former names and other names: *Council of Ministers of Health for GCC States* – former; *Executive Board of the Health Ministers' Council for the Gulf Cooperation Council States* – former; *Gulf Health Council for Cooperation Council States* – former. **Aims** Coordinate efforts by member states to combat infectious diseases; coordinate primary health care programmes; develop maternal and child health services; promote public health and health education; unify the efforts of the Gulf Cooperation Council States and strengthen relations for the sake of development of health services and provision of the highest possible standard of health for their citizens. **Structure** Health Ministers' Conference (annual Ministerial Council); Executive Board; Executive Body; Technical Committees and Work Teams (currently 24). **Languages** Arabic, English. **Staff** 55.00 FTE, paid. **Finance** Budget shared by member countries. Budget not fixed. **Activities** Research and development; events/meetings; awareness raising. **Events** *Annual Conference* Riyadh (Saudi Arabia) 2001. **Publications** *Role of Evidence-based Public Health in Controlling Emerging Infectious Diseases* (2015) by Tawfik A M Khoja et al; *Environmental Health Standards in Accrediting Hospitals and Healthcare Facilities* (2013); *Nurse's Role in Implementing Principles of Quality and Patient Safety – 1st ed* (2013); *The Way Forward to Public Health in Gulf Cooperation Council (GCC) Countries: A Need for Public Health Systems and Law* (2013) by Tawfik A M Khoja et al; *Working Together for Better Health Technical Cooperation among the Gulf States in the Field of Health Through the Health Ministers' Council for Cooperation Council States – 6th ed* (2013). Directories; glossaries; guidelines; regulations; studies.
Members Ministers of Health of 7 countries:
Bahrain, Kuwait, Oman, Qatar, Saudi Arabia, United Arab Emirates, Yemen.
NGO Relations Member of (1): *International Council on Harmonisation of Technical Requirements for Registration of Pharmaceuticals for Human Use (ICH, #13027)* (Observer). [2020/XF0700/**F***]

♦ Gulf Health Council for Cooperation Council States / see Gulf Health Council (#10830)

♦ Gulf Heart Association (GHA) **10831**
Contact 907 Dusseldorf Business Point, Al Barsha 1, Dubai, United Arab Emirates. E-mail: helpdesk@gulfheart.org.
URL: http://www.gulfheart.org/
History 2002, Doha (Qatar), during *Gulf Cooperation Council (GCC, #10826)* Cardiovascular Symposium. **Aims** Improve the quality of *cardiac* care in the GCC states. **Structure** Board of Directors. Working Groups: Fetal Heart; Intervention; *Gulf Heart Rhythm Society*; Lipid. **Activities** Events/meetings; standards/guidelines. **Events** *Conference* Doha (Qatar) 2018, *Gulf Arrhytmia Congress* Dubai (United Arab Emirates) 2018, *Conference* Muscat (Oman) 2017, *Conference* Kuwait (Kuwait) 2015, *Conference* Manama (Bahrain) 2014. **Publications** *Heart Views* (4 a year) – journal.
Members Full in 7 countries:
Bahrain, Kuwait, Oman, Qatar, Saudi Arabia, United Arab Emirates, Yemen.
NGO Relations Affiliate of: *European Society of Cardiology (ESC, #08536).* [2019/XM3390/**E**]

♦ Gulf International Bank (GIB) **10832**
CEO GIB Head Office, Al-Dowali Bldg, 3 Palace Avenue, PO Box 1017, Manama, Bahrain. T. +97317534000. Fax +97317530030.
URL: https://www.gib.com/en/
History Established 13 Nov 1975, by international treaty among member GCC governments. Operations commenced 1976. **Aims** Become the leading universal *bank* in the Gulf Cooperation Council (GCC) states. **Structure** Board of Directors; Branch Offices (5): London (UK); New York NY (USA); Cayman Is; Riyadh (Saudi Arabia); Jeddah (Saudi Arabia). Representative Offices (2): Beirut (Lebanon); Abu Dhabi (United Arab Emirates). Includes Gulf International Bank (UK) Limited. **Languages** Arabic, English. **Finance** Governments of the 6 countries comprising *Gulf Cooperation Council (GCC, #10826)* own the Bank – Bahrain (0.44%); Kuwait (0.73%); Oman (0.44%); Qatar (0.73%); Saudi Arabia (97.22%); United Arab Emirates (0.44%); As at 2010: capital – US$ 2,500 million; total assets – US$ 15,500 million; shareholders' equity – US$ 1,218 million; net profit US$ 100.4 million. **Activities** Provides client-led, innovative financial products and services including project and trade finance, syndications, investment banking and asset management. Main services: asset management; corporate and project finance; structured and acquisition finance; deposits and placements; spot and forward trading; foreign exchange and interest rate derivatives; private equity; Islamic banking. **Publications** Annual Report.
Members Governments of 6 countries:
Bahrain, Kuwait, Oman, Qatar, Saudi Arabia, United Arab Emirates.
Banking members (4):
Bankers Society of Bahrain; *Financial Markets Association (FMA, #09767); Union of Arab Banks (UAB, #20349).*
IGO Relations Shareholder in: *Arab Trade Financing Programme (ATFP, #01060). Islamic Development Bank (IsDB, #16044).* **NGO Relations** Member of: *Accounting and Auditing Organization for Islamic Financial Institutions (AAOIFI, #00062); International Capital Market Association (ICMA, #12438).* [2019/XF1804/e/**F***]

♦ Gulf Intervention Society (GIS) **10833**
Contact Office Damac Business Tower, Elabraj stBusiness bay Burj, Khalifa Community, Office 1003, PO Box 9859, Dubai, United Arab Emirates. T. +97144307892. E-mail: admin@gisonline.org.
URL: https://gisonline.org/
Aims Lead the Gulf interventional cardiovascular community through education, research, and quality patient care. **Structure** Executive Board. **Activities** Events/meetings; training/education. **Events** *Annual Conference* Dubai (United Arab Emirates) 2022, *Annual Conference* Dubai (United Arab Emirates) 2021. [2022/AA2741/**D**]

♦ Gulf Investment Corporation (GIC) **10834**
CEO PO Box 3402, 13035 Safat, Kuwait. T. +96522225000. E-mail: info@gic.com.kw.
URL: http://www.gic.com.kw/
History 10 Nov 1983. Established when Ministers of Finance of member states of *Gulf Cooperation Council (GCC, #10826)* signed the GIC's Agreement of Incorporation and Articles of Association. Registered, 5 Jun 1983, in the State of Kuwait. **Aims** Develop private *enterprise* and foster *economic* growth in the Gulf Cooperation Council (GCC) region. **Structure** Board of Directors; Executive Committee; Audit Committee; CEO/GM. **Finance** Authorized capital: US$ 2,100 million, equally subscribed by member countries; paid-up capital: US$ 750 million. **Activities** Financial and/or material support. **Events** *Seminar on stock exchanges in Gulf Cooperation Council* Bahrain 1990. **Publications** *GIC Newsletter* (4 a year); *GCC Economic Statistics* (annual) in English. Annual report in Arabic/English.
Members Governments of 6 countries:
Bahrain, Kuwait, Oman, Qatar, Saudi Arabia, United Arab Emirates.
IGO Relations Member of: *Gulf Aluminium Rolling Mill Company (GARMCO, no recent information).* **NGO Relations** Member of: *International Capital Market Association (ICMA, #12438).* [2020/XF3070/e/**F***]

♦ Gulf Marketing Association (inactive)

♦ Gulfmet **10835**
Pres Al Ghadir, Riyadh 13311, Saudi Arabia. T. +966112746655. E-mail: info@gulfmet.org.
URL: https://www.gulfmet.org/
History 2 Jun 2010, Kuwait. A Regional Metrology Organization (RMO) established under the auspices of *GCC Standardization Organization (GSO, #10084).* Former names and other names: *Gulf Association for Metrology* – full title. **Aims** Enhance the metrological infrastructure and activities within member states; ensure the technical capabilities of national metrology institutes and designated institutes participating in the GULFMET as an RMO. **Structure** Steering Committee; Presidency; Secretariat. Technical Committees; Working Groups.
Members National Metrological institutes of 6 Gulf countries:
Bahrain, Kuwait, Oman, Qatar, Saudi Arabia, United Arab Emirates.
Associate members in 5 countries and territories:
Bosnia-Herzegovina, Egypt, Hong Kong, Korea Rep, Türkiye. [2022/AA1825/**E***]

◆ **Gulf Neurosurgical Society (GNS)** 10836
Contact King Faisal Specialist Hosp, Dept of Neurosciences, MBC 76 P O Box 3354, Riyadh 11211, Saudi Arabia.
History 2005, Kuwait. **Events** *Congress* Dubai (United Arab Emirates) 2015, *Congress* Doha (Qatar) 2013, *Interdisciplinary World Congress on Low Back and Pelvic Pain* Dubai (United Arab Emirates) 2013, *Congress* Riyadh (Saudi Arabia) 2011, *Congress* Muscat (Oman) 2009. [2014/XJ5496/**D**]

◆ Gulf News Agency (inactive)
◆ Gulf Obesity Surgery Society (unconfirmed)

◆ **Gulf Organization for Industrial Consulting (GOIC)** 10837
Organisation des ingénieurs-conseils des industries du Golfe – Organización del Golfo para la Asesoria Industrial
SG PO Box 5114, Doha, Qatar. T. +9744858888. Fax +9744831465. E-mail: sg@goic.org.qa – goic@goic.org.qa.
URL: http://www.goic.org.qa/
History 26 Feb 1976, Doha (Qatar), at a conference of Ministers of Industry of the States of the Arabian Gulf, now comprising *Gulf Cooperation Council (GCC, #10826)*. **Aims** Promote industrial cooperation and coordination among its members and foster industrial development both at public and private sector levels, through: collection and publication of data and information on industrial projects and policies; suggestion of viable industrial projects that can by implemented by the GCC States on a joint-venture basis; submission of recommendations with regard to the coordination and integration of industrial projects in the GCC States; enhancement of economic and technical cooperation among operating and/or planned industrial establishments; assistance in the preparation and/or evaluation of industrial studies; industrial data analysis and studies. **Structure** Board of Directors. Executive Management, headed by Secretary General. **Languages** Arabic, English. **Staff** 96.00 FTE, paid. **Finance** Committed shares of Member States. Other sources: optional donations; revenues from GOIC's work. **Activities** Meeting activities; training/education; guidance/assistance/consulting; networking/liaising; research/documentation. **Events** *Biennial Gulf Industrialists' Conference* Oman 2014, *Biennial Gulf Industrialists' Conference* Riyadh (Saudi Arabia) 2011, *Biennial Gulf Industrialists' Conference* Doha (Qatar) 2009, *Biennial Gulf Industrialists' Conference* Abu Dhabi (United Arab Emirates) 2008, *Biennial Gulf Industrialists' Conference* Kuwait 2005. **Publications** *Gulf Industrial Bulletin*. Annual Report in English/Arabic; research papers; studies; specialized magazines; books; directories; brochures. **Information Services** *Experts and Consulting Houses Data Base*; *Foreign Trade Statistics Data Base*; *Gulf Industries Data Base (GID)*; *Industrial Market Intelligence Dept* – set up 1979, comprising Library, Data Collection and Analysis Unit, Applications Unit and Systems Operation and Management Unit; *Investment Opportunities Data Base*; *Library Information System (LIS)*; *OSCAR – On-line System for Citations and Abstracts Retrieval Data Base*; *Socio-Economic Data Base*; *Technology Data Base*.
Members Arab countries of the Gulf (7):
Bahrain, Kuwait, Oman, Qatar, Saudi Arabia, United Arab Emirates, Yemen.
IGO Relations Special agreement with: *UNESCO (#20322)*; *UNIDO (#20336)*. [2014/XD6633/t/**D***]

◆ **Gulf Petrochemical Industries Company (GPIC)** 10838
Pres PO Box 26730, Manama, Bahrain. T. +97317731777. Fax +97317731047. E-mail: gpic@gpic.com.
URL: http://www.gpic.com/
History 5 Dec 1979.
Members Governments of 3 countries:
Bahrain, Kuwait, Saudi Arabia. [2017.07.05/XM1068/et/**F***]

◆ **Gulf Petrochemicals and Chemicals Association (GPCA)** 10839
SG PO Box 123055, Vision Tower – Business Bay, Dubai, United Arab Emirates. T. +97144510666. Fax +97144510777.
URL: http://www.gpca.org.ae/
History Officially launched, 1 Mar 2006, Dubai (United Arab Emirates). **Aims** Represent the non-commercial activities of the Gulf region's petrochemicals and chemicals industry; serve as a platform for information exchange. **Structure** General Assembly. Board of Directors. Executive Committee. Committees (6). **Languages** Arabic, English. **Staff** 20.00 FTE, paid. **Finance** Members' dues. **Activities** Events/meetings. **Events** *GPCA Supply Chain Conference* Dubai (United Arab Emirates) 2022, *Conference* Riyadh (Saudi Arabia) 2022, *GPCA Forum* Riyadh (Saudi Arabia) 2022, *Annual Forum* Dubai (United Arab Emirates) 2019, *Supply Chain Conference* Dubai (United Arab Emirates) 2019. **Publications** *GPCA Insight Newsletter*. Research studies. **Members** Companies (250) in 33 countries. Membership countries not specified. **NGO Relations** Full member of: *International Council of Chemical Associations (ICCA, #13003)*. Associated member of: *World Chlorine Council (WCC, #21274)*; *World Plastics Council (WPC, #21730)*. [2022/XM1615/**D**]

◆ Gulf Research Centre (internationally oriented national body)

◆ **Gulf Society for Maintenance Professionals (GSMP)** 10840
Main Office Office 43 Bldg 1033, Road 2721, Area 327, Manama, Bahrain. T. +97317180398. E-mail: info@gsmp-online.org.
URL: http://gsmp-online.org/
History Jan 2010, following discussions initiated in 2007. **Aims** Provide a platform for promoting world class maintenance by sharing knowledge and exchanging best practices among maintenance professionals. **Structure** Board of Directors, comprising Chairman, Vice-Chairman, Secretary, Finance Officer and 3 members. **Activities** Organizes: *Middle East Maintenance Conference and Exhibition (MaintCon)*. **Events** *MaintCon* Bahrain 2010. **NGO Relations** Founding member of: *Global Forum on Maintenance and Asset Management (GFMAM, #10374)*. [2015/XM4072/t/**D**]

◆ **Gulf Society of Pediatric Respirology (GSPR)** 10841
Vice-Pres College of Medicine, King Saud Univ, PO Box 245, Riyadh 11411, Saudi Arabia.
Events *Gulf thoracic congress* Abu Dhabi (United Arab Emirates) 2011, *Gulf thoracic congress* Abu Dhabi (United Arab Emirates) 2010. [2010/XJ2118/**D**]

◆ Gulf Society of Radiology (unconfirmed)
◆ Gulf Society for Stem Cell Research and Regenerative Medicine (unconfirmed)
◆ Gulf States Health Organization (inactive)
◆ GUMR – Groupement des utilisateurs de matériaux réfractaires (inactive)
◆ **GUNI** Global University Network for Innovation (#10641)
◆ Gurdjieff Studies (internationally oriented national body)
◆ **GURS** Society of Genitourinary Reconstructive Surgeons (#19564)
◆ **GUS** Gemeinschaft der Unabhängigen Staaten (#04341)
◆ Gustav E von Grunebaum Center for Near Eastern Studies (internationally oriented national body)
◆ Gustav Mahler Jugendorchester (internationally oriented national body)
◆ Gustav Mahler Youth Orchestra (internationally oriented national body)
◆ GUTA Association – Association of Environmental Lawyers of Central and Eastern Europe and Newly Independent States (inactive)
◆ Gütegemeischaft Kerzen (internationally oriented national body)
◆ Gutenberg-Gesellschaft – Internationale Vereinigung für Geschichte und Gegenwart der Druckkunst / see International Gutenberg Society (#13766)
◆ Gutenberg Society – International Association for Past and Present History of the Art of Printing / see International Gutenberg Society (#13766)
◆ Güteschutzgemeinschaft Hartschaum (internationally oriented national body)
◆ **GuT** Gemeinschaft Umweltfreundlichen Teppichboden (#02489)
◆ **GUTMA** Global UTM Association (#10644)
◆ Guttmacher Institute (internationally oriented national body)
◆ GUUAM Group / see Organization for Democracy and Economic Development (#17861)
◆ GVC – Gruppo di Volontariato Civile (internationally oriented national body)
◆ GVDA – Global Voluntary Development Association (internationally oriented national body)
◆ **GVDN** Global Vaccine Data Network (#10645)
◆ GVEP International / see Energy 4 Impact (#05465)

◆ **GVF** 10842
Headquarters 63-66 Hatton Garden, 5th Floor, Suite 23, London, EC1N 8LE, UK. E-mail: info@gvf.org.
Regional Office 1177 22nd Street NW, Suite 8A, Washington DC 20037, USA.
URL: https://gvf.org/
History 5 Aug 1997, Rome (Italy). Launched 31 Mar 1998, Rome (Italy) as *Global VSAT Forum (GVF)*. VSAT stands for *Very Small Aperture Terminal*. Now known only by acronym. Registered in accordance with UK law. **Aims** Facilitate expanded access to satellite-based connectivity solutions globally. **Structure** General Assembly (annual); Board of Directors; Secretariat, headed by Secretary General. **Languages** English. **Staff** 3.00 FTE, paid. **Finance** Sources: fees for services; members' dues; sponsorship. Annual budget: 500,000 GBP. **Activities** Awareness raising; events/meetings; humanitarian/emergency aid; networking/liaising; projects/programmes; research and development; training/education. **Events** *Defence Satellites Conference* Brussels (Belgium) 2016, *Annual Conference* London (UK) 2013.
Members Full; Associate. Members in 30 countries:
Argentina, Australia, Belgium, Botswana, Brazil, Cameroon, Canada, China, France, Germany, India, Indonesia, Japan, Jordan, Luxembourg, Malaysia, Mauritius, Nigeria, Norway, Russia, Saudi Arabia, Singapore, South Sudan, Spain, Sweden, Tanzania UR, UK, United Arab Emirates, USA, Zimbabwe.
Included in the above, 3 organizations listed in this Yearbook:
Arab Satellite Communications Organization (ARABSAT, #01037); *International Mobile Satellite Organization (IMSO, #14174)*; *Intersputnik International Organization of Space Communications (#15976)*.
NGO Relations Member of: *Emergency Telecommunications Cluster (ETC, #05438)*.
[2022.05.04/XJ7474/y/**F**]

◆ GVG / see European Transport Workers' Federation (#08941)
◆ GVI Charitable Trust – Global Vision International Charitable Trust (internationally oriented national body)
◆ GVL / see Human Variome Project (#10992)
◆ **GVM** Global Volcano Model Network (#10649)
◆ GVN / see Bamboo Foundation
◆ **GVN** Global Virus Network (#10647)
◆ GV-NOK / see Association of National Olympic Committees (#02819)
◆ GVPE / see Group of the Greens – European Free Alliance (#10781)
◆ **GV-SOLAS** Gesellschaft für Versuchstierkunde (#19585)
◆ **GV-SOLAS** Society for Laboratory Animal Science (#19585)
◆ **GVU** Global Virtual University (#10646)
◆ **G-WADI** Water and Development Information for Arid Lands Global Network (#20826)
◆ **GWA** Gender and Water Alliance (#10102)
◆ **GWA** Global Wordnet Association (#10661)
◆ **GWC** Global WASH Cluster (#10651)
◆ GWC – Global Water Challenge (internationally oriented national body)
◆ GWC – Green World City Organisation (unconfirmed)
◆ **GWEC** Global Wind Energy Council (#10656)
◆ GWEI – Gandhi Worldwide Education Institute (internationally oriented national body)
◆ GWF – Geospatial World Forum (meeting series)
◆ GW – Global Witness (internationally oriented national body)
◆ **GWIC** Global Warming International Center (#10650)
◆ **GWIC** Gravitational Wave International Committee (#10697)
◆ Gwich'in Council International (internationally oriented national body)
◆ GWI – Global Wellness Institute (internationally oriented national body)
◆ **GWI** Graduate Women International (#10688)
◆ GWiiN – Global Women Inventor and Innovator Network (internationally oriented national body)
◆ **GWLG** Gottfried-Wilhelm-Leibniz-Gesellschaft (#10683)
◆ **GWNET** Global Women's Network for the Energy Transition (#10659)
◆ **GWO** Global Wind Organisation (#10657)
◆ **GWOPA** Global Water Operators' Partnerships Alliance (#10652)
◆ **GWP** Global Water Partnership (#10653)
◆ **GWPR** Global Women in PR (#10658)
◆ **GWRC** Global Water Research Coalition (#10654)
◆ GWSE – Global Women Social Enterprise (unconfirmed)
◆ **GWS** Global Water Solidarity (#10655)
◆ **GWS** Global Women's Strike (#10660)
◆ GWUP – Gesellschaft zur wissenschaftlichen Untersuchung von Parawissenschaften (internationally oriented national body)
◆ GX – Global Exchange (internationally oriented national body)
◆ **GYA** Global Young Academy (#10662)
◆ GYAN – Global Youth Action Network (internationally oriented national body)
◆ **GYBN** Global Youth Biodiversity Network (#10664)
◆ GYCC – Global Youth Coalition Against Cancer (unconfirmed)
◆ **GYG** Global Young Greens (#10663)
◆ GYIN – Global Youth Innovation Network (internationally oriented national body)
◆ GYLA – Global Young Leaders Academy (unconfirmed)
◆ Gymnastic Association of the Northern Countries (inactive)
◆ Gyngres Geltaidd (#03632)

◆ **Gypsy Lore Society (GLS)** 10843
Pres 5607 Greenleaf Rd, Cheverly MD 20785, USA. E-mail: gls.gypsyloresociety@gmail.com.
Sec address not obtained.
URL: http://www.gypsyloresociety.org/
History 1888, UK. Moved head office to USA, 1989. **Aims** Promote the study of Gypsy peoples and analogous *itinerant* or *nomadic* groups; disseminate information of Gypsy *culture*; establish close contacts among Gypsy scholars. **Structure** Board of Directors. **Staff** 15.00 FTE, voluntary. **Finance** Sources: members' dues. **Events** *Annual Meeting and Conference* Belgrade (Serbia) 2022, *Annual Meeting and Conference* Prague (Czechia) 2021, *Annual Meeting and Conference* Prague (Czechia) 2020, *Annual Meeting and Conference* Reykjavik (Iceland) 2019, *Annual Meeting and Conference* Bucharest (Romania) 2018. **Publications** *Newsletter of the Gypsy Lore Society* (4 a year); *Romani Studies* (2 a year). Books.
Members Organizations and libraries in 16 countries:
Australia, Bulgaria, Canada, Czechia, Finland, France, Germany, Hungary, Italy, Japan, Norway, Portugal, Sweden, Switzerland, UK, USA.
Individuals in 34 countries and territories:
Albania, Australia, Austria, Brazil, Bulgaria, Canada, Croatia, Czechia, Finland, Germany, Greece, Hungary, Iceland, India, Ireland, Italy, Latvia, Moldova, Netherlands, Norway, Poland, Portugal, Romania, Russia, Scotland, Serbia, Slovakia, Slovenia, Spain, Sweden, Switzerland, Türkiye, UK, USA. [2022.05.03/XF5849/**F**]

◆ Gyvos Baltijos Juros Fondas (internationally oriented national body)
◆ **GZ** Global Zero (#10666)
◆ **GZM** Internationale Gesellschaft für Ganzheitliche Zahn-Medizin (#13239)
◆ GZO-PI – Gaston Z Ortigas Peace Institute (internationally oriented national body)
◆ H3ABioNet – Pan African Bioinformatics Network for H3Africa (unconfirmed)
◆ H4+ / see H6 (#10844)

◆ **H6** 10844
Address not obtained.
URL: http://h6partners.wordpress.com/
History Set up 2008, as *H4+*. Current title adopted Mar 2016. **Aims** Leverage the strengths and capacities of member *United Nations* agencies so as to support *high-burden* countries in their efforts to improve the survival, *health* and *well-being* of every *woman*, *newborn*, *child* and adolescent. **Activities** Financial and/or material support.

Members A partnership of 6 UN agencies:
Joint United Nations Programme on HIV/AIDS (UNAIDS, #16149); The World Bank Group (#21218); UNICEF (#20332); United Nations Population Fund (UNFPA, #20612); UN Women (#20724); WHO (#20950).
NGO Relations *Global Financing Facility (GFF, #10360); Every Woman Every Child (EWEC, #09215).*
[2017/XM6253/**E***]

- ♦ H-8-Group – Humanitarian 8 (no recent information)
- ♦ Haager Konferenz für Internationales Privatrecht / see The Hague Conference on Private International Law (#10850)
- ♦ **Haager Kreis** International Konferenz der Waldorf/Steiner Pädagogik (#13653)
- ♦ Ha'amota Leidud Vekidum Shmirat Hateva Bamizrach Hatichon (internationally oriented national body)
- ♦ HAARAN – Horn of Africa Aid and Rehabilitation Action Network (internationally oriented national body)
- ♦ Habitat Pro Association (internationally oriented national body)
- ♦ Habitat for Humanity International (internationally oriented national body)

♦ Habitat International Coalition (HIC) 10845

Coalition Internationale de l'Habitat – Coalición Internacional de Habitat

Gen Sec HIC General Sec, 12 Tiba St – 2nd Fl, Muhandisin, Giza, Egypt. E-mail: gs@hic-net.org.
Pres C/ de Huatasco 59, Roma Sur, Mexico City CDMX, Mexico. E-mail: hic-al@hic-al.org.
URL: http://www.hic-net.org/

History 1976, following United Nations Conference on Human Settlements, 1976, Vancouver (Canada), as *NGO Committee on Human Settlements*. Name subsequently changed to *Habitat International Council – Conseil international habitat*. Revised Constitution and present name adopted 7 Jun 1987. **Aims** Struggle for social justice, gender equality and environmental sustainability; work in defence, promotion and realization of human rights related to housing and land in both rural and urban areas. **Structure** General Assembly (annual); Board. **Languages** English, French, Spanish. **Finance** Members' dues. Grants for individual projects. **Activities** Training/education; knowledge management/information dissemination; guidance/assistance/consulting; events/meetings. **Events** *World Social Forum* Tunis (Tunisia) 2015, *Meeting on social production of habitat* Barcelona (Spain) 2004, *Workshop* Berlin (Germany) 1996, *NGO forum* Istanbul (Turkey) 1996, *Towards a city for life* Quito (Ecuador) 1995. **Publications** *HIC News Bulletin* (6 a year). Annual Report/.
Members Nongovernmental and community-based organizations, professional bodies, voluntary agencies, research, scientific and educational institutions. Individual 'Friends of Habitat International Coalition'. Members in 84 countries and territories:
Afghanistan, Algeria, Angola, Argentina, Australia, Azerbaijan, Bangladesh, Belgium, Benin, Bolivia, Botswana, Brazil, Burkina Faso, Cameroon, Canada, Chile, Colombia, Congo Brazzaville, Congo DR, Costa Rica, Côte d'Ivoire, Cuba, Denmark, Dominican Rep, Ecuador, Egypt, El Salvador, Ethiopia, France, Germany, Ghana, Guatemala, Guinea, Honduras, Hong Kong, India, Indonesia, Iran Islamic Rep, Iraq, Israel, Jamaica, Jordan, Kenya, Korea Rep, Malaysia, Mali, Mauritania, Mauritius, Mexico, Morocco, Namibia, Netherlands, Nicaragua, Niger, Norway, Pakistan, Palestine, Panama, Papua New Guinea, Peru, Philippines, Russia, Senegal, Sierra Leone, South Africa, Spain, Sudan, Sweden, Switzerland, Syrian AR, Tanzania UR, Thailand, Togo, Trinidad-Tobago, Tunisia, Türkiye, Uganda, UK, Uruguay, USA, Venezuela, Yemen, Zambia, Zimbabwe.
Members (230), of which 23 organizations listed in this Yearbook:
- *African Peace Network (APNET);*
- *Alternatives for Sustainable Development (ASDE);*
- *Arab Organization for Human Rights (AOHR, #01020);*
- *Arab Women's Habitat Network;*
- *Asian Coalition for Housing Rights (ACHR, #01381);*
- *Association internationale de techniciens, experts et chercheurs (AITEC, #02745);*
- *Center for Development Studies and Promotion (DESCO);*
- *Centre for African Settlement Studies and Development (CASSAD);*
- *Christian Institute for the Study of Religion and Society (CISRS);*
- *Collectif interafricain des habitants (CIAH);*
- *Fondo Andaluz de Municipios para la Solidaridad Internacional (FAMSI);*
- *Global Communities;*
- *Habitat et participation;*
- *Institute for Housing and Urban Development Studies (IHS);*
- *Instituto de Estudios Politicos para América Latina y Africa (IEPALA);*
- *Instituto para el Desarrollo Económico y Social de América Latina;*
- *International Association 'Znanie';*
- *International Institute for Environment and Development (IIED, #13877);*
- *International Network for Urban Research and Action (INURA, #14338);*
- *International Union of Tenants (IUT, #15822);*
- *Mission Sahel (MS);*
- *Society for Development Alternatives;*
- *World Shelter Organization.*

Consultative Status Consultative status granted from: *ECOSOC (#05331)* (Special). **IGO Relations** Accredited by: *United Nations Office at Vienna (UNOV, #20604).* **NGO Relations** Member of: *EarthAction (EA, #05159); ETO Consortium (ETOs, #05560); European Anti-Poverty Network (EAPN, #05908); International NGO Committee on Human Rights in Trade and Investment (INCHRITI, no recent information); Right to Food and Nutrition Watch Consortium (#18943). World Social Forum (WSF, #21797).* Housing and Land Rights Network (HLRN) is member of *International Network for Economic, Social and Cultural Rights (ESCR-Net, #14255).* Supports: *Global Call for Action Against Poverty (GCAP, #10263).* [2017/XE7548/y/**F**]

- ♦ Habitat International Council / see Habitat International Coalition (#10845)
- ♦ Habitat et participation (internationally oriented national body)
- ♦ Habitat / see United Nations Human Settlements Programme (#20572)
- ♦ HABM / see European Union Intellectual Property Office (#08996)
- ♦ HAC – The Hague Academic Coalition (internationally oriented national body)
- ♦ Hackers and Developers (inactive)
- ♦ Hacking Health (unconfirmed)
- ♦ HACOT – Humanitarian and Charitable ONE Trust (internationally oriented national body)
- ♦ HACU – Hispanic Association of Colleges and Universities (internationally oriented national body)
- ♦ Hadassah (internationally oriented national body)
- ♦ Hadassah-Brandeis Institute (internationally oriented national body)
- ♦ Hadassah International Research Institute on Jewish Women / see Hadassah-Brandeis Institute
- ♦ HAEC / see Historical Archives of the European Union (#10927)
- ♦ **HAE** Hire Association Europe (#10922)
- ♦ HAEI / see HAE International (#10846)
- ♦ **HAEi** HAE International (#10846)

♦ HAE International (HAEi) 10846

CEO Strandkaervej 30-1, 8700 Horsens, Denmark. E-mail: info@haei.org.
Registered address 10560 Main St, Ste PS40, Fairfax VA 22030, USA.
URL: https://haei.org/

History Oct 2003, Milan (Italy). Founded on signature of charter and mission, following earlier congress, Sep 2002, Palermo (Italy). Former names and other names: *Hereditary Angioedema International Association (HAEI)* – full title. Registration: Start date: 2014, Switzerland; Start date: Nov 2004, France. **Aims** Promote cooperation, coordination and information sharing between *hereditary angioedema* (HAE) specialists and national HAE patient associations so as to help facilitate availability of effective diagnosis and management of C1 inhibitor deficiencies worldwide. **Structure** General Assembly; Executive Committee. **Events** *Global Conference* 2020, *Scandinavian Conference* Oslo (Norway) 2019, *Global Conference* Vienna (Austria) 2018, *Scandinavian Conference* Stockholm (Sweden) 2017, *Global Conference* Madrid (Spain) 2016. **NGO Relations** *EURORDIS – Rare Diseases Europe (#09175).* [2019/XJ2039/**C**]

♦ Haematology Nurses & Healthcare Professionals Group (HNHCP) . . 10847

Pres PO Box 29, 8408 Winterthur ZH, Switzerland. E-mail: hnhcp@hemcare.org.
URL: https://hemcare.org/

History Former names and other names: *HEMCARE* – alias. Registration: Switzerland. **Aims** Support nurses and other health care professionals through the rapidly evolving landscape of haematology; enable them to deliver optimal care to patients and support their families. **Structure** Board of Directors. [2019/AA1827/**D**]

- ♦ **HAEU** Historical Archives of the European Union (#10927)
- ♦ Hagop Kevorkian Center for Near Eastern Studies, New York (internationally oriented national body)
- ♦ The Hague Academic Coalition (internationally oriented national body)
- ♦ The Hague Academy Centre for Studies and Research in International Law and International Relations (internationally oriented national body)
- ♦ The Hague Academy of International Law (internationally oriented national body)
- ♦ The Hague Agreement Concerning the International Deposit of Industrial Designs (1925 treaty)

♦ Hague Appeal for Peace (HAP) 10848

Address not obtained.

History Oct 1996, New York NY (USA), to sponsor a civil society organized summit on peace, by *International Association of Lawyers Against Nuclear Arms (IALANA, #11994), International Physicians for the Prevention of Nuclear War (IPPNW, #14578), International Peace Bureau (IPB, #14535)* and *World Federalist Movement – Movement for a Just World Order through a Strengthened United Nations (WFM, #21404).* **Aims** Seek to de-legitimize *war* and refocus on a world *vision* in which *violent conflict* is publicly acknowledged as illegitimate, *illegal* and fundamentally *unjust*; strengthen international *human rights* and *humanitarian* law and institutions; advance *peaceful settlement* of *disputes*, including *conflict prevention* and *peace building*; link and develop substantive issues in *disarmament*, including abolition of *nuclear weapons*; create a culture of peace and alleviate root causes of war. **Structure** Board of Directors. Officers. International Advisory Committee; Honorary 6 Committee; International Advisory Committee of the Global Campaign for Peace Education. **Languages** English. **Staff** 3.00 FTE, paid. **Events** *Peace education conference* Tirana (Albania) 2004, *African regional conference on non-violent conflict resolution and reconciliation* Cape Town (South Africa) 2001. **IGO Relations** Associated with the Department of Global Communications of the United Nations.
NGO Relations Member of: *Abolition 2000 – Global Network to Eliminate Nuclear Weapons (Abolition 2000, #00006); Global Partnership for the Prevention of Armed Conflict (GPPAC, #10538); NGO Committee on Disarmament, Peace and Security, New York NY (#17106).* Instrumental in setting up: *Global Campaign for Peace Education (#10266); International Action Network on Small Arms (IANSA, #11585); International Campaign for Economic Justice (ICEJ, no recent information); Alliance Against Genocide (AAG, #00655).*
Represented on the Organizing Committee as of Oct 2000 (" indicates participating observer):
- *African Law Students and Young Lawyers Association (APAED, no recent information);*
- *African League of Human Rights and Peace Culture, France (no recent information);*
- *Amnesty International (AI, #00801);*
- *Arab Coordination Center for NGOs (ACCN, no recent information);*
- *Arab Lawyers' Union (ALU, #01002);*
- *Armenian Relief Society (ARS, #01111);*
- *Asian Forum for Human Rights and Development (FORUM-ASIA, #01491);*
- *Centre for Peacemaking and Community Development (CPCD, no recent information);*
- *EarthAction (EA, #05159);*
- *Economists for Peace and Security (EPS, #05322);*
- *European Action Council for Peace in the Balkans (no recent information);*
- *The European Law Students' Association (ELSA, #07660);*
- *Fourth World Center for the Study of Indigenous Law and Politics, Denver CO (no recent information);*
- *Friends of the Earth International (FoEI, #10002);*
- *Fundación Ecuatoriana de Relaciones Internacionales y Estratégicas (FERIS, no recent information);*
- *Global Partnership for the Prevention of Armed Conflict Foundation (GPPAC Foundation);*
- *The Hague International Model United Nations (THIMUN);*
- *Helsinki Citizens' Assembly (hCa, #10905);*
- *Human Rights First;*
- *Inter-African Network for Human Rights and Development (Afronet, inactive);*
- *International Association of Lawyers Against Nuclear Arms (IALANA, #11994);*
- *International Committee of the Red Cross (ICRC, #12799) ();*
- *International Federation for Human Rights (#13452);*
- *International Fellowship of Reconciliation (IFOR, #13586);*
- *International Institute for Peace through Tourism (IIPT);*
- *International Network of Engineers and Scientists for Global Responsibility (INES, #14260);*
- *International Peace Bureau (IPB, #14535);*
- *International Physicians for the Prevention of Nuclear War (IPPNW, #14578);*
- *Lawyers Committee on Nuclear Policy (LCNP);*
- *Mahatma M K Gandhi Foundation for Non-Violent Peace (no recent information);*
- NGO Committee on Disarmament, Peace and Security, New York NY;
- *Norwegian Peace Council;*
- *Nuclear Age Peace Foundation;*
- *Nuclear-Free and Independent Pacific Movement (NFIP Movement, #17617);*
- *Pan-African Reconciliation Council (PARC, #18063);*
- *Parliamentarians for Global Action (PGA, #18208);*
- *Pax Christi – International Catholic Peace Movement (#18266);*
- *Peace Boat;*
- *Pugwash Conferences on Science and World Affairs (#18574);*
- *Religions for Peace (RfP, #18831);*
- *Saferworld;*
- *SERVAS International (#19234);*
- *Servicio Paz y Justicia en América Latina (SERPAJ-AL, #19247);*
- *Society for International Development (SID, #19581);*
- *UMTAPO Centre – Peace Education Centre;*
- *United Network of Young Peacebuilders (UNOY, #20653);*
- *Unrepresented Nations and Peoples Organization (UNPO, #20714);*
- *Women for Peace, Switzerland;*
- *Women's Environment and Development Organization (WEDO, #21016);*
- *Women's International League for Peace and Freedom (WILPF, #21024);*
- *World Federalist Movement – Movement for a Just World Order through a Strengthened United Nations (WFM, #21404);*
- *World Order Models Project (WOMP, #21684);*
- *The World Veterans Federation (WVF, #21900).* [2010.09.20/XF4980/**E**]

- ♦ The Hague Centre for Strategic Studies (internationally oriented national body)
- ♦ **Hague Circle** International Forum for Steiner/Waldorf-Education (#13653)

♦ The Hague Club 10849

Address not obtained.

History 1971, Turin (Italy). Registered in accordance with Dutch law, as a foundation ('stichting') in 1980. **Aims** Function as an informal gathering (in their personal capacities) of the chief executive officers of a number of *European* foundations which have both a *professional* nature and an international dimension. **Structure** Meeting (annual since 1985). Steering Committee of 4 members. Closed meetings. **Languages** English. **Staff** None. **Finance** Members' dues. Budget (annual): about euro 7,500. **Activities** Organizes annual meetings hosted by member countries. **Events** *Annual Meeting* Lisbon (Portugal) 2019, *Meeting* Madrid (Spain) 2012, *Meeting* Turin (Italy) 2011, *Meeting* Stockholm (Sweden) 2010, *Annual meeting* The Hague (Netherlands) 2009.
Members Chief executives of foundations (23) in 11 countries:
Belgium, Finland, Germany, Italy, Netherlands, Norway, Portugal, Spain, Sweden, Switzerland, UK.
Included in the above, 9 organizations listed in this Yearbook:
Adriano Olivetti Foundation; Calouste Gulbenkian Foundation; Fritz Thyssen Foundation; King Baudouin Foundation (KBF); Leverhulme Trust; Robert Bosch Foundation; Volkswagen Foundation; Wellcome Trust; Wihuri Foundation for International Prizes.
Corresponding members (6) in 6 countries:
Australia, Belgium, China, Romania, Switzerland, USA. [2015/XF0229/y/**F**]

- ♦ Hague Code of Conduct Against Ballistic Missile Proliferation (treaty)

♦ The Hague Conference on Private International Law (HCCH) 10850

Conférence de La Haye de droit international privé

Contact Churchillplein 6b, 2517 JW The Hague, Netherlands. Fax +31703604867. E-mail: secretariat@hcch.net.
URL: http://www.hcch.net/

History 15 Jul 1955, The Hague (Netherlands). First Session of the Hague Conference on Private International Law convened, 1893 by the Government of the Netherlands, at the initiative of T.M.C. Asser (Nobel Peace Prize 1911). The Conference would meet five more times before the outbreak of the Second World War, in 1894, 1900, 1904, 1925 and 1928. At 7th Session, 1951, participating States agreed on adoption of a Statute reflecting the Conference's permanent character. Statute entered into force, 15 July 1955, HCCH becoming a permanent intergovernmental organization. HCCH meets in principle every four years in plenary session (Diplomatic Session) to negotiate and adopt Conventions and decide upon future work; most recent Session held, 2019. Several times per year Special Commissions or working groups organised to conduct preparatory work for adoption of new Conventions and review the operation and effective implementation of existing Conventions. Former names and other names: *HCOPIL* – former; *CODIP* – former; *Conferencia de La Haya de Derecho Internacional Privado* – former; *Haager Konferenz für Internationales Privatrecht* – former. **Aims** Work toward progressive unification of the rules of private international law through development and effective implementation of Conventions and other multilateral legal instruments. **Structure** Permanent Bureau, with headquarters in The Hague; Regional Offices in Buenos Aires (Argentina) and Hong Kong. **Languages** English, French. **Staff** 28.00 FTE, paid. **Finance** Sources: contributions of member/participating states; revenue from activities/projects. Budget approved every year by the Council of Diplomatic Representatives of Member States.

Activities HCCH works towards progressive unification of the rules of private international law. This involves finding internationally-agreed approaches – primarily through negotiation and servicing of multilateral Conventions – to issues such as jurisdiction of the courts, applicable law, and recognition and enforcement of judgments in a wide range of areas, from commercial law and finance law to international civil procedure and from child protection to matters of marriage and personal status.

Permanent Bureau facilitates relations between Member States; prepares background information and performs research on subjects related to potential or existing Conventions; provides post-Convention services and assistance to requesting Members or Contracting Parties; provides assistance or referrals to private entities and individuals; promotes the work of the HCCH.

Conventions and instruments adopted under the auspices of the HCCH:

1. Statute of the Hague Conference on Private International Law;
2. *Convention Relating to Civil Procedure, 1954 (1954)*;
3. *Convention on the Law Applicable to International Sales of Goods (1955)*;
4. *Convention on the Law Governing Transfer of Title in International Sales of Goods (1958)*;
5. *Convention sur la compétence du for contractuel en cas de vente à caractère international d'objets mobiliers corporels (1958)*;
6. *Convention Relating to the Settlement of the Conflicts between the Law of Nationality and the Law of Domicile (1955)*;
7. *Convention Concerning the Recognition of the Legal Personality of Foreign Companies, Associations and Institutions (1956)*;
8. *Convention on the Law Applicable to Maintenance Obligations Towards Children (1956)*;
9. *Convention Concerning the Recognition and Enforcement of Decisions Relating to Maintenance Obligations Towards Children (1958)*;
10. *Convention Concerning the Powers of Authorities and the Law Applicable in Respect of the Protection of Infants (1961)*;
11. *Convention on the Conflicts of Laws Relating to the Form of Testamentary Dispositions (1961)*;
12. *Convention Abolishing the Requirement of Legalisation for Foreign Public Documents (1961)*;
13. *Convention on Jurisdiction, Applicable Law and Recognition of Decrees Relating to Adoptions (1965)*;
14. *Convention on the Service Abroad of Judicial and Extrajudicial Documents in Civil or Commercial Matters (1965)*;
15. *Convention on the Choice of Court (1965)*;
16. *Convention on the Recognition and Enforcement of Foreign Judgements in Civil and Commercial Matters (1971)*;
17. *Supplementary Protocol to the Convention on the Recognition and Enforcement of Foreign Judgments in Civil and Commercial Matters (1971)*;
18. *Convention on the Recognition of Divorces and Legal Separations (1970)*;
19. *Convention on the Law Applicable to Traffic Accidents (1971)*;
20. *Convention on the Taking of Evidence Abroad in Civil or Commercial Matters (1970)*;
21. *Convention Concerning the International Administration of the Estates of Deceased Persons (1973)*;
22. *Convention on the Law Applicable to Products Liability (1973)*;
23. *Convention on the Recognition and Enforcement of Decisions Relating to Maintenance of Obligations (1973)*;
24. *Convention on the Law Applicable to Maintenance Obligations (1973)*;
25. *Convention on the Law Applicable to Matrimonial Property Regimes (1978)*;
26. *Convention on Celebration and Recognition of the Validity of Marriages (1978)*;
27. *Convention on the Law Applicable to Agency (1978)*;
28. *Convention on the Civil Aspects of International Child Abduction (1980)*;
29. *Convention on the International Access to Justice (1980)*;
30. *Convention on the Law Applicable to Trusts and on Their Recognition (1985)*;
31. *Convention on the Law Applicable to Contracts for the International Sale of Goods (1986)*;
32. *Convention on the Law Applicable to Succession to the Estates of Deceased Persons (1989)*;
33. *Convention on Protection of Children and Cooperation in Respect of Intercountry Adoption (1993)*;
34. *Convention on Jurisdiction, Applicable Law, Recognition, Enforcement and Cooperation in Respect of Parental Responsibility and Measures for the Protection of Children (1996)*;
35. *Convention on the International Protection of Adults (2000)*;
36. *Convention on the Law Applicable to Certain Rights in Respect of Securities Held with an Intermediary (2002)*;
37. *Convention on Choice of Court Agreements (2005)*;
38. *Convention on the International Recovery of Child Support and other Forms of Family Maintenance (2007)*;
39. *Protocol on the Law Applicable to Maintenance Obligations (2007)*;
40. Principles on Choice of Law in International Commercial Contracts;
41. *Convention on the Recognition and Enforcement of Foreign Judgements in Civil or Commercial Matters (2019)*, 2 July 2019.

Events *Meeting* The Hague (Netherlands) 2019, *Asia Pacific Week Meeting* Seoul (Korea Rep) 2017, *Regional Seminar on Protecting the Best Interests of the Child in Cross-Border Family Disputes* Doha (Qatar) 2016, *International Forum on the electronic Apostille Program* The Hague (Netherlands) 2016, *Meeting* The Hague (Netherlands) 2016. **Publications** *HCCH International Family Law Briefings* (4 a year); *Judges' Newsletter on International Child Protection* (2 a year). Explanatory reports; practical handbooks; guides to good practice.

Members Members (91):
Albania, Andorra, Argentina, Armenia, Australia, Austria, Azerbaijan, Belarus, Belgium, Bosnia-Herzegovina, Brazil, Bulgaria, Burkina Faso, Canada, Chile, China, Costa Rica, Croatia, Cyprus, Czechia, Denmark, Dominican Rep, Ecuador, Egypt, El Salvador, Estonia, Finland, France, Georgia, Germany, Greece, Honduras, Hungary, Iceland, India, Ireland, Israel, Italy, Japan, Jordan, Kazakhstan, Korea Rep, Latvia, Lithuania, Luxembourg, Malaysia, Malta, Mauritius, Mexico, Moldova, Monaco, Mongolia, Montenegro, Morocco, Namibia, Netherlands, New Zealand, Nicaragua, North Macedonia, Norway, Panama, Paraguay, Peru, Philippines, Poland, Portugal, Romania, Russia, Saudi Arabia, Serbia, Singapore, Slovakia, Slovenia, South Africa, Spain, Sri Lanka, Suriname, Sweden, Switzerland, Thailand, Tunisia, Türkiye, UK, Ukraine, Uruguay, USA, Uzbekistan, Venezuela, Vietnam, Zambia.
European Union (EU, #08967). [2022.10.12/XE1006/y/**F***]

- ♦ The Hague Convention, 1954 – Convention for the Protection of Cultural Property in the Event of Armed Conflict (1954 treaty)
- ♦ The Hague Institute for Global Justice (internationally oriented national body)
- ♦ The Hague Institute – The Hague Institute for Global Justice (internationally oriented national body)
- ♦ Hague Institute for Innovation of Law (internationally oriented national body)
- ♦ Hague Institute for the Internationalisation of Law / see Hague Institute for Innovation of Law
- ♦ The Hague International Model United Nations (internationally oriented national body)
- ♦ Hague School of European Studies (internationally oriented national body)
- ♦ **The Hague Union** Union for the International Deposit of Industrial Designs (#20417)
- ♦ HA – Hermanitas de la Asunción (religious order)
- ♦ HA – Humanitarian Affairs (unconfirmed)

♦ HAI Africa 10851

Contact PO Box 66054, Nairobi, 00800, Kenya. T. +254203860434.
URL: http://www.haiafrica.org/

History As the regional coordinating office of *Health Action International (HAI, #10868).* **Aims** Work for equitable access to affordable quality *health care* and essential medicines, especially for the poor and disadvantaged, so they may exercise their *human right* to health. **Structure** Informal network with Board of Directors and Working Groups. **Languages** English. **Activities** Research and developemnt; advocacy/lobbying/activism; knowledge management/information dissemination. **NGO Relations** Member of: *Reproductive Health Supplies Coalition (RHSC, #18847).* [2007.07.24/XK2272/**E**]

- ♦ **HAIAP** HAI – Asia-Pacific (#10852)

♦ HAI – Asia-Pacific (HAIAP) 10852

Contact address not obtained.
URL: http://www.haiasiapacific.org/

History Mar 1986, Penang (Malaysia), as *Action for Rational Drugs in Asia (ARDA)*, after a summit meeting of consumer, health care professional, groups and activists from 8 Asian countries in Asia. Current name adopted, 7 Feb 2002, when registered in accordance with the law of Sri Lanka as Asia-Pacific chapter of *Health Action International (HAI, #10868).* **Aims** Increase access to essential medicines and improve their rational use through research excellence and evidence-based advocacy; strive for health for all. **Structure** General Meeting (annual); Governing Council. **Languages** English. **Staff** 0.50 FTE, voluntary. **Finance** Financial support from donor agencies. **Activities** Advocacy/lobbying/activism. **Events** *Workshop* Colombo (Sri Lanka) 1992, *Rational prescribing; challenge to medical educators* Vellore (India) 1991, *Consumer health and drug information and education* Penang (Malaysia) 1990. **Publications** *HAIAP News* (3 a year). Proceedings.

Members Individuals (17); National, international organizations (20) and associate (21). Members in 18 countries:
Afghanistan, Australia, Bangladesh, Cambodia, China, Egypt, India, Indonesia, Iran Islamic Rep, Malaysia, Maldives, Nepal, New Zealand, Pakistan, Philippines, Sri Lanka, Thailand, Vietnam.

NGO Relations Member of: *People's Health Movement (PHM, #18305).* Associate member of: *International Society of Drug Bulletins (ISDB, #15066).* [2019/XF1595/**F**]

- ♦ HAIB – Hawaii Association of International Buddhists (internationally oriented national body)
- ♦ **HAI Europe** Health Action International – Europe Association (#10869)
- ♦ **HAI** Health Action International (#10868)
- ♦ HAI – Health Alliance International (internationally oriented national body)
- ♦ HAI – Heartland Alliance International (internationally oriented national body)
- ♦ HAI – Helicopter Association International (internationally oriented national body)
- ♦ HAIT – High Arab Institute for Translation (internationally oriented national body)

♦ Hakluyt Society 10853

Administration c/o Map Library – British Library, 96 Euston Road, London, NW1 2DB, UK. T. +447568468066. E-mail: office@hakluyt.com.
URL: http://www.hakluyt.com/

History 1846, London (UK). Registration: Charity Commission, No/ID: 313168, England and Wales. **Aims** Advance education by publication of scholarly editions of records of voyages, travels and other *geographical* material of the past. **Structure** Annual General Meeting, always in London (UK); Council. **Languages** English. **Staff** 1.00 FTE, paid. **Finance** Sources: donations; grants; members' dues; sale of publications. **Activities** Events/meetings; publishing activities. **Events** *Annual General Meeting* London (UK) 2023, *Annual General Meeting* London (UK) 2021, *Annual General Meeting* London (UK) 2020, *Annual General Meeting* London (UK) 2008, *Annual General Meeting* London (UK) 2007. **Publications** *Journal of the Hakluyt Society.* Book Series (First, Second, Third and Extra). Annual Report; lectures. **Members** Organizations; Individuals. Membership countries not specified. [2022.12.05/XE3319/**E**]

- ♦ Halal Food Council of Europe (internationally oriented national body)
- ♦ Halcrow Foundation (unconfirmed)
- ♦ Halifax International Security Forum (internationally oriented national body)
- ♦ Hallmarking convention – Convention on the Control and Marking of Articles of Precious Metals (1972 treaty)
- ♦ HALO Trust (internationally oriented national body)
- ♦ Halveti-Jerrahi Order of Dervishes (religious order)
- ♦ Halveti-Jerrahi tariqa (religious order)
- ♦ Hamburgisches WeltWirtschafts Institut (internationally oriented national body)
- ♦ Hamburg Symposia / see European Group on Tumour Markers (#07438)
- ♦ HAMC / see Hell's Angels Motorcycle Club (#10903)
- ♦ Hammer Forum (internationally oriented national body)

♦ Hammer Skin Nation (HSN) 10854

Address not obtained.
URL: http://www.hammerskins.net/

History 1988. A neo-Nazi skinhead group.
Members Mainly North American membership. Chapters in 8 countries:
Australia, Canada, France, Germany, Hungary, Italy, Portugal, Spain, Switzerland, UK. [2015/XM0476/s/**F**]

- ♦ Handa Foundation (internationally oriented national body)
- ♦ Handbell Society of Australasia (internationally oriented national body)

♦ Hand in Hand International (HiH International) 10855

Contact Caparo House, 101-103 Baker Street, London, W1U 6LN, UK. T. +442075145091.
URL: http://www.hihinternational.org/

History 2006. UK Registered Charity: 1113868. **Aims** Eliminate *poverty* through an integrated *community development* programme. **Structure** Board of Trustees. **Activities** Active in: Afghanistan, Cambodia, Eswatini, India, Kenya, Lesotho, South Africa, Zimbabwe. [2018.06.13/XJ5516/**F**]

- ♦ Hand in Hand tegen Racisme (internationally oriented national body)
- ♦ HandiCapacités (internationally oriented national body)
- ♦ Handicap International / see Humanity and Inclusion (#10975)
- ♦ Handicapped People in Europe Living Independently in Open Society (inactive)
- ♦ Handicapped Scuba Association International (internationally oriented national body)
- ♦ Handikapporganisationernes Nordiska Råd (no recent information)
- ♦ Handmaids of Charity (religious order)
- ♦ Handmaids of Mary – Sisters Servants of Mary (religious order)
- ♦ Handmaids of the Sacred Heart of Jesus (religious order)
- ♦ Handpump Technology Network / see Rural Water Supply Network (#19006)
- ♦ Hands On Europe / see Hands On ! International Association of Children's Museums (#10856)
- ♦ Hands to Hearts International (internationally oriented national body)

♦ Hands On ! International Association of Children's Museums (HO!I) 10856

Secretariat Friedrichgasse 34, 8010 Graz, Austria. E-mail: secretariat@hands-on-international.net.
URL: https://www.hands-on-international.net/

History 1998, Lisbon (Portugal). Founded following the activities of an informal network since 1994. Head office moved to Italy, 2007. Former names and other names: *European Association of Children's Museums (Hands On Europe)* – former (1998). **Aims** Promote the development of children's museums in Europe. **Structure** General Assembly (every 2 years); Board of Directors. **Languages** English. **Staff** 0.50 FTE, paid; 5.00 FTE, voluntary. **Finance** Members' dues. **Events** *Online Conference* 2021, *Conference* Frankfurt-Main (Germany) 2019, *Conference* Pisek (Czechia) / Pilsen (Czechia) / Prague (Czechia) 2017, *Conference* Amsterdam (Netherlands) 2015, *Conference* Stockholm (Sweden) 2013.

Members Institutional; Corporate. Members in 37 countries:
Austria, Belgium, Bosnia-Herzegovina, Brazil, Bulgaria, Canada, Czechia, Denmark, France, Gambia, Germany, Ghana, Greece, India, Ireland, Israel, Italy, Jordan, Korea Rep, Kosovo, Latvia, Luxembourg, Mexico, Netherlands, Norway, Philippines, Portugal, Russia, Slovakia, Slovenia, Spain, Switzerland, Thailand, Türkiye, UK, United Arab Emirates, USA.
Included in the above, 1 organization listed in this Yearbook:
Royal Museum for Central Africa (KMMA).

NGO Relations *International Council of Museums (ICOM, #13051).* [2021/XM1542/y/**D**]

♦ Hands Off Cain – Citizens' and Parliamentarians' League for the Abolition of the Death Penalty Worldwide (Hands Off Cain) 10857

Nessuno Tocchi Caino

Sec Via di Torre Argentina, 76, 00186 Rome RM, Italy. T. +393358000577. E-mail: info@nessunotocchicaino.it.
Registered Office Avenue de Terveueren 152/B5, B-1150 Brussels, 1150 Brussels, Belgium. T. +32475825085.
URL: http://www.handsoffcain.info/

History Dec 1994, Brussels (Belgium). Founded at World Congress. Former names and other names: *International League for the Abolition of the Death Penalty by the Year 2000* – former (Dec 1994); *Lega Internazionale per l'Abolizione della Pena di Morte entro il 2000* – former (Dec 1994); *Hands Off Cain – Citizens' and Parliamentarians' League for the Abolition of the Death Penalty Worldwide by 2000* – former; *Nessuno Tocchi Caino* – former. **Aims** Abolish all constitutional *laws* and articles providing for the death penalty to be inflicted following a sentence pronounced by a legally constituted *court*; establish strict and progressive *penal* regulations. **Structure** General Assembly (every 2 years, at Conference); Management Council; Executive Secretariat. **Languages** English, French, Italian. **Staff** 6.00 FTE, paid. 6 **Finance** Sources: members' dues. **Activities** Advocacy/lobbying/activism.
Members Founder; Regular (individuals); Confederate (associations or groups). Individuals and organizations in 45 countries:
Albania, Algeria, Argentina, Armenia, Belgium, Bolivia, Bosnia-Herzegovina, Brazil, Bulgaria, Burkina Faso, Canada, Côte d'Ivoire, Croatia, Cuba, Czechia, Estonia, France, Georgia, Germany, Hungary, Israel, Italy, Kazakhstan, Latvia, Lithuania, Luxembourg, Mali, Moldova, Netherlands, North Macedonia, Philippines, Poland, Portugal, Romania, Russia, Senegal, Serbia, Slovakia, Slovenia, South Africa, Spain, Sweden, Tunisia, UK, USA.
Offices in 27 countries and territories:
Albania, Azerbaijan, Belarus, Belgium, Bulgaria, Burkina Faso, Côte d'Ivoire, Croatia, Czechia, Estonia, France, Georgia, Hungary, Italy, Kazakhstan, Lithuania, Malta, Northern Ireland, Poland, Portugal, Romania, Russia, South Africa, Spain, Tunisia, Ukraine, USA.
NGO Relations Cooperates with (2): *Nonviolent Radical Party, Transnational and Transparty (PRNTT, #17154)*; *Unrepresented Nations and Peoples Organization (UNPO, #20714).* [2022.11.20/XF3441/**F**]

- Hands Off Cain – Citizens' and Parliamentarians' League for the Abolition of the Death Penalty Worldwide by 2000 / see Hands Off Cain – Citizens' and Parliamentarians' League for the Abolition of the Death Penalty Worldwide (#10857)
- **Hands Off Cain** Hands Off Cain – Citizens' and Parliamentarians' League for the Abolition of the Death Penalty Worldwide (#10857)

♦ Hands-on Science Network (HSCI) 10858

Pres Rua 1 de Maio 2 – 2o, 4730-734 Vila Verde, Portugal. E-mail: president@hsci.info.
URL: http://www.hsci.info/
History Supported by the *Associação Hands-on Science Network* registered in accordance with Portuguese law. **Aims** Promote development of science education and scientific literacy in society. **Activities** Events/meetings. **Events** *Annual International Conference* Burgos (Spain) 2022, *Hands-on Science Education Activities – Challenges and Opportunities of Distant and Online Teaching and Learning* Vila Verde (Portugal) 2021, *Science education – discovering and understanding the wonders of nature* Vila Verde (Portugal) 2020, *Conference* Kharkiv (Ukraine) 2019, *Conference* Barcelona (Spain) 2018. **NGO Relations** Member of (1): *International Council of Associations for Science Education (ICASE, #12997).* [2021.06.01/XM8354/**F**]

- Handvest van de grondrechten van de Europese Unie (2000 treaty)

♦ Hand and Wrist Biomechanics International (HWBI) 10859

Contact 9500 Euclid Avenue, ND20, Cleveland OH 44195, USA. E-mail: info@hwbi.org.
URL: https://www.hwbi.org/
History 2012. Founded by International Advisory Board of the International Symposium on Hand and Wrist Biomechanics, initiated in 1992. **Aims** Further enhance the development of hand and wrist biomechanics and its clinical applications. **Structure** Board of Directors. **Events** *Hand and Wrist Biomechanics International Symposium* Cleveland, OH (USA) 2021, *Hand and Wrist Biomechanics International Symposium* Cleveland, OH (USA) 2020, *Hand and Wrist Biomechanics International Symposium* Berlin (Germany) 2019, *Hand and Wrist Biomechanics International Symposium* Brisbane, QLD (Australia) 2017, *International Hand and Wrist Biomechanics Symposium* Yokohama (Japan) 2012. **NGO Relations** Affiliated with (2): *International Federation of Societies for Surgery of the Hand (IFSSH, #13551)*; *International Society of Biomechanics (ISB, #14966).* [2020/AA0739/c/**E**]

- Hangzhou International Centre on Small Hydro-Power / see International Centre on Small Hydro-Power
- Hanlingsorgan for Borgernes Europa / see European Citizen Action Service (#06555)
- Hanns Seidel Foundation (internationally oriented national body)
- Hanns-Seidel-Stiftung (internationally oriented national body)
- Hanseatic League (inactive)
- Hanwang Forum (unconfirmed)
- **HAP** Hague Appeal for Peace (#10848)
- HAP International – Humanitarian Accountability Partnership International (inactive)
- Hapoel Hamizrachi Women's Organization / see World Emunah Religious Zionist Women's Organization (#21378)
- Happy Child International Foundation / see It's a Penalty
- Happy Science (internationally oriented national body)
- **HAPUA** Forum of Heads of ASEAN Power Utilities/Authorities (#09917)

♦ Harakat ul-Ansar (HUA) 10860

Address not obtained.
History Oct 1993, on merger of 2 Pakistani political activist groups: *'Harakat ul-Jihad al-Islami'* and *'Harakat ul-Mujahedin'.* **Aims** Fight for accession of Kashmir to Pakistan; in general, continue the armed struggle against non-Muslims and anti-*Islamic forces*, by *terrorist* or other means. **Structure** Core militant group plus several thousand other armed members. **Finance** For humanitarian assistance work and relief supplies: governments of Gulf and Islamic states. For military purposes: sympathetic Arab countries and wealthy individuals. **Activities** Insurgent and terrorist operations in Kashmir, Myanmar, Tajikistan, Bosnia-Herzegovina. Training of local Muslims in handling of weapons and guerrilla warfare. Humanitarian assistance to Muslims in Tajikistan, Myanmar and Kashmir. **Members** Membership countries not available. [2009/XN7823/s/**F**]

- Harare Protocol – Protocol on Patents and Industrial Designs within the Framework of ARIPO (1982 treaty)
- Harbour Masters of North Western Europe / see European Harbour Masters' Committee (#07449)
- Harmadik Vilag Szegényeinek Szolgai Missziós Mozgalmat (religious order)
- HARMNST – International Workshop on High Aspect Ratio Micro and Nano System Technology (meeting series)
- **HARMO** Initiative on Harmonisation within Atmospheric Dispersion Modelling for Regulatory Purposes (#11210)
- Harmonisierungsamt für den Binnenmarkt – Marken, Muster und Modelle / see European Union Intellectual Property Office (#08996)

♦ Harm Reduction International (HRI) 10861

Exec Dir 61 Mansell St, Aldgate, London, E1 8AN, UK. T. +442073243535. E-mail: office@hri.global.
URL: https://www.hri.global/
History 1996, Hobart, TAS (Australia). Founded at the 7th International Conference on the Reduction of Drug-Related Harm. Trades under the above title. Took over activities of *International Coalition on Alcohol and Harm Reduction (ICAHRE, inactive).* Former names and other names: *International Harm Reduction Association (IHRA)* – former (1996 to 2011); *International Harm Reduction Network* – alias. Registration: Charity Commission, No/ID: 1117375, England and Wales; Companies House, No/ID: 3223265, England and Wales. **Aims** Promote evidence-based harm reduction policies and practices on a global basis for all psychoactive substances, including illicit *drugs, tobacco* and *alcohol.* **Structure** Executive Committee. Offices in: London (UK); Melbourne (Australia). **Languages** English. **Staff** 6.00 FTE, paid. **Finance** Members' dues. Other sources: donations; conference proceeds; project grants. **Activities** Events/meetings; advocacy/lobbying/activism; research/documentation; networking/liaising; knowledge management/information dissemination. **Events** *International Harm Reduction Conference (HR23)* Melbourne, VIC (Australia) 2023, *International Harm Reduction Conference* Porto (Portugal) 2019, *International Harm Reduction Conference* Montréal, QC (Canada) 2017, *International Harm Reduction Conference* Kuala Lumpur (Malaysia) 2015, *Annual International Harm Reduction Conference* Vilnius (Lithuania) 2013. **Publications** *IHRA E-Newsletter* (12 a year); *International Journal of Drug Policy* (6 a year); *Harm Reduction Journal* – online.
Members Premium; Individual; Institutional. Members in 101 countries and territories:
Afghanistan, Albania, Andorra, Argentina, Armenia, Australia, Austria, Azerbaijan, Bangladesh, Barbados, Belarus, Belgium, Bolivia, Brazil, Bulgaria, Cambodia, Canada, Chile, China, Colombia, Costa Rica, Croatia, Cuba, Czechia, Denmark, Dominica, Ecuador, Egypt, El Salvador, Finland, France, Germany, Greece, Grenada, Hong Kong, Hungary, Iceland, India, Indonesia, Iran Islamic Rep, Iraq, Ireland, Israel, Italy, Japan, Jordan, Kazakhstan, Kenya, Korea Rep, Kuwait, Kyrgyzstan, Laos, Latvia, Lebanon, Lithuania, Luxembourg, Malaysia, Maldives, Malta, Mauritius, Mexico, Moldova, Monaco, Mongolia, Myanmar, Nepal, Netherlands, New Zealand, Nicaragua, Nigeria, North Macedonia, Norway, Pakistan, Palestine, Paraguay, Peru, Philippines, Poland, Portugal, Romania, Russia, Singapore, Slovenia, South Africa, Spain, Sri Lanka, Sweden, Switzerland, Taiwan, Tajikistan, Thailand, Türkiye, UK, Ukraine, United Arab Emirates, Uruguay, USA, Uzbekistan, Venezuela, Vietnam, Zimbabwe.
Consultative Status Consultative status granted from: *ECOSOC (#05331)* (Special). **NGO Relations** Member of: *Civil Society Forum on Drugs (CSFD, #03968)*; *End Corporal Punishment (#05457)*; *UK Consortium on AIDS and International Development.* Coordinates: *European Harm Reduction Network (EuroHRN, #07450).* Similar regional networks: *Asian Harm Reduction Network (AHRN, #01501)*; *Caribbean Harm Reduction Coalition (CHRC, #03513)*; *Correlation – European Harm Reduction Network (C-EHRN, #04848)*; *Middle East and North Africa Harm Reduction Network (MENAHRA, #16780).* Instrumental in setting up: *International Network Women and Drugs (no recent information).* [2021/XF4727/**F**]

- **HARRPA** Hydrocarbon and Rosin Resins Producers Association (#10996)
- Harry Benjamin International Gender Dysphoria Association / see World Professional Association For Transgender Health (#21739)
- Harry Frank Guggenheim Foundation (internationally oriented national body)
- Harry S Truman Library Institute for National and International Affairs (internationally oriented national body)
- Harry S Truman Research Institute for the Advancement of Peace (internationally oriented national body)
- HART – Humanitarian Aid Relief Trust (internationally oriented national body)
- Harvard Project for Asian and International Relations (internationally oriented national body)
- Harvard University Asia Center (internationally oriented national body)
- Harvest House International Church (religious order)

♦ HarvestPlus 10862

Contact c/o IFPRI, 2033 K St NW, Washington DC 20006-1002, USA. T. +12028625600. Fax +12024674439.
URL: http://www.harvestplus.org/
History 2002, as one of 3 pioneer Challenge Programmes of *CGIAR System Organization (CGIAR, #03843)* Micronutrients Project. Officially launched 2004, when it became the first recipient of funding for bio-fortification research granted by *Bill and Melinda Gates Foundation (BMGF).* Co-convened by *International Centre for Tropical Agriculture (#12527)* and *International Food Policy Research Institute (IFPRI, #13622).* **Aims** Reduce hidden *hunger* and provide *micronutrients* to people directly through the staple *foods* that they eat. **Finance** Original funding from *Bill and Melinda Gates Foundation (BMGF).* Research and implementation funded through donations from: *Asian Development Bank (ADB, #01422)*; Austrian Ministry of Finance; Bill and Melinda Gates Foundation; *Canadian International Development Agency (CIDA, inactive)*; *DANIDA*; *Department for International Development (DFID, inactive)* (R4D for DFID-funded research); *International Bank for Reconstruction and Development (IBRD, #12317)* (World Bank); International Fertilizer Group; *International Life Sciences Institute (ILSI, #14044)*; *Swedish International Development Cooperation Agency (Sida)*; *United States Agency for International Development (USAID)*; United States Department of Agriculture. **Activities** Cooperates with over 200 agricultural and nutrition scientists around the world. [2011.07.08/XJ1812/**E**]

♦ Hashomer Hatzair – World Movement for Zionist Youth 10863

SG Hayasmin 1 St, 52960 Ramat Efal, Israel. E-mail: central-office@hashomer-hatzair.org.
URL: http://www.hashomer-hatzair.net/
History Known also as: *Hashomer Hatzair World Zionist Youth Organization* and *World Youth Movement of Hashomer Hatzair.* **Structure** General Secretary; Treasurer; Desk Coordinator; Regional Representatives. **Languages** English, Portuguese, Spanish. **Activities** Training/education. **Events** *World seminar* Jerusalem (Israel) 1999.
Members Individuals in 21 countries:
Argentina, Australia, Austria, Belarus, Belgium, Brazil, Bulgaria, Canada, Chile, France, Germany, Hungary, Israel, Italy, Mexico, Netherlands, Switzerland, Ukraine, Uruguay, USA, Venezuela. [2018.08.05/XE7851/v/**E**]

- Hashomer Hatzair World Zionist Youth Organization / see Hashomer Hatzair – World Movement for Zionist Youth (#10863)
- HASI / see Church of Scientology International (#03922)
- Hastinapura Foundation (#10023)
- **HASTQB** Hispanic America Software Testing Qualifications Board (#10923)

♦ Hasumi International Research Foundation (HIRF) 10864

Chairman/CEO 2200 Pennsylvania Avenue NW, 4th Floor East, Washington DC 20037, USA. T. +12029736459.
URL: http://www.hasumi-foundation.org/
History 29 Jan 1999, Philadelphia PA (USA). Registered in the State of Pennsylvania. Named after Dr Kiichiro Hasumi. **Aims** Conduct and support research in connection with finding a cure for various forms of *cancer*, particularly with the use of *immunotherapy.* **Events** *International Cancer Vaccine Symposium / Symposium* Florence (Italy) 2012, *International Cancer Vaccine Symposium / Symposium* New York, NY (USA) 2008, *International cancer vaccine symposium / Symposium* Vienna (Austria) 2007, *International cancer vaccine symposium / Symposium* Washington, DC (USA) 2006, *International cancer vaccine symposium / Symposium* London (UK) 2004. [2012/XM2607/f/**E**]

- **HAT** – Frontline Homeopathy / Homeopathy Action Trust (internationally oriented national body)
- **HaT** Health and Trade Network (#10890)
- Haut Commissaire aux minorités nationales (#17901)
- Haut-Commissariat des Nations Unies aux droits de l'homme (#17697)
- Haut commissariat des Nations Unies pour les réfugiés (#20327)
- Haut Commissariat pour les réfugiés de la Société des Nations (inactive)
- Haut conseil de La Francophonie (inactive)
- Haute commission de l'Afrique orientale (inactive)
- Haute commission alliée pour l'Allemagne (inactive)
- Haute école populaire internationale (internationally oriented national body)
- HAVOYOCO – Horn of Africa Voluntary Youth Committee (internationally oriented national body)
- Hawaii Association of International Buddhists (internationally oriented national body)
- Hawaii International Conference on System Sciences (meeting series)
- HAWK-Produktions-und Logistikorganisation (no recent information)
- HawkWatch International (internationally oriented national body)
- HAXPES – International Conference on Hard X-ray Photoelectron Spectroscopy (meeting series)
- Hazardous Areas Life-Support Organisation / see HALO Trust
- Hazardous Materials Advisory Council / see Dangerous Goods Advisory Council (#05001)
- Hazardous Waste Europe (unconfirmed)
- HBA – Healthcare Businesswomen's Association (internationally oriented national body)
- **HbbTV Association** Hybrid broadcast broadband TV Association (#10995)
- **HBGI** Healthy Brains Global Initiative (#10892)
- HBIA – Hot Briquetted Iron Association (inactive)
- HBIGDA / see World Professional Association For Transgender Health (#21739)
- **HBSC** Health Behaviour in School-Aged Children (#10871)
- HBS – Holy Bible Society (internationally oriented national body)
- HBSRA – Healthcare and Biological Sciences Research Association (internationally oriented national body)
- **hCa** Helsinki Citizens' Assembly (#10905)
- **HCA** Human Cell Atlas (#10962)
- HCA – Hydrographic Commission on Antarctica (see: #13825)

- hCa International / see Helsinki Citizens' Assembly (#10905)
- **HCCE** Historic Conference Centres of Europe (#10928)
- **HCC** Healthy Caribbean Coalition (#10893)
- **HCCH** The Hague Conference on Private International Law (#10850)
- **HCDH** Haut-Commissariat des Nations Unies aux droits de l'homme (#17697)
- **HCDM** Human Cell Differentiation Molecules (#10963)
- **HCEC** / see European Hospital and Healthcare Federation (#07501)
- **HCF** – Haut conseil de La Francophonie (inactive)
- **HCFI** Healthcare Christian Fellowship International (#10873)
- **HCIEE** High Council of Islamic Economy in Europe (#10913)
- **HCI** Healthcare Caterers International (#10872)
- **HCI** – Human Concern International (internationally oriented national body)
- **HCI** International Conference (meeting series)
- **HCI** – International Conference on the Physics of Highly Charged Ions (meeting series)
- **HCIMA** / see Institute of Hospitality (#11269)
- **HCIM** – Healthcare Clowning International Meeting (meeting series)
- **HCJB** Global / see Reach Beyond
- **HCJB** World Radio / see Reach Beyond
- **HCNM** OSCE High Commissioner on National Minorities (#17901)
- **HCOC** – Hague Code of Conduct Against Ballistic Missile Proliferation (treaty)
- **HCOPIL** / see The Hague Conference on Private International Law (#10850)
- **HCPC Europe** Healthcare Compliance Packaging Council Europe (#10874)
- **HCP** – Health Communication Partnership (internationally oriented national body)
- **HCP** – Heirloom Cacao Preservation Fund (internationally oriented national body)
- **HCP** / see WHO European Healthy Cities Network (#20936)
- **HCR** Haut commissariat des Nations Unies pour les réfugiés (#20327)
- **HCSA** – Humanitarian Coalition on Small Arms (internationally oriented national body)
- **HCSE** – International Conference on Health Care Systems Engineering (meeting series)
- **HCSS** – The Hague Centre for Strategic Studies (internationally oriented national body)
- **HCV** – International Symposium on Hepatitis C Virus and Related Viruses (meeting series)

♦ **HCV Network Ltd (HCV Network)** 10865
Global Dir c/o Critchleys Llp, Beaver House, 23-38 Hythe Bridge Street, Oxford, OX1 2EP, UK. E-mail: secretariat@hcvnetwork.org.
URL: https://www.hcvnetwork.org/
History 2006. Former names and other names: *High Conservation Value Resource Network (HCV Resource Network)* – former. **Aims** Promote consistent implementation of the High Conservation Value approach, a tool used as part of responsible production of *food, paper* and *timber*. **Structure** Management Committee; Members; Supporters; Secretariat. **Languages** English, French, Indonesian, Portuguese, Spanish. **Staff** 10.00 FTE, paid. **Finance** Sources: donations; members' dues. Other sources: income from the HCV Assessor Licensing Scheme. **Activities** Certification/accreditation; guidance/assistance/consulting; knowledge management/information dissemination; networking/liaising; research/documentation.
Members Organizations (27), including 12 organizations listed in this Yearbook:
Deutsche Gesellschaft für Internationale Zusammenarbeit (GIZ); Fauna & Flora International (FFI, #09277); Forest Peoples Programme (FPP, #09865); Forest Stewardship Council (FSC, #09869); Greenpeace International (#10727); Rainforest Alliance; Round Table on Responsible Soy Association (RTRS, #18983); Roundtable on Sustainable Palm Oil (RSPO, #18986); Social Agriculture Network (SAN, #19333); The Nature Conservancy (TNC); World Resources Institute (WRI, #21753); World Wide Fund for Nature (WWF, #21922).
NGO Relations Memorandum of Understanding with (1): *Aquaculture Stewardship Council (ASC, #00885).* Member of (2): *Better Cotton Initiative (BCI, #03218); Global Platform for Sustainable Natural Rubber (GPSNR, #10552).* Partner of (1): *Tropical Forest Alliance (TFA, #20249).* Subscriber to: *ISEAL (#16026).* Also links with national organizations.
[2022.10.24/XJ9345/y/F]

- **HCV Network** HCV Network Ltd (#10865)
- HCV Resource Network / see HCV Network Ltd (#10865)
- **HCWH-Asia** Health Care Without Harm-Asia (#10876)
- **HCWH Europe** Health Care Without Harm Europe (#10877)
- **HCWH** Health Care Without Harm (#10875)
- **HDCA** Human Development and Capability Association (#10964)
- The HD Centre – Centre for Humanitarian Dialogue (internationally oriented national body)
- **HD** – Hackers and Developers (inactive)
- **HDH** – Humanidades Digitales Hispanicas – Sociedad Internacional (internationally oriented national body)
- **HD** Human Dignity (#10965)
- **HDI** – Health and Development International (internationally oriented national body)
- **HDLP** – Hermanitas de los Pobres (religious order)
- **HdlS** – Hijas de la Sabiduria (religious order)
- **HDRA** – Henry Doubleday Research Association (internationally oriented national body)
- +he Academy / see European Academy of Gynaecological Surgery (#05795)
- Head and Neck European Society (inactive)
- Heads of Audit Offices of the South Pacific / see Pacific Association of Supreme Audit Institutions (#17935)
- Heads of European Nature Conservation Agencies / see European Network of Heads of Nature Conservation Agencies (#07917)

♦ **Heads of the European Radiological Protection Competent Authorities (HERCA)** 10866
Secretariat 15 rue Louis Lejeune, CS 70013, 92541 Montrouge CEDEX 6, France. E-mail: secretariat@herca.org.
URL: http://www.herca.org/
History 2007. Terms of Reference signed 8 Dec 2008, Paris (France); revised 1 Dec 2010, 12 Jun 2014 and 21 Oct 2014. **Aims** Initiate an exchange of knowledge and experiences so as to facilitate practical and harmonized solutions to important regulatory issues in *radiation* protection. **Structure** Board; Technical Secretariat. Working Groups; Task Forces; Networks. **Activities** Research/documentation; training/education.
Events *Med Inspector workshop* Stockholm (Sweden) 2018. **Publications** Papers.
Members Authorities (56) in 32 countries:
Austria, Belgium, Bulgaria, Croatia, Cyprus, Czechia, Denmark, Estonia, Finland, France, Germany, Greece, Hungary, Iceland, Ireland, Italy, Latvia, Lithuania, Luxembourg, Malta, Netherlands, Norway, Poland, Portugal, Romania, Serbia, Slovakia, Slovenia, Spain, Sweden, Switzerland, UK.
Observer organizations (5):
European Commission (EC, #06633); Food and Drug Administration (FDA); *International Atomic Energy Agency (IAEA, #12294); Nuclear Energy Agency (NEA, #17615); WHO (#20950).*
[2022/XM6604/D]

- Heads of Medicines Agencies (unconfirmed)
- Heads of National Drug Law Enforcement Agencies (meeting series)

♦ **Heads of University Management and Administration Network in Europe (HUMANE)** 10867
Secretariat Rue Théodore de Cuyper 100, 1200 Brussels, Belgium. T. +32493501836. E-mail: secretariat@humane.eu – contact@humane.eu.
URL: http://www.humane.eu/
History 1997. Founded within the framework of *SOCRATES Programme (inactive),* currently Lifelong Learning Programme. Former names and other names: *European Round Table of Senior Administrators* – former. Registration: ASBL/VZW, Belgium. **Aims** Build global networks, foster innovation in higher education services and drive professional excellence in higher education management. **Structure** Round Table (General Assembly); Executive Committee (Board). **Languages** English. **Activities** Events/meetings; training/education.

Events *Digital transformation is getting ready for higher education, but is higher education ready for digital transformation?* Aveiro (Portugal) 2018, *Annual Conference* Malmö (Sweden) 2018, *Contemporary student activism in European universities* Trento (Italy) 2018, *The leadership of people, knowledge and change – the contribution of the administration to institutional sustainability* Frascati (Italy) 2017, *Annual Conference* Paris (France) 2017.
Members Universities; associations. Members in 28 countries:
Austria, Belgium, Croatia, Cyprus, Czechia, Denmark, Estonia, Finland, France, Germany, Greece, Hungary, Iceland, Ireland, Italy, Latvia, Lithuania, Netherlands, Norway, Poland, Portugal, Romania, Slovakia, Slovenia, Spain, Sweden, Switzerland, UK.
[2022/XF5643/E]

- HeadWaters International (internationally oriented national body)
- HEAL Africa (unconfirmed)
- Healey International Relief Foundation (internationally oriented national body)
- HealeyIRF – Healey International Relief Foundation (internationally oriented national body)
- **HEAL** Health and Environment Alliance (#10879)
- Heal The Planet – Global Organisation (internationally oriented national body)

♦ **Health Action International (HAI)** 10868
Action santé internationale (ASI) – Acción para la Salud Internacional
Contact Overtoom 60-II, 1054 HK Amsterdam, Netherlands. T. +31204124523. E-mail: info@haiweb.org.
URL: http://www.haiweb.org/
History Founded 29 May 1981, Geneva (Switzerland), as a coalition of consumer, health, women's and developing countries groups at an International NGO Seminar on Pharmaceuticals. Registered as a Foundation under Dutch law, 1986. EU Transparency Register: 44361352681-84. **Aims** Advance policies that enable access to medicines and rational medicine use for people around the world. **Structure** Foundation Board. **Languages** English. **Staff** 16.00 FTE, paid. **Finance** Project grants from governments and foundations. Annual budget: about US$ 2,000,000. **Activities** Healthcare; publishing activities; events/meetings; training/education; research and development; capacity building; advocacy/lobbying/activism; politics/policy/regulatory.
Events *Annual General Meeting* Berlin (Germany) 2013, *Annual General Meeting* Amsterdam (Netherlands) 2012, *Europe annual general meeting / Annual General Meeting* Cork (Ireland) 2011, *Europe annual general meeting / Annual General Meeting* Amsterdam (Netherlands) 2010, *Europe annual general meeting* Brussels (Belgium) 2007. **Publications** *Briefing Papers.* Policy papers; issue fact sheets; press releases.
Members Consumer, development and public interest groups. Participants in 70 countries and territories:
Argentina, Armenia, Australia, Bangladesh, Belgium, Bolivia, Brazil, Canada, Chile, Colombia, Cuba, Cyprus, Dominican Rep, Ecuador, Estonia, Ethiopia, Finland, France, Germany, Ghana, Greece, Hong Kong, Hungary, India, Indonesia, Ireland, Italy, Jamaica, Japan, Kazakhstan, Kenya, Korea Rep, Kyrgyzstan, Latvia, Lebanon, Lithuania, Malaysia, Mauritius, Mexico, Moldova, Mozambique, Namibia, Netherlands, New Zealand, Norway, Pakistan, Panama, Peru, Philippines, Poland, Portugal, Russia, Rwanda, Senegal, Spain, Sri Lanka, Sweden, Switzerland, Tajikistan, Tanzania UR, Thailand, Trinidad-Tobago, Türkiye, Uganda, UK, Uruguay, USA, Venezuela, Zambia, Zimbabwe.
Included in the above, 13 organizations listed in this Yearbook:
Acción Internacional por la Salud – Latinoamérica and Caribe (AIS-LAC, #00056); Commons Network; HAI Africa (#10851); HAI – Asia-Pacific (HAIAP, #10852); Health Action International – Europe Association (HAI Europe, #10869); International Society of Drug Bulletins (ISDB, #15066); Medicines for Europe (#16633); Medico International; Oxfam International (#17922); Public Eye; Salud por Derecho; T1International, WEMOS.
Consultative Status Consultative status granted from: *WHO (#20950)* (Official Relations). **NGO Relations** Member of: *European Alliance for Responsible R and D and Affordable Medicines (#05879); European Public Health Alliance (EPHA, #08297).*
[2019/XF0934/y/F]

♦ **Health Action International – Europe Association (HAI Europe)** 10869
Sec c/o HAI, Overtoom 60(2), 1054 HK Amsterdam, Netherlands.
URL: http://haiweb.org/hai-europe-assoication/
History 1994. Within *Health Action International (HAI, #10868).* **Aims** Promote rational health *policies* and appropriate *drug* use in developing and developed countries; support networks, countries, NGOs and individuals with the same objective. **Structure** Annual General Meeting; Board. **NGO Relations** Member of: *International Society of Drug Bulletins (ISDB, #15066).*
[2018/XM6406/E]

- Health Alliance International (internationally oriented national body)

♦ **Health for Animals** 10870
Exec Dir Avenue de Tervuren 168, Boîte 8, 1150 Brussels, Belgium. T. +3225410111 – +3225410119. E-mail: carel@healthforanimals.org – info@healthforanimals.org.
URL: http://healthforanimals.org/
History Founded as *Worldwide Council of the Animal Health Industry – Consultation mondiale de l'industrie de la santé animale.* Subsequently changed name to *Worldwide Confederation of the Animal Health Industry – Confédération mondiale de l'industrie de la santé animale (COMISA),* Dec 1997; *International Federation for Animal Health (IFAH),* Mar 2001. Current name adopted Jun 2015. Registered in accordance with Belgian law. **Aims** Create a harmonized, science-based regulatory and trade framework that supports a global animal health industry which is economically viable and high-technology driven, contributing to a healthy and safe *food* supply. **Structure** General Assembly (annual). **Activities** Standards/guidelines; politics/policy/regulatory.
Events *Annual General Assembly* Brussels (Belgium) 2006, *Annual General Assembly* Brussels (Belgium) 2002, *Seminar* Madrid (Spain) 2002.
Members Full animal health industry associations; global companies (10). Member in South East Asia (countries not specified) and in 27 other countries:
Argentina, Australia, Belgium, Brazil, Canada, Chile, Denmark, France, Germany, India, Indonesia, Ireland, Italy, Japan, Korea Rep, Mexico, Netherlands, New Zealand, Paraguay, Portugal, South Africa, Spain, Sweden, Switzerland, Thailand, UK, USA.
Also member, one organization listed in this Yearbook:
AnimalhealthEurope (#00837).
Consultative Status Consultative status granted from: *FAO (#09260)* (Liaison Status). **NGO Relations** Member of: *European Network of Agricultural Journalists (ENAJ, #07864).* Partner of: *Livestock Environmental Assessment and Performance Partnership (LEAP, #16500).*
[2016.10.18/XD2583/y/F]

♦ **Health Behaviour in School-Aged Children (HBSC)** 10871
Intl Coordinator MRC/CSO Social and Public Health Sciences Unit, Univ of Glasgow, 200 Renfield Street, Glasgow, G2 3AX, UK. E-mail: info@hbsc.org.
URL: http://www.hbsc.org/
History Originated 1982, when English, Finnish and Norwegian researchers agreed to develop a shared protocol to survey school children. HBSC study adopted by *WHO Regional Office for Europe (#20945),* 1983. **Aims** Gain new insight into, and increase understanding of health behaviours, health, well-being, lifestyles and social contexts of young people in different countries. **Structure** Principal Investigator's Assembly. Centres: International Coordinating; Support Centre for Publications; Data Management; WHO Collaborating. Coordinating Committee; Scientific Development Group; Methodology Development Group; Policy Development Group; Focus Groups. **Activities** Research/documentation; knowledge management/information dissemination; monitoring/evaluation; events/meetings. **Publications** Articles; reports; fact sheets.
Members Full in 48 countries and territories:
Albania, Armenia, Austria, Azerbaijan, Belgium/Flemish Region, Belgium/Wallonia Region, Bulgaria, Canada, Croatia, Czechia, Denmark, England, Estonia, Finland, France, Georgia, Germany, Greece, Greenland, Hungary, Iceland, Ireland, Israel, Italy, Kazakhstan, Latvia, Lithuania, Luxembourg, Malta, Moldova, Netherlands, North Macedonia, Norway, Poland, Portugal, Romania, Russia, Scotland, Serbia, Slovakia, Slovenia, Spain, Sweden, Switzerland, Türkiye, Ukraine, USA, Wales.
[2018/XM7493/F]

- Health Books International (internationally oriented national body)
- HealthBridge (internationally oriented national body)
- HealthBridge Foundation of Canada / see HealthBridge
- Health Builders (internationally oriented national body)
- Healthcare and Biological Sciences Research Association (internationally oriented national body)
- Healthcare Businesswomen's Association (internationally oriented national body)

♦ **Healthcare Caterers International (HCI)** **10872**
Main Office 406 SUrrey Woods Dr, St Charles IL 60174, USA. T. +16305876336. Fax +16305876308.
Chairman address not obtained. E-mail: mherrera.lhc@salud.madrid.org.
URL: http://www.hciglobal.org/
History Jul 2004. **Aims** Represent caterers and foodservice managers in healthcare industries. **Publications** *Healthcare Caterer.*
Members National organizations (9) in 7 countries:
Australia, Canada, Ireland, Norway, Sweden, UK, USA.
Regional organization (1):
Middle East Dietary Association (MEDA, no recent information). [2011.10.03/XM2215/**D**]

♦ **Healthcare Christian Fellowship International (HCFI)** **10873**
Main Office PO Box 11955, Rynfield, Johannesburg, 1514, South Africa. T. +27119691971. Fax +27119694822. E-mail: president@hcfglobal.org.
Coordinator Vincent van Goghstraat 15, 3781 XM Voorthuizen, Netherlands.
URL: http://www.hcfi.info/
History 1936, South Africa. Founded by Francis Grim. Former names and other names: *International Hospital Christian Fellowship* – former (1936 to 1999). **Structure** Includes Caribbean section. **Events** *Conference* Manila (Philippines) 2011, *Conference* South Africa 1995, *Conference* Kössen (Austria) 1992, *Conference* Vienna (Austria) 1992. **NGO Relations** Associate member of: *World Evangelical Alliance (WEA, #21393).* [2020/XD2755/**D**]

♦ Healthcare Clowning International Meeting (meeting series)

♦ **Healthcare Compliance Packaging Council Europe (HCPC Europe)** . **10874**
Contact c/o NVC Netherlands Packaging Centre, PO Box 164, 2800 AD Gouda, Netherlands. T. +31182512411.
URL: http://www.hcpc-europe.org/
History Founded 2004, when registered in accordance with Belgian law, 2004. **Aims** Achieve demonstrable improvement in patient compliance through implementation of packaging-related initiatives; improve patients' lives. **Structure** General Assembly; Board. **Languages** English. **Staff** 1.00 FTE, paid. **Activities** Advocacy/lobbying/activism; knowledge management/information dissemination; standards/guidelines; networking/liaising. **Events** *General Assembly* Freiburg (Germany) 2019, *General Assembly* Eltville am Rhein (Germany) 2018, *General Assembly* Eltville am Rhein (Germany) 2017, *General Assembly* Eltville am Rhein (Germany) 2015, *Conference* Copenhagen (Denmark) 2007. **Publications** *HCPC Europe Newsletter* (4 a year); *Packaging that improves patients' lives* (annual). White paper.
Members Companies (17) in 9 countries:
Austria, France, Germany, India, Ireland, Italy, Netherlands, Switzerland, UK.
NGO Relations Member of: *International Alliance of Patients' Organizations (IAPO, #11633).* Partner of: *European Alliance for Access to Safe Medicines (EAASM, #05859).* [2017.03.14/XM3295/**D**]

♦ **Health Care Without Harm (HCWH)** **10875**
D'abord ne pas nuire (DNPN) – Salud sin Daño – Salute Senza Danno
Global Secretariat 1 Rue de la Pepiniere, 1000 Brussels, Belgium. T. +3225034911. E-mail: europe@hcwh.org.
Intl Dir Program and Strategy address not obtained. T. +14157521658. E-mail: josh@hcwh.org.
URL: http://www.noharm.org/
History Sep 1996, Bolinas CA (USA). **Aims** Transform healthcare worldwide so it reduces its environmental footprint; become a community anchor for sustainability and a leader in the global movement for environmental health and justice. **Structure** Boards of Directors (4): Latin-America; *Health Care Without Harm-Asia (HCWH-Asia, #10876)*; *Health Care Without Harm Europe (HCWH Europe, #10877)*; US and Canada. Offices (4): Arlington VA (USA); Brussels (Belgium); Buenos Aires (Argentina); Manila (Philippines). **Activities** Events/meetings. **Events** *CleanMed Europe : International Healthcare Congress on Sustainable Products and Practices in Europe* Copenhagen (Denmark) 2016, *CleanMed : health care conference on environmentally preferable products and green buildings* Boston, MA (USA) 2013, *CleanMed Europe : international healthcare congress on sustainable products and practices in Europe* Oxford (UK) 2013, *CleanMed Conference* Denver, CO (USA) 2012, *CleanMed Conference* Denver, CO (USA) 2011.
Members Organizations (over 500) in 57 countries:
Argentina, Armenia, Australia, Austria, Bangladesh, Belarus, Belgium, Brazil, Cambodia, Cameroon, Canada, Costa Rica, Croatia, Czechia, Denmark, Egypt, El Salvador, France, Germany, India, Iran Islamic Rep, Ireland, Italy, Kenya, Lebanon, Liberia, Malaysia, Mexico, Moldova, Morocco, Mozambique, Nepal, Netherlands, Nigeria, North Macedonia, Pakistan, Philippines, Poland, Romania, Russia, Saudi Arabia, Senegal, Slovakia, Slovenia, South Africa, Spain, Sweden, Switzerland, Syrian AR, Tanzania UR, Thailand, Togo, Uganda, UK, Ukraine, USA, Zambia.
Included in the above, 10 organizations listed in this Yearbook:
Commonweal; *Earth Economics*; *Environmental Defense Fund (EDF)*; *Greenpeace International (#10727)*; *HORIZON International*; *International Council of Nurses (ICN, #13054)*; *International Physicians for the Prevention of Nuclear War (IPPNW, #14578)*; *International Society of Doctors for the Environment (ISDE, #15065)*; *Medact*; *Women Engage for a Common Future (WECF, #20992).*
NGO Relations Member of: *EDC Free Europe (#05355)*; *Federation of European and International Associations Established in Belgium (FAIB, #09508)*; *Global Climate and Health Alliance (GCHA, #10288)*; *Nordic Center for Sustainable Healthcare (NCSH, #17229)*; *Planetary Health Alliance (PHA, #18383).* Partner of: *1% for the Planet*; *Global Call for Climate Action (GCCA, inactive).* Europe is member of: *Environmental Coalition on Standards (ECOS, #05499).* [2019/XF6059/y/**F**]

♦ **Health Care Without Harm-Asia (HCWH-Asia)** **10876**
Dir Unit 203 – Kalayaan Ctr Bldg, 65 V Luna Road cor Kalayaan Avenue, Brgy Pinyahan, 1101 Quezon City, Philippines. T. +6329287572. Fax +6329262649. E-mail: mon@no-harm.org – pats@no-harm.org.
URL: http://noharm-asia.org/
History 2003, within *Health Care Without Harm (HCWH, #10875).* **Aims** Transform the health sector, without compromising patient safety or care, so that it becomes ecologically sustainable and a leading advocate for environmental health and justice. **Structure** Board of Trustees; Regional Advisory Council. **Activities** Advocacy/lobbying/activism. [2019/XM6772/**E**]

♦ **Health Care Without Harm Europe (HCWH Europe)** **10877**
Exec Dir Rue de l'Industrie 10, 1000 Brussels, Belgium. T. +3225030481. E-mail: edward.bennett@hcwh.org – europe@hcwh.org.
URL: http://noharm-europe.org/
History 2003. Set up within *Health Care Without Harm (HCWH, #10875).* Registration: Banque-Carrefour des Entreprises, No/ID: 0767.799.441, Start date: 4 May 2021, Belgium, Brussels; EU Transparency Register, No/ID: 57514749088-82, Start date: 4 Jul 2012. **Aims** Transform healthcare so that it reduces its environmental footprint, becomes a community anchor for sustainability and a leader in the global movement for environmental health and justice. **Structure** Board. **Staff** 22.00 FTE, paid. **Finance** Annual budget: 1,760,000 EUR (2022). **Activities** Advocacy/lobbying/activism; guidance/assistance/consulting; training/education.
Members 90 members across 19 countries:
Austria, Belgium, Czechia, Denmark, Finland, France, Germany, Greece, Iceland, Ireland, Italy, Netherlands, Norway, Poland, Portugal, Spain, Sweden, Switzerland, UK.
NGO Relations Member of (1): *Federation of European and International Associations Established in Belgium (FAIB, #09508).* [2023.02.14/XM6771/y/**E**]

♦ Healthcare Infection Society (internationally oriented national body)

♦ **Healthcare Information For All (HIFA)** **10878**
Contact c/o GHI-Net, Corner House, Market Str, Charlbury, OX7 3PN, UK. T. +441608811899. E-mail: admin@hifa.org.
URL: https://www.hifa.org/
History Oct 2006, Mombasa (Kenya). Founded at 10th Congress of *Association for Health Information and Libraries in Africa (AHILA, #02630)*, under the title: *Healthcare Information For All by 2015 (HIFA2015).* One of 5 initiatives within *HIFA Global Forums.* **Aims** Create a world where every person and every health worker has access to healthcare information needed to protect their own health and the health of those for whom they are responsible. **Structure** Steering Group; Advisory Panel. Administered by: *Global Healthcare Information Network (GHI-net).* **Languages** English, French, Portuguese, Spanish. **Staff** 1.50 FTE, paid. **Finance** Donations from health and development organizations. Budget (annual): pounds40,000. **Activities** Events/meetings; advocacy/lobbying/activism. **Events** *International Conference* Dar es Salaam (Tanzania UR) 2014, *International Conference* London (UK) 2011. **Information Services** *HIFA Voices.* **Members** Full (over 12,000) representing over 2,500 organizations in 170 countries. Membership countries not specified. **NGO Relations** Associated member of: *European Forum for Primary Care (EFPC, #07326).* Support from: *Universala Medicina Esperanto-Asocio (UMEA, #20672).* [2014.06.24/XJ7110/**E**]

♦ Healthcare Information For All by 2015 / see Healthcare Information For All (#10878)
♦ Healthcare Information and Management Systems Society (internationally oriented national body)
♦ Health Communication Partnership (internationally oriented national body)
♦ Health Council on Osteoporosis (inactive)
♦ Health and Development International (internationally oriented national body)
♦ Health and Development Policy Project / see Center for Health and Gender Equity

♦ **Health and Environment Alliance (HEAL)** **10879**
Exec Dir Avenue des Arts 7/8, 1210 Brussels, Belgium. T. +3223290080. E-mail: info@env-health.org.
URL: https://www.env-health.org/
History 2003. Founded, on the initiative of Génon K Jensen, as the environmental wing of *European Public Health Alliance (EPHA, #08297).* Former names and other names: *EPHA Environment Network (EEN)* – former. Registration: EU Transparency Register, No/ID: 00723343929-96, Start date: 26 Apr 2016. **Aims** Monitor policy within EU institutions to identify threats and opportunities for environment and health; run advocacy campaigns to bring the voice of the health community to policy makers; follow policy-relevant research and make it accessible; facilitate public and stakeholder participation; build capacity. **Structure** General Assembly; Executive Committee. **Languages** English. **Staff** 11.00 FTE, paid. **Finance** Sources: members' dues. Other sources. Supported by: *European Commission (EC, #06633).* **Activities** Advocacy/lobbying/activism; capacity building; events/meetings; politics/policy/regulatory; projects/programmes; publishing activities; research/documentation. **Events** *International congress of the Paris Appeal at UNESCO* Paris (France) 2006. **Publications** Press releases; letters; position papers. **Members** Members (over 90) include international and Europe-wide organizations, as well as national and local groups. Membership countries not specified. **Consultative Status** Consultative status granted from: *UNEP (#20299).* **IGO Relations** Links with EU institutions including: *Council of the European Union (#04895)*; *European Chemicals Agency (ECHA, #06523)*; *European Commission (EC, #06633)*; *European Parliament (EP, #08146).* **NGO Relations** Member of (5): *EDC Free Europe (#05355)*; *EU Civil Society Contact Group (CSCG, #05572)*; *Global Climate and Health Alliance (GCHA, #10288)*; *International Pollutants Elimination Network (IPEN, #14616)*; *The Green 10 (#10711).* Also member of: EU and WHO Expert Groups and Task Forces. [2023.02.16/XM1613/y/**F**]

♦ Health and Environment Justice Support (unconfirmed)

♦ **Health Evidence Network (HEN)** **10880**
Contact WHO Regional Office for Europe, UN City, Marmorvej 51, 2100 Copenhagen, Denmark. T. +4545337000. Fax +4545337001. E-mail: euhen@who.int.
URL: http://www.euro.who.int/en/what-we-do/data-and-evidence/evidence-informed-policy-making/health-evidence-network-hen/
History Comes within *WHO Regional Office for Europe (#20945).* **Aims** Support public health decision-makers to use the best available evidence in their own decision-making; ensure links between evidence, health policies and improvements in public health. **Structure** Part of Division of Information, Evidence, Research and Innovation at WHO/Europe. **Languages** English, French, German, Russian. **Staff** 1.50 FTE, paid. **Finance** Mainly financed by WHO regular budget and voluntary donations. **Activities** Research/documentation; knowledge management/information dissemination; politics/policy/regulatory; healthcare. **Events** *Meeting* Copenhagen (Denmark) 2004, *Meeting* Copenhagen (Denmark) 2003. **Publications** Evidence synthesis report series. **NGO Relations** Cooperates with: *European Network for Health Technology Assessment (EUnetHTA, #07921).* [2021/XF7030/y/**F**]

♦ **Health First Europe (HFE)** **10881**
Exec Dir Rue du Trône 60, 1st Floor, 1050 Brussels, Belgium. T. +3226261999. Fax +3226269501. E-mail: info@healthfirsteurope.org.
URL: http://www.healthfirsteurope.org/
History Mar 2004. Registration: EU Transparency Register, No/ID: 69743997841-11. **Aims** Encourage reflection and dialogue on the future of healthcare in Europe; ensure that equitable access to modern, innovative and reliable medical technology and healthcare is regarded as a vital investment in the future of Europe. **Structure** Executive Committee; Secretariat. **Activities** Awareness raising. **Events** *New Horizons Congress* Brussels (Belgium) 2008.
Members Organizations (24):
– *Active Citizenship Network (ACN)*;
– Aktion Meditech;
– *European Alliance for Medical and Biological Engineering and Science (EAMBES, #05873)*;
– *European Confederation of Care-Home Organizations (ECHO, #06700)*;
– *European Federation of Associations of Patients with Haemochromatosis (EFAPH, #07056)*;
– *European Federation of Crohn's and Ulcerative Colitis Associations (EFCCA, #07095)*;
– *European Federation of Employees in Public Services (EUROFEDOP, #07106)*;
– *European Federation of National Associations of Orthopaedics and Traumatology (EFORT, #07169)*;
– *European Health Chamber*;
– *European Health Management Association (EHMA, #07458)*;
– *European Health Telematics Association (EHTEL, #07463)*;
– *European Institute of Women's Health (EIWH, #07574)*;
– *European Medical Association (EMA, #07761)*;
– *European Specialist Nurses Organisation (ESNO, #08808)*;
– *Heart Failure Policy Network (HF Policy Network, #10899)*;
– *International Alliance of Patients' Organizations (IAPO, #11633)*;
– *International Diabetes Federation Europe (IDF Europe, #13165)*;
– *International Organization for Standardization (ISO, #14473)*;
– *International Patient Organization for Primary Immunodeficiencies (IPOPI, #14533)*;
– *International Society for Neonatal Screening (ISNS, #15292)*;
– Medical Technology Group;
– *MedTech Europe (#16692)*;
– Pelvic Pain;
– *Union européenne de l'hospitalisation privée (UEHP, #20397).* [2022/XM0432/y/**F**]

♦ Health GAP – Health Global Access Project (internationally oriented national body)
♦ Health Global Access Project (internationally oriented national body)
♦ Health and Global Policy Institute (internationally oriented national body)

♦ **HEALTHGRAIN Forum (HGF)** **10882**
Sec c/o VTT, Tietotie 2, FI-02044 Espoo, Finland. E-mail: office@healthgrain.org.
URL: https://healthgrain.org/
History 6 May 2010, Lund (Sweden). Current statutes adopted Apr 2016. Registration: Finland. **Aims** Promote science based concepts fully unlocking the health promoting potential in the entire grain food production chain to obtain healthy, convenient and appealing foods. **Structure** General Assembly; Board. **Finance** Sources: members' dues. **Events** *Meeting* Vienna (Austria) 2014. **Publications** *HGF Newsletter.*
Members Organizations in 14 countries:
Austria, Belgium, Denmark, Finland, France, Germany, Ireland, Italy, Netherlands, Norway, Sweden, Switzerland, UK, USA.
NGO Relations Member of (1): *Whole Grain Initiative (WGI, #20939).* [2021/AA1296/**F**]

♦ **HealthGrid Association** **10883**

Exec Dir 36 rue Charles-de-Montesquieu, 63430 Pont-du-Château, France. T. +33473405155. Fax +33473405002.
URL: http://www.healthgrid.org/

History France. Statutes adopted during General Assembly, 2003, Lyon (France). Registered in accordance with French law. **Aims** Promote awareness and use of the Grid technologies in the *biomedical* sector. **Structure** General Meeting (annual, during Conference). Board of Directors. **Languages** English, French. **Activities** Runs the *HealthGrid Initiative*. **Events** *Conference* Amsterdam (Netherlands) 2012, *Conference* Paris (France) 2010, *Conference* Berlin (Germany) 2009, *Conference* Chicago, IL (USA) 2008, *Conference* Geneva (Switzerland) 2007. [2011/XJ2324/**F**]

♦ **Health Informatics in Africa (HELINA)** **10884**

Regional Representative c/o Kassenärztliche Vereinigung Hamburg, Humboldtstrasse 56, 22083 Hamburg, Germany.
URL: http://www.helina-online.org/

History 1993. **Activities** Organizes International Working Conference on Health Informatics in Africa. **Events** *Conference* Accra (Ghana) 2014, *Conference* Nigeria 2011, *Health information systems – scaling up solutions to transform healthcare delivery in Africa* Yaoundé (Cameroon) 2011, *Conference* Abidjan (Côte d'Ivoire) 2009, *Conference* Cairo (Egypt) 2002.
Members National societies. Full members in 6 countries:
Côte d'Ivoire, Ethiopia, Malawi, Mali, Nigeria, South Africa.
Corresponding members in 9 countries:
Algeria, Cameroon, Congo DR, Egypt, Kenya, Madagascar, Tanzania UR, Uganda, Zimbabwe.
NGO Relations Member of: *International Medical Informatics Association (IMIA, #14134)*. [2013/XJ1966/**D**]

♦ Health Information Network Europe (internationally oriented national body)
♦ Health Innovation Pathways / see Health Innovation in Practice (#10885)
♦ Health Innovation for People / see Health Innovation in Practice (#10885)

♦ **Health Innovation in Practice (HIP)** **10885**

Dir Dr Martine Berger, c/o WCC, Route de Morillons 1-5, 1211 Geneva 2, Switzerland. T. +41227989852. E-mail: mberger@hip3.org.
Co-Dir address not obtained.
URL: http://www.hip3.org/

History Also referred to as *Health Innovation Pathways* and *Health Innovation for People*. Current statutes adopted 5 Mar 2011, Geneva (Switzerland). Registered in accordance with Swiss Civil Code. **Aims** Promote and facilitate policy action around needs-driven innovation for health at country and regional levels, as well as across countries. **Structure** General Assembly; Board; Advisory Group. [2015/XM7258/**F**]

♦ **Health Level Seven International (HL7)** **10886**

CEO 3300 Washtenaw Ave, Ste 227, Ann Arbor MI 48104, USA. T. +17346777777. Fax +17346776622. E-mail: hq@hl7.org.
URL: http://www.hl7.org/

History 1987. **Aims** Provide standards that empower global health data interoperability. **Structure** Board of Directors; Advisory Council; International Council; Technical Steering Committee. **Activities** Standards/guidelines; awards/prizes/competitions; certification/accreditation; events/meetings; training/education. **Events** *Working Group Meeting* Sydney, NSW (Australia) 2020, *Working Group Meeting* San Antonio, TX (USA) 2019, *Working Group Meeting* Baltimore, MD (USA) 2018, *Working Group Meeting* Cologne (Germany) 2018, *Working Group Meeting* New Orleans, LA (USA) 2018. **Members** Full (over 1,600) from over 50 countries. Membership countries not specified. [2021/XM5467/**F**]

♦ HealthLink360 (internationally oriented national body)
♦ Healthmatch International (inactive)
♦ Health of Mother Earth Foundation (internationally oriented national body)
♦ Health Net (see: #15807)

♦ **Health On the Net Foundation (HON)** **10887**

Exec Dir c/o HUG-Belle-Idée, Chemin du Petit-Bel-Air 2, 1225 Chêne Bourg GE, Switzerland. T. +41223726250. Fax +41223055728. E-mail: honsecretariat@healthonnet.org.
URL: http://www.healthonnet.org/

History Founded 8 Sep 1995, Geneva (Switzerland), by participating organizations of an international meeting. Operations commenced in 1996. Registered in accordance with Swiss Civil Code. **Aims** Guide Internet users to reliable health information sources online. **Structure** Foundation Council; Advisory Board; Executive Board; Departments (5). **Languages** 35. **Staff** 8.00 FTE, paid. **Finance** Members' dues. Public and private sector donations and research grants. **Activities** Advocacy/lobbying/activism; knowledge management/information dissemination; certification/accreditation. **Events** *MEDNET : annual world congress on the internet in medicine* Geneva (Switzerland) 2003. **Publications** Articles; survey; pamphlet. Information Services: Health websites database; international database of conferences and events related to health (including CME courses).
Consultative Status Consultative status granted from: *ECOSOC (#05331)* (Special); *WHO (#20950)* (Official). [2019.02.12/XF3942/f/**F**]

♦ HealthNet International / see HealthNet TPO
♦ HealthNet TPO (internationally oriented national body)
♦ Health Oceans, Healthy People (internationally oriented national body)
♦ Health Organization of the League of Nations (inactive)
♦ Health Outreach to the Middle East (internationally oriented national body)
♦ Health Poverty Action (internationally oriented national body)
♦ HealthProm (internationally oriented national body)
♦ HealthRight International (internationally oriented national body)

♦ **Health Systems Global** **10888**

Secretariat c/o Curatio, 0179 Kavsadze Str 3, Office 5, Tbilisi, Georgia. E-mail: info@healthsystemsglobal.org.
URL: http://www.healthsystemsglobal.org/

History Legally set up 26 Oct 2012. Launched Nov 2012, Beijing (China), at 2nd Global Symposium on Health Systems Research. Registration: Start date: Nov 2015, Switzerland. **Aims** Convene researchers, policy-makers and implementers from around the world to develop the field of health systems research and unleash their collective capacity to create, share and apply knowledge to strengthen health systems. **Structure** Board of 11. Secretariat, including Director and Coordinator. **Languages** English. **Staff** 1.00 FTE, paid. **Finance** Members' dues. Other sources: contributions from University of Copenhagen (Denmark) and *Centre for Tropical Veterinary Medicine, Edinburgh (CTVM)*; symposium proceeds. **Events** *Global Symposium on Health Systems Research* Nagasaki (Japan) 2024, *Global Symposium on Health Systems Research* Liverpool (UK) 2018, *Global Symposium on Health Systems Research* Vancouver, BC (Canada) 2016, *Global Symposium on Health Systems Research* Cape Town (South Africa) 2014, *Global Symposium on Health Systems Research* Beijing (China) 2012. [2018/XJ8507/**E**]

♦ **Health Technology Assessment International (HTAi)** **10889**

Main Office #1280 5555 Calgary Trail, Edmonton AB T6H 5P9, Canada. E-mail: info@htai.org.
URL: http://www.htai.org/

History 25 Jun 2003, Canmore, AB (Canada). Founded to succeed *International Society of Technology Assessment in Health Care (ISTAHC, inactive)*. **Aims** Improve health outcomes worldwide by advancing and promoting health technology assessment. **Structure** International Board of Directors; Executive Committee; Advisory Committees; Working Groups; Secretariat. **Languages** English. **Staff** 10-12 FTE, paid. **Finance** Members' dues. Other sources: events; sponsorship activities. **Activities** Awards/prizes/competitions; awareness raising; capacity building; certification/accreditation; events/meetings; healthcare; networking/liaising; politics/policy/regulatory; projects/programmes; publishing activities; research/documentation; standards/guidelines; training/education. **Events** *Annual Meeting* Adelaide, SA (Australia) 2023, *Annual Meeting* Utrecht (Netherlands) 2022, *Annual Meeting* Manchester (UK) 2021, *Annual Meeting* Beijing (China) 2020, *Annual Meeting* Cologne (Germany) 2019. **Publications** *International Journal of Technology Assessment in Health Care (IJTAHC)* (4 a year).
Members For-profits (16) and Not-for-profits (53) in 37 countries:
Australia, Austria, Belgium, Brazil, Canada, China, Czechia, Denmark, Estonia, Finland, France, Germany, Greece, Hungary, India, Indonesia, Ireland, Israel, Italy, Japan, Korea Rep, Malaysia, Netherlands, New Zealand, Nigeria, Norway, Philippines, Poland, Romania, Singapore, South Africa, Spain, Sweden, Switzerland, Thailand, UK, USA.
Consultative Status Consultative status granted from: *WHO (#20950)* (Official). [2022/XF6998/**F**]

♦ Health Technology Assessment Network of the Americas (#18655)

♦ **Health and Trade Network (HaT)** **10890**

Contact address not obtained. E-mail: info@healthandtradenetwork.org.
URL: http://www.healthandtradenetwork.org/

History 2015. Registered in accordance with Belgian law. **Aims** Advocate for health wherever trade *agreements* are negotiated; force trade agreements to prove their benefit to health before they can be supported. **Structure** Board. **Activities** Advocacy/lobbying/activism.
Members Organizations in Europe and USA. Membership countries not specified. Members include 4 organizations listed in this Yearbook:
Commons Network; *Health Action International (HAI, #10868)*; *SOLIDAR (#19680)*; *WEMOS*.
NGO Relations Member of: *European Alliance for Responsible R and D and Affordable Medicines (#05879)*. [2018/XM6409/**F**]

♦ Health Unlimited / see Health Poverty Action
♦ Health Volunteers Overseas (internationally oriented national body)

♦ **Health and Water African Foundation (HWAF)** **10891**

Fondation africaine de l'eau et de la santé (FAES)
Address not obtained.
URL: http://www.faes-hwaf.org/

History 1999. **Aims** Improve access to drinking water and sanitation services in Africa; fight against water borne diseases; improve the setting hygiene. **Publications** Books.
Members Regional Offices in 3 countries:
Benin, Burkina Faso, Congo DR.
NGO Relations Member of: *Freshwater Action Network (FAN, inactive)*. [2009/XM2721/f/**F**]

♦ **Healthy Brains Global Initiative (HBGI)** **10892**

Communications Officer address not obtained. E-mail: info@hbgi.org.
URL: https://www.hbgi.org/

History 2020. Registration: 501(c)(3), USA. **Aims** Improve the lives of people affected by neurological and mental health problems. **Structure** Board of Directors; Management Team; Lived Experience Council. **Activities** Financial and/or material support. **NGO Relations** Partner of (1): *World Economic Forum (WEF, #21367)*. [2022.10.12/AA1158/**F**]

♦ **Healthy Caribbean Coalition (HCC)** **10893**

Secretariat Culloden Office Complex, Culloden Road, St Michael BB14018, ST MICHAEL BB14018, Barbados. E-mail: hcc@healthycaribbean.org.
URL: http://www.healthycaribbean.org/

History 2008. Registration: Start date: 2012, Barbados. **Aims** Harness the power of civil society, in collaboration with government, private enterprise, academia, and international partners, as appropriate, in the development and implementation of plans for the prevention and management of chronic diseases among Caribbean people.
Members Voluntary associations and informal networks; individuals. Members in 18 countries and territories:
Antigua, Bahamas, Barbados, Belize, Bermuda, Cayman Is, Dominica, Grenada, Guadeloupe, Guyana, Haiti, Jamaica, Montserrat, St Kitts-Nevis, St Lucia, St Maarten, Suriname, Trinidad-Tobago.
Included in the above, 3 organizations listed in this Yearbook:
Caribbean Cardiac Society (CCS, #03467); *Caribbean College of Family Physicians (CCFP, #03474)*; *InterAmerican Heart Foundation (IAHF, #11432)*.
Consultative Status Consultative status granted from: *ECOSOC (#05331)* (Special). **IGO Relations** Memorandum of Understanding with (1): *Caribbean Public Health Agency (CARPHA, #03544)*. Official Relations with *Pan American Health Organization (PAHO, #18108)*. **NGO Relations** Member of (2): *The NCD Alliance (NCDA, #16963)*; *World Heart Federation (WHF, #21562)*. [2021/XJ7628/**D**]

♦ Healthy Cities Project / see WHO European Healthy Cities Network (#20936)
♦ Healthy, Happy, Holy Organization / see 3HO Foundation (#22046)

♦ **Healthy Newborn Network (HNN)** **10894**

Secretariat c/o Save the Children, 501 Kings Hwy E, Ste 900, Fairfield CT 06825, USA. T. +12032214030 – +12032214000. Fax +12032275667.
URL: http://www.healthynewbornnetwork.org/

History Apr 2010, as an online community, on the initiative of *Save the Children Federation (SCF)* – Saving Newborn Lives Program. **Aims** Address critical gaps in newborn *health*.
Members Partners, including the following organizations listed in this Yearbook (17):
African Mothers Health Initiative (AMHI); *Circle of Health International (COHI)*; *Council of International Neonatal Nurses (COINN, #04904)*; *Global Alliance to Prevent Prematurity and Stillbirth (GAPPS)*; *Global Organization for Maternal and Child Health (Go-MCH)*; *Health Alliance International (HAI)*; *International Confederation of Midwives (ICM, #12863)*; *International Stillbirth Alliance (ISA, #15608)*; *IntraHealth International*; *Neonatal Nursing Association of Southern Africa (NNASA)*; *PATH (#18260)*; *PMNCH (#18410)*; *Save the Children Federation (SCF)*; *Swedish Organization for Global Health (SOGH)*; *United States Agency for International Development (USAID)*; *White Ribbon Alliance for Safe Motherhood (WRA, #20934)*; *World Vision International (WVI, #21904)*.
NGO Relations Cooperates with: *European Foundation for the Care of Newborn Infants (EFCNI, #07344)*. [2021/XJ4554/y/**F**]

♦ Healthy Newborn Partnership / see PMNCH (#18410)
♦ **Healthy Stadia** European Healthy Stadia Network (#07464)

♦ **Hearing International** **10895**

Main Office Univ of Colorado, Anschutz Medical Campus, 12631 E 17th Ave, Aurora CO 80045, USA.
URL: http://hearinginternational.org/

History 20 Jun 1993, Istanbul (Turkey), by *International Federation of Oto-Rhino-Laryngological Societies (IFOS, #13496)*. Replaces *International Agency for the Promotion of Ear Care (IAPEC, inactive)*, set up Sep 1984, as *IFOS Standing Committee for Worldwide Prevention of Hearing Impairment (WOPHIC)*, from 10 Nov 1987 known as *International Agency for the Prevention of Deafness (IAPD)*, and also known as *IFOS International Agency for the Promotion of Ear Care*. **Aims** Promote prevention of deafness; seek to mobilize public and political interest with the aim of getting practical resources for the creation of *public health audiology* and *otology* facilities; offer active support and cooperation to WHO by implementing a global programme at international, regional and national levels, particularly in *developing countries*. **Structure** Executive Board, comprising President, Vice-President, Treasurer, Secretary General and 15 members. **Finance** Members' dues. Donations. **Activities** Works with the WHO Regional Offices to set up regional Prevention of Deafness Programmes, to be included in Primary Health Care Programmes; represents medical and social bodies, expert in ear diseases and hearing impairment, offering their cooperation and services to governmental bodies and to WHO; participates in IFOS-sponsored international and regional meetings. **Events** *Scientific conference and general assembly* Bangkok (Thailand) 2009, *Scientific conference / General Assembly and Scientific Conference* Pattaya (Thailand) 2007, *Scientific conference and general assembly* Manila (Philippines) 2006, *General assembly / General Assembly and Scientific Conference* Manila (Philippines) 2005, *Scientific conference* Manila (Philippines) 2005. **Publications** *Hearing International Newsletter* (4 a year).
Members Organizations and individuals in 39 countries and territories:
Australia, Bangladesh, Belgium, Canada, Chile, China, Colombia, Denmark, Germany, Greece, Hong Kong, India, Indonesia, Iran Islamic Rep, Israel, Italy, Kenya, Korea Rep, Malaysia, Mexico, Myanmar, Netherlands, Nigeria, Pakistan, Philippines, Samoa, Saudi Arabia, Singapore, South Africa, Spain, Sri Lanka, Sweden, Switzerland, Taiwan, UK, USA, Venezuela, Vietnam, Zimbabwe.
International organizations (5):

IMPACT – International Initiative Against Avoidable Disablement (#11137); International Association of Logopedics and Phoniatrics (IALP, #12005); International Association of Physicians in Audiology (IAPA, #12084); International Federation of Oto-Rhino-Laryngological Societies (IFOS, #13496); International Society of Audiology (ISA, #14948).
IGO Relations Represented on Executive Board of: *WHO (#20950); IMPACT – International Initiative Against Avoidable Disablement (#11137).* Cooperates with: *UNESCO Office, Jakarta – Regional Bureau for Sciences in Asia and the Pacific (#20313).* **NGO Relations** Represented on Executive Board of: *Council for International Organizations of Medical Sciences (CIOMS, #04905); Hearing International (#10895); International Association of Physicians in Audiology (IAPA, #12084); International Federation of Hard of Hearing People (IFHOH, #13435); International Federation of Oto-Rhino-Laryngological Societies (IFOS, #13496); Nordic Audiological Society (#17210).* [2019/XF2797/y/**F**]

♦ Heartbeat International Foundation 10896

Exec Vice-Pres 2810 West Saint Isabel St, Ste 100, Tampa FL 33607, USA. T. +18132591213. Fax +18132591215. E-mail: connect@heartbeatsaveslives.org.
URL: http://www.heartbeatsaveslives.org/

History 2007. Founded as a non-profit organization next to *Heartbeat International Worldwide (HBIWW)*, set up 19 Oct 1984. Registration: 501(c)(3), No/ID: 26-0330887, USA. **Aims** Save lives globally by providing *cardiovascular* implantable devices and treatment to the needy people of the world. **Structure** Board of Directors. **Activities** Projects/programmes; healthcare. [2020/XJ5870/f/**F**]

♦ HEART – European Association for Research in Transportation (HEART) 10897

Chair EPFL ENAC IIC LUTS, Station 18, 1015 Lausanne VD, Switzerland. T. +41216932481.
URL: http://www.heart-web.org/

History 2012, Lausanne (Switzerland). **Aims** Promote excellence in transportation research in Europe, with a strong emphasis on the promotion of PhD students and young researchers. **Structure** Steering Committee. Scientific Committee. **Languages** English. **Staff** None paid. **Finance** No budget. **Activities** Events/meetings; networking/liaising; knowledge management/information dissemination. **Events** *Symposium* Lyon (France) 2021, *Symposium* Budapest (Hungary) 2019, *Symposium* Athens (Greece) 2018, *Symposium* Haifa (Israel) 2017, *Symposium* Delft (Netherlands) 2016.
Members Full in 15 countries:
Belgium, Denmark, France, Germany, Greece, Hungary, Israel, Italy, Netherlands, Norway, Portugal, Spain, Sweden, Switzerland, UK.
IGO Relations None. **NGO Relations** None. [2019/XJ8905/**D**]

♦ Heart Failure Association of the ESC 10898

Contact European Heart House, Les Templiers, 2035 Route des Colles, CS 80179 BIOT, 06903 Sophia Antipolis, France. T. +33492947600. Fax +33492947601.
URL: http://www.escardio.org/HFA/

History Founded Aug 2004, Munich (Germany), replacing ESC Working Group on Heart Failure. Registered branch of *European Society of Cardiology (ESC, #08536).* **Aims** Improve quality of life and longevity, through better prevention, diagnosis and treatment of heart failure. **Structure** Executive Committee; Board; Committees (12). **Languages** English. **Staff** Provided by *European Society of Cardiology (ESC, #08536).* **Activities** Events/meetings; training/education; knowledge management/information dissemination; awareness raising. **Events** *Annual Heart Failure Congress* Madrid (Spain) 2022, *Joint Congress on Heart Failure and Acute Heart Failure* Florence (Italy) 2021, *Annual Heart Failure Congress* Barcelona (Spain) 2020, *World Congress on Acute Heart Failure* Barcelona (Spain) 2020, *Annual Heart Failure Congress* Athens (Greece) 2019. **Publications** *Guidelines for Acute and Chronic Heart Failure and Device Therapy in Heart Failure; Heart Failure: Preventing Disease and Death Worldwide; Heart Failure Specialist Curriculum.* **Members** Basic; Online; Full. Members (8,000) worldwide. Membership countries not specified. [2015.02.16/XJ4096/**E**]

♦ Heart Failure Policy Network (HF Policy Network) 10899

Secretariat c/o Health Policy Partnership, 68-69 St Martin's Lane, London, WC2N 4JS, UK.
URL: http://www.hfpolicynetwork.eu/

History Launched 29 Sep 2015. **Aims** Lead significant policy changes that may improve the lives of people with heart failure (HF).
Members Individuals in 11 countries:
Belgium, Finland, France, Germany, Ireland, Italy, Netherlands, Romania, Spain, Sweden, UK.
NGO Relations Member of: *Health First Europe (HFE, #10881).* [2018/XM6893/**F**]

♦ Heart Friends Around the World (HFATW) 10900

Exec Dir Strada della Boffalora 1, 24060 Bianzano BG, Italy.
URL: http://www.hfatw.org/

Aims Promote *prevention* and *rehabilitation* of heart disease. **Structure** General Assembly; Assembly of Ordinary Members; Board of Directors; Board of Trustees. **Events** *Annual Congress* Puerto Rico 2009, *Annual Congress* Mexico 2008, *Annual Congress* Nairobi (Kenya) 2007, *Annual Congress* Albena (Bulgaria) 2006, *Annual Congress* Porto (Portugal) 2005. **Members** Cardiologists (1,000) in 100 countries. Membership countries not specified. **NGO Relations** Associate member of: *World Heart Federation (WHF, #21562).* Member of: *The NCD Alliance (NCDA, #16963).* [2013/XF5887/**F**]

♦ **HEART** HEART – European Association for Research in Transportation (#10897)
♦ Heart to Heart International (internationally oriented national body)
♦ Heart to Heart International (internationally oriented national body)
♦ HEART – International Symposium on Highly-Efficient Accelerators and Reconfigurable Technologies (meeting series)
♦ Heartland Alliance International (internationally oriented national body)
♦ Heartnet International (internationally oriented national body)
♦ Heart's Home (#02863)
♦ Heart-Team Education Association (unconfirmed)

♦ Heart Valve Society (HVS) 10901

Main Office 500 Cummings Center, Suite 4400, Beverly MA 01915, USA. T. +19789278330. Fax +19785240498.
URL: https://heartvalvesociety.org/

Aims Promote awareness, advance knowledge and innovate to reduce the burden of heart valve disease with a global and multidisciplinary approach. **Structure** Board of Directors. **Finance** Sources: members' dues. **Events** *Annual Meeting* Miami, FL (USA) 2021, *Annual Meeting* Abu Dhabi (United Arab Emirates) 2020, *Annual Meeting* Barcelona (Spain) 2019, *Annual Meeting* New York, NY (USA) 2018, *Annual Meeting* Monaco (Monaco) 2017. [2020/AA0628/**C**]

♦ Hear the World Foundation (internationally oriented national body)
♦ Heavenly Culture, World Peace, Restoration of Light (internationally oriented national body)
♦ Heaven's Magic / see The Family International (#09253)
♦ Heavily Indebted Poor Countries Initiative / see Enhanced Heavily Indebted Poor Countries Initiative (#05483)
♦ HEBO / see Hague School of European Studies
♦ Hebrew Immigrant Aid Society / see HIAS
♦ HEDCO – Higher Education for Development Cooperation (internationally oriented national body)
♦ HEDLA – International Conference on High Energy Density Laboratory Astrophysics (meeting series)
♦ **HEDNA** Hotel Electronic Distribution Network Association (#10951)
♦ HEDON Household Energy Network (internationally oriented national body)
♦ Hedrologicum Conlegium – Société internationale pour l'étude des maladies du côlon et du rectum (inactive)
♦ HEDS – International Conference on High Energy Density Sciences (meeting series)
♦ HEduBT – European Association for Higher Education in Biotechnology (inactive)
♦ **HE** Helsinki España – Dimensión Humana (#10906)
♦ HEI / see École supérieure d'études internationales
♦ Heidelberger Institut für Global Health (internationally oriented national body)
♦ Heidelberg Institute of Global Health (internationally oriented national body)
♦ Heifer International (internationally oriented national body)
♦ Heifer Project International / see Heifer International
♦ Heifers for Relief / see Heifer International
♦ Heilsarmee (#19041)
♦ Heinrich Böll Foundation (internationally oriented national body)
♦ Heinrich Böll Stiftung (internationally oriented national body)
♦ Heinz Schwarzkopf Foundation for European Youth / see Schwarzkopf Foundation Young Europe (#19136)
♦ Heinz-Schwarzkopf-Stiftung Junges Europa / see Schwarzkopf Foundation Young Europe (#19136)
♦ Heirloom Cacao Preservation Fund (internationally oriented national body)
♦ **HEIRNET** History Educators International Research Network (#10931)
♦ **HEIRS** History of European Integration Research Society (#10932)
♦ HEJSupport – Health and Environment Justice Support (unconfirmed)
♦ HEK – Hilelista Esperanto-Komunumo (internationally oriented national body)
♦ HEKS – Hilfswerk der Evangelischen Kirchen der Schweiz (internationally oriented national body)
♦ **HELCOM** Baltic Marine Environment Protection Commission – Helsinki Commission (#03126)
♦ Helen Dwight Reid Educational Foundation (internationally oriented national body)

♦ Helen Keller International (HKI) 10902

Pres/CEO One Dag Hammarskjold Plaza, Floor 2, New York NY 10017, USA. T. +12125320544. Fax +12125326014. E-mail: info@hki.org.
URL: http://www.hki.org/

History 1915, Paris (France). American branch of the Fund incorporated 1919, in the State of New York (USA). *'American Foundation for the Blind'*, set up 1921, in the State of Delaware (USA), affiliated with ABP in 1945. Former names and other names: *Permanent Blind Relief War Fund* – former (1915 to 1925); *American Braille Press for War and Civilian Blind (ABP')* – former (1925); *American Foundation for Overseas Blind (AFOB)* – former (1946); *Permanent Blind Relief War Fund for Soldiers & Sailors of the Allies* – former (1919). **Aims** Address the causes and consequences of *blindness* and *malnutrition* for the most vulnerable and disadvantaged; provide primary eye care; prevent eye diseases and blindness; restore the sight of cataract victims; develop long-term, sustainable solutions to malnutrition; combat neglected tropical diseases; using technical assistance approach, help people to help themselves. **Structure** Board of Trustees; Helen Keller International Europe (HKIE) Board; Executive Committee; Technical Advisory Committee; Senior Management Team, comprising President and CEO, Vice President and Regional Director for Africa, Vice President and Regional Director for Asia-Pacific, Senior Vice President/Programs, COO, Vice President/Eye Health, Vice President/Development and Communications and Managing Director HKIE. **Languages** English, French. **Staff** 638 full-time and part-time, paid. **Finance** Individual donations; corporate and private grants; government grants; gifts in kind. **Activities** Programmes in 22 countries. Eye Health programmes address several major causes of preventable blindness and low vision, including: cataract; trachoma; onchocerciasis; vitamin A deficiency; refractive error; diabetic retinopathy. In addition to trachoma and onchocerciasis, also combats soil-transmitted helminths, schistosomiasis, and lymphatic filariasis. Nutrition programmes include: micronutrient supplementation to combat vitamin A, iron/folate, zinc and other diet deficiencies; food fortification; homestead food production (including community and school gardening); infant and young child feeding; community-based management of acute malnutrition; school health education initiatives. **Events** *World conference on services to deafblind persons* Paipa (Colombia) 1997, *World conference on services to deafblind persons* Osimo (Italy) 1993, *World conference on services to deaf-blind persons* Stockholm (Sweden) 1989. **Publications** *Worldview Newsletter.* Annual Report; training material. **Members** Not a membership organization. **Consultative Status** Consultative status granted from: *ECOSOC (#05331)* (Ros C); *UNICEF (#20332); WHO (#20950)* (Official Relations).
IGO Relations Participates as observer in the activities of: *Codex Alimentarius Commission (CAC, #04081).* Accredited by: *United Nations Office at Vienna (UNOV, #20604).* Partner of:
- *Australian Aid (inactive);*
- *Canadian International Development Agency (CIDA, inactive);*
- *FAO (#09260);*
- *International Bank for Reconstruction and Development (IBRD, #12317)* (World Bank);
- *Japan International Cooperation Agency (JICA);*
- *Management of Social Transformations (MOST, #16562);*
- *UNDP (#20292);*
- *United States Agency for International Development (USAID);*
- *West African Health Organization (WAHO, #20881);*
- *World Food Programme (WFP, #21510).*

NGO Relations Member of (10): *CORE Group; Global Impact; InsideNGO (inactive); International Coalition for Trachoma Control (ICTC, #12624); International Council for Education of People with Visual Impairment (ICEVI, #13015); Neglected Tropical Diseased NGO Network (NNN, #16969); NGO Committee on UNICEF (#17120); NonProfit Organizations Knowledge Initiative (NPOKI); PMNCH (#18410); World Blind Union (WBU, #21234).* Instrumental in setting up (2): *VISION 2020 – The Right to Sight (inactive); World Federation of the Deafblind (WFDB, #21426).*
Partner of:
- *1,000 Days;*
- *Action Against Hunger (#00086);*
- *American Council for Voluntary International Action (InterAction);*
- *Bread for the World, USA (BFW);*
- *Cambodia Action;*
- *CARE International (CI, #03429);*
- *The Carter Center;*
- *Catholic Relief Services (CRS, #03608);*
- *ChildFund International (#03869);*
- *Church World Service (CWS);*
- *Concern Worldwide* (Ireland);
- *Counterpart International (FSP);*
- *EngenderHealth;*
- *Fred Hollows Foundation;*
- *German Catholic Bishops' Organisation for Development Cooperation (MISEREOR);*
- *Global Alliance for Improved Nutrition (GAIN, #10202);*
- Global Alliance for Vitamin A;
- *Health Poverty Action (HPA);*
- *Humanity and Inclusion (HI, #10975);*
- *IMA World Health (IMA);*
- *International Rescue Committee (IRC, #14717);*
- *International Science and Technology Institute, Arlington VA (ISTI, no recent information);*
- *Lions Clubs International (LCI, #16485);*
- *Mercy Corps International (MCI);*
- national organizations and universities;
- *Nutrition International (#17627);*
- *Opportunities Industrialization Centers International (OICI, #17775);*
- *Organisation pour la prévention de la cécité (OPC);*
- *Oxfam Novib;*
- *Partners for Development (PFD);*
- *Peace Corps;*
- *Plan International (#18386);*
- *Rotary International (RI, #18975);*
- *RTI International;*
- *Save the Children International (#19058);*
- *Seva Foundation (SF);*
- *Sightsavers International (#19270);*
- *SIMAVI;*
- *World Vision International (WVI, #21904).* [2021/XF1898/**E**]

♦ Helen Kellogg Institute for International Studies (internationally oriented national body)
♦ Helen Suzman Foundation (internationally oriented national body)
♦ Helferinnen der Seelen im Fegfeuer (religious order)

- ♦ Helicobacter Pathogenesis and Immunology / see European Study Group on Pathogenesis and Immunology in Helicobacter Infections (#08851)
- ♦ Helicopter Association International (internationally oriented national body)
- ♦ HELICS – Hospitals in Europe Link for Infection Control through Surveillance (no recent information)
- ♦ **HELINA** Health Informatics in Africa (#10884)
- ♦ **HeliOffshore** International Offshore Helicopter Association (#14400)
- ♦ HELIOS – Handicapped People in Europe Living Independently in Open Society (inactive)
- ♦ Hellenic Centre for European Studies (internationally oriented national body)
- ♦ Hellenic Foundation for European and Foreign Policy (internationally oriented national body)
- ♦ Hellerwork International (internationally oriented national body)
- ♦ **HELLIS** WHO South-East Asia Region Health Literature, Library and Information Services Network (#20948)
- ♦ Hello Tomorrow (internationally oriented national body)
- ♦ **Hell's Angels MC** Hell's Angels Motorcycle Club (#10903)

♦ Hell's Angels Motorcycle Club (Hell's Angels MC) 10903

Sec Hells Angels MC Oakland, 4019 Foothill Blvd, Oakland CA 94601, USA. T. +15105350404.
URL: http://www.hells-angels.com/

History First chapter founded in USA, 1948. Also referred to as *HAMC*. **Events** *Annual Congress* Hämeenlinna (Finland) 2000.
Members Chapters (approx 280) in 22 countries:
Argentina, Australia, Austria, Brazil, Canada, Czechia, Denmark, Finland, France, Germany, Greece, Italy, Liechtenstein, Netherlands, Norway, Portugal, South Africa, Spain, Sweden, Switzerland, UK, USA. [2010/XF3256/s/**F**]

- ♦ Help and Action Coordination Committee (inactive)
- ♦ Help Africa / see Help International, UK
- ♦ Help the Aged, UK / see Age UK

♦ HelpAge International 10904

Contact PO Box 78840, London, SE1 7RL, UK. T. +442072787778. E-mail: info@helpage.org.
Registered Address 35-41 Lower Marsh, 4th Floor, London, SE1 7RL, UK.
URL: http://www.helpage.org/

History Oct 1983, London (UK). Derived from the setting up, 1961, of Help the Aged (UK), now *Age UK*, to raise funds for the needs of elderly people in disasters worldwide. Registration: Charity Commission, No/ID: 288180, England and Wales; EU Transparency Register, No/ID: 071230647405-02, Start date: 18 Aug 2022. **Aims** Work towards a world in which all *older people* can lead dignified, active, healthy and secure lives; cooperate with partners to ensure that people everywhere understand how much older people contribute to society and that they must enjoy their right to healthcare, social services and economic and physical security. **Structure** Leadership group includes UK-based directors and regional directors. Board of Trustees. Member organizations participate on an equal basis while retaining their own national decision-making structure and independence. **Finance** Members' dues. Other sources: donations from Governments, national and international organizations and foundations, including: *AARP International*; *Australian Aid (inactive)*; *CARE International (CI, #03429)*; *Catholic Organization for Relief and Development (Cordaid)*; *Comic Relief*; *Commonwealth Foundation (CF, #04330)*; ECHO; *European Commission (EC, #06633)*; Help the Aged, UK; *Inter-American Development Bank (IDB, #11427)*; *International Bank for Reconstruction and Development (IBRD, #12317)* (World Bank); *International NGO Training and Research Centre, Oxford (INTRAC)*; *Swedish International Development Cooperation Agency (Sida)*; *Swiss Agency for Development and Cooperation (SDC)*; *UNICEF (#20332)*; WHO. **Activities** Advocacy/lobbying/activism; projects/programmes. **Events** *World Congress on Healthy Ageing* Kuala Lumpur (Malaysia) 2012, *World NGO forum on ageing* Madrid (Spain) 2002, *Global meeting of generations* Washington, DC (USA) 1999, *Meeting* Harare (Zimbabwe) 1994, *Workshop* Prague (Czechoslovakia) 1992. **Publications** Newsletters; reports; manuals; films; guidelines.
Members Organizations (119) in 74 countries and territories:
Albania, Antigua-Barbuda, Argentina, Armenia, Australia, Bangladesh, Barbados, Belize, Bolivia, Bosnia-Herzegovina, Cambodia, Cameroon, Canada, Chile, China, Colombia, Costa Rica, Czechia, Denmark, Dominica, Dominican Rep, Ethiopia, Fiji, Finland, Germany, Ghana, Grenada, Haiti, Hong Kong, India, Indonesia, Ireland, Jamaica, Kenya, Korea Rep, Kyrgyzstan, Lebanon, Lesotho, Malaysia, Malta, Mauritius, Moldova, Mongolia, Montserrat, Mozambique, Netherlands, Nigeria, Pakistan, Palestine, Peru, Philippines, Russia, Serbia, Sierra Leone, Singapore, Slovenia, South Africa, South Sudan, Spain, Sri Lanka, St Lucia, Sudan, Suriname, Sweden, Switzerland, Tanzania UR, Thailand, Uganda, UK, Ukraine, USA, Vietnam, Zambia, Zimbabwe.
Included in the above, 4 organizations listed in this Yearbook:
Age International; *Catholic Organization for Relief and Development (Cordaid)*; *WorldGranny*.
Consultative Status Consultative status granted from: *ECOSOC (#05331)* (General); *United Nations Population Fund (UNFPA, #20612)*; *WHO (#20950)* (Official Relations); *African Commission on Human and Peoples' Rights (ACHPR, #00255)* (Observer). **IGO Relations** Accredited by: *United Nations Office at Vienna (UNOV, #20604)*. Associated with Department of Global Communications of the United Nations.
NGO Relations Member of:
- *Association for African Medicinal Plants Standards (AAMPS, no recent information)*;
- *Conference of Non-Governmental Organizations in Consultative Relationship with the United Nations (CONGO, #04635)*;
- *Conseil européen de l'industrie chimique (CEFIC, #04687)*;
- *Council for Education in the Commonwealth (CEC)*;
- *Global Alliance for the Rights of Older People (#10226)*;
- *Global Coalition on Women and AIDS (GCWA, #10297)*;
- *Grow Up Free from Poverty Coalition*;
- *InsideNGO (inactive)*;
- *Inter-Agency Task Team on Children affected by AIDS (IATT, #11394)*;
- *International Disability and Development Consortium (IDDC, #13177)*;
- *International Institute on Ageing, United Nations – Malta (INIA, #13860)*;
- *National Council for Voluntary Organizations (NCVO)*;
- *Partnership Committee to the WHO Programme for the Prevention of Blindness (Partnership Committee, no recent information)*;
- *Regional Inter-Agency Task Team on Children and AIDS in Eastern and Southern Africa (RIATT-ESA, #18791)*;
- *SDG Watch Europe (#19162)*;
- *Start Network (#19969)*;
- *UK Consortium on AIDS and International Development*;
- *Vienna NGO Committee on the Family (#20774)*.

Partner of: *Global Call for Climate Action (GCCA, inactive)*. Participates in: *Global Meeting of Generations (GMG)*. Shareholder of: *International Civil Society Centre (#12589)*. Instrumental in setting up: *ACAPS (#00044)*. Support from: *Charities Aid Foundation of America (CAF America)*.
Links with:
- *Consortium of Christian Relief and Development Association (CCRDA)*;
- *Cooperation Committee for Cambodia (CCC)*;
- *ECHO – International Health Services*;
- *European Exchange Centre on Gerontology (EECG, no recent information)*;
- *International Association of Gerontology and Geriatrics (IAGG, #11920)*;
- *International Federation on Ageing (IFA, #13345)*, through *International Federation of Medical Students' Associations (IFMSA, #13478)*;
- *International Social Security Association (ISSA, #14885)*;
- *Japan Foundation*;
- *London School of Hygiene and Tropical Medicine (LSHTM)*;
- *NGO Forum on Cambodia (#17124)*;
- *Terre des hommes Foundation (Tdh Foundation, #20132)*;

Dhaka Ahsania Mission (DAM); *Global Legal Empowerment Network (#10457)*. [2022/XF0233/y/**F**]

- ♦ Help for the Andes Foundation (internationally oriented national body)
- ♦ Help a Child (internationally oriented national body)
- ♦ Help for Children in Need (internationally oriented national body)
- ♦ Help – Hilfe zur Selbsthilfe (internationally oriented national body)
- ♦ Help Honduras Foundation / see Horizons of Friendship
- ♦ Helping Other People (internationally oriented national body)
- ♦ Helping to Reach Many Through Direct Assistance in Development / see Hermandad
- ♦ Helping the World's Cleft Children / see Cleft-Children International (#03994)
- ♦ Help International, UK (internationally oriented national body)
- ♦ Help International, USA (internationally oriented national body)
- ♦ Help for the Persecuted Church (internationally oriented national body)
- ♦ Help the Poor International (internationally oriented national body)
- ♦ Helsingfors kriminalpolitiska institut verksamt i anslutning till Förenta Nationerna / see European Institute for Crime Prevention and Control affiliated with the United Nations (#07550)
- ♦ Helsingin Yliopisto, Kehitysmaatutkimuksen Laitos (internationally oriented national body)
- ♦ Helsinki Accords – Helsinki Final Act of the Conference on Security and Cooperation in Europe (1975 treaty)

♦ Helsinki Citizens' Assembly (hCa) 10905

Contact c/o hCa Turkey, Gümüssuyu Mah, Aga Çiragi Sok No 7, Pamir Apt D3, 34437 Istanbul/Istanbul, Türkiye. T. +902122926842 – +902122926843. Fax +902122926844. E-mail: iletisim@hyd.org.tr.
URL: http://www.hyd.org.tr/

History 19 Oct 1990, Prague (Czechia). 19-21 Oct 1990, Prague (Czech Rep). Also referred to as *hCa International*. **Aims** As a an international coalition of civil society initiatives, work for integration of a wider Europe from the citizens' level, especially in issues connected with basic values of democracy – tolerance, mutual understanding and confidence, human rights and political and economic reconstruction; carry out projects addressing issues of peace and integration among citizens. **Structure** General Assembly (every 1 to 2 years); International Coordinating Committee (ICC). **Languages** English. **Finance** Independent administrative and financial structures for each affiliated organization. **Activities** Networking/liaising; training/education; projects/programmes. **Events** *Séminaire international sur l'identité, la famille, clan et citoyenneté* Algajola (France) 2000, *General Assembly* Baku (Azerbaijan) 2000, *International Trans-Caucasian youth dialogue* Echevan (Armenia) / Kazakh (Armenia) 1997, *International conference* Tuzla (Bosnia-Herzegovina) 1995, *General Assembly* Tuzla (Turkey) 1995. **Publications** *Collage* – youth magazine; *hCA Newsletter*. Books; booklets; reports.
Members Groups and/or individual activists in 20 countries:
Armenia, Azerbaijan, Belgium, Bosnia-Herzegovina, Bulgaria, Czechia, Denmark, France, Georgia, Germany, Greece, Moldova, Netherlands, Norway, Russia, Slovakia, Slovenia, Türkiye, UK, Ukraine.
Affiliated national organizations in 10 countries:
Armenia, Azerbaijan, Bosnia-Herzegovina, France, Georgia, Germany, Moldova, Serbia, Türkiye, UK.
Included in the above, 2 organizations listed in this Yearbook:
European Assembly of Citizens (EAC, #05922); European Dialogue.
Consultative Status Consultative status granted from: *Council of Europe (CE, #04881)* (Participatory Status). **NGO Relations** Represented on the Organizing Committee of: *Hague Appeal for Peace (HAP, #10848)*. Member of: *European Council on Refugees and Exiles (ECRE, #06839)*; *UNITED for Intercultural Action – European Network Against Nationalism, Racism, Fascism and in Support of Migrants and Refugees (UNITED, #20511)*. Instrumental in setting up: *European Dialogue (ED)*; *Inter Citizens Conferences Network (no recent information)*; *International Network for Democratic Solidarity (no recent information)*. Participating organizations include: *American Friends Service Committee (AFSC)*; *Amnesty International (AI, #00801)*; *Conference of European Churches (CEC, #04593)*; European Group for Ecological Action; *Global Partnership for the Prevention of Armed Conflict (GPPAC, #10538)*; *Mediterranean Citizens' Forum (no recent information)*; *World Wide Fund for Nature (WWF, #21922)*. [2020/XF2254/**F**]

- ♦ Helsinki Commission / see Commission on Security and Cooperation in Europe
- ♦ Helsinki Convention, 1974 – Convention on the Protection of the Marine Environment of the Baltic Sea Area (1974 treaty)
- ♦ Helsinki Convention, 1992 – Convention on the Protection of the Marine Environment of the Baltic Sea Area, 1992 (1992 treaty)
- ♦ Helsinki Convention, 1999 – Convention on the Protection of the Marine Environment of the Baltic Sea Area, 1999 (1999 treaty)

♦ Helsinki España – Dimensión Humana (HE) 10906

Main Office Santa Cruz de Marcenado 11, 1º piso B, 28015 Madrid, Spain. E-mail: helsinkiespana@helsinkiespana.org.
URL: https://helsinkiespana.org/

History 1990. Founded under the umbrella of *Helsinki Final Act of the Conference on Security and Cooperation in Europe (Helsinki Accords, 1975)*. Former names and other names: *Helsinki España – Human Dimension* – alias. **Aims** Disseminate and promote principles of Helsinki Final Act of Organization for Security and Cooperation in Europe (OSCE) related to the human dimension. **Structure** Board of Trustees; Executive Committee. **Languages** English, Spanish. **Staff** 4.00 FTE, paid; 50.00 FTE, voluntary. **Finance** Private and public sponsors. **Activities** Training/education; events/meetings; awareness raising. **Events** *Global University Forum* Santiago de Compostela (Spain) 2018, *Universities for Poverty Alleviation International Congress of Rectors* Madrid (Spain) 2015, *Meeting* New York, NY (USA) 2009, *Meeting on the 60th anniversary of the Universal Declaration of Human Rights* Valencia (Spain) 2008. **Publications** Analyses; conference proceedings. **Members** Universities (140) in 53 countries. Membership countries not specified. **IGO Relations** Cooperates with: *European Union (EU, #08967)*; *NATO (#16945)*; *Organization for Security and Cooperation in Europe (OSCE, #17887)*; *United Nations (UN, #20515)*. **NGO Relations** Cooperates with: *International Committee of the Red Cross (ICRC, #12799)*. [2021/XM2965/**F**]

- ♦ Helsinki España – Human Dimension / see Helsinki España – Dimensión Humana (#10906)
- ♦ Helsinki Final Act of the Conference on Security and Cooperation in Europe (1975 treaty)
- ♦ Helsinki Institute for Crime Prevention and Control affiliated with the United Nations / see European Institute for Crime Prevention and Control affiliated with the United Nations (#07550)
- ♦ Helsinki Literature and the City Network / see Association for Literary Urban Studies
- ♦ Helsinki Treaty – Treaty of Cooperation between Denmark, Finland, Iceland, Norway and Sweden (1962 treaty)
- ♦ Helsinkskij Institut po Preduprezdeniju Prestupnosti i Borbe s nej svjazannyj s Organizaciej Obedinennyh Nacij / see European Institute for Crime Prevention and Control affiliated with the United Nations (#07550)
- ♦ HELVETAS Swiss Intercooperation (internationally oriented national body)
- ♦ HEMCARE / see Haematology Nurses & Healthcare Professionals Group (#10847)
- ♦ **Hemispheric Institute** Hemispheric Institute of Performance and Politics (#10907)

♦ Hemispheric Institute of Performance and Politics (Hemispheric Institute) 10907

Instituto Hemisférico de Performance y Politica – Instituto Hemisférico de Performance e Politica
Main Office c/o New York Univ, 20 Cooper Square, 5th Floor, New York NY 10003, USA. T. +12129981631. Fax +12129954423.
URL: http://hemisphericinstitute.org/

History 1998, USA. Founded on the initiative of Diana Taylor. **Structure** Board, consisting of Steering Committee and one individual of each member institution. Steering Committee. **Finance** Funding from *Ford Foundation (#09858)*. **Events** *Meeting* Montréal, QC (Canada) 2014. **Publications** *e-misférica* (2 a year) – online journal.
Members Institutions in 9 countries:
Brazil, Canada, Chile, Colombia, Costa Rica, Mexico, Peru, Puerto Rico, USA. [2021/XJ6487/j/**D**]

- ♦ Hemispheric Insurance Conference / see Federación Interamericana de Empresas de Seguros (#09331)
- ♦ Hemispheric Social Alliance (#00635)
- ♦ The Hemostasis and Oxygenation Research Network / see Trauma Hemostasis & Oxygenation Research (#20229)
- ♦ **HEN** Health Evidence Network (#10880)
- ♦ **Les Hénokiens** Association Internationale d'Entreprises Familiales and Bicentenaires (#11723)
- ♦ **The Henokiens** International Association of Bicentenary Family Companies (#11723)
- ♦ Henri Capitant Association for the French Legal System (#02631)
- ♦ Henri La Fontaine Foundation (internationally oriented national body)
- ♦ Henry Doubleday Research Association (internationally oriented national body)

Henry Dunant Centre
10907
alphabetic sequence excludes
For the complete listing, see Yearbook Online at

- ♦ Henry Dunant Centre for Humanitarian Dialogue / see Centre for Humanitarian Dialogue
- ♦ Henry L Stimson Center (internationally oriented national body)
- ♦ Henry Luce Foundation (internationally oriented national body)
- ♦ Henry Martyn Centre for the Study of Mission and World Christianity / see Cambridge Centre for Christianity Worldwide
- ♦ Henry M Jackson School of International Studies (internationally oriented national body)

♦ Henry Sweet Society for the History of Linguistic Ideas 10908

Administrator School of Arts, English and Languages, Queen's University Belfast, Belfast, BT7 1NN, UK.
URL: https://www.henrysweet.org/

History 1984. **Aims** Promote and encourage the study of the history of all branches of linguistic thought, theoretical and applied, and including non-European traditions. **Structure** Annual General Meeting; Executive Committee. **Activities** Awards/prizes/competitions; events/meetings. **Events** *Annual Colloquium* Leuven (Belgium) 2022, *Annual Colloquium* London (UK) 2021, *Annual Colloquium* 2020, *Annual Colloquium* Edinburgh (UK) 2019, *Annual Colloquium* Maynooth (Ireland) 2018. **Publications** *Language & History* (3 a year).
[2022/AA2213/**E**]

♦ HEPA Europe 10909

Programme Manager WHO Regional Office, UN City, Marmorvej 51, 2100 Copenhagen, Denmark. T. +4545336822. Fax +4545337001. E-mail: hepaeurope@who.int.
URL: http://www.euro.who.int/hepaeurope/

History 2005, collaborating closely with *WHO Regional Office for Europe (#20945)*. Replaces *European Network on Health-Enhancing Physical Activity (HEPA, inactive)*. Full title: *HEPA Europe – European network for the promotion of health-enhancing physical activity.* **Aims** Strengthen and support efforts and actions that increase participation and improve the conditions favourable to a healthy *lifestyle*, in particular with respect to health-enhancing *physical activity*. **Structure** Steering Committee, comprising Chair and 14 members. **Languages** English, Russian. **Activities** Advocacy/lobbying/activism. **Events** *Annual Meeting* Odense (Denmark) 2019, *Conference* Odense (Denmark) 2019, *Annual Meeting* London (UK) 2018, *Annual Meeting* Zagreb (Croatia) 2017, *Conference* Zagreb (Croatia) 2017. **Publications** *HEPA Europe Newsletter* (2-4 times a year). Reports; booklets; articles.
Members Institutions (140) and individuals (4) in 33 countries:
Austria, Belgium, Bosnia-Herzegovina, Bulgaria, Croatia, Cyprus, Czechia, Denmark, Finland, France, Georgia, Germany, Greece, Hungary, Iceland, Ireland, Israel, Italy, Lithuania, Malta, Netherlands, North Macedonia, Norway, Poland, Portugal, Russia, Slovenia, Spain, Sweden, Switzerland, Türkiye, UK, Ukraine.
NGO Relations Regional Network of: *Agita Mundo Network (#00560).* [2021/XM3376/**F**]

- ♦ HEPA Europe – European network for the promotion of health-enhancing physical activity / see HEPA Europe (#10909)

♦ Hepatitis B and C Public Policy Association 10910

Corporate Sec 19 rue Eugène Ruppert, L-2453 Luxembourg, Luxembourg. T. +393396596105. Fax +35226644848. E-mail: info@hepbcppa.org.
URL: http://www.hepbcppa.org/

History Apr 2009. Former names and other names: *Hepatitis B and C Summit Conferences Association* – former (Jun 2011). Registration: No/ID: F7987, Luxembourg. **Aims** Bring together thought leaders and stakeholders from across the board to reflect on recent advances and challenges in understanding, measuring, preventing, diagnosing and treating hepatitis B and C and develop policy responses that can effectively and measurably address these challenges. **Structure** Board of Directors. **Activities** Events/meetings. **Events** *HCV Policy Summit* Spain 2021.
Members Individuals in 14 countries:
Austria, Belgium, Canada, China, Egypt, France, Italy, Portugal, Slovenia, Spain, Switzerland, Türkiye, UK, USA.
NGO Relations Member of (1): *ACHIEVE (#00068)* (Founding). Cooperates with (1): *Liver Patients International (LPI, #16498).* [2021/AA2336/v/**D**]

- ♦ Hepatitis B and C Summit Conferences Association / see Hepatitis B and C Public Policy Association (#10910)

♦ HEPiX Forum 10911

Contact address not obtained. E-mail: hepix-board@hepix.org.
URL: http://www.hepix.org/

History 1991, Tsukuba (Japan). **Aims** Bring together worldwide *Information Technology* staff from high energy physics and nuclear physics laboratories and institutes, to foster a learning and sharing experience between sites facing scientific *computing* and *data* challenges. **Structure** Board; 2 Co-Chairs. Working Groups. **Activities** Events/meetings. **Events** *Forum* Amsterdam (Netherlands) 2019, *Forum* Barcelona (Spain) 2018. **Members** Individuals working at IT departments. Membership countries not specified.
[2019/XM8355/**F**]

- ♦ **HEPTech** High Energy Physics Technology Transfer Network (#10914)
- ♦ **HERACLES** Forum Mondial Heracles (#09925)
- ♦ HERA – International Centre of Health Protection (internationally oriented national body)
- ♦ Heraldiska Sällskapet (#19442)
- ♦ Heraldisk Selskab (#19442)
- ♦ Heraldisk Selskap (#19442)
- ♦ Herbert Vere Evatt Memorial Foundation / see Evatt Foundation
- ♦ **HERCA** Heads of the European Radiological Protection Competent Authorities (#10866)
- ♦ HERDSA – Higher Education Research and Development Society of Australasia (internationally oriented national body)
- ♦ Hereditary Angioedema International Association / see HAE International (#10846)
- ♦ Hereditary Hemorrhagic Telangiectasia Foundation International (internationally oriented national body)
- ♦ **HEREIN Association** International Association of the European Heritage Network (#11881)
- ♦ **HEREIN Project** European Information Network on Cultural Heritage Policies (#07533)
- ♦ Herfah – First Multipurpose Women Cooperative in Gassim (internationally oriented national body)
- ♦ HERIMED – Association for the Documentation, Preservation and Enhancement of the Euro-Mediterranean Cultural Heritage (no recent information)
- ♦ Heritage Africa (internationally oriented national body)
- ♦ Heritage in Asia Research Group / see Cultural Heritage Asia Pacific Network
- ♦ **Heritage Europe** European Association of Historic Towns and Regions (#06068)
- ♦ Heritage Foundation (internationally oriented national body)
- ♦ Hermanas Agustinas Misioneras (religious order)
- ♦ Hermanas del Amor de Dios (religious order)
- ♦ Hermanas Betlemitas (religious order)
- ♦ Hermanas del Bueno Socorro (religious order)
- ♦ Hermanas de la Caridad Cristiana, Hijas de la Beata Virgen Maria de la Inmaculada Concepción (religious order)
- ♦ Hermanas de la Caridad de Jesús y Maria (religious order)
- ♦ Hermanas de la Caridad de Montreal (religious order)
- ♦ Hermanas de la Caridad de Nevers (religious order)
- ♦ Hermanas de la Caridad de Nuestra Señora de las Mercedes (religious order)
- ♦ Hermanas de la Caridad de Santa Ana (religious order)
- ♦ Hermanas Carmelitas del Sagrado Corazón de Jesús (religious order)
- ♦ Hermanas Carmelitas de San José (religious order)
- ♦ Hermanas Franciscanas de la Inmaculada Concepción (religious order)
- ♦ Hermanas Grises – Hermanas de la Caridad de Montreal (religious order)
- ♦ Hermanas Mercedarias Misioneras de Bérriz (religious order)
- ♦ Hermanas de la Misericordia de las Américas (religious order)
- ♦ Hermanas Misioneras de la Inmaculada Concepción (religious order)
- ♦ Hermanas Misioneras de San Carlos Borromeo (religious order)
- ♦ Hermanas del Niño Jesús, Puy (religious order)
- ♦ Hermanas de Notre Dame (religious order)
- ♦ Hermanas Oblatas del Santisimo Redentor (religious order)
- ♦ Hermanas de la Providencia (religious order)
- ♦ Hermanas de la Sagrada Familia (religious order)
- ♦ Hermanas del Sagrado Corazón de Jesús (religious order)
- ♦ Hermanas de la Santa Cruz (religious order)
- ♦ Hermanas del Santo Angel de la Guarda (religious order)
- ♦ Hermanas Terciarias Capuchinas de la Sagrada Familia (religious order)
- ♦ Hermanas Terciarias Dominicanas de la Congregación de Nuestra Señora del Santisimo Rosario (religious order)
- ♦ Hermanas de la Virgen Maria del Monte Carmelo – Hermanas Terciarias Carmelitas de Orihuela (religious order)
- ♦ Hermandad (internationally oriented national body)
- ♦ Hermandad de la Virgen del Carmel (religious order)
- ♦ Hermanitas de los Ancianos Desamparados (religious order)
- ♦ Hermanitas de la Asunción (religious order)
- ♦ Hermanitas de los Pobres (religious order)
- ♦ Hermanitos de Jesús (religious order)
- ♦ Hermann-Gmeiner-Fonds, Deutschland (internationally oriented national body)
- ♦ Hermann Gmeiner Funds, Germany (internationally oriented national body)
- ♦ Hermanos de la Caridad (religious order)
- ♦ Hermanos de los Hombres / see Brothers to All Men (#03339)
- ♦ Hermanos Misioneros de la Caridad (religious order)
- ♦ Hermanos de Nuestra Señora de Lourdes (religious order)
- ♦ Hermes Community / see HIT Rail (#10933)
- ♦ Hermes Information Technology / see HIT Rail (#10933)
- ♦ Hernstein International Management Institute (internationally oriented national body)
- ♦ Herriarte (internationally oriented national body)
- ♦ HESI – Higher Education Sustainability Initiative (unconfirmed)
- ♦ **HESPEL** Hôte européen pour les services publics (#09911)
- ♦ Hesperian Foundation / see Hesperian Health Guides
- ♦ Hesperian Health Guides (internationally oriented national body)
- ♦ Hessische Stiftung Friedens- und Konfliktforschung / see Peace Research Institute Frankfurt
- ♦ HE Symposium – International Symposium Hydrogen & Energy (meeting series)
- ♦ **HETI** Federation of Horses in Education and Therapy International (#09593)
- ♦ **HETL** International Higher Education Teaching and Learning Association (#13795)
- ♦ **HEUG** Higher Education User Group (#10915)
- ♦ **HEUNI** European Institute for Crime Prevention and Control affiliated with the United Nations (#07550)
- ♦ Hewlett Foundation / see The William and Flora Hewlett Foundation
- ♦ Hexagonal / see Central European Initiative (#03708)
- ♦ Hexagonale / see Central European Initiative (#03708)
- ♦ Hexagonal Initiative / see Central European Initiative (#03708)

♦ Hezbollah Internationale 10912

Address not obtained.

History 1982, during the Lebanon War, when a group of Lebanese Shi'ite Muslims declared themselves to be the *Party of God – Hizb Allah.* Closely allied with the Islamic Revolution in Iran. Also referred to as: *Hizballah*; *Islamic Jihad for the Liberation of Palestine*; *Organization of the Oppressed on Earth*; *Revolutionary Justice Organization.* **Aims** As an international network of *Islamic extremist* groups, resist the Israeli invasion of the Lebanon; eventually create an Islamic republic in Lebanon and remove all non-Islamic influences from the area. **Structure** Main operations in Beirut (Lebanon). Cells in Europe, Africa, North America and South America. Current Secretary-General is Sheikh Sayyed Hassan Nasrallah. **Finance** Funding and other assistance from the government of Iran Islamic Republic. **Activities** Wages the holy war *Islamic Jihad for the Liberation of Palestine.* Anti-Israel and anti-USA terrorist attacks. **Members** Several thousand individuals. Membership countries not available. [2008/XF4017/s/**F**]

- ♦ HFA – Hope for Africa (internationally oriented national body)
- ♦ **HFATW** Heart Friends Around the World (#10900)
- ♦ HFAW – Hope Foundation for African Women (internationally oriented national body)
- ♦ **HFCC** High Frequency Coordination Conference (#10916)
- ♦ HFCE – Halal Food Council of Europe (internationally oriented national body)
- ♦ **HFC** "Hope for Children" CRC Policy Center (#10943)
- ♦ **HFE** Health First Europe (#10881)
- ♦ **HFE** Hindu Forum of Europe (#10920)
- ♦ HFE – Hope for Europe (internationally oriented national body)
- ♦ **HFES-EUR** Human Factors and Ergonomics Society – Europe Chapter (#10967)
- ♦ HFES GCC – Human Factors and Ergonomics Society GCC Chapter (unconfirmed)
- ♦ HFES – Human Factors and Ergonomics Society (internationally oriented national body)
- ♦ HFHI – Habitat for Humanity International (internationally oriented national body)
- ♦ HF – Honda Foundation (internationally oriented national body)
- ♦ HFIAW / see International Association of Heat and Frost Insulators and Allied Workers
- ♦ HFIAW – International Association of Heat and Frost Insulators and Allied Workers (internationally oriented national body)
- ♦ **HF Policy Network** Heart Failure Policy Network (#10899)
- ♦ **HFSJG** Internationale Stiftung Hochalpine Forschungsstationen Jungfraujoch und Gornergrat (#13671)
- ♦ **HFSJG** International Foundation of the High Altitude Research Stations Jungfraujoch and Gornergrat (#13671)
- ♦ **HFSPO** International Human Frontier Science Program Organization (#13819)
- ♦ **HFT** International Symposium on Human Factors in Telecommunications (#15642)
- ♦ **HFTN** Hope for the Nations (#10944)
- ♦ **HGF** HEALTHGRAIN Forum (#10882)
- ♦ **HGF** The Historic Gardens Foundation (#10929)
- ♦ HGPI – Health and Global Policy Institute (internationally oriented national body)
- ♦ HGSA – Human Genetics Society of Australasia (internationally oriented national body)
- ♦ **HGVS** Human Genome Variation Society (#10969)
- ♦ **HHE** Historic Hotels of Europe (#10930)
- ♦ HHGFAA / see International Association of Movers
- ♦ HH Humanitarian Relief Foundation (internationally oriented national body)
- ♦ HHI Church – Harvest House International Church (religious order)
- ♦ HHI – Hands to Hearts International (internationally oriented national body)
- ♦ HHI – Heart to Heart International (internationally oriented national body)
- ♦ HHS – Society of the Helpers of the Holy Souls (religious order)
- ♦ HHT Europe (unconfirmed)
- ♦ HHT Foundation – Hereditary Hemorrhagic Telangiectasia Foundation International (internationally oriented national body)
- ♦ HI-12 – High Twelve International (internationally oriented national body)
- ♦ HIARG / see Cultural Heritage Asia Pacific Network
- ♦ HIAS (internationally oriented national body)
- ♦ HIAS-JCA Emigration Association (inactive)
- ♦ HIC / see International Centre on Small Hydro-Power
- ♦ HICEM – HIAS-JCA Emigration Association (inactive)
- ♦ **HIC** Habitat International Coalition (#10845)
- ♦ **HiCN** Households in Conflict Network (#10955)
- ♦ HICOG – Allied High Commission for Germany (inactive)

♦ HICS / see Holt International
♦ HICSS – Hawaii International Conference on System Sciences (meeting series)
♦ HIDA / see Association for Overseas Technical Cooperation and Sustainable Partnerships
♦ HidroEx – Fundação Centro Internacional de Educação, Capacitação e Pesquisa Aplicada em Aguas (internationally oriented national body)
♦ Hieronymites – Order of St Jerome (religious order)
♦ HIFA2015 / see Healthcare Information For All (#10878)
♦ **HIFA** Healthcare Information For All (#10878)
♦ Higgs Hunting – Workshop "Higgs Hunting" (meeting series)
♦ High Arab Institute for Translation (internationally oriented national body)
♦ High Conservation Value Resource Network / see HCV Network Ltd (#10865)

♦ High Council of Islamic Economy in Europe (HCIEE) 10913

Main Office Kattenberg 100, 2140 Antwerp, Belgium.
URL: http://www.mabenyaich.org/
Structure General Assembly (annual). Board of Directors, including President, Vice-President, Secretary and Treasurer. **Finance** Members' dues.
Members Individuals (7) in 3 countries:
Belgium, France, Morocco. [2012/XD8300/**D**]

♦ High Energy Physics Technology Transfer Network (HEPTech) 10914

Chairman GSI Helpholtzzentrum für Schwerionenforschung, Planckstrasse 1, 64291 Darmstadt, Germany.
Communication Officer address not obtained.
URL: http://heptech.web.cern.ch/
History 2006. Founded by *European Organization for Nuclear Research (CERN, #08108)* Council. **Aims** Enhance technology transfer from fundamental research in physics to society. **Structure** Board; Coordination Team. **Languages** English. **Staff** 0.50 FTE, paid. **Finance** Sources: members' dues. Annual budget: 55,000 EUR. **Activities** Events/meetings; knowledge management/information dissemination. **Events** *European Cryogenic Days* Lund (Sweden) 2019, *Annual Symposium* Szeged (Hungary) 2018, *Annual Symposium* Darmstadt (Germany) 2017, *Annual Symposium* Bucharest (Romania) 2016, *European Cryogenics Days* Geneva (Switzerland) 2016. **Publications** *HEPTech Newsletter*. Press releases.
Members Research institutions active in particle, astro-particle and nuclear physics in 13 countries:
Bulgaria, Czechia, Germany, Greece, Hungary, Italy, Portugal, Romania, Slovakia, Spain, Sweden, Switzerland, UK.
Included in the above, 2 organizations listed in this Yearbook:
European Organization for Nuclear Research (CERN, #08108); *European Spallation Source ERIC (ESS, #08804)*.
IGO Relations *European Organization for Nuclear Research (CERN, #08108)*; *Joint Research Centre (JRC, #16147)*. **NGO Relations** *Cryogenics Society of Europe (CSE, #04975)*; *Enterprise Europe Network (EEN, #05493)*; *European Spallation Source ERIC (ESS, #08804)*. [2020.05.12/XM4930/y/**F**]

♦ Higher Education for Development Cooperation (internationally oriented national body)
♦ Higher Education Research and Development Society of Australasia (internationally oriented national body)
♦ Higher Education Sustainability Initiative (unconfirmed)

♦ Higher Education User Group (HEUG) 10915

Exec Dir address not obtained. T. +16026330734. E-mail: support@heug.org.
URL: http://www.heug.org/
History 1997. Set up as an international organization consisting of Higher Education institutions that use application software from the Oracle Corporation. Registration: 501(c)(3) non-profit, USA. **Aims** Provide a mechanism for sharing information and experience on selection, implementation and cost-effective use of Oracle application *software*. **Structure** Board of Directors. **Activities** Networking/liaising; events/meetings. **Events** *Alliance* Seattle, WA (USA) 2022, *Alliance* 2021, *Asia Alliance Conference* Singapore (Singapore) 2019, *European, Middle East and Africa Annual Conference* Barcelona (Spain) 2017, *Arab Alliance Conference* Abu Dhabi (United Arab Emirates) 2016. [2021/XM5230/**F**]

♦ Higher Institute of Emergency Planning / see Higher Institute of Emergency Planning – European Centre Florival
♦ Higher Institute of Emergency Planning – European Centre Florival (now national)
♦ Higher Institute of International Relations 'Raúl Roa Garcia' (internationally oriented national body)
♦ High Frequency Coordination Committee / see High Frequency Coordination Conference (#10916)

♦ High Frequency Coordination Conference (HFCC) 10916

Chairman Vinohradska 12, 120 99 Prague 2, Czechia. E-mail: info@hfcc.org.
URL: http://www.hfcc.org/
History 1990, as *High Frequency Coordination Committee*. Registered in accordance with Czech law. **Aims** Promote efficient and economic use of the *short-wave radio* spectrum; improve radio reception of short-wave *broadcast* transmissions world-wide. **Structure** Plenary Meeting (twice a year). Steering Board, comprising chairman, Vice-Chairman, Systems Development Coordinator and Rapporteur. Secretariat. **Languages** English. **Staff** 1.00 FTE, paid; 0.50 FTE, voluntary. **Finance** Members' dues. Conferences also partly paid by sponsorship. **Events** *High Frequency Coordination Conference* Kuala Lumpur (Malaysia) 2018, *Biannual Meeting* Kuala Lumpur (Malaysia) 2014, *Biannual Meeting* Sofia (Bulgaria) 2014, *Biannual Meeting* Bratislava (Slovakia) 2013, *Biannual Meeting* Tunis (Tunisia) 2013.
Members Broadcasting companies and organizations in 50 countries:
Albania, Algeria, Austria, Belarus, Belgium, Bulgaria, China, Croatia, Czechia, Ecuador, Egypt, France, Germany, Greece, Holy See, Hungary, Iran Islamic Rep, Israel, Italy, Jordan, Kuwait, Libya, Lithuania, Madagascar, Mauritania, Morocco, Netherlands, Nigeria, Norway, Oman, Philippines, Poland, Qatar, Romania, Russia, Saudi Arabia, Singapore, Slovakia, South Africa, Spain, Sudan, Sweden, Syrian AR, Tunisia, Türkiye, UK, Ukraine, United Arab Emirates, USA, Uzbekistan.
Included in the above, 5 organizations listed in this Yearbook:
Adventist World Radio (see: #10109); *Far East Broadcasting Company*; *International Broadcasting Bureau (IBB)*; *Reach Beyond*; *Trans World Radio (TWR)*.
IGO Relations Sector member of *International Telecommunication Union (ITU, #15673)* in the category of Regional and International Organizations. [2014/XF3718/y/**F**]

♦ HIGH – Heidelberg Institute of Global Health (internationally oriented national body)
♦ High Level Forum on Aid Effectiveness (meeting series)
♦ High-Level Inter-American Network on Decentralization, Local Government and Citizen Participation (#18691)

♦ High Level Panel for a Sustainable Ocean Economy (Panel) 10917

Secretariat c/o WRI, 10 G St NE, Ste 800, Washington DC 20002, USA. E-mail: info@oceanpanel.org.
URL: https://www.oceanpanel.org/
History 24 Sep 2018, New York, NY (USA). Inaugural meeting, 24 Sep 2018. New York NY (USA). **Aims** Advance a new contract between humanity and the sea that protects the Ocean and optimizes its value to humankind. **Structure** Advisory Network; Expert Group; Secretariat, based at *World Resources Institute (WRI, #21753)*. **Activities** Advocacy/lobbying/activism.
Members Advisory Network members: Businesses; NGOs; IGOs; Initiatives; Foundations. Included in the above, 69 organizations listed in this Yearbook:
- *5 Gyres Institute (5GYRES)*;
- *African Development Bank (ADB, #00283)*;
- *Aquaculture Stewardship Council (ASC, #00885)*;
- *Asian Development Bank (ADB, #01422)*;
- *Asian Infrastructure Investment Bank (AIIB, #01512)*;
- *Asia-Pacific Economic Cooperation (APEC, #01887)*;
- *Bloomberg Philanthropies*;
- *Blue Finance (#03283)*;
- *Caribbean Community (CARICOM, #03476)*;
- *Centre for Livelihoods, Ecosystems, Energy, Adaptation and Resilience in the Caribbean (CLEAR Caribbean)*;
- *Climate Bonds Initiative (#04006)*;
- *Coastal Oceans Research and Development – Indian Ocean (CORDIO East Africa, #04073)*;
- *Conservation International (CI)*;
- *Deep Sea Conservation Coalition (DSCC, #05024)*;
- *EAT (#05267)*;
- *Environmental Defense Fund (EDF)*;
- *European Bank for Reconstruction and Development (EBRD, #06315)*;
- *FAO (#09260)*;
- *Fauna & Flora International (FFI, #09277)*;
- *Global Environment Facility (GEF, #10346)*;
- *Global Fishing Watch (GFW)*;
- *Global Maritime Forum (#10465)*;
- *Global Penguin Society (GPS)*;
- *Global Salmon Initiative (GSI, #10585)*;
- *Global Sustainable Tourism Council (GSTC, #10619)*;
- *ILO (#11123)*;
- *Indian Ocean Rim Association (IORA, #11161)*;
- *Inter-American Development Bank (IDB, #11427)*;
- *Intergovernmental Oceanographic Commission (IOC, #11496)*;
- *International Alliance of Marine-Related Institutions (IAMRI, #11630)*;
- *International Bank for Reconstruction and Development (IBRD, #12317)* (World Bank);
- *International Chamber of Shipping (ICS, #12535)*;
- *International Coalition of Fisheries Associations (ICFA, #12614)*;
- *International Collective in Support of Fishworkers (ICSF, #12639)*;
- *International Council for the Exploration of the Sea (ICES, #13021)*;
- *International Maritime Organization (IMO, #14102)*;
- *International Pole and Line Foundation (IPNLF, #14610)*;
- *International Renewable Energy Agency (IRENA, #14715)*;
- *International Seafood Sustainability Foundation (ISSF)*;
- *International Union for Conservation of Nature and Natural Resources (IUCN, #15766)*;
- *Marine Stewardship Council (MSC, #16580)*;
- *MarViva Foundation (#16591)*;
- *Minderoo Foundation*;
- *Natural Capital Coalition (NCC, #16952)*;
- *Nordic Development Fund (NDF, #17271)*;
- *Oceana*;
- *Ocean Conservancy*;
- *Oceano Azul Foundation*;
- *Ocean Outcomes (O2)*;
- *Ocean Policy Research Institute (OPRI)*;
- *Ocean Unite*;
- *Partnerships in Environmental Management for the Seas of East Asia (PEMSEA, #18242)*;
- *Pew Charitable Trusts*;
- *Rare*;
- *Regional Organization for the Conservation of the Environment of the Red Sea and Gulf of Aden (PERSGA, #18804)*;
- *REV Ocean*;
- *Secretariat of the Convention of Wetlands (#19200)*;
- *Secretariat of the Convention on Biological Diversity (SCBD, #19197)*;
- *Sustainable Ocean Alliance (SOA)*;
- *The Coral Reef Alliance (CORAL)*;
- *The Nature Conservancy (TNC)*;
- *The Ocean Foundation (TOF)*;
- *UNCTAD (#20285)*;
- *United Nations Economic Commission for Latin America and the Caribbean (ECLAC, #20556)*;
- *United Nations Office of the High Representative for the Least Developed Countries, Landlocked Developing Countries and Small Island Developing States (UN-OHRLLS, #20599)*;
- *Western and Central Pacific Fisheries Commission (WCPFC, #20912)*;
- *World Forum of Fish Harvesters and Fishworkers (WFF, #21518)*;
- *World Resources Institute (WRI, #21753)*;
- *World Trade Organization (WTO, #21864)*. [2020/XM8929/y/**F**]

♦ High North Dialogue (meeting series)

♦ High Seas Alliance (HSA) 10918

Contact c/o Ecology Action Centre, 2705 Fern Lane, Halifax NS B3K 4L3, Canada. E-mail: info@highseasalliance.org.
URL: http://highseasalliance.org/
History 2011, Washington, DC (USA). **Aims** Conserve the world's high seas. **Structure** Assembly. Steering Group. Coordination Team, headed by Executive Director. Advisory Committee. **Finance** Sources: international organizations. Supported by: *The Ocean Foundation (TOF)* (sponsorship).
Members Organizations (24) including the following 15 listed in this Yearbook:
Antarctic and Southern Ocean Coalition (ASOC, #00849); *BirdLife International (#03266)*; *Greenpeace International (#10727)*; *Intergovernmental Committee for the Global Ocean Observing System (I-GOOS, #11473)*; *International Ocean Institute (IOI, #14394)*; *International Union for Conservation of Nature and Natural Resources (IUCN, #15766)*; *Marine Conservation Institute*; *Migratory Wildlife Network (Wild Migration)*; *Oceana*; *OceanCare*; *Tethys Research Institute*; *Turtle Island Restoration Network (TIRN)*; *Whale and Dolphin Conservation (WDC)*; *Wildlife Conservation Society (WCS)*; *World Wide Fund for Nature (WWF, #21922)*. [2020/XJ5896/y/**C**]

♦ High Twelve International (internationally oriented national body)
♦ **HiH International** Hand in Hand International (#10855)
♦ HI / see Humanity and Inclusion (#10975)
♦ **HI** Humanity and Inclusion (#10975)
♦ HIIA – Hungarian Institute of International Affairs (internationally oriented national body)
♦ HIIL / see Hague Institute for Innovation of Law
♦ HIIL – Hague Institute for Innovation of Law (internationally oriented national body)
♦ Hijas del Espiritu Santo (religious order)
♦ Hijas de Jesús, Salamanca (religious order)
♦ Hijas de Maria (religious order)
♦ Hijas de la Natividad de Maria (religious order)
♦ Hijas de la Pasión de Jesucristo y de Maria Dolorosa (religious order)
♦ Hijas de la Sabiduria (religious order)
♦ Hijas de Santa Ana (religious order)
♦ Hijos de la Sagrada Familia (religious order)
♦ Hilelista Esperanto-Komunumo (internationally oriented national body)
♦ Hilfe für Brüder International (internationally oriented national body)
♦ Hilfsaktion Märtyrerkirche (internationally oriented national body)
♦ Hilfswerk Austria / see Hilfswerk International
♦ Hilfswerk der Evangelischen Kirchen der Schweiz (internationally oriented national body)
♦ Hilfswerk International (internationally oriented national body)
♦ Hillel International (see: #03290)
♦ HiMA / see International Association of Gay and Lesbian Martial Artists
♦ Himalayan Languages Symposium (meeting series)
♦ HIMSS – Healthcare Information and Management Systems Society (internationally oriented national body)
♦ HinD / see Women in Dialogue

♦ Hindemith Foundation 10919

Fondation Hindemith – Hindemith-Stiftung
Contact Champ Belluet 41, 1807 Blonay VD, Switzerland. T. +41219430528. Fax +41219430529. E-mail: administration@hindemith.org.
Pres Siebengebirgsweg 51, 53424 Remagen-Oberwinter, Germany.
URL: http://www.hindemith.org/

History 1968. **Aims** Maintain *musical* and *literary* heritage of Paul Hindemith; encourage interest and research in the field of music, in particular *contemporary music*, and diffusion of the results of this research. **Activities** Events/meetings; research/documentation; training/education. **Publications** *Hindemith General Original Edition*. Yearbook. **Information Services** *Hindemith Institut Frankfurt* – centre for archives, documentation and publication. [2022.02.14/XF3182/f/**F**]

♦ Hindemith-Stiftung (#10919)

♦ Hindu Forum of Europe (HFE) 10920

Contact Avenue d'Auderghem 197, 1040 Brussels, Belgium. T. +3222185800. E-mail: info@hinduforum.eu.
URL: http://hinduforum.eu/

History 2006. **Aims** Promote shared values of European citizenship, interfaith friendship and peaceful coexistence; provide support to European governments and citizens in building communities that are cohesive and integrated; preserve European *values* of human *dignity* by drawing on the Hindu ethos rooted in respect for all traditions, cultures, religions and beliefs. **Structure** Board of Directors.
Members Full in 8 countries:
Belgium, Hungary, Italy, Netherlands, Portugal, Spain, Sweden, UK.
NGO Relations Member of: *European Network on Religion and Belief (ENORB, #07985)*. [2017/XM6430/**F**]

♦ HINE – Health Information Network Europe (internationally oriented national body)
♦ HIN – Hoger Instituut voor de Noodplanning – Studiecentrum Europe (now national)
♦ HIPA – Honey and the International Packers Association (internationally oriented national body)
♦ HIPC Initiative / see Enhanced Heavily Indebted Poor Countries Initiative (#05483)
♦ **HIPC Initiative** Enhanced Heavily Indebted Poor Countries Initiative (#05483)
♦ **HiPEAC** European Network on High-performance Embedded Architecture and Compilation (#07922)
♦ Hipertensievereniging van Suider-Afrika (internationally oriented national body)
♦ **HIP** Health Innovation in Practice (#10885)
♦ HIP – Hispanics in Philanthropy (unconfirmed)

♦ Hipólito Unanue Agreement 10921

Convention Hipólito Unanue – Convenio Hipólito Unanue (CONHU)

Exec Sec c/o Organismo Internacional de Caracter Subregional, Av Paseo de la República 3832, Piso 3, San Isidro, Lima, Peru. T. +5112210074. Fax +5116113700.
URL: http://www.orasconhu.org/

History Founded 18 Dec 1971, Lima (Peru), at 1st Meeting of Ministers of Health. as an Andean integration organ of the *Andean Subregional Integration Agreement (Cartagena Agreement, 1969)*. A Social Agreement of *Sistema Andino de Integración (SAI, #19292)* within the framework of *Andean Community (#00817)* to complement integration efforts in the economic and trade sectors with action in the health field. Also referred to also under the acronym *CHU*. **Aims** Harmonize and shape policies; provide a space for sharing of experiences; devise strategies in response to common *health* problems. **Structure** *Meeting of Ministers of Health in the Andean Region (REMSAA)* (annual), integrated by the Ministers of Health each country. Coordinating Committee, COCONHU, (meets at least twice a year), consisting of a representative of each member country. Executive Secretariat, headed by Executive Secretary. Advisory Commissions. **Languages** Spanish. **Finance** Financed by governments annual payment of US$ 91,633. Budget (annual): US$ 549,798. **Activities** Strategic areas: health integration; epidemiological shield; access to medicines; human resources; social determinants of health; universal health systems. **Events** *Ordinary Meeting of Ministers of Health* Bogota (Colombia) 2012, *Extraordinary Meeting* Lima (Peru) 2011, *Ordinary Meeting of Ministers of Health* Santiago (Chile) 2011, *Ordinary Meeting of Ministers of Health* Buenos Aires (Argentina) 2010, *Meeting of the ministers of health of the Andean region / Ordinary Meeting of Ministers of Health / Extraordinary Meeting* Lima (Peru) 2009. **Publications** *Salud Andina* (4 a year). *Alerta Bibliografica* (1994); *Apuntes de Medicina Tradicional*; *Catalogo de Referencias Bibliograficas*; *Instrumentos Juridicos del Convenio Hipólito Unanue*; *Politica Andina de Equipamiento Técnico Saniatrio*; *Politica Andina de Salud*; *Propuesta Estratégica de Fortalecimiento de la Cooperación Andina de Salud*. Meeting resolutions.
Members Member countries of the Andean Group (9):
Bolivia, Chile, Colombia, Ecuador, Guyana, Paraguay, Peru, Uruguay, Venezuela.
Observer countries (5):
Argentina, Brazil, Cuba, Panama, Spain.
IGO Relations Cooperation with: *Andean Parliament (#00820)*; *Convenio Andrés Bello de integración educativa, científica y cultural de América Latina y España (Convenio Andrés Bello, #04785)*; *Pan American Health Organization (PAHO, #18108)*. Instrumental in setting up: *Institute of Odontological Resources for the Andean Area (inactive)*. Secretariat participates in: *Andean Cooperation in Health (CAS, no recent information)*. [2018/XF5032/**F***]

♦ Hire Association Europe (HAE) 10922

CEO 2450 Regents Court, The Crescent, Birmingham Business Park, Solihull, B37 7YE, UK. T. +441213804600. E-mail: enquiries@hae.org.uk – membership@hae.org.uk.
PA to CEO address not obtained.
URL: http://www.hae.org.uk/

History 1974. **Aims** Promote throughout Europe and the rest of the world the interests of participants in the *hiring* of goods and equipment. **Structure** Board of Directors. **Finance** Sources: members' dues. **Activities** Awards/prizes/competitions; events/meetings. **Events** *Conference* Birmingham (UK) 2019, *Annual Conference* Dublin (Ireland) 2002. **Publications** *Hire Standard*.
Members Organizations (900) in 8 countries:
Australia, Belgium, France, Ireland, Netherlands, South Africa, Spain, UK.
NGO Relations Member of (1): *European Rental Association (ERA, #08358)*. Instrumental in setting up (1): *Portable Sanitation Europe (PSE)*. [2021/XD7080/**D**]

♦ **HIRF** Hasumi International Research Foundation (#10864)
♦ HIRIJW / see Hadassah-Brandeis Institute
♦ Hiroshima Institute of Research Workers on Peace Education / see Hiroshima Peace Institute
♦ Hiroshima Peace Culture Foundation (internationally oriented national body)
♦ Hiroshima Peace Institute (internationally oriented national body)
♦ Hirugarren Mundua Ta Bakea / see Fundación Mundubat
♦ HIS – Healthcare Infection Society (internationally oriented national body)
♦ HIS – Hyperheritage International Seminar (meeting series)
♦ **HIS** Hypospadias International Society (#11001)
♦ His Nets (internationally oriented national body)
♦ HISPA – International Association for the History of Physical Education and Sport (inactive)
♦ **HISPAMEF** Asociación Hispanoamericana de Medicina del Fútbol (#02131)

♦ Hispanic America Software Testing Qualifications Board (HASTQB) 10923

Sec address not obtained. E-mail: info@hastqb.org.
Pres address not obtained.
URL: http://hastqb.org/

History 2008. Former names and other names: *Latin American Testing Board* – former. **Aims** Support the ISTQB qualification scheme aimed at software and system testing professionals in Latin America. **Structure** Executive Committee; Board of Directors; Working Groups. **Activities** Certification/accreditation; training/education.
Members Full in 15 countries:
Argentina, Bolivia, Chile, Colombia, Costa Rica, Cuba, Dominican Rep, Ecuador, El Salvador, Mexico, Panama, Paraguay, Peru, Uruguay, Venezuela.
NGO Relations Member of (1): *International Software Testing Qualifications Board (ISTQB, #15559)*. [2020/XM3094/**D**]

♦ Hispanic Association of Colleges and Universities (internationally oriented national body)
♦ Hispanic Digital Humanities – International Association (internationally oriented national body)
♦ Hispanics in Philanthropy (unconfirmed)
♦ Hispano-American Association of Acupuncture (internationally oriented national body)
♦ Hispano-American Association of Research Centers and Telecommunications Enterprises / see Asociación Interamericana de Empresas de Telecomunicaciones (#02160)
♦ Hispano-American Network of Researchers in Globalization and Territory (#18670)

♦ Hispano-Luso-American Institute of International Law 10924

Institut hispano-luso-américain de droit international – Instituto Hispano-Luso-Americano de Derecho Internacional (IHLADI)

Contact Fac of Law, Univ of Granada, Plaza de la Universidad s/n, 18071 Granada, Spain. E-mail: ihladi@ugr.es.
URL: http://www.ihladi.org/

History 1951, Madrid (Spain). **Aims** Promote study and progress of principles, institutions, systems and instruments of international law in the Hispano-Luso-American community of nations. **Structure** Executive Council; Commissions; National Branches. **Languages** Portuguese, Spanish. **Staff** 1.00 FTE, voluntary. **Finance** Members' dues. **Events** *Congress* Santiago (Chile) 2022, *Congress* Managua (Nicaragua) 2014, *Congress* San Juan (Puerto Rico) 2012, *Congress* Santo Domingo (Dominican Rep) 2010, *Congress* Córdoba (Argentina) 2008. **Publications** *Anuario Hispano-Luso-Americano de Derecho Internacional (AHLADI)* – 22 vols to date. Proceedings.
Members Ordinary; Honorary; Associate; Observer. Members in 24 countries and territories:
Argentina, Bolivia, Brazil, Chile, Colombia, Costa Rica, Cuba, Dominican Rep, Ecuador, El Salvador, Guatemala, Honduras, Mexico, Nicaragua, Panama, Paraguay, Peru, Philippines, Portugal, Puerto Rico, Spain, Uruguay, USA, Venezuela.
IGO Relations Consultative relations with: *United Nations (UN, #20515)*. [2022/XD3867/jv/**E**]

♦ Hispano-Luso-American-Philippine Assembly on Tourism (inactive)
♦ HISPASAT / see Asociación de Televisión Educativa Iberoamericana (#02303)
♦ HISRECO – History of Recent Economics Conference (meeting series)
♦ Histamine Club / see European Histamine Research Society (#07489)
♦ HIST / see International Centre on Space Technologies for Natural and Cultural Heritage (#12517)
♦ **HIST** International Centre on Space Technologies for Natural and Cultural Heritage (#12517)

♦ Histiocyte Society (HS) 10925

Secretariat 332 North Broadway, Pitman NJ 08071, USA. T. +18565896606. Fax +18565896614. E-mail: secretariat@histiocytesociety.org.
Pres Dana Farber Cancer Institute, 450 Brookline Ave, Boston MA 02284-9168, USA.
URL: http://www.histiocytesociety.org

History 1985. **Aims** Promote the study of histiocytosis and histiocyte-related disorders. **Structure** Executive Board, comprising President, Past-President, Treasurer, Secretary and 2 Members-at-Large. **Activities** Committees (2): Education; Scientific. Working Groups (10): Adult Histiocytosis; Epidemiology; HLH; Late Effects; LCH III; LCH-CNS; LCH-HCT; LCH-S; Malignant Disorders; Pathology. **Events** *Annual Meeting* Stockholm (Sweden) 2022, *Annual Meeting* Pitman, NJ (USA) 2021, *Annual Meeting (First Part)* 2020, *Annual Meeting (Second Part)* 2020, *Annual Meeting* Memphis, TN (USA) 2019. **Members** Individuals (over 220) in 40 countries. Membership countries not specified. [2013/XN8467/v/**D**]

♦ Histocity Network 10926

Scientist in Charge Univ degli Studi di Florence, TxP Research UniFI c/o DIDA – Dipto di Architettura, Via San Niccolo 93, 50125 Florence FI, Italy. T. +39552491560. Fax +39552347152.
URL: http://www.txpresearch.wordpress.com/

History 13 Jan 1997, as a network of the 11 partners of *Geographical Information Systems International Group (GISIG, #10133)* and GIS users – universities, public bodies and companies. The number of subscribers grew up to 75 belonging to 17 countries, 42 organizations and 36 different scientific disciplines. **Aims** In the framework of Geographical Information Systems (GIS): conduct studies; diffuse information, methods of *analysis* and *design*; train young researchers on the application of design technology to *sustainable development* of *historical cities*. **Structure** Organizational Committee, comprising the 11 GISIG Partners; Event Scientific Board (appointed annually at Euro-Conference); Working Groups (6). Officers: President; Scientist in Charge. **Languages** English, Italian, Spanish. **Staff** 4.00 FTE, voluntary. 1 trainee; additional staff hired on the basis of specific project needs. **Finance** Sources: University of Florence (Italy); Training and Mobility of Researchers (TMR) Programmes of *European Commission (EC, #06633)*; private companies (design offices, engineering and building companies). **Activities** Operates through: mailing lists; working groups; seminars, meetings participation in EC programmes; consultants in large urban revitalization projects (Comune de Florence); short training courses and specialization courses; application projects. Formerly organized annual Euro-Conference. Operates as a research and consulting network. Working Groups (7): Urban Mobility; Urban Pollution; Historical Building Assets and Historical Spaces; Public Spaces Design and Historical Parks Renovation; Sector Planning (urban commerce revitalization; Natural Commercial Centres planning and design); Remote Sensing for Urban Land Use/Land Cover Recognition for Planning Design. The Network assists exchange of young researchers between partners of different organization types so as to help the applied research training process through case-study and Geographical Information Systems (GIS) application design based on: different source data acquisition and integration with traditional data (radar and optical); remote-sensing data acquisition; multidisciplinary modelling for urban architectural design; conceptual schema design for complex problem simulation and problem solving in urban architectural design (traffic flow, etc); standard metadata gathering methods. Target groups: architects operating in urban architectural design or in conservation and restoration of monuments or expert in such restoration; engineers operating in traffic/transportation design/management or in pollution analysis; economists; historians; urban remote sensing experts; satellite image processing experts; urban geographers; database analysts and designers. **Events** *Annual Euro-Conference* Seville (Spain) 2000, *Annual European conference / Annual Euro-Conference* Siracusa (Italy) 1999, *Annual European conference / Annual Euro-Conference* Florence (Italy) 1998. **Publications** *Histocity Book*.
Members Researchers (72) in 17 countries (also in former Yugoslavia, although member country not specified):
Belgium, Czechia, France, Germany, Greece, Hungary, Italy, Poland, Portugal, Russia, Slovakia, Spain, Sweden, UK, Ukraine, USA.
IGO Relations *Council of Europe (CE, #04881)*; *European Environment Agency (EEA, #06995)*; *UNESCO (#20322)*. **NGO Relations** *International Council on Monuments and Sites (ICOMOS, #13049)*. [2013.07.25/XF4780/**F**]

♦ Historical Archives of the European Communities / see Historical Archives of the European Union (#10927)

♦ Historical Archives of the European Union (HAEU) 10927

Archives historiques de l'Union européenne (AHUE)

Dir Villa Salviati, Via Bolognese 156, 50139 Florence FI, Italy. T. +390554685649. E-mail: archiv@eui.eu.
Main Website: https://www.eui.eu/en/academic-units/historical-archives-of-the-european-union

History 1983. Founded following regulation by *Council of the European Union (#04895)*, then the Council of the European Communities, and *European Commission (EC, #06633)*, then the Commission of the European Communities to open their archives to the public. A subsequent agreement, 1984, between the Commission of the European Communities and *European University Institute (EUI, #09034)* laid the groundwork for establishing the Archives in Florence (Italy). Opened to researchers and the public, 1986. Memorandum of Understanding between EUI and EC reinforced Historical Archives' role, 2011. Council of European Union amended regulations, Mar 2015. New Framework Partnership Agreement between EUI and EC signed, 15 Apr 2015; renewed 2019. Former names and other names: *Historical Archives of the European Communities (HAEC)* – former; *Archives historiques des Communautés européennes (AHCE)* – former. **Aims** Preserve and make accessible for research the archives deposited by EU institutions; collect and preserve private papers of individuals, movements and international organizations involved in European integration; facilitate research on the history of the European Union by providing on site and online access to archival material; promote public interest in European integration; enhance transparency in the functioning of EU Institutions. **Languages** English, French, German, Italian, Slovene, Spanish. **Staff** 18.00 FTE, paid. **Finance** General budget of the European Union. **Activities** Knowledge management/information dissemination; research/documentation; training/education. European Union. **Events** *History of the European Parliament: research* *projects, sources and historical memory,1979-2019* Brussels (Belgium) 2019, *Conference of the network of European Documentation Centres* Florence (Italy) 2019, *The Audiovisual Heritage of the European Integration Process* Florence (Italy) 2019, *Conference on Setting an Agenda for Historical Research in European Law* Florence (Italy) 2015, *Conference on the Building of a European Civil Society in the Context of Equality between Women and Men* Florence (Italy) 2015. **Publications** Books and documentation; image and audio collection; archival holdings. **IGO Relations** Member of (1): *European University Institute (EUI, #09034)*. **NGO Relations** Cooperates with (6): *European Movement*; *European Science Foundation (ESF, #08441)*; *European Society of Culture (#08576)*; *Fondation Jean Monnet pour l'Europe (#09825)*; Fondazione Alcide De Gasperi; *International Council on Archives (ICA, #12996)*. [2022.11.11/XE2818/**E**]

- ♦ Historical Metallurgy Group of the Iron and Steel Institute / see Historical Metallurgy Society
- ♦ Historical Metallurgy Society (internationally oriented national body)

♦ Historic Conference Centres of Europe (HCCE) 10928

Main Office PO Box 703, Huntingdon, PE29 9LT, UK. T. +442033979630.
URL: http://www.hcce.com/

History Oct 1996, Graz (Austria). **Aims** As a marketing focused association, promote conference and convention centres in heritage buildings and the destinations in which they are located. **Structure** General Assembly (annual). **Languages** English. **Staff** 1.00 FTE, paid. **Activities** Awareness raising. **Events** *General Assembly* Luxembourg (Luxembourg) 2014, *General Assembly* Villa Era (Italy) 2013, *General Assembly* Merano (Italy) 2012, *General Assembly* Zeist (Netherlands) 2011, *General Assembly* Pau (France) 2010. **Publications** *HCCE Member Guide*.
Members Conference centres (19) in 11 countries:
Austria, Belgium, France, Germany, Greece, Ireland, Italy, Luxembourg, Malta, Poland, Switzerland. [2018/XM1233/**D**]

♦ The Historic Gardens Foundation (HGF) 10929

Main Office 34 River Court, Upper Ground, London, SE1 9PE, UK. T. +442076339165.
URL: http://www.historicgardens.org/

History Feb 1995, London (UK). Registered, Feb 1995, UK, as an educational charity. **Aims** Promote the cause of historic parks and gardens worldwide; create links between people involved in historic parks and gardens in all countries; encourage good practice in garden restoration and maintenance. **Structure** Board of Directors; Trustees. **Languages** English, French, Italian, Spanish. **Staff** Paid; voluntary. **Finance** Subscriptions; donations. **Activities** Networking/liaising; publishing activities. **Events** *Conference and forum* Arnhem (Netherlands) 1999. **Publications** *HGF Newsletter* (4 a year); *Historic Gardens Review* (2 a year). Information leaflets.
Members Organizations and individuals in 36 countries:
Australia, Austria, Belgium, Bosnia-Herzegovina, Canada, Croatia, Czechia, Denmark, Estonia, Finland, France, Germany, Greece, Hungary, Ireland, Israel, Italy, Japan, Liechtenstein, Luxembourg, Malta, Netherlands, New Zealand, Norway, Poland, Portugal, Romania, Russia, Slovakia, South Africa, Spain, Sweden, Switzerland, Türkiye, UK, USA.
[2019.12.15/XF4348/f/**F**]

♦ Historic Hotels of Europe (HHE) 10930

Main Office Via Borsieri 8, 28832 Belgirate VB, Italy. T. +393355363405. E-mail: info@historichotelsofeurope.com.
Registered Office HHE Limited, Unit 53, The Cubes, Beacon South Quarter, Sandyford, Dublin, CO. DUBLIN, Ireland.
URL: http://www.historichotelsofeurope.com/

History 1997. Founded as *European Federation of Traditional Accommodation and Historic Houses – Fédération européenne d'hébergements historiques (FEHH) – Federación Europea de Alojamientos Históricos – Europäische Vereinigung Tradizioneller Beherbergungsbetriebe*. Present name adopted, 2003.
Members National organizations (10) in 9 countries:
Austria, Denmark, France, Ireland, Italy, Portugal, Spain, Sweden, UK. [2022/XD7265/**D**]

♦ History Educators International Research Network (HEIRNET) 10931

Contact Cherry Dodwell, Postgrad School of Ed, St Luke's Campus, Exeter, EX1 2LU, UK. E-mail: heirnet@exeter.ac.uk – heirnet@gmail.com.
URL: http://www.history.org.uk/

Aims Act as a forum for researchers to meet, share research findings, explore issues of joint concern and contribute towards professional development of colleagues from a range of countries. **Activities** Events/meetings. **Events** *Conference* London (UK) 2015, *Conference* Ljubljana (Slovenia) 2014, *Conference* Nicosia (Cyprus) 2013. **Publications** *International Journal of Historical Learning, Teaching and Research (IJHLTR)* (2 a year). **Members** Membership countries not specified. [2015/XJ0414/**F**]

♦ History of European Integration Research Society (HEIRS) 10932

Contact address not obtained.
Contact address not obtained.
URL: https://heirsweb.wordpress.com/

History 2004. **Aims** Foster collaboration among postgraduate researchers across Europe with an interest in European integration history. **Structure** Steering Committee. **Activities** Events/meetings; networking/liaising; research/documentation. **Events** *HEIRS Conference* 2021, *Colloquium* Paris (France) 2019, *Colloquium* Portsmouth (UK) 2015, *Conference / Colloquium* Maastricht (Netherlands) 2014, *Conference / Colloquium* Sønderborg (Denmark) 2013. **NGO Relations** Partner of (1): *International Research Network of Young Historians of European Integration (RICHIE Association, #14739)*. Represented at meetings of: *European Union Liaison Committee of Historians (#09000)*. [2021/XM1662/**D**]

- ♦ History NGO Forum – History NGO Forum for Peace in East Asia (internationally oriented national body)
- ♦ History NGO Forum for Peace in East Asia (internationally oriented national body)
- ♦ The History of Philosophy of Science Working Group / see International Society for the History of Philosophy of Science (#15174)
- ♦ History of Recent Economics Conference (meeting series)
- ♦ History of Science Society (internationally oriented national body)
- ♦ Hitachi Foundation (internationally oriented national body)

♦ HIT Rail 10933

Dir Corporate Affairs Leidseveer 4, 3511 SB Utrecht, Netherlands. E-mail: info@hitrail.com.
Gen Dir address not obtained.
URL: http://www.hitrail.com/

History 1978. Founded under the patronage of *International Union of Railways (#15813)*. Currently independent. Former names and other names: *Hermes Community* – former (1978 to 1990); *Hermes Information Technology* – former; *Information Technology Services for the European Railways* – former (1990). **Aims** Provide efficient and secure data connections to support railway business processes; facilitate connectivity and interoperability between railways' business applications; build the *Hermes* Ecosystem and the *HEROS* interoperability framework as a network of stakeholders in each of the *railway* markets (passengers, freight and infrastructure). **Structure** Supervisory Board; Management Board. **Languages** Czech, Dutch, English, French, German, Italian, Spanish. **Staff** 2.00 FTE, paid. **Finance** Sources: fees for services. Fees for network and HEROS services paid by railway members and customers. **Activities** Events/meetings. **Publications** Technical documents; management handbooks.
Members Railway companies and associations of companies (49) in 23 countries:
Austria, Belgium, Croatia, Czechia, Denmark, Finland, France, Germany, Hungary, Italy, Luxembourg, Netherlands, Poland, Romania, Russia, Slovakia, Slovenia, Spain, Sweden, Switzerland, Türkiye, UK, Ukraine.
NGO Relations Raildata. [2020.05.09/XF0865/e/**F**]

- ♦ Hives Save Lives – Africa (internationally oriented national body)
- ♦ HIV in Europe / see EuroTEST (#09188)
- ♦ HIV-NAT – HIV Netherlands Australia Thailand Research Collaboration (internationally oriented national body)
- ♦ HIV Netherlands Australia Thailand Research Collaboration (internationally oriented national body)
- ♦ Hivos – Humanistisch Instituut voor Ontwikkelingssamenwerking (internationally oriented national body)

♦ HIV Outcomes 10934

Secretariat address not obtained. T. +3226132828. E-mail: nikos.dedes@eatg.org – secretariat@hivoutcomes.eu.
URL: http://www.hitoutcomes.eu/

History Created 2016. **Aims** Improve the long-term health outcomes and quality of life of all people living with HIV across Europe – and thereby improve the sustainability of European healthcare systems. **Structure** Steering Group. **Activities** Knowledge management/information dissemination; advocacy/lobbying/activism; events/meetings. **Events** *Meeting* Brussels (Belgium) 2018. **IGO Relations** Observer: *European Centre for Disease Prevention and Control (ECDC, #06476)*. **NGO Relations** Partners include: *AIDS Action Europe (#00590)*; *AIDS Foundation East-West (AFEW)*; *East European and Central Asian Union of PLWH (ECUO, #05257)*; *European AIDS Treatment Group (EATG, #05850)*; *Gilead Foundation*. [2019/XM7790/**F**]

- ♦ HIV Research Net (internationally oriented national body)

♦ HIV Research Trust (HIVRT) 10935

Registered Office 437 & 439 Caledonian Road, London, N7 9BG, UK. E-mail: hivresearchtrust@tht.org.uk.
URL: http://www.hivresearchtrust.org.uk/

History 2002, UK. *International Congress on Drug Therapy in HIV Infection* set up in 1992. The Scientific Committee decided that unspent funds should be transferred to a charity whose remit was to support researchers in resource-limited countries in obtaining further training and expertise in developing their research programmes. The HIV Research Trust (HIVRT) was established and 4 appointing bodies were agreed: University College London Medical School (UK); Karolinska Institute (Sweden); Amsterdam Medical Centre (Netherlands); International AIDS Society (Italy). Trustees were appointed to oversee the allocation of the funding of competitive scholarships open to researchers in all specialties concerned with HIV infection. In 2021, became a subsidiary of *Terrence Higgins Trust*. Registration: Charity Commission, No/ID: 1123611, England and Wales; Companies House, No/ID: 06020633, England and Wales. **Aims** Build capacity in HIV in low and lower-middle income countries by promoting study into the prevention and treatment of HIV infection to further the knowledge of early to mid-career healthcare professionals working in resources limited settings. Long-term objective: improve outcomes for patients and people living with HIV in these regions. **Structure** Board of Trustees. **Languages** English. **Staff** None. **Finance** Income from International Congress; education grants from corporate sponsors. **Activities** Awards/prizes/competitions; research/documentation; financial and/or material support. **Publications** None. **Members** Not a membership organization. [2021/XM5228/**F**]

- ♦ **HIVRT** HIV Research Trust (#10935)
- ♦ Hizballah / see Hezbollah Internationale (#10912)

♦ Hizb ut-Tahrir (HuT) 10936

Islamic Liberation Front
Address not obtained.
URL: http://www.hizbuttahrir.org/

History 1953, East Jerusalem, by 2 Muslim clerics and Sheikh Taqiuddin Nahbani, as a secret offshoot of *Muslim Brotherhood (#16915)*. After being banned in Egypt, Jordan, Lebanon and Syrian AR, began operating from the Federal Republic of Germany in 1977. **Aims** Resume the Islamic way of life by establishing an Islamic State or caliphate that executes the systems of Islam worldwide. [2011/XF3343/s/**F**]

- ♦ Hjalparstofnun Kirkjunnar (internationally oriented national body)
- ♦ HKH-FRIEND – FRIEND / Hindu Kush-Himalayan (see: #13826)
- ♦ HKIAC – Hong Kong International Arbitration Centre (internationally oriented national body)
- ♦ HKIAPS – Hong Kong Institute of Asia-Pacific Studies (internationally oriented national body)
- ♦ **HKI** Helen Keller International (#10902)
- ♦ **HL7** Health Level Seven International (#10886)
- ♦ HLB / see HLB International
- ♦ HLB – The Global Advisory and Accounting Network / see HLB International
- ♦ HLB International (internationally oriented national body)
- ♦ HLF – High Level Forum on Aid Effectiveness (meeting series)
- ♦ **HLI** Human Life International (#10977)
- ♦ HLS – Himalayan Languages Symposium (meeting series)
- ♦ HMAC / see Dangerous Goods Advisory Council (#05001)
- ♦ HMA – Heads of Medicines Agencies (unconfirmed)
- ♦ HMC / see Cambridge Centre for Christianity Worldwide
- ♦ **HMEI** Association of Hydro-Meteorological Industry (#02636)
- ♦ HMK – Hilfsaktion Märtyrerkirche (internationally oriented national body)
- ♦ HMM – International Symposium on Hysteresis Modeling and Micromagnetics (meeting series)
- ♦ HMS – Historical Metallurgy Society (internationally oriented national body)
- ♦ HMSS / see Healthcare Information and Management Systems Society
- ♦ **HNHCP** Haematology Nurses & Healthcare Professionals Group (#10847)
- ♦ HNI / see HealthNet TPO
- ♦ **HNN** Healthy Newborn Network (#10894)
- ♦ HNR – Handikapporganisationernes Nordiska Råd (no recent information)
- ♦ **HNSA** HomeNet South Asia (#10940)
- ♦ **HNSEA** HomeNet South-East Asia (#10941)
- ♦ HNS – International Convention on Liability and Compensation for Damage in Connection with the Carriage of Hazardous and Noxious Substances by Sea (1996 treaty)
- ♦ HNS PROT 2010 – Protocol of 2010 to Amend the International Convention of Liability and Compensation for Damage in Connection with the Carriage of Hazardous and Noxious Substances by Sea (2010 treaty)
- ♦ **HoA-REN** Horn of Africa Regional Environment Centre and Network (#10946)
- ♦ Hoffnung für Europa (internationally oriented national body)
- ♦ HOF – Horizons of Friendship (internationally oriented national body)
- ♦ Hof van Justitie van de Europese Gemeenschappen / see Court of Justice of the European Union (#04938)
- ♦ Hof van Justitie van de Europese Unie (#04938)
- ♦ Hogendorp Centre for European Constitutional Studies (internationally oriented national body)
- ♦ Hogendorp Centrum voor Europese Constitutionele Studies / see Hogendorp Centre for European Constitutional Studies
- ♦ Hogendorpcentrum voor Europese Constitutionele Studies (internationally oriented national body)
- ♦ Hogere Europese Beroepen Opleiding / see Hague School of European Studies
- ♦ Hoger Instituut voor de Noodplanning / see Higher Institute of Emergency Planning – European Centre Florival
- ♦ Hoger Instituut voor de Noodplanning – Studiecentrum Europe (now national)
- ♦ HOGIC – House of Galilee International Church and Ministries (internationally oriented national body)
- ♦ HOGUT – Rådgivningsgruppen för Nordiskt Samarbete inom Högre Utbildning (inactive)
- ♦ **HO!I** Hands On ! International Association of Children's Museums (#10856)
- ♦ Holt International (internationally oriented national body)
- ♦ Holt International Children's Services / see Holt International
- ♦ Holy Alliance Treaty, 1684 (1684 treaty)
- ♦ Holy Alliance Treaty, 1815 (1815 treaty)
- ♦ Holy Bible Society (internationally oriented national body)
- ♦ Holy Childhood (internationally oriented national body)
- ♦ Holy Community of Mount Athos (religious order)
- ♦ Holy Earth Foundation / see Earthstewards Network

Holy Great Council
10937

alphabetic sequence excludes
For the complete listing, see Yearbook Online at

♦ **Holy and Great Council** **10937**
Address not obtained.
URL: http://www.holycouncil.org/
History Proposed 1951-1952. Process of preparation launched 1961, Rhodes (Greece). Pre-conciliar conferences held 1976, 1982, 1986, 2009 and 2015. Opening of the Council, Jun 2016, Crete (Greece). Former names and other names: *Holy and Great Council of the Orthodox Church* – full title. **Structure** Synaxis; Panorthodox Council Secretariat. **Languages** Arabic, English, French, Irish Gaelic, Russian. **Activities** Events/meetings. **Events** *Synod of Bishops* Kolymbari (Greece) 2016.
Members Churches in 15 countries:
Albania, Bulgaria, Cyprus, Czechia, Egypt, Georgia, Greece, Israel, Poland, Romania, Russia, Serbia, Slovakia, Syrian AR, Türkiye.
Churches include:
Ecumenical Patriarchate of Constantinople (#05349); Greek Orthodox Patriarchate of Alexandria and All Africa (#10709); Greek Orthodox Patriarchate of Antioch and All the East (#10710). [2016/XM5103/F]

- ♦ Holy and Great Council of the Orthodox Church / see Holy and Great Council (#10937)
- ♦ Holy Land Christian Mission International / see Children International
- ♦ Holy League Treaty, 1495 (1495 treaty)
- ♦ Holy League Treaty, 1511 (1511 treaty)
- ♦ Holy League Treaty, 1526 (1526 treaty)

♦ **Holy Qu'ran Memorization International Organization** **10938**
Gen Sec King Abdullah Road, Naseem District, Jeddah 21312, Saudi Arabia. T. +9665522252012. Fax +9666611640012. E-mail: info@hqmi.org.sa.
URL: http://www.hqmi.org/
History Also referred to as *International Organization of Memorizing the Holy Quran (IOMHQ).* **Activities** Organizes conferences, seminars and contests. **IGO Relations** Cooperates with: *Islamic World Educational, Scientific and Cultural Organization (ICESCO, #16058).* [2020/XJ1908/E]

- ♦ Holy Spirit Association for the Unification of World Christianity (religious order)
- ♦ Holy Spirit Association for the Unification of World Christianity Foundation
- ♦ HOM / see Aim for Human Rights
- ♦ HOMEF – Health of Mother Earth Foundation (internationally oriented national body)
- ♦ HOME – Health Outreach to the Middle East (internationally oriented national body)
- ♦ Homeless International / see Reall

♦ **Homeless World Cup Foundation (HWC)** **10939**
Contact 1 Broughton Market, Edinburgh, EH3 6NU, UK. T. +441312902241. E-mail: info@homelessworldcup.org.
URL: http://www.homelessworldcup.org/
Aims Use football to support and inspire people who are homeless to change their own lives; change perceptions and attitudes towards people who are experiencing homelessness. **Activities** Sporting activities. **Events** *Tournament* Amsterdam (Netherlands) 2015, *Tournament* Santiago (Chile) 2014, *Tournament* Poznań (Poland) 2013, *Tournament* Mexico City (Mexico) 2012, *Tournament* Graz (Austria) 2003.
Members National partners in 73 countries and territories:
Argentina, Australia, Austria, Belgium, Bosnia-Herzegovina, Brazil, Bulgaria, Burkina Faso, Cambodia, Cameroon, Canada, Chile, Costa Rica, Côte d'Ivoire, Croatia, Czechia, Denmark, Egypt, England, Finland, France, Germany, Ghana, Greece, Grenada, Guatemala, Guinea, Haiti, Honduras, Hong Kong, Hungary, India, Indonesia, Ireland, Israel, Italy, Japan, Kenya, Korea Rep, Kyrgyzstan, Liberia, Lithuania, Luxembourg, Malawi, Mali, Mexico, Namibia, Netherlands, Nigeria, Northern Ireland, Norway, Pakistan, Paraguay, Peru, Philippines, Poland, Portugal, Romania, Russia, Scotland, Slovenia, South Africa, Spain, Sweden, Switzerland, Togo, Uganda, Ukraine, USA, Venezuela, Wales, Zambia, Zimbabwe.
NGO Relations Partners include: *International Network of Street Papers (INSP, #14330); Schwab Foundation for Social Entrepreneurship.* [2018.09.06/XJ5300/f/F]

- ♦ HomeNet SEA / see HomeNet South-East Asia (#10941)

♦ **HomeNet South Asia (HNSA)** **10940**
Liaison Office Flat-6, 32 Shamnath Marg, Opp V Sabha Metro, Civil Lines, Delhi 110054, DELHI 110054, India. E-mail: janhavi.hnsa@gmail.com – homenetsouthasia@gmail.com.
Registered Office c/o Rogers Cap Trustee Serv, Sr Louis Business Ctr, Cnr Desoreches / St Louis Streets, Port Louis, Mauritius.
URL: http://hnsa.org.in/
History 2000, as a project supported by (Indian) Self Employed Women's Association (SEWA) and *United Nations Development Fund for Women (UNIFEM, inactive).* Registered as a charitable trust in Mauritius, 19 oct 2006; with Liaison office stationed in Ahmedabad (India). Officially launched 17 Jan 2007. **Aims** Make *homebased workers* and their issues more visible; advocate national policies for homebased workers in each country; strengthen grass roots, particularly membership-based, organizations of homebased workers in each country; create and strengthen the South Asia network of homebased workers and their organizations. **Structure** Trustee Board. Advisory Committee. Finance Committee.
Members Full in 4 countries:
Bangladesh, India, Nepal, Pakistan.
NGO Relations Member of: *Women in Informal Employment: Globalizing and Organizing (WIEGO, #21003).* [2018/XJ5068/D]

♦ **HomeNet South-East Asia (HNSEA)** **10941**
Regional Coordinator 680/48 Soi Wuttaram, Nahmuang Road, Khon Kaen, 40000, Thailand. T. +6643321427. E-mail: sunnewomen@gmail.com.
URL: http://www.homenetseasia.org/
History 1997. Also referred to as *HomeNet SEA.* **Aims** Empower *homebased workers* in the subregion.
Members Full in 7 countries:
Cambodia, Indonesia, Laos, Malaysia, Philippines, Thailand, Vietnam.
NGO Relations Member of: *Women in Informal Employment: Globalizing and Organizing (WIEGO, #21003).* [2012/XJ5067/D]

- ♦ Homeopaten Zonder Grenzen / see Homeopaths Without Borders France (#10942)
- ♦ Homéopathes sans frontières / see Homeopaths Without Borders France (#10942)
- ♦ Homéopathes sans frontières France (#10942)
- ♦ Homeopaths Without Borders / see Homeopaths Without Borders France (#10942)

♦ **Homeopaths Without Borders France (HWB)** **10942**
Homéopathes sans frontières France (HSF)
Main Office 17 avenue Victor Hugo, 31800 Labarthe-Rivière, France. T. +33561953604. E-mail: hsf@hsf-france.com.
URL: https://hsf-france.com/
History 1984, France, as *Homeopaths Without Borders (HWB) – Homéopathes sans frontières (HSF) – Homeopaten Zonder Grenzen.* Name changed to current title after encouraging constitution of other associations in other countries, at which time it was decided to add the countries name to the title. Working towards creation of an international federation.
Members Works in 9 countries:
Benin, Burkina Faso, Cambodia, Cameroon, Congo DR, Lebanon, Madagascar, Senegal, Togo. [2020/XF6893/F]

- ♦ Homeopathy One (unconfirmed)
- ♦ Homeplanet Alliance
- ♦ Home Rule Globally (internationally oriented national body)
- ♦ Home-Start International (internationally oriented national body)
- ♦ Home Study Institute / see Griggs University and International Academy
- ♦ Home Study International / see Griggs University and International Academy
- ♦ HomeWorkers Worldwide (internationally oriented national body)
- ♦ L'homme contre les virus (see: #05781)
- ♦ Homosexuals in the Martial Arts / see International Association of Gay and Lesbian Martial Artists
- ♦ Honda Foundation (internationally oriented national body)
- ♦ HONDURAS GLOBAL (internationally oriented national body)
- ♦ Honey Bee Network (internationally oriented national body)
- ♦ Honey and the International Packers Association (internationally oriented national body)
- ♦ Hong Kong Christian Aid to Refugees / see Christian Action
- ♦ Hong Kong Convention – Hong Kong International Convention for the Safe and Environmentally Sound Recycling of Ships, 2009 (2009 treaty)
- ♦ Hong Kong Institute of Asia-Pacific Studies (internationally oriented national body)
- ♦ Hong Kong International Arbitration Centre (internationally oriented national body)
- ♦ Hong Kong International Convention for the Safe and Environmentally Sound Recycling of Ships, 2009 (2009 treaty)
- ♦ **HON** Health On the Net Foundation (#10887)
- ♦ HONLEA – Heads of National Drug Law Enforcement Agencies (meeting series)
- ♦ Hoover Institution on War, Revolution and Peace (internationally oriented national body)
- ♦ HOPE '87 – Hundreds of Original Projects for Employment (internationally oriented national body)
- ♦ Hope for Africa (internationally oriented national body)
- ♦ Hope for Children (internationally oriented national body)

♦ **"Hope for Children" CRC Policy Center (HFC)** **10943**
Dir Gen 75 Limassol Avenue Office 201, 2nd Floor, CY-2121 Nicosia, Cyprus. T. +35722103234. Fax +35722104024. E-mail: info@uncrcpc.org.
URL: https://www.uncrcpc.org/
Aims Advocate and protect children's rights based on the standards and principles of the UN Convention on the Rights of the Child and European Union Law. **Structure** Senior Advisory Board. Headquarters in Cyprus. Offices: USA, Portugal; Denmark; Italy; Hungary; Romania; UK; Nigeria. **Activities** Advocacy/lobbying/activism; projects/programmes. **Consultative Status** Consultative status granted from: *Council of Europe (CE, #04881)* (Participatory Status). **IGO Relations** *Council of Europe (CE, #04881); United Nations Convention on the Rights of the Child (CRC, 1989).* **NGO Relations** Member of: *Destination Unknown (#05047); European Federation for Missing and Sexually Exploited Children (Missing Children Europe, #07166).* [2019/XM8807/E]

- ♦ Hope for Europe (internationally oriented national body)
- ♦ **HOPE** European Hospital and Healthcare Federation (#07501)
- ♦ Hope Foundation for African Women (internationally oriented national body)
- ♦ HOPe – Helping Other People (internationally oriented national body)
- ♦ Hope and Homes for Children (internationally oriented national body)
- ♦ **HOPE** Hospital Organization of Pedagogues in Europe (#10949)
- ♦ HOPE International (internationally oriented national body)
- ♦ Pro-Hope International (internationally oriented national body)
- ♦ Hope International Development Agency (internationally oriented national body)

♦ **Hope for the Nations (HFTN)** **10944**
Address not obtained.
Contact Arquen House, 4-6 Spicer Street, St Albans, AL3 4PQ, UK. T. +441727834481. E-mail: info@hftn.co.uk.
URL: http://www.hopeforthenations.com/
History 1994, Kelowna, BC (Canada). Registered in over 20 countries. Former names and other names: *Hope for the Nations Children's Charity* – legal name. Registration: Canada Revenue Agency, No/ID: 898759931 RR 0001, Start date: 9 Aug 1994, Canada; Charity Commission, No/ID: 1098715, England and Wales. **Aims** Create hope in the lives of *children* at Risk in developing countries. **Structure** Board of Directors. **NGO Relations** Allied partner of: *Financial Transparency Coalition (FTC, #09772).* [2020/XJ1097/F]

- ♦ Hope for the Nations Children's Charity / see Hope for the Nations (#10944)
- ♦ Hope Unlimited (internationally oriented national body)
- ♦ Hope Worldwide (internationally oriented national body)
- ♦ Hôpitaux en liaison européenne pour la lutte contre l'infection par la surveillance (no recent information)
- ♦ **HOPOS** International Society for the History of Philosophy of Science (#15174)
- ♦ Hoppets Stjärna Stiftelsen (#19967)
- ♦ **HORATIO** European Psychiatric Nurses (#08291)
- ♦ Horizon 2007 (internationally oriented national body)
- ♦ HORIZON Communications / see HORIZON International
- ♦ HORIZON International (internationally oriented national body)
- ♦ Horizons d'amitié (internationally oriented national body)
- ♦ Horizons de Armistad (internationally oriented national body)
- ♦ Horizons of Friendship (internationally oriented national body)
- ♦ HORIZONT 3000 (internationally oriented national body)

♦ **Horizontal Technical Cooperation Group of Latin America and the Caribbean on HIV/AIDS (HTGC)** **10945**
Grupo de Cooperación Técnica América Latina y Caribe en VIH/SIDA – Grupo de Cooperação Técnica Horizontal da América Latina e Caribe sobre o HIV/Aids (GCTH)
Admin Sec Ciudad del Saber, Edif 178, Av Carlos Renato Lara, Panama, Panamá, Panama PANAMá, Panama. T. +5073055571.
Pres Min de Salud, Av 18 de Julio 1892, Montevideo, Uruguay. T. +59824088296. E-mail: mlosi@adinet.com.uy.
Aims Improve response to the challenges of the epidemic in a context of horizontal technical cooperation partnership, strengthening prevention strategies and management ability of the National AIDS Programmes. **Structure** Comprised of representatives of Governmental HIV/AIDS Control and Prevention Programmes. Pro Tempore rotating secretariat for one year, with possible extension of another year. Sub-regional rotating coordinators represent different areas of the region: Argentina (MERCOSUL); Venezuela (Andean Region); El Salvador (Central America); Dominican Republic (Caribbean). The Technical Secretariat and Sub-Regional Co-ordinators jointly establish the workplan for one year. **Activities** Organizes: Horizontal Technical Cooperation Conference; Annual Meeting; other conferences, fora and workshops. **Events** *Annual Meeting* Santa Cruz (Bolivia) 2000, *Annual Meeting* Caracas (Venezuela) 1998, *Annual Meeting* Buenos Aires (Argentina) 1997.
Members HIV/AIDS Control and Prevention Programmes in 20 Latin American and Caribbean countries:
Argentina, Bolivia, Brazil, Chile, Colombia, Costa Rica, Cuba, Dominican Rep, Ecuador, El Salvador, Guatemala, Haiti, Honduras, Mexico, Nicaragua, Panama, Paraguay, Peru, Uruguay, Venezuela.
NGO Relations Partner of: *International Community of Women Living with HIV/AIDS (ICW, #12826)* – Latin America Chapter; *Association for an Integral Health and Citizenship of Latin America and the Caribbean (#02651); Latin American and Caribbean Council of AIDS Service Organizations (LACCASO, #16272); Latin American Network of People Living with HIV/AIDS (RED LA+, #16355); Movimiento Latinoamericano y del Caribe de Mujeres Positivas Regional Argentina (MLCM+, no recent information); Red de Latinoamérica y El Caribe de Personas Trans (REDLACTRANS, #18699); Red de Trabajadoras Sexuales de América Latina y el Caribe (REDTRASEX, #18731).* [2010/XM3589/D]

- ♦ Horn of Africa Aid and Rehabilitation Action Network (internationally oriented national body)

♦ **Horn of Africa Regional Environment Centre and Network (HoA-REN)** **10946**
Head office College of Natural Science, Addis Ababa Univ, PO Box 80773, Addis Ababa, Ethiopia. T. +251116550226. E-mail: info@hoarec.org.
URL: http://www.hoarec.org/
History 2006, as *Horn of Africa Regional Environment Network.* **Aims** Strengthen and advocate initiatives related to environmental *conservation* and natural resource management; enhance environmental governance and management; contribute to *sustainable development*; improve livelihoods within the region. **Structure** Autonomous institution under Addis Ababa University. Horn of Africa Regional Environment Centre serves as Secretariat for the Network. **Languages** Amharic, English. **Events** *MESA international conference* Nairobi (Kenya) 2008.
Members Active in 7 countries:
Djibouti, Eritrea, Ethiopia, Kenya, Somalia, South Sudan, Sudan.
NGO Relations *Wetlands International (#20928).* [2018/XM2643/D]

♦ Horn of Africa Regional Environment Network / see Horn of Africa Regional Environment Centre and Network (#10946)
♦ Horn of Africa Relief and Development Organization / see African Development Solutions (#00287)
♦ Horn of Africa Voluntary Youth Committee (internationally oriented national body)
♦ Horn Relief / see African Development Solutions (#00287)
♦ Horodia ton Evropaikon Kinotiton / see European Union Choir (#08980)
♦ Horodia tis Evropaikis Enosis / see European Union Choir (#08980)
♦ Horticulture Research International / see Warwick HRI
♦ **HOSPEEM** European Hospital and Healthcare Employers' Association (#07500)
♦ Hospitalarias del Sagrado Corazón de Jesús (religious order)
♦ Hospital Committee of the Common Market / see European Hospital and Healthcare Federation (#07501)
♦ Hospital Committee of the European Community / see European Hospital and Healthcare Federation (#07501)
♦ Hospitalières de Besançon (religious order)
♦ Hospital Infection Society / see Healthcare Infection Society

♦ HOSPITALITY EUROPE 10947

SG Rue Guimard 1, 1040 Brussels, Belgium. T. +3225070536. Fax +3225099606.
URL: http://www.hospitality-europe.eu/

History Set up to represent *Ordine Ospedaliero di San Giovanni di Dio (Fatebenefratelli)* and *Sisters Hospitallers of the Sacred Heart of Jesus.* Operational since 2012. Registered in accordance with Belgian law. EU Transparency Register: 330135316980-44. **Aims** Represent the *hospitals* and *social/welfare* facilities of both orders; liaise with the institutions of the European Union. **Structure** Structure and coordination jointly by General Councils of the Order and the Sisters Hospitallers, General Assembly of the association as well as European Provinces of both institutes. **Publications** *HOSPITALITY EUROPE Newsletter.* **NGO Relations** Member of: *Forum of Catholic Inspired NGOs (#09905).* [2018/XM5763/**E**]

♦ Hospitality Sales and Marketing Association International (HSMAI) 10948

Main Office 7918 Jones Branch Dr, Ste 300, McLean VA 22102, USA. T. +17035063280. Fax +17035063266. E-mail: info@hsmai.org.
URL: http://www.hsmai.org/

History 1927, USA. Former names and other names: *International Hotel Sales Management Association (HSMA)* – former (1927 to 1983); *Hotel Sales and Marketing Association International* – former (1983); *Association de marketing pour les hôtels* – former (1983); *Verband für Marketing im Hotelwesen* – former (1983); *HSMAI Global* – alias. **Aims** Grow business for hotels and their partners by fueling sales, inspiring marketing and optimizing revenue. **Structure** Global Board, comprised of delegates from 3 Regions: Americas; Asia Pacific; Europe. Additional Chapter: United Arab Emirates. *HSMAI Foundation,* set up 1983, as research and educational arm. **Events** *Asia Pacific Revenue Optimization Conference* Singapore (Singapore) 2022, *HSMAI ROC ME Conference* Dubai (United Arab Emirates) 2021, *Asia Pacific Revenue Optimization Conference* Singapore (Singapore) 2021, *Americas Curate* Montréal, QC (Canada) 2020, *Asia Pacific Revenue Optimization Conference* Hong Kong (Hong Kong) 2019. **Members** Individuals (nearly 7,000) from 35 countries. Membership countries not specified. **NGO Relations** Member of: *Events Industry Council (EIC, #09212); Hotel Technology Next Generation (HTNG, #10952).* [2020/XG0177/**C**]

♦ Hospitaller Order of St John of God (religious order)
♦ Hospitaller Sisters of St John of Jerusalem (religious order)
♦ Hospitallers of the Order of the Holy Ghost (inactive)
♦ Hospital Management Systems Society / see Healthcare Information and Management Systems Society

♦ Hospital Organization of Pedagogues in Europe (HOPE) 10949

Treas Our Lady's Hospital School, Crumlin, Dublin, CO. DUBLIN, Ireland. T. +35314096414. E-mail: secretary@hospitalteachers.eu.
Registered address Bondgenotenlaan 134 Bus 4, 3000 Leuven, Belgium.
URL: http://www.hospitalteachers.eu/

History 1989, Ljubljana (Yugoslavia), as *European Association of Hospital Pedagogues (EAHP).* Present title adopted 1993. Also referred to as *European Association of Hospital Teachers (EAHT).* Registered in accordance with Belgian law. **Aims** Promote development of hospital pedagogy and raise its image at a professional level; act as a forum for all disciplines involved within hospital teaching and publicize examples of good practice; promote and encourage research in all aspects of hospital pedagogy. **Structure** General Assembly (every 2 years); Committee; Bureau. **Languages** English, French, German. **Staff** Voluntary. **Finance** Members' dues. **Events** *Congress* Milan (Italy) 2023, *Congress* Milan (Italy) 2022, *Congress* Tallinn (Estonia) 2020, *Congress* Poznań (Poland) 2018, *Congress* Vienna (Austria) 2016. **Publications** *HOPE Newsletter* (4 a year).
Members Individual Effective; Associate; Honorary. Collective membership. Individual members in 23 countries:
Armenia, Austria, Belgium, Croatia, Denmark, Estonia, Finland, France, Germany, Greece, Hungary, Iceland, Ireland, Italy, Luxembourg, Netherlands, Norway, Romania, Slovenia, Spain, Sweden, Switzerland, UK.
NGO Relations Formal contacts with: *European Association for Special Education (EASE, no recent information).* [2018.01.10/XF2277/**D**]

♦ Hospitals in Europe Link for Infection Control through Surveillance (no recent information)

♦ Hostelling International 10950

CEO 7 Bell Yard, London, WC2A 2JR, UK. E-mail: info@hihostels.com.
URL: http://www.hihostels.com/

History 1932. Reorganized 1946. Former names and other names: *International Youth Hostels' Association* – former (1932); *Union internationale des auberges pour la jeunesse (1932)* – former; *Internationale Arbeitsgemeinschaft für Jugendherbergen (1932)* – former; *International Youth Hostel Federation (IYHF)* – former (1946); *Fédération internationale des auberges de la jeunesse (FIAJ)* – former (1946); *Federación Internacional de Albergues de la Juventud* – former (1946); *Internationaler Jugendherbergsverband (1946)* – former. **Aims** Promote education of all young people of all nations, but especially young people of limited means, by encouraging in them a greater knowledge, love and care of the countryside and an appreciation of the cultural values of towns and cities in all parts of the world; provide hostels or other accommodation in which there shall be no distinction of origin, nationality, colour, religion, sex, class or political opinions and thereby develop a better understanding of their fellow men, both at home and abroad. **Structure** Conference (every 2 years); Board of Trustees; Task and Working Groups. **Languages** English. **Staff** 10.00 FTE, paid. **Finance** Sources: donations; members' dues; sale of products; sale of publications. Annual budget: 3,000,000 USD. **Activities** Advocacy/lobbying/activism; awareness raising; capacity building; certification/accreditation; events/meetings; guidance/assistance/consulting; knowledge management/information dissemination; networking/liaising; projects/programmes; standards/guidelines; training/education. **Events** *Biennial Conference* Doha (Qatar) 2022, *Biennial Conference* 2020, *Biennial Conference* Reykjavik (Iceland) 2018, *Biennial Conference* London (UK) 2016, *North American Managers Meeting* Montréal, QC (Canada) 2015. **Publications** Annual Report; miscellaneous international publications.
Members Full in 58 countries and territories:
Algeria, Australia, Austria, Bahrain, Belgium/Wallonia Region, Bolivia, Bosnia-Herzegovina, Brazil, Canada, Chile, China, Croatia, Czechia, Denmark, Egypt, England and Wales, Finland, Flanders, France, Germany, Hong Kong, Iceland, India, Ireland, Israel, Italy, Japan, Jordan, Korea Rep, Kuwait, Lebanon, Libya, Luxembourg, Malaysia, Malta, Morocco, Netherlands, New Zealand, Northern Ireland, Norway, Pakistan, Philippines, Poland, Portugal, Qatar, Romania, Saudi Arabia, Scotland, Serbia, Slovenia, Spain, Sudan, Switzerland, Taiwan, Taiwan, Tunisia, United Arab Emirates, Uruguay, USA.
Associate organizations in 2 countries:
Greece, Syrian AR.
Consultative Status Consultative status granted from: *ECOSOC (#05331)* (Special); *UNESCO (#20322)* (Consultative Status). **IGO Relations** Accredited by (1): *United Nations Office at Vienna (UNOV, #20604).* Member of (1): *World Tourism Organization (UNWTO, #21861).* **NGO Relations** Member of: *Global Sustainable Tourism Council (GSTC, #10619); STAY WYSE (inactive).* [2022.12.01/XB2828/**B**]

♦ Hot Briquetted Iron Association (inactive)
♦ Hôte européen pour les services publics (#09911)
♦ Hotel, Catering and Institutional Management Association / see Institute of Hospitality (#11269)

♦ Hotel Electronic Distribution Network Association (HEDNA) 10951

Contact 1000 Westgate Dr, Ste 252, St Paul MN 55114, USA. T. +16512906291. Fax +16512902266. E-mail: info@hedna.org.
URL: http://www.hedna.org/

History 1991. **Aims** Work to optimize the use of technologies while influencing development of current and emerging distribution channels. **Structure** Board of Directors. **Activities** Events/meetings. **Events** *Global Distribution Conference* Miami, FL (USA) 2021, *Half-Yearly Meeting* Miami, FL (USA) 2021, *Half-Yearly Meeting* Amsterdam (Netherlands) 2020, *Half-Yearly Meeting* Los Angeles, CA (USA) 2020, *Half-Yearly Meeting* Madrid (Spain) 2019. **Publications** *President's Letter* (2-3 a year); *Working Groups Newsletter* (2-3 a year). Annual Report; white papers; hotel chain code matrix; industry guidelines; educational resources. **Members** Companies representing all areas of the electronic distribution industry. Membership countries not specified. [2019.06.03/XM0613/**D**]

♦ Hotel Sales and Marketing Association International / see Hospitality Sales and Marketing Association International (#10948)

♦ Hotel Technology Next Generation (HTNG) 10952

Exec VP/CEO 650 E Algonquin Rd, Ste 207, Schaumburg IL 60173, USA. T. +18473035560.
URL: http://www.htng.org/

History 2002. Incorporated as HTNG Illinois (NFP) in the State of Illinois (USA). Operates under the above trading name. **Aims** Through collaboration and partnership, foster development of next-generation systems and solutions to enable hoteliers and their technology vendors to do business globally in the 21st century. **Structure** Board of Governors; Executive Advisors; Forum Chairs; Regional Coordinators; Vendor Advisory Council. **Finance** Members' dues. **Activities** Events/meetings. **Events** *Asia Pacific Regional Conference* Singapore (Singapore) 2017, *Asia Pacific Regional Conference* Bangkok (Thailand) 2016, *European Conference* Barcelona (Spain) 2016, *Middle East Regional Conference* Dubai (United Arab Emirates) 2016, *European Regional Conference* Nice (France) 2015.
Members Hospitality Companies; Corporate Industry Partners; Association Partners; Allied Members. Association partners include 6 organizations listed in this Yearbook:
Confederation of National Associations of Hotels, Restaurants, Cafés and Similar Establishments in the European Union and European Economic Area (HOTREC, #04569); Hospitality Sales and Marketing Association International (HSMAI, #10948); International Card Manufacturers Association (ICMA); International Hospitality Information Technology Association (iHITA); International Hotel and Restaurant Association (IH&RA, #13813); Open Group (#17755). [2018.06.25/XJ9019/y/**F**]

♦ **HOTREC** Confédération des associations nationales de l'hôtellerie et de la restauration de la Communauté européenne (#04569)
♦ **HOTREC** Confederation of National Associations of Hotels, Restaurants, Cafés and Similar Establishments in the European Union and European Economic Area (#04569)

♦ In House Competition Lawyers' Association (ICLA) 10953

Contact address not obtained. E-mail: info@inhousecompetitionlawyers.com.
URL: http://competitionlawyer.co.uk/ICLA/INTRO.html

History Founded Oct 2005, as an informal gathering. Initially a UK organization, but expanded 2010. **Aims** Share legal and compliance related to development at national and supranational level; discuss matters of common interest. **Structure** Board. Chapters (7): EU; UK; Italy; Asia; Nordic countries; Germany; Netherlands. **Activities** Events/meetings.
Members Full (over 360) in 23 countries. Membership mainly in 9 countries:
Belgium, Denmark, Finland, Germany, Italy, Netherlands, Spain, Sweden, UK. [2021/XM7625/**C**]

♦ In-house Counsel Worldwide (ICW) 10954

Secretariat c/o CCASA, 75 King Street, Berario, Northcliff, Johannesburg, 2195, South Africa. E-mail: info@ccasa.co.za.
URL: https://inhousecounselworldwide.com/

History Founded Oct 2011. **Aims** Unite the in-house legal community for the benefit of all in-house counsel, their organizations and the profession, through cooperation and collaboration. **Structure** Annual General Meeting; Executive Committee. **Events** *Summit* Toronto, ON (Canada) 2018.
Members Full in 11 countries:
Belgium, Brazil, Canada, France, Germany, India, Malaysia, New Zealand, Singapore, South Africa, UK. [2020/XM8028/**C**]

♦ House of Galilee International Church and Ministries (internationally oriented national body)
♦ Household Goods Forwarders Association of America / see International Association of Movers

♦ Households in Conflict Network (HiCN) 10955

Co-Dir Inst of Development Studies – Univ of Sussex, Falmer, Brighton, BN1 9RE, UK. T. +441273915819. Fax +441273621202. E-mail: info@hicn.org.
URL: http://www.hicn.org/

Aims Undertake collaborative research into the causes and effects of violent conflict at the household level. **Finance** Supported by: *Institute of Development Studies, Brighton (IDS); International Security and Development Center (ISDC); Leverhulme Trust;* Université Libre de Bruxelles. **Activities** Knowledge management/information dissemination; research/documentation. **Events** *Annual Workshop* Paris (France) 2019. **Publications** *HiCN Quarterly Newsletter* (4 a year). Working Papers. [2020/AA0920/j/**F**]

♦ House of Jacobs International (internationally oriented national body)
♦ Housewives in Dialogue / see Women in Dialogue

♦ Housing Europe – The European Federation for Public Cooperative and Social Housing (Housing Europe) 10956

SG Square de Meeûs 18, 1050 Brussels, Belgium. T. +3225410562. Fax +3225410569. E-mail: communications@housingeurope.eu.
URL: http://www.housingeurope.eu/

History 4 Mar 1988, Brussels (Belgium). Original statutes adopted 4 Mar 1988. Statutes modified: 8 Nov 1990, Venice (Italy); 18 May 1993, Santiago de Compostella (Spain); 4 Oct 1994, Faro (Portugal). Derives from *European Committee of Housing Cooperatives (inactive),* set up May 1986, by national housing cooperatives (5) in France, Germany FR and Italy. Former names and other names: *Comité européen de coordination de l'habitat social (CECODHAS)* – former; *European Liaison Committee for Social Housing* – former; *Europäischer Verbindungsausschuss zur Koordinierung der Sozialen Wohnungswirtschaft* – former. Registration: EU Transparency Register, No/ID: 794469327833-17, Start date: 24 Jul 2017. **Aims** Provide access to decent and affordable housing for all throughout Europe in communities which are socially, economically and environmentally sustainable and where everyone is enabled to reach their full potential. **Structure** General Assembly; Board; Executive Committee; Working Groups. Includes Research branch: *European Social Housing Observatory (#08502).* **Languages** English. **Staff** 7.00 FTE, paid. **Finance** Members' dues. **Activities** Advocacy/lobbying/activism; events/meetings; knowledge management/information dissemination; networking/liaising; research/documentation. **Events** *Boosting Energy Communities in the EU* Brussels (Belgium) 2022, *Renovation Summit* Brussels (Belgium) 2022, *General Assembly* Helsinki (Finland) 2022, *General Assembly* Brussels (Belgium) 2021, *Annual Conference and General Assembly* Glasgow (UK) 2020. **Publications** *Housing Europe News* (22 a year). Studies.
Members National and regional federations (44) gathering about 43,000 public, social and cooperative housing provides, altogether managing over 26 million homes, about 11% of existing dwellings in the EU. Members in 23 countries:
Albania, Armenia, Austria, Belgium, Czechia, Denmark, Estonia, Finland, France, Germany, Hungary, Ireland, Italy, Luxembourg, Netherlands, Norway, Poland, Portugal, Spain, Sweden, Switzerland, Türkiye, UK.
NGO Relations Member of: *Coalition for Energy Savings (#04056); EU Alliance for a democratic, social and sustainable European Semester (EU Semester Alliance, #05565); European Housing Forum (EHF, #07504); Finance Watch (#09764); SDG Watch Europe (#19162); Social Platform (#19344); Spring Alliance (inactive).* Cooperative Section member of: *Cooperatives Europe (#04801).* Cooperates with: *Covenant of Mayors for Climate and Energy (#04939).* Instrumental in setting up: *IGLOO Europe (no recent information).* [2022/XE0564/**E**]

♦ **Housing Europe** Housing Europe – The European Federation for Public Cooperative and Social Housing (#10956)
♦ Housing Initiative for Easter Europe (internationally oriented national body)
♦ Housing Initiative for Eastern Europe for the Promotion of a Market-oriented and Ecological Development of the Housing and Construction Sectors in Eastern Europe / see Initiative Wohnungswirtschaft Osteuropa

♦ **Housing Nordic (NBO)** **10957**
Nordiska Kooperativa och Allmännyttiga Bostadsföretags Organisation (NBO)
Pres Studiestraede 50, 1554 Copenhagen, Denmark. T. +4533762000. E-mail: bma@bl.dk.
Sec address not obtained.
URL: http://www.nbo.nu/
History 1950. Former names and other names: *Organization of Nordic Cooperative and Public Utility Housing Enterprises* – former; *Nordic Housing Companies' Organization* – former; *Organization of Nordic Cooperative and Municipal Housing Enterprises (NBO)* – former. **Aims** Promote financially, ecologically, and socially sustainable housing for everyone in the Nordic countries; improve growth of municipalities and regions, lively and safe residential areas and freedom of choice for residents. **Structure** Board (meets 3 times a year). **Languages** Danish, English, Norwegian, Swedish. **Staff** Secretariat functions managed by one of the member organizations. **Finance** Sources: members' dues. **Activities** Awards/prizes/competitions; events/meetings; knowledge management/information dissemination; politics/policy/regulatory. **Events** *Biennial Conference* Sweden 2024, *Biennial Conference* Oslo (Norway) 2022, *Biennial Conference* Copenhagen (Denmark) 2020, *Biennial Conference* Stockholm (Sweden) 2018, *Biennial Conference* Helsinki (Finland) 2016. **Publications** *Med Gemensamma Regler Tygger vi Billigare. State of Housing in the Nordic Countries 2020* (2020); *NBO Housing Statistics – October 2019.* **Information Services** *Affordable Housing Models in the Nordic Countries.* **Members** Organizations (one or more per country), representing over 2,400,000 dwellings, in 5 countries: Denmark, Finland, Iceland, Norway, Sweden.
IGO Relations *Nordic Council (NC, #17256).* **NGO Relations** *Housing Europe – The European Federation for Public Cooperative and Social Housing (Housing Europe, #10956).* [2023.02.21/XD0092/D]

♦ **HoverAid** **10958**
UK Office Units 1-2 Warrior Ct, 9-11 Mumby Rd, Gosport, PO12 1BS, UK. T. +442081442338.
Netherlands Office V d Duynlaan 17, 2761 VR Zevenhuizen, Netherlands. T. +31180631104.
Madagascar Office BP 132, Ivato Aeroport (105), Antananarivo, Madagascar.
URL: http://uk.hoveraid.org/
History Nov 1991, as a charity. Madagascar office set up 2006; Netherlands office set up 2007. Currently a federation of independent country based organizations with local boards, but plans to create *HoverAid International*, as overall coordinating body. Hoveraid Trust is a UK Registered Charity: 1005977. **Aims** Use *hovercraft* to reach remote communities and address the injustice, oppression, *poverty*, and hunger, which are a result of poor access. **Structure** Boards in 3 countries: UK; Netherlands; Madagascar. [2011/XJ4545/F]

♦ Howard Center for Family, Religion and Society (internationally oriented national body)
♦ Howard League for Penal Reform (internationally oriented national body)
♦ Howard Liga für die Reform des Strafvollzugs (internationally oriented national body)
♦ How to Change the World (unconfirmed)
♦ HPA – Health Poverty Action (internationally oriented national body)
♦ HPA – Homeplanet Alliance
♦ HPAIR – Harvard Project for Asian and International Relations (internationally oriented national body)
♦ HPBB – International Association of High Pressure Bioscience and Biotechnology (unconfirmed)
♦ HPC Asia – International Conference on High Performance Computing in Asia-Pacific Region (meeting series)
♦ HPCF – Hiroshima Peace Culture Foundation (internationally oriented national body)
♦ HPH / see International Network of Health Promoting Hospitals and Health Services (#14277)
♦ **HPH** International Network of Health Promoting Hospitals and Health Services (#14277)
♦ HPI / see Heifer International
♦ HPI / see European Study Group on Pathogenesis and Immunology in Helicobacter Infections (#08851)
♦ HPI – Help the Poor International (internationally oriented national body)
♦ HPIS – International Hemipteran-Plant Interactions Symposium (meeting series)
♦ HPLC – International Symposium on High Performance Liquid Phase Separations and Related Techniques (meeting series)
♦ **HPN** Humanitarian Practice Network (#10973)
♦ **HPP** International Humana People to People Movement (#13817)
♦ HPSG – International Conference on Head-Driven Phrase Structure Grammar (meeting series)
♦ HPSP – International Conference on High Pressure Semiconductor Physics (meeting series)
♦ HPTH Europe – Hypoparathyroidism Europe (inactive)
♦ **HQAI** Humanitarian Quality Assurance Initiative (#10974)
♦ HQ Kosovo Force / see KFOR (#16187)
♦ HRAF – Human Relations Area Files (internationally oriented national body)
♦ HRA – Human Rights Advocates (internationally oriented national body)
♦ HRAS – Human Rights at Sea (internationally oriented national body)
♦ HRCA – Human Rights Centre of Azerbaijan (internationally oriented national body)
♦ HRC – Human Rights Committee (internationally oriented national body)
♦ HRC – Nordiska Unionen för Hotell-, Café- och Restauranganställda (inactive)
♦ **HRC** United Nations Human Rights Council (#20571)
♦ **HRDN** Human Rights and Democracy Network (#10980)
♦ HREA – Human Rights Education Associates (internationally oriented national body)
♦ HRES – European Network on Human Response to Environmental Stress (see: #05333)
♦ **HREYN** Human Rights Education Youth Network (#10982)
♦ HRFA – Human Rights for Africa (internationally oriented national body)
♦ HRF – Human Relief Foundation (internationally oriented national body)
♦ HRF – Human Rights Foundation (internationally oriented national body)
♦ HRFN – Human Rights Funders Network (internationally oriented national body)
♦ HRG – Home Rule Globally (internationally oriented national body)
♦ HRI / see Warwick HRI
♦ **HRI** Harm Reduction International (#10861)
♦ **HRI** Human Rights Internet (#10986)
♦ HRJGI / see Human Rights and Justice Group International
♦ **HRMI** Human Rights Measurement Initiative (#10987)
♦ HRN – Human Rights Now (internationally oriented national body)
♦ HRRCA / see Human Rights Resource Centre (#10989)
♦ **HRRC** Human Rights Resource Centre (#10989)
♦ **HRWF** Human Rights without Frontiers International (#10983)
♦ **HRW** Human Rights Watch (#10990)
♦ HSA – Handbell Society of Australasia (internationally oriented national body)
♦ **HSA** Hemispheric Social Alliance (#00635)
♦ **HSA** High Seas Alliance (#10918)
♦ HSA International – Handicapped Scuba Association International (internationally oriented national body)
♦ HSA-UWC – Holy Spirit Association for the Unification of World Christianity (religious order)
♦ **HSB** Hydrographic Society Benelux (#10999)
♦ HSC – Human Security Collective (internationally oriented national body)
♦ **HSCI** Hands-on Science Network (#10858)
♦ HSF – Helen Suzman Foundation (internationally oriented national body)
♦ **HSF** Homéopathes sans frontières France (#10942)
♦ HSF / see Homeopaths Without Borders France (#10942)
♦ HSF – Hydraulique sans frontières (internationally oriented national body)
♦ HSFK / see Peace Research Institute Frankfurt
♦ HSFK – Leibniz-Institut Hessische Stiftung Friedens- und Konfliktforschung (internationally oriented national body)
♦ **HS** Histiocyte Society (#10925)
♦ **HSI** Humane Society International (#10966)
♦ HSMA / see Hospitality Sales and Marketing Association International (#10948)
♦ HSMAI Global / see Hospitality Sales and Marketing Association International (#10948)
♦ **HSMAI** Hospitality Sales and Marketing Association International (#10948)
♦ **HSN** Hammer Skin Nation (#10854)
♦ **HSPA** Hydrocarbon Solvents Producers Association (#10997)
♦ HSS – History of Science Society (internationally oriented national body)
♦ HSS / see Schwarzkopf Foundation Young Europe (#19136)
♦ **HTAi** Health Technology Assessment International (#10889)

♦ **HTAsiaLink** **10959**
Secretariat Namsam Square 7F, 173 Toegye-ro, Jung-gu, Seoul, Korea Rep. T. +82221742700. Fax +8227474916.
URL: http://htasialink.org/
Aims Support collaboration among *Asian health technology assessment* agencies. **Events** *Annual Conference* Seoul (Korea Rep) 2019. **Publications** *HTAsiaLink Newsletter.* **Members** Full in 11 countries and territories:
Australia, Bhutan, China, Korea Rep, Malaysia, Philippines, Singapore, Taiwan, Thailand, UK, Vietnam.
NGO Relations *international HealthTechScan (i-HTS, #13784).* [2017/XM5806/F]

♦ HTC KL / see Regional Humid Tropics Hydrology and Water Resources Centre for South East Asia and the Pacific (#18787)
♦ HTCMC – International Conference on High Temperature Ceramic Matrix Composites (meeting series)
♦ **HTC** Regional Humid Tropics Hydrology and Water Resources Centre for South East Asia and the Pacific (#18787)
♦ HTEA – Heart-Team Education Association (unconfirmed)
♦ **HTGC** Horizontal Technical Cooperation Group of Latin America and the Caribbean on HIV/AIDS (#10945)
♦ **HTNG** Hotel Technology Next Generation (#10952)
♦ HTP – Heal The Planet – Global Organisation (internationally oriented national body)
♦ **HTR-TN** European High Temperature Reactor Technology Network (#07487)
♦ HU / see Health Poverty Action
♦ **HUA** Harakat ul-Ansar (#10860)

♦ **Huairou Commission** **10960**
Chair 249 Manhattan Ave, Brooklyn NY 11211-4905, USA. T. +17183888915. Fax +17183880285.
URL: http://www.huairou.org/
History Founded, 1995, Beijing (China), during the 4th World Conference on Women. **Aims** Promote the institutional transformation needed to engender local community development and governance. **Finance** Supported by: *American Jewish World Service (AJWS); Global Ministries Of The United Methodist Church (GM-UMC); World Urban Campaign (WUC, #21893); Stanley Center for Peace and Security; UNDP (#20292); United Nations Human Settlements Programme (UN-Habitat, #20572); United States Agency for International Development (USAID).* **Events** *International conference on women's safety* Delhi (India) 2010, *South Asia planning meeting on advancing grassroots women's leadership in community resilience* Kathmandu (Nepal) 2010, *Annual Women's Land Link Africa grassroots women's land academy* Lusaka (Zambia) 2010, *Annual Women's Land Link Africa grassroots women's land academy* Accra (Ghana) 2009, *Grassroots women's international academy* Johannesburg (South Africa) 2009.
Members International organizations (6):
Asian Women and Shelter Network (AWAS, inactive); Grassroots Organizations Operating Together in Sisterhood (GROOTS); HIC Women and Shelter Network (WAS, no recent information); International Council of Women (ICW, #13093); Women for Peace Network (no recent information); Women in Cities International.
Consultative Status Consultative status granted from: *ECOSOC (#05331)* (Special). **NGO Relations** Partners: *OWEN – Mobile Academy for Gender Democracy and Promotion of Peace (OWEN, #17920);* national organizations. Partner of: *Global Coalition on Women and AIDS (GCWA, #10297); World Urban Campaign (WUC, #21893).* Member of: *Global Gender and Climate Alliance (GGCA, no recent information).* [2014/XE2955/y/E]

♦ Hubbard Association of Scientologists International / see Church of Scientology International (#03922)
♦ Hudson Institute (internationally oriented national body)
♦ **HUGO** Human Genome Organization (#10968)
♦ Les huit / see Group of Eight (#10745)
♦ Hulp van St-Andries aan de Derde Wereld (internationally oriented national body)
♦ Hulp aan de Verdrukte Kerk (internationally oriented national body)
♦ Humains Associés (#02339)
♦ Humana / see International Humana People to People Movement (#13817)

♦ **Human Appeal** **10961**
UK Office Pennine House, 1 Cheadle Point, Carrs Road, Cheadle, SK8 2BL, UK. T. +441612250225. Fax +441612250226. E-mail: customercare@humanappeal.org.uk.
URL: http://humanappeal.org.uk/
History Nov 1984, UK. Founded by young social workers wishing to offer urgent relief to African people suffering the effects of famine due to desertification. Former names and other names: *Charity Organization* – former; *Human Appeal International* – former (Sep 1991). Registration: Charity, No/ID: 1154288, England and Wales; Charity, No/ID: SC046481, Scotland. **Aims** Deliver immediate relief aid to disaster affected areas and follow internationally recognized guidelines for humanitarian response including the SPHERE Humanitarian Charter and the International Red Cross Codes of Conduct. **Structure** Board of Trustees; Chief Executive Officer. **Languages** English. **Staff** Over 150 FTE, paid; 2,000 voluntary at head office level; 500 voluntary in countries of operations. **Finance** Funding from: institutional donors; trusts; foundations; banks; investments; contributions; donations. Annual budget: pounds35,000,000. **Activities** Humanitarian/emergency aid; projects/programmes; financial and/or material support; research and development.
Members Active in 16 countries and territories:
Bangladesh, India, Iraq, Jordan, Kenya, Lebanon, Myanmar, Pakistan, Palestine, Senegal, Somalia, Sri Lanka, Sudan, Syrian AR, Türkiye, Yemen.
Consultative Status Consultative status granted from: *ECOSOC (#05331)* (Special). **IGO Relations** Relations with the following United Nations agencies: *UNHCR (#20327); UNICEF (#20332); World Food Programme (WFP, #21510).* **NGO Relations** Member of (3): *Active Learning Network for Accountability and Performance in Humanitarian Action (ALNAP, #00101); CHS Alliance (#03911); International Council of Voluntary Agencies (ICVA, #13092).* [2017.06.22/XF5112/F]

♦ Human Appeal International / see Human Appeal (#10961)
♦ Human Asia (internationally oriented national body)

♦ **Human Cell Atlas (HCA)** **10962**
Contact address not obtained. E-mail: hca@humancellatlas.org.
URL: https://www.humancellatlas.org/
History Founded Oct 2016, London (UK). **Aims** Create comprehensive reference maps of all human cells – the fundamental units of life – as a basis for both understanding human health and diagnosing, monitoring, and treating disease. **Structure** Organizing Committee; Executive Office. Working Groups (3): Analysis; DCP Governance; Standards and Technology. **Activities** Research/documentation; events/meetings. **Events** *General Meeting* Barcelona (Spain) 2019, *Asia Meeting* Singapore (Singapore) 2019, *General Meeting* Tokyo (Japan) 2019, *General Meeting* Cambridge, MA (USA) 2018, *Asia Meeting* Jeju (Korea Rep) 2018. [2019/XM8312/F]

♦ **Human Cell Differentiation Molecules (HCDM)** **10963**

Registered Address Vyšehradská 320/49, Nové Město, 128 00 Prague 2, Czechia. E-mail: tomas.kalina@lfmotol.cuni.cz.
Pres Numancia 73 7° C2, 08029 Barcelona, Spain. T. +34933633954.
URL: http://www.hcdm.org/

Aims Characterize the structure, function and distribution of leucocyte surface molecules and other molecules of the immune system. **Structure** Council. **Activities** Events/meetings. **Events** *International Leukocyte Differentiation Antigen Workshop* Sydney, NSW (Australia) 2014, *International Conference on Human Leukocyte Differentiation Antigens* Barcelona (Spain) 2010. **NGO Relations** Sponsors include: *International Union of Immunological Societies (IUIS, #15781).* [2019/AA2188/c/**F**]

♦ Human Concern International (internationally oriented national body)

♦ **Human Development and Capability Association (HDCA)** **10964**

Association pour le développement humain et l'approche

Administrator PO Box 1051, Brewster MA 02631, USA. E-mail: admin@hd-ca.org.
URL: https://hd-ca.org/

History Sep 2004. **Aims** Promote research in the interconnected areas of human development and capability. **Structure** Executive Council; Fellows. Committees (6): Nominating; Conference Advisory; Conference Program; Sen/Haq Lecture Series; Affiliation; Finance. **Languages** English. **Staff** 5.00 FTE, paid. **Finance** Members' dues; reduced dues for members in developing countries. **Activities** Events/meetings. **Events** *International Conference* Auckland (New Zealand) 2020, *International Conference* London (UK) 2019, *International Conference* Buenos Aires (Argentina) 2018, *International Conference* Cape Town (South Africa) 2017, *Conference* Kunitachi (Japan) 2016. **Publications** *Journal of Human Development and Capabilities* (4 a year). **Members** in over 70 countries. Membership countries not specified. [2020/XM0561/**C**]

♦ HumanDHS – Human Dignity and Humiliation Studies (internationally oriented national body)

♦ **Human Dignity (HD)** **10965**

Contact 22 rue du Sergent Bauchat, 75012 Paris, France. E-mail: info@hdignity.org.
URL: http://www.hdignity.org/

History Founded Jan 2014. **Aims** Advance economic, social and cultural rights in Sub-Saharan Africa. **Structure** Board. **Consultative Status** Consultative status granted from: *ECOSOC (#05331)* (Special). [2019/XM7196/**F**]

♦ Human Dignity and Humiliation Studies (internationally oriented national body)
♦ Human Dignity Trust (internationally oriented national body)
♦ Humane Africa Trust (internationally oriented national body)
♦ **HUMANE** Heads of University Management and Administration Network in Europe (#10867)
♦ The Humane League (unconfirmed)

♦ **Humane Society International (HSI)** **10966**

Pres 1255 23rd Street NW, Suite 450, Washington DC 20037, USA. T. +12024521100. E-mail: info@hsi.org.
HSI Europe Kunstlaan 50, 1000 Brussels, Belgium.
URL: http://www.hsi.org/

History 1991. Founded as the international arm of *'The Humane Society of the United States (HSUS)'*. Registration: No/ID: 52-1769464, USA; Charity Commission, No/ID: 1098925, England and Wales; Banque-Carrefour des Entreprises, No/ID: 0562.718.279, Belgium. **Aims** Promote humane treatment of *animals*; foster respect, understanding and compassion for all creatures; promote *responsible pet* ownership. **Structure** Board of Directors. Offices: Australia; Canada; Europe (Brussels, Belgium); Global (USA); India; Latin America (Costa Rica); UK; USA. **Activities** Events/meetings. **Events** *Annual Conference* Anaheim, CA (USA) 2006, *Annual Conference* Atlanta, GA (USA) 2005, *Annual Conference* Dallas, TX (USA) 2004, *Companion animals – issues and answers* Moscow (Russia) 2003, *Annual Conference* Reno, NV (USA) 2003. **Publications** *All Animals* (4 a year); *Wildlife Tracks* (4 a year); *Wild Neighbors News* (4 a year); *Animal Sheltering* (24 a year).
Members Individuals in 50 countries and territories:
Albania, Algeria, Argentina, Australia, Austria, Belarus, Belgium, Brazil, Canada, Cayman Is, Colombia, Costa Rica, Czechia, Denmark, Dominican Rep, France, Georgia, Germany, Greece, Grenada, Honduras, Hong Kong, India, Indonesia, Iran Islamic Rep, Ireland, Israel, Italy, Jamaica, Japan, Korea Rep, Mexico, Monaco, Netherlands, Norway, Panama, Peru, Philippines, Portugal, Russia, Saudi Arabia, South Africa, Spain, Sri Lanka, Sweden, Taiwan, UK, Ukraine, Venezuela.
IGO Relations Accredited by: *International Whaling Commission (IWC, #15879).* Observer at: *Commission for the Conservation of Southern Bluefin Tuna (CCSBT, #04207).* Member of: *Standing Committee to the Bern Convention on the Conservation of European Wildlife and Natural Habitats (#19949).*
NGO Relations Member of:
- *Alliance for Zero Extinction (AZE, #00730);*
- *American Council for Voluntary International Action (InterAction);*
- *Ape Alliance (#00871);*
- *Asia Canine Protection Alliance (ACPA, #01257);*
- *InsideNGO (inactive);*
- *International Coalition for Animal Welfare (ICFAW, #12607);*
- *International Tiger Coalition (ITC);*
- *LEDS Global Partnership (LEDS GP, #16435);*
- *Species Survival Network (SSN, #19916);*
- *Turtle Conservation Fund (TCF, #20263).*

Affiliate Member of: *Fur Free Alliance (FFA, #10043).* Partner of: *1% for the Planet*; *Global Call for Climate Action (GCCA, inactive).* [2022/XE3646/v/**E**]

♦ Human Factors and Ergonomics Society (internationally oriented national body)

♦ **Human Factors and Ergonomics Society – Europe Chapter (HFES-EUR)** **10967**

Sec c/o LJMU – Psychology, Tom Reilly Building, Byrom Street, Liverpool, L3 3AF, UK. E-mail: secretary@hfes-europe.org.
URL: http://www.hfes-europe.org/

History 25 Jan 1983, Soesterberg (Netherlands). Founded on approval of by-laws, as European Chapter of *Human Factors and Ergonomics Society (HFES).* **Aims** Through exchange of knowledge and methodology in *behavioural*, biological and physical sciences, promote and advance understanding and application of the understanding of human factors involved in design, acquisition and use of hardware, software and personnel aspects of tools, devices, machines, equipment, computers, vehicles, systems and artificial environments of all kinds. **Structure** Executive Council; Committees (5). **Languages** English. **Staff** 7.00 FTE, voluntary. **Finance** Members' dues. **Activities** Networking/liaising; events/meetings. **Events** *Annual Meeting* Liverpool (UK) 2022, *Annual Meeting* Nantes (France) 2019, *Annual Meeting* Berlin (Germany) 2018, *Annual Meeting* Paris (France) 2017, *Annual Meeting* Prague (Czechia) 2016. **Publications** *Newsletter of the Europe Chapter HFES.* Conference proceedings.
Members Fellow; Member; Associate; Colleague; Student. Individuals in 30 countries and territories:
Australia, Austria, Belgium, Canada, Finland, France, Germany, Greece, Iceland, India, Ireland, Israel, Italy, Japan, Latvia, Malaysia, Malta, Netherlands, Norway, Poland, Portugal, Romania, Serbia, Slovenia, Spain, Sweden, Switzerland, Türkiye, UK, USA. [2021/XE3804/v/**E**]

♦ Human Factors and Ergonomics Society GCC Chapter (unconfirmed)
♦ Human Genetics Society of Australasia (internationally oriented national body)

♦ **Human Genome Organization (HUGO)** **10968**

Organisation du génome humain

Admin Officer Graduate Bldg No 101, Ewhayeodaegil-52, Seodaemun-gu, Seoul 03760, Korea Rep. T. +82232774750. E-mail: admin@hugo-international.org.
URL: http://www.hugo-international.org/

History Apr 1988, Cold Spring Harbor NY (USA). Registered in accordance with Swiss Civil Code. **Aims** Promote fundamental genomic research within nations and throughout the world; foster scientific exchange in genomics with a particular emphasis on scientifically developing and emerging countries; support discourse in the ethics of genetics and genomics with a global perspective. **Structure** Council; Secretariat, located in Singapore (Singapore). **Languages** English. **Staff** 2.00 FTE, paid. **Finance** Members' dues. Other source: meeting revenue. Annual budget: US$ 250,000. **Activities** Awards/prizes/competitions; knowledge management/information dissemination; events/meetings. **Events** *Annual Meeting* Tel Aviv (Israel) 2022, *Annual Meeting* Tel Aviv (Israel) 2021, *Annual Meeting* Perth, WA (Australia) 2020, *Annual Meeting* Seoul (Korea Rep) 2019, *Annual Meeting* Yokohama (Japan) 2018. **Publications** *The HUGO Journal.*
Members Individuals in 37 countries:
Argentina, Australia, Belgium, Brazil, Brunei Darussalam, Canada, China, Cyprus, Czechia, Denmark, Ecuador, Egypt, Estonia, France, Germany, India, Indonesia, Israel, Italy, Japan, Korea Rep, Malaysia, Mexico, Netherlands, Philippines, Russia, Saudi Arabia, Singapore, South Africa, Sweden, Switzerland, Taiwan, Tanzania UR, Thailand, UK, USA, Vietnam.
IGO Relations *OECD (#17693)*; *WHO (#20950).* **NGO Relations** Member of: *Global Alliance for Genomics and Health (GA4GH, #10199). International Association of Law, Ethics and Science (Milazzo Group, no recent information)* is an observer member. [2017.10.16/XD2443/v/**D**]

♦ **Human Genome Variation Society (HGVS)** **10969**

Exec Sec c/o Genomic Disorders Research Ctr, Level 2, 161 Barry St, Carlton South VIC 3053, Australia. T. +61383441831. Fax +61393476842.
URL: http://www.hgvs.org/

Aims Foster discovery and characterization of genomic variations including population distribution and phenotypic associations; promote collection, documentation and free distribution of genomic variation information and associated clinical variations; foster the development of the necessary methodology and informatics. **Structure** Board of Director, comprising President, Secretary/Treasurer and members. **Activities** Organizes scientific meetings. **Events** *Meeting on informatics for next generation sequencing* Montpellier (France) 2010, *Conference on exploring the functional consequences of genomic variation* Washington, DC (USA) 2010, *Symposium on genome wide association studies* Vienna (Austria) 2009. **Publications** *Human Mutation* – journal. **NGO Relations** Affiliated with: *International Federation of Human Genetics Societies (IFHGS, #13451).* [2013/XM3785/**D**]

♦ Humanic Relief (internationally oriented national body)
♦ Humanidades Digitales Hispanicas – Sociedad Internacional (internationally oriented national body)
♦ Human Info NGO (internationally oriented national body)

♦ **Humanist** **10970**

SG Ifsttar Lyon-Bron, 25 avenue François Mitterrand, Case 24, Cité des mobilités, 69675 Bron CEDEX, France. T. +33472142315. E-mail: secretariat@humanist-vce.eu.
URL: http://www.humanist-vce.eu/

History Founded 2003. Full title: *Humanist – Virtual Centre of Excellence – European Network for Research on Human Factors in Transport.* **Structure** Board. **Activities** Events/meetings; training/education; research/documentation. **Events** *Conference* The Hague (Netherlands) 2018. **NGO Relations** Partner of (1): *European Transport Research Alliance (ETRA, #08939).* [2019/XM7840/**F**]

♦ **Humanistica** **10971**

Sec MESHS, 2 rue des Canonniers, 59000 Lille, France. E-mail: humanisticadh@gmail.com.
Registered Address Rue d'Egmont 5, 1000 Brussels, Belgium.
URL: http://www.humanisti.ca/

History 2014. Proposed 2012. Former names and other names: *Association francophone des humanités numériques/digitales (Humanistica)* – full title. Registration: Banque-Carrefour des Entreprises, No/ID: 0555.722.995, Start date: 5 Jul 2014, Belgium. **Aims** Gather and federate the francophone community of digital humanities; represent the community nationally and internationally. **Structure** General Assembly; Coordinating Committee; Bureau. **Activities** Events/meetings. **Events** *Colloquium Humanistica* Montréal, QC (Canada) 2022, *Colloquium Humanistica* Rennes (France) 2021, *Colloquium Humanistica* Bordeaux (France) 2020. **Publications** *Humanités numériques* (2 a year).
Members Full in 14 countries:
Belgium, Cameroon, Canada, Croatia, France, Germany, Italy, Lebanon, Luxembourg, Netherlands, Romania, Switzerland, Tunisia, USA. [2022/AA2537/**C**]

♦ Humanistic Institute for Cooperation with Developing Countries / see Humanistisch Instituut voor Ontwikkelingssamenwerking
♦ Humanist Institute for Cooperation with Developing Countries (internationally oriented national body)
♦ Humanistisch Instituut voor Ontwikkelingssamenwerking (internationally oriented national body)

♦ **Humanists International** **10972**

Chief Exec 272 Bath Street, Glasgow, G4 2JR, UK. E-mail: office@humanists.international – comms@humanists.international.
Registered Address 1821 Jefferson Pl NW, Washington DC 20036, USA.
URL: https://humanists.international/

History 26 Aug 1952, Amsterdam (Netherlands). Founded after 1st International Congress on Humanism and Ethical Culture. Former names and other names: *International Humanist and Ethical Union (IHEU)* – former (1952); *Union internationale humaniste et laïque* – former; *Unión Internacional Humanista y Etica* – former; *Internationale Humanistische und Ethische Union* – former; *Humanists International 2020* – legal name. Registration: Scottish Charity Regulator, No/ID: SC050629, Start date: 14 Dec 2020, Scotland; Companies House, No/ID: SC682230, Start date: 27 Nov 2020, Scotland; Start date: 12 Aug 1953, USA, New York. **Aims** Build and represent global Humanist movement that defends human rights; promote Humanist values world-wide; influence international policy through representation and information; build the humanist network and let the world know about the worldview of Humanism. **Structure** General Assembly; Board. Headquarters in London (UK). Youth section: *Young Humanists International (#21993).* **Languages** English, French, German, Italian, Spanish. **Staff** London (UK): 3 FTE; Brussels (Belgium): 1 FTE. **Finance** Sources: contributions; members' dues. **Activities** Events/meetings; knowledge management/information dissemination; networking/liaising. **Events** *World Humanist Congress* Copenhagen (Denmark) 2023, *General Assembly* Glasgow (UK) 2022, *General Assembly* Kathmandu (Nepal) 2021, *World Humanist Congress* Miami, FL (USA) 2020, *General Assembly* Reykjavik (Iceland) 2019. **Publications** *IHEU Member and Supporter Newsletters* (12 a year); *IHEU Freedom of Thought Report* (annual). *1952-2002: Past present and future* (2002); *International Humanist and Ethical Union and its Member Organizations* (1974); *Challenge of Out Time* (1960) by J P van Praag; *Radioactive Fall-out and Human Progress* (1958) by H J Muller; *Bibliography of Humanism* (1957) by Kwee Swan Liat; *An Ethical Humanist Approach to Peace and Practical Suggestion for Implementation* by Sudney H Scheuer; *Aspectos del Humanismo Contemporaneo* by F Subidé; *Declaration of Global Interdependence: A New Global Ethics*; *Humanism* by J P van Praag; *Humanist Counselling* by P A Pols; *The Humanist Himself* by H J Blackham. Congress proceedings.
Members Full in 24 countries:
Argentina, Belgium, Canada, Denmark, Finland, France, Germany, Iceland, India, Ireland, Italy, Kenya, Malawi, Nepal, Netherlands, New Zealand, Nigeria, Norway, Slovakia, Sweden, Switzerland, Uganda, UK, USA.
Included in the above, 2 organizations listed in this Yearbook:
LGBT Humanists; *Young Humanists International (#21993).*
Associate in 27 countries:
Austria, Bangladesh, Belgium, Brazil, Canada, Czechia, Egypt, Finland, France, Greece, Hungary, India, Italy, Luxembourg, Malawi, Nepal, New Zealand, Peru, Philippines, Poland, Romania, Russia, South Africa, Sweden, Uganda, UK, USA.
Included in the above, 1 organization listed in this Yearbook:
Mouvement Europe et laïcité.
Specialist in 3 countries:
India, Netherlands, USA.
Included in the above, 1 organization listed in this Yearbook:
Humanistisch Instituut voor Ontwikkelingssamenwerking (Hivos).
Applicant in 5 countries:
Canada, Colombia, Indonesia, Kenya, Singapore.

Consultative Status Consultative status granted from: *ECOSOC (#05331)* (Special); *UNESCO (#20322)* (Consultative Status); *UNICEF (#20332)*; *Council of Europe (CE, #04881)* (Participatory Status); *African Commission on Human and Peoples' Rights (ACHPR, #00255)* (Observer). **IGO Relations** Accredited by: *United Nations Office at Vienna (UNOV, #20604)*. Participant in Fundamental Rights Platform of *European Union Agency for Fundamental Rights (FRA, #08969)*. Associated with Department of Global Communications of the United Nations. **NGO Relations** Member of (2): *Conference of INGOs of the Council of Europe (#04607)*; *NGO Committee on UNICEF (#17120)*. Cooperates with (3): *Committee for Skeptical Inquiry (CSI)*; *International Association for Intercultural Education (IAIE, #11969)*; *Unitarian Universalist Association (UUA, #20494)*. Instrumental in setting up (5): *African Humanist Alliance (AHAL, no recent information)*; *European Humanist Professionals (EHP, #07508)*; *Institute for the Secularization of Islamic Society (ISIS)*; *International Secretariat for Growth and Development (see: #10972)*; *South Asian Humanist Network (see: #10972)*.
[2022/XC2112/y/**C**]

- ♦ Humanists International 2020 / see Humanists International (#10972)
- ♦ Humanist – Virtual Centre of Excellence – European Network for Research on Human Factors in Transport / see Humanist (#10970)
- ♦ Humanitarian 8 (no recent information)
- ♦ Humanitarian Accountability Partnership International (inactive)
- ♦ Humanitarian Affairs (unconfirmed)
- ♦ Humanitarian Aid Network for Distribution (internationally oriented national body)
- ♦ Humanitarian Aid Relief Trust (internationally oriented national body)
- ♦ Humanitarian Association of Turkmens of the World, Ashgabat (no recent information)
- ♦ Humanitarian and Charitable ONE Trust (internationally oriented national body)
- ♦ Humanitarian Coalition on Small Arms (internationally oriented national body)
- ♦ Humanitarian Crisis Hub (internationally oriented national body)
- ♦ Humanitarian Demining Information Center / see Mine Action Information Center
- ♦ Humanitarian Foundation of People Against Landmines / see People Against Landmines
- ♦ Humanitarian Medicine Brock Chisholm Trust / see International Association for Humanitarian Medicine Chisholm-Gunn (#11946)

♦ Humanitarian Practice Network (HPN) 10973

Contact c/o Overseas Development Institute, 203 Blackfriars Rd, London, SE1 8NJ, UK. T. +442079220334 – +442079220399. E-mail: hpn@odi.org.uk.
URL: http://www.odihpn.org/

History 1994, as *Relief and Rehabilitation Network (RRN)*, following recommendations, 1993, of research undertaken by *Overseas Development Institute (ODI)* on the changing role of NGOs in relief and rehabilitation operations and consultation with other ODI networks. Now an independent network operating within Humanitarian Policy Group of ODI. Current name adopted 2000. **Aims** Stimulate critical analysis, advance professional learning and development, and improve practice on the part of those engaged in and around humanitarian action and assistance; improve aid policy and practice as applied in complex political emergencies; commission, publish and disseminate analysis and reflection on issues of good practice in policy and programming of humanitarian operations. **Finance** Free membership to those engaged in humanitarian action. Organizational donors include: *CARE International (CI, #03429)*; *DANIDA*; *Department for International Development (DFID, inactive)*; *Migrant Forum in Asia (MFA, #16798)*; *Save the Children UK (SC UK)*; *Swedish International Development Cooperation Agency (Sida)*; *UNDP (#20292)*; *United Nations Office for the Coordination of Humanitarian Affairs (OCHA, #20593)*; *World Food Programme (WFP, #21510)*. **Activities** Produces information, analysis, debate and practical resources on aspects of conflict, management, disaster prevention, relief and development linkages, humanitarian policy initiatives and protection; targets individuals and organizations actively engaged in humanitarian action and those involved in the improvement of performance at international, national and local level. **Publications** *Humanitarian Exchange* (4 a year) – magazine; *Good Practice Review* (occasional); *Network Papers* (3-4 a year).
Members Covers 89 countries and territories:
Afghanistan, Algeria, Argentina, Australia, Austria, Bangladesh, Belgium, Bosnia-Herzegovina, Botswana, Brazil, Burkina Faso, Burundi, Cambodia, Cameroon, Canada, Central African Rep, Chile, China, Congo Brazzaville, Congo DR, Côte d'Ivoire, Croatia, Czechia, Denmark, Djibouti, Egypt, Eritrea, Ethiopia, Finland, France, Gambia, Germany, Ghana, Guinea, Hong Kong, India, Iran Islamic Rep, Iraq, Ireland, Israel, Italy, Japan, Jordan, Kazakhstan, Kenya, Kyrgyzstan, Liberia, Luxembourg, Madagascar, Malawi, Malta, Mexico, Morocco, Mozambique, Nepal, Netherlands, New Zealand, Nigeria, Norway, Pakistan, Panama, Peru, Philippines, Poland, Portugal, Russia, Rwanda, Serbia, Sierra Leone, Slovakia, Slovenia, Somalia, South Africa, Spain, Sri Lanka, Sudan, Sweden, Switzerland, Tajikistan, Tanzania UR, Thailand, Türkiye, Uganda, UK, Ukraine, USA, Vietnam, Zambia, Zimbabwe.
[2014/XF4423/**F**]

♦ Humanitarian Quality Assurance Initiative (HQAI) 10974

Co-Exec Dir Chemin de Balexert 7-9, Châtelaine, 1219 Geneva, Switzerland. T. +41225661399. E-mail: contact@hqai.org.
URL: https://www.hqai.org/

History 2015. Set up as a follow-up of the certification review of the *Steering Committee for Humanitarian Response (SCHR, #19978)*, the publication of the Core Humanitarian Standard, Dec 2014, and the merger of the *Humanitarian Accountability Partnership and People in Aid*. Registration: Swiss Civil Code, Switzerland. **Aims** Provide professional independent quality assurance services to improve the work of humanitarian and development organizations. **Structure** Board of Directors; Advisory and Complaint Board; Subsidy Fund Management Committee; Secretariat. **Languages** English, French, Spanish. **Staff** 8.00 FTE, paid. **Finance** Sources: government support. Supported by: *DANIDA*; *Department for International Development (DFID, inactive)*; GFFO Germany; *Luxembourg Agency for Development Cooperation (LUXDEV)*; *Swiss Agency for Development and Cooperation (SDC)*. Annual budget: 1,300,000 CHF (2021). **Activities** Awareness raising; capacity building; certification/accreditation; knowledge management/information dissemination; monitoring/evaluation; standards/guidelines; training/education. **Publications** Annual Report; system documents; standards.
Members Individuals in 7 countries:
Australia, France, India, Japan, South Africa, Switzerland, UK.
NGO Relations Member of (4): *CHS Alliance (#03911)*; *Disasters Emergency Committee (DEC)*; H2H; *International Council of Voluntary Agencies (ICVA, #13092)*.
[2022.05.12/XM5053/**F**]

- ♦ Humanitarian Tools Foundation / see Radio Benevolencija Foundation
- ♦ Humanité 2000 (inactive)
- ♦ Humanity 3000 Programme (internationally oriented national body)
- ♦ Humanity in Action (internationally oriented national body)

♦ Humanity and Inclusion (HI) 10975

Contact Rue de l'Arbre Benit 44, boite 1, 1050 Brussels, Belgium. T. +3222801601. Fax +3222306030. E-mail: info@belgium.hi.org.
Contact 138 avenue des Frères Lumière, CS 88379, 69371 Lyon CEDEX 08, France.
URL: http://hi.org/

History 19 Jul 1982, Lyon (France), as *Operation Handicap International – Opération handicap internationale (OHI)*. Subsequently changed title to *Handicap International (HI)*. Current title adopted 24 Jan 2018. Individual countries may still use old title. current bylaws updated and approved Jun 2016. Registered in Belgium, 10 Sep 1986. French section has taken over activities of *Action Nord Sud (inactive)*. **Aims** Reduce risk-factors which lead to incapacity or increased *vulnerability*; develop individuals' abilities and independence in order to help them fulfil their life goals; adapt environmental, social and physical factors so to improve quality and access to services; develop social participation in order to reduce situations of disability, vulnerability or exclusion. **Structure** National Associations (8); Relief Department. **Languages** Dutch, English, French. **Staff** 230.00 FTE, voluntary. **Finance** International and national organizations; individual donations; sponsorship; partnership. **Activities** Advocacy/lobbying/activism; awareness raising. **Events** *Colloque international sur Simone Weil, l'Europe et l'universel* Lyon (France) 2009, *Colloque international sur le rôle et l'avenir des ONG dans la nouvelle gouvernance mondiale* Lyon (France) 2008, *Assemblée générale* Brussels (Belgium) 2007, *Landmine conference* Brussels (Belgium) 2000, *Create and recrete the museum – the place and the role of the disabled in the museums* Grenoble (France) 1995. **Publications** *Handicap International* (4 a year). Each section has an Annual Report, liaison letters and technical publications. **Members** Categories Adherent; Active; Honorary. Membership countries not specified. **Consultative Status** Consultative status granted from: *ECOSOC (#05331)* (Special); *WHO (#20950)* (Official). **NGO Relations** Member of Board of: *Voluntary Organisations in Cooperation in Emergencies (VOICE, #20809)*. Founding member of: *Global Rehabilitation Alliance (#10565)*. Member of: *Campaign to Stop Killer Robots (#03405)*; *Confédération européenne des ong d'urgence et de développement (CONCORD, #04547)*; *Coordination SUD*; *Fédération francophone et germanophone des associations de coopération au développement (ACODEV, #09587)*; *Global Health Council (GHC, #10402)*; *ILO Global Business and Disability Network (GBDN, #11122)*; *International Campaign to Ban Landmines – Cluster Munition Coalition (ICBL-CMC, #12427)*; *International Council of Voluntary Agencies (ICVA, #13092)*; *International Network on Explosive Weapons (INEW, #14266)*. Partner of: *Global Health Cluster (GHC, #10401)*.
[2019/XF0223/**F**]

♦ Humanity's Team 10976

Dir PO Box 58, Fort Collins CO 80522, USA. T. +19706720017. E-mail: info@humanitysteam.org.
Main Website: http://www.humanitysteam.com/

History 2003, USA. Registration: Section 501(c)(3), USA. **Aims** Make conscious living pervasive worldwide by 2040. **Languages** English, French, Spanish.
Members Teams in 56 countries and territories:
Australia, Austria, Bangladesh, Belgium, Bolivia, Brazil, Bulgaria, Canada, Chile, Colombia, Costa Rica, Croatia, Denmark, Dominican Rep, Ecuador, Estonia, France, Germany, Greece, Honduras, Hungary, India, Iraq, Ireland, Italy, Japan, Kazakhstan, Korea Rep, Liberia, Mexico, Nepal, Netherlands, New Zealand, Nigeria, Norway, Panama, Paraguay, Peru, Poland, Portugal, Romania, Rwanda, Saudi Arabia, Scotland, Serbia, Singapore, South Africa, Spain, Switzerland, Taiwan, Trinidad-Tobago, Tunisia, Turkey, UK, USA, Venezuela.
[2022.10.19/XM0301/**F**]

- ♦ Humanity United (internationally oriented national body)

♦ Human Life International (HLI) 10977

Vie humaine internationale – Vida Humana Internacional – Vita Umana Internazionale

Main Office 4 Family Life Ln, Front Royal VA 22630, USA. T. +15406357884. Fax +15406226247. E-mail: hli@hli.org.
URL: http://www.hli.org/

History 1981, Washington DC (USA). Registered in accordance with USA law. **Aims** Serve as a research, educational, and service program offering positive alternatives to *anti-life/anti-family* movement; explore and comment on various dimensions of human life issues. **Structure** Officers: President, Treasurer, Secretary, Director of Publications, Special Consultant, Director of Communications, Director – Population Research Institute, 2 Latin American Coordinators and Director of Development. Board of Advisors of 24 members. **Languages** Croatian, English, French, German, Polish, Portuguese, Spanish, Tamil. **Staff** 50.00 FTE, paid. **Finance** Donations. Budget (annual): US$ 4.7 million. **Activities** Guidance/assistance/consulting; training/education; events/meetings. **Events** *Asia Pacific Congress on Faith, Life and Family* Kodakara (India) 2020, *Asia Pacific Congress on Faith, Life and Family* Nakhon Pathom (Thailand) 2017, *Asia Pacific Congress on Faith, Life and Family* Taipei (Taiwan) 2015, *Asia Pacific Congress on Faith, Life and Family* Kota Kinabalu (Malaysia) 2013, *Congress* Vienna (Austria) 2012. **Publications** *HLI Reports* (12 a year); *HLI Special Reports* (12 a year); *HLPL Reports* (12 a year); *Prolife and Pro-Family Parish Notes* (12 a year); *Escoge la Vida* (6 a year); *Population Research Institute Review* (6 a year). *And Now Euthanasia*; *Confessions of a Pro-Life Missionary*; *Eight Reasons You Should Consider Having One More Child*; *Is Contraception a Sin ?*; *Population Control Goes to School*; *Population Control of the Family*; *RU-486: The Rest of the Story*; *The Deadly New Colonialism*; *Their Plans for Your Children*; *USAID's Agenda of Fear*.
Members Head Office in USA. Organizations (); Individuals, in 125 countries and territories:
Angola, Argentina (*), Australia (*), Austria (*), Bahamas, Bangladesh, Barbados (*), Belgium (*), Belize, Benin, Bolivia, Botswana, Brazil (*), Bulgaria, Burkina Faso, Burundi, Cameroon, Central African Rep, Chile (*), China, Colombia (*), Congo Brazzaville, Congo DR, Costa Rica (*), Croatia (*), Cyprus, Czechia (*), Denmark (*), Dominican Rep, Ecuador (*), Egypt, El Salvador, Eswatini, Ethiopia, Fiji, Finland, France, Gambia, Georgia (*), Germany, Ghana, Greece, Grenada, Guatemala, Guinea, Guyana, Haiti, Holy See, Honduras, Hong Kong, Hungary (*), Iceland, India (*), Indonesia, Iraq, Ireland (*), Israel, Italy, Jamaica, Japan, Kenya (*), Kiribati, Korea Rep, Kuwait, Latvia, Lebanon, Lesotho, Liberia, Liechtenstein, Lithuania, Luxembourg, Madagascar, Malawi, Malaysia (*), Mali, Malta, Mauritius, Mexico, Monaco, Morocco, Mozambique, Myanmar, Namibia (*), Nepal, Netherlands (*), New Zealand, Nicaragua, Nigeria (*), Norway, Pakistan, Panama, Papua New Guinea, Paraguay (*), Peru, Philippines (*), Poland (*), Portugal, Puerto Rico (*), Romania, Russia (*), Rwanda, Saudi Arabia, Senegal, Seychelles, Sierra Leone, Singapore (*), Solomon Is, South Africa (*), Spain, Sri Lanka (*), Sudan, Sweden (*), Switzerland (*), Taiwan, Tanzania UR, Thailand, Tonga, Trinidad-Tobago, Uganda, UK (* – 2), Uruguay, USA, Venezuela, Zambia, Zimbabwe (*).
Consultative Status Consultative status granted from: *ECOSOC (#05331)* (Special).
[2017/XF0144/**F**]

♦ Human Proteome Organization (HUPO) 10978

Address not obtained.
Registered Address c/o ICS, 10685-B Hazelhurst Dr, Ste 26427, Houston TX 77043, USA.
URL: http://www.hupo.org/

History 8 Feb 2001. **Aims** Define and promote proteomics through international cooperation and collaborations by fostering development of new technologies, techniques and training to better understand human disease. **Structure** Council of 45 members. Executive Committee, comprising Vice-Presidents who are chairs of various standing committees. Officers: President; Secretary-General; Treasurer. Committees (13). **Languages** English. **Staff** 2.00 FTE, paid. **Finance** Members' dues. Other sources: sponsorship; proceeds from annual congress and other activities. **Activities** Initiatives (11): Human Liver Proteome Project (HLPP); Human Brain Proteome Project (HBPP); Proteomic Standards Initiative (PSI); Human Antibody Initiative (HAI); Plasma Proteome Project (PPP); Human Disease Glycomics/Proteome Initiative (HGPI); HUPO Cardiovascular Initiative (HUPO CVI); Proteome Biology of Stem Cells Initiative; Disease Biomarkers Initiatives (DBI); Mouse Models of Human Disease (MMHD); Kidney and Urine Initiative (HKUPP). Committees (13): Executive; Initiatives; Industrial Advisory Board; Nomination and Elections; New Technology and Resources; Education and Training; Ethics; Meetings; Membership Awards; Finance; Publications; By-Laws. **Events** *World Congress* Cancún (Mexico) 2022, *World Congress* 2021, *Connect Congress* Stockholm (Sweden) 2020, *World Congress* Adelaide, SA (Australia) 2019, *Annual World Congress* Orlando, FL (USA) 2018.
Members National societies in 11 countries:
Canada, China, France, Germany, Italy, Japan, Korea Rep, Russia, Sweden, UK, USA.
Regional societies (2), listed in this Yearbook:
Asia Oceania Human Proteome Organization (AOHUPO, #01801); *Latin American Human Proteome Organization (LAHUPO, no recent information)*.
[2021/XD8914/**D**]

- ♦ Human Relations Area Files (internationally oriented national body)
- ♦ Human Relief / see Humanic Relief
- ♦ Human Relief Foundation (internationally oriented national body)
- ♦ Human Rights Advocates (internationally oriented national body)
- ♦ Human Rights for Africa (internationally oriented national body)
- ♦ Human Rights Association (internationally oriented national body)
- ♦ Human Rights Centre (internationally oriented national body)
- ♦ Human Rights Centre of Azerbaijan (internationally oriented national body)
- ♦ Human Rights Committee (internationally oriented national body)

♦ Human Rights Committee (CCPR) 10979

Comité des droits de l'homme

Secretariat Human Rights Treaties Div (HRTD), OHCHR, Palais Wilson, Rue des Pâquis 52, 1201 Geneva, Switzerland. T. +41229179261. Fax +41229179008. E-mail: ccpr@ohchr.org.
URL: http://www.ohchr.org/EN/HRBodies/CCPR/Pages/CCPRIndex.aspx

History Sep 1976. Established as an organ of the member states of the *United Nations (UN, #20515)* under article 28 of *International Covenant on Civil and Political Rights (ICCPR, 1966)*, adopted by General Assembly resolution 2200 A 'XXI' of 16 Dec 1966, and which entered into force 23 Mar 1976, in accordance with article 49 of the Covenant. Based at *United Nations Office at Geneva (UNOG, #20597)*. Functions as a treaty body of: *Office of the United Nations High Commissioner for Human Rights (OHCHR, #17697)*. **Aims** Monitor implementation of the Covenant; examine individual complaints under optional protocol procedure; adopt General Comments (interpretations) on articles of the Covenant. **Structure** Committee comprises 18 members, elected in their personal capacity for 4-year terms by states party to the Covenant, from among their nationals. Bureau; Secretariat in Geneva (Switzerland), headed by Secretary. **Languages** English, French, Spanish. **Staff** One; several staff assigned to treaty bodies. **Finance** On the regular budget of the United Nations. **Activities** Periodically examines reports submitted by State Parites on implementation of the

Covenant under article 40 of the same treaty. Under the Optional Protocol to the Covenant and for States Parties to the treaty, also considers confidential communications from individuals claiming to be victims of violations of any rights proclaimed under the Convenant. Carries out functions of interpreting the Covenant through development and adoption of general comments which clarify the scope and meaning of the Covenant provisions. Holds one session in New York NY (USA) and two in Geneva (Switzerland) each year, each session preceded by a one-week working group session. **Events** *Session* Geneva (Switzerland) 2020, *Session* Geneva (Switzerland) 2019, *Session* Geneva (Switzerland) 2019, *Session* Geneva (Switzerland) 2019, *Session* Geneva (Switzerland) 2018. **Publications** *Selected Decisions of the Human Rights Committee under the Optional Protocol* – vol I, II, III, IV, V, VI. Annual report to the General Assembly; reports from states parties to the Covenant; books; brochures.
Members Individuals: nationals of 18 states parties to the Covenant (with term of expiry indicated):
Albania (2022), Canada (2020), Chile (2022), Egypt (2020), France (2022), Germany (2020), Greece (2022), Guyana (2022), Israel (2020), Japan (2022), Latvia (2020), Mauritania (2020), Paraguay (2020), Portugal (2020), Slovenia (2022), South Africa (2020), Tunisia (2022), Uganda (2022).
States Parties to Covenant as of Aug 2020 (173):
Afghanistan, Albania, Algeria, Andorra, Angola, Antigua-Barbuda, Argentina, Armenia, Australia, Austria, Azerbaijan, Bahamas, Bahrain, Bangladesh, Barbados, Belarus, Belgium, Belize, Benin, Bolivia, Bosnia-Herzegovina, Botswana, Brazil, Bulgaria, Burkina Faso, Burundi, Cambodia, Cameroon, Canada, Cape Verde, Central African Rep, Chad, Chile, Colombia, Congo Brazzaville, Congo DR, Costa Rica, Côte d'Ivoire, Croatia, Cyprus, Czechia, Denmark, Djibouti, Dominica, Dominican Rep, Ecuador, Egypt, El Salvador, Equatorial Guinea, Eritrea, Estonia, Eswatini, Ethiopia, Fiji, Finland, France, Gabon, Gambia, Georgia, Germany, Ghana, Greece, Grenada, Guatemala, Guinea, Guinea-Bissau, Guyana, Haiti, Honduras, Hungary, Iceland, India, Indonesia, Iran Islamic Rep, Iraq, Ireland, Israel, Italy, Jamaica, Japan, Jordan, Kazakhstan, Kenya, Korea DPR, Korea Rep, Kuwait, Kyrgyzstan, Laos, Latvia, Lebanon, Lesotho, Liberia, Libya, Liechtenstein, Lithuania, Luxembourg, Madagascar, Malawi, Maldives, Mali, Malta, Marshall Is, Mauritania, Mauritius, Mexico, Moldova, Monaco, Mongolia, Montenegro, Morocco, Mozambique, Namibia, Nepal, Netherlands, New Zealand, Nicaragua, Niger, Nigeria, North Macedonia, Norway, Pakistan, Palestine, Panama, Papua New Guinea, Paraguay, Peru, Philippines, Poland, Portugal, Qatar, Romania, Russia, Rwanda, Samoa, San Marino, Sao Tomé-Principe, Senegal, Serbia, Seychelles, Sierra Leone, Slovakia, Slovenia, Somalia, South Africa, Spain, Sri Lanka, St Vincent-Grenadines, Sudan, Suriname, Sweden, Switzerland, Syrian AR, Tajikistan, Tanzania UR, Thailand, Timor-Leste, Togo, Trinidad-Tobago, Tunisia, Türkiye, Turkmenistan, Uganda, UK, Ukraine, Uruguay, USA, Uzbekistan, Vanuatu, Venezuela, Vietnam, Yemen, Zambia, Zimbabwe. [2020/XE0429/**E***]

♦ Human Rights Council of Australia (internationally oriented national body)
♦ Human Rights and Democracy Link Africa (internationally oriented national body)

♦ Human Rights and Democracy Network (HRDN) 10980

Contact address not obtained. E-mail: troika@hrdn.eu.
URL: http://www.hrdn.eu/
History Set up as an informal network of NGOs. **Aims** Influence the EU and member state human rights policies and the programming of their funding instruments to promote democracy, human rights and sustainable peace. **Structure** Troika, composed of representatives of 3 member organizations. **Languages** English. **Staff** None. **Finance** Members' dues. Annual budget: about euro 6,000. **Events** *EU NGO Forum on Human Rights* Brussels (Belgium) 2018, *EU NGO Forum on Human Rights* Brussels (Belgium) 2012.
Members International organizations (50), including the following 42 listed in this Yearbook:
- *ACT Alliance EU (#00082)*;
- *Amnesty International (AI, #00801)*;
- *Association for the Prevention of Torture (APT, #02869)*;
- *Christian Blind Mission (CBM)*;
- *Coalition for the International Criminal Court (CICC, #04062)*;
- *Conference of European Churches (CEC, #04593)*;
- *CSW*;
- *DEMAS – Association for Democracy Assistance and Human Rights*;
- *EuroMed Rights (#05733)*;
- *European Association for the Defence of Human Rights (AEDH, no recent information)*;
- *European Partnership for Democracy (EPD, #08156)*;
- *European Peacebuilding Liaison Office (EPLO, #08176)*;
- *Fair Trials (#09242)*;
- *Front Line Defenders (FLD, #10008)*;
- *Human Rights Watch (HRW, #10990)*;
- *Human Rights without Frontiers International (HRWF, #10983)*;
- *ILGA-Europe (#11118)*;
- *International Center for Transitional Justice (ICTJ)*;
- *International Dalit Solidarity Network (IDSN, #13129)*;
- *International Federation for Human Rights (#13452)*;
- *International Federation of ACATs – Action by Christians for the Abolition of Torture (#13334)*;
- *International Partnership for Human Rights (IPHR)*;
- *International Rehabilitation Council for Torture Victims (IRCT, #14712)*;
- *International Rescue Committee (IRC, #14717)*;
- *La Strada International (LSI, #20002)*;
- *Light for the World (#16474)*;
- *Minority Rights Group International (MRG, #16820)*;
- *Nonviolent Peaceforce (NP, #17153)*;
- *Open Society Foundations (OSF, #17763)*;
- *PartnersGlobal*;
- *Peace Brigades International (PBI, #18277)*;
- *Penal Reform International (PRI, #18290)*;
- *Plan International (#18386)* (EU Office);
- *Platform for International Cooperation on Undocumented Migrants (PICUM, #18401)*;
- *Protection International (PI, #18548)*;
- *Quaker Council for European Affairs (QCEA, #18587)*;
- *Save the Children Federation (SCF)*;
- *Search for Common Ground (SFCG)*;
- *Terre des Hommes International Federation (TDHIF, #20133)*;
- *World Coalition Against the Death Penalty (#21281)*;
- *World Organisation Against Torture (OMCT, #21685)*;
- *World Vision International (WVI, #21904)*.

NGO Relations Member of: *EU Civil Society Contact Group (CSCG, #05572)*. [2017.03.09/XM1641/y/**F**]

♦ Human Rights and Development Trust of Southern Africa (Huridetsa) 10981

Contact address not obtained. T. +2634774233. Fax +2634752012.
URL: http://www.huridetsa.co.zw/
History Jun 2008. **Aims** Promote human rights, good governance and development in the SADC sub-region through human rights training and capacity building of various stakeholders. **NGO Relations** Member of: *UNCAC Coalition (#20283)*. [2010/XJ1119/**F**]

♦ Human Rights Education Associates (internationally oriented national body)

♦ Human Rights Education Youth Network (HREYN) 10982

Registered Address Avenue de Tervueren 138, 1150 Sint-Pieters-Woluwe, Belgium. E-mail: contact@hreyn.net.
URL: https://www.hreyn.net/
History 2006. Previously registered under Spanish law. Registration: Banque-Carrefour des Entreprises, No/ID: 0731.650.907, Start date: 29 Jul 2019, Belgium. **Aims** Contribute to the development of human rights education with young people. **Structure** General Assembly (annual); Board; Committees; Executive Officer. **Consultative Status** Consultative status granted from: *Council of Europe (CE, #04881)* (Participatory Status). **IGO Relations** Member of (1): *European Youth Centres (EYCs, #09138)*. **NGO Relations** Member of (1): *Conference of INGOs of the Council of Europe (#04607)*. [2023.03.01/XM2866/**F**]

♦ Human Rights First (internationally oriented national body)
♦ Human Rights Foundation (internationally oriented national body)

♦ Human Rights without Frontiers International (HRWF) 10983

Droits de l'homme sans frontières
Dir Av d'Auderghem 61, 1040 Brussels, Belgium. T. +3223456145. E-mail: international.secretariat.brussels@hrwf.org.
URL: http://hrwf.eu/
History Jan 2001. Developed from *Bruxelles-Droits de l'homme – Brussels-Human Rights – Brüssel-Menschenrechte*, founded 1989. Registration: EU Transparency Register, No/ID: 91170255848-52; Belgium. **Aims** Monitor, research and analyse in the field of human rights, as well as promote democracy and the rule of law on national and international levels. **Finance** Members' dues. Swiss foundations. **Activities** Knowledge management/information dissemination; advocacy/lobbying/activism; events/meetings. **Events** *Geneva Summit for Human Rights, Tolerance and Democracy* Geneva (Switzerland) 2010, *Geneva Summit for Human Rights, Tolerance and Democracy* Geneva (Switzerland) 2009, *Seminar on freedom of religious conscience in Greece* Athens (Greece) 1993. **Publications** *Religious Discrimination and Intolerance* (5 a week) – electronic news service; *Democracy, Rule of Law and Human Rights* – in China, Korea DPR, Iraq, Ukraine, Turkey.
Members Individuals in 11 countries:
Albania, Belgium, Canada, Denmark, France, Germany, Greece, Latvia, Romania, Switzerland, USA.
IGO Relations Participant in Fundamental Rights Platform of: *European Union Agency for Fundamental Rights (FRA, #08969)*. Formal contact with: *Council of Europe (CE, #04881)*; *European Commission (EC, #06633)*; *European Parliament (EP, #08146)*; *Organization for Security and Cooperation in Europe (OSCE, #17887)*; *United Nations (UN, #20515)*. **NGO Relations** Full member of: *European Network on Religion and Belief (ENORB, #07985)*; *Human Rights and Democracy Network (HRDN, #10980)*. Member of: *EarthAction (EA, #05159)*; *International Coalition to Stop Crimes Against Humanity in North Korea (ICNK, #12622)*; *UNITED for Intercultural Action – European Network Against Nationalism, Racism, Fascism and in Support of Migrants and Refugees (UNITED, #20511)*. Member of Advisory Board of: *European Parliament Platform for Secularism in Politics (EPPSP, #08152)*. Contact with numerous NGOs worldwide (not specified). [2020/XE4557/v/**E**]

♦ Human Rights Funders Network (internationally oriented national body)

♦ Human Rights House Foundation 10984

Dir Mariboes gate 13, 0183 Oslo, Norway. T. +4746848850. E-mail: info@humanrightshouse.org.
URL: http://www.humanrightshouse.org/
History 1992. Founded following establishment of the first Human Rights House in Oslo (Norway), 1989. **Aims** Protect, empower and support human rights defenders and their organizations locally, and unite them in an international network of Human Rights Houses. **Events** *Network meeting* Zagreb (Croatia) 2019, *Network Meeting* Tbilisi (Georgia) 2018, *Network Meeting* Belgrade (Serbia) 2016, *Network Meeting* Oslo (Norway) 2015, *Network Meeting* Chernihiv (Ukraine) / Kiev (Ukraine) 2014.
Members Human Rights Houses (17) in 11 countries:
Armenia, Azerbaijan, Belarus, Croatia, Georgia, Norway, Poland, Russia, Serbia, UK, Ukraine.
Consultative Status Consultative status granted from: *Council of Europe (CE, #04881)* (Participatory Status). [2021.05.27/XM0448/**F**]

♦ Human Rights Information and Documentation Systems, International (HURIDOCS) 10985

Systèmes d'information et de documentation sur les droits de l'homme, international – Sistemas de Documentación y de Información sobre Derechos Humanos, Internacional
Exec Dir Rue de Varembé 3 – 4th Floor, 1202 Geneva, Switzerland. T. +41227555252. E-mail: hello@huridocs.org.
URL: https://www.huridocs.org/
History Founded 1979, by an ad hoc international working group of people with experience in human rights and documentation. Formally established, 24 July 1982, iStrasbourg (France), when Constitution was adopted. Constitution most recently revised by Extraordinary General Assembly, 2015. Registration: IDE, No/ID: CHE-114.361.924, Start date: 19 Jun 2008, Switzerland. **Aims** Help human rights groups gather, organize and use information to create positive change in the world. **Structure** Board of Advisors; International Secretariat. **Languages** Arabic, English, French, German, Russian, Spanish. **Staff** 20.00 FTE, paid. **Finance** Sources: donations; fees for services; government support; grants; international organizations; private foundations. Annual budget: 1,500,000 USD (2020). **Activities** Guidance/assistance/consulting; knowledge management/information dissemination; projects/programmes; standards/guidelines; training/education. **Events** *Conference / General Assembly* Geneva (Switzerland) 2009, *General Assembly* Geneva (Switzerland) 2009, *General Assembly* Tunis (Tunisia) 1998, *International conference / General Assembly* Tunis (Tunisia) 1998, *General Assembly* Crete (Greece) 1992. **Consultative Status** Consultative status granted from: *African Commission on Human and Peoples' Rights (ACHPR, #00255)* (Observer); *UNESCO (#20322)* (Consultative Status); *ECOSOC (#05331)* (Special).
NGO Relations Member of: *Child Rights International Network (CRIN, #03885)*; *Fédération des Institutions Internationales établies à Genève (FIIG, #09599)*; *World Organisation Against Torture (OMCT, #21685)*. Together with: *Arab Institute for Human Rights (AIHR, #00983)*; *Arab Lawyers' Union (ALU, #01002)*; and *Arab Organization for Human Rights (AOHR, #01020)*, set up: *Arab Human Rights Documentation and Information Network (AHRINET, no recent information)*. Supports: *West African Human Rights Defenders' Network (WAHRDN, #20882)*. Contacts with a large number of organizations worldwide, including the following bodies listed in this Yearbook:
- *African Centre for Democracy and Human Rights Studies (ACDHRS, #00239)*;
- *African Centre for Treatment and Rehabilitation of Torture Victims (ACTV)*;
- *American Association for the Advancement of Science (AAAS)*;
- *Asian Research Centre for Migration (ARCM)*;
- *Ecumenical Documentation and Information Centre in Southern Africa (EDICISA, #05346)*;
- *Environnement et développement du Tiers-monde (enda, #05510)*;
- *European Coordination Committee on Human Rights Documentation (ECCHRD, #06791)*;
- *Ford Foundation (#09858)*;
- *International Alert (#11615)*;
- *International Commission of Jurists (ICJ, #12695)*;
- *International Institute for Human Rights, Environment and Development (INHURED International, #13886)*;
- *The International Movement Against All Forms of Discrimination and Racism (IMADR, #14191)*;
- *International Refugee Documentation Network (IRDN, no recent information)*;
- *International Rehabilitation Council for Torture Victims (IRCT, #14712)*;
- *Netherlands Institute of Human Rights (SIM)*;
- *Red de Informatica y Documentación en Derechos Humanos para América Latina y el Caribe (RIDHUALC, inactive)*.

[2021.09.06/XF4158/**F**]

♦ Human Rights Institute, Moscow (internationally oriented national body)

♦ Human Rights Internet (HRI) 10986

Chair address not obtained. T. +16137897407. Fax +16137897414. E-mail: info@hri.ca.
URL: http://www.hri.ca/
History 1976, USA. Founded as an international communications network and clearinghouse on human rights with universal coverage. Former names and other names: *INTERNET International Human Rights Documentation Network* – former; *INTERNET Réseau international de documentation sur les droits humains* – former; *INTERNET Red Internacional de Documentación sobre los Derechos Humanos* – former. **Aims** As a consulting and capacity building organization, promote human rights in the areas of social justice, good governance and conflict prevention. **Structure** Board of Directors. **Languages** English, French, Spanish. **Staff** 9.00 FTE, paid. **Finance** Grants and project contributions from private foundations and government agencies. **Activities** Conflict resolution; advocacy/lobbying/activism. **Events** *Vienna plus five international NGO forum* Ottawa, ON (Canada) 1998. **Publications** *Human Rights Tribune/Tribune des droits humains* (3 a year) – online. **Members** Not a membership organization. **Consultative Status** Consultative status granted from: *African Commission on Human and Peoples' Rights (ACHPR, #00255)* (Observer); *UNICEF (#20332)*. **IGO Relations** Associated with Department of Global Communications of the United Nations. **NGO Relations** Founder member of: *International Federation of Human Rights Archives and Documentation Centers (no recent information)*. Member of: *CIVICUS: World Alliance for Citizen Participation (#03962)*; *World Organisation Against Torture (OMCT, #21685)*. Cooperates with: *International Council for Adult Education (ICAE, #12983)*. [2020/XF1399/**F**]

♦ Human Rights and Justice Group International (internationally oriented national body)

♦ **Human Rights Measurement Initiative (HRMI)** **10987**

Contact Motu Economic and Public Policy Research, Level 1, 97 Cuba St, PO Box 24390, Wellington 6142, New Zealand. E-mail: thalia.kehoerowden@motu.org.nz.
URL: https://humanrightsmeasurement.org/

History 2016. **Aims** Produce world-changing human rights data tools that track the human rights performance of countries. **Languages** Chinese, English, French, Portuguese, Russian, Spanish. **Finance** Sources: international organizations; private foundations. **Activities** Knowledge management/information dissemination; monitoring/evaluation; research/documentation. [2022.05.04/AA0052/j/**F**]

♦ **Human Rights in Mental Health (FGIP)** **10988**

Chief Exec PO Box 1956, 1200 BZ Hilversum, Netherlands. T. +31651534123.
URL: http://www.gip-global.org/

History Dec 1980, as *International Association on the Political Use of Psychiatry (IAPUP) – Association internationale contre l'utilisation de la psychiatrie à des fins politiques – Internationale Vereinigung gegen die Politische Verwendung der Psychiatrie*, following the setting up, 1975, of an *Initiating Committee Against Abuses of Psychiatry for Political Purposes – Comité d'initiative contre les abus de la psychiatrie à des fins politiques – Initiativkomitee gegen den Missbrauch der Psychiatrie zu Politischen Zwecken*, which became a Swiss national association in Mar 1976. Previously also known under the full title: *Geneva Initiative on Psychiatry – International Foundation for the Abolition and Prevention of Political Psychiatry (GIP)*. Subsequently changed title to *Geneva Initiative on Psychiatry*, 1991. Subsequently change title to *Global Initiative on Psychiatry (GIP)*, 4 Mar 2005, with full title: *Global Initiative on Psychiatry – an international foundation for the promotion of humane, ethical and effective mental health care throughout the world*. Also referred to as *Federation Global Initiative on Psychiatry*. Registered in accordance with Dutch law. **Aims** Promote humane, ethical and effective *mental health care* throughout the world; support a global network of individuals and organizations to develop, advocate for and carry out necessary reforms; campaign against political abuse of psychiatry wherever it occurs. **Structure** Federation Council; General Board (meeting once a year). **Languages** Albanian, Armenian, Bulgarian, Czech, English, Estonian, French, Georgian, German, Latvian, Lithuanian, Romanian, Russian, Slovakian, Ukrainian. **Activities** Projects/programmes; training/education; events/meetings. **Events** *International conference on reforming psychiatry in Eastern Europe* Soesterberg (Netherlands) 1999, *Meeting* Netherlands 1998, *Meeting of reformers in psychiatry / Meeting* Prague (Czech Rep) 1995, *Meeting of reformers in psychiatry / Meeting* Driebergen (Netherlands) 1994. **Publications** *Mental Health Reforms* (2 a year). Annual Report; information pamphlets; books; translations. **Members** Organizations in 5 countries:
Bulgaria, Georgia, Lithuania, Netherlands, USA.
Consultative Status Consultative status granted from: *WHO (#20950)* (Official). **IGO Relations** Agreement signed concerning cooperation with: *WHO Regional Office for Europe (#20945)*. [2019.02.17/XD0004/**F**]

♦ Human Rights Now (internationally oriented national body)
♦ Human Rights Organization of Nepal (internationally oriented national body)

♦ **Human Rights Resource Centre (HRRC)** **10989**

Exec Dir Univ of Indonesia, Guest House Complex/Ex Rumah Dinas Rektor UI, No 4, Depok Campus, Depok 16424, Indonesia. T. +62217866720. Fax +62217866720. E-mail: info@hrrca.org.
URL: http://hrrca.org/

History 2010. Founded by original members of *Working Group for an ASEAN Human Rights Mechanism (Working Group)* and other human rights advocates and academics. Former names and other names: *Human Rights Resource Centre for ASEAN (HRRCA)* – former. **Aims** Support a rights-based approach to ASEAN integration. **Structure** Governing Board; Advisory Council. **Finance** Sources: contributions. Supported by: *Canadian International Development Agency (CIDA, inactive)*; *East-West Center (EWC, #05263)*; *MacArthur Foundation*; *United States Agency for International Development (USAID)*. **Activities** Events/meetings; research/documentation; training/education. **IGO Relations** Consultative Status with: *ASEAN (#01141)* – Intergovernmental Commission on Human Rights (AICHR). [2020/AA0953/**E**]

♦ Human Rights Resource Centre for ASEAN / see Human Rights Resource Centre (#10989)
♦ Human Rights at Sea (internationally oriented national body)

♦ **Human Rights Watch (HRW)** **10990**

Exec Dir 350 Fifth Ave, 34th floor, New York NY 10118-3299, USA. T. +12122904700. Fax +12127361300.
URL: http://www.hrw.org/

History 1987, USA, 'Helsinki Watch' having been set up 1978. EU Transpanrecy Register: 56362448807-46. **Aims** Report on human rights practices; document imprisonment, censorship, disappearances, due process of law, murder, prison conditions, torture, violation of laws of war and other abuses of internationally recognized human rights; by documenting and publicizing discrepancies between pretence and practice use public embarrassment to press governments to cease abusive practices; create multiple and reinforcing sources of pressure to curb human rights violations. **Structure** Board of Directors (meets 4 times a year). Divisions (17), each with its own Executive Director. **Staff** 280, including lawyers, journalists, linguists and over 120 country specialists. **Finance** Financed by private individuals and foundations. No direct or indirect government funding. Budget (annual): US$ 40 million. **Activities** Politics/policy/regulator; advocacy/lobbying/activism; financial and/or material support. **Events** *Global Summit* Kyoto (Japan) 2017, *Global Summit* Berlin (Germany) 2016, *International conference on child soldiers* Amman (Jordan) 2001. **Publications** *Human Rights Watch Update* (10 a year); *Human Rights Watch World Report* (annual). *Human Rights Reports* – series; *Struggling for Ethnic Identity* – series – published by Europe and Central Asia Division. *A Modern Form of Slavery: Trafficking of Burmese Women and Girls into Brothels in Thailand* (1993) – published by Asia Division; *The Human Rights Crisis in Kashmir: A Pattern of Impunity* (1993) – published by Asia Division. Country reports. Divisions produce their own publications. **Members** Introductory; Participating; Contributing. Based in USA; membership countries not specified. **Consultative Status** Consultative status granted from: *ECOSOC (#05331)* (Special); *UNICEF (#20332)*; *Council of Europe (CE, #04881)* (Participatory Status). **IGO Relations** Observer status with: *African Commission on Human and Peoples' Rights (ACHPR, #00255)*; *International Organization for Migration (IOM, #14454)*. Accredited by: *United Nations Office at Vienna (UNOV, #20604)*. European division is participant in Fundamental Rights Platform of: *European Union Agency for Fundamental Rights (FRA, #08969)*. Associated with Department of Global Communications of the United Nations. **NGO Relations** Member of:
- *Advocacy Network for Africa (ADNA)*;
- *Alliance of NGOs on Crime Prevention and Criminal Justice (#00709)*;
- *ATHENA Network (ATHENA, #03004)*;
- *Campaign to Stop Killer Robots (#03405)*;
- *Child Rights Connect (#03884)*;
- *Child Rights International Network (CRIN, #03885)*;
- *Council for Global Equality*;
- *EarthAction (EA, #05159)*;
- *ETO Consortium (ETOs, #05560)*;
- *European NGO Platform Asylum and Migration (EPAM, #08051)*;
- *Girls not Brides (#10154)*;
- *End Corporal Punishment (#05457)*;
- *Global Network Initiative (GNI)*;
- *Global Partnership for the Prevention of Armed Conflict (GPPAC, #10538)*;
- *Human Rights and Democracy Network (HRDN, #10980)*;
- *IFEX (#11100)*;
- *International Campaign to Ban Landmines – Cluster Munition Coalition (ICBL-CMC, #12427)*;
- *International Coalition against Enforced Disappearances (ICAED, #12605)*;
- *International Code of Conduct Association (ICoCA, #12629)*;
- *International Dalit Solidarity Network (IDSN, #13129)*;
- *International Drug Policy Consortium (IDPC, #13205)*;
- *International Network on Explosive Weapons (INEW, #14266)*;
- *International NGO Platform on the Migrant Workers' Convention (IPMWC, #14367)*;
- *International Treatment Preparedness Coalition (ITPC, #15729)*;
- *NGO Working Group for Women, Peace and Security (NGOWG, #17129)*;
- *PMNCH (#18410)*;
- *UNITED for Intercultural Action – European Network Against Nationalism, Racism, Fascism and in Support of Migrants and Refugees (UNITED, #20511)*;
- *Watchlist on Children and Armed Conflict (Watchlist)*;
- *World Coalition Against the Death Penalty (#21281)*.

Founding member of: *Consortium of Minority Resources (COMIR, no recent information)*; *International Coalition for the Responsibility to Protect (ICRtoP, #12620)*; *International Coalition to Stop Crimes Against Humanity in North Korea (ICNK, #12622)*. Participates in: *Global Partnership on Children with Disabilities (GPcwd, #10529)*; *International Working Group on Satellite-Based Emergency Mapping (IWG-SEM, #15911)*. Steering Committee member of: *International Corporate Accountability Roundtable (ICAR, #12968)*. Associate member of: *EuroMed Rights (#05733)*. Signatory to the 'Publish What You Pay' appeal of: *Publish What You Pay Coalition (PWYP, #18573)*. Cooperates with: *African Democracy Forum (ADF, #00281)*; *Amnesty International (AI, #00801)*; *Crisis Action (#04957)*; *ICASO (#11040)*; *ILGA World (International Lesbian, Gay, Bisexual, Trans and Intersex Association, #11120)*; *REDRESS*. On Board of: *Initiative for Responsible Mining Assurance (IRMA, #11212)*. Instrumental in setting up: *Global Centre for the Responsibility to Protect (GCR2P, #10277)*. Supports: *Global Call for Action Against Poverty (GCAP, #10263)* [2019/XF2418/**F**]

♦ The Human Safety Net (unconfirmed)
♦ Human Security Collective (internationally oriented national body)
♦ Human Security Network in Latin America and the Caribbean (#19218)

♦ **Human Service Information Technology Applications (HUSITA)** **10991**

Chair School of Social Sciences, Open Polytechnic of New Zealand, 3 Cleary St, Waterloo, Lower Hutt 5011, New Zealand.
URL: http://www.husita.org/

History Founded 1981, as (US) Computer Use In Social Services Network (CUSSN). Present name adopted 1983. A virtual association of human service professionals interested in applying information and communication technology to solve human problems. **Aims** Promote ethical and effective use of information technology to better serve humanity. **Structure** Board of Directors. **Languages** English. **Staff** None. **Finance** Journal royalties. **Activities** Events/meetings; publishing activities; knowledge management/information dissemination; research/documentation. **Events** *Conference* Melbourne, VIC (Australia) 2014, *Conference* Hong Kong (Hong Kong) 2010, *Conference* India 2009, *Information technology and diversity in human services – promoting strength through difference* Toronto, ON (Canada) 2007, *Social development and digital inclusion* Hong Kong (Hong Kong) 2004. **Publications** *Journal of Technology in Human Services*. **Members** Individuals. Membership countries not specified. [2016.10.19/XF7204/**F**]

♦ Humantem – Banque de matériel médical pour l'aide humanitaire (internationally oriented national body)

♦ **Human Variome Project (HVP)** **10992**

Intl Project Coordinator Inst of Genetic Medicine, Newcastle Univ, Intl Cntr for Life, Central Parkway, Newcastle upon Tyne, NE1 3BZ, UK. T. +441912418983.
WHO Liaison address not obtained.
URL: http://www.humanvariomeproject.org/

History 2006. Founded resulting from various groups started as early as 1992. Former names and other names: *Human Variome Project International Limited* – legal name (2016); *Global Variome Limited (GVL)* – legal name (2016). Registration: Private Limited Company by guarantee, No/ID: 10269298, Start date: 7 Aug 2016, England. **Aims** Work with national governments and international organizations to embed the collection, curation, interpretation and sharing of *genomic* knowledge into routine clinical practice. **Structure** Scientific Advisory Committee; Coordinating Office; Advisory Councils (2). **Languages** English. **Staff** 2.00 FTE, paid. **Finance** Support from national governments; grants; philanthropic donations. **Activities** Research/documentation; training/education; events/meetings. **Events** *Biennial Meeting* Paris (France) 2016, *Biennial Meeting / Meeting* Paris (France) 2014, *Biennial Meeting / Meeting* Paris (France) 2012, *Biennial meeting / Meeting* Paris (France) 2010, *Educational strategy meeting* Washington, DC (USA) 2010.
Members Country nodes in 31 countries:
Argentina, Australia, Austria, Bangladesh, Belgium, Brazil, Canada, China, Congo DR, Cyprus, Czechia, Egypt, Italy, Korea Rep, Kuwait, Malaysia, Mexico, Mozambique, Nepal, Netherlands, New Zealand, Nigeria, Philippines, Portugal, South Africa, Spain, Sweden, UK, USA, Venezuela, Vietnam.
Consortium members (over 1,100) in 80 countries and territories:
Argentina, Armenia, Australia, Austria, Belgium, Brazil, Canada, Chile, China, Colombia, Congo DR, Costa Rica, Croatia, Cyprus, Czechia, Denmark, Ecuador, Egypt, Estonia, Ethiopia, Finland, France, Germany, Greece, Guatemala, Hong Kong, Hungary, India, Indonesia, Iran Islamic Rep, Ireland, Israel, Italy, Japan, Kazakhstan, Korea Rep, Kuwait, Latvia, Lebanon, Malaysia, Mexico, Mozambique, Myanmar, Nepal, Netherlands, New Zealand, Nigeria, North Macedonia, Norway, Oman, Pakistan, Palestine, Philippines, Poland, Portugal, Qatar, Romania, Russia, Rwanda, Saudi Arabia, Serbia, Sierra Leone, Singapore, South Africa, Spain, Sri Lanka, Sweden, Switzerland, Taiwan, Thailand, Tunisia, Türkiye, Uganda, UK, Ukraine, United Arab Emirates, USA, Venezuela, Vietnam, Zimbabwe.
Consultative Status Consultative status granted from: *UNESCO (#20322)* (Associate Status). [2021/XJ1831/**E**]

♦ Human Variome Project International Limited / see Human Variome Project (#10992)
♦ Human-Wildlife Female and male African lionConflict Collaboration / see Center for Conservation Peacebuilding
♦ humedica (internationally oriented national body)
♦ humedica Internationale Hilfe / see humedica

♦ **Humentum** **10993**

CEO 1120 20th St, NW, Suite 520 S, Washington DC 20036, USA. E-mail: contact@humentum.org – connect@humentum.org.
URL: https://humentum.org/

History Jul 2017. Founded on merger of *InsideNGO (inactive)*, LINGOs and Mango. **Aims** Partner with the global development community to be an equitable, accountable, and resilient force for social good. **Structure** Board. **Activities** Advocacy/lobbying/activism; guidance/assistance/consulting; training/education.
Members Sustaining members include 23 organizations listed in this Yearbook:
- *American Near East Refugee Aid (ANERA)*;
- *Americares Foundation*;
- *Catholic Relief Services (CRS, #03608)*;
- *Coral Triangle Initiative on Coral Reefs, Fisheries and Food Security (CTI-CFF, #04833)*;
- *Elizabeth Glaser Pediatric AIDS Foundation (EGPAF)*;
- *FHI 360*;
- *Global Fund to End Modern Slavery (GFEMS)*;
- *Humanity and Inclusion (HI, #10975)*;
- *International Youth Foundation (IYF)*;
- *Last Mile Health*;
- *Mercy Corps International (MCI)*;
- *Nascent Solutions*;
- *Nuru International*;
- *Peace Winds* (America);
- *Population Council (#18458)*;
- *Project HOPE*;
- *Relief International*;
- *Resolve to Save Lives*;
- *Splash International (Splash)*;
- *Teach For All (#20108)*;
- *The Carter Center*;
- *ThinkWell*;
- *Winrock International*.

All members include 139 organizations listed in this Yearbook:
- *350.org*;
- *ACCION International*;
- *ACDI/VOCA*;
- *Action Against Hunger (#00086)*;
- *Adventist Development and Relief Agency International (ADRA, #00131)*;
- *America-Mideast Educational and Training Services (AMIDEAST)*;
- *Amref Health Africa (#00806)*;
- *Asia Foundation*;
- *Aspen Network of Development Entrepreneurs (ANDE, #02310)*;

- Bioversity International (#03262);
- Blumont International;
- Bureau international des Médecins sans frontières (MSF International, #03366);
- CARE International (CI, #03429);
- Catholic Medical Mission Board (CMMB);
- Center for International Private Enterprise (CIPE);
- Center for Victims of Torture (CVT);
- CGIAR System Organization (CGIAR, #03843);
- ChildFund International (#03869);
- Children International;
- Children's HeartLink (CHL);
- Church World Service (CWS);
- CLASP (#03979);
- Community Organized Relief Effort (CORE);
- Community Partners International (CPI);
- Concern Worldwide;
- Conservation International (CI);
- CORE Group;
- Counterpart International (FSP);
- Cultivating New Frontiers in Agriculture (CNFA);
- Democracy International (DI);
- DevWorks International;
- D-tree International;
- Education Development Center (EDC);
- Episcopal Relief and Development;
- Food for the Hungry (fh, #09845);
- Global Communities;
- Global Health Corps (GHC);
- Habitat for Humanity International (HFHI);
- Heifer International;
- Helen Keller International (HKI, #10902);
- Holt International;
- HOPE International;
- Hunger Project (#10994);
- ICAP;
- Institute of International Education (IIE);
- International AIDS Vaccine Initiative (IAVI, #11602);
- International Centre for Tropical Agriculture (#12527);
- International Food Policy Research Institute (IFPRI, #13622);
- International Maize and Wheat Improvement Center (#14077);
- International Medical Corps (IMC);
- International Orthodox Christian Charities (IOCC);
- International Potato Center (#14627);
- International Republican Institute (IRI);
- International Rescue Committee (IRC, #14717);
- International Research and Exchanges Board (IREX);
- International Water Management Institute (IWMI, #15867);
- IntraHealth International;
- IPAS (#16010);
- Jane Goodall Institute (JGI, #16089);
- Johns Hopkins Program for International Education in Gynecology and Obstetrics (JHPIEGO);
- Light for the World (#16474);
- Making Cents International;
- Management Sciences for Health (MSH);
- MEDAIR;
- Medical Care Development International (MCDI);
- Medical Teams International (MTI);
- Mennonite Central Committee (MCC);
- Mennonite Economic Development Associates (MEDA);
- Meridian International Center (MIC);
- MiracleFeet (#16824);
- mothers2mothers (m2m, #16859);
- MSI Reproductive Choices;
- Namati (#16931);
- Near East Foundation (NEF);
- No Means No Worldwide (NMNW);
- Norwegian People's Aid (NPA);
- Norwegian Refugee Council (NRC);
- Oceana;
- Open Government Partnership (OGP, #17753);
- Operation Smile;
- Opportunity International (#17776);
- ORBIS International (#17786);
- Pact (#18016);
- PAI (#18025);
- Pan American Development Foundation (PADF, #18094);
- Partners for Development (PFD);
- PartnersGlobal;
- Partners in Health (PIH);
- Partners of the Americas;
- PATH (#18260);
- PCI Global;
- Plan International (#18386);
- Population Reference Bureau (PRB);
- PSI (#18555);
- PYXERA Global;
- Rainforest Alliance;
- Refugees International (RI);
- Results for Development (R4D, #18923);
- ReSurge International;
- Rise Against Hunger;
- Room to Read;
- RTI International;
- Salvation Army World Service Office (SAWSO, see: #19041);
- Samaritan's Purse (#19047);
- Save the Children Federation (SCF);
- School-to-School International (STS);
- Seeds of Peace;
- Sesame Workshop;
- Sightsavers International (#19270);
- Social Science Research Council (SSRC);
- Solidarity Center;
- Special Olympics International (SOI, #19910);
- Synergos (#20082);
- Task Force for Global Health (TFGH, #20098);
- Tearfund, UK;
- TechnoServe (#20120);
- The END Fund (#05459);
- The Freedom Fund;
- The Lutheran World Federation (LWF, #16532);
- The Nature Conservancy (TNC);
- Tostan (#20176);
- Trickle Up Program (TUP, #20236);
- VillageReach;
- Vital Strategies;
- Voluntary Service Overseas (VSO);
- War Child International (#20817);
- Water for People (WFP);
- White Ribbon Alliance for Safe Motherhood (WRA, #20934);
- Wildlife Conservation Society (WCS);
- Witness;
- Women for Women International (WFWI);
- Women's Refugee Commission (WRC);
- World Agroforestry Centre (ICRAF, #21072);
- World Learning;
- World Relief;
- World Renew;
- World Resources Institute (WRI, #21753);
- World Vision International (WVI, #21904);
- World Wide Fund for Nature (WWF, #21922).

Subscribers include 17 organizations listed in this Yearbook:
ActionAid (#00087); African Population and Health Research Center (APHRC, #00420); Catholic Agency for Overseas Development (CAFOD); Center for Reproductive Rights; Christian Blind Mission (CBM); CIVICUS: World Alliance for Citizen Participation (#03962); Compassion International (CI, #04413); Danish Refugee Council (DRC); Free Wheelchair Mission (FWM); GOAL; Greenpeace International (#10727); Human Appeal (#10961); International Development Law Organization (IDLO, #13161); Islamic Relief Worldwide (IRWW, #16048); Self Help Africa (SHA, #19220); Trocaire – Catholic Agency for World Development; WorldFish (#21507). [2022/AA2831/y/C]

♦ Humid Tropics Centre Kuala Lumpur / see Regional Humid Tropics Hydrology and Water Resources Centre for South East Asia and the Pacific (#18787)
♦ Humorforskernettverk i Norden (no recent information)
♦ HundrED (unconfirmed)
♦ The Hundred to continue Living/For World Disarmament and Peace (internationally oriented national body)
♦ Hungarian Institute of International Affairs (internationally oriented national body)
♦ Hungarian Institute of International Relations / see Hungarian Institute of International Affairs
♦ Hungarian Interchurch Aid (internationally oriented national body)
♦ Hungarian International Development Assistance (internationally oriented national body)
♦ Hungarian Peace Association (internationally oriented national body)
♦ Hungarian Peace Council / see Hungarian Peace Association
♦ Hungarológus Oktatók Nemzetközi Tarsasaga (no recent information)
♦ Hungary Platform / see EDEN Digital Learning Europe (#05356)

♦ **Hunger Project** **10994**
Projet faim – Proyecto Hambre – Hunger Projekt
Mailing Address 110 West 30th St, 6th fl, New York NY 10001, USA. T. +12122519100. Fax +12125329785. E-mail: info@thp.org.
URL: http://www.thp.org/
History 1977. **Aims** Achieve the *sustainable* end of world hunger; empower people to achieve lasting *progress* in health, education, nutrition and family income; identify and transform the entrenched *social conditions* that give rise to hunger, most notably the severe subjugation of women. **Structure** Global Board of Directors. **Finance** Budget (annual): about US$ 8 million. **Activities** Events/meetings; training/education; advocacy/lobbying/activism; awards/prizes/competitions. **Events** Annual global meeting New York, NY (USA) 2005. **Publications** Newsletter (12 a year). Annual Report. Reports on programmes and issues.
Members Activities in 23 countries:
Australia, Bangladesh, Benin, Bolivia, Burkina Faso, Canada, Ethiopia, Germany, Ghana, India, Japan, Malawi, Mexico, Mozambique, Netherlands, New Zealand, Peru, Senegal, Sweden, Switzerland, Uganda, UK, USA.
Consultative Status Consultative status granted from: *ECOSOC* (#05331) (Ros A). **IGO Relations** Accredited by: *United Nations Office at Vienna (UNOV, #20604)*. Associated with Department of Global Communications of the United Nations. Invited to Governing Council sessions of: *International Fund for Agricultural Development (IFAD, #13692)*. **NGO Relations** Member of: *American Council for Voluntary International Action (InterAction); Verband Entwicklungspolitik und Humanitäre Hilfe e.V. (VENRO); Association for Women's Rights in Development (AWID, #02980); Conference of Non-Governmental Organizations in Consultative Relationship with the United Nations (CONGO, #04635); Fédération des Institutions Internationales établies à Genève (FIIG, #09599); Girls not Brides (#10154); InsideNGO (inactive); Japanese NGO Center for International Cooperation (JANIC); PMNCH (#18410)*. Partner of: *1,000 Days*. [2020/XF1561/F]

♦ Hunger Projekt (#10994)
♦ HUN-IDA – Hungarian International Development Assistance (internationally oriented national body)
♦ **HUPO** Human Proteome Organization (#10978)
♦ **Huridetsa** Human Rights and Development Trust of Southern Africa (#10981)
♦ **HURIDOCS** Human Rights Information and Documentation Systems, International (#10985)
♦ HURIGHTS Osaka – Asia Pacific Human Rights Information Center (internationally oriented national body)
♦ HURON – Human Rights Organization of Nepal (internationally oriented national body)
♦ HURPEC International Network (internationally oriented national body)
♦ **HUSITA** Human Service Information Technology Applications (#10991)
♦ **HuT** Hizb ut-Tahrir (#10936)
♦ HVK – Hulp aan de Verdrukte Kerk (internationally oriented national body)
♦ HVO – Health Volunteers Overseas (internationally oriented national body)
♦ **HVP** Human Variome Project (#10992)
♦ **HVS** Heart Valve Society (#10901)
♦ **HWAF** Health and Water African Foundation (#10891)
♦ **HWB** / see Homeopaths Without Borders France (#10942)
♦ **HWB** Homeopaths Without Borders France (#10942)
♦ **HWBI** Hand and Wrist Biomechanics International (#10859)
♦ **HWCC** / see Center for Conservation Peacebuilding
♦ **HWC** Homeless World Cup Foundation (#10939)
♦ HWE – Hazardous Waste Europe (unconfirmed)
♦ HWI – HawkWatch International (internationally oriented national body)
♦ HWI – HeadWaters International (internationally oriented national body)
♦ HWI – Hellerwork International (internationally oriented national body)
♦ HWPL – Heavenly Culture, World Peace, Restoration of Light (internationally oriented national body)
♦ **HWRP** WMO Hydrology and Water Resources Programme (#20977)
♦ HWW – HomeWorkers Worldwide (internationally oriented national body)
♦ HWWI – Hamburgisches WeltWirtschafts Institut (internationally oriented national body)

♦ **Hybrid broadcast broadband TV Association (HbbTV Association)** .. **10995**
Contact c/o EBA, L'Ancienne-Route 17A, Grand-Saconnex, 1218 Geneva, Switzerland. T. +41227172735. Fax +41227474735. E-mail: eo@hbbtv.org.
URL: http://www.hbbtv.org/
History Activities of *Open IPTV Forum (OIPF, inactive)* transferred to HbbTV Association, Jun 2014. **Aims** Harmonize the broadcast and broadband delivery of entertainment services to consumers through connected TVs, set-top boxes and multiscreen devices. **Structure** Steering Group. Groups (5): Certification; Marketing; Specification; Requirements; Testing. **Finance** Members' dues. **Activities** Events/meetings. **Events** Annual Symposium Athens (Greece) 2019, Annual Symposium Berlin (Germany) 2018, Annual Symposium Madrid (Spain) 2016, Annual Symposium London (UK) 2015. **NGO Relations** European Broadcasting Union (EBU, #06404). [2016/XM5306/D]

♦ Hydraulics Without Border / see Hydraulique sans frontières
♦ Hydraulique sans frontières (internationally oriented national body)

♦ **Hydrocarbon and Rosin Resins Producers Association (HARRPA)** .. **10996**
Secretariat c/o CEFIC, Rue Belliard 40, Box 15, 1040 Brussels, Belgium. E-mail: jwi@cefic.be – kco@cefic.be.
URL: http://www.harrpa.eu/

History A sector group of *Conseil européen de l'industrie chimique (CEFIC, #04687)*. Previously referred to as *Association of Rosin and Hydrocarbon Resins Producers (ARHRP)*. **Aims** Represent European based producers of resins; maintain a positive image for the products by promoting their safe and proper use; monitor environmental, health and dafety EU regulations and promote their applications. **Structure** General Assembly; Sections (2); Technical Committees (2). **Activities** Advocacy/lobbying/activism; monitoring/evaluation.
Members Hydrocarbon and rosin resins producers (19) in 12 countries:
Austria, Belgium, Bulgaria, Finland, France, Germany, Greece, Netherlands, Portugal, Spain, Sweden, UK.
[2019/XE2171/**E**]

♦ Hydrocarbon Solvents Producers Association (HSPA) 10997

Dir Gen Rue Belliard 40, Bte 15, 1040 Brussels, Belgium. T. +3224369300. E-mail: cti@cefic.be – hco@cefic.be.
URL: http://www.esig.org/

History Founded as a sector group of *Conseil européen de l'industrie chimique (CEFIC, #04687)*. **Aims** Bring together producers of hydrocarbon solvents in Europe; foster the perception of hydrocarbon solvents as valuable, eco-efficient, safe solutions which serve the needs of downstream industry as well as consumers. **Structure** General Assembly; Technical Committee. **Languages** English. **Staff** 2.00 FTE, paid. **Finance** Sources: members' dues. **Activities** Knowledge management/information dissemination.
Members Hydrocarbon producers (9) in 9 countries:
Belgium, Finland, France, Germany, Greece, Italy, Netherlands, Spain, UK. [2022.05.04/XE3483/**E**]

♦ Hydrocephalus Society / see International Society for Hydrocephalus and Cerebrospinal Fluid Disorders (#15187)

♦ Hydrogen Europe 10998

SG Avenue de la Toison d'Or 56-60, 1060 Brussels, Belgium. T. +3225408775. E-mail: secretariat@hydrogeneurope.eu.
URL: http://hydrogeneurope.eu/

History 2009. Took over functions of *World Fuel Cell Council (inactive)* and *Fuel Cell Europe (FCEu, inactive)*, 2012, as *New Energy World Industry Grouping (NEW-IG)*. Previous full title: *New Energy World IG – fuel cells and hydrogen for sustainability*. Current title adopted Nov 2015. Registration: Banque-Carrfour des Entreprises, No/ID: 0890.025.478, Start date: 28 Mar 2007, Belgium; EU Transparency Register, No/ID: 77659588648-75, Start date: 23 Apr 2012. **Aims** Bring together diverse industry players, large companies and SMEs, who support the delivery of hydrogen and fuelcells technologies. **Structure** General Assembly (annual); Board; Secretariat. Technical Committees; Working Groups; Task Forces. **Events** *European Hydrogen Week Meeting* Brussels (Belgium) 2022, *European Zero Emission Bus Conference* Paris (France) 2021, *How to scale up zero-emission commercial vehicles?* Brussels (Belgium) 2020, *General Assembly* Espoo (Finland) 2019.
Members Full in 23 countries:
Austria, Belgium, Czechia, Denmark, Estonia, Finland, France, Germany, Greece, Iceland, Ireland, Italy, Luxembourg, Netherlands, Norway, Poland, Portugal, Slovakia, Slovenia, Spain, Sweden, Switzerland, UK.
NGO Relations Member of: *Industry4Europe (#11181)*. [2020/XJ8945/**F**]

♦ Hydrographic Commission on Antarctica (see: #13825)
♦ Hydrographic Society, The / see International Federation of Hydrographic Societies (#13453)

♦ Hydrographic Society Benelux (HSB) 10999

Sec Hellestraat 13, 9800 Deinze, Belgium. E-mail: hvdkaaij@visual-hydrography.nl.
URL: http://www.hydrographicsocietybenelux.eu/

Structure Board, comprising Chairman, Treasurer, Secretary and 4 members. **Activities** Active in: Belgium, Luxembourg, Netherlands. **NGO Relations** Founding member of: *International Federation of Hydrographic Societies (IFHS, #13453)*. [2022/XJ5157/**D**]

♦ **HYDROLARE** International Data Centre on Hydrology of Lakes and Reservoirs (#13137)
♦ **HYDROMAG** International Association for Hydromagnetic Phenomena and Applications (#11955)
♦ Hydrometeorological Research Institute of Uzhydromet (internationally oriented national body)
♦ HYEL – International Conference on Hydroelasticity in Marine Technology (meeting series)
♦ **HyER** European Association for Hydrogen and fuel cells and Electro-mobility in European Regions (#06076)
♦ Hyperheritage International Seminar (meeting series)

♦ Hyper-Kamiokande Collaboration 11000

Leader address not obtained.
Co-Leader King's College London, Strand, London, WC2R 2LS, UK.
URL: http://www.hyperk.org/

Structure Project Leader and Co-Leader; Steering Committee; International Board of Representatives. Boards (2): Conveners; Speakers. **Activities** Events/meetings. **Events** *General Meeting* Madrid (Spain) 2018.
Members Collaborating institutes in 15 countries:
Armenia, Brazil, Canada, France, Italy, Japan, Korea Rep, Poland, Russia, Spain, Sweden, Switzerland, UK, Ukraine, USA.
[2019/XM7698/**F**]

♦ hypoPARA Norge (inactive)
♦ Hypoparathyroidism Europe (inactive)
♦ Hypophosphatasie Europe (unconfirmed)

♦ Hypospadias International Society (HIS) 11001

Contact Max-Planck-Str 2, 63500 Seligenstadt, Germany. T. +491742056913. E-mail: assistant@hypospadias-society.org.
URL: https://www.hypospadias-society.org/

History 2018. **Aims** Provide an international forum for all disciplines and persons interested in the field of hypospadias. **Structure** Scientific Committee; Executive Board. **Activities** Events/meetings; training/education. **Events** *Hypospadias International Congress* Vienna (Austria) 2020. [2021/AA1671/**C**]

♦ HyRaMP / see European Association for Hydrogen and fuel cells and Electro-mobility in European Regions (#06076)
♦ **HySafe** International Association for Hydrogen Safety (#11952)
♦ **I10H** International Commission of Military History (#12705)
♦ **i2a** International Antimony Association (#11657)
♦ I2CCNER – International Institute for Carbon-Neutral Energy Research (internationally oriented national body)
♦ I2SM – International Symposium on Sediment Management (meeting series)
♦ I2U2 (unconfirmed)
♦ I2UD – Institute for International Urban Development (internationally oriented national body)
♦ **I3AE** International Institute of Innovative Acoustic Emission (#13891)
♦ I3M – International Multidisciplinary Modelling & Simulation Multiconference (meeting series)
♦ **I3PM** International Institute for Intellectual Property Management (#13893)
♦ I4ADA – Institute for Accountability in the Digital Age (internationally oriented national body)
♦ IA / see Instituto de Derecho de Autor
♦ IA / see International Association of Sheet Metal, Air, Rail and Transportation Workers
♦ IAAAC – International Association of Athletic Administrators and Coaches (unconfirmed)
♦ IAAAD – International Association of Athletes Against Drugs (no recent information)
♦ **IAAA** International Association of Astronomical Artists (#11718)
♦ IAAAM – International Association for Aquatic Animal Medicine (internationally oriented national body)
♦ IAAB / see International Association of Broadcasting (#11738)
♦ **IAACA** International Association of Anti-Corruption Authorities (#11703)
♦ **IAACD** International Alliance of Academies of Childhood Disability (#11619)
♦ **IAAC** Inter-American Accreditation Cooperation (#11396)
♦ IAACI / see World Allergy Organization – IAACI (#21077)
♦ **IAACS** International Association for the Advancement of Curriculum Studies (#11685)
♦ IAADADT / see International Association against Drug Trafficking and Drug Abuse (#11693)
♦ IAADFS – International Association of Airport Duty Free Stores (internationally oriented national body)
♦ **IAAD** International Academy for Adhesive Dentistry (#11534)
♦ IAADP – International Association of Assistance Dog Partners (internationally oriented national body)
♦ **IAADS** International Athletic Association for Persons with Down Syndrome (#12289)
♦ IAAE / see Autism-Europe (#03040)
♦ **IAAE** International Association of Agricultural Economists (#11695)
♦ **IAAE** International Association of Airport Executives (#11697)
♦ **IAAE** International Association for Applied Econometrics (#11704)
♦ **IAAEM** International Association of Aquaculture Economics and Management (#11706)
♦ IAAER / see Association mondiale des sciences de l'éducation (#02811)
♦ **IAAER** International Association for Accounting Education and Research (#11682)
♦ IAAEU / see Institut für Arbeitsrecht und Arbeitsbeziehungen in der Europäischen Union
♦ IAAEU – Institut für Arbeitsrecht und Arbeitsbeziehungen in der Europäischen Union (internationally oriented national body)
♦ **IAA Europe** International Association of Art – Europe (#11711)
♦ IAAFA – Inter-American Air Forces Academy (internationally oriented national body)
♦ IAAF / see World Athletics (#21209)
♦ IAAGT – International Association for the Advancement of Gestalt Therapy (internationally oriented national body)
♦ **IAAH** International Association for Adolescent Health (#11683)
♦ IAAHPC – International Association for Animal Hospice and Palliative Care (internationally oriented national body)
♦ **IAAIA** International Association of Airline Internal Auditors (#11696)
♦ iAAID / see International Conference of Occlusion Medicine (#12884)
♦ **IAAI** International Association for the Advancement of Innovative Approaches to Global Challenges (#11687)
♦ IAAI – International Association of Arson Investigators (internationally oriented national body)
♦ **IAAIL** International Association for Artificial Intelligence and Law (#11712)
♦ **IAA** INSEAD Alumni Association (#11229)
♦ IAA – Institute of African Affairs, Hamburg (internationally oriented national body)
♦ **IAA** Inter-American Accounting Association (#11395)
♦ **IAA** International Academy of Architecture (#11535)
♦ **IAA** International Academy of Astronautics (#11536)
♦ IAA – International Academy of Ayurveda (internationally oriented national body)
♦ **IAA** International Actuarial Association (#11586)
♦ **IAA** International Advertising Association (#11590)
♦ IAA – International Aerosol Association (inactive)
♦ IAA – International Ammunition Association (internationally oriented national body)
♦ **IAA** International Aquathlon Association (#11662)
♦ IAA – International Arthroscopy Association (inactive)
♦ IAA – International Arts Association (no recent information)
♦ **IAA** International Association for Aerobiology (#11691)
♦ **IAA** International Association for Aesthetics (#11692)
♦ IAA – International Association of Agriculturalists (inactive)
♦ **IAA** International Association of Art (#11710)
♦ **IAA** International Association of Astacology (#11717)
♦ IAAIP / see Asociación Interamericana de la Propiedad Intelectual (#02161)
♦ IAALD – International Association of Agricultural Information Specialists (inactive)
♦ IAAM / see International Association of Venue Managers
♦ IAAMC / see AMC Institute
♦ **IAAM** International Association of Advanced Materials (#11684)
♦ IAAMRH / see International Association of Rural Health and Medicine (#12140)
♦ IAAMSAD – International Association for the Advancement of Methods for System Analysis and Design (no recent information)
♦ IAAND – International Affiliate of the Academy of Nutrition and Dietetics (internationally oriented national body)
♦ **IAAO** International Association of Assay Offices (#11715)
♦ IAAO – International Association of Assessing Officers (internationally oriented national body)
♦ IAAOM / see International Academy of Orthopedic Medicine (#11565)
♦ **IAAPA** International Association of Amusement Parks and Attractions (#11699)
♦ IAAPC – International Association of Arab Pharmacy Colleges (inactive)
♦ **IAAPEA** International Association Against Painful Experiments on Animals (#11694)
♦ **IAAP** International Association of Accessibility Professionals (#11680)
♦ IAAP – International Association of Administrative Professionals (internationally oriented national body)
♦ IAAP / see International Association of Amusement Parks and Attractions (#11699)
♦ **IAAP** International Association for Analytical Psychology (#11700)
♦ IAAP – International Association of Anthroposophic Pharmacists (internationally oriented national body)
♦ **IAAP** International Association of Applied Psychology (#11705)
♦ IAAPS – Indian Association for Asian and Pacific Studies (internationally oriented national body)
♦ **IAAPS** International Association for Asia Pacific Studies (#11714)
♦ **IAAPS** International Association of Aviation Personnel Schools (#11721)
♦ **IAAPT** International Acupuncture Association of Physical Therapists (#11587)
♦ IAARA – Ibero-American Animal Reproduction Association (no recent information)
♦ **IAARC** International Association for Automation and Robotics in Construction (#11719)
♦ **IAASB** International Auditing and Assurance Standards Board (#12296)
♦ IAASEES / see Inter-American Association of Sanitary and Environmental Engineering (#11400)
♦ IAAS – Institute for African American Studies, University of Connecticut (internationally oriented national body)
♦ IAAS – Institute of African and Asian Studies, Khartoum (internationally oriented national body)
♦ IAAS – Institute of Asian and African Studies (internationally oriented national body)
♦ IAAS – Institute of Asian and African Studies, Moscow State University (internationally oriented national body)
♦ **IAAS** International Association of Academies of Sciences (#11679)
♦ IAAS – International Association for Agricultural Sustainability (unconfirmed)
♦ **IAAS** International Association for Ambulatory Surgery (#11698)
♦ **IAAS** International Association for Anselm Studies (#11701)
♦ **IAAS** International Association of Students in Agricultural and Related Sciences (#12191)
♦ **IAASM** International Academy of Aviation and Space Medicine (#11537)
♦ IAASP / see InterPortPolice (#15963)
♦ IAASR – International Association of Asylum Seekers and Refugees (unconfirmed)
♦ IAASSE / see International Association of Academicians (#11678)
♦ **IAASSE** International Association of Academicians (#11678)
♦ **IAASS** International Association for the Advancement of Space Safety (#11689)
♦ IAATE – International Association of Avian Trainers and Educators (internationally oriented national body)
♦ **IAATI** International Association of Auto Theft Investigators (#11720)
♦ IAAT – International Association Against Torture (no recent information)
♦ IAATM / see International Traffic Medicine Association (#15713)
♦ IAATO / see Global Alliance of Assistive Technology Organizations (#10185)
♦ **IAATO** International Association of Antarctica Tour Operators (#11702)
♦ IAAW – International Association of African Writers (inactive)
♦ IAAY – International Association of African Youths (unconfirmed)
♦ **IABA** Inter-American Bar Association (#11401)
♦ IABA – Inter-American Board of Agriculture (see: #11434)

- ♦ IABA – International Association of Aircraft Brokers and Agents (inactive)
- ♦ **IABA** International Auto/Biography Association (#12299)
- ♦ IABB – International Association of Baby Boxes (unconfirmed)
- ♦ IABC – International Association for Biologically Closed Electric Circuits in Biomedicine (inactive)
- ♦ **IABC** International Association of Buddhist Culture (#11742)
- ♦ **IABC** International Association of Business Communicators (#11747)
- ♦ **IABCR** International Association for Breast Cancer Research (#11733)
- ♦ IABE – Internacia Asocio de Bankistoj Esperantistaj (inactive)
- ♦ **IABE** International Academy of Business and Economics (#11538)
- ♦ IABE / see International Association of Butterfly Exhibitors and Suppliers (#11749)
- ♦ **IABEM** International Association for Boundary Element Methods (#11732)
- ♦ **IABES** International Association of Butterfly Exhibitors and Suppliers (#11749)

♦ IAB Europe 11002

CEO Rond-Point Schuman 11, 1040 Brussels, Belgium. T. +3222577533. E-mail: communication@iabeurope.eu.
URL: http://www.iabeurope.eu/

History 1998, as *Interactive Advertising Bureau Europe (IAB Europe)*. Current title adopted when merged with *European Interactive Advertising Association (EIAA, inactive)*, 18 May 2011. EU Transparency Register: 43167137250-27. **Aims** Support and promote the growth of the European *digital* and interactive *marketing* industry. **Structure** General Assembly; Board. **Languages** English. **Staff** Central unit: 8 FTE; national chapters: 125 FTE. **Finance** Members' dues. **Activities** Advocacy/lobbying/activism; networking/liaising. **Events** *INTERACT Congress* Lisbon (Portugal) 2022, *INTERACT Congress* Lisbon (Portugal) 2021, *INTERACT Congress* Brussels (Belgium) 2020, *INTERACT Congress* Milan (Italy) 2018, *INTERACT Congress* Amsterdam (Netherlands) 2017. **Publications** *Digital Dialogue* (12 a year) – newsletter. Surveys; reports; studies.
Members National IAB associations in 27 countries:
Austria, Belgium, Bulgaria, Croatia, Czechia, Denmark, Finland, France, Germany, Greece, Hungary, Ireland, Italy, Netherlands, Norway, Poland, Romania, Russia, Serbia, Slovakia, Slovenia, Spain, Sweden, Switzerland, Türkiye, UK, Ukraine.
NGO Relations Member of: *European Advertising Standards Alliance (EASA, #05829)*; *European Interactive Digital Advertising Alliance (EDAA, #07582)*; *IAB Global Network (#11003)*. Partners include: *Online Publishers Association Europe (OPA Europe, #17742)*; *Search and Information Industry Association (Siinda, #19188)*.
[2020/XD9013/**D**]

- ♦ IABG – International Association of Biomedical Gerontology (no recent information)
- ♦ **IABG** International Association of Botanic Gardens (#11731)

♦ IAB Global Network 11003

Main Office 116 East 27th St, 6th Fl, New York NY 10016, USA. T. +12123804700.
URL: http://www.iab.com/

History Set up to bring together all licensees of the *Interactive Advertising Bureau*. **Aims** Share challenges, develop global solutions and advance the digital advertising industry worldwide.
Members Organizations (over 40) in 17 countries and territories:
Argentina, Australia, Brazil, Canada, Chile, China, Colombia, Ecuador, Hong Kong, India, Japan, Mexico, New Zealand, Peru, South Africa, Uruguay, USA.
European organizations grouped into one regional organization:
IAB Europe (#11002). [2019/XM7622/y/**F**]

- ♦ **IABIN** Inter-American Biodiversity Information Network (#11402)
- ♦ **IAB** International Association of Bioethics (#11725)
- ♦ **IAB** International Association of Bookkeepers (#11728)
- ♦ **IAB** International Association of Broadcasting (#11738)
- ♦ **IAB** International Association of Bryologists (#11741)
- ♦ **IAB** Internationale Akademie für Bäder-, Sport-, und Freizeitbauten (#13211)
- ♦ IABLA – Inter-American Bibliographical and Library Association (inactive)
- ♦ IABL – International Association for Blended Learning (unconfirmed)
- ♦ **IABMAS** International Association for Bridge Maintenance and Safety (#11736)
- ♦ **IABM** International Association of Broadcasting Manufacturers (#11739)
- ♦ **IABM** International Association of Broadcast Meteorology (#11740)
- ♦ **IABMS** International Association of Botanical and Mycological Societies (#11730)
- ♦ IABO – Internacia Asocio de Bibliistoj kaj Orientalistoj (inactive)
- ♦ **IABO** International Association of Biological Oceanography (#11726)
- ♦ IABPAD – International Academy of Business and Public Disciplines (internationally oriented national body)
- ♦ IABPFF – International Association of Black Professional Fire Fighters (internationally oriented national body)
- ♦ **IABP** International Arctic Buoy Programme (#11667)
- ♦ **IABP** International Association of Building Physics (#11746)
- ♦ IABP – International Association of Business and Parliament (inactive)
- ♦ **IABR** International Association for Breath Research (#11734)
- ♦ **IABSE** International Association for Bridge and Structural Engineering (#11737)
- ♦ IABS / see International Alliance for Biological Standardization (#11622)
- ♦ **IABS** International Alliance for Biological Standardization (#11622)
- ♦ **IABS** International Association of Buddhist Studies (#11743)
- ♦ **IABS** International Association for Business and Society (#11748)
- ♦ **IABS** International Association of Byron Societies (#11750)
- ♦ IABSOIW / see International Association of Bridge, Structural, Ornamental and Reinforcing Iron Workers
- ♦ **IABU** International Association of Buddhist Universities (#11744)
- ♦ IABYT – International Black Yoga Teachers Association (internationally oriented national body)
- ♦ IAC / see Gays and Lesbians in Alcoholics Anonymous
- ♦ IAC / see International Academy of Consciousness
- ♦ IAC / see International Health Academy
- ♦ IAC / see Inter-African Committee on Traditional Practices Affecting the Health of Women and Children (#11384)
- ♦ IAC2 – International Association of Certified Indoor Air Consultants (internationally oriented national body)
- ♦ IACA / see Airlines International Representation in Europe (#00608)
- ♦ **IACAC** Inter-American Commercial Arbitration Commission (#11410)
- ♦ **IACAC** International Association of Civil Aviation Chaplains (#11774)
- ♦ **IACACT** International Association of Communication Activists (#11791)
- ♦ IACA – International A-Catamaran Association (see: #21760)
- ♦ **IACA** International Anti-Corruption Academy (#11654)
- ♦ **IACA** International Association for Caribbean Archaeology (#11756)
- ♦ **IACA** International Association of Consulting Actuaries (#11813)
- ♦ IACA – International Association for Court Administration (internationally oriented national body)
- ♦ **IACAPAP** International Association for Child and Adolescent Psychiatry and Allied Professions (#11766)
- ♦ **IACAP** International Association for Computing and Philosophy (#11805)
- ♦ IACAT – International Association for Computerized Adaptive Testing (internationally oriented national body)
- ♦ **IACB** International Association of Catholic Bioethicists (#11758)
- ♦ **IACBT** International Association of Cognitive Behavioral Therapy (#11781)
- ♦ IACC (internationally oriented national body)
- ♦ **IACC Council** International Anti-Corruption Conference Council (#11655)
- ♦ IACCE / see Inter-American Catholic Education Association (#11403)
- ♦ **IACChE** Inter-American Confederation of Chemical Engineering (#11417)
- ♦ **IACC** Ibero-American Association of Chambers of Commerce (#11014)
- ♦ IACC – Inter-American Confederation of Cattlemen (no recent information)
- ♦ IACC – International Anti-Corruption Conference (meeting series)
- ♦ **IACC** International Anticounterfeiting Coalition (#11656)
- ♦ **IACC** International Assembly of Capitals and Cities (#11677)
- ♦ IACC – International Association for Cell Culture (inactive)
- ♦ IACC – International Association of Colour Consultants/Designers (unconfirmed)
- ♦ **IACC** International Association for Computers and Communications (#11804)
- ♦ **IACCM** International Association of Cross-Cultural Competence and Management (#11827)
- ♦ IACCM / see World Commerce and Contracting (#21284)
- ♦ IACCP – Inter-American Council of Commerce and Production (no recent information)
- ♦ **IACCP** International Association for Cross-Cultural Psychology (#11828)
- ♦ IACD / see Van Hall Larenstein University of Applied Sciences
- ♦ IACD / see International Society of Computerized Dentistry
- ♦ IACDF – Inter-American Culture and Development Foundation (internationally oriented national body)
- ♦ IACD – Institute of Asian Culture and Development (internationally oriented national body)
- ♦ **IACD** Inter-American Agency for Cooperation and Development (#11397)
- ♦ **IACD** International Academy of Cosmetic Dermatology (#11542)
- ♦ **IACD** International Association for Community Development (#11793)
- ♦ **IACDS** International Association of Concrete Drillers and Sawers (#11806)
- ♦ IACE / see International Air Cadet Exchange Association (#11607)
- ♦ **IACEA** International Air Cadet Exchange Association (#11607)
- ♦ **IACEE** International Association for Continuing Engineering Education (#11817)
- ♦ **IACE** Institut arabe des chefs d'entreprises (#11236)
- ♦ IACE / see International Association for Cognitive Education and Psychology (#11782)
- ♦ **IACEP** International Association for Cognitive Education and Psychology (#11782)
- ♦ **IACES** International Association of Civil Engineering Students (#11776)
- ♦ IACET – International Association for Continuing Education and Training (internationally oriented national body)
- ♦ IACFA – International Association of Cystic Fibrosis Adults (inactive)
- ♦ IACF – International Association for Cultural Freedom (inactive)
- ♦ **IACFM** International Association of Clinical Forensic Medicine (#11779)
- ♦ IACFP – International Association for Correctional and Forensic Psychology (internationally oriented national body)
- ♦ **IACFP** International Association of Couple and Family Psychoanalysis (#11822)
- ♦ **IACFS** International Association of Centers for Federal Studies (#11761)
- ♦ IACG – European Academic Conference on Internal Audit and Corporate Governance (meeting series)
- ♦ IACHEI – International Association of Consultants in Higher Education Institutions (inactive)
- ♦ IACH – International Academy for Clinical Hematology (unconfirmed)
- ♦ IACHP – International Association of Circumpolar Health Publishers (inactive)
- ♦ **IACHR** Inter-American Commission on Human Rights (#11411)
- ♦ IACHS / see International Federation of Cardio HIIT BodyWeight Exercise
- ♦ IACI / see Istituto Agronomico per l'Oltremare, Italy
- ♦ **IACI** Inter-American Children's Institute (#11406)
- ♦ **IACI** International Association of Craniofacial Identification (#11823)
- ♦ IACI – International Association of Creativity and Innovation (unconfirmed)
- ♦ **IAC** Insurance Association of the Caribbean (#11360)
- ♦ **IAC** InterAction Council (#11378)
- ♦ **IAC** Inter-African Committee on Traditional Practices Affecting the Health of Women and Children (#11384)
- ♦ **IAC** International Academy of Ceramics (#11540)
- ♦ IAC – International Academy of Consciousness (internationally oriented national body)
- ♦ **IAC** International Academy of Cytology (#11544)
- ♦ IAC – International Action Center, New York (internationally oriented national body)
- ♦ IAC – International Aerobatic Club (internationally oriented national body)
- ♦ IAC – International ANTOR Committee (inactive)
- ♦ **IAC** International Association of Community and Further Education Colleges (#11794)
- ♦ **IAC** International Association for Counselling (#11821)
- ♦ IAC – International Association for Cyanophyte Research (inactive)
- ♦ IAC – International Asthma Council (inactive)
- ♦ **IAC** International Auschwitz Committee (#12297)
- ♦ IAC / see Interstate Aviation Committee (#15977)
- ♦ **IAC** Interstate Aviation Committee (#15977)
- ♦ **IACIPP** International Association of CIP Professionals (#11772)
- ♦ **IACIS** International Association of Colloid and Interface Scientists (#11788)
- ♦ IACIT – International Association of Conference Interpreters and Translators (inactive)
- ♦ **IACK** International Alliance of Catholic Knights (#11624)
- ♦ **IACLAM** International Association of Colleges of Laboratory Animal Medicine (#11787)
- ♦ IACLE / see International Association of Contact Lens Educators (#11815)
- ♦ **IACLE** International Association of Contact Lens Educators (#11815)
- ♦ **IACL** International Association of Chinese Linguistics (#11768)
- ♦ **IACL** International Association of Constitutional Law (#11811)
- ♦ **IACL** International Association for Consumer Law (#11814)
- ♦ **IACLSC** International Association of Comparative Literature, Society and Culture (#11796)
- ♦ **IACMAG** International Association for Computer Methods and Advances in Geomechanics (#11802)
- ♦ **IACME** Inter-American Committee of Mathematics Education (#11413)
- ♦ IAC and ME – International Association of Coroners and Medical Examiners (internationally oriented national body)
- ♦ IACME – International Association of Crafts and Small and Medium-Sized Enterprises (inactive)
- ♦ IACM / see International Association for Cannabinoid Medicines (#11754)
- ♦ **IACM** International Association for Cannabinoid Medicines (#11754)
- ♦ **IACM** International Association of Catholic Missiologists (#11760)
- ♦ IACM – International Association of Color Manufacturers (internationally oriented national body)
- ♦ **IACM** International Association for Comparative Mythology (#11797)
- ♦ **IACM** International Association for Computational Mechanics (#11800)
- ♦ **IACM** International Association for Conflict Management (#11808)
- ♦ **IACM** International Association of Customs Museums (#11831)
- ♦ **IACMS** International Association of Catholic Medical Schools (#11759)
- ♦ **IACNDR** Inter-American Committee on Natural Disaster Reduction (#11414)
- ♦ **IACNET** Inter-American Citrus Network (#11407)
- ♦ IACNRE – International Association for Conservation of Natural Resources and Energy (inactive)
- ♦ **IACO** Inter-African Coffee Organization (#11383)
- ♦ **IACO** International Alliance of Carer Organizations (#11623)
- ♦ IACOLE – International Association for Civilian Oversight of Law Enforcement (inactive)
- ♦ **IACORDS** International Association of Cold Regions Development Studies (#11786)
- ♦ IACP&AP / see International Association for Child and Adolescent Psychiatry and Allied Professions (#11766)
- ♦ **IACP** Association internationale des chefs de police (#11765)
- ♦ IACP / see Association internationale villes et ports – réseau mondial des villes portuaires (#02751)
- ♦ **IACPB** International Association of Comparative Physiology and Biochemistry (#11798)
- ♦ IACP – Inter-African Council for Philosophy (no recent information)
- ♦ **IACP** International Academy of Collaborative Professionals (#11541)
- ♦ **IACP** International Association of Chiefs of Police (#11765)

♦ IACP / see International Association for Child and Adolescent Psychiatry and Allied Professions (#11766)
♦ **IACP** International Association of Claim Professionals (#11777)
♦ IACP / see International Association of Cognitive Behavioral Therapy (#11781)
♦ **IACPM** International Association of Credit Portfolio Managers (#11824)
♦ **IACPP** International Advisory Commission on the Principle of Precaution (#11591)
♦ **IACPS** International Association of Centres for Peirce Studies (#11762)
♦ IACPT – International Association for Cultivated Plant Taxonomy (inactive)
♦ IACREOT – International Association of Clerks, Recorders, Election Officials and Treasurers (internationally oriented national body)
♦ **IACR** Inter-American College of Radiology (#11409)
♦ **IACR** International Association of Cancer Registries (#11753)
♦ **IACR** International Association for Critical Realism (#11826)
♦ **IACR** International Association for Cryptologic Research (#11830)
♦ IACR Rothamsted International / see Rothamsted International
♦ IACSC / see Controlled Environment Building Association (#04783)
♦ **IACSC** International Academic Consortium for Sustainable Cities (#11532)
♦ **IACSEE** International Association for Citizenship, Social and Economics Education (#11773)
♦ **IACS** International Academy of Cardiovascular Sciences (#11539)
♦ **IACS** International Academy of Cosmetic Surgery (#11543)
♦ **IACS** International Alliance for the Control of Scabies (#11625)
♦ IACS – International Alliance for Cooperation among Schools (inactive)
♦ **IACS** International Association of Catalysis Societies (#11757)
♦ **IACS** International Association for Children's Spirituality (#11767)
♦ **IACS** International Association of Classification Societies (#11778)
♦ **IACS** International Association for Cognitive Science (#11783)
♦ **IACS** International Association for Cognitive Semiotics (#11785)
♦ **IACS** International Association of Combative Sports (#11789)
♦ IACS – International Association for Comparative Semitics (unconfirmed)
♦ **IACS** International Association for Coptic Studies (#11820)
♦ **IACS** International Association of Cryospheric Sciences (#11829)
♦ IACSM – International Association of Collectors of Slag Minerals (inactive)
♦ IACSP – International Association of Counterterrorism and Security Professionals (internationally oriented national body)
♦ **IACSR** International Association for the Cognitive Science of Religion (#11784)
♦ IACSS / see Inter-American Conference on Social Security (#11419)
♦ **IACSS** International Association of Computer Science in Sport (#11803)
♦ **IACS Society** Inter-Asia Cultural Studies Society (#11456)
♦ IACST / see International Association for Commodity Science and Technology (#11790)
♦ **IACST** International Association for Convergence Science and Technology (#11819)
♦ iACT (internationally oriented national body)
♦ IACT – International Association of Certified Thermographers (internationally oriented national body)
♦ **IACT** International Association on Chemical Thermodynamics (#11764)
♦ IACT – International Association for Clean Technology (inactive)
♦ I-act – International Association for Creation and Training (internationally oriented national body)
♦ **IACToR** International Association of CyberPsychology, Training, and Rehabilitation (#11832)
♦ IACVB / see Destinations International (#05046)
♦ IACVB – International Association of Crime Victim Compensation Boards (inactive)
♦ IACVS – International Association of Certified Valuation Specialists (internationally oriented national body)
♦ IACWGE / see Inter-Agency Network on Women and Gender Equality (#11388)
♦ **IACW** International Association of Crime Writers (#11825)
♦ **IADAA** International Association of Dealers in Ancient Art (#11835)
♦ IADAC – International Academy of Dialogue Among Cultures and Civilizations (internationally oriented national body)
♦ IADA – International Association for the Defence of Artists (inactive)
♦ **IADA** International Association for Dialogue Analysis (#11847)
♦ **IADA** Internationale Arbeitsgemeinschaft der Archiv-, Bibliotheks- und Graphikrestauratoren (#11729)
♦ IADAP – Instituto Andino de Artes Populares (no recent information)
♦ IADAT – International Association for the Development of Advances in Technology (internationally oriented national body)
♦ **IADB** Inter-American Defense Board (#11425)
♦ **IADC** Inter-Agency Space Debris Coordination Committee (#11392)
♦ **IADC** Inter-American Defense College (#11426)
♦ **IADC** International Association of Dredging Companies (#11852)
♦ IADC – International Association of Drilling Contractors (internationally oriented national body)
♦ IADC / see International Association of Paediatric Dentistry (#12064)
♦ **IADDM** International Academy for Digital Dental Medicine (#11546)
♦ IAdEM – Internacia Asocio de Esperantistaj Matematikistoj (no recent information)
♦ IADF – Inter-American Association for Democracy and Freedom (inactive)
♦ **IADH** Institut arabe des droits de l'homme (#00983)
♦ IADH / see International Association for Disability and Oral Health (#11848)
♦ **iADH** International Association for Disability and Oral Health (#11848)
♦ **IADI** Institut africain de droit international (#00341)
♦ **IADI** International Association of Deposit Insurers (#11843)
♦ IAD – Inter-American Dialogue (internationally oriented national body)
♦ **IAD** International Association of Designers (#11844)
♦ IAD – International Association of Documentalists and Information Officers (inactive)
♦ **IAD** Internationale Arbeitsgemeinschaft Donauforschung (#11834)
♦ **IADIP** Institut africain du droit international privé (#11234)
♦ IADIWU – International Association for the Development of International and World Universities (no recent information)
♦ **IADL** International Association of Democratic Lawyers (#11837)
♦ IADL – International Association for Distance Learning (internationally oriented national body)
♦ **IADMFR** International Association of Dento-Maxillo-Facial Radiology (#11841)
♦ IADM – Internationale Assoziation Deutschsprachiger Medien (inactive)
♦ **IADMS** International Association for Dance Medicine and Science (#11833)
♦ **IADN** Inter-American Democracy Network (#18692)
♦ IADP – International Association of Dynamic Psychotherapy (internationally oriented national body)
♦ IADPPNW / see International Architects, Designers, Planners for Social Responsibility (#11666)
♦ **IADPSG** International Association of the Diabetes and Pregnancy Study Groups (#11846)
♦ **IADR** International Association for Dental Research (#11838)
♦ IADR-NOF / see Scandinavian Association for Dental Research (#19070)
♦ IADR-PER / see Continental European Division of the International Association for Dental Research (#04780)
♦ **IADSA** International Alliance of Dietary Food Supplement Associations (#11627)
♦ IADS – Initiative action pour le développement au Sahel (internationally oriented national body)
♦ **IADS** International Association of Dental Students (#11839)
♦ **IADS** International Association of Department Stores (#11842)
♦ **IADTDA** International Association against Drug Trafficking and Drug Abuse (#11693)
♦ **IADT** International Association of Dental Traumatology (#11840)
♦ IADT – Internationale Arbeitsgemeinschaft Deutschsprachiger Theater (no recent information)
♦ **IAEAC** International Association of Environmental Analytical Chemistry (#11876)
♦ **IAEA-EL** IAEA Environment Laboratories (#11004)

♦ IAEA Environment Laboratories (IAEA-EL) 11004

Dir PO Box 100, 1400 Vienna, Austria. T. +43126000. Fax +43126007. E-mail: official.mail@iaea.org.
URL: http://www.iaea.org/monaco/page.php

History 1961, as *International Laboratory of Marine Radioactivity (ILMR)*, on conclusion of a tripartite agreement between *International Atomic Energy Agency (IAEA, #12294)*, the Government of the Principality of Monaco and the Oceanographic Institute of France. Now bipartite between IAEA and the Government of the Principality of Monaco. Subsequently referred to as *IAEA Marine Environment Laboratories (IAEA-MEL)*. Previously also known as *IAEA Marine Environment Laboratory*. Martine laboratories in Monaco and Terrestrial Laboratory in Seibersdorf (Austria) consolidated under current title. **Aims** Assist IAEA Member States understand, monitor and protect the marine and *terrestrial* environment from *radioactive* and non-radioactive *pollution*; coordinate technical aspects of international ocean protection, training and assistance programmes; use nuclear techniques to assist in answering marine and terrestrial environmental questions. **Structure** Director; Director's Secretary; Administration; Electronic and Engineering Support Services. Laboratories (4): Radiometrics, including measurements, mapping, modelling and radiological assessment of marine radioactivity, analytical quality assurance, global database, methods development, training; Radio-ecology, including vertical transport, bioaccumulation, training; Marine Environmental Studies (MESL), including reference methods, instrument servicing, non-radioactive pollution, training; Terrestrial Environment Laboratories (TEL), including measurements, mapping, modelling and radiological assessment of terrestrial radioactivity. **Languages** English, French. **Staff** About 60 scientists, technicians and administrative personnel. **Finance** On the budget of IAEA, with Member States providing about US$ 6,000,000 as regular budget. Extra-budgetary funds (about US$ 1,600,000) from: different Member States. **Activities** Training/education; knowledge management/information dissemination. **Events** *International symposium on marine pollution* Monte Carlo (Monaco) 1998. **Information Services** *Global Marine Radioactivity Database (GLOMARD)*; *Marine Information Systems (MARIS)*. **IGO Relations** Tripartite Memorandum of Understanding with: *UNEP (#20299)* and *Intergovernmental Oceanographic Commission (IOC, #11496)* including joint coordinated planning of common programmes. [2018.08.29/XF1135/**F***]

♦ IAEA – Inter-American Education Association (inactive)
♦ IAEA – Internacia Agrikultura Esperanto-Asocio (no recent information)
♦ IAEA – International Agricultural Exchange Association (inactive)
♦ **IAEA** International Arts and Entertainment Alliance (#11676)
♦ **IAEA** International Association for Educational Assessment (#11861)
♦ **IAEA** International Association of Empirical Aesthetics (#11867)
♦ **IAEA** International Atomic Energy Agency (#12294)
♦ IAEA Marine Environment Laboratories / see IAEA Environment Laboratories (#11004)
♦ IAEA Marine Environment Laboratory / see IAEA Environment Laboratories (#11004)
♦ IAEA-MEL / see IAEA Environment Laboratories (#11004)
♦ IAEA Staff Association / see Staff Association of the International Atomic Energy Agency (#19938)
♦ IAECE – International Association of Early Childhood Education (internationally oriented national body)
♦ **IAEC** International Association of Educating Cities (#11860)
♦ IAEC – International Association of Evangelical Chaplains (internationally oriented national body)
♦ IAE CIS / see International Association of Exchanges of the Commonwealth of Independent States Countries (#11884)
♦ IAEDB / see Deafblind International (#05014)
♦ IAED – International Academies of Emergency Dispatch (internationally oriented national body)
♦ IAED – International Agency for Economic Development (internationally oriented national body)
♦ **IAEE** International Association for Earthquake Engineering (#11855)
♦ **IAEE** International Association for Education in Ethics (#11863)
♦ **IAEE** International Association of Elevator Engineers (#11866)
♦ **IAEE** International Association for Energy Economics (#11869)
♦ **IAEE** International Association of Ethnopsychologists and Ethnopsychotherapists (#11880)
♦ IAEE – International Association of Exhibitions and Events (internationally oriented national body)
♦ IAEEL – International Association for Energy-Efficient Lighting (inactive)
♦ IAEF – Internacia Asocio de la Esperantistaj Fervojistoj (inactive)
♦ **IAEF** International Association for Engineering and Food (#11871)
♦ IAEG / see Alliance Against Genocide (#00655)
♦ IAEG / see International Association of Engineering Geology and the Environment (#11872)
♦ **IAEG** International Association of Engineering Geology and the Environment (#11872)
♦ IAEGTD – Afro-Asian Region – International Association on Electricity Generation, Transmission and Distribution – Afro-Asian Region (no recent information)
♦ IAE – International AIDS Empowerment (internationally oriented national body)
♦ **IAE** International Association of Egyptologists (#11865)
♦ IAE – International Association of Exorcists (internationally oriented national body)
♦ IAE / see International Travel Insurance Alliance e.V. (#15728)
♦ **IAEJ** International Alliance of Equestrian Journalists (#11628)
♦ **IAELC** International Association for Ethical Literary Criticism (#11879)
♦ **IAEL** International Association of Entertainment Lawyers (#11875)
♦ IAELPS – International Academy of Ecology and Life Protection Sciences (internationally oriented national body)
♦ IAEM / see International Association of Exhibitions and Events
♦ **IAEMGS** International Association of Environmental Mutagenesis and Genomics Societies (#11877)
♦ IAEM – International Association of Emergency Managers (internationally oriented national body)
♦ IAEMS / see International Association of Environmental Mutagenesis and Genomics Societies (#11877)
♦ **IAEN** International AIDS Economics Network (#11600)
♦ IAEP – International Association of Educators for Peace (internationally oriented national body)
♦ IAEP – International Association for Emergency Psychiatry (no recent information)
♦ **IAESB** International Accounting Education Standards Board (#11582)
♦ **IAESCSI** International Association of Economic and Social Councils and Similar Institutions (#11858)
♦ IAESDO – International Association of English Speaking Directors' Organizations (inactive)
♦ IAES – International Academy of Environmental Safety (internationally oriented national body)
♦ **IAES** International Association of Endocrine Surgeons (#11868)
♦ **IAES** International Association of Evidence Science (#11883)
♦ **IAES** International Atlantic Economic Society (#12291)
♦ IAESL – International Association for East Slavonic Lexicography (no recent information)
♦ IAES and PH – International Academy of Environmental Sanitation and Public Health (internationally oriented national body)
♦ **IAESS** International Association of Education in Science and Snowsports (#11864)
♦ **IAESTE** International Association for the Exchange of Students for Technical Experience (#11885)
♦ **IAEVG** International Association for Educational and Vocational Guidance (#11862)
♦ IAEWP – International Association of Educators for World Peace (internationally oriented national body)
♦ IAEWP – International Association – Epics of the World's Peoples (no recent information)
♦ **IAEx of CIS** International Association of Exchanges of the Commonwealth of Independent States Countries (#11884)
♦ IAFAE2 – International Association of Food and Agro-industrial Economy (inactive)
♦ IAFA – International Association of Football Agents (no recent information)
♦ IAFC / see Aussie Rules International
♦ IAFC – International Association of Fire Chiefs (internationally oriented national body)
♦ **IAFCMandF** International Association of Former Child Migrants and their Families (#11903)
♦ IAFCT / see Coésio – Destinations Francophone de Congrès (#04082)
♦ IAFE / see International Association of Fire Chiefs
♦ **IAFEI** International Association of Financial Executives Institutes (#11890)

♦ IAFE – International Association of Fairs and Expositions (internationally oriented national body)
♦ **IAFEP** International Association for the Economics of Participation (#11859)
♦ IAFESM / see International Association for the Economics of Participation (#11859)
♦ **IAFFE** International Association for Feminist Economics (#11889)
♦ IAFF – International Association of Fire Fighters (internationally oriented national body)
♦ IAF / see Futuribles International (#10052)
♦ IAFHR – International Association for Halitosis Research (unconfirmed)
♦ **IAFI** International Association of Fish Inspectors (#11894)
♦ **IAFI** International Association for Forensic Institutes (#11895)
♦ **IAF** Inter-American Foundation (#11431)
♦ **IAF** International Abilympic Federation (#11530)
♦ IAF – International Abolitionist Federation (inactive)
♦ **IAF** International Accreditation Forum (#11584)
♦ **IAF** International Aikido Federation (#11605)
♦ IAF – International Anglican Fellowship (see: #20193)
♦ **IAF** International Apparel Federation (#11659)
♦ **IAF** International Association of Facilitators (#11887)
♦ **IAF** International Association for Falconry and Conservation of Birds of Prey (#11888)
♦ **IAF** International Astronautical Federation (#12286)
♦ **IAF** International Athletics Foundation (#12290)
♦ **IAF** International Authors Forum (#12298)
♦ **IAFL** International Academy of Family Lawyers (#11548)
♦ **IAFL** International Association of Forensic Linguists (#11896)
♦ **IAFMHS** International Association of Forensic Mental Health Services (#11897)
♦ IAFM – International Association of Flagmakers (inactive)
♦ **IAFM** International Association for Mediterranean Forests (#02699)
♦ IAFMM / see The Marine Ingredients Organisation (#16579)
♦ **IAFN** International Agri-Food Network (#11599)
♦ **IAFN** International Analog Forestry Network (#11650)
♦ IAFN – International Anglican Family Network (see: #00827)
♦ IAFN – International Association of Forensic Nurses (internationally oriented national body)
♦ **IAFOR** International Academic Forum (#11533)
♦ IAFOR Research Foundation / see International Academic Forum (#11533)
♦ **IAFPA** International Association for Forensic Phonetics and Acoustics (#11898)
♦ **IAFPA** International Aviation Fire Protection Association (#12303)
♦ **IAFP** International Association for Financial Participation (#11891)
♦ IAFP / see International Association for Forensic Phonetics and Acoustics (#11898)
♦ **IAFP** International Association for Forensic Psychotherapy (#11899)
♦ **IA-FramCoS** International Association on Fracture Mechanics of Concrete and Concrete Structures (#11905)
♦ IAFR – International Association of Forensic Radiographers (internationally oriented national body)
♦ IAFS – International Association of Family Sociology (no recent information)
♦ **IAFS** International Association of Forensic Sciences (#11900)
♦ **IAFSM** International Association of Forensic and Security Metrology (#11901)
♦ **IAFSS** International Association for Fire Safety Science (#11892)
♦ **IAFTCC** International Federation of Associations of Textile Chemists and Colourists (#13365)
♦ IAFWNO – Inter-American Federation of Working Newspapermen's Organizations (inactive)
♦ IAGA / see International Association of Gaming Advisors (#11907)
♦ **IAGA** International Association of Gaming Advisors (#11907)
♦ **IAGA** International Association for Genetics in Aquaculture (#11911)
♦ **IAGA** International Association of Geomagnetism and Aeronomy (#11916)
♦ IAGA – International Association of Golf Administrators (internationally oriented national body)
♦ IAGC – International Academy of Gynecological Cytology (inactive)
♦ IAGC / see International Association of GeoChemistry (#11913)
♦ **IAGC** International Association of GeoChemistry (#11913)
♦ **IAGC** International Association of Geophysical Contractors (#11918)
♦ IAGD – International Association for Geoscience Diversity (internationally oriented national body)
♦ IAGE – International Association for Green Energy (unconfirmed)
♦ **IAGETH** International Association for Geoethics (#11915)
♦ IAGF / see International Automotive Glass Federation (#12300)
♦ **IAGG** International Association of Gerontology and Geriatrics (#11920)
♦ IAG'i – International Association of Geo-Informatics (unconfirmed)
♦ **IAG** Inter-Africa Group – Centre for Dialogue on Humanitarian, Peace and Development Issues in the Horn of Africa (#11381)
♦ **IAG** International Academy of Genealogy (#00028)
♦ **IAG** International Association of Geoanalysts (#11912)
♦ **IAG** International Association of Geodesy (#11914)
♦ **IAG** International Association of Geomorphologists (#11917)
♦ **IAG** International Association of Gerodontology (#11919)
♦ IAG / see International Association of Gerontology and Geriatrics (#11920)
♦ **IAG** International Association for Gnotobiology (#11921)
♦ IAGLMA – International Association of Gay and Lesbian Martial Artists (internationally oriented national body)
♦ IAGOD Commission on Industrial Minerals and Rocks (see: #11910)
♦ IAGOD Commission on Ore Deposits in Mafic and Ultramafic Rocks (see: #11910)
♦ IAGOD Commission on Paragenesis (see: #11910)
♦ IAGOD Commission on Placer Deposits (see: #11910)
♦ IAGOD Commission on Tectonics of Ore Deposits (see: #11910)
♦ IAGOD Commission on Thermodynamics of Ore Forming Fluids (see: #11910)
♦ **IAGOD** International Association on the Genesis of Ore Deposits (#11910)
♦ **IAGP** International Association for Greek Philosophy (#11925)
♦ **IAGP** International Association for Group Psychotherapy and Group Processes (#11926)
♦ **IAGR** International Association of Gaming Regulators (#11908)
♦ **IAGR** International Association for Gondwana Research (#11923)
♦ **IAGSA** International Airborne Geophysics Safety Association (#11606)
♦ **IAGSDC** International Association of Gay Square Dance Clubs (#11909)
♦ IAGS – International Association of Genocide Scholars (internationally oriented national body)
♦ **IAGSP** International Association for the Study of German Politics (#12200)
♦ **IAGTO** International Association of Golf Tour Operators (#11922)
♦ IAGU – Institut africain de gestion urbaine (internationally oriented national body)
♦ IAHA / see Airport Services Association (#00613)
♦ IAHA – Inter-American Hotel Association (no recent information)
♦ **IAHA** International Association of Historians of Asia (#11932)
♦ **IAHAIO** International Association of Human-Animal Interaction Organizations (#11944)
♦ **IAHB** International Association of Human Biologists (#11945)
♦ **IAHCCJ** International Association for the History of Crime and Criminal Justice (#11934)
♦ IAHC – International Association of Headwater Control (no recent information)
♦ IAHCSMM – International Association of Healthcare Central Service Material Management (internationally oriented national body)
♦ **IAHD** International Association for Handicapped Divers (#11928)
♦ IAHD – International Association of the History of Dentistry (no recent information)
♦ IAHECL – International Association of Humanist Educators, Counsellors and Leaders (inactive)
♦ IAHE – International Alliance of Healthcare Educators (internationally oriented national body)
♦ IAHE – International Association of Hotel Executives (internationally oriented national body)
♦ **IAHE** International Association for Hydrogen Energy (#11951)
♦ IAHF / see InterAmerican Heart Foundation (#11432)
♦ **IAHF** InterAmerican Heart Foundation (#11432)
♦ IAHF – International Amateur Handball Federation (inactive)
♦ iAHFME – International Association of Hospitality Financial Management Education (unconfirmed)
♦ IAHGM – International Association of Hotel General Managers (unconfirmed)
♦ IAHH – International Association for Humane Habitat (internationally oriented national body)
♦ IAHI / see IHG Owners Association (#11112)
♦ **IAH** International Association of Hydatidology (#11949)
♦ **IAH** International Association of Hydrogeologists (#11953)
♦ **IAH** Internationale Arbeitsgemeinschaft für Hymnologie (#13213)
♦ IAHLS – International Archaeology and Historical Linguistics Society (unconfirmed)
♦ **IAHM** International Association for Humanitarian Medicine Chisholm-Gunn (#11946)
♦ IAHMS – International Association of Hotel Management Schools (inactive)
♦ **IAHN** International Association for the History of Nephrology (#11935)
♦ IAHO – International Association for Hyperthermic Oncology (inactive)
♦ **IAHPC** International Association for Hospice and Palliative Care (#11941)
♦ **IAHPE** International Association of Health Policy in Europe (#11931)
♦ **IAHP** Institutes for Achievement of Human Potential (#11292)
♦ IAHP – International Association of Healthcare Practitioners (internationally oriented national body)
♦ **IAHP** International Association of Health Policy (#11930)
♦ IAHP / see International Association Interactions of Psychoanalysis (#11968)
♦ IAHPSTC / see Association of Sport Performance Centres (#02929)
♦ **IAHR** International Academy of Human Reproduction (#11551)
♦ **IAHR** International Association for the History of Religions (#11936)
♦ **IAHR** International Association for Hydro-Environment Engineering and Research (#11950)
♦ **IAHSA** International Association of Homes and Services for the Ageing (#11938)
♦ **IAHS** International Association of Hairdressing Schools (#11927)
♦ **IAHS** International Association for Housing Science (#11943)
♦ **IAHS** International Association for Hungarian Studies (#11948)
♦ **IAHS** International Association of Hydrological Sciences (#11954)
♦ **IAHSSJH** International Association of Historical Societies for the Study of Jewish History (#11933)
♦ IAHTI – International Association of Human Trafficking Investigators (internationally oriented national body)
♦ **IAHV** International Association for Human Values (#11947)
♦ IAI / see Ingénieurs assistance internationale
♦ IAIABC – International Association of Industrial Accident Boards and Commissions (internationally oriented national body)
♦ **IAIA** International Association for Impact Assessment (#11956)
♦ IAIA – International Association 'Interaction' – East-West Partnerships for a Better World (inactive)
♦ IAIAS / see Inter-American Institute for Cooperation on Agriculture (#11434)
♦ IAIB – International Association of Islamic Banks (no recent information)
♦ IAI / see buildingSMART International (#03353)
♦ **IAIC** International Arabidopsis Informatics Consortium (#11664)
♦ IAICM – International Association of Independent Corporate Monitors (internationally oriented national body)
♦ IAIDPA – International Association of Information and Documentation in Public Administration (inactive)
♦ IAIDQ / see Information Quality International (#11197)
♦ IAIE – International Association for Integrative Education (inactive)
♦ **IAIE** International Association for Intercultural Education (#11969)
♦ IAIFA – International Association of Insurance Fraud Agencies (no recent information)
♦ IAIGC / see Arab Investment and Export Credit Guarantee Corporation (#00997)
♦ IAI – Ibero-America Institute for Economic Research of the University of Göttingen (internationally oriented national body)
♦ IAI – Ibero-Amerikanisches Institut Preussischer Kulturbesitz (internationally oriented national body)
♦ **IAI** Institut africain d'informatique (#11235)
♦ **IAI** Inter-American Institute for Global Change Research (#11437)
♦ IAI – International Acupuncture Institute (internationally oriented national body)
♦ **IAI** International African Institute (#11596)
♦ IAI – International Alliance of Inhabitants (unconfirmed)
♦ **IAI** International Aluminium Institute (#11643)
♦ IAI – International Association for Identification (internationally oriented national body)
♦ IAI – International Automotive Institute (inactive)
♦ IAI / see International Biochar Initiative (#12342)
♦ IAI / see International Society of the Built Environment (#14985)
♦ IAI – Istituto Affari Internazionali, Roma (internationally oriented national body)
♦ IAIJ – International Association of Independent Journalists (internationally oriented national body)
♦ **IAIM** International Association of Infant Massage (#11962)
♦ IA – Inclusion Africa (unconfirmed)
♦ **IAIN** International Association of Institutes of Navigation (#11965)
♦ IA – Inter aide (internationally oriented national body)
♦ **IA** Interciencia Association (#11459)
♦ IA-IP – International Academy of Investigative Psychology (inactive)
♦ **IAIP** International Association of Individual Psychology (#11960)
♦ **IAIP** International Association Interactions of Psychoanalysis (#11968)
♦ **IAIR** International Association of Insolvency Regulators (#11964)
♦ IA – Irmãzinhas da Assunção (religious order)
♦ IA – Irrigation Association (internationally oriented national body)
♦ IAIS – Institute of Arab and Islamic Studies (internationally oriented national body)
♦ **IAIS** International Association of Inflammation Societies (#11963)
♦ **IAIS** International Association of Insurance Supervisors (#11966)
♦ IAIS – Internationale Allianz Iranischer Studenten (internationally oriented national body)
♦ IAIS – International Institute of Advanced Islamic Studies, Malaysia (internationally oriented national body)
♦ **IAITL** International Association of IT Lawyers (#11972)
♦ **IAITPTF** International Alliance of the Indigenous Tribal Peoples of the Tropical Forests (#11629)
♦ IAIW – Ibero-Amerika Institut für Wirtschaftsforschung der Universität Göttingen (internationally oriented national body)
♦ **IAJBS** International Association of Jesuit Business Schools (#11974)
♦ IAJC – Inter-American Juridical Committee (see: #17629)
♦ IAJFCM / see International Association of Youth and Family Judges and Magistrates (#12283)
♦ **IAJGS** International Association of Jewish Genealogical Societies (#11976)
♦ **IAJ** International Association of Judges (#11978)
♦ IAJLJ / see International Association of Jewish Lawyers and Jurists (#11977)
♦ IAJP – International Association for Japanese Philosophy (internationally oriented national body)
♦ **IAJS** International Association of Jaspers Societies (#11973)
♦ **IAJS** International Association of Jungian Studies (#11979)
♦ **IAJU** International Association of Jesuit Universities (#11975)
♦ IAK / see Institute of African Affairs, Hamburg
♦ IAKF / see International Traditional Federation of Karate (#15711)
♦ **IAK** Internationales Auschwitz-Komitee (#12297)
♦ **IAKM** International Association for the Karlstad Model (#11980)
♦ **IAKM** International Association for Knowledge Management (#11981)

IAKSA
11004

alphabetic sequence excludes
For the complete listing, see Yearbook Online at

♦ IAKSA – International Amateur Kickboxing Sport Association (inactive)
♦ **IAKS** Internationale Vereinigung Sport- und Freizeiteinrichtungen (#13319)
♦ IAL / see Institute of Latin America of the Russian Academy of Sciences
♦ IALA – International African Law Association (inactive)
♦ **IALA** International Association of Landscape Archaeology (#11985)
♦ **IALA** International Association of Marine Aids to Navigation and Lighthouse Authorities (#12013)
♦ IALA – International Auxiliary Language Association (inactive)
♦ **IALANA** International Association of Lawyers Against Nuclear Arms (#11994)
♦ **IALB** International Association Language and Business (#11987)
♦ **IALB** Internationale Akademie land- und hauswirtschaftlicher Beraterinnen und Berater (#13212)
♦ IALC / see Association internationale de la critique littéraire (#02679)
♦ **IALCCE** International Association for Life-Cycle Civil Engineering (#12001)
♦ IALC – International Arid Lands Consortium (internationally oriented national body)
♦ **IALC** International Association of Language Centres (#11988)
♦ IALC – International Association of Library Centres (inactive)
♦ **IALC** International Association of Lyceum Clubs (#12007)
♦ IALD – International Association of Lighting Designers (internationally oriented national body)
♦ IALEI / see International Network of Education Institutes (#14256)
♦ **IALE** International Association for Landscape Ecology (#11986)
♦ **IALFS** International Association of Law and Forensic Sciences (#11991)
♦ **IALHA** International Andalusian and Lusitano Horse Association (#11652)
♦ **IALHI** International Association of Labour History Institutions (#11982)
♦ **IALIC** International Association for Languages and Intercultural Communication (#11989)
♦ **IALI** International Association of Labour Inspection (#11983)
♦ IAL – Instituto de Latinoamérica de la Academia de Ciencias de Rusia (internationally oriented national body)
♦ **IAL** International Association of Legislation (#11998)
♦ **IAL** International Association for Lichenology (#12000)
♦ IAL / see International Society of Limnology (#15232)
♦ **IALJS** International Association for Literary Journalism Studies (#12003)
♦ IALL / see International Association for Language Learning Technology
♦ **IALL** International Academy of Linguistic Law (#11556)
♦ **IALL** International Association of Law Libraries (#11992)
♦ IALLT – International Association for Language Learning Technology (internationally oriented national body)
♦ **IALMH** International Academy of Law and Mental Health (#11554)
♦ **IALM** International Academy of Legal Medicine (#11555)
♦ **IALMS** International Academy of Laser Medicine and Surgery (#11553)
♦ **IALP** International Association of Logopedics and Phoniatrics (#12005)
♦ IALRI – International Association of Legal Research and Investigators (no recent information)
♦ **IALRW** International Association of Liberal Religious Women (#11999)
♦ **IALS** International Association for Ladakh Studies (#11984)
♦ **IALS** International Association of Law Schools (#11993)
♦ **IALS** International Association of Legal Science (#11997)
♦ **IALS** International Association of Linguistics Students (#12002)
♦ **IALS** International Association of Literary Semantics (#12004)
♦ IALSM – International Association for Laser and Sports Medicine (inactive)
♦ **IALSP** International Association of Language and Social Psychology (#11990)
♦ IALTA – International Alliance on Land Tenure and Administration (internationally oriented national body)
♦ IALTA – International Green Automotive Lightweight Technology Alliance (unconfirmed)
♦ IALU / see International Association of La Salle Universities (#12142)
♦ **IALU** International Association of La Salle Universities (#12142)
♦ IAMA – International Abstaining Motorists' Association (inactive)
♦ **IAMA** International Artist Managers' Association (#11673)
♦ IAMA – International Arts-Medicine Association (inactive)
♦ IAMA / see International Food and Agribusiness Management Association (#13619)
♦ IAMAM / see International Committee of Museums and Collections of Arms and Military History (#12790)
♦ IAMANEH – International Association for Maternal and Neonatal Health (inactive)
♦ IAMAP / see International Association of Meteorology and Atmospheric Sciences (#12031)
♦ IAMAP International Commission on Atmospheric Chemistry and Global Pollution / see International Commission on Atmospheric Chemistry and Global Pollution (#12664)
♦ IAMAP International Commission on Atmospheric Electricity / see International Commission on Atmospheric Electricity (#12665)
♦ IAMAP International Commission on Clouds and Precipitation / see International Commission on Clouds and Precipitation (#12672)
♦ IAMAP International Commission on the Meteorology of the Upper Atmosphere / see International Commission on Middle Atmosphere Science (#12704)
♦ IAMAP International Commission on Planetary Atmospheres and their Evolution / see International Commission on Planetary Atmospheres and their Evolution (#12715)
♦ IAMAP International Commission on Polar Meteorology / see International Commission on Polar Meteorology (#12718)
♦ IAMAP International Radiation Commission / see International Radiation Commission (#14684)
♦ **IAMAS** International Association of Meteorology and Atmospheric Sciences (#12031)
♦ IAMAS International Commission on Dynamical Meteorology / see International Commission on Dynamical Meteorology (#12679)
♦ IAMAS International Ozone Commission / see International Ozone Commission (#14495)
♦ IAMAT – International Association for Medical Assistance to Travellers (internationally oriented national body)
♦ IAMAW / see International Association of Machinists and Aerospace Workers
♦ IAMB / see Mediterranean Agronomic Institute of Bari (#16641)
♦ **IAM Bari** Institut agronomique méditerranéen de Bari (#16641)
♦ IAMBE – International Association of Medicine and Biology of the Environment (inactive)
♦ IAMB – International Antimilitarist Bureau Against War and Reaction (inactive)
♦ IAMC' / see AMC Institute
♦ **IAMC** Integrated Assessment Modeling Consortium (#11366)
♦ IAMCM – International Association for Mathematical and Computer Modelling and Scientific Computing (no recent information)
♦ **IAMCR** International Association for Media and Communication Research (#12022)
♦ **IAMCS** International Alliance of Messianic Congregations and Synagogues (#11631)
♦ **IAME** International Association of Maritime Economists (#12014)
♦ **IAMFA** International Association of Museum Facility Administrators (#12039)
♦ **IAMFE** International Association on Mechanization of Field Experiments (#12021)
♦ **IAMFN** Ibero-American Model Forest Network (#18659)
♦ IAMFS / see International College for Maxillo-Facial Surgery (#12645)
♦ IAMFSP – International Association of Military Flight Surgeon Pilots (no recent information)
♦ IAMG / see International Association for Mathematical Geosciences (#12017)
♦ **IAMG** International Association for Mathematical Geosciences (#12017)
♦ **IAMH** International Association of Museums of History (#12040)
♦ **IAMHIST** International Association for Media and History (#12023)
♦ **IAM** Iberoamerican Academy of Management (#11012)
♦ IAMIC – International Association for Museums and Collections of Musical Instruments (inactive)
♦ **IAMIC** International Association of Music Information Centres (#12041)
♦ IAMI – International Association of Marine Investigators (internationally oriented national body)
♦ **IAMI** International Association of Maritime Institutions (#12015)
♦ IAM – Institut Afrique Monde (internationally oriented national body)
♦ IAM – International Academy of Management (internationally oriented national body)
♦ IAM – International Association of Machinists and Aerospace Workers (internationally oriented national body)
♦ **IAM** International Association of Meiobenthologists (#12029)
♦ **IAM** International Association of Memory (#12030)
♦ IAM – International Association of Movers (internationally oriented national body)
♦ **IAM** International Association of Multilingualism (#12038)
♦ IAMLA / see International Association of Medical Regulatory Authorities (#12026)
♦ **IAmLearn** International Association for Mobile Learning (#12033)
♦ IAML / see International Academy of Family Lawyers (#11548)
♦ **IAML** International Association of Music Libraries, Archives and Documentation Centres (#12042)
♦ IAMLT / see International Federation of Biomedical Laboratory Science (#13372)
♦ **IAMM** International Association for Music and Medicine (#12043)
♦ **IAMMM** International Academy of Manual/Musculoskeletal Medicine (#11557)
♦ IAMNC / see World Winter Cities Association for Mayors (#21940)
♦ IAMO / see Leibniz-Institut für Agrarentwicklung in Transformationsökonomien
♦ IAMO – Leibniz-Institut für Agrarentwicklung in Transformationsökonomien (internationally oriented national body)
♦ IAMO – Leibniz Institute of Agricultural Development in Transition Economies (internationally oriented national body)
♦ **IAMOT** International Association for Management of Technology (#12010)
♦ **IAMP** International Association of Mathematical Physics (#12018)
♦ IAMP – International Association of Muslim Psychologists (unconfirmed)
♦ IAMPOV – International Symposium on Innovations and Applications of Monitoring Perfusion, Oxygenation and Ventilation (meeting series)
♦ **IAMRA** International Association of Medical Regulatory Authorities (#12026)
♦ **IAMRI** International Alliance of Marine-Related Institutions (#11630)
♦ IAMS / see International Union of Muslim Scholars
♦ IAMSCU – International Association of Methodist Schools, Colleges and Universities (internationally oriented national body)
♦ **IAMSE** International Association of Medical Science Educators (#12027)
♦ IAMS – International Airway Management Society (unconfirmed)
♦ **IAMS** International Association of Manichaean Studies (#12011)
♦ **IAMS** International Association for Media in Science (#12024)
♦ **IAMS** International Association for Mission Studies (#12032)
♦ **IAMS** International Association for Mongol Studies (#12035)
♦ IAMS / see International Union of Microbiological Societies (#15794)
♦ **IAMSLIC** International Association of Aquatic and Marine Science Libraries and Information Centers (#11707)
♦ IAM / see SOLIDAR (#19680)
♦ **IAMSR** International Association of Management, Spirituality & Religion (#12009)
♦ **IAMT** International Association for Machine Translation (#12008)
♦ IAMT – Internationale Assoziation für Medizintechnik (no recent information)
♦ **IAMTN** International Association of Money Transfer Networks (#12034)
♦ **IAMU** International Association of Maritime Universities (#12016)
♦ IAMV – Internationaler Anti-Militaristischer Verein (inactive)
♦ IAMWF – Inter-American Mine Workers Federation (inactive)
♦ IAM de Zaragoza / see Mediterranean Agronomic Institute of Zaragoza (#16644)
♦ **IAMZ** Instituto Agronómico Mediterraneo de Zaragoza (#16644)
♦ **IANA** International Academy on Nutrition and Aging (#11560)
♦ IANA – Internet Assigned Numbers Authority (internationally oriented national body)
♦ **IANAS** InterAmerican Network of Academies of Science (#11441)
♦ **IAN-BD** Iberoamerican Network for Bipolar Disorder (#11026)
♦ IANC – International Airline Navigators Council (inactive)
♦ **IANDS** International Association for Near-Death Studies (#12047)
♦ IANEC – Inter-American Nuclear Energy Commission (inactive)
♦ IANGEL – International Action Network for Gender Equity and Law (internationally oriented national body)
♦ IANGV / see NGV Global (#17131)
♦ IAN – International Affairs Network (inactive)
♦ **IAN** International Aquarium Network (#11661)
♦ **IAN** International Association for Neuropterology (#12049)
♦ **IAN** Internationals amis de la nature (#14780)
♦ **IANLS** International Association for Neo-Latin Studies (#12048)
♦ IANOS – International Assembly of National Organizations of Sport (inactive)
♦ **IANPHI** International Association of National Public Health Institutes (#12044)
♦ **IANP** International Association of Nature Pedagogy (#12046)
♦ IANR – International Association of Neurorestoratology (unconfirmed)
♦ **IANSA** International Action Network on Small Arms (#11585)
♦ **IANS** International Anal Neoplasia Society (#11649)
♦ IANVS – International Association for Non-Violent Sport (no recent information)
♦ **IANWGE** Inter-Agency Network on Women and Gender Equality (#11388)
♦ **IANYS** International Association for National Youth Service (#12045)
♦ **IAOA** International Association for Ontology and its Applications (#12055)
♦ **IAOCO** International Academy of Olympic Chiropractic Officers (#11561)
♦ IAOD – International Association of Opera Directors (inactive)
♦ **IAOE** International Association of Online Engineering (#12054)
♦ IAOHRA – International Association of Official Human Rights Agencies (internationally oriented national body)
♦ IAOIA / see International Antimony Association (#11657)
♦ IAOI – International Association of Organizational Innovation (internationally oriented national body)
♦ IAO – Institut d'Asie orientale (internationally oriented national body)
♦ **IAO** International Academy of Orthokeratology (#11564)
♦ **IAO** International Academy of Osteopathy (#11566)
♦ **IAO** International Association for Orthodontics (#12058)
♦ **IAO** Inter-Parliamentary Assembly on Orthodoxy (#15959)
♦ IAO – Istituto Agronomico per l'Oltremare, Italy (internationally oriented national body)
♦ **IAOLE** International Association of Legal Ethics (#11995)
♦ IAOL – International Association of Orientalist Librarians (inactive)
♦ IAOMC / see International Academy of Orthokeratology (#11564)
♦ IAOMC – International Association of Medical Colleges (no recent information)
♦ **IAOMED** International Academy of Orthopedic Medicine (#11565)
♦ **IAOM** International Academy of Oral Medicine (#11562)
♦ IAOM – International Academy of Osteopathic Medicine (inactive)
♦ IAOM – International Association of Operative Millers (internationally oriented national body)
♦ IAOMO – International Association of Olympic Medical Officers (inactive)
♦ **IAOMS** International Association of Oral and Maxillofacial Surgeons (#12057)
♦ IAOMT – International Academy of Oral Medicine and Toxicology (internationally oriented national body)
♦ **IAOO** International Academy of Oral Oncology (#11563)
♦ **IAOPA** International Council of Aircraft Owner and Pilot Associations (#12988)

- **IAOP** International Association of Oral and Maxillofacial Pathologists (#12056)
- **IAOP** International Association of Outsourcing Professionals (#12062)
- IAOPN – International Association for the Optimization of Plant Nutrition (inactive)
- **IAOSEH** International Association for Ottoman Social and Economic History (#12061)
- **IAOS** International Association for Obsidian Studies (#12051)
- **IAOS** International Association for Official Statistics (#12052)
- IAOUG – European Association of Underwater Games (inactive)
- **IAP2** International Association for Public Participation (#12117)
- **IAP3** / see International Association for Public Participation (#12117)

♦ IAPA 11005
CEO 120 Moorgate, London, EC2M 6UR, UK. T. +441252267880. E-mail: admin@iapa.net.
URL: http://www.iapa.net/
History 1979. Former names and other names: *International Association for Practising Accountants (IAPA)* – former; *International Association of Professional Accountants (IAPA)* – former; *IAPA International* – alias. Registration: Companies House, No/ID: 05166917, Start date: 30 Jun 2004, England and Wales. **Aims** Support members in providing clients with a diverse range of professional, comprehensive and cost-effective business solutions, regardless of sector or location. **Structure** International Board; Executive Board; Regional Boards. **Languages** English. **Staff** 3.00 FTE, paid. **Finance** Sources: members' dues. **Activities** Events/meetings; guidance/assistance/consulting. Active in all member countries. **Events** *Global Conference* London (UK) 2022, *International Conference* London (UK) 2020, *Europe, Middle East and Africa Regional Conference* Palma (Spain) 2019, *International Conference* Singapore (Singapore) 2019, *International Conference* Miami, FL (USA) 2018. **Publications** *IAPA Newsletter*. Tax bulletins; promotional materials. **Members** Independent accounting, audit, tax, legal, advisory, financial, immigration and technology services firms (over 200) in over 75 countries. Membership countries not specified. **NGO Relations** Member of (2): *Association of International Law Firm Networks (AILFN, #02753); European Group of International Accounting Networks and Associations (EGIAN, #07426)*.
[2022.11.01/XD6823/**D**]

- IAPAC / see International Association of Providers of AIDS Care
- IAPAC – International Association of Providers of AIDS Care (internationally oriented national body)
- **IAPAE** International Academy of Physician Associate Educators (#11571)
- IAP / see African Private Equity and Venture Capital Association (#00425)
- IAPA / see IAPA (#11005)
- **IAPA** Inter American Press Association (#11444)
- IAPA International / see IAPA (#11005)
- **IAPA** International Airline Passengers Association (#11609)
- **IAPA** International Association of Physicians in Audiology (#12084)
- **IAPA** International Association of Physiological Anthropology (#12086)
- IAPA – International Association of Professional Advisers (inactive)
- **IAPA** International Au Pair Association (#14500)
- IAPAO – International Association of Performance Art Organizers (no recent information)
- **IAPB** International Agency for the Prevention of Blindness (#11597)
- **IAPB** International Association of Plant Biotechnology (#12090)
- **IAPBT** International Association of Piano Builders and Technicians (#12088)
- IAPCC – International Association of Private Career Colleges (unconfirmed)
- IAPCD – International Association for Pain and Chemical Dependency (inactive)
- IAPCHE / see International Network for Christian Higher Education (#14241)
- **IAPC** International Association of Political Consultants (#12094)
- **IAPC** International Association of Press Clubs (#12099)
- IAPC / see International Auditing and Assurance Standards Board (#12296)
- IAPC – Internationaler Aero-Philatelisten Club (internationally oriented national body)
- **IAPCO** International Association of Professional Congress Organisers (#12103)
- **IAPCS** International Association for Phenomenology and the Cognitive Sciences (#12077)
- IAPD / see International Association of Plastics Distribution
- IAPD / see Hearing International (#10895)
- **IAPD** International Association of Paediatric Dentistry (#12064)
- IAPD – International Association for Participatory Development (internationally oriented national body)
- IAPD – International Association of Plastics Distribution (internationally oriented national body)
- IAPDM – International Association of Professionals in Disability Management (unconfirmed)
- **IAPDO** International Alliance of Dermatology Patient Organizations (#11626)
- **IAPESGW** International Association of Physical Education and Sport for Girls and Women (#12081)
- IAPES / see International Association of Workforce Professionals (#12278)
- **IAPF** International Anti-Poaching Foundation (#11658)
- **IAPF** International Association of Peace Foundations (#12071)
- IAPFoN – International Association for the Psychology of Food and Nutrition (inactive)
- **IAPG** International Aquatic Plants Group (#11663)
- **IAPG** International Association for Promoting Geoethics (#12107)
- IAPHC – International Association of Printing House Craftsmen (internationally oriented national body)
- **IAPH** International Association of Ports and Harbors (#12096)
- **IAPh** Internationale Assoziation von Philosophinnen (#12269)
- IAPHLSR / see Healthcare and Biological Sciences Research Association
- **IAP** InterAcademy Partnership (#11376)
- **IAP** International Academy of Pathology (#11567)
- IAP – International Accountability Project (internationally oriented national body)
- **IAP** International Association of Pancreatology (#12065)
- **IAP** International Association of Phonosurgery (#12080)
- **IAP** International Association of Phytoplankton Taxonomy and Ecology (#12087)
- IAP – International Association of Planetology (inactive)
- IAP – International Association of Police (internationally oriented national body)
- **IAP** International Association of Prosecutors (#12111)
- IAP – International Association of Pteridologists (no recent information)
- IAPIP / see International Association for the Protection of Intellectual Property (#12112)
- **IAPL** International Association of Penal Law (#12074)
- **IAPL** International Association of People's Lawyers (#12076)
- **IAPL** International Association of Practising Lawyers (#12097)
- **IAPL** International Association for Procedural Law (#12102)
- **IAPLL** International Association for the Psychology of Language Learning (#12115)
- **IAPMA** International Association of Hand Papermakers and Paper Artists (#11929)
- **IAPMC** International Association of Peace Messenger Cities (#12073)
- **IAPMD** International Association For Premenstrual Disorders (#12098)
- **IAPM** International Academy of Perinatal Medicine (#11568)
- IAPM – International Association of Medical Prosthesis Manufacturers (inactive)
- IAPMO – International Association of Plumbing and Mechanical Officials (internationally oriented national body)
- **IAPN** International Association of Professional Numismatists (#12104)
- **IAPO** Interamerican Association of Pediatric Otorhinolaryngology (#11399)
- **IAPO** International Alliance of Patients' Organizations (#11633)
- IAPO / see International Association for the Physical Sciences of the Oceans (#12082)
- IAPOP – International Association of Process Oriented Psychology (unconfirmed)
- IAPP / see Academy of Criminal Justice Sciences
- IAPP – International Association for Plant Physiologists (inactive)
- IAPP – International Association of Privacy Professionals (internationally oriented national body)
- IAPP – Internationale Akademie für Positive und Transkulturelle Psychotherapie (internationally oriented national body)
- **IAPPP** International Amateur-Professional Photoelectric Photometry (#11645)
- IAPPP / see International Association for Public Participation (#12117)
- **IAPPS** International Association for the Plant Protection Sciences (#12091)
- **IAPRD** International Association of Parkinsonism and Related Disorders (#12068)
- **IAPRI** International Association of Packaging Research Institutes (#12063)
- **IAPR** International Association for Pattern Recognition (#12069)
- **IAPR** International Association for the Psychology of Religion (#12116)
- IAPR – International Association for Psychotronic Research (no recent information)
- **IAPSAM** International Association for Probabilistic Safety Assessment and Management (#12101)
- **IAPSAS** International Association for Protein Structure Analysis and Proteomics (#12114)
- **IAPSC** International Association of Pipe Smokers Clubs (#12089)
- IAPSF / see Association of Pension and Social Funds of the CIS (#02856)
- **I-APS** Inter-American Photochemical Society (#11443)
- **IAPS** International Academy of Philosophy of Sciences (#11570)
- **IAPS** International Association of Patristic Studies (#02692)
- **IAPS** International Association for People-Environment Studies (#12075)
- **IAPS** International Association for the Philosophy of Sport (#12078)
- **IAPS** International Association of Physics Students (#12085)
- IAPS / see International Association for the Properties of Water and Steam (#12110)
- **IAPS** International Association of Protective Structures (#12113)
- IAPS – International Association of Social Scientists, Architects and Planners (inactive)
- **IAPSIT** International Association of Professionals in Sugar and Integrated Technologies (#12105)
- **IAPSO** International Association for the Physical Sciences of the Oceans (#12082)
- **IAPSS** International Association for Political Science Students (#12095)
- IAPTC and B / see International Association of Plant Biotechnology (#12090)
- **IAPTC** International Association of Peacekeeping Training Centres (#12072)
- IAPTC / see International Association of Plant Biotechnology (#12090)
- **IAPTI** International Association of Professional Translators and Interpreters (#12106)
- **IAPT** International Association for the Philosophy of Time (#12079)
- **IAPT** International Association for Plant Taxonomy (#12092)
- IAPUP / see Human Rights in Mental Health (#10988)
- **IAPWE** International Association for the Promotion of Women of Europe (#12109)
- IAPWO – International Association of Public Works Officials (inactive)
- **IAPWS** International Association for the Properties of Water and Steam (#12110)
- **IAQG** International Aerospace Quality Group (#11594)
- **IAQ** International Academy for Quality (#11573)
- **IAQMS** International Academy of Molecular Quantum Sciences (#11558)
- IAQVEC – International Conference on Indoor Air Quality, Ventilation and Energy Conservation in Buildings (meeting series)
- IAR / see Asia Research Institute
- IARA – Institute for Anthropological Research in Africa (internationally oriented national body)
- IARA – Inter-Allied Reparations Agency (inactive)
- **IARA** International Aerosol Research Assembly (#11593)
- **IARA** International Association of Rebekah Assemblies (#12123)
- **IARAN** Inter-Agency Research and Analysis Network (#11391)
- **IARCA** Iglesia Anglicana de la Region Central de América (#11108)
- IARCA / see International Community Corrections Association (#12822)
- **IARC** International Agency for Research on Cancer (#11598)
- IARC – International Amateur Radio Club (internationally oriented national body)
- IARC – International Aphasia Rehabilitation Conference (meeting series)
- IARC / see International Approval and Registration Centre (#11660)
- **IARC** International Approval and Registration Centre (#11660)
- IARC – International Automobile Recycling Congress (meeting series)

♦ IARC Staff Association 11006
Contact c/o IARC Secretariat, 150 Cours Albert Thomas, 69372 Lyon CEDEX 08, France. T. +33472738485. Fax +33472738575. E-mail: staffassociation@iarc.fr.
History 1968, to represent staff members of *International Agency for Research on Cancer (IARC, #11598)*. **Aims** Safeguard the collective and individual rights and interests of staff members. **Structure** Annual General Assembly; Committee of Staff Association; Auditor. **Languages** English, French. **Staff** As of Dec 2005: 136 fixed-term; 65 short-term. **Finance** Members' dues. Contributions. **Members** Individuals (201) in 17 countries. Membership countries not specified. **NGO Relations** Close cooperation with: *Federation of International Civil Servants' Associations (FICSA, #09603)*. Also collaborates closely with WHO staff associations: *Association of Former WHO Staff Members (AFSM, #02604); Staff Association of the WHO Regional Office for Africa (no recent information); WHO Eastern Mediterranean Region Staff Association, Cairo (EMRSA, no recent information); WHO-HQ Staff Association, Geneva (WHO-HQ SA, #20938); WHO Staff Association for South-East Asia Region (no recent information); WHO/WPR Staff Association (no recent information)*.
[2012/XE2196/v/**E**]

- **IARD** International Alliance for Responsible Drinking (#11638)
- **IARD** International Association for Relativistic Dynamics (#12128)
- **IAREP** International Association for Research in Economic Psychology (#12132)
- **IARF** International Association for Religious Freedom (#12130)
- IARF / see International Racquetball Federation (#14683)
- IARHH – International Association for Research in Hospital Hygiene (no recent information)
- **IARIGAI** International Association of Research Organizations for the Information, Media and Graphic Arts Industries (#12136)
- **IAR** Institut africain de réadaptation (#00437)
- IAR – Institute of Asian Research, Vancouver BC (internationally oriented national body)
- IAR – International Animal Rescue (internationally oriented national body)
- **IAR** International Association of Radiopharmacology (#12121)
- IAR – International Authority for the Ruhr (inactive)
- **IARIW** International Association for Research in Income and Wealth (#12134)
- **IARJ** International Association of Religion Journalists (#12129)
- **IARLA** International Alliance of Research Library Associations (#11636)
- **IARLD** International Academy for Research in Learning Disabilities (#11574)
- IARLJ / see International Association of Refugee and Migration Judges (#12126)
- **IARM** International Association of Ropeway Manufacturers (#12139)
- **IARM** International Association of Rural Health and Medicine (#12140)
- **IARMJ** International Association of Refugee and Migration Judges (#12126)
- **IARMM** International Association of Risk Management in Medicine (#12138)
- IARNSC – International Association for the Rights of Needy and Suffering Children (internationally oriented national body)
- **IARO** International Air Rail Organization (#11612)
- IARO – International Autistic Research Organization (inactive)
- **IARP** International Advanced Robotics Programme (#11589)
- IARPP – International Association for Relational Psychoanalysis and Psychotherapy (internationally oriented national body)
- **IARR** International Association for Radiation Research (#12119)
- **IARR** International Association for Relationship Research (#12127)
- IARSAF – International Association of Research Fellows and Scholars (internationally oriented national body)
- IARS – Institute of African Research and Studies, University of Cairo (internationally oriented national body)
- IARS – International Anesthesia Research Society (internationally oriented national body)
- **IARS** International Association for Reconciliation Studies (#12124)

- ♦ IARSTL – International Association of Research, Scientific and Technical Libraries (inactive)
- ♦ IARTC – International Academic Research and Technology Center (internationally oriented national body)
- ♦ **IARTEM** International Association for Research on Textbooks and Educational Media (#12137)
- ♦ **IARU** International Alliance of Research Universities (#11637)
- ♦ **IARU** International Amateur Radio Union (#11646)
- ♦ IARUS – International Association for Regional and Urban Statistics (inactive)
- ♦ **IARW** International Association of Refrigerated Warehouses (#12125)
- ♦ IAS / see Institute of Economic and Social Research
- ♦ IAS / see International Aid Services
- ♦ IAS / see GIGA Institut für Asien-Studien
- ♦ IASA / see Alliance for Sustainability
- ♦ IASAA – International Agricultural Students Association of the Americas (inactive)
- ♦ Iasa Global (internationally oriented national body)
- ♦ IASA – Ibero-American Society for Anatomy (inactive)
- ♦ IASAIL / see International Association for the Study of Irish Literatures (#12201)
- ♦ IASA – International Administrative Science Association (internationally oriented national body)
- ♦ IASA – International Air Safety Association (inactive)
- ♦ **IASA** International Air and Shipping Association (#11613)
- ♦ **IASA** International American Studies Association (#11648)
- ♦ IASA – International Association of Schools in Advertising (inactive)
- ♦ **IASA** International Association of Sound and Audiovisual Archives (#12172)
- ♦ IASA – International Association for the Study of Antisemitism (inactive)
- ♦ IASA – International Association for Sustainable Aviation (internationally oriented national body)
- ♦ **IASAJ** International Association of Supreme Administrative Jurisdictions (#12215)

♦ IAS Asia Pacific Federation 11007

SG c/o Natl Center for Geriatrics and Gerontology, 7-430 Morioka-cho, Obu AICHI, Japan. T. +81562462311. Fax +81562870115. E-mail: ias_ap@j-athero.or.jp.
Chair Fac of Medicine, Macau Univ of Science and Technology, Avda Wai Long, Taipa, Macau. T. +85388972415. Fax +85328825057.
URL: http://www.athero.org/asia.asp/

History as a regional federation of *International Atherosclerosis Society (IAS, #12288)*. Also referred to as *Asia-Pacific Federation of the International Atherosclerosis Society* and *International Atherosclerosis Society Regional Federation for Alia-Pacific*. **Aims** Promote scientific understanding of the etiology, prevention and treatment of *atherosclerosis* in the region. **Structure** Board. **Languages** English. **Staff** 1.00 FTE, voluntary. **Finance** Corporate donations. **Activities** Awards/prizes/ceremonies; knowledge management/information dissemination; training/education; events/meetings.
Members Full in 6 countries and territories:
Australia, China, Japan, Korea Rep, Philippines, Taiwan. [2019.12.12/XJ2103/**E**]

- ♦ **IASAS** International Association of Student Affairs and Services (#12189)
- ♦ **IASB** International Accounting Standards Board (#11583)
- ♦ IASB – International Association of Speakers Bureaus (internationally oriented national body)
- ♦ IASBM – International Association of Surgical Blade Manufacturers (inactive)
- ♦ **IASBS** International Association of Shin Buddhist Studies (#12163)
- ♦ **IASCA** International Arab Society of Certified Accountants (#11665)
- ♦ **IASCA Worldwide** International Auto Sound Challenge Association (#12302)
- ♦ IASC Foundation' / see International Accounting Standards Board (#11583)
- ♦ IASC Foundation / see International Financial Reporting Standards Foundation (#13603)
- ♦ **IASC** Inter-Agency Standing Committee (#11393)
- ♦ IASC – Inter-American Safety Council (no recent information)
- ♦ IASC – Inter-American Society for Chemotherapy (no recent information)
- ♦ IASC / see International Accounting Standards Board (#11583)
- ♦ **IASC** International Arctic Science Committee (#11668)
- ♦ IASC – International Association of Seed Crushers (inactive)
- ♦ **IASC** International Association for Statistical Computing (#12183)
- ♦ IASC / see International Association for Structural Control and Monitoring (#12186)
- ♦ **IASC** International Association for the Study of the Commons (#12195)
- ♦ **IASC** International Association for the Study of Controversies (#12196)
- ♦ **IASC** International Association of Supercomputing Centers (#12214)
- ♦ **IASCL** International Association for the Study of Child Language (#12194)
- ♦ **IASCM** International Association for Structural Control and Monitoring (#12186)
- ♦ IASCP / see International Association for the Study of the Commons (#12195)
- ♦ **IASCUD** International Association for Science and Cultural Diversity (#12150)
- ♦ **IASCYS** International Academy for Systems and Cybernetic Sciences (#11578)
- ♦ IASD – Interafricaine socialiste et démocratique (inactive)
- ♦ **IASD** International Association for the Study of Dreams (#12197)
- ♦ **IASDR** International Association of Societies of Design Research (#12170)
- ♦ IASEE – International Association for Solar Energy Education (inactive)
- ♦ **IASE** International Association for Special Education (#12174)
- ♦ **IASE** International Association of Sport Economists (#12177)
- ♦ **IASE** International Association for Statistics Education (#12184)
- ♦ IASEM – International Association of Structural Engineering and Mechanics (internationally oriented national body)
- ♦ IASEN – International Association of Specialists in Energy (no recent information)
- ♦ **IASFCP** International Association for the Study of Fossil Cnidaria and Porifera (#12199)
- ♦ **IASFM** International Association for the Study of Forced Migration (#12198)
- ♦ IAS – GIGA Institut für Asien-Studien (internationally oriented national body)
- ♦ IAS – GIGA Institute for Asian Studies (internationally oriented national body)
- ♦ IASG / see International Association of Surgeons, Gastroenterologists and Oncologists (#12216)
- ♦ **IASGO** International Association of Surgeons, Gastroenterologists and Oncologists (#12216)
- ♦ IASHGNA – Ibero-American Society of Human Genetics of North America (internationally oriented national body)
- ♦ **IASH** Inter-American Society of Hypertension (#11449)
- ♦ **IASH** International Association for Small Hydro (#12165)
- ♦ **IASH** International Association for Stability, Handling and Use of Liquid Fuels (#12182)
- ♦ **IASIA** International Association of Schools and Institutes of Administration (#12147)
- ♦ **IASI** Inter-American Statistical Institute (#11452)
- ♦ **IASI** International Association for Sports Information (#12179)
- ♦ **IASIL** International Association for the Study of Irish Literatures (#12201)
- ♦ **IASIM** International Association for Spectral Imaging (#12176)
- ♦ IAS – Initiative pour une Afrique solidaire (internationally oriented national body)
- ♦ IAS – Institute of African Studies at Columbia University, New York (internationally oriented national body)
- ♦ IAS – Institute of African Studies, Rabat (internationally oriented national body)
- ♦ IAS – Institute for African Studies, University of Bayreuth (internationally oriented national body)
- ♦ IAS – Institute of Andean Studies (internationally oriented national body)
- ♦ IAS – Institute of Asian Studies, Bangkok (internationally oriented national body)
- ♦ IAS – Institute for Asian Studies, Madras (internationally oriented national body)
- ♦ IAS – Instituto Andino de Sistemas (internationally oriented national body)
- ♦ **IAS** Intelligent Autonomous Systems Society (#11373)
- ♦ **IAS** International Abalone Society (#11529)
- ♦ IAS – International Acupuncture Society (internationally oriented national body)
- ♦ **IAS** International Adsorption Society (#11588)
- ♦ IAS – International Aid Services (internationally oriented national body)
- ♦ **IAS** International AIDS Society (#11601)
- ♦ **IAS** International Allelopathy Society (#11618)
- ♦ **IAS** International Aroid Society (#11670)
- ♦ **IAS** International Arthurian Society (#11671)
- ♦ IAS – International Association of Scientologists (see: #03922)
- ♦ **IAS** International Association of Sedimentologists (#12155)
- ♦ IAS / see International Association of Seismology and Physics of the Earth's Interior (#12157)
- ♦ IAS – International Association of Somatotherapy (no recent information)
- ♦ **IAS** International Association of Sufism (#12212)
- ♦ **IAS** International Atherosclerosis Society (#12288)
- ♦ **IAS** International Avocado Society (#12304)
- ♦ **IAS** Internationaler Arbeitskreis Sicherheit beim Skilauf (#15443)
- ♦ **IASIS** International Association for Student Insurance Services (#12190)
- ♦ **IAS** Islamic World Academy of Sciences (#16057)
- ♦ IASIT – International Association of Safe Injection Technology (inactive)
- ♦ **IASJ** International Association of Schools of Jazz (#12148)
- ♦ **IASK** International Association of Specialized Kinesiologists (#12175)
- ♦ **IASK** International Association of Sport Kinetics (#12178)
- ♦ **IASL** Associació Internacional del Dret de l'Esport (#12180)
- ♦ **IASLC** International Association for the Study of Lung Cancer (#12204)
- ♦ IASL – Institute of Air and Space Law, Montréal (internationally oriented national body)
- ♦ **IASL** International Association of School Librarianship (#12146)
- ♦ IASL – International Association for the Semiotics of Law (inactive)
- ♦ **IASL** International Association of Sports Law (#12180)
- ♦ **IASL** International Association for the Study of the Liver (#12203)
- ♦ **IASMEN** International Association for Surgical Metabolism and Nutrition (#12217)
- ♦ **IASMiRT** International Association for Structural Mechanics in Reactor Technology (#12187)
- ♦ **IASMM** International Association for the Study of Maritime Mission (#12205)
- ♦ **IASN** Iberoamerican Society of Neonatology (#11031)
- ♦ **IASNR** International Association for Society and Natural Resources (#12171)
- ♦ IASOC – International Association for the Study of Organized Crime (internationally oriented national body)
- ♦ **IASO** Ibero-American Stroke Organization (#19365)
- ♦ IASOM – International Association for Studies of Men (no recent information)
- ♦ IASO / see World Obesity (#21678)
- ♦ IASP / see Inter-American Society of Psychology (#11450)

♦ IASPEI/IAVCEI Commission on Volcano Seismology 11008

Co-Chair School of Earth Sciences, Univ of Leeds, Leeds, LS2 9JT, UK. T. +441133436769. Fax +441132335259. E-mail: locko@earth.leeds.ac.uk.
Co-Chair Natl Research Inst for Earth Science and Disaster Prevention, 3-1 Tennodai, Tsukuba-shi, Ibaraki OSAKA, 305 Japan. T. +81298637606. Fax +81298540629.
URL: http://www.iavcei.org/

History Jul 1995, Boulder CO (USA), at XXI General Assembly of *International Union of Geodesy and Geophysics (IUGG, #15776)*, as a joint commission of *International Association of Seismology and Physics of the Earth's Interior (IASPEI, #12157)* and *International Association of Volcanology and Chemistry of the Earth's Interior (IAVCEI, #12259)*. Also referred to as *IASPEI/IAVCEI Joint Committee on Volcano Seismology*. **Aims** Promote volcano seismology as a tool to gain a better understanding of the dynamics of explosive volcanoes and improve the ability to predict their behaviour; facilitate collaborations among scientists and institutions investigating volcanic processes and structures; facilitate the transfer of knowledge, tools and training between scientists and volcano observatories, especially in developing countries; promote the use of state-of-the-art seismic equipment, such as broadband sensors and high dynamic range date-loggers, in routine volcanic monitoring and seismic experiments; promote conferences, seminars and high-level education aimed at familiarizing researchers with modern theoretical and experimental seismic methods used in the interpretation of volcanic processes and structures; promote funding from international organizations. **Events** *Symposium on Volcano Seismology* Birmingham (UK) 1999, *Symposium on Volcano Seismology* Puerto Vallarta (Mexico) 1997, *Symposium on Volcano Seismology* Thessaloniki (Greece) 1997. [2018/XE2832/v/**E**]

- ♦ IASPEI-IAVCEI Inter-Association Commission on Physical and Chemical Properties of Materials of the Earth's Interior / see IASPEI/IAVCEI Joint Commission on Physics and Chemistry of Earth Materials (#11009)

♦ IASPEI/IAVCEI Joint Commission on Physics and Chemistry of Earth Materials 11009

Chair IASPEI HPSTAR and CeSMEC, Florida Intl Univ, 11200 SW 8th St, Miami FL 33174, USA.
Co-Chair IAVCEI Bayerisches Geoinstitut, Univ of Bayreuth, Universitätsstr 30, 95447 Bayreuth, Germany.
Co-Chair IAGA Scripps Inst of Oceanography, Inst of Geophysics and Planetary Physics, La Jolla CA 92093, USA.
URL: http://www.iaspei.org/commissions/CPCEM.html

History Founded 1996, as a joint commission of *International Association of Seismology and Physics of the Earth's Interior (IASPEI, #12157)* and *International Association of Volcanology and Chemistry of the Earth's Interior (IAVCEI, #12259)*, replacing *IASPEI Commission on Physical and Chemical Properties of Materials of the Earth's Interior (inactive)*. Previously also referred to as *IASPEI-IAVCEI Inter-Association Commission on Physical and Chemical Properties of Materials of the Earth's Interior*. Previously also co-chaired by *International Association of Geomagnetism and Aeronomy (IAGA, #11916)*. **Aims** Encourage and facilitate both experimental and theoretical interdisciplinary research and discussion on the nature and dynamics of the Earth's interior; further understanding of the planet's evolution since creation, notably through characterization of the nature and dynamics of materials, melts and magmas that make up the interior; further appreciation of geophysical and geochemical measurements and the uncertainties in them so as to facilitate informed application of the constraints they impose in models developed in *geophysics*, *geochemistry*, *petrology* and *volcanology*. **Structure** Small committee of volunteers organizes symposia at appropriate scientific meetings, comprising Chair Co-Chairs and association representatives form IAGA, IAVCEI and IASPEI. **Languages** English. **Staff** Part-time, voluntary. **Finance** Variable funding from: *International Association of Seismology and Physics of the Earth's Interior (IASPEI, #12157)*; *International Association of Geomagnetism and Aeronomy (IAGA, #11916)*; *International Association of Volcanology and Chemistry of the Earth's Interior (IAVCEI, #12259)*. **Activities** Events/meetings. **Publications** Symposium proceedings; meeting reports.
Members Individuals in 11 countries:
Australia, Canada, China, France, Germany, Italy, Japan, Poland, Russia, UK, USA. [2017.01.23/XE2723/v/**E**]

- ♦ IASPEI/IAVCEI Joint Committee on Volcano Seismology / see IASPEI/IAVCEI Commission on Volcano Seismology (#11008)
- ♦ **IASPEI** International Association of Seismology and Physics of the Earth's Interior (#12157)
- ♦ IASP – International Association of Safety Professionals (internationally oriented national body)
- ♦ IASP – International Association of Scholarly Publishers (inactive)
- ♦ IASP / see International Association of Science Parks and Areas of Innovation (#12151)
- ♦ **IASP** International Association of Science Parks and Areas of Innovation (#12151)
- ♦ IASP – International Association for Scottish Philosophy (internationally oriented national body)
- ♦ IASP – International Association for Social Progress (inactive)
- ♦ IASP – International Association of Spiritual Psychiatry (inactive)
- ♦ **IASP** International Association for the Study of Pain (#12206)
- ♦ IASP – International Association for the Study of Peace and Prejudice (no recent information)
- ♦ **IASP** International Association for Suicide Prevention and Crisis Intervention (#12213)
- ♦ IASPM – International Association of Scientific Paper Makers (inactive)
- ♦ **IASPM** International Association for the Study of Popular Music (#12207)
- ♦ **IASPN** Inter-American Social Protection Network (#11447)
- ♦ IASPPV – International Association of Former Soviet Political Prisoners and Victims of the Communist Regime (internationally oriented national body)

- ♦ **IASPRR** International Association of Sexual Plant Reproduction Research (#12161)
- ♦ IASPS / see Bernoulli Society for Mathematical Statistics and Probability (#03212)
- ♦ **IASQ** International Association on Social Quality (#12168)
- ♦ **IASRB** International Atlantic Salmon Research Board (#12292)
- ♦ **IASRG** International Association of Sleep Research in Gerontology (#12164)
- ♦ **IASR** International Academy of Sex Research (#11575)
- ♦ **IASR** International Academy of Suicide Research (#11577)
- ♦ IASR – International Association for the Study of Racism (inactive)
- ♦ **IASSA** International Arctic Social Sciences Association (#11669)
- ♦ IASSA – Investment Analysts Society of Southern Africa (internationally oriented national body)
- ♦ IASS-AIS / see International Association for Semiotic Studies (#12160)
- ♦ **IASS-AIS** International Association for Semiotic Studies (#12160)
- ♦ **IASSAR** International Association for Structural Safety and Reliability (#12188)
- ♦ IASSCS – International Association for the Study of Sexuality, Culture and Society (inactive)
- ♦ **IASSIDD** International Association for the Scientific Study of Intellectual and Developmental Disabilities (#12153)
- ♦ IASSID / see International Association for the Scientific Study of Intellectual and Developmental Disabilities (#12153)
- ♦ IASS – International Academy of Social Sciences (unconfirmed)
- ♦ IASS – International Adam Smith Society (internationally oriented national body)
- ♦ **IASS** International Association of Sanskrit Studies (#12143)
- ♦ **IASS** International Association for Scandinavian Studies (#12145)
- ♦ **IASS** International Association for Shell and Spatial Structures (#12162)
- ♦ **IASS** International Association of Survey Statisticians (#12218)
- ♦ **IASSIST** International Association for Social Science Information Service and Technology (#12169)
- ♦ **IASSL** International Association for the Study of Scottish Literatures (#12208)
- ♦ IASSMD / see International Association for the Scientific Study of Intellectual and Developmental Disabilities (#12153)
- ♦ IASSP / see International Association for the Semiotics of Space and Time (#12159)
- ♦ **IASSp+T** International Association for the Semiotics of Space and Time (#12159)
- ♦ **IASST** International Association for Safety and Survival Training (#12141)
- ♦ **IASSW** International Association of Schools of Social Work (#12149)
- ♦ IAST / see International Academy for the Study of Tourism (#11576)
- ♦ **IASTAM** International Association for the Study of Traditional Asian Medicine (#12209)
- ♦ IASTAR-Europe – International Association of Student Television and Radio (no recent information)
- ♦ IASTBI – International Association for the Study of Traumatic Brain Injury (inactive)
- ♦ **IASTE** International Association for the Study of Traditional Environments (#12210)
- ♦ IASTG – International Association of Structural / Tectonic Geologists (inactive)
- ♦ **IAST** International Association to Save Tyre (#12144)
- ♦ IAST – International Association for Social Tourism (no recent information)
- ♦ **IASUHM** Ibero-American Association for School and University Health and Medicine (#11017)
- ♦ IAS-UN – Institute for Advanced Studies on the United Nations (internationally oriented national body)
- ♦ **IASWECE** International Association for Steiner/Waldorf Early Childhood Education (#12185)
- ♦ IASWG – International Association for Social Work with Groups (unconfirmed)
- ♦ **IASWS** International Association for Sediment Water Science (#12156)
- ♦ IASWS – International Association of Severe Weather Specialists (no recent information)
- ♦ **IASYM** International Association for the Study of Youth Ministry (#12211)
- ♦ IATAFI – International Association for Technology Assessment and Forecasting Institutions (inactive)
- ♦ **IATA** International Air Transport Association (#11614)
- ♦ IATAN – International Airlines Travel Agent Network (internationally oriented national body)
- ♦ IATAS – International Academy of Television Arts and Sciences (internationally oriented national body)
- ♦ **IATBLT** International Association for Task-Based Language Teaching (#12220)
- ♦ **IATBR** International Association for Travel Behaviour Research (#12240)
- ♦ IATCA / see International Personnel Certification Association (#14560)
- ♦ IATC / see Association of Traumatic Stress Specialists (#02961)
- ♦ IATC – Inter-American Congress of Ministers and High-Level Authorities of Tourism (see: #11423)
- ♦ **IATC** International Association of Theatre Critics (#12226)
- ♦ IATD – International Association of Telecommunications Dealers (no recent information)
- ♦ IATD – International Association of Tontine Development (internationally oriented national body)
- ♦ **IATDMCT** International Association for Therapeutic Drug Monitoring and Clinical Toxicology (#12227)
- ♦ IATEC – International Antiviral Therapy Evaluation Center (internationally oriented national body)
- ♦ IATED – International Association of Technology, Education and Development (internationally oriented national body)
- ♦ **IATEFL** International Association of Teachers of English as a Foreign Language (#12222)
- ♦ IATE – International Association of Television Editors (inactive)
- ♦ **IATE** International Association for Tourism Economics (#12230)
- ♦ IATEO – International Aviation Training and Education Organisation (unconfirmed)
- ♦ **IATF** Inter-American Theosophical Federation (#11453)
- ♦ **IATF** International Airline Training Fund (#11611)
- ♦ IATH – International Association of Teachers of Hungarian (no recent information)
- ♦ **IATI** International Aid Transparency Initiative (#11604)
- ♦ **IAT** International Academy of Telepathology (#11579)
- ♦ IAT – International AIDS Trust (internationally oriented national body)
- ♦ IAT – International Association for Transformation (internationally oriented national body)
- ♦ **IAT** International Association of Trichologists (#12242)
- ♦ **IATIS** International Association for Translation and Intercultural Studies (#12236)
- ♦ **IATJ** International Association of Tax Judges (#12221)
- ♦ **IATM** International Association of Tour Managers (#12231)
- ♦ **IATM** International Association of Transport and Communications Museums (#12237)
- ♦ **IATMO** International Academy of Tumor Marker Oncology (#11580)
- ♦ IATOCA – International Association of Tourist Organizations Operating in Central Asia (inactive)
- ♦ IATO – International Association of Theatre Public Organization (inactive)
- ♦ IATOUR – International Association for Tourism Policy (unconfirmed)
- ♦ IATP – Institute for Agriculture and Trade Policy (internationally oriented national body)
- ♦ IATP – International Affiliation of Tongue-tie Professionals (internationally oriented national body)
- ♦ IATP – International Agricultural Training Programme (internationally oriented national body)
- ♦ **IATP** International Airlines Technical Pool (#11610)
- ♦ IATP – International Association of Trampoline Parks (internationally oriented national body)
- ♦ **IATP** International Association for Transport Properties (#12238)
- ♦ IATRC – International Agricultural Trade Research Consortium (internationally oriented national body)

♦ Iatrogenic Europe Unite – Alliance (IEU) 11010

Chairwoman Wevelaan 45, 3571 XS Utrecht, Netherlands.

History Former names and other names: *Stichting Iatrogenic Europe Unite-Alliance* – legal name; *Stichting IEU-Alliance* – trading name. Registration: No/ID: 30218429, Netherlands, Utrecht. **Aims** Improve the position of victims of *medical* errors, the so called iatrogenic patients and to improve *patient* safety in general. **Structure** Board, including Chair. **NGO Relations** Member of: *International Alliance of Patients' Organizations (IAPO, #11633)*. [2020/XM1048/**D**]

- ♦ IATROS – Organisation mondiale des médecins indépendants (inactive)
- ♦ IATSE – International Alliance of Theatrical Stage Employees, Moving Picture Technicians, Artists and Allied Crafts of the United States, its Territories and Canada (internationally oriented national body)
- ♦ IATSIC / see International Association for Trauma Surgery and Intensive Care (#12239)
- ♦ **IATSIC** International Association for Trauma Surgery and Intensive Care (#12239)
- ♦ **IATS** International Association for Tibetan Studies (#12228)
- ♦ **IATSO** International Association for the Treatment of Sexual Offenders (#12241)
- ♦ **IATSS** International Association of Traffic and Safety Sciences (#12235)
- ♦ IATT-CABA / see Inter-Agency Task Team on Children affected by AIDS (#11394)
- ♦ **IATTC** Inter-American Tropical Tuna Commission (#11454)
- ♦ **IATT** Inter-Agency Task Team on Children affected by AIDS (#11394)
- ♦ **IATTO** International Association of Trade Training Organizations (#12233)
- ♦ IATUL / see International Association of University Libraries (#12247)
- ♦ **IATUL** International Association of University Libraries (#12247)
- ♦ **IATUR** International Association for Time Use Research (#12229)
- ♦ IATVPM – International Association of Teachers of Veterinary Preventive Medicine (inactive)
- ♦ IATWS – International Association of Traditional Wrestling Sports (no recent information)
- ♦ **IAUAFMW** International Amalgamation of Unions of Automobile and Farm Machinery Workers (#11644)
- ♦ **IAUA** International Association of Unions of Architects (#12245)
- ♦ **IAUC** International Association for Urban Climate (#12251)
- ♦ IAUD – International Association for the Union of Democracies (inactive)
- ♦ IAUD – International Association for Universal Design (internationally oriented national body)
- ♦ IAUED – International Association of Used Equipment Dealers (inactive)
- ♦ IAUG – International Avaya Users Group (internationally oriented national body)
- ♦ IAU – Institute for American Universities, Aix-en-Provence (internationally oriented national body)
- ♦ IAU – International Antiterrorism Unity (internationally oriented national body)
- ♦ **IAU** International Association of Ultrarunners (#12244)
- ♦ **IAU** International Association of Universities (#12246)
- ♦ **IAU** International Astronomical Union (#12287)
- ♦ **IAU** Internationale Armbrustschützen Union (#13117)
- ♦ IAUL – Inter-African Union of Lawyers (inactive)
- ♦ **IAUPE** International Association of University Professors of English (#12249)
- ♦ **IAUP** International Association of University Presidents (#12248)
- ♦ **IAUPL** International Association of University Professors and Lecturers (#12250)
- ♦ IAURRE – International Association for Urban and Regional Research and Education (inactive)
- ♦ **IAUS** International Association of Ukrainian Studies (#12243)
- ♦ IAVAC – International Association for Video in Arts and Culture (inactive)
- ♦ **IAVCEI** International Association of Volcanology and Chemistry of the Earth's Interior (#12259)
- ♦ **IAVD** International Association for Vehicle Design (#12254)
- ♦ IAVE – International Association of Veterinary Editors (unconfirmed)
- ♦ **IAVE** International Association for Volunteer Effort (#12260)
- ♦ IAV / see European Waterproofing Association (#09084)
- ♦ IAVFH / see World Association of Veterinary Food Hygienists (#21204)
- ♦ **IAVH** International Association for Veterinary Homeopathy (#12256)
- ♦ IAVI / see International Association for Identification
- ♦ **IAVI** International AIDS Vaccine Initiative (#11602)
- ♦ IAVM – International Association of Venue Managers (internationally oriented national body)
- ♦ **IAVRPT** International Association of Veterinary Rehabilitation and Physical Therapy (#12257)
- ♦ **IAVSD** International Association for Vehicle System Dynamics (#12255)
- ♦ **IAVS** International Association for Vegetation Science (#12253)
- ♦ **IAVS** International Association for Visual Semiotics (#12258)
- ♦ IAWA – International Airport Watch Association (unconfirmed)
- ♦ IAWA – International Archive of Women in Architecture (internationally oriented national body)
- ♦ IAWA – International Association of Women in the Arts (internationally oriented national body)
- ♦ **IAWA** International Association of Wood Anatomists (#12273)
- ♦ **IAWBH** International Association on Workplace Bullying and Harassment (#12279)
- ♦ **IAWC** International AIDS Women's Caucus (#11603)
- ♦ **IAWD** International Association of Water Service Companies in the Danube River Catchment Area (#12264)
- ♦ **IAWD** Internationale Arbeitsgemeinschaft der Wasserwerke im Donaueinzugsgebiet (#12264)
- ♦ **IAWE** International Association of Wind Engineering (#12266)
- ♦ **IAWE** International Association for World Englishes (#12280)
- ♦ IAWERA – International Association of Waterborne Emergency Response Activities (inactive)
- ♦ **IAWF** International Association of Wildland Fire (#12265)
- ♦ IAWGD – Inter-Agency Working Group on Desertification (inactive)
- ♦ **IAWG** International Affiliation of Writers' Guilds (#11595)
- ♦ IAWG / see United Nations Evaluation Group (#20560)
- ♦ **IAW** International Alliance of Women (#11639)
- ♦ **IAWIS** International Association of Word and Image Studies (#12276)
- ♦ **IAWJ** International Association of Women Judges (#12267)
- ♦ IAWL / see International Association for Water Law (#12263)
- ♦ **IAWMH** International Association for Women's Mental Health (#12272)
- ♦ **IAWM** International Alliance for Women in Music (#11641)
- ♦ **IAWM** International Association of Women Ministers (#12268)
- ♦ IAWN – International Anglican Women's Network (see: #00827)
- ♦ **IAWN** International Asteroid Warning Network (#12285)
- ♦ **IAWPA** International Association of World Peace Advocates (#12281)
- ♦ **IAWP** International Association of Women Police (#12270)
- ♦ **IAWP** International Association of Workforce Professionals (#12278)
- ♦ **IAWPS** International Association of Wood Products Societies (#12274)
- ♦ IAWQ – International Association on Water Quality (inactive)
- ♦ **IAWR** Internationale Arbeitsgemeinschaft der Wasserwerke im Rheineinzugsgebiet (#13215)
- ♦ IAWR / see International Water Resources Association (#15871)
- ♦ **IAWRT** International Association of Women in Radio and Television (#12271)
- ♦ **IAWS** International Academy of Wood Science (#11581)
- ♦ IAYC / see International Workshop for Astronomy (#15913)
- ♦ **IAYFJM** International Association of Youth and Family Judges and Magistrates (#12283)
- ♦ **IAYMH** International Association for Youth Mental Health (#12284)
- ♦ IAYP – International Association of Young Philosophers (inactive)
- ♦ IAYSC – International Association of Yoga Science Centres (no recent information)
- ♦ IB²MAC – International Brick and Block Masonry Conference (meeting series)
- ♦ IBAA – Europe / see European Business Aviation Association (#06415)
- ♦ IBAC / see International Bioacoustics Society (#12341)
- ♦ **IBAC** International Bioacoustics Society (#12341)
- ♦ **IBAC** International Business Aviation Council (#12418)
- ♦ IBAC Society / see International Bioacoustics Society (#12341)
- ♦ IBAF – International Baseball Federation (inactive)
- ♦ IBA Forum / see International Forum on Industrial Bioprocesses (#13640)
- ♦ **IBAGS** International Basal Ganglia Society (#12325)
- ♦ IBAH / see Interafrican Bureau for Animal Resources (#11382)
- ♦ **IBAHRI** International Bar Association's Human Rights Institute (#12322)
- ♦ IBA-IFIBiop / see International Forum on Industrial Bioprocesses (#13640)
- ♦ **IBA** International Association for Bear Research and Management (#11722)
- ♦ IBA – International Banana Association (no recent information)
- ♦ IBA – International Bankers Association (no recent information)
- ♦ **IBA** International Bar Association (#12320)
- ♦ **IBA** International Bartenders Association (#12324)
- ♦ **IBA** International Battery Materials Association (#12327)
- ♦ IBA – International Bauxite Association (inactive)

- ♦ **IBA** International Biennial Association (#12339)
- ♦ **IBA** International Biographical Association (#12350)
- ♦ **IBA** International Blackcurrant Association (#12357)
- ♦ IBA – International Bodyflight Association (unconfirmed)
- ♦ **IBA** International Bodyguard Association (#12376)
- ♦ **IBA** International BodyTalk Association (#12378)
- ♦ **IBA** International Boxing Association (#12385)
- ♦ IBA – International Breeders Association (inactive)
- ♦ **IBA** International Bryozoology Association (#12403)
- ♦ IBA / see International Institute for Bioenergetic Analysis (#13863)
- ♦ **IBAME** International Board on the Applications of the Mössbauer Effect (#12365)
- ♦ **IBANGS** International Behavioural and Neural Genetics Society (#12332)
- ♦ IBANGS Society / see International Behavioural and Neural Genetics Society (#12332)
- ♦ IBAR / see Interafrican Bureau for Animal Resources (#11382)
- ♦ Ibaraki International Association (internationally oriented national body)
- ♦ IBAR – International Bank for Arms Regulation (unconfirmed)
- ♦ IBAS – International Ban Asbestos Secretariat (internationally oriented national body)
- ♦ IBA / see World Bamboo Organization (#21214)
- ♦ IBBA – Institut bolivien de biologie d'altitude (internationally oriented national body)
- ♦ IBBA – International Brangus Breeders Association (internationally oriented national body)
- ♦ IBBH – Internationaler Bund der Bau- und Holzarbeiter (inactive)
- ♦ IBB – International Book Bank (internationally oriented national body)
- ♦ **IBB** International Brain Bee (#12390)
- ♦ IBB – International Broadcasting Bureau (internationally oriented national body)
- ♦ IBB – Internationales Bildungs- und Begegnungswerk (internationally oriented national body)
- ♦ **IBB** Internationale des travailleurs du bâtiment et du bois (#03355)
- ♦ **IBBS** The International Biodeterioration and Biodegradation Society (#12344)
- ♦ **IBBS** International Brain Barriers Society (#12389)
- ♦ **IBBY** International Board on Books for Young People (#12366)
- ♦ IBC / see International Boundary and Water Commission

♦ IBC 11011

CEO The Brew Eagle House, 163 City Road, London, EC1V 1NR, UK. T. +442045341000. E-mail: marketing@ibc.org.
URL: https://www.ibc.org/

History 1967. An independent body, owned by: *International Association of Broadcasting Manufacturers (IABM, #11739)*; *Society for Broadband Professionals (SCTE)*; *Institute of Electrical and Electronics Engineers (IEEE, #11259)* – Broadcast Technology Society; *Institution of Engineering and Technology (IET, #11320)*; *Society of Motion Picture and Television Engineers (SMPTE)*; Royal Television Society. Former names and other names: *International Broadcasting Convention (IBC)* – former. **Structure** Council; Steering Group; Board; Management Team. **Activities** Events/meetings. **Events** *International Broadcasting Convention (IBC)* Amsterdam (Netherlands) 2023, *International Broadcasting Convention (IBC)* Amsterdam (Netherlands) 2022, *International Broadcasting Convention* Amsterdam (Netherlands) 2017, *International Broadcasting Convention* Amsterdam (Netherlands) 2014, *International Broadcasting Convention* Amsterdam (Netherlands) 2011.
[2022/AA3002/c/**E**]

- ♦ **IBCA** International Braille Chess Association (#12388)
- ♦ **IBCE** International Board of Chiropractic Examiners (#12367)
- ♦ **IBC-IC** Inflammatory Breast Cancer International Consortium (#11189)
- ♦ IBC / see International Ballistics Society (#12308)
- ♦ **IBC** International Baptist Convention (#12318)
- ♦ **IBC** International Bioethics Committee of UNESCO (#12348)
- ♦ IBC – International Biographical Centre (internationally oriented national body)
- ♦ IBC – International Blue Crescent (internationally oriented national body)
- ♦ **IBC** International Blue Cross (#12364)
- ♦ **IBC** International Borzoi Council (#12383)
- ♦ IBC – International Botanical Congress (meeting series)
- ♦ **IBC** International Buddhist Confederation (#12405)
- ♦ IBC – International Bunker Conference (meeting series)
- ♦ **IBC** International Business Congress (#12419)
- ♦ **IBC** International Butchers' Confederation (#12421)
- ♦ **IBC** International Old Catholic Bishops' Conference (#14403)
- ♦ IBCMC / see Institute of Career Certification International
- ♦ **IBCMT** International Board of Clinical Metal Toxicology (#12368)
- ♦ **IbCN** Iberoamerican Cochrane Network (#18641)
- ♦ **IBCN** International Bladder Cancer Network (#12360)
- ♦ **IBCR** International Bureau for Children's Rights (#12412)
- ♦ **IBCSG** International Breast Cancer Study Group (#12394)
- ♦ **IBCS** International Board of Cosmetic Surgery (#12369)
- ♦ IBCT – Institute of Balkan Studies and Center of Thracology (internationally oriented national body)
- ♦ IBCT / see International Board of Clinical Metal Toxicology (#12368)
- ♦ **IBDA** International Banknote Designers Association (#12315)
- ♦ **IBDA** International BioDynamic Association (#12346)
- ♦ **IBDA** Internationaler Verein für Biologisch-Dynamische Landwirtschaft (#12346)
- ♦ **IBDC** International Committee Buchenwald Dora and Commandos (#12749)
- ♦ IBD – International Brewers' Guild (internationally oriented national body)
- ♦ IBD – International Bureau for Declarations of Death (inactive)
- ♦ **i-BEC** Interbalkan Environment Center (#11458)
- ♦ **IBEC** International Bank for Economic Co-operation (#12310)
- ♦ IBEDC – International Business and Economic Development Center (internationally oriented national body)
- ♦ IBED / see Interafrican Bureau for Animal Resources (#11382)
- ♦ IBED – Inter-African Bureau of Epizootic Diseases (inactive)
- ♦ **IBEF** International Bitumen Emulsion Federation (#12356)
- ♦ iBEGIN – International Business, Economic Geography and Innovation (unconfirmed)
- ♦ IBEI – Fundació Institut Barcelona d'Estudis Internacionals (internationally oriented national body)
- ♦ **IBE** International Bureau of Education (#12413)
- ♦ **IBE** International Bureau for Epilepsy (#12414)
- ♦ **IBEP** International Bioenergy Platform (#12347)
- ♦ IBERAMIA / see Iberoamerican Society of Artificial Intelligence (#11029)
- ♦ **IBERAMIA** Sociedad Iberoamericana de Inteligencia Artificial (#11029)
- ♦ Iberian Conference on Perception (meeting series)
- ♦ Iberian Latin American Society of Neuroradiology (#19381)
- ♦ IBERI – International Biology and Environment Research Institute (unconfirmed)
- ♦ Ibero-America Institute for Economic Research of the University of Göttingen (internationally oriented national body)
- ♦ Ibero-American Academy of Criminal and Forensic Studies (#00012)

♦ Iberoamerican Academy of Management (IAM) 11012

Contact 7225 W Oakland St, Chandler AZ 85226-2433, USA. Fax +14808581802.
URL: http://www.iberoacademy.org/

History 1997, as an affiliate of the US Academy of Management. **Aims** Foster general advancement of knowledge in theory and practice of management among Iberoamerican scholars and/or academics interested in Iberoamerican issues; perform and support educational activities contributing to intellectual and operational *leadership* in the field of management within an Iberoamerican context. **Structure** Executive Committee, comprising President and 3 Vice-Presidents. Advisory Board. Committees (8). **Events** *International Conference* Santiago (Chile) 2015, *International Conference* Sao Paulo (Brazil) 2013, *International Conference* Lima (Peru) 2011, *International Conference* Buenos Aires (Argentina) 2009, *International Conference* Santo Domingo (Dominican Rep) 2007. **Publications** *Management Research* – journal. [2011/XJ6689/**D**]

♦ Iberoamerican Academy of Pediatric Neurology 11013

Academia Iberoamericana de Neurologia Pediatrica (AINP)

Pres Sierra De Las Palomas 305, CP 20120 Aguascalientes, Mexico. Fax +5249171930. E-mail: neuronags@hotmail.com – contacto.ainp@gmail.com.
URL: http://www.ainponline.org/

History 1992, Avila (Spain). **Events** *Congress* Asunción (Paraguay) 2022, *Annual Congress* Madrid (Spain) 2016, *Annual Congress* Campos do Jordão (Brazil) 2015, *Annual Congress* Tegucigalpa (Honduras) 2014, *Annual Congress* Valencia (Spain) 2013. **Publications** *Acta Neuropediatrica* (4 a year) in English, Spanish.
Members Full in 24 countries:
Argentina, Bolivia, Brazil, Canada, Chile, Colombia, Costa Rica, Cuba, Dominican Rep, Ecuador, El Salvador, France, Honduras, Mexico, Neth Antilles, Nicaragua, Panama, Paraguay, Peru, Portugal, Spain, Uruguay, USA, Venezuela. [2022/XJ0128/**E**]

- ♦ Iberoamerican Air Transportation Research Society (#18669)
- ♦ Ibero-American Animal Reproduction Association (no recent information)
- ♦ Ibero-American Association of Aerospace Medicine (#02147)
- ♦ Iberoamerican Association Against Thyroid Cancer (#02136)

♦ Ibero-American Association of Chambers of Commerce (IACC) 11014

Association ibéroaméricaine des chambres de commerce – Asociación Iberoamericana de Camaras de Comercio (AICO)

SG Av Balderas 144-4o piso, Del Cuauhtémoc, Mexico City CDMX, Mexico. E-mail: aico@aico.org.
URL: http://www.aico.org/

History Nov 1974, Mexico City (Mexico). Formally established in Jun 1975, Madrid (Spain). Current Statutes include modifications approved by: 7th Assembly, 1980, Guatemala (Guatemala); 10th Assembly, 1983, Caracas (Venezuela); 12th Assembly, Seville (Spain) 1985. Previously known under the acronym *AICC*. **Aims** Defend the rights of private enterprise and of national and international free trade between Spanish and Portuguese speaking countries, in particular between enterprises and businessmen; study matters of concern to economic activity and international trade, with special reference to the Ibero-American area; define ideas, studies, projects and initiatives that encourage growth and stability of private enterprise; promote meetings of chambers of commerce and related agencies and business meetings within the Ibero-American area; establish agreements strengthening friendship, cooperation and solidarity both among members and between AICO and international institutions and organizations; promote solution and settlement of conflicts and claims between businessmen by means of International Commercial Arbitration. **Structure** Assembly (annual); Directive Council; Board of Directors; Regional Secretariats (4). **Languages** English, Portuguese, Spanish. **Staff** 6.00 FTE, paid. **Finance** Members' dues. Other sources: subsidies from various institutions and organizations; income from activities and services. **Events** *Annual General Assembly* Lisbon (Portugal) 2018, *Annual General Assembly* Madrid (Spain) 2017, *Annual General Assembly* Seville (Spain) 2016, *Annual General Assembly* Bogota (Colombia) 2015, *Annual General Assembly / Annual Assembly* Mexico City (Mexico) 2014. **Publications** *International Bulletin of Trade Opportunities* (12 a year); *Ibero-American Directory of Chambers of Commerce and other Institutions* (annual); *Ibero-American Economic Statistics* (annual); *Market Profiles*. **Information Services** *IACO Trade Link Network – Red de Información Comercial AICO* – computerized information system, currently located at the Chamber of Commerce of Bogota.
Members Full; Honorary: Chambers of Commerce, Industry and Navigation and related bodies (over 400) in 23 countries:
Andorra, Argentina, Bolivia, Brazil, Chile, Colombia, Costa Rica, Dominican Rep, Ecuador, El Salvador, Guatemala, Honduras, Mexico, Nicaragua, Panama, Paraguay, Peru, Portugal, Puerto Rico, Spain, Uruguay, USA, Venezuela.
Consultative Status Consultative status granted from: *UNCTAD (#20285)* (General Category); *OAS (#17629)*.
NGO Relations Through Global Chamber Platform, links with: *Association des chambres de commerce et d'industrie européennes (EUROCHAMBRES, #02423)*. Memorandum of Understanding with: *Asociación de las Camaras de Comercio e Industria del Mediterraneo (ASCAME, #02112)*; *World Chambers Federation (WCF, #21269)*. [2017.07.18/XD9228/**D**]

- ♦ Iberoamerican Association of Family Dentistry (inactive)
- ♦ Iberoamerican Association of Flower Therapists (no recent information)
- ♦ Iberoamerican Association of Geological and Mining Surveys (#02297)
- ♦ Iberoamerican Association of Institutions on Civil Defence and Protection (#02150)
- ♦ Iberoamerican Association of Insurance Information and Professional Promotion (no recent information)
- ♦ Ibero-American Association of Medicine and School and University Health / see Ibero-American Association for School and University Health and Medicine (#11017)
- ♦ Iberoamerican Association of Olympic Academies / see Pan-Iberican Association of Olympic Academies (#18181)

♦ Ibero-American Association for Open University Education 11015

Association ibéroaméricaine de l'enseignement supérieur à distance – Asociación Iberoamericana de Educación Superior a Distancia (AIESAD)

Exec Dir Calle 14 Sur 14–23, Bogota, Bogota DC, Colombia. E-mail: info@aiesad.org.
Permanent Sec c/o UNED, C/ Bravo Murillo 38, 7ª Planta, 28015 Madrid, Spain.
URL: http://www.aiesad.org/

History Oct 1980, Madrid (Spain). Founded at 1st *Symposium of Open University Rectors*. **Aims** Assist in information, cooperation and coordination among member organizations; promote study and application of new techniques and facilitate their use by members; encourage the training of teachers and staff; assist in the application and adaptation to local requirements of methods and materials; design educational and cultural programmes; represent needs of distance education with national and international bodies, reducing obstructions and difficulties in its development. **Structure** General Assembly (every 2 years); Board (meets once a year); Permanent and Executive Secretariats. **Languages** Spanish. **Staff** 1.00 FTE, paid. **Finance** Members' dues. Other sources: grants, subsidies and donations from governments, international bodies and public institutions. **Activities** Events/meetings. **Events** *Meeting* Madrid (Spain) 2016, *Meeting* Lisbon (Portugal) 2009, *Meeting* Dominican Rep 2007, *Virtual Educa : international conference on education, training and new technologies* São José dos Campos (Brazil) 2007, *International meeting on higher education / Meeting* Mexico City (Mexico) 2005. **Publications** *Revista Iberoamericana de Educación Superior a Distancia* (2 a year).
Members Universities and institutes (43) in 17 countries:
Argentina, Bolivia, Brazil, Chile, Colombia, Costa Rica, Cuba, Dominican Rep, Ecuador, Mexico, Panama, Paraguay, Peru, Portugal, Spain, Uruguay, Venezuela.
IGO Relations *Agencia Española de Cooperación Internacional para el Desarrollo (AECID)*. **NGO Relations** *Instituto Latinoamericano y del Caribe de Calidad en Educación Superior a Distancia (CALED, #11342)*.
[2022/XD8073/**D**]

- ♦ Iberoamerican Association of Pediatric Surgery (#02134)
- ♦ Iberoamerican Association of Postgraduate Universities (#02307)
- ♦ Ibero-American Association of Printing Houses for the Visually Handicapped (inactive)
- ♦ Ibero-American Association of Professional for Quality and Development (unconfirmed)
- ♦ Iberoamerican Association of Public Defence Counsels / see Asociación Interamericana de Defensorias Públicas (#02159)
- ♦ Ibero-American Association of Public Prosecutors (#02149)
- ♦ Ibero-American Association for the Rehabilitation of Disabled (inactive)
- ♦ Ibero-American Association of Ricoeur Studies (unconfirmed)

♦ Ibero-American Association of Roman Law 11016

Asociación Iberoamericana de Derecho Romano (AIDROM)

Sec Fac Derecho Univ Oviedo, C/ Valentin Andrés Alvarez s/n, 33006 Oviedo, Asturias, Spain. E-mail: clrendo@uniovi.es.
URL: http://www.aidrom.com/

History 1994. **Aims** Study and disseminate Roman Law in its strict sense both in the field of the legal tradition and its projection in European legislation and Ibero-Americana. **Structure** Board of Directors, comprising Honorary President, President, 3 Vice-Presidents, Secretary and 11 members. **Languages** Italian, Portuguese, Spanish. **Staff** 230.00 FTE, paid. **Finance** Sources: members' dues. **Events** *Ibero-American Congress of Roman Law* Buenos Aires (Argentina) 2021, *International Congress* Buenos Aires (Argentina) 2021, *Ibero-American Congress of Roman Law* Oviedo (Spain) 2019, *International Congress* Oviedo (Spain) 2019, *Ibero-American Congress of Roman Law* Porto (Portugal) 2018. **Publications** *RIDROM – International Review of Roman Law* (2 a year) in English, Spanish – electronic. *Fundamentos Romanísticos del Derecho Contemporáneo. Varios vols.* (1st ed 2021) by Prof Dr Carmen Lopez-Rendo Rodriguez and Prof Dr Maria Jose Azaustre Fernandez et al; *Fundamentos Romanísticos del Derecho Europeo e Iberoamericano. 2 Vols* (1ed 2020) by Prof Carmen Lopez-Rendo Rodriguez in English, Portuguese, Spanish. Articles also in French, German, Italian, Portuguese.
Members Full in 11 countries:
Argentina, Bolivia, Brazil, Italy, Mexico, Netherlands, Peru, Portugal, Puerto Rico, Spain, Uruguay. [2021.08.31/XM3755/**D**]

♦ Ibero-American Association for School and University Health and Medicine (IASUHM) 11017

Asociación Iberoamericana de Medicina y Salud Escolar y Universitaria

Contact Calle Amorós 3 – 1o A, 28040 Madrid, Spain. E-mail: saludescolar@telefonica.net.
URL: http://www.saludescolar.net/

History 2007, Juarez (Mexico). Originally also referred to in English as *Ibero-American Association of Medicine and School and University Health.* **Aims** Promote health in schools and universities. **Structure** International Council (meets every 2 years), comprising Country Presidents and Executive Members. Executive (2 year terms), comprising President, regional Vice-Presidents (Europe, North America, Latin America and Caribbean, and South America), Scientific Secretary, International Treasurer. **Languages** Spanish. **Staff** Voluntary. **Finance** Country contributions. **Activities** Co-organizes congress and other events. **Events** *International congress of health promoting universities* Pamplona (Spain) 2009. **Publications** *Promoción de la Salud Universitaria* (2011) by J A Saez Crespo and López Iglesias; *Entornos Saludables para los Escolares – Hacia Una Mayor Equidad* (2010) by J A Saez Crespo; *Epidemiologia y Prevención del Maltrato Infantil* (2008) by J A Saez Crespo. **Members** Membership countries not specified. [2012.06.01/XJ0677/**F**]

- ♦ Ibero-American Association for Sports Information (no recent information)
- ♦ Ibero-American Association for the Study of Alcohol and Drug Problems (no recent information)

♦ Ibero-American Astronomy League 11018

Ligue ibéroaméricaine d'astronomie – Liga Iberoamericana de Astronomia (LIADA)

Sec Observatorio Astronómico CODE, Av Almirante Brown 4998, Costanera Oeste, S3002GVP Santa Fé, Argentina. T. +54342155001236. E-mail: ssliada@gmail.com.
URL: https://sites.google.com/site/webliada/

History 12 Dec 1982, Montevideo (Uruguay). Founded at 1st Congress, taking over the activities of *Liga Latino Americana de Astronomia (LLADA, inactive)*, set up in 1958 but which had since ceased to exist. **Aims** Promote study of astronomy in areas of scientific significance; unite Spanish and Portuguese speaking observers of the planet Earth; promote and expand respect and appreciation of the Earth as a planet; promote exchange of ideas among professionals and amateurs; publish members' work. **Structure** General Council; Executive Officers; Section Coordinators. **Languages** Portuguese, Spanish. **Staff** 16.00 FTE, paid. **Finance** Members' dues: US$ 15 to US$ 30 depending on membership category. Other sources: grants from governmental, scientific and educational organizations. **Events** *Congreso Internacional Pro-Am LIADA* 2017, *Congress* Buenos Aires (Argentina) 2006, *Congress* Córdoba (Argentina) 2003, *Congress* Villa Carlos Paz (Argentina) 2003, *Congress* Asunción (Paraguay) 2001. **Publications** *RedLIADA – Boletin Semanal de Astronoticias* (weekly); *Revista Universo Anuario* (annual); *Revista Universo Digital.*
Members Student; Individual; Professional; Benefactor. Individuals and associations in 25 countries and territories:
Argentina, Belgium, Bolivia, Brazil, Chile, Colombia, Costa Rica, Cuba, Dominican Rep, Ecuador, El Salvador, France, Guatemala, Honduras, Italy, Mexico, Nicaragua, Panama, Peru, Portugal, Puerto Rico, Spain, Uruguay, USA, Venezuela. [2020/XD7427/**D**]

- ♦ Ibero-American Athletic Association (inactive)
- ♦ Ibero-American Bureau of Education / see Organization of Ibero-American States for Education, Science and Culture (#17871)
- ♦ Ibero-American Business Council (#04708)
- ♦ Ibero-American and Caribbean Best Practices Forum – Human Settlements for a More Sustainable Future / see Ibero-American and Caribbean Forum of Best Practices (#11019)
- ♦ Ibero-American and Caribbean Ecological Restoration Network (inactive)
- ♦ Ibero-American and Caribbean Ecological Restoration Society (#19362)

♦ Ibero-American and Caribbean Forum of Best Practices 11019

Foro Iberoamericano y del Caribe de Mejores Practicas

Secretariat c/o Gobierno de España, Min de Fomento, Paseo de la Caltellana 67, 28017 Madrid, Spain.
Facebook: https://www.facebook.com/foroiberoamericano/

History 1997. Former names and other names: *Ibero-American and Caribbean Best Practices Forum – Human Settlements for a More Sustainable Future* – alias. **Aims** Increase *citizen* participation in focusing of *human settlement policy.* **Structure** Regional arm of UN-HABITAT Best Practices and Local Leadership Programme in Latin America. Sub-regional Nodes (4): Centro de la Vivienda y Estudios Urbanos (CENVI) – Mexico and Central America; Brazilian Institute for Municipal Administration (IBAM); El Agora – Southern Cone of South America sub-region; Fundación Habitat Colombia (FHC) – Andean countries. Focal points (4): Costa Rica; El Salvador; Bolivia; Chile. **Languages** Spanish. **Staff** None. **Finance** No budget. **Activities** Annual Action Plan. [2022/XD6794/**D**]

- ♦ Ibero-American Center for the Elderly (internationally oriented national body)
- ♦ Iberoamerican Center for Strategic Urban development (#03800)
- ♦ Iberoamerican Chitin Society (#19378)
- ♦ Iberoamerican Cochrane Centre (internationally oriented national body)
- ♦ Iberoamerican Cochrane Network (#18641)

♦ Ibero-American College of Rheumatology 11020

Colegio Ibero-Americano de Reumatologia (CIAR)

Pres Durand Gen Hosp Univ BA, Av Salvador M del Carril 4165, 1419 Buenos Aires, Argentina. T. +541145040950. Fax +541145040950.
Chairperson address not obtained.

History 1981, as *Associação Comite Ibero-Americano de Reumatologia.* **NGO Relations** Member of: *International Osteoporosis Foundation (IOF, #14490).* [2015/XD8516/**D**]

- ♦ Ibero-American Confederation of Catholic Students (inactive)
- ♦ Ibero-American Confederation of Christian Communicators, Mass Media, Pastors and Leaders (#04449)
- ♦ Iberoamerican Confederation of Family Medicine (#04450)
- ♦ Ibero-American Confederation of National Committees, Councils and Commissions on Disability (no recent information)
- ♦ Iberoamerican Confederation of Young Entrepreneurs / see Federación Iberoamericana de Jóvenes Empresarios (#09314)
- ♦ Ibero-American Conference on Constitutional Justice (#04652)
- ♦ Ibero-American Congress on Crystallography (meeting series)
- ♦ Iberoamerican Congress on Membrane Science and Technology (meeting series)
- ♦ Ibero-American Congress on Sensors (meeting series)
- ♦ Ibero-American Copyright Organization (#17840)
- ♦ Ibero-American Cornea Society / see Pan-American Cornea Society (#18090)
- ♦ Iberoamerican Corporation of State Lotteries and Betting (#04838)
- ♦ Ibero-American Council of Associations of Architects (no recent information)
- ♦ Iberoamerican Cultural Center 'House of the Americas', Madrid (internationally oriented national body)
- ♦ Ibero-American Down Syndrome Association (inactive)
- ♦ Iberoamerican Educational Television Association (#02303)
- ♦ Ibero-american Electrochemical Society (#19364)
- ♦ Ibero-American Endodontic Federation (inactive)
- ♦ Ibero-American Equine Veterinary Association (no recent information)
- ♦ Ibero-American Ethical Humanist Association (no recent information)

♦ Ibero-American Federation of Acoustics 11021

Federación Iberoamericana de Acústica – Federação Iberoamericana de Acústica (FIA)

Acting Pres Lab de Acustica y Luminotecnia LAL-CIC, Camino Centenario y calle 506, (1897) Manuel B Gonnet, B1897AVB Buenos Aires, Argentina.
URL: http://www.fia.ufsc.br/

History Oct 1995, Valdivia (Chile). **Aims** Develop acoustics science and technology areas in Spanish and Portuguese speaking countries. **Structure** Council. **Languages** Portuguese, Spanish. **Staff** Part-time, voluntary. **Activities** Events/meetings. **Events** *Congress* Santiago (Chile) 2024, *Congress* Florianópolis (Brazil) 2022, *Congress* Florianópolis (Brazil) 2020, *Congress* Cadiz (Spain) 2018, *Congress* Buenos Aires (Argentina) 2016.
Members Acoustical societies in Spanish or Portuguese speaking countries. National associations (11) in 11 countries:
Argentina, Brazil, Chile, Colombia, Ecuador, Mexico, Peru, Portugal, Spain, Uruguay, Venezuela.
NGO Relations Member of (3): *International Commission for Acoustics (ICA, #12658)* (as Affiliate member of); *International Institute of Acoustics and Vibration (IIAV, #13858)* (as Affiliate member of); *International Institute of Noise Control Engineering (IINCE, #13903)* (as Observer member of). [2022.10.31/XD7253/**D**]

- ♦ Iberoamerican Federation of Business Women (#09316)
- ♦ Ibero-American Federation of Cinematographic and Audiovisual Producers (#09318)
- ♦ Iberoamerican Federation of Early Stimulation (no recent information)
- ♦ Iberoamerican Federation of Economic History Associations (no recent information)

♦ Ibero-American Federation of Exchanges 11022

Fédération ibéroaméricaine des bourses – Federación Iberoamericana de Bolsas (FIAB)

Contact 25 de mayo 347, Piso 4, Of 413 C1002, Buenos Aires, Argentina. T. +541143167140. E-mail: correo@fiabnet.org.
URL: http://www.fiabnet.org/

History Founded 27 Sep 1973, Rio de Janeiro (Brazil), as *Ibero-American Federation of Stock Exchanges (FIABV).* Statutes approved by General Assembly, 24-27 Sep 1973, Rio de Janeiro. Registered 20 Sep 1983, Buenos Aires (Argentina). **Aims** Encourage establishment of rules and procedures ensuring solvency, competence, legitimacy and fair information disclosure to all savers investing through Member Exchanges. **Structure** General Assembly (annual); Executive Committee; Presidency; Secretariat. **Languages** English, Portuguese, Spanish. **Staff** 3.50 FTE, paid. **Finance** Member's dues. **Activities** Research and development; events/meetings; publishing activities. **Events** *Annual General Assembly* Rosario (Argentina) 2019, *Annual General Assembly* Asunción (Paraguay) 2018, *Annual General Assembly* Santa Cruz (Bolivia) 2017, *Annual General Assembly* Panama (Panama) 2015, *Annual General Assembly* Buenos Aires (Argentina) 2014. **Publications** *Anuario Estadistico – Fact Book* in English, Spanish; *Informe Mensual – Monthly Information* in English, Spanish; *Memoria Anual* in Spanish. Institutional brochures; handbook in English/Spanish. Information Services: Comprehensive Documentation Centre (DC) accessible by phone, fax and electronic mail. On-line bibliographical database. Statistical database accessible through the Internet.
Members Stock and derivatives exchanges in major cities of 17 countries:
Argentina, Bolivia, Brazil, Chile, Colombia, Costa Rica, Dominican Rep, Ecuador, El Salvador, Mexico, Panama, Paraguay, Peru, Portugal, Spain, Uruguay, Venezuela.
IGO Relations Interchange of mutual information and publications with: *Institute for the Integration of Latin America and the Caribbean (#11271).* [2017.10.11/XD2304/**D**]

- ♦ Ibero-American Federation of Financial Associations (no recent information)
- ♦ Ibero-American Federation of Franchising (#09310)
- ♦ Iberoamerican Federation of Informatic Law Associations (#09303)
- ♦ Ibero-American Federation of Ombudsmen (#09317)
- ♦ Ibero-American Federation of the Periodical Press (inactive)
- ♦ Iberoamerican Federation of Physics Societies (#09321)
- ♦ Iberoamerican Federation of Psychology Associations (#09305)
- ♦ Iberoamerican Federation of Small Animal Veterinary Associations (#09306)
- ♦ Ibero-American Federation of Stock Exchanges / see Ibero-American Federation of Exchanges (#11022)

♦ Ibero-American Federation of the World Council for Gifted and Talented Children 11023

Federación Iberoamericana del Consejo Mundial del Niño Dotado y Talentoso (FICOMUNDYT)

Secretariat Centro Huerta del Rey, C/Pio del Rio Hortega 10, 47014 Valladolid, Spain. T. +34983341382. E-mail: c_h_rey@cop.es.
URL: http://www.ficomundyt.com/

History within *World Council for Gifted and Talented Children (WCGTC, #21328).* **Aims** Promote educational programmes for gifted and talented children; foster research and studies on gifted and talented people's problems. **Structure** General Assembly (every 2 years); Executive Committee; Standing Committees (5). **Languages** Portuguese, Spanish. **Finance** Sources: members' dues. **Events** *Ibero-American Congress* 2017, *Ibero-American Congress* Foz do Iguaçu (Brazil) 2014, *Ibero-American Congress* Buenos Aires (Argentina) 2012, *Ibero-American Congress* León (Mexico) 2010, *Ibero-American Congress* Lima (Peru) 2008. **Publications** *Boletin de FICOMUNDYT.* Books; conference proceedings.
Members National and regional associations; universities, parents; investigators and professors in 12 countries:
Argentina, Brazil, Chile, Colombia, Costa Rica, Ecuador, Mexico, Peru, Portugal, Spain, Uruguay, Venezuela. [2022/XD6465/**D**]

- ♦ Iberoamerican Federation of Young Entrepreneurs (#09314)
- ♦ Ibero-American and Filipino Confederation of Sugar Cane Growers (no recent information)
- ♦ Iberoamerican Forum for Evangelical Dialogue / see Latin Evangelical Alliance (#16397)
- ♦ Iberoamerican Forum of Radiological and Nuclear Regulatory Organisations (#09878)
- ♦ Iberoamerican Foundation for Quality Management (#10026)
- ♦ Ibero-American Foundations Confederation (no recent information)
- ♦ Iberoamerican Fund for Integration in Science and Technology (unconfirmed)

♦ Ibero-American General Secretariat 11024

Secretaria General Iberoamericana (SEGIB) – Secretaria Geral Ibero-Americana

SG Paseo de Recoletos 8, 28001 Madrid, Spain. T. +34915901980. Fax +34915901981. E-mail: info@segib.org.
Central America Office Avenida Universidad 1200, Planta Baja, Cuadrante 1-A, Colonia Xoco, 03330 Mexico City CDMX, Mexico. E-mail: mexico@segib.org.
URL: https://www.segib.org/

History 2003, Bolivia. Founded during 13th *Ibero-American Summit of Chiefs of State and Government*, Summits having been organized since 1991. One of 5 organizations within *Comité de Dirección Estratégica de los Organismos Iberoamericanos (CoDEI, #04149)*. **Aims** Serve as the permanent body to organize the *Summits*. **Structure** Officers: Secretary, Vice-Secretary; Committees (3); Divisions (6). **Languages** Portuguese, Spanish. **Finance** Sources: contributions; in-kind support. **Activities** Events/meetings; networking/liaising. **Events** *Summit* Santo Domingo (Dominican Rep) 2023, *Summit* Andorra la Vella (Andorra) 2021, *SMEs Business Forum* Buenos Aires (Argentina) 2019, *SMEs Business Forum* Madrid (Spain) 2019, *Summit* Antigua (Guatemala) 2018. **Publications** *Iberoamérica en Marcha* – newsletter. *Anuario Iberoamérica-Asia Pacifico* (2010). Reports; meeting proceedings.
Members Governments of 22 countries:
Andorra, Argentina, Bolivia, Brazil, Chile, Colombia, Costa Rica, Cuba, Dominican Rep, Ecuador, El Salvador, Guatemala, Honduras, Mexico, Nicaragua, Panama, Paraguay, Peru, Portugal, Spain, Uruguay, Venezuela.
Organizations cooperating within the Registro de Redes Iberoamericano / Ibero-American Network Registry (15):
Asociación Iberoamericana de Ministerios Públicos (AIAMP, #02149); Conferencia de Directores Iberoamericanos del Agua (CODIA); Red/Consejo Iberoamericano de Donación y Trasplante (RCIDT, #18642); Red de Autoridades en Medicamentos de Iberoamérica (Red EAMI, #18636); RedEmprendia; Red Iberoamericana de Bosques Modelo (RLABM, #18659); Red Iberoamericana de Cooperación Jurídica Internacional (IberRed, #18662); Red Iberoamericana de Estudios Internacionales (RIBEI, #18665); Red Iberoamericana de Garantias (REGAR, #18667); Red Iberoamericana de Migraciones Profesionales de Salud (RIMPS, #18675); Red Iberoamericana de Organismos y Organizaciones contra la Discriminación (RIOOD, #18678); Red Iberoamericana de Organizaciones no Gubernamentales que Trabajan en Drogodependencias (RIOD, #18679); Red Iberoamericana de Protección de Datos (RIPD, #18681); Red Iberoamericana Ministerial de Aprendizaje e Investigación en Salud (RIMAIS, #18676); Red Intergubernamental Iberoamericana de Cooperación Técnica para el Desarrollo de Politicas de Atención a personas con Discapacidad y Adultos Mayores (RIICOTEC, #18697).
IGO Relations Observer to: *International Organization for Migration (IOM, #14454); Regional Conference on Migration (RCM, #18769); United Nations (UN, #20515); ECOSOC (#05331).* Special agreement with: *Latin American Faculty of Social Sciences (#16316).* Supports: *Latin American and Caribbean Demographic Centre (#16273).* **NGO Relations** Hosts secretariat of: *Virtual Educa (#20787).* [2023/XM2387/**E***]

- ♦ Iberoamerican Go Federation (#09311)
- ♦ Iberoamerican Group of Orthogonal Polynomials and Applications (#10806)
- ♦ Iberoamerican Group of Radiation Protection Societies (no recent information)
- ♦ Ibero-American Guarantees Network (#18667)
- ♦ Ibero-American Institute / see Nordic Institute of Latin American Studies
- ♦ Ibero-American Institute of Aeronautic and Space Law and Commercial Aviation (#11332)
- ♦ Ibero-American Institute of Agrarian Law and Agrarian Reform (no recent information)
- ♦ Ibero-American Institute of The Hague (internationally oriented national body)
- ♦ Ibero-American Institute of Maritime Law (internationally oriented national body)
- ♦ Ibero-American Institute on Procedural Law (internationally oriented national body)
- ♦ Ibero-American Institute Prussian Cultural Heritage Foundation (internationally oriented national body)
- ♦ Ibero-American Institute Prussian Heritage Foundation / see Ibero-Amerikanisches Institut Preussischer Kulturbesitz
- ♦ Iberoamerican Institute, Sophia University (internationally oriented national body)
- ♦ Iberoamerican Institute of Stock Exchanges (#11333)

♦ Ibero-American and Inter-American Network of Science and Technology Indicators 11025

Red Iberoamericana e Interamericana de Indicadores de Ciencia y Tecnologia (RICYT)
Main Office c/o REDES, Mansilla 2698, 2o piso, 1425 BPD Buenos Aires, Argentina. T. +541143123750 – +541143123692. Fax +541143123750 – +541143123692. E-mail: ricyt@ricyt.org.
URL: http://www.ricyt.org/
History Apr 1995, Quito (Ecuador). Previously referred to as *Ibero American Network of Science and Technology Indicators – Red Iberoamericana de Indicadores de Ciencia y Tecnologia.* **Activities** Organizes seminars. **Events** *Congress* Lisbon (Portugal) 2021, *Congress* San José (Costa Rica) 2017, *Congress* Bogota (Colombia) 2013, *Congress* Madrid (Spain) 2010. **IGO Relations** *UNESCO Institute for Statistics (UIS, #20306).* [2020/XF6589/**F**]

- ♦ Iberoamerican Intergovernmental Network for Technical Cooperation (#18697)
- ♦ Iberoamerican Juvenile Association (inactive)
- ♦ Ibero-American Lawyers' Union (#20411)
- ♦ Ibero-American League of Civil Society Organizations (#16470)
- ♦ Iberoamerican LP Gas Association (#02143)
- ♦ Ibero American Maintenance Federation (#09315)
- ♦ Iberoamerican Mechanical Engineering Federation (#09313)
- ♦ Iberoamerican Medical Law Association (no recent information)
- ♦ Ibero-American Mission Alliance (#04791)
- ♦ Ibero-American Model Forest Network (#18659)
- ♦ Ibero-American Municipal Secretariat (no recent information)
- ♦ Ibero-American National Library Association / see Association of Ibero-American States for the Development of National Libraries (#02638)
- ♦ Iberoamerican Network for Bioinformatics (inactive)
- ♦ Ibero-American Network of Biosphere Reserves and MAB Committees (#18661)

♦ Iberoamerican Network for Bipolar Disorder (IAN-BD) 11026

Exec Dir ISBD, PO Box 7168, Pittsburgh PA 15213, USA. T. +14126244402.
URL: http://www.isbd.org/
Aims Facilitate contact and collaborations in the field of bipolar disorders among centers, clinicians, investigators and advocacy groups from IberoAmerican countries (Latin America, Spain and Portugal) as well as the United States and Italy. **Activities** Training and research. **NGO Relations** Affiliated to: *International Society for Bipolar Disorders (ISBD, #14977).* [2014/XJ6677/**D**]

- ♦ Ibero-American Network of Communications and Cultural Journals (#18682)
- ♦ Iberoamerican Network/Council on Donation and Transplantation (#18642)
- ♦ Iberoamerican Network on Data Protection (#18681)
- ♦ Iberoamerican Network of Family Hypercholesterolemia (#18668)
- ♦ Ibero American Network Marketing in Health (#18674)
- ♦ Ibero-American Network of Nongovernmental Organizations working on Drug Addiction (#18679)
- ♦ Ibero-American Network of Organizations and Persons with Disabilities / see Latin American Network of Non-Governmental Organizations of Persons with Disabilities and their Families (#16354)
- ♦ Ibero-American Network of Postgraduate Programmes on Territorial Policies and Studies (#18680)
- ♦ Ibero American Network of Science and Technology Indicators / see Ibero-American and Inter-American Network of Science and Technology Indicators (#11025)
- ♦ Iberoamerican Network of Senior Citizens Associations (#18658)
- ♦ Ibero-American Network for Teaching and Research on Pulp and Paper (#18664)
- ♦ Ibero-American NMR Meeting (meeting series)
- ♦ Ibero American Oculoplastic Society (#19376)
- ♦ Ibero-American Organization of Inter-Municipal Cooperation (#17839)
- ♦ Ibero-American Organization of Private Health Service Providers (#17841)
- ♦ Ibero-American Philosophical Society (no recent information)
- ♦ Ibero-American Pilots' Organization (no recent information)
- ♦ Ibero-American Ports and Coasts Association (inactive)
- ♦ Ibero-American Programme of Science and Technology for Development (#18524)
- ♦ Ibero-American Road Safety Observatory (#17641)

♦ Ibero-American Science and Technology Education Consortium (ISTEC) 11027

Consorcio Iberoamericano para la Educación en Ciencia y Tecnologia – Consórcio Iberoamericano para la Educação em Ciência e Tecnologia
Main Office MSC01 1100, 1 Univ of New Mexico, Albuquerque NM 87131-0001, USA. T. +15052772412. Fax +15052778298. E-mail: presidente@istec.org – contact@istec.org.
URL: http://www.istec.org/
History Dec 1990, Albuquerque, NM (USA). Registration: Section 501(c)(3), Start date: 1999, USA. **Aims** Promote scientific, technological and engineering education, joining international research and development efforts; provide a profitable vehicle for the application and transfer of technology to the region, identifying needs for achieving technological advancement in Latin America and the Iberian Peninsula. **Structure** General Assembly (annual); Board of Directors; Executive Offices (3), located at: Universidad de Vigo, Vigo (Spain); Universidade de Campinas, Campinas (Brazil); University of New Mexico, Albuquerque NM (USA). **Languages** English, Portuguese, Spanish. **Finance** Sources: members' dues. **Activities** Knowledge management/information dissemination; networking/liaising; research and development; training/education. **Events** *World Engineering Education Forum* Cartagena de Indias (Colombia) 2013, *General Assembly* Porto Alegre (Brazil) 2011, *General Assembly* Loja (Ecuador) 2007, *Annual General Assembly* Loja (Ecuador) 2006, *General Assembly* Sao Paulo (Brazil) 2005. **Publications** *ISTEC Quarterly Message* – electronic.
Members Full A – Educational institutions, B – Non-profit organizations, C – Industry; Honorary; Institutional; Collaborator. Universities and educational institutions (60) in 20 countries:
Argentina, Bolivia, Brazil, Chile, Colombia, Costa Rica, Cuba, Dominican Rep, Ecuador, El Salvador, Guatemala, Mexico, Panama, Paraguay, Peru, Puerto Rico, Spain, Uruguay, USA, Venezuela.
Included in the above, 2 universities listed in this Yearbook:
Andes University (ULA); Universidad Centroamericana José Simeón Cañas (UCA).
NGO Relations Secretariat provided by: *Latin American and Iberian Institute, Albuquerque (LAII).* Member of: *Engineering for the Americas (EftA, no recent information); International Federation of Engineering Education Societies (IFEES, #13412).* [2022.05.09/XF4356/y/**F**]

- ♦ Ibero-American Seminar on Water & Drainage Networks (meeting series)
- ♦ Ibero-American Social Security Office / see Ibero-American Social Security Organization (#11028)

♦ Ibero-American Social Security Organization 11028

Organisation ibéroaméricaine de sécurité sociale – Organización Iberoamericana de Seguridad Social (OISS) – Organização Iberoamericana de Segurança Social
SG Velazquez 105 – 1a planta, 28006 Madrid, Spain. T. +34915611747 – +34915611955. Fax +34915645633. E-mail: sec.general@oiss.org – oiss@oiss.org.
URL: http://www.oiss.org/
History 1950, Madrid (Spain). Founded at 1st Ibero-American Social Security Congress. Structure changed at 2nd Congress, 1954, Lima (Peru), on approval of constitutional plan by *ILO (#11123), OAS (#17629), International Social Security Association (ISSA, #14885)* and the governments of 21 countries. Statutes ratified, 1958, Quito (Ecuador), at 3rd Congress. One of 5 organizations withing *Comité de Dirección Estratégica de los Organismos Iberoamericanos (CoDEI, #04149).* Former names and other names: *Ibero-American Social Security Office* – former (1950 to 1954); *Comisión Iberoamericana de Seguridad Social* – former (1950 to 1954). **Aims** Improve economic and social *welfare* of the peoples of Ibero-America and elsewhere by promoting coordination, exchange and use of their mutual experience in the social security sphere. **Structure** Congress of delegates of full members; Management Committee; Standing Committee; General Secretariat. Economic Commission. Standing Technical Commissions. Institutional Technical Commissions (regional perspective): Central America – Caribbean; Cono Sur; Andean countries; non-American countries. Regional activity centres (3): Buenos Aires (Argentina); Bogota (Colombia); San José (Costa Rica). National Delegations (2): La Paz (Bolivia); San José. Technical Departments (3): Training of Experts; Cooperation and Assistance; Studies and Reports. **Languages** Portuguese, Spanish. **Finance** Members' quotas. Subventions. **Activities** Advocacy/lobbying/activism; events/meetings; guidance/assistance/consulting; knowledge management/information dissemination; research/documentation; training/education. Maintains database. **Events** *Congress* Salvador (Brazil) 2004, *Congress* Salvador (Brazil) 2004, *Congress* Santiago (Chile) 1999, *Congress* Punta del Este (Uruguay) 1995, *Congress* Santa Cruz (Bolivia) 1991. **Publications** *Revista de la Seguridad Social Iberoamericana* (annual); *Boletín Informativo de la Organización Iberoamericana de Seguridad Social (BIOISS)* in Spanish. Congress reports; reports on legislation; social security bibliography; listing of social security experts in Ibero-American countries. **Information Services** *Banco de Información de los Sistemas de Seguridad Social en Iberoamérica (BISSI)* – databank on Ibero-American social security systems, including statistics and other information; *Información Comparativa de los Sistemas de Seguridad Social (INCOSSI).*
Members Governments and social security institutions of 22 countries:
Argentina, Bolivia, Brazil, Chile, Colombia, Costa Rica, Cuba, Dominican Rep, Ecuador, El Salvador, Equatorial Guinea, Guatemala, Honduras, Mexico, Nicaragua, Panama, Paraguay, Peru, Portugal, Spain, Uruguay, Venezuela.
IGO Relations Cooperates with (5): *Conferencia de Ministros de Justicia de los Países Iberoamericanos (COMJIB, #04656); Ibero-American General Secretariat (#11024); Ibero-American Youth Organization (#11036); OAS (#17629); Organization of Ibero-American States for Education, Science and Culture (#17871).* [2020/XD1017/**D***]

- ♦ Ibero-American Society for Anatomy (inactive)

♦ Iberoamerican Society of Artificial Intelligence 11029

Sociedad Iberoamericana de Inteligencia Artificial (IBERAMIA)
Chair address not obtained. E-mail: iberamia@iberamia.org.
URL: http://www.iberamia.org/
History Former names and other names: *Comité Coordinador de las Sociedades Iberoamericanas de Inteligencia Artificial (IBERAMIA)* – former. **Aims** Promote scientific and technological activities related to Artificial Intelligence in Ibero-American and Spanish and Portuguese-speaking countries; strengthen ties with scientific institutions as well as companies, institutions, public administrations and other international organizations; support teaching, research and technological transfer and innovation related to Artificial Intelligence; coordinate with Artificial Intelligence Associations of the Ibero-American countries, promoting activities and projects that help promote and disseminate Artificial Intelligence. **Structure** Executive Committee, including President and Secretary. **Activities** Events/meetings; financial and/or material support; knowledge management/information dissemination; networking/liaising; publishing activities; research and development; training/education. **Events** *Biennial Conference* Santiago (Chile) 2014, *Biennial Conference* Cartagena de Indias (Colombia) 2012, *Biennial Conference* Bahia Blanca (Argentina) 2010, *Biennial Conference* Lisbon (Portugal) 2008, *Biennial conference* Ribeirão Preto (Brazil) 2006.
Members National organizations (8) in 8 countries:
Argentina, Brazil, Chile, Cuba, Mexico, Portugal, Spain, Venezuela. [2023.02.15/XM2212/**E**]

- ♦ Iberoamerican Society for Bioinformatics (#19361)
- ♦ Ibero-American Society for Cell Biology (inactive)
- ♦ Iberoamerican Society of Contamination and Environmental Toxicology (unconfirmed)
- ♦ Ibero-American Society for the Development of Biorefineries (#19363)
- ♦ Ibero-American Society of Digital Graphics (#19370)
- ♦ Ibero-American Society of Environmental Physics and Chemistry (#19369)
- ♦ Ibero-American Society of Gynecological Endoscopy / see Ibero-American Society of Gynecological Endoscopy and Images (#11030)

♦ Ibero-American Society of Gynecological Endoscopy and Images . . 11030

Société ibéroaméricaine de endoscopie et imagénologie gynécologique – Sociedad Iberoamericana de Endoscopia Ginecológica e Imagenes (SIAEGI)
Pres Calle 60 7-25, Monteria 230002, Córdoba, Colombia. E-mail: franciscocarmonasl@gmail.com.
History 1984, as *Ibero-American Society of Gynecological Endoscopy – Sociedad Iberoamericana de Endoscopia Ginecológica (SIAEG).* Registered in accordance with Spanish law. **Aims** Develop and teach endoscopial and *ultrasound* techniques in the Ibero-American background; improve collaboration among member societies. **Structure** Executive Board, comprising President, Vice-President, Secretary General,

Deputy Secretary, Treasurer and Deputy Treasurer. National Secretaries. **Languages** English, Portuguese, Spanish. **Staff** 5.00 FTE, paid. **Finance** Members' dues. Other sources: grants; other support. **Activities** Organizes: biennial congress; project meetings; seminars. **Events** *International Congress on Gynaecological Endoscopy and Human Reproduction* Lima (Peru) 2015, *International Congress on Gynaecological Endoscopy and Human Reproduction* Cartagena de Indias (Colombia) 2013, *Congress* Cartagena de Indias (Colombia) 2009, *Congress / International Congress on Gynaecological Endoscopy and Human Reproduction* Panama (Panama) 2007, *Congress / International Congress on Gynaecological Endoscopy and Human Reproduction* Quito (Ecuador) 2004.
Members Full in 23 countries:
Argentina, Bolivia, Brazil, Chile, Colombia, Costa Rica, Cuba, Dominican Rep, Ecuador, El Salvador, France, Guatemala, Honduras, Italy, Mexico, Panama, Paraguay, Peru, Portugal, Spain, Uruguay, USA, Venezuela. [2015/XD0680/**D**]

- ♦ Ibero-American Society of Human Genetics of North America (internationally oriented national body)
- ♦ Iberoamerican Society of Interventional Radiology (#19373)
- ♦ Iberoamerican Society of Lingual Orthodontics (no recent information)
- ♦ Ibero American Society of Medical Law (no recent information)

♦ Iberoamerican Society of Neonatology (IASN) 11031
Sociedad Ibero-Americana de Neonatologia (SIBEN)
Dir Gen address not obtained. T. +5491136023876. E-mail: info@siben.net.
Dir of Operations address not obtained.
URL: http://www.siben.net/
History Mar 2004, Galapagos (Ecuador). **Aims** Improve the quality of life of newborns and their families in the Iberoamerican population. **Structure** Board of Directors, comprising President, Past President, Vice-President, Secretary and Treasurer. **Events** *Annual Congress* Mérida (Mexico) 2022, *Annual Congress* 2020, *Annual Congress* Quito (Ecuador) 2019, *Annual Congress* San Pedro Sula (Honduras) 2018, *Annual Congress* Santa Cruz (Bolivia) 2017. [2022/XM3451/**D**]

- ♦ Ibero-American Society for Neurochemistry (inactive)
- ♦ Ibero-American Society of Numismatic Research (#19367)

♦ Iberoamerican Society of Osteology and Mineral Metabolism 11032
Sociedad Iberoamericana de Osteologia y Metabolismo Mineral (SIBOMM)
Pres address not obtained.
Pres Elect address not obtained.
Sec address not obtained.
URL: http://www.sibommin.com/
History 1992. **Aims** Bring together Latin-American, Spanish and Portuguese scientific societies related with bone and mineral research. **Structure** Executive Committee, comprising President, President Elect, Past President, Secretary and Treasurer. **Languages** Spanish. **Finance** Members' dues. **Events** *Congress* Panama (Panama) 2019, *Congress* Lima (Peru) 2017, *Congress* Lisbon (Portugal) 2015, *Congress* Madrid (Spain) 2011, *Congress* Foz do Iguaçu (Brazil) 2009.
Members National organizations (26) in 16 countries:
Argentina, Brazil, Chile, Colombia, Costa Rica, Cuba, Dominican Rep, Ecuador, Mexico, Panama, Peru, Portugal, Puerto Rico, Spain, Uruguay, Venezuela.
NGO Relations Member of: *International Association of Asylum Seekers and Refugees (IAASR)*. [2016/XD8273/**D**]

♦ Iberoamerican Society of Paediatric Urology 11033
Sociedad Iberoamericana de Urologia Pediatrica (SIUP)
Sec address not obtained. E-mail: miguel.castell@gmail.com – jcprietos@hotmail.com.
URL: http://www.siupurol.com/
History 1995, Santiago (Chile). **Aims** Promote research and increase the knowledge of this discipline to improve awareness of paediatric patients with congenital anomalies and related diseases. **Events** *Congress* Guayaquil (Ecuador) 2020, *Congress* Buenos Aires (Argentina) 2019, *Congress* Panama (Panama) 2016, *Congress* Cancún (Mexico) 2015, *Congress* Punta del Este (Uruguay) 2014. [2015/XJ0549/**D**]

- ♦ Iberoamerican Society of Pneumonology / see Asociación Latinoamericana del Tórax (#02273)
- ♦ Ibero-American Society of Prenatal Diagnosis and Treatment (no recent information)
- ♦ Iberoamerican Society for Scientific Information (#19372)
- ♦ Ibero-American Stroke Organization (#19365)
- ♦ Ibero-American Table Tennis Federation (#09322)
- ♦ Ibero-American Television Organization / see Organización de Telecomunicaciones de Iberoamérica (#17851)
- ♦ Ibero-American Transpersonal Association (#02304)

♦ Ibero-American Union of Municipalists 11034
Unión Iberoamericana de Municipalistas (UIM)
SG Plaza Mariana Pineda 9, 18009 Granada, Spain. T. +34958215047. Fax +34958229767. E-mail: uim@uimunicipalistas.org – info@uimunicipalistas.org.
URL: https://www.uimunicipalistas.org/
History 19 Feb 1990. Former names and other names: *Latin American Organization of Intermunicipal Cooperation* – alias. **Aims** Promote cooperation and exchange among municipalities, staff working in *local government* and specialists and researchers in local development and autonomy in Spain and Latin America; foster activities favouring development of local autonomy; encourage active participation of neighbours and citizens in their own interests; protect community interests and activities with respect to national and international bodies; improve education and capabilities of local administration management and civil servants. **Structure** General Assembly. Council, comprising President, Executive Secretary, Executive Vice-Secretary and 12 further members including President of *Centro de Estudios Municipales y de Cooperación Internacional (CEMCI)*, where Technical Office is located. Networks include: Red Iberoamericana de Profesionales por la Comunicación Pública (IBERCOMP); Red UIM de Cooperación Internacional al Desarrollo Local (RUDICEL); Red UIM de Instituciones Iberoamericanas para el Desarrollo Local (RIIDEL); Red UIM de Empresas Colaboradoras al Desarrollo Local (ENCODEL); Red Iberoamericana de Universidades y Centros Académicos sobre Investigación, Innovación, Desarrollo Tecnológico y Transferencia del Conocimiento Municipal (REDUNI). **Languages** Spanish. **Staff** None. **Finance** Members' dues. Other sources: grants from *Agencia Española de Cooperación Internacional para el Desarrollo (AECID)*. **Activities** Advanced training programme leading to master's degree provided in: Córdoba (Argentina); Antigua; Guatemala (Guatemala); Maracaibo (Venezuela); Guanajuato (Mexico). Other training programmes: local authorities encounter; local management workshops; local information and documentation; technical assistance. **Events** *Encuentro Iberoamericano de Comunicación Pública* Malaga (Spain) 2022, *Cumbre Iberoamericanas de Agendas Locales de Género*, Cuenca (Ecuador) 2018, *Congreso Iberoamericanos de Municipalistas* Manizales (Colombia) 2017, *Cumbre Iberoamericanas de Agendas Locales de Género* Santiago (Chile) 2016, *Congreso Iberoamericanos de Municipalistas* San Juan (Puerto Rico) 2014. **Publications** *Cuadernos de Documentación e Información Municipal* – series. Collections: EDIL. Studies; commentaries; syntheses; monographies; historical reserach.
Members Full in 24 countries:
Argentina, Bolivia, Brazil, Chile, Colombia, Costa Rica, Cuba, Dominica, Dominican Rep, Ecuador, El Salvador, Guatemala, Honduras, Mexico, Nicaragua, Panama, Paraguay, Peru, Portugal, Puerto Rico, Spain, Uruguay, USA, Venezuela.
IGO Relations Accredited by: *OAS (#17629)*. [2022/XD6989/**D**]

♦ Ibero-American Union of Parents 11035
Union ibéroaméricaine des parents – Unión Iberoamericana de Padres de Familia y Padres de Alumnos (UNIAPA)
Pres C/ Alfonso XI 4, 28014 Madrid, Spain. T. +34915325865. Fax +34915315983. E-mail: concapa@concapa.org.
History Mar 1988, Madrid (Spain). **Aims** Promote the lasting values of the family, especially in its educational function. **Structure** General Assembly. Permanent Commission, consisting of a representative for each member country. Officers: President, 2 Vice-Presidents, Secretary General, Treasurer. **Languages** Portuguese, Spanish. **Staff** 5.00 FTE, voluntary. **Finance** Members' dues. Budget (annual): US$ 16,500. **Activities** Congresses; conferences; seminars. **Events** *Congress* Madrid (Spain) 1992, *Congress* Bolivia 1991, *Congress* Chile 1991, *Congress* Saragossa (Spain) 1991, *Congress* Mexico City (Mexico) 1990. **Publications** *La Participación de los Padres en los Centros Educativos* (1990).
Members Parents' associations, grouping 25 million parents of pupils, in 12 countries:
Argentina, Bolivia, Chile, Colombia, Ecuador, Mexico, Paraguay, Peru, Portugal, Spain, Uruguay, Venezuela. [2012/XD1692/**D**]

- ♦ Ibero-American University for Graduate Studies / see Asociación Universitaria Iberoamericana de Postgrado (#02307)
- ♦ Ibero-American University, Mexico (internationally oriented national body)

♦ Ibero-American Youth Organization 11036
Organización Iberoamericana de Juventud (OIJ)
Contact Paseo de Recoletos 8, First Floor, 28001 Madrid, Spain. T. +34913690284. E-mail: secretariageneral@oij.org.
URL: http://www.oij.org/
History 1996, Buenos Aires (Argentina). Founded during 8th Iberoamerican Conference of Ministers of Youth. One of 5 organizations within *Comité de Dirección Estratégica de los Organismos Iberoamericanos (CoDEI, #04149)*. **Aims** Improve life quality for youngsters in the region; facilitate and promote cooperation among members, as well as IGOs and NGOs working in the field of youth; strengthen governmental structures concerning youth affairs; work towards interinstitutional and intersectoral coordination; formulate and execute programs and projects; act as a consultative body for the execution and administration of programs and projects in youth affairs and for the adoption of positions and strategies on youth subjects. **Structure** Ibero-American Conference of Ministers of Youth; Directive Council; Office of Secretary General. **Languages** English, Portuguese, Spanish. **Finance** Member States' contributions. **Activities** Events/meetings; networking/liaising; projects/programmes; training/education. **Events** *European Union – Latin America and the Caribbean youth summit* Madrid (Spain) 2010, *Conference* Santo Domingo (Dominican Rep) 2010, *FEULAT : Euro-Latin American youth forum* Mollina (Spain) 2009, *Conference* Santiago (Chile) 2009, *FEULAT : Euro-Latin American youth forum* Mollina (Spain) 2006. **Publications** *Ibero-American Report on Youth Entrepreneurship*. Summit conclusions and other documents; Conference declarations.
Members Governments of 21 countries:
Argentina, Bolivia, Brazil, Chile, Colombia, Costa Rica, Cuba, Dominican Rep, Ecuador, El Salvador, Guatemala, Honduras, Mexico, Nicaragua, Panama, Paraguay, Peru, Portugal, Spain, Uruguay, Venezuela.
IGO Relations Observer status with (2): *Council of Europe (CE, #04881)*; *United Nations (UN, #20515)* (General Assembly). Cooperates with (4): *Conferencia de Ministros de Justicia de los Países Iberoamericanos (COMJIB, #04656)*; *Ibero-American General Secretariat (#11024)*; *Ibero-American Social Security Organization (#11028)*; *Organization of Ibero-American States for Education, Science and Culture (#17871)*. Cooperation agreement with: *Development Bank of Latin America (CAF, #05055)*; *ILO (#11123)*; *OECD (#17693)*; *United Nations Economic Commission for Latin America and the Caribbean (ECLAC, #20556)*; *United Nations Population Fund (UNFPA, #20612)*; *United Nations Volunteers (UNV, #20650)*. Supports activities of: *Latin American and Caribbean Demographic Centre (#16273)*. Participates in: Central American Youth Forum; *Comunidade dos Paises de Lingua Portuguesa (CPLP, #04430)*; Pacific Alliance. [2018.06.20/XD6023/**D***]

- ♦ Ibero-Amerika Institut für Wirtschaftsforschung / see Ibero-America Institute for Economic Research of the University of Göttingen
- ♦ Ibero-Amerika Institut für Wirtschaftsforschung der Universität Göttingen (internationally oriented national body)
- ♦ Ibero-Amerikanisches Institut Preussischer Kulturbesitz (internationally oriented national body)
- ♦ **IBEROAQUA** Asociación Iberoamericana de las Tecnologias del Agua y Riego (#02153)
- ♦ IBEROEKA – Proyectos de Innovación IBEROEKA (see: #18524)
- ♦ Ibero-Latin American Academy of Craniomandibular Disorders (internationally oriented national body)
- ♦ Ibero-Latin American Association of Endodontists / see Asociación Iberolatinoamericana de Endodoncia (#02157)
- ♦ Ibero-Latin American College of Dermatology (#04093)
- ♦ Ibero-Latin American Endodontic Association (#02157)
- ♦ Ibero-Latin American Federation of Medical Societies of Acupuncture (#09327)
- ♦ Ibero-Latin-American Federation of Performers (#09325)
- ♦ Ibero-Latin American Federation of Plastic Surgery (#09326)
- ♦ Ibero-Latin American Federation of Training and Development Organizations / see Federación Iberoamericana de Capacitación y Desarrollo (#09308)
- ♦ Ibero-Latinoamerican Academy of Bodily Damage Evaluation (unconfirmed)
- ♦ **IberoMAB** Red Iberoamericana de Comités MAB y Reservas de la Biósfera (#18661)
- ♦ IberoPanamerican Federation of Periodontics (#09328)
- ♦ **IberRed** Red Iberoamericana de Cooperación Jurídica Internacional (#18662)
- ♦ Ibersensor – Congreso Iberoamericano de Sensores (meeting series)
- ♦ IBESA – International Battery and Energy Storage Alliance (unconfirmed)
- ♦ **IBES** International Bronchoesophagological Society (#12401)
- ♦ IBEW – International Brotherhood of Electrical Workers (internationally oriented national body)
- ♦ IBF / see Bears in Mind
- ♦ IBF / see International Banking Federation (#12311)
- ♦ **IBFAN** International Baby Food Action Network (#12305)
- ♦ IBF / see Badminton World Federation (#03060)
- ♦ **IBFD** International Bureau of Fiscal Documentation (#12415)
- ♦ **IBFed** International Banking Federation (#12311)
- ♦ **IBFEG** Internationaler Bund Freier Evangelischer Gemeinden (#13433)
- ♦ IBFES – International Board of Forensic Engineering Sciences (internationally oriented national body)
- ♦ IBF / see Federation of International Bandy (#09601)
- ♦ IBFG – Internationaler Bund Freier Gewerkschaften (inactive)
- ♦ **IBF** International Balint Federation (#12307)
- ♦ IBF – International Balut Federation (no recent information)
- ♦ IBF – International Bicycle Fund (internationally oriented national body)
- ♦ IBF – International Booksellers Federation (inactive)
- ♦ **IBF** International Bowling Federation (#12384)
- ♦ **IBF** International Boxing Federation (#12386)
- ♦ **IBF** International Breathwork Foundation (#12396)
- ♦ IBF – International Buddhist Foundation (internationally oriented national body)
- ♦ **IBF** International Buffalo Federation (#12408)
- ♦ IBF – Internationale Budo Federatie (inactive)
- ♦ **I-BFM-SG** International BFM Study Group (#12335)
- ♦ **IBFRA** International Boreal Forest Research Association (#12382)
- ♦ IBF/USBA / see International Boxing Federation (#12386)
- ♦ IBG' / see Royal Geographical Society – with the Institute of British Geographers
- ♦ **IBGA** International Blind Golf Association (#12362)
- ♦ **IBG** Intelligent Building Group (#11374)
- ♦ IBG / see International Brecht Society (#12397)
- ♦ IBG / see International Bureau of Strata Mechanics (#12417)
- ♦ IBG – Internationale Begegnung in Gemeinschaftsdiensten (internationally oriented national body)
- ♦ **IBG** Internationales Büro für Gebirgsmechanik (#12417)
- ♦ IBG / see International Union of Soil Sciences (#15817)
- ♦ IBGS – International Barley Genetics Symposium (meeting series)
- ♦ IBHA – International Big History Association (unconfirmed)
- ♦ **IBHA** International Buckskin Horse Association (#12404)
- ♦ **IBHRE** International Board of Heart Rhythm Examiners (#12370)
- ♦ **IBIA** Internatioanl Betting Integrity Association (#11527)
- ♦ **IBIA** International Brain Injury Association (#12391)
- ♦ **IBIA** International Bunker Industry Association (#12411)
- ♦ **IBICA** International Brethren in Christ Association (#12398)
- ♦ IBIC – International Buffalo Information Centre (internationally oriented national body)
- ♦ IBI – Intergovernmental Bureau for Informatics (inactive)

- ♦ IBI – International Banking Institute, Sofia (internationally oriented national body)
- ♦ IBI – International Banking Institute, St Petersburg (internationally oriented national body)
- ♦ **IBI** International Biochar Initiative (#12342)
- ♦ IBI – Internationales Burgen-Institut (inactive)
- ♦ IBI / see International Institute of Communications (#13870)
- ♦ Ibike / see International Bicycle Fund
- ♦ IB – Institut Belleville (internationally oriented national body)
- ♦ **IB** International Baccalaureate (#12306)
- ♦ IB – International Børnehjaelp (internationally oriented national body)
- ♦ IB – International Symposium on Integrative Bioinformatics (meeting series)
- ♦ Ibis – Denmark (internationally oriented national body)
- ♦ **IBIS** International Bioiron Society (#12351)
- ♦ IBIS – International Book Information Service (internationally oriented national body)
- ♦ Ibis Reproductive Health (internationally oriented national body)
- ♦ IBITA – An international association for adult neurological rehabilitation / see International Bobath Instructors Training Association (#12373)
- ♦ IBITAH / see International Bobath Instructors Training Association (#12373)
- ♦ **IBITA** International Bobath Instructors Training Association (#12373)
- ♦ IBKAB – Internationaler Bund Katholischer Arbeitnehmer-Bewegungen (inactive)
- ♦ **IBKA** Internationaler Bund der Konfessionslosen und Atheisten (#14020)
- ♦ **IBK** Internationale Bodenseekonferenz (#13217)
- ♦ **IBK** Internationalen Altkatholischen Bischofskonferenz (#14403)
- ♦ IBLA – International Boatmen's Linesmen's Association (unconfirmed)
- ♦ IBLA / see Pontifical Institute for Arabic and Islamic Studies (#18448)
- ♦ **IBLCE** International Board of Lactation Consultant Examiners (#12371)
- ♦ **IBLC** International Business Law Consortium (#12420)
- ♦ IBLF Global (internationally oriented national body)
- ♦ **IBMA** International Biocontrol Manufacturers Association (#12343)
- ♦ IBMA – International Bluegrass Music Association (internationally oriented national body)
- ♦ IBMATA – International Border Management and Technologies Association (unconfirmed)
- ♦ IBMEC – International Business and Management Education Centre (internationally oriented national body)
- ♦ **IBM** International Brotherhood of Magicians (#12402)
- ♦ IBMM – International Conference on Ion Beam Modification of Materials (meeting series)
- ♦ **IBMS** International Bone and Mineral Society (#12379)
- ♦ IBN – International Benefits Network (unconfirmed)
- ♦ Ibn Khaldoun Center for Development Studies, Cairo (internationally oriented national body)
- ♦ IBNLP – International Business NLP Association (unconfirmed)
- ♦ **IBNS** International Bank Note Society (#12316)
- ♦ **IBNS** International Behavioral Neuroscience Society (#12331)
- ♦ IBO / see International Baccalaureate (#12306)
- ♦ **IBO** Internationale Bouworde (#11745)
- ♦ **IBO** Internationaler Bauorden (#11745)
- ♦ **iBOL** International Barcode of Life (#12323)

♦ IBON International 11037

Dir 3rd Floor, IBON Center, 114 Timog Ave, 1103 Quezon City, Philippines. T. +6329277060 – +6329277061 – +6329277062. Fax +6329276981. E-mail: atujan@iboninternational.org – international@iboninternational.org.
URL: http://www.iboninternational.org/

History Set up as the international arm of *IBON Foundation*. Name derives from the Filipino word for 'bird'. **Aims** Respond to international demand to provide support in research and education to people's movements and *grassroots empowerment* and advocacy, and link these to international initiatives and networks. **Structure** Head offices in: Manila (Philippines); Andhra Pradesh (India); Brussels (Belgium); Nairobi (Kenya). Regional programme units: Africa; Asia; South Asia; Europe. **Activities** Guidance/assistance/consulting; knowledge management/information dissemination. **Events** *International Assembly of Migrants and Refugees / International Assembly of Migrants and Refugees – IAMR* Manila (Philippines) 2008. **Consultative Status** Consultative status granted from: *ECOSOC (#05331)* (Special); *UNEP (#20299)*. **IGO Relations** Accredited by: *Green Climate Fund (GCF, #10714)*. **NGO Relations** Hosts: *Asia-Pacific Research Network (APRN, #02013)*; *CSO Partnership for Development Effectiveness (CPDE, #04976)*; *The Reality Of Aid (ROA, #18626)*; Water for the People Network (WPN). Member of: *People's Coalition on Food Sovereignty (PCFS, #18303)*.
[2018/XJ0535/f/**E**]

♦ IBOS Association 11038

Managing Dir Golden Cross House, 8 Duncannon St, London, WC2N 4JF, UK. T. +442074845387.
URL: http://www.ibosbanks.com/

History Originally started as a for-profit joint venture between Banco Santander (Spain) and the Royal Bank of Scotland (UK). Original title: *International Banking – One Solution (IBOS Association)*. Previously also referred to as *Inter-Bank Online System (IBOS)* and *International Banking Assocdiation (IBOS)*. **Aims** Enable member banks to service *corporate* customers with a wide range of international *banking* services.
Members Banks. Full in 10 countries:
Belgium, Finland, France, Germany, Ireland, Italy, Portugal, Spain, UK, USA.
Associate members in 19 countries:
Austria, Brazil, Bulgaria, Chile, Croatia, Czechia, Denmark, Finland, Hungary, Italy, Mexico, Netherlands, Norway, Poland, Romania, Russia, Slovakia, Slovenia, Sweden.
[2019.04.23/XJ8169/**F**]

- ♦ IBOS / see IBOS Association (#11038)
- ♦ **IBPA** International Bridge Press Association (#12399)
- ♦ IBPA – International Bullying Prevention Association (internationally oriented national body)
- ♦ IBPAT / see International Union of Painters and Allied Trades
- ♦ IBPGR / see Bioversity International (#03262)
- ♦ **IBP** International Budget Partnership (#12406)
- ♦ IBPMA – International Biodegradable Products Manufacturers Association (inactive)
- ♦ IBPO – International Brotherhood of Police Officers (internationally oriented national body)
- ♦ IBPSA – International Boarding and Pet Services (unconfirmed)
- ♦ **IBPSA** International Building Performance Simulation Association (#12409)
- ♦ IBPSA World / see International Building Performance Simulation Association (#12409)
- ♦ IBRA / see IBRA Media
- ♦ **IBRA** International Bee Research Association (#12330)
- ♦ **IBRA** International Bible Reading Association (#12337)
- ♦ **IBRA** International Bone Research Association (#12380)
- ♦ IBRA – International Buckwheat Research Association (unconfirmed)
- ♦ IBRA Media (internationally oriented national body)
- ♦ IBRA Radio / see IBRA Media
- ♦ IBRC – International Bat Research Conference (meeting series)
- ♦ IBRD Economic Development Institute / see World Bank Institute (#21220)
- ♦ **IBRD** International Bank for Reconstruction and Development (#12317)
- ♦ IBREA Foundation (internationally oriented national body)
- ♦ **IBREAM** Institute for Breeding Rare and Endangered African Mammals (#11243)
- ♦ IBRF / see International Rhino Foundation (#14752)
- ♦ **IBRG** International Biodeterioration Research Group (#12345)
- ♦ IBRI – Instituto Brasileiro de Relações Internacionais (internationally oriented national body)
- ♦ IBR – International Bird Rescue (internationally oriented national body)
- ♦ **IBRO** International Brain Research Organization (#12392)
- ♦ IBRO – International Buddhist Relief Organization (internationally oriented national body)
- ♦ IBRRC / see International Bird Rescue
- ♦ IBRU – International Boundaries Research Unit (internationally oriented national body)
- ♦ IBS / see Biblica
- ♦ IBS / see International Society for Utilitarian Studies
- ♦ **IBSA** International Banking Security Association (#12312)
- ♦ **IBSA** International Bible Students Association (#12338)
- ♦ **IBSA** International Blind Sports Federation (#12363)
- ♦ IBS / see Barents Euro-Arctic Council (#03177)
- ♦ IBSCC – International Bureau for the Suppression of Counterfeit Coins (internationally oriented national body)

♦ IB Schools Australasia 11039

Mailing Address PO Box 3143, North, Ivanhoe VIC 3079, Australia. E-mail: office@ibaustralasia.org.
URL: https://ibaustralasia.org/

History Former names and other names: *Association of Australasian International Baccalaureate Schools* – alias; *Association of Australasian IB Schools (AAIBS)* – former. **Aims** Support the goals and objectives of the International Baccalaureate Office and International Baccalaureate World Schools in Australasia. **Structure** Standing Committee, comprising Chair, Treasurer, Secretary and 7 members. **Languages** English. **Staff** 5.00 FTE, voluntary. **Finance** Members' dues. **Activities** Provides support for the International Baccalaureate Diploma, Middle Years and Primary Years Programmes for IB schools in Australasia; liaises on behalf of AAIBS member schools with Ministries and Departments of Education, universities and professional educational organizations in Australasia; acts upon request or when deemed necessary so as to promote recognition of the International Baccalaureate Diploma as a qualification for entry to universities in Australasia; supports professional development programmes of the International Baccalaureate, in particular those sponsored by the International Baccalaureate Organization and originating in member schools; promotes research into the benefits of the International Baccalaureate Programme and assessment. Organizes annual conference (July). **Events** *Annual Conference* Melbourne, VIC (Australia) 2012, *Annual Conference* Auckland (New Zealand) 2010, *Annual Conference* Adelaide, SA (Australia) 2009, *Annual Conference* Sydney, NSW (Australia) 2008, *Annual Conference* Canberra, ACT (Australia) 2007. **Publications** *AAIBS Newsletter*. **NGO Relations** Partner of (1): *International Baccalaureate (IB, #12306)*.
[2022/XE2575/**E**]

- ♦ IBSC – International Bird Strike Committee (inactive)
- ♦ **IBSC** International Black Sea Club (#12358)
- ♦ **IBSC** International Boys' Schools Coalition (#12387)
- ♦ **IBSES** International Board of Shoulder and Elbow Surgery (#12372)
- ♦ IBSFC – International Baltic Sea Fishery Commission (internationally oriented national body)
- ♦ **IBSF** International Billiards and Snooker Federation (#12340)
- ♦ **IBSF** International Bobsleigh and Skeleton Federation (#12375)
- ♦ IBS – Institute of Baltic Studies (internationally oriented national body)
- ♦ **IBS** International Ballistics Society (#12308)
- ♦ **IBS** International Biogeography Society (#12349)
- ♦ IBS – International Biohydrometallurgy Symposium (meeting series)
- ♦ **IBS** International Biometals Society (#12353)
- ♦ **IBS** International Biotherapy Society (#12355)
- ♦ IBS – International Boethius Society (internationally oriented national body)
- ♦ **IBS** International Brecht Society (#12397)
- ♦ IBS – International Broadcasters Society (inactive)
- ♦ IBS – International Broadcasting Society (inactive)
- ♦ IBS – International Rail Freight Business Association (unconfirmed)
- ♦ IBS – Istanbul International Brotherhood and Solidarity Association (internationally oriented national body)
- ♦ IBSL – Internationaler Bund der Schuh- und Lederarbeiter (inactive)
- ♦ **IBSM** International Bureau of Strata Mechanics (#12417)
- ♦ IbSN – Ibero-American Society for Neurochemistry (inactive)
- ♦ IBSN / see International Cancer Screening Network (#12435)
- ♦ IBSO – International Businesses Standards Organization (internationally oriented national body)
- ♦ **IBSSA** International Bodyguard and Security Services Association (#12377)
- ♦ IBS-STL Global / see Biblica
- ♦ IBSU – International Black Sea University (internationally oriented national body)
- ♦ IBSV / see International Blind Sports Federation (#12363)
- ♦ IBTA – International Basement Tectonics Association (inactive)
- ♦ **IBTA** International Brain Tumour Alliance (#12393)
- ♦ **IBTC** International Biomass Torrefaction Council (#12352)
- ♦ IBT – International Broadcasting Trust (internationally oriented national body)
- ♦ IBT – International Brotherhood of Teamsters (internationally oriented national body)
- ♦ **IBTN** International Behavioural Trials Network (#12333)
- ♦ IBTS Centre Amsterdam / see International Baptist Theological Study Centre, Amsterdam (#12319)
- ♦ **IBTSC** International Baptist Theological Study Centre, Amsterdam (#12319)
- ♦ **IBTTA** International Bridge, Tunnel and Turnpike Association (#12400)
- ♦ IBTU – Internationella Byggnads- och Träindustriarbetar-Unionen (inactive)
- ♦ **IBUG** International Blaise Users Group (#12361)
- ♦ **IBU** International Biathlon Union (#12336)
- ♦ IBU – Internationale Binnenschiffahrts Union (inactive)
- ♦ **IBU** Internationale Bodenkundliche Union (#15817)
- ♦ **IBU** Islamic Broadcasting Union (#16033)
- ♦ **IBUS** International Breast Ultrasound School (#12395)
- ♦ IBV – Internationale Buchhändler-Vereinigung (inactive)
- ♦ IBV – Internationaler Bergarbeiterverband (inactive)
- ♦ **IBVPA** International Beach Volleyball Players' Association (#12329)
- ♦ IBVS / see European Board of Veterinary Specialisation (#06375)
- ♦ IBWA – International Bottled Water Association (internationally oriented national body)
- ♦ IBWC – International Boundary and Water Commission (internationally oriented national body)
- ♦ IBWG / see International Federation of Biosafety Associations (#13373)
- ♦ IBZ / see World House, Bielefeld
- ♦ **IBZ** Informations- und Bildungszentrum Schloss Gimborn (#12877)
- ♦ IBZ – Internationale Bibliothek für Zukunftsfragen, Salzburg – Robert-Jungk Stiftung (internationally oriented national body)
- ♦ IC / see International Circle of Educational Institutes for Graphic Arts Technology and Management (#12573)
- ♦ ICAAD – International Center for Advocates Against Discrimination (internationally oriented national body)
- ♦ ICA Agricultural Committee / see International Co-operative Agricultural Organisation (#12943)
- ♦ ICAA – International Civil Airports Association (inactive)
- ♦ **ICAA** International Committee on Activation Analysis (#12739)
- ♦ ICAA – International Confederation of Artists Associations (inactive)
- ♦ ICAA – International Conference on Aluminium Alloys (meeting series)
- ♦ ICAA – International Council on Active Aging (internationally oriented national body)
- ♦ **ICAA** International Council on Alcohol and Addictions (#12989)
- ♦ ICAA / see International Council for Evangelical Theological Education (#13020)
- ♦ ICAAMC / see International Compressor Applications And Machinery Committee (#12834)
- ♦ **ICAAMC** International Compressor Applications And Machinery Committee (#12834)
- ♦ ICAAR – International Conference on Alkali Aggregate Reaction in Concrete (meeting series)
- ♦ **ICAAS** International Council on Amino Acid Science (#12991)
- ♦ ICA / see Association for European Life Science Universities (#02519)
- ♦ **ICA** Association for European Life Science Universities (#02519)

♦ **ICABEEP** International Confederation for the Advancement of Behavioral Economics and Economic Psychology (#12842)
♦ ICAB – International Council Against Bullfighting (inactive)
♦ **ICABR** International Consortium on Applied Bioeconomy Research (#12904)
♦ ICABT – International Conference on Agriculture and Biotechnology (meeting series)
♦ ICACBR – International Centre for the Advancement of Community-Based Rehabilitation (internationally oriented national body)
♦ ICA Central Banking Committee / see International Cooperative Banking Association (#12945)
♦ **ICACGP** International Commission on Atmospheric Chemistry and Global Pollution (#12664)
♦ **ICAC** Institute of Chartered Accountants of the Caribbean (#11245)
♦ **ICAC** International Cotton Advisory Committee (#12979)
♦ ICACM – International Conference on Advanced Composite Materials (meeting series)
♦ ICA Committee for Consumer Co-operatives / see Consumer Co-operatives Worldwide (#04770)
♦ ICA Consumer Committee / see Consumer Co-operatives Worldwide (#04770)
♦ ICACS – International Conference on Atomic Collisions in Solids (meeting series)
♦ ICACT – International Congress on Anti-Cancer Treatment (meeting series)
♦ **ICADA** International Committee on Allergic Diseases of Animals (#12744)
♦ ICADA – International Cosmetic and Device Association (unconfirmed)
♦ ICAD – Interagency Coalition on AIDS and Development (internationally oriented national body)
♦ **ICAD** International Community for Auditory Display (#12820)
♦ ICAD – International Conference on Axiomatic Design (meeting series)
♦ ICADS – Institute for Central American Development Studies (internationally oriented national body)
♦ **ICADS** International Coalition of Art Deco Societies (#12608)
♦ **ICADTS** International Council on Alcohol, Drugs and Traffic Safety (#12990)
♦ ICAD / see World DanceSport Federation (#21354)
♦ **ICAEA** International Civil Aviation English Association (#12580)
♦ **ICAEC** Institute of Chartered Accountants of the Eastern Caribbean (#11246)
♦ **ICAED** International Coalition against Enforced Disappearances (#12605)
♦ **ICAE** International Commission on Atmospheric Electricity (#12665)
♦ ICAE – International Conference on Applied Energy (meeting series)
♦ **ICAE** International Council for Adult Education (#12983)
♦ ICAEP / see Institut de la Culture Afro-européenne à Paris
♦ ICAEP – Institut de la Culture Afro-européenne à Paris (internationally oriented national body)
♦ **ICAES** Instituto Centroamericano de Estudios Sociales (#11326)
♦ ICAFE – Intergovernmental Collaborative Action Fund for Excellence (internationally oriented national body)
♦ ICAF espace francophone / see Institut pour la coopération audiovisuelle francophone
♦ ICAFFH – International Committee for the Anthropology of Food and Food Habits (inactive)
♦ ICAF – Institut pour la coopération audiovisuelle francophone (internationally oriented national body)
♦ ICAF – International Child Art Foundation (internationally oriented national body)
♦ ICAF / see International Committee on Aeronautical Fatigue and Structural Integrity (#12741)
♦ **ICAF** International Committee on Aeronautical Fatigue and Structural Integrity (#12741)
♦ ICAF – International Congress of African Studies (inactive)
♦ ICA Fisheries Committee / see International Cooperative Fisheries Organization (#12946)
♦ **ICA Foundation** International Contraceptive Access Foundation (#12936)
♦ ICAGL – International Colloquium on Ancient Greek Linguistics (meeting series)
♦ ICAHM / see ICOMOS International Scientific Committee on Archaeological Heritage Management (#11073)
♦ **ICAHM** ICOMOS International Scientific Committee on Archaeological Heritage Management (#11073)
♦ ICA Housing / see Co-operative Housing International (#04799)
♦ ICA Housing Cooperatives / see Co-operative Housing International (#04799)
♦ ICAHS – International Conference on Animal Health Surveillance (meeting series)
♦ ICAICONF – International Conference on Innovation in Computer Science and Artificial Intelligence (meeting series)
♦ ICAI – Institut canadien des affaires internationales (internationally oriented national body)
♦ **ICAI** Institute of Cultural Affairs International (#11251)
♦ **ICA** Infrastructure Consortium for Africa (#11206)
♦ ICA – Institut culturel africain (inactive)
♦ **ICA** Institute for Connectivity in the Americas (#11249)
♦ **ICA Institute** India China and America Institute (#11157)
♦ **ICA** Interarab Cambist Association (#11455)
♦ **ICA** Inter-Cultural Association (#11465)
♦ ICA – International Cardijn Association (internationally oriented national body)
♦ **ICA** International Cartographic Association (#12446)
♦ ICA – International Carwash Association (internationally oriented national body)
♦ **ICA** International Cellulosics Association (#12465)
♦ ICA / see International Ceramic Federation (#12530)
♦ ICA – International Chiropractors Association (internationally oriented national body)
♦ **ICA** International Christian Association (#12556)
♦ **ICA** International Chrysotile Association (#12570)
♦ **ICA** International Clarinet Association (#12590)
♦ **ICA** International Cluttering Association (#12603)
♦ ICA – International Coke Association (no recent information)
♦ **ICA** International College of Angiology (#12640)
♦ ICA / see International Commission for Acoustics (#12658)
♦ **ICA** International Commission for Acoustics (#12658)
♦ **ICA** International Communication Association (#12814)
♦ ICA – International Compliance Association (internationally oriented national body)
♦ **ICA** International Confectionery Association (#12840)
♦ **ICA** International Confederation of Accordionists (#12841)
♦ ICA – International Congress of Accountants (meeting series)
♦ **ICA** International Congress of Americanists (#12890)
♦ **ICA** International Co-operative Alliance (#12944)
♦ **ICA** International Copper Association (#12962)
♦ **ICA** International Cotton Association (#12980)
♦ **ICA** International Council on Archives (#12996)
♦ **ICA** International Council for Information Technology in Government Administration (#13033)
♦ **ICA** International CPTED Association (#13101)
♦ ICA – International Crisis Aid (internationally oriented national body)
♦ **ICA** International Currency Association (#13123)
♦ ICAIR / see Gateway Antarctica
♦ ICAIS – International Conference on Aquatic Invasive Species (meeting series)
♦ ICA – Islamic Cement Association (inactive)
♦ ICAITI – Instituto Centroamericano de Investigación y Tecnologia Industrial (inactive)
♦ ICAIT – International Conference on Advanced Infocomm Technology (meeting series)
♦ **ICAK** International College of Applied Kinesiology (#12641)
♦ ICALEPCS – International Conference on Accelerator and Large Experimental Physics Control Systems (meeting series)
♦ ICAMAS / see CIHEAM – International Centre for Advanced Mediterranean Agronomic Studies (#03927)
♦ **ICAMC** International Committee on Automation of Mines and Quarries (#12747)
♦ ICAMC – International Conference on Architecture, Materials and Construction (meeting series)
♦ ICAMCyL – International Center for Advanced Materials and raw materials of Castilla y León (internationally oriented national body)
♦ ICAMD – International Commission on Antigens and Molecular Diagnostics (see: #15794)
♦ ICAME / see International Board on the Applications of the Mössbauer Effect (#12365)
♦ ICAMES – Inter-University Consortium for Arab Studies and Middle Eastern Studies (internationally oriented national body)
♦ ICAMET – International Conference on Advanced Material Engineering & Technology (meeting series)
♦ ICAMG – International Conference on Asian Marine Geology (meeting series)
♦ **ICAMI** International Committee Against Mental Illness (#12742)
♦ **ICAM** International Companion Animal Management Coalition (#12828)
♦ **ICAM** International Confederation of Architectural Museums (#12846)
♦ ICAM – International Conference on Arctic Margins (meeting series)
♦ **ICAM** International Council for Applied Mineralogy (#12993)
♦ ICAMT – ICOM International Committee for Architecture and Museum Techniques (see: #13051)
♦ ICAMT – International Centre for Advancement of Manufacturing Technology, Bangalore (see: #20336)
♦ **ICANAS** International Congress of Asian and North African Studies (#12891)
♦ **ICAN** Infection Control Africa Network (#11184)
♦ ICAN – Institute of Cardiometabolism And Nutrition (internationally oriented national body)
♦ **ICAN** International Campaign to Abolish Nuclear Weapons (#12426)
♦ ICAN – International Cancer Advocacy Network (unconfirmed)
♦ ICAN – International Citizen debt Audit Network (unconfirmed)
♦ **ICAN** International Civil Society Action Network (#12588)
♦ ICAN – International Coalition for Advocacy on Nutrition (unconfirmed)
♦ **ICANNA** International Institute for Cannabinoids (#13865)
♦ **ICANN** Internet Corporation for Assigned Names and Numbers (#15949)
♦ ICANN Studienkreis (unconfirmed)
♦ **ICANS** International Collaboration on Advanced Neutron Sources (#12636)
♦ ICANS – International Conference on Amorphous and Nano-crystalline Semiconductors (meeting series)
♦ **ICAO** International Civil Aviation Organization (#12581)
♦ **ICAO** International Co-operative Agricultural Organisation (#12943)
♦ **ICAO Staff Association** Staff Association of the International Civil Aviation Organization (#19939)
♦ ICAP (internationally oriented national body)
♦ **ICAPA** International Coalition for Aging and Physical Activity (#12606)
♦ **ICAPE** International Confederation of Associations for Pluralism in Economics (#12849)
♦ ICAP – Global – Health – Action / see ICAP
♦ **ICAP** Instituto Centroamericano de Administración Pública (#03670)
♦ **ICAP** International Carbon Action Partnership (#12440)
♦ ICAP – International Conference on Atomic Physics (meeting series)
♦ **ICAPO** International Council on Animal Protection in OECD Programmes (#12992)
♦ **ICAPP** International Conference of Asian Political Parties (#12874)
♦ ICAPPS – International Conference of Asian-Pacific Planning Societies (meeting series)
♦ ICAR / see Jimmy and Rosalynn Carter School for Peace and Conflict Resolution
♦ **ICARA** International Confederation of Alcohol, Tobacco and other Drug Research Associations (#12843)
♦ **ICARDA** International Center for Agricultural Research in the Dry Areas (#12466)
♦ ICARE – International Christian Aid Relief Enterprises (internationally oriented national body)
♦ ICARE / see International Confederation of Associations for Pluralism in Economics (#12849)
♦ ICARE – Internet Centre Anti-Racism Europe (internationally oriented national body)
♦ **ICARHMA** International Council of Air-Conditioning, Refrigeration, and Heating Manufacturers Associations (#12987)
♦ ICAR – International Cannabis Alliance for Reform (inactive)
♦ ICAR – International Coalition for Agunah Rights (internationally oriented national body)
♦ **ICAR** International Commission for Alpine Rescue (#12662)
♦ **ICAR** International Committee for Animal Recording (#12746)
♦ ICAR – International Conference on Adoption Research (meeting series)
♦ **ICAR** International Corporate Accountability Roundtable (#12968)
♦ ICARMA / see International Council of Air-Conditioning, Refrigeration, and Heating Manufacturers Associations (#12987)
♦ ICARMO – International Council of the Architects of Historical Monuments (inactive)
♦ ICARSAH / see ICOMOS International Scientific Committee on Analysis and Restoration of Structures of Architectural Heritage (#11072)
♦ **ICARUS** International Centre for Archival Research (#12477)
♦ ICAR / see Women's Global Network for Reproductive Rights (#21019)
♦ ICASAC – International Congo Aid-Smile African Children (internationally oriented national body)
♦ **ICASA** International Collaboration on ADHD and Substance Abuse (#12635)
♦ ICASALS – International Center for Arid and Semiarid Land Studies (internationally oriented national body)
♦ **ICASC** International Committee for Airspace Standards and Calibration (#12743)
♦ ICASC / see Women's Global Network for Reproductive Rights (#21019)
♦ ICASEA – International Copper Association Southeast Asia (internationally oriented national body)
♦ **ICASE** International Council of Associations for Science Education (#12997)
♦ **ICASI** International Committee of Analysis for Steel and Iron Industry (#12745)
♦ **ICAS** Instituto Centro Americano de la Salud (#11328)
♦ ICAS – International Centre for Asian Studies (internationally oriented national body)
♦ ICAS – International Conference on Advanced Steels (meeting series)
♦ ICAS – International Convention of Asia Scholars (internationally oriented national body)
♦ **ICAS** International Council for Advertising Self-Regulation (#12984)
♦ **ICAS** International Council of the Aeronautical Sciences (#12985)
♦ **ICAS** International Council of Arbitration for Sport (#12994)

♦ ICASO 11040

Exec Dir 120 Carlton St, Ste 311, Toronto ON M5A 4K2, Canada. T. +14169210018. E-mail: icaso@icaso.org.
URL: http://www.icaso.org/

History Nov 1990, Paris (France). Founded during 2nd international conference of AIDS-related non-governmental organizations. Most recent by-laws amended 2012, Ottawa (Canada). Former names and other names: *International Council of AIDS Mexico City (ICASO)* – former; *Réseau international d'organisations d'entraide et de lutte contre le SIDA* – former; *Internationale Rat von AIDS-Service-Organisationen* – former. Registration: Charity, No/ID: 895549178 RR 0001, Start date: 1 Jan 2001, Canada, Ontario. **Aims** Facilitate inclusion and leadership of communities in the effort to bring about an end to the *HIV pandemic*, recognizing the importance of promoting health and human rights as part of this undertaking; encourage policy analysis and strategic information-gathering, with a particular focus on community-based research; build the capacity of community leaders to act as strong advocates and stewards of community-based structures for HIV mobilization and engagement; advocate for accountability, evidence-based and human rights-based approaches, and strategic use of HIV resources for maximum impact; develop networks to support an HIV mouvement that contributes more broadly to health, human rights and gender equality. **Structure** General Meeting (annual, always in Canada); Board. **Languages** English, French, Russian, Spanish. **Staff** 6.00 FTE, paid. **Finance** Sources: international organizations. Supported by: *Bill and Melinda Gates Foundation (BMGF)*; *Canadian International Development Agency (CIDA, inactive)*; Capital for Good; *Deutsche Gesellschaft für Internationale Zusammenarbeit (GIZ)*; *Global Fund to Fight AIDS, Tuberculosis and Malaria (Global Fund, #10383)*; *International AIDS Society (IAS, #11601)*; *International Civil Society Support (ICSS)*; *Joint United Nations Programme on HIV/AIDS (UNAIDS, #16149)*; Open Society Foundation. Annual budget: 900,000 EUR. **Activities** Advocacy/lobbying/activism; capacity building; events/meetings; knowledge management/information dissemination; research/documentation; training/education. **Events** *International AIDS Conference* Montréal, QC (Canada) 2022, *International AIDS Conference* 2020, *International AIDS Conference* Amsterdam

(Netherlands) 2018, *International AIDS Conference* Durban (South Africa) 2016, *International AIDS conference* Melbourne, VIC (Australia) 2014. **Publications** Action/Advocacy Alerts; Discussion Papers; Analytical Reports; Toolkits; Guidance Notes; Policy Briefs; Lessons Learned. **Consultative Status** Consultative status granted from: *ECOSOC (#05331)* (Roster). **IGO Relations** Cooperates with: *Global Fund to Fight AIDS, Tuberculosis and Malaria (Global Fund, #10383)*; *Joint United Nations Programme on HIV/AIDS (UNAIDS, #16149)*; *WHO (#20950)*.
NGO Relations Cooperates with:
- *Accountability International (#00059)*;
- *African Council of AIDS Service Organizations (AfriCASO, #00272)*;
- *Caribbean Vulnerable Communities Coalition (CVC, #03565)*;
- *Centre pour le développement des peuples, Accra (CEDEP, no recent information)*;
- *Eastern African Network of AIDS Service Organizations (EANNASO, see: #00272)*;
- *Ecumenical Advocacy Alliance (EAA, inactive)*;
- *Frontline AIDS (#10007)*;
- *MPact Global Action for Gay Men's Health and Rights (MPact, #16875)*;
- *Global Network of People Living with HIV/AIDS (GNP+, #10494)*;
- *Global Network of Sex Work Projects (NSWP, #10498)*;
- *Health Global Access Project (Health GAP)*;
- *HIV Young Leaders Fund (HYLF, no recent information)*;
- *Human Rights Watch (HRW, #10990)*;
- *Interagency Coalition on AIDS and Development (ICAD)*;
- *International AIDS Society (IAS, #11601)*;
- *International Community of Women Living with HIV/AIDS (ICW, #12826)* – Global and East Africa;
- *International Network of People who Use Drugs (INPUD, #14301)*;
- *International Treatment Preparedness Coalition (ITPC, #15729)*;
- John Hopkins Center for Public Health and Human Rights (CPHHR);
- national organizations in Malawi and Uganda;
- *SRHR Africa Trust (SAT, #19934)*. [2020/XC0013/**C**]

- ♦ ICA Specialized Organization on Agricultural Co-operation / see International Co-operative Agricultural Organisation (#12943)
- ♦ ICASP – International Conference on Advances in Solidification Processes (meeting series)
- ♦ **ICASSI** International Committee for Adlerian Summer Schools and Institutes (#12740)
- ♦ ICASS – International Conference on Advanced Structural Steels (meeting series)
- ♦ ICASS – International Conference on Advances in Steel Structures (meeting series)
- ♦ iCAST – International Center for Appropriate and Sustainable Technology (internationally oriented national body)
- ♦ ICAST – International Conference on Adaptive Structures and Technologies (meeting series)
- ♦ iCatCare – International Cat Care (internationally oriented national body)
- ♦ **ICAT** International Committee for Abrasive Technology (#12738)
- ♦ **ICATU** International Confederation of Arab Trade Unions (#12845)
- ♦ ICAU – International Centre for Underwater Archaeology in Zadar (internationally oriented national body)
- ♦ ICA / see World Alliance for Decentralized Energy (#21081)
- ♦ **ICAZ** International Council for Archaeozoology (#12995)
- ♦ **ICBA** International Carbon Black Association (#12441)
- ♦ **ICBA** International Center for Biosaline Agriculture (#12468)
- ♦ **ICBA** International Cooperative Banking Association (#12945)
- ♦ **ICBA** International Council of Beverages Associations (#12999)
- ♦ ICBA – International Council of Biotechnology Associations (unconfirmed)
- ♦ ICBBE – International Conference on Biomedical and Bioinformatics Engineering (meeting series)
- ♦ ICBB / see International Commission for Plant-Pollinator Relationships (#12716)
- ♦ **ICBCG** International Center for Banking and Corporate Governance (#12467)
- ♦ ICBDMS / see International Clearinghouse for Birth Defects Surveillance and Research (#12594)
- ♦ **ICBDSR** International Clearinghouse for Birth Defects Surveillance and Research (#12594)
- ♦ ICBD / see World Dance Council (#21353)
- ♦ ICBEC – International Conference on Biology, Environment and Chemistry (meeting series)
- ♦ ICBEIT – International Conference on Business, Economics and Information Technology (meeting series)
- ♦ **ICBEN** International Commission on Biological Effects of Noise (#12668)
- ♦ ICBEST – International Conference for Building Envelope Systems and Technology (meeting series)
- ♦ ICBF – Stiftung Internationales Centrum für Begabungsforschung (internationally oriented national body)
- ♦ ICBG – International Cooperative Biodiversity Groups (internationally oriented national body)
- ♦ ICBIC – International Conference on Biological Inorganic Chemistry (meeting series)
- ♦ ICB – Industrial Coordination Bureau (inactive)
- ♦ ICB – International Christian Broadcasters (inactive)
- ♦ **ICB** International Committee on Bionomenclature (#12748)
- ♦ **ICB** International Criminal Bar (#13107)
- ♦ **ICBL-CMC** International Campaign to Ban Landmines – Cluster Munition Coalition (#12427)
- ♦ **ICBL** International Conference on the Bioscience of Lipids (#12875)
- ♦ ICBM / see International Commission of the Meuse (#12702)
- ♦ **ICBM** International Consortium for Brain Mapping (#12905)
- ♦ ICBMM – International Conference on Building Materials and Materials Engineering (meeting series)
- ♦ ICBN / see International Committee on Systematics of Prokaryotes (#12807)
- ♦ ICBP / see BirdLife International (#03266)
- ♦ ICBP – International Conference on Bio-based Polymers (meeting series)
- ♦ ICBP' / see World Working Group on Birds of Prey and Owls (#21945)
- ♦ ICBR – International Centre for Bamboo and Rattan (internationally oriented national body)
- ♦ ICBR – International Conference on Building Resilience (meeting series)
- ♦ ICBR – International Congress for Battery Recycling (meeting series)
- ♦ **ICBR** Internationale Commissie ter Bescherming van de Rijn (#12721)
- ♦ ICBS / see Blue Shield International (#03286)
- ♦ **ICBS** International Chemical Biology Society (#12540)
- ♦ ICBS / see International Commission of the Schelde River (#12727)
- ♦ ICBSP – International Conference on Boar Semen Preservation (meeting series)
- ♦ **ICBSS** International Centre for Black Sea Studies (#12478)
- ♦ **ICBUW** International Coalition to Ban Uranium Weapons (#12609)
- ♦ **ICBWA** International Council of Bottled Water Associations (#13001)
- ♦ ICC / see International Charismatic Consultation (#12537)
- ♦ ICCA / see CLIA Australasia

♦ ICCA Consortium 11041

Consortium APAC – Consorcio TICCA

Global Coordinator address not obtained. E-mail: info@iccaconsortium.org.
Administration Coordinator address not obtained.
URL: http://www.iccaconsortium.org/

History 2008, Barcelona (Spain). Founded during 4th World Conservation Congress. Registration: Start date: Jul 2010, Switzerland. **Aims** Promote the appropriate recognition and support to ICCAs – *Indigenous peoples' and Community Conserved Areas* and territories, in the regional, national and global arena. **Structure** General Assembly. Steering Committee. Regional Coordinators. **Languages** English, French, Spanish. **Events** *General Assembly* Valdeavellano de Tera (Spain) 2013, *General Assembly* Andhra Pradesh (India) 2012, *General Assembly* Bogor (Indonesia) 2011, *General Assembly* Nagoya (Japan) 2011, *General Assembly* Whakatane (New Zealand) 2011. **Publications** *ICCA Consortium Newlsetter*, *ICCA Registry* – online database. Annual Report.
Members Indigenous People Organizations (IPOs); Community-based Organizations (CBOs); civil society organizations; Honorary (individuals). Organizations in 30 countries and territories:
Argentina, Bolivia, Brazil, Canada, Chile, China, Colombia, Congo DR, Croatia, Ethiopia, Guatemala, India, Iran Islamic Rep, Italy, Jordan, Kenya, Madagascar, Malaysia, Nepal, Netherlands, Niger, Panama, Philippines, Russia, Senegal, South Africa, Taiwan, Tanzania UR, UK, USA.
Included in the above, 11 organizations listed in this Yearbook:
African Biodiversity Network (ABN, #00222); *Crown Commonwealth League of Rights (CCLR, no recent information)*; *Forest Peoples Programme (FPP, #09865)*; *Gaia Foundation*; *Global Diversity Foundation (GDF)*; *Global Forest Coalition (GFC, #10368)*; *Indigenous Peoples of Africa Coordinating Committee (IPACC, #11163)*; *International Collective in Support of Fishworkers (ICSF, #12639)*; *Non-Timber Forest Products Exchange Programme for South and Southeast Asia (NTFP-EN, #17151)*; *Sacred Natural Sites Initiative (SNSI)*; *World Alliance of Mobile Indigenous Peoples (WAMIP)*.
NGO Relations Member of: *GEF CSO Network (GCN, #10087)*. [2023/XJ8497/y/**C**]

- ♦ ICCAE – Instituto Centroamericano de Capacitación Aeronautica (see: #04837)
- ♦ ICCAE – International Cooperation Centre for Agricultural Education (internationally oriented national body)
- ♦ **ICCAIA** International Coordinating Council of Aerospace Industry Associations (#12956)
- ♦ **ICCA** Institute for Corporate Culture Affairs (#11250)
- ♦ ICCA – International Cabin Crew Association (inactive)
- ♦ ICCA – International Chemistry Conference in Africa (meeting series)
- ♦ **ICCA** International Community Corrections Association (#12822)
- ♦ ICCA / see International Computer Games Association (#12836)
- ♦ **ICCA** International Congress and Convention Association (#12892)
- ♦ ICCA – International Corporate Chefs Association (internationally oriented national body)
- ♦ **ICCA** International Correspondence of Corkscrew Addicts (#12972)
- ♦ **ICCA** International Corrugated Case Association (#12974)
- ♦ **ICCA** International Council of Chemical Associations (#13003)
- ♦ **ICCA** International Council for Commercial Arbitration (#13010)
- ♦ **ICCA** Inter-parliamentary Coalition for Combating Antisemitism (#15960)
- ♦ **ICC Americas** Cricket Council of the Americas (#04952)
- ♦ ICCAM – International Committee of Children's and Adolescents' Movements (inactive)
- ♦ **ICC-Angkor** International Coordinating Committee on the Safeguarding and Development of the Historic Site of Angkor (#12954)
- ♦ ICCAP – International Conference on Child and Adolescent Psychopathology (meeting series)
- ♦ ICCAP – International Coordination Committee for the Accountancy Profession (inactive)
- ♦ ICCAS – International Conference on Culinary Arts and Science (meeting series)
- ♦ ICCATCI / see Coatings Societies International (#04075)
- ♦ **ICCAT** International Commission for the Conservation of Atlantic Tunas (#12675)
- ♦ **ICCBA** International Criminal Court Bar Association (#13109)

♦ ICCBBA 11042

Exec Dir PO Box 11309, San Bernardino CA 92423-1309, USA. T. +19097936516. Fax +19097936214. E-mail: support@isbt128.org – iccbba@iccbba.org.
Main Website: http://www.isbt128.org

History 1994. Former names and other names: *International Council for Commonality in Blood Banking Automation (ICCBBA)* – former (1994). Registration: 501(c)(3), USA. **Aims** Enhance *patient safety* by promoting and managing the ISBT 128 international information standard for use with *medical products* of human origin including blood, stem cells, tissues, organs and human milk. **Structure** Board of Directors. **Languages** English. **Finance** Funded entirely from licensing fees. **Activities** Awards/prizes/competitions; monitoring/evaluation; standards/guidelines. **Consultative Status** Consultative status granted from: *WHO (#20950)* (Official). **NGO Relations** Member of (1): *Worldwide Network for Blood and Marrow Transplantation (WBMT, #21929)*. [2023.03.03/XE3517/**E**]

- ♦ ICCBR – International Conference on Case-Based Reasoning (meeting series)
- ♦ ICCBS – International Center for Chemical and Biological Sciences (internationally oriented national body)
- ♦ ICCCAD – International Centre for Climate Change and Development (internationally oriented national body)
- ♦ ICC / see Caritas Internationalis (#03580)
- ♦ **ICCCASU** International Conference on Canadian, Chinese and African Sustainable Urbanization (#12876)
- ♦ ICC Centre for Maritime Cooperation (see: #12534)
- ♦ ICCCI – International Conference on Characterization and Control of Interfaces for High Quality Advanced Materials (meeting series)
- ♦ ICCC – International Center for Complexity and Conflict (internationally oriented national body)
- ♦ **ICCC** International Centre for Comparative Criminology (#12482)
- ♦ **ICCC** International Christian Chamber of Commerce (#12558)
- ♦ ICCC – International Concentration Camp Committee (no recent information)
- ♦ ICCC – International Conference Centers Consultants (inactive)
- ♦ ICCC – International Conference on Coordination Chemistry (meeting series)
- ♦ ICCC – International Congresses on the Communication of Culture through Architecture, Arts and Mass Media (inactive)
- ♦ ICCC – International Council for Caring Communities (internationally oriented national body)
- ♦ **ICCC** International Council of Christian Churches (#13005)
- ♦ ICCC – International Council of Community Churches (internationally oriented national body)
- ♦ ICC Commercial Crime Bureau / see ICC Financial Investigation Bureau (#11046)
- ♦ ICC Commercial Crime Services (see: #12534)
- ♦ ICC – Corrosion Institute of Southern Africa (internationally oriented national body)

♦ ICC Counterfeiting Intelligence Bureau (CIB) 11043

Bureau d'enquêtes de la CCI sur la contrefaçon (BEC)

Contact Cinnabar Wharf, 26 Wapping High Street, London, E1W 1NG, UK. T. +442074236960. Fax +442074236961. E-mail: ccs@icc-ccs.org.
URL: http://www.icc-ccs.org/icc/cib/

History 3 Dec 1984. Founded by the Executive Board and Council of *International Chamber of Commerce (ICC, #12534)*. One of 3 offices comprising *ICC Commercial Crime Services (CCS, see: #12534)*. **Aims** Investigate and seek to prevent counterfeiting of *trademarked goods* and trade dress, as well as of *patents*, *copyrights* and industrial designs and models; protect industry from damage done by counterfeiting networks by gathering intelligence. **Structure** Board of Directors. **Finance** Members' dues: ordinary (medium-sized companies); major (multinational corporations and government agencies). **Activities** Knowledge management/information dissemination; guidance/assistance/consulting; training/education; events/meetings. **Events** *Conference – Product counterfeiting protection* San Francisco, CA (USA) 1999. **Members** Manufacturers, individuals, trade associations and other organizations. Membership countries not specified. [2022/XE3580/**E**]

- ♦ ICCCPO / see Childhood Cancer International (#03871)
- ♦ ICCCR – International Center for Cooperation and Conflict Resolution (internationally oriented national body)
- ♦ **ICCCS** International Confederation of Contamination Control Societies (#12855)
- ♦ ICCC / see World Organisation of Systems and Cybernetics (#21686)
- ♦ ICCD / see Clubhouse International (#04035)
- ♦ **ICCD** International Chess Committee of the Deaf (#12544)
- ♦ ICCD – International Committee for a Community of Democracies (inactive)
- ♦ **ICCDPP** International Centre for Career Development and Public Policy (#12479)

♦ ICCDU International Scientific Committee 11044

Conference Chair EMS Energy Inst, Pennsylvania State Univ – C-211 CUL, University Park PA 16802-2323, USA. T. +18148654575. Fax +18148637432.
URL: http://www.energy.psu.edu/ICCDU/

History 1991. **Structure** Comprises Permanent Secretary and 17 members. **Activities** Organizes *International Conference on Carbon Dioxide Utilization (ICCDU).* **Events** *International Conference on Carbon Dioxide Utilization* Singapore (Singapore) 2021, *Biennial International Conference on Carbon Dioxide Utilization* Singapore (Singapore) 2015, *Biennial International Conference on Carbon Dioxide Utilization* Alexandria, VA (USA) 2013, *Biennial International Conference on Carbon Dioxide Utilization* Dijon (France) 2011, *Biennial International Conference on Carbon Dioxide Utilization* Tianjin (China) 2009. [2013/XJ6467/c/**E**]

- ♦ ICCEC – International Conference on Clinical Ethics and Consultation (meeting series)
- ♦ **ICCEES** International Council for Central and East European Studies (#13002)
- ♦ **ICCE** Imaging Consumables Coalition of Europe, Middle-East and Africa (#11124)
- ♦ **ICCE** Inter-American Catholic Education Association (#11403)
- ♦ ICCE – International Center for Contemporary Education (internationally oriented national body)
- ♦ **ICCE** International Centre for Coast Ecohydrology (#12481)
- ♦ ICCE – International Conference on Chemical Education (meeting series)
- ♦ ICCE – International Conference on Clean Energy (meeting series)
- ♦ ICCE – International Conference on Coastal Engineering (meeting series)
- ♦ ICCE – International Congress on Comparative Endocrinology (meeting series)
- ♦ **ICCE** International Consortium for Court Excellence (#12908)
- ♦ ICCE / see International Council for Coaching Excellence (#13008)
- ♦ **ICCE** International Council for Coaching Excellence (#13008)
- ♦ ICCE – International Council of Commerce Employers (inactive)
- ♦ ICCE / see International Council for Open and Distance Education (#13056)
- ♦ Ic-Centru Kongunt Ghar-Ricerka (#16147)
- ♦ ICCES – International Centre of Climate and Environmental Sciences (internationally oriented national body)
- ♦ ICCES – International Conference on Computational & Experimental Engineering and Sciences (meeting series)
- ♦ ICCEU – International Conference on Combustion & Energy Utilization (meeting series)
- ♦ ICC – European Language Network / see ICC – the international language association (#11050)
- ♦ **ICC Europe** International Cricket Council Europe Region (#13106)
- ♦ ICCFAA / see International Council of Investment Associations (#13034)
- ♦ ICCFD – International Conference on Computational Fluid Dynamics (meeting series)

♦ The ICCF Group 11045

US Office 25786 Georgetown Station, Washington DC 20027, USA. E-mail: hq@iccfoundation.us.
UK Office 71-75 Shelton Street, Convent Garden, London, WC2H 9JQ, UK. E-mail: hq@iccf-uk.org.
URL: https://www.internationalconservation.org/

History A group of ICCF offices, each established as a separate legal entity, registered in the host country, with its own Board of Directors. Former names and other names: *International Conservation Caucus Foundation (ICCF)* – former. Registration: 501(c)3, No/ID: EIN 83-0449176, USA; Charity Commission, No/ID: 1191764, England and Wales; Companies House, No/ID: 12291141, Start date: 31 Oct 2019, England and Wales; No/ID: 900650926-8, Colombia. **Aims** Advance conservation governance by building political willproviding on-the-ground solutions. **Structure** Offices in: Washington DC (USA); London (UK); Nairobi (Kenya); Bogotá (Colombia); Bangkok (Thailand).
Members Conservation Council comprising public and private sector representatives. Included, 10 organizations listed in this Yearbook:
African Wildlife Foundation (AWF, #00498); FAO (#09260); Global Coalition Against Child Pneumonia (#10290); Global Environment Facility (GEF, #10346); International League of Conservation Photographers (iLCP); Panthera; Rainforest Alliance; The Nature Conservancy (TNC); WILD Foundation (WILD, #20956); Wildlife Conservation Society (WCS).
Consultative Status Consultative status granted from: *UNEP (#20299).* **NGO Relations** *Global Parks.* [2022/XJ1611/fy/**F**]

- ♦ ICCF / see The ICCF Group (#11045)

♦ ICC Financial Investigation Bureau (FIB) 11046

Main Office Cinnabar Wharf, 26 Wapping High Street, London, E1W 1NG, UK. T. +442074236960. Fax +442074236961. E-mail: fib@icc-ccs.org.
URL: http://www.icc-ccs.org/icc/fib/

History Jan 1992, as *ICC Commercial Crime Bureau (CCB) – Bureau de la CCI contre le crime commercial (BCC)*, by Executive Board and Council of *International Chamber of Commerce (ICC, #12534).* One of 4 units of *ICC Commercial Crime Services (CCS, see: #12534).* Present name adopted Jan 2004. **Aims** Combat the increase in *commercial fraud* and *malpractice* in both public and private sectors worldwide; promote cooperation between *business* and *law enforcement.* **Structure** Director; Assistant Director. **Finance** Members' dues: Major Membership – pounds3,100; Ordinary Membership – pounds1,470. **Activities** Fraud consultancy service; vetting and authentication of documents; analysis of financial transactions; investigations; training; seminars and lectures. Holds an annual workshop on fraud prevention for banks. **Events** *Annual conference on fraud and money laundering prevention for the financial sector* London (UK) 2002. **Publications** *Commercial Crime International* (12 a year); *FIB Confidential Bulletin* (12 a year) – for members only. Special reports; warnings. Information Services: Confidential data base on all aspects of banking fraud, including reports on suspected fraudsters operating throughout the world; cheque fraud registry. **Members** Financial institutions; financial regulators; insurance companies; law enforcement agencies; trading houses in 70 countries. Membership countries not specified. **NGO Relations** Close working relationship with: *International Maritime Bureau (IMB, #14097).* [2013/XK0453/**E**]

- ♦ **ICCF** International Classic Cosmoenergy Federation (#12591)
- ♦ ICCF – International Concealed Carry Federation (internationally oriented national body)
- ♦ ICCF – International Conference on Condensed Matter Nuclear Science (meeting series)
- ♦ **ICCF** International Correspondence Chess Federation (#12971)
- ♦ **ICCFM** International Confederation of Christian Family Movements (#12851)
- ♦ **ICCFR** International Commission on Couple and Family Relations (#12676)
- ♦ ICCGE – International Conference on Clean and Green Energy (meeting series)
- ♦ **ICCG** International Catholic Centre of Geneva (#12449)
- ♦ **ICCG** International Catholic Conference of Guiding (#12452)
- ♦ ICCG – International Center for Climate Governance (internationally oriented national body)
- ♦ ICCG – International Conference on Construction Grammar (meeting series)
- ♦ ICC / see Global Alliance of National Human Rights Institutions (#10214)
- ♦ ICCGS – International Conference on Collision and Grounding of Ships and Offshore Structures (meeting series)
- ♦ ICCH – International Catholic Confederation of Hospitals (inactive)
- ♦ ICCH – International Conference on Culture and History (meeting series)
- ♦ ICCH – International Council for Classical Homeopathy (inactive)
- ♦ ICCHMT – International Conference on Computational Heat, Mass and Momentum Transfer (meeting series)
- ♦ ICCHNR – International Collaboration for Community Health Nursing Research (internationally oriented national body)
- ♦ ICCHP – International Conference on Computers Helping People with Special Needs (meeting series)
- ♦ ICCHRA – International Centre for Conflict and Human Rights Analysis (internationally oriented national body)
- ♦ **ICCIA** Islamic Chamber of Commerce, Industry and Agriculture (#16036)
- ♦ ICCICA – Interim Coordinating Committee for International Commodity Arrangements (inactive)
- ♦ ICC / see ICC – the international language association (#11050)
- ♦ **ICC** ICC – the international language association (#11050)
- ♦ ICCICE / see Islamic Chamber of Commerce, Industry and Agriculture (#16036)
- ♦ ICCIDD / see Iodine Global Network (#16004)
- ♦ ICCIDD Global Network / see Iodine Global Network (#16004)
- ♦ ICCI Europe / see International Cryosphere Climate Initiative (#13119)
- ♦ ICCI – Institut Català de Cooperació Iberoamericana (internationally oriented national body)
- ♦ ICCI – International Cannabis and Cannabinoids Institute (internationally oriented national body)
- ♦ **ICCI** International Cryosphere Climate Initiative (#13119)
- ♦ ICCI / see Islamic Chamber of Commerce, Industry and Agriculture (#16036)
- ♦ ICC Institute of International Business Law and Practice / see ICC Institute of World Business Law (#11047)

♦ ICC Institute of World Business Law 11047

Institut du droit des affaires internationales d'ICC

Dir c/o ICC, 33-34 av de Président Wilson, 75116 Paris, France. T. +33149532828. Fax +33149533030. E-mail: institute@iccwbo.org.
Chair address not obtained.
URL: http://www.iccwbo.org/about-icc/organisation/institute-of-world-busine ss-law/

History Mar 1979, Paris (France). Founded by *International Chamber of Commerce (ICC, #12534).* Former names and other names: *ICC Institute of International Business Law and Practice* – former; *Institut du droit et des pratiques des affaires internationales de la CCI* – former. **Aims** Provide research, training and dissemination of information among practitioners and scholars in the field of international business law, with particular attention given to international *commercial arbitration.* **Structure** Council; Secretariat. **Languages** English, French. **Activities** Awards/prizes/competitions; events/meetings; training/education. **Events** *Annual Meeting* Paris (France) 2022, *Annual Meeting* Paris (France) 2021, *Annual Meeting* Paris (France) 2020, *Annual Meeting* Paris (France) 2019, *Annual Meeting* Paris (France) 2018. **Publications** *Dossiers of the Institute* – series. Reports.
Members Practitioners in international business law in 48 countries and territories:
Algeria, Australia, Bahrain, Belgium, Bolivia, Brazil, Bulgaria, Canada, China, Colombia, Croatia, Czechia, Denmark, Egypt, France, Germany, Greece, Guatemala, Hong Kong, India, Indonesia, Iran Islamic Rep, Italy, Japan, Jordan, Lebanon, Lithuania, Luxembourg, Netherlands, Nigeria, Pakistan, Poland, Portugal, Romania, Russia, Singapore, Spain, Sri Lanka, Sweden, Switzerland, Togo, Tunisia, Türkiye, UK, United Arab Emirates, Uruguay, USA, Venezuela.
IGO Relations Collaborates with: *Council of Europe (CE, #04881); European Commission (EC, #06633); International Institute for the Unification of Private Law (UNIDROIT, #13934); International Trade Centre (ITC, #15703); OECD (#17693); UNDP (#20292); United Nations Commission on International Trade Law (UNCITRAL, #20531); UNIDO (#20336).* **NGO Relations** Collaborates with: *Chartered Institute of Arbitrators (CIArb); International Bar Association (IBA, #12320); International Council for Commercial Arbitration (ICCA, #13010); ICC International Court of Arbitration (#11049);* various arbitration centres. [2021.05.25/XE6744/j/**E**]

♦ ICC – International Association for Cereal Science and Technology 11048

Association internationale des sciences et technologies céréalières – Asociación Internacional para la Ciencia y la Tecnologia Cerealistas – Internationale Gesellschaft für Getreidewissenschaft und -technologie

Acting Pres Stubenring 12, 1010 Vienna, Austria. T. +43170772020. E-mail: office@icc.or.at.
URL: http://www.icc.or.at/

History 1955, Hamburg (Germany). Founded on the occasion of 3rd International Bread Congress. Former names and other names: *International Association for Cereal Chemistry* – former; *Association internationale de chimie cérçalière* – former; *Asociación Internacional de Quimica de los Cereales* – former; *Internationale Gesellschaft für Getreidechemie* – former; *Mezdunarodnoe Obscestvo po Himii Zerna* – former. **Aims** Contribute to advancement of cereal science and technology in all its aspects; study and standardize test methods in cereal science and related fields, including flour chemistry and milling; relate the results of scientific and technological research to the more efficient utilization of cereals; establish and maintain contacts among cereal scientists and technologists. **Structure** General Assembly (every 2 years); Governing Committee; Executive Committee; Technical Committee; Working Groups of experts. **Languages** Chinese, English, French, German, Italian, Russian, Spanish. **Staff** 4.50 FTE, paid. **Finance** Sources: members' dues. **Activities** Events/meetings; guidance/assistance/consulting; knowledge management/information dissemination; networking/liaising; research/documentation; standards/guidelines. **Events** *International Cereal and Bread Congress* Nantes (France) 2024, *International Dietary Fibre Conference* Leuven (Belgium) 2022, *Vienna ICC Conference* Vienna (Austria) 2022, *International Cereal and Bread Congress* 2021, *Whole Grain Summit* 2021. **Publications** *ICCe-Newsletter. Multilingual Dictionary of Cereal Science and Technology* (2006) in Chinese, English, French, German, Italian, Russian, Spanish; *History of ICC 60 Years 1955-2015.* Annual Report; congress proceedings; press releases; reports.
Members Public or private institutions in 26 countries and territories:
Argentina, Australia, Austria, Belgium, Canada, China, Croatia, Finland, France, Germany, Greece, Ireland, Italy, Japan, Lebanon, Lithuania, Netherlands, New Zealand, Romania, Russia, Sweden, Switzerland, Taiwan, Türkiye, UK, USA.
Consultative Status Consultative status granted from: *ECOSOC (#05331)* (Ros C); *UNIDO (#20336); FAO (#09260)* (Liaison Status). **IGO Relations** Observer status with (1): *Codex Alimentarius Commission (CAC, #04081).* Cooperates with (3): *International Atomic Energy Agency (IAEA, #12294); International Organization of Legal Metrology (#14451); World Customs Organization (WCO, #21350).* **NGO Relations** Member of (1): *Whole Grain Initiative (WGI, #20939).* Cooperates with (4): *American Oil Chemists' Society (AOCS); AOAC INTERNATIONAL (#00863); Cereals and Grains Association (#03830); International Organization for Standardization (ISO, #14473).* [2021.09.07/XC1179/**C**]

- ♦ ICC International Centre for ADR (see: #12534)
- ♦ **ICC** International Chamber of Commerce (#12534)
- ♦ **ICC** International Charismatic Consultation (#12537)
- ♦ **ICC** International Children's Care (#12551)
- ♦ ICC – International Children's Center (internationally oriented national body)
- ♦ **ICC** International China Concern (#12554)
- ♦ ICC – International Chornobyl Centre (internationally oriented national body)
- ♦ ICC – International Chrysanthemum Council (no recent information)
- ♦ ICC – International Coaching Community (internationally oriented national body)
- ♦ **ICC** International Coconut Community (#12628)
- ♦ ICC – International Code Council (internationally oriented national body)
- ♦ **ICC** International College of Cardiology (#12642)
- ♦ ICC – International Color Consortium (internationally oriented national body)
- ♦ **ICC** International Committee for Crimea (#12758)
- ♦ **ICC** International Communist Current (#12818)
- ♦ **ICC** International Computing Centre (#12839)
- ♦ ICC – International Congregational Council (inactive)
- ♦ **ICC** International Coordinating Committee for the Presentation of Science and the Development of Out-of-School Scientific Activities (#12953)
- ♦ **ICC** International COPD Coalition (#12961)
- ♦ ICC – International Coronary Congress (internationally oriented national body)
- ♦ **ICC** International Corrosion Council (#12973)

♦ ICC International Court of Arbitration 11049

Cour internationale d'arbitrage de la Chambre de commerce internationale

SG 33-43 av President Wilson, 75116 Paris, France. T. +33149532800. E-mail: arb@iccwbo.org.
Main: https://iccwbo.org/

History 1923, Paris (France). Founded by *International Chamber of Commerce (ICC, #12534).* Former names and other names: *ICC International Court of Arbitration* – former; *Cour internationale d'arbitrage de la CCI* – former. **Aims** Provide for settlement of *disputes* by arbitration in accordance with the Rules of Arbitration of the International Chamber of Commerce. **Structure** Court; Secretariat. **Languages** English, French, German, Portuguese, Spanish. **Staff** 80.00 FTE, paid. **Finance** On the overall budget of ICC, including the arbitration administration fees paid by parties in a dispute. **Activities** Events/meetings; guidance/assistance/consulting; training/education. **Events** *International Forum on Online Dispute Resolution* Paris (France) 2017, *Asia Pacific ADR Conference* Seoul (Korea Rep) 2015, *Asia Regional Conference on International Arbitration* Singapore (Singapore) 2015, *Asia Pacific Conference* Seoul (Korea Rep) 2014, *Conference on investment state arbitration in Latin America* Mexico City (Mexico) 2010. **Publications** *ICC Disputes Resolution Bulletin*

(3 a year). Multilingual collection of ICC dispute resolution rules (arbitration, mediation, experts, dispute boards, DOCDEX); Reports of the ICC Commission on Arbitration and ADR. **Information Services** *ICC Dispute Resolution Library*. **Members** Companies, chambers of commerce and business associations in over 130 countries. Membership countries not specified. **IGO Relations** Observer status with (1): *United Nations (UN, #20515)*. [2022.05.06/XF5206/v/**F**]

- ♦ **ICC** International Cricket Council (#13105)
- ♦ **ICC** International Criminal Court (#13108)
- ♦ ICC International – Institute of Career Certification International (internationally oriented national body)

♦ ICC – the international language association (ICC) 11050

Chair Postfach 10 12 28, 44712 Bochum, Germany. T. +4923462347100. E-mail: info@icc-languages.eu.
URL: http://www.icc-languages.eu/

History 1994, Germany. Former names and other names: *International Certificate Conference (ICC)* – former (1994); *ICC – European Language Network* – former alias; *International Language Network* – former alias; *International Certificate Conference – The International Language Association* – full title. Registration: Germany. **Aims** Promote excellence in teaching and learning of languages by: defining professional standards for teachers and learners; recognizing quality and best practice across a wide range of educational environments; disseminating these standards and practice to the widest possible public. **Structure** Board. **Languages** English, German. **Staff** 1.00 FTE, paid; 12.00 FTE, voluntary. **Finance** Members' contributions and donations; projects; training programme fees. **Activities** Training/education. **Events** *Conference* 2022, *Conference* Belgrade (Serbia) 2020, *Annual Conference* Berlin (Germany) 2019, *Annual conference* Santorini Is (Greece) 2018, *Annual Conference* Graz (Austria) 2017. **Publications** *Training Language and Culture* (4 a year). Educational materials; surveys.
Members Organizations (24) in 16 countries:
Bulgaria, China, Czechia, Finland, Germany, Greece, Italy, Mexico, Romania, Russia, Serbia, Sweden, Switzerland, Türkiye, UK, USA.
NGO Relations Member of: *European Civil Society Platform for Multilingualism (ECSPM, #06569)*; *Federación Internacional de Estudios sobre América Latina y el Caribe (FIEALC, #09338)*. [2022/XM3669/**F**]

- ♦ ICC International Maritime Bureau / see International Maritime Bureau (#14097)
- ♦ ICC – International Public Safety Consortium (meeting series)
- ♦ ICC / see Inuit Circumpolar Council (#15995)
- ♦ **ICC** Inuit Circumpolar Council (#15995)
- ♦ **ICCIP** International Climate Change Information Programme (#12597)
- ♦ **ICCIR** International Coordination Committee for Immunology of Reproduction (#12958)
- ♦ ICCJ – International Committee for Cooperation of Journalists (inactive)
- ♦ **ICCJ** International Council of Christians and Jews (#13006)
- ♦ ICCLA – International Committee on Christian Literature for Africa (inactive)
- ♦ ICCLC – International Civil and Commercial Law Centre Foundation (internationally oriented national body)
- ♦ **ICCL** International Committee on Computational Linguistics (#12752)
- ♦ **ICCL** International Committee on Contaminated Land (#12756)
- ♦ ICCLR – International Centre for Criminal Law Reform and Criminal Justice Policy (internationally oriented national body)
- ♦ **ICCMC** International Committee on Concrete Model Code for Asia (#12753)
- ♦ ICCM – International Centre for Choral Music (internationally oriented national body)
- ♦ **ICCM** International Committee on Composite Materials (#12751)
- ♦ **ICCM** International Committee for the Conservation of Mosaics (#12755)
- ♦ ICCM – International Conference on Computational Methods (meeting series)
- ♦ ICCM – International Conference on Computing and Missions (meeting series)
- ♦ **ICCMO** International College of Cranio-Mandibular Orthopedics (#12643)
- ♦ IC-CMTP – International Conference on Competitive Materials and Technology Processes (meeting series)
- ♦ **ICCM** UNUM OMNES International Council of Catholic Men (#20720)
- ♦ ICCN – International Centre on Conflict and Negotiation (internationally oriented national body)
- ♦ ICCOC-GTL – International Conference on Coordination on Organometallic Chemistry of Germanium, Tin and Lead (meeting series)
- ♦ ICCO / see Consumer Co-operatives Worldwide (#04770)
- ♦ ICCO – Interchurch Organization for Development Cooperation (internationally oriented national body)
- ♦ ICCO – Interkerkelijke Organisatie voor Ontwikkelingssamenwerking (internationally oriented national body)
- ♦ ICCO – International Carpet Classification Organization (no recent information)
- ♦ **ICCO** International Cocoa Organization (#12627)
- ♦ **ICCO** International Communications Consultancy Organisation (#12815)
- ♦ **ICCON** International Consortium for Cooperation on the Nile (#12907)
- ♦ ICCO – Organisation inter-Eglises de coopération au développement (internationally oriented national body)
- ♦ ICCOPS – International Centre for Coastal and Ocean Policy Studies (internationally oriented national body)
- ♦ **IC Council** Council of International Lawn Tennis Clubs (#04903)
- ♦ ICCOWE / see International Charismatic Consultation (#12537)
- ♦ ICCPA – International Conference on Carbonaceous Particles in the Atmosphere (meeting series)
- ♦ ICCPB / see International Association of Comparative Physiology and Biochemistry (#11798)
- ♦ **ICCPCA** International Confederation of Cleft Lip and Palate and Related Craniofacial Anomalies (#12852)
- ♦ ICCP / see International Christian Medical and Dental Association (#12562)
- ♦ ICCP – International Climate Change Partnership (internationally oriented national body)
- ♦ **ICCP** International Commission on Clouds and Precipitation (#12672)
- ♦ **ICCP** International Committee for Coal and Organic Petrology (#12750)
- ♦ **ICCP** International Council for Children's Play (#13004)
- ♦ **ICCP** International Council of Coloproctology (#13009)
- ♦ **ICCPM** International Centre of Complex Project Management (#12484)
- ♦ **ICCPPC** International Commission of Catholic Prison Pastoral Care (#12670)
- ♦ ICCPR – International Conference on Cultural Policy Research (meeting series)
- ♦ ICCPR – International Covenant on Civil and Political Rights (1966 treaty)
- ♦ **ICCRA** International Critical Control Rooms Alliance (#13112)
- ♦ ICCRH / see International Bone and Mineral Society (#12379)
- ♦ ICCR – Interfaith Center on Corporate Responsibility (internationally oriented national body)
- ♦ **ICCR** International Collaboration on Cancer Reporting (#12637)
- ♦ ICCR – International Committee for Coal Research (no recent information)
- ♦ **ICCR** International Confederation of Container Reconditioners (#12854)
- ♦ ICCR – International Conference on the Use of Computers in Radiation Therapy (meeting series)
- ♦ **ICCR** International Cooperation on Cosmetics Regulation (#12939)
- ♦ **ICCROM** International Centre for the Study of the Preservation and Restoration of Cultural Property (#12521)
- ♦ **ICCrPT** International Confederation of Cardiorespiratory Physical Therapists (#12850)
- ♦ ICCSA – International Conference on Computational Science and Applications (meeting series)
- ♦ ICCS / see European Democrat Students (#06901)
- ♦ **ICCS** Intereuropean Commission on Church and School (#11469)
- ♦ **ICCS** International Catholic Conference of Scouting (#12453)
- ♦ ICCS – International Centre for Cultural Studies (internationally oriented national body)
- ♦ **ICCS** International Children's Continence Society (#12552)
- ♦ ICCS – International Clinical Cytometry Society (internationally oriented national body)
- ♦ **ICCS** International Commission on Civil Status (#12671)
- ♦ ICCS – International Conference on Composite Structures (meeting series)
- ♦ ICCS – International Congress of Celtic Studies (meeting series)
- ♦ ICCS – International Consumers for Civil Society (no recent information)
- ♦ ICCS – International Council for Canadian Studies (internationally oriented national body)
- ♦ ICCSO – International Council of Customer Service Organisations (unconfirmed)
- ♦ ICCST – International Conference on the Chemistry of Selenium and Tellurium (meeting series)
- ♦ ICCTA / see International Chemical Trade Association (#12543)
- ♦ **ICCTF** International Cognition and Cancer Task Force (#12632)
- ♦ ICCT – International Centre for Counter-Terrorism – The Hague (internationally oriented national body)
- ♦ ICCT – International Cold Chain Technology (internationally oriented national body)
- ♦ ICCT – International Conference on Convergence Technology (meeting series)
- ♦ **ICCT** International Council on Clean Transportation (#13007)
- ♦ ICCT – Islamic Chamber Council for Textile (inactive)
- ♦ ICC / see Unity-and-Diversity World Council (#20670)
- ♦ ICCV/NAZEMSE – Initiative Communautaire Changer la Vie/NAZEMSE (internationally oriented national body)
- ♦ **ICCWC** International Consortium on Combating Wildlife Crime (#12906)
- ♦ ICCWS – International Conference on Cyber Warfare and Security (meeting series)
- ♦ ICDAA – International Criminal Defence Attorneys Association (inactive)
- ♦ ICDAD – International Committee for Museums and Collections of Decorative Arts and Design (see: #13051)
- ♦ **ICdA** International Cadmium Association (#12424)
- ♦ **ICDA** International Chromium Development Association (#12567)
- ♦ **ICDA** International Circulation Directors Association (#12576)
- ♦ **ICDA** International Common Disease Alliance (#12812)
- ♦ **ICDA** International Confederation of Dietetic Associations (#12856)
- ♦ ICDAM – International Conference on Diet and Activity Methods (meeting series)
- ♦ ICDAPS – International Conference on Design and Analysis of Protective Structures (meeting series)
- ♦ **ICDBL** International Committee for the Defence of the Breton Language (#12761)
- ♦ ICDC – International Code Documentation Centre (see: #12305)
- ♦ ICDCS / see Comité permanent inter-Etats de lutte contre la sécheresse dans le Sahel (#04195)
- ♦ ICDD – International Centre for Diffraction Data (internationally oriented national body)
- ♦ ICDDPS – International Conference on Data-Driven Plasma Science (meeting series)

♦ ICDDR,B 11051

Exec Dir GPO Box 128, Dhaka 1000, Bangladesh. T. +88029827001. E-mail: info@icddrb.org.
URL: http://www.icddrb.org/

History 1978, Dhaka (Bangladesh). Founded as successor to *Cholera Research Laboratory*. Former names and other names: *International Centre for Diarrhoeal Disease Research, Centre for Health and Population Research* – full title; *International Centre for Diarrhoeal Disease Research, Bangladesh* – alias. **Aims** Solve public health problems through innovative scientific research. **Structure** Board of Trustees; Senior Leadership Team. **Languages** English. **Staff** 4500.00 FTE, paid. **Finance** Research supported by bilateral donors and grant income. Revenue sources for restricted and unrestricted grants include: *Bill and Melinda Gates Foundation (BMGF)*; *Department for International Development (DFID, inactive)*; *European Commission (EC, #06633)*; *Global Fund to Fight AIDS, Tuberculosis and Malaria (Global Fund, #10383)*; Government of Bangladesh; *Swedish International Development Cooperation Agency (Sida)*; *United States Agency for International Development (USAID)*. **Activities** Research and development; research/documentation; healthcare; training/education; knowledge management/information dissemination; events/meetings. **Events** *Scientific conference / Annual Scientific Conference* Dhaka (Bangladesh) 2011, *Scientific conference* Dhaka (Bangladesh) 2009, *Scientific conference* Dhaka (Bangladesh) 2007, *Asian Congress on Diarrhoeal Diseases and Nutrition* Bangkok (Thailand) 2006, *Asian conference on diarrhoeal diseases* Dhaka (Bangladesh) 2003. **Publications** *Glimpse* (4 a year) in English – magazine; *Health and Science Bulletin* (4 a year) in Bengali, English; *Shasthya Sanglap* (4 a year); *Chronic Disease News* (2 a year); *Equity Dialogue*; *HDSS Annual Report*; *Shahjadpur Integrated MNH Project Newsletter*; *SUZY News*. Annual Report; working papers; scientific reports; special publications; monographs. **Members** Not a membership organization. [2021/XE5776/**E***]

- ♦ ICDE / see International Council for Open and Distance Education (#13056)
- ♦ **ICDE** International Council for Open and Distance Education (#13056)
- ♦ **ICDF** International Christian Dance Fellowship (#12559)
- ♦ ICDF – International Cooperation and Development Fund (internationally oriented national body)
- ♦ **ICDHS** International Committee on Design History and Studies (#12763)
- ♦ ICDI / see International Drug Awareness Research Foundation
- ♦ ICDI – International Centre for Development Initiatives (internationally oriented national body)
- ♦ ICDI – International Child Development Initiatives (internationally oriented national body)
- ♦ ICDI – International Climate Development Institute (internationally oriented national body)
- ♦ **ICD** Institute for Cultural Diplomacy (#11252)
- ♦ **ICD** International College of Dentists (#12644)
- ♦ ICD – International Communes Desk (internationally oriented national body)
- ♦ ICD / see Internationale des coiffeurs de dames (#13218)
- ♦ ICD – Islamic Corporation for the Development of the Private Sector (see: #16044)
- ♦ **ICDIWU** International Community of Defence Industry Workers' Unions (#12823)

♦ ICDL Europe 11052

Contact c/o ICS, 87-89 Pembroke Road, Ballsbridge, Dublin, 4, CO. DUBLIN, Ireland. E-mail: info@icdl.ie.
URL: https://icdleurope.org/

History 1997. Founded by *Council of European Professional Informatics Societies (CEPIS, #04893)*. Former names and other names: *European Computer Driving Licence Foundation (ECDL Foundation)* – former. Registration: EU Transparency Register, No/ID: 44018642457-83. **Aims** Enable proficient use of Information and Communication Technology (ICT) that empowers individuals, organizations and society, through development, promotion and delivery of quality certification programmes throughout the world. **Structure** National partners appointed to implement certification programmes at national level. **Languages** English. **Staff** 30.00 FTE, paid. **Activities** Awareness raising; events/meetings; guidance/assistance/consulting; research and development. **Events** *Forum* Prague (Czechia) 2018, *Forum* Oslo (Norway) 2012, *Chief executive officers forum* Vienna (Austria) 2008. **Publications** *ICDL Newsletter* (12 a year).
Members Computer societies and approved organizations, licensed by ECDL Foundation, in 110 countries and territories:
Albania, Argentina, Australia, Austria, Bangladesh, Barbados, Belarus, Belgium, Bermuda, Bhutan, Bosnia-Herzegovina, Botswana, Brunei Darussalam, Bulgaria, Cambodia, Canada, Chile, China, Croatia, Cyprus, Czechia, Denmark, Dubai, Egypt, Estonia, Eswatini, Fiji, Finland, France, Germany, Ghana, Greece, Grenada, Hong Kong, Hungary, Iceland, India, Indonesia, Ireland, Italy, Jamaica, Japan, Jordan, Kenya, Korea DPR, Korea Rep, Kuwait, Laos, Latvia, Lesotho, Liechtenstein, Lithuania, Luxembourg, Malaysia, Maldives, Malta, Marshall Is, Mauritius, Micronesia FS, Mongolia, Mozambique, Myanmar, Namibia, Nepal, Netherlands, New Zealand, North Macedonia, Norway, Pakistan, Palau, Palestine, Papua New Guinea, Philippines, Poland, Portugal, Romania, Russia, Samoa, Serbia, Singapore, Slovakia, Slovenia, Solomon Is, South Africa, Spain, Sri Lanka, St Kitts-Nevis, St Vincent-Grenadines, Sudan, Sweden, Switzerland, Syrian AR, Taiwan, Tanzania UR, Thailand, Tonga, Trinidad-Tobago, Tunisia, Türkiye, Tuvalu, Uganda, UK, Ukraine, United Arab Emirates, USA, Vanuatu, Vietnam, Yemen, Zambia, Zimbabwe.
IGO Relations Cooperates with (9): *International Bank for Reconstruction and Development (IBRD, #12317)* (World Bank); *Joint United Nations Programme on HIV/AIDS (UNAIDS, #16149)*; *UNDP (#20292)*; *UNESCO (#20322)* (Chair in Water Resources); *UNHCR (#20327)*; *United Nations Relief and Works Agency for Palestine Refugees in the Near East (UNRWA, #20622)*; *United Nations (UN, #20515)*; *United States Agency for International Development (USAID)*; *WHO (#20950)*. **NGO Relations** Member of (2): *Council of European Professional Informatics Societies (CEPIS, #04893)*; *European Alliance on Skills for Employability (#05883)*. [2021/XF5000/f/**F**]

- ♦ **ICDLI** International Committee of the Decorative Laminates Industry (#12760)
- ♦ **ICDM** International Commission on Dynamical Meteorology (#12679)

♦ **ICDM** International Confederation of Drum Manufacturers (#12857)
♦ **ICDO** International Civil Defence Organization (#12582)
♦ ICDO – International Cultural Diversity Organization (unconfirmed)
♦ ICDP / see International Forum for Innovative Northeast Asia Strategy
♦ **ICDP** International Child Development Programme (#12548)
♦ **ICDP** International Commission against the Death Penalty (#12659)
♦ **ICDP** International Committee for Dermatopathology (#12762)
♦ ICDP – International Confederation for Disarmament and Peace (inactive)
♦ **ICDP** International Continental Scientific Drilling Program (#12935)
♦ ICDRB – International Centre for the Documentation and Research of Basketball, Alcobendas (internationally oriented national body)
♦ **ICDRG** International Contact Dermatitis Research Group (#12933)
♦ ICDR / see International Confederation of Container Reconditioners (#12854)
♦ ICDSC – International Conference on Digital Satellite Communications (meeting series)
♦ ICDS – Ibn Khaldoun Center for Development Studies, Cairo (internationally oriented national body)
♦ **ICDS** International Cell Death Society (#12462)
♦ ICDS – International Centre for Defence and Security (internationally oriented national body)
♦ ICDS – International Conference on Defects in Semiconductors (meeting series)
♦ ICDT – International Centre for Democratic Transition (internationally oriented national body)
♦ ICDT – International Conference on Database Theory (meeting series)
♦ **ICDT** Islamic Centre for Development of Trade (#16035)
♦ **ICDV** International Council for the Day of VESAK (#13012)
♦ ICDVRAT – International Conference on Disability, Virtual Reality and Associated Technologies (meeting series)
♦ ICE / see Central European Initiative (#03708)
♦ ICEAA – International Cost Estimating and Analysis Association (internationally oriented national body)
♦ **ICEAC** International Court of Environmental Arbitration and Conciliation (#13096)
♦ **ICEA** International Childbirth Education Association (#12546)
♦ ICEA – International Community Education Association (inactive)
♦ ICEA – International Confucian Ecological Alliance (unconfirmed)
♦ ICEBAC / see International Council of Employers of Bricklayers and Allied Craftworkers
♦ **ICEB** International Consortium for Electronic Business (#12910)
♦ ICEBY / see International Council for Education of People with Visual Impairment (#13015)
♦ **ICEC** International Centre for Electronic Commerce (#12488)
♦ ICEC – International Communication Enhancement Center (inactive)
♦ ICEC – International Conference on Environmental Catalysis (meeting series)
♦ **ICEC** International Consortium for Emergency Contraception (#12911)
♦ **ICEC** International Cost Engineering Council (#12976)
♦ **ICEC** International Cryogenic Engineering Committee (#13118)
♦ ICECN – International Conference on EEG and EMG Data Processing (meeting series)
♦ **ICE Council** Council for International Congresses of Entomology (#04900)
♦ **ICECSA** Islamic Commission for Economic, Cultural and Social Affairs (#16038)
♦ IceCube – South Pole Neutrino Observatory (unconfirmed)
♦ **ICEDD** International Committee of Editors of Diplomatic Documents (#12765)
♦ ICEDI – Instituto Canario de Estudios de Derecho Internacional (internationally oriented national body)
♦ ICED – Instituto Caribeño para el Estado de Derecho (internationally oriented national body)
♦ ICED / see International Centre for Environment Audit and Sustainable Development (#12489)
♦ **iCED** International Centre for Environment Audit and Sustainable Development (#12489)
♦ ICED – International Centre for Evidence in Disability (internationally oriented national body)
♦ **ICED** International Consortium for Educational Development (#12909)
♦ ICED – International Council for Educational Development (inactive)
♦ **ICEDIS** International Committee on EDI for Serials (#12764)
♦ **ICEDOC** International Campaign for Establishment and Development of Oncology Centres (#12428)
♦ **ICEDR** International Consortium for Executive Development Research (#12913)
♦ ICEE / see Brien Holden Vision Institute
♦ **ICEED** International Council on Environmental Economics and Development (#13017)
♦ ICEED – International Research Center for Energy and Economic Development (internationally oriented national body)
♦ ICEE – ICOM International Committee for Exhibition Exchange (see: #13051)
♦ ICEENN – International Conference on the Environmental Effects of Nanoparticles and Nanomaterials (meeting series)
♦ **ICEEP** International Committee on Equine Exercise Physiology (#12767)
♦ **ICEERS** International Center for Ethnobotanical Education Research and Service (#12469)
♦ ICEFA – International Conference on Electrical Fuses and their Applications (meeting series)
♦ **ICEFAT** International Convention of Exhibition and Fine Art Transporters (#12937)
♦ **ICEFI** Instituto Centroamericano de Estudios Fiscales (#11325)
♦ ICEF – Innovation for Cool Earth Forum (meeting series)
♦ **ICEF** International Committee for Research and Study of Environmental Factors (#12801)
♦ ICEF – International Conferences on Environmental Future (meeting series)
♦ **ICEF** International Court of the Environment Foundation (#13097)
♦ ICEF – International Federation of Chemical, Energy and General Workers' Unions (inactive)
♦ ICEG / see Alliance Against Genocide (#00655)
♦ ICEGE – International Conference on Earthquake Geotechnical Engineering (meeting series)
♦ ICEHA / see Global Medic Force
♦ **ICE-HBV** International Coalition to Eliminate HBV (#12611)
♦ ICEH – International Centre for Eye Health (internationally oriented national body)
♦ ICEH / see International Network on Children's Health, Environment and Safety (#14240)
♦ ICEHM – International Centre of Economics, Humanities and Management (unconfirmed)
♦ **ICEHO** International Consortium of Environmental History Organizations (#12912)
♦ **ICEIGATM** International Circle of Educational Institutes for Graphic Arts Technology and Management (#12573)
♦ ICEI – Instituto Complutense de Estudios Internacionales (internationally oriented national body)
♦ ICEI – Istituto per la Cooperazione Economica Internazionale (internationally oriented national body)
♦ **ICE** Institution of Civil Engineers (#11319)
♦ **ICE** Intercoop Europe (#11464)
♦ ICE – International Centre for Eremology (internationally oriented national body)
♦ ICE – International Conference on Education (meeting series)
♦ ICE – International Council of Employers of Bricklayers and Allied Craftworkers (internationally oriented national body)
♦ **ICE** International Council of Ethologists (#13019)
♦ ICEIS – International Conference on Enterprise Information Systems (meeting series)
♦ ICE – Islamic Council of Europe (no recent information)
♦ **ICEJ** International Christian Embassy Jerusalem (#12560)
♦ Icelandic Church Aid (internationally oriented national body)
♦ Icelandic Human Rights Centre (internationally oriented national body)
♦ Icelandic Lutheran Mission (internationally oriented national body)
♦ Icelandic Mission Society / see Samband Islenskra Kristnibodsfélaga
♦ ICEL / see Instituto Internacional de Estudios Legislativos del FOPREL (#11338)
♦ **ICEL** International Commission on English in the Liturgy (#12681)
♦ ICEL – International Conference on Electroluminescence and Optoelectronic Devices (meeting series)
♦ ICEL – International Conference on End-of-Life Law, Ethics, Policy, and Practice (meeting series)
♦ ICEL / see International Council of Environmental Law (#13018)
♦ **ICEL** International Council of Environmental Law (#13018)
♦ **ICEM** International Confederation for Electroacoustic Music (#12858)
♦ **ICEM** International Council for Educational Media (#13014)
♦ ICEM – International Federation of Chemical, Energy, Mine and General Workers' Unions (inactive)
♦ ICEM / see International Organization for Migration (#14454)
♦ **ICEMS** International Commission for Electromagnetic Safety (#12680)
♦ ICEMS – International Conference on Electrical Machines and Systems (meeting series)
♦ ICEM Steering Committee / see International Conference on Electrical Machines Steering Committee (#12878)
♦ ICEMU – International Committee of Entertainment and Media Unions (inactive)
♦ ICENECDEV – International Centre for Environmental Education and Community Development (internationally oriented national body)
♦ ICENS – International Centre for Environmental and Nuclear Sciences (internationally oriented national body)
♦ ICE Observatory – International Care Ethics Observatory (internationally oriented national body)
♦ ICEO – International Cultural Exchange Organization (internationally oriented national body)
♦ ICEOS – International Congress on Early Onset Scoliosis and the Growing Spine (meeting series)
♦ ICEP / see aicep Portugal Global – Trade and Investment Agency
♦ ICEP – Institut zur Cooperation bei Entwicklungs-Projekte (internationally oriented national body)
♦ ICEPO / see Dana Center for Preventive Ophthalmology (#04997)
♦ ICEPP – International Center for Elementary Particle Physics, Tokyo (internationally oriented national body)
♦ ICEPS – Istituto per la Cooperazione Economica Internazionale e i Problemi dello Sviluppo (internationally oriented national body)
♦ ICEQ – International Quantum Electronics Conference (meeting series)
♦ ICERC – International Cetacean Education Research Centre (internationally oriented national body)
♦ **ICER** International Confederation of Energy Regulators (#12859)
♦ ICER / see International Society for Eye Research (#15111)
♦ ICERM – International Center for Ethno-Religious Mediation (internationally oriented national body)
♦ ICESC / see Islamic Commission for Economic, Cultural and Social Affairs (#16038)
♦ ICESC – International Committee for European Security and Cooperation (inactive)
♦ ICESC – International Council for Economic and Social Cooperation (inactive)
♦ **ICESCO** Islamic World Educational, Scientific and Cultural Organization (#16058)
♦ **ICESCO** Organisation du Monde Islamique pour l'Education (#16058)
♦ ICESCR – International Covenant on Economic, Social and Cultural Rights (1966 treaty)
♦ ICES Foundation – International Centre for Earth Simulation (unconfirmed)
♦ **ICESI** International Coalition for Energy Storage and Innovation (#12613)
♦ **ICES** International Centre of Educational Systems (#12487)
♦ **ICES** International Centre for Ethnic Studies (#12490)
♦ **ICES** International Collaboration for Essential Surgery (#12638)
♦ ICES – International Conference on Economics and Security (meeting series)
♦ ICES – International Conference on Environmental Systems (meeting series)
♦ **ICES** International Cooperation on Education About Standardization (#12940)
♦ ICES – International Council of Electrophoresis Societies (no recent information)
♦ **ICES** International Council for the Exploration of the Sea (#13021)
♦ ICESPS – International Centre for Environmental Social and Policy Studies (internationally oriented national body)
♦ **ICETE** International Council for Evangelical Theological Education (#13020)
♦ **ICET** International Centre for Earth Tides (#12486)
♦ **ICET** International Coalition to End Torture (#12612)
♦ **ICET** International Council on Education for Teaching (#13016)
♦ ICETT – International Center for Environmental Technology Transfer (internationally oriented national body)
♦ ICEVH / see International Council for Education of People with Visual Impairment (#13015)
♦ **ICEVI** International Council for Education of People with Visual Impairment (#13015)
♦ ICEVS – Internationaal Comité voor Europese Veiligheid en Samenwerking (inactive)
♦ ICF / see International Cardijn Association
♦ ICFAD – International Council of Fine Arts Deans (internationally oriented national body)
♦ **ICFA** International Coalition of Fisheries Associations (#12614)
♦ **ICFA** International Committee for Future Accelerators (#12774)
♦ ICFA – International Committee for Museums and Collections of Fine Arts (see: #13051)
♦ ICFAM – International Centre for Food Micro-Algae Against Malnutrition (internationally oriented national body)
♦ **ICFAW** International Coalition for Animal Welfare (#12607)
♦ ICfC – International Center for Conciliation (internationally oriented national body)
♦ ICFED – International Centre for Financial and Economic Development, Moscow (internationally oriented national body)
♦ ICFEM – International Conference on Formal Engineering Methods (meeting series)
♦ ICFG – International Church of the Foursquare Gospel (internationally oriented national body)
♦ **ICFG** International Cold Forging Group (#12634)
♦ **ICFI** International Committee of the Fourth International (#12771)
♦ **ICF** Instituto de Ciencias Familiares (#11330)
♦ **ICF** International Cablemakers Federation (#12422)
♦ **ICF** International Camping Fellowship (#12431)
♦ **ICF** International Canoe Federation (#12437)
♦ **ICF** International Carrom Federation (#12444)
♦ ICF / see International Casting Sport Federation (#12447)
♦ **ICF** International Catholic Foundation for the Service of Deaf Persons (#12457)
♦ **ICF** International Ceramic Federation (#12530)
♦ **ICF** International Coach Federation (#12604)
♦ **ICF** International Communications Forum (#12816)
♦ ICF – International Community Foundation (internationally oriented national body)
♦ **ICF** International Congregational Fellowship (#12889)
♦ **ICF** International Congress on Fracture (#12894)
♦ ICF – International Corn Foundation (internationally oriented national body)
♦ **ICF** International Crane Foundation (#13102)
♦ **ICF** International Cremation Federation (#13104)
♦ **ICF** International Crystal Federation (#13120)
♦ ICF – International Cystinuria Foundation (internationally oriented national body)
♦ **ICF** Investment Climate Facility for Africa (#15998)
♦ ICFIS – International Conference on Forensic Inference and Statistics (meeting series)
♦ ICFJ / see International Center for Journalists
♦ ICFJ – International Center for Journalists (internationally oriented national body)
♦ ICFLC / see Fellowship of the Least Coin (#09728)
♦ ICFMA – International Cystic Fibrosis / Mucoviscidosis / Association (inactive)
♦ ICFM / see Confederación Iberoamericana de Medicina Familiar (#04450)
♦ **ICFMH** International Committee on Food Microbiology and Hygiene (#12770)
♦ ICFM – International Commission on Food Mycology (see: #15794)
♦ ICFM – International Conference on Flood Management (meeting series)
♦ **ICFMO** Islamic Countries Forensic Medicine Organization (#16042)
♦ **ICFO** International Committee on Fundraising Organizations (#12773)
♦ **ICFO** International Cooperative Fisheries Organization (#12946)
♦ ICF-PADA – International Christian Federation for the Prevention of Alcoholism and Drug Addiction (no recent information)
♦ **ICFPA** International Council of Forest and Paper Associations (#13023)
♦ ICFPE – International Conference on Flexible and Printed Electronics (meeting series)

- ♦ ICFPT – International Conference on Field Programmable Technology (meeting series)
- ♦ ICFPW – International Confederation of Former Prisoners of War (inactive)
- ♦ ICFS – International Conference on Fluvial Sedimentology (meeting series)
- ♦ ICFT – International Conference on Fish Telemetry (meeting series)
- ♦ ICFTU African Regional Organization / see International Trade Union Confederation – African Regional Organization (#15709)
- ♦ ICFTU Asian and Pacific Regional Organization / see ITUC – Asia Pacific (#16076)
- ♦ ICFTU Inter-American Regional Organization of Workers / see Confederación Sindical de Trabajadores y Trabajadoras de las Américas (#04480)
- ♦ ICFTU – International Confederation of Free Trade Unions (inactive)
- ♦ ICFU – International Council on the Future of the University (inactive)
- ♦ **ICFV** International Committee for a Free Vietnam (#12772)
- ♦ ICF-WASI / see International Congress on Fracture (#12894)
- ♦ ICF / see World Curling Federation (#21348)
- ♦ ICG / see International Crisis Group (#13111)
- ♦ **ICGA** International Chewing Gum Association (#12545)
- ♦ **ICGA** International Computer Games Association (#12836)
- ♦ ICGA – International Conference on Governance and Accountability (meeting series)
- ♦ **ICG/CARIBE EWS** Intergovernmental Coordination Group for Tsunami and Other Coastal Hazards Warning System for the Caribbean and Adjacent Regions (#11483)
- ♦ ICGC – Institute for Conscious Global Change (internationally oriented national body)
- ♦ **ICGC** International Cancer Genome Consortium (#12432)
- ♦ ICGCR – International Council on Global Conflict Resolution (internationally oriented national body)
- ♦ **ICGdR** International Consortium on Geo-disaster Reduction (#12914)
- ♦ ICG-EAC / see International Cooperative Group on Environmentally-Assisted Cracking (#12947)
- ♦ **ICG-EAC** International Cooperative Group on Environmentally-Assisted Cracking (#12947)
- ♦ **ICGEB** International Centre for Genetic Engineering and Biotechnology (#12494)
- ♦ **ICGEM** International Centre for Global Earth Models (#12495)
- ♦ ICG / see European International Contractors (#07586)
- ♦ **ICGFM** International Consortium on Governmental Financial Management (#12915)
- ♦ ICGG – International Centre on Global-Scale Geochemistry (internationally oriented national body)
- ♦ **ICGG** International Critical Geography Group (#13113)
- ♦ **ICGH** International Confederation of Genealogy and Heraldry (#04561)
- ♦ ICGH – International Conference on Gas Hydrates (meeting series)
- ♦ ICGHP – International Council for Global Health Progress (no recent information)
- ♦ ICGI / see Goodwill Industries International
- ♦ ICGI – International Coalition for Genital Integrity (unconfirmed)
- ♦ **ICGI** International Cotton Genome Initiative (#12981)
- ♦ ICG – International Centre for Geohazards (internationally oriented national body)
- ♦ **ICG** International Commission on Glass (#12683)
- ♦ **ICG** International Committee on Global Navigation Satellite Systems (#12775)
- ♦ ICG – International Consultative Group for Peace and Disarmament (inactive)
- ♦ **ICG IOTWS** Intergovernmental Coordination Group for the Indian Ocean Tsunami Warning and Mitigation System (#11480)
- ♦ **ICGLR** International Conference on the Great Lakes Region (#12880)
- ♦ **ICGMA** International Council of Grocery Manufacturers Associations (#13026)
- ♦ **ICG/NEAMTWS** Intergovernmental Coordination Group for the Tsunami Early Warning and Mitigation System in the North-eastern Atlantic, the Mediterranean and Connected Seas (#11482)
- ♦ **ICGN** International Corporate Governance Network (#12969)
- ♦ **ICG/PTWS** Intergovernmental Coordination Group for the Pacific Tsunami Warning and Mitigation System (#11481)
- ♦ ICGR – International Conference on Gender Research (meeting series)
- ♦ ICGS / see International Chromosome and Genome Society (#12568)
- ♦ **ICGS** International Chromosome and Genome Society (#12568)
- ♦ ICGS – International Corporate Governance Society (unconfirmed)
- ♦ **ICGTD** International Council on Grapevine Trunk Diseases (#13025)
- ♦ ICGT – International Colloquium on Graph Theory and Combinatorics (meeting series)
- ♦ ICGT – International Conference on Graph Transformation (meeting series)
- ♦ ICGTMP – International Colloquium on Group Theoretical Methods in Physics (meeting series)
- ♦ ICHA – International Cardiovascular Health Alliance (unconfirmed)
- ♦ ICHARM – International Centre for Water Hazard and Risk Management (internationally oriented national body)
- ♦ ICHCA – International Cargo Handling Coordination Association (inactive)

♦ ICHCA International Limited (IIL) 11053

CEO Ste 5 Meridian House, 62 Station Road, London, E4 7BA, UK. T. +44233277560.
URL: http://www.ichca.com/

History May 2002, when legally established as a non-profit company by a representative number of members of the former *International Cargo Handling Coordination Association (ICHCA, inactive)*. Launched 1 Jan 2003. **Aims** Represent the *cargo* handling world on an international basis. **Structure** Board; International Safety Panel. **Staff** 1.00 FTE, paid. **Events** *Bigger ships, greater challenges* Barcelona (Spain) 2016, *Annual International AusIntermodal Conference* Sydney, NSW (Australia) 2013, *International Cargo Handling Seminar* Tokyo (Japan) 2013, *Biennial conference* Melbourne, VIC (Australia) 2012, *Biennial Conference* Casablanca (Morocco) 2010. **Publications** *Cargo World – The Newsletter* (6 a year); *Cargo World* (annual). *IIL Information papers* – series; *IIL Technical Reports* – series; *International Safety Panel Briefing Pamphlets* – series; *International Safety Panel Research Papers* – series. **Members** Membership countries not specified. **Consultative Status** Consultative status granted from: *International Maritime Organization (IMO, #14102)*. **IGO Relations** Recognized by: *ILO (#11123)*. The former ICHCA was in specialized consultative status with: *FAO (#09260)*. **NGO Relations** Close cooperation with: *International Association of Ports and Harbors (IAPH, #12096)*. Recognized by: *International Organization for Standardization (ISO, #14473)*.

[2017.07.03/XF6886/**F**]

- ♦ **ICHCAP** International Information and Networking Centre for Intangible Cultural Heritage in the Asia-Pacific Region under the auspices of UNESCO (#13847)
- ♦ ICHC – International Conference on the History of Cartography (meeting series)
- ♦ ICHDA – International Cooperative Housing Development Association (inactive)
- ♦ ICHD – International Centre for Human Development (internationally oriented national body)
- ♦ **ICHD** International Commission on Historical Demography (#12684)
- ♦ ICHD – International Conference on Hydrodynamics (meeting series)
- ♦ ICHD – International Council of Human Duties (no recent information)
- ♦ **ICHE** International Council for Higher Education (#13030)
- ♦ **IChemE** Institution of Chemical Engineers (#11318)
- ♦ ICHEM – International Centre for Higher Education Management (internationally oriented national body)
- ♦ ICHET – International Centre for Hydrogen Energy Technologies (internationally oriented national body)
- ♦ ICHF / see Child Health Foundation
- ♦ ICHF – International Children's Heart Foundation (internationally oriented national body)
- ♦ ICHG – International Child Health Group (internationally oriented national body)
- ♦ ICHG – International Collaboration for Hypermesis Gravidarum Research (unconfirmed)
- ♦ ICHG – International Conference of Historical Geographers (meeting series)
- ♦ ICH – International Centre for Hydropower (internationally oriented national body)
- ♦ ICH – International Conference on Hydrogenases and other redox biocatalysts for energy conversion (meeting series)
- ♦ **ICH** International Council on Harmonisation of Technical Requirements for Registration of Pharmaceuticals for Human Use (#13027)
- ♦ **ICH** International Council for Homeopathy (#13031)
- ♦ ICH – Interstate Council on Hydrometeorology of the Countries of the Commonwealth of Independent States (unconfirmed)
- ♦ ICHLC – International Corporate Health Leadership Council (internationally oriented national body)
- ♦ ICHLD – International Center for Health Leadership Development (internationally oriented national body)
- ♦ ICHLE – International Center for Health, Law and Ethics, University of Haifa (internationally oriented national body)
- ♦ **ICHM** Foundation of the International Congress on Hyperbaric Medicine (#09962)
- ♦ **ICHM** International Commission on the History of Mathematics (#12686)
- ♦ **ICHM** International Commission on History of Meteorology (#12687)
- ♦ **ICHM** International Committee for Historical Metrology (#12776)
- ♦ **ICHMT** International Centre for Heat and Mass Transfer (#12496)
- ♦ ICHNR – International Congress of Head and Neck Radiology (meeting series)
- ♦ ICHoLS – International Conference on the History of the Language Sciences (meeting series)
- ♦ ICHOM – International Consortium for Health Outcomes Measurement (internationally oriented national body)
- ♦ ICHOU / see Institute of Caribbean Insurance Risk Managers (#11244)
- ♦ ICHPER / see International Council for Health, Physical Education, Recreation, Sport and Dance (#13028)
- ♦ **ICHPER-SD** International Council for Health, Physical Education, Recreation, Sport and Dance (#13028)
- ♦ ICHR – International Council for Human Rights (internationally oriented national body)
- ♦ ICHRPI / see International Commission for the History of State Assemblies (#12689)
- ♦ ICHRP – International Coalition for Human Rights in the Philippines (unconfirmed)
- ♦ ICHS – Inter-African Committee for Hydraulic Studies (inactive)
- ♦ ICHS – International Centre for Human Sciences, Byblos (internationally oriented national body)
- ♦ **ICHS** International Clinical Hyperthermia Society (#12600)
- ♦ **ICHS** International Committee of Historical Sciences (#12777)
- ♦ ICHS – International Council of Homehelp Services (inactive)
- ♦ **ICHS** International Immunocompromised Host Society (#13835)
- ♦ **ICHSLTA** International Council of Hides, Skins and Leather Traders Associations (#13029)
- ♦ ICHSPP – International Congress on High Speed Photography and Photonics (meeting series)
- ♦ **ICHTH** International Commission for the History and Theory of Historiography (#12690)
- ♦ ICHTS / see International Chinese Musculoskeletal Research Society
- ♦ **ICHTT** International Commission for the History of Travel and Tourism (#12692)
- ♦ Ichud Olami / see World Labour Zionist Movement (#21615)
- ♦ ICI / see Dirección General de Cooperación con Iberoamérica
- ♦ ICIA / see Audiovisual and Integrated Experience Association
- ♦ **ICIA** International Council of Investment Associations (#13034)
- ♦ ICIA / see International Credit Insurance & Surety Association (#13103)
- ♦ **ICIAM** International Council for Industrial and Applied Mathematics (#13032)
- ♦ ICIBCA – International Council of Intermediate Bulk Container Associations (internationally oriented national body)
- ♦ ICIC / see Iranian Christians International
- ♦ ICICHE / see International Network for Christian Higher Education (#14241)
- ♦ **ICICH** ICOMOS International Committee on Intangible Cultural Heritage (#11064)
- ♦ ICICIC – International Conference on Innovative Computing, Information and Control (meeting series)
- ♦ ICIC – International Conference for the Information Community (meeting series)
- ♦ **ICIC** Islamic Committee for International Crescent (#16039)
- ♦ ICI-CNR / see Istituto di Studi Giuridici Internazionali
- ♦ ICICS – International Conference on Information and Communications Security (meeting series)
- ♦ **ICID** International Commission on Irrigation and Drainage (#12694)
- ♦ ICIDS – International Conference on Interactive Digital Storytelling (meeting series)
- ♦ **ICIEC** Islamic Corporation for the Insurance of Investment and Export Credit (#16041)
- ♦ ICIEE – International Centre for Indoor Environment and Energy (internationally oriented national body)
- ♦ **ICIE** International Centre for Innovation in Education (#12497)
- ♦ **ICIE** International Congress of Industrialists and Entrepreneurs (#12895)
- ♦ ICIE – International Council for Innovation in Higher Education (internationally oriented national body)
- ♦ ICIFI – International Council of Infant Food Industries (inactive)
- ♦ ICIF / see International Cooperative and Mutual Insurance Federation (#12948)

♦ ICI Global 11054

Headquarters 70 Gracechurch Street, Suite 318, 3rd Floor, London, EC3V 0HR, UK. E-mail: icipubcomm@ici.org.
Pres/CEO 1401 H Street NW, Washington DC 20005, USA.
URL: https://www.ici.org/iciglobal

History Officially launched 2011 to carry out the work of *Investment Company Institute*. **Aims** Adhere to high ethical standards, promote public understanding and advance interests of regulated investment funds, their managers and investors. **Structure** Board of Governors; Global Policy Council; Executive Committee. **Languages** Chinese, English, French. **Staff** 180.00 FTE, paid. **Finance** Members' dues. **Activities** Politics/policy/regulatory; knowledge management/information dissemination; events/meetings. **Events** *Annual General Meeting* Washington, DC (USA) 2021, *Annual General Meeting* Washington, DC (USA) 2020, *Annual General Meeting* Washington, DC (USA) 2019, *Annual General Meeting* Washington, DC (USA) 2018, *Annual General Meeting* Washington, DC (USA) 2017. **Publications** Research and policy publications; statistical reports. **Members** Funds publicly offered to investors in jurisdictions worldwide. Membership countries not specified.

[2021/XJ6904/**E**]

- ♦ ICIIL – International Centre for Innovation and Industrial Logistics (internationally oriented national body)
- ♦ **ICI** Inter-American Cooperative Institute (#11420)
- ♦ **ICI** Inter-American Copyright Institute (#11421)
- ♦ **ICI** International Association of Coaching Institutes (#11780)
- ♦ **ICI** International Childbirth Initiative (#12547)
- ♦ ICI – International Climate Initiative (internationally oriented national body)
- ♦ **ICI** International Cocoa Initiative (#12626)
- ♦ ICI – International Communicology Institute (internationally oriented national body)
- ♦ ICI – Iranian Christians International (internationally oriented national body)
- ♦ ICIJ – International Consortium of Investigative Journalists (internationally oriented national body)
- ♦ ICIKM – International Conference on Innovation, Knowledge, and Management (meeting series)
- ♦ ICIL – International Conference on Iranian Linguistics (meeting series)
- ♦ ICIM / see European Federation of Managers in the Steel Industry (#07162)
- ♦ ICIM – International Conference on Inorganic Membranes (meeting series)
- ♦ **ICIMOD** International Centre for Integrated Mountain Development (#12500)
- ♦ ICIMP – International Conference on Information Management and Processing (meeting series)
- ♦ IC – Institutum Charitatis (religious order)
- ♦ **ICIPE** International Centre of Insect Physiology and Ecology (#12499)
- ♦ **ICIP** ICOMOS International Committee on Interpretation and Presentation (#11065)
- ♦ **ICIP** International Consortium for Intergenerational Programmes (#12916)
- ♦ **ICIRM** Institute of Caribbean Insurance Risk Managers (#11244)
- ♦ ICIS / see International Centre for Integrated Assessment and Sustainable Development
- ♦ ICISA – International Communications and Information Security Association (inactive)
- ♦ **ICISA** International Credit Insurance & Surety Association (#13103)
- ♦ ICISF – International Critical Incident Stress Foundation (internationally oriented national body)
- ♦ ICIS – Institute for Comparative and International Studies (internationally oriented national body)

- **ICIS** International Cancer Imaging Society (#12433)
- ICIS – International Centre for Integrated Assessment and Sustainable Development (internationally oriented national body)
- **ICIS** International Committee for Imaging Science (#12779)
- ICIS – International Congress of Infant Studies (internationally oriented national body)
- **ICIS** International Construction Information Society (#12925)
- **ICIS** International Cytokine and Interferon Society (#13127)
- ICIT – International Centre for Island Technology (internationally oriented national body)
- ICIWaRM – International Center for Integrated Water Resources Management (internationally oriented national body)
- ICJA / see International Cultural Youth Exchange (#13122)
- ICJHE – International Center for Jesuit Higher Education (internationally oriented national body)
- **ICJ** International Commission of Jurists (#12695)
- **ICJ** International Court of Justice (#13098)
- **ICJW** International Council of Jewish Women (#13036)
- ICK / see Kneipp Worldwide (#16197)
- **ICKL** International Council of Kinetography Laban (#13038)
- ICKSF – International Chinese Kuo Shu Federation (inactive)
- ICLAC – International Cell Line Authentication Committee (unconfirmed)
- **ICLA** In House Competition Lawyers' Association (#10953)
- **ICLA** International Civil Liberties Alliance (#12584)
- **ICLA** International Cognitive Linguistics Association (#12633)
- **ICLA** International Comparative Literature Association (#12829)
- **ICLA** International Construction Law Association (#12926)
- ICLA / see International Council for Laboratory Animal Science (#13039)
- ICLAM / see International Committee for Insurance Medicine (#12780)
- **ICLAM** International Committee for Insurance Medicine (#12780)
- ICLARM / see WorldFish (#21507)
- **ICLARS** International Consortium for Law and Religion Studies (#12918)
- **ICLAS** International Council for Laboratory Animal Science (#13039)
- ICLASS International / see Institute for Liquid Atomization and Spray Systems (#11278)
- **ICLC** International Centre for Local Credit (#12501)
- ICLD – International Center for Law in Development (internationally oriented national body)
- ICLD – Swedish International Centre for Local Democracy (internationally oriented national body)
- ICLEE – International Consortium of Landscape and Ecological Engineering (unconfirmed)
- ICLEI / see Local Governments for Sustainability (#16507)
- **ICLEI** Local Governments for Sustainability (#16507)
- ICLE – International Conference on Lymphocyte Engineering (meeting series)
- ICLG – Groupe de bibliothéconomie internationale et comparée / see International Library and Information Group (#14037)
- ICLG – International Conference on Local Government (meeting series)
- **ICLHE** Integrating Content and Language in Higher Education (#11371)
- Iclif – The Iclif Leadership and Governance Centre (internationally oriented national body)
- The Iclif Leadership and Governance Centre (internationally oriented national body)
- **ICL** International Consortium on Landslides (#12917)
- ICL / see International Lithosphere Program (#14059)
- **ICLMG** – International Civil Liberties Monitoring Group (internationally oriented national body)
- ICLM – ICOM International Committee for Literary Museums (see: #13051)
- ICLM – Infanoj Chirkaw la Mondo (internationally oriented national body)
- ICLN – International Criminal Law Network (internationally oriented national body)
- ICLOCA – International Center for Letter of Credit Arbitration (internationally oriented national body)
- **ICLP** International Conference on Lightning Protection (#12882)
- ICLR – International Conference on Learning Representations (meeting series)
- ICLR – International Conference of Legal Regulators (meeting series)
- ICLRS – International Center for Law and Religion Studies, Provo UT (internationally oriented national body)
- ICLS – International Council for the Life Sciences (unconfirmed)
- **ICLS** International Courtly Literature Society (#13100)
- ICLSO / see International Medical Contact Lens Council (#14131)
- ICLTA – International Cognitive Load Theory Association (unconfirmed)
- ICLT / see Tibet Justice Center (#20159)
- ICMAA – International Conference on Matrix Analysis and Applications (meeting series)
- **ICMAC** Iuris Canonici Medii Aevi Consociatio (#19593)
- ICMAH – ICOM International Committee for Museums and Collections of Archaeology and History (see: #13051)
- **ICMA** International Capital Market Association (#12438)
- ICMA – International Card Manufacturers Association (internationally oriented national body)
- **ICMA** International Christian Maritime Association (#12561)
- **ICMA** International City / County Management Association (#12579)
- ICMA / see International Classified Marketplace Association (#12592)
- **ICMA** International Classified Marketplace Association (#12592)
- **ICMA** International Commission on Middle Atmosphere Science (#12704)
- **ICMA** International Computer Music Association (#12837)
- ICMA – International Congress of Maritime Arbitrators (meeting series)
- ICMA – International Consortium for Medical Abortion (inactive)
- ICMAN – International Conference on Mechanisms of Action of Nutraceuticals (meeting series)
- ICMAP – International Conference on Microelectronics and Plasma Technology (meeting series)
- **ICMAP** International Council for Medicinal and Aromatic Plants (#13047)
- **ICMART** International Committee Monitoring Assisted Reproductive Technologies (#12787)
- **ICMART** International Council of Medical Acupuncture and Related Techniques (#13046)
- ICMASS – International Conference on Maritime Autonomous Surface Ship (meeting series)
- **ICMB** International Centre for Monetary and Banking Studies (#12506)
- **ICMC – Europe** International Catholic Migration Commission – Europe (#12460)
- **ICMCI** International Council of Management Consulting Institutes (#13042)
- **ICMC** International Catholic Migration Commission (#12459)
- **ICMC** International Committee for Marine Conservation (#12781)
- **ICMC** International Consortium for Male Contraception (#12919)
- **ICMDA** International Christian Medical and Dental Association (#12562)
- ICMDA – International Conference on Materials Design and Applications (meeting series)
- **ICMEC** International Centre for Missing and Exploited Children (#12505)
- ICME – ICOM International Committee for Museums and Collections of Ethnography (see: #13051)
- **ICME** International Council on Materials Education (#13045)
- ICME – International Council on Metals and the Environment (inactive)
- ICMEM – International Conference on Material Engineering and Manufacturing (meeting series)
- **IC MEMO** International Committee of Memorial Museums for the Remembrance of Victims of Public Crimes (#12784)
- ICMEO – International Conference on Men and Equal Opportunities (meeting series)
- ICMEP – International Conference on Manufacturing Engineering and Processes (meeting series)
- ICMF / see International Cancer Microenvironment Society (#12434)
- ICMF – International Conference on Magnetic Fluids (meeting series)
- ICMF – International Conference on Multiphase Flow (meeting series)
- **ICMFS** International College for Maxillo-Facial Surgery (#12645)
- ICMFS – International Colloquium on Magnetic Films and Surfaces (meeting series)
- ICM Geneva Headquarters Staff Association / see IOM Global Staff Association Committee (#16008)
- **ICMG** International Committee of the Mediterranean Games (#12783)
- ICMGP – International Conference on Mercury as a Global Pollutant (meeting series)
- **ICMHD** International Centre for Migration, Health and Development (#12502)
- ICMH – International Center for Mental Health (internationally oriented national body)
- ICMH / see International Centre for Migration, Health and Development (#12502)
- **ICMICA** Pax Romana, International Catholic Movement for Intellectual and Cultural Affairs (#18267)
- **ICMIF/Américas** Federação internacional de Cooperativas e Mutualidades de Seguros / Associação Regional para As Américas (#12949)
- **ICMIF/Américas** Federación Internacional de Cooperativas y Mutuales de Seguros / Asociación Regional para Las Américas (#12949)
- **ICMIF/Americas** International Cooperative and Mutual Insurance Federation / Regional Association for The Americas (#12949)
- **ICMIF/Amériques** Fédération Internationale des Coopératives et Mutuelles d'Assurance / Association Régionale pour les Amériques (#12949)
- **ICMIF** International Cooperative and Mutual Insurance Federation (#12948)
- **ICMI** International Commission on Mathematical Instruction (#12700)
- **ICMI** International Committee on Measurements and Instrumentation (#12782)
- **ICM** Internacional de Trabajadores de la Construcción y la Madera (#03355)
- ICM – International Centre of Martial Arts (internationally oriented national body)
- ICM – International Centre for Materials Technology Promotion (see: #20336)
- **ICM** International Confederation of Midwives (#12863)
- **ICM** International Congress on Mechanical Behaviour of Materials (#12897)
- ICM / see International Organization for Migration (#14454)
- ICMJE – International Committee of Medical Journal Editors (unconfirmed)
- **iCMLf** International Chronic Myeloid Leukemia Foundation (#12569)
- ICML – International Congress on Medical Librarianship (meeting series)
- ICML – International Council for Machinery Lubrication (internationally oriented national body)
- ICMMA – International Council of the Museum of Modern Art (internationally oriented national body)
- **ICMM** International Committee of Military Medicine (#12785)
- **ICMM** International Congress of Maritime Museums (#12896)
- **ICMM** International Council on Mining and Metals (#13048)
- ICM – Missionary Sisters of the Immaculate Heart of Mary (religious order)
- ICMMP / see International Committee of Military Medicine (#12785)
- ICMNS – International Conference on Mathematical Neuroscience (meeting series)
- ICMOVPE – International Conference on Metal Organic Vapor Phase Epitaxy (meeting series)
- ICMP/CIEM / see International Confederation of Music Publishers (#12864)
- ICMPC – International Conference on Music Perception and Cognition (meeting series)
- **ICMPD** International Centre for Migration Policy Development (#12503)
- **ICMPE** International Center of Mental Health Policy and Economics (#12470)
- **ICMP** International Commission on Missing Persons (#12706)
- **ICMP** International Confederation of Music Publishers (#12864)
- **ICMRA** International Coalition of Medicines Regulatory Authorities (#12616)
- **ICMRBS** International Council on Magnetic Resonance in Biological Systems (#13041)
- ICMR – International Center for Materials Research (internationally oriented national body)
- ICMR – International Conference on Materials and Reliability (meeting series)
- ICMRM – International Conference on Magnetic Resonance Microscopy (meeting series)
- ICMRS – International Chinese Musculoskeletal Research Society (internationally oriented national body)
- ICMR / see World Mountain Running Association (#21659)
- ICMSB – International Conference on Molecular Systems Biology (meeting series)
- **ICMS Board** International Critical Management Studies Board (#13114)
- ICMS Coalition / see International Cost Management Standard Coalition (#12978)
- **ICMS Coalition** International Cost Management Standard Coalition (#12978)
- ICMSET – International Conference on Material Science and Engineering Technology (meeting series)
- **ICMSF** International Commission on Microbiological Specifications for Foods (#12703)
- ICMS – ICOM International Committee for Museum Security (see: #13051)
- ICMS – International Centre for Mathematical Sciences (internationally oriented national body)
- ICMS – International Congress on Musical Signification (meeting series)
- ICMS / see International Society for Mushroom Science (#15286)
- **ICMSSE** International Committee of Mine Safety Science and Engineering (#12786)
- ICMT – International Conference on Mechatronics Technology (meeting series)
- ICMUA / see International Commission on Middle Atmosphere Science (#12704)
- ICMV – International Conference On Matrix Vesicles (meeting series)
- ICNAF – International Commission for the Northwest Atlantic Fisheries (inactive)
- **ICNA** International Child Neurology Association (#12550)
- ICNA – International Cooperation Networking Association (inactive)
- ICNAS – International Conference on Non-Aqueous Solutions (meeting series)
- ICNATAS / see International Academy of Television Arts and Sciences
- ICNB – International Conference on Nanomaterials and Biomaterials (meeting series)
- ICNC – International Center on Nonviolent Conflict (internationally oriented national body)
- ICNCP – International Commission for the Nomenclature of Cultivated Plants (see: #15760)
- ICNDST – International Conference on the New Diamond Science and Technology (meeting series)
- **ICNDT** International Committee on Non-Destructive Testing (#12793)
- ICNE – Congrès international pour une nouvelle évangélisation (meeting series)
- ICNEM – Internacia Centro de la Neutrala Esperanto Movado (inactive)
- ICNI – International Conference on Noncovalent Interactions (meeting series)
- **ICN** International Cleantech Network (#12593)
- ICN – International College of Nutrition (internationally oriented national body)
- **ICN** International Competition Network (#12832)
- **ICN** International Council of Nurses (#13054)
- **ICNIRP** International Commission on Non-Ionizing Radiation Protection (#12707)
- **ICNIRS** International Council for Near Infrared Spectroscopy (#13053)
- **ICNK** International Coalition to Stop Crimes Against Humanity in North Korea (#12622)
- ICNL-Budapest / see European Center for Not-for-Profit Law (#06463)
- **ICNL** International Center for Not-for-Profit Law (#12471)
- **ICNLP International** International Community of NLP (#12825)
- ICNMD – International Congress of Neuromuscular Diseases (meeting series)
- ICNME – International Conference on Nanomaterials and Materials Engineering (meeting series)
- ICNM – International Centre for New Media (internationally oriented national body)
- **ICNM** International Committee on Nanostructured Materials (#12791)
- **ICNM** International Congress on Naturopathic Medicine (#12898)
- **ICNMP** International College of Nuclear Medicine Physicians (#12646)
- ICNRD – International Conference on New or Restored Democracies (meeting series)
- ICNS – International Conference on Nitride Semiconductors (meeting series)
- ICNSO – International Confederation of Nutrition Support Organizations (inactive)
- **ICNT** International Competence Network for Tourism Research and Education (#12831)
- ICOAM – International Conference on Optical Angular Momentum (meeting series)
- **ICoBC** International Council on Badges and Credentials (#12998)
- ICoCA / see International Code of Conduct Association (#12629)
- **ICoCA** International Code of Conduct Association (#12629)
- ICO Center – International Catholic Organizations Information Center (internationally oriented national body)
- ICOCI – International Conference on Computing and Informatics (meeting series)
- ICOC – International Churches of Christ (internationally oriented national body)

ICOC International Commission
11054

alphabetic sequence excludes
For the complete listing, see Yearbook Online at

- ♦ **ICOC** International Commission for Orders of Chivalry (#12711)
- ♦ **ICOC** International Conference on Oriental Carpets (#12885)
- ♦ **ICoD** Euro-Mediterranean Centre on Insular Coastal Dynamics (#05718)
- ♦ **ICODIMS** International Committee on Databases in Multiple Sclerosis (#12759)
- ♦ **ICoD** International Council of Design (#13013)
- ♦ ICOD – International Council on Disability (inactive)
- ♦ ICOFA – International Scientific Commission on the Family (inactive)
- ♦ ICOFM / see Islamic Countries Forensic Medicine Organization (#16042)
- ♦ ICOFOM – ICOM International Committee for Museology (see: #13051)
- ♦ **ICOFORT** ICOMOS International Scientific Committee on Fortifications and Military Heritage (#11076)
- ♦ Icograda / see International Council of Design (#13013)
- ♦ **ICOH** International Commission on Occupational Health (#12709)
- ♦ **ICOHTEC** International Committee for the History of Technology (#12778)
- ♦ **ICOI** International Congress of Oral Implantologists (#12899)
- ♦ **ICO** International Coastal and Ocean Organization (#12625)
- ♦ **ICO** International Coffee Organization (#12630)
- ♦ **ICO** International Commission for Optics (#12710)
- ♦ **ICO** International Council of Ophthalmology (#13057)
- ♦ **ICO** Joint IUBMB-IUPAC International Carbohydrate Organization (#16138)
- ♦ **ICOLC** International Coalition of Library Consortia (#12615)
- ♦ **ICOLD** International Commission on Large Dams (#12696)
- ♦ ICOLF – International Center of Law, Life, Faith and Family (internationally oriented national body)
- ♦ **ICOMAM** International Committee of Museums and Collections of Arms and Military History (#12790)
- ♦ ICOM-ARAB – ICOM Regional Alliance for Arab Countries (see: #13051)
- ♦ ICOM Asia-Pacific Regional Alliance (see: #13051)
- ♦ ICOM-ASPAC – ICOM Asia-Pacific Regional Alliance (see: #13051)
- ♦ **ICOMBO** International Council of Multiple Birth Organisations (#13050)
- ♦ ICOM-CC – ICOM International Committee for Conservation (see: #13051)
- ♦ ICOMC – International Conference on Organometallic Chemistry (meeting series)
- ♦ ICOM Comité internacional para museos y colecciones de instrumentos y de música (see: #13051)
- ♦ ICOM Comité international pour les musées et collections d'instruments et de musique (see: #13051)
- ♦ ICoME – International Conference for Media in Education (meeting series)
- ♦ ICOM European Regional Alliance (see: #13051)
- ♦ ICOM-Europe – ICOM European Regional Alliance (see: #13051)
- ♦ ICOMH – International Committee on Occupational Mental Health (inactive)
- ♦ **ICOMIA** International Council of Marine Industry Associations (#13044)
- ♦ ICOM / see International Christian Organisation of the Media (#12563)
- ♦ **ICOM** International Christian Organisation of the Media (#12563)
- ♦ ICOM International Committee for Architecture and Museum Techniques (see: #13051)
- ♦ ICOM International Committee for Audiovisual and New Technologies of Image and Sound (see: #13051)

♦ ICOM International Committee for Collecting (COMCOL) 11055

Sec Western Cape Museum Service, Private Bag X9067, Cape Town, 8000, South Africa. E-mail: comcol.secretary@gmail.com.
URL: http://network.icom.museum/comcol/

History as an international committee of *International Council of Museums (ICOM, #13051)*. **Aims** Deepen discussions and share knowledge on the practice, theory and ethics of collecting and *collections* (both tangible and intangible) development. **Structure** Executive Board. **Languages** English, French, Portuguese, Spanish. **Activities** Events/meetings; publishing activities. **Events** *Annual Conference* Umeå (Sweden) 2017, *Annual Conference* Milan (Italy) 2016, *Annual Conference* Seoul (Korea Rep) 2015, *Annual Conference* Celje (Slovenia) 2014, *Annual Conference* Rio de Janeiro (Brazil) 2013. **Publications** *COMCOL Newsletter* (3 a year). Articles; conference proceedings.

Members Organizations in 16 countries:
Austria, Belgium, Brazil, China, Czechia, Finland, France, Germany, Hungary, Korea Rep, Poland, Russia, Slovakia, Sweden, UK, USA.

Individuals in 57 countries:
Argentina, Armenia, Australia, Austria, Belarus, Belgium, Bosnia-Herzegovina, Botswana, Brazil, Cameroon, Canada, Chile, China, Colombia, Costa Rica, Croatia, Cyprus, Denmark, Estonia, Finland, France, Germany, Greece, Guatemala, Iceland, India, Iran Islamic Rep, Ireland, Israel, Italy, Japan, Kenya, Latvia, Luxembourg, Malta, Mongolia, Montenegro, Morocco, Namibia, Netherlands, Niger, Norway, Poland, Qatar, Serbia, Singapore, Slovenia, South Africa, Spain, Sweden, Switzerland, Thailand, Türkiye, UK, USA, Venezuela, Zimbabwe. [2019/XJ2618/**E**]

♦ ICOM International Committee for the Collections and Activities of Museums of Cities (CAMOC) 11056

Sec Hellenic Ministry of Culture and Tourism, Directorate of Museums/Exhibitions/Education Programmes, 6 Saripolou St, 101 86 Athens, Greece. T. +302102858675. Fax +302108212942.
Pres History Foundation of Turkey, Zindankapi Degirmen Sokak 15, Eminonu, 34134 Istanbul/Istanbul, Türkiye. T. +902125220202. Fax +902125135400.
URL: http://camoc.icom.museum/

History 2005, Moscow (Russia), on the initiative of Moscow City Museum and museum professionals in other countries who felt the need for a committee which would focus on museums of the city. Committee was approved by the Executive Council of *International Council of Museums (ICOM, #13051)* during the ICOM General Conference held in Seoul (Korea Rep), Oct 2004. At a meeting in Moscow (Russia), Apr 2005, delegates form 13 countries drafted the Committee's aims and objectives and elected an Executive Board. **Aims** Serve as a forum for all who are interested and involved in cities, where they can share knowledge and experience, exchange ideas and explore partnerships across national boundaries; be recognized as an international authority on the subject and a think-tank for ICOM on cities and city museums. **Structure** Executive Board of 15 members, including Chairperson, 2 Vice Chairpersons and Secretary. **Languages** English, French, Spanish. **Staff** Executive Board members, all voluntary. **Activities** Organizes annual scientific conference; develops a database for the operation of city museums worldwide; establishes joint projects between city museums as well as city museums and other organizations regarding the role of city museums in tackling social, financial and environmental issues in the life of their cities; networks between different stakeholders, shares information and determines best practices as well the undertakes research on city regeneration and city development on environmental issues and on urban municipal projects and their connection to city museums; organizes training and educational programmes in developing countries, through which members share, teach and exchange experiences with people on how to develop city programmes; raises funds to support city museums; publishes academic works on city museums. **Events** *Annual Conference* Kyoto (Japan) 2019, *Annual Conference* Kyoto (Japan) 2019, *Annual Conference* Frankfurt-Main (Germany) 2018, *Migration:Cities Workshop* Athens (Greece) 2017, *Annual Conference* Mexico City (Mexico) 2017. **Publications** *CAMOC News* – electronic. *City Museums and City Development* (2008); *City Museums and the Future of the City* (2008) in English, Korean; *Museum International: Urban Life and Museums – vol 58* (2006) in Arabic, Chinese, English, French, Spanish. **Members** Voting (149); Non-Voting; Corresponding 39 from Russia; 59 from Europe (France – 11, Turkey – 4); 16 from North America (USA – 13); 12 from South America (Brazil – 9); 6 from Australasia (Australia – 5, New Zealand – 1). **NGO Relations** Links with other International Committees of ICOM.
[2015/XJ0228/**E**]

- ♦ ICOM International Committee for Conservation (see: #13051)
- ♦ ICOM International Committee for Documentation (see: #13051)
- ♦ ICOM International Committee for Education and Cultural Action (see: #13051)
- ♦ ICOM International Committee for Egyptology (see: #13051)
- ♦ ICOM International Committee for Exhibition Exchange (see: #13051)

♦ ICOM International Committee for Historic House Museums (DEMHIST) 11057

Comité International pour les Demeures Historiques- Musée – Comité Internacional por las Residencias Históricas-Museo

Sec-Treas address not obtained.
Pres address not obtained.
URL: https://icom-demhist.org/

History Founded as an international committee of *International Council of Museums (ICOM, #13051)*. **Aims** Provide a forum for historic house museum professionals in order to share problems and solutions specific to this kind of museum. **Structure** Executive Board, comprising President, 2 Vice-Presidents, Secretary-Treasurer and 5 members. **Languages** English, French, Spanish. **Staff** None. **Finance** Through subscriptions to ICOM. **Activities** Organizes annual conferences. **Events** *Annual Conference* Chicago, IL (USA) 2018, *Annual Conference* London (UK) 2017, *Annual Conference* Milan (Italy) 2016, *Annual Conference* Mexico City (Mexico) 2015, *Annual Conference* Compiègne (France) 2014. **Publications** Proceedings. **Members** Worldwide. Membership countries not specified. [2021/XE3854/**E**]

- ♦ ICOM International Committee for Literary Museums (see: #13051)
- ♦ ICOM International Committee for Marketing and Public Relations (see: #13051)
- ♦ ICOM International Committee for Money and Banking Museums (see: #13051)
- ♦ ICOM International Committee for Museology (see: #13051)
- ♦ ICOM International Committee for Museum Management (see: #13051)
- ♦ ICOM International Committee for Museums and Collections of Archaeology and History (see: #13051)
- ♦ ICOM International Committee for Museums and Collections of Costume (see: #13051)
- ♦ ICOM International Committee for Museums and Collections of Ethnography (see: #13051)
- ♦ ICOM International Committee for Museums and Collections of Glass (see: #13051)
- ♦ ICOM International Committee of Museums and Collections of Instruments and Music (see: #13051)
- ♦ ICOM International Committee for Museums and Collections of Natural History (see: #13051)
- ♦ ICOM International Committee for Museums and Collections of Science and Technology (see: #13051)
- ♦ ICOM International Committee for Museum Security (see: #13051)
- ♦ ICOM International Committee for Regional Museums (see: #13051)
- ♦ ICOM International Committee for the Training of Personnel (see: #13051)

♦ ICOM International Committee for University Museums and Collections (UMAC) 11058

Chair Macquarie Univ, Balaclava Rd, Macquarie Park, Sydney NSW 2109, Australia. T. +61298501802. E-mail: secretary@umac.icom.museum – chair.umac@icom.museum.
Sec address not obtained.
URL: http://umac.icom.museum/

History Jun 2000. Created by ICOM Executive Council following proposition by an international group of university museum professionals to face different issues encountered by university museums and collections. First annual conference in 2001, Barcelona (Spain). Constitution adopted 2 July 2001. Current by-laws adopted Sept 2017. **Aims** Following the values and principles enshrined in the ICOM Code of Ethics (2013) and the Magna Carta Universitatum (Bologna, 1988), contribute to society by sustaining the continued development of university museums and collections as essential resources devoted to research, education, and the preservation of cultural, historic, natural and scientific heritage. **Structure** General Meeting (annual and every 3 years in conjunction with ICOM General Assembly); Board; Board Committees; Working Groups. **Languages** English, French, Spanish. **Staff** None. **Finance** Sources: contributions; donations; grants; revenue from activities/projects; sponsorship. **Activities** Advocacy/lobbying/activism; awards/prizes/competitions; awareness raising; events/meetings; research and development. **Events** *University museums and collections as cultural hubs – the future of tradition* Kyoto (Japan) 2019, *Tokyo Seminar* Tokyo (Japan) 2019, *Conference* Miami, FL (USA) 2018, *Conference* Jyväskylä (Finland) / Helsinki (Finland) 2017, *University museums, collections and cultural landscapes* Milan (Italy) 2016. **Publications** *University Museums and Collection Journal*. *ICOM Study Series*. Conference proceedings.

Members Full in 55 countries and territories:
Albania, Argentina, Armenia, Australia, Austria, Belarus, Belgium, Brazil, Canada, Chile, China, Colombia, Czechia, Denmark, Egypt, El Salvador, Estonia, Finland, France, Georgia, Germany, Greece, Guatemala, Iran Islamic Rep, Ireland, Israel, Italy, Japan, Korea Rep, Latvia, Lithuania, Malta, Mexico, Morocco, Nepal, Netherlands, Norway, Pakistan, Peru, Philippines, Poland, Portugal, Russia, Senegal, Serbia, South Africa, Spain, Sri Lanka, Sweden, Switzerland, Taiwan, Thailand, UK, Ukraine, USA.

IGO Relations Memorandum of Understanding with (1): *World Customs Organization (WCO, #21350)* (through ICOM). Agreement with: *International Criminal Police Organization – INTERPOL (ICPO-INTERPOL, #13110)*. Associated with Department of Global Communications of the United Nations. **NGO Relations** Instrumental in setting up (1): *Répertoire international d'iconographie musicale (RIdIM, #18844)* (together with IAML and IMS). [2022/XK2285/v/**E**]

- ♦ ICOM – International Communications Agency Network (internationally oriented national body)
- ♦ ICOM – International Conference on Memory (meeting series)
- ♦ **ICOM** International Conference of Occlusion Medicine (#12884)
- ♦ ICOM – International Congress on Membranes and Membrane Processes (meeting series)
- ♦ **ICOM** International Council of Museums (#13051)
- ♦ ICOM-LAC – ICOM Latin American and Caribbean Regional Alliance (see: #13051)
- ♦ ICOM Latin American and Caribbean Regional Alliance (see: #13051)
- ♦ ICOM NATHIST – ICOM International Committee for Museums and Collections of Natural History (see: #13051)
- ♦ ICOMON – ICOM International Committee for Money and Banking Museums (see: #13051)
- ♦ ICOMOS CIB / see ICOMOS International Wood Committee (#11085)
- ♦ **ICOMOS CIVVIH** ICOMOS International Committee on Historic Cities, Towns and Villages (#11063)
- ♦ ICOMOS-IFLA International Committee of Cultural Landscapes / see ICOMOS – IFLA International Scientific Committee on Cultural Landscapes (#11059)
- ♦ ICOMOS-IFLA International Committee of Historic Gardens-Cultural Landscapes / see ICOMOS – IFLA International Scientific Committee on Cultural Landscapes (#11059)

♦ ICOMOS – IFLA International Scientific Committee on Cultural Landscapes (ISCCL) 11059

Comité Scientifique International de Paysages Culturels – Comite Cientifico Internacional de Paisajes Culturales

Pres Heritage Landscapes LLC, Preservation Planners and Landscape Architects, PO Box 321, Charlotte VT 05445, USA. E-mail: president.icomosiflaisccl@gmail.com.
SG address not obtained. E-mail: secretarygeneral.isccl@gmail.com.
URL: https://landscapes.icomos.org/

History 1970. A Scientific Committee of *International Council on Monuments and Sites (ICOMOS, #13049)*, in partnership with *International Federation of Landscape Architects (IFLA, #13467)*. Statutes adopted 1983. *Florence Charter* approved by ICOMOS General Assembly 1981. Former names and other names: *ICOMOS International Committee of Historic Gardens and Sites* – former; *Comité international pour les jardins et les sites historiques* – former; *ICOMOS-IFLA International Committee of Historic Gardens-Cultural Landscapes* – former; *Comité international pour les jardins historiques-paysages culturels* – former; *ICOMOS-IFLA International Committee of Cultural Landscapes* – former; *Comité international pour les paysages culturels d'ICOMOS-IFLA* – former. **Aims** Promote worldwide cooperation in the identification, increased awareness, study, education and training for protection, preservation, restoration, monitoring, management of cultural landscapes. **Structure** Bureau. **Activities** Events/meetings; monitoring/evaluation; training/education. **Events** *Meeting* Coimbra (Portugal) 2006, *International seminar on historic gardens* Buenos Aires (Argentina) 2001, *International congress on gardening* Madrid (Spain) 1992, *International seminar on the restoration of historical gardens* Barcelona (Spain) 1989. **Publications** Newsletter; symposium proceedings. **Members** Individuals over 200). Membership countries not specified. [2020/XE0471/v/**E**]

- ♦ ICOMOS International c Committee on Industrial Heritage (unconfirmed)
- ♦ ICOMOS International Committee on Aerospace Heritage (unconfirmed)
- ♦ ICOMOS International Committee on Archaeological Heritage Management / see ICOMOS International Scientific Committee on Archaeological Heritage Management (#11073)
- ♦ ICOMOS International Committee for Architectural Photogrammetry / see CIPA Heritage Documentation (#03929)

♦ ICOMOS International Committee on Cultural Routes 11060

Comité international des itinéraires culturels – Comité Internacional de Itinerarios Culturales

Pres Nicolás Bravo 906, 31000 Chihuahua, Mexico. E-mail: ciicicomos.pres@gmail.com – ciicicomos.org@gmail.com.
SG address not obtained. E-mail: ciicicomos.sec@gmail.com.
URL: https://ciicicomos.org/

History 1998. A Scientific Committee of *International Council on Monuments and Sites (ICOMOS, #13049)*. Former names and other names: *ICOMOS International Scientific Committee on Cultural Routes* – former (1998); *Comité international des itinéraires culturels de l'ICOMOS (CIIC)* – former (1998); *Comité Internacional de Itinerarios Culturales ICOMOS* – former (1998). **Aims** Promote: identification, study and enhancement of cultural routes; protection, maintenance and conservation of *monuments*, groups of buildings, *archaeological* remains, cultural landscapes and sites as they are connected through cultural values and historical links. **Structure** Board of Directors. **Finance** Supported by Spanish National Committee of ICOMOS. **Events** *Scientific Symposium* Florence (Italy) / Ravello (Italy) 2023, *World heritage international exchange symposium* Ise (Japan) 2009, *International seminar on cultural routes and intangible heritage within universal context* Spain 2001, *Cultural routes and intangible heritage* Spain 2000. **Publications** *CIIC Scientific Magazine*. **Members** Individuals. Membership countries not specified. [2023/XK1884/v/E]

♦ ICOMOS International Committee on Cultural Tourism / see ICOMOS International Cultural Tourism Committee (#11070)

♦ ICOMOS International Committee on Earthen Architectural Heritage 11061

Comité international sur le patrimoine de l'architecture de terre de l'ICOMOS

Pres DICAAR – Univ degli Studi di Cagliari, Via Santa Croce 59, 09123 Cagliari, Italy.
SG address not obtained.
URL: https://isceah.icomos.org/

History 1987. A Scientific Committee of *International Council on Monuments and Sites (ICOMOS, #13049)*. Former names and other names: *ICOMOS International Committee for the Study and Conservation of Earthen Architecture* – former; *Comité international pour l'étude et la conservation de l'architecture de terre de l'ICOMOS* – former. **Aims** Advise ICOMOS on policy and programme in the domain; promote cooperation of ICOMOS with activities of other organizations specialized in this domain, in particular by establishing a network to monitor it; facilitate establishment of specialized national sub-committees within the framework of ICOMOS national committees; serve as a channel of communication. **Structure** Bureau; Board of Directors. **Activities** Events/meetings; guidance/assistance/consulting; training/education. **Events** *TERRA World Congress on Earthen Architecture* Santa Fe, NM (USA) 2022, *TERRA World Congress on Earthen Architecture* Santa Fe, NM (USA) 2021, *TERRA Conference on the Study and Conservation of Earthen Architectural Heritage* Lyon (France) 2016, *TERRA conference on the study and conservation of earthen architectural heritage* Lima (Peru) 2012, *TERRA Conference on the study and conservation of earthen architecture / Conference* Bamako (Mali) 2008. **Members** Individuals. Membership countries not specified. [2022/XE2230/v/E]

♦ ICOMOS International Committee on Economics of Conservation .. 11062

Comité international sur l'économie de la conservation de l'ICOMOS

Contact Univ of Naples Federico II, Dpt of Conservation of Architectural and Environmental Assets, Via Rome 402, 80134 Naples NA, Italy. T. +39812538650. Fax +39812538649.

History Apr 1988. A Scientific Committee of *International Council on Monuments and Sites (ICOMOS, #13049)*. Statutes were adopted 1988. **Aims** Make better use of all kinds of limited resources which are available for conservation, so that the quality of the *cultural heritage* that is produced is higher, and less open to danger than would otherwise be the case. **Members** Individuals. Membership countries not specified. [2008.11.04/XE1346/v/E]

♦ ICOMOS International Committee on Historic Cities, Towns and Villages (ICOMOS CIVVIH) 11063

Pres Rue de la Victoire 192c, 1060 Brussels, Belgium.
URL: https://civvih.icomos.org/

History 13 Dec 1982, Paris (France). Founded by the Executive Committee of *International Council on Monuments and Sites (ICOMOS, #13049)*. *International Charter of Historic Towns* adopted 5 Dec 1986, approved by ICOMOS General Assembly 1987. Former names and other names: *Comité international de Eger sur les villes historiques* – former; *ICOMOS International Committee on Historic Towns* – former (1984); *Comité international sur les villes historiques de l'ICOMOS (CIVIH)* – former (1984); *ICOMOS International Committee on Historic Towns and Villages* – former; *Comité international des villes et villages historiques de l'ICOMOS (CIVVIH)* – former; *Történeti Varosok és Falvak Nemzetközi Bizottsaga* – former. **Aims** Contribute to the *protection* of historic towns and ensembles on all continents. **Structure** Bureau. **Languages** English, French. **Staff** 1.00 FTE, paid; 1.00 FTE, voluntary. **Activities** Promotes the carrying out of the Charter. Exhibitions. Annual meeting/summer university/seminar in Eger (Hungary). **Events** *Annual Meeting* Brussels (Belgium) 2022, *Annual Meeting* Seoul (Korea Rep) 2016, *Meeting* Patras (Greece) 2006, *Annual meeting* Rauma (Finland) 2006, *Annual meeting* Istanbul (Turkey) 2005.

Members Individuals Permanent (10); Associate (27); Honorary (1); Permanently invited (1). Members in 26 countries:
Argentina, Austria, Bulgaria, Canada, Croatia, Czechia, Denmark, Finland, France, Germany, Ghana, Hungary, Ireland, Israel, Italy, Luxembourg, Norway, Poland, Portugal, Romania, Russia, Serbia, Sweden, Tunisia, UK, USA. [2023/XE7798/v/E]

♦ ICOMOS International Committee of Historic Gardens and Sites / see ICOMOS – IFLA International Scientific Committee on Cultural Landscapes (#11059)

♦ ICOMOS International Committee on Historic Towns / see ICOMOS International Committee on Historic Cities, Towns and Villages (#11063)

♦ ICOMOS International Committee on Historic Towns and Villages / see ICOMOS International Committee on Historic Cities, Towns and Villages (#11063)

♦ ICOMOS International Committee on Intangible Cultural Heritage (ICICH) 11064

Comité international sur le patrimoine culturel immatériel

Pres 93 Triveni Apartments, West Enclave, Pitampura, Delhi 110034, DELHI 110034, India.
URL: https://icich.icomos.org/

History 2005. A Scientific Committee of *International Council on Monuments and Sites (ICOMOS, #13049)*. **Structure** Bureau. [2023/XM2879/v/E]

♦ ICOMOS International Committee on Interpretation and Presentation (ICIP) 11065

Comité international sur l'interpretation et présentation de l'ICOMOS

Pres C/- SHP, 2/204 Turner Street, Port Melbourne VIC 3207, Australia.
SG address not obtained.
URL: http://icip.icomos.org/

History A Scientific Committee of *International Council on Monuments and Sites (ICOMOS, #13049)*. **Aims** Study the evolving technologies and techniques of public interpretation and presentation, evaluating their potential to enrich contemporary historical discourse; heighten sensitivity to the universal values and particular modes of human expression embodied in cultural heritage sites. **Languages** English, French. **Events** *Annual Ename international colloquium* Ghent (Belgium) 2008. [2021/XM2877/v/E]

♦ ICOMOS International Committee on Risk Preparedness / see ICOMOS International Scientific Committee on Risk Preparedness (#11080)

♦ ICOMOS International Committee on Rock Art 11066

Comité international pour l'art rupestre de l'ICOMOS (CAR)

Coordinator UWA – Fac of Arts, Archaeology, Mailbag 257, Crawley WA 6009, Australia.
URL: https://www.isc-car.org/

History Oct 1980, Warsaw (Poland). A Scientific Committee of *International Council on Monuments and Sites (ICOMOS, #13049)*. Original statutes adopted, Oct 1980; new statutes adopted, 2014. **Aims** Promote international cooperation in the field of rock art; counsel ICOMOS organs in the elaboration of its programme in this field. **Structure** Annual Meeting; Bureau. **Languages** English, French. **Finance** Donations. **Activities** Events/meetings; guidance/assistance/consulting; knowledge management/information dissemination; publishing activities. **Events** *Joint annual symposium* Valcamonica (Italy) 2004, *Joint annual symposium* Valcamonica (Italy) 2000, *Joint annual symposium* Valcamonica (Italy) 1999, *Joint annual symposium* Valcamonica (Italy) 1998, *Joint annual symposium* Valcamonica (Italy) 1995. **Publications** *International Newsletter on Rock Art (INORA)* (3 a year).

Members Individuals in 63 countries and territories (* indicates national coordinator):
Albania, Algeria, Angola, Argentina (*), Australia (*), Austria, Belgium, Bolivia, Bosnia-Herzegovina, Brazil, Canada, Chile, China (*), Colombia (*), Costa Rica, Croatia, Cuba, Czechia, Denmark, Dominican Rep, Egypt, Ethiopia, Finland, France (*), Germany (*), Greece, Hong Kong, India, Italy (*), Japan (*), Jordan, Kenya (*), Kuwait, Lesotho, Malawi, Mexico (*), Morocco, Mozambique, Netherlands (*), New Zealand, Niger, Norway (*), Peru, Poland, Portugal (*), Russia (*), Saudi Arabia (*), Serbia, Slovakia, Slovenia, South Africa (*), Spain (*), Sweden (*), Switzerland, Tajikistan, Tanzania UR (*), Tunisia, Türkiye, UK, Uruguay (*), USA, Venezuela, Zimbabwe.

IGO Relations *UNESCO (#20322)*. **NGO Relations** Links with many organizations working in the field of rock art and cultural heritage conservation, not specified. [2022/XE1540/v/E]

♦ ICOMOS International Committee on Stained Glass / see ICOMOS International Scientific Committee for the Conservation of Stained Glass (#11074)

♦ ICOMOS International Committee on Stone / see ICOMOS International Scientific Committee for Stone (#11082)

♦ ICOMOS International Committee for the Study and Conservation of Earthen Architecture / see ICOMOS International Committee on Earthen Architectural Heritage (#11061)

♦ ICOMOS International Committee on Theory and Philosophy of Conservation and Restoration (TheoPhilos) 11067

Comité international sur le théorie et philosophie de la conservation et de la restauration de l'ICOMOS

Pres The Royal Castle, Pl Zamkowy 4, 02-227 Warsaw, Poland. Fax +48226224159. E-mail: theophilos@icomos.org.
URL: https://theophilos.icomos.org/

History 2005, Xian (China). A Scientific Committee of *International Council on Monuments and Sites (ICOMOS, #13049)*. **Aims** Provide a forum for developing the relation of conservation theory to practice in dialogue with all parts of the conservation community. **Structure** Bureau. **Activities** Events/meetings. **Events** *Seminar on Terrorist Analysts* Singapore (Singapore) 2011. [2022/XM2880/v/E]

♦ ICOMOS International Committee on Twentieth Century Heritage (see: #13049)

♦ ICOMOS International Committee on the Underwater Cultural Heritage 11068

Comité international sur le patrimoine culturel sous-marin de l'ICOMOS

Pres Charcas 3321-9A, 1425 Buenos Aires, Argentina.
SG address not obtained.
URL: https://icuch.icomos.org/

History A Scientific Committee of *International Council on Monuments and Sites (ICOMOS, #13049)*. Charter Nov 1991. Relevant treaty: *Convention on the Protection of the Underwater Cultural Heritage (2001)*. Original statutes adopted 1991. **Aims** Promote international cooperation in the identification, *protection* and *conservation* of underwater cultural heritage *sites*; advise ICOMOS on the development and implementation of programmes in the field. **Activities** Advocacy/lobbying/activism; events/meetings; knowledge management/information dissemination; standards/guidelines; training/education. **Publications** *Underwater Cultural Heritage*.

Members Individuals in 19 countries:
Argentina, Australia, Canada, Cayman Is, Denmark, France, Honduras, India, Israel, Kenya, Malaysia, Mexico, Netherlands, Philippines, Russia, Sri Lanka, Sweden, UK, USA. [2022/XK0697/v/E]

♦ ICOMOS International Committee for Vernacular Architecture 11069

Comité international pour l'architecture vernaculaire de l'ICOMOS (CIAV)

Pres 7 Inott Furze, Oxford, OX3 7ES, UK. E-mail: icomosciav@gmail.com.
URL: https://ciav.icomos.org/

History 1976, Plovdiv (Bulgaria). Founded as an International Specialized Committee for scientific, methodological and theoretical research and conservation in the field of vernacular, folkloric and popular architecture of *International Council on Monuments and Sites (ICOMOS, #13049)*. Statutes adopted 1983; restructured 1994. **Aims** Promote international cooperation in the identification, study, protection and conservation of vernacular architecture, including vernacular *monuments*, groups of buildings and sites. **Structure** Bureau. **Languages** English, French. **Staff** Voluntary. **Finance** Financed by: contributions of National Committees of ICOMOS. **Activities** Events/meetings; knowledge management/information dissemination. **Events** *Thailand International Conference on Timber Heritage and Cultural Tourism* Bangkok (Thailand) 2015, *Annual meeting* Québec, QC (Canada) 2008, *Annual meeting* Cameroon 2007, *Annual meeting* San Antonio, NL (Mexico) 2006, *Annual meeting* Xian (China) 2005. **Publications** *CIAV Newsletter*. *Vernacular Architecture* (2002); *Conservation and Revitalization of Vernacular Architecture* (1997); *Conservation Management Training in Cultural Landscape* (1993) in English, French; *L'architecture traditionnelle des Balkans* (1992) by D Pavlovich. Papers; studies.

Members Voting members in 41 countries:
Armenia, Australia, Austria, Belgium, Bulgaria, Cameroon, Canada, Chile, Croatia, Cuba, Czechia, Denmark, Dominican Rep, Finland, Germany, Guatemala, Hungary, Israel, Japan, Korea Rep, Lithuania, Mexico, Netherlands, North Macedonia, Norway, Paraguay, Philippines, Poland, Romania, Russia, Slovakia, South Africa, Spain, Sweden, Switzerland, Tanzania UR, Thailand, Togo, Türkiye, UK, USA.

Honorary members in 5 countries:
Australia, Finland, Germany, Guatemala, Switzerland.

Associated members in 15 countries:
Argentina, Bulgaria, Canada, Dominican Rep, Finland, Greece, Israel, Japan, Mexico, Norway, Portugal, Romania, South Africa, Spain, Thailand.

Coopted members in 4 countries and territories:
Greece, Mexico, Palestine, Tonga.

NGO Relations Cooperates with several scientific committees of ICOMOS. [2022/XE0486/E]

♦ ICOMOS International Committee on Wall Paintings / see ICOMOS International Scientific Committee on Mural Paintings (#11078)

♦ **ICOMOS** International Council on Monuments and Sites (#13049)

♦ ICOMOS International Cultural Tourism Committee (ICTC) 11070

Pres 69 Chemin Juniper, Chelsea QC J9B 1T3, Canada. E-mail: info@icomosictc.org.
SG address not obtained.
URL: https://www.icomosictc.org/

History 1969. A Scientific Committee of *International Council on Monuments and Sites (ICOMOS, #13049)*. An international scientific committee since the early 1980s. *Charter of Cultural Tourism*, 1976; Oct 1999. Former names and other names: *ICOMOS International Scientific Committee on Cultural Tourism* – alias; *ICOMOS International Committee on Cultural Tourism* – former; *Comité international du tourisme culturel de l'ICOMOS* – former. **Aims** Work with host countries and communities, other international organizations and the tourism industry to encourage growth of a sustainable worldwide cultural tourism industry. **Structure** Bureau. **Languages** English. **Staff** All voluntary. **Finance** Fees received through preparation of publications for *World Tourism Organization (UNWTO, #21861)*. No annual budget. **Activities** Events/meetings; guidance/assistance/consulting; knowledge management/information dissemination. **Events** *Annual Meeting* Bangkok (Thailand) 2022, *Annual Meeting* Vigan (Philippines) 2012, *Impact of mass tourism on historical and traditional villages* Seoul (Korea Rep) / Andong (Korea Rep) 2006, *Annual meeting* Rhodes Is (Greece) 2003. **Publications** *Communicating Heritage – A Handbook for the Tourism Sector – WTO* (2011); *Tourism Congestion Management at Natural and Cultural Sites – WTO* (2005); *International Cultural Tourism Charter* (1999).

ICOMOS International Polar
11071
alphabetic sequence excludes
For the complete listing, see Yearbook Online at

Members Individuals (110) in 35 countries and territories:
Australia, Bahrain, Belgium, Canada, China, Croatia, Denmark, Finland, France, Germany, Greece, Hungary, India, Indonesia, Italy, Japan, Korea Rep, Malta, Mauritius, Mexico, Netherlands, Northern Cyprus, Norway, Philippines, Portugal, Seychelles, Spain, Sri Lanka, Sweden, Syrian AR, Thailand, Trinidad-Tobago, UK, USA, Vietnam. [2022/XE0448/v/E]

♦ ICOMOS International Polar Heritage Committee (IPHC) 11071

Comité international pour le patrimoine historique polaire de l'ICOMOS

Pres 84 Ballarat Street, Fisher, Canberra ACT 2611, Australia. E-mail: iphc@icomos.org.
SG address not obtained.
URL: https://www.iphc-icomos.org/home

History 1 Nov 2000. A Scientific Committee of *International Council on Monuments and Sites (ICOMOS, #13049)*. **Aims** Promote international cooperation in the protection and conservation of non-indigenous heritage in the Arctic and Antartic; consult and cooperate with Arctic indigenous peoples regarding heritage of cross cultural significance; provide a forum for interchange of experience, ideas, knowledge and the results of research between administrators, archaeologists, conservators, historians, legislators and other professionals; promote international studies and projects; expand technical cooperation by fostering links with specialized institutions. **Languages** English. **Staff** Voluntary. **Activities** Events/meetings; knowledge management/information dissemination; publishing activities. **NGO Relations** Memorandum of Understanding with (1): *Scientific Committee on Antarctic Research (SCAR, #19147)*. [2023/XK2276/v/E]

♦ ICOMOS International Scientific Committee on Analysis and Restoration of Structures of Architectural Heritage (ISCARSAH) 11072

Comité international pour l'analyse et la restauration des structures du patrimoine architectural de l'ICOMOS

SG 11 rue du Séminaire de Conflans, 94220 Charenton-le-Pont, France. E-mail: iscarsah@gmail.com.
URL: https://iscarsah.org/

History 1996. A Committee of *International Council on Monuments and Sites (ICOMOS, #13049)*. By-laws most recently revised June 2020. Former names and other names: *ICARSAH* – former. **Aims** Promote international cooperation in the establishment of a world body gathering the various specializations of professionals in conservation and restoration concerned with integrating the contribution of structural engineering into conservation knowledge; establish guidelines and/or formulate general recommendations; disseminate the knowledge acquired for the development of competency in conservation of historic structures in different countries. **Structure** Bureau. **Finance** No budget. **Events** *Annual Meeting* Seoul (Korea Rep) 2022.
Members Individuals in 28 countries:
Australia, Belgium, Benin, Brazil, Canada, Czechia, Egypt, Finland, France, Georgia, Germany, Greece, Israel, Italy, Japan, Luxembourg, Netherlands, New Zealand, Peru, Romania, Senegal, Spain, Sri Lanka, Tunisia, Türkiye, UK, USA, Zambia. [2022/XK1655/v/E]

♦ ICOMOS International Scientific Committee on Archaeological Heritage Management (ICAHM) 11073

Admin Sec 11 ure du Séminarie de Conflans, 94220 Charenton-le-Pont, France.
Pres address not obtained.
URL: https://icahm.icomos.org/

History 1985. A Scientific Committee of *International Council on Monuments and Sites (ICOMOS, #13049)*. Statutes adopted 1986. *Charte international pour la gestion du patrimoine archéologique*, 1990. Current by-laws adopted May 2020. Former names and other names: *ICOMOS International Committee on Archaeological Heritage Management (ICAHM)* – former; *Comité international de la gestion du patrimoine archéologique de l'ICOMOS* – former. **Aims** Promote the need to preserve and enhance archaeological *sites*; reach a greater public with the results of archaeological research; promote exchange of experience, ideas and research methods and interventions at an international level. **Structure** Bureau. **Activities** Events/meetings; training/education. **Events** *Annual Meeting* Dublin (Ireland) 2022, *Annual Meeting and Symposium* Cusco (Peru) 2012, *Asia Pacific regional network meeting* Alice Springs, NT (Australia) 2001. **Publications** *Directory of Archaeological Heritage Management* (1990) by Pauline Desjardins. **Members** Individuals. Membership countries not specified. [2022/XE0463/v/E]

♦ ICOMOS International Scientific Committee for the Conservation of Stained Glass (ISCCSG) 11074

Comité scientifique international pour la conservation des vitraux

Pres address not obtained.
URL: http://sgc.lrmh.fr/

History 1984. A Scientific Committee of *International Council on Monuments and Sites (ICOMOS, #13049)*. Charter *Guidelines for the Conservation of Ancient Monumental Stained and Painted Glass*. Former names and other names: *ICOMOS International Committee on Stained Glass* – former; *Comité international pour le vitrail de l'ICOMOS* – former. **Aims** Promote *conservation* of stained and painted glass. **Activities** Events/meetings; guidance/assistance/consulting. **Publications** *Directory of Archaeological Heritage Management*. Newsletter. **Members** Individuals. Membership countries not specified. [2018/XE1119/v/E]

♦ ICOMOS International Scientific Committee on Cultural Routes / see ICOMOS International Committee on Cultural Routes (#11060)
♦ ICOMOS International Scientific Committee on Cultural Tourism / see ICOMOS International Cultural Tourism Committee (#11070)

♦ ICOMOS International Scientific Committee on Energy and Sustainability (ISCES) 11075

Pres 11 rue du Séminaire de Conflans, 94220 Charenton-le-Pont, France. T. +33141941759. E-mail: isces@icomos.org.
URL: https://isces.icomos.org/

History A Scientific Committee of *International Council on Monuments and Sites (ICOMOS, #13049)*. **Aims** Research and promote the understanding, protection, conservation and management of built cultural heritage through consideration of the requirements of energy, sustainability and climate change. **Structure** Bureau. **Activities** Events/meetings; knowledge management/information dissemination. **Events** *Symposium* 2022. [2022/AA3297/v/E]

♦ ICOMOS International Scientific Committee on Fortifications and Military Heritage (ICOFORT) 11076

Pres No706 UNESCO House, 26 Myeongdong-gil, Jung-gu, Seoul 04536, Korea Rep. E-mail: contact@icofort.org.
SG address not obtained.
URL: https://www.icofort.org/

History 8 Feb 2005, Paris (France). A Scientific Committee of *International Council on Monuments and Sites (ICOMOS, #13049)*. Bylaws most recently updated Aug 2019. **Aims** Promote the knowledge of the resources, including their historical, architectural, artistic and scientific values, and to encourage the preservation and maintenance of fortifications, military and naval structures, fortress landscapes and other objects and sites connected with the military heritage. **Structure** Bureau. **Languages** English, French. **Events** *Meeting* Valletta (Malta) 2005, *Meeting* Xian (China) 2005.
Members Individuals in 12 countries:
Australia, Canada, Cuba, France, Hungary, Malta, Mauritius, Norway, Poland, Spain, UK, USA. [2021/XM1970/v/E]

♦ ICOMOS International Scientific Committee on Legal, Administrative and Financial Issues 11077

Comité international de l'ICOMOS pour les questions de droit, d'administration et de finances – Comité Internacional ICOMOS de Asuntos Legales, Administrativos y Financieros

Contact address not obtained. E-mail: iclafi.info@gmail.com.
URL: https://iclafi.icomos.org/

History 18 Apr 1997. A Scientific Committee of *International Council on Monuments and Sites (ICOMOS, #13049)*. Former names and other names: *Comité international aux questions légales, administratives et financiers de l'ICOMOS* – alias. **Aims** Promote international cooperation in the identification, study and solution of legal, administrative and financial issues in connection with the protection, maintenance and conservation of monuments, groups of building and sites. **Activities** Events/meetings; guidance/assistance/consulting; networking/liaising; research/documentation. **Events** *Meeting on legal issues related to archaeology* Brussels (Belgium) 2005. [2021/XK1658/v/E]

♦ ICOMOS International Scientific Committee on Mural Paintings (ISCMP) 11078

Pres address not obtained. E-mail: muralpainting@icomos.org.
SG address not obtained.
URL: https://muralpainting.icomos.org/

History 1994. A Scientific Committee of *International Council on Monuments and Sites (ICOMOS, #13049)*. Former names and other names: *ICOMOS International Committee on Wall Paintings* – former; *Comité international des peintures murales de l'ICOMOS* – former. **Aims** Promote international co-operation in the identification, protection and conservation of wall and mural paintings. **Structure** Bureau. [2023/XK1656/v/E]

♦ ICOMOS International Scientific Committee on Places of Religion and Ritual (PRERICO) 11079

Pres 101-1410 (Samhwam Apt Chungdam-dong), No49 Hakdong-ro 77gil, Gangnam-gu, Seoul 06067, Korea Rep.
SG address not obtained.
URL: https://prerico.icomos.org/

History 2014. **Aims** Research and provide specialised interests in Monuments and Sites of Religions and Ritual, including places of world religions and local traditions and beliefs, religious heritage and sacred places including their intangible significance. [2022/AA3298/v/E]

♦ ICOMOS International Scientific Committee on Risk Preparedness (ICORP) 11080

SG Yildiz Technical Univ, Fac of Architecture, Restoration Dept, Room 205, 34349 Istanbul/Istanbul, Türkiye. T. +902123832630. Fax +902123832653. E-mail: icorp@icomos.org.
International Secretariat 11 rue du Séminaire de Conflans, 94220 Charenton-le-Pont, France. T. +33141941759. Fax +33148931916.
URL: https://icorp.icomos.org/

History 1997. A Scientific Committee of *International Council on Monuments and Sites (ICOMOS, #13049)*. Former names and other names: *ICOMOS International Committee on Risk Preparedness* – former; *Comité international sur la préparation aux risques de l'ICOMOS* – former. **Aims** Integrate the protection of cultural property into international and national disaster management, preparedness planning, mitigation and relief; stimulate and support ICOMOS national and international committees for improving risk preparedness for cultural heritage on the national and local level. **Events** *International Symposium* Istanbul (Turkey) 2012. [2022/XK1657/v/E]

♦ ICOMOS International Scientific Committee on Shared Built Heritage (SBH ISC) 11081

Pres Rua Carlos Oliveira 8, Edificio Mozart, 1600-029 Lisbon, Portugal.
URL: https://sbh.icomos.org/

History Sep 1998, Stockholm (Sweden). A Scientific Committee of *International Council on Monuments and Sites (ICOMOS, #13049)*. Original statutes adopted, 1998. Former names and other names: *ICOMOS Scientific Committee on Shared Colonial Architecture and Town Planning* – former; *Comité scientifique de l'architecture et urbanisme coloniaux partagés de l'ICOMOS* – former; *ICOMOS Scientific Committee on Shared Built Heritage* – former. **Aims** Identify and value/revalue monuments, sites and landscapes of mutual heritage; stimulate and pioneer preservation and restoration/renewal projects; encourage integration into planning and development programmes; publish and present results of research, design and advisory work; provide technical assistance in relevant territories and sites. **Structure** Committee. **Languages** English. **Staff** 0.50 FTE, voluntary. **Finance** Annual forum paid by attendees with support of guest city. **Activities** Events/meetings; guidance/assistance/consulting. **Events** *International Seminar on Interpreting Shared Heritage through Time* Helsinki (Finland) 2018, *Round table forum* Melaka (Malaysia) 2004, *Africa-Europe regional meeting* Ghana 2002, *Asia regional meeting* Bandung (Indonesia) 2001, *Africa-Europe regional meeting* Genadendal (South Africa) 2001. **Publications** Annual reports on internal meetings.
Members Individuals in 22 countries and territories:
Argentina, Barbados, Belgium, Cameroon, Côte d'Ivoire, Denmark, France, Germany, Ghana, Indonesia, Malaysia, Mauritius, Morocco, Netherlands, Portugal, South Africa, Suriname, Sweden, Uganda, UK, USA. [2022/XK1883/v/E]

♦ ICOMOS International Scientific Committee for Stone (ISCS) 11082

Pres 11 rue du Séminaire de Conflans, 94220 Charenton-le-Pont, France. T. +33141941759. Fax +33148931916. E-mail: iscs@icomos.org.
SG address not obtained.
URL: https://iscs.icomos.org/

History 1967. A Scientific Committee of *International Council on Monuments and Sites (ICOMOS, #13049)*. Statutes adopted 2001. Former names and other names: *ICOMOS International Committee on Stone* – former; *Comité international pour la pierre de l'ICOMOS* – former. **Aims** Promote *knowledge* and *preservation* of stone materials in cultural heritage. **Structure** Annual meeting; Board (meets at least annually. **Languages** English. **Staff** Voluntary. **Finance** Committee members pay their own costs for Committee activities and meetings. **Activities** Advocacy/lobbying/activism; events/meetings; networking/liaising. **Events** *Meeting* 2023, *International Conference on Conservation of Stone and Earthen Architectural Heritage* Gongju (Korea Rep) 2014. **Publications** *Diagnostic par effet non destructif* (1993) by Marc Mamillan.
Members ICOMOS members with specific competences in stone conservation. Voting Representatives of national committees in 21 countries:
Australia, Belgium, Canada, Czechia, Finland, France, Germany, Greece, Hungary, Japan, Korea Rep, Malta, Netherlands, Portugal, Spain, Sweden, Switzerland, Thailand, Türkiye, UK, USA.
Associates in 8 countries:
Austria, Belgium, Chile, France, Germany, India, Italy, USA.
NGO Relations *Réunion internationale des laboratoires d'essais et de recherches sur les matériaux et les constructions (RILEM, #18930)*. [2023/XE0464/E]

♦ ICOMOS International Scientific Committee on Water and Heritage (ISCWater) 11083

Contact address not obtained. E-mail: iscwater@icomos.org.
URL: https://water.icomos.org/

History A Scientific Committee of *International Council on Monuments and Sites (ICOMOS, #13049)*. **Aims** Progress comprehension and dissemination of the knowledge and experience contained in the World's water heritage and harness it to sustainably address the water-related concerns of the present and future. [2022/AA3301/E]

♦ ICOMOS International Training Committee 11084

Comité international pour la formation de l'ICOMOS (CIF)

Pres c/o ADCRU – Dept of Architecture, Univ of Strathclyde, Glasgow, G1 1XJ, UK. E-mail: cif@icomos.org.
URL: https://cif.icomos.org/

History 1985. A Scientific Committee of *International Council on Monuments and Sites (ICOMOS, #13049)*. **Aims** Produce guidelines and standards for education and training in the *conservation* and *restoration* of the *cultural heritage* in *monuments, sites, historic towns* and areas and *man-made landscape*; develop an international network of conservation teachers related to university and post-university education and training, training at an international level, and training of trainers. **Structure** Bureau. **Activities** Events/meetings; standards/guidelines; training/education. **Events** *Symposium* Florence (Italy) 2022, *Conference on dangerous liaisons* Helsinki (Finland) 2001, *Meeting* Brazil 1998. **Members** Individuals. Membership countries not specified. [2022/XE0451/v/E]

articles and prepositions
http://www.brill.com/yioo
ICPVTR
11086

♦ ICOMOS International Wood Committee (IIWC) 11085

Comité international du bois de l'ICOMOS (CIB)

Pres 7 Dalai Lama st, Via della Scala 93, 01015 Vitoria-Gasteiz, Álava, Spain. E-mail: icomos.wood.committee@gmail.com – icomos.iwc.president@gmail.com.
URL: https://www.icomoswood.org/

History 1975. A Specialist Committee of *International Council on Monuments and Sites (ICOMOS, #13049)* concerned with the problems of the conservation of wood in historic monuments. Former names and other names: *ICOMOS IWC / CIB* – former; *ICOMOS IWC* – former; *ICOMOS CIB* – former. **Aims** Promote international cooperation in the field of *preservation* of wood in *buildings* and structures. Advise on development of ICOMOS programs in the field. Coordinate, study and disseminate knowledge concerning: *timber* structures, including *ships* and *boats* and their preservation; *conservation* of timber as a secondary structural member in buildings constructed of another material; conservation of wood auxiliary parts in buildings, such as integrated decorations, windows, staircases, shingle *roofing*. **Structure** Managing Group. **Languages** English, French. **Finance** Sources: book sales; support from 'Government of Canada. **Activities** Events/meetings; knowledge management/information dissemination; standards/guidelines. **Events** *International Symposium Wooden Heritage Conservation* Chiloe Is (Chile) 2022, *International symposium* Istanbul (Turkey) 2006, *International Symposium* Russia 2002, *International congress on performance of traditional architecture in seismic zones* Istanbul (Turkey) 2000, *International Symposium* Vietnam 2000. **Publications** Conference and Symposium proceedings; handbooks.

Members Corresponding; Coopted. Individuals (over 100) in 41 countries:
Argentina, Australia, Belgium, Bosnia-Herzegovina, Bulgaria, Canada, China, Croatia, Cuba, Cyprus, Czechia, Denmark, Egypt, Ethiopia, Finland, France, Germany, Haiti, Israel, Italy, Japan, Kenya, Korea Rep, Lithuania, Mexico, Nepal, Netherlands, New Zealand, Norway, Poland, Russia, Serbia, Spain, Sri Lanka, Sweden, Switzerland, Tanzania UR, Thailand, Tunisia, Türkiye, UK, USA, Zambia. [2022/XE0711/v/**E**]

- ♦ ICOMOS / ISPRS Committee for Documentation of Cultural Heritage / see CIPA Heritage Documentation (#03929)
- ♦ ICOMOS IWC / see ICOMOS International Wood Committee (#11085)
- ♦ ICOMOS IWC / CIB / see ICOMOS International Wood Committee (#11085)
- ♦ ICOMOS Scientific Committee on Shared Built Heritage / see ICOMOS International Scientific Committee on Shared Built Heritage (#11081)
- ♦ ICOMOS Scientific Committee on Shared Colonial Architecture and Town Planning / see ICOMOS International Scientific Committee on Shared Built Heritage (#11081)
- ♦ ICOM Periodicals (inactive)
- ♦ **ICOMP** Initiative for a Competitive Online Marketplace (#11209)
- ♦ **ICOMP** International Council on the Management of Population Programs (#13043)
- ♦ ICOM Regional Alliance for Arab Countries (see: #13051)
- ♦ ICOM Regional Alliance for South East Europe (see: #13051)
- ♦ ICOM SEE – ICOM Regional Alliance for South East Europe (see: #13051)
- ♦ ICoMST – International Congress of Meat Science and Technology (meeting series)
- ♦ **ICOMVIS** Instituto Internacional en Conservación y Manejo en Vida Silvestre (#11336)
- ♦ ICOMW – International Committee on Offensive Microwave Weapons (internationally oriented national body)
- ♦ ICON / see International Catholic Organizations Information Center
- ♦ ICONE – International Conference on Nuclear Engineering (meeting series)
- ♦ ICO Network / see International Catholic Organizations Information Center
- ♦ ICONIC HOUSES (internationally oriented national body)
- ♦ **ICONICS** International Committee On New Integrated Climate change assessment Scenarios (#12792)
- ♦ ICON – International Conference of Cognitive Neuroscience (meeting series)
- ♦ Icons of Europe (internationally oriented national body)
- ♦ **ICON-S** International Society of Public Law (#15404)
- ♦ ICOOPMA – International Conference on Optical, Optoelectronic and Photonic Materials and Applications (meeting series)
- ♦ ICO / see Organization of Islamic Capitals and Cities (#17875)
- ♦ ICOPA / see International Circle of Penal Abolitionists (#12574)
- ♦ **ICOPA** International Circle of Penal Abolitionists (#12574)
- ♦ ICOP – International Commission on Protozoology (no recent information)
- ♦ ICOP – International Committee on Proteolysis (inactive)
- ♦ ICOP – International Conference on Ophthalmic Photography (meeting series)
- ♦ ICOP – International Conference of Producer Organisations (meeting series)
- ♦ ICOPRAPA / see International Nonviolent Initiatives
- ♦ **ICORD Society** International Conference on Rare Diseases and Orphan Drugs (#12886)
- ♦ ICORE – International Community for Open Research and Education (unconfirmed)
- ♦ **ICORN** International Cities of Refuge Network (#12578)
- ♦ **ICORP** ICOMOS International Scientific Committee on Risk Preparedness (#11080)
- ♦ ICORR – International Consortium on Rehabilitation Robotics (unconfirmed)
- ♦ ICORS / see International Combined Orthopaedic Research Societies (#12657)
- ♦ **I-CORS** International Combined Orthopaedic Research Societies (#12657)
- ♦ ICORS – International Conference on Raman Spectroscopy (meeting series)
- ♦ ICORS – International Conference on Robust Statistics (meeting series)

♦ ICOS 11086

Contact address not obtained. T. +3224033660. Fax +3224033750.
URL: http://icosgroup.net/

History May 2002, Senlis (France), as *Senlis Council – Conseil de Senlis – Consejo de Senlis*, by Mercator Fund, a project of *Network of European Foundations (NEF, #17019)*. Subsequently changed title to: *International Council on Security and Development (ICOS)*. Currently only known under acronym. **Aims** Combine *research* and *innovation* at the intersections of social and economic *development*. **Structure** Offices in: Kabul (Afghanistan); Brussels (Belgium); Rio de Janeiro (Brazil); London (UK); Dubai (United Arab Emirates). **Languages** Arabic, Dari, English, Pashto, Portuguese, Spanish. **Staff** 40.00 FTE, paid. **Activities** ICOS Labs; ICOS Cultural Analysis Studies. **Publications** Reports; studies; technical documents. [2015/XJ3210/**E**]

- ♦ ICOSA / see North America Maritime Ministry Association
- ♦ ICOSAHOM – International Conference on Spectral and High Order Methods (meeting series)
- ♦ **ICOSA** International Coffee Organization Staff Association (#12631)
- ♦ ICO – Salvation Army International College for Officers (see: #19041)
- ♦ ICOSE – International Conference on Software Engineering (meeting series)
- ♦ **ICOSEP** International Coalition for Organizations Supporting Endocrine Patients (#12618)
- ♦ ICOS ERIC / see Integrated Carbon Observation System (#11368)
- ♦ **ICOSI** Institut de coopération sociale internationale (#11237)
- ♦ **ICOS** Integrated Carbon Observation System (#11368)
- ♦ **ICOS** International Council of Onomastic Sciences (#13055)
- ♦ ICOS – Irish Council for International Students (internationally oriented national body)
- ♦ **ICOSPA** International Council of Sheet Metal Presswork Associations (#13073)
- ♦ ICOS-RI / see Integrated Carbon Observation System (#11368)
- ♦ ICO Staff Association / see International Coffee Organization Staff Association (#12631)
- ♦ ICoTA / see Intervention and Coiled Tubing Association
- ♦ ICoTA Global / see Intervention and Coiled Tubing Association
- ♦ ICoTA – Intervention and Coiled Tubing Association (internationally oriented national body)
- ♦ ICOT – ICOT – The International Conference on Thinking (meeting series)
- ♦ ICOT – International Center for Otologic Training (internationally oriented national body)
- ♦ ICOT – The International Conference on Thinking (meeting series)
- ♦ ICOTOM – International Conference on Textures of Materials (meeting series)
- ♦ **ICOWHI** International Council on Women's Health Issues (#13094)
- ♦ ICPA / see Comité International des Plastiques en Agriculture (#04185)
- ♦ **ICPAE** International Commission on Planetary Atmospheres and their Evolution (#12715)
- ♦ **ICPA-Forum** International Comparative Policy Analysis Forum (#12830)
- ♦ **ICPAFR** International Council for Physical Activity and Fitness Research (#13062)
- ♦ ICPA – International Commercial Property Associates (inactive)
- ♦ ICPA – International Commission on Penicillium and Aspergillus (see: #15794)
- ♦ **ICPA** International Commission for the Prevention of Alcoholism and Drug Dependency (#12719)
- ♦ ICPA – International Conference on Positron Annihilation (meeting series)
- ♦ ICPA / see International Corrections and Prisons Association for the Advancement of Professional Corrections (#12970)
- ♦ **ICPA** International Corrections and Prisons Association for the Advancement of Professional Corrections (#12970)
- ♦ ICPA – International Cotton Producers Association (inactive)
- ♦ **ICPALA** Asociación Internacional de Prisiones y Correcciones Capitulo Latinoamericano (#02168)
- ♦ ICPBR / see International Commission for Plant-Pollinator Relationships (#12716)
- ♦ **ICPCC** International Council on Pastoral Care and Counselling (#13059)
- ♦ ICPCHE / see International Network for Christian Higher Education (#14241)
- ♦ **ICPC** International Cable Protection Committee (#12423)
- ♦ ICPC – International Center for Policy and Conflict (internationally oriented national body)
- ♦ **ICPC** International Centre for the Prevention of Crime (#12508)
- ♦ ICPC – International Children's Peace Council (internationally oriented national body)
- ♦ ICPC / see International Confederation of Popular Banks (#12867)
- ♦ **ICPCM** International College of Person-Centered Medicine (#12647)
- ♦ **ICPCN** International Children's Palliative Care Network (#12553)
- ♦ **ICPD** International Center for Peace and Development (#12472)
- ♦ ICPD – International Center for Professional Development (internationally oriented national body)
- ♦ **ICPD** International Commission on Physics for Development (#12713)
- ♦ **ICPDR** International Commission for the Protection of the Danube River (#12720)
- ♦ ICPEAC – International Conference on Photonic, Electronic and Atomic Collisions (meeting series)
- ♦ **ICPE** International Centre for Promotion of Enterprises (#12509)
- ♦ **ICPE** International Commission on Physics Education (#12714)
- ♦ ICPEMC – International Commission for Protection Against Environmental Mutagens and Carcinogens (inactive)
- ♦ **ICPE Mission** Institute for World Evangelisation (#11303)
- ♦ **ICPEN** International Consumer Protection and Enforcement Network (#12930)
- ♦ **ICPER** International Commission for the Protection of the Elbe River (#13249)
- ♦ **ICPerMed** International Consortium for Personalised Medicine (#12920)
- ♦ ICPES / see World Society of Arrhythmias (#21799)
- ♦ ICPFFI – International Conference on Physiology of Food and Fluid Intake (meeting series)
- ♦ ICPF / see International Center for Peace and Development (#12472)
- ♦ **ICPF** International Cleft Lip and Palate Foundation (#12595)
- ♦ ICPFR / see International Council for Physical Activity and Fitness Research (#13062)
- ♦ ICPH – International Conference on Physician Health (meeting series)
- ♦ ICPH – International Conference on Polyphenols and Health (meeting series)
- ♦ ICPHS / see International Council for Philosophy and Human Sciences (#13061)
- ♦ ICPHSO – International Consumer Product Health and Safety Organization (internationally oriented national body)
- ♦ **ICPIC** International Council for Philosophical Inquiry with Children (#13060)
- ♦ ICPIM / see International Institute of Business
- ♦ **ICP-IM** International Cooperative Programme on Integrated Monitoring of Air Pollution Effects on Ecosystems (#12951)
- ♦ **ICP** International Cities of Peace (#12577)
- ♦ **ICP** International College of Prosthodontists (#12648)
- ♦ **ICP** International Confederation of Principals (#12868)
- ♦ ICP – International Conference on Paleoceanography (meeting series)
- ♦ **ICP** International Council of Psychologists (#13065)
- ♦ ICP / see International Federation of Palynological Societies (#13498)
- ♦ **ICP International** Inline Certification Program International (#11218)
- ♦ ICPIP – Interstate Council on the Protection of Industrial Property (inactive)
- ♦ ICPJ – International Council for Peace and Justice (internationally oriented national body)
- ♦ **ICPLA** International Clinical Phonetics and Linguistics Association (#12601)
- ♦ **ICPLR** International Centre for Physical Land Resources (#12507)
- ♦ **ICPMA** International Construction Project Management Association (#12927)
- ♦ ICPMAT – International Conference on the Physical Properties and Application of Advanced Materials (meeting series)
- ♦ **ICPM** International College of Psychosomatic Medicine (#12649)
- ♦ **ICPM** International Commission on Polar Meteorology (#12718)
- ♦ ICPM – International Conference on Prospective Memory (meeting series)
- ♦ **ICPM** Rotman International Centre for Pension Management (#18977)
- ♦ **ICPMS** International Commissions for the Protection of the Moselle and Saar (#12729)
- ♦ IC-PMS – International Conference on Polyol Mediated Synthesis (meeting series)
- ♦ ICPMS – International Council of Prison Medical Services (no recent information)
- ♦ ICPN / see International Plant Nutrition Council (#14592)
- ♦ **ICPOF** International Cooperative of Plastic Optical Fiber (#12950)
- ♦ **ICPO** International Commission for the Protection of the Odra River against Pollution (#13250)
- ♦ ICPO – International Council of Producers' Organizations (inactive)
- ♦ **ICPO-INTERPOL** International Criminal Police Organization – INTERPOL (#13110)
- ♦ ICPPB – International Conference on Plant Pathogenic Bacteria (meeting series)
- ♦ **ICPP** International Commission on Plasma Physics (#12717)
- ♦ ICPP – International Confederation of Plastics Packaging Manufacturers (internationally oriented national body)
- ♦ ICPP – International Conferences on Philosophical Practice (meeting series)
- ♦ IC-PPMH / see International Organization of Physical Therapists in Mental Health (#14461)
- ♦ **ICPPR** International Commission for Plant-Pollinator Relationships (#12716)
- ♦ ICPP / see World Association for Positive and Transcultural Psychotherapy (#21174)
- ♦ **ICPRA** International Council of Police Representative Associations (#13063)
- ♦ **ICPRBI** International Committee for Promotion of Research in Bio-Impedance (#12797)
- ♦ **ICPR** International Commission for the Protection of the Rhine (#12721)
- ♦ ICPRP / see International Commission for the Protection of the Rhine (#12721)
- ♦ ICPRR – International Council on Public Relations in Rehabilitation (inactive)
- ♦ ICPS / see International Centre for Pesticides and Health Risk Prevention
- ♦ ICPSC – International Consumer Product Safety Caucus (inactive)
- ♦ **ICPS** Inter-American College of Physicians and Surgeons (#11408)
- ♦ ICPS – International Centre for Parliamentary Studies (internationally oriented national body)
- ♦ ICPS – International Centre for Policy Studies, Kiev (internationally oriented national body)
- ♦ ICPS – International Centre for Prison Studies, London (internationally oriented national body)
- ♦ **ICPS** International Cerebral Palsy Society (#12531)
- ♦ ICPSR – Inter-University Consortium for Political and Social Research (internationally oriented national body)
- ♦ ICPS – Trade Unions International of Chemical, Oil and Allied Workers (inactive)
- ♦ **ICPT** International Committee on Pavement Technology (#12794)
- ♦ ICPT – International Conference on Planarization/CMP Technology (meeting series)
- ♦ ICPVR – International Conference on Plasmodium vivax Research (meeting series)
- ♦ **ICPVT** International Council for Pressure Vessel Technology (#13064)
- ♦ ICPVTR – International Centre for Political Violence and Terrorism Research (internationally oriented national body)

- ♦ **ICQC** International Carbohydrate Quality Consortium (#12439)
- ♦ **ICQFD** International Council for Quality Function Deployment (#13067)
- ♦ **ICQHS** International Center on Qanats and Historic Hydraulic Structures, Yazd (#12473)
- ♦ ICQL – International Council for the Quality of Working Life (inactive)
- ♦ ICR / see Build Africa
- ♦ ICRA / see International Cleaning and Restoration Association
- ♦ ICRAA – International Committee for Rehabilitation Aid to Afghanistan (internationally oriented national body)
- ♦ **ICRAC** International Committee for Robot Arms Control (#12803)
- ♦ ICRAF / see World Agroforestry Centre (#21072)
- ♦ **ICRAF** World Agroforestry Centre (#21072)
- ♦ **ICRA** International Catholic Rural Association (#12461)
- ♦ **ICRA** International Center for Relativistic Astrophysics (#12474)
- ♦ ICRA – International Centre for Development Oriented Research in Agriculture (internationally oriented national body)
- ♦ ICRA – International Cleaning and Restoration Association (internationally oriented national body)
- ♦ **ICRA** International Collegium of Rehabilitative Audiology (#12651)
- ♦ ICRA – International Conference on Representations of Algebras (meeting series)
- ♦ ICRA – International Cooperation Research Association (internationally oriented national body)
- ♦ **ICRA International** International Commission for the Rights of Aboriginal Peoples (#12726)
- ♦ **ICRANet** International Center for Relativistic Astrophysics Network (#12475)
- ♦ **ICRAN** International Coral Reef Action Network (#12964)
- ♦ ICRAP / see International Commission for the Protection of the Rhine (#12721)
- ♦ ICRAPHE – International Conference on Risk Assessment of Pharmaceuticals in the Environment (meeting series)
- ♦ **ICRARD** International Committee on Regulatory Authority Research and Development (#12800)
- ♦ ICRAR – International Centre for Radio Astronomy Research (internationally oriented national body)
- ♦ ICRB – International Centre of Rural Broadcasting (inactive)
- ♦ ICRB – International Cooperative Reinsurance Bureau (inactive)
- ♦ ICRBM – International Conference on Rodent Biology and Management (meeting series)
- ♦ **ICRCC** International Colorectal Cancer Club (#12654)
- ♦ **ICRC** International Committee of the Red Cross (#12799)

♦ ICRC MoveAbility Foundation (MoveAbility) 11087

Exec Dir Avenue de la Paix 19, 1202 Geneva, Switzerland. T. +41227302357 – +41227302401. E-mail: moveability@icrc.org.
URL: http://moveability.icrc.org/

History Set up 1983, as *ICRC Special Fund for the Disabled*, by *International Committee of the Red Cross (ICRC, #12799)*. Became an independent foundation, 2001. Current title adopted Jan 2017. Registered in accordance with Swiss Civil Code. **Aims** Improve *rehabilitation* services in low- and middle-income countries so as to promote *social inclusion* of persons with *disabilities*. **Structure** Board; Executive. **NGO Relations** *International Committee of the Red Cross (ICRC, #12799)*; *International Red Cross and Red Crescent Movement (#14707)*. Member of: *Global Rehabilitation Alliance (#10565)*. [2019.02.21/XM7373/f/**F**]

- ♦ ICRC Special Fund for the Disabled / see ICRC MoveAbility Foundation (#11087)
- ♦ ICRD / see International Institute for Child Rights and Development
- ♦ ICRD – International Center for Religion and Diplomacy (internationally oriented national body)
- ♦ **ICREA** International Computer Room Experts Association (#12838)
- ♦ ICREA – International Consortium of Real Estate Associations (internationally oriented national body)
- ♦ **ICREFH** International Commission for Research into European Food History (#12725)
- ♦ **ICRE** International Commission on Radiological Education (#12723)
- ♦ **ICRF** International Coalition for Religious Freedom (#12619)
- ♦ ICRF – International Conference on Ingot Casting, Rolling and Forging (meeting series)
- ♦ ICRH – International Centre for Reproductive Health (internationally oriented national body)
- ♦ **ICRIC** Islamic Chamber Research and Information Center (#16037)
- ♦ ICR – ICOM International Committee for Regional Museums (see: #13051)
- ♦ ICRIER – Indian Council for Research on International Economic Relations (internationally oriented national body)
- ♦ ICRI – International Child Resource Institute, Berkeley (internationally oriented national body)
- ♦ **ICRI** International Coral Reef Initiative (#12965)
- ♦ ICR – International Centre for Reconciliation, Coventry (internationally oriented national body)
- ♦ ICR – International Centre of the Roerichs (internationally oriented national body)
- ♦ **ICR** International Committee on Rheology (#12802)
- ♦ ICR – International Conference on Romanticism (internationally oriented national body)
- ♦ ICR – International Congress of Radiology (meeting series)
- ♦ **ICR** International Council of Reflexologists (#13068)
- ♦ ICR – International Council for Reprography (inactive)
- ♦ **ICRISAT** International Crops Research Institute for the Semi-Arid Tropics (#13116)
- ♦ **ICRL** International Consciousness Research Laboratories (#12903)
- ♦ **ICRM** International Committee for Radionuclide Metrology (#12798)
- ♦ **ICRN** International Cholangiocarcinoma Research Network (#12555)
- ♦ **ICROA** International Carbon Reduction and Offset Alliance (#12442)
- ♦ ICROD / see International Centre for Research in Organizational Discourse, Strategy and Change (#12512)
- ♦ **ICRODSC** International Centre for Research in Organizational Discourse, Strategy and Change (#12512)
- ♦ **ICROFS** International Centre for Research in Organic Food Systems (#12511)
- ♦ **ICRO** International Cell Research Organization (#12463)
- ♦ ICROSS – International Community for the Relief of Starvation and Suffering (internationally oriented national body)
- ♦ **ICRP** International Commission on Radiological Protection (#12724)
- ♦ ICRP – International Conference on Reactive Plasmas (meeting series)
- ♦ ICRPMA / see International Committee for Animal Recording (#12746)
- ♦ ICRPN / see Children's Rights International (#03879)
- ♦ ICRPRD – International Conference on Reproduction, Pregnancy and Rheumatic Diseases (meeting series)
- ♦ ICRSE / see European Sex Workers' Rights Alliance (#08472)
- ♦ **ICRS** International Cannabinoid Research Society (#12436)
- ♦ ICRS / see International Cartilage Regeneration & Joint Preservation Society (#12445)
- ♦ **ICRS** International Cartilage Regeneration & Joint Preservation Society (#12445)
- ♦ ICRSW / see European Sex Workers' Rights Alliance (#08472)
- ♦ I-CRT – International Campaign for Responsible Technology (internationally oriented national body)
- ♦ **ICRT** International Centre for Responsible Tourism (#12513)
- ♦ **ICRT** International Consortium for Rehabilitation Technology (#12921)
- ♦ **ICRT** International Consumer Research and Testing (#12931)
- ♦ **ICRtoP** International Coalition for the Responsibility to Protect (#12620)
- ♦ ICRTS – International Centre for Research and Training on Seabuckthorn (internationally oriented national body)
- ♦ ICRT-WA – International Centre for Responsible Tourism-West Africa (unconfirmed)
- ♦ **ICRU** International Commission on Radiation Units and Measurements (#12722)
- ♦ ICRW – International Center for Research on Women (internationally oriented national body)
- ♦ ICS / see Institute of Commonwealth Studies, London
- ♦ ICS (internationally oriented national body)
- ♦ ICSA / see The Chartered Governance Institute of UK and Ireland
- ♦ ICSA / see International Memorialization Supply Association
- ♦ ICSAC – Inter-American Catholic Social Action Confederation (inactive)
- ♦ ICSA – International Career Support Association (internationally oriented national body)
- ♦ **ICSA** International Cell Senescence Association (#12464)
- ♦ **ICSA** International Christian Studies Association (#12565)
- ♦ **ICSA** International Coalition for Sustainable Aviation (#12623)
- ♦ **ICSA** International Communal Studies Association (#12813)
- ♦ ICSA – International Correspondence Society of Allergists (no recent information)
- ♦ **ICSA** International Council of Securities Associations (#13071)
- ♦ **ICSA** International Council for Sustainable Agriculture (#13082)
- ♦ **ICSA** International Cultic Studies Association (#13121)
- ♦ ICSB / see International Committee on Systematics of Prokaryotes (#12807)
- ♦ **ICSB** International Council for Small Business (#13075)
- ♦ ICSCE – International Conference on Spontaneous Coherence in Excitonic Systems (meeting series)
- ♦ ICS / see Churchill Centre, The (#03914)
- ♦ ICS/CI / see International Clarinet Association (#12590)
- ♦ ICSC – International Catholic Stewardship Council (internationally oriented national body)
- ♦ ICSC – International Centre for Sustainable Cities, Vancouver (internationally oriented national body)
- ♦ ICSC / see International Chess Committee of the Deaf (#12544)
- ♦ **ICSC** International Civil Service Commission (#12587)
- ♦ **ICSC** International Climate Science Coalition (#12598)
- ♦ **ICSC** International Coalition of Sites of Conscience (#12621)
- ♦ ICSC – International Computer Science Conventions (internationally oriented national body)
- ♦ ICSC – International Conference on Solution Chemistry (meeting series)
- ♦ **ICSC** International Council of Shopping Centers (#13074)
- ♦ ICSC – International Cycling Safety Conference (meeting series)
- ♦ ICSCRM – International Conference on Silicon Carbide and Related Materials (meeting series)

♦ ICSC – World Laboratory 11088

Pres CERN – Bldg 29, 1211 Geneva 23, Switzerland. T. +41227679957. Fax +41227679965.

History Founded 1986, Geneva (Switzerland). Also referred to as *International Centre for Scientific Culture World Laboratory*. **Aims** Promote East-West and North-South technical and scientific cooperation for research without secrecy and without frontiers; favour the free circulation of scientific information, scientists and researchers, in particular by means of fellowships and visiting scientists programmes; carry out projects in the scientific, technical and medical fields, in particular for the benefit of developing countries, associating thereto researchers from other organizations and institutions without any discrimination, whether geographical, political, ideological, religious or racial; establish National Scholarship Programmes; fight planetary emergencies. **Structure** General Assembly; Executive Committee; Scientific Committee; Committee of Project Directors; Auditing Body. **Languages** English. **Staff** 8.00 FTE, paid; 600.00 FTE, voluntary. **Finance** Members' dues. Other sources: voluntary contributions, subsidies, donations or legacies from members or from other individuals or legal entities who wish to support the overall activity of the Organization, or specific programmes or projects carried out in the framework and under the Organization's responsibility. **Activities** Projects/programmes; financial and/or material support. Twelve thousand highly qualified scientists voluntarily engaged in the projects; 20 governmental agreements signed; 62 scientific cooperation agreements signed; 39 permanent centres and 6 branches; implementation of 89 projects and project phases in 20 scientific fields in 50 developing countries for the mitigation of planetary emergencies.

Members Individual founding members scientists (12) in 6 countries:
France, Italy, Sweden, Switzerland, UK, USA.
Branches in 6 countries:
China, Estonia, Georgia, Italy, Lithuania, Ukraine.
Institutional founding members (9), of which 3 listed in this Yearbook:
African Academy of Sciences (AAS, #00193); *Comité permanent inter-Etats de lutte contre la sécheresse dans le Sahel (CILSS, #04195)*.

Consultative Status Consultative status granted from: *ECOSOC (#05331)* (Ros B). [2015.06.01/XF2198/y/**F**]

- ♦ ICSDC – Institute of Caribbean Studies, Washington DC (internationally oriented national body)
- ♦ **ICSD** International Committee of Sports for the Deaf (#12805)
- ♦ **ICSD** International Consortium for Social Development (#12922)
- ♦ ICSDSRA / see International Council of Securities Associations (#13071)
- ♦ ICSDW / see Socialist International Women (#19341)
- ♦ ICSEAD / see Asian Growth Research Institute
- ♦ ICSEAF – International Commission for the Southeast Atlantic Fisheries (inactive)
- ♦ ICSEES / see International Council for Central and East European Studies (#13002)
- ♦ **ICSEI** International Congress for School Effectiveness and Improvement (#12900)
- ♦ **ICSE** International Committee for Solvent Extraction (#12804)
- ♦ ICSE – International Conference on Spectroscopic Ellipsometry (meeting series)
- ♦ **ICSE** Internation Council for Sustainable Energy (#15947)
- ♦ **ICSERA** International Council of Voluntarism, Civil Society, and Social Economy Researcher Associations (#13091)
- ♦ **ICSF** International Casting Sport Federation (#12447)
- ♦ ICSF – International Centre for Social Franchising (internationally oriented national body)
- ♦ **ICSF** International Collective in Support of Fishworkers (#12639)
- ♦ ICSFS – International Conference on Solid Films and Surfaces (meeting series)
- ♦ **ICSFT** International Council Supporting Fair Trial and Human Rights (#13081)
- ♦ ICSG – International Center of Social Gerontology (inactive)
- ♦ **ICSG** International Copper Study Group (#12963)
- ♦ ICSHB – International Committee for Standardization in Human Biology (inactive)
- ♦ **ICSH** International Council for Standardization in Haematology (#13078)
- ♦ ICSHMO – International Conference on Southern Hemisphere Meteorology and Oceanography (meeting series)
- ♦ ICSHP / see International Centre on Small Hydro-Power
- ♦ IC-SHP – International Centre on Small Hydro-Power (internationally oriented national body)
- ♦ **ICSID** International Centre for Settlement of Investment Disputes (#12515)
- ♦ Icsid / see World Design Organization (#21358)
- ♦ **iCSi** International Consumer Support for Infertility Community (#12932)
- ♦ ICS – Institute for Cooperation in Space (internationally oriented national body)
- ♦ **ICS** Intercontinental Church Society (#11460)
- ♦ **ICS** International Camellia Society (#12425)
- ♦ ICS – International Centre for Science and High Technology (inactive)
- ♦ **ICS** International Chamber of Shipping (#12535)
- ♦ ICS – International Chemometrics Society (inactive)
- ♦ ICS / see International Clarinet Association (#12590)
- ♦ ICS – International Cogeneration Society (inactive)
- ♦ **ICS** International College of Surgeons (#12650)
- ♦ **ICS** International Collie Society (#12652)
- ♦ ICS / see International Commission of the Schelde River (#12727)
- ♦ **ICS** International Commission on Stratigraphy (#12730)
- ♦ ICS – International Communication Society (internationally oriented national body)
- ♦ **ICS** International Compumag Society (#12835)
- ♦ **ICS** International Continence Society (#12934)
- ♦ ICS / see International Coronelli Society for the Study of Globes (#12967)
- ♦ ICS – International Council of Sqay (internationally oriented national body)
- ♦ ICS – Investing in Children and their Societies / see ICS
- ♦ ICS – Italian Consortium of Solidarity (internationally oriented national body)
- ♦ ICSMA – International Conference on the Strength of Metals and Alloys (meeting series)
- ♦ ICSM – International Conference on the Science and Technology of Synthetic Metals (meeting series)

- ♦ **ICSMS** International Committee on Morphological Sciences (#12789)
- ♦ **ICSN** International Cancer Screening Network (#12435)
- ♦ **ICSOBA** International Committee for the Study of Bauxite, Alumina and Aluminium (#12806)
- ♦ ICSOB – International Conference on Software Business (meeting series)
- ♦ ICSO / see INTERNATIONAL CYBER POLICING ORGANIZATION (#13125)
- ♦ ICSOM – International Conference of Symphony and Opera Musicians (internationally oriented national body)
- ♦ ICSOP / see Center for Justice and Peacebuilding
- ♦ ICSoR – International Conference on the Survivors of Rape (meeting series)
- ♦ ICSOS – International Conference on the Structure of Surfaces (meeting series)
- ♦ ICSPA – International Cyber Security Protection Alliance (internationally oriented national body)
- ♦ ICSPE-CIEPS / see International Council of Sport Science and Physical Education (#13077)
- ♦ ICSPFT / see International Council for Physical Activity and Fitness Research (#13062)
- ♦ **ICSPI** International Council for the Study of the Pacific Islands (#13079)
- ♦ ICSP / see International Committee for Imaging Science (#12779)
- ♦ **ICSP** International Committee on Systematics of Prokaryotes (#12807)
- ♦ **ICSP** International Council on Shared Parenting (#13072)
- ♦ ICSP – International Council of Societies of Pathology (no recent information)
- ♦ ICSPRO – Inter-Secretariat Committee on Scientific Programmes Relating to Oceanography (inactive)
- ♦ ICSPS – International College of Spiritual and Psychic Sciences (internationally oriented national body)
- ♦ ICSR / see European Council for Maritime Applied R and D (#06829)
- ♦ ICSR – International Centre for the Study of Radicalisation (unconfirmed)
- ♦ **ICSR** International Centre for the Study of Radicalization (#12522)
- ♦ ICSR – International Conference on Shellfish Restoration (meeting series)
- ♦ ICSR – International Conference on Social Responsibility, Ethics and Sustainable Business (meeting series)
- ♦ ICSR – International Conference on Social Robotics (meeting series)
- ♦ ICSR / see International Society for the Sociology of Religions (#15451)
- ♦ ICSSA – Infection Control Society of Southern Africa (internationally oriented national body)
- ♦ ICSSA – International Conference on Software Security and Assurance (meeting series)
- ♦ ICSSCO – International Collaborative Society for Supportive Care in Oncology (inactive)
- ♦ **ICSS** Inter-American Conference on Social Security (#11419)
- ♦ **ICSS** International Centre for Sport Security (#12518)
- ♦ ICSS – International Civil Society Support (internationally oriented national body)
- ♦ ICSS – International Congress on Science and Skiing (meeting series)
- ♦ **ICSS** International Crop Science Society (#13115)
- ♦ ICSS / see International Sociology of Sport Association (#15554)
- ♦ ICSS – Interuniversity Centre for Scandinavian Studies, Ghent (internationally oriented national body)
- ♦ ICSSN – International Conference on Superlattices, Nanostructures and Nanodevices (meeting series)
- ♦ **ICSSPE** International Council of Sport Science and Physical Education (#13077)
- ♦ ICSSUR – International Conference on Squeezed States and Uncertainty Relations (meeting series)
- ♦ **ICSTI** International Centre for Scientific and Technical Information (#12514)
- ♦ ICSTI – International Congress on Science and Technology of Ironmaking (meeting series)
- ♦ **ICSTI** International Council for Scientific and Technical Information (#13070)
- ♦ **ICST** Institute for Computer Sciences, Social-Informatics and Telecommunications Engineering (#11248)
- ♦ ICSU AB / see International Council for Scientific and Technical Information (#13070)
- ♦ **ICSUD** International Centre for Studies on Urban Design (#12520)
- ♦ ICSU – International Council for Science (inactive)
- ♦ ICSVE – International Center for the Study of Violent Extremism (internationally oriented national body)
- ♦ ICSV – Internationale Christelijke Sociale Vereniging (inactive)
- ♦ **ICSW** International Council on Social Welfare (#13076)
- ♦ ICSWSE – International Centre for Space Weather Science and Education (unconfirmed)
- ♦ ICT / see International Institute for Counter-Terrorism
- ♦ ICT4Peace Foundation (internationally oriented national body)
- ♦ ICT4Peace – ICT4Peace Foundation (internationally oriented national body)
- ♦ ICT4S – ICT for Sustainability (meeting series)
- ♦ ICTA / see World Food Travel Association
- ♦ ICTA Association / see Tropical Agriculture Association
- ♦ **ICTAC** International Confederation for Thermal Analysis and Calorimetry (#12871)
- ♦ ICTAC – International Conference on Theoretical Aspects of Catalysis (meeting series)
- ♦ ICTA – International Center for Technology Assessment (internationally oriented national body)
- ♦ **ICTA** International Chemical Trade Association (#12543)
- ♦ ICTA – International Christian Technologists' Association (internationally oriented national body)
- ♦ ICTA – International Cinema Technology Association (unconfirmed)
- ♦ ICTA / see International Confederation for Thermal Analysis and Calorimetry (#12871)
- ♦ ICTAR – International Centre for Terrestrial Antarctic Research (internationally oriented national body)
- ♦ **ICTC** ICOMOS International Cultural Tourism Committee (#11070)
- ♦ **ICTC** International Coalition for Trachoma Control (#12624)
- ♦ ICTC – International Conference on Toxic Cyanobacteria (meeting series)
- ♦ iCT – Conference on Industrial Computed Tomography (meeting series)
- ♦ **ICTCT** International Cooperation on Theories and Concepts in Traffic Safety (#12942)
- ♦ **ICTD** International Centre for Tax and Development (#12523)
- ♦ ICTE / see Whitney R Harris World Ecology Center
- ♦ ICTEHV – International Conference of Tissue-Engineering Heart Valves (meeting series)
- ♦ ICTE – International Conference on Technology Education in the Asia-Pacific Region (meeting series)
- ♦ **ICTF** Association of International Credit and Trade Finance Professionals (#02660)
- ♦ ICTF – International Cocoa Trades Federation (inactive)
- ♦ **ICTF** International Commission on the Taxonomy of Fungi (#12734)
- ♦ ICTI CARE Foundation / see ICTI Ethical Toy Program (#11089)

♦ ICTI Ethical Toy Program 11089

CEO Room 528, Star House, 3 Salisbury Road, Hong Kong, Central and Western, Hong Kong. T. +85221112462. Fax +85221112126. E-mail: info@ethicaltoyprogram.org.
URL: http://www.ethicaltoyprogram.org

History 2004. Former names and other names: *ICTI CARE Foundation* – former. **Aims** Focus on safe work environments, ensuring that toy factory workers are treated fairly with respect and dignity and that factories operate ethically. **Structure** Governance Board; Executive Committee; Technical Advisory Council; Offices in Asia, Europe and North America. **Languages** Chinese, English. **Activities** Awareness raising; capacity building; certification/accreditation; events/meetings; guidance/assistance/consulting; knowledge management/information dissemination; monitoring/evaluation; networking/liaising; standards/guidelines; training/education. **NGO Relations** Affiliated with (1): *International Council of Toy Industries (ICTI, #13086).*

[2022.05.04/XM5564/f/**F**]

- ♦ **ICTI** International Council of Toy Industries (#13086)
- ♦ **ICT** International Campaign for Tibet (#12429)
- ♦ ICT – International Children's Trust (internationally oriented national body)
- ♦ ICT – International College of Thermology (no recent information)
- ♦ **ICT** International Council of Tanners (#13084)
- ♦ ICT – International Institute for Counter-Terrorism (internationally oriented national body)
- ♦ ICTJ – International Center for Transitional Justice (internationally oriented national body)
- ♦ ICTLL – International Conference on Sino-Tibetan Langauges and Linguistics (meeting series)
- ♦ ICTMC – International Conference on Ternary and Multinary Compounds (meeting series)
- ♦ **ICTM** International Council for Traditional Music (#13087)
- ♦ ICTMM – International Congress for Tropical Medicine and Malaria (meeting series)
- ♦ ICTMT – International Conference on Technology in Mathematics Teaching (meeting series)
- ♦ ICTO – International Cooperative Trading Organization (inactive)
- ♦ ICTOP – ICOM International Committee for the Training of Personnel (see: #13051)
- ♦ **ICTP** Abdus Salam International Centre for Theoretical Physics (#00005)
- ♦ ICTP – International Council of Tourism Partners (internationally oriented national body)
- ♦ ICTPPO – International Conference on the Tetrapyrrole Photoreceptors of Photosynthetic Organisms (meeting series)
- ♦ ICTP Society of African Physicists and Mathematicians / see African Physical Society (#00417)
- ♦ ICTR – International Conference on Tourism Research (meeting series)
- ♦ ICTR – International Criminal Tribunal for Rwanda (inactive)
- ♦ **ICTSD** International Centre for Trade and Sustainable Development, Geneva (#12524)
- ♦ **ICTSG** International Council of Traditional Sports and Games (#13088)
- ♦ ICTS – International Center for Terrorism Studies (internationally oriented national body)
- ♦ ICTS – International Conference on Thai Studies (meeting series)
- ♦ **ICTS** International Congresses on Thermal Stresses (#12893)
- ♦ **ICTS** International Consortium for Telemetry Spectrum (#12923)
- ♦ ICT for Sustainability (meeting series)
- ♦ ICTT – International Conference on Transport Theory (meeting series)
- ♦ **ICTUR** International Centre for Trade Union Rights (#12525)
- ♦ ICTV – International Committee on Taxonomy of Viruses (see: #15794)
- ♦ ICTVTR / see Islamic University of Technology (#16055)
- ♦ ICTWS – International Conference on Thin-Walled Structures (meeting series)
- ♦ ICTY – International Criminal Tribunal for the former Yugoslavia (inactive)
- ♦ ICTY Staff Union / see United Nations Criminal Tribunals Staff Union (#20550)
- ♦ ICUAE – International Congress of University Adult Education (inactive)
- ♦ **ICUD** International Consultation on Urological Diseases (#12928)
- ♦ ICUE – International Consortium for Universities of Education in East Asia (unconfirmed)
- ♦ ICUERP – International Conference on University Education for Public Relations (inactive)
- ♦ ICUH – International Center for Urban Water Hydroinformatics Research and Innovation (internationally oriented national body)
- ♦ **ICUH** International Cyber University for Health (#13126)
- ♦ **ICUIL** International Committee on Ultrahigh Intensity Lasers (#12810)
- ♦ **ICU** Instituto para la Cooperación Universitaria (#11331)
- ♦ **ICU** International Cheer Union (#12539)
- ♦ ICU – International Christian University (internationally oriented national body)
- ♦ **ICU** International Congress on Ultrasonics (#12901)
- ♦ **ICU** International Cooperative University (#12952)
- ♦ ICU – International Culture University (internationally oriented national body)
- ♦ **ICU** Internationalist Communist Union (#13965)
- ♦ **ICUMSA** International Commission for Uniform Methods of Sugar Analysis (#12736)
- ♦ ICUP / see International Christian Organisation of the Media (#12563)
- ♦ ICUP – International Conference on Urban Pests (meeting series)
- ♦ ICUSD – International Conference on Ultrafast Structural Dynamics (meeting series)
- ♦ ICUS – International Centre for Urban Safety Engineering (internationally oriented national body)
- ♦ ICUSS – International Council for United Services to Seamen (inactive)
- ♦ **ICUSTA** International Council of Universities in the Spirit of St Thomas Aquinas (#13090)
- ♦ **ICUT** International Consortium for Uncertainty Theory (#12924)
- ♦ **ICUU** International Council of Unitarians and Universalists (#13089)
- ♦ ICUUW / see International Women's Convocation (#15896)
- ♦ **ICVA** International Council of Voluntary Agencies (#13092)
- ♦ ICVGE – International Conference on Vapour Growth and Epitaxy (meeting series)
- ♦ ICVG / see International Council for the Study of Virus and Virus-like Diseases of the Grapevine (#13080)
- ♦ **ICVG** International Council for the Study of Virus and Virus-like Diseases of the Grapevine (#13080)
- ♦ ICVH – International Council on Ventilation Hygiene (no recent information)
- ♦ ICV – International Cruise Victims (internationally oriented national body)
- ♦ **ICV** Internationaler Controller Verein (#13292)
- ♦ ICVolontaires (#12817)
- ♦ ICVoluntarios (#12817)
- ♦ ICVolunteers / see International Communications Volunteers (#12817)
- ♦ **ICVolunteers** International Communications Volunteers (#12817)
- ♦ ICVPME – International Conference on the Valuation of Plant, Machinery and Equipment (meeting series)
- ♦ **ICVS** International Colour Vision Society (#12656)
- ♦ ICVS – International Conference on Visual Storytelling (meeting series)
- ♦ ICVT – International Congress of Voice Teachers (meeting series)
- ♦ ICW / see International Chemical Workers Union Council
- ♦ ICWA – Indian Council of World Affairs (internationally oriented national body)
- ♦ ICWA – Institute of Current World Affairs (internationally oriented national body)
- ♦ IC Water – International Centre of Water for Food Security (internationally oriented national body)
- ♦ ICWC – International Centre for Water Cooperation (internationally oriented national body)
- ♦ ICWC – International Centre for Women and Child (internationally oriented national body)
- ♦ ICWC – International Research and Documentation Centre for War Crimes Trials (internationally oriented national body)
- ♦ **ICWC** Inter-State Commission for Water Coordination of Central Asia (#15979)
- ♦ **ICWEA** International Community of Women living with HIV Eastern Africa (#12827)
- ♦ ICW Eastern Africa / see International Community of Women living with HIV Eastern Africa (#12827)
- ♦ iCWEE – International Conference on Water and Environmental Engineering (meeting series)
- ♦ ICWF / see International Disciples Women's Ministries
- ♦ ICWFD – International Commission on Workforce Development (internationally oriented national body)
- ♦ ICWF – International Center for Work and Family (internationally oriented national body)
- ♦ ICWG – International Confocal Working Group (unconfirmed)
- ♦ ICWG – International Cooperative Women's Guild (inactive)
- ♦ **ICW** In-house Counsel Worldwide (#10954)
- ♦ **ICW** International Community of Women Living with HIV/AIDS (#12826)
- ♦ **ICW** International Council of Women (#13093)
- ♦ ICW – Internationales Centrum für Weltmission (internationally oriented national body)
- ♦ ICWL – International Conference on Web-based Learning (meeting series)
- ♦ **ICWO** Infections Control World Organization (#11185)
- ♦ ICWO – International Canals and Waterways Organization (inactive)
- ♦ ICWO – International Child Welfare Organization (internationally oriented national body)
- ♦ **ICWP** International Centre for Women Playwrights (#12529)
- ♦ ICWP – International Conference on World Peace (meeting series)
- ♦ **ICWRGC** International Centre for Water Resources and Global Change (#12528)
- ♦ ICWS – Institute of Commonwealth Studies, London (internationally oriented national body)
- ♦ **ICWTWU** International Confederation of Water Transport Workers' Unions (#12873)
- ♦ ICWUC – International Chemical Workers Union Council (internationally oriented national body)
- ♦ ICXRL – International Conference on X-Ray Lasers (meeting series)
- ♦ **ICYCW** International Coordination of Young Christian Workers (#12960)
- ♦ ICYDICT – International Centre for Youth Development on Information Communication Technology (internationally oriented national body)
- ♦ **ICYE Federation** International Cultural Youth Exchange (#13122)
- ♦ ICYE / see International Cultural Youth Exchange (#13122)

♦ ICYER – International Centre for Yoga Education and Research (internationally oriented national body)
♦ **ICYF-DC** Islamic Conference Youth Forum for Dialogue and Cooperation (#16040)
♦ ICYF – International Catholic Youth Federation (inactive)
♦ ICYGMB – International Conference on Yeast Genetics and Molecular Biology (meeting series)
♦ ICY – International Commission on Yeasts (see: #15794)
♦ ICY – International Congress on Yeasts (meeting series)
♦ **ICYLS** International Club of Young Laparoscopic Surgeons (#12602)
♦ **ICYRnet** International Childhood and Youth Research Network (#12549)
♦ **ICZ** International Congress of Zookeepers (#12902)
♦ ICZM Protocol – Protocol on Integrated Coastal Zone Management in the Mediterranean (2008 treaty)
♦ **ICZN** International Commission on Zoological Nomenclature (#12737)
♦ IDA / see Institut de la Culture Afro-européenne à Paris
♦ IDACE / see Specialised Nutrition Europe (#19909)
♦ **IDAC** IDA Council (#11090)
♦ IDAC – Institut d'action culturelle (internationally oriented national body)
♦ IDAC – International Draft Animal Consultants (internationally oriented national body)

♦ IDA Council (IDAC) 11090

Sec Aalto Univ, PO Box 11000, FI-00076 Aalto, Finland.
URL: http://www.ida-society.org/

History Governing body of *International Conference on Intelligent Data Analysis (IDA)*. **Aims** Ensure that Intelligent *Data Analysis* conferences meet high scientific standards; promote a sense of community. **Structure** Officers: Chairman; Treasurer; Secretary. **Activities** Events/meetings. **Events** *Biennial International Symposium on Intelligent Data Analysis* Porto (Portugal) 2021, *Biennial International Symposium on Intelligent Data Analysis* Konstanz (Germany) 2020, *Biennial International Symposium on Intelligent Data Analysis* 's Hertogenbosch (Netherlands) 2018, *Biennial international symposium on intelligent data analysis* Lisbon (Portugal) 2001. [2019/XE3143/**E**]

♦ IDAD – Insan Dogasini Arastirma Dernegi (internationally oriented national body)

♦ IDA Foundation 11091

CEO PO Box 37098, 1030 AB Amsterdam, Netherlands. T. +31204033051. Fax +31204031854. E-mail: info@idafoundation.org.
URL: http://www.idafoundation.org/

History Founded 1972, Amsterdam (Netherlands), by a group of pharmacy students. Original title was *International Drug Association*; changed name, 1975, to *International Dispensary Association (IDA Foundation)*. Also referred to as *Stichting IDA*. **Aims** Ensure health care providers have access to quality products at a fair price. **Structure** Offices (4); represented by locally-based agents in over 30 markets. **Languages** Dutch, English, French, Portuguese, Russian, Spanish. **Staff** 281.00 FTE, paid. **Finance** Independent and self-supporting. **Activities** Humanitarian/emergency aid. **Publications** *IDA Price Indicator* (annual). **NGO Relations** Member of: *PMNCH (#18410)*. [2016.12.19/XN1646/f/**F**]

♦ **IDAG** International DMB Advancement Group (#13184)
♦ IDA – Initiative for the Development of Africa (internationally oriented national body)
♦ IDA – International Conference on Intelligent Data Analysis (meeting series)
♦ IDA – International Dark-Sky Association (internationally oriented national body)
♦ **IDA** International DART 18 Association (#13135)
♦ **IDA** International Desalination Association (#13152)
♦ **IDA** International Development Association (#13155)
♦ **IDA** International Diabolo Association (#13166)
♦ **IDA** International Disability Alliance (#13176)
♦ **IDA** International Documentary Association (#13187)
♦ IDA – International Doll Association (inactive)
♦ IDA – International Downtown Association (internationally oriented national body)
♦ IDA – International Dragon Association (see: #21760)
♦ IDA – International Dyslexia Association (internationally oriented national body)
♦ **IDAN** International Divers Alert Network (#13181)
♦ IDAP – Institut de développement pour l'Asie et le Pacifique (inactive)
♦ **IDARS** International Drug Abuse Research Society (#13204)
♦ IDATE – Institut de l'audiovisuel et des télécommunications en Europe (internationally oriented national body)
♦ **IDAWG** Immunogenomics Data-Analysis Working Group (#11132)
♦ IDAY International / see International Day of the African Child and Youth (#13140)
♦ IDAY / see International Day of the African Child and Youth (#13140)
♦ **IDAY** International Day of the African Child and Youth (#13140)
♦ IDB / see Inter-American Development Bank (#11427)
♦ IDBA / see Deaf International Basketball Federation (#05017)
♦ **IDBF** International Dragon Boat Federation (#13197)
♦ **IDB** Inter-American Development Bank (#11427)
♦ IDB Invest / see Inter-American Investment Corporation (#11438)
♦ IDBRA – International Drivers' Behaviour Research Association (inactive)

♦ IDB Staff Association 11092

Contact 1300 New York Ave, Washington DC 20577, USA. T. +12026231000. Fax +12026233096. E-mail: pic@iadb.org.

History Oct 1963, Washington DC (USA), to represent staff members of *Inter-American Development Bank (IDB, #11427)*. **Aims** Promote the welfare of members through consultations, advisory services, activities associated with human and *labour* relations and contact with similar associations of other international or national organizations.
Members Branches in 25 countries:
Argentina, Barbados, Bolivia, Brazil, Chile, Colombia, Costa Rica, Dominican Rep, Ecuador, El Salvador, France, Guatemala, Guyana, Haiti, Honduras, Jamaica, Mexico, Nicaragua, Panama, Paraguay, Peru, Trinidad-Tobago, UK, Uruguay, Venezuela.
NGO Relations Consultative Status with: *Federation of International Civil Servants' Associations (FICSA, #09603)*. [2010/XE1635/v/**E**]

♦ IDC / see Instytut Studiów Regionalnych i Globalnych
♦ IDCA – International Development Centre for Africa (internationally oriented national body)
♦ **IDCA** International Digestive Cancer Alliance (#13174)
♦ IDC / see Centrist Democrat International (#03792)
♦ IDC – In Defence of Christians (internationally oriented national body)
♦ **IDC** Internacional Demócrata de Centro (#03792)
♦ IDC – International Dairy Committee (inactive)
♦ **IDC** International Delphic Council (#13146)
♦ **IDC** International Detention Coalition (#13154)
♦ **IDC** International Diaconate Centre (#13167)
♦ IDC – International Diagnostics Centre (internationally oriented national body)
♦ **IDC** International Diamond Council (#13170)
♦ IDC / see International Disability and Development Consortium (#13177)
♦ IDC – International Discussion Club – Initiative for International Development and Cooperation (internationally oriented national body)
♦ **IDC** International Drycleaners Congress (#13207)
♦ IDCJ – International Development Centre of Japan (internationally oriented national body)
♦ IDCN – International Design Centre, Nagoya (internationally oriented national body)
♦ IDCS / see Deaf Child Worldwide
♦ **IDDC** International Disability and Development Consortium (#13177)
♦ **IDDC** International Dryland Development Commission (#13208)
♦ **IDDO** Infectious Diseases Data Observatory (#11187)
♦ **IDDRG** International Deep Drawing Research Group (#13143)
♦ IDDRI – Institut du développement durable et des relations internationales (internationally oriented national body)
♦ IDE / see Institute of Developing Economies, Japan External Trade Organization
♦ IDEA / see International Downtown Association
♦ IDEA / see Instituto Internacional de Estudios Avanzados, Caracas
♦ IDEA / see Dance and the Child International (#04999)
♦ **IDEA Europe** International Diving Educators Association – Europe (#13182)
♦ **IDEA Internacional** Instituto Internacional para la Democracia y la Asistencia Electoral (#13872)
♦ **IDEA** International Association for Integration, Dignity and Economic Advancement (#11967)
♦ IDEA – International Data Exchange Association (inactive)
♦ **IDEA** International Debate Education Association (#13142)
♦ IDEA – International Defence Economics Association (inactive)
♦ **IDEA** International Dermato-Epidemiology Association (#13150)
♦ IDEA – International Desalination and Environmental Association (inactive)
♦ **IDEA** International Development Ethics Association (#13157)
♦ IDEA – International Dialogue for Environmental Action (internationally oriented national body)
♦ IDEA – International District Energy Association (internationally oriented national body)
♦ IDEA – International Diving Educators Association (internationally oriented national body)
♦ **IDEA** International Drama/Theatre and Education Association (#13198)
♦ IDEAL – International Conference on Intelligent Data Engineering and Automated Learning (meeting series)
♦ **Idealliance** International Digital Enterprise Alliance (#13175)
♦ **IDEALS** International Dental Ethics and Law Society (#13149)
♦ IDEAS Centre (internationally oriented national body)
♦ iDEAS – Initiatives for Development and Eco Support (internationally oriented national body)
♦ IDEAS – International Database Engineering and Applications Symposium (meeting series)
♦ IDEAs – International Development Economics Associates (internationally oriented national body)
♦ IDEAS – International Development Education Association of Scotland (internationally oriented national body)
♦ **IDEAS** International Development Evaluation Association (#13158)
♦ IDEASS – Innovation for Development and South-South cooperation (unconfirmed)
♦ IDEA WILD (internationally oriented national body)
♦ **IDEC** Institut pour le droit européen de la circulation (#11262)
♦ IDEC – International Democratic Education Conference (meeting series)
♦ IDEC – International Drug Enforcement Conference (meeting series)
♦ IDEEA – International Defense Equipment Exhibitors Association (internationally oriented national body)
♦ IDEE Institute for Democracy in Eastern Europe / see Institute for Democracy in Eastern Europe
♦ IDEE – Institute for Democracy in Eastern Europe (internationally oriented national body)
♦ IDEE Instytut na Rzecz Demokracji w Europie Wschodniej / see Institute for Democracy in Eastern Europe
♦ **IDEF** Institut international de droit d'expression et d'inspiration françaises (#11310)
♦ **IDEG** International Diabetes Epidemiology Group (#13163)
♦ IDEI – Instituto de Estudios Internacionales, Lima (internationally oriented national body)
♦ IDE – Institut international des droits de l'enfant (internationally oriented national body)
♦ IDE-International / see International Development Enterprises (#13156)
♦ IDE – International Deaf Emergency (internationally oriented national body)
♦ **IDE** International Development Enterprises (#13156)
♦ IDE-JETRO – Institute of Developing Economies, Japan External Trade Organization (internationally oriented national body)
♦ IDELA – Instituto de Estudios Latinoamericanos, Costa Rica (internationally oriented national body)
♦ IDEM / see Instituto Paulo Freire
♦ **IDEMA** International Disk Drive Equipment and Materials Association (#13179)
♦ IDEMEC – Institut d'ethnologie méditerranéenne et comparative (internationally oriented national body)
♦ IDEN – International Democratic Education Network (unconfirmed)
♦ Idente Youth (internationally oriented national body)
♦ Identification of Dark Matter (meeting series)
♦ Identity Movement / see Christian Identity
♦ **IDEP** Institut Africain de Développement Economique et de Planification des Nations Unies (#20518)
♦ **IDERS** Institute for Dynamics of Explosions and Reactive Systems (#11256)
♦ IDESAC / see Instituto para el Desarrollo Económico y Social de América Latina
♦ IDESAM – Instituto Para el Desarrollo Social Andino y Amazónico (internationally oriented national body)
♦ IDES – Instituto de Desarrollo Económico y Social (internationally oriented national body)
♦ IDESMAC – Instituto para el Desarrollo Sustentable en Mesoamérica, Mexico (internationally oriented national body)
♦ IDESUF – Institut pour le développement de l'enseignement supérieur francophone, Bordeaux (internationally oriented national body)
♦ IDE / see World Bank Institute (#21220)
♦ IDEX – International Development Exchange (internationally oriented national body)
♦ IDFA – International Dairy Foods Association (internationally oriented national body)
♦ **IDFB** International Down and Feather Bureau (#13195)
♦ IDFC / see European Travel Retail Confederation (#08945)
♦ **IDFC** International Development Finance Club (#13159)
♦ **IDF Europe** International Diabetes Federation Europe (#13165)
♦ **IDFF** Internationale Demokratische Frauenföderation (#21022)
♦ **IDF** Industrial Development Fund (#11173)
♦ **IDF** International Dairy Federation (#13128)
♦ **IDF** International Diabetes Federation (#13164)
♦ **IDF** International Dialogues Foundation (#13168)
♦ **IDF** International DOI Foundation (#13188)
♦ **IDF** International Downhill Federation (#13196)
♦ **IDF** International Draughts Federation (#13199)
♦ IDGCA – International Dangerous Goods and Containers Association (internationally oriented national body)
♦ IDGC – International Digital Games Committee (unconfirmed)
♦ IDG – Initiative pour la démocratie globale (internationally oriented national body)
♦ **IDHAE** Institut des droits de l'Homme des Avocats européens (#11240)
♦ IDHDP – International Doctors for Healthier Drug Policies (internationally oriented national body)
♦ IDHL – Institut des droits de l'homme, Lyon (internationally oriented national body)
♦ IDHP – Institut des droits de l'homme et de la paix en Afrique (internationally oriented national body)
♦ IDH / see The Sustainable Trade Initiative (#20070)
♦ **IDH** The Sustainable Trade Initiative (#20070)
♦ IDIA – Institute for Domestic and International Affairs (internationally oriented national body)
♦ iDICs – International Digital Image Correlation Society (internationally oriented national body)
♦ IDI – Inclusive Development International (internationally oriented national body)
♦ **IDI** Institut de Droit international (#11276)
♦ IDI – International Development Institute (unconfirmed)
♦ **IDI** International Distribution Institute (#13180)
♦ IDIN – International Development Innovation Network (internationally oriented national body)
♦ ID – Initiative développement (internationally oriented national body)
♦ IDJC / see International Dressage Officials Club (#13200)
♦ **IdK** Internationale der Kriegsdienstgegner/innen/ (#20818)

♦ IDLC LINK / see International Institute of Management LINK
♦ IDLI / see International Development Law Organization (#13161)
♦ **IDL** International Database on Longevity (#13136)
♦ **IDLO** International Development Law Organization (#13161)
♦ **IDLSoc** International Data Links Society (#13138)
♦ IDMA – International Destination Management Association (inactive)
♦ **IDMA** International Diamond Manufacturers Association (#13171)
♦ IDM / see Association of International Dental Manufacturers (#02661)
♦ **IDM** Association of International Dental Manufacturers (#02661)
♦ IDMAT / see ASEED International Institute of Development Management Technology
♦ IDM-BLS / see Institute of Development Management (#11253)
♦ **IDMC** Internal Displacement Monitoring Centre (#11526)
♦ IDMC – International Dystrophia Myotonica Consortium (unconfirmed)
♦ IDM – Identification of Dark Matter (meeting series)
♦ IdM – Ingénieurs du monde (internationally oriented national body)
♦ IDM – Institut für den Donauraum und Mitteleuropa (internationally oriented national body)
♦ **IDM** Institute of Development Management (#11253)
♦ IDMJI – Iglesia de Dios Ministerial de Jesucristo Internacional (religious order)
♦ IDMRCS – International Discussion Meeting on Relaxations in Complex Systems (meeting series)
♦ **IDMSC** International Disability Management Standards Council (#13178)
♦ IDNG / see International Skin-Care Nursing Group (#14872)
♦ IDNIYRA – Europe – International DN Ice Yacht Racing Association – Europe (see: #13185)
♦ **IDNIYRA** International DN Ice Yacht Racing Association (#13185)
♦ IDNIYRA-North America – International DN Ice Yacht Racing Association-North America (see: #13185)
♦ IDO (internationally oriented national body)
♦ **IDOC** International Dressage Officials Club (#13200)
♦ **IDOCO** Internationale des organisations culturelles ouvrières (#13285)
♦ **IDO** International Dance Organization (#13131)
♦ IDP / see IDP Education
♦ IDPA – International Dart Players Association (internationally oriented national body)
♦ IDPA – International Developmental Pediatrics Association (unconfirmed)
♦ **IDPA** International Diatomite Producers Association (#13172)
♦ IDPC Consortium / see International Drug Policy Consortium (#13205)
♦ **IDPC** International Drug Policy Consortium (#13205)
♦ IDP Education (internationally oriented national body)
♦ IDP Education Australia / see IDP Education
♦ IDP Foundation (internationally oriented national body)
♦ IDP Foundation – Innovation-Development-Progress / see IDP Foundation
♦ **IDP** International Dunhuang Project (#13209)
♦ IDP – Irmãzinhas dos Pobres (religious order)
♦ IDPP / see Institute on Disability and Public Policy (#11255)
♦ **IDPP** Institute on Disability and Public Policy (#11255)
♦ IDRA – Intercultural Development Research Association (internationally oriented national body)
♦ **IDRC** International Development Research Centre (#13162)
♦ **IDRC** International Dressage Riders Club (#13201)
♦ IDRF – International Development and Relief Foundation (internationally oriented national body)
♦ **IDRIART** Institut pour le développement des relations interculturelles par l'art (#11238)
♦ **IDRI** Infectious Disease Research Institute (#11186)
♦ IDRI – International Dispute Resolution Institute (unconfirmed)
♦ Idrima Karnavalion ton Evropaikon Poleon / see Federation of European Carnival Cities (#09496)
♦ **IDRiM Society** International Society for Integrated Disaster Risk Management (#15205)
♦ IDRO – International Deaf Rugby Organization (no recent information)
♦ IDRP – Institut de documentation et de recherche sur la paix (internationally oriented national body)
♦ **IDRS** International Double Reed Society (#13194)
♦ IDSA – Institute for Defence Studies and Analyses (internationally oriented national body)
♦ **IDSA** International Dance Sport Association (#13132)
♦ **IDSA** International Data Spaces Association (#13139)
♦ **IDSA** International Diving Schools Association (#13183)
♦ IDSF – International Dwarf Sports Federation (unconfirmed)
♦ IDSF / see World DanceSport Federation (#21354)
♦ **IDS** Immunology of Diabetes Society (#11133)
♦ IDs – Information Diffusion Europe Associations (inactive)
♦ IDS – Institute of Development Studies, Brighton (internationally oriented national body)
♦ IDS – Institute of Development Studies, Dar es Salaam (internationally oriented national body)
♦ IDS – Institute of Development Studies, Harare (internationally oriented national body)
♦ IDS – Institute of Development Studies, Helsinki (internationally oriented national body)
♦ IDS – International Dendrimer Symposium (meeting series)
♦ **IDS** International Dendrology Society (#13148)
♦ **IDS** International Dermoscopy Society (#13151)
♦ **IDS** International Dielectric Society (#13173)
♦ **IDS** International DORIS Service (#13192)
♦ **IDS** International Dostoevsky Society (#13193)
♦ **IDSN** International Dalit Solidarity Network (#13129)
♦ IDSS / see S Rajaratnam School of International Studies
♦ IDSSA – Infectious Diseases Society of Southern Africa (internationally oriented national body)
♦ **IDTA** International Dance Teachers' Association (#13133)
♦ **IDTC** International Dressage Trainers Club (#13202)
♦ IDTR / see Institut de formation et de recherche démographiques (#11304)
♦ **IDUG** International DB2 Users Group (#13141)
♦ **IDU** International Democrat Union (#13147)
♦ **IDUM** International Dialogue on Underwater Munitions (#13169)
♦ **IDV** Internationale Deutschlehrerverband / Der (#13228)
♦ **IDWF** International Domestic Workers Federation (#13190)
♦ **IDW** International Dolphin Watch (#13189)
♦ IDWM – International Disciples Women's Ministries (internationally oriented national body)
♦ IDWN / see International Domestic Workers Federation (#13190)
♦ **IDYM** International Dominican Youth Movement (#13191)
♦ IDZ – Internationales Design Zentrum, Berlin (internationally oriented national body)
♦ **IDZ** Internationales Diakonatszentrum (#13167)
♦ IEA / see Institute of International European Affairs, Dublin
♦ **IEAAF** International Euro-Asian Aikido Federation (#13310)
♦ IEAA – International Education Association of Australia (internationally oriented national body)
♦ IEAC – Institute of Euro-Asian Culture (internationally oriented national body)
♦ IEA The Clean Coal Centre / see IEA Clean Coal Centre (#11093)

♦ IEA Clean Coal Centre 11093

Contact Apsley House, Third Floor, 176 Upper Richmond Road, London, SW15 2SH, UK. T. +442039053870. E-mail: mail@iea-coal.org.
URL: http://www.iea-coal.org/

History Established 1975, London (UK), as *IEA Coal Research*, under the auspices of the *International Energy Agency (IEA, #13270)*. Changed name to *IEA Coal Research – The Clean Coal Centre*, Jan 1997. Previous name *IEA The Clean Coal Centre* adopted 25 Apr 2002. **Aims** Provide information and analysis on clean coal technology for *power* generation, including *carbon capture* and storage, co-firing, coal supply and use, the control of mercury, gaseous and particulate *emissions* and fundamental coal science. **Structure** Executive Committee. **Languages** English. **Staff** 16.00 FTE, paid. **Finance** Members' dues. Consultancy work. **Activities** Research/documentation; events/meetings; publishing activities. **Events** *Workshop on Cofiring Biomass with Coal* Kitakyushu (Japan) 2020, *Mercury and Multi-Pollutant Emissions from Coal Workshop* Hanoi (Vietnam) 2019, *International Conference on Clean Coal Technologies* Houston, TX (USA) 2019, *Workshop on Cofiring Biomass with Coal* Copenhagen (Denmark) 2018, *Mercury and Multi-Pollutant Emissions from Coal Workshop* Krakow (Poland) 2018. **Publications** Technical/analytical reports (about 15 a year); Annual Review; executive summaries. Information Services: Emissionas standards database; library of reports.

Members Representatives of 14 countries:
Australia, China, Germany, India, Italy, Japan, Poland, Russia, South Africa, Spain, Thailand, UK, United Arab Emirates, USA.
Representatives of: [2020/XE0571/**E***]

♦ IEA Coal Research / see IEA Clean Coal Centre (#11093)
♦ IEA Coal Research – The Clean Coal Centre / see IEA Clean Coal Centre (#11093)
♦ **IEACS** Institut Européen des Armes de Chasse et de Sport (#11299)
♦ IEAEC – International Environmental Analysis and Education Center (internationally oriented national body)

♦ IEA European Epidemiology Federation (EEF) 11094

Chairman address not obtained. E-mail: councillor@iea-europe.org.
URL: http://www.iea-europe.org/

History Aug 1996, Nagoya (Japan), as IEA European Group, within *International Epidemiological Association (IEA, #13287)*. **Structure** Board. Executive Committee of 6 members. Chairman. **Finance** Subscriptions. **Events** *Congress* Maastricht (Netherlands) 2015, *Congress* Aarhus (Denmark) 2013, *Congress* Cork (Ireland) 2007, *Epidemiology and health care practice* Utrecht (Netherlands) 2006, *Congress* Porto (Portugal) 2004. [2018/XE4631/**E**]

♦ IEAI – Irish in Europe Association (internationally oriented national body)
♦ IEA – Institut des études africaines, Rabat (internationally oriented national body)
♦ IEA – Institut européen des affaires (internationally oriented national body)
♦ **IEA Interatomenergo** International Economic Association Interatomenergo (#13223)
♦ **IEA** International Association for the Evaluation of Educational Achievement (#11882)
♦ **IEA** International Economic Association (#13222)
♦ **IEA** International Emergency Action (#13258)
♦ **IEA** International Energy Agency (#13270)
♦ **IEA** International Enneagram Association (#13276)
♦ **IEA** International Epidemiological Association (#13287)
♦ **IEA** International Ergonomics Association (#13294)
♦ IEAJ – Internacia Esperanto-Asocio de Juristoj (inactive)
♦ **IEAP** Institut européen d'administration publique (#07569)
♦ IEAPS – Institute for East Asia Peace Studies (internationally oriented national body)
♦ **iEARN** International Education and Resource Network (#13231)
♦ IEARS – Institute of East Asian Regional Studies, Seoul (internationally oriented national body)
♦ IEASA – International Education Association of South Africa (internationally oriented national body)
♦ IEAS – Institute of East Asian Studies, Berkeley CA (internationally oriented national body)
♦ IEAS – Institute of European and American Studies, Taiwan (internationally oriented national body)
♦ IEASMA – International Electronic Article Surveillance Manufacturers' Association (no recent information)
♦ IEBA – International Entertainment Buyers Association (internationally oriented national body)
♦ **IEB** Inner Ear Biology (#11219)
♦ IEB – Institut européen de bioéthique (internationally oriented national body)
♦ IEB – International Environmental Bureau (inactive)
♦ IECAH – Instituto de Estudios sobre Conflictos y Acción Humanitaria (internationally oriented national body)
♦ **IECA** International E coli Alliance (#13219)
♦ **IECA** International Energy Credit Association (#13271)
♦ **IECA** International Environmental Communication Association (#13278)
♦ **IECA** International Erosion Control Association (#13297)
♦ IECA / see International Prestressed Hollowcore Association (#14638)
♦ IECCC – Institut Européen Conflits Cultures Coopérations (internationally oriented national body)
♦ IECC / see Global Express Association (#10351)
♦ IECCI – Indo-European Chamber of Commerce and Industry (internationally oriented national body)
♦ IECD (internationally oriented national body)
♦ IECDF / see International Cooperation and Development Fund
♦ IECEE / see IEC System of Conformity Assessment Schemes for Electrotechnical Equipment and Components (#11096)
♦ **IECEE** IEC System of Conformity Assessment Schemes for Electrotechnical Equipment and Components (#11096)
♦ IECER – Interdisciplinary European Conference on Entrepreneurship Research (meeting series)
♦ **IECEx System** International Electrotechnical Commission System for Certification to Standards Relating to Equipment for use in Explosive Atmospheres (#13256)
♦ **IECG** Internationale Ernst Cassirer Gesellschaft (#13295)
♦ IEC – Institute of Eastern Culture (internationally oriented national body)
♦ IEC – Institute for European Cultures (internationally oriented national body)
♦ IEC – Instituto de Estudios Caribeños (internationally oriented national body)
♦ IEC – International Echinoderm Conference (meeting series)
♦ **IEC** International Eczema Council (#13227)
♦ **IEC** International Egg Commission (#13245)
♦ **IEC** International Electrotechnical Commission (#13255)
♦ IEC – Inter-State Ecological Council (no recent information)
♦ **IECnet** International Association of Accountants, Auditors and Tax Consultants (#11681)
♦ IECOB / see Institute for East-Central Europe and the Balkans
♦ IECOB – Istituto per l'Europa Centro-Orientale e Balcanica (internationally oriented national body)
♦ IECPL – Institute of European and Comparative Private Law (internationally oriented national body)
♦ IECQ-CECC / see IEC Quality Assessment System for Electronic Components (#11095)
♦ **IECQ** IEC Quality Assessment System for Electronic Components (#11095)

♦ IEC Quality Assessment System for Electronic Components (IECQ) . 11095

Système CEI d'assurance de la qualité des composants électroniques

Exec Sec c/o IEC Sydney Office, Executive Centre, Australia Square – Level 33, 264 George St, Sydney NSW 2000, Australia. T. +61246284690. Fax +61246275285. E-mail: info@iecq.org.
URL: http://www.iecq.org/

History Founded 21 May 1976, Nice (France), within *International Electrotechnical Commission (IEC, #13255)*. Merged with *CENELEC Electronic Components Committee (CECC, inactive)*, 1 Apr 2003. Previously known under the acronym *IECQ-CECC*. **Aims** Give users confidence in the quality of electronic components (including processes and services), through independent auditing of product quality. **Structure** Management Committee, comprising delegates of Member Bodies, nominates Officers for appointment by IEC Conformity Assessment Board. Conformity Assessment Bodies Committee advises Management Committee and supervises uniform application of rules concerning quality assessment. Meetings closed. **Languages** English, French. **Staff** 2.00 FTE, paid. **Finance** Members' dues. Each member organization pays a share of the central costs and its own expenses arising from IECQ activities. **Activities** Standards/guidelines. **Events** *International Supply Chain Management Conference* Paris (France) 2016, *Annual Meeting* Singapore (Singapore) 2015, *Annual Meeting* London (UK) 2014, *Annual Meeting* Singapore (Singapore) 2013, *Annual Meeting* Busan (Korea Rep) 2012. **Publications** *IECQ Specifications List – QC 001004*. **Information Services** *IECQ Online Certificate Database*.

Members National organizations in 16 countries:
Australia, Austria, China, Denmark, Finland, France, Germany, India, Japan, Korea Rep, Norway, Russia, Serbia, Singapore, UK, USA. [2016/XF3867/**F**]

♦ IEC System for the Certification to Standards for Electrical Equipment for Explosive Atmospheres / see International Electrotechnical Commission System for Certification to Standards Relating to Equipment for use in Explosive Atmospheres (#13256)

♦ IEC System of Conformity Assessment Schemes for Electrotechnical Equipment and Components (IECEE) 11096

Secretariat c/o IEC Central Office, Rue de Varembé 3, PO Box 131, 1211 Geneva 20, Switzerland. T. +41229190252 – +41229190211. Fax +41229190300. E-mail: tsm@iec.ch.
URL: http://www.iecee.org/

History 21 Oct 1946, Amsterdam (Netherlands). Founded in succession to 'Installationsfragen- Kommission (IFK)', set up 15 Apr 1926, Berlin (Germany). Reorganized 1 Jan 1980. In Sep 1985, integrated with *International Electrotechnical Commission (IEC, #13255).* Former names and other names: *International Commission on Rules for the Approval of Electrical Equipment* – former (1926 to 1980); *Commission internationale de réglementation en vue de l'approbation de l'équipement électrique* – former (1926 to 1980); *International Commission for Conformity Certification of Electrical Equipment (CEE)* – former (1980); *Commission internationale de certification de conformité de l'équipement électrique* – former (1980); *IEC System for Conformity Testing to Standards for Safety of Electrical Equipment* – former; *Système CEI d'essais de conformité aux normes de sécurité de l'équipement électrique* – former; *IEC System for Conformity Testing and Certification of Electrical Equipment (IECEE)* – former (1998); *Système CEI d'essais de conformité et de certification des équipements électriques* – former (1998); *IEC System for Conformity Testing and Certification of Electrical Equipment and Components* – former; *IEC System for Conformity Testing and Certification of Electrotechnical Equipment and Components (IECEE)* – former. **Aims** Under the authority of the IEC, in conformity with Statutes: facilitate international trade in electrical equipment primarily used in homes, offices, workshops, healthcare facilities and similar locations. **Structure** Certification Management Committee; Conformity Assessment Board; Committees (4). Meetings closed. **Languages** English, French. **Staff** 6.00 FTE, paid. **Finance** Sources: members' dues. Each member organization pays a share of the central costs and its own expenses arising from IECEE activities. **Activities** Standards/guidelines. **Events** *Annual meting* Milwaukee, WI (USA) 2023, *Annual Meeting* Halifax, NS (Canada) 2022, *Annual Meeting* Geneva (Switzerland) 2021, *Annual Meeting* Geneva (Switzerland) 2020, *Annual Meeting* Santiago (Chile) 2019.
Members National organizations in 54 countries:
Argentina, Australia, Austria, Bahrain, Belarus, Belgium, Brazil, Bulgaria, Canada, Chile, China, Colombia, Côte d'Ivoire, Croatia, Czechia, Denmark, Finland, France, Germany, Greece, Hungary, India, Indonesia, Israel, Italy, Japan, Kenya, Korea Rep, Malaysia, Mexico, Netherlands, New Zealand, Nigeria, Norway, Pakistan, Poland, Portugal, Russia, Saudi Arabia, Serbia, Singapore, Slovakia, Slovenia, South Africa, Spain, Sweden, Switzerland, Thailand, Türkiye, UK, Ukraine, United Arab Emirates, USA, Vietnam. [2023.02.13/XD1569/**F**]

♦ IEC System for Conformity Testing and Certification of Electrical Equipment / see IEC System of Conformity Assessment Schemes for Electrotechnical Equipment and Components (#11096)
♦ IEC System for Conformity Testing and Certification of Electrical Equipment and Components / see IEC System of Conformity Assessment Schemes for Electrotechnical Equipment and Components (#11096)
♦ IEC System for Conformity Testing and Certification of Electrotechnical Equipment and Components / see IEC System of Conformity Assessment Schemes for Electrotechnical Equipment and Components (#11096)
♦ IEC System for Conformity Testing to Standards for Safety of Electrical Equipment / see IEC System of Conformity Assessment Schemes for Electrotechnical Equipment and Components (#11096)
♦ **IECU** International Europe Class Union (#13312)
♦ IEDA Relief – International Emergency and Development Aid (internationally oriented national body)
♦ IEDC / see IEDC – Bled School of Management
♦ IEDC – Bled School of Management (internationally oriented national body)
♦ IEDC – International Economic Development Council (internationally oriented national body)
♦ **IEDDH** instrument européen pour la démocratie et les droits de l'Homme (#07576)
♦ Ieder Voor Allen (internationally oriented national body)
♦ IEDES – Institut d'études du développement économique et social (internationally oriented national body)
♦ IED – Innovations, environnement, développement Afrique (internationally oriented national body)
♦ IED – Institute for Economic Democracy (internationally oriented national body)
♦ **IED** Institute of European Democrats (#11260)
♦ IED – Instituto de Estudos para o Desenvolvimento, Lisboa (internationally oriented national body)
♦ IED – Istituto Europeo di Design (internationally oriented national body)
♦ **IEDMS** International Educational Data Mining Society (#13229)
♦ IEDRO – International Environmental Data Rescue Organization (internationally oriented national body)
♦ **IEDTA** International Experiential Dynamic Therapy Association (#13323)
♦ IEDW – Communauté d'intérêts des anciens résistants dans les pays occupés par le fascisme (inactive)
♦ IEECP – Institute for European Energy and Climate Policy (unconfirmed)
♦ **IEEE** Institute of Electrical and Electronics Engineers (#11259)
♦ **IEEE** Institut Européen de l'expertise et de l'expert (#07015)
♦ IEEFI – Institut européen pour l'étude des fibres industrielles (inactive)
♦ **IEEF** Institut européen d'éducation familiale (#07554)
♦ IEEI – Institut d'études européennes et internationales du Luxembourg (internationally oriented national body)
♦ IEEI – Instituto de Estudos Econômicos e Internacionais (internationally oriented national body)
♦ IEEI – Instituto de Estudos Estratégicos e Internacionais, Lisboa (internationally oriented national body)
♦ IEEI – Instituto Europeo de Estudios Internacionales (internationally oriented national body)
♦ IEE – Institut d'études européennes, Louvain-la-Neuve (internationally oriented national body)
♦ IEE – Institut d'études européennes, ULB (internationally oriented national body)
♦ I.E.E. – Institut Européen d'Ecriture (internationally oriented national body)
♦ IEE / see Institution of Engineering and Technology (#11320)
♦ IEEL – Institut Européen Emmanuel Levinas (unconfirmed)
♦ IEEM – Institute of European Studies of Macau (internationally oriented national body)
♦ **IEEP** Institute for European Environmental Policy (#11261)
♦ **IEEPS** Institut européen d'éducation et de politique sociale (#07551)
♦ IEEP – UNESCO/UNEP International Environmental Education Programme (inactive)
♦ **IEES** International Ecological Engineering Society (#13220)
♦ IE / see European Association for Heritage Interpretation (#06067)
♦ IEF / see Europe Institute, Vienna
♦ IEFA – International Economic Forum of the Americas (internationally oriented national body)
♦ IEFC – Institut européen de la forêt cultivée (internationally oriented national body)
♦ IEFG – International Education Funders Group (unconfirmed)
♦ **IEF** International Ecumenical Fellowship (#13226)
♦ IEF – International Egg Foundation (unconfirmed)
♦ IEF – International Elephant Foundation (internationally oriented national body)
♦ **IEF** International Energy Forum (#13272)
♦ **IEF** International Energy Foundation (#13273)
♦ **IEF** International Environment Forum (#13283)
♦ **IEF** International Eye Foundation (#13324)
♦ IEFP – Institut européen pour la formation professionnelle (inactive)
♦ **IEFR** International Emergency Food Reserve (#13259)
♦ IEG – Institute of Economic Growth – Research Centre on Social and Economic Development in Asia (internationally oriented national body)
♦ IEHA / see Institut européen d'histoire et des cultures de l'alimentation (#11300)
♦ **IEHA** International Economic History Association (#13224)
♦ IeHA – International eHealth Association (no recent information)
♦ **IEHCA** Institut européen d'histoire et des cultures de l'alimentation (#11300)
♦ IEH – International Environment House (internationally oriented national body)
♦ **IEHSC** International Environmental & Health Sciences Consortium (#13279)
♦ **IEHS** International Endo Hernia Society (#13268)
♦ IEI / see Institute of Earth Systems, Malta
♦ **IEIAS** Institut européen interuniversitaire de l'action sociale (#15988)
♦ **IEI** Internacia Esperanto-Instituto (#13302)
♦ **IEI** International Enamellers Institute (#13267)
♦ **IEI** International Esperanto Institute (#13302)
♦ **IEIIS** International Endotoxin and Innate Immunity Society (#13269)
♦ **IE** Integral Europe (#11365)
♦ **IE** Internacional de la Educación (#05371)
♦ **IE** Internationale de l'éducation (#05371)
♦ IEIP – Institute of European Integration and Policy (internationally oriented national body)
♦ **IEIP** Institut européen des industries de la pectine (#11301)
♦ **IEISW** Inter-University European Institute on Social Welfare (#15988)
♦ IEKV – Internationale Eisenbahn-Kongressvereinigung (inactive)
♦ **IELA** International E-Learning Association (#13253)
♦ IELA / see International Exhibition Logistics Association (#13322)
♦ **IELA** International Exhibition Logistics Association (#13322)
♦ IELRC – International Environmental Law Research Centre (internationally oriented national body)
♦ IELSG – International Extranodal Lymphoma Study Group (internationally oriented national body)
♦ IEMA – International 8 Metre Association (see: #21760)
♦ IEMANYA OCEANICA (internationally oriented national body)
♦ IEMed – Institut Europeu de la Mediterrània (internationally oriented national body)
♦ IEMI / see Global Democracy Initiative
♦ IEMI – Institut européen de management international (internationally oriented national body)
♦ IEM – Institut évangélique de missiologie (internationally oriented national body)
♦ **IEMO** International Emergency Management Organization (#13260)
♦ **IEMO** International Energy and Mines Organization (#13274)
♦ **IEMSS** International Environmental Modelling and Software Society (#13280)
♦ **IENE** Infrastructure Ecology Network Europe (#11207)
♦ IEN – Institut d'Estudis Nord-Americans (internationally oriented national body)
♦ IEN – Instituto de Estudios Norteamericanos (internationally oriented national body)
♦ **IEOA** International Equestrian Organisers' Alliance (#13289)
♦ **IEOC** International Equine Ophthalmology Consortium (#13290)
♦ **IEOC** International Eventing Officials Club (#13313)
♦ IEO / see European Institute for Wood Preservation (#07575)
♦ IEO – Istituto Europeo de Oncologia, Milano (internationally oriented national body)
♦ IEOM Society International (unconfirmed)
♦ IEOSC / see Committee on Earth Observation Satellites (#04249)

♦ IEPA Early Intervention in Mental Health 11097

Exec Officer PO Box 143, Parkville VIC 3052, Australia. T. +61399669147. E-mail: secretariat@iepa.org.au.
URL: http://iepa.org.au/

History 1996, Melbourne (Australia), as *International Early Psychosis Association (IEPA).* Present name adopted 2015. **Aims** Enhance awareness of early *psychosis* and the process of recovery. **Structure** President; 3 Vice-Presidents (Europe, North America, Asia Pacific); Treasurer. **Languages** English. **Staff** 5.00 FTE, paid. **Events** *Conference* Lausanne (Switzerland) 2023, *Conference* Singapore (Singapore) 2022, *Conference* Parkville, VIC (Australia) 2020, *Conference* Rio de Janeiro (Brazil) 2020, *Conference* Boston, MA (USA) 2018.
Publications *Early Intervention in Psychiatry Journal.* [2020/XD8307/**D**]

♦ IEPA / see IEPA Early Intervention in Mental Health (#11097)
♦ IEPALA – Instituto de Estudios Politicos para América Latina y Africa (internationally oriented national body)
♦ IEPC – International Electric Propulsion Conference (meeting series)
♦ IEPF / see Institut de la Francophonie pour le développement durable (#11305)
♦ **IEPF** International Eurasia-Press Fund (#13309)
♦ IEPFPD / see European Parliamentary Forum for Sexual & Reproductive Rights (#08149)
♦ IEPG – Independent European Programme Group (inactive)
♦ **IEP** Institute for Economics and Peace (#11257)
♦ IEP – Institut d'études politiques de Paris (internationally oriented national body)
♦ IEP – Institut für Europäische Politik, Berlin (internationally oriented national body)
♦ IEPRI – Instituto de Estudios Politicos y Relaciones Internacionales, Bogota (internationally oriented national body)
♦ IEQ-GA / see Indoor Environmental Quality – Global Alliance (#11168)
♦ **IEQ Global Alliance** Indoor Environmental Quality – Global Alliance (#11168)
♦ **IERA** International Employment Relations Association (#13266)
♦ IERAL – Instituto de Estudios Económicos sobre la Realidad Argentina y Latinoamericana (internationally oriented national body)
♦ **IERASG** International Evoked Response Audiometry Study Group (#13320)
♦ IERB – Islamic Economics Research Bureau (internationally oriented national body)
♦ IERC – International Electronics Recycling Congress (meeting series)
♦ **IERE** International Electrical Research Exchange (#13254)
♦ IER – Institutul European din România (internationally oriented national body)
♦ IER / see Organization for International Economic Relations (#17873)
♦ **IERPE** Institut européen de recherche sur la politique de l'eau (#07570)
♦ IERS – Institute for Euroregional Studies (internationally oriented national body)
♦ Iers Instituut voor Europese Zaken, Leuven / see Leuven Institute for Ireland in Europe
♦ IERS / see International Earth Rotation and Reference Systems Service (#13216)
♦ **IERS** International Earth Rotation and Reference Systems Service (#13216)
♦ IERS – International Symposium on Equine Reproduction (meeting series)
♦ Iers Minderbroederscollege / see Leuven Institute for Ireland in Europe
♦ IESA / see International Experiential Dynamic Therapy Association (#13323)
♦ **IESBA** International Ethics Standards Board for Accountants (#13306)
♦ **IESB** International Environmental Specimen Bank Group (#13281)
♦ IESC / see International Ethics Standards Coalition (#13307)
♦ IESCARIBE – Red de Institutos de Investigación Económica y Social de la Cuenca del Caribe (internationally oriented national body)
♦ IESC – International Executive Service Corps (internationally oriented national body)
♦ **IES Coalition** International Ethics Standards Coalition (#13307)
♦ IESE Business School, University of Navarra (internationally oriented national body)
♦ IESE – Instituto de Estudios Superiores de la Empresa (internationally oriented national body)
♦ **IESF** International Esports Federation (#13304)
♦ **IESF** International Esports Federation (#13303)
♦ **IESF** International Executive Search Federation (#13321)
♦ IESH – Institut européen des sciences humaines (see: #09682)
♦ IES – Illuminating Engineering Society (internationally oriented national body)
♦ IES – Institute of Earth Systems, Malta (internationally oriented national body)
♦ IES – Institute for Economic Studies – Europe (internationally oriented national body)
♦ IES – Institute for Environmental Security (internationally oriented national body)
♦ IES – Institute for European Studies, Montréal (internationally oriented national body)
♦ IES – Institute of European Studies, Toronto (internationally oriented national body)
♦ IES – Institut d'études slaves (internationally oriented national body)

- IES / see International Endotoxin and Innate Immunity Society (#13269)
- **IES** International Eosinophil Society (#13286)
- **IES** International EPR Society (#13288)
- **IES** International Euphorbia Society (#13308)
- IESNA / see Illuminating Engineering Society
- **IESP** Information Economy and Society Partnership (#11196)
- IEST – Institute of Environmental Sciences and Technology (internationally oriented national body)
- IESW – Instytut Europy Srodkowo-Wschodniej (internationally oriented national body)
- **IETA** International Emissions Trading Association (#13262)
- **IETC** International Environmental Technology Centre (#13282)
- IETF – International Essential Tremor Foundation (internationally oriented national body)
- **iEthanol** European Industrial & Beverage Ethanol Association (#07523)
- IET – Institut européen de télémédecine (internationally oriented national body)
- **IET** Institution of Engineering and Technology (#11320)
- **IETL** Institute for European Traffic Law (#11262)
- IETM / see IETM – International Network for Contemporary Performing Arts (#11098)

◆ IETM – International Network for Contemporary Performing Arts .. 11098
IETM – Réseau international pour les arts du spectacle
SG Square Sainctelette 19, 1000 Brussels, Belgium. T. +3222010915. Fax +3222030226. E-mail: ietm@ietm.org.
URL: http://www.ietm.org/
History Founded 1981, Italy, as *Informal European Theatre Meeting (IETM)*. Since 1989 registered in accordance with Belgian law. EU Transparency Register: 55642894775-05. **Aims** Stimulate the quality, development and contexts of contemporary performing arts in a global environment, by initiating and facilitating professional networking and communication, information exchange, know-how transfer and presentations of examples of good practice. **Structure** General Assembly (at least annually); Advisory Board; Board of Directors. **Languages** English, French. **Staff** 4.00 FTE, paid. **Finance** Members' dues. International funding bodies: *European Commission (EC, #06633)*. National funding bodies: Ministry of Culture – Flemish Community (Belgium). Project grants from: EC; Flemish Community (Belgium); Creative Scotland. **Activities** Events/meetings. **Events** *Annual Spring Plenary Meeting* Hull (UK) 2019, *Annual Autumn Plenary Meeting* Munich (Germany) 2018, *Annual Spring Plenary Meeting* Porto (Portugal) 2018, *Annual Autumn Plenary Meeting* Brussels (Belgium) 2017, *Annual Autumn Plenary Meeting* Valencia (Spain) 2016. **Publications** *IETM Inform* – newsletter. Books; manuals; studies.
Members Organizations (about 550), professionally engaged in the performing arts field, in 48 countries and territories:
Albania, Armenia, Australia, Austria, Azerbaijan, Belarus, Belgium, Bosnia-Herzegovina, Brazil, Bulgaria, Cambodia, Canada, Chile, Congo Brazzaville, Croatia, Czechia, Denmark, Finland, France, Georgia, Germany, Greece, Hungary, Iceland, Ireland, Italy, Japan, Korea Rep, Latvia, Lithuania, Malta, Netherlands, North Macedonia, Norway, Poland, Portugal, Romania, Russia, Serbia, Slovakia, Slovenia, Spain, Sweden, Switzerland, Türkiye, UK, Ukraine, USA.
Included in the above, 3 organizations listed in this Yearbook:
Arts International; *British Council*; *International Cultural Desk (ICD, no recent information)*.
NGO Relations Member of: *European Alliance for Culture and the Arts (#05866)*; *On the Move (OTM, #16868)*; *A Soul for Europe (ASF, #19697)*. [2019/XF1751/y/**F**]

- IETM – Réseau international pour les arts du spectacle (#11098)
- IETP Association – International Engineering and Technology Publication Association (unconfirmed)
- IETS / see International Embryo Technology Society (#13257)
- **IETS** International Embryo Technology Society (#13257)
- **IEU** Iatrogenic Europe Unite – Alliance (#11010)
- IEUSS – Institute for European Union Studies at SUNY (internationally oriented national body)
- IEVA – Independent European Vaping Alliance (unconfirmed)
- **IEVR** Institut für Europäisches Verkehrsrecht (#11262)
- IEW – Evangelical International Workers' Union (inactive)
- **IEWG** International Elbow Working Group (#13252)
- IEW – International Energy Workshop (meeting series)
- IEWS / see EastWest Institute (#05264)
- IF / see International Federation for Spina Bifida and Hydrocephalus (#13552)
- **IF20** G20 Interfaith Forum Association (#10055)
- **iF3** International Functional Fitness Federation (#13691)
- IFA / see GIGA Institut für Asien-Studien
- IFAA / see International Communications Agency Network
- IFAAET – International Federation of Anthroposophic Arts and Eurythmy Therapies (internationally oriented national body)
- **IFAA** Institute for African Alternatives (#11241)
- **IFAA** International Federation of Adjusting Associations (#13340)
- **IFAA** International Federation of Associations of Anatomists (#13361)
- **IFAA** International Field Archery Association (#13595)
- **IFAA** International Fossil Algae Association (#13662)
- **IFAAMAS** International Foundation for Autonomous Agents and Multiagent Systems (#13664)
- IFAAO – International Food Authenticity Assurance Organization (unconfirmed)
- IFABC / see International Federation of Audit Bureaux of Certification (#13366)
- **IFABC** International Federation of Audit Bureaux of Certification (#13366)
- IFABE – International Federation of Associations of Business Economists (inactive)
- **i-FAB** International Foot and Ankle Biomechanics Community (#13624)
- IFAB – International Football Association Board (see: #13360)
- IFABS – International Finance and Banking Society (internationally oriented national body)
- **IFACCA** International Federation of Arts Councils and Culture Agencies (#13358)
- **IFAC** International Federation of Accountants (#13335)
- **IFAC** International Federation of Automatic Control (#13367)
- IFAC – International Food Additives Council (internationally oriented national body)
- IFAC – International Foundation for African Children (unconfirmed)
- **IFAD** International Fund for Agricultural Development (#13692)

◆ IFAD Staff Association 11099
Address not obtained.
History to represent staff of *International Fund for Agricultural Development (IFAD, #13692)*. **NGO Relations** Member of: *Federation of International Civil Servants' Associations (FICSA, #09603)*. [2012/XE1506/v/**E**]

- IFAE – Inter-American Federation for Adult Education (inactive)
- **IFAE** International Federation of Automobile Experts (#13368)
- IFAF Europe (inactive)
- **IFAF** International Federation of American Football (#13354)
- IFAG / see École supérieure de la francophonie pour l'administration et le management (#05298)
- **IFAGG** International Federation of Aesthetic Group Gymnastics (#13343)
- IFAH-Europe / see AnimalhealthEurope (#00837)
- IFAH / see Health for Animals (#10870)
- **IFAHR** International Federation of Arabian Horse Racing (#13356)
- IFAID Aquitaine – Institut de formation et d'appui aux initiatives de développement (internationally oriented national body)
- **IFAI** Industrial Fabrics Association International (#11174)
- **IFAIMA** International Federation of Aeronautical Information Management Associations (#13341)
- ifa – Institut für Auslandsbeziehungen, Stuttgart (internationally oriented national body)
- IFA – International Factoring Association (internationally oriented national body)
- **IFA** International Federation on Ageing (#13345)
- **IFA** International Federation of Airworthiness (#13352)
- IFA – International Federation Alysh (no recent information)
- IFA – International Federation of Armsports (internationally oriented national body)
- IFA – International Federation of Aromatherapists (internationally oriented national body)
- IFA / see International Federation of Fertility Societies (#13426)
- IFA / see International Fertilizer Association (#13589)
- **IFA** International Fertilizer Association (#13589)
- IFA – International Filariasis Association (inactive)
- IFA – International Finn Association (see: #21760)
- **IFA** International Fiscal Association (#13608)
- **IFA** International Fistball Association (#13609)
- **IFA** International Fluency Association (#13617)
- iFA – International Fluid Academy (internationally oriented national body)
- **IFA** International Forwarding Association (#13660)
- IFA – International Franchise Association (internationally oriented national body)
- **IFA** International Freight Association (#13683)
- IFA – International Fructose Association (inactive)
- IFA / see International Islamic Fiqh Academy (#13960)
- IFA / see International Trade and Forfaiting Association (#15705)
- **IFAJ** International Federation of Agricultural Journalists (#13346)
- **IFALDA** International Federation of Airline Dispatchers' Associations (#13348)
- **IFALPA** International Federation of Air Line Pilots' Associations (#13349)
- **IFAMA** International Food and Agribusiness Management Association (#13619)
- IFAN – Institut fondamental d'Afrique noire – Cheikh Anta Diop (internationally oriented national body)
- IFAN / see International Federation of Standards Users (#13558)
- **IFAN** International Federation of Standards Users (#13558)
- **IFAO** International Federation for Artificial Organs (#13357)
- **IFAPA** International Federation of Adapted Physical Activity (#13338)
- IFAPAO / see Asia Pacific Council of Optometry (#01876)
- IFAP – Information for All Programme (see: #20322)
- IFAP – International Federation of Agricultural Producers (inactive)
- IFAPO / see Institut français du Proche-Orient
- **IFAPP** International Federation of Associations of Pharmaceutical Physicians (#13363)
- IFARD – International Federation of Agricultural Research Systems for Development (no recent information)
- IFAR – International Foundation for Art Research (internationally oriented national body)
- IFAR – International Fund for Agricultural Research (internationally oriented national body)
- **IFASA** International Fur Animal Scientific Association (#13695)
- IFASIC – International Fine Art and Specie Insurance Conference (unconfirmed)
- IFAS – International Federation of Associations of Specialists in Occupational Safety and Industrial Hygiene (no recent information)
- **IFAS** International Fund for Saving the Aral Sea (#13694)
- IFASS – International Forum of Accounting Standard Setters (unconfirmed)
- **IFATCA** International Federation of Air Traffic Controllers' Associations (#13350)
- IFATE / see International Federation of Airworthiness (#13352)
- **IFATSEA** International Federation of Air Traffic Safety Electronic Associations (#13351)
- **IFATS** International Federation for Adipose Therapeutics and Science (#13339)
- IFAT / see World Fair Trade Organization (#21396)
- **IFAW** International Fund for Animal Welfare (#13693)
- **IFAWPCA** International Federation of Asian and Western Pacific Contractors' Associations (#13359)
- **IFBA** International Federation of Biosafety Associations (#13373)
- **IFBA** International Food and Beverage Alliance (#13620)
- **IFBA** International Food and Beverage Association (#13621)
- IFBB / see International Fitness and Bodybuilding Federation (#13610)
- **IFBB** International Fitness and Bodybuilding Federation (#13610)
- IFBC / see International Blue Cross (#12364)
- **IFBDO** International Federation of Blood Donor Organizations (#13374)
- IFBEC / see International Forum on Business Ethical Conduct (#13631)
- **IFBEC** International Forum on Business Ethical Conduct (#13631)
- IFBF – International Flow Battery Forum (meeting series)
- **IFB** Institute of Forest Biosciences (#11263)
- IFB – International Federation of the Blind (inactive)
- **IFB** International Foundation for Biosynthesis (#13665)
- **IFBLS** International Federation of Biomedical Laboratory Science (#13372)
- **IFBMA** International Federation of Bike Messenger Associations (#13371)
- IFBO – Intercontinental Federation of Behavioural Optometry (inactive)
- IFBP / see Eyewitness Palestine
- IFBPW – FIFCLC – FIMNP / see International Federation of Business and Professional Women (#13376)
- **IFBSO** International Federation of Boat Show Organisers (#13375)
- IFBWW – International Federation of Building and Wood Workers (inactive)
- IFC / see Training Center for Tropical Resources and Ecosystems Sustainability
- IFCA / see IFCA International
- **IFCAA** International Fire Chiefs' Association of Asia (#13605)
- IFCAD – Institut de formation de cadres pour le développement (internationally oriented national body)
- IFCAI – International Federation of Commercial Arbitration Institutions (internationally oriented national body)
- IFCA International (internationally oriented national body)
- **IFCA** International Financial Cryptography Association (#13601)
- **IFCA** International Forum of Catholic Action (#09919)
- IFCA – International Funboard Class Association (see: #21760)
- **IFCARS** International Foundation for Computer Assisted Radiology and Surgery (#13666)
- IFCATI / see International Textile Manufacturers Federation (#15679)
- **IFCBA** International Federation of Customs Brokers Associations (#13400)
- **IFCB** International Federation for Cell Biology (#13382)
- **IFCCD** International Federation of Coalitions for Cultural Diversity (#13394)
- IFCC – Intergovernmental Follow-up and Coordination Committee of the Group of 77 on Economic Cooperation among Developing Countries (see: #10732)
- **IFCC** International Federation of Christian Churches (#13389)
- IFCC / see International Federation of Clinical Chemistry and Laboratory Medicine (#13392)
- **IFCC** International Federation of Clinical Chemistry and Laboratory Medicine (#13392)
- IFCC – International Federation of Culture Collection of Microbic Types (inactive)
- IFCE / see Halal Food Council of Europe
- **IFCES** International Federation of Comparative Endocrinological Societies (#13396)
- IFC – Fédération internationale de la corderie (inactive)
- IFCG – International Film Conciliation Group (inactive)
- IFC Global Corporate Governance Forum (inactive)
- **IFCHC** International Federation of Community Health Centres (#13395)
- IFCH – International Federation of Cardio HIIT BodyWeight Exercise (internationally oriented national body)
- IFCI / see International Financial Risk Institute
- **IFC** International Federation of Cheerleading (#13386)
- IFC – International Federation of Master-Craftsmen (inactive)
- **IFC** International Finance Corporation (#13597)

- IFC / see International Fortress Council (#13629)
- IFC International Fortress Council (#13629)
- IFC Irving Fisher Committee on Central Bank Statistics (#16020)
- IFCJ – International Federation of Catholic Journalists (inactive)
- IFCJ – International Fellowship of Christians and Jews (internationally oriented national body)
- IFCLA International Federation of Computer Law Associations (#13398)
- IFCL / see Internationale des Forums – Ecole de Psychanalyse des Forum du Champ Lacanien (#13234)
- IFCL – International Fixed Calendar League (inactive)
- IFCMC / see International Federation of Bike Messenger Associations (#13371)
- IFCM International Federation for Choral Music (#13388)
- IFCN (internationally oriented national body)
- IFCN – Dairy Data – Knowledge – Inspiration / see IFCN
- IFCN International Federation of Clinical Neurophysiology (#13393)
- IFCO International Foster Care Organization (#13663)
- IFCO – Interreligious Foundation for Community Organization (internationally oriented national body)
- IFCoLog International Federation for Computational Logic (#13397)
- IFCO/Pastors for Peace / see Pastors for Peace
- IFCPA International Federation of Centres for Puppetry Arts (#13384)
- IFCPC International Federation for Cervical Pathology and Colposcopy (#13385)
- IFCR – International Foundation for CDKL5 Research (internationally oriented national body)
- IFCS – Intergovernmental Forum on Chemical Safety (inactive)
- IFCS International Federation of Chopin Societies (#13387)
- IFCS International Federation of Classification Societies (#13391)
- IFCU International Federation of Catholic Universities (#13381)
- IFCW International Federation of Celtic Wrestling (#13383)
- IFCW International Forum for Child Welfare (#13633)
- IFDA International Family Doctors Association (inactive)
- IFDA / see International Federation of Daseinsanalysis (#13401)
- IFDA International Federation of Daseinsanalysis (#13401)
- IFDA International Fog and Dew Association (#13618)
- IFDA – International Foundation for Development Alternatives (inactive)
- IFDAS International Federation of Dental Anesthesiology Societies (#13403)
- IFDAT – International Forum for Drug and Alcohol Testing (unconfirmed)
- IFDC – Internacional Femenina Demócrata Cristiana (inactive)
- IFDC – Internationale des femmes démocrates-chrétiennes (inactive)
- IFDC International Fertilizer Development Center (#13590)
- IFDCO – International Family Day Care Organization (inactive)
- IFDCO – International Flying Dutchman Class Organization (see: #21760)
- IFDD Institut de la Francophonie pour le développement durable (#11305)
- IFDEA International Federation of Dental Educators and Associations (#13404)
- IFDE – Independent Food Distributors of Europe (inactive)
- IFDH International Federation of Dental Hygienists (#13405)
- IFDI – International Fibre Drum Institute (internationally oriented national body)
- IFD Internationale Föderation des Dachdeckerhandwerks (#13534)
- IFD International Foundation for Dermatology (#13668)
- IFDO International Federation of Data Organizations for the Social Sciences (#13402)
- IFDO – International Friendship Development Organization (internationally oriented national body)
- IFDP / see Institute for Food and Development Policy
- IFDS International Association for Disabled Sailing (#11849)
- IFDT International Forum on Diplomatic Training (#13634)
- IFDU / see International Federation of Professional and Technical Engineers
- IFEA-E International Festivals and Events Association Europe (#13591)
- IFEA – Instituto Francés de Estudios Andinos (internationally oriented national body)
- IFEA International Federation of Endodontic Associations (#13411)
- IFEA – International Festivals and Events Association (internationally oriented national body)
- IFEAS – Institut für Ethnologie und Afrika-Studien (internationally oriented national body)
- IFEAT The International Federation of Essential Oils and Aroma Trades (#13416)
- IFEC / see Association Rencontre CEFIR
- IFEC – Institut franco-européenne de chiropratique (internationally oriented national body)
- IFEDEC – Instituto de Formación Demócrata Cristiana (internationally oriented national body)
- IFED International Federation of Esthetic Dentistry (#13417)
- IFED International Forum on Engineering Decision Making (#13635)
- IFEES International Federation of Engineering Education Societies (#13412)
- IFEES – Islamic Foundation for Ecology and Environmental Sciences (internationally oriented national body)
- IFE / see European Forest Institute (#07297)
- IFEF Institut de la Francophonie pour l'éducation et la formation (#11306)
- IFEF Internacia Fervojista Esperanto Federacio (#13415)
- IFEH International Federation of Environmental Health (#13414)
- IfE – Initiative for Equality (internationally oriented national body)
- IFE Initiative Féministe Euroméditerranéenne (#05715)
- IFE – Institut de la francophonie pour l'entrepreneuriat (internationally oriented national body)
- IFE Institution of Fire Engineers (#11321)
- IFE / see International Federation Icestocksport (#13455)
- IFE International Föderation Eisstock Sport (#13455)
- IFE – International Friendship Evangelism (internationally oriented national body)
- IFE – Ivory For Elephants (internationally oriented national body)
- IFEJ – International Federation of Environmental Journalists (inactive)
- IFEM / see Institut de la francophonie pour l'entrepreneuriat
- IFEM International Federation for Emergency Medicine (#13409)
- IFEO – International Flight Engineers' Organization (inactive)
- IFEPAG International Fellowship of Paediatric and Adolescent Gynaecology (#13585)
- IFEPT International Federation for Enteric Phage Typing (#13413)
- IFERA International Family Enterprise Research Academy (#13328)
- IFER – Internationale Föderation der Eisenbahn-Reklame-Gesellschaften (inactive)
- IFERPECO – Initiatives pour la formation européenne et les relations avec les pays de l'Europe centrale et orientale (internationally oriented national body)
- IFESCCO Intergovernmental Foundation for Educational, Scientific and Cultural Cooperation (#11485)
- IFESH – International Foundation for Education and Self-Help (internationally oriented national body)
- IFES – Institute of Far Eastern Studies (internationally oriented national body)
- IFES International Federation of Exhibition and Event Services (#13420)
- IFES International Fellowship of Evangelical Students (#13583)
- IFES International Field Emission Society (#13596)
- IFES International Foundation for Electoral Systems (#13669)
- IFESS International Functional Electrical Stimulation Society (#13690)
- IFET / see Fédération Internationale de Tourisme Équestre (#09666)
- IFETB – International Federation of Eye and Tissue Banks (inactive)
- IFET International Federation for East Timor (#13408)
- IFEW – Inter-American Federation of Entertainment Workers (inactive)

- IFEX 11100

Exec Dir IFEX Secretariat, PO Box 61041, Eglinton/Dufferin RO, Toronto ON M6E 3S0, Canada. E-mail: media@ifex.org – campaigns@ifex.org.
URL: http://www.ifex.org/
History May 1992, Montréal, QC (Canada). Originally funded by *UNESCO (#20322)*. Former names and other names: *International Freedom of Expression Exchange (IFEX)* – full title. **Aims** Promote and defend the right to freedom of expression and information. **Structure** General Meeting; Council; Secretariat. **Languages** Arabic, English, French, Spanish. **Staff** 20.00 FTE, paid. **Finance** Supported by: *Ford Foundation (#09858)*; Fritt Ord; Government of Canada; Norwegian Ministry of Foreign Affairs; *Open Society Foundations (OSF, #17763)*; Sigrid Rausing Trust; Swedish International Development Cooperation Agency (Sida); *UNESCO (#20322)*. **Activities** Advocacy/lobbying/activism; awareness raising; financial and/or material support; knowledge management/information dissemination; networking/liaising; projects/programmes. **Events** General Meeting Berlin (Germany) 2019, General Meeting Montréal, QC (Canada) 2017, General Meeting Port-of-Spain (Trinidad-Tobago) 2015, General Meeting Phnom Penh (Cambodia) 2013, General Meeting Beirut (Lebanon) 2011. **Publications** *IFEX This Week* (weekly).
Members Freedom-of-expression groups (over 100) in 69 countries and territories: Afghanistan, Albania, Argentina, Australia, Austria, Azerbaijan, Bahrain, Bangladesh, Belarus, Belgium, Bolivia, Bosnia-Herzegovina, Brazil, Cambodia, Canada, Chile, Colombia, Congo DR, Costa Rica, Ecuador, Egypt, Fiji, France, Ghana, Greece, Honduras, Hong Kong, Hungary, India, Indonesia, Kazakhstan, Kyrgyzstan, Lebanon, Liberia, Malaysia, Mexico, Moldova, Mongolia, Myanmar, Namibia, Nepal, Netherlands, Nigeria, North Macedonia, Norway, Pakistan, Palestine, Paraguay, Peru, Philippines, Romania, Samoa USA, Senegal, Serbia, South Africa, South Sudan, Sri Lanka, Switzerland, Syrian AR, Thailand, Trinidad-Tobago, Tunisia, Türkiye, Uganda, UK, Ukraine, Uruguay, USA, Venezuela.
Included in the above, 30 organizations listed in this Yearbook:
– Africa Freedom of Information Centre (AFIC, #00175);
– Arabic Network for Human Rights Information (ANHRI, #00979);
– ARTICLE 19 (#01121);
– Association mondiale des radiodiffuseurs communautaires (AMARC, #02810);
– Association of Caribbean Media Workers (ACM, #02408);
– Cairo Institute for Human Rights Studies (CIHRS, #03397);
– Cartoonists Rights Network International (CRN International, #03594);
– Child Rights International Network (CRIN, #03885);
– Committee to Protect Journalists (CPJ, #04280);
– Electronic Frontier Foundation (EFF);
– Freedom House;
– Globe International;
– Human Rights Watch (HRW, #10990);
– Index on Censorship (Index);
– Inter American Press Association (IAPA, #11444);
– International Federation of Journalists (IFJ, #13462);
– International Federation of Library Associations and Institutions (IFLA, #13470);
– International Foundation for Protection of Freedom of Speech – Adil Soz;
– International PEN (#14552) (including Norwegian PEN, PEN American Center USA and PEN Canada);
– International Press Centre (IPC);
– International Press Institute (IPI, #14636);
– International Publishers Association (IPA, #14675);
– Media Foundation for West Africa (MFWA, #16617);
– Media Institute of Southern Africa (MISA, #16619);
– Pacific Islands News Association (PINA, #17975);
– Privacy International (PI, #18504);
– Reporters sans frontières (RSF, #18846);
– South East European Network for Professionalisation of the Media (SEENPM, #19817);
– South East Europe Media Organisation (SEEMO, #19823);
– West African Journalists' Union (#20885).
Consultative Status Consultative status granted from: *Council of Europe (CE, #04881)* (Participatory Status).
IGO Relations Partner of (1): *OAS (#17629)*. [2021.09.02/XF3406/y/F]

- IFFAD – International Foundation for Fair Trade and Development (internationally oriented national body)
- IFFA International Family Forestry Alliance (#13329)
- IFFA International Frozen Food Association (#13686)
- IFFAMPAC / see Families of the Missing
- IFFAS International Federation of Foot and Ankle Societies (#13431)
- IFFC Asian-Pacific Regional Research and Training Centre for Integrated Fish Farming (#01628)
- IFFD International Federation for Family Development (#13423)
- IFFEC International Federation of Free Evangelical Churches (#13433)
- IFFF / see Women's International League for Peace and Freedom (#21024)
- IFFH International Federation for Family Health (#13424)
- IFFHS International Federation of Football History and Statistics (#13432)
- IFFIm International Finance Facility for Immunisation (#13598)
- IFF International Feldenkrais Federation (#13582)
- IFF International Finance Forum (#13599)
- IFF International Floorball Federation (#13615)
- IFF / see International Fur Federation (#13696)
- IFF International Fur Federation (#13696)
- IFFJ – International Federation of Free Journalists (inactive)
- IFFLP – International Federation for Family Life Promotion (inactive)
- IFFO / see The Marine Ingredients Organisation (#16579)
- IFFO The Marine Ingredients Organisation (#16579)
- IFFPO – International Frozen Food Press Organization (no recent information)
- IFFPS / see Global Speakers Federation (#10612)
- IFFPSS International Federation of Facial Plastic Surgery Societies (#13422)
- IFFS International Federation of Fertility Societies (#13426)
- IFFS International Federation of Film Societies (#13430)
- IFFTI International Foundation of Fashion Technology Institutes (#13670)
- IFFTU – International Federation of Free Teachers' Unions (inactive)
- IFGA – International Federation of Grocers' Associations (inactive)
- IFGICT – International Federation of Global & Green Information Communication Technology (unconfirmed)
- IFGI – International Federation for the Graphical Industries – WCL (inactive)
- IFG – International Federation of Glucose Industries (inactive)
- IFG International Forum on Globalization (#13637)
- IFGK – Institut für Friedensarbeit und Gewaltfreie Konfliktaustragung (internationally oriented national body)
- IFGMA / see International Council of Grocery Manufacturers Associations (#13026)
- IFGO / see Fédération Internationale de Gynécologie et d'Obstétrique (#09638)
- IFGU Institut de la Francophonie pour la gouvernance universitaire (#11307)
- IFGVP – International Federation of Gastronomical, Vinicultural and Touristic Press (inactive)
- IFHA International Federation of Hainan Associations (#13434)
- IFHA International Federation of Helicopter Associations (#13444)
- IFHA International Federation of Horseracing Authorities (#13449)
- IFHA International Forum for Hypertension Control and Prevention in Africa (#13638)
- IFHE / see International Federation of Healthcare Engineering (#13439)
- IFHE International Federation of Healthcare Engineering (#13439)
- IFHE International Federation for Home Economics (#13447)
- IFHEMA International Federation for Historical European Martial Arts (#13446)
- IFHGS International Federation of Human Genetics Societies (#13451)
- IFHHRO International Federation of Health and Human Rights Organisations (#13440)
- IFHIMA International Federation of Health Information Management Associations (#13441)
- IFH – Internationale Föderation des Handwerks (inactive)

- ♦ IFH – International Scientific Forum on Home Hygiene (internationally oriented national body)
- ♦ **IFHNOS** International Federation of Head and Neck Oncologic Societies (#13438)
- ♦ IFHOH-Europe / see European Federation of Hard of Hearing People (#07136)
- ♦ **IFHOH** International Federation of Hard of Hearing People (#13435)
- ♦ **IFHOHYP** International Federation of Hard-of-Hearing Young People (#13436)
- ♦ **iFHP** International Federation of Health Plans (#13442)
- ♦ IFHP / see International Federation for Housing and Planning (#13450)
- ♦ **IFHP** International Federation for Housing and Planning (#13450)
- ♦ IFHPSM – International Federation for Hygiene, Preventive and Social Medicine (inactive)
- ♦ **IFHRA** International Federation of Horse Racing Academies (#13448)
- ♦ IFHR / see International Federation for Human Rights (#13452)
- ♦ IFHRO / see International Federation of Health Information Management Associations (#13441)
- ♦ IFHSB-Europe – International Federation for Hydrocephalus and Spina Bifida – Europe (inactive)
- ♦ **IFHS** International Federation of Highrise Structures (#13445)
- ♦ **IFHS** International Federation of Hydrographic Societies (#13453)
- ♦ IFHT / see International Federation for Heat Treatment and Surface Engineering (#13443)
- ♦ **IFHTSE** International Federation for Heat Treatment and Surface Engineering (#13443)
- ♦ IFHV – Institut für Friedenssicherungsrecht und Humanitares Volkerrecht, Bochum (internationally oriented national body)
- ♦ IFIA – Inter-African Forest Industries Association (inactive)
- ♦ IFIA / see International Federation of Hardware and Housewares Associations (#13437)
- ♦ IFIA – International Federation of Inspection Agencies (inactive)
- ♦ **IFIA** International Federation of Inventors' Associations (#13461)
- ♦ **IFIAR** International Forum of Independent Audit Regulators (#13639)
- ♦ IFIAS – International Federation of Institutes for Advanced Study (inactive)
- ♦ **IFIBiop** International Forum on Industrial Bioprocesses (#13640)
- ♦ **IFIC** International Federation of Infection Control (#13457)
- ♦ IFIC – International Food Information Council (internationally oriented national body)
- ♦ **IFIC** International Foundation for Integrated Care (#13672)
- ♦ **IFIEC – Europe** International Federation of Industrial Energy Consumers, Europe (#13456)
- ♦ IFIEC – International Federation of Industrial Energy Consumers (inactive)
- ♦ **IFIE** International Forum for Investor Education (#13642)
- ♦ IFIESR / see International Society of Occupational Ergonomics and Safety Research
- ♦ **IFIF** International Feed Industry Federation (#13581)
- ♦ IFIG / see Centre international de recherches et d'information sur l'économie publique, sociale et coopérative (#03764)
- ♦ IFIGE – Union internationale francophone pour la formation des informaticiens et gestionnaires d'entreprise (no recent information)
- ♦ **IFIGS** International Forum of Insurance Guarantee Schemes (#13641)
- ♦ **IFI** Institut de finance internationale (#11275)
- ♦ IFI – International Fabricare Institute (internationally oriented national body)
- ♦ **IFI** International Federation Icestocksport (#13455)
- ♦ IFI / see International Federation of Interior Architects / Designers (#13460)
- ♦ **IFI** International Federation of Interior Architects / Designers (#13460)
- ♦ **IFI** International Flood Initiative (#13613)
- ♦ IFI – International Forestry Institute, Russia (unconfirmed)
- ♦ IFI / see International Francophone Institute (#13682)
- ♦ **IFI** International Francophone Institute (#13682)
- ♦ IFI – International Fund for Ireland (internationally oriented national body)
- ♦ **IFIMES** International Institute for Middle East and Balkan Studies (#13901)
- ♦ i-FINER / see International Society for Immunonutrition (#15194)
- ♦ IFINS – International Forum for Innovative Northeast Asia Strategy (internationally oriented national body)
- ♦ IF / see Institut Africain pour le Développement Economique et Social – Centre Africain de Formation (#11233)
- ♦ IF – International Forum (internationally oriented national body)
- ♦ IFIPAC / see International Federation of Centres for Puppetry Arts (#13384)
- ♦ IFIPA – International Federation of Infertility Patient Associations (inactive)
- ♦ **IFIP** International Federation for Information Processing (#13458)
- ♦ IFIP – International Funders for Indigenous Peoples (internationally oriented national body)

♦ IFIS 11101

Head of Marketing and Engagement Ground Floor, 115 Wharfedale Road, Winnersh Triangle, Wokingham, RG41 5RB, UK. T. +441189883895.
URL: http://www.ifis.org/

History 1968. Founded by the collaboration of 4 organizations: *CABI (#03393)* (UK); Deutsche Landwirtschafts-Gesellschaft eV (DLG); Institute of Food Technologists (USA); Centrum voor Landbouw Publikaties en Landbouwdocumentatie (PUDOC), Netherlands. Former names and other names: *International Food Information Service (IFIS Publishing)* – full title. Registration: Charity Commission, No/ID: 1068176, England and Wales. **Aims** Fundamentally understand and best serve the information needs of the food community. **Structure** Board of Trustees; Management Team. **Languages** English. **Staff** 20.00 FTE, paid. **Finance** Sources: fees for services; sale of products. **Activities** Knowledge management/information dissemination; monitoring/evaluation. **Events** *International conference on food science and technology information* Budapest (Hungary) 1989, *International conference on food science and technology information* Berlin (Germany FR) 1987. **Publications** *FSTA Thesaurus*; *IFIS Dictionary of Food Science and Technology*. Whitepapers; articles. **Information Services** *Food Science and Technology Abstracts (FSTA)*. **Members** Not a membership organization. **NGO Relations** Member of (2): *Association of Learned and Professional Society Publishers (ALPSP, #02786)*; Research4Life programmes.. [2020.10.13/XF2731/**F**]

- ♦ **IFISA** International Flight Information Service Association (#13612)
- ♦ IFIS – International Flight Inspection Symposium (meeting series)
- ♦ **IFISO** Informal Forum of International Student Organizations (#11193)
- ♦ IFIS Publishing / see IFIS (#11101)
- ♦ IFITA / see International Network for Information Technology in Agriculture (#14287)
- ♦ IFIT – Institute for Integrated Transitions (unconfirmed)
- ♦ **IFITT** International Federation of Information Technology and Tourism (#13459)
- ♦ IFIUS – International Federation for Interuniversity Sport (inactive)
- ♦ IFIWA – International Federation of Importers and Wholesale Grocers Associations (inactive)
- ♦ IFJC – Internationales Forum Junge Chormusik (internationally oriented national body)
- ♦ **IFJ** International Federation of Journalists (#13462)
- ♦ IFJO – International Flying Junior Organization (see: #21760)
- ♦ **IFJS** International Forum of Jewish Scouts (#13643)
- ♦ IFJU / see International Fruit and Vegetable Juice Association (#13687)
- ♦ IFKAB – Internationale Federatie van Katholieke Arbeiders Bewegingen (inactive)
- ♦ IFKF / see International Federation of Kidney Foundations – World Kidney Alliance (#13463)
- ♦ IFKF – International Fight Kickboxing Federation (unconfirmed)
- ♦ **IFKF-WKA** International Federation of Kidney Foundations – World Kidney Alliance (#13463)
- ♦ IFK – Internationale Filmkammer (inactive)
- ♦ **IFKO** International Federation of Kitesports Organizations (#13464)
- ♦ **IFKT** International Federation of Knitting Technologists (#13465)
- ♦ **IFKWVA** International Federation of the Korean War Veterans' Associations (#13466)
- ♦ IFLAC / see IFLAC – International Forum for the Literature and Culture of Peace (#11102)
- ♦ **IFLAC** IFLAC – International Forum for the Literature and Culture of Peace (#11102)

♦ IFLAC – International Forum for the Literature and Culture of Peace (IFLAC) 11102

Founder-Pres 1A Gdalyahou Street, 3258701 Haifa, Israel.
Vice-Pres address not obtained.
Main: http://www.iflac.org/

History Founded 1975, Haifa (Israel), as *The Bridge: Jewish and Arab Women for Peace. 'The Bridge'* is currently the women's branch of IFLAC. Subsequently referred to as *International Forum of Culture and Literature for Paving Peace (IFLAC), International Forum for the Culture of World Peace, IFLAC PAVE PEACE – International Forum for the Literature and Culture of Peace* and *Friends of Literature Association.* 'Creative Statutes' for the Millennium adopted in 2000. Registered as a Voluntary Association, in accordance with Israeli law, 1987. In 1999, registered as a Voluntary Association, in accordance with Israeli law as *International Forum for the Literature and Culture of Peace (IFLAC).* **Aims** Promote peace and mutual respect between people and nations; promote social, cultural and religious *tolerance* between people; eliminate violence in all its forms; organize peace culture researchers, writers, intellectuals and friends of literature; encourage creativity that promotes culture and peace; promote the status of women; develop creative aspects of women leadership and peace. **Structure** General Assembly (annual, in Haifa, Israel); Board; Honorary Advisory Committee; Subgroups include: *The Bridge: Jewish and Arab Women for Peace in the Middle East (see: #11102)*; League of Women Against Discrimination (LENA); *Writers International and Friends of Literature and Culture Association (WIFLAC, see: #11102).* World Centre in Israel; International Branches (12). **Languages** Arabic, English, French, Hebrew, Hungarian, Romanian, Russian, Spanish. **Staff** All voluntary. **Finance** None; uses costless model under which all projects, activities and publishing are on a purely voluntary basis. **Activities** Events/meetings; projects/programmes. Produces music and peace poems put to music which are sung on radio and television programmes. **Events** *Conference* Netanya (Israel) 2014, *International Congress* Netanya (Israel) 2014, *Conference / International Congress* Ramat Gan (Israel) 2011, *Conference / International Congress* Ramat Gan (Israel) 2009, *Conference / International Congress* Haifa (Israel) 2006. **Publications** *Daily IFLAC Peace Culture Digest* – newsletter; *Horizon: PAVE PEACE* – magazine. *Anti-Terror and Peace IFLAC Anthology* (2016); *From the Nile to the Jordan: A Historical Peace Novel* by Ada Aharoni; *Galim-Waves: Literature, Culture, Art and Society* – anthology; *Lirit Anthology* in English, Hebrew. Peace books, including by IFLAC writers and poets worldwide; blogs; novels; poetry; articles; children's books; memoirs; historical novels; plays; films; videos; websites.
Members Branches, comprising about 100,000 members, in 35 countries and territories:
Argentina, Australia, Austria, Belgium, Bosnia-Herzegovina, Brazil, Cameroon, Canada, China, Egypt, France, Greece, Haiti, Hong Kong, India, Israel, Italy, Japan, Kenya, Korea Rep, Mexico, Norway, Pakistan, Palestine, Peru, Romania, Russia, Rwanda, South Africa, Spain, Switzerland, Taiwan, Türkiye, UK, Uruguay.
Members in all states in Latin America. ot all membership countries not specified.
IGO Relations None. [2016.10.18/XF4597/**F**]

- ♦ IFLAC PAVE PEACE – International Forum for the Literature and Culture of Peace / see IFLAC – International Forum for the Literature and Culture of Peace (#11102)

♦ IFLA Europe 11103

Exec Sec c/o WAO, Rue Lambert Crickx 19, 1070 Brussels, Belgium. T. +32492319451. E-mail: secretariat@iflaeurope.eu.
SG address not obtained. E-mail: sgeneral@iflaeurope.eu.
URL: http://iflaeurope.eu/

History 4 Apr 1989, Brussels (Belgium). Previously changed title to *European Federation for Landscape Architecture (EFLA) – Fédération européenne pour l'architecture du paysage (FEAP),* to take over activities of *Komitee der Europäischen Garten- und Landschaftsarchitekten (CEGAP, inactive).* Serves as European Region of *International Federation of Landscape Architects (IFLA, #13467).* Former names and other names: *European Foundation for Landscape Architecture* – former (4 Apr 1989 to 13 Feb 1990); *Fondation européenne pour l'architecture du paysage* – former (4 Apr 1989 to 13 Feb 1990); *European Federation for Landscape Architecture (EFLA)* – former (13 Feb 1990 to Feb 2013); *Fédération européenne pour l'architecture du paysage (FEAP)* – former (13 Feb 1990 to Feb 2013). Registration: Belgium. **Aims** Establish, support and promote the *landscape architectural* profession across Europe, contributing to international discourse, shaping and disseminating European initiatives and facilitating exchange of information while promoting excellence in professional practice, education and research culminating in a culturally rich, diverse and sustainable Europe. **Structure** General Assembly; Executive Committee; Management Board; Committees (2); Working Groups. **Languages** English, French. **Staff** Paid; voluntary. **Finance** Sources: donations; members' dues; sponsorship. **Activities** Events/meetings; guidance/assistance/consulting; training/education. **Events** *Europe General Assembly* London (UK) 2018, *Europe General Assembly and Conference* Bucharest (Romania) 2017, *Europe General Assembly* Brussels (Belgium) 2016, *Europe General Assembly* Lisbon (Portugal) 2015, *European Urban Green Infrastructure Conference* Vienna (Austria) 2015. **Publications** *IFLA Europe Yearbook* (annual). *Collaboration to Landscape Architecture Europe.* Reports.
Members National associations in 34 countries:
Austria, Belgium, Bulgaria, Croatia, Czechia, Denmark, Estonia, Finland, France, Germany, Greece, Hungary, Iceland, Ireland, Israel, Italy, Latvia, Lithuania, Luxembourg, Netherlands, Norway, Poland, Portugal, Romania, Russia, Serbia, Slovakia, Slovenia, Spain, Sweden, Switzerland, Türkiye, UK, Ukraine.
Individuals in 5 countries. Membership countries not specified.
Consultative Status Consultative status granted from: *Council of Europe (CE, #04881)* (Participatory Statuts).
IGO Relations Accredited by (2): *European Commission (EC, #06633)*; *UNESCO (#20322).* **NGO Relations** Member of (1): *European Heritage Alliance 3.3 (#07477).* [2020.05.11/XF1697/f/**E**]

- ♦ IFLAIC / see Latin American Forestry Institute
- ♦ IFLA – Instituto Forestal Latinoamericano (internationally oriented national body)
- ♦ **IFLA** International Federation of Landscape Architects (#13467)
- ♦ **IFLA** International Federation of Library Associations and Institutions (#13470)
- ♦ **IFLA** International Finance and Leasing Association (#13600)
- ♦ **IFLBP** International Federation of Little Brothers of the Poor (#13471)
- ♦ **IFL** International Friendship League (#13685)
- ♦ IFL – International Futures Library, Salzburg – Robert-Jungk Foundation (internationally oriented national body)
- ♦ **IFLN** International Financial Litigation Network (#13602)
- ♦ **IFLN** International Freight and Logistics Network (#13684)
- ♦ IFLRY / see International Federation of Liberal Youth (#13469)
- ♦ **IFLRY** International Federation of Liberal Youth (#13469)
- ♦ IFLS – International Federation of Law Students (inactive)
- ♦ **IFLS** International Federation of Logistics and SCM Systems (#13472)
- ♦ **IFMAD** International Forum on Mood and Anxiety Disorders (#13646)
- ♦ **IFMA** International Facility Management Association (#13325)
- ♦ **IFMA** International Farm Management Association (#13333)
- ♦ IFMA – International Federation of Margarine Associations (inactive)
- ♦ **IFMA** International Federation of Muaythai Associations (#13482)
- ♦ **IFMA** International Federation of Multimedia Associations (#13483)
- ♦ IFMA – International Foodservice Manufacturers Association (internationally oriented national body)
- ♦ IFMA – International Forensic Medicine Association (unconfirmed)
- ♦ **IFMANT** International Federation of Medical Associations of Neural Therapy (#13476)
- ♦ **IFMAR** International Federation of Model Auto Racing (#13479)
- ♦ **IFMBE** International Federation for Medical and Biological Engineering (#13477)
- ♦ IFMCA – International Family Ministries and Counseling Association (no recent information)
- ♦ IFMCH – International Foundation for Mother and Child Health (internationally oriented national body)
- ♦ IFMC / see International Council for Traditional Music (#13087)
- ♦ iFM Conference – International Conference on integrated Formal Methods (meeting series)
- ♦ IFMCP – International Federation of Married Catholic Priests (inactive)
- ♦ IFME / see International Federation of Municipal Engineering (#13484)
- ♦ **IFME** International Federation of Municipal Engineering (#13484)
- ♦ **IFM** International Association of Infant Food Manufacturers (#11961)

- ♦ IFM / see International Falcon Movement – Socialist Educational International (#13327)
- ♦ IFM – International Federation of Mallyuddha (unconfirmed)
- ♦ IFM – International Federation of Mammalogists (see: #15760)
- ♦ IFMMS – International Federation of Mining and Metallurgical Students (inactive)
- ♦ IFMP – International Federation of Maritime Philately (inactive)
- ♦ IFMP – International Federation of Match Poker (unconfirmed)
- ♦ IFMP / see International Federation for Psychotherapy (#13523)
- ♦ **IFMRS** International Federation of Musculoskeletal Research Societies (#13485)
- ♦ **IFMSA** International Federation of Medical Students' Associations (#13478)
- ♦ **IFM-SEI** International Falcon Movement – Socialist Educational International (#13327)
- ♦ IFMS – International Federation of Micromount Societies (no recent information)
- ♦ **IFMS** International Forum of Meteorological Societies (#13644)
- ♦ IFMSO / see Marfan World (#16574)
- ♦ IFMSS – Fédération internationale des associations de la sclérose en plaques – Internationale Vereinigung der Multiple Sklerose Gesellschaften – Federación Internacional de Sociedades contra la Esclerosis Múltiple / see Multiple Sclerosis International Federation (#16899)
- ♦ **IFMT** Institut de la francophonie pour la médecine tropicale (#11308)
- ♦ IFMT – Internationell Förening Mot Tortyren (no recent information)
- ♦ IFMW – International Federation of Mazdaznan Women (inactive)
- ♦ IFM / see World Monuments Fund (#21657)
- ♦ **IFNA** International Family Nursing Association (#13330)
- ♦ **IFNA** International Federation of Nonlinear Analysts (#13491)
- ♦ **IFNA** International Federation of Nurse Anesthetists (#13492)
- ♦ IFNA / see World Netball (#21668)
- ♦ IFND / see International Federation of Non-Government Organizations for the Prevention of Drug and Substance Abuse (#13490)
- ♦ **IFNEC** International Framework for Nuclear Energy Cooperation (#13681)
- ♦ **IFNE** International Federation on Neuroendoscopy (#13489)
- ♦ **IFNet** International Flood Network (#13614)
- ♦ **IFNGO** International Federation of Non-Government Organizations for the Prevention of Drug and Substance Abuse (#13490)
- ♦ IFN – Institut de la Francophonie numérique (inactive)
- ♦ IFN / see Internationals amis de la nature (#14780)
- ♦ **IFNS** International Federation of Nematology Societies (#13488)
- ♦ IFNTF – International Federation of National Teaching Fellows (unconfirmed)
- ♦ IFOA – International Family Office Association (internationally oriented national body)
- ♦ **IFOA** International Forward Osmosis Association (#13661)
- ♦ IFOAM EU Group / see IFOAM Organics Europe (#11104)
- ♦ IFOAM / see IFOAM – Organics International (#11105)
- ♦ **IFOAM** IFOAM – Organics International (#11105)

♦ IFOAM Organics Europe 11104

Dir Rue du Commerce 124, 1000 Brussels, Belgium. T. +3222801223. Fax +3227357381. E-mail: info@organicseurope.bio.
URL: https://www.organicseurope.bio/

History Feb 2000. An independent regional group within *IFOAM – Organics International (IFOAM, #11105).* Superseded *EU Working Group*, formed in 1990. Since 2003, operates with an office in Brussels. Former names and other names: *IFOAM EU Group* – former. Registration: Start date: 2002, Sweden. **Aims** Promote within the EU the principles and practices of *organic agriculture* and *food* production as set out in the IFOAM Standards; coordinate and represent IFOAM members in EU countries, within IFOAM, in the EU and elsewhere; enable exchange of information both among IFOAM members in EU countries and with other bodies worldwide; assist in coordination and dissemination of research in organic food production throughout the EU; work towards establishment of common policies within the Group in relation to the above. **Structure** General Assembly; Council; Board; Office; Working and Interest Groups. **Activities** Standards/guidelines; research/documentation. **Events** *European Organic Congress* Bordeaux (France) 2022, *European Organic Congress* Lisbon (Portugal) 2021, *European Organic Congress* Brussels (Belgium) 2020, *European Organic Congress* Bucharest (Romania) 2019, *Organic Innovation Days* Brussels (Belgium) 2018. **Publications** *IFOAM EU Group Newsletter.* Annual Report; newsletter; position papers; official letters and dossiers; fact sheets. **Members** Organic establishments, including consumer, farmer and processor associations; research, education and advisory organizations; certification bodies; commercial organic companies. Organizations (over 300) in EU countries, accession countries and EFTA. **NGO Relations** Partner of: *Conseil européen des jeunes agriculteurs (CEJA, #04689); Ecologica International Association (#05299); Eurogroup for Animals (#05690); Euromontana (#05737); European Community of Consumer Cooperatives (EURO COOP, #06678); European Environmental Bureau (EEB, #06996); European Federation of Food, Agriculture and Tourism Trade Unions (EFFAT, #07125); European NGO Network on Genetic Engineering (GENET, #08050); European Organic Certifiers Council (EOCC, #08094); Friends of the Earth Europe (FoEE, #10001); International Research Association for Organic Food Quality and Health (FQH, #14719); International Society of Organic Farming Research (ISOFAR, #15331).* Member of: *TP Organics – European Technology Platform (TP Organics, #20180).* [2022/XJ0664/**E**]

♦ IFOAM – Organics International (IFOAM) 11105

Exec Dir Charles-de-Gaulle-Str 5, 53113 Bonn, Germany. T. +492289265010. Fax +492289265099. E-mail: contact@ifoam.bio.
URL: http://www.ifoam.bio/

History Nov 1972, Versailles (France). Former names and other names: *International Federation of Organic Agriculture Movements (IFOAM)* – former; *Fédération internationale des mouvements d'agriculture biologique* – former; *Federación Internacional de los Movimientos de Agricultura Biológica* – former; *Internationale Vereinigung Biologischer Landbaubewegungen* – former; *Internationale Vereinigung Biologischer Landwirtschaftsbewegungen* – former. Registration: Local Court Bonn, Germany Register Court, No/ID: No: VR 8726, Germany, NRW. **Aims** Work towards true sustainability in agriculture, from the field, through the value chain to the consumer; promote worldwide adoption of *ecologically*, socially and economically sound systems based on principles of organic agriculture; represent the organic movement in parliamentary, administrative and policy-making fora. **Structure** General Assembly (every 3 years at Conference); World Board; Executive Board; Executive Director; Task Forces; Working Groups. Self-Organized Structures (SoS): Regional Bodies (6): *AgroBioMediterraneao (ABM, #00579); IFOAM Organics Europe (#11104); IFOAM Latin America; IFOAM Asia; IFOAM Euro-Asia; IFOAM Southern African Network (ISAN).* National Bodies (3): France; Japan; Iran. Sector Platforms (7): *Intercontinental Network of Organic Farmers Organizations (INOFO);* IFOAM Aquaculture; IFOAM Animal Husbandry Alliance (IAHA); IFOAM Apiculture; IFOAM Seeds; Technology Innovation Platform of IFOAM (TIPI). Daughter Organization: *IOAS (#16001).* **Languages** Arabic, Dutch, English, French, German, Hindi, Italian, Polish, Portuguese, Spanish. **Staff** 15.00 FTE, paid. **Finance** Sources: donations; fees for services; members' dues; revenue from activities/projects. **Activities** Advocacy/lobbying/activism; events/meetings; knowledge management/information dissemination; networking/liaising; standards/guidelines; training/education. **Events** *Organic World Congress* Rennes (France) 2021, *Asian Local Governments for Organic Agriculture (ALGOA) International Summit on Organic Agriculture Policy* Goesan (Korea Rep) 2019, *International Conference of Wheat Landraces for Healthy Food Systems* Bologna (Italy) 2018, *BIOFACH Conference* Delhi (India) 2018, *Organic World Congress* Delhi (India) 2017. **Publications** *IFOAM Insider* (10 a year) – newsletter; *The World of Organic Agriculture: Statistics and Emerging Trends* (annual). Members' directory; conference proceedings; books; videos.

Members Full: associations of producers, processors, traders and consultants and institutions involved in research, training and information; Associate: individuals and private companies. Members (833) in 118 countries and territories:
Albania, Argentina, Armenia, Australia, Austria, Azerbaijan, Bangladesh, Belarus, Belgium, Belize, Benin, Bolivia, Bosnia-Herzegovina, Brazil, Burkina Faso, Burundi, Cambodia, Cameroon, Canada, Chile, China, Colombia, Congo DR, Costa Rica, Côte d'Ivoire, Croatia, Cyprus, Czechia, Denmark, Ecuador, Egypt, Estonia, Ethiopia, Fiji, Finland, France, Georgia, Germany, Ghana, Greece, Guatemala, Hong Kong, Hungary, Iceland, India, Indonesia, Iran Islamic Rep, Iraq, Ireland, Israel, Italy, Jamaica, Japan, Kenya, Korea DPR, Korea Rep, Kyrgyzstan, Latvia, Lithuania, Luxembourg, Madagascar, Malawi, Malaysia, Malta, Mauritius, Mexico, Mongolia, Morocco, Myanmar, Namibia, Nepal, Netherlands, New Caledonia, New Zealand, Nicaragua, Nigeria, Norway, Pakistan, Palestine, Panama, Paraguay, Peru, Philippines, Poland, Polynesia Fr, Portugal, Qatar, Romania, Russia, Rwanda, Samoa, Saudi Arabia, Senegal, Serbia, Singapore, Slovenia, South Africa, Spain, Sri Lanka, Sudan, Sweden, Switzerland, Syrian AR, Taiwan, Tanzania UR, Thailand, Togo, Trinidad-Tobago, Tunisia, Türkiye, Uganda, UK, Ukraine, United Arab Emirates, USA, Venezuela, Vietnam, Zimbabwe.
Included in the above, one organization listed in this Yearbook:

Consultative Status Consultative status granted from: *ECOSOC (#05331)* (Ros A); *FAO (#09260)* (Liaison Status); *ILO (#11123)* (Special List); *UNCTAD (#20285)* (Special Category); *UNEP (#20299).* **IGO Relations** Accredited to the Conference of the Parties of: *Secretariat of the United Nations Convention to Combat Desertification (Secretariat of the UNCCD, #19208).* Accredited by: *United Nations Framework Convention on Climate Change – Secretariat (UNFCCC, #20564); United Nations Office at Vienna (UNOV, #20604).* Participates as observer in the activities of: *Codex Alimentarius Commission (CAC, #04081).* Observer: *International Fund for Agricultural Development (IFAD, #13692).* Consultative status with: *Deutsche Gesellschaft für Internationale Zusammenarbeit (GIZ).* **NGO Relations** Member of: *SDG Watch Europe (#19162); World Fair Trade Organization (WFTO, #21396); More and Better (#16855).* Charter member of: *Global Landscapes Forum (GLF, #10451).* In liaison with technical committees of: *International Organization for Standardization (ISO, #14473).* Cooperates with: *Fairtrade International (FLO, #09240); Social Accountability International (SAI); Social Agriculture Network (SAN, #19333). Ecologica International Association (#05299)* is member. Instrumental in setting up: *ISEAL (#16026).* Supports: *Global 100% RE (#10160).* Partner of: *1% for the Planet.* Associate of: *WFTO-Europe (#20930).* Subscriber to: *ISEAL (#16026).* [2022.10.11/XC4625/**B**]

- ♦ **IFOC** International Federation of Orgonomic Colleges (#13494)
- ♦ IFOC – International Fellowship of Chaplains (internationally oriented national body)
- ♦ IFOF – Institut für Ökumenische und Interreligiöse Forschung (internationally oriented national body)
- ♦ IFOFSAG / see International Scout and Guide Fellowship (#14812)
- ♦ IFOMA / see The Marine Ingredients Organisation (#16579)
- ♦ IFOM / see International Academy of Oral Medicine (#11562)
- ♦ **IFOMPT** International Federation of Orthopaedic Manipulative Physical Therapists (#13495)
- ♦ IFOMT / see International Federation of Orthopaedic Manipulative Physical Therapists (#13495)
- ♦ IFOPA – International Fibrodysplasia Ossificans Progressiva Association (internationally oriented national body)
- ♦ **IFORD** Institut de formation et de recherche démographiques (#11304)
- ♦ **IFOR** International Fellowship of Reconciliation (#13586)
- ♦ **IFORS** International Federation of Operational Research Societies (#13493)
- ♦ IFORVU – International Federation of Recreational Vehicle Users (inactive)
- ♦ IFOSA – International Federation of Scoliosis Associations (inactive)
- ♦ IFOSA – International Federation of Stationery, Office Machines and Furniture Associations (inactive)
- ♦ IFOS International Agency for the Promotion of Ear Care / see Hearing International (#10895)
- ♦ IFOS – International Federation of Ophthalmological Societies (inactive)
- ♦ **IFOS** International Federation of Oto-Rhino-Laryngological Societies (#13496)
- ♦ IFOSSS – International Foundation of Security and Safety Sciences (internationally oriented national body)
- ♦ IFOS Standing Committee for Worldwide Prevention of Hearing Impairment / see Hearing International (#10895)
- ♦ IFOTES / see International Federation of Telephone Emergency Services (#13567)
- ♦ **IFOTES** International Federation of Telephone Emergency Services (#13567)
- ♦ **IFoU** International Forum on Urbanism (#13658)
- ♦ IFPAAW – International Federation of Plantation, Agricultural and Allied Workers (inactive)
- ♦ IFPA – Institute for Foreign Policy Analysis (internationally oriented national body)
- ♦ IFPa – International Federation of Pankration Athlima (inactive)
- ♦ IFPA / see International Federation of Placenta Associations (#13513)
- ♦ **IFPA** International Federation of Placenta Associations (#13513)
- ♦ IFPA – International Federation of Professional Aromatherapists (internationally oriented national body)
- ♦ **IFPA** International Federation of Psoriasis Associations (#13520)
- ♦ **IFPA** International Fuel and Power Association (#13688)
- ♦ I.F.P.B. – International Federation for Proprioceptive and Biomechanical Therapies (internationally oriented national body)
- ♦ **IFPB** International Forum of Psychosis and Bipolarity (#13647)
- ♦ **IFPC** International Federation for Peace and Conciliation (#13501)
- ♦ IFPC / see International Federation for Produce Standards (#13518)
- ♦ IFPC – International Fund for the Promotion of Culture (inactive)
- ♦ **IFPCM** Industrial Federation Paints and Coats of Mercosul (#11175)
- ♦ IFPCM – International Federation of Professional Coaches and Mentors (inactive)
- ♦ **IFPCRN** International Federation of Primary Care Research Networks (#13516)
- ♦ **IFPCS** International Federation of Pigment Cell Societies (#13512)
- ♦ IFPCW – International Federation of Petroleum and Chemical Workers (inactive)
- ♦ **IFPD** International Foundation for Population and Development (#13674)
- ♦ **IFPE** International Federation for Parent Education (#13499)
- ♦ **IFPE** International Federation of Psychiatric Epidemiology (#13521)
- ♦ IFP / see Forus (#09934)
- ♦ **IFPH** International Federation for Public History (#13524)
- ♦ IFPH – International Forum for Public Health (unconfirmed)
- ♦ IFPIA – Independent Film Producers International Association (no recent information)
- ♦ **IFPI** International Federation of the Phonographic Industry (#13508)
- ♦ **IFP** Inorganic Feed Phosphates (#11226)
- ♦ **IFP** International Federation of Pedestrians (#13502)
- ♦ IFP / see International Federation of Podiatrists (#13514)
- ♦ **IFP** International Federation of Podiatrists (#13514)
- ♦ **IFP** International Federation for Psychotherapy (#13523)
- ♦ IFP – International Federation of Purchasing (inactive)
- ♦ IFP – Interns for Peace (internationally oriented national body)
- ♦ IFPLAA – Internationale Föderation der Plantagen, Land- und Anverwandten Arbeiter (inactive)
- ♦ **IFPMA** International Federation of Pharmaceutical Manufacturers and Associations (#13505)
- ♦ IFPM / see Federación Interamericana de Asociaciones de Gestión Humana (#09329)
- ♦ IFPMM / see International Federation of Purchasing and Supply Management (#13525)
- ♦ IFPMO – International Federation of the Psychological-Medical Organizations (inactive)
- ♦ IFPMR – International Federation of Physical Medicine and Rehabilitation (inactive)
- ♦ **IFPN** International Federation of Perioperative Nurses (#13503)
- ♦ IFPNT – International Federation of Practitioners of Natural Therapeutics (inactive)
- ♦ IFPO – Institut français du Proche-Orient (internationally oriented national body)
- ♦ **IFPOS** International Federation of Paediatric Orthopaedic Societies (#13497)
- ♦ IFPRA / see Inter-American Confederation of Public Relations (#11418)
- ♦ IFPRA – International Federation of Park and Recreation Administration (inactive)
- ♦ IFPRERLOM – International Federation for the Protection of the Rights of Ethnic, Religious, Linguistic and Other Minorities (inactive)
- ♦ **IFPRI** International Fine Particle Research Institute (#13604)
- ♦ **IFPRI** International Food Policy Research Institute (#13622)
- ♦ **IFPR** International Foundation for Production Research (#13675)
- ♦ IFPRO – European Association of Importers of Finished Products (inactive)
- ♦ IFPS / see International Federation of Popular Sports (#13515)
- ♦ IFPSD – International Federation for Peace and Sustainable Development (internationally oriented national body)
- ♦ **IFPS** International Federation of Palynological Societies (#13498)
- ♦ **IFPS** International Federation for Produce Standards (#13518)
- ♦ **IFPS** International Federation of Psychoanalytic Societies (#13522)

- ♦ IFPS – International Free Press Society (inactive)
- ♦ IFPS – International Freight Pipeline Society (inactive)
- ♦ **IFPSM** International Federation of Purchasing and Supply Management (#13525)
- ♦ **IFPTA** International Forest Products Transport Association (#13627)
- ♦ IFPTE – International Federation of Professional and Technical Engineers (internationally oriented national body)
- ♦ **IFPTOHE** International Federation of Physical Therapists working in Occupational Health and Ergonomics (#13511)
- ♦ IFPTO – International Federation of Popular Travel Organizations (inactive)
- ♦ **IFPU** International Forum of Public Universities (#13648)
- ♦ **IFPW** International Federation of Pharmaceutical Wholesalers (#13506)
- ♦ **IFQC** International Fuel Quality Center (#13689)
- ♦ IFRAA – International Federation of Regional Airlines Associations (inactive)
- ♦ IFRA – Institut français de recherche en Afrique (internationally oriented national body)
- ♦ **IFRA** International Fragrance Association (#13680)
- ♦ IFRA-Nairobi / see Institut français de recherche en Afrique
- ♦ **IFRAO** International Federation of Rock Art Organizations (#13533)
- ♦ IFRB – International Frequency Registration Board (inactive)
- ♦ IFRC / see International Federation of Red Cross and Red Crescent Societies (#13526)
- ♦ IFRC – International Fusion Research Council (see: #12294)
- ♦ IFREDOC – Institut européen de formation continue en réparation et évaluation du dommage corporel (unconfirmed)
- ♦ IFRE – Instituts de recherches français à l'étranger (internationally oriented national body)
- ♦ Ifremer (internationally oriented national body)
- ♦ IFREMT – International Federation of Registered Equine Massage Therapists (unconfirmed)
- ♦ **IFRF** International Flame Research Foundation (#13611)
- ♦ IFRG / see Resource Alliance (#18914)
- ♦ IFRI – Institut français des relations internationales (internationally oriented national body)
- ♦ IFRI – International Financial Risk Institute (internationally oriented national body)
- ♦ IFRI – International Forestry and Resources Institutions (internationally oriented national body)
- ♦ **IFRIMA** International Federation of Risk and Insurance Management Associations (#13531)
- ♦ IFR – Internationaler Förderkreis für Raumfahrt Hermann Oberth-Wernher von Braun (internationally oriented national body)
- ♦ **IFR** International Federation of Robotics (#13532)
- ♦ IFR – International Front Runners (internationally oriented national body)
- ♦ IFRR – International Federation of Renal Registries (no recent information)
- ♦ **IFRR** International Foundation of Robotics Research (#13676)
- ♦ IFRRO / see International Federation of Reproduction Rights Organizations (#13527)
- ♦ **IFRRO** International Federation of Reproduction Rights Organizations (#13527)
- ♦ **IFRS Foundation** International Financial Reporting Standards Foundation (#13603)
- ♦ **IFRS** International Fibrinogen Research Society (#13594)
- ♦ **IFRTD** International Forum for Rural Transport and Development (#13650)
- ♦ **IFRTT** International Forum for Road Transport Technology (#13649)
- ♦ **IFRWH** International Federation for Research in Women's History (#13528)
- ♦ IFSA / see International Flight Services Association
- ♦ IFSA – IInternational Conference on Inertial Fusion Sciences and Applications (meeting series)
- ♦ **IFSA** International Farming Systems Association (#13332)
- ♦ IFSA – International Federation of Sports Acrobatics (inactive)
- ♦ IFSA / see International Fire Suppression Alliance (#13607)
- ♦ **IFSA** International Fire Suppression Alliance (#13607)
- ♦ IFSA – International Flight Services Association (internationally oriented national body)
- ♦ **IFSA** International Forensic Strategic Alliance (#13626)
- ♦ **IFSA** International Forestry Students' Association (#13628)
- ♦ IFSA – International Frequency Sensor Association (internationally oriented national body)
- ♦ **IFSA** International Fuzzy Systems Association (#13697)
- ♦ IFSA – International Salmon Farmers Association (no recent information)
- ♦ **IFSAM** International Federation of Scholarly Associations of Management (#13536)
- ♦ **IF SBH** International Federation for Spina Bifida and Hydrocephalus (#13552)
- ♦ IFSB – International Flying Saucer Bureau (inactive)
- ♦ **IFSB** Islamic Financial Services Board (#16045)
- ♦ **IFSCC** International Federation of Societies of Cosmetic Chemists (#13545)
- ♦ **IFSC** International Federation of Sport Climbing (#13553)
- ♦ **IFSC** International Federation of Surgical Colleges (#13560)
- ♦ **IFSCO** International Federation of Scout and Guide Stamp Collecting Organizations (#13537)
- ♦ **IFSDA** International Federation of Stamp Dealers' Associations (#13557)
- ♦ IFSDP – International Federation of the Socialist and Democratic Press (no recent information)
- ♦ IFSE – International Federation of Scientific Editors (no recent information)
- ♦ IFSEM / see International Federation of Societies for Microscopy (#13550)
- ♦ **IFSES** International Federation of Societies of Endoscopic Surgeons (#13546)
- ♦ IFS-Eurogroup – International Federation of Settlements Eurogroup (see: #13538)
- ♦ **IFSF** International Forecourt Standards Forum (#13625)
- ♦ **IFSHC** International Federation of Societies for Histochemistry and Cytochemistry (#13548)
- ♦ IFSH – Institut für Friedensforschung und Sicherheitspolitik, Hamburg (internationally oriented national body)
- ♦ IFSH – International Federation of Sound Hunters (inactive)
- ♦ IFSHJ – International Federation for Secular and Humanistic Judaism (inactive)
- ♦ **IFSHT** International Federation of Societies for Hand Therapy (#13547)
- ♦ ifs – ifs internationale filmschule köln (internationally oriented national body)
- ♦ **IFSI** International Federation of Snowsport Instructors (#13542)
- ♦ **IFSI** International Forum for Social Innovation (#13651)
- ♦ **IFSI** International Society for the Study of Itch (#15478)
- ♦ ifs internationale filmschule köln (internationally oriented national body)
- ♦ IFS – Internationale Föderation des Seilerhandwerks (inactive)
- ♦ **IFS** International Federation of Settlements and Neighbourhood Centres (#13538)
- ♦ **IFS** International Ferrocement Society (#13587)
- ♦ **IFS** International Fertiliser Society (#13588)
- ♦ **IFS** International Feuchtwanger Society (#13593)
- ♦ ifs international film school cologne (internationally oriented national body)
- ♦ **IFS** International Foundation for Science (#13677)
- ♦ IFS – International Frankenstein Society (internationally oriented national body)
- ♦ **IFS** International Sumo Federation (#15624)
- ♦ **IFSMA** International Federation of Shipmasters Associations (#13539)
- ♦ IFSMC – International Federation of Small and Medium-Sized Commercial Enterprises (inactive)
- ♦ IFSMI – International Federation of Small and Medium-Sized Industrial Enterprises (inactive)
- ♦ **IFSM** International Federation of Societies for Microscopy (#13550)
- ♦ IFSNC / see International Federation of Settlements and Neighbourhood Centres (#13538)
- ♦ **IFSN** International Food Security Network (#13623)
- ♦ **IFSO** International Federation for Sports Officials (#13555)
- ♦ **IFSO** International Federation for the Surgery of Obesity and Metabolic Disorders (#13559)
- ♦ **IFSPD** International Foundation for Sustainable Peace and Development (#13678)
- ♦ IFSP / see International Federation of Sports Physical Therapy (#13556)
- ♦ IFSPO – International Federation of Senior Police Officers (no recent information)
- ♦ **IFSPT** International Federation of Sports Physical Therapy (#13556)
- ♦ **IFSR** International Federation for Systems Research (#13564)
- ♦ **IFSS Coalition** International Fire Safety Standards Coalition (#13606)
- ♦ **IFSSH** International Federation of Societies for Surgery of the Hand (#13551)
- ♦ **IFSS** International Federation of Sleddog Sports (#13541)
- ♦ IFSS – International Federation for Sterile Supply (inactive)
- ♦ **IFSSO** International Federation of Social Science Organizations (#13543)
- ♦ IFSTAD – Islamic Foundation for Science, Technology and Development (inactive)
- ♦ **IFSTA** International Federation of Swimming Teachers' Association, UK (#13563)
- ♦ IFSTP – International Federation of Societies of Toxicologic Pathologists (no recent information)
- ♦ **IFSUA** International Forum for Sustainable Underwater Activities (#13654)

♦ IFSW Europe 11106

Pres address not obtained. E-mail: europe@ifsw.org.
URL: http://www.ifsweurope-ifsweurope.blogspot.com/

History Founded as the regional organization of *International Federation of Social Workers (IFSW, #13544)*. Registered as an independent legal entity. **Aims** Promote social work as a profession; promote formation of organizations or trade unions for social workers; support national organizations to promote participation in social planning and the inclusion of social workers in formulation of social legislation. **Structure** Delegates Meeting (annual); Executive Committee. **Languages** English. **Finance** Sources: meeting proceeds; members' dues. **Activities** Events/meetings; projects/programmes; publishing activities. **Events** *European Social Work Conference* Prague (Czechia) 2023, *Delegates Meeting* Yerevan (Armenia) 2012, *Delegates Meeting* Brussels (Belgium) 2011, *Delegates Meeting* Valletta (Malta) 2010, *Delegates Meeting* Dubrovnik (Croatia) 2009. **Publications** *IFSW Europe Newsletter* (2 a year).
Members Associations in 39 countries:
Armenia, Austria, Azerbaijan, Belarus, Belgium, Bulgaria, Croatia, Cyprus, Czechia, Denmark, Faeroe Is, Finland, France, Georgia, Germany, Greece, Iceland, Ireland, Israel, Italy, Kosovo, Lithuania, Luxembourg, Malta, Moldova, Netherlands, North Macedonia, Norway, Poland, Portugal, Romania, Russia, Slovakia, Spain, Sweden, Switzerland, Türkiye, UK, Ukraine.
NGO Relations Member of (3): *European Anti-Poverty Network (EAPN, #05908)*; *European Network for Social Action (ENSACT, #08003)*; *Social Platform (#19344)*. [2022.09.28/XJ1234/**E**]

- ♦ **IFSWF** International Forum of Sovereign Wealth Funds (#13652)
- ♦ **IFSW** International Federation of Social Workers (#13544)
- ♦ IFTAC – International Federation for Toys and Childhood (inactive)
- ♦ IFTA – Independent Film and Television Alliance (internationally oriented national body)
- ♦ **IFTA** International Family Therapy Association (#13331)
- ♦ IFTA – International Federation of Teachers' Associations (inactive)
- ♦ **IFTA** International Federation of Technical Analysts (#13566)
- ♦ **IFTA** International Federation of Television Archives (#13568)
- ♦ **IFTA** International Federation of Thanatologists Associations (#13569)
- ♦ IFTA – International Font Technology Association (inactive)
- ♦ IFTB – International Federation of Terminology Banks (inactive)
- ♦ IFTC – Institute of Tropical Forest Conservation (internationally oriented national body)
- ♦ **IFTC** International Council for Film, Television and Audiovisual Communication (#13022)
- ♦ IFTC-WCL – International Federation Textile and Clothing (inactive)
- ♦ IFTDH / see Terre des Hommes International Federation (#20133)
- ♦ **IFTDO** International Federation of Training and Development Organizations (#13573)
- ♦ **IFTE** International Federation for the Teaching of English (#13565)
- ♦ IFTF – Institute for the Future (internationally oriented national body)
- ♦ IFTF / see International Fur Federation (#13696)
- ♦ IFTGA / see International Tobacco Growers' Association (#15694)
- ♦ IFT – Institute of Food Technologists (internationally oriented national body)
- ♦ IFT – International Foundation for Telemetering (internationally oriented national body)
- ♦ IFTK-WVA – Internationale Federatie Textiel en Kleding (inactive)
- ♦ **IFTM** International Federation for Tropical Medicine (#13575)
- ♦ **IFTO** International Federation of Tour Operators (#13571)
- ♦ **IFToMM** International Federation for the Promotion of Mechanism and Machine Science (#13519)
- ♦ **IFTR** International Federation for Theatre Research (#13570)
- ♦ IFTS – International Federation of Teratology Societies (inactive)
- ♦ **IFTTA** International Forum of Travel and Tourism Advocates (#13657)
- ♦ IFTU – International Federation of Trade Unions (inactive)
- ♦ IFTwA – International Federation of Tiddlywinks Associations (internationally oriented national body)
- ♦ IFU / see Investeringsfonden for Udviklingslande
- ♦ IFU / see International Fruit and Vegetable Juice Association (#13687)
- ♦ **IFU** International Fruit and Vegetable Juice Association (#13687)
- ♦ IFU – Investeringsfonden for Udviklingslande (internationally oriented national body)
- ♦ IFUSCO – International Finno-Ugric Students' Conference (meeting series)
- ♦ IFUW / see Graduate Women International (#10688)
- ♦ IFVHSF / see International Federation of Health Plans (#13442)
- ♦ IFV / see International Fistball Association (#13609)
- ♦ **IFVTCC** Internationale Föderation der Vereine der Textilchemiker und Coloristen (#13365)
- ♦ IFWA – International Federation for Weeks of Art (inactive)
- ♦ IFWA – International Federation of Youth Hostel Wardens Associations (inactive)
- ♦ **IFWA** International Foundation for Women Artists (#13679)
- ♦ **IFWEA** International Federation of Workers' Education Associations (#13580)
- ♦ IFWHA – International Federation of Women's Hockey Associations (inactive)
- ♦ IfW – Institut für Weltwirtschaft, Kiel (internationally oriented national body)
- ♦ IFWL / see International Federation of Women Lawyers (#13578)
- ♦ IFWLA – International Federation of Warehousing and Logistics Associations (inactive)
- ♦ IFWLA – International Federation of Women's Lacrosse Associations (inactive)
- ♦ **IFWLC** International Federation of Women in Legal Careers (#13579)
- ♦ IFWP – International Federation of Wildlife Photography (inactive)
- ♦ **IFWS** Internationale Föderation von Wirkerei- und Strickerei-Fachleuten (#13465)
- ♦ IFWTO – International Federation of Women's Travel Organizations (inactive)
- ♦ IGA / see International Island Games Association (#13962)
- ♦ IGAB / see International Association of Speakers Bureaus
- ♦ **IGAC** International Global Atmospheric Chemistry Project (#13721)
- ♦ IgA Club / see International IgA Nephropathy Network (#13833)
- ♦ IGADD – Inter-Governmental Authority on Drought and Development (inactive)
- ♦ **IGAD** Intergovernmental Authority on Development (#11472)
- ♦ IGAEA / see Graphic Communications Education Association
- ♦ **IGAeM** Internationale Gesellschaft für Aerosole in der Medizin (#14907)
- ♦ **IGAFIT** Interest Group on Algorithmic Foundations of Information Technology (#11468)
- ♦ IGA / see ILGA World (#11120)
- ♦ IGA – Internacia Geografa Asocio (inactive)
- ♦ **IGA** International Gaucher Alliance (#13701)
- ♦ **IGA** International Genetic Alliance (#13709)
- ♦ **IGA** International Geothermal Association (#13717)
- ♦ **IGA** International Glaucoma Association (#13719)
- ♦ **IGA** International Glima Association (#13720)
- ♦ IGA – International Glove Association (internationally oriented national body)
- ♦ **IGA** International Goat Association (#13725)
- ♦ **IGA** International Gothic Association (#13729)
- ♦ IGA – International Grains Agreement (treaty)
- ♦ **IGA** International Greeter Association (#13737)
- ♦ **IGALA** International Gender and Language Association (#13706)
- ♦ **IGAL** Intercontinental Grouping of Accountants and Lawyers (#11462)

IGAL
11106

alphabetic sequence excludes
For the complete listing, see Yearbook Online at

♦ IGAL – Welt Interessen Gemeinschaft Alterer Langstvecken Läufer (inactive)
♦ IGAM – Internationale Gesellschaft für Allgemeinmedizin (inactive)
♦ **IGAMT** International Group on Aviation and Multimodal Transport Research (#13741)
♦ **I-GAP** Internationale Gesellschaft für angewandte Präventionsmedizin (#13236)
♦ IGAP / see International Federation for Psychotherapy (#13523)
♦ IGAS – International Genetics of Ankylosing Spondylitis Conference (meeting series)
♦ IGAS – International Graphic Arts Society (inactive)
♦ **IGASS** International Group for Advancement in Spinal Science (#13740)
♦ **IGBA** International Generic and Biosimilar Medicines Association (#13708)
♦ IGB / see International Co-operative Alliance (#12944)
♦ **IGB** Internationaler Genossenschaftsbund (#12944)
♦ **IGB** Internationaler Gewerkschaftsbund (#15708)
♦ IGBK – Internationale Gesellschaft der Bildende Künste (internationally oriented national body)
♦ **IGCA** International Garden Centre Association (#13698)
♦ **IGCA** International Gastric Cancer Association (#13699)
♦ **IGCAT** International Institute of Gastronomy, Culture, Arts and Tourism (#13883)
♦ IGCC – Institute on Global Conflict and Cooperation (internationally oriented national body)
♦ IGCC – Investor Group on Climate Change (internationally oriented national body)
♦ IGCCT – Intergovernmental Commission for Cooperation of Socialist Countries in the Field of Computer Technology (inactive)
♦ IGCI – Internationale Gesellschaft für Chemo- und Immunotherapie (inactive)
♦ IGCI – International Global Change Institute, Hamilton (internationally oriented national body)
♦ **IGC** Intergovernmental Committee of the Universal Copyright Convention (#11478)
♦ IGC / see Inter-Governmental Consultations on Migration, Asylum and Refugees (#11479)
♦ **IGC** Inter-Governmental Consultations on Migration, Asylum and Refugees (#11479)
♦ **IGC** International Gemmological Conference (#13704)
♦ **IGC** International Gender Champions (#13705)
♦ IGC – International Geological Congress (meeting series)
♦ **IGC** International Grains Council (#13731)
♦ **IGC** International Group of Controlling (#13742)
♦ IGC – International Guides' Club (inactive)
♦ **IGC** Inter Nordic Guide Club (#15954)
♦ IGC – Inuvialuit Game Council, Canada (internationally oriented national body)
♦ IGCP / see International Gorilla Conservation Programme
♦ **IGCP** International Geoscience Programme (#13715)
♦ IGCP – International Gorilla Conservation Programme (internationally oriented national body)
♦ IGCR – Intergovernmental Committee on Refugees (inactive)
♦ **IGCS** International Gynecologic Cancer Society (#13767)
♦ IGDA – International Game Developers Association (internationally oriented national body)
♦ **IGDF** International Guide Dog Federation (#13763)
♦ IGD – Initiative for Global Development (internationally oriented national body)
♦ IGDO / see International Opticians Association (#14415)
♦ **IGDS** Intercontinental Group of Department Stores (#11461)
♦ **IGEB** Internationale Gesellschaft zur Erforschung und Förderung der Blasmusik (#13237)
♦ IGEH – Internationale Gesellschaft zur Erforschung von Hirntraumata (inactive)
♦ IGE – Institute for Global Economics (internationally oriented national body)
♦ **IGEL** Internationale Gesellschaft für Empirische Literaturwissenschaft (#15085)
♦ **IGeLU** International Group of Ex Libris Users (#13745)
♦ IGEM – Internationale Ärztegesellschaft für Energiemedizin (no recent information)
♦ **IGEO** International Geoscience Education Organization (#13714)
♦ **IGEPA** Internationale Gewerkschaft im Europäischen Patentamt (#19944)
♦ **IGEP** International Group of Educational Publishers (#13743)
♦ **IGEQ** International Group for Equestrian Qualifications (#13744)
♦ **IGES** Institute for Global Environmental Strategies (#11266)
♦ IGES – Institute of Global Environment and Society (internationally oriented national body)
♦ **IGES** International Genetic Epidemiology Society (#13710)
♦ IGESIP – Instituto Galego de Estudos de Seguranza Internacional e da Paz (internationally oriented national body)
♦ IGFA – International Game Fish Association (internationally oriented national body)
♦ **IGFAP** Internationale Gesellschaft für Analytische Psychologie (#11700)
♦ **IGfH** Internationale Gesellschaft für Erzieherische Hilfen (#09622)
♦ **IGF** Intergovernmental Forum on Mining, Minerals, Metals and Sustainable Development (#11484)
♦ **IGF** International Foundation for the Conservation of Wildlife (#13667)
♦ **IGF** International Genetics Federation (#13711)
♦ IGF – International Gerbil Federation (no recent information)
♦ **IGF** International Go Federation (#13726)
♦ **IGF** International Golf Federation (#13727)
♦ IGF – International Graphical Federation (inactive)
♦ **IGF** International Guarantee Fund (#13761)
♦ **IGF** Internet Governance Forum (#15950)
♦ **IGFM** Internationale Gesellschaft für Menschenrechte (#15183)
♦ **IGFSA** International Governance Forum Support Association (#13730)
♦ IGFS – International Geriatric Fracture Society (internationally oriented national body)
♦ **IGF Society** International Society for IGF Research (#15191)
♦ IGfW – Internationale Gesellschaft für Weltwirtschaft (internationally oriented national body)
♦ **IGG on Hard Fibres** Intergovernmental Group on Hard Fibres (#11489)
♦ **IGG on Jute, Kenal and Allied Fibres** Intergovernmental Group on Jute, Kenaf and Allied Fibres (#11490)
♦ IGGMED – Internationale Gesellschaft für Ganzheitsmedizin (unconfirmed)
♦ **IGGP** Inclusive Green Growth Partnership (#11146)
♦ **IGHA** Internationale Gesellschaft für historische Alpenforschung (#02990)
♦ IGHA – International Generic Horse Association (no recent information)
♦ **IGhB** Internationale Gesellschaft heilpädagogischer Berufs- und Fachverbände (#13240)
♦ IGHD – Institute for Global Health and Development, Edinburgh (internationally oriented national body)
♦ **IGHEM** International Group for Hydraulic Efficiency Measurement (#13748)
♦ IGHH – Internationale Gesellschaft für Homöopathie und Homotoxikologie (internationally oriented national body)
♦ IGH – Institute of Global Homelessness (internationally oriented national body)
♦ IGH – UCL Institute for Global Health (internationally oriented national body)

♦ IGI – The Global Wallcoverings Association (IGI) 11107

Exec Dir Chée de Louvain 426, 1380 Lasne, Belgium. T. +3227200009. E-mail: info@igiwallcoverings.org.
URL: http://www.igiwallcoverings.org/

History 1950, Zurich (Switzerland). Statutes amended: 1981; 1995. Former names and other names: *Groupement international des fabricants de papiers peints* – former; *Internationaler Verein der Tapetenfabrikanten* – former; *International Wallcovering Manufacturers Association (IGI)* – former; *Groupement international des fabricants de revêtements muraux* – former; *Internationaler Verband der Wandbekleidungsfabrikanten* – former. Registration: Banque-Carrefour des Entreprises, No/ID: 0418.885.095, Start date: 29 Nov 1978, Belgium. **Aims** Increase the ability of wallcovering industry members to solve their business problems by providing a forum for discussion, disseminating information and representing the industry before government and standards bodies. **Structure** General Assembly; Officers; Committees (3). **Languages** English, French. **Finance** Sources: members' dues. **Activities** Knowledge management/information dissemination; research/documentation; standards/guidelines; training/education. **Events** *Annual General Assembly* Budapest (Hungary) 2019, *Annual General Assembly* Albufeira (Portugal) 2018, *Annual General Assembly* Santa Cruz de Tenerife (Spain) 2017, *Annual General Assembly* Barcelona (Spain) 2016, *Annual General Assembly* Sintra (Portugal) 2015. **Publications** *IGI Newsletter* (3 a year). Annual Report.
Members Individual companies (manufacturers); Associate membership (suppliers). Members in 20 countries:
Belgium, China, Denmark, Finland, France, Germany, Italy, Japan, Korea Rep, Lithuania, Netherlands, Norway, Russia, Spain, Sweden, Switzerland, Türkiye, UK, Ukraine, USA.
NGO Relations In liaison with technical committees of: *Comité européen de normalisation (CEN, #04162)*. Member of: *Federation of European and International Associations Established in Belgium (FAIB, #09508)*.
[2021.06.10/XD2806/**D**]

♦ IGI / see IGI – The Global Wallcoverings Association (#11107)
♦ **IGI** IGI – The Global Wallcoverings Association (#11107)
♦ **IG** Internationale Gerbervereinigung (#13084)
♦ **IGIP** Internationale Gesellschaft für Ingenieurpädagogik (#15089)
♦ IGJ – Institute for Global Justice (internationally oriented national body)
♦ **IGKB** Internationale Gewässerschutzkommission für den Bodensee (#13244)
♦ **IGLA** International Gay and Lesbian Aquatics (#13702)
♦ IGLA / see International Library and Information Group (#14037)
♦ IGLCC – International Gay and Lesbian Chamber of Commerce (no recent information)
♦ **IGLC** International Group for Lean Construction (#13749)
♦ IGLD – International Grand Lodge of Druidism (religious order)
♦ Iglesia Anglicana del Cono Sur de América / see The Anglican Church of South America (#00825)

♦ Iglesia Anglicana de la Region Central de América (IARCA) 11108

Anglican Church of Central America
Primate Box R, Balboa, Panamá, Balboa PANAMá, Panama.
Facebook: https://www.facebook.com/IARCA.OFICIAL/

History within the framework of *Anglican Communion (#00827)*. **IGO Relations** Partner of: *UNHCR (#20327)*. **NGO Relations** Member of: *Lambeth Conference of Bishops of the Anglican Communion (#16224)*; *Primates Meeting of the Anglican Communion (#18497)*. [2020/XE3414/**E**]

♦ Iglesia de Dios Ministerial de Jesucristo Internacional (religious order)
♦ Iglesia Internacional del Evangelio Cuadrangular (internationally oriented national body)
♦ La Iglesia Metodista Unida (#20514)
♦ Iglesia Reformada en America (internationally oriented national body)
♦ **IGLFA** International Gay and Lesbian Football Association (#13703)
♦ IGLHRC / see OutRight Action International
♦ IGLTA – International Gay and Lesbian Travel Association (internationally oriented national body)
♦ **IGLU** Institut de gestion et de leadership universitaires (#11298)
♦ **IGLU-Leaders** Institute of University Management and Leadership (#11298)
♦ IGLYO / see International Lesbian, Gay, Bisexual, Transgender, Queer and Intersex Youth and Student Organization (#14032)
♦ **IGLYO** International Lesbian, Gay, Bisexual, Transgender, Queer and Intersex Youth and Student Organization (#14032)
♦ **IGMG** Internationale Gustav Mahler Gesellschaft (#13765)
♦ IGM – Internationale Gesellschaft für Moorforschung (inactive)
♦ **IGM** International Society of Gender Medicine (#15137)
♦ IGMOF – Internationale Gesellschaft für Mittel- und Osteuropaforschung, Wien (internationally oriented national body)
♦ **IGMS** International Gustav Mahler Society (#13765)
♦ IGMSP / see International Federation for Psychotherapy (#13523)
♦ IGMW / see International Musicological Society (#14201)
♦ Ignacio Martin-Baró Fund for Mental Health and Human Rights / see Martín-Baró Initiative for Wellbeing and Human Rights
♦ **IGNC** International Good Neighbour Council (#13728)
♦ **IGN** Internationale Gesellschaft für Nutztierhaltung (#15236)
♦ **IGN** International Guardianship Network (#13762)
♦ **IGN** Iodine Global Network (#16004)
♦ IGNIS – Institute for Global Networking, Information and Studies (internationally oriented national body)
♦ Ignitus Worldwide (internationally oriented national body)
♦ **IGNM** Internationale Gesellschaft für Neue Musik (#15035)
♦ **IGO Conference** Intergovernmental Organizations Conference (#11498)
♦ IGO – Institute of Global Responsibility (internationally oriented national body)
♦ **IGO** International Glycoconjugate Organization (#13723)
♦ IGO / see International Opticians Association (#14415)
♦ **I-GOOS** Intergovernmental Committee for the Global Ocean Observing System (#11473)
♦ **IGORR** International Group of Research Reactors (#13754)
♦ IGPA / see International Generic and Biosimilar Medicines Association (#13708)
♦ **IGPF** Internationale Gesellschaft für Photogrammetrie und Fernerkundung (#15362)
♦ **IGP** Internationale Föderation für Psychotherapie (#13523)
♦ **IGP** International Group for Paper Distribution Quality (#13750)
♦ IGP – Internet Governance Project (internationally oriented national body)
♦ IGPME / see International Group for the Psychology of Mathematics Education (#13753)
♦ **IGPN** International Green Purchasing Network (#13736)
♦ **IGRAC** International Groundwater Resources Assessment Centre (#13739)
♦ IGRA – International Green Roof Association (inactive)
♦ IGRC – International Gas Research Conference (meeting series)
♦ IGRDM – International Group on Radiation Damage Mechanisms (meeting series)
♦ Igreja de Deus Deus Ministerial de Jesus Cristo Internacional (religious order)
♦ Igreja Internacional do Evangelho Quadrangular Edição (internationally oriented national body)
♦ **IGROF** Internationale Rorschach-Gesellschaft (#15430)
♦ **IGSA** International Gravity Sports Association (#13735)
♦ IGSBi / see Internationale Gesellschaft für Schulbuch- und Bildungsmedienforschung (#13242)
♦ **IGSBi** Internationale Gesellschaft für Schulbuch- und Bildungsmedienforschung (#13242)
♦ IGSC / see International Association of Surgeons, Gastroenterologists and Oncologists (#12216)
♦ IGSC – International Geosciences Student Conference (meeting series)
♦ IGSD – Institute for Governance and Sustainable Development (internationally oriented national body)
♦ **IGS** Institute of General Semantics (#11264)
♦ IGS – Institute for Global Studies (internationally oriented national body)
♦ **IGS** The International Edvard Grieg Society (#13232)
♦ IGS – International Gender Studies Centre, Oxford (internationally oriented national body)
♦ **IGS** International Geosynthetics Society (#13716)
♦ IGS – International Geranium Society (internationally oriented national body)
♦ **IGS** International Glaciological Society (#13718)
♦ IGS / see International GNSS Service (#13724)
♦ **IGS** International GNSS Service (#13724)
♦ **IGS** International Gramsci Society (#13733)
♦ **IGS** International Graphonomics Society (#13734)
♦ IGSO – Institute for Globalization Studies and Social Movements, Moscow (internationally oriented national body)
♦ **IGSO** International Geodetic Students Organization (#13712)
♦ **IGSP** Internationale Gesellschaft der Schriftpsychologie (#15398)
♦ **IGSRP** Internationale Gesellschaft der Stadt- und Regionalplaner (#15012)
♦ **IGSRV** International Group of Specialist Racing Veterinarians (#13756)

- ♦ IGST – Integrability in Gauge and String Theory (meeting series)
- ♦ IGSV – Internationaler Gras Ski Verband (inactive)
- ♦ IGT / see Gas Technology Institute
- ♦ IGTA / see International Gay and Lesbian Travel Association
- ♦ **IGTA** International Group of Treasury Associations (#13759)
- ♦ **IGTC** International Glutamate Technical Committee (#13722)
- ♦ **IGTC** International Grain Trade Coalition (#13732)
- ♦ **IGTF** International Grid Trust Federation (#13738)
- ♦ **IGTI** ASME International Gas Turbine Institute (#02107)
- ♦ IGTI – Internationale Gesellschaft für Thymologie und Immunotherapie (inactive)
- ♦ IGT – Internationale Gesellschaft fur Tiefenpsychologie (internationally oriented national body)
- ♦ **IGTM** Internationale Gesellschaft für Theologische Mediävistik (#13243)
- ♦ **IGTN** International Gender and Trade Network (#13707)
- ♦ IGTYF – International Good Templar Youth Federation (inactive)
- ♦ Igualdad Ya (#05518)
- ♦ **IGU** Internationale Gesellschaft für Umweltschutz (#15097)
- ♦ IGU – Internationale Gewerbeunion (inactive)
- ♦ **IGU** International Gas Union (#13700)
- ♦ **IGU** International Geographical Union (#13713)
- ♦ **IGUS** International Group of Experts on the Explosion Risks of Unstable Substances (#13746)
- ♦ IGVF / see International Cooperative and Mutual Insurance Federation (#12948)
- ♦ IGV – Internationale Gebedsvereniging (religious order)
- ♦ IGV – Internationale Gebetsvereinigung (religious order)
- ♦ **IGV** Internationale Gussasphalt-Vereinigung (#14119)
- ♦ IGWMC – International Ground Water Modelling Center (internationally oriented national body)
- ♦ **IG-WRDRR** International Group for Wind-Related Disaster Risk Reduction (#13760)
- ♦ **IGWT** Internationale Gesellschaft für Warenwissenschaften und Technologie (#11790)
- ♦ IGZ / see SGF International (#19252)
- ♦ IHAB – International Halal Authority Board (unconfirmed)
- ♦ **IHAF** International Halal Accreditation Forum (#13769)
- ♦ IHA Foundation for the Future / see IHRA Foundation for the Future (#11113)
- ♦ **IHA** International Federation of Hardware and Housewares Associations (#13437)
- ♦ IHA – International Hahnemannian Association (inactive)
- ♦ **IHA** International Halliwick Association (#13770)
- ♦ IHA – International H-Boat Class Association (see: #21760)
- ♦ IHA – International Health Academy (internationally oriented national body)
- ♦ IHA – International Hemp Association (no recent information)
- ♦ **IHA** International Hobbes Association (#13800)
- ♦ IHA / see International Hotel and Restaurant Association (#13813)
- ♦ IHA – International House Association (inactive)
- ♦ **IHA** International Housing Association (#13815)
- ♦ **IHA** International Huntington Association (#13824)
- ♦ **IHA** International Hydropower Association (#13828)
- ♦ **IHAN** International Health Awareness Network (#13778)
- ♦ IHATIS – International Hide and Allied Trades Improvement Society (inactive)
- ♦ **IHBA** International Hemp Building Association (#13789)
- ♦ **IHB** Internationales Hopfenbaubüro (#13807)
- ♦ IHB / see International Hydrographic Organization (#13825)
- ♦ IHBPA / see International Hepato-Pancreato-Biliary Association (#13790)
- ♦ IHCA / see Instituto de História de Nicaragua y Centroamérica
- ♦ **IHCA** International Hansa Class Association (#13773)
- ♦ **IHCA** International Hobie Class Association (#13801)
- ♦ IHCA / see International Messianic Jewish Alliance (#14148)

♦ IHCF African Christian Hospitals 11109

Stiftung zur Förderung der Gesundheit – IHCF

Exec Dir 102 N Locust St, Searcy AR 72143, USA. T. +15012689511. Fax +15012683811.
URL: http://www.ihcf.net/index.html

History Original title: *African Christian Hospitals Foundation.* Subsequent title in English: *International Health Care Foundation (IHCF).* **Aims** Facilitate translation of scientifically based *preventive oral* care into efficacious health care. **Structure** Executive Board, comprising 6 members; Scientific Board; Working Groups (4): Advanced training and publications; Management of practical and insurance-related aspects of prevention; Product testing; Use of the logo. **Languages** English, German. **Events** *Annual Congress* Berlin (Germany) 2010, *Annual Congress* Lindau (Germany) 2009, *Annual Congress* Lindau (Germany) 2008, *Annual Congress* Lindau (Germany) 2007, *Annual congress* Lindau (Germany) 2006.
Members Individuals and companies in 16 countries:
Austria, China, Finland, France, Germany, Ireland, Italy, Japan, Liechtenstein, Netherlands, Poland, Spain, Sweden, Switzerland, UK, USA. [2016/XD6539/f/**F**]

- ♦ IHCF / see IHCF African Christian Hospitals (#11109)
- ♦ IHC Global – International Housing Coalition (internationally oriented national body)
- ♦ IHCI – International Conference on Intelligent Human Computer Interaction (meeting series)
- ♦ **IHC** International Harmonization Council (#13775)
- ♦ IHC – International Hydrodynamics Committee (see: #15318)
- ♦ **IHCNO** International Home Care Nurses Organization (#13805)
- ♦ **IHCO** International Health Cooperative Organization (#13779)
- ♦ IHCSA – International Hospitality and Conference Service Association (internationally oriented national body)
- ♦ IHCTAS / see International Society of Vascularized Composite Allotransplantation (#15536)
- ♦ **i-HD** European Institute for Innovation through Health Data (#07561)
- ♦ IHD International (internationally oriented national body)
- ♦ IHDLN / see International Population Data Linkage Network (#14620)
- ♦ IHDP – International Human Development Project (internationally oriented national body)
- ♦ **iHEA** International Health Economics Association (#13780)
- ♦ IHEA / see International Health Evaluation and Promotion Association (#13781)
- ♦ IHEAL – Institut des hautes études de l'Amérique latine (internationally oriented national body)
- ♦ **IHEC** International Human Epigenome Consortium (#13818)
- ♦ IHE Delft / see IHE Delft Institute for Water Education (#11110)

♦ IHE Delft Institute for Water Education 11110

Rector PO Box 3015, 2601 DA Delft, Netherlands. T. +31152151715. Fax +31152122921. E-mail: info@un-ihe.org.
Street Address Westvest 7, 2611 AX Delft, Netherlands.
URL: http://www.un-ihe.org/

History 1957. Founded jointly by Delft University of Technology and *Netherlands Organization for International Cooperation in Higher Education (NUFFIC).* At 31st General Conference of *UNESCO (#20322),* 5 Nov 2001, Paris (France), establishment of IHE as an UNESCO institute endorsed. Previously integral part of UNESCO. Former names and other names: *International Institute for Hydraulic and Environmental Engineering* – former; *Institut international pour l'hydraulique et l'environnement* – former; *Internationaal Instituut voor Waterbouwkunde en Milieubeheer* – former; *International Institute for Infrastructural, Hydraulic and Environmental Engineering (IHE Delft)* – former; *UNESCO – IHE Institute for Water Education* – former (5 Nov 2001); *Institut UNESCO-IHE pour l'éducation relative à l'eau* – former (5 Nov 2001). Registration: No/ID: KVK 41146484, Start date: 1993, Netherlands, South Holland. **Aims** Contribute to the education and training of professionals; build the capacity of sector organizations, knowledge centres and other institutions active in the fields of *water,* the *environment* and infrastructure in *developing countries* and countries in transition. **Structure** Governing Board, appointed by DG UNESCO. Foundation Board; Rectorate; Academic Board; Management Team. Academic Departments (3). **Languages** English. **Staff** 194.00 FTE, paid. Over 350 guest lecturers. **Finance** Subsidy from Dutch Ministry of Education; fellowships; contract training and research; consultancy services. Budget (2013): euro 36,337 million. **Activities** Capacity building; research/documentation; training/education. **Events** *From Capacity Development to Implementation Science* Delft (Netherlands) 2020, *International Conference on Amphibious Architecture, Design and Engineering* Waterloo, ON (Canada) 2017, *International Conference on Amphibious Architecture, Design and Engineering* Bangkok (Thailand) 2015, *LINKS Annual Meeting* Delft (Netherlands) 2014, *Working on Assessment of Capacity Development Resources for Water and Sanitation Operators* Delft (Netherlands) 2014. **Publications** *Newsletter* (annual). *Lecture Notes Series.* Conference proceedings; monographs; over 350 scientific publications a year. **Members** Not a membership organization but over 15,000 alumni in over 160 countries worldwide. **IGO Relations** Member of: *Regional Centre on Urban Water Management, Teheran (RCUWM, #18761).* Partner of: *Group on Earth Observations (GEO, #10735).* **NGO Relations** Leads: *Africa-EU Innovation Alliance for Water and Climate (AfriAlliance, #00169).* Member of:
- *European Water Partnership (EWP, #09083);*
- *Global Clean Water Desalination Alliance (GCWDA, #10285);*
- *Global Development Learning Network (GDLN, #10317);*
- *International Office for Water (IOW, #14399);*
- *Sustainable Sanitation Alliance (SuSanA, #20066);*
- *United Nations Academic Impact (UNAI, #20516);*
- *Water and Development Information for Arid Lands Global Network (G-WADI, #20826);*
- *Water Integrity Network (WIN, #20830);*
- *WaterNet (#20832);*
- *World Water Council (WWC, #21908).*

Founding partner of: *Network for Capacity Building in Integrated Water Resources Management (CAP-Net, #17000); Water Footprint Network (WFN, #20829).* Partner of: *UNLEASH; Wetlands International (#20928).* Participates in: *Movement of Spiritual Inner Awareness (MSIA). IRC (#16016)* is member. [2022/XE3965/jv/**E**]

♦ IHE-Europe 11111

Europe Coordinator c/o ECR Gmbh, Am Gestade 1, 1010 Vienna, Austria. T. +431533406443. Fax +4315334064448. E-mail: secretariat@ihe-europe.net.
Registered Address Bluepoint Bldg, Boulevard Ryers 80, 1030 Brussels, Belgium. E-mail: office@ihe-europe.net.
URL: http://www.ihe-europe.net/

History Set up to coordinate European activities of *Integrating Healthcare Enterprise International (IHE International, #11372).* Registration: Banque-Carrefour des Entreprises, No/ID: 0898.675.997, Start date: 19 Jun 2008, Belgium. **Aims** Coordinate European input to international IHE development activities and IHE activities in Europe; engage clinicians, health authorities, industry and users to improve *healthcare interoperability* in Europe. **Structure** Executive Committee. Committees (3): MarCom; IHE-Services; European Affairs. **Events** *Moving forward digital health with cybersecurity* Rennes (France) 2019, *Getting the basics right, key success factors in interoperability* The Hague (Netherlands) 2018, *Interoperability in eHealth Marches Ahead* Venice (Italy) 2017. [2022/XM7838/**E**]

- ♦ **IHEG** Internationale Hanns Eisler Gesellschaft (#13246)
- ♦ IHEID – Institut de hautes études internationales et du développement (internationally oriented national body)
- ♦ IHE – International Health Exchange (internationally oriented national body)
- ♦ **IHE International** Integrating Healthcare Enterprise International (#11372)
- ♦ IHEI / see Sustainable Hospitality Alliance (#20061)
- ♦ IHEMI / see International Health Policy and Management Institute (#13782)
- ♦ IHENU – Institut des Hautes Etudes sur les Nations Unies (internationally oriented national body)
- ♦ **IHEO** International Honey Export Organization (#13806)
- ♦ **IHEPA** International Health Evaluation and Promotion Association (#13781)
- ♦ IHERC / see International Relations Center
- ♦ **IHES** International Hydrologic Environment Society (#13827)
- ♦ IHEU / see Humanists International (#10972)
- ♦ IHEYO / see Young Humanists International (#21993)
- ♦ IHF / see International Hockey Federation (#13802)
- ♦ IHFA / see Adventist Health Food Association (#00132)
- ♦ IHFA – International Health and Fitness Association (unconfirmed)
- ♦ **IHFC** International Heat Flow Commission (#13786)
- ♦ **IHFFC** International Humanitarian Fact-Finding Commission (#13820)
- ♦ **IHF** International Handball Federation (#13771)
- ♦ IHF – International Hapkido Federation (internationally oriented national body)
- ♦ **IHF** International Hospital Federation (#13812)
- ♦ IHF – International Humanity Foundation (internationally oriented national body)
- ♦ IHFM / see Adventist Health Food Association (#00132)
- ♦ **IHGC** International Hop Growers' Convention (#13807)
- ♦ **IHG** Institute on the Holocaust and Genocide (#11268)

♦ IHG Owners Association 11112

CEO Three Ravinia Drive, Suite 100, Atlanta GA 30346, USA. T. +17706045555. Fax +17706045684.
Events Manager address not obtained.
URL: https://www.owners.org/

History 26 May 1956. Founded by *'Holiday Inns of America',* a forerunner of the *Holiday Inn Worldwide,* as an association of hotel owners. Incorporated in 1976 as an independent organization. Former names and other names: *National Association of Holiday Inns* – former; *International Association of Holiday Inns* – former (1963 to 2011); *International Association of Bass Hotels and Resorts (IAHI)* – former. **Aims** Maximize the investment a member makes in an IHG-branded hotel. **Structure** Annual Meeting; Board of Directors. **Finance** Funded by a combination of members' dues, system funds and expense allocations from Holiday Inn Worldwide. **Activities** Advocacy/lobbying/activism. **Events** *International committee meeting* Rome (Italy) 1990, *Franchise owners annual conference* Seattle, WA (USA) 1988. **Members** Hotel owners (4400) in 65 countries. Membership countries not specified. [2021/XM1065/e/**C**]

- ♦ **IHHA** International Heavy Haul Association (#13787)
- ♦ IHH Insani Yardim Vakfi (internationally oriented national body)
- ♦ **IHhS** International Hyperhidrosis Society (#13829)
- ♦ **IHHWA** International Housing and Home Warranty Association (#13816)
- ♦ IHI – Internationales Hilfskomitee für Intellektuelle (inactive)
- ♦ IH – Internationaler Hilfsfonds (internationally oriented national body)
- ♦ iHITA – International Hospitality Information Technology Association (internationally oriented national body)
- ♦ IHIVF – International HIV Fund (internationally oriented national body)
- ♦ IHJ – International House of Japan (internationally oriented national body)
- ♦ **IHJR** Institute for Historical Justice and Reconciliation (#11267)
- ♦ **IHLADI** Instituto Hispano-Luso-Americano de Derecho Internacional (#10924)
- ♦ **IHMA** International Harbour Masters' Association (#13774)
- ♦ **IHMA** International Hologram Manufacturers Association (#13804)
- ♦ IHMA – International Humanistic Management Association (unconfirmed)
- ♦ IHMC – International Human Microbiome Consortium (unconfirmed)
- ♦ IHME – Institute for Health Metric and Evaluation (internationally oriented national body)
- ♦ Ihmisoikeuksien yleismaailmallinen julistus (1948 treaty)
- ♦ Ihmisoikeusinstituutti (internationally oriented national body)
- ♦ Ihmisoikeusliitto – Förbundet för Mänskliga Rättigheter / see Finnish League for Human Rights
- ♦ Ihmisoikeusliitto Ry (internationally oriented national body)
- ♦ IHMN – International Human Motricity Network (unconfirmed)
- ♦ IHM – Sisters Servants of the Immaculate Heart of Mary of Scranton (religious order)
- ♦ IHNCA – Instituto de História de Nicaragua y Centroamérica (internationally oriented national body)
- ♦ IHN / see European Heart Network (#07467)

♦ IHN – Interactive Health Network (internationally oriented national body)
♦ **IHN** International Haemovigilance Network (#13768)
♦ IHNW / see International Health Awareness Network (#13778)
♦ **IHO** International Hydrographic Organization (#13825)
♦ IHPA / see International Wood Products Association
♦ **IHPA** International HCH and Pesticides Association (#13776)
♦ IHPA – International Health Professions Association (inactive)
♦ IHPA – International Humanistic Psychology Association (internationally oriented national body)
♦ **IHPBA** International Hepato-Pancreato-Biliary Association (#13790)
♦ IHPC – International Hydrolyzed Protein Council (internationally oriented national body)
♦ IHP-HELP Centre for Water Law, Policy and Science / see UNESCO Centre for Water Law, Policy and Science
♦ IHP – International Health Partners (internationally oriented national body)
♦ **IHP** International Hydrological Programme (#13826)
♦ **IHPMI** International Health Policy and Management Institute (#13782)
♦ IHPRS – International Husserl and Phenomenological Research Society (see: #21725)
♦ IHPS / see International Society of Psychology of Handwriting (#15398)
♦ **IHPST** International History, Philosophy, and Science Teaching Group (#13799)
♦ IHP+ / see UHC2030 (#20277)
♦ **IHPVA** International Human-Powered Vehicle Association (#13822)
♦ IHRAAM – International Human Rights Association of American Minorities (internationally oriented national body)
♦ **IH&RA** Association internationale de l'hôtellerie et de la restauration (#13813)

♦ IHRA Foundation for the Future (FFF) 11113

Fondation IHRA pour l'avenir

Pres Av Thedore Flournoy 5, 1207 Geneva, Switzerland. T. +41797676436. Fax +41225948145.

History 1989, as *IHA Foundation for the Future – Fondation AIH pour l'avenir*, with an initial donation of *American Express Foundation*, and managed by *International Hotel and Restaurant Association (IH&RA, #13813)*, together with another fund *IH and RA Fund for the Future (inactive)* (set up in 1987 and closed down 1998). Present name adopted Nov 1996. Registered in accordance with the Swiss Civil Code since 1989, when also became managed by an independent Board. Since Jan 2016, operated by Aidi Charitable Foundation. **Aims** Provide support to the *hospitality* industry through education, research and award programmes aimed at improving the quality and technology of *hotel* and *tourism services* worldwide. **Structure** Board of Trustees; Executive Committee; Secretariat. **Languages** English, French. **Staff** 1.00 FTE, paid. **Finance** Financial resources administered through a charitable foundation headquartered in Zurich (Switzerland). **Activities** Financial and/or material support; training/education; awards/prizes/competitions. **Members** All IHRA members. [2016.12.13/XF1574/f/**E**]

♦ IHRA / see Harm Reduction International (#10861)
♦ IHRA – International High-Speed Rail Association (internationally oriented national body)
♦ **IHRA** International Holocaust Remembrance Alliance (#13803)
♦ **IH&RA** International Hotel and Restaurant Association (#13813)
♦ IHRA – International Hot Rod Association (internationally oriented national body)
♦ IHRAS – International Human Rights and Anti-Corruption Society (internationally oriented national body)
♦ IHRB – Institute for Human Rights and Business (internationally oriented national body)
♦ IHRC – Islamic Human Rights Commission (internationally oriented national body)
♦ IHRCP – International Human Rights Committee for Protection (internationally oriented national body)
♦ IHRDA – Institute for Human Rights and Development in Africa (internationally oriented national body)
♦ IHRFG / see Human Rights Funders Network
♦ IHRI – Institut hongrois des affaires internationales (internationally oriented national body)
♦ IHRLI – International Human Rights Law Institute (internationally oriented national body)
♦ IHRM – International Human Resource Management Conference (meeting series)
♦ IHRO – International Human Rights Observer (internationally oriented national body)
♦ IHRPG – International Human Rights Protector's Group (internationally oriented national body)
♦ **IHRSA** International Health, Racquet and Sportsclub Association (#13783)
♦ IHS / see Institute for Housing and Urban Development Studies
♦ **IHSA** International Humanitarian Studies Association (#13821)
♦ Ihsan Foundation for West Africa (internationally oriented national body)
♦ IHSAN – International Hadith Study Association Network (internationally oriented national body)
♦ IHSART – International Health and Safety Association for Radio and Television (no recent information)
♦ IHSC / see International Association for Disabled Sailing (#11849)
♦ **IHSC** International Horse Sports Confederation (#13811)
♦ **IHSG** International Herbage Seed Group (#13791)
♦ IHS Global (internationally oriented national body)
♦ **IHSI** International Horizon Scanning Initiative (#13808)
♦ IHS – Institute for Housing and Urban Development Studies (internationally oriented national body)
♦ **IHS** International Headache Society (#13777)
♦ IHS – International Hibernation Society (inactive)
♦ **IHS** International Hip Society (#13797)
♦ **IHS** International Hormone Society (#13809)
♦ **IHS** International Horn Society (#13810)
♦ IHS / see International Immunocompromised Host Society (#13835)
♦ IHSPRG / see International Herbage Seed Group (#13791)
♦ IHSRC – International Human Science Research Conference (meeting series)
♦ **IHSS** International Humic Substances Society (#13823)
♦ IHTA – International Health and Temperance Association (internationally oriented national body)
♦ IHTMS – International Hypothermia and Temperature Management Symposium (meeting series)
♦ IHTSDO / see SNOMED International (#19330)
♦ i-HTS / see international HealthTechScan (#13784)
♦ **i-HTS** international HealthTechScan (#13784)
♦ **IHU** Internationale Hunde-Union (#20370)
♦ IHV – Internationaler Hotelbesitzer-Verein (inactive)
♦ **IHWG** International Histocompatibility Working Group (#13798)
♦ **IHWO** International House World Organization (#13814)
♦ IHZ Zorg in the Buitenland (internationally oriented national body)
♦ IIAA / see Center for Latin American Studies, Gainesville
♦ IIAAC – International Independent Authors and Artists Consortium (unconfirmed)
♦ IIAA – International Institute of Applied Aesthetics (internationally oriented national body)
♦ IIAEM – International Institute for Adult Education Methods (no recent information)
♦ IIAG – Institut international d'agriculture (inactive)
♦ IIA – Ibaraki International Association (internationally oriented national body)
♦ **IIA** Institute of Internal Auditors (#11272)
♦ **IIA** Institut international des assurances, Yaoundé (#11309)
♦ **iiA** International Irradiation Association (#13954)
♦ IIAL – International Institute of Arts and Letters (inactive)
♦ **IIAPC** International and Interdisciplinary Association on the Pharmaceutical Life Cycle (#02707)
♦ IIAP – Insurance Institute for Asia and the Pacific (internationally oriented national body)
♦ IIAPS – International Institute for Advanced Purchasing and Supply (internationally oriented national body)
♦ IIAR – International Institute of Ammonia Refrigeration (internationally oriented national body)
♦ IIAR – International Institute of Anticancer Research (internationally oriented national body)
♦ **IIASA** Internationales Institut für Angewandte Systemanalyse (#13861)
♦ **IIASA** International Institute for Applied Systems Analysis (#13861)
♦ **IIAS** International Institute of Administrative Sciences (#13859)
♦ IIAS – International Institute for Advanced Studies in Systems Research and Cybernetics (internationally oriented national body)
♦ **IIAS** International Institute for Archival Science of Trieste and Maribor (#13862)
♦ IIAS – International Institute for Asian Studies, Leiden (internationally oriented national body)
♦ **IIAV** International Institute of Acoustics and Vibration (#13858)
♦ **IIBA** International Institute for Bioenergetic Analysis (#13863)
♦ **IIBA** International Institute of Business Analysis (#13864)
♦ **IIBC** International Indoor Bowls Council (#13839)
♦ IIBH – Institute of International Harmonization for Building and Housing (internationally oriented national body)
♦ IIB – Institut international des brevets (inactive)
♦ IIB – International Conference on Intergranular and Interphase Boundaries (meeting series)
♦ IIB – International Institute of Business (internationally oriented national body)
♦ **IIB** International Investment Bank (#13951)
♦ IIBLP – Institute of International Banking Law and Practice (internationally oriented national body)
♦ IIBT – International Institute of Business Technologies (internationally oriented national body)
♦ IICAB – Institute for International Cooperation in Animal Biologics (internationally oriented national body)
♦ **IICA** Institut interaméricain de coopération pour l'agriculture (#11434)
♦ **IICA** Instituto Interamericano de Cooperação para a Agricultura (#11434)
♦ **IICA** Instituto Interamericano de Cooperación para la Agricultura (#11434)
♦ IICA / see Inter-American Institute for Cooperation on Agriculture (#11434)
♦ **IICA** Inter-American Institute for Cooperation on Agriculture (#11434)
♦ IICA – International Ice Cream Association (internationally oriented national body)
♦ **IICAS** International Institute for Central Asian Studies (#13868)
♦ **IICBA** UNESCO – International Institute for Capacity Building in Africa (#20308)
♦ IICBEE – International Institute of Chemical, Biological and Environmental Engineering (unconfirmed)
♦ IICCB – Informal International Conference of Christian Broadcasting (inactive)
♦ **IICC** International Infection Control Council (#13842)
♦ IICC – International Institute for Commercial Competition (inactive)
♦ IICD / see One World Center
♦ IICDM – International Institute of Creative Design and Media (unconfirmed)
♦ IICE – International Institute of Concurrent Engineering (internationally oriented national body)
♦ IICHG / see Institute on the Holocaust and Genocide (#11268)
♦ IICIF / see Institute for International Criminal Investigations (#11274)
♦ **IICI** Institute for International Criminal Investigations (#11274)
♦ IICI – Institut international de coopération intellectuelle (inactive)
♦ IIC – India International Centre (internationally oriented national body)
♦ IIC / see Industry IoT Consortium (#11182)
♦ **IIC** Industry IoT Consortium (#11182)
♦ **IIC** Instituto Internacional de Custos (#12977)
♦ IIC – Intellectbase International Consortium (internationally oriented national body)
♦ **IIC** Inter-American Investment Corporation (#11438)
♦ **IIC** International Institute of Communications (#13870)
♦ **IIC** International Institute for Conservation of Historic and Artistic Works (#13871)
♦ IIC – International Institute for Cotton (inactive)
♦ IIC – International Interfaith Centre, Oxford (internationally oriented national body)
♦ IIC – International Investment Centre (internationally oriented national body)
♦ **IICL** Institute of International Container Lessors (#11273)
♦ IICLO – International Institute for Children's Literature, Osaka (internationally oriented national body)
♦ IICM / see Connected International Meeting Professionals Association
♦ **IICO** International Infertility Counseling Organization (#13843)
♦ **IICO** International Islamic Charitable Organization (#13957)
♦ **IICPSR** International Islamic Centre for Population Studies and Research (#13956)
♦ IICRD – International Institute for Child Rights and Development (internationally oriented national body)
♦ IICS / see Global Scholars
♦ IICT – Instituto de Investigação Cientifica Tropical (internationally oriented national body)
♦ **IICWG** International Ice Charting Working Group (#13830)
♦ IICY – International Independent Christian Youth (no recent information)
♦ IIDACC – International Institute for Dialogue among Cultures and Civilizations (internationally oriented national body)
♦ IIDAC – International Institute for the Development of the Citizenship (internationally oriented national body)
♦ **IIDA** Institut interaméricain de droit d'auteur (#11421)
♦ **IIDA** Instituto Interamericano de Derecho de Autor (#11421)
♦ **IIDA** Instituto Interamericano de Direito de Autor (#11421)
♦ **IIDA** International Interior Design Association (#13946)
♦ IIDARA – Instituto Iberoamericano de Derecho y Reforma Agraria (no recent information)
♦ **IIDD** Institut international du développement durable (#13930)
♦ **IIDEA** International Institute for Developing Engineering Academics (#13873)
♦ IIDET – International Institute of Dental Ergonomics and Technology (inactive)
♦ **IIDH** Institut international de droit humanitaire (#13885)
♦ **IIDH** Institut international des droits de l'homme – Fondation René Cassin (#13887)
♦ **IIDH** Instituto Interamericano de Derechos Humanos (#11334)
♦ IIDH – International Institute for Digital Humanities (internationally oriented national body)
♦ IIDH / see International Institute of Human Rights – Fondation René Cassin (#13887)
♦ **IIDI** Inter-American Institute on Disability and Inclusive Development (#11435)
♦ IID – Institut international de la démocratie (inactive)
♦ IID / see Inter-American Institute on Disability and Inclusive Development (#11435)
♦ IIDLC / see International Academy of Linguistic Law (#11556)
♦ IIDMA – Instituto Internacional de Derecho y Medio Ambiente (internationally oriented national body)
♦ IIDM – Instituto Iberoamericano de Derecho Maritimo (internationally oriented national body)
♦ IIDS – Institute for Integrated Development Studies (internationally oriented national body)
♦ **IIDU** Istituto Internazionale di Diritto Umanitario (#13885)
♦ IIE / see Peterson Institute for International Economics, Washington
♦ **IIEAC** Institut International d'Etudes d'Asie Centrale (#13868)
♦ IIEA – Institute of International European Affairs, Dublin (internationally oriented national body)
♦ IIEA – Instituto Internacional de Estudios Avanzados, Caracas (internationally oriented national body)
♦ IIEA – International Institute for Ecological Agriculture (internationally oriented national body)
♦ **IIEB** Institut international d'études bancaires (#12313)
♦ IIEB – Instituut voor Internationaal en Europees Beleid (internationally oriented national body)
♦ IIEC-Europe – International Institute for Energy Conservation – Europe (see: #13875)
♦ **IIEC** International Institute for Energy Conservation (#13875)
♦ IIED-AL / see IIED América-Latina (#11114)

♦ IIED América-Latina 11114

Contact CP1429, Ramallo 1975, 1D CABA, Buenos Aires, Argentina. T. +54959118008. Fax +541147012805. E-mail: iied-al@iied-al.org.ar.
URL: http://www.iied-al.org.ar/

History 2 May 1988, Buenos Aires (Argentina), as *International Institute for Environment and Development – Latin America – Instituto Internacional de Medio Ambiente y Desarrollo – América Latina (IIED-AL)*, to continue the work programme initiated in 1979 when a regional office of *International Institute for Environment and Development (IIED, #13877)* was formed in Buenos Aires. **Aims** Contribute to the development of more just, participative, *democratic* and *sustainable* societies; carry out studies and research on critical *environmental* and *development* issues such as land tenure, access to infrastructure, housing, rights to the city, disaster risk reduction, *climate change*, resilience and urban transformation; further networking among interested NGOs. **Structure** Executive Committee; Executive Director. **Languages** English, Spanish. **Finance** Source: international funding agencies and national organizations. **Activities** Research/documentation; guidance/assistance/consulting; knowledge management/information dissemination. **Publications** *Medio Ambiente y Urbanización* (2 a year). Annual Report; books. [2018.11.27/XE5903/j/E]

♦ **IIED Europe** International Institute for Environment and Development – Europe (#13878)
♦ IIEDH – Institut international d'études des droits de l'homme, Trieste (internationally oriented national body)
♦ **IIED** International Institute for Environment and Development (#13877)
♦ IIEES – International Institute of Earthquake Engineering and Seismology (internationally oriented national body)
♦ IIE / see Institute of Industrial and Systems Engineers (#11270)
♦ IIE – Institute of International Education (internationally oriented national body)
♦ IIE – Institute of International Exchange (internationally oriented national body)
♦ **IIE** Institut international d'espéranto (#13302)
♦ IIE – International Institute of Embryology (inactive)
♦ IIE / see International Society of Developmental Biologists (#15052)
♦ **IIEL-FOPREL** Instituto Internacional de Estudios Legislativos del FOPREL (#11338)
♦ **IIEL** Institut international d'études ligures (#11311)
♦ **IIEL** Instituto Internacional de Estudios Laborales (#13897)
♦ **IIEMCA** International Institute for Ethnomethodology and Conversation Analysis (#13879)
♦ IIEO – International Islamic Economic Organization (inactive)
♦ IIEP – International Information and Ecology Parliament (internationally oriented national body)
♦ **IIEP** International Institute for Educational Planning (#13874)
♦ IIEPS – Institute for International Economic and Political Studies, Moscow (internationally oriented national body)
♦ IIES – Institute for International Economic Studies (internationally oriented national body)
♦ **IIES** Institut international d'études sociales (#13897)
♦ **IIES** International Institute for Environmental Studies (#13876)
♦ IIFA – International Institute of Films on Art (inactive)
♦ **IIFA** International Investment Funds Association (#13952)
♦ **IIFA** International Islamic Fiqh Academy (#13960)
♦ **IIFB** International Indigenous Forum on Biodiversity (#13837)
♦ **IIFC** International Institute for FRP in Construction (#13882)
♦ IIFE / see International Federation Icestocksport (#13455)
♦ IIFE – International Institute for Franchise Education (internationally oriented national body)
♦ IIFES / see International Board of Forensic Engineering Sciences
♦ **IIFET** International Institute of Fisheries Economics & Trade (#13880)
♦ **IIF** Institute of International Finance (#11275)
♦ **IIF** Institut international du froid (#13918)
♦ **IIF** Internationales Institut für den Frieden (#13907)
♦ IIF – International Iguana Foundation (internationally oriented national body)
♦ IIF – International Immigrants Foundation (internationally oriented national body)
♦ **IIF** International Institute of Forecasters (#13881)
♦ **IIF** International Insulin Foundation (#13937)
♦ **IIFM** International Islamic Financial Market (#13959)
♦ **IIFP** Institut international de finances publiques (#13915)
♦ IIFSO – International Islamic Federation of Student Organizations (inactive)
♦ IIFWP / see Universal Peace Federation (#20681)
♦ **IIGA** International Island Games Association (#13962)
♦ **IIgANN** International IgA Nephropathy Network (#13833)
♦ IIGBM – Institut international de génie biomédical (inactive)
♦ **IIGCC** Institutional Investors Group on Climate Change (#11317)
♦ IIG – Instituto Internacional de Gobernabilidad (internationally oriented national body)
♦ IIGL – International Institute for Global Leadership (internationally oriented national body)
♦ IIGRS – International Indology Graduate Research Symposium (meeting series)
♦ IIH / see Instituto Iberoamericano de la Haya
♦ IIHA – Institute of International Humanitarian Affairs (internationally oriented national body)
♦ IIHA – International Institute of the Hylean Amazon (inactive)
♦ **IIHA** International Intelligence History Association (#13942)
♦ IIHCP – International Institute for Health Care Professionals (internationally oriented national body)
♦ IIHD / see Institute for Global Health and Development, Edinburgh
♦ **IIHF** International Ice Hockey Federation (#13831)
♦ IIH – Instituto Iberoamericano de la Haya (internationally oriented national body)
♦ **IIH** International Institute for Hermeneutics (#13884)
♦ **IIHL** International Institute of Humanitarian Law (#13885)
♦ **IIHN** Institut international d'histoire du notariat (#11312)
♦ IIHR / see International Institute of Human Rights – Fondation René Cassin (#13887)
♦ **IIHR** International Institute of Human Rights – Fondation René Cassin (#13887)
♦ IIHRS – International Institute for Human Rights Studies, Trieste (internationally oriented national body)
♦ **III-CAB** Instituto Internacional de Integración del Convenio Andrés Bello (#13940)
♦ **IIIC** International Intra-Ocular Implant Club (#13948)
♦ IIID / see Dialogue Institute
♦ IIID – International Institute for Information Design (internationally oriented national body)
♦ IIIEE – International Institute for Industrial Environmental Economics (internationally oriented national body)
♦ **IIIE** International Institute of Inspiration Economy (#13892)
♦ IIIE – International Institute of Islamic Economics (internationally oriented national body)
♦ **III GLOBAL** International Insolvency Institute (#13857)
♦ IIIHS – International Institute of Integral Human Sciences (internationally oriented national body)
♦ III – International Isocyanate Institute, New York (internationally oriented national body)
♦ **II** Ikebana International (#11115)
♦ III Millennio Foundation (internationally oriented national body)
♦ IIIM – International Institute of Islamic Medicine (internationally oriented national body)
♦ **iIIRG** International Investigative Interviewing Research Group (#13950)
♦ **IIIRR** International Institute for Infrastructure Resilience and Reconstruction (#13890)
♦ IIIS – Institute for International Integration Studies (internationally oriented national body)
♦ IIIS – Institut international de l'image et du son (internationally oriented national body)
♦ **IIIS** International Institute of Informatics and Systemics (#13889)
♦ IIITEC – International Institute of Innovation and Technology (unconfirmed)
♦ **IIIT** International Institute of Islamic Thought (#13894)
♦ IIJC – International Institute of Journalism and Communication (internationally oriented national body)
♦ **IIJE** International Institute for Justice Excellence (#13895)
♦ **IIJ** International Institute for Justice and the Rule of Law (#13896)
♦ **IIJM** Istituto Internazionale Jacques Maritain (#13967)
♦ IIK / see Institut für Lateinamerika-Studies
♦ **IILACE** International Institute of Law Association Chief Executives (#13898)
♦ **IILA** Instituto Italo-Latinoamericano (#16071)
♦ IILG – International Internet Leathercrafter's Guild (internationally oriented national body)
♦ **IIL** ICHCA International Limited (#11053)
♦ **IILI** Instituto Internacional de Literatura Iberoamericana (#13888)
♦ IILJ – Institute for International Law and Justice (internationally oriented national body)
♦ IILL / see Kyiv International University
♦ **IILP** Instituto Internacional de Lingua Portuguesa (#11339)
♦ IILS – Institute of International Legal Studies, Quezon City (internationally oriented national body)
♦ **IILS** International Institute for Labour Studies (#13897)
♦ IILSR – International Institute of Labour and Social Relations (internationally oriented national body)
♦ IIM / see European University, Belgrade
♦ IIM-Africa – Institute of Information Management (internationally oriented national body)
♦ **IIMA** International Iron Metallics Association (#13953)
♦ IIMA – Istituto Internazionale Maria Ausiliatrice delle Salesiane di Don Bosco (internationally oriented national body)
♦ IIMCB – International Institute of Molecular and Cell Biology, Warsaw (internationally oriented national body)
♦ IIMC – Instituto Interamericano de Mercados de Capital (inactive)
♦ IIMC – International Institute of Municipal Clerks (internationally oriented national body)
♦ IIMCR – Institute for International Mediation and Conflict Resolution (internationally oriented national body)
♦ **IIMDP** International Institute of Monitoring Democracy Development, Parliamentarianism and Suffrage Protection for the Citizens of the IPA CIS Member Nations (#13902)
♦ IIME – Institute for International Medical Education (internationally oriented national body)
♦ IIMEPSA – Islamic and Interfaith Middle Eastern Peace Studies Association (internationally oriented national body)
♦ **IIMHL** International Initiative for Mental Health Leadership (#13852)
♦ IIMI / see International Water Management Institute (#15867)
♦ IIM / see Institut international de la marionnette (#11314)
♦ **IIM** Institut international de la marionnette (#11314)
♦ IIM LINK – International Institute of Management LINK (internationally oriented national body)
♦ **IIMSAM** Intergovernment Institution for the use of Micro-Algae Spirulina against Malnutrition (#11504)
♦ **IIMS** International Institute of Marine Surveyors (#13900)
♦ IIMT – International Institute of Management in Technology (internationally oriented national body)
♦ **IIMV** Instituto Iberoamericano de Mercados de Valores (#11333)
♦ **IINAS** Internationales Institut für Nachhaltigkeitsanalysen und -strategien (#13929)
♦ IINA / see Union of OIC News AGencies (#20467)
♦ **IINCE** International Institute of Noise Control Engineering (#13903)
♦ **IIN** Instituto Interamericano del Niño, la Niña y Adolescentes (#11406)
♦ **IINS** International Institute for Non-Aligned Studies (#13904)
♦ IInternational Conference on Inertial Fusion Sciences and Applications (meeting series)
♦ **IIOA** International Input-Output Association (#13856)
♦ **IIOC** Independent International Organization for Certification (#11149)
♦ IIO – International Islamic Organization (no recent information)
♦ **IIOM** International Institute of Obsolescence Management (#13905)
♦ **IION** International Interfaith Organizations Network (#13945)
♦ IIPAC – International IP ADR Center (unconfirmed)
♦ IIPA – International Intellectual Property Alliance (internationally oriented national body)
♦ IIPCC – International IP Commercialization Council (unconfirmed)
♦ IIPC – International Institute for Popular Culture (internationally oriented national body)
♦ **IIPC** International Institute of Projectiology and Conscientiology (#13912)
♦ IIPC – International Interfaith Peace Corps (internationally oriented national body)
♦ **IIPC** International Internet Preservation Consortium (#13947)
♦ IIPDEP – Indian Institute for Peace, Disarmament and Environmental Protection (internationally oriented national body)
♦ **IIPDS** International Institute of Peace and Development Studies (#13908)
♦ IIPE – Institute of International Politics and Economics, Belgrade (internationally oriented national body)
♦ **IIPE** Institut international de planification de l'éducation (#13874)
♦ **IIPE** Instituto Internacional de Planeamiento de la Educación (#13874)
♦ IIPE – International Institute on Peace Education (internationally oriented national body)
♦ **IIPE** International Institute for Public Ethics (#13914)
♦ **IIPF** International Institute of Public Finance (#13915)
♦ IIPI – International Intellectual Property Institute (internationally oriented national body)
♦ **IIP** Institut international de philosophie (#13910)
♦ IIP – Institut international de photographie (inactive)
♦ **IIP** Institut international de la presse (#14636)
♦ **IIP** International Ice Patrol (#13832)
♦ IIP – International Initiative for Peace (internationally oriented national body)
♦ IIP – International Institute for Peace (internationally oriented national body)
♦ **IIP** International Institute for Peace (#13907)
♦ **IIP** International Institute of Philosophy (#13910)
♦ IIP / see International Institute of Projectiology and Conscientiology (#13912)
♦ IIP – International Intervisitation Programme (meeting series)
♦ **IIPLA** International Intellectual Property Law Association (#13941)
♦ **IIPPE** International Initiative for Promoting Political Economy (#13853)
♦ **IIPP** Institut international de promotion et de prestige (#11315)
♦ **IIPSGP** International Institute of Peace Studies and Global Philosophy (#13909)
♦ IIPS – Institute for International Policy Studies, Tokyo (internationally oriented national body)
♦ IIPS – International Institute of Peace Studies (internationally oriented national body)
♦ IIPS – International Institute of Political Sciences (internationally oriented national body)
♦ IIPS / see International Institute for Population Sciences (#13911)
♦ **IIPS** International Institute for Population Sciences (#13911)
♦ IIPT – International Institute for Peace through Tourism (internationally oriented national body)
♦ IIPU / see Parliamentary Union of the OIC Member States (#18220)
♦ **IIQM** International Institute for Qualitative Methodology (#13916)
♦ IIR / see Diplomatic Academy of Vietnam
♦ IIRA / see International Labour and Employment Relations Association (#13997)
♦ **IIRA** Islamic International Rating Agency (#16046)
♦ IIRAP / see Burkle Center for International Relations
♦ IIRB / see International Institute of Sugar Beet Research (#13928)
♦ **IIRB** International Institute of Sugar Beet Research (#13928)
♦ **IIRCA** Institut international de l'UNESCO pour le renforcement des capacités en Afrique (#20308)
♦ IIRE – International Institute for Research and Education (internationally oriented national body)
♦ IIRF – Institut internationale de recherche et de formation, Amsterdam (internationally oriented national body)
♦ **IIRF** Institut islamique de recherches et de formation (#16050)
♦ **IIRF** International Institute for Religious Freedom (#13919)
♦ IIRF – International Investor Relations Federation (inactive)
♦ IIRI – Ilmin International Relations Institute (internationally oriented national body)
♦ IIR – Institute of International Relations, Prague (internationally oriented national body)
♦ IIR – Institute of International Relations, Taipei (internationally oriented national body)

♦ IIR – Institut of International Relations, Athens (internationally oriented national body)
♦ IIR – Institut islamique de recherche (internationally oriented national body)
♦ IIR – International Institute of Reflexology, Walkley (internationally oriented national body)
♦ **IIR** International Institute of Refrigeration (#13918)
♦ **IIRM** International Institute for Race Medicine (#13917)
♦ IIRO – International Islamic Relief Organization (internationally oriented national body)
♦ IIROSA / see International Islamic Relief Organization
♦ IIRPS – Institute of International Relations and Political Sciences, Vilnius (internationally oriented national body)
♦ **IIRR** Institut international de recherche sur le riz (#14754)
♦ **IIRR** International Institute of Rural Reconstruction (#13921)
♦ IIRSA – IIRSA Technical Forum (inactive)
♦ IIRSA Technical Forum (inactive)
♦ **IIRSM** International Institute of Risk and Safety Management (#13920)
♦ IIS / see Freeman Spogli Institute for International Studies
♦ IISA / see International Institute of Concurrent Engineering
♦ **IISA** Institut international des Sciences administratives (#13859)
♦ IISA / see Inter-American Institute for Cooperation on Agriculture (#11434)
♦ **IISART** International Industry Society in Advanced Rehabilitation Technology (#13840)
♦ **iiSBE** International Initiative for a Sustainable Built Environment (#13854)
♦ IISCOR – Institute for International Security and Conflict Resolution (internationally oriented national body)
♦ **IISD** International Institute for Sustainable Development (#13930)
♦ **IISE** Institute of Industrial and Systems Engineers (#11270)
♦ IISE – International Institute of Social Economics (inactive)
♦ IISE – International Institute for Special Education (internationally oriented national body)
♦ **IISES** International Institute of Social and Economic Sciences (#13924)
♦ IISF – International Inbound Services Forum (unconfirmed)
♦ IISG – Internationaal Instituut voor Sociale Geschiedenis (internationally oriented national body)
♦ IISHI – Institut international des sciences humaines intégrales (internationally oriented national body)
♦ **IISHJ** International Institute for Secular Humanistic Judaism (#13923)
♦ IISI – Internationales Institut für Sozio-Informatik (internationally oriented national body)
♦ IIS – Institute of Intelligent Systems (unconfirmed)
♦ IIS – Institute of International Studies, Berkeley CA (internationally oriented national body)
♦ **IIS** Institut international de statistique (#15603)
♦ **IIS** International Institute of Sociology (#13925)
♦ **IIS** International Insurance Society (#13939)
♦ **IIS** International Isotope Society (#13964)
♦ IISI / see World Steel Association (#21829)
♦ **IISJ** Instituto Internacional de Sociologia Juridica de Oñati (#17725)
♦ **IISL** International Institute of Space Law (#13926)
♦ **IISL** Istituto Internazionale di Studi Liguri (#11311)
♦ **IISL** Oñati International Institute for the Sociology of Law (#17725)
♦ IISNC – International Institute for the Study of Nomadic Civilizations (internationally oriented national body)
♦ IISNFP / see Institute for Reproductive Health
♦ IISR – International Institute for the Study of Religions (internationally oriented national body)
♦ **IISRP** International Institute of Synthetic Rubber Producers (#13931)
♦ **IISS** International Image Sensor Society (#13834)
♦ **IISS** International Institute for the Science of Sintering (#13922)
♦ **IISS** International Institute for Strategic Studies (#13927)
♦ IISSM – International Institute of Security and Safety Management (internationally oriented national body)
♦ IIST / see Center for International Economic Collaboration
♦ **IITA** International Institute of Tropical Agriculture (#13933)
♦ **IITC** International Indian Treaty Council (#13836)
♦ IITD – Institute of International Trade and Development (internationally oriented national body)
♦ IITEA / see Fundatia Institutul International de Tehnologie si Economie Apicola
♦ **IITE** UNESCO Institute for Information Technologies in Education (#20304)
♦ **IITF** Internationales Institut für Terminologieforschung (#13932)
♦ IITF – International Institute of Tropical Forestry (internationally oriented national body)
♦ IIT/FM – International Conference on Information Integration Theory and Functional Measurement (meeting series)
♦ IIT – Institute for International Trade (internationally oriented national body)
♦ IIT – Institut interafricain du travail (inactive)
♦ **IIT** Institut International du Théâtre (#15683)
♦ IIT / see Islamic University of Technology (#16055)
♦ IITM – Institut international du théâtre de la Méditerranée (internationally oriented national body)
♦ IITM – International Institute for Traditional Music (inactive)
♦ IITTSS – International Intradiscal and Transforaminal Therapy Society (internationally oriented national body)
♦ IIUE – International Institute for the Urban Environment (internationally oriented national body)
♦ IIUEPS – International Independent University of Environmental and Political Sciences, Moscow (internationally oriented national body)
♦ IIU / see International Islamic University Malaysia (#13961)
♦ **IIUM** International Islamic University Malaysia (#13961)
♦ IIUOP – Internationale Unabhangige Universitat fur Okologie und Politilogie (internationally oriented national body)
♦ **IIV** Institut international de vaccins (#15839)
♦ **IIWC** ICOMOS International Wood Committee (#11085)
♦ **IIWF** International Indigenous Women's Forum (#13838)
♦ IIWGHA – International Indigenous Working Group on HIV and AIDS (unconfirmed)
♦ **IIWG** International Industry Working Group (#13841)
♦ **IIW** International Inner Wheel (#13855)
♦ **IIW** International Institute of Welding (#13935)
♦ IIWP – Institute for Individual and World Peace (internationally oriented national body)
♦ IIWR-MB – Institute for International Women's Rights – Manitoba (internationally oriented national body)
♦ IIYL-AYDC – International Islamic Youth League – African Youth Development Centre (unconfirmed)
♦ IIZAT – Internationales Institut für Zahnärztliche Arbeitswissenschaft und Technologie (inactive)
♦ IJA / see Institute for Jewish Policy Research
♦ IJA Forum – International Justice Analysis Forum (internationally oriented national body)
♦ IJA – International Judicial Academy (internationally oriented national body)
♦ **IJAN** Internationale des jeunes amis de la nature (#15929)
♦ IJAN – International Jewish Anti-Zionist Network (unconfirmed)
♦ IJA World / see International Judicial Academy
♦ IJBBA – International Junior Brangus Breeders Association (internationally oriented national body)
♦ **IJB** Internationale Jugendbibliothek (#15936)
♦ IJCAI / see International Joint Conferences on Artificial Intelligence (#13973)
♦ **IJCAI** International Joint Conferences on Artificial Intelligence (#13973)
♦ IJCAR – International Joint Conference on Automated Reasoning (meeting series)
♦ **IJCIC** International Jewish Committee on Interreligious Consultations (#13970)
♦ IJCIEOM – International Joint Conference on Industrial Engineering and Operations Management (meeting series)
♦ IJC – International Joint Commission (internationally oriented national body)
♦ IJCIR / see International Jewish Committee on Interreligious Consultations (#13970)
♦ IJD – Institut Jacques Delors (internationally oriented national body)
♦ IJES – International Jacques Ellul Society (internationally oriented national body)
♦ **IJF** Internationale Journalisten-Föderation (#13462)
♦ IJF – International Jazz Federation (inactive)
♦ **IJF** International Jendo Federation (#13968)
♦ **IJF** International Judo Federation (#13975)
♦ IJF – International Jukskei Federation (unconfirmed)
♦ IJGD – Internationale Jugendgemeinschaftsdienste (internationally oriented national body)
♦ IJIPA – Institut juridique international pour la protection des animaux (inactive)
♦ IJJO – International Juvenile Justice Observatory (internationally oriented national body)
♦ **IJL** International Association of Jewish Lawyers and Jurists (#11977)
♦ IJM – International Justice Mission (internationally oriented national body)
♦ IJO Asia / see International Jurist Organization (#13979)
♦ **IJOC** International Jumping Officials Club (#13976)
♦ IJO – International Juridical Organization for Environment and Development (no recent information)
♦ **IJO** International Jurist Organization (#13979)
♦ IJO – International Jute Organization (inactive)
♦ IJP / see Center for Justice and Peacebuilding
♦ IJPC-SE / see International Network for Epidemiology in Policy (#14264)
♦ IJP – International Justice Project (internationally oriented national body)
♦ **IJRC** International Jumping Riders Club (#13977)
♦ IJRC – International Justice Resource Center (internationally oriented national body)
♦ **IJRU** International Jump Rope Union (#13978)
♦ IJSBA / see International Jet Sports Boating Association (#13969)
♦ **IJSBA** International Jet Sports Boating Association (#13969)
♦ IJSG – International Jute Study Group (no recent information)
♦ **IJUBOA** International Jack-Up Barge Operators' Association (#13966)
♦ **IJVS** International Jewish Vegetarian and Ecological Society (#13971)
♦ IKAA Europe / see International Korean Adoptee Associations (#13991)
♦ **IKAA** International Korean Adoptee Associations (#13991)
♦ **IKA** International Kiteboarding Class Association (#13987)
♦ **IKA** International Kurash Association (#13993)
♦ **IKAM** Internationale Koordination Anthroposophische Medizin (#12957)
♦ IKAP – Indigenous Knowledge and Peoples Network (inactive)
♦ **IKAR** Internationale Kommission für Alpines Rettungswesen (#12662)
♦ **IKBD** Internationale Komitee Buchenwald-Dora und Kommandos (#12749)
♦ **IKBF** Internationale Krachtbalfederatie (#13251)
♦ IKC / see Bear Information Centre
♦ **IKCC** International Kidney Cancer Coalition (#13983)
♦ IKCEST – International Knowledge Centre for Engineering Sciences and Technology under the Auspices of UNESCO (unconfirmed)
♦ **IKC** International Kinesiology College (#13986)
♦ IKDB – International Kenaf Development Board (unconfirmed)
♦ **IKD** Internationale Kommission der Detektiv-Verbände (#13364)

♦ Ikebana International (II) 11115

Headquarters Misaki Bldg – 5th fl, 3-28-9 Kanda Ogawamachi, Chiyoda-ku, Tokyo, 101-0052 Japan. T. +81332938188. Fax +81332942272. E-mail: ikebana@ikebanahq.org.
URL: http://www.ikebanahq.org/

History 17 Aug 1956, Tokyo (Japan). Founded on the initiative of Ellen Gordon Allen. **Aims** Promote and encourage appreciation of ikebana, the *Japanese art of flower* arrangement, and related arts; use ikebana and love of nature to unite all peoples. **Structure** Regional Groupings (7): (I) Africa; (II) Asia; (III) Australia/ New Zealand; (IV) Europe; (V) Middle East; (VI) North and Central America; (VII) South America. Chapters (1615). **Languages** English. **Staff** 2.50 FTE, paid. **Finance** Sources: grants; members' dues. **Activities** Events/meetings. **Events** *North and Central American Regional Conference* Philadelphia, PA (USA) 2024, *Asian Regional Conference* Hyderabad (India) 2023, *Quinquennial World Convention* Tokyo (Japan) 2022, *Asian Regional Conference* Hyderabad (India) 2020, *North American Regional Conference* Dallas, TX (USA) 2019. **Publications** *I I Activities* (3 a year) – newsletter; *Ikebana International* (3 a year) – magazine; *Sakursa News* (3 a year). **Members** Individuals (about 7,600) in 161 chapters in about 50 countries. Membership countries not specified. [2022/XC5492/**C**]

♦ IKED – International Organisation for Knowledge Economy and Enterprise Development (internationally oriented national body)
♦ **IKEF** Internacia Komerca kaj Ekonomia Fakgrupo (#11522)
♦ **IKEK** Internacia Komunista Esperantista Kolektivo (#12819)
♦ **IKEL** Internacia Komitato por Etnaj Liberecoj (#11523)
♦ IKEWM / see International Committee for Animal Recording (#12746)
♦ IKF / see International Kendo Federation (#13982)
♦ IKFF / see Women's International League for Peace and Freedom (#21024)
♦ **IKF** International Kempo Federation (#13981)
♦ **IKF** International Korfball Federation (#13992)
♦ Ikhwan al-Muslimin (#16915)
♦ Al Ikhwan al Muslimum / see Muslim Brotherhood (#16915)
♦ IKI – Internationale Klimaschutzinitiative (internationally oriented national body)
♦ IKK / see Kneipp Worldwide (#16197)
♦ **IKKP** Internationale Katholische Konferenz des Pfadfindertums (#12453)
♦ IKMAS – Institut Kajian Malaysia dan Antarabangsa (internationally oriented national body)
♦ IKMB – Internationale Katholische Mittelstandsbewegung (inactive)
♦ IKMF – International Krav Maga Federation (unconfirmed)
♦ **IKMG** International Kidney & Monoclonal Gammopathy Research Group (#13984)
♦ IKM – Internationaler Kongress über Anwendungen der Mathematik in den Ingenieurwissenschaften (meeting series)
♦ **iKNOW Politics** International Knowledge Network of Women in Politics (#13989)
♦ IKO – International Kiteboarding Organization (unconfirmed)
♦ **IKO** International Kiwifruit Organization (#13988)
♦ Ikonomikis ke Kinonikis Epitropis / see European Economic and Social Committee (#06963)
♦ Ikonomikis ke Kinonikis Epitropis ton Evropaikon Kinotiton / see European Economic and Social Committee (#06963)
♦ IKOS – Institutt for Kulturstudies og Orientalske Språk (internationally oriented national body)
♦ IKR / see Instytut Studiów Regionalnych i Globalnych
♦ **IKRK** Internationales Komitee vom Roten Kreuz (#12799)
♦ **IKSD** Internationale Kommission zum Schutz der Donau (#12720)
♦ **IKSE** Internationale Kommission zum Schutz der Elbe (#13249)
♦ IKS – Internacia Kultura Servo (internationally oriented national body)
♦ **IKS** Internationale Kommunistische Stroming (#12818)
♦ **IKS** International Kierkegaard Society (#13985)
♦ **IKS** International Kodaly Society (#13990)
♦ **IKSJ** Internationale Katholische Studierende Jugend (#15926)
♦ IKSM / see International Commission of the Meuse (#12702)
♦ **IKSMS** Internationale Kommissionen zum Schutze von Mosel und Saar (#12729)
♦ IKSO / see Internationale Kommission zum Schutz der Oder gegen Verunreinigung (#13250)
♦ **IKSOgV** Internationale Kommission zum Schutz der Oder gegen Verunreinigung (#13250)
♦ **IKSR** Internationale Kommission zum Schutz des Rheins (#12721)

♦ IKT International Association of Curators of Contemporary Art 11116

Internationale Kunstausstellungsleitertagung (IKT)

Acting Gen Sec c/o MOSTYN, 12 Vaughan Street, Llandudno, LL30 1AB, UK. T. +4401492879201. E-mail: mail@iktsite.org.
URL: http://www.iktsite.org/

History 1973. Former names and other names: *International Association of Art-Exhibition-Directors* – former (1978 to 1993). **Aims** Facilitate and stimulate the debate concerning the conception and realization of contemporary art *exhibitions.* **Activities** Events/meetings. **Events** *Annual Conference* Louisville, KY (USA) 2022, *Annual Conference* Osnabrück (Germany) 2021, *Annual Conference* Osnabrück (Germany) 2020, *Annual Conference* Miami, FL (USA) 2019, *Annual Conference* Gdansk (Poland) / Vilnius (Lithuania) 2018. **Members** Membership countries not specified. [2022.05.11/XD9085/**D**]

- ♦ **IKT** Internationale Kunstausstellungsleitertagung (#11116)
- ♦ IKU / see Childhood Education International
- ♦ **IKUE** Internacia Katolika Unuigo Esperantista (#12455)
- ♦ **IKUMA** International Karate Do and Martial Arts Union (#13980)
- ♦ Ikumenikon Patriarhion (#05349)
- ♦ IKUWA – Internationaler Kongreß für Unterwasserarchäologie (meeting series)
- ♦ IKV / see PAX
- ♦ **IKVI** Internationale Komitee der Vierten Internationale (#12771)
- ♦ **IKV** Internationale Kartographische Vereinigung (#12446)
- ♦ IKV – Internationale Kriminalistische Vereinigung (inactive)
- ♦ IKV Pax Christi / see PAX
- ♦ **IKYF** International Kyudo Federation (#13994)
- ♦ IKYTA – International Kundalini Yoga Teachers Association (see: #22046)
- ♦ ILA / see Institute of Latin America of the Russian Academy of Sciences
- ♦ ILAA – International Lawyers in Alcoholics Anonymous (internationally oriented national body)
- ♦ ILAA – International Legal Aid Association (inactive)
- ♦ **ILAB** International League of Antiquarian Booksellers (#14015)
- ♦ ILACIF / see Organization of Latin American and Caribbean Supreme Audit Institutions (#17877)
- ♦ **ILAC** International Laboratory Accreditation Cooperation (#13995)
- ♦ **ILAC** International Legal Assistance Consortium (#14025)
- ♦ ILADC – Ibero-Latin American Academy of Craniomandibular Disorders (internationally oriented national body)
- ♦ **ILADES** Instituto Latinoamericano de Doctrinas y Estudios Sociales (#11345)
- ♦ ILADS – International Lyme and Associated Diseases Society (internationally oriented national body)
- ♦ **ILADT** Instituto Latinoamericano de Derecho Tributario (#11344)
- ♦ **ILAE** International League Against Epilepsy (#14013)
- ♦ ILAFA / see Asociación Latinoamericana del Acero (#02176)
- ♦ ILAFP / see Federación Iberolatinoamericana de Artistas Intérpretes y Ejecutantes (#09325)
- ♦ **ILAG** International Legal Aid Group (#14024)
- ♦ **ILAI** Italian-Latin American Institute (#16071)
- ♦ **ILA** Independent Learning Association (#11150)
- ♦ ILA – Informationsstelle Lateinamerika (internationally oriented national body)
- ♦ ILA – Institute of Latin America of the Russian Academy of Sciences (internationally oriented national body)
- ♦ **ILA** Internacia Laboristo Asocio (#15906)
- ♦ **ILA** International Law Association (#14003)
- ♦ **ILA** International Lead Association (#14009)
- ♦ **ILA** International Leadership Association (#14010)
- ♦ **ILA** International Leprosy Association (#14029)
- ♦ **ILA** International Light Association (#14045)
- ♦ **ILA** International Lime Association (#14049)
- ♦ ILA – International Listening Association (internationally oriented national body)
- ♦ **ILA** International Liszt Association (#14056)
- ♦ **ILA** International Literacy Association (#14057)
- ♦ ILA / see International Lodging Association (#14063)
- ♦ **ILA** International Lodging Association (#14063)
- ♦ ILA – International Longshoremen's Association (internationally oriented national body)
- ♦ **ILA** International Lupin Association (#14068)
- ♦ ILAIS / see Institute of Latin American Studies, New York
- ♦ **ILAMA** International Lifesaving Appliance Manufacturers Association (#14039)
- ♦ ILAM – Instituto Latinoamericano de Museos (internationally oriented national body)
- ♦ ILAM – International Library of African Music (internationally oriented national body)
- ♦ **ILANUD** Instituto Latinoamericano de las Naciones Unidas para la Prevención del Delito y Tratamiento del Delincuente (#11347)
- ♦ ILAR / see Asociación Latinoamericana de Autocuidado Responsable (#02184)
- ♦ **ILAR** Asociación Latinoamericana de Autocuidado Responsable (#02184)
- ♦ **ILAR** International League of Associations for Rheumatology (#14016)
- ♦ ILAS / see Teresa Lozano Long Institute of Latin American Studies, Austin
- ♦ ILASE – Internacia Ligo de Agrikulturaj Specialistoj-Esperantistoj (inactive)
- ♦ ILAS – Institute of Latin American Studies, Bundoora (internationally oriented national body)
- ♦ ILAS – Institute of Latin American Studies, New York (internationally oriented national body)
- ♦ ILAS – Institut für Lateinamerika-Studies (internationally oriented national body)
- ♦ ILAS – Instituto Latinoamericano de Salud Mental y Derechos Humanos (internationally oriented national body)
- ♦ ILAS – Instituto Latino Americano da Sepse (internationally oriented national body)
- ♦ **ILAS** International Linear Algebra Society (#14051)
- ♦ ILASS-Americas – Institute for Liquid Atomization and Spray Systems, North and South America (internationally oriented national body)
- ♦ **ILASS-Asia** Institute for Liquid Atomization and Spray Systems – Asia (#11279)
- ♦ **ILASS-Europe** Institute for Liquid Atomisation and Spray Systems – Europe (#11277)
- ♦ **ILASS International** Institute for Liquid Atomization and Spray Systems (#11278)
- ♦ IL – Association of Fire Testing Laboratories of European Industries (inactive)
- ♦ ILATES – Instituto Latinoamericano de Estudios Sociales 'Humberto Valdez' (inactive)
- ♦ **ILATID** Instituto Latinoamericano de Alta Tecnologia, Informatica y Derecho (#11341)
- ♦ ILBF / see Bodhimitra – International Lay Buddhist Forum (#03298)
- ♦ ILBF – International Law Book Facility (internationally oriented national body)
- ♦ ILC / see International Center for Law in Development
- ♦ ILCAA – Institute for the Study of Languages and Cultures of Asia and Africa (internationally oriented national body)
- ♦ **ILCAC** International Light-Cone Advisory Committee (#14046)
- ♦ ILCA – International Labor Communications Association (internationally oriented national body)
- ♦ ILCA – International Lactation Consultant Association (internationally oriented national body)
- ♦ ILCA – International Lightning Class Association (see: #21760)
- ♦ **ILCA** International Liver Cancer Association (#14060)
- ♦ **ILCE** Instituto Latinoamericano de la Comunicación Educativa (#11343)
- ♦ **ILC Global Alliance** International Longevity Centre Global Alliance (#14064)
- ♦ **ILC** International Catholic-Jewish Liaison Committee (#12458)
- ♦ ILC – International Labelling Centre (inactive)
- ♦ **ILC** International Land Coalition (#13999)
- ♦ **ILC** International Law Commission (#14004)
- ♦ **ILC** International Limousin Council (#14050)
- ♦ **ILC** International Linear Collider (#14052)
- ♦ **ILC** International Lutheran Council (#14069)
- ♦ ILCOP / see International Peace Bureau (#14535)
- ♦ **ILCOR** International Liaison Committee on Resuscitation (#14036)
- ♦ iLCP – International League of Conservation Photographers (internationally oriented national body)
- ♦ **ILCS** International Liquid Crystal Society (#14055)
- ♦ ILCU Foundation – Irish League of Credit Unions International Development Foundation (internationally oriented national body)
- ♦ ILCU International Development Foundation (internationally oriented national body)
- ♦ **ILDA** International Laser Display Association (#14002)
- ♦ ILDAV / see International Doctors – ILDAV (#13186)
- ♦ ILDC – International Legal Defense Counsel (internationally oriented national body)
- ♦ ILD – Internationaler Ländlicher Entwicklungsdienst (internationally oriented national body)
- ♦ **ILDIS** Instituto Latinoamericano de Investigaciones Sociales (#11346)
- ♦ ILDS / see International Committee for Dermatopathology (#12762)
- ♦ **ILDS** International League of Dermatological Societies (#14018)
- ♦ ILEA – International Live Events Association (internationally oriented national body)
- ♦ **ILEAP** International Lawyers and Economists Against Poverty (#14006)
- ♦ ILECI – Institut de l'économie et du commerce international (internationally oriented national body)
- ♦ ILEC / see Instituto Latinoamericano de la Comunicación Educativa (#11343)
- ♦ **ILEC** International Lake Environment Committee Foundation (#13998)
- ♦ ILEI / see ESPERANTO + EDUKADO (#05544)
- ♦ **ILEI** ESPERANTO + EDUKADO (#05544)
- ♦ **ILEP** International Federation of Anti-Leprosy Associations (#13355)
- ♦ **ILERA** Internacia Ligo de Esperantistaj Radio-Amatoroj (#11524)
- ♦ **ILERA** International Labour and Employment Relations Association (#13997)
- ♦ ILERI – Institut d'étude des relations internationales (internationally oriented national body)
- ♦ Iles de paix / see Friends of the Islands of Peace
- ♦ Iles de paix – Amis d'Iles de Paix (internationally oriented national body)
- ♦ ILEX / see International Learning Exchange in Social Education
- ♦ ILEX – International Learning Exchange in Social Education (internationally oriented national body)
- ♦ ILFA – International Lawyers for Africa (internationally oriented national body)
- ♦ **ILFCAAE** International League for Teaching, Education and Popular Culture (#14023)
- ♦ **ILFGA** International Lexical Functional Grammar Association (#14033)
- ♦ ILFI – International Labour Film Institute (inactive)
- ♦ ILFI – International Living Future Institute (internationally oriented national body)
- ♦ ILF – International Legal Forum (internationally oriented national body)
- ♦ **ILF** International Legal Foundation (#14026)
- ♦ **ILF** International Lymphoedema Framework (#14070)
- ♦ ILF / see International Maritime Rescue Federation (#14104)

♦ ILGA Asia 11117

Exec Dir address not obtained. E-mail: info@ilgaasia.org.
URL: https://www.ilgaasia.org/

History 2002, Mumbai (India). A regional structure of *ILGA World (International Lesbian, Gay, Bisexual, Trans and Intersex Association, #11120).* **Aims** Promote universal respect for and observance of human rights and fundamental freedoms; work for the equality of all people regardless of sexual orientation or gender identity / expression and sex characteristic, as well as liberation from all forms of discrimination and stigmatization; empower and support LGBTI communities, organizations and individuals in Asia. **Structure** Regional Conference; Executive Board. **Staff** 5.00 FTE, paid. **Activities** Advocacy/lobbying/activism; capacity building; networking/liaising. **Events** *Conference* Seoul (Korea Rep) 2019.
Members Organizations (over 100) in 38 countries and territories:
Afghanistan, Bahrain, Bangladesh, Bhutan, Brunei Darussalam, Cambodia, China, India, Indonesia, Iran Islamic Rep, Iraq, Israel, Japan, Jordan, Korea DPR, Korea Rep, Kuwait, Laos, Lebanon, Malaysia, Maldives, Mongolia, Myanmar, Nepal, Pakistan, Palestine, Philippines, Qatar, Saudi Arabia, Singapore, Sri Lanka, Syrian AR, Taiwan, Thailand, Timor-Leste, United Arab Emirates, Vietnam, Yemen. [2020/AA1246/**E**]

♦ ILGA-Europe 11118

Exec Dir Rue du Trône 60, 1050 Brussels, Belgium. T. +3226095410. Fax +3226095419. E-mail: info@ilga-europe.org.
URL: http://www.ilga-europe.org/

History 1996. Founded as the European regional branch of *ILGA World (International Lesbian, Gay, Bisexual, Trans and Intersex Association, #11120).* Registration: Banque-Carrefour des Entreprises, No/ID: 0476.617.319, Start date: 10 Aug 2001, Belgium; EU Transparency Register, No/ID: 11977456675-84, Start date: 14 Sep 2011. **Aims** Work towards equality and human rights for *lesbian, gay, bisexual, trans* and *intersex* (*LGBTI*) people. **Structure** Executive Board. **Languages** English. **Staff** 20.00 FTE, paid. **Finance** Sources: donations; private foundations; sponsorship. Supported by: *European Commission (EC, #06633).* **Activities** Europe and Central Asia. **Events** *Conference* Sofia (Bulgaria) 2022, *Gathering Online Meeting* Brussels (Belgium) 2021, *Annual Conference* 2020, *Gathering Online Meeting* Brussels (Belgium) 2020, *Annual Conference* Prague (Czechia) 2019. **Publications** Annual Review; Rainbow Map.
Members Full: organizations (over 700) in 52 countries:
Albania, Andorra, Armenia, Austria, Azerbaijan, Belarus, Belgium, Bosnia-Herzegovina, Bulgaria, Croatia, Cyprus, Czechia, Denmark, Estonia, Finland, France, Georgia, Germany, Greece, Hungary, Iceland, Ireland, Italy, Kazakhstan, Kosovo, Kyrgyzstan, Latvia, Liechtenstein, Lithuania, Luxembourg, Malta, Moldova, Montenegro, Netherlands, North Macedonia, Norway, Poland, Portugal, Romania, Russia, San Marino, Serbia, Slovakia, Slovenia, Spain, Sweden, Switzerland, Tajikistan, Türkiye, UK, Ukraine, Uzbekistan.
Included in the above, 10 organizations listed in this Yearbook:
Association of Nordic and Pol-Balt LGBTQ Student Organizations (ANSO, #02832); Egalité (#05393); European Forum of Lesbian, Gay, Bisexual and Transgender Christian Groups (Forum LGBT, #07318); European LGBT Police Association (EGPA, #07686); Gay Christian Europe (GCE); Global Alliance of Lesbian, Gay, Bisexual and Transgender Education (GALE); International Lesbian, Gay, Bisexual, Transgender, Queer and Intersex Youth and Student Organization (IGLYO, #14032); Network of European LGBTIQ Families Associations (NELFA, #17021); Organisation Intersex International Europe (OII Europe, #17812); TGEU (#20138).
Consultative Status Consultative status granted from: *Council of Europe (CE, #04881)* (Participatory Status). **IGO Relations** Participant in Fundamental Rights Platform of: *European Union Agency for Fundamental Rights (FRA, #08969).* **NGO Relations** Full member of: *Human Rights and Democracy Network (HRDN, #10980).* Member of: *European NGO Platform Asylum and Migration (EPAM, #08051); Social Platform (#19344).* [2022.11.07/XK2033/y/**D**]

- ♦ ILGA / see ILGA World (#11120)
- ♦ **ILGALAC** Asociación Internacional de Lesbianas, Gays, Bisexuales, Trans e Intersex para América Latina y el Caribe (#02166)
- ♦ ILGA Mundo (#11120)
- ♦ ILGA North America & Caribbean (unconfirmed)

♦ ILGA Oceania 11119

Contact address not obtained. E-mail: ilgaoceania@gmail.com.
Contact address not obtained.
URL: https://ilgaoceania.life/

History A regional structure of *ILGA World (International Lesbian, Gay, Bisexual, Trans and Intersex Association, #11120).* **Structure** Board. **Events** *Conference* Nouméa (New Caledonia) 2020. [2020/AA1249/**E**]

- ♦ ILGA World (#11120)

♦ ILGA World (International Lesbian, Gay, Bisexual, Trans and Intersex Association) 11120

ILGA World (Association internationale des lesbiennes, gays, bisexuels, trans et intersexes) – ILGA Mundo (Asociación Internacional de Lesbianas, Gays, Bisexuales, Trans e Intersex) – ILGA World (Associação Internacional de Lésbicas, Gays, Bissexuais, Trans e Intersexo)

Exec Dir Rue Rothschild 20, 1202 Geneva, Switzerland. E-mail: info@ilga.org.
URL: https://ilga.org/

History 1978, Coventry (UK). Founded by regional and national associations. Subsequently changed title, at 8th Annual Conference, Copenhagen (Denmark). Current title adopted Mar 2019, Wellington (New Zealand), at 30th World Conference. Former names and other names: *International Gay Association (IGA)* – former (1978 to 1986); *Association gay internationale* – former (1978 to 1986); *Asociación Gay Internacional* – former (1978 to 1986); *International Lesbian and Gay Association (ILGA)* – former (Jul 1986 to 2019); *Association internationale des gays et des lesbiennes* – former (Jul 1986 to 2019); *Asociación Lesbia y Gay Internacional* – former (Jul 1986 to 2019); *Asociación Internacional de Lesbianas y Gays* – former (Jul 1986 to 2019). Registration: Banque-Carrefour des Entreprises, No/ID: 0896.799.840, Start date: 31 Mar 2008, Belgium; No/ID: CH-660-1-166-015-4, Switzerland. **Aims** Campaign for lesbian, gay, bisexual, trans and intersex *human rights*. **Structure** World Conference; Board; Head Office in Geneva (Switzerland). Regional structures; Regional branches: *Pan Africa ILGA (PAI, #18032)*; *ILGA Asia (#11117)*; *ILGA-Europe (#11118)*; *ILGA North America & Caribbean*; *ILGA Oceania (#11119)*; *Asociación Internacional de Lesbianas, Gays, Bisexuales, Trans e Intersex para América Latina y el Caribe (ILGALAC, #02166)*. Steering Committees (5): Bisexual; Intersex; Trans; Women's; Youth. **Languages** English, Spanish. **Staff** 15.00 FTE, paid. **Finance** Sources: donations; grants; members' dues. **Activities** Advocacy/lobbying/activism; events/meetings; knowledge management/ information dissemination; training/education. **Events** *World Conference* Long Beach, CA (USA) 2022, *World Conference* Los Angeles, CA (USA) 2021, *Asia Regional Conference* Seoul (Korea Rep) 2019, *World Conference* Wellington (New Zealand) 2019, *World Conference* Bangkok (Thailand) 2016. **Publications** *The week in LGBTI news of the world* (weekly) – online. Newsletters; reports; maps; annual global survey on attitudes towards LGBTI people.

Members Full and Associate: mostly non-profit LGBTI associations (1,881). Members in 163 countries and territories:
Åland, Albania, Algeria, Angola, Argentina, Armenia, Australia, Austria, Azerbaijan, Bangladesh, Barbados, Belarus, Belgium, Belize, Benin, Bolivia, Bonaire Is, Bosnia-Herzegovina, Botswana, Brazil, Bulgaria, Burkina Faso, Burundi, Cambodia, Cameroon, Canada, Central African Rep, Chile, China, Colombia, Congo Brazzaville, Congo DR, Cook Is, Costa Rica, Côte d'Ivoire, Croatia, Cuba, Curaçao, Cyprus, Czechia, Denmark, Dominica, Dominican Rep, Ecuador, Egypt, El Salvador, Equatorial Guinea, Estonia, Eswatini, Ethiopia, Fiji, Finland, France, Gambia, Georgia, Germany, Ghana, Greece, Guatemala, Guyana, Haiti, Honduras, Hong Kong, Hungary, Iceland, India, Indonesia, Iran Islamic Rep, Iraq, Ireland, Israel, Italy, Jamaica, Japan, Jersey, Kazakhstan, Kenya, Kiribati, Korea Rep, Kosovo, Kyrgyzstan, Latvia, Lebanon, Liberia, Libya, Lithuania, Luxembourg, Madagascar, Malawi, Malaysia, Maldives, Mali, Malta, Mauritania, Mexico, Moldova, Mongolia, Montenegro, Morocco, Mozambique, Myanmar, Namibia, Nepal, Netherlands, New Caledonia, New Zealand, Nicaragua, Nigeria, Niue, North Macedonia, Norway, Pakistan, Palestine, Panama, Papua New Guinea, Paraguay, Peru, Philippines, Poland, Polynesia Fr, Portugal, Romania, Russia, Rwanda, Saba, Samoa, Samoa USA, Senegal, Serbia, Sierra Leone, Singapore, Slovakia, Slovenia, Somalia, South Africa, Spain, Sri Lanka, St Eustatius, St Lucia, Sudan, Suriname, Sweden, Switzerland, Taiwan, Tajikistan, Tanzania UR, Thailand, Togo, Tonga, Trinidad-Tobago, Tunisia, Türkiye, Uganda, UK, Ukraine, United Arab Emirates, Uruguay, USA, Uzbekistan, Venezuela, Vietnam, Zambia, Zimbabwe.

Consultative Status Consultative status granted from: *ECOSOC (#05331)* (Special). **NGO Relations** Member of (1): *ProtectDefenders.eu (#18546)*. Cooperates with (7): *Amnesty International (AI, #00801)*; COC Netherlands; *Global Action for Trans Equality (GATE, #10169)*; *Human Rights Watch (HRW, #10990)*; *Institute for Human Rights and Business (IHRB)* (Centre for Sports and Human Rights); *International Gay and Lesbian Travel Association (IGLTA)*; *International Service for Human Rights (ISHR, #14841)*. [2023.02.16/XD7249/y/**C**]

♦ ILGTH – International Liaison Group on Tobacco and Health (internationally oriented national body)
♦ Ilhas de Paz / see Friends of the Islands of Peace
♦ Ilhas de Paz – Amigos da Ilhas de Paz (internationally oriented national body)
♦ **ILH** International League of Humanists for Peace and Tolerance (#14019)
♦ **ILHMFLT** International Laboratory of High Magnetic Fields and Low Temperatures (#13996)
♦ ILHM – International Lutheran Hour Ministries (internationally oriented national body)
♦ **ILI – ACLE** International Law Institute – African Centre for Legal Excellence (#14005)
♦ ILIG / see International Library and Information Group (#14037)
♦ ILI – Inter-African Labour Institute (inactive)
♦ ILI / see International Law Institute – African Centre for Legal Excellence (#14005)
♦ ILI – International Law Institute, Washington DC (internationally oriented national body)
♦ **ILI** International Lignin Institute (#14047)
♦ ILI – International Literacy Institute (internationally oriented national body)
♦ **I-LISS** International Library and Information Science Society (#14038)
♦ ILLA – International Language and Law Association (internationally oriented national body)
♦ ILL / see Institute Max von Laue – Paul Langevin (#11283)
♦ **ILL** Institute Max von Laue – Paul Langevin (#11283)
♦ Ill-Kummissjoni Ewropea (#06633)
♦ ILLL – International Lutheran Layman's League (internationally oriented national body)
♦ **ILLS** International Laparoscopic Liver Society (#14001)
♦ Illuminating Engineering Society (internationally oriented national body)
♦ Illuminating Engineering Society of North America / see Illuminating Engineering Society

♦ Illustrious Pontifical Academy of Fine Arts and Letters of the Virtuosi of the Pantheon 11121

Pontificia Insigne Accademia di Belle Arti e Lettere dei Virtuosi al Pantheon

Sec Via Rovigo 4, 00161 Rome RM, Italy.
Pres Via della Conciliazione 5, 00193 Rome RM, Italy. T. +39669882292.
URL: http://www.vatican.va/roman_curia/pontifical_councils/cultr/

History Recognized by Pope Paul III, 15 Oct 1542. Comes within *Administrative Hierarchy of the Roman Catholic Church (#00117)*. **Aims** Promote the study, exercise and improvement of fine arts and letters, with special attention for the literature of Christian inspiration and sacred art in all its expressions; promote spiritual elevation of the artists, in connection with the Pontifical Council of the Culture. **Structure** Academic Council. **Languages** Italian. **Publications** *CineArte on Line* (4 a year) – magazine. *Storia della Compagnia de San Giuseppe de Terra Santa* by Vitaliano Tiberia – in 4 vols. *Il Film Sull'Arte di Soggetto Sacro, Documenti di Ricerca e Studio* – catalogue. [2010.08.23/XM4663/**F**]

♦ ILMA – Instituto Latinoamericano de Mercadeo Agricola (inactive)
♦ ILMC – International Lead Management Center (internationally oriented national body)
♦ ILMG – Israel-Lebanon Monitoring Group (no recent information)
♦ Ilmin International Relations Institute (internationally oriented national body)
♦ ILMR / see IAEA Environment Laboratories (#11004)
♦ **ILNA** International League of Non-Religious and Atheists (#14020)
♦ **ILN** International Lawyers Network (#14007)
♦ ILNSS – International Labour Network of Solidarity and Struggles (unconfirmed)
♦ **ILOA** International Lunar Observatory Association (#14067)
♦ ILO Central American Multidisciplinary Technical Advisory Team (see: #11123)

♦ ILO Global Business and Disability Network (GBDN) 11122

Secretariat Route des Morillons 4, 1211 Geneva, Switzerland. E-mail: businessanddisability@ilo.org.
URL: http://www.businessanddisability.org/

History 2010. **Aims** Create a global workforce culture that is respectful and welcoming of people with disabilities; make sure that employment policies and practices in companies of all types are inclusive of people with disabilities around the world; increase awareness about the positive relationship between disability inclusion and business success. **Structure** Steering Committee; Technical Secretariat hosted by the International Labour Organization (ILO). **Activities** Guidance/assistance/consulting; knowledge management/ information dissemination. **Events** *Business opportunities in Africa: Inclusion of talent with disabilities* 2022, *Global Annual Conference* 2022, *Disability & Digitalisation: Business Opportunities in Asia and the Pacific* Bangkok (Thailand) 2021, *Making the Future of Work Inclusive of Persons with Disabilities* Geneva (Switzerland) 2019. **Publications** *GBDN News*. *Publications and tools*.

Members Companies (36); not-for-profit organizations (8); national business and disability networks (33). Not-for-profit organizations include 5 organizations listed in this Yearbook:
Christian Blind Mission (CBM); *Humanity and Inclusion (HI, #10975)*; *International Disability Alliance (IDA, #13176)*; *Light for the World (#16474)*; *Sightsavers International (#19270)*.

National networks in 34 countries:
Australia, Austria, Bangladesh, Brazil, Chile, China, Costa Rica, Egypt, El Salvador, Ethiopia, France, Germany, India, Indonesia, Kenya, Mauritius, Mexico, New Zealand, Nigeria, Paraguay, Peru, Philippines, Poland, Saudi Arabia, South Africa, Spain, Sri Lanka, Switzerland, Uganda, UK, Uruguay, USA, Vietnam, Zambia.

IGO Relations Affiliated with (1): *ILO (#11123)*. [2022.10.19/XM9004/**E**]

♦ **ILO** Instituto Latino Americano del Ombudsman (#16342)

♦ ILO – International Labour Organization 11123

Organisation internationale du travail (OIT) – Organización Internacional del Trabajo (OIT)

Dir Gen Route des Morillons 4, 1211 Geneva 22, Switzerland. T. +41227996111. Fax +41227988685. E-mail: ilo@ilo.org – communication@ilo.org.
Liaison Office with the UN 220 East 42nd St, Suite 3101, New York NY 10017, USA.
URL: http://www.ilo.org/

History Established 28 Jun 1919, Versailles (France), by Part XIII (Labour) of *Treaty of Peace between the Allied and Associated Powers and Germany (Treaty of Versailles, 1919)*, taking over the activities of *'International Labour Office (BIT)'*, set up in 1901, Basel (Switzerland), as an autonomous body, by *International Association for Labour Legislation, 1889 (inactive)*, formed 9 Sep 1889, Paris (France). The International Labour Office is now the Secretariat of the ILO. Subsequently associated with the *League of Nations (SDN, inactive)*, as an autonomous part of the League. Constitution became operative 11 Apr 1919. In 1944 took over the activities of *International Technical Training Office (inactive)*, created 27 Sep 1931. On 14 Dec 1946, became the first specialized agency associated with the *United Nations (UN, #20515)* as a Specialized Agency within *United Nations System (#20635)* linked to *ECOSOC (#05331)*, under the terms of an agreement which recognized the responsibility of ILO in its own field of competence. The International Labour Conference, held in 1944, Philadelphia PA (USA), adopted a Declaration redefining the aims and purposes. Instruments amending the original Constitution were adopted by the Conference in 1945, 1946, 1953, 1962 and 1972, and came into effect respectively in 1946, 1948, 1954, 1963 and 1975. Last Amendments to the Standing Orders of the International Labour Conference were adopted by the Conference at its 82nd Session, Jun 1995. Directors-General: Albert Thomas, France (1919-1932); Harold Butler, UK (1932-1938); John G Winant, USA (1939-1941); Edward J Phelan, Ireland (1941-1948); David A Morse, USA (1948-1970); Wilfred Jenks, UK (1970-1973); Francis Blanchard, France (1974-1989); Michel Hansenne (1989-1999); Juan Somavia (1999-2011); Guy Ryder (2012-present). Headquarters established at Geneva (Switzerland) in 1920. From 1940 until 1948 ILO activities were directed from a working centre at Montréal QC (Canada). On its 50th anniversary in 1969 it was awarded the Nobel Peace Prize. **Aims** Promote opportunities of decent work for all; promote and realize standards and fundamental principles and rights at work; create greater opportunities for women and men to secure decent employment and income; enhance coverage and effectiveness of social protection for all; strengthen tripartism and social dialogue.

Structure *'International Labour Conference (ILC) – Conférence internationale du travail – Conferencia Internacional del Trabajo'*, composed of national delegations comprising 4 delegates (2 from government, 1 worker and 1 employer), each of which may be accompanied by technical advisers. *'Governing Body'* comprises 56 persons, 28 representing governments, 14 representing workers and 14 representing employers. Countries which are of chief industrial importance hold 10 of the 28 government seats while the remaining 18 are filled by election. *'International Labour Office'* is the secretariat of the Organization and comprises the Director General's Office and 6 departments: Standards and Fundamental Principles; Employment; Social Protection; Social Dialogue; Regions and Technical Cooperation; Support Services. Industrial Committees (8): Building, Civil Engineering and Public Works; Coal Mines; Chemical Industries; Iron and Steel; Metal Trades; Petroleum; Textiles; Inland Transport. Tripartite committees (work on plantations, salaried employees and professional workers). Joint Maritime Commission; Joint Committee on the Public Service; Rural Development Committee. Permanent expert bodies: Committee of Experts on the Application of Conventions and Recommendations; Committee of Social Security Experts; panels of consultants concerned with special problems; *Joint ILO/WHO Committee on Health of Seafarers (no recent information)*; *Global Coalition for Occupation Safety and Health (#10294)*.

Multidisciplinary teams (17):
– *'Africa'*:
– *ILO Decent Work Team for West Africa (DWT/CO, Dakar)*;
– *ILO East Africa Multidisciplinary Advisory Team (ILO/EAMAT)*;
– *ILO North Africa Multidisciplinary Team*;
– *ILO Southern Africa Multidisciplinary Advisory Team (ILO/SAMAT)*;
– *Equipe multidisciplinaire consultative de l'OIT pour l'Afrique sahélienne (BSR-Dakar)*;
– *ILO Central and West Africa Multidisciplinary Advisory Team (OIT/EMACO)*.
– *'America'*:
– *ILO Subregional Office for the Andean Countries (SRO-Lima / OSR-Lima)*;
– *ILO Central American Multidisciplinary Technical Advisory Team (OIT/ETM San José)*;
– *ILO Multidisciplinary Technical Advisory Team, Santiago (OIT/ETM Santiago)*.
– *'Asia'*:
– *ILO East Asia Multidisciplinary Advisory Team (ILO/EASMAT)*;
– *ILO South Asia Multidisciplinary Advisory Team (ILO/SAAT)*;
– *ILO Subregional Office for South-East Asia and the Pacific*.
– *'Europe'*:
– *ILO Decent Work Technical Support Team and Country Office for Central and Eastern Europe (DWT/CO-Budapest)*;
– *Multidisciplinary Team for Eastern Europe and Central Asia (ILO/EECAT)*.
– *'Arab States'*:
– *ILO Arab States Multidisciplinary Advisory Team (ILO/ARMAT)*.

Languages Arabic, Chinese, English, French, German, Russian, Spanish. **Staff** Personnel negotiations through: *Staff Union of the International Training Centre of the ILO (ITCILO Staff Union)*; *Staff Union of the International Labour Office (#19945)*. The *Administrative Tribunal of the International Labour Organization (ILO Tribunal, #00118)* is competent to settle disputes. **Finance** Assessments on Member States. Annual budget: 363,350,000 USD.

Activities Knowledge management/information dissemination; management of treaties and agreements; networking/liaising; research/documentation; standards/guidelines.

Manages the following treaties/agreements:
– *Convention Concerning Accommodation of Crews, 1970 (1970)*;
– *Convention Concerning Accommodation on Board Fishing Vessels (1966)*;
– *Convention Concerning Annual Holidays with Pay, 1936 (1936)*;
– *Convention Concerning Annual Holidays with Pay (1970)*;
– *Convention Concerning Annual Holidays with Pay for Seamen, 1936 (1936)*;
– *Convention Concerning Annual Leave with Pay for Seafarers (1976)*;
– *Convention Concerning Basic Aims and Standards of Social Policy (1962)*;
– *Convention Concerning Benefits in the Case of Employment Injury (1964)*;
– *Convention Concerning Compulsory Invalidity Insurance for Persons Employed in Agricultural Undertakings (1933)*;
– *Convention Concerning Compulsory Invalidity Insurance for Persons Employed in Industrial or Commercial Undertakings, in the Liberal Professions, and for Outworkers and Domestic Servants (1933)*;
– *Convention Concerning Compulsory Old-age Insurance for Persons Employed in Agricultural Undertakings (1933)*;
– *Convention Concerning Compulsory Old-age Insurance for Persons Employed in Industrial or Commercial Undertakings, in the Liberal Professions, and for Outworkers and Domestic Servants (1933)*;
– *Convention Concerning Compulsory Widows' and Orphans' Insurance for Persons Employed in Agricultural Undertakings (1933)*;
– *Convention Concerning Compulsory Widows' and Orphans' Insurance for Persons Employed in Industrial or Commercial Undertakings, in the Liberal Professions and for Outworkers and Domestic Servants (1933)*;
– *Convention Concerning Conditions of Employment of Plantation Workers (1958)*;
– *Convention Concerning Continuity of Employment of Seafarers (1976)*;
– *Convention Concerning Crew Accommodation on Board Ship, 1946 (1946)*;
– *Convention Concerning Crew Accommodation on Board Ship, 1949 (1949)*;
– *Convention Concerning Discrimination in Respect of Employment and Occupation (1958)*;
– *Convention Concerning Employment and Conditions of Work and Life of Nursing Personnel (1977)*;
– *Convention Concerning Employment of Women During the Night, 1919 (1919)*;
– *Convention Concerning Employment of Women During the Night, 1934 (1934)*;
– *Convention Concerning Employment Policy (1964)*;
– *Convention Concerning Employment Promotion and Protection Against Unemployment (1988)*;
– *Convention Concerning Equality of Treatment for National and Foreign Workers as Regards Workmen's Compensation for Accidents (1925)*;
– *Convention Concerning Equality of Treatment of Nationals and Non-nationals in Social Security (1962)*;

- Convention Concerning Equal Opportunities and Equal Treatment for Men and Women Workers: Workers with Family Responsibilities (1981);
- Convention Concerning Equal Remuneration for Men and Women Workers for Work of Equal Value (1951);
- Convention Concerning Fee-charging Employment Agencies, 1933 (1933);
- Convention Concerning Fee-charging Employment Agencies, 1949 (1949);
- Convention Concerning Fishermen's Articles of Agreement (1959);
- Convention Concerning Fishermen's Certificates of Competency (1966);
- Convention Concerning Food and Catering for Crews on Board Ship (1946);
- Convention Concerning Forced or Compulsory Labour (1930);
- Convention Concerning Freedom of Association and Protection of the Right to Organize (1948);
- Convention Concerning Health Protection and Medical Care for Seafarer (1987);
- Convention Concerning Holidays with Pay in Agriculture (1952);
- Convention Concerning Home Work (1996);
- Convention Concerning Hours of Work and Rest Periods in Road Transport (1979);
- Convention Concerning Hours of Work on Board Ship and Manning (1936);
- Convention Concerning Hygiene in Commerce and Offices (1964);
- Convention Concerning Indigenous and Tribal Peoples in Independent Countries (1989);
- Convention Concerning Invalidity, Old-age and Survivors' Benefits (1967);
- Convention Concerning Labour Administration: Role, Functions and Organization (1978);
- Convention Concerning Labour Clauses in Public Contracts (1949);
- Convention Concerning Labour Inspection in Agriculture (1969);
- Convention Concerning Labour Inspection in Industry and Commerce (1947);
- Convention Concerning Labour Inspectorates in Non-metropolitan Territories (1947);
- Convention Concerning Labour Standards in Non-metropolitan Territories (1947);
- Convention Concerning Labour Statistics (1985);
- Convention Concerning Maternity Protection (1952);
- Convention Concerning Medical Care and Sickness Benefits (1969);
- Convention Concerning Medical Examination for Fitness for Employment in Industry of Children and Young Persons (1946);
- Convention Concerning Medical Examination of Children and Young Persons for Fitness for Employment in Non-industrial Occupations (1946);
- Convention Concerning Medical Examination of Young Persons for Fitness for Employment Underground in Mines (1965);
- Convention Concerning Migration for Employment (1949);
- Convention Concerning Migrations in Abusive Conditions and the Promotion of Equality of Opportunity and Treatment of Migrant Workers (1975);
- Convention Concerning Minimum Age for Admission to Employment (1973);
- Convention Concerning Minimum Standards in Merchant Ships (1976);
- Convention Concerning Minimum Standards of Social Security (1952);
- Convention Concerning Minimum Wage Fixing Machinery in Agriculture (1951);
- Convention Concerning Minimum Wage Fixing, with Special Reference to Developing Countries (1970);
- Convention Concerning Night Work (1990);
- Convention Concerning Night Work in Bakeries (1925);
- Convention Concerning Night Work of Women Employed in Industry (1948);
- Convention Concerning Occupational Health Services (1985);
- Convention Concerning Occupational Safety and Health and the Working Environment (1981);
- Convention Concerning Occupational Safety and Health in Dock Work (1979);
- Convention Concerning Organizations of Rural Workers and Their Role in Economic and Social Development (1975);
- Convention Concerning Paid Educational Leave (1974);
- Convention Concerning Part-time Work (1994);
- Convention Concerning Penal Sanctions for Breaches of Contracts of Employment by Indigenous Workers (1939);
- Convention Concerning Prevention and Control of Occupational Hazards Caused by Carcinogenic Substances and Agents (1974);
- Convention Concerning Private Employment Agencies (1997);
- Convention Concerning Protection Against Hazards of Poisoning Arising from Benzene (1971);
- Convention Concerning Protection and Facilities to be Afforded to Workers' Representatives in the Undertaking (1971);
- Convention Concerning Protection of the Rights to Organize and Procedures for Determining Conditions of Employment in the Public Service (1978);
- Convention Concerning Safety and Health in Construction (1988);
- Convention Concerning Safety and Health in Mines (1995);
- Convention Concerning Safety in the Use of Asbestos (1986);
- Convention Concerning Safety in the Use of Chemicals at Work (1990);
- Convention Concerning Safety Provisions in the Building Industry (1937);
- Convention Concerning Seafarers' Hours of Work and the Manning of Ships (1996);
- Convention Concerning Seafarers' National Identity Documents (1958);
- Convention Concerning Seafarers' Pensions (1946);
- Convention Concerning Seafarers' Welfare at Sea and in Port (1987);
- Convention Concerning Seamen's Articles of Agreement (1926);
- Convention Concerning Sickness Insurance for Agricultural Workers (1927);
- Convention Concerning Sickness Insurance for Seamen (1936);
- Convention Concerning Sickness Insurance for Workers in Industry and Commerce and Domestic Servants (1927);
- Convention Concerning Social Policy in Non-metropolitan Territories (1947);
- Convention Concerning Social Security for Seafarers, 1946 (1946);
- Convention Concerning Social Security for Seafarers, 1987 (1987);
- Convention Concerning Statistics of Wages and Hours of Work in the Principal Mining and Manufacturing Industries, Including Building and Construction, and in Agriculture (1938);
- Convention Concerning Termination of Employment at the Initiative of the Employer (1982);
- Convention Concerning the Abolition of Forced Labour (1957);
- Convention Concerning the Abolition of Penal Sanctions for Breaches of Contract of Employment by Indigenous Workers (1955);
- Convention Concerning the Age for Admission of Children to Employment in Agriculture (1921);
- Convention Concerning the Age for Admission of Children to Non-industrial Employment, 1932 (1932);
- Convention Concerning the Age for Admission of Children to Non-industrial Employment, 1937 (1937);
- Convention Concerning the Application of the Principles of the Right to Organize and to Bargain Collectively (1949);
- Convention Concerning the Application of the Weekly Rest in Industrial Undertakings (1921);
- Convention Concerning the Certification of Able Seamen (1946);
- Convention Concerning the Certification of Ships' Cooks (1946);
- Convention Concerning the Compulsory Medical Examination of Children and Young Persons Employed at Sea (1921);
- Convention Concerning the Creation of Minimum Wage-fixing Machinery (1928);
- Convention Concerning the Employment of Women before and After Childbirth (1919);
- Convention Concerning the Employment of Women on Underground Work in Mines of all Kinds (1935);
- Convention Concerning the Establishment of an International Scheme for the Maintenance of Rights under Invalidity, Old-age and Widows' and Orphans' Insurance (1936);
- Convention Concerning the Establishment of an International System for the Maintenance of Rights in Social Security (1982);
- Convention Concerning the Guarding of Machinery (1963);
- Convention Concerning the Inspection of Seafarers' Working and Living Conditions (1996);
- Convention Concerning the Liability of the Shipowner in Case of Sickness, Injury or Death of Seamen (1936);
- Convention Concerning the Marking of the Weight on Heavy Packages Transported by Vessels (1929);
- Convention Concerning the Maximum Length of Contracts of Employment of Indigenous Workers (1947);
- Convention Concerning the Maximum Permissible Weight to be Carried by One Worker (1967);
- Convention Concerning the Medical Examination of Fishermen (1959);
- Convention Concerning the Medical Examination of Seafarers (1946);
- Convention Concerning the Minimum Age for Admission to Employment as Fishermen (1959);
- Convention Concerning the Minimum Age for Admission to Employment Underground in Mines (1965);
- Convention Concerning the Minimum Requirement of Professional Capacity for Masters and Officers on Board Merchant Ships (1936);
- Convention Concerning the Night Work of Young Persons Employed in Industry, 1919 (1919);
- Convention Concerning the Night Work of Young Persons Employed in Industry, 1948 (1948);
- Convention Concerning the Organization of the Employment Service (1948);
- Convention Concerning the Partial Revision of the Conventions Adopted by the General Conference of the International Labour Organisation (1961);
- Convention Concerning the Prevention of Occupational Accidents to Seafarers (1970);
- Convention Concerning the Prohibition and Immediate Action for the Elimination of the Worst Forms of Child Labour (1999);
- Convention Concerning the Promotion of Collective Bargaining (1981);
- Convention Concerning the Protection Against Accidents of Workers Employed in Loading or Unloading Ships, 1929 (1929);
- Convention Concerning the Protection and Integration of Indigenous and other Tribal and Semi-tribal Populations in Independent Countries (1957);
- Convention Concerning the Protection of Wages (1949);
- Convention Concerning the Protection of Workers Against Ionising Radiations (1960);
- Convention Concerning the Protection of Workers Against Occupational Hazards in the Working Environment Due to Air Pollution, Noise and Vibration (1977);
- Convention Concerning the Protection of Workers' Claims in the Event of the Insolvency of Their Employer (1992);
- Convention Concerning the Recruitment and Placement of Seafarers (1996);
- Convention Concerning the Recruitment, Placing and Conditions of Labour of Migrants for Employment (1939);
- Convention Concerning the Reduction of Hours of Work in Glass-bottle Works (1935);
- Convention Concerning the Reduction of Hours of Work in the Textile Industry (1937);
- Convention Concerning the Reduction of Hours of Work on Public Works (1936);
- Convention Concerning the Reduction of Hours of Work to Forty a Week (1935);
- Convention Concerning the Regulation of Certain Special Systems of Recruiting Workers (1936);
- Convention Concerning the Regulation of Hours of Work and Rest Periods in Road Transport (1939);
- Convention Concerning the Regulation of Hours of Work in Commerce and Offices (1930);
- Convention Concerning the Regulation of Written Contracts of Employment of Indigenous Workers (1939);
- Convention Concerning the Repatriation of Seafarers, 1987 (1987);
- Convention Concerning the Repatriation of Seamen, 1926 (1926);
- Convention Concerning the Restriction of Night Work of Children and Young Persons in Non-industrial Occupations (1946);
- Convention Concerning the Revision of the Maternity Protection Convention (2000);
- Convention Concerning the Right of Association and the Settlement of Labour Disputes in Non-metropolitan Territories (1947);
- Convention Concerning the Rights of Association and Combination of Agricultural Workers (1921);
- Convention Concerning the Simplification of the Inspection of Emigrants on Board Ship (1926);
- Convention Concerning the Social Repercussions of New Methods of Cargo Handling in Docks (1973);
- Convention Concerning the Use of White Lead in Painting (1921);
- Convention Concerning Tripartite Consultations to Promote the Implementation of International Labour Standards (1976);
- Convention Concerning Unemployment (1919);
- Convention Concerning Unemployment Indemnity in Case of Loss or Foundering of the Ship (1920);
- Convention Concerning Vacation Holidays with Pay for Seafarers, 1946 (1946);
- Convention Concerning Vacation Holidays with Pay for Seafarers, 1949 (1949);
- Convention Concerning Vocational Guidance and Vocational Training in the Development of Human Resources (1975);
- Convention Concerning Vocational Rehabilitation and Employment (1983);
- Convention Concerning Wages, Hours of Work on Board Ship and Manning, 1946 (1946);
- Convention Concerning Wages, Hours of Work on Board Ship and Manning, 1949 (1949);
- Convention Concerning Wages, Hours of Work on Board Ship and Manning, 1958 (1958);
- Convention Concerning Weekly Rest in Commerce and Offices (1957);
- Convention Concerning Working Conditions in Hotels, Restaurants and Similar Establishments (1991);
- Convention Concerning Workmen's Compensation for Accidents (1925);
- Convention Concerning Workmen's Compensation for Occupational Diseases, 1925 (1925);
- Convention Concerning Workmen's Compensation for Occupational Diseases, 1934 (1934);
- Convention Concerning Workmen's Compensation in Agriculture (1921);
- Convention Ensuring Benefit or Allowances to the Involuntarily Unemployed (1934);
- Convention Fixing the Minimum Age for Admission of Children to Employment at Sea, 1920 (1920);
- Convention Fixing the Minimum Age for Admission of Children to Industrial Employment, 1919 (1919);
- Convention Fixing the Minimum Age for Admission of Children to Industrial Employment, 1937 (1937);
- Convention Fixing the Minimum Age for the Admission of Children to Employment at Sea, 1936 (1936);
- Convention Fixing the Minimum Age for the Admission of Young Persons to Employment as Trimmers or Stokers (1921);
- Convention for Establishing Facilities for Finding Employment for Seamen (1920);
- Convention for the Regulation of Hours of Work in Automatic Sheet-glass Works (1934);
- Convention Limiting Hours of Work in Coal Mines, 1931 (1931);
- Convention Limiting Hours of Work in Coal Mines, 1935 (1935);
- Convention Limiting the Hours of Work in Industrial Undertakings to Eight in the Day and Forty-eight in the Week (1919);
- Convention on the Prevention of Major Industrial Accidents (1993);
- Final Articles Revision Convention (1946);
- Maritime Labour Convention (2006);
- Promotional Framework for Occupational Safety and Health Convention (2006);
- Protection Against Accidents / Dockers, 1932 (1932);
- Safety and Health in Agriculture Convention (2001);
- Seafarers' Identity Documents Convention (2003);
- Violence and Harassment Convention, 2019 (2019).

Events Triennial World Congress on Safety and Health at Work Sydney, NSW (Australia) 2023, Round Table on Labor Migration in Asia Bangkok (Thailand) 2022, Global Conference on Sustained Eradication of Child Labour Durban (South Africa) 2022, Session of the International Labour Conference Geneva (Switzerland) 2022, Vision Zero Summit Tokyo (Japan) 2022. **Publications** International Labour Review (4 a year) in French, Spanish; International Journal of Labour Research (annual) in English, French, Spanish; World of Work Magazine (annual) in English, French, Spanish; ILO InfoStories (2-4 a year) in Arabic, Chinese, English, French, German, Russian, Spanish. Reports; trends; outlooks; overviews; conference proceedings. Information Services: Library of over 1 million books regularly receives over 8,000 periodicals and items of legislation from most member states. Other information services: International Institute for Labour Studies (IILS, #13897); International Training Centre of the ILO (ITC, #15717); International Occupational Safety and Health Knowledge Network (no recent information). **Information Services** Clearinghouse on Conditions of Work; International Integrated System of Labour Information (ILIS); LABORDOC, Labour Information Database (LABORINFO).
Members Membership in the League of Nations carried with it membership in ILO. Between 1919 and 1945 some states, including USA in 1934, were admitted though not being members of the League. Present Constitution declares that the members are those states which were members on 1 Nov 1945, and those which join under the terms of the Constitution. These provide that a member of the United Nations may become a member of the ILO by accepting the obligations of membership, and that the admission of non-members of the United Nations must be approved by the General Conference by a two-thirds majority. Member states (187): Afghanistan, Albania, Algeria, Angola, Antigua-Barbuda, Argentina, Armenia, Australia, Austria, Azerbaijan, Bahamas, Bahrain, Bangladesh, Barbados, Belarus, Belgium, Belize, Benin, Bolivia, Bosnia-Herzegovina, Botswana, Brazil, Brunei Darussalam, Bulgaria, Burkina Faso, Burundi, Cambodia, Cameroon, Canada, Cape Verde, Central African Rep, Chad, Chile, China, Colombia, Comoros, Congo Brazzaville, Congo DR, Cook Is, Costa Rica, Côte d'Ivoire, Croatia, Cuba, Cyprus, Czechia, Denmark, Djibouti, Dominica, Dominican Rep, Ecuador, Egypt, El Salvador, Equatorial Guinea, Eritrea, Estonia, Eswatini, Ethiopia, Fiji, Finland, France, Gabon, Gambia, Georgia, Germany, Ghana, Greece, Grenada, Guatemala, Guinea, Guinea-Bissau, Guyana, Haiti, Honduras, Hungary, Iceland, India, Indonesia, Iran Islamic Rep, Iraq, Ireland, Israel, Italy, Jamaica, Japan, Jordan, Kazakhstan, Kenya, Kiribati, Korea Rep, Kuwait, Kyrgyzstan, Laos, Latvia, Lebanon, Lesotho, Liberia, Libya, Lithuania, Luxembourg, Madagascar, Malawi, Malaysia, Maldives, Mali, Malta, Marshall Is, Mauritania, Mauritius, Mexico, Moldova, Mongolia, Montenegro, Morocco, Mozambique, Myanmar, Namibia, Nepal, Netherlands, New Zealand, Nicaragua, Niger, Nigeria, North Macedonia, Norway, Oman, Pakistan, Palau, Panama, Papua New Guinea, Paraguay, Peru, Philippines, Poland, Portugal, Qatar, Romania, Russia, Rwanda, Samoa, San Marino, Sao Tomé-Principe, Saudi Arabia, Senegal, Serbia, Seychelles, Sierra Leone, Singapore, Slovakia, Slovenia, Solomon Is, Somalia, South Africa, South Sudan, Spain, Sri Lanka, St Kitts-Nevis, St Lucia, St Vincent-Grenadines, Sudan, Suriname, Sweden, Switzerland, Syrian AR, Tajikistan, Tanzania UR, Thailand, Timor-Leste, Togo, Tonga, Trinidad-Tobago, Tunisia, Türkiye, Turkmenistan, Tuvalu, Uganda, UK, Ukraine, United Arab Emirates, Uruguay, USA, Uzbekistan, Vanuatu, Venezuela, Vietnam, Yemen, Zambia, Zimbabwe.
IGO Relations Cooperates with: FAO (#09260); UNDP (#20292); UNEP (#20299); UNESCO (#20322); UNHCR (#20327); UNICEF (#20332); UNIDO (#20336); United Nations Economic Commission for Latin America and the Caribbean (ECLAC, #20556) (through the Regional Office for Latin America and the Caribbean); United Nations Girls' Education Initiative (UNGEI, #20566); United Nations Group on the Information Society (UNGIS, #20570); WHO (#20950). Member of: United Nations Alliance of Civilizations (UNAOC, #20520); United Nations Sustainable Development Group (UNSDG, #20634); UN-OCEANS (#20711); UN-Water (#20723). Supports: United Nations Non-Governmental Liaison Service (NGLS, #20591). Together with OAU, instrumental in setting up: African Rehabilitation Institute (ARI, #00437). Instrumental in setting up: Comité Latinoamericano de Derecho Bancario; ILO Central American Multidisciplinary Technical Advisory Team (OIT/ETM San José, see: #11123).
NGO Relations 'General Consultative Status' is granted to 6 organizations:
- Business Africa (BUSINESSAFRICA, #03377); International Co-operative Alliance (ICA, #12944); International Organisation of Employers (IOE, #14428); International Trade Union Confederation (ITUC, #15708); Organisation of African Trade Union Unity (OATUU, #17798); World Federation of Trade Unions (WFTU, #21493).

'Regional Consultative Status' is granted to a further 14 organizations:
- ASEAN Confederation of Employers (ACE, #01158);
- Caribbean Congress of Labour (CCL, #03480);
- Caribbean Employers' Confederation (CEC, #03495);
- Confederación Sindical de Trabajadores y Trabajadoras de las Américas (CSA, #04480);
- Confederation of Asia-Pacific Employers (CAPE, #04513);
- European Trade Union Confederation (ETUC, #08927);
- General Confederation of Trade Unions (GCTU, #10108);
- International Confederation of Arab Trade Unions (ICATU, #12845);
- International Trade Union Confederation – African Regional Organization (#15709);
- Latin American Industrialists Association (#16341);
- Permanent Congress of Trade Union Unity of Latin American Workers (CPUSTAL, inactive);
- Union of Arab Chambers (UAC, #20350).

ILO 11123

alphabetic sequence excludes
For the complete listing, see Yearbook Online at

'Special List' covers organizations having an interest in one or more topics of relevance to ILO:
- African Commission of Health and Human Rights Promoters (ACHHRP);
- African Union of Broadcasting (AUB, #00490);
- AIESEC (#00593);
- Amnesty International (AI, #00801);
- Anti-Slavery International (#00860);
- Arab Lawyers' Union (ALU, #01002);
- Assemblée parlementaire de la Francophonie (APF, #02312);
- Association internationale de la mutualité (AIM, #02721);
- Association internationale des universités du troisième âge (AIUTA, #02749);
- AVSI Foundation;
- Caritas Internationalis (CI, #03580);
- Centre international de recherches et d'information sur l'économie publique, sociale et coopérative (CIRIEC, #03764);
- Center for Migration Studies, New York (CMS);
- Commission Internationale de l'Eclairage (CIE, #04219);
- Consultative Council of Jewish Organizations (CCJO, no recent information);
- Coordinating Board of Jewish Organizations (CBJO, #04813);
- Defence for Children International (DCI, #05025);
- Disabled Peoples' International (DPI, #05097);
- European Disability Forum (EDF, #06929);
- International Federation of Women Lawyers (FIDA, #13578);
- Graduate Women International (GWI, #10688);
- Grupo Latinoamericano para la Participación, la Integración y la Inclusión de las Personas con Discapacidad (GLARP IIPD, no recent information);
- IFOAM – Organics International (IFOAM, #11105);
- Inclusion International (#11145);
- Indigenous World Association (#11166);
- Institution of Occupational Safety and Health (IOSH);
- Institution of Occupational Safety and Health, Wigston (UK);
- International Actuarial Association (IAA, #11586);
- CIDSE (CIDSE, #03926);
- International Alliance of Orchestra Associations (IAOA, no recent information);
- International Alliance of Women (IAW, #11639);
- International Association for Community Development (IACD, #11793);
- International Association of Conference Interpreters (#11807);
- International Association for Counselling (IAC, #11821);
- International Association for Educational and Vocational Guidance (IAEVG, #11862);
- International Association for the Exchange of Students for Technical Experience (IAESTE, #11885);
- International Association of Judges (IAJ, #11978);
- International Association of Labour Inspection (IALI, #11983);
- International Association for Media and Communication Research (IAMCR, #12022);
- International Association of Ports and Harbors (IAPH, #12096);
- International Association of Rural Health and Medicine (IARM, #12140);
- International Catholic Committee of Nurses and Medico-social Assistants (#12451);
- International Catholic Migration Commission (ICMC, #12459);
- International Centre for Trade Union Rights (ICTUR, #12525);
- International Christian Maritime Association (ICMA, #12561);
- International Collective in Support of Fishworkers (ICSF, #12639);
- International Commission of Jurists (ICJ, #12695);
- International Commission on Non-Ionizing Radiation Protection (ICNIRP, #12707);
- International Commission on Occupational Health (ICOH, #12709);
- International Confederation of Midwives (ICM, #12863);
- International Coordination of Young Christian Workers (ICYCW, #12960);
- International Council for Adult Education (ICAE, #12983);
- International Council on Alcohol and Addictions (ICAA, #12989);
- International Council for Educational Media (ICEM, #13014);
- International Council of Jewish Women (ICJW, #13036);
- International Council of Nurses (ICN, #13054);
- International Council on Social Welfare (ICSW, #13076);
- International Council of Voluntary Agencies (ICVA, #13092);
- International Council of Women (ICW, #13093);
- International Ergonomics Association (IEA, #13294);
- International Federation on Ageing (IFA, #13345);
- International Federation of Business and Professional Women (BPW International, #13376);
- International Federation of Hard of Hearing People (IFHOH, #13435);
- International Federation for Human Rights (#13452);
- International Federation of Non-Government Organizations for the Prevention of Drug and Substance Abuse (IFNGO, #13490);
- International Federation of Persons with Physical Disability (FIMITIC, #13504);
- International Federation of Red Cross and Red Crescent Societies (#13526);
- International Federation of Senior Police Officers (IFSPO, no recent information);
- International Federation of Shipmasters Associations (IFSMA, #13539);
- International Federation of Social Workers (IFSW, #13544);
- International Federation of Training and Development Organizations (IFTDO, #13573);
- International Federation of Women in Legal Careers (IFWLC, #13579);
- International Federation of Workers' Education Associations (IFWEA, #13580);
- International Institute of Administrative Sciences (IIAS, #13859);
- International League for Human Rights (ILHR, inactive);
- International Movement of Apostolate of Children (IMAC, #14192);
- International Movement ATD Fourth World (#14193);
- International Occupational Hygiene Association (IOHA, #14391);
- International Organization for Standardization (ISO, #14473);
- International Planned Parenthood Federation (IPPF, #14589);
- International Radiation Protection Association (IRPA, #14686);
- International Social Science Council (ISSC, inactive);
- International Social Service (ISS, #14886);
- International Social Tourism Organisation (ISTO, #14889);
- International Union Against Tuberculosis and Lung Disease (The Union, #15752);
- International Union for the Scientific Study of Population (IUSSP, #15814);
- International Union of Socialist Youth (IUSY, #15815);
- International Work Group for Indigenous Affairs (IWGIA, #15907);
- International Young Christian Workers (IYCW, #15927);
- Junior Chamber International (JCI, #16168);
- KOLPING INTERNATIONAL (#16203);
- Life Institute (no recent information);
- Mouvement International de la jeunesse agricole et rurale catholique (MIJARC, #16865);
- Observatoire des missions publiques en Europe (OMIPE, no recent information);
- Pan African Institute for Development (PAID, #18053);
- Pan African Women's Organization (PAWO, #18074);
- PAI (#18025);
- Population Council (#18458);
- RI Global (#18948);
- Saami Council (#19012);
- Save the Children International (#19058);
- Secrétariat international des ingénieurs, des agronomes et des cadres économiques catholiques (SIIAEC, #19203);
- Socialist International Women (SIW, #19341);
- Société de législation comparée (#19500);
- Society for International Development (SID, #19581);
- SOLIDAR (#19680);
- Soroptimist International (SI, #19686);
- Special Olympics International (SOI, #19910);
- Survival International (#20047);
- Terre des Hommes International Federation (TDHIF, #20133);
- Union of International Associations (UIA, #20414);
- Union internationale des architectes (UIA, #20419);
- Union internationale des Avocats (UIA, #20422);
- United Seamen's Service (USS, #20661);
- Women's International Democratic Federation (WIDF, #21022);
- Women's International League for Peace and Freedom (WILPF, #21024);
- Workability International (#21049);
- World Alliance of Young Men's Christian Associations (YMCA, #21090);
- World Assembly of Youth (WAY, #21113);
- World Association of Girl Guides and Girl Scouts (WAGGGS, #21142);
- World Association for Psychosocial Rehabilitation (WAPR, #21178);
- World Association of Public Employment Services (WAPES, #21179);
- World Association for the School as an Instrument of Peace (#21184);
- World Association for Small and Medium Enterprises (WASME, #21189);
- World Blind Union (WBU, #21234);
- World Council of Churches (WCC, #21320);
- World Council of Credit Unions (WOCCU, #21324);
- World Design Organization (WDO, #21358);
- World Family Organization (WFO, #21399);
- World Federation of the Deaf (WFD, #21425);
- World Federation of Democratic Youth (WFDY, #21427);
- World Federation for Mental Health (WFMH, #21455);
- World Federation of Methodist and Uniting Church Women (WFM and UCW, #21457);
- World Federation of People Management Associations (WFPMA, #21474);
- World Federation of United Nations Associations (WFUNA, #21499);
- World Jewish Congress (WJC, #21599);
- World Jurist Association (WJA, #21604);
- World Leisure Organization (WLO, #21624);
- World Medical Association (WMA, #21646);
- World Movement of Christian Workers (WMCW, #21660);
- World Organisation Against Torture (OMCT, #21685);
- World ORT (WO, #21698);
- World Peace Council (WPC, #21717);
- World Savings Banks Institute (WSBI, #21764);
- World Union of Catholic Women's Organisations (WUCWO, #21876);
- World Union of Professions (WUP, #21882);
- The World Veterans Federation (WVF, #21900);
- World Vision International (WVI, #21904);
- World Young Women's Christian Association (World YWCA, #21947);
- WorldSkills International (WSI, #21791);
- Zonta International (#22038). [2020.03.26/XB2183/**B***]

♦ ILO-IPEC / see International Programme on the Elimination of Child Labour and Forced Labour (#14652)
♦ ILO / see Latin American Institute for the Ombudsman (#16342)
♦ Ilopango Agreement Concerning Inspection Procedures with the Objective of Guaranteeing the Safety of Flight Operations in Central America, Panama and Belize (1995 treaty)
♦ ILO Staff Union / see Staff Union of the International Labour Office (#19945)
♦ **ILO Tribunal** Administrative Tribunal of the International Labour Organization (#00118)
♦ ILO Turin Centre / see International Training Centre of the ILO (#15717)
♦ ILO Turin Centre ITC Staff Union / see Staff Union of the International Training Centre of the ILO
♦ ILPA / see International Labor Communications Association
♦ ILPA – Institutional Limited Partners Association (internationally oriented national body)
♦ ILPC — International Labour Process Conference (meeting series)
♦ **ILPES** Instituto Latinoamericano y del Caribe de Planificación Económica y Social (#16279)
♦ ILPES / see Latin American and Caribbean Institute for Economic and Social Planning (#16279)
♦ ILPH / see World Horse Welfare
♦ ILP / see International Lithosphere Program (#14059)
♦ **ILP** International Lithosphere Program (#14059)
♦ **ILPS** International League of Peoples' Struggle (#14021)
♦ ILP Vegetable – International Licensing Platform Vegetable (internationally oriented national body)
♦ ILRC – ABA-UNDP International Legal Resource Centre (internationally oriented national body)
♦ ILRERF / see Global Labor Justice-International Labor Rights Forum
♦ ILRF / see Global Labor Justice-International Labor Rights Forum
♦ ILRG – International Landslide Research Group (internationally oriented national body)
♦ ILRIG – International Labour Research and Information Group (internationally oriented national body)
♦ **ILRI** International Livestock Research Institute (#14062)
♦ ILRS — International Laser Ranging Service (see: #11914)
♦ **ILRS** International League of Religious Socialists (#14022)
♦ ILSA / see Latin American Institute for and Alternative Society and an Alternative Law
♦ ILSA – Instituto Latinoamericano para una Sociedad y un Derecho Alternativos (internationally oriented national body)
♦ **ILSA** Inter-American Legal Services Association (#11439)
♦ ILSA – International Law Students Association (internationally oriented national body)
♦ ILSAM / see International Life Saving Federation – Americas (#14041)
♦ **ILSAP** International Life Saving Federation – Asia/Pacific (#14042)
♦ **ILSE** International Life Saving Federation of Europe (#14043)
♦ ILSI Global / see International Life Sciences Institute (#14044)
♦ **ILSI** International Life Sciences Institute (#14044)
♦ ILS International Conference – International Conference on Information Systems, Logistics and Supply Chain (meeting series)
♦ **ILS** International Legume Society (#14027)
♦ **ILS** International Leptospirosis Society (#14031)
♦ **ILS** International Life Saving Federation (#14040)
♦ **ILS** International Lilac Society (#14048)
♦ ILS LEDA – International Links and Services for Local Economic Development Agencies (unconfirmed)
♦ ILSMH EA / see Inclusion Europe – European Association of Societies of Persons with Intellectual Disability and their Families (#11144)
♦ ILSMH European Association / see Inclusion Europe – European Association of Societies of Persons with Intellectual Disability and their Families (#11144)
♦ ILSMH / see Inclusion International (#11145)
♦ ILSSA – International Legislative Support Services Association (no recent information)
♦ **ILTA** International Language Testing Association (#14000)
♦ ILTA – International Liquid Terminals Association (internationally oriented national body)
♦ **ILTER** International Long-Term Ecological Research Network (#14065)
♦ **ILTS** International Liver Transplantation Society (#14061)
♦ **ILU** International Leprosy Union (#14030)
♦ ILU / see International Underwriting Association (#15748)
♦ ILWC – International League of Women Composers (inactive)
♦ ILWML – International Lutheran Women's Missionary League (internationally oriented national body)
♦ ILWU – International Longshore and Warehouse Union (internationally oriented national body)
♦ **ILZRO** International Lead Zinc Research Organization (#14011)
♦ **ILZSG** International Lead and Zinc Study Group (#14012)
♦ IM4DC – International Mining for Development Centre (internationally oriented national body)
♦ IMA / see IMA World Health
♦ IMA / see Islamic Medical Association of North America
♦ IMA / see International Medical Assistance Foundation
♦ **IMAA** International Mastic Asphalt Association (#14119)
♦ IMAAN – International Muslim Association for Animals and Nature (inactive)
♦ IMAB – Comité européen des importateurs de machines à bois (inactive)
♦ IMACA / see Asian Mycological Association (#01545)
♦ IMACE / see European Margarine Association (#07736)
♦ **IMACE** European Margarine Association (#07736)
♦ **IMAC** International Movement of Apostolate of Children (#14192)
♦ **IMACO** International Mask Arts and Culture Organization (#14111)
♦ IMA Committee for Asia / see Asian Mycological Association (#01545)
♦ **IMACS** International Association for Mathematics and Computers in Simulation (#12019)
♦ IMACS – International Myositis Assessment & Clinical Studies Group (unconfirmed)

- ♦ **IMADR** The International Movement Against All Forms of Discrimination and Racism (#14191)
- ♦ IMAECSED – International Movement for Advancement of Education Culture Social and Economic Development (internationally oriented national body)
- ♦ IMAEM / see International Maritime Association of the Mediterranean (#14096)
- ♦ **IMA Europe** Industrial Minerals Association – Europe (#11179)
- ♦ **IMAFD** International Martial Arts Federation of the Deaf (#14109)
- ♦ **IMAF** International Martial Arts Federation (#14108)
- ♦ Imagine H20 (internationally oriented national body)
- ♦ ImagineNations (internationally oriented national body)
- ♦ Imaging Consumables Coalition of Europe / see Imaging Consumables Coalition of Europe, Middle-East and Africa (#11124)

♦ Imaging Consumables Coalition of Europe, Middle-East and Africa (ICCE) 11124

Main Office OKI Europe, Blays House, Wick Road, Egham, TW20 0HJ, UK.
URL: https://icce.net/

History 1997. Former names and other names: *Imaging Consumables Coalition of Europe* – former. Registration: Companies House, No/ID: 03426589, Start date: Aug 1997, England and Wales. **Aims** Fight counterfeit goods; influence public policy. **Publications** *ICCE Newsletter*. **Members** Members (9) representing 10 brands. **IGO Relations** Member of (1): *World Customs Organization (WCO, #21350)*. **NGO Relations** Partner of (1): *Transnational Alliance to Combat Illicit Trade (TRACIT)*. *Imaging Supplies Coalition for International Intellectual Property Protection (ISC)*. [XF6005/**F**]

♦ Imaging and Perimetric Society (IPS) 11125

Sec Dept of Optometry and Vision Sciences, Univ of Melbourne, Level 4 Alice Hoy Building, Monash Rd, University of Melbourne Parkville Campus, Parkville, Melbourne VIC 3010, Australia.
URL: http://www.perimetry.org/

History 1974, as *International Perimetric Society*. **Aims** Promote the study of normal and abnormal *visual* function and of *ocular* imaging; ensure and facilitate the cooperation and friendship of scientists of different countries working and interested in these disciplines. **Structure** Board. **Languages** English. **Finance** Sources: members' dues. **Events** *Biennial Symposium* Berkeley, CA (USA) 2021, *Biennial Symposium* Berkeley, CA (USA) 2020, *Biennial Symposium* Kanazawa (Japan) 2018, *International Visual Field and Imaging Symposium* Kanazawa (Japan) 2018, *Biennial Symposium* Udine (Italy) 2016. **Publications** Symposia proceedings; standards documents.

Members Individuals (about 150) in 29 countries:
Argentina, Australia, Austria, Belgium, Brazil, Canada, China, Denmark, Egypt, Finland, France, Germany, Greece, Ireland, Israel, Italy, Japan, Korea Rep, Netherlands, New Zealand, Norway, Russia, Spain, Sweden, Switzerland, Tunisia, Türkiye, UK, USA. [2019/XD1287/v/**C**]

- ♦ Imaging Supplies Coalition for International Intellectual Property Protection (internationally oriented national body)
- ♦ Imaging the World (internationally oriented national body)
- ♦ IMAGO / see International Federation of Cinematographers (#13390)
- ♦ **IMAGO** International Federation of Cinematographers (#13390)
- ♦ IMAGRI – International Migration and Gender Research Institute (unconfirmed)
- ♦ IMA – IMA World Health (internationally oriented national body)
- ♦ IMA – Institute of International Maritime Affairs (internationally oriented national body)
- ♦ IMA – Institut Madeleine Aulina (religious order)
- ♦ **IMA** Institut du monde arabe (#11324)
- ♦ **IMA** International Magnesium Association (#14073)
- ♦ **IMA** International Maintenance Association (#14076)
- ♦ **IMA** International Management Assistants (#14081)
- ♦ **IMA** International Marangoni Association (#14087)
- ♦ **IMA** International Marinelife Alliance (#14093)
- ♦ **IMA** International Maxi Association (#14122)
- ♦ IMA – International Measurement Association (unconfirmed)
- ♦ **IMA** International Mechanochemical Association (#14126)
- ♦ IMA – International Mentoring Association (internationally oriented national body)
- ♦ **IMA** International Microsimulation Association (#14158)
- ♦ **IMA** International Migrants Alliance (#14161)
- ♦ IMA – International Milling Association (inactive)
- ♦ **IMA** International Mineralogical Association (#14165)
- ♦ IMA – International Mobility Alliance (unconfirmed)
- ♦ **IMA** International Monorail Association (#14182)
- ♦ **IMA** International Mycological Association (#14203)
- ♦ IMA / see International Yehudi Menuhin Foundation (#15922)
- ♦ **IMAK** International Medical Society for Applied Kinesiology (#14139)
- ♦ Imam Al-Khoei Benevolent Foundation (internationally oriented national body)
- ♦ Imam Al-Khoei Foundation / see Imam Al-Khoei Benevolent Foundation
- ♦ Imamia Medics International (internationally oriented national body)
- ♦ **IMAM** International Maritime Association of the Mediterranean (#14096)
- ♦ Imam Muhammad Ibn Saud Islamic University (internationally oriented national body)
- ♦ Imam Ouzai College of Islamic Studies (internationally oriented national body)
- ♦ IMAMPC – International Meeting on Atomic and Molecular Physics and Chemistry (meeting series)

♦ Imam Reza Network 11126

Address not obtained.
URL: http://www.imamreza.net/

History 6 Nov 1999. **Aims** As a non-profit *Internet*-based group, present the ideals and teachings of *Islam* with particular emphasis on the holy life and works of Hazrat Emam Abul Hasan Ali ibn Musa ar-Reza, the 8th holy *Shi'ite* Emam. **Information Services** *Aalul Bayt Global Centre for Information*. [2018/XF6493/**F**]

- ♦ Imams and Rabbis for Peace (internationally oriented national body)
- ♦ IMANA – Islamic Medical Association of North America (internationally oriented national body)
- ♦ IManf – The Institute of Manufacturing (internationally oriented national body)
- ♦ Imani Africa Communities Development Agency (internationally oriented national body)
- ♦ **IMAO** Institut monétaire de l'Afrique de l'ouest (#20888)
- ♦ IMAP – International Meeting on Antimicrobial Peptides (meeting series)
- ♦ **IMAPS** International Microelectronics Assembly and Packaging Society (#14156)
- ♦ IMarE / see Institute of Marine Engineering, Science and Technology (#11280)
- ♦ **IMarEST** Institute of Marine Engineering, Science and Technology (#11280)
- ♦ **imars** International Maillard Reaction Society (#14075)
- ♦ IMASIE – Institut des mondes asiatiques (internationally oriented national body)
- ♦ IMAS – Institute for Marine and Antarctic Studies (internationally oriented national body)
- ♦ IMATA – International Marine Animal Trainers Association (internationally oriented national body)
- ♦ **IMAU** International Martial Arts Union (#14110)
- ♦ IMAU – International Movement for Atlantic Union (inactive)
- ♦ IMAV – International Micro Air Vehicle Conference (meeting series)
- ♦ IMA World Health (internationally oriented national body)
- ♦ **IMBA Europe** International Mountain Bicycling Association Europe (#14189)
- ♦ IMBA / see Insurope (#11363)
- ♦ **IMBA** International Marine Biotechnology Association (#14090)
- ♦ **IMBA** International Mountain Bicycling Association (#14188)
- ♦ **IMBCO** International MotherBaby Childbirth Organization (#14185)
- ♦ IMBE – Institut Méditerranéen de Biodiversité et d'Ecologie marine et continentale (internationally oriented national body)
- ♦ **IMBF** International Mortgage Broker Federation (#14183)
- ♦ IMB – Institute of International Relations, Kiev (internationally oriented national body)
- ♦ IMB – Internationaler Metallgewerkschaftsbund (inactive)
- ♦ **IMB** International Maritime Bureau (#14097)
- ♦ IMB – International Mission Board (internationally oriented national body)
- ♦ **IMBISA** Inter-Regional Meeting of Bishops of Southern Africa (#15971)
- ♦ IMB Piracy Reporting Centre / see Piracy Reporting Centre, Kuala Lumpur (#18373)
- ♦ IMB PRC / see Piracy Reporting Centre, Kuala Lumpur (#18373)
- ♦ IMC / see International Medical University, Malaysia
- ♦ IMC / see Artsen Zonder Vakantie
- ♦ IMC / see CEU Business School
- ♦ **IMCA** IMCA International Marine Contractors Association (#11127)
- ♦ IMCA – International Management Centres Association (inactive)

♦ IMCA International Marine Contractors Association (IMCA) 11127

CEO 66 Buckingham Gate, London, SW1E 6AU, UK. T. +442078245520. Fax +442078245521. E-mail: imca@imca-int.com – communications@imca-int.com.
URL: http://www.imca-int.com/

History 1972. 1995 merged with the *Dynamic Positioning Vessel Owners Association (DPVOA)*, founded 1990. Former names and other names: *International Association of Offshore Diving Contractors (AODC)* – former (1972); *AODC International Association of Underwater Engineering Contractors* – former; *IMCA Trading Ltd* – legal name. Registration: Comapnies House, No/ID: 07169292, England and Wales. **Aims** Improve performance in the marine contracting industry. **Structure** Board; CEO; Operations Committee; Core Committees; Division Committees; Region Committees; Workgroups. **Languages** English. **Activities** Events/meetings; networking/liaising; politics/policy/regulatory; publishing activities; standards/guidelines. **Events** *Offshore Technology Conference (OTC)* Houston, TX (USA) 2021, *Annual Seminar* London (UK) 2020, *Health, Safety and Environment Seminar* Amsterdam (Netherlands) 2019, *Asia-Pacific Meeting* Singapore (Singapore) 2019, *Annual Seminar* The Hague (Netherlands) 2018. **Publications** *IMCA Digest* (12 a year); *Making Waves* – newsletter. Guidance documents; technical reports; briefing notes; notifications; safety flashes; dynamic positioning bulletins.

Members Global Contractor; International Contractor; Contractor; Supplier; Corresponding. Members (about 1,000) in 65 countries and territories:
Angola, Argentina, Australia, Austria, Azerbaijan, Bahrain, Belgium, Brazil, Brunei Darussalam, Cameroon, Canada, China, Congo Brazzaville, Croatia, Cyprus, Denmark, Egypt, Estonia, Faeroe Is, Finland, France, Gabon, Germany, Greece, Hong Kong, India, Indonesia, Ireland, Italy, Japan, Kazakhstan, Korea Rep, Kuwait, Malaysia, Malta, Mexico, Monaco, Myanmar, Netherlands, New Zealand, Nigeria, Norway, Oman, Philippines, Poland, Portugal, Qatar, Romania, Russia, Saudi Arabia, Singapore, South Africa, Spain, Sweden, Switzerland, Thailand, Trinidad-Tobago, Tunisia, Türkiye, UK, Ukraine, United Arab Emirates, USA, Vietnam, Zambia.

Consultative Status Consultative status granted from: *International Maritime Organization (IMO, #14102)*. **NGO Relations** Member of (4): *European Diving Technology Committee (EDTC, #06932)*; *Global Wind Energy Council (GWEC, #10656)*; International Offshore Marine Operations Organisations Forum (IOMOOF); *World Federation of Pipe Line Industry Associations (WFPIA, #21475)*. Partner of (1): *Asia Wind Energy Association (#02106)*. [2022/XD7634/**C**]

- ♦ IMCA – International Mirror Class Association (see: #21760)
- ♦ IMCA Trading Ltd / see IMCA International Marine Contractors Association (#11127)
- ♦ IMCCA – Interactive Multimedia and Collaborative Communications Alliance (internationally oriented national body)
- ♦ IMCC / see Global Mayors' Forum (#10467)
- ♦ **IMCC** Integrated Marketing Communications Council of Europe (#11369)
- ♦ IMCC – International Medical Cooperation Committee (internationally oriented national body)
- ♦ **IMCG** International Mire Conservation Group (#14169)
- ♦ IMCHF – International Maternal and Child Health Foundation Canada (unconfirmed)
- ♦ **IMCI** International Marine Certification Institute (#14091)
- ♦ IMC – Institutum Missionum a Consolata (religious order)
- ♦ **IMC** Intermediterranean Commission (#11521)
- ♦ **IMC** Internationale Maascommissie (#12702)
- ♦ IMC – International Information Management Congress (inactive)
- ♦ IMC – International Marine Centre (internationally oriented national body)
- ♦ **IMC** International Mauthausen Committee (#04179)
- ♦ IMC – International Medical Corps (internationally oriented national body)
- ♦ IMC – International Missionary Council (inactive)
- ♦ **IMC** International Music Council (#14199)
- ♦ **IMC** Investment Migration Council (#15999)
- ♦ IMCJ / see Nation Center for Global Health and Medicine
- ♦ **IMCLC** International Medical Contact Lens Council (#14131)
- ♦ **IMCL Council** International Making Cities Livable Council (#14078)
- ♦ IMCL – International Movement of Catholic Lawyers (inactive)
- ♦ IMCO / see International Maritime Organization (#14102)
- ♦ IMCOM – International Conference on Ubiquitous Information Management and Communication (meeting series)
- ♦ **IMCoS** International Map Collectors' Society (#14084)
- ♦ **IMCPC** International Medical Cannabis Patients Coalition (#14130)
- ♦ IMCS – International Meeting on Chemical Sensors (meeting series)
- ♦ **IMCS** Pax Romana, International Movement of Catholic Students (#18268)
- ♦ **IMDA** International Management Development Association (#14082)
- ♦ IMDA / see International Map Industry Association (#14085)
- ♦ IMDC – International Marine Design Conference (meeting series)
- ♦ IMDI – International Mushroom Dye Institute (unconfirmed)
- ♦ IMD – Internationales Musikinstitut Darmstadt (internationally oriented national body)
- ♦ IMD – International Institute for Management Development (internationally oriented national body)
- ♦ **IMD** International Methods Time-Measurement Directorate (#14154)
- ♦ IMD – Netherlands Institute for Multiparty Democracy (internationally oriented national body)
- ♦ **IMDRF** International Medical Device Regulators Forum (#14132)
- ♦ **IMDSA** International Mosaic Down Syndrome Association (#14184)
- ♦ IMEA / see Institut de Médecine et d'Epidémiologie Appliquée
- ♦ IMEA – Institute of Materials Engineering, Australasia (internationally oriented national body)
- ♦ IMEA – Institut de Médecine et d'Epidémiologie Appliquée (internationally oriented national body)
- ♦ IMEA – International Marine Electronics Alliance (unconfirmed)
- ♦ IMEBESS – International Meeting on Experimental and Behavioral Social Sciences (meeting series)
- ♦ IMEC / see International Maritime Employers' Council (#14098)
- ♦ **IMEC** International Maritime Employers' Council (#14098)
- ♦ IMEC – International Medical Equipment Collaborative (internationally oriented national body)
- ♦ IMEC – International Mountain Explorers Connection (internationally oriented national body)
- ♦ IMED – Istituto per il Mediterraneo (internationally oriented national body)
- ♦ IMEHA / see International Maritime History Association (#14100)
- ♦ IMEI / see Mexican International Studies Association
- ♦ **IME** Institut méditerranéen de l'eau (#11323)
- ♦ IME – Institut monétaire européen (inactive)
- ♦ IME – International Congress on Insurance: Mathematics and Economics (meeting series)
- ♦ IMEIS – Institute for Middle Eastern and Islamic Studies, Durham (internationally oriented national body)
- ♦ **IMEKO** Internationale Messtechnische Konföderation (#14124)
- ♦ **IMEKO** International Measurement Confederation (#14124)
- ♦ IMEMO – Institut Mirovoj Ekonomiki i Mezdunarodnyh Otnosenij Rossijskoj Akademii Nauk (internationally oriented national body)

IMEOF International Medical
11127
alphabetic sequence excludes
For the complete listing, see Yearbook Online at

- ♦ **IMEOF** International Medical Ozone Federation (#14136)
- ♦ IMEO – International Methane Emission Observatory (unconfirmed)
- ♦ IMEPI – Institut Mezdunarodnyh Ekonomiceskih i Politiceskih Issledovanij (internationally oriented national body)
- ♦ IMEP – Institut méditerranéen d'écologie et paléoécologie (internationally oriented national body)
- ♦ IMERCSA – India Musokotwane Environment Resource Centre for Southern Africa (internationally oriented national body)
- ♦ IMESA – Institute of Municipal Engineering of Southern Africa (internationally oriented national body)
- ♦ IMES – GIGA Institute of Middle East Studies, Hamburg (internationally oriented national body)
- ♦ **IMES** International Metabolic Engineering Society (#14149)
- ♦ IMET2000 – International Medical Education Trust 2000 (internationally oriented national body)
- ♦ **IMFC** International Monetary and Financial Committee (#14179)
- ♦ IMFE and FPT – Institute of Mediterranean Forest Ecosystems and Forest Products Technology (internationally oriented national body)
- ♦ IMFF – International Mini-Football Federation (inactive)
- ♦ IMF Institute (see: #14180)
- ♦ IMF – Institut méditerranéen de formation et recherche en travail social (internationally oriented national body)
- ♦ IMF – Internationale Ménière Federatie (inactive)
- ♦ **IMF** International Marketing Federation (#14106)
- ♦ IMF – International Ménière Federation (inactive)
- ♦ IMF – International Metalworkers' Federation (inactive)
- ♦ **IMF** International Monetary Fund (#14180)
- ♦ **IMF** International Myeloma Foundation (#14204)
- ♦ IMF – Internationella Metallarbetarfederationen (inactive)
- ♦ **IMFN** International Model Forest Network (#14175)
- ♦ IMFNS / see International Model Forest Network (#14175)
- ♦ IMFP – International Meeting on Fundamental Physics (meeting series)
- ♦ IMFS – International Marie de France Society (internationally oriented national body)

♦ IMF Staff Association 11128

Contact c/o IMF, 700 19th St NW, Room 3-103 Ext 37650, Washington DC 20431, USA. T. +12026237650. Fax +12026234073. E-mail: imfsac@imf.org.
Contact address not obtained.

History Founded in 1948, to represent staff of *International Monetary Fund (IMF, #14180)*. **Aims** Represent and promote the interests and general welfare of the staff on matters related to compensation, benefits, working conditions, and personnel policies; engage in dialogue with staff associations of international financial institutions. **Structure** Staff Association Committee (SAC), comprised of 7 Principals elected annually by the Staff Association (SA) membership. **Languages** English. **Staff** About 4,300 employees, of which 2,175 are members of Staff Association. **Finance** Members' dues: 0.02% of annual net salary. **Activities** Networking/liaising. **Publications** *Sacnews* (4-6 a year). **Members** Staff employed by: International Monetary Fund (IMF) in its 189 member countries (not specified). **NGO Relations** Consultative status with: *Federation of International Civil Servants' Associations (FICSA, #09603).* [2019.09.11/XE1526/v/**E**]

- ♦ **IMGA** International Masters Games Association (#14117)
- ♦ **IMGA** International Medical Geology Association (#14133)
- ♦ **IMGC** International Martial Art Games Committee (#14107)
- ♦ IMGEAV / see Medizinische Gesellschaft für System- und Regulationsdiagnostik (#16689)
- ♦ IMGF / see World Minigolf Sport Federation (#21653)
- ♦ **IMG** Internationale Mosel-Gesellschaft mbH (#13263)
- ♦ IMG – Islamic Missionaries Guild of the Caribbean and South America (inactive)
- ♦ **IMGL** International Masters of Gaming Law (#14118)
- ♦ **IMHA** International Maritime Health Association (#14099)
- ♦ **IMHA** International Maritime History Association (#14100)
- ♦ IMHE – OECD Higher Education Programme (inactive)
- ♦ IMH – Internationale Medienhilfe (internationally oriented national body)
- ♦ IMHO – International Medical Health Organization (internationally oriented national body)
- ♦ IMHPA – European Network for Mental Health Promotion and Mental Disorder Prevention (inactive)
- ♦ IMHRD – International Workshop on Methane Hydrate Research and Development (meeting series)
- ♦ **IMIA** International Association of Engineering Insurers, The (#11874)
- ♦ **IMIA** International Map Industry Association (#14086)
- ♦ **IMIA** International Map Industry Association (#14085)
- ♦ **IMIA** International Medical Informatics Association (#14134)
- ♦ IMIA – International Medical Interpreters Association (unconfirmed)
- ♦ **IMIA-LAC** International Medical Informatics Association for Latin America and the Caribbean (#14135)
- ♦ IMIEU – Institute for Infrastructure, Environment and Innovation (unconfirmed)
- ♦ IMIF – International Maritime Industries Forum (inactive)
- ♦ **IMIG** International Mesothelioma Interest Group (#14147)
- ♦ IMI – Imamia Medics International (internationally oriented national body)
- ♦ **IMI** Innovative Medicines Initiative (#11221)
- ♦ **IMI** International Mahayana Institute (#14074)
- ♦ IMI – International Masonry Institute (internationally oriented national body)
- ♦ **IMI** International Mediation Institute (#14129)
- ♦ IMI – International Migration Institute (unconfirmed)
- ♦ IMI – International Mine Initiative (internationally oriented national body)
- ♦ IMI – International Myopia Institute (unconfirmed)
- ♦ IMI-Kiev – International Management Institute, Kiev (internationally oriented national body)
- ♦ IM – Individuell Människohjälp (internationally oriented national body)
- ♦ IM – InfluenceMap (internationally oriented national body)
- ♦ **IMIR** International Centre for Minority Studies and Intercultural Relations (#12504)

♦ IMISCOE Research Network 11129

Network Officer Social Sciences EUR, Room T17-16, PO Box 1738, 3000DR Rotterdam, Netherlands. E-mail: imiscoe@fsw.eur.nl.
URL: http://www.imiscoe.org/

History Also referred to as *International Migration, Integration and Social Cohesion in Europe.* Originally a Network of Excellence within the Framework Programme for Research of *European Commission (EC, #06633)*, for the period 1 Apr 2004 – 1 Apr 2010. Continued under current name as of 1 Apr 2009. 'IMISCOE' stands for: *International Migration, Integration and Social Cohesion Europe.* **Aims** Create a joint research programme on *migration, integration* and *social cohesion* in *Europe.* **Structure** Executive Board; Board of Directors; Committees (5); Research Clusters (20). **Finance** Members' dues. **Activities** Research/documentation; training/education; knowledge management/information dissemination; events/meetings; awards/prizes/competitions. **Events** *Annual Conference* Oslo (Norway) 2022, *Annual Conference* Esch-sur-Alzette (Luxembourg) 2021, *Annual Conference* Esch-sur-Alzette (Luxembourg) 2020, *Annual Conference* Malmö (Sweden) 2019, *Annual Conference* Barcelona (Spain) 2018. **Publications** *IMISCOE Newsletter.* Book Series; Policy Briefs; Working Papers.
Members Institutes (35) in 18 countries:
Austria, Belgium, Czechia, Denmark, Finland, France, Germany, Italy, Luxembourg, Netherlands, Norway, Poland, Portugal, Spain, Sweden, Switzerland, Türkiye, UK.
NGO Relations Partner of: *Open Access Publishing in European Networks (OAPEN, #17746).*
[2016.12.14/XJ3750/y/**F**]

- ♦ IMIS – Institute for Migration Research and Intercultural Studies (internationally oriented national body)
- ♦ IMIS – Institut für Migrationsforschung und Interkulturelle Studien (internationally oriented national body)
- ♦ IMIS – International Conference on Innovative Mobile and Internet Services in Ubiquitous Computing (meeting series)
- ♦ IMISP – International Management Institute, St Petersburg (internationally oriented national body)
- ♦ IMIU – Imam Muhammad Ibn Saud Islamic University (internationally oriented national body)
- ♦ **IMJA** International Messianic Jewish Alliance (#14148)
- ♦ IMJM – International Mahavira Jain Mission (internationally oriented national body)
- ♦ **IMK** Internationale Maaskommission (#12702)
- ♦ **IMK** Internationales Mauthausen Komitee (#04179)
- ♦ **IMLA** International Maritime Lecturers' Association (#14101)
- ♦ **IMLA** International Media Lawyers Association (#14127)
- ♦ IMLAS – International Musculoskeletal Laser Society (no recent information)
- ♦ IMLAST / see International Movement for Leisure Activities in Science and Technology
- ♦ IMLAST – International Movement for Leisure Activities in Science and Technology (internationally oriented national body)
- ♦ IMLB – International Meeting on Lithium Batteries (meeting series)
- ♦ **IMLC** International Medieval Latin Committee (#14140)
- ♦ **IMLI** IMO International Maritime Law Institute (#11134)
- ♦ IML / see IML Walking Association (#11130)
- ♦ **IML** IML Walking Association (#11130)
- ♦ **IML** International Institute for the Management of Logistics and Supply Chain (#13899)
- ♦ IMLS – International Machine Learning Society (internationally oriented national body)

♦ IML Walking Association (IML) 11130

Contact address not obtained. E-mail: info@imlwalking.org.
URL: http://www.imlwalking.org/

History 1987, as *International Marching League (IML).* Present name adopted 2006. Registered in accordance with Dutch law. **Aims** Promote health; encourage friendship between people worldwide by promoting and encouraging multi-days walking events internationally. **Structure** General Meeting; Board. **Languages** English. **Finance** Sources: members' dues; sponsorship. Other sources: sales. **Activities** Awards/prizes/competitions; sporting activities. **Events** *General Meeting* Vaasa (Finland) 2001. **Publications** *IML Newsletter.*
Members Full in 26 countries and territories:
Australia, Austria, Belgium, China, Czechia, Denmark, Finland, France, Germany, Indonesia, Ireland, Israel, Italy, Japan, Korea Rep, Lithuania, Luxembourg, Netherlands, New Zealand, Norway, Spain, Sweden, Switzerland, Taiwan, UK, USA.
NGO Relations Member of: *The Association for International Sport for All (TAFISA, #02763).*
[2019/XN9979/**C**]

- ♦ **IMMAA** International Mixed Martial Arts Association (#14172)
- ♦ **IMMAF** International Mixed Martial Arts Federation (#14173)
- ♦ IMMA – International Menuhin Music Academy (internationally oriented national body)
- ♦ **IMMA** International Mesostructured Materials Association (#14146)
- ♦ **IMMA** International Motorcycle Manufacturers Association (#14186)
- ♦ iMMAP (internationally oriented national body)
- ♦ IMMC – International Metallurgy and Materials Congress (meeting series)
- ♦ IMMC – International Museum Membership Conference (meeting series)
- ♦ **IMMC** International Scientific Committee of the International Medicinal Mushroom Conference (#14802)
- ♦ **IMMDA** International Marathon Medical Directors Association (#14088)
- ♦ **IMMF** International Music Managers' Forum (#14200)
- ♦ IMM – Foundation for Mediterranean Studies (internationally oriented national body)
- ♦ **IMMFWG** International Mass Marketing Fraud Working Group (#14115)
- ♦ Immigration and Refugee Services of America / see US Committee for Refugees and Immigrants
- ♦ IMM – Institute of Marketing and Management (internationally oriented national body)
- ♦ IMM – International Media Ministries (see: #10110)
- ♦ IMM – International Miners' Mission (internationally oriented national body)
- ♦ IMM – International Morphology Meeting (meeting series)
- ♦ IMMOA – International Mercantile Marine Officers' Association (inactive)
- ♦ IMMS – International Marine Minerals Society (internationally oriented national body)
- ♦ **IMMS** International Military Music Society (#14162)
- ♦ IMMTA – International MultiModal Transport Association (inactive)

♦ Immunization Partners in Asia Pacific (IPAP) 11131

Pres Ste 17D Univ Towers, 728 Pedro Gil St, ERmita, 1000 Manila, Philippines. T. +6327084561. Fax +6327084561. E-mail: ipap.inc@ymail.com.
URL: http://www.ip-ap.net/

History Jul 2011, Jakarta (Indonesia). Founded during 3rd Asian Vaccine Conference (ASVAC). **Aims** Engender collaboration, cooperation and partnerships to develop a dynamic, reliable and effective advocacy campaign to increase, expand and improve the immunization coverage in the region for all preventable *diseases.* **Activities** Events/meetings. **Events** *ASVAC : Asian Vaccine Conference* Colombo (Sri Lanka) 2022, *ASVAC : Asian Vaccine Conference* Yangon (Myanmar) 2019, *ASVAC : Asian Vaccine Conference* Singapore (Singapore) 2017, *ASVAC : Asian Vaccine Conference* Hanoi (Vietnam) 2015, *ASVAC : Asian Vaccine Conference* Cebu City (Philippines) 2013. [2020/XJ8962/**D**]

- ♦ Immunocompromised Host Society / see International Immunocompromised Host Society (#13835)

♦ Immunogenomics Data-Analysis Working Group (IDAWG) 11132

Contact UCSF Dept of Pediatrics, 5700 MLK Jr Way, Oakland CA 94609-1673, USA. E-mail: idawg@immunogenomics.org.
URL: http://igdawg.org/

History as an international collaborative effort of researchers concerned with issues of immunogenomics data management and analysis. **Aims** Facilitate sharing of immunogenomic data; foster consistent analysis and interpretation of such data by the immunogenomics and larger genomics communities. **Languages** English. **Activities** Events/meetings; knowledge management/information dissemination; research and development.
Members Full in 10 countries:
Australia, Austria, Brazil, France, Germany, India, Korea Rep, Thailand, UK, USA.
NGO Relations Participates in meetings of: American Society for Histocompatibility and Immunogenetics (ASHI); *Asia Pacific Histocompatibility and Immunogenetics Association (APHIA, #01927); European Federation for Immunogenetics (EFI, #07141).* [2023.02.13/XJ8171/**E**]

♦ Immunology of Diabetes Society (IDS) 11133

Sec Clinical Sci Dept, Skåne University Hosp, Lund University, SE-205 02 Malmö, Sweden.
URL: http://www.immunologyofdiabetessociety.com/

Aims Foster research related to the genetics and pathogenesis, prevention and cure of type 1 diabetes; act as an international forum for scientific discussion of all aspects of the immunology of insulin-dependent diabetes, including studies of the genetics, immunology, prediction and prevention of the disease and of pancreatic transplantation, in animal models and humans. **Structure** General Assembly. Executive Council, including President, Treasurer and Secretary. **Finance** Sources: members' dues. **Activities** Organizes regular scientific meetings and workshops. **Events** *Congress* Paris (France) 2023, *Congress* Nashville, TN (USA) 2021, *Congress* Beijing (China) 2020, *Congress* London (UK) 2018, *Congress* San Francisco, CA (USA) 2017. **Publications** *IDS Newsletter.*
Members Individuals in 21 countries:
Australia, Austria, Belgium, Canada, China, Czechia, Denmark, Finland, France, Germany, India, Israel, Italy, Japan, Korea Rep, New Zealand, Norway, Sweden, Switzerland, UK, USA. [2018/XJ2645/v/**C**]

- ♦ ImmunoRad – International Conference on Immunotherapy Radiotherapy Combinations (meeting series)
- ♦ iMNC – international MicroNano Conference (meeting series)
- ♦ **IMnI** International Manganese Institute (#14083)
- ♦ IMNRC – International Multidisciplinary Neuroscience Research Centre (internationally oriented national body)

- ♦ IMO / see Institute for Development and International Relations
- ♦ **IMOA** International Molybdenum Association (#14178)
- ♦ IMOCA – International Monohull Open Classes Association (see: #21760)
- ♦ IMODEV – Institut du Monde et du Développement pour la Bonne Gouvernance Publique (internationally oriented national body)
- ♦ IMO/FAO/JUNESKO-MOK/VMO/VOZ/MAGATE/OON/JUNEP Obedinennaja Gruppa Ekspertov po Naucnym Aspektam Zascity Morskoj Sredy / see Joint Group of Experts on the Scientific Aspects of Marine Environmental Protection (#16131)
- ♦ IMO/FAO/UNESCO-IOC/WMO/WHO/IAEA/UN/UNEP Joint Group of Experts on the Scientific Aspects of Marine Environmental Protection / see Joint Group of Experts on the Scientific Aspects of Marine Environmental Protection (#16131)
- ♦ **IMOF** International Mathematical Olympiad Foundation (#14120)

♦ IMO International Maritime Law Institute (IMLI) 11134

Institut de droit maritime international de l'OMI

Dir c/o Univ of Malta, University Heights, Tal-Qroqq, Msida, MSD 2080, Malta. T. +35621319343 – +35621310816. Fax +35621343092. E-mail: info@imli.org – imlidirector@imli.org.
URL: http://www.imli.org/

History 1988. Founded under the auspices of *International Maritime Organization (IMO, #14102)*, a specialized agency of the UN. Officially inaugurated 4 Nov 1989. **Aims** Enhance capacity building in all states, particularly developing states; promote safe, secure, environmentally sound, efficient and sustainable shipping through cooperation; promote the International Maritime Law and the general Law of the Sea, with special reference to IMO regulations and procedures. **Structure** Governing Board; Academic Committee; Financial and Human Resources Committee; Director. **Languages** English. **Staff** 19.00 FTE, paid. **Finance** Sources: contributions; donations; government support; in-kind support; international organizations; private foundations; sponsorship. Support from ITF Seafarers' Trust; Lloyd's Register Foundation; Transport Malta; CMI Charitable Trust. Supported by: *International Maritime Organization (IMO, #14102)*; *Nippon Foundation.* **Activities** Capacity building; guidance/assistance/consulting; knowledge management/information dissemination; standards/guidelines; training/education. IMLI has provided quality training and education to over 150 States and territories. **Events** *Maritime Transport Seminar* Msida (Malta) 2021, *International Workshop on The Role of Maritime Law in East Asian Maritime Relations* Msida (Malta) 2019, *Maritime Transport Seminar* Msida (Malta) 2019, *Symposium on international maritime labour law* Tal Qroqq (Malta) 2000, *International conference on Consolato di Mare and chambers of Commerce* Valletta (Malta) 1998. **Publications** *IMLI Newsletter*, *MLI E-News. 30 Years in the Service of the Rule of International Maritime Law. IMLI Manual on International Maritime Law;; IMLI Studies in International Maritime Law*, *MLI Treatise on Global Ocean Governance.* Annual Report; essays in honour of Professor David Joseph Attard; brochures; directory; special publications. **NGO Relations** Member of (1): *Comité maritime international (CMI, #04192)* (consultative). Also links with national maritime law associations and educational centres. [2022.05.12/XE1602/j/**E**]

- ♦ **IMO** International Maritime Organization (#14102)
- ♦ IMO – International Meteorological Organization (inactive)
- ♦ **IMO** International Meteor Organization (#14152)
- ♦ IMO – International Miners' Organization (no recent information)
- ♦ **IMoLIN** International Money Laundering Information Network (#14181)
- ♦ IMoSEB – International Mechanism of Scientific Expertise on Biodiversity (unconfirmed)
- ♦ IMO-SPHINX – International Academy IMOS – Interallied Military Organization 'Sphinx' (internationally oriented national body)
- ♦ **iMOSS** International Molecular Moss Science Society (#14176)

♦ IMO Staff Association 11135

Main Office c/o IMO, 4 Albert Embankment, London, SE1 7SR, UK. T. +442075873197. Fax +442075873210. E-mail: staffassociation@imo.org.
URL: http://www.imo.org/

History 1969, London (UK). Founded to represent staff members of *International Maritime Organization (IMO, #14102)*. Former names and other names: *IMO Staff Union* – former; *Syndicat du personnel de l'OMI* – former; *Sindicato del Personal de la OMI* – former. **Aims** Represent staff in their relations with appropriate authorities of IMO and appropriate bodies outside IMO; safeguard the rights and protect the interests of staff and improve their *working conditions.* **Structure** Staff Assembly (meets annually); Staff Committee. **Finance** Sources: members' dues. **Events** *Conference of staff associations of international organizations* London (UK) 2002. **Publications** *IMO Staff Association Newsletter* (irregular). **Members** Open to all dues-paying members of the staff of IMO. [2021/XE1964/v/**E**]

- ♦ IMO Staff Union / see IMO Staff Association (#11135)
- ♦ IMOWF – International Muslim Organization for Woman and Family (unconfirmed)
- ♦ **IMPACS** CARICOM Implementation Agency for Crime and Security (#03573)

♦ IMPACT 11136

Exec Dir 331 Cooper St, Ste 600, Ottawa ON K2P 0G5, Canada. T. +16132376768. E-mail: info@impacttransform.org.
URL: http://impacttransform.org/

History 1986. Former names and other names: *Partnership Africa Canada (PAC)* – former (1986 to 2017); *Partenariat Afrique Canada (PAC)* – former (1986 to 2017). **Aims** Transform how natural resources are managed in areas where security and human rights are at risk; investigate and develop approaches for natural resources to improve security, development and equality. **Structure** Board of Directors; Field Level Project Managers; Head Office in Ottawa ON (Canada). **Languages** English, French. **Staff** 36.00 FTE, paid. **Finance** Support from governments; international institutions; private sector companies; investment bodies; NGOs; IGOs; universities; labour unions; charities; foundations. Annual budget (2018-2019): Canadian $ 3,497,753. **Activities** Research and development; networking/liaising. **Events** *Annual General Assembly* Ottawa, ON (Canada) 1996, *Joint meeting* Dakar (Senegal) 1994, *Joint meeting* Dakar (Senegal) 1993, *Joint meeting* Dakar (Senegal) 1993. **Publications** Research reports; policy briefs.
Members Voting; Observer. National and international organizations located in Canada, including 65 organizations listed in this Yearbook:
- *Africa Community Technical Service (ACTS)*;
- *African Society for Humanitarian Aid and Development (ASHAD, no recent information)*;
- *Aga Khan Foundation (AKF, #00545)* (Canadian office);
- *Age UK* (Canadian office);
- *Alternatives – Action and Communication Network for International Development*;
- *Amref Health Africa (#00806)* (Canadian office);
- *Association québécoise des organismes de coopération internationale (AQOCI)*;
- *Broadcasting for International Understanding (BIU, no recent information)*;
- *Camrose International Institute (CII, inactive)*;
- *Canada-Africa International Forestry Association (CAIFA, no recent information)*;
- *Canada World Youth (JCM)*;
- *Canadian Baptist Ministries (CBM)*;
- *Canadian Bureau for International Education (CBIE)*;
- *Canadian Crossroads International (CCI)*;
- *Canadian Foodgrains Bank (CFGB)*;
- *Canadian Physicians for Aid and Relief (CPAR)*;
- *CARE International (CI, #03429)* (Canadian office);
- *Carrefour d'éducation à la solidarité internationale – Québec (CESIQ)*;
- *Carrefour de solidarité internationale (CSI)*;
- *Centre estrien de ressources en développement international (no recent information)*;
- *Centre international de solidarité ouvrière (CISO)*;
- *ChildFund International (#03869)* (Canadian office);
- *Children's Aid Direct (inactive)* (Canadian office);
- *Coady International Institute (CII)*;
- *CODE*;
- *Compassion International (CI, #04413)* (Canadian office);
- *Development and Peace (CCODP)*;
- *Développement international des étudiants des collèges et des universités bénévolés du Québec (DIBEC, no recent information)*;
- *Equality Fund (EF)*;
- *European Partnership for Responsible Minerals (EPRM, #08159)*;
- *Global Aid Foundation (#10175)* (Canadian office);
- *Hope International Development Agency*;
- *Institute of Peace and Conflict Studies, Waterloo ON (IPACS)*;
- *International Committee of the Red Cross (ICRC, #12799)* (Canadian office);
- *International Council for Adult Education (ICAE, #12983)*;
- *International Development and Relief Foundation (IDRF)*;
- *International Development Education Resource Association (IDERA, no recent information)*;
- *International Family Farm Exchange Association (Farmers Helping Farmers, no recent information)*;
- *International Federation for Home Economics (IFHE, #13447)* (Canadian office);
- *International Solidarity Centre, Saguenay Lac-Saint-Jean (CSI)*;
- *Inter Pares*;
- *Lutheran World Relief (LWR)* (Canadian office);
- *MBMS International*;
- *Mennonite Economic Development Associates (MEDA)*;
- *Mission Aviation Fellowship (MAF, #16829)* (Canadian office);
- *Mission Inclusion*;
- *North-South Institute (NSI)*;
- *Operation Eyesight Universal*;
- OXFAM – Québec;
- *PATH (#18260)* (Canadian office);
- *Peacefund Canada (no recent information)*;
- *People to People International (PTPI, #18300)* (Canadian office);
- *Primate's World Relief and Development Fund (PWRDF)*;
- *Salvation Army (#19041)* (Canadian office);
- *Save the Children International (#19058)* (Canadian office);
- *SeedChange*;
- *SIM International* (Canadian office);
- *SUCO*;
- *Terre sans frontières (TSF)*;
- *Transforming Education Through Information Technologies (EDUCAUSE)* (Canadian office);
- *Victoria International Development Education Association (VIDEA)*;
- *Vues d'Afrique*;
- *World ORT (WO, #21698)* (Canadian office);
- *World Renew*;
- *World Vision International (WVI, #21904)*.

Consultative Status Consultative status granted from: *ECOSOC (#05331)* (Special). **IGO Relations** Observer: *Minamata Convention on Mercury (2013).* **NGO Relations** Member of (1): *Environmental Peacebuilding Association (EnPAx, #05509).* Cooperates with (1): *Publish What You Pay Coalition (PWYP, #18573).* Instrumental in setting up: *Africa Information Afrique (AIA, no recent information).* [2019.12.11/XG4921/y/**F**]

- ♦ Impact Académique (#20516)
- ♦ Impact Carbon (internationally oriented national body)
- ♦ **ImpactEng** International Society of Impact Engineering (#15195)
- ♦ IMPACT – Initiative internationale contre les incapacités évitables (#11137)
- ♦ **IMPACT** Initiative de mobilisation panafricaine de controle de tabac (#11211)
- ♦ IMPACT Initiatives (unconfirmed)

♦ IMPACT – International Initiative Against Avoidable Disablement .. 11137

IMPACT – Initiative internationale contre les incapacités évitables

CEO 151 Western Road, Haywards Heath, RH16 3LH, UK. T. +441444457080. Fax +441444457877. E-mail: impact@impact.org.uk.
Int Coordinator c/o WHO, Avenue Appia 20, 1211 Geneva 27, Switzerland. T. +41227913732. Fax +41227910746.
URL: http://www.impact.org.uk/

History 2 Oct 1983, India, by *UNDP (#20292)*, *UNICEF (#20332)* and *WHO (#20950)*. **Aims** In cooperation with UN agencies, governments and international NGOs, prevent and, where possible, reverse causes of *disability* which affect massive populations throughout the *developing world.* **Structure** Nationally, managed by each national IMPACT Foundation. **Finance** Private donations. **Activities** Advocacy/lobbying/activism; humanitarian/emergency aid. **Publications** *Impact Newsletter.* Annual Review.
Members IMPACT foundations are active in 14 countries:
Bangladesh, Cambodia, India, Kenya, Nepal, Norway, Pakistan, Philippines, Sri Lanka, Sweden, Switzerland, Tanzania UR, Thailand, UK. [2014.06.01/XF0850/**F***]

- ♦ **IMPACT** International Multilateral Partnership Against Cyber Threats (#14196)
- ♦ Impacto Académico (#20516)
- ♦ IMPA / see Intergraf (#11505)
- ♦ **IMPA** International Marine Purchasing Association (#14094)
- ♦ **IMPA** International Maritime Pilots' Association (#14103)
- ♦ IMPA – International Movement for Peace Action (inactive)
- ♦ IMPA – International Music Publishers Association (inactive)
- ♦ **IMPALA** Independent Music Companies Association (#11151)
- ♦ **IMPCA** International Methanol Producers and Consumers Association (#14153)
- ♦ IMPC – International Mechanical Pulping Conference (meeting series)
- ♦ **IMPC** International Mineral Processing Council (#14166)
- ♦ IMPD – International Movement of Parliamentarians for Democracy (see: #21661)
- ♦ **IMPEL** European Union Network for the Implementation and Enforcement of Environmental Law (#09005)
- ♦ Imperial College of Tropical Agriculture / see Tropical Agriculture Association
- ♦ Imperial Communications Advisory Committee / see Commonwealth Telecommunications Organisation (#04365)
- ♦ Imperial Conference / see Commonwealth Heads of Government Meeting (#04337)
- ♦ Imperial Conference of the British Empire / see Commonwealth Heads of Government Meeting (#04337)
- ♦ Imperial Cricket Conference / see International Cricket Council (#13105)
- ♦ Imperial Institute / see The Commonwealth Education Trust (#04323)
- ♦ Imperial Order Daughters of the Empire and Children of the Empire Junior Branch / see IODE
- ♦ Imperial War Graves Commission / see Commonwealth War Graves Commission (#04367)
- ♦ **IMPF** Independent Music Publishers Forum (#11152)
- ♦ **IMP Group** Industrial Marketing and Purchasing Group (#11178)
- ♦ **IMPHOS** Institut mondial du phosphate (#21728)
- ♦ **IMPI** International Microwave Power Institute (#14160)
- ♦ **IMP** International Mito Patients (#14171)
- ♦ Implementation of Certain Provisions Concerning Nationality (1969 treaty)
- ♦ **IMPO** International Medical Parliamentarians Organization (#14137)
- ♦ Imported Hardwood Plywood Association of America / see International Wood Products Association
- ♦ Imported Hardwood Products Association / see International Wood Products Association
- ♦ IMPR Humanitarian Aid and Relief Center (internationally oriented national body)
- ♦ IMPR HUMANITARIAN – IMPR Humanitarian Aid and Relief Center (internationally oriented national body)
- ♦ Improve International (internationally oriented national body)
- ♦ Improving Outcomes in the Treatment of Opioid Dependence Conference (meeting series)

♦ Impunity Watch 11138

Exec Dir Alexanderveld 5, 2585 DB The Hague, Netherlands. T. +31622367199. E-mail: info@impunitywatch.org.
URL: https://www.impunitywatch.org/

History 2004. Originally a project within the *SOLIDARIDAD Network (#19681)*. Since Jan 2008, an independent foundation. Registration: ANBI/RSIN, No/ID: 8190.96.337, Start date: 2008, Netherlands. **Aims** Promote accountability for past atrocities, notably in countries emerging from a violent past. **Structure** Board of Directors. [2020/AA1528/t/**F**]

- ♦ IMRA / see Retail Industry Leaders Association
- ♦ **IMRA** International Medical Research Association (#14138)
- ♦ **IMRB** International Mine Rescue Body (#14167)
- ♦ IMRET – International Conference of Microreaction Technology (meeting series)
- ♦ **IMRF** International Maritime Rescue Federation (#14104)
- ♦ IMRF – International Membrane Research Forum (meeting series)
- ♦ **IMRF** International Multisensory Research Forum (#14198)
- ♦ IMRI – Institut Marocain des Relations Internationales (internationally oriented national body)
- ♦ IMR – Internationaler Missionsrat (inactive)
- ♦ IMS / see Artsen Zonder Vakantie
- ♦ IMS / see Rensselaerville Institute
- ♦ IMSA – International Medical Sciences Academy (internationally oriented national body)
- ♦ IMSA – International Memorialization Supply Association (internationally oriented national body)
- ♦ **IMSA** International Mind Sports Association (#14164)
- ♦ **IMSCOGS** International Multiple Sclerosis Cognition Society (#14197)
- ♦ IMSCO – International Multiracial Shared Cultural Organization (internationally oriented national body)
- ♦ **IMSD** International Association for Multibody System Dynamics (#12037)
- ♦ IMSE / see International Steering Committee on Integral Methods in Science and Engineering (#15604)
- ♦ **IMSE** International Steering Committee on Integral Methods in Science and Engineering (#15604)
- ♦ **IMSF** International Marine Simulator Forum (#14095)
- ♦ **IMSF** International Maritime Statistics Forum (#14105)
- ♦ **IMSF** International Mass Spectrometry Foundation (#14116)
- ♦ IMS Forum – IP Multimedia Subsystems Forum (internationally oriented national body)
- ♦ IMS Global Learning Consortium (internationally oriented national body)
- ♦ IMS – IMS Global Learning Consortium (internationally oriented national body)
- ♦ IMS – Institute of Management Specialists (internationally oriented national body)
- ♦ **IMS** Institute of Mathematical Statistics (#11282)
- ♦ **IMS** Institut mondial des sciences (#21590)
- ♦ **IMS** Intelligent Manufacturing Systems (#11375)
- ♦ IMS – International Machiavelli Society (unconfirmed)
- ♦ **IMS** International Masonry Society (#14114)
- ♦ **IMS** International Meat Secretariat (#14125)
- ♦ **IMS** International Media Support (#14128)
- ♦ **IMS** International Medieval Society, Paris (#14142)
- ♦ **IMS** International Meningioma Society (#14144)
- ♦ **IMS** International Menopause Society (#14145)
- ♦ **IMS** International Metallographic Society (#14151)
- ♦ IMS – International Microencapsulation Society (inactive)
- ♦ IMS – International Micropatrological Society (inactive)
- ♦ **IMS** International Mountain Society (#14190)
- ♦ IMS – International Multihull Society (inactive)
- ♦ **IMS** International Musicological Society (#14201)
- ♦ **IMS** International Myeloma Society (#14205)
- ♦ **IMS** International MYOPAIN Society (#14206)
- ♦ IMS / see International Social Service (#14886)
- ♦ IMSN / see International Consumer Protection and Enforcement Network (#12930)
- ♦ **IMSO** International Mobile Satellite Organization (#14174)
- ♦ IMSoP / see International Spinal Cord Society (#15581)
- ♦ **IMSPG** International Microgravity Strategic Planning Group (#14157)
- ♦ IMSS / see International Mass Spectrometry Foundation (#14116)
- ♦ **IMSS** International Microsurgery Simulation Society (#14159)
- ♦ **IMSSS** International Medieval Sermon Studies Society (#14141)
- ♦ **IMSSU** International Metallic Silhouette Shooting Union (#14150)
- ♦ IMST – International Mushroom Society for the Tropics (inactive)
- ♦ **IMTAC** International Music Therapy Assessment Consortium (#14202)
- ♦ IMTA / see INTERFERRY (#11470)
- ♦ IMTA / see International Map Industry Association (#14085)
- ♦ IMTA – International Medical Travel Association (inactive)
- ♦ **IMTA** International Military Testing Association (#14163)
- ♦ IMTALAP / see International Museum Theatre Alliance Asia Pacific
- ♦ IMTAL Asia Pacific – International Museum Theatre Alliance Asia Pacific (internationally oriented national body)
- ♦ IMTAL-Europe – International Museum Theatre Alliance for Europe (internationally oriented national body)
- ♦ IMTAL – International Museum Theatre Alliance (internationally oriented national body)
- ♦ IMTC – International Money Transfer and Payments Conferences (meeting series)
- ♦ IMTCO – International Multilateral Trade Cooperation Organization (unconfirmed)
- ♦ IMTD – Institute for Multi-Track Diplomacy (internationally oriented national body)
- ♦ IMTEC Foundation (#19988)
- ♦ IMTEC – International Movements Towards Educational Change / see Stiftelsen IMTEC (#19988)
- ♦ **IMTF** International Malnutrition Task Force (#14079)
- ♦ **IMTG** Internationale Gesellschaft für Moor- und Torfkunde (#14538)
- ♦ **IMT-GT** Indonesia-Malaysia-Thailand Growth Triangle (#11167)
- ♦ IMT – Institut de médecine tropicale Prince Léopold (internationally oriented national body)
- ♦ IMT – Instituto del Mundo del Trabajo (internationally oriented national body)
- ♦ IMT – International Meeting on Thermodiffusion (meeting series)
- ♦ IMU / see European Metal Union (#07785)
- ♦ **IMU** International Mathematical Union (#14121)
- ♦ IMU – International Medical University, Malaysia (internationally oriented national body)
- ♦ IMU – International Monarchist Union (no recent information)
- ♦ IMU – Irish Missionary Union (internationally oriented national body)
- ♦ IMUNA – International Model United Nations Association (internationally oriented national body)
- ♦ IMUSA – International Office of Musicians (inactive)
- ♦ IMVF – Instituto Marquês de Valle Flôr (internationally oriented national body)
- ♦ **IMV** Internationaler Metzgermeister-Verband (#12421)
- ♦ **IMV** Internationaler Milchwirtschaftverband (#13128)
- ♦ IMWAC / see We Are Church International (#20841)
- ♦ **IMWA** International Mine Water Association (#14168)
- ♦ **IMWF** International Mediterranean Women's Forum (#14143)
- ♦ **IMW** Institute of Masters of Wine (#11281)
- ♦ IMXA – Institute for Balkan Studies, Thessaloniki (internationally oriented national body)
- ♦ IMYM – International Mazdaznan Youth Movement (inactive)
- ♦ IMZ Internationales Musik + Medienzentrum (#11139)

♦ IMZ International Music + Media Centre 11139

IMZ Internationales Musik + Medienzentrum

SG Stiftgasse 29, 1070 Vienna, Austria. T. +4318890315. Fax +431889031577. E-mail: office@imz.at.
URL: http://www.imz.at/

History 3 Jul 1961, Vienna (Austria). Former names and other names: *International Music Centre* – former (3 Jul 1961); *Centre international de la musique* – former (3 Jul 1961); *Internationales Musikzentrum* – former (3 Jul 1961). **Aims** Promote and disseminate music and dance in *audio-visual media*: television, films, radio and records; reinforce artistic dialogue in the media and stimulate international cooperation; act as a forum and information network for music, *dance* and media professionals and assist them in keeping pace with the changing requirements of music and media worlds. **Structure** General Assembly; Executive Board; Secretariat in Vienna (Austria). **Languages** English, French, German. **Staff** 7.00 FTE, paid. **Finance** Sources: fees for services; grants; members' dues. **Activities** Awards/prizes/competitions; events/meetings; knowledge management/information dissemination; networking/liaising. **Events** *Annual General Assembly* Cannes (France) 2007, *Annual General Assembly* Cannes (France) 2006, *Annual General Assembly* Cannes (France) 2005, *Annual General Assembly* Cannes (France) 2004, *Workshop on facts and figures of making arts and music films* Amman (Jordan) 2003. **Publications** *Dance screen on tour catalogues* (every 2 years); *AVANT Première* – IMZ Directory. *Music and Entertainment in Cultural Policy and the Public Conscious* (1987); *Musik in den technischen Medien: Probleme und Perspektiven der Aus- und Fortbildung von Medien-Mitarbeitern* (1979); *Radio und Neue Musik* (1979); *Music in Film and Television, 1964-1974* (1975); *50 Jahre Musik im Hörfunk* (1973); *International Anthology of Recorded Music* (1971); *Ten Years of Films on Ballet and Classical Dance 1956-1965* (1968).

Members totalling 150 public service broadcasters, independent production companies, record companies, radio stations, artists' agents, opera houses, concert halls, museums, educational institutions, dance companies, festivals and music publishers. Full; Associate; Affiliate; Individual; Honorary. Members in 32 countries:
Australia, Austria, Belgium, Brazil, Canada, China, Croatia, Czechia, Denmark, Estonia, Finland, France, Germany, Ghana, Hungary, Ireland, Israel, Italy, Japan, Latvia, Netherlands, Norway, Poland, Portugal, Russia, Slovenia, Spain, Sweden, Switzerland, UK, United Arab Emirates, USA.

NGO Relations Member of (2): *European Music Council (EMC, #07837)*; *International Music Council (IMC, #14199)*. Cooperates with (3): *European Broadcasting Union (EBU, #06404)*; *International Council for Traditional Music (ICTM, #13087)*; *International Society for Music Education (ISME, #15287)*. Cooperates with: Music Information Centre Austria (MICA). [2023/XC2276/**E**]

♦ INAA Group 11140

Main Office Rue de la Presse 4, 1000 Brussels, Belgium. T. +3222291912. Fax +3222184131. E-mail: secretariat@inaa.org.
URL: http://www.inaa.org/

History Apr 1992. Former names and other names: *International Network of Accountants and Auditors* – former; *INAA GROUP – International Association of Independent Accounting Firms* – full title. **Aims** Establish an international association primarily of accountants and auditors suitably qualified in their countries of origin; facilitate liaison between member firms so they can obtain advice on international matters affecting their clients and the *accountancy* profession internationally; facilitate referral of professional work on an exclusive basis between member firms. **Structure** General Meeting (annual); Board. **Languages** English. **Staff** None. **Finance** Members' dues (annual). Referral fees. **Events** *Intermediate Meeting* Budapest (Hungary) 2022, *Intermediate Meeting* Barcelona (Spain) 2019, *Annual General Meeting* Cape Town (South Africa) 2018, *Intermediate Meeting* Copenhagen (Denmark) 2018, *Annual General Meeting* San Francisco, CA (USA) 2017.

Members in 50 countries and territories:
Algeria, Argentina, Australia, Austria, Belgium, Bosnia-Herzegovina, Brazil, Canada, Chile, Croatia, Cyprus, Denmark, Egypt, France, Germany, Guernsey, Hong Kong, India, Indonesia, Ireland, Israel, Italy, Kazakhstan, Kenya, Korea Rep, Kuwait, Luxembourg, Malta, Mauritius, Mexico, Netherlands, Nigeria, Norway, Peru, Poland, Portugal, Romania, Russia, Serbia, Singapore, Slovenia, Spain, Switzerland, Tunisia, Türkiye, UK, United Arab Emirates, Uruguay, USA, Venezuela.
[2021/XF7177/**F**]

- ♦ INAA GROUP – International Association of Independent Accounting Firms / see INAA Group (#11140)
- ♦ **INACH** International Network Against Cyber Hate (#14229)
- ♦ INACSL – International Nursing Association for Clinical Simulation and Learning (internationally oriented national body)
- ♦ INADES / see Center of Research and Action for Peace (#03651)
- ♦ **INADES-Formation** Institut Africain pour le Développement Economique et Social – Centre Africain de Formation (#11233)
- ♦ INAFORM – International Association for Forest Resources Management (inactive)
- ♦ **INAHTA** International Network of Agencies for Health Technology Assessment (#14230)
- ♦ INAI – Fundación Instituto para las Negociaciones Agricolas Internacionales (internationally oriented national body)
- ♦ INA – International Academy for Innovative Pedagogy, Psychology and Economics, Free University of Berlin (internationally oriented national body)
- ♦ INA – Internationale Akademie für Innovative Pädagogik, Psychologie und Ökonomie, Freien Universität Berlin (internationally oriented national body)
- ♦ **INA** International Naikan Association (#14207)
- ♦ **INA** International Nannoplankton Association (#14208)
- ♦ **INA** International Neonatology Association (#14224)
- ♦ **INA** International Neuropsychiatric Association (#14356)
- ♦ **INA** International Neurotoxicology Association (#14359)
- ♦ **INA** International Neurotoxin Association (#14360)
- ♦ INA – International Nightlife Association (unconfirmed)
- ♦ INA – Iraqi National Accord (internationally oriented national body)
- ♦ **INAISE** International Association of Investors in the Social Economy (#11971)
- ♦ INALCO – Institut national des langues et civilisations orientales (internationally oriented national body)
- ♦ **INANE** International Academy of Nursing Editors (#11559)
- ♦ **INAP** International Network for Acid Prevention (#14227)
- ♦ **INAP** International Network of Affiliated Ports (#14228)
- ♦ INARA – International Network for Aid Relief and Assistance (internationally oriented national body)
- ♦ INARI – International Agency for Rural Industrialization (no recent information)
- ♦ INAR – International Network of Address Research (unconfirmed)
- ♦ INAS / see Centre for Nepal and Asian Studies
- ♦ INASCON – International Nanoscience Student Conference (meeting series)
- ♦ **InASEA** International Association for Southeast European Anthropology (#12173)
- ♦ INASEN – International Assembly of NGOs concerned with the Environment (inactive)
- ♦ INAS-FID / see Virtus: World Intellectual Impairment Sport (#20793)
- ♦ INAS-FMH / see Virtus: World Intellectual Impairment Sport (#20793)
- ♦ **INAS** Internationale Arbeitsgemeinschaft Sozialmanagement / Sozialwirtschaft (#13214)
- ♦ **INAS** International Network of Analytical Sociologists (#14231)
- ♦ **INAS** International Network for Autonomous Ships (#14232)
- ♦ **INASP** International Network for the Availability of Scientific Publications (#14233)
- ♦ **INASTE** International Network for Academic Steiner Teacher Education (#14226)
- ♦ INATBA – International Association of Trusted Blockchain Applications (unconfirmed)
- ♦ **INAUCO** Instituto Intercultural para la Autogestión y la Acción Comunal (#11335)
- ♦ Inayati Order (religious order)
- ♦ Inayatiyya – Inayati Order (religious order)
- ♦ **INBA** Inter-Islamic Network on Biosaline Agriculture (#11506)
- ♦ INBA – International Network of Business Advertising Agencies (inactive)
- ♦ INBAM / see International Network of Business and Management Journal Editors (#14237)
- ♦ **INBAM** International Network of Business and Management Journal Editors (#14237)
- ♦ **INBAR** International Network for Bamboo and Rattan (#14234)
- ♦ **INBO** International Network of Basin Organizations (#14235)

♦ INCAE Business School 11141

Rector Walter Kissling Campur, Apartado 960, Alajuela, Alajuela, Alajuela, 4050, Costa Rica. T. +50624372392. Fax +50624339798. E-mail: rectoria@incae.edu.

URL: http://www.incae.ac.cr/
History Founded 1964, Managua (Nicaragua), by Harvard Business School; second campus opened, 1983, Alajuela (Costa Rica). Original title: *Central American Institute for Business Administration – Instituto Centroamericano de Administración de Empresas (INCAE).* **Aims** Promote comprehensive development of the countries served; educate leaders in key sectors by improving their practices, attitudes and values. **Structure** Board of Directors. **Languages** English, Spanish. **Finance** Sources: private and public contributions; tuition. **Activities** Research/documentation; training/education; knowledge management/information dissemination. Together with *United States Agency for International Development (USAID)*, administers a fund for sponsoring scholarly studies on economic and political development of Central America. **Events** *International conference on marketing and development* San José (Costa Rica) 1993. **Publications** *Alumni Magazine*; *INCAE Business Review*. Books by faculty. Information Services: Campus in Costa Rica and in Nicaragua have each their own library for a total of 75,000 volumes; Collection of 3,000 teaching case materials on Latin America.
Members Managing Board members from 19 countries:
Argentina, Bolivia, Chile, Colombia, Costa Rica, Dominican Rep, Ecuador, El Salvador, Guatemala, Honduras, Mexico, Nicaragua, Panama, Paraguay, Peru, Spain, Uruguay, USA, Venezuela.
IGO Relations *Central American Common Market (CACM, #03666)*; *Central American Monetary Council (#03672)*; *International Nickel Study Group (INSG, #14370)*; *Puebla-Panama Plan (PPP, no recent information).* **NGO Relations** *Center for Sustainable Development in the Americas (CSDA)*; *Centro Latinoamericano para la Competitividad y el Desarrollo Sostenible (CLACDS)*; *Earth Council Alliance (ECA, inactive)*; *EFMD – The Management Development Network (#05387)*; *Federación de Entidades Privadas de Centroamérica, Panama y Republica Dominica (FEDEPRICAP, #09300)*; *Ford Foundation (#09858)*; *International Center for Economic Growth (ICEG, inactive)*; *LatinoAméricaPosible (LAP, #16402)*; *Tinker Foundation*; *World Business Council for Sustainable Development – Latin America (WBCSD-LA, no recent information).* [2013.07.30/XF0222/**E**]

- ♦ INCAE / see INCAE Business School (#11141)
- ♦ **INCA** International Neuroendocrine Cancer Alliance (#14348)
- ♦ **INCANA** Inter-regional Network on Cotton in Asia and North Africa (#15972)
- ♦ **INCAP** Institute of Nutrition of Central America and Panama (#11285)
- ♦ **INCASUR** Instituto Internacional de Estudios y Capacitación Social del Sur (#11337)
- ♦ INCATEL – Instituto Centroamericano de Telecomunicaciones (inactive)
- ♦ **INCB** International Narcotics Control Board (#14212)
- ♦ **INCCA** International Network of Centres for Computer Applications (#14239)
- ♦ **INCCA** International Network for the Conservation of Contemporary Art (#14245)
- ♦ INCC – International Network for Caregiving Children (unconfirmed)
- ♦ INCE / see Central European Initiative (#03708)
- ♦ **INCEDES** Instituto Centroamericano de Estudios Sociales y Desarrollo (#11327)
- ♦ INCED – International Centre for Education in Development, Coventry (internationally oriented national body)
- ♦ INCE Europe (internationally oriented national body)
- ♦ INCEP – Instituto Centroamericano de Estudios Politicos (internationally oriented national body)
- ♦ **INCF** International Neuroinformatics Coordinating Facility (#14351)
- ♦ INC-Forests – Intergovernmental Negotiating Committee for a Legally Binding Agreement on Forests in Europe (inactive)
- ♦ **INCHE** International Network for Christian Higher Education (#14241)
- ♦ **INCHES** International Network on Children's Health, Environment and Safety (#14240)
- ♦ INCHR – International Network for Circumpolar Health Research (inactive)
- ♦ INCIDI – Institut international des civilisations différentes (inactive)
- ♦ INCIID – InterNational Council for Infertility Information Dissemination (no recent information)
- ♦ INCI / see International Chemical Information Network (#12542)
- ♦ INC – International Inflammatory Neuropathy Consortium (see: #18314)
- ♦ **INC** International Neonatal Consortium (#14223)
- ♦ INC / see International Numismatic Council (#14385)
- ♦ **INC** International Numismatic Council (#14385)
- ♦ INC / see International Nut and Dried Fruit Council Foundation (#14387)
- ♦ **INC** International Nut and Dried Fruit Council Foundation (#14387)
- ♦ INCIPE – Instituto de Cuestiones Internacionales y Politica Exterior, Madrid (internationally oriented national body)
- ♦ **INCLEN-ASIA** International Clinical Epidemiology Network – Asia (#12599)
- ♦ INCLEN / see INCLEN Trust International (#11142)
- ♦ INCLEN-SEA / see International Clinical Epidemiology Network – Asia (#12599)

♦ INCLEN Trust International 11142

Exec Dir Executive Office India, F-1/5 2nd Floor, Okhla Industrial Area, Phase I, Delhi 110020, DELHI 110020, India. T. +911147730000. Fax +911147730001. E-mail: ieodelhi@inclentrust.org.
URL: http://www.inclentrust.org/
History 1980. Founded as a project of *The Rockefeller Foundation (#18966)*. Became an independent organization registered in the State of Pennsylvania *USA*, 1988. Leadership shifted to Low and Middle Income Countries, 2000, when current title was adopted. Former names and other names: *International Clinical Epidemiology Network (INCLEN)* – former. **Aims** Attain equity in health for development through essential research and training in global health and related disciplines. **Structure** Governing Body; Board of Trustees. Regional networks (7): CanUSACLEN; ChinaCLEN; *French Language Network for International Clinical Epidemiology (#09992)* / Euro-MediterraneanCLEN; *INCLEN Africa (IA, no recent information)*; IndiaCLEN; *International Clinical Epidemiology Network – Asia (INCLEN-ASIA, #12599)*; *Latin American Clinical Epidemiology Network (#16298)*. Also includes: *INCLEN Institute of Global Health (IIGH)*, set up 2015. **Languages** English. **Staff** 150.00 FTE, paid. **Finance** *The Rockefeller Foundation (#18966)* provided initial core financial support until 1999. Since 2000, revenue through research and capacity building activities. Sources also include multilateral, bilateral funding and government funding agencies. **Activities** Capacity building; projects/programmes; research and development; training/education. **Events** *Annual meeting* Agra (India) 2004, *Annual Meeting* Kunming (China) 2003, *Annual meeting* Sharm el Sheikh (Egypt) 2002, *Annual meeting* Bangkok (Thailand) 2001, *Annual meeting* Bangkok (Thailand) 2000. **Publications** *INCLEN Newsletter* (annual). *INCLEN Monograph Series on Critical International Health Issues* (irregular). Annual Report; programmes and abstracts of annual meetings; brochure. **Members** Clinical Epidemiology Resource and Training Centers (31), Clinical Epidemiology Units (59), clinical faculty members, biostatisticians, epidemiologists, clinical economists and social scientists (1,843) in 34 countries. Membership countries not specified. **IGO Relations** Recognized by: *WHO (#20950)* – Strategic Advisory Group of Experts on Immunization; *WHO (#20950)* – Working Group on Science and Evidence for Ending Childhood Obesity. **NGO Relations** Member of (1): *Global Vaccine Data Network (GVDN, #10645)*. Recognized by (1): *European Association for the Study of Obesity (EASO, #06234)*. Supports (2): *Global Network for Perinatal and Reproductive Health (GNPRH, #10495)*; *International Epidemiological Association (IEA, #13287).* [2023/XF1155/**F**]

- ♦ **INCLO** International Network of Civil Liberties Organizations (#14242)

♦ Include Network 11143

Conference Dir Helen Hamlyn Centre, Royal College of Art, Kensington Gore, London, SW7 2EU, UK. T. +44275904242. Fax +44275904244. E-mail: include@rca.ac.uk – hhcd@rca.ac.uk.
URL: http://www.hhc.rca.ac.uk/210/all/1/Network.aspx
History superseding the *European Design for Ageing Network (DAN)*, set up Jul 1994, and coordinated by the *'DesignAge'* programme of the Royal College of Art, London (UK). Incorporated into the Helen Hamlyn Centre at the RCA. **Aims** Support people working to promote inclusive *design* – open to *old* and young and to people of all abilities and *disabilities*. **Languages** English. **Activities** Biennial conference; workshops; seminars. **Events** *Biennial Conference* Hong Kong (Hong Kong) 2013, *Biennial Conference* London (UK) 2011, *Biennial Conference* London (UK) 2009, *Biennial conference* London (UK) 2007, *Biennial Conference* London (UK) 2005. **Publications** Conference papers; DVD; CD-ROM; Books.
Members Full (over 300) in 33 European countries and territories:
Australia, Austria, Belgium, Canada, China, Colombia, Croatia, Denmark, Finland, France, Germany, Ghana, Hong Kong, India, Iran Islamic Rep, Ireland, Israel, Italy, Japan, Korea Rep, Lithuania, Malaysia, Netherlands, Poland, Portugal, South Africa, Spain, Sweden, Switzerland, Taiwan, Thailand, UK, USA.
IGO Relations *European Commission (EC, #06633)* (funding up to 1998); *European Cooperation in Science and Technology (COST, #06784)*; *SOCRATES Programme (inactive)* (Erasmus). [2010.06.01/XF3568/**F**]

- ♦ Inclusion Africa (unconfirmed)
- ♦ Inclusion Europe – L'Association Européenne des Organisations des Personnes Handicapées Mentales et leur Familles (#11144)

♦ Inclusion Europe – European Association of Societies of Persons with Intellectual Disability and their Families (Inclusion Europe) 11144

Inclusion Europe – L'Association Européenne des Organisations des Personnes Handicapées Mentales et leur Familles
Dir Avenue des Arts 3-4-5, 1210 Brussels, Belgium. T. +3225022815. E-mail: secretariat@inclusion-europe.org.
URL: https://www.inclusion-europe.eu/
History 1988. Founded within the framework of *Inclusion International (#11145)*, as a sub-group of its European Affairs Committee. Former names and other names: *ILSMH European Association (ILSMH EA)* – former; *Association européenne de l'ILSMH* – former; *European Association of the International League of Societies for Persons with Mental Handicap (Inclusion Europe)* – former; *Association européenne de la Ligue internationale des associations pour les personnes handicapées mentales* – former. Registration: Banque-Carrefour des Entreprises, No/ID: 0438.050.317, Start date: 2 Aug 1989, Belgium. **Aims** Encourage collaboration between member countries; cooperate with like-minded organizations; enhance opportunities for people with intellectual disability and their families; compare legislation and services around Europe; exchange information. **Structure** General Assembly (annual); Board; Secretariat, headed by Director; Main Office in Brussels (Belgium); Regional Office in Prague (Czech Rep); Units (3); Working Groups (9). Includes: European Platform of Self-Advocates (EPSA). **Finance** Sources: members' dues. **Activities** Events/meetings; knowledge management/information dissemination. **Events** *Europe in Action Conference* Brussels (Belgium) 2022, *Europe in Action Conference* Tampere (Finland) 2021, *Europe in Action Conference* Vienna (Austria) 2020, *Hear our Voices Conference* Graz (Austria) 2019, *Europe in Action Conference* Vilnius (Lithuania) 2019. **Publications** *Include* (6 a year) in English, French; *Human Rights Observer* in English, French; *Weekly Information Letter* in English, French. *European Directory of Self-advocacy Organizations*. Annual Report.
Members Full; Affiliate; Self-advocate organizations; Associate; Subscribing. Organizations in 38 countries and territories:
Albania, Austria, Belgium, Bosnia-Herzegovina, Bulgaria, Croatia, Cyprus, Czechia, Denmark, Estonia, Faeroe Is, Finland, France, Germany, Greece, Hungary, Iceland, Ireland, Israel, Italy, Latvia, Lithuania, Luxembourg, Malta, Netherlands, North Macedonia, Norway, Poland, Portugal, Romania, Russia, Serbia, Slovakia, Slovenia, Spain, Sweden, Switzerland, UK.
European organization (3):
Down Syndrome Education International (DSE); *European Cooperation in Anthroposophical Curative Education and Social Therapy (ECCE, #06783)*; Special Olympics Europe Euroasia.
Consultative Status Consultative status granted from: *Council of Europe (CE, #04881)* (Participatory Status). **IGO Relations** *European Commission (EC, #06633)*; *European Parliament (EP, #08146)*. Participant in Fundamental Rights Platform of: *European Union Agency for Fundamental Rights (FRA, #08969)*. **NGO Relations** Coordinator for the sector Intellectual Impairment within: *European Disability Forum (EDF, #06929)*. Member of: *Federation of European and International Associations Established in Belgium (FAIB, #09508)*. Instrumental in setting up: *European Coalition for Community Living (ECCL, #06590).* [2022/XD1918/**E**]

- ♦ Inclusion Europe / see Inclusion Europe – European Association of Societies of Persons with Intellectual Disability and their Families (#11144)
- ♦ **Inclusion Europe** Inclusion Europe – European Association of Societies of Persons with Intellectual Disability and their Families (#11144)

♦ Inclusion International 11145

Coordinator The Foundry, 17 Oval Way, London, SE11 5RR, UK. E-mail: info@inclusion-international.org.
Exec Dir address not obtained.
URL: http://www.inclusion-international.org/
History 1960. Constitution revised at General Assembly, Nov 1988, Mexico City (Mexico); further revised after General Assembly, 1994, Delhi (India); Oct 2016, USA. Former names and other names: *European League of Societies for the Mentally Handicapped* – former (1960 to Oct 1962); *Ligue européenne des associations d'aide aux handicapés mentaux* – former (1960 to Oct 1962); *International League of Societies for the Mentally Handicapped* – former (Oct 1962 to 31 Mar 1981); *Ligue internationale des associations d'aide aux handicapés mentaux* – former (Oct 1962 to 31 Mar 1981); *Liga Internacional de Asociaciones pro Deficientes Mentales* – former (Oct 1962 to 31 Mar 1981); *Internationale Liga von Vereinigungen zugunsten Geistig Behinderter* – former (Oct 1962 to 31 Mar 1981); *International League of Societies for Persons with Mental Handicap (ILSMH)* – former (31 Mar 1981 to 1994); *Ligue internationale des associations pour les personnes handicapées mentales* – former (31 Mar 1981 to 1994); *Liga Internacional de Asociaciones en favor de las Personas con Deficiencia Mental* – former (31 Mar 1981 to 1994); *Internationale Liga von Vereinigungen für Menschen mit Geistiger Behinderung* – former (31 Mar 1981 to 1994). Registration: Charity Commission, No/ID: 1106715, England and Wales; Companies House, No/ID: 5072000, England and Wales; Switzerland. **Aims** Advocate for the human rights of people with intellectual disabilities. **Structure** Assembly (every 2 years); Council. Includes: *Inclusion Africa (IA)*; *Inclusion Europe – European Association of Societies of Persons with Intellectual Disability and their Families (Inclusion Europe, #11144)*. **Languages** English, French, German, Spanish. **Staff** 2.00 FTE, paid. **Finance** Sources: members' dues. **Activities** Advocacy/lobbying/activism. **Events** *World Congress* 2022, *World Congress* Birmingham (UK) 2018, *World Congress* Nairobi (Kenya) 2014, *Meeting* Brussels (Belgium) 2012, *International Meeting of Families* Cali (Colombia) 2012. **Publications** *Newsletter* (periodical). Reports.
Members Full; Associate. Full in 82 countries and territories:
Albania, Algeria, Australia, Austria, Bangladesh, Belarus, Belgium, Belize, Benin, Brazil, Bulgaria, Burkina Faso, Cameroon, Canada, Chile, China, Colombia, Congo Brazzaville, Côte d'Ivoire, Croatia, Cuba, Cyprus, Czechia, Denmark, Dominican Rep, Ecuador, El Salvador, Estonia, Eswatini, Ethiopia, Faeroe Is, Finland, Germany, Ghana, Greece, Guatemala, Honduras, Hungary, Iceland, India, Indonesia, Ireland, Israel, Japan, Kuwait, Lebanon, Lesotho, Lithuania, Luxembourg, Malawi, Mali, Mauritius, Mexico, Moldova, Mongolia, Morocco, Nepal, New Zealand, Nicaragua, North Macedonia, Norway, Panama, Peru, Philippines, Poland, Portugal, Romania, Scotland, Senegal, Slovakia, Slovenia, South Africa, Spain, Sweden, Switzerland, Tanzania UR, Tunisia, Uganda, UK, Uruguay, Zambia, Zimbabwe.
Affiliate in 58 countries and territories:
Angola, Argentina, Bahrain, Belarus, Bolivia, Chile, Congo DR, Curaçao, Cyprus, Ecuador, Egypt, France, Germany, Ghana, Greece, Haiti, Hong Kong, India, Ireland, Israel, Italy, Jordan, Kenya, Korea Rep, Latvia, Lebanon, Madagascar, Malaysia, Malta, Mauritania, Moldova, Morocco, Netherlands, New Zealand, Nicaragua, Niger, Nigeria, Pakistan, Philippines, Portugal, Romania, Russia, Rwanda, Singapore, Slovakia, South Africa, Spain, Sri Lanka, Sudan, Taiwan, Thailand, Togo, Türkiye, Uganda, Ukraine, United Arab Emirates, USA, Zimbabwe.
Associate Member Organizations (federations of national societies and international – or regional – organizations) (2), listed in this Yearbook:
Asian Federation on Intellectual Disabilities (#01461); *Pan African Federation of Associations for Persons with Mental Handicap (FEPAPHAM, no recent information).*
Consultative Status Consultative status granted from: *ECOSOC (#05331)* (Special); *UNESCO (#20322)* (Consultative Status); *ILO (#11123)* (Special List); *UNICEF (#20332)*. **NGO Relations** Works with: *International Association for the Scientific Study of Intellectual and Developmental Disabilities (IASSIDD, #12153)*. Member of: *End Corporal Punishment (#05457)*; *Global Partnership to End Violence Against Children (End Violence Against Children, #10533)*. Founding member of: *International Disability Alliance (IDA, #13176)*; *NGO Committee on UNICEF (#17120)*. Participates in: *Global Partnership on Children with Disabilities (GPcwd, #10529)*. Special links with: *RI Global (#18948)*; *World Blind Union (WBU, #21234).* [2022/XB2221/y/**B**]

- ♦ Inclusive Development International (internationally oriented national body)

♦ Inclusive Green Growth Partnership (IGGP) 11146

Contact c/o GGGI, Seoul Headquarters, 19-F Jeongdong Bldg, 21-15 Jeongdong-gil, Jung-gu, Seoul 100-784, Korea Rep. T. +82220969991. Fax +82220969990. E-mail: info@gggi.org.
URL: http://gggi.org/inclusive-green-growth-partnership/
History Launched 7 Dec 2015, Paris (France), at 21st Conference of Parties of *United Nations Framework Convention on Climate Change (UNFCCC, 1992)*. A joint inititaive of *Global Green Growth Institute (GGGI, #10392)* and multilateral development banks and UN regional commissions. **Aims** Support *developing countries* in identifying green growth opportunities and *investments* that promote inclusive, shared prosperity and equitable growth that creates employment and raises the incomes of the poorest. **Events** *Global Green Growth Week Meeting* Jeju (Korea Rep) 2016.

Members Founding members (8):
African Development Bank (ADB, #00283); Asian Development Bank (ADB, #01422); Global Green Growth Institute (GGGI, #10392); Inter-American Development Bank (IDB, #11427); United Nations Economic and Social Commission for Asia and the Pacific (ESCAP, #20557); United Nations Economic and Social Commission for Western Asia (ESCWA, #20558); United Nations Economic Commission for Africa (ECA, #20554); United Nations Economic Commission for Latin America and the Caribbean (ECLAC, #20556). [2015/XM4617/y/**F**]

♦ **Inclusive Growth Forum** **11147**

Treas Rue Henri-Mussard 11, 1208 Geneva, Switzerland. E-mail: info@inclusivegrowthforum.org.
URL: http://inclusivegrowthforum.org/

History Registered in accordance with Swiss Civil Code. **Aims** Encourage and promote awareness and adoption of inclusive *innovation* so as to generate inclusive growth; promote collaboration and knowledge-sharing between different actors, researchers and innovators so as to proactively influence inclusive growth. **Structure** General Assembly; Board of Directors; Bureau; Audit. **Languages** English, French. **Staff** 15.00 FTE, voluntary. None paid. **Activities** Advocacy/lobbying/activism; awards/prizes/competitions; certification/accreditation; guidance/assistance/consulting; knowledge management/information dissemination; events/meetings; monitoring/evaluation; networking/liaising; publishing activities; research/documentation. **IGO Relations** *Mekong Institute (MI, #16701).* [2018.05.29/XM6739/**F**]

♦ INCM – Institut de neurosciences cognitives de la méditerranée (internationally oriented national body)
♦ Incomindios / see International Committee for the Indigenous Peoples of the Americas
♦ Incomindios – International Committee for the Indigenous Peoples of the Americas (internationally oriented national body)

♦ **Incontri Internazionali Uomini e Religioni** **11148**

Association for International Meetings People and Religions – Association pour les Rencontres internationales Hommes et religions

Contact c/o Communità di S Egidio, Piazza Sant'Egidio 3, 00153 Rome RM, Italy.

History in the 1980s, on the initiative of *Community of Sant'Egidio.* **Aims** Intensify dialogue among religions; promote cooperation and solidarity among peoples for the growth of *peace* and *social justice*; develop cultural activities to promote mutual *understanding* and dialogue among different religions and other cultural realities. **Activities** Organizes meetings among institutions, associations, groups and representatives of different religions, including annual world-wide meeting for peace, with participation of the Christian Churches and the great religions. Has set up a network of relationships among people and organizations in 90 countries, with different faiths and cultures, linked by common aspirations to justice and peace. Organizes study and friendship trips and prepares seminars for foreigners in Italy. **Events** *Annual International Meeting* Milan (Italy) 1993, *Annual international meeting* Brussels (Belgium) / Leuven (Belgium) 1992, *Annual International Meeting* Malta 1991, *Annual International Meeting* Bari (Italy) 1990, *Annual International Meeting* Warsaw (Poland) 1989. [2015/XF5066/**F**]

♦ **INCOPA** European Inorganic Coagulants Producers Association (#07542)
♦ INCORE – International Conflict Research Institute (see: #20642)
♦ Incorporated Brewers' Guild / see International Brewers' Guild
♦ Incorporated Commonwealth Chambers of Commerce and Industry of the Caribbean / see Caribbean Association of Industry and Commerce (#03448)
♦ Incorporated Research Institutions for Seismology (internationally oriented national body)
♦ **INCORVUZ-XXI** International Coordination Council of Educational Institutions Alumni (#12959)
♦ **INCOSE** International Council on Systems Engineering (#13083)
♦ **INCP** International Network on Cultural Policy (#14246)
♦ INCRA / see International Copper Association (#12962)
♦ InCRC – International Child Rights Center (internationally oriented national body)
♦ INCRESE – International Centre for Reproductive Health and Sexual Rights (internationally oriented national body)
♦ INCS – International Nuclear Chemistry Society (inactive)
♦ **INCSOC** International Network of Civil Society Organizations on Competition (#14243)
♦ **INCTR** International Network for Cancer Treatment and Research (#14238)
♦ **INCU** International Network of Customs Universities (#14248)
♦ INDEFI / see International Delegates on Filtration (#13144)
♦ **INDEFI** International Delegates on Filtration (#13144)
♦ **INDEN** International Network for Doctoral Education in Nursing (#14252)
♦ Independant Pan European Digital Association (unconfirmed)
♦ Independent Aviation Handlers Association / see Airport Services Association (#00613)
♦ Independent European Programme Group (inactive)
♦ Independent European Vaping Alliance (unconfirmed)
♦ Independent Film Producers International Association (no recent information)
♦ Independent Film and Television Alliance (internationally oriented national body)
♦ Independent Food Distributors of Europe (inactive)
♦ Independent Fundamental Churches of America / see IFCA International

♦ **Independent International Organization for Certification (IIOC)** **11149**

CEO address not obtained. T. +447508722501.
Sec Technical Committee address not obtained. T. +447880743769.
URL: http://www.iioc.org/

History 1993. **Aims** Create a strong, credible representative network representing the certification industry; draw the worlds of standardization, certification and accreditation closer together to the benefit of the business community; raise awareness of the benefits of accredited certification. **Structure** Board; Technical Committee; IIOC Food and Aerospace Colleges. **Languages** English. **Staff** 1.00 FTE, paid. **Finance** Members' dues. **Activities** Awareness raising; knowledge management/information dissemination; research/documentation; certification/accreditation. **Members** Accredited certification bodies. Membership countries not specified. **NGO Relations** Associate member of: *International Accreditation Forum (IAF, #11584).* Recognized stakeholder of: *European Cooperation for Accreditation (EA, #06782).* Liaison to a number of Committees at: *International Organization for Standardization (ISO, #14473).* [2018/XD4920/**D**]

♦ **Independent Learning Association (ILA)** **11150**

Contact c/o English Language Centre, Hong Kong Polytechnic, Hung Hom, Kowloon, Hong Kong. T. +85227667500. Fax +85223342141.

Aims Promote the advancement of research and practice in independent *language* learning. **Events** *Developing Learner Autonomy in Language Learning* Mexico City (Mexico) 2021, *Biennial Conference* Kobe (Japan) 2018, *Biennial Conference* Wuhan (China) 2016, *Biennial Conference* Bangkok (Thailand) 2014, *Biennial Conference* Wellington (New Zealand) 2012. **Publications** Conference proceedings. [2021/XM8140/**D**]

♦ **Independent Music Companies Association (IMPALA)** **11151**

Secretariat Coudenberg 70, 1000 Brussels, Belgium. T. +3225033138. Fax +3225032391. E-mail: info@impalamusic.org.
URL: http://www.impalamusic.org/

History Nov 2000. Former names and other names: *Independent Music Publishers and Labels Association* – alias. Registration: Banque-Carrefour des Entreprises, No/ID: 0453.683.450, Start date: 1 Aug 1994, Belgium. **Aims** Grow the independent music sector, return more value to artists, promote cultural diversity and entrepreneurship, improve political access and modernize perceptions of the music sector. **Structure** General Assembly; Board; Secretariat. **Languages** English, French. **Staff** 4.00 FTE, paid. **Finance** Sources: members' dues. **Activities** Advocacy/lobbying/activism; awards/prizes/competitions.

Members Members (nearly 6,000). Independent music companies and national associations in 20 countries:
Austria, Belgium, Czechia, Denmark, Finland, France, Germany, Hungary, Israel, Italy, Netherlands, Norway, Poland, Portugal, Romania, Spain, Sweden, Switzerland, Türkiye, UK.
RUNDA (#18999).

Consultative Status Consultative status granted from: *World Intellectual Property Organization (WIPO, #21593)* (Permanent Observer Status). **NGO Relations** Member of (2): *Pro-music; Worldwide Independent Network (WIN, #21925).* Supports (1): *Music Climate Pact.* [2022/XD9109/y/**D**]

♦ **Independent Music Publishers Forum (IMPF)** **11152**

Contact Rue Saint-Laurent 36, 1000 Brussels, Belgium. E-mail: secretariat@impforum.org.
URL: http://www.impforum.org/

History 2013, Brussels (Belgium). Registration: Banque-Carrefour des Entreprises, Belgium; EU Transparency Register, No/ID: 907923020842-83. **Aims** Provide a network and meeting place for independent music publishers. **Structure** General Assembly; Board; Executive Board. **Languages** English, French. **Staff** 3.00 FTE, paid; 20.00 FTE, voluntary. **Finance** Sources: members' dues. Annual budget: 110,000 EUR. **Activities** Advocacy/lobbying/activism; awareness raising; capacity building; events/meetings; guidance/assistance/consulting; knowledge management/information dissemination; monitoring/evaluation; networking/liaising; politics/policy/regulatory; publishing activities. Active in: Australia, Belgium, Brazil, Canada, Finland, France, Germany, Greece, Italy, Japan, Netherlands, Norway, Poland, Romania, Sweden, Switzerland, Türkiye, UK, USA. **Publications** *IMPF Newsletter* (12 a year). **Members** Individuals (106) in 36 countries. Membership countries not specified. **NGO Relations** Member of (3): *Confédération internationale des sociétés d'auteurs et compositeurs (CISAC, #04563); International Confederation of Music Publishers (ICMP, #12864); Pro-music.* [2022.02.08/XM5770/**C**]

♦ Independent Music Publishers and Labels Association / see Independent Music Companies Association (#11151)
♦ Independent Order of Odd Fellows (religious order)
♦ Independent Organic Inspectors Association / see International Organic Inspectors Association (#14421)
♦ Independent Organization International (unconfirmed)
♦ Independent Oxygen Manufacturers Association / see International Oxygen Manufacturers Association (#14493)

♦ **Independent Power Producers Forum (IPPF)** **11153**

SG Ste 711, 7th Floor – Block E, 13-15 Hong Shing Str, Quarry Bay, Hong Kong, Central and Western, Hong Kong. T. +85228948105. Fax +85225775817. E-mail: info@ippfpowerasia.com.
URL: http://www.ippfpowerasia.com/

Aims Work toward best practices in the power generation industry across the Asia / Pacific region. **Structure** Executive Committee. Secretariat. Committees. **Activities** Meeting activities. **Events** *Asian Nuclear Power Briefing Meeting* Tokyo (Japan) 2018, *Biogas and Waste to Energy Forum* Bangkok (Thailand) 2017.

Members Companies. Chapters in 19 countries and territories:
Australia, China, Hong Kong, India, Japan, Jordan, Korea Rep, Pakistan, Philippines, Russia, Saudi Arabia, Singapore, Sweden, Taiwan, Thailand, UK, United Arab Emirates, USA, Vietnam. [2020/XJ7983/**F**]

♦ **Independent Retail Europe** **11154**

Dir Gen Av des Gaulois 3 – Bte 3, 1040 Brussels, Belgium. T. +3227324660. E-mail: info@independentretaileurope.eu.
URL: http://www.independentretaileurope.eu/

History 22 Nov 1963, Frankfurt-Main (Germany). Statutes modified: 20 May 1975, Copenhagen (Denmark); 21 Oct 1976, Paris (France); 18 Dec 1986, Brussels (Belgium); 12 Oct 1995; 11 Nov 1999. Former names and other names: *Association of Retailer-Owned Wholesalers in Foodstuff (AROW)* – former (22 Nov 1963 to 25 Feb 1987); *Union des groupements d'achat de l'alimentation* – former (22 Nov 1963 to 25 Feb 1987); *Union der Genossenschaftlichen Einkaufsorganisationen für Lebensmittel (UGEL)* – former (22 Nov 1963 to 25 Feb 1987); *Association of Retailer-Owned Wholesalers of Europe* – former (25 Feb 1987 to 13 May 1995); *Union des Groupements d'Achat coopératifs de Détaillants de l'Europe* – former (25 Feb 1987 to 13 May 1995); *Union der Genossenschaftlichen Einkaufsorganisationen Europas* – former (25 Feb 1987 to 13 May 1995); *Union of Independent Retailer's Groups in Europe* – former (13 May 1995 to 13 Jun 2002); *Union des groupements de commerçants détaillants indépendants de l'Europe* – former (13 May 1995 to 13 Jun 2002); *Union der Verbundgruppen von Selbständigen Einzelhändlern Europas* – former (13 May 1995 to 13 Jun 2002); *Union des groupements de détaillants indépendants de l'Europe (UGAL)* – former (13 Jun 2002 to 16 Oct 2013); *Union of Groups of Independent Retailers of Europe* – former (13 Jun 2002 to 16 Oct 2013); *Union der Verbundgruppen selbständiger Einzelhändler Europas* – former (13 Jun 2002 to 16 Oct 2013). Registration: Belgium; EU Transparency Register, No/ID: 034546859-02. **Aims** Ensure European Union regulations include and contribute to economic, political and legal promotion of independent retailers through their groups, and entitle them to a free choice of the most appropriate solutions for coping with competition. **Structure** General Assembly (annual); Board of Directors; Secretariat. **Languages** English, French, German. **Staff** 5.00 FTE, paid. **Finance** Sources: members' dues. **Events** *Annual General Assembly* Barcelona (Spain) 2015, *Annual General Assembly* London (UK) 2014, *Annual General Assembly* Hamburg (Germany) 2013, *Annual General Assembly* Marrakech (Morocco) 2012, *Annual General Assembly* Vienna (Austria) 2012.

Members Full – organizations (17); cooperation agreement; associated members (6). Full in 9 countries:
Austria, Finland, France, Germany, Italy, Netherlands, Spain, Sweden, Switzerland.
Associate in 6 countries:
Czechia, Hungary, Ireland, Romania, Spain, UK.

IGO Relations Accredited by (2): *European Commission (EC, #06633); European Economic and Social Committee (EESC, #06963).* [2022.05.13/XD0159/y/**D**]

♦ Independent Scholars of Asia (internationally oriented national body)
♦ Independent Schools Association of Southern Africa (unconfirmed)
♦ Independent Schools Council Bursars' Association / see Southern African Bursars of Independent Schools Association

♦ **Independent Social Research Foundation (ISRF)** **11155**

Head Office Johannes Vermeerplein 11, 1071 DV Amsterdam, Netherlands. E-mail: stuart.wilson@isrf.org.
London Office 62 Bayswater Road, London, W2 3PS, UK. T. +442072620196.
URL: http://www.isrf.org/

History Founded 2008. Registered in accordance with Dutch law. **Aims** Advance social sciences through the promotion of new modes of inquiry and the development of interdisciplinary expertise and methods, and through better understanding of social entities and processes. **Structure** Board; Academic Board; Executive Team. **Activities** Financial and/or material support; networking/liaising; research/documentation; events/meetings. **Events** *Annual Workshop* Oxford (UK) 2019, *Annual Workshop* Berlin (Germany) 2018, *Annual Workshop* Amsterdam (Netherlands) 2017, *Annual Workshop* London (UK) 2016, *Annual Workshop* Edinburgh (UK) 2015. **Publications** *ISRF Bulletin.* [2019/XM8375/f/**F**]

♦ Independent South Asian Commission on Poverty Alleviation (see: #19721)
♦ Independent Union of the European Lubricant Industry / see Union Européenne de l'Industrie des Lubrifiants (#20398)

♦ **INDEPTH Network** **11156**

Exec Dir PO Box KD 213, Kanda, Accra, Ghana. T. +233302519394. Fax +233302519395. E-mail: info@indepth-network.org.
URL: http://www.indepth-network.org/

History 9 Nov 1998, Dar es Salaam (Tanzania UR). 9-12 Nov 1998, Dar es Salaam (Tanzania UR), during founding meeting. Formally constituted, 2002. Name derives from 'International Network for the Demographic Evaluation of Populations and Their Health in developing countries'. **Aims** Be an international platform of sentinel *demographic* sites that provides health and demographic data and research to enable *developing countries* to set *health* priorities and policies based on longitudinal evidence. **Structure** Annual General Meeting; Board of Trustees; Secretariat; Scientific Advisory Committee; Working Groups; Projects. **Languages** English, French. **Staff** 22.00 FTE, paid. **Finance** Budget (2014): US$ 5.8 million. Supporters include: *Bill and Melinda Gates Foundation (BMGF); DANIDA; The William and Flora Hewlett Foundation; The Rockefeller Foundation (#18966); Swedish International Development Cooperation Agency (Sida); Swiss Tropical and Public Health Institute (Swiss TPH); Wellcome Trust.* **Activities** Projects/programmes; capacity building; training/education. **Events** *Annual General Meeting* Addis Ababa (Ethiopia) 2015, *Scientific Conference* Addis Ababa (Ethiopia) 2015, *Scientific Conference* Johannesburg (South Africa) 2013, *Annual General Meeting* Pune (India) 2009, *Annual General Meeting* Dar es Salaam (Tanzania UR) 2008. **Publications** *INDEPTH Resource Kit; INDEPTH Slides; INDEPTH Tools; Policy Lessons.* Articles.

Members Health and Demographic Surveillance System (HDSS) sites (52) in 20 countries:
Bangladesh, Burkina Faso, Côte d'Ivoire, Ethiopia, Gambia, Ghana, Guinea-Bissau, India, Indonesia, Kenya, Malawi, Mozambique, Nigeria, Papua New Guinea, Senegal, South Africa, Tanzania UR, Thailand, Uganda, Vietnam.
IGO Relations Collaborates with: *ICDDR,B (#11051)*. Partner of: *West African Science Service Center on Climate Change and Adapted Land Use (WASCAL, #20897)*. **NGO Relations** Founding member of: *International Network for Climate and Health for Africa (Clim-HEALTH Africa, #14244)*. Supports: *Council on Health Research for Development (COHRED, no recent information)*. [2017/XM4559/**F**]

- ♦ **INDES** Inter-American Institute for Economic and Social Development (#11436)
- ♦ Index on Censorship (internationally oriented national body)
- ♦ Index – Index on Censorship (internationally oriented national body)
- ♦ IND EX – Intercontinental Association of Experts for INDustrial EXplosion Protection (unconfirmed)

♦ India China and America Institute (ICA Institute) 11157

Exec Dir 1000 Chastain Rd, Office BB476, Coles College of Business, Kennesaw State Univ, Kennesaw GA 30144, USA. T. +17704236580.
URL: http://www.icainstitute.org/
History 2004. **Aims** Foster economic growth through innovation, entrepreneurship and inclusiveness within India, China and America (ICA) and *trade* and *investment* among these economies. **Structure** Advisory Board. Executive Director. [2012/XJ5763/j/**E**]

- ♦ India International Centre (internationally oriented national body)
- ♦ India Musokotwane Environment Resource Centre for Southern Africa (internationally oriented national body)
- ♦ Indian Association for Asian and Pacific Studies (internationally oriented national body)
- ♦ Indian Council for Research on International Economic Relations (internationally oriented national body)

♦ Indian Council of South America 11158

Conseil indien sudaméricain – Consejo Indio de Sudamérica (CISA)
Contact Maison des Associations, 15 rue des Savoises, 1205 Geneva, Switzerland. T. +41223211033. Fax +41223211033.
URL: http://www.puebloindio.org/
History Mar 1980, Cusco (Peru), during 1st Congress of South American Movements. **Aims** Seek and maintain unity of Indian peoples; combat genocide and *ethnocide*, defend human *rights*; strengthen economies of Indian communities; strengthen base organizations, rendering them self-financing, and maintain an exchange of information on forms of organization and experience; fight for defence and *recuperation* of lands taken and for development; promote cultural exchange. **Structure** Congress; General Assembly; Directive Council, consisting of General Coordinator, Secretary General, Treasurer and alternates. Divisions (3): Legal and Technical Assistance; Social and Productive Projects; Administrative. **Languages** Spanish. **Staff** Professional, technical and support staff. **Finance** Grants from a number of national and international development agencies. **Activities** Areas of activity: human resources; productive projects, research and legal aspects; women's affairs; dissemination of information; refugees; regional assemblies. Assessment: education; health; feasibility study on projects for commercialization of products and producing of handicrafts. Organizes seminars, meetings, meeting groups. **Events** *General Assembly* Peru 2001, *General Assembly* La Paz (Bolivia) 1994, *General Assembly* Tromsø (Norway) 1992, *Meeting between Indian leaders and religious leaders of the Catholic Church in South America* Brasilia (Brazil) 1989, *Meeting of representatives of trade unions confederations, of the Peruvian Government and of the organizations of Indians in South America* Lima (Peru) 1989. **Publications** *Boletin Informativo CISA* (6 a year) in Spanish; *Pueblo Indio* (4 a year) in Spanish; *CISA News Bulletin* (3 a year) in English. *El Génesis de la Cultura Andina* by Carlos Milla Villena; *El Yuyo y el Ataqo en la Alimentación del Hombre Andino* by Luz Huayhualla; *Historia Oficial para Acabar con un Pueblo* by Yvon Sondag; *Hombre Nacional y Pan Ajeno* by Manuel Lajo; *Medicina Popular Peruana* by Emilio Valdizan; *Sistemas de Oposición de las Comunidades Sarhua* by Salvador Palomino Flores; *Tawantinsuyo* by Ramiro Reynaga.
Members Associations in 10 countries:
Argentina, Bolivia, Brazil, Chile, Colombia, Ecuador, Paraguay, Peru, Suriname, Venezuela.
Consultative Status Consultative status granted from: *ECOSOC (#05331)* (Ros A). **IGO Relations** Representatives with: *FAO (#09260)*; *ILO (#11123)*; *WHO (#20950)*. Accredited by: *United Nations Office at Vienna (UNOV, #20604)*. Associated with Department of Global Communications of the United Nations. **NGO Relations** CISA coordinates its activities with the following regional organizations: *ICCO – Interchurch Organization for Development Cooperation*; *International Committee for the Indigenous Peoples of the Americas (Incomindios)*; *Saami Council (#19012)*; *WCIP Regional Council for North America (no recent information)*; *WCIP Pacific Regional Council (no recent information)*. Member of: *World Association for Christian Communication (WACC, #21126)*. [2017/XD4178/**D**]

- ♦ Indian Council of World Affairs (internationally oriented national body)
- ♦ Indian Institute for Peace, Disarmament and Environmental Protection (internationally oriented national body)
- ♦ Indian Law Resource Center (internationally oriented national body)
- ♦ Indian Ocean Commission (#04236)

♦ Indian Ocean Comparative Education Society (IOCES) 11159

Sec c/o WCCES ED, UNESCO International Bureau of Education, 15, Route des Morillons, 1218 Le Grand-Saconnex, 1218 Geneva, Switzerland. E-mail: secretary@ioces.org – contact@ioces.org.
URL: https://www.ioces.org/
Aims Promote studies and researches on comparative education, in particular on educational institutions and systems of the countries effacing the Indian Ocean privileging historical and interdisciplinary approaches. **Structure** General Assembly. Executive Committee, comprising President, 2 Vice-Presidents, Secretary-Treasurer, 3 members and 1 co-opted member. **Languages** English. **Activities** Events/meetings. Active in all member countries. **Events** *IOCES International Conference* Geneva (Switzerland) 2022, *IOCES International Conference* Geneva (Switzerland) 2021, *IOCES International Conference* Lisbon (Portugal) 2020, *IOCES International Conference* Johannesburg (South Africa) 2018, *IOCES International Conference* Bangalore (India) 2015. **Publications** Selected papers of conferences. **NGO Relations** Member of (1): *World Council of Comparative Education Societies (WCCES, #21322)*. [2022.11.26/XJ6306/**D**]

- ♦ Indian Ocean Islands Association for Environmental Assessment (inactive)
- ♦ Indian Ocean MOU – Memorandum of Understanding on Port State Control in the Indian Ocean (1998 treaty)

♦ Indian Ocean Research Group (IORG) 11160

Vice Chair Geopolitics Cntr, Poli Sci Dept, Arts Block VI Panjab Univ, Chandigarh 160 014, CHANDIGARH 160 014, India. T. +911722534757. Fax +911722784695. E-mail: csgiorg@gmail.com.
Sec Dept génie civil et de génie des eaux, Pavillon Adrien-Pouliot – local 2982, Univ Laval, Québec QC G1K 7P4, Canada. T. +14186562131ext2868. Fax +14186562928.
URL: http://www.iorgroup.org/
History Nov 2002, Chandigarh (India). Registered in the State of Western Australia (Australia), 22 Jun 2007. **Aims** Initiate a policy-oriented dialogue among academics, governments, industries, NGOs and communities, so as to work towards a shared, peaceful, stable and prosperous future for the Indian Ocean region. **Structure** General Meeting (annual). Committee of Management, comprising Chairperson, Vice-Chairperson, Secretary, Treasurer and 4 members. **Events** *Climate change in the Indian ocean region – geopolitics, energy and security* Hyderabad (India) 2009, *Marine biodiversity and fisheries in the Indian ocean region – opportunities and threats in Oman* Muscat (Oman) 2007, *Conference* Kuala Lumpur (Malaysia) 2005, *Energy security in the Indian ocean* Teheran (Iran Islamic Rep) 2004, *The Indian ocean in a globalizing world – critical perspectives on the 21st century* Chandigarh (India) 2002. **Publications** *Journal of the Indian Ocean Region (JIOR)*. Books.
IGO Relations Observer Status with: *Indian Ocean Rim Association (IORA, #11161)*. [2011.01.14/XM3890/**E**]

♦ Indian Ocean Rim Association (IORA) 11161

SG 3rd Floor Tower I, NeXTeracom Bldg Cybercity, Ebene, Mauritius. T. +2304541717. Fax +2304681161. E-mail: hq@iora.int.
URL: https://www.iora.int/
History 6 Mar 1997, Port Louis (Mauritius). Formally launched at 1st Ministerial Meeting, when Charter was adopted. Former names and other names: *Indian Ocean Rim Association for Regional Cooperation (IOR-ARC)* – former. **Aims** Promote sustainable growth and balanced development of the region and member states; focus on areas of economic cooperation which provide maximum opportunities for development, shared interest and mutual benefit; promote trade liberalization, remove impediments and lower barriers towards a freer and enhanced flow of goods, services, investment and technology within the Indian Ocean rim. **Structure** Council of (Foreign) Ministers (meets annually). Committee of Senior Officials, composed of government officials of member states. Indian Ocean Rim Academic Group; Indian Ocean Rim Business Forum (IORBF). Troika; Secretariat. **Languages** English. **Staff** 11.00 FTE, paid. **Finance** Members' contribution (annual). Special fund for specific projects. **Activities** Projects/programmes; events/meetings. **Events** *Meeting* Colombo (Sri Lanka) 2019, *Blue Economy Ministerial Conference* Dhaka (Bangladesh) 2019, *Meeting* Durban (South Africa) 2019, *Modernising Trade in the Indian Ocean Rim Conference* Durban (South Africa) 2019, *Workshop on Improving Knowledge for Research on Blue Carbon in the Western Indian Ocean* Toliara (Madagascar) 2019.
Members Governments of 22 countries:
Australia, Bangladesh, Comoros, India, Indonesia, Iran Islamic Rep, Kenya, Madagascar, Malaysia, Maldives, Mauritius, Mozambique, Oman, Seychelles, Singapore, Somalia, South Africa, Sri Lanka, Tanzania UR, Thailand, United Arab Emirates, Yemen.
Dialogue Partner States (9):
China, Egypt, France, Germany, Japan, Korea Rep, Türkiye, UK, USA.
IGO Relations Observer status with (1): *United Nations (UN, #20515)* (General Assembly). **NGO Relations** Observer status granted to: *Indian Ocean Research Group (IORG, #11160)*; *Indian Ocean Tourism Organisation (IOTO, no recent information)*. [2021/XD7435/**D***]

- ♦ Indian Ocean Rim Association for Regional Cooperation / see Indian Ocean Rim Association (#11161)
- ♦ Indian Ocean Tourism Organisation (no recent information)

♦ Indian Ocean Tuna Commission (IOTC) 11162

Commission des thons de l'océan Indien
Exec Sec PO Box 1011, Victoria, Mahe, Seychelles. T. +248225494. E-mail: iotc.secretariat@fao.org.
URL: http://www.iotc.org/
History 25 Nov 1993, Rome (Italy). Established on acceptance of a draft agreement presented at Conference of *FAO (#09260)*, following: recommendations, 1989, Rome, of a technical conference; opening for signature, 19 Jun 1991, of Convention establishing *Western Indian Ocean Tuna Organization (no recent information)*; proposal at Diplomatic Conference, Jun 1992. Agreement came into force on acceptance by 10 states, 27 Mar 1996. Established under Article XIV of the FAO constitutions, establishment having been assisted in particular by *Tuna Fisheries Development and Management in the Indian Ocean and the Pacific off Southeast Asia (IPTP, inactive)*. First session: 21-24 Mar 1997. **Aims** Manage tuna and tuna-like species in the Indian Ocean and adjacent seas by promoting cooperation among Members with a view to ensuring, through appropriate management, conservation and optimum utilization of stocks covered by the Agreement and encouraging sustainable development of fisheries based on such stocks. **Structure** Annual Session; Commission Contracting Parties; Commission Cooperating Non-Contracting Parties; Sub-Commissions; Committees (3); Working Parties; Secretariat. **Languages** English, French. **Finance** Contributions from Contracting Parties. **Activities** Management of treaties and agreements; politics/policy/regulatory. Manages the following treaties/agreements: *Convention on the Protection of the Marine Environment of the Baltic Sea Area, 1992 (Helsinki Convention, 1992, 1992)*. **Events** *Working Party on Ecosystems and Bycatch Session* Victoria (Seychelles) 2020, *Session* Eden Is (Seychelles) 2016, *Management Procedures Dialogue* Saint-Denis (Réunion) 2016, *Session* Saint-Denis (Réunion) 2016, *Session* Saint-Denis (Réunion) 2016.
Members Membership open to Indian Ocean coastal countries and to countries or regional economic economic organizations which are members of the UN or one of its specialized agencies and are fishing for tunas in this ocean. Contracting Parties (29):
Australia, Bangladesh, China, Comoros, Eritrea, France, India, Indonesia, Iran Islamic Rep, Japan, Kenya, Korea Rep, Madagascar, Malaysia, Maldives, Mauritius, Mozambique, Oman, Pakistan, Philippines, Seychelles, Somalia, South Africa, Sri Lanka, Sudan, Tanzania UR, Thailand, UK, Yemen.
European Union (EU, #08967).
Cooperating Non-Contracting Parties (1):
Liberia.
IGO Relations Over 45 observers are registered with IOTC, not specified. **NGO Relations** Over 45 observers are registered with IOTC, not specified. [2023.02.19/XE2029/**E***]

- ♦ Indian School of International Studies / see School of International Studies, Delhi
- ♦ Indian Society for Afro-Asian Studies (internationally oriented national body)
- ♦ Indian Society of International Law (internationally oriented national body)
- ♦ Indian Society of Naturalists / see International Society of Naturalists
- ♦ Indigenous Affairs / see International Work Group for Indigenous Affairs (#15907)
- ♦ Indigenous Knowledge and Peoples Network (inactive)
- ♦ Indigenous Peasant Office of Central American Community Forestry / see Asociación Coordinadora Indigena y Campesina de Agroforesteria Comunitaria (#02120)

♦ Indigenous Peoples of Africa Coordinating Committee (IPACC) 11163

Comité de coordination des peuples autochtones d'afrique
Head Office 21 Palmer Rd, Muizenberg, Cape Town, 7945, South Africa. T. +27829045736 – +27740495100. E-mail: admipacc@gmail.com – ipacc@iafrica.com.
URL: http://www.ipacc.org.za/
History First constitution adopted, 1997. **Aims** Unite diverse community based indigenous peoples' organisations into a network and alliance for effective advocacy. **Structure** General Meeting (annual); Executive Committee; Secretariat. **Members** Indigenous peoples' organizations (150) in 20 countries. Membership countries not specified. **Consultative Status** Consultative status granted from: *African Commission on Human and Peoples' Rights (ACHPR, #00255)* (Observer); *ECOSOC (#05331)* (Special); *UNESCO (#20322)* (Consultative Status); *UNEP (#20299)*. **IGO Relations** Accredited to the Conference of the Parties of: *Secretariat of the United Nations Convention to Combat Desertification (Secretariat of the UNCCD, #19208)*. **NGO Relations** Member of (3): *ICCA Consortium (#11041)*; *International Union for Conservation of Nature and Natural Resources (IUCN, #15766)*; *World Heritage Watch (WHW)*. [2021.05.27/XM3678/**E**]

♦ Indigenous Peoples' Biodiversity Network (IPBN) 11164

Red de Biodiversidad de los Pueblos Indígenas
International Coordinator Calle Ruinas 451, Appartado Postal 567, Cusco, Peru. T. +5184232603.
IGO Relations *Secretariat of the Convention on Biological Diversity (SCBD, #19197)*. **NGO Relations** *Cultural Survival*. [2008/XF3956/**F**]

- ♦ Indigenous Peoples' Center for Documentation, Research and Information (internationally oriented national body)
- ♦ Indigenous Peoples' International Centre for Policy Research and Education (internationally oriented national body)

♦ Indigenous Peoples Movement for Self-determination and Liberation (IPMSDL) 11165

Communications Officer 275 E Rodriguez Sr, Barangay Kalusugan, 1112 Quezon City, Philippines. T. +6383548157. E-mail: info@ipmsdl.org.
Main Website: https://www.ipmsdl.org/
History 8 Nov 2010, Baguio (Philippines). Founded during International Conference on Indigenous Peoples Rights, Alternatives and Solutions to the Climate Crisis held in Baguio City, Philippines, 5-8 Nov 2010. **Aims** Upholdsthe right of Indigenous Peoples to govern themselves free from imperialism, state oppression and human rights violations; work to empower Indigenous Peoples, respecting the legitimacy of the different forms of struggle and self-determination that Indigenous Peoples opt to employ. **Structure** Board of Directors; Solidarity and Coordinative Mechanism; Global Secretariat. **Languages** English, Filipino, French, Spanish. **Activities** Advocacy/lobbying/activism; capacity building; monitoring/evaluation; networking/liaising; politics/policy/regulatory; publishing activities; research/documentation. **Events** *International Meeting of Native Indigenous Peoples of Guatemala and Latin America* Cobán (Guatemala) 2019. [2023.02.14/XM4181/**F**]

♦ Indigenous Peoples Survival Foundation (internationally oriented national body)
♦ Indigenous Women's Biodiversity Network (unconfirmed)
♦ Indigenous Women's Network (internationally oriented national body)

♦ Indigenous World Association 11166

Association du monde indigène – Asociación Indigena Mundial

Contact UN/ECOSOC, PO Box 2069, Kahnawake QC J0L 1B0, Canada. T. +15145916704. Fax +14506358479.

History Dec 1981. **Aims** Provide education about the application of international *human rights* initiatives, law and processes; promote rule of law domestically and internationally in relation to the rights of indigenous peoples, *ethnic minorities* and *uprooted people*; inform those groups and general public in various countries about the achievements and work of the United Nations system in those fields. **Languages** English. **Activities** Disseminates documentation and information in English and Spanish; organizes conferences, seminars and other forums, emergency meetings on urgent situations; consults Governments, international and intergovernmental organizations, private institutions, religious bodies, regarding the rights of vulnerable peoples.

Members Full in 7 countries:
Argentina, Canada, Chile, Costa Rica, El Salvador, St Lucia, USA.

Consultative Status Consultative status granted from: *ECOSOC (#05331)* (Special); *ILO (#11123)* (Special List). **IGO Relations** Accredited by: *International Whaling Commission (IWC, #15879)*; *United Nations Office at Vienna (UNOV, #20604)*. Associated with Department of Global Communications of the United Nations.
[2009.06.01/XF0408/**F**]

♦ Individual Self-esteem and Transition to Adolescence with Respect Research Network (unconfirmed)
♦ Individuell Människohjälp (internationally oriented national body)
♦ INDJ – Institut Notre-Dame de la Joie (religious order)
♦ Indochinese Refugee Information Centre / see Asian Research Centre for Migration
♦ Indo-European Chamber of Commerce and Industry (internationally oriented national body)

♦ Indonesia-Malaysia-Thailand Growth Triangle (IMT-GT) 11167

Address not obtained.
URL: http://www.imtgt.org/

History Initiated by former Prime Minister of Malaysia, H E Tun Dr Mahathir Mohammad. Formalisation endorsed 1993, Langwaki (Malaysia). Original title: *Growth Triangle*. Previously also referred to as *Growth Triangle of Singapore, Malaysia's Jamore State and Indonesia's Riau Province (SIJORI)*. **Aims** Facilitate location of websites with *trade*, investment, and economic information. **Structure** Includes *Centre for IMT-GT Subregional Cooperation (CIMT)*, set up Aug 2007. **Events** *UNINET Conference* Melaka (Malaysia) 2018.

Members Governments of 3 countries:
Indonesia, Malaysia, Thailand. [2017/XF3566/**F***]

♦ Indonesian Students Association for International Studies (internationally oriented national body)
♦ Indoor Air International / see International Society of the Built Environment (#14985)

♦ Indoor Environmental Quality – Global Alliance (IEQ Global Alliance) 11168

Contact Rue Washington 40, 1050 Brussels, Belgium.
URL: https://ieq-ga.net/

History 2014. Founded by Italian Association of Air Conditioning, Ventilation and Refrigeration (AiCARR), American Industrial Hygiene Association, *Air Infiltration and Ventilation Centre (AIVC, #00603)* , American Society of Heating, Refrigerating and Air-Conditioning Engineers (ASHRAE), Indian Society of Heating, Refrigerating, and Air Conditioning Engineers and *Federation of European Heating, Ventilation and Air-Conditioning Associations (REHVA, #09507)*. Former names and other names: *IEQ-GA* – alias. **Aims** Provide an acceptable indoor environmental quality (thermal environment-indoor air quality-lighting-acoustic) to occupants in buildings and places of work around the world; make sure the knowledge from research on IEQ get to be implemented in practice. **Structure** Board of Directors.

Members Full (7).
India, Italy, USA.
Air Infiltration and Ventilation Centre (AIVC, #00603); *Federation of European Heating, Ventilation and Air-Conditioning Associations (REHVA, #09507)*.
Affiliate:
USA.
Air and Waste Management Association (A and WMA). [AA0022/y/**C**]

♦ Indo-Pacific Association of Law, Medicine and Science (INPALMS) . 11169

Congress Secretariat SOVO Amcorp, Ste 1208, Level 12, Amcorp Tower, Amcorp Trade Ctr, 18 Persiaran Barat, 46050 Petaling Jaya, Selangor, Malaysia. T. +60379485307. Fax +60379556363. E-mail: atmadjads2016@gmail.com.
URL: http://inpalms.org/

History 1983, Singapore (Singapore), by medico-legal society of Singapore together with those of Japan, Thailand, Sri Lanka, India and Bangladesh. Also referred to as *Asian and Pacific Area Medico-Legal Society*. **Aims** Promote national and international cooperation in matters of education and research in the fields of legal medicine, *forensic* science and law enforcement. **Structure** Council, comprising 12 members. Officers: President; 10 Vice-Presidents; Secretary-General; Treasurer. **Languages** English. **Staff** Voluntary. **Finance** Each member pays own expenses, including organization of Congress in own country. **Activities** Organizes and holds meetings, conferences, lectures, workshops and seminars. **Events** *Triennial Indo-Pacific Congress on Legal Medicine and Forensic Sciences* Bali (Indonesia) 2016, *Triennial Indo-Pacific Congress on Legal Medicine and Forensic Sciences / Triennial Indo-Pacific Congress* Kuala Lumpur (Malaysia) 2013, *Triennial Indo-Pacific congress on legal medicine and forensic sciences / Triennial Indo-Pacific Congress* Delhi (India) 2010, *Triennial Indo-Pacific congress on legal medicine and forensic sciences / Triennial Indo-Pacific Congress* Colombo (Sri Lanka) 2007, *Triennial Indo-Pacific congress on legal medicine and forensic sciences / Triennial Indo-Pacific Congress* Manila (Philippines) 2004. **Publications** *INMPALM's Newsletter* (annual).

Members Medico-legal societies and individuals in 21 countries and territories:
Australia, Bahrain, Bangladesh, China, Fiji, Hong Kong, India, Indonesia, Iran Islamic Rep, Israel, Japan, Malaysia, Nepal, New Zealand, Philippines, Qatar, Saudi Arabia, Singapore, Sri Lanka, Taiwan, Thailand.

NGO Relations *Asia-Pacific Medico-Legal Association (APMLA, #01954).* [2016/XD3377/**D**]

♦ Indo-Pacific Conservation Alliance (internationally oriented national body)

♦ Indo-Pacific Economic Framework for Prosperity (IPEF) 11170

Address not obtained.

History 23 May 2022, Tokyo (Japan). Launched by US President Joe Biden. **Aims** Strengthen ties in the region to define the coming decades for technological innovation and the global economy. **Activities** Politics/policy/regulatory. **Events** *Launch Summit* Tokyo (Japan) 2022.

Members Participating States (14):
Australia, Brunei Darussalam, Fiji, India, Indonesia, Japan, Korea Rep, Malaysia, New Zealand, Philippines, Singapore, Thailand, USA, Vietnam. [2022/AA2916/**F***]

♦ Indo-Pacific Fisheries Council / see Asia-Pacific Fishery Commission (#01907)
♦ Indo-Pacific Fishery Commission / see Asia-Pacific Fishery Commission (#01907)

♦ Indo-Pacific Prehistory Association (IPPA) 11171

Association de préhistoire de la région Indo-Pacifique

SG School of Archaeology and Anthropology, Australian National Univ, Banks Bldg, 44 Linnaeus Way, Acton ACT 2601, Australia. E-mail: secgen@ippasecretariat.org.
URL: https://www.ippasecretariat.org/home/

History 1953. Organizational activities commenced 1929. Former names and other names: *Far-Eastern Prehistory Association* – former (1953 to 1976). **Aims** Promote cooperation in the study of archaeology and related subjects of Indo-Pacific region; help maintain direct communication among scholars working in the field; uphold and improve scientific methods in archaeological and related research. **Structure** Congress (every 4 years); Executive Committee; Editorial Board. **Languages** English. **Staff** 1.00 FTE, voluntary. **Finance** Sources: contributions; meeting proceeds. **Activities** Events/meetings. **Events** *Congress* Chiang Mai (Thailand) 2022, *Congress* Hue (Vietnam) 2018, *Congress* Siem Reap (Cambodia) 2014, *Congress* Hanoi (Vietnam) 2009, *Congress* Manila (Philippines) 2006. **Publications** *IPPA Bulletin* (at least annual) – online.

Members National organizations; other institutions; individuals; students. Members in 397 countries and territories:
Australia, Bangladesh, Brunei Darussalam, Cambodia, Canada, Chile, China, Denmark, Fiji, France, Germany, Hong Kong, India, Indonesia, Italy, Japan, Korea Rep, Laos, Malaysia, Myanmar, Netherlands, New Caledonia, New Zealand, Norway, Pakistan, Papua New Guinea, Philippines, Polynesia Fr, Russia, Singapore, Solomon Is, Sri Lanka, Sweden, Switzerland, Taiwan, Thailand, UK, USA, Vietnam. [2021.08.31/XC0072/**C**]

♦ Indo-Pacific Theosophical Federation (IPTF) 11172

Secretariat 60B Riro Street, Point Chavalier, Auckland 1022, New Zealand. E-mail: john@theosophy.org.nz.

History Founded 1978, Yogyakarta (Indonesia), after preliminary talks held in Sydney (Australia). A federation of *Theosophical Society (TS, #20141)*. **Aims** Promote cooperation among the various theosophical societies in the Indo-Pacific area. **Languages** English. **Staff** Voluntary. **Finance** Members' dues. **Activities** Events/meetings. **Events** *Conference* Diliman (Philippines) 2019, *Triennial Conference* Manila (Philippines) 2007, *Triennial Conference* Sydney, NSW (Australia) 2001, *Triennial conference* Kuala Lumpur (Malaysia) 1997, *Triennial Conference* India 1995. **Publications** *IPTF Newsletter*.

Members Individuals in 13 countries:
Australia, Bangladesh, India, Indonesia, Japan, Korea Rep, Malaysia, Myanmar, New Zealand, Pakistan, Philippines, Singapore, Sri Lanka. [2016.06.28/XD7322/v/**D**]

♦ **INDR** International Network on Displacement and Resettlement (#14251)
♦ **INDRUM** International Network for Didactic Research in University Mathematics (#14250)
♦ INDUP / see Dances of Universal Peace International (#05000)
♦ Industria Latinoamericana de Automedicación Responsable / see Asociación Latinoamericana de Autocuidado Responsable (#02184)
♦ Industrial Coordination Bureau (inactive)

♦ Industrial Development Fund (IDF) 11173

Fonds pour le développement industriel (FDI)

Contact c/o UNIDO, Vienna Int Centre, PO Box 300, 1400 Vienna, Austria. T. +431260265022. Fax +431260266881.
URL: http://www.unido.org/

History Dec 1976, as *United Nations Industrial Development Fund (UNIDF) – Fonds des Nations Unies pour le développement industriel (FNTDI)*, by the General Assembly of the United Nations, Resolutions 31/202 and 31/203, following initiative of the Industrial Development Board of *UNIDO (#20336)*. Commenced operations in 1978 and, 1 Jan 1986, adopted the present name when UNIDO assumed the status of a specialized agency of the United Nations (art 17 – UNIDO Constitution). **Aims** Promote sustainable industrial development in countries with developing economies and transition economies; harness the joint force of government and the private sector to foster competitive industrial production, develop international partnership and promote socially equitable and environmentally friendly industrial development. **Structure** Managed by UNIDO; Industrial Development Board (IDB); Secretariat at *Vienna International Centre (VIC)*. **Languages** Arabic, Chinese, English, French, Russian, Spanish. **Staff** 870.00 FTE, paid. **Finance** Voluntary contributions from governments and from intergovernmental and nongovernmental sources (including private enterprises). Has "desirable funding level" of US$ 50 million annually. **Activities** Financial and/or material support; capacity building. **Publications** *Industrial Development Report*. **Members** Not a membership organization.
[2019.02.12/XF8361/ft/**F***]

♦ Industrial Fabrics Association International (IFAI) 11174

Pres/CEO 1801 County Rd B W, Ste 100, Roseville MN 55113, USA. T. +16512256986. Fax +16516319334. E-mail: generalinfo@ifai.com.
Chairman address not obtained.
URL: http://www.ifai.com/

History 1912, Denver, CO (USA). Primarily North American membership. Former names and other names: *Canvas Products Association International (CPA)* – former; *National Tent & Awning Association* – former (1912); *National Canvas Goods Manufacturers Association* – former. **Aims** Represent companies in the international specialty fabrics marketplace. **Structure** Board of Directors. Regional Offices (3): IFAI Canada; IFAI Japan; IFAI New Zealand. Divisions: Advanced Textile Products division (ATP); Equipment Division (EQP); Fabric Graphics Association (FGA); Fabric Structures Association (FSA); Geosynthetic Materials Association (GMA); Makers Division (MAKERS); Marine Fabricators Association (MFA); Military Division (MIL); Narrow Fabrics Institute (NFI); Professional Awning Manufacturers Association (PAMA); Tarp Association; Tent Rental Division (TRD); United States Industrial Fabrics Institute (USIFI). **Languages** English. **Staff** 60.00 FTE, paid. **Finance** Members' dues. Other sources: magazine advertising; exhibit revenue. Annual revenue: US$ 9,000,000. **Activities** Events/meetings. **Events** *Marine Fabricators Conference* New Orleans, LA (USA) 2023, *Marine Fabricators Conference* Isle of Palms SC, SC (USA) 2022, *Outlook Conference* Hilton Head, SC (USA) 2021, *Geosynthetics Conference* Kansas City, MO (USA) 2021, *Marine Fabricators Conference* New Orleans, LA (USA) 2021. **Publications** *Specialty Fabrics Review* (12 a year) – magazine; *Geosynthetics* (6 a year) – magazine; *InTents* (6 a year) – magazine; *Marine Fabricator* (6 a year) – magazine; *Fabric Architecture* (annual) – magazine; *Advanced Textiles Source*.

Members Companies ranging in size from one-person shops to multinational corporations in 40 countries and territories:
Australia, Austria, Barbados, Belgium, Bermuda, Brazil, Canada, China, Colombia, Czechia, Denmark, Dominican Rep, Finland, France, Germany, India, Ireland, Israel, Italy, Jamaica, Japan, Korea Rep, Malaysia, Mexico, Netherlands, New Zealand, Poland, Qatar, Singapore, South Africa, Spain, St Lucia, Sweden, Switzerland, Taiwan, Trinidad-Tobago, Türkiye, UK, United Arab Emirates, USA. [2021/XD2144/t/**D**]

♦ Industrial Federation Paints and Coats of Mercosul (IFPCM) 11175

Contact Av Santo Amaro 62273, 3o 32 Sto Amaro, Sao Paulo SP, 04701100, Brazil. T. +551155213185. Fax +551155230113.

History Also referred to as *Federation Industrial Paints and Coats of Mercosul*. **Aims** Defend the interests of the Mercosul paint industry. **Structure** Direction, comprising President, Vice-President, Secretary and 5 Directors.

Members National organizations in 4 countries:
Argentina, Brazil, Paraguay, Uruguay.

IGO Relations *Southern Common Market (#19868)*; *United Nations Committee of Experts on the Transport of Dangerous Goods and on the Globally Harmonized System of Classification and Labelling of Chemicals (Committee of Experts on TDG and GHS, #20543).* [2009/XJ1413/t/**D**]

♦ Industrial Internet Consortium / see Industry IoT Consortium (#11182)
♦ Industrialiseringsfonden for Udviklingslandene / see Investeringsfonden for Udviklingslande
♦ Industrialization Fund for Developing Countries / see Investeringsfonden for Udviklingslande

♦ industriAll European Trade Union (industriALL Europe) 11176

Gen Sec c/o ITUH, Boulevard du Roi Albert II 5, 1210 Brussels, Belgium. T. +3222260050. Fax +3222175963. E-mail: info@industriall-europe.eu.
URL: http://www.industriall-europe.eu/

History Founding Congress, 16 May 2012, Brussels (Belgium), resulting from a merger of *European Metalworkers' Federation (EMF, inactive)*, *European Mine, Chemical and Energy Workers' Federation (EMCEF, inactive)* and *European Trade Union Federation for Textiles, Clothing and Leather (ETUF-TCL, inactive)*. EU Transparency Register: 358284014848-82. **Aims** Protect and advance the rights of working men and women across supply chains in the *manufacturing*, *mining* and *energy* sectors across Europe. **Structure** Congress (every 4 years); Steering Committee (meets twice a year); Executive Committee (meets twice a year). **Languages** English, French, German. **Staff** 23.00 FTE, paid. **Finance** Members' dues. **Activities** Events/meetings. **Events** *Congress* Thessaloniki (Greece) 2020, *Congress* Madrid (Spain) 2016.

Members Affiliates in 38 countries:
Albania, Austria, Belgium, Bosnia-Herzegovina, Bulgaria, Croatia, Cyprus, Czechia, Denmark, Estonia, Finland, France, Germany, Greece, Hungary, Iceland, Ireland, Italy, Kosovo, Latvia, Lithuania, Luxembourg, Monaco, Montenegro, Netherlands, North Macedonia, Norway, Poland, Portugal, Romania, Serbia, Slovakia, Slovenia, Spain, Sweden, Switzerland, Türkiye, UK.
NGO Relations Member of (1): *European Trade Union Confederation (ETUC, #08927).* [2019/XJ7253/t/**D**]

♦ **industriALL Europe** industriAll European Trade Union (#11176)

♦ IndustriALL Global Union (IndustriALL) 11177

Gen Sec ACACIAS, Route des Acacias 54 bis, 1227 Geneva, Switzerland. T. +41223085050. E-mail: info@industriall-union.org.
Pres address not obtained.
URL: http://www.industriall-union.org/

History 19 Jun 2012, Copenhagen, on merger of *International Metalworkers' Federation (IMF, inactive), International Federation of Chemical, Energy, Mine and General Workers' Unions (ICEM, inactive)* and *International Textile, Garment and Leather Workers' Federation (ITGLWF, inactive).* Registered in accordance with Swiss Civil Code. **Aims** Represent blue collar and white collar men and women workers in the metal, chemical, energy, mining, textile and related industries throughout the world. **Structure** Congress; Executive Committee; Finance Committee; Secretariat; Regional Offices (5). **Languages** English, French, German, Japanese, Russian, Spanish. **Staff** 40.00 FTE, paid. **Finance** Sources: contributions; members' dues. **Activities** Advocacy/lobbying/activism; events/meetings; networking/liaising; research/documentation. **Events** *Congress* Cape Town (South Africa) 2021, *Congress* Cape Town (South Africa) 2020, *Asia-Pacific Trade and Industrial Policy Meeting* Singapore (Singapore) 2019, *Women World Conference* Vienna (Austria) 2015. **Publications** Research; reports. **Members** Free, independent and democratic trade unions (680), representing 50 million workers in 140 countries in the mining, energy and manufacturing sector. Membership countries not specified. **IGO Relations** Represents members in: *ILO (#11123); International Bank for Reconstruction and Development (IBRD, #12317); International Monetary Fund (IMF, #14180); OECD (#17693); World Trade Organization (WTO, #21864).* **NGO Relations** Member of (8): *Aluminium Stewardship Initiative (ASI, #00758); European Network on Silica (NEPSI, #08001); European Responsible Investment Network (ERIN); Global Labour University (GLU, #10448); Global Union Federations (GUF, #10638); GoodElectronics (#10679); Initiative for Responsible Mining Assurance (IRMA, #11212); ResponsibleSteel (#18921).* [2019/XJ6079/t/**B**]

♦ **IndustriALL** IndustriALL Global Union (#11177)

♦ Industrial Marketing and Purchasing Group (IMP Group) 11178

Contact address not obtained. E-mail: admin@impgroup.org.
URL: https://www.impgroup.org/

History Founded as an informal network of scholars. **Structure** Board. **Activities** Events/meetings; research/documentation. **Events** *Industrial Marketing and Purchasing Conference* Florence (Italy) 2022, *Industrial Marketing and Purchasing Conference* Paris (France) 2019. [2020/AA0921/t/**F**]

♦ Industrial Minerals Association – Europe (IMA Europe) 11179

Dir-Gen Rue des Deux Eglises 26, Box 2, 1000 Brussels, Belgium. T. +3222104420 – +3222104410. E-mail: secretariat@ima-europe.eu.
Pres address not obtained.
URL: http://www.ima-europe.eu/

History 15 Dec 1993, Brussels (Belgium). Registration: AISBL/IVZW, Belgium; EU Transparency Register, No/ID: 14190001484-01. **Aims** Study all non-commercial issues concerning the minerals industries represented in the Association, especially the scientific, technical, documentary and institutional fields. **Structure** General Assembly (annual); Board of Directors; Secretariat. Industrial Minerals Chief Executive Council (IMCEC); IMA Technical Board Administrative Council; Executive Committee. **Languages** English, French, German. **Staff** 9.50 FTE, paid. **Finance** Members' dues. **Activities** Knowledge management/information dissemination; awards/prizes/competitions. **Events** *Biennial Conference* Brussels (Belgium) 2018, *European Minerals Day Meeting* Brussels (Belgium) 2017, *Biennial Conference* Brussels (Belgium) 2016, *Biennial Conference* Brussels (Belgium) 2014, *Biennial Conference* Brussels (Belgium) 2012. **Publications** Annual Report; minerals report (every 2 years).
Members Effective (including founders); associations or companies; Adhering. Members belong to the section(s) with which they are most concerned and include companies in 16 countries:
Austria, Belgium, Czechia, Denmark, Finland, France, Germany, Italy, Netherlands, Norway, Portugal, Spain, Sweden, Switzerland, Türkiye, UK.
Regional members (10):
Calcium Carbonate Association – Europe (CCA-Europe, #03399); European Association of Feldspar Producers (EUROFEL, #06037); European Association of Industrial Silica Producers (EUROSIL, #06082); European Bentonite Producers Association (EUBA, #06328); European Borates Association (EBA, #06382); European Kaolin and Plastic Clays Association (KPC Europe, #07623); European Lime Association (EuLA, #07699); European Speciality Minerals Association (ESMA, #08811); International Diatomite Producers Association (IDPA, #13172); Scientific Association of European Talc Industry (Eurotalc, #19146).
NGO Relations Member of: *European Network on Silica (NEPSI, #08001); European Policy Centre (EPC, #08240); Federation of European and International Associations Established in Belgium (FAIB, #09508); Industry4Europe (#11181).* In liaison with technical committees of: *Comité européen de normalisation (CEN, #04162); International Organization for Standardization (ISO, #14473).* Houses: *European Kaolin and Plastic Clays Association (KPC Europe, #07623).* [2020/XD3606/ty/**D**]

♦ Industrial Property Organization for English-Speaking Africa / see African Regional Intellectual Property Organization (#00434)
♦ Industrial Workers of the World (internationally oriented national body)

♦ Industrianställda i Norden 11180

Pohjoismaiden Teollisuustyöntekijät – Nordic IN

SG Olof Palmes Gata 11, SE-105 52 Stockholm, Sweden. T. +4687868000. E-mail: post@nordic-in.org.
URL: http://www.nordic-in.org/

History 1 Jan 2006. Founded by merger of *Nordiska Industriarbetare Federationen (NIF, inactive)* and *Nordic Metal (inactive).* **Aims** Act as coordinating body for Nordic trade unions representing workers in the industrial sector. **Structure** Nordic Forum; Executive Committee; Secretariat. **Languages** Danish, English, Finnish, Norwegian, Swedish. **Staff** 3.75 FTE, paid. **Finance** Sources: members' dues. Annual budget: 7,000,000 SEK (2022).
Members Trade Unions (21), representing 1 million individual members, in 5 countries:
Denmark, Finland, Iceland, Norway, Sweden. [2022.05.10/XM2192/t/**D**]

♦ Industria Petrolera Internacional para la Conservación del Medio Ambiente (#14562)
♦ Industribageriernes Internationale Forening (#02674)
♦ Industrie mondiale de l'automédication responsable / see Global Self-Care Federation (#10588)
♦ Industrie pétrolière internationale pour la conservation de l'environnement (#14562)
♦ Industrieverband Kunststoffbahnen (unconfirmed)

♦ Industry4Europe 11181

Contact address not obtained. E-mail: contact@industry4europe.eu.
URL: https://www.industry4europe.eu/

Aims Campaign for an ambitious EU *industrial* strategy. **Publications** Reports; studies; manifesto.
Members Organizations (153):
– *AEGIS Europe;*
– *Aerospace and Defence Industries Association of Europe (ASD, #00146);*
– *Aggregates Europe (UEPG, #00558);*
– *AnimalhealthEurope (#00837);*
– *APPLiA – Home Appliance Europe (#00877);*
– *A.SPIRE (#02311);*
– *Association des constructeurs européens de motocycles (ACEM, #02450);*
– *Association européenne des métaux (EUROMETAUX, #02578);*
– *Association of European Automative and Industrial Battery Manufacturers (EUROBAT, #02498);*
– *Association of European Candle Makers (AECM, inactive);*
– *Association of Plastics Manufacturers in Europe (Plastics Europe, #02862);*
– *Association of the European Rail Supply Industry (UNIFE, #02536);*
– *Association technique de l'industrie européenne des lubrifiants (ATIEL, #02950);*
– *Bio-based Industries Consortium (BIC, #03238);*
– *Bioenergy Europe (#03247);*
– *Bromine Science and Environmental Forum (BSEF, #03337);*
– *Bureau international du béton manufacturé (BIBM, #03363);*
– *CEMBUREAU – The European Cement Association (CEMBUREAU, #03634);*
– *CIRFS – European Man-made Fibres Association (#03944);*
– *CO2 Value Europe (CVE, #04042);*
– *Comité européen des constructeurs d'instruments de pesage (CECIP, #04151);*
– *Committee for European Construction Equipment (CECE, #04254);*
– *Confédération Européenne de l'Industrie de la Chaussure (CEC, #04544);*
– *Confédération européenne des industries du bois (CEI Bois, #04545);*
– *Confederation of European Paper Industries (CEPI, #04529);*
– *Confederation of the European Bicycle Industry (CONEBI, #04519);*
– *Conseil européen de l'industrie chimique (CEFIC, #04687);*
– *Conseil européen de l'industrie des peintures, des encres d'imprimerie et des couleurs d'art (CEPE, #04688);*
– *Construction Products Europe AISBL (#04761);*
– *Cosmetics Europe – The Personal Care Association (#04852);*
– *CropLife Europe (#04965);*
– *EDANA, the voice of nonwovens (EDANA, #05353);*
– *Energy Technologies Europe (#05477);*
– *EU ProSun;*
– *EURATEX – The European Apparel and Textile Confederation (EURATEX, #05616);*
– *Euroalliages (#05629);*
– *Eurogas (#05682);*
– *Europacable (#05743);*
– *European Agricultural Machinery Association (CEMA, #05846);*
– *European Aliphatic Isocyanates Producers Association (ALIPA);*
– *European Aluminium (#05893);*
– *European Asphalt Pavement Association (EAPA, #05920);*
– *European Association for Coal and Lignite (EURACOAL, #05978);*
– *European Association for Passive Fire Protection (EAPFP, #06143);*
– *European Association of Automotive Suppliers (CLEPA, #05948);*
– *European Association of Bioindustries (EuropaBio, #05956);*
– *European Association of Gas and Steam Turbine Manufacturers (EUTurbines, #06050);*
– *European Association of Internal Combustion Engine Manufacturers (EUROMOT, #06090);*
– *European Association of Mining Industries, Metal Ores and Industrial Minerals (EUROMINES, #06122);*
– *European Association of Plaster and Plaster Product Manufacturers (EUROGYPSUM, #06152);*
– *European Association of Technical Fabrics producers (TECH-FAB Europe);*
– *European Association of the Machine tool Industries and related Manufacturing Technologies (CECIMO, #06113);*
– *European Autoclaved Aerated Concrete Association (EAACA, #06297);*
– *European Automobile Manufacturers' Association (ACEA, #06300);*
– *European Bicycle Manufacturers Association (EBMA);*
– *European Boating Industry (EBI, #06377);*
– *European Brands Association (#06397);*
– *European Breakfast Cereal Association (CEEREAL, #06399);*
– *European Calcium Silicate Producers Association (ECSPA, #06430);*
– *European Carbon and Graphite Association (ECGA, #06447);*
– *European Ceramic Industry Association (CERAME-UNIE, #06506);*
– *European Ceramic Tile Manufacturers' Federation (CET, #06508);*
– *European Coil Coating Association (ECCA, #06601);*
– *European Composites Industry Association (EuCIA, #06692);*
– *European Concrete Paving Association (EUPAVE, #06697);*
– *European Coordination Committee of the Radiological, Electromedical Healthcare IT Industry (COCIR, #06792);*
– *European Dairy Association (EDA, #06883);*
– *European Diisocyanate and Polyol Producers Association (ISOPA, #06926);*
– *European Domestic Glass (EDG, #06938);*
– *European Elevator Association (#06976);*
– *European Engineering Industries Association (EUnited, #06991);*
– *European Engine Power Plants Association (EUGINE);*
– *European Expanded Clay Association (EXCA, #07013);*
– *European Federation for Construction Chemicals (EFCC, #07088);*
– *European Federation of Catering Equipment Manufacturers (EFCEM, #07068);*
– *European Federation of Ceramic Sanitaryware Manufacturers (#07073);*
– *European Federation of Concrete Admixtures Associations (EFCA, #07085);*
– *European Federation of Corrugated Board Manufacturers (#07091);*
– *European Federation of Pharmaceutical Industries and Associations (EFPIA, #07191);*
– *European Federation of Steel Wire Rope Industries (EWRIS, #07221);*
– *European Flavour Association (EFFA, #07269);*
– *European Flour Millers' Association (#07272);*
– *European Furniture Industries Confederation (EFIC, #07369);*
– *European Garage Equipment Association (EGEA, #07377);*
– *European General Galvanizers Association (EGGA, #07383);*
– *European Heat Pump Association (EHPA, #07469);*
– *European Manufacturers of Expanded Polystyrene (EUMEPS, #07732);*
– *European Mortar Industry Organization (EMO, #07822);*
– *European Panel Federation (EPF, #08137);*
– *European Partnership for Energy and the Environment (EPEE, #08157);*
– *European Photonics Industry Consortium (EPIC, #08205);*
– *European Plastics Converters (EuPC, #08216);*
– *European Powder Metallurgy Association (EPMA, #08260);*
– *European Power Tool Association (EPTA, #08264);*
– *European Precious Metals Federation (EPMF, #08267);*
– *European Ready Mixed Concrete Organization (ERMCO, #08330);*
– *European Refractories Producers Federation (#08339);*
– *European Semiconductor Industry Association (ESIA, #08462);*
– *European Shipyards' and Maritime Equipment Association (SEA Europe, #08479);*
– *European Special Glass Association (ESGA, #08807);*
– *European Steel Association (EUROFER, #08835);*
– *European Steel Tube Association (ESTA, #08837);*
– *European Suppliers of Waste to Energy Technology (ESWET, #08858);*
– *European Technical Ceramics Federation (EuTeCer, #08878);*
– *European Tyre and Rubber Manufacturers' Association (ETRMA, #08963);*
– *European Union Road Federation (ERF, #09014);*
– *European Ventilation Industry Association (EVIA, #09052);*
– *European Wind Tower Association (EWTA);*
– *EU Specialty Food Ingredients (#09200);*
– *Fédération Européenne des Aérosols (FEA, #09557);*
– *Fédération européenne des fabricants d'aliments composés pour animaux (FEFAC, #09566);*
– *Fédération européenne des industries de colles et adhésifs (FEICA, #09572);*
– *Fédération européenne des industries de corderie ficellerie et de filets (EUROCORD, #09573);*
– *Fédération européenne des industries de porcelaine et de faience de table et d'ornementation (FEPF, #09574);*
– *Fédération européenne des producteurs d'enveloppes (FEPE, #09578);*
– *Fédération européenne du commerce chimique (Fecc, #09563);*
– *Fédération européenne du verre d'emballage (FEVE, #09583);*
– *Federation of European Producers of Abrasives (FEPA, #09532);*
– *Federation of European Rice Millers (FERM, #09537);*
– *Federation of European Rigid Polyurethane Foam Associations (PU Europe, #09538);*
– *FEFANA – EU Association of Specialty Feed Ingredients and their Mixtures (#09720);*
– *Fertilizers Europe (#09738);*
– *FEUGRES – European Clay Pipe Association (FEUGRES e.V., #09741);*
– *Flame Retardants Europe (FRE, #09791);*
– *FoodDrinkEurope (#09841);*
– *FTA Europe (#10012);*
– *FuelsEurope (#10014);*
– *Glass Alliance Europe (#10156);*
– *GlassFibreEurope (#10158);*
– *Glass for Europe (#10157);*

Industry IoT Consortium
11182

alphabetic sequence excludes
For the complete listing, see Yearbook Online at

- *Hydrogen Europe (#10998)*;
- *Industrial Minerals Association – Europe (IMA Europe, #11179)*;
- *Intergraf (#11505)*;
- *International Association for Soaps, Detergents and Maintenance Products (#12166)*;
- *International Association of Oil and Gas Producers (IOGP, #12053)*;
- *International Confederation of Paper and Board Converters in Europe (CITPA, #12866)*;
- *International Federation of Industrial Energy Consumers, Europe (IFIEC – Europe, #13456)*;
- *LightingEurope (#16472)*;
- *Medicines for Europe (#16633)*;
- *MedTech Europe (#16692)*;
- *Nanotechnology Industries Association (NIA, #16933)*;
- *nucleareurope (#17616)*;
- *Ocean Energy Europe (EU-OEA, #17649)*;
- *Plastics Recyclers Europe (PRE, #18394)*;
- *Primary Food Processors (PFP, #18496)*;
- *RECHARGE (#18627)*;
- *SEMI (#19225)* (Europe);
- *Solar Heat Europe (SHE, #19674)*;
- *Tiles and Bricks Europe (TBE, #20163)*;
- *Union européenne du commerce du bétail et de la viande (UECBV, #20394)*;
- *WindEurope (#20965)*. [2019/XM8883/ty/**F**]

♦ Industry IoT Consortium (IIC) 11182
CEO 9C Medway Rd, PMB 274, Milford MA 01757, USA. T. +17814440404. E-mail: info@iiconsortium.org.
Events Manager address not obtained.
URL: http://www.iiconsortium.org
History Mar 2014, USA. Part of the *Object Management Group (OMG)*. Former names and other names: *Industrial Internet Consortium (IIC)* – former. Registration: USA. **Aims** Deliver transformative business value to industry, organizations and society by accelerating adoption of a trustworthy internet of things. **Structure** Steering Committee; Industry Leadership Council. Working Groups. **Languages** English, Japanese. **Events** *IOT Solutions World Congress* Barcelona (Spain) 2022, *IOT Solutions World Congress* Barcelona (Spain) 2021, *IOT Solutions World Congress* Barcelona (Spain) 2020, *Internet of Things Solutions World Congress* Barcelona (Spain) 2015. **Members** Large and small industry, entrepreneurs, academics and government organizations. Membership countries not specified. **NGO Relations** Partner of (1): *Augmented Reality for Enterprise Alliance (AREA)*. [2022/XM5051/t/**C**]

♦ Industry Standardisation for Institutional Trade Communication Committee / see ISITC Europe (#16032)
♦ INEA – Internationaler Elektronik-Arbeitskreis (inactive)
♦ INEAS – Institute of Near Eastern and African Studies (internationally oriented national body)
♦ IN-EAST – Institute for East Asian Studies, Duisburg (internationally oriented national body)
♦ INEB International Network of Engaged Buddhists (#14259)
♦ INEBRIA International Network on Brief Interventions for Alcohol and Other Drugs (#14236)

♦ INEC – Association of Producers of Carob Bean Gum (INEC) 11183
Vereinigung der Hersteller von Johannisbrotkernmehl (INEC)
Admin Sec c/o Polygal AG, Weinfelderstrasse 13, 8560 Marstetten TG, Switzerland.
Pres address not obtained.
URL: http://inec.biz/
History 14 Feb 1972, Brussels (Belgium). INEC (Belgium) was dissolved at the General Assembly 2004. Former names and other names: *Institut européen des industries de la gomme de caroube (INEC)* – former (14 Feb 1972 to Nov 2003). Registration: Swiss Civil Code, No/ID: CHE-110.262.482, Start date: Nov 2003, Switzerland; EU Transparency Register, No/ID: 072692941225-13, Start date: 4 Feb 2021. **Aims** Pursue scientific studies related to research, production and use of carob bean gum – locust bean gum; collect documentation and advise on carob bean gum and its uses; represent interests of the industry with intergovernmental organizations; induce and support programmes to: protect the carob tree, encourage new plantations and improve economics of harvesting and utilization. **Structure** General Assembly (annual); Board; Executive Committee; Technical Committee. **Languages** English. **Staff** Part-time, voluntary. **Finance** Sources: members' dues. **Activities** Events/meetings; research/documentation. **Events** *Annual General Meeting* Fez (Morocco) 2014, *Annual Genberal Meeting / Annual General Meeting* Dresden (Germany) 2013, *Annual General Meeting* Palma (Spain) 2012, *Annual General Meeting* Interlaken (Switzerland) 2011, *Annual General Meeting* Palermo (Italy) 2010.
Members Private companies in 5 countries:
Italy, Portugal, Spain, Switzerland, Türkiye.
IGO Relations Accredited by (1): *European Commission (EC, #06633)*. **NGO Relations** Member of (1): *EU Specialty Food Ingredients (#09200)*. [2020.05.11/XD0296/**F**]

♦ INECE International Network for Environmental Compliance and Enforcement (#14261)
♦ INEC / see INEC – Association of Producers of Carob Bean Gum (#11183)
♦ INEC INEC – Association of Producers of Carob Bean Gum (#11183)
♦ INEC Vereinigung der Hersteller von Johannisbrotkernmehl (#11183)
♦ INEE Inter-agency Network for Education in Emergencies (#11387)
♦ INEE Polis – International Network in Environmental Education (#18421)
♦ INEES Institut européen de l'économie solidaire (#07572)
♦ INEF – Institut für Entwicklung und Frieden, Duisburg (internationally oriented national body)
♦ INEF International Network of Environmental Forensics (#14262)
♦ INEI International Network of Education Institutes (#14256)
♦ INE Inland Navigation Europe (#11216)
♦ INEMAP – Institut européen de management public, Charleroi (internationally oriented national body)
♦ INEM International Network for Economic Method (#14254)
♦ INEM International Network for Environmental Management (#14263)
♦ INEOA – International Narcotic Enforcement Officers Association (internationally oriented national body)
♦ INEPA – International Exchange Promotion Association (internationally oriented national body)
♦ INEP International Network for Epidemiology in Policy (#14264)
♦ INEPS International Network of Productive Learning Projects and Schools (#14308)
♦ Iner-American Association of Public Defenders (#02159)
♦ INERELA+ International Network of Religious Leaders Living with or Personally Affected by HIV and AIDS (#14315)
♦ INESAP – International Network of Engineers and Scientists Against Proliferation (see: #14260)
♦ INES International Network of Engineers and Scientists for Global Responsibility (#14260)
♦ INESOR – Institute of Economic and Social Research (internationally oriented national body)
♦ INESPE – International Network of Engineers and Scientists' Projects on Ethics (see: #14260)
♦ INET – Institute for New Economic Thinking (unconfirmed)
♦ INET International Networking for Educational Transformation (#14289)
♦ INET – International Network for Lesbian, Gay and Bisexual Concerns and Transgender Issues in Psychology (internationally oriented national body)
♦ INEUCS International Network of Employers and University Careers Services (#14257)
♦ INEVAWG International Network to End Violence Against Women and Girls (#14258)
♦ INEW International Network on Explosive Weapons (#14266)
♦ INEX / see INEX – Association of Voluntary Activities
♦ INEX – Association of Voluntary Activities (internationally oriented national body)
♦ INEX – International Network for Educational Exchange (internationally oriented national body)
♦ INEX-SDA – INEX - Sdruzeni dobrovolnych aktivit (internationally oriented national body)
♦ INEX – Sdruzeni dobrovolnych aktivit (internationally oriented national body)
♦ INF / see Nevin Scrimshaw International Nutrition Foundation
♦ INFACT / see Corporate Accountability International
♦ InFACT International Forum for Acute Care Trialists (#13630)

♦ INFA International Faculty for Artificial Organs (#13326)
♦ INFA International Federation of Aestheticians (#13344)
♦ INFA – International NF Association (inactive)
♦ INFAL Inter-American Network of Food Analysis Laboratories (#18694)
♦ Infanoj Chirkaw la Mondo (internationally oriented national body)
♦ Infante Sano / see World Connect
♦ Infant Feeding Action Coalition / see Corporate Accountability International
♦ Infant Jesus Sisters – Nicolas Barré (religious order)
♦ INFANTS – INternational Federation of Acute Neonatal Transport Services (unconfirmed)
♦ Infarma – European Pharmacies Conference (meeting series)
♦ INFCE – International Nuclear Fuel Cycle Evaluation (inactive)
♦ INFDC / see Nevin Scrimshaw International Nutrition Foundation

♦ Infection Control Africa Network (ICAN) 11184
Admin Officer Stellenbosch Univ, PO Box 19063, Tygerberg, 7505, South Africa. T. +27219385054. Fax +27219315065. E-mail: orasslan@gmail.com.
URL: http://www.icanetwork.co.za/
History Jun 2008, Accra (Ghana), as *Infection Prevention and Control Africa Network (IPCAN)*, following proposal at annual meeting of *Safe Injection Global Network (SIGN, #19028)*, 2007, Geneva (Switzerland). **Aims** Establish support in training, operational research and high standards of healthcare practice in healthcare facilities under one umbrella. **Events** *Congress* Harare (Zimbabwe) 2014, *Congress* Windhoek (Namibia) 2011, *Congress* South Africa 2010, *African congress on infection prevention and control* Kampala (Uganda) 2009, *Congress* Uganda 2009. **NGO Relations** Member of: *International Federation of Infection Control (IFIC, #13457)*; *World Federation for Hospital Sterilisation Sciences (WFHSS, #21438)*. [2014/XJ2066/**D**]

♦ Infection Control Society of Southern Africa (internationally oriented national body)
♦ Infection Prevention and Control Africa Network / see Infection Control Africa Network (#11184)

♦ Infections Control World Organization (ICWO) 11185
Contact address not obtained. E-mail: icwo@sympatico.ca.
URL: http://www3.sympatico.ca/kurstak/
History Includes activities of *International Comparative Virology Organization (inactive)*. **Aims** Promote discussions, exchange of information and international cooperation to develop *vaccines* and improve *immunization* for prevention and control of infectious diseases. **Events** *World Congress on Vaccines, Immunisation and Immunotherapy* Genoa (Italy) 2014, *World Congress on Vaccines, Immunisation and Immunotherapy* Barcelona (Spain) 2012, *World Congress on Vaccines, Immunisation and Immunotherapy* Berlin (Germany) 2010, *World Congress on Vaccines, Immunisation and Immunotherapy* Milan (Italy) 2008, *World congress on vaccines, immunisation and immunotherapy* Montréal, QC (Canada) 2006. [2018.06.30/XD8821/**D**]

♦ Infectious Disease Research Institute (IDRI) 11186
Contact 1616 Eastlake Ave E, Ste 400, Seattle WA 98102, USA. T. +12063810883. E-mail: office@idri.org.
URL: http://www.idri.org/
History 1993. **Aims** Apply innovative science to develop products to eliminate infectious diseases of global importance. **Structure** Board of Directors. **Staff** 115.00 FTE, paid. **Finance** Annual budget: US$ 25,000,000. **NGO Relations** Member of: *Global Health Technologies Coalition (GHTC)*. [2019.02.15/XJ7315/j/**D**]

♦ Infectious Diseases Data Observatory (IDDO) 11187
Dir Ctr for Tropical Medicine and Global Health, New Richards Bldg, Old Road Campus, Roosevelt Drive, Headington, OX3 7LG, UK. T. +441865612948. E-mail: comms@iddo.org.
URL: https://www.iddo.org/
History 2016. **Aims** Provide methods, governance and infrastructure to translate data into evidence that improves outcomes for patients worldwide. **Structure** Board; Scientific Advisory Committee; Executive Management Team. *Centre for Tropical Medicine, Oxford* operates as coordinating centre. **Staff** 33.00 FTE, paid. **Finance** Supported by: *Bill and Melinda Gates Foundation (BMGF)*; Drugs for Neglected Diseases Initiative (DNDi); *UNICEF/UNDP/World Bank/WHO Special Programme for Research and Training in Tropical Diseases (TDR, #20331)*. **Activities** Capacity building; knowledge management/information dissemination; research and development. [2021.01.04/AA1042/**F**]

♦ Infectious Diseases Society of Southern Africa (internationally oriented national body)
♦ INFEDOP International Federation of Employees in Public Services (#13410)
♦ INFEMIT / see International Fellowship for Mission as Transformation (#13584)
♦ INFEMIT International Fellowship for Mission as Transformation (#13584)
♦ INfG International Network for Girls (#14273)
♦ INFID International NGO Forum on Indonesian Development (#14366)

♦ Infinite Way 11188
Voie infinie
Mailing Address PO Box 8260, Moreno Valley CA 92552, USA.
URL: https://joelgoldsmith.com/
Aims Apply the *spiritual* teachings of Joel S Goldsmith (1892-1964) to daily life. **Activities** Group meetings receive advice. **Events** *Annual Forum* Ottawa, ON (Canada) 2002. **Publications** *La Voie Infinie*; *Lettres d'enseignements mensuels de Joël S Goldsmith*.
Members Groups in 6 countries:
Belgium, France, Germany, Switzerland, UK, USA. [2012/XF2746/**F**]

♦ INFINITI Conference on International Finance (meeting series)
♦ INFINITI – INFINITI Conference on International Finance (meeting series)
♦ INF International Naturist Federation (#14219)
♦ INF – International Nepal Fellowship (internationally oriented national body)
♦ INF International Neuroendocrine Federation (#14349)
♦ Infirmité motrice cérébrale association internationale pour le sport et la récréation (#03833)
♦ INFITA International Network for Information Technology in Agriculture (#14287)

♦ Inflammatory Breast Cancer International Consortium (IBC-IC) 11189
Contact 710 N Fairbanks Ct, Olson Pavilion, Ste 8-250A, Chicago IL 60611, USA. E-mail: contact@ibcic.org.
URL: http://www.ibcic.org/
History First encounter 2008. Founded as a non-profit 2014. **Aims** Foster collaboration among inflammatory breast cancer researchers and clinicians. **Structure** Officers. **Events** *International Symposium* Madrid (Spain) 2018. [2019/XM7694/**C**]

♦ Inflammatory Skin Disease Summit (meeting series)
♦ InfluenceMap (internationally oriented national body)
♦ INF – Nevin Scrimshaw International Nutrition Foundation (internationally oriented national body)
♦ INfoAndina Latin American Network on Andean Mountains (#16350)
♦ INFO/CAR Centre d'Activités Régionales pour l'Information et la Communication de la Convention de Barcelone (#18745)
♦ INFOCLIMA – WMO Climate Data Information Referral Service (see: #21649)
♦ InfoComm International / see Audiovisual and Integrated Experience Association
♦ InFocus Programme on Safety and Health at Work and the Environment (see: #11123)

♦ infoDev 11190
Contact c/o World Bank, 1818 H St NW, Washington DC 20433, USA. T. +12024732414. Fax +12025223186.
URL: http://www.infodev.org/

History 1995, as a global multilateral donor program administered by *International Bank for Reconstruction and Development (IBRD, #12317)*. Full title: *Information for Development Program – infoDev*. **Aims** Help *developing countries* and their international partners to maximize the impact of information and *communication technologies* (ICTs) in combating *poverty* and promoting broad-based *sustainable development*. **Structure** Coordinated by Secretariat, housed at Global ICT Department (GICT) of World Bank. **Finance** Donors: governments, public and private organizations. Current donors include: governments of Brazil, Finland, Germany, India, Ireland, Japan, Korea Rep, Sweden, Switzerland, UK; *European Commission (EC, #06633)*; World Bank. **Activities** Funds projects in the field. Since its creation, received 782 proposals for projects, 148 of which have been funded. Launching an intensive programme of support for research, analysis and evaluation, impact monitoring and toolkit development focused on distilling the lessons of experience from the past 10 years on the impact of ICT on poverty, with a particular focus on mainstreaming and scaling up successful ICT approaches and applications. In light of the new strategy, infoDev has suspended core grant and iCSF programmes and is no longer accepting proposals for either programme. Conference Scholarship Fund (iCSF). **Events** *Global Forum on Innovative and Technology Entrepreneurship* Helsinki (Finland) 2011, *Global Forum* Brazil 2009, *Conference on open source* Washington, DC (USA) 2002. **Publications** *infoDev eXchange* (4 a year) – newsletter. *Year 2000 Grant Program Information* in English, French, Spanish. Quarterly and annual reports; books; handbooks; background papers; donor list; staff profiles; news. **Information Services** *direct internet links to infoDev projects*; *INFODEV-L* – electronic discussion list; *live proposal and project database – updated hourly*. **IGO Relations** *Commonwealth of Learning (COL, #04346)*.
[2018/XF4851/f/**F**]

♦ INFOE – Institut für Ökologie und Aktions-Ethnologie (internationally oriented national body)
♦ **INFOFISH** Intergovernmental Organization for Marketing Information and Technical Advisory Services for Fishery Products in the Asia and Pacific Region (#11497)
♦ **INFO** International Natural Fiber Organization (#14215)
♦ **INFOJEUNESSE** INFOJEUNESSE – Réseau mondial d'information sur les questions de jeunesse (#11204)
♦ INFOJEUNESSE – Réseau mondial d'information sur les questions de jeunesse (#11204)
♦ INFOJUVE / see INFOYOUTH – Worldwide Information Network on Youth Related Issues (#11204)
♦ INFOLAC – Information Society Program for Latin America and the Caribbean (inactive)
♦ Infonomics Society (unconfirmed)
♦ **INFOODS** International Network of Food Data Systems (#14271)

♦ INFOPECHE 11191

Dir Tour C, 19ème étage, Cité Administrative, Abidjan 01, Côte d'Ivoire. T. +22520360497 – +22520360507 – +22520213198. Fax +22520218054. E-mail: infopeche@aviso.ci – infopech@gmail.com.
URL: http://infopeche.org/

History 1985, Abidjan (Côte d'Ivoire), by *FAO (#09260)*. **Aims** Assist communications between producers and exporters of *fish* and *seafood* in *Africa* and potential buyers throughout the world. **Structure** Sub office: INFOSA covers South African Development Committee (SADC) region. Secretariat located at Windhoek (Namibia). **Finance** Members' dues. **Activities** Promotes sales of African fish, particularly within Africa, by putting sellers and buyers in touch with each other; keeps fish producers and exporters in Africa up-to-date on marketing trends and opportunities; offers expert technical advice to African producers in all phases of handling, storing and marketing their products; commissions studies by expert consultants covering topics of interest to African producers and governments; sponsors regular training courses on post-harvesting aspects of fishing industry operations; maintains up-to-date world rosters of fisheries experts and consulting firms specializing in the post-harvesting phase of fishing industry operations; organizes *'CAPE TOWN International Fisheries Conference'*, Buyers and Sellers Meetings and other conferences, seminars and workshops. Consultancy services cover: marketing information on fisheries products, including sales opportunities and supply prospects, within and outside Africa; advice on technological developments, product specifications, processing methods and quality standards in accordance with market requirements; assistance in identifying new products and promoting under-utilized species; training of staff in governments, institutions and the fishing industry in marketing development. **Events** *World pelagics conference* Cape Town (South Africa) 2003, *International small pelagic conference* Agadir (Morocco) 2001, *Conférence sur les petites pélagiques et merlu* Cape Town (South Africa) 1995. **Publications** *INFOPECHE Trade News* (bi-weekly) in English, French; *INFOFISH International (II)* (6 a year) in English – with summaries in Arabic/French/Spanish – jointly with other network members. Catalogues; reports; directories. Information Services: Computerized and constantly updated register of buyers of fish products throughout the world; similar register of African producers and exporters, together with detailed information about regular product lines and current offerings.
Members Member States (18):
Cameroon, Congo Brazzaville, Côte d'Ivoire, Eritrea, Gabon, Gambia, Ghana, Guinea, Guinea-Bissau, Liberia, Mauritania, Morocco, Mozambique, Namibia, Nigeria, Senegal, Sierra Leone, Togo.
IGO Relations Cooperation agreement with: FAO; *Ministerial Conference on Fisheries Cooperation Among African States Bordering the Atlantic Ocean (ATLAFCO, #16816)*; *UNIDO (#20336)*. Part of *FAO GLOBEFISH (#09261)*, also comprising: *International Organisation for the Development of Fisheries and Aquaculture in Europe (EUROFISH, #14427)* (Europe); *Intergovernmental Organization for Marketing Information and Technical Advisory Services for Fishery Products in the Asia and Pacific Region (INFOFISH, #11497)* (Asia and the Pacific); *INFOPESCA (#11192)* (Latin America and the Caribbean); *INFOSA (#11203)* (Southern Africa); *Centre for Marketing Information and Advisory Services for Fishery Products in the Arab Region (INFOSAMAK, #03772)* (Arab countries); *'INFOYU'* (China).
[2018/XF2121/**F***]

♦ INFOPESCA 11192

Dir Julio Hererra y Obes 1296, Casilla de Correo 7086, 11200 Montevideo, Uruguay. T. +59829028701. Fax +59829030501. E-mail: infopesca@infopesca.org.
URL: http://www.infopesca.org/

History Jun 1977, as a regional project of *FAO (#09260)*, following operations from 1975 on the initiative of *UNDP (#20292)*. **Aims** Promote development of *fisheries* and *aquaculture* projects in *Latin America* and the *Caribbean*; provide an international fish marketing service for the region by establishing contacts between private and governmental exporters and importers; provide technical assistance and indirect assistance through publications. **Structure** Permanent and multidisciplinary team of experts with international experience; liaison officers in all Latin America and the Caribbean countries; worldwide network of specialized consultancy enterprises; network of associated experts. **Languages** English, French, Portuguese, Spanish. **Staff** 10.00 FTE, paid; 30.00 FTE, voluntary. **Finance** International, national and private financing. Sources: private industry and government institutions in member countries; subscriptions to INFOPESCA publications; subscriptions to other projects of the Global Network; international funding agencies (projects). Budget (annual): about US$ 500,000. **Activities** Main fields of activity: information on marketing of seafood; processing and quality control; production, development strategy; provision of information on world markets for fishery products through direct communication or publications. Assists with technical advice on processing, handling, packaging, regulations; organizes seminars, conferences and workshops. **Events** *Meeting on seafood networks in Latin America* Mar del Plata (Argentina) 2005, *Pan American meeting on inspection and quality control of products* Porlamar (Venezuela) 2003, *Pan American meeting on fish inspection and quality control* Cartagena de Indias (Colombia) 2000, *Seafood conference* Kyoto (Japan) 1990. **Publications** *INFOPESCA Noticias Comerciales (INC)* (bi-weekly) in Spanish – also available online; *INFOPESCA International* (4 a year) – magazine. Conference and symposium reports; studies; directories; manuals.
Members Governments of 11 countries:
Argentina, Belize, Brazil, Colombia, Costa Rica, Dominican Rep, Honduras, Mexico, Nicaragua, Uruguay, Venezuela.
IGO Relations Cooperation agreement with FAO. Part of *FAO GLOBEFISH (#09261)*, which also includes: *International Organisation for the Development of Fisheries and Aquaculture in Europe (EUROFISH, #14427)* (Europe); *Intergovernmental Organization for Marketing Information and Technical Advisory Services for Fishery Products in the Asia and Pacific Region (INFOFISH, #11497)* (Asia and the Pacific); *INFOPECHE (#11191)* (Africa); *INFOSA (#11203)* (Southern Africa); *Centre for Marketing Information and Advisory Services for Fishery Products in the Arab Region (INFOSAMAK, #03772)* (Arab countries); *'INFOYU'* (China). **NGO Relations** Coordinates: *Network of Latin American Women of the Fishery Sector (#17046)*. Provides secretariat for: *Pan-American Network of Fish Inspection, Quality Control and Technology (#18122)*.
[2012.09.18/XF0645/**F***]

♦ INFO/RAC / see Regional Activity Centre for Information and Communication of the Barcelona Convention (#18745)
♦ **INFO/RAC** Regional Activity Centre for Information and Communication of the Barcelona Convention (#18745)
♦ Inforce Foundation – International Forensic Centre of Excellence for the Investigation of Genocide (internationally oriented national body)
♦ Información Comunitaria, Empoderamiento y Transparencia (internationally oriented national body)
♦ Información Comunitaria y Tecnologias Epidemiológicas / see Community Information, Empowerment and Transparency
♦ Informal Consultative Meeting of Regional and International Students Structures (meeting series)
♦ Informal European Theatre Meeting / see IETM – International Network for Contemporary Performing Arts (#11098)

♦ Informal Forum of International Student Organizations (IFISO) 11193

Management Team address not obtained. E-mail: management.ifiso@gmail.com.
URL: https://managementifiso.wixsite.com/ifiso

History 2004. **Aims** Provide a platform where leaders of international student organizations come together to share ideas, best practices and network. **Structure** Meeting (twice a year); Management Team, elected at each meeting by partner organizations. **Languages** English. **Staff** 4.00 FTE, voluntary. **Finance** Financed through cooperation with companies and universities. **Activities** Events/meetings. **Events** *Spring Meeting* 2021, *Forum* 2020, *Autumn Meeting* Brussels (Belgium) 2019, *Spring Meeting* Budapest (Hungary) 2015, *Autumn Meeting* Zurich (Switzerland) 2015.
Members Partners (21):
- *Association des états généraux des étudiants de l'Europe (AEGEE-Europe, #02495)*;
- *Board of European Students of Technology (BEST, #03294)*;
- *Electrical Engineering STudents' European assoCiation (EESTEC, #05416)*;
- *Erasmus Student Network (ESN, #05529)*;
- *European Association of Aerospace Students (EUROAVIA, #05930)*;
- *European Dental Students Association (EDSA, #06904)*;
- *European Federation of Psychology Students' Associations (EFPSA, #07200)*;
- *European Geography Association for Students and Young Geographers (EGEA, #07388)*;
- *European Medical Students' Association (EMSA, #07764)*;
- *European Pharmaceutical Students' Association (EPSA, #08197)*;
- *European Students of Industrial Engineering and Management (ESTIEM, #08846)*;
- *International Association for Political Science Students (IAPSS, #12095)*;
- *International Association of Physics Students (IAPS, #12085)*;
- *International Association of Students in Agricultural and Related Sciences (IAAS, #12191)*;
- *International Federation of Medical Students' Associations (IFMSA, #13478)*;
- *International Forestry Students' Association (IFSA, #13628)*;
- *International Pharmaceutical Students' Federation (IPSF, #14568)*;
- *International Students of History Association (ISHA, #15613)*;
- *International Veterinary Students' Association (IVSA, #15851)*;
- *Junior Enterprises Europe (JE Europe, #16169)*;
- *The European Law Students' Association (ELSA, #07660)*.

[2021.09.09/XJ3873/cy/**F**]

♦ Informal International Conference of Christian Broadcasting (inactive)
♦ Informasjonsarbeidere for Fred (internationally oriented national body)

♦ Informatics Europe 11194

Exec Dir Binzmühlestrasse 14, 8050 Zurich ZH, Switzerland. T. +41446354357. E-mail: administration@informatics-europe.org.
URL: http://www.informatics-europe.org/

History Set up following 2 European Computer Science Summits (ECSS), Oct 2005 and Oct 2006, Zurich (Switzerland). **Aims** Foster quality research, education and knowledge transfer in informatics in Europe. **Structure** General Assembly; Executive Board; Secretary-General. **Languages** English. **Staff** 4.00 FTE, paid. **Finance** Sources: fees for services; grants; members' dues; sponsorship. **Activities** Awards/prizes/competitions; awareness raising; events/meetings; knowledge management/information dissemination; monitoring/evaluation; networking/liaising; projects/programmes; research and development; research/documentation; training/education. **Events** *European Computer Science Summit* Madrid (Spain) 2021, *European Computer Science Summit* Gothenburg (Sweden) 2018, *European Computer Science Summit* Lisbon (Portugal) 2017, *European Computer Science Summit* Budapest (Hungary) 2016, *European Computer Science Summit* Vienna (Austria) 2015. **Publications** *Informatics Europe Members' Bulletin* (6 a year). Reports. **Information Services** *Informatics Hgher Education Data Portal*; *Informatics Job Platform*; *Informatics Research and Education Directory*.
Members University departments; faculties and schools; research laboratories. Industrial; Industrial Associate. Members (over 150) in 32 countries:
Austria, Belgium, Bosnia-Herzegovina, Bulgaria, Croatia, Czechia, Denmark, Estonia, Finland, France, Germany, Greece, Hungary, Ireland, Italy, Latvia, Lithuania, Luxembourg, Netherlands, Norway, Poland, Portugal, Romania, Russia, Serbia, Slovakia, Slovenia, Spain, Sweden, Switzerland, Türkiye, UK.
NGO Relations Member of (2): *European Forum for ICST (#07316)*; *Initiative for Science in Europe (ISE, #11214)*.
[2021.06.10/XJ1266/**D**]

♦ Informatics for the Third World (inactive)
♦ Informatienetwerk voor Onderwijs in Europa (inactive)
♦ Information Africa (unconfirmed)
♦ Information for All Programme (see: #20322)
♦ Information Bureau of Communist and Workers' Parties (inactive)
♦ Information Bureau for Peace Work (internationally oriented national body)

♦ Information Centre for Bilingual and Plurilingual Education (CeBiPE) 11195

Centre d'information sur l'éducation bilingue et plurilingue (CIEBP) – Centro de Información sobre Educación Bilingüe e Plurilingüe – Informationszentrum für Zweisprachige und Mehrsprachige Erziehung – Centro di Informazione sull' Educazione Bilingua e Plurilingue – Centr Informacii po Dvuhjazycnomu Obrazovaniju

Coordination Bureau c/o Univda – Sci Humaine, Strada Cappuccini 2/A, 11100 Aosta AO, Italy.
Registered Office c/o MSH, 54 Boulevard Raspail, 75006 Paris, France.
URL: https://ciebp.org/

History 1972, Aosta (Italy), as a specialized agency within the framework of *World Federation of United Cities (UTO, inactive)*. Original title: *World Information Centre for Bilingual Education (WICBE) – Centre mondial d'information sur l'éducation bilingue (CMIEB) – Centro Mundial de Información sobre Educación Bilingüe – Welt-Informationszentrum für Zweisprachige Erziehung – Centro Mondiale di Informazione sull' Educazione Bilingua – Vsemirnyj Centr Informacii po Dvuhjazycnomu Obrazovaniju*. Also previously known as *World Information Centre for Bilingual and Plurilingual Education (WICBPE) – Centre mondial d'information sur l'éducation bilingue et plurilingue (CMIEBP) – Centro Mundial de Información sobre Educación Bilingüe e Plurilingüe – Welt-Informationszentrum für Zweisprachige und Mehrsprachige Erziehung – Centro Mondiale di Informazione sull' Educazione Bilingua e Plurilingue – Vsemirnyj Centr Informacii po Dvuhjazycnomu Obrazovaniju*. Registered in accordance with French law. **Aims** Promote a system of bi- and plurilingual education for international and European *schools*; encourage establishment of bilingual departments at education institutions; facilitate exchange of information. **Structure** Officers: President; 2 Vice-Presidents; Secretary; Treasurer. Board of Administrators. **Languages** English, French, German, Italian, Spanish. **Staff** Voluntary. **Finance** Financed by: Aosta Valley Government. **Activities** Research/documentation; events/meetings. **Events** *Meeting* Paris (France) 2014, *Meeting* Aosta (Italy) 2013, *Meeting* Paris (France) 2012, *Meeting* Aosta (Italy) 2011, *Meeting* Paris (France) 2010. **Publications** *Education and Plurilingual Societies/Education et Sociétés Plurilingues/Educazione e Società Plurilingui* (2 a year) in English, French, German, Italian, Spanish – journal.
Members Full individuals in 12 countries:
Belarus, Belgium, France, Germany, Italy, Luxembourg, Portugal, Romania, Spain, Switzerland, UK, Ukraine.
Correspondents in 35 countries:

Albania, Algeria, Belarus, Belgium, Bulgaria, Burkina Faso, Canada, Chad, France, Gabon, Germany, Ghana, Greece, Hungary, Israel, Jamaica, Japan, Luxembourg, Malta, Moldova, Niger, Nigeria, Peru, Portugal, Romania, Senegal, Slovenia, Spain, Sweden, Switzerland, Tanzania UR, Trinidad-Tobago, UK, Ukraine, USA.
NGO Relations Member of: *European Observatory for Plurilingualism (EOP).* [2019/XE2660/v/**E**]

♦ Information Centre of the International Catholic Organizations / see International Catholic Centre of Geneva (#12449)
♦ Information for Development Program – infoDev / see infoDev (#11190)
♦ Information Diffusion Europe Associations (inactive)
♦ Information and Documentation Centre on the Council of Europe (internationally oriented national body)

♦ Information Economy and Society Partnership (IESP) 11196

Address not obtained.
URL: http://www.icegec-memo.hu/iesp/index.htm
History Coordinated by *ICEG European Centre (inactive).* **Aims** Share knowledge and experience in the field of information and communication technology.
Members Institutions (9) in 9 countries:
Cyprus, Czechia, Estonia, Hungary, Latvia, Lithuania, Poland, Slovakia, Slovenia.
Included in the above, 2 organizations listed in this Yearbook:
Baltic International Centre for Economic Policy Studies (BICEPS); ICEG European Centre. [2007/XM2627/**F**]

♦ Information, Koordination, Tagungen zu Themen des Nord-Süd-Konflikts und der Konziliaren Bewegung / see INKOTA Network
♦ Information Network Development Policy (internationally oriented national body)
♦ Information Network on Education in Europe (inactive)
♦ Information Network Focus on Religious Movements (internationally oriented national body)
♦ Information Network on Higher Education Studies in Latin America and the Caribbean (see: #18084)

♦ Information Quality International (IQ International) 11197

Administration 6920 Brookmill Rd, Baltimore MD 21215, USA. T. +14104840304. E-mail: services@iqint.org.
URL: https://www.iqint.org/
History 2004, as *International Association for Information and Data Quality (IAIDQ).* Current bylaws adopted Jun 2017. **Aims** Advance the quality of information around the world by building a community, supporting learning and sharing knowledge for the benefit of the profession and information consumers. **Structure** Board of Directors; Advisory Council; Executive Officer. **Finance** Sources: members' dues. **Activities** Certification/accreditation; events/meetings; knowledge management/information dissemination. **Events** *Conference* Baltimore, MD (USA) 2015, *Conference* Richmond, VA (USA) 2014, *Conference* Little Rock, AR (USA) 2013, *Conference* San Diego, CA (USA) 2012, *Data governance and information quality conference / Conference* San Diego, CA (USA) 2011. **Publications** *IQ International Journal.* **Members** Individual; corporate about 400. Membership countries not specified. **NGO Relations** *Electronic Commerce Code Management Association (ECCMA, #05424).* [2018/XJ4036/**C**]

♦ Information et réseau d'action pour le droit à se nourrir (#09743)
♦ Informations- und Bildungszentrum Schloss Gimborn (#12877)
♦ Information scandinave sur les OVNI (#19127)

♦ Information Security Forum (ISF) 11198

Dir 10 Eastcheap, London, EC3M 1AJ, UK. T. +442038756868. Fax +442038756909. E-mail: info@securityforum.org.
Registered Office 42-50 Hersham Road, Walton-on-Thames, KT12 1RZ, UK.
URL: http://www.securityforum.org/
History 15 May 1989. Constitutional changes: 1 Dec 1992; 1 Nov 1998. Former names and other names: *European Security Forum (ESF)* – former. **Aims** Support members to protect their *business information* from *cyber* security threats. **Structure** Council; Executive. **Languages** English. **Finance** Sources: members' dues. **Activities** Guidance/assistance/consulting; monitoring/evaluation; projects/programmes; standards/guidelines; training/education. **Events** *Annual Congress* London (UK) 2020, *Annual Congress* Dublin (Ireland) 2019, *Annual Congress* Las Vegas, NV (USA) 2018, *Annual Congress* Cannes (France) 2017, *Annual Congress* Berlin (Germany) 2016. **Publications** Guides; standards.
Members Businesses, governmental agencies and academic institutions (480) in 36 countries and territories:
Argentina, Australia, Austria, Belgium, Brazil, Canada, China, Denmark, Dominican Rep, Ethiopia, Finland, France, Germany, Ghana, Greece, India, Ireland, Italy, Japan, Latvia, Malaysia, Netherlands, New Zealand, Nigeria, Norway, Qatar, Saudi Arabia, Scotland, Singapore, South Africa, Spain, Sweden, Switzerland, Türkiye, Uganda, USA.
IGO Relations Attends meetings of Committee for Information, Computer and Communications Policy of: *OECD (#17693).* **NGO Relations** Instrumental in setting up (1): *INFOSEC Business Advisory Group (IBAG, inactive).* [2020.10.28/XF1179/y/**F**]

♦ Information Security Solutions Europe (meeting series)
♦ Informationsnettet om Uddannelse i Europa (inactive)
♦ Informationsnetz zum Bildungswesen in Europa (inactive)
♦ Information Society Program for Latin America and the Caribbean (inactive)
♦ Information Society Technologies / see IST-Africa (#16070)
♦ Informationsstelle für Friedensarbeit (internationally oriented national body)
♦ Informationsstelle Lateinamerika (internationally oriented national body)
♦ Informationsverbund Entwicklungspolitik (internationally oriented national body)

♦ Information System on Occupational Exposure (ISOE) 11199

Joint Secretariat OECD NEA – Div of Radiological Protection and Human Aspects of Nuclear Safety, 46 quai Alphonse le Gallo, 92100 Boulogne-Billancourt, France. T. +33173212936. E-mail: isoe.secretariat@oecd-nea.org.
Joint Secretariat IAEA – Div of Radiation/Transport/Waste Safety, PO Box 100, 1400 Vienna, Austria. T. +431260026173.
URL: http://www.isoe-network.net/
History Created 1992. **Aims** Improve the management of occupational exposure at *nuclear* power plants by exchanging broad and regularly updated information, data and experience on methods to optimize occupational *radiological* protection. **Structure** Management Board; Bureau. Technical Centres (4): Europe; North America; Asia; IAEA. **Finance** Jointly sponsored by: *Nuclear Energy Agency (NEA, #17615); International Atomic Energy Agency (IAEA, #12294).* **Activities** Knowledge management/information dissemination. **Events** *International Symposium* Tours (France) 2021, *North American Symposium* Key West, FL (USA) 2020, *International Symposium* Tours (France) 2020, *International Symposium on Occupational Exposure Management at Nuclear Facilities* Beijing (China) 2019, *International Symposium* Beijing (China) 2019.
Members Representatives from nuclear licensees (78) national regulatory authorities (27). Utilities in 28 countries:
Armenia, Belgium, Brazil, Bulgaria, Canada, China, Czechia, Finland, France, Hungary, Italy, Japan, Korea Rep, Lithuania, Mexico, Netherlands, Pakistan, Romania, Russia, Slovakia, Slovenia, South Africa, Spain, Sweden, Switzerland, Ukraine, United Arab Emirates, USA.
Authorities in 27 countries:
Armenia, Belarus, Belgium, Brazil, Bulgaria, Canada, China, Finland, France, Germany, Japan, Korea Rep, Lithuania, Mexico, Netherlands, Pakistan, Romania, Slovakia, Slovenia, South Africa, Spain, Sweden, Switzerland, UK, Ukraine, United Arab Emirates, USA.
IGO Relations Framework of Cooperation with: *United Nations Scientific Committee on the Effects of Atomic Radiation (UNSCEAR, #20624).* **NGO Relations** Technical Cooperation Agreements with: national entities. Special Liaison Organization Status with: *International Commission on Radiological Protection (ICRP, #12724).* [2020.02.18/XM7881/**E**]

♦ Information Systems Audit and Control Association / see ISACA (#16022)

♦ Information Systems Research in Scandinavia (IRIS) 11200

Sec address not obtained.
URL: https://communities.aisnet.org/scandinavia/home
History Aug 1997. Functions as regional chapter of *Association for Information Systems (AIS, #02645).* **Aims** Promote research and education in the use, development and management of information systems in Scandinavia. **Structure** Steering Committee, including Chairman; Editorial Board; Secretariat. **Finance** Members' dues. **Activities** Events/meetings. *IRIS (Information systems research seminar in Scandinavia)* and the *Scandinavian Conference on Information Systems (SCIS)* are held as a joint conference. **Events** *Annual Scandinavian Conference on Information Systems* Orkanger (Norway) 2021, *Annual Conference* Sundsvall (Sweden) 2020, *Annual Scandinavian Conference on Information Systems* Sundsvall (Sweden) 2020, *Annual Conference* Tampere (Finland) 2019, *Annual Conference* Oulu (Finland) 2015. **Publications** *Scandinavian Journal of Information Systems.*
Members in 6 countries:
Denmark, Finland, Netherlands, Norway, Sweden, UK. [2021/XF6837/**F**]

♦ Information Systems for Telecommunications '92 / see ETIS – Global IT Association for Telecommunications (#05559)
♦ Informationszentrum für Zweisprachige und Mehrsprachige Erziehung (#11195)
♦ Information Technology Agreement (1996 treaty)
♦ Information Technology for Humanitarian Assistance, Cooperation and Action (internationally oriented national body)
♦ Information Technology Services for the European Railways / see HIT Rail (#10933)
♦ Information Unit for Conventions /Environmental/ (inactive)
♦ Information Workers for Peace (internationally oriented national body)
♦ Informatique pour les Tiers-mondes (inactive)
♦ INFORM – Information Network Focus on Religious Movements (internationally oriented national body)

♦ Informing Science Institute (ISI) 11201

Exec Dir 131 Brookhill Court, Santa Rosa CA 95409, USA. T. +17073243171.
Exec Dir address not obtained.
Main Website: http://informingscience.org/
History 2000. Registration: US IRS Non-profit, No/ID: 83-313 1083, Start date: 2018, USA, California. **Aims** Advance multidisciplinary study of informing systems that draws together people who teach, research and use information technologies to inform clients for the purpose of sharing knowledge. **Structure** Board of Governors. **Languages** English. **Staff** 3.00 FTE, paid; 250.00 FTE, voluntary. **Finance** Sources: members' dues; sponsorship. **Activities** Events/meetings; publishing activities. **Events** *InSITE Conference* 2022, *InSITE Conference* 2021, *InSITE Conference* 2020, *InSITE Conference* Jerusalem (Israel) 2019, *InSITE Conference* La Verne, CA (USA) 2018. **Publications** Journals; books; articles; conference proceedings. **Members** Individuals in about 50 countries and territories. Membership countries not specified. **IGO Relations** Cooperates with (1): *International Civil Aviation Organization (ICAO, #12581).* **NGO Relations** Cooperates with (1): *International Institute of Informatics and Systemics (IIIS, #13889).* Also links with educational institutions and universities. [2022.05.03/XJ6683/j/**F**]

♦ **INFORM** International Network for Fatty Acid Oxidation Research and Management (#14269)
♦ INFORM – International Reference Organization in Forensic Medicine (inactive)

♦ InformNorden 11202

Contact c/o HSL Helsinki Region Transport, Opastinsilta 6 A, PL 100, 00077 HSL, Helsinki, Finland. T. +358947664379. E-mail: magnus.arnstrom@gmail.com.
URL: http://www.informnorden.org
History 1998 by the public transport authorities in Scandinavia. **Aims** Stimulate information exchange on the use of *information technology* in *public transport.* **Structure** Steering Group. **Events** *Annual International Conference* Stockholm (Sweden) 2019, *Annual International Conference* Stockholm (Sweden) 2018, *Annual International Conference* Aalborg (Denmark) 2017, *Annual International Conference* Helsinki (Finland) 2016, *Annual International Conference* Reykjavik (Iceland) 2015. **Publications** *InformNorden Newsletter.*
Members Full in 5 countries:
Denmark, Finland, Iceland, Norway, Sweden. [2016/XM3748/**F**]

♦ **INFORMS** Institute for Operations Research and the Management Sciences (#11286)
♦ **INFORSE** International Network for Sustainable Energy (#14331)

♦ INFOSA 11203

Contact PO Box 23523, Windhoek, Namibia. T. +26461279430. Fax +26461279434. E-mail: infosa@infosa.org.na.
URL: http://www.infosa.org.na/
History Established 2003, within the framework of *FAO (#09260).* Full title: *INFOSA – Marketing Information and Technical Advisory Services for the Fisheries Industry in Southern Africa. INFOPECHE (#11191)* Unit in the *Southern African Development Community (SADC, #19843)* region. Hosted by the Government of Namibia. **Aims** Promote and develop fish *trade* in Southern Africa; contribute to the development and modernization of the fisheries sector in Southern Africa; contribute to a more balanced supply of fisheries products in the region; contribute to the development of aquaculture in Southern Africa; make best use of the *export* opportunities within and outside Africa; promote technical and economic cooperation among contracting partners. **Structure** Head Office in Windhoek (Namibia); National Liaison Offices in member countries. **Languages** English, French, Portuguese. **Staff** 6.50 FTE, paid. Several part-time (on consultancy basis). **Finance** Donor contributions from Government of Norway; hosting contributions from the Government of Namibia; project financing from *FAO (#09260);* other income from conferences and consultancies. **Activities** Assists companies in the industry to find buyers for their products or to find suppliers for those who are in the market to buy through: maintaining an updated computerized register of regional producers and international buyers of seafood products; organizing buyer-seller meetings in the region; participating in international exhibitions and fairs to promote seafood products from the SADC region. Keeps the industry updated through: publishing of a newsletter; participation in the global Fish Info Network. Publishes market studies on products of interest to the SADC region, in cooperation with other regional services. Offers technical advice to producers in the region, ranging from product development, efficiency improvements, to quality control systems. Advises industry and small-scale sectors on aquaculture from production to harvesting and marketing. Advice is available on request, and covers such issues as: plant design and layout; quality assurance systems; HACCP; ISO; reduction of post harvest losses; better utilization of raw material; product development; new and more efficient technology. Offers specialized consulting services. Organizes: occasional regional and international events; training courses and technical seminars in Quality Assurance, Marketing and Aquaculture in member countries. **Publications** *Market Reports* (12 a year); *Africa's Fish Industry* (annual) – magazine; *ITN – INFOSA Trade News* (24 a year). Guidelines; manuals.
Members in 14 countries:
Angola, Botswana, Congo DR, Lesotho, Madagascar, Malawi, Mauritius, Mozambique, Namibia, Seychelles, South Africa, Tanzania UR, Zambia, Zimbabwe.
IGO Relations *Centre for Marketing Information and Advisory Services for Fishery Products in the Arab Region (INFOSAMAK, #03772)* (Arab countries); *Common Fund for Commodities (CFC, #04293); International Organisation for the Development of Fisheries and Aquaculture in Europe (EUROFISH, #14427)* (East European region); *FAO GLOBEFISH (#09261);* INFOPECHE (Sub-Saharan Africa); *INFOPESCA (#11192)* (Latin America); *Intergovernmental Organization for Marketing Information and Technical Advisory Services for Fishery Products in the Asia and Pacific Region (INFOFISH, #11497)* (Asia and the Pacific); *'INFOYU'* (China); *New Partnership for Africa's Development (NEPAD, #17091); Southern African Development Community (SADC, #19843).* [2014.01.15/XM1117/**F***]

♦ **INFOSAMAK** Centre for Marketing Information and Advisory Services for Fishery Products in the Arab Region (#03772)
♦ INFOSA – Marketing Information and Technical Advisory Services for the Fisheries Industry in Southern Africa / see INFOSA (#11203)
♦ **INFOSAN** FAO/WHO International Food Safety Authorities Network (#09270)
♦ **infosyon** Internationales Forum für System-Aufstellungen in Organisationen und Arbeitskontexten (#13656)

♦ **INFOTERM** International Information Centre for Terminology (#13846)
♦ INFOTERRA – Global Environmental Information Exchange Network (inactive)
♦ **INFOYOUTH** INFOYOUTH – Worldwide Information Network on Youth Related Issues (#11204)

♦ INFOYOUTH – Worldwide Information Network on Youth Related Issues (INFOYOUTH) 11204

INFOJEUNESSE – Réseau mondial d'information sur les questions de jeunesse (INFOJEUNESSE)

Coordinator c/o INJEP, 95 avenue de France, 75650 Paris CEDEX 13, France. T. +33170989400.
Programme Specialist 1 rue Miollis, 75732 Paris, France. T. +33145683666. Fax +33145685583.

History 1992, within the framework of *UNESCO (#20322)*, as an international information and data exchange network on youth. Previously also referred to as *UNESCO Infoyouth Network – Réseau Infojeunesse de l'UNESCO – Red Infojuve de la UNESCO (INFOJUVE)*. **Aims** Support universal access to information, local content production and regional and inter-regional interaction by means of *ICTs* in order to create knowledge, experience and analyses underlying youth *policies* and issues and make them available to all; enable decision-makers to keep up to date on current trends and issues relating to *young people*; promote cultural and language diversity; provide access to information and preventative education support in the global effort against HIV/AIDS; raise awareness and facilitate initiation and training of young people in ICT skills, particularly in disadvantaged areas and post-conflict zones; support efforts of youth to foster a culture of peace, tolerance, sustainable development and quality of life. **Structure** Steering Committee, comprising representatives from UNESCO and French individuals. Operated by Institut national de la jeunesse et de l'éducation populaire (INJEP), France. **Activities** Disseminates and exchanges data on and for young people. Promotes exchanges between field workers, associations, institutional partners and researchers. Backs innovative projects aimed at stimulating the participation of young people in the political, economic and cultural life of society. Facilitates the design of appropriate policies and programmes for young people. Organizes seminars.

Members Full in 23 countries and territories:
Armenia, Bangladesh, Brazil, Bulgaria, Burkina Faso, China, Colombia, Czechia, France, Gabon, Germany, India, Korea Rep, Mali, Palestine, Peru, Poland, Senegal, South Africa, Tunisia, UK, Uruguay, USA.
Included in the above, 2 organizations listed in this Yearbook:
Centro Latinoamericano sobre Juventud (CELAJU); International Foundation for Human Development (IFHD, no recent information).

NGO Relations Cooperates with national and international youth organizations, institutions, research and information agencies, including: *Circle for Youth Research Cooperation in Europe (CYRCE, no recent information).* [2011/XK0510/y/**E**]

♦ **INFPD** International Network on Family Poultry Development (#14267)
♦ Infrared Data Association (internationally oriented national body)

♦ Infrared and Raman Users' Group (IRUG) 11205

Regional Chair Philadelphia Museum of Art, 2600 Benjamin Franklin Pkwy, Philadelphia PA 19130, USA.
Regional Chair Victoria and Albert Museum, Cromwell Road, London, SW7 2RL, UK. T. +442079422116. Fax +442079422092.
URL: http://www.irug.org/

History 1993, USA. Registration: Start date: 2001, USA, Pennsylvania. **Aims** Stimulate professional development of members by providing a forum for exchange of infrared (IR) and Raman *spectroscopic* information, reference spectra and materials. **Structure** Board of 11 members. **Events** *Biennial Conference* Amersfoort (Netherlands) 2021, *Biennial Conference* Amersfoort (Netherlands) 2020, *Biennial Conference* Sydney, NSW (Australia) 2018, *Biennial Conference* Chalkidiki (Greece) 2016, *Biennial Conference* Boston, MA (USA) 2014. **Publications** Information Services: Database of spectra of artists' and related materials. [2021/XM3759/**E**]

♦ Infrastructure Consortium for Africa (ICA) 11206

Consortium pour les infrastructures en Afrique

Secretariat Coordinator c/o African Development Bank, Avenue Jean-Paul II, 01 BP 1387, Abidjan 01, Côte d'Ivoire. T. +22520264280. E-mail: icasecretariat@afdb.org.
URL: http://www.icafrica.org/

History Jul 2005, following the *Group of Eight (G-8, #10745)* Summit in Gleneagles (UK). Inaugural meeting 6 Oct 2005, London (UK). **Aims** Help improve lives and economic well-being of Africa's people through encouraging, supporting and promoting increased investment in sustainable infrastructure in Africa, from public and private sources. **Structure** Hosted by: *African Development Bank (ADB, #00283)*. **Languages** English, French. **Staff** Staffed by permanent staff of African Development Bank and experts on secondment from ICA member countries. **Finance** Voluntary contributions from members. **Activities** Advocacy/lobbying/activism; knowledge management/information dissemination; events/meetings; networking/liaising; training/education; capacity building. **Events** *Workshop on Urban Transport and Mobility Development* Accra (Ghana) 2017, *Workshop on Urban Transport and Mobility Development* Addis Ababa (Ethiopia) 2017, *Annual Meeting* Rome (Italy) 2017, *Annual Meeting* Abidjan (Côte d'Ivoire) 2016, *Annual Meeting* Abidjan (Côte d'Ivoire) 2015. **Publications** *Infrastructure Financing Trends in Africa*. Annual Report; reports; studies; books.

Members Government and development agencies of all G8 countries and one G20 country:
Canada, France, Germany, Italy, Japan, Russia, South Africa, UK, USA.
Organizations (5):
African Development Bank (ADB, #00283); Development Bank of Southern Africa (DBSA); European Commission (EC, #06633); European Investment Bank (EIB, #07599); The World Bank Group (#21218).

IGO Relations Participate as observers in ICA meetings: *African Union (AU, #00488)* Commission; *New Partnership for Africa's Development (NEPAD, #17091)*; regional economic communities, development banks and power pools. [2017.06.01/XM2960/y/**E***]

♦ Infrastructure Ecology Network Europe (IENE) 11207

Chair 195 Rue Saint-Jacques, 75005 Paris, France. E-mail: info@iene.info.
URL: http://www.iene.info/

History 1996. Founded at the initiative of the Dutch Government. Re-established, 2008. **Aims** Promote a safe and *sustainable* pan-European *transport infrastructure* through recommending measures and planning procedures to conserve biodiversity, counteract landscape fragmentation, and reduce *vehicle accidents* and *animal casualties*. **Structure** General Assembly; Steering Committee; Scientific Expert Committee; Secretariat; Working Groups. **Languages** English. **Events** *Conference* Evora (Portugal) 2021, *Conference* Evora (Portugal) 2020, *International Conference* Eindhoven (Netherlands) 2018, *International Conference* Lyon (France) 2016, *International Conference* Malmö (Sweden) 2014. **Publications** *IENE Declaration 2018.* in English – Connecting Europe, Connecting Nature – Building bridges and crossing borders for the defragmentation of Europe.

Members in 48 countries and territories:
Armenia, Australia, Austria, Belgium, Bosnia-Herzegovina, Brazil, Bulgaria, Canada, China, Croatia, Czechia, Denmark, Estonia, Finland, France, Georgia, Germany, Greece, Hungary, India, Iraq, Ireland, Israel, Italy, Kenya, Kosovo, Latvia, Lithuania, Mexico, Netherlands, Nigeria, Norway, Pakistan, Poland, Portugal, Romania, Slovakia, Slovenia, South Africa, Spain, Sweden, Switzerland, Taiwan, Thailand, Tunisia, Türkiye, UK, USA.

IGO Relations Member of: *Standing Committee to the Bern Convention on the Conservation of European Wildlife and Natural Habitats (#19949).* [2020.04.29/XF6091/**F**]

♦ e-Infrastructure Reflection Group (e-IRG) 11208

Secretariat NWO – Science Domain, PO Box 93460, 2509 AL The Hague, Netherlands. T. +31630369904. E-mail: secretariat@e-irg.eu.
Street Address Laan van Nieuw Oost-Indië 300, 2509 AL The Hague, Netherlands.
URL: http://e-irg.eu/

History 2003. Established as a body advising the EC and national governments on policies related to the European Research e-Infrastructures. **Aims** Pave the way towards a general-purpose European e-infrastructure enabling flexible cooperation and optimal use of all electronically available resources. **Structure** Plenum; Delegates' Meeting (4 times a year); Executive Board. **Languages** English. **Staff** None. e-IRG Support Project (e-IRGSP) facilitates operations which has about 5 staff working on a project basis. **Finance** None. Members' costs of participating in meetings and work done covered by the country of each delegate. Operation support through EU funded Project e-IRGSP. **Activities** Events/meetings; projects/programmes; research/documentation. **Events** *Delegates Meeting* Portugal 2021, *e-IRG Workshop* Portugal 2021, *Delegates Meeting* Helsinki (Finland) 2019, *Workshop* Budapest (Hungary) 2011, *Workshop* Poznań (Poland) 2011. **Publications** *e-IRG Newsletter*. White papers; roadmaps; guidelines.

Members Representatives of the following governments (33):
Austria, Belgium, Bosnia-Herzegovina, Bulgaria, Croatia, Czechia, Denmark, Estonia, Finland, France, Germany, Greece, Hungary, Ireland, Italy, Latvia, Lithuania, Luxembourg, Malta, Netherlands, Norway, Poland, Romania, Serbia, Slovakia, Slovenia, Spain, Sweden, Switzerland, Türkiye, UK, Ukraine.
Regional body (1):
European Union (EU, #08967). [2021.03.10/XJ3955/**E***]

♦ INFRC – International Nature Farming Research Center (internationally oriented national body)
♦ **INFV** International Network on Family Violence (#14268)
♦ Inga Foundation (internationally oriented national body)
♦ INGA – International NaB Golf Association (internationally oriented national body)
♦ INGA – International Network on Genetics in Aquaculture (see: #21507)
♦ INGAR – International Natural Gums Association for Research (inactive)
♦ **INGEDE** Internationale Forschungsgemeinschaft Deinking-Technik (#13233)
♦ Ingénieurs assistance internationale (internationally oriented national body)
♦ Ingénieurs-conseils dans les pays nordiques (no recent information)
♦ Ingénieurs du monde (internationally oriented national body)
♦ Ingénieurs sans frontières / see Ingénieurs assistance internationale
♦ Ingénieurs sans frontières (internationally oriented national body)
♦ Ingénieurs sans frontières international (#05481)
♦ Ingenieurs Zonder Grenzen (internationally oriented national body)
♦ Ingenieurs Zonder Grenzen Internationaal (#05481)
♦ INGER – International Network for Genetic Evaluation of Rice (see: #14754)
♦ **INGID** International Nursing Group for Immunodeficiencies (#14386)
♦ INGI / see International NGO Forum on Indonesian Development (#14366)
♦ INGO DMW / see Diplomaten International (#05088)
♦ INGRACE / see International Groundwater Resources Assessment Centre (#13739)
♦ INGRADNET – International Network of Graduate Surveys (unconfirmed)
♦ **INGRED** Institute for Geopolitical Research and Development (#11265)
♦ Ingrid Renard Fonds (internationally oriented national body)
♦ **INGSA** International Network for Government Science Advice (#14274)
♦ INGSM – International Nuclear Graphite Specialist Meeting (meeting series)
♦ Inha Center for International Studies (internationally oriented national body)
♦ Inhaled Therapies for Tuberculosis and Other Infectious Diseases Conference (meeting series)
♦ **INHH** International Network for the History of Hospitals (#14282)
♦ **INHIGEO** International Commission on the History of Geological Sciences (#12685)
♦ **INHN** International Network for the History of Neuropsychopharmacology (#14283)
♦ **INHOPE** International Association of Internet Hotlines (#11970)
♦ **INHPF** International Network of Health Promotion Foundations (#14278)
♦ **INHPH** International Network for the History of Public Health (#14284)
♦ **INHR** International Network of Human Rights (#18891)
♦ **INHS** International Network for Hate Studies (#14275)
♦ INHS / see International Society for the Prevention and Mitigation of Natural Hazards (#15386)
♦ INHSU / see International Network on Health and Hepatitis in Substance Users (#14276)
♦ **INHSU** International Network on Health and Hepatitis in Substance Users (#14276)
♦ INHURED / see International Institute for Human Rights, Environment and Development (#13886)
♦ **INHURED International** International Institute for Human Rights, Environment and Development (#13886)
♦ **INHWE** International Network for Health Workforce Education (#14279)
♦ **INHWTS** International Network to Promote Household Water Treatment and Safe Storage (#14309)
♦ **INIA** International Institute on Ageing, United Nations – Malta (#13860)
♦ **INICC** International Nosocomial Infection Control Consortium (#14376)
♦ Iniciativa de Comercio Etico (internationally oriented national body)
♦ Iniciativa de Comunicación (internationally oriented national body)
♦ Iniciativa para los Derechos y Recursos (#18947)
♦ Iniciativa Global por los Derechos Económicos, Sociales y Culturales (internationally oriented national body)
♦ Iniciativa Global de Justicia, Verdad y Reconciliación (unconfirmed)
♦ Iniciativa Interamericana de Capital Social, Etica y Desarrollo (see: #11427)
♦ Iniciativa de Micronutrientes / see Nutrition International (#17627)
♦ Iniciativa de Salud Oral del Caribe (#03534)
♦ Iniciativas Mundiales de Apoyo a Donantes (#21926)
♦ Iniciativa para la Transparencia de las Industrias Extractivas (#09229)
♦ Iniciativa Una ONU Asociación para el Aprendizaje sobre el Cambio Climatico / see One UN Climate Change Learning Partnership (#17735)
♦ INIC / see International Foundation for Integrated Care (#13672)
♦ **INI** International Nitrogen Initiative (#14372)
♦ INI – International Nonviolent Initiatives (internationally oriented national body)
♦ InIIS – Institut für Interkulturelle und Internationale Studien (internationally oriented national body)
♦ Inimõiguste Instituut (internationally oriented national body)
♦ **IN** International Association of NLP Institutes (#12050)
♦ IN / see International Needs (#14222)
♦ **IN** International Needs (#14222)
♦ IN – Intuition Network (internationally oriented national body)
♦ INIRC / see International Commission on Non-Ionizing Radiation Protection (#12707)
♦ **INIRE** International Network for Interreligious Research and Education (#14290)
♦ **INIS** International Nuclear Information System (#14378)
♦ INISTE – International Network for Information in Science and Technology Education (inactive)
♦ INIST – International Institute for Sustainable Transportation (internationally oriented national body)
♦ Initiatief Duurzame Handel / see The Sustainable Trade Initiative (#20070)
♦ Initiative 360 (internationally oriented national body)
♦ Initiative Action for Development in the Sahel (internationally oriented national body)
♦ Initiative action pour le développement au Sahel (internationally oriented national body)
♦ Initiative pour une Afrique solidaire (internationally oriented national body)
♦ Initiative pour les Amériques / see Enterprise for the Americas Initiative and Tropical Forest Conservation Act
♦ Initiative du bassin du Nil (#17140)
♦ Initiative Communautaire Changer la Vie/NAZEMSE (internationally oriented national body)

♦ Initiative for a Competitive Online Marketplace (ICOMP) 11209

Chairman address not obtained.
URL: http://www.i-comp.org/

History Registered in accordance with UK law. **Aims** As an industry initiative for organizations and businesses involved in Internet commerce, work towards a transparent and competitive Internet that is responsive to *consumer* interests and law-abiding. **Structure** Council of Members determines the general programme. Council Chair; Secretariat. **Events** *Meeting on online Search* Brussels (Belgium) 2011.

Members Signatories; Council Members; Trustees. Companies, trade associations, consumer organizations and individuals involved in Internet commerce, including online publishers; advertisers; Internet service and network providers; agencies active in online advertising. Members (over 70) in 18 countries:
Australia, Austria, Belgium, Brazil, Czechia, France, Germany, Greece, India, Ireland, Israel, Italy, Lithuania, Poland, Portugal, Spain, UK, USA.
Included in the above, 1 organization listed in this Yearbook:
Coordination of European Picture Agencies, Press Stock Heritage (CEPIC, #04825). [2018/XJ0831/y/**F**]

♦ Initiative pour la démocratie globale (internationally oriented national body)
♦ Initiative for the Development of Africa (internationally oriented national body)

♦ Initiative développement (internationally oriented national body)
♦ Initiative pour les Droits et Ressources (#18947)
♦ Initiative: Eau (internationally oriented national body)
♦ Initiative for Equality (internationally oriented national body)
♦ Initiative d'éthique commerciale (internationally oriented national body)
♦ Initiative Féministe Euroméditerranéenne (#05715)
♦ Initiative für Frieden (internationally oriented national body)
♦ Initiative for Global Development (internationally oriented national body)

♦ Initiative on Harmonisation within Atmospheric Dispersion Modelling for Regulatory Purposes (HARMO) 11210

Contact address not obtained. E-mail: harmo@isac.cnr.it.
URL: http://www.harmo.org/
History 1991. **Aims** Increase cooperation and standardization of atmospheric dispersion models for regulatory purposes. **Structure** Steering Committee. **Activities** Events/meetings. **Events** *Conference on Harmonization within Atmospheric Dispersion Modelling for Regulatory Purposes* Bruges (Belgium) 2019. [2020/AA0085/**F**]

♦ Initiative hexagonale / see Central European Initiative (#03708)
♦ initiative for integrated virtual product creation / see ProSTEP iViP Association
♦ Initiative internationale pour les récifs coralliens (#12965)
♦ Initiative internationale pour la transparence de l'aide (#11604)
♦ Initiative pour les micronutrients – Iniciativa para los Micronutrientes / see Nutrition International (#17627)
♦ Initiative pour les micronutriments / see Nutrition International (#17627)

♦ Initiative de mobilisation panafricaine de controle de tabac (IMPACT) 11211

Contact BP 400, Yaoundé, Cameroon. T. +2379566554. Fax +2372235614. E-mail: impactafrica55@gmail.com.
SG address not obtained.
URL: http://blogsofbainbridge.typepad.com/impact/
History 2004, as *Coalition panafricaine d'études et d'actions de contrôle de tabac (CPEACT)*. [2008/XM2782/**F**]

♦ Initiative mondiale pour l'asthme (#10422)
♦ Initiative mondiale pour l'horticulture (#10412)
♦ Initiative mondiale pour la justice, la vérité et la réconciliation (unconfirmed)
♦ Initiative multilatérale sur le paludisme (#16886)
♦ Initiative des Nations Unies pour l'éducation des filles (#20566)
♦ Initiative pour un Pacte Climat européen (unconfirmed)
♦ Initiative for Peace (internationally oriented national body)
♦ Initiative for Peace and Cooperation in the Middle East / see Search for Common Ground in the Middle East
♦ Initiative for Peace Studies in the University of London (internationally oriented national body)
♦ Initiative pentagonale / see Central European Initiative (#03708)
♦ Initiative for Policy Dialogue (internationally oriented national body)
♦ **Initiative PRI** Principes pour l'investissement responsable (#18499)
♦ Initiative quadrilatérale / see Central European Initiative (#03708)
♦ Initiative for Quiet diplomacy (internationally oriented national body)
♦ Initiative and Referendum Institute Europe (internationally oriented national body)
♦ Initiative Régionale pour la Lutte contre le Tabac en Afrique (#00524)

♦ Initiative for Responsible Mining Assurance (IRMA) 11212

Contact PO Box 289, Port Townsend WA 98368, USA. E-mail: info@responsiblemining.net.
URL: http://www.responsiblemining.net/
History 2006, Vancouver, BC (Canada). Former names and other names: *Responsible Mining Assurance Initiative (RMAI)* – former. **Aims** Create market incentives for improvement and drive value for best practices through a mine-site focused multi-stakeholder standard for industrial-scale mining. **Structure** Board. **Languages** English. **Staff** 4.00 FTE, paid. **Finance** Sources: members' dues. Other sources: supply chain fees; philanthropic contributions. Annual budget: 700,000 USD. **Activities** Standards/guidelines; certification/accreditation; research and development; projects/programmes; monitoring/evaluation; events/meetings. **Publications** *Standard for Responsible Mining* (2018).
Members Mining companies; companies that purchase mined materials; civil society organizations; labour unions; financial institutions; communities impacted by mining. Members include the following 5 organizations listed in this Yearbook:
Earthworks; Fauna & Flora International (FFI, #09277); Human Rights Watch (HRW, #10990); IndustriALL Global Union (IndustriALL, #11177); Pact (#18016).
NGO Relations Member of (1): *ResponsibleSteel (#18921)* (associate). Board member representatives: *Earthworks; Human Rights Watch (HRW, #10990).* Subscriber to: *ISEAL (#16026).* [2019.12.11/XJ2185/y/**F**]

♦ Initiatives Pour un Autre Monde (internationally oriented national body)
♦ Initiatives canadiennes oecuméniques pour la justice (internationally oriented national body)
♦ Initiatives of Change / see Initiatives of Change International – Caux (#11213)

♦ Initiatives of Change International – Caux (IofC) 11213

Main Office 1 rue de Varembé, Case Postale 3, 1211 Geneva 20, Switzerland. T. +41227491620. Fax +41227330267. E-mail: ia-secretariat@iofc.org.
URL: http://www.iofc.org/
History 1921, London (UK), by Frank N D Buchman, with the title *Oxford Group*. Became known as *Moral Re-Armament (MRA) – Réarmement moral – Rearme Moral – Moralische Aufrüstung* on 4 Jun 1938. Name changed to *Initiatives of Change* in 2001 and to current title in Apr 2002. Registered in accordance with Swiss Civil Code. **Aims** Inspire, equip and connect people to address world needs, starting with themselves. **Structure** International Council; Principal regional offices (4); Regional offices (11); Administrative Committees for international programmes (6); Conference Centres (3); Secretariat located in Geneva (Switzerland). **Languages** English, French, German. **Finance** Donations; grants. **Activities** Networking/liaising; events/meetings; projects/programmes. **Events** *Caux Forum* Caux (Switzerland) 2019, *Caux Forum* Caux (Switzerland) 2018, *Asia Pacific Youth Conference* Pahang (Malaysia) 2018, *International Forum* Tokyo (Japan) 2018, *Caux Forum* Caux (Switzerland) 2017. **Publications** *Network Focus* (4 a year) – newsletter. Videos and literature in support of programmes.
Members National societies in 23 countries:
Australia, Brazil, Canada, Denmark, Finland, France, Germany, Ghana, India, Japan, Kenya, Malaysia, Netherlands, New Zealand, Nigeria, Norway, South Africa, Sweden, Switzerland, Tanzania UR, Uganda, UK, USA.
Consultative Status Consultative status granted from: *ECOSOC (#05331)* (Special); *Council of Europe (CE, #04881)* (Consultative Status). **IGO Relations** Accredited to the Conference of the Parties of: *Secretariat of the United Nations Convention to Combat Desertification (Secretariat of the UNCCD, #19208).* Associated with Department of Global Communications of the United Nations. **NGO Relations** Founding member of: *NGO Forum on Environment (FOE, #17125).* Member of: *Conference of Non-Governmental Organizations in Consultative Relationship with the United Nations (CONGO, #04635); International Network for a Culture of Nonviolence and Peace (#14247); Network for Religious and Traditional Peacemakers (#17054).* [2020/XF3455/**F**]

♦ Initiative for Science in Europe (ISE) 11214

Exec Coordinator 1 quai Lezay-Marnesia, 67000 Strasbourg, France. E-mail: contact@initiative-se.eu.
URL: https://initiative-se.eu/
History Nov 2003, Dublin (Ireland). EU Transparency Register: 263249337259-15. **Aims** Promote mechanisms to support basic science at a European level; involve scientists in the design and implementation of European science policies; advocate strong independent scientific advice in European policy making. **Structure** Group, comprising Chair, Secretary and members. **Publications** *ISE Newsletter*.
Members Organziations (18):
Continental European Division of the International Association for Dental Research (CED-IADR, #04780); EIROforum (#05401); European Acoustics Association (EAA, #05824); European Aeronautics Science Network (EASN, #05835); European Association of Social Anthropologists (EASA, #06209); European Association of Social Psychology (EASP, #06210); European Biophysical Societies' Association (EBSA, #06341); European Calcified Tissue Society (ECTS, #06429); European Conference for Aero-Space Sciences (EUCASS, #06728); European Council of Doctoral Candidates and Junior Researchers (EURODOC, #06815); European Educational Research Association (EERA, #06967); European Molecular Biology Organization (EMBO, #07816); European Physical Society (EPS, #08207); European Plant Science Organization (EPSO, #08211); Informatics Europe (#11194); Marie Curie Alumni Association (MCAA, #16576); Society for Experimental Biology (SEB); Young Academy of Europe (YAE, #21979).
IGO Relations Instrumental in setting up: *European Research Council (ERC, #08364).* [2020/XM0990/y/**E**]

♦ Initiatives for Development and Eco Support (internationally oriented national body)
♦ Initiatives des Femmes Africaines de la Nonviolence Active pour le changement social (#00502)
♦ Initiatives pour la formation européenne et les relations avec les pays de l'Europe centrale et orientale (internationally oriented national body)
♦ Initiatives for International Dialogue (internationally oriented national body)
♦ Initiatives, Researches, Experiences for a New Europe (internationally oriented national body)
♦ Initiative pour la Transparence dans les Industries Extractives (#09229)

♦ Initiative Transport Europe (ITE) 11215

ITE European Transport Initiative – ITE Europäische Verkehrsinitiative – ITE Iniziativa Europea delle Trasporti
Secretariat c/o Alpen-Initiative, Herrengasse 2, Postfach 28, 6460 Altdorf UR, Switzerland. T. +41418709781. Fax +41418709788.
URL: http://www.ite-euro.com/
History Apr 1995, France. Founded Apr 1995, Mouhans-Sartoux (France). **Aims** Reduce harmful effects of freight transport; encourage transport policies in Europe which respect human beings and the environment. **Structure** General Assembly and Conference (annual); Board; International Secretariat. **Languages** English, French, German, Italian, Slovene. **Events** *Annual General Assembly and Conference* Pollegio (Switzerland) 2012, *General Assembly and Conference* Ticino (Switzerland) 2012, *Annual General Assembly and Conference / General Assembly and Conference* Steinach am Brenner (Austria) 2011, *Annual General Assembly and Conference / General Assembly and Conference* Cuneo (Italy) 2010, *General Assembly and Conference* Flüelen (Switzerland) 2009. **Publications** *ITEnews*.
Members Full in 8 countries:
Austria, France, Germany, Hungary, Italy, Liechtenstein, Slovenia, Switzerland.
NGO Relations Partner of: *1% for the Planet.* Links with a large number of organizations, including: *CIPRA International (#03930).* [2018.09.07/XG5121/**F**]

♦ Initiative Welt-Zukunftsrat / see World Future Council Foundation (#21533)
♦ Initiative Wohnungswirtschaft Osteuropa (internationally oriented national body)
♦ Initiative Wohnungswirtschaft Osteuropa zur Förderung marktwirtschaftlichers Strukturen in der Bau- und Wohnungswirtschaft in Osteuropa / see Initiative Wohnungswirtschaft Osteuropa
♦ **INIT** Inter Islamic Network on Information Technology (#11508)
♦ **INIVE** International Network for Information on Ventilation and Energy Performance (#14288)
♦ Iniziativa da las Alps (internationally oriented national body)
♦ Iniziative, Ricerche, Esperienze per una Nuova Europa (internationally oriented national body)
♦ **INK** International Network in Kangaroo Mother Care (#14291)
♦ INKOTA Network (internationally oriented national body)
♦ INKOTA Netzwerk (internationally oriented national body)
♦ INLAC – Instituto Latinoamericano de la Calidad (internationally oriented national body)
♦ **INLA** International Nuclear Law Association (#14379)
♦ Inland Navigation Congresses (inactive)

♦ Inland Navigation Europe (INE) 11216

SG Koning Albert II laan 20, Box 22, 1000 Brussels, Belgium. E-mail: info@inlandnavigation.eu.
URL: https://www.inlandnavigation.eu/
History 16 Oct 2000. Former names and other names: *European Federation for Inland Water Transport* – former; *Fédération européenne de promotion des transports par voie navigable* – former. Registration: Banque-Carrefour des Entreprises, Belgium; EU Transparency Register, No/ID: 1811573195-25. **Aims** Promote waterway transport; contribute to long-term strategies for sustainable transportation by moving more goods by water in EU regions and cities with accessible and navigable rivers and canals. **Structure** General Assembly (annual); Board of Directors; Secretariat, located in Brussels (Belgium). **Languages** English. **Staff** 2.00 FTE, paid. **Finance** Sources: members' dues. **Activities** Politics/policy/regulatory; research and development. **Publications** Activity reports; statements; brochures.
Members Executive; Effective; Corresponding. Members in 14 countries:
Austria, Belgium, France, Germany, Hungary, Italy, Luxembourg, Netherlands, Poland, Portugal, Romania, Serbia, Slovakia, Sweden. [2022.05.12/XD8506/**D**]

♦ Inland South America Missionary Union / see South America Mission
♦ Inland Transport Committee / see Committee on Inland Transport (#04262)

♦ Inland Waterways International (IWI) 11217

Pres Transmanche Consultants, Espace Col'Inn, 34 av Félix Viallet, 38000 Grenoble, France. E-mail: dem@transmanche.net.
Registered Address Ingles Manor, Castle Hill Ave, Folkestone, CT20 2RD, UK. E-mail: info@inlandwaterwaysinternational.org.
URL: https://inlandwaterwaysinternational.org/
History 1994. Founded as *International Association for Inland Waterways*. Present title adopted 1996. **Aims** Conserve, use, develop and manage inland waterways worldwide; raise public awareness of benefits of using waterways for commercial carrying and recreational use; promote restoration, where appropriate, of waterways which have become derelict. **Structure** Council, reporting to members at Annual General Meeting. **Languages** English, French. **Staff** Voluntary. **Finance** Members' dues. Fees for services paid by World Canals Conference host. Annual budget: about pounds10,000. **Activities** Advocacy/lobbying/activism; events/meetings. **Events** *World Canals Conference* Leipzig (Germany) 2022, *World Canals Conference* Hagerstown, MD (USA) 2021, *World Canals Conference* Leipzig (Germany) 2020, *World Canals Conference* Wuxi (China) / Yangzhou (China) 2019, *World Canals Conference* Athlone (Ireland) 2018. **Publications** *IWI Newsletter* (2 a year); *World Wide Waterways magazine* (2 a year). Online archives.
Members Commercial organizations, voluntary organizations, navigation authorities and individuals in 23 countries:
Australia, Austria, Belgium, Canada, China, Czechia, Finland, France, Germany, Hungary, India, Ireland, Italy, Netherlands, New Zealand, Nigeria, Poland, Romania, Serbia, Sweden, Switzerland, UK, USA.
IGO Relations Involvement in EU-funded programmes on inland waterways, in which IWI corporate members are partners or associate partners. **NGO Relations** Member of: *World Historic and Cultural Canal Cities Cooperation Organization (WCCO, #21570).* [2022/XF4849/**F**]

♦ INLAP – Institute for Law and Peace, London (internationally oriented national body)

♦ Inline Certification Program International (ICP International) 11218

Exec Dir c/o NISS, 27931 Gilchrist Dr, Cleveland OH 44132, USA. E-mail: info@inlinecertificationprogram.org.
URL: https://www.inlinecertificationprogram.org/
History 1991. Founded following the certification programmes of *International Inline Skating Association (IISA, inactive).* **Aims** Promote ICP as the standard for inline *skating instructors.* **Members** Membership countries not specified. [2023/XJ8151/**E**]

♦ INL – International Iberian Nanotechnology Laboratory (internationally oriented national body)
♦ **INLPTA** International Neuro-Linguistic Programming Trainer's Association (#14352)
♦ **INLW** International Network of Liberal Women (#14294)

- ♦ INMA / see International News Media Association (#14363)
- ♦ **INMA** International News Media Association (#14363)
- ♦ Inmarsat / see International Mobile Satellite Organization (#14174)
- ♦ Inmarsat Mobile / see International Mobile Satellite Organization (#14174)
- ♦ **INMD** International Network on Migration and Development (#14296)
- ♦ INMED / see INMED Partnerships for Children
- ♦ INMED Partnerships for Children (internationally oriented national body)
- ♦ **INMP** International Network of Museums for Peace (#14297)
- ♦ INNA – International Newsreel and News Film Association (no recent information)
- ♦ **INNCO** International Network of Nicotine Consumer Organisations (#14298)

♦ Inner Ear Biology (IEB) 11219

Contact Univ of Tübingen, Dept of Otolaryngology, Section of Physiological Acoustics and Communication, Elfriede-Aulhorn-Str 5, 72076 Tübingen, Germany. T. +4970712988191. Fax +497071294174.
URL: http://www.innerearbiology.eu/

Aims Provide the opportunity for an open exchange of ideas. **Finance** Registration fees. **Events** *Annual Inner Ear Biology Workshop* Padua (Italy) 2019, *Annual Inner Ear Biology Workshop* Berlin (Germany) 2018, *Annual Inner Ear Biology Workshop* Hannover (Germany) 2017, *Annual Inner Ear Biology Workshop* Montpellier (France) 2016, *Annual Inner Ear Biology Workshop* Rome (Italy) 2015. [2018/XJ6962/c/**E**]

♦ Inner Peace Movement (IPM) 11220

Mouvement de la paix intérieure

Contact PO Box 681757, San Antonio TX 78268, USA. T. +12109808490. E-mail: ipmtx@copper.net.
URL: http://www.innerpeacemovement.org/

History 1964, by 7 individuals, including Dr Francisco Coll. **Aims** Provide personal *leadership* training and better understanding of innate abilities of *clairvoyance, intuition* and *perception.* **Structure** International Board of Directors; Autonomous Groups; Network of Leaders. **Activities** Events/meetings; training/education. **Publications** *EXPRESSION* – magazine.
Members Individuals (over 500,000) in 40 countries and territories, including the following 16 countries and territories:
Australia, Canada, Dominican Rep, France, Germany, Haiti, Ireland, Italy, Japan, Korea Rep, Mexico, New Zealand, Philippines, Puerto Rico, UK, USA.
Members also in Africa. Membership countries not specified. [2019.02.13/XF5195/**F**]

- ♦ Inner Trip Reiyukai International (internationally oriented national body)
- ♦ IN Network / see International Needs (#14222)
- ♦ INNGE – International Network of Next-Generation Ecologists (unconfirmed)
- ♦ **INN** Inter-Islamic Network of Nanotechnology (#11509)
- ♦ Innocent Foundation (internationally oriented national body)
- ♦ INNOTECH / see SEAMEO Regional Center for Educational Innovation and Technology (#19168)
- ♦ Innovaciones y Redes para el Desarrollo (#05057)
- ♦ Innovate Plantain – Banana Research Network for West and Central Africa (unconfirmed)
- ♦ Innovatie en Praktijk Centrum Groene Ruimte, Arnhem (internationally oriented national body)
- ♦ Innovation for Cool Earth Forum (meeting series)
- ♦ Innovation for Development and South-South cooperation (unconfirmed)
- ♦ Innovations, environnement, développement Afrique (internationally oriented national body)
- ♦ Innovations for Poverty Action (internationally oriented national body)
- ♦ Innovations et réseaux pour le développement (#05057)

♦ Innovative Medicines Initiative (IMI) 11221

Exec Dir IMI JU, TO 56, 1049 Brussels, Belgium. T. +3222218181. E-mail: infodesk@imi.europa.eu.
Street address Av de la Toison d'Or 56-60, 1060 Brussels, Belgium.
URL: http://imi.europa.eu/

History 2008. Launched as a partnership between *European Union (EU, #08967)* – represented by *European Commission (EC, #06633)* and European pharmaceutical industry – represented by *European Federation of Pharmaceutical Industries and Associations (EFPIA, #07191).* Second phase 'IMI2', launched Jul 2014. **Aims** Improve health by speeding up development of, and *patient* access to, innovative medicines, particularly in areas where there is an unmet medical or social need. **Structure** Governing Board; Scientific Committee; States Representatives Group; Strategic Governing Groups; Executive Director; Stakeholder Forum. **Staff** 56.00 FTE, paid. **Finance** Sources: *European Commission (EC, #06633)* – FP7 and Horizon 2020; *European Federation of Pharmaceutical Industries and Associations (EFPIA, #07191)* companies; contributions from associated partners. **Activities** Research and development; projects/programmes. **Events** *Forum* Brussels (Belgium) 2019, *Forum* Brussels (Belgium) 2018. **Publications** *IMI Newsletter.* Brochures. **NGO Relations** Member of (1): *EU Agencies Network (EUAN, #05564).* [2018.09.19/XM5100/**F**]

♦ Innovative Therapies for Children with Cancer Consortium (ITCC) . . 11222

Pres Inst Gustave Roussy, 114 rue Edouard Vaillant, 94805 Villejuif, France. T. +33142116741 – +33142116033. Fax +33142114963. E-mail: itcc.network@gmail.com.
URL: http://www.itcc-consortium.org/

History 25 Mar 2003. Registration: RNA, No/ID: W943002935, Start date: 24 Sep 2011, France; EU Transparency Register, No/ID: 193382825960-65, Start date: 9 Mar 2017. **Aims** Develop novel therapies for the treatment of paediatric and adolescent cancers in cooperation with regulatory bodies, pharmaceutical companies, parents and patients. **Structure** Executive Committee; Committees (4); Office. **Languages** English. **Staff** 3.00 FTE, paid. **Events** *ACCELERATE Paediatric Oncology Conference* Brussels (Belgium) 2021, *ACCELERATE Paediatric Oncology Conference* Brussels (Belgium) 2020, *ACCELERATE Paediatric Oncology Conference* Brussels (Belgium) 2019, *ACCELERATE Paediatric Oncology Conference* Brussels (Belgium) 2018, *ACCELERATE Paediatric Oncology Conference* Brussels (Belgium) 2017. **Publications** Studies; reports.
Members European Paediatric Oncology Departments (55) in 13 countries:
Austria, Belgium, Denmark, Finland, France, Germany, Ireland, Israel, Italy, Netherlands, Spain, Switzerland, UK.
NGO Relations Member of (1): *European Network of Paediatric Research at the European Medicines Agency (Enpr-EMA, #07963).* Instrumental in setting up (1): *ACCELERATE (#00046).* [2019.10.02/XJ4780/**D**]

♦ Innovative Vector Control Consortium (IVCC) 11223

COO address not obtained. T. +441517053268.
URL: http://www.ivcc.com/

History Initially set up as a research consortium of 5 public health institutions in UK, USA and South Africa with a grant from *Bill and Melinda Gates Foundation (BMGF).* Since 2008, UK Registered Charity. **Aims** Improve public health by increasing effectiveness and efficiency of the control of *insects* which transmit *disease.* **Structure** Board of Trustees. Management Committee of 7. External Scientific Advisory Committees (ESACs). **NGO Relations** Member of: *Global Health Technologies Coalition (GHTC).* Original founding members include: *Liverpool School of Tropical Medicine (LSTM); London School of Hygiene and Tropical Medicine (LSHTM).* [2013/XJ7316/**E**]

♦ InnovaWood (IW) 11224

SG European Forestry House, Rue du Luxembourg 66, 1000 Brussels, Belgium. T. +3222392300. Fax +3222192191. E-mail: office@innovawood.com.
URL: http://www.innovawood.com/

History Set up by merger of *European Association of Furniture Technology Institutes (EURIFI, inactive), European Network for the Forest and Wood Sector Industries (EUROFORTECH, inactive), European Network of Timber Technical Centres and Research Institutes (Eurowood, inactive)* and Euroligna. **Aims** Provide a forum to contribute more effectively to the *forest, wood* based and *furniture* industries sector; increase collaboration between members, industrial stakeholders, technology platforms and European institutions; facilitate and support involvement of members in research and innovation support programmes on international and transnational level in Europe. **Structure** General Assembly (annual). Executive Board; Managing Board. Thematic Groups (4); Permanent secretariat in Brussels (Belgium). **Languages** English. **Staff** 2.00 FTE, paid. **Finance** Members' dues. Projects. **Events** *Annual General Assembly* Hamburg (Germany) 2019, *Annual General Assembly* Ljubljana (Slovenia) 2018, *Annual General Assembly* Tuusula (Finland) 2017, *Annual General Assembly* Montpellier (France) 2016, *Annual General Assembly* Zagreb (Croatia) 2015.
Members Institutes and organizations (over 50) in 26 countries:
Australia, Austria, Belgium, Bulgaria, Croatia, Czechia, Denmark, Finland, France, Germany, Hungary, Ireland, Italy, Latvia, Luxembourg, Netherlands, North Macedonia, Norway, Poland, Portugal, Slovakia, Slovenia, Spain, Sweden, Switzerland, UK.
NGO Relations Member of (2): *Woodrise Alliance (#21045); Wood Sector Alliance for the New European Bauhaus (Wood4Bauhaus, #21046)* (Founding). [2020/XF6787/**F**]

- ♦ **INNOVEMOS** Latin American and Caribbean Education Innovation Network (#16275)
- ♦ INNS – International Neural Network Society (internationally oriented national body)
- ♦ INOC / see Inter-Islamic Science and Technology Network on Oceanography (#11514)
- ♦ **INOC** International Non-Olympic Committee (#14374)
- ♦ **INoEA** International Network of Esophageal Atresia (#14265)
- ♦ **INOE** Internacia Naturista Organizo Esperantista (#14220)
- ♦ **INOE** International Naturist Organization for Esperanto (#14220)

♦ INOGATE Programme 11225

Technical Secretariat 26-28 Kudriavskaya Street, Kiev, 04053, Ukraine. T. +380442302754. Fax +380442302753. E-mail: secretariat.kiev@inogate.org – k.mirianashvili@inogate.org.
URL: http://www.inogate.org/

History 1996, within the framework of *Tacis Programme (inactive).* A programme of *European Commission (EC, #06633).* Also known as *INOGATE Technical Assistance Programme.* INOGATE derives from 'Interstate Oil and Gas Transport to Europe'. **Aims** Address priority projects for *oil* and *gas transport* from the *Caspian Sea* region to Central and *Eastern Europe.* **Activities** Complementary feasibility studies; priority emergency investment in oil and gas infrastructure; institutional support and strengthening of regional cooperation. **IGO Relations** Supports: *Energy Community (#05468).* **NGO Relations** Supports: *Energy Regulators Regional Association (ERRA, #05476).* [2016/XK1784/**E***]

- ♦ INOGATE Technical Assistance Programme / see INOGATE Programme (#11225)
- ♦ **INOGE** Inter-Islamic Network on Genetic Engineering and Biotechnology (#11507)
- ♦ **INoPSU** International Network of Paediatric Surveillance Units (#14300)

♦ Inorganic Feed Phosphates (IFP) 11226

Contact c/o CEFIC, Rue Belliard 40, 1040 Brussels, Belgium.
URL: http://www.feedphosphates.org/

History 1972, as a sector group of *Conseil européen de l'industrie chimique (CEFIC, #04687),* with the title *Inorganic Feed Phosphates International Technical Bureau.* **Aims** Develop a coordinated approach to represent and defend the interests of inorganic feed phosphate producers; promote the use, quality, bioavailability of inorganic feed phosphates; follow up trade, scientific research, legislation, technical and environmental issues. **Structure** General Assembly; Chairman; General Secretary.
Members Companies in 8 countries:
Belgium, Bulgaria, Finland, France, Lithuania, Netherlands, Serbia, Spain. [2019.06.18/XE4048/**E**]

- ♦ Inorganic Feed Phosphates International Technical Bureau / see Inorganic Feed Phosphates (#11226)
- ♦ **INORMS** International Network of Research Management Societies (#14317)
- ♦ INOS – International Neuro Ophthalmology Society (inactive)
- ♦ INOU – International Non-Olympic University (internationally oriented national body)

♦ INPACT International 11227

Exec Dir Tavistock House South, Tavistock Square, London, WC1H 9LG, UK. T. +442073874741. Fax +442076874715.
URL: https://inpactglobal.org/

History 1989, London (UK). **Aims** Build a world-class *accounting* alliance. **Structure** Board of Directors; Executive Office; INPACT Americas. **Languages** Bulgarian, English, Spanish. **Staff** 4.00 FTE, paid. **Finance** Sources: members' dues. **Activities** Events/meetings; guidance/assistance/consulting; networking/liaising; training/education. **Events** *EMEA-CSA-IAP Conference* Amsterdam (Netherlands) 2022, *Stronger Better Together 2.0* London (UK) 2021, *EMEA-CSA-IAP Conference* London (UK) 2020, *World Conference* Prague (Czechia) 2018, *Future proofing your firm* Athens (Greece) 2017. **Publications** *E-Tax Bulletin* (2 a year); *Global Executive Update (GEU)* (3-4 a year).
Members Independent accounting firms in 67 countries and territories:
Argentina, Australia, Austria, Bangladesh, Belgium, Brazil, Bulgaria, Canada, Chile, China, Cyprus, Denmark, Dominican Rep, Ecuador, Finland, France, Germany, Greece, Guatemala, Honduras, Hong Kong, Hungary, India, Indonesia, Ireland, Italy, Japan, Jordan, Kenya, Korea Rep, Kuwait, Lesotho, Luxembourg, Malaysia, Malta, Mauritania, Mauritius, Morocco, Netherlands, New Zealand, Nigeria, Norway, Pakistan, Panama, Paraguay, Peru, Philippines, Poland, Portugal, Romania, Saudi Arabia, Senegal, Singapore, South Africa, Spain, Sweden, Switzerland, Taiwan, Tunisia, Türkiye, UK, Ukraine, United Arab Emirates, Uruguay, USA, Vietnam, Yemen.
NGO Relations Member of (1): *European Group of International Accounting Networks and Associations (EGIAN, #07426).* [2022.04.21/XJ9125/**C**]

- ♦ **INPA** International Neurological Physical Therapy Association (#14353)
- ♦ **INPALMS** Indo-Pacific Association of Law, Medicine and Science (#11169)
- ♦ INPARR / see International Pension Research Association (#14556)
- ♦ INPCM / see International College of Person-Centered Medicine (#12647)
- ♦ INPCS – International Neuropalliative Care Society (internationally oriented national body)
- ♦ **INPDA** International Niemann-Pick Disease Alliance (#14371)
- ♦ INPDW – International Network of Psychology and the Developing World (see: #15807)
- ♦ **INPEA** International Network for the Prevention of Elder Abuse (#14307)
- ♦ **INPE** International Network of Philosophers of Education (#14302)
- ♦ INPFC – International North Pacific Fisheries Commission (inactive)
- ♦ **INPIQS** International Network for Planning and Improving Quality and Safety in Health Systems in Africa (#14304)
- ♦ INPM – International Network on Personal Meaning (internationally oriented national body)
- ♦ **INPP** International Network for Philosophy and Psychiatry (#14303)
- ♦ **INPROL** International Network to Promote the Rule of Law (#14310)
- ♦ **INPRRF** International Nobel Peace Prize Recommendation Forum (#14373)
- ♦ **INPS** International Neuropeptide Society (#14355)
- ♦ **INPSSE** Intercontinental Network for the Promotion of the Social Solidarity Economy (#11463)
- ♦ **INPUD** International Network of People who Use Drugs (#14301)
- ♦ **INPUT** International Public Television (#14674)
- ♦ **INQAAHE** International Network of Quality Assurance Agencies in Higher Education (#14312)
- ♦ **INQUA** International Union for Quaternary Research (#15811)
- ♦ **INRA** International Nuclear Regulators Association (#14380)
- ♦ INRATIP – International Network of Religious Against Trafficking in Persons (unconfirmed)
- ♦ INRA / see UNU Institute for Natural Resources in Africa (#20718)
- ♦ **INRC** International Narcotics Research Conference (#14213)
- ♦ **INRES** Inter-Islamic Network on Renewable Energy Sources (#11510)
- ♦ **INREV** European Association for Investors in Non-listed Real Estate Vehicles (#06093)
- ♦ **INRICH** International Network for Research on Inequalities in Child Health (#14316)
- ♦ **INRIC** International Network of Resource Information Centers (#14320)
- ♦ INRO – International Natural Rubber Organization (inactive)
- ♦ **INRO** International Naval Research Organization (#14221)
- ♦ INRO – International Neurotrauma Research Organization (inactive)
- ♦ **INRouTe** International Network on Regional Economics, Mobility and Tourism (#14314)
- ♦ **INRUD** International Network for Rational Use of Drugs (#14313)
- ♦ INRULED – UNESCO International Research and Training Centre for Rural Education (internationally oriented national body)
- ♦ INSA / see Global Health Action
- ♦ INSAF – International Network for Safety Assurance of Fuel Cycle Industries (unconfirmed)
- ♦ INSAG / see International Nuclear Safety Group (#14381)
- ♦ **INSAG** International Nuclear Safety Group (#14381)
- ♦ **INSAH** Institut du Sahel (#11357)

- ♦ **INSA** International Network for School Attendance (#14322)
- ♦ INSA – International Nuclear Non-proliferation and Security Academy (internationally oriented national body)
- ♦ INSA – International Shipowners' Association (inactive)
- ♦ **INSAM** International Society for Agricultural Meteorology (#14912)
- ♦ Insan Dogasini Arastirma Dernegi (internationally oriented national body)
- ♦ Insanligi Birlestiren Bilgiyi Yayma Vakfi (internationally oriented national body)
- ♦ **INSARAG** International Search and Rescue Advisory Group (#14816)
- ♦ **INSCA** International Natural Sausage Casing Association (#14216)
- ♦ **INSC** International Nuclear Societies Council (#14382)

♦ INSEAD 11228

Contact INSEAD Europe Campus, Bd de Constance, 77305 Fontainebleau CEDEX, France. T. +33160724000. Fax +33160745500.
INSEAD Asia Campus 1 Ayer Rajah Avenue, Singapore 138676, Singapore. T. +6567995388. Fax +6567995399.
INSEAD Abu Dhabi Campus Muroor Road, Street No 4, PO Box 48049, Abu Dhabi, United Arab Emirates. T. +97126515200. Fax +97124439461.
URL: http://www.insead.edu/

History 1957, Fontainebleau (France), on the initiative of General Georges Doriot and the 'Chambre de commerce et d'industrie de Paris'. Full title: *European Institute of Business Administration – Institut européen d'administration des affaires – Europäisches Institut für Unternehmensführung.* **Aims** Promote a non-dogmatic learning environment that brings together people, cultures and ideas from around the world to: develop responsible, thoughtful *business* leaders and *entrepreneurs* whose actions create value for their organizations and their communities; create and disseminate management knowledge that expands the frontiers of academic thought and informs business practice. **Structure** Board; INSEAD Foundation Board; International Council; Advisory Committee for Management Education; *INSEAD Alumni Association (IAA, #11229)*; Committee of Deans; Committee of External Relations; Executive Committee; Committee of Area Coordinators; Asia Campus; Europe Campus. **Languages** English. **Staff** Dean; permanent faculty – 150; visiting faculty – 80; administrative staff – 616. **Finance** Tuition; revenue from programmes; gifts and endowments. **Activities** Training/education; knowledge management/information dissemination; research and development. **Events** *Asian Private Equity and Venture Capital Conference* Singapore (Singapore) 2020, *Changemakers Summit* Singapore (Singapore) 2020, *Seminar on Limited Partner Strategies for a Post-COVID Clinate* Singapore (Singapore) 2020, *Seminar on Limited Partner Strategies for a Post-COVID Clinate* Singapore (Singapore) 2020, *Seminar on Private Equity* Singapore (Singapore) 2020. **Publications** Annual Report in English. Programme brochures; books; case studies; working papers; articles. **Information Services** *INSEAD Knowledge* – online summaries, videos of recent INSEAD research organized into themes; *INSEAD Online* – online courses, simulations and communication tools.
Members National councils in 21 countries:
Australia, Austria, Belgium, Brazil, Canada, Denmark, Finland, France, Germany, Italy, Japan, Netherlands, Norway, Portugal, Singapore, South Africa, Spain, Sweden, Switzerland, UK, USA.
NGO Relations Member of: *AACSB International – Association to Advance Collegiate Schools of Business; EFMD – The Management Development Network (#05387); Global Business School Network (GBSN, #10260); Global Network for Advanced Management (GNAM); Globally Responsible Leadership Initiative (GRLI, #10462); Graduate Management Admission Council (GMAC, #10687); International Consortium for Executive Development Research (ICEDR, #12913); Principles for Responsible Management Education (PRME, #18500).* Associate member of: *Asian Venture Philanthropy Network (AVPN, #01778).* Instrumental in setting up: *Asia Pacific Decision Sciences Institute (APDSI).* [2020/XF0090/j/F]

♦ INSEAD Alumni Association (IAA) 11229

Pres bd de Constance, 77305 Fontainebleau CEDEX, France. T. +33160724000.
URL: http://www.insead.edu/alumni/

History 1961, by the alumni of *INSEAD (#11228).* Also referred to as: *INSEAD Association of Former Students; INSEAD International Alumni Association.* Registered in accordance with French law. **Aims** Bring together the alumni of INSEAD. **Structure** Board. **Events** *Workshop* Singapore (Singapore) 2008, *Presidents' Meeting* Belgium 2005, *Presidents Meeting* France 2004, *Presidents meeting / Presidents' Meeting* Zurich (Switzerland) 2003, *Presidents meeting / Presidents' Meeting* Singapore (Singapore) 2002. **Publications** *INSEAD Address Book* – confidential. Alumni career service, alumni memberships. **Information Services** *INSEAD Alumni Online (IAO).* **Members** National associations and individuals in 176 countries. Membership countries not specified. [2020/XE4788/E]

- ♦ INSEAD Association of Former Students / see INSEAD Alumni Association (#11229)
- ♦ INSEAD International Alumni Association / see INSEAD Alumni Association (#11229)
- ♦ **INSEA** International Society for Education through Art (#15074)
- ♦ **INSeCT** International Network of Societies for Catholic Theology (#14328)
- ♦ INSEE – International Society of Extension Education (internationally oriented national body)
- ♦ INSEIT – International Society for Ethics and Information Technology (internationally oriented national body)
- ♦ Insel-Kommission (#16061)
- ♦ **INSG** International Nickel Study Group (#14370)
- ♦ **INSHED** International Network for Standardization of Higher Education Degrees (#14329)
- ♦ **IN-SHP** International Network on Small Hydro Power (#14324)
- ♦ **INSHPO** International Network of Safety and Health Practitioner Organisations (#14321)
- ♦ INSHS – International Network of Sport and Health Science (unconfirmed)

♦ Inside Industry Association (Inside) 11230

SG High Tech Campus 69-3, 5656 AG Eindhoven, Netherlands. T. +31880036188. E-mail: info@inside-association.eu.
URL: https://www.inside-association.eu/

History Jun 2004. Founded as a legal body, 2007. ARTEMIS stands for *Advanced Research and Technology for EMbedded Intelligent Systems.* Former names and other names: *ARTEMIS European Technology Platform* – former; *ARTEMIS Industry Association* – former (2007 to 2021). Registration: Handelsregister, No/ID: KVK 17201341, Netherlands; EU Transparency Register, No/ID: 310026619668-24, Start date: 24 Nov 2015. **Aims** Strengthen Europe's position in embedded intelligent systems; attain world-class leadership in this domain to support the European industry. **Structure** General Assembly; Steering Board; Praesidium. **Languages** English. **Finance** Members' dues. **Activities** Events/meetings. **Events** *Electronic Components and Systems Brokerage Event* Brussels (Belgium) 2022, *Electronic Components and Systems Brokerage Event* Eindhoven (Netherlands) 2021, *European Forum for Electronic Components and Systems (EFECS)* Netherlands 2021, *Electronic Components and Systems Brokerage Event* Brussels (Belgium) 2020, *Embedded intelligent systems within Europe* Amsterdam (Netherlands) 2019. **Publications** *ARTEMIS Magazine* (2 a year).
Members Full (over 195) in 20 countries:
Austria, Belgium, Czechia, Denmark, Finland, France, Germany, Hungary, Ireland, Italy, Latvia, Netherlands, Norway, Poland, Portugal, Romania, Russia, Spain, Sweden, UK.
IGO Relations Partner of (1): *Eureka Association (Eureka, #05621).* **NGO Relations** Member of (1): *European Partnership for Key Digital Technologies (KDT, #08158).* Partner of (2): *Association for European NanoElectronics ActivitieS (AENEAS, #02525); European Technology Platform on Smart Systems Integration (EPoSS, #08892).* [2023/XM5607/t/D]

- ♦ **Inside** Inside Industry Association (#11230)
- ♦ INSIDE – Instituto Internacional de Dirección de Empresas (internationally oriented national body)
- ♦ **InSiGHT** International Society for Gastrointestinal Hereditary Tumours (#15136)
- ♦ **INSI** International News Safety Institute (#14364)
- ♦ INS – Institut Nord-Sud (internationally oriented national body)
- ♦ **INS** International Napoleonic Society (#14211)
- ♦ **INS** International Neuroethics Society (#14350)
- ♦ **INS** International Neuromodulation Society (#14354)
- ♦ INS / see International Neuropsychological Society (#14358)
- ♦ **INS** International Neuropsychological Society (#14358)
- ♦ **INSME** International Network for Small and Medium Sized Enterprises (#14325)
- ♦ **INSNA** International Network for Social Network Analysis (#14326)

♦ INSOL Europe 11231

CEO PO Box 7149, Clifton, Nottingham, NG11 6WD, UK. T. +447951022978.
URL: http://www.insol-europe.org/

History 1981. Former names and other names: *European Insolvency Practitioners Association (EIPA)* – former; *Association européenne des praticiens des procédures collectives (AEPPC)* – former. Registration: SIREN, No/ID: 844 433 425 00015, France. **Aims** Contribute to the work of European and international official bodies on insolvency, bankruptcy and business recovery. **Structure** Council; Officers: President, Deputy President, Vice President and Treasurer; Secretariat. **Languages** English. **Staff** 4.00 FTE, paid. **Finance** Sources: members' dues. Annual budget: 250,000 EUR. **Activities** Events/meetings; knowledge management/information dissemination; research and development; training/education. **Events** *Academic Conference* Dublin (Ireland) 2024, *Annual Congress* Sorrento (Italy) 2024, *Annual Congress* Amsterdam (Netherlands) 2023, *INSOL Europe Eastern European Countries' Committee Conference* Vilnius (Lithuania) 2023, *Annual Congress* Dubrovnik (Croatia) 2022. **Publications** *INSOL Newsletter* (12 a year); *EUROFENIX* (4 a year). Technical series of conference papers.
Members Full; Associate. Individuals (about 1,250) in 48 countries and territories:
Argentina, Australia, Austria, Belgium, Bermuda, Bulgaria, Canada, Cayman Is, Channel Is, Croatia, Cyprus, Czechia, Denmark, Estonia, Finland, France, Germany, Gibraltar, Greece, Hungary, Iceland, Ireland, Israel, Italy, Kosovo, Latvia, Liechtenstein, Lithuania, Luxembourg, Malaysia, Moldova, Netherlands, North Macedonia, Norway, Poland, Portugal, Romania, Russia, Serbia, Slovakia, Slovenia, South Africa, Spain, Sweden, Switzerland, UK, Ukraine, USA.
NGO Relations Member of (1): *International Federation of Restructuring, Insolvency and Bankruptcy Professionals (INSOL International, #13530).* [2022.05.17/XD6760/v/D]

- ♦ INSOL International / see International Federation of Restructuring, Insolvency and Bankruptcy Professionals (#13530)
- ♦ **INSOL International** International Federation of Restructuring, Insolvency and Bankruptcy Professionals (#13530)
- ♦ INSONA – International Society of Naturalists (internationally oriented national body)
- ♦ Inspection, Cleaning and Restoration Association / see International Cleaning and Restoration Association
- ♦ Inspectorans Rerum Publicarum Europaeorum Pharmacopopularum Societas (no recent information)
- ♦ INSP / see International Network of Street Papers (#14330)
- ♦ **INSP** International Network of Street Papers (#14330)

♦ Inspire – the European Partnership for Sexual and Reproductive Health and Rights (Inspire) 11232

Address not obtained.
URL: http://www.inspire-partnership.org/

History Set up as an action-oriented alliance without organizational status, following *International Conference on Population and Development (ICPD),* Sep 1994, Cairo (Egypt). First declaration of common goals passed, Oct 1995, Hannover (Germany). Original title: *European Non-Governmental Organizations for Sexual and Reproductive Health and Rights, Population and Development (EuroNGOs) – ONGs européennes pour la santé et les droits de la reproduction, la population et le développement – Europäische NROs für Sexuelle und Reproduktive Gesundheit und Rechte, Bevölkerung und Entwicklung.* Current title adopted 2018. Ceased to exist 31 Dec 2019. **Aims** Act to ensure sexual and reproductive health and rights for all. **Structure** Steering Committee; Rotating Chairmanship. **Staff** 3.00 FTE, paid. **Finance** Sources: different national and international private and public funding; membership contributions. **Activities** Knowledge management/information dissemination; capacity building; events/meetings; advocacy/lobbying/activism; projects/programmes; financial and/or material support. **Events** *Annual Meeting* Ghent (Belgium) 2018, *Annual Meeting* Brussels (Belgium) 2017, *Annual Meeting* Paris (France) 2016, *Annual Meeting* Oslo (Norway) 2015, *Annual Meeting* Madrid (Spain) 2014. **Publications** *Inspire Newsletter.*
Members NGOs (34) in 23 countries:
Armenia, Austria, Belgium, Bulgaria, Denmark, Finland, France, Germany, Hungary, Ireland, Italy, Latvia, Lithuania, Netherlands, Norway, Portugal, Romania, Serbia, Spain, Sweden, Switzerland, Türkiye, UK.
Consultative Status Consultative status granted from: *United Nations Population Fund (UNFPA, #20612).* [2019.03.04/XE3525/y/E]

- ♦ **Inspire** Inspire – the European Partnership for Sexual and Reproductive Health and Rights (#11232)
- ♦ **INSPIRE** Integrated Spatial Potential Initiative for Renewables in Europe (#11370)
- ♦ **INSPIRE** International Spine Research Foundation (#15584)
- ♦ **INSSA** International NGO Safety and Security Association (#14368)
- ♦ Installation européenne de rayonnement synchrotron / see European Synchrotron Radiation Facility (#08868)
- ♦ Instance permanente sur les questions autochtones (#20609)
- ♦ Instâncias Africanas de Regulação e da Comunicação (#00259)
- ♦ Institución contra el Trafico de Mujeres / see Coördinatiecentrum Mensenhandel
- ♦ Institución Magdalena Aulina (religious order)
- ♦ Institución de la Seguridad y la Salud en el Trabajo (internationally oriented national body)
- ♦ Institución Teresiana (religious order)
- ♦ Institut d'action culturelle (internationally oriented national body)
- ♦ Institut des affaires culturelles internationales (#11251)
- ♦ Institut d'affaires internationales, Rome (internationally oriented national body)
- ♦ Institut africain / see Instytut Studiów Regionalnych i Globalnych
- ♦ Institut africain-américain islamique (internationally oriented national body)
- ♦ Institut africain, Bruxelles / see Institut africain, Tervuren
- ♦ Institut africain de développement (#00286)
- ♦ Institut Africain de Développement Economique et de Planification des Nations Unies (#20518)
- ♦ Institut africain pour le développement économique et social / see Center of Research and Action for Peace (#03651)

♦ Institut Africain pour le Développement Economique et Social – Centre Africain de Formation (INADES-Formation) 11233

African Institute for Economic and Social Development – African Training Centre

Gen Sec 08 BP 8, Abidjan 08, Côte d'Ivoire. T. +22522400216. Fax +22522400230. E-mail: ifsiege@inadesfo.net.
URL: http://www.inadesfo.net/

History Founded 26 Jan 1977, Abidjan (Côte d'Ivoire), when became an independent association under the present name. An offshoot of *'African Institute for Economic and Social Development (INADES)',* currently *Center of Research and Action for Peace (CERAP, #03651).* Derives from INADES training department, which had been operating independently since 1972, INADES having been engaged in adult education since its inception in 1962. Recognized, 1979, as an association 'in the public interest' by the Government of Côte d'Ivoire, with which it signed a cooperation agreement in 1982. Also referred to as *International Association of Inades-Formation (IF).* **Aims** Train *rural adults* – men, women, youth – so as to promote their social and economic advancement while emphasizing their knowledge and know-how; work for a society in which equitable relations prevail between men and women and in which men and women *farmers* are organized, have genuine power to promote law and order and influence *local* and national development policy, control and manage natural resources on a continuing basis, master agricultural produce channels and ensure food self-reliance and increase their financial autonomy. **Structure** General Assembly (every 3 years). Governing Council (meeting twice a year) comprises President, Delegate-Administrator, Secretary-Treasurer and 6 members. Head Office in Abidjan (Côte d'Ivoire) comprises Director General, Secretary General and 2 sections each with Director: Administration and Finance; Research-Evaluation-Pedagogy. National Offices either under direct authority of Inades-Formation or linked by agreement through the relevant national association. Includes *African Rural Development Fund (Fondafrica, see: #11233).* **Languages** English, French. **Staff** 267.00 FTE, paid. Staff includes experts in agronomy, social sciences, communication, economics, management, literacy, environment and animal husbandry.

Finance Funding partners (over 30) include the following organizations listed in this Yearbook:
- *Agriculteurs français et développement international (AFDI)*;
- *Associazione di Cooperazione Rurale in Africa e America Latina (ACRA)*;
- *Canadian International Development Agency (CIDA, inactive)*;
- *Catholic Central Agency for Development Aid*;
- *Comité Catholique contre la Faim et pour le Développement-Terre Solidaire (CCFD-Terre Solidaire)*;
- *Catholic Organization for Relief and Development (Cordaid)* (formerly Bilance);
- *Coordination in Development (CODEL, inactive)*;
- *Development and Peace (CCODP)*;
- *Economic Community of West African States (ECOWAS, #05312)*;
- *European Commission (EC, #06633)*;
- *FAO (#09260)*;
- *German Catholic Bishops' Organisation for Development Cooperation (MISEREOR)*;
- *IMPACT (#11136)*;
- *INTERMON OXFAM*;
- *International Development Research Centre (IDRC, #13162)*;
- *International Fund for Agricultural Development (IFAD, #13692)*;
- *Norwegian Church Aid*;
- *Oxfam GB*;
- *UNDP (#20292)*.

Budget (annual): French Fr 2,500 million.
Activities From 1965 onwards, INADES focused on on rural development through *Agri-service – Afrique* correspondence courses and seminars. Current fields of intervention: structuring and management of farm organizations; animation/communication: mobilization of financial resources; agricultural production; environment; project management; context analysis; drawing up plans of action and orientations. Methods of intervention, including correspondence courses and workshops, are based on self-help education and involve: study of training needs; identification of training needs; distance training with field visits; local workshops in trainees' villages; exchange trips. Functions through a decentralized system of training, in which most educational materials are produced by national offices and which benefits 50,000 to 60,000 people annually. Target audience: rural groups of literate or illiterate adults (women, youth, men); leaders of village associations; leaders of NGOs; rural animators; development agents. **Events** *General Assembly* Kenya 2013, *General Assembly* Machakos (Kenya) 2013, *General Assembly* Côte d'Ivoire 2010, *Triennial general assembly* 2001, *Workshop / General Assembly* Côte d'Ivoire 1998. **Publications** *Agri-Congo* (4 a year) in French – Congo; *Essor Paysan* (4 a year) – Côte d'Ivoire; *Terimbere* (4 a year) – in Kirundi – Burundi; *Venegda* (4 a year) – in Moore – Burkina Faso; *Courrier de l'abonné* in French – Chad; *Inter-Info* in French – Kenya; *Kisomo Na Vitendo* in French – also in Kiswahili – Kenya; *La voix du paysan* in French – Chad; *Rural Development Review* in French – Cameroon; *Tumenyane* in French – also in Kirundi – Burundi. Educational materials: booklets; audiovisual aids – in French, English, Amharique, Oromo, Kiswahili, Kinyarwanda, Kirundi, Lingala, Cibula, Moore.
Members National Offices (NOs) in 10 countries:
Burkina Faso, Burundi, Cameroon, Chad, Congo DR, Côte d'Ivoire, Kenya, Rwanda, Tanzania UR, Togo.
Individuals in a further 5 countries:
Belgium, Central African Rep, France, Guinea, Madagascar.
NGO Relations Member of: *Environment Liaison Centre International (ELCI, no recent information)*. Partner of: *Development Innovations and Networks (#05057)*; Agri-Service Ethiopia. [2014/XE3642/j/**E**]

♦ Institut africain de droit international (#00341)

♦ Institut africain du droit international privé (IADIP) 11234

African Institute of Private International Law – Istituto Africano di Diritto Internazionale Privato
Address not obtained.
History 28 Mar 1968, Addis Ababa (Ethiopia). **Aims** Harmonize private law in Africa; conduct research and programming studies with a view to facilitating African countries' economic and social development; realize social and health projects, multifunctional health structures, schools and houses for poor people. **Structure** General Meeting (every 2 years). Council; Executive Committee, including Chairman, General Secretary. Economic Affairs Department. **Languages** English, French, Italian. **Staff** 6.00 FTE, paid. **Finance** Members' dues. Other sources: donations; project financing. **Activities** Studies on problems relating to limits on discretion in commercial contracts between Africa and other parts of the world; courses in African international trade law; compiling documentation on the national and international trade law of the African countries. Instituted the International Award "Trophy for Peace". **Events** *Conference* Parma (Italy) 1993, *Conference* Addis Ababa (Ethiopia) 1987, *Seminar* Lomé (Togo) 1986, *Conference* Lomé (Togo) 1985, *Conference* Venice (Italy) 1982. **Publications** *Africa and Law* – magazine.
Members Founding members; individuals in 4 countries:
Guinea, Jordan, Lebanon, Mali.
IGO Relations Advisory Status with: *ECOSOC (#05331)*. **NGO Relations** Instrumental in setting up: *East-European Association for International Private Law (no recent information)*. [2013.06.01/XF0779/j/**F**]

♦ Institut africain de gestion urbaine (internationally oriented national body)

♦ Institut africain d'informatique (IAI) 11235

African Institute of Informatics – Instituto Africano de Informatica
Dir Gen BP 2263, Libreville, Gabon. T. +241720005. Fax +241720011. E-mail: contact@iaisiege.com.
URL: http://iaisiege.com/
History 29 Jan 1971, Libreville (Gabon), on signature of a Convention, under the aegis of the then Afro-Malagasy Union for Economic Cooperation (UAMCE), subsequently *African and Mauritian Common Organization (OCAM, inactive)*. **Aims** Carry out education and training, post-experience training, and research in the field of *data processing*. **Structure** General Assembly (every 2 years). Administrative Council (meets annually), consisting of government ministers of member states. Council of Advanced Training, consisting of representatives of national data processing centres. Executive Board, consisting of Director General, General Secretary, Study Director, Administrative and Finance Director, Research and Development Director, Management Controller. Council of Professors; Students' Committee. **Languages** French. **Staff** 56.00 FTE, paid. **Finance** Student fees paid by member states. Other sources: Government of France; donations; subventions; legacies; remuneration for services; interest; loans. **Activities** Training for computer programmers, analysts and engineers. Research activities, especially in the fields of information systems, data bases, image processing and parallelism. Seminars. Founder of: *Laboratoire africain de recherche en mathématique et informatique applicatives (LARMIA, no recent information)*. **Events** *Colloque* Libreville (Gabon) 1996.
Members Membership open to all states which accept provisions of the agreement establishing IAI. Governments of 11 countries:
Benin, Burkina Faso, Cameroon, Central African Rep, Chad, Congo Brazzaville, Côte d'Ivoire, Gabon, Niger, Senegal, Togo.
NGO Relations Member of: *Agence universitaire de La Francophonie (AUF, #00548)*. [2015/XE2537/j/**E***]

♦ Institut Africain International (#11596)
♦ Institut africain des Nations Unies pour la prévention du crime et le traitement des délinquants (#20519)
♦ Institut africain pour la prévention du crime et le traitement des délinquants / see United Nations African Institute for the Prevention of Crime and the Treatment of Offenders (#20519)
♦ Institut africain de réadaptation (#00437)
♦ Institut africain des sciences de la gestion (internationally oriented national body)
♦ Institut africain, Tervuren (internationally oriented national body)
♦ Institut africain pour les transfert de fonds (unconfirmed)
♦ Institut für Afrika-Kunde, Hamburg / see Institute of African Affairs, Hamburg
♦ Institut für Afrikanistik, Leipzig (internationally oriented national body)
♦ Institut für Afrikanistik, Vienna / see Institut für Afrikawissenschaften, Wien
♦ Institut für Afrika-Studien, Hamburg (internationally oriented national body)
♦ Institut für Afrikastudien, Universität Bayreuth (internationally oriented national body)
♦ Institut für Afrikawissenschaften, Wien (internationally oriented national body)
♦ Institut Afriki Akademii Nauk SSSR / see Institute for African Studies of the Russian Academy of Sciences
♦ Institut Afriki Rossijskoj Akademii Nauk (internationally oriented national body)
♦ Institut de l'Afrique de l'Académie des Sciences de l'URSS / see Institute for African Studies of the Russian Academy of Sciences
♦ Institut Afrique Monde (internationally oriented national body)
♦ Institut d'Afrique orientale pour la recherche médicale (inactive)
♦ Institut Afro-Arabe pour la Culture et les Etudes Stratégiques (#00534)
♦ Institut agraire international (inactive)
♦ Institut für Agrarentwicklung in Mittel- und Osteuropa / see Leibniz-Institut für Agrarentwicklung in Transformationsökonomien
♦ Institut agronomique méditerranéen de Bari (#16641)
♦ Institut agronomique méditerranéen de Chania (#16642)
♦ Institut agronomique méditerranéen de Montpellier (#16643)
♦ Institut agronomique méditerranéen de Zaragoza (#16644)
♦ Institut pour l'alimentation et la politique de développement (internationally oriented national body)
♦ Institut allemand de développement / see Deutsches Institut für Entwicklungspolitik
♦ Institut allemand d'études orientales (internationally oriented national body)
♦ Institut des alternatives africaines (#11241)
♦ Institut andin des arts populaires (no recent information)
♦ Institut Antarabangsa Pemikiran dan Tamadun Islam (internationally oriented national body)

♦ Institut arabe des chefs d'entreprises (IACE) 11236

Arab Institute of Business Managers
International Relations Officer La Maison de l'Entreprise, Blvd principale, Les Berges du Lac 1053, Tunis, Tunisia. T. +21671962331. Fax +21671962516. E-mail: contact@iace.org.tn.
URL: http://www.iace.tn/
History 30 Oct 1984, Tunis (Tunisia). **Aims** Promote the private sector. **Structure** Executive Committee, headed by President. **Languages** Arabic, English, French. **Staff** 30.00 FTE, paid. **Finance** Sources: fees for services; members' dues; subsidies. Annual budget: 1,500,000 USD. **Activities** Events/meetings; projects/programmes; research/documentation; training/education. **Publications** Research studies; articles.
Members Full in 11 countries:
Algeria, France, Germany, Italy, Libya, Mali, Marshall Is, Mauritania, Togo, Tunisia, USA.
NGO Relations Member of: *Arab Forum for Young Entrepreneur Associations (AFYE, #00961)*. Institutional partner of: *Institut de Prospective économique du Monde Méditerranéen (IPEMED, #11352)*. Allied partner of: *Financial Transparency Coalition (FTC, #09772)*. [2022.02.02/XU5036/j/**E**]

♦ Institut arabe pour le développement urbain (#01071)
♦ Institut arabe des droits de l'homme (#00983)
♦ Institut arabe d'éducation ouvrière et de recherches sur le travail (#00984)
♦ Institut arabe d'études forestières (no recent information)
♦ Institut arabe de formation de l'industrie pétrolière (no recent information)
♦ Institut arabe de formation et de recherches statistiques (#00987)
♦ Institut arabe de planification (#01027)
♦ Institut für Arbeitsrecht und Arbeitsbeziehungen in der Europäischen Union (internationally oriented national body)
♦ Institut de l'argent (#19282)
♦ Institut of the Arid Regions, Tunisia (internationally oriented national body)
♦ Institut Aristides Calvani / see Instituto de Formación Demócrata Cristiana
♦ Institut asiatique de technologie (#01519)
♦ Institut d'Asie et de l'Extrême-Orient pour la prévention du délit et le traitement du délinquant / see United Nations Asia and Far East Institute for the Prevention of Crime and the Treatment of Offenders (#20521)
♦ Institut für Asienkunde / see GIGA Institut für Asien-Studien
♦ Institut d'Asie orientale (internationally oriented national body)
♦ Institut de l'Asie et du Pacifique pour le développement des émissions radiophoniques (#01934)
♦ Institut d'Asie du Sud, Heidelberg (internationally oriented national body)
♦ Institut Aspen (#02309)
♦ Institut atlantique (internationally oriented national body)
♦ Institut de l'audiovisuel et des télécommunications en Europe (internationally oriented national body)
♦ Institut des auditeurs internes (#11272)
♦ Institut für Auslandsbeziehungen / see Institute for Development and International Relations
♦ Institut für Auslandsbeziehungen, Stuttgart (internationally oriented national body)
♦ Institut automobile international (inactive)
♦ Institut pour l'avenir (internationally oriented national body)
♦ Institut de la banque mondiale (#21220)
♦ Institut Battelle (#03187)
♦ Institut der beim Europäischen Patentamt zugelassenen Vertreter (#11288)
♦ Institut des belles lettres arabes / see Pontifical Institute for Arabic and Islamic Studies (#18448)
♦ Institut Belleville (internationally oriented national body)
♦ Institut biblique pontifical (#18437)
♦ Institut de la Bienheureuse Vierge Marie (religious order)
♦ Institut des bioénergies (internationally oriented national body)
♦ Institut de la BIRD pour le développement économique / see World Bank Institute (#21220)
♦ Institut bolivien de biologie d'altitude (internationally oriented national body)
♦ Institut du Caire pour les études des droits de l'Homme (#03397)
♦ Institut canadien des affaires internationales (internationally oriented national body)
♦ Institut canadien d'études stratégiques (internationally oriented national body)
♦ Institut canadien pour l'ordre international (internationally oriented national body)
♦ Institut Caraïbéen pour l'Etat de Droit (internationally oriented national body)
♦ Institut caraïbéen de périnatologie (no recent information)
♦ Institut des Caraïbes pour l'alimentation et la nutrition (inactive)
♦ Institut caribéen et régional de l'information et de la traduction (#03548)
♦ Institut Caritas Christi (religious order)
♦ Institut Català de Cooperació Iberoamericana (internationally oriented national body)
♦ Institut Cavanis – Congrégation des Prêtres des Ecoles de Charité (religious order)
♦ Institut centroaméricain d'administration publique (#03670)
♦ Institut centroaméricain de technologie, Santa Tecla (internationally oriented national body)
♦ Institut centroaméricain de télécommunications (inactive)
♦ Institut chrétien pour l'étude de la religion et de la société (internationally oriented national body)
♦ Institut pour la connectivité dans les Amériques (#11249)
♦ Institut coopératif interaméricain (#11420)
♦ Institut pour la coopération audiovisuelle francophone (internationally oriented national body)
♦ Institut de coopération économique internationale (internationally oriented national body)
♦ Institut pour la coopération économique internationale et le développement (internationally oriented national body)
♦ Institut zur Cooperation bei Entwicklungs-Projekte (internationally oriented national body)
♦ Institut pour la coopération intercontinentale, 1977 (inactive)
♦ Institut pour la coopération intergouvernementale dans la recherche scientifique (#04098)
♦ Institut de coopération internationale de la Confédération allemande pour l'éducation des adultes (internationally oriented national body)

♦ Institut de coopération sociale internationale (ICOSI) 11237

Institute of International Social Cooperation
SG 30 rue des Epinettes, 75017 Paris, France. E-mail: info@icosi.org.
URL: https://www.icosi.org/

History 1983, Paris (France). Former names and other names: *Institut der Internationalen Sozialen Kooperation* – former alias; *Institut Mezdunarodnoj Socialnoj Kooperacii* – former alias. Registration: France. **Aims** Promote values of social economy – *solidarity*, respect for the principles and modalities of democratic management, combination of economic development, sustainable development and social justice; promote dissemination and defence of human rights, democracy and international labour standards; promote *workers' cooperatives*; collaborate with partners to lobby public institutions, so as to promote solidarity-based solutions and place the human being at the heart of economic choices. **Structure** General Assembly; Executive Board. **Languages** English, French. **Staff** 4.00 FTE, paid. **Finance** Sources: contributions; members' dues; subsidies. Logistic and financial support from organizations constituting General Assembly and Executive Board. Annual budget: 400,000 EUR. **Activities** Advocacy/lobbying/activism; guidance/assistance/consulting; networking/liaising; research and development; training/education. France, Algérie, Bénin, Maroc, Tunisie, Comores, Sénégal, Europe. **Events** *Conférence Euro-Mediterranéenne / Conference* Casablanca (Morocco) 2013, *Colloque sur l'Economie Sociale et le Logement en Europe* Paris (France) 2013, *European conference on social economy* Strasbourg (France) 2008, *Séminaire franco-roumain sur le handicap* Bucharest (Romania) 2002, *Rencontre franco-bulgare sur le tourisme associatif* Sofia (Bulgaria) 2002.
Members Organizations considered "traditional" social economy institutions (cooperatives, associations, foundations, mutual insurance companies, etc) and collective welfare institutions in 10 countries:
Algeria, Belgium, France, Italy, Mali, Morocco, Portugal, Senegal, Spain, Tunisia.
Included in the above, 1 organization listed in this Yearbook:
Pour la Solidarité (PLS).
IGO Relations Contacts with: *ILO (#11123)*. **NGO Relations** Member of: *Comité pour les Partenariats avec l'Europe Continentale (Comité PECO)*. Collaborates with: *Association internationale de la mutualité (AIM, #02721)*; *Centre international de recherches et d'information sur l'économie publique, sociale et coopérative (CIRIEC, #03764)*; *Confédération européenne des coopératives de travail associé, des coopératives sociales et des entreprises sociales et participatives (CECOP, #04541)*; *European Trade Union Confederation (ETUC, #08927)*; *Friedrich-Ebert-Stiftung (FES)*; *International Trade Union Confederation (ITUC, #15708)*; *International Organisation of Industrial and Service Cooperatives (CICOPA, #14429)*. [2023.02.23/XE1955/j/E]

- Institut pour la coopération universitaire (#11331)
- Institut de la Culture Afro-européenne à Paris (internationally oriented national body)
- Institut de la Culture Euro-Asiatique (internationally oriented national body)
- Institut culturel africain (inactive)
- Institut culturel danois (internationally oriented national body)
- Institut des cultures afro-européennes à Paris / see Institut de la Culture Afro-européenne à Paris
- Institut des cultures européennes (internationally oriented national body)
- Institut danois d'information sur le Danemark et de coopération culturelle avec les autres nations / see Danish Cultural Institute
- Institut Destrée (internationally oriented national body)
- Institut pour le développement et l'aménagement des télécommunications et de l'économie / see Institut de l'audiovisuel et des télécommunications en Europe
- Institut de développement pour l'Asie et le Pacifique (inactive)
- Institut du développement durable et des relations internationales (internationally oriented national body)
- Institut de développement économique / see World Bank Institute (#21220)
- Institut pour le développement de l'enseignement supérieur francophone, Bordeaux (internationally oriented national body)
- Institut de développement harmonique de l'homme (inactive)

♦ Institut pour le développement des relations interculturelles par l'art (IDRIART) 11238

Institute for the Development of Intercultural Relations through the Arts – Institut zur Förderung der Interkulturellen Beziehungen durch die Kunst

Contact ECOCULTURES SECS, Rue Gabriel Lippmann 13, L-5365 Munsbach, Luxembourg.
History 1983, Chartres (France), by Miha Pogacnik. Registered in accordance with Swiss law. **Aims** Rediscover the possibility for the arts to educate the noblest in the individual instead of to merely entertain the most ignoble in the masses; find in the arts the tools which politics have failed to provide – tools to build lasting bridges which span the gulf of ideological, social and economic differences between people form different nations. **Activities** Organizes Arts Festivals worldwide, accompanied by lectures, concerts, discussions, workshops, masterclasses and seminars.
Members Represented in 38 countries:
Australia, Austria, Belgium, Botswana, Brazil, Bulgaria, Canada, China, Czechia, Denmark, Finland, France, Germany, Greece, Hungary, Iceland, India, Indonesia, Ireland, Israel, Italy, Japan, Luxembourg, Mexico, Netherlands, New Zealand, Norway, Peru, Philippines, Poland, Romania, Serbia, South Africa, Spain, Sweden, Switzerland, UK, USA.
Represented also in the former USSR; countries not specified. [2019/XF1994/j/F]

- Institut pour le développement et les relations internationales / see Institute for Development and International Relations
- Institut de la diaspora africaine / see Institut de la Culture Afro-européenne à Paris

♦ Institut für die Wissenschaften vom Menschen (IWM) 11239

Institute for Human Sciences

Dir Spittelauer Lände 3, 1090 Vienna, Austria. T. +431313580. Fax +4313135860. E-mail: iwm@iwm.at.
URL: http://www.iwm.at/
History 1982, Vienna (Austria). USA affiliate: *'Institute for Human Sciences at Boston University'*, founded 2001. An associated institute of *European Cultural Foundation (ECF, #06868)*. Registered in accordance with Austrian law. **Aims** As an independent, interdisciplinary institute for advanced study in the *humanities* and *social sciences*: support free exchange of ideas so as to help overcome dividing lines and mechanisms of *exclusion* within and between societies; help strengthen *civil societies* and contribute to their self-understanding. **Structure** Board of Directors; Board of Trustees; Academic Advisory Board; Board of Patrons. **Languages** English, German. **Staff** 12.50 FTE, paid. **Finance** Sources: Austrian Federal Ministry of Education, Science and Research; City of Vienna (Austria); international cultural and scientific foundations; other grant-making institutions. Annual budget: about euro 3,000,000. **Activities** Training/education; events/meetings; knowledge management/information dissemination. **Events** *Conference on conditions for international solidarity* Vienna (Austria) 2007, *International conference* Vienna (Austria) 2002, *International conference* Vienna (Austria) 2000, *Meeting on Central Europe and the EU* Vienna (Austria) 2000, *International conference* Vienna (Austria) 1998. **Publications** *IWMpost Magazine* (3 a year) in English, German; *Transit* – journal. Books; conference proceedings; working papers. **NGO Relations** Close cooperation with academic institutions in East Central Europe. [2018.08.07/XF2956/j/E]

- Institut de documentation et de recherche sur la paix (internationally oriented national body)
- Institut für den Donauraum und Mitteleuropa (internationally oriented national body)
- Institut de Dret Privat Europeu i Comparat (internationally oriented national body)
- Institut de droit aérien et spatial (internationally oriented national body)
- Institut du droit des affaires internationales d'ICC (#11047)
- Institut pour le droit en Europe (internationally oriented national body)
- Institut pour le droit européen de la circulation (#11262)
- Institut de droit européen et de droit comparé (internationally oriented national body)
- Institut du droit européen des médias (internationally oriented national body)
- Institut de Droit international (#11276)
- Institut de droit international public et des relations internationales de Thessalonique (internationally oriented national body)
- Institut de droit maritime international de l'OMI (#11134)
- Institut du droit et des pratiques des affaires internationales de la CCI / see ICC Institute of World Business Law (#11047)

♦ Institut des droits de l'Homme des Avocats européens (IDHAE) 11240

European Bar Human Rights Institute

SG 57 av Bugeaud, 75116 Paris, France.
Registered office Rue de Vianden 10, L-2680 Luxembourg, Luxembourg.
URL: http://www.idhae.org/
History 2001, Luxembourg, to study human rights and in particular *Convention for the Protection of Human Rights and Fundamental Freedoms (1950)* and its protocols and *Charter of Fundamental Rights of the European Union (2000)*. **Aims** Monitor human rights protection, particularly under the European Convention of Human Rights and Fundamental Freedoms of November 4th, 1950 and its Protocols as well as the Charter of Fundamental rights of the European Union. **Structure** Board, comprising President, 2 Vice-Presidents, Secretary-General and Treasurer. **Languages** English, French. **Finance** Members' dues. Annual budget: euro 7,000. **Activities** Awards/prizes/competitions; monitoring/evaluation; events/meetings; training/education. **Publications** *Le Journal des droits de l'homme* (12 a year).
Members Members in 11 countries:
Austria, Belgium, France, Germany, Greece, Italy, Luxembourg, Netherlands, Poland, Spain, Switzerland.
IGO Relations Participant in Fundamental Rights Platform of: *European Union Agency for Fundamental Rights (FRA, #08969)*. [2018/XJ6196/j/D]

- Institut des droits de l'homme, Lyon (internationally oriented national body)
- Institut des droits de l'homme et de la paix en Afrique (internationally oriented national body)
- Institut pour les droits humains et le développement en afrique (internationally oriented national body)
- Institut de droit du travail et des relations industrielles dans la Communauté Européenne / see Institut für Arbeitsrecht und Arbeitsbeziehungen in der Europäischen Union
- Institut de droit du travail et des relations industrielles dans l'Union Européenne (internationally oriented national body)
- The Institute / see Global CCS Institute (#10274)
- Institute for Accountability in the Digital Age (internationally oriented national body)
- Institute for Advanced Studies on the United Nations (internationally oriented national body)
- Institute of African Affairs, Hamburg (internationally oriented national body)

♦ Institute for African Alternatives (IFAA) 11241

Institut des alternatives africaines

Contact 10A Hilgrove Road, London, NW6 4TN, UK. E-mail: ifaanet@gn.apc.org.
URL: http://www.ifaanet.org/
History Jan 1986, as a network institute for policy research on alternative development strategies for the African continent, with links to NGOs in the North and South and grassroots organizations in Africa. **Aims** Conduct and facilitate research on problems of Africa and the processes necessary for *social transformation*. **Structure** Network research institute with centres in 5 African countries (Nigeria, Senegal, South Africa, Tanzania UR, Zimbabwe) and one centre in the United Kingdom. **Finance** Members' dues. **Activities** Arranges conferences, workshops and seminars; maintains ongoing contacts with the official bodies concerned with Africa, development policy and Third World problems and participates in their work; represents African perspectives in various fora and campaigns in and outside Africa; conducts residential training programmes and courses; runs courses for certification on African related subjects in conjunction with various universities. **Events** *Understanding conflict resolution in Africa* Addis Ababa (Ethiopia) 1995, *Pan African congress* Kampala (Uganda) 1994, *Conference on African women in cooperatives* Addis Ababa (Ethiopia) 1990, *Conference on the impact of the IMF and world bank policies on the people of Africa* London (UK) 1987. **Publications** *IFAA-UK News* (4 a year). Reports; conference proceedings; lectures; occasional papers; books.
Members Supporting; Ordinary; Student. Organizations in 5 countries:
Kenya, Nigeria, Senegal, South Africa, Tanzania UR.
Individuals in 23 countries:
Australia, Austria, Belgium, Botswana, Canada, Eritrea, Ethiopia, Gabon, Germany, Ghana, Italy, Malawi, Mozambique, Namibia, Netherlands, Sudan, Sweden, Switzerland, Uganda, UK, USA, Zambia, Zimbabwe.
Consultative Status Consultative status granted from: *ECOSOC (#05331)* (Ros A). **IGO Relations** *United Nations Economic Commission for Africa (ECA, #20554)*. **NGO Relations** Member of: *Jubilee Research (#16158)*. [2008.04.14/XF5051/j/F]

- Institute for African American Studies, University of Connecticut (internationally oriented national body)
- Institute of African and Asian Studies, Khartoum (internationally oriented national body)
- Institute for African Development, Ithaca NY (internationally oriented national body)
- Institute for African Medicine and Epidemiology / see Institut de Médecine et d'Epidémiologie Appliquée
- Institute of African Research and Studies, University of Cairo (internationally oriented national body)
- Institute of African Studies / see Instytut Studiów Regionalnych i Globalnych
- Institute of African Studies at Columbia University, New York (internationally oriented national body)
- Institute of African Studies, Hamburg / see Institute of African Affairs, Hamburg
- Institute of African Studies, Legon (internationally oriented national body)
- Institute for African Studies, Lusaka / see Institute of Economic and Social Research
- Institute of African Studies, Rabat (internationally oriented national body)
- Institute for African Studies of the Russian Academy of Sciences (internationally oriented national body)
- Institute for African Studies, University of Bayreuth (internationally oriented national body)
- Institute of Afro-Asian Studies, Beijing (internationally oriented national body)
- Institute of Agricultural Development in Central and Eastern Europe / see Leibniz-Institut für Agrarentwicklung in Transformationsökonomien
- Institute of Agricultural and Zootechnical Research (no recent information)
- Institute for Agriculture and Trade Policy (internationally oriented national body)
- Institute of Air and Space Law, Montréal (internationally oriented national body)
- Institute of Air Transport (inactive)
- Institute of American Culture / see Institute of European and American Studies, Taiwan
- Institute of American Economy (inactive)
- Institute for American Universities, Aix-en-Provence (internationally oriented national body)
- Institute of the Americas (internationally oriented national body)
- Institute of Andean Studies (internationally oriented national body)
- Institute for Anthropological Research in Africa (internationally oriented national body)
- Institute of Apostolic Oblates (religious order)
- Institute of Applied Metaphysics (inactive)

♦ Institute of Appropriate Technology Transfer to Marginal Sectors of the Andrés Bello Convention 11242

Institut du transfert des technologies appropriées pour les secteurs marginaux de la Convention Andrés Bello – Instituto de Transferencia de Tecnologia Apropiada para Sectores Marginales del Convenio Andrés Bello (ITACAB)

Secretariat Avenida de las Artes Norte No 819, San Borja, 41, Lima, Peru. Fax +5112257225 – +5112257760. E-mail: itacab@itacab.org.
URL: http://www.itacab.org/
History 1 Dec 1986, Panama, as a body of the Principal Advisory Commission of *Convenio Andrés Bello de integración educativa, científica y cultural de América Latina y España (Convenio Andrés Bello, #04785)*, by resolution PREMECAB No 02-86 of the President of *Reunión de Ministros de Educación del Convenio Andrés Bello (REMECAB)*. **Aims** Formulate sustainable development models for marginal sectors and carry out programs; foster development, rescue and use of appropriate technology in agroecology, renewable energy, creation of enterprises and other fields of interest for the implementation of sustainable development models. **Structure** Management Board; Technical Committee. **Languages** Spanish. **Finance** Sources: Secretaria Ejecutiva del Convenio Andrés Bello (SECAB); Ministry of Education of Peru. **Activities** Focuses attention on projects in the following fields: education; science and technology; culture and communication; sustainable development; information. **Events** *Meeting* Lima (Peru) 1988. **Publications** Monographs; handbooks; studies. Information Services: Maintains a documentation centre.

Members Governments of 9 countries:
Bolivia, Chile, Colombia, Cuba, Ecuador, Panama, Peru, Spain, Venezuela.
IGO Relations *Andean Community (#00817)*; *Deutsche Gesellschaft für Technische Zusammenarbeit (GTZ, inactive)*; *OAS (#17629)*; *UNESCO (#20322)*; *UNICEF (#20332)*. [2014.01.20/XE5997/j/**E***]

♦ Institute of Arab and Islamic Studies (internationally oriented national body)
♦ Institute of Arab Manuscripts (no recent information)
♦ Institute of Arab Research and Studies (no recent information)
♦ The Institute of Arbitrators / see Chartered Institute of Arbitrators
♦ Institute of Arctic Medicine, Oulu / see Centre for Arctic Medicine, Oulu
♦ Institute of Asian Affairs / see GIGA Institut für Asien-Studien
♦ Institute of Asian and African Studies / see Institute of West Asian and African Studies, Beijing
♦ Institute of Asian and African Studies (internationally oriented national body)
♦ Institute of Asian and African Studies, Moscow State University (internationally oriented national body)
♦ Institute of Asian Cultural Studies, Tokyo (internationally oriented national body)
♦ Institute of Asian Culture and Development (internationally oriented national body)
♦ Institute of Asian Cultures, Tokyo (internationally oriented national body)
♦ Institute for Asian Research / see Asia Research Institute
♦ Institute of Asian Research, Vancouver BC (internationally oriented national body)
♦ Institute of Asian Studies, Bangkok (internationally oriented national body)
♦ Institute for Asian Studies, Madras (internationally oriented national body)
♦ Institute for Asian Studies, Portland (internationally oriented national body)
♦ Institute of Asian and Transcultural Studies (internationally oriented national body)
♦ Institute of Asian Worlds (internationally oriented national body)
♦ Institute of Asia-Pacific Studies, Beijing (internationally oriented national body)
♦ Institute of Asia-Pacific Studies Waseda University (internationally oriented national body)
♦ Institute of Association Management Companies / see AMC Institute
♦ Institute of Balkan Studies and Center of Thracology (internationally oriented national body)
♦ Institute for Balkan Studies, Thessaloniki (internationally oriented national body)
♦ Institute for Baltic Sea Research / see Baltic Sea Research Institute
♦ Institute of Baltic Studies (internationally oriented national body)
♦ Institute of Bankers, London / see International Banking Summer School (#12314)
♦ Institute for Bible Translation (internationally oriented national body)
♦ Institute for Bioenergetic Analysis / see International Institute for Bioenergetic Analysis (#13863)
♦ Institute of the Blessed Virgin Mary (religious order)
♦ Institute of the Blessed Virgin Mary, Irish Branch (religious order)

♦ Institute for Breeding Rare and Endangered African Mammals (IBREAM) 11243

Research Dir Fac of Veterinary Medicine, Dept of Equine Sciences, Yalelaan 114, 3584 CM Utrecht, Netherlands. T. +31302531331. Fax +31302537970.
URL: http://ibream.org/
Aims Protect endangered African mammals from extinction. **Structure** Board of 2 Directors. Advisory Board. [2020/XJ2062/j/**D**]

♦ Institute of Brewing / see International Brewers' Guild
♦ Institute of British Geographers / see Royal Geographical Society – with the Institute of British Geographers
♦ Institute of the Brothers of the Sacred Heart (religious order)
♦ Institute for Business History (inactive)
♦ Institute of Cardiometabolism And Nutrition (internationally oriented national body)
♦ Institute of Career Certification International (internationally oriented national body)
♦ Institute of Caribbean Home Office Underwriters / see Institute of Caribbean Insurance Risk Managers (#11244)

♦ Institute of Caribbean Insurance Risk Managers (ICIRM) 11244

Secretariat 1 Pearl Gardens Crescent, Pearl Gardens, Pearl Gardens, Petit Valley, Trinidad-Tobago. T. +18687841144.
URL: http://www.icirm.org/
History 1995, as *Institute of Caribbean Home Office Underwriters (ICHOU)*. **Aims** Act as a forum for continuing education for underwriters, claims technicians and medical professionals. **Structure** Committee. **Events** *Conference* Port-of-Spain (Trinidad-Tobago) 2014, *Conference* Aruba 2010. [2014/XJ9040/j/**D**]

♦ Institute of Caribbean Studies (internationally oriented national body)
♦ Institute of Caribbean Studies, Kingston (internationally oriented national body)
♦ Institute of Caribbean Studies, Washington DC (internationally oriented national body)
♦ Institute for Central American Development Studies (internationally oriented national body)
♦ Institute for Central Asian Studies / see International Institute for Central Asian Studies (#13868)
♦ Institute and Centre for Research of Air and Space Law, Montréal / see Institute of Air and Space Law, Montréal
♦ Institute of Charity (religious order)

♦ Institute of Chartered Accountants of the Caribbean (ICAC) 11245

Pres 6 Lockett Avenue, Kingston, Jamaica. T. +18769223223. Fax +18769486610. E-mail: admin@icacorg.com.
URL: http://www.icac.org.jm/
History Founded 28 Oct 1988, Kingston (Jamaica), on signature of the Memorandum and Articles of Association, by 7 founding institutes. Registered under the Companies Act of Jamaica. **Aims** Be the internationally recognized body for the accountancy profession in the Caribbean, with an expanding influence in the region; regulate the profession and promote the highest standards of professional and ethical conduct. **Structure** Board; Executive Officers; Committees (6); Sub-committees (2); Governance Taskforce. **Languages** English. **Staff** 3.00 FTE, paid. **Finance** Members' dues. Other sources: conference, seminar and workshop proceeds; funding from national and international agencies and affiliates. **Activities** Training/education; monitoring/evaluation; events/meetings. **Events** *Annual Conference* Grenada 2023, *Annual Conference* Kingston (Jamaica) 2022, *Annual Conference* Miami, FL (USA) 2021, *Annual Conference* Miami, FL (USA) 2020, *Annual Conference* Kingston (Jamaica) 2019. **Publications** *ICAC Newsletter* (3 a year). Annual Report.
Members Institutes in 13 countries and territories:
Antigua-Barbuda (*), Bahamas, Barbados, Belize, Dominica (*), Grenada (*), Guyana, Jamaica, St Kitts-Nevis (*), St Lucia (*), St Vincent-Grenadines (*), Suriname (*), Trinidad-Tobago (*).
'*' indicates member of: Institute of Chartered Accountants of the Eastern Caribbean (ICAEC).
Affiliate members (3) in 3 countries:
Canada, UK, USA.
Included in the above, 1 organization listed in this Yearbook:
Associate member in 1 territory:
Turks-Caicos.
IGO Relations Represented on: *Caribbean Court of Justice (CCJ, #03486)* Trust Fund. **NGO Relations** Represented on: *Caribbean Actuarial Association (CAA, #03433)*. Regional group of: *Caribbean Association of Industry and Commerce (CAIC, #03448)*; *International Federation of Accountants (IFAC, #13335)*. Observer status with: *Inter-American Accounting Association (IAA, #11395)*. [2023/XD1965/j/**D**]

♦ Institute of Chartered Accountants of the Eastern Caribbean (ICAEC) 11246

Main Office PO Box 1515, Castries, St Lucia. E-mail: icaecslu@gmail.com.
URL: http://icaec.org/
History 17 Jun 2004. **Structure** Council, comprising President, Vice-President, Treasurer, Secretary and 3 members.
Members Full in 9 countries and territories:
Anguilla, Antigua-Barbuda, Dominica, Grenada, Montserrat, St Kitts-Nevis, St Lucia, St Vincent-Grenadines, Virgin Is UK.
NGO Relations Member of: *Institute of Chartered Accountants of the Caribbean (ICAC, #11245)*. [2016/XM1573/j/**F**]

♦ Institute of Chartered Secretaries and Administrators / see The Chartered Governance Institute of UK and Ireland

♦ Institute of Chartered Shipbrokers 11247

Dir 85 Gracechurch Street, London, EC3V 0AA, UK. T. +442076231111. Fax +442076238118. E-mail: enquiries@ics.org.uk.
URL: http://www.ics.org.uk/
History 1911. Incorporated by Royal Charter 21 Jan 1920. Supplemental Charter: 25 Jul 1984. **Aims** Educate, examine and qualify those who wish to enter the profession of shipbroking and commercial *shipping* worldwide. **Structure** Controlling Council; Executive Council; Education and Training Committee; Membership Committee; Federation Council. **Languages** English. **Finance** Members' dues. Student and examination fees. **Activities** Training/education. **Publications** *Shipping Network* – magazine.
Members Individuals; Branches and Teaching Centres. Individuals in 91 countries and territories:
Argentina, Australia, Austria, Bahamas, Bahrain, Bangladesh, Barbados, Belarus, Belgium, Belize, Brazil, Brunei Darussalam, Bulgaria, Cameroon, Canada, Chile, China, Colombia, Costa Rica, Cyprus, Denmark, Ecuador, Egypt, Eritrea, Estonia, Finland, France, Georgia, Germany, Ghana, Gibraltar, Greece, Hong Kong, Iceland, India, Indonesia, Ireland, Italy, Jamaica, Kenya, Korea Rep, Kuwait, Latvia, Malaysia, Malta, Mauritius, Mexico, Monaco, Mozambique, Myanmar, Namibia, Netherlands, New Zealand, Nigeria, Norway, Oman, Pakistan, Panama, Papua New Guinea, Peru, Philippines, Poland, Portugal, Qatar, Romania, Russia, Saudi Arabia, Sierra Leone, Singapore, South Africa, Spain, Sri Lanka, St Lucia, Sweden, Switzerland, Taiwan, Tanzania UR, Thailand, Trinidad-Tobago, Tunisia, Türkiye, UK, Ukraine, United Arab Emirates, Uruguay, USA, Venezuela, Vietnam, Yemen, Zambia, Zimbabwe.
Branches and Teaching Centres in 23 countries and territories:
Australia, Bulgaria, Cameroon, Canada, China, Cyprus, Denmark, Germany, Ghana, Greece, Hong Kong, India, Ireland, Italy, Kenya, New Zealand, Norway, Pakistan, Singapore, South Africa, Sri Lanka, Sweden, UK.
Consultative Status Consultative status granted from: *UNCTAD (#20285)* (Special Category). **NGO Relations** Founder member of: *Federation of National Associations of Shipbrokers and Agents (FONASBA, #09694)*. Associate Member of: *International Association of Independent Tanker Owners (INTERTANKO, #11959)*. [2016.12.16/XF1493/j/**F**]

♦ Institute for Child Rights and Development / see International Institute for Child Rights and Development
♦ Institute of Christian Culture – Oriental Religions (internationally oriented national body)
♦ Institute of Commonwealth Studies, London (internationally oriented national body)
♦ Institute for Comparative and International Studies (internationally oriented national body)

♦ Institute for Computer Sciences, Social-Informatics and Telecommunications Engineering (ICST) 11248

Office Begijnhoflaan 93, 9000 Ghent, Belgium. T. +3293299425. E-mail: info@icst.org.
URL: http://www.icst.org/
History Set up as *International Communication Sciences and Technology Association*. Registered in accordance with Belgian law. **Aims** Support research, innovation and technology transfer in information technologies, their management, and their applications in the service of the Institute members and the global society. **Structure** Board, comprising President, Scientific Council Chair, Secretary, Executive Director and Treasurer. Scientific Council; SIB Councils; Student Councils. Committees (7): Technical Activities Planning; Publication; Events; Internationalization; Technology Challenges Planning; Institute and Membership Activities; IT. World Chapters (5): Americas; Asia/Pacific; Australia; Europe; Africa/Middle East. **Activities** Meeting activities; grants and awards. **Events** *International Conference on Body Area Networks* Sydney, NSW (Australia) 2015, *International Conference on Intelligent Technologies for Interactive Entertainment* Chicago, IL (USA) 2014, *International Conference on Simulation Tools and Techniques* Lisbon (Portugal) 2014, *International Conference on Body Area Networks* Boston, MA (USA) 2013, *International Conference on Quantum Communication and Quantum Networking* Budapest (Hungary) 2012. **Publications** *ICST Transaction* – journal. *Lecture Notes of ICST* – series. **IGO Relations** Collaborates with: *European Commission (EC, #06633)*. **NGO Relations** Member of: *European Alliance for Innovation (EAI, #05872)*. Collaborates with: *Association for Computing Machinery (ACM, #02447)*; *Institute of Electrical and Electronics Engineers (IEEE, #11259)*; national organizations. [2014/XM1210/j/**E**]

♦ Institute for Conflict Analysis and Resolution, Fairfax / see Jimmy and Rosalynn Carter School for Peace and Conflict Resolution
♦ Institute for Conflict Studies and Peacebuilding / see Center for Justice and Peacebuilding

♦ Institute for Connectivity in the Americas (ICA) 11249

Institut pour la connectivité dans les Amériques – Instituto para la Conectividad en las Americas – Instituto para a Conectividade nas Américas

Dir 250 Albert Street, PO Box 8500, Ottawa ON K1G 3H9, Canada. T. +16132366163ext2354. Fax +16135677749.
Regional Office Avenida Brasil 2655, CP 11400 Montevideo, Uruguay. T. +59827090042. Fax +59827086776.
History Apr 2001. Founded by the Canadian Government, during Summit of the Americas. **Aims** Promote implementation of innovative uses of information and communication technologies for development. **Structure** IDRC Advisory Board of Governors. Working Group. Regional office: Montevideo (Uruguay). **Languages** English, French, Portuguese, Spanish. **Staff** 7.00 FTE, paid. **Finance** Funded by the Government of Canada, institutions and foundations. **Activities** Supports initiatives that deliver innovative uses of information and communication technologies for development in 4 core areas: e-Economy; e-Education; e-Health; e-Citizenship. **Events** *Seminar on ICT for development* San Salvador (El Salvador) 2008. **NGO Relations** Relations and cooperation with: *Bellanet Alliance of Social Entrepreneurs (BASE, #03196)*. [2007.01.02/XK2256/j/**E***]

♦ Institut d'économie américaine (inactive)
♦ Institut de l'économie et du commerce international (internationally oriented national body)
♦ Institut d'économie européenne (inactive)
♦ Institut pour l'économie mondiale de l'Académie hongroise de sciences (internationally oriented national body)
♦ Institut d'économie mondiale, Budapest / see Institute for World Economics of the Hungarian Academy of Sciences
♦ Institut pour l'économie mondiale, Kiel (internationally oriented national body)
♦ Institut d'économie mondiale et des relations internationales de l'Académie des sciences de la Russie (internationally oriented national body)
♦ Institut d'économie mondiale et des relations internationales de l'Académie des sciences de l'URSS / see Institut Mirovoj Ekonomiki i Mezdunarodnyh Otnosenij Rossijskoj Akademii Nauk
♦ Institut des économies en développement / see Institute of Developing Economies, Japan External Trade Organization
♦ Institute for Conscious Global Change (internationally oriented national body)
♦ Institute of Consolata Missionaries (religious order)
♦ Institute for Contemporary Asian Studies / see Monash Asia Institute
♦ Institute for Cooperation with Arabian, Mediterranean and Developing Countries / see Dirección General de Cooperación con Africa, Asia y Europa Oriental
♦ Institute for Cooperation in Development Projects (internationally oriented national body)
♦ Institute for Cooperation with Latin America / see Dirección General de Cooperación con Iberoamérica
♦ Institute for Cooperation in Space (internationally oriented national body)

♦ Institute for Corporate Culture Affairs (ICCA) 11250

Address not obtained.
General: http://www.cca-institute.org/
History Mar 2003, by merger of *Centre for European Business History (CEBH, inactive)* and *Institute for Business History (SEBH, inactive)*. **Aims** Increase awareness of corporate social responsibility (CSR); provide services for proper CSR integration in international companies. **Languages** English, German. **Activities** Organizes symposia, workshops and conferences. **Events** *The history of corporate social responsibility in companies and banks* Frankfurt-Main (Germany) 2008, *Conference* Berlin (Germany) 2007, *Conference* Düsseldorf (Germany) 2007, *Conference* London (UK) 2007, *Brand and image in the history of European*

business Warsaw (Poland) 2007. **Publications** *This Week in CSR* (weekly); *CSR Briefing Notes* (12 a year). *The A to Z of CSR: A Complete Reference Guide to Concepts, Codes and Organizations* (2007); *ICCA Handbook of Corporate Social Responsibility* (2006). Reports from meetings. **Information Services** *CSR Globe* – online database. [2011/XM2539/j/**E**]

♦ Institute for Cultural Action (internationally oriented national body)

♦ Institute of Cultural Affairs International (ICAI) 11251

Institut des affaires culturelles internationales – Instituto Internacional de Asuntos Culturales – Institut für Kulturelle Weiterbildung – Internationaal Instituut voor Kulturele Zaken

Pres c/o ICA Canada, 401 Richmond St W, Ste 405, Toronto ON M5V 3A8, Canada. T. +14166912316. Fax +14166912491.

URL: http://www.ica-international.org/

History 1977, Brussels (Belgium). Founded as an international, non profit, association to facilitate activities of a network of autonomous national member institutes. The first national *Institute of Cultural Affairs (ICA) – Institut des affaires culturelles – Instituto de Asuntos Culturales*, founded in Chicago IL (USA), 1973, emerged as a result of the activities of a related body created 1964, also in Chicago, the *Ecumenical Institute (EI, no recent information)*, which focused on training church leaders for church renewal and relevant social action. Relocated to Canada, 2006. Registration: No/ID: 849849161RR0001, Start date: 2006, Canada. **Aims** As a global community of non-profit organizations advancing human development worldwide, facilitate peer-to-peer interchange, learning and mutual support across the network, for greater and deeper impact. **Structure** General Assembly (GA); Board of Directors. Operates with responsibility for priority global functions delegated and appropriated by national ICAs. **Languages** English, French, Spanish. **Staff** Voluntary. **Finance** Sources: donations; grants; members' dues. **Activities** Capacity building; events/meetings; guidance/assistance/consulting; knowledge management/information dissemination; networking/liaising; projects/programmes; research and development; training/education. **Events** *Quadrennial Global Conference* Kathmandu (Nepal) 2012, *Quadrennial General Assembly* Talegaon Dabhade (India) 2010, *Quadrennial Global Conference* Takayama (Japan) 2008, *Quadrennial global conference* Tokyo (Japan) 2008, *Quadrennial General Assembly* Toronto, ON (Canada) 2006. **Publications** *IERD Series – Vol III: Approaches that Work in Rural Development* (1988); *IERD Series – Vol I: Directory of Rural Development Projects* (1985); *IERD Series – Vol II: Voices of Rural Practitioners* (1985). *Changing Lives Changing Societies: ICA's experience in Nepal and in the world* (2012); *Beyond Prince and Merchant: The Rise of Civil Society* (1996) by John Burbidge.

Members Organizations and related groups in 34 countries and territories:
Australia, Bangladesh, Benin, Cameroon, Canada, Chile, China, Côte d'Ivoire, Egypt, France, Germany, Ghana, Guatemala, India, Japan, Kenya, Korea Rep, Nepal, Netherlands, Nigeria, Peru, Philippines, South Africa, Spain, Sri Lanka, Taiwan, Tanzania UR, Togo, Uganda, UK, Ukraine, USA, Zambia, Zimbabwe.

Consultative Status Consultative status granted from: *ECOSOC (#05331)* (Special); *FAO (#09260)* (Liaison Status); *UNESCO (#20322)* (Consultative Status); *UNICEF (#20332)*. **IGO Relations** Working relations with: *WHO (#20950)*. **NGO Relations** Member of (1): *CIVICUS: World Alliance for Citizen Participation (#03962)*. [2022.06.03/XF7747/j/**F**]

♦ Institute for Cultural Diplomacy (ICD) 11252

Dir/Founder Genthinerstr 20, D-10785, Berlin, Germany. T. +493023607680. Fax +4930236076811. E-mail: info@culturaldiplomacy.org.

URL: http://www.culturaldiplomacy.org/

History Founded 1999. Registered in accordance with German and USA laws. **Aims** Promote global peace and stability by strengthening and supporting *intercultural relations* at all levels; extend current research, programmes and practices in the field; create a platform to promote and sustain inter-cultural dialogue at all levels. **Structure** Advisory Board; Secretariat. Includes: Organization for Youth Education and Development (OYED); Center for Cultural Diplomacy Studies (CCDS); *Inter-Parliamentary Alliance for Human Rights and Global Peace*. **Languages** English. **Finance** Participation costs; individual grants; contributions; donations; sponsorship; in-kind support. **Activities** Advocacy/lobbying/activism; events/meetings. **Events** *Annual Conference* Berlin (Germany) 2016, *Europe Meets Russia Conference* Brussels (Belgium) 2012. **NGO Relations** Partner of: *International Studies Association (ISA, #15615)*. [2014.11.04/XJ2925/j/**F**]

♦ Institute of Current World Affairs (internationally oriented national body)
♦ Institute for the Danube Region and Central Europe (internationally oriented national body)
♦ Institute of Defence and Strategic Studies, Singapore / see S Rajaratnam School of International Studies
♦ Institute for Defence Studies and Analyses (internationally oriented national body)
♦ Institute for Democracy in Eastern Europe (internationally oriented national body)
♦ Institute for Demographic Training and Research / see Institut de formation et de recherche démographiques (#11304)
♦ Institute for Developing Countries / see Institute for Development and International Relations
♦ Institute of Developing Countries, Warsaw / see Instytut Studiów Regionalnych i Globalnych
♦ Institute of Developing Economies / see Institute of Developing Economies, Japan External Trade Organization
♦ Institute of Developing Economies, Japan External Trade Organization (internationally oriented national body)
♦ Institute of Developing Economies Law / see Institute of Developing Economies, Japan External Trade Organization
♦ Institute for Development, Environment and Peace (internationally oriented national body)
♦ Institute for the Development of Intercultural Relations through the Arts (#11238)
♦ Institute for Development and International Relations (internationally oriented national body)

♦ Institute of Development Management (IDM) 11253

Regional Office Carbo Centre, Riverwalk, PO Box 60167, Gaborone, Botswana. T. +2673906433. Fax +2673913423. E-mail: directorcs@idmbls.com.

URL: http://www.idmbls.com/

History 1974, as a regional management development institution of *Association of Management Training Institutions of Eastern and Southern Africa (AMTIESA, no recent information)*. Became fully autonomous in 1979. Also referred to as *Institute of Development Management – Botswana, Lesotho and Swaziland (IDM-BLS)*. **Structure** Governing Board, consisting of 12 members. Regional Office, headed by Regional Director, located in Gaborone (Botswana). Country Directors (3) and Assistant Registrars (3). **Staff** 35.00 FTE, paid. **Activities** Provides education and training for middle and senior managers and administrators in all sectors of civil service, parastatal organizations and private sector in Botswana, Lesotho and Eswatini. Maintains a Management Resource Centre, undertakes management consultancies and related research to assist management within the region. Executive Development Unit (EDU) provides specialized programmes and courses, including Top Executive Seminar Series, to other SADC countries in the Southern African region. **Events** *Conference* Lesotho 2015. **IGO Relations** *Commonwealth Fund for Technical Cooperation (CFTC, #04331)*. [2020/XE0213/j/**E**]

♦ Institute of Development Management – Botswana, Lesotho and Swaziland / see Institute of Development Management (#11253)
♦ Institute for Development and Peace, Duisburg (internationally oriented national body)
♦ Institute of Development Policy and Management, University of Antwerp (internationally oriented national body)
♦ Institute for Development Research and Development Policy (internationally oriented national body)
♦ Institute of Development Studies, Brighton (internationally oriented national body)
♦ Institute of Development Studies, Dar es Salaam (internationally oriented national body)
♦ Institute of Development Studies, Harare (internationally oriented national body)
♦ Institute of Development Studies, Helsinki (internationally oriented national body)
♦ Institute of Development Studies, Jaipur (internationally oriented national body)

♦ Institute of Directors (IoD) 11254

Main Office 116 Pall Mall, London, SW1Y 5ED, UK. T. +442078391233. Fax +442079301949. E-mail: enquiries@iod.com.

URL: http://www.iod.com/

History 1903, UK. Royal Charter awarded in 1906. Registration: Royal Charter, No/ID: RC000252, UK. **Aims** Provide an effective voice to represent interests of members; bring experience of *business leaders* to bear on conduct of public affairs for the common good; encourage and help members improve their professionalism as business leaders. **Activities** Events/meetings; networking/liaising. **Publications** *Director* (10 a year) – magazine.

Members Full; Member; Associate. Individuals (nearly 40,000) and national organizations mainly in UK but in a total of 14 countries:
Belgium, Bermuda, Cyprus, France, Germany, Gibraltar, Hong Kong, Ireland, Malta, Monaco, Netherlands, Nigeria, UK, Zimbabwe.

NGO Relations Member of: *EFMD – The Management Development Network (#05387)*. [2020/XF2682/j/**F**]

♦ Institute on Disability and Public Policy (IDPP) 11255

Exec Dir address not obtained.

URL: http://www.aseanidpp.org/

History Launched 4 Apr 2011 Full title: *Institute on Disability and Public Policy for the ASEAN Region (IDPP)*. Set up in accordance with *ASEAN (#01141)* Vision 2020. **Aims** Improve the circumstances of persons with disabilities in ASEAN countries. **Structure** Executive Committee; Advisory Board. **Finance** Support from: *Nippon Foundation*. **Activities** Financial and/or material support; capacity building; research/documentation. **NGO Relations** *Global Forum on Law, Justice and Development (GFLJD, #10373)*. [2017/XM5743/j/**E**]

♦ Institute on Disability and Public Policy for the ASEAN Region / see Institute on Disability and Public Policy (#11255)
♦ Institute for Domestic and International Affairs (internationally oriented national body)
♦ Institut d'éducation UNRWA/UNESCO (no recent information)

♦ Institute for Dynamics of Explosions and Reactive Systems (IDERS) 11256

Contact ME 513, EEEL 403 – Schulich School of Engineering, Univ of Calgary, 2500 Univ Drive NW, Calgary AB T2N 1N4, Canada.

URL: http://www.icders.org/

History Set up as the sponsoring organization of *International Colloquium on the Dynamics of Explosions and Reactive Systems (ICDERS)*. Registered in the State of Washington DC (USA). **Structure** Board of Directors. **Activities** Events/meetings; awards/prizes/competitions. **Events** *Biennial Colloquium* Boston, MA (USA) 2017, *Biennial Colloquium* Leeds (UK) 2015, *Biennial Colloquium* Taipei (Taiwan) 2013, *Colloquium* Taipei (Taiwan) 2013, *Biennial Colloquium* Irvine, CA (USA) 2011. **Publications** Abstracts. [2017/XM4501/c/**E**]

♦ Institute of Earthquake Engineering and Engineering Seismology (internationally oriented national body)
♦ Institute of Earth Systems, Malta (internationally oriented national body)
♦ Institute of East Asian Regional Studies, Seoul (internationally oriented national body)
♦ Institute of East Asian Studies (internationally oriented national body)
♦ Institute of East Asian Studies, Bangkok (internationally oriented national body)
♦ Institute of East Asian Studies, Berkeley CA (internationally oriented national body)
♦ Institute for East Asian Studies, Duisburg (internationally oriented national body)
♦ Institute for East Asia Peace Studies (internationally oriented national body)
♦ Institute for East-Central Europe and the Balkans (internationally oriented national body)
♦ Institute on East Central Europe, New York NY / see East Central Europe Center, New York NY
♦ Institute of Eastern Culture (internationally oriented national body)
♦ Institute for Eastern Europe / see Osteuropa-Institut
♦ Institute for Eastern European Studies, Free University of Berlin / see Osteuropa-Institut
♦ Institute of Eastern Studies / see Deadong Institute for Korean Studies
♦ Institute for East European Research / see Osteuropa-Institut
♦ Institute for East European Studies (internationally oriented national body)
♦ Institute for East and Southeast European Studies (internationally oriented national body)
♦ Institute for East West Security Studies / see EastWest Institute (#05264)
♦ Institute for East-West Studies / see EastWest Institute (#05264)
♦ Institute for Ecology and Action Anthropology (internationally oriented national body)
♦ Institute for Economic Democracy (internationally oriented national body)
♦ Institute of Economic Growth – Research Centre on Social and Economic Development in Asia (internationally oriented national body)
♦ Institute for Economic and International Studies (internationally oriented national body)
♦ Institute of Economic and Social Research (internationally oriented national body)

♦ Institute for Economics and Peace (IEP) 11257

Dir Partnerships 205 Pacific Hwy, St Leonards, Sydney NSW 2065, Australia. T. +61299018500. E-mail: info@economicsandpeace.org.

USA Office 3 East 54th St, New York NY 10022, USA.

Europe Office Cours Saint Michel 30b, Hive 5, 1040 Brussels, Belgium.

URL: http://www.economicsandpeace.org/

History 2007. Founded by Steve Killelea. Registration: Australia; USA; Netherlands. **Aims** Create a paradigm shift in the way the world thinks about peace by using data driven research; develop metrics to analyse peace and to quantify its economic benefits; promote better understanding of social and economic factors that develop a more peaceful society. **Structure** Offices: Sydney (Australia); New York NY (USA); Mexico City (Mexico); The Hague (Netherlands); Brussels (Belgium); Harare (Zimbabwe). **Languages** Dutch, English, French, German, Spanish. **Staff** 26.00 FTE, paid. **Activities** Events/meetings; guidance/assistance/consulting; research/documentation; training/education. **Events** *Annual Positive Peace Conference* Stanford, CA (USA) 2017. **Publications** *Business and Peace*; *Economic Value of Peace*; *Global Peace Index (GPI)*; *Global Terrorism Index (GTI)*; *Mexico Peace Index*; *Positive Peace Report*; *SDG16 Progress Report*; *The Ecological Threat Register*. **Consultative Status** Consultative status granted from: *ECOSOC (#05331)* (Special). **IGO Relations** Partner of (8): Australian Department of Foreign Affairs and Trade; *Commonwealth Secretariat (#04362)*; *European Commission (EC, #06633)*; *International Bank for Reconstruction and Development (IBRD, #12317)* (World Bank); *OECD (#17693)*; *UNDP (#20292)*; *UNICEF (#20332)*; *United Nations (UN, #20515)*.

NGO Relations Partner of (22):
- *Alliance for Peacebuilding*;
- Australian National University (ANU) – Crawford School;
- *Center for Strategic and International Studies, Washington DC (CSIS)*;
- *Danish Refugee Council (DRC)*;
- *Earth Institute at Columbia University*;
- *Geneva Centre for Security Policy (GCSP)*;
- *Global Community Engagement and Resilience Fund (GCERF, #10303)*;
- *Global Partnership for the Prevention of Armed Conflict (GPPAC, #10538)*;
- *International Union of Painters and Allied Trades (IUPAT)*;
- *Mercy Corps International (MCI)*;
- *Network of European Peace Scientists (NEPS, #17026)*;
- Order of Malta;
- Peace and Security Funders Group;
- Ramon Llull University – Blanquerna (Spain);
- *Religions for Peace (RfP, #18831)*;
- *Rotary International (RI, #18975)*;
- *Stockholm International Peace Research Institute (SIPRI, #19994)*;
- United Nations Association of Australia;
- *United Nations Global Compact (#20567)*;
- United States Institute for Peace;
- *Universal Peace Federation (UPF International, #20681)*;
- *World Leadership Alliance – Club de Madrid (WLA-CdM, #21619)*. [2021.09.02/XJ2766/j/**F**]

♦ Institute of Economic Studies of Argentine and Latin American Reality (internationally oriented national body)
♦ Institute for Economic Studies – Europe (internationally oriented national body)
♦ Institute of Economics of the World Socialist System / see Institute for International Economic and Political Studies, Moscow

♦ Institute for Ecumenical and Interreligious Research (internationally oriented national body)
♦ Institute for Ecumenical Research / see Institut für Ökumenische und Interreligiöse Forschung

♦ Institute for Ecumenical Research, Strasbourg 11258

Centre d'études oecuméniques, Strasbourg – Institut für Ökumenische Forschung, Strasbourg

Dir 8 rue Gustave-Klotz, 67000 Strasbourg, France. T. +33388152575. Fax +33388152570. E-mail: stras-ecum@wanadoo.fr – strasecum@ecumenical-institute.org.
URL: http://www.strasbourginstitute.org/

History 1 Feb 1965, Strasbourg (France). Founded by *Lutheran Foundation for Interconfessional Research (#16529)*, under the auspices of *The Lutheran World Federation (LWF, #16532)*. **Aims** Contribute to fulfillment of the *Lutheran* Church's ecumenical responsibility in the area of *theology*; conduct research in areas where Christian churches are divided in matters of *doctrine* and church order and where theological questions are a matter of controversy. **Structure** Board of Trustees; Research Staff; Director. **Languages** English, French, German. **Staff** None. **Finance** Sources: contributions; donations; investments. **Activities** Events/meetings; guidance/assistance/consulting; research/documentation; training/education. **Events** *International Seminar* Strasbourg (France) 2021, *International Seminar* Strasbourg (France) 2019, *International Seminar* Strasbourg (France) 2018, *International Seminar* Strasbourg (France) 2017, *International Seminar* Strasbourg (France) 2017. **Publications** *Newsletter* (irregular). *Oecumenica (1966-1972)*; *Ökumenische Dokumentation (1974-)*; *Ökumenisches Perspektiven (1972-1977)*. Books; statements; reports. Information Services: Maintains a library of 30,000 volumes and over 100 journals, focused on the Reformation and on Lutheran, Roman Catholic and ecumenical theology. [2021.05.25/XE0796/j/**E**]

♦ Institute of Education / see European Institute of Education and Social Policy (#07551)

♦ Institute of Electrical and Electronics Engineers (IEEE) 11259

Exec Dir IEEE Operations Center, 445 Hoes Ln, PO Box 1331, Piscataway NJ 08855-1331, USA. Fax +17329811721. E-mail: executivedirector@ieee.org – society-info@ieee.org – contactcenter@ieee.org.
Pres and CEO address not obtained. E-mail: president@ieee.org.
URL: http://www.ieee.org/

History 1884, USA. Founded under current name, 1Jan 1963, on merger of (USA) *Institute of Radio Engineers (IRE)*, founded 1912, and the American Institute of Electrical Engineers (AIEE), founded 1884. Constitution most recently amended, 15 Dec 1998. Registration: EU Transparency Register, No/ID: 79856747620-58; USA. **Aims** Advance the theory and practice of electrical, electronics and computer engineering and *computer science*. **Structure** Assembly (annual); Board of Directors. Offices (7) in: China; Germany; India; Japan; Singapore; USA. Technical Societies (38) comprising sub-disciplines / interest areas. **Staff** 1200.00 FTE, paid. **Activities** Events/meetings; networking/liaising; projects/programmes. **Events** *Asia-Pacific Microwave Conference* China 2027, *International Symposium on Antennas and Propagation and URSI Radio Science Joint Meeting* Kyoto (Japan) 2027, *Asia-Pacific Microwave Conference* Fukuoka (Japan) 2026, *Asia-Pacific Microwave Conference* Jeju (Korea Rep) 2025, *International Conference on E-health Networking, Application & Services* Kanazawa (Japan) 2024. **Publications** *IEEE Technical Activities Guide*. Journals; magazines; standards. **Information Services** *IEEE Xplore Digital Library*. **Members** Member; Senior Member; Fellow; Associate; Student. Electrical and electronics engineers (over 423,000) in over 160 countries and territories. Membership countries not specified. **IGO Relations** Accredited by (1): *United Nations Framework Convention on Climate Change – Secretariat (UNFCCC, #20564)*. Participates in: *Group on Earth Observations (GEO, #10735)*. **NGO Relations** Member of (9): *ABET*; *DataCite (#05011)*; *Engineering for the Americas (EftA, no recent information)*; *Global Innovation Exchange (The Exchange, inactive)*; *International Federation for Medical and Biological Engineering (IFMBE, #13477)*; *International Federation of Engineering Education Societies (IFEES, #13412)*; *International Society for Geometry and Graphics (ISGG, #15141)*; *Knowledge4Innovation (K4I, #16198)*; *ORCID (#17790)*. Affiliate member of: *International Federation of Robotics (IFR, #13532)*. In liaison with technical committees of: *International Organization for Standardization (ISO, #14473)*. Joint meetings with: *SPIE (#19919)*. Collaboration agreement with: *Institute for Systems and Technologies of Information, Control and Communication (INSTICC)*. Technical co-sponsorship of: *International Society of Infrared, Millimeter and Terahertz Waves (IRMMW-THz, #15204)*. [2021/XF1848/jv/**F**]

♦ Institute of Environmental Sciences and Technology (internationally oriented national body)
♦ Institute for Environmental Security (internationally oriented national body)
♦ Institute for Environment and Sustainability (inactive)
♦ Institute for Ethnology and African Studies, Munich (internationally oriented national body)
♦ Institute of Euro-Asian Culture (internationally oriented national body)
♦ Institute of European Affairs, Dublin / see Institute of International European Affairs, Dublin
♦ Institute of European and American Studies, Taiwan (internationally oriented national body)
♦ Institute of European and Comparative Law, Oxford (internationally oriented national body)
♦ Institute of European and Comparative Private Law (internationally oriented national body)
♦ Institute of European Cultural History (internationally oriented national body)
♦ Institute for European Cultures (internationally oriented national body)

♦ Institute of European Democrats (IED) 11260

Contact Rue de l'Industrie 4, 1000 Brussels, Belgium. T. +3222130010. Fax +3222130019. E-mail: info@iedonline.eu.
URL: http://www.iedonline.eu/

History Set up Sep 2007, as an independent research institute. Registered in accordance with Belgian law. **Aims** Promote a better understanding of the main aspects of the European *integration* process; play actively in strengthening the confidence of European citizens towards European institutions and, above all, the idea of a united Europe. **Structure** Board of Directors; Scientific Committee. **Languages** Dutch, English, French, German, Hungarian, Italian, Portuguese, Spanish. **Staff** 2.00 FTE, paid. **Finance** Members' dues. Funded by *European Parliament (EP, #08146)*. **Activities** Events/meetings; research/documentation. **Publications** *IED Newsletter*. Working papers. **NGO Relations** Formally affiliated to: *European Democratic Party (EDP, #06900)*. [2019.02.15/XM6471/j/**E**]

♦ Institute of European Economics (inactive)
♦ Institute for European Energy and Climate Policy (unconfirmed)

♦ Institute for European Environmental Policy (IEEP) 11261

Institut pour une politique européenne de l'environnement – Instituto para la Politica Ambiental Europea – Institut für Europäische Umweltpolitik – Instituut voor Europees Milieubeleid

Exec Dir Rue Joseph II 36-38, 1000 Brussels, Belgium. T. +3227387482. Fax +3227324004.
Contact 25EP, 25 Eccleston Place, Belgravia, London, SW1W 9NF, UK. T. +442045249900.
URL: http://www.ieep.eu/

History 1 Jan 1976, Bonn (Germany). Founded by *European Cultural Foundation (ECF, #06868)*. Functions independently from ECF since 1 Jan 1990. Successor to *Network of Institutes for International and European Environmental Policy (inactive)*, set up 1989 and coordinated by *Foundation for European Environmental Policy (FEEP, see: #11261)*. Former names and other names: *Institute for European Environmental Research* – former. Registration: No/ID: 0678767990, Belgium; Charity Commission, No/ID: 802956, England and Wales; EU Transparency Register, No/ID: 934329423960-72; Companies House, No/ID: FC035126, England and Wales. **Aims** Produce evidence-based research and policy insight through collaboration between stakeholders from public, civil, academic and industrial institutions, and a team of economists, scientists and lawyers; advance impact-driven sustainability policy across the EU and the world. **Structure** Board; Advisory Council. **Languages** English. **Staff** 30.00 FTE, paid. **Activities** Knowledge management/information dissemination; politics/policy/regulatory; research/documentation; training/education. **Events** *Think2030 Conference* Paris (France) 2022, *Think2030 Conference* 2020, *Pegasus Project Final Conference* Brussels (Belgium) 2018, *Think2030 conference* Brussels (Belgium) 2018, *Workshop on applying integrated environmental assessment to EU waste policy* Brussels (Belgium) 2004. **Publications** Annual Report; other reports; papers; other publications.

Members Organizations (8):
BC3 Basque centre for climate change; *Ecologic Institut (#05303)*; *Institut du développement durable et des relations internationales (IDDRI)*; *International Institute for Sustainable Development (IISD, #13930)*; *Stockholm Environment Institute (SEI, #19993)*; The Green Tank; TMG Think Tank for Sustainability; *WiseEuropa*.

Consultative Status Consultative status granted from: *UNEP (#20299)*. **NGO Relations** Member of (3): *Climate Action Network (CAN, #03999)*; *Climate Action Network Europe (CAN Europe, #04001)*; *European Forum on Integrated Environmental Assessment (EFIEA, no recent information)*. [2021.09.01/XE6380/j/**E**]

♦ Institute for European Environmental Research / see Institute for European Environmental Policy (#11261)
♦ Institute of European Integration and Policy (internationally oriented national body)
♦ Institute for European Integration Research / see Centre for European Integration Research
♦ Institute of European Media Law (internationally oriented national body)
♦ Institute for European Policy (internationally oriented national body)
♦ Institute for European Politics, Berlin (internationally oriented national body)
♦ Institute of European Postgraduate Studies / see College of Europe (#04105)
♦ Institute for European Social Protection (internationally oriented national body)
♦ Institute of European Studies 'Alcide de Gasperi' (internationally oriented national body)
♦ Institute of European Studies, Bilbao (internationally oriented national body)
♦ Institute for European Studies, Bruxelles (internationally oriented national body)
♦ Institute for European Studies, Cornell University (internationally oriented national body)
♦ Institute of European Studies, Karachi / see Area Study Centre for Europe, Karachi
♦ Institute of European Studies – Law Department – of Saarland University / see Europa-Institut at Saarland University
♦ Institute of European Studies, Ljubljana (internationally oriented national body)
♦ Institute of European Studies, Louvain-la-Neuve (internationally oriented national body)
♦ Institute of European Studies of Macau (internationally oriented national body)
♦ Institute for European Studies, Malta (internationally oriented national body)
♦ Institute for European Studies, Montréal (internationally oriented national body)
♦ Institute of European Studies, Toronto (internationally oriented national body)
♦ Institute of European Teacher Education, Berlin (internationally oriented national body)
♦ Institute for European Tort Law (internationally oriented national body)

♦ Institute for European Traffic Law (IETL) 11262

Institut pour le droit européen de la circulation (IDEC) – Institut für Europäisches Verkehrsrecht (IEVR)

Contact Rue de Mamer 75, L-8055 Bertrange, Luxembourg. T. +35226311204. Fax +35226311206. E-mail: info@idec.lu.
URL: http://www.ietl.org/

History Founded 26 Nov 2003, Trier (Germany), at *Academy of European Law (#00035)*. Seat moved to Bertrange (Luxembourg), Jun 2011. **Aims** Serve research, politics, business and consumer protection in all areas of national and international traffic law. **Structure** Board of Directors; Management Director; Secretariat. **Languages** English, French, German. **Activities** Organizes European Traffic Law Days, always in Luxembourg. **Events** *European Traffic Law Days* Vienna (Austria) 2017, *European traffic law days* Luxembourg (Luxembourg) 2009, *Conference on third party motor liability insurance* Turin (Italy) 2009, *European traffic law days* Luxembourg (Luxembourg) 2008, *European traffic law days* Luxembourg (Luxembourg) 2007. [2013.06.25/XM0673/j/**E**]

♦ Institute for European Union Studies at SUNY (internationally oriented national body)
♦ Institute européen de la communication et de la culture (internationally oriented national body)
♦ Institute européen de recherches spatiales / see ESRIN (#05546)
♦ Institute of Europe, Moscow (internationally oriented national body)
♦ Institute of Europe Russian Academy of Sciences / see Institute of Europe, Moscow
♦ Institute for Euroregional Studies (internationally oriented national body)
♦ Institute of Exchange Associations, 1925 (inactive)
♦ Institute of Executive Training for Development (internationally oriented national body)
♦ Institute for Family Policies International Federation (internationally oriented national body)
♦ Institute of Family Sciences (#11330)
♦ Institute of Far Eastern Studies (internationally oriented national body)
♦ Institute of Ferro-Alloy Producers in Western Europe (inactive)
♦ Institute for Food and Development Policy (internationally oriented national body)
♦ Institute of Food Technologists (internationally oriented national body)
♦ Institute for Foreign Cultural Relations, Stuttgart (internationally oriented national body)
♦ Institute for Foreign Policy Analysis (internationally oriented national body)
♦ Institute for Foreign and Security Studies, Bratislava (internationally oriented national body)

♦ Institute of Forest Biosciences (IFB) 11263

Pres 140 Preston Executive Dr, Ste 100G, Cary NC 27513, USA.
URL: http://forestbio.org/

History 2000, State of North Carolina (USA). 2000, in the State of North Carolina (USA) as *Institute of Forest Biotechnology*, where it is registered. **Aims** Foster use of science and technologies that create healthier and more productive forests. **Structure** Board of Directors. **Languages** English. **Staff** 2.00 FTE, paid. **Finance** Grants; donations; in-kind contributions. Annual budget: about US$ 350,000. **Activities** Events/meetings; knowledge management/information dissemination; awards/prizes/competitions. Active in: Brazil, Canada, Chile, New Zealand, USA. **Publications** Books; whitepapers; reports.

Members National organizations in 6 countries:
Belgium, Brazil, Canada, Chile, New Zealand, USA. [2018.07.27/XJ8351/j/**F**]

♦ Institute of Forest Biotechnology / see Institute of Forest Biosciences (#11263)
♦ Institute of Forest Conservation / see Training Center for Tropical Resources and Ecosystems Sustainability
♦ Institute of Fundamental Black African Studies (internationally oriented national body)
♦ Institute for the Future (internationally oriented national body)
♦ Institute for Futures Studies, Copenhagen / see Copenhagen Institute for Futures Studies
♦ Institute for Futures Studies, Stockholm (internationally oriented national body)
♦ Institute of Gas Technology / see Gas Technology Institute

♦ Institute of General Semantics (IGS) 11264

Contact 72-11 Austin St, Ste 233, Forest Hills NY 11375, USA. T. +1212729797. Fax +12127932527.
URL: http://www.generalsemantics.org/

History 1938, Chicago IL (USA). **Aims** Promote and up-to-date understanding of how humans process language and other symbol systems, with specific regard to the resulting behaviours and attitudes. **Structure** Board, including President, Vice-President, Secretary and Treasurer. **Activities** Conducts educational seminars, workshops and conferences; publishes journals and books. **Events** *Conference* Fort Worth, TX (USA) 2006, *General semantics seminar-workshop* Las Vegas, NV (USA) 2003, *International conference on general semantics / Conference* Las Vegas, NV (USA) 2003. **Publications** *ETC: A Review of General Semantics* (4 a year) – journal; *General Semantics Bulletin* (annual). Books.

Members Individuals (700, mostly in USA) in 22 countries:
Argentina, Australia, Barbados, Belgium, Canada, France, Germany, Honduras, India, Ireland, Israel, Italy, Japan, Netherlands, New Zealand, Norway, Portugal, Spain, Sweden, Switzerland, UK, Uruguay. [2012/XF3788/jv/**F**]

♦ Institute of Geography of Developing Countries / see Instytut Studiów Regionalnych i Globalnych

♦ Institute for Geopolitical Research and Development (INGRED) 11265

Chairman August Vermeylenlaan 3, Bus 28, 2050 Antwerp, Belgium. E-mail: info@ingred.org.
URL: http://www.ingred.org/

History 2011. Former names and other names: *Global Governance Foundation (GGF)* – former. Registration: Banque-Carrefour des Entreprises, Start date: 2011, Belgium; EU Transparency Register, No/ID: 523228735333-92. **Aims** Provide assistance in developing projects ideas into a professional and bankable business plan. **Structure** Board. **Languages** Dutch, English, French, German, Polish. **Finance** Sources: fees for services; sponsorship. Annual budget: 75,000 EUR. **Activities** Guidance/assistance/consulting; publishing activities; training/education. **Publications** Books.

Members Full in 19 countries and territories:
Bangladesh, Belgium, Congo DR, Curaçao, Egypt, Gambia, Germany, Ghana, Guinea-Bissau, India, Indonesia, Kenya, Malta, Netherlands, Philippines, Poland, Senegal, Tanzania UR, Uganda.
IGO Relations *European Union (EU, #08967); United Nations (UN, #20515).* [2021.08.31/XM8449/f/**F**]

♦ Institute on Global Conflict and Cooperation (internationally oriented national body)
♦ Institute for Global Economics (internationally oriented national body)
♦ Institute of Global Education (internationally oriented national body)

♦ Institute for Global Environmental Strategies (IGES) 11266

Chair 2108-11 Kamiyamaguchi, Hayama KANAGAWA, 240-0115 Japan. T. +81468553700. Fax +81468553709. E-mail: iges@iges.or.jp.
URL: https://www.iges.or.jp

History 31 Mar 1998, Japan. Founded as an initiative of the Japanese government. Since Apr 2012, a Public Interest Incorporated Foundation. Registration: Japan. **Aims** Achieve a new paradigm for civilization and conduct innovative policy development and strategic research for environmental measures, reflecting research results into political decisions for realizing sustainable development both in the Asia-Pacific region and globally. **Structure** Board of Directors; Board of Trustees; Satellite Offices (4). **Languages** English, Japanese. **Staff** 190.00 FTE, paid. **Activities** Research/documentation; events/meetings; knowledge management/information dissemination. **Events** *Climate and SDGs Conference* Tokyo (Japan) 2022, *Conference on Sustainability Science (ICSS)* Tokyo (Japan) 2022, *Global Conference on Strengthening Synergies between the Paris Agreement and the 2030 Agenda for Sustainable Development* Tokyo (Japan) 2022, *High Level Seminar on Environmentally Sustainable Cities* Tokyo (Japan) 2022, *Zero Carbon City International Forum* Tokyo (Japan) 2022. **Information Services** *Internet Researchers Database.*

Members Signatory government ministries, organizations and institutions of the founding charter. National Administrative Organizations (16):
Australia, Cambodia, Canada, China, India, Indonesia, Japan, Korea Rep, Laos, Malaysia, Mongolia, Nepal, New Zealand, Philippines, Thailand, Vietnam.
International organizations (7):
International Tropical Timber Organization (ITTO, #15737); UNEP (#20299); United Nations Centre for Regional Development (UNCRD, #20526); United Nations Economic and Social Commission for Asia and the Pacific (ESCAP, #20557); United Nations Institute for Training and Research (UNITAR, #20576); United Nations University Institute for the Advanced Study of Sustainability (UNU-IAS, #20643).
Research and academic institutions (26) in 17 countries:
Austria, Canada, China, Costa Rica, Finland, Germany, India, Japan, Korea Rep, Malaysia, New Zealand, Singapore, Sweden, Switzerland, Thailand, UK, USA.
Included in the above, 14 organizations listed in this Yearbook:
Asia-Pacific Centre for Environmental Law, Singapore (APCEL); Center for International Environmental Law (CIEL); Earth Council Alliance (ECA, inactive); Energy and Resources Institute (TERI); Global Industrial and Social Progress Research Institute (GISPRI); Institute of Development Studies, Brighton (IDS); Institute of Strategic and International Studies, Malaysia (ISIS); International Global Change Institute, Hamilton (IGCI); International Institute for Applied Systems Analysis (IIASA, #13861); International Institute for Sustainable Development (IISD, #13930); ISEAS – Yusof Ishak Institute (ISEAS); Potsdam Institute for Climate Impact Research (PIK); World Resources Institute (WRI, #21753); Wuppertal Institute for Climate, Environment and Energy.

Consultative Status Consultative status granted from: *ECOSOC (#05331)* (Special). **IGO Relations** Accredited by (2): *Green Climate Fund (GCF, #10714); UNEP (#20299).* Houses: *Water Environment Partnership in Asia (WEPA, #20827).* **NGO Relations** Member of (2): *Climate Chain Coalition (CCC, #04008); International Partnership for the Satoyama Initiative (IPSI, #14525).* [2020/XN9300/jy/**E**]

♦ Institute of Global Environment and Society (internationally oriented national body)
♦ Institute for Global Health and Development, Edinburgh (internationally oriented national body)
♦ Institute of Global Homelessness (internationally oriented national body)
♦ Institute on Globalization and the Human Condition (internationally oriented national body)
♦ Institute of Globalization and Social Movements / see Institute for Globalization Studies and Social Movements, Moscow
♦ Institute of Globalization Studies, Moscow / see Institute for Globalization Studies and Social Movements, Moscow
♦ Institute for Globalization Studies and Social Movements, Moscow (internationally oriented national body)
♦ Institute for Global Justice (internationally oriented national body)
♦ Institute for Global Learning, Seaside CA (internationally oriented national body)
♦ Institute for Global Networking, Information and Studies (internationally oriented national body)
♦ Institute of Global and Regional Studies, Warsaw (internationally oriented national body)
♦ Institute of Global Responsibility (internationally oriented national body)
♦ Institute for Global Studies (internationally oriented national body)
♦ Institute for Global Studies, Minneapolis (internationally oriented national body)
♦ Institute of Global Studies, Nankai University (internationally oriented national body)
♦ Institute for a Global Sustainable Information Society (The) (internationally oriented national body)
♦ Institute for Governance and Sustainable Development (internationally oriented national body)
♦ Institute for the Harmonious Development of Man (inactive)
♦ Institute for Healthcare Improvement (internationally oriented national body)
♦ Institute for Health Metric and Evaluation (internationally oriented national body)
♦ Institute of Higher European Studies / see Hague School of European Studies
♦ Institute de Higiene e Medicina Tropical, Universidade Nova e Lisboa (internationally oriented national body)

♦ Institute for Historical Justice and Reconciliation (IHJR) 11267

Exec Dir IHJR c/o Humanities, Postbox 9515, 2300 RA Leiden, Netherlands. E-mail: info@ihjr.org.
URL: http://historyandreconciliation.org/

History 2004, Netherlands. **Aims** Promote reconciliation, tolerance, and understanding in historically divided societies. **Structure** Executive Committee, comprising Chairman, Vice-Chairman and 3 members. Advisory Board. **Publications** *IHJR Newsletter.* Annual Report. [2016/XJ7082/j/**E**]

♦ Institute on the Holocaust and Genocide (IHG) 11268

Exec Dir PO Box 10311, 91102 Jerusalem, Israel. T. +97226720424. Fax +97226720424. E-mail: encygeno@gmail.com.
Magazine: http://www.genocidepreventionnow.org/

History 1979, as *Institute of the International Conference on the Holocaust and Genocide (IICHG)*, when was announced the International Conference on the Holocaust and Genocide which was held in 1982, Tel Aviv. Present (shortened) name adopted in 1989. **Aims** Bridge between memorial of the Holocaust of the Jewish people and the genocides suffered by all other peoples; bring together many fields of scholarship and many professions in an interdisciplinary network devoted to the study and prevention of genocide; translate memorials of past genocides and scholarship on the history and nature of genocide towards a new focus on intervention in emerging genocidal situations and the prevention of genocide in future. **Structure** Founding Members (3); Executive Director; Associate Director; Assistant Director; Council of 36 members. **Languages** English, Hebrew. **Activities** Research/documentation; monitoring/evaluation; knowledge management/information dissemination. **NGO Relations** Member of: *Genocide Watch; Alliance Against Genocide (AAG, #00655); International Association of Genocide Scholars (IAGS).* Supports the creation of: *United Nations International Lifesaving Army (no recent information).* [2014.12.09/XF0099/j/**F**]

♦ Institute of Hospitality 11269

Contact Counting House, 14 Palmerston Road, Sutton, SM1 4QL, UK. T. +442086614900. Fax +442086614901. E-mail: info@instituteofhospitality.org.
URL: http://www.instituteofhospitality.org/

History 1971. Previous to this, there were only two professional bodies in catering industry – Hotel and Catering Institute (HCI), created 1949, and Institutional Management Association (IMA), created 1938. HCIMA was created in response to the need for a strong professional body to represent industry interests as a whole. Former names and other names: *Hotel, Catering and Institutional Management Association (HCIMA)* – former (1971 to 2 Apr 2007). Registration: Charity, No/ID: 326180, England and Wales. **Aims** Promote the highest professional standards of management and education in the international hospitality industry. **Structure** General Meeting (annual); Executive Council. **Languages** English. **Staff** 16.00 FTE, paid. **Finance** Sources: fees for services; members' dues; sale of publications. Other sources: Awarding Body, Accreditation and Endorsement; professional activities; Education Membership Scheme (EMS); Business Partner Programme. **Activities** Awards/prizes/competitions; certification/accreditation; events/meetings; financial and/or material support; monitoring/evaluation; standards/guidelines; training/education. **Events** *Annual General Meeting* London (UK) 2014, *Annual general meeting / Annual Conference* London (UK) 2009, *Annual Conference* London (UK) 2008, *Extraordinary general meeting / Annual Conference* London (UK) 2007, *Annual general meeting / Annual Conference* London (UK) 2006. **Publications** *Hospitality Magazine (HQ); Insight Newsletter.* Guides; reports; e-resources.

Members Branches in 6 countries and territories:
Cyprus, Hong Kong, Malta, Nigeria, Sri Lanka, UK. [2021.06.10/XD3532/jv/**D**]

♦ Institute for Housing Studies / see Institute for Housing and Urban Development Studies
♦ Institute for Housing and Urban Development Studies (internationally oriented national body)
♦ Institute for Human Rights and Business (internationally oriented national body)
♦ Institute for Human Rights and Development in Africa (internationally oriented national body)
♦ Institute for Human Rights, Environment and Development / see International Institute for Human Rights, Environment and Development (#13886)
♦ Institute on Human Rights and the Holocaust (internationally oriented national body)
♦ Institute of Human Rights, Moscow / see Human Rights Institute, Moscow
♦ Institute of Human Rights and Peace in Africa (internationally oriented national body)
♦ Institute for Human Rights, Turku (internationally oriented national body)
♦ Institute for Human Sciences (#11239)
♦ Institute of Ibero-American Studies, Hamburg / see Institut für Lateinamerika-Studies
♦ Institute of Iberoamerican Thought, Salamanca (internationally oriented national body)
♦ Institute for Inclusive Security (internationally oriented national body)
♦ Institute for Individual and World Peace (internationally oriented national body)
♦ Institute of Industrial Engineers / see Institute of Industrial and Systems Engineers (#11270)

♦ Institute of Industrial and Systems Engineers (IISE) 11270

CEO 3577 Parkway Ln, Ste 200, Norcross GA 30092, USA. T. +17704490460. Fax +17704413295. E-mail: cs@iienet.org.
URL: http://www.iise.org/

History 1948, Columbus, OH (USA). Former names and other names: *American Institute of Industrial Engineers (AIIE)* – former (1948 to 1981); *Institute of Industrial Engineers (IIE)* – former (1981 to 2016). Registration: USA. **Aims** Advance technical and managerial excellence of industrial and systems engineers; provide members with information on the profession and continuing education opportunities. **Structure** Board of Trustees; Senior Chapters and University Chapters organized in geographic regions and represented by 15 Regional Vice Presidents; Societies (3); Networking Communities (13). **Languages** English. **Finance** Members' dues. Other sources: sale of products and services. Annual budget: US$ 5,000,000. **Activities** Events/meetings; training/education; financial and/or material support; awards/prizes/competitions. **Events** *Annual Conference* Seattle, WA (USA) 2022, *Annual Conference* Montréal, QC (Canada) 2021, *Annual Conference* New Orleans, LA (USA) 2020, *Conference on Manufacturing Modeling, Management, and Control* Berlin (Germany) 2019, *Annual Conference* San Juan (Puerto Rico) 2019. **Publications** *IISE Transactions* (12 a year) – technical journal; *ISE Magazine* (12 a year); *Industrial Management* (6 a year) – magazine; *IISE Transactions on Healthcare Systems Engineering* (4 a year) – technical journal; *IISE Transactions on Occupational Ergonomics and Human Factors* (4 a year) – technical journal; *Journal of Enterprise Transformation* (4 a year); *The Engineering Economist* (4 a year) – technical journal.

Members Individuals (14,000) in 83 countries and territories:
Argentina, Australia, Austria, Bahamas, Bahrain, Barbados, Belgium, Bolivia, Botswana, Brazil, Brunei Darussalam, Canada, Cayman Is, Chile, China, Colombia, Costa Rica, Cyprus, Denmark, Dominican Rep, Ecuador, Egypt, El Salvador, Finland, France, Germany, Greece, Grenada, Guam, Guatemala, Honduras, Hong Kong, Iceland, India, Indonesia, Iran Islamic Rep, Ireland, Israel, Italy, Jamaica, Japan, Jordan, Kenya, Korea Rep, Kuwait, Libya, Malaysia, Malta, Mexico, Morocco, Netherlands, New Zealand, Nigeria, Norway, Oman, Pakistan, Panama, Peru, Philippines, Portugal, Puerto Rico, Saudi Arabia, Singapore, Slovakia, South Africa, Spain, Sri Lanka, St Vincent-Grenadines, Sweden, Switzerland, Taiwan, Thailand, Trinidad-Tobago, Tunisia, Türkiye, Uganda, UK, Ukraine, United Arab Emirates, USA, Venezuela, Zambia, Zimbabwe.
Chapters, mainly in USA but in a total of 15 countries and territories:
Argentina, Australia, Canada (11), Costa Rica, Egypt, Hong Kong, Indonesia, Ireland, Italy, Korea Rep, Mexico (2), Philippines, Saudi Arabia, Singapore, USA (155).

NGO Relations Member of (1): *ABET.* Affiliated with: *World Organisation of Systems and Cybernetics (WOSC, #21686).* [2018.06.01/XF3784/jtv/**F**]

♦ Institute of Information Management (internationally oriented national body)
♦ Institute for Infrastructure, Environment and Innovation (unconfirmed)
♦ Institute for Integrated Development Studies (internationally oriented national body)
♦ Institute for Integrated Transitions (unconfirmed)

♦ Institute for the Integration of Latin America and the Caribbean ... 11271

Institut pour l'intégration de l'Amérique latine et des Caraïbes – Instituto para la Integración de América Latina y el Caribe (INTAL) – Instituto para a Integração da América Latina e do Caribe

Dir Esmeralda 130 – piso 16, Casilla de Correo 39, Sucursal 1, 1401 Buenos Aires, Argentina. T. +541143232350. Fax +541143232365. E-mail: intal@iadb.org.
URL: http://www.iadb.org/en/intal/

History 1965, pursuant to agreement between *Inter-American Development Bank (IDB, #11427)* and the Government of Argentina. Part of IDB Vice-Presidency of Countries (VPC). **Aims** Promote and consolidate Latin American and Caribbean integration at the sub-regional, regional, inter-regional, hemispheric and international levels through: *capacity-building* in *trade* and integration; support to research networks for sustaining policy reforms to reinforce efficiency of research centres and individual experts, thus facilitating decision-making on integration and trade-related issues in the public and private sectors; public outreach. **Structure** Director; Senior Trade and Integration Economist; Officials in charge of Library/Documentation Center, Publications, Fora and Technical Cooperation Projects, Events and Databases. **Languages** English, Portuguese, Spanish. **Staff** 15.00 FTE, paid. **Finance** Grants from IDB and Government of Argentina; voluntary contributions from other Latin American and Caribbean countries. **Activities** Works mainly in the framework of the Joint IDB/INTAL-WTO Program to Support Trade Negotiations in Latin America and the Caribbean. Focus is on the following thematic areas: development of physical infrastructure; legal aspects of integration agreements; macroeconomic coordination and convergence; integration and changes in the Latin American and Caribbean productive structure; social issues at the sub-regional level; integration and development of border areas; readiness of the region's countries to adhere to NAFTA or relate to the European Union or APAC and participate in hemispheric convergence; intra-sub-regional direct investment flows promoted by integration and economic complementation agreements; harmonization of services market regulations; development of sub-regional information systems. Organizes specialized training programmes for government officials and civil society representatives in trade and integration matters; provides technical assistance to increase efficiency in government consultations with civil society for formulation and enforcement of trade and integration policies; supports research networks; carries out research work; provides technical assistance to governments and institutions at academic and business levels; provides training in support of regional integration and cooperation processes; organizes workshops, fora and special events. Since 2001, hosts Technical Coordination Committee Secretariat of the *'Initiative for Regional Infrastructure Integration in South America'*, made up of IDB, CAF and FONPLATA. **Events** *Seminario sobre los procesos de integracion en la encrucijada* Santiago (Chile) 2006, *Forum on the academic incomes of the first conference of the Euro-Latin Study Network on Integration and Trade* Buenos Aires (Argentina) 2004, *Seminar on opportunities and challenges of Latin America for a closer link with Asia* Buenos Aires (Argentina) 2004, *Workshop on*

macroeconomic coordination in MERCOSUR Buenos Aires (Argentina) 2004, *Technical workshop* Buenos Aires (Argentina) 2003. **Publications** *Alerta Bibliografico: Novedades en Integración* (weekly) in Spanish; *Integration and Trade* (2 a year) in English, Spanish – journal; *MERCOSUR Report* (annual) in English, Portuguese, Spanish; *INTAL Monthly Newsletter* in English, Portuguese, Spanish. **Information Services** *Basic Instruments of Economics Integration in Latin America and the Caribbean* in Spanish – data base containing organized basic juridical texts relevant to regional economic integration in Latin America; *DATAINTAL* – foreign trade data from 1992-2010 encompassing 31 countries; *INTAL Documentation Center (CDI)* – information in integration, trade, infrastructure, development and relating topics in Latin America and the Caribbean.
Members Representatives of governments of 21 countries:
Argentina, Barbados, Bolivia, Brazil, Chile, Colombia, Costa Rica, Dominican Rep, Ecuador, El Salvador, Guatemala, Honduras, Jamaica, Mexico, Nicaragua, Panama, Paraguay, Peru, Trinidad-Tobago, Uruguay, Venezuela.
NGO Relations Supports: Integration Research Centers Network (RedInt); *Latin America-Caribbean and Asia-Pacific Economics and Business Association (LAEBA, no recent information)*; *Euro-Latin Study Network on Integration and Trade (ELSNIT, #05701)*; *Red de Centros de Estudio de América Latina y el Caribe sobre Asia Pacifico (REDEALAP)*. [2023/XD1025/j/**E***]

- ♦ Institute of Intelligent Systems (unconfirmed)
- ♦ Institute for Inter-American Affairs / see Center for Latin American Studies, Gainesville
- ♦ Institute for Interconnecting and Packaging Electronic Circuits / see IPC
- ♦ Institute for Intercontinental Cooperation, 1977 (inactive)
- ♦ Institute for Intercultural and International Studies (internationally oriented national body)

♦ Institute of Internal Auditors (IIA) 11272

Institut des auditeurs internes – Instituto de Auditores Internos

Mailing Address 1035 Greenwood Blvd, Ste 401, Lake Mary FL 32746, USA. T. +14079371111. Fax +14079371101. E-mail: customerrelations@theiia.org.
URL: http://www.theiia.org/

History Dec 1941, New York, NY (USA). Current statutes approved 1983. Former names and other names: *Institut des vérificateurs internes* – alias. Registration: USA, New York. **Aims** Define and maintain professional internal auditing *standards*; research, disseminate and promote knowledge and information concerning internal auditing, including internal control and related subjects. **Structure** Meeting (annual). Board of Directors, consisting of Executive Committee and 27 Directors. Executive Committee, comprising International Chairman of the Board, Senior Vice Chairman, 4 Vice Chairmen, Secretary and Treasurer, together with the 2 Immediate Past Chairmen. Board or Chairman appoints Audit Committee, Nominating Committee and Technical and Special Committees. Centres (3): Advocacy, Operating and Administration Practices; Learning; Business. **Languages** English, French, Spanish. **Staff** 100.00 FTE, paid. **Finance** Members' dues. Other sources: sale of publications; fees for attending seminars and conferences; certification examination fees for internal auditing; video programmes. **Activities** Provides professional development certification and guidance for internal auditors on an international basis, organizes annual regional conferences. Each chapter and institute hold frequent meetings throughout the year. Chapter and membership services include: *'Certification'* – twice yearly written examinations; *'Professional Development'* – including conferences, seminars, in-house training, chapter education programmes and media-assisted training courses; *'Professional Issues'* – reports to members on major trends, issues, technological innovations and opportunities and identification of projects to be funded by Institute of Internal Auditors Research Foundation, set up in 1976; *'Quality Auditing Services'* – including quality assurance review service and GAIN, a bench-marking service for internal auditing departments; educational products; standards and ethics, including assistance to members, governments and other organizations in developing, approving and adopting code of ethics and standards; endorses universities; technology practices; customer service centre; finance and administration; marketing/public relations; information services. Speciality offerings for Control Self-Assessment; Gaming Auditors; Financial Services Auditors; Chief Audit Executives. **Events** *Financial Services Exchange Conference* Washington, DC (USA) 2023, *Chief Audit Executive Conference* Abu Dhabi (United Arab Emirates) 2022, *International Conference* Chicago, IL (USA) 2022, *Financial Services Exchange Conference* Washington, DC (USA) 2022, *Financial Services Exchange Conference* Washington, DC (USA) 2021. **Publications** *AuditWire* (6 a year) – electronic; *Internal Auditor* (6 a year); *The Educator* (4 a year) – electronic; *ITAUDIR'dot'org* – continuous electronic newsletter. *International Standards for the Professional Practice of Internal Auditing*; *Practice Advisories*. Directories; research reports; textbooks; self study courses.
Members Regular, Educational, Audit Group, Sustaining Organization, Student and Retired members individuals (100,000, one half in North America), forming 280 chapters and institutes in 97 countries and territories:
Algeria, Argentina, Australia, Austria, Azerbaijan, Bahamas, Barbados, Belgium, Bermuda, Bolivia, Botswana, Brazil, Bulgaria, Cameroon, Canada, Chile, China, Colombia, Congo DR, Costa Rica, Curaçao, Cyprus, Czechia, Denmark, Dominican Rep, Ecuador, Egypt, Estonia, Ethiopia, Fiji, Finland, France, Germany, Ghana, Greece, Guyana, Haiti, Honduras, Hong Kong, Hungary, Iceland, India, Indonesia, Israel, Italy, Jamaica, Japan, Kenya, Korea Rep, Kyrgyzstan, Latvia, Lebanon, Lithuania, Luxembourg, Malawi, Malaysia, Mali, Mexico, Morocco, Netherlands, New Zealand, Nicaragua, Nigeria, Norway, Oman, Pakistan, Papua New Guinea, Paraguay, Peru, Philippines, Poland, Portugal, Puerto Rico, Qatar, Romania, Russia, Senegal, Singapore, Slovenia, South Africa, Spain, Sweden, Switzerland, Taiwan, Thailand, Trinidad-Tobago, Tunisia, Türkiye, Uganda, UK, Ukraine, United Arab Emirates, Uruguay, USA, Venezuela, Zambia, Zimbabwe.
IGO Relations Accredited by: *United Nations Office at Vienna (UNOV, #20604)*. Associated with Department of Global Communications of the United Nations. [2020/XC1031/j/**F**]

- ♦ Institute for International Affairs (internationally oriented national body)
- ♦ Institute of International Affairs – Centre for Small State Studies (internationally oriented national body)
- ♦ Institute for International Affairs and Foreign Policy, Madrid (internationally oriented national body)
- ♦ Institute for International Affairs Studies, Milano / see Italian Institute for International Political Studies
- ♦ Institute for International Agricultural Negotiations (internationally oriented national body)
- ♦ Institute of International Bankers (internationally oriented national body)
- ♦ Institute of International Banking Law and Practice (internationally oriented national body)
- ♦ Institute of the International Conference on the Holocaust and Genocide / see Institute on the Holocaust and Genocide (#11268)

♦ Institute of International Container Lessors (IICL) 11273

Institut des loueurs internationaux de conteneurs – Instituto de Arrendadores Internacionales de Contenedores

Dir – Marketing and Admin 1120 Connecticut Avenue, Ste 440, Washington DC 20036-3946, USA. T. +12022239800. Fax +12022239810. E-mail: emena@iicl.org – info@iicl.org.
Chairman address not obtained.
URL: http://www.iicl.org/

History 1971. Registration: Incorporated, USA, Delaware. **Aims** Act as *trade* association for the international container and *chassis leasing* industry. **Structure** Board of Directors (elected annually). President; Director Technical Services; Director Marketing and Administration. Committees (3): Technical; Tax; Legal. **Languages** English. **Staff** 3.00 FTE, paid. **Activities** Container testing, inspector certification, technical publishing, EDI, environmental concerns; also active in regulatory, tax, customs and other technical fields. Annual leased container fleet survey. Participated in development of *International Convention for Safe Containers (CSC, 1972)*. **Events** *International conference on containers and goods / Conference* St Petersburg (Russia) 2005, *International conference on containers and goods* St Petersburg (Russia) 2004, *Annual Conference* San Francisco, CA (USA) 1991. **Publications** *IICL Inspection Directory* (annual); *IICL News*. *General Guide for Refrigerated Container Inspection and Repair* (3rd ed); *Guide for Chassis Inspection and Maintenance* (4th ed); *Guide for Container Cleaning* (2nd ed); *Guide for Container Damage Measurement*; *Guide for Flatrack Container Inspection*; *Guide for Flatrack Container Repair*; *Guide for Floorboard Quality Assurance Program*; *Guide for Open Top Container Equipment Inspection*; *IICL/ICS Guide for Container Equipment Inspection* (5th ed); *Pocket Edition of the Container Inspection Tables*; *Repair Manual for Steel Freight Containers* (5th ed); *Supplement on Container Inspection and Repair: Gray Areas*. CSC pamphlet. **Members** Container and Chassis leasing companies (10), representing about 90% of the leasing Industry and about 50% of the world container fleet. Membership countries not specified. **Consultative Status** Consultative status granted from: *ECOSOC (#05331)* (Ros A); *UNCTAD (#20285)* (Special Category); *International Maritime Organization (IMO, #14102)*. **IGO Relations** Accredited by: *United Nations Office at Vienna (UNOV, #20604)*. Associated with Department of Global Communications of the United Nations. **NGO Relations** Core Partner in: *Global Cold Chain Alliance (GCCA, #10299)*. [2023/XF1101/j/**F**]

- ♦ Institute for International Cooperation in Animal Biologics (internationally oriented national body)
- ♦ Institute for International Cooperation and Development / see One World Center
- ♦ Institute for International Cooperation of the German Adult Education Association (internationally oriented national body)

♦ Institute for International Criminal Investigations (IICI) 11274

Exec Dir Anna Paulownastraat 101, 2518 BC The Hague, Netherlands. T. +31703644660. Fax +31703632300. E-mail: info@iici.global.
Contact 899 Ellis Str, San Francisco CA 94109, USA. T. +14154870737. Fax +14154870748.
URL: http://www.iici.info/

History 2003, The Hague (Netherlands). Incorporated in the State of California (USA). *International Criminal Investigations Foundation (IICIF)* is registered as a foundation in the Netherlands. **Aims** Train professionals in the investigation of *genocide*, *war* crimes and crimes against humanity; support international criminal justice and fact-finding mechanisms with training and deployment of multidisciplinary investigative teams to scenes of war crimes around the world. **Structure** Board of Directors; Council of Advisors. **Languages** English. **Staff** 4.00 FTE, paid. **Finance** Sources: grants; members' dues. Other sources: projects; tuition fees. Annual budget: 700,000 EUR. **Activities** Training/education. [2015.09.10/XJ8536/j/**C**]

- ♦ Institute of International Culture, Tokyo (internationally oriented national body)
- ♦ Institute for International Development / see Opportunity International (#17776)
- ♦ Institute for International and Developmental Studies, University of Windsor / see Windsor International, University of Windsor
- ♦ Institute for International Economic Cooperation (internationally oriented national body)
- ♦ Institute for International Economic Cooperation and Development (internationally oriented national body)
- ♦ Institute for International Economic Cooperation and Development Problems / see Istituto per la Cooperazione Economica Internazionale e i Problemi dello Sviluppo
- ♦ Institute for International Economic and Political Studies, Moscow (internationally oriented national body)
- ♦ Institute for International Economic Studies (internationally oriented national body)
- ♦ Institute for International Economics, Washington / see Peterson Institute for International Economics, Washington
- ♦ Institute of International Education (internationally oriented national body)
- ♦ Institute of International European Affairs, Dublin (internationally oriented national body)
- ♦ Institute for International and European Policy (internationally oriented national body)
- ♦ Institute of International Exchange (internationally oriented national body)

♦ Institute of International Finance (IIF) 11275

Institut de finance internationale (IFI)

Main Office 1333 H St NW, Ste 800E, Washington DC 20005-4770, USA. T. +12028573600. Fax +12027751430. E-mail: info@iif.com.
URL: http://www.iif.com/

History Jan 1983, Washington DC (USA), by 30 international banks from 10 countries. EU Transparency Register: 48714858158-06. **Aims** Improve the timeliness and quality of information available on sovereign *borrowers*; encourage better communications between official and private *creditors*; foster a greater public understanding of the role of *banks* in supporting countries' external financing requirements. **Structure** Meetings of members and associate members twice a year. Economic Advisory Committee of senior economists from member banks (meets twice a year). Other Working Parties as required. **Finance** Members' dues. Budget: about US$ 5 million. **Activities** Knowledge management/information dissemination; events/meetings. **Events** *European Summit* Brussels (Belgium) 2022, *Emerging Markets Central Banking Summit* Brussels (Belgium) 2020, *European Summit* Brussels (Belgium) 2019, *Spring Meeting* Tokyo (Japan) 2019, *MENA Chief Risk Officer Forum* Dubai (United Arab Emirates) 2018. **Publications** *IIF Overview* (4 a year).
Members Full (124) in 36 countries and territories:
Argentina, Australia, Austria, Bahrain, Belgium, Brazil, Canada, Czechia, Denmark, Finland, France, Germany, Greece, India, Indonesia, Ireland, Italy, Japan, Korea Rep, Kuwait, Malaysia, Mexico, Netherlands, Norway, Poland, Portugal, Saudi Arabia, Slovenia, Spain, Sweden, Switzerland, Taiwan, Türkiye, UK, USA, Venezuela.
Associate (48) in 22 countries and territories:
Australia, Belgium, Bermuda, Brazil, Canada, Finland, France, Germany, India, Italy, Japan, Korea Rep, Luxembourg, Netherlands, Saudi Arabia, Spain, Sweden, Switzerland, Taiwan, Thailand, UK, USA. [2020/XF0153/j/**F**]

- ♦ Institute for International and Foreign Trade Law / see International Law Institute, Washington DC
- ♦ Institute for International Government / see World Policy Institute
- ♦ Institute of International Harmonization for Building and Housing (internationally oriented national body)
- ♦ Institute for International Health and Development, Edinburgh / see Institute for Global Health and Development, Edinburgh
- ♦ Institute of International Humanitarian Affairs (internationally oriented national body)
- ♦ Institute of International Integration and Industrial Economics (internationally oriented national body)
- ♦ Institute for International Integration Studies (internationally oriented national body)

♦ Institute of International Law 11276

Institut de Droit international (IDI)

Secretariat c/o IHEID, Chemin Eugène-Rigot 2, CP 1672, 1211 Geneva 21, Switzerland. T. +41229084407.
URL: http://www.idi-iil.org/

History 11 Sep 1873, Ghent (Belgium). Revised statutes adopted; 2 Apr 1910 Paris (France); amended 1913 Oxford (UK), 1947 Lausanne, 1961 Salzburg, 1971 Zagreb (Yugoslavia), 1977 Oslo (Norway), 1993 Milan (Italy), 1995 Lisbon (Portugal), 2005 Krakow (Poland), 2007 Santiago (Chile), 2009 Naples (Italy). Received Nobel Peace Prize in 1904. **Aims** Promote the progress of international law by: striving to formulate the general principles of this law, lending its cooperation in the gradual and progressive codification of international law; issuing reasoned legal opinions in doubtful or controversial cases; implement, through various means, the principles of *justice* and *humanity*. **Structure** Bureau; Members and Associates (with a maximum of 132). **Languages** English, French. **Finance** Sources: members' dues. The assets of the Institute are kept in the form of a trust fund, *Fondation auxiliaire de l'IDI*, Basel (Switzerland). **Activities** Awards/prizes/competitions; events/meetings. **Events** *Biennial Plenary Session* Geneva (Switzerland) 2021, *Biennial Plenary Session* The Hague (Netherlands) 2019, *Biennial Plenary Session* Hyderabad (India) 2017, *Biennial Plenary Session* Tallinn (Estonia) 2015, *Biennial Plenary Session* Tokyo (Japan) 2013. **Publications** *Annuaire de l'Institut de droit international* – 78 vols to date. *Tableau des résolutions adoptées 1957-1991* (1992); *Livre du centenaire (1873-1973)* (1973); *Tableau général des résolutions de l'Institut de droit international (1873-1956)* (1957).
Members Titular and Associate in 61 countries:
Algeria, Argentina, Australia, Austria, Belgium, Bosnia-Herzegovina, Bulgaria, Burundi, Cameroon, Canada, Chile, China, Colombia, Croatia, Cyprus, Czechia, Egypt, Estonia, Finland, France, Germany, Ghana, Greece, Hungary, India, Indonesia, Iran Islamic Rep, Israel, Italy, Japan, Korea Rep, Lebanon, Madagascar, Mexico, Morocco, Nepal, Netherlands, New Zealand, Nigeria, Norway, Peru, Philippines, Poland, Portugal, Romania, Russia, Senegal, Sierra Leone, Slovakia, Somalia, South Africa, Spain, Sri Lanka, Sweden, Switzerland, Tanzania UR, Thailand, Tunisia, UK, Uruguay, USA.
Consultative Status Consultative status granted from: *ECOSOC (#05331)* (General); *International Civil Aviation Organization (ICAO, #12581)*. **IGO Relations** *The Hague Conference on Private International Law (HCCH, #10850)*. [2022.06.15/XC1032/j/**C**]

- ♦ Institute of International Law and International Relations, Graz (internationally oriented national body)
- ♦ Institute for International Law and Justice (internationally oriented national body)
- ♦ Institute of International Law, Kiel / see Walther-Schücking-Institute for International Law
- ♦ Institute for International Law of Peace and Armed Conflict, Bochum (internationally oriented national body)
- ♦ Institute of International Legal Studies, Quezon City (internationally oriented national body)
- ♦ Institute of International Management, MBA University / see European University, Belgrade
- ♦ Institute of International Maritime Affairs (internationally oriented national body)
- ♦ Institute for International Mediation and Conflict Resolution (internationally oriented national body)

Institute International Medical
11276

alphabetic sequence excludes
For the complete listing, see Yearbook Online at

♦ Institute for International Medical Education (internationally oriented national body)
♦ Institute for International Order / see World Policy Institute
♦ Institute of International Peace Leaders (internationally oriented national body)
♦ Institute of International Peace Research, Hiroshima / see Hiroshima Peace Institute
♦ Institute for International Policy Studies, Tokyo (internationally oriented national body)
♦ Institute for International Policy, Washington DC / see Center for International Policy
♦ Institute of International Politics and Economics, Belgrade (internationally oriented national body)
♦ Institute of International Public Law and International Relations of Thessaloniki (internationally oriented national body)
♦ Institute of International Relations / see Institute of International Relations and Political Sciences, Vilnius
♦ Institute of International Relations / see China Institute of International Studies
♦ Institute of International Relations and Area Studies, Kyoto (internationally oriented national body)
♦ Institute of International Relations, Beijing (internationally oriented national body)
♦ Institute of International Relations, Chengchi University (internationally oriented national body)
♦ Institute for International Relations, Hamburg (internationally oriented national body)
♦ Institute for International Relations, Hanoi / see Diplomatic Academy of Vietnam
♦ Institute of International Relations, Kiev (internationally oriented national body)
♦ Institute of International Relations and Policy / see Burkle Center for International Relations
♦ Institute of International Relations and Political Sciences, Vilnius (internationally oriented national body)
♦ Institute of International Relations, Prague (internationally oriented national body)
♦ Institute for International Relations, Sofia (internationally oriented national body)
♦ Institute of International Relations, St Augustine (internationally oriented national body)
♦ Institute of International Relations, Taipei (internationally oriented national body)
♦ Institute for International Relations, Zagreb / see Institute for Development and International Relations
♦ Institute for International Scientific and Technological Cooperation (internationally oriented national body)
♦ Institute for International Security and Conflict Resolution (internationally oriented national body)
♦ Institute of International Social Cooperation (#11237)
♦ Institute of International Sociology, Gorizia (internationally oriented national body)
♦ Institute of International and Strategic Studies, Albania (internationally oriented national body)
♦ Institute of International Studies, Berkeley CA (internationally oriented national body)
♦ Institute for International Studies of Communication in Environmental Matters / see Académie d'environnement d'expression francophone, philosophique et scientifique
♦ Institute for International Studies in Education, Pittsburgh PA (internationally oriented national body)
♦ Institute of International Studies, Joplin MO (internationally oriented national body)
♦ Institute of International Studies, Lima (internationally oriented national body)
♦ Institute of International Studies, Minneapolis / see Institute for Global Studies, Minneapolis
♦ Institute for International Studies of Natural Family Planning / see Institute for Reproductive Health
♦ Institute for International Studies, Notre Dame / see Helen Kellogg Institute for International Studies
♦ Institute of International Studies, Peoria (internationally oriented national body)
♦ Institute for International Studies, Stanford / see Freeman Spogli Institute for International Studies
♦ Institute for International Studies and Training / see Center for International Economic Collaboration
♦ Institute of International Studies of the University of Chile (internationally oriented national body)
♦ Institute for International Studies, Warsaw (internationally oriented national body)
♦ Institute of International Studies, Wroclaw (internationally oriented national body)
♦ Institute for International Trade (internationally oriented national body)
♦ Institute of International Trade and Development (internationally oriented national body)
♦ Institute for International Urban Development (internationally oriented national body)
♦ Institute for International Women's Rights – Manitoba (internationally oriented national body)
♦ Institute for Interreligious, Intercultural Dialogue / see Dialogue Institute
♦ Institute of Island Studies (internationally oriented national body)
♦ Institute of Jewish Affairs / see Institute for Jewish Policy Research
♦ Institute for Jewish Policy Research (internationally oriented national body)
♦ Institute for Justice and Peacebuilding / see Center for Justice and Peacebuilding
♦ Institute of Labor Economics (unconfirmed)
♦ Institute of Labour Law and Industrial Relations in the European Community / see Institut für Arbeitsrecht und Arbeitsbeziehungen in der Europäischen Union
♦ Institute for Labour Law and Industrial Relations in the European Union (internationally oriented national body)
♦ Institute of Latin America of the Academy of Sciences of the USSR / see Institute of Latin America of the Russian Academy of Sciences
♦ Institute of Latin American and Iberian Studies, New York / see Institute of Latin American Studies, New York
♦ Institute of Latin American Studies, Austin / see Teresa Lozano Long Institute of Latin American Studies, Austin
♦ Institute of Latin American Studies, Bundoora (internationally oriented national body)
♦ Institute of Latin American Studies, Chapel Hill NC (internationally oriented national body)
♦ Institute for Latin American Studies, Costa Rica (internationally oriented national body)
♦ Institute for Latin American Studies, Freie Universität Berlin (internationally oriented national body)
♦ Institute of Latin American Studies, Hamburg (internationally oriented national body)
♦ Institute of Latin American Studies, Milan (internationally oriented national body)
♦ Institute of Latin American Studies, New York (internationally oriented national body)
♦ Institute of Latin American Studies, Stockholm / see Nordic Institute of Latin American Studies
♦ Institute of Latin America of the Russian Academy of Sciences (internationally oriented national body)
♦ Institute for Law and Peace, London (internationally oriented national body)
♦ Institute for Legal Studies on the International Community of the National Research Council, Rome (internationally oriented national body)

♦ Institute for Liquid Atomisation and Spray Systems – Europe (ILASS-Europe) 11277

Chair c/o LITEC, Maria de Luna 10, 50018 Saragossa, Spain.
URL: http://ilasseurope.org/

History 1983, within *Institute for Liquid Atomization and Spray Systems (ILASS International, #11278)*. Registered in accordance with Italian law. **Aims** Promote the science and application of liquid atomization and spray systems. **Structure** Assembly (annual); Committee: Officers. **Languages** English. **Staff** None. **Finance** Members' dues. **Activities** Events/meetings; awards/prizes/competitions. **Events** *European Conference on Liquid Atomization and Spray Systems* Venice (Italy) 2023, *European Conference on Liquid Atomization and Spray Systems* 2022, *European Conference on Liquid Atomization and Spray Systems* Tel Aviv (Israel) 2020, *Annual Conference* Paris (France) 2019, *Annual Conference* Valencia (Spain) 2017. **Publications** *ILASS Europe Newsletter* (2-3 a year). [2020/XE2904/j/E]

♦ Institute for Liquid Atomization and Spray Systems (ILASS International) 11278

Pres UCI Combustion Laboratory, Univ of California, Irvine CA 92697-3550, USA. T. +19498245950 ext121.
Vice-Pres Universität Bremen, Fachgebiet Verfahrenstechnik, Badgasteiner Str 3, 28359 Bremen, Germany. T. +494212183663. Fax +494212187011. E-mail: ufri@iwt.uni-bremen.de.
URL: http://www.ilass.org/

History Previously also referred to as *International Council of Institutes for Liquid Atomization and Spray Systems (ICLASS International)*. **Aims** Promote research and development and education in the field of atomization and sprays. **Structure** Includes: *Institute for Liquid Atomization and Spray Systems – Asia (ILASS-Asia, #11279)*; *Institute for Liquid Atomisation and Spray Systems – Europe (ILASS-Europe, #11277)*; *Institute for Liquid Atomization and Spray Systems, North and South America (ILASS-Americas)*. **Languages** English. **Events** *International Conference on Liquid Atomization and Spray Systems* Shanghai (China) 2024, *International Conference on Liquid Atomization and Spray Systems* Edinburgh (UK) 2021, *International Conference on Liquid Atomization and Spray Systems* Chicago, IL (USA) 2018, *Korea Workshop* Hongcheon (Korea Rep) 2018, *Conference* Jeju (Korea Rep) 2018. **Publications** *Atomization and Sprays* – journal. Conference proceedings. [2019/XD8104/F]

♦ Institute for Liquid Atomization and Spray Systems – Asia (ILASS-Asia) 11279

Contact address not obtained. E-mail: ilassasia@ilassasia.org.
URL: http://ilassasia.org/

History 1991. Founded within *Institute for Liquid Atomization and Spray Systems (ILASS International, #11278)*. **Aims** Promote science and technology of liquid atomization and spray systems in the region. **Activities** Awards/prizes/competitions; events/meetings. **Events** *Annual Conference* Jeju (Korea Rep) 2023, *Annual Conference* Indore (India) 2022, *Annual Conference* ZhenJiang (China) 2020, *Annual Conference* Ube City (Japan) 2019, *Annual Conference* Jeju (Korea Rep) 2017. **Publications** Proceedings of conferences.
Members in 4 countries:
China, Japan, Korea Rep, Taiwan.
NGO Relations *Institute for Liquid Atomization and Spray Systems, North and South America (ILASS-Americas)*; *Institute for Liquid Atomisation and Spray Systems – Europe (ILASS-Europe, #11277)*. [2023/XG8503/j/E]

♦ Institute for Liquid Atomization and Spray Systems, North and South America (internationally oriented national body)
♦ Institute of London Underwriters / see International Underwriting Association (#15748)
♦ Institute of Malaysian and International Studies (internationally oriented national body)
♦ The Institute of Management Sciences / see Institute for Operations Research and the Management Sciences (#11286)
♦ Institute of Management Specialists (internationally oriented national body)
♦ Institute on Man and Science / see Rensselaerville Institute
♦ The Institute of Manufacturing (internationally oriented national body)
♦ Institute for Marine and Antarctic Studies (internationally oriented national body)

♦ Institute of Marine Engineering, Science and Technology (IMarEST) 11280

Chief Executive 1 Birdcage Walk, London, SW1H 9JJ, UK. T. +442073822600. E-mail: marketing@imarest.org.
URL: http://www.imarest.org/

History 1889, London (UK). Former names and other names: *Institute of Marine Engineers (IMarE)* – former. Registration: Royal Charter, Start date: 1933, UK; UK Registered Charity, No/ID: 212992, England and Wales. **Aims** Work with the global marine community to promote scientific development of marine engineering, science and technology; provide opportunities for exchange of ideas and practices; uphold the status, standards and expertise of marine professionals worldwide. **Structure** Board of Trustees; Council; Executive; Membership Committee; Professional Affairs and Education Committee; Proceedings Supervisory Board; Technical Leadership Board; Offices: Asia-Pacific, China, Europe. **Activities** Events/meetings; guidance/assistance/consulting. **Events** *International Naval Engineering Conference* London (UK) 2020, *Seminar on Advanced Hull Integrity Management Systems to Reduce Technical Operation Costs* Singapore (Singapore) 2020, *Seminar on Prediction and Analysis of Ship Performance and Fuel Efficiency with a Proper Selection of Foulin Control Coatings* Singapore (Singapore) 2020, *Technical Seminar on Hydrogen as a Source of Power for Marine Applications* Singapore (Singapore) 2020, *Tropical Storms – Risks And Costs In Offshore Operations* Singapore (Singapore) 2020. **Publications** *Journal of Marine Engineering and Technology (JMET)*; *Journal of Operational Oceanography (JOO)*; *Marine Professional*. Transactions of the IMarEST. **Members** Marine engineers, scientists and technologists (about 22,000), in over 120 countries. Membership countries not specified. **Consultative Status** Consultative status granted from: *ECOSOC (#05331)* (Ros C); *International Maritime Organization (IMO, #14102)*. **IGO Relations** Observer status with (3): *Intergovernmental Oceanographic Commission (IOC, #11496)*; *Intergovernmental Panel on Climate Change (IPCC, #11499)*; *International Hydrographic Organization (IHO, #13825)*. **NGO Relations** Affiliation agreements with similar national bodies in: Brazil, USA. [2023.02.16/XN3554/jv/D]

♦ Institute of Marine Engineers / see Institute of Marine Engineering, Science and Technology (#11280)
♦ Institute of Maritime and Tropical Medicine, Gdynia (internationally oriented national body)
♦ Institute of Marketing and Management (internationally oriented national body)

♦ Institute of Masters of Wine (IMW) 11281

Office Coordinator 6 Riverlight Quay, Kirtling Street, London, SW11 8EA, UK. T. +442073839130. E-mail: info@mastersofwine.org.
Exec Dir address not obtained.
URL: https://www.mastersofwine.org/

History 1953, UK. **Aims** Promote excellence, interaction and learning across all sectors of the global wine community. **Activities** Events/meetings; training/education. **Events** *International Symposium* Wiesbaden (Germany) 2023, *International Symposium* Adelaide, SA (Australia) 2022, *International Symposium* Logroño (Spain) 2018, *International Symposium* Florence (Italy) 2014, *International Symposium* Bordeaux (France) 2010.
Members Masters of Wine in 27 countries and territories:
Argentina, Australia, Austria, Belgium, Canada, China, Croatia, Egypt, Finland, France, Germany, Greece, Hong Kong, Hungary, India, Indonesia, Ireland, Israel, Japan, Netherlands, New Zealand, Singapore, South Africa, Sweden, Switzerland, UK, USA. [2022/AA0481/v/C]

♦ Institute of Materials Engineering, Australasia (internationally oriented national body)

♦ Institute of Mathematical Statistics (IMS) 11282

Institut de statistiques mathématiques

Exec Sec PO Box 22718, Beachwood OH 44122, USA. T. +12162952340. Fax +12162955661. E-mail: erg@imstat.org – ims@imstat.org.
URL: http://www.imstat.org/

History 12 Sep 1935, Ann Arbor MI (USA). **Aims** Encourage the development, dissemination and application of mathematical statistics and probability theory. **Structure** General Meeting (annual). Council of 15 members elected for 3-year term. **Languages** English. **Staff** 1.50 FTE, paid. **Finance** Sources: members' dues; sale of publications. **Events** *International Conference on Statistics and Data Science (ICSDS)* Florence (Italy) 2022, *Annual General Meeting* Seattle, WA (USA) 2021, *Annual General Meeting* Seoul (Korea Rep) 2021, *Annual General Meeting* Seoul (Korea Rep) 2020, *Annual General Meeting* Denver, CO (USA) 2019. **Publications** *Annals of Statistics* (6 a year); *IMS Bulletin* (6 a year); *Annals of Applied Probability* (4 a year); *Annals of Probability* (4 a year); *Statistical Science* (4 a year).
Members Individuals (3,300); Fellows (800), in 113 countries and territories:
Albania, Algeria, Andorra, Angola, Argentina, Armenia, Australia, Austria, Azerbaijan, Bahamas, Bahrain, Bangladesh, Barbados, Belarus, Belgium, Bosnia-Herzegovina, Botswana, Brazil, Brunei Darussalam, Bulgaria, Burkina Faso, Cameroon, Canada, Chile, China, Colombia, Congo DR, Côte d'Ivoire, Croatia, Cuba, Cyprus, Czechia, Denmark, Ecuador, Egypt, El Salvador, Estonia, Finland, France, Georgia, Germany, Greece, Guyana, Hong Kong, Hungary, Iceland, India, Indonesia, Iran Islamic Rep, Iraq, Ireland, Israel, Italy, Jamaica, Japan, Jordan, Kazakhstan, Kenya, Korea Rep, Kuwait, Kyrgyzstan, Latvia, Lithuania, Madagascar, Malawi, Malaysia, Malta, Mauritius, Mexico, Moldova, Morocco, Nepal, Netherlands, New Zealand, Nigeria, North Macedonia, Norway, Oman, Pakistan, Peru, Philippines, Poland, Portugal, Romania, Russia, Rwanda, Saudi Arabia, Senegal, Serbia-Montenegro, Singapore, Slovenia, South Africa, Spain, Sri Lanka, Sweden, Switzerland, Taiwan, Tajikistan, Tanzania UR, Thailand, Trinidad-Tobago, Tunisia, Türkiye, Turkmenistan, UK, Ukraine, Uruguay, USA, Uzbekistan, Venezuela, Vietnam, Zambia, Zimbabwe.
NGO Relations Affiliated with: *International Statistical Institute (ISI, #15603)*. [2019/XE1034/jv/B]

♦ Institute Max von Laue – Paul Langevin (ILL) 11283

Institut Max von Laue – Paul Langevin

Head Communication Unit 71 av des Martyrs, CS 20156, 38042 Grenoble CEDEX 9, France. T. +33476207179. Fax +33476483906. E-mail: cico@ill.eu – communication@ill.eu – welcome@ill.eu.

Dir address not obtained.
URL: http://www.ill.eu/

History Established Jan 1967, Grenoble (France), with the signature of an intergovernmental convention between France and the Federal Republic of Germany. The United Kingdom joined as third Associate partner on 1 Jan 1973. Spain acceded to 'Scientific Membership' on 1 Jan 1987, Switzerland became a Scientific Member in May 1988, Austria in Apr 1990, Italy in 1996, Czech Rep in 1999, Sweden in 2005 and Hungary and Belgium in 2006, Denmark and Slovakia in 2009, and India in 2011. Also referred to as *Institut Laue – Langevin (ILL)*. Registered in accordance with French law. Intergovernmental Convention between France, Germany and UK has been extended for another 10 years until 31 Dec 2023. **Aims** Provide scientists with a very high flux of neutrons feeding some 40 state-of-the-art instruments which are constantly being developed and upgraded; make facilities and expertise available to visiting scientists. **Structure** Steering Committee; Scientific Council. Associate countries (3) are represented by 4 Associates (2 for France, 1 for Germany and 1 for UK). **Languages** English, French, German. **Staff** 500.00 FTE, paid. **Finance** Annual budget: about euro 100,000,000. **Activities** Research and development; knowledge management/information dissemination; events/meetings. **Events** *Joint workshop on surfaces* Grenoble (France) 1993, *Workshop on neutrons and X-rays in the study of magnetism* Grenoble (France) 1993, *Workshop on quasicrystals* Grenoble (France) 1993, *Workshop on the dynamics of disordered materials* Grenoble (France) 1993, *Workshop on applications of high resolution gamma-spectroscopy in studies of atomic collisions and nuclear lifetimes* Grenoble (France) 1992. **Publications** *ILL Newsletter* (4 a year); *Science in School* (4 a year). Annual Report; peer-reviewed scientific publications.

Members National scientific organizations of 13 countries:
Austria, Belgium, Czechia, Denmark, France, Germany, Italy, Poland, Slovakia, Spain, Sweden, Switzerland, UK.

IGO Relations Links with other partners of EIROforum: *European Consortium for the Development of Fusion Energy (EUROfusion, #06753)*; *European Molecular Biology Laboratory (EMBL, #07813)*; *European Organization for Nuclear Research (CERN, #08108)*; *European Organization for Astronomical Research in the Southern hemisphere (ESO, #08106)*; *European Space Agency (ESA, #08798)*; *European Synchrotron Radiation Facility (ESRF, #08868)*; *European X-Ray Free-Electron Laser Facility (European XFEL, #09127)*. **NGO Relations** Member of: *EIROforum (#05401)*. [2019.12.11/XF4747/j/**E***]

- ♦ Institute of Mediterranean Forest Ecosystems and Forest Products Technology (internationally oriented national body)
- ♦ Institute for Mediterranean Studies (internationally oriented national body)
- ♦ Institute of Metals and Materials Australasia / see Institute of Materials Engineering, Australasia
- ♦ Institute for Middle Eastern and Islamic Studies, Durham (internationally oriented national body)
- ♦ Institute for Migration Research and Intercultural Studies (internationally oriented national body)
- ♦ Institute for Millimetre Radio Astronomy (#11353)
- ♦ Institute for Multi-Track Diplomacy (internationally oriented national body)
- ♦ Institute of Municipal Engineering of Southern Africa (internationally oriented national body)
- ♦ Institute for Natural Resources in Africa / see UNU Institute for Natural Resources in Africa (#20718)
- ♦ Institute of Near Eastern and African Studies (internationally oriented national body)
- ♦ Institute of Nepal and Asian Studies / see Centre for Nepal and Asian Studies
- ♦ Institute of Nepal Studies / see Centre for Nepal and Asian Studies
- ♦ Institut de l'énergie et de l'environnement de la francophonie / see Institut de la Francophonie pour le développement durable (#11305)
- ♦ Institute for New Economic Thinking (unconfirmed)

♦ Institute of Noetic Sciences (IONS) 11284

CEO 101 San Antonio Rd, Petaluma CA 94952, USA. T. +17077753500. Fax +17077817420. E-mail: membership@noetic.org.
URL: http://www.noetic.org/

History 1973, by Apollo 14 astronaut Edgar D Mitchell. **Aims** Support individuals to learn, grow and evolve so that the *collective consciousness* of our planet can be transformed to create a better future for all. **Structure** Board of Directors, consisting of Founder, Chair, Vice-Chair, President, Secretary, Treasurer, 15 regular members and 2 ex-officio members representing the Stewardship Council. **Staff** Over 30 full- and part-time; voluntary. **Finance** Members' dues (annual): 10 categories, dues ranging from US$ 35 to US$ 50,000 and above. **Activities** Provides seed grants for leading-edge scientific and scholarly research; organizes lectures and sponsors conferences, workshops and study groups. Publishing activity. Programmes: *'Research'* – Extended Human Capacities, Integral Health and Healing and Emerging World Views; *'Education'* – engages the public, organizes biennial international conference and sponsors transformative retreats, workshops and lectures; *'Community Groups'* – supports 280 groups worldwide, including designing and implementation of programmes; *'Temple Awards for Creative Altruism'*; *'IONS Travel Programme'*. **Events** *Quest for global healing conference* Ubud (Indonesia) 2006, *International conference on science and consciousness* Albuquerque, NM (USA) 2001, *International conference* Palm Springs, CA (USA) 2001, *International conference* Los Angeles, CA (USA) 2000, *International Conference* St Louis, MO (USA) 2000. **Publications** *iConnect* (12 a year) – electronic newsletter; *SHIFT: At the Frontiers of Consciousness* (4 a year) – journal. **Information Services** *Noetic Café* – online discussion forum.

Members As of Jul 2004 individuals (25,693, mainly in the USA) in 55 countries and territories:
Argentina, Australia, Austria, Bahamas, Belgium, Brazil, Canada, China, Croatia, Cyprus, Czechia, Denmark, Fiji, Finland, France, Germany, Greece, Guatemala, Hong Kong, Hungary, India, Indonesia, Ireland, Israel, Italy, Japan, Kenya, Korea Rep, Liechtenstein, Mexico, Mozambique, Netherlands, New Zealand, Nicaragua, Nigeria, Norway, Philippines, Portugal, Russia, Singapore, South Africa, Spain, Sweden, Switzerland, Taiwan, Tanzania UR, Thailand, Trinidad-Tobago, Türkiye, UK, Ukraine, United Arab Emirates, USA, Venezuela.

NGO Relations Affiliate: *Intuition Network (IN)*. [2010/XF1554/jv/**F**]

- ♦ Institute of North American Studies (internationally oriented national body)
- ♦ Institut für Entwicklung und Frieden, Duisburg (internationally oriented national body)
- ♦ Institut für Entwicklungsforschung und Entwicklungspolitik (internationally oriented national body)

♦ Institute of Nutrition of Central America and Panama (INCAP) 11285

Institut de nutrition de l'Amérique centrale et de Panama – Instituto de Nutrición de Centro América y Panama

Dir Calzada Roosevelt 6-25, Zona 11, Apartado Postal 1188, 01011 Guatemala, Guatemala. T. +50223157900. Fax +50224736529. E-mail: e-mail@incap.int.
URL: http://www.incap.int/

History 16 Sep 1949. 1Established on official inauguration as a technical regional organization, on modification of an agreement signed 20 Feb 1946, by representatives of the governments of Costa Rica, El Salvador, Guatemala, Honduras, Nicaragua and Panama, and of *Pan American Sanitary Bureau (PASB, #18129)*, executive body of *Pan American Health Organization (PAHO, #18108)*. Permanent Agreement signed 17 Dec 1953. Belize became a member in 1991; Dominican Rep in 2006. Part of *Central American Integration System (#03671)*. **Aims** Promote nutrition and *food security* in member countries, with a culture based on important motivations, strongly collective, with leadership, dynamism, managerial capacity and scientific and technical excellence developed through its basic functions of research, information and communication, technical assistance, formation and human resources development and mobilization of resources. **Structure** Directing Council; Advisory Council; Director; Technical Units; Technical Representatives; Institutional Ethics Committee (IEC). **Languages** English, Spanish. **Staff** 67 professional staff; 108 technical and service personnel. **Finance** Sources: contributions of member/participating states; donations; fees for services; revenue from activities/projects. Supported by: Central American and Dominican Republic Member States. Annual budget: 1,764,000 USD. **Activities** Knowledge management/information dissemination; projects/programmes; research and development; training/education. **Events** *Seminar* Guatemala (Guatemala) 2021, *Seminar* Guatemala (Guatemala) 2021, *Seminar* Guatemala (Guatemala) 2021, *Meeting* 1999. **Publications** Annual Report; scientific articles – in English, Spanish; education leaflets; technical notes; monographs; various other documents. **Information Services** *Virtual Library in Food and Nutrition Security*.

Members Governments of 8 countries:
Belize, Costa Rica, Dominican Rep, El Salvador, Guatemala, Honduras, Nicaragua, Panama.

IGO Relations Observer status with (1): *Codex Alimentarius Commission (CAC, #04081)*. **NGO Relations** Memorandum of Understanding with (3): *Iodine Global Network (IGN, #16004)*; national institutes; universities. [2021.09.27/XD1035/j/**E***]

- ♦ Institut de l'environment durable (inactive)
- ♦ Institut de l'Environnement et de la Sécurité Humaine de l'Université des Nations Unies (#20645)
- ♦ Institute for Ocean Conservation Science (internationally oriented national body)
- ♦ Institute for the Officialization of Esperanto (inactive)

♦ Institute for Operations Research and the Management Sciences (INFORMS) 11286

Headquarters 5521 Research Park Dr, Ste 200, Catonsville MD 21228, USA. T. +14437573500. E-mail: informs@informs.org.
URL: http://www.informs.org/

History 1 Dec 1953, New York NY (USA), as *The Institute of Management Sciences (TIMS) – Institut des sciences de gestion*, by 69 charter members. Incorporated under the laws of the State of California (USA) as a not-for-profit corporation, 2 Sep 1954. Present name adopted 1 Jan 1995, on merger with the Operations Research Society of America. **Aims** Improve operational processes, *decision-making* and management through application of methods from science and *mathematics*. **Structure** Board of Directors, comprising President, President-elect, Secretary, Treasurer, Past-President, 10 Vice-Presidents (Chapters/Fora; Education; Marketing, Communication and Outreach; Information Technology; International Activities; Meetings; Membership and Professional Recognition; Practice Activities; Publications; Sections/Societies) and Executive Director. Departments (11): Executive; Board Services; Human Resources; Finances/Accounting; Member Services; Information Technology; Marketing; Meeting Services; Publications; Public Relations; Subdivisions. **Languages** English. **Staff** 43.00 FTE, paid. **Finance** Members' dues. Other sources: Sale of publications; meeting proceeds. Budget: US$ 8.6 million. **Activities** Organizes: international meetings; research symposia; management science roundtables. Makes awards. **Events** *Annual Conference on Business Analytics and Operations Research* Aurora, CO (USA) 2023, *Annual Meeting* Phoenix, AZ (USA) 2023, *Annual Conference on Business Analytics and Operations Research* Houston, TX (USA) 2022, *Annual Meeting* Indianapolis, IN (USA) 2022, *Annual Meeting* Anaheim, CA (USA) 2021. **Publications** *Management Science* (12 a year) – journal; *Interfaces* (6 a year) – journal; *Marketing Science* (6 a year) – journal; *Operations Research* (6 a year) – journal; *Organization Science* (6 a year) – journal; *OR/MS Today* (6 a year) – magazine; *Decision Analysis* (4 a year) – journal; *Information Systems Research* (4 a year) – journal; *Informs Journal on Computing* (4 a year); *Manufacturing and Service Operations Management* (4 a year) – journal; *Mathematics of Operations Research* (4 a year) – journal; *Transportation Science* (4 a year) – journal; *Informs Transactions on Education* (periodical) – electronic journal; *PubsOnLine Suite* (54 a year) – electronic updates of 10 online journals.

Members Full members: practitioners, academics, business and industrial executives; Student members: full-time students. Members (10,500) in 91 countries and territories:
Argentina, Australia, Austria, Bangladesh, Belgium, Bolivia, Brazil, Burundi, Canada, Chile, China, Colombia, Congo Brazzaville, Costa Rica, Cyprus, Czechia, Denmark, Dominica, Dominican Rep, Ecuador, Egypt, El Salvador, Eswatini, Fiji, Finland, France, Germany, Ghana, Greece, Guyana, Honduras, Hong Kong, Hungary, Iceland, India, Indonesia, Iran Islamic Rep, Iraq, Ireland, Israel, Italy, Japan, Jordan, Kenya, Korea Rep, Kuwait, Lebanon, Luxembourg, Malawi, Malaysia, Mauritius, Mexico, Monaco, Morocco, Netherlands, New Zealand, Niger, Nigeria, Norway, Pakistan, Panama, Peru, Philippines, Poland, Portugal, Qatar, Russia, Rwanda, Saudi Arabia, Senegal, Serbia, Singapore, Slovakia, South Africa, Spain, Sri Lanka, Sudan, Sweden, Switzerland, Taiwan, Thailand, Trinidad-Tobago, Tunisia, Türkiye, Uganda, UK, United Arab Emirates, Uruguay, USA, Venezuela, Zambia.

NGO Relations Member of: *International Federation of Operational Research Societies (IFORS, #13493)*. Associate member of: *Association of European Operational Research Societies (EURO, #02528)*. [2020/XB1033/jv/**F**]

- ♦ Institute of Oriental Languages / see Institute of Asian and African Studies, Moscow State University
- ♦ Institute of Our Lady of Life (religious order)
- ♦ Institute of Our Lady of Mercy (religious order)
- ♦ Institute for Palestine Studies (internationally oriented national body)
- ♦ Institute of Peace and Conflicts, Granada (internationally oriented national body)
- ♦ Institute of Peace and Conflict Studies (internationally oriented national body)
- ♦ Institute of Peace and Conflict Studies, Waterloo ON (internationally oriented national body)
- ♦ Institute for Peace, Development and Integration (internationally oriented national body)
- ♦ Institute for Peace Research and Documentation (internationally oriented national body)
- ♦ Institute for Peace Research and Security Policy, Hamburg (internationally oriented national body)
- ♦ Institute for Peace Science, Hiroshima University / see Hiroshima Peace Institute
- ♦ Institute for Peace Work and Nonviolent Settlement of Conflict (internationally oriented national body)
- ♦ Institute of Physics and Engineering in Medicine (internationally oriented national body)

♦ Institute for Planetary Synthesis (IPS) 11287

Institut pour une synthèse planétaire – Instituto para la Sintesis Planetaria – Instituto para a Sintese Planetaria – Institut für Planetarische Synthese

SG Chemin de l'Etang 37, 1219 Châtelaine, Switzerland. T. +41227338876. E-mail: ipsbox@ipsgeneva.com.
URL: http://www.ipsgeneva.com/

History 19 May 1981, Geneva (Switzerland). **Aims** Reawaken an awareness of *spiritual* values in daily life; promote planetary awareness which leads to planetary citizenship; analyse and help solve world problems on the basis of spiritual values and planetary awareness. **Structure** General Assembly (every 3 years), always in Geneva (Switzerland); Executive Committee; Consultative Committee; Arbitration Tribunal. Includes: *'Maitreya Project: Fund for the Preparation of the Reappearance of the Christ'*, since 24 Dec 1988. **Languages** English, French, German, Portuguese, Russian, Spanish. **Staff** 3.00 FTE, voluntary. **Finance** Sources: donations. Annual budget: 10,000 CHF. **Activities** Events/meetings; guidance/assistance/consulting; knowledge management/information dissemination; training/education. **Events** *General Assembly* Geneva (Switzerland) 2023, *General Assembly* 2020, *General assembly* Geneva (Switzerland) 2017, *General Assembly* Geneva (Switzerland) 2008, *General Assembly* Geneva (Switzerland) 2005. **Information Services** *Ten Seed Group* – Geneva (Switzerland).

Members Individuals or groups in 63 countries:
Algeria, Angola, Argentina, Australia, Austria, Bangladesh, Belarus, Belgium, Bolivia, Brazil, Bulgaria, Chile, Colombia, Congo Brazzaville, Congo DR, Costa Rica, Côte d'Ivoire, Croatia, Czechia, Denmark, Estonia, Finland, France, Gambia, Germany, Ghana, Greece, Hungary, India, Indonesia, Ireland, Israel, Italy, Jordan, Kazakhstan, Kenya, Madagascar, Mali, Mexico, Moldova, Morocco, Namibia, Nepal, Netherlands, Nigeria, Pakistan, Philippines, Poland, Romania, Russia, Samoa, Sierra Leone, Slovenia, Spain, Sweden, Switzerland, Togo, Uganda, UK, Ukraine, USA, Uzbekistan, Zimbabwe.

Consultative Status Consultative status granted from: *ECOSOC (#05331)* (Ros A); *UNEP (#20299)*. **IGO Relations** Accredited by (4): *UNEP (#20299)*; *United Nations Office at Geneva (UNOG, #20597)*; *United Nations Office at Vienna (UNOV, #20604)*; *United Nations (UN, #20515)*. Involved in preparations for: *United Nations Conference on Environment and Development (UNCED) – Earth Summit* and *World Summit for Social Development*. **NGO Relations** Founding member of: *NGO Forum on Environment (FOE, #17125)*. Links with national organizations. [2022.10.19/XF0178/j/**F**]

- ♦ Institute for Policy Studies, Singapore (internationally oriented national body)
- ♦ Institute for Policy Studies, Washington DC (internationally oriented national body)
- ♦ Institute for Political and International Studies, Teheran (internationally oriented national body)
- ♦ Institute for Political Science, Innsbruck / see Department of Political Science, Innsbruck
- ♦ Institute of Political Science, Zurich (internationally oriented national body)
- ♦ Institute for Political Studies on Latin America and Africa (internationally oriented national body)
- ♦ Institute for Politics and International Studies (internationally oriented national body)
- ♦ Institute for Polynesian Studies / see Jonathan Napela Center for Hawaiian and Pacific Islands Studies
- ♦ Institute of Postcolonial Studies (internationally oriented national body)
- ♦ Institute for Poverty Alleviation and International Development (internationally oriented national body)
- ♦ Institute of Prado (religious order)
- ♦ Institute for the Preservation of Medical Traditions (internationally oriented national body)
- ♦ Institute for Printed Circuits / see IPC
- ♦ Institute for Private and Public International Law, International Commercial Arbitration and European Law / see TMC Asser Institute – Centre for International and European Law
- ♦ Institute for Productive Learning in Europe (internationally oriented national body)

♦ **Institute of Professional Representatives before the European Patent Office (epi)** 11288
Institut des mandataires agréés près l'Office européen des brevets – Institut der beim Europäischen Patentamt zugelassenen Vertreter
Gen Manager Bayerstrasse 83, 80335 Munich, Germany. T. +49892420520. Fax +4989242052220.
SG address not obtained. E-mail: secretarygeneral@patentepi.org.
URL: http://www.patentepi.org/
History 21 Oct 1977, Munich (Germany FR), according to Article 134, para 8 (b) *European Patent Convention*, by the Administrative Council of the European Patent Organization. 1st meeting of the Council: Apr 1978, Munich. Also referred to as *European Patent Institute*. **Aims** Collaborate with the European Patent Organization on matters relating to the patent *profession, intellectual property*, disciplinary matters and on European qualifying examination. **Structure** Council (meets twice a year); Board; Presidium; Committees; Secretariat. **Languages** English, French, German. **Staff** 13.00 FTE, paid. **Finance** Members' dues. **Activities** Knowledge management/information dissemination; training/education. **Events** *Half-Yearly Meeting* Lisbon (Portugal) 2019, *Half-Yearly Meeting* Helsinki (Finland) 2018, *Half-Yearly Meeting* Athens (Greece) 2016, *Half-Yearly Meeting* Berlin (Germany) 2016, *Half-yearly meeting* Prague (Czech Rep) 2013. **Publications** *epi Information* (4 a year) – journal. Brochures.
Members Individuals (about 12,800) in 38 countries:
Albania, Austria, Belgium, Bulgaria, Croatia, Cyprus, Czechia, Denmark, Estonia, Finland, France, Germany, Greece, Hungary, Iceland, Ireland, Italy, Latvia, Liechtenstein, Lithuania, Luxembourg, Malta, Monaco, Netherlands, North Macedonia, Norway, Poland, Portugal, Romania, San Marino, Serbia, Slovakia, Slovenia, Spain, Sweden, Switzerland, Türkiye, UK.
Consultative Status Consultative status granted from: *World Intellectual Property Organization (WIPO, #21593)* (Permanent Observer Status). **IGO Relations** Observer status at: Administrative Council of *European Patent Organisation (#08167)*; Select Committee of *European Commission (EC, #06633)*. **NGO Relations** Formal contacts with all types of organizations for the patent profession, including: American Intellectual Property Law Association (AIPLA); *ASEAN Patent Attorney Association (no recent information)*; *Asian Patent Attorneys Association (APAA, #01655)*; *Committee of National Institutes of Patent Agents (CNIPA, #04274)*; *European Federation of Agents of Industry in Industrial Property (#07042)*; *Fédération Internationale des Conseils en Propriété Intellectuelle (FICPI, #09624)*; *International Association for the Protection of Intellectual Property (#12112)*; *Union of European Practitioners in Intellectual Property (UNION, #20392)*.
[2020.01.29/XE2366/jtv/**E**]

♦ Institute for the Promotion and Support of Development (internationally oriented national body)

♦ **Institute for Psychohistory** 11289
Dir 140 Riverside Drive, New York NY 10024-2605, USA. T. +12127995207. Fax +12128730994. E-mail: psychhst@gmail.com – heinsusan@aol.com.
Aims Study the science of historical motivation. **Activities** Events/meetings. **Publications** *Journal of Psychohistory* (4 a year).
Members Branches in 13 countries:
Australia, Austria, Brazil, Canada, Finland, France, Germany, New Zealand, Nigeria, Romania, Switzerland, UK, USA.
NGO Relations Affiliated with: *International Psychohistorical Association (IPA)*. [2017.03.09/XM0284/j/**E**]

♦ Institute of Psychotraumatology and Mediation (unconfirmed)
♦ Institute for Public Administration and European Integration (internationally oriented national body)
♦ Institute of Public Health, Heidelberg / see Heidelberg Institute of Global Health
♦ Institute of Public International Law, Utrecht / see Utrecht Centre for International Legal Studies
♦ Institute of Public Service International, University of Connecticut / see Global Training and Development Institute

♦ **The Institute of Quarrying** 11290
Head Office National Stone Centre, Porter Lane, Wirksworth, Matlock, DE4 4LS, UK. T. +441159729995. E-mail: mail@quarrying.org.
URL: http://www.quarrying.org/
History 1917. Former names and other names: *Quarry Managers' Association* – former (1917 to 1927). **Aims** Promote education and training within the industry in order to encourage improvements in all aspects of quarry operation and business management, from the initial *extraction* to processing, marketing, restoration and after-use. **Structure** International Branches (5): Australia; Hong Kong; Malaysia; New Zealand; South Africa. **Activities** Advocacy/lobbying/activism; events/meetings; training/education. **Events** *Annual Conference* Gateshead (UK) 1995, *Quarrying – a customer focus* Sydney, NSW (Australia) 1994, *Quarrying and public accountability* Torquay (UK) 1994, *International symposium* Buxton (UK) 1993, *Asia Pacific conference* Hong Kong (Hong Kong) 1992. **Publications** *Quarry Management* (12 a year). **Members** Fellow; Member; Technical Member; Associate; Student. Individuals (about 6,000) in about 70 countries (mostly in UK). Membership countries not specified. [2022.10.21/XF5478/j/**F**]

♦ Institute of Race Relations (internationally oriented national body)
♦ Institute for Regional and International Studies, Sofia (internationally oriented national body)
♦ Institute for Regional and Local Studies / see Centre for European Regional and Local Studies
♦ Institute of Regional Studies, Islamabad (internationally oriented national body)
♦ Institute of Regional Studies, Seoul / see Institute of East Asian Regional Studies, Seoul
♦ Institute of the Regions of Europe (internationally oriented national body)
♦ Institute on Religion in an Age of Science (internationally oriented national body)
♦ Institute for Reproductive Health (internationally oriented national body)
♦ Institute of Research Against Counterfeit Medicines (internationally oriented national body)
♦ Institute for Research and Application of Development Methods (internationally oriented national body)
♦ Institute for Research and Debate on Governance (internationally oriented national body)

♦ **Institute for Research, Extension and Training in Agriculture (IRETA)** 11291
Dir USP, Fac of Business and Economics, Private Bag, Apia, Samoa. T. +68521882. Fax +68522372.
URL: http://www.usp.ac.fj/
History 1980, as an institute of the *University of the South Pacific (USP, #20703)*. **Aims** Contribute to sustainable growth and development of South Pacific countries by responding to their needs for research, information and training in the broad fields of agriculture and rural development. **Structure** Departments (4): Administration; Development Media; Information and Networking; Capacity Development. **Finance** Funded by: *European Community (inactive)*; *FAO (#09260)*; *Centre technique de coopération agricole et rurale (CTA, inactive)*; *United States Agency for International Development (USAID)*; USP. **Activities** Research; media development; information dissemination; capacity development. **Events** *Regional meeting on indigenous nuts in the Pacific* Port Vila (Vanuatu) 1994. **Publications** *IRETA's South Pacific Agricultural News (SPAN)* (12 a year) – newsletter; *Journal of South Pacific Agriculture (JOSPA)* (2 a year). Annual Report; annual research report; pamphlets; workshops proceedings; technical manuals; videos; video library catalogue. Information Services: Bibliographic database searches. IRETA Electronic Media Unit provides video, audio and USPNET satellite services to facilitate and implement IRETA programs on research, extension, training and distance learning programs of the School of Agriculture and University Extension. Also provides consultancies on video productions and training.
Members in 22 countries and territories:
Australia, Fiji, Germany, Hong Kong, India, Kiribati, Marshall Is, Micronesia FS, Nauru, Netherlands, New Zealand, Palau, Papua New Guinea, Philippines, Samoa, Solomon Is, South Africa, Tokelau, Tonga, Tuvalu, USA, Vanuatu.
IGO Relations Member of: *CABI (#03393)*; *International Information System for the Agricultural Sciences and Technology (AGRIS, #13848)*. **NGO Relations** *Mouvement international de la jeunesse agricole et rurale catholique (MIJARC, #16865)*; *Royal Tropical Institute (KIT)*. [2010/XE1493/j/**E***]

♦ Institute for Research on Public Policy (internationally oriented national body)
♦ Institute of Research and Study on the Arab and Islamic Worlds (#11354)
♦ Institute for Research on World Systems (internationally oriented national body)
♦ Institute of Risk Management (internationally oriented national body)
♦ Institute for Russian and East European Studies, Seoul (internationally oriented national body)

♦ **Institutes for Achievement of Human Potential (IAHP)** 11292
Organisation mondiale pour le potentiel humain
Dir 8801 Stenton Avenue, Wyndmoor PA 19038, USA. T. +12152332050. Fax +12152339312. E-mail: institutes@iahp.org.
URL: http://www.iahp.org/
History Founded 1968, as *World Organization for Human Potential (WOHP) – Organisation mondiale pour le potentiel humain*. **Aims** Act as spokesman for the children of the world when social, cultural and political customs and practices are discovered that tend to foster and accelerate the progress of children toward the achievement of their potential; do everything possible to make known such customs and practices and encourage them by means of appropriate action; conversely, help publicize, prevent and/or correct customs and practices which diminish or slow down the progress of children. **Structure** Includes *Institutes for the Achievement of Human Potential*. **Activities** Events/meetings, always in Philadelphia PA (USA). **Events** *Conference* Philadelphia, PA (USA) 1999, *Conference* Philadelphia, PA (USA) 1998, *Conference* Philadelphia, PA (USA) 1996, *Conference* Philadelphia, PA (USA) 1994, *Conference* Philadelphia, PA (USA) 1993. **Publications** *Kids Who Start Ahead, Stay Ahead* by Neil Harvey.
Members Individuals (physicians, anthropologists, educators of brain-injured and gifted children) in 103 countries and territories:
Afghanistan, Argentina, Australia, Austria, Belgium, Belize, Bermuda, Bolivia, Botswana, Brazil, British Caribbean Terr, Cameroon, Canada, Canaries, Chile, China, Colombia, Costa Rica, Côte d'Ivoire, Cuba, Cyprus, Czechia, Denmark, Dominican Rep, Ecuador, Egypt, El Salvador, England, Estonia, Ethiopia, Fiji, Finland, France, Gabon, Germany, Greece, Guatemala, Guiana Fr, Haiti, Honduras, Hong Kong, Hungary, Iceland, India, Indonesia, Iran Islamic Rep, Ireland, Israel, Italy, Jamaica, Japan, Kenya, Korea Rep, Laos, Lebanon, Libya, Lithuania, Luxembourg, Malaysia, Martinique, Morocco, Mozambique, Myanmar, Namibia, Netherlands, New Zealand, Nicaragua, Nigeria, Norway, Pakistan, Panama, Paraguay, Peru, Philippines, Poland, Portugal, Puerto Rico, Romania, Samoa, Saudi Arabia, Scotland, Serbia, Singapore, South Africa, Spain, Sweden, Switzerland, Tahiti Is, Taiwan, Tanzania UR, Thailand, Trinidad-Tobago, Tunisia, Türkiye, Uganda, Uruguay, USA, Venezuela, Virgin Is USA, Wales, Zambia, Zimbabwe. [2016/XC4609/v/**F**]

♦ Institute for Science and International Security (internationally oriented national body)

♦ **Institute for Scientific Information on Coffee (ISIC)** 11293
SG van Boetzelaerlaan 21, 2581 AA The Hague, Netherlands. T. +31702170082. E-mail: isic@isic-coffee.org.
URL: http://www.coffeeandhealth.org/
History 1990. Registration: Handelsregister, No/ID: 77478177, Netherlands. **Aims** Support, study, evaluate and disseminate scientific research on coffee and health. **Finance** Sources: members' dues. **Members** European coffee companies. Membership countries not specified. [2022.05.04/XG0448/j/**E**]

♦ Institute for the Secularization of Islamic Society (internationally oriented national body)
♦ Institute of Secular Missionaries (religious order)
♦ Institute for Security and Cooperation in Outer Space / see Institute for Cooperation in Space
♦ Institute for Security and Development Policy (internationally oriented national body)
♦ Institute of Security and International Studies, Bangkok (internationally oriented national body)
♦ Institute for Security and International Studies, Sofia (internationally oriented national body)
♦ Institute for Security Studies (internationally oriented national body)
♦ Institute of Slavic, East European and Eurasian Studies, Berkeley CA (internationally oriented national body)
♦ Institute for Social Banking (unconfirmed)
♦ Institute of Social and Economic Research / see Sir Arthur Lewis Institute of Social and Economic Studies

♦ **Institute for Social and Environmental Transition–International (ISET-International)** 11294
CEO 4770 Lee Circle, Boulder CO 80303, USA.
URL: https://www.i-s-e-t.org/
History 1997. **Aims** Catalyze transformative changes toward a more resilient and equitable future. **Structure** Board of Directors. **Activities** Advocacy/lobbying/activism; guidance/assistance/consulting; research/documentation; training/education. **NGO Relations** Member of (1): *Climate Chain Coalition (CCC, #04008)*.
[2021/AA1980/**F**]

♦ Institute of Social and Ethical Accountability / see AccountAbility (#00058)
♦ Institute for Social and European Studies (internationally oriented national body)
♦ Institute for Social Inventions (internationally oriented national body)
♦ Institute of Social Training of the 'Cono Sur' (#11337)
♦ Institute of Sociology of Law for Europe (inactive)
♦ Institute of South Asian Studies (internationally oriented national body)
♦ Institute of Southeast Asian Studies / see ISEAS – Yusof Ishak Institute
♦ Institute for Southeast Asian Studies, Hanoi (internationally oriented national body)
♦ Institute of South-East Asian Studies, Nagasaki (internationally oriented national body)
♦ Institute for Soviet and East European Studies, Tel Aviv / see Cummings Center for Russian and East European Studies
♦ Institutes for Strategic and International Studies / see ASEAN Institutes for Strategic and International Studies (#01200)

♦ **Institute on Statelessness and Inclusion (ISI)** 11295
Co-Dir/Sec Gestelsestr 134, 5615 LJ Eindhoven, Netherlands. E-mail: info@institutesi.org.
Co-Dir/Chair address not obtained.
URL: http://www.institutesi.org/
History 2014. Registered in accordance with Dutch law. **Aims** Promote human rights of stateless persons; foster inclusion to ultimately end statelessness. **Structure** International Board of Trustees; Executive Board; Advisory Council. **Staff** 6.00 FTE, paid. **Activities** Research/documenation; capacity building; networking/liaising; knowledge management/information dissemination; advocacy/lobbying/activism. **NGO Relations** *Global Campaign for Equal Nationality Rights (#10265)*; *Equal Rights Trust (#05520)*; *European Network on Statelessness (ENS, #08013)*. [2015/XM4202/**D**]

♦ Institute for Strategic and Defense Studies, Budapest / see Center for Strategic and Defense Studies, Budapest
♦ Institute for Strategic and Development Studies, Quezon City (internationally oriented national body)

♦ **Institute for Strategic Dialogue (ISD)** 11296
Exec Dir PO Box 7814, London, W1C 1YZ, UK. T. +442074939333. E-mail: info@strategicdialogue.org.
URL: http://www.strategicdialogue.org/
History mid-1990s, as *Club of Three*, bringing together individuals from UK, France and Germany. Structure reorganized, 2006, with the current title as umbrella for various programmes, including the Club of Three. UK Registered Charity under name Trialogue Educational Trust, No 1076660. **Aims** Develop multi-country responses to current major *security* and *socio-economic* challenges; enhance the capacity of *Europe* to act effectively in the global arena. **Structure** Board of Trustees; Policy Board. **NGO Relations** Instrumental in setting up: *European Muslim Professionals Network (CEDAR, #07840)*. [2016/XJ4761/j/**F**]

♦ Institute for Strategic and International Studies, Lisbon (internationally oriented national body)
♦ Institute of Strategic and International Studies, Malaysia (internationally oriented national body)
♦ Institute for Strategic and Regional Studies, Tashkent (internationally oriented national body)
♦ Institute for Strategic Studies / see International Institute for Strategic Studies (#13927)
♦ Institute for Strategic Studies, Brno (internationally oriented national body)
♦ Institute for Strategic Studies, Ulaanbaatar (internationally oriented national body)
♦ Institute of Studies on Conflicts and Humanitarian Action (internationally oriented national body)
♦ Institute for Studies on the Mediterranean (internationally oriented national body)
♦ Institute of Studies on Mediterranean Societies / see Istituto di Studi sul Mediterraneo
♦ Institut d'Estudis Nord-Americans (internationally oriented national body)
♦ Institute for the Study of the Americas (internationally oriented national body)

♦ Institute for the Study of Diplomacy (internationally oriented national body)
♦ Institute for the Study of English in Africa (internationally oriented national body)
♦ Institute for the Study of Europe, New York / see Blinken European Institute, Columbia University, New York
♦ Institute for the Study of Genocide, New York (internationally oriented national body)
♦ Institute for the Study of Global Antisemitism and Policy (internationally oriented national body)
♦ Institute for the Study of Human Rights, Columbia University (internationally oriented national body)
♦ Institute for the Study of International Development (internationally oriented national body)

♦ Institute for the Study of Islam and Christianity (ISIC) 11297

Contact, USA 6729 Curran St, McLean VA 22101, USA.
Contact, UK Moscrop Centre, River St, Pewsey, SN9 5DB, UK.
URL: http://www.isic-centre.org/

History Founded 1989. **Aims** In view of increasing tensions between Islam and the West, present an objective, robust and rigorous *understanding* of the relevant issues and their implications for Islamic and western societies. **Activities** Provides research and publications on Islam, including its sources, history, Islamic law, Muslim minorities in the West, Muslim-Christian relations and non-Muslims in Muslim-majority societies. **Events** *Consultation on gospel contextualisation revisited* Haslev (Denmark) 1997. **Publications** *ISIC Bulletin.* [2013/XJ1281/j/F]

♦ Institute for the Study of Languages and Cultures of Asia and Africa (internationally oriented national body)
♦ Institute for the Study of Multi-ethnicity / see ISMU Foundation – Foundation for Initiatives and Studies on Multi-ethnicity
♦ Institute for the Study of Transport in European Integration (internationally oriented national body)
♦ Institute of Sudanese Studies / see Institute of African Research and Studies, University of Cairo
♦ Institute for Sustainable Communities (internationally oriented national body)
♦ Institute for Sustainable Development in Mesoamerica, Mexico (internationally oriented national body)
♦ Institute for Sustainable Power (internationally oriented national body)
♦ Institute for Sustainable Rural Development Foundation (internationally oriented national body)
♦ Institut d'Etat des relations internationales de Moscou (internationally oriented national body)
♦ Institutet för Framtidsstudier (internationally oriented national body)
♦ Institut ethnographique international (inactive)
♦ Institut für Ethnologie und Afrikanistik (internationally oriented national body)
♦ Institut für Ethnologie und Afrika-Studien (internationally oriented national body)
♦ Institut d'ethnologie méditerranéenne et comparative (internationally oriented national body)
♦ Institutet för Internationell Ekonomi (internationally oriented national body)
♦ Institutet för Mänskliga Rättigheter (internationally oriented national body)
♦ Institute for Tourism and Development (internationally oriented national body)
♦ Institute for Tourism and Recreational Research in Northern Europe (internationally oriented national body)
♦ Institute for Training in Non-Violence (inactive)
♦ Institute for Transnational Arbitration (internationally oriented national body)
♦ Institute of Transport / see Chartered Institute of Logistics and Transport (#03856)
♦ Institute for Transportation and Development Policy (internationally oriented national body)
♦ Institute of Tropical Forest Conservation (internationally oriented national body)
♦ Institute for Tropical and Medical Hygiene, University of Lisbon (internationally oriented national body)
♦ Institute of Tropical Medicine Antwerp (internationally oriented national body)
♦ Institute of Tropical Medicine, Berlin / see Institut für Tropenmedizin und Internationale Gesundheit
♦ Institute of Tropical Medicine and International Health (internationally oriented national body)
♦ Institute for Tropical Ophthalmology in Africa (inactive)
♦ Institute of Tropical and Subtropical Agriculture / see Institute of Tropics and Subtropics, Prague
♦ Institute of Tropics and Subtropics, Prague (internationally oriented national body)
♦ Institut d'étude du développement international (internationally oriented national body)
♦ Institut d'étude des îles (internationally oriented national body)
♦ Institut d'étude des pays en développement / see Institut d'études du développement, Louvain-la-Neuve
♦ Institut d'étude des relations internationales (internationally oriented national body)
♦ Institut d'études africaines de l'Academie des sciences de la Russie (internationally oriented national body)
♦ Institut des études Africaines et Asiatique, Khartoum (internationally oriented national body)
♦ Institut d'études africaines, Hambourg (internationally oriented national body)
♦ Institut d'études africaines, Legon (internationally oriented national body)
♦ Institut des études africaines, Rabat (internationally oriented national body)
♦ Institut d'études de l'Amérique Latine, Stockholm / see Nordic Institute of Latin American Studies
♦ Institut d'études et analyses sur la défense (internationally oriented national body)
♦ Institut d'études de l'Asie du Sud-Est / see ISEAS – Yusof Ishak Institute
♦ Institut d'études du développement, Dar es Salaam (internationally oriented national body)
♦ Institut d'études du développement économique et social (internationally oriented national body)
♦ Institut d'études sur le développement, Helsinki (internationally oriented national body)
♦ Institut d'études du développement, Louvain-la-Neuve (internationally oriented national body)
♦ Institut d'études économiques internationales (internationally oriented national body)
♦ Institut d'études européennes 'Alcide de Gasperi' (internationally oriented national body)
♦ Institut des études européennes, Bilbao (internationally oriented national body)
♦ Institut d'études européennes – CEPSE / see National-European Communitarian Party
♦ Institut d'études européennes et internationales du Luxembourg (internationally oriented national body)
♦ Institut d'études européennes, Louvain-la-Neuve (internationally oriented national body)
♦ Institut d'études européennes, Montréal (internationally oriented national body)
♦ Institut d'études européennes Nation Europe / see National-European Communitarian Party
♦ Institut des études européennes, Paris (internationally oriented national body)
♦ Institut d'études européennes – Section droit – de l'Université de la Sarre / see Europa-Institut at Saarland University
♦ Institut d'études européennes, ULB (internationally oriented national body)
♦ Institut d'études européennes, ULB (internationally oriented national body)
♦ Institut d'études internationales de la communication sur l'environnement / see Académie d'environnement d'expression francophone, philosophique et scientifique
♦ Institut des études internationales, Peoria (internationally oriented national body)
♦ Institut d'études latinoaméricaines (internationally oriented national body)
♦ Institut des études latinoaméricaines, Hambourg / see Institut für Lateinamerika-Studies
♦ Institut des études palestiniennes (internationally oriented national body)
♦ Institut pour les études de politique internationale / see Italian Institute for International Political Studies
♦ Institut d'études politiques sur l'Amérique latine et l'Afrique (internationally oriented national body)
♦ Institut d'études politiques de Paris (internationally oriented national body)
♦ Institut d'études politiques, Washington DC (internationally oriented national body)
♦ Institut des études et des recherches arabes (no recent information)
♦ Institut d'études des relations internationales contemporaines et de recherches diplomatiques / see Institut d'étude des relations internationales
♦ Institut d'études de sécurité de l'Union européenne (#08994)
♦ Institut d'études slaves (internationally oriented national body)
♦ Institut d'études sociales d'Amérique centrale (#11326)
♦ Institut d'études stratégiques / see International Institute for Strategic Studies (#13927)
♦ Institut d'études stratégiques et internationales, Lisbonne (internationally oriented national body)

♦ Institut pour l'étude des transports dans l'intégration européenne (internationally oriented national body)
♦ Institute for Twenty-First Century Studies / see Millennium Institute
♦ Institute for University Cooperation (#11331)

♦ Institute of University Management and Leadership (IGLU-Leaders) 11298

Institut de gestion et de leadership universitaires (IGLU) – Instituto de Gestión y Liderazgo Universitario – Instituto de Gestão e Liderança Universitaria

Exec Dir c/o IOHE, 3744 Jean-Brillant, bureau 592, Montréal QC H3t 1P1, Canada. T. +15143436980. E-mail: info@oui-iohe.org.
URL: https://oui-iohe.org/en/iglu/

History Nov 1983, Rio de Janeiro (Brazil). Founded as a program of *Inter-American Organization for Higher Education (IOHE, #11442).* **Aims** Contribute to the training of professional development for university executives in Latin America and the Caribbean; ensure greater relevance and a more important role for universities within their immediate environment; contribute to the transformation of the university into an instrument of sustainable development. **Structure** Superior Council; Board of Directors; Executive Director; General Executive Secretary. **Languages** English, Portuguese, Spanish. **Staff** 2.00 FTE, paid. **Finance** Supported by IOHE institutional members; self-funding activities; funded projects. **Activities** Training/education; events/meetings; awards/prizes/competitions. **Publications** Books.

Members Member universities cover 24 countries:
Argentina, Bolivia, Brazil, Canada, Chile, Colombia, Costa Rica, Cuba, Dominican Rep, Ecuador, El Salvador, Guatemala, Guyana, Haiti, Honduras, Mexico, Nicaragua, Panama, Paraguay, Peru, Puerto Rico, Uruguay, USA, Venezuela.

IGO Relations Formal links with: *OAS (#17629).* **NGO Relations** Supported by: *Institute of University Management and Leadership (IGLU-Leaders, #11298).* Activities supported by: *Inter-American Organization for Higher Education (IOHE, #11442).* [2021/XE6067/j/E]

♦ Institut für Europäische Integrationsforschung / see Centre for European Integration Research
♦ Institut für Europäische Kulturen (internationally oriented national body)
♦ Institut für Europäische Kulturgeschichte (internationally oriented national body)
♦ Institut für Europäische Politik, Berlin (internationally oriented national body)
♦ Institut für Europäische Rechtswissenschaft (internationally oriented national body)
♦ Institut für Europäisches Medienrecht (internationally oriented national body)
♦ Institut für Europäisches Verkehrsrecht (#11262)
♦ Institut für Europäische Umweltpolitik (#11261)
♦ Institut für Europarecht, Osnabrück / see European Legal Studies Institute
♦ Institut für Europarecht und Rechtsvergleichung (internationally oriented national body)
♦ Institut europeen pour une politique culturelle progressive (internationally oriented national body)
♦ Institut de l'Europe de centre-est, Lublin (internationally oriented national body)
♦ Institut européen d'administration des affaires / see INSEAD (#11228)
♦ Institut européen d'administration publique (#07569)
♦ Institut européen des affaires (internationally oriented national body)

♦ Institut Européen des Armes de Chasse et de Sport (IEACS) 11299

European Institute of Hunting and Sporting Weapons

Contact Viale dell'Astronomia 30, 00144 Rome RM, Italy. T. +3965903510. Fax +39654282691. E-mail: ieacs@anpam.it.
Registered Office Rue Th De Cuyper 100, 1200 Brussels, Belgium.
URL: https://www.ieacs.eu/

History 1977, Brussels (Belgium). Most recent statutes adopted 1996. Registration: Banque-Carrefour des Entreprises, No/ID: 0416.718.136, Start date: 12 Jan 1977, Belgium; EU Transparency Register, No/ID: 208929410103-47, Start date: 12 Nov 2012. **Aims** Encourage scientific research on hunting and sporting weapons; facilitate exchange of information; ensure representation to international institutions, particularly those of the European communities. **Structure** General Assembly (annual). Board of at least 5 (currently 8) members, including President and Vice-President. Secretary-General. **Languages** French. **Finance** Members' dues.

Members Manufacturers/importers of hunting and sporting weapons and their accoutrements; national associations of such manufacturers/importers. Members in 6 countries:
Finland, France, Germany, Italy, Spain, UK.
Associate members (2):
Association of European Manufacturers of Sporting Ammunition (#02522); Association of European Manufacturers of Sporting Firearms (ESFAM, #02523).

IGO Relations Recognized by: *European Commission (EC, #06633).* **NGO Relations** Member of (1): *World Forum on Shooting Activities (WFSA, #21523).* [2020/XD0148/j/D]

♦ Institut européen de bioéthique (internationally oriented national body)
♦ Institut Européen Conflits Cultures Coopérations (internationally oriented national body)
♦ Institut européen de coopération et de développement, Paris / see IECD
♦ Institut européen de corporate governance (#06799)
♦ Institut européen de l'économie solidaire (#07572)
♦ Institut Européen d'Ecriture (internationally oriented national body)
♦ Institut européen d'éducation familiale (#07554)
♦ Institut européen d'éducation et de politique sociale (#07551)
♦ Institut européen pour l'égalité entre les hommes et les femmes (#07557)
♦ Institut Européen Emmanuel Levinas (unconfirmed)
♦ Institut européen Est-Ouest (internationally oriented national body)
♦ Institut européen pour l'étude des fibres industrielles (inactive)
♦ Institut Européen de l'expertise et de l'expert (#07015)
♦ Institut européen de la forêt cultivée (internationally oriented national body)
♦ Institut européen de formation continue en réparation et évaluation du dommage corporel (unconfirmed)
♦ Institut européen de formation et de coopération / see Association Rencontre CEFIR
♦ Institut européen pour la formation professionnelle (inactive)
♦ Institut européen pour la formation à la sûreté de l'aviation (#06304)
♦ Institut européen, Gand (internationally oriented national body)
♦ Institut européen d'histoire de l'alimentation / see Institut européen d'histoire et des cultures de l'alimentation (#11300)

♦ Institut européen d'histoire et des cultures de l'alimentation (IEHCA) 11300

European Institute for the History and Culture of Food

Dir Villa Rabelais, 116 bvd Béranger, 37000 Tours, France. T. +33247059030. Fax +33247609075. E-mail: contact@iehca.eu.
URL: http://www.iehca.eu/

History Dec 2000, as *Institut européen d'histoire de l'alimentation (IEHA) – European Institute of Food History.* Registered in accordance with French law. **Aims** Increase knowledge of food history and food cultures; promote dissemination of research in the field. **Structure** Board, including President and Secretary. **Activities** Organizes annual conference, forums and Summer school. **Events** *Annual Conference* Bologna (Italy) 2003, *Annual Conference* Tours (France) 2002, *Annual Conference* Strasbourg (France) 2001. [2020/XM0628/j/E]

♦ Institut européen des industries de la gomme de caroube / see INEC – Association of Producers of Carob Bean Gum (#11183)

♦ Institut européen des industries de la pectine (IEIP) 11301

European Institute of the Pectin Industries

Gen Sec Turnstrasse 37, 75305 Neuenbürg, Germany. T. +4970827913700. Fax +4970827913701. E-mail: secretary-general@ieip.eu.

Institut européen intérêt
11301

alphabetic sequence excludes
For the complete listing, see Yearbook Online at

History 1967, Brussels (Belgium). Registered in accordance with Belgian law, 12 Aug 1968. **Aims** Collect scientific studies at European Union level relevant to research, production and applications of pectins; supply documentation and advice; ensure representation of the Common Market pectin industry with the European Economic Community and other international organizations; ensure representation of the pectin industry within the European Common Market and European Economic Community. **Structure** General Meeting; Board. **Languages** English, French, German. **Staff** 0.50 FTE, paid. **Finance** Members' dues. **Events** *Annual General Assembly* Brussels (Belgium) 1986.
Members Manufacturers situated in a Member-State of the European Economic Community. Members in 7 countries:
Czechia, Denmark, France, Germany, Italy, Poland, Spain.
IGO Relations Recognized by: *European Commission (EC, #06633).* [2017.11.06/XE0785/jt/**E**]

- ♦ Institut européen pour l'intérêt de l'enfant (internationally oriented national body)
- ♦ Institut européen interuniversitaire de l'action sociale (#15988)
- ♦ Institut européen des itinéraires culturels (internationally oriented national body)
- ♦ Institut européen de management international (internationally oriented national body)
- ♦ Institut européen de management public, Charleroi (internationally oriented national body)
- ♦ Institut européen des matériels industriels de fixation mécanique (#07524)
- ♦ Institut européen de la méditerranée (internationally oriented national body)
- ♦ Institut européen des normes de télécommunication (#08897)
- ♦ Institut européen de l'ombudsman (#08085)
- ♦ Institut européen du papier (inactive)
- ♦ Institut européen pour la prévention du crime et la lutte contre la délinquance affilié à l'Organisation des Nations Unies (#07550)
- ♦ Institut européen de recherche pour l'aménagement régional et urbain (inactive)
- ♦ Institut européen de recherche comparative sur la culture (#07547)
- ♦ Institut européen de recherche et d'information sur la paix et la sécurité / see Groupe de recherche et d'information sur la paix et la sécurité
- ♦ Institut européen de recherche sur la politique de l'eau (#07570)
- ♦ Institut européen de recherches et d'études supérieures en management (#07544)
- ♦ Institut européen de recherches pour les problèmes de consommation (#08363)
- ♦ Institut européen des sciences humaines (see: #09682)
- ♦ Institut européen de sécurité sociale (#07571)
- ♦ Institut européen de technologie / see European Institute of Innovation and Technology (#07562)
- ♦ Institut européen de télémédecine (internationally oriented national body)
- ♦ Institut de l'Europe pour l'imprégnation du bois (#07575)
- ♦ Institut de l'Europe occidentale pour l'imprégnation du bois / see European Institute for Wood Preservation (#07575)
- ♦ Institut Europeu de la Mediterrània (internationally oriented national body)
- ♦ Institut évangélique de missiologie (internationally oriented national body)
- ♦ Institute Vienna Circle (internationally oriented national body)
- ♦ Institute Vienna Circle – Society for the Advancement of the Scientific World Conception / see Institut Wiener Kreis
- ♦ Institut za Evropske Studije, Ljubljana (internationally oriented national body)
- ♦ Institut pro evropskou politiku (internationally oriented national body)

♦ Institute for War and Peace Reporting (IWPR) 11302

IWPR Europe 48 Grays Inn Road, London, WC1X 8LT, UK. T. +442078311030. Fax +442078311050. E-mail: iwpr-nl@iwpr.net.
USA Office 729 15th St NW, Suite 500, Washington DC 20005, USA. E-mail: iwpr-us@iwpr.net.
URL: http://www.iwpr.net/

History 1991. Registration: Charity Commission, No/ID: 1027201, England and Wales; Companies House, No/ID: 2744185, Start date: 1 Sep 1992, England and Wales; No/ID: EIN 43-1962561, USA; Handelsregister, No/ID: KVK 27307022, Netherlands. **Aims** Support recovery and development in crisis zones by providing professional training, financial assistance and an international platform to independent *media, human rights* activists and other local democratic voices. **Structure** Board of Trustees. **Finance** Supported by a number of organizations, including: *European Commission (EC, #06633); Ford Foundation (#09858); MacArthur Foundation; Swedish International Development Cooperation Agency (Sida); United States Institute of Peace (USIP).* **Activities** Engages local reporters in crisis areas for training, research and reporting projects; builds local networks, engages in extensive editing and hosts workshops and discussion sessions. **Publications** *Afghan Recovery Report* in English; *Africa Report* in English; *Caucasus Reporting Service* in English, Russian; *International Justice Report* in Arabic, English, French; *Iraqi Crisis Report* in English; *IWPR Monthly Newsletter* in English; *Tribunal Update* in Bosnian, Croatian, English, Serbian. Various special reports. **NGO Relations** Partners: *Kazakhstan International Bureau for Human Rights and Rule of Law (KIBHR, no recent information);* national human rights organizations. Member of: *Extractive Industries Transparency Initiative (EITI, #09229).* Supports: *International News Safety Institute (INSI, #14364).* [2020/XG4253/j/**F**]

- ♦ Institute of War and Peace Studies / see Saltzman Institute of War and Peace Studies
- ♦ Institute of West Asian and African Studies, Beijing (internationally oriented national body)
- ♦ Institute for Western Affairs, Poznan (internationally oriented national body)
- ♦ Institute on Western Europe, New York / see Blinken European Institute, Columbia University, New York
- ♦ Institute for Women's Studies in the Arab World (internationally oriented national body)
- ♦ Institute of World Affairs (internationally oriented national body)
- ♦ Institute for World Cultures, Paris / see Maison des Cultures du Monde
- ♦ Institute for World Economics, Budapest / see Institute for World Economics of the Hungarian Academy of Sciences
- ♦ Institute for World Economics of the Hungarian Academy of Sciences (internationally oriented national body)
- ♦ Institute for World Economics and International Management, Bremen (internationally oriented national body)
- ♦ Institute of World Economics and International Relations / see Institut Mirovoj Ekonomiki i Mezdunarodnyh Otnosenij Rossijskoj Akademii Nauk
- ♦ Institute for World Economics, Kiel / see Kiel Institute for the World Economy
- ♦ Institute of World Economics and Politics (internationally oriented national body)
- ♦ Institute of World Economics and Politics – Chinese Academy of Social Sciences / see Institute of World Economics and Politics
- ♦ Institute of World Economics and Politics, Hanoi (internationally oriented national body)
- ♦ Institute of World Economy / see Institute of World Economics and Politics
- ♦ Institute of World Economy and International Relations of the Academy of Sciences of the USSR / see Institut Mirovoj Ekonomiki i Mezdunarodnyh Otnosenij Rossijskoj Akademii Nauk
- ♦ Institute of World Economy and International Relations of the Russian Academy of Sciences (internationally oriented national body)

♦ Institute for World Evangelisation (ICPE Mission) 11303

Pres International Office, Via Licio Giorgieri 64, 00165 Rome RM, Italy. T. +39666512891. E-mail: internationaloffice@icpe.org.
URL: http://www.icpe.org/

History 1985, Valletta (Malta). Recognized by the Holy See as an international association of the faithful of pontifical right. Former names and other names: *International Catholic Programme of Evangelization* – former. **Aims** Train Catholics as effective evangelists and send them into the world to win it for *Christ*; uphold and maintain the universal nature of the *Catholic Church*. **Structure** Council. **Languages** English, German, Italian, Korean, Polish, Spanish. **Staff** 149.00 FTE, voluntary. **Finance** Sources: grants. Financially autonomous. **Activities** Projects/programmes; religious activities; training/education. Active in: Colombia, Germany, Ghana, India, Italy, Korea Rep, Malaysia, Malta, New Zealand, Philippines, Singapore, USA. **Events** *Meeting on How to Deal with Money as Christians* Seoul (Korea Rep) 2012, *Meeting* Seoul (Korea Rep) 2012, *What is humility?* Seoul (Korea Rep) 2012, *Meeting* Brescia (Italy) 1995, *European leaders congress* Bern (Switzerland) 1990. **Publications** *ICPE Newsletter.* Booklets; pamphlets.

Members Schools, missions and participants in 25 countries:
Albania, Austria, Belgium, Czechia, Germany, Ghana, India, Indonesia, Ireland, Italy, Kenya, Korea Rep, Malaysia, Malta, Mexico, Netherlands, New Zealand, Nigeria, Philippines, Poland, Russia, Singapore, Switzerland, UK, USA.
[2023.02.14/XF1941/j/**F**]

- ♦ Institute for World Order / see World Policy Institute
- ♦ Institute of World Politics (internationally oriented national body)
- ♦ Institute for World Politics and Economy (internationally oriented national body)
- ♦ Institute for World Society Studies (internationally oriented national body)
- ♦ Institute for Zero Waste in Africa (internationally oriented national body)
- ♦ Institut du facteur 10 (#09236)
- ♦ Institut des femmes d'Asie (inactive)
- ♦ Institut de finance internationale (#11275)
- ♦ Institut de financement du développement du Maghreb Arabe, Tunis (internationally oriented national body)
- ♦ Institut du FMI (see: #14180)
- ♦ Institut fondamental d'Afrique noire / see Institut fondamental d'Afrique noire – Cheikh Anta Diop
- ♦ Institut fondamental d'Afrique noire – Cheikh Anta Diop (internationally oriented national body)
- ♦ Institut zur Förderung der Interkulturellen Beziehungen durch die Kunst (#11238)
- ♦ Institut forestier européen / see European Forest Institute (#07297)
- ♦ Institut de formation et d'appui aux initiatives de développement (internationally oriented national body)
- ♦ Institut de formation de cadres pour le développement (internationally oriented national body)
- ♦ Institut de formation démocrate-chrétien (internationally oriented national body)
- ♦ Institut de formation européen et de cooperation / see Association Rencontre CEFIR
- ♦ Institut de formation à la non-violence (inactive)

♦ Institut de formation et de recherche démographiques (IFORD) . . . 11304

Contact BP 1556, Yaoundé, Cameroon. T. +23722232947 – +23722222471. Fax +23722226893. E-mail: iford@iford-cm.org.
Ngoa Ekelle Campus address not obtained. T. +23722034412. Fax +23722226793.
URL: http://www.iford-cm.org/

History Nov 1972, Yaoundé (Cameroon). Established following an agreement, 9 Nov 1971, between *United Nations (UN, #20515)* (which financed and managed the Institute until Jun 1982) and the Government of Cameroon. On 1 Jul 1982, regionalization of the Institute started with the decentralization of the management of ILFORD to *United Nations Economic Commission for Africa (ECA, #20554).* Second reorganization ran from 1992 to 1994 with academic attachment of IFORD to the University of Yaoundé II, Jul 1992. On 31 Dec 1999, *United Nations Population Fund (UNFPA, #20612)* principal funding partner of the Institute, withdrew itself. Became an intergovernmental institution, 2001. Reorganized between 1 Jul 2005 – Feb 2007. New era started 2008. Former names and other names: *Institute for Demographic Training and Research (IDTR)* – alias. **Aims** Train senior staff and undertake and publish the results of research in *population, demography* and related fields; provide technical support to member states and partners. **Structure** Council of Ministers (meets every 2 years); Board of Directors; Executive Director. **Languages** French. **Staff** 5.00 FTE, paid. **Finance** Sources: annual contributions of Member States; subsidies from funding organizations and partners; income from technical support activities, research projects, training. **Activities** Training/education; research/documentation; knowledge management/information dissemination; guidance/assistance/consulting; events/meetings. **Events** *Seminar* Yaoundé (Cameroon) 2010, *Seminar* Yaoundé (Cameroon) 2009, *Seminar* Yaoundé (Cameroon) 2008, *Seminar* Yaoundé (Cameroon) 2007, *International Symposium* Yaoundé (Cameroon) 2006. **Publications** *Annales de l'IFORD* (2 a year); *IFORD-Infos* – electronic. *Enquêtes sur la mortalité infantile et juvenile (Enquêtes EMIJ)* – series. *Les cahiers de l'IFORD.* Pedagogical documents; seminar, conference and symposium proceedings. Information Services: Specialized library.
Members Governments of 23 countries:
Algeria, Benin, Burkina Faso, Burundi, Cameroon, Central African Rep, Chad, Comoros, Congo Brazzaville, Congo DR, Côte d'Ivoire, Djibouti, Equatorial Guinea, Gabon, Guinea, Madagascar, Mali, Mauritania, Morocco, Niger, Rwanda, Senegal, Togo.
[2016.06.01/XE8248/j/**E***]

- ♦ Institut de formation sociale du Cône Sud (#11337)
- ♦ Institut français d'archéologie de Beyrouth / see Institut français du Proche-Orient
- ♦ Institut français d'archéologie du Proche-Orient / see Institut français du Proche-Orient
- ♦ Institut français d'études et de terminologie de l'environnement / see Académie d'environnement d'expression francophone, philosophique et scientifique
- ♦ Institut français du Proche-Orient (internationally oriented national body)
- ♦ Institut français de recherche en Afrique (internationally oriented national body)
- ♦ Institut français de recherche pour l'exploitation de la mer / see Ifremer
- ♦ Institut français des relations internationales (internationally oriented national body)
- ♦ Institut franco-européenne de chiropratique (internationally oriented national body)
- ♦ Institut Francophone International (#13682)
- ♦ Institut de la Francophonie pour l'Administration et la Gestion / see École supérieure de la francophonie pour l'administration et le management (#05298)

♦ Institut de la Francophonie pour le développement durable (IFDD) . 11305

Dir 200 chemin Sainte-Foy, Bureau 1-40, Québec QC G1R 1T3, Canada. T. +14186925727. Fax +14186925644. E-mail: ifdd@francophonie.org.
URL: http://www.ifdd.francophonie.org/

History Dec 1987, Paris (France). Established by *Agence intergouvernementale de La Francophonie (inactive),* currently *Organisation internationale de la Francophonie (OIF, #17809).* Former names and other names: *Institut de l'énergie et de l'environnement de la francophonie (IEPF)* – former. **Aims** Contribute in the design and implantation of *sustainable development* strategies. **Structure** A subsidiary organ of *Organisation internationale de la Francophonie (OIF, #17809).* **Languages** French. **Staff** 20.00 FTE, paid. **Finance** Mainly through OIF. Annual budget: 5,600,000 CAD. **Activities** Events/meetings. **Events** *Colloque sur les défis énergétiques et environnementaux* Québec, QC (Canada) 2008, *Conférence internationale – Québec 2008* Québec, QC (Canada) 2008, *Workshop on legal support for the implementation of the Ramsar Convention in West and Central Africa* Yaoundé (Cameroon) 2006, *African forum of biomass energy* 1997, *Journées scientifiques internationales sur l'électrification rurale* Abidjan (Côte d'Ivoire) 1993. **Publications** *Liaison Énergie-Francophonie* (4 a year) in French. *Fiches techniques PRISME* (2021) in French – Programme international de soutien à la maîtrise de l'énergie (PRISME); *Guide des négociations – Guide to the negotiations* (2021) in English, French; *Revue Africaine de Droit de l'Environnement (RADE)* (2021) in French. Handbooks; conference proceedings. **Members** OIF Member States. **IGO Relations** Accredited by (1): *European Union (EU, #08967).* Partner of (3): *Green Climate Fund (GCF, #10714); UNEP (#20299); Union économique et monétaire Ouest africaine (UEMOA, #20377).* **NGO Relations** Member of (1): *Global Alliance for Buildings and Construction (GlobalABC, #10187).* Partner of (1): *International Union for Conservation of Nature and Natural Resources (IUCN, #15766).* [2022.02.02/XE1235/j/**E***]

♦ Institut de la Francophonie pour l'éducation et la formation (IFEF) . 11306

Dir Pointe des Almadies, 12500 Dakar, Senegal. T. +221338592258. E-mail: ifef@francophonie.org – akaag@francophonie.org.
URL: https://ifef.francophonie.org/

History 12 Oct 2017. Proposed at 15th Summit of *Organisation internationale de la Francophonie (OIF, #17809),* Nov 2014, Dakar (Senegal) and reaffirmed at *World Education Forum (#21371),* May 2015, Incheon (Korea Rep). Functions as a programme of OIF. **Aims** Implement cooperation programmes in the education sector; contribute to the development, implementation, monitoring and evaluation of national policies; propose and organize capacity building activities; strengthen the capacities of member states and governments and its partners so as to improve the quality of teaching programmes of and in French. **Activities** Training/education.
[2022.01.18/AA2314/**E***]

- ♦ Institut de la francophonie pour l'entrepreneuriat (internationally oriented national body)
- ♦ Institut de la francophonie pour l'entrepreneuriat de Maurice / see Institut de la francophonie pour l'entrepreneuriat

♦ Institut de la Francophonie pour la gouvernance universitaire (IFGU) 11307

Contact Campus universitaire de Ngoa-Ekelle, BP 8114, Yaoundé, Cameroon. E-mail: ifgu@auf.org.
URL: http://ifgu.auf.org/

History Launched Jul 2009, Paris (France), evolving from a project called *Panafrican Institute of University Governance (PAIUG) – Institut panafricain de gouvernance universitaire (IPAGU)*, set up Jul 2008, Paris (France), by *Agence universitaire de La Francophonie (AUF, #00548)* and *Association of Commonwealth Universities, The (ACU, #02440)*. **Aims** Support, advise and provide expertise in order to contribute to the good performance of higher education in universities of the Francophonie by deploying tools of governance, quality, planification, strategic steering and evaluation. **Structure** Board. **Languages** French. **Activities** Monitoring/evaluation; guidance/assistance/consulting; research/documentation. **Publications** *IFGU Newsletter*. **IGO Relations** Partners include: *African and Malagasy Council for Higher Education (#00364)*. **NGO Relations** Partners include: *Agence universitaire de La Francophonie (AUF, #00548)*; *Association of Commonwealth Universities, The (ACU, #02440)*; *Groupement international des secrétaires généraux des universités francophones (GISGUF, #10763)*. [2018.06.11/XJ4839/j/**E**]

♦ Institut de la Francophonie pour l'Informatique / see International Francophone Institute (#13682)
♦ Institut de la Francophonie pour l'Innovation / see International Francophone Institute (#13682)

♦ Institut de la francophonie pour la médecine tropicale (IFMT) 11308

Main Office c/o Ministry of Health, Ban thatkhao, Sisattanack District, Rue Simeuang, 01030 Vientiane, Laos. T. +85621214000.

History Initially within the framework of *Agence universitaire de La Francophonie (AUF, #00548)*, as an international francophone training and research institute. **Aims** Provide practical and theoretical *tertiary education* in the field of *tropical diseases* whose frequency or gravity cause them to have significant impact on *peri-equatorial* regions, so as to train practitioners and experts in research, education and treatment, particularly those based in or coming from *Southeast Asian* countries; develop research specific to regional priorities; set up a network using modern communications systems permitting interaction among all French-speakers. **Activities** Training/education. [2017/XE3858/j/**E**]

♦ Institut de la Francophonie numérique (inactive)
♦ Institut des Frères de la Sainte-Famille de Belley (religious order)
♦ Institut für Friedensarbeit und Gewaltfreie Konfliktaustragung (internationally oriented national body)
♦ Institut für Friedensforschung und Sicherheitspolitik, Hamburg (internationally oriented national body)
♦ Institut für Friedenssicherungsrecht und Humanitares Volkerrecht, Bochum (internationally oriented national body)
♦ Institut des futurs africains (#00327)
♦ Institut géographique international (inactive)
♦ Institut 'Georg Eckert' Centre international de recherches sur les manuels scolaires (internationally oriented national body)
♦ Institut de gestion pour l'Afrique orientale et l'Afrique australe (#05254)
♦ Institut de gestion et de leadership universitaires (#11298)
♦ Institut des hautes études de l'Amérique latine (internationally oriented national body)
♦ Institut des hautes études européennes / see Hague School of European Studies
♦ Institut de hautes études internationales et du développement (internationally oriented national body)
♦ Institut des Hautes Etudes sur les Nations Unies (internationally oriented national body)
♦ Institut d'Helsinki pour la prévention du crime et la lutte contre la délinquance affilié à l'Organisation des Nations Unies / see European Institute for Crime Prevention and Control affiliated with the United Nations (#07550)
♦ Institut hispano-luso-américain de droit international (#10924)
♦ Institut für Höhere Europäische Studien / see Hague School of European Studies
♦ Institut pour l'homme et la science / see Rensselaerville Institute
♦ Institut hongrois des affaires internationales (internationally oriented national body)
♦ Institut Hudson (internationally oriented national body)
♦ Institut humaniste de coopération avec les pays en voie de développement (internationally oriented national body)
♦ Institut ibéroaméricain du droit aéronautique et de l'espace et de l'aviation commerciale (#11332)
♦ Institut ibéroaméricain de droit agraire et de réforme agraire (no recent information)
♦ Institut für Iberoamerika-Kunde, Hamburg / see Institut für Lateinamerika-Studies
♦ Institut de l'Infrastructure Environnement et Innovation (unconfirmed)
♦ Institut pour l'intégration de l'Amérique latine et des Caraïbes (#11271)
♦ Institut interafricain du travail (inactive)
♦ Institut interaméricain de coopération pour l'agriculture (#11434)
♦ Institut interaméricain de droit d'auteur (#11421)
♦ Institut interaméricain des droits de l'homme (#11334)
♦ Institut interaméricain de l'enfant (#11406)
♦ Institut interaméricain des études internationales juridiques (inactive)
♦ Institut interaméricain d'études syndicales (inactive)
♦ Institut interaméricain d'histoire municipale et institutionnelle (inactive)
♦ Institut interaméricain des marchés de capitaux (inactive)
♦ Institut interaméricain de musique (inactive)
♦ Institut interaméricain des sciences agricoles / see Inter-American Institute for Cooperation on Agriculture (#11434)
♦ Institut interaméricain des services juridiques alternatifs (#11439)
♦ Institut interaméricain de statistique (#11452)
♦ Institut interculturel Timisoara (internationally oriented national body)
♦ Institut für Interkulturelle und Internationale Studien (internationally oriented national body)
♦ Institut intermédiaire international (inactive)
♦ Institut international de l'administration de l'eau (see: #14399)
♦ Institut international d'agriculture (inactive)
♦ Institut international d'agriculture tropicale (#13933)
♦ Institut international d'alimentation (inactive)
♦ Institut international d'alphabétisation (internationally oriented national body)
♦ Institut international d'aluminium (#11643)
♦ Institut international d'aluminium primaire / see International Aluminium Institute (#11643)
♦ Institut international pour l'analyse des systèmes appliqués / see International Institute for Applied Systems Analysis (#13861)
♦ Institut international d'appui au développement (internationally oriented national body)
♦ Institut international d'art public (inactive)
♦ Institut international des arts et des lettres (inactive)

♦ Institut international des assurances, Yaoundé (IIA) 11309

International Institute of Insurance, Yaoundé

Dir Gen BP 1575, Bastos, Yaoundé, Cameroon. T. +23722207152. E-mail: contact@iiayaounde.com.
URL: http://www.iiayaounde.com/

History 1972, Yamoussoukro (Côte d'Ivoire), pursuant to provisions of the convention of cooperation regarding control of insurance companies and operations. The constitutive act of Yamoussoukro in 1972 was modified by the Treaty instituting the *Inter-African Conference on Insurance Markets (#11385)*, signed 10 Jul 1992, Yaoundé (Cameroon), by the Ministers for Finance of Member States. Comes within the framework of CIMA. **Aims** Train and improve *executives* of all levels and specializations for insurance enterprises and control authorities; promote research in the field; offer technical assistance to insurance companies and organisms in the form of missions, consultations and specific studies. **Structure** Council of Ministers, consisting of Ministers in charge of the insurance sector. Administrative Council; Pedagogical Council; Directorate-General; Council of Professors. **Languages** French. **Staff** 3.00 FTE, paid. **Finance** Member's dues. Budget (2010): Franc CFA 848 million. **Activities** Provides training; organizes seminars on legal, financial, accounting, technical and other aspects of insurance enterprises; provides assistance in the field; carries out research; publishing activity. **Events** *Seminar* Abidjan (Côte d'Ivoire) 2006, *Seminar* Abidjan (Côte d'Ivoire) 2006, *Seminar* Bamako (Mali) 2006, *Agrément d'une société d'assurance – spécialisation des sociétés d'assurances* Dakar (Senegal) 2001, *L'assurance incendie – pertes d'exploitation* Douala (Cameroon) 2001. **Publications** *Afrique assurance* – magazine. *Assur Echo* – supplement to the Annual Report 2015. Seminar proceedings; course materials; guides; documents. Information Services: Library.

Members Governments of 14 countries:
Benin, Burkina Faso, Cameroon, Central African Rep, Chad, Congo Brazzaville, Côte d'Ivoire, Equatorial Guinea, Gabon, Guinea-Bissau, Mali, Niger, Senegal, Togo.

IGO Relations Member of: *Commission régionale de contrôle des assurances dans les Etats africains (CRCA, see: #11385)*. Partner of: *African and Malagasy Council for Higher Education (#00364)*; CIMA; *Compagnie commune de réassurance des Etats membres de la CICA (CICA-RE, no recent information)*. **NGO Relations** Member of: *Agence universitaire de La Francophonie (AUF, #00548)*. Partner of: *Association internationale des établissements francophones de formation à l'assurance (AIEFFA, #02687) Federation of African National Insurance Companies (#09408)*. [2018/XK0671/j/**E***]

♦ Institut international de bibliographie sociale (inactive)
♦ Institut international de biologie moléculaire et cellulaire, Varsovie (internationally oriented national body)
♦ Institut international des brevets (inactive)
♦ Institut international canadien de la negotiation pratique (internationally oriented national body)
♦ Institut international de catéchèse et de pastorale (#13867)
♦ Institut international Chanoine Triest (#13866)
♦ Institut international des châteaux historiques (inactive)
♦ Institut international de christianisme social (inactive)
♦ Institut international du cinématographe éducatif (inactive)
♦ Institut international des civilisations différentes (inactive)
♦ Institut international de collaboration philosophique / see International Institute of Philosophy (#13910)
♦ Institut international du commerce (inactive)
♦ Institut international des communications (#13870)
♦ Institut international pour la conservation des objets d'art et d'histoire (#13871)
♦ Institut international pour la conservation des objets de musée / see International Institute for Conservation of Historic and Artistic Works (#13871)
♦ Institut international de coopération intellectuelle (inactive)
♦ Institut international du coton (inactive)
♦ Institut international des coûts (#12977)
♦ Institut international de la démocratie (inactive)
♦ Institut international pour la démocratie et l'assistance électorale (#13872)
♦ Institut international du développement durable (#13930)
♦ Institut international pour la diffusion des expériences sociales (inactive)
♦ Institut international de droit du développement / see International Development Law Organization (#13161)

♦ Institut international de droit d'expression et d'inspiration françaises (IDEF) 11310

International Institute of Law of the French-Speaking Countries – Instituto Internacional de Derecho de Expresión y Inspiración Franceses – Internationales Institut für Rechtsfragen Französisch-sprechenden Staaten

SG 60 boulevard de la Tour Maubourg, 75007 Paris, France. E-mail: institut.idef@gmail.com.
URL: http://www.institut-idef.org/

History 9 Jun 1964, Paris (France). Founded at the suggestion of Alain Plantey and René Cassin. First congress, Jan 1966, Fort-Lamy. Statutes most recently modified 21 Jun 1995. Former names and other names: *Institut international de droit des pays d'expression française* – former. Registration: RNA, No/ID: W751016088, France. **Aims** Establish links and facilitate exchange of ideas among individuals and organizations concerned with study or practice of *law* in countries that are wholly or partially French-speaking; promote and organize cultural exchange and cooperation between individuals and institutions of different nationalities concerned with legal problems. **Structure** General Assembly (annual); Governing Board; Bureau; General Secretariat. **Languages** French. **Staff** 5.00 FTE, voluntary. **Finance** Sources: grants; members' dues. **Activities** Events/meetings; publishing activities. **Events** *Congress* Sharjah (United Arab Emirates) 2017, *Annual Congress / Regional Colloquium* Montréal, QC (Canada) 2013, *Congress* Paris (France) 2003, *Congress* Cairo (Egypt) 2000, *Annual congress / Congress / Regional Colloquium* Beirut (Lebanon) 1999. **Publications** *Indépendance et coopération* (4 a year) – journal; *Bulletin de l'IDEF* (2 a year). Congress and colloquium proceedings.

Members National sections and correspondents in 53 countries:
Algeria, Belgium, Benin, Bulgaria, Burkina Faso, Burundi, Cambodia, Cameroon, Canada, Central African Rep, Chad, Comoros, Congo Brazzaville, Congo DR, Côte d'Ivoire, Czechia, Djibouti, Dominican Rep, Egypt, France, Gabon, Guinea, Guyana, Haiti, Hungary, India, Iran Islamic Rep, Jordan, Laos, Lebanon, Luxembourg, Madagascar, Mali, Mauritania, Mauritius, Moldova, Monaco, Morocco, Niger, Poland, Romania, Russia, Rwanda, Senegal, Seychelles, Switzerland, Syrian AR, Thailand, Togo, Tunisia, USA, Vanuatu, Vietnam.

IGO Relations *UNESCO (#20322)*. **NGO Relations** Member of (1): *Association francophone d'amitié et de liaison (AFAL, #02605)*. Partner of: *Global Forum on Law, Justice and Development (GFLJD, #10373)*. [2022/XC2151/j/**C**]

♦ Institut international de droit humanitaire (#13885)
♦ Institut international de droit linguistique comparé / see International Academy of Linguistic Law (#11556)
♦ Institut international de droit des pays d'expression française / see Institut international de droit d'expression et d'inspiration françaises (#11310)
♦ Institut international de droit public (inactive)
♦ Institut International pour les Droits et le Développement (unconfirmed)
♦ Institut international des droits de l'enfant (internationally oriented national body)
♦ Institut international pour les droits des enfants et le développement (internationally oriented national body)
♦ Institut international pour les droits des groupes ethniques et pour le régionalisme (#13300)
♦ Institut international des droits de l'homme / see International Institute of Human Rights – Fondation René Cassin (#13887)
♦ Institut international des droits de l'homme – Fondation René Cassin (#13887)
♦ Institut international des droits de l'Homme et de la paix (internationally oriented national body)
♦ Institut international de droit spatial (#13926)
♦ Institut für Internationale Angelegenheiten, Hamburg (internationally oriented national body)
♦ Institut International de l'Écologie Industrielle and de l'Économie Verte (internationally oriented national body)
♦ Institut international d'économie humaine (inactive)
♦ Institut international d'économie sociale (inactive)
♦ Institut international d'émailleurs (#13267)
♦ Institut international d'embryologie / see International Society of Developmental Biologists (#15052)
♦ Institut international d'embryologie (inactive)
♦ Institut international d'énergie par les micro-ondes (#14160)
♦ Institut international pour l'enseignement supérieur en Amérique latine et dans les Caraïbes / see UNESCO International Institute for Higher Education in Latin America and the Caribbean (#20309)
♦ Institut der Internationalen Sozialen Kooperation / see Institut de coopération sociale internationale (#11237)
♦ Institut international pour l'environnement et le développement (#13877)
♦ Institut Internationale de la pensée Islamique / see International Institute of Islamic Thought (#13894)
♦ Institut internationale de recherche et de formation, Amsterdam (internationally oriented national body)

- ♦ Institut international d'ergonomie et technologie dentaire (inactive)
- ♦ Institut für Internationales Geistiges Eigentum (internationally oriented national body)
- ♦ Institut international d'espéranto (#13302)
- ♦ Institut für Internationales Recht, Kiel / see Walther-Schücking-Institute for International Law
- ♦ Institut international d'esthétique appliquée (internationally oriented national body)
- ♦ Institut international pour l'étude des causes des maladies mentales et leur prophylaxie (inactive)
- ♦ Institut international d'étude et de documentation en matière de concurrence commerciale (inactive)
- ♦ Institut international d'études administratives de Montréal (internationally oriented national body)
- ♦ Institut international d'études afro-américaines (inactive)
- ♦ Institut International d'Etudes d'Asie Centrale (#13868)
- ♦ Institut international d'études bancaires (#12313)
- ♦ Institut international d'études des classes moyennes (inactive)
- ♦ Institut international pour les études de défense sociale / see International Society of Social Defence and Humane Criminal Policy (#15447)
- ♦ Institut international d'études des droits de l'homme, Trieste (internationally oriented national body)
- ♦ Institut international d'études européennes Antonio Rosmini (internationally oriented national body)
- ♦ Institut international d'études généalogiques et d'histoire des familles (internationally oriented national body)

♦ Institut international d'études ligures (IIEL) 11311

International Institute for Ligurian Studies – Istituto Internazionale di Studi Liguri (IISL)

Dir Via Romana 39, 18012 Bordighera IM, Italy. T. +39184263601. Fax +39184266421. E-mail: iisl.segreteria@gmail.com.
URL: http://www.iisl.it/

History 1947, Bordighera (Italy). Established to carry on the work of: *Bicknell International Library and Museum*, set up in 1888; Società Storica Archeologica Ingauna e Intemelia, created in 1932; Istituto di Studi Liguri, formed in 1941. Registration: Start date: 7 Mar 1947, Italy. **Aims** Promote research and appreciation of prehistoric, archaeological, linguistic, underwater *archaeology* and historical aspects of ancient monuments and regional traditions in the North-West arc of the *Mediterranean* (Northern Italy, Southern France, Spain). **Structure** General Assembly; Council; Officers. Membership subject to acceptance by Selection Committee. **Languages** French, Italian, Spanish. **Staff** 14.00 FTE, paid; 2.00 FTE, voluntary. **Finance** Sources: government support; grants; members' dues; sale of publications. **Activities** Events/ meetings; training/education. **Events** *Museo Navale Romano Di Albenga – A Project for the New Millenium* Albenga (Italy) 2019, *Italian and French Riviera – Similarities and Differences* France 2019, *La Valorisation de l'Archéologie Sous-Marine en Italie* Albenga (Italy) / Genoa (Italy) 2018, *Monstres, Artisanat et Saints dans les Plafonds en Bois Médieval* Bordighera (Italy) 2018, *Congress* Albenga (Italy) 2006. **Publications** *Cahiers Ligures*; *Cahiers Rhodaniens*; *Forma Maris Antiqui*; *Giornale Storico della Lunigiana* in French, Italian, Spanish; *Ligures*; *Quaderni SIMA*; *Rivista di Archeologia, Storia, Arte e Cultura Ligure*; *Rivista di Studi Liguri* in English, French, Italian, Spanish; *Rivista Ingauna e Intemelia*; *Studi Genuensi*. Monographs; various collections; congress proceedings. Reviews published by member sections. Information Services: Maintains a Central Library (over 116,000 vols).

Members Sections (11), composed of municipalities and individuals (about 1,000), in 8 countries:
Austria, Belgium, France, Germany, Italy, Monaco, Spain, Switzerland. [2021.05.26/XD2127/j/**E**]

- ♦ Institut international d'études sociales (#13897)
- ♦ Institut international d'études stratégiques (#13927)
- ♦ Institut international des experts maritimes (#13900)
- ♦ Institut für Internationale Zusammenarbeit des Deutschen Volkshochschul-Verbandes (internationally oriented national body)
- ♦ Institut international du film sur l'art (inactive)
- ♦ Institut international des films du travail (inactive)
- ♦ Institut international de finances publiques (#13915)
- ♦ Institut international du froid (#13918)
- ♦ Institut international de génie biomédical (inactive)
- ♦ Institut international de hautes études, Caracas (internationally oriented national body)

♦ Institut international d'histoire du notariat (IIHN) 11312

SG-Treas 60 bd de la Tour-Maubourg, 75007 Paris, France. T. +33144903025. Fax +33144903030. E-mail: gnomon@notaires.fr.
Pres address not obtained.
URL: http://www.notaires.fr/fr/institut-international-dhistoire-du-notariat-iihn/

History 1974, Paris (France). Former names and other names: *Le Gnomon* – alias. Registration: France. **Aims** Bring together those interested in the history of the profession of notary and in collecting related items. **Structure** General Assembly (annual); Board of Directors. **Languages** French. **Staff** 1.00 FTE, paid. **Finance** Sources: members' dues; subscriptions. **Activities** Awards/prizes/competitions. **Events** *L'Histoire de l'Authenticité, Pilier de la Sécurité Juridique* Paris (France) 2022, *General Assembly* France 2019, *1918, le prix de la paix* Paris (France) 2018, *General Assembly* 2008, *Colloquium* Paris (France) 2008. **Publications** *Le Gnomon – Revue internationale d'histoire du notariat* (4 a year).

Members Notaries; Universities; Correspondents. Notaries in 45 countries and territories:
Algeria, Argentina, Austria, Belgium, Benin, Brazil, Bulgaria, Burkina Faso, Cameroon, Canada, Chile, Colombia, Congo DR, Côte d'Ivoire, Czechia, Dominican Rep, Ecuador, Estonia, Gabon, Georgia, Germany, Greece, Guinea, Haiti, Hungary, Italy, Lithuania, Luxembourg, Mali, Mexico, Morocco, Netherlands, Niger, Poland, Puerto Rico, Romania, Russia, Senegal, Slovakia, Spain, Switzerland, Tunisia, Türkiye, Uruguay, USA.

NGO Relations Member of (2): Association Française pour l'Histoire de la Justice; *International Council on Archives (ICA, #12996)*. [2021.05.26/XE0972/j/**E**]

- ♦ Institut international d'histoire de la Révolution française (inactive)
- ♦ Institut international d'histoire sociale (internationally oriented national body)
- ♦ Institut international pour l'hydraulique et l'environnement / see IHE Delft Institute for Water Education (#11110)
- ♦ Institut international de l'hyléa amazonienne (inactive)
- ♦ Institut international de l'image et du son (internationally oriented national body)

♦ Institut International d'Ingénierie de l'Eau et de l'Environnement (2iE) 11313

International Institute for Water and Environmental Engineering (2iE)

Dir Gen Rue de la Science – 01 BP 594, Ouagadougou 01, Burkina Faso. T. +22625492800. Fax +22625492801. E-mail: 2ie@2ie-edu.org – admission@2ie-edu.org.
URL: http://www.2ie-edu.org/

History 2004. Founded on merger of *Inter-State Organization for Advanced Technicians of Hydraulics and Rural Equipment (ETSHER, inactive)* and *Inter-State School of Rural Equipment Engineers (inactive)*. Former names and other names: *Inter-State Institution of Higher Learning and Research in the Areas of Water, Energy, Environment and Public Work (EIER-ETSHER)* – former. **Aims** Contribute to the regional integration of men and knowledge for development in Western and Central Africa; increase economical growth of member states in the field of *water, energy, environment* and public works. **Structure** General Assembly (annual); Board of Directors; Scientific Committee; Management Committee. **Languages** French. **Staff** 105 teachers-researchers; 105 support and administrative staff. **Finance** Sources: donations; government support. Other sources: scholarship fees; governments of Burkina Faso, Canada, France, Switzerland. Supported by: *African Development Bank (ADB, #00283)*; *African Union (AU, #00488)*; *European Union (EU, #08967)*; *International Bank for Reconstruction and Development (IBRD, #12317)* (World Bank); *Union économique et monétaire Ouest africaine (UEMOA, #20377)*; *United States Agency for International Development (USAID)* (HED). **Activities** Certification/accreditation; knowledge management/information dissemination; research/ documentation; training/education. **Events** *International symposium on global campus for sustainability education* Sapporo (Japan) 2010.

Members Governments of 16 countries:
Benin, Burkina Faso, Cameroon, Central African Rep, Chad, Congo Brazzaville, Congo DR, Côte d'Ivoire, Gabon, Guinea, Guinea-Bissau, Mali, Mauritania, Niger, Senegal, Togo.

IGO Relations Member of (1): *African and Malagasy Council for Higher Education (#00364)*. Partner of (1): *West African Science Service Center on Climate Change and Adapted Land Use (WASCAL, #20897)*. Partnership agreements with: *Institut de recherche pour le développement (IRD)*; *Centre de coopération internationale en recherche agronomique pour le développement (CIRAD, #03733)*; *International Development Research Centre (IDRC, #13162)*; *UNESCO (#20322)*; national organizations. **NGO Relations** Member of (6): *Association of African Universities (AAU, #02361)*; *Global Water Partnership (GWP, #10653)*; *Higher Education Sustainability Initiative (HESI)*; *International Commission of Agricultural and Biosystems Engineering (#12661)*; national associations; *World Water Council (WWC, #21908)*. Partner of (2): *Africa-EU Innovation Alliance for Water and Climate (AfriAlliance, #00169)*; *Green Growth Knowledge Platform (GGKP, #10719)*. Partnership agreement with: *Oxfam Novib*. [2021.10.27/XM1276/j/**F***]

- ♦ Institut international d'intégration de la Convention Andrés Bello (#13940)
- ♦ Institut international des interprètes (inactive)
- ♦ Institut international Jacques Maritain (#13967)
- ♦ Institut international de journalisme et communication (internationally oriented national body)
- ♦ Institut international de journalisme, Ecole de solidarité / see International Institute of Journalism, Berlin – Brandenburg
- ♦ Institut international de journalisme 'José Marti' (#11340)
- ♦ Institut international de journalisme 'Werner Lamberz', Ecole de solidarité / see International Institute of Journalism, Berlin – Brandenburg
- ♦ Institut International pour La Justice et l'Etat de Droit (#13896)
- ♦ Institut international de langue arabe à Kharthoum (no recent information)
- ♦ Institut international des langues et civilisations africaines / see International African Institute (#11596)
- ♦ Institut international pour la littérature enfantine, juvénile et populaire / see International Institute for Children's Literature and Reading Research (#13869)
- ♦ Institut international de littérature ibéroaméricaine (#13888)
- ♦ Institut international pour la littérature juvénile et de la recherche sur la lecture (#13869)
- ♦ Institut international Mahayana (#14074)
- ♦ Institut international de management de l'irrigation / see International Water Management Institute (#15867)
- ♦ Institut international du manganèse (#14083)
- ♦ Institut international de la marionnette / see Institut international de la marionnette (#11314)

♦ Institut international de la marionnette (IIM) 11314

Dir 7 place Winston Churchill, 08000 Charleville-Mézières, France. T. +33324337250. E-mail: institut@marionnette.com.
URL: http://www.marionnette.com/

History 1981. Established in tight collaboration with *Union internationale de la marionnette (UNIMA, #20430)*. Former names and other names: *International Puppet Institute* – former; *International Institute of Puppetry* – former; *Institut international de la marionnette (IIM)* – former. Registration: France. **Aims** Promote research, *artistic* education and training on puppetry arts in connection with other arts. **Structure** Departments (4): Initial training and professional continuing education; Research and innovation; Arts and cultural education; Documentation and collections centre. **Languages** English, French, Spanish. **Activities** Events/meetings; publishing activities; research and development; training/education. **Events** *European encounter of higher schools of puppetry arts* Charleville-Mézières (France) 2007, *Meeting* Bialystok (Poland) 2006, *International encounter for teaching of the arts* Charleville-Mézières (France) 1999, *Rencontre internationale des enseignements artistiques* Charleville-Mézières (France) 1996, *Rencontre internationale des professeurs d'histoire et de théorie du théâtre et de la marionnette intervenants dans l'enseignement supérieur* Charleville-Mézières (France) 1995. **Publications** *Puck Review* in French – previous issues in German, Spanish. Specialized publications; bibliographies; studies; monographs; reports; proceedings. **Information Services** *Centre de documentation sur les arts de la marionnette*.

Members Individual and institutional membership covers 77 countries and territories:
Albania, Algeria, Argentina, Australia, Austria, Belgium, Bolivia, Bosnia-Herzegovina, Brazil, Bulgaria, Cameroon, Canada, Chile, China, Colombia, Congo Brazzaville, Congo DR, Costa Rica, Côte d'Ivoire, Croatia, Cuba, Czechia, Denmark, Egypt, El Salvador, Estonia, Finland, France, Georgia, Germany, Greece, Guatemala, Honduras, Hong Kong, Hungary, Iceland, India, Indonesia, Iran Islamic Rep, Iraq, Ireland, Israel, Italy, Kenya, Lithuania, Luxembourg, Madagascar, Mali, Moldova, Montenegro, Morocco, Netherlands, Nicaragua, Niger, Norway, Paraguay, Peru, Poland, Portugal, Romania, Russia, Serbia, Slovakia, Slovenia, South Africa, Spain, Sri Lanka, Sweden, Switzerland, Togo, Tunisia, Türkiye, Ukraine, Uruguay, USA, Venezuela, Vietnam.

NGO Relations Set up, 1987, the French 'Ecole nationale supérieure des arts de la marionnette' which accepts foreign students, and originated the *International Convention of Puppetry Schools (#12938)*, signed 1990, Charleville-Mézières, during the first 'Rencontre internationale des écoles de marionnette'. Proposed the setting up of a *Réseau international des sources de recherche sur la marionnette*. [2022.10.20/XF0010/j/**F**]

- ♦ Institut international de mécanoculture (inactive)
- ♦ Institut international du médiateur / see International Ombudsman Institute (#14411)
- ♦ Institut international pour les méthodes d'alphabétisation des adultes (no recent information)
- ♦ Institut international de musique, Darmstadt (internationally oriented national body)
- ♦ Institut international pour la musique traditionnelle (inactive)
- ♦ Institut international des observateurs électoraux / see Global Democracy Initiative
- ♦ Institut international de l'océan (#14394)
- ♦ Institut international olympique (inactive)
- ♦ Institut international de l'Ombudsman (#14411)
- ♦ Institut international d'optimalisation stochastique (inactive)
- ♦ Institut international de l'organisation scientifique du travail (inactive)
- ♦ Institut international de la paix / see International Institute for Peace (#13907)
- ♦ Institut international de la paix, Monaco (inactive)
- ♦ Institut international pour la paix par le tourisme (internationally oriented national body)
- ♦ Institut international de pédagogie familiale (inactive)
- ♦ Institut international de philosophie (#13910)
- ♦ Institut international de philosophie du droit et de sociologie juridique (inactive)
- ♦ Institut international de photographie (inactive)
- ♦ Institut international de planification de l'éducation (#13874)
- ♦ Institut international de plasmogène et de biologie universelles (inactive)
- ♦ Institut international de politique publique (internationally oriented national body)
- ♦ Institut international de la potasse (#14626)
- ♦ Institut international de la presse (#14636)
- ♦ Institut international pour les problèmes humains du travail (inactive)
- ♦ Institut international de producteurs de caoutchouc synthétique (#13931)

♦ Institut international de promotion et de prestige (IIPP) 11315

International Institute for Promotion and Prestige – Internationales Institut für Förderung und Ansehen

Pres address not obtained. E-mail: info@iipp.org.
Hon Pres Rue Varembé 1, 1202 Geneva, Switzerland.
URL: http://www.iipp.org/

History 1963, Geneva (Switzerland). Founded as an International Committee. New constitution and present title adopted 12 Oct 1968. Registration: Switzerland. **Aims** Pay tribute to and promote international recognition of those individuals, groups, companies or institutions who work for the advancement of human knowledge, scientific and technological progress and the enrichment of Man's cultural and artistic heritage. **Structure** General Assembly; Governing Board; Executive Committee. Committees (2): Consultative (advises on awards); Honorary. Co-Presidents (2) of the Scientific Sector. Commissions (2): Research; Awards. **Languages** English, French. **Staff** 17.00 FTE, paid. **Finance** Sources: sponsorship. **Activities** Awards/prizes/competitions. Awards the 'Trophée international' in various fields, the 'Prix de promotion internationale', the 'Médaille internationale humanitaire', the 'Mérite au développement'in various fields, the 'Médaille internationale art et création', as medals, cultural awards. **Events** *Ecology – economy* Paris (France) 1992.

Members Active; Honorary; Benefactor – consultative. Individuals (1023) in 75 countries and territories:

Algeria, Argentina, Austria, Belgium, Brazil, Bulgaria, Cameroon, Canada, Central African Rep, Chile, China, Colombia, Côte d'Ivoire, Croatia, Denmark, Estonia, Finland, France, Gabon, Germany, Greece, Grenada, Haiti, Honduras, Hong Kong, Hungary, India, Indonesia, Iran Islamic Rep, Ireland, Israel, Italy, Japan, Kosovo, Kuwait, Lebanon, Luxembourg, Madagascar, Mali, Mauritania, Mauritius, Mexico, Monaco, Montenegro, Morocco, Netherlands, Nicaragua, Niger, Nigeria, North Macedonia, Norway, Philippines, Poland, Portugal, Romania, Russia, Rwanda, Senegal, Serbia, Singapore, Slovakia, Slovenia, Somalia, Spain, Sweden, Switzerland, Taiwan, Togo, Tunisia, Türkiye, UK, Ukraine, USA, Venezuela, Zambia. [2022/XF3416/jv/**F**]

- ♦ Institut international de psychagogie et de psychothérapie: Charles Baudouin / see International Institute of Psychoanalysis and Psychotherapy Charles Baudouin (#13913)
- ♦ Institut international de psychanalyse et de psychothérapie Charles Baudouin (#13913)
- ♦ Institut international de radiotélédiffusion / see International Institute of Communications (#13870)
- ♦ Institut international de recherche sur les cultures des zones tropicales semi-arides (#13116)
- ♦ Institut international de recherche, de documentation et de formation pour la prévention et la lutte contre la falsification des produits de santé (internationally oriented national body)
- ♦ Institut international de recherche sur la paix de Stockholm (#19994)
- ♦ Institut international de recherche sur les politiques alimentaires (#13622)
- ♦ Institut international de recherche sur le riz (#14754)
- ♦ Institut International de Recherches Betteravières / see International Institute of Sugar Beet Research (#13928)
- ♦ Institut international de recherches sur l'étain / see International Tin Association (#15692)
- ♦ Institut international de recherches sur la paix à Genève (internationally oriented national body)
- ♦ Institut international des recherches sur la terminologie (#13932)
- ♦ Institut international pour la reconstruction rurale (#13921)
- ♦ Institut of International Relations, Athens (internationally oriented national body)
- ♦ Institut international des relations industrielles (inactive)
- ♦ Institut International Sainte Marcelline (religious order)
- ♦ Institut international pour la santé global de l'UNU (#20719)
- ♦ Institut international pour la science de frittage (#13922)
- ♦ Institut international de la science politique (inactive)
- ♦ Institut international des Sciences administratives (#13859)
- ♦ Institut international des sciences humaines intégrales (internationally oriented national body)
- ♦ Institut international des sciences théoriques (internationally oriented national body)
- ♦ Institut international de sexoanalyse (internationally oriented national body)
- ♦ Institut international de sociologie (#13925)
- ♦ Institut international de sociologie juridique d'Oñati (#17725)
- ♦ Institut international de sociologie et de réformes politiques et sociales (inactive)
- ♦ Institut international du son (inactive)
- ♦ Institut international du soufre (#20034)
- ♦ Institut international de statistique (#15603)
- ♦ Institut international de sténographie (inactive)
- ♦ Institut international de techno-bibliographie (inactive)
- ♦ Institut international de la technologie de contrôle du bruit (#13903)
- ♦ Institut international de technologie et d'économie apicoles / see Fundatia Institutul International de Tehnologie si Economie Apicola
- ♦ Institut International du Théâtre (#15683)
- ♦ Institut international du théâtre de la Méditerranée (internationally oriented national body)
- ♦ Institut international de théologie pour la pastorale de la santé (#13906)
- ♦ Institut International de l'UNESCO pour l'enseignement supérieur en Amérique latine et dans les Caraïbes (#20309)
- ♦ Institut international de l'UNESCO pour le renforcement des capacités en Afrique (#20308)
- ♦ Institut international pour l'unification du droit privé (#13934)
- ♦ Institut international de l'UNU pour la technologie des logiciels / see United Nations University Institute on Computing and Society (#20644)
- ♦ Institut international de vaccins (#15839)
- ♦ Institut international sur le vieillissement des Nations Unies / see International Institute on Ageing, United Nations – Malta (#13860)
- ♦ Institut international sur le vieillissement, Nations Unies -Malte (#13860)
- ♦ Institut interrégional de recherche des Nations Unies sur la criminalité et la justice (#20580)

♦ Institutional Development Programme between European and Latin American Universities (COLUMBUS Association) 11316

Exec Dir 114 rue du Rhône, Case Postale 3174, 1211 Geneva 3, Switzerland.
URL: http://www.columbus-web.org/

History 1987, by *Association of European Universities (CRE, inactive)* and *Association of Universities of Latin America and the Caribbean (#02970)*. Originally also referred to as *Collaboration on University Management – a Bridge between Universities and Scholars in Europe and Latin America*. Previously also referred to as *COLUMBUS Project* and *COLUMBUS Programme*. **Aims** Promote multilateral cooperation in higher education; disseminate innovative experience in key areas of *institutional management*; guide *universities* through the process of adaptation and internationalization; foster multilateral cooperation in *higher education*; track key developments; identify institutional innovation; facilitate exchange of experience; support change processes; stimulate projects of common interest among member universities. **Structure** General Assembly; Governing Board. **Languages** English, French, German, Italian, Portuguese, Spanish. **Finance** Members' dues. Other sources: UNESCO; European Commission; European and Latin American governments. **Activities** Training/education; networking/liaising; guidance/assistance/consulting; events/meetings. **Events** *The internationalization of higher education, the emergence of regional spaces* Turin (Italy) 2000. **Publications** Documents; collections; manuals.
Members Universities (48) in 14 countries:
Argentina, Belgium, Brazil, Chile, Colombia, Costa Rica, Ecuador, Ireland, Italy, Mexico, Peru, Portugal, Spain, Venezuela.
IGO Relations Sponsoring organizations: *European Commission (EC, #06633)*; *UNESCO (#20322)*.
[2017.10.30/XE2332/**E**]

♦ Institutional Investors Group on Climate Change (IIGCC) 11317

Chief Exec Adam House, 7-10 Adam Street, The Strand, London, WC2N 6AA, UK. T. +442075209302. E-mail: info@iigcc.org.
Registered address c/o JS2, One Crowns Square, Woking, GU21 6HR, UK.
URL: http://www.iigcc.org/

History Registration: Private company limited by guarantee, No/ID: 07921860, Start date: 24 Jan 2012, England. **Aims** Provide investors with a collaborative platform to encourage public policies, investment practices and corporate behaviour that address long-term risks and opportunities associated with climate change. **Structure** Board. Secretariat. **Events** *Annual General Meeting* London (UK) 2015. **Members** Mainstream investors (over 140) in 11 countries. Membership countries not specified. **NGO Relations** Member of (1): *Global Investor Coalition on Climate Change (GIC, #10434)*. Cooperates with (1): *We Mean Business*. Instrumental in setting up (1): *Climate Investment Coalition (CIC, #04014)*. [2020/XJ9742/**F**]

- ♦ Institutional Limited Partners Association (internationally oriented national body)
- ♦ Institution Arabe de Navigation (#00985)

♦ Institution of Chemical Engineers (IChemE) 11318

Head Office Davis Bldg, Railway Terrace, Rugby, CV21 3HQ, UK. T. +441788578214. Fax +441788560833. E-mail: customerservices@icheme.org.
URL: http://www.icheme.org/

History 1922, UK. Registration: Charity Commission, No/ID: 214379, England and Wales; Charity Commission, No/ID: SC039661, Scotland. **Aims** Set standards for chemical and process safety engineering professionals; advance the contribution of chemical engineering for the good of society. **Structure** Board of Trustees; Congress. **Languages** English. **Staff** 100.00 FTE, paid. Voluntary. **Finance** Sources: members' dues. **Activities** Awards/prizes/competitions; events/meetings. **Events** *KIHSSE : Kuwait International Health, Safety, Security and Environment Conference* Kuwait (Kuwait) 2019, *Hazards Conference* Singapore (Singapore) 2016, *European Gasification Conference* Rotterdam (Netherlands) 2014, *Nuclear fuel cycle conference* Manchester (UK) 2012, *European gasification conference* Amsterdam (Netherlands) 2010. **Publications** *The Chemical Engineer* (10 a year) – magazine; *Loss Prevention Bulletin*. *Chemical Engineering Research and Design*; *Forms of Contract*; *Process Safety and Environmental Protection*; *Sustainable Production and Consumption*. **Members** Individuals (over 40,000) in over 100 countries. Membership countries not specified.
[2020/XM3922/j/**C**]

♦ Institution of Civil Engineers (ICE) 11319

Contact 1 Great George Street, Westminster, London, SW1P 3AA, UK.
URL: http://www.ice.org.uk/

History Founded 1818. UK Registered Charity: 210252. **Aims** Support civil engineers and technicians. **Structure** Board of Trustees; Council. **Activities** Awards/prizes/competitions; events/meetings; knowledge management/information dissemination; training/education. **Events** *European Local Associations Conference* Paris (France) 2016, *Coastal Management Conference* Amsterdam (Netherlands) 2015, *Forum on Resilient Society and Social Infrastructure Development Policy in Accordance with People's Attitudes* Tokyo (Japan) 2012, *International conference on sustainable construction materials and technologies* Ancona (Italy) 2010, *Conference on coasts, marine structures and breakwaters* Edinburgh (UK) 2009. [2020/XW0456/j/**C**]

- ♦ Institution de coordination nordique des questions relatives à la population lapone et à l'élevage de rennes (no recent information)
- ♦ Institution of Electrical Engineers / see Institution of Engineering and Technology (#11320)
- ♦ Institutionen för Freds-och Konfliktforskning vid Uppsala Universitet (internationally oriented national body)
- ♦ Institutionen för Freds- och Utvecklingsforskning, Göteborgs Universitet (internationally oriented national body)

♦ Institution of Engineering and Technology (IET) 11320

Chief Exec/Sec c/o Michael Faraday House, Six Hills Way, Stevenage, SG1 2AY, UK. T. +441438313311. E-mail: postmaster@theiet.org.
INSPEC Contact – Americas 379 Thornall St, Edison NJ 08837, USA. T. +17323215575. Fax +17323215702. E-mail: inspec@inspecinc.com.
URL: http://www.theiet.org/

History 1871, UK. Current name adopted when merged with Institution of Incorporated Engineers (IIE) in 2006. Incorporated in UK by Royal Charter, 15 Aug 1921; most recent amendment Nov 2007. By-laws adopted 23 Mar 1922; most recently amended Nov 2007. Former names and other names: *Institution of Electrical Engineers (IEE)* – former (1871 to 2006). **Aims** Promote the advancement of science, engineering and technology; facilitate the exchange of knowledge and ideas on these subjects. **Structure** General Meeting (annual). Board of Trustees. Chief Executive; Secretary. Branches. **Finance** Sources: members' dues; revenue from activities/projects. Annual budget: 50,000,000 GBP. **Activities** Certification/accreditation; events/meetings; training/education. **Events** *International Conference on Radar Systems* Edinburgh (UK) 2022, *International Conference on Renewable Power Generation* London (UK) 2022, *ISAP : International Symposium on Antennas and Propagation* Stevenage (UK) 2021, *ISAP : International Symposium on Antennas and Propagation* Osaka (Japan) 2020, *International Topical Meeting on Microwave Photonics* Stevenage (UK) 2020. **Publications** *Electronics Letters* (bi-weekly) – journal; *Physics Abstracts (PA)* (bi-weekly); *Computers and Control Abstracts (CCA)* (12 a year); *Electrical and Electronics Abstracts (EEA)* (12 a year); *Key Abstracts* (12 a year); *IET Research Journals* (6 a year) – also online; *Electronics Education* (3 a year); *Wiring Matters* (2 a year); *IET Careers* (23 a year) – newspaper. *Current Papers in Electrical and Electronics Engineering*; *Current Papers in Physics*; *Current Papers on Computing and Control*. Book series in the following fields: BTexact Communication Technology; Telecommunications; Electromagnetic Waves; Radar, Sonar, Navigation and Avionics; Circuits, Devices and Systems (EMIS); EMIS Processing; Materials and Devices; Energy; Power and Energy; Control; Professional Applications of Computing; Electrical Measurement; History of Technology; Manufacturing. Distance Learning Series: Communications (C Series); Manufacturing (I and ME Series); Management for Engineers (M Series); Regulations, Standards, Codes of Practice, Safety (R Series); Software Engineering (S Series). Annual Review. Conference proceedings. Other publications on: Wiring Regulations and Associate Trade; Engineering Policy. Information Services: Library and electronic library. **Information Services** *IET Information Service*; *Information Services for the Physics and Engineering Communities (INSPEC)*; *INFOTRIEVE*; *INSPEC Database* – over 10 million scientific and technical papers; *INSPEC Direct*; *INSPEC Site Licensing*; *SDI* – Customised Search Profiles; *Topics*.
Members Individuals (about 153,000, 80% in UK) in several categories according to Charter. Members in 131 countries and territories:
Algeria, Argentina, Australia, Austria, Bahamas, Bahrain, Bangladesh, Barbados, Belarus, Belgium, Belize, Bermuda, Botswana, Brazil, Brunei Darussalam, Bulgaria, Cambodia, Cameroon, Canada, Central African Rep, Chile, China, Colombia, Congo DR, Costa Rica, Côte d'Ivoire, Croatia, Cyprus, Czechia, Denmark, Ecuador, Egypt, El Salvador, Estonia, Eswatini, Ethiopia, Fiji, Finland, France, Gabon, Gambia, Germany, Ghana, Gibraltar, Greece, Guinea, Guyana, Hong Kong, Hungary, Iceland, India, Indonesia, Iran Islamic Rep, Iraq, Ireland, Israel, Italy, Jamaica, Japan, Jordan, Kenya, Korea DPR, Korea Rep, Kuwait, Laos, Latvia, Lebanon, Lesotho, Libya, Luxembourg, Macau, Madagascar, Malawi, Malaysia, Malta, Mauritius, Mexico, Monaco, Morocco, Mozambique, Myanmar, Namibia, Nepal, Netherlands, New Zealand, Nigeria, North Macedonia, Norway, Oman, Pakistan, Papua New Guinea, Peru, Philippines, Poland, Portugal, Puerto Rico, Qatar, Romania, Russia, Saudi Arabia, Senegal, Serbia, Seychelles, Sierra Leone, Singapore, Slovakia, South Africa, Spain, Sri Lanka, Sudan, Sweden, Switzerland, Syrian AR, Taiwan, Tanzania UR, Thailand, Togo, Tonga, Trinidad-Tobago, Türkiye, Uganda, UK, Ukraine, United Arab Emirates, Uruguay, USA, Venezuela, Yemen, Zambia, Zimbabwe.
NGO Relations Member of (1): *International Cost Management Standard Coalition (ICMS Coalition, #12978)*. Instrumental in setting up (1): *IBC (#11011)*. Joint meetings with: *SPIE (#19919)*. [2022/XF5191/jv/**F**]

♦ Institution of Fire Engineers (IFE) 11321

Sec c/o IFE House, 64-66 Cygnet Court, Timothy's Bridge Road, Stratford-upon-Avon, CV37 9NW, UK. T. +441789261463. Fax +441789296426. E-mail: info@ife.org.uk.
Registered Office Scottish Fire and Rescue Service, 93 McDonald Road, Edinburgh, UK.
URL: http://www.ife.org.uk/

History 31 Oct 1918, Leicester (UK). First Memorandum, Articles of Association and By-Laws approved, and initial membership fees fixed at 2nd meeting, 2 Jan 1919. **Aims** Pomote, encourage and improve the science, practice and professionalism of fire engineering, acting as a beacon of established expertise and guiding the way to a fire safe future. **Languages** English. **Staff** 24.00 FTE, paid. **Activities** Certification/accreditation; events/meetings; training/education. **Events** *Annual General Conference / Annual Conference* London (UK) 2015, *Annual General Conference / Annual Conference* Stratford-upon-Avon (UK) 2014, *Fire Seminar* Singapore (Singapore) 2013, *Annual Conference* Stratford-upon-Avon (UK) 2013, *Annual Conference* Stratford-upon-Avon (UK) 2012. **Publications** *International Fire Professional Journal* (4 a year); *E-newsletter* (8 a year). *A Guide to Fire Investigation* by Patrick G Cox; *A Political Analysis of the British Fire Service* by L Leckie; *Culture, Identity and Change in the Fire and Rescue Service: Leadership Lessons for the 21st Century* by Dr Brian Allaway; *Disasters and Emergencies: Managing the Response* by W R Tucker; *Elementary Fire Engineering Handbook* (4th ed); *Equal Opportunities* by Margaret Southworth; *Introduction to Total Quality Management* by Glenys Southworth; *Level 4 Certificate Self Study Guide*; *Risk Assessment of the Emergency Services* by R A Klein. **Members** Individuals (over 10,000). Membership countries not specified. **NGO Relations** Member of (1): *International Fire Safety Standards Coalition (IFSS Coalition, #13606)*.
[2022.02.09/XD3070/jv/**F**]

- ♦ Institution internationale de l'éducation physique (inactive)
- ♦ Institution internationale pour l'électronique appliquée (inactive)
- ♦ Institution of Municipal Engineering of Southern Africa / see Institute of Municipal Engineering of Southern Africa
- ♦ Institution de la Mutuelle Panfricaine de Gestion de Risques (#00442)
- ♦ Institution nordique de coordination de l'information scientifique (inactive)
- ♦ Institution nordique pour la coordination de la recherche agricole / see Nordic Joint Committee for Agricultural and Food Research (#17332)
- ♦ Institution of Occupational Safety and Health (internationally oriented national body)
- ♦ Institution of Permanent Way Inspectors / see Permanent Way Institution
- ♦ Institution de la sécurité et de la santé au travail (internationally oriented national body)

Institution Structural Engineers
11322

alphabetic sequence excludes
For the complete listing, see Yearbook Online at

♦ Institution of Structural Engineers (IStructE) 11322

Chief Exec International HQ, 47-58 Bastwick Street, London, EC1V 3PS, UK. T. +442072354535. E-mail: mail@istructe.org.
URL: http://www.istructe.org/

History 1908, London (UK), as *Concrete Institute*. Current title adopted 1922. Previously also known under the acronym *ISE*. Registered Charity in England and Wales: 233392. Registered Charity in Scotland: SC038263. **Aims** Drive and support continuing development of the structural engineering profession and hold it to the highest standards. **Structure** Council; Board; President; Committees; Panels. **Languages** English. **Staff** 60.00 FTE, paid. **Activities** Awards/prizes/competitions; events/meetings; training/education. **Events** *International Conference* Singapore (Singapore) 2015, *ICSA : International Conference on Structures and Architecture* Guimarães (Portugal) 2013, *Conference on structural marvels* Singapore (Singapore) 2010, *International Kerensky conference* Hong Kong (Hong Kong) 1997, *International Kerensky conference* Singapore (Singapore) 1994. **Publications** *The Structural Engineer* (11 a year). Reports; ttechnical guides; manuals. **Members** Individuals (over 27,000) in 105 countries. Membership countries not specified. [2019.04.30/XN3602/jv/**B**]

♦ Institutip nittartagaanut tikilluarit / see Danish Institute for Human Rights
♦ Institut irlandais des affaires européennes, Louvain / see Leuven Institute for Ireland in Europe
♦ Institut islamique de recherche (internationally oriented national body)
♦ Institut islamique de recherches et de formation (#16050)
♦ Institut islamique de technologie / see Islamic University of Technology (#16055)
♦ Institut italien pour la recherche sur la paix (internationally oriented national body)
♦ Institut italo-latinoaméricain (#16071)
♦ Institut Jacob Blaustein pour le progrès des droits de l'homme (internationally oriented national body)
♦ Institut Jacques Delors (internationally oriented national body)
♦ **Institut für Jugendliteratur** Internationales Institut für Jugendliteratur und Leseforschung (#13869)
♦ Institut Jules-Destrée / see Institut Destrée
♦ Institut juridique international pour la protection des animaux (inactive)
♦ Institut Kajian Malaysia dan Antarabangsa (internationally oriented national body)
♦ Institut von Karman de dynamique des fluides (#16182)
♦ Institut für Kulturelle Weiterbildung (#11251)
♦ Institut kurde de Bruxelles (internationally oriented national body)
♦ Institut kurde pour la défense d'une culture millénaire en péril / see Kurdish Institute of Paris (#16212)
♦ Institut kurde de Paris (#16212)
♦ Institut für Lateinamerika-Studies (internationally oriented national body)
♦ Institut latinoaméricain et des Caraïbes de planification économique et sociale (#16279)
♦ Institut latinoaméricain de communication éducative (#11343)
♦ Institut latinoaméricain de la doctrine et des études sociales (#11345)
♦ Institut latinoaméricain de droit comparé (inactive)
♦ Institut latinoaméricain du droit des taxes (#11344)
♦ Institut latinoaméricain d'étude du marketing agricole (inactive)
♦ Institut latinoaméricain d'études sociales 'Humberto Valdez' (inactive)
♦ Institut Latinoaméricain du Fer et de l'Acier / see Asociación Latinoamericana del Acero (#02176)
♦ Institut latinoaméricain de haute technologie, d'informatique et de droit (#11341)
♦ Institut latinoaméricain de recherches sociales (#11346)
♦ Institut Laue – Langevin / see Institute Max von Laue – Paul Langevin (#11283)
♦ Institut Leonard Davis pour les relations internationales (internationally oriented national body)
♦ Institut libre d'étude des relations internationales / see Institut d'étude des relations internationales
♦ Institut des loueurs internationaux de conteneurs (#11273)
♦ Institut Madeleine Aulina (religious order)
♦ Institut Maghreb-Europe (internationally oriented national body)
♦ Institut des mandataires agréés près l'Office européen des brevets (#11288)
♦ Institut des manuscrits arabes (no recent information)
♦ Institut Marga (internationally oriented national body)
♦ Institut Marocain des Relations Internationales (internationally oriented national body)
♦ Institut Max von Laue – Paul Langevin (#11283)
♦ Institut de médecine et d'épidémiologie africaines / see Institut de Médecine et d'Epidémiologie Appliquée
♦ Institut de Médecine et d'Epidémiologie Appliquée (internationally oriented national body)
♦ Institut de médecine tropicale Bernhard Nocht (internationally oriented national body)
♦ Institut de médecine tropicale Prince Léopold (internationally oriented national body)
♦ Institut des médias d'Afrique australe (#16619)
♦ Institut de la Méditerranée (internationally oriented national body)
♦ Institut de la Méditerranée, Marseille / see Université de la Méditerranée, Marseille
♦ Institut méditerranéen (internationally oriented national body)
♦ Institut Méditerranéen de Biodiversité et d'Ecologie marine et continentale (internationally oriented national body)

♦ Institut méditerranéen de l'eau (IME) 11323

Mediterranean Water Institute – Instituto Mediterraneo del Agua – Akdeniz Su EnstitüsÜ

Exec Dir Immeuble "Le Schuman", 18/20 avenue Robert Schuman, 13002 Marseille, France. T. +33491598777. E-mail: info@ime-eau.org.
URL: http://www.ime-eau.org/

History 1982, Rabat (Morocco). Registered in accordance with French law. **Aims** Develop multilateral and trans-Mediterranean cooperation between local and territorial authorities, professionals and individuals concerned about the problem of water and *sanitation* in the Mediterranean. **Structure** General Assembly; Board of Directors; Bureau; General Secretariat. **Languages** Arabic, English, French, Spanish. **Staff** 4.00 FTE, paid. **Finance** Members' dues. Other sources: subvention from local, national and regional authorities; partnership agreements with international organizations. **Activities** Events/meetings; projects/programmes; networking/liaising; knowledge management/information dissemination. **Events** *Mediterranean Water Forum* Malta 2020, *Mediterranean Water Forum* Cairo (Egypt) 2018, *Réunion sur le Projet de Plate-Forme Méditerranéenne des Connaissances sur l'Eau* Barcelona (Spain) 2014, *Mediterranean Water Forum* Murcia (Spain) 2014, *SESAME : Séminaire International sur l'Eau et la Sécurité Alimentaire en Méditerranée* Montpellier (France) 2013. **Publications** *IME Information Letter*.
Members Active; Honorary; Associate; Observer. Local and Regional Authorities, Technical Departments of Water Ministries, public or private management organizations, associations, NGOs, research and training centres and private individuals. About 100 members in 11 countries and territories:
Algeria, France, Germany, Italy, Jordan, Lebanon, Morocco, Palestine, Spain, Tunisia, Türkiye.
IGO Relations Accredited by: *United Nations Office at Vienna (UNOV, #20604)*. **NGO Relations** Member of: *International Office for Water (IOW, #14399)*; *World Water Council (WWC, #21908)*. [2021/XE0040/j/**E**]

♦ Institut méditerranéen d'écologie et paléoécologie (internationally oriented national body)
♦ Institut méditerranéen de formation et recherche en travail social (internationally oriented national body)
♦ Institut za Medjunarodnu Politiku i Privredu, Belgrade (internationally oriented national body)
♦ Institut za Medunarodne Odnose, Zagreb / see Institute for Development and International Relations
♦ Institut for Menneskerettigheder (internationally oriented national body)
♦ Institut de métaphysique appliquée (inactive)
♦ Institut Mezdunarodnoj Socialnoj Kooperacii / see Institut de coopération sociale internationale (#11237)
♦ Institut po Mezdunarodnomu Sotrudnicestvu Nemeckoj Associacii Narodnyh Universitetov (internationally oriented national body)
♦ Institut Mezdunarodnyh Ekonomiceskih i Politiceskih Issledovanij (internationally oriented national body)
♦ Institut für Migrationsforschung und Interkulturelle Studien (internationally oriented national body)
♦ Institut für Migrations- und Rassismusforschung, Hamburg (internationally oriented national body)
♦ Institut Mirovoj Ekonomiki i Mezdunarodnyh Otnosenij Akademii Nauk SSSR / see Institut Mirovoj Ekonomiki i Mezdunarodnyh Otnosenij Rossijskoj Akademii Nauk
♦ Institut Mirovoj Ekonomiki i Mezdunarodnyh Otnosenij Rossijskoj Akademii Nauk (internationally oriented national body)
♦ Institut des Missionnaires de la Consolata (religious order)

♦ Institut du monde arabe (IMA) 11324

Arab World Institute

Contact 1 rue des Fossés-Saint-Bernard, 75236 Paris CEDEX 05, France. T. +33140513839. Fax +33143547645.
URL: http://www.imarabe.org/

History 23 Jun 1980, Paris (France), on agreement between France and several Arab states. **Aims** Develop and extend the study, knowledge and understanding of the Arab world in *France*, and of its *languages*, civilization and approach to development; promote *cultural* exchanges, communication and cooperation between France and the Arab world, particularly in the field of science and technology; contribute to the development of relations between the Arab world and Europe. **Structure** Council, consisting of: one representative of each founder member; Board of Directors, comprising 6 French and 6 Arab administrators. French President; Arab Director-General. **Staff** 158.00 FTE, paid. **Finance** Members' contributions. Budget (annual): French Fr 100 million. **Activities** Facilities include: museum of Islamic art; computerized library (70,000 volumes); reading and meeting rooms; L'Espace Image et Son for consultation of photographs and documentary films and for audiovisual archives; auditorium; audiovisual centre; computer centre; Language and Civilization Centre, providing courses in Arabic language studies. Organizes exhibitions, musical evenings, film shows, literary debates and colloquia. **Events** *Euro-Arab dialogue forum* Paris (France) 2006, *International Conference on Computers Helping People with Special Needs* Paris (France) 2004, *Colloque international sur les dynamiques des sociétés civiles* Paris (France) 1995, *International meeting* Paris (France) 1995, *Colloque sur l'Islam dans ses rapports avec l'Europe* Paris (France) 1992. **Publications** *Qantara* (4 a year) – cultural magazine; *Al-Moukhtarat* (3 a year). Educational Bibliography. Brochures presenting Arabic languages and cultures. Diverse publications covering Arab literature, history and culture. **Information Services** *EDINFO Databank* – list of publishing houses specialising exclusively or partially in the Arab world; *JARID Databank* – scientific information; *RIMA Databank* – libraries and documentation bodies with information on Arab world.
Members Governments of 21 countries:
Algeria, Bahrain, Djibouti, Egypt, France, Iraq, Jordan, Kuwait, Lebanon, Libya, Mauritania, Morocco, Oman, Qatar, Saudi Arabia, Somalia, Sudan, Syrian AR, Tunisia, United Arab Emirates, Yemen.
IGO Relations Cooperates with: *Islamic World Educational, Scientific and Cultural Organization (ICESCO, #16058)*. **NGO Relations** Library is member of: *International Federation of Library Associations and Institutions (IFLA, #13470)*. Cooperates with: *Arab Urban Development Institute (AUDI, #01071)*; *Institut de recherches et d'études sur le monde arabe et musulman (IREMAM, #11354)*. [2009/XE3974/j/**E***]

♦ Institut du Monde et du Développement pour la Bonne Gouvernance Publique (internationally oriented national body)
♦ Institut des mondes asiatiques (internationally oriented national body)
♦ Institut mondial des amis / see Global College, Long Island University
♦ Institut mondial des caisses d'épargne (#21764)
♦ Institut mondial des hautes études phénoménologiques / see World Phenomenology Institute (#21725)
♦ Institut mondial de phénoménologies – Weltinstitut für Phaenomenologie (#21725)
♦ Institut mondial du phosphate (#21728)
♦ Institut mondial de recherche sur l'économie du développement (#20722)
♦ Institut mondial des sciences (#21590)
♦ Institut monétaire de l'Afrique de l'ouest (#20888)
♦ Institut monétaire européen (inactive)
♦ Institut montréalais d'études sur le génocide et les droits de la personne (internationally oriented national body)
♦ Institut multinational de formation professionnelle des postes et télécommunications, Blantyre (no recent information)
♦ Institut national des langues et civilisations orientales (internationally oriented national body)
♦ Institut des Nations Unies d'Asie et de l'Extrême-Orient pour la prévention du délit et le traitement du délinquant / see United Nations Asia and Far East Institute for the Prevention of Crime and the Treatment of Offenders (#20521)
♦ Institut des Nations Unies pour la Formation et la Recherche (#20576)
♦ Institut des Nations Unies pour la recherche sur le désarmement (#20575)
♦ Institut néerlandais des droits de l'homme (internationally oriented national body)
♦ Institut de neurosciences cognitives de la méditerranée (internationally oriented national body)
♦ Institut nigérien pour les relations internationales (internationally oriented national body)
♦ Institut nordic de navigation (#17323)
♦ Institut nordique d'Åland (internationally oriented national body)
♦ Institut nordique pour le contrôle des matériaux dentaires (#17485)
♦ Institut nordique de droit maritime (#17515)
♦ Institut nordique d'études asiatiques / see NIAS-Nordisk Institut for Asienstudier (#17132)
♦ Institut nordique d'études sur la condition féminine et la recherche sur l'égalité des sexes / see Nordic Information for Gender Knowledge (#17317)
♦ Institut nordique pour la formation continue dans le domaine des conditions de travail (#17321)
♦ Institut nordique au Groenland (internationally oriented national body)
♦ Institut nordique pour la physique théorique (#17324)
♦ Institut nordique de recherches sur la peinture et l'imprimerie (inactive)
♦ Institut nordique à Reykjavik (internationally oriented national body)
♦ Institut nordique de technologie de l'information (inactive)
♦ Institut nordique de volcanologie / see Nordic Volcanological Center (#17463)
♦ Institut Nord-Sud (internationally oriented national body)
♦ Institut de Notre-Dame (religious order)
♦ Institut Notre-Dame de la Joie (religious order)
♦ Institut de Notre-Dame du Travail (religious order)
♦ Institut Notre-Dame de Vie (religious order)
♦ Institut de nutrition de l'Amérique centrale et de Panama (#11285)
♦ Instituto Africano de Informatica (#11235)
♦ Instituto Africano de Remessas (unconfirmed)
♦ Instituto Agronómico Mediterraneo de Zaragoza (#16644)
♦ Instituto Aleman de Desarrollo / see Deutsches Institut für Entwicklungspolitik
♦ Instituto de Alimentación y Nutrición del Caribe (inactive)
♦ Instituto de América Latina de la Academia de Ciencias de la URSS / see Institute of Latin America of the Russian Academy of Sciences
♦ Instituto Andino de Artes Populares (no recent information)
♦ Instituto Andino de Ecologia y Desarrollo (internationally oriented national body)
♦ Instituto Andino de Sistemas (internationally oriented national body)
♦ Instituto Aristides Calvani / see Instituto de Formación Demócrata Cristiana
♦ Instituto de Arrendadores Internacionales de Contenedores (#11273)
♦ Instituto Aspen (#02309)
♦ Instituto de Auditores Internos (#11272)
♦ Instituto Austriaco para América Latin (internationally oriented national body)
♦ Instituto Autor – Instituto de Derecho de Autor (internationally oriented national body)
♦ Instituto del Azufre (#20034)
♦ Instituto del Banco Mundial (#21220)
♦ Instituto Boliviano de Biologia de la Altura (internationally oriented national body)
♦ Instituto Brasileiro de Relações Internacionais (internationally oriented national body)
♦ Instituto del Canal de Panama y Estudios Internacionales (internationally oriented national body)

♦ Instituto Canario de Estudios de Derecho Internacional (internationally oriented national body)
♦ Instituto Caribeño para el Estado de Derecho (internationally oriented national body)
♦ Instituto Catalan de Cooperación Iberoamericana (internationally oriented national body)
♦ Instituto Catalan de Cultura Hispanica / see Institut Català de Cooperació Iberoamericana
♦ Instituto Centroamericano de Administración de Empresas / see INCAE Business School (#11141)
♦ Instituto Centroamericano de Administración Pública (#03670)
♦ Instituto Centroamericano de Capacitación Aeronautica (see: #04837)

♦ Instituto Centroamericano de Estudios Fiscales (ICEFI) 11325

Exec Dir 7 Avda 5-45 zona 4, Edificio XPO1, oficinas 505 y 506, 01004 Guatemala, Guatemala. T. +50225056363. E-mail: info@icefi.org.
URL: https://icefi.org/

History 2005. **Aims** Serve as a research centre that specializes in assessing fiscal policy in each Central American country, and in the region; generate knowledge to develop proposals and discussions on fiscal issues that contributes to formulation and implementation of fair, transparent and efficient public policies in Central America. **Structure** Advisory Board; Board of Directors. **Languages** English, Spanish. **Staff** 14.00 FTE, paid. **Finance** Supported by: *Christian Aid*; *International Bank for Reconstruction and Development (IBRD, #12317)* (World Bank); *Irish Aid*; *Swedish International Development Cooperation Agency (Sida)*; *UNICEF (#20332)*. **Activities** Guidance/assistance/consulting; knowledge management/information dissemination; networking/liaising; research/documentation; training/education. Active in: Costa Rica, El Salvador, Guatemala, Honduras, Nicaragua, Panama. **Publications** *Central American Fiscal Watch* (bi-weekly); *Central American Fiscal Lens* – newsletter; *Contamos! Fiscal Policy Bulletin*. *Fiscal Policy At the Crossroads: The case of Central America* – fiscal policy report; *Fiscal Policy in Times of Crises* – fiscal policy report. Fiscal studies bulletins; fiscal policy bulletins; public finances analysis papers; research; reports; other publications. **NGO Relations** Member of (1): *Red de Justicia Fiscal de América Latina y el Caribe*. Cooperates with (2): EUROsociAL; *Fundación Henry Dunant América Latina (FuHD – AL, #10024)*. [2022.05.11/XJ9327/j/**D**]

♦ Instituto Centroamericano de Estudios Legislativos / see Instituto Internacional de Estudios Legislativos del FOPREL (#11338)
♦ Instituto Centroamericano de Estudios Politicos (internationally oriented national body)

♦ Instituto Centroamericano de Estudios Sociales (ICAES) 11326

Institut d'études sociales d'Amérique centrale – Central American Institute of Social Studies

Address not obtained.
Twitter: https://twitter.com/icaesca

History Founded Feb 1964, Guatemala (Guatemala), as sub-regional institute of *Latin American Central of Workers (CLAT, inactive)*. **Aims** Contribute to promotion and development of people's organizations in the Central American region by providing technical assistance, educational programmes and information. **Events** *Central America conference on social security* San José (Costa Rica) 1988, *Seminario Centroamericano para los principales dirigentes de las organizaciones de trabajadores de la agricultura y la alimentacion* San José (Costa Rica) 1987. [2016/XE5910/j/**E**]

♦ Instituto Centroamericano de Estudios Sociales y Desarrollo (INCEDES) 11327

Contact 0 Calle 16-26 zona 15, Colonia El Maestro, 01015 Guatemala, Guatemala. T. +50223692774. E-mail: información@incedes.org.gt – incedes.programas@gmail.com.
URL: http://www.incedes.org.gt/

History Feb 2005. **Aims** Strengthen networks of thought and action for promotion of changes in social and institutional realities that foster human mobility in the Central-North America *migration* system from the perspective of human rights, gender equity, access to justice and sustainable development. **Structure** General Assembly; Executive Board; Consultative Council. **Languages** Spanish. **Staff** 10.00 FTE, paid. **Finance** Also support from: national foundations; universities. Supported by: *Catholic Relief Services (CRS, #03608)*; *ILO (#11123)*; *Instituto Interamericano de Derechos Humanos (IIDH, #11334)*; *International Organization for Migration (IOM, #14454)*; *MacArthur Foundation*; *Pan American Development Foundation (PADF, #18094)*; *Save the Children International (#19058)*; *Trocaire – Catholic Agency for World Development*; *UNICEF (#20332)*; *United Nations Population Fund (UNFPA, #20612)*.
Members Associated researchers in 7 countries:
Costa Rica, El Salvador, Guatemala, Honduras, Mexico, Nicaragua, USA.
NGO Relations Also links with national organizations. [2021/XM2338/j/**D**]

♦ Instituto Centroamericano de Investigación y Tecnologia Industrial (inactive)

♦ Instituto Centro Americano de la Salud (ICAS) 11328

Central American Health Institute

Costa Rica Office Apartado 6-2010, Zapote, San José, San José, Costa Rica. T. +5062215278. Fax +5062583943. E-mail: costarica@icas.net.
URL: http://www.icas.net/

Members in 5 countries:
Costa Rica, El Salvador, Guatemala, Honduras, Nicaragua.
NGO Relations Member of: *The NCD Alliance (NCDA, #16963)*; *Union for International Cancer Control (UICC, #20415)*. [2009/XE3535/j/**E**]

♦ Instituto Centroamericano de Telecomunicaciones (inactive)

♦ Instituto Cervantes 11329

Dir Alcala 49, 28014 Madrid, Spain. T. +34914367600. Fax +34914367691. E-mail: director@cervantes.es – informa@cervantes.es.
URL: http://www.cervantes.es/

History 1991, Alcala de Henares (Spain). **Aims** Promote the teaching of *Spanish* around the world; spread Spanish – Spain and Latin American – culture, in cooperation with all Spanish-speaking countries. **Structure** Trust (meets annually). Executive Board; Administration Board. **Languages** Basque, Catalan, Galician, Spanish. **Finance** Mainly public funding. Other sources: licenses of online programmes. Budget (2010): about euro 100 million. **Activities** Organizes: courses on general subjects, and particularly on the Spanish language; cultural activities on Spain and Latin America; exhibitions; concerts; film showings; theatre; conferences; round table discussions. Delivers certificates and diplomas; organizes examinations for the Official Diploma of Spanish as a Foreign Language; updates teaching methods and teacher training; participates in programmes for the promotion of the Spanish language. **Events** *Sistema Internacional de Certification del Espanol Internacional Congreso* Alcala de Henares (Spain) 2016, *World Congress of Teachers of Spanish* 2011.
Members Regional centres (75) in 42 countries:
Algeria, Australia, Austria, Belgium, Brazil, Bulgaria, Canada, China, Croatia, Czechia, Egypt, France, Germany, Greece, Hungary, Iceland, India, Indonesia, Ireland, Israel, Italy, Japan, Jordan, Lebanon, Malaysia, Morocco, Netherlands, Philippines, Poland, Portugal, Romania, Russia, Serbia, Slovakia, Slovenia, Sweden, Syrian AR, Tunisia, Türkiye, UK, USA, Vietnam. [2012/XE3635/j/**E**]

♦ Instituto de Ciencias Familiares (ICF) 11330

Institute of Family Sciences

Contact Puntas de Santiago 1615, 11500 Montevideo, Uruguay. T. +59826000331 – +598259899313326. Fax +59826000331.
Facebook: https://www.facebook.com/institutodecienciasfamiliares/

History Founded 1965, Lima (Peru), as *Centro de Investigaciones y Estudios Familiares (CIEF)*, at Latin American General Assembly of the *International Confederation of Christian Family Movements (ICCFM, #12851)*. **Aims** Coordinate on a Latin American scale scientific research and studies in the various disciplines concerned with family life; contribute to formation of family leaders and family counsellors; make a strong emphasis on teaching and promoting Natural *Family Planning* and *sex education* in the Pro-life culture. **Structure** General Assembly (every 2 years); Governing Council; Executive Committee. Technical Departments (5). **Languages** English, French, Spanish. **Staff** 2.00 FTE, paid; 6.00 FTE, voluntary. **Finance** Donations; fees. Annual budget: US$ 30,000. **Activities** Training/education. **Events** *Congress* Tegucigalpa (Honduras) 2008, *Congress* Montevideo (Uruguay) 2002, *Congress* Montevideo (Uruguay) 1987, *Congress* Buenos Aires (Argentina) 1986, *Congress* Caracas (Venezuela) 1985.
Members Individuals in 6 countries and territories:
Argentina, Brazil, Chile, Italy, Spain, USA. [2017.06.01/XF4508/jv/**F**]

♦ Instituto Complutense de Estudios Internacionales (internationally oriented national body)
♦ Instituto Comunitario das Variedades Vegetais (#04404)
♦ Instituto para la Conectividad en las Americas (#11249)
♦ Instituto para a Conectividade nas Américas (#11249)
♦ Instituto para la Cooperación Economica Internacional (internationally oriented national body)
♦ Instituto de Cooperación Iberoamericana / see Dirección General de Cooperación con Iberoamérica
♦ Instituto de la Cooperación Internacional de la Asociación Alemana para Educación de Adultos (internationally oriented national body)
♦ Instituto de Cooperación con el Mundo Arabe, Mediterraneo y Paises en Desarrollo / see Dirección General de Cooperación con Africa, Asia y Europa Oriental
♦ Instituto de Cooperación para la Seguridad Hemisférica (internationally oriented national body)
♦ Instituto para la Cooperación de Seguridad del Hemisferio Occidental / see Western Hemisphere Institute for Security Cooperation

♦ Instituto para la Cooperación Universitaria (ICU) 11331

Institut pour la coopération universitaire – Institute for University Cooperation – Istituto per la Cooperazione Universitaria

SG Viale G Rossini 26, 00198 Rome RM, Italy. T. +39685300722. Fax +3968554646. E-mail: info@icu.it.
URL: http://www.icu.it/

History 1966, Italy, by a group of Italian scholars. Registered in accordance with Italian law. **Aims** Promote international development in the fields of economic, social, cultural and human development; convey the know-how, skills and other resources of European and local universities to developing countries. **Structure** Officers: President, Vice President, Secretary General, Executive Director. Headquarters in Rome (Italy). Offices in: Brussels (Belgium), Beirut (Lebanon), Yerevan (Armenia), Guangzhou (China), Hong Kong, Lima (Peru), Manila (Philippines). Representatives in: El Salvador, Guatemala (Guatemala), Jerusalem (Israel), Kinshasa (Congo DR), Lagos (Nigeria), Nairobi (Kenya), Delhi (India), Santiago (Chile), Tirana (Albania). **Staff** Professionals: 37 FTE; technical and administrative workers: 11. **Finance** Development cooperation programmes sponsored by the Government of Italy, international foundations and: *UNDP (#20292)*; *WHO (#20950)*; *European Commission (EC, #06633)*. **Activities** Projects/programmes; research/documentation; publishing activities; training/education. **Events** *International university congress* Rome (Italy) 2006, *International university congress* Rome (Italy) 2004, *International university congress* Rome (Italy) 1999, *University Congress* Rome (Italy) 1999, *International Colloquium* Palermo (Italy) / Catania (Italy) 1996. **Publications** Bulletins; books; audiovisual material on development issues in Europe.
Members Organizations () and individuals in 58 countries and territories:
Albania (*), Argentina, Armenia (*), Australia, Austria, Belgium (*), Bolivia, Brazil, Canada, Chile (*), China (*), Colombia, Congo DR (*), Costa Rica, Côte d'Ivoire, Czechia, Dominican Rep, Ecuador, El Salvador (*), Estonia, Ethiopia (*), Finland, France, Germany, Guatemala (*), Honduras, Hong Kong (*), Ireland, Israel (*), Italy (*), Japan, Kenya (*), Lebanon (*), Lithuania, Mexico, Netherlands, New Zealand, Nicaragua, Nigeria, Paraguay, Peru (*), Philippines (*), Poland, Portugal, Puerto Rico, Singapore, Slovakia, Spain, Sweden, Switzerland, Taiwan, Trinidad-Tobago, Tunisia, Uganda, UK, Uruguay, USA, Venezuela. [2015.06.01/XF4206/j/**F**]

♦ Instituto Cooperativo Interamericano (#11420)
♦ Instituto de Cuestiones Internacionales y Politica Exterior, Madrid (internationally oriented national body)
♦ Instituto de Cultura Hispanica / see Dirección General de Cooperación con Iberoamérica
♦ Instituto Cultural Africano (inactive)
♦ Instituto de Derecho de Autor (internationally oriented national body)
♦ Instituto de Derecho Privado Europeo y Comparado (internationally oriented national body)
♦ Instituto de Derechos Humanos y Relaciones Internacionales Alfredo Vazquez Carrizosa (internationally oriented national body)
♦ Instituto de Desarrollo Comunitario / see Center for Development Studies and Promotion
♦ Instituto de Desarrollo Económico / see World Bank Institute (#21220)
♦ Instituto de Desarrollo Económico y Social (internationally oriented national body)
♦ Instituto para el Desarrollo Económico y Social de América Centra / see Instituto para el Desarrollo Económico y Social de América Latina
♦ Instituto para el Desarrollo Económico y Social de América Latina (internationally oriented national body)
♦ Instituto para el Desarrollo y las Relaciones Internacionales / see Institute for Development and International Relations
♦ Instituto Para el Desarrollo Social Andino y Amazónico (internationally oriented national body)
♦ Instituto para el Desarrollo Sustentable en Mesoamérica, Mexico (internationally oriented national body)
♦ Instituto para o Desenvolvimento, Meio Ambiente e Paz (internationally oriented national body)
♦ Instituto de Economia Americana (inactive)
♦ Instituto de Economias en Desarrollo / see Institute of Developing Economies, Japan External Trade Organization
♦ Institut oecuménique de recherches théologiques (#20096)
♦ Instituto de Estudios Caribeños (internationally oriented national body)
♦ Instituto de Estudios sobre Conflictos y Acción Humanitaria (internationally oriented national body)
♦ Instituto de Estudios de Desarrollo Centroamericana (internationally oriented national body)
♦ Instituto de Estudios Económicos sobre la Realidad Argentina y Latinoamericana (internationally oriented national body)
♦ Instituto de Estudios Europeos, Bilbao (internationally oriented national body)
♦ Instituto de Estudios Europeos, ULB (internationally oriented national body)
♦ Instituto de Estudios Hispanicos de Barcelona / see Institut Català de Cooperació Iberoamericana
♦ Instituto de Estudios Iberoamericanos, Hamburgo / see Institut für Lateinamerika-Studies
♦ Instituto de Estudios Iberoamericanos, Stockholm / see Nordic Institute of Latin American Studies
♦ Instituto de Estudios de Iberoamérica y Portugal / see Instituto Interuniversitario de Estudios de Iberoamérica y Portugal
♦ Instituto de Estudios Internacionales, Lima (internationally oriented national body)
♦ Instituto de Estudios Internacionales de la Universidad de Chile (internationally oriented national body)
♦ Instituto de Estudios Latinoamericanos, Costa Rica (internationally oriented national body)
♦ Instituto de Estudios Latinoamericanos, Freie Universität Berlin (internationally oriented national body)
♦ Instituto de Estudios Latinoamericanos, Stockholm / see Nordic Institute of Latin American Studies
♦ Instituto de Estudios Norteamericanos (internationally oriented national body)
♦ Instituto de Estudios Politicos para América Latina y Africa (internationally oriented national body)
♦ Instituto de Estudios Politicos y Relaciones Internacionales, Bogota (internationally oriented national body)
♦ Instituto de Estudios Superiores de la Empresa (internationally oriented national body)
♦ Instituto de Estudos da América Latina, Stockholm / see Nordic Institute of Latin American Studies
♦ Instituto de Estudos para o Desenvolvimento, Lisboa (internationally oriented national body)
♦ Instituto de Estudos Econômicos e Internacionais (internationally oriented national body)
♦ Instituto de Estudos Estratégicos e Internacionais, Lisboa (internationally oriented national body)
♦ Instituto de Estudos Europeus, Lisboa (internationally oriented national body)
♦ Instituto de Estudos Latinoamericanos, Freie Universität Berlin (internationally oriented national body)
♦ Instituto de Estudos Orientais (internationally oriented national body)
♦ Instituto Europeo para el Estudio de las Fibras Industriales (inactive)
♦ Instituto Europeo de Estudios Internacionales (internationally oriented national body)
♦ Instituto Europeo para la Formación Profesional (inactive)
♦ Instituto Europeo de Investigación Cultural Comparativa (#07547)
♦ Instituto Europeo del Mediterraneo (internationally oriented national body)
♦ Instituto Europeo del Ombudsman (#08085)
♦ Instituto Europeo de Seguridad Social (#07571)
♦ Instituto Europeo de Tecnologia / see European Institute of Innovation and Technology (#07562)

- ♦ Instituto Europeu de Tecnologia / see European Institute of Innovation and Technology (#07562)
- ♦ Instituto Fernand Braudel de Economia Mundial (internationally oriented national body)
- ♦ Institut pour l'officialisation de l'espéranto (inactive)
- ♦ Instituto de Filosofia da Libertação (internationally oriented national body)
- ♦ Instituto del FMI (see: #14180)
- ♦ Instituto Forestal Latinoamericano (internationally oriented national body)
- ♦ Instituto Forestal Latinoamericano de Investigación y Capacitación / see Latin American Forestry Institute
- ♦ Instituto de Formación Demócrata Cristiana (internationally oriented national body)
- ♦ Instituto de Formación Superior Profesional Europeo / see Hague School of European Studies
- ♦ Instituto Francés de Estudios Andinos (internationally oriented national body)
- ♦ Instituto Galego de Estudos de Seguranza Internacional e da Paz (internationally oriented national body)
- ♦ Instituto de Gestão e Liderança Universitaria (#11298)
- ♦ Instituto de Gestión y Liderazgo Universitario (#11298)
- ♦ Instituto Hemisférico de Performance y Politica (#10907)
- ♦ Instituto Hemisférico de Performance e Politica (#10907)
- ♦ Instituto Hispano-Luso-Americano de Derecho Internacional (#10924)
- ♦ Instituto Hispano-Luso-Americano de Derecho Maritimo / see Instituto Iberoamericano de Derecho Maritimo
- ♦ Instituto de História de Nicaragua y Centroamérica (internationally oriented national body)
- ♦ Instituto Histórico Centroamericano, Managua / see Instituto de História de Nicaragua y Centroamérica
- ♦ Instituto Holandés de Derechos Humanos (internationally oriented national body)
- ♦ Instituto sobre el Hombre y la Ciencia / see Rensselaerville Institute
- ♦ Instituto Humanista para la Cooperación con los Paises en Desarrollo (internationally oriented national body)

♦ Instituto Iberoamericano de Derecho Aeronautico y del Espacio y de la Aviación Comercial 11332

Ibero-American Institute of Aeronautic and Space Law and Commercial Aviation – Institut ibéroaméricain du droit aéronautique et de l'espace et de l'aviation commerciale

Main Office c/o ETSIA – UPM, Plaza Cardenal Cisneros 3, 28040 Madrid, Spain. T. +34913366374. Fax +34915439859. E-mail: secretaria@instibaerospa.org.
URL: https://derechoaeroespacial.org/

History 24 Apr 1964, Salamanca (Spain). Registered in accordance with Spanish law, 25 Sep 1968. **Aims** Study, coordinate and promote the development of aeronautic and space law, commercial aviation and related fields; promote, through scientific investigation and practical work, harmonization and unification of aeronautic and space legislation in Latin American countries; establish ties with national and international, public and private institutions that relate to the aims of the Institute; exchange information and documentation and issue publications; promote standardization of aeronautical regulations. **Structure** General Assembly (usually together with 'Ibero-American Days', organized by the Institute). Executive Committee, consisting of President, 4 Vice-Presidents, Honorary President, Secretary General and 12 members. General Secretariat in Madrid (Spain). Coordinators in each country. **Languages** Portuguese, Spanish. **Staff** 12.00 FTE, voluntary. **Finance** Contributions from members and associates; grants from governments for seminars of aviation law. **Activities** Organizes courses for civil aviation technicians; carries out scientific and experimental work. Research Centre. **Events** *Ibero-American Days* Buenos Aires (Argentina) 2018, *Ibero-American Days* Santiago (Chile) 2017, *Ibero-American Days* Madrid (Spain) 2016, *Ibero-American Days* Madrid (Spain) 2014, *Ibero-American Day* Buenos Aires (Argentina) 2010. **Publications** *Revista del Instituto Iberoamericano de Derecho Aeronautico y del Espacio y de la Aviación Comercial. Ensayo para un Diccionario de Derecho Aeronautico* (1991) by Luis Tapii Salinas and Enrique Mpelli. Yearbooks; convention proceedings.

Members Full Individual (academics, company executives, civil aviation officials) or Collective (universities and aeronautical companies), in Spanish or Portuguese-speaking countries; Associate Individual or Collective, in other countries; Corresponding. Members (over 400) in 26 countries and territories:
Argentina, Bolivia, Brazil, Chile, Colombia, Costa Rica, Cuba, Dominican Rep, Ecuador, El Salvador, France, Guatemala, Honduras, Israel, Mexico, Neth Antilles, Nicaragua, Panama, Paraguay, Peru, Portugal, Puerto Rico, Spain, Uruguay, USA, Venezuela.

IGO Relations Observer status with: *Committee on the Peaceful Uses of Outer Space (COPUOS, #04277)*; *Latin American Civil Aviation Commission (LACAC, #16297)*. Associated with Department of Global Communications of the United Nations. **NGO Relations** Cooperation agreement with: *Ibero-American Pilots' Organization (OIP, no recent information)*; *International Forum of Travel and Tourism Advocates (IFTTA, #13657)*.
[2021/XD4431/j/**D**]

- ♦ Instituto Iberoamericano de Derecho Maritimo (internationally oriented national body)
- ♦ Instituto Iberoamericano de Derecho Procesal (internationally oriented national body)
- ♦ Instituto Iberoamericano de Derecho y Reforma Agraria (no recent information)
- ♦ Instituto Ibero-Americano Fundación Patrimonio Cultural Prusiano (internationally oriented national body)
- ♦ Instituto Iberoamericano de la Haya (internationally oriented national body)
- ♦ Instituto Iberoamericano de la Haya – para la Paz, los Derechos Humanos y la Justicia Internacional / see Instituto Iberoamericano de la Haya
- ♦ Instituto Iberoamericano de Investigaciones Económicas de la Universidad de Gotinga (internationally oriented national body)

♦ Instituto Iberoamericano de Mercados de Valores (IIMV) 11333

Iberoamerican Institute of Stock Exchanges

Sec C/Edison 4, 28006 Madrid, Spain. T. +34915850901. E-mail: acf@iimv.org – mdr@iimv.org.
URL: http://www.iimv.org/

History 20 May 1999, by the Spanish Government. **Aims** Encourage progress and modernization of the securities markets in Latin America. **Structure** Council; Board, including Chair. **Languages** Spanish. **Activities** Programmes (2): Training and Research; Communication and Cooperation. **Publications** *Revista Iberoamericana de Mercados de Valores.* Studies.

Members Full in 20 countries:
Argentina, Bolivia, Brazil, Chile, Colombia, Costa Rica, Dominican Rep, Ecuador, El Salvador, Guatemala, Honduras, Mexico, Nicaragua, Panama, Paraguay, Peru, Portugal, Spain, Uruguay, Venezuela.

NGO Relations Member of: *Council of Securities Regulators of the Americas (#04918)*. [2014/XE4517/j/**E**]

- ♦ Instituto Iberoamericano del Patrimonio Cultural Prusiano / see Ibero-Amerikanisches Institut Preussischer Kulturbesitz
- ♦ Instituto Iberoamericano, Universidad Sofia (internationally oriented national body)
- ♦ Instituto de Imprensa da Sociedade Interamericana de Imprensa (see: #11444)
- ♦ Instituto de Información y Traducción para la Región del Caribe (#03548)
- ♦ El Instituto: Institute of Latina/o, Caribbean and Latin American Studies (internationally oriented national body)
- ♦ Instituto para a Integração da América Latina e do Caribe (#11271)
- ♦ Instituto para la Integración de América Latina y el Caribe (#11271)
- ♦ Instituto Interamericano de Ciencias Agricolas / see Inter-American Institute for Cooperation on Agriculture (#11434)
- ♦ Instituto Interamericano de Cooperação para a Agricultura (#11434)
- ♦ Instituto Interamericano de Cooperación para la Agricultura (#11434)
- ♦ Instituto Interamericano da Criança (#11406)
- ♦ Instituto Inter-Americano sobre Deficiência (#11435)
- ♦ Instituto Interamericano de Derecho de Autor (#11421)

♦ Instituto Interamericano de Derechos Humanos (IIDH) 11334

Institut interaméricain des droits de l'homme – Inter-American Institute of Human Rights – Instituto Interamericano de Direitos Humanos

Exec Dir Aptdo Postal 10081, San José, San José, San José, 11501, Costa Rica. T. +50622340404. Fax +50622340378. E-mail: direccionejecutiva@iidh.ed.cr.
URL: http://www.iidh.ed.cr/

History 30 Jul 1980, San José (Costa Rica). Founded on signature of an agreement between *Corte Interamericana de Derechos Humanos (Corte IDH, #04851)* and the Government of Costa Rica, as an autonomous international academic institution. **Aims** Promote and strengthen respect for human rights set out in the "American Convention on Human Rights"; contribute to consolidation of *democracy* in the Americas through education, research, political mediation, programmes for training, technical assistance in the field of human rights and dissemination of knowledge. **Structure** General Assembly of 40 members, including *Corte Interamericana de Derechos Humanos (Corte IDH, #04851)* judges and *Inter-American Commission on Human Rights (IACHR, #11411)* members. Steering Committee of 11 members, including President and 2 Vice-Presidents. Executive Directorate, headed by Executive Director. Directorates (3): Mexico and the Caribbean and *Centre for Electoral Promotion and Assistance (CAPEL, see: #11334)*; South America and the Cooperation Office; Central America, and Women's Human Rights. Regional Office at Montevideo (Uruguay); National Office at Bogota (Colombia). **Languages** English, Spanish. **Staff** 17.00 FTE, paid. **Finance** Sources: government support; international organizations; private foundations. Contributions from the Governments of Argentina, Costa Rica, Denmark, Netherlands, Norway, Sweden, USA, Uruguay, and Venezuela. Supported by: *Canadian International Development Agency (CIDA, inactive)*; *Ford Foundation (#09858)*; *Friedrich Naumann Foundation for Freedom*; *Inter-American Commission on Human Rights (IACHR, #11411)*; *International Development Research Centre (IDRC, #13162)*; *Jacob Blaustein Institute for the Advancement of Human Rights (JBI)*; *UNDP (#20292)*; *United States Agency for International Development (USAID)*; *World Council of Churches (WCC, #21320)*. **Activities** Capacity building; research and development; training/education. Active in all member countries. **Events** *The role of media in process of transition and consolidation of democracy in Latin America* Managua (Nicaragua) 1994, *Workshop on administration of criminal law and the indigenous peoples of the Americas* San José (Costa Rica) 1990, *Meeting of electoral organisms of Central America and the Caribbean* Costa Rica 1989, *Los elementos esenciales de un proceso democratico de elecciones* Venezuela 1989. **Publications** *IIHR in the Americas* (bi-weekly) – newsletter; *Boletin Electoral Latinoamericano* (2 a year) in English, Spanish; *Revista IIDH* (2 a year); *Cuadernos CAPEL.* Books. Information Services: Documentation center; online courses; digital library. **Information Services** *Aula Interamericana Virtual* – online courses in Spanish, English and Portuguese; *Electoral Network of the Americas: Women's Rights and Indigenous and Afrodescendent Rights*; *Integrated Information and Communication System for Ombudsman Offices in Latin America and the Caribbean (OMBUDSNET)*.

Members Individuals, by invitation of the Board, in 20 countries:
Argentina, Barbados, Bolivia, Brazil, Canada, Chile, Colombia, Costa Rica, Ecuador, El Salvador, Guatemala, Guyana, Honduras, Jamaica, Mexico, Paraguay, Peru, Uruguay, USA, Venezuela.

IGO Relations Cooperates with (1): *International Institute for Democracy and Electoral Assistance (International IDEA, #13872)*. **NGO Relations** Member of (1): *Global Partnership for the Prevention of Armed Conflict (GPPAC, #10538)*. Partner of (1): *Red Latinoamericana para Educación e Investigación en Derechos Humanos (RedLEIDH, #18712)* (Founding Partner). Cooperates with (1): *Centre for Research on Latin America and the Caribbean (CERLAC)*. Supports (1): *Instituto Centroamericano de Estudios Sociales y Desarrollo (INCEDES, #11327)*. [2022.10.18/XE0020/jv/**E**]

- ♦ Instituto Interamericano para el Desarrollo Económico y Social (#11436)
- ♦ Instituto Interamericano para el Desarrollo Social / see Inter-American Institute for Economic and Social Development (#11436)
- ♦ Instituto Interamericano de Direito de Autor (#11421)
- ♦ Instituto Interamericano de Direitos Humanos (#11334)
- ♦ Instituto Interamericano sobre Discapacidad (#11435)
- ♦ Instituto Interamericano de Estadistica (#11452)
- ♦ Instituto Interamericano de Estudios Juridicos Internacionales (inactive)
- ♦ Instituto Interamericano de Estudios Sindicales (inactive)
- ♦ Instituto Interamericano de Historia Municipal e Institucional (inactive)
- ♦ Instituto Interamericano para la Investigación del Cambio Global (#11437)
- ♦ Instituto Interamericano de Mercados de Capital (inactive)
- ♦ Instituto Interamericano del Niño / see Inter-American Children's Institute (#11406)
- ♦ Instituto Interamericano del Niño, la Niña y Adolescentes (#11406)

♦ Instituto Intercultural para la Autogestión y la Acción Comunal (INAUCO) 11335

Intercultural Institute for Self-Management and Community Action

Dir FADE-UPV, Camino de Vera s/n, 46022 Valencia, Spain. E-mail: ancovia@urb.upv.es – inauco@upvnet.upv.es.
URL: http://www.upv.es/inauco/

History 1978, Valencia (Spain). A centre created by *'Fundación Libre Académica para la Enseñanza y la Cultura (FLAPE)'*. An interuniversity education and research centre with Universidad Politécnica de Valencia (Spain). **Aims** Carry out research, education, publishing and technical assistance around the concepts of autonomy, self-organization and self-management in economics, politics, education and the social sciences. **Structure** Patronage of 6 international research centres, foundations and institutions. **Languages** Portuguese, Spanish. **Staff** Voluntary. **Finance** Sources: post-graduate courses; publications. **Activities** Research/documentation; training/education; networking/liaising. **Events** *Latin America-Europe colloquium* Madrid (Spain) 1996. **Publications** *Revista Iberoamericana de Autogestión y Acción Comunal (RIDAA)* (4 a year). Monographs.

Members Organizations and individuals in 9 countries:
Argentina, Brazil, Chile, Colombia, Germany, Israel, Mexico, Spain, Venezuela.
Individuals in 15 countries:
Argentina, Brazil, Chile, Colombia, Ecuador, France, Guatemala, Italy, Mexico, Peru, Portugal, Spain, Uruguay, USA, Venezuela.

NGO Relations Presidency of: *Consejo Español de Estudios Iberoamericanos (CEEIB, no recent information)*. Member of: *Federación Internacional de Estudios sobre América Latina y el Caribe (FIEALC, #09338)*.
[2017.06.01/XF3022/j/**F**]

- ♦ Instituto Internacional de Agricultura Tropical (#13933)
- ♦ Instituto Internacional del Algodón (inactive)
- ♦ Instituto Internacional Americano de Protección a la Infancia / see Inter-American Children's Institute (#11406)
- ♦ Instituto Internacional de Artes y Letras (inactive)
- ♦ Instituto Internacional de Asuntos Culturales (#11251)
- ♦ Instituto Internacional de Capacitación Social del Sur / see Instituto Internacional de Estudios y Capacitación Social del Sur (#11337)
- ♦ Instituto Internacional de Cinematografia Educativa (inactive)
- ♦ Instituto Internacional de Civilizaciones Diferentes (inactive)

♦ Instituto Internacional en Conservación y Manejo en Vida Silvestre (ICOMVIS) 11336

Dir Universidad Nacional, Apartado 1350-3000, Heredia, Heredia, Heredia, Costa Rica. T. +5062377039. Fax +5062377036.
URL: http://www.icomvis.una.ac.cr/

History Founded Oct 1984, as *Regional Wildlife Management Program for Meso-America and the Caribbean – Programa Regional en Manejo de Vida Silvestre para Mesoamérica y el Caribe (PRMVS)*. Declared an International Research Institute, 2005. **Aims** Train professionals in neotropical wildlife management and conservation; develop methods and techniques which enable humans to use, control and conserve wildlife within the sustainable development strategies of each country; develop a scientific and technical basis for planning, monitoring and organizing wildlife resources with special emphasis on improving rural developments in Latin America. **Languages** English, Spanish. **Staff** 13.00 FTE, paid. **Finance** Major funding agencies: USFWS, German Academic Exchange Service. Donations from national and international organizations, including the

following bodies listed in this Yearbook: *Dirección General de Cooperación con Iberoamérica*; Universidad Nacional de Costa Rica; United States Fish and Sild Service (USFWS); German Academic Exchange Service (DAAD). Budget (annual): about US$ 650,000. **Activities** Training/education.
Members Professors and researchers; associate professors and researchers; administrative staff; associate staff; students. Individuals in 21 countries:
Argentina, Bolivia, Brazil, Chile, Colombia, Costa Rica, Ecuador, El Salvador, Germany, Guatemala, Honduras, Japan, Mexico, Nicaragua, Panama, Paraguay, Peru, Spain, Uruguay, USA, Venezuela. [2014.11.10/XF3791/jv/**F**]

- ♦ Instituto Internacional de Custos (#12977)
- ♦ Instituto Internacional para la Democracia y la Asistencia Electoral (#13872)
- ♦ Instituto Internacional de Derecho para el Desarrollo / see International Development Law Organization (#13161)
- ♦ Instituto Internacional de Derecho de Expresión y Inspiración Franceses (#11310)
- ♦ Instituto Internacional de Derecho y Medio Ambiente (internationally oriented national body)
- ♦ Instituto Internacional para los Derechos de Grupos Etnicos y Regionalismo (#13300)
- ♦ Instituto Internacional de Derechos Humanos / see International Institute of Human Rights – Fondation René Cassin (#13887)
- ♦ Instituto Internacional De Derechos Humanos (internationally oriented national body)
- ♦ Instituto Internacional de Derechos Humanos – Fondation René Cassin (#13887)
- ♦ Instituto Internacional para el Desarrollo de la Ciudadania (internationally oriented national body)
- ♦ Instituto Internacional para o Desenvolvimento da Cidadania (internationally oriented national body)
- ♦ Instituto Internacional de Dirección de Empresas (internationally oriented national body)
- ♦ Instituto Internacional para la Educación Superior en América Latina y el Caribe / see UNESCO International Institute for Higher Education in Latin America and the Caribbean (#20309)
- ♦ Instituto Internacional de Estadistica (#15603)
- ♦ Instituto Internacional de Estudio y Documentación en Materia de Competencia Comercial (inactive)
- ♦ Instituto Internacional de Estudios Administrativos de Montreal (internationally oriented national body)
- ♦ Instituto Internacional de Estudios Avanzados, Caracas (internationally oriented national body)
- ♦ Instituto Internacional para Estudios Avanzados en Investigación de Sistemas y Cibernética (internationally oriented national body)
- ♦ Instituto Internacional de Estudios Bancarios (#12313)

♦ Instituto Internacional de Estudios y Capacitación Social del Sur (INCASUR) 11337

Institute of Social Training of the 'Cono Sur' – Institut de formation sociale du Cône Sud
Dir Alberti 36, 1082 Buenos Aires, Argentina. T. +54119532776. Fax +54119532776. E-mail: administracion@incasur.org – comunicacion@incasur.org.
URL: http://www.incasur.org/
History Also referred to as *Instituto Internacional de Capacitación Social del Sur*. **Events** *Seminar on new training strategies and technologies in the knowledge society* Buenos Aires (Argentina) 2004, *Communication seminar on design and creation of Southern Cone communication network* Porto Alegre (Brazil) 2004, *Latin American conference on technological progress in the economic, social and communication field and industrial relations* Buenos Aires (Argentina) 1987. [2014/XF5005/j/**F**]

- ♦ Instituto Internacional de Estudios de Clases Medias (inactive)
- ♦ Instituto Internacional de Estudios sobre la Familia (internationally oriented national body)
- ♦ Instituto Internacional de Estudios Genealógicos y de Historia Familiar (internationally oriented national body)
- ♦ Instituto Internacional de Estudios Laborales (#13897)

♦ Instituto Internacional de Estudios Legislativos del FOPREL (IIEL-FOPREL) 11338

Contact Lomas de Monserrat, Casa D-1, Apartado A-78, Managua, Nicaragua. T. +5052773848. Fax +5052443758.
URL: https://foprel.digital/iiel/
History Feb 1995. A permanent and auxiliary body of *Foro de presidentes y presidentas de Poderes Legislativos de Centroamérica y el Caribe (FOPREL, #09887)*. Restructured 2021. Former names and other names: *Instituto Centroamericano de Estudios Legislativos (ICEL)* – former. **Aims** Contribute to the processes of modernization of the legislative powers and harmonization of regulatory frameworks. [2022/XG9163/j/**E**]

- ♦ Instituto Internacional de Filosofia (#13910)
- ♦ Instituto Internacional del Frio / see International Institute of Refrigeration (#13918)
- ♦ Instituto Internacional de Gobernabilidad (internationally oriented national body)
- ♦ Instituto Internacional de Hacienda Pública (#13915)
- ♦ Instituto Internacional Henry Dunant (see: #10024)
- ♦ Instituto Internacional sobre Informatica y Sistemas (#13889)
- ♦ Instituto Internacional de Integración del Convenio Andrés Bello (#13940)
- ♦ Instituto Internacional de Investigación de Cultivos para las Zonas Tropicales Semiaridas (#13116)
- ♦ Instituto Internacional de Investigación de Encharcamiento y Salinidad (internationally oriented national body)
- ♦ Instituto Internacional de Investigaciones sobre Politicas Alimentarias (#13622)
- ♦ Instituto Internacional Jacques Maritain (#13967)

♦ Instituto Internacional de Lingua Portuguesa (IILP) 11339

Main Office Avenida Andrade Corvo no 8, Platô, Praia, Santiago, Cape Verde. T. +2382619504. E-mail: iilpblog@gmail.com – iilp.chf.sec@gmail.com.
URL: http://iilp.cplp.org/
History 31 Jul 2001, Sao Tomé-Principe. An institution of *Comunidade dos Paises de Lingua Portuguesa (CPLP, #04430)*, with legal personality and administrative autonomy. **Structure** General Assembly; Scientific Council; Executive Board. **Events** *International Colloquium on the Portuguese on the Internet and the Digital World* Ceará (Brazil) 2012, *General Assembly* Praia (Cape Verde) 2003. **Publications** *Plato* – review.
Members Governments (9):
Angola, Brazil, Cape Verde, Equatorial Guinea, Guinea-Bissau, Mozambique, Portugal, Sao Tomé-Principe, Timor-Leste. [2022/XK2358/j/**E***]

- ♦ Instituto Internacional de Literatura Iberoamericana (#13888)
- ♦ Instituto Internacional de Medio Ambiente y Desarrollo (#13877)
- ♦ Instituto Internacional de Medio Ambiente y Desarrollo – América Latina / see IIED América-Latina (#11114)
- ♦ Instituto Internacional del Ombudsman (#14411)
- ♦ Instituto Internacional pro Paz / see International Institute for Peace (#13907)
- ♦ Instituto Internacional de Periodismo y Comunicación (internationally oriented national body)

♦ Instituto Internacional de Periodismo 'José Marti' (IPJM) 11340

Institut international de journalisme 'José Marti' – José Marti International Institute of Journalism
Contact Avenida de los Presidentes no 503, entre 21 y 23, Vedado CP 10 400, CP 10 400 Havana, Cuba. T. +5378320566 – +5378320567. E-mail: loenrinda@gmail.com – eventos@prensaip.co.cu.
URL: http://www.prensaip.co.cu/
History 17 Oct 1983, Havana (Cuba), by the Unión de Periodistas de Cuba (UPEC), *International Organization of Journalists (IOJ, inactive)* and *Federación Latinoamericana de Periodistas (FELAP, #09359)*. **Aims** Contribute to the scientific qualification of *Latin American* journalists; improve their *professional* skills. **Activities** Courses (annually 2 courses of 2 months each). **Events** *Ibero American meeting on gender and communication* Havana (Cuba) 2008. [2010/XE6153/j/**E**]

- ♦ Instituto Internacional de Periodismo 'Werner Lamberz', Escuela de la Solidaridad / see International Institute of Journalism, Berlin – Brandenburg
- ♦ Instituto Internacional de Planeamiento de la Educación (#13874)
- ♦ Instituto Internacional de la Potasa (#14626)
- ♦ Instituto Internacional de la Prensa (#14636)
- ♦ Instituto Internacional de Productores de Caucho Sintético (#13931)
- ♦ Instituto Internacional de Projeciologia / see International Institute of Projectiology and Conscientiology (#13912)
- ♦ Instituto Internacional de Projeciologia e Conscienciologia (#13912)
- ♦ Instituto Internacional de Proyecciologia / see International Institute of Projectiology and Conscientiology (#13912)
- ♦ Instituto Internacional de Proyecciologia y Conscientiologia (#13912)
- ♦ Instituto Internacional de Reconstrucción Rural (#13921)
- ♦ Instituto Internacional de Recursos Fitogenéticos / see Bioversity International (#03262)
- ♦ Instituto Internacional de Recursos Renovables (internationally oriented national body)
- ♦ Instituto Internacional San Telmo (internationally oriented national body)
- ♦ Instituto Internacional de Sociologia (#13925)
- ♦ Instituto Internacional de Sociologia Juridica de Oñati (#17725)
- ♦ Instituto Internacional de Sociologia y Reformas Politicas y Sociales (inactive)
- ♦ Instituto Internacional del Teatro Mediterraneo (internationally oriented national body)
- ♦ Instituto Internacional de Tecnologia y Economia Apicolas / see Fundatia Institutul International de Tehnologie si Economie Apicola
- ♦ Instituto Internacional de Teologia Pastoral Sanitaria (#13906)
- ♦ Instituto Internacional de la UNESCO para la Educación Superior en América Latina y el Caribe (#20309)
- ♦ Instituto Internacional para la Unificación del Derecho Privado (#13934)
- ♦ Instituto Internacional de Vacunas (#15839)
- ♦ Instituto Interregional de las Naciones Unidas para Investigaciones sobre la Delincuencia y la Justicia (#20580)
- ♦ Instituto Interuniversitario de Estudios de Iberoamérica y Portugal (internationally oriented national body)
- ♦ Instituto Interuniversitario de Iberoamérica / see Instituto Interuniversitario de Estudios de Iberoamérica y Portugal
- ♦ Instituto de Investigação Cientifica Tropical (internationally oriented national body)
- ♦ Instituto de Investigación y Debate sobre la Gobernanza (internationally oriented national body)
- ♦ Instituto de Investigación Económica y Social de la Cuenca del Caribe / see Network of Institutes for Socioeconomic Studies of the Caribbean Basin
- ♦ Instituto de Investigaciones de las Naciones Unidas para la Defensa Social / see United Nations Interregional Crime and Justice Research Institute (#20580)
- ♦ Instituto de Investigación de las Naciones Unidas para el Desarrollo Social (#20623)
- ♦ Instituto Italo-Latinoamericano (#16071)
- ♦ Institut für Ökologie und Aktions-Ethnologie (internationally oriented national body)
- ♦ Institut für Ökumenische Forschung / see Institut für Ökumenische und Interreligiöse Forschung
- ♦ Institut für Ökumenische Forschung, Strasbourg (#11258)
- ♦ Institut für Ökumenische und Interreligiöse Forschung (internationally oriented national body)
- ♦ Instituto de Latinoamérica de la Academia de Ciencias de Rusia (internationally oriented national body)

♦ Instituto Latinoamericano de Alta Tecnologia, Informatica y Derecho (ILATID) 11341

Institut latinoaméricain de haute technologie, d'informatique et de droit – Latin American High Tech, Computer and Law Institute
Pres Suipacha 1111, 5 Floor, C1008AAW Buenos Aires, Argentina. T. +541152977000.
History 1987, Buenos Aires (Argentina). Previously also referred to as *Latin American Institute for Advanced Technology, Computer Science and Law*. **Aims** Develop studies and research in high technology, informatics and legal fields; cooperate with research and teaching institutions for the development of joint projects in the field; establish cooperation, consultation and support relationships with competent international organizations to study and recommend valid legislative solutions at the regional or national level. **Structure** General Assembly (every 2 years); Administration Council. **Languages** English, Spanish. **Activities** Training/education. **Events** *Conference of the Americas* Santo Domingo (Dominican Rep) 2004, *Meeting* Buenos Aires (Argentina) 1994, *Meeting* Lisbon (Portugal) 1994.
Members Individuals or national centers in 9 countries:
Argentina, Bolivia, Brazil, Chile, Colombia, Mexico, Paraguay, Uruguay, Venezuela.
Consultative Status Consultative status granted from: *World Intellectual Property Organization (WIPO, #21593)* (Permanent Observer Status). **NGO Relations** Cooperates with: *Centre for Interdisciplinary Research on Development, Brussels (CIRD, no recent information)*. Instrumental in setting up: *International Federation of Computer Law Associations (IFCLA, #13398)*. [2014.06.01/XD2918/j/**E**]

- ♦ Instituto Latinoamericano de la Calidad (internationally oriented national body)

♦ Instituto Latinoamericano y del Caribe de Calidad en Educación Superior a Distancia (CALED) 11342

Dir San Cayetano Alto, AP 11-01-608, Loja, Ecuador. Fax +59372673158. E-mail: caled@caledead.org.
URL: http://www.caled-ead.org/
Aims Contribute to the improvement of the quality of teaching in all institutions in Latin America and the Caribbean. **Structure** Board of Directors; Advisory Council; Academic Council.
Members Universities in 9 countries:
Chile, Colombia, Dominican Rep, Ecuador, Mexico, Panama, Peru, Puerto Rico, Venezuela.
IGO Relations *OAS (#17629)*; *Organization of Ibero-American States for Education, Science and Culture (#17871)*. **NGO Relations** *Association of Universities of Latin America and the Caribbean (#02970)*; *Ibero-American Association for Open University Education (#11015)*; *Inter-American Distance Education Consortium (#11428)*; *Inter-American Organization for Higher Education (IOHE, #11442)*; *Ibero-American Science and Technology Education Consortium (ISTEC, #11027)*; *International Council for Open and Distance Education (ICDE, #13056)* – Latin America. [2019/XM7746/**D**]

- ♦ Instituto Latinoamericano y del Caribe de Planificación Económica y Social (#16279)
- ♦ Instituto Latinoamericano de Ciencias Fiscalizadoras / see Organization of Latin American and Caribbean Supreme Audit Institutions (#17877)
- ♦ Instituto Latinoamericano de la Cinematografia Educativa / see Instituto Latinoamericano de la Comunicación Educativa (#11343)

♦ Instituto Latinoamericano de la Comunicación Educativa (ILCE) ... 11343

Institut latinoaméricain de communication éducative – Latin American Institute of Educational Communication
Dir Gen Calle del Puente 45, Colonia Ejidos de Huipulco, Delegación Tlalpan, 14380 Mexico City CDMX, Mexico. T. +525555949106 – +525555944061. Fax +525555949683. E-mail: vinculacion@ilce.edu.mx.
URL: http://www.ilce.edu.mx/
History 30 May 1956, Mexico City (Mexico). Founded on signature of an agreement by the Mexican government and *UNESCO (#20322)*, following decision of UNESCO General Conference, 1954, Montevideo (Uruguay). Agreement was initially for 2 years but was later renewed. Restructured, and objectives and scope restated, 31 May 1978, on signature of a convention for cooperation by 13 Latin America and Caribbean countries. Statutes registered in *'UNTS 1/20439'*. Former names and other names: *Latin American Institute of Educational Cinema* – former (1956); *Instituto Latinoamericano de la Cinematografia Educativa* – former (1956); *Latin American Educational Film Institute* – alias; *Latin American Institute of Communication Education* – former; *Instituto Latinoamericano para la Educación por la Comunicación (ILEC)* – former. **Aims** Enhance education through different *media* – publication, software and audiovisual; promote regional cooperation

in research, experimentation, production and distribution of *audiovisual* materials; secure preparation and training of *human resources* in the field of educational technology. **Structure** Executive Board, consisting of an accredited representative of each Latin American country which has signed and ratified the Convention. **Languages** English, Spanish. **Finance** Regular contributions of Member States. **Activities** Trains personnel in the fields of educational technology and communication for educational and cultural purposes; produces and distributes audiovisual materials to meet specific needs of the region; conducts research and experiments on appropriate use of educational technology and the media in promoting open and distance education, job training and cultural dissemination; organizes regional seminars and other meetings; collaborates with distance education activities of the Mexican Ministry of Education. *Center for Training and Advanced Studies on Educational Communication* provides training leading to a Master's Degree in Educational Technology or a Specialized Degree on Educational Communication and organizes training workshops and courses in: radio, television, audiovisual materials production; educational software production; educational administration; educational communication; teaching strategies. **Events** *Virtual Educa : international conference on education, training and new technologies* São José dos Campos (Brazil) 2007, *ONLINE EDUCA : international conference on technology based education and training* Madrid (Spain) 2006, *Latin American meeting on the training of educators for young people and adults* Patzcuaro (Mexico) 2003. **Publications** *Tecnologia y Comunicación Educativas* (2 a year). Books; monographs; manuals; minutes of meetings. Information services: Operates *Center of Audiovisual Documentation for Latin America (CEDAL, no recent information).* Maintains library of 31,000 volumes. **Information Services** *Educational Satellite Network (EDUSAT) – Red Satelital de Televisión Educativa* – Since 5 Sep 1994, broadcasts educational and cultural programmes.
Members Governments of 13 countries:
Bolivia, Colombia, Costa Rica, Ecuador, El Salvador, Guatemala, Haiti, Honduras, Mexico, Nicaragua, Panama, Paraguay, Venezuela.
IGO Relations Invited to sessions of Intergovernmental Council of: *International Programme for the Development of Communication (IPDC, #14651).* **NGO Relations** Member of: *Asociación de Televisión Educativa Iberoamericana (ATEI, #02303); Association internationale des télévisions d'éducation et de découverte (AITED, no recent information); Consejo de Educación de Adultos de América Latina (CEAAL, #04707); Inter-American Distance Education Consortium (#11428); Worlddidac Association (#21361).* Functions as regional representative of: *Asociación de Investigación y Especialización sobre Temas Iberoamericanos (AIETI).*
[2020.03.04/XD2873/j/**E***]

♦ Instituto Latinoamericano de Derecho Comparado (inactive)

♦ Instituto Latinoamericano de Derecho Tributario (ILADT) 11344

Institut latinoaméricain du droit des taxes – Latin American Tax Law Institute

Secretariat Cerrito 461, Piso 4, 11000 Montevideo, Uruguay. T. +59829005675. Fax +59829005675. E-mail: iladt@iladt.org.
URL: http://www.iladt.org/

History 1958, Mexico. **Aims** Promote the study and technical and legal improvement of tax law; bring about the creation of specialized scientific institutions in Latin American countries; maintain permanent contacts with universities, teaching institutions, specialized institutes, lawyers and other similar institutions; organize an Information Office on matters relative to the object of the institute reuniting corresponding informative material and a library. **Structure** General Assembly. Executive Council, comprising member representatives, electing a President and Vice-President from among them. Secretary General. **Languages** Spanish. **Finance** Members' dues. **Activities** Organizes "Jornadas ILADTH" (ILADT Days). **Events** *Biennial Symposium* Santiago de Compostela (Spain) 2012, *Biennial Symposium* Cartagena de Indias (Colombia) 2010, *Biennial Symposium* Porlamar (Venezuela) 2008, *Biennial Symposium* Córdoba (Argentina) 2006, *Biennial Symposium* Quito (Ecuador) 2004. **Publications** *Revista ILADT.*
Members Founding; Active; Honorary; Corresponding institutes in 16 countries:
Argentina, Bolivia, Brazil, Chile, Colombia, Costa Rica, Ecuador, Guatemala, Italy, Mexico, Paraguay, Peru, Portugal, Spain, Uruguay, Venezuela.
NGO Relations *Inter-American Centre for Tax Administrations (#11405).* [2012.06.01/XE4045/jv/**E**]

♦ Instituto Latinoamericano de Doctrinas y Estudios Sociales (ILADES) 11345

Latin American Institute of Social Theory and Social Studies – Institut latinoaméricain de la doctrine et des études sociales

Contact Univ Alberto Hurtado, Erasmo Escala 1835, Santiago, Santiago Metropolitan, Chile. E-mail: ecoadmi@uahurtado.cl.

History 27 Sep 1965, Santiago (Chile). **Aims** Promote the study, dissemination and renovation of the social thought of the *Church*, in accordance with new challenges and the various situations existing on the Latin American continent. **Structure** ILADES Foundation administered by Board, consisting of President Emeritus, Honorary President, 5 Directors and 5 Alternate Directors. ILADES Institute executive organization: Director of ILADES; 4 Departments. **Activities** Departments (5): Academic Department (Postgraduate Program in Development Sciences; Postgraduate Program in Economy); Research and Labour Activity Department; Training and Publications Department; Pastoral Department; Administration Department. **Events** *Pluralist society and religious diversity* Santiago (Chile) 1995, *International seminar* Córdoba (Argentina) 1988, *International seminar* Santiago (Chile) 1988. **Publications** *Persona y Sociedad* (2 a year); *Revista de Analisis Económico* (2 a year) – together with Georgetown University, Washington DC. Monographs; mimeographed material. **Information Services** *DOCLA – Documentación Social Católica Latinoamericana.* **IGO Relations** Participating institution of: *Latin American and Caribbean Research Network (#16284).* **NGO Relations** Member of: *Association of Universities Entrusted to the Society of Jesus in Latin-America (#02969); International Center for Economic Growth (ICEG, inactive).* [2010/XF0333/j/**F**]

♦ Instituto Latinoamericano para la Educación por la Comunicación / see Instituto Latinoamericano de la Comunicación Educativa (#11343)
♦ Instituto Latinoamericano de Estudios Sociales 'Humberto Valdez' (inactive)
♦ Instituto Latinoamericano de Ferro e Aço / see Asociación Latinoamericana del Acero (#02176)
♦ Instituto Latinoamericano del Fierro y el Acero / see Asociación Latinoamericana del Acero (#02176)

♦ Instituto Latinoamericano de Investigaciones Sociales (ILDIS) 11346

Institut latinoaméricain de recherches sociales – Latin American Institute for Social Research

Contact Casilla 17-03-367, Quito, Ecuador. T. +59322562103. Fax +59322504337. E-mail: info@fes-ecuador.org.
URL: http://www.ildis.org.ve/

History Founded 30 Apr 1974, Quito (Ecuador), on signature of a cooperation agreement in the field of economic and social sciences between the Government of Ecuador and *Friedrich-Ebert-Stiftung (FES).* Forms part of the research department of the latter. **Aims** Promote and conduct research in the field of social sciences, particularly in the areas of *economics, sociology, political sciences* and education. **Activities** Training/education; research/documentation; events/meetings; knowledge management/information dissemination. **Events** *Congreso Internacional sobre Comunicacion, Decolonizacion y Buen ,Vivir* Quito (Ecuador) 2015. **Publications** *Materiales de Trabajo* – series. Books; pamphlets. **IGO Relations** Member of: *Latin American and Caribbean Research Network (#16284).* [2016/XD0416/j/**E**]

♦ Instituto Latinoamericano de Mercadeo Agricola (inactive)
♦ Instituto Latinoamericano de Museos (internationally oriented national body)

♦ Instituto Latinoamericano de las Naciones Unidas para la Prevención del Delito y Tratamiento del Delincuente (ILANUD) 11347

United Nations Latin American Institute for the Prevention of Crime and the Treatment of Offenders – Instituto Latinoamericano das Nações Unidas para a Precenção do Delito e Tratamento do Delinquente

Dir Gen Avenidas 6 y 8 calles 17 y 19, Tercer piso Edificio Plaza de la Justicia, San José, San José, San José, 10108, Costa Rica. T. +50622575826. Fax +50622337175.
URL: http://www.ilanud.or.cr/

History 11 Jul 1975, San José (Costa Rica). Established pursuant to an agreement between the *United Nations (UN, #20515)* and the Government of Costa Rica and in compliance with resolutions 731-F (XXVII) and 1584 (L) of *ECOSOC (#05331).* Agreement ratified by Costa Rican Legislative Assembly, 7 Dec 1977, and supplemented by bilateral cooperation agreements with countries of the region. **Aims** In accordance with provisions of foundational charter: collaborate with governments in the balanced economic and social development of Latin American countries through the formulation and incorporation into national development plans of adequate policies and action instruments in the field of crime prevention and criminal justice. *'Objectives'*: focus on the legal system as a whole; study and solve problems that have a regional, subregional or national impact on the political consensus needed for introducing changes in conception, organization and operation and the theoretical and doctrinal underpinning of justice systems; improve the legal, technical and administrative capacity of justice system institutions. *'Principles'*: (1) support region-wide efforts to coordinate and harmonize policies and approaches to improving administration of justice; (2) provide research and training for individuals involved in administering justice. (3) upgrade national capabilities to bring legal systems in line with international instruments; (4) set up centres to provide the public with statistical and scholarly information; (5) highlight the particular problems of administering justice for minors, women and ethnic minorities; (6) emphasize areas enjoying special protection under the *law*, such as the environment and freedom from social unrest. **Languages** English, Portuguese, Spanish. **Staff** 10.00 FTE, paid. **Finance** Sources: government support. Support from governments of Latin America and the Caribbean. **Activities** Guidance/assistance/consulting; knowledge management/information dissemination; research and development; research/documentation; training/education. **Publications** Biennial report. Books, articles and monographs, many available in electronic form, on: criminal justice policy; crime and population safety; juvenile criminal justice; women, justice and gender; domestic violence; organized and transnational crime; prison system; alternatives to prison; alternative conflict resolution; comparative statistics; crime data and victimology; drug abuse prevention; controlling production and trafficking of illicit drugs; control of money and assets laundering and related crimes; female criminality; Latin American criminality; training of judicial personnel; legislative reform; the correctional system. **Information Services** *Centro de Documentación sobre Politica Criminal Latinoamericana CEDO/ILANUD; Administration of Justice Information System* – 8 databases covering areas relating to administration of justice in the Latin American region.
Members Participating countries and territories (33):
Antigua-Barbuda, Argentina, Bahamas, Barbados, Belize, Bermuda, Bolivia, Brazil, Chile, Colombia, Costa Rica, Cuba, Dominica, Dominican Rep, Ecuador, El Salvador, Grenada, Guatemala, Guyana, Haiti, Honduras, Jamaica, Mexico, Nicaragua, Panama, Paraguay, Peru, St Kitts-Nevis, St Lucia, St Vincent-Grenadines, Trinidad-Tobago, Uruguay, Venezuela.
IGO Relations Cooperates with (1): *OAS (#17629).* **NGO Relations** Member of (1): *International Centre for the Prevention of Crime (ICPC, #12508).* [2021.11.08/XE7803/j/**E***]

♦ Instituto Latinoamericano das Nações Unidas para a Precenção do Delito e Tratamento do Delinquente (#11347)
♦ Instituto Latino Americano del Ombudsman (#16342)
♦ Instituto Latinoamericano del Ombudsman – Defensor del Pueblo / see Latin American Institute for the Ombudsman (#16342)
♦ Instituto Latinoamericano de Planificación Económica y Social / see Latin American and Caribbean Institute for Economic and Social Planning (#16279)
♦ Instituto Latinoamericano de Salud Mental y Derechos Humanos (internationally oriented national body)
♦ Instituto Latino Americano da Sepse (internationally oriented national body)
♦ Instituto Latino Americano de Sepse (internationally oriented national body)
♦ Instituto Latinoamericano de Servicios Legales (#11439)
♦ Instituto Latinoamericano de Servicios Legales Alternativos / see Latin American Institute for and Alternative Society and an Alternative Law
♦ Instituto Latinoamericano para una Sociedad y un Derecho Alternativos (internationally oriented national body)
♦ Instituto Lusiada de Estudos Europeus / see Instituto de Estudos Europeus, Lisboa
♦ Instituto Marquês de Valle Flôr (internationally oriented national body)
♦ Instituto de Medicina Tropical Principe Leopoldo (internationally oriented national body)
♦ Instituto de Medio Ambiente y Seguridad Humana de la Universidad de las Naciones Unidas (#20645)
♦ Instituto para el Mediterraneo (internationally oriented national body)
♦ Instituto para o Mediterrâneo (internationally oriented national body)
♦ Instituto Mediterraneo del Agua (#11323)
♦ Instituto Mexicano de Estudios Internacionales / see Mexican International Studies Association
♦ Instituto Missionario da Consolata (religious order)
♦ Instituto Mondiale de Altos Estudios Fenomenologicos / see World Phenomenology Institute (#21725)
♦ Instituto Mundial de los Amigos / see Global College, Long Island University
♦ Instituto Mundial de Investigaciones de Economia del Desarrollo (#20722)
♦ Instituto Mundo Libre (internationally oriented national body)
♦ Instituto del Mundo del Trabajo (internationally oriented national body)
♦ Instituto de las Naciones Unidas para la Formación Profesional e Investigaciones (#20576)
♦ Instituto Nórdico en Estudios de la Mujer e Investigaciones de Género / see Nordic Information for Gender Knowledge (#17317)
♦ Instituto de Nutrición de Centro América y Panama (#11285)
♦ Instituto Oceanico Internacional (#14394)
♦ Instituto por Oficialigo de Esperanto (inactive)
♦ Instituto para Oficialización del Esperanto (inactive)
♦ Instituto Panafricano de Desarrollo (#18053)
♦ Instituto Panamericano de Alta Dirección de Empresa / see IPADE Business School

♦ Instituto Panamericano de Educación Fisica (IPEF) 11348

Pan American Institute on Physical Education

Dir Universidad de Panama, Campus Harmodio Arias Madrid, Av Juan Pablo II, Albrook, Panama, Panamá, Panama PANAMá, Panama.

History 1987, when took on the organization of *Congreso Panamericano de Educación Fisica (CPEF),* which had been previously (1947-1952) been organized by *Permanent Secretariat of the Pan American Congress of Physical Education (inactive).* **Aims** Offer courses and programs in the fields of physical education, sports, recreation and related areas. **Languages** English, Spanish. **Activities** Training/education. **Events** *Pan-American congress* Caracas (Venezuela) 2001, *Pan-American Congress* Panama (Panama) 1999, *Pan-American congress on physical education / Pan-American Congress* Quito (Ecuador) 1997, *Congress on women sport* Maracaibo (Venezuela) 1996, *International conference on recreation and sport for all* Mérida (Venezuela) 1995.
Members National delegations in 23 countries and territories:
Argentina, Aruba, Bolivia, Brazil, Canada, Chile, Colombia, Costa Rica, Cuba, Dominica, Ecuador, El Salvador, Guatemala, Honduras, Mexico, Nicaragua, Panama, Paraguay, Peru, Puerto Rico, Uruguay, USA, Venezuela. [2017/XD6371/j/**E**]

♦ Instituto Panamericano de Engenharia Naval (#11349)
♦ Instituto Panamericano de Geografia e Historia (#18113)
♦ Instituto Panamericano de Ingeneria de Minas y Geologia (inactive)

♦ Instituto Panamericano de Ingenieria Naval (IPIN) 11349

Pan American Institute of Naval Engineering – Institut panaméricain de l'industrie navale – Instituto Panamericano de Engenharia Naval (IPEN)

Pres Av Rio Branco 124, Grupo 1701, Rio de Janeiro RJ, 20040-001, Brazil. T. +552122246047. E-mail: ipen@ipen.org.br.
URL: http://www.ipen.org.br/

History 1966. **Aims** Promote, on the American continent, the progress of naval engineering and techniques of *transportation* by water, and of all sectors related to shipbuilding activities. **Structure** General Assembly (every 2 years); Consultative Council; Board of Directors. **Languages** English, Portuguese, Spanish. **Staff** 3.00 FTE, paid. **Finance** Members' dues. **Activities** Events/meetings. **Events** *Biennial Congress on Naval Engineering, Maritime Transportation and Port Engineering / Biennial General Assembly* Montevideo (Uruguay) 2015,

Biennial Congress on Naval Engineering, Maritime Transportation and Port Engineering Porlamar (Venezuela) 2013, *Biennial General Assembly* Porlamar (Venezuela) 2013, *Biennial congress on naval engineering, maritime transportation and port engineering / Biennial General Assembly* Buenos Aires (Argentina) 2011, *Biennial General Assembly* Montevideo (Uruguay) 2009. **Publications** *IPinternet News* (10 a year); *Glossary of Naval Technical Terms* in English, Portuguese, Spanish; *IPEN Journal* – proceeding. Proceedings of congresses and symposiums.
Members Individuals; Supporting (companies related to the naval industry); Navies (Patronal Members). Members in 22 countries:
Argentina, Australia, Bolivia, Brazil, Canada, Chile, Colombia, Cuba, Dominican Rep, Ecuador, France, Mexico, Netherlands, Panama, Paraguay, Peru, Portugal, Spain, UK, Uruguay, USA, Venezuela. [2014.06.01/XD1253/jt/**F**]

♦ Instituto Paulo Freire (internationally oriented national body)
♦ Instituto de la Paz y los Conflictos, Granada (internationally oriented national body)
♦ Instituto Pedagógico Latinoamericano y del Caribe (unconfirmed)
♦ Instituto del Pensamiento Iberoamericano, Salamanca (internationally oriented national body)
♦ Instituto de Pesquisa Ambiental da Amazônia (internationally oriented national body)
♦ Instituto Petroquimico Latinoamericano / see Asociación Petroquimica y Quimica Latinoamericana (#02294)
♦ Institut d'ophtalmologie tropicale africaine (inactive)
♦ Instituto de Población (internationally oriented national body)
♦ Instituto para la Politica Ambiental Europea (#11261)
♦ Instituto Politica Familiar Federación Internacional (internationally oriented national body)
♦ Instituto Português de Relações Internacionais (internationally oriented national body)
♦ Instituto Português de Relações Internacionais e Segurança (internationally oriented national body)
♦ Instituto de Prensa de la Sociedad Interamericana de Prensa (see: #11444)
♦ Instituto de Promoción y Apoyo al Desarrollo (internationally oriented national body)
♦ Instituto de Radio-Astronomia Milimétrica (#11353)
♦ Instituto de Relaciones Internacionales y de Investigación para la Paz (internationally oriented national body)
♦ Instituto de Relaciones Internacionales, St Augustine (internationally oriented national body)
♦ Instituto para las Relaciones Internacionales, Zagreb / see Institute for Development and International Relations
♦ Instituto de Relações Internacionais (internationally oriented national body)
♦ Institut orientaliste, Louvain-la-Neuve (internationally oriented national body)
♦ Instituto de Salud Global Barcelona (internationally oriented national body)
♦ Instituto de Salud Reproductiva (internationally oriented national body)
♦ Instituto Secolare " Serve di Gesù Sacerdote" (religious order)
♦ Instituto Secular Pio X (#18376)
♦ Instituto Secular "Servas de Jesus Sacerdote" (religious order)
♦ Instituto Sindical para América Central y el Caribe (internationally oriented national body)
♦ Instituto Sindical de Cooperación al Desarrollo, Madrid (internationally oriented national body)
♦ Instituto para a Sintese Planetaria (#11287)
♦ Instituto para la Sintesis Planetaria (#11287)
♦ Instituto Smart City Business América (#19318)
♦ Institut für Ostasienwissenschaften, Duisburg (internationally oriented national body)
♦ Institut für Ostseeforschung Warnemünde (internationally oriented national body)
♦ Institut für Ost- und Südosteuropaforschung (internationally oriented national body)
♦ Instituto Superior Ecuménico Andino de Teologia (internationally oriented national body)
♦ Instituto Superior de Relaciones Internacionales 'Raúl Roa Garcia' (internationally oriented national body)
♦ Instituto Svizzero di Studi Internazionali (internationally oriented national body)
♦ Instituto Tecnológico Centroamericano, Santa Tecla (internationally oriented national body)
♦ Instituto Tecnológico y de Estudios Superiores de Occidente (internationally oriented national body)

♦ Instituto Teológico Pastoral para América Latina (ITEPAL) 11350

Contact Avda Boyaca No 169 D-75, Bogota, Bogota DC, Colombia. T. +5716770110667005O. Fax +5716776521. E-mail: cebitepalencontacto@celam.org – itepalcelam@gmail.com – itepal@celam.org.
URL: http://www.celam.org/
History 1972. Founded by 14th Ordinary Meeting of: *Consejo Episcopal Latinoamericano (CELAM, #04709)*, at which 4 Church training centres in Latin America were merged. Became functional, 4 Mar 1974, Medellin (Colombia), and was transferred, 1989, to Bogota (Colombia). **Aims** Act as a *training* center serving pastoral agents from Latin America, operated by Latin American Episcopal Conference – CELAM. **Structure** Episcopal Commission, comprising 2 Bishops and one Archbishop. Managing Team, consisting of Rector, Academic Vice Rector, Pastoral Vice Rector and Administrator. **Activities** Training/education; events/meetings. **Publications** *Medellin – Teologia y Pastoral para América Latina* – magazine.
Members National Bishops Conferences in 22 countries:
Argentina, Bolivia, Brazil, Chile, Colombia, Costa Rica, Cuba, Dominican Rep, Ecuador, El Salvador, Guatemala, Haiti, Honduras, Mexico, Neth Antilles, Nicaragua, Panama, Paraguay, Peru, Puerto Rico, Uruguay, Venezuela.
One ational Conference covers the Caribbean region. [2019/XE2043/j/**E**]

♦ Instituto del Tercer Mundo, Montevideo (internationally oriented national body)
♦ Instituto de Transferencia de Tecnologia Apropiada para Sectores Marginales del Convenio Andrés Bello (#11242)
♦ Instituto del Transporte Aéreo (inactive)
♦ Instituto de la UNESCO para la Educación / see UNESCO Institute for Lifelong Learning (#20305)
♦ Instituto Unificado de Investigaciones Nucleares / see Joint Institute for Nuclear Research (#16134)
♦ Instituto Universitario de Estudios Internacionales / see Centre for International Information and Documentation, Barcelona
♦ Instituto de Viena para el Desarrollo y la Cooperación / see Vienna Institute for International Dialogue and Cooperation
♦ Institut pacifique (internationally oriented national body)
♦ Institut pour la paix, le développement et l'innovation (internationally oriented national body)
♦ Institut pakistanais de développement de l'économie (internationally oriented national body)
♦ Institut panafricain pour le développement (#18053)

♦ Institut panafricain de géopolitique (IPAG) 11351

Dir and Registered Office Bibliothèque Droit, 11 Place Carnot, 54042 Nancy CEDEX, France. T. +33667680824. Fax +33145169096.
Paris Office 74 place Saint Jacques, 75014 Paris, France. T. +33143315009. Fax +33143367862.
History Apr 1986. Registered in accordance with French law. **Aims** Constitute a laboratory of ideas where new instruments of analysis of the present challenges and future strategies of the African continent emerge; promote a new Panafrican spirit; contribute to the strengthening of new solidarities between all the African *civilizations.* **Structure** Managing Board, consisting of President, Vice-President, Director and Secretary General. Scientific Council of 4 members. Scientific Committee of the 'Cahiers de l'IPAG', currently composed of 6 persons. **Languages** French. **Staff** 150.00 FTE, paid. **Finance** Members' dues. Other sources: sale of publications; service charge. Budget (annual): euro 150,000. **Activities** Organizes symposia. **Events** *Colloque international sur les problèmes et perspectives de l'industrie minière en Afrique* Paris (France) 1989, *Symposium* Paris (France) 1989. **Publications** *Cahiers de l'IPAG* – series. Monographs.
Members Individuals in 20 countries:
Algeria, Belgium, Benin, Brazil, Cameroon, Canada, Chad, Congo Brazzaville, Congo DR, Côte d'Ivoire, France, Gabon, Ghana, Kenya, Liberia, Morocco, Switzerland, Togo, USA, Zimbabwe.
IGO Relations *African Union (AU, #00488); Organisation internationale de la Francophonie (OIF, #17809); UNESCO (#20322); United Nations (UN, #20515).* [2010/XF1417/jv/**F**]

♦ Institut panaméricain de génie minier et de géologie (inactive)
♦ Institut panaméricain de géographie et d'histoire (#18113)
♦ Institut panaméricain de l'industrie navale (#11349)
♦ Institut Pasteur (internationally oriented national body)
♦ Institut Pasteur International Network / see Pasteur Network (#18256)
♦ Institut Pasteur d'outre-mer / see Pasteur Network (#18256)
♦ Institut pastoral de l'AMECEA (#00771)
♦ Institut pastoral de l'Asie orientale (#05207)
♦ Institut des pays en développement, Varsovie / see Instytut Studiów Regionalnych i Globalnych
♦ Institut pour les pays en voie de développement / see Institute for Development and International Relations
♦ Institut de pêche du Golfe et des Caraïbes (#10823)
♦ Institut pédagogique centroaméricain (inactive)
♦ Institut des Petites Soeurs de Bethléem (religious order)
♦ Institut des Petites Soeurs des Maternités Catholiques (religious order)
♦ Institut Pierre Richet (no recent information)
♦ Institut für Planetarische Synthese (#11287)
♦ Institut Plavi Svijet – Blue World Institute of Marine Research and Conservation (internationally oriented national body)
♦ Institut pluridisciplinaire d'études sur l'Amérique latine à Toulouse / see Institut Pluridisciplinaire pour les Études sur les Amériques à Toulouse
♦ Institut Pluridisciplinaire pour les Études sur les Amériques à Toulouse (internationally oriented national body)
♦ Institut polaire international (inactive)
♦ Institut für Politikwissenschaft, Innsbruck (internationally oriented national body)
♦ Institut für Politikwissenschaft, Zürich (internationally oriented national body)
♦ Institut de politique et d'économie internationales, Belgrade (internationally oriented national body)
♦ Institut de politique européenne, Berlin (internationally oriented national body)
♦ Institut pour une politique européenne de l'environnement (#11261)
♦ Institut de politique et de gestion du développement, Université Anvers (internationally oriented national body)
♦ Institut polonais des affaires internationales (internationally oriented national body)
♦ Institut pontifical d'archéologie chrétienne (#18449)
♦ Institut pontifical d'études arabes / see Pontifical Institute for Arabic and Islamic Studies (#18448)
♦ Institut pontifical d'études arabes et d'islamologie (#18448)
♦ Institut pontifical d'études orientales / see Pontifical Institute for Arabic and Islamic Studies (#18448)
♦ Institut pontifical de musique sacrée (#18455)
♦ Institut pontifical oriental (#18451)
♦ Institut pour la prévention du crime et le traitement des délinquants en Asie et en Extrême-Orient (#20521)
♦ Institut des producteurs de ferro-alliages d'Europe occidentale (inactive)
♦ Institut de production télévisée commune des Etats du Golfe arabe (inactive)
♦ Institut für Produktives Lernen in Europa (internationally oriented national body)

♦ Institut de Prospective économique du Monde Méditerranéen (IPEMED) 11352

Pres 104 bd du Montparnasse, 75014 Paris, France. T. +33156543838. Fax +33156543051. E-mail: communication@ipemed.coop.
URL: http://www.ipemed.coop/
History 2006. Registered in accordance with French law. **Aims** Bring the 2 sides of the Mediterranean closer together using economics; make a concrete contribution to building an integrated, sustainable and socially responsible Euro-Mediterranean area. **Structure** General Assembly; Board of Directors; Scientific Committee; Supervisory Board / *Euro-Mediterranean Competitiveness Council (EMCC)*; Political Sponsorship Committee. **Languages** English, French. **Events** *Forum des Diaspora Africaines* Paris (France) 2018. **Publications** *IPEMED News.*
Members Founding members in 7 countries:
Algeria, France, Jordan, Lebanon, Mauritania, Spain, Tunisia.
IGO Relations Institutional partners: *European University Institute (EUI, #09034); Plan Bleu pour l'environnement et le développement en Méditerranée (Plan Bleu, #18379).* **NGO Relations** Institutional partners include: *Institut arabe des chefs d'entreprises (IACE, #11236); Institut Europeu de la Mediterrània (IEMed); Mediterranean Agronomic Institute of Montpellier (CIHEAM Montpellier, #16643).* Member of: *ANIMA Investment Network (#00833). Association of Organisations of Mediterranean Businesswomen (#02840)* is member. [2016.11.25/XJ6606/j/**D**]

♦ Institut de la protection sociale européenne (internationally oriented national body)
♦ Institut de Psychotraumatologie et Médiation (unconfirmed)
♦ Institut québécois des hautes études internationales / see École supérieure d'études internationales
♦ Institut für Radio-Astronomie im Millimeterbereich (#11353)

♦ Institut de radio-astronomie millimétrique (IRAM) 11353

Institute for Millimetre Radio Astronomy – Institut für Radio-Astronomie im Millimeterbereich – Instituto de Radio-Astronomia Milimétrica
Dir 300 rue de la Piscine, Domaine Universitaire, 38406 Saint-Martin-d'Hères, France. T. +33476824900. Fax +33476515938. E-mail: moreau@iram.fr – zacher@iram.fr.
Manager Avda Divina Pastora 7, Núcleo Central, 18012 Granada, Spain. T. +34958805454. Fax +34958222363.
URL: http://www.iram-institute.org/
History 1979. Founded by *Max Planck Society for the Advancement of Science (MPG)* and Centre National de la Recherche Scientifique (CNRS). **Aims** Cover all aspects of *radio astronomy* at millimetre wavelengths, including development of instrumentation and software for the benefit of the astronomical community. **Structure** Steering Committee; Scientific Advisory Committee; Program Committee. **Languages** English, French, German, Spanish. **Staff** 125.00 FTE, paid. **Finance** Annual budget: 16,900,000 EUR. **Activities** Events/meetings; research and development; training/education. **Publications** Annual Report; brochures; conference proceedings.
Members Research institutes in 3 countries:
France, Germany, Spain.
NGO Relations Also links with observatories and universities. [2023.02.20/XE2903/j/**E**]

♦ Institut za Rasvoj i Medunarodne Odnose (internationally oriented national body)
♦ Institut za Razvoj i Medunarodne Odnose / see Institute for Development and International Relations
♦ Institut de recherche de l'agriculture biologique (#18857)
♦ Institut de recherche agronomique et zootechnique (no recent information)
♦ Institut de recherche sur l'Asie du Sud-Est contemporaine (internationally oriented national body)
♦ Institut de recherche et débat sur la gouvernance (internationally oriented national body)
♦ Institut de recherche pour le développement (internationally oriented national body)
♦ Institut de recherche et de développement agricoles des Caraïbes (#03436)
♦ Institut de recherche économique sur la production et le développement / see Institute of International Integration and Industrial Economics
♦ Institut de recherche et d'études du monde arabe et méditerranéen / see Institut de recherches et d'études sur le monde arabe et musulman (#11354)
♦ Institut de recherche pour la gestion des associations et des coopératives, Fribourg (internationally oriented national body)
♦ Institut de recherche sur le Maghreb contemporain, Tunis (internationally oriented national body)
♦ Institut de recherche des Nations Unies sur la défense sociale / see United Nations Interregional Crime and Justice Research Institute (#20580)
♦ Institut de recherche des Nations Unies pour le développement social (#20623)
♦ Institut de recherche pour la paix dans le monde, Oslo / see Peace Research Institute Oslo
♦ Institut de recherche pour la paix, Oslo (internationally oriented national body)

- ♦ Institut de recherche en politiques publiques (internationally oriented national body)
- ♦ Institut de recherche sur la résolution non-violente des conflits (internationally oriented national body)
- ♦ Institut de recherches et d'applications des méthodes de développement (internationally oriented national body)
- ♦ Institut de recherches et d'études africaines, Université du Caire (internationally oriented national body)
- ♦ Institut de recherches et d'études sur les migrations et les rapports interculturels (internationally oriented national body)

♦ Institut de recherches et d'études sur le monde arabe et musulman (IREMAM) 11354

Institute of Research and Study on the Arab and Islamic Worlds

Dir c/o MMSH UMR 7310, 5 rue du Chateau de l'Horloge, CS 90412, 13097 Aix-en-Provence CEDEX 2, France. T. +33442524162. Fax +33442524980.

URL: http://iremam.cnrs.fr/

History 1964, Aix-en-Provence (France), as a unity of the 'Centre national de la recherche scientifique' attached to Universités d'Aix-Marseille I and III (France). From 1986, took over activities of *Groupement d'intérêt scientifique-sciences humaines sur l'aire méditerranéenne (GIS)*, set up 1980. Also integrates: *Centre d'études et de recherches sur l'Orient arabe contemporain (CEROAC, inactive)*; *Centre de recherches et d'études sur les sociétés méditerranéennes (CRESM, inactive)*; *Groupe de recherches et d'études sur le Proche-Orient (GREPO, inactive)*. Former names and other names: *Institut de recherche et d'études du monde arabe et méditerranéen* – alias. **Aims** Carry out research on the Arab and Muslim worlds including Arab and Muslim minorities in the Diaspora. **Structure** Mixed unit of research associating the National Scientific Research Center (CNRS), University of Marseille (AMU) and the Institute of Political Studies of Aix (IEP). **Languages** Arabic, English, French. **Staff** About 40 academics; 8 administrative and technical staff. **Finance** Annual donations: euro 64,000 from the CNRS; euro 64,000 from Aix-Marseille University. Other sources: specific research contracts. **Activities** Research/documentation; training/education; knowledge management/information dissemination; events/meetings. **Events** *Congrès des Etudes sur le Moyen-Orient et les Mondes Musulmans* Paris (France) 2019, *Rencontres franco-egyptiennes de politologie* Aix-en-Provence (France) 2006, *Table ronde* Aix-en-Provence (France) 2006, *Colloque international sur l'immigration, le transit et la rétention* Marseille (France) 2006, *La France et l'Egypte à l'époque des vice-rois (1805-1882)* Aix-en-Provence (France) 1998. **Publications** *Anti Atlas Journal*; *Arabian Humanities*; *L'Année du Maghreb*; *L'Encyclopédie berbère*; *Revue des mondes musulmans et de la Méditerranée*.

Members Researchers in 12 countries:
Algeria, Egypt, France, Italy, Jordan, Lebanon, Morocco, Palestine, Spain, Syrian AR, Tunisia, Yemen.

NGO Relations Cooperates with: *GIGA Institute of Middle East Studies, Hamburg (IMES)*. [2022/XF0236/jv/**E**]

- ♦ Institut de recherches interculturelles (see: #04692)
- ♦ Institut de recherche sur les sociétés contemporaines, Paris (internationally oriented national body)
- ♦ Institut de recherches et technologie industrielles pour l'Amérique centrale (inactive)
- ♦ Institut de recherche sur le sud-est Asiatique (internationally oriented national body)
- ♦ Institut de recherche touristique et balnéaire en Europe du Nord (internationally oriented national body)
- ♦ Institut Régional Africain pour la Science et la Technologie de l'Information Géospatiale (#00433)
- ♦ Institut régional de coopération et de développement (internationally oriented national body)
- ♦ Institut régional pour l'enseignement supérieur et le développement / see SEAMEO Regional Centre for Higher Education and Development (#19174)

♦ Institut Régional d'Enseignement Supérieur et de Recherche en Développement Culturel (IRES-RDEC) 11355

Regional Institute of Higher Education and Research in Cultural Development

Dir Gen 01 BP 3253, Lomé, Togo. T. +22822224433. Fax +22822207245.

URL: http://iresrdec.org/

History May 1976, Dakar (Senegal), as an affiliated body of *African Cultural Institute (ACI, inactive)*, in accordance with a convention adopted by ACI Executive Committee at its 5th Session, when statutes were adopted. Original title: *Regional Centre for Cultural Action (RCCA) – Centre régional d'action culturelle (CRAC)*. Previously also referred to in English as *Regional Cultural Action Centre*. **Aims** Promote endogenous processes of *development* by broadening participation in cultural activities and strengthening the cultural dimension of national plans for *integrated development*; provide ACI member States with cultural officials trained in the *African* milieu; promote greater understanding of African cultural realities; teach effective mastering of traditional and modern forms of *artistic expression*; develop contacts, communications and organizational skills. **Structure** Conference of Ministers. **Languages** French. **Staff** 8.00 FTE, paid. **Finance** Tuition fees. **Activities** Training/education; events/meetings. **Publications** *Ingénierie culturelle* – review. Proceedings; papers; CDs; DVDs.

Members States with institutions having registered students in the Institute (9):
Algeria, Benin, Burkina Faso, Central African Rep, Côte d'Ivoire, Equatorial Guinea, Gabon, Niger, Togo.

IGO Relations *Organisation internationale de la Francophonie (OIF, #17809)*; *African Union (AU, #00488)*; *UNESCO (#20322)*. [2018.09.10/XE0540/**E***]

- ♦ Institut sous-régional multisectoriel de technologie appliquée, de planification et d'évaluation de projets (no recent information)

♦ Institut sous-régional de statistique et d'économie appliquée (ISSEA) 11356

Dir BP 294, Yaoundé, Cameroon. T. +237220134. Fax +2372229521. E-mail: isseacemac@yahoo.fr.

Contact address not obtained.

History 19 Dec 1984, Brazzaville (Congo Brazzaville), a *Centre international de formation statistique (CIFS)* having been created, Nov 1961, Yaoundé (Cameroon), for the particular needs of the Central African states and an *Institut de formation statistique (IFS)*, having been formed, Jan 1969, Yaoundé, for all the African francophone countries (the latter became, 1975, a national institution, under the title 'Institut de statistique, de planification et d'économie appliquée (ISPEA)'). ISSEA is placed under the auspices of *Union douanière et économique de l'Afrique centrale (UDEAC, inactive)*. **Aims** Provide the *training* of statisticians whose task is to create, manage and utilize statistical information for drawing up decisions of economic and social nature concerning the nation, the region or the enterprise. **Structure** Management Board, consisting of 2 representatives of CACEU member states (including one Minister per member state), 2 representatives of the General Secretariat of CACEU (including Secretary General) and representatives of ISSEA. Council of Improvement. General Direction, comprising Director General, Administrative and Financial Director and Director of Studies. Council of Professors; Council of Students; Council of Discipline. **Activities** Training cycles (3).

Members CACEU member states (6):
Cameroon, Central African Rep, Chad, Congo Brazzaville, Equatorial Guinea, Gabon. [2010/XE1552/j/**E***]

- ♦ Institut der Regionen Europas (internationally oriented national body)
- ♦ Institut des régions arides, Tunisia (internationally oriented national body)
- ♦ Institut des relations internationales, Athènes (internationally oriented national body)
- ♦ Institut des relations internationales du Cameroun (internationally oriented national body)
- ♦ Institut des relations internationales de Moscou / see Moskovskij Gosudarstvennyj Institut Mezdunarodnyh Otnosenij
- ♦ Institut de relations internationales, Prague (internationally oriented national body)
- ♦ Institut de relations internationales et de recherche pour la paix (internationally oriented national body)
- ♦ Institut de relations internationales et stratégiques (internationally oriented national body)
- ♦ Institut des relations internationales, Taipei (internationally oriented national body)
- ♦ Institut pour les relations internationales, Zagreb / see Institute for Development and International Relations
- ♦ Institut Religieux Apostolique de Marie-Immaculée (religious order)
- ♦ Institut Religieux Sainte-Croix de Jérusalem (religious order)
- ♦ Institut Robert Schuman pour l'Europe (#18959)
- ♦ Institut Royal Colonial Belge / see Royal Academy of Overseas Sciences
- ♦ Institut royal des relations internationales / see Egmont Institute
- ♦ Institut royal des tropiques (internationally oriented national body)
- ♦ Institut du Sacré-Coeur de Marie, Vierge-Immaculée (religious order)

♦ Institut du Sahel (INSAH) 11357

Sahel Institute

Gen Dir BP 1530, Bamako, Mali. T. +22320222148 – +22320223043 – +22320224706. Fax +22320227831. E-mail: administration.insah@cilss.int.

URL: http://insah.cilss.int/

History 1976, Bamako (Mali). Established as as a result of a proposal in Sep 1973, Ouagadougou (Burkina Faso), at the first meeting of *Comité permanent inter-Etats de lutte contre la sécheresse dans le Sahel (CILSS, #04195)*. **Aims** Provide *food security* in a balanced *ecological environment*; promote, harmonize and coordinate agricultural research programmes and scientific information; contribute to better knowledge of human environments in Sahelian countries. **Structure** Technical and Management of Technical Departments Committee; Scientific Committee; Meeting of INRA General Directors; meeting of focal points in research on population and development. Food Market Program; Departments (3): Agriculture, Environment and Market Research Department (DREAM); *Centre for Applied Research on Population and Development (CERPOD, no recent information)* – Department of Population and Studies Research; Seed, Pesticide, Reglementation Department (DRIAR). Management Support Units (2): Communication, Information and Documentation Unit (UCID); Administration, Finances, Accounting and Human Resources Unit (UAFC/RH). Scientific Coordination Cell. **Languages** Arabic, English, French, Portuguese. **Staff** 28.00 FTE, paid. **Finance** Sources: contributions of member/participating states; donations. Supported by: *European Commission (EC, #06633)*; *International Bank for Reconstruction and Development (IBRD, #12317)* (World Bank); *United States Agency for International Development (USAID)*. **Activities** Events/meetings; research/documentation. Coordinates, harmonizes and promotes studies and research on agriculture, the environment, markets and population and development. **Events** *Atelier régional de validation des résultats sur la réglementation commune des semences* Bamako (Mali) 2003, *Session* Bamako (Mali) 2003, *Conférence internationale sur la transformation de l'agriculture en Afrique sub-saharienne* Abidjan (Côte d'Ivoire) 1995, *Atelier sur l'impact de la dévaluation du franc CFA sur les revenus et la sécurité alimentaire en Afrique de l'Ouest* Bamako (Mali) 1995, *Colloque international sur l'intensification agricole au Sahel* Bamako (Mali) 1995. **Publications** *Liaison Sahel*; *Nouvelles du CERPOD*; *POP-Sahel*; *Sahel IPM*. *Agronomie et Agroforesterie*; *Agronomie et Agroforesterie au Sahel*; *Lait Sain pour le Sahel*; *La Santé de la Reproduction des Adolescents au Sahel*; *Lueurs d'Espoir*; *Mobilité et VIH/SIDA*; *Regional Synthesis on the 2002-2003 Cropping Season*; *Synthèse de la Campagne Agricole 2002-2003*. Annual Report; meeting reports; research reports; brochures; cataglogue of publications.

Members Governments of 13 countries:
Benin, Burkina Faso, Cape Verde, Chad, Côte d'Ivoire, Gambia, Guinea, Guinea-Bissau, Mali, Mauritania, Niger, Senegal, Togo.

NGO Relations Member of: *International Foundation for Science (IFS, #13677)*; *Sustainable Development Solutions Network (SDSN, #20054)*. [2023/XE6031/j/**E***]

- ♦ Institut de la santé reproductive (internationally oriented national body)
- ♦ Institut scandinave d'études africaines / see Nordic Africa Institute (#17168)
- ♦ Institut des sciences de gestion / see Institute for Operations Research and the Management Sciences (#11286)
- ♦ Institut des sciences et des techniques de l'équipement et de l'environnement pour le développement (internationally oriented national body)
- ♦ Institut Séculier Dominicain d'Orléans (religious order)
- ♦ Institut Séculier Féminin du Coeur de Jésus (religious order)
- ♦ Institut Séculier Masculin du Coeur de Jésus (religious order)
- ♦ Institut séculier Pie X (#18376)
- ♦ Institut Séculier des Prêtres du Coeur de Jésus (religious order)
- ♦ Institut Séculier de Saint-François de Sales (religious order)
- ♦ Instituts für europäische Lehrerbildung, Berlin (internationally oriented national body)

♦ Institut Sexocorporel International (ISI) 11358

Contact Via Monte Boglia 5, 6900 Lugano TI, Switzerland. T. +41919714222. E-mail: info@doctorj.ch.

URL: http://www.sexocorporel.com/

History 28 Apr 2004, Geneva (Switzerland). **Structure** Officers: Honorary President; President; Vice-President; Secretary; Treasurer. **Languages** English, French, German, Italian, Spanish. **Events** *Congress* Saint-Malo (France) 2015, *Scientific Days* Saint-Malo (France) 2015, *General Assembly* Paris (France) 2012, *Scientific Days* Paris (France) 2012, *Meeting* Vienna (Austria) 2009. **Publications** *Santé sexuelle* – review.

Members Individuals in 6 countries:
Belgium, Canada, France, Italy, Mexico, Switzerland. [2015/XJ1357/jv/**D**]

- ♦ Institut de la sidérurgie du Sud-Est asiatique (#19756)
- ♦ Institut social d'Asie (internationally oriented national body)
- ♦ Institut de sociologie du droit pour l'Europe (inactive)
- ♦ Institut des Soeurs Franciscaines Missionnaires de la Nativité de Notre-Dame (religious order)
- ♦ Institut pour la solidarité internationale des femmes (#19298)
- ♦ Instituts Panos / see Panos Network (#18183)
- ♦ Instituts de recherches français à l'étranger (internationally oriented national body)
- ♦ Institut de statistique pour l'Asie et le Pacifique (#19972)
- ♦ Institut de statistiques mathématiques (#11282)
- ♦ Institut de statistique de l'UNESCO (#20306)
- ♦ Institut suédois des études de la politique européenne (internationally oriented national body)
- ♦ Institut suisse pour le développement / see Swiss Academy for Development
- ♦ Institut suisse de recherches internationales (internationally oriented national body)
- ♦ Institut Supérieur Arabe de Traduction (internationally oriented national body)
- ♦ Institut supérieur de commerce international de Dunkerque (internationally oriented national body)
- ♦ Institut supérieur international du tourisme (internationally oriented national body)
- ♦ Institut supérieur panafricain d'économie coopérative / see African University for Cooperative Development (#00494)
- ♦ Institut supérieur de planification d'urgence / see Higher Institute of Emergency Planning – European Centre Florival
- ♦ Institut supérieur de planification d'urgence – Centre d'étude Europa (now national)
- ♦ Institut supérieur du tourisme de Tanger / see Institut supérieur international du tourisme
- ♦ Institut syndical européen (#08928)
- ♦ Institut pour une synthèse planétaire (#11287)
- ♦ Institut technique européen du bois-énergie / see Bioenergy Institute
- ♦ Institut technique international des officiers mécaniciens de l'aviation civile (inactive)
- ♦ Institut technique latinoaméricain d'intégration coopérative (inactive)
- ♦ Institutet for Fremtidsforskning (internationally oriented national body)
- ♦ Institutt for fredsforskning, Oslo (internationally oriented national body)
- ♦ Institutt for globalt nettverksarbeid, informasjon og studier (internationally oriented national body)
- ♦ Institut Thomas More (#20154)
- ♦ Institutt for Kulturstudies og Orientalske Språk (internationally oriented national body)
- ♦ Institut du tourisme asiatique (#01521)
- ♦ Institut für Tourismus- und Bäderforschung in Nordeuropa (internationally oriented national body)
- ♦ Institut du transfert des technologies appropriées pour les secteurs marginaux de la Convention Andrés Bello (#11242)
- ♦ Institut du transport aérien (inactive)
- ♦ Institut du Travail d'Afrique Centrale (unconfirmed)
- ♦ Institut für Tropenmedizin, Berlin / see Institut für Tropenmedizin und Internationale Gesundheit

♦ Institut für Tropenmedizin und Internationale Gesundheit (internationally oriented national body)
♦ Institut tropical et de santé publique suisse (internationally oriented national body)
♦ Institut tropical suisse / see Swiss Tropical and Public Health Institute
♦ Institut tropického a subtropického zemedelstvi / see Institute of Tropics and Subtropics, Prague
♦ Institut Tropického a Subtropického Zemědělství, Praha (internationally oriented national body)
♦ Institutul European din România (internationally oriented national body)
♦ Institutul pentru Politici si Reforme Europene (internationally oriented national body)
♦ Institutul Român de Studii Internationale – Nicolae Titulescu (internationally oriented national body)
♦ Institutul Unificat de Cercetari Nucleare / see Joint Institute for Nuclear Research (#16134)
♦ Institutum Charitatis (religious order)
♦ Institutum Filiarum Mariae (religious order)
♦ Institutum Fratrum Beatae Mariae Virginis a Misericordia (religious order)
♦ Institutum Fratrum Filiorum Sancti Iosephi, vulgo Bayozefiti (religious order)
♦ Institutum Fratrum Franciscalium a Santa Cruce (religious order)
♦ Institutum Fratrum Instructionis Christianae de Ploërmel (religious order)
♦ Institutum Fratrum Instructionis Christianae a Sancto Gabriele (religious order)
♦ Institutum Fratrum Maristarum a Scholis (religious order)
♦ Institutum Fratrum a Sancta Familia de Bellicio (religious order)
♦ Institutum Fratrum Scholarum Christianarum (religious order)
♦ Institutum Missionariorum Opificum (religious order)
♦ Institutum Missionum a Consolata (religious order)
♦ Institutum Oblatorum Sancti Francisci Salesii (religious order)
♦ Institutum Parvulorum Fratrum Iesu (religious order)
♦ Institutum Patrum Josephitarum Gerardimontensium (religious order)
♦ Institutum Tropologicum Helveticum / see Swiss Tropical and Public Health Institute
♦ Institutum Yarumalense pro Missionibus ad Exteras Gentes (religious order)
♦ Institut UNESCO pour l'application des technologies de l'information à l'éducation (#20304)
♦ Institut de l'UNESCO pour l'apprentissage tout au long de la vie (#20305)
♦ Institut de l'UNESCO pour l'éducation / see UNESCO Institute for Lifelong Learning (#20305)
♦ Institut UNESCO-IHE pour l'éducation relative à l'eau / see IHE Delft Institute for Water Education (#11110)
♦ Institut unifié des recherches nucléaires (#16134)
♦ Institut universitaire d'études européennes, Torino (internationally oriented national body)
♦ Institut universitaire européen (#09034)
♦ Institut Universitaire Intergouvernemental pour la Coopération (internationally oriented national body)
♦ Institut universitaire international de Luxembourg (internationally oriented national body)
♦ Institut Universitari d'Estudis Europeus (internationally oriented national body)
♦ Institut Universitari d'Estudis Internacionals / see Centre for International Information and Documentation, Barcelona
♦ Institut de l'UNU pour les ressources naturelles en Afrique (#20718)
♦ Institut des vérificateurs internes / see Institute of Internal Auditors (#11272)
♦ Institut de Vienne pour le développement et la coopération / see Vienna Institute for International Dialogue and Cooperation
♦ Institut für Völkerkunde / see Institut für Ethnologie und Afrika-Studien
♦ Institut für Völkerkunde und Afrikanistik / see Institut für Ethnologie und Afrikanistik
♦ Institut für Völkerrecht und Internationale Beziehungen (internationally oriented national body)
♦ Institut Voluntas Dei (religious order)
♦ Institut für Weltgesellschaft (internationally oriented national body)
♦ Institut für Weltwirtschaft und Internationales Management, Bremen (internationally oriented national body)
♦ Institut für Weltwirtschaft, Kiel (internationally oriented national body)
♦ Institut Wiener Kreis (internationally oriented national body)
♦ Institut Wiener Kreis – Verein zur Förderung Wissenschaftlicher Weltauffassung / see Institut Wiener Kreis
♦ Institut za Zemlje u Razvoju / see Institute for Development and International Relations
♦ Instituut voor Europees Milieubeleid (#11261)
♦ Instituut voor Internationaal en Europees Beleid (internationally oriented national body)
♦ Instituut voor Internationaal Privaat- en Publiekrecht, Internationale Handelsarbitrage en Europees Recht / see TMC Asser Institute – Centre for International and European Law
♦ Instituut voor Ontwikkelingsbeleid en -beheer, Universiteit Antwerpen (internationally oriented national body)
♦ Instituut voor Strategische and Internationale Studies, Lissabon (internationally oriented national body)
♦ Instituut voor de Vorming van Kaders voor de Ontwikkeling (internationally oriented national body)
♦ INSTR – International Symposium on Transport Network Reliability (meeting series)

♦ Instruct-ERIC 11359

Coordinator Oxford House, Parkway Court, John Smith Drive, Oxford, OX4 2JY, UK. T. +441865988639. E-mail: admin@instruct-eric.eu.
URL: https://instruct-eric.eu/

History 2012. Started as a group of professors across Europe working together through the Structural Proteomics in Europe (SPINE) project. Established during the European Research Infrastructure Preparatory Phase of the ESFRI roadmap. Since Jul 2018, granted ERIC (European Research Infrastructure Consortium) status by *European Commission (EC, #06633)*. **Aims** Promote innovation in biomedical science. **Structure** Council; Executive Committee; Advisory Committees. **Finance** Sources: contributions of member/participating states. Also external funding through EU and other programmes. **Activities** Events/meetings; training/education. **Events** *Biennial Structural Biology Conference* Utrecht (Netherlands) 2022, *Biennial Structural Biology Conference* Madrid (Spain) 2019.
Members Member countries (13):
Belgium, Czechia, Denmark, Finland, France, Israel, Italy, Latvia, Netherlands, Portugal, Slovakia, Spain, UK.
European Molecular Biology Laboratory (EMBL, #07813).
Observer country:
Greece. [2020/AA0559/**E**]

♦ instrument européen pour la démocratie et les droits de l'Homme (#07576)
♦ Instrument Rating / see PPL/IR Europe
♦ Instrument Society of America / see International Society of Automation
♦ Instytut Afrykanistyczny / see Instytut Studiów Regionalnych i Globalnych
♦ Instytut Europy Srodkowo-Wschodniej (internationally oriented national body)
♦ Instytut Gospodarki Swiatowej (internationally oriented national body)
♦ Instytut Krajów Rozwiajacych / see Instytut Studiów Regionalnych i Globalnych
♦ Instytut Polsko-Skandynawski (#18420)
♦ Instytut na Rzecz Demokracji w Europie Wschodniej (internationally oriented national body)
♦ Instytut Studiów Miedzynarodowych (internationally oriented national body)
♦ Instytut Studiów Regionalnych i Globalnych (internationally oriented national body)
♦ Instytut Zachodni, Poznan (internationally oriented national body)
♦ **INSULEUR** Network of the Insular Chambers of Commerce and Industry of the European Union (#17040)

♦ Insurance Association of the Caribbean (IAC) 11360

Manager Thomas Peirce Bldg, Lower Collymore Rock, St Michael BB11115, ST MICHAEL BB11115, Barbados. T. +2464275608. Fax +2464277277. E-mail: info@iac-caribbean.com.
URL: http://iac-caribbean.com/

History 1974, Kingston (Jamaica), following discussions initiated in 1972. **Aims** Protect, promote and foster the advancement of the insurance industry of the Caribbean. **Events** *Annual Caribbean Insurance Conference / Caribbean Insurance Conference* Montego Bay (Jamaica) 2015, *Annual Caribbean Insurance Conference / Caribbean Insurance Conference* Willemstad (Curaçao) 2014, *Caribbean Insurance Conference* Cancún (Mexico) 2013, *Caribbean Insurance Conference* St Thomas Is (Virgin Is USA) 2012, *Caribbean Insurance Conference* Trinidad-Tobago 2011. [2015/XN2613/**D**]

♦ Insurance Broker Network (Euribron) 11361

Contact Koninklijkelaan 74, 2600 Antwerp, Belgium.
URL: http://www.euribron.com/

History Founded 1994. Registered in accordance with Belgian law. **Structure** Board. Committees (3). **Languages** English. **Activities** Events/meetings. **Events** *International Conference* Madrid (Spain) 2017, *International Conference* Paris (France) 2011. **Members** Firms (27) in 61 countries. Membership countries not specified. [2014.06.24/XJ5080/**F**]

♦ Insurance Council of the ASEAN Countries / see ASEAN Insurance Council (#01201)

♦ Insurance Europe 11362

Spokesperson Rue du Champ de Mars 23, 1050 Brussels, Belgium. T. +3228943000. E-mail: info@insuranceeurope.eu.
URL: https://www.insuranceeurope.eu/

History 6 Mar 1953. Founded during plenary meeting of national insurance associations of Western Europe, following preliminary meetings in Jan 1950, Paris (France) and June 1951, Brussels (Belgium). Former names and other names: *Comité européen des assurances (CEA)* – former (6 Mar 1953 to Mar 2012). Registration: Banque-Carrefour des Entreprises, No/ID: 0893.193.420, Start date: 31 Oct 2007, Belgium; EU Transparency Register, No/ID: 33213703459-54, Start date: 15 Apr 2010. **Aims** Draw attention to issues of strategic interest to all European *insurers* and reinsurers in a sustainable manner; raise awareness of insurers' and reinsurers' roles in providing insurance protection and security to the community, as well as in contributing to economic growth and development; promote a competitive and open market to the benefit of the European consumer, as well as corporate clients. **Structure** General (Plenary) Assembly (annual); with International Conference; Executive Committee; Strategic Board; Departments; Committees. **Languages** English. **Staff** 41.00 FTE, paid. **Finance** Sources: members' dues. **Activities** Knowledge management/information dissemination; networking/liaising. **Events** *International Insurance Conference* Paris (France) 2023, *International Insurance Conference* Prague (Czechia) 2022, *Conference on Tackling the Pension Challenge* Brussels (Belgium) 2020, *International Insurance Conference* Brussels (Belgium) 2020, *International Insurance Conference* Bucharest (Romania) 2019. **Publications** *European Insurance in Figures* (annual); *Indirect Taxation on Insurance Contracts* (annual); *Key Facts* (annual). Position papers; press releases; statistical publications; technical specifications. **Members** National insurance associations (36), representing over 4,900 insurance undertakings. Membership countries not specified. **Consultative Status** Consultative status granted from: *UNCTAD (#20285)* (Special Category). [2023.02.15/XD0788/**D**]

♦ Insurance Hall of Fame (internationally oriented national body)
♦ Insurance Institute for Asia and the Pacific (internationally oriented national body)
♦ Insurance Workers International Union / see United Food and Commercial Workers Union

♦ Insurope 11363

CEO Insurope Secretariat, Av des Arts 9, 1210 Brussels, Belgium. T. +3222865086. E-mail: info@insurope.com.
URL: https://www.insurope.com/

History 1968, Brussels (Belgium). Founded as a worldwide network of life insurers, specializing in group insurance benefits for employees of multinational companies. Former names and other names: *Insurope – Multinational Benefits Association (IMBA)* – former. **Aims** Provide professional advice and solutions in employees' benefit plans in their respective local insurance markets. **Structure** Executive Committee; Regional Coordinating Offices (8); Secretariat in Brussels (Belgium). **Languages** English. **Staff** 50.00 FTE, paid. **Activities** Knowledge management/information dissemination; networking/liaising. **Events** *Annual Sales Meeting* Brussels (Belgium) 2022, *General Meeting* Paris (France) 2020, *General Meeting* Dubai (United Arab Emirates) 2018, *General Meeting* Leipzig (Germany) 2014, *Annual Sales Meeting* Lisbon (Portugal) 2013. **Publications** *INSUROPE News*. **Members** Group insurance and pension companies in over 100 countries. Membership countries not specified. [2022.02.24/XF0586/e/**F**]

♦ Insurope – Multinational Benefits Association / see Insurope (#11363)
♦ INSWaP / see European Network of Steiner Waldorf Parents (#08014)

This alphabetical listing is continued in Volume 1B.

La suite de cette séquence alphabétique se trouve dans le Volume 1B.

DISCLAIMER. The organizations described in this Yearbook are invited annually to update their profiles. By updating or approving a profile, the organization gives its fully informed permission to the Union of International Associations (UIA) to collect, save and use the data the organization thus submits, in order to execute UIA's core activities as set out in https://uia.org/core-activities. At any time an organization described in this Yearbook may ask UIA to remove, free of charge, its contact details by writing to uia@uia.org. UIA is responsible for processing the data it receives in accordance with the *General Data Protection Regulation* of the European Union. UIA will take all reasonable measures to ensure the protection of the data it holds. Those who submit data acknowledge and agree that the transmission of data is never without risk and therefore potential damage due to the unlawful use of information by third parties cannot be claimed from UIA. For more information, please see https://uia.org/privacypolicy

Appendix 1
Contents of organization descriptions

Order of descriptions
The descriptions of organizations in this volume appear in alphabetic order of the first title. In the case of a few intergovernmental organizations known more usually by their initials (eg WHO, UNESCO), the abbreviation is used instead of the title.

Listed in the one alphabetic sequence are all titles and abbreviations of the organizations in this edition, their former titles and abbreviations, and titles and abbreviations of subsidiary bodies mentioned in their descriptions. The index in Volume 3 also lists keywords in titles.

Each description is identified by a sequence number assigned for this edition. The sequence number follows the alphabetic sequence.

For some types of organization no description is included in this edition due to limitations imposed by printing and binding. In such cases, no sequence number is assigned and an explanatory comment is given instead of the description (for example: "no longer active"; "meeting series"; "treaty"). All descriptions can be found in the Yearbook Online.

A description may be abridged when sufficient information has not yet been obtained, or when the organization is classified as one of the types for which extensive information is either not collected or not included in the book version due to limitations imposed by printing and binding; see below under "Codes", or the Appendix "Types of organization" for further information.

Descriptions always include the following information.

Organization name
The organization's name is given in all languages in which it is available. Normally the names are given in the order:
- European languages (starting with English, French, Spanish, German)
- transliterated languages (Arabic, Russian, Japanese, etc)
- artificial languages (Esperanto, Ido, Occidental, etc)
- historical languages (Latin, etc)

The order may be changed to reflect the organization's concern with a particular language. For example, an organization promoting the use of Latin may have its Latin name in the first position.

Abbreviations follow the appropriate name.

When an organization does not have an official name in English or French, the editors may provide translated versions. An asterisk then follows the unofficially translated name.

Organization number
The number to the right of each title (eg •00123) is a sequence number with no significance other than as a fixed point of reference in the sequence of organizations in this edition of the Yearbook. Cross-references in organization descriptions, other volumes in this series and indexes refer to this number. The order and numbering of the organizations is of no significance other than alphabetical access.

Descriptions may include the following information.

Addresses
The main address for correspondence is inset beneath the organization names. Telephone, fax, e-mail and other media addresses are also given when available.

Secondary addresses are inset in smaller type below the main address. Included here are registered offices, continental regional offices, information offices and addresses for secondary correspondence.

The address of the organization's home page is given, if known, with an indication as to which aspect of the organization it refers where appropriate.

Address locations are indexed by country in Volume 2.

For various reasons no address is given for some organizations. In such cases, the reason for this absence is given.

History
The date and location of founding or of establishment are indicated under this heading. In the absence of a precise legal date, the date of the first General Meeting is given. Other information on the history and changes in structure or name of the organization is also given.

Where another organization is cited, if it has a description included in this edition, its first title is given, followed by its abbreviation and the sequence number allotted to it for this edition. If it has no description included in this edition (eg former names, subsidiary bodies), all its titles and abbreviations are given, but no sequence number; these titles are included in the overall alphabetical sequence with a reference to this description.

Aims
Principal objectives are summarized, wherever possible on the basis of the organization's statutes. In some cases keywords are given in italics. These are then used to determine classification of the organization in Volume 3.

Structure
The key organs and commissions of the organization are enumerated, together with some indication of the frequency of their meetings and of composition of the executive body. Where another organization is cited, it is treated as explained under "History" above.

Languages
Official and working languages used by the organization are listed.

Staff
The numbers of paid and voluntary staff are given.

Finance
Sources of funding and the annual budget figures are given.

Where another organization is cited, it is treated as explained under "History" above.

Activities
Under this heading appears a summary of the main activities and programme concerns of each organization. Special emphasis is placed on developmental activities, where relevant.

Where another organization is cited, it is treated as explained under "History" above.

Events
Listed here are the dates and locations of previous and future periodic meetings or other events. For a fuller list of events, for more details on the events listed here, and for full indexes to them, users are directed to the *International Congress Calendar*.

Publications
Listed here are the titles of major periodical and non-periodical publications of the organization. Titles in italics are indexed and classified in Volume 4.

Information Services
Listed here are the names of libraries, databanks and library and publications consultancy services operated by the organization. Websites of these services are listed with the organization's address (see above). Titles in italics are indexed and classified in Volume 4.

Members
Listed here are the types of membership and numbers of members. This may include the list of countries represented or in which members are located. These countries are indexed and cross-referenced in Volume 2.

Where another organization is cited, it is treated as explained under "History" above.

Note on country names
It is not the intention of the editors to take a position with regard to the political or diplomatic implications of geographical names or continental groupings used.

The geographical names used in this publication are chosen for the sake of brevity and common usage. Wherever possible, the country (or territory) name preferred by the organization concerned is used, providing this is possible within the limits of standardization required for mailing or statistical purposes. It is important to note that some organizations insist on the inclusion of territories on the same basis as countries, or on the inclusion of countries or territories that are not recognized by other organizations.

Political changes over the years may lead to some questions in an organization's description. Briefly: countries referred to in an organization's description retain their old form when referring to a date prior to the change. For example, towns referred to in events prior to 1991 still retain their country as German DR (Democratic Republic) or Germany FR (Federal Republic), while subsequent dates refer simply to Germany.

Consultative Status
Where the organization has an officially recognized relationship to a major intergovernmental organization, this is indicated. Cited organizations are treated as explained under "History" above.

IGO Relations
Where the organization has a special relationship to an intergovernmental organization, this is indicated. Cited organizations are treated as explained under "History" above. It should be noted that tenuous links, or links that have not been confirmed by both parties, have been omitted from the printed descriptions, although they are available in the Yearbook Online and are included in the statistics.

NGO Relations
Where the organization has a special relationship with international non-governmental organizations, this is indicated. Cited organizations are treated as explained under "History" above. It should be noted that tenuous links, or links that have not been confirmed by both parties, have been omitted from the printed descriptions, although they are available in the Yearbook Online and are included in the statistics.

Date
The last line of the description includes the date on which the most recent information has been received. Two forms are used:
- 2023.02.16: the organization checked the description and returned it on that date;
- 2021: the organization has not checked the description since that date, but information has been received in the given year from another reliable source (which may be the organization's own website).

Old dates, or no date, may be an indication that an organization is becoming inactive.

Codes
Organizations are coded by type, indicated by a single upper case letter printed in bold at the end of the description. The upper case type code may be preceded by a letter code printed in lower case. The type code of Intergovernmental organizations is followed by an asterisk, '*'. For further information, see the Appendix: "Types of organization".

Appendix 4
Editorial problems and policies

Coverage

The Yearbook attempts to cover all "international organizations", according to a broad range of criteria. It therefore includes many bodies that may be perceived, according to narrower definitions, as not being fully international or as not being of sufficient significance to merit inclusion. Such bodies are nevertheless included, so as to enable users to make their own evaluation in the light of their own criteria. For some users, these bodies may even be of greater interest.

The editors are sensitive to the existence of forms of social organization that may substitute for the creation of a more formal conventional organization. A conference series with no continuing committee is one example. Such "organizations" are generally included in one of the Special Types (see the Appendix "Types of Organization).

The definition of profit-making, and the extent to which any non-profit organization may incidentally or deliberately make a profit as defined by particular tax regimes, cannot be unambiguously resolved. This grey area has been treated in a variety of ways with the sensitivity it merits. The editors are attentive to the non-profit objectives of an organization registered under for-profit legal status. Especially problematic are the professional and trade organizations whose existence is in part justified, in their members' eyes, by the extent to which they defend or improve the members' income.

The editors acknowledge that some types of organization may be totally absent or under-reported within the database, for example virtual organizations associated with the internet (including those of otherwise conventional structure, but also "usenets", web discussion groups, "listserv" communities etc.), criminal networks, cartels and price-fixing rings, mercenary-groups, spy and undercover organizations, terrorist organizations, secret societies, religious sects, family and fraternity groups, bodies with no formal structure or fixed address or associations essentially constituted by a journal subscribership.

The editors have always given priority to bodies that are not focused on, or deriving from, a particular country. This may be construed as under-reporting of certain forms of aid, missionary activity, language and cultural activities, etc.

The editors have traditionally stressed the importance of involvement of three countries on a more-or-less equal footing, to the exclusion of bilateral international bodies and those in which a particular country is dominant. Indications of "internationality" are distribution of board members, location of meetings, rotation of secretariat, source of finance in addition to membership and other such relevant information.

Although in many ways under-reported, and not included in the categories of conventional international bodies, some level of recognition is given to these organization forms in the types clustered under "Other International Bodies" and "Special Types".

The central concern of the Yearbook has always been that of maintaining comprehensive coverage of international bodies that correspond to its criteria of Types A to D (see the Appendix: Types of organization). The coverage of types E to G is not comprehensive for the following reasons:

- Type E: commissions of international bodies. Only those cited by other bodies, or which appear to have some degree of independent "outer-directed" action are included. A deliberate search for them is not usually made. Less independent bodies are classified as Type K; the least independent are cited only in the "mother" organization's entry.

- Type F: new forms of organization, organizational experiments and organizational substitutes. Forms most frequently arising in recent years have been networks and, currently, bodies existing only on internet. The emergence of such "bodies" is a constant and useful challenge to any selection criteria. Type F has also been used as a transitional category: it previously contained religious orders (now Type R), and meeting series (now Type S). It currently holds many financing and funding organizations and others with a self-styled structure.

- Type G: national bodies perceived as "internationally active" by international organizations. Clearly it is difficult to define the limits in such a case. In practice, only those which appear international (due to their name or preoccupations), or which are cited with other international bodies, are included. A deliberate search for them is not made.

Change in editorial policy and practice

While every effort is made to maintain continuity of types of organization, over the period of production of the Yearbook series some new types have been added to the classification system in order to complete the coverage and evolution of the range of organizational forms. This is relevant to understanding the international community of organizations. The editors usually prefer to add a new type to the classification system, rather than modify the definitions of pre-existing types, in order to minimize disruption to the core statistical series.

New types of international organization are usually one of two forms: new kinds of organization (networks, virtual organizations, etc.) which have no implications for historical statistics; or an acknowledgement of previously neglected types with a long historical record (e.g. religious orders).

Sources

The descriptions of organizations in this Yearbook are based on information received from a variety of sources. Priority is normally given to information received from the organizations themselves. Questionnaires are sent out between May of any given year and February of the following year (the reporting year). The replies received may neglect to mention significant events (e.g. relocation of the secretariat) that will take place later in the reporting year. Such gaps in information will be corrected only in the following reporting year.

Every effort is made by the editors to check this primary source information against other sources (periodicals, official documents, media, etc.). Equally, and especially when no primary source information is received, the profile of the organization may be updated by consulting secondary sources (print media, websites, documents of collaborating organizations, etc.). This information is submitted to the organizations concerned for verification in the following reporting year.

Organizations may over time change their purpose or characteristics. Some changes will have an effect on classification and on statistical reporting. The editors therefore use information from a variety of sources to present the most appropriate static picture of what is essentially a dynamic situation.

Reliability of sources

Because an organization's view of itself has been given priority, and because secondary sources are not always available or reliable, the editors cannot take responsibility for any resulting inaccuracies in the information presented. The editors apologize for any inconvenience this might cause the user.

The information received, even if from a primary source, does not always originate from the person most competent to provide it. From year to year, different people, of different competence or experience within an organization, may be responsible for replying to Yearbook questionnaires. They may be inadequately informed of the complexities of their organization, or unwilling to take responsibility for more than generalities, or lacking the authority or confidence to give information on an evolving, politically sensitive structure. As a result, the information received may be of inconsistent quality.

Organizations in a process of restructuring may be reluctant to provide information or announce anticipated changes. Organizations that have a radical change of policy may evidence some embarrassment at the reality of their own history and may seek to modify this information. Some organizations, or some people within organizations, will deliberately deliver false information. Some organizations report incompletely and/or infrequently because of lack of administrative resources and/or motivation.

It may take a second reporting year, or more, to remedy misleading reporting. A more detailed update of inadequate information initially obtained may necessitate a reclassification of organizational type, thus affecting statistical reporting.

Information collection

The number and variety of organizations in this Yearbook are sufficient indication of the information collection problem. Documenting many organizations is difficult for reasons such as the following.

- Regional proliferation and functional specialization is such that, frequently, organizational "neighbours" do not know of each other's existence.

- The "creation" of an organization is often the subject of widely-reported resolutions of an international conference, but such resolutions are not always acted upon very effectively – the intent being of greater significance (or practicability) than later implementation.

- Many organizations are ephemeral creations or are only "activated" for infrequent meetings, events or projects.

- A significant number of bodies have secretariats rotated among annually elected officers, making continuing contact somewhat problematic.

- The differing (mis)translations of the name of a body (further complicated by name changes) make it difficult to determine whether one or more bodies exist.

- Many bodies are reluctant to publicise their activities.

- Many active "international" bodies do not perceive themselves as "international" or as sufficiently formalized to be mentioned in the same context those that are legally established.

- Information on the existence, or change in status, of an organization may take time to filter through communication networks and be registered by the editors.

- Organizations may not respond to questionnaires, or may omit significant information from their replies, in which case outdated information from previous periods will be treated as current.

- Information on the creation, existence or formal dissolution of an organization may only be received after the current reporting year, thus affecting reporting by year.

In such a dynamic environment, the time required for information collection may even be greater than the effective life of organization.

Dating information

Organizations may form gradually. A formal organization that evolves from a network or series of meetings may not have a clear date of foundation. There may be several dates that could be considered as the date of founding (*e.g.* first statutes, first officers, first address, first members). Representatives of the organization may have differing views on when the organization started. Similarly the dissolution of an organization may be progressive, rather than formally indicated at a particular date. It is therefore not always evident, even with hindsight, in which reporting year its dissolution should be correctly indicated.

Description length

How much space can be devoted to a particular organization? As a general guide, more information is desirable for organizations in Type B than in Type C; an absolute minimum is the rule for most of those in Type G. However, large, active or structurally complex organizations of any type generally warrant longer descriptions, while relatively inactive or simple bodies merit less space, especially when the aims are evident from the title. This obviously gives rise to difficulties due to the tendency of organizations to inflate their importance according to normal public relations practice. In the case of exaggerated claims, however, when they are briefly stated they can effectively be used to define the organization. This is not the case when organizations claim large membership in many countries. Some supporting evidence is therefore sought although there is a limit to what can be usefully demanded. Normally, however, exaggerated claims are easy to detect and can be handled by limiting the amount of information given and allocating the organization to the appropriate type.

Since it is difficult to obtain information from organizations that do not wish to supply it, some elements of a description may remain incomplete (e.g. budget and staff). The organization may even request that information, such as the country list of membership, should be suppressed because of its political or other significance.

When no information is available, the problem is one of how long to allow entries to remain un-updated before considering the organization inactive. Generally, there is a delay of several years before it is assumed that the body is no longer functioning.

Censorship

Users should be aware that the editors are subject to pressure from some international bodies to suppress certain categories of information. Reasons given include: (a) the body does not belong with "international organizations", possibly because it is an informal network (personal not public) or because it is in some way transcendental to the mundane organization of the international community (as is the case of certain religious bodies); (b) the body is of "no possible interest" to anyone else (as is the case of some staff associations of major intergovernmental organizations); (c) mention of the body, or of its normal relationships, attracts unwelcome attention (as in the case of some military bodies in countries where terrorism is a problem); (d) mention of membership of the body may subject members to victimization (as is the case of trade unions with members in countries with severe human rights problems); (e) organizations wish to avoid unsolicited mail (especially "junk mail"). In most cases, the editors resist these pressures; in some cases, the entry is reworded to respect the concern of the body in question. No entries have been eliminated as a result of such pressure.

Evaluation

It has never been the intention of the editors to evaluate the significance of the organizations described or to provide interpretation of the information supplied by an organization. The guiding principle has been to portray the organization as it sees itself usually in words from its own documents, as far as this is possible. The editors cannot verify the claims made in documents received.

The final evaluation of the information presented here must be left to the users of this volume. Users may be assisted in this assessment by whether a full description is included, by the amount of information it has been considered useful to include in the description, by the last date on which information has been received, and by the organization type. See the Appendices "Contents of organization descriptions" and "Types of organization" for further information.

Some organizations included are perceived as highly suspect by other bodies, whether because of dubious academic standing, questionable values, or as a threat to public order. The editors do not act on such judgements, which may be contradicted by others. However, in the case of the very small minority of bodies that seek to mislead through false claims, to defraud or to engage in covert operations, the editors endeavour to juxtapose items of information that draw attention to the questionable aspects of these organizations. The final assessment is left to the user.

Error control policy

It would be unrealistic to expect a Yearbook of this size to be error free. There are various kinds of possible error.

- Errors in information supplied: As noted above, the entries attempt to describe the organizations as they wish themselves to be perceived. Whilst it is possible to detect exaggeration in some claims, it is not always possible to detect errors in information such as budgets, date of foundation, etc.

- Errors due to out-of-date information: Portions of organization descriptions can quickly become out-of-date (especially when the secretariat address rotates among members). Every effort is made to include the most recent information and to date entries accordingly.

- Errors in editorial treatment: Since the editorial treatment of an organization may involve weighing alternative possibilities in documents from different sources, this can result in errors of judgement, which can only be corrected when the organization next receives its entry for updating or other information is received from other sources.

- Errors in keyboarding/proof-reading: Whilst every effort is made to reduce the number of such errors, it is not cost-effective to do this beyond a certain point when there is a print deadline to be met.

- Duplicate entries: Tracing organizations whose names may be (mis)reported in a variety of languages can result in duplicates being detected too late to be eliminated.

Country names

It is not the intention of the editors to take a position with regard to the political or diplomatic implications of geographical names or continental groupings used in this Yearbook.

The names of countries used may not be the complete official names of those countries. The geographical names used are chosen for the sake of brevity and common usage.

Wherever possible, the country (or territory) name preferred by the organization concerned is used, providing this is possible within the limits of standardization required for mailing or statistical purposes.

It is important to note that some organizations insist on the inclusion of territories on the same basis as countries, or on the inclusion of geographical areas that are not recognized – whether under the specified name or indeed as a definable area at all – by other organizations.

Giving precedence as much as possible to the organization's preferences may lead to what appears to be duplication, as one geographical area may, according to some parties, have more than one possible name.

Some geographical names used in this publication may not, strictly speaking, even refer to geographical areas. An example is groups "in exile", namely a group identifying itself by the name of a sovereign State but not actually present in that State.

Political changes over the years may lead to some questions in an organization's description. Briefly: countries referred to in an organization's description retain their old form when referring to a date prior to the change. For example, towns referred to in events prior to 1991 still retain their country as German DR (Democratic Republic) or Germany FR (Federal Republic), while subsequent dates refer simply to Germany.